Africa
South of
the Sahara
2023

Africa South of the Sahara 2023

52nd Edition

Taylor & Francis Group

LONDON AND NEW YORK

52nd edition published 2022
by Routledge
4 Park Square, Milton Park, Abingdon, Oxon, OX14 4RN

and by Routledge
605 Third Avenue, New York, NY 10158

Routledge is an imprint of the Taylor & Francis Group, an informa business

First published 1971

ISBN: 978-1-032-27297-9
ISSN: 0065-3896

Typeset in New Century Schoolbook
by Data Standards Limited, Frome, Somerset

Regional Editor: Iain Frame

Regional Organizations Editor: Helen Canton

Senior Editor, Statistics: Philip McIntyre

Editorial Assistants: Lucy Pritchard, Avi Sharma

Editorial Research Manager: Surabhi Srivastava

Statistics Researchers: Mohd Khalid Ansari (Senior Team Leader), Akansha Gusain, Syed Zaki Mehdi (Senior Researchers), Ankita Nigam, Anjishtha Sharma

Directory Editorial Researchers: Aditi Kapoor (Team Leader), Birendra Pratap Nayak (Senior Researcher), Sakshi Bansal, Richa Chhabra, Vani Devraj, Manmeet Kaur, Waqar Momin, R. Prajapathy

Contributing Editors: Imogen Gladman, Catriona Holman (Regional Organizations), Catriona Marcham, Gareth Vaughan (Commodities)

Publisher: Juliet Love

Printed and bound by CPI Group (UK) Ltd, Croydon, CR0 4YY

FOREWORD

The main political and economic developments in each of the 53 countries and territories of the region, are comprehensively narrated and examined in this volume, the 52nd edition of AFRICA SOUTH OF THE SAHARA. Readers' perspectives are further expanded by the General Survey, a collection of introductory essays providing in-depth analysis of current economic trends, an assessment of aid and development initiatives over the past 100 years, an examination of France's ongoing involvement in Africa and the phenomenon of *Françafrique*, and an investigation of the upholding, and, in some cases, breakdown, of the rule of law in sub-Saharan Africa.

In addition to contributions by specialist authors, researchers and commentators, all statistical and directory material in the new edition has been extensively updated, revised and expanded. A calendar of the key political events of 2021–22 provides convenient rapid reference to the year's main developments. Comprehensive coverage of international organizations and research bodies active in Africa is included, together with detailed background information on the continent's major agricultural and mineral commodities. Select bibliographies of relevant books and periodicals are also provided.

The entire content of the print edition of AFRICA SOUTH OF THE SAHARA is available online at www.europaworld.com. This prestigious resource incorporates sophisticated search and browse functions as well as specially commissioned visual and statistical content. An ongoing programme of updates of key areas of information ensures currency of content, and enhances the richness of the coverage.

The period under review in this edition of AFRICA SOUTH OF THE SAHARA has been marked by ongoing political and economic turbulence, particularly in the Sahel subregion. Burkina Faso experienced two military takeovers within eight months: the armed forces ousted President Roch Marc Christian Kaboré in January 2022, citing his failure effectively to respond to the escalating security crisis in the country, and the leader of that coup, Lt-Col Paul-Henri Sandaogo Damiba, was himself deposed in September. In neighbouring Mali the military-led transitional authorities continued to grapple with a worsening political crisis, which has also had significant economic, social and humanitarian impacts. Diplomatic tensions with France (and other European nations) regarding the presence of peacekeeping troops in Mali escalated during early 2022, culminating in June in the dismantling of the French-led Takuba Task Force and the withdrawal of Mali from the regional G5 Sahel grouping. Although France pledged to continue anti-jihadist operations in the wider Sahel, and increased its military co-operation with Niger, by the end of August all French troops had left Mali. Nevertheless, some progress was made towards the restoration of constitutional order in Mali with an agreement that the transitional period would be brought to a conclusion in March 2024, while similar headway was made in Chad (where the military had seized power in April 2021); upon the conclusion of a national dialogue it was agreed that the transitional period would end in October 2024.

Sub-Saharan Africa was perhaps less affected, in terms of case numbers and deaths, by the COVID-19 pandemic than most other areas of the world, and the region's gross domestic product (GDP) rebounded strongly in 2021, to grow by 4.7%, according to the International Monetary Fund. Within that figure there were, however, wide disparities, and the nascent recovery was threatened by rising food and energy prices exacerbated by the Russian Federation's invasion of Ukraine, tightening global financial conditions, and, in many countries, the existence of unsustainable government debt-to-GDP ratios. Furthermore, food insecurity has rapidly increased across the region since the beginning of the pandemic, and it was estimated that as many as 120m. people in sub-Saharan Africa would experience acute food insecurity by the end of 2022, with the countries of the Horn of Africa and the Sahel among those most severely affected.

The Editors are once again thankful to all the contributors for their articles and advice, and to the numerous governments and organizations that have returned questionnaires and provided statistical and other information.

October 2022

ACKNOWLEDGEMENTS

The Editors gratefully acknowledge the interest and co-operation of all the contributors to this volume, and of numerous national statistical and information offices, and embassies and high commissions, whose valued assistance in updating the material contained in AFRICA SOUTH OF THE SAHARA is greatly appreciated.

The editors owe special thanks for the co-operation, interest and advice of all the authors who contributed to this volume. We are also indebted to many organizations connected with the region, particularly the national statistical offices. The editors gratefully acknowledge particular indebtedness for permission to reproduce material from the following sources: the United Nations' statistical databases and *Demographic Yearbook, Statistical Yearbook* and *Monthly Bulletin of Statistics*; the United Nations Educational, Scientific and Cultural Organization's Institute for Statistics database; the *Human Development Report* of the United Nations Development Programme; the Food and Agriculture Organization of the United Nations' statistical database; the statistical databases of the World Health Organization; the statistical databases of the UNCTAD/WTO International Trade Centre; the International Labour Office's statistical database; the World Bank's statistical databases, especially the World Development Indicators database and the *World Development Report*; the International Monetary Fund's statistical database, *International Financial Statistics* and *Government Finance Statistics Yearbook*; the African Development Bank's *African Statistical Yearbook 2021*; the World Tourism Organization's *Tourism Highlights* and *Yearbook of Tourism Statistics, 2022 edition*, UNWTO, Madrid; the US Geological Survey; the International Telecommunication Union; Lloyd's List; and *The Military Balance 2022*, a publication of the International Institute for Strategic Studies, Arundel House, 6 Temple Place, London, WC2R 2PG, United Kingdom.

HEALTH AND WELFARE STATISTICS: SOURCES AND DEFINITIONS

Total fertility rate Source: WHO Global Health Observatory. The number of children that would be born per woman, assuming no female mortality at child-bearing ages and the age-specific fertility rates of a specified country and reference period.

Under-5 mortality rate Source: WHO Global Health Observatory. Defined by WHO as the probability of a child born in a specific year or period dying before reaching the age of five, if subject to the age-specific mortality rates of that year or period.

HIV/AIDS Source: UNAIDS. Estimated percentage of adults aged 15 to 49 years living with HIV/AIDS. < indicates 'fewer than'.

COVID-19 Sources: Center for Systems Science and Engineering (CSSE) at Johns Hopkins University (JHU) via Our World In Data: Hannah Ritchie, Edouard Mathieu, Lucas Rodés-Guirao, Cameron Appel, Charlie Giattino, Esteban Ortiz-Ospina, Joe Hasell, Bobbie Macdonald, Diana Beltekian and Max Roser (2020)—'Coronavirus Pandemic (COVID-19)'. Published online at OurWorldInData.org. (Retrieved from https://ourworldindata.org/coronavirus); Our World in Data: Mathieu, E., Ritchie, H., Ortiz-Ospina, E. et al. 'A global database of COVID-19 vaccinations' (Nature Human Behaviour, 2021). For reasons of comparability, UN population estimates have been used for most calculations.
Cumulative confirmed deaths (per 100,000 persons)
Attribution of cause of death to COVID-19 is based on classifications from the World Health Organization's International Statistical Classification of Diseases and Related Health Problems (ICD) guidelines, supported by national advice to health practitioners. Data refer to confirmed deaths only, actual numbers are likely to be greater.
Fully vaccinated population (% of total population)
'Fully vaccinated' denotes receipt of all doses prescribed by specific vaccination regimes, this may vary depending on the vaccine. Alternative definitions of fully vaccinated, including receipt of only part of a dosing regime, or recovery from illness, have been disregarded. For the sake of best comparison, rates are based on the total rather than eligible population in each case.

Domestic health expenditure Source: WHO Global Health Expenditure database. Covering the provision of health services (preventive and curative), family planning activities and nutrition activities. Public sources include domestic revenue as internal transfers and grants, transfers, subsidies to voluntary health insurance beneficiaries, non-profit institutions serving households (NPISH) or enterprise financing schemes as well as compulsory prepayment and social health insurance contributions. External grants or loans for health care, provided by international agencies and other national authorities, are not included.
US $ per head (PPP)
International dollar estimates. Current domestic general government expenditures as a ratio of total population.
% of GDP
The share of current domestic general government resources used to fund health expenditures, given as a percentage of the economy as measured by gross domestic product (GDP).
Public expenditure % of total current expenditure
Share of current health expenditures funded from general government sources, social health insurance and compulsory prepayment.

Access to water and sanitation Source: WHO/UNICEF Joint Monitoring Programme on Water Supply, Sanitation and Hygiene (JMP) (*Progress on Household Drinking Water, Sanitation and Hygiene, 2000–2020*). Defined in terms of the percentage of the population using improved facilities in terms of the type of technology and levels of service afforded. For water, this includes house connections, public standpipes, boreholes with handpumps, protected dug wells, protected spring and rainwater collection; allowance is also made for other locally defined technologies. Sanitation is defined to include connection to a sewer or septic tank system, pour-flush latrine, simple pit or ventilated improved pit latrine, again with allowance for acceptable local technologies. Access to water and sanitation does not imply that the level of service or quality of water is 'adequate' or 'safe'.

Carbon dioxide emissions Source: World Bank, World Development Indicators database, citing CAIT data. Climate Watch. 2020. GHG Emissions. Washington, DC: World Resources Institute. Available at: https://climatewatchdata.org/ghg-emissions. Emissions comprise those resulting from the burning of fossil fuels (including those produced during consumption of solid, liquid and gas fuels and from gas flaring) and from the manufacture of cement, but exclude emissions resulting from land-use transformation and forestry.

Human Development Index (HDI) Source: UNDP, *Human Development Report* (2021–22). A summary of human development measured by three basic dimensions: prospects for a long and healthy life, measured by life expectancy at birth; access to knowledge, measured by a combination of mean years of schooling for adults and expected years of schooling for children; and standard of living, measured by GNI per head (PPP US $). The index value obtained lies between zero and one. A value above 0.800 indicates very high human development, between 0.700 and 0.799 high human development, between 0.550 and 0.699 medium human development and below 0.550 low human development. A centralized data source for all three dimensions was not available for all countries. In some cases other data sources were used to calculate a substitute value; however, this was excluded from the ranking. Other countries, including non-UNDP members, were excluded from the HDI altogether. In total, 191 countries were ranked for 2021.

CONTENTS

CONTENTS

CONTENTS

PART THREE
Regional Information

MAJOR COMMODITIES OF AFRICA

CALENDARS

RESEARCH INSTITUTES CONCERNED WITH AFRICA

SELECT BIBLIOGRAPHY (BOOKS)

SELECT BIBLIOGRAPHY (PERIODICALS)

INDEX OF REGIONAL ORGANIZATIONS

THE CONTRIBUTORS

J. A. Allan. Late Professor of Geography, School of Oriental and African Studies, University of London, United Kingdom.

Manorama Akung. Senior Lecturer in History, Head of Centre for Research on Slavery and Indenture, University of Mauritius.

L. Berry. Former Professor of Geography, University of Dar es Salaam, Tanzania.

E. A. Boateng. Environmental consultant and educationalist.

George M. Bob-Milliar. Senior Lecturer, Department of History and Political Studies, Kwame Nkrumah University of Science and Technology, Kumasi, Ghana.

Anna Bruzzone. Stipendiary Lecturer in European and World History, University of Oxford, United Kingdom.

Marisé Castro. Researcher, Amnesty International, International Secretariat, London, United Kingdom.

Ismaila Ceesay. Senior Lecturer in Political Science and Head of the Political Science Unit, University of The Gambia, Serrekunda, The Gambia.

Tony Chafer. Professor of African and French Studies, Centre for European and International Studies, University of Portsmouth, United Kingdom.

Christopher Clapham. Centre of African Studies, University of Cambridge, United Kingdom.

John I. Clarke. Late Professor of Geography, University of Durham, United Kingdom.

Julian Cooke. Editor of the *Anglo-Malagasy Society Newsletter*.

Devon E. A. Curtis. Lecturer in Politics and International Studies, University of Cambridge, United Kingdom.

Moudwe Daga. Usawa Fellow, Department of Politics and International Studies, SOAS University of London, United Kingdom.

Juan Fandos-Rius. Encyclopaedist and historian of the Central African Republic.

Sheereen Fauzel. Researcher, PhD in Development Economics, University of Mauritius.

Marie Gibert. Visiting Fellow, Centre for European and International Studies Research, University of Portsmouth, United Kingdom.

Solomon M. Gofie. Associate Professor, Department of Political Science and International Relations, Addis Ababa University, Ethiopia.

Pierre Gourou. Late Professor of Geography, Université Libre de Bruxelles, Belgium, and Collège de France, Paris, France.

Stephen Harmon. Late Professor of History, Pittsburg State University, Pittsburg KS, USA.

R. J. Harrison Church. Late Professor of Geography, London School of Economics, United Kingdom.

David Hilling. Late Honorary Research Fellow, University of Greenwich, United Kingdom.

A. MacGregor Hutcheson. Former Lecturer in Geography, Aberdeen College of Education, United Kingdom.

Abdourahmane Idrissa. Assistant Professor, African Studies Centre, Leiden University, Netherlands, and Humboldt Researcher, University of Göttingen, Germany.

Michael Jennings. Senior Lecturer in International Development, SOAS University of London, United Kingdom.

Warka Solomon Kahsay. Saint Francis Xavier University, Antogonish, Canada.

George Kay. Head of the Department of Geography and Recreation Studies, Staffordshire University, United Kingdom.

Teresia Kaulihowa. Associate Professor of Economics, Namibia University of Science and Technology, Windhoek, Namibia.

Fred van der Kraaij. Economist specializing in Liberia and the Western Sahel.

B. W. Langlands. Late Professor of Geography, Makerere University College, Kampala, Uganda.

I. M. Lewis. Late Professor of Anthropology, London School of Economics, United Kingdom.

Robert E. Looney. International consultant specializing in economic development and Distinguished Professor, Naval Postgraduate School, Monterey, CA, USA.

Akin L. Mabogunje. Late Professor of Geography, University of Ibadan, Nigeria.

Hugh Macmillan. Research Associate, African Studies Centre, University of Oxford, United Kingdom.

Giuseppe Maimone. Adjunct Professor, Department of Political Science and International Relations, University of Palermo, Italy.

Albert Makochekanwa. Lecturer, Department of Economics, University of Zimbabwe, Harare, Zimbabwe.

Malefa Rose Malefane. Associate Professor, Department of Economics, University of South Africa, Pretoria, South Africa.

Paul Melly. Journalist specializing in francophone Africa and Associate Fellow of the Africa Programme at Chatham House (The Royal Institute of International Affairs), United Kingdom.

Peter K. Mitchell. Honorary Senior Research Fellow, Centre of West African Studies, University of Birmingham, United Kingdom.

Ticky Monekosso. Journalist and researcher specializing in human rights, development issues and related humanitarian affairs in Africa, and founder of Afromedi@net.

W. T. W. Morgan. Former Senior Lecturer, Department of Geography, University of Durham, United Kingdom.

Katharine Murison. Former Editor of *Africa South of the Sahara*.

Essa Njie. Lecturer in Political Science, University of The Gambia, Serrekunda, The Gambia.

Jacob M. Nyambe. Associate Professor of Economics and Executive Dean, Faculty of Commerce, Management and Law, University of Namibia, Windhoek, Namibia.

René Pélissier. Author specializing in contemporary Spanish-speaking and Portuguese-speaking Africa.

Bram Posthumus. Writer, broadcaster and correspondent covering francophone West Africa.

Luca Raineri. Research Fellow in Security Studies, Sant'Anna School of Advanced Studies, Pisa, Italy.

Brad Safarik. Lecturer in Political Science and International Relations, Université Catholique de l'Ouest, Angers, France, and Associate Researcher, Les Afriques dans le Monde, Institute d'Etudes Politiques de Bordeaux, France.

Christopher Saunders. Emeritus Professor, Department of Historical Studies, University of Cape Town, South Africa.

Boopen Seetanah. Professor, Co-Chair of the WTO Chair Programme and Director of Research at the International Centre for Sustainable Tourism and Hospitality, University of Mauritius.

Gerhard Seibert. Associate Researcher, Centre for International Studies, ISCTE—Lisbon University Institute, Portugal.

Max Siollun. Historian and author specializing in Nigeria's political and military history.

Sishuwa Sishuwa. Lecturer in African History, University of Zambia, Lusaka, Zambia.

Miles Smith-Morris. Writer specializing in developing countries.

Donald L. Sparks. Emeritus Professor of International Economics, The Citadel, Charleston SC, USA, and Lecturer in International Business, Management Centre Innsbruck, Austria.

Leighann Spencer. PhD candidate, Charles Sturt University, Australia, and Tutor in Justice Studies, La Trobe University, Australia.

David Styan. Department of Politics, Birkbeck, University of London, United Kingdom.

Verena Tandrayen-Ragoobur. Associate Professor of Economics and Statistics, University of Mauritius.

Virginia Thompson. Writer specializing in francophone Africa.

Valdemar J. Undji. Lecturer, Department of Economics, University of Namibia, Windhoek, Namibia.

Helen Ware. Professor of Peace Studies, School of Humanities, University of New England, Armidale, Australia.

Jörg Wiegratz. Lecturer in Political Economy of Global Development, School of Politics and International Studies, University of Leeds, United Kingdom.

Geoffrey J. Williams. Former Professor of Geography, University of Zambia, Lusaka, Zambia.

Duncan Woodside. Journalist and analyst specializing in economics and conflict in the Great Lakes of Africa.

ABBREVIATIONS

Acad.	Academician; Academy		Dr.	Drive
ACP	African, Caribbean and Pacific (States)		Dra	Doctora
ADF	African Development Fund		dwt	dead weight tons
Adm.	Admiral		E	East; Eastern; Emalangeni (Swaziland currency)
Admin.	Administration; Administrative; Administrator		€	Euro (currency)
AEC	African Economic Community		EAC	East African Community
AfCFTA	African Continental Free Trade Area		EC	European Community
AfDB	African Development Bank		ECA	Economic Commission for Africa (UN)
AG	Aktiengesellschaft (limited company)		ECF	Extended Credit Facility
AGOA	African Growth and Opportunity Act		ECOWAS	Economic Community of West African States
a.i.	ad interim		ECU	European Currency Unit(s)
AIDS	acquired immunodeficiency syndrome		Ed.(s)	Editor(s)
AM	Amplitude Modulation		EDF	European Development Fund
Apdo	Apartado (Post Box)		edn	edition
Apt	Apartment		EEZ	Exclusive Economic Zone
ARV	advanced retroviral		e.g.	exempli gratia (for example)
Ass.	Assembly		EIB	European Investment Bank
Asscn	Association		EME	emerging market economy
Assoc.	Associate		Eng.	Engineer; Engineering
Asst	Assistant		EP	Empresa Pública
ATM	automated teller machine		EPZ	Export Processing Zone
AU	African Union		ESAF	Enhanced Structural Adjustment Facility
Aug.	August		est.	established; estimate; estimated
auth.	authorized		etc.	etcetera
Av.	Avenida (Avenue)		EU	European Union
Ave	Avenue		EVD	Ebola Virus Disease
			excl.	excluding
BCEAO	Banque Centrale des Etats de l'Afrique de l'Ouest		Exec.	Executive
Bd	Board		exhbn(s)	exhibition(s)
b/d	barrels per day		Ext.	Extension
BEAC	Banque des Etats de l'Afrique Centrale			
Bldg(s)	Building(s)		f.	founded
Blk	Block		FAO	Food and Agriculture Organization
Blvd	Boulevard		FDI	foreign direct investment
BOAD	Banque Ouest-Africaine de Développement		Feb.	February
BP	Boîte Postale (Post Box)		Fed.	Federation; Federal
br.(s)	branch(es)		FG	Guinea Franc
Brig.	Brigadier		FIDES	Fonds d'Investissement et de Développement Economique et Social
C	Centigrade; Cedi(s) (Ghana currency)		FIFA	Fédération Internationale de Football Association
c.	circa		Flt	Flight
cap.	capital		FMD	foot-and-mouth disease
Capt.	Captain		FMG	Malagasy Franc
CEMAC	Communauté Economique et Monétaire de l'Afrique Centrale		fmr(ly)	former(ly)
Cen.	Central		f.o.b.	free on board
CEO	Chief Executive Officer		Fr	Father
cf.	confer (compare)		Fr.	Franc(s)
CFA	Communauté Financière Africaine; Coopération Financière en Afrique Centrale		Fri.	Friday
			ft	foot (feet)
Chair.	Chairman/woman		FTA	free trade agreement/area
Cie	Compagnie			
c.i.f.	cost, insurance and freight		g	gram(s)
C-in-C	Commander-in-Chief		GDP	gross domestic product
circ.	circulation		Gen.	General
cm	centimetre(s)		GMO(s)	genetically modified organism(s)
cnr	corner		GMT	Greenwich Mean Time
c/o	care of		GNI	gross national income
Co	Company; County		GNP	gross national product
Col	Colonel		Gov.	Governor
Comm.	Commission		Govt	Government
Commdr	Commander		GPO	General Post Office
Commr	Commissioner		grt	gross registered ton(s)
Conf.	Conference		GWh	gigawatt hour(s)
Confed.	Confederation			
COO	Chief Operating Officer		ha	hectare(s)
Corpn	Corporation		HDI	Human Development Index
CP	Caixa Postal, Case Postale (Post Box)		HIPC	heavily indebted poor country
Cpl	Corporal		HIV	human immunodeficiency virus
Cttee	Committee		hl	hectolitre(s)
cu	cubic		HLTF	High Level Task Force
cwt	hundredweight		HM	His/Her Majesty
			HPAI	highly pathogenic avian influenza
Dec.	December		HQ	Headquarters
Del.	Delegate		HYV	high-yielding variety
Dem.	Democratic			
Dep.	Deputy		ibid.	ibidem (from the same source)
dep.	deposits		IBRD	International Bank for Reconstruction and Development (World Bank)
Dept	Department			
Devt	Development		ICT	information and communication technology
Dir	Director		IDA	International Development Association
Div.	Division(al)		IDPs	Internally Displaced Persons
Dr	Doctor		i.e.	id est (that is to say)
			IGAD	Intergovernmental Authority on Development
			ILO	International Labour Organization/Office

IMF	International Monetary Fund		pl.	place (square)
in	inch (inches)		PLC	Public Limited Company
Inc	Incorporated		PMB	Private Mail Bag
incl.	include, including		PO	Post Office
Ind.	Independent		POB	Post Office Box
Ing.	Engineer		PPP	purchasing-power parity
Insp.	Inspector		Pres.	President
Inst.	Institute		PRGF	Poverty Reduction and Growth Facility
Int.	International		Prin.	Principal
Is	Islands		Prof.	Professor
ISIC	International Standard Industrial Classification		Prov.	Province; Provincial
ISP	internet service provider		PSI	Policy Suport Instrument, Poverty Strategies Initiative
ITUC	International Trade Union Confederation		Pte	Private
IUU	illegal, unreported and unregulated		Pty	Proprietary
			p.u.	paid up
Jan.	January		publ.(s)	publication(s); published
Jr	Junior		Publr	Publisher
Jt	Joint		Pvt.	Private
K	Kwacha (Malawi and Zambia currencies)		q.v.	quod vide (to which refer)
kg	kilogram(s)		R	Rand (South African currency)
km	kilometre(s)		Rd	Road
kW	kilowatt(s)		RECs	regional economic communities
kWh	kilowatt hour(s)		regd	registered
			reorg.	reorganized
lb	pound(s)		Rep.	Representative
Lda	Limitada (limited company)		Repub.	Republic
LDCs	Least Developed Countries		res	reserves
Le.	Leone (Sierra Leone currency)		retd	retired
LGBT	lesbian, gay, bisexual and transgender		Rev.	Reverend
LLC	Limited Liability Company		Rm	Room
LNG	Liquefied natural gas		RMS	Royal Mail Steamer
LPG	Liquefied petroleum gas		Rs	Rupee(s) (Mauritius currency)
Lt	Lieutenant		Rt	Right
Ltd	Limited			
			S	South; Southern
M	Maloti (Lesotho currency)		SA	Société Anonyme, Sociedad Anónima (limited company); South Africa
m	metre(s)			
m.	million		SADC	Southern African Development Community
Maj.	Major		SARL	Sociedade Anônima de Responsabilidade Limitada (limited company)
Man.	Manager; Managing			
MB/s	megabits per second		Sat.	Saturday
MDG	Millennium Development Goal		SDR	Special Drawing Right(s)
MDRI	multilateral debt relief initiative		Sec.	Secretary
Me	Maître		Secr.	Secretariat
mem.	member		Sept.	September
MFA	Multi-fibre Arrangement		Sgt	Sergeant
Mfg	Manufacturing		SITC	Standard International Trade Classification
mfrs	manufacturers		SME	small and medium-sized enterprises
mg	milligram(s)		Soc.	Society
Mgr	Monseigneur, Monsignor		Sq.	Square
Mil.	Military		sq	square (in measurements)
mm	millimetre(s)		SR	Seychelles Rupee(s)
Mon.	Monday		Sr	Senior
MP	Member of Parliament		St	Street; Saint, San, Santo
MSS	manuscripts		Sta	Santa
Mt	Mount		Ste	Sainte
MV	Motor Vessel		STI(s)	sexually transmitted infection(s)
MW	megawatt(s); medium wave		Stn	Station
MWh	megawatt hour(s)		Sun.	Sunday
			Supt	Superintendent
N	North; Northern			
₦	Naira (Nigerian currency)		tech.	technical, technology
NA	National Association (banking)		trans.	translator, translated
n.a.	not available		Treas.	Treasurer
Nat.	National		TV	Television
NCO	Non-Commissioned Officer			
NEPAD	New Partnership for Africa's Development		UA	Unit(s) of Account
n.e.s.	not elsewhere specified		UEE	Unidade Económica Estatal
NGO	non-governmental organization		UEMOA	Union Economique et Monétaire Ouest-Africaine
No.	number		UK	United Kingdom
Nov.	November		ul.	ulitsa (street)
nr	near		UM	Ouguiya(s) (Mauritania currency)
nrt	net registered ton(s)		UN	United Nations
NV	Naamloze Vennootschap (limited company)		UNAIDS	United Nations Joint Programme on HIV/AIDS
			UNCTAD	United Nations Conference on Trade and Development
OAU	Organization of African Unity		UNDP	United Nations Development Programme
Oct.	October		UNESCO	United Nations Educational, Scientific and Cultural Organization
OECD	Organisation for Economic Co-operation and Development			
OIC	Organization of the Islamic Conference, Organization of Islamic Cooperation		UNHCR	United Nations High Commissioner for Refugees
			Univ.	University
OMVS	Organisation pour la Mise en Valeur du Fleuve Sénégal		UNWTO	World Tourism Organization
OPEC	Organization of the Petroleum Exporting Countries		US(A)	United States (of America)
opp.	opposite		USAID	United States Agency for International Development
Org.(s)	Organization(s)		USSR	Union of Soviet Socialist Republics
oz	ounce(s)			
			Vol.(s)	Volume(s)
P	Pula (Botswana currency)			
p.	page		W	West; Western
p.a.	per annum		WHO	World Health Organization
Parl.	Parliament(ary)		WSSD	World Summit on Sustainable Development
Perm.	Permanent		WTO	World Trade Organization
PGM	platinum-group metals		yr(s)	year(s)

INTERNATIONAL TELEPHONE CODES

To make international calls to telephone numbers listed in *Africa South of the Sahara*, dial the international code of the country from which you are calling, followed by the appropriate country code for the organization you wish to call (listed below), followed by the area code (if applicable) and telephone number listed in the entry.

	Country code		Country code
Angola	244	Malawi	265
Ascension Island	247	Mali	223
Benin	229	Mauritania	222
Botswana	267	Mauritius	230
British Indian Ocean Territory	246	Mayotte	262
Burkina Faso	226	Mozambique	258
Burundi	257	Namibia	264
Cabo Verde	238	Niger	227
Cameroon	237	Nigeria	234
The Central African Republic	236	Réunion	262
Chad	235	Rwanda	250
The Comoros	269	Saint Helena	290
Congo, Democratic Republic	243	São Tomé and Príncipe	239
Congo, Republic	242	Senegal	221
Côte d'Ivoire	225	Seychelles	248
Djibouti	253	Sierra Leone	232
Equatorial Guinea	240	Somalia	252
Eritrea	291	South Africa	27
Eswatini (Swaziland)	268	South Sudan	211*
Ethiopia	251	Sudan	249
Gabon	241	Tanzania	255
The Gambia	220	Togo	228
Ghana	233	Tristan da Cunha	290
Guinea	224	Uganda	256
Guinea-Bissau	245	Zambia	260
Kenya	254	Zimbabwe	263
Lesotho	266		
Liberia	231		
Madagascar	261		

*Some telephone numbers for South Sudan use the country code for Sudan (249) or Uganda (256).

EXPLANATORY NOTE ON THE
DIRECTORY SECTION

The Directory section of each chapter is arranged under the following headings, where they apply:

THE CONSTITUTION

THE GOVERNMENT
  HEAD OF STATE
  CABINET/COUNCIL OF MINISTERS
  MINISTRIES

PRESIDENT

LEGISLATURE

ELECTION COMMISSION

POLITICAL ORGANIZATIONS

DIPLOMATIC REPRESENTATION

JUDICIAL SYSTEM

RELIGION

THE PRESS

PUBLISHERS

BROADCASTING AND COMMUNICATIONS
  TELECOMMUNICATIONS
  RADIO
  TELEVISION

FINANCE

CENTRAL BANK
NATIONAL BANKS
COMMERCIAL BANKS
DEVELOPMENT BANKS
MERCHANT BANKS
SAVINGS BANKS
INVESTMENT BANKS
FINANCIAL INSTITUTIONS
STOCK EXCHANGE
INSURANCE

TRADE AND INDUSTRY
  GOVERNMENT AGENCIES
  DEVELOPMENT ORGANIZATIONS
  CHAMBERS OF COMMERCE
  INDUSTRIAL AND TRADE ASSOCIATIONS
  EMPLOYERS' ORGANIZATIONS
  UTILITIES
  MAJOR COMPANIES
  CO-OPERATIVES
  TRADE UNIONS

TRANSPORT
  RAILWAYS
  ROADS
  INLAND WATERWAYS
  SHIPPING
  CIVIL AVIATION

TOURISM

DEFENCE

EDUCATION

POLITICAL EVENTS IN AFRICA SOUTH OF THE SAHARA, 2021–22

1 **Angola** President João Manuel Gonçalves Lourenço appointed Mário Caetano de Sousa as Minister of Economy, replacing Sérgio Mendes dos Santos.

1 **Nigeria** President Maj.-Gen. (retd) Muhammadu Buhari dismissed Minister of Power Saleh Mamman and Minister of Agriculture and Rural Development Mohammed Sabo Nanono, subsequently appointing Abubakar Aliyu and Dr Muhammad Mahmoud Abubakar as their respective replacements.

2 **Lesotho** Machesetsa Mofomobe, the leader of the Basotho National Party, was appointed Minister of Small Business Development, Co-operatives and Marketing.

5 **Guinea** President Alpha Condé was detained by disaffected members of an elite military unit, the Groupement des Forces Spéciales, led by Col Mamady Doumbouya, who announced the creation of a ruling Comité National du Rassemblement et du Développement, the suspension of the Constitution, and the dissolution of the Government and the legislature.

5 **São Tomé and Príncipe** In the presidential election run-off Carlos Vila Nova secured victory, gaining 57.6% of the vote to defeat Guilherme Pósser da Costa. Vila Nova was sworn in as President on 2 October.

7 **Zambia** A new Government was sworn in following Hakainde Hichilema's victory at a presidential election held on 12 August. Stanley Kakubo, Ambrose Lufuma and Jack Mwiimbu assumed the key portfolios of foreign affairs, defence and home affairs, respectively.

9 **South Sudan** Beatrice Khamisa Wani-Noah was replaced by Mayiik Ayii Deng as Minister of Foreign Affairs and International Co-operation.

11 **Tanzania** In a government reorganization Stergomena Lawrence Tax was appointed Minister of Defence and National Service.

24 **Chad** A 93-member Conseil National de Transition (CNT), which was to serve as an interim legislative body, was appointed, with the election of Dr Haroun Kabadi as CNT President following on 5 October.

30 **Zimbabwe** President Emmerson Mnangagwa effected a reorganization of the Cabinet, appointing hitherto Minister of Primary and Secondary Education Cain Mathema as Minister without Portfolio in the Office of the President and Cabinet. Mathema was replaced by Dr Evelyn Ndlovu, who previously served as Minister of State in the Office of the Vice-President.

OCTOBER 2021

1 **Guinea** Doumbouya was inaugurated as Transitional President. On 6 October Mohamed Béavogui was appointed Prime Minister, and the formation of a new Government, primarily comprising technocrats, was completed in early November.

4 **Ethiopia** Dr Abiy Ahmed Ali was sworn in as Prime Minister for a second term. On 6 October he named a new 22-member Cabinet, which included, *inter alia*, Dr Abraham Belay as Minister of National Defence and Binalf Andualem as Minister of Peace.

13 **Lesotho** Prime Minister Moeketsi Majoro effected a cabinet reorganization, appointing Nkaku Kabi as Minister of Agriculture, Food Security and Marketing, Likopo Mahase as Minister in the Prime Minister's Office and Kemiso Mosenene as Minister of Water.

13 **São Tomé and Príncipe** Engrácio do Sacramento Soares da Graça was named as Minister of Planning, Finance and the Blue Economy, replacing Osvaldo Tavares dos Santos Vaz.

17 **Cabo Verde** A presidential election was held, at which former Prime Minister José Maria Neves won 51.7% of the vote, defeating his closest rival, Carlos Veiga, who took 42.4%. Neves was sworn in as President on 9 November.

20 **Zimbabwe** President Mnangagwa appointed Sibangumuzi Sixtone Khumalo as Minister of State in the Office of the Vice-President.

25 **Sudan** Gen. Abdel Fattah al-Burhan Abdelrahman announced the dissolution of the Transitional Government and it was reported that Prime Minister Abdalla Hamdok had been detained, along with the civilian members of the Sovereign Council. On 11 November Abdelrahman reformed the Sovereign Council and on 21 November Adelrahman and Hamdok signed an agreement which provided for the latter's reinstatement as Prime Minister.

NOVEMBER 2021

9–11 **Mozambique** In a series of changes to the Council of Ministers President Filipe Nyusi dismissed Amade Miquidade as Minister of the Interior, Jaime Bessa Neto as Minister of National Defence and Adelaide Anchia Amurane as Minister in the Presidency. Arsénia Massingue, Maj.-Gen. Cristóvão Chume and Constantino Alberto Bacela were appointed as their respective replacements.

12 **South Sudan** President Salva Kiir Mayardit dismissed Minister of Finance and Economic Planning Athian Diing Athian and Minister of the Interior Paul Mayom Akech. They were replaced by Agak Achuil Lual and Mahmoud Solomon Agok, respectively.

18 **Burundi** A reorganization of the Council of Ministers was announced with appointments including Domine Banyankimbona as Minister of Justice and Marie Chantal Nijimbere as Minister of Commerce, Transport, Industry and Tourism.

20 **Somalia** As part of a wider ministerial reorganization, Mohamed Abdirizak Mohamud was replaced by Abdisaid Muse Ali as Minister of Foreign Affairs and International Co-operation.

29 **Niger** In a reorganization of the Council of Ministers Hamadou Adamou Souley was named as Minister of the Interior and Decentralization, replacing Alkache Alhada, who became Minister of Trade.

DECEMBER 2021

4 **The Gambia** At a presidential election the incumbent, Adama Barrow of the National People's Party, secured a second term with 53.2% of the vote, defeating his nearest challenger, Ousainou Darboe of the United Democratic Party, who received 27.7%.

5 **Lesotho** Nkaku Kabi was dismissed as Minister of Agriculture, Food Security and Marketing.

8 **Burkina Faso** Prime Minister Christophe Dabiré tendered the resignation of his Government. Two days later, Lassina Zerbo was named as his replacement. On 13 December a new 25-member Government was appointed, including Rosine Sori-Coulibaly as Minister of Foreign Affairs, Regional Co-operation and Burkinabè Abroad.

10 **Rwanda** President Maj.-Gen. Paul Kagame effected a reorganization of the Cabinet, appointing Alfred Gasana as Minister of the Interior.

20 **Guinea-Bissau** The Minister of Justice and Human Rights, Mamadú Iaia Djaló, passed away.

24 **Botswana** Mpho Balopi resigned from his position as Minister of Employment, Labour Productivity and Skills Development.

26 **Somalia** Two government ministers exchanged portfolios—Abdulkadir Mohamed Nur 'Jama' becoming Minister of Defence, and Hassan Hussein Haji becoming Minister for Minister of Justice and Constitutional Affairs. On the following day President Mohamed Abdullahi Mohamed suspended the powers of Prime Minister Mohamed Hussein Roble on suspicion of corruption and of interfering with a defence ministry investigation. However, Roble defied the President's order, denouncing it as unconstitutional and an attempted coup.

31 **Guinea** The Keeper of the Seals, Minister of Justice, Fatoumata Yarie Soumah, was replaced by Moriba Alain Koné.

JANUARY 2022

2 **Djibouti** President Ismaïl Omar Guelleh effected a minor reorganization of the Council of Ministers. Isman Ibrahim Robleh, hitherto Minister of Labour, in charge of Formalization and Social Protection, was named as Minister of the Budget. He was replaced in his former post by Omar Abdi Said.

2 **Sudan** Prime Minister Hamdok announced his resignation, citing the need for discussions on a new transitional timetable.

8 **Tanzania** President Samia Suluhu Hassan carried out a reorganization of the Cabinet. Most notably, Hamad Masauni was appointed Minister of Home Affairs, while Dr Ashatu Kachwamba Kijaji became head of the newly established Ministry of Investment, Industry and Trade.

10 **Zimbabwe** Minister of State for National Security Owen Ncube was dismissed.

22 **Guinea** In conformity with the transition charter of 27 September 2021, the 81 members of the transitional legislative body, the Conseil National de la Transition (CNT), were appointed by Transitional President Doumbouya. The CNT was officially installed on 5 February.

24 **Botswana** As part of a cabinet reorganization carried out by President Dr Mokgweetsi Masisi, Minister of Local Government and Rural Development Eric Molale was reassigned to the infrastructure and housing development portfolio.

24 **Burkina Faso** A group of dissident officers, the Mouvement Patriotique pour la Sauvegarde et la Restauration, led by Lt-Col Paul-Henri Sandaogo Damiba, announced the arrest of President Roch Marc Christian Kaboré, the suspension of the 1991 Constitution, and the dissolution of the Government

and the National Assembly. On 16 February Damiba was sworn in as Transitional President.

24 **Malawi** President Lazarus Chakwera dismissed the Government. In the new Cabinet sworn in on 30 January, Nancy Tembo became Minister of Foreign Affairs and Sosten Gwengwe Minister of Finance and Economic Affairs.

26 **Guinea-Bissau** President Umaro Sissoco Embaló announced a major reorganization of the Council of Ministers, in which a number of ministers were dismissed; notable appointments included that of Teresa Alexandrina da Silva as Minister of Justice and Human Rights.

31 **Rwanda** President Kagame appointed Dr Ernest Nsabimana as Minister of Infrastructure, replacing Claver Gatete.

FEBRUARY 2022

1 **São Tomé and Príncipe** President Vila Nova effected a reorganization of the Council of Ministers, appointing, *inter alia*, Jorge Amado as Minister of National Defence and Cilcio Pires dos Santos as Minister of Justice, Internal Administration and Human Rights.

4 **Central African Republic** Henri-Marie Dondra resigned as Prime Minister. On 7 February he was succeeded by Félix Moloua, who also retained the economy, planning and international co-operation portfolio.

11 **Madagascar** Herilaza Imbiki resigned as Keeper of the Seals, Minister of Justice.

21 **Mali** The Conseil National de Transition adopted a charter allowing the military authorities to rule for up to five years. Thereafter Transitional President Col Assimi Goïta was to be barred from standing as a candidate in the presidential election.

22 **Eswatini** The Minister of Natural Resources, Peter Bhembe, passed away. Minister of Agriculture Jabulani Mabuza was subsequently given charge of his portfolio in an acting capacity.

25 **Chad** A government reorganization took place. Among the notable changes, Idriss Dokony Adiker was appointed Minister of Public Security and Immigration, while Djerassem Le Bemadjiel was named as Minister of Petroleum and Energy. Dr Abdoulmadjid Abderahim assumed responsibility for the health and national solidarity portfolio.

MARCH 2022

1 **Côte d'Ivoire** Gilbert Koné Kafana was appointed Minister of State at the Presidency of the Republic, in charge of Relations with the Institutions of the Republic.

3 **Burkina Faso** Transitional President Damiba named Albert Ouédraogo as Prime Minister. A Transitional Government was announced on 5 March, including Olivia Ragnaghnèwendé Rouamba as Minister of Foreign Affairs, Regional Co-operation and Burkinabè Abroad and Séglaro Abel Somé as Minister of the Economy, Finance and Planning. Gen. Aimé Barthélemy Simporé retained the defence and war veterans portfolio.

3 **Mozambique** President Nyusi effected a reorganization of the Cabinet. Most notably, hitherto Minister of the Economy and Finance Adriano Maleiane was appointed as the Prime Minister, replacing Carlos Agostinho do Rosário, who had been dismissed on

the previous day. Ernesto Max Elias Tonela, who previously served as Ministry of Mineral Resources and Energy, took charge of Maleiane's former portfolio.

8 **Gabon** A government reorganization was carried out, in which Michael Moussa Adamo was appointed Minister of Foreign Affairs, while Félicité Ongouori Ngoubili was named as Minister of National Defence.

8 **Tanzania** The President of Zanzibar, Dr Hussein Ali Mwinyi, announced a number of changes to the Zanzibar Government of National Unity.

16 **Madagascar** President Andry Nirina Rajoelina effected a reorganization of the Council of Ministers. Among the new appointments were those of Richard Randriamandrato as Minister of Foreign Affairs, Justin Tokely as Minister of the Interior and Decentralization, and François Rakotozafy as Keeper of the Seals, Minister of Justice.

20 **Uganda** The Speaker of Parliament, Jacob Oulanyah, passed away. Anita Annet Among was subsequently elected as his replacement.

30 **Democratic Republic of the Congo** Jean-Marie Kalumba was removed from the post of Minister of the Economy by a vote of the National Assembly.

31 **Mauritania** Prime Minister Mohamed Ould Bilal tendered the resignation of his Government. He was subsequently reappointed as Prime Minister and a new Council of Ministers was announced. Most notably, Mohamed Mahmoud Ould Cheikh Abdoullah Ould Boyé was appointed Minister of Justice, while Dr Mohamed Salem Ould Merzoug was named as Minister of Foreign Affairs, Co-operation and Mauritanians Abroad.

31 **Namibia** Leon Jooste resigned Minister of Public Enterprises; Minister of Finance Iipumbu Shiimi was given additional charge of the portfolio on an interim basis.

APRIL 2022

4 **South Africa** President Cyril Ramaphosa appointed Thulas Nxesi as Acting Minister of Public Service and Administration, in addition to his role as Minister of Employment and Labour, following Ayanda Dlodlo's appointment as an Executive Director at the World Bank.

7 **Lesotho** Prime Minister Majoro reorganized his Cabinet, appointing *inter alia* Keketso Sello as Minister of Agriculture, Food and Security and Moshe Leoma as Minister of Local Government and Chieftainship Affairs.

13 **Côte d'Ivoire** Prime Minister Patrick Achi submitted the resignation of his Government. He was reappointed to the premiership on 19 April. On the same day Tiémoko Meyliet Koné, hitherto Governor of the Banque Centrale des Etats de l'Afrique de l'Ouest, was appointed as Vice-President. On 20 April a largely unchanged new Government was announced.

14 **The Gambia** Fabakary Tombong Jatta was elected Speaker of the National Assembly.

22 **Botswana** President Masisi effected a major reorganization of the Cabinet, including changes to the structure of numerous ministries. Most notably, Machana Ronald Shamukuni was appointed as head of the newly-created Ministry of Justice.

23 **Niger** President Mohamed Bazoum implemented a reorganization of the Council of Ministers, appointing, *inter alia*, Ibrahim Yacouba Minister of State,

Minister of Energy and Renewable Energy Sources, and Prof. Ibrahim Natatou Minister of National Education.

MAY 2022

4 **Liberia** Ruth Coker-Collins became Minister of Public Works.

7 **Côte d'Ivoire** The President of the National Assembly, Amadou Soumahoro, passed away owing to ill health. On 7 June Adama Bictogo was elected to replace him.

9 **Comoros** President Col Assoumani Azali announced a reorganization of the Council of Ministers, in which Mze Abdou Mohamed Chanfiou was appointed Minister of Finance, the Budget and the Banking Sector. Among other notable changes, Ahmed Ali Bazi was named as Minister of the Economy, Industry and Investment, with responsibility for Economic Integration, while Djae Ahamada Chanfi became Minister of Justice, Islamic Affairs and the Civil Service.

12 **Guinea-Bissau** Victor Mandinga was dismissed as Minister of the Economy, Planning and Regional Integration.

15 **Somalia** Hassan Sheikh Mohamud was elected President of Somalia in a ballot which was conducted on an electoral college basis, with the 274 members of House of the People and the 54 members of the Upper House casting their votes. He took office on 23 May.

16 **Guinea-Bissau** President Embaló announced the dissolution of the Assembleia Nacional Popular. On 24 May he reappointed Nuno Gomes Nabiam as Prime Minister, and on 9 June announced the formation of a new, 36-member Council of Ministers.

26 **Senegal** Minister of Health and Social Action Abdoulaye Diouf Sarr was dismissed.

JUNE 2022

13 **Mozambique** Janfar Abdulai was dismissed as Minister of Transport and Communications; Mateus Magala was appointed as his replacement.

15 **Somalia** President Mohamud named Hamza Abdi Barre as the new Prime Minister. He was sworn in on 30 June.

24 **Gabon and Togo** Gabon and Togo joined the Commonwealth as its 55th and 56th members, respectively.

24 **The Gambia** In a cabinet reorganization Ousman A. Bah was named as Minister of Communication and the Digital Economy.

JULY 2022

4 **Guinea-Bissau** President Embaló appointed Ilídio Vieira Té Minister of Finance.

6 **Nigeria** President Buhari effected a minor cabinet reorganizationMu'azu Jaji Sambo became Minister of Transportation, while Adeleke Mamora was allocated the science and technology portfolio.

8 **Guinea** Alphonse Charles Wright was named as Keeper of the Seals, Minister of Justice.

9 **Chad** A minor government reorganization took effect. Moussa Batraki, hitherto Minister of Land Management, Housing Development and Town Planning, was named as Minister of the Economy, Development Planning and International Co-operation. His vacated portfolio was assumed by Ndolenodji Alixe Naïmbaye.

10 **Republic of the Congo** The first round of legislative elections were held, followed by a second on 31 July. According to the final results, the Parti Congolais du Travail obtained 112 out of the 151 seats in the National Assembly, while the Union des Démocrates Humanistes-Yuki and the Union Panafricaine pour la Démocratie Sociale won seven seats each. The Mouvement d'Action et pour le Renouveau took four seats.

19 **Zimbabwe** Minister of State for Provincial Affairs for Harare Oliver Chidawu died.

21 **Uganda** In a cabinet reorganization Norbert Mau was appointed Minister of Justice and Constitutional Affairs.

31 **Senegal** Legislative elections were held, at which Benno Bokk Yaakaar obtained 82 of the 165 seats in the National Assembly, while Yewwi Askan Wi secured 56 seats. Wallu Sénégal took 24 seats.

AUGUST 2022

2 **Somalia** Prime Minister Barre named a 75-member Council of Ministers, which included Salah Ahmed Jama as Deputy Prime Minister and Dr Elmi Mohamud Nur as Minister of Finance.

9 **Kenya** Presidential and legislative elections took place. In the former William Samoei Arap Ruto was declared the victor, having secured 50.5% of the vote. His closest challenger, Raila Amollo Odinga, received 48.9%. At elections to the National Assembly, Ruto's United Democratic Alliance won 140 of the contested 337 seats, while the Orange Democratic Movement obtained 83. Ruto was sworn in as President on 13 September.

13 **Saint Helena, Ascension and Tristan da Cunha** Nigel Phillips was sworn in as Governor.

20 **Guinea** The Minister of Trade, Industry and Small and Medium-sized Enterprises Dr Bernard Goumou, who had been appointed Acting Prime Minister on 16 July following Béavogui's illness, was confirmed in his post. In a subsequent reorganization of the Council of Ministers the Minister of the Economy, Finance and Planning, Dr Lancinè Condé, and the Minister of the Budget, Moussa Cissé, exchanged positions.

21 **Mali** Lt-Col Abdoulaye Maïga, Minister of Territorial Administration and Decentralization, was named as Interim Prime Minister, in addition to his hitherto ministerial portfolio.

23 **Réunion** Jérôme Filippini took office as Prefect.

24 **Angola** At a general election the Movimento Popular de Libertação de Angola (MPLA) secured the highest representation with 51.2% of the total valid votes cast, while the União Nacional para a Independência Total de Angola came second with 44.0% of votes. João Lourenço, the incumbent President representing the MPLA, was thus re-elected to the position. On 15 September Lourenço was sworn in for his second term and he installed a new Cabinet, with most outgoing members retaining their previous positions. Also on that day Carolina Cerqueira was appointed as the new President of the National Assembly, replacing Fernando da Piedade Dias dos Santos.

SEPTEMBER 2022

6 **Mauritania** President Mohamed Ould Cheikh Mohamed Ahmed Ould Ghazouani carried out a reorganization of the Council of Ministers. Among the new appointees were Nany Ould Chrougha (Minister of Equipment and Transport), Moctar Ahmed Yedaly (Minister of Digital Transformation, Innovation and the Modernization of the Administration) and Yahya Ould Ahmed el-Waghef (Minister of Agriculture).

7 **Burundi** Gervais Ndirakobuca, hitherto Minister of the Interior, Community Development and Public Security, was named as Prime Minister, replacing Alain-Guillaume Bunyoni. On the following day a government reorganization took place, in which Ndirakobuca's former portfolio was allocated to Martin Niteretse, while Audace Niyonzima became the new Minister of Finance, the Budget and Economic Planning.

12 **Burkina Faso** Transitional President Damiba dismissed Simporé as Minister of Defence and War Veterans and assumed his portfolio.

12 **Liberia** Minister of State for Presidential Affairs Nathaniel F. McGill announced his resignation. He was replaced in an acting capacity on 30 September by George Wesseh Blamoh.

17 **Senegal** President Macky Sall appointed Amadou Ba to the reinstated post of Prime Minister. On that day a new Council of Ministers was announced, with Amadou Moustapha Bâ named as Minister of Finance and the Budget. Aïssata Tall Sall and Antoine Félix Abdoulaye Diome remained Minister of Foreign Affairs and Senegalese Nationals Abroad and Minister of the Interior, respectively.

19 **Chad** Chérif Mahmat Zene resigned as Minister of Foreign Affairs, African Integration and Chadians Abroad.

24 **Republic of the Congo** President Gen. Denis Sassou Nguesso announced a new Council of Ministers. Among the most notable appointments were those of Jean Baptiste Ondaye as Minister of the Economy and Finance, and Jean-Claude Gakosso as Minister of Foreign Affairs, Francophone Affairs and Congolese Nationals Abroad.

25 **São Tomé and Príncipe** Legislative elections were held, at which the Acção Democrática Independente obtained 30 of the 55 seats, while the Movimento de Libertação de São Tomé e Príncipe—Partido Social Democrata took 18.

26 **Mauritania** President Ghazouani announced a minor reorganization of the Council of Ministers, appointing, *inter alia*, Brahim Vall Ould Mohamed Lemine Minister of National Education and the Reform of the Education System and Zeinabou Mint Hmednah Minister of the Civil Service and Labour.

27 **Kenya** President Ruto announced a new Cabinet, comprising 22 Cabinet Secretaries and four Cabinet-level officials. Among the notable appointments were those of Prof. Abraham Kithure Kindiki (Secretary for the Interior and National Administration), Prof. Njuguna Ndung'u (Secretary for National Treasury and Planning), Aden Bare Duale (Secretary for Defence) and Alfred Mutua (Secretary for Foreign and Diaspora Affairs).

30 **Burkina Faso** Transitional President Damiba was removed from his position by junior members of the armed forces. Their leader, Capt. Ibrahim Touré, stated that they had acted due to Damiba's inability to quell the ongoing insurgency by Islamist militants in the country. The Ouédraogo-led Transitional Government was dissolved as was the 71-member Transitional National Assembly.

PART ONE

General Survey

ECONOMIC TRENDS IN AFRICA SOUTH OF THE SAHARA

DONALD L. SPARKS

INTRODUCTION AND RECENT ECONOMIC DEVELOPMENTS

Sub-Saharan Africa faces strong economic headwinds in 2022–23, led by the impact of the Russian Federation's invasion of Ukraine in February 2022 and the continued COVID-19 pandemic. The International Monetary Fund (IMF) predicts that the region's gross domestic product (GDP) will increase by only 3.8% in 2022 and 4.0% in 2023 (see *Table 2*). This less-than-expected growth in 30 countries means that more people in the region will fall into poverty; indeed, the IMF estimated that 39m. people slipped into poverty in 2020 and 2021. This is particularly concerning for countries such as Ethiopia, Liberia, Madagascar, Niger, Sierra Leone and the Democratic Republic of the Congo (DRC), where large numbers are already at risk of hunger. Furthermore, drought in the Horn of Africa and conflict in the Sahel area exacerbate this problem. Indeed, the Secretary-General of the United Nations (UN) recently remarked after a visit to the Sahel, 'Leaders told me that, because of the war in Ukraine, on top of the other crises they face, they fear this dangerous situation could tip into catastrophe'.

Direct trade links between sub-Saharan Africa and Russia and Ukraine are relatively moderate, comprising less than 3% of the region's trade with the rest of the world. However, the conflict has had (and will continue to have) dramatic effects on commodities. The region imports some 85% of its wheat, and for several countries Russia and Ukraine are the main suppliers. Besides supply disruptions, prices have increased dramatically. In addition, Russia is a major supplier of fertilizer and natural gas (an important input for fertilizer), and reduced access will constrain agricultural output and is likely to drive food prices even higher. According to the World Bank's June 2022 *Global Economic Prospects*, '. . . prolonged disruptions to the food supply chain across the region could significantly increase poverty, hunger, and malnutrition, while persistent inflation could ignite stagflation risks and further limit policy space to support recoveries. An elevated cost of living could increase the risk of social unrest, especially in the low-income countries.'

While the human and economic costs of the COVID-19 pandemic have not been as severe as initially feared, they none the less have had important negative impacts in a number of key areas, tourism being most notable. The health effects of COVID-19 have been more acute in some countries than in others. According to the World Health Organization (WHO), at mid-2022 the number of cumulative recorded cases of COVID-19 for sub-Saharan Africa was over 8.6m., with 172,381 deaths. It should be noted, perhaps, that the region accounts for less than 2% of confirmed cases and less than 1% of deaths reported worldwide. However, because of reporting delays and poor statistical gathering in general in the region, many experts suspect that this figure under-represents the actual number of cases and deaths (for example, most people in the region die at home, not in hospitals, and many deaths are not recorded in official systems). However, WHO studies suggest that about two-thirds of the population of most sub-Saharan African countries have antibodies to COVID-19. For the vast majority of these, the antibodies have resulted from infection, as the vaccination rate is so low (as discussed below). In addition, with a median age of 19 years (compared with 43 years in Europe), many young Africans are asymptomatic. None the less, *The Economist* journal estimates that there have been between 1m. and 2.9m. excess deaths due to the pandemic. Most countries in the region have depended on the COVID-19 Vaccines Global Access (COVAX) for vaccines, as their domestic production is limited or non-existent. Furthermore, the distribution has been hindered by transportation and other logistical challenges (such as keeping the vaccines cold).

Table 1. Laboratory-confirmed COVID-19 Cases and Deaths in Sub-Saharan Africa (as of June 2022)

	2021	2022
Cases	5,356,859	8,618,824
Deaths	128,931	172,239
Case Fatality Rate (%)	2.4	2.0

Sources: World Health Organization Africa Region, *Weekly Bulletin on Outbreaks and Other Emergencies*, 2 June 2022.

Between 1961 and 1975 the region generally experienced solid economic growth (above 5% in most cases), but this was followed by two decades of stagnation in the 1980s and 1990s. However, from the early 1990s sub-Saharan Africa's economic output expanded at nearly twice the global rate until 2015. In 2015 and 2016 economic growth slowed to its lowest levels in nearly 20 years, with the region's GDP in 'real' terms, i.e. taking inflation into account, growing by 3.3% in 2015, barely above the rate of population growth, and down from 5.0% in 2014. The IMF reported that GDP increased by 3.1% in 2019, but declined by 1.7% in 2020, with a recovery in growth of 4.5% in 2021, and a projected increase of 3.8% in 2022 and 4.0% in 2023, as mentioned above (see *Table 2)*.

Table 2. Regional GDP Growth Rates (annual % change, in real terms)

	2010–18	2020	2021	2022*	2023*
Sub-Saharan Africa	4.2	−1.7	4.5	3.8	4.0
Sub-Saharan Africa, excluding Nigeria and South Africa	5.2	0.0	4.8	4.6	5.2
Oil exporting countries	3.5	−2.3	2.9	3.5	3.2
CFA Franc Zone	4.4	0.6	4.2	7.8	5.6
EAC	5.6	0.9	6.2	5.3	5.6
ECOWAS	4.7	−0.6	4.2	4.1	4.2
SACU	2.1	−6.5	5.1	2.1	1.6
SADC	3.1	−4.4	4.4	3.1	3.0

* Projections.

Source: IMF, *Regional Economic Outlook: Sub-Saharan Africa (April 2022)*.

Table 3. Sub-Saharan Africa's Fastest Growing Economies (annual real GDP % change, in market prices)

	2022
Benin	5.9
Cabo Verde	5.5
DRC	6.0
Côte d'Ivoire	5.7
The Gambia	5.6
Ghana	5.6
Kenya	5.5
Mauritius	5.9
Niger	5.2
Rwanda	6.8
Tanzania	5.3
Togo	5.0

Source: World Bank, *Global Economic Prospects*, June 2022.

There were significant differences between economic growth in individual countries and regions in 2022. A total of 12 countries were forecast to grow by more than 5% (see *Table 3*). For the largest economies, the performance was mixed. South Africa experienced its third wave of COVID-19 cases in the third quarter of 2021 and its growth slowed to less than a projected 2% by 2022 (below the rate of population growth). Nigeria's economic growth improved to an expected 3.4% in 2022, due to increases in international oil prices. However, it faced a number of short-term challenges, including low vaccination rates, inflation and heightened security risks. After five consecutive years of recession, Angola's economy was expected to grow by 3%, due to higher oil prices. However, its oil sector has experienced a number of setbacks that have limited its growth in recent years. Ethiopia's economic growth was forecast to slow to 3.8% in 2022 from 6.3%, due to the continued conflict in the north and the impact of reduced wheat imports from Ukraine.

Several countries that rely on tourism were predicted to perform well in 2022, due to their higher vaccination rates (such as Seychelles and Mauritius), while the region's fragile economies (see *Table 4*) were expected to show slight increases in growth, from an average of 4.6% in 2021 to 4.8% in 2022.

Table 4. Sub-Saharan Africa's Fragile Economies

Burundi	CAR	Chad
Comoros	Republic of the Congo	DRC
Côte d'Ivoire	Eritrea	The Gambia
Guinea	Guinea-Bissau	Liberia
Madagascar	Malawi	Mali
São Tomé and Príncipe	Sierra Leone	South Sudan
Togo	Zimbabwe	

Source: IMF, *Regional Economic Outlook: Sub-Saharan Africa*, April 2022.

Unfortunately for the region, its generally overall positive GDP growth in recent years has not correlated with poverty reduction as had been hoped. Furthermore, sub-Saharan Africa is being confronted by daunting challenges in the near term, as discussed above. The effects of the COVID-19 pandemic will be exacerbated by slower expansion in other emerging markets (especially the People's Republic of China) and Europe, as strong growth in the region has been supported by the demand (principally for mineral commodities) from these economies.

Importantly, sub-Saharan Africa has great diversities and the 49 countries of the region range significantly in terms of population, size and economic scale. Nigeria has the largest population (an estimated 216.7m. at mid-2022), and Seychelles has the smallest population, of just 99,202 (at mid-2021). The region's total population was estimated by the World Bank at 1,165.6m. in 2021, and Africa's population is growing more rapidly than that of any other region worldwide; for many African countries the population is doubling each generation, while some 42% of the region's population were under 15 years of age in 2020. Climate and topography vary greatly and include Mediterranean, tropical and semi-tropical, desert, rainforest, savannah, mountains and plains. Some sub-Saharan countries, including South Africa, the DRC, Botswana, Namibia and Zimbabwe, are relatively well endowed with natural resources, while others, for example Niger and Somalia, have few such assets.

Most Africans (some 60%) live in rural areas, although some countries are more intensively urbanized than others. Djibouti's urban population, for example, represents some 78% of the country's total, while in Burundi it accounts for only 14%. Generally, the region has a very low population density (45 people per sq km), which increases the cost of providing infrastructure and services. Namibia has the lowest density, with 3 people per sq km, and Mauritius the highest, with 623 people per sq km. GDP per head (on an international purchasing-power parity basis) in 2021 ranged from US $793 in Burundi to $29,838 in Seychelles, while the average for sub-Saharan Africa was $4,121.

Educational levels also vary greatly: nearly 100% of children in the appropriate age-group are enrolled in primary schools, although the completion rate remains at only 69%, while enrolment in secondary schools averaged 44% in 2019. The region's adult literacy rate was 66% in 2020, while the youth literacy rate was 77%, both representing the lowest levels of any region globally. In Benin, Burkina Faso, Chad, the Central African Republic (CAR), Guinea, Guinea-Bissau, Liberia, Mali, Niger, Sierra Leone, Somalia and South Sudan fewer than one-half of all adult males were able to read and write. Seychelles and Mauritius, with youth literacy rates of 99%, ranked highest, while the rate in Chad was only 31%. Expenditure on education is low, at an annual average of less than US $50 per pupil.

Life expectancy at birth was 62 years in 2020. For females it varied, from 56 years in the CAR, Chad, Nigeria and Sierra Leone to 82 years in Seychelles, with a regional average of only 64 years, some 12 years less than the world average and more than 20 years lower than in many advanced economies. For males, the data is even worse, with an average life expectancy of 60. In many countries, particularly in those most affected by HIV/AIDS, such as Eswatini and Botswana, average life expectancy has been reduced by more than 20 years since the mid-1980s.

The countries of the region do however share many common characteristics: they are, for the most part, poor and fragile. The region has been caught in a 'poverty trap' where low incomes lead to low savings, which lead to low investment and consumer demand; low investment results in lower productivity and lower demand leads to less revenue, both of which lead back to poverty. In 2021 sub-Saharan Africa accounted for just 3% of world trade and perhaps 1% of global GDP. The region is poor: according to the World Bank, its combined adjusted gross national income (GNI) at current prices was US $1,839,229m. in 2021.

Unlike other parts of the developing world, sub-Saharan Africa had more people living in poverty in 2017 (413m.) than in 1990 (278m.), despite having reduced the percentage of people living on less than $1.90 per day from 54% of the total population in 1990 to 38% in 2019. Just over one-half of the world's population living under the international poverty line resides in sub-Saharan Africa and the region is probably home to more very poor people than in the rest of the world combined. Furthermore, sub-Saharan Africa's output per head is lower than it was 30 years earlier, having declined by about 50% in some countries. It is also the only region in which child malnutrition has not been declining in recent years.

Table 5. Population Living on Less Than US $1.90 per day (2011 purchasing-power parity basis, % of total population)

	1990	2008	2013	2018
East Asia and Pacific . .	61.4	15.2	3.7	1.0
Eastern Europe and Central Asia . .	1.7	3.1	2.2	1.0
Latin America and Caribbean	16.0	7.1	4.9	3.7
Middle East and North Africa	6.2	2.7	2.3	7.0
South Asia	44.6	29.4	14.7	15.2
Sub-Saharan Africa . .	54.3	49.6	41.0	40.4
World	34.8	13.7	10.7	9.3

Source: World Bank, *World Development Indicators 2020*.

Table 6. Population Living on Less Than US $1.90 per day (2011 purchasing-power parity basis, millions)

	1990	2017
East Asia and Pacific	984	74
Eastern Europe and Central Asia .	8	10
Latin America and Caribbean . .	70	30
Middle East and North Africa . .	14	8
South Asia	506	249
Sub-Saharan Africa	278	413
World	1,865	769

Source: World Bank, *World Development Indicators 2020*.

Sub-Saharan Africa has the world's second most unequal distribution of income, after Latin America. None the less, the region is seeing an emerging middle class and the retail sector shows promising potential as consumer spending is expected to almost double over the next decade. Furthermore, surprising to many, there has been an increase in the number of millionaires and billionaires (measured in current US dollars). In 2022 Forbes listed nine billionaires in sub-Saharan Africa. South Africa and Nigeria each had five billionaires, while the richest was Aliko Dangote of Nigeria, worth US \$13,900m. In 2016 there were some 90,000 millionaires in the region, with South Africa heading the list with 40,400, followed by Nigeria with 12,300 and Kenya with 9,400. Ethiopia (with 3,100 millionaires), once thought of by many outsiders as a land of famine, has been creating millionaires at a faster rate than any other country in the region. With an economy ranked in the 10 fastest growing in the world, Ethiopia more than doubled its number of millionaires from 1,300 in 2007 to 3,100 in 2016. However, the region has the fewest 'ultra high net worth' individuals (whose assets are at least \$30m.), with 894 in 2017, compared with 3,012 in Latin America, 18,138 in China, 31,938 in Europe and 74,982 in North America.

The World Bank classifies 32 countries as 'fragile and conflict-affected' states, with 19 of these in sub-Saharan Africa. These countries are 'characterized by a legacy of severe social and political turmoil, economic instability, and in some cases, violent conflict', and their economic challenges 'are often exacerbated by socio-political, governance and security problems' (see *Table 7*).

Given this vast diversity, it is, accordingly, difficult to draw general conclusions about the continent's economic performance as a whole during any given year. Additionally, the lack of current statistics for several countries makes it difficult to provide accurate assessments of economic conditions. Nevertheless, some broad comparisons can be made: of the world's developing areas, sub-Saharan Africa has the worst record in virtually all of the most important social and economic indicators (see *Table 8*). The region has the lowest GNI per head, the lowest life expectancy at birth, the lowest youth literacy rate, the highest rate of adult HIV infection and the highest number of children not living past five years of age. Since 1971 the UN has viewed Least Developed Countries (LDCs) as a category of states that are considered to be highly disadvantaged in their development process. Of the 46 LDCs, 33 are in sub-Saharan Africa. Furthermore, of the 31 countries included within the 'low human development' category in the UN Development Programme's (UNDP) *Human Development Report 2021/2022*, 28 were in sub-Saharan Africa (not including Somalia which was not ranked, but would be in that category). Angola, Botswana, Cabo Verde, Cameroon, Congo, Eswatini, Equatorial Guinea, Ghana, Kenya, Namibia, São Tomé and Príncipe, Zambia and Zimbabwe were ranked in the 'medium human development' category, while Gabon, Seychelles and South Africa were included within the 'high' category, and only Mauritius was ranked in the 'very high' category.

The factors underlying Africa's parlous economic and social condition can be broadly categorized either as 'external' or 'internal'. The major external factors have included adverse movements in the terms of trade (including petroleum and other non-fuel commodities), low levels and low value-added of exports, declines in foreign aid and low levels of foreign investment and external shocks, like the COVID-19 pandemic and the effects of the war in Ukraine. The internal factors include small, fragmented economies, high levels of ethnic diversity, poor soils, widely fluctuating and harsh climates, widespread civil strife which often spills over borders, inadequate human and physical infrastructure, large number of landlocked states, rapid urbanization and population growth, environmental degradation, poor business climates, ineffective (and often corrupt) government and inappropriate public economic policies.

EXTERNAL TRENDS

Trade, Regional Co-operation and South-South Linkages

Sub-Saharan Africa occupies a minor role in global trade (although it is a major source of several key, strategic minerals, as will be discussed below). The region has generally imported more goods than it has exported, resulting in overall trade deficits. However, in 2014 imports were constrained and the overall trade balance moved into surplus (see *Table 9*). The balance returned to deficits in 2015, 2016 and 2017, before achieving a small surplus in 2018 and then returning to deficit in 2019.

One of the most serious of the external factors Africa faces is its inability to diversify its trade. For approximately two-thirds of the countries in the region, 60% of their exports come from only one or two products. In 13 countries, one product constitutes 75% or more of total exports. In addition, the region has generally seen declining traditional exports and increasing imports, both in terms of value and volume, although recent years have been out of step with those trends. Of total exports,

Table 7. Fragile and Conflict-Affected Countries

High-Intensity Conflict	Medium Intensity Conflict	High Institutional and Social Fragility
Somalia	Burkina Faso	Burundi
	Cameroon	Republic of the Congo
	CAR	Eritrea
	Chad	The Gambia
	DRC	Guinea-Bissau
	Mali	Liberia
	Mozambique	Sudan
	Niger	Zimbabwe
	Nigeria	
	South Sudan	

Source: World Bank.

Table 8. Social and Economic Indicators in the Developing World

	Arab States	East Asia/ Pacific	East Europe/ Central Asia	Latin America/ Caribbean	South Asia	Sub-Saharan Africa
Human Development Index value (2020)	0.70	0.74	0.79	0.76	0.64	0.54
Life expectancy (years at birth, 2020) .	72	76	77	76	70	62
Mean years of schooling (2018) . .	7.3	8.1	10.4	8.7	6.5	5.8
GNI per capita, purchasing-power parity basis (US \$, 2019) . . .	14,869	14,710	17,934	14,812	6,532	3,686
Prevalence of undernourishment, stunting (% of population under 5 years, 2017)	15.0	12.2	n.a.	9.6	35.0	34.1
Under-5 mortality rate (per 1,000 live births, 2018)	22	15	5	16	42	78
Maternal mortality rate (deaths per 1,000 births, 2017)	135	73	20	73	149	535
Youth literacy rate (% of persons aged 15–24, 2018)	90	99	100	99	89	77

Sources: IMF, *Regional Economic Outlook: Sub-Saharan Africa 2021*; UNDP, *Human Development Report 2020*; and World Bank, *World Development Indicators 2021*.

Table 9. Sub-Saharan Africa's Trade Balance (US $'000 million at current prices)

	2014	2016	2017	2018	2019
Exports . . .	344.7	239.5	287.7	327.3	241.4
Imports . . .	321.8	286.2	297.3	316.0	253.4
Trade balance .	22.9	−46.7	−9.6	11.3	−12.0

Source: World Bank, *World Integrated Trade Solution*, 2021.

raw materials continued as the most valuable export in 2019 (with 43.6% of the total), compared with 32.4% for intermediate goods. Consumer goods contributed 17.1% of the total, and capital goods 6.7% (see *Table 10*).

Table 10. Composition of Sub-Saharan Africa's Exports and Imports (US $ million, 2019)

	Exports	Imports
Raw materials	105,328	28,431
Intermediate goods . . .	78,308	52,026
Consumer goods . . .	41,207	94,927
Capital goods	16,134	69,684
Total (incl. others) . . .	241,362	253,395

Source: World Bank, *World Integrated Trade Solution*, 2021.

Most of the region's export growth has been driven by natural resources, with petroleum, ores, base metals and gold being the most important. The IMF has identified 20 'resource rich' countries in sub-Saharan Africa: eight are oil exporters (Angola, Cameroon, Chad, Congo, Equatorial Guinea, Gabon, Nigeria, and South Sudan) and 10 non-fuel mineral exporters (Botswana, the DRC, Guinea, Liberia, Mauritania, Namibia, Niger, Sierra Leone, South Africa and Zambia). Others have resource potential, including Mozambique, São Tomé and Príncipe and Uganda (oil and gas) and Malawi (uranium). It should be noted that there has often been a link between resource wealth and lack of development (the so-called 'resource curse'), increased corruption and poverty. (Nigeria with vast oil and gas resources is a prime example.) The resource rich countries recorded average GDP growth of 3.1% before the pandemic, considerably lower than the average of 5.9% experienced by the non-resource rich countries. Furthermore, as a whole they have generally not benefited; for example, they often have lower life expectancies, extreme poverty is higher and education levels are lower. However, if resources are well managed, they can have positive effects (such as Botswana with its diamond resources). A total of 50 countries (27 from sub-Saharan Africa—although Equatorial Guinea has been delisted) have signed up to the Extractive Industries Transparency Initiative (EITI), which helps to ensure that earnings are shared in a more equitable and transparent manner.

A generation ago, Brazil, Russia, India and China accounted for perhaps 1% of African trade, with the European Union (EU), the USA and Japan commercially dominant. Since 2000 the overall growth of African exports to emerging markets in the Global South (particularly China, India and Brazil) has equalled and surpassed that of shipments to developed markets (this is called 'South–South' trade). Indeed, by 2012 exports to China, India and Brazil had exceeded those to the EU. Furthermore, China is now by far the major purchaser of the region's petroleum, and total trade with that country reached US $45,548m. in 2019, some 18% of the total (see *Table 11*). About 70% of the region's exports to China are commodities (oil, metals and other minerals). A sharp slow-down in China's growth and related reduced demand will have measurable negative effects for sub-Saharan Africa. The United Kingdom's departure from the EU (Brexit) also has implications for the region. The UK will have to make new trade agreements with sub-Saharan African countries to replace those in place while it was part of the EU. Although trade with the region in the past was important to the UK, in 2018 it fell to $46,000m. (about 2% of the UK's total trade). None the less, South Africa is an important trading partner for the UK, with that country importing around 10% of South

Africa's wine exports and the UK is the second largest market for Kenya's fresh cut flowers.

Table 11. Sub-Saharan Africa's Major Trade Partners (US $'000 million, 2019)

	Exports to	Imports from
China	25,987	45,548
India	18,494	17,087
South Africa	14,765	17,303
USA	12,460	16,407
Netherlands	11,338	6,913
Germany	9,673	12,397

Source: World Bank, *World Integrated Trade Solution*, 2021.

The import policies of the Western industrialized countries have played a major, and often negative, role in Africa's export performance. In 2000 the Cotonou Agreement replaced successive Lomé Conventions between the EU and the group of African, Caribbean and Pacific (ACP) states. Under the new agreement, the preferential treatment currently in force was to be retained initially, but thereafter trade between ACP countries and the EU was to be gradually liberalized over a period of 12–15 years. A new generalized system of preferences introduced by the European Commission came into effect in 2005. The scheme offers duty-free access to the EU market for 80% of tariff lines from countries that adhere to international conventions on human rights, labour, good governance and the environment. In 2007 trade talks at the EU-Africa Summit in Lisbon, Portugal, promoted a new accord, known as the Economic Partnership Agreements (EPAs), under which bilateral agreements would phase out the remaining preferential trade pacts. In 2016 SADC was the first regional bloc to sign an EPA (Angola has an option to join in the future) and this became fully operational in February 2018. ECOWAS and UEMOA have also signed a partnership agreement. A number of other regions are currently negotiating EPAs, although some countries were resisting agreeing as they feared competition from advanced and well-established European firms and also the loss of tariff revenue. The EU has also concluded the 'Everything but Arms' agreement with many African states. Under the agreement, they are allowed to export all products, other than weapons, into the EU without having to pay tariffs. As a result, these countries do not face significant economic consequences if they choose not to join an EPA. Meanwhile, in 2004 the USA extended its Africa Growth and Opportunity Act (AGOA) which provides the 38 eligible sub-Saharan African countries with duty-free access to the US market covering some 1,800 products, although it has at various points suspended AGOA with a number of countries, including Burundi, the DRC, Eswatini, The Gambia and Rwanda, because of governance issues. The programme is due to expire in 2025.

Notwithstanding the above and the benefits of these protocols, protectionism and restrictive agricultural practices (including subsidies to farmers), particularly in the EU and (to a lesser extent) the USA, have resulted in an oversupply of some agricultural commodities, and have thus inhibited worldwide demand and weakened world prices. Tariff and non-tariff barriers to trade erected by the Western industrialized countries have discouraged value-added or semi-processed agricultural imports from African states. In addition to the decreased demand owing to protectionism from the developed nations, as their incomes increase, consumer demand for agricultural products does not advance proportionately. Industry is increasingly turning to substitutes, such as fibre optics for copper wires in telecommunications and beet sugar for cane sugar. As agricultural prices decline, Western consumers do not increase their consumption. Furthermore, even in countries that have dynamic export sectors such as Kenya (which exports cut flowers) and Lesotho (apparel), benefits for employment and diversification of their respective economies remain low. Finally, many African nations rely on import taxes as major sources of government revenues and are thus hesitant to reduce such barriers.

Although trade between African states is low, this is an improving area: the combined intra-trade of the three largest regional economic communities (RECs) grew from

US \$30,000m. in 2004 to \$102,600m. in 2014 and intra-African exports grew by 50% between 2010 and 2013, with manufacturing goods constituting nearly 40% of intra-African trade. In 2016 members of SADC had the highest proportion of intra-regional trade (around 21% of total trade is between its members, see *Table 12*).

Table 12. Share of Total Trade of African RECs (%, 2016)

	REC members	Rest of Africa	Rest of the World
SADC	21.0	2.7	76.2
EAC	11.5	10.1	78.4
ECOWAS	10.7	5.6	83.7
COMESA	7.0	9.3	83.7
CEN-SAD	7.5	4.1	88.4
IGAD	7.3	8.0	84.8

Source: UNCTAD, *Key Statistics and Trends in Regional Trade in Africa, 2019*.

Most African states produce similar products for export, generally unprocessed primary agricultural or mineral commodities, and, as most of the value-added is carried out in Western industrialized countries, there is little African demand for these products. African states themselves have often discouraged trade by their strongly inward-oriented, import-substitution development strategies, including over-valued exchange rates and protectionist trade policies. Their transport infrastructure (which is often inadequate in any event) is geared towards export to the EU, Japan and North America (and more recently towards China), rather than to nearby countries. Finally, since the landlocked countries' trade is principally with Europe, neighbouring countries are often viewed as competitive obstacles rather than potential markets.

African states have tried various methods of improving their trade performance, and of developing overall regional economic co-operation. There have been several attempts to form free trade areas or customs unions, and the New Partnership for Africa's Development (NEPAD) has adopted regional integration as one of its core objectives. In early 1997 the Organization of African Unity (OAU) inaugurated the African Economic Community, with the eventual goal of uniting the region's existing economic organizations into a single institution similar to the EU. The OAU was formally replaced by a new African Union (AU) in July 2002. In June 2015 the AU heads of state launched the proposed African Continental Free Trade Area (AfCFTA), which, when implemented, will be the world's largest free trade area by number of countries (54). As of mid-2022 35 countries had ratified the AfCFTA Agreement, thus fulfilling the requirements for the agreement to come into effect. Once in full operation the AfCFTA will eliminate tariffs on 90% of intra-regional trade flows and establish a market of 1,200m. people with a combined GDP of US \$250,000m. In addition, the pact will also reduce or eliminate many non-tariff barriers, as well as standardize the trade process through digitalization, which may prove to be more important in the long term. The abolition of tariffs on 90% of existing intra-regional trade flows (including North Africa) would increase trade by about 16%, according to the IMF. Yet it should be noted that reducing tariffs alone are not enough to significantly boost intra-regional trade. Other impediments include poor trade logistics and road infrastructure and cumbersome border customs clearance procedures. However, in another positive development, the recent Pan-African Payment and Settlement Scheme should help to reduce currency risks and facilitate regional transactions and payments.

In addition to the AfCFTA, Africa has 14 trading blocs with overlapping members. Most countries belong to at least two blocs, and many belong to three (see *Table 13*). The Southern African Customs Union (SACU), comprising Botswana, Eswatini, Lesotho, Namibia and South Africa, is the world's oldest existing customs union—it celebrated the 100th anniversary of its foundation in 2010. It is also perhaps the most successful regional organization in sub-Saharan Africa. SACU permits free trade among its members and provides a common external tariff. Customs revenue is generally collected by South Africa and allocated to individual members according to a formula based on members' share of total trade. Such revenues are often the largest source of funding for the budgets of Eswatini, Lesotho and Namibia.

Table 13. Member Countries of Major Regional Groupings in Sub-Saharan Africa

Organization	Member countries
Union Economique et Monétaire Ouest-Africaine	Benin, Burkina Faso, Côte d'Ivoire, Guinea-Bissau, Mali, Niger, Senegal and Togo
Communauté Economique et Monétaire de l'Afrique Centrale	Cameroon, CAR, Chad, Congo, Equatorial Guinea and Gabon
Common Market for East and Southern Africa	Burundi, Comoros, DRC, Djibouti, Eritrea, Eswatini, Ethiopia, Kenya, Madagascar, Malawi, Mauritius, Rwanda, Seychelles, Somalia, Sudan, Uganda, Zambia and Zimbabwe
East African Community	Burundi, Kenya, Rwanda, South Sudan, Tanzania and Uganda
Southern African Development Community	Angola, Botswana, Comoros, DRC, Eswatini, Lesotho, Madagascar, Malawi, Mauritius, Mozambique, Namibia, Seychelles, South Africa, Tanzania, Zambia and Zimbabwe
Southern African Customs Union	Botswana, Eswatini, Lesotho, Namibia and South Africa
Common Monetary Area (Rand Zone)	Eswatini, Lesotho, Namibia and South Africa
Intergovernmental Authority on Development	Djibouti, Ethiopia, Somalia, Eritrea, Sudan, South Sudan, Uganda

Source: African Union, African Development Bank and UN Economic Commission for Africa *Africa Regional Integration Report 2019*.

The two groupings which command good prospects are SADC and ECOWAS. The latter has as its eventual goal the removal of barriers to trade, employment and movement between its 15 member states, as well as the rationalization of currency and financial payments among its members. Owing to the political and economic disparity of its members, it is likely to be many years before the above objectives are fully met. SADC was established initially as the Southern African Development Co-ordination Conference (SADCC) to provide a counter, during the era of apartheid, to South Africa's economic hegemony over the region. SADCC did not initially seek an economic association or customs union, but rather to function as a subregional planning centre to rationalize development planning. Its reconstitution in 1992 as SADC placed binding obligations on member countries with the aim of promoting economic integration towards a fully developed common market. Despite SADC's desire to reduce and eventually remove trade barriers, some members have not eliminated tariffs as stipulated by the agreement, and in some cases countries that removed tariffs later reimposed them.

In 2008 three regional economic communities formed the COMESA-EAC-SADC Tripartite Free Trade Area (TFTA), with a total of 26 member states. The three RECs make up nearly one-half of the AU's membership of 55 countries, contribute more than 58% of the continent's GDP and account for around 57% of the total population of the AU.

Another important grouping, the CFA Franc Zone, was formed in 1948 and it comprises, together with France, 12 former French colonies, Equatorial Guinea (a former Spanish colony) and Guinea-Bissau (a former Portuguese possession) with a total population of 155m. people. It operates with four general principles: fixed parity exchange rates; convertibility guaranteed by the French Treasury; free movement of capital; and a central foreign exchange reserve. As the CFA franc is pegged to the euro, investors from the euro area and other countries are more likely to invest in the Franc Zone, since they are protected against exchange rate risks. Excluding France, each of the Zone's members are small states, none with a population exceeding 24m., and most are poor. A few, such as

Cameroon, Congo, Equatorial Guinea and Gabon, are heavily reliant on petroleum export revenues. In May 2019 France announced that the UEOMA Franc Zone agreement was being ended (with no changes to CEMAC). Plans were announced to adopt a new regional currency, the eco, which will remain pegged to the value of the euro, although there will be no requirement to keep 50% of the group's reserve with the Bank of France.

The other currency area is the Common Monetary Area (known as the Rand Zone), comprising Eswatini, Lesotho, Namibia and South Africa. All the members peg their currencies at par value to the South African Rand. Countries in a monetary area receive benefits as well as face costs. For example, a fixed exchange rate can reduce transaction costs and ensure stability (at least in the short term). On the other hand, member countries lose control over their monetary policies, and cannot allow their currencies to devaluate individually, thus at times making their exports relatively more expensive and thus less competitive.

Foreign Debt, Aid and Foreign Investment

Three of the most obvious manifestations of external difficulties are foreign debt, fluctuating levels of international aid and the problem of attracting outside investment. In 2010 sub-Saharan Africa's level of official (non-concessional) external debt amounted to US $278,450m., compared with $198,900m. in 2009 and $216,250m. in 2005. Nevertheless, in 2013 total external debt was equivalent to 28.5% of GDP, which compared favourably with other developing regions. The ratio of public debt to GDP has increased, on average, by some 10% since 2014 to reach an average of 42% (and a median of 51%) of GDP in 2016. This is the highest percentage since many countries received debt relief in the 2000s under the Initiative for Heavily Indebted Poor Countries (HIPC) and the Multilateral Debt Relief Initiative (MDRI). Indeed, according to the World Bank, by 2021 over 60% of countries in the region were in or at high risk of debt distress. This was largely due to fiscal imbalances and increased indebtedness (and higher repayment costs resulting from the US dollar's appreciation) caused by the COVID-19 pandemic.

In 2018 government debt-to-GDP ratios rose to 60% in one-third of the countries in the region. Largely as a consequence of the COVID-19 pandemic, the region's public debt increased to almost 58% of GDP by 2020, the highest level in 20 years and a 6% increase over the previous year. Its ratio of debt service to exports increased from 16.1% in 2019 to 21% in 2020. In 2020 external debt as a percentage of exports was 202.9%, compared with 154.5% in 2019, and the region's long-term external debt stood at US $702,407.5m.

It should be noted that the composition of public debt has changed over the past few years. Countries have recently been relying on domestic bank and non-bank financing, much of it on commercial terms (with interest rates still at almost historic lows). As official development assistance (ODA) has declined for many countries, they have turned to non-concessional sources for funding. Non-concessional debt now accounts for more than one-half of the total public debt in many countries (for example, Côte d'Ivoire, Ghana, Congo, Sudan, Zambia and Zimbabwe). In recent years higher-cost private debt has begun to supplement loans from official sources such as the international financial institutions (the World Bank and the IMF). However, almost one-half of public debt is financed in foreign currencies (mostly US dollars), making it sensitive to foreign exchange fluctuations and recently more expensive to finance given the US dollar's appreciation. In addition, countries adversely affected by commodity price declines have become unable to service their debts.

The majority of the world's 'most debt-distressed countries' are in sub-Saharan Africa, and in May 2022 14 regional states were classified as being at high risk of debt distress: Burundi, Cameroon, Cabo Verde, the CAR, the Comoros, Djibouti, Ethiopia, Gambia, Ghana, Guinea-Bissau, Kenya, Malawi, Sierra Leone, South Sudan, Zambia and Zimbabwe. Furthermore, Chad, the DRC, Mozambique, São Tomé and Príncipe Somalia and Zimbabwe were classified as being in high distress.

The Group of 20 (G20) Debt Service Suspension Initiative has provided some relief for countries suffering from the COVID-19 pandemic, by temporarily deferring debt payments (but without reducing the total debt levels). Participating countries have saved an estimated US $5,500m. Furthermore, Chad, Ethiopia and Zambia have applied for debt restructuring under the group's Common Framework agreement, although all countries have had difficulty producing tangible results. In addition, the IMF in 2021 allocated US $23,000m. of special drawing rights (SDR) funds to 22 countries in the region. So far, a number of countries (including Chad, Gambia, Niger, Rwanda and Sierra Leone) have used some of their SDR funding for essential pandemic-related needs. The region's poorest countries received debt service relief through the Catastrophic Containment and Relief Trust which ended in April 2022. The G20 has pledged $100,000m. for vulnerable countries in the region.

The region's debt service paid to official bilateral creditor nations in 2019 was US $34,133m. During the past two decades there has been a continuing debate on how best to reduce poor countries' debt burdens and how to fund such reductions. In 1996 the World Bank and the IMF launched the HIPC to help ensure that 40 of the world's poorest countries could reduce their debts to 'sustainable levels'. The HIPC Initiative was supplemented in 2005 by the MDRI, which allows for 100% relief on eligible debts by the IMF, the World Bank and the African Development Fund. The HIPC guidelines required a candidate country to complete a three-year reform programme, following which the country was then permitted a further three years to carry out additional adjustments to obtain the actual debt reductions. Both the World Bank and the IMF are working on a major debt forgiveness programme in light of the COVID-19 pandemic and on 1 May 2020 announced the start of debt payment suspension for recipients of the International Development Association (IDA) of the World Bank. In addition, in March the World Bank created a $14,000m. fast-track facility with 25 project grants to assist 10 countries in the region.

Many countries in the region have been some of the largest recipients of aid, which has, in many cases, been equivalent to 10%–20% of GDP, and sometimes higher. The largest recipient of bilateral aid in 2017 was Ethiopia, which received US $2,172m., although it should be noted that only Ethiopia was in the top 10 recipients worldwide of ODA in 2017 and sub-Saharan Africa accounted for just 22% of worldwide ODA. Total ODA receipts to the region amounted to $46,766m. in 2017, rising slightly to $47,843m. in 2018, before increasing more significantly to $52,630 in 2019. (see *Table 14*).

Table 14. Sub-Saharan Africa's Net ODA Receipts (US $ million)

2015	2016	2017	2018	2019
42,840	41,830	46,766	47,843	52,630

Source: OECD, *Statistics on Resource Flows to Developing Countries 2022*.

The composition of ODA has also changed in recent years: less is now targeted for long-term economic development and a greater proportion is being devoted to short-term emergency food aid and peacekeeping activities. By 2019 the sub-Saharan region's major bilateral donors were the USA (US $9,235m.), Germany ($3,290m.), the United Kingdom ($3,276m.) France ($2,426m.) and Japan ($1,309m.). The European Development Fund entered into force in 2015 and was endowed with €30,500m. for the period 2014–20. EU institutions provided $5,174m. in ODA in 2019 while the IDA contributed $10,841m.

It is a widely held view among economists that foreign aid is effective in stimulating growth in countries with sound macroeconomic environments, but it can be unproductive and detrimental in countries with weak policy environments. Also, many states have become 'aid dependent'. Sub-Saharan Africa's per head ODA totalled US $50 in 2019, the second highest among the developing world after the Middle East and North Africa (at $64 per head). Aid is often given for political reasons and includes construction of physical projects, such as roads and dams, with little provided for recurrent costs. Additionally, these projects are generally carried out in an uncoordinated way, funded by multiple donor agencies.

Remittances from expatriates are also important for the region, having reached US $47,959m. in 2019 but declined to $42,428m. in 2020. The decline has been caused by a combination of factors (notably, of course, the COVID-19 pandemic) in key destinations where African migrants reside, including the EU, the USA, the Middle East and China. These large economies host a large share of sub-Saharan African migrants and are a source of nearly one-quarter of total remittances sent to the region.

Sub-Saharan Africa accounts for a modest 2% of global foreign direct investment (FDI), attracting US $30,148m. in 2020, down slightly from $31,759m. in 2019. Most of this is from private capital, both direct and portfolio investments. FDI can bring many benefits to developing countries, and a lack of capital can be, and has been, a major impediment to development. FDI contributes to capital formation, human capital development, technology transfer, increased managerial skills and market expansion. Generally, there is a strong correlation between higher FDI and economic growth. Since the late 1980s increased levels of FDI to developing countries have generated more intense competition for new FDI. Negotiations between host countries and potential investors generally produce an outcome more favourable to the investor, as the host country does not want to lose the deal, and often provides substantial incentives, including 'tax holidays' or lower taxes, direct subsidies and other arrangements (sometimes referred to as a 'race to the bottom'). In any event, until very recently sub-Saharan Africa had a poor record of attracting such investment. According to the 2021 *EY Africa Attractiveness Report*, in 2020 the largest recipients of FDI were Nigeria ($6,600m.), South Africa ($3,800m.) and Angola ($3,100m.). Other significant (greater than $1,000m.) FDI destinations included Ghana, Angola and Congo. However, levels were already experiencing a decline and UNCTAD stated in mid-2020 that this would be exacerbated by the dual shock of the COVID-19 pandemic and low prices of many commodities.

Traditionally over one-half of FDI to the region has come from the UK (the largest single investor), France, the Netherlands, South Africa and the USA. However, in recent years China had become the region's major investor: China's FDI surged from US $75m. in 2003 to $5,400m. in 2018 and most of that investment has been in the oil producing states of Nigeria and Sudan, or in South Africa and Zambia. None the less, according to the 2021 *EY Africa Attractiveness Report*, France and the USA were the largest investors (measured by FDI projects) in 2019–20, overtaking China.

While foreign investors are attracted by the region's vast raw materials, potential high returns and low-wage economies, they are fearful of internal political volatility and the uncertainty of securing the enforcement of commercial contracts. These considerations, combined with the deteriorating human and physical infrastructure, significantly diminished investor confidence. Investor perception is of major importance. Investors appeared more confident about improvements in tariffs, the rule of law and access to financing. Increased investment in recent years has arisen partly because governments have worked hard to make life easier for investors.

A further major problem is that African capital flight is huge. An estimated US $1,200,000m. of illicit financial flows fled the region between 1980 and 2009, roughly equal to the region's current economic output. Such flows are generated from tax evasion, bribes, money laundering and transactions from cross-border smuggling. Added to this capital flight is a large 'brain drain' of skilled human resources due to the lack of suitable jobs at home (or to a variety of other reasons, including personal security). Significantly, the attraction of the industrial countries is likely to grow, and health care is but one illustration of the severe problems caused when the very skilled people trained and needed to develop a country leave for better opportunities. On the positive side, however, there are signs of increasing numbers of professional Africans returning home (a 'reverse brain drain'). Finally, a recent UN report estimated that Africans hold as much as 40% of their financial portfolios outside Africa. If these funds returned, the region would increase its capital stock by about two-thirds.

South Africa was in 1995 the first country of the region' to issue sovereign bonds, also known as Eurobonds (although a few countries are denominating these bonds in local currencies). In 2006 Seychelles became the second sub-Saharan African country to join the Eurobond market. By 2021 some 21 countries in the region had issued bonds with a total value of over US $155,000m. These bonds are attractive because their yields are much higher (because of the high risk) than those found in safer, more traditional markets of the advanced economies. However, the potential negative to this trend is that should the economies stall, the countries will be hard pressed to service the bonds, and this is likely to be the case in the coming years, especially given the budgetary constraints posed by the COVID-19 pandemic. In 2021 the credit rating agency Fitch Ratings estimated that such wealth funds contracted by 2.1% in 2020, although it forecast growth to resume in 2021 to 4%. It has downgraded seven of the 19 rated sovereign wealth funds.

INTERNAL TRENDS

Africa also faces a number of 'internal' economic problems, which, in the view of many analysts, outweigh the 'external' factors discussed above. Many countries in sub-Saharan Africa are still suffering from a crisis of statehood and a crisis of capability. An urgent priority is to rebuild state effectiveness through an overhaul of public institutions, the resurrection of the rule of law, and credible checks on abuse of state power. Indeed, as far back as 1989 a World Bank study on sub-Saharan Africa's quest for sustainable growth suggested that 'underlying the litany of Africa's problems is 'a crisis of governance'. This, unfortunately, is still the case in all too many countries.

Governance, Parastatal Organizations, the Business Environment and the Informal Sector

In sub-Saharan Africa most of the post-independence parastatal organizations operated in natural monopoly areas: large infrastructure projects (highways, railways and dams) and social service facilities (schools, hospitals and medical clinics). Government soon moved into areas that had previously been dominated by the private sector (or, at least, traditionally dominated by the colonial sector in most 'mixed' economies), and parastatal bodies accounted for more than one-third of employment in many countries. However, most analysts generally considered parastatal organizations to have failed, at least in terms of economic efficiency criteria. After independence most African countries expanded the size of their civil service more rapidly than their economic growth justified. This expansion was designed to provide employment, but civil servants received lower and lower real wages, and many governments became bloated and corrupt. For most states the need for better governance became critical and many governments have scaled back the role of parastatals in recent years. Related to better governance is fiscal discipline: putting government debt on a sustainable track. In many cases government revenue projections are overly optimistic and spending levels unrealistic. The result has too often been large and unstainable budget deficits. Reforms have helped but the African Development Bank (AfDB) lists several remaining challenges: weak tax and customs administrations; lack of transparency; low taxpayer morale; and hard to tax sectors (e.g. the informal sector, see below).

The general perception is that the region has not developed an appropriate enabling environment for the private sector to grow and flourish. Indeed, it lags behind other regions in providing a quality business environment, although that is changing. The World Bank's 2020 *Doing Business* report cited a record number of reforms (107), making it easier to do business. (The Bank has subsequently suspended publication of this report, due to charges of impropriety in research methodology). However, compared to the previous year, sub-Saharan African economies raised their average ease of doing business score by just one percentage point. Mauritius was ranked 13th on the Bank's list of the easiest places to do business, just ahead of Australia, while Rwanda (at 38th place) was the next highest African country. Indeed, Rwanda, which 25 years ago experienced a brutal genocide, was considered friendlier to investors than the Netherlands. None the less, of the 40 countries (out of a total of 190) that ranked as the hardest in which to conduct business, 22 were in sub-Saharan Africa.

The World Economic Forum's *2019 Global Competitiveness Report* ranked sub-Saharan Africa as the world's least competitive region. Mauritius was ranked as the most competitive country in the region (52nd out of 141 countries worldwide). Of the 30 countries ranked at the bottom of the list, 28 were from sub-Saharan Africa. South Africa, the second most competitive in the region, moved to 60th position, while Namibia (94th), Rwanda (100th), Uganda (115th) and Guinea (122nd) made significant improvements. Kenya (95th) and Nigeria (116th) also improved their performances. It should be noted that of the 25 countries that have improved their health pillar score by two points or more, 14 are from sub-Saharan Africa, making strides to close the gaps in longer life expectancy. The *Global Competitiveness Report Special Edition 2020* changed its ranking methodology and provided eleven major policy areas of 'transformation readiness'. The only category where a country from sub-Saharan Africa ranked highly was 'shift to more progressive taxation. rethinking how corporations. wealth and labour are taxed. nationally and in an international cooperative framework'. In that category South Africa was the highest ranked.

Registering property is difficult and costly (although it is becoming faster), and in addition to the delays owing to excessive bureaucracy, there are often further delays caused by poor infrastructure, as discussed below. Many countries in the region also ranked poorly in Transparency International's *Corruption Perceptions Index*; in 2021 only four countries—Seychelles (23rd), Cabo Verde (39th), Botswana (45th) and Mauritius (49th)—ranked in the top 50 least corrupt countries worldwide. Of the 20 countries listed as most corrupt, 11 were from sub-Saharan Africa.

The informal sector accounts for nearly 90% of non-agricultural employment and accounts for 40% of official GDP. Many small firms see no advantage in joining the formal sector. For example, formal employment usually entails taxation and rigid employment contracts making the recruitment and dismissal of employees difficult. The majority of workers in the informal sector lack income security and employment benefits while life expectancy is lower and poverty higher than for those working in the formal sector. Most informal sector workers (and their families) will not have adequate access to health care during the COVID-19 pandemic.

Many business owners have poor proof of title, and without adequate property rights and contract enforcement, lenders are hesitant to extend credit. While the types of activities carried out in the informal sector existed prior to colonialism, independence brought in the distinction between informal and formal activities, as countries around the region sought to formalize or 'modernize' their economies. The focus then (and indeed to some degree today) was rapid industrialization. Although the informal sector has declined in a few countries (e.g., Botswana, Ethiopia, Malawi, Rwanda and Tanzania), for much of the region it is the informal sector, not the formal sector that is the growth engine. Thus, how governments treat the informal sector has profound impacts on employment, growth, equity and sustainability.

Agriculture and the Urban Bias

Sub-Saharan Africa possesses perhaps one-half of the world's uncultivated land surface and the growth potential in the sector is enormous. According to the World Bank, 'in sub-Saharan Africa, growth in agriculture and services is more effective at reducing poverty than growth in industry'. Unfortunately, a leading factor behind the declines in African economies and the high levels of malnutrition has been the poor performance of agriculture. This sector basically comprises two components: food production for local consumption (often at the subsistence level), and export commodities. Indeed, 90% of the region's agricultural output is produced by smallholders on farms averaging 2.5 ha in size. Agriculture (including forestry and fishing) accounted for only 17.2% of GDP for the region as a whole in 2021, according to the World Bank, but provided 53% of total employment in 2019. Agricultural labour productivity

is quite low, and failure to transform agriculture has resulted in millions of rural Africans being trapped in a cycle of under-employment, underproduction, low incomes and chronic poverty. Access to land (particularly by women, who produce up to 80% of all basic food products) remains a large problem, and insecure land tenure rights prevent farmers from investing in new technology which would increase output. Agricultural productivity is the lowest in the world: value-added per worker in 2010 was US $322 compared with the world average of $992. Nevertheless, agriculture was projected to become an industry worth $1,000,000m. by 2030, up from $313,000m. in 2010.

For virtually all African economies the major agricultural exports consist of one, or perhaps two or three, primary products (cash crops such as coffee, cocoa, tea, sugar and sisal), the prices of which fluctuate widely from year to year on the world market. The region also produces large amounts of domestic food crops, which are generally not as important for export (see Table 15)

Table 15. Major Cash Crops (% of world production, 2019)

Yams	97
Cassava	63
Plantains	64
Sorghum	49
Sweet potatoes	30
Maize	7
Sugar cane	5
Rice	5
Wheat	5

Source: USDA, *Foreign Agriculture Service*, 2021.

Unfortunately, Africa's share of world agricultural exports has declined since the 1970s. Food import costs have increased dramatically, from US $5,433m. in 1980 to $8,352m. in 2000, and averaged some $40,000m. per year by the late 2000s. Commodity prices enjoyed considerable increases prior to the 2008 crash, and indeed for some years after. However, that boom has now ended. The value of many exports (including oil, gold and coffee) declined between 2014 and 2016. While prices of oil and metals recovered in 2016 and 2017, they fell dramatically in 2019. Indeed, as noted earlier, oil prices were at historic lows in mid-2020 although they had recovered to pre-2019 price levels by mid-2021.

Food security remains a serious issue for much of the region. Sub-Saharan Africa is the world's most vulnerable area to food insecurity, and acute famine still persists in the region. On average, food imports account for some 20% of total imports in the region, almost twice as high as in other developing markets. Sub-Saharan Africa has the largest number of food insecure people, and highest share of any region—about 22% of the population was food insecure in 2019. While food security is expected to improve by 2029, according to the United States Department of Agriculture's Economic Research Service, the region will still account for over 70% (287m. people) of the food insecure people in the developing world.

While grain production is projected to grow at a little over 2% per year over the next 10 years (through increased productivity and area expansion), this is slower than the increase in demand for grains, which usually increases with rising population and higher incomes. One-half of the calories consumed come from grains that are generally rain-fed and thus highly vulnerable to climatic change, which is likely to intensify. Smallholders, who typically grow only one or two crops, are subject to various shocks, including weather and declining commodity prices, and even a modest decline in harvests can be devastating for household food security. Since a large share of family income is spent on food, poor households are vulnerable to food price increases and recent rises due to supply interruption, especially of wheat from Russia and Ukraine, have already had a serious impact, as noted above.

Famine can result from several factors, although production failures are perhaps the most common cause. Since 2000 there have been four severe famines—in Ethiopia (in 2000), Malawi (2002), Niger (2005), and in Somalia and Ethiopia (in 2011–12), affecting some 10m. people. In 2015–16 the El Niño drought severely affected large areas in East and Southern Africa. The

2020 locust infestation in East Africa as well as the consequences of the COVID-19 pandemic will only exacerbate the problem. Another factor can be classified as a response failure by governments and the international community, and can include indifference by governments that, in any event, have a limited capacity to deliver basic services. In addition, many governments have reduced agricultural extension and research services as part of structural adjustments. Finally, poor roads make it difficult for farmers to get their crops to market, and, during times of famine, present obstacles to the effective distribution of emergency food aid. Few governments have robust early warning systems, or food buffer stocks.

Until quite recently, many governments implemented economic policies that were designed to keep urban wages and living conditions high and farm prices low by maintaining the value of currencies at high, unrealistic rates of exchange. This is understandable and obvious: political power in Africa rests in the city, not in the village or countryside. This 'urban bias' was sometimes a deliberate strategy, at other times more a result of planned rural neglect, and on many occasions was endorsed by the international development community.

In addition to this 'urban bias', producers were often bound by prices fixed by their governments, and at times these 'producer' prices failed to cover input costs. This resulted in farmers reducing their production for sale and reverting to subsistence agriculture. It should be noted that investment in agriculture has traditionally been low. For example, agriculture typically receives less than 10% of public spending. Also, as much as three-quarters of the region's farmland has become degraded owing to erosion and other results of population pressures, resulting, for example, in grain yields stagnating at one metric ton per ha, compared with the world average of about three tons per ha. Productivity growth will require a number of changes, and improvements in soil fertility, improved seeds and water and pest management have been long overdue.

CIVIL STRIFE

Social and political stability are generally associated with higher economic growth rates. Since independence, more than one-half of sub-Saharan African countries have been caught up in civil wars, uprisings, mass migrations and famine. It has been suggested that the typical civil war in the region has lasted about seven years and caused GDP to decline by more than 2% for each year of strife. Furthermore, it typically takes a country about 14 years after the end of the conflict to recover to its pre-war growth levels, resulting in long lasting social damage. Many post-conflict governments continue to spend heavily on their military, thus reducing the potential peace dividend. Conflicts can be both a cause and consequence of poverty and some observers have termed this the 'conflict trap'. The IMF suggest that these conflicts can arise from weak political systems, inter-community tensions, poor governance and country-specific triggers such as election tensions. In 2019 there were approximately 18m. displaced persons in the region.

Although the intensity of conflict is now lower than during the 1990s, strife continues to plague many areas of the region, with conflicts sometimes involving neighbouring countries and thus inhibiting economic growth for the entire subregion. Conflict tends to reduce the tax base while at the same time increasing government expenditure, to the detriment of much-needed social services. Between 2020 and early 2022 the military took control in Burkina Faso, Chad, Guinea and Mali, and coups were attempted in Guinea-Bissau and Niger. Moreover, 'traditional' wars have been replaced by non-state based conflicts. For example, the militant Islamist group Boko Haram has continued its activities in Nigeria and neighbouring countries, although at a lower level than a few years ago. Other countries with elevated security concerns include Burkina Faso, Cameroon, the CAR, Chad, Ethiopia, Mali and Mozambique.

HEALTH, POPULATION, EDUCATION, THE NATURAL ENVIRONMENT AND CLIMATE CHANGE

Life expectancy in the region was 62 years in 2020, falling well below the 80 years in the advanced economies. Perhaps the leading factor causing this is inadequate heath care: virtually all African states face significant problems in providing health services (especially during the COVID-19 pandemic), and the region's total health expenditure was 5.0% of its GDP in 2019 (compared with a world average of 9.8%). This expenditure has been unevenly distributed among countries: for example, in 2018, according to the World Bank, Congo spent the least on health care as a percentage of its GDP (2.1%), while Sierra Leone spent the greatest proportion (16.6%). Moreover, care was unevenly distributed throughout many countries, with most health facilities concentrated in urban areas. In 2016 Seychelles led the region with 1 physician per 1,000 people, contrasted with the region's average of 0.3.

The COVID-19 pandemic dramatically illustrated the lack of health care infrastructure. According to WHO, there are some 2,000 working ventilators in the region (compared to more than 170,000 in the USA). WHO also noted the shortage of intensive care hospital beds: with an estimated five beds per 1m. people, compared to about 4,000 beds per 1m. in Europe.

Vaccination rates in the region continue to lag behind other developing areas of the world. Indeed, by May 2022 only 15% of the region's population had been fully vaccinated, compared with an average of over 60% in other developing countries. In some of the most populous countries, such as the DRC and Nigeria, less than 10% have been fully vaccinated. Furthermore, the cost of vaccinating 60% of the population is equivalent to about a 50% increase in their health spending. Most countries in the region have depended on COVAX (as discussed earlier) to obtain much-needed vaccines. This is a pooled procurement initiative that can charge as little as US $2 per dose for low-income countries. The AU has launched its own initiative, the African Vaccine Acquisition Task Team, to provide some 1,100m. doses. In addition, a handful of vaccine production facilities have been set up in Ghana, Rwanda, Senegal and South Africa. None the less, major logistical constraints are massive, including storage, delivery and adequate health care personnel. The Omicron variant of COVID-19 that hit the region at the end of 2021 caused confirmed cases to rise rapidly, reaching the highest level since the pandemic began.

Regulations under the 1995 TRIPS agreement and the 2001 Doha Declaration allow governments to compel drug developers to license critical medicines, such as the various COVID-19 vaccines, at competitive market rates, as has been the case for HIV medications. The World Health Assembly has appealed for 'a global guarantee which ensures that, when a safe and effective vaccine is developed, it is produced rapidly at scale and made available for all people, in all countries, free of charge. The same applies for all treatments, diagnostics, and other technologies for COVID-19'. However, even if a multilateral approach is adopted, there is no mechanism to guide how vaccines will be distributed or who will get first access. While several countries are supportive (including the USA), it is unclear if such intellectual property relaxation would speed up vaccination delivery on the ground.

Less than one-third of the region's population has access to adequate sanitation, and in some nations this is as low as 8%–15%. Proper hygiene is one of the most effective ways to prevent the spread of disease, and this became even more evident during the COVID-19 pandemic. The United Nations University notes that no country in the region has achieved what it classifies as the highest level of national water security. That study suggests the 10 indicators of water security are access to drinking water, sanitation and hygiene facilities, per capita water availability, water use efficiency, water infrastructure and governance, wastewater treatment, disaster risk and water dependency on neighbouring countries. Niger, Chad and Somalia are the least water secure in the region.

The UN's Sustainable Development Goals (SDGs) are monitoring the percentage of people who have facilities to wash their hands at home with soap and water and recent related studies indicate that access to water and soap for handwashing

Economic Trends in Africa South of the Sahara

varies immensely in the 70 countries with data available: in Seychelles 100% of the population have access to sanitation, while only 20% do in Chad and Ethiopia. About 40% of the region's population lack sanitation. In 2015 68% of the total sub-Saharan African population had access to clean water (compared to 47% in 1990), and among the urban population the figure is 87%. Significantly, some 80% of illness in Africa's LDCs can be associated with inadequate water supplies or poor sanitation. Indeed, every day, about 500 children in sub-Saharan Africa die due to diarrheal diseases. Urban sanitation access ranges from a high of 89% of the population in Angola's cities, to 20% in Ghana with the region's average at 30% (up from 24% in 1990).

HIV/AIDS is a major public health and economic development concern and cause of death in many parts of sub-Saharan Africa. Although the continent is home to only about 15% of the world's population, sub-Saharan Africans alone accounted for an estimated 70% of all people living with HIV and 70% of all AIDS deaths in 2011, and by 2012 some 70% of new infections. Indeed, by 2013 of the 1.5m. AIDS-related deaths worldwide, 1.2m. were in sub-Saharan Africa. The majority of HIV/AIDS is concentrated in eastern and southern Africa, where some 20.6m. people were infected in 2020, while central and western Africa had 4.7m. cases (see *Table 16*).

Table 16. Regional HIV/AIDS Treatment Coverage (2020)

	East and Southern Africa	West and Central Africa
Pregnant women accessing ARVs (%)	95	56
Adults (aged 15 and over) living with HIV accessing ARVs	78	77
Children (aged 0–14) living with HIV accessing ARVs (%)	57	35
People living with HIV accessing ARVs (%) . .	77	73
Number of people living with HIV (million)	20.6	4.7

Source: UNAIDS, *Fact Sheet 2020*.

HIV/AIDS, malaria and deaths from conflicts have contributed to a decline in life expectancy in several states, particularly those hardest hit in southern Africa. The region saw a dramatic drop in life expectancy around 1990, which coincided with the rise of HIV/AIDS. In Botswana life expectancy fell by a decade and in Eswatini it fell by two decades. However, since the early 2000s, as progress has been made on tackling HIV, life expectancy has been rising again, although it is only now approaching the levels reached prior to the HIV pandemic. While this has slowed dramatically in the region (the death rate fell by 39% between 2005 and 2013), HIV/AIDS remains a threatening health problem in many countries, and more than 20m. Africans have died from the disease.

AIDS in Africa generally affects young adults (aged 20–45 years) in their most economically productive years, and in Africa the educated, urban elite have been hardest hit. The number of HIV positive people in Africa receiving anti-retroviral therapy rose from 1m. to 7.1m. between 2005 and 2012. By the end of 2017 15.3m. people living with HIV/AIDS in the region had access to life-saving anti-retroviral drugs (ARVs), representing 70% of the 21.7m. people accessing ARVs globally, according to WHO. In eastern and southern Africa, 95% of pregnant women had access to ARVs in 2020, while in central and western Africa only 56% did (see *Table 16*).

The International Partnership Against AIDS in Africa was launched in 1999, with the participation of African governments, the UN, international donors, and the private and community sectors. The Partnership has campaigned for, and 10 states have received, access to lower-cost generic drugs to fight HIV/AIDS and South Africa has successfully negotiated agreements with pharmaceutical companies to produce drugs domestically. In 2000 the USA agreed to allow African states to develop generic AIDS vaccines without regard to US patent protections and the drastic fall in prices mentioned above has subsequently enabled treatment expansion.

Although HIV/AIDS and COVID-19 attract most of the attention, approximately 11% of disease-induced deaths in Africa are caused by malaria, and malaria will probably kill more people than COVID-19 in sub-Saharan Africa this year, according to WHO. The region accounts for 93% of malaria cases and 94% of the 405,000 malaria deaths annually (mostly children) worldwide. A child dies every minute from malaria in sub-Saharan Africa. Some researchers believe that had malaria been eradicated 30 years ago, the region's GDP would now be one-third higher than it is, and the World Bank estimates that malaria takes US $12,000m. of Africa's GDP every year. However, there are promising signs with a new antimalarial drug being developed in Kenya. None the less, WHO's *World Malaria Report 2020* stated that the success in controlling the disease over the past 20 years had been delayed, with the COVID-19 pandemic diverting resources such as insecticide-treated mosquito nets, diagnostics and medicines. In addition, a warmer climate will likely make malaria more deadly.

African trypanosomiasis (sleeping sickness), which had been virtually eradicated in the early 1960s, reappeared in 1970 and is now widespread, occurring in 36 sub-Saharan African countries. Owing to a lack of screening and treatment, and regional conflict, this disease has become the greatest cause of mortality in areas of South Sudan, Angola and the DRC. None the less, there have been some successful attempts to combat disease in the region. For example, onchocerciasis (river blindness) has been virtually eliminated in West Africa; WHO estimated that its programme for the control of the disease (concluded in 2002) prevented 600,000 new cases and only 977 cases were recorded in 2018.

African countries have some of the highest annual average population growth rates in the world, with a regional average of 2.7% in 2019. Most of sub-Saharan Africa is undergoing a demographic transition, owing to declining infant mortality and fertility rates. Sub-Saharan Africa's population, numbering 1,165.6m. in 2021 (according to the World Bank), is projected to rise to 2,000m. by 2050 and to 3,700m. by 2100. By 2035 the number of sub-Saharan Africans reaching working age (15–64), currently at about 14% of the world total, will exceed that of the rest of the world combined. Sub-Saharan Africa's share of the global labour force is thus projected to increase from 10% in 2010 to 37% by 2100. Indeed, the region will need to create jobs at an extraordinary rate, about 20m. per year until 2035, in order to absorb the growing labour force. While the demographic transition may ensure the labour supply side of growth, a more diversified and robust economy means that labour demand is needed to turn the transition into a 'demographic dividend'. Many parts of Africa could enjoy the benefits of the 'youth bulge' (as happened in many countries in East and South Asia). However, failure to seize the opportunity is likely to result in even greater numbers of unemployed people along with increasingly negative social and economic consequences.

The demographic changes are projected to vary across sub-Saharan Africa. The biggest increase in population will occur in the eastern and western areas, while population growth will remain largely flat in the southern subregion, reflecting the demographic transitions of its largest economy, South Africa. Nigeria is expected to have the largest increase in population. As the African population grows in size, it will also alter in shape: the median age now is 20 years, compared with 30 in Asia and 40 in Europe. Africa's dependency ratio (the ratio of working-age population to dependants) is close to 1:1, compared with East Asia's ratio of 2:1.

Most African countries have family planning programmes, and some have set targets for population growth. Stemming rapid population growth in Africa is difficult because of social as well as economic factors. Most Africans live in rural areas on farms and require large numbers of helpers. The cheapest way of obtaining such assistance is for a farmer to have more children. Owing to the high infant mortality rate (resulting from poor health and nutrition), rural couples tend to want, and have, more babies. Additionally, most African countries do not have organized old-age support schemes, and children are often viewed as potential providers of support for the elderly.

However, Africa now seems to be on the path toward smaller families that has occurred in much of the world, although at a very slow rate. One important success is the recent huge decline in child mortality (the number of deaths of children under five per 1,000 live births). Indeed, the rates of decline in African child mortality are the highest in the world in the past 30 years. None the less, while the under five years old mortality rate of 180 per 1,000 live births in 1990 declined to 73 in 2020, this is still the world's highest and remains almost double the world average.

There has been a direct link between education and growth—between 1960 and 1980 the African countries that had higher percentages of children enrolled in primary school also had higher economic growth rates. Low primary school enrolment hampers economic development. The percentage of malnourished children rose from 31% in 1992 to 35% in 2015, the only region in the world to witness such an increase: children who do not have enough to eat perform poorly in school. A further key factor is that of increased education for women, which is clearly associated with lower fertility rates. A study by the World Bank found that the three countries with declining fertility—Botswana, Kenya and Zimbabwe—had the highest levels of female schooling and the lowest rates of child mortality. The study also indicated that in the Sahel, where female schooling rates are lowest, both fertility rates and child mortality have remained high.

Shortly after independence most countries of the sub-Saharan region initiated programmes aimed at establishing universal primary education. Nearly 100% of children in the appropriate age-group are enrolled in primary schools (compared with 79% in 1999), while 44% were enrolled in secondary schools in 2020. Access to tertiary education, while increasing in recent years, still remains the lowest in the world, with only 9% of the relevant aged population enrolled in 2019. And while the gender gap in education has narrowed (especially in primary schools) in many countries, there are areas where fewer than three girls are enrolled in secondary education for every four boys. The COVID-19 lockdowns prevented many children from attending school. Indeed, the World Bank estimated that perhaps 90% of all students have been impacted by the pandemic. And, unlike most countries in the developed world, there is scant opportunity for online learning in much of sub-Saharan Africa.

Rapid urbanization has also imposed stresses on many African economies. Africa is still very largely rural and agricultural. In 1980 about 75% of the region's population lived in rural areas, but that figure has declined to around 60%. However, approximately 70% of Africa's poorest live in rural areas. Urbanization has increased at an alarming pace, and it has been forecast that by 2025 Africa's urban population will be three times larger than in 2000, with more than one-half of the population living in cities. More than 45% of all urban-dwelling sub-Saharan Africans reside in cities with more than 500,000 inhabitants, compared with only 8% in 1960, when there were only two cities in the region with populations exceeding 500,000. Unemployment and underemployment are rampant in every major city of Africa and living conditions in virtually every city have worsened over the last two decades. In addition, the cost of living is relatively more expensive in Africa than in many other developing regions.

Until relatively recently most African governments did not regard rapid population growth or environmental degradation as matters for concern. Indeed, until fairly recently most areas of the region practised what is known as 'slash and burn' agriculture, a technique that can only succeed where land is abundant. However, a succession of countries, realizing that their resources cannot service their population growth, have begun to recognize the necessity for environmental protection.

Africa's environment has been under intense pressure, particularly since the beginning of the 21st century. With the increases in population discussed above, overcultivation and overgrazing have turned vast areas into virtual wastelands. Also, wood is collected for heating and cooking, supplying 70% of domestic energy needs. During 1990–2005 sub-Saharan Africa had the highest annual average rate of deforestation in the world. During 1990–2007 forest area as a percentage of total land area declined from 29.4% to 26.2%, with old growth

forests in the region being cut down at more than 4m. ha per year, twice the world's deforestation average. According to the World Bank, African forests are believed to contain 45% of the world's biodiversity, while forest-related activities account for at least 10% of GDP for 17 nations in the region. In addition, the region contains about 15% of the world's remaining forests, second to South America in the amount of tropical forests that are the most effective in removing carbon from the air. Across the Sahel population increases and changes in settlement patterns are putting pressure on fragile ecosystems. Fertile land is turning into dust, as people living in the transitional zone between the Sahel and the Sahara cut down trees for charcoal and send their animals further out in search of pasture.

It is predicted that climate change will affect sub-Saharan Africa more seriously than any other area in the world, although the region produces only about 7% of the world's greenhouse gases. Greater rainfall variability will contribute to both more flooding and droughts, and exacerbate the malaria problem. In 2007 the UN's Intergovernmental Panel on Climate Change predicted a minimum increase in temperature of 2.5°C by 2030, suggesting that food security will be severely compromised. The *Africa Adaptation Gap* report published by the UN Environment Programme in 2015 warned that climate change could reduce crop output by as much as 20% by 2070, while sea level rises would have dire economic consequences. For example, the projected 70 cm rise by 2070 could devastate the city of Dar es Salaam (Tanzania), East Africa's major port. It should be noted, however, that climate change could bring benefits; for example, eastern Africa could see increased rainfall in its parched highland areas, although extreme rainfall also causes problems Furthermore, climate change offers opportunities for the region to diversify and create green jobs. In 2022 below average rainfall and above average temperatures have intensified droughts in several areas, such as southern Ethiopia, Kenya and Uganda, while planting delays are likely to reduce harvests in Burundi, Madagascar, Malawi and Mozambique. Drought is threatening cocoa harvests in Côte d'Ivoire and Ghana.

Many government leaders in the past suggested that the achievement of economic growth was inconsistent with environmental protection, and that African development could only advance at the expense of its environment. It has only been in recent years that the two goals have been recognized as not mutually exclusive. Indeed, it is now generally accepted that sustained economic growth is impossible without adequate environmental protection. Specifically, many countries, such as Kenya, Tanzania and South Africa, increasingly depend on tourism based on wildlife and undisturbed natural habitats. However, no country in the region ranked highly on the 2019 Travel and Tourism Competitiveness Index: Mauritius was the highest ranking country, with a global rank of 54th, followed by South Africa at 61st and Seychelles at 62nd. Of the 140 countries ranked, 19 of the bottom 20 are from sub-Saharan Africa. While attracting only 6% of the world's tourists, the region has the potential for significant growth.

With the exception of 2020 (when the COVID-19 pandemic struck), the number of visitors and their related expenditures has increased considerably since 2009 (see *Table 17*). In 2019 sub-Saharan Africa attracted 55m. visitors, compared with 6.7m. visitors in 1990, and its receipts from tourism for the same year amounted to more than US $38,000m., or 2.8% of the region's GDP. According to the World Tourism and Travel Council, the direct contribution of travel and tourism to regional GDP was $40,100m. (2.6% of total GDP) in 2016, and was forecast to increase to $66,900m. (2.7% of total GDP) by 2027. However, as a result of the COVID-19 pandemic, international arrivals to sub-Saharan Africa declined by 63% in 2020. It is unclear when the economic damage to the tourism sector will be repaired, but it is unlikely that the sector will return to its 2019 levels until 2023.

PHYSICAL INFRASTRUCTURE, THE STRUCTURE OF THE ECONOMIES AND EMPLOYMENT

For most countries in the region physical infrastructure—including transportation, electricity and communications—

Table 17. International Tourism in Sub-Saharan Africa

	2009	2019
Inbound tourists ('000)	28,335	55,251
Inbound tourism expenditures (US $ million)	24,022	38,739

Source: World Bank, *World Development Indicators 2021.*

has generally deteriorated since the achievement of independence in the early and mid-1960s. With 16 landlocked countries, high transportation costs have hampered growth. Additionally, essential services such as electric power, water, roads, railways, ports and communications have been neglected, particularly in rural areas. Indeed, the region's energy infrastructure is tiny and fragile, and service is unpredictable. The region has what the World Bank has branded an 'infrastructure deficit'. There have been some recent positive developments: the region is now spending almost US $7,000m. on road paving and the 4,500-km Trans-Sahara Highway (linking Lagos north to Algiers) is currently 85% paved (the rest is sand). Major rail projects (generally financed by China) are being completed, including a recent link between Angola, Zambia and the DRC, and a new electric rail line between Addis Ababa (Ethiopia) and Djibouti was opened, while a light rail system was brought into operation in the Ethiopian capital in 2015.

An integrated and well-maintained road system is vital for a country's economic growth and development. The region has approximately 1m. km of classified road network, another 492,000 km of unclassified roads and about 193,000 km of urban roads, according to the World Bank, making them some of the most valuable state assets. However, in spite of their importance, roads have been badly managed and over one-half of the roads in sub-Saharan Africa are in very poor condition; in many countries the road network is woefully inadequate. Even in countries where the road network is good, for example in South Africa, recent budgetary constraints have delayed much-needed maintenance and expansion. Poor transportation affects all facets of African life, from commerce to health care to schooling. Some 70% of Africa's rural population lives more than a mile from an all-season road. Poor roads add to the costs of production in a region with the world's highest poverty rates, and the costs of transporting goods in Africa are the highest in the world. Poor road conditions can increase fuel consumption and the need for vehicle maintenance due to damage, and reduce the life of tyres and of vehicles. Owing to lower speeds, vehicles are not as efficient as they could be.

Higher transportation expenses raise the costs of doing business, impede private investment and add another barrier to Africa's ability to take advantage of the rapid growth in world trade. Trade is highly sensitive to transport costs: a 10% decrease in such costs could increase Africa's trade by 25%. Of all the world's regions, intra-regional trade is lowest in sub-Saharan Africa. While there are many reasons for this (e.g. tariff and non-tariff barriers, cumbersome customs procedures, lack of product diversification, the similarity in production among neighbouring countries), poor roads play a major role. For many areas it is a lack of sufficient maintenance rather than a lack of infrastructure itself that hinders business growth and, even where the infrastructure exists, it is often of poor quality. The cost of exporting or importing a standard cargo container of goods costs about US $2,000, or twice the amount in other regions of the world. The World Bank estimated that the region requires $22,000m. annually for both capital and maintenance expenditures. To address these problems, regional leaders and their private sector counterparts met in Dakar, Senegal, in 2014 to agree on how to finance 16 regional infrastructure projects they considered as priorities. The Dakar Agenda for Action appealed for a public-private partnership to work with the AfDB to find innovative ways for funding.

Sub-Saharan Africa has been confronted by a number of serious energy challenges, mainly related to insufficient generation capacity and an over-reliance on fossil fuels. Due to the region's small, fragmented energy markets, electrical supply systems cannot take advantage of economies of scale, and

electricity is thus expensive (although often heavily subsidized). The region's entire electric generation capacity (63 GW) is comparable to that of Spain. The region (excluding South Africa) has the world's lowest per capita consumption of electricity at 150 kWh), compared with a world average of 3,133 kWh. Indeed, some 500m. people are without electricity and less than one in five Africans are connected to a national energy grid (compared with 40% in low-income economies elsewhere). Furthermore, the price of energy is quite high in sub-Saharan Africa (especially when using average salaries as a measure). Unfortunately, the region has low access to diversified, sustainable energy. While the region has vast potential to develop alternative energy sources such as hydro, wind, solar, thermal and tidal, most countries have yet to successfully adopt them. Senegal, which has an estimated 1,200 MW capacity for hydroelectric power is currently only producing 260 MW at its Manantali plant. There are some exceptions: for example, in South Africa renewable energy is becoming more widely used as costs have come down.

The region uses only 3% of its renewable water for electricity generation, compared with 52% in South Asia. In addition, climate change will render hydrology more difficult as water levels will probably vary more greatly than in the past. Currently there are several dam projects being completed for electricity generation: the Grand Ethiopian Renaissance Dam will be the largest in the continent when completed. The Grand Inga Dam in the DRC will generate even more capacity, but it is still in the conceptual stages. The EU budgeted some €2,000m. for 2015–20 towards renewable energy projects, while additional assistance valued at €5,000m. is provided by individual EU member states.

Structural transformation involves large-scale changes in the actual make up of a country's or region's production. Such transformation can take decades. The underlying structure of sub-Saharan Africa's economies has not changed dramatically since independence. In 1965 agriculture accounted for 24% of GDP, industry 30% (of which manufacturing comprised 17%) and services 46%, according to the World Bank. By 2015 agriculture contributed 18% of GDP, while industry contributed 25%, manufacturing 11% and services 58%. Most countries tended to use vertical diversification to take advantage of their comparative advantage, for example, Ethiopia's recent moves into textiles. However, many countries have not diversified and have remained unable to take advantage of global value chains. In 2019 manufacturing as a percentage of GDP remained at 11% for the region and only about one-fifth of the total manufactured goods are exported to countries in the region. Within the region the distribution of manufacturing activity is highly skewed with just one country, South Africa, accounting for 27.3% of total manufacturing value-added (MVA) in sub-Saharan Africa and registering significant growth over the past two decades. There are some other examples; for instance, Ghana has attracted automobile manufacturing plants from Nissan and Volkswagen. However, for most countries there has been a loss in their share of global manufacturing output as production costs in the region are generally higher than other regions. Another problem for the region is the poor level of productivity in general, and of investment productivity in particular, as measured by a capital input-output ratio. Thus, even if Africa can attract more foreign investment, it must make that investment more productive.

Furthermore, the region lags behind other developing regions in almost all its industry-related indices. World Bank data indicates that with a few exceptions (Botswana, Cabo Verde, Eswatini, Madagascar, Namibia, Seychelles and South Africa) industrial output per capita as measured by the dollar MVA per population has been stagnant over the past three decades or has even declined. Further analysis by the UN Industrial Development Organization of trends in industrial output suggests that MVA in Africa has grown at a rate exceeding the world average (although falling well short of the phenomenal growth rates achieved in East and South Asia). However, in per head terms, growth in Africa's MVA remains below the global average.

The region annually supplies 10%–15% of the world's petroleum. It should be noted that, with the exception of Congo,

Nigeria, Angola, Gabon and Equatorial Guinea, none of the other states are members of the Organization of Petroleum Exporting Countries (OPEC), and thus are not subject to output limits. Recent discoveries of petroleum, natural gas and minerals in Ghana, Uganda, Kenya, Tanzania and Mozambique have again raised the question of how better to manage the earnings from those resources. A total of 19 African countries are members of the EITI, as discussed above, which promotes voluntary standards for showing payments made by companies and revenues collected by governments related to gains from extractive resources. None the less, the oil-rich countries in the region have a poor record of directing such revenues towards social development. For example, the oil producing states of Equatorial Guinea and Gabon, with per head incomes of some US \$14,600 and \$14,420, respectively, in 2019, have some of the lowest child immunization rates in the region. The World Bank cited four paradoxes relative to the region's energy crisis: abundant energy but little power; higher prices but high production costs; inefficient reform in the energy sector; and inadequate financing. By mid-2020 international oil prices were at historic lows, trading at times in negative territory (as there was an excess supply and inadequate storage available), and threatened to become a major issue for the oil producing countries, many of which have borrowed heavily against future income from newly discovered oil and gas reserves.

While the region lacks some of the information and communication technology available in many other parts of the world (for example, only one African per 100 people had a fixed-line telephone in 2019), between 1999 and 2004 the region's mobile phone market grew faster than in any other region worldwide, and between 2012 and 2013 mobile data use doubled. The region by 2020 had 83 mobile phone subscriptions per 100 people (compared with the world average of 106 per 100 people). While lower than the world average, it should be noted that the World Bank estimates that every day more than 90,000 new users connect to the internet for the first time. This has important potential for economic growth and inclusion. In 2020 Seychelles had the largest number of mobile phone subscribers per 100 people (at 187), with South Africa next (at 162). The CAR had the lowest number of mobile phones, with 38 per 100 people. Mobile users in the region prefer using their devices for a variety of activities that are normally performed on laptops or desktops in industrial countries: mobile phones allow access to banking to people who otherwise would be without it, and provide other important services, such as information on the weather and crop prices. However, internet use is relatively low, with just 30% of the region's population being internet users in 2020 (the world average is 60%). Seychelles had the highest proportion of internet users (79% of the population), followed by South Africa (70%).

The region's total labour force in 2021 was 447.4m. Given the size of the informal sector, as discussed above, estimates for formal sector unemployment vary so greatly that it is impossible to provide precise data, although the World Bank estimated that unemployment in the region for 2019 was 6.1%. It is worth noting, however, that estimates of official unemployment in the formal sector are as high as 30% in some countries, while unofficial estimates are higher still. And, as noted earlier, the informal sector is the main source of employment for most of the region.

CONCLUSION

During the 1970s and early 1980s African governments responded to increasing pressure from a variety of sources to 'liberalize' their economic policies. The World Bank, the IMF, the USA and other donors began to insist on 'conditionality' for their support. The IMF, in particular, required specific macroeconomic policy changes, usually in the area of exchange rates (i.e. devaluation), and reductions in government spending before a new loan agreement could be granted. Other required measures included the privatization of state-owned enterprises, public sector reform, reduction in the civil service and liberalization of agricultural marketing boards. In 1998 a total of 35 African countries launched structural adjustment programmes or borrowed from the IMF to support reform policies. Although these programmes (subsequently termed Poverty Reduction and Growth Facility and Extended Credit Facility arrangements) have many common points, they are actually varied. Additional pressures, known as the 'Washington Consensus' came from the World Bank and the United States Agency for International Development. Specifically, a landmark 1981 World Bank study proposed four critical policy changes: namely (i) the correction of overvalued exchange rates; (ii) the improvement of price incentives for exports and agriculture; (iii) the protection of industry in a more uniform and less direct way; and (iv) the reduction of direct governmental controls. Other pressures originated and grew internally, as more people became increasingly dissatisfied with their low standard of living and the poor economic performance in their own countries.

Many economists believe that these economic and political reforms did, in general, led to improved economic performance. Indeed, for nearly 20 years starting in the mid-1990s when most of the reforms were robust, most African countries saw stronger economic growth and development performance. However, the gains were not equally shared nor was poverty reduced as much as projected or hoped. Furthermore, structural adjustment is very controversial, and some studies have failed to demonstrate a definite linkage between reform and growth. Economic assistance to the region has been made increasingly dependent upon economic reform, and the major donor countries of the Organisation for Economic Co-operation and Development have generally reallocated most of their economic assistance to countries implementing reform programmes. Additionally, the major multilateral donors were also reallocating their resources on this basis.

As sub-Saharan Africa moves forward, its governments have begun to realize that, while many economic problems were inherited, responsibility must be taken for problems that are soluble. Rather than being hostile to foreign investment and entrepreneurs, most African governments are now actively seeking foreign commercial involvement.

However, an important question remains: how sustainable are the region's political and economic improvements? In the past, periods of economic growth were often (in some cases usually) followed by periods of significant decline. Yet, the region in 2022 is much different from that of 1990 when it emerged from two oil price shocks, a plunge of commodity prices and a decade of economic stagnation. For example, during the 1970s growth was based on a commodity boom, which had come to an end by the 1980s with little to show for it. During the recent growth period previously discussed, the region has witnessed perhaps a more sustainable path forward: economic growth is starting to come from other sources (almost one-half of the growth came from the services sector, with a fast-growing middle class). Manufacturing output is expanding as quickly as the rest of the economy. Growth is even faster in services, and many countries, including Ethiopia, Ghana, Kenya, Mozambique and Nigeria, have recently revised their estimates of GDP to account for their growing non-resource sectors.

As noted above, the IMF has projected low economic growth for the region in 2022–23, due to the COVID-19 pandemic and the impact of the war in Ukraine. In addition, the global economic slowdown will reduce demand from key trading partners, especially the USA and China, which accounts for 20% of the region's exports. In around one-half of the fragile and conflict-affected countries per-capita incomes are forecast to remain below pre-pandemic levels during 2023. School closures across the region have jeopardized economic prospects for perhaps a decade. Perhaps equally worrisome, the gap between sub-Saharan Africa and the wealthier industrial economies has grown.

In the longer term, there are a number of indicators that suggest the region is poised to effect economic transformation. The African Union (AU) Commission has identified five 'mega trends' that will offer tremendous opportunities (and challenges) for the region:

1 Demographic changes (with a growing young workforce and middle class, greater potential for savings and investment);

2 Rapid urbanization (opportunities for more efficient use of resources and social innovation, with an increasing middle class leading to greater demand);

3 Climate change (potential for new employment in green industries and green technologies);

4 The new 'industrial revolution' (increased efficiencies at the corporate level with lower costs, new innovations in manufacturing, and the growth of niche markets);

5 Shifting terms of trade (increased FDI into the region, transfers of technology and skills, along with diversification of the export market).

In addition to these trends, the region is taking important steps towards greater co-operation and integration. Since most of the region's economies are small, such co-operation is vital to the achievement of enlarged markets, to increase economies of scale and to attract FDI. The most important of these—and another 'game changer'—is the AfCFTA, as discussed earlier. Most small firms will benefit from reduced tariffs, the harmonization of customs clearance procedures and a lowering of other trade barriers. Furthermore, several regional economic communities are working to strengthen regional value chains and to identify potential regional 'clusters'. For example, SADC's Industrialization Strategy and Roadmap 2015–2063 has prioritized six key clusters. These clusters are selected areas that governments can utilize as a means to focus resources (e.g. infrastructure and financing) and thereby encourage knowledge transfers and other associated spillovers that should enhance countries' specialization and comparative advantages. While such examples of economic clusters are common in the industrial economies (such as high technology in California's Silicon Valley or garment manufacturing in northern Italy), they are less common in sub-Saharan Africa. None the less, there are increasing numbers of examples, including Ethiopia's eastern industrial zone and flagship Hawassa Industrial Park, and Rwanda's Kigali special economic zone, which have attracted world-class multinational corporations whose operations include textiles, garment manufacturing and shoe production.

Furthermore, the AU Commission lists nine important ongoing pan-African initiatives which could help to usher in economic transformation:

1 Agenda 2063;

2 The AU's Action Plan for the Accelerated Industrial Development of Africa;

3 The UN's Third Industrial Development Decade for Africa;

4 The Programme for Infrastructure Development in Africa;

5 The Science, Technology and Innovation Strategy for Africa 2024;

6 The African Agrobusiness and Agro-industries Development Initiative;

7 The Comprehensive Africa Agriculture Development Programme;

8 The African Mining Vision;

9 The African Productive Capacity Initiative.

However, given the COVID-19 pandemic and global geopolitical uncertainties, it is difficult to say when these initiatives will bear fruit.

The SDGs replaced the Millennium Development Goals (MDGs) when they expired at the end of 2015. In 2014 the UN General Assembly's Open Working Group on SDGs forwarded a proposal for the SDGs to the Assembly that contained 17 goals with 169 targets (and 304 indicators) covering a broad range of sustainable development issues. These included ending poverty and hunger, improving health and education, making cities more sustainable, combating climate change, and protecting oceans and forests. As the region did not fully meet the MDGs, it is hoped that they will be able to achieve more of these SDGs.

For sub-Saharan Africa's future a number of serious questions remain, the most important of course currently being how well the countries respond to the COVID-19 pandemic. Other questions include: Will real peace and stability finally come to Mali, South Sudan, Sudan, Somalia and other strife-ridden areas? Will sub-Saharan Africa continue to be marginalized, or can it find ways to integrate more successfully into the global economy? How can the negative effects of globalization be minimized? As China's economy and those of other nations slow, how will that affect those countries for which mineral exports are so important to their continued growth? Can richly endowed countries avoid the 'resource curse'? Will the industrialized countries open their agricultural markets to competition from the region and provide more necessary economic assistance? Will the region find more ways to improve cooperation and integrate its economies, including improving its transportation infrastructure? Will more employment opportunities in the formal and informal sectors emerge? Will the countries begin to invest in an often overlooked resource: their own people, particularly their women? Will the 'youth bulge' turn out to be an engine for growth or a time bomb for disaster?

This is a resilient region, one with great potential and enormous untapped resources. While there have been setbacks in recent years, there have also been a significant number of positive developments, as discussed above. It is safe to say that this region is on the verge of effecting economic and social transformation. While it may be difficult to reach this goal, it is attainable.

BEYOND *FRANÇAFRIQUE*—THE STATE OF RELATIONS BETWEEN FRANCE AND AFRICA

TONY CHAFER

INTRODUCTION: THE CONTEXT OF FRANCO-AFRICAN RELATIONS

From the early 20th century the possession of a colonial empire became the benchmark of the French claim to great power status. Africa was central to this claim, not least because of the increasingly important economic ties between France and its African colonies and the key role played by African troops who fought for France during the two world wars. Confronted with the emergence of the two new superpowers on the global stage, namely the USA and the Soviet Union, after the humiliations of the Second World War the maintenance of empire became even more important to France's continuing claim to world power status. This was to lead France into two hugely destructive wars of decolonization, which put paid to any hope of a peaceful, negotiated redefinition of the imperial relationship in Indochina and Algeria. The question of how to maintain France's world power status thus became all the more urgent. Morocco and Tunisia were granted independence in 1956 and, with the situation in Algeria deteriorating rapidly and France desperate to avoid the opening of a 'second front' in sub-Saharan Africa, the Government embarked on a programme of political reform in its colonies south of the Sahara that was designed to defuse the nationalist threat and show their populations that they had a viable future as French overseas territories (as the colonial empire was now called). Following an attempted coup by army officers in Algiers, Charles de Gaulle returned to power in 1958 and quickly realized that, if France was to maintain good relations with, and influence in, Africa, it would need to ride the anti-colonial tide that had been sweeping across Asia and Africa and grant its sub-Saharan African colonies independence.

De Gaulle's strategy for maintaining France's world power status in the post-colonial era had four pillars: the development of an independent nuclear deterrent; the retention of France's permanent seat on the United Nations (UN) Security Council; the positioning of France alongside Germany at the heart of the project to construct a new Europe; and the maintenance of a sphere of influence in Africa. It was this latter pillar that laid the basis for the 'special relationship' with Africa—often referred to as *la Françafrique*—that emerged after France's colonies in sub-Saharan Africa gained their independence in 1960. The first use of the term has been widely attributed to Félix Houphouët-Boigny, the first President of Côte d'Ivoire, who was an enthusiastic supporter of close relations with France. However, there is no evidence that he ever actually used the term. It was François-Xavier Verschave who gave currency to the term with his 1998 book *La Françafrique: le plus long scandale de la République*. For him the term referred to a range of corrupt practices that characterized French Africa policy. Beneath the image of France as the best friend of Africa, committed to a new partnership for development, the reality of the Franco-African 'special relationship', according to Verschave, was quite different. Jacques Foccart, de Gaulle's 'man in the shadows' and special adviser on African affairs, was given the task of maintaining France's position in Africa. To achieve this, he was accused of having used various methods to place, or keep, in power African heads of state who were 'friends of France', for example through war (in Cameroon), military intervention, electoral fraud, political assassinations, or other operations designed to maintain francophone African countries' dependency on France. The term *Françafrique*, through its homonym 'France à fric'[1], also refers to the misappropriation of funds, ranging from the payment of kickbacks to African political leaders and illegal funding of political parties to the illicit use of debt relief and development aid to finance Franco-African political-business networks.

In essence, *Françafrique* became shorthand for a neocolonial relationship that was rooted in illicit, sometimes criminal, practices designed to maintain France's former colonies in a relationship of dependency. Underpinning this relationship was a language of partnership—*coopération*—and a dense array of official links that bound France to its former colonies in sub-Saharan Africa. These included defence and military assistance accords, economic aid, political and cultural links—the latter in particular through *la Francophonie*—and the maintenance of a common currency zone (see below).

These official links were accompanied by a range of semi-official and unofficial family-like ties that were epitomized by the Franco-African summits, instituted at the instigation of President Hamani Diori of Niger in 1973, which brought the French President together with African and French political leaders in an annual celebration of their special relationship. These meetings were traditionally more like a family gathering than an official summit meeting, as there was no published agenda and no final communiqué was issued. Networks of personal relationships, the most notorious of which were the shadowy *réseaux Foccart*[2], regular French presidential visits to Africa and visits by African presidents to Paris further strengthened the ties between France and francophone African countries.

The close inter-linking of these official, semi-official, unofficial and illicit dimensions of the relationship, and support for them at the summit of the French state, no matter which of the main parties of the left or right was in power, was the key to their enduring nature. Moreover, somewhat less tangibly but no less importantly, French and African governing elites cultivated a sense of association and common heritage between France and Africa which served to cement the links between them. Both during and after the colonial period the projection of the 'universal' French republican values of liberty, equality and fraternity offered generations of francophone Africans the hope of progress and the prospect of a partnership with France to bring it about. At the same time, the idea that, thanks to their shared history and experience, France has a special understanding of Africa and Africans has had a powerful influence in shaping the attitudes and mind-sets of governing elites in both France and Africa.

THE 'SPECIAL RELATIONSHIP' AND THE ESTABLISHMENT OF A FRENCH PRIVILEGED SPHERE OF INFLUENCE IN AFRICA

Once it became clear that political independence was inevitable, the priority was to ensure that decolonization did not mark an end, but rather a restructuring, of the imperial relationship in sub-Saharan Africa (Chafer, 2016a). In Indochina and Algeria, where France fought two wars of decolonization, political independence marked a real watershed in relations. South of the Sahara, with the notable exceptions of Cameroon, where a little known war of decolonization resulted in up to 100,000 deaths, and Guinea, where Ahmed Sekou Touré's decision to defy de Gaulle and declare immediate independence in 1958 led to a more turbulent transition, the transfer of power was largely peaceful and smooth. France's former colonies in West and Central Africa—the so-called *pays du champ*—were to be at the centre of its *pré carré* (privileged sphere of influence) on the continent[3].

This was achieved in a number of different ways. The Franc Zone tied the French franc to the currency of its former colonies in Africa at a fixed rate and obliged the countries using the CFA franc to deposit the majority of their foreign currency reserves with the Banque de France in Paris[4]. There was a Ministry of Co-operation, successor to the colonial Ministry for Overseas France, whose minister had a seat on the Council of Ministers; this ministry was effectively a ministry for sub-Saharan francophone Africa and as such represented a symbol of France's continuing commitment to Africa. Two-thirds of French development aid went to France's former colonies in sub-Saharan Africa. France also signed cultural, technical and military co-operation accords with most of its former colonies at independence. The sending of large numbers of *coopérants* as teachers, university lecturers and educational advisers to former French Africa served to maintain, and indeed reinforce, the position of the French language and the French cultural presence in these countries. In addition, other specialists, such as financial and military advisers, were sent to Africa to work for the newly independent governments. Defence agreements set the framework within which French military interventions—some 35 between 1960 and 1994—were undertaken. France also maintained a dense network of embassies across the continent. Finally, with the establishment of the Fifth Republic in 1958, Africa policy became the *domaine réservé* of the President, which meant that decision making largely bypassed the Ministry of Foreign Affairs; instead, Africa policy was largely made by the President in close consultation with his 'Africa cell' of special advisers and was not subject to the normal processes of parliamentary scrutiny. This personalization of policymaking was an important vehicle for the cultivation of regional friends among Africa's political leaders, a practice that was facilitated by the fact that many of the leaders of the newly independent states of francophone Africa had been elected members of the Assemblée Nationale (National Assembly), and even become French government ministers, in Paris under the Fourth Republic.

CHALLENGES TO FRANÇAFRIQUE IN THE 1990s

At the international level, the political context within which *la Françafrique* had thrived changed after 1990. At the same time, at the domestic level, cracks began to appear in the 'Gaullist consensus' that had underpinned French Africa policy since 1960. During the Cold War Washington saw France's continuing presence, in a part of the world that was not a strategic priority and that it did not know well, as desirable to ensure that the region did not fall into the clutches of Moscow. This tacit division of responsibilities suited both France and the USA for the duration of the Cold War and afforded France a 'space' on the international stage in which it was able to present itself as the guarantor of Western interests in sub-Saharan Africa. However, it is important to recognize that France's motives in developing this special relationship with francophone Africa were in practice fundamentally different from those of the USA in allowing it to do so: whereas US policy was driven by Cold War concerns, France was motivated above all by the strategic need to maintain a privileged sphere of influence in Africa. Thus, while the USA saw the maintenance of a French sphere of influence as essential to the containment of communism in Africa, successive French governments saw the *pré carré* as a means of containing 'Anglo-Saxon'—for which read US and British—influence.

The change in the geopolitical context following the end of the Cold War made it much more difficult for France to maintain this stance. At the same time, the end of the Cold War provoked a rapid transition to multi-partyism, which resulted in a notably less stable policy environment. In several West and Central African states, increased conflict and political fragmentation, combined with the debt crisis and severe economic problems, threatened French influence and raised the cost to France of maintaining its *pré carré*. At the same time, in the context of the post-1990 neoliberal world order, the overt exercise of French power in support of political allies, which derives from the notion of an interventionist state and had since 1960 been the traditional hallmark of the French presence in Africa, became more problematic as a means of projecting French influence.

Alongside these international developments, changes in Paris were also affecting the context within which policymaking on Africa was formulated. In the aftermath of the fall of the Berlin Wall and the subsequent democratic revolutions in Central and Eastern Europe, questions were asked about the desirability of maintaining close relations with African dictators who had poor human rights records. Recognizing that France could no longer be seen to be supporting these authoritarian regimes, President François Mitterrand signalled a significant break with past French practice at the

1990 Franco-African summit in La Baule by stating that in future France intended to reward those governments that committed themselves to political reform. Political conditionality in this form had traditionally never been part of French Africa policy and, even if the application of the policy was in practice extremely uneven, the speech nevertheless sent a warning shot across the bows of African leaders who refused to undertake reforms (Cumming, 1996). Questions were also being raised in Paris about the value and effectiveness of French development aid, which had signally failed to promote economic take-off even though France had spent large sums of money since independence in 1960 supporting its former colonies (see, for example, Brunel, 1993).

Against this background, two developments in the mid-1990s marked a clear watershed in French Africa policy. The first of these was the announcement by Prime Minister Edouard Balladur of the so-called 'Abidjan doctrine', whereby French budgetary support for African states became conditional upon the prior conclusion of structural adjustment agreements with the International Monetary Fund (IMF) and the World Bank. This required states in the *pré carré* to restructure their economies 'in accordance with the principles of international liberalism or accept their decline and marginalization' (Bourmaud, 1996). Importantly, the adoption of this doctrine marked an end to one of the distinguishing features of *la Françafrique*: the provision of financial assistance to countries in the *pré carré* without any formal economic conditions attached. From now on, only countries undertaking an IMF/World Bank-sponsored reform programme would be eligible for French aid.

Following the death of the Ivorian President Houphouët-Boigny in December 1993, the CFA franc was devalued by 50% in January 1994, a measure which he had resisted for a number of years. This produced an immediate reduction in the cost to France of its Africa policy, resulting in a sharp reduction in the bilateral development aid budget between 1995 and 2001, in both value (down from €4,137,000m. to €2,653,000m.) and percentage terms (the proportion of bilateral aid to multilateral aid went down from 73% to 59.7%). The devaluation was experienced by many African leaders in the *pré carré* as a betrayal of the Franco-African special relationship. The subsequent closure of the Ministry of Co-operation, which African leaders of the *pré carré* had traditionally seen as 'their' ministry, and its merger in 1998 with the Ministry of Foreign Affairs, further contributed to the impression that the Franco-African special relationship— *la Françafrique*—was changing.

If the adoption of the Abidjan doctrine and the subsequent devaluation of the CFA franc represented the first significant new policy initiative towards Africa in response to the post-Cold War policy environment, it was France's questionable role in the events leading up to and following the Rwandan genocide of 1994 that provoked the most far-reaching re-evaluation of French Africa policy (Chafer, 2005; Kroslak, 2007). Following the shooting down of Rwandan President Juvenal Habyarimana's plane in April 1994, his supporters were responsible for the killing of some 800,000 Rwandan Tutsis and moderate Hutus within the space of two months. Although domestic criticism of French involvement in Rwanda was, at the time, relatively muted, there was widespread, and well-publicized, condemnation of France in the foreign press and by international non-governmental organizations (see in particular Human Rights Watch, 1995) because it had, from 1990–94, been the main external supporter of the Habyarimana regime. As a result, members of France's governing elites and sections of the French press increasingly questioned the benefits to France of the Franco-African special relationship and the Ministry of Defence, stung by international criticism of the French armed forces' role in Rwanda and keen to shed France's image as the 'gendarme' of Africa (Vallin, 2015), launched a wide-ranging review of the French military presence and its role in sub-Saharan Africa. This led to the idea of creating, with French support, an African peacekeeping force, driven on the one hand by the need to maintain international acceptance for France's military effort on the continent, and on the other by the desire to reduce the risks, both military and political, of this effort. The decision was also taken to reduce the number of French troops stationed in Africa, with two bases in the Central

African Republic (CAR) being closed in 1999[5]. Finally, as part of its strategy to reduce the risk and forestall international criticism of its military interventions, successive French governments have, since 1994, sought the approval of the UN Security Council and of Africa's regional or subregional organizations, such as the African Union (AU) and the Economic Community of West African States (ECOWAS), for French military operations on the continent.

FROM UNILATERALISM TO MULTILATERALISM

Until the mid-1990s France had adopted a unilateral approach to Africa. Relations with its former colonies were conducted on the basis of bilateral agreements. This was as true of its aid policy as it was of its military policy. With an array of bilateral defence and military assistance accords signed with its former colonies at independence and up to 10,000 soldiers either stationed or taking part in military operations in its former colonies 30 years after independence, France undertook at least 30 unilateral, direct military interventions on the continent between 1964 and 1995 and pursued a policy of substitution for, rather than partnership with, African military forces in its post-colonial sphere of influence, the *pré carré*.

This began to change in the late 1990s. At the December 1998 Franco-British summit in Saint-Malo, France, the British and French Governments declared their intention to set aside a century of rivalry, to 'harmonise policies towards Africa and pursue close cooperation on the ground ... [and] promote subregional integration, in particular between networks of anglophone and francophone countries'. This opened the door to French co-operation with the United Kingdom. At the same time, there was convergence between the USA, the UK and France on the need to train African troops for peacekeeping duties on the African continent, with the USA in particular reluctant to undertake military interventions in Africa following its recent humiliation in Somalia. All three countries now supported the aim to enhance the capacity of African military forces to provide effective peacekeeping or humanitarian relief operations on the continent. Thus, in 1996, the USA launched its African Crisis Response Initiative programme and in 1997 the UK launched its African Peacekeeping Training Support Programme, while France introduced its RECAMP (Renforcement des Capacités Africaines de Maintien de la Paix) programme, with similar objectives to the US and British programmes, in the same year. This marked a watershed in French policy as it sought to move away from its traditional approach of direct, unilateral, military intervention by French troops towards a policy of supporting Africans to undertake peacekeeping operations themselves. This convergence was one of the factors that led to the establishment in 1997 of the so-called 'P3' initiative, an informal grouping which brought the USA, the UK and France together at the level of the UN Security Council in an effort to co-ordinate their positions and harmonize their peacekeeping capacity-building programmes in Africa.

In West Africa the civil war in Liberia (and its regional spillover) was a further catalyst for the French change to a more multilateral approach. Following Charles Taylor's 1997 presidential election victory, opposition to his brutal and repressive regime grew and the country's second civil war broke out in 1999, threatening once again to engulf the entire region. This danger, as well as the threat to British expatriates, led to the British Government's decision to send troops to Sierra Leone in 2000 and the French Government's decision to relinquish its support for Taylor, as it feared that the conflict could impact on security throughout the region and undermine the stability of key French regional allies such as Côte d'Ivoire. This increased French readiness to work with the USA and the UK and opened the door to British-French-US collaboration in the region (Chafer, 2013).

An early example of co-ordination at the level of the 'P3' was the series of UN Security Council resolutions on the Mano River countries in 2002–03. Continuing conflict and instability in Liberia, Sierra Leone and, from 2002, Côte d'Ivoire, were a concern for the USA, the UK and France. All three countries recognized that the conflicts were not confined to one country, that there was potential for 'regional contagion' and that they

could not be resolved on an individual country basis. Importantly also, the 'P3' saw that they could benefit from working together on peace and security issues in the region. Thus, thanks to its close links with the country, the UK had a comparative advantage in dealing with Sierra Leone, while France had a similar comparative advantage in Côte d'Ivoire and the USA in Liberia. The various UN Security Council resolutions from 1999 onwards, on Sierra Leone, Liberia and Côte d'Ivoire respectively, provided an example of the 'P3' working in concert, in the first instance bilaterally with key regional actors such as Nigeria and Senegal and then, via them, to influence other ECOWAS member states.

The attacks on the World Trade Center and the Pentagon in the USA in September 2001 ('9/11') reinforced this converging focus on security issues between France, the UK and the USA, as Africa became a key arena of the 'war on terror'. This subsequently led to further co-operation at the level of the 'P3' on African security issues; for example, Security Council Resolution 1498 in August 2003 renewed authorization for French and West African forces operating in Côte d'Ivoire, and this was followed by a series of further resolutions from 2004 onwards, establishing the United Nations Operation in Côte d'Ivoire (UNOCI), renewing the mandate of French and West African forces and reinforcing the sanctions regime in the country.

In addition to sharing the costs and risks of French African policy, this new, multilateral approach reflected the fact that France was operating in an increasingly multipolar and competitive global environment, in which its position in Africa was coming under challenge from emerging powers such as the People's Republic of China and India. The adoption of a multilateral approach, working with international and regional partners and combined with close bilateral relations with key individual countries, was now seen as the most effective way for France as a medium-sized power to maintain its position as a key player on the continent.

DOMESTIC PRESSURES FOR CHANGE

The changed international context not only made it more difficult for France to act alone in Africa, but also greatly reduced the political dividends from doing so because of the growing criticism, both internationally and from within Africa, of French policy. In parallel with these developments the domestic political context also changed. The 'Gaullist consensus' on Africa policy broke down and Africa policy became the subject of disagreements between the so-called 'traditionalists' (*les anciens*) and 'modernizers' (*les modernes*) (Bourmaud, 1996; Gounin, 2009). While both sides agreed that France should maintain an active role on the continent, the 'traditionalists' clung to the old ways and advocated maintaining the unilateral approach that had served France well until the 1990s, whereas the 'modernizers' believed that France needed to move with the times and change its approach if it was to continue to be a significant player on the continent.

Other developments on the domestic stage contributed to this change. During the 1990s two periods of political 'cohabitation', between a president of the Left and a prime minister of the Right (Mitterrand and Balladur, 1993–95) and then between a president of the Right and a prime minister of the Left (Jacques Chirac and Lionel Jospin, 1997–2002) meant that Africa policy became less exclusively a presidential *domaine réservé*. We have already seen how prime minister Balladur pushed through a major change in French economic policy towards Africa. Similarly, in 1997, Prime Minister Jospin was determined not to leave Africa policy to President Chirac. A 'modernizer' in terms of Africa policy, Jospin pushed through the abolition of the Ministry of Co-operation and a significant reduction in the French bilateral aid budget. During his premiership, the notion of *pays du champ*, considered too redolent of the outdated notion of a French colonial 'backyard', was abandoned in favour of the idea of a Zone de Solidarité Prioritaire. All 54 countries in the zone, of which 44 were in Africa, would henceforth be eligible for French aid. This was supposed to dilute the family-like special relationship with Africa, as the 44 included former British and Portuguese colonies that were not part of France's traditional *pré carré*.

Jospin also reduced the number of French troops stationed in Africa and refused to send troops to Côte d'Ivoire in December 1999 to support President Henri Konan Bédié, who was overthrown in a military coup. President Chirac's African adviser, Michel Dupuch, wanted to intervene in support of Bédié who, with French support, had succeeded long-time French ally Houphouët-Boigny as President in 1993. However, Jospin overruled him, thereby challenging the notion of Africa as a presidential *domaine réservé*, where the President both called the policy shots and was the unchallenged spokesman on French Africa policy. Some commentators at the time saw this as another step away from the traditional family-like relationship with francophone Africa and towards the 'normalization' of French policy.

Finally, the cost of the French military presence and interventions in Africa is substantial. Against the background of growing pressure on public finances and reductions in the defence budget, burden-sharing represented the only possibility for France to meet the costs of its desire to maintain its military position on the continent.

TOWARDS THE 'EUROPEANIZATION' OF AFRICA POLICY?

As part of the shift towards a multilateral approach, 'Europeanization' meant that the European Union (EU) would in principle play a greater role in the design and implementation of Africa policy. From a French perspective, this had the advantage in the military sphere both of sharing the costs and risks of its Africa policy with other EU member states and of helping France to avoid the charge of neocolonialism, insofar as an EU military operation did not have the same direct association with France as a solely French operation.

Successive French governments have, since the turn of the century, argued that Europe, because of its proximity to the continent, has key security concerns in Africa, arising from the threat of terrorism, international crime, migration pressures, weapons proliferation, instability and conflict. President Chirac (2002–07) made efforts to Europeanize military missions to Africa and his successor, Nicolas Sarkozy (2007–12), oversaw the 'Europeanization' of the RECAMP programme, which was renamed EURORECAMP in 2008 and placed under the European Council. This coincided with the EU developing its European Security and Defence Policy (ESDP), for which Africa rapidly emerged as a key theatre. As a result, during the Chirac and Sarkozy presidencies there were three French-inspired ESDP military missions on African soil: Operation Artemis in the Democratic Republic of Congo (DRC) from June to September 2003; EUFOR, also in the DRC, from July to November 2006; and EUFOR Chad/CAR, from January 2008 to March 2009 (Chafer and Cumming, 2010; Barrios, 2010). In addition, an EU naval operation, EU NAVFOR Operation Atalanta, was launched in December 2008, with France and the UK taking the lead, to fight piracy off the coast of Somalia. Following the Saint-Malo and Cahors (2001) Franco-British summits, the British and French Governments played a key role in gaining EU member states' support for these missions. They also played a key role in the EU's adoption, for the first time, of an Africa strategy in 2005.

However, having been persuaded to take part in French-led military operations on the continent under the ESDP from 2003–09, some EU member states, in particular Germany, became sceptical about the value of direct EU military interventions in African crises. Wary of France seeking to implicate them in 'its' African problems, they preferred to leave military actions involving the deployment of combat troops to France, as it has troops on the ground and is clearly willing and able to intervene. As a result, there were no further deployments of combat troops from other EU member states to Africa after EUFOR Chad/CAR until Operation Takuba (see below) and France was forced to rethink its 'Europeanization' strategy for military intervention on the continent.

The shift in French policy from a bilateral to a multilateral approach was not limited to the security field, but also extended to the field of development aid, with an increased proportion of French overseas development assistance (ODA) now channelled through multilateral organizations, in

particular the EU. Multilateral aid as a proportion of France's total aid budget rose strongly in the first decade of the 21st century and by 2010 reached nearly 40% of the total aid budget, 50% of which went to the EU (OECD, 2013). These percentages remained more or less stable during the 2010s, with 42% of its total aid budget of US $11,400m. being multilateral in 2017 (53% of which went to the EU) (Sénat, 2018). France also drew up a 'Multilateral Aid Strategy 2017–2021' in response to recommendations contained in the 2013 OECD Development Assistance Committee peer review of French ODA (OECD, 2018).

From the French perspective, the channelling of a significant proportion of its ODA through multilateral organizations has several advantages. It provides the opportunity for France to play a leading role in international debates on development. This enables French governments both to influence policy and leverage further resources from bilateral and multilateral donors in support of its policy priorities. It also means that France can exercise influence in countries and regions beyond the reach of its bilateral assistance. These advantages can be seen at the level of the EU where France, as the second largest contributor to the European Development Fund, has been able to promote convergence with its priority geographic areas for development assistance in sub-Saharan Africa and its priority sectors for intervention, such as health, education, climate change, gender equality and economic infrastructure (OECD, 2018).

It should be noted that these developments were part of a wider trend in EU-Africa relations, as they marked a move away from an essentially 'technical' relationship between the EU and Africa. This relationship was traditionally managed as part of the African-Caribbean-Pacific (ACP) group of countries, in which the European Commission took the policy lead; however, following the first Africa-Europe summit in 2000 in Cairo, the EU-Africa relationship evolved into a much more wide-ranging, overtly political and security-focused relationship, for which the AU would become the EU's privileged interlocutor. Moreover, reflecting the EU's ambition to play a greater role on the global stage as a foreign policy actor, the European Council took the leading role in driving EU-Africa policy, a shift that was confirmed by the signature of the Africa-EU Strategic Partnership at the AU-EU summit in Lisbon in 2007. This shift towards intergovernmentalism, which placed France, with its long history of involvement in the African continent, at the centre of EU policymaking on Africa, meant that the French Government had to consult more widely on Africa policy with its partners than it had done in the past, but also afforded France new opportunities to enlist support from other EU member states for its African initiatives.

'AFRICAN SOLUTIONS TO AFRICAN PROBLEMS': FORGING A NEW FRANCO-AFRICAN SECURITY PARTNERSHIP

The African peace and security context has radically altered in recent years. The end of the Cold War and changing realities on the ground, such as the increased activism of the USA, China, India, the Russian Federation and other emerging powers on the continent, have placed limits on French interventionism. At the same time, the increased salience of security concerns on the continent post-'9/11' has created new opportunities for France. Its position as a permanent member of the UN Security Council and one of the most important member states of the EU, combined with its pre-positioned troops stationed at strategic locations on the continent and long experience of military action on the continent, have all provided 'comparative advantage' for France when it comes to responding to Africa's security challenges. Thus, following the period of cohabitation between President Chirac and Prime Minister Jospin which ended in 2002[6], there was a marked increase in French military activism on the continent.

Two features that have been a constant of Africa policy under presidents Sarkozy, François Hollande and Emmanuel Macron are the stated commitment to multilateralization and the language of partnership with Africa. Like 'Europeanization', the forging of a new partnership with Africa to promote 'African solutions to African problems' is also about sharing the risks and costs of French military interventions on the continent. This means ensuring that any military intervention has received approval from the UN Security Council and been endorsed by the relevant African regional organization such as the AU or ECOWAS. It has also meant, as we have seen, a commitment to the reorientation of French military actions on the continent towards building African peacekeeping capacity, so that African forces are able to take greater responsibility for peace and security on the continent.

In 2008 President Sarkozy gave a clear indication of France's commitment to move away from exclusive, bilateral defence relations towards a more multilateral approach when he acknowledged that the defence agreements France had signed with the governments of newly independent African states were no longer fit for purpose: 'Their wording is obsolete. It is now unthinkable, for example, for us to be drawn into domestic conflicts' (Sarkozy, 2008). Specifically, he proposed: first, that the agreements should be renegotiated through discussion with African governments in order to adapt them to 'the realities of the present'; second, that, contrary to what had happened in the past, the new agreements must be based on transparency, with no secret clauses and with the French Parliament involved in the process; third, that the role of French forces should not be to intervene directly in African conflicts, but to help the AU achieve its aim of establishing the continent's own collective security arrangements by building African peacekeeping capacity—this was a key aim of the RECAMP/EURORECAMP programme; and finally, in keeping with this objective, to make Europe a major partner for bringing about peace and security in Africa. The promise to renegotiate the agreements was carried out and the new texts were published. Yet, despite this commitment to multilateralism and a new partnership for African security that was supposed to reduce the need for direct intervention by French troops, French military interventions continued. Military interventions took place in Chad in support of President Idriss Deby Itno (2006, 2008 and 2019), in Côte d'Ivoire to remove President Laurent Gbagbo (2011) and in Libya, which resulted in the removal of Col Muammar al-Qaddafi (2011) from power. These were followed by further interventions in Mali and the CAR under President Hollande: although he had previously promised not to deploy combat troops to these countries, Hollande launched Operation Serval in Mali in January 2013 and Operation Sangaris in the CAR in December of the same year. Subsequently, in 2014, the operation in Mali and the ongoing Operation Epervier (which had started in Chad in 1986 under the terms of the bilateral defence accord between the two countries) were consolidated into the Sahel-wide Operation Barkhane (see below).

Believing that Islamists were on the point of taking over the country and that Mali was on the verge of becoming a fundamentalist Islamist state where drug trafficking and religious extremism could flourish, on 11 January 2013 President Hollande launched Operation Serval, involving the deployment of 4,000 French troops to the country, supported by 2,000 Chadians. The UN Security Council had passed three resolutions in 2011–12 identifying terrorism as one of the greatest threats to global peace and security and Resolution 2085 on Mali referred specifically to the threat of terrorist networks in the country. As a permanent member of the Security Council, with troops on the ground who had on many occasions demonstrated their capacity to intervene in African crises, and with France having played a key role in drawing international attention to the terrorist threat in the country, President Hollande decided that it was France's responsibility to intervene. Moreover, key French allies, notably President Macky Sall of Senegal and President Mahamadou Issoufou of Niger, had appealed for French intervention, fearing that an Islamist takeover in Mali would have serious security implications for their countries.

Operation Serval was a military success and very quickly chased the Islamists from the cities and main towns in the north of the country. It was terminated on 31 July 2014 and replaced by Operation Barkhane on 1 August. This new operation retained the troops involved in Operations Serval and Epervier, but its theatre of engagement now stretched across the whole of the francophone Sahara-Sahel region, spanning

five countries (Mauritania, Mali, Burkina Faso, Niger and Chad—referred to as the 'G5 Sahel'). It comprised 4,500 troops, some 200 armoured carriers, six fighter planes, 20 helicopters, 10 transport planes and several drones. Its stated aim was to support the armed forces of the participating countries in their interventions against armed terrorist groups across the Sahel and to help prevent the re-establishment of terrorist sanctuaries in the region. However, while the policy discourse regarding Barkhane was very much one of partnership with African forces, the reality was that the capacity to intervene of the armed forces of the G5 Sahel countries most affected by the violence (Mali, Niger, Burkina Faso) without the support of French troops was limited. Moreover, despite the deployment of Barkhane, the security situation across the region continued to deteriorate, with attacks by Islamist extremists spreading from the north of Mali to the centre of the country and also to neighbouring countries. Thus, like its attempt to 'Europeanize' its military strategy in the early 2000s, the French plan to forge a new security partnership with African countries to enable them to take greater responsibility for their own security was not producing the hoped-for results.

MACRON'S AFRICA STRATEGY

Like his predecessors, Sarkozy and Hollande, President Macron promised an end to *Françafrique* and the establishment of a new partnership with Africa. Like them, he has also made regular official visits to Africa: his first, in May 2017 shortly after his election, was to French troops in Mali to reaffirm France's commitment to Operation Barkhane. Underlining the continuity between his and Hollande's presidency in the area of security policy, in his August 2017 address to French ambassadors he made it clear that his Government's diplomatic priority was the struggle against terrorism and he paid tribute to President Hollande's efforts to combat terrorism and prevent the Sahel becoming a sanctuary for terrorists. At the same time, faced with a deteriorating security situation in the Sahel, Macron was concerned that his predecessor had not put in place a credible exit strategy for Barkhane. He was therefore active in promoting the creation of the G5 Sahel Joint Force and played a key role in lobbying the international community to provide financial support, which resulted in the EU and Saudi Arabia both pledging €100m., the United Arab Emirates €30m., and the USA, Japan and Norway also promising support, although there are question marks over how much of this money actually arrived.

Despite these pledges and the creation of the G5 Sahel Joint Force in 2017, the ongoing deployment of 4,500 Barkhane troops across the Sahel was not able to deliver peace and security. Indeed, by 2019, in central Mali and Burkina Faso the violence had got much worse and there was no realistic prospect that France would, in the short or medium term, be able to transfer responsibility for security in the region to the G5 Sahel Joint Force. At the same time there was no question of withdrawing French forces, as Macron had promised France's allies in the G5 Sahel that it would stay until the jihadist groups were under control. However, it was clear that a new approach was needed. The areas to which the violence had spread were much more populous than northern Mali and the tactics of the armed groups had changed over the five years since Barkhane was launched. They increasingly sought to win over the local population, and largely avoided open battles. They focused instead on roadside attacks on the UN Multidimensional Integrated Stabilization Mission in Mali (MINUSMA) peacekeeping force and on killing, or threatening to kill, government officials in the areas of the country they controlled, in order to disrupt attempts to restore government services and reopen schools.

With the violence escalating, Macron decided that the military effort needed to be strengthened. However, at the same time he was angered by the growing expressions of anti-French sentiment in the region, both on the streets of Bamako (Mali), Niamey (Niger) and Ouagadougou (Burkina Faso), and on social media, especially following the loss of the lives of 13 French troops when two helicopters of Operation Barkhane crashed on 25 November 2019. In response to these developments, he summoned the G5 Sahel leaders to a summit in Pau,

France, at which he made it clear that he expected them to reaffirm their support for Operation Barkhane.

The Pau summit was postponed, after an armed attack on the Nigerien military base at Inates on 10 December 2019 which resulted in the deaths of 71 Nigerien soldiers, and eventually took place on 13 January 2020. The way in which they were summoned to Pau by President Macron, demanding that they 'clarify' formally their support for France's intervention, was experienced by G5 leaders as a summons and seen as disrespectful. Nevertheless, the summit went ahead, with the Nigerien Minister of Foreign Affairs proposing an increase in the military effort. The major new initiative announced at the summit was the creation of the international Coalition for the Sahel, which included the launch of Takuba, a European military task force composed of European special forces under the leadership of France. The Coalition has four pillars: the fight against armed terrorist groups; building the capacities of the armed forces of the region; supporting the return of the state and administrations and improving access to basic services; and assisting development. Takuba played a key role in the first of these pillars, where its role was to advise and accompany the Malian armed forces, in co-ordination with their G5 Sahel partners, in their fight against armed terrorist groups, with a particular focus on the tri-border area between Mali, Niger and Burkina Faso. The second pillar is essentially a fleshing out of the Partnership for Security and Stability in the Sahel (P3S), which was announced at the 2019 Biarritz Group of Seven (G7) summit with the aim to identify security needs and increase efforts in the fields of defence and internal security, while the third pillar represents an effort to identify the priority needs of the P3S and co-ordinate training and equipment assistance for national internal security forces (police, gendarmerie, national guard). The fourth pillar centres on the Sahel Alliance. Originally launched on 13 July 2017 by France, Germany and the EU, it aims to attract development assistance to the region and improve the effectiveness of aid by co-ordinating the actions of major development partners. Finally, Macron announced 600 extra troops for Operation Barkhane, bringing its total complement to 5,100.

In August 2020 a military coup removed the Malian President, Ibrahim Boubacar Keïta, and he was replaced by a military-backed transitional government that subsequently opened negotiations with armed jihadist groups. This further complicated the political landscape and raised questions about previous claims of political progress within the country. Moreover, with French troop losses above 50, costs rising and facing a potentially difficult election in 2022, Macron was under growing pressure to bring forward an exit strategy after nearly eight years of military operations in the region. None the less, Macron drew back from announcing a widely predicted reduction in French troop numbers at the G5 Sahel summit in Chad on 15–16 February 2021. However, the delay in announcing the drawdown of French troops proved to be only temporary as, on 10 June 2021, in advance of the G7 summit in the UK, Macron announced the end of Operation Barkhane.

Following this announcement, events on the ground moved quickly, obliging Macron to rethink France's Sahel strategy. Mali suffered a second military coup in May 2021, as the army sought to reassert control over the political transition, and in January 2022 a military coup toppled Burkinabè President Roch Marc Christian Kaboré. Also in January, the Malian Government expelled the French ambassador from the country and Danish troops, who had arrived in the country to join the Takuba task force, were told to leave. In the meantime, troops belonging to the Russian private security company, Wagner, arrived in the country in December 2021 and started undertaking military operations alongside the Malian military forces. The Malian Government then announced the country's withdrawal from the G5 Sahel, accusing it of being under 'foreign' (for which read French) influence. Following these developments, Takuba closed down at the end of June 2022 and all French troops left the country by the end of August. Macron's plan post-Barkhane is for a lighter, more discreet, French military presence in the region, based in Niger, with some 2,500 French troops providing intelligence, equipment and training at the express request of African governments.

French Africa policy, however, is not limited to the security field. Beyond security policy, during his first term Macron launched initiatives to promote the French language and reinvigorate Francophonie. He sees Africa as key to the future of the French language and believes that there is the opportunity for French to become the third most spoken language in the world thanks to the continent's rapid population growth. During his presidency he has made a series of interventions to promote Francophonie on the continent, although these have not always been well received by African intellectuals, such as Alain Mabanckou, who view them as a renewed expression of French neocolonial ambitions on the continent.

In his first major speech in Africa, in front of 800 students at Ouagadougou University (Burkina Faso) in November 2017, Macron not only restated the promise to put an end to *Françafrique* but went further and paid homage to the country's former President, Thomas Sankara, assassinated in 1987, who was a vigorous opponent and strong critic of France's neocolonial policies and the *Françafrique* networks that underpinned them. Pointing out that he, like them, was of a generation that had not known Africa under colonialism, Macron appealed directly to the youth of Africa as the future of the continent and, quoting Sankara, invited them to build 'the future that you dare to invent'. To enable this, he promised to create an investment fund directed at young African entrepreneurs.

Underlining his change in approach to Africa, Macron has sought to address the legacy of France's colonial past in Africa, for example by expressing his readiness to consider the restitution of artefacts looted or illegally taken out of Africa during the colonial period. He also became the first French President to visit the two major anglophone countries in West Africa, Ghana (November 2017) and Nigeria (July 2018). There was not only a political, but also an economic logic to this. France has long had difficult relations with Nigeria thanks to de Gaulle's support for Biafran secession during the Nigerian civil war (1967–70), but it is the economic powerhouse of West Africa with a huge potential market, while Ghana has one of the strongest economies in the region. However, the visit had a wider significance, as it was also about sending out a message to African political leaders and civil society that France has changed and that it wants to create new partnerships with Africa beyond its traditional *pré carré* through culture, sport and economic development. Significantly therefore, after visiting the capital Abuja and meeting President Muhammadu Buhari to discuss security, he travelled on to Lagos, where he visited the famous New Afrika Shrine nightclub, formerly run by the legendary Afrobeat musician Fela Kuti who was frequently imprisoned during the 1970s and 1980s for his outspoken criticism of Nigerian military rule. As in Ouagadougou, Macron again appealed directly to African youth, to encourage them to get involved in politics: 'Fela was not just a musician. He was a politician who wanted to change society', Macron told the young audience from the stage. 'So if I have one message for young people, it's this: yes, politics is important; yes, be involved'. During his first term, Macron also visited Ethiopia and Kenya, also both outside France's traditional African *pre carré*.

In addition, there was a change of approach with regard to the CFA Franc zone. In December 2019, at a joint press conference in Abidjan, Macron and the Ivorian President, Alassane Ouattara, announced reforms to the West African CFA franc zone. For long criticized as a neocolonial construct—a relic of the *Françafrique* era—the announced reform sought to address three of the most widely made criticisms of the zone. First, the name of the currency would change from the CFA franc, considered too redolent of its colonial origins, to the eco. Second, the requirement for member states to deposit 50% of their foreign reserves with the Bank de France would be ended. Third, French officials would be withdrawn from the central bank's board, although some have suggested that the significance of this change should not be overestimated, as they will be replaced by a formal reporting mechanism that will allow the French Treasury to maintain its oversight of the zone's finances. Other aspects remain unchanged: in particular, the fixed parity with the euro will be maintained and Paris will retain its role as guarantor of the currency for the eight member countries of the Union Economique et Monétaire Ouest-Africaine. It should also be noted that these reforms apply only to the eight countries in the West African zone and not to the six in the Central African zone. In any case, it seems clear that these changes have not gone far enough to satisfy the zone's increasingly vocal critics and even the name change may not happen any time soon. The 'eco' was the name that ECOWAS had chosen in June 2019 for its planned single currency and Nigeria in particular was affronted that a group of francophone countries had, from its perspective, hijacked the plan for a West African single currency.

Following his re-election as President in May 2022, Macron has sought to reset Africa policy following the failure in Mali. Yet, apart from the shift in emphasis away from the military dimension, much of the new Africa policy represents continuity with his first term. Macron has promised to consolidate relations with France's 'historic partners', while also developing relations with countries outside the traditional *pré carré*. He has promised support for youth employment and enterprise; to work with European partners, in particular to finance infrastructure projects; and to build new partnerships with African youth and civil society, while maintaining bilateral relations with African governments[7]. His first visit to Africa after his re-election was also in keeping with the theme of change with continuity: in July 2022 he visited Cameroon, whose President Paul Biya has been in power for over 40 years and is a long-standing French ally; Benin, another francophone country, that has been subject to a series of terrorist attacks from armed groups coming over the border from Burkina Faso; and Guinea-Bissau, a former Portuguese colony that is not part of the French *pré carré* and at the time of writing holds the presidency of ECOWAS.

In sum, under President Macron there has been a shift in both presidential style and policy discourse. There has been a real effort to extend French engagement beyond France's traditional sphere of influence in francophone Africa, to enhance economic diplomacy and strengthen French 'soft power' on the continent. In other respects, however, especially if we consider French African policy *sur la longue durée*, while the policy tools have had to be adapted to the new policymaking context, Macron's Africa strategy is in one respect not radically different from that of his predecessors, insofar as its central aim remains, the recent setbacks in Mali notwithstanding, to maintain France's geopolitical position as a pivotal actor in the region through a combination of economic, military and cultural power and political activism.

CONCLUSION

France has had to adapt its African policy to a new geopolitical context in which the USA as well as new external actors, such as China, India, Russia, Turkey and other Middle Eastern countries, have been stepping up their interest in the continent. Africa remains important for France as a privileged arena for the projection of French power overseas. This is partly a product of history: the centrality of Africa to France's colonial empire, the nature of French decolonization in sub-Saharan Africa and the dense array of links that France has maintained with the region since political independence. These include the large number of French citizens and French dual nationals who live in Africa, particularly in francophone Africa; the permanent French military presence and frequent military interventions on the continent; the density of its diplomatic presence; and the Franc Zone. France also has significant economic interests in West and Central Africa: petroleum (Gabon, the Republic of the Congo, Gulf of Guinea); uranium (Niger); trade in cocoa and coffee (Côte d'Ivoire); as well as banking, transport and other services (water, communications, telephony) throughout the region. In addition, African countries play a central role in the Organisation Internationale de la Francophonie and are crucially important to the maintenance of French as a world language.

Efforts have certainly been made to reconfigure France's special relationship with Africa and there have been changes in approach and language. Thus, for example, the old-style unilateral military interventions, which were increasingly criticized from the 1990s both domestically and from within Africa, were rejected in favour of a more multilateral approach. The move to 'Europeanize' its interventions in the early 2000s was designed primarily to reduce the financial costs and political risks of unilateral French operations. In the same vein, the language of humanitarianism and partnership with Africa, the importance attached to gaining the prior approval of African regional and international organizations for any proposed military intervention and the stated commitment to working in partnership with African forces were a significant new departure.

The profound changes in the international context since the end of the Cold War have thus had a significant impact on the nature of the Franco-African relationship. France does not have the leverage that it once had on the continent and the old-style *Françafrique* networks are a thing of the past. However, because of its continuing geopolitical significance for France and given the common history and density of links between France and its former colonies in Africa, the Franco-African relationship remains in many respects a special one. It is also the case that, against the background of the emergence of Africa as a key focus, post-'9/11', of international efforts to combat terrorism, fighting alongside allies to counter the spread of terrorism as part of the 'global war on terror', provided new opportunities and a new legitimacy for French military actions on the continent (Chafer, 2016b, Ndiaye, 2014). Owing to its position within the EU, its permanent seat on the UN Security Council, its long experience and knowledge of West and Central Africa, its pre-positioned troops stationed on the continent and its capacity to intervene militarily, France has been able to leverage both regional and international support for its initiatives in that part of Africa. As a result, France has been able to establish itself as the pivotal actor, at the head of an assemblage of regional and international actors intervening in that part of the continent. However, this has not prevented a growing rejection of what many Africans see as French interference on the continent: its military presence, the maintenance of the CFA franc and the continuation of what are seen as paternalistic attitudes among its governing elites are particular bones of contention for francophone African intellectuals and many of the younger generation of Africans. The frequency of anti-French street demonstrations and of campaigns in the press and on social media in recent years suggest that France's political leaders have some way to go if they are to succeed in their stated ambition to reset the country's relationship with the continent and escape the accusations of neocolonialism. Following the recent setbacks in Mali, they will also need to rethink the French military presence on the continent.

FOOTNOTES

[1] In French, 'fric' is slang for 'cash' or 'money'.

[2] After de Gaulle's resignation, Foccart subsequently also acted as adviser to presidents Georges Pompidou and Jacques Chirac.

[3] One of the many specificities of *Françafrique* is that it has traditionally had a language of its own. These are two examples. *Réseaux* ('networks') is another term that has specific connotations in this context.

[4] The CFA franc is now pegged to the euro rather than the franc. 14 countries in West and Central Africa are members of the Franc Zone, which was created in 1945. Franc Zone countries were formerly required to deposit 50% of their foreign currency reserves with the Banque de France, but it was announced in December 2019 that this would no longer be the case for the West African zone.

[5] In 1997 French forces in Africa numbered some 8,000 soldiers in seven states: Cameroon, the CAR, Chad, Djibouti, Gabon, Côte d'Ivoire, and Senegal. By 2000 this had been reduced to 5,600 (Charbonneau, 2008).

[6] Jospin described his policy as '*ni ingérence, ni indifférence*' ('neither interference, nor indifference').

[7] This was also the theme of the new-format Africa-France summit that took place in Montpellier, France, in October 2021, to which 'actors of change' (entrepreneurs, intellectuals, artists, sportspeople and influencers) were invited, but no African heads of state.

BIBLIOGRAPHY

Barrios, C. 'France in Africa: from paternalism to pragmatism', in *Fride Policy Brief*, No. 58, 2010. www.files.ethz.ch/isn/130902/PB_58_Eng_France_in_Africa.pdf. Accessed 27 July 2020.

Bourmaud, D. 'La politique africaine de Jacques Chirac: les anciens contre les modernes', in *Modern and Contemporary France*, 4(4), pp. 431–442, 1996.

Brunel, S. *Le gaspillage de l'aide publique*. Paris, Seuil, 1993.

Chafer, T. 'Chirac and "la Françafrique": no longer a family affair', in *Modern and Contemporary France*, 13(1), pp. 7–23, 2005.

'The UK and France in West Africa: towards convergence?', in *African Security*, 6(3–4), pp. 234–256, 2013.

'French African policy in historical perspective', in *Readings in the International Relations of Africa*, Young, T., (Ed.), Bloomington, Indiana University Press, 2016a.

'France in Mali: towards a new Africa strategy', in *International Journal of Francophone Studies*, 19(2), pp. 119–141, 2016b.

Chafer, T., and Cumming, G. 'Beyond Fashoda: Anglo-French security cooperation in Africa since St-Malo', in *International Affairs*, 86(5), pp. 1129–1147, 2010.

Charbonneau, B. *France and the New Imperialism: Security Policy in Sub-Saharan Africa*. Aldershot, Ashgate, 2008.

The Dilemmas of International Intervention in Mali. Montréal, Centre FrancoPaix, 2017.

Cumming, G. 'French aid to Africa: a changing agenda?', in *France: From the Cold War to the New World Order*, Chafer, T., and Jenkins, B. (Eds), Basingstoke, Macmillan, 1996.

Gounin, Y. *La France en Afrique: le combat des anciens et des modernes*. Brussels, De Boeck, 2009.

G5 Sahel. 'Conférence de presse des Chefs d'État à l'issue du Sommet de Pau', 13 January 2020. www.elysee.fr/emmanuel-macron/2020/01/13/sommet-de-pau-declaration-conjointe-des-chefs-detat. Accessed 15 August 2022.

Human Rights Watch. www.hrw.org/reports/1995/WR95/AFRICA-08.htm. Accessed 27 July 2020.

Kroslak, D. *The Role of France in the Rwandan Genocide*. London, Hurst and Company, 2007.

'La difficile évolution de l'approche française en Afrique', *Le Monde*, 29 July 2022.

'Macron visits Fela Kuti-founded nightclub during Nigeria visit', *The Guardian*, 4 July 2018.

N'Diaye, B. 'Still "getting away with it": France's Africa defense and security policy', in *Routledge Handbook of African Security*, Hentz, J. (Ed.), Abingdon, Routledge, 2014.

Organisation for Economic Co-operation and Development. *Development Co-operation Peer Review: France 2013*. Paris, OECD, 2013.

Development Co-operation Peer Review: France 2018. Paris, OECD, 2018.

Pérouse de Montclos, M. 'France's fiasco in the Sahel', *Le Monde diplomatique*, October 2021.

Sarkozy, N. 'Discours de M. le Président de la République devant le Parlement Sud-Africain.' 2008. www.diplomatie.gouv.fr/fr/IMG/pdf/PARLEMENT_AS.pdf. Accessed 27 August 2020.

Sénat. 'Sur le système multilatéral de l'aide publique au développement'. *Rapport d'information n° 112*. Le Sénat, 2018.

Taylor, I. 'France à fric: the CFA zone in Africa and neocolonialism', in *Third World Quarterly*, 40(6), pp. 1064–1088, 2019.

United Nations. United Nations Stabilization Mission in Mali. peacekeeping.un.org/en/mission/minusma. Accessed 17 August 2021.

Vallin, V. 'France as the Gendarme of Africa, 1960–2014', in *Political Science Quarterly*, 130(1), pp. 79–101, 2015.

Verschave, F. *La Françafrique: le plus long scandale de la République*. Paris, Stock, 1998.

'Why a celebrated Francophone Africa writer said no to president Macron's Francophone project', *Quartz Africa*, 20 January 2018. qz.com/africa/1184735/frances-macron-turned-down-by-congo-writer-alain-mabanckou-for-francophone-project. Accessed 13 August 2021.

A CENTURY OF DEVELOPMENT: POLICY AND PROCESS IN SUB-SAHARAN AFRICA

MICHAEL JENNINGS

INTRODUCTION

The last 100 or so years have been the century of 'development' in Africa. National governments, external powers, development consultants, policymakers and analysts have drawn up plans and implemented programmes designed to reduce poverty and improve the socioeconomic lives of the continent's inhabitants. Aid policies and structures have emerged and evolved to pay for development activity. Societies have been transformed through the imposition of colonial rule, the birth of nation-states, incorporation into the global capitalist system, and by donor-imposed economic and governmental structures. Vast sums of money have been spent on developing Africa, entire professions have emerged concerned solely with poverty alleviation, and the line of politicians who have declared poverty in Africa to be the world's most pressing issue stretches back through the decades.

Yet, for all the effort, energy and words expended on development in Africa, what has been achieved? Life expectancy for someone living in sub-Saharan Africa was 58 years in 1960. In 2013 it was still 58 years, having risen from its fall to 46 years in 2004. In 2014 some 227m. people were suffering from hunger in sub-Saharan Africa, 24m. more than in 2002, and 57m. more than in the early 1990s. Over one-half of all maternal deaths in the world occur in sub-Saharan Africa. One could be forgiven for assuming that development has achieved little in the continent. Certainly the levels of suffering are almost beyond imagination, reduced to statistics showing in stark numbers the realities of life for millions of people.

Since 2005 the issue of development in Africa has achieved unprecedented prominence on the world stage. The international community has held numerous meetings to discuss poverty alleviation, aid policy and poor-country debt. Major reports have sought to highlight the immediacy of the crisis and define new approaches to development, while from 2006, the emergence of a potential new major player in African development—the People's Republic of China—raised questions about current policy paradigms.

'Development' has largely been presented as a monolithic, universally understood concept that has stood unchanging across the decades. In reality, the meaning of development, in terms of planned development, and the question of how it should be achieved, has shifted during the course of the century of development. In particular, two main questions have exercised those who plan or set policy for, or analyse, development in Africa. First, which agency should be responsible for planning and implementing development? Second, what are the objectives of development? Or in other words, what does 'development' actually mean? The answers to these questions have changed over the past century, and continue to play central roles in the debates about aid and support for current and future African development.

A HISTORY OF DEVELOPMENT IN AFRICA

The Beginnings: Colonial Development to 1939

'Development' in Africa, in the sense of planned interventions in society and economy, began for much of the region with the onset of colonialism. Colonial powers were determined that the newly acquired territories not be a drain on metropolitan treasuries, and that they become sources of income. Early colonial planners regarded Africa as lacking in the vital accoutrements of 'civilization': capitalist social and economic structures (in particular a cash economy); modern communications and transport; and a centralized administration. The colonial task, as it liked to present itself at least, was to mould these new societies and 'develop' them, in order to create modern societies operating within a global market. 'Development' was defined by European perceptions of social organization, European economic need, and the requirements of colonial administrations to maintain power and control.

Reflecting the Victorian division of society into rigidly delineated public, private and philanthropic spheres, early colonial development planning relied on the private sector as the engine of change and development. Capitalist investment would create the required modern institutions and structures, with the state providing the rule of law and order. Welfare activities could be left to the charitable sector (in this case the missions) which would provide the bulk of health and education services to the African population. However, the failure of the anticipated private investment to arrive in the new colonies forced the state to accept responsibility for creating the infrastructure—in particular the ports and railways—essential for the colonial development vision.

For most African countries, agriculture was identified as the critical sector which would drive economic growth and expansion. Development planning, by the early 20th century, had thus become a question of how to increase agricultural output. Administrations faced two broad constraints (one real, one contrived by colonial depictions of Africans) in meeting this objective: a poor infrastructure inhibiting the movement of crops from the field to their end destination in Europe; and a belief that traditional land-use practices could not sustain a massive increase in production for the new export market. The first could be met through government investment. Over 90% of British government loans to the colonies, for example, were for the construction of the railways. By the 1930s a network of roads and rail tracks integrated cash cropping rural hinterlands to the global market. Those areas deemed unproductive were largely ignored and forced to rely on migrant labour as the main opportunity for cash generation.

The second constraint was to be met by encouraging African farmers to change their practices, adopt 'modern' (i.e. European) techniques and new crops. Colonial depictions of African peasantry as inherently conservative and unwilling to change were used to justify compulsion and, in some cases, force. In Uganda in the early 20th century, for example, farmers were forced (often with physical violence) to grow cotton in certain districts. Development was therefore regarded as a fundamentally conflictual process: means were sought to persuade people that the priorities of the colonial state ought to be respected, with such persuasion turning to force where argument alone failed.

Thus over the course of the first two decades of the 20th century, several important characteristics of 'development' had emerged. First, it was defined almost exclusively in economic terms. Second, the characterization of African societies as resistant to modernizing demands created a mindset that development implied conflict between planners and target communities. Development was to be a process of encouraging or forcing people to change, regardless of whether they accepted the logic of externally imposed values. Third, development was a process largely set and controlled by the state. However reluctantly, governments had assumed greater responsibility for development planning and financing. Nevertheless, that financing was to be the responsibility of individual territories, not a burden on the taxpayers of the European powers. Until colonial territories had sufficient incomes to pay for their development, European loans, not grants, would provide the necessary funds. Between 1896 and 1923 some 98% of British government funds for colonial development (across all of the British Empire) were in the form of loans. Colonial assistance (or 'aid' as we would now call it) was to be extremely limited.

By the mid-1920s politicians in Europe, especially in France and the UK, were appealing for an interventionist policy, and improved funding mechanisms for the required modernizations. The foundations of modern official development aid were laid at the end of the 1920s with the British Colonial Development Act (CDA) of 1929. For the first time, taxpayers of one country were to support sustained development of those in another, and largely through aid in the form of grants rather than loans. Over 60% of CDA funds were provided in the form of grants, and of the loan element, around 80% was on easy repayment terms (generally with an interest-free period of three or four years and low rates thereafter).

This was of great significance for future development funding. The principle that development should only be funded through internal revenues was broken, and metropolitan regimes accepted that they had a responsibility to provide aid. Moreover, the types of intervention that the CDA envisaged supporting signalled a new departure in the defining of development. The 'development as economic growth' paradigm was gradually replaced with a model that sought to include welfare concerns. Aid was increasingly understood as a social investment as much as economic. Public health schemes in particular became a significant focus of aid allocations (16% of CDA schemes by 1939, the second highest proportion after communication and transport schemes). Advisory committees reviewing project proposals came to the conclusion that living standards were as important a responsibility of colonial development as increasing productivity and, indeed, could contribute to the latter.

By the end of the 1930s the foundations of the modern development era had been laid. First, the state had gradually accepted responsibility for planning, directing and funding development, abandoning its earlier position that private investment was to be the main driving engine. Second, the definition of what constituted development had widened from almost exclusively economic dimensions to incorporate a social welfare agenda that regarded improving living standards as essential to the developmental mandate.

The Primacy of the State, 1945–70s

Global depression in the 1930s and the onset of war in 1939 impeded the efforts to implement fully the new principles underlying development planning and aid that had emerged by the end of the 1930s. Such efforts were postponed until 1945, from which point colonial and metropolitan governments began to put into effect a more interventionist development policy. Post-war development was characterized by three elements: the absolute primacy of the state in directing, implementing and managing all aspects of development policy; a fuller incorporation of social development/welfarist principles; and the rise of international organizations to prominence in policy setting and funding of development.

The experiences of central planning during the war suggested to the European colonial powers that micromanagement of colonial economies was the most efficient means of ensuring development objectives were met. Colonial administrations devised long-term development plans, used marketing boards to set producer prices and purchase entire crops, increased the number of agricultural advisers, and sought to change laws governing land use, labour migration and urban settlement, pursuing measures designed primarily rapidly to 'modernize' colonial societies. The state was able to exert its full authority over development. Following independence from the late 1950s to the mid-1960s for the majority of sub-Saharan African states, this trend was continued.

But the role of the state in development was founded on more than inherited structures and mechanisms for enforcing control. It also rested on a consensus that development was best left to the state. The creation of a large public sphere was not only tolerated, but encouraged by donors. International overseas development assistance (ODA) was directed through government departments and treasuries across Africa. Government ministers were expected to formulate development plans. The Bretton Woods institutions undertook projects with governments for the large part, rather than private investors or voluntary agencies.

As the state assumed full control over development processes, the breadth of aims to which its activity was directed continued to expand. The definition of 'development' had fully accepted social welfare principles by this period, culminating in the late 1960s with the emergence of 'social development' as

an objective in itself. Social welfare schemes came to dominate colonial aid spending in Africa, a trend continued following independence. The new national governments assumed responsibility for the provision of welfare services. The rise to dominance of social development at the national level reflected broader shifts in the international community: the United Nations (UN) International Development Strategy in 1970 which put social objectives at the heart of the developmental mandate; and the announcement by the President of the World Bank, Robert McNamara, of the 'dethronement of gross national product' as a marker for progress.

Colonial development policy had been geared towards benefiting the metropolitan economy as much as (if not more than) the colonial territories. The independent governments had no such dualistic imperatives to consider in their development policy. However, the departure of colonial administrations left a vacuum into which the emergent international development organizations could enter. While African governments to a large extent could set national policies reflecting their own interpretations of needs and priorities, the International Monetary Fund (IMF), the World Bank, other UN agencies, as well as powerful new donor countries such as the USA and the Soviet Union were increasingly important partners in the process. African countries had since the onset of colonialism been subject to the policies of those who controlled access to funds. With the massive expansion in aid for development, particularly from the 1960s, they became subject to a broader range of interests. While economies grew, significant power over development remained at the national level in Africa. However, the apparent strength of the state in Africa masked a growing vulnerability. Should economic crisis emerge, the authority of those states could be challenged by the new masters of development.

Rolling Back the State, 1980s–90s

From the mid-1970s a global slump in trade, collapsing commodity prices, and the economic shock of successive oil crises undid the advances made by African governments and led to a fundamental reappraisal of international development policy. The weakening economic position of African governments left them less able to meet the rising costs of social welfare and development spending. The sudden rise in interest rates led to the African debt crisis with governments now unable to meet the repayments for loans they were encouraged to take out in the more affluent 1960s and early 1970s. Unable to mitigate the effects of economic crisis themselves, African governments could not sustain internal control over development processes, and from the mid-1980s to the early 1990s they saw a gradual transfer of their power to external donors and international organizations.

The state, identified as the driver of development for over 60 years, was now regarded as its chief brake: states were too big, too unwieldy and too inflexible to the demands of the global market. International donors began to call for the public sector to downsize and to undo its network of controls over economy and society. The market was resurgent, and private investment held up as the solution to poverty and new engine of development. The structural adjustment programmes imposed upon African governments called for the state to act as a manager of development and welfare, not the deliverer. The principles of the free market were to be adopted as African regimes were encouraged to sell off parastatals, cut the number of civil servants and public officials, eliminate subsidies and price supports and open up their economies.

The 'Washington consensus'—a phrase coined by the economist John Williamson in relation to Latin America—came to characterize the new orthodoxy underlying development policy worldwide. Among its key tenets, governments were to impose fiscal discipline, remove controls over interest and exchange rates, liberalize trade, and privatize uncompetitive public assets. While it was never truly a 'consensus' (not all of its policy recommendations were accepted, indeed some were vigorously opposed by the emerging anti-globalization campaigners), its promulgation through organizations such as the World Bank and the IMF and major donors gave it power and authority. Individual countries were forced through economic and political crisis to accept these terms in order to receive continued ODA. The combination of a government crippled by an economic crisis, and Organisation for Economic Co-operation and Development (OECD) member countries prepared to use their aid policies to support the promotion of a new orthodoxy, left many African states few options other than to cede to the demands of international donors. Aid had become a tool for control as much as for development.

The State Resurgent? The Good Governance Agenda

The hoped for massive inflow of private capital following liberalization and structural adjustment did not occur, and development indicators for much of sub-Saharan Africa during the 1990s seemed to go into reverse. As the HIV/AIDS pandemic swept across Africa, with debt levels increasingly unsustainable, along with a series of crop failures, droughts and famines associated with the El Niño effect, it was becoming increasingly clear that the power of the market alone was not sufficient to break through the development bottleneck. Just as the early colonial development planners had been forced to recognize the limits of private investment, the World Bank acknowledged that it had been overzealous in pursuing the rolling back of the state and had unwittingly undermined the ability of states to pursue development.

Governance became the new watchword of development, with the adoption in the early 1990s of the 'good governance' agenda by the World Bank and national and international donors. The 1992 *World Development Report* coined the phrase 'good governance' and placed it at the heart of international development policy, highlighting four key areas: public sector management; accountability; a sound legal framework for development; and transparency.

During the 1990s the technocratic model of the World Bank was refined by major donors and institutions such as the UN, focusing in particular on the democratic deficit in many African countries, the link between human rights and development and the link between effective and efficient states and the provision of equitable and universal social services. Good governance came to be defined as a democratic system, an independent judiciary, transparent structures, with a strong civil society able to participate fully in public life. Development could be achieved, the new orthodoxy suggested, through the use of aid and international development policies to reinforce good governance across the region. As the 1990s drew to a close international funds that a decade earlier had been channelled through non-official agencies, bypassing government ministries, agencies and treasuries, were now to be directed once more through state institutions. Governments across Africa were required by international donors to draw up Sector-Wide Approaches (SWAPs) and Poverty Reduction Strategy Papers (PRSPs) to illustrate a commitment to spending their national income to improve both the developmental prospects of the country and the lives of the most vulnerable.

By the 2000s governance had become the new established orthodoxy of development, and remains so today: development was held to follow the establishment of good governance, and without it, could not flourish. As a result donors invested increasing proportions of aid into governance and civil society programmes. However, evidence for this new orthodoxy is contested, with critics of the 'development follows governance' model pointing to the example of countries such as the Republic of Korea (South Korea), Taiwan and others, where democracy, reductions in corruption and increased transparency followed economic development. Indeed, even the evidence that corruption undermines economic development has been challenged and shown to be far from conclusive.

A more challenging critique of the good governance agenda, however, has been that while it has indeed seen a resurgence of the state, it has not replaced the former pro-market understanding of drivers of development, but actually served to harden reliance on market-based solutions: for the ideal type of governance that donors envisioned in their prescriptions for African reforms in this period were designed not to return to the statism of the 1970s and earlier, but to establish governments capable of creating and maintaining stability and rule of law that would encourage investment. In other words, the logic of good governance in no way challenged the underlying precepts that had driven Washington Consensus-era policies

across Africa. They were, in fact, designed to make those policies more realizable.

Ownership

Accompanying the focus on the institutions and processes of recipient governments under the good governance agenda, donors looked to another (related) issue which they held responsible for poor development performance: ownership. Development, it was argued, would be more successful if recipients 'owned' the policy reforms and programmes they were implementing. The Paris Declaration of 2005, and the Accra Agenda for Action in 2008 requested that donors and recipient countries (now called 'partners' to emphasize this supposed conceptual shift) allow countries to exercise greater leadership over development policy and its implementation. Donors were expected to respect priorities set by partner countries, and to invest in their institutional capacity to deliver.

Ownership was reflected in two new development mechanisms: PRSPs that governments were to draw up through a process of participatory discussions; and SWAPs that were developed in the 1990s to build government capacity in particular sectors such as health, education, agriculture, etc.

PRSPs also built on a growing consensus that development interventions lacked local legitimacy (linking in through this to the good governance agenda), were too short-term in their focus, and failed to build on best practice. Accordingly, PRSPs were established on five key principles: they should be country-driven (enhancing local ownership); they were to be result-oriented; they were to be comprehensive in their definitions of poverty and assessment of the causes of that poverty; they were to be partnership-oriented (i.e. multi-stakeholder in delivery, bringing together public, private and volunteer sectors); and they were to adopt a long-term perspective in their planning. Built into the PRSP process was pro-poor planning: interventions, plans to encourage economic growth, efforts at diversification and increasing foreign direct investment, etc., were all to take into account the needs of the poorest.

Under SWAPs, individual government ministries took responsibility for developing policy and managing expenditure, supported by the SWAP. National governments would establish priorities, engage with stakeholders in drawing up policies and programmes, and disperse and account for donor funding. Health ministries were to receive funds earmarked for public health projects; government agencies responsible for water and sanitation projects were once more put in charge of implementing schemes and programmes.

The concept of ownership raised the issue of donor conditionality. How could national ownership of development be reconciled with donor conditions upon the use of aid? The World Bank and IMF continued to see no major contradiction between the two, but embedded with the Paris Declaration and subsequent agreements was a commitment to reduce *ante-hoc* conditionality.

Reducing conditions, embedding ownership over development policy, and building the institutional capacity of governments to manage and implement development were central planks of the London Agenda of the mid-2000s. Built around the confluence in 2005 of the publication of the Commission for Africa's report, Jeffrey Sachs's *The End of Poverty*, and the Gleneagles Group of Eight leading industrial countries (G8) meeting, donors agreed that they would commit to increased aid flows to facilitate pro-poor development policies in line with the development objectives and priorities focused around the UN Millennium Development Goals (MDGs). All this seemed to reinforce the apparent commitment to building up the African state both through giving it greater control over development processes within its borders and increasing aid to support long-term programming, with African governments committing themselves in return to boosting their ability to undertake this challenge through improving their own governance institutions and processes in line with the good governance agenda.

The result in the early years of the 21st century has been to revive the power of the state to manage development from its moribund condition of the late 1980s and early 1990s, but not so completely as seriously to challenge the power of those who hold the purse strings. The state has been resurgent, not victorious. Moreover, by the end of the 2000s the global financial crisis (which obliged donors to better account for aid delivery and results to an increasingly sceptical public), and perceptions of continued and growing endemic corruption in many of the so-called 'donor darlings' (such as Tanzania and Uganda) led to pressure on donors to return to more directed aid models, rather than the general budgetary support advocated so strongly at the start of the decade.

Rights, Security and Development
If the period from the late 1990s saw a partial return to earlier notions of the role of the state in promoting and directing development, the scope of what the state was supposed to manage continued to evolve. One of the most significant of these shifts was the rights-based approach. During the 1980s human rights organizations began to consider issues of development as part of their mandate. At the same time non-governmental organizations and non-official development-sector workers began to consider how the poor and marginalized could best be guaranteed access to particular services and expectations. Gradually the two merged, creating an understanding that one central task of development was to ensure that all people had access to a range of services and opportunities to which all had a right under an emerging consensus of universal human rights. Thus the right to a certain level of education, to a particular level of health care and to a sustainable livelihood became not responsibilities of a national government to provide, but the right of all people to expect. By framing development objectives as 'rights', governments which had signed up to the new international treaties that were drafted throughout the 1990s could be held to account.

The UN Development Programme's 1994 *Human Development Report* introduced the notion of human security, which was to continue the broadening of the definition of poverty. Human security, the report suggested, consisted of seven areas: economic security, food security, health security, environmental security, personal security, community security and political security. Linked into this, government and international organizations were advised to focus on meeting 'basic needs' as part of a growing emphasis on meeting the needs of the poorest of the poor. These concerns found their way into the pro-poor planning systems that emerged in the mid- to late 1990s (and were encapsulated in the new PRSPs), and were incorporated into the formulation of the MDGs that were to shape development objectives from 2000.

However, at the same time, a rival construction of the link between 'security' and 'development' emerged. With the rise of the securitization of development discourse in the 1990s, poverty and global security concerns became conflated. Development became increasingly defined as a global security concern, and interventions characterized as protecting Western interests from instability as much as reducing the impact of poverty on the poor and poor countries themselves. The result was that the social and economic concerns of donor agencies became increasingly intertwined with the security concerns of donor foreign policy. In the USA the State Department became an increasingly important deliverer of aid, with control over a significant aid budget. Military forces have become used with greater frequency in delivering aid and implementing programmes. Non-governmental organizations have expressed concern over the conflation of humanitarian and military objectives in intervention in conflicts, a process highlighted by the experiences of working in Somalia from 1992. This process continued into the 2000s, accelerated (but not initiated) by the September 2001 terrorist attacks in the USA.

It was not just poverty that was increasingly securitized: health issues too became imbued with a security prism. In 2000 the UN declared HIV/AIDS to constitute a security risk, while in 2002 the US National Intelligence Council released a report outlining the diseases presenting a potential security risk for US interests (the Central Intelligence Agency had suggested HIV/AIDS constituted such a threat as early as 1987, but for different, and as it turned out, unfounded, reasons).

To return to the two questions that have formed the basis of development debates over the course of the past century—

those of agency and of objective—one can see that the argument has come full circle in the case of the former. In current debates it is the state that is dominant in managing and implementing development. There is a broad consensus, however, that it must be a particular type of state: one that is transparent and democratic; that pursues sound macroeconomic management; that puts poverty alleviation and eradication at the heart of its agenda; that guarantees the rule of law; and that protects the rights of its citizens. In terms of the objectives towards which this state is oriented, however, the definition of development has continued to widen, incorporating new ideas, notions, priorities and trends. Development no longer means economic growth from which all else will flow: it incorporates broad social objectives; notions of people's right to certain opportunities, services and levels of care; and issues of sustainability and security. Development has come to mean the creation of an entirely different society, where absolute poverty is eradicated, where all people have access to the same opportunities and where all live without fear. But 'development' in Africa is also presented as a means to ensure stability and security in the global North; and to ensure a more stable environment in which investors from the global North and rising powers such as China can be more certain of the safety of those investments. The question is whether these are complementary, or contradictory, claims for what development is and should be in Africa.

AID AND DEVELOPMENT IN AFRICA TODAY
At the turn of the century, the international community moved towards larger scale targets for eradicating poverty. The MDGs (2000–15) were a set of eight goals divided into specific targets around absolute poverty, hunger, education, and maternal and child mortality. In 2015 the Sustainable Development Goals (SDGs) replaced the MDGs: a wider set of 17 goals and 169 targets for tackling poverty, inequality, injustice and (seen as a critically important addition) the climate emergency by 2030. Both have been criticized for reinforcing the power of international organizations and donors in setting development priorities, and reducing the policy space for African governments to operate in.

The SDGs marked a shift from 'international' to 'global' development. Under international development, power remained vested in donors and the global North, which controlled policy and funding, and situated the 'problem' to be addressed in the global South. Global development was built upon a principle that development problems were global, and that true collaboration and partnerships were essential to the eradication of poverty, improving lives and protecting the planet.

Nevertheless, some continued to argue that the SDGs remained embedded in an economic growth model of development, with insufficient attention paid to the issue of inequalities in the distribution of, and access to, resources. Others argued that the model still gave too much power to institutions in the global North, and did not live up to its promise to share power more equitably. Despite these criticisms, the SDGs were deemed to have been successful in shaping global development priorities in Africa (and worldwide) until the events of 2020 forced a radical reorientation of those priorities.

Progress was made towards the SDGs in 2015–20 in Africa, notably in relation to: SDG3 (good health and wellbeing); SDG4 (quality education); SDG6.1 (access to clean water); and SDG7.1 (access to electricity). However, even before the outbreak of the COVID-19 pandemic, concerns were growing about the relatively slow pace of progress in eradicating poverty (SDG1) and ending hunger (SDG2).

With global attention currently focused on how to manage the COVID-19 crisis, less attention has been paid to the longer-term implications for broader development. The most immediate impact of COVID-19 was on short- to medium-term development financing. With most official donor aid tied to gross national income, the economic impact of the pandemic was already reducing development finance before several donors (in particular the UK, Australia and Japan) reduced their official aid spending to prioritize their own economic needs.

These cuts came at a time of increased requirement, as the pandemic reversed a general downward trend in global poverty, with the majority of countries likely to see this reversal over the medium term concentrated in sub-Saharan Africa[1]. With sub-Saharan Africa as a region experiencing a recession as a result of the pandemic[2], and with a decline in global trade and investment in the region, millions will be pushed into poverty, and more people will be reliant on a declining trend in official development assistance.

One consequence for global development is likely to be an increased focus on inequality, as the pandemic exacerbates existing, and creates new forms of, inequality and vulnerability. There is also likely to be a greater emphasis on social infrastructure and protection as against economic growth as a core focus for development interventions.

The biggest shift, however, is likely to come from the impact of the climate emergency. As evidence of climate change induced crises continued to mount from the 2000s, in the form of the increased frequency of droughts, heavier rains and flooding, crop failures and shifting health environments as new areas became more conducive to disease carrying vectors, climate change mitigation is becoming increasingly central (although still not central enough) to global development policy and aid.

The failure of many health, education and other systems during the COVID-19 crisis also drew increased attention to resilient systems, and systems capable of withstanding shocks and crises are only going to become more common as a result of the climate emergency.

THE RISE OF NEW DEVELOPMENT ACTORS?

In the late 2000s a new group of donors, largely from the emerging economies and led primarily by China, began to make a greater impact on African development and aid. At the beginning of 2006 China declared its intention to extend and deepen its links with sub-Saharan Africa, through its 'Africa Policy'. Japan too has increased the scale of its commitment to sub-Saharan Africa, announcing in May 2008 that it would double its aid to Africa by 2012 to US $3,500m., as well as providing access to $4,000m. of low-interest rate loans. India and Saudi Arabia have also increased aid to Africa. Turkey, too, has used aid, alongside diplomacy, foreign investment and support for Islam, as a means to increase its presence across sub-Saharan Africa. Turkey spent around 1.1% of its gross national income (GNI) in development aid in 2018[3].

The rise of new donors, and China in particular, has caused concern among OECD donors over the potential impact on its policy of linking good governance, 'pro-poor' growth and development. China's willingness to respect national sovereignty and internal political decisions is viewed in some quarters as giving rise to a 'Beijing consensus' that challenges the insistence of western donors on attaching conditions to development aid. Sudan and Zimbabwe, both recipients of significant amounts of Chinese aid, are held up as examples of how China is allegedly subverting international efforts to promote change.

Although there was little prospect of new donors replacing the traditional OECD-group of donors (the Chinese Government, for example, is developing African programmes in partnership with the World Bank), some have detected a return to the Cold War politics of aid and development, where aid was used as a diplomatic and strategic tool for leveraging support.

FROM REGIONS TO FRAGILE STATES

If from the mid-2000s the focus amongst donors on global development challenges had turned, in rhetoric if not always followed by the money, to sub-Saharan Africa, in the mid-2010s gains (questionable as some may be) made during the MDG process in reducing certain markers of poverty, and the rise of former low-income states (including Ghana, Nigeria, Zambia, Senegal and Cameroon) to middle-income country (MIC) status or near middle-income status—Kenya, Rwanda, Sierra Leone and Zimbabwe are forecast to become MICs by 2025—led to new questions about aid. In particular, whether aid

should be more targeted at the remaining pockets of extreme poverty—colloquially known as fragile and conflict states. Fragile states and conflict states were more likely, donors argued, to be tipped into a crisis as a result of adverse economic, social, political or environmental events. Moreover, they were less able to escape the cycle of crisis and poverty and move towards middle-income status.

However, middle-income status, which formally begins when economies reach the US $1,005 per capita GNI mark, is problematic as a guide for aid flows. Firstly, the benchmark is still very low, and recent entries to that group are still poor by global standards. Gabon is in theory well above the MIC threshold, for example, with a per capita GNI of $6,610[4]. Yet almost one-third of its population remains vulnerable; under-5 mortality is 47.4 per 1,000 live births, which is lower than low-income country Tanzania (57 per 1,000 births)[5] but not substantially so. Similarly, GNI per head for Equatorial Guinea is $8,250[6], but immunization rates for measles are just 30%; the under-5 mortality rate is 90.9 per 1,000 live births; and one-quarter of the population do not have access to an improved water source[7]. Middle-income status can therefore hide ongoing vulnerability. Secondly, the concept of 'fragile state' has increasingly engaged with pockets of internal fragility, further undermining national-based assessments. Thirdly, how a country has reached middle-income status is important. Mature MICs such as Botswana, Mauritius and South Africa have had longer transitions to ensure their economies are resilient, and their governments are able to respond to domestic development needs (although, as South Africa has shown over the past decade, this is not unproblematic).

CONCLUSION: THE CHALLENGE FOR THE FUTURE

To return to the question posed at the beginning of the essay: has development failed in Africa? It is true that many human development indicators remain poor, and millions remain affected by hunger, easily treatable health issues, and lack of access to resources and services, which together undermine their capacity to escape poverty. The story of development also appears to be one in which voices from Africa have been silenced by successive external powers. But, as ever, external aid and development policy devised in the USA and in Europe is but one aspect of Africa's hope for the future. Ultimately the answers lie, as they always have, within the continent itself. Development policy has too often been implemented with the interests of non-Africans at its heart. Policies have been started and abruptly stopped as trends and debates have shifted. The developed world has forced African countries to accept free markets while continuing to impose restrictions in their own. But through the constantly shifting international policies, the citizens of Africa have sought to improve their daily lives in small, incremental ways.

This essay has focused on the broad debates and shifting agendas in African development. However, it would be wrong to conclude that the sole story of development is located there. Self-help and community groups across Africa, civil society organizations, local faith and secular development groups have undertaken local schemes and projects with little, if any, external assistance. Colonial and international policies have been resisted and refined by those living with the consequences. African governments have in the recent past sought to address in concert some of the problems facing the continent. Through the establishment of the New Partnership for Africa's Development, the African Union, the creation of an African peacekeeping force, through free trade zones and other institutional unions, Africa is gradually restoring a measure of control over its own destiny. Of course, not all is positive. Corruption and violence continue to undermine development efforts. Violent conflict takes its toll in life and human misery. The lack of resources means many states are unable to meet their commitments, even where willing. However, should, as the past tells us is likely, the world avoid its responsibilities and once more push African poverty to the back of the international agenda, the prospects for development and poverty alleviation will continue to lie with Africans themselves.

FOOTNOTES

[1] Kharas, H., and Dooley, M. 'Long-run impacts of COVID-19 on extreme poverty'. www.brookings.edu/blog/future-development/ 2021/06/02/long-run-impacts-of-covid-19-on-extreme-poverty, 2 June 2021. Accessed 21 July 2021.

[2] World Bank. 'World Bank confirms economic downturn in sub-Saharan Africa'. www.worldbank.org/en/news/press-release/2020/ 10/08/world-bank-confirms-economic-downturn-in-sub-saharan-africa-outlines-key-polices-needed-for-recovery, 8 October 2020. Accessed 21 July 2021.

[3] OECD. 'Development aid drops in 2018, especially to neediest countries'. www.oecd.org/newsroom/development-aid-drops-in-2018-especially-to-neediest-countries.htm, 10 April 2019. Accessed 30 July 2020.

[4] data.worldbank.org/country/gabon.

[5] data.unicef.org/country/gab/.

[6] data.worldbank.org/country/equatorial-guinea.

[7] data.unicef.org/country/gnq/.

AN ANALYSIS OF THE RULE OF LAW IN SUB-SAHARAN AFRICA

LEIGHANN SPENCER

INTRODUCTION

The rule of law, in its simplest connotation, accords the law supremacy and sees it applied to all persons, institutions and entities, including the state itself. The characteristics of the rule of law include, but are not necessarily limited to, the following:

i) the law must be adopted through an established process;

ii) the law must be transparent and accessible;

iii) the law must be consistently applied (certainty before the law);

iv) the law must be applied with procedural fairness;

v) that no one is above the law (all are equal before the law).

This essay will first outline the ideas and debates floated about the rule of law before providing an overview as to how modern sub-Saharan Africa has fared on upholding this ideal. It will then delve deeper into key components of the rule of law with specific case studies from the continent, and a discussion as to why failures to uphold said components have occurred. Stemming from the case studies, it will identify some of the broader consequences of the breakdown of the rule of law. Finally, this essay provides recommendations as to promoting the rule of law in sub-Saharan Africa

The rule of law as both a theoretical and practical concept is contentious. The origin of the concept is elusive; the phrase has been stated to have been in use since the 17th century, from John Locke's *Two Treatises of Government*, becoming popular from the 19th century with the works of Albert Venn Dicey. However, the philosophical underpinnings can be drawn back to the likes of Aristotle in ancient Greece. This Westernized version of the history of the rule of law is a point of contention, with the argument that components of the rule of law can be found throughout many societies and cultures over the ages. This is an important consideration, as perceptions of the rule of law as a Western concept can have implications for its implementation in African (and other) nations.

For now, it is safe to say that the concept has somewhat existed globally for centuries. Yet what it entails is hardly settled. That is not to say the idea itself is contested; as put by Stewart (2004, p. 136), the rule of law is generally seen as necessary 'because if we stop believing in it, the ideals that it represents will cease to exist and the practical effects would be disastrous'. Rather, it is the scope and utility that are still subject to debate. In terms of scope, some restrict the concept to a formalist framework, while others look to substantive frameworks. The formalist framework posits that the rule of law requires certain procedural attributes, these being transparent and accessible laws, an effective judicial system and effective law enforcement agencies. The substantive framework broadens this to examine the ends to the means of the rule of law, conflating the concept with other liberal ideals such as democracy and human rights.

Related to this is the utility of the rule of law. As some argue, upholding procedural attributes does not necessarily equal a good political regime nor provide an effective model for assessing performance. Those most critical, for instance within Marxist and feminist fields of thought, consider it as a legitimating ideology that serves the class-or-gender-based function of the law. The same can be said for regimes of systematic racism and religious intolerance. As such, there have been calls for the abolishment of the 'outdated' concept. Conversely, many prefer to turn to the substantive approach to consider the actual content and consequences of law. For instance, the United Nations (UN) addresses the rule of law by its intersection with three pillars: peace and security; human rights; and development. Several protocols, including the Universal Declaration of Human Rights, include aspects of both formalist and substantive rule of law. This essay does not intend to dismiss potential shortcomings of the rule of law, nor the importance of related liberal ideals. However, for sake of space and clarity, it largely analyses the components of the rule of law across sub-Saharan Africa in the formalist sense.

Before doing so it is important to return to the perception of the rule of law as a Western-centric import that has no application to countries such as those in Africa, or that it may be a neocolonial assertion of control or suppression. To combat such perceptions, African scholars have drawn attention to alternate histories of the concept and how it can be underscored by African values such as Ubuntu, and to the recent use of the rule of law to obtain liberation, good governance and human rights. Indeed, the African Union's (AU) Agenda 2063 envisions the rule of law as a precursor to broader ideals, and the rule of law is embedded in regional protocols such as the African Charter on Human Rights and the African Charter on Democracy, Elections and Governance. It is imperative that one considers the African context when addressing the rule of law on the continent.

HOW DOES SUB-SAHARAN AFRICA FARE ON THE RULE OF LAW?

As an elusive concept, the rule of law is difficult to measure. Several indexes monitoring democracy, development, and human rights include it as an indicator, considering factors such as judicial independence, due process, access to information, and equality in laws and politics[1]. Most pertinently, the World Justice Project (WJP) specifically monitors the rule of law worldwide and will be the mode of general measure here. Its annual Rule of Law Index looks at eight factors: constraints on government powers, being effective limitation of executive over-reach; absence of corruption in all government branches; open government, including access to information and complaint processes; fundamental rights; order and security surrounding crime and conflict; regulatory enforcement, being effective administrative proceedings; effective civil justice; and effective criminal justice.

Across 139 countries ranked in the 2021 Rule of Law Index, Rwanda (42nd), Namibia (44th), and Mauritius (45th) are the only African countries to make the top 50. In the bottom 25 countries, sub-Saharan Africa is represented by the Democratic Republic of the Congo (DRC, 137th), Cameroon (135th), Mauritania (133rd), Zimbabwe (127th), Uganda (125th), Mozambique (123rd), Ethiopia (122nd), Nigeria (121st), Guinea (120th), the Republic of the Congo (118th), Sudan (116th) and Mali (115th). The majority of countries in the region saw a decrease or no change in ranking since the year prior. This snapshot shows that a lack of rule of law is a pervasive problem across sub-Saharan Africa.

According to the WJP, notably worrying trends across sub-Saharan Africa are: corruption; lack of sanctions for official misconduct; limited access to information; the likelihood for violence to redress grievances; and issues with criminal justice including lack of due process, ineffective investigations and government influence on its application. This has been exacerbated by state of emergency measures and the diversion of resources to combat COVID-19. These trends can be linked to the formalist framework and the three procedural aspects necessary for rule of law. These are:

i) effective judicial systems;

ii) effective law enforcement agencies (both these and the judicial systems must be honest, impartial, and able to provide procedural fairness and certainty and equality before the law, and be in place alongside);

iii) transparent and accessible law, including access to information as well as access to the judicial system and law enforcement.

These would also reduce the likelihood for violence which occurs when conventional methods are considered illegitimate.

The following sections take a closer look at the three procedural aspects in modern sub-Saharan Africa.

JUDICIAL EFFECTIVENESS

Arguably, an effective judicial system is the foremost attribute to engender the rule of law via application of laws in a procedural, consistent, and equal manner. It is a vital mechanism for oversight, important to consider in the context of emergency powers utilized during COVID-19. Central to judicial effectiveness is that it remains an autonomous authority. A core principle of democracy is the separation of powers: the requirement of an executive arm; a legislative arm; and a judicial arm of government, all of which are independent and thus can provide checks and balances against one another. The separation of legislative and executive powers was expounded by Locke as key to the rule of law, with Montesquieu including the judiciary soon after in *The Spirit of Laws*. Despite being a long-held principle, a regular concern when it comes to the rule of law in Africa is executive over-reach. This section focuses on executive interference into the judiciary with reference to Peter VonDoepp and Rachel Ellett's six tactics.

The first tactic is general institutional assaults. This involves institutional restructuring to restrict the issues a court can rule on, the bypassing of the judiciary, or a failure to abide by its rulings. This tactic is ripe across sub-Saharan Africa. For instance, in Nigeria, it has been calculated that President Muhammadu Buhari has ignored court decisions on at least 40 occasions since coming to power in May 2015[2]. These included ignoring release orders for Islamic Movement of Nigeria leader Sheikh Ibrahim Zakzaky, who was been held in unlawful detention for over six years. While he was finally discharged in July 2021, there have been continued efforts to delay court proceedings to provide Zakzaky and his wife with passports to obtain medical attention abroad, leading to large-scale 'free Zakzaky' protests. Buhari has also ignored orders to divulge financial details in relation to corruption allegations. Judicial oversight for corruption took on a further dimension during the pandemic, with allegations of mismanaged funds which were donated to combat COVID-19 in countries such as Nigeria, Cameroon, Uganda, Kenya, Uganda and Malawi. In short, institutional assaults create impunity for some, and a lack of due process for others.

The second tactic is personal manipulation, which revolves around judicial appointments, primarily by appointing judges who support the executive and purging those who make dissenting decisions. In several sub-Saharan countries, judges—or at least the highest echelons of the judiciary—are explicitly appointed by the executive. These include Rwanda, Angola, Cameroon, Senegal, Mali, Gabon, Equatorial Guinea and Eritrea[3]. This is a direct subversion of the separation of powers and thus the rule of law. By appointing judges, the executive can ensure arbiters are those who will make decisions in line with the regime's will. For instance, in Gabon, Marie-Madeleine Mborantsuo has been the President of the Constitutional Court since its inception in 1991, and prior to that was President of the Supreme Court. Mborantsuo was the mistress of Omar Bongo Ondimba, former President of Gabon and father of current President Ali Bongo Ondimba. She has played a direct role in numerous controversial decisions.

In other sub-Saharan countries, the tactic of personal manipulation is more covert. In Kenya the independent Judicial Service Commission (JSC) nominates judges and lawyers. However, they are then sworn in by the executive. In 2019 President Uhuru Kenyatta refused to swear in 41 nominees on the grounds of 'integrity concerns'—and this was not the first occasion on which this had happened. When the JSC requested further details it was refused, and the case was taken to court. In February 2020 the High Court ordered the executive to swear in the judges and lawyers within 14 days. This was not carried out until June 2021—whereupon Kenyatta still refused six of the 41 nominees—demonstrating an overlap of personal manipulation and institutional assaults.

Personal manipulation is linked to the third tactic, which is remuneration manipulation, or the control of judicial salaries to reward or punish personnel. Although difficult to ascertain exact instances of remuneration manipulation, the majority of African judiciaries depend on the executive for their budgets, affecting salaries alongside overall efficiency. In 2018 Kenyatta reduced the Kenyan judicial budget by US $30m., purportedly in retaliation for the court's 2017 annulment of the presidential election results. In 2019 the budget was again cut by $29m., although this was restored in 2020 just days after the Chief Justice accused the executive of deliberately undermining the judiciary. Nevertheless, tensions remain, particularly with the court making another critical ruling against Kenyatta in May 2021. This stated that in the President's bid to amend the Constitution to create new executive positions and constituencies, he failed to meet the leadership and integrity threshold[4].

The fourth tactic used by the executive to interfere with the judiciary is personal attacks; the public badgering of, or personal threats against, judicial personnel by the head of state or government or other politicians. This can include investigations or threats of investigations, all which work to delegitimize or intimidate the judiciary. For instance, several Constitutional Court judges in Malawi were threatened and bombarded with unsubstantiated allegations of bribery when they ruled for an annulment of the 2019 presidential election. In 2020, when a High Court judge made several rulings against the will of then President Prof. Arthur Peter Mutharika, including an injunction against a COVID-19 lockdown until measures were put in place to protect those of low socio-economic class, he faced public harassment declaring that he was responsible for spreading the virus.

Personal attacks can be found elsewhere. In South Africa the judiciary is regularly criticized by members of the ruling African National Congress (ANC). Although in this context, former President and ANC member Jacob Zuma was held to account for contempt of court in 2021 and sentenced to 15 months' imprisonment. The Court stated that its 'scurrilous and unfounded attacks on the judiciary and its members were intolerable and could not be met with impunity'. This conviction demonstrated the importance of an independent judiciary and was considered a win for the rule of law. None the less, personal attacks are damaging, and can even turn physical as seen with the 2020 murder of a DRC judge who presided over the corruption trial of the President's chief of staff.

The fifth and sixth tactics identified by VonDoepp and Ellett are patronage, and personal links and communications. The former relates to the presence of patronage politics and how this can extend to the judiciary as a form of control; the latter concerns structural links such as regular consultations between the executive and the judiciary. In Equatorial Guinea patronage politics has created a judicial system loyal to President Gen. (retd) Obiang Nguema Mbasogo, and has played a role in him becoming the longest-serving president in the world. In Angola senior judicial positions are often filled by those with personal links to the ruling party. We can also see this in the case of Gabon's Mborantsuo. Material coercion and secret consultations with the judiciary by both those within and outside of government is further problematic. This all impacts the ability of the judiciary to make fair and consistent decisions based on law.

These categories are comprehensive and cover various types of interference which occur in sub-Saharan Africa. However, some have criticized the focus on 'judicial interference', arguing that in some countries there is no judicial arm of government to begin with. As Kamga (2019, p. 60) argues: 'if the executive power in Cameroon was to interfere with the judiciary, it would be similar to colluding with its own shadow'. The same could be said for all of the above-mentioned countries in which judges are explicitly appointed by the executive. Cameroon is such a country as Section 37(3) of the Constitution provides the President with the power to 'appoint members of the [judicial] bench and for the legal department'. This has been the case since independence in 1960; executive control of the judiciary is well and truly entrenched. Such control has contributed to the marginalization of those from the anglophone regions, and by extension, to the current conflict in the nation[5].

Cameroon is also a prime example of executive control of the legislative arm. Laws are more often than not adopted by presidential decree rather than through established legislative procedure. When the legislature is involved, it largely acts merely to rubber stamp the wishes of President Paul Biya. Rule by decree further became a concern worldwide when countries enacted state of emergencies to deal with the COVID-19 pandemic. Although allowing extraordinary executive powers is a routine response to emergencies, it is ripe for exploitation, as has been the case in countries such as Togo, Guinea, the DRC, Rwanda, Angola, Zimbabwe and Malawi. In this last the virus could not have emerged at a better time for President Mutharika, who was facing nationwide protests and general unpopularity in the lead up to June's presidential election re-run. Immediately after declaring a state of emergency, Mutharika used his extraordinary powers to ban opposition protests and rallies.

The fact that Malawi had an election re-run is, however, an example of good judicial workings. The May 2019 presidential election was beset with irregularities, and in February 2020, the Constitutional Court nullified the results and demanded that the poll be reheld. In May the Supreme Court upheld this decision. In June, just days before the election re-run was to take place, the Government placed the Chief Justice and the second most senior justice on leave pending retirement. This attempt at personal manipulation was overturned after an extensive backlash. The repeat poll, held on 23 June, resulted in a victory for the opposition candidate, Dr Lazarus Chakwera, who secured 59.3% of the valid votes cast, and was well received by Malawians. The role of the judiciary in facilitating the election re-run followed in the footsteps of Kenya, where the Supreme Court annulled the 2017 presidential election due to irregularities. As shown, both countries' judiciaries faced executive backlash for these decisions. This substantiates a common proposition as to why the executive chooses to interfere with the judiciary: the judicialization of politics.

This refers to the extent to which judiciaries become arbitrators in political decisions and their behaviour when doing so[6]. Interestingly, research has also shown that it is when judiciaries are quasi-independent that post-election violence is most likely to flare as an annulment is perceived possible but only with public assertion. Such violence has been apparent in both Malawi and Kenya in the lead up to annulments. This highlights the need for full independence of the courts in order to promote democracy without the need for violent redress. None the less, Malawi and Kenya have set important precedents for judiciaries as a check against state power and thus as guardians of the rule of law. These two countries have accordingly scored high on the WJP Rule of Law Index. However, there are certainly many instances in sub-Saharan Africa where irregular elections have been upheld by courts which are fully non-independent.

In Gabon decisions by Mborantsuo have included upholding election results in favour of the Bongo family. Thus, the executive appointment of judges has had a direct impact on democratic electoral processes. In Uganda popular opposition leader Robert Kyagulanyi Ssentamu (known as Bobi Wine) attempted to contest the 2021 re-election of President Yoweri Museveni, but later withdrew his case citing court bias. In a similar vein, fully non-independent courts have seen the extension of presidential term limits, a successful strategy in 18 African countries since 2000[7]. The 2018 removal of the age limit in Uganda, upheld by the Supreme Court, paved the way for Museveni to rule for life. In 2015 in Burundi the Constitutional Court upheld the right of Pierre Nkurunziza to run for a third presidential term; it was subsequently revealed that the judges had been forced into this decision. Both Uganda and Burundi have experienced ongoing unrest with serious human rights violations as a result. This is a notable trend when term limits are prolonged, with the latest casualty being Guinea in 2020. This shows how failures of the rule of law can stunt the promotion of broader liberal ideals.

POLICE EFFECTIVENESS

Just as effective judiciaries are vital for the rule of law to function, so are the gatekeepers to the justice system: the police. And similar to judiciaries, police effectiveness is hindered by issues of corruption, patronage, and low budgets. These issues affect certainty and equality before the law, not to mention procedural fairness, arguably the most visible failure of the rule of law across many African nations. It is important to note that these issues can be found in other state security agencies such as the military. However, the focus here is on police forces.

A 2022 survey by LexisNexis showed that 52% of respondents viewed corruption as the biggest impediment to the rule of law in Africa, with 6% stating that this increased with the pandemic. Corruption is perceived to be greatest amongst police forces, with citizens often having to pay bribes to receive services. This is related to patronage, which creates security for the highest bidder and has been observed in several countries such as Uganda, Kenya, the DRC, Nigeria, Sierra Leone, and South Africa[8]. For instance, the Zondo Commission of Inquiry (COI) in South Africa, better known as the Commission into State Capture, which concluded in January 2022, aimed to reveal the extent to which state organs and resources have been appropriated to enrich private citizens causing a collapse in state functions for the majority. The Zondo COI included investigations into criminal justice mechanisms such as the South African Police Service (SAPS). Witness testimonies alleged that SAPS runs on a network of patronage and is compromised at the highest levels: promotions are based on favours to senior officers, who make corrupt deals with service providers, while resources are diverted to protect the elite in and outside of SAPS, and this goes unfettered as officers are forced to play the game or resign.

While the South African elite are protected and enriched by the SAPS, disparities are perpetuated among the general population. In 2019 a ground-breaking judgement was made by the Western Cape Equality Court: the allocation of police resources in the province discriminated against people on the basis of race and socioeconomic status. This stemmed from evidence revealed during the O'Regan COI which concluded in 2014. For instance, whereas the affluent, predominantly white Camps Bay area had a police to population ratio of 1:113, the poor, predominantly black Harare area ratio was 1:719. However, despite the O'Regan COI and the Equality Court judgement, change has yet to be shown. What has been shown is how this affects order and security, as those areas with low police resources have the highest crime rates.

Policing inequalities can be seen elsewhere, such as in Nigeria where many officers are delegated as personal guards for the wealthy. Corruption is rampant here also. During the COVID-19 lockdowns and restrictions on movement, both police and military officials were reported to have taken bribes to allow people to pass through checkpoints. At the same time, a young man was killed in Warri after he failed to stop at a checkpoint. This highlights the lack of certainty and equality before the law. As to police budgets designated by the executive, this can perpetuate issues: for example, poor salaries result in officers turning to alternate payment routes, and poor regional funds see an unequal distribution across stations. And again, to reiterate the above point, ineffective law enforcement and security agencies lead to poor order and security, as seen with the spate of kidnappings and armed burglaries, and the enduring herder–farmer conflict and Boko Haram insurgency in Nigeria.

In addition to, and often related to, the above factors, is the lack of due process displayed by police across the continent. This includes the exertion of excessive force, arbitrary arrests, and illegal detention. Excessive force was utilized to enforce COVID-19 lockdowns in countries such as Nigeria, Kenya, Rwanda, and South Africa. Within five days of the announcement of Nigeria's lockdown in April 2020, 18 people had been extrajudicially killed by the police, including the young man in Warri, and a further 105 human rights violations were reported. By the time the lockdown ended in May, more Nigerians had died at the hands of the police than had died due to COVID-19. It has been speculated that the heavy-handed lockdown enforcement will impact community-police relations far beyond the pandemic. Indeed, longstanding grievances against the Nigerian Special Anti-Robbery Squad (SARS) resurfaced in late 2020 during the Black Lives Matter protests elsewhere. The Nigerian protests, dubbed #EndSARS, were met with live bullets killing at least 12. Over 1,500 were arrested, and the media was restricted from reporting on the issue. Although the Government eventually agreed to disband the SARS, concerns remain given that their mandate and personnel have been allocated elsewhere and little more has been done to improve the force. As such, the #EndSARS movement continues with the goal of overall police reform.

Similarly, protests against police brutality exploded in South Africa when an unarmed 16-year-old boy with Down's syndrome was shot dead in August 2020. As noted, the months prior to this incident had seen excessive force used to implement COVID-19 restrictions. However, the statistics show that 2020 was not an unusual year. In fact, the SAPS average about 430 killings every year. In 2020 in Kenya a total of 168 people were killed by police—compared to 145 in 2019 (pre-COVID-19), and to 219 in 2021 when restrictions had lifted[9]. It is important to recognize that although carried out under a new pretext with COVID-19, these were not new or isolated cases. The same goes for Rwanda, which came under scrutiny in 2020 when numerous people were arbitrarily arrested for COVID-19 infractions and detained in stadiums without due process. Yet for years Rwandan authorities have illegally detained citizens. From 2017 legal frameworks have enabled two months detention for anyone exhibiting 'deviant behaviours' without any further legal justification.

Arbitrary arrests and illegal detention have become commonplace to ruling regimes when dealing with opposition. In Uganda the January 2021 election and Museveni's securing of a sixth term in office led to hundreds of arrests of opposition members and supporters. The primary opposition leader, Wine, was illegally held under house arrest for almost two weeks. Furthermore, there were hundreds of enforced disappearances 2019–21, including children and women. People have been abducted from the streets or their homes, detained and beaten, and accused of political crimes. The Ugandan parliamentary human rights committee released a report revealing unofficial facilities across the country, known as 'safe houses', where incommunicado detention, forced labour and torture was rampant. In 2021 some detainees were released due to public pressure, although claim to be subject to ongoing surveillance and threats. Moreover, many remain missing, and Museveni has undermined investigations by denying the enforced disappearances have occurred.

Another example of state-sponsored violence is that of Ethiopia, where ethno-political tensions have consistently resulted in abuse by various security agencies. In 2020 this exploded into a full-blown conflict with the federal intention to eradicate the Tigray People's Liberation Front. Fighting has largely occurred in Tigray and the neighbouring Afar and Amhara regions, with reports of massacres and widespread sexual violence. Over 2.6m. people have been displaced. Furthermore, Tigrayans across the country have been targeted. Between December 2021 and February 2022 over 1,500 arbitrary arrests and detentions were documented. In early March the UN appointed investigators to collect evidence for prosecutions at the International Criminal Court. By end of that month Prime Minister Dr Abiy Ahmed Ali declared a humanitarian truce. However, whether this is working is contentious, with claims that the federal Government is still restricting provision of aid. And should the conflict end, it is almost certain that inequality before the law will remain. Indeed, in sub-Saharan Africa, large scale abuses by police and other security agencies are often due to longstanding identity politics, highlighting the impacts on broader liberal ideals.

Another impacted liberal ideal is that of press freedom. Journalists have been threatened and arrested in Ethiopia for covering the aforementioned abuses. In May 2022 at least 18 were arrested, with two facing the death penalty. International journalists have also been targeted; *The Economist*'s correspondent in Addis Ababa was expelled in May 2022 after his accreditation was revoked. This came a year after the *New York Times'* correspondent was forced to leave. Similar tactics have been used in countries such as Uganda, Eritrea, Nigeria, Mali, Benin, Burkina Faso and the DRC. In this last three journalists were arrested after covering protests against the Equateur provincial governor: one in November 2021, and two in January 2022. The former was only released in July 2022 and the two others remain in detention. These cases

demonstrate the influence of executive over-reach on the justice system.

The issues hindering police effectiveness as outlined in this section impact certainty and equality before the law, and procedural fairness for citizens in many sub-Saharan African countries. While police forces may see disregarding the rule of law as a necessary trade-off for order and security, research shows that order and security is inextricably linked to upholding the rule of law. Finally, it should be stressed that police accountability is practically non-existent. There are various reasons for this, such as lack of evidence, poor resources and regulations for investigation and prosecution, state interference, unwilling witnesses due to fear of retaliation, and the fact that it is generally police investigating police. In essence, this means that the police are often held above the law.

ACCESSIBLE LAW

The final precondition to formalist rule of law is that the law must be transparent and accessible. This is often conceptualized as access to justice. The issues described thus far regarding judicial and police effectiveness not only create inequalities and uncertainty before the law; they also affect access to justice. Afrobarometer surveys reveal disturbing figures conveying a lack of access to justice across Africa. One survey, which looked at perceptions of police, found that 56% of respondents who had been victims of crime did not report it due to the belief that the police could not/would not help or would demand a bribe. In addition, 59% of overall respondents stated that it was not easy to obtain assistance from the police, and 32% stated that women were faced with unequal treatment by police.

Another Afrobarometer survey, which looked at perceptions of the courts, found that 43% of respondents trusted the courts 'not at all' or 'just a little'. Of those who had contact with courts, 30% had paid a bribe, 38% had been unable to pay legal costs and 47% could not understand legal procedures. Furthermore, 60% had experienced long delays. In terms of demographics, low socioeconomic class was the greatest indicator of poor access to legal redress, while residing in a rural area also played a role. These issues have been exacerbated by COVID-19. Most countries either suspended or severely limited court proceedings, impeding access to justice particularly for these demographics, such as those without internet where proceedings moved online. (A total of 16 African countries have less than one-quarter of their population online.) Backlogs endured once the courts returned to full capacity. For example, in 2022 a Ugandan judge noted that 'in the Court of Appeals we have for the 11 justices a workload of about 7,500 to 8,000 matters sitting on our tables'. For these reasons, many Africans avoid court contact.

COVID-19 restrictions also obstructed legal assistance. For instance, in Zimbabwe lawyers were not considered an essential service and thus could not meet with clients. A lack of access to information is a major problem. When citizens are unaware of their legal rights, or when there is a lack of transparency around the law and government actions, neither formalist rule of law nor other liberal ideals, such as development, democracy and human rights, can be realized. These ideals are stated in the African Platform on Access to Information Declaration of 2011, overseen by the UN and the AU. Yet in 2022 just 21 sub-Saharan African countries have access to information laws[10], with Ghana and The Gambia only joining this number in the past three years. These are not always effective either. For instance, South Africa has, in theory, a good Access to Information Act. However, in practice, there is little knowledge of this legislation among the public, and poor record keeping has led to many refusals to provide information. In an extreme case, the Zimbabwe Access to Information Act has been predominantly used to stifle press freedom rather than uphold accessibility.

One could also consider issues such as attacks on press freedom and internet shutdowns as detrimental to access to information and thus the rule of law. As tracked by Access Now, Africa experienced 25 internet shutdowns across 14 countries in 2021. This was an increase from 18 internet shutdowns across 11 countries in 2020. In sub-Saharan Africa the countries experiencing shutdowns in 2021 included Chad, Gabon, Congo, Uganda, Ethiopia, South Sudan, Zambia, Eswatini, Nigeria, Niger, Burkina Faso, Senegal and Sudan. Internet shutdowns typically occurred when protests or elections were taking place: for instance, during the elections in Uganda, Zambia, Niger and Congo. Internet shutdowns took on a new dimension during the COVID-19 crisis, with citizens then kept in the dark about state of emergency laws, as well as health information and services. Some countries, such as Ethiopia, specifically restricted reporting on COVID-19 under the pretence of 'avoiding terror and distress'. Indeed, the state of press freedom in Ethiopia and other countries has been relayed, including aspects of judicial and police effectiveness. All three of the procedural attributes of the rule of law are inter-related and have considerable impacts on society.

Thus far, some of the consequences of rule of law failures have been given, alluding to the substantive approach. As mentioned, a comprehensive overview is outside the scope of this essay. None the less, the link to broader ideals cannot be ignored. Dereliction of rule of law attributes have undoubtedly played a role in unrest, conflict, and even civil war in sub-Saharan Africa. Furthermore, such circumstances can then hamper the rule of law for years to come. A prime example is that of Sierra Leone, with which it has been argued that corruption, patronage politics and executive over-reach set the scene for the 1991 civil war. Despite the war coming to an end in 2002, there are lasting deficiencies within the police and judicial system. Sierra Leone and neighbouring Liberia, which experienced two civil wars over 1989 to 2003, ranked worst in the recent Afrobarometer surveys suggesting that post-conflict states face the greatest challenges to access to justice.

Another consequence of inaccessible law is that it is motivation for the use of vigilantism to obtain justice and provide security. Judicial and police ineffectiveness (particularly the latter) has been cited in vigilantism studies from *inter alia* South Africa, Zimbabwe, Rwanda, Nigeria, Sierra Leone and Liberia. To grasp the extent of the problem, one can look to South Africa where the SAPS includes murder by vigilantism in their annual crime statistics, recording 1,202 in the most recent report. The actual count would be higher, as it can be difficult to discern which killings are due to vigilantism, and it excludes punitive actions which have not resulted in death such as beatings and banishment. Vigilantism in South Africa and elsewhere has been found to most likely occur in rural areas and amongst those of low socioeconomic class, and these are factors which also serve as indicators for lack of access to conventional justice. On a related point, as the Afrobarometer surveys indicate, citizens often prefer to turn to traditional justice mechanisms. However, one must not disregard traditional justice in the upholding of rule of law, as will be discussed in the following section.

WHAT CAN BE DONE TO IMPROVE THE RULE OF LAW IN SUB-SAHARAN AFRICA?

Considering the extent of issues in sub-Saharan Africa, improving the rule of law may appear a daunting task. Naturally, with many of the discussed problems being so entrenched there is a need to address underlying governmental culture and even perceptions amongst the general population. None the less, there is a case for optimism, with 40% of the LexisNexis survey respondents holding the belief that the rule of law will improve in their home jurisdictions over the next five years. Research does show concrete actions that can be taken to improve judicial effectiveness, police effectiveness and access to the law. This section outlines such actions with an emphasis on the African context. Although there is undoubtedly a role to be played by international, and particularly regional, institutions, the focus here is implementation on the national level.

The most immediate hindrance to judicial effectiveness is executive interference and there is a need for urgent reform to the practice of arbitrary appointments by the executive. Countries where the judiciary is fully non-independent are those which do not have a separate commission for judicial appointments. Placing the mandate onto independent persons is imperative: this could consist of experts in the judicial field, or of persons nominated by a democratic public process. Quotas

for representation could further assist in improving the rule of law. Any commission must also be responsible for judicial discipline and transfers. However, independence from the executive should not detract from co-operation between the two arms; governments must ensure compliance with judicial decisions and relationships must be cordial. Furthermore, those quasi-independent courts are not exempt from the need for reform, as shown with the cases of Malawi and Kenya.

Advocates for judicial independence do stress holistic measures. One prominent measure is for judges to become social and political actors: agents of change rather than simply decision makers. Although judicialization of politics can see retaliatory interference and potential electoral violence, evidence shows that it is ultimately fruitful; and, if combined with the above recommendation, would limit avenues for interference. Thus, judges should be at the forefront of calls for independence and play an active role in the promotion of liberal ideals. This could include: regional judge associations to engender communication and comradeship[11]; greater interaction with stakeholders; giving lectures or writing articles to educate and raise awareness; and participating in the training of incoming court officials. In addition, judicial budgets need to be sufficient and free from manipulation. Lifting judge salaries would remove the need for corruption, and an increase in resources would improve the overall effectiveness of case processing.

With regards to police reform, sufficient budgets are arguably the priority. Poor salaries are continuously found to be cause for police corruption and for low police morale. The latter is also affected by a general lack of resources available to police when fighting crime: stations go without adequate personnel, vehicles, computers and investigative equipment. As shown, this can perpetuate inequalities when the meagre resources held are delegated to elites or 'the highest bidder'. Furthermore, a lack of conventional means is often what translates into police brutality. As such, the Nigerian #EndSARS movement includes calls to improve police welfare. However, addressing underlying police culture cannot be dismissed, particularly when it comes to those that are militarized. The police need to be seen as a service to the community, not a force against it, and this is particularly important when it comes to the reminiscence of historical injustices[12].

Improving community-police relations more generally is an important aspect of police reform. This involves breaking down misconceptions on either side to allow mutual understanding. Methods include: involvement of the community in policing; police participation in community events, of which sport has proved a successful example; police officers being representative of the communities in which they work; education in the community; and enhanced training for police officers. Training should involve curriculums on human rights and conflict resolution, as well as on local contexts where representation is difficult. Many problems have arisen in Nigeria where officers from the federally structured police force do not know the culture, language or terrain in which they operate.

Additionally, effective oversight mechanisms are essential to ensure that police are not held above the law. While many sub-Saharan African nations do have police oversight mechanisms, these too require reform. They must be independent; current mechanisms tend to consist of former police officers or others with links to the polity. Whether or not this affects their decisions is irrelevant, as perceived independence can be just as important as genuine independence. Resources are again a factor. For instance, the Kenyan Independent Police Oversight Authority only finalized four cases within its first six years of operation due to meagre resources. Improving this is imperative to swift yet effective decision making. Current mechanisms are also often delegating investigative capacities to police as they do not have the resources[13], nor mandate, to do so themselves. On a similar note, mandates should be extended to allow oversight mechanisms to assume disciplinary measures and implement recommendations.

By reforming the judiciary and police as independent and effective institutions, the law would become more accessible. As noted, citizens frequently do not employ the courts or police as they believe they would not/could not help them. The state must prioritize resources to bring these services up to standard. Enhancing internet access—through the investment in infrastructure and provision of affordable services—would assist. Not only would this ameliorate access to information, but it would also allow streamlined administration of justice. For instance, it could facilitate digital hearings to address COVID-19 induced court backlogs. In Rwanda public computers were introduced during the pandemic to ensure that persons belonging to disadvantaged groups had access, a commended initiative. Then there are other aspects of accessible law, such as functional Access to Information Acts and secure press freedom.

Taking into account the atmosphere in many African nations, civil society has the greatest role to play in promoting these aspects, to urge government compliance and to educate the general population. Education on the law and on human rights would empower citizens to not only access justice but to hold their governments to account. Improving access to legal aid as per the African Commission on Human and Peoples' Rights' Lilongwe Declaration would also safeguard access to the law. Certainly, to improve the rule of law it is important to consider various actors, whether it be international, regional or national institutions, governmental organs or independent mandated institutions, and civil society or ordinary citizens. This additionally involves consideration of traditional actors.

Scholars and practitioners working on judicial reform, police reform, and overall rule of law in Africa argue for the inclusion of traditional justice mechanisms. This is particularly the case in post-conflict nations such as Sierra Leone and Liberia. By focusing solely on 'conventional' formal mechanisms, this is taking a Western-centric approach, and, moreover, fails to account for their colonial and post-colonial histories[14], alongside current on-the-ground realities including their ineffectiveness. Such research and ideas about the need to consider traditional justice does not completely exclude conventional means nor the need to implement aforementioned reforms, rather the point is that a hybrid approach would work best. This is important as traditional mechanisms themselves are not devoid of issues relating to political manipulation, lack of due process or violation of human rights.

Those who argue for a hybrid approach appeal for a hierarchical system with traditional justice as a broad bottom tier. Reform therefore includes the expansion of traditional justice to all sectors of society which may not have readily available access to formal mechanisms. Although a main benefit of traditional justice is that it is already more accessible to rural populations, other benefits include: the low cost; a conversational nature, particularly beneficial for illiterate or semi-literate populations; a less daunting atmosphere; and cultural and social legitimacy. There also tends to be a focus on reconciliation and repatriation rather than punitive measures which can feed into inequalities. However, this is not always the case, and as such calls for hybridization emphasize restrictions on the types of cases which traditional mechanisms have jurisdiction over, and on the types of punishments they may apply. Thus, the hierarchical aspect allows formal mechanisms as higher tiers which can be accessed for more serious crimes and can act as appeal system for lower tier decisions. There is also an emphasis on the traditional as a voluntary tier.

By this, it is still necessary to reform the judiciary and police, and to co-implement other measures to improve access to justice. It is also worth stating that those who advocate traditional justice typically incorporate vigilante groups. Here, the line is drawn between spontaneous and punitive mob lynchings, and organized vigilante groups who, despite being reputed for punitive actions, can provide efficient, non-punitive justice and security. For instance, several vigilante groups in Nigeria are known as more accessible means for such, and a focus has been put on transitioning them into accountable and regulated community policing groups. Traditional justice ties in to appeals for devolution to remove concentration of power from the executive; however, clear mandates and jurisdictions, alongside ample training and oversight is key to ensuring that failures of conventional rule of law are not simply perpetuated[15].

CONCLUSION

The rule of law is a vital component of modern states. This essay has shown that despite some successes, the three aspects of formalist rule of law require much improvement across sub-Saharan Africa. These three aspects are inter-related. Judicial ineffectiveness, which is very much a case of executive interference, has created an atmosphere where government officials and other elites are granted impunity for their actions. Simultaneously, it creates a lack of procedural fairness for others, particularly those who pose a threat to the regime. There becomes no certainty or equality before the law. Police ineffectiveness sees similar consequences, and additionally allows disorder and insecurity to go unabated. Without effective judiciaries or effective police, the law becomes inaccessible for much of the population. This is compounded by a general lack of access to information, including insufficient press freedom and internet.

With the case examples within this essay, broader implications of rule of law failures become apparent. As a vital component of modern states, a lack of the rule of law negates the potential for democracy, development, human rights, and peace and security. Nevertheless, tangible measures can be taken to improve the situation across sub-Saharan Africa. Such measures should consider a multitude of actors across the international, regional, national and local spheres. In particular, traditional actors should not be discounted. It is vital that reform of any aspect, those being judicial effectiveness, police effectiveness, or accessible law, moves beyond Western-centric views of what the rule of law entails, and, moreover, addresses perceptions that African nations did not or would not have the rule of law without Western imposition.

FOOTNOTES

[1] For instance, Freedom House's *Freedom Around the World* and The Fund for Peace's Fragile States Index.

[2] Calculated by Olaniyan, K., in 'Rule of Law? What Rule of Law?' mg.co.za/article/2019-11-22-00-rule-of-law-what-rule-of-law, 22 November 2019. Accessed 16 June 2020.

[3] As outlined by Freedom House *Freedom Around the World 2021*.

[4] See, for instance, Omondi, A. 'Ex-Supreme Court Judge Who Ruled Election Petition in Uhuru's Favour Lands Plum State Job'. www.tuko.co.ke/357339-ex-supreme-court-judge-jackton-ojwang-ruled-election-petition-uhurus-favour-plum-state-job.html, 16 May 2020. Accessed 16 June 2020.

[5] See, for instance, Spencer, L. 'Executive Control Through Judicial Appointments in Turkey and Cameroon'. www.iacl-democracy-2020.org/blog/2016/3/23/blog-post-sample-9wntn-6ye75-hwawc-xx9lz-p6k2z, 16 November 2020. Accessed 20 June 2021.

[6] As for interference into other judiciaries, see VonDoepp and Ellett for suggested reasons.

[7] Calculated by Zounmenou, D. in 'Third Terms for Presidents of Cote d'Ivoire and Guinea must be Stopped'. issafrica.org/iss-today/third-terms-for-presidents-of-cote-divoire-and-guinea-must-be-stopped, 30 September 2020. Accessed 30 June 2022.

[8] See Kimani, M. (2009). 'Security for the Highest Bidder'. Africa Renewal and The Editors. (2016). 'Patronage and Ethnic Divisions Hobble Sierra Leone's Political Parties'. World Politics Review.

[9] See Missing Voices (missingvoices.or.ke) for a comprehensive breakdown.

[10] The African Freedom of Expression Exchange provides a list of countries with access to information laws.

[11] This can include Associations for specific agendas, such as the International Association of Women Judges who work on gendered issues.

[12] South Africa had some success in rebranding the Police Force as the Police Service post-Apartheid. For a breakdown of what demilitarization should look like, see the work by Peter Kraska.

[13] For a comprehensive overview of the issues with Kenyan investigations, see Spencer, L. 'Obtaining Justice for Extrajudicial Killings in Kenya'. democracyinafrica.org/obtaining-justice-extrajudicial-killings-kenya, 14 November 2018. Accessed 16 June 2020.

[14] However, it has been argued that some forms of 'traditional justice' were also perpetuated or assimilated by colonialism.

[15] Of particular concern is traditional actors perpetuating gender, class, ethnic or religious based divisions.

BIBLIOGRAPHY

Access Now. 'Internet Shutdowns in 2021: The Return of Digital Authoritarianism'. www.accessnow.org/cms/assets/uploads/2022/05/2021-KIO-Report-May-24-2022.pdf, 24 May 2022. Accessed 9 July 2022.

Baker, B. 'Who do People Turn to for Policing in Sierra Leone?', in *Journal of Contemporary African Studies*, 23(3), pp. 371–390, 2005.

'Beyond the Tarmac Road: Local Forms of Policing in Sierra Leone & Rwanda', in *Review of African Political Economy*, 118, pp. 555–570, 2008.

Bayley, D. 'Law Enforcement and the Rule of Law: Is there a Tradeoff?', in *Criminology and Public Policy*, 2(1), pp. 133–154, 2002.

Buchard, S., and Simati, M. 'The Role of the Courts in Mitigating Election Violence in Nigeria', in *Cadernos de Estudos Africanos*, 38, pp. 123–144, 2019.

Center for Advancement of Rights and Democracy. 'The Digital Divide'. www.cardeth.org/digital-divide/, 16 May 2022. Accessed 6 June 2022.

Dicey, A. V. *Introduction to the Study of the Law of the Constitution*. (8th Edn). London, Macmillan, 1915.

Freedom House. *Freedom Around the World 2021*.

Haruna, B. A., and A. M. Yusuf. 'A Conceptual Analysis of the Rule of Law in Nigeria', in *Bayero Journal of International Law & Jurisprudence*, 1(1), pp. 101–127, 2016.

Human Rights Watch. 'I Only Need Justice: Unlawful Detention and Abuse in Unathorized Places of Detention in Uganda.' www.hrw.org/report/2022/03/22/i-only-need-justice/unlawful-detention-and-abuse-unauthorized-places-detention, 22 March 2022. Accessed 14 June 2022.

Iloh, E. C., and Nwokedi, M. E. 'Non-State Actors and Internal Security Management in Nigeria: The Case of Vigilante Groups', in Oshita, O., Alumona, I. M., and Onuoha, F. C. (Eds). *Internal Security Management in Nigeria*. Singapore, Palgrave Macmillan, 2019.

International Crisis Group. 'Watchmen of Lake Chad: Vigilante Groups Fighting Boko Haram'. www.crisisgroup.org/africa/west-africa/nigeria/244-watchmen-lake-chad-vigilante-groups-fighting-boko-haram, 23 February 2017. Accessed 16 June 2020.

International Institute for Democracy and Electoral Assistance. *Challenges to the Rule of Law in Africa: Workshop Report*. Pretoria, 2016.

Kamga, G. E. K. 'The Political (In)Dependence of the Judiciary in Cameroon: Fact or Fiction?', in *Africa Review* 11(1), pp. 46–62, 2019.

Kantor, A, and Persson, M. 'Understanding Vigilantism: Informal Security Providers and Security Sector Reform in Liberia.' fba.se/contentassets/59ce4a18f4db4484ad1a4b8bcd1cbaf0/understanding-vigilantism-ssr-liberia-2.pdf. Accessed 16 June 2020.

Kposowa, A. 'Erosion of the Rule of Law as a Contributing Factor in Civil Conflict: The Case of Sierra Leone', in *Police Practice and Research*, 7(1), pp 35–48, 2006.

Laslett, P. (Ed.) *Locke: Two Treatises of Government*. Cambridge, Cambridge University Press, 1988.

LexisNexis. *Advancing the Rule of Law in Africa 2022*.

Logan, C. 2017. 'PP39: Ambitious SDG Goal Confronts Challenging Realities: Access to Justice is Still Elusive for Many Africans'. afrobarometer.org/publications/pp39-access-to-justice-in-africa, 13 March 2017. Accessed 16 June 2020.

Marais, E. 'The Police-Community Relationship', in Glanz, L. (Ed.) *Managing Crime in the New South Africa: Selected Readings*, pp. 113–136. Pretoria, HSRC Publishers. 1993.

Martin, J. 2012. 'Vigilantism and State Crime in South Africa', in *State Crime*, 1(2), pp. 217–234, 2012.

Masengu, T. 'The Vulnerability of Judges in Contemporary Africa: Alarming Trends', in *Africa Today*, 63(4), pp. 3–19, 2017.

Maunga, M., Mugari, I., and Tundu, M. 'Perspectives on Vigilantism in the Republic of Zimbabwe', in *Mediterranean Journal of Social Sciences*, 6(5), pp. 323–334, 2015.

Cohler, A., Miller, C., and Stone, H. (Eds). *Montesquieu: The Spirit of Laws*. Cambridge, Cambridge University Press, 1989.

Mutua, M. 2016. 'Africa and the Rule of Law', in *Sur International Journal on Human Rights*, 13(23), pp. 159–173, 2016.

O'Regan, C. 'Towards a Safer Khayelitsha'. www.khayelitsha-commission.org.za/images/towards_khaye_docs/Khayelitsha_Commission_Report_WEB_FULL_TEXT_C.pdf, August 2014. Accessed 16 June 2020.

Obarrio, J. 'Traditional Justice as Rule of Law in Africa', in Sriram, C. L., Martin-Ortega, O. and Herman, J. (Eds). *Peacebuilding and Rule of Law in Africa: Just Peace?*. Routledge, Abingdon, 2011.

Pring, C., and Vrushi, J. 'Global Corruption Barometer—Africa 2019: Citizens' views and experiences of corruption'. www.afrobarometer.org/publications/global-corruption-barometer-africa-2019-citizens-views-and-experiences-corruption, 12 July 2019. Accessed 16 June 2020.

Shomade, S. *Colonial Legacies and the Rule of Law in Africa*. Routledge, Abingdon, 2022.

Simati, M. *Post-Election Violence in Africa: The Impact of Judicial Independence*. Routledge, Abingdon, 2020.

Sriram, C. L. '(Re)Building the Rule of Law in Sierra Leone', in Sriram, C. L., Martin-Ortega, O. and Herman, J. (Eds). *Peacebuilding and Rule of Law in Africa: Just Peace?* Routledge, Abingdon, 2011.

Stewart, C. 'The Rule of Law and the Tinkerbell Effect: Theoretical Considerations, Criticisms and Justifications for the Rule of Law', in *Macquarie Law Journal*, 4, pp. 135–164, 2004.

Super, G. 'Volatile Sovereignty: Governing Crime through the Community in Khayelitsha', in *Law & Society Review*, 50(2), pp. 450–483, 2016.

United Nations Human Rights Council. 'The Coronavirus Disease (COVID-19) Pandemic: Impact and Challenges for Independent Justice'. independence-judges-lawyers.org/wp-content/uploads/2021/06/A_HRC_47_35_English.pdf, June 2021. Accessed 29 June 2022.

United Nations Office of the High Commissioner for Human Rights. 'Oral Update on the Situation of Human Rights in the Tigray Region of Ethiopia and on progress Made in the Context of the Joint Investigation'. www.ohchr.org/en/statements/2022/03/oral-update-situation-human-rights-tigray-region-ethiopia-and-progress-made, 7 March 2022. Accessed 6 July 2022.

VonDoepp, P, and Ellett, R. 'Reworking Strategic Models of Executive-Judicial Relations: Insights from New African Democracies', in *Comparative Politics*, 43(2), pp. 147–165, 2011.

Wambua, P. 2015. 'AD57: Call the police? Across Africa, citizens point to police and government performance issues on crime'. afrobarometer.org/publications/ad57-call-police-across-africa-citizens-point-police-and-government-performance-issues, 9 November 2015. Accessed 16 June 2020.

World Justice Project. Rule of Law Index 2021.

Zondo, R. Judicial Commission of Inquiry into State Capture. www.gov.za/sites/default/files/gcis_document/202206/electronic-state-capture-commission-report-part-v-vol-i.pdf, June 2022. Accessed 3 July 2022.

PART TWO
Country Surveys

ANGOLA

Physical and Social Geography

RENÉ PÉLISSIER

PHYSICAL FEATURES

The Republic of Angola, covering an area of 1,246,700 sq km (481,354 sq miles), is the largest Portuguese-speaking state in Africa. It is composed of 18 provinces, one of which, Cabinda (formerly known as Portuguese Congo), is separated from the others by the oceanic outlet of the Democratic Republic of the Congo (DRC, formerly Zaire) and the delta of the River Congo. On its landward side Cabinda is surrounded by the DRC and the Republic of the Congo. Greater Angola is bordered to the north and east by the DRC, to the east by Zambia and to the south by Namibia. Excluding the Cabinda enclave, Angola extends 1,277 km from the northern to the southern border, and 1,236 km from the mouth of the Cunene river to the Zambian border.

Two-thirds of Angola is a plateau. The average elevation is 1,050 m–1,350 m above sea level, with higher ranges and massifs reaching above 2,000 m. The highest point of Angola is Mt Moco (2,620 m) in Huambo province. Through the central part of the inland plateau runs the watershed of Angola's rivers. The coastal plain on the Atlantic is separated from this plateau by a sub-plateau zone, which varies in breadth from about 160 km in the north to 25 km–40 km in the centre and south. The Namib desert occupies the coastal plain at a considerable height above Namibe. Towards the Cuango (Kwango) basin, in Zaire province, a sedimentary hollow forms the Cassange depression, in which cotton is cultivated. The north-western section of the Angolan plateau has jungle-covered mountains, which are suitable for the cultivation of coffee. The Mayombe range in Cabinda is covered by equatorial jungle.

Except for the Cuanza (Kwanza) river, which is navigable up to Dondo (193 km upstream), Angolan rivers do not provide easy access to the interior from the coast. On the other hand, they are harnessed for the production of electricity and for irrigation. The main rivers are, above the Cuanza, the Chiloango (Cabinda), the Congo, the M'bridge, the Loge, the Dange and the Bengo. The Cassai (Kasai), Cuilo (Kwilu) and Cuango rivers are known more for their importance to the DRC than for their upper reaches in Angola, although many tributaries of the Kasai intersect the Angolan plateau, exposing rich deposits of alluvial diamonds in the Lunda provinces.

Angola has a tropical climate, locally tempered by altitude. The Benguela current, along the coast, influences and reduces rainfall in that part of the country, which is arid or semi-arid. The interior uplands in the provinces of Bié, Huambo and Huíla enjoy an equable climate.

POPULATION

According to the census held in 2014 (the first to be conducted since 1970), Angola had 25,789,024 inhabitants. The United Nations (UN) estimated the population at 33,086,278 in mid-2022, with a population density of 26.5 persons per sq km. Angola has considerable ethnic diversity, although all indigenous groups, of which the Ovimbundu and Mbundu are the most numerous, are of Bantu stock. An important characteristic of the population is its youth, as about 44.9% are under 15 years old and only 2.5% are over 65. According to World Bank figures, the average life expectancy at birth in 2020 was 61.5 (males 58.7; females 64.4). In 2011–20 Angola's population increased at an estimated average annual rate of 3.4%.

Following the onset of civil strife in the mid-1970s, Angola experienced considerable economic dislocation, accompanied by a widespread regrouping of African populations, brought about by insecurity and massacres. The population is predominantly engaged in food-crop farming and, in the south, in cattle raising. Only in areas where coffee, cotton and maize are cultivated are Angolans engaged to any extent in commercial agriculture. An estimated 46.4% of the economically active population were employed in the agricultural sector in 2019. Serious food shortages and periods of famine periodically beset central and southern Angola. The lengthy civil conflict created problems of 'internal' refugees (a total of 4.3m. were believed to have been displaced by the conflict), and in late 2006 it was estimated that there were some 171,393 Angolan refugees in surrounding countries, despite the return of almost 400,000 since the ceasefire of April 2002. By mid-2012 the number of Angolan refugees remaining in the region had decreased to approximately 120,000 and in June 2012 the office of the UN High Commissioner for Refugees declared that Angolan exiles who had fled from the various conflicts since 1965 would no longer be considered refugees, owing to the relative stability of Angola's political climate and the availability of repatriation options. Efforts continued thereafter to normalize the status of the remaining former Angolan refugees or to encourage their return to Angola.

The population of the capital, Luanda (which was 480,613 at the 1970 census), had grown to an estimated 2.8m by mid-2022, and the city has experienced a boom in construction since 2000. The urban centres of Benguela and Lobito were among those most seriously damaged by the war, and the port of Lobito suffered from the disruption of traffic with the DRC and Zambia. Huambo, formerly an important centre for rail traffic to the eastern regions and to the DRC and Zambia, and for road traffic to Luanda and Namibia, was once again expected to become a focal point of economic activity. Other centres, such as Namibe, Lubango, Cuito and Luena, also suffered from the war and local disorder. The city of Cabinda has benefited from the exploitation of offshore petroleum resources, while pioneer towns such as Menongue and Saurimo may eventually assume new importance as regional centres.

History

BRAD SAFARIK

INTRODUCTION

The turn of the 21st century marked a major turning point in the history of Angola as the civil war (1975–2002) pitting the Movimento Popular de Libertação de Angola (MPLA) against the União Nacional para a Independência Total de Angola (UNITA) came to end. The death of UNITA's charismatic leader Jonas Savimbi allowed the country's leadership to quickly reinvent itself amid the growing narrative across the continent of an 'Africa Rising', and from the civil war's divisions came national unity. UNITA was itself originally composed of former members of the Frente Nacional de Libertação de Angola (FNLA), who broke off and claimed to represent ethnic groups not integrated in the Bakongo nationalist FNLA or the Creole- and Mbundu-dominant MPLA programmes, later consolidating around the Ovimbundu peoples and setting itself up as the main opposition to the MPLA. Set along the Atlantic Ocean in southern Africa and sharing a border with the Democratic Republic of the Congo (DRC) to the north, Zambia to the east and Namibia to the south, Angola's 1.2m. sq km area, 1,600 km of coastline and abundant natural resources have provided the country with the geopolitical potential to further cement its role as a major regional player in sub-Saharan Africa. Much of this economic clout is derived from its vital oil wealth, principally sourced from the waters outside the detached territorial enclave of Cabinda to the north.

The regional influence of Angola is most evident from its major role in achieving the independence of its southern neighbour, Namibia, on 22 March 1990. This historical moment in Southern Africa was the fruit of one of the continent's major military battles in the small bush town of Cuito Cuanavale in January and February 1988. Vital Cuban military support dealt apartheid South Africa's first decisive military defeat against another African army as it sought to interfere with Angola's internal power struggles. The negotiations held in New York, USA, on 22 December 1988 secured the withdrawal of Cuba's protective force of 50,000 troops on Angolan soil, under the condition that South Africa not only withdraw its troops but also allow its colony, then known as South-West Africa (itself a legacy of German colonization), to accede to independence. The famous battle marked a definitive turning point in Angola's civil war, although the two remaining military forces would continue to fight in a long and protracted civil conflict.

The official end of the war in 2002 marked a point of self-reflection and self-restoration. The rebuilding process was accompanied by the legacy of decades of nearly constant war that would leave deep physical and psychological scars across the country after the death of an estimated 500,000 Angolans. The abrupt turn to rehabilitation quickly became a monumental task. Rising revenues of a burgeoning oil sector provided the financial foundations to enact a nationwide social and economic reconstruction effort, although foreign and international aid and assistance was also required to rebuild the country's devastated infrastructure and hollowed out government apparatus.

This herculean task fell to the war's ultimate victors, the _nomenklatura_ of insider elites aligned with then President José Eduardo dos Santos as the central nexus who was determined to single-handedly transform his role from the 'architect of peace' to the 'architect of reconstruction'. Heavy-handed authoritarian tactics remained in place to suppress dissent, being justified as necessary means to maintain the fragile social stability within a population exhausted from conflict. The exponential concentration of power within the inner elite circle of dos Santos led the Government quickly to expand its control and influence over the country's resources, anchored in a system of patrimonial distribution in exchange for loyalty and regime continuation. These authoritarian tactics were not unique to the consolidated clan in power, but rather learned and studied strategies of Angola's first President, Dr Agostinho Neto, himself a student of the oppressive Portuguese colonial regime that left heavy impressions in the path the country is currently set upon.

COLONIAL PASTS INFORMING FUTURE SPACES

A confluence of events led Portugal to experience unique pressures in the late 1950s and early 1960s that produced rapid institutional changes across its empire, leading to historic repercussions on the viability of its overseas projects. Domestically, the colonies were putting heavy financial pressures on a country with an underdeveloped economy unable to cope. Likewise, international criticism led by the rise of a strong self-determination sentiment within the newly founded United Nations (UN—established in October 1945), backed by the two anti-colonialist superpowers, also put Portugal in an increasingly difficult position in its insistence to preserve its colonies, leading it officially to change its administrative nature in 1949 from a colonial empire to a 'pluri-continental nation', including its 'overseas provinces'. In December 1960 tensions were further escalated with the UN's Declaration on the Granting of Independence to Colonial Countries and Peoples. At the same time that the international environment became increasingly hostile to the idea of colonial possessions, domestic turmoil began to reach its breaking point.

In an effort to preserve its colonial empire and quell rising social grievances, the economist-turned-dictator, António de Oliveira Salazar, imposed stricter financial reforms designed to alleviate the heavy fiscal burden of the colonies by adopting coercive measures of fiscal capture. The laser-like focus on finances created a form of 'financial dictatorship' at home and abroad. Economic performance quickly took precedence in the peripheral spaces as Portugal's development plan laid out in 1953 focused almost exclusively on the construction of the infrastructure necessary (roads, ports, hydroelectric projects) to allow for the installation of settlers and the extraction of their production to overseas markets. At the particular juncture in the world economy recovering from the massive disruptions of the two World Wars ravaging Europe, North Africa and parts of Asia, colonial Angola found itself well situated in the recovering global marketplace in the production of a small range of commercial crops (maize, beans, sugar, sisal) and natural resources (timber), with the coffee bean emerging as the most prized natural resource.

The mounting pressures focused on export stirred up mounting animus against colonial authorities by both the native Angolan populations and the European settlers. This growing social unrest led to a transformation of the colony's political economy in the 1960s to place greater importance on developing the internal investment in the overseas province itself and, at least theoretically, improving living standards through an incremental industrialization of the colonial economies. The retooling of the vision of Portugal's colonial empire took shape as its previous 'Colonial Pact' policy was rebranded as the 'Portuguese Economic Space', thereby eliminating the semantic differentiation between the territories while formulating a stronger economic integration strategy which triggered a greater emphasis on industrializing Angola. Administrative reforms designed to allow for more internal economic development accrued to the groups already favourably positioned in the colonial social order, leaving the African population increasingly sidelined from the benefits of growth while still under obligation to pay into a predatory colonial system.

This growing chasm of social inequalities would subsequently set up a long and bloody path towards independence, sparked in large part by a rural uprising beginning on 4 January 1961 by forced indentured rural peasants working cotton fields in Baixa de Cassanje, costing the lives of an estimated 40,000 people. Another major outbreak of violence in a prison in the capital, Luanda, on 4 February 1961, led by FNLA sympathizers, marked the beginning of the struggle for independence. These events placed major pressure on colonial authorities to walk back their forced labour models as it severely disrupted the social and economic lifestyles of the African populations. Yet these uprisings merely represented an early warning sign, as grievances swelled under the authoritarian yoke of the Salazar dictatorship.

The ensuing colonial war marked a clear break in the history of Portugal's empire as well as the foundations of Angolan nationalism. This led Portugal to abolish its colonial social caste system, a principal source of the rising pressures of local grievance and rebellion. In particular, the 1899 Statute of the Portuguese Natives of the Provinces of Angola, Mozambique and Guinea, which separated the native population into an *indígena* category separate from the 'civilized' European or the rarely granted status of *assimilado* blacks or mestiços who enjoyed the same rights as the Portuguese. This *indigenato* regime codified the daily life of the native populations and stipulated that natives were legally required to work in order to provide the material means of their survival. Their exploitation through taxation created additional burdens on these populations and led to generalized resistance against the colonial regime. The weight of living and operating under the *indígena* regime and its mechanisms of marginalization were central motivators for the local pockets of resistance against the colonial system.

Angolans would not achieve independence until the colonial dictatorship was overthrown, triggered by a *coup d'état* engineered by the military and later supported by the Portuguese people themselves, motivated in part by the costly and deadly colonial wars. The Carnation Revolution began on 2 April 1974 and paved the way for a power-sharing agreement between the main political parties having led the arduous war for independence: the MPLA under Agostinho Neto, the FNLA under Holden Roberto and UNITA under Jonas Savimbi. While the official independence date of Angola is 11 November 1975, the transitional government began its creation on 31 January 1975 through the Alvor Agreement signed on 15 January between the post-Salazarist Portuguese Government and the three political groups it officially recognized. Angola would be the last of Portugal's African colonies to set up a transitional government, but its creation quickly broke down due to internal power struggles amid the nearly nine-month delay between independence and the first elections, originally scheduled for October 1975.

CIVIL WAR AND FOREIGN INFLUENCE

As the Alvor Agreement negotiations slowly collapsed and the transitional government's demise became clearer, the emerging political parties each began to consolidate their respective political and military allies, culminating in a 'Scramble for Angola'. A battle for the control of the capital quickly ensued, exacerbated by the intervention of foreign interference motivated by geopolitical concerns of the future composition of a soon to be independent Angola. However, rather than a product of the Cold War, the root causes of the civil war originated long before independence and solidified within the social, geographic and ethnic divisions built into the three Angolan nationalist movements, themselves largely forged through the colonial experience.

The foreign actors joining this complex sociological matrix descending on Angola with the goal of positioning themselves for its future independence had no real idea how the combination of their respective interventions would dramatically escalate the conflict. As foreign arrivals increased, the ultimate endgame of power and authority became diluted in the amalgam of conflicting interests. Many of the military partnerships initially forged would waver, crumble and renew throughout the ensuing civil war, further exacerbating the war's divisions.

The status of allies and enemies was rarely clear in the heat of war. On the one hand, some allies did remain loyal. Cuba and Yugoslavia never wavered in their support for their 'socialist' ally. The People's Republic of China gave temporary, limited support to both UNITA and the FNLA. Chinese military instructors were on the ground by mid-1974 and left on 27 October 1975, positioning themselves in Zaire (as the DRC was then known) without crossing into Angola, while instructors from the Democratic People's Republic of Korea (North Korea), who were already on the ground in Zaire

training President Joseph-Désiré Mobutu's elite forces, also assisted in the training of UNITA troops. As an ideological battleground of the Cold War, military and political support was not unconditional. The Union of Soviet Socialist Republics (USSR) even temporarily withdrew its support for the MPLA between 1973 and 1975 due to a temporary power-sharing agreement between Neto and Roberto's FNLA group, which was perceived by the USSR as ceding too much political control given the FNLA's close ties to Mobutu's Zaire as well as the growing threat of South African forces that had invaded the territory from the southern border in August 1975. The MPLA's victory over the latter at the battle of Quifangondo on 10 November 1975 secured its control over Luanda and its historic place as the forebearer of independence. The weakened FNLA retreated to Zaire, where its protector eventually pulled its support in 1978, as Mobutu sought to engage with the new Angolan Government.

On the other hand, some allies changed sides as the power struggle evolved. The USA provided assistance to both UNITA and the FNLA at various points in the war before pulling its support, notably after the South Africans began their retreat, the fall of the USSR reduced the threat of communism spreading, and the USA no longer saw strategic interest in supporting the guerrilla war. For its part, South Africa supported both the FNLA and UNITA at different times. The South African Government had multiple interests in influencing internal Angolan politics, most notably its fear of a Marxist, anti-apartheid government giving shelter to the South West Africa People's Organization of Namibia (SWAPO) independent movement on its southern border, which had been operating there since the mid-1960s. Likewise, the development of a hydroelectric project on the Cunene river was set to provide irrigation and electricity to the arid regions of modern-day northern Namibia. Ultimately, it was the South African troop invasion across the southern border in mid-October 1975 that convinced Cuba's Prime Minister, Fidel Castro, to send troops into Angola in support of the ideologically aligned MPLA. This decisive decision was taken solely by Castro, only later supported by the USSR. Ironically, apartheid South Africa also produced mercenary soldiers that at once fought against the MPLA forces, the Forças Armadas de Angola (FAA), before being pulled across the battle lines as soldiers of fortune selling their mercenary services in support of the MPLA.

The accumulation of wavering commitments, weak alliances and self-interested actors accentuated the seasoned mindset of Angola's elites with the reality that true loyalty is a rare resource in the political arena, and reinforced the fact that the most effective currency for maintaining allies and alliances was money and access to power. As evidenced by its duration and intensity, the Angolan civil war was an extremely complex phenomenon bringing together national, regional and international forces. However, the role and influence of foreign actors have tended to overshadow the deep endogenous roots of the conflict. The attempted *coup d'état* shortly after independence would bring home this hard reality in the early years of the Republic.

AUTHORITARIAN 'SOCIALISM'

Having won control of Luanda, MPLA leader Neto unilaterally proclaimed the new country's independence on 11 November 1975. For their part, UNITA and the FNLA similarly declared their own Democratic People's Republic of Angola in Huambo (formerly Nova Lisboa), at the time the country's second largest city, though it was never officially recognized. Although President Neto would only hold power until 1979, his influence was vitally important in locking in the country's ideological path that its independent foundations would be built upon. The 'socialist' revolution that he purportedly sought for Angola's transformation was quickly undermined by the *coup d'état* on 27 May 1977, led by Alves Bernardo Batista (more commonly known as Nito Alves) and José Van Dunem, quelled in large part by Cuban forces already in the country. This quickly descended into a violent purge of factions of MPLA adherents deemed disloyal to the MPLA's main political programme. The ideals of the 'socialist' revolution quickly withered away under the increasing adoption of the same authoritarianism tactics of

Salazar's Portugal as the MPLA purged its party of the 'Nitistas' and the influences that Nito Alves championed.

While this episode was a mostly urban affair, the authoritarian tendencies that sprang from it would consolidate across the territory. In particular, the MPLA moved in 1977 to dismantle the revolutionary 'people's power' organizations that had been established under the Law on People's Power in 1975. Despite the misleading name of the law, its actual purpose was to effectively usurp the public's ability to exercise popular autonomy which had begun to take form upon independence. This law had allowed for the organization of elections of various organizations, including trade unions, student associations and even political parties. Although these organizations could channel popular sentiment, they remained appendages beholden to the MPLA's political party structure.

Being perceived as complicit in the organization of the *coup d'état*, these organizations were disbanded, with the Law on People's Power being rescinded as well. While the internal political purge was still active, during 4–11 December 1977 the MPLA convened its first congress, where it officially adopted its 'Marxist-Leninist' character and its 'socialist' production model. These two events colliding in history imbued the MPLA's 'Marxism-Leninism' with the cold authoritarian streak already engrained by the colonial experience. This political crackdown and consolidation in 1977 further cemented the MPLA's approach to controlling and manipulating popular initiatives, whether led by the consolidating urban civil society or later adopted to counter emerging civil society organizations (CSOs) and non-governmental organization (NGO) influences.

During his short reign in power, a critical component of Neto's tenure in regard to rebuilding the country is that of absence. Independence and the ensuing civil war provoked the exodus of nearly all of the Portuguese settlers, taking what they could with them, and even sabotaging what they could not. This led to the complete disarticulation of the rural economy, and severely hindered the technical and logistical know-how required to pursue its continuation. Under the constant pressure of war, this dismantling created the need to finance foodstuffs, organize a distribution network for goods and services, and rebuild the institutions left idle or crumbling in the wake of independence. Across the board, deterioration reigned and massive structural difficulties loomed large. Among the most pressing issues was the relationship of the rural communities, at the time comprising approximately 80% of the total population, to the newly established state in a post-colonial society still devoid of formed notions of a nation.

The widespread weakened links to social commonalities were in large part a result of the geographic marginalization of wide swaths of the country. The political system tasked with taking on these enormous issues was an approach based on a colonial authoritarian heritage mixed within a 'socialist' bureaucracy and run by stalled institutions nationwide. With this system, the MPLA would have to start anew with little to no time for preparation. Feeding a hungry nation became a major priority to gain legitimacy in the eyes of its people, as well as to secure the energy necessary to overcome both foreign invasion and domestic turmoil. The weak transitional government would need a foundational structure in order to achieve the monumental task of not only feeding its population, but also running a nascent country. Given the extreme social turbulence, however, national food production plummeted. Outside of urban enclaves, the institutionalization of the new Angolan state and the expansion of its authority could be measured alongside the tyre tracks of food distribution networks.

The new Government sought to rebuild the country while the civil war continued unabated. The institutional framework began to take concrete form after the resolution on economic policy passed by the Central Committee of the Party in October 1976. The Law of State Intervention (Law no. 17 of 1977) led the Government to begin setting up the nationalized state enterprises allowing for the nationalization and confiscation of private property. This nationalization process of Angola's resources post-independence gave omnipresent power to the governing party, which was now in charge of remaking the entire political economy in its image with little, if any, opposition. Many of these takeovers were later formed into

monopolistic companies dominant in specific sectors of the economy, representing a feature and not a bug in the 'socialist' system.

The organization of the rural economy, lauded for its colonial prowess, followed the centralizing social and productive forces through the ideals of 'Marxism-Leninism', upholding the farmer as an idealized symbol of the hard-working masses powering the engine of the country's growth. This idolization is featured prominently on the national flag adopted upon independence, symbolized by the principal tool of the peasantry, the machete, in effect sharpening the gears of the imminent industrialization of the country. The strategy was two-fold: 1) nationalize and reactivate the colonial-era farms, and (2) organize peasants into associations and co-operatives, the latter being overseen and directed by the Government through the Confederation of Associations of Peasants and Agro-livestock Co-operatives of Angola, created in 1980. In the same way that the Law on People's Power was in reality a tool to reduce the autonomous spaces of the population and guide them into controlled and supervised groups better aimed at furthering the Government's power and influence, the peasant associative and co-operative movement appeared to be the rural version of this strategy. Such desires for a state-led centralized agricultural system would have to be nearly completely rebuilt, but its strategy would be based on its colonial heritage. The incoming MPLA leaders were adept students of the Salazarian model of authoritarian governance, having grown up within its system.

Nationalizing the colonial farms permitted the party to keep key productive resources under its strict control, while the associative and co-operative movements gave the Government oversight and control over the country's most productive rural economic actors. Measures of total control of the rural economy, notably its productive economic agents, were the order of the day. Not only was the 'socialist' system a pretext for control over social organization and economic development, but it was also used as a political system to usurp agency and autonomy from the peasantry. Autonomous capital accumulation and social organizing represented an unacceptable political risk, particularly with the civil war breaking out, unleashing political forces that resigned the rural populations to a position of exclusion politically, socially, economically, institutionally and even symbolically. The urban/rural divide of the conflict, with UNITA's strongholds spread throughout the countryside, represented a major obstacle to implementing any coherent rural policies.

The historical reality of senior MPLA officials making policies to develop the peripheral areas of Angola is that those areas were, during significant time periods in contemporary history, overrun, ruled and pillaged through a combination of forces intent on the destruction of the MPLA and thus by extension the very seed of 'revolution' that liberated the country from external oppression. While the war was won at heavy cost, this internationalization of the countryside by destructive military actions through the aforementioned Scramble for Angola not only released primal forces that changed the course of the civil war, but similarly left an enduring legacy that has unleashed further fundamental forces of social control that remain difficult to discern, but palpable none the less. The death of President Neto on 10 September 1979 led to the arrival of José Eduardo dos Santos, who would remain in power until 26 September 2017. He would inherit this legacy of absence, mistrust, urban bias, and a dilapidated party-state fighting for survival.

ELECTIONS, WAR AND PEACE
Working from their political stronghold of Luanda, both Neto and dos Santos eventually moved from loosely held dogmatic beliefs to pragmatic positions, focusing their attention on maintaining semblances of stability among the populations of their rapidly growing urban strongholds during the increasingly costly civil war. As a guerrilla movement, UNITA was established by Jonas Savimbi in March 1966 as an organization that claimed to represent first and foremost the rural African populations, thereby positioning itself in opposition to the urban-based, mulatto-dominated MPLA. While its identity

was established with its rural roots in the central highlands, UNITA's ideological belief structure was much more pragmatic than fundamentalist.

Savimbi's 'anti-colonial' message was a rhetorical political tool, but it did not stop him from partnering with apartheid South Africans in violating the country's territorial sovereignty or from accepting assistance from the USA's Central Intelligence Agency. Instead, he constructed a 'nativist' nationalist discourse to project a self-crafted image to position himself as a political counterpower capable of championing the marginalized peoples across the countryside. Marginalization was chiefly identified as the distance from the social hierarchy established through the legacy of colonial rule, although pragmatism pushed him to accept certain rural social groups that found themselves once part of or connected to the colonial regime, yet cut off post-independence. By having partnered with the Portuguese before 1974 to fight against the MPLA and later working in tandem with the South Africans from 1975, UNITA demonstrated how *realpolitik* trumped any core ideology. Rather, these actions were the pure pursuit of power seeking to install an Afro-centrist nationalist power structure elevating rural indigenous culture over the supposedly imported urbanized model projected by the MPLA.

Until relatively recently, the main lines weaving together UNITA's historical narrative have been distilled into a two-stage evolution between its 1980s conventional Cold War character, morphing in the 1990s into a destructive resource war of attrition, wherein UNITA controlled up to 80% of the mostly rural national territory with important areas rich in diamonds to finance their war effort. The notion of 'control' is relative, however, as the loss and gain of territory was in constant flux in bordering areas. This notion extends to the populations that lived near or under UNITA operations, as fragile territorial control translates to a weakened capacity to impose any durable sense of authority and adhesion to a common political cause.

Even in spaces under de facto UNITA control, its lack of overall resources, organizational capacity and its difficulties in setting up reliable supply chains made its ability to secure and institutionalize a permanent presence extremely difficult. Furthermore, this territorial instability was a part of UNITA's military strategy itself, upending the livelihoods of certain populations to cause additional logistical problems for the MPLA receiving them, thereby making migration a de facto instrument of war. Much of UNITA's nation-building project was implemented to varying degrees depending on the geographical location of the spaces, the infrastructural heritage of the urban areas occupied in the 1990s, and their relative connections with their limited supply chains and logistics capacities. The strategic alliance with South Africa along the southern border provided a much-improved logistics network, making its unofficial capital in Jamba a natural headquarters for the factional group.

While the Angolan civil war is often understood as essentially lasting from 1975 until 2002, it did have momentary lapses of fragile ceasefires in 1991–92 and 1994–98. The first peace process in 1991, known as the Bicesse Accords, set up the country's first multi-party parliamentary elections on 12 September 1992, which were narrowly won by the MPLA (with 49.6% of the votes cast) and rejected by UNITA (which received 40.1%). The UN considered the process mostly free and fair, although errors due to inexperience were also noted. According to the results, both parties handily won their provincial strongholds, including Benguela, Bié, Huambo and Kuando Kubango for UNITA, and Luanda, Bengo, Kwanza-Norte and Malanje for the MPLA. Despite the largely urban/rural divide between the warring sides, the distribution of votes appeared much more complex, with the MPLA also scoring major victories in largely rural, interior provinces such as Lunda-Norte, Lunda-Sul and Cunene that were far from the MPLA's sphere of immediate influence. Following the ethnic distribution across the territory, UNITA's belligerent ethno-nationalism seemed to be rejected by a majority of voters in those areas where Ovimbundus are not numerous. As a result, the MPLA emerged from the 1992 elections as a regionally and ethnically integrated party.

Nevertheless, the election results did codify an important ideological marker in the country's political landscape as the provinces staked out their first official political positions. The dark cloud hanging over the countryside since the 1992 general elections that saw many rural areas vote UNITA persisted in the MPLA's spirit like a foggy casualty of war and an affront to its 'revolutionary' colonial fight. The rural character of UNITA's stronghold based in the central highlands, headquartered first in the provincial capital of Huambo until 1993, when it was forced to find refuge in Jamba, in Kuando Kubango province, made the Luanda-based MPLA deeply distrustful of large swaths of the rural populations having voted for UNITA. Moreover, the 'blood and soil' nationalism of Jonas Savimbi and his claims that the Ovimbundu people were the 'real Angolans' raised further hesitations of how to approach and later integrate those followers into the MPLA's national project. This political reality led the dos Santos regime to double down on its urban political power centres, despite only approximately 37% of Angolans living in cities in 1990.

In a return to war in 1992, after UNITA rejected the election results, the following two years witnessed some of the worst fighting experienced in the country. More of the Angolan population died between October 1992 and November 1994 than in the previous 16 years of conflict. The intensifying battle moving from the countryside to the cities destroyed what remained of the economy. The second attempt at a peaceful resolution came in 1994 with the Lusaka Protocol, promoting political reconciliation and the integration of UNITA military forces into the national army. The conditions for the ceasefire were never fully met and the process broke down in 1998. The MPLA then made a concerted push to overtake UNITA's stronghold in the central highlands and by the end of the century many of its bases along the Zambian border had also been captured, straining UNITA's safe territory to resupply its dwindling resources. Savimbi's death in February 2002 led UNITA to sign a peace treaty on 4 April, officially bringing the civil war to a close, although the Cabinda insurgency endured. After securing the international borders, the total territorial sovereignty of the country under one Government was finally achieved.

THE GREAT RECONSTRUCTION

The UN's various peacekeeping missions beginning in 1989 played a marginal role in maintaining the peace, alongside the work of numerous NGOs, CSOs, and religious organizations. The UN missions overall were largely seen as failures, as they were unable to bring any prolonged stability to the country or to protect civilians from attack. The missions were criticized both by the Angolan population for their inability to stop the conflict and by both warring parties, which ultimately demanded their withdrawal in 1999, leaving behind only 30 workers in the UN Office in Angola.

The pursuit of peace became one of the most important historical conjunctures bringing together groups of actors that had previously been operating separately in their own areas of influence, spearheaded by the initiative of religious institutions. Having previously advocated for peace separately, the major Protestant organizations of the Council of Christian Churches of Angola, founded in February 1977, and the Angolan Evangelical Alliance, as well the Angolan Catholic Church's Episcopal Conference of Angola and São Tomé, became involved in the founding of the Peacebuilding Programme in 1998. These different civic and religious organizations later merged to create the Inter-Ecclesial Committee for Peace in Angola in 1999 in order to unite forces as a demonstration of hope to overcome historical tensions and rivalries for the common good. Coming from a serious democratic deficit, the pro-peace movements spurred major social organizing initiatives across the country and became part of the first attempts at healing the brutal scars left behind by the war. Further collaborative efforts continued to evolve with the needs on the ground during reconstruction, thereby consolidating and energizing civil society initiatives faced with an authoritarian regime determined to control the direction of the national dialogue, by force if necessary.

The sociological schisms resulting from 41 years of war, between fighting for independence and the subsequent civil war, has definitively marked the ethos of the country for the foreseeable future. War has been a central influence in the construction of Angola's post-colonial state as it profoundly influenced the organization and structure of the political powers. Immediately after the civil war, the MPLA deployed a heavily authoritarian security apparatus throughout the country in order to re-establish both state and human security, given that it controlled only 40% of the territory prior to the end of the conflict. Alongside the security presence, a massive deployment of public resources was enacted, destined for a nationwide reconstruction effort focused on transportation networks, schools, government offices and medical posts.

This resource deployment was accompanied by the implantation of government officials, effectively establishing the MPLA as the legitimate modern-legal authority throughout the territory. The population, worn down by war, sought more than anything else a return to social stability. However, the bleak presence of the Government at the local level and its disconnect from the populations it is tasked to nominally serve undermine both its attempts to spread its capacity outside of urban areas and its ability to effect structural change in the lives of everyday Angolans. This neglect would grow to become another central feature of the MPLA's governance model more generally, as peacetime spending levels in basic services such as education and health mirrored those during wartime, despite the oil boom of the 2000s providing the potential resources.

A lack of transparency and the widespread use of patronage and clientelism were a major impediment for the engagement of international financial institutions when strategizing how to engage with Angola's fractured political environment. The greatest asset to the world economy that Angola possesses is its vast oil wealth, managed by the state behemoth Sociedade Nacional de Combustíveis de Angola (SONANGOL) and jealously guarded by the inner elite circle of the MPLA-led Government. A major point of reform requested from Western donors was transparency of all the actors linked to the sector, which simultaneously financed the Government's weakened capacity to run the country, powered the MPLA's war machine, and held the financial power behind the hopes of rebuilding once the war ended. It was particularly this third purpose that drew the majority of calls for systemic reforms and transparency.

Such demands were warranted. According to the International Monetary Fund (IMF), in the final years of the war between 1997 and 2002, US $4,220m. went entirely unaccounted for, diverted through opaque networks operating with the support of a cadre of politically connected Angolans and a small cadre of Western-based facilitators. The serial misuse of resources has had a wide-ranging impact on the relationship between the Government, the international community and increasingly Angolans themselves. The entrance of China's financial diplomacy into Angola in March 2004, just as the country was emerging from its civil war, allowed the former its initial foothold in Africa in exchange for massive oil-backed loans. This financing would help fuel major reconstruction efforts but also provoke internal power struggles as to who would benefit most from this massive infusion of money into the opaque Reconstruction Office in charge of the rebuilding projects.

While many donors remained committed to humanitarian and emergency assistance after the war, as the years of peacetime grew and the economy boomed, buoyed by rising oil prices, international donors began to pull out of the country. Angola became to be seen as too 'wealthy' in resources to merit intensive donor activity. Simultaneously, the continued lack of transparency or serious reform by the Angolan authorities caused other organizations to consider whether picking up where the Government should be performing was ultimately the best strategy for the country. The fact that the Government has continued to attribute paltry sums to the key sectors of health and education, with minimal difference from wartime to peacetime, gives credence to the idea that these sectors would have remained underfunded with or without the presence of non-state actors providing basic services normally reserved for the Government. It cannot be known for sure, but the Government certainly has not proven otherwise in the two decades since.

A general review of the major economic and social indicators of Angola in the 21st century allows us a broad understanding of how economic growth has translated to social progress during the reign of President José Eduardo dos Santos throughout the period of peacetime. The sustainability of the noted improvements remains an open question, given the extreme volatility the country has experienced in the last two decades, spurred on by boom and bust cycles of international oil prices. Angola has one of the world's least diversified export economies, being almost wholly reliant on diamonds and oil for access to foreign currency revenue, while these economic conditions are responsible for providing for a total population that has nearly doubled since 2000.

The phenomenon of rural flight, more prevalent than other regional countries due to the intense civil war, has continued apace, with the urban population growing by nearly 145% over the last two decades as rural populations grew by 30%. Over the same period life expectancy has improved significantly (by nearly 15 years, representing a 30.5% increase), although the country was ranked 148th out of 189 countries in 2019, according to the Human Development Index (HDI) produced by the UN Development Programme. The fight against poverty, the measure of which is living on less than US $1.90 per day based on 2011 purchasing-power parity, has stalled alongside rapid population growth, increasing in absolute numbers throughout the period of peacetime. Nationally, 47.6% of the Angolan population lives in poverty, but the rate is significantly higher in rural areas (73%) than urban (32%). While the number of undernourished people has been halved in the last two decades, over 5.5m. people remain unable to correctly feed themselves.

A major culprit of this entrenched poverty and consistent malnourishment is the weak institutional articulation between policies and programmes aimed at reducing these numbers, as well as climatic instability with recurrent droughts gravely affecting the southern provinces. The country has made some progress on the HDI, but this again has been modest. Between 2000 and 2019 its HDI score has grown from 0.394 to 0.581, representing a 47% increase. Given that the country was emerging from nearly 40 years of war at the turn of the century, it should come as no surprise that Angola has gained considerable ground in these various indicators. Stagnating indicators invite serious criticism of the MPLA's long rule due to Angola's continued languishing among the bottom ranks of the world.

THE ARRIVAL OF JOÃO LOURENÇO: TRANSITIONS AND TRANSFORMATIONS?

In 2010 significant changes were made to the Constitution in the distribution of power and authority through a modification of the electoral system to mirror that of South Africa. Direct presidential elections were replaced by parliamentary elections, whereby the party winning the most seats in the Assembleia Nacional (National Assembly) would de facto win the presidency. The legislative elections of 23 August 2017 set in motion an historic power transfer from dos Santos, in power for 38 years, to Gen. João Manuel Gonçalves Lourenço. Lourenço had spent his professional career deep within the military structure, joining the Central Committee of the MPLA in 1985 and becoming a member of the Politiburo in 1990. He was President of the MPLA parliamentary group from 1991 to 1998 and occupied the role of first Vice-President of the National Assembly from 2003 to 2014. In the latter year he was nominated by presidential decree to become Minister of National Defence, a role he held until the electoral campaign in 2017.

In the mean time, Lourenço became Vice-President of the MPLA in 2016. He was therefore integrated into the military and security services, which provided him with a strong internal support mechanism in his eventual attempts at taking over the helm of the party and the Government as a whole, while his long history in the inner political circle allowed him an intimate seat at the table of state power. This insider knowledge and deep military and political connections would become his greatest assets in taking over the party from the entrenched dos Santos clan, whose family members had been nominated to key positions throughout the Government during his last years in power to maintain influence after the President's departure.

Beyond underfinancing development, one of the most nefarious political realities consolidated by the elite circle directed by dos Santos was the creation of an effective party-state where MPLA interests merged the public and private spheres within the country. This had the effect of not only normalizing a culture of endemic corruption among elites, siphoning off public funds for private gain, but also cementing a reputation of corruption, mismanagement and lack of transparency among international financial institutions and major donor agencies. This has severely damaged Angola's institutional reputation among these key organizations. Rectifying this degraded image was a principal task of Lourenço's first mandate as he embarked on a pseudo anti-corruption campaign largely seen as inadequate given the severity of the problem.

So far, however, any truly structural change remains superficial as the MPLA remains unopposed across the state apparatus, and few major figures have paid serious penalties outside of the immediate dos Santos family and some of their closest advisers. Centralizing corruption in political discourse during his first campaign has, however, energized the civil society actors advocating for the end of elite impunity, more transparency, investment in better social services, and the adoption of good governance practices. In fact, Angola's civil society has grown increasingly vocal throughout the last decade, with anti-Government protests beginning to emerge in 2011, expanding in 2013 and 2014 amid plummeting oil prices and economic turmoil, and ultimately simmering until the elections in 2017.

The momentous arrival of the new President aroused much hope among the masses that structural changes were finally on the horizon. However, improvements have hardly materialized and for some Angolans the situation has continued to degrade. Lourenço has not been able to rely upon high oil revenues until relatively recently, leaving his administration unable to enact considerable investments in social programmes. Furthermore, the overall economy has been weakened by the corrosive effects of the COVID-19 pandemic. Overcoming these difficult conditions became the main reason why the country's latest elections were seen as so consequential.

The public's mounting frustrations with the MPLA's authoritarian rule over a country stagnating under poverty and mismanagement was on full display in the lead up to the country's fifth multi-party elections of 24 August 2022. UNITA nominated a charismatic, 60-year-old leader Adalberto Costa Júnior and his popularity was evident as he used his communication skills to mobilize massive shows of support during the campaign, notably in the major coastal cities. Positioning himself as the candidate of hope and change, UNITA had never come so close to finally garnering an electoral majority and thus capturing the presidency. However, fundamental political change would not arrive in 2022.

Shortly after the parliamentary elections, the National Electoral Commission (CNE) declared that the MPLA had won a slim majority of votes (51.2%) with UNITA placed second (with 44.0%). These results were further confirmed by the Constitutional Court, with both institutions under firm control of the Government. Each voting precinct was supposed to have provided a paper count of the total votes cast and UNITA contested the elections requesting the publication of these official results. The electoral win was ultimately upheld without providing any transparency in the vote counting. Exit polls conducted by UNITA and a new civil society organization Movimento Cívico Mudei both showed UNITA winning the majority, although with only limited access to voter information. Without the transparency of publishing primary data sources, the true results cannot be confirmed.

UNITA's leader continued to contest election 'irregularities' but never overtly claimed the presence of electoral fraud. This

balancing act allowed Costa Júnior to maintain pressure on the Government, preserve legitimacy in the eyes of his voters, while also facilitating the position of his party members taking their seats inside the National Assembly. UNITA gained 39 seats compared with the 2017 election, for a total of 90, while the MPLA lost 26 for a total of 124. This calculation leaves the MPLA with only a relative majority. This is considerable because the National Assembly will now require political compromise if Lourenço's administration is to pass any significant legislation.

Ultimately, the election results show a steady decline in the MPLA's electoral performance, systematically lowering their score by some 10% each election. The MPLA lost heavily in Luanda, with UNITA earning 63% of the votes to the MPLA's 33%. The erosion of the MPLA's support among urban citizens represents a major change in the composition of the parties' respective electoral bases. UNITA traditionally positioned itself as a rural-based coalition focused on the inner provinces but has since extended its support to the younger urban masses desperate for change. The MPLA therefore owes its contested victory to the votes of Angolans averse to major change, dependent on, or beneficiary to, the current social structures, as well rural and provincial voters. The latter categories are significant as they represent areas of the country the Government has traditionally neglected in favour of a modernist urban bias agenda.

CONCLUSION

According to recent estimates, nearly 80% of Angola's population is 34 years of age or younger, meaning that the oldest of this group would have been 15 when the peace accords were signed in 2002. This youth bulge is coming of age in a time of post-civil war and with connection to the internet and social media. For these Angolans the years of war and destruction are felt through painful family histories of suffering rather than personal experience. During the 2022 elections and in their aftermath, different security services were frequently mobilized as a show of force, violently dispersing and arresting demonstrators. While the resort to state violence remains a useful tool for authoritarian rule, the use and abuse of force are far less accepted by average Angolans today who are more willing to speak out and push back against such measures. These changing demographics represent a serious challenge for the Government to channel this enormous human capital into positive directions, calling upon the need for major social and economic reforms as the status quo creates ever-rising tensions.

The next major political issue facing the country will be the decision to organize the country's first elections at the local level. Planned for 2020, they were cancelled supposedly due to complications from COVID-19 and never revived. The aversion to going forward with these elections is a strong indication that the Government fears a popular backlash against their stranglehold on power and control at all levels of government. In the current system, local officials are appointed by the provincial government, and the provincial governors, the most senior executives, are appointed by the President. Local elections therefore have the potential to finally grant control of decision-making to opposing parties.

Now that President João Lourenço is no longer seen as a novel actor capable of bringing positive change to a sclerotic system, his second mandate is likely to be even more fraught with difficulties. The frustration in the streets is palpable as Angolans now prepare for five more years under MPLA rule. The combination of economic stagnation, growing discontent among the masses, and a President now perceived as a continuation of the same policies failing the majority of Angolans has increased the stakes for the political class leading the country. Across the aisle, the burgeoning opposition is entrenching itself to take advantage of one of its best opportunities to influence one of Africa's major regional powers.

Economy

BRAD SAFARIK

INTRODUCTION

Angola's petroleum sector dominates its economy, which is the second largest in sub-Saharan Africa. Today the sector comprises roughly one-third of total gross domestic product (GDP), 60% of government revenue and approximately 90% of total exports. In a solemn end-of-year speech on 18 December 2015, former President José Eduardo dos Santos admitted that the policies guiding his and his party's vision had failed at any true sense of economic diversification capable of moving the economy out of its chronic dependence on oil exports, while still claiming that it was not too late to start. This revealing statement, coming from the head of state whose authoritarian administration had single-handedly guided government policy since 1979, serves as a clear evidentiary signpost detailing the continued domination of the oil sector in the country's overall political economy as well as the narrow state-building agenda which the Movimento Popular de Libertação de Angola (MPLA) has enacted throughout its time in power. Recently rising oil prices provide a crucial opportunity to finance much needed economic reforms and investment, a central campaign theme of President João Manuel Gonçalves Lourenço after winning the country's fifth multi-party elections held on 24 August 2022.

KEY CURRENT INDICATORS

Since the beginning of the 21st century, favourable conditions of global economic expansion have resulted in Angola's GDP increasing significantly. Starting from US $9,130m. in 2000, GDP peaked at $145,700m. in 2014, although it fell back to $88,820m. in 2019. The massive increase in GDP has effectively translated into a rise in gross national income (GNI) by 58% since 2000 to $6,550 per capita. However, the country's high cost of living, persistent inflation and limited supply chains all contribute to making the GNI increase relative for the average Angolan.

The booming oil market of the 2000s allowed the economy to grow to such an extent that it became eligible in 2012 to graduate from its status as a least developed country (LDC) based on the criteria of income alone. At the time of consideration, GNI per capita was estimated at US $4,518, far above the threshold for graduation set at $1,242 in 2016. Angola was recommended to graduate to lower-middle income status in 2016, with its transition planned for 2021. However, the era of booming oil prices came to an abrupt end in 2014, which left the economy in a recession from 2016 until 2021, exacerbated by the global COVID-19 pandemic. Both the International Monetary Fund (IMF) and the World Bank have predicted a return to growth in 2022. Yet, due to this sombre economic outlook, the country's graduation from LDC status has been pushed back to 2024, although it remains classified as a lower-middle income economy.

While Angola's socioeconomic conditions have registered significant improvements since the turn of the century, the overall economy continues to underperform. The country ranked 148th out of 189 countries in the United Nations (UN) Development Programme's Human Development Index for 2020 despite noted improvements since the official end of the civil war in 2002. The significant increases in the macro economy provided a brief decrease in overall inequalities, although sustainable improvements remained elusive. The Gini index, which measures inequalities through the distribution of income among individuals or households, has hardly improved since its 2000 score of 52. These structural weaknesses have been recognized and a new Programme for Strengthening Social Protection (KWENDA), has been set up in partnership with the World Bank for the country's most vulnerable. However, providing a fixed monthly allowance of 8,500 kwanza to qualifying beneficiaries will have minimal structural impacts for the rising numbers of Angolans living in poverty. (It is estimated that 56% of the population lives below the US $1.90 per day international poverty line.)

Angola's deep dependency on oil exports links its economic health to global markets, leaving the economy facing significant headwinds. The combination of the pandemic, weak investment in oil exploration and infrastructure alongside endemic corruption has severely hampered economic recovery. Transparency International ranked Angola 142nd out of 180 countries on its Corruption Perceptions Index in 2020. The overall business environment is classified among the worst in the world, according to the World Bank's 2020 *Doing Business* report, ranking the country at 177th out of 190 countries. Furthermore, although rich in material wealth, Angola's economic performance has become decoupled from the development of its human capital. In the pivotal years from the 1991 Bicesse Accords until 2015 and the sustained drop in oil prices, the economy increased in real value by 229%, while employment only increased by 116%.

The overall population has nearly doubled since 2000, reaching 33.1m. in 2022. Angola has experienced greater urbanization than its regional neighbours because of the decades of civil war, creating increasing pressures on urban infrastructure, even though 37% of the population still resides in the countryside. Despite this rural flight, rural populations continue to increase in absolute numbers. Nevertheless, the human masses flowing towards urban centres represent a potent organic symbol of the MPLA's continued inability to provide a viable socioeconomic base for rural communities. The roots of Angola's extraverted economy and subsequent social inequalities were established during the long Portuguese colonial period and hardened through the decades of civil war that further distorted the national economy, furthering the trends of concentrating economic growth within narrow sectors of society.

COLONIAL LEGACY

In important structural aspects, Portugal's approach to developing its labour-intensive colonial economy differed significantly from its counterparts on the continent, particularly due to systemic deficiencies and the inability of the settlers to produce commercially without the recourse to forced labour. The massive exportation of slaves to the New World led an already sparsely populated territory to seriously lack able-bodied workers to sustain an overseas colony. The cessation of slavery, approved by decree in 1858 and finally extinguished by 1878, took away a vital source of the workforce for the Portuguese overseas colonies and made the settlers' agricultural production model obsolete, as paying the workers for their labour was untenable.

Unable to compete with the endogenous production, the settlers instead monopolized the commercialization process of the goods produced. Behind the protection inferred by their privileged social status provided by the colonial government, they engaged in often unfair trade practices in attempts to take advantage of, and further marginalize, the local populations. Angola's colonial system was thus able to insert itself into global markets through a number of monoculture cash crops, first through the forced production of cotton, but later including coffee, corn, sisal and sugar. Authorities had to walk a fine line by enabling policies that promoted endogenous production essential to the colony's growth, development and social stability, while simultaneously exploiting this labour through coercive monocultural export schemes.

Agricultural practices had already been significantly developed by the native populations, varying in techniques throughout the territory depending on the geographic and climatic conditions. Subsistence farmers were mostly concentrated in a few specific areas divided between the Kwanza river. In the northern region around the modern-day Malanje plateau was where the Bakongo and the Dembos peoples were most densely populated, due to favourable growing conditions for traditional crops such as cassava, rice and coffee, as well as potatoes, bananas, beans and grains. South of the Kwanza river, geography dictated different social structures.

The imposing mountainous plateau of the Central Highlands sits at a high altitude (5,000 ft–6,000 ft above sea level) and has been a main source for the production of cassava, rice, beans and potatoes. The semi-arid region below the plateau (lower Huíla and Cunene provinces) allows for more diverse economic activities with the practice of subsistence agriculture, the planting of certain cash crops (notably maize), various local cereals such as millet and sorghum, as well as ideal conditions for cattle herding and pastoralism, which has become a pivotal economic and cultural activity of the regional populations including the Ambo, Nyaneka-Nkumbi and Herero peoples.

The first official study of Angola's colonial agricultural production was conducted in 1950, focused on the main colonial exports. A decade later, in 1962, the Missão de Inquéritos Agrícolas de Angola (Board of Agricultural Surveys) created the first national map identifying the various agricultural zones throughout the territory. Subsequent studies produced the vital statistics that would underscore the significant capacity of Angola's agricultural sector. Before the Second World War, maize became the principal export crop. About 90% of the colonial production was spread out across African *lavras* (planting fields) located throughout the Benguela-Bié plateau and sold through Portuguese middlemen onto the port of Lobito, which was specialized in the exportation of agricultural goods—including beans, manioc, rice and sisal—that were sown by the natives on lands largely owned by Europeans.

The rising value of the coffee bean in the post-war period quickly made it by far the most important cash crop during the late colonial period. Once the word began to spread about coffee cultivation, more European farmers sought to control the lands where it could be grown but did so reluctantly, mostly due to the tropical diseases associated with its semi-tropical forests and savannas, coupled with the fierce resistance of the local populations. The main coffee growing region was north of the Kwanza river, encompassing nearly 80% of the total area and 80% of its ultimate production. Today production areas have spread further, covering the provinces of Uíge and Kwanza-Norte, but also includes parts of Malanje and Kwanza-Sul.

Leading up to the Second World War, colonial Angola achieved the highest coffee production in Africa, making it a national priority of Portugal to create the conditions to allow it to prosper. Production peaked in the 1970s at around 250,000 metric tons annually. However, amid the rising tensions and social instability sparking the war for liberation from colonial rule, the European colonialists fled the country en masse upon independence, often sabotaging what they could not take with them. This chaotic transition decimated coffee production, while the international market simultaneously expanded with new competitors. The sector still holds great potential, with an ever-increasing market of global consumption. Considerable efforts have been made to revitalize the sector, though production levels remain far diminished from their colonial-era heights.

According to the Food and Agricultural Organization of the UN (FAO), the area planted with coffee has increased five-fold since 2002, rising from 10,000 ha to over 50,000 ha in 2018. This has led to a modest production of 15,000 metric tons in 2018 (and a similar figure was produced in the two following years) due to a lack of technical capacity and investment in proper inputs. Similar to other crops, overall yields have flatlined during the same period, being among the worst in the region. Nevertheless, given the historical importance of the coffee sector to the country's economy, reinvesting in coffee production is seen to have particular potential for diversifying exports and the colonial era lays out a potential template to follow. A caveat must be made regarding the reliability of official statistics of the agricultural sector. Their proper compilation has long been a major concern of development partners, as official statistics remain largely opaque and lack rigorous scientific testing.

The colonial political economy therefore emphasized building up the backbone of the colony through the modernization of its agricultural sector, consequently feeding, both literally and figuratively, the rest of the economy and its nascent manufacturing sector. However, this economic machine was purposefully built to prevent the capacity to lay an independent foundation for national growth and development. Instead, the system was conceived and pre-configured for a controlled growth model in the service of providing for foreign economies, specifically that of Portugal and the major Western investors in the colonial economy—including England, France and Belgium.

Once Angolans achieved political independence, economic growth became dependent on foreign investment, expertise, and control over logistical operations, most notably in the oil sector. Western companies moved to establish partnerships with the newly formed state-owned enterprise (SOE) Sociedade Nacional de Combustíveis de Angola (SONANGOL), nationalized from the Portuguese company SACOR/Petrogal. Given its oversized importance to the stabilization of the country, the oil sector was the only one spared from the socialist policies of resource nationalism, and the company retained most of its original Portuguese employees. This practice of outsourcing major industries has since shaped the state's capacity and engagement during the reconstruction period through private contracts with foreign companies forged through historic links including Brazil and Portugal, but also with emerging players such as the People's Republic of China, the Russian Federation, the Republic of Korea (South Korea), the USA and Israel.

Angola's subordinate position as a passive producer of natural resources sought by growing Western economies conditioned the degree of independence the post-colonial country could exercise in decision-making and policy positions, with the permanent interaction between the material foundations and the politico-institutional superstructure governing it eventually morphing into a formidable force against structural change. Locked into this dynamic, the dependence on natural resource rents has created a two-tier social class system, the minority positioned to manage and exploit the rents (rent-seekers), and the majority condemned either to push the exploitative system along, or worse, being completely marginalized by it.

A NASCENT RURAL ECONOMY

Inspired by the Soviet bloc, the new MPLA Government nationalized the totality of Angola's natural resources upon independence in 1975 and established a centralized, planned economy around the nascent oil sector. However, the 'socialist' nature of the regime was only officially ratified in October 1976 by the first Congress and was thus not written into the original Constitution of the Republic in 1975. The Government clearly lacked the means and capacity to rebuild the economy funnelled through a weakened state apparatus, but the goal of dominating the productive, commercial and distributive flows of resources was achieved.

Revitalizing the agricultural sector was originally seen as a vital springboard to wider economic growth, although taking complete control of such a complex economic sector while being wholly bereft of the means to properly manage it is a recipe for dissolution. The reality was that resources were scarce, the incoming bureaucracy disorganized, and logistics hampered. Furthermore, the plethora of newly established governmental entities had hardly any qualified staff to manage them. The Ministry of Agriculture, for example, had only 1% of its own personnel trained, a similar 1% of the total rural labour force was classified as technically trained, and most of the new agricultural schools were closed due to a lack of resources.

The first statistics of independent Angola's agricultural production began to be compiled in 1977, though the numbers should be regarded with scepticism given the overall chaotic environment in which they began to be compiled and the lack of technical expertise in amassing the data. Centrally planned, ambitious targets were set and missed. Entirely beholden to the state, the agricultural sector experienced profound structural weaknesses due to systemic shortages across the board. The enormous divide between set production targets and actual production (sometimes only reaching 10% of their target) reveals an agricultural sector in complete disarray, accompanied by a newly formed Government incapable of turning it around. As the country descended into civil war, the hopes of reviving the agricultural sector quickly ceded to the reality that an already established offshore oil economy would be the most important sector for the future of the country.

THE DOMINATION OF THE OIL SECTOR

The nationalized oil company SONANGOL, created in June 1976, has been the key economic actor in Angola since independence, responsible for negotiating contracts with foreign firms and managing the sector's immense wealth production. Since 1985 oil has been officially recognized as the main source of financing for the country and has therefore become the focus and priority of the Government, much to the detriment of the other economic sectors. Dependence on the sector leaves Angola's economy and its government revenue strongly tied to the whims of the volatile oil market.

Oil profits financed the war machine as it absorbed nearly one-half of the Government's total expenditure in the late 1980s and further increased with the heightening of hostilities post-1992. In the 1990s alone, the Government spent nearly four times the amount on military expenditures as that allocated for the health and education sector combined. The first discovery of ultra-deep water oil fields in 1996 incited a huge interest by foreign investors. During the reconstruction period the oil and gas sectors dominated foreign direct investment (FDI), amounting to 82% overall between 2003 and 2017. Despite this heavy investment, crude output has been in decline since 2008.

Upstream investment in developing technology has been insufficient, leading to considerable reservoir depletion in fields currently exploited. The proven reserves are estimated at 7,800m. barrels of crude oil as of 2020. Domestic refinery capacity is low, estimated at 65,000 barrels per day, although three further refineries are currently under development. Without further exploration, reserves are expected to effectively run dry by 2040. Furthermore, as a member of the Organization of the Petroleum Exporting Countries (OPEC), the Angolan Government has come under pressure to follow the group's decision to lower production and ease exports in order to better balance the supply and demand equilibrium in a world suddenly awash with oil as the global economic recovery struggles to take hold in some major economies.

The enormous power and wealth concentrated within SONANGOL has also attracted considerable scrutiny over serious irregularities in the accounting of the company's finances. A 2011 audit by the IMF found a US $32,000m. discrepancy in account activity of SONANGOL not registered in official budgetary accounts. While the dominant oil sector gave Angolan leaders their principal point of leverage in seeking loans and building alliances, the sector also drew the most scrutiny from international institutions seeking reforms of transparency within a country afflicted with pervasive poverty. In a bid to reverse the decline in this all-important sector, the SOE has undergone a significant restructuring since 2017 and is currently preparing for 30% of its equity stake to be set for an initial public offering within the next five years.

INSIPID INVESTMENT

A major impediment to achieving sustained economic growth not reliant on the global oil market is the fact that Angola's growth model is centred on the exploitation of natural resources without a strategy to convert gains into other forms of capital. Public funds are not significantly invested in diversified vehicles for further wealth creation, instead being mostly destined for the ageing oil and mining sector, two areas of the economy that already attract the most FDI. This imbalance has long been flagged as a major structural risk for the country's overall stability.

The lack of diversification in the economy has likewise disincentivized private venture capital investments in other sectors, leading to a situation wherein the country as a whole registers one of the worst disinvestment rates in sub-Saharan Africa. Tight controls over foreign investments in specific sectors have further hampered the introduction of much needed financial resources. Current laws limit foreign

participation to 49% for companies in the oil and gas sector, 50% for insurance and 10% for the banking, although some exceptions to the rule exist.

Alongside FDI, officials have long depended on official development assistance (ODA) from abroad to make up for their own lack of investment, notably in the sectors of health, education and agriculture. However, with the establishment of social stability and the availability of oil revenue, organizations providing ODA have begun to move on. Angola came to be seen as too 'wealthy' in resources to merit intensive donor activity. The continued lack of transparency and serious reform by the Angolan authorities caused other organizations to reconsider their roles in providing basic services in sectors where the Government should be the central actor.

As GDP and GNI have increased, a direct correlation has been established with foreign donors and development institutions pulling out of the country. Net ODA has nearly halved in the past two decades, from US $302.2m. in 2000 to $159.4m. in 2018. Furthermore, the combination of a weak bureaucratic system, few enforceable regulations, and a limited amount of formal companies adhering to the tax regime has seen tax revenue as a percentage of total GDP drop from 28.7% in 2000 to 9.2% in 2018. In response, the Government has not moved to fill the void left by the departing non-governmental organizations (NGOs), further exacerbating problems.

Low investment in the health, education and agricultural sectors have all contributed to Angola's stagnation in global development rankings. Once believed to be a product of the war, this lack of investment in the human capital of its own people has continued throughout peacetime, thereby dismantling the argument that were if not for the war, the Government would have funnelled considerably more resources into these sectors. The evidence piled up from the past two decades of budget allocation does not support this claim. During the decade following the end of the war, the country had never before been so endowed with financial resources. Nevertheless, that wealth was not invested in any meaningful way for a long-term strategy in these three key sectors. In sum, the decades of peacetime have brought social stability and improvements for the wealthy and well-connected, while lacking widespread material benefits and meaningful investment in human capital.

STATE-DRIVEN PRIVATE SECTOR GROWTH

Despite announced attempts at economic reform, an engrained political desire for authoritarian control has impeded the emergence of a dynamic private sector free from government influence. The 1990s brought significant changes to the country as the Government began an incremental abandonment of the tenuous 'Marxist-Leninist' character of its governing philosophy. However, the omnipresence of SOEs throughout the economy has led many businesses to rely on public contracts for their operations or put them in direct competition with companies supported by the state. Faced with this difficult business climate, the persistence of underperforming SOEs throughout the economy further disincentivizes private investment, both foreign and national.

Historically, the main vehicle influencing the normalization of public-private partnerships (PPPs) was President dos Santos himself, through his Fundação Eduardo dos Santos (FESA) set up in March 1996. Modelled on the philanthropic foundations of developed countries, the institution has sought to complement government policies of economic development through partnerships with companies supported by state patronage. The sources of the FESA's funds are vague, however, with most of them coming from private national and international companies operating in Angola that have felt compelled to contribute to the foundation to keep in the Government's good graces, while some of the funds come from the state itself. This combination of mixed foreign capital, government officials (current and/or former) and public companies has consolidated a new emerging class of Angolans who were able to access and accumulate capital through their connections and demark themselves further from the population at large. For some, the FESA reinforced the powers of an authoritarian President through a generalized system of clientelism. Anyone accruing a significant amount of private wealth would need to remain loyal to the ruling party.

This public/private funded FESA model would later be expanded upon with the creation in 2012 of a sovereign wealth fund, the Fundo Soberano de Angola (FSDEA). Directed by the then President's son, José Filomeno dos Santos, the fund was endowed with US $5,000m. in public funds and initially invested primarily in mining, infrastructure, basic services, real estate and the agricultural sector alongside financial vehicles and instruments. The distribution of the funds throughout the economy eventually fed into the private interests of Angola's elites as their investments sprawled across the major sectors of the economy.

The arrival of the current President, João Lourenço, in 2017 saw various policy measures enacted to spur economic growth and at least performative attempts at combating endemic corruption, with varying degrees of success. The publication of the Panama Papers in 2016 revealed self-serving investments and mismanagement of public funds by the company in charge of the FSDEA's management, Quantum Global, which was run by a close friend of the former President's son, Jean-Claude Bastos de Morais. In January 2018 the new President dismissed the son of the former President and cut ties with the asset manager Quantum Global by April of the same year. During the process the Angolan Government declared that it had recovered US $3,350m. in financial and non-financial assets. The FSDEA remains in operation and has attempted to provide further transparency through annual audits and adoption of the International Financial Reporting Standards.

AGRO-BUSINESS

Agro-business has been identified as a critical sector for generating economic growth as well as being a vehicle for broader development potential. The largely informal agricultural sector employs almost one-half of the country's workforce, although only 3% of those workers are formal workers. Despite its strategic importance for employment and food security, the sector has averaged a mere 6% of FDI between 2003 and 2016. While modest, the overall trend in investments has been positive in the broader agricultural, livestock and fisheries sector. FDI has increased steadily since 1988, when it stood at 1.4% of total foreign investment, to approximately US $700m. in 2015, representing 20% of the total. This is a considerable sum given the extremely low budgetary allocation to the Ministry of Agriculture and Fisheries, representing only $205m. in 2015, for example. Aside from the FDI, available credit from the national banking sector destined for agricultural development represents less than 5% of all credit allocated.

The sector remains beset by a host of difficulties, namely degraded infrastructure, disorganized supply chains, and the lack of a formal food distribution network for most producers. Furthermore, major climatic challenges have also frustrated attempts at renewal. Erratic rainfall leaves the southern portion of the country vulnerable to cyclical periods of drought, thus creating conditions for malnourishment, increased indices of poverty and an underperforming regional economy. Between 2011 and 2013 harvests were severely impacted across central and southern Angola, affecting over 1.8m. people. According to the Famine Early Warning System Network in 2013, 20% of the population in the provinces of Cunene and neighbouring Namibe experienced severe food insecurity wherein they were only able to meet basic alimentary requirements.

While the situation was the worst in Cunene and Namibe, the drought had a far-reaching impact across neighbouring provinces as well. During the same time period the drought led to the loss of nearly the entire production of cereal and vegetable production for large areas across Cunene, Namibe, Benguela, Kwanza-Sul and southern Huíla, with northern Huíla only able to recover 40% of its harvests. Southern Angola has remained in severe drought conditions ever since, currently experiencing its worst in 40 years. The scarcity of water is becoming an ever more rising concern among regional economic actors, inflaming social tensions between the few commercial actors in the region and the rural populations. The

development and expansion of private ranches have further aggravated the situation, due not only to the limited water sources but also increased land grabbing practices of communal lands that traditionally serve rural communities for vital subsistence agriculture.

Since 2000, the Government has never allocated more than 2% of its total budget to public investments in the agricultural sector. This underinvestment remains far below purported goals. Angola joined the Comprehensive Africa Agriculture Development Programme Compact in August 2014, which sought a goal of dedicating 10% of national budgets for the proper development of the agricultural sector across the continent in order to spark a continent wide 'green revolution'. This goal is clearly far from reality. The continued underfunding of the agricultural sector is a clear indicator that the discourse of its revival will continue to encounter serious complications as it remains severely under resourced, structured as such throughout the decades set by political priorities.

CHINESE-BUILT FARMS

Foreign investment is made even more important given these realities. Within the agricultural sector specifically, China has been a key partner in attempts at modernizing the sector, although the results have been underwhelming. The budding relationship with China demonstrated the *realpolitik* needs at the time, as the MPLA held China as 'enemy number one' (on par with the USA) for many years because of its former support of the hostile regime of President Mobutu Sese Seko in Zaire and the União Nacional para a Independência Total de Angola (UNITA) under Jonas Savimbi. Putting their differences aside, Angola found itself awash in oil production and in need of loans for reconstruction.

Taking advantage of this situation, China has positioned itself for a long-term presence in Angola by building political capital with the Government through its use of favourable loan terms, often backed with oil guarantees. In 2004 China offered its most ambitious oil-backed loan to any country at the time: a US $2,000m. line of credit with an interest rate one percentage point lower than that offered by Western financial institutions, with a built-in grace period included. This loan marked a major turning point in Sino-Angolan relations for its sheer scale and crucial timing in the reconstruction efforts of the country. The sudden infusion of money similarly sparked internal infighting within the leadership regarding the allocation and disbursement of the new financing.

In the rural economy, the partnership took the form of various infrastructure projects including transportation networks, water irrigation canals, industrial farms and machinery. The construction of seven agro-industrial state farms in particular constituted a massive investment by the Government into an area that had been largely neglected until the establishment of this new partnership. The farms were built by Chinese companies between 2011 and 2014. However, due to a complex process of managerial and financial instability provoked by Angola's political class, the farms have underperformed and significantly degraded in few years following their construction. Two of the farms were eventually handed over to the army, the Forças Armadas de Angola, while nearly all the rest have since been set up for privatization as the Government looks to offload these public investments to private investors.

More oil-backed loans followed, reaching US $4,500m. worth of credit extended by China's Eximbank. The reconstruction programme was managed through the Gabinete de Reconstrução Nacional (Angola's Reconstruction Office), run by the President's inner circle and ultimately placing him at the heart of the country's rebuilding. The policies pursued via these loans would reveal the priorities of the Angolan elite as they sought to solidify their positions of dominance while setting the path for the country's emergence into peacetime. However, the Chinese loans are not accounted for in the national budget and instead follow the opaque nature of Angolan finances overall.

FISHERIES AND FORESTRY

Angola is favourably positioned geographically, with an extensive coastline of 1,650 km located between the Benguela

current system in the south and the Guinea current system in the north. The main species fished are shrimp, horse mackerel, tuna and sardinella. The latter is particularly abundant and remains at sustainable levels. The sector is enormously important as a source of economic activity, both formal and informal, as well as food security. While 6m. Angolans suffer from insufficient nourishment, fish proteins are a vital source of nutrition for the population with access to these resources.

Fishing production levels rose consistently until 2017, when they peaked at 531,575 metric tons, but have fallen back since then with some 379,000 tons landed in 2020. Very little is exported internationally—only about 5%—though exports have tripled since 2012. Total catches are divided between industrial sources (60%) and artisanal fisheries (40%). Industrial fishing is mostly run by foreign vessels, dominated by Russians, Europeans (Italy, Portugal, Spain), and Asians (South Korea, Taiwan, China).

Beyond its expansive coastline, the country's 66.6m. ha of forests also hold significant economic potential, though only about 5% of credit goes to the forestry industry. Between 2010 and 2021 Angola registered the biggest net loss in forested area in southern Africa, at a rate of 548,000 ha per year. A significant part of this loss is linked to smallholder farming, illegal logging, and the burning of wood for charcoal production among rural communities. The laws governing the exploitation of the country's forests were updated in 2017, replacing the colonial-era regulations of the 1950s. The agriculture, fisheries and forestry sectors combined accounted for approximately 9.4% of overall GDP in 2020.

MINING

The mining sector contributes significantly to the national economy, although similarly to the oil sector it produces relatively few jobs by employing barely over 1% of the total workforce. Angola is the world's seventh largest producer of diamonds, comprising around 7% of global output. Diamond exploitation is the most developed mining commodity and the country's second main source of export revenue and thus foreign currency. Foreign investment in the sector is hampered however by the fact that corporate practices do not follow the Extractive Industries Transparency Initiative, although the Government has expressed its intentions to present its candidacy in 2022. The sector has long been tarnished by allegation of corruption and cronyism linked to the sale of 'blood diamonds' during the civil war and opaque connections to former President dos Santos's family since. Official extraction, concession and allocation has been managed by the state-owned Empresa Nacional de Diamantes de Angola (ENDIAMA), while the commercialization was funnelled through the state-owned Empresa Nacional de Comercialização de Diamantes de Angola (SODIAM).

Although the country is now party to the Kimberley Process (an initiative aimed at preventing the sale of blood diamonds on international markets), illegal artisanal mines remain commonplace. Informal mining is often worked by Congolese miners migrating between the border with the Democratic Republic of the Congo. Nearly all of the exploited mines are located in the northern provinces of Lunda-Norte and Lunda-Sul, although large swathes of territory remain unexplored. Significant transparency reforms of the sector were enacted by President Lourenço in order to increase overall production. SODIAM's bidding process was previously limited to a select few companies but has since been widened to include over 100 companies. Likewise, ENDIAMA was planning for a public offering of a 30% stake in 2022 in order to boost investment and production in the sector.

Alongside diamonds, a vast array of industrial and precious metal deposits has been identified throughout the territory, including gold, iron, copper, zinc, lead, phosphate and manganese, but none has been seriously exploited on an industrial scale. Certain mineral deposits and commodities have seen recent development, including cement, crushed stone, granite, limestone, marble, quartz, salt, sand and gypsum. The full potential of Angola's mineral resource wealth remains understudied.

MANUFACTURING AND SERVICES

Driven in large part by banking and telecommunications, the services sector has seen the largest constant increase in job creation in recent years, adding over 1m. jobs between 2008 and 2014. However, a general lack of technical and skilled labour leaves out an important section of Angolans who are unable to occupy advanced positions that are instead often held by foreigners. Major portions of the population also lack access to basic services, including health and education. During the civil war many public services were provided by NGOs, but as they have slowly retreated since peacetime, the Government has been slow or unable to assume these vital responsibilities.

Domestic manufacturing has increased significantly, powered in large part by the rise in the services sector. Increased consumption in food and beverages has concentrated the most activity, although manufacturing of plastics, paper, pulp and industrial chemicals has also expanded. The sector makes up 6% of GDP and provides employment for 6% of the formal workforce, although it remains fragile. Beyond unfair competition with underperforming SOEs, the private sector faces deep structural impediments to competitive and sustainable growth due to difficulties in procuring affordable and reliable inputs, including the most basic: electricity, transportation, telecommunications and financial capital.

Despite a massive reconstruction effort, only around one-third of the population has access to reliable electricity (43% urban, 8% rural) with blackouts not uncommon even in the major cities. The World Bank ranked the country 156th out of 190 in electricity access as increased capacity has not translated into improved distribution, although officials are aiming to provide a 60% national electrification rate by 2025. To improve coverage, a second telecommunications satellite, Angosat-2, was due to be launched in March 2021 after the first one lost contact soon after its launch in December 2017. The official launch date of the new satellite has been constantly delayed, and is now scheduled for October 2022. Approximately one-quarter of the population are internet users and one-half uses mobile phones, serviced by four different companies (Unitel, Movicel, Angola Telecom and the newest addition, Africell). The telecommunications sector has traditionally been dominated by the state and the politico-military elite.

The existence of 77 river basins and 43 hydrological basins throughout the territory provides significant potential for hydroelectricity, which currently produces nearly 60% of energy needs. Only around 20% of the 75,000-km road network is paved, leaving many areas of the country largely inaccessible during seasonal flooding. The 2,750 km of railway lines built in the colonial era remain in use, with three main lines transporting goods from the east to the western port cities of Lobito, Luanda and Namibe.

OPENING BORDERS

Tourism has been identified as a potential area for growth, but the sector lacks basic infrastructure and trained human resources. The current administration made major changes to the visa regime, facilitating entry requirements for tourists from a number of specific countries, as well as streamlining authorizations to invest and carry out business activities in the country for extended periods. Along these lines, Angola has adhered to the African Continental Free Trade Area, which was inaugurated in May 2019. While still too early to measure its effectiveness, the hope is to reduce custom tariffs, facilitate trade within the region, and improve the overall business climate. The emergence of the COVID-19 pandemic has severely hampered the administration's plans for opening borders to business, trade, and tourism.

REFORMS AND MONETARY POLICY

The era of reconstruction has left Angola's leaders with a massive debt to pay off, two-thirds of which is held in foreign currencies. Economic difficulties since 2015 have led to lower economic output and considerable depreciation of the kwanza, which has in turn led to a considerable increase in the debt-to-GDP ratio: from 57% in 2015 to over 120% in 2020. Rising inflation rates had been brought under control by the central bank, the Banco Nacional de Angola (BNA), since the end of the war, but have returned since 2014. Peaking at 40% in December 2016, inflation slowly declined to approximately 17% in 2019 though has since risen again to 26% in 2021. Servicing external debts was estimated to exceed 100% of total fiscal revenues in 2020 as the country looks to negotiate repayment deals with its lenders. The financial difficulties have also led the Government to reduce fuel subsidies since 2014. Positive economic reforms implemented by the administration of João Lourenço led to three credit rating upgrades between September 2021 and 2022.

The COVID-19 pandemic exacerbated these issues through a trifecta of shocks, with the slowdown in global output leading to an economic crisis, which is degrading a woefully under-resourced national health system. Fiscal policies implemented by the BNA, supported by the IMF, had been attempting to ease the economic stress even prior to the pandemic, but the margins to act are limited. Since mid-October 2019 the official currency, the kwanza, has been converted to a flexible exchange rate regime. The former policy had led to a significant overvaluation of the currency because of the overwhelming role that the oil sector plays in the national economy. Commercial banks have also been ordered to increase minimum capital requirements to ensure financial stability.

The depreciation of the currency has played a positive role, absorbing the shocks due to the volatility of the oil market as well as the COVID-19 pandemic. Anti-corruption reforms combating money laundering, restrictive monetary policies, further transparency of financial transactions, and a more streamlined process for investors have eased access to foreign and international lenders. In the fight against corruption, the current administration implemented a no-questions-asked repatriation programme of funds illegally held overseas, backed up with the threat of imprisonment for non-compliance. Despite some arrests of significant officials, including various members of the previous President's family, the money recuperation effort has claimed over 700 cases being pursued. While some of the military and political elites linked to cases of corruption during the former administration have been pursued by the judicial system, others have maintained close ties with the current Government. The MPLA's dominance across all spheres of government has created a political system of conflicting interests that represent a major hurdle in implementing serious economic reform measures.

RESTRUCTURING DEBTS

In bilateral relations, China is by far Angola's biggest creditor, having loaned the large majority of the more than US $20,000m. in bilateral aid which requires paying back. However, the economic fallout from the COVID-19 pandemic is putting additional pressure on this Sino-Angolan partnership. The oil payments with China were indexed to a higher price per barrel at the time of negotiating the loans, meaning that Angola must send oil in much higher volumes in order to compensate for the lower market prices.

These oil-for-loans partnerships were ultimately counterproductive for Angola, leaving it with significant debt and new infrastructure that has not brought the desired added value to the economy. In some cases, the poor quality of construction has left these relatively new infrastructure projects in need of further investment. Under the administration of President Lourenço, Angola began to reduce the amount of oil shipped to China as part of paying off its debts, in an attempt to send a signal to Beijing that it hoped to renegotiate the terms of the loan repayments. Chinese lenders ultimately agreed to a three-year debt moratorium in June 2020.

Angola has long served as Beijing's major entrance point into Africa in its loan diplomacy. Its principal interest in maintaining a flexible relationship with Luanda was both its privileged access to oil as well as the signing of major infrastructure contracts favouring Chinese firms.

Due to the volatility in the oil market and the sub-par investment projects, Angola's difficulties in paying off their Chinese debt burden could put the traditional oil-for-loans model to the test moving forward. Searching for new financing

opportunities has led the administration into new negotiations with the IMF. Lourenço established an agreement with the Fund for a loan valued at US $3,700m., the largest such loan for an African country. In exchange, Angola had to open up the Government's accounting books to periodic review as well as reconsider the indebting practice of oil-for-infrastructure loans practised extensively with China. No longer able to follow his predecessor's finance and investment model, President Lourenço has had to create his own pathway to economic growth. This latest round of negotiations will likely have significant repercussions on the Sino-Angolan relationship.

UNLOADING STATE ASSETS: 'SOCIALIST' PASTS LINGER IN A LIBERALIZING ECONOMY

The 'socialist' legacy of the nationalization of the economy has remained visible throughout, both as an ideological marker but also as a tool of political control. In 1980 President dos Santos declared that the development and consolidation of the private sector constituted an imminent danger to the socialist revolution, although in practice these claims were contradictory (private property and investment, as long as it served the common good, were protected by the Constitution), paradoxical (the Government should have been prioritizing means of improving efficiency in the ailing state-run national economy) and even absurd (the Law on Foreign Investment had already been published in 1979, aimed at attracting private foreign investment), while the Government overtly welcomed private investment in certain sectors.

Private and public interests have long been a major source of friction, as the MPLA has blurred the lines between its formation as a political party and the construction of the state, effectively merging the two. Furthermore, this friction has become further engrained due to the ambiguity between the modern laws established by the Constitution and the customary laws that had been respected before the arrival of the Portuguese. While remaining operational, they have been considerably weakened and undermined by often ambiguous legislation left up to interpretation. What is clear, however, is that this vague line between the modern state and the manipulation of traditional customary practices, has created an legal environment characterized by instability and precariousness in strengthening the economy.

Marking a new development strategy on the recommendation of the IMF and the World Bank, the administration of President Lourenço has begun preparations to unload the extensive portfolio of public companies and infrastructure assets that have been weighing heavily on public finances. As the World Bank has demonstrated, SOEs have been extremely costly to state finances. Between 2013 and 2016 the Government spent nearly 1% of total GDP covering general operational costs and salaries of SOEs, about 2.5% of GDP on state subsidies, while losing nearly US $848m. in 2015 and $221m. in 2016 through company underperformance, if you subtract the lucrative state oil company SONANGOL.

To rectify this situation, the Government has created the Programa de Privatizações. The new privatization policy was approved through a presidential decree in August 2019, conducted via the Instituto de Gestão de Activos e Participações do Estado (Institute of Asset Management and State Holdings) in June 2018, alongside the Ministry of Finance and with a recommended mandate of four years. It was created with the specific mandate to reduce the influence of SOEs in the economy and increase the quality and variety of services available to the population. This process has marked a fundamental change in the character of the state as it cedes influence of various sectors of the economy to private actors, although it remains to be seen which private actors will ultimately take over these state assets.

In total the Government announced its intention to privatize in full or in part 195 public companies across the sectors of finance, agro-industry, fisheries, tourism, telecommunications, health, transportation, oil, construction, industry and real estate. The ambition of this privatization policy is vast and fraught with risks, given that the current global economic outlook and Angola's itself are far from ideal. Much too ambitious, the programme remains operational but far behind schedule with around one third of the state companies privatized to mainly local investors. The vast list of assets assigned for privatization produced in 2019 reveals the extent to which public companies have continued to play an enormous role in the national economy, far removed from its 'socialist' past, further revealing the limits of the 'liberalization' supposedly under way since the 1990s.

CONCLUSION

The MPLA-led Government deserves credit for establishing both social and political stability in Angola, but it also invites serious criticism over the country's continued languishing among the bottom ranks of the world in social development indicators. The GDP expansion in the last two decades (an increase of 1,010%) has been massive, but the streamlined, vertical nature of oil rents combined with the systematic misuse of these funds has contributed to equally massive social inequalities. Having been in power since independence, the MPLA's grip on power is becoming ever more tenuous as the population grows restless. Too many Angolans feel excluded by the authoritarian political system that rules their lives through fear, intimidation, disrespect, and marginalization. The contested electoral results of September 2022, at which the MPLA won 51.4% of the vote, reveal a deep divide in the Government's policies and a strong will for political change. Whether the MPLA party-state, in power since independence, is capable of fundamental change will be the key question hanging over the country as a five-year mandate begins anew.

Statistical Survey

Sources (unless otherwise stated): Instituto Nacional de Estatística, Av. Ho Chi Minh, CP 1215, Luanda; tel. 226420730; e-mail geral@ine.gov.ao; internet www.ine.gov.ao; Ministério da Economia e Planeamento, Edificio CIF One, Av. I, Congresso do MPLA, Luanda; tel. 222668889; e-mail gcii@mep.gov.ao; internet www.mep.gov.ao.

Area and Population

AREA, POPULATION AND DENSITY

Area (sq km)	1,246,700*
Population (census results)	
15 December 1970	5,646,166
16–31 May 2014	
Males	12,499,041
Females	13,289,983
Total	25,789,024
Population (official estimates at mid-year)	
2020	31,127,674
2021	32,097,671
2022	33,086,278
Density (per sq km) at mid-2022	26.5

* 481,354 sq miles.

POPULATION BY AGE AND SEX
(official estimates at mid-2022)

	Males	Females	Total
0–14 years	7,394,424	7,464,627	14,859,051
15–64 years	8,391,577	9,010,908	17,402,485
65 years and over	361,644	463,098	824,742
Total	16,147,645	16,938,633	33,086,278

PROVINCES
(official population estimates at mid-2022)

	Area (sq km)	Population	Density (per sq km)
Bengo	31,370	497,721	15.9
Benguela	31,788	2,749,300	86.5
Bié	70,314	1,883,101	26.8
Cabinda	7,283	894,276	122.8
Cunene	89,342	1,271,638	14.2
Huambo	34,274	2,645,080	77.2
Huíla	75,002	3,185,244	42.5
Kuando Kubango . . .	199,049	677,430	3.4
Kwanza-Norte . . .	24,190	554,749	22.9
Kwanza-Sul . . .	55,658	2,370,936	42.6
Luanda	2,416	9,079,811	3,758.2
Lunda-Norte . . .	102,782	1,090,897	10.6
Lunda-Sul	45,647	690,073	15.1
Malanje	97,600	1,247,509	12.8
Moxico	223,023	964,426	4.3
Namibe	58,137	650,500	11.2
Uíge	58,696	1,867,157	31.8
Zaire	40,129	766,430	19.1
Total	1,246,700	33,086,278	26.5

PRINCIPAL TOWNS
(official population estimates at mid-2022 unless otherwise indicated)

Luanda (capital) .	2,831,280	Benguela . . .	692,202
Viana	2,092,439	Uíge	653,640
Cacuaco . . .	1,408,589	Malanje	641,011
Belas	1,400,163	Cuito	583,479
Cazenga	1,151,206	Saurimo . . .	567,922
Lubango . . .	990,165	Lobito	484,351
Huambo	934,127	Cuanhama . . .	480,975
Cabinda	739,182*	Luena	454,409

* At mid-2020.

BIRTHS AND DEATHS
(annual averages, UN estimates)

	2005–10	2010–15	2015–20
Birth rate (per 1,000)	46.8	44.2	40.9
Death rate (per 1,000)	13.5	10.1	8.3

Source: UN, *World Population Prospects: The 2019 Revision.*

2011 (official figures, provisional): Live births 15,011; marriages 1,842; registered deaths 15,379.

Life expectancy (years at birth, estimates): 61.5 (males 58.7; females 64.4) in 2020 (Source: World Bank, *World Development Indicators* database).

ECONOMICALLY ACTIVE POPULATION
(persons aged 15 years and over, average of 12 months to February 2019)

	Males	Females	Total
Agriculture, forestry and fishing .	1,949,729	2,505,787	4,455,516
Industry (excl. construction) . .	345,901	97,528	443,429
Construction	338,912	3,522	342,434
Wholesale and retail trade; repair of motor vehicles and motorcycles	580,332	1,464,967	2,045,299
Transport, storage and communications	422,516	66,970	489,486
Financial intermediation, real estate and consulting services .	52,089	21,579	73,668
Public administration and defence; compulsory social security . .	701,448	182,331	883,779
Education	222,916	114,697	337,613
Human health and social work activities	47,659	41,600	89,259

—continued	Males	Females	Total
Households with employed persons and extraterritorial organizations	118,715	329,213	447,928
Sub-total	4,780,217	4,828,194	9,608,411
Not classified by economic activity	39,220	42,743	81,963
Total employed	4,819,435	4,870,937	9,690,372
Unemployed	1,817,126	2,143,544	3,960,670
Total labour force . . .	6,636,561	7,014,481	13,651,042

Note: Totals may not be equal to the sum of components, owing to rounding.

Health and Welfare

KEY INDICATORS

Total fertility rate (children per woman, 2020)	5.4
Under-5 mortality rate (per 1,000 live births, 2020) . . .	71.5
HIV/AIDS (% of persons aged 15–49, 2020)	1.8
COVID-19: Cumulative confirmed deaths (per 100,000 persons at 31 August 2022)	5.6
COVID-19: Fully vaccinated population (% of total population at 28 August 2022)	22.6
Physicians (per 1,000 head, 2017)	0.2
Hospital beds (per 1,000 head, 2005)	0.8
Domestic health expenditure (2019): US $ per head (PPP) .	73.4
Domestic health expenditure (2019): % of GDP . . .	1.0
Domestic health expenditure (2019): public (% of total current expenditure)	41.2
Access to improved water resources (% of persons, 2020) .	57
Access to improved sanitation facilities (% of persons, 2020) .	52
Total carbon dioxide emissions ('000 metric tons, 2018) . .	27,340
Carbon dioxide emissions per head (metric tons, 2018) . .	0.9
Human Development Index (2021): ranking	148
Human Development Index (2021): value	0.586

Note: For data on COVID-19 vaccinations, 'fully vaccinated' denotes receipt of all doses specified by approved vaccination regime (Sources: Johns Hopkins University and Our World in Data). Data on health expenditure refer to current general government expenditure in each case. For more information on sources and further definitions for all indicators, see Health and Welfare Statistics: Sources and Definitions section (europaworld.com/credits).

Agriculture

PRINCIPAL CROPS
('000 metric tons)

	2018	2019	2020
Bananas	3,954	4,037	4,115*
Beans, dry*	326	363	373
Cabbages and other brassicas* .	339	338	338
Cassava (Manioc)	8,731	9,000	8,782*
Coffee, green*	15	15	15
Groundnuts, with shell . . .	212	212	232*
Maize	2,765	2,819	2,300†
Millet	59*	56*	55†
Onions and shallots, green* . .	27	27	27
Pineapples*	598	588	595
Potatoes	458	455	446†
Rice, paddy	10	10	10†
Sorghum	40	32	60†

—continued	2018	2019	2020
Soybeans (Soya beans) . . .	35	37	41*
Sugar cane*	639	750	808
Sunflower seed*	12	12	12
Sweet potatoes	1,688	1,680	1,728*
Tomatoes*	17	17	17
Wheat*	3	3	3

* FAO estimate(s).
† Unofficial figure.

Aggregate production ('000 metric tons, may include official, semi-official or estimated data): Total cereals 2,877 in 2018, 2,920 in 2019, 2,428 in 2020; Total fruit (primary) 5,008 in 2018, 5,080 in 2019, 5,175 in 2020; Total oilcrops 553 in 2018, 555 in 2019, 580 in 2020; Total roots and tubers 10,877 in 2018, 11,136 in 2019, 10,956 in 2020; Total vegetables (primary) 746 in 2018, 743 in 2019, 744 in 2020.

Source: FAO.

LIVESTOCK
('000 head, year ending September, FAO estimates)

	2018	2019	2020
Cattle	5,100	5,078	5,120
Chickens	37,670	44,362	47,306
Goats	4,495	4,603	4,711
Pigs	3,326	3,537	3,740
Sheep	1,136	1,156	1,173

Source: FAO.

LIVESTOCK PRODUCTS
('000 metric tons, FAO estimates)

	2018	2019	2020
Cattle hides, fresh	15.1	15.2	15.3
Cattle meat	103.8	104.3	104.9
Cattle offals, edible	16.6	16.7	16.8
Cows' milk	218.8	218.2	219.7
Chicken meat	41.6	49.0	52.2
Game meat	9.5	9.4	9.4
Goat meat	20.5	20.9	21.4
Pig meat	133.9	141.8	149.8
Hen eggs	5.1	5.1	5.2
Honey (natural)	23.5	23.5	23.5

Source: FAO.

Forestry

ROUNDWOOD REMOVALS
('000 cubic metres, excluding bark, FAO estimates)

	2017	2018	2019
Sawlogs, veneer logs and logs for sleepers	200	200	200
Other industrial wood	1,050	1,050	1,050
Fuel wood	4,677	4,773	4,872
Total	5,927	6,023	6,122

2020: Production assumed to be unchanged from 2019 (FAO estimates).
Source: FAO.

SAWNWOOD PRODUCTION
('000 cubic metres, including railway sleepers, FAO estimates)

	2018	2019	2020
Total (all broadleaved) . . .	20	50	30

Source: FAO.

Fishing

('000 metric tons, live weight)

	2018	2019	2020
Capture*	443.1	400.8	377.3
Freshwater fishes . . .	29.0	15.0*	9.8
West African croakers . .	3.3	3.3	2.5
Dentex	19.7	1.6	1.9
Cunene horse mackerel . .	37.0	64.3	71.0
Pilchards and sardinellas . .	137.9	170.7	131.7
Chub mackerel	15.0*	26.6	30.9
Aquaculture	1.8	1.9	2.1
Total catch (incl. others)* . .	444.8	402.7	379.4

* FAO estimate(s).

Source: FAO.

Mining

	2016	2017	2018
Crude petroleum ('000 42-gallon barrels)	640,575	611,010	559,910
Salt (unrefined, '000 metric tons)*.	43	45	40
Diamonds ('000 carats)† . . .	9,021	9,439	8,409

* Estimates.

† Reported figures, based on estimates of 10% of production at industrial grade.

Source: US Geological Survey.

Crude petroleum ('000 metric tons, estimates): 69,070 in 2019; 64,220 in 2020; 56,607 in 2021 (Source: BP, *Statistical Review of World Energy*).

Industry

SELECTED PRODUCTS

('000 metric tons unless otherwise indicated)

	2017	2018	2019
Palm fruit oil*†	280	281	281
Cement‡	4,600	5,000	n.a.
Jet fuels	279	189	285
Motor gasoline (petrol) . . .	35	5	39
Naphthas	278	39	333
Kerosene	52	36	24
Distillate fuel oils	607	436	615
Residual fuel oils	947	614	1,072
Electrical energy (million kWh) .	10,737	12,869	15,474

* Data from FAO.

† FAO estimates.

‡ Data from US Geological Survey, estimates.

Source: mainly UN Energy Statistics Database.

Finance

CURRENCY AND EXCHANGE RATES

Monetary Units
100 lwei = 1 kwanza.

Sterling, Dollar and Euro Equivalents (31 May 2022)
£1 sterling = 532.963 kwanza;
US $1 = 423.356 kwanza;
€1 = 453.541 kwanza;
1,000 kwanza = £1.88 = $2.36 = €2.20.

Average Exchange Rate (kwanza per US $)
2019   364.826
2020   578.259
2021   631.442

Note: In April 1994 the introduction of a new method of setting exchange rates resulted in an effective devaluation of the new kwanza, to US $1 = 68,297 new kwanza, and provided for an end to the system of multiple exchange rates. Further substantial devaluations followed, and in July 1995 a 'readjusted' kwanza, equivalent to 1,000 new kwanza, was introduced. The currency, however, continued to depreciate. Between July 1997 and June 1998 a fixed official rate of US $1 = 262,376 readjusted kwanza was in operation. In May 1999 the central bank announced its decision to abolish the existing dual currency exchange rate system. In December 1999 the readjusted kwanza was replaced by a new currency, the kwanza, equivalent to 1m. readjusted kwanza.

BUDGET

('000 million kwanza)

Revenue*	2020	2021†	2022†
Taxes	6,605	9,904	11,869
Petroleum revenue . . .	3,612	6,043	7,352
Non-petroleum revenue . .	2,993	3,862	4,517
Social contributions	320	328	336
Other revenue	123	170	278
Total	7,049	10,403	12,483

Expenditure‡	2020	2021†	2022†
Current	5,918	7,347	9,149
Wages and salaries	2,067	2,484	2,675
Goods and services	965	1,512	2,047
Interest payments	2,300	2,456	2,715
Domestic	1,008	1,221	1,307
External	1,292	1,236	1,408
Subsidies	38	210	1,049
Other expenses	547	685	663
Acquisition of non-financial assets	1,773	1,743	1,935
Total	7,691	9,090	11,085

* Excluding grants received ('000 million kwanza): 4 in 2020; 1 in 2021 (projection); 1 in 2022 (projection).

† Projections.

‡ Excluding lending minus repayments ('000 million kwanza): −638 in 2020; 1,314 in 2021 (projection); 1,399 in 2022 (projection).

Source: IMF, *Angola: 2021 Article IV Consultation and Six Review under the Extended Arrangement of the Extended Fund Facility and Request for a Waiver of Nonobservance of a Performance Criterion; Press Release; Staff Report; and Statement by the Executive Director for Angola* (January 2022).

INTERNATIONAL RESERVES

(US $ million at 31 December)

	2019	2020	2021
IMF special drawing rights . .	288.06	269.54	1,190.39
Reserve position in IMF . . .	157.07	163.55	158.91
Foreign exchange	15,889.72	13,348.91	13,118.81
Total	16,334.85	13,781.99	14,468.11

Source: IMF, *International Financial Statistics*.

MONEY SUPPLY
(million kwanza at 31 December)

	2019	2020	2021
Currency outside depository corporations	418,992	404,596	401,789
Transferable deposits	4,520,367	5,939,266	5,318,626
Other deposits	5,275,046	6,353,875	5,792,832
Securities other than shares	4,746	4,746	5,066
Broad money	10,219,151	1,2702,483	11,518,313

Source: IMF, *International Financial Statistics.*

COST OF LIVING
(Consumer Price Index; base: December 2014 = 100)

	2017	2018	2019
Food and non-alcoholic beverages	180.6	209.3	244.0
Clothing and footwear	187.2	245.9	296.8
Housing and utilities	144.5	170.3	209.0
All items (incl. others)	179.1	214.3	250.9

Source: International Monetary Fund (IMF).

Cost of Living (Consumer Price Index; base: December 2020 = 100): All items 73.9 in 2019; 90.4 in 2020; 113.7 in 2021.

NATIONAL ACCOUNTS
(million kwanza at current prices)

Expenditure on the Gross Domestic Product

	2018	2019	2020
Government final consumption expenditure	2,684,389	3,263,514	3,115,695
Private final consumption expenditure	14,444,171	18,206,546	21,838,013
Gross capital formation	4,579,529	5,393,114	6,852,618
Total domestic expenditure	21,708,090	26,863,174	31,806,326
Exports of goods and services	10,465,419	12,834,624	12,712,846
Less Imports of goods and services	6,545,767	8,137,370	9,847,418
Statistical discrepancy	—	1,061,270	1,357,767
GDP in purchasers' values	25,627,742	32,621,698	36,029,521

Gross Domestic Product by Economic Activity

	2018	2019	2020
Agriculture, forestry and fishing	2,205,970	2,172,835	3,397,502
Mining and utilities	7,967,792	9,139,544	9,279,659
Manufacturing	1,571,283	2,437,724	2,346,938
Construction	2,744,697	4,729,266	4,500,542
Wholesale and retail trade; restaurants and hotels	5,278,726	5,846,236	7,008,739
Transport, storage and communication	864,676	1,118,275	1,262,610
Other services	4,929,553	5,709,131	6,642,869
Sub-total	25,562,697	31,153,011	34,438,858
Indirect taxes on products (net)*	65,045	1,468,687	1,590,663
GDP in purchasers' values	25,627,742	32,621,698	36,029,521

* Figures obtained as a residual.

Source: UN National Accounts Main Aggregates Database.

BALANCE OF PAYMENTS
(US $ million)

	2019	2020	2021
Exports of goods	34,725.6	20,937.4	33,581.5
Imports of goods	−14,127.1	−9,543.1	−11,794.8
Balance on goods	20,598.5	11,394.3	21,786.6
Exports of services	454.6	67.0	93.5
Imports of services	−8,172.3	−5,602.5	−7,050.4
Balance on goods and services	12,880.8	5,858.8	14,829.8
Primary income received	692.6	535.8	354.8
Primary income paid	−8,208.9	−5,459.9	−6,138.7
Balance on goods, services and primary income	5,364.5	934.6	9,045.8
Secondary income received	11.8	56.9	29.2
Secondary income paid	−239.0	−119.6	−675.6
Current balance	5,137.4	871.9	8,399.5
Capital account (net)	2.0	1.2	2.0
Direct investment assets	2,349.4	−90.5	1,057.4
Direct investment liabilities	−4,098.5	−1,866.5	−4,355.1
Portfolio investment assets	−1,324.1	1,640.4	−34.7
Portfolio investment liabilities	3,000.0	0.0	0.0
Financial derivatives and employee stock options (net)	0.7	20.1	−18.9
Other investment assets	−1,761.7	−2,205.2	−6,044.5
Other investment liabilities	−1,879.6	−1,928.1	366.5
Net errors and omissions	−953.6	−871.7	−1,306.3
Reserves and related items	472.1	−4,428.4	−1,934.3

Source: IMF, *International Financial Statistics.*

External Trade

SELECTED COMMODITIES
(distribution by HS, million kwanza)

Imports	2019	2020	2021
Live animals and animal products	273,162	267,477	302,988
Meat and edible meat offal	160,010	176,333	219,901
Vegetables and vegetable products	312,436	482,791	524,224
Animal or vegetable fats and oils, and products thereof	136,339	189,158	196,971
Prepared foodstuffs; beverages, spirits, vinegar; tobacco and articles thereof	312,055	324,634	323,562
Beverages, spirits and vinegar	48,734	60,680	54,619
Mineral products	735,560	546,266	1,204,235
Mineral fuels, oils, distillation products, etc.	722,395	535,730	1,191,383
Chemicals and related products	383,687	501,649	626,306
Plastics, rubber, and articles thereof	230,730	280,963	340,182
Plastic and articles thereof	171,657	210,511	255,757
Pulp of wood, paper and paperboard, and articles thereof	173,222	166,965	197,170

Imports—*continued*	2019	2020	2021
Textiles and textile articles .	115,277	133,704	255,578
Iron and steel, other base metals and articles of base metal	317,703	410,479	577,002
Machinery and mechanical appliances; electrical equipment; parts thereof .	986,386	1,216,908	1,623,663
Machinery, boilers, etc. .	686,403	875,416	1,133,875
Electrical, electronic equipment .	299,983	341,492	489,788
Vehicles, aircraft, vessels and associated transport equipment . .	805,896	530,201	562,998
Vehicles other than railway, tramway	257,063	312,082	491,344
Ships and other floating structures	495,047	21,016	15,523
Optical, medical apparatus, etc.; clocks and watches; musical instruments; parts thereof	80,035	141,117	174,454
Total (incl. others)	5,067,401	5,392,911	7,149,360

Exports	2019	2020	2021
Live animals and animal products	8,998	45,556	27,962
Mineral products . .	12,186,788	11,402,696	19,812,042
Wood, wood charcoal, cork, and articles thereof . . .	10,856	19,872	31,359
Pearls, precious or semi-precious stones, precious metals, and articles thereof .	448,721	640,780	970,750
Machinery and mechanical appliances; electrical equipment; parts thereof .	48,611	47,515	53,199
Total (incl. others)	12,788,140	12,234,837	21,001,890

PRINCIPAL TRADING PARTNERS
(million kwanza)

Imports c.i.f.	2019	2020	2021
Belgium	333,840	232,585	245,653
Brazil	205,780	305,159	344,764
China, People's Republic . . .	739,221	829,590	1,066,007
France	638,540	176,541	259,317
India	173,081	262,427	470,883
Italy	n.a.	134 627	269,371
Korea, Republic	277,253	164,707	n.a.
Netherlands	n.a.	74 679	272,846
Portugal	666,389	748,428	857,346
South Africa	183,535	225,864	n.a.
Thailand	94,600	145,611	n.a.
Togo	143,408	55,739	434,238
Türkiye	107,067	137,108	n.a.
United Arab Emirates . . .	141,969	n.a.	n.a.
United Kingdom . . .	152,511	249,739	328,303
USA	243,079	350,147	329,142
Total (incl. others)	5,067,401	5,392,911	7,149,360

Exports f.o.b.	2019	2020	2021
China, People's Republic . . .	7,857,065	7,641,925	12,665,530
Chile	n.a.	49,656	327,255
France	219,278	203,764	n.a.
India	1,231,993	931,875	1,899,565
Indonesia	n.a.	15,319	280,522
Italy	284,562	173,060	398,383
Netherlands	72,884	135,128	290,622
Portugal	404,393	149,933	n.a.
Singapore	122,151	245,161	474,921
South Africa	123,745	109,333	316,982
Spain	457,091	305,572	420,401
Taiwan	72,957	173,439	n.a.
Thailand	230,253	506,818	634,497
United Arab Emirates . . .	412,035	545,688	879,465
USA	321,257	215,111	290,319
Total (incl. others)	12,788,140	12,234,837	21,001,890

Transport

GOODS TRANSPORT
(million metric tons)

	2002	2003	2004
Air	646.4	248.6	21,745.0
Road	7,505.7	4,635.5	19,031.0
Railway	253.6	129.3	54.0
Water	3,523.8	4,259.7	1,189.0

Source: Portais Governo de Angola.

PASSENGER TRANSPORT
(million passenger-km)

	2002	2003	2004
Air	804.9	978.4	21,229.0
Road	235,208.0	1,112,272.0	1,188,063.0
Railway	2,975.2	3,708.4	192.0
Water	—	—	1,522.0

Source: Portais Governo de Angola.

ROAD TRAFFIC
(motor vehicles in use at 31 December, estimates)

	1997	1998	1999
Passenger cars	103,400	107,100	117,200
Lorries and vans	107,600	110,500	118,300
Total	211,000	217,600	235,500

2000–02: Data assumed to be unchanged from 1999 (estimates).
Source: UN, *Statistical Yearbook*.

SHIPPING

Flag Registered Fleet
(at 31 December)

	2019	2020	2021
Number of vessels	125	132	133
Total displacement (grt) . . .	202,633	211,401	211,914

Source: Lloyd's List Intelligence (www.bit.ly/LLintelligence).

CIVIL AVIATION
(traffic on scheduled services)

	2013	2014	2015
Kilometres flown (million) . .	25	26	25
Passengers carried ('000) . . .	1,322	1,410	1,244
Passenger-km (million) . . .	3,711	4,024	3,535
Total ton-km (million)	70	66	46

Source: UN, *Statistical Yearbook*.

2020 (domestic and international): Departures 3,792; Passengers carried 0.4m.; Freight carried 29m. ton-km (Source: World Bank, World Development Indicators database).

Tourism

FOREIGN TOURIST ARRIVALS

Country of residence	2018	2019	2020
Brazil	18,501	14,638	5,759
China, People's Republic . . .	20,418	17,193	1,634
France	10,208	13,928	4,804
India	5,374	7,719	2,501
Lebanon	2,369	3,517	1,448
Namibia	6,180	6,876	2,483
Portugal	59,709	65,701	25,019
South Africa	8,710	5,401	1,731
United Kingdom	7,744	8,404	2,523
USA	6,808	6,659	2,193
Total (incl. others)	217,866	217,512	63,617

Tourism receipts (US $ million, excl. passenger transport): 880 in 2017; 544 in 2018; 384 in 2019 (provisional).

Source: World Tourism Organization.

Communications Media

	2018	2019	2020
Telephones ('000 main lines in use)	171.9	124.7	119.2
Mobile telephone Subscriptions ('000)	13,288.4	14,830.2	14,645.1
Broadband subscriptions, fixed ('000)	109.6	119.1	230.6
Broadband subscriptions, mobile ('000)	5,820.2	6,740.4	6,637.3
Internet users (% of population) .	35.0	36.0	n.a.

Source: International Telecommunication Union.

Education

(2015/16 unless otherwise indicated)

	Teachers	Students		
		Males	Females	Total
Pre-primary	12,440	416,069	368,312	784,381
Primary	95,827	2,986,710*	2,634,205*	5,620,915*
Secondary:				
general	65,129*	1,064,386	682,164	1,746,550
vocational	7,730*	165,796	121,804	287,600
Higher	8,660*	137,403	115,884	253,287

* 2014/15.

Source: UNESCO Institute for Statistics.

Pupil-teacher ratio (primary education, UNESCO estimate): 50.0 in 2014/15 (Source: UNESCO Institute for Statistics).

Adult literacy rate (UNESCO estimates): 71.2% (males 82.0%; females 60.7%) in 2015 (Source: UNESCO Institute for Statistics).

Directory

The Constitution

The main provisions of the Constitution promulgated on 5 February 2010 are summarized below:

BASIC PRINCIPLES

The Republic of Angola shall be a sovereign and independent state whose prime objective shall be to build a free and democratic society of peace, justice and social progress. It shall be a democratic state based on the rule of law, founded on national unity, the dignity of human beings, pluralism of expression and political organization, respecting and guaranteeing the basic rights and freedoms of persons, whether as individuals or as members of organized social groups. Sovereignty shall be vested in the people, which shall exercise political power through periodic universal suffrage.

The Republic of Angola shall be a unitary and indivisible state. Economic, social and cultural solidarity shall be promoted between all the Republic's regions for the common development of the entire nation and the elimination of regionalism and tribalism.

Religion

The Republic shall be a secular state and there shall be complete separation of the state and religious institutions. All religions shall be respected.

The Economy

The economic system shall be based on the coexistence of diverse forms of property—public, private, mixed, co-operative and family— and all shall enjoy equal protection. The state shall protect foreign investment and foreign property, in accordance with the law. The fiscal system shall aim to satisfy the economic, social and administrative needs of the state and to ensure a fair distribution of income and wealth. Taxes may be created and abolished only by law, which shall determine applicability, rates, tax benefits and guarantees for taxpayers.

Education

The Republic shall vigorously combat illiteracy and obscurantism and shall promote the development of education and of a true national culture.

FUNDAMENTAL RIGHTS AND DUTIES

The state shall respect and protect the human person and human dignity. All citizens shall be equal before the law. They shall be subject to the same duties, without any distinction based on colour, race, ethnic group, sex, place of birth, religion, level of education, or economic or social status.

All citizens aged 18 years and over, other than those legally deprived of political and civil rights, shall have the right and duty to take an active part in public life, to vote and be elected to any state organ, and to discharge their mandates with full dedication to the cause of the Angolan nation. The law shall establish limitations in respect of non-political allegiance of soldiers on active service, judges and police forces, as well as the electoral incapacity of soldiers on active service and police forces.

Freedom of expression, of assembly, of demonstration, of association and of all other forms of expression shall be guaranteed. Groupings whose aims or activities are contrary to the constitutional order and penal laws, or that, even indirectly, pursue political objectives through organizations of a military, paramilitary or militarized nature shall be forbidden. Every citizen has the right to a defence if accused of a crime. Individual freedoms are guaranteed. Freedom of conscience and belief shall be inviolable. Work shall be the right and duty of all citizens. The state shall promote measures necessary to ensure the right of citizens to medical and health care, as well as assistance in childhood, motherhood, disability, old age, etc. It shall also promote access to education, culture and sports for all citizens.

STATE ORGANS

President of the Republic

The President of the Republic shall be the Head of State, Head of Government and Commander-in-Chief of the Angolan armed forces. The leader of the political party, or coalition of political parties, obtaining a majority vote in the general elections shall be named President of the Republic and shall be assisted by a Vice-President; the position of Vice-President shall be filled by the deputy leader of the ruling party. The President may serve a maximum of two five-year terms. The President of the Republic shall have the following powers:

- to appoint and dismiss Ministers and other government officials determined by law
- to appoint the judges of the Supreme Court
- to preside over the Council of Ministers
- to declare war and make peace, following authorization by the National Assembly
- to sign, promulgate and publish the laws of the National Assembly, government decrees and statutory decrees
- to preside over the National Defence Council
- to decree a state of siege or state of emergency
- to announce the holding of general elections
- to issue pardons and commute sentences
- to perform all other duties provided for in the Constitution.

National Assembly

The National Assembly is the supreme state legislative body, to which the Government is responsible. The Assembly shall be composed of 220 deputies, elected for a term of five years. The Assembly shall convene in ordinary session twice yearly and in special session on the initiative of the President of the Assembly, the Standing Commission of the Assembly or of no less than one-third of its deputies. The Standing Commission shall be the organ of the Assembly that represents and assumes its powers between sessions.

Government

The Government shall comprise the President of the Republic, the ministers and the secretaries of state, and other members whom the law shall indicate, and shall have the following functions:

- to organize and direct the implementation of state domestic and foreign policy, in accordance with the decision of the National Assembly and its Standing Commission
- to ensure national defence, the maintenance of internal order and security, and the protection of the rights of citizens
- to prepare the draft National Plan and General State Budget for approval by the National Assembly, and to organize, direct and control their execution.

The Council of Ministers shall be answerable to the National Assembly. In the exercise of its powers, the Council of Ministers shall issue decrees and resolutions.

Judiciary

The organization, composition and competence of the courts shall be established by law. Judges shall be independent in the discharge of their functions.

Local State Organs

The organs of state power at provincial level shall be the Provincial Assemblies and their executive bodies. The Provincial Assemblies shall work in close co-operation with social organizations and rely on the initiative and broad participation of citizens. The Provincial Assemblies shall elect commissions of deputies to perform permanent or specific tasks. The executive organs of Provincial Assemblies shall be the Provincial Governments, which shall be led by the Provincial Governors. The Provincial Governors shall be answerable to the President of the Republic, the Council of Ministers and the Provincial Assemblies.

National Defence

The state shall ensure national defence. The National Defence Council shall be presided over by the President of the Republic, and its composition shall be determined by law. The Angolan armed forces, as a state institution, shall be permanent, regular and non-partisan. Defence of the country shall be the right and the highest indeclinable duty of every citizen. Military service shall be compulsory. The forms in which it is fulfilled shall be defined by the law.

The Government

HEAD OF STATE

President: João Manuel Gonçalves Lourenço (took office 26 September 2017; re-elected 24 August 2022).

Vice-President: Bornito de Sousa Baltazar Diogo.

COUNCIL OF MINISTERS
(October 2022)

President: João Manuel Gonçalves Lourenço.

Vice-President: Bornito de Sousa Baltazar Diogo.

Minister of State and Chief of Staff in the Presidency: Adão Francisco Correia de Almeida.

Minister of State for Economic Co-ordination: Manuel José Nunes Júnior.

Minister of State for Social Affairs: Dalva Maurícia Calombo Ringote Allen.

Minister of State and Head of Security in the Presidency: Francisco Pereira Furtado.

Minister of National Defence and War Veterans: João Ernesto dos Santos.

Minister of the Interior: Eugénio César Laborinho.

Minister of External Relations: Téte António.

Minister of Territorial Administration: Dionísio Manuel da Fonseca.

Minister of Justice and Human Rights: Marcy Cláudio Lopes.

Minister of Finance: Vera Esperança dos Santos Daves de Sousa.

Minister of the Economy and Planning: Mário Caetano João.

Minister of Public Administration, Labour and Social Security: Teresa Rodrigues Dias.

Minister of Agriculture and Forestry: António Francisco de Assis.

Minister of Fisheries and Marine Resources: Carmen Sacramento Neto.

Minister of Industry and Commerce: Victor Francisco dos Santos Fernandes.

Minister of Mineral Resources, Petroleum and Gas: Diamantino Pedro Azevedo.

Minister of Transport: Ricardo Daniel Sandão Queirós Veigas d'Abreu.

Minister of Energy and Water: João Baptista Borges.

Minister of Public Works, Urbanism and Housing: Carlos Alberto Gregório dos Santos.

Minister of Telecommunications, Information Technology and Social Communication: Mario Augusto da Silva Oliveira.

Minister of Higher Education, Science, Technology and Innovation: Maria do Rosário Bragança Sambo.

Minister of Education: Luísa Maria Alves Grilo.

Minister of Health: Sílvia Paula Valentim Lutucuta.

Minister of Social Action, Families and the Promotion of Women: Ana Paula do Sacramento Neto.

Minister of Culture and Tourism: Filipe Silvino de Pina Zau.

Minister of the Environment: Ana Paula Chantre Luna de Carvalho.

Minister of Youth and Sports: Palmira Leitão Barbosa.

Secretary of the Council of Ministers: Ana Maria da Silva Sousa e Silva.

In addition, there were 48 secretaries of state.

MINISTRIES

Office of the President: Rua 17 de Setembro, Palácio do Povo, Luanda; tel. 222332939; internet fb.com/PresidedaRepublica.

Office of the Vice-President: Largo 17 de Setembro, Luanda; tel. 222396501; internet governo.gov.ao.

Ministry of Agriculture and Forestry: Largo António Jacinto, CP 527, Luanda; tel. 222322377; internet www.minagrif.gov.ao.

Ministry of Culture and Tourism: Edif. 4, Complexo Administrativo-Clássicos do Talatona, Rua do MAT, TalatonaLuanda; tel. 222322070; e-mail gcii@mcta.gov.ao; internet mcta.gov.ao.

Ministry of Economy and Planning: Edif. CIF 1, 10º andar, Av. I, Congresso do MPLA, Luanda; tel. 930091708; e-mail geral@mep.gov.ao; internet www.mep.gov.ao.

Ministry of Education: Edif. MED, Largo António Jacinto, Rua Comandante Gika 82, CP 1281, Luanda; tel. 222321236; e-mail oficial.med@med.gov.ao; internet med.gov.ao.

Ministry of Energy and Water: Rua Cónego Manuel das Neves 234, CP 2229, Luanda; tel. 222430227; e-mail geral@minea.gov.ao; internet www.minea.gov.ao.

Ministry of the Environment: Edif. Zimbo Tower 2–6A, Rua dos Enganos, Luanda; tel. 222334761; e-mail geral@minamb.gov.ao; internet www.minamb.gov.ao.

Ministry of External Relations: Palácio do Comércio, Rua Maj. Kanhangulo, Luanda; tel. 226430546; e-mail geral@mirex.gov.ao; internet mirex.gov.ao.

Ministry of Finance: Largo da Mutamba, Luanda; tel. 222706000; e-mail gci.minfin@minfin.gov.ao; internet www.minfin.gov.ao.

Ministry of Fisheries and Marine Resources: Luanda.

Ministry of Health: Rua 17 de Setembro, CP 1201, Luanda; tel. 222330473; internet minsa.gov.ao.

Ministry of Higher Education, Science, Technology and Innovation: Edif. MED, Largo António Jacinto, Rua Comandante Gika 82, Luanda; tel. 222999999; e-mail geral@mescti.gov.ao; internet mescti.gov.ao.

Ministry of Industry and Commerce: Rua Cerqeira Lukoki 25, Luanda; tel. 222334700; internet www.mind.gov.ao.

Ministry of the Interior: Av. 4 de Fevereiro, Luanda; tel. 945716517; e-mail geral@minint.gov.ao; internet minint.gov.ao.

Ministry of Justice and Human Rights: Rua 17 de Setembro, CP 2250, Luanda; tel. 222336045; internet www.minjusdh.gov.ao.

Ministry of Mineral Resources, Petroleum and Gas: Av. 4 de Fevereiro 105, CP 1279, Luanda; tel. 226421216; e-mail geral@mirempet.gov.ao; internet mirempet.gov.ao.

Ministry of National Defence and War Veterans: Rua 17 de Setembro, Luanda; tel. 222330354; e-mail geral@mindenvp.gov.ao; internet mindenvp.gov.ao.

Ministry of Public Administration, Labour and Social Security: Largo dos Ambiente, Rua do Municipios, Portugueses-Ingombota, Luanda; tel. 222333095; e-mail contacto@maptss.gov.ao; internet www.maptss.gov.ao.

Ministry of Public Works, Urbanism and Housing: Luanda.

Ministry of Social Action, Families and the Promotion of Women: Palácio de Vidro, Largo 4 de Fevereiro, Luanda; tel. 222311728; e-mail geral@masfamu.gov.ao; internet masfamu.gov.ao.

Ministry of Telecommunications, Information Technology and Social Communication: Av. 4 de Fevereiro, Rua da Alfândega 10, Luanda; tel. 222210740; e-mail geral@minttics.gov.ao; internet minttics.gov.ao.

Ministry of Territorial Administration: Complexo Administrativo Clássicos de Talatona, Luanda; tel. 937116515; e-mail geral@mat.gov.ao; internet www.mat.gov.ao.

Ministry of Transport: Av. 4 de Fevereiro 42, Luanda; tel. 937279804; e-mail geral@mintrans.gov.ao; internet mintrans.gov.ao.

Ministry of Youth and Sports: Av. Comandante GIKA, Largo António Jacinto, Bloco 3, 2° andar, Ala Esquerda, Maianga, Luanda; tel. 942517450; e-mail minjud@minjud.gov.ao; internet www.minjud.gov.ao.

PROVINCIAL GOVERNORS
(October 2022)

All Provincial Governors are ex officio members of the Government.

Bengo: MARIA ANTÓNIA NELUMBA.

Benguela: LUÍS MANUEL DA FONSECA NUNES.

Bié: PEREIRA ALFREDO.

Cabinda: MARA REGINA DA SILVA BAPTISTA DOMINGOS QUIOSA.

Cunene: GERDINA ULIPAME DIDALEWA.

Huambo: LOTTI NOLIKA.

Huíla: NUNO BERNABÉ MAHAPI DALA.

Kuando Kubango: JOSÉ MARTINS.

Kwanza-Norte: PEDRO MAQUITA ARMANDO JÚLIA.

Kwanza-Sul: JOB PEDRO CASTELO CAPAPINHA.

Luanda: MANUEL GOMES DA CONCEIÇÃO HOMEM.

Lunda-Norte: DEOLINDA ÓDIA PAULO SATULA VILARINHO.

Lunda-Sul: DANIEL FÉLIX NETO.

Malanje: MARCOS ALEXANDRE NHUNGA.

Moxico: ERNESTO MUANGALA.

Namibe: AUGUSTO ARCHER DE SOUSA MANGUEIRA.

Uíge: JOSÉ CARVALHO DA ROCHA.

Zaire: ADRIANO MENDES DE CARVALHO.

Legislature

National Assembly: Av. Dr Antonio Agostinho Neto, Praia do Bispo, Luanda; tel. 222679700; e-mail assembleianacional@parlamento.ao; internet www.parlamento.ao.

President: CAROLINA CERQUEIRA.

General Election, 24 August 2022

Party	Valid votes	% of valid votes	Seats
Movimento Popular de Libertação de Angola (MPLA) .	3,209,429	51.17	124
União Nacional para a Independência Total de Angola (UNITA)	2,756,786	43.95	90
Partido de Renovação Social (PRS)	71,351	1.14	2
Frente Nacional de Libertação de Angola (FNLA)	66,337	1.06	2
Partido Humanista de Angola (PHA)	63,749	1.02	2
Convergência Ampla de Salvação de Angola-Coligação Eleitoral (CASA-CE)	47,446	0.76	—
Aliança Patriótica Nacional (APN)	30,139	0.48	—
Partido Nacionalista para a Justiça em Angola (P-NJANGO)	26,867	0.43	—
Total	6,272,104*	100.00	220

* There were, in addition, a total of 182,005 invalid and blank votes.

Election Commission

Comissão Nacional Eleitoral (CNE): Edif. Margaret Anstee, Coqueiros, Luanda; tel. 990000000; e-mail geral@cne.com; internet www.cne.ao; f. 2005; govt agency; Pres. MANUEL PEREIRA DA SILVA.

Advisory Council

Conselho Económico e Social: Luanda; f. 2020; autonomous body; 45 mems.

Political Organizations

In 2022 there were 13 legally recognized political parties in Angola, six of which were grouped in a formal coalition.

Aliança Patriótica Nacional (APN): Luanda; e-mail aliancapatrioticanacional@gmail.com; f. 2015; Pres. QUINTINO ANTÓNIO MOREIRA.

Convergência Ampla de Salvação de Angola-Coligação Eleitoral (CASA-CE): Sagrada Família, Rua Cabral Moncada 179, Junto ao INE Garcia Neto, Luanda; e-mail ce.sen@hotmail.com; internet casa-ce.org; f. 2012; Leader MANUEL FERNANDES; Exec. Sec. LEONEL GOMES.

Bloco Democrático: Bairro Azul, Samba, Luanda; tel. 928554655; e-mail blocodemocraticoluanda2015@gmail.com; internet blocodemocraticoangola.com; f. 2010; Pres. FILOMENO VIEIRA LOPES; Sec.-Gen. MUATA SEBASTIÃO.

Partido de Aliança Livre de Maioria Angolana (PALMA): Pres. MANUEL FERNANDES; Sec.-Gen. CASIMIRO ANTÓNIO FRANCISCO.

Partido de Apoio para Democracia e Desenvolvimento de Angola—Aliança Patriótica (PADDA-AP): Luanda; tel. 992058169; e-mail padda.apsenoc@gmail.com; internet fb.com/PADDA.AP1; f. 2010; Pres. ALEXANDRE SEBASTIÃO ANDRÉ; Sec. Gen. ANTÓNIO GONÇALVES JURANTE.

Partido Democrático para o Progresso de Aliança Nacional Angolana (PDP—ANA): Rua n° 6, Casa n° 73, Quarterão 6, Bairro Palanca, Municipio de Kilamba Kiaxi; tel. 926013905; e-mail pdpana@pdp-ana.org; f. 1991; Pres. ABREU CAPITÃO BERNARDO; Sec.-Gen. ZISSALA PULULU.

Partido Nacional de Salvação de Angola (PNSA): Pres. SIKONDA LULENDO ALEXANDRE; Sec.-Gen. BOKOLO KABUIKU MANUEL.

Partido Pacífico Angolano (PPA): Pres. FELÊ ANTÓNIO; Sec.-Gen. PEDRO LUNDEMBA.

Frente Nacional de Libertação de Angola (FNLA) (National Liberation Front of Angola): Av. Hoji Va Henda (ex Av. do Brasil) 91/306, CP 151, Luanda; e-mail fnlangola@gmail.com; f. 1962; Pres. NIMI A SIMBI; Sec.-Gen. PEDRO MUCOMBE DALA.

Movimento Popular de Libertação de Angola (MPLA) (Popular Movement for the Liberation of Angola): Av. Ho Chi Minh 34, Luanda; e-mail sede@mpla-angola.org; internet www.mpla.ao; f. 1956; in 1961–74 conducted guerrilla operations against Portuguese rule; governing party since 1975; known as Movimento Popular de Libertação de Angola—Partido do Trabalho (MPLA—PT) (People's Movement for the Liberation of Angola—Workers' Party) 1977–92; in Dec. 1990 replaced Marxist-Leninist ideology with commitment to 'democratic socialism'; absorbed the Fórum Democrático Angolano (FDA) in 2002; Chair. JOÃO MANUEL GONÇALVES LOURENÇO; Sec.-Gen. PAULO POMBOLO.

Partido Humanista de Angola (PHA): Rua Nelito Soares C7 de Baixo 26, Zona 14, Luanda; tel. 998043712; e-mail info@humanistas.co; internet humanistas.co; f. 2020 following split from UNITA; Leader FLORBELA MALAQUIAS.

Partido Nacionalista para a Justiça em Angola (P-NJANGO) (Nationalist Justice Party of Angola): Luanda; f. 2022; Leader EDUARDO JONATÃO SAMUEL CHINGUNGI.

Partido de Renovação Social (PRS): Rua n°1, Martires de Kifangondo n° 33D; tel. 222326293; e-mail sede@prs-angola.com; internet prsangola.com; f. 1990; Pres. JOÃO BENEDITO DANIEL; Sec.-Gen. RUI MALOPA MIGUEL.

União Nacional para a Independência Total de Angola (UNITA): Rua 28 de Maio, 1A Travessa 2, Maianga, Luanda; tel. 222331215; e-mail info@unitaangola.org; internet www.unitaangola.com; f. 1966; Pres. ADALBERTO COSTA JÚNIOR; Sec.-Gen. FRANCO MARCOLINO NHANY.

Diplomatic Representation

EMBASSIES IN ANGOLA

Algeria: Edif. Siccal, Rua Rainha Ginga, CP 1389, Luanda; tel. 222332881; e-mail ambalg@netangola.com; Ambassador ABDERLHAKIM MIHOUB.

Argentina: Rua Comandante Stona 190, Bairro Alvalade, Luanda; tel. 222323286; e-mail eango@mrecic.gov.ar; internet eango.cancilleria.gob.ar; Ambassador ALEJANDRO GUILHERMO VERDIER.

Belgium: Rua Houari Boumedienne 100, Miramar, Luanda; tel. 222449396; e-mail luanda@diplobel.fed.be; internet angola.diplomatie.belgium.be; Ambassador JOZEF SMETS.

Brazil: Av. Presidente Houari Boumedienne 132, Miramar, CP 5428, Luanda; tel. 222442010; e-mail secretariado.luanda@itamaraty.gov.br; internet www.gov.br/mre/pt-br/embaixada-luanda; Ambassador RAFAEL VIDAL.

Cabo Verde: Rua Emílio M'Bidi 3, Luanda; tel. 222321765; e-mail embaixadacaboverde.luanda@gmail.com; internet embaixada-de-cabo-verde-em-angola.odoo.com; Ambassador JORGE FIGUEREDO.

China, People's Republic: Rua Houari Boumedienne 196, Miramar, CP 52, Luanda; tel. 226435015; e-mail chinaemb_ao@mfa.gov.cn; internet ao.china-embassy.gov.cn; Ambassador GONG TAO.

Congo, Democratic Republic: Rua Cesário Verde 24, Luanda; tel. 222361953; Ambassador DIDIER KAZADI NYEMBWE.

Congo, Republic: Av. 4 de Fevereiro 3, Luanda; tel. 222310293; e-mail ambaco@netangola.com; Ambassador CHRIST BONAVENTURE ENGOBO.

Côte d'Ivoire: Rua Samuel Bernado 52, Bairro Ingombota, CP 432, Luanda; tel. 222440878; e-mail ambaciango@yahoo.fr; internet angola.diplomatie.gouv.ci; Ambassador SANTIÉRO JEAN-MARIE SOMET.

Cuba: Rua Eduardo Mondlane 202, Maianga, CP 3005, Luanda; tel. 222336949; e-mail secretaria.ang@embacuba.co.ao; internet misiones.minrex.gob.cu/es/angola; Ambassador ESTHER ARMENTEROS CÁRDENAS.

Egypt: Rua Comandante Stona 247, Alvalade, CP 3704, Luanda; tel. 222321591; e-mail embassy.luanda@mfa.gov.eg; Ambassador MOHAMED SAFWAT RAMADAN ATTA.

Equatorial Guinea: Luanda; tel. 222353939; e-mail embajsecretaria@gmail.com; Ambassador PROTASIO EDU EDJANG NNAGA.

France: Rua Reverendo Pedro Agostinho Neto 31–33, CP 584, Luanda; tel. 222334335; e-mail cad.luanda-amba@diplomatie.gouv.fr; internet ao.ambafrance.org; Ambassador DANIEL VOSGIEN.

Gabon: Rua Eng. Armindo de Andrade, Luanda; tel. 222042943; e-mail ambagabonluanda@hotmail.com; internet fb.com/ambagabonangola; Ambassador GUY NAMBO WEZET.

Germany: Rua de Benguela 17, Bairro de Cruzeiro, CP 1295, Luanda; tel. 222430404; e-mail info@luanda.diplo.de; internet luanda.diplo.de; Ambassador Dr STEFAN TRAUMANN.

Ghana: Rua Houari Boumedienne 52, CP 1012, Luanda; tel. 222447044; e-mail luanda@mfa.gov.gh; internet ghanaembassy-angola.com; Ambassador MAVIS ESI KUSORGBOR.

Guinea: Rua I, Casa W24, Bairro Cassenda, Luanda; tel. 222359366; e-mail ibsthiam@yahoo.fr; Ambassador Gen. EDOUARD THÉA.

Guinea-Bissau: Luanda; Ambassador APOLINÁRIO MENDES DE CABRAL.

Holy See: Rua Luther King 123, CP 1030, Luanda; tel. 222330532; e-mail nunc.nuncio@gmail.com; Apostolic Nuncio Rev. MONSIGNOR GIOVANNI GASPARI (Titular Archbishop of Alba Maritima).

Hungary: Condomínio Zenith Towers, VIA AL-16 S/N, Torre 1, Talatona, Luanda; tel. 222778597; e-mail mission.lad@mfa.gov.hu; internet luanda.mfa.gov.hu; Ambassador ZSOLT MARIS.

India: Rua Commandante Nzaji 47, Alvalade, Luanda; tel. 222017618; e-mail amb.luanda@mea.gov.in; internet www.indembangola.gov.in; Ambassador PRATIBHA PARKAR.

Israel: Edif. Siccal, Rua Rainha Ginga 187, Luanda; tel. 222395295; e-mail consular@luanda.mfa.gov.il; internet embassies.gov.il/luanda; Ambassador SHIMON SOLOMON.

Italy: Rua Américo Boavida 51, Ingombotas, CP 6220, Luanda; tel. 222331245; e-mail ambasciata.luanda@esteri.it; internet ambluanda.esteri.it; Ambassador CRISTIANO GALLO.

Japan: Torres Loanda 2F, Rua Gamal Abdel Nasser, Ingombota, Luanda; tel. 923167090; e-mail emb@ln.mofa.go.jp; internet www.angola.emb-japan.go.jp; Ambassador JIRO MARUHASHI.

Kenya: Villa 2, Four Villas, Av. Principal de Talatona, Talatona, Luanda; tel. 255300233; e-mail luanda@mfa.go.ke; internet kenyaembassyangola.com; Ambassador CLEMENT NZOMO (designate).

Korea, Democratic People's Republic: Rua Montepio Ferroviário, S/N, Luanda; tel. 222409290; Ambassador JO PYONG CHOL.

Korea, Republic: Condominio Zenith Torre 1, 3° andar, Via AL 16, Luanda; tel. 222006067; e-mail korembassy_angola@mofa.go.kr; internet overseas.mofa.go.kr/ao-ko/index.do; Ambassador KIM CHANG-SIK.

Mali: Rua Alfredo Felner 5, Nelito Souares 11, Luanda; tel. 222440317; e-mail ambamali@netangola.com; Ambassador DIAMOU KEITA.

Mauritania: Luanda; Ambassador MOHAMED OULD MEKHALLA.

Morocco: Edif. Siccal, 10° andar, Rua Rainha Ginga, CP 20, Luanda; tel. 222393708; e-mail aluanda@supernet.ao; Ambassador SAADIA ALAOUI.

Mozambique: Rua Salvador Alende 55, Luanda; tel. 222332883; e-mail embamoc.angola@minec.gov.mz; Ambassador OSVALDA JOANA.

Namibia: Rua dos Coqueiros 37, CP 953, Luanda; tel. 222395483; e-mail embnam@netangola.com; Ambassador PATRICK NANDANGO.

Netherlands: Empreendimento Comandante Gika, Torre B Piso 8, Travessa Ho Chi Minh, Alvalade, CP 3624, Luanda; tel. 923120200; e-mail lua@minbuza.nl; internet www.nederlandwereldwijd.nl/landen/angola; Ambassador TSJEARD HOEKSTRA.

Nigeria: Rua Ndunduma 6, Miramar, CP 479, Luanda; tel. 222344085; e-mail enquiries@nigeriaembluanda.com; internet nigeriaembluanda.com; Ambassador Prof. MONIQUE OSHAME EKPONG.

Norway: Rua Garcia Neto 9, Miramar, CP 3835, Luanda; tel. 222449936; e-mail emb.luanda@mfa.no; internet www.norway.no/angola; Ambassador BJØRNAR DAHL HOTVEDT.

Poland: Rua Damião de Góis 64, Alvalade, CP 1340, Luanda; tel. 222327199; e-mail luanda.amb.sekretariat@msz.gov.pl; internet www.gov.pl/web/angola; Ambassador PIOTR JÓZEF MYŚLIWIEC.

Portugal: Av. de Portugal 50, CP 1346, Luanda; tel. 222331079; e-mail luanda@mne.pt; internet luanda.embaixadaportugal.mne.pt; Ambassador FRANCISCO ALEGRE DUARTE.

Romania: Rua Ramalho Ortigão 30, Bairro Alvalade, Luanda; tel. 222321076; e-mail ambromania@netcabo.co.ao; internet luanda.mae.ro; Chargé d'affaires a.i. FLORIN TUDORIE.

Russian Federation: Rua Houari Boumedienne 170, CP 3141, Luanda; tel. 222445028; e-mail russembangola@gmail.com; internet angola.mid.ru; Ambassador VLADIMIR TARAROV.

Rwanda: Condomínio Four Villas, Av. Central (Samora Machel), Talatona, CP 10602, Luanda; tel. 944202193; e-mail ambaluanda@minaffet.gov.rw; internet angola.embassy.gov.rw; Ambassador WELLARS GASAMAGERA.

São Tomé and Príncipe: Rua Comandante N'zagi 64–66, Luanda; tel. 222328663; Ambassador CARLOS GUSTAVO DOS ANJOS.

Serbia: Rua Comandante N'zagi 25–27, Alvalade, CP 3278, Luanda; tel. 222321421; e-mail serbiaemb@netcabo.co.ao; internet luanda .mfa.gov.rs; Ambassador MILOS PERISIĆ.

South Africa: Rua Premio Dubai, Condominio Ouro Verde, Municipio da Samba, Sector ZRGA, CP 6212, Luanda; tel. 222460732; e-mail saemb.finance@nexus.ao; Ambassador OUPA MONARENG.

Spain: Av. 4 de Fevereiro 95, 1° andar, CP 3061, Luanda; tel. 222391166; e-mail emb.luanda@maec.es; internet www.exteriores .gob.es/embajadas/luanda; Ambassador MANUEL MARÍA LEJARRETA LOBO.

Sudan: Luanda; Ambassador (vacant).

Sweden: Rua Garcia Neto 9, Miramar, CP 1130, Luanda; tel. 222447522; e-mail ambassaden.luanda@gov.se; internet www .swedenabroad.se/luanda; Ambassador EWA POLANO.

Switzerland: Edif. Garden Towers, Torre B, Av. Ho Chi Minh, Alvalade, CP 3163, Luanda; tel. 912501396; e-mail luanda@eda .admin.ch; internet www.eda.admin.ch/luanda; Ambassador LUKAS JOHANNES GASSER.

Türkiye (Turkey): Av. Pedro de Castro Van-Dúnem Loy, 535 Mundo Verda-Talatona, Luanda; tel. 939765336; internet luanda.be.mfa .gov.tr; Ambassador ALP AY.

Ukraine: Rua Companhia de Jesus 35, Miramar, Luanda; tel. 222716758; e-mail emb_ao@mfa.gov.ua; internet angola.mfa.gov .ua; Chargé d'affaires a.i. ANDRII P. CHORNOPYSKYI.

United Arab Emirates: Rua 7A, Talatona, Via S, Luanda; tel. 931736840; e-mail luandaemb@mofaic.gov.ae; Ambassador KHALID SALEM ALI BIN GHALAITAH ALMHEIRI.

United Kingdom: Rua 17 de Setembro, CP 1244, Ingombotas, Luanda; tel. 222334583; e-mail britishembassy.luandageral@fco .gov.uk; internet www.gov.uk/world/organisations/ british-embassy-luanda; Ambassador ROGER STRINGER.

Uruguay: Rua 28 de Maio, No. 7/8, Bairro Maianga, Luanda; tel. 222323360; e-mail uruangola@mrree.gub.uy; Ambassador Dr ÁLVARO ENRIQUE GONZÁLEZ OTERO.

USA: Rua Houari Boumedienne 32, Miramar, CP 6468, Luanda; tel. 222641000; e-mail consularluanda@state.gov; internet ao .usembassy.gov; Ambassador Dr TULINABO SALAMA MUSHINGI.

Venezuela: Rua de 28 de Agosto, Casa FZ 22, Futungo de Belas, Luanda; tel. 222020681; e-mail embve.aolda@mppre.gob.ve; Ambassador MARLON PENÄ LABRADOR.

Viet Nam: Rua Houari Boumediene 74, Miramar, CP 1774, Luanda; tel. 222010697; e-mail vnemb.angola@mofa.gov.vn; internet vnembassy-luanda.mofa.gov.vn; Ambassador VU NGOC MINH.

Zambia: Rua Rei Katyavala 106–108, CP 1496, Luanda; tel. 222331145; e-mail zambianembassyluanda@yahoo.com; Ambassador LAWRENCE CHAMA CHALUNGUMANA.

Zimbabwe: Edif. Secil, Av. 4 de Fevereiro 42, CP 428, Luanda; tel. 222449938; e-mail zimluanda@zimfa.gov.zw; Ambassador THANDO MADZVAMUSE.

Judicial System

The country's highest judicial body is the Constitutional Court (Tribunal Constitucional), while there is also a Supreme Court (Tribunal Supremo), an Audit Court (Tribunal de Contas) and a Supreme Military Court (Supremo Tribunal Militar). There are also civil and criminal courts at the provincial level.

Constitutional Court (Tribunal Constitucional): Palácio da Justiça, Rua 17 de Setembro, Bairro do Saneamento, Luanda; tel. 222370877; e-mail info@tribunalconstitucional.ao; internet www .tribunalconstitucional.ao; f. 2008; Pres. LAURINDA CARDOSO.

Supreme Court (Tribunal Supremo): Rua 17 de Setembro e Pinheiro Furtado, Cidade Alta, Luanda; tel. 222339079; e-mail geral@ tribunalsupremo.ao; internet tribunalsupremo.ao; Pres. Dr JOEL LEONARDO.

Audit Court (Tribunal de Contas): Cidade Alta, Rua 17 de Setembro, Luanda; tel. 222371920; e-mail info@tcontas.ao; internet www .tcontas.ao; Pres. Dr EXALGINA RENÉE VICENTE OLAVO GAMBÔA.

Office of the Attorney-General: Rua 17 de Setembro, Luanda; tel. 222333171; Attorney-General Gen. HÉLDER FERNANDO PITTA GRÓZ.

Religion

CHRISTIANITY

Conselho de Igrejas Cristãs em Angola (CICA) (Council of Christian Churches in Angola): Rua 15 24, Bairro Cassenda, CP 1301/1659, Luanda; tel. 222719223; f. 1977 as Conselho Angolano de Igrejas Evangélicas; 22 mem. churches; Gen. Sec. Rev. DEOLINDA TECA.

The Anglican Communion

A new Anglican province for Angola and Mozambique—the Igreja Anglicana de Moçambique e Angola—was formed in September 2021, with four of the 12 dioceses in Angola.

Igreja Anglicana de Moçambique e Angola (IAMA): Luanda; f. 2021; Acting Presiding Bishop CARLOS MATSINHE.

Other Protestant Churches

Igreja Evangélica Congregacional em Angola (Evangelical Congregational Church in Angola—IECA): Morro Bento II, Rua do Condomínio das Mangueirinhas 40, CP 1552, Luanda; tel. 222355108; e-mail iecageral@gmail.com; internet www.iecaecca .com; f. 1880; Pres. BONIFÁCIO CHIWALE CASSOMA; Gen. Sec. Most Rev. ANDRÉ CANGOVI EURICO.

Igreja Evangélica Lutherana de Angola (Evangelical Lutheran Church of Angola): CP 222, Lubango; tel. 22228428; e-mail iela_lubango@yahoo.com.br; Pres. Rev. TOMÀS NDAWANAPO.

Igreja Universal do Reino de Deus, Angola (IURD): Luanda; internet www.universal.org; Leader ALBERTO SEGUNDA.

Other active denominations include the African Apostolic Church, the Church of Apostolic Faith in Angola, the Church of Our Lord Jesus Christ in the World, the Evangelical Baptist Church, the Evangelical Church in Angola, the Evangelical Church of the Apostles of Jerusalem, the Evangelical Reformed Church of Angola, the Kimbanguist Church in Angola, the Maná Church and the United Methodist Church.

The Roman Catholic Church

Angola comprises five archdioceses and 14 dioceses.

Bishops' Conference: Rua Comandante Bula, Bairro São Paulo, CP 3579, Luanda; tel. 222443686; e-mail cecasp@gmail.com; internet www.ceastangola.org; f. 1967; Pres. Most Rev. FILOMENO DO NASCIMENTO VIEIRA DIAS (Archbishop of Luanda).

Archbishop of Huambo: Most Rev. ZEFERINO ZECA MARTINS, Arcebispado, CP 10, Huambo; tel. 241220133.

Archbishop of Luanda: Most Rev. FILOMENO DO NASCIMENTO VIEIRA DIAS, Arcebispado, Largo do Palácio 9, CP 87, 1230-C, Luanda; tel. 222334640; e-mail spastoral@snet.com.ao.

Archbishop of Lubango: Most Rev. GABRIEL MBILINGI, Arcebispado, CP 231, Lubango; tel. 261224140.

Archbishop of Malanje: Most Rev. LUZIZILA KIALA, Bispado, CP 192, Malanje; tel. 251231708; e-mail diocesemalanje@ceastangola .org.

Archbishop of Saurimo: Most Rev. JOSÉ MANUEL IMBAMBA, Bispado, Rua do Cemiterio, CP 52, Saurimo; tel. 923312623; internet diocesesaurimo@ceastangola.org.

The Press

STATE-OWNED NEWSPAPER GROUP

Edições Novembro: Rua Rainha Ginga 12-26, CP 1312, Luanda; tel. 261224215; e-mail ednovembro.dg@nexus.ao; internet fb.com/ edicoesnovembro; f. 1923; Chair. DRUMOND ALCIDES JAIME MAFUTA.

DAILY NEWSPAPERS (PRINT AND ONLINE)

Jornal de Angola: Rua Rainha Ginga 12–26, CP 1312, Luanda; tel. 222036578; e-mail redaccao@jornaldeangola.ao; internet www .jornaldeangola.ao; f. 1975; publ. by Edições Novembro; state-owned; Chair. DRUMOND ALCIDES JAIME MAFUTA.

O País: Rua do MAT, Condomínio Alfa, Edif. 6, Talatona, Luanda; tel. 943023747; e-mail comercial@medianova.co.ao; internet opais.co .ao; f. 2008; Dir DANIEL COSTA.

PERIODICALS

O Apostolado: Rua Comandante Bula 118, São Paulo, CP 3579, Luanda; tel. 222443093; e-mail jornalapostolado@gmail.com; f. 1935; current and religious affairs; Dir MAURÍCIO AGOSTINHO CAMUTO.

Chocolate: Condomínio Alpha Escritórios, Edif. 5, Talatona, Luanda; tel. 222398565; e-mail gerson.iven@chocolate.co.ao; internet www.chocolate.co.ao; f. 2005; monthly; publ. by Media Nova; lifestyle; Dir GERSON IVEN.

Cultura: Luanda; tel. 222337690; internet www.jornaldeangola.ao; Dir and Editor-in-Chief JOSÉ LUÍS MENDONÇA.

Diário da República: Rua Henrique de Carvalho 2, Cidade Alta, CP 1306, Luanda; tel. 217810870; official govt bulletin; joint initiative by Imprensa Nacional EP and Edições Jurídicas Lda.

Economia and Finanças: Rua Rei Katyavala 126B, Ingombota, Luanda; tel. 222447354; e-mail redaccaoeconomia@gmail.com; internet www.jornaldeangola.ao; Dir AGOSTINHO CHITATA.

EXAME Angola: Zona Residencial ZR6-B, Lote 32, Sector de Talatona, Luanda Sul; tel. 222003275; e-mail exameangola@gmail .com; internet exame.com; Editor JAIME FIDALGO.

Folha 8: Apt 19, 5° andar, Rua Conselheiro Júlio de Vilhena 21, CP 6527, Luanda; tel. 222391943; e-mail kuibao@hotmail.com; internet jornalf8.net; f. 1994; bi-weekly; Dir WILLIAM TONET; Editor-in-Chief PEDRO TECA.

Jornal dos Desportos: Rua Rainha Ginga 18–24, CP 1312, Luanda; tel. 222335531; e-mail jornaldosdesportos@hotmail.com; internet www.jornaldeangola.ao; f. 1994; bi-weekly; Dir MATIAS ADRIANO.

Novo Jornal: Edif. Condomínio Bengo, Bloco B, Escritórios 01, Vila Alice, Rua Fernão Sousa, Luanda; tel. 921358582; e-mail geral@ novojornal.co.ao; internet novojornal.co.ao; Dir CARLOS FERREIRA.

NEWS AGENCIES

Agência Angola Press (ANGOP): Rua Rei Katyavala 120/122, CP 2181, Luanda; tel. 222446901; e-mail comercial@angop.ao; internet www.angop.ao; f. 1975 as Agência Nacional Angola Press (ANAP); Chair. JOSUÉ SALUSUVA ISAÍAS.

Centro de Imprensa Anibal de Melo (CIAM): Rua Cerqueira Lukoki 124, CP 2805, Luanda; tel. 922259272; e-mail geral@ciam.gov .ao; internet www.ciam.gov.ao; f. 1976; govt press centre; Dir-Gen. ANTÓNIO RODRIGUES MASCARENHAS.

Publishers

Chá de Caxinde: Av. do 1° Congresso do MPLA 20–24, CP 5731, Luanda; tel. 222390936; e-mail geral@chadecaxinde.net; internet chadecaxinde.net; f. 1989; Dir JAQUES ARLINDO DOS SANTOS.

Plural Editores: Centro Logístico de Talatona, Loja C-3; tel. 924351990; e-mail plural@pluraleditores.co.ao; internet www .pluraleditores.co.ao; f. 2005; 100% owned by Porto Editora (Portugal); technical and educational; Dir-Gen. PAULO MACHADO RIBEIRO.

União dos Escritores Angolanos (UEA): Av. Ho-Chi-Min, Largo das Escolas 1° de Maio, CP 2767, Luanda; tel. 222322421; internet www.ueangola.com; f. 1975; Sec.-Gen DAVID CAPELENGUELA.

GOVERNMENT PUBLISHING HOUSE

Imprensa Nacional, UEE: Rua Henrique de Carvalho 2, Cidade Alta, Ingombota, CP 1306, Luanda; tel. 222336139; e-mail geral .comercial@imprensanacional.gov.ao; internet www .imprensanacional.gov.ao; f. 1845; Pres. LANDO SEBASTIÃO TETA.

Broadcasting and Communications

TELECOMMUNICATIONS

Africell Angola: Luanda; internet www.africell.ao; f. 2021; CEO CHRISTOPHER LUNDH.

Angola Telecom (AT): Rua das Quipacas 186, 3° andar, CP 625, Luanda; tel. 222700000; e-mail info@angolatelecom.ao; internet www.angolatelecom.com; f. 1992 by a merger of former state-owned enterprises Enatel and EPTEL; partial privatization pending; fixed-line and mobile services; Chair. ADILSON MIGUEL DOS SANTOS; Exec. Dir EDSON SALEK FRANCISCO PEREIRA.

Movicel Telecomunicações, Lda: Edif. Kwando Kubango, Av. de Talatona, Belas Business Park, Luanda; tel. 222692000; e-mail support19191@movicel.co.ao; internet www.movicel.co.ao; f. 2003; mobile telephone operator; shares acquired by Angola Telecom in 2021; CEO ADILSON MIGUEL DOS SANTOS.

Mundo StarTel: Rua da Polícial, Bairro dos Correios, Município do Rangel, Luanda; tel. 227227227; e-mail negocios@startel.ao; internet www.startel.ao; f. 2004.

Net One: Rua dos Enganos 1, 1° andar, Luanda; tel. 226450450; e-mail netone@netone.co.ao; internet www.netone.co.ao; internet service provider.

Unitel SARL: Rua Kwamme Nkrumah 53A, Talatona Sector, Via CS3, Luanda Sul; tel. 923199100; e-mail support.client@unitel.co.ao; internet www.unitel.ao; f. 1998; private mobile telephone operator; Dir-Gen. MIGUEL GERALDS.

Regulatory Authority

Instituto Angolano das Comunicações (INACOM): Av. Dr António Agostinho Neto 25, Zona C, Praia do Bispo, CP 1459, Luanda; tel. 222210666; e-mail geral@inacom.gov.ao; internet

www.inacom.gov.ao; f. 1999; monitoring and regulatory authority; Chair. PASCOAL BORGES ALÉ FERNANDES.

BROADCASTING
Radio

Rádio Nacional de Angola: CP 1329, Luanda; tel. 946441484; e-mail rna@rna.ao; internet www.rna.ao; f. 1975; state-controlled; operates Canal A, Radio 5, RNA Internacional, Rádio Luanda and N'gola Yetu; broadcasts in Portuguese, English, French, Lingala and vernacular languages (Chokwe, Kikongo, Kimbundu, Kwanyama, Fiote, Ngangela, Luvale, Songu, Umbundu); Chair PEDRO AFONSO CABRAL.

Luanda Antena Comercial (LAC): Rua Luther King 5, CP 3521, Luanda; tel. 222339917; e-mail info@lacluanda.co.ao; internet www .lacluanda.co.ao; f. 1992; popular music; Gen. Man LUÍSA FANÇONY.

Rádio Escola: Rua Luther King 5, 123/4, Luanda; tel. 222337409; e-mail geral@cefojor.sapo.ao; internet radios.sapo.ao/radio-escola; f. 2003; commercial station, provides journalistic training; Dir-Gen. IKUMA JOSÉ BAMBA.

Rádio Ecclésia—Emissora Católica de Angola: Rua Comandante Bula 118, São Paulo, CP 3579, Luanda; tel. 222447153; e-mail marketingecclesia@sapo.ao; internet www.radioecclesia.org; f. 1955; Dir-Gen. Fr AUGUSTO EPALANGA.

Rádio Mais: Rua Projecto Nova Vida, 4° andar, Luanda; tel. 928006929; e-mail comercialmarketing@radiomais.co.ao; internet www.radiomais.co.ao.

The Voice of America (internet www.ebonet.net/voa) also broadcasts from Luanda.

Television

Televisão Pública de Angola (TPA): Av. Ho Chi Minh, CP 2604, Luanda; tel. 222320025; internet tpa.sapo.ao; f. 1975; state-controlled; 3 channels; broadcasts in Portuguese; Chair. JOSÉ FERNANDO GONÇALVES GUERREIRO.

TV Cabo Angola: Av. Pedro de Castro Van-Dúnem Loy, Morro Bento, Luanda; tel. 222680000; e-mail tvcabo@tvcabo.co.ao; internet www.tvcabo.co.ao; f. 2006; provider of digital television and internet services; Man. Dir FRANCISCO FERREIRA.

TV Zimbo: Luanda; tel. 922225918; internet fb.com/ informacaotvzimbo; f. 2008; private; owned by Medianova; Dir FRANCISCO MENDES.

ZAP: Edif. ZAP, Via A4A, Talatona-Município de Samba, Luanda; tel. 935555500; e-mail apoio.cliente@zap.co.ao; internet www.zap.co .ao; f. 2010; Gen. Man. JOSÉ CARLOS LOURENÇO.

Finance

BANKING

In 2022 there were 25 banks authorized by the Banco Nacional de Angola to be operating in the country.

Central Bank

Banco Nacional de Angola: Av. 4 de Fevereiro n° 151, CP 1243, Luanda; tel. 222679200; internet www.bna.ao; f. 1976; bank of issue; Gov. JOSÉ DE LIMA MASSANO.

Commercial Banks

Banco BIC SA: Bairro de Talatona, Município da Samba, Luanda; tel. 923130000; e-mail bancobic@bancobic.ao; internet www .bancobic.ao; f. 2005; 25% owned by Fidel Kiluange Assis Araujo; 20% owned by Fernando Mendes Teles; Chair. FERNANDO MENDES TELES.

Banco Comercial Angolano SA (BCA): Av. Comandante Valódia 83A, CP 6900, Luanda; tel. 222641330; e-mail apoioaocliente@bca.co .ao; internet www.bca.co.ao; f. 1997; Pres. FRANCISCO DA SILVA CRISTOVÃO; CEO MATEUS FILIPE MARTINS.

Banco Económico: Rua 1, Congresso do MPLA 8, Bairro Ingombota, Luanda; tel. 222693600; e-mail directo@bancoeconomico.ao; internet www.bancoeconomico.ao; f. 2002 as Banco Espírito Santo Angola; present name adopted in 2014; Chair. Dr PEDRO LUÍS DA FONSECA; CEO Dr JOÃO SALVADOR QUINTAS.

Banco de Fomento Angola (BFA): Rua Amílcar Cabral 56, Maianga, Luanda; tel. 923120120; e-mail bfa@bfa.ao; internet www.bfa.ao; f. 1993 as Banco Fomento Exterior; present name adopted in 2001; 51.9% owned by Unitel and 48% owned by Banco BPI, SA, Portugal; Chair. RUI MANGUEIRA; CEO LUÍS ROBERTO FERNANDES GONÇALVES.

Banco Keve SA: Edif. Garden Towers, Rua Ho Chi Minh, Alvalade, Luanda; e-mail ikeve@bancokeve.ao; internet www

.bancokeve.ao; f. 2003; Chair. ELSA DALILA AZEVEDO DA SILVA; CEO BRUNO GRILO.

Banco Millennium Atlântico: Edif. Atlântico, Bloco 7/8, Rua do Centro de Convenções de Talatona, Bairro Talatona, Luanda; tel. 226460460; e-mail info@atlantico.ao; internet www.atlantico.ao; f. 2016 by merger of Banco Privado Atlântico and Banco Millennium Angola; Chair. ANTÓNIO JOÃO ASSIS DE ALMEIDA; CEO DANIEL SANTOS.

Banco de Poupança e Crédito SA (BPC): Largo Major Saydi Mingas, CP 1343, Luanda; tel. 226423000; e-mail bpc@bpc.ao; internet www.bpc.ao; f. 1956 as Banco Comercial de Angola; present name adopted in 1991; 99% state-owned, 1% owned by the Instituto Nacional de Segurança Social; Chair. ANDRÉ LOPES.

Banco Sol: Gaveto da Rua Frederico Welvitch 47 e Rua Lourenço Mendes da Conceição 7, Luanda; tel. 923637000; internet www .bancosol.ao; f. 2001; 55% owned by SANSUL; Chair. ROSÁRIO SIMÃO JACINTO.

Development Banks

Banco de Comércio e Indústria SA: Rua Rainha Ginga, Largo do Atlético 79–83, POB 1395, Luanda; tel. 227333000; e-mail apoioaocliente@bci.ao; internet www.bci.ao; f. 1991; provides loans to businesses in all sectors; Chair. ZENAIDA GERTRUDES DOS SANTOS RAMOS ZUMBI.

Banco de Desenvolvimento de Angola (BDA): Av. 4 de Fevereiro 113, Rua Robert Shields 3, Luanda; tel. 222692800; internet bda.ao; f. 2006; Chair. MARIA DO CARMO BASTOS CORTE REAL BERNARDO; CEO ELIZABETH FERNANDA JOÃO SUNGANI DAVID KINANGA.

Standard Bank de Angola: Edif. Kuando Kubango, 8º andar, Condomínio Belas Business Park, Luanda; tel. 923190888; e-mail apoiocliente@standardbank.co.ao; internet www.standardbank.co .ao; f. 2010; CEO LUIS TELES.

Investment Banks

Banco Angolano de Investimentos SA (BAI): Travessa Ho Chi Minh, Edif. Garden Towers, Maianga, Torre BAI, Luanda; tel. 222693800; e-mail baidirecto@bancobai.ao; internet bancobai.ao; f. 1996; fmrly Banco Africano de Investimentos SARL; present name adopted in 2011; 8.95% owned by BAI Treasury Stock; 8.5% owned by SONANGOL; Chair. Dr JOSÉ CARLOS DE CASTRO PAIVA; CEO LUIS FILIPE RODRIGUES LÉLIS.

STOCK EXCHANGE

Bolsa da Dívida e Valores de Angola (Bodiva): Edif. Sky Business Tower, 8º andar, Rua Marechal Brós Tito 41, Luanda; tel. 225420300; e-mail institutional@bodiva.ao; internet www.bodiva.ao; f. 2014; CEO OTTONIEL DOS SANTOS; Chair. ANTÓNIO FURTADO.

INSURANCE

In 2022 there were 22 insurance companies licensed to operate in Angola.

AAA Seguros SA: Rua Lenine 58, Ingombota, 5500 Luanda; tel. 222691200; e-mail website@aaa.co.ao; internet fb.com/AAA.Seguros .Pensoes; f. 2000; life and non-life; Pres. and CEO Dr CARLOS MANUEL DE SÃO VICENTE.

Confiança Seguros SA: Edif. Beira, Patriota Financial Zone, Luanda; tel. 226426226; e-mail info@confiancaseguros.co.ao; internet www.confiancaseguros.co.ao; f. 2008.

ENSA Seguros de Angola: Av. 4 de Fevereiro 93, CP 5778, Luanda; tel. 222671000; e-mail segurado@ensa.co.ao; internet www.ensa.co .ao; f. 1978; state-owned; to be privatized; Chair. MÁRIO MOTA LEMOS.

Fidelidade Angola: Condomínio Cidade Financeira, Via S8, Prédio 10, 3º e 4º andares, Talatona, Luanda; tel. 923167240; e-mail info@ fidelidade.co.ao; internet www.fidelidade.co.ao; f. 2009; fmrly Universal Seguros, SA; present name adopted in 2017; life and non-life; Chair. JOSÉ MANUEL ALVAREZ QUINTERO.

Global Seguros: Edif. Garden Towers, Travessa Ho Chi Minh, Torre B, Piso 13, Alvalade, Luanda; tel. 923166900; e-mail apoio .cliente@globalseguros.ao; internet www.globalseguros.ao; f. 2006; Pres. AMÍLCAR SILVA; CEO RUI COSTA CAMPOS.

Nova Sociedade de Seguros de Angola SA (Nossa Seguros): Av. Pedro de Castro Van-Dúnem Loy, Academia BAI, Bloco C, 4º andar, Morro Bento, Luanda; tel. 222670700; e-mail info@nossaseguros.ao; internet www.nossaseguros.ao; f. 2004; Chair. LUIS LÉLIS; CEO ALEXANDRE CARREIRA.

Saham Angola Seguros: Edif. Cabinda, 4º andar, Belas Business Park 1, Talatona, Luanda; tel. 222653300; e-mail info@ sahamseguros.co.ao; internet www.sahamseguros.co.ao; f. 2005; fmrly GA Seguros; present name adopted in 2016; owned by Saham Group (Morocco); Chair. RAYMOND FARHAT; CEO PHILIPPE ALLIALI.

Tranquilidade Corporação: Edif. ESCOM, 15º andar, Rua Marechal Brós Tito 35, Luanda; tel. 226434510; e-mail apoio@ tranquilidade.co.ao; internet www.tranquilidade.co.ao; f. 2012; part of Apollo Global Management; Chair. ARTUR DUARTE.

Regulatory Authority

Agência de Regulação e Supervisão de Seguros (ARSEG): Edif. Torre Maculusso, 10º andar, Rua Frederick Welwitsch 84, CP 2795, Luanda; tel. 222444084; e-mail geral@arseg.ao; internet www .arseg.ao; Chair. ELMER VIVALDO DE SOUSA SERRÃO.

Insurance Association

Associação de Seguradoras de Angola (ASAN): Edif. G do Complexo Sigma, 1º andar, Rua Centro de Convencoes, Talatona, Luanda; tel. 927212522; e-mail geral@asan.co.ao; internet asan.co .ao; f. 2012; Pres. CARLOS DUARTE.

Trade and Industry

GOVERNMENT AGENCIES

Agência de Investimento Privado e Promoção das Exportações (AIPEX): Rua Kwame Nkrumah 10, KN10, Município de Belas, Luanda; tel. 222391434; e-mail geral@aipex.gov.ao; internet www .aipex.gov.ao; f. 2018 to replace Agência para a Promoção do Investimento e Exportações (APIEX) and, prior to 2015, Agência Nacional para o Investimento Privado (ANIP); under the Ministry of the Economy and Planning; Chair. ANTÓNIO DA RESSURREIÇÃO HENRIQUES DA SILVA.

Gabinete de Obras Especiais (GOE): Luanda; f. 2011; Dir-Gen. LEONEL CRUZ.

Instituto Angolano da Propriedade Industrial: Rua Cerqueira Lukoki 25, 6º andar, CP 3840, Luanda; tel. 222004991; e-mail prudencia.silva@yahoo.com.br; Dir ANA PAULA MIGUEL.

Instituto de Desenvolvimento Industrial de Angola (IDIA): Rua Cerqueira Lukoki 25, 8º andar, CP 594, Luanda; tel. 222338492; e-mail geral@india.gov.ao; internet idia.gov.ao; f. 1995; promotes industrial devt; Dir-Gen. DÁRIO CAMATI.

Instituto Nacional de Apoio as Micro, Pequenas e Médias Empresas (INAMPEM): Largo 1º Maio, Edif. Torres Dipanda, Lado A, 4º andar, Luanda; tel. 937537383; internet www.inapem.gov.ao; responsible for implementation of policies and strategies in the field of training and financing of micro, small and medium-sized enterprises; Chair. JOÃO NKOSSI.

Instituto Nacional de Cereais (INCER): Clássicos de Talatona, Prédio nº2, 6º e 7º andares, Rua do MAT, Luanda; tel. 936702118; e-mail geral@ciencia.ao; internet ciencia.ao; promotes cereal crops; Dir-Gen. Dr BENJAMIM ÁLVARO CASTELO.

Instituto Regulador dos Serviços de Electricidade e de Água (IRSEA): Edif. Complexo Clássicos do Talatona 5, 6º andar, Rua do MAT, Luanda; tel. 222747707; e-mail irsea.irsea@irsea.gov.ao; internet www.irsea.gov.ao; Chair. LUÍS MOURÃO DA SILVA.

CHAMBERS OF COMMERCE

Câmara de Comércio e Indústria de Angola (CCIA) (Angolan Chamber of Commerce and Industry): Largo do Kinaxixi 14, 1º andar, CP 92, Luanda; tel. 938872540; e-mail CCIANGOLA2021@ gmail.com; internet www.cciangola.com; f. 1988; Chair. Eng. VICENTE SOARES; Exec. Sec. ANTÓNIO TIAGO GOMES.

INDUSTRIAL AND TRADE ASSOCIATIONS

Associação Industrial de Angola (AIA): Rua Manuel Fernando Caldeira 6, CP 61227, Luanda; tel. 222330624; e-mail contactos@ aiangola.net; f. 1930; suspended operations between 1976 and 1992; re-launched 1992; Pres. JOSÉ SEVERINO.

Associação dos Empreendedores de Angola (AEA): Município de Belas Via AL3, Luanda; tel. 939648142; e-mail info@ empreendedoresangola.org; internet www.empreendedoresangola .org.

STATE TRADING ORGANIZATIONS

Empresa Nacional de Comercialização de Diamantes de Angola (SODIAM EP): Edif. Endiama/De Beers, 7º andar, Rua Rainha Ginga 87, CP 1072, Luanda; tel. 222396786; e-mail geral@ sodiam.co.ao; internet www.sodiam.co.ao; f. 1999; part of the ENDIAMA group; Chair. EUGÉNIO PEREIRA BRAVO DA ROSA.

STATE INDUSTRIAL ENTERPRISES

Agência Nacional de Recursos Minerais: Luanda; f. 2020 to replace FERRANGOL; CEO JACINTO FERREIRA DOS SANTOS ROCHA.

Agência Nacional de Petróleo, Gás e Biocombustíveis (ANPG): Edif. Torres do Carmo, Torre 2, Rua Lopes Lima, Distrito

Urbano da Ingombota, CP 3279, Luanda; tel. 226428000; e-mail comunicacao@anpg.co.ao; internet anpg.co.ao; f. 2019; Chair. PAULINO JERÓNIMO.

Empresa Nacional de Diamantes de Angola, UEE (ENDIAMA): Rua Major Kanhangulo nº 100, CP 1247, Luanda; tel. 222334585; e-mail endiama.invest@endiama.co.ao; internet www.endiama.co.ao; f. 1981; commenced operations 1986; diamond mining; a number of subsidiaries incl. SODIAM, ENDITRADE and ALFA 5; Chair. JOSÉ MANUEL GANGA JÚNIOR.

Instituto Regulador dos Derivados de Petróleo (IRDP): Rua João de Deus 55, Vila Alice, Distrito Urbano do Rangel, Luanda; tel. 936715021; e-mail informa@irdp.gov.ao; internet www.irdp.gov.ao; Dir-Gen. ALBINO FERREIRA.

Sociedade Nacional de Combustíveis de Angola (SONANGOL): Rua Rainha Ginga 22, nº 29-31, Luanda; tel. 222334448; e-mail secretariageral@sonangol.co.ao; internet www.sonangol.co.ao; f. 1976; exploration, production and refining of crude petroleum, and marketing and distribution of petroleum products; sole concessionary in Angola, supervises on- and offshore operations of foreign petroleum cos; Chair. SEBASTIÃO PAI QUERIDO GASPAR MARTINS.

Sonangalp, Lda: Largo 17 de Setembro 3, 1º Esq., Presidente Business Center, Luanda; tel. 222310830; e-mail geral@sonangalp.co.ao; f. 1994; 51% owned by SONANGOL, 49% owned by Galp Energia (Portugal); fuel distribution; Dir-Gen. FRANCISCO LIMA AIRES.

UTILITIES

Electricity

Empresa Nacional de Distribuiçãode Electricidade (ENDE): Rua Cónego Manuel das Neves 234, Luanda; tel. 222641750; internet www.ende.co.ao; f. 2014; responsible for the distribution of electricity; Chair. HÉLDER DE JESUS GARCIA ADÃO.

Empresa Pública de Produção de Electricidade (PRODEL): nr TPA Production Centre, Luanda; tel. 913953111; e-mail geral@prodel.co.ao; internet www.prodel.co.ao; f. 2014; responsible for the operation of power stations; Chair. JOAQUIM VENTURA.

Rede Nacional de Transporte de Electricidade (RNT): nr TPA Production Centre, Luanda; tel. 222704404; e-mail geral@rnt.co.ao; internet www.rnt.co.ao; f. 2014; responsible for the management of the transmission grid; Chair. RUI PEREIRA DO AMARAL GOURGEL.

Water

Empresa Pública de Água de Luanda (EPAL): Rua Frederico Engels 3, 1387 Luanda; tel. 942454831; e-mail geral@epal.co.ao; internet www.epal.co.ao; f. 1995; state-owned; Chair. MANUEL SILVA LOPES DA CRUZ.

MAJOR COMPANIES

Agroquímica de Angola SARL (AGRAN): Av. de Portugal 71–1º, Luanda; tel. 924812853; e-mail info@agran-angola.com; internet www.agran-angola.com; f. 1960; 98.7% owned by Finertec, Portugal; manufacture of agricultural chemicals.

Azule Energy: Av. 4 de Fevereiro 197, Torres Atlantico, Luanda,; tel. 222637440; e-mail info@azule-energy.com; internet www.azule-energy.com; f. 2022; jt venture between BP PLC (UK) and Eni (Angola); CEO ADRIANO MONGINI.

Chevron: Av. Dr. Agostinho Neto, CP 2950, Luanda; tel. 222692600; e-mail clocal@chevron.com; internet angola.chevron.com; owns Cabinda Gulf Oil Co (CABGOC); Man. Dir DEREK MAGNESS.

Cimenfort: Estrada Nacional 100, Rua Cimenteira, Bairro da Thaka, Catumbella, Benguela; tel. 943099172; e-mail vendas@cimenfort.com; internet cimenfort.com; cement producer; Dir-Gen. PAUL HENG.

Companhia Fabril e Comercial de Angola SARL (COMFABRIL): Av. 4 de Fevereiro 79, 3º andar, Ingombota, CP 859, Luanda; tel. 938380010; e-mail geral@comfabril.com; internet comfabril.com; f. 1954; manufacture and sale of chemicals; Gen. Man. PEDRO ALVES.

Grupo Nov Angola: Rua do Complexo de Escolas do Cazenga 25, Cazenga, Luanda; tel. 222395601; e-mail geral@gruponov.co.ao; internet www.gruponov.com; f. 2006; subsidiaries incl. Lena Engenharia e Construções, Abrantina Sucursal, Angola Investimento Imobiliária SA, Jonasbel-Angola Empreendimentos Lda, TEC Lda. Lenindústria Angola SA; Group Chair. JOAQUIM PAULO DA CONCEIÇÃO.

Nova Cimangola SA (Empresa de Cimentos de Angola): Av. 4 de Fevereiro 42, 2º andar, CP 2532, Luanda; tel. 222310190; f. 1957; 49% owned by Ciminvest,; 40% state-owned; 10% Banco Angolano de Investimento; production of cement and plaster; CEO SINDIKA MANUEL DA SILVA PACAVIRA, Jr.

Petrogal Angola SA: Av. 4 de Fevereiro 3–4, Luanda; tel. 222397987; part of Galp Energia Group; exploration, production and distribution of petroleum; CEO ANDY BROWN.

Petromar Lda: Rua Rodrigo Miranda Henriques, 15B Bairro Maculusso, Luanda; tel. 923167620; e-mail geral@petromar.co.ao; internet www.petromar.co.ao; f. 1984; pre-fabrication, construction, installation and maintenance of oil equipment; 70% owned by Saipem SA and 30% owned by Sonangol Holdings 30%; Dir Eng. BRAVO NETO.

Sociedade Mineira de Catoca, Lda: Talatona, Luanda; tel. 222624700; e-mail geral@catoca.com; internet www.catoca.com; f. 1992; jt diamond mining and exploration operation owned by ENDIAMA, Alrosa (Russia) and Lev Leviev International (China); Chair. and Man. Dir Dr BENEDITO PAULO MANUEL.

TRADE UNIONS

Sindicato dos Jornalistas Angolanos (SJA): Rua Francisco Tavora, CP 2805, Luanda; tel. 923310455; e-mail sindicatodosjornalistas_sja92@hotmail.com; internet fb.com/SindicatoDosJornalistasAngolanos; f. 1992 by fmr mems of the União dos Jornalistas Angolanos; Sec.-Gen. CÂNDIDO TEIXEIRA.

Sindicato Nacional de Professores (Sinprof): Apt 407, Prédio 72, 4º andar, Rua da Missão 71, Luanda; tel. 222739025; e-mail info@sinprof.co.ao; internet sinprof.co.ao; f. 1996; teachers' union; Pres. GUILHERME SILVA; Sec.-Gen. ADMAR GINGUMA.

União Nacional das Associações de Camponeses Angolanos (UNACA): Rua Major Kanhangulo 146, 1º andar, CP 2465, Luanda; tel. 938302794; e-mail unaca2@gmail.com; internet fb.com/UNACAparaCamponeses; f. 1990; peasants' asscn and agro-livestock co-operatives; Pres. (vacant); Gen. Sec. SEBASTIÃO JOÃO DA COSTA.

União Nacional dos Trabalhadores Angolanos-Confederação Sindical (UNTA-CS) (National Union of Angolan Workers): Av. Rainha Ginga 23, CP 28, Luanda; tel. 222334670; e-mail info@unta-cs.org; internet unta-cs.org; f. 1960; Sec.-Gen. MANUEL AUGUSTO VIAGE.

Transport

The transport infrastructure was severely dislocated by the civil war that ended in 2002. Subsequently, major rebuilding and upgrading projects have been undertaken.

RAILWAYS

There are three main railway lines in Angola: the Benguela railway, which runs from the coast to the Zambian border; the Luanda–Malange line; and the Moçâmedes line, which connects Namibe and Kuando Kubango. Following the end of the civil war in mid-2005 a project for rebuilding and upgrading the railway system was approved by the Southern African Development Community (SADC). The 424-km Luanda–Malange line was completed in mid-2010; passenger services resumed in January 2011 and goods transport (between Luanda and Dondo) in May 2013. The Benguela line—a significant export route—reopened in 2011, following demining and reconstruction work by Chinese workers. The Moçâmedes line was reopened in mid-2012.

Instituto Nacional dos Caminhos de Ferro de Angola (INCFA): Av. 4 de Fevereiro 42, 4º andar, Luanda; tel. 222336340; Dir-Gen. JÚLIO BANGO JOAQUIM.

Benguela Railway (Caminho de Ferro de Benguela—Empresa Pública) (CFB): Praça 11 Novembro 3, CP 32, Lobito, Benguela; tel. 272222645; e-mail cfbeng@ebonet.net; owned by Govt of Angola; line carrying passenger and freight traffic from the port of Lobito across Angola, via Huambo and Luena, to the border of the Democratic Republic of the Congo (DRC); 1,344 track-km; Chair. LUÍS TEIXEIRA.

Caminho de Ferro de Moçâmedes (Moçâmedes Railways—CFM): Av. 4 de Fevereiro, Bairro Sto. António, CP 130, Lubango; tel. 261221752; e-mail gab.dir.cfm@netangola.com; f. 1905; main line from Namibe to Menongue, via Lubango; br. lines to Chibia and iron ore mines at Cassinga; 838 track-km; Chair. DANIEL JOÃO QUIPAXE.

Luanda Railway (Empresa de Caminho de Ferro de Luanda, UEE) (CFL): Rua Major Kanhangulo 1, Bungo, CP 1250-C, Luanda; tel. 923001100; e-mail cfl@cfl.co.ao; internet www.cfl.co.ao; f. 1886; serves an iron-, cotton- and sisal-producing region between Luanda and Malange; 536 track-km; Chair. JÚLIO BANGO JOAQUIM.

ROADS

Direcção Nacional dos Transportes Rodoviárias: Rua Rainha Ginga 74, 1° andar, Luanda; tel. 228742171; e-mail dntr@mintrans.gov.ao; Dir NOÉLIA CONCENTINA SACHICAGO.

Instituto Nacional de Estradas de Angola (INEA): Rua Amílcar Cabral 35, 3° andar, CP 5667, Luanda; tel. 222332828; Dir-Gen. HENRIQUE VICTORINO.

SHIPPING

The main harbours are at Lobito, Luanda and Namibe.

Instituto Marítimo e Portuário de Angola (IMPA): Rua Rainha Ginga 74, 4° andar, Bairro dos Coqueiros, Luanda; tel. 222390034; internet www.portal-impa.co; Dir-Gen. MANUEL NAZARETH NETO.

Empresa Portuária do Lobito, UEE: Av. da Independência 16, Lobito, Benguela; tel. 272222710; e-mail quintino.trinta@eplobito.net; internet www.eplobito.net; long-distance sea transport; CEO CELSO RODRIGUES DE LEMOS ROSAS.

Empresa Portuária de Luanda: Av. 4 de Fevereiro, CP 1224, Luanda; tel. 226431121; e-mail geral@portoluanda.co.ao; internet www.portoluanda.co.ao; CEO ALBERTO ANTÓNIO BENGUE.

Orey Angola: Largo 17 de Setembro 7, Luanda; tel. 943721456; e-mail oreao@orey.co.ao; internet www.orey-angola.co.ao; int. shipping, especially to Portugal.

Porto do Namibe, UEE: Av Mondlaine, CP 49, Namibe; tel. 264260643; e-mail geral@portodonamibe.co.ao; internet portodonamibe.co.ao; long-distance sea transport; CEO ANTÓNIO SAMUEL.

CIVIL AVIATION

Angola's airport system is well developed, but suffered some damage in the later years of the civil war. The 4 de Fevereiro international airport in Luanda underwent modernization in the late 2000s, while a new international airport, at Lubango was opened in January 2010. During the late 2000s airports at Luanda, Lobito, Soyo, Namibe, Saurimo, Uíge, Huambo and Bié also underwent rehabilitation. In August 2012 a new international airport, built at a cost of US $250m., was inaugurated at Catumbela, Benguela province, while construction of a new international airport serving Luanda was expected to be completed by 2023.

Autoridade Nacional da Aviação Civil (ANAC): Luanda; Chair. AMÉLIA CRISTINA DE SOUSA DOMINGUES KUVÍNGUA.

Empresa Nacional de Navegação Aerea: Av. 21 de Janeiro 21, CCR, Aeroporto Internacional, 4 de Fevereiro, CP 841, Luanda; tel. 222330791; e-mail info@enna.co.ao; internet enna.co.ao; administers air traffic and air navigational safety; Chair. MANUEL AGOSTINHO FILIPE JUNIOR.

Instituto Nacional da Aviação Civil: Rua Miguel de Melo 96, 6° andar, Luanda; tel. 222335936; internet www.inavic.gv.ao; Dir-Gen. Dr CARLOS MANUEL DAVID.

Sociedade Nacional de Gestão de Aeroportos de Angola: Luanda; internet www.enana.co.ao; administers management and operation of the national airports; Chair. MÁRIO MIGUEL DOMINGUES; Man. Dir NATANIEL ALBERTO DOS SANTOS DOMINGOS.

SONAIR SARL: Aeroporto Internacional 4 de Fevereiro, CP 2675 Luanda; tel. 226691133; e-mail snr.dai.ext@sonangol.co.ao; internet www.sonair.co.ao; f. 1998; subsidiary of SONANGOL; operates direct flights between Luanda and Houston, USA; Chair. SEBASTIÃO PAI QUERIDO GASPAR MARTINS; CEO RUBEN MONTEIRO DA COSTA.

TAAG—Linhas Aéreas de Angola: Rua da Missão 123, CP 79, Luanda; tel. 923190001; e-mail info.taag@flytaag.com; internet www.taag.com; f. 1938; internal scheduled passenger and cargo services, and services from Luanda to destinations within Africa and to Europe and South America; Chair. (vacant).

Angola Air Charter: Aeroporto Internacional 4 de Fevereiro, CP 3010, Luanda; tel. 222330994; f. 1987; subsidiary of TAAG Angola Airlines; CEO A. DE MATOS.

Tourism

Instituto de Fomento Turístico: Rua do MAT, Complexo Administrativo Clássicos, Luanda; tel. 226431391; e-mail instituto.fomento.turistico@hotmail.com; Dir-Gen. SIMÃO MANUEL PEDRO.

Defence

As assessed at November 2021, the Forças Armadas de Angola had an estimated total strength of 107,000: army 100,000, navy 1,000 and air force 6,000. In addition, there was a paramilitary force numbering an estimated 10,000. In 2021 a total of 113 troops were stationed abroad.

Defence Budget: 627,000m. kwanza in 2021.

Chief of General Staff of the Armed Forces: Gen. ANTÓNIO EGÍDIO DE SOUSA SANTOS.

Chief of General Staff of the Army: Gen. MATIAS LIMA COELHO.

Chief of General Staff of the National Air Force: Gen. ALTINO CARLOS JOSÉ DOS SANTOS.

Chief of General Staff of the Navy: Gen. JORGE MANUEL DOS SANTOS.

Education

Education is officially compulsory for eight years, between seven and 15 years of age, and is provided free of charge by the Government. Primary education begins at seven years of age and lasts for four years. Secondary education, beginning at the age of 11, lasts for up to six years, comprising two cycles of three years each. According to estimates by the United Nations Educational, Scientific and Cultural Organization (UNESCO), enrolment at pre-primary institutions in 2015/16 was equivalent to 40% of children (boys 42%; girls 37%) in the relevant age-group, while enrolment at primary schools in 2010/11 included 82% of children in the relevant age-group (boys 92%; girls 71%). Secondary enrolment in 2015/16 was equivalent to 51% of children in the relevant age-group (boys 62%; girls 40%).

Bibliography

Andresen Guimarães, F. *The Origins of the Angolan Civil War: Foreign Intervention and Domestic Political Conflict*. Basingstoke, Palgrave, 2001.

Anstee, M. *Orphan of the Cold War: The Inside Story of the Collapse of the Angolan Peace Process*. London, Macmillan, and New York, St Martin's Press, 1996.

Bender, G. J. *Angola Under the Portuguese: The Myth and the Reality*. Lawrenceville, NJ, Africa World Press, 2004.

Birmingham, D. *Empire in Africa: Angola and its Neighbors*. Columbus, OH, Ohio State University Press, 2006.

Short History of Modern Angola. Oxford, Oxford University Press, 2015.

Bridgland, F. *Jonas Savimbi: A Key to Africa*. Edinburgh, Mainstream, 1986.

The War for Africa: 12 Months that Transformed a Continent. Oxford, Casemate, 2017.

Cann, J. P. *The Flechas. Insurgent Hunting in Eastern Angola, 1965–1974*. Solihull, Helion and Co., 2013.

Capoco, Z. *Nacionalismo e Construção do Estado-Angola (1945–1975)*. Lobito, Angola, Escolar Editora, 2012.

Chabal, P., and Videl, N. (Eds). *Angola: The Weight of History*. New York, Columbia University Press, 2007.

Cilliers, J., and Dietrich, C. (Eds) *Angola's War Economy: The Role of Oil and Diamonds*. Pretoria, Institute for Security Studies, 2000.

Conçalves, J. *Economics and Politics of the Angolan Conflict: The Transition Re-Negotiated*. Bellville Centre for Southern Africa Studies, University of the Western Cape, 1995.

Corkin, L. *Uncovering African Agency: Angola's Management of China's Credit Lines*. Farnham, Ashgate, 2013.

De Oliveira, R. S. *Magnificent and Beggar Land: Angola since the Civil War*. Oxford, Oxford University Press, 2015.

Faria, P. C. J. *The Post-War Angola: Public Sphere, Political Regime and Democracy*. Newcastle-upon-Tyne, Cambridge Scholars, 2013.

Galliani, F. *Portrait of the New Angola*. Milan, Skira Editore, 2012.

García Rodríguez, J.-L., García Rodríguez, F. J., and Castilla Gutiérrez, C. *Power of Oil in Angola*. New York, Nova Science Publishers, 2014.

George, E. *The Cuban Intervention in Angola (1965–1991), from Che Guevara to Cuito Cuanavale*. London, Frank Cass, 2005.

Hatzky, C. _Cubans in Angola: South-South Cooperation and Transfer of Knowledge, 1976–1991_. Madison, WI, University of Wisconsin Press, 2015.

Heywood, L. _Contested Power in Angola, 1840s to the Present_. Rochester, NY, University of Rochester Press, 2000.

Hodges, T. _Angola: Anatomy of an Oil State_. Oxford, James Currey Publrs, 2004.

Júnior, M. _Angola: The Failure of Operation Savannah 1975_. Bloomington, IN, AuthorHouse, 2015.

Kisalu Kiala, A. _Angola, La Trajectoire Dramatique d'Un Pays_. Paris, L'Harmattan, 2015.

MacQueen, N. _The Decolonization of Portuguese Africa: Metropolitan Revolution and the Dissolution of Empire_. Harlow, Longman, 1997.

Maier, K. _Angola: Promises and Lies_. London, Serif Books, 2007.

Martin, J. W. _A Political History of the Civil War in Angola, 1974–90_. New Brunswick, NJ, Transaction Publishers, 1992.

Mendes, P. R. _Bay of Tigers: A journey through war-torn Angola_. London, Granta, 2004.

Moorman, J. _Powerful Frequencies: Radio, State Power, and the Cold War in Angola, 1931–2002_. Athens. OH, Ohio University Press, 2010.

Pawson, L. _In the Name of the People: Angola's Forgotten Massacre_. London, I.B. Tauris, 2014.

Pearce, J. _An Outbreak of Peace: Angola's Situation of 'Confusion'_. Cape Town, New Africa Books, 2005.

Political Identity and Conflict in Central Angola, 1975–2002. Cambridge, Cambridge University Press, 2015.

Power, M., and Alves, A. (Eds). _China and Angola: A Marriage of Convenience?_ Oxford, Pambazuka Press, 2012.

Roque, P. C. _Governing in the Shadows: Angola's Securitised State_. London, Hurst & Co., 2021.

Shaxson, N. _Poisoned Wells: The Dirty Politics of African Oil_. London, Palgrave Macmillan, 2008.

Scholz, L. _The Battle of Cuito Cuanavale: Cold War Angolan Finale, 1987-1988_. Solihull, Helion & Co, 2016.

Venter, A. J. _Battle for Angola: The End of the Cold War in Africa c1975-89_. Solihull, Helion & Co, 2017.

Weigert, S. _Angola: A Modern Military History, 1961–2002_. Basingstoke, Palgrave Macmillan, 2011.

Wheeler, D. L., and Pélissier, R. _Angola_. London, Greenwood Press, 1978.

World Bank. _Angola: Oil, Broad-based Growth, and Equity_. Washington, DC, 2013.

Wright, G. _The Destruction of a Nation: United States Policy towards Angola since 1945_. London, Pluto Press, 1997.

BENIN

Physical and Social Geography

R. J. HARRISON CHURCH

The Republic of Benin, bordered on the east by Nigeria, on the west by Togo and to the north by Burkina Faso and Niger, covers an area of 114,763 sq km (44,310 sq miles). From a coastline of some 100 km on the Gulf of Guinea, the republic extends inland about 650 km to the Niger river. According to the census of May 2013, the population was 10,008,749, giving an average population density of 88.9 inhabitants per sq km. The population of Cotonou, the political capital and major port, was estimated at 679,012 at the census, and that of Porto-Novo, the official capital, was 264,320. Other large cities include Abomey-Calavi (656,358), Djougou (267,812), Parakou (255,478) and Banikoura (246,575). At mid-2022 the United Nations projected that the population of Benin had increased to 12,784,728.

The coast is a straight sandbar, pounded by heavy surf on the seaward side and backed by one or more lagoons and former shorelines on the landward side. Rivers flow into these lagoons, Lakes Ahémé and Nokoué being estuaries of two rivers whose seaward exits are obstructed by the sandbar. A lagoon waterway is navigable for barges to Lagos, Nigeria.

North of Lake Nokoué the Ouémé river has a wide marshy delta, with considerable agricultural potential. Elsewhere the lagoons are backed northward by the Terre de Barre, a fertile and intensively farmed region of clay soils. North again is the seasonally flooded Lama swamp. Beyond are areas comparable with the Terre de Barre, and the realm of the pre-colonial kingdom of Dahomey.

Most of the rest of the country is underlain by Pre-Cambrian rocks, with occasional bare domes, laterite cappings on level surfaces, and poor soils. In the north-west are the Atacora mountains, whose soils, although less poor, are much eroded. On the northern borders are primary and other sandstones; soils are extremely infertile and short of water.

Deposits of low-grade iron ores, chromium, rutile, phosphates, kaolin and gold occur in the north of the country. Extraction of petroleum from a small oilfield, off shore from Cotonou, at Sémé, ceased in late 1998, although new discoveries were made in the early 2010s. Limestone and marble are currently mined.

Southern Benin has an equatorial climate, most typical along the coast, although with a low rainfall of some 1,300 mm. Away from the coast the dry months increase until a tropical climate prevails over the northern half of the country. The dry season alternates with a wet one, the latter being of seven months in the centre and four months in the north.

In the colonial period the Fon and Yoruba of the south enjoyed educational advantages and were prominent in administration throughout French West Africa. After independence many were expelled to Benin, where there is great unemployment or underemployment of literates. The northern peoples, such as the Somba and Bariba, are less Westernized. The Fon were the most numerous ethnic group in the country, accounting for 39.2% of the population in 2002, followed by the Adja (15.2%) and Yoruba (12.3%).

History

PAUL MELLY

DEEP HISTORICAL AND CULTURAL ROOTS

As a modern independent state Benin has existed since 1960 when it gained independence under the name Dahomey. However, both of these names in fact reflect the deep historical roots of a country whose territory encompasses regions that were among the more important kingdoms of pre-colonial West Africa and have left a legacy that still shapes identity and the nature of society today. Geography was also a powerful influence, with northern savannah-Sahelian areas mainly populated by ethnic groups such as the Bariba, Zarma, Haoussa, Mossi and Peul (Fulani), while the more humid tropical south was inhabited mainly by the Fon, Goun, Yoruba and Aja-Ewé. Southern areas were also heavily impacted by the transatlantic slave trade, and the consequent growth of religious and cultural connections with Brazil and the Caribbean.

Traditional chieftancies predominated but from the 15th century onwards more substantial kingdoms began to emerge, with Sunin Séro, for example, establishing the Bariba kingdom of Nikki, whose soldiers fought alongside the Yorubas against the Peul in the early 19th century. Bariba society had a strict social hierarchy, with slaves and craftsmen ranking below praise poets and singers (griots) and yeoman farmers, and the warrior nobility having the highest status. The Yoruba were largely predominant in the east, with two major kingdoms, Shabê-Okpa and Kétou, while more western zones were the preserve of the Aja-Ewé, with the kingdoms of Savi and Davié (now Allada), from which, in the late 17th century, the kingdom of Dahomey developed, establishing a capital at Abomey. Notable for its contingent of female warriors (amazones),

who were largely former elephant hunters, Dahomey extended its authority as far as Ouidah on the coast, where it developed trading ties with the European mariners, who regularly visited from the 15th century onwards. Trade in slaves developed, with the English and French building forts at Ouidah to protect their interests in this traffic. The kingdom of Dahomey was highly organized, if violent, and incorporated human sacrifice into royal funeral rituals. The slave trade was a channel of two way-influence and connection, with natives of southern Benin shipped across the Atlantic taking their voudon religion to Haiti and Brazil, while some freed former slaves eventually returned to the land of their ancestors. In the early 19th century King Ghézo introduced new crops of Americas origin—tomatoes, maize, groundnuts and tobacco.

However, Dahomey's predominance generated the resentment of Toffa, ruler of the vassal kingdom of Xogbonou (today's Porto Novo), which had signed a friendship treaty with France in 1851. Subsequently, the nearby Cotonou area was actually ceded to French rule and then in 1886 Toffa signed a treaty to make his territory a French protectorate. This provoked Béhanzin, King of Dahomey, into launching an attack on the French which was initially successful but ultimately proved a failure. Béhanzin surrendered in 1894 and was deported to the French Caribbean island of Martinique.

Meanwhile, France formally established Dahomey as a colony, gradually extending its territorial control and overcoming fierce resistance from the kingdom of Nikki; the boundaries of the new colonial territory were formalized through agreements with the Germans, who were taking over Togo to the west, and with the British, now in control of Nigeria. Dahomey was incorporated as a unit of the wider French West Africa territory and became one of its most important centres for education, leading to the emergence of a growing intellectual and political class and a steadily growing campaign for independence. In the 1950s there was gathering momentum for greater self-government in France's African colonies and, like many others, Dahomey became an autonomous state within the French Community in 1958. However, it soon became clear that such arrangements could not satisfy spreading local demands for the outright independence of sub-Saharan territories. Dahomey, like many of its neighbours, secured full independence just two years later in 1960.

INDEPENDENCE AND ARMY RULE

Established on 1 August 1960 the newly independent republic was soon consumed by destabilizing rivalries within the mainly southern political elite, and in October 1963 Col Christophe Soglo led a military putsch that deposed the first President, Hubert Maga, amid social discontent and radical complaints about bad governance and the cost of living. Soglo soon stood aside, but seized power again in 1965 only to be deposed himself two years later. Further putsches followed in quick succession until Maj. Mathieu Kérékou, a northerner, seized power in October 1972. Two years later he introduced Marxism-Leninism as the official ideology, establishing a one-party system and seeking to marginalize traditional tribal authorities; nationalization and the promotion of co-operative agriculture were at the heart of economic strategy. Kérékou also discarded the country's name in a bid to erode the legacy influence of the southern Dahomey cultural inheritance: in 1975 it was renamed the People's Republic of Benin, thus taking the name of the important pre-colonial state in neighbouring western Nigeria.

Kérékou left the army in January 1987 to become a civilian head of state but soon had to fend off army resentments, with attempted coups in March and June 1988. Meanwhile, the economy was in deep trouble, with customs revenues slashed when Nigeria imposed a prolonged shutdown of the border, leaving the state unable to pay public servants' salaries. Benin had to seek the support of the International Monetary Fund (IMF), which insisted on drastic spending curbs and a 10% cut in public sector pay in 1987, followed by further austerity measures two years later. This triggered a wave of popular protest which placed the regime under severe pressure at a time when urban populations across francophone Africa could view television coverage of how 'people power' mass protest was overturning the communist regimes in eastern Europe. With discreet French encouragement, Kérékou resisted the temptation to order a crackdown on demonstrations, opting instead for a radical process of liberalization and agreeing to the organization of a national conference of the 'active forces of the nation', encompassing representatives from a broad range of political and civil society voices, to debate a new route forward for the country.

CONSENSUAL DEMOCRATIC REFORM

In February 1990 the national conference voted to abolish the existing Marxist one-party structure of state institutions, to rename the country the Republic of Benin and to organize multi-party democratic legislative and presidential elections. Nicéphore Soglo, a former World Bank official, was designated interim Prime Minister and new legislation was promulgated to permit the registration of political parties.

In a referendum in December 1990, Beninois voters approved a new Constitution, which included age limits for presidential candidates that disqualified several former heads of state. Legislative elections in February 1991 saw a pro-Soglo alliance gain the most seats (12) in a 64-member Assemblée Nationale (National Assembly) and in the presidential contest the following month Soglo defeated Kérékou in a second round of voting, with a decisive 67.7% of the vote.

This peaceful and voluntary end to autocratic one-party rule and the subsequent relatively consensual establishment of a genuine multi-party democracy, with a change of government achieved through the ballot box, set a precedent widely followed across francophone Africa. This was an achievement of genuinely historic significance that gave Benin totemic status,

particularly among francophone countries, and across West Africa more widely, as a pioneer of sub-Saharan democracy—a status that has rendered the country's recent slide back towards authoritarianism all the more shocking in the eyes of many citizens and those watching on from other francophone African societies.

The genuinely pluralistic and contesting nature of Benin's democratic life was demonstrated in November 1994 when the National Assembly ignored opposition from President Soglo and approved the creation of an independent electoral commission, the Commission Electorale Nationale Autonome (CENA), and an increase in the number of deputies to 83. Legislative elections followed in March 1995 and, after by-elections for 13 seats where irregularities forced a re-run, Soglo's party, La Renaissance du Bénin (RB), was left in a minority: RB won 20 seats and other parties supporting the head of state secured a further 13. However, the opposition won 49 seats, of which the largest component was the 19 seats won by the Parti du Renouveau Démocratique (PRD).

THE RETURN OF KÉRÉKOU, 1996–2006

In the March 1996 presidential election Soglo topped the first round poll, with 35.7% of the valid votes, but only just ahead of Kérékou, staging an impressive comeback with 33.9% although well ahead of the PRD's Adrien Houngbédji on 19.7%. In the run-off Kérékou—perhaps rewarded by voters for his graceful acquiescence in the transition to democracy five years earlier—nudged ahead of Soglo to secure victory with 52.5%. However, politics remained tightly contested and in the March 1999 legislative elections opposition parties captured 42 of the 83 seats, just ahead of pro-Kérékou parties with 41.

The next presidential election, in March 2001, became enveloped in controversy: Kérékou won 45.4% of the first round votes, far ahead of Soglo (27.1%), Houngbédji (12.6%) and Bruno Amoussou, leader of the Parti Social-Démocrate (PSD), on 8.6%. Soglo disputed the results and when the Constitutional Court rejected his appeal for a re-run he pulled out of the race altogether, as did Houngbédji. However, Amoussou, who had already pledged his second round support for Kérékou, then agreed to stay in the race, thus ensuring there was a contested second round, which bolstered the credibility of the President's now almost inevitable re-election. Kérékou duly crushed Amoussou in the 22 March second round ballot, securing 84.1% of the votes.

It was not until 2003 that legislative elections produced a clear pro-presidential majority for the first time since the establishment of democracy 12 years earlier: Kérékou supporters secured 52 of the 83 seats, a position soon further bolstered to 63 seats when Houngbédji's PRD switched to ally with the Government. The RB was reduced to just 15 seats.

THE YAYI PRESIDENCY, 2006–16

Kérékou respected the limit of two consecutive presidential terms and thus stood down in 2006. In the election to succeed him Thomas Boni Yayi, until recently President of the Banque Ouest-Africaine de Développement (BOAD), won the first round with 35.6%, followed by Houngbédji on 24.1% and Amoussou with 16.2%. In the 19 March second ballot Boni Yayi secured a decisive victory over Houngbédji with 74.5%. In legislative elections one year later the Force Cauris pour un Bénin Emergent (FCBE), a pro-presidential coalition of some 20 parties, won 35 of the 83 seats, ahead of the Alliance pour une Dynamique Démocratique—comprising the RB and the PSD, among others—with 20 seats, and the PRD with 10. The remainder were shared by smaller parties or alliances.

The March 2011 presidential polls produced a clear victory for Boni Yayi, with 53.1%, over Houngbédji (35.6%), this time standing as the candidate of the Union Fait la Nation (UFN) alliance of the PRD, the PSD and the RB. Third place went to Abdoulaye Bio Tchané, a respected former finance minister who had gone on to become Africa director of the IMF and then head of BOAD. At legislative elections the following month the FCBE maintained its position as the largest political force, with 41 of the 83 seats, while the UFN obtained 30. The remaining 12 seats were divided among six political movements. However, the Government's political base was consolidated when a number of parties, including the RB, joined the presidential majority, which ended up with 61 of the 83 legislative seats.

The following year saw the emergence of a bizarre conspiracy saga: Boni Yayi's own niece, Zoubérath Kora-Séké, his personal physician, Dr Ibrahim Mama Cissé, and the Director-General of the Société de Développement du Coton, Moudjaïdou Soumanou, were arrested in October 2012 over allegations of a plot to poison the President. Then in December the French authorities briefly detained Patrice Talon, one of Benin's wealthiest business figures, with huge interests in cotton and the import sector, over allegations that he had instigated the plot. Talon, a former supporter of Boni Yayi, was placed under judicial supervision while the Benin authorities sought his extradition. The mood of suspicion deepened when the authorities announced that they had foiled a February 2013 coup plot and arrested a former head of the Cotonou gendarmerie and a cousin of Talon. Angelo Houssou, an examining magistrate (*juge d'instruction*) who dismissed the charges against the poisoning and plot suspects was then himself detained while trying to leave Benin and the suspects were kept in detention even after the Court of Appeal in Cotonou had upheld Houssou's judgment. The magistrate himself finally fled to the USA in November 2013 and in the following month a French appeals court rejected Benin's request for the extradition of Talon. In May 2014 the Benin Supreme Court ordered a resumption of legal proceedings only for Boni Yayi to then pardon all those implicated in the poisoning and coup attempts.

At legislative elections in April 2015 the FCBE secured 33 of the 83 seats in the National Assembly, while the opposition UFN and PRD took 13 and 10 seats, respectively; eight other parties also won seats. Voter turnout was 65.9%. In June 2015 Boni Yayi appointed a new Government headed by Lionel Zinsou, a Franco-Beninois economist and banker close to the former French Prime Minister, Laurent Fabius. The President had originally hoped to abandon the constitutional term limit, so that he could seek a third mandate; but eventually he backed away from the idea, instead choosing the technocratic Zinsou as the FCBE succession candidate for the 2016 presidential election.

TALON'S ELECTION AND PRESIDENCY

In the first round of the election, held on 6 March 2016, Zinsou, who also had the support of the PRD and the RB, headed the poll with 28.4% of the vote. However, he faced fierce competition from two business tycoon politicians: Talon, who had returned to Benin from exile in France five months earlier, took 24.7%, just ahead of Sébastien Ajavon (23.0%). More traditional political figures, Bio Tchané and former Prime Minister Pascal Koupaki, trailed behind on 8.7% and 5.9% respectively. In the run-off held on 20 March Talon, campaigning on his image as a can-do businessman and 'local boy made good', secured 65.4% of the vote to inflict a crushing defeat on the more establishment Zinsou, whose image was not helped by his French connections. Talon's second round campaign had also been aided by endorsements from Bio Tchané, Koupaki and Ajavon.

Talon, probably Benin's most substantial business figure, now held the levers of political power too. New to government, he shrewdly appointed the experienced Koupaki as Secretary-General of the Presidency with senior State Minister rank and the internationally respected Bio Tchané as State Minister for Planning and Development, effectively his chief economic strategist. Talon acted swiftly to assert his authority, abrogating some 20 decrees signed by Boni Yayi, replacing or deposing a number of senior officials and mayors and appointing a commission to recommend political and institutional reforms. Talon also ordered the restitution to his own business group of cotton sector ginning assets that had been seized by the Boni Yayi Government and restored a Cotonou port import inspection contract that had been removed from his firm, Benin Control, by the previous administration.

Talon also began to marginalize or neuter political threats. Ajavon was briefly detained in October 2016 on suspicion of drug trafficking, while four opposition-linked broadcasters,

including two owned by Ajavon, were shut down. In August 2017 Ajavon companies were accused of tax evasion and he was ordered to pay 167,000m. francs CFA and two months later he was charged with forgery and fraud, proceedings that Ajavon viewed as politically motivated. Former President Soglo's son, Léhady Soglo, was removed as leader of the RB and as mayor of Cotonou, Benin's main city and the seat of government. He fled to exile in France.

Meanwhile, the President was pushing forward proposals for constitutional change: a single six-year presidential term, public funding for political parties and positive discrimination for women in politics. However, the plans met with widespread suspicion and 18 opposition parties, trade unions and civil society organizations formed the Front de Sursaut Patriotique to oppose them, while the National Assembly refused even to discuss the package. The Government also faced demonstrations over the cost of living and against the planned privatization of some state-owned enterprises.

At first Talon backed off, announcing the abandonment of the constitutional plans—this bought him some political room for manoeuvre and enabled the Government to secure National Assembly approval for controversial legislation banning strikes in the security, health and justice sectors in December 2017. When the Constitutional Court ruled that the new measure was unconstitutional, justice minister Joseph Djogbénou was quickly installed as President of the Court, which then reversed its stance and approved the strike ban in June 2018.

Faced with Talon's strongly assertive approach to Government, opponents began to reorganize. In March 2018 Ajavon launched the Union Sociale Libérale (USL). Meanwhile the FCBE transformed itself from an alliance of movements into a single party, with Boni Yayi as honorary President and Valentin Djènontin, a former justice minister, as leader (National Executive Secretary).

Talon hit back ordering audits that left various political figures looking vulnerable. Djènontin and two other opposition deputies, Idrissou Bako and Atao Hinnouho, were implicated in allegations of alleged mismanagement, trafficking in fake medicines and customs fraud. In July 2018 the National Assembly lifted their immunity and in November Hinnouho was sentenced to more than six years' imprisonment over the fake medicines scandal.

Moreover, Talon was still pushing forward various proposals for reshaping political life, although he sought approval of these from the increasingly compliant National Assembly rather than risking a referendum. In July 2018 some 62 of the 83 deputies voted in favour of the constitutional amendments, which represented strong support, although still short of the four-fifths' majority required for adoption. However, finally, in September 2018, he managed to nudge the National Assembly into approving a new electoral code, which set out stringent and detailed requirements for parties to secure official registration and the right to contest elections. The deposits to be paid by presidential and legislative candidates were increased and parties were henceforth required to obtain at least 10% of the total national vote to win legislative seats. All this was presented as rendering Benin's famously diverse and lively political life more simple, structured and clear; but the practical consequence was to hamper political opposition. Other new legislation limited workers' right to strike to just 10 days a year, thus weakening the protest capacity of civil society.

The Government had meanwhile set up an anti-corruption court, the Court for the Suppression of Economic Offences and Terrorism (Cour de Répression des Infractions Economiques et du Terrorisme—CRIET). And in October 2018 this convicted Ajavon, *in absentia*, of drug trafficking and sentenced him to 20 years' imprisonment and a fine of 5m. francs CFA; in April 2019 he was granted political asylum in France. The Soleil FM radio station owned by Ajavon was ordered to suspend broadcasting. The African Court on Human and Peoples' Rights (ACHPR) ruled that several of Ajavon's rights, including that to a fair trial, had been violated. Meanwhile, the Beninois authorities also accused a former finance minister, Komi Koutché, of financial misconduct, issuing an international warrant for his arrest. He was detained in Spain in December 2018 but a Spanish court subsequently refused his extradition. In April 2020 the CRIET convicted him *in absentia* and sentenced him to 20 years in prison and a fine of 500m. francs CFA.

THE 2019 LEGISLATIVE ELECTIONS

As the 2019 legislative elections approached, pro-Talon factions merged into two parties, the Union Progressiste (UP, absorbing the UFN) and the Bloc Républicain (BR), which were both registered under the stringent new requirements. However, opposition parties struggled to satisfy the new requirements and in March 2019 the electoral commission decided that only the UP and the BR could contest the polls. For many Beninois, and many watching on across francophone West Africa, this was a severe shock, because of the totemic pioneer role Benin had played in leading the region-wide trend towards democracy in 1990. A country celebrated for the diversity of its political life was now seeing the abolition of meaningful electoral choice.

Some 20,000 peopled attended a protest march in Cotonou on 11 March 2019 organized by the FCBE and the USL. However, the Constitutional Court upheld the CENA's ruling. Protests continued and former Presidents Boni Yayi and Soglo urged Talon to halt the electoral process and, when their appeal was ignored, they demanded a boycott of the polls. However, the authorities pressed ahead with the polls on 28 April, soured by a record low turnout, of just 27.1%, and with internet access blocked; voting did not take place at all in 39 of the country's 546 districts owing to local 'incidents', while civil society groups reported two deaths in polling violence. The UP secured 47 of the 83 seats and the BR the remaining 36, creating a de facto monochrome legislature.

After the results had been announced, opposition demonstrators clashed with troops and riot police in Cotonou. On 1 May 2019 soldiers were deployed in the city to break up barricades erected by protesters, and the next day the security forces stormed Boni Yayi's residence, reportedly firing on the crowd outside. The opposition claimed that five people had died in the Cotonou clashes and two more in Kandi, in the north. In mid-June there were further protests and clashes in Tchaourou, Boni Yayi's home town, and Savé, leaving at least two dead. The authorities accused Boni Yayi of incitement, but he refused to co-operate with the investigation and, after Ivorian and Nigerian mediation, he was released from house arrest on 22 June and allowed to leave Benin for medical treatment. These events came as a huge shock to many Beninois: in a country noted for its free climate of political and media debate, large numbers of people were being detained, often without proper due process, while the security forces had used lethal force against protesters—the sort of crackdown Beninois were used to hearing about in countries with a long history of repression but not seeing on their own urban streets. Independent media were muzzled through threats or the loss of public sector advertising.

Meanwhile, the judicial system continued to be deployed to disqualify or intimidate potential opponents. In August 2019 former Prime Minister Zinsou, now living in France, was sentenced *in absentia* to a six-month suspended prison term, fined 50m. francs CFA and forbidden from standing for political office for five years, for supposedly exceeding expense limits and using false documents in his 2016 election campaign. (The ban was reduced to four years after the documents charges were thrown out.) The FCBE was finally granted official recognition in September 2019, but only after the now exiled Djènontin and Koutché had been dropped from the party executive, a decision that split the party into an officially recognized wing, led by new National Executive Secretary Paul Hounkpè, and a faction loyal to Boni Yayi and Djènontin. In November Djènontin too was convicted *in absentia*, for stealing and disseminating a state document and sentenced to two years' imprisonment.

Supposedly to defuse tension and listen to opposition views the Government organized a political dialogue in early October 2019; however, only the nine parties that had been prepared to go through the legal registration process were invited, which split the FCBE between one faction prepared to register and another that felt that would amount to 'selling out'. The

dialogue did reportedly recommend amendments to the electoral law and the charter of political parties, the release of political prisoners and the abandonment of political prosecutions. Yet the talks fell far short of what committed opponents felt would be acceptable and therefore the parties that had been excluded organized a counter-dialogue of their own, chaired by former President Soglo, and demanded fresh legislative elections open to all parties, the return of political exiles and the release of political detainees.

CONSTITUTIONAL REFORMS AND COMMUNAL ELECTIONS

On 1 November 2019 the National Assembly—no longer including any opposition members—adopted constitutional amendments to implement the recommendations of the official dialogue, some of which bore close resemblance to the ideas originally put forward by Talon. The principal revisions were the consolidation of presidential, legislative, communal and local elections from 2026; an increase in the duration of deputies' mandates from four to five years, henceforth renewable only twice; the creation of an elected post of Vice-President; and the abolition of the death penalty. The limit of two presidential terms of office was retained and made lifelong. Furthermore, on 7 November the Assembly approved an amnesty for those still detained after the April 2019 unrest and 63 political prisoners were released, while the summons issued against Boni Yayi was annulled. On 14 November 2019 the Assembly adopted the political parties charter and a reform of the electoral code and increased the number of legislative seats to 109 (from 83), of which 24 were reserved for women.

On the face of it these changes largely seemed like a liberal modernization. Yet the critical requirements and exclusions that had hampered the opposition's ability to challenge were kept in place or reinforced: the controversial requirements for party participation in legislative elections were maintained and while the deposit for presidential candidates was cut from 250m. francs CFA to just 50m. francs CFA, candidates were henceforth required to secure the sponsorship of at least 10% of deputies and mayors—a tough requirement for any opposition challenger, given the Government's monopoly of parliamentary seats.

The scale of the obstacles facing opponents became even more clear with the approach of the May 2020 elections to Benin's 77 municipal councils. The new rules required that parties secure at least 10% of the vote nationally to be eligible for council seats, thus effectively excluding parties with localized support of individual and independent candidates. Some 34 parties had contested the 2015 municipal polls, but in 2020 only nine parties applied to take part and four of those were excluded. The USL remained unauthorized while the Restaurer l'Espoir party of former minister Candide Azannaï decided to boycott the elections as 'not credible' even though it had actually managed to secure official recognition. The FCBE was still split and so Boni Yayi decided to quit the movement that had originally been founded as a vehicle for his support.

Ajavon took his complaint about exclusion to the ACHPR, which then requested the postponement of the elections until it had given its ruling on the issue. However, the Government had already moved to forestall such pressure by initiating the withdrawal of Beninois individuals' and non-governmental organizations' right to submit complaints direct to the ACHPR (a move that would take formal effect in late March 2022). Unsurprisingly, given the many constraints on the opposition, the communal elections of 17 May 2022 produced a comprehensive victory for the pro-Talon parties, which secured 1,555 of the 1,815 council seats: the UP won 820, the BR some 735 and the compliant wing of the FCBE 260. Turnout was officially reported as 49.1%. The PRD and the Union Démocratique pour un Bénin Nouveau, also allied to the presidential camp, failed to meet the 10% vote threshold and thus won no seats. The results left the UP with 41 mayoralties, including Cotonou and Porto-Novo—Benin's formal capital and seat of the National Assembly—while the BR had won 29 but the FCBE just seven.

Meanwhile, like other West African countries Benin acted rapidly to confront the novel threat posed by COVID-19 in early 2020. The first confirmed case was reported on 16 March 2020, just five days after the World Health Organization (WHO) had declared a pandemic. The Government imposed quarantine on arriving air travellers, tightened land border controls and banned public gatherings, shutting down schools, universities and places of worship. In late March restrictions on movement were imposed in the most exposed southern urban centres, including Cotonou and Porto-Novo, but from mid-May restrictions were gradually relaxed. Case numbers declined in the second half of 2020, before picking up again in early 2021, and the experiencing a further decline. As in many other countries, the progress of the vaccination programme launched in early 2021 was hampered both by a shortage of vaccine supplies and some scepticism among the public—in part a reflection of the fact that COVID-19 had a relatively limited health impact compared with longstanding challenges such as malaria and malnutrition. By late August 2022 some 27,638 cases had been recorded but only 163 deaths; limited access to testing suggests the true figures were probably higher. However, the greatest impact of the pandemic was probably economic in slowing trade, tourism and commerce, and thus depressing incomes and disrupting livelihoods, particularly in urban trade and the informal sector.

After media reports of a failed coup attempt in late June 2020, the Government detained nine soldiers and civilians for suspected 'acts contrary to peace', referred the cases to the CRIET. In July it sentenced the exiled Léhady Soglo *in absentia* to 10 years' imprisonment for abuse of office; his lawyer argued that the proceedings were politically motivated.

THE 2021 PRESIDENTIAL ELECTION

Looking for ways to mount effective opposition within Benin's tightly constricted new political framework, Boni Yayi and other former FCBE members developed a new political party, Les Démocrates, led by Eric Houndété from La Résistance (an opposition movement formed in the aftermath of the 2019 legislative polls). In July 2020 the group applied for official registration, taking great pains to ensure that it satisfied all the new requirements. Official recognition was finally granted in December. Meanwhile, civil society organizations, human rights groups, opposition parties and even the Roman Catholic Church pressed for the abolition of the sponsorship rules that threatened to prevent parties other than the UP and the BR from presenting candidates in the 11 April 2021 presidential election. Lacking representation in the National Assembly, opposition candidates would otherwise have to secure the sponsorship of at least 16 of the 77 new mayors and the Constitutional Court refused to strike down these tough new qualification requirements. However, subsequent events were to demonstrate that even if all the regulatory hurdles were satisfied, any serious opponent might still find their path into the presidential race blocked.

In November and December 2020 the ACHPR ordered the repeal of the November 2019 constitutional changes and subsequent election legislation, as these had been introduced without the national consensus required by the African Union's African Charter on Democracy, Elections and Governance; the African court accused Benin of violating its commitment to the independence of the Constitutional Court and also ordered the repeal of legislation against strikes, an amnesty for offences committed during the 2019 legislative elections and the reversal of the rule removing recognition from political parties that fail to present candidates for two consecutive parliamentary elections. However, the Government had already ignored numerous ACHPR rulings and seemed likely to do so again.

In 2016 Talon had advocated a single presidential term of office, a proposal later repeated though never legislated for. Yet in January 2021, to little surprise, he confirmed that he would in fact stand for another term, and it soon became clear that no serious rival challenge would be allowed. The CENA validated only three of the 20 presidential nominees: Talon himself—with the sponsorship of 118 National Assembly deputies and mayors—and two token opponents who were helpfully granted some sponsorship signatures from politicians in the UP and the BR (the two pro-government parties that held all the parliamentary seats). Former minister Alassane Soumanou stood for

the now tamed FCBE, while Corentin Kohoué, a member of Les Démocrates but standing in a personal capacity, was also a candidate.

Of the 17 excluded would-be candidates two represented particularly serious political threats to Talon—the highly regarded constitutional law professor, Joël Aïvo, representing the opposition Front pour la Restauration de la Démocratie (FRD) alliance, and Boni Yayi's charismatic former justice minister Reckya Madougou; the latter had been selected by Les Démocrates, who had opted to contest the election separately despite being part of the FRD. That the Constitutional Court rejected all appeals against the exclusions was unsurprising. However, there was widespread shock in Benin and the broader region when Madougou, in March, and then Aïvo in April, were arrested. (Both men were subsequently charged with state security offences, and convicted; Aïvo received a gaol term of 10 years for money laundering and plotting against the state, while Madougou was sentenced to 20 years in jail for complicity in terrorism, in nakedly political trials that removed two resilient and powerful critics from the public scene.) This was a level of ruthlessness in suffocating political opposition almost unparalleled in 21st century West Africa and clearly in blatant breach of Economic Community of West African States (ECOWAS) democratic governance principles.

As the election approached, tensions rose further, with exiled opposition figures accusing Talon of over-running his five-year mandate by six days. Demonstrations took place in towns in the north and centre of the country and two people were reportedly killed in a security forces crackdown. The FRD appealed for its supporters to boycott the poll, which took place on 11 April 2021 at which, with all serious challengers excluded, Talon cruised to a massive victory, with 86.3% of the valid votes cast. Soumanou took 11.4%, while Kohoué trailed on 2.3%. However, popular scepticism was evidenced by the turnout of 50.6%—low by Benin standards—and voting did not take place at all in 13 of the 546 districts. Nevertheless, the fact that turnout reached even this level, and that Talon got such a hefty share, was evidence of the appeal of his core sales pitch, focused on his success in sustaining economic growth through the COVID-19 pandemic, curbing petty corruption and improving basic services and infrastructure. For many Beninois, these achievements outweighed the political discomfort of the erosion of democratic liberties.

Talon promised to prosecute those supposedly responsible for pre-election violence and by the end of April 2021 more than 100 arrests had been made. Human rights groups, opposition figures, the US Department of State and the Roman Catholic Church expressed concern, but the authorities took a hard line.

Talon now permitted only compliant opposition to operate within Benin's tightly redrawn political system. In May 2021 he had designated the FCBE's Paul Hounkpè as the country's first official Leader of the Opposition. A measure of the weakness of officially recognized opposition is that the FCBE, its largest force, had just seven mayors and no members of the National Assembly.

Talon was sworn in to serve a second term of office on 23 May 2021, subsequently appointing a new Government little changed from the previous ministerial team. Speaking at an event in July Talon promised to leave power in 2026, at the end of his current mandate, but many observers remain to be convinced he will honour this commitment.

SECURITY, REGIONAL RELATIONS AND EXTERNAL AFFAIRS

Regional relationships within West Africa are crucial for Benin, as a small country heavily reliant on trade and the partnerships with its neighbours in the 15-member ECOWAS. While the partnership with the seven other members of the West African CFA franc single currency bloc is particularly close, for Benin the relationship with its large eastern neighbour Nigeria—Africa's most populous country and largest economy—is absolutely key. While economic and social networks are fundamental to Benin's role within West Africa, security has also increasingly become a major priority in recent years.

Like other coastal West African states Benin has become exposed to the risk of infiltration and attack by the violent jihadist groups now active across the central Sahel and increasingly probing southwards from Burkina Faso into the northern reaches of Benin, Togo and Côte d'Ivoire. This security threat has become a major preoccupation for the Government, faced with a growing danger to its own citizens and territory. What started as a contribution to a regional security effort has now developed a strong domestic national defence dimension.

For many years Benin has participated in efforts to stabilize Mali and tackle militant groups there: it contributed 300 troops to AFISMA (African-led International Support Mission to Mali), the African force that intervened alongside the French Operation Serval to liberate northern Malian towns from jihadist occupation in early 2013, and when AFISMA was upgraded to become the United Nations (UN) peacekeeping force MINUSMA (Multidimensional Integrated Stabilization Mission in Mali) Benin remained a participant; in May 2022 it had some 250 troops and 136 police deployed with the UN mission. This was very much in Benin's longstanding tradition of participation in ECOWAS and UN intervention and peace-keeping missions (in Côte d'Ivoire, Liberia, the Central African Republic, Chad, the Democratic Republic of the Congo, Sudan and South Sudan). Benin also contributed 150 troops to the Multinational Joint Task Force fighting Boko Haram in north-east Nigeria and the wider Lake Chad basin, a move perhaps also intended as a goodwill gesture towards improved relations with Nigeria.

However, in recent year the Government has also had to reinforce its domestic security effort in the face of infiltration and raids by jihadists now well implanted in neighbouring Burkina Faso. The first serious raid came in May 2019 when suspected Islamist militants kidnapped two French tourists in the Pendjari National Park (PNP), adjacent to the Burkina border. The tourists' local guide was killed. The French military succeeded in rescuing the hostages 10 days later, but lost two of their own soldiers in the mission. This jihadist attack, and their readiness to simply murder the Beninois guide, caused genuine shock in Benin, which had hitherto escaped the direct impact of terrorist violence. Despite its northern location the PNP had been regarded as relatively safe. The attack destroyed such perceptions, with tourists henceforth advised to stay away from the PNP and the large cross-border W National Park further east, with a devastating impact on local communities that depended heavily on income from wildlife guiding, the sale of handicrafts and service activities.

The Government responded by deploying additional troops to the far north, to patrol the border with Burkina and protect local communities. Benin also co-operated with Togo, Ghana, Côte d'Ivoire and Burkina in the Accra Initiative, launched in 2017, to co-ordinate their military efforts against a southwards expansion of jihadist activity. Moreover, France has also stepped up its security support, partly through the redeployment of resources that it pulled out of Mali in the first half of 2022, and joint cross-border military operations have targeted groups of militants, with some success. However, these reinforced security precautions have not prevented a steady trickle of further attacks; the Beninois authorities indicated that by the end of June 2022 the country had suffered at least 21 such raids, and there had also been attacks in northern Côte d'Ivoire and Togo. Benin has stated that it will bring home the troops it has contributed to MINUSMA in stages in November 2022 and November 2023; this may reflect both concern over the deteriorating security and political environment in Mali and a strategic judgement that these forces are more urgently needed back home to reinforce protection of the northern border.

Meanwhile, like other coastal states, Benin also faces persistent piracy in the Gulf of Guinea, a threat to Cotonou port's role as a trade gateway. Joint efforts at tackling the problem have been steadily reinforced, with Benin and Nigeria instigating joint maritime patrols in 2011, regional states adopting a common code of conduct in 2013 and the 2015 inauguration of an ECOWAS Maritime Co-ordination Centre in Cotonou. The frequency of attacks reduced from 2012 to 2017 but then accelerated again, with increased kidnapping of crew members.

Benin maintains generally good relations with West African neighbours, agreeing with both Burkina Faso and Niger to refer border disputes to the International Court of Justice (ICJ) at The Hague. There was a delay in formally submitting the difference with Burkina to the Court, with the two countries leaving a joint committee to administer the 68-sq km Kourou/Koalou as a neutral zone in the meantime. The difference with Niger was resolved more rapidly, with a July 2005 ICJ ruling that 16 of 25 disputed small islands in the Niger river, including Lété, in fact belonged to Niger. Moreover, the governments in Cotonou and Niamey recognize the strong shared interest in maintaining a smooth relationship: Benin is a major trade gateway for Niger and they have built a one-stop integrated frontier post on their main border crossing between Malanville and Gaya. Moreover, the Chinese are now building an oil pipeline from the Agadem field in Niger to an export terminal at Sémé on the Benin coast, a project set to come on stream by the end of 2022 and that will generate revenue for both countries. The relationship of mutual trust was further reconfirmed in April 2021 when the Beninois authorities arrested three soldiers suspected of participating in an alleged attempted coup in Niger.

Relations with Nigeria are inevitably more complex and delicate, because of the ethnic and societal ties between the two countries, political mistrust and the huge flows of both formal and informal trade across their shared border. For some years the two countries had mounted shared border patrols and in 2005 they signed an agreement aimed at curbing informal trade and cross-border crime while boosting formal trade; a bilateral treaty on their maritime boundary was signed the next year. However, the efforts to promote more formalized economic relations have been constantly undermined by economic reality and by the policies of both governments: Cotonou port offers lower costs and faster handling times than the main terminals in Lagos—and until the 2015 harmonization of West African tariffs it also offered a more favourable tariff regime. These factors lead many businesses to import Nigeria-bound goods into Benin at Cotonou and then move them informally over the border into the Nigerian market. Meanwhile, Nigeria subsidises fuel prices, whereas Benin does not, which means that Benin attracts a constant smuggled inflow of cheap Nigerian fuel, which is then openly resold informally at roadsides in Benin. These issues have been constant irritants, particularly for the Nigerian authorities, which incline towards a protectionist stance. Matters came to a head in August 2019 when Nigeria unilaterally closed trade through the land border, supposedly to curb weapons trafficking; this had a painful economic impact on southern Benin. Nigeria did not reopen its land borders until December 2020, and even then continued to restrict trade. At talks in January 2021 President Talon suggested that Nigeria could station its own police and customs officers in his country, to inspect goods destined for export across the border; his Nigerian counterpart Muhammadu Buhari agreed that the two governments should study this idea. In the following month villages around Pobé in southern Benin hosted almost 5,000 Nigerians seeking refuge from inter-communal violence.

In the long term the African Continental Free Trade Area (AfCFTA) may help to smooth the flow of cross-border trade within the continent and Benin signed the agreement on its creation in July 2019. However, it had still not ratified the accord by May 2022, in contrast to the majority of states on the continent.

Beyond its region, Benin's most important external relationships remain with France and Europe more generally, the People's Republic of China for economic development and, within Africa, Rwanda, whose model of business efficient development Talon admires. But for Beninois critics Rwanda's highly authoritarian culture offers a troubling political model.

The tightening of political space over recent years has also caused tensions in the relationship with the European Union (EU). In November 2019 the Beninois authorities expelled the EU ambassador Oliver Nette for supposed 'subversive activities' after he held meetings with opposition parties and civil society organizations. The EU quickly hit back, declaring the head of Benin's mission to the EU persona non grata.

France has also been concerned about Talon's increasing authoritarianism but fears being accused of neo-colonial interference if it speaks out publicly on this issue. Matters are complicated by the need for France and Benin to co-operate closely in the effort to contain the spread of violent jihadist activity. Therefore President Emmanuel Macron has adopted a pro-active positive approach to relations: Benin was one of the states selected for the early return of cultural artefacts looted by French forces in the colonial era. Some 26 artefacts were formally transferred to Benin's ownership in November 2021, while culture, security and educational co-operation were the main items on the agenda when Macron made an official visit to Cotonou in July 2022.

Economy
PAUL MELLY

INTRODUCTION

For Benin, as for most sub-Saharan African nations, the COVID-19 pandemic and its aftermath have posed serious challenges. Previously buoyant real gross domestic product (GDP) growth tailed off sharply in 2020, although a recession was avoided and the first half of 2021 saw signs of a tentative economic resurgence.

For the past two decades diversity has been a key strength of the Beninois economic model: agriculture, the mainstay of rural production and livelihoods, is complemented by the role of Cotonou port and city as a regional trade gateway, particularly for Nigeria, the most populous country in Africa. Maritime and related commercial and transport activity has sustained huge volumes of business income, government revenue and formal and informal employment. However, this has been seriously impacted by the events of the past two years: in August–September 2019 the Nigerian Government suspended all trade across its land borders, a severe curb on the landing of cargo at Cotonou port for onwards transit to Nigeria—and on Benin's own agricultural exports to this huge consumer market. Although the official frontier closure could not entirely suppress the substantial informal flow of goods across the border, the overall impact on business activity and livelihoods was significant. Six months later COVID-19 arrived, forcing the Benin Government to impose social distancing and lockdown measures that depressed domestic urban activity and thus further cooled the already slowing rates of growth. The Nigerian border was not officially reopened until January 2021, while the impacts of COVID-19 have persisted for many months more.

Although the mainly rural economy of northern Benin was less severely affected by the Nigerian border shutdown, it was already suffering from the overspill impacts of the security crisis in the Sahel: in May 2019 militants kidnapped two French tourists—later rescued—from the Pendjari National Park and killed their local guide. The fragile security climate is an impediment to overall investor confidence and development efforts in the north, already the poorest part of the country.

President Patrice Talon's erosion of democratic freedoms and move towards a more authoritarian style rule of rule has without doubt affected the business climate and overall mood in Benin, but the impact on economic activity is hard to measure with any accuracy. His style of government certainly inhibits free debate and effective scrutiny of government or business by the Assemblée Nationale (National Assembly), civil society or the independent media. Furthermore, it has scarred the intellectual self-confidence and freedom of research and policy discussion of a society that had been long accustomed to free expression and genuine democratic choice, fostering an environment in which policy research by think-tanks and other independent voices flourished. The restriction of public voice and political choice has alienated sections of Beninois opinion, particularly the educated urban youth, and thus threatens to erode the aspirations of many talented Beninois; this fuels increased outward migration from a poor country whose strong educational and intellectual traditions had been a powerful asset. In more specific terms there have been both positive and negative evolutions in the business environment: Talon has placed a strong focus on enhanced efficiency and effectiveness in economic management, the construction of public infrastructure, the provision key public services—for example, there is a drive to provide school meals for children in poor regions, in co-ordination with the United Nations, UN—and on curbing petty corruption by officials. There is a hotline for members of the public to report when they are harassed for bribes. However, there has also been an unstated but painfully felt trend towards the concentration of economic advantage and business opportunity in the hands of those closely aligned with the regime, which can suffocate alternative independent entrepreneurial enterprise and reinforces the predominance of favoured vested interests.

However, in the short term, and before the pandemic, any influence from these deeper governance cultural factors was more than outweighed by the positive impact of Talon's focus on public service efficiency consolidation of public finances and pursuit of a firmly pro-business national economic strategy: real GDP growth was 6.9% in 2019.

Almost one-half of Benin's population now lives in the Cotonou conurbation and other urban areas, where the foundations of the economy are public administration and services, private sector commercial and service activity and informal business and services. The city's Dantokpa market is one of the largest in West Africa and there has also been significant commercial development in areas extending east from the city to the key border crossing with Nigeria at Sémé-Kraké. Hitherto much of the cross-border trade has been informal, with goods smuggled into Nigeria (and cheap Nigerian fuel smuggled back into Benin). This traffic has caused serious annoyance in Abuja, and Benin must find a way to overhaul its economic model to reduce reliance on informal cross-border trade, stimulating instead the growth of formalized service activities that may still cater for Nigerian customers, but within a framework of legal regulation and taxation that thus avoids friction with the Abuja authorities. However, the fractious and increasingly repressive political, intellectual and media climate is a constraint on the expansion of knowledge and ideas-based sectors.

In southern rural areas, with a humid tropical climate, crops such as pineapple, yam and coconut are grown; forestry and offshore and lagoon fishing are also important. In central regions with drier savannah conditions, the economy is dominated by the smallholder farming of cereals and cotton, and the local ginning plants that process this key cash crop are Benin's main industrial activity. The economy of the far north, fringing the Sahel, is based around agriculture and livestock husbandry. In non-pandemic times, tourism has been a significant earner, with visitors drawn to sites in Ouidah and Porto-Novo related to the voodoo religion or the legacy of slavery, the stilt lagoon village of Ganvié and the royal palace in Abomey; the uplands of the Atakora massif in the north-west attract visitors for its cooler climate. The wildlife of the W and Pendjari national parks along the northern border was a major attraction, but their proximity to highly insecure areas of eastern Burkina Faso is now a deterrent to visitors.

The regional setting for Benin's economic activity is provided by its membership of both the eight-member Union Economique et Monétaire Ouest-Africaine (UEMOA) single currency bloc and the 15-country Economic Community of West African States (ECOWAS). All UEMOA states are also members of

ECOWAS and UEMOA's CFA franc and the Nigerian naira are the two predominant currencies of the West African region.

Established in 1975, ECOWAS was originally conceived as a framework for economic integration. However, when the developing Liberian civil war confronted the bloc with stability and security challenges in a member state, it assumed an interventionist security and peacekeeping mandate, deploying its first ever intervention force into Liberia in 1990, to prevent that country's civil war from sliding towards large-scale genocide. Subsequent deployments to Sierra Leone and Guinea-Bissau followed, gradually establishing a culture of collective security management that remains strikingly resilient. Countries across the region came to accept that major political or security crisis in one member state was in fact the affair of all. This means that member governments are willing to quickly meet and decide how to handle crises that crop up in member states and, in cases of serious security need, they are willing to despatch troops to take part in intervention force missions, either under the aegis of ECOWAS itself or the African Union or the UN. In 2002 ECOWAS adopted its democracy and good governance protocol, setting out some fundamental criteria for member states. Most notably the bloc refuses to recognize governments in any of the 15 member states that come to power through a coup or war—and this has been the basis for ECOWAS' use of sanctions or the threat of sanctions in an attempt to pressure the military juntas that seized power in Mali, Guinea and Burkina Faso in 2020 and 2021 into agreeing timetables for the restoration of constitutional governments via multi-party elections. Nevertheless, the degree to which the broader democratic good governance principles have been honoured varies widely, and in practice governments that were originally elected have enjoyed considerable latitude to tinker with constitutions, manipulate term limits or use authoritarian techniques to curb opposition challenge and abuse power, as President Talon has done in Benin. This has provoked widespread disillusion with ECOWAS particularly among urban young people who increasingly view it as a club for incumbent presidents. Bloc leaders have implicitly recognised this flaw and have asked Jean-Claude Kassi Brou, President of the ECOWAS Commission, to look at how the protocol could be strengthened. these have in practice been honoured has varied and member governments have now accepted that the rules need to be tightened up, to strengthen protections against abuse of power. Still, ECOWAS core principles of good governance and collective crisis management have certainly helped to sustain the stability of West Africa during an era of severe challenge—and this has had economic consequences in helping the region to continue to attract foreign aid and investment despite facing serious security challenges.

ECOWAS has also renewed its interest in economic issues with the introduction, from 2015 onwards, of a Common External Tariff (CET) to replace the UEMOA common import tariff regime and the individual national regimes operated by other ECOWAS states. UEMOA tariffs had generally been lower than Nigeria's so the adoption of the CET reduced Cotonou's cost competitive advantage over Lagos as a trade gateway to the vast Nigerian market, with goods formally imported into Benin but then smuggled into Nigeria. ECOWAS has also tried to liberalize trade between member states themselves, for example by banning tariffs on cross-border trade in food. Benin does export substantial volumes of locally grown food to Nigeria, and it is also a route for the informal trafficking of Asian rice and Italian pasta into Nigeria. Furthermore, the bloc has also set up a common market regime for the cross-border trading of electricity—of particular relevance to Benin as an electricity importing country. However, large obstacles towards deeper integration persist, notably the absence of harmonized technical and product standards and the refusal of the Central Bank of Nigeria (CBN) and UEMOA central bank (Banque Centrale des Etats de l'Afrique de l'Ouest—BCEAO) to allow direct electronic cross-border payments in local CFA franc or naira currencies between UEMOA and Nigeria; this rule is a serious impediment to the formalization of cross-border trade by local small businesses that operate only in the West African market and have no income flow in international hard currency.

UEMOA, the other key regional framework for the Beninois economy, is one of two blocs using the CFA franc, a currency inherited from the period of French colonial rule that ended in 1960. The bloc has eight member countries: Benin, Burkina Faso, Côte d'Ivoire, Guinea-Bissau, Mali, Niger, Togo and Senegal. Six central African countries also use a version of the CFA franc, but the two blocs operate quite separately. The cornerstone of the UEMOA system is the CFA franc's fixed peg to the euro, at a rate guaranteed by the French Treasury. The peg is derived from an original peg to the French franc, which was of course absorbed into the euro in 2002. This means that the monetary policy pursued by the BCEAO—which is headquartered in Dakar, Senegal, with branches in member states—is closely aligned with the conservative monetary stance of the European Central Bank. This generally holds inflation low, except in periods of exceptional surge in the price of key imported commodities, such as West Africa experienced in 2022 after the Russian Federation's invasion of Ukraine. In 2019 UEMOA and France agreed a reform of rules originally set up to underpin the currency and fixed peg, which required member countries to deposit one-half of their foreign exchange reserves in a special Operations Account at the French Treasury and allocated France seats on the governing boards of the UEMOA core institutions. That these requirements were no longer felt necessary is a measure of the monetary credibility that UEMOA has earned through the BCEAO's tight stewardship. The bloc also has a central commission based in Ouagadougou, Burkina Faso, to oversee its framework of close economic co-operation and data sharing and common system of banking regulation. The bloc also operates a regional capital market and electronic stock exchange and all member states also belong to OHADA, a harmonized system of business law covering most francophone African countries, which has an independent supranational appeals tribunal.

The CFA franc system has proved resilient, adjusting to the only devaluation in its history, in 1994, and withstanding the stress imposed by the 2002–10 crisis in Côte d'Ivoire, UEMOA's largest economy. However, the use of a currency with post-colonial associations has become increasingly unpopular among sections of West African opinion, particularly progressive intellectuals and the urban youth. Moreover, being tied to a currency as strong as the euro has kept the CFA franc's value high, and this has a tendency to squeeze the competitiveness of local producers, while keeping imports cheap. In the early 1990s this became an acute problem, triggering the 50% devaluation of the currency in 1994, with support from the International Monetary Fund (IMF), France and the World Bank; this dramatically restored the competitiveness of local agriculture and helped launch a sustained trend of economic recovery and growth that continued until the COVID pandemic hit. However, there has been a resurgence in recent years of the problem of a guaranteed value strong currency sucking in imports, and favouring the international interests of a small urban elite. Although the situation is less acute than in the early 1990s, the case for a fresh reform has gained growing adherence. In 2017 France's President, Emmanuel Macron, declared that France would support reform if that was the wish of UEMOA states. The bloc charged Côte d'Ivoire's President, Alassane Ouattara—a former deputy managing director of the IMF—to draft proposals. The result was the plan, agreed with Macron, to abolish the foreign exchange deposit requirement and for France to give up its board seats. Ouattara also proposed renaming the CFA franc as the eco—a move clearly designed to disarm domestic political critics, although this proposal was fiercely criticized by Nigeria and some other ECOWAS states, because this name had already been agreed by all ECOWAS countries as the name of a planned single currency covering the whole bloc.

ECOWAS has long been formally committed to the goal of creating a single currency that would be adopted by all its 15 member states, including UEMOA members and those not in the CFA franc bloc. However, progress towards concrete implementation of the common currency plan was slow and 2020 had to be dropped as the target year for its launch. Member states were cautious about addressing some of the most difficult issues, such as the location and the operating framework of the future central bank: both the CBN and the BCEAO are strong institutions that will probably be hugely reluctant to surrender their prerogatives or be subordinated to a supreme regional central bank authority. However, before the disagreement over the naming of the currency could be resolved, the COVID-19 pandemic intervened. In June 2021 ECOWAS agreed a fresh timetable for the monetary union, setting 2027 as the launch date, with a preparatory framework for monetary and fiscal convergence by member states running through to the end of 2026. Even so, many expert observers are sceptical that even this timetable will be honoured, because of the technical and political difficulty of merging Nigeria's central banking and monetary systems with those of other member states fearful they would simply end up as weak elements of an enlarged zone of Nigerian monetary influence.

AN EVOLVING ECONOMIC STRATEGY

Shortly after independence in 1960 Benin adopted a state-socialist system. However, the advent of multi-party democracy in 1990–91 and election of Nicéphore Soglo as President opened the door to a gradual economic liberalization, supported by the IMF, a process of change accelerated by the 1994 devaluation, which bolstered the competitiveness of Benin's farmers and livestock herders. When the former one-party socialist ruler Mathieu Kérékou regained power in the 1996 election he opted to continued the liberalizing trend, underpinned by tight fiscal discipline and, eventually, debt relief granted by the international community under the Heavily Indebted Poor Countries Initiative and the Multilateral Debt Relief Initiative. The debt relief also released more resources for health, education and poverty reduction measures. The strategy remained broadly the same under President Thomas Boni Yayi (2006–16) until a short-lived and ill-judged spending binge in the run-up to the 2016 election, which left his successor, Talon, with a looming fiscal and debt service crisis. Talon's new Minister of Planning and Development, Abdoulaye Bio Tchané, a former director of the IMF African department, was obliged to launch a drive for financial consolidation, to put public finances and investment strategy back on a sustainable basis.

However, Talon was also one of Benin's most important business actors, heavily involved in the cotton sector, while his company Benin Control had at one stage been awarded the contract for verification of imports at Cotonou port, a crucial part of the economy. Talon's relationship with Boni Yayi deteriorated, and his Government then transferred the import verification to a rival provider and also seized six of the 10 cotton ginning plants controlled by Talon's business empire. Upon acceding to the presidency Talon established hands-off arrangements for the day-to-day management of his businesses, but he also used his power, as head of the Government, to immediately reinstate Benin Control's import verification contract and restore the expropriated cotton sector operations to his business group. Moreover, political opponents and media critics have subsequently alleged that key government policy decisions tend to favour commercial entities to which he is linked.

The privatization of strategic economic operations that were once in state hands has been a fairly consistent theme of government policy since Soglo's presidency in the early 1990s, but it has been implemented on a pragmatic case by case basis, tailored to the specific circumstances in each sector. With the Société Béninoise d'Energie Electrique struggling to keep pace with rising demand, Boni Yayi overhauled the energy sector in an effort to attract the private sector to invest in generating capacity, while Cotonou port's two container terminals are operated by Bolloré and APM Terminals, and the Talon Government has entrusted overall management of the port as a whole to the Port of Antwerp (Belgium). However, policy has not always followed a linear track: the 1999 sale of a 55% stake in the parastatal Société Nationale de Commercialisation des Produits Pétroliers (SONACOP) was followed by a return to public sector control nine years later, as the company struggled to compete against cheap imports smuggled from Nigeria. Meanwhile, political sensitivities often influence policy towards the cotton sector, which is a critical source of cash income for many farmers and a rare source of formal employment in the countryside: policy has fluctuated between experiments in privatization, a restructured relationship with private sector ginning companies, the restoration of a major role for the state and then, after Talon's election as President in 2016, the transfer of many ginning assets back to the private sector.

MACROECONOMIC AND FISCAL SITUATION

Under successive governments Benin sustained macroeconomic progress under, with real GDP rising by an average of 4.1% per annum over 2010–16, underpinned by a stable fiscal and monetary stance. Yet, as previously noted, Benin's economy is heavily influenced by conditions in Nigeria and thus was adversely affected when the 2014 oil price slump hurt its hydrocarbons producing neighbour. Boni Yayi sought to counter the slowdown with a surge in spending and borrowing, which jeopardized financial stability. Therefore, when Talon took power in 2016 he initially had to reassert a conservative fiscal stance.

The Boni Yayi administration approved contracts for off-budget projects worth almost 24% of GDP outside standard procurement procedures, leaving Talon to inherit a schedule of debt service payments equal to 41% of government revenue, with arrears piling up and a public service salary bill that consumed one-half of the Government's income, and which left only 9% of revenues to cover all other spending needs. Talon's vigorous drive to consolidate public finances, supported by a new IMF three-year Extended Credit Facility (ECF) programme, managed to contain the domestic fiscal deficit (excluding donor aid) at 6.6% of GDP in 2016, sinking to 5.6% by 2018. The following year the deficit shrank to 2.2% of GDP on the old measure and just 0.6% of the new 'rebased' GDP figure.

Moreover, throughout this tough period of consolidation, headline real GDP growth actually continued to rise, and helped by his shrewd pro-business policies it reached 5.7% in 2017, then 6.7% in 2018 and 6.9% in 2019. Trend data for 2017–19 should be treated with some caution, as the Government, the IMF, the World Bank and other key institutions 'rebased' the calculation of economic output and national accounts, to better capture the full scale of activity in an economy where informal and semi-formal activities play a major role. Growth figures are now measured from the starting point of the rebased 2018 and 2019 data. In gauging the real value of output, allowance also has to be made for shifts in the exchange rate of the euro—and thus the CFA franc—against the dollar, which may partly explain marked fluctuations in World Bank figures for real GDP per capita in 2018–20. Even so, real growth in economic output probably did outstrip the average 2.7% annual rise in Benin's population and thus provided at least the fundamental platform for improvement in living standards for many Beninois in 2018 and 2019.

In 2020 the pace of growth was almost halved by the twin impacts of Nigeria's closure of its land border to trade (from August 2019 to January 2021) and the lockdown measures imposed by Talon's Government to curb the COVID-19 pandemic. Nevertheless, Benin's performance was resilient, with real GDP still rising by 3.8%, and in 2021 there was a strong resurgence, with growth at 6.6%. The impact of the Russian invasion of Ukraine, pushing up world grain prices but also injecting increased oil income into the Nigerian economy, has had complex effects on activity in Benin in 2022. However, by September the IMF was still able to project real GDP growth for the year at 5.9%.

Yet headline growth figures are not the whole story. Poverty remains widespread, especially in the rural north, even though Benin has made steady progress towards the UN Sustainable Development Goals, with average life expectancy, at 61 years for men and 64 years for women, above the average for West and Central Africa. With inflation reaching 3% in 2020 and projected at 4.6% in 2022, the cost of living imposes serious pressures on lower income households, particularly those in urban areas unable to grow their own food or cook on wood outdoors and thus totally reliant on the food and fuel they can afford to buy.

By mid-2022 Benin was coming under serious pressure on several fronts as the increased cost of living and the scars left by the slowdown triggered by the COVID-19 pandemic coincided with the broadening impact of jihadist terrorist attacks on the far north of the country. These not only damaged communities in the northernmost regions, Atakora and Alibori, where wildlife tourism in the Pendjari and W national parks had been a significant source of livelihoods, and undermined the security of public services and administration. The spreading violence, and the increasingly insecure condition of neighbouring regions of Togo, Burkina Faso, Niger and Nigeria, also threatened wider damage to investment confidence in Benin.

Therefore in July 2022 the IMF approved US $650m. in support, provided simultaneously through its Extended Fund Facility (EFF) and the ECF—a package that was four times the value of Benin's quota at the IMF and was one of the Fund's largest interventions in the region. Benin thus became the first country worldwide to be supported under the IMF's new High Combined Credit Exposure (HCCE) policy, which assists states that face exceptional balance of payments pressures but do have sufficient institutional strength to implement Fund programmes higher in value than they would normally be entitled to under a routine combined package of EFF and ECF support. The programme provided a rapid early injection of support for government finances, totalling $300m., of which $143m. was disbursed immediately. However, the Government also sees the IMF package as longer term support for its National Development Plan (NDP). The plan's main themes include measures to strengthen governance, pursue structural reform and improve the wellbeing of the population. There would be a strong focus on technical and vocational education to promote agriculture, tourism, digital sectors and the knowledge economy. Although unstated, this hinted at an attempt to shift the southern urban economy away from its heavy reliance on smuggling into Nigeria. Meanwhile, in the north, the aim is to pre-empt the growing terrorist threat by strengthening the presence of the state and public services, such as the provision of clean water, while also supporting the growth and diversification of the rural economy through rehabilitating rural roads, giving farmers easier access to microcredit. The NDP also includes key social measures such as the school feeding programme and cash transfers to encourage girls to remain in school.

The platform for Benin's resilience during the pandemic was the steady consolidation of public finances over the preceding years and this has perhaps also underpinned the IMF's recent confidence in the country's capacity to make effective use of the large funding package approved in July 2022. Total revenues climbed from just 745,700m. francs CFA in 2016 to 1,088,000m. francs CFA in 2019 and to 1,142,100m. francs CFA in 2020, equivalent to 12.7% of GDP. Within this overall total, non-fiscal revenue more than doubled in 2017, reaching 231,600m. francs CFA, but subsequently declined to 194,200m. francs CFA in 2020. By contrast, there has been a steady rise in fiscal receipts: these had slipped from 713,100m. francs CFA in 2015 to just 641,000m. francs CFA the next year, but have since followed a steady upward trend, increasing from 712,800m. francs CFA in 2017 to 811,300m. francs CFA in 2018, then to 893,300m. francs CFA the year after that and to 947,800m. francs CFA in 2020. Expenditure, which had sunk from 1,222,200m. francs CFA in 2015 to 1,080,700m. francs CFA the following year, rebounded to 1,311,700m. francs CFA in 2017, but was tightly controlled over the following two years, falling to 1,303,400m. francs CFA in 2018 and to 1,231,200m. francs CFA in 2019; however, 2020 brought a sharp rebound, to 1,718,100m. francs CFA as the Government sought to cope with the impacts of COVID-19. Within that total, current expenditure has slowly risen, from 781,100m. francs CFA in 2016 to 900,800m. francs CFA in 2019 and 1,095,600m. francs CFA in 2020, although as a proportion of GDP it declined from 11.2% in 2016 to 10.7% in 2019 before rebounding in 2020, to 12.7%, as the Government stepped up its spending in response to the pandemic, at a time when economic growth was slowing down sharply.

Salaries and public service other staff benefits accounted for a large share of current expenditure, at 395,100m. francs CFA in 2020, while interest payments on domestic debt cost 105,700m. francs CFA that year and interest payments to foreign creditors totalled 70,600m. francs CFA.

POPULATION AND SOCIAL CONTEXT

Development trends in Benin are strongly influenced by demography. The country had a population of 12.8m. in 2022 and the UN Population Fund estimates that it is increasing by an average 2.6% per annum, although the rate of growth is slowing gradually. Therefore demography exerts real demand pressure both on Benin's natural resources of land and water and the state's capacity to provide essential services and infrastructure; however, it also drives economic expansion, as the number of consumers increases and more young people enter the labour market each year. The fertility rate—the number of children that would be born to each woman if she lived to the end of her child-bearing years, giving birth at the national average rate—is 4.6 children, more than double the rate of 2.1 children that maintains a stable population. Just 14% of women aged 15–49 use modern contraception and only 34% of the demand for modern contraceptives is currently being met.

High population growth makes for a youthful society. Some 42% of Beninois are aged under 15, while 23% are aged between 10 and 19. Such figures confirm the huge demands for education and basic public child health care, and the need for Benin's economy to generate more jobs, or at least more informal sector livelihood opportunities. Urban areas are now home to some 49% of Beninois, where labour market and cost of living pressures are intense; this is particularly the case in the Cotonou conurbation, which is home to more than 2.3m. people.

Key development indicators reveal steady progress. Average life expectancy continues to rise, while the incidence of maternal mortality, at 397 deaths per 100,000 live births in 2017, was well below the regional average, a reflection of the fact that 78% of all births are attended by trained personnel, significantly higher than the West and Central African norm (55%). Yet there are still serious problems: 71% of children aged between six and 59 months are anaemic and in 2020 some 7% of the total population was undernourished. Some 59% of girls and 65% of boys complete primary education; and while the vast majority of these do enrol in secondary school, it is less clear how many actually continue for long enough to attain a significant level of secondary education. Particularly in Cotonou, there is a relatively large cadre of younger adults sufficiently educated to work with information technology or specialist technical and commercial matters. The Government's development strategy implicitly acknowledges the need to generate more such skilled employment, both to provide livelihoods for educated young Beninois and to diversify the economy.

However, inequality remains a serious problem: the poorest 20% of Beninois hold only 7% of the country's income. Only 7% of the rural population have access to improved sanitation (compared with 36% in urban areas), but 72% of rural residents do have access to improved water supply, not far behind the figure for urban populations (85%).

AGRICULTURE, FORESTRY AND FISHERIES

While Cotonou's urban trading economy is a crucial source of state revenues and livelihoods, the rural sectors remain hugely important: agriculture, livestock, forestry, hunting and fishing account for 30% of Benin's GDP. As its territory extends from the tropical coastal belt to the fringes of the Sahel, the country can produce a diverse range of crops; this is all the more important because, unlike all its immediate neighbours, it does not have significant mining or hydrocarbons activity to generate revenues and employment in provincial areas. Besides producing the main commercialized crops, rural household also grow vegetables and fruit, raise poultry and small livestock or earn revenues from small scale trading and crafts.

The major southern tropical crops include cassava, coconuts, yam, cocoa, pineapple and a small quantity of Robusta coffee; there are also commercial timber plantations, and fishing—both offshore and in lagoons—is an important source of income and nutrition. Further north, in the savannah belt, the farming economy is built around the production of cereals and cotton—

annual crops that are complementary and can be grown in rotation—and livestock husbandry, particularly for semi-nomadic groups such as the Peul. In the far north, large barely populated areas are set aside as wildlife reserves or national parks, but insecurity has drastically curbed normal tourism activity in the areas.

In the savannah and Sahelian regions the annual weather cycle is a crucial foundation: there is a single annual rainy season, from late June to early September, when crops are planted and grazing vegetation replenished; but the annual rains are vulnerable to annual fluctuations, droughts and the longer term impacts of climate change, which has rendered the weather less predictable. To manage these risks Benin participates in the regional network for data monitoring and crisis early warning systems overseen by the Comité Permanent Inter-Etats de Lutte Contre la Sécheresse dans le Sahel (Permanent Interstate Committee for Drought Control in the Sahel).

Most farmers are smallholders, relying on manual techniques or oxen-drawn ploughs. As in most West African countries, Government and development partners support efforts to improve yields and food and farm incomes through the use of improved seed, fertilizer and better cultivation, storage and processing techniques. Benin is mostly self-sufficient in the core food crops and is able to export surplus output to Nigeria.

Cotton, grown in the centre and north of the country, is Benin's most important export crop and a crucial source of cash income for many rural families. It plays a key role in the annual farming cycle of the main producing regions, which also grow cereals such as millet, sorghum and maize: cotton and the cereals are annual crops that can be grown in rotation and when cereals are planted on land that was used for cotton the previous year they benefit from the residues of the fertilizer that had been applied to boost the cotton yields. Farmers can adjust the way they split their land between cotton and cereals from year to year, depending on which is crop is attracting better prices, and that is influenced by the levels of state support for cotton (producer prices and the supply of inputs). For example, in the 2015/16 season the cotton harvest slumped by almost one-third, after a delay in the delivery of key inputs persuaded many farmers to switch more of their land to cereals; in the next year production rebounded. Harvests of both cotton and maize, by far the most important cereal crop, have been rising steadily since the 2017/18 season; production of millet and sorghum was also rising but slipped back somewhat in 2020/21.

After sinking to just 1.29m. metric tons in the 2015/16 agricultural year maize output has steadily grown, to 1.38m. tons in 2016/17 then to 1.58m. tons in 2019/20 and to 1.61m. tons in 2020/21. Millet and sorghum are produced in smaller volumes, although they cope well with the more difficult conditions in arid northern regions: output rose from 123,900 tons in 2014/15 to 154,800 tons in 2016/17, and then surged to 180,300 tons in 2017/18, and to 186,300 tons in 2019/20; however, it slipped back to 175,500 tons in 2020/21. The Government has also been encouraging the production of paddy rice, frequently planted in the north in low-lying seasonally irrigated troughs. Large volumes are exported informally into Nigeria—where demand for West African rice often outstrips supply—which means that official output data probably fails to capture the full picture. Nevertheless, even officially recorded production surged from 204,300 tons in 2015/16 to 281,400 tons in 2016/17 and to 361,300 tons in 2017/18 before reaching 406,100 tons in 2019/20 and 411,600 tons in 2020/21. Groundnuts are also an important crop that can be produced in both savannah and Sahelian areas as well as more humid tropical conditions: the harvest sank to just 134,300 tons in 2015/16, before gently rebounding to 137,200 tons the following season and then climbing to 156,900 tons in 2017/18 and to 172,600 tons in 2020/21.

Cassava and yams are grown in the tropical south and in the Atacora highlands in the north, where altitude moderates hot season temperatures. The cassava crop rose from 3.89m. metric tons in 2016/17 to 4.53m. tons in 2019/20, but slipped back to 4.16m. tons in 2020/21. Significant volumes are transformed into tapioca and gari (flour), some of which is exported to Nigeria and other countries in the region. Yam is also a major

crop in the tropical south: harvests rose from 3.04m. tons in 2016/17 to 3.37m. tons in 2019/20, before falling back to 3.15m. tons in 2020/21.

While food crops are grown mainly for domestic consumption and export to Nigeria, cotton is mostly produced for the international market, particularly as Benin's local textile industry has been squeezed hard by the competitive pressure of cheap imports from the People's Republic of China. The cotton sector represents as much as 12%–13% of GDP and ginning, the first stage processing of the crop, accounts for more than one-half of the country's industrial output and is a key source of formal sector employment in provincial areas. Because of cotton's importance as a source of cash income for so many rural households the crop is of real political significance, which adds to the sensitivities surrounding Talon's position as a major actor in the sector. During the Yayi presidency Talon secured majority control of the main ginning and marketing company, Société de Développement du Coton (SODECO), and the then Government agreed a development strategy with the Association Interprofessionnelle du Coton (AIC), the main representative of the private sector and producers, of which Talon was Vice-Chair; this prioritized the supply of improved seed, fertilizer and pesticide subsidies and a rise in the producer price paid to growers. However, after Yayi and Talon fell out the Government suspended the AIC, requisitioned six of the 10 SODECO ginning plants and itself took over responsibility for inputs supply, which it then mismanaged, leading to the 2015/16 slump in output. After Talon was himself elected President, in 2016, this rift was rapidly resolved, to the benefit both of farmers and his personal business interests. He quickly reinstated the accord with the AIC and ordered the settlement of 19,500m. francs CFA in overdue payments to growers, restoring their confidence in cotton as a source of income; they responded by allocating more land to the crop, triggering a rebound in output that has been sustained since the 2016/17 season. Talon also cancelled the requisition of the six SODECO ginning plants and ordered the payment of 12,000m. francs CFA in requisition royalty payments.

The cotton producer price output was set at 260 francs CFA per kg in 2016/17 but was increased to 265 francs CFA per kg for 2018/19; for the following two seasons the price was kept stable, but in a country where rates of inflation have been generally low that does not seem to have been a disincentive to farmers. Indeed, production continued on a steady upward trend. Harvest volumes are of course also influenced by other factors—the weather, affordable access to inputs and the relative attractiveness of local market prices for alternative annual crops such as cereals. Cotton output reached a nadir of 269,200 metric tons in 2013/14. However, thereafter the trend has been one of steady growth, assisted by mostly good rainfall and by the Talon Government's sustained focus on boosting the sector. In 2018/19 the area of land planted with cotton reached 656,000 ha, more than double the area allocated to the crop three seasons earlier, while yields have also improved, perhaps helped by fertilizer and other technical measures. Output surged reached 594,000 tons in 2017/18, 714,700 tons in 2019/20, before climbing to 731,100 tons in 2020/21 and an estimated 766,000 tons in 2021/22. The Government has set a target of eventually pushing output to 850,000 tons and the value of cotton exports soared from 161,600m. francs CFA in 2015 to 361,900m. francs CFA in 2020.

Meanwhile, Benin does produce a range of other crops and the Government is trying to encourage further diversification competitiveness, setting a target for the revamp of 135,000 ha of cashew plantations and 10,000 ha of banana plantations. Agriculture accounts for 70% of livelihoods and 75% of home-produced exports, and so increased output and the development of more value-added processing and marketing activity could significantly bolster rural employment and incomes. For example, cashew nut output has risen from 91,608 metric tons in 2015 to an estimated 180,000 tons in 2021, ranking cashews as Benin's second largest cash crop, accounting for 9% of domestically produced exports. For the 2020 season some 70 trading houses registered to export cashews. Yet only about 30,000 tons are processed locally at present. In an effort to push the sector into developing the Government has announced that the export of unprocessed cashews will be banned from April

2024 and aims to push total output to 350,000 tons. Benin already has a reputation for producing particularly high quality pineapples, many of which are exported to Nigeria, and efforts are now underway to develop organic production, which could attract an extra price premium in European markets. Moreover, one-half of the pineapple crop is already processed in Benin itself, adding extra value and employment. Producers and traders have lobbied for protection from Asian competition for Benin's cashews and pineapples; but securing ECOWAS agreement on effective region-wide measures could be difficult. Other southern cash crops include cocoa, coffee, palm oil and sugar cane, while mangoes, tomatoes and sheanuts (*karité*) are grown in the centre and north.

The Government encourages farmers to plant improved varieties of oil palm and cocoa bush, while oil processing plants have been privatized. UEMOA paid for 24 warehouses to store produce, while the Food and Agriculture Organization of the UN (FAO) is supporting a range of projects for agriculture, the environment and livestock—particularly important in northern areas. Villagers typically rely on a blend of arable farming, market gardening and livestock husbandry. In July 2020 the Government strengthened credit arrangements for farmers and decided to sell off many small local agro-processing plants in a bid to boost competitive efficiency.

As in most of coastal West Africa, fish is a key source of protein for Beninois. Annual consumer demand reaches 120,000 metric tons yet the national catch falls far short of this. Locally-based industrial deep sea boats land only a few thousands tons a year. The mainstay of the catch comes from the 5,000 or so coastal artisanal fishermen, using some 850 canoes and landing around 10,000 tons a year, and the 60,000 or so people employed in the artisanal fishing of rivers, coastal lagoons and lakes such as Lake Nokoué and processing the catch, of around 30,000 tons per year. Aquaculture is little developed so far.

With few deep-sea fishing vessels, Benin is unable to take full advantage of its 200 mile offshore economic zone, which is poorly guarded and widely poached by foreign vessels and has seen the disappearance of some species. (Neighbouring Togo protects its waters more effectively and lands around 100,000 metric tons, more than double that of Benin.) Artisanal coastal fishing communities have exclusive rights to the waters up to 9.5 km offshore, but some have been displaced to make way for coastal tourist projects. Lagoon fishermen tend to use small mesh nets that sweep up too many juvenile fish, threatening reproduction and future stocks, while water hyacinth—which sucks out the oxygen fish need to survive—has spread across considerable tracts of lake or lagoon. FAO is supporting the restoration of mangroves, to improve lagoon water health, and it also believes the coastal catch could be increased to 15,000 tons without damaging biomass.

MINING AND POWER

Although Nigeria and many other West African countries have substantial oil and gas reserves, few discoveries have been made in Benin, with production limited to small volumes of crude oil from the Sémé field in the 1990s. The Government introduced a new hydrocarbons code in January 2019, in the hope of stimulating fresh investor interest in exploration. So Benin is totally dependent on imported oil and gas. The national fuel distributor SONACOP, reliant on supplies purchased at world market prices, often struggles to compete against cheap imports smuggled in from the heavily subsidized Nigerian domestic market and sold informally at roadside stalls. In 2020 Nigeria abolished subsidies, thus significantly eroding the rationale for smuggling into Benin; however. after Russia's invasion of Ukraine sent world prices soaring again, Nigeria decided once again to heavily subsidize domestic sales of fuel, to keep its cost well below the market level. This restored the powerful economic rationale for smuggling into Benin. Benin does officially import gas from Nigeria, through the West African Gas Pipeline (which continues to Togo and Ghana).

The mining sector is small in scale. There are deposits of marble (which have sometimes been quarried) and chromium,

gold, iron ore, kaolin, phosphates and rutile. Limestone is quarried to supply the cement industry.

Some 41.4% of Benin's population now has access to electricity. As small neighbouring countries sharing some electricity generating potential—notably, the lower reaches of the Mono river—Benin and Togo set up the Communauté Electrique du Bénin (CEB) as a joint entity to manage generation and transmission infrastructure: the 66-MW Nangbeto hydro power station, two 20-MW thermal plants, a 1,763-km high tension distribution network, two interconnectors between Benin and Togo and a supply link from Nigeria. However, the CEB, operational from 1968, was unable to meet steadily rising demand. Benin has to import more than two-thirds of its electricity from Ghana—where generating capacity at the Akosombo hydro plant can be depressed in periods of low rainfall—and Côte d'Ivoire. To better meet their energy needs the two countries gradually began to develop separate national strategies, with Benin deciding to create its own national power generation company. They agreed to dissolve the CEB, a proposal formally adopted by the CEB board in March 2021.

Benin has therefore been pursuing a drive to boost its own generating capacity. The thermal generation site at Maria Gléta, north of Cotonou, is being expanded from its original 127 MW to an eventual 390 MW, to be fuelled with liquified natural gas (LNG) supplied by Total through a floating offshore terminal and pipeline under a July 2021 deal with the Government and national power utility Société Béninoise d'Energie Electrique (SBEE). Meanwhile Sinohydro Africa (of China) has been developing the 147-MW Adjarala hydro plant, while Voith Hydro, from Germany, has been rehabilitating Nangbeto. In July 2022 SBEE's 25-MW solar power plant at Illoulofin, built by RMT Eiffage of France, entered service; co-financed by the EU and the Agence Française de Développement (AFD) it has the capacity to supply 180,000 people and is connected to the national grid. Additional hydrogenerating capacity is also planned. Moreover, supply security has been enhanced by the 2018 creation of a West Africa integrated regional electricity market, overseen by the ECOWAS Regional Electricity Regulatory Authority and facilitating regional trade in power on transparent and to some extent standardized terms.

MANUFACTURING

Benin has a thin manufacturing base. The ginning of cotton (the key stage in the preparation of the crop for export) is the main contributor to manufacturing's average share of GDP of 14% in 2014–18. Besides the export trade, the ginneries also supply makers of downstream products such as cotton thread. Although cheap imports from China flood the textile market, the Government is trying to revive local production, to cater for the strong local demand for cotton clothing and rising European and North American demand for goods made from African hand-picked and often organic cotton. Cotton fibres that are too short to make thread are used to produce cooking oil and biofuel. The drive to develop the value-added processing of other crops, such as cashews, should gradually diversify the manufacturing sector.

Cement is produced by the Nouvelle Cimenterie du Bénin—with capacity to produce 1.5m. metric tons per year—and Onigbolo Cement, a Lafarge/Dangote joint venture, with a capacity of 600,000 tons. Beer and soft drinks, palm oil, construction materials and simple consumer goods are also made. Chinese interests run the Sucrerie de Complant du Benin sugar factory at Savé.

THE SERVICES SECTOR

Besides the main rural sectors, the urban importing and trading economy centred on Cotonou is a major pillar of output and employment, both formal and informal. The city is a trade gateway for both Nigeria and landlocked Sahelian countries, particularly Niger, and commercial services, banking and insurance accounted for 20% of GDP in 2015–19; if unrecorded informal activity were factored in, the true figure would probably be larger still. The flow of imported goods through Cotonou port feeds numerous warehouses across the city, where containers—many declared officially as imports into Benin itself—are unpacked, ready for goods to be moved onward into Nigeria, often through informal channels). Cotonou's main market is Dantokpa, in the city; but a second market was developed at Missebo, close to the Sémé-Kraké border post on the main highway to Lagos, specifically to cater for traders supplying Nigeria. The decision of Nigeria to close its land borders with Benin and Niger to the transit of goods, from August 2019 to the end of December 2020, had a substantial impact on formal trading activity, as did the COVID-19 pandemic; but it is difficult to gauge how much informal trade continued to flow across the border through the usual smuggling channels.

Beninois rely mainly on mobile telephones, with 92 subscriptions per 100 people. MTN and Moov are the country's longest established mobile operators, while the national utility, Société Béninoise d'Infrastructures Numériques (SBIN), runs the fixed-line network and the international submarine cable connections. To further diversify the mobile telecoms market, in May 2021 the Government awarded Société Nationale des Télécommunications du Sénégal—a national utility with long experience of providing mobile services—a management contract to run SBIN. There is also a programme of upgrades to the fixed-line network, with a 222-km loop around Cotonou and 235 km of fibre-optic connection; China's Huawei has built a 974-km high speed fibre-optic network, with 30 access points in the Cotonou area and at least 67 of Benin's 77 municipalities now have high speed broadband.

The country has 15 banks – and one other registered financial institution—including offshoots of groups owned or based in Burkina Faso (Coris), Cameroon (First Afriland), Côte d'Ivoire (NSIA), Gabon (BGFI), France (Société Générale), Morocco (CBAO Attijariwafa), Niger (Sonibank), Nigeria (Ecobank and UBA) and Togo (Banque Atlantique and Orabank). There are 4.74 ATM machines per 100,000 people, and in 2019 bank lending rose by 16.6%. The sector proved resilient in the face of the COVID-19 induced slowdown in growth in 2020: the proportion of its loan book that was non-performing or doubtful actually fell to 15.1% (from 16.8% in 2019), while the ratio of provisioning cover against such potential bad debts rose to 64.4% (from 58% in 2019). The solvability ratio also improved. However, the banking network is heavily tilted towards the Cotonou area and probably less than one-fifth of the population have an account at a financial institution, while only 2% of people have a mobile banking account—compared with 12% in Mali and 6% in Senegal.

Transport Infrastructure

Cotonou port has long been a trade gateway for Niger and Burkina Faso as well as Nigeria, offering modern facilities and easy road access, and competitive charges and electricity tariffs (to service refrigerated containers). It has two container terminals, operated by Bolloré and APM Terminals, and a roll-on-roll-off vehicles terminal. The port is a major employer and generator of spin-off jobs in the Cotonou trading and transport economy, typically generating 40% of the Government's fiscal receipts, as well as much revenue for Bénin Control, the company responsible for import verification, which is part of the Talon business empire. Thanks to its competitive pricing, efficiency and ease of access, Cotonou port became the second largest trade gateway to Nigeria, surpassed only by Lagos port itself; but this business—and particularly vehicle importation—was hit hard by Nigeria's closure of its land borders in 2019–20. Nevertheless, in 2021 the port handled 12.3m. metric tons of cargo and it remains one of West Africa's leading freight hubs.

However, the regional competition between ports is steadily intensifying: Lomé port, in Togo, has hugely expanded, while a major new container terminal is being developed at Lekki, east of Lagos. Therefore, in 2017 the Benin Government appointed the Port of Antwerp, one of Europe's largest, to manage Cotonou port and design a modernization plan, to expand the fuel terminal and increase the number of container gantry cranes from four to 16. In July 2022 a consortium led by the French engineering group Eiffage was awarded a €160m. contract to modernize and expand the port—a project that will take four years to complete but will equip Cotonou to accept the giant 'post-Panamax' container vessels.

Benin's road links are also being improved: much of the Benin section of the West African coastal highway from Lagos to Abidjan (Côte d'Ivoire) has been converted to dual carriageway. Integrated and modernized border crossings, designed to boost efficiency and reduce scope for corruption, have been opened at the Malanville/Gaya crossing into Niger and the Sémé-Kraké crossing on the main Cotonou–Lagos highway. However, uncertainty still hangs over plans to upgrade the rail line from Cotonou to Parakou, in central Benin, and extend this to Niamey.

The existing airport at Cotonou sits within the city, with little room for expansion. However, in June 2021 the Government confirmed that financing is now in place for China Aviation Industry Corporation, overseen by France's Groupe ADP, to build a new airport at Glo-Djigbé, with direct links to the main highways to Lomé and Lagos. No major regional carrier is based at Cotonou, so the new airport will struggle to compete with the established regional hubs—Lomé, home to ASKY, or Abidjan, the base for Air Ivoire.

FOREIGN TRADE AND PAYMENTS

Official trade figures provide only a partial picture because so much trade flows informally across the Nigeria border. Many goods declared officially as imports into Benin are subsequently re-exported, yet only part of this traffic shows up in official data.

Officially recorded imports rose from 1,293,600m. francs CFA in 2015 to 2,166,200m. francs CFA in 2018, before declining slightly to 2,051,400m. francs CFA, in 2019 and then dropping sharply, to just 1,668,500m. CFA, in 2020, the year of the pandemic and a resulting economic slowdown. Food accounts for the largest share of this trade, at 413,000m. francs CFA in 2020, ahead of imports of petroleum products worth 288,400m. CFA and imports of capital goods, including vehicles, worth 231,300m. francs CFA, all significantly down on 2019, both because of the COVID-19 slowdown and the impact of Nigerian restrictions on the official import of goods originally landed in Cotonou, such as vehicles. Benin's officially recorded imports of fuel do not include the large volumes smuggled from Nigeria.

Benin's official exports rose from 995,100m. francs CFA in 2015 to 1,857,600m. francs CFA in 2018, before falling back to 1,788,000m. francs CFA in 2019 and a mere 1,330,200m. francs CFA in 2020. Cotton remains the backbone of Benin's home produced export trade, with sales climbing steadily from just 60,700m. francs CFA in 2011 to 161,600m. francs CFA in 2015; problems in the sector reduced exports to 97,800m. francs CFA in 2016 but 2017 brought a sharp rebound, to 243,700m. francs CFA in 2017, followed by further continued growth, with cotton exports reaching 325,500m. francs CFA in 2019 and then 361,900m. francs CFA in 2020.

Exports of cashew nuts have fluctuated sharply, declining from 42,500m. francs CFA in 2015 to 23,100m. francs CFA in the following year, before rebounding to 48,300m. francs CFA in 2017 and 76,200m. francs CFA in 2018, only to plunge back to 44,700m. francs CFA in 2019 and a mere 19,500m. francs CFA in 2020; however, the shift towards more value added processing of cashews may also have an impact on the trend. Plantation production of teak is important in south-central Benin and exports of wood and wood products reached 8,700m. francs CFA in 2013, before sinking to just 400m. francs CFA in 2018 and then rebounding to 14,900m. francs CFA in 2019 and 15,600m. francs CFA in 2020. After deepening from 298,500m. francs CFA in 2015 to 396,800m. francs CFA in 2016 and to 494,600m. francs CFA in 2017, the deficit in merchandise trade shrank sharply to 308,600m. francs CFA in 2018 and only 263,300m. francs CFA the year after, before deepening once more, to 338,300m. francs CFA in 2020. Benin's largest export markets are the United Arab Emirates (which took an average of 22% of annual exports in 2015–19), India (19%) and China (6.3%). Official data show that only 19.7% went to other African countries, but this figure does not include the vast volumes of goods that move into Nigeria through informal channels and are not officially measured or recorded.

The overall balance of payments has a structural deficit of fluctuating size. It reached 539,700m. francs CFA in 2017, but fell to 360,400m. francs CFA in 2018 and 340,200m. francs CFA the year after, before edging back up to 353,500m. francs CFA in 2020, equivalent to 3.9% of GDP. Within this total remittance payments from the Beninois diaspora reached 125,200m. francs CFA in 2019; and, contrary to what had seemed likely, remittances actually rose slightly, to 126,100m. francs CFA in 2020, despite the recession caused by COVID-19 lockdown measures in France and other economies where expatriate Beninois live. Budget support from external donors more than doubled in 2020, to 123,800m. francs CFA, as key partners sought to help African countries cope with the impact of the pandemic. Net foreign direct investment flows, which also reflect fluctuations in the timing of specific projects or business transactions such as takeovers, fell from 112,000m. francs CFA in 2019 to 87,200m. francs CFA in 2020. However, interest payments on the Government's international debt surged dramatically, to 86,900m. francs CFA in 2020.

ECONOMIC PROSPECTS

Although the Beninois economy has rebounded strongly from the pandemic, the country still has vulnerabilities. The Nigerian border closure from August 2019 to the end of 2020 highlighted the fragility of the Cotonou re-export economy, both of official shipments, which were blocked, and informal movements that Nigerian border patrols tried to curb. This experience reminded Benin of the need to develop a more diverse, modern and formalized base of urban activity. With a large pool of highly educated professionals, Benin is well equipped to act as a service hub and bridge between Nigeria and its francophone neighbours. However, the growth of knowledge and service businesses, which tend to flourish in an open intellectual climate, could be hampered by the curbs on political choice and free expression that have developed since 2019 and by the cronyist constraints on independent entrepreneurialism. Yet if these pressures can be overcome, there is good potential for growth in the service, research and analysis sector.

Moreover, these economic prospects will be supported by the expansion of Cotonou port and construction of the city's new airport and, potentially, the construction of a rail line to Niger.

However, for the majority rural population, what will matter most is progress in diversifying agriculture and related downstream value-added activity. Benin certainly has the potential to further expand farm output, develop the processing of products such as cashews and pineapples, targeting European export markets. There is also scope to reinvigorate the textile sector, focusing on high quality products using local cotton and design skills, to cater for the domestic, West African and European markets.

Furthermore, the growing security threat posed by jihadists infiltrating from Burkina Faso represents a real danger for efforts to strengthen public services and economic diversification in northern areas. Concerns about insecurity could also weaken the investor confidence so important for a country such as Benin, which has few mineral or hydrocarbon extractive resources to bolster government revenues or the balance of payments and must rely strongly on its farming, trading and services skills.

Statistical Survey

Source (unless otherwise stated): Institut National de la Statistique et de l'Analyse Economique, BP 323, Cotonou; tel. 21-30-82-43; e-mail insae@insae-bj.org; internet www.insae-bj.org.

Area and Population

AREA, POPULATION AND DENSITY

Area (sq km)	114,763*
Population (census results)	
11 February 2002	6,769,914
11 May 2013	
Males	4,887,820
Females	5,120,929
Total	10,008,749
Population (UN estimates at mid-year)†	
2020	12,123,198
2021‡	12,451,031
2022‡	12,784,728
Density (per sq km) at mid-2022‡	111.4

* 44,310 sq miles.
† Source: UN, *World Population Prospects: The 2019 Revision.*
‡ Projection.

POPULATION BY AGE AND SEX
('000, UN projections at mid-2022)

	Males	Females	Total
0–14 years	2,689.9	2,613.7	5,303.6
15–64 years	3,514.2	3,542.3	7,056.5
65 years and over	184.8	239.8	424.6
Total	**6,389.0**	**6,395.8**	**12,784.7**

Note: Totals may not be equal to the sum of components, owing to rounding.

Source: UN, *World Population Prospects: The 2019 Revision.*

ADMINISTRATIVE DIVISIONS
(population at 2013 census)

Département	Area (sq km)	Population	Population density (per sq km)
Alibori	26,242	867,463	33.1
Atacora	20,499	772,262	37.7
Atlantique	3,233	1,398,229	432.5
Borgou	25,856	1,214,249	47.0
Collines	13,931	717,477	51.5
Couffo	2,404	745,328	310.0
Donga	11,126	543,130	48.8
Littoral	79	679,012	8,595.1
Mono	1,605	497,243	309.8
Ouémé	1,281	1,100,404	859.0
Plateau	3,264	622,372	190.7
Zou	5,243	851,580	162.4
Total	**114,763**	**10,008,749**	**87.2**

PRINCIPAL TOWNS
(population at 2013 census)

Cotonou . . .	679,012		Seme-Kpodji . .	222,701
Abomey-Calavi . .	656,358		Bohicon . . .	171,781
Djougou	267,812		Aplahoué . . .	171,109
Porto-Novo (capital)	264,320		Kalalé . . .	168,882
Parakou . . .	255,478		Malanville . .	168,641
Banikoara . . .	246,575		Ketou . . .	157,352
Tchaourou . . .	223,138		Savalou . . .	144,549

BIRTHS AND DEATHS
(annual averages, UN estimates)

	2005–10	2010–15	2015–20
Birth rate (per 1,000)	40.0	38.4	36.4
Death rate (per 1,000)	10.6	9.7	9.0

Source: UN, *World Population Prospects: The 2019 Revision*.

Birth rate: 34.6 per 1,000 in 2018 (Source: African Development Bank).

Death rate: 6.7 per 1,000 in 2018 (Source: African Development Bank).

Life expectancy (years at birth, estimates): 62.1 (males 60.5; females 63.6) in 2020 (Source: World Bank, World Development Indicators database).

ECONOMICALLY ACTIVE POPULATION
('000, FAO estimates at mid-year)

	2013	2014	2015
Agriculture, etc.	1,769	1,782	1,795
Total labour force (incl. others) .	4,268	4,399	4,534

Source: FAO.

2002 (census results): Total employed 2,811,753 (males 1,421,474, females 1,390,279); Unemployed 19,123 (males 12,934, females 6,189); Total labour force 2,830,876 (males 1,434,408, females 1,396,468).

Health and Welfare

KEY INDICATORS

Total fertility rate (children per woman, 2020)	4.7
Under-5 mortality rate (per 1,000 live births, 2020) . . .	85.9
HIV/AIDS (% of persons aged 15–49, 2020)	0.9
COVID-19: Cumulative confirmed deaths (per 100,000 persons at 31 August 2022)	1.3
COVID-19: Fully vaccinated population (% of total population at 14 August 2022)	20.7
Physicians (per 1,000 head, 2019)	0.7
Hospitals (per 100,000 head, 2013)	0.41
Domestic health expenditure (2019): US $ per head (PPP) .	18.6
Domestic health expenditure (2019): % of GDP . . .	0.5
Domestic health expenditure (2019): public (% of total current expenditure)	22.7
Access to improved water resources (% of persons, 2020) .	65
Access to improved sanitation facilities (% of persons, 2020) .	17
Total carbon dioxide emissions ('000 metric tons, 2018) . .	7,910
Carbon dioxide emissions per head (metric tons, 2018) . .	0.7
Human Development Index (2021): ranking	166
Human Development Index (2021): value	0.525

Note: For data on COVID-19 vaccinations, 'fully vaccinated' denotes receipt of all doses specified by approved vaccination regime (Sources: Johns Hopkins University and Our World in Data). Data on health expenditure refer to current general government expenditure in each case. For more information on sources and further definitions for all indicators, see Health and Welfare Statistics: Sources and Definitions section (europaworld.com/credits).

Agriculture

PRINCIPAL CROPS
('000 metric tons)

	2018	2019	2020
Bananas*	19.8	19.9	19.8
Beans, dry	140.5	132.5	134.9
Cashew nuts, with shell . .	115.6	130.3	190.0
Cassava (Manioc)	3,819.8	4,525.5	4,161.7
Chillies and peppers, green .	49.1	86.8	108.9
Coconuts	14.4†	14.0*	13.9*
Cotton lint	277.8*	300.0*	n.a.
Groundnuts, with shell . .	225.7	170.5	172.6
Maize	1,509.8	1,580.8	1,611.6
Millet	26.1	26.3	27.3
Oil palm fruit*	591.7	588.2	590.1

—continued	2018	2019	2020
Okra	63.3	46.1	55.1
Onions, dry	23.5	66.9	77.4
Pineapples	374.6	350.3	440.2
Rice, paddy	459.3	406.1	411.6
Seed cotton	677.7	714.7	728.0
Sorghum	319.2	160.0	148.2
Soybeans (Soya beans) . . .	222.0	257.0	254.0
Sugar cane	10.0†	10.0†	12.1*
Sweet potatoes	64.7	59.4	56.9
Tomatoes	253.2	360.3	261.1
Yams	2,944.9	3,365.5	3,150.2

* FAO estimate(s).
† Unofficial figure.

Aggregate production ('000 metric tons, may include official, semi-official or estimated data): Total cereals 2,320.8 in 2018, 2,177.8 in 2019, 2,203.1 in 2020; Total fruit (primary) 562.3 in 2018, 537.2 in 2019, 627.3 in 2020; Total oilcrops 1,756.2 in 2018, 1,769.2 in 2019, 1,783.4 in 2020; Total pulses 189.6 in 2018, 181.0 in 2019, 183.7 in 2020; Total roots and tubers 6,830.5 in 2018, 7,952.3 in 2019, 7,370.7 in 2020; Total treenuts 118.1 in 2018, 132.1 in 2019, 191.6 in 2020; Total vegetables (primary) 606.5 in 2018, 795.9 in 2019, 702.8 in 2020.

Source: FAO.

LIVESTOCK
('000 head, year ending September)

	2018	2019	2020
Cattle	2,462	2,526	2,592
Chickens	21,304	21,986	22,690
Goats	1,921	1,965	2,010
Pigs	504	524	545
Sheep	954	974	994

Source: FAO.

LIVESTOCK PRODUCTS
('000 metric tons)

	2018	2019	2020
Cattle hides, fresh*	6.9	7.0	7.2
Cattle meat	41.9	42.9	44.1
Cattle offals, edible*	8.4	8.6	8.8
Cows' milk	122.0	125.1	128.4
Chicken meat	14.6	15.0	15.5
Game meat*	8.2	8.2	8.2
Goat meat*	6.0	6.1	6.2
Goats' milk*	27.2	27.6	28.0
Pig meat*	6.6	6.8	7.1
Hen eggs	15.4	15.9	16.9

* FAO estimates.

Source: FAO.

Forestry

ROUNDWOOD REMOVALS
('000 cubic metres, excl. bark)

	2017	2018	2019
Sawlogs, veneer logs and logs for sleepers	133	133	133
Other industrial wood	252	252	252
Fuel wood	6,567	6,600	6,633
Total	6,952	6,984	7,018

2020: Production assumed to be unchanged from 2019 (FAO estimates).

Source: FAO.

SAWNWOOD PRODUCTION
('000 cubic metres, incl. railway sleepers, FAO estimates)

	2018	2019	2020
Total (all broadleaved) . . .	134	184	154

Source: FAO.

Fishing

('000 metric tons, live weight)

	2018	2019	2020
Capture	55.0	73.5*	74.0*
Tilapias	13.0	14.0*	13.7*
Torpedo-shaped catfishes . .	5.6	5.0*	5.2*
Diadromous clupeoids . . .	1.9	1.0*	1.3*
Lesser African threadfin . .	2.4	2.7	2.6*
West African croakers . . .	1.6	2.4	2.2*
West African Spanish mackerel	3.0	5.2	4.5*
Little tunny	4.0	4.5	4.4*
Guachanche barracuda . . .	n.a.	6.0	6.0*
Flyingfishes	2.1	n.a.	0.7
Freshwater crustaceans . .	2.8	2.6	2.7*
Aquaculture	5.1	5.7	3.0
Nile tilapia	2.8	2.8	1.6
Total catch (incl. others) . .	60.1	79.2*	77.0*

* FAO estimate.

Note: Figures exclude catches by Beninois canoes operating from outside the country.

Source: FAO.

Mining

	2006	2007	2008
Clay ('000 metric tons)	72.2	77.3	77.0
Gold (kg)	24	19	20
Gravel ('000 cu m)	10.6	25.3	25.0

2009–11: Production assumed to be unchanged from 2008 (estimates).

Source: US Geological Survey.

Industry

SELECTED PRODUCTS
('000 metric tons unless otherwise indicated)

	2017	2018	2019
Cement (hydraulic)	1,373	2,530	2,500*
Beer of barley†	106.5	106.5	105.0
Palm oil	70	75	78
Palm kernel oil†	9.1	9.8	10.2
Electrical energy (million kWh) .	331	202	529

* Estimate.
† Unofficial figures.

Sources: US Geological Survey; FAO; UN Energy Statistics Database.

Finance

CURRENCY AND EXCHANGE RATES

Monetary Units
100 centimes = 1 franc de la Communauté Financière Africaine (CFA).

Sterling, Dollar and Euro Equivalents (31 May 2022)
£1 sterling = 770.825 francs CFA;
US $1 = 612.300 francs CFA;
€1 = 655.957 francs CFA;
10,000 francs CFA = £12.97 = $16.33 = €15.25.

Average Exchange Rate (francs CFA per US $)
2019   585.951
2020   574.295
2021   554.603

Note: An exchange rate of 1 French franc = 50 francs CFA, established in 1948, remained in force until January 1994, when the CFA franc was devalued by 50%, with the exchange rate adjusted to 1 French franc = 100 francs CFA. This relationship to the French currency remained in effect with the introduction of the euro on 1 January 1999. From that date, accordingly, a fixed exchange rate of €1 = 655.957 francs CFA has been in operation.

BUDGET
('000 million francs CFA)

Revenue	2018	2019*	2020†
Tax revenue	811.4	893.3	829.9
Taxes on international trade and transactions‡	331.9	358.0	315.0
Direct and indirect taxes . .	479.4	535.3	514.9
Non-tax revenue	217.2	194.8	168.8
Grants	47.2	97.7	218.6
Total	1,075.8	1,185.7	1,217.3

Expenditure	2018	2019*	2020†
Salaries	356.7	369.7	394.7
Pensions and scholarships . .	92.2	90.5	103.0
Other expenditure and current transfers	283.0	306.0	451.8
Investment	445.6	330.4	531.8
Budgetary contribution . .	279.1	228.3	296.8
Financed from abroad . . .	166.5	102.1	235.0
Interest due	126.0	134.6	189.3
Internal	108.8	106.8	102.4
External	17.1	27.8	86.9
Net lending	2.5	−3.9	—
Total	1,305.9	1,227.3	1,670.6

* Estimates.
† Projections.
‡ Including value added taxes on imports.

Source: IMF, *Benin: Requests for Disbursement Under the Rapid Credit Facility and Purchase Under the Rapid Financing Instrument—Press Release; Staff Report; and Statement by the Executive Director for Benin* (January 2021).

INTERNATIONAL RESERVES
(excluding gold, US $ million at 31 December)

	2019	2020	2021
IMF special drawing rights . .	104.0	412.5	566.1
Reserve position in IMF . . .	25.2	26.2	25.6
Foreign exchange	1.1	2.0	3.3
Total	130.3	440.7	595.0

Source: IMF, *International Financial Statistics*.

MONEY SUPPLY
('000 million francs CFA at 31 December)

	2019	2020	2021
Currency outside depository corporations	569.4	713.7	757.7
Transferable deposits . . .	878.4	1,040.5	1,393.8
Other deposits	894.2	993.8	1,048.2
Broad money	2,342.0	2,747.9	3,199.7

Source: IMF, *International Financial Statistics*.

COST OF LIVING
(Consumer Price Index for African households in Cotonou; base: 2014 = 100)

	2019	2020	2021
Food and non-alcoholic beverages .	100.4	103.4	109.5
Clothing and footwear	104.6	106.7	109.0
Housing, fuel and other utilities .	99.9	102.8	100.8
All items (incl. others) . . .	101.1	104.2	106.0

NATIONAL ACCOUNTS
('000 million francs CFA at current prices)

Expenditure on the Gross Domestic Product

	2018	2019	2020
Government final consumption expenditure	825	872	871
Private final consumption expenditure	5,581	5,772	5,897
Gross fixed capital formation . .	2,052	2,123	2,436
Change in inventories . . .	38	38	38
Total domestic expenditure .	8,496	8,805	9,243
Exports of goods and services . .	2,161	2,499	1,617
Less Imports of goods and services	2,735	2,871	2,127
GDP in purchasers' values .	7,922	8,432	8,732
GDP in constant 2015 prices .	7,845	8,383	8,551

Gross Domestic Product by Economic Activity

	2018	2019	2020
Agriculture, hunting, forestry and fishing	2,223	2,266	2,428
Mining and utilities	86	95	98
Manufacturing	726	832	834
Construction	348	449	409
Wholesale and retail trade, restaurants and hotels . . .	1,255	1,287	1,374
Transport, storage and communication	883	981	989
Other activities	1,729	1,781	1,865
Sub-total	7,249	7,691	7,996
Indirect taxes (net)*	673	741	736
GDP in purchasers' values .	7,922	8,432	8,732

* Figures obtained as a residual.

Source: UN National Accounts Main Aggregates Database.

BALANCE OF PAYMENTS
(US $ million)

	2018	2019	2020
Exports of goods	3,344.4	3,056.5	2,995.8
Imports of goods	−3,899.9	−3,500.9	−3,152.1
Balance on goods	−555.6	−444.5	−156.2
Exports of services . . .	503.3	528.5	510.4
Imports of services . . .	−768.8	−805.7	−789.9
Balance on goods and services	−821.0	−721.7	−435.7
Primary income received . . .	106.8	124.0	212.3
Primary income paid	−161.9	−194.8	−333.6
Balance on goods, services and primary income	−876.1	−792.5	−557.1
Secondary income received . .	314.4	302.2	392.9
Secondary income paid . .	−87.1	−85.3	−128.2

—*continued*	2018	2019	2020
Current balance	−648.8	−575.6	−292.5
Capital account (net)	196.7	198.5	19.7
Direct investment assets . .	−9.8	−27.1	−21.5
Direct investment liabilities . .	194.1	218.2	174.0
Portfolio investment assets . .	92.9	−190.7	−790.7
Portfolio investment liabilities .	−92.5	215.6	280.6
Other investment assets . .	207.3	−296.3	−214.7
Other investment liabilities . .	300.3	465.2	840.2
Net errors and omissions . . .	−5.3	19.1	19.5
Reserves and related items .	234.8	26.7	14.6

Source: IMF, *International Financial Statistics*.

External Trade

PRINCIPAL COMMODITIES
(distribution by HS, US $ million)

Imports c.i.f.	2019	2020	2021
Live animals and animal products	226.1	204.2	240.6
Meat and meat products . . .	105.3	79.7	109.2
Meat and edible offal of poultry .	104.9	79.3	108.2
Fish, crustaceans, molluscs, and aquatic invertebrates . . .	104.8	110.7	114.2
Frozen fish (excluding fish fillets and other fish meat) . . .	104.5	110.4	113.9
Vegetables and vegetable products	642.0	470.9	731.8
Cereals	582.4	401.4	663.4
Rice	572.4	392.8	640.9
Animal or vegetable fats and oils, and products thereof .	122.7	71.5	80.2
Palm oil and its fractions, whether or not refined (excluding chemically modified)	121.8	69.7	7.6
Prepared foodstuffs; beverages, spirits, vinegars; tobacco and articles thereof	136.8	134.3	159.1
Mineral products	636.6	546.2	497.9
Mineral fuels, oils, distillation products, etc.	582.7	495.6	425.7
Petroleum oils	363.4	346.2	334.1
Electrical energy	140.7	96.0	—
Chemicals and related products	338.1	323.1	287.9
Pharmaceutical products . . .	124.2	125.2	146.6
Medicaments consisting of mixed or unmixed products for therapeutic or prophylactic uses	109.3	106.6	125.3
Fertilizers	111.4	83.6	52.3
Iron and steel; other base metals and articles of base metal .	141.7	156.3	240.6
Iron and steel	92.1	88.4	142.4
Machinery and mechanical appliances; electrical equipment; parts thereof .	237.6	247.8	310.2
Machinery, boilers, etc.	148.9	125.9	162.5
Electrical, electronic equipment .	88.7	121.9	147.7
Vehicles, aircraft, vessels and associated transport equipment	212.3	218.0	339.7
Vehicles other than railway, tramway	209.3	216.8	312.6
Total (incl. others)	2,936.1	2,660.6	3,188.2

Exports f.o.b.	2019	2020	2021
Live animals and animal products	21.3	0.6	0.6
Meat and edible meat offal	19.7	0.0	0.0
Vegetables and vegetable products	143.5	123.1	105.9
Edible fruit, nuts, peel of citrus fruit, melons	77.6	60.1	52.3
Brazil nuts, cashew nuts and coconuts	76.3	57.0	48.7
Oil seeds and oleaginous fruits, miscellaneous grains, seeds and fruit	62.5	61.2	50.8
Animal or vegetable fats and oils, and products thereof	33.2	17.3	21.9
Prepared foodstuffs; beverages, spirits, vinegars; tobacco and articles thereof	32.4	51.2	47.4
Mineral products	50.5	56.1	49.0
Mineral fuels, oils, distillation products, etc.	25.6	37.8	37.4
Petroleum oils	24.9	37.2	37.1
Textiles and textile articles	467.6	474.7	641.5
Cotton	466.9	472.5	637.3
Cotton, not carded or combed	450.4	450.9	625.2
Pearls, precious stones, metals, coins, etc.	14.8	14.8	15.3
Gold unwrought or in semi-manufactured forms	14.8	14.8	15.3
Iron and steel; other base metals and articles of base metal	32.0	33.4	64.3
Iron and steel	23.6	24.7	50.4
Machinery and mechanical appliances; electrical equipment; parts thereof	10.1	36.2	23.5
Machinery, boilers, etc.	6.1	13.9	16.1
Total (incl. others)	850.6	845.4	1,024.2

Source: Trade Map-Trade Competitiveness Map, International Trade Centre, marketanalysis.intracen.org.

PRINCIPAL TRADING PARTNERS
(US $ million)

Imports c.i.f.	2019	2020	2021
Argentina	46.5	2.3	3.4
Belgium	111.0	165.5	177.8
Brazil	46.6	51.5	48.0
China, People's Republic	325.1	305.1	374.3
Côte d'Ivoire	56.6	78.3	38.2
France	259.2	274.5	350.2
Germany	41.8	38.8	42.4
Ghana	43.2	37.7	33.7
India	400.1	304.0	547.3
Indonesia	37.3	15.7	51.9
Italy	25.6	37.4	47.2
Malaysia	34.1	31.6	42.5
Mauritania	61.4	29.8	32.3
Morocco	83.9	39.9	75.5
Netherlands	76.5	47.8	47.5
Nigeria	61.1	45.2	67.3
Pakistan	34.0	26.4	24.2
Russian Federation	76.2	115.6	68.4
Singapore	13.0	45.0	43.3
Spain	39.5	47.2	42.0
Switzerland	10.2	35.2	56.7
Thailand	158.0	75.2	102.9
Togo	317.4	221.5	133.3
Türkiye	67.9	101.6	108.7
Ukraine	33.7	10.7	30.8
United Arab Emirates	99.8	57.0	126.9
United Kingdom	25.7	56.3	66.3
USA	71.1	89.1	84.8
Total (incl. others)	2,936.1	2,660.6	3,188.2

Exports f.o.b.	2019	2020	2021
Bangladesh	229.0	325.6	427.4
Burkina Faso	19.6	20.8	15.8
Chad	5.5	13.3	36.6
China, People's Republic	62.8	56.1	100.7
Côte d'Ivoire	11.1	12.7	11.6
Denmark	30.3	31.6	23.8
Egypt	29.3	14.8	27.5
India	120.7	100.3	102.0
Malaysia	25.1	39.9	15.6
Mali	4.2	8.6	6.1
Netherlands	9.4	11.0	4.8
Niger	26.5	23.0	29.8
Nigeria	48.1	8.5	8.7
Pakistan	0.3	9.6	20.8
Singapore	16.0	3.3	2.9
Togo	6.7	8.9	14.9
Türkiye	15.0	3.3	16.4
Ukraine	18.5	39.7	22.2
United Arab Emirates	15.4	30.3	21.0
USA	15.6	8.1	2.5
Viet Nam	88.3	25.6	51.3
Total (incl. others)	850.6	845.4	1,024.2

Source: Trade Map-Trade Competitiveness Map, International Trade Centre, marketanalysis.intracen.org.

Transport

ROAD TRAFFIC
(new motor vehicles registered)

	2017	2018	2019
Passenger cars	20,529	19,374	19,119
Buses and coaches	737	521	424
Lorries and vans	6,146	4,490	5,124
Motorcycles and mopeds	117,792	173,344	192,933
Other vehicles	5	0	1,518

RAILWAYS
(traffic)

	2004	2005	2006
Passenger-km (million)	45.4	17.0	—
Freight ton-km (million)	33.8	23.0	28.9

Source: mainly IMF, *Benin: Selected Issues and Statistical Appendix* (August 2008).

SHIPPING

Flag Registered Fleet
(at 31 December)

	2019	2020	2021
Number of vessels	6	6	7
Total displacement (grt)	991	991	991

Source: Lloyd's List Intelligence (www.bit.ly/LLintelligence).

International Seaborne Freight Traffic
(at Cotonou, including goods in transit, '000 metric tons)

	2009	2010	2011
Goods loaded	731.2	719.7	1,032.0
Goods unloaded	5,967.1	6,239.6	5,756.7

CIVIL AVIATION
(scheduled services)

	2010	2011	2012
Passengers carried ('000)	413	433	446
Total freight carried (metric tons)	7,097	6,823	6,962

Tourism

FOREIGN VISITORS BY COUNTRY OF ORIGIN*

	2018	2019	2020
Burkina Faso	14,960	15,236	15,366
Cameroon	8,390	9,521	9,618
Congo, Republic	8,042	8,785	8,744
Côte d'Ivoire	12,140	13,125	13,467
China, People's Republic	10,233	10,494	11,256
France	14,645	14,724	13,870
Ghana	8,255	8,460	7,240
Mali	4,522	4,830	4,969
Netherlands	10,915	11,130	10,230
Niger	16,920	17,099	17,620
Nigeria	29,085	31,708	32,150
Senegal	12,020	11,886	10,270
Switzerland	8,466	8,566	9,600
Togo	15,600	15,188	15,426
Total (incl. others)	294,753	309,491	324,966

* Arrivals of non-resident tourists at national borders, by country of residence.

Tourism receipts (US $ million, excl. passenger transport): 123 in 2016; 150 in 2017; 162 in 2018.

Source: World Tourism Organization.

Communications Media

	2018	2019	2020
Telephones (main lines in use)	48,508	35,917	32,386
Mobile telephone subscriptions ('000)	9,461.9	10,349.8	11,140.9
Broadband subscriptions, fixed ('000)	27.0	25.4	30.0
Broadband subscriptions, mobile ('000)	2,273.6	2,532.3	3,300.0
Internet users (% of persons)	19.0	22.4	25.8

Source: International Telecommunication Union.

Education

(2019/20 unless otherwise indicated)

	Institutions*	Teachers	Students ('000)		
			Males	Females	Total
Pre-primary	2,866	6,535	78.9	77.8	156.7
Primary	11,154	57,002	1,149.1	1,033.6	2,182.7
Secondary	1,791	48,785	495.6	390.8	886.4
Tertiary†	n.a.	2,672	90.8	41.6	132.4

* 2018/19.
† 2017/18.

Source: UNESCO Institute for Statistics.

Pupil-teacher ratio (qualified teaching staff, primary education, UNESCO estimate): 38.3 in 2019/20 (Source: UNESCO Institute for Statistics).

Adult literacy rate (UNESCO estimates): 42.4% (males 54.0%; females 31.1%) in 2018 (Source: UNESCO Institute for Statistics).

Directory

The Constitution

A new Constitution was approved in a national referendum on 2 December 1990. Its main provisions, including amendments adopted in November 2019, are summarized below:

PREAMBLE

The Beninois People reaffirm their opposition to any political regime founded on arbitrariness, dictatorship, injustice and corruption, reassert their attachment to the principles of democracy and human rights, as defined in the United Nations Charter, the Universal Declaration of Human Rights and the African Charter of the Rights of Man and Peoples, proclaim their attachment to the cause of African Unity and solemnly adopt this new Constitution as the supreme Law of the State.

I. THE STATE AND SOVEREIGNTY

Articles 1–6: The State of Benin is an independent, sovereign, secular, democratic Republic. The capital is Porto-Novo. The official language is French. The principle of the Republic is 'government of the People, by the People and for the People'. National sovereignty belongs to the People and is exercised through elected representatives and by referendums. Political parties operate freely, as determined by the Charter of Political Parties, and must respect the principles of national sovereignty, democracy, territorial integrity and the secular basis of the state. Suffrage is universal, equal and secret.

II. RIGHTS AND DUTIES OF THE INDIVIDUAL

Articles 7–40: The state is obliged to respect and protect the sacred and inviolable rights of the individual, and ensures equal access to health, education, culture, information, vocational training and employment. Primary education is compulsory. The state progressively assures the provision of free public education. Private schools are permitted. Torture and the use of cruel or degrading punishment are prohibited, and detention is subject to strict limitations. All persons have the right to property ownership, to freedom of conscience and expression. The state guarantees the freedoms of movement and association. All are equal before the law. The state recognizes the right to strike. Military service is compulsory.

III. THE EXECUTIVE

Articles 41–78: The President of the Republic is the head of state. Candidates for the presidency must be of Beninois nationality by birth or have been naturalized for at least 10 years, and must be aged 40–70 years. The President is elected (together with a Vice-President) for a mandate of five years, renewable only once, by an absolute majority of votes cast. If no candidate receives an absolute majority, a second round is to be held between the two highest placed candidates. The Constitutional Court oversees the regularity of voting and announces the results. No President may serve more than two mandates.

The President of the Republic holds executive power and is head of the Government. Following consultation with the Bureau of the National Assembly, he or she names the members of the Government, who may not hold any parliamentary mandate. The President of the Republic chairs the Council of Ministers and has various defined powers of appointment.

The President of the Republic promulgates laws adopted by the National Assembly, and may demand the resubmission of a law to the National Assembly prior to its promulgation. In the event that the President of the Republic fails to promulgate a law, the Constitutional Court may, in certain circumstances, declare the law as binding.

After consultation with the President of the National Assembly and the President of the Constitutional Court, the President of the Republic may call a referendum on matters pertaining to human rights, subregional or regional integration or the organization of public powers. The President of the Republic is the Supreme Chief of the Armed Forces.

The President of the Republic may delegate certain specified powers to ministers. The President of the Republic or any member of his or her Government may be called to account by the National Assembly.

In the event of the presidency becoming vacant as a result of the death, resignation or impeachment of the President, the Vice-President automatically assumes the presidency.

IV. THE LEGISLATURE

i. The National Assembly

Articles 79–93: Parliament exercises legislative power and controls the activities of the Government. Deputies of the National Assembly, who must be civilians, are elected by direct universal suffrage for five years, and may be re-elected twice. The National Assembly elects its President and a Bureau. Deputies enjoy various conditions of immunity from prosecution.

ii. Relations between the National Assembly and the Government

Articles 94–113: Members of the Government may attend sessions of the National Assembly. Laws are approved by a simple majority, although organic laws require an absolute majority and approval by the Constitutional Court. The National Assembly authorizes any declaration of war. States of siege and of emergency are declared in the Council of Ministers, although the National Assembly must approve the extension of any such state beyond 15 days.

Deputies may, by a three-quarters' majority, decide to submit any question to referendum. If the National Assembly has not approved a balanced budget by 31 December of any year, the measures foreseen by the finance law may be implemented by ordinance.

V. THE CONSTITUTIONAL COURT

Articles 114–124: The Constitutional Court is composed of seven members, of whom four are named by the Bureau of the National Assembly and three by the President of the Republic, each for a mandate of five years, renewable only once. The President of the Constitutional Court is elected by his or her peers for a period of five years and is a senior magistrate or lawyer. The decisions of the Constitutional Court are not subject to appeal.

VI. THE JUDICIARY

Articles 125–130: The judiciary is independent of the legislature and of the executive. It consists of the Supreme Court, and other courts and tribunals created in accordance with the Constitution. Judges may not be removed from office. The President of the Republic appoints magistrates and is the guarantor of the independence of the judiciary, assisted by the Higher Council of Magistrates, the composition, attributes, organization and function of which are fixed by an organic law.

i. The Supreme Court

Articles 131–134: The Supreme Court is the highest jurisdiction of the state in administrative and judicial matters. The decisions of the Court are not subject to appeal. The President of the Supreme Court is appointed for five years by the President of the Republic. The President of the Supreme Court may not be removed from office during his or her mandate, which is renewable only once.

ii. The High Court of Justice

Articles 135–138: The High Court of Justice comprises the members of the Constitutional Court (other than its President), six deputies of the National Assembly and the President of the Supreme Court. The High Court of Justice elects a President from among its members and is competent to try the President of the Republic and members of the Government in cases of high treason, crimes committed during the exercise of their functions and plots against state security. In the event of an accusation of high treason or of contempt of the National Assembly, and in certain other cases, the President of the Republic and members of the Government are to be suspended from their functions. In the case of being found guilty of such charges, they are dismissed from their responsibilities.

VII. THE ECONOMIC AND SOCIAL COUNCIL

Articles 139–141: The Economic and Social Council advises on proposed laws, ordinances or decrees that are submitted to it. Proposed laws of an economic or social nature must be submitted to the Council.

VIII. THE HIGH AUTHORITY FOR BROADCASTING AND COMMUNICATION

Articles 142–143: The High Authority for Broadcasting and Communication assures the freedom of the press and all other means of mass communication. It oversees the equitable access of political parties, associations and citizens to the official means of communication and information.

IX. INTERNATIONAL TREATIES AND ACCORDS

Articles 144–149: The President of the Republic negotiates and ratifies international treaties and accords. Peace treaties, those relating to international organization or territorial changes and to certain other matters must be ratified by law.

X. LOCAL AUTHORITIES

Articles 150–152: The local authorities of the Republic are created by law and are freely administered by elected councils. Their development is overseen by the state.

XI. GENERAL ELECTIONS

Articles 153–157: Legislative and communal elections are held on the second Tuesday in January. The presidential election is held on the second Tuesday in April.

The Government

HEAD OF STATE

President: PATRICE TALON (inaugurated 6 April 2016; re-elected 11 April 2021).

COUNCIL OF MINISTERS
(October 2022)

President: PATRICE TALON.

Minister of State, Minister of Development and Co-ordination of Government Actions: ABDOULAYE BIO TCHANÉ.

Minister of State, Minister of the Economy and Finance: ROMUALD WADAGNI.

Keeper of the Seals, Minister of Justice and Legislation: SÉVÉRIN LUDOVIC MAXIME QUENUM.

Minister of Foreign Affairs and Co-operation: AURÉLIEN AMAH AGBÉNONCI.

Minister of the Interior and Public Security: ALASSANE SEIDOU.

Minister of Quality of Life and Sustainable Development: JOSÉ DIDIER TONATO.

Minister of Agriculture, Stockbreeding and Fisheries: COSSI GASTON DOSSOUHOUI.

Minister of Decentralization and Local Government: RAPHAËL DOSSOU AKOTEGNON.

Minister of Labour and the Civil Service: ADIDJATOU ALAYI MATHYS.

Minister of Social Affairs and Microfinance: VÉRONIQUE TOGNIFODE MEWANOU.

Minister of Health: BENJAMIN IGNACE BODOUNRIN HOUNKPATIN.

Minister of Higher Education and Scientific Research: ELÉONORE YAYI LADEKAN.

Minister of Secondary and Technical Education and Professional Training: YVES KOUARO CHABI.

Minister of Nursery and Primary Education: SALIMANE KARIMOU.

Minister of Tourism, Culture and the Arts: BABALOLA JEAN-MICHEL HERVÉ ABIMBOLA.

Minister of Digital Technology and Digitalization: AURÉLIE ADAM SOULÉ ZOUMAROU.

Minister of Infrastructure and Transport: HERVÉ YVES HEHOMY.

Minister of Industry and Trade: SHADIYA ALIMATOU ASSOUMAN.

Minister of Energy: DONA JEAN-CLAUDE HOUSSOU.

Minister of Water and Mining: SAMOU SEÏDOU ADAMBI.

Minister of Small and Medium-sized Enterprises and the Promotion of Employment: MODESTE TIHUNTÉ KÉRÉKOU.

Minister of Sport: OSWALD HOMEKY.

Minister-delegate to the President of the Republic, in charge of National Defence: FORTUNET ALAIN NOUATIN.

MINISTRIES

Office of the President: BP 1288, Cotonou; tel. 21-30-00-90; internet presidence.bj.

Ministry of Agriculture, Stockbreeding and Fisheries: 03 BP 2900, Cotonou; tel. 21-30-04-10; internet agriculture.gouv.bj.

Ministry of Decentralization and Local Government: Cotonou; tel. 21-30-40-30; e-mail decentralisation.infos@gouv.bj; internet decentralisation.gouv.bj.

Ministry of Development and Co-ordination of Government Actions: Route de l'Aéroport, 08 BP 755, Cotonou; tel. 21-30-07-42; e-mail mdc.info@gouv.bj; internet developpement.gouv.bj.

Ministry of Digital Technology and Digitalization: 01 BP 120, Cotonou; tel. 21-31-22-27; e-mail ministre@communication.gouv.bj; internet numerique.gouv.bj.

Ministry of the Economy and Finance: Route de l'Aéroport, 01 BP 301, Cotonou; tel. 21-30-87-85; e-mail contact@finances.bj; internet finances.bj.

Ministry of Energy: ave Jean-Paul II, 04 BP 1412, Cotonou; tel. 21-31-29-07; e-mail contact.me@gouv.bj; internet energie.gouv.bj.

Ministry of Foreign Affairs and Co-operation: pl. des Martyrs, route de l'Aéroport, 06 BP 318, Cotonou; tel. 21-30-04-00; e-mail contact@diplomatie.gouv.bj; internet diplomatie.gouv.bj.

Ministry of Health: Immeuble ex-MCAT, 01 BP 882, Cotonou; tel. 21-33-21-63; e-mail sante.infos@gouv.bj; internet sante.gouv.bj.

Ministry of Higher Education and Scientific Research: 01 BP 348, Cotonou; tel. 21-30-06-81; e-mail contact.mesrs@gouv.bj; internet enseignementsuperieur.gouv.bj.

Ministry of Industry and Trade: BP 363, Cotonou; tel. 21-30-76-45; internet commerce.gouv.bj.

Ministry of Infrastructure and Transport: 01 BP 372, Cotonou; tel. 21-31-46-64; internet transports.bj.

Ministry of the Interior and Public Security: BP 925, Cotonou; tel. 21-30-11-06.

Ministry of Justice and Legislation: ave Pape Jean Paul 2, BP 2493, Cotonou; tel. 21-31-31-46; e-mail justice@gouv.bj; internet justice.gouv.bj.

Ministry of Labour and the Civil Service: BP 907, Cotonou; tel. 21-33-23-30; e-mail mtfp.usager@gouv.bj; internet travail.gouv.bj.

Ministry of Nursery and Primary Education: 01 BP 10, Porto-Novo; tel. 20-21-33-27.

Ministry of Quality of Life and Sustainable Development: rue 637, Cotonou; tel. 21-31-50-58; internet cadredevie.gouv.bj.

Ministry of Secondary and Technical Education and Professional Training: 10 BP 348, Cotonou; tel. 21-30-06-81; internet enseignementsecondaire.gouv.bj.

Ministry of Small and Medium-sized Enterprises and the Promotion of Employment: Cotonou; internet pmepe.gouv.bj.

Ministry of Social Affairs and Microfinance: Cotonou; tel. 60-42-02-02; e-mail spmicrofinance@gouv.bj; internet social.gouv.bj.

Ministry of Sport: Cotonou; internet fb.com/msportbenin.

Ministry of Tourism, Culture and the Arts: Route de l'Aéroport, BP 2037, Cotonou; tel. 21-30-70-13; e-mail mtca.sp@gouv.bj; internet fb.com/tourismebj229.

Ministry of Water and Mining: Immeuble Loko, Cadjèhoun, BP 1412, Cotonou; tel. 21-30-45-10; e-mail eaumines@gouv.bj; internet eau-mines.gouv.bj.

President

Presidential Election, 11 April 2021

Candidate	Valid votes	% of valid votes
Patrice Talon	1,982,534	86.30
Alassane Soumanou	261,096	11.37
Corentin Kohoué	53,685	2.34
Total	**2,297,315***	**100.00**

* Excluding 134,099 invalid votes.

Legislature

National Assembly: BP 371, Porto-Novo; tel. 20-21-36-44; e-mail infos@assemblee-nationale.bj; internet assemblee-nationale.bj.

President: Louis Gbéhounou Vlavonou.

General Election, 28 April 2019

Party	Seats
Union Progressiste	47
Bloc Républicain	36
Total	**83**

Election Commission

Commission Electorale Nationale Autonome (CENA): 01 BP 443, Cotonou; tel. 21-31-41-24; e-mail contact@cena.bj; internet www.cena.bj; f. 1994; 5 mems appointed by the National Assembly; Pres. Sacca Lafia.

Advisory Council

Economic and Social Council (Conseil Economique et Social—CES): ave Jean-Paul II, 08 BP 679, Cotonou; tel. 21-30-03-91; e-mail contact@ces.bj; internet ces.bj; f. 1994; 30 mems, representing the executive, legislature and 'all sections of the nation'; reviews all legislation relating to economic and social affairs; competent to advise on proposed economic and social legislation, as well as to recommend economic and social reforms; Pres. Augustin Tabé Gbian; Sec.-Gen. Charlemagne Tomavo.

Political Organizations

Alliance Nationale pour la Démocratie et le Développement (AND): Cotonou; composed of 18 political orgs; Nat. Co-ordinator Valentin Aditi Houdé.

Alliance Soleil: Cotonou; f. 2014; Pres. Sacca Lafia.

  Force Espoir: Cotonou; Leader Antoine Dayori.

Bloc Républicain (BR): tel. 60-60-32-33; e-mail ecrire@blocrepublicain.co; internet www.blocrepublicain.co; f. 2018; led by a 59-mem. political bureau comprising political leaders and personalities supportive of Pres. Patrice Talon; Nat. Sec.-Gen. Abdoulaye Bio Tchané.

Congrès pour la Mobilisation des Valeurs Citoyennes (CMVC): Pres. Etienne Kossi.

Les Démocrates: Saint-Michel, Cotonou; tel. 97000000; e-mail contact@lesdemocrates.bj; internet lesdemocrates.bj; f. 2020; Pres. Eric Houndété.

Force Cauris pour un Bénin Emergent (FCBE): tel. 95861100; Nat. Exec. Sec. Valentin Djènontin.

Mouvement Africain pour la Démocratie et le Progrès (MADEP): BP 1509, Cotonou; tel. 21-31-31-22; f. 1997; Leader El Hadj Séfou L. Fagbohoun.

Mouvement pour le Développement et la Solidarité (MDS): BP 73, Porto-Novo; Leader Sacca Moussédikou Fikara.

Mouvement des Ecologistes du Bénin (MEB-Les Verts): BP 3492, Abomey-Calavi; tel. 97-86-41-41; internet fb.com/meblesverts; Pres. Florent Tokin.

La Nouvelle Alliance (LNA): Cotonou; f. 2021; Pres. Théophile Yarou Kora Woodi; Sec.-Gen. Dr Faton : de Laure Laurent.

Parti Démocrate: Cotonou; f. 2016; Pres. Martin Rodriguez.

Parti du Progrès de la Démocratie Béninoise (PPDB): Pres. Emmanuel Koï.

Parti Social-Démocrate–Golou wing (PSD): BP 2205, Cotonou; Leader Emmanuel Golou.

Réveil Patriotique: Leader Janvier Yahouédéhou.

Union des Forces Démocratiques (UFD): Parakou; f. 1994; Leader Sacca Georges Zimé.

Union Progressiste le Renouveau (UPR): Cotonou; internet fb.com/unionprogressiste1; f. 2022 following merger of Union Progressiste and Parti du Renouveau Démocratique; pro-Pres. Patrice Talon; Pres. Joseph Djogbénou.

Les Verts du Bénin—Parti Écologiste du Bénin: 06 BP 1336, Cotonou; tel. 21-35-19-47; e-mail greensbenin@yahoo.fr; f. 1995; Pres. Toussaint Hinvi.

Diplomatic Representation

EMBASSIES IN BENIN

Belgium: Les Cocotiers, Lot 12N, 01 BP 1881, Cotonou; tel. 21-30-18-75; e-mail cotonou@diplobel.fed.be; internet benin.diplomatie.belgium.be; Ambassador (vacant).

Brazil: Residence Laico, Villa B16, blvd CEN SAD, 01 BP 534, Cotonou; tel. 21-31-55-16; e-mail brasemb.cotonou@itamaraty.gov.br; internet www.gov.br/mre/pt-br/embaixada-cotonou; Ambassador Luís Regina Célia de Oliveira Bittencourt.

China, People's Republic: 2 route de l'Aéroport, 01 BP 196, Cotonou; tel. 21-30-12-92; e-mail chinaemb_bj@mfa.gov.cn; internet bj.china-embassy.gov.cn; Ambassador Peng Jingtao.

Congo, Democratic Republic: Lot 1158, Haie-vive, 01 BP 130, Cotonou; tel. 21-30-91-78; Chargé d'affaires a.i. AZIMBA MINDIA.

Cuba: Carré 4234, Lot 572, Quartier Zongo-Ehuzu, 01 BP 948, Cotonou; tel. 67010027; e-mail embajador@bj.embacuba.cu; internet misiones.minrex.gob.cu/es/benin; Ambassador YENIELYS VILMA REGUEIFEROS LINARES.

Egypt: Lot G26, route de l'Aéroport, BP 1215, Cotonou; tel. 21-30-08-42; e-mail embassy.cotonou@mfa.gov.eg; Ambassador AMAL AFIFI.

France: 2235 ave Jean-Paul II, BP 966, Cotonou; tel. 21-36-55-33; e-mail secretariat.cotonou-amba@diplomatie.gouv.fr; internet bj.ambafrance.org; Ambassador MARC VIZY.

Germany: 1438 ave Jean-Paul II, 01 BP 504, Cotonou; tel. 21-31-29-67; e-mail info@cotonou.diplo.de; internet cotonou.diplo.de; Ambassador MICHAEL DERUS.

Ghana: route de l'Aéroport, Lot F, Les Cocotiers, BP 488, Cotonou; tel. 21-30-07-46; e-mail ghcotonou@yahoo.com; internet www.ghanaembassybenin.com; Ambassador CHRISTINE CHURCHER.

Holy See: 08 BP 400, Cotonou; tel. 21-30-03-08; e-mail nonciaturebenin@gmail.com; Apostolic Nuncio MARK GERARD MILES (Titular Archbishop of Città Ducale).

Japan: Zone Résidentielle de Cotonou, Djomehountin Cotonou; tel. 21-30-59-86; internet www.bj.emb-japan.go.jp; Ambassador TAKAHISA TSUGAWA.

Kuwait: derrière l'hôtel Novotel Cotonou, Villa Roc Fleuri No. 2, Cotonou; tel. 21-00-29-01; e-mail ambassade.koweit.benin@gmail.com; Ambassador MESHAL AHMAD AL-MANSOUR (designate).

Libya: Carré 36, BP 405, Cotonou; tel. 21-30-04-52; e-mail busheha2015@gmail.com; Ambassador OMAR ABDEL HADI AL-FARGANY.

Morocco: Cotonou; tel. 97724251; e-mail ambmacoo.benin@gmail.com; Ambassador RACHID RGUIBI.

Netherlands: ave Jean-Paul II, route de l'Aéroport, derrière le Tri Postal, 08 BP 0783, Cotonou; tel. 21-30-04-39; e-mail cot@minbuza.nl; internet www.paysbasmondial.nl/pays/benin; Ambassador TO TJOELKER-KLEVE.

Niger: derrière l'Hôtel de la Plage, BP 352, Cotonou; tel. 21-31-56-65; e-mail aissataamadou2@gmail.com; Ambassador SIDI ABDOU.

Nigeria: blvd de la CENSAD, BP 2019, Cotonou; tel. 21-30-11-42; e-mail nigembctn@ymail.com; Ambassador Lt-Gen. (retd) TUKUR YUSUFU BURATAI.

Qatar: Quartier Djomehountin, Lot 1, Allee Aphrodite 1, Cotonou; tel. 21-50-07-26; e-mail cotonou@mofa.gov.qa; internet cotonou.qa; Ambassador (vacant).

Russian Federation: Zone Résidentielle, ave de la Marina, face Hôtel du Port, BP 2013, Cotonou; tel. 21-31-28-34; e-mail benin@mid.ru; internet benin.mid.ru; Ambassador IGOR DMITRIEVICH EVDOKIMOV.

South Africa: BP 7696, Cotonou; tel. 21-30-72-17; e-mail cotonou.dha@dirco.gov.za; Ambassador ROBINA P. MARKS.

Togo: SIKE CODJI, rue Marina, Carré 908, 01 BP 89, Cotonou; tel. 60651111; e-mail blcotonouambassade@gmail.com; Ambassador LÉNÉ DIMBAN.

Türkiye (Turkey): Benin Marina Hotel, blvd de la Marina, 01 BP 1901, Cotonou; tel. 21-30-01-40; e-mail ambassade.cotonou@mfa.gov.tr; internet kotonu.be.mfa.gov.tr; Ambassador KEMAL ONUR ÖZÇERI.

USA: ave Marina, 01 BP 2012, Cotonou; tel. 21-30-06-50; e-mail irccotonou@state.gov; internet bj.usembassy.gov; Ambassador BRIAN W. SHUKAN.

Venezuela: Lot 646, Parcelle D, 08 BP 564, Cotonou; tel. 21-30-23-88; e-mail embve.bjctn@mppre.gob.ve; internet benin.embajada.gob.ve; Ambassador BELÉN TERESA ORSINI PIC.

Judicial System

The judicial system consists of a Constitutional Court, a Supreme Court, a High Court of Justice, a Court of Suppression of Economic Offences and Terrorism, three Courts of Appeal (located at Abomey, Cotonou and Parakou), a Tribunal of Commerce and other local tribunals.

Constitutional Court: rue 637, Ganhi, 01 BP 2050, Cotonou; tel. 21-31-16-10; e-mail contact@courconstitutionnelle.bj; internet courconstitutionnelle.bj; f. 1990; inaug. 1993; 7 mems; 4 appointed by the National Assembly, 3 by the President of the Republic; exercises highest jurisdiction in constitutional affairs; determines the constitutionality of legislation, oversees and proclaims results of national elections and referendums, responsible for protection of individual and public rights and obligations, charged with regulating functions of organs of state and authorities; Pres. RAZAKI AMOUDA (acting), (vacant); Sec.-Gen. Dr GILLES SÈGNON BADET.

High Court of Justice: 01 BP 2958, Porto-Novo; tel. 20-21-26-81; tel. contact@hcj-benin.org; internet fb.com/hcjbenin; f. 1990; officially inaugurated in 2001; competent to try the President of the Republic and members of the Government in cases of high treason, crimes committed in, or at the time of, the exercise of their functions, and of plotting against state security; Pres. CÉCILE MARIE-JOSÉ DE DRAVO ZINZINDOHOUÉ.

Revenue Court: Cotonou; f. 2021; Pres. ISMATH BIO TCHANÉ.

Supreme Court: 01 BP 330, Cotonou; tel. 20-21-26-77; internet www.coursupreme.bj; f. 1960; highest juridical authority in administrative and judicial affairs; competent in disputes relating to local elections; advises the executive on jurisdiction and administrative affairs; comprises a President (appointed by the President of the Republic, after consultation with the President of the National Assembly, senior magistrates and jurists), presidents of the component chambers, a public prosecutor, 4 assistant procurators-fiscal, counsellors and clerks; Pres. VICTOR DASSI ADOSSOU.

Tribunal of Commerce of Cotonou: rue 651A, Cotonou; tel. 21-31-31-46; e-mail presidence-tcc@tribunalcommercecotonou.bj; internet tribunalcommercecotonou.bj; f. 2017; Pres. WILLIAM KODJOH-KPAKPASSOU.

Religion

Religious and spiritual cults, which were discouraged under the military regime, re-emerged as a prominent force in Beninois society during the 1990s. At the time of the 2013 census it was estimated that some 49% of the population were Christians (mainly Roman Catholics), 28% were Muslims, and 12% followed the traditional *vodoun* religion, with a further 3% being adherents of other traditional religions.

CHRISTIANITY

The Roman Catholic Church

Benin comprises two archdioceses and eight dioceses. An estimated 25.5% of the population were Roman Catholics at the time of the 2013 census.

Bishops' Conference: Conférence Episcopale du Bénin, Archevêché, 01 BP 491, Cotonou; tel. 21-30-66-48; internet eglisecatholiqueaubenin.org; Pres. Most Rev. VICTOR AGBANOU (Bishop of Lokossa).

Archbishop of Cotonou: Most Rev. ROGER HOUNGBÉDJI, Archevêché, 01 BP 491, Cotonou; tel. 21-30-01-45; e-mail mhlagbot@yahoo.fr.

Archbishop of Parakou: PASCAL N'KOUÉ, Archevêché, BP 75, Parakou; tel. 23-61-02-54; e-mail archeveche@borgou.net.

Protestant Church

Eglise Protestante Méthodiste en République du Bénin (EPMB): 54 ave Mgr Steinmetz, 01 BP 34, Cotonou; internet epmbenin.org; tel. 21-31-11-42; f. 1843; Pres. Rev. Dr AMOS HOUNSA; Sec. Rev. Dr ZABULON ANDRÉ DJARRA.

VODOUN

The origins of the traditional *vodoun* religion can be traced to the 14th century. Its influence is particularly strong in Latin America and the Caribbean, owing to the shipment of slaves from the West African region to the Americas in the 18th and 19th centuries.

Communauté Nationale du Culte Vodoun du Bénin (CNCVB): Ouidah; Pres. ADANYROH AGASSA GUÈDÉHOUNGUÈ II.

ISLAM

Union Islamique du Bénin (UIB): Cotonou; internet fb.com/unionislamiquedubenin; Pres. Imam ASSIFATOU MOHAMMED ALI; Sec.-Gen. Imam ABDOU DJALIL YESSOUF.

BAHÁ'Í FAITH

National Spiritual Assembly: BP 1252, Cotonou.

The Press

DAILY NEWSPAPERS (PRINT AND ONLINE)

Actu-Express: 01 BP 2220, Cotonou; tel. 97981047; e-mail lactuexpress2013@yahoo.fr; internet fb.com/Actu-Express-1972471836366588; Dir of Publication MÉDÉRIC FRANÇOIS GOHOUNGO.

L'Adjinakou: Lot AC, Parcelle 1 Avakpa-Tokpa, Immeuble Radio école APM, 03 BP 105, Porto-Novo; tel. 20-22-06-76; e-mail adjinakou2004@yahoo.com; internet www.journal-adjinakou-benin .net; f. 2003; Dir of Publication MAURILLE AGBOKOU.

L'Araignée: siège du cyber DOPHIA, face Cité Houeyiho, 10 BP 1199, Cotonou; tel. 95953458; e-mail info@laraignee.org; f. 2001; online only; politics, public affairs, culture, society, sport; Dir of Publishing FÉLIX ANIWANOU HOUNSA.

L'Autre Quotidien: Zone de la Pharmacie Camp Guézo, 01 BP 6659, Cotonou; tel. 21-31-01-99; e-mail lautreredaction@yahoo.fr; Dir ROMAIN TOÏ; Editor-in-Chief LÉON BRATHIER.

Banouto: Cotonou; tel. 96-25-12-44; e-mail redaction@banouto.info; internet www.banouto.bj; f. 2017; online only; Dir of Publication OLIVIER RIBOUIS; Editor-in-Chief YAO HERVÉ KINGBEWE.

Le Confrère de la Matinée: Esplanade du Stade de l'Amitié, Cotonou; tel. 21-38-30-30; Dir of Publication FAUSTIN BABATOUNDÉ ADJAGBA.

Djakpata: Quartier Todote C/410, Maison Bokononhui, 02 BP 2744, Cotonou; tel. 21-32-43-73; e-mail quotidiendjakpata@yahoo.fr; Editor CYRILLE SAÏZONOU.

Fraternité: face Station Menontin, 05 BP 915, Cotonou; tel. 21-38-47-70; e-mail contact@fraternitebj.info; internet www.fraternitebj .info; Dir of Publication BRICE U. HOUSSOU; Editor-in-Chief GÉRARD GANSOU.

L'Informateur: Etoile Rouge, Bâtiment Radio Star, Carré 1072c, 01 BP 5421, Cotonou; tel. 95956488; internet fb.com/ LInformateur-B%C3%A9nin-222929167719583; f. 2001; Dir CLÉMENT ADÉCHIAN; Editor-in-Chief BRICE GUÈDE.

Le Matin: C/791 Ḥ. Sikècodji, 06 BP 2217, Cotonou; tel. 21-32-32-33; e-mail lematin@yahoo.fr; internet www.quotidienlematin.net; f. 1994; independent; Dir-Gen. MOÏSE DATO; Editorial Dir IGNACE FANOU.

Matin Libre: Immeuble Aïssi, Carré No 486 Bar Tito, Cotonou; tel. 21-32-60-60; e-mail info@matinlibre.com; internet matinlibre.com; Dir-Gen. CHÉRIF OLATOUNDJI RIWANOU; Dir of Publication MAXIMIN TCHIBOZO.

Le Matinal: Carré 153–154, Atinkanmey, 06 BP 1989, Cotonou; tel. 90948332; e-mail infodumatinal@yahoo.fr; internet quotidien-lematinal.info; f. 1997; daily; Dir-Gen. MAXIMIN TCHIBOZO; Editor-in-Chief NAPOLÉON MAFORIKAN.

La Nation: Cadjèhoun, 01 BP 1210, Cotonou; tel. 21-30-02-99; e-mail redaction@lanationbenin.info; internet lanation.bj; f. 1990; official newspaper; Dir of Publication PAUL AMOUSSOU (acting); Editor-in-Chief HUBERT O. AKPONIKPE.

La Nouvelle Tribune: Immeuble Zonon, Lot 1498, Quartier Missogbè à Vêdoko, 09 BP 336, Cotonou; tel. 63942465; e-mail contact@ lanouvelletribune.info; internet lanouvelletribune.info; f. 2001; Dir-Gen. and Dir of Publication VINCENT FOLY; Web Editor E. FOLY.

Les Pharaons: Cotonou; tel. 97487294; e-mail eudesnathan@gmail .com; internet www.lespharaons.com; f. 2004; reappeared 2014; independent.

La Presse du Jour: Quartier Missité, 01 BP 1719, Cotonou; tel. 21-30-51-75; e-mail lapressedujour@yahoo.fr; internet quotidienlapressedujour.com; Dir of Publication PASCAL HOUNKPATIN.

Le Progrès: 05 BP 708, Cotonou; tel. 21-32-52-73; e-mail contact@ leprogresinfo.net; internet leprogresinfo.net; Dir of Publication LUDOVIC AGBADJA.

Le Soleil Bénin: 02 BP 767, Cotonou; tel. 95106458; internet lesoleilbenin.com.

La Tribune de la Capitale: Lot 03-46, Parcelle E, Houinmè, Maison Onifadé, Catchi, 01 BP 1463, Porto-Novo; tel. 20-22-55-69; e-mail latribunedelacapitale@yahoo.fr; internet www .latribunedelacapitale.com; Dir of Publication SETH EVARISTE HODONOU; Editor-in-Chief KPAKOUN CHARLES.

PERIODICALS

La Croix du Bénin: Centre Paul VI, 01 BP 105, Cotonou; tel. 21-32-12-07; e-mail contactcroixdubenin@gmail.com; internet croixdubenin.com; f. 1946; weekly; Roman Catholic; Dir of Publication SERGE N. BIDOUZO; Editor-in-Chief ALAIN SESSOU; circ. 3,000.

La Gazette du Golfe: Immeuble La Gazette du Golfe, Carré 902E, Sikècodji, 03 BP 1624, Cotonou; tel. 95010054; e-mail golfetvafrica@ hotmail.com; internet golfegroupe.com; f. 1987; weekly; Dir ISMAËL Y. SOUMANOU; Editor MARCUS BONI TEIGA.

Le Héraut: 03 BP 3417, Cotonou; tel. 21-36-00-64; e-mail franck .kouyami@auf.org; internet leherautbenin.info; monthly; current affairs; analysis; produced by students at Université Nationale du Bénin; Dir GEOFFREY GOUNOU N'GOYE; Editor-in-Chief GABRIEL DIDEH.

Le Journal de Notre Epoque: Cotonou; tel. 97086865; e-mail contact@notreepoque.bj; internet www.notreepoque.bj; Dir of Publication PRUDENCE SEKODO; Editorial Dir HERVÉ PRUDENCE HESSOU.

Journal Officiel de la République du Bénin: BP 59, Porto-Novo; tel. 20-21-39-77; f. 1890; present name adopted 1990; official govt bulletin; fortnightly; Dir AFIZE DÉSIRÉ ADAMO.

Les Scoops du Jour: 01 BP 2587, Cotonou; tel. 97960657; e-mail lesscoopsdujou@yahoo.fr; internet fb.com/lesscoopsdujour; 2 a week.

Press Associations

Conseil National du Patronat de la Presse et de l'Audiovisuel (CNPA): Carré 1248, Gbèdjromédé, 01 BP 7370, Cotonou; e-mail patronat_pressebenin@yahoo.fr; Pres. BASILE TCHIBOZO; Dir-Gen. FORTUNÉ ASSOGBA.

Union des Professionnels des Médias du Bénin (UPMB): Maison des Médias Thomas Mègnassan Carré 1248, Gbèdjromèdé 2, 03 BP 4365, Cotonou; tel. 21-32-61-99; f. 1992; asscn of media employees; Pres. ZAKIATH LATOUNDJI.

Publishers

AFRIDIC: 01 BP 269, 01 Porto-Novo; tel. 20-22-32-28; f. 1996; poetry, essays, fiction; Dir ADJIBI JEAN-BAPTISTE.

Les Éditions du Flamboyant: 08 BP 271 Cotonou; tel. 21-31-02-20; Dir DOROTHÉE GÉRARD HOUESSOU.

Editions Le Perroquet: BP 1671, Cotonou; tel. 66267107; e-mail contact@editionsleperroquet.com; internet www .editionsleperroquet.com; f. 2013.

Editions Ruisseaux d'Afrique: 04 BP 1154, Cotonou; tel. 21-38-31-86; internet www.ruisseauxdafrique.com; f. 1992; children's literature; Dir BÉATRICE GBADO.

GOVERNMENT PUBLISHING HOUSE

Office National d'Imprimerie et de Presse (ONIP): 01 BP 1210, Cotonou; tel. 21-30-02-99; f. 1975; Dir-Gen. BERTIN SOWAKOUDÉ (acting).

Broadcasting and Communications

TELECOMMUNICATIONS

ISOCEL: Tour de la Miséricorde, 7e étage, ave Clozel, 01 BP 3366, Cotonou; tel. 97217258; e-mail info@isoceltelecom.com; internet isoceltelecom.com; f. 2008; internet service provider; Dir-Gen. ROBERT AOUAD.

Moov Africa Bénin: Immeuble Etisalat-Bénin, ave Jean Paul II, Zone Résidentielle, 01 BP 8052, Cotonou; tel. 95353535; e-mail contact@moovafrica.bj; internet moov-africa.bj; f. 2000 as Telcel Bénin; name changed as above in 2021; mobile telephone operator in Cotonou, Porto-Novo, Abomey, Lokossa, other regions of southern Benin and in Parakou; Dir-Gen. OMAR NAHLI; 5.1m. subscribers (Dec. 2021).

MTN Bénin: 01 BP 5293, Cotonou; tel. 21-31-66-41; internet www .mtn.bj; f. 2000 as BéninCell; renamed as Areeba in 2005; mobile telephone operator in Cotonou, Porto-Novo and Parakou under network name Areeba; owned by Mobile Telephone Network International (South Africa); CEO UCHE UFODILE; 7.6m. subscribers (Dec. 2021).

Regulatory Authority

Autorité de Régulation des Communications Electroniques et de la Poste (ARCEP): Immeuble Maersk House, Zone OCBN, Lot 531, Parcelle B, 01 BP 2034, Cotonou; tel. 21-31-01-65; e-mail contacts@arcep.bj; internet arcep.bj; f. 2014 to replace the Autorité Transitoire de Régulation des Postes et Télécommunications; Pres. FLAVIEN BACHABI; Exec. Sec. HERVÉ COOVI GUEDEGBE.

BROADCASTING

Haute Autorité de l'Audiovisuel et de la Communication (HAAC): 01 BP 3567, Cotonou; tel. 21-31-17-43; e-mail contact@ haac.bj; internet www.haac.bj; f. 1994; Pres. RÉMI PROSPER MORETTI.

Radio

Office de Radiodiffusion et de Télévision du Bénin (ORTB): route de l'Aéroport, 01 BP 366, Cotonou; tel. 21-30-00-48; e-mail contact@ortb.bj; internet ortb.bj; state-owned; radio programmes broadcast from Cotonou and Parakou in French, English and 18 local languages; Dir-Gen. JEAN-PHILIPPE ERICK ABRAHAM; Dir of Radio OGOUCHINA KOUNDÉ.

    Atlantic FM: Cotonou; tel. 21-30-00-48; internet ortb.bj/ radioatlanticfm.html.

Radio Bénin: BP 366, Cotonou; tel. 21-30-10-96; internet ortb.bj/radiobenin.html; f. 1953; Dir OGOUCHINA KOUNDÉ.

CAPP FM (FM 99.6): Abokicodji, en face du Centre Lazaret, Cotonou; tel. 21-33-35-03; e-mail info@cappfm.com; internet cappfm.com; f. 1998; general radio; Dir-Gen. JÉRÔME CARLOS.

Frissons Radio (95.2 FM): Cotonou; tel. 61282828; e-mail frissonsradioinfo@gmail.com; internet www.frissonsradiocotonou.com.

Radio Carrefour: 01 BP 440, Bohicon; tel. 22-51-16-55; e-mail radiocarrefour91.7@gmail.com; internet fb.com/radiocarrefour91.7; f. 1999; production and broadcast of radio and television programmes; Dir-Gen. CHRISTOPHE DAVAKAN.

Radio Maranatha: 03 BP 4113, Cotonou; tel. 21-32-58-82; operated by the Conseil des Eglises Protestantes Evangéliques du Bénin; Dir Rev. CLOVIS ALFRED KPADE.

Radio Tokpa: Dantokpa, Cotonou; tel. 21-31-45-32; e-mail contact@radiotopka.info; internet radiotokpa.info; Dir-Gen. GUY KPAKPO.

Radio Wêkê: 05 BP 436, Cotonou; tel. 20-21-38-40; e-mail issabadarou@hotmail.com; Promoter ISSA BADAROU-SOULÉ.

Soleil FM: PK 16,5 Autoroute du Nigéria, Djèffa, BP 0897, Cotonou; tel. 94550978; Dir DONKLAM ABALO.

Television

ORTB: (see Radio); Dir of Television ABIATH OUMAROU (acting).

Canal 3 Bénin: Cotonou; tel. 69235555; e-mail info@canal3television.com; internet canal3television.com; Dir-Gen. BERTHE CAKPOSSA.

Éden TV: Fondation Espace Afrique CIEVRA, Golo Djigbé, Cotonou; tel. 62793232; e-mail info@benineden.tv; internet benin-eden.tv.

Golfe TV: Immeuble La Gazette du Golfe Carré, 902 E. Quartier Sikècodji, 03 BP 1624, Cotonou; tel. 95243000; e-mail gazettedugolfe@gmail.com; internet golfegroupe.com; Pres. ISMAËL SOUMANOU.

TVC Bénin: Cotonou; tel. 21-30-37-44; e-mail contact@tvcbenin.com; internet fb.com/carrefourtv; f. 2004; Dir-Gen. CHRISTOPHE DAVAKAN.

Finance

BANKING

Central Bank

Banque Centrale des Etats de l'Afrique de l'Ouest (BCEAO): ave Jean-Paul II, BP 325, Cotonou; tel. 21-36-46-00; e-mail akangni@bceao.int; internet www.bceao.int; HQ in Dakar, Senegal; f. 1962; bank of issue for the mem. states of the Union Economique et Monétaire Ouest-Africaine (UEMOA, comprising Benin, Burkina Faso, Côte d'Ivoire, Guinea-Bissau, Mali, Niger, Senegal and Togo); Gov. JEAN-CLAUDE KASSI BROU; Dir in Benin EMMANUEL ASSILAMEHOO.

Commercial Banks

In 2021 there were 14 banks operating in Benin.

Bank of Africa—Bénin (BOAB): ave Jean-Paul II, 08 BP 0879, Cotonou; tel. 21-31-32-28; e-mail information@boabenin.com; internet www.boabenin.com; f. 1990; Chair. PAULIN L. COSSI; Dir-Gen. SADIO CISSÉ.

Banque Atlantique du Bénin: rue du Gouverneur Bayol, 08 BP 0682, Cotonou; tel. 21-31-10-18; e-mail babn_support@banqueatlantique.net; internet www.banqueatlantique.net; Chair. LUCIEN KONAN; Dir-Gen. KHADY BOYE HANNE.

Banque Internationale pour l'Industrie et le Commerce (BIIC): Lot No. 374, Plot C, blvd St Michel, 01 BP 7744, Cotonou; tel. 21-31-22-00; e-mail info@biic-bank.com; internet www.biic-bank.com; f. 2015; established through merger of Banque Internationale du Bénin (f. 1989) and Banque Africaine pour l'Industrie et le Commerce; Pres. RIZWAN HAÏDER; Dir-Gen. CLAUDE EMMANUEL ACAKPO.

Banque Sahélo-Saharienne pour l'Investissement et le Commerce (BSIC): Lot 26F, 106 rue Dako Donou, Guinkomey, 08 BP 485, Cotonou; tel. 21-31-87-07; e-mail bsic.benin@bsicbank.com; internet fb.com/bsicbeninsa; Pres. SALIF NAMBALA KEÏTA; Dir-Gen. JÉRÔME YODA.

BGFIBank Bénin: Immeuble COOP, Ganhi, 01 BP 4270, Cotonou; tel. 21-31-33-48; e-mail benin@bgfi.com; internet benin.groupebgfibank.com; Pres. HENRI-CLAUDE OYIMA; Dir-Gen. PASCAL COVE.

CCEI Bank Benin: Quartier Ganhi, Carré 524C, rue du Gouverneur Bayol, 01 BP 7766, Cotonou; tel. 21-36-59-10; e-mail contact@cceibankbenin.com; internet www.cceibankbenin.com; f. 2015; Pres. MARCELINO OWONO EDU; Dir-Gen. HERVÉ BORNA.

Coris Bank International: Lot 122, Parcelle ZA, 01 BP 5783, Cotonou; tel. 21-36-00-54; e-mail corisbank-bj@coris-bank.com; internet benin.coris.bank; f. 2016; Pres. IDRISSA NASSA; Dir-Gen. JEAN JACQUES GOLOU.

Ecobank Bénin: rue du Gouverneur Bayol, 01 BP 1280, Cotonou; tel. 21-31-40-23; e-mail ecobankbj@ecobank.com; internet www.ecobank.com; f. 1989; 79% owned by Ecobank Transnational Inc (operating under the auspices of the Economic Community of West African States); Chair. VINCENT MAFORIKAN; Man. Dir LAZARE NOULEKOU.

NSIA Banque: 308 rue du Révérend Père Colineau, 01 BP 955, Cotonou; tel. 21-31-97-97; e-mail ecoute@groupensia.com; internet www.groupensia.com/bj/fr/; f. 2001; fmrly Diamond Bank Bénin; Chair. JANINE KACOU DIAGOU; Dir-Gen. OSSEY EUGÈNE AMONKOU.

Orabank Bénin SA (FBB): ave du Gouverneur Général Ponty, 01 BP 2700, Cotonou; tel. 21-31-31-00; internet www.orabank.net; f. 1989; 93.18% owned by Oragroup (Togo), 5.11% owned by Caisse Nationale de Sécurité Sociale; Pres. ALAIN FAGNON KOUTANGNI; Dir-Gen. JOSIANE SALOMÉ TCHOUNGUI.

Société Générale Bénin (SGBBE): Lot 4153, ave Clozel, Placodji-Kpodji, 01 BP 585, Cotonou; tel. 21-31-83-00; e-mail banque.sgb@socgen.com; internet societegenerale.bj; f. 2002; 77% owned by SG Financial Services Holding, a wholly-owned subsidiary of Groupe Société Générale (France); Dir-Gen. Eladji YERY SECK.

UBA Bénin: ave Jean-Paul II, Carrefour des Trois Banques, 01 BP 2020, Cotonou; tel. 21-31-24-24; e-mail cfcbenin@ubagroup.com; internet www.ubabenin.com; f. 1993 to assume activities of Crédit Lyonnais Bénin; fmrly Continental Bank—Bénin (La Continentale); present name adopted 2012; Pres. FOGAN SOSSAH; Dir-Gen. GBENGA MAKINDE.

Savings Bank

Caisse Nationale d'Epargne: Cadjèhoun, route Inter-Etat Cotonou-Lomé, Cotonou; tel. 21-30-18-35; Dir-Gen. Prof. JUDITH GLIDJA.

Credit Institutions

FECECAM: 08 BP 0843, Cotonou; tel. 21-04-86-77; e-mail fececam@yahoo.fr; internet www.fececam.org; f. 1977.

Finadev Bénin: Immeuble Orabank, en face de la Préfecture de Cotonou, 01 BP 6335, Cotonou; tel. 21-31-40-81; e-mail info.bj@finadev-groupe.com; f. 2000; majority-owned by Oragroup; Pres. FERDINAND NGON KEMOUM.

Vital Finance: Sarre 0548D, Zone Residentielle, Cotonou; tel. 21-31-26-23; internet www.vitalfinance.com; f. 1998.

Financial Institution

Caisse Autonome d'Amortissement: BP 59, Cotonou; tel. 21-31-47-81; e-mail caabenin@caabenin.org; internet www.caabenin.net; f. 1966; govt-owned; manages state funds; Dir-Gen. HUGUES OSCAR LOKOSSOU.

Banking Association

Association Professionnelle des Banques et Etablissements Financiers du Bénin (APBEF—Benin): Immeuble Ecobank, 3e étage, ave Steinmetz, 08 BP 200, Cotonou; tel. 21-31-75-14; e-mail info@apbef-bj.org; internet apbef-bj.org; Pres. LAZARE KOMI NOULEKOU; Exec. Dir COSME AHOUANSOU.

STOCK EXCHANGE

Bourse Régionale des Valeurs Mobilières (BRVM): Antenne Nationale des Bourses du Bénin, Immeuble Chambre de Commerce et d'Industrie du Bénin, ave Charles de Gaulle, 01 BP 2985, Cotonou; tel. 21-31-21-26; e-mail patioukpe@brvm.org; internet www.brvm.org; f. 1998; nat. branch of BRVM (regional stock exchange based in Abidjan, Côte d'Ivoire, serving the member states of UEMOA); Man. in Benin PAULINE ATIOUKPE.

INSURANCE

Africaine des Assurances: ave Jean-Paul II (AV-5078), place du Souvenir, 01 BP 3128, Cotonou; tel. 21-30-04-83; e-mail directiongenerale@africaine-assur.com; internet www.africaine-assur.com; Pres. AHMED DE DRAVO; Dir-Gen. KENNETH ELÉGBÉDÉ.

Assurance Mutuelle Agricole du Bénin (AMAB): Immeuble Adjété, blvd des Armées, Cotonou; tel. 21-30-11-38; e-mail info@amab.bj; agricultural insurance; Dir-Gen. TIBURCE KOUTON.

Atlantique Assurances Bénin Vie: ave Steinmetz, Lot 103, Parcelle H, 04 BP 0851, Cadjehoun, Cotonou; tel. 21-30-56-43; e-mail aabvie@aabvie.net; internet www.aabvie.net; life; Dir-Gen.

CORINNE GBENOU FOURN; also **Atlantique Assurance Bénin IARD**, general.

CIF Assurance Vie Bénin: 08 BP 0843, Cotonou; tel. 66660151; e-mail infos@cif-vie.bj; internet cif-vie.bj; f. 2012; life insurance; Dir-Gen. FÉLIX EDOUARD LADEKAN.

La Générale des Assurances du Bénin (GAB): Immeuble GAB, blvd St Michel, 01 BP 3573, Cotonou; tel. 21-33-82-30; e-mail info@gabassurance.com; internet gabassurance.com; Dir-Gen. CHRISTIAN AFFAGNON.

Nouvelle Société Interafricaine d'Assurances du Bénin: Immeuble Kougblénou, ave Mgr Steinmetz, 08 BP 0258, Cotonou; tel. 21-31-33-69; f. 1997; Dir-Gen. (vacant).

Sanlam Assurance Vie Bénin: Lot 505D, Quartier Les Cocotiers, 04 BP 1419, Cotonou; tel. 21-30-85-23; e-mail contact@bj.sanlam.com; internet bj.sanlam.com; fmrly Colina Vie Bénin, subsequently Saham Vie Bénin; present name adopted 2020; Dir-Gen. MARIAM NASSIROU; also **Sanlam Assurance Bénin**.

Sunu Assurances Vie Bénin: Immeuble SUNU Assurances, Lot 37 Patte d'Oie, pl. du Souvenir, 08 BP 70, Cotonou; tel. 21-30-06-90; e-mail benin.vie@sunu-group.com; internet benin.vie.sunu-group.com; f. 1994; fmrly Union Béninoise d'Assurance-Vie; name changed as above in 2015; merger of Avie Assurances and Sunu Assurances Vie Bénin in 2016; 84.9% owned by Groupe SUNU (France); Man. Dir LASSINA COULIBALY; also Sunu Assurances IARD Bénin (fmrly Allianz Bénin Assurances).

Insurance Association

Association des Sociétés d'Assurance du Bénin (ASA-Benin): 01 BP 5508, Cotonou; tel. 21-30-00-40; e-mail secretariat@asabenin.org; internet asabenin.org; f. 1999; Pres. MOUFTAOU SOUHOUIN.

Trade and Industry

GOVERNMENT AGENCIES

Agence Nationale d'Aménagement du Territoire (ANAT): Vodjè, Pavillon Bleu, Cotonou; tel. 21-30-98-75; e-mail anat.infos@gouv.bj; internet anat.bj; f. 2018; Dir-Gen. COCOU EDMOND ODIDI.

Agence de Promotion des Investissements et des Exportations (APIEx): Immeuble APIEx/ANAEP, Lot 368, 01 BP 5160, Cotonou; tel. 21-31-07-04; e-mail contact@apiex.bj; internet apiex.bj; f. 2014 following merger of Agence Béninoise pour la Promotion des Echanges Commerciaux, the Guichet Unique de Formalité des Entreprises and the Centre de Promotion des Investissements; facilitates creation of new cos; Dir-Gen. LAURENT GANGBÈS.

Centre Béninois de la Recherche Scientifique et de l'Innovation (CBRSI): 03 BP 1665, Cotonou; tel. 21-32-12-63; e-mail cbrsi@cbrsi-benin.org; f. 1986; promotes scientific and technical research and training; Dir-Gen. BIAOU FIDÈLE DIMON.

Centre de Promotion de l'Artisanat (CPA): à côté du Hall des Arts et de la Culture, 01 BP 2651, Cotonou; tel. 21-30-34-32; f. 1987; Dir LATIFOU ALASSANE.

Centre de Promotion et d'Encadrement des Petites et Moyennes Entreprises (CePEPE): face à la Mairie de Xlacondji, 01 BP 2093, Cotonou; tel. 21-31-22-61; e-mail cepepe@cepepe.org; internet www.cepepe.org; f. 1989; promotes business and employment; offers credits and grants to small businesses; undertakes management training and consultancy; publishes bi-monthly journal, *Initiatives*; Dir-Gen. DOROTHÉ GOUNON.

Institut National de Recherches Agricoles du Bénin (INRAB): Godomey, Route IITA, 01 BP 884, Cotonou; tel. 64283702; e-mail sp.inrab@inrab.org; internet inrab.org; f. 1992; undertakes research into agricultural improvements; publicizes advances in agriculture; Dir (vacant).

Institut National de la Statistique et de l'Analyse Economique (INSAE): route de l'aéroport, 01 BP 323, Cotonou; tel. 21-30-82-44; e-mail webmaster@insae.bj; internet www.insae.bj; f. 1973; Dir-Gen. LAURENT MAHOUNOU HOUNSA.

Office Béninois de Recherches Géologiques et Minières (OBRGM): rue 858, Placodji, 01 BP 249, Cotonou; tel. 21-31-03-09; e-mail nestorved@yahoo.fr; internet eau-mines.gouv.bj/structure/6/office-beninois-recherches-geologiques-minieres; f. 1996 as govt agency responsible for mining policy, exploitation and research; Dir-Gen. ALASSANE OSSENI INOUSSA.

Office National du Bois (ONAB): PK 3,5 route de Porto-Novo, 01 BP 1238, Cotonou; tel. 21-33-16-32; f. 1983; reorganized and partially privatized in 2002; forest devt and management, manufacture and marketing of wood products; industrial activities privatized in 2009; Dir-Gen. DAOUDA TAKPARA.

DEVELOPMENT ORGANIZATIONS

Agence Béninoise pour la Réconciliation et le Développement (ABRD): Haie Vive, Les Cocotiers, 04 BP 1063, Cotonou; tel. 21-00-75-48; Dir-Gen. FLORE DOVONOU MEHINTO.

Agence Française de Développement (AFD): 1506 blvd de France, 01 BP 38, Cotonou; tel. 21-31-35-80; e-mail afdcotonou@afd.fr; internet www.afd.fr; fmrly Caisse Française de Développement; Country Dir JÉRÔME BERTRAND-HARDY.

Agence Nationale du Domaine et du Foncier (ANDF): Cotonou; internet www.andf.bj; f. 2013; Dir-Gen. VICTORIEN D. KOUGBLENOU.

Centre Songhaï: Route de Ouando, 01 BP 597, Porto-Novo; tel. 60933334; e-mail songhai@songhai.org; internet www.songhai.org; devt of agriculture; Dir GODFREY NZAMUJO.

Conseil des Investisseurs Privés au Bénin (CIPB): Immeuble Kougblénou, 85 ave Steinmetz, Tokpa Hoho, 03 BP 4304, Cotonou; tel. 95429042; e-mail info@cipb.bj; internet cipb.bj; f. 2002; Pres. ROLAND RIBOUX; Sec.-Gen. ROLAND METINHOUE.

France Volontaires: Supermarché Du Pont, 1er étage, 4032 ave de la Francophonie, 01 BP 344, Cotonou; tel. 94413958; e-mail ev.benin@france-volontaires.org; internet www.france-volontaires.org; f. 1964; name changed as above in 2009; Nat. Rep. EUGÈNE KOUNKER SOMÉ.

Projet d'Appui au Développement des Micro-entreprises (PADME): C/226 F-Jéricho, 08 BP 712, Cotonou; tel. 21-32-48-02; e-mail padme@padmebenin.org; internet www.padmebenin.org; f. 1994; Dir-Gen. DOSSOU THIERRY AGOSSA.

SNV Bénin (Organisation Néerlandaise de Développement): Carré 107, Zone Résidentielle, Rue du PNUD, 01 BP 1048, Cotonou; tel. 21-31-21-42; e-mail benin@snv.org; internet snv.org/country/benin; f. 1970; Country Dir JEANNETTE DE REGT.

CHAMBERS OF COMMERCE

Chambre de Commerce et d'Industrie du Bénin (CCIB): ave du Général de Gaulle, 01 BP 31, Cotonou; tel. 21-31-20-81; e-mail info@ccib.bj; internet www.ccibenin.org; f. 1908; present name adopted 1962; Pres. ARNAULD AKAKPO; Gen. Sec. RAYMOND ADJAKPA ABILE; brs at Parakou, Mono-Zou, Natitingou and Porto-Novo.

EMPLOYERS' ORGANIZATIONS

Conseil National des Chargeurs du Bénin (CNCB): Zone Résidentielle, Lot 557, Parcelle B, 06 BP 2528, Cotonou; tel. 21-31-59-47; internet www.besc-benin.com; f. 1983; represents interests of shippers; Dir-Gen. CODJO GAUTHIER ABLET.

Conseil National du Patronat du Bénin (CNP): 01 BP 1260, Cotonou; tel. 21-31-77-90; e-mail contact@cnpbenin.com; f. 1984 as Organisation Nationale des Employeurs du Bénin; Pres. SÉBASTIEN GERMAINE AJAVON.

Fédération des Unions de Producteurs du Bénin (FUPRO): rue en face des Sapeurs Pompiers, Quartier Honmeho, BP 372, Bohicon; tel. 22-11-18-52; e-mail fuproben@yahoo.fr; internet www.fuprobenin.org; f. 1994; Pres. ATHANASE AGUIYA; Sec.-Gen. MARTIAL KOUDÉRIN.

UTILITIES

Agence Béninoise d'Electrification Rurale et de Maîtrise d'Energie (ABERME): rue 2602, Cotonou; tel. 21-31-38-63; internet www.aberme.bj; Dir-Gen. JEAN-FRANCIS TCHÉKPO.

Autorité de Régulation de l'Electricité: Quartier Haie-Vive, Villa No 186, Cotonou; tel. 21-13-86-96; e-mail info@are.bj; internet are.bj; f. 2015; regulatory authority; Pres. CLAUDE GBAGUIDI GBÉDONOUGBO.

Société Béninoise d'Energie Electrique (SBEE): ave du Gouverneur Général Ponty, 01 BP 123, Cotonou; tel. 94010262; e-mail info@sbee.bj; internet www.sbee.bj; f. 1973; state-owned; distribution of electricity; Dir-Gen. FRANCIS PERANI (acting).

Société Béninoise de Production Electrique (SBPE): Cotonou; e-mail contact@sbpe.bj; internet www.sbpe.bj; f. 2020; electricity production; Dir-Gen. EMÉRIC TOKOUDAGBA.

Société Nationale des Eaux du Bénin (SONEB): 92 ave Jean-Paul II, 01 BP 216, RP Cotonou; tel. 21-31-62-58; e-mail info@soneb.bj; internet www.soneb.bj; f. 2003 to assume water activities of Société Béninoise d'Electricité et d'Eau; operates under supervision of Ministry of Water and Mining; utilizes about 60 systems of drinkable water adductions, feeding 69 municipalities; Dir-Gen. CAMILLE DANSOU.

MAJOR COMPANIES

The following are among the largest companies in terms of either capital investment or employment.

Agence d'Exécution des Travaux Urbains SA (AGETUR): 01 BP 2780, Cotonou; tel. 21-30-39-21; e-mail agetur@intnet.bj; internet www.agetur.bj; civil construction; Pres. and Dir-Gen. LAMBERT KOTY.

Agence Privé d'Investigations et d'Analyses Stratégiques (APIAS): Carré 1115, Quartier Wologuèdè, 01 BP 6468, Cotonou; tel. 21-32-05-49; e-mail apias.apias@yahoo.fr; internet www.apiasbenin.com; financial and information technology solutions; Dir-Gen. CLOVIS ADANZOUNON.

AGETIP Benin: Lot 1181, XC, Cadjèhoun 2, 01 BP 413, Cotonou; tel. 21-30-13-05; e-mail agetipbeninsa@yahoo.fr; internet www.agetip-benin.com; civil construction; Dir-Gen. RAYMOND ADEKAMBI.

Cajaf Comon: PK 16, 5 Autoroute du Nigeria, Djèffa; 03 BP 0879, Cotonou; tel. 20-24-02-41; e-mail contact@comoncajaf.com; importer and distributor of food items; Dir-Gen. SÉBASTIEN ADJAVON.

CAMIN SA—Centrale de l'Automobile et de Matériel Industriel: PK3,5, Akpakpa, route de Porto-Novo, Zone Industrielle, 01 BP 2636, Cotonou; tel. 21-33-01-95; e-mail societe_camin@yahoo.fr; f. 1986; import and export of motorcycles, vehicles, components and parts, and agricultural and industrial equipment; Chair. and Man. Dir RÉMY GAUDENS YESSOUFOU.

CIMBENIN SA—Cimenterie du Bénin: PK8, route de Porto Novo, BP 1224, Cotonou; tel. 21-33-07-32; e-mail cimbenin@hcafrica.com; internet www.heidelbergcement.com; f. 1991; mfrs of cement and wholesalers of bldg materials; 54% owned by HeidelbergCement Group (Germany); Man. Dir DICKSON KWESI.

Colas-Bénin: PK4, route de Porto-Novo, 01 BP 228, Cotonou; tel. 21-33-40-10; e-mail secretariat@colasbenin.bj; internet www.colas.com; construction; mem. of Groupe Colas (France); Dir STÉPHANE KNEBEL.

Compagnie Béninoise de Négoce et de Distribution (CBND): ave Pierre Delorme, 01 BP 07, Cotonou; tel. 97383010; e-mail info@cbndgroupe.com; internet www.cbndgroupe.com; f. 1973; fmrly CFAO Bénin; import, export and distribution of consumer goods; Pres. and Dir-Gen. EMMANUEL KOUTON.

Fludor Benin SA: Immeuble Kougblénou, ave Steinmetz, 03 BP 4304, Cotonou; tel. 21-31-65-31; e-mail info@fludorbenin.com; internet fludorbenin.com; f. 1996; agro-based; Pres. and Dir-Gen. ROLAND RIBOUX.

Grands Moulins du Bénin (GMB): Zone Industrielle d'Akpakpa, 01 BP 949, Cotonou; tel. 21-33-08-17; f. 1971; owned by Chagoury Group (Nigeria); wheat milling; Chair. GILBERT RAMEZ CHAGOURY; Chief Exec. RONALD CHAGOURY.

Pharmaquick: Zone Industrielle d'Akpakpa, 06 BP 713, Cotonou; tel. 21-33-07-58; e-mail aahphqk@wanadoo.fr; internet pharmaquick-benin.com; f. 1982; mfrs of pharmaceutical preparations; Dir-Gen. CHARLES ADJALLA.

SCB—Société des Ciments du Bénin: Xwlacodji, rue 657, 01 BP 448, Cotonou; tel. 21-31-37-03; e-mail serviceclient@cimentbouclier.com; internet www.cimentbouclier.com; produces and distributes cement; owned by Amida Group (France); Pres. PIERRE AMIDA.

SCB-Lafarge: Résidence des Cocotiers 01 BP 1557, Cotonou; tel. 20-30-61-81; e-mail scb.lafarge@scb-lafarge.bj; f. 1999 to replace Société des Ciments d'Onigbolo; 50% owned by Société des Ciments du Bénin, 50% by Société Financière Lafarge (France); produces and markets cement; Man. Dir MARIUS ELÉGBÉDÉ.

Société Béninoise de Brasserie (SOBEBRA): PK 2.5, route de Porto-Novo, BP 135, Cotonou; tel. 21-33-11-24; e-mail infos@sobebra.bj; internet sobebra.bj; f. 1957; production and marketing of beer, soft drinks and ice; Dir-Gen. SÉBASTIEN YVES-MÉNAGER.

Société de Commerce d'Automobile et de Réprésentation (SOCAR Bénin): rue 1200 Apakpa, 01 BP 6, Cotonou; tel. 97979436; e-mail louis.besancenot@socar-benin.com; internet www.socar-benin.com; wholesale trade in motor vehicles and spare parts; Dir-Gen. GEOFFREY FADOUL.

Société Nationale de Commercialisation des Produits Pétroliers (SONACOP): ave Jean Paul II, 01 BP 245, Cotonou; tel. 21-31-22-90; internet sonacopsa.com/bj; f. 1974; imports and distributes petroleum products; Dir-Gen. BIO GOUNOU SINA.

Société Nationale de Mécanisation Agricole (SoNaMA): BP 01, Ouidah; tel. 51209085; e-mail contact@sonama.bj; internet sonama.bj; f. 2021 to replace Agence Nationale de Mécanisation Agricole; Dir-Gen. ERIC RENAUD.

TotalEnergies Bénin: ave Jean Paul II, 08 BP 701, Cotonou 08; tel. 21-30-65-47; distribution of petroleum; fmrly Total Bénin; present name adopted 2021; Dir-Gen. PHILIPPE PRUDENT.

TRADE UNIONS

Centrale Syndicale des Travailleurs du Bénin (CSTB): 03 BP 0989, Cotonou; tel. 21-30-13-15; actively opposes privatization and the influence of the international financial community; linked to the Parti Communiste du Bénin; Sec.-Gen. NAGNINI KASSA MAMPO.

Centrale des Syndicats Autonomes du Bénin (CSA—Bénin): 1 blvd Saint-Michel, Bourse du Travail, 04 BP 1115, Cotonou; tel. 97476720; e-mail csabenin2020@gmail.com; internet fb.com/syndicatcsabenin; principally active in private sector enterprises; Sec.-Gen. ANSELME AMOUSSOU.

Centrale des Syndicats du Secteur Privé et Informel du Bénin (CSPIB): 03 BP 2961, Cotonou; tel. 21-33-53-53; Sec.-Gen. (vacant).

Centrale des Syndicats Unis du Bénin (CSUB): Cotonou; tel. 21-33-10-27; Sec.-Gen. CHRISTOPHE HOUÉSSIONON.

Confédération Générale des Travailleurs du Bénin (CGTB): 06 BP 2449, Cotonou; tel. 21-31-73-11; e-mail cgtbpdd@bow.intnet.bj; principally active in public administration; Sec.-Gen. MOUDACHIROU BACHABI.

Confédération des Organisations Syndicales Indépendantes du Bénin (COSI—Benin): Bourse du Travail, 03 BP 1218, Cotonou; tel. 96065006; Sec.-Gen. NOËL CHADARÉ.

Union Nationale des Syndicats de Travailleurs du Bénin (UNSTB): 1 blvd Saint-Michel, BP 69, Recette Principale, Cotonou; tel. 21-30-36-13; Sec.-Gen. APPOLINAIRE AFFÉWÉ.

Transport

RAILWAYS

In March 2015 a project was formally launched to extend the Cotonou–Parakou line to Niamey, Niger, and Kaya, close to the Burkina Faso capital Ouagadougou.

Bénirail: BP 16, Cotonou; tel. 21-31-28-57; f. 2015 to replace Organisation Commune Bénin-Niger des Chemins de Fer et des Transports; 40% owned by Groupe Bolloré, 10% by Govt of Benin, 10% by Govt of Niger; total of 579 track-km; main line runs for 438 km from Cotonou to Parakou in the interior; br. line runs westward via Ouidah to Segboroué (34 km); also line of 107 km from Cotonou via Porto-Novo to Pobé (near the Nigerian border); extension to the Republic of Niger, Burkina Faso and Togo proposed; Dir-Gen. THIERY BALLARD.

ROADS

Agence Générale de Transit et de Consignation (AGETRAC): blvd Maritime, BP 1933, Cotonou; tel. 21-31-32-22; f. 1967; goods transportation and warehousing.

Bolloré Bénin: Route du Collège de l'Union, Z.I. d'Akpakpa, 01 BP 433, Cotonou; e-mail bernard.de-buor@bollore.com; tel. 21-33-11-23; f. 1947; Dir-Gen. BERNARD DE BUOR.

Société des Infrastructures Routières du Bénin (SIRB): Cotonou; f. 2018.

SHIPPING

The main port is at Cotonou, which handled a total of 10.0m. metric tons in 2019.

Port Autonome de Cotonou (PAC): ave de la Marina, BP 927, Cotonou; tel. 21-31-28-90; e-mail contact@pac.bj; internet www.portdecotonou.com; f. 1965; state-owned port authority; Dir-Gen. JORIS THYS.

Maersk Bénin: Maersk House, Zone OCBN Lot 531, Parcelle B, 01 BP 2826, Cotonou; tel. 21-31-43-30; e-mail bnncsidir@maersk.com; internet www.maersk.com/local-information/benin; subsidiary of Maersk Line (Denmark); Dir DAVID SKOV.

Société Béninoise des Manutentions Portuaires (SOBEMAP): blvd de la Marina, BP 35, Cotonou; tel. 21-31-41-45; e-mail sobemap@sobemap.com; internet www.sobemap.com; f. 1969; state-owned; Dir-Gen. BERNARD AMOUSSOU-SOSSOU.

CIVIL AVIATION

There is an international airport at Cotonou-Cadjehoun and secondary airports at Parakou, Natitingou, Kandi, Savè, Porga and Djougou. In mid-2021 the Government confirmed plans to construct a new international airport north of Cotonou at Glo-Djigbé.

Agence Nationale de l'Aviation Civile: 01 BP 305, Cotonou; tel. 21-30-92-17; e-mail anacaero@anac.bj; internet anac.bj; f. 2004; Pres. PAUL GONGO; Dir-Gen. KARL LEGBA.

Trans Air Bénin (TAB): ave Jean Paul II, Lot No 14, Les Cocotiers, Cotonou; tel. 21-00-61-65; e-mail transairbenin@aol.com; f. 2000; regional flights; Dir BRICE KIKI.

Tourism

Agence Nationale de Promotion des Patrimoines et de Développement du Tourisme (ANPT): Palais de la Marina, 01 BP 2028, Cotonou; tel. 95188282; e-mail info@anpt.presidence.bj; Chair. BABALOLA JEAN-MICHEL HERVÉ ABIMBOLA.

Direction de la Promotion et des Professions Touristiques: BP 2037, Cotonou; tel. 21-32-68-24; internet www.tourismebenin.bj.

Defence

As assessed at November 2021, the Beninois Armed Forces numbered an estimated 7,250 active personnel (land army 6,500, navy about 500, air force 250). Paramilitary forces comprised a 4,800-strong republican police force. Military service is by selective conscription, and lasts for 18 months. In 2021 a total of 432 troops were stationed abroad.

Defence Budget: 125,000m. francs CFA in 2021.

Chief of General Staff of the Armed Forces: Gen. FRUCTUEUX CANDIDE AHODEGNON GBAGUIDI.

Chief of Staff of the Army: Gen. ABOU ISSA.

Chief of Staff of the Navy: Capt. JEAN LÉON OLATOUNDJI.

Chief of Staff of the Air Force: Lt-Col HERMANN WILLIAM AVOCANH.

Education

The Constitution of Benin obliges the state to make a quality compulsory primary education available to all children. Primary education was declared free of charge in 2006. Primary education begins at six years of age and lasts for six years. Secondary education, beginning at 12 years of age, lasts for up to seven years, comprising a first cycle of four years and a second of three years. According to estimates by the United Nations Educational, Scientific and Cultural Organization (UNESCO), in 2019/20 enrolment at the pre-primary level was equivalent to 22% of children in the relevant age-group (males 22%; females 22%), while primary enrolment in 2018/19 included 94% of children in the appropriate age-group (males 97%; females 90%). Enrolment at secondary schools in 2015/16 was equivalent to 59% of children in the appropriate age-group (males 67%; females 51%). The Université Nationale du Bénin, at Cotonou, was founded in 1970 and a second university, in Parakou, opened in 2001. According to UNESCO estimates, in 2018 spending on education represented 17.7% of total government expenditure.

Bibliography

Adekounte, F. L. *Entreprises publiques Béninoises: la descente aux enfers.* Cotonou, Les Editions du Flamboyant, 1996.

Adjovi, V. E. *Une élection libre en Afrique: la présidentielle du Bénin, 1996.* Paris, Editions Karthala, 1998.

Banégas, R. *La démocratie à pas de caméléon. Transition et imaginaires politiques au Bénin.* Paris, Editions Karthala, 2003.

Bio Tchané, A., and Montigny, P. *Lutter contre la corruption: un impératif pour le développement du Bénin dans l'économie internationale.* Paris, L'Harmattan, 2000.

Coovi Anignikin, S. *Les origines du mouvement national en Afrique noire. Le cas du Bénin, 1900–1939.* Paris, L'Harmattan, 2015.

Cornevin, R. *La République populaire du Bénin, des Origines dahoméennes à nos jours.* Paris, Académie des Sciences d'Outremer, 1984.

Dissou, M. *Le Bénin et l'épreuve démocratique: leçons des élections de 1991 à 2001.* Paris, L'Harmattan, 2002.

Dovenon, N. *Bénin: Quelles solutions pour un développement durable?* Paris, L'Harmattan, 2010.

Eades, J. S., and Allen, C. *Benin.* Oxford, Clio, 1996.

Gbago, B. G. *Le Bénin et les droits de l'homme.* Paris, L'Harmattan, 2001.

Hado, P., and Opoubor, A. *Boni Yayi, société civile et dynamique du changement au Bénin.* Paris, L'Harmattan, 2007.

Harding, L. *Das Königreich Benin: Geschichte, Kultur, Wirtschaft.* München, Oldenbourg Wissenschaftsverlag, 2010.

Harman, A. *Benin 900-1897 CE.* London, Wayland, 2014.

Harrison Church, R. J. *West Africa.* 8th edn. London, Longman, 1979.

Heilbrunn, J. R. *Markets, Profits and Power: The Politics of Business in Benin and Togo.* Bordeaux, Centre d'étude d'Afrique noire, 1996.

Houngnikpo, M. C. *Determinants of Democratization in Africa: A Comparative Study of Benin and Togo.* Lanham, MD, University Press of America, 2001.

Houngnikpo, M. C., and Decalo, S. *Historical Dictionary of Benin.* Lanham, MD., Scarecrow Press, 2013.

Manning, P. *Slavery, Colonialism and Economic Growth in Dahomey, 1640–1960.* Cambridge, Cambridge University Press, 1982.

Ngango Youmbi, E. *La Justice Constitutionnelle au Bénin: Logiques Politique et Sociale.* Paris, L'Harmattan, 2016.

Noudjenoume, P. *La démocratie au Bénin, 1988–1993: bilans et perspectives.* Paris, L'Harmattan, 1999.

Les Frontières Maritimes du Bénin. Paris, L'Harmattan, 2004.

Okunlola, O., and Laleye, M. *La Décentralisation et le Développement des Territoires au Bénin.* Paris, L'Harmattan, 2003.

Onibon, Y. O. *Les Femmes Béninoises: de l'étalage a la conquête du marché international.* Paris, Université de Paris, 1995.

Padonou, O., and Quenum, E. C. *Le Bénin et les operations de paix. Pour une capitalisation des expériences.* Paris, L'Harmattan, 2012.

Passot, B. *Le Bénin: guide pratique.* Paris, L'Harmattan, 2005.

Rush, D. *Vodun in Coastal Benin: Unfinished, Open-Ended, Global.* Nashville, TN, Vanderbilt University Press, 2017.

Topanou, P. V. *Boni Yayi ou le grand malentendu.* Paris, L'Harmattan, 2012.

Introduction à la sociologie politique du Bénin. Paris, L'Harmattan, 2013.

Pfeiffer, V. *Agriculture au Sud Bénin.* Paris, L'Harmattan, 1988.

Pliya, J. *L'histoire de mon pays le Bénin.* Librairie Notre Dame, Cotonou, 1997.

Van Ufford, P. Q. *Trade and Traders: The Making of the Cattle Market in Benin.* Amsterdam, Thela Thesis, 1999.

BOTSWANA

Physical and Social Geography

A. MacGregor Hutcheson

PHYSICAL FEATURES

The Republic of Botswana is a landlocked country, bordered by Namibia to the west and by that country's Zambezi Region (formerly known as the Caprivi Strip) to the north, by Zimbabwe to the north-east, and by South Africa to the south and south-east. Botswana occupies 581,730 sq km (224,607 sq miles) of the downwarped Kalahari Basin of the great southern African plateau, which has here an average altitude of 900 m above sea level. Gentle undulations to flat surfaces, consisting of Kalahari sands overlying Archean rocks, are characteristic of most of the country but the east is more hilly and broken. Most of southern Botswana is without surface drainage and, apart from the bordering Limpopo and Chobe rivers, the rest of the country's drainage is interior and does not reach the sea. Flowing into the north-west from the Angolan highlands, the perennial Okavango river is Botswana's major system. The Okavango drains into a depression in the plateau, 145 km from the border, to form the Okavango swamps and the ephemeral Lake Ngami. From this vast marsh, covering 16,000 sq km, there is a seasonal flow of water eastwards along the Botletle river 260 km to Lake Xau and thence into the Makarakari salt pan. Most of the water brought into Botswana by the Okavango is lost through evaporation and transpiration in the swamps.

The Kalahari Desert dominates southern and western Botswana. From the near-desert conditions of the extreme south-west with an average annual rainfall of around 130 mm, there is a gradual increase in precipitation towards the north (635 mm) and east (380 mm–500 mm). There is an associated transition in the natural vegetation from the sparse thornveld of the Kalahari Desert to the dry woodland savannah of the north and east, and the infertile sands give way eastwards to better soils developed on granitic and sedimentary rocks.

POPULATION AND RESOURCES

The eastern strip, the best-endowed and most developed region of Botswana, is home to about 80% of the population, which totalled 2,346,179, according to provisional results of the census of March 2022. Seven of the eight Batswana tribes, and most of the Europeans and Asians, are concentrated in the east. A substantial number of Batswana (the figure is unrecorded) are employed in South Africa, many of them in mining, although this figure declined dramatically in the 2000s. The absence of these workers helps to ease pressure on resources and contributes to the country's income through deferred pay and remittances sent home to their families. However, as a large proportion of the population is less than 15 years of age, there is a pressing need for improvements in agricultural productivity and in other sectors of the economy to provide work for the growing number of young people who are entering the labour market.

Shortage of water, resulting from the low annual rainfall and aggravated by considerable fluctuations in the monthly distribution and total seasonal rainfall, is the main hindrance to the development of Botswana's natural resources, although a number of projects have improved water supply to the main centres of economic activity. Limitations imposed by rainfall make much of the country more suitable for the rearing of livestock, especially cattle, but it has been estimated that in eastern Botswana 4.45m. ha are suitable for cultivation, of which only about 10% is actually cultivated. Although in the east the irrigation potential is limited, the Okavango-Chobe swamps offer substantial scope for irrigation (as much as an estimated 600,000 ha).

In recent years Botswana's economic base has been considerably widened. Exploitable deposits of diamonds (of which Botswana was the world's second largest producer by both value and volume in the late 2010s), gold, silver, uranium, copper, nickel, coal, manganese, asbestos, common salt, potash, soda ash and sodium sulphate have been identified, and some of these minerals are currently being mined. In particular, the major developments of diamond mining at Orapa, Letlhakane and Jwaneng, and copper-nickel mining focused on Selebi-Phikwe, with their attendant infrastructural improvements, are assisting in the diversification of the predominantly agricultural economy.

History

CHRISTOPHER SAUNDERS

What today is the Republic of Botswana was the northern portion of the territory that the British Government declared a protectorate in 1885, at the request of local Tswana rulers who wished to deter Boer encroachment from the Transvaal in the east. In 1895 the southern portion was incorporated into the Cape Colony, but the large northern protectorate continued to be ruled directly by the United Kingdom through the High Commissioner. The sparsely populated territory remained under direct British rule until it gained independence as Botswana in 1966, with over 80% of its land still under tribal control.

In 1960 the first nationalist party, the Bechuanaland People's Party, was founded, with links to the African National Congress of South Africa (ANC). Two years later the most influential figure in the country, Seretse (later Sir Seretse) Khama, paramount chief of the Ngwato, the largest Tswana grouping, formed the Bechuanaland (later Botswana) Democratic Party (BDP). In the territory's first direct general election under universal adult suffrage, held in 1965, the BDP won 28 of the 31 seats; Khama became Prime Minister. Independence followed on 30 September 1966, when Bechuanaland became the Republic of Botswana, with Khama as President. At independence, Botswana was one of the world's poorest countries. However, significant deposits of diamonds were then discovered, and by the early 1980s Botswana was the largest supplier of diamonds to the global market. Botswana achieved a consistent rate of economic growth, and it became known as Africa's most stable democracy. The BDP remains the ruling party today.

Upon the death of Khama in July 1980, his Vice-President, Dr Quett (later Sir Quett) Ketumile Masire, became President. As Minister of Finance and Development Planning, Masire had played an important role in the country's economic development. In March 1992 Festus Mogae, who in the same ministerial post had gained a reputation for fiscal prudence and sound economic management, was appointed Vice-President. In 1997 several constitutional amendments were adopted, introducing a two-term presidential limit and providing for the Vice-President to succeed automatically in the event of the death or resignation of the President. The electoral system was reformed, the voting age was reduced to 18 years, and an independent electoral commission was established. On 31 March 1998 Masire retired from politics, and the following day Mogae was inaugurated as President.

THE MOGAE PRESIDENCY

The only new minister in Mogae's Cabinet was Lt-Gen. Seretse Khama Ian Khama, the oldest son of Sir Seretse Khama, and paramount chief of the Ngwato. A military man, he was Commander of the Botswana Defence Force (BDF) but received the portfolio of presidential affairs and public administration, and was designated as Vice-President, subject to his election to the National Assembly.

In the general election of 1994 the opposition Botswana National Front (BNF) had unexpectedly won 37.7% of the votes, but hostility between its founder and leader, Kenneth Koma, and his deputy, Michael Dingake, split the party in 1998. Koma, supported by dissident members, expelled leading members, some of whom formed the Botswana Congress Party (BCP). This became the official opposition after 11 of the BNF's 13 deputies chose to join the new party. Despite discontent in the BDP over corruption and the selection of candidates for the October 1999 general election, the BDP won 33 of the 40 seats in that election, the BNF six and the BCP only one.

Following the recommendations of a commission established in July 2000 to investigate allegations of discrimination against minority ethnic groups, the Government presented several draft constitutional amendments to Parliament. The House of Chiefs, Botswana's second legislative chamber, was renamed the Ntlo ya Dikgosi, and its membership increased from 15 to 35, comprising 30 members elected every five years by senior tribal authorities and five specially appointed members. The National Assembly was enlarged from 40 seats to 57, with effect from the 2004 general election.

By 2000 the HIV/AIDS pandemic had become the Government's primary health concern. Although Botswana was the first country in Africa to distribute antiretroviral drugs (ARVs) for those with HIV, by 2003 an estimated 300,000 people were HIV-positive, with some 37% of 15–49-year-olds infected, the highest proportion anywhere in the world. As a result, life expectancy fell to 40 years by early 2006, the second lowest globally. However, this began to change as free ARVs were rolled out along with counselling, targeting priority groups of HIV-positive people, including pregnant women, children older than six months and patients with tuberculosis. Voluntary test centres were established, HIV prevalence among pregnant women began to decline, and mother-to-child transmission decreased dramatically. By the end of 2007 over 90,000 people were receiving ARVs. Yet by the late 2010s, although AIDS-related deaths and new infections had declined significantly, and life expectancy had risen considerably, around 23% of the adult population was still living with HIV.

From the late 1990s the Botswana Government provoked much international criticism for its attempts to relocate some 3,000 San, often referred to by the derogatory term Basarwa, meaning 'people without cattle', from their ancestral lands in the Central Kalahari Game Reserve (CKGR) to new settlements elsewhere. A 1985 government study had found that the San were abandoning their traditional means of hunting on foot and that permanent, settled agricultural communities with grazing livestock were being established, which the study concluded was not consistent with the land-use patterns envisaged when the CKGR was formed. In an attempt to persuade the San to move, the Government began to disconnect water supplies, and offered them compensation if they relocated. The UK-based minority-rights group Survival International (SI), which took up the case of the San, claimed that the policy of resettlement had been devised to allow diamond mining to take place in the reserve, where a number of diamond companies were awarded prospecting licences, while other licences were granted to drill methane.

The issue of the forced removal of the San was highlighted again in January 2002, when the Government cut off water supplies to those who had refused to leave the CKGR. In April

243 San, assisted financially by SI, began legal action, requesting a ruling that the termination of basic services was illegal and that they had been forcefully deprived of their land. The case was taken to the High Court, which in December 2006 ruled that the Government's refusal to issue the San with hunting licences for the reserve was unlawful and that they had the right to remain on their ancestral land. Although it accepted the judgment, the Government refused to help the San to return, and San continued to be detained for hunting in the reserve. In June 2008 President Khama reiterated that the authorities would not provide the San with any amenities. Meanwhile, diamond companies had begun prospecting, and in early 2009 the Government admitted that mining would take place in the reserve. SI continued to claim that the security forces were arresting and intimidating San in the CKGR. When a group of San who had returned were prevented from drawing water from a well, they lodged a formal complaint at the High Court. Although in 2010 that court rejected their right to the water, the Court of Appeal overturned this decision in January 2011. The Government accepted the judgment and pledged to continue efforts to resolve the issue with the San through dialogue. From January 2014 all hunting in Botswana except on game farms or ranches was banned, representing another major setback for the San.

Meanwhile, in February 2005 Kenneth Good, an Australian-born professor of political science at the University of Botswana, was given 48 hours to leave the country owing to the widespread belief that he had supported SI's attempt to have Botswana's diamonds labelled 'blood diamonds' (diamonds obtained in situations of conflict) because of the removal of the San from the CKGR. President Mogae and his Government were strong supporters of the Kimberley Process Certification Scheme, which regulates the trade in rough diamonds, and Botswana maintained that the country could account for the origin of its diamonds. Although Good challenged his deportation order in court, he failed to have the decision overturned.

At the general election held in October 2004, the ruling BDP won 44 of the 57 seats with 51.7% of the vote. Mogae was sworn in for a second term on 2 November. The President was able to appoint four members of the Assembly, and his selection of two defeated BDP candidates was criticized for breaking an unwritten rule that prevented such appointments. However, the Mogae Government was much praised, with the Mo Ibrahim Foundation in 2007 ranking Botswana first in Africa for adherence to the rule of law, transparency and lack of corruption, and Transparency International (TI) naming Botswana as the least corrupt African country. (After Mogae's second term as President ended, he was awarded the 2008 Ibrahim Prize for Achievement in African Leadership, granted for good governance.) Mogae relinquished the presidency on 31 March 2008, and the following day Khama was inaugurated as head of state. Some observers feared that Khama's leadership style would be authoritarian, given his military background. However, most commentators were impressed by the peaceful nature of the handover, a stark contrast to neighbouring Zimbabwe, where President Robert Mugabe was increasingly using force to retain power.

THE PRESIDENCY OF IAN KHAMA

In 2008 the Director of Public Prosecutions brought corruption charges against the former Managing Director of Debswana Diamond Co (Pty) Ltd, Louis Nchindo, and a number of that company's senior employees. Debswana, a 50:50 joint venture between the Botswana Government and De Beers Centenary AG of Switzerland, contributed more than 80% of Botswana's foreign earnings through its diamond sales and 50% of the country's public revenue. In February 2010 Nchindo was found dead in a remote game reserve, shortly before the much-delayed case against him was to be heard. Former President Mogae was to have given evidence for the prosecution, amid allegations that De Beers had funded the BDP over many years. Nchindo's death was registered as suicide, although some believed that he could have been murdered to prevent the case from proceeding. By then several extrajudicial killings had taken place of people whom the state referred to as suspected criminals, while other allegations of official corruption were made.

Prior to the general election held in October 2009, the Barata-Phathi ('We Love the Party') faction of the BDP accused President Khama of acting dictatorially. However, Khama retained widespread support, especially in rural areas, and easily secured his first full, five-year presidential term. The BDP won 45 of the 57 seats in the National Assembly, having received 53.3% of the vote; the BNF secured six seats, with 21.9% of the vote; and the BCP won four seats, with 19.2%. Nevertheless, tensions within the BDP remained, and in April 2010 prominent members of the Barata-Phathi faction left to form the Botswana Movement for Democracy (BMD), which four members of Parliament joined.

In April 2011 public sector workers commenced industrial action demanding higher wages, their salaries having remained stagnant since 2008. President Khama contended that the Government, which remained the single largest employer in the country, could not afford to meet the workers' demands owing to the budgetary deficit; this was forecast to increase in the 2011/12 fiscal year, largely owing to the impact of the global recession on state revenues and to reduced revenues from the Southern African Customs Union (SACU). Almost 1,500 government employees in essential services were dismissed, and a number of hospitals and schools were closed. The trade unions demanded the unconditional reinstatement of those dismissed. By mid-May 2011 over 90,000 workers were involved, and the strike threatened to undermine the country's image as an African success story. Khama held firm, however, and the strike ended after eight weeks. The Government then expanded the areas of work regarded as essential and in which workers could not take industrial action (these included teachers and diamond workers). However, it reinstated most of the public sector workers who had been dismissed, following legal action by the labour unions.

The opposition parties failed to capitalize on the opportunity that the strike provided, although the leading public sector trade union urged them to enter an electoral alliance ahead of the 2014 general election. While the BMD, the BNF, the BCP and the Botswana People's Party (BPP) agreed to co-operate electorally, in December 2011 the BCP withdrew from unity talks due to a dispute over the allocation of parliamentary constituencies. The BDP, which in 2012 celebrated its 50th anniversary, continued to present itself as the natural party of government. In response, the BNF, the BMD and the BPP formed a loose alliance, the Umbrella for Democratic Change (UDC), but the opposition lacked the resources to mount an effective challenge to the ruling party. It did, however, criticize the Government for corruption, poor service delivery, and the use of increasingly authoritarian measures.

The general election held on 24 October 2014 again returned the BDP to power with a considerable majority, winning 37 of the 57 elected seats. However, for the first time since independence it gained less than 50% of the vote (46.5%). While the party retained its traditional support among rural and older voters, it was clearly losing support among younger voters and the urban middle class. The UDC—under the forceful leadership of Duma Boko, a former law lecturer at the University of Botswana and a human rights activist—won 30.0% of the vote, securing 17 seats, while the BCP won 20.4% and three seats. Having won a second term in office, President Khama asked members of Parliament to vote on his nomination for Vice-President by a show of hands and not by secret ballot. This led to fears that he intended to name his younger brother, Tshekedi Khama, as his deputy and likely successor, and the High Court ruled that the vote should be held by secret ballot to protect lawmakers from undue influence by the President. Parliament then approved the appointment of the Minister of Education and Skills Development, Mokgweetsi Masisi, as the country's eighth Vice-President. Meanwhile, a new Cabinet was appointed shortly after President Khama's inauguration on 28 October. Masisi's position within the BDP was strengthened after he became party chairperson at the congress held in July 2015. Although his position was not unchallenged, it was widely assumed therefore that Masisi would be Khama's successor.

In July 2014 President Khama launched Bot50, which was to organize nationwide activities until September 2016, Botswana's 50th anniversary of independence, to celebrate the country's achievements over the five decades. A negative note was struck, however, when the US-based organization Freedom House, which monitors levels of political freedom across the world, downgraded Botswana's ranking, claiming that freedom of expression was under attack. In May 2015 officials from the Directorate on Corruption and Economic Crime detained staff of the *Botswana Gazette*, after the newspaper reported alleged links between the Directorate on Intelligence and Security Services (DISS) and the BDP to secure illegal oil and diamond deals with a South African petroleum company. More positively, the Ibrahim Index of African Governance listed Botswana as first on the continent in the category of safety and security, and third overall. In 2015–17 it was the least corrupt African country on the TI Corruption Perception Index. The Government congratulated itself on the progress that had been made in meeting the United Nations (UN) Millennium Development Goals, especially in reducing poverty and achieving universal access to HIV treatment, and signed on to the UN's new Sustainable Development Goals.

By 2016 Botswana had come to be regarded as a successful example of democratic stability and socioeconomic progress, having seemingly avoided the 'resource curse' that afflicted so many other African countries. However, a number of problems remained. As a largely semi-arid country, with limited water resources, Botswana continued to import 90% of its food, mostly from South Africa. Climate change seemed likely to exacerbate food supply problems, and rising food prices were a significant issue in a country with one of the most inequitable income distributions in the world, and large unemployment. Although Botswana was a middle-income country, the median per head household income in Gaborone, the capital, was little more than US $2 per day. Furthermore, the mining industry remained under stress and the Government acknowledged the need to diversify the economy; tourism received considerable private and public investment. Yet the main tourist attraction, the Okavango Delta, was threatened by Angola's use of water from the Kavango river for new plantations, an issue that was under discussion. Although President Khama was criticized for his authoritarianism, for failing to promote internal democracy and for not doing enough to diversify the economy, Botswana retained its reputation for good governance and for being the least corrupt country in the Southern African Development Community (SADC—see *External Relations*). Nevertheless, in his last months in office Khama was accused of corruption and linked to a case involving the alleged looting of the National Petroleum Fund.

THE PRESIDENCY OF MOKGWEETSI MASISI

In March 2017 Khama had announced that he would resign the presidency in March 2018, after completing two terms in office. Another peaceful transition followed, with Masisi taking over as President on 1 April 2018. He quickly began to assert himself against Khama, and relations between the two men became increasingly acrimonious. Masisi restricted Khama's privileges, including the use of official aircraft, and overturned the ban on hunting that Khama had supported, allowing controlled culling of Botswana's large elephant population, while Masisi also relaxed some of the strict alcohol laws Khama had imposed. Khama had expected Masisi to appoint his younger brother, Tshekedi, to the vice-presidency, but instead Masisi moved him from the important tourism portfolio to that of youth empowerment, sport and culture development. Furthermore, Masisi replaced the much-feared DISS Director-General, Isaac Kgosi, a close ally of Ian Khama, and Kgosi was then very publicly arrested in January 2019 on charges of alleged tax evasion.

By early 2019 Ian Khama was openly supporting Dr Pelonomi Venson-Moitoi, who had served under him as Minister of International Affairs and Co-operation, for the BDP's presidential nomination for the forthcoming general election. This was the first time that an incumbent President had been challenged for his party's nomination as candidate in a forthcoming election. Khama argued that unless Venson-Moitoi was chosen, the BDP might split, fail to win a majority in the election and might thus have to enter a coalition with other parties. However, on the eve of the BDP's elective congress in April, Venson-Moitoi withdrew her candidacy, claiming that the process was rigged against her, with some of her supporters disqualified from attending. (A last-minute court bid to block the conference from taking place had also been dismissed.) Thus, Masisi became the BDP's presidential candidate. Khama continued to oppose Masisi by endorsing opposition parliamentary candidates, and allegedly leading a shadowy BDP faction called New Jerusalem. In late May, after Masisi had rescinded a ban on elephant trophy hunting, Khama announced that he had left the BDP, had made a mistake in choosing Masisi as his successor, and would support the opposition UDC in the election.

In the elections for the National Assembly held on 23 October 2019, the ruling BDP won 52.7% of the vote and 38 of the 57 elected seats. This represented an improvement on the party's performance in 2014. Masisi was subsequently elected by the Assembly for a further presidential term. The UDC won 35.9% of the vote and 15 seats, a slight improvement in its share of the popular vote but a decline in its parliamentary representation. The party Khama backed—the Botswana Patriotic Front, BPF—received 4.4% of the vote and three seats. Although SADC and African Union (AU) observer missions found no fault with the elections, UDC leader Boko and Khama complained of 'massive electoral discrepancies'. In December 2019 the High Court dismissed a challenge to the results in 16 constituencies, on the grounds that there was insufficient evidence to prove fraud. The Court of Appeal also rejected the challenge in January 2020.

In February 2019 Botswana had acceded to the African Peer Review Mechanism (APRM). In anticipation of the visit of an APRM team to Botswana in 2020, non-governmental organizations launched an APRM popular sensitization project, which produced a report outlining where Botswana fell short on governance, respect for human rights and the welfare of its citizens. The coronavirus disease (COVID-19) pandemic then put the APRM process on hold. At the end of March 2020, after the first cases were confirmed in Botswana, President Masisi declared a state of public emergency, and announced a strict nationwide lockdown from 2 April for 21 days: gatherings were restricted, along with domestic and international travel, schools were closed, and the sale of alcohol was banned. The National Assembly approved the state of emergency, although the UDC maintained that it would grant too much power to Masisi. All members of Parliament were forcibly placed in quarantine after a health worker who had screened them for the virus was found to have COVID-19. To ameliorate the socioeconomic impact of the pandemic, the Government approved wage subsidies and tax relief, and in early May eased certain restrictions. Some mines began to resume production. However, in June, as infections rose, Gaborone was declared a high-risk area and travel in and out of the city was strictly controlled. In September the National Assembly agreed to extend the state of emergency for another six months (as also occurred in April 2021), despite further objections from the opposition alliance, which cited the major impact it was having on the economy. When the BDP lost seats in a series of by-elections during late 2021 and early 2022, it was thought that Masisi's popularity had suffered because of the economic hardships caused by the lockdown.

The COVID-19 pandemic had particularly serious consequences for mining and tourism, the most important sectors of Botswana's economy. For a time the Government faced sharply reduced revenues from the lockdown and the fall-off in diamond sales. Buyers from diamond cutting and polishing centres in Europe, India and the People's Republic of China were unable to enter the country to buy diamonds from Debswana. Although Botswana was ranked best placed by *The Economist* in early May 2020 out of 66 emerging economies potentially in financial peril as a result of the pandemic (largely as a result of its low debt and strong foreign exchange reserves), the Minister of Finance and Economic Development, Dr Thapelo Matsheka, warned that the mining sector might contract by over 30% in 2020 and the economy as a whole by 13%, and that the budget deficit would widen significantly (see

Economy). Debswana later reported that its earnings almost halved in 2020. Botswana relied heavily on imports from South Africa, and these were negatively affected by controls at the border. By late June Botswana was experiencing a severe shortage of fuel. At that point the country had only one reported death from COVID-19, and at the end of 2020 Botswana had fewer than 15,000 confirmed cases and only 42 deaths from the virus. Cases then spiked, and by mid-2022 there had been over 300,000 confirmed cases and some 2,700 reported deaths. But by then, with relatively few new cases, with most restrictions having been lifted and with a revival of international travel, tourism had begun to recover fast.

Of even greater importance for the economy was the recovery in mineral sales. In 2021 Debswana sold 61% more diamonds by value (US $3,300m.) than in 2020. As the global market for diamonds recovered, Debswana increased production. It extended the lifespan of its flagship mine, Jwaneng, to 2034, and drew up plans to make it the world's largest underground mine. Then in early 2022 came the Russian invasion of Ukraine, which led to the imposition of sanctions on the Russian Federation and its mining conglomerate. As Russia was the world's largest producer of diamonds, this promised to give Botswana, the world's second largest producer, a greater share of Western markets and to boost the country's ambition to become a key regional centre for the cutting, polishing and trading of diamonds. Botswana asserted that it should host the permanent headquarters and secretariat for the Kimberley Process to combat trade in 'blood diamonds'. A 10-year diamond agreement between the Government and De Beers, which had expired in 2020 was extended to the end of June 2022, and then for a further year while negotiations continued. The Government pressed for greater tax revenues and more say over the whole diamond chain, from production and cutting to sales.

However, concern about its heavy dependence on diamonds led the Government to promote investment in other minerals, in particular coal, despite its role in climate change. The country was estimated to have 200,000m. metric tons in untapped reserves. As environmental concerns made coal an unattractive investment for many, Botswana hoped that China might take the lead as investor and customer. Demand for coal increased because of the war in Ukraine, and Botswana stepped up production. From April 2022 coal from Botswana began to be exported via Maputo, Mozambique.

Botswana continued to have the largest elephant population of any country, estimated at more than 130,000, and the Government decided controversially in early 2021 to lift a five-year ban on hunting elephants The main justification given for allowing some 300 to be shot was that local communities wanted elephant numbers reduced because of the damage they did to crops, and that allowing hunting would benefit such communities financially.

In November 2021 the Court of Appeal unanimously upheld a June 2019 ruling decriminalizing same-sex relationships. The Government had appealed the ruling, arguing that Botswana's people did not agree with it, but the Court ruled that such relationships should have constitutional protection.

Having made it clear that he wanted to oust Masisi, whom he accused of trying to get rid of him as a contender before the 2024 general election, Khama moved to South Africa in November 2021. When he was charged in a Gaborone court, along with three other leading Botswana figures, with possessing illegal firearms and other offences, he did not appear, stating that he had not been served with a summons. When the case was heard again in June 2022, without him, the state told the court that it would seek his extradition but by September this had not been requested. Khama continued to live in South Africa, claiming that he was planning to return to Botswana, but also that he believed it would be at the risk of his life. After the BDP performed badly in by-elections in July, Khama was seen celebrating in a video in which he wore the yellow colours of the BPF, which agreed in early August formally to become part of the UDC. Khama charged that President Masisi was using law enforcement measures, including arbitrary detentions, to purge political foes, and he predicted that the BDP would be defeated in the 2024 general election. Many observers were, however, sceptical that an opposition coalition would hold together before in the run-up to that election.

EXTERNAL RELATIONS

After the unilateral declaration of independence by Rhodesia (now Zimbabwe) in 1965, Seretse Khama voiced his opposition to the illegal regime, but his country remained dependent on the Rhodesian-owned railways for its economic survival. Khama, nevertheless, played an important role in the alliance of 'front-line' states against the apartheid regime in South Africa from the mid-1970s. Botswana was a founder member of the Southern African Development Co-ordination Conference (SADCC), formed in 1980 to encourage regional development and reduce its members' economic dependence on South Africa. In the 1970s and 1980s Botswana accommodated South African refugees, while preventing them from using the country as a base for attacks on South Africa. With the relaxation of the political climate within South Africa from 1990, bilateral relations gradually improved, and full diplomatic relations were established in June 1994. SADCC was reorganized in 1992 as the treaty organization SADC (see *The Presidency of Ian Khama*), with its headquarters in Gaborone, and South Africa joined SADC in August 1994.

In 1992 a border dispute developed between Botswana and Namibia regarding their rival territorial claims over a small island in the Chobe river, which Namibia called Kasikili and Botswana Sedudu. In early 1995 both countries agreed to present the case for arbitration at the International Court of Justice (ICJ) in The Hague, Netherlands, and in December 1998 the Court awarded the island to Botswana. What were perceived as attempts by Botswana to extend the role and capabilities of its armed forces (including the completion of a large new airbase at Molepolole in 1995) were, for a time, a source of friction with Namibia, although Botswana emphasized that it only sought to expand its regional and international peacekeeping role. A Namibian proposal to construct a pipeline to take water from the Okavango river, which feeds the Okavango Delta, an important habitat for Botswana's varied wildlife, created further tension. However, in August 2011 Botswana joined Namibia, Angola, Zimbabwe and Zambia in establishing the Kavango-Zambezi Transfrontier Conservation Area to protect wildlife, especially elephants, and encourage and manage tourism.

With the worsening of Zimbabwe's economic crisis from the mid-1990s, many Zimbabweans moved into Botswana, and several violent incidents took place along the border. In July 2003 Botswana and Zimbabwe began operating joint patrols intended to prevent the passage of refugees into Botswana, and by 2004 Botswana was repatriating some 2,500 illegal immigrants—mainly Zimbabweans—each month; it was unclear how many remained. President Mogae stated that Zimbabwe suffered from a 'drought of leadership', but hesitated to criticize the country openly. Shortly after Khama took office as President, amid record oil prices, the Botswana Government banned the export of bulk fuel to Zimbabwe, and Khama requested that the media expose the plight of refugees from Zimbabwe, for whom a temporary refugee camp had been set up in Francistown. Following the disputed presidential election in Zimbabwe in March 2008, Morgan Tsvangirai, leader of the opposition Movement for Democratic Change, who claimed to have won the election, was granted temporary refuge in Gaborone. Khama announced that he would not attend SADC meetings to which Mugabe had been invited. In June the Botswana Government condemned the Mugabe regime's campaign of violence and intimidation against opposition supporters ahead of the run-off poll. Khama then reluctantly supported the power-sharing arrangement subsequently reached in Zimbabwe, but described the July 2013 as neither free nor fair and criticized SADC for accepting the outcome. Khama subsequently declared that Botswana would not participate in any future SADC election observer missions because they were a waste of resources.

Following a ferry accident in 2003, Botswana and Zambia sought funding for a bridge across the Zambezi river at Kazungula, to replace the ferry service, which created a bottleneck for tourist traffic and trade. Zimbabwe initially raised objections because part of the bridge would straddle its territory, and Botswana and Zambia decided to proceed, bypassing Zimbabwe. In March 2012 the African Development Bank and Japan's Development Assistance Agency agreed to provide loans to finance the construction of a road and rail bridge, at a cost of US $230m., to be paid for by Botswana and Zambia in equal proportions. Construction began in 2014. In March 2018, after the accession to power of President Emmerson Mnangagwa in Zimbabwe, Botswana and Zambia agreed that Zimbabwe could join the second phase of the project. After a delay caused in part by the COVID-19 pandemic, the bridge was finally opened in May 2021.

Although a large building was erected in Gaborone to house the SADC secretariat, Botswana's attitude to SADC was ambivalent. In 2004 SADC agreed that an early-warning centre to collect information on developing crises in the region would be located in Botswana. President Khama was a low-key chair of SADC from August 2015, but broke ranks with both SADC and the AU when he criticized an AU resolution that sought immunity for sitting heads of state at the International Criminal Court (ICC), while in February 2016 the Botswana Minister of International Affairs and Co-operation, Dr Pelonomi Venson-Moitoi, spoke of the ICC as a 'noble idea' and a means to protect the powerless from abuse by rulers. She was the SADC candidate to take over the AU Commission chair when Nkosazana Dlamini-Zuma stepped down in 2017, but received only lukewarm backing from South Africa.

President Khama welcomed Mugabe's departure as President of Zimbabwe in November 2017 and in February 2018 invited the new President for a state visit, during which Mnangagwa spoke of a new special bilateral relationship and announced that Zimbabwe would in future process its diamonds in Botswana. Under President Masisi relations with Zimbabwe continued to improve, although efforts to stop illegal immigration from Zimbabwe largely failed, as many who were deported subsequently returned to Botswana.

After initially signing its own interim Economic Partnership Agreement (EPA) with the European Union (EU) in June 2009, Botswana agreed in 2010 to join the other SACU countries and Mozambique in presenting a united front to the EU, and after lengthy negotiations Botswana was one of the countries that in July 2014 signed a joint SADC-EU EPA. Botswana was concerned when South Africa pressed for a revision of the revenue-sharing formula in SACU because its earnings from SACU were its second largest source of revenue after minerals. Within SACU Botswana argued for a common industrialization policy, claiming that SACU had benefited South African industry at the expense of all others in the region.

In 2003 Botswana and South Africa agreed to form a joint permanent commission to meet biannually and carry out studies in agriculture, livestock, water affairs, mining and tourism. A Botswana-South Africa Joint Permanent Commission on Defence and Security also met annually on a rotational basis. Relations between the two countries suffered when in late 2011 Julius Malema, who headed the ANC Youth League, appealed for regime change in Botswana, calling the Government a 'puppet' of US 'imperialism' and out of line with other countries in southern Africa on Zimbabwe and other regional matters. The Youth League declared that it would work towards uniting the Botswana opposition against the BDP. South African President Jacob Zuma criticized this, and Malema was expelled from the ANC. To improve relations, a formal South Africa-Botswana Bi-National Commission was inaugurated in Pretoria, South Africa, in November 2013. Co-chaired by the respective Presidents, it was supposed to meet annually to monitor progress in implementing bilateral agreements. After some years in which it did not meet, in part because of the COVID-19 pandemic, it convened for the fifth time in April 2022 and the two parties proclaimed how good relations were.

From April 2019, however, cordial relations between Botswana and South Africa were strained after a Botswana newspaper alleged that Bridgette Motsepe-Radebe, a South African with mining interests in Botswana, wife of the South African Minister of Energy and sister-in-law of President Cyril Ramaphosa, had flown to the Victoria Falls to give Ian Khama a large sum of money to be used in support of the campaign by Venson-

Moitoi to become the BDP's presidential candidate in the election. Ramaphosa dispatched his Minister of International Relations and Co-Operation to Botswana to assure Masisi that the South African Government was not involved in the matter, but the Botswana authorities informed Motsepe-Radebe that she would need to apply for a visa if she wished to visit the country. From June 2020 AfriForum, a conservative South African lobby group, was hired to assist the Botswana authorities in pursuing charges of money laundering and fraud against her. She denied the allegations and threatened to sue, while AfriForum accused the South African authorities of failing to provide information about her business affairs. AfriForum's chief prosecutor, Gerrie Nel, brought a case in a South African court against a Botswana intelligence agent on charges of terrorism and money-laundering, but when the case came to court in August 2021 it was thrown out, with the judge finding that the accounts alleged to have been used for laundering money had never existed.

President Ian Khama had been critical of China for its substandard and costly work on a coal-fired power station and its sensitivity over any recognition of the Dalai Lama, the head of Tibet's Buddhist clergy and the region's spiritual leader. When Masisi visited China soon after becoming head of state, he confirmed that the Dalai Lama would not be allowed to visit Botswana, and when Khama travelled to meet the Dalai Lama in March 2019, the Masisi Government made clear its displeasure.

In early 2021 members of the indigenous San communities of both Botswana and Namibia protested against the two Governments allowing a Canadian firm, ReconAfrica, to begin an exploratory test for oil and gas in the Kavango Basin, which straddled the two countries and was part of the Kavango-Zambezi Transfrontier Conservation Area. While ReconAfrica spoke of a 25-year project that would extract some 120,000m. barrels of oil equivalent, creating jobs for the local population, critics said that the environmental impact assessment procedures were flawed and that, although the exploration licence area did not include the most sensitive areas, crucial water supplies would be contaminated, threatening Botswana's main tourist attraction, the Okavango Delta—designated by the UN Educational, Scientific and Cultural Organization (UNESCO) as a World Heritage Site.

In 2022 Botswana increased co-operation with neighbouring Namibia. In August the two countries stopped agricultural imports from South Africa to protect their local agricultural industries and in September President Masisi welcomed the President of Namibia in Gaborone for the inaugural meeting of a Botswana-Namibia Bi-National Commission, which was expected to meet on a regular basis.

Economy

ROBERT E. LOONEY

INTRODUCTION

Botswana's economy is an African success story and often considered a role model for other sub-Saharan African countries. In contrast to the poor economic record of most landlocked countries in the region, Botswana's relatively small population (2.3m. in 2022) has not hindered it in sustaining high economic growth rates over the last 30 years. The keys to the country's success have been creating and maintaining elevated levels of governance, stable institutions, and the application of conservative monetary and fiscal policies. This policy mix enabled the country to overcome many of its impediments when achieving independence in 1966.

Before independence, Botswana was the British protectorate of Bechuanaland. The British governed the area, assuming that South Africa would eventually absorb the territory. Insufficient investment took place during the colonial period, and it was not until 1957 that the British invested significantly in the protectorate's infrastructure and education. When Botswana became independent, per capita incomes were only around US $100. Cattle herding was the primary economic activity, with little in the way of an industrial base, skilled workers, or a middle class. However, since independence Botswana has been a prosperous, democratic model for the rest of sub-Saharan Africa. Today diamond mining is the leading industry and the economy's primary driver. However, diamonds have been a mixed blessing. Diamond revenues have financed much of the country's infrastructure while putting the Government's finances on a solid footing. Concurrently, they have made the economy vulnerable to external developments, mainly outside the country's control, and highlighted the need for diversification to sustain high levels of economic performance.

After expanding at an average annual rate of 8.7% in the 1960s, economic growth accelerated to 15.4% in the 1970s. Since then, growth in gross domestic product (GDP), while still satisfactory by international standards, has gradually declined. The country has experienced average annual expansion rates of 7.8% in the 1980s and 1990s, falling to 3.5% during 2000–21. By the end of 2021 this expansion had propelled Botswana's per capita income to US $16,167 on a purchasing-power parity (PPP) basis (2017 international dollars), qualifying the country for membership in the World Bank's group of upper-middle-income countries. Botswana is sub-Saharan Africa's 20th largest economy, slightly smaller than Gabon but larger than Mozambique. Botswana's population was 2.3m. according to the provisional results of the March 2022 census, with a relatively low projected growth rate of 1.8% for 2020–25. However, the population's demographic structure is favourable for economic growth. The ratio of the working-age group (15–64 years) is expected to increase from 62.1% in 2020 to 65.4% in 2030 and to 67.3% in 2040.

Recent years have seen high growth volatility, with recorded rates of economic expansion of 6.8% (2011), 0.2% (2012), 11.1% (2013) and 5.7% (2014), before a contraction of 4.9% in 2015. Growth recovered in 2016, with the economy expanding by 7.2%, only to slip to 4.1% in 2017 and 4.2% in 2018. In 2019 growth fell back to 3.0% because of a severe drought. Traditionally, growth volatility has stemmed from droughts and developments in the mining sector. However, the country's economic situation changed dramatically in 2020 with the global spread of novel coronavirus disease (COVID-19). Not only did the economy contract by 8.5%, but many of the country's vulnerabilities—including overdependence on sectors such as mining and tourism—became immediately apparent. Sharp contractions occurred in mining (26.2%), manufacturing (8.7%), construction (11.0%), trade, hotels and restaurants (14.8%), and transport and communications (7.7%). However, the country experienced a strong recovery in 2021, with GDP growth reaching 12.1%, with industry, mainly diamonds, leading the expansion at 26.7%.

Before the COVID-19 pandemic, the country's economic performance appeared satisfactory. However, the World Bank had classified Botswana, along with 18 other African countries, as 'underperforming' as the country's growth (of 2.6%) in 2015–19 declined from what it had been during 1995–2008 (5.3%). This weakening occurred across all the economy's sub-sectors, with the most significant reductions occurring in mining (growth of 3.5% in 1995–2008 compared with a decrease of 6.1% in 2015–19), manufacturing (an increase of 7.1% compared with 2.6%), and trade, hotels and restaurants (growth of 10.2% compared with 5.2%). In 2020 unemployment increased to 17.7%, the third highest in the region, following South Africa and Sudan.

Under President Mokgweetsi Masisi (who assumed office in April 2018), the Government appears determined to arrest the economy's recent slippage by attempting to reduce unemployment, through diversifying the economy away from minerals and mining.

However, the Government has found that diversification and employment generation goals often clash. For example, recently the Government found countless elephants in the country were a threat to improved economic growth and community livelihoods—elephants can destroy crops when they encroach onto farmland. However, the proposed culling led to the cancellation of many tourist groups and intense international condemnation.

The COVID-19 pandemic hit the country hard, with cases increasing well into 2022. One wave started on 1 July 2021, with cases rising from 71,443 to 186,594 by 31 October. Another wave increased cases from 204,701 in December to 302,752 by 26 March 2022. However, the World Bank was optimistic that growth in Botswana will remain steady, at 4.1% in 2022 and 4.0% in 2023.

In part, optimism stems from a faster rollout of vaccines than expected, with the country successfully meeting the World Health Organization's global target of vaccinating 40% of the population by the end of December 2021. Also, the Omicron variant of COVID-19, first discovered by both Botswana and South Africa in late November 2021, caused a record low number of COVID-related hospitalizations and deaths. These factors point toward an economic recovery that should sustain growth in 2022.

DEVELOPMENT AND GOVERNANCE INDICATORS

Botswana's solid economic performance has improved several significant socioeconomic indicators in recent years. The United Nations Development Programme (UNDP)'s *Human Development Report (HDR) 2020* showed Botswana having a Human Development Index (HDI) ranking of 100th out of 189 countries, up from 108th in 2015. This improvement also elevated Botswana into the UN's 'high human development' group. However, Botswana's HDI ranking was 27 places lower than that for gross national income, suggesting that the country's overall prosperity did not translate directly into socioeconomic improvements. Also, Botswana's advances in this area have slowed down over the past decade. Between 2000 and 2010 the country's HDI scores improved at an average annual rate of 1.33% before falling to 1.15% in 2010–19.

Botswana ranked 82nd out of 167 countries on the Legatum Institute's 2021 Prosperity Index. The country's strengths included governance (38th), economic quality (53rd) and personal freedom (57th), while its weaknesses included the natural environment (141st), health (131st) and living conditions (114th).

The World Bank characterizes the country's growth as pro-poor, and in its most recent (March 2015) Botswana Poverty Assessment documented that between 2002/03 and 2009/10, poverty decreased steadily from 29.8% to 18.2%. During this period the incidence of extreme poverty declined from 22.7% to 13.8%. Between 2002/03 and 2009/10 rural areas accounted for 87% of the poverty reduction. For 2015/16, UNDP's *HDR 2020* showed that 17.2% of the population suffered from multidimensional poverty and 3.5% from severe multidimensional poverty. Approximately 19.7% were vulnerable to multidimensional poverty. Health contributed 30.3% to the country's multidimensional poverty, with education accounting for 16.5% and standard of living 53.2%. The World Bank's figures for 2021 estimated that at US $1.90 per person per day (in 2011 international PPP prices), 12.3% of the population were in poverty. At $3.20, the rate increased to 33.1% and at $5.50, it was 56.6%.

Poverty reduction in Botswana involved a combination of equitable growth and a fall in fertility rates. Other poverty-reducing actions included increased credit and the expansion of social assistance programmes. Also, Botswana is an anomaly in sub-Saharan Africa in that both redistribution and growth have contributed to reducing poverty. The consumption per capita growth rate for the bottom 40th percentile of the population was considerably higher than those in the top 60th percentile.

Despite the gains in poverty alleviation, the country's income distribution remains highly unequal. However, estimates vary. In 2017 Botswana had a Gini coefficient (a measure of inequality in income distribution) of 0.61 in 2017, the third highest in sub-Saharan Africa. As of 2021, the country had reached none of the UN's 17 Sustainable Development Goals, and it faced significant challenges in 10 of the goals.

Botswana's development and its long-run economic expansion reflect its robust governance structures. However, while Botswana generally scores well in the major areas of governance, as ranked on the World Bank's Governance Index, recent years have seen a reversal of gains made earlier, with the country falling from the 74th percentile in 1996 to the 61st in 2020. Furthermore, while Botswana is the least corrupt country in sub-Saharan Africa, the World Bank's control of corruption measure has shown a downward trend since 2003, when Botswana ranked very high at the 85th percentile. By 2019 the country had fallen to the 72nd percentile. Another area of concern is government effectiveness, where Botswana's ranking dropped from the 71st percentile in 2016 to the 63rd in 2020.

AGRICULTURE

Botswana's topography is far from ideal for agricultural production. Most of the country's land comprises semi-desert and savannah with erratic rainfall and relatively poor soils, making it more suitable for grazing than crop production. The country's water stress ranking in 2020 was 55th globally, just behind Eritrea but ahead of Eswatini. Currently, changing rain patterns threaten crop plantings and yields, leading to food shortages and the need to rely on imports. There has been a decline in agricultural productivity since the mid-1900s. After reaching US $4,257 (constant 2010 prices), value-added per worker in agriculture declined to only $1,749 by 2019.

Botswana's principal crops are maize, sorghum, millet, beans, sunflowers, groundnuts, roots and tubers, and pulses. Maize production, which stood at 12.3m. metric tons in 2017, increased to 24.6m. tons in 2018 before falling to 7.7m. tons in 2019. Despite rising considerably in 2020, to 61.9m. tons, production is still significantly below consumption, which averages around 300m. tons per year, with the shortfall made up through imports. Sorghum production has fluctuated even more dramatically in recent years, increasing to 48.6m. tons in 2018 from 6.0m. tons in 2017. Production then fell to 36.0m. tons in 2018 before rising to 87.8m. tons in 2020.

As in most growing emerging economies, agriculture in Botswana has declined as a share of GDP. Given the country's limited prospects for expanding the acreage under cultivation or irrigation, this contraction has been more rapid than is usually the case. Growth declined sharply in the 1980s and 1990s, averaging only 1.5% and 1.6% per year, respectively, before recovering briefly in the 2000s to 2.8% per year. However, in 2010–21 growth fell to an average annual rate of 1.4%.

Agriculture's average share of GDP fell from 38.9% in the 1960s to 23.7% in the 1970s. By the 1980s agriculture accounted for only 8.7% of GDP, falling to 4.3% in the 1990s. Since 2000 the agricultural sector has averaged around 2.0% of GDP per year, accounting for 2.1% in 2021. In sharp contrast to the sectorial patterns found in most developing economies, agriculture has increased its share of the employed workforce, expanding from 17.2% in the 1990s to 22.3% in the 2000s and reaching an average of 22.6% during 2010–19. However, the agricultural sector still retains a significant share of the labour force because of its falling worker productivity.

Advocates for more governmental emphasis on agriculture often argue that it still provides employment and income for most of its rural population, despite the sector's stagnant productivity. Income generated in the industry has also provided an essential means of reducing poverty because Botswana's agricultural methods are relatively labour-intensive.

Botswana has invested significantly in agricultural research and development, hoping to improve the sector's productivity and performance. Agriculture will be a significant beneficiary of the conflict in Ukraine following its invasion by the Russian Federation in February 2022, with global prices of maize elevated through much of 2022. With the Russia–Ukraine conflict, escalating maize prices accelerated their upward trend from September 2021, stemming from the increased cost of energy used in fertilizers. Maize is a fertilizer-intensive crop, and if the war continues, its price may offset any profitability gains from the higher maize prices.

MINERALS AND MINING

Over the last four decades, Botswana's mining sector has, on average, generated approximately 85% of the country's foreign exchange earnings and over one-third of government revenues. Botswana's primary area of mining is diamonds. Other minerals extracted include coal, copper and soda ash. The country also possesses untapped deposits of uranium, lead and zinc. Currently, Botswana contains over 60% of Africa's identified untapped coal reserves. In contrast with many of Africa's mineral producers, the business environment has been favourable to investment in the sector with low taxes, minimal political interference, and streamlined licensing procedures.

Large-scale mineral exploration began in 1971, and diamonds swiftly became the critical sector of the economy and the ultimate source of the country's rapid economic expansion. Botswana is consistently among the world's three largest diamond producers, along with Russia and the People's Republic of China. In 2018 Botswana produced nearly 24.4m. carats of diamonds, with production declining to 23.7m. carats in 2019. Although classified as essential services, allowing mining operations to continue despite the country's lockdowns against COVID-19, diamond production fell to just under 16.8m. carats in 2020. However, the dominant diamond producer, Debswana, increased its output in 2021, bringing production back to 21.0m. carats with a forecast of 22.0m. carats in 2022. In 2021 Botswana was the world's fourth largest producer of industrial diamonds, with 6m. carats produced, following Russia (15m. carats), the Democratic Republic of the Congo (11m. carats) and Australia (8m. carats). In 2020 Botswana was the world's second largest diamond producer, albeit distant from Russia's output of 32.1m. carats.

Despite its importance in generating foreign exchange and government revenues, the mining sector's overall size in the economy has been declining. Mining averaged 25.8% of GDP in 2004 before falling to 19.2% in 2010 and 11.5% in 2020. Because of its capital-intensive nature, the mining sector only employs about 6% of the country's formal labour force.

In recent years the mining sector has experienced erratic growth, contracting by 5.8% in 2012 before expanding by 24.2% in 2013. The industry then entered a decline, growing by only 0.5% in 2014 before contracting by 19.6% in 2015, 3.5% in 2016 and 11.2% in 2017. It expanded by 7.5% in 2018, only to contract again by 4.0% in 2019 and by 26.2% in 2020. The sharp decline in 2020 stemmed, in part, from travel restrictions related to COVID-19, which prevented international buyers from purchasing diamonds in Botswana. The primary diamond corporation, De Beers, cancelled its diamond sales in Gaborone in March 2020 and has since needed to expand its e-commerce into selling rough gems online outside of Botswana.

Botswana's diamond mines are currently owned and managed by Debswana, which has a similar share ownership arrangement between the Botswana Government and De Beers Centenary. Botswana's Jwaneng mine is the world's largest mine, producing 15% of the global supply in 2017. Jwaneng and another mine, Orapa, currently account for 92% of the country's diamond production.

Continued investment in the diamond sector bodes well for the sector's long-term outlook. In April 2021 Debswana confirmed that it is undergoing a significant expansion through developing an underground mine. Expansions are also scheduled for Canada's Lucara Diamond operations at Karowe.

Botswana's Government is attempting to bring more value to its diamond sector by increasing the number of De Beers diamonds cut and polished domestically. Botswana currently relies on gems for 90% of its exports and hopes to move up the value chain. The country's exports of polished diamonds as a percentage of total gem exports have been climbing in recent years, but they only reached US $846m. in 2018, compared with $5,100m. for exports of rough diamonds.

With the recent global increase in copper prices, there is interest in reviving several of the country's idled mines. The Government is taking steps to sell BCL Mine Limited, which went into liquidation in 2015 due to low copper prices and high operating costs. Several copper mines have stopped running in recent years because of high operating costs and low copper prices. Botswana averaged about 39,000 metric tons of mined copper during 2009–13 (or 0.3% of global output) before production slowed and halted in recent years.

New projects are making progress. Botswana's most recently opened and only operational copper mine, the Khoemacau mine, has an annual output of 60,000–65,000 metric tons of copper concentrate and 2m. oz of silver metal. US-based private equity firm Cupric Canyon owns the mine.

Since identifying the exploitation of the country's considerable coal reserves as a national objective, the Government is working to supply the infrastructure to allow for increased production and exports. Botswana has extensive coal reserves and the potential to become a major coal producer on a global scale. In the early 1990s coal production averaged slightly less than 1.0m. metric tons. However, production increased rapidly, rising from 1.0m. tons in 2010 to 2.1m. tons in 2015, 2.5m. tons in 2018 and 3.1m. tons in 2021.

In recent years Botswana's coal mining projects have continued to progress. For example, privately owned Minergy announced in 2019 that its Masama coal mine was now fully operational. It had produced its first saleable coal and exported it to South Africa and Namibia. The company intends to produce 100,000 metric tons per month in the coming years. Other projects are currently in the development stage. However, growing funding challenges mean that coal project financing will become increasingly reliant on funding coming from China.

TOURISM

Concern over Botswana's dependence on the diamond sector for most of the country's foreign exchange earnings and much of the Government's revenue has prompted efforts at economic diversification, particularly in the tourism industry. Botswana's advantage in this area is its unique ecosystem, the Okavango Delta, where tourists can find various game and birds. A large herd of elephants lives in the Chobe Game Reserve. The Central Kalahari Game Reserve (CKGR) offers unspoiled wilderness besides a variety of game. Popular safaris occur regularly in the Chobe National Park and the Moremi Game Reserve in the Okavango Delta.

With these resources to draw on, there is a great potential to attract an increasing number of international tourists to Botswana. However, since 2014 Botswana's tourism sector has come under severe criticism from Survival International (SI, see *History*), which started a significant advertising campaign advocating a boycott of tourism to the country. SI claimed that the Botswana Government was attempting to promote tourism in the CKGR while seeking to move the remaining members of the San from their homes in the Reserve. Despite some concessions by the Botswana Government, the boycott remains in effect.

In early 2019 the Government's consideration of revoking a five-year hunting ban sparked a global outcry with tourist groups, particularly those from Western countries, expressing severe misgivings. Despite warnings of tourist cancellations, the Government lifted the ban in May 2019, with hunting rights sold in packages of 10 elephants each. However, at the national level, the sale of these licences will have a minimal effect on fiscal revenue and the tourism sector and may cause many tourists to switch destinations.

In 2019 tourism contributed 9.6% of GDP and accounted for 8.4% of total employment. Tourism was second only to mining in generating government revenues and foreign exchange earnings in that year. However, as a result of the COVID-19-related travel restrictions and domestic lockdowns, tourism's contribution to GDP declined to 5.3% in 2020 and the sector employed just 6.6% of the workforce. International visitor expenditure, which accounted for 9.2% of total exports in 2019, fell to 2.7% in 2020. Tourist arrivals reached 2.7m. in 2019, but fell to 500,400 in 2020 and 433,000 in 2021. Because of lingering COVID-19 concerns and a likely slowdown in the global economy stemming from Russia's invasion of Ukraine, many experts forecast that arrivals will not return to their 2019 level until at least 2024.

MANUFACTURING

Manufacturing in Botswana has never played a prominent role in the economy. The sector has experienced periods of high growth, albeit from a low base. In the 1970s it expanded at an average annual rate of 21.1%, only to average 10.6% in the 1980s. From 1995 to 2009 the sector expanded at an average yearly rate of 7.1% but grew by only 3.0% during 2009–20. Growth in recent years slowed, with rates of 1.6% (2016), 2.2% (2017), 3.4% (2018) and 2.8% (2019), before declining by 8.7% in 2020. With these rates of growth, manufacturing has maintained a relatively constant share of GDP, although it declined from 5.6% in 2004 to 5.4% in 2020.

The limited development of manufacturing in Botswana stems from several impediments. These include location—it is distant from seaports, which affects the sourcing of raw materials and, therefore, export costs. There is also only a small domestic market, minimal availability of water and power, and a lack of competitiveness. On 1 January 2022 the country's minimum wage, at US $152 per month, was the fourth highest in sub-Saharan Africa. In 2020 Botswana ranked sixth in the region on the World Bank's Ease of Doing Business index, despite its stalled reforms.

The country has several structural deficiencies in critical areas that limit firm competitiveness and profitability. The World Economic Forum's *Global Competitiveness Report 2019* ranked the country's competitiveness at 91st out of 141 countries. However, this was a decline of 27 places from 2017. While the country has relatively good supporting institutions, ranking first in macroeconomic stability and 12th in future orientation of Government, it rates much lower in terms of infrastructure (108th), health (111th), skills (94th), innovative capability (99th) and flexibility of wage determination (111th). Botswana's domestic competition ranked 97th.

Several unfavourable aspects of the country's business climate and barriers to entrepreneurship continue to slow manufacturing's growth and diversification. Specifically, Botswana ranked 104th in overall business dynamism. It also ranked 132nd in time to start a business, 113th in developing innovative companies, and 104th in attitudes towards entrepreneurial risk.

While Heritage House classifies Botswana as having the third highest level of economic freedom in sub-Saharan Africa, there has been a slippage in recent years. Botswana's economic freedom reached a peak in 2014 and has been trending downward since. As a result, the country has declined from the top half of the 'moderately free' category to the lower half. Fiscal health, a previous strength, caused a large share of this erosion. There is little doubt that advances in competitiveness and economic freedom would improve the manufacturing environment and lead to higher investment rates and growth.

POWER AND WATER

Rapid growth in the economy and the population resulted in an equally swift expansion in demand for energy and water. In 2020 Botswana had one of the highest levels of electrification in sub-Saharan Africa, with rates of 72% overall, 90.7% in urban areas and 26.4% in rural areas. Thermal power, which currently makes up 99% of electricity generated, dominates generating capacity, with coal-fired power comprising the vast majority.

However, Botswana's power sector faces several difficulties that impede its ability to meet the rising demand. Losses from the grid are high, at around 16.2% in 2020, because of the rudimentary condition of the transmission lines and widespread theft from the system. A lack of domestic generating capacity means that the country is highly dependent on imported electricity, which is susceptible to interruptions.

Since 2006 the state-owned Botswana Power Corporation has undertaken a continuing programme of capacity expansion. However, delays have occurred, with load shedding becoming increasingly common. Policymakers were slow to respond to the looming shortages and adopted some emergency measures such as high-cost diesel generation to augment

domestic supplies. The contribution from renewables is currently minimal but will expand with the development of the small solar power segment, although this will depend to a large extent on foreign investment.

Proposed upgrades in the power sub-sector involve two transport-related projects, one to improve rail infrastructure linkage to South Africa and one to connect with Zambia, through which Botswana will gain a gateway to Central African markets. The improved rail links to South Africa could unlock Botswana's extensive coal reserves. Botswana has the second largest untapped coal reserves in sub-Saharan Africa, but a lack of infrastructure has been holding back investment in the sector.

The performance of the water sub-sector continues to be relatively poor due to water restrictions arising from periodic droughts and inadequate infrastructure to deliver water to the areas of most use. For an arid country such as Botswana, the provision of water is a formidable challenge. Still, approximately 96% of the population now has access to clean drinking water.

TRANSPORT AND COMMUNICATIONS

Botswana's landlocked status causes over-reliance on a few neighbouring ports, translating into longer trade times and transport costs. The situation poses a significant disadvantage for investors and foreign businesses in the country. Combined with the still rudimentary air freight transport links, the Government is under continual pressure to maintain, upgrade and expand Botswana's road and rail networks.

Botswana's transport and communications sector has shown steady growth since the mid-1990s, increasing at an average annual rate of 6.2% between 1995 and 2008, and by an average of 6.3% during 2009–20, despite contracting by 7.7% in 2020. As a result, the sector increased its contribution to total GDP from 3.4% in 2004 to 5.8% in 2020. Both transport and communications are fundamentally different from at the time of independence in 1965. Telecommunications were very primitive, and there were few paved roads; however, since 1964, the authorities have been able to link all the country's major towns by paved highways. Similarly, air traffic lagged until the establishment of a major airport in Gaborone in 1984.

Since independence, Botswana has made notable strides in enhancing the quality and extent of its roads. The country has 9,810 km of paved roads and 21,937 km that are unpaved. Botswana's roads remain in good condition because of the Government's large-scale investments in expanding and rehabilitating the network, even in more isolated rural areas. This effort enables the country to compete with the well-developed national road networks in South Africa and Namibia. Roads are the primary transport mode for freighted goods, with major roads linking neighbouring countries with main urban areas and economic centres, and therefore providing vital supply chain links for businesses.

Botswana's rail network is relatively underdeveloped compared with the national road network. However, it remains vital to supply chains in heavy industries. With 888 km of standard gauge track, the network comprises one primary line connecting major cities in the east to South Africa and Zimbabwe. However, in October 2018 Botswana Railways announced a planned expansion to add 520 km to the country's network.

In time, Botswana should emerge as a significant transportation gateway for the region's North–South Corridor, which will help support trade growth in Southern Africa—particularly once the African Continental Free Trade Area (AfCFTA) Agreement enters full operation and paves the way for investment into transport infrastructure.

Regulatory reform in the telecommunications sector has resulted in Botswana developing into one of the most liberalized markets in sub-Saharan Africa. Botswana currently has one of Africa's highest mobile market penetration rates. The state-run Botswana Telecommunications Corporation Ltd underwent partial privatization to further increase competition and innovation, with an initial public offer in 2016. Although three mobile operators should ensure a healthy level of competition, data rates remain high because of the country's landlocked setting and thus more limited access to international bandwidth than its neighbours.

BANKING AND FINANCE

Banking in Botswana began with the establishment of Standard Chartered Bank Botswana in 1897, later joined by Barclays Bank Botswana in the 1950s. Both banks functioned as branches of their South Africa headquarters before being incorporated in 1975 as independent entities. That year also marked the creation of the country's central bank, the Bank of Botswana (BoB), followed by introducing a national currency, the pula, in 1976. There are 10 commercial banks in Botswana, two small state-owned statutory banks, and one building society. Concentration is high, with four banks holding about 80% of total assets. All are foreign owned. Given the country's limited population and the small size of some banks, consolidation is likely. In a challenging environment, the banking sector remains relatively sound. Larger banks are more profitable because of economies of scale, but there remain some concerns about the potential instability caused by smaller banks with deteriorating asset quality levels.

Two laws govern the supervision of banks in Botswana: the Bank of Botswana Act 1996 (BoBA) and the Banking Act 1995 (BA). The BoBA regulates the role of the central bank, its powers, and its objectives. Under this, the BoB can make bylaws and issue directives to regulate the sector. The BoBA replaced earlier legislation, passed in 1975, that established the central bank. A new legislative framework dealt with substantial foreign exchange reserves and the maturity of the financial sector. The BA enables the BoB to licence, supervise, and regulate banks operating in Botswana to enhance competition.

There have been no banking failures, and the sector appears liberalized by sub-Saharan African standards. There are no direct controls over interest rates. The BoB has also created a relatively inflation-free environment, thus reducing a significant source of banking risk.

Finance and business services have shown steady growth since the mid-1990s, averaging 5.4% per year in 1995–2008 and 5.8% in 2009–2020, with banks willing to assume higher risks in lending. As a result, the sector has increased its share of GDP from 12.7% in 2004 to 13.4% in 2010 and to 15.3% in 2020.

Historically, banks heavily depended on household lending, with that sector accounting for most commercial bank loans. Profitability levels within the banking sector are respectable but have remained on the low side due to low interest rates in recent years. Recently, because of the pandemic, credit growth has declined because of a more cautious approach to lending in an environment of slower personal income growth and rising household debt-to-income levels.

The BoB has traditionally pursued conventional monetary policies and, in doing so, has created a stable price environment for banks to expand their portfolios. During the commodity boom of the mid-2000s, inflation increased slightly, with rates of 11.6% in 2006 and 12.6% in 2008. In recent years inflation has begun falling back to safe levels: it reached 3.1% in 2015 and 2.8% in 2016, before rising slightly to 3.1% in 2017 and 3.2% in 2018, declining to 2.8% in 2019 and 1.9% in 2020. However, inflation jumped to 6.7% in 2021 and was expected to rise further in 2022.

The BoB's recent monetary policy actions have attempted to support economic activity suffering from the effects of the COVID-19 pandemic. At its monetary policy meeting at the end of February 2021, the BoB kept its key policy rate at 3.75%. The move followed two rate cuts (of 50 basis points each) in 2020. In 2020 the BoB reduced the primary reserve requirements for commercial banks by 50% to 2.5% and the capital adequacy ratio to 12.5% (from 15%) to improve liquidity in the banking system. The BoB also lowered the downward rate of crawl for the pula to 2.87% from 1.51%, allowing the currency to depreciate faster to increase exports. At the meeting of its monetary policy committee held on 24 February 2022, the BoB maintained its main policy rate at 3.75%—a historic low—despite annual inflation, which reached a 13-year high of 10.6% in January. This action suggests that Botswana is maintaining an expansive monetary policy in real terms in its efforts to support an economic recovery, despite the continued upward pressure on prices (in particular, energy prices).

In 2018 Botswana amended its Financial Intelligence Agency Act to crack down on money laundering and terrorism financing. The reforms required newly registered companies to identify all their beneficiaries while requiring existing companies to comply, starting in July 2019. The move came after the European Union (EU) included Botswana in a list of jurisdictions it intended to blacklist because of concerns about money laundering and terrorism financing.

FOREIGN TRADE AND BALANCE OF PAYMENTS

Botswana has a reasonably open trade regime, with tariffs averaging around 0.5%. It is the third placed sub-Saharan country (after Guinea and Mauritius) in terms of its reliance on trade, with imports and exports in 2020 equal to 76% of GDP. Diamonds make up around three-quarters of the country's exports, with imports mainly comprising transport equipment, machinery, consumer goods and food. In 2020 21.5% of Botswana's exports went to the United Arab Emirates (UAE), followed by Belgium (21.4%), India (21.0%) and South Africa 13.4%. South Africa accounted for 58.6% of imports, followed by Belgium (7.8%), Namibia (7.6%) and the UAE (4.4%).

The country belongs to the Southern African Customs Union (SACU), whose member countries include Eswatini, Namibia, Lesotho and South Africa. SACU's goal is to lower trade barriers and encourage the expansion of trade between the member countries. Botswana also belongs to the Southern African Development Community (SADC), which promotes economic co-operation and integration. In November 2018 Botswana became the 51st country to sign the AfCFTA.

Botswana's foreign trade has several significant trends. Exports of goods and services grew at an average annual rate of 6.9% before the international financial crisis (1980–2008) but declined to an average of 3.7% in 2009–21. Because of their predominance, developments in the diamond market account for much of the recent decline in export growth, with Botswana's exports of goods contracting by 8.1% in 2015, 8.9% in 2016 and 6.3% in 2017 before recovering to 14.1% in 2018. Another sharp contraction of 8.5% occurred in 2019 and the value declined by 14.3% in 2020 before exports recovered to expand by 42.0% in 2021.

Imports of goods and services have seen more stability, with an average annual increase of 6.3% in 1980–2008, falling to 6.0% in 2009–21. Import and export patterns have carried over somewhat to Botswana's current account, particularly the trade component, with surpluses averaging 5.5% of GDP per year from 1980 to 2008 before contracting at an annual rate of 0.4% during 2009–21. However, with the slowdown in exports, the country had a current account deficit of 7.6% of GDP in 2019, the first deficit since 2008. With diamonds making up 77.0% of the country's total exports in 2019, the external account is highly vulnerable to fluctuations in global diamond prices, which plummeted further with the international lockdown measures, reducing demand for luxury goods, including diamonds. As a result, the country ran a current account deficit of 10.8% of GDP in 2020. With a global recovery under way in 2021, Botswana's current account deficit recovered to only 0.5% of GDP in 2021.

Foreign direct investment (FDI) flows to Botswana, which have never been considerable, are declining, with new inflows falling from 3.3% of GDP in 2014 to 1.7% in 2018 and to 0.6% in 2021. By comparison, during 2018–20 South Africa's FDI averaged 4.6% of GDP, and that of Ghana 2.9%, Nigeria 1.8%, Kenya 1.0% and Rwanda 0.3%.

GOVERNMENT FINANCE

Historically, the Botswana Government has pursued a conservative, prudent approach to the country's budget. Government expenditures show prolonged stability, with debt levels manageable. Data from the IMF shows that government expenditures averaged 40.1% of GDP in 2000–08, before declining to 37.8% in 2009–21. However, the drop in revenues was higher, falling from 42.8% of GDP in 2000–08 to 34.2% in 2009–21. Because of these trends, the Government ran a healthy surplus of 2.8% of GDP during 2000–08, before deteriorating to an average annual deficit of 3.5% of GDP in 2009–21. The Government's primary deficit, which excludes interest payments, experienced a dramatic increase from 0.6% of GDP in 2017 to 4.5% of GDP in 2018, 7.9% in 2019 and 10.4% in 2020 before falling back to 4.0% in 2021. Despite the increase in fiscal deficits in recent years, the Government's debt is still very low by developing country standards. In 2018 government debt as a share of GDP was only 14.9%. By 2021 it had still reached only 21.3%.

Part of the increased deficit stems from an April 2020 fiscal stimulus by the Government to offset the effects of the COVID-19 pandemic. The 2,000m. pula expenditure plan included funds to support family incomes, assist struggling companies, and investments in affected sectors such as agriculture, transport and health.

As noted, Botswana derives a significant portion (40%–50%) of its government revenues from the mineral, mainly diamond, sector. Also, Botswana receives substantial payments as part of its membership in the SACU. Member countries deposit all excise, customs and additional duties into a revenue pool to be shared using a formula. SACU revenues typically account for around 30% of Botswana's revenues.

A fiscal rule diverts much of the Government's chronic budgetary surpluses to the country's sovereign wealth fund, the Pula Fund. The Fund comprises the Government Investment Account (GIA) and the BoB account, both held by the central bank. The GIA contains funds raised through fiscal surpluses generated chiefly through the budgetary rule that spending must not exceed 40% of GDP and a Sustainable Budget Index, a ratio of recurrent expenditure to non-mineral revenues. The Pula Fund uses an allocation strategy that has, over recent years, devoted around 60%–65% of its resources to long-term fixed income and 35%–40% to equities.

The Pula Fund has suffered from lower diamond prices and declining domestic diamond reserves. In 2017 the Fund's value came to around 58,000m. pula (US $5,600m.), and it has seen a decline in recent years. (By early 2020 the Fund was worth $4,900m.) A fund of this size cannot sustain the economy as diamond revenues diminish. While the Fund could support growth in the short term, government forecasts show that diamond reserves will be exhausted by 2040. At that time, Botswana will need to have a sovereign wealth fund with sufficient assets to ensure that the country can continue its economic transformation while catering to the needs of a growing population.

PROSPECTS

Before the COVID-19 pandemic, Botswana faced several potential short-term risks. Water scarcity is increasingly constraining growth, with many companies, especially in the agriculture sector, facing crippling water shortages. Also, expansion of activity was likely to be constrained by the dearth of local technical and creative skills. The Government was under increased pressure from the business community to undertake broad-based reforms to reverse the decline in the country's business environment and competitiveness.

In response, the Government has developed Vision 2036, a forward-looking document that outlines the general direction of government policy during the intervening years. The Vision expects Botswana's future to be built on four pillars: sustainable economic development; human and social development; sustainable environment; and good governance, peace, and security. The intent is to give direction to a country that seems to be drifting in its transition away from minerals.

During the coming years, these goals are likely to translate into a focus on economic recovery and addressing the fiscal deficit. Infrastructure projects are aimed at enhancing long-term productive capacity. Emphasis will be on generating employment and improving social infrastructure (such as healthcare). However, limited diversification away from diamonds and copper is likely to occur.

Still, many uncertainties will make it difficult to chart the course of the economy in the medium term. More adverse weather affecting crop production is a distinct possibility, for which there is currently no answer. Commodity prices and global demand patterns could fluctuate adversely depending on the fresh waves of COVID-19 or developments stemming from the conflict in Ukraine. Botswana faces the risk that mineral deposits will become exhausted in the longer term. Furthermore, failure to effectively tackle high-income inequality and unemployment could increase the risks of social unrest and erode popular support for the ruling Botswana Democratic Party.

Statistical Survey

Source (unless otherwise stated): Statistics Botswana, Plot 8843, Finance House, Khama Crescent, Gaborone; tel. 3671300; e-mail info@statsbots.org.bw; internet www.statsbots.org.bw.

Area and Population

AREA, POPULATION AND DENSITY

Area (sq km)	581,730*
Population (census results)	
9–18 August 2011	
Males	989,128
Females	1,035,776
Total	2,024,904
18–31 March 2022†	2,346,179
Density (per sq km) at 2022 census†	4.0

* 224,607 sq miles.
† Preliminary.

POPULATION BY AGE AND SEX
('000, UN projections at mid-2022)

	Males	Females	Total
0–14 years	402.9	393.6	796.5
15–64 years	735.9	791.6	1,527.5
65 years and over	46.1	71.0	117.2
Total	**1,185.0**	**1,256.2**	**2,441.2**

Note: Totals may not be equal to the sum of components, owing to rounding; UN projections not adjusted to take account of results of 2022 census.

Source: UN, *World Population Prospects: The 2019 Revision.*

DISTRICTS AND SUB-DISTRICTS
(population at 2022 census, preliminary)

Central			Kweneng West . .	57,261
Bobonong . . .	76,922		*North-East*	
Boteti . . .	74,099		Francistown . .	102,444
Mahalapye . .	130,530		North-East . . .	68,910
Orapa . . .	8,614		*North-West*	
Selebi-Phikwe . .	41,839		Chobe	28,388
Serowe/Palapye .	201,775		Ngamiland West .	73,122
Sowa Town . .	2,901		Ngamiland East† .	123,452
Tutume . . .	164,228		*South-East*	

Ghanzi			Gaborone . . .	244,107
Ghanzi* . . .	55,884		Lobatse	29,457
Kgalagadi			South-East . . .	111,474
Kgalagadi North .	23,215		*Southern*	
Kgalagadi South .	35,160		Barolong . . .	58,394
Kgatleng			Jwaneng . . .	18,576
Kgatleng . . .	121,411		Ngwaketse . .	140,321
Kweneng			Ngwaketse West .	23,253
Kweneng East . .	330,442		**Total**	2,346,179

* Including Central Kalahari Game Reserve (CKGR) sub-district.
† Including Delta sub-district.

PRINCIPAL TOWNS AND VILLAGES
(population at 2022 census, preliminary)

Gaborone (capital) .	244,107	Molepolole . . .	74,719
Francistown . .	102,444	Tlokweng* . . .	55,517
Mogoditshane . .	88,098*	Serowe	55,484
Maun	85,293	Palapye	52,398

* Part of the Gaborone conurbation.

BIRTHS, MARRIAGES AND DEATHS

	Registered live births		Marriages		Registered deaths	
	Number	Rate (per 1,000)	Number	Rate (per 1,000)	Number	Rate (per 1,000)
2015 . .	46,765	21.4	6,677	6.1	13,030	6.0
2016 . .	49,984	22.5	6,051	5.5	12,825	5.8
2017 . .	43,290	19.2	6,203	5.5	12,386	5.5
2018 . .	54,023	23.6	5,489	4.8	12,609	5.5
2019 . .	54,100	23.3	6,097	5.3	13,185	5.7

2020: Marriages 6,518 (marriage rate 5.5 per 1,000).

Life expectancy (years at birth, estimates): 69.8 (males 66.7; females 72.6) in 2020 (Source: World Bank, World Development Indicators database).

EMPLOYMENT
(multi-topic survey, October—December 2021, persons aged 15 years and over)

	Males	Females	Total
Agriculture, hunting, forestry and fishing	42,419	11,411	53,830
Mining and quarrying	9,384	2,653	12,037
Manufacturing	31,516	25,286	56,802
Electricity, gas and water supply .	5,961	4,202	10,163
Construction	46,223	3,225	49,449
Wholesale and retail trade; repair of motor vehicles, motorcycles and personal and household goods	55,657	78,779	134,436
Hotels and restaurants . . .	11,751	14,335	26,086
Transport, storage and communications	27,139	6,693	33,831
Financial intermediation . . .	3,203	8,189	11,392
Real estate, renting and business services	38,363	28,484	66,846
Public administration and defence; compulsory social security . .	41,948	71,570	113,518
Education	20,171	55,954	76,125
Health and social work . . .	9,730	21,409	31,139
Other community, social and personal service activities . .	6,523	7,541	14,064
Private households with employed persons	5,296	21,457	26,753
Extraterritorial organizations and bodies	487	459	946
Total employed	355,771	361,647	717,418

Health and Welfare
KEY INDICATORS

Total fertility rate (children per woman, 2020)	2.8
Under-5 mortality rate (per 1,000 live births, 2020) . . .	44.8
HIV/AIDS (% of persons aged 15–49, 2020)	19.9
COVID-19: Cumulative confirmed deaths (per 100,000 persons at 31 August 2022)	107.3
COVID-19: Fully vaccinated population (% of total population at 7 August 2022)	58.4
Physicians (per 1,000 head, 2018)	0.3
Hospitals (per 100,000 head, 2013)	1.3
Domestic health expenditure (2019): US $ per head (PPP) .	881.1
Domestic health expenditure (2019): % of GDP	4.7
Domestic health expenditure (2019): public (% of total current expenditure)	78.5
Access to improved water resources (% of persons, 2020) .	92
Access to improved sanitation facilities (% of persons, 2020).	80
Total carbon dioxide emissions ('000 metric tons, 2018) . .	8,210
Carbon dioxide emissions per head (metric tons, 2018) . .	3.6
Human Development Index (2021): ranking	117
Human Development Index (2021): value	0.693

Note: For data on COVID-19 vaccinations, 'fully vaccinated' denotes receipt of all doses specified by approved vaccination regime (Sources: Johns Hopkins University and Our World in Data). Data on health expenditure refer to current general government expenditure in each case. For more information on sources and further definitions for all indicators, see Health and Welfare Statistics: Sources and Definitions section (europaworld.com/credits).

Agriculture
PRINCIPAL CROPS
('000 metric tons)

	2018	2019	2020
Cabbages and other brassicas .	14.8	14.4	16.3*
Maize	24.6	7.3	61.9
Onions, dry	7.9	9.0	9.7*
Oranges	3.9	4.0	4.0*
Potatoes	12.3	1.8	5.3*
Sorghum	48.6	36.0	87.8
Sunflower seed	0.8	0.1	0.3*
Tomatoes	6.4	8.8	8.5*
Watermelons	11.1	16.7	22.3*

* FAO estimate.

Aggregate production ('000 metric tons, may include official, semi-official or estimated data): Total cereals 81.0 in 2018, 48.5 in 2019, 162.2 in 2020; Total fruit (primary) 20.8 in 2018, 26.5 in 2019, 32.2 in 2020; Total pulses 8.5 in 2018, 2.3 in 2019, 20.7 in 2020; Total roots and tubers 117.1 in 2018, 107.5 in 2019, 112.6 in 2020; Total vegetables (primary) 75.3 in 2018, 78.7 in 2019, 81.4 in 2020.

Source: FAO.

LIVESTOCK
('000 head, year ending September)

	2018*	2019	2020*
Asses	125	140*	130
Cattle	1,100	935	1,045
Goats	1,315	1,229	1,293
Horses	23	27*	25
Pigs	3	3*	2
Poultry	807	822*	780
Sheep	238	243	240

* FAO estimate(s).

LIVESTOCK PRODUCTS
('000 metric tons, FAO estimates)

	2018	2019	2020
Cattle hides, fresh	4.6	4.6	3.9
Cattle meat	34.0	34.0	28.3
Cattle offals, edible	4.6	4.6	3.9
Cows' milk	235.6	279.1	267.7
Chicken meat	3.9	3.9	3.7
Game meat	26.1	25.7	25.9
Goat meat	4.8	4.1	4.4
Goats' milk	12.5	12.0	12.4
Hen eggs	3.7	3.7	3.4

Source: FAO.

Forestry

ROUNDWOOD REMOVALS
('000 cubic metres, excl. bark, FAO estimates)

	2017	2018	2019
Industrial wood	105.0	105.0	105.0
Fuel wood	699.3	699.4	699.5
Total	804.3	804.4	804.5

2020: Total production assumed to be unchanged from 2019.

Source: FAO.

Fishing

(capture in metric tons, live weight, FAO estimates)

	2018	2019	2020
Capture	38	38	33
Tilapias	35	35	30
Torpedo-shaped catfishes	2	2	2
Other freshwater fishes	1	1	1
Aquaculture	25	35	146
Total catch	63	73	179

Source: FAO.

Mining

(metric tons unless otherwise indicated)

	2018	2019	2020
Hard coal	2,482,313	2,110,891	1,923,990
Gold (kg)	1,105	862	780
Salt	367,988	383,779	418,379
Diamonds ('000 carats)	24,378	23,686	16,868
Soda ash (natural)	297,237	264,119	238,476

2011 ('000 cu m, estimate): Sand and Gravel 3,000 (Source: US Geological Survey).

2016 (metric tons): Copper ore 13,120; Nickel ore 16,878; Cobalt 281. Note: Figures refer to the metal content of matte; product smelted was granulated nickel-copper-cobalt matte.

Source (unless otherwise stated): Bank of Botswana, *Annual Report 2020*.

Industry

SELECTED PRODUCTS

	2001	2002	2003
Beer ('000 hl)	1,692	1,396	1,198
Soft drinks ('000 hl)	431	389	405
Electrical energy (million kWh)	1,035	1,044	936

Electrical energy (million kWh): 2,205 in 2019; 2,004 in 2020; 2,144 in 2021.

Source: partly UN Industrial Commodity Statistics Database.

Finance

CURRENCY, EXCHANGE RATES AND FISCAL YEAR

Monetary Units
100 thebe = 1 pula (P).

Sterling, Dollar and Euro Equivalents (31 May 2022)
£1 sterling = 15.061 pula;
US $1 = 11.963 pula;
€1 = 12.816 pula;
100 pula = £6.64 = $8.36 = €7.80.

Average Exchange Rate (pula per US $)
2019   10.7559
2020   11.4562
2021   11.0873

Fiscal Year
The fiscal year ends on 31 March.

BUDGET
(million pula, fiscal year)

Revenue*	2016/17	2017/18	2018/19
Taxation	50,847.2	52,992.2	51,057.2
Mineral revenue	22,495.9	18,686.3	18,467.7
Customs and excise	11,773.3	17,864.4	14,788.5
Non-mineral income taxes	9,572.2	8,200.3	9,900.1
Other taxes	7,005.8	8,241.3	7,900.8
General sales tax/VAT	6,642.7	7,776.4	7,374.1
Other current revenue	6,395.0	3,047.3	2,335.0
Interest	536.8	52.5	122.6
Other property income	66.8	107.3	116.8
Bank of Botswana revenues	2,842.0	1,573.2	740.0
Fees, charges, etc.	2,879.1	1,236.1	1,310.7
Sales of fixed assets and land	70.5	78.2	44.9
Total	57,242.2	56,039.5	53,392.2

Expenditure†	2016/17	2017/18	2018/19
General services (incl. defence)	15,799.8	15,076.6	16,745.2
Social services	25,343.6	26,683.5	28,240.1
Education	12,839.8	13,174.1	13,952.9
Health	6,355.1	7,137.5	7,438.5
Housing, urban and regional development	2,541.7	1,939.3	2,486.4
Food and social welfare programme	1,859.1	2,551.4	2,449.3
Other community and social services	1,747.8	1,881.3	1,913.0
Economic services	10,804.0	11,513.9	11,946.6
Agriculture, forestry and fishing	1,247.8	2,019.5	2,217.2
Mining	1,132.0	939.9	349.0

Expenditure†—continued	2016/17	2017/18	2018/19
Electricity and water supply .	5,048.0	4,800.9	4,315.1
Transport	2,270.0	2,658.5	3,201.3
Others	1,106.3	1,095.1	1,864.1
Transfers	4,327.4	5,118.9	5,418.8
Deficit grants to local authorities	3,449.6	4,129.4	4,327.9
Interest on public debt . . .	877.8	989.5	1,090.9
Total	56,274.8	58,392.9	62,350.6

* Excluding grants received (million pula): 156.2 in 2016/17; 371.5 in 2017/18; 77.9 in 2018/19.

† Including net lending (million pula): –52.1 in 2016/17; 85.05 in 2017/18; –382.2 in 2018/19.

2019/20 (budget figures): *Revenue:* Mineral revenue 14,555; Non-mineral revenue 39,749; Total 54,304. *Expenditure:* Recurrent expenditure 51,813 (Wages and salaries 26,252, Grants and subventions 13,823, Public debt interest 1,204, Other charges 10,534); Development expenditure 13,644; Net lending –57; Total 65,400.

2020/21 (budget figures): *Revenue:* Mineral revenue 6,561; Non-mineral revenue 41,767; Total 48,328. *Expenditure:* Recurrent expenditure 57,204 (Wages and salaries 26,909, Grants and subventions 17,725, Public debt interest 1,427, Other charges 11,142); Development expenditure 12,228; Net lending –76; Total 69,356.

2021/22 (budget figures): *Revenue:* Mineral revenue 23,199; Non-mineral revenue 41,379; Total 64,578. *Expenditure:* Recurrent expenditure 56,047 (Wages and salaries 28,768, Grants and subventions 14,959, Public debt interest 1,579, Other charges 10,740); Development expenditure 14,753; Net lending –190; Total 70,610.

Source: Bank of Botswana, *Annual Report 2020.*

INTERNATIONAL RESERVES
(US $ million at 31 December)

	2019	2020	2021
IMF special drawing rights . .	81.87	85.46	347.62
Reserve position in IMF . . .	54.99	68.80	69.65
Foreign exchange	6,033.36	4,786.64	4,384.34
Total	6,170.22	4,940.89	4,801.61

Source: IMF, *International Financial Statistics.*

MONEY SUPPLY
(million pula at 31 December)

	2019	2020	2021
Currency outside depository corporations	1,883	2,409	2,418
Transferable deposits	18,148	21,106	21,981
Other deposits	64,743	66,247	69,869
Broad money	84,774	89,762	94,268

Source: IMF, *International Financial Statistics.*

COST OF LIVING
(Consumer Price Index; base: December 2018 = 100)

	2019	2020	2021
Food	101.8	105.6	111.9
Clothing (incl. footwear) . . .	100.7	102.9	106.5
Housing	100.8	105.9	114.1
All items (incl. others) . . .	101.4	103.3	110.2

NATIONAL ACCOUNTS
(million pula at current prices)
Expenditure on the Gross Domestic Product

	2019	2020	2021
Government final consumption expenditure	56,924	61,946	64,941
Private final consumption expenditure	79,612	83,503	90,986
Change in inventories	3,546	8,735	2,018
Gross fixed capital formation . .	51,901	47,356	54,518
Total domestic expenditure .	191,983	201,540	212,463
Exports of goods and services . .	66,722	53,628	87,131
Less Imports of goods and services	82,764	79,478	97,388
Statistical discrepancy	3,640	–4,648	–6,916
GDP in purchasers' values .	179,580	171,042	195,290
GDP at constant 2016 prices	183,762	167,726	186,787

Gross Domestic Product by Economic Activity

	2019	2020	2021
Agriculture, hunting, forestry and fishing	3,748	3,784	3,363
Mining and quarrying	24,163	14,956	22,203
Manufacturing	10,960	9,699	10,868
Water and electricity	1,642	2,084	2,181
Construction	20,387	18,370	22,727
Trade, restaurants and hotels .	25,217	23,616	28,458
Transport, post and telecommunications	8,338	8,476	9,502
Finance, insurance, real estate and business services	25,519	25,409	28,199
Administrative and support activities	31,923	35,582	36,680
Education	9,211	9,928	10,202
Human health and social work .	5,624	6,115	6,701
Other services	4,310	4,138	4,526
GDP at basic prices	171,041	162,157	185,608
Indirect taxes (net)	8,539	8,885	9,682
GDP in purchasers' values	179,580	171,042	195,290

BALANCE OF PAYMENTS
(US $ million)

	2018	2019	2020
Exports of goods	6,594.5	5,242.6	4,216.0
Imports of goods	–6,108.3	–6,324.8	–6,263.9
Balance on goods	486.2	–1,082.2	–2,047.8
Exports of services	937.8	968.7	470.5
Imports of services	–1,254.1	–1,370.0	–1,085.3
Balance on goods and services	169.9	–1,483.5	–2,662.7
Primary income received . . .	242.1	293.0	146.8
Primary income paid . . .	–1,826.2	–1,169.0	–395.5
Balance on goods, services and primary income . . .	–1,414.2	–2,359.5	–2,911.4
Secondary income received . .	1,619.7	1,387.5	1,561.0
Secondary income paid . . .	–147.6	–201.5	–275.3
Current balance	57.9	–1,173.6	–1,625.7
Direct investment assets . . .	–82.1	19.8	16.9
Direct investment liabilities . .	286.0	93.6	80.1
Portfolio investment assets . .	684.6	–962.4	–964.0
Portfolio investment liabilities .	–56.6	35.3	–19.1
Financial derivatives and employee stock options (net) . . .	34.7	2.8	2.4
Other investment assets . . .	–608.3	457.8	269.3
Other investment liabilities . .	45.5	–82.9	–66.6
Net errors and omissions . . .	–772.2	490.2	549.3
Reserves and related items .	–410.5	–1,119.3	–1,757.5

Source: IMF, *International Financial Statistics.*

External Trade

PRINCIPAL COMMODITIES
(million pula)

Imports c.i.f.	2019	2020	2021
Food, beverages and tobacco . .	9,003.4	9,521.1	10,719.2
Fuels	8,863.6	9,669.4	11,119.9
Chemicals and rubber products .	6,344.4	6,998.8	8,782.4
Textiles and footwear	1,677.5	1,495.2	1,976.7
Metals and metal products . .	3,549.9	3,001.5	4,362.8
Machinery and electrical			
equipment	8,775.1	8,302.1	10,215.0
Vehicles and transport equipment	6,819.7	6,452.7	6,765.2
Diamonds	20,050.1	23,070.6	32,485.9
Total (incl. others)	70,621.4	74,558.4	92,956.9

Exports (incl. re-exports) f.o.b.	2019	2020	2021
Meat and meat products . . .	663.5	222.6	159.6
Diamonds	51,088.2	43,304.5	73,990.4
Gold	436.5	572.4	387.7
Machinery and electrical			
equipment	1,581.1	1,637.8	1,871.3
Vehicles and transport equipment	443.7	294.5	206.9
Textiles and footwear	161.7	162.3	72.4
Total (incl. others)	56,578.1	49,115.5	18,888.6

PRINCIPAL TRADING PARTNERS
(US $ million)

Imports c.i.f.	2018	2019	2020
Belgium	110.8	215.6	507.5
Canada	533.1	453.8	207.4
China, People's Republic . . .	109.5	125.6	160.7
France	55.5	180.6	87.9
Germany	64.8	48.1	36.3
India	201.1	269.7	163.0
Israel	75.4	18.5	38.8
Japan	45.7	52.9	72.2
Namibia	425.4	520.6	496.1
Russian Federation	41.3	140.3	98.1
South Africa	3,743.9	3,799.1	3,811.5
Switzerland	13.6	57.1	125.1
UAE	41.3	33.8	283.2
United Kingdom	58.9	71.2	26.7
USA	73.9	120.7	45.3
Zambia	19.7	91.1	23.7
Total (incl. others)	5,921.3	6,558.5	6,503.3

Exports f.o.b.	2018	2019	2020
Belgium	1,240.2	1,026.1	912.1
Hong Kong	349.1	303.5	186.3
India	1,198.0	1,131.4	891.9
Israel	453.2	374.1	208.1
Namibia	177.1	159.1	66.8
Singapore	526.3	287.6	259.1
South Africa	592.6	503.3	569.0
Switzerland	147.3	176.8	34.3
UAE	891.7	952.9	916.9
USA	198.9	78.4	58.6
Viet Nam	42.8	58.4	22.4
Total (incl. others)	6,122.4	5,238.1	4,256.0

Source: Trade Map-Trade Competitiveness Map, International Trade Centre, marketanalysis.intracen.org.

Transport

RAILWAYS
(traffic)

	2017	2018	2019
Number of passengers ('000) . .	134.7	232.1	246.2
Freight ('000 metric tons) . . .	1,542.4	1,549.2	1,220.5

2020: Freight ('000 metric tons) 1,205.0.

ROAD TRAFFIC
(registered vehicles)

	2018	2019	2020
Cars	350,757	388,767	369,161
Light duty vehicles	110,254	113,013	12,820
Trucks	32,389	35,681	35,956
Buses	21,109	22,316	19,953
Tractors	6,766	6,773	6,952
Others (incl. trailers, motorcycles			
and tankers)	32,373	34,640	34,947
Total	553,648	601,190	579,789

CIVIL AVIATION
(traffic on scheduled services)

	2018	2019	2020
Aircraft movements	16,215	16,759	4,575
Passengers carried ('000) . . .	645	683	166

2018: Freight carried (metric tons) 396.9.

Tourism

FOREIGN TOURIST ARRIVALS

Country of origin	2016	2017	2018
Germany	32,587	47,808	46,830
Namibia	190,654	191,372	191,421
South Africa	740,802	687,607	762,661
United Kingdom	31,531	30,449	36,361
USA	49,684	55,732	68,530
Zambia	214,027	181,367	250,190
Zimbabwe	755,742	689,804	752,982
Total (incl. others)	2,401,786	2,305,205	2,587,511

2020: Germany 4,509; Namibia 26,340; South Africa 161,345; United Kingdom 5,502; USA 6,637; Zambia 72,351; Zimbabwe 175,700; *Total* 500,434.

Tourism receipts (US $ million, excl. passenger transport): 578 in 2016; 704 in 2017; 574 in 2018 (Source: World Tourism Organization).

Communications Media

	2018	2019	2020
Telephones ('000 main lines in use)	142.5	142.6	139.9
Mobile telephone subscriptions ('000)	3,381.2	3,746.8	3,819.0
Broadband subscriptions, fixed ('000)	40.0	49.3	71.9
Broadband subscriptions, mobile ('000)	1,749.1	2,037.4	2,193.6
Internet users (% of population)	58.0	61.0	n.a.

Source: International Telecommunication Union.

Education

(2017 unless otherwise indicated)

	Institutions	Teachers	Students
Pre-primary*	645	2,934	33,425
Primary	821	13,969	359,193
Secondary	290	15,093	178,985
General programmes	n.a.	15,418†	169,489‡
Technical and vocational programmes	43§	1,121‖	9,627‖
Tertiary¶	44	3,105	53,930

* 2014.
† 2012/13.
‡ 2014/15.
§ 2008.
‖ 2007.
¶ 2018/19.

Sources: Ministry of Education, Gaborone; UNESCO Institute for Statistics.

Agricultural college (2006): Teachers 106; students 960.

University (2017/18 unless otherwise indicated): Teachers 914 (2013/14); students 12,886 (Source: University of Botswana).

Pupil-teacher ratio (primary education): 25.7 in 2017.

Adult literacy rate (UNESCO estimates): 88.2% (males 87.2%; females 89.2%) in 2015 (Source: UNESCO Institute for Statistics).

Directory

The Constitution

The Constitution of the Republic of Botswana took effect at independence on 30 September 1966. Its main provisions, with subsequent amendments, are summarized below:

EXECUTIVE

President

Executive power lies with the President of Botswana, who is also Commander-in-Chief of the armed forces. Election for the office of President is linked with the election of members of the National Assembly. The President is restricted to two terms of office. Presidential candidates must be over 30 years of age and receive at least 1,000 nominations. If there is more than one candidate for the presidency, each candidate for office in the Assembly must declare support for a presidential candidate. The candidate for President who commands the votes of more than one-half of the elected members of the Assembly will be declared President. In the event of the death or resignation of the President, the Vice-President will automatically assume the presidency. The President, who is an ex officio member of the National Assembly, holds office for the duration of Parliament. The President chooses four members of the National Assembly.

Cabinet

There is also a Vice-President, whose office is ministerial. The Vice-President is appointed by the President and deputizes in the absence of the President. The Cabinet consists of the President, the Vice-President and other Ministers, including Assistant Ministers, appointed by the President. The Cabinet is responsible to the National Assembly.

LEGISLATURE

Legislative power is vested in Parliament, consisting of the President and the National Assembly, acting after consultation in certain cases with the Ntlo ya Dikgosi. The President may withhold assent to a Bill passed by the National Assembly. If the same Bill is again presented after six months, the President is required to assent to it or to dissolve Parliament within 21 days.

Ntlo ya Dikgosi

Formerly known as the House of Chiefs, the Ntlo ya Dikgosi comprises no more than 35 members, five of which are appointed by the President. Bills and motions relating to chieftaincy matters and alterations of the Constitution must be referred to the Ntlo ya Dikgosi, which may also deliberate and make representations on any matter.

National Assembly

The National Assembly consists of 57 members directly elected by universal adult suffrage, together with four members who are elected by the National Assembly from a list of candidates submitted by the President; the President and the Speaker are also ex officio members of the Assembly. The life of the Assembly is five years.

The Constitution contains a code of human rights, enforceable by the High Court.

The Government

HEAD OF STATE

President: Dr Mokgweetsi Eric Keabetswe Masisi (took office 1 April 2018; re-elected 25 October 2019).

Vice-President: Slumber Tsogwane.

CABINET

(October 2022)

The Government is formed by the Botswana Democratic Party.

President: Dr Mokgweetsi Eric Keabetswe Masisi.

Vice-President: Slumber Tsogwane.

Minister for State President: Neale Sechele Morwaeng.

Minister of Defence and Security: Kagiso Thomas Mmusi.

Minister of Foreign Affairs: Dr Lemogang Kwape.

Minister of Justice: Machana Ronald Shamukuni.

Minister of Local Government and Rural Development: Kgotla Kenneth Autlwetse.

Minister of Finance: Peggy Onkutlwile Serame.

Minister of Transport and Public Works: Eric Mothibi Molale.

Minister of Lands and Water Affairs: Kefentse Mzwinila.

Minister of Agriculture: Fidelis Macdonald Molao.

Minister of Labour and Home Affairs: Annah Maria Mokgethi.

Minister of Education and Skills Development: Dr Douglas Letsholathebe.

Minister of Health: Dr Edwin Gorataone Dikoloti.

Minister of Minerals and Energy: Lefhoko Maxwell Maogi.

Minister of Trade and Industry: Mmusi Kgafela.

Minister of Communications, Knowledge and Technology: Thulagano Merafe Segoko.

Minister of Youth, Gender, Sport and Culture: Tumiso Macdonald Rakgare.

Minister of Environment and Tourism: PHILDA KERENG.

Minister of Entrepreneurship: KARABO SOCRAAT GARE.

In addition, there were 10 Assistant Ministers. The Attorney-General and the Permanent Secretary to the Presidency were also *ex officio* members of the Cabinet.

MINISTRIES

Office of the President: PMB 001, Gaborone; tel. 3950800; e-mail bgcis@gov.bw; internet www.gov.bw.

Office of the Vice-President: PMB 001, Gaborone.

Ministry for State President: State House Dr., Government Enclave, PMB 001, Gaborone; tel. 3950800; e-mail op-pr-office@gov.bw.

Ministry of Agriculture: Plot 4701, Mmaraka Rd, PMB 003, Gaborone; tel. 33689000; e-mail moa17755@gov.bw; internet fb.com/AgrinewsMagazineMoa.

Ministry of Communications, Knowledge and Technology: West Gate Mall, Gaborone; tel. 3612000; e-mail mtc@gov.bw.

Ministry of Defence and Security: Plot 54355, PMB 00384, Gaborone; tel. 3698200; e-mail mdjs@gov.bw; internet fb.com/MDSBOTSWANA.

Ministry of Education and Skill Development: Govt Enclave, Blk 6 Bldg, PMB 005, Gaborone; tel. 3715100; internet fb.com/EducationandSkillsDevelopmentBotswana.

Ministry of Entrepreneurship: Khama Cres., Gaborone; tel. 3631300; internet fb.com/Ministry-of-Entrepreneurship-114524161247425.

Ministry of the Environment and Tourism: Plot 13064, Government Enclave, PMB BO199, Gaborone; tel. 3647900; e-mail ment_pr@gov.bw; internet fb.com/www.mewt199.co.bw.

Ministry of Finance: Government Enclave, Khama Cres., Blk 25, State Dr., PMB 008, Gaborone; tel. 3950100; e-mail MoF-PRO@gov.bw; internet www.finance.gov.bw.

Ministry of Foreign Affairs: Government Enclave, PMB 00368, Gaborone; tel. 3600700; e-mail miacpdrpa@gov.bw.

Ministry of Health: Plot 54069, 24 Amos St, PMB 0038, Gaborone; tel. 3632500; e-mail health@gov.bw; internet www.moh.gov.bw.

Ministry of Justice: PMB 002200, Gaborone; tel. 3718000; e-mail justiceenquiries@gov.bw; internet www.justice.gov.bw.

Ministry of Labour and Home Affairs: Govt Enclave, Blk 8, Gaborone; tel. 3611118.

Ministry of Lands and Water Affairs: Plot 1108, AKD Bldg, PMB 00434, Gaborone; tel. 3682000; e-mail mlwsfeedbak@gov.bw; internet fb.com/MlwsBotswana.

Ministry of Local Government and Rural Development: PMB 006, Gaborone; tel. 3658400.

Ministry of Minerals and Energy: Plot 50676, Blk C, Fairground Office Park, PMB 0018, Gaborone; tel. 3656600; internet fb.com/mmgebotswana.

Ministry of Trade and Industry: Plot 54380, CBD, Gaborone; tel. 3601202; e-mail mitipru@gov.bw; internet fb.com/mitiBw.

Ministry of Transport and Public Works: PMB 54, Gaborone; tel. 3911758; e-mail mtcpro@gov.bw; internet fb.com/MTPWBotswana.

Ministry of Youth, Gender, Sport and Development: Plot 54372, Y2K Bldg, Central Business District, PMB 00514, Gaborone; tel. 3682667; e-mail myscpro@gov.bw; internet fb.com/bwmysc.

Legislature

NTLO YA DIKGOSI

Following a review, in December 2005 the membership of the Ntlo ya Dikgosi was increased from 15 to 35 members.

Ntlo ya Dikgosi: Parliament Bldg, POB 240, Gaborone; tel. 3616800; internet www.parliament.gov.bw.

Chairperson: Chief KGOSI PUSO GABORONE.

NATIONAL ASSEMBLY

National Assembly: Parliament Bldg, POB 240, Gaborone; tel. 3616800; internet www.parliament.gov.bw.

Speaker: PHANDU SKELEMANI.

General Election, 23 October 2019

Party	Votes	% of votes	Seats
Botswana Democratic Party .	406,561	52.65	38
Umbrella for Democratic Change*	277,121	35.87	15
Alliance for Progressives . .	39,561	5.12	1
Botswana Patriotic Front . .	34,028	4.41	3
Others	14,937	1.93	—
Total	772,208	100.00	57†

* An alliance comprising the Botswana Movement for Democracy, the Botswana National Front and the Botswana People's Party.
† The President and the Speaker are also ex officio members of the National Assembly. In addition, there were four specially elected members, all of whom represented the Botswana Democratic Party.

Election Commission

Independent Electoral Commission (IEC): Fair Ground Holdings, Plot 63726, Gaborone; tel. 3612400; e-mail info@iec.bw; internet www.iec.gov.bw; f. 1997; Chair. BARNABAS NYAMADZABO.

Political Organizations

Alliance for Progressives (AP): Queens Rd, Gaborone; e-mail afprogressives@gmail.com; internet fb.com/AllianceForProgressives; f. 2017; breakaway faction of Botswana Movement for Democracy; Chair. Maj.-Gen. PIUS MOKGWARE; Pres. NDABA GAOLATHE.

Botswana Democratic Party (BDP) (Domkrag): Plot 695, behind Tsholetsa House, POB 28, Gaborone; tel. 3952564; f. 1962 as the Bechuanaland Democratic Party; Chair. SLUMBER TSOGWANE; Pres. Dr MOKGWEETSI ERIC KEABETSWE MASISI; Sec.-Gen. MPHO BALOPI.

Umbrella for Democratic Change (UDC): 10139 Kaunda Rd, POB 0065, Gaborone; tel. 3167392; e-mail info@udc.org.bw; internet udc.org.bw; f. 2012; an alliance of opposition parties in Botswana; Leader DUMA BOKO.

Botswana Congress Party (BCP): Plot 364, Ext. 4, Independence Ave, Gaborone; POB 2918, Gaborone; tel. 3181805; e-mail monchomk@gmail.com; f. 1998 following split from the BNF; merged with Botswana Alliance Movement to form BCP in 2010; Nat. Chair. (vacant); Pres. DUMELANG SALESHANDO; Sec.-Gen. GORETETSE KEKGONEGILE.

Botswana Movement for Democracy (BMD): POB 1300, Gaborone; tel. 75533777; f. 2010 by fmr mems of the Botswana Democratic Party; a faction known as Alliance for Progressives (AP) launched by Ndaba Gaolathe in Sept. 2017; Pres. SIDNEY PILANE; Sec.-Gen. TSELENG BOTLHOLE (acting).

Botswana National Front (BNF): POB 40065, Gaborone; tel. 3182921; e-mail botswananationalfront@yahoo.com; f. 1966; incl. fmr mems of the United Socialist Party (PUSO), which split from the BNF in 1994 later to re-affiliate in 2005; Pres DUMA BOKO; Sec.-Gen. KETLHALEFILE MOTSHEGWA.

Botswana People's Party (BPP): POB 685, Francistown; tel. 2416161; f. 1960; Pres. MOTLATSI MOLAPISI; Sec.-Gen. NONO KGAFELA-MOKOKA.

Diplomatic Representation

EMBASSIES AND HIGH COMMISSIONS IN BOTSWANA

Angola: Plot 13232, Khama Cres., Nelson Mandela Rd, PMB BR 111, Gaborone; tel. 3900204; e-mail embassy@angola.co.bw; internet angolaembassybw.com; Ambassador BEATRIZ ANTÓNIA MANUEL DE MORAIS.

Brazil: Plot 1124–5, Main Mall, Standard House, 3rd Floor, Queen's Rd, PMB 475, Gaborone; tel. 3951061; e-mail brasemb.gaborone@itamaraty.gov.br; internet www.gov.br/mre/pt-br/embaixada-gaborone; Ambassador FLÁVIO LIMA ROCHA.

China, People's Republic: Plot 3096 North Ring Rd, POB 1031, Gaborone; tel. 3952209; e-mail chinaemb_bw@mfa.gov.cn; internet bw.china-embassy.gov.cn; Ambassador WANG XUEFENG.

Cuba: Plot 5504, Kolobe Rd, Gaborone; tel. 3911485; e-mail embajada@bw.embacuba.cu; internet misiones.minrex.gob.cu/botswana; Ambassador ORLANDO ERNESTO ÁLVAREZ ÁLVAREZ.

France: 761 Robinson Rd, POB 1424, Gaborone; tel. 3680800; e-mail frambbots@orangemail.co.bw; internet bw.ambafrance.org; Ambassador OLIVIER BROCHENIN (designate).

Germany: Plot 1079–84, Main Mall, Queens Rd, POB 315, Gaborone; tel. 3953143; e-mail info@gaborone.diplo.de; internet gaborone .diplo.de; Ambassador MARGIT HELLWIG-BÖTTE.

India: Plot 5375, President's Dr., POB 249, Gaborone; tel. 3972676; e-mail hoc.gaborone@mea.gov.in; internet www.hcigaborone.gov.in; High Commissioner RAJESH RANJAN.

Japan: Plot 8842, Barclays House, 4th Floor, Khama Cres., PMB 00222, Gaborone; tel. 3914456; e-mail information@gr.mofa.go.jp; internet www.botswana.emb-japan.go.jp; Ambassador TAKASHI HOSHIYAMA.

Kenya: Plot 2615, Zebra Way, off Chuma Dr., PMB 297, Gaborone; tel. 3951408; e-mail info@khcbotswana.org.bw; internet www .khcbotswana.org.bw; High Commissioner MOHAMED M. SHIDIYE.

Libya: Plot 8851, Government Enclave, POB 180, Gaborone; tel. 3952481; Ambassador ABDELMATLOB BUHAWIA.

Mozambique: Phuti Cres. 2638, POB 00215, Gaborone; tel. 3191251; e-mail embamoc.botswana@minec.gov.mz; High Commissioner DOMINGOS ESTÊVÃO FERNANDES.

Namibia: Plot 186, Morara Close, POB 987, Gaborone; tel. 3902181; e-mail namibhc@botsnet.bw; High Commissioner ASSER KUVERI KAPERE.

Nigeria: Plot 1086–92, Queens Rd, The Mall, POB 274, Gaborone; tel. 3913561; e-mail nigeriabotswana@it.bw; High Commissioner (vacant).

Russian Federation: Plot 4711, Tawana Close, POB 81, Gaborone; tel. 3953389; e-mail botswana@mid.ru; internet botswana.mid.ru; Ambassador ANDREY KEMARSKY.

South Africa: Plot 29, Queens Rd, PMB 00402, Gaborone; tel. 3904800; e-mail gaborone.dha@dirco.gov.za; internet fb.com/ SAHCBotswana; High Commissioner THANINGA PANDIT SHOPE-SOUMAH.

Türkiye (Turkey): Plot 8842, Old Barclays House, 3rd Floor, PMB 12 AAD, Gaborone; tel. 3903612; e-mail embassy.gaborone@mfa.gov.tr; internet gaboron.be.mfa.gov.tr; Ambassador MELTEM BÜYÜKKARAKAŞ.

United Kingdom: Plot 1079–1084, Main Mall, off Queens Rd, PMB 0023, Gaborone; tel. 3952841; e-mail gaborone.enquiries@fco.gov .uk; internet www.gov.uk/world/organisations/british-high -commission-gaborone; High Commissioner SIAN PRICE.

USA: Embassy Dr., Government Enclave, off Khama Cres., POB 90, Gaborone; tel. 3953982; e-mail consulargaborone@state.gov; internet bw.usembassy.gov; Chargé d'affaires AMANDA S. JACOBSEN.

Zambia: Plot 1120, Queens Rd, The Mall, POB 362, Gaborone; tel. 3951951; e-mail zamhico@mega.bw; High Commissioner (vacant).

Zimbabwe: Plot 8850, Orapa Close Government Enclave, POB 1232, Gaborone; tel. 3914495; e-mail zimembassy@zimgaborone .gov.zw; internet www.zimgaborone.gov.zw; Ambassador BATIRAI MUKONOWESHURO MANDIGORA.

Judicial System

Appeals lie to the Court of Appeal of Botswana, which is the highest court in the country. The High Court has unlimited jurisdiction and is headed by a Chief Justice. The Chief Justice and the President of the Court of Appeal are appointed by the President. There is also an Industrial Court that oversees labour disputes and holds an equal rank to the High Court, and a Magistrate Court in each district.

Chief Justice: TERENCE RANNOWANE.

Court of Appeal: PMB 220, Gaborone; tel. 3718000; e-mail justiceenquiries@gov.bw; internet www.justice.gov.bw; Pres. TEBOGO TAU.

High Court: PMB 220, Gaborone; tel. 3718000; internet www .justice.gov.bw; brs at Lobatse, Francistown and Maun; Registrar and Master MICHAEL MOTLHABI.

Office of the Attorney-General: Plot 50762, Government Enclave, PMB 009, Gaborone; internet www.agc.gov.bw; tel. 3613600; e-mail agcinfodesk@gov.bw; internet www.agc.gov.bw; Attorney-Gen. ABRAHAM M. KEETSHABE.

Religion

According to the 2011 census, the majority of the population were Christians (some 79%); an estimated 4% held animist beliefs. There are Islamic mosques in Gaborone and Lobatse. Hinduism, Rastafarianism and the Bahá'í Faith are also represented.

CHRISTIANITY

Botswana Council of Churches (Lekgotla la Dikereke mo Botswana): Plot 3283, Ext. 12, POB 335, Gaborone; tel. 3951981; f. 1966; Pres. Rt Rev. METLHAYOTLHE BELEME; Gen. Sec. Rev. GABRIEL TSUANENG; 24 mem. churches and orgs.

The Anglican Communion

Anglicans are adherents of the Church of the Province of Central Africa, covering Botswana, Malawi, Zambia and Zimbabwe. The Church comprises 15 dioceses, including one in Botswana. The current Archbishop of the Province is the Bishop of Northern Zambia. The Province was established in 1955, and the diocese of Botswana was formed in 1972.

Bishop of Botswana: Rt Rev. METLHAYOTLHE RAWLINGS BELEME, Plot 5349, Church Rd, POB 769, Gaborone; tel. 3953779; e-mail info@ anglicanbotswana.org.bw; internet www.diobot.org.

Protestant Churches

Evangelical Lutheran Church in Botswana (Kereke ya Luthere ya Efangele mo Botswana): Plot 28570, Serotologane St, POB 1976, Gaborone; tel. 3164612; e-mail elcb@info.bw; f. 1979; Bishop MOTHUSI LETLHAGE.

Evangelical Lutheran Church in Southern Africa (Botswana Diocese): Bontleng, POB 201012, Gaborone; tel. 302144; f. 1982; Bishop Rev. G. EKSTEEN.

Methodist Church of Southern Africa—Botswana: Plot 3176-3179, ZK Cres., Ext 12, POB 260, Gaborone; tel. 3167627; Circuit Supt Rev. ODIRILE E. MERE.

Other denominations active in Botswana include the Church of God in Christ, the Dutch Reformed Church, the Mennonite Church, the United Methodist Church and the Seventh-day Adventists.

The Roman Catholic Church

Botswana comprises two dioceses. The metropolitan see is Pretoria, South Africa. The church was established in Botswana in 1928. The Bishops participate in the Southern African Catholic Bishops' Conference, currently based in Pretoria.

Bishop of Francistown: Rt Rev. ANTHONY PASCAL REBELLO, St Francis House, Tsie Rd, 14061 Area W, POB 702, Francistown; tel. 2413601; e-mail info@dioceseoffrancistown.com; internet dioceseoffrancistown.com.

Bishop of Gaborone: Most Rev. FRANKLYN NUBUASAH (Archbishop *ad personam*), Bishop's House, Plot 162, Queens Rd, POB 218, Gaborone; tel. 3913192; e-mail gabs.diocese@botsnet.bw.

The Press

DAILY NEWSPAPERS (PRINT AND ONLINE)

Daily News: Plot 37795, Mass Media Complex, cnr Wellie Seboni Rd and KT Motsete Rd, PMB BR137, Gaborone; tel. 3653500; e-mail dailynews@gov.bw; internet fb.com/DailyNews.BW; f. 1964; Mon.–Fri.; publ. by Dept of Information and Broadcasting; English; Co-Editors BAAITSE MOLAPO, EDWARD ROBERT.

Mmegi: Plot 767, The Main Mall, Tati Rd, Ext. 2, PMB BR50, Gaborone; tel. 3912667; e-mail online@mmegi.bw; internet www .mmegi.bw; f. 1984 as *Mmegi wa Dikgang*; daily; publ. by Dikgang Publishing Co; Setswana and English; Man. Dir TITUS MBUYA; Editor RYDER GABATHUSE; also publishes the weekly *Mmegi Monitor* (f. 2000).

PERIODICALS

The Botswana Gazette: Plot 125, Sedimosa House, Gaborone International Finance Park, POB 1605, Gaborone; tel. 3912833; e-mail editorial@gazettebw.com; internet www.thegazette.news; f. 1985; weekly; publ. by News Co Botswana; Man. Editor SHIKE OLSEN; Editor LAWRENCE SERETSE.

Botswana Guardian: Plot 121, Finance Park, PMB 00153, Gaborone; tel. 3908408; e-mail comments@guardiansun.co.bw; internet guardiansun.co.bw; f. 1983; weekly; publ. by CBET (Pty)LTD; English.

The Business Weekly and Review: Plot 145, Unit 14, Kgale Court, Gaborone International Finance Park, Gaborone; tel. 3170615; e-mail info@businessweekly.co.bw; internet businessweekly.co.bw; economic and financial weekly; f. 2014; Editor TSHIRELETSO MOTLOGELWA.

Kutlwano: Plot 37795, Willie Sebonie Rd, PMB BR137, Gaborone; tel. 3653500; e-mail kutlwanoonline@gov.bw; internet www .kutlwano.gov.bw; f. 1962; monthly; publ. by Dept of Information Services; Setswana and English; Editor THOMAS NKHOMA.

The Midweek Sun: Plot 121, Finance Park, PMB 00153, Gaborone; tel. 3908408; e-mail comments@guardiansun.co.bw; internet www.themidweeksun.co.bw; f. 1989; weekly; English; publ. by CBET (Pty) Ltd.

The Ngami Times: Mabudutsa Ward, PMB BO30, Maun; tel. 6864807; e-mail thengamitimes@gmail.com; f. 1999; weekly; owned by The Ngami Times Printing and Publishing Co Botswana (Pty) Ltd; English; Editor KETO SEGWAI.

The Oriental Post: Plot 22120, POB 81066, Gaborone; tel. 3163003; e-mail gmmg@gmmg.com; f. 2009; twice a month; Chinese; Pres. MILES NAN.

Sunday Standard: Plot 104, Unit 21, Gaborone International Commerce Park, Moores Rowland, POB 1079AAD, Gaborone; tel. 3188784; e-mail editors@sundaystandard.co.bw; internet www.sundaystandard.info; Editor OUTSA MOKONE.

WeekendPost: Plot 125, Unit 13, Gaborone International Finance Park, Kgale Mews, POB AD717, Gaborone; tel. 3908849; e-mail editor@weekendpost.co.bw; internet www.weekendpost.co.bw; ATD Media Corpn (Pty) Ltd.

The Voice: Plot 142, Unit 4, Gaborone International Finance Park, POB 40415, Gaborone; tel. 3161585; e-mail info@thevoicebw.com; internet news.thevoicebw.com; f. 1993 as *The Francistowner*; weekly; Editor EMANG BOKHUTLO.

NEWS AGENCIES

Botswana Press Agency (BOPA): PMB BR139, Gaborone; tel. 3653525; e-mail bopa@gov.bw; f. 1981.

PRESS ORGANIZATIONS

Press Council of Botswana: Samdef House, POB 301315, Tlokweng, Gaborone; tel. 3500378; f. 2002; Chair. ABREY LUTE.

Publishers

Bay Publishing: POB 502503, Gaborone; tel. 3105955; e-mail lene@baybookpublishers.com; internet www.baybookpublishers.com; f. 1994; Man. Dir JODE N. ANDERSON.

The Botswana Society (BotSoc): Plot 184, Tlale House, Unit 3, Matsitama St, Mainmall, POB 71, Gaborone; tel. 3919745; e-mail tbsbotsoc@gmail.com; internet www.thebotswanasociety.net; f. 1968; archaeology, arts, history, law, sciences; Chair. Prof. BOJOSI OTLHOGILE.

Heinemann Educational Botswana (Pty) Ltd: Plot 20695, Unit 4, Magochanyana Rd, POB 10103, Village Post Office, Gaborone; tel. 3972305.

Macmillan Botswana Publishing Co (Pty) Ltd: Plot 131, Nkwe Sq., Unit 9, Gaborone International Finance Park, POB 1155, Gaborone; tel. 3911770; e-mail vatib@macmillan.bw; internet www.macmillan.bw; f. 1981; Man. Dir WIM UITERWIJK.

Mmegi Publishing House (MPH): Plot 767, Tati Rd, The Main Mall, Ext. 2, PMB BR 50, Gaborone; tel. 3974784; e-mail dikgang@mmegi.bw; internet www.mmegi.bw; owned by Dikgang Publishing Co; academic and general; Man. Dir TITUS MBUYA.

Pearson Botswana: Plot 14386, West Industrial Site, New Lobatse Rd, POB 1083, Gaborone; tel. 3922969; e-mail chris.koveya@pearson.com; internet www.pearson.com/africa/countries/botswana.html; f. 1981; subsidiary of Pearson Education, UK; educational; Man. Dir CHRIS KOVEYA.

Printing and Publishing Co (Botswana) (Pty) Ltd (PPCB): Plot 5647, Nakedi Rd, Broadhurst Industrial, POB 130, Gaborone; tel. 3166059; e-mail info@ppcb.co.bw; internet www.ppcb.co.bw; f. 1971; educational.

GOVERNMENT PUBLISHING HOUSE

Department of Government Printing and Publishing Service: cnr Mokolwane and Lejara Rds, Broadhurst Industrial, PMB 0081, Gaborone; tel. 3685200.

Broadcasting and Communications

TELECOMMUNICATIONS

Botswana Telecommunications Corpn Ltd (BTC): Plot 50350, Megaleng, Khama Cres., POB 700, Gaborone; tel. 3958000; e-mail crm@btc.bw; internet www.btc.bw; f. 1980; 54.16% state-owned; fixed-line and mobile telecommunications provider; merged its fixed-line and mobile operations (BTC Mobile) under BTC banner in 2016; Chair. LORATO BOAKGOMO-NTAKHWANA; Man. Dir ANTHONY MASUNGA.

Mascom: Plot 4705–6, Tsholetsa House, Botswana Rd, Main Mall, Bontleng, PMB BO298, Gaborone; tel. 3903396; e-mail digitaladmins@mascom.bw; internet fb.com/mascom.bw; f. 1998; mobile telecommunications provider; CEO DZENE MAKHWADE-SEBONI.

Orange Botswana: Plot 43002–1, Camphill Bldg, PMB BO64, Bontleng, Gaborone; tel. 3693700; e-mail customerservice@orange.com; internet www.orange.co.bw; f. 1998 as Vista Cellular; present name adopted in 2003; 49% owned by Orange SA, France; 46% owned by Mosokelatsebeng Cellular; mobile telecommunications provider; CEO NÉNÉ MAÏGA.

Regulatory Authority

Botswana Communications Regulatory Authority (BOCRA): Plot 50671, Independence Ave, PMB 00495, Gaborone; tel. 3957755; e-mail info@bocra.org.bw; internet www.bocra.org.bw; f. 1996; Chair. TSAONE RUTH THEBE; CEO MARTIN MOKGWARE.

BROADCASTING

Department of Broadcasting Services: PMB 0060, Gaborone; tel. 3658000; e-mail otsiang@btv.gov.bw; internet www.dib.gov.bw; f. 1978 following merger between Information Services and Radio Botswana; Dir LESOLE OBONYE.

Radio

Duma FM: Plot 59140, Blk 7, POB 1823, Gaborone; tel. 3500131; internet fb.com/DumaFM; f. 2007; Programme Man. DONALD SEBERANE.

Radio Botswana (RB1): PMB 0060, Gaborone; tel. 3952541; f. 1965; state-owned; fmrly Radio Bechuanaland; present name adopted 1966; culture, entertainment, news and current affairs programmes; Gen. Man. KEITIRELE MATHAPE.

Radio Botswana (RB2) (FM 103): PMB 0060, Gaborone; tel. 3653000; e-mail mmphusu@gov.bw; f. 1992; contemporary entertainment; Station Man. SAKAEYO JANE.

GABZ FM 96.2: Plot 64516, 2nd Floor, Showgrounds Close, PMB 319, Gaborone; tel. 3170905; e-mail info@gabzfm.co.bw; internet www.gabzfm.com; f. 1999; owned by Thari Investment; entertainment, news and politics; broadcasts in Setswana and English; Programmes Man KENNETH MOENG.

Yarona FM: Plot 28562, Unit F18, Fairgrounds Shopping Mall, Samora Machel Dr., POB 1607, Gaborone; tel. 3912305; e-mail info@yaronafm.co.bw; internet www.yaronafm.co.bw; f. 1999; available in Gaborone, Francistown, Lobatse, Serowe, Palapye, Selibe Phikwe, Maun, Mahalapye, Sojwe, Hukuntsi, Letlhakane/Orapa, Takatokwane, Salajwe and Malwelwe; owned by Copacabana Investment; Station Man. KELLY RAMPUTSWA-TLALE.

Television

Botswana Television (BTV): 28483 Batsadi, Gaborone; tel. 3658000; e-mail botswanatelevision@gmail.com; internet fb.com/BotswanaTelevision; f. 2000; Gen. Man. BONTLE MOGOTLLWANA.

E-Botswana: Plot 53996, Suite 168, Broadhurst Industrial Estate, Gaborone; POB AD 69 ABE, Gaborone; tel. 3957654; e-mail info@ebotswana.co.bw; internet www.ebotswana.co.bw; f. 1988; present name adopted 2010; operated by Gaborone Broadcasting Co (Pty) Ltd; Setswana and English.

Finance

BANKING

Central Bank

Bank of Botswana (BoB): 17938 Khama Cres., PMB 154, Gaborone; tel. 3606000; e-mail webmaster@bob.bw; internet www.bankofbotswana.bw; f. 1975; bank of issue; Gov. MOSES DINEKERE PELAELO.

Commercial Banks

Absa Bank Botswana Ltd: Barclays House, 6th Floor, Plot 8842, Khama Cres., POB 478, Gaborone; tel. 3159575; e-mail botswanacustomerservice@absa.africa; internet www.absa.co.bw; f. 1975 as local successor to Barclays Bank Int. Ltd; fmrly Barclays Bank of Botswana Ltd; present name adopted 2020; Chair. NEO MOROKA; Man. Dir KEABETSWE PHEKO-MOSHAGANE.

Access Bank Botswana: BancABC House, Plot 62433, Fairground Office Park, POB 00303, Gaborone; tel. 3674300; e-mail info@bancabc.com; internet botswana.accessbankplc.com; f. 1989 as ulc (Pty) Ltd; name changed to African Banking Corpn (Pty) Ltd in 2001; fmrly BankABC, present name adopted in 2021; financial services and investment banking; operates in Botswana, Mozambique, South

Africa, Tanzania, Zambia and Zimbabwe; owned by ABC Holdings Ltd (part of Atlas Mara Ltd); Group Man. Dir SANJEEV ANAND.

Bank of Baroda (Botswana) Ltd: Plot 14456, Postnet Kgale View, Kamoshungo Rd, POB AD216, Gaborone; tel. 3992710; e-mail md .botswana@bankofbaroda.com; internet www.bankofbaroda.co.bw; f. 2001; subsidiary of the Bank of Baroda, India; Chair. SERETSE BAGONI; Man. Dir SANJAY JOSHI.

Bank Gaborone Ltd: Plot 74768, cnr 2nd Commercial Rd and Western Commercial Rd, CBD, PMB 00325, Gaborone; tel. 3671500; e-mail info@bankgaborone.co.bw; internet www.bankgaborone.co .bw; f. 2006; subsidiary of Capricorn Investment Holdings (Botswana) Ltd; Chair. PETER COLLINS; Man. Dir S. A. COETZEE.

Bank SBI Botswana Ltd: Plot 54351, Exponential, 2nd Floor, CBD, POB 505243, Gaborone; tel. 3919778; internet www .sbibotswana.co.bw; 100% owned subsidiary of State Bank of India; Man. Dir PRAMOD PAL.

First Capital Bank Ltd: First Capital House, Plot 74768, 2nd Commercial Rd, New CBD, Gaborone; tel. 3158659; e-mail feedback@firstcapitalbank.co.bw; internet firstcapitalbank.co.bw; f. 2007; fmrly Capital Bank Ltd; current name adopted in 2018; part of FMB Group (Malawi); Chair. HITESH ANADKAT; CEO JACO VILJOEN.

First National Bank of Botswana Ltd (FNBB): Plot 54362, CBD, POB 1552, Gaborone; tel. 3706000; internet www.fnbbotswana.co .bw; f. 1991; 69.5% owned by First Nat. Bank Holdings Botswana Ltd; Chair. JOHN KIENZLEY MACASKILL; CEO STEVEN L. BOGATSU.

Stanbic Bank Botswana Ltd: Stanbic House, Plot 50672, Fairgrounds Office Park, PMB 00168, Gaborone; tel. 3987801; e-mail cccbw@stanbic.com; internet www.stanbicbank.co.bw; f. 1992; subsidiary of Standard Bank Investment Corpn Africa Holdings Ltd; CEO SAMUEL MINTA.

Standard Chartered Bank Botswana Ltd (SCBB): Standard House, 5th Floor, Plots 1124–1127, The Mall, POB 496, Gaborone; tel. 3601672; e-mail contactus.bw@sc.com; internet www.sc.com/bw/; f. 1975; 75% owned by Standard Chartered Holdings (Africa) BV, Amsterdam; CEO MPHO CALVIN MASUPE.

Other Banks

Botswana Savings Bank (BSB): Tshomarelo House, Plot 53796, cnr Lekgarapa and Letswai Rds, Broadhurst Mall, POB 1150, Gaborone; tel. 3670000; e-mail info@bsb.bw; internet www.bsb.bw; f. 1963 as the Post Office Savings Bank; present name adopted 1992; Chair. KEALEBOGA MOLELOWOTLADI; CEO NIXON MARUMOLOA.

Letshego Botswana (Letshego Financial Services Botswana): Letshego Pl., Plot 22, Khama Cres., POB 381, Gaborone; tel. 3643000; e-mail info@letshego.com; internet www.letshego.com/ botswana; f. 1998; micro-finance; Chair. PHILIP ODERA; CEO FERGUS FERGUSON.

National Development Bank: Development House, Plot 1123, The Mall, POB 225, Gaborone; tel. 3952801; e-mail enquiries@ndb.bw; internet www.ndb.bw; f. 1963; state-owned; Chair. WILFRED MPAI; CEO LORATO C. MORAPEDI.

STOCK EXCHANGE

Botswana Stock Exchange: Fairscape Precinct, 4th Floor, Plot 70667, Fairgrounds, POB 00417, Gaborone; tel. 3674400; e-mail info@bse.co.bw; internet www.bse.co.bw; f. 1989; commenced formal functions of a stock exchange in 1995; Chair. Lt-Gen. (retd) TEBOGO MASIRE; CEO THAPELO TSHEOLE; 24 domestic cos listed in 2021.

INSURANCE

Alpha Direct Insurance Co: Botswana Innovation Hub, 1st Floor, Bar 1, Plot 69184, POB 26ADC, Gaborone; tel. 3928264; e-mail godirect@alphadirect.co.bw; internet alphadirect.co.bw; f. 2014; Chair. KIRAN C. PATEL; CEO ARUN P. IYER.

Botswana Insurance Co Ltd: BIC House, Gaborone Business Park, Plot 50372, Gaborone Business Park, POB 715, Gaborone; tel. 3600500; e-mail enquiries@bic.co.bw; internet www.bic.co.bw; f. 1975; CEO NEWTON JAZIRE.

Botswana Insurance Holdings Ltd (BIHL): Plot 66458, Blk A, 3rd Floor, Fairgrounds Office Park, POB 336, Gaborone; tel. 3707000; e-mail tkeepetsoe@bihl.co.bw; internet www.bihl.co.bw; f. 1975; 58% owned by Sanlam Group, South Africa; Acting Chair. MAHUBE MPUGWA; CEO CATHERINE LESETEDI-LETEGELE.

> **Botswana Life Insurance Ltd:** Plot 50676, Blk A, Fairgrounds Office Park, POB 00296, Gaborone; tel. 3645100; e-mail webmaster@blil.co.bw; internet www.botswanalife.co.bw; f. 1975; subsidiary of BIHL; life insurance; CEO RONALD JAMES SAMUELS.

Hollard Botswana: Plot 70667, 2nd Floor, Bldg 2, Fairscape Precinct, Fairgrounds, Gaborone; tel. 3958023; internet www.hollard.co .bw; acquired Regent Insurance Botswana 2017; owned by Hollard Group, South Africa; Man. Dir JANE TSELAYAKGOSI.

Liberty Life Botswana: Fairscape Precinct, 6th Floor, Plot 70667, Fairgrounds, PMB 00168, Gaborone; tel. 3180262; e-mail customervoice@libertygroup.co.bw; internet www.liberty.co.bw; f. 2008; owned by Liberty Holdings, South Africa; 165 corporate clients; Man. Dir LULU RASEBOTSA.

Metropolitan Botswana Ltd: Plot 54352, East Tower, Zambezi Towers, CBD, PMB 231, Gaborone; tel. 3624400; e-mail omothibatsela@metropolitan.co.bw; internet www.metropolitan.co .bw; f. 1996; 75% owned by Metropolitan South Africa, 25% owned by the Botswana Devt Corpn; Man. Dir FRIKKIE AUGUSTYN.

Old Mutual Botswana: Plot 64511, Fairgrounds, PMB 347, Gaborone; tel. 3995700; e-mail contactus@oldmutual.co.bw; internet www .oldmutual.co.bw; f. 1994; Man. Dir KUSHATHA MOSWELA.

Insurance Association

Insurance Institute of Botswana: Plot 70667, Fairscape Precinct, Fairgrounds, POB 715, Gaborone; tel. 3980450; e-mail admin@iib.co .bw; internet www.iib.co.bw; f. 2016; training and development of insurance sector; Chair. DZIKI NGANUNU.

Regulatory Authority

Non-Bank Financial Institutions Regulatory Authority (NBFIRA): Plot 54351, Exponential Bldg, 3rd Floor, New CBD, off PG Matante Rd, PMB 00314, Gaborone; tel. 3686100; e-mail info@ nbfira.org.bw; internet www.nbfira.org.bw; f. 2006; Chair. MOTLALEPULA KABOMO; CEO ODUETSE MOTSHIDISI.

Trade and Industry

GOVERNMENT AGENCIES

Botswana Housing Corpn (BHC): Plot 5129, cnr Pilane and Queens Rds, POB 412, Gaborone; tel. 3605100; e-mail info@bhc .bw; internet www.bhc.bw; f. 1971; provides housing for govt and local authority needs and assists with private sector housing schemes; Acting Chair. MOEMEDI GABANA; Acting CEO PASCALINE SEFAWE.

Citizen Entrepreneurial Development Agency (CEDA): Plot 54350, PG Matante Rd, Four Thirty Sq., Gaborone; tel. 3170895; e-mail feedback@ceda.co.bw; internet www.ceda.co.bw; f. 2001; develops and promotes citizen-owned enterprises; provides business training and financial assistance; Chair. Dr ALFRED TSHEBOENG; CEO THABO THAMANE.

Competition and Consumer Authority: Plot 28, Matsitama Rd, Main Mall, PMB 00101, Gaborone; tel. 3934278; e-mail ca@ competitionauthority.co.bw; internet www.competitionauthority.co .bw; f. 2011; monitors, controls and prohibits anti-competitive trade or business practices; Chair. Dr MALEBOGO BAKWENA; CEO TEBELELO PULE.

Local Enterprise Authority: Lot 70667, Bldg 1, Ground Floor, Unit 2A, Fairscape Precinct, Fairgrounds Office Park, PMB 191, Gaborone; tel. 3644000; e-mail botsalea@lea.co.bw; internet www.lea .co.bw; promotes citizen entrepreneurship; provides business development services through training and mentoring; Chair. LORATO NTAKHWANA; CEO Dr RACIOUS M. MOATSHE.

Public Enterprises Evaluation and Privatisation Agency (PEEPA): Plot 64511, Fairground Office Park, PMB 00510, Gaborone; tel. 3980000; e-mail enquiries@peepa.co.bw; internet www .peepa.co.bw; f. 2001; responsible for commercializing and privatizing public parastatals; Chair. TINY KGATLHWANE; CEO ISHMAEL JOSEPH (acting).

DEVELOPMENT ORGANIZATIONS

Botswana Council of Non-Governmental Organisations (BOCONGO): Plot 54513, Unit 5, Courtyard Village, Gaborone; tel. 3911319; e-mail info@bocongo.org; internet www.bocongo.org; f. 1995; Exec. Dir MONAMETSI SOKWE.

Botswana Development Corpn Ltd: Plot 70667, Fairscape Precinct, Tower Fairgrounds Office Park, PMB 160, Gaborone; tel. 3651300; e-mail enquiries@bdc.bw; internet www.bdc.bw; f. 1970; Chair. MALEHO MOTHIBATSELA; Man. Dir CROSS KGOSIDIILE.

Botswana Investment and Trade Centre (BITC): Plot 54351, Exponential Bldg, off P. G. Matante Rd, Private Bag 00445, Gaborone; tel. 3633300; e-mail enquiries@bitc.co.bw; internet www .gobotswana.com; f. 2012 following merger of the Botswana Export Development and Investment Authority (BEDIA) and the Botswana International Financial Services Centre; promotes and facilitates local and foreign investment, and the devt of cross-border financial services based in Botswana; Chair. TERRENCE DAMBE; CEO KELETSOSITSE OLEBILE.

INDUSTRIAL AND TRADE ASSOCIATIONS

Botswana Agricultural Marketing Board (BAMB): Plot 130, Nkwe Sq., Unit 3 and 4, Gaborone International Finance Park, PMB 0053, Gaborone; tel. 3951341; e-mail info@bamb.co.bw; internet www.bamb.co.bw; Chair. TALLY TSHEKISO; CEO Dr BENJAMIN DITSELE (acting).

Botswana Meat Commission (BMC): Plot 621, 1 Khama Ave, PMB 4, Lobatse; tel. 5340000; e-mail communications@bmc.bw; internet www.bmc.bw; f. 1965; slaughter of livestock, export of hides and skins, carcasses, frozen and chilled boneless beef; operates tannery and beef products cannery; Chair. BOYCE MHUTSIWA; CEO Dr BOITUMELO MOGOME-MASEKO (acting).

EMPLOYERS' ORGANIZATIONS

Botswana Chamber of Mines (BCM): Plot 165, Capricorn House, Pilane Rd, POB 2130, Gaborone; tel. 3914685; e-mail bcm@info.bw; internet www.bcm.org.bw; Pres. MONTY MPHATHI; CEO CHARLES SIWAWA; 39 mem cos.

Botswana Teachers' Union (BTU): Kgale Courts, Unit 21, nr Game City, Gaborone; PMB 0019, Mogoditshane; tel. 3906774; e-mail headoffice@btu.org.bw; internet btu.org.bw; f. 1937 as the Bechuanaland Protectorate African Teachers' Asscn; present name adopted 1966; Pres. GOTLAMANG OITSILE; Sec.-Gen. AGANG GABANA.

Business Botswana: Business Botswana House, Luthuli Rd, POB 432, Gaborone; tel. 3953459; e-mail publicrelations@bb.org.bw; internet www.bb.org.bw; f. 1971 as Botswana Confederation of Commerce, Industry and Manpower (BOCCIM); present name adopted in 2015; Pres. GOBUSAMANG KEEBINE; CEO NORMAN MOLEELE.

UTILITIES

Regulatory Authority

Botswana Energy Regulatory Authority (BERA): Plot 8842, Extension Town Centre, Lobatse; tel. 5330932; e-mail info@bera.co.bw; internet www.bera.co.bw; f. 2017; responsible for economic regulation of energy supply sector in Botswana; Chair. THEBE JUSTICE MOILWA; CEO ROSE NUNU SERETSE.

Electricity

Botswana Power Corpn (BPC): Motlakase House, Macheng Way, POB 48, Gaborone; tel. 3607000; e-mail contactcentre@bpc.bw; internet www.bpc.bw; f. 1970; parastatal; operates power station at Morupule (132 MW); Chair. Prof. OBOETSWE MOTSAMAI; CEO DAVID S. KGOBOKO.

Water

Department of Water Affairs: Plot 25019, Old Lobatse Rd, PMB 0029, Gaborone; tel. 3607100; e-mail folesitse@gov.bw; internet www.water.gov.bw; water resources management.

Water Utilities Corpn: Plot 17530, Luthuli Rd, PMB 00276, Gaborone; tel. 3604400; e-mail contactcentre@wuc.bw; internet www.wuc.bw; f. 1970; state-owned; supplies water to main urban centres; Chair. NOBLE KATSE; CEO GASELEMOGWE SENAI.

MAJOR COMPANIES

The following are among the leading companies in Botswana in terms of capital investment and employment.

Botswana Oil Corpn Ltd: Plot 54373, Petroleum House, Matante Mews, PMB BO173, Bontleng, Gaborone; tel. 3981700; e-mail enquiries@botswanaoil.co.bw; internet www.botswanaoil.co.bw; sale of petroleum products to customers in Botswana; state-owned; Chair. MARTIN MAKGATLHE; CEO MESHACK TSHEKEDI.

Chobe Holdings Ltd: Chobe National Park, POB 32, Kasane; tel. 77000854; e-mail info@chobeholdings.co.bw; internet www.chobeholdings.co.bw; f. 1983; eco-tourism; interests in Botswana and Namibia; subsidiaries include: Desert & Delta Safaris (Pty) Ltd, The Bookings Co, Ker and Downey Botswana (Pty) Ltd; Chair. MYRA SEKGOROROANE; Group Man. Dir LEMPHEDITSE ODUMETSE.

Choppies Enterprises Ltd: Plot 169, GICP, Gaborone; tel. 3186657; e-mail info@choppies.co.bw; internet choppies.co.bw; f. 1986; grocery retailer; operates outlets in Kenya, Tanzania, Namibia, Mozambique, Zambia, South Africa and Zimbabwe; Chair. UTTUM COREA; CEO RAMACHANDRAN OTTAPATHU.

Debswana Diamond Co (Pty) Ltd: Plot 64288, Airport Rd, Blk 8, POB 329, Gaborone; tel. 3614200; e-mail corporateAffairs@debswana.bw; internet www.debswana.com; f. 1968; owned equally by the Botswana Govt and De Beers Centenary AG, Switzerland; sole diamond mining interest in Botswana; operates mines in Orapa, Jwaneng, Letlhakane and Damtshaa; Chair. BRUCE CLEAVER; Man. Dir ANDREW MAATLA MOTSOMI.

Engen Botswana Ltd: Plot 54026, Western Bypass, Gaborone West, POB 867, Gaborone; tel. 3635300; internet engen.co.za; fmrly Mobil; subsidiary of Engen Petroleum Ltd, South Africa; suppliers of petroleum-based fuels and lubricants; Chair. AHMAD ADLY ALIAS; Man. Dir BRIAN FARAYI SAMEKE (acting).

G4S Botswana Ltd: Plot 20584, Blk 3 Industrial, Western Bypass, POB 1488, Gaborone; tel. 3698000; e-mail head.office@bw.g4s.com; internet www.g4s.com/en-bw; f. 2003 following acquisition of Inco Group; subsidiary of G4SPLC, UK; fmrly Securicor Botswana Ltd; security and cash transportation services; Chair. L. M. MPOTOKWANE; Man. Dir MOTHUSI MOLOKOMME.

Lucara Botswana (Pty) Ltd: Plot 67782, Diamond Technology Park, Blk 8 Industrial, POB AE 668, AEH-Postnet, Gaborone; tel. 3922310; e-mail info@lucaradiamond.com; internet lucaradiamond.com; Man. Dir NASEEM LAHRI.

Minergy Ltd: Plot 75782, Bldg 3, Unit 2, Ground Floor, Pinnacle Park, Setlhoa, POB 2330 ABG, Broadhurst, Gaborone; tel. 3972891; internet www.minergycoal.com; coal mining; CEO MORNÉ DU PLESSIS.

MRI Botswana: Plot 60601, Blk 7, Mogoditshane, PMB BR256, Gaborone; tel. 3903066; e-mail enquiries@mri.co.bw; internet www.mri.co.bw; f. 1992; suppliers of medical and rescue services; Chair. LEBOGANG T. MATALE; Man. Dir THAPELO L. LIPPE.

Northern Textile Mills (Pty) Ltd: Plot 9807, Phase 4 Industrial Area, POB 1508, Francistown; tel. 2414773; e-mail info@nortex.co.bw; internet www.nortex.co.za; f. 1990; mfrs of household textiles; exports to Mauritius, South Africa, Tanzania, Zimbabwe and the USA; Chair. and Man. Dir MUKESH JOSH.

Okavango Diamond Co: Plot 67782, Diamond Technology Park, Blk 8 Industrial, POB 2258 ABG Sebele, Gaborone; tel. 3992300; e-mail info@odc.co.bw; internet www.odc.co.bw; jt venture between the Govt and De Beers; Man. Dir MMETLA MASIRE.

Puma Energy Botswana: Plot 682/3, Botswana Rd, Main Mall, POB 183, Gaborone; tel. 3610300; e-mail botswana@pumaenergy.com; internet pumaenergy.com; f. 2010; fmrly BP Botswana (Pty) Ltd; petroleum exploration and production; Gen. Man. MAHUBE MPUNGWA.

RDC Properties Ltd: Plot 5624, Lejara Rd, Broadhurst Industrial, POB 405391, Gaborone; tel. 3901654; e-mail rdc@rdc.bw; internet rdcbw.com; f. 1992; property management, devt and retail; interests in Botswana, Madagascar and South Africa; Chair. and Man. Dir GUIDO R. GIACHETTI; CEO JACOPO PARI.

RPC Data Ltd: Plot 39, Unit 5, International Commerce Park, PMB BR 42, Gaborone; tel. 3903644; e-mail info@rpcdata.com; internet www.rpcdata.com; f. 1989 as Rob Pool Computing (Pty) Ltd; present name adopted in 1994; management consultancy and information technology services; operates in Botswana, South Africa, Uganda and Zambia; Exec. Chair. ROB POOL; Man. Dir KOMAL RAO.

Sechaba Brewery Holdings Ltd (SBHL): Plot 70667, Fairscape Precinct, 8th Floor, Fairgrounds Office Park, PMB 160, Gaborone; tel. 3651410; e-mail sechaba@bdc.bw; 25.6% owned by Botswana Devt Corpn, 16.8% owned by SABMiller Africa BV, Netherlands; mfrs of clear beer and soft drinks; distributors of wines and spirits (Kgalagadi Breweries Ltd) and traditional beers (Botswana Breweries Ltd); Chair. BAFANA MOLOMO; Man. Dir MABU NTETA.

Sefalana Holding Co Ltd: Plot 10038, cnr Nelson Mandela Dr. and Kubu Rd, Broadhurst Industrial Site, PMB 0080, Gaborone; tel. 3913661; e-mail info@sefalana.com; internet www.sefalana.com; f. 1974; miller, processor and distributor of cereals (Foods Botswana); motor vehicle dealership and travel agency (M. F. Holdings Ltd); soap production (Kgalagadi Soap Industries Ltd); Chair. JENNIFER MARINELLI; Man. Dir CHANDRAKANTH D. CHAUHAN.

> **Sefalana Cash and Carry Ltd (SEFCASH):** Plot 10238, cnr Lejara and Moporoporo Rds, Broadhurst Ext 20, PMB 00422, Gaborone; tel. 3681700; f. 1994; wholesale retailer; fully owned by Sefalana; Man. Dir HANS WERNER KAMPMANN.

Turnstar Holdings Ltd: Plot K09, Turnstar House, Farm Forest Hill, Game City, Gaborone; tel. 3936105; e-mail info@turnstar.co.bw; internet turnstar.co.bw; f. 2002; property investment; Chair. BUTLER PHIRIE; Man. Dir GULAAM HUSAIN ABDOOLA.

TRADE UNIONS

Botswana Federation of Trade Unions (BFTU): Plot 4220/2, Ext. 14, POB 440, Gaborone; tel. 3952534; e-mail admin@bftu.org.bw; internet www.bftu.org.bw; f. 1977; Pres. MARTHA MOLEMA; Sec.-Gen. THUSANG BUTALE; 25 affiliated mems.

Affiliated Unions

Affiliated unions include: the Air Botswana Employees' Union; the Botswana Bank Employees' Union; the Botswana Diamond Workers' Union; the Botswana Housing Corpn Workers' Union; the Botswana Textile Manufacturing and Packaging Workers' Union; the Botswana Meat Industry Workers Union; the Botswana Mine Workers'

Union; the Botswana National Development Bank Employees Union; the Botswana Postal Services Workers' Union; the Botswana Power Corporation Workers' Union; the Botswana Private Medical and Health Services Workers' Union; the Botswana Railways and Allied Workers' Union; the Botswana Savings Bank Employees' Union; the Botswana Telecommunications Employees' Union; the Botswana Vaccine Institute Staff Union; the Botswana Government Workers' Union; the Botswana Diamond Workers' Union; the Botswana National Productivity Centre Support Staff Union; the Trainers and Allied Workers' Union; the University of Botswana Non-Academic Staff Union; the University of Botswana Senior Support Staff Union; Botswana Wholesalers Furniture and Retail Workers' Union; Botswana Public Employees Union; the Footballers Union of Botswana and the Central Bank Union.

Principal Non-affiliated Unions

Botswana Land Boards and Local Authorities Health Workers Union (BLLAHWU): Plot 178, Unit 3, Commerce Park, Gaborone; tel. 3932399; e-mail bllahwuinfo@mokaulengwe.co.bw; internet bllahwu.com; f. 1972; fmrly the Botswana Unified Local Govt Service Asscn; Sec.-Gen. KETLHALEFILE MOTSHEGWA.

Botswana Sectors of Educators Trade Union (BOSETU): Robinson Rd, Gaborone; tel. 3937472; e-mail info@bosetu.org.bw; internet bosetu.org.bw; f. 1986 as Botswana Fed. for Secondary School Teachers (BOFESETE); Pres. WINSTON RADIKOLO; Sec.-Gen. TOBOKANI RARI.

The BLLAHWU, the BOSETU and three other unions (the Botswana Public Employees Union, the Botswana Teachers Union and the National Amalgamated Local Government, and Central Government and Parastatals Union) form the Botswana Federation of Public Service Unions (BOFEPUSU).

Transport

RAILWAYS

The railway line from Mafikeng, South Africa, to Bulawayo, Zimbabwe, passes through Botswana and has been operated by Botswana Railways (BR) since 1987. Through its links with Transnet, which operates the South African railways system, and the National Railways of Zimbabwe, BR provides connections with Namibia and Eswatini to the south, and an uninterrupted rail link to Zambia, the Democratic Republic of the Congo, Angola, Mozambique, Tanzania and Malawi to the north. A 1,100-km railway project linking Botswana (and Zimbabwe) with a new port at Ponta Techobanine in southern Mozambique was in development. Botswana has a Dry Port in Namibia, which started operating in 2015. The Dry Port receives and dispatches commodities either destined for Botswana or the region.

Botswana Railways (BR): A1 Mahalapye Main Rd, Mowana Ward, PMB 52, Mahalapye; tel. 4711375; e-mail info@botrail.bw; internet www.botswanarailways.co.bw; f. 1986; Chair. MMOLOKI RAMAEBA; CEO CHELESILE MALELE (acting).

ROADS

Department of Road Transport and Safety: PMB 0054, Gaborone; tel. 3688600; responsible for national road network; Dir BOKHUTLO MODUKANELE.

CIVIL AVIATION

The main international airport is at Gaborone. The five other major airports are located at Kasane, Maun, Francistown, Selebi Phikwe and Ghantsi. Scheduled services of Air Botswana are supplemented by an active charter and business sector.

Civil Aviation Authority of Botswana (CAAB): Plot 61920, Letsema Office Park, POB 250, Fairgrounds, Gaborone; tel. 3688200; e-mail caab@caab.co.bw; internet www.caab.co.bw; f. 2009; Chair. MPHO JUDITH DIMBUNGU; CEO Dr BAO MOSINYI.

Air Botswana: POB 92, Sir Seretse Khama Airport, Gaborone; tel. 3688400; internet www.airbotswana.co.bw; f. 1972; 45% state-owned; domestic services and regional services to countries in eastern and southern Africa; Chair. Lt-Gen. (retd) TEBOGO CARTER MASIRE; Gen. Man. AGNES KHUNWANA.

BlueSky Airways: Private Bag SK11, Gaborone; tel. 3181544; e-mail info@blueskyairways.co.bw; internet www.blueskyairways .co.bw; Man. Dir MARK SPICER.

Kalahari Air Services: Sir Seretse Khama Airport, Gaborone; tel. 3951804; e-mail kas@kalahariair.co.bw; internet www.kalahariair .co.bw; f. 1968; Man. Dir NOEL FITZGERALD.

Moremi Air: Maun Airport Bldg, 1st Floor, PMB 187, Maun; tel. 6863632; e-mail info@moremiair.com; internet www.moremiair .com; f. 1997; air charter operator; domestic and regional services; Gen. Man. KELLY SEROLE.

Tourism

Botswana Tourism Organisation (BTO): Plot 50676, Fairground Office Park, Blk B, Ground Floor, Gaborone; tel. 3913111; e-mail board@botswanatourism.co.bw; internet www.botswanatourism.co .bw; f. 2009 to replace Botswana Tourism Board; joined the World Travel and Tourism Council (WTTC) in 2018; Chair. BOITUMELO SEKWABABE; CEO (vacant).

Hospitality and Tourism Association of Botswana (HATAB): PMB 00423, Gaborone; tel. 3957144; e-mail hatab@hatab.bw; internet www.hatab.bw; f. 1982; fmrly Hotel and Tourism Asscn of Botswana; Chair. JOE MOTSE; CEO LILY RAKORONG.

Defence

Military service is voluntary. Botswana established a permanent defence force in 1977. As assessed at November 2021, the total strength of the Botswana Defence Force (BDF) was some 9,000, comprising an army of 8,500 and an air force of 500. In 2007 Botswana began recruiting women into the BDF for the first time.

Defence Budget: P5,760m. in 2021.

Defence Force Commander: Lt-Gen. PLACID SEGOKO.

Education

Although education is not compulsory, enrolment ratios are high. Primary education begins at six years of age and lasts for up to seven years. Secondary education, beginning at the age of 13, lasts for a further five years, comprising a first cycle of three years and a second of two years. According to estimates by the United Nations Educational, Scientific and Cultural Organization (UNESCO), enrolment at pre-primary institutions in 2014/15 included 18% of children in the relevant age-group (boys 18%; girls 18%). Enrolment at primary schools in 2013/14 included 89% of children in the relevant age-group (boys 88%; girls 90%). Tertiary education is provided by the University of Botswana and the affiliated College of Technical and Vocational Education. There are also technical and vocational training centres, including the Institute of Health Sciences, the Botswana College of Agriculture, the Roads Training College, the Colleges of Education (Primary and Secondary), and the Botswana Institute of Administration and Commerce. Expenditure on education by the central Government in 2021/22 was budgeted at P14,120m. (representing 20.0% of total projected expenditure and net lending in that year).

Bibliography

Alexander, K., and Kaboyakgosi, G. (Eds). *A Fine Balance. Assessing the Quality of Governance in Botswana*. Pretoria, Institute for Democracy in South Africa, 2012.

Bolaane, M., and Mgadla, P. T. *Batswana*. New York, Rosen Publishing Group Inc, 1997.

Dale, R. *Botswana's Search for Autonomy in Southern Africa*. Westport, CT, Greenwood Press, 1995.

Dingake, M. *The Politics of Confusion: The BNF Saga 1984–1998*. Gaborone, Bay Publishing (Pty) Ltd, 2004.

Düsing, S. *Traditional Leadership and Democratisation in Southern Africa: A Comparative Study of Botswana, Namibia, and Southern Africa*. London, Lit, 2002.

Good, K. *Diamonds, Dispossession & Democracy in Botswana*. Woodbridge, James Currey, 2008.

Gulbrandsen, Ø. *The State and the Social: State Formation in Botswana and its Pre-Colonial and Colonial Genealogies*. New York, Berghahn Books, 2012.

Hillbom, E., and Bolt, J. *Botswana - A Modern Economic History: An African Diamond in the Rough*. Cham, Palgrave Macmillan, 2018.

Jackson, A. *Botswana, 1939–1945: An African Country at War*. Oxford, Clarendon Press, 1999.

Jalata, A. *Cultural Capital and Prospects for Democracy in Botswana and Ethiopia*. Abingdon, Routledge, 2021.

Leith, J. C. *Why Botswana Prospered*. Montreal, QC, McGill-Queen's University Press, 2005.

Livingston, J. *Debility and the Moral Imagination in Botswana*. Bloomington, IN, Indiana University Press, 2005.

McCaig, B. *Stuck in the Middle? Structural Change and Productivity Growth in Botswana*. Cambridge, MA, National Bureau of Economic Research, 2015.

Makgatla, J. *Elite Conflict in Botswana: A History*. Pretoria, Africa Institute of South Africa, 2006.

Masire, K. *Very Brave or Very Foolish? Memoirs of an African Democrat*. Gaborone, Macmillan Botswana, 2006.

Maundeni, Z. *40 Years of Democracy in Botswana, 1965–2005*. Gaborone, Mmegi Publishing House, 2005.

Mazonde, I. N. (Ed.). *Minorities in the Millennium: Perspectives from Botswana*. Gaborone, Lightbooks, 2002.

Morton, B., and Ramsay, J. *Historical Dictionary of Botswana*, 5th edn. Lanham, MD, Rowman & Littlefield, 2018.

Motzafi-Haller, P. *Fragmented Worlds, Coherent Lives: The Politics of Difference in Botswana*. Westport, CT, Bergin and Garvey, 2002.

Peters, P. E. *Dividing the Commons: Politics, Policy and Culture in Botswana*. London, University of Virginia Press, 1994.

Phirinyane, M. *Elections and the Management of Diversity in Botswana*. Gaborone, Botswana Institute for Development Policy Analysis, 2013.

Rakner, L. *Botswana: 30 Years of Economic Growth, Democracy and Aid*. Bergen, CMI, 1996.

Schmidt, D. A. *The Bechuanaland Pioneers and Gunners*. Westport, CT, Praeger, 2006.

Selolwane, O. *Poverty Reduction and Changing Policy Regimes in Botswana*. Basingstoke, Palgrave Macmillan, 2012.

Siphambe, H. K., et al. *Economic Development of Botswana: Facets, Policies, Problems and Prospects*. Gaborone, Bay Publishing (Pty) Ltd, 2005.

Stedman, S. J. *Botswana: The Political Economy of Democratic Development*. Boulder, CO, Lynne Rienner Publishers, 1993.

Tlou, T., et al. *Seretse Khama, 1921–1980*. Johannesburg, Macmillan, 1995.

Vanqa, T. P. *The Development of Education in Botswana*. Gaborone, Lightbooks Publishers, 2001.

Vaughn, O. *Chiefs, Power and Social Change: Chiefship and Modern Politics in Botswana, 1880s–1990s*. Trenton, NJ, Africa World Press, 2003.

Werbner, R. P. *Reasonable Radicals and Citizenship in Botswana* Bloomington, IN, Indiana University Press, 2004.

    The Making of an African Working Class. Politics, Law, and Cultural Protest in the Manual Workers' Union of Botswana. London, Pluro Press, 2014.

Williams, A. S. *Colour Bar: The Triumph of Seretse Khama and His Nation*. London, Allen Lane, 2006.

Wiseman, J. *Botswana*. Oxford, ABC Clio, 1992.

THE BRITISH INDIAN OCEAN TERRITORY (BIOT)

The British Indian Ocean Territory (BIOT) was formed in November 1965, through the amalgamation of the former Seychelles islands of Aldabra, Desroches and Farquhar with the Chagos Archipelago, a group of islands 1,930 km north-east of Mauritius, previously administered by the Governor of Mauritius. Aldabra, Desroches and Farquhar were ceded to Seychelles when that country was granted independence in June 1976. Since then BIOT has comprised only the Chagos Archipelago, including the coral atoll Diego Garcia, with a total land area of 60 sq km (23 sq miles).

BIOT was established to meet British and US defence requirements in the Indian Ocean. An agreement concluded in 1966 between the United Kingdom and the USA provided for BIOT to be used by both countries over an initial period of 50 years, with the option of extending this for a further 20 years. The UK undertook to cede the Chagos Archipelago to Mauritius when it was no longer required for defence purposes.

Following the purchase of the islands' privately owned coconut plantations by the British Crown in 1966, they ceased to operate and the inhabitants were offered the choice of resettlement in Mauritius or in Seychelles. The majority (numbering about 1,200 individuals) went to Mauritius.

In November 2000 the High Court of England and Wales ruled that the Chagos islanders (Chagossians or Ilois) had been illegally evicted from the Chagos Archipelago, and quashed Section 4 of the 1971 Immigration Ordinance, which prevented the return of the Chagossians to BIOT. During the case it transpired that the British Government had apparently termed the Chagossians 'contract workers' in order to persuade the United Nations (UN) that the islanders were not an indigenous population with democratic rights. However, memorandums of the Foreign and Commonwealth Office (FCO) revealed government knowledge of some of the Chagossians living in the Chagos Archipelago for two generations. The British Government declined an appeal, thereby granting the islanders an immediate right to return to BIOT. A new ordinance, issued in January 2001, permitted the former residents to return to any of the islands in the Archipelago, except Diego Garcia.

In June 2004 the British Government issued two decrees under the Royal Prerogative explicitly stating the UK's resumption of full control of immigration services within the archipelago and banning the Chagossians from returning. In May 2006 the High Court of England and Wales ruled that the exclusion of the islanders (many of whom had moved to the UK) from their territory was unlawful. The British Government commenced proceedings to overturn the ruling at the Court of Appeal in February 2007; however, in May that court upheld the displaced islanders' immediate right to return. In November the House of Lords granted the British Government the right to appeal against the Court of Appeal's decision. The appeal was heard in mid-2008 and in November the House of Lords ruled in favour of the Government, thus denying the Chagossians the right to return, and citing as its main reason the fact that the UK would have been obliged to meet the costs of economic, social and educational advancement of the residents. The ruling also stated that the British Government had no further obligations towards the Chagossians. In June 2015 the Chagossians appealed to the UK Supreme Court (which assumed the judicial functions formerly exercised by the House of Lords in 2009) to overturn the 2008 decision. However, in July 2016 the UK Supreme Court ruled to uphold the 2008 decision.

In April 2010 the British Government announced that it had designated the Chagos Archipelago a Marine Protected Area (MPA), within which all fishing and other activities were to be prohibited. The conservation area, covering some 544,000 sq km, was to be patrolled by a ship vested with the powers to arrest fleets caught fishing illegally. In December the Mauritian Government announced that it had taken a case against the UK to the UN International Tribunal for the Law of the Sea (UNITLS) on the grounds that the MPA was not compatible with the UN Convention on the Law of the Sea (UNCLOS). The Mauritian case against the UK was heard by a five-member Arbitral Tribunal of the Permanent Court of Arbitration in April–May 2014, and in March 2015 the Tribunal ruled that the British Government had acted illegally in declaring the MPA. The UK was ruled to have breached its obligations under UNCLOS to consult Mauritius before declaring the MPA, and had illegally deprived that country of fishing rights. In June 2017 the Chagossians challenged the creation of the MPA in the British Supreme Court, arguing that it infringed upon their rights to their native land, including fishing rights.

Meanwhile, in July 2013 the British Government announced its intention to commission a new feasibility study into the resettlement of the Chagossians on BIOT. FCO officials met with a wide range of parties, including Chagossian communities in Mauritius, the UK and in Seychelles. The professional services company KPMG was appointed as an independent consultant by the FCO and released its final report into Chagossian resettlement in February 2015. This assessed three options for potential resettlement and suggested that the most likely options for any initial return would either be a pilot, small-scale resettlement or a medium-scale resettlement. The former would involve resettling some 150 Chagossians, while the latter envisaged resettling around 500 people. The report stated that this would 'probably' be on Diego Garcia with 'possible later expansion' to the outer islands, which could involve the large-scale resettlement of 1,500 Chagossians. The report also stated that there were no fundamental legal obstacles to a resettlement of BIOT proceeding, but maintained that the needs of the returning population would have to be balanced with environmental concerns and the use of the territory for defence purposes. In August–October the British Government carried out a consultation exercise that sought the view of Chagossians on potential return options. According to the Government's summary of its findings, released in January 2016, some 98% of Chagossians supported the resettlement of their homeland.

However, in November 2016 the British Government stated that it would not be proceeding with a pilot resettlement 'on the grounds of feasibility, defence and security interests, and cost to the British taxpayer'. At the same time a funding package to the value of £40m. to 'support improvements to the livelihoods of Chagossians in the communities where they now live' was also announced. (In mid-2020 it was reported that only around £500,000 of this funding package had been disbursed, while the FCO confirmed that no mechanism had yet been put in place to 'implement a plan for the Chagossian community.) The decision to refuse resettlement was widely criticized and in December hundreds of Chagossians protested outside the office of the British Prime Minister. A legal challenge to the decision to refuse resettlement was dismissed by the High Court of England and Wales, but in July 2019 the Chagossians were granted permission to take their case to the Court of Appeal. In late July 2020 the Court dismissed the claim. Meanwhile, in early 2017 it was confirmed that the agreement between the UK and the USA providing for BIOT to be used by both countries had been extended until 2036.

In recent years Diego Garcia has frequently been used as a base for US aircraft carrying out air strikes on Iraq and Afghanistan. In February 2008 the British Government admitted that, contrary to previous statements, a number of so-called rendition flights (the transfer of detainees by the US Central Intelligence Agency to third countries where it was possible that they might be subjected to torture during interrogation) had used facilities at Diego Garcia.

In April 2004 the Mauritius Government renewed the campaign to reclaim sovereignty over the Chagos Archipelago after specialists in international law advised that the decree by which the UK separated the Chagos Archipelago from Mauritius was illegal. An attempt was made to block the Mauritian Government from pursuing the case at the International Court of Justice (ICJ) on the basis of a longstanding ruling, whereby members of the Commonwealth could not take the UK to court; in July the ruling was extended to former members of the Commonwealth, in order to prevent Mauritius from circumventing the obstacle by withdrawing from that organization. Mauritius announced that it would pursue the matter at the General Assembly of the UN. The Mauritian case was strengthened by the fact that, at that time, the 1966 agreement establishing the US base on Diego Garcia was due to expire at the end of 2016. Following the Permanent Court of Arbitration's ruling in March 2015 (see above), the Mauritian Prime Minister, Aneerood Jugnauth, wrote to his British counterpart, David Cameron, proposing negotiations on the Chagos Archipelago and senior British and Mauritian officials held inconclusive talks in November and again in May 2016. Jugnauth requested in May that the UK agree to return control of the Chagos Archipelago to Mauritius by a certain date (to be mutually agreed on) and issued an ultimatum: if the UK did not reply to this request by the end of June, Mauritius would take action at the international level, including at the UN. In June 2017 a motion, proposed by Mauritius, to refer the UK to the ICJ with regards to the validity of that nation's sovereignty claim over the Chagos Islands, was passed, with 94 members of the UN General Assembly voting in its favour. (15 countries voted against the motion, while 65 abstained.) On 25 February 2019 the ICJ ruled that the UK must return sovereignty of the Chagos Islands to Mauritius as rapidly as possible, as the continued British occupation of the islands was illegal, and the transfer of sovereignty in 1965 had not represented a 'free and genuine expression of the people concerned'. However, the ruling was advisory and non-binding, and the UK dismissed it, arguing that the BIOT military installations helped to protect the region from terrorism, piracy and organized crime. In a further non-binding vote in May, the UN General Assembly adopted a resolution (by 116 countries to six, with 56 abstentions) demanding that the UK uphold the ICJ advisory opinion and relinquish administration of the Chagos Archipelago. In November the British Government issued a statement reinforcing its claim to sovereignty over the Chagos Islands, and again rejected the ICJ's advisory ruling. In June 2020 an official world map produced by the UN identified the Chagos Islands as Mauritian territory. In January 2021 the UNITLS ruled (in a case regarding a dispute between the Maldives and Mauritius over maritime borders) that the UK did not have sovereignty over the Chagos Islands. In August, in a symbolic move that further exposed the UK's growing international isolation, the UN Universal Postal Union overwhelmingly voted in favour of withdrawing recognition of postage stamps issued by BIOT, with all future mail from the Chagos Islands required to use Mauritian stamps. In an additional assertion of its sovereignty over the islands, in February 2022 the Mauritian Government threatened to initiate legal action against a British company that had minted coins for BIOT, accusing the firm of 'a serious violation of international law'. Later that month the Mauritian Government chartered a vessel to conduct a survey of the outer reefs of the Chagos Archipelago to gather data to support its maritime boundary case against the Maldives. The ship also transported a group of Chagossians and the Mauritian ambassador to the UN, Jagdish Koonjul, who planted Mauritian flags on two of the outer atolls. The UK responded by removing the flags and reaffirming its sovereignty over the islands, while dismissing the Mauritian expedition as a 'political stunt'. Meanwhile, measures included in the UK's Nationality and Borders Bill would allow the descendants of the Chagos Islanders to apply for British citizenship and British Overseas Territory citizenship; the Bill received Royal Assent in April 2022.

The civil administration of BIOT is the responsibility of a non-resident commissioner in the Foreign, Commonwealth and Development Office (as the FCO had become in June 2020) in London, UK, represented on Diego Garcia by a Royal Navy commander and a small British naval presence. A chief justice, a senior magistrate and a principal legal adviser (who performs the functions of an attorney-general) are resident in the UK.

Land Area about 60 sq km (Diego Garcia 44 sq km).

Population There are no permanent inhabitants.

Currency The official currency is the pound sterling, but the US dollar is also accepted.

Commissioner: Paul Candler, Director of Overseas Territories, Foreign, Commonwealth and Development Office, King Charles St, London, SW1A 2AH, UK; tel. (20) 7008-2691.

Deputy Commissioner and Head of BIOT Policy Team: Becky Richards, Overseas Territories Dept, Foreign, Commonwealth and Development Office, King Charles St, London, SW1A 2AH, UK; tel. (20) 7008-2691.

Administrator: Balraj Dhanda, Overseas Territories Dept, Foreign, Commonwealth and Development Office, King Charles St, London, SW1A 2AH, UK; tel. (20) 7008-2691.

Commissioner's Representative: Commdr Colvin Osborn, RN, Diego Garcia, c/o BFPO Ships.

BURKINA FASO

Physical and Social Geography

R. J. HARRISON CHURCH

Burkina Faso (formerly the Republic of Upper Volta) is a landlocked state of West Africa and is situated north of Côte d'Ivoire, Ghana and Togo. Burkina has an area of 273,187 sq km (105,478 sq miles). The 2019 census recorded a total population of 20,505,155, giving an average density of 75.1 inhabitants per sq km. By mid-2022, according to United Nations estimates, this had risen to 22,102,838 and a density of 80.9 inhabitants per sq km. In the early 2000s there was large-scale emigration to neighbouring Côte d'Ivoire and Ghana by people seeking work on farms, in industries and in the service trades, although economic and political difficulties in these host countries (particularly the former) prompted the return of large numbers of migrant workers to Burkina. The main ethnic groups are the Mossi in the north and the Bobo in the south-west. Along the northern border are the semi-nomadic Fulani, who are also present in the east of the country. The capital city, Ouagadougou, had a population of 2,415,266 at the 2019 census.

Towards the south-western border with Mali there are primary sandstones, terminating eastward in the Banfora escarpment. As in Guinea, Mali and Ghana, where there are also great expanses of these rocks, their residual soils are poor and water percolates deep within them. Although most of the rest of the country is underlain by granite, gneisses and schists, there is much loose sand or bare laterite; consequently, there are extensive infertile areas. Moreover, annual rainfall is only some 635 mm–1,145 mm, and comes in a rainy season of at the most five months. Water is scarce except by the rivers or in the Gourma swampy area; by the former the simulium fly, whose bite leads to blindness, has been the target of extensive eradication projects, while in the latter the tsetse, a fly that can cause sleeping sickness, is found. Given the grim physical environment, the density of population in the north-central Mossi area is remarkable. The area is, in fact, one of the oldest indigenous kingdoms of West Africa, dating back to the 11th century. Islam first penetrated the area during the 14th–16th centuries. At the end of the 18th century some local rulers, notably the leader of the Mossi, adopted Islam, but traditional religious practices among the population remained strong. Islam's expansion was facilitated by the circumstances of French rule, and by the time of the 2019 census, more than 63% of the population were Muslims.

Burkina Faso has valuable deposits of gold, manganese and zinc, industrial exploitation of which is in progress or is planned. Reserves of silver, nickel, lead, phosphates and vanadium have also been identified.

History

BRAM POSTHUMUS

INDEPENDENCE AND INTERMITTENT MILITARY RULE

Following the September 1958 referendum organized by the French colonial authorities in order to establish the status of each one of its colonies on the African continent, Upper Volta (which was renamed Burkina Faso in 1984) opted to become a self-governing republic within the French Community. Two years later, on 5 August 1960, the country was granted full independence.

The first President of the First Republic was Maurice Yaméogo, who upon assuming power banned all political parties except his own Union Démocratique Voltaïque (UDV). His autocratic style, perhaps in reaction to the instability that surrounded independence, but also his ostentatious lifestyle, in combination with the stringent austerity he imposed on the population at large led to strikes and protests, and he was deposed in a coup, on 3 January 1966, led by Lt-Col Aboubacar Sangoulé Lamizana.

Initially, Lamizana's reign was more autocratic than Yaméogo's; however, in 1969 political parties were given permission to operate. A new Constitution was adopted by referendum in June 1970, ushering in a short-lived Second Republic. An elected civilian administration took office in December but effective power remained with the army. Lamizana confirmed this in 1974 by taking the reins once again. It was a coup in all but name.

In November 1977 the Government went through the motions of organizing another constitutional referendum, which marked the start of the Third Republic. In the following year legislative and presidential elections took place. Lamizana won the latter but he came under increasing pressure as salaries remained unpaid and the cost of living increased. Numerous strikes were organized, in spite of the President's efforts to have trade unions banned. In a situation that resembled the 1966 uprising and coup, Lamizana was deposed by Col Saye Zerbo in November 1980. His reign lasted a mere two years before another coup brought to the fore a new strongman in November 1982, Jean-Baptiste Ouédraogo, an army medic. Ouédraogo appointed an army captain, Thomas Sankara, as Prime Minister, who held that post for just five months, until his arrest in May 1983.

THOMAS SANKARA'S RISE AND MURDER

Sankara, arguably the most emblematic public figure in Burkina Faso's history, grew up in various parts of the country, went to school in Bobo-Dioulasso, the second largest city, and pursued a military education in his own country, Cameroon, Madagascar and Morocco. He co-founded a left-leaning collective of army officers and maintained a strong pan-African and anti-colonial ideology. It was this hard line that resulted in his detention in May 1983, much to the consternation of his allies in the army, some political parties and the very influential trade unions, which demanded his release. When this did not happen the army contingent based in Pô, near the Ghanaian border and Sankara's duty station, marched on the capital, Ouagadougou, and took power. Among the main leaders of that uprising was another captain, Blaise Compaoré.

Sankara was made President on 4 August 1983 and instituted the Conseil Nationale de la Révolution (CNR). Precisely one year later he renamed the country Burkina Faso, a name that combines the two main languages in the country (Moré and Dioula) and projects a positive image: the name means 'Land of the Upright People'. However, Sankara's rule was not without controversy. His efforts to make the country self-sufficient in food, his concerns for women and the environment, and his refusal to use state resources for personal wealth were rated positively. However, his decision to diminish the authority of the country's traditional leaders in the name of progress was deeply resented, as were his increasingly intolerant and authoritarian tendencies. The CNR and its local offshoots were implicated in serious human rights abuses, including murder. The border war with Mali in December 1985 revealed tensions within the ruling revolutionary committee, and brought the already deep personal differences with his deputy, Compaoré, further to the fore.

On 15 October 1987 Sankara and 12 others were murdered during one of their weekly CNR meetings. The instigator was Compaoré, who in April 2022 received a life sentence *in absentia* for his role in the assassinations (see *Trials of High-ranking Operatives of the Compaoré Era*). Regional and international complicities have always been suspected (particularly the roles of Côte d'Ivoire's President, Félix Houphouët-Boigny, and Mali's Moussa Traoré, who were openly hostile to Sankara, France and a future Liberian warlord, Prince Yormie Johnson) although there has been no conclusive evidence of their involvement.

COMPAORÉ AND THE FOURTH REPUBLIC

Upon taking power, Compaoré disbanded the CNR and began a policy that he named the 'rectification' of the revolution. It consisted principally of restoring the traditional leaders, the '*chefferie*', which became his principal electoral agency especially in the rural areas. Another key plank was re-establishing a cordial relationship with Côte d'Ivoire, home to a large Burkinabè population. He then set about rearranging the institutional configuration of the country, away from the revolutionary fervour of his predecessor. In terms of state finances, Structural Adjustment Programmes were agreed with the International Monetary Fund (IMF) and the World Bank and a number of state enterprises were privatized.

In April 1989 the Organisation pour la Démocratie Populaire/Mouvement du Travail (ODP/MT) was formed, a precursor to the Congrès pour la Démocratie et le Progrès (CDP). Roch Marc Christian Kaboré became the designated leader of the ODP/MT. Those who refused to affiliate to the ODP/MT were removed from office. In September 1989 a plot was said to have been discovered involving four leaders associated with the 1983 revolution. They were summarily executed.

On 2 June 1991 a draft Constitution, which provided for a multi-party political system was put to a referendum and endorsed by 93% of those who voted. The Fourth Republic was born. Kaboré became the most senior member of a transitional Council of Ministers. At the end of that year Compaoré—who had resigned his army commission—was elected President with more than 90% of the votes cast, although he was the only candidate as the opposition boycotted proceedings. In May 1992 the ODP/MT took 78 of the available 107 seats in a newly created legislature, the Assemblée des Députés du Peuple (ADP—Assembly of People's Deputies); the opposition attributed their loss to electoral fraud. President Compaoré appointed an economist, Youssouf Ouédraogo, as Prime Minister.

Ouédraogo resigned in March 1994, after trade unions denounced as inadequate the measures he had proposed to offset the adverse effects of the 50% devaluation of the CFA franc in January, pushed through by France at the instigation of the IMF and the World Bank. Kaboré, who had made a career in banking before entering politics, assumed the premiership but in 1996 he was replaced by anther banker, Kadré Désiré Ouédraogo. Meanwhile, the ODP/MT folded into the newly formed CDP; Kaboré became the party's first Vice-President, a post he combined with being Special Presidential Adviser.

In January 1997 the ADP approved constitutional changes, including the removal of the clause restricting the number of presidential mandates. It also increased the number of seats to 111. In May 1997 parliamentary elections for what was now called the Assemblée Nationale (National Assembly) resulted in a victory for the CDP, which took 101 seats. In the following year Compaoré was comfortably re-elected for another seven year presidential term. On each of these occasions voter participation was weak at well below 50%, and the opposition did not present a candidate in the presidential ballot.

The Murder of Norbert Zongo

On 13 December 1998 the investigative journalist and editor of the newspaper *L'Indépendant*, Norbert Zongo, was assassinated in his car with three other passengers including his brother. The quadruple murder, ascribed to the presidential guard (Régiment de Sécurité Présidentiel—RSP), precipitated the first major political crisis of the Compaoré presidency. Zongo, a frequent critic of Compaoré, had been investigating the death (by torture at the hands of the RSP) of David Ouédraogo, a chauffeur employed by François Compaoré, the President's younger brother. After a trial lasting nearly five years, a military tribunal sentenced two RSP elements to 20 years in prison and one to a 10-year term in August 2020 for David Ouédraogo's murder.

REFORMS, ELECTIONS AND MUTINY

In April 2000 the National Assembly revised the electoral code. Under the new regulations 90 deputies were to be elected from regional lists while 21 would be elected from a national list. Deputies also approved a reduction in the presidential mandate from seven years to five, renewable only once. The opposition was of the opinion that this meant that Compaoré could no longer run, having already completed two terms; however, the Constitutional Court ruled that the amendments approved by the National Assembly could not be applied retroactively, thus clearing the way for Compaoré to present himself for a fresh term of office in 2005 and again in 2010.

In November 2000 Kadré Désiré Ouédraogo resigned and was replaced as premier by Paramanga Ernest Yonli, hitherto Minister of the Civil Service and Institutional Development. A total of 12 members of the opposition were brought into the new, 36-member Government. Ouédraogo embarked on a diplomatic career, with an ambassadorship in Belgium between 2001 and 2011 and then moved to Nigeria, where he held the post of President of the Commission of the Economic Community of West African States (ECOWAS) from 2012 to 2016, before returning to Burkinabè politics.

At the 2002 parliamentary elections the CDP narrowly retained its majority, winning 57 out of the 111 available seats. The ADF—RDA (a fusion of the Alliance pour la Démocratie et la Fédération and the Rassemblement Démocratique Africain) secured 17 seats; 11 other parties were represented in the new legislature.

In October 2003 the Government announced that it had prevented a coup. Its presumed leader, Capt. Luther Ouali, was sentenced to 10 years in prison in April 2004. In November 2005 Compaoré was again comfortably re-elected to the presidency, taking 80.4% of the vote. Voter turnout was reported to be 57.5%. This was repeated at the next parliamentary election, held in May 2007, when reported turnout stood at 56.4%. The CDP increased its majority, thanks in no small part to the traditional '*chefferie*', which Compaoré had come to rely upon for issuing voting instructions to the large rural population. The CDP took 73 seats and the ADF—RDA 14, while 11 other parties secured representation. Tertius Zongo, a former ambassador to the USA, was appointed Prime Minister in June. In 2010 Compaoré once again secured a large victory at the presidential election, obtaining 80.2% of the votes cast.

Another death, in February 2011, triggered the second major political crisis Compaoré faced, marked by a series of violent protests, mutinies and looting sprees. There had been protests before against police brutality and the cost of living (in 1998, 2006 and 2008, *inter alia*); however, the economic situation in particular had been exacerbated by the return of hundreds of thousands of Burkinabè, who had fled the violent conflicts in neighbouring Côte d'Ivoire between late 2002 and early 2011. The death in police custody of a student, Justin Zongo, in the town of Koudougou provoked mass riots, initially in that town, where government buildings were set on fire and the protests were violently repressed, resulting in seven deaths. The riots spread and reached other urban centres including Ouagadougou as well as Ouahigouya and Bobo-Dioulasso. Six more deaths were reported.

Late at night on 22 March 2011 soldiers joined the protests, voicing their dissatisfaction with the incarceration of some of their colleagues. They stormed the military prison in

Ouagadougou, freed their colleagues and engaged in a looting spree. The unrest prompted the Government to declare a dusk to dawn curfew on 30 March. Tensions escalated still further on 14 April when elements of the RSP mutinied over unpaid housing and food allowances, prompting Compaoré to flee Ouagadougou briefly to his fief of Ziniaré. There existed animosity between the army and the RSP but on this occasion they operated together and looted shops and businesses. Violence and looting spread around the country and even the dismissal of the Government by the President, who had subsequently returned to the capital, nor his removal of the Chief of the General Staff of the Armed Forces and his promise to pay all arrears to the RSP, halted the unrest.

Business owners whose properties had been damaged by the mutinous troops attacked public buildings, while thousands of people participated in fresh protests over high food and fuel prices. On 18 April 2011 Luc Adolphe Tiao, hitherto ambassador to France, was appointed Prime Minister, while Compaoré himself assumed responsibility for the defence portfolio. In May the Government introduced emergency measures to allay public discontent over the high cost of living but the unrest took a while to die down, with soldiers in Bobo-Dioulasso and 11 other towns staging mutinies in May and June that were quelled by forces loyal to the President, essentially the RSP. In July 566 soldiers were discharged from the army and 217 were detained on charges of rebellion, desertion and looting. Some members of the RSP left the force following these events, including Lt-Col Paul-Henri Sandaogo Damiba, who was to become a significant figure in subsequent events.

ARTICLE 37 AND COMPAORÉ'S FORCED DEPARTURE

In April 2012 the National Assembly approved its enlargement from 111 to 127 seats. In June it also agreed upon the introduction of lower and upper age limits for presidential candidates (35 and 75 years, respectively) and immunity from prosecution for all heads of state since independence. The opposition boycotted the vote.

At legislative elections held in April 2012 the CDP retained its majority, taking 70 of the 127 available seats. A new party, firmly of the opposition (unlike the ADF—RDA and other parties that generally supported Compaoré's policies), obtained 19 seats. The Union pour le Progrès et le Changement (UPC) was created in 2010 by former finance minister Zéphirin Diabré, who had left the country to work for the United Nations (UN) Development Programme and then the French nuclear group Areva before returning to Burkina Faso and politics. Voter participation was high at around 76%. Tao retained his job as Prime Minister and there was inclusion, once again, of members of the nominal opposition (not the UPC); however on this occasion the ADF—RDA found itself excluded from the Government.

In May 2013 the National Assembly adopted legislation that would lead to the creation of a Senate; however the opposition, including the ADF—RDA rejected the bill because they feared that the Government's ultimate agenda was to revise Article 37 of the Constitution, which in its current form stipulated that Compaoré could no longer present himself for the next presidential election. The proposed composition of the Senate indicated that the objective would have full congressional support (National Assembly and Senate) for Compaoré's plan as of the 89 members, 29 would be appointed by the President, 39 would be elected by regional councillors (almost all pro-Compaoré) and 21 would be nominated by 'civil society', i.e. traditional leaders (also pro-Compaoré since he gave them their authority back in 1987), religious leaders, trade unions, the business community and Burkinabè expatriates. Under pressure from renewed demonstrations and opposition agitation Compaoré shelved the project in August 2013.

Nevertheless, Compaoré was not going to abandon his ambition to remain in power. On 21 October 2013 the Council of Ministers approved draft legislation that would enable him to stand for re-election. Mass demonstrations occurred on 30 October during which many buildings were attacked, including the national radio and television station, the prestigious Hotel L'Indépendance, the adjacent building of the

National Assembly and the nearby CDP party headquarters; these last two were set alight, while the hotel was ransacked. Compaoré relented ·and announced that the bill was to be withdrawn: he would no longer be a presidential candidate. Unappeased, the protesters demanded his immediate resignation. On 31 October they marched on the presidential palace and during clashes with the RSP several demonstrators were killed. (Official figures stated that 33 people lost their lives during these events.) Compaoré resigned and drove in a convoy to his old military base at Pô, where he was picked up by a French helicopter and flown into exile in Côte d'Ivoire.

A TURBULENT TRANSITION

On the same day that Compaoré fled to Côte d'Ivoire, the Chief of the General Staff of the Armed Forces, Gen. Nabéré Honoré Traoré, declared himself head of state. However, several hours later there came a rival claim by Lt-Col Yacouba Isaac Zida, the second-in-command of the RSP, after Gen. Gilbert Diendéré, who was also Compaoré's former Special Chief of Staff. Zida received the support of some of the protesters and crucially that of the military. Both auto-declarations were in breach of the Constitution, with Article 43 stating that in case of a vacancy the President of the National Assembly would become transitional head of state with the task of organizing elections within 90 days. Zida managed to sway the crowds that had gathered in Ouagadougou's Place de la Nation; Traoré retracted his claim and Zida became interim head of state.

Amid pressure from the African Union, ECOWAS and the UN, Zida began talks with opposition politicians, representatives of civil society instrumental in deposing Compaoré (especially the youth movement Balai Citoyen, or Citizens' Broom, which had been in the forefront of the protests), and religious and traditional leaders. The objective was to arrive at a timetable for a return to civilian rule. The Constitution was reinstated on 15 November 2014 and a Transitional Charter was signed the following day. A career diplomat, Michel Kafando, was sworn in as Interim President on 18 November. He was a consensus candidate, regarded as mostly non-political and he appointed Zida as Prime Minister.

The next step was the creation of an interim legislative body, the Conseil National de la Transition (CNT). It was composed of 90 members: 30 from the former opposition parties, 25 from the armed and security forces, 25 from civil society and 10 from the former governing party. It was convened for the first time on 27 November 2014.

In a bid to gradually dismantle the old Compaoré system, 12 of the country's 13 regional governors were dismissed, as well as Diendéré. There were rumours that the RSP would be dissolved and its 1,300 elements re-integrated in the regular army. Resentment in the regular army over the privileges that the RSP members enjoyed (including better equipment and remuneration) was rife. When these plans were confirmed to be part of the Government's agenda, RSP elements disrupted cabinet meetings on several occasions, demanding the resignation of Zida, who was viewed as a high-ranking member of the RSP who had betrayed the group. They did not succeed but obtained a compromise: former Compaoré associates were appointed presidential Chief of Staff and RSP commander. This triggered further demonstrations and demands for the immediate dissolution of the RSP.

In January 2015 Kafando announced that presidential and legislative elections would be held on 11 October. In April the CNT adopted a new electoral code, which excluded from any election deputies who had supported the amendment of Article 37 and thus Compaoré's renewed presidential bid. The ECO-WAS Court of Justice ruled in July that these exclusions violated basic human rights and had to be removed but in August Burkina Faso's Constitutional Council ruled that six of the potential 22 presidential candidates—including the new CDP leader, Eddie Komboïgo—and 42 parliamentary candidates were ineligible to stand. In September the Council also rejected the presidential candidacies of former foreign minister Djibril Bassolé and former sports minister Yacouba Ouédraogo. However, the candidacies of former Prime Minister Kaboré and opposition leader Diabré were approved.

The September 2015 Coup Attempt

A Commission de la Reconciliation Nationale et des Réformes (CRNR), which had held its first meetings in March 2015, proposed the definitive dissolution of the RSP on 14 September. Two days later members of the RSP once again interrupted a meeting of the Council of Ministers and detained Interim President Kafando, Zida and two other ministers. Diendéré, the leader of the coup attempt, declared himself head of a Conseil National de la Démocratie, which announced the dissolution of the interim authorities. The putschists cited the exclusion of Compaoré's allies from the forthcoming elections as justification for their move but this was all about the survival of the RSP. Young Burkinabè mounted a spirited resistance to the RSP, which tried to violently repress it, resulting in at least 14 deaths. In various urban centres in the country (including Bobo-Dioulasso) the people appealed for the regular army to march on Ouagadougou and dislodge the RSP from their camp behind the presidential palace, Naaba Koom. Diendéré's house in the small town of Yako was set on fire. On 18 September ECOWAS dispatched the Presidents of Senegal (Macky Sall) and Benin (Boni Yayi) to mediate an end to the crisis, which began with the liberation of the hostages. Putschists and mediators met again on 20 and 21 September and negotiated under severe pressure from Balai Citoyen protesters and the army, which had begun to encircle the RSP base. On 22 September an agreement was signed that provided for the restoration to power of Kafando and the transitional bodies that had been temporarily suspended. The RSP was dissolved on 25 September and four days later the army took control of its camp. Diendéré, who had taken refuge in an embassy, surrendered on 1 October.

Most of the 1,300 elements in the RSP were integrated, with some difficulty, into the regular army. In February 2018 the trial commenced in a military court of 84 individuals connected with the failed coup, and in early September the court condemned Diendéré to 20 years in prison and his main political accomplice, Bassolé, to at 10-year term; nine other defendants received prison sentences ranging from 10 to 19 years, while a further eight individuals being tried *in absentia* were also convicted of involvement in the coup. The longest prison sentences, of 30 years, were given to Diendéré's wife Fatoumata, former government minister René Emile Kaboré and businessman Abdoul Karim André Traoré. In January 2020 the military court ordered the perpetrators of the coup to pay 947m. francs CFA in damages to civil parties.

THE KABORÉ PRESIDENCY

In early November 2015, the CNT adopted several amendments to the Constitution, including a clause that limited the number of presidential mandates to two. Meanwhile, as a result of the failed September coup the presidential and legislative elections were rescheduled and eventually took place on 29 November. They were largely free from incident and the former resulted in a win for Kaboré, who secured 53.5% of the vote in the first round with his closest rival Diabré taking 29.6%. The participation rate was reported to be around 60%. In the elections to the 127-seat re-established National Assembly, Kaboré's Mouvement du Peuple pour le Progrès (MPP) failed to obtain an outright majority, winning 55 seats; Diabré's UPC came second with 33 while the former ruling CDP secured 18. Eleven other parties secured seats; several among them, holding a combined total of 14 seats, formed a group allied to the MPP. While ideologically more left-leaning than the CDP, the MPP inherited structures and methods that resembled those of the CDP. These included a large party infrastructure, support from traditional leaders who could be relied upon to instruct rural voters whom to vote for and vote buying if and when necessary. The MPP was still a very young party so securing majorities on the scale that the CDP formerly obtained was always going to be a challenge. However, with the alliance in the National Assembly in place, Kaboré would not have to worry about 'co-habitation', i.e. working with a hostile legislature. Furthermore, during the municipal elections in May 2016, the MPP performed much better than expected, taking 11,167 seats from a total of 19,222 and taking control of most major cities and towns.

Kaboré was sworn in as President on 29 December 2015, formally marking the end of the transition. On 6 January 2016 Kaboré appointed an economist, Paul Kaba Thiéba, as Prime Minister. Combating corruption was identified as a key priority of the new Government. However, very early on in the Kaboré presidency other priorities imposed themselves.

Jihadist-related Violence Increases

Armed attacks ascribed to self-declared jihadist outfits were beginning to spill across the northern border with Mali. The first such incident took place in April 2015 at the Romanian-owned Tambao manganese mine in the north of Burkina when suspected Islamists kidnapped a security officer. In October three gendarmes were killed in Samorogouan, in the west of the country and some 30 km from the Malian border. When French troops based just outside Ouagadougou were called in to help end the deadly siege at the Radisson hotel in the Malian capital, Bamako, astute Burkinabè observers noted that this may have been the trigger the Islamist insurgents were waiting for. Whatever the merits of their observations, 18 days into the Kaboré presidency the Burkinabè capital was hit by an unprecedented attack that had three principal targets: the Splendid Hotel, the Cappuccino coffee bar and a bar called Taxi Brousse, all located on a busy crossroads between the capital's prestigious Avenue Kwame Nkrumah and a nameless street. (The fourth corner, not attacked was occupied by the burnt-out CDP headquarters.) The assailants entered the Cappuccino and shot randomly at the clients and the owner's family, and took hostages in the Splendid Hotel where several meetings and conferences were in progress. The assailants were dislodged in the early hours of the next morning. Some of them ran through the Taxi Brousse brandishing their guns and hid in the nearby Yibi Hotel, which was then also besieged by Burkinabè and French forces. The attack left 30 people dead and was the worst Ouagadougou had ever witnessed. Two Mali-based groups with roots and leadership from Algeria (al-Qa'ida in the Islamic Maghreb and its affiliate, al-Mourabitoun) claimed responsibility for the attack. Fully one-third of the victims were Burkinabè, while six were from Canada and four from Ukraine.

The attacks in the border areas also continued. In October 2016 a military post was attacked at Intangom; four soldiers were killed. This action was claimed by Islamic State in the Greater Sahara (ISGS), a new group that had emerged in 2015 from an outfit that had briefly controlled Gao, in Mali. However, there was also home-grown terrorism. On 16 December 2016 an attack on an army and gendarmerie base at Nassoumbou killed 12 troops. Ansaroul Islam, a Djibo-based group led by a radical preacher Malam Ibrahim Dicko claimed responsibility. Later that month, the Chief of the General Staff of the Armed Forces was replaced and a February 2017 government reorganization mainly affected the ministries concerned with the security sector. Nevertheless, the security situation in the northern regions continued to deteriorate, with jihadist gangs attacking military posts, police facilities and schools. Increasingly, the border region with Niger was affected. Burkinabè, Malian and French troops undertook offensives in the Sahel region in April 2017 with Dicko believed to have died on Malian territory. His younger brother Jafar succeeded him.

A second major attack in Ouagadougou occurred a short distance from the place of the first and targeted a Turkish-owned restaurant, Aziz Istanbul, where in mid-August 2017 two assailants opened fire killing 19 people, two of whom were prominent Kuwaiti imams and three others their Burkinabè students. The standoff with the assailants and Burkinabè security forces lasted all night and ended with the former, both very young men in their early twenties, dead. Despite social media reports claiming this was the work of the newly formed coalition of convenience JNIM (Jama'at Nusrat al-Islam wal-Muslimeen—Group for the Support of Islam and Muslims), responsibility for the attack was never claimed.

Meanwhile, the Government announced a plan to stem jihadist-related violence by introducing an emergency programme for the Sahel region. The Government pledged to build much-needed infrastructure, alleviate poverty and marginalization in an effort to discourage participation in militant groups. Following (principally French) military offensives in the border region of Burkina Faso, Mali and Niger starting in early 2018, elements of ISGS moved into largely unprotected border areas between Niger and Burkina Faso and crossed over into Burkina Faso, where they took hold of the lucrative artisanal gold business.

On 2 March 2018 co-ordinated attacks were launched on the army headquarters and the French embassy in Ouagadougou in which nine assailants and seven soldiers were killed. JNIM claimed that it had carried out the attack in retaliation for a French airstrike in Mali in February that had killed several of its leaders. Given the sophistication of the multiple attacks and the short time lapse between the air strikes and the claimed revenge attacks, JNIM's claim has limited credibility. The fact that the army headquarters was the main target has given rise to the theory that this could very well have been a violent manifestation of existing divisions within the army, made worse by the ongoing difficult integration of RSP elements into the regular armed forces. In October 2016 the Government revealed that it had foiled a coup plot involving former RSP members, two of whom had been shot by gendarmes.

Throughout 2018 and into 2019, attacks on the security forces, government officials, magistrates, teachers and civilians continued to increase in frequency, with a spate of roadside bomb and gun attacks recorded in the east of Burkina in September resulting in at least 29 deaths. In May Human Rights Watch (HRW) accused the Burkinabè security forces of carrying out extrajudicial killings during their operations against suspected armed Islamist groups in 2017 and 2018. The Government pledged to investigate the allegations but then adopted legislation in June 2019 which seriously restricted independent reporting on actions taken against armed groups by the security forces. The new law encompassed a change in the penal code, which provided for jail terms of up to 10 years if individuals reported on military operations.

Meanwhile, officials had started to abandon their posts in the northern and eastern areas; the town of Djibo was coming under repeated attack to the point of being cut off from the rest of the country. In December 2018 the Government declared a state of emergency in 14 provinces.

Project for a New Constitution on Hold

In September 2016 a commission was inaugurated, tasked with drafting a new constitution that would, once approved by referendum, serve as the basic law for a future Fifth Republic. The commission had 92 members, drawn from political parties, civil society organizations, trade unions, the security forces, religious and traditional leaders, business organizations and Burkinabè of the diaspora. The commission presented a revised draft constitution in December 2017, which stipulated the maximum time in office for the President to be two terms of five years. It also proposed the strengthening of the role of Prime Minister, would replace the Constitutional Council with a nine-member Constitutional Court (only two of these were to be nominated by the President), would abolish the death penalty and would guarantee Burkinabè living abroad the right to representation in the National Assembly and the right to vote.

In July 2019 a political dialogue took place, in which representatives of the almost 40 parties supporting the presidential majority and the opposition (principally the CDP and the UPC) discussed plans for a constitutional referendum, as well as the forthcoming 2020 general elections. The security situation also came under discussion, especially its expected impact on the polls. The constitutional project briefly returned when Kaboré announced in November 2020 that a referendum would be held in 2021 but as of August 2022 the project remained paused.

Violence Escalates Further

On 31 December 2019 at least 49 deaths were reported following an attack on the village of Yirgou, in Sanmatenga province. Village militias, mostly belonging to predominantly Mossi self-defence groups collectively known as *koglwéogo*, carried out reprisals and attacked several camps belonging to nomadic Peul (or Fulani) herdsman, accusing them of being accomplices to jihadist terror groups. These revenge attacks, born out of a guilt-by-association reflex were to become a recurring pattern in Burkina Faso. The *koglwéogo* were originally established as law-and-order restoration militias at the time of the MPP

takeover of government and soon became a law unto themselves. They were publicly endorsed by former security minister Simon Compaoré (no relation to the deposed President), which outraged human rights activists and civil society groups. In August 2019 several *koglwéogo* were arrested in connection with reprisal attacks against the Peul.

Meanwhile, in January 2019 Prime Minister Thiéba and his Government resigned under public pressure over the deteriorating security situation. Christophe Joseph Marie Dabiré, a former government minister under Blaise Compaoré, was appointed Prime Minister. The ministers responsible for defence and security were both replaced. Following another attack on the northern village of Kain, in which 14 civilians died, the military launched an offensive in which it claimed to have killed 146 'terrorists'. A national human rights organization (the Mouvement Burkinabè des Droits de l'Homme et des Peuples) later stated that some 60 of those 146 had been summarily executed. In March HRW again accused the security forces of extrajudicial killings, alleging that between mid-2018 and February 2019 it had executed some 116 people, mostly ethnic Peul. In March 2019 the Kaboré Government imposed a curfew on the eastern region of the country.

The killing of an important religious leader in a village near Arbinda, in the much-affected northern Soum province, led to inter-communal violence that left 62 people dead. In late April 2019 a Protestant church was attacked for the first time in the Sahel town of Silgadji, leaving five dead, including the pastor. Increasingly, there emerged a pattern of killings in which Christian clerics were targeted as well as imams considered not sufficiently radical. In August that year, again in Soum province, at least 24 soldiers lost their lives in an attack on a military post in Koudougou. ISGS claimed to have carried out the raid. Furthermore, Sanmatenga and Bam provinces, in the Centre-Nord region, were repeatedly hit by attacks. The increasing violence and insecurity prompted a demonstration in Ouagadougou on September 16, a first clear manifestation of public discontent over what protesters termed 'a security, social and economic crisis' in the country. Police used tear gas to disperse the march.

The Government's policy of replacing senior army officers and regional governors changed little. Those parts of the country living under a state of emergency often also had dusk to dawn curfews imposed on them, as was the case in Loroum province and all four provinces in the Sahel region. However, the attacks continued and were claimed either by JNIM or by ISGS. In Soum province, up to 40 people lost their lives in several attacks, prompting many to flee to the already besieged provincial capital Djibo. In an ambush in early November 2019 Oumarou Dicko, the deputy mayor of Djibo and a member of the National Assembly, was killed. In the east of the country 39 civilians died in an ambush on a bus carrying local employees of the Canadian gold firm Semafo. In December Arbinda came under attack again and in the ensuing massacres and reprisals a total of 122 people lost their lives, among them soldiers, civilians and supposed terrorists. The start of 2020 was marked by more attacks in Soum and Sanmatenga provinces.

Gendarmes, private company and government workers, government officials and civilians continued to be victims of terrorist attacks and reprisals at the hands of government forces or supposedly self-regulating militias like the *koglwéogo*. On 21 January 2020 the National Assembly added another group, by approving the creation of Volontaires pour la Défense de la Patrie (VDPs). Their creation had been the idea of defence minister Chérif Sy and the VDPs were to be recruited at village level and would, after a brief period of military training, be issued with an AK-47 assault rifle and asked to assist the military in the fight against terrorist insurgents. Human rights groups voiced concerns, maintaining that arming poorly trained civilians would in all likelihood increase insecurity, potentially exacerbate already existing ethnic tensions and lead to more human rights abuses, as such groups tend to become a law unto themselves. It was also pointed out that the presence of VDPs was likely to turn the localities where they were operating into preferred targets for armed criminals and/or jihadist insurgents. The warnings were not heeded.

The violence increased further in 2020, as Islamist insurgent activity persisted in numerous regions, while members of the Peul community found themselves increasingly on the receiving end of violent actions from the security forces, *koglwéogo* and the VDPs, who accused them of collaborating with jihadist armed groups. In one particularly violent incident more than 100 civilians were killed in two villages in the northern Yatenga province, of whom 43 were Peul. Summary executions of Peul civilians around Djibo by the security forces continued and in spite of regular condemnations by President Kaboré and promises that these and other abuses would be investigated, the pattern did not fundamentally change. To complicate matters further clashes began to be reported between JNIM fighters and those of ISGS. (Nominally, ISGS had been subsumed under the Islamic State of West Africa Province—ISWAP—from March 2019 but communication between it and ISWAP, which is concentrated in the Lake Chad Basin, is patchy. To all intents and purposes it is ISGS that still operates in Burkina Faso.)

In early March 2020 the introduction of a new tax on allowances and bonuses for civil service workers provoked five days of strike action and demonstrations in Ouagadougou and other urban centres by some 200,000 public sector workers. Subsequent marches and rallies were suspended or called off by the trade unions, following the introduction of government restrictions on mass meetings in response to the COVID-19 pandemic (see *The COVID-19 Pandemic and its Impact*.

In June 2020, the Observatoire pour la Démocratie et les Droits de l'Homme (ODDH), a local monitoring group, made an assessment of the situation since 2015. It concluded that between April 2015 and May 2020 at least 580 attacks had been perpetrated by jihadist terrorist groups, causing the deaths of 1,219 civilians and 436 members of the security forces. The ODDH added that over the same period the security forces had killed 588 civilians; mostly from the Peul (Fulani) group. In July HRW published a report in which it accused the security forces of involvement in 180 extrajudicial killings since November 2019. The dead were mainly members of the Peul community, whose bodies had been found in mass graves near Djibo.

The COVID-19 Pandemic and its Impact

The death on 18 March 2020 of the Second Vice-President of the National Assembly, Rose Marie Compaoré, was the first recorded fatality in sub-Sahara Africa from the COVID-19 virus, which had been declared a worldwide pandemic by the World Health Organization (WHO) one week earlier. Measures were quickly introduced to curb the spread of the virus. These included a ban on large gatherings (affecting the public sector workers' manifestations), a travel ban between cities and the closing of borders, the closure of schools and universities, and a nationwide curfew. Later that year, some of these restrictions were gradually lifted, including the travel ban (in May), the curfew (June) and the ban on international flights (August). However, the land borders remained closed. Educational institutions reopened in October. Having seen a sharp increase in cases at the beginning of 2021, the numbers decreased gradually in the ensuing months. A vaccination campaign began in June 2021, with the AstraZeneca vaccine provided under the WHO's COVAX initiative. 21,128 cases had been confirmed as of August 2022, resulting in 387 deaths. The number of people fully vaccinated stood at 1,640,349 or 7.9% of the population.

The 2020 Elections

Presidential and legislative elections were scheduled for 22 November 2020 and during the course of the year several candidates emerged. In May the CDP selected Eddie Komboïgo to stand, causing a rift in the party, with longstanding party loyalist and stalwart Léonce Koné changing camp in June and joining Kadré Désiré Ouédraogo, who had returned to the country and founded the Mouvement Agir Ensemble pour le Burkina Faso. President Kaboré was officially endorsed as the MPP's candidate in July, while the UPC nominated Zéphirin Diabré as its candidate.

In August 2020 the National Assembly approved a controversial amendment to the Electoral Code, which stipulated that if voting could not proceed in certain areas because of the security situation the results for the relevant constituencies would be based on the polling stations that were able to open, no matter how few or how low the turnout. Those who had been displaced by violence were to vote in their current place of residence.

Voter registration had been halted in some places because of the insecurity and been complicated in others owing to a large influx of displaced persons wanting to register. Meanwhile, the violence continued with attacks in Gourma province; notably Souaibou Cissé, the grand imam of Djibo was abducted and murdered. An army offensive in the Centre-Nord, Nord and Sahel regions changed little; jihadist attacks continued throughout. Just under two weeks before the elections, on 11 November 2020, 14 Burkinabè soldiers were killed during an ambush in Oudalan province.

The electoral campaign was dominated by the security situation; as domestic and sometimes international military efforts had failed to stem the tide, several opposition candidates suggested breaking a longstanding taboo and opening talks with the jihadist insurgents.

The elections took place as scheduled on 22 November 2020. It was decided that 1,318 of the 21,154 polling stations would not open, which meant that 596,756 voters (or 9.5% of the electorate) were disenfranchised. A further 926 polling stations remained closed on polling day, as they came under threat of jihadist violence. Kaboré was re-elected with 57.7% of the vote; Komboïgo came second with 15.5% and Diabré third with 12.5%. Voter turnout was low, at 50.2%. In the new National Assembly the MPP almost exactly repeated its performance in the 2015 poll, gaining one seat to take a total of 56. The CDP performed remarkably well and gained 20 seats, two more than in 2015. The main disappointment was the UPC, which declined from 33 seats to only 12. An otherwise marginal pro-presidential party, Nouveau Temps pour la Démocratie, a creation of Vincent Dabilgou, the Minister of Transport, Urban Mobility and Road Safety, increased its presence from three to 13, thus solving the MPP's majority problem. The remaining 26 seats were shared between 11 other parties. President Kaboré was inaugurated for a second and final term of office on 28 December 2020.

FURTHER ATTACKS; KABORÉ DEPOSED

Kaboré pledged to restore security and stability and promised that Burkina Faso's estimated 1m. internally displaced persons would be able to return home. He also pledged to work towards national reconciliation. In January 2021 he reappointed Dabiré as Prime Minister and his new Government included the UPC's Diabré, as Minister to the President, responsible for National Reconciliation and Social Cohesion. When Dabiré was sworn in on 4 February he replied to a question from an opposition deputy with language to the effect that he would not immediately rule out talks with the jihadist insurgents. This attracted considerable attention, since Kaboré, in particular, had always strictly opposed any such contact. Indeed, the Government denied having contacts with the jihadists, in spite of persistent reports that had circulated since October 2020 that there had been informal talks, notably with JNIM and its Malian leader, Iyad ag Agaly.

However, insecurity persisted throughout 2021 and spread to border areas with three out of four Burkina Faso's southern neighbours, Côte d'Ivoire, Benin and Togo; only Ghana was spared jihadist incursions. More than 730 people lost their lives in 2021, the highest since the crisis began. JNIM continues to mount attacks against villages in the Nord region, while ISGS concentrates its violent attacks in Estregion. Both are active in Sahel, the only Burkinabè region that borders both neighbouring countries (Mali and Niger) heavily affected by jihadist-linked violence.

Repeated operations by the armed forces in the Nord and Sahel regions failed to stop the attacks, which increased in intensity. On the night of 4–5 June 2021 the deadliest incident took place since the trouble began in 2015, in the village of Solhan in the north-eastern province of Yagha where more than 160 people lost their lives. Many of the dead were VDPs, who were resting in their camp. The assailants targeted the VDP positions first and then proceeded to the village homes.

JNIM denied responsibility for the attack. This violence gave rise to more demonstrations in Dori, Kaya and Titao. The protesters decried the Government's inability and inaction in addressing the growing menace. In early July Kaboré dismissed Chérif Sy from the defence portfolio and briefly took responsibility for this himself before handing it to Brig.-Gen. Aimé Barthélémy Simporé in October. However, protest marches continued to be held in Ouagadougou and several other parts of the country.

By the end of 2021 jihadist insurgents, armed groups or terrorists (still the preferred term in Burkina Faso) controlled or had free access to 40% of the national territory, which constituted one of the fastest deteriorations in security anywhere in the world. The worst attack against the security forces was perpetrated near Inata, a northern town, when 49 gendarmes and four civilians lost their lives.

Towards the end of 2021 there were signs that the security forces, unhappy with the absence of any progress in the fight against the armed groups, were preparing another coup. On 10 January 2022 Lt-Col Emmanuel Zoungrana was among a group of eight officers who were detained on suspicion of plotting one. Hearing of these arrests, Burkinabè youth took to the streets in Ouagadougou and other cities demanding their release. On 23 January an army mutiny broke out in three camps across Ouagadougou, which in the intervening overnight hours became a coup that garnered support on the streets of Kaya and Ouahigouya, two towns close to intense jihadist activity. On the following day, national television broadcast a statement to the effect that Kaboré had resigned and that a new body, the Mouvement Patriotique pour la Sauvegarde et la Restauration (MPSR), had taken over. A former RSP member, Lt-Col Paul-Henri Sandaogo Damiba took the reins and became the new interim head of state. The junta suspended the Constitution and the National Assembly, announced a three-year transition and promised to deliver peace and security to the country. A new Chief of General Staff of the Armed Forces was appointed and the head of the gendarmerie and the land army were also replaced, answering longstanding complaints from the rank and file troops. Rumours circulated that a possible entry of the Russian mercenary outfit Wagner could have been a factor in the coup (in that Damiba is alleged to have suggested this to Kaboré, which the latter subsequently refused) but this cannot be independently confirmed. It is, however, plausible to qualify the Inata attack as the final trigger that caused Damiba and his men to move.

After the coup the violence continued to spread. HRW issued a report in May 2022, documenting the extreme cruelty and destructiveness of JNIM and ISGS, their use of child soldiers and improvised explosive devices, but also the extrajudicial killings carried out by the security forces and the VDPs. According to the 2022 Global Terrorism Index, JNIM is the fastest growing terrorist network in the world while Islamic State-affiliated organizations, including ISGS and ISWAP, are among the deadliest. One of the worst attacks of 2022 occurred in Seytenga, in the north of the country, where 89 civilians were murdered in June. According to the UN Office for the Coordination of Humanitarian Affairs, by the end of June 2022 the violence had displaced 1.9m. Burkinabè in their own country, while just over 25,000 had fled abroad. Furthermore, 4,258 schools had been closed, affecting 708,000 students.

THE RETURN OF BLAISE COMPAORÉ: ANGER AND QUESTIONS

On 7 July 2022 Compaoré made a brief return to Burkina Faso and was allowed to return to exile in Abidjan 48 hours later, in a chain of events that enraged Burkinabè civil society and lawyers for the Sankara family, who reproached the military junta for a complete disregard for the rule of law by allowing the passage through the country of a convicted murderer. Compaoré's visit was ostensibly designed to prepare for another political dialogue and find a way out of the security crisis. However, many others perceived the visit as a step towards restoring the old Compaoré systems and networks, while some observers regarded this as a preparation for the retirement of Compaoré, who was visibly in poor health, at his home in Ziniaré.

DAMIBA REMOVED

On 2 October 2022 Damiba signed his resignation as head of state following an attack on his base on 30 September and a tense two-day standoff between armed groups supporting him and the man who replaced him, a junior army officer Capt. Ibrahim Traoré. At issue was, once again, the ever deteriorating security situation in the country; the direct trigger was an attack on a food convoy in Soum province that was intended to provide relief for the jihadi-besieged provincial capital of Djibo. Upon obtaining Damiba's resignation—he subsequently departed for Togo—following lengthy negotiations involving the country's influential religious and traditional leaders, Traoré promised to redouble efforts to rid the country of the jihadist groups.

TRIALS OF HIGH-RANKING COMPAORÉ ERA OPERATIVES

The death of former President Thomas Sankara on 15 October 1987 dominated Burkinabè political life in the ensuing decades. In October 2021 the trial commenced of 14 individuals suspected to have been involved in his assassination. Among this number was Blaise Compaoré, Sankara's successor and in exile in Côte d'Ivoire since late October 2014, who was being tried *in absentia*, although an international warrant for his arrest had been issued in December 2015. Also outside detention was the then head of Compaoré's security detail, Chief Warrant Officer Hyacinthe Kafando. However, Kafando's superior, Diendéré, who just over two years earlier had been sentenced to 20 years in prison for his involvement in the 2015 failed coup, was able to be tried in person. All three received life terms on April 6 2022.

No other case, apart from the Sankara murder, signified the Compaoré era as the violent death in 1998 at the hands of RSP operatives of Norbert Zongo. In May 2017 an international arrest warrant in connection with Zongo's murder was issued by the Burkinabè authorities for François Compaoré, who was interrogated by French police in October that year, as he arrived at Paris Charles de Gaulle airport from Abidjan. France ordered that he be extradited to Burkina Faso in February 2020. Having exhausted all available appeal procedures in France, including their appeal to the French Council of State, François Compaoré's legal representatives took the matter to the European Court for Human Rights (ECHR), where they obtained a stay of extradition in August 2021. Several Burkinabè and international non-governmental organizations requested the incarceration of François but this did not happen. Following the January 2022 coup, the ECHR demanded that France ensured that the Burkinabè authorities respect Compaoré's rights in case of an extradition. The procedure was still ongoing in August 2022.

Meanwhile, in April 2017 the trial began before the High Court of Justice in Ouagadougou of more than 30 ministers over the deaths of several protesters during the October 2014 popular uprising that toppled Blaise Compaoré. (Compaoré himself was tried *in absentia*.) The trial was set up to render the politicians involved accountable for the events of October 2014. However, in June 2017 the Constitutional Court ruled that the law governing the High Court was illegal, as the legislation in question lacked provisions for an appeals procedure. That law was amended in July and the High Court had an appeals chamber attached to it in October but as at August 2022 the trial was yet to resume.

FOREIGN RELATIONS

In 1974 Burkina Faso and Mali clashed over the 160-km Agacher Strip in the Sahel; a five-day war over the territory ensued in late December 1985, which ended in a mediated ceasefire. In December 1986 the International Court of Justice, based at The Hague, Netherlands, allocated equal parts of the strip, the dispute over which was a colonial heritage, to each country, which they accepted.

Burkina Faso contributed 1,261 personnel (including 1,080 troops) to the UN's Multidimensional Integrated Stabilization Mission in Mali. This was established in July 2013 as the continuation of the regional ECOWAS mission to Mali, which had been put into place to protect Malian civilians against violence from Islamist extremists and other armed groups that invaded Mali in 2012 and subsequently spread to other parts of the country before spilling over into Burkina Faso and Niger. As a result of the increasing violence, Burkina Faso and Mali have been receiving each others' refugees, with some 26,600 Malians in Burkina Faso and 24,500 Burkinabè in Mali at September 2022.

Relations with Côte d'Ivoire have been influenced by a shared French colonial history and the way in which they have interfered in each others' domestic politics, beginning with the removal of Thomas Sankara, widely believed to have been instigated by the then Ivorian President Houphouët-Boigny (and with tacit French approval). Hostility against the estimated 2.3m. Burkinabè living and working in Côte d'Ivoire by 1998 had been flaring up occasionally, starting as far back as the 1980s, but matters came to a head when the Burkina Faso Government provided a safe haven for the leaders of the rebellious forces that occupied the northern half of Côte d'Ivoire between 2002 and 2011. The region served as a conduit for the contraband with which the rebels financed their movement. Having been accused by Laurent Gbagbo's Ivorian Government of siding with the rebels, at least 200,000 Burkinabè returned to their country as refugees. When peace returned to Côte d'Ivoire in 2011, the migratory movements resumed, and by the early 2020s there were an estimated 3.5m. Burkinabè in Côte d'Ivoire (many with Ivorian nationality either acquired through administrative procedures or by being born there) and 500,000 Ivorians in Burkina Faso.

Relations were always volatile but received a boost in July 2008 when Gbagbo visited Ouagadougou and the two countries signed a co-operation and friendship treaty, an instrument of diplomacy, economic and cultural co-operation that has worked remarkably well. Former President Kaboré met with Gbagbo's successor, Alassane Ouattara, regularly and treaty-related meetings continued to be held almost every year. In 2017 it was decided to rehabilitate the 1,260-km railway between Ouagadougou and Abidjan, a lifeline for Burkinabè traders. In May 2018 the Prime Ministers of Burkina Faso, Mali and Côte d'Ivoire launched a special economic zone in their respective regions of Bobo-Dioulasso (Burkina Faso), Sikasso (Mali) and Korhogo/Man (Côte d'Ivoire). The ninth treaty-related meeting between the Burkina and Ivorian Governments was held in Abidjan in July 2021 and centred on issues of commerce and transport, the fight against terrorism and the issue of child trafficking. Ivorian and Burkinabè forces had already conducted a joint operation called Comoé (in the region of the same name) in May 2020, killing eight suspected jihadists and dismantling a suspected terrorist base at Alidougou in Burkina Faso. Armed men staged a retaliatory attack at an Ivorian army post at Kafolo, close to the border with Burkina Faso, killing 14 Ivorian soldiers.

Burkina Faso and Benin sought to resolve a longstanding border issue in 2008 by agreeing to take the matter to the ICJ, although the case had not been formally submitted by August 2022. In the mean time, the disputed region (a 68-sq km area called Kourou/Koalou) was to remain neutral and to be administered by a joint management committee, which meets regularly.

In April 2013 the Governments of Burkina Faso and Niger accepted an ICJ judgment concerning the demarcation of part of their common border. In May 2015 plans were announced to exchange sovereignty over 18 towns, 14 to be assigned to Burkina Faso and four to Niger. However, the upsurge of armed violence in the area has seriously delayed execution of these plans.

French participation in counter-terrorist operations in Burkina Faso has been relatively small-scale and discreet, with the exception of the January 2016 siege in central Ouagadougou and some French troop participation in offensive action in the Sahel region and into Mali. France maintains a special forces base near Ouagadougou, as part of the counter-terrorist 5,000 strong Operation Barkhane, which was launched in August 2014. However, Barkhane had to be reconfigured, following its departure from Mali, its principal operations theatre, in 2022.

France sought a different, and preferably smaller, Barkhane even before it fell out with the Malian junta. It pushed hard for a regional replacement force, the Force Conjointe du G5 Sahel (FC-G5S), which was an offshoot of the G5 Sahel, a 2014 initiative by the Presidents of Mauritania, Chad, Mali, Niger and Burkina Faso, to collaborate more closely on security issues and combating terrorism. The new force staged its first operation in the tri-border area of Niger, Mali and Burkina Faso in November 2017. This was followed two years later by Operation Bourgou IV, during which the FC-G5S worked with French troops and killed or captured 24 suspected jihadists. The tri-border area had become the principal operation area of ISGS and the theory was to combat them in that region. Ultimately, however, it succeeded only in dispersing them into Niger and Burkina Faso.

In the light of rising anti-French sentiment in the region, French President Emmanuel Macron invited the G5 heads of state to a summit in the French military town of Pau in January 2020, in order to reinforce co-operation and allay fears of waning loyalties. The manner in which the invitation had been conveyed and the fact that the G5 heads of state had to make their way to France was badly received in the region. Following the 2020 and 2021 coups in Mali and the rapidly increasing animosity between the military junta there and France, in part exacerbated by Macron's resistance to any idea of dialogue with jihadists—an idea that was gaining currency in Mali and Burkina Faso—Macron announced Barkhane's departure from Mali in July 2021. The force was to be reduced to perhaps 2,500 or 3,000 and redeployed to Niger by late 2022. The hostility to France's military presence on the ground was emphasized in November 2021 when a French convoy with supplies, coming from Abidjan and destined for Gao in Mali, was held up on several occasions by protesters in both Burkina Faso and Niger.

Meanwhile, a new task force, Takuba, was officially launched in March 2020 and subsequently began to take shape and work to combat terrorism as a pan-European effort. However, there was little enthusiasm for the idea of having special forces from various European countries co-operate in the Sahel under French command. Following the deterioration in relations between France and Mali, the operation was discreetly terminated on 1 July 2022. Meanwhile, in mid-May the Malian Government had announced that it was pulling out of the FC-G5S effort, effectively also pulling the plug on that operation.

In the light of the jihadist terrorist threat travelling further south and crossing the borders of Burkina Faso and its four southern neighbours with large cities on the coast (Côte d'Ivoire, Ghana, Togo and Benin), the five countries launched the Accra Initiative in September 2017, with the principal objectives of preventing spillage into the coastal states of terrorist activity and to address cross-border organized crime (the two are very closely linked). It is a self-funded mechanism, a network, not heavy on administration. The exchange of intelligence, the training of security forces and conducting joint operations are its three pillars.

There have, so far been four such military operations, code-named Koudanglou. They were held in May and November 2018, November 2019 and November 2021 and always involved Burkina Faso and two of its three neighbours. A fifth, provisionally codenamed 'Strengthened Koudanglou' is in preparation. While the operations have not been able to stop the incursions of armed groups into Côte d'Ivoire, Togo and Benin, the model is considered promising since it lacks the cumbersome superstructure of the GC-G5S, is based on co-operation and sharing intelligence, and has no foreign-based command structure.

In March 2018 Burkina Faso signed an agreement to establish the African Continental Free Trade Area (AfCFTA), which entered into force in May 2019. Trading under AfCFTA commenced on 1 January 2021 and by August 2022 it had been signed by 54 countries (excepting Eritrea) and ratified by 43, including Burkina Faso.

Economy

PAUL MELLY

INTRODUCTION

Landlocked and located at the heart of the Sahel, Burkina Faso has always faced the challenges of an arid climate with a starkly seasonal pattern of rainfall. Rapid population growth imposes severe pressure on resources of water, land and biomass, while high transport costs constrain economic competitiveness. However, over the past decade the country has been gradually enveloped by the security crisis that has spread ever wider across the Sahel.

For years the north and the east has experienced frequent attacks by jihadist and criminal groups, disrupting economic activity and forcing the closure of more than 1,900 schools. Yet the violence is now spreading even more widely, with militant groups even infiltrating parts of the south. This has had a hugely disruptive practical impact on everyday life in many rural areas, disrupting local commerce and the state's provision of public services. Burkina is proud of its strong development track record, but senior government strategists concede that over recent years the outlying northern and eastern areas probably have not benefited from as much development activity and public service support as they should have done. This may have contributed to the social pressures and disenchantment that leads some young men and even young teenagers to join armed groups, a recruitment pitch often reinforced with the offer of a motorcycle or some money. As the violence has accelerated, this has actually impeded efforts to continue providing essential services or relaunch development efforts, creating a vicious circle: socioeconomic conditions worsen, populations are displaced or become isolated, insecurity spreads and it then becomes even harder for the state to provide services and foster economic opportunity; this climate of insecurity and a reversal of development progress also fuels inter-ethnic mistrusts and alienation that can then further fuel the violence. The United Nations (UN) reported that by March 2022 some 1.85m people in the country were internally displaced, with the number rising by 2%–10% every month; the UN assessed that 3.5m. people—out of a total population of 22.1m.—were in humanitarian need. Conditions are most difficult in northern regions such as Soum and Sanmatenga and eastern regions such as Séno and Gourma. The spread of violence and atmosphere of an accelerating slide ever deeper into crisis has eroded the sense of security underpinning everyday life, public services and development in many rural areas.

Jihadist violence sometimes overlaps with non-ideological criminal banditry or localized grievances over issues such as access to resources of land and minerals. Some parts of the security forces were weakened by politicization or vested interests under President Blaise Compaoré (1997–2014) and the coup of 30 September–1 October 2022 exposed the depth of the rifts within parts of the military. Meanwhile, in some rural areas the inadequacy of official justice and policing services has stimulated the emergence of informal community militias (*kolwéogos*), with the risk that the marginalized or unpopular fall victim to vindictive punishments or even lynchings.

Yet in many respects Burkina's technical public service apparatus remains among the strongest in the Sahel, with many committed and highly trained personnel in key roles, particularly in sectors such as rural development and food security. In parts of the country local communities manage to sustain their smallholder farming and livestock economy and it has also proved possible to protect most of the industrial gold mines that produce Burkina's dominant export and generate much of its fiscal revenue. The urban economy has also proved resilient, although terrorist attacks in 2016, 2017 and 2018, and the COVID-19 pandemic of 2020, came as severe blows to tourism in Ouagadougou—a city whose image still owes much to memories of the now distant radical progressive regime of Capt. Thomas Sankara (1983–87) and to its internationally reputed Pan-African Film and Television Festival (FESPACO).

Headline economic performance has proved surprisingly strong. The rate of real gross domestic product (GDP) growth was 5.7% in 2019. The following year it fell sharply, to 1.9%, as the economy felt the impact of lockdown measures to fight COVID-19, combined with the pressure of ongoing violence. In 2021 growth rebounded to 6.9%; however, this figure should be treated with caution as the Government, the International Monetary Fund (IMF) and the World Bank had 'rebased' the calculation of national output to more comprehensively assess the extent of informal sector activity—a reappraisal that in African countries usually does lead to a marked upward revision of the IMF's estimate of real GDP, because the informal sector accounts for so much economic activity. A full sense of the trend in Burkina's economic output will only become fully clear once several years' worth of data has been produced, calculated on the new basis. The IMF's projection of real GDP growth of 4.7% in 2022 does indicate that headline economic output is still growing strongly, albeit at a slightly slower pace than the figures for recent years might have suggested. Yet there are further caveats: the highly productive industrial gold mining sector accounts for considerable economic output, exports and government tax revenue, but the industrial mines are islands of intense activity, and they do not always have a major spin-off impact on neighbouring rural communities. Moreover, given the current security conditions, in some areas it is now harder than usual for officials to carry out the field research required to get a full picture of agricultural and livestock sector activity and other related rural economic output.

FUNDAMENTALS OF THE ECONOMY

Burkina Faso remains an overwhelmingly rural society, and even most city dwellers have close family connections to farming villages, which means that the security crisis in provincial areas is acutely felt by most people. Moreover, it has driven a significant number of villagers to see refuge in Ouagadougou, scraping a living from begging or the fringes of the informal economy. Agriculture and livestock husbandry, local commerce and services, cotton ginning and gold mining (both industrial and artisanal) are the foundations of national output; brewing and cotton textile production are the main manufactures. The Government and the service sector are major employers in Ouagadougou and Burkina's second city, Bobo-Dioulasso, which has an important university. While formal employment in the private sector is estimated at 400,000, some 80,000 are employed in the public sector. Ouagadougou hosts the commission of the UEMOA (Union Economique et Monétaire Ouest-Africaine) single currency bloc and the headquarters of the regional food security early warning network, CILSS (Permanent Interstate Committee for Drought Control in the Sahel). The city is also an important base for development partners working in the Sahel.

As a landlocked country, Burkina depends heavily on its on rail and road links with coastal economies—Côte d'Ivoire, Ghana, Togo and Benin, and now even Mauritania—whose ports are the gateway to international markets and sources of supply. Coastal countries are also an important market for Burkina's exports of livestock, while their cities and the plantations of the Ivorian cocoa belt attract numerous Burkinabè migrant workers. Between 2m.–4m Burkinabè work abroad, particularly in Côte d'Ivoire and France, and they sent home 240,400m. francs CFA in remittances in 2019 and 242,000m. francs CFA in 2020—sums that in both years outstripped the value of Burkina's second largest export, cotton.

Despite the worsening security crisis and the impact of COVID-19, Burkina's headline macroeconomic performance has proved resilient, with sustained positive real GDP growth and low inflation—consumer prices actually contracted by 3.4% in 2019, before rebounding by 1.9% in 2020 and 3.9% the following year. In the aftermath of the Russian Federation's invasion of Ukraine the pressure on global supplies pushed up prices for imported grain and fuel and the IMF projected an overall inflation rate of 6.0% for the year 2022 as a whole. The fiscal deficit was contained at 3.2% of GDP in 2019. It expanded to 5.3% in 2020, but mainly because of the impacts of the COVID-19 pandemic, the cost of which the IMF estimated at 2.3% of GDP. Burkina managed to sustain a modest rate of real GDP growth in 2020, but this fell well short of the 2.9% annual increase in population, which meant that average per capita income fell in real terms.

Although gold mining is a significant contributor to exports and government revenues, more than two-thirds of Burkina's population still lives in rural communities, dependent mainly on smallholder agriculture, pastoralism, hunting, fishing and forestry, and these activities accounted for the largest average share of GDP over the period 2016–20, at 23.4%, just ahead of services (22.1%), with commerce and hospitality (12.1%) the third largest element. The majority of Burkinabè households depend on farming and livestock husbandry, and related activities, and most inhabitants of cities and towns retain close personal ties to relatives still living in their families' home villages. Industrial gold mines and cotton ginneries are rare islands of formal sector employment in provincial areas, while large numbers of people—and not always locals—engage in artisanal mining, which injects cash into the grassroots economy but can cause social dislocation and also damage health and the environment. Farming households generally produce food both for both home consumption and commercial sale; cotton is the main pure cash export crop and, as an annual crop it can be planted in complementary rotation with cereals such as maize or millet; villagers also produce vegetables and tree-crops such as sheanuts (*karité*) and mangoes. Most rural households have some poultry or livestock and in the more arid northern areas many families live mainly from pastoralism, with patterns of local or long-distance seasonal transhumance reflecting the availability of grazing.

Burkina lies entirely within the Sahelian belt that fringes the Sahara and the rural economy is shaped by the annual weather cycle: beginning usually in late June or early July, the rainy season extends into early September, but is briefest in the north and longest in the south; it is followed by nine dry months, sometimes punctuated by short, light rains in April. Cereal crops and cotton, providing the mainstay of the Burkinabè diet and the main cash income for farming households, are planted early in the wet season and then harvested from September onwards. The food and income generated by this brief agricultural season must sustain families through the following 12 months, until the next harvests. Pressures on villagers' food supply and household finances can become intense during the final four or five months before crops are ready for harvest; during this lean season (*la soudure*) many families have to seek grain from community or government reserve stocks released at subsidized prices and supplemented sometimes with food aid from foreign donors. Vegetables and a small amount of cereals are grown through the dry season on market garden plots watered from wells. Drought has always been a risk, and the rains can fall short or completely fail. Climate change has brought new challenges: the weather is becoming even hotter and less predictable and sometimes there can even be heavy rains at unexpected times of the year, when farmers are not equipped to take advantage, because their fields are not prepared and they do not have seeds or fertilizer to hand.

After devastating droughts in the early 1970s, the countries of the Sahel agreed on the need to prepare ahead of time for the probability of future crises. They recognized the need to develop systems for early warning of potential food crisis and the management of emergency food bank reserves, with individual national efforts supported by a regional body, and so they established CILSS. Over time, these systems have evolved to make the most of the latest technology, and harmonized data standards and strengthened independent central oversight of the efforts of each country's national food security system. Today, weather, agricultural, livestock and health data are collected by officials and communities at local level and transmitted to the provincial and eventually national level, for collation and analysis by central government. National systems are overseen by CILSS, which ensures

that data is assessed on a common harmonized basis and in partnership with the Paris-based OECD (Organization for Economic Co-operation and Development) and co-ordinates the partnership between Sahelian countries and the international development and donor community through the framework of the Food Crisis Prevention Network (RPCA). Ouagadougou hosts the CILSS headquarters, while its technical assessment and standards auditing arm is based in Niamey, Niger. The group has gradually expanded and now comprises 13 full-time member states, with further co-operation links with countries such as Nigeria that have yet to join. Of the full members, Burkina, Niger and Mali are widely regarded as having the most advanced early warning systems, increasingly collecting data by smartphone and operating a network of local and regional food banks. Although the system was developed to enable Burkina and its neighbours to cope with weather crises, in recent times it has proved invaluable in monitoring the development and humanitarian impact of the security crisis that has spread across the central Sahel, providing the Burkina Government and donors with detailed up to date information about where communities' food supply position is insecure or in crisis.

Industrial gold mining provides formal employment, and generates spin-off economic activity, but is concentrated in a relatively small number of locations; artisanal gold digging accounts for a smaller share of production but is more widely scattered, and thus has a significant social and economic footprint. Despite the disruptive impacts of COVID-19 and the security crisis, gold output surged to 66.9 metric tons in 2020, from just 50 tons the previous year. Manganese and zinc is also mined. Burkina's other main industries are cotton ginning, brewing and some import substitution.

Burkina has never formally broken with the revolutionary culture of the Sankara era, but in reality the country gradually edged towards a market oriented economic model over the course of the 1990s, supported by a disciplined fiscal stance and close development partnerships with the IMF and World Bank, the African Development Bank (AfDB) and the European Union (EU); with its track record of focus on basic development, the country has been strongly supported by European bilateral donors. After the 2014 democratic revolution this approach was maintained by President Roch Marc Christian Kaboré (elected in December 2015), and the IMF agreed a new Extended Credit Facility (ECF) programme for 2018–20. The successive military regimes that seized power in January 2022 and then October of the same year have not challenged these basic strategic economic connections.

Burkina Faso belongs to a supportive constellation of regional partnerships—the 15-member Economic Community of West African States (ECOWAS), the eight-strong West African CFA franc zone UEMOA and the G5 Sahel grouping (formed in 2014). The latter co-ordinates cross-border military operations against jihadist groups. Donors have agreed to fund a list of 40 development projects across the G5, largely in outlying areas close to frontiers where the lack of economic options can nudge some youths towards joining criminal or terrorist groups; but in Burkina it is unclear how many projects can go ahead amid the prevailing insecurity in northern and eastern areas.

Established in 1975, ECOWAS is gradually deepening regional economic integration—particularly important for a landlocked country such as Burkina. A common external tariff was introduced from 2015 onwards, border procedures have been simplified to encourage trade flows and in 2018 the bloc created a regional market for trading electricity; this could be particularly helpful to Burkina, whose hydropower generation capacity is vulnerable to drought. ECOWAS decided to create a single currency and set up a system for monitoring member states' compliance with a set of technical convergence criteria. Members chose eco as the name for the new currency and set 2020 as a launch date. However, they made much slower progress towards resolving politically difficult issues such as the location and operating framework of the future central bank. Both the Central Bank of Nigeria (CBN) and the UEMOA central bank, the Banque Centrale des Etats de l'Afrique de l'Ouest (BCEAO, headquartered in Dakar, Senegal), are strong institutions reluctant to become subordinated to a supreme regional central bank authority. By 2019 it had become clear that the timetable for launching the currency might have to slip until these institutional issues could be resolved. The advent of the COVID-19 pandemic then obliged Burkina and all fellow member governments to concentrate on more immediate health and economic priorities. In June 2021 an ECOWAS summit in Accra, Ghana, agreed a revised and more realistic timetable for monetary union, with an adjusted set of monetary and fiscal convergence criteria. Countries' performance in complying with these would be monitored through to the end of 2026, prior to the launching of the new currency in 2027. However, the Accra meeting left the complex institutional obstacles to the new currency still to be resolved.

The UEMOA single currency bloc, created in 1960, has eight member states: Benin, Burkina Faso, Côte d'Ivoire, Guinea-Bissau, Mali, Niger, Togo and Senegal, all using the CFA franc inherited from the era of French colonial rule. There is also a six-country central African CFA franc bloc (Communauté Economique et Monétaire de l'Afrique Centrale—CEMAC), but the two operate quite separately. UEMOA has a central commission (based in Ouagadougou) to oversee its framework of economic co-operation, as well as a common bank regulatory regime, a regional money market and also an electronic regional stock market (Bourse Régionale des Valeurs Mobilières), based in Abidjan, Côte d'Ivoire. UEMOA states, and many other francophone African countries, share a harmonized framework of business law (the Organisation pour l'Harmonisation en Afrique du Droit des Affaires, OHADA), with a supranational disputes tribunal providing a measure of independent jurisdiction for investors.

The CFA franc system has seen only one devaluation in its history, in 1994, and it even coped well with the stress imposed by the 2002–10 crisis in Côte d'Ivoire, UEMOA's largest economy. However, the use of a currency with post-colonial associations has become increasingly unpopular among sections of West African opinion, particularly progressive intellectuals and urban youth. Moreover, the CFA's high value—the consequence of the currency peg—has kept imports cheap to the benefit of the most affluent consumers, while squeezing the competitiveness of local farmers. This problem became particularly acute in the early 1990s, triggering the decision to devalue the CFA franc by 50% in 1994, with support from the IMF, France and the World Bank; this dramatically restored the competitiveness of local agriculture and helped launch a sustained trend of economic recovery and growth that continued until the COVID-19 pandemic hit. However, recent years have seen a resurgence of the problem, with the strong local currency sucking in imports at a favourable exchange rate, to the benefit of a small urban elite. Although the situation is less acute than in the early 1990s, the case for a fresh reform has gained growing adherence and in 2017 France's President, Emmanuel Macron stated that his country would support reform if that was the wish of UEMOA states. The bloc charged Côte d'Ivoire's President, Alassane Ouattara, to draft proposals, resulting in a plan, agreed with Macron, to abolish the foreign exchange deposit requirement and for France to give up its board seats. Ouattara also proposed renaming the CFA franc as the eco—a move clearly designed to disarm domestic political critics; but this proposal was fiercely criticized by Nigeria and some other ECOWAS states, because this name had already been agreed by all ECOWAS countries as the name of a planned single currency covering the whole bloc. That issue remains to be resolved.

SOCIETY

Burkina Faso has made significant development progress, but remains among the world's poorest countries. Moreover, the spreading security crisis has seriously set back development progress in many areas, as schools are closed and local economic activity disrupted; by April 2022 some 1.85m. people (of whom probably more than one-half were children) had been displaced from their homes and usual livelihoods. In 2021 real per capita GDP was US $918.2, compared with $594.9 in Niger and $917.9 in Mali. Gross national income per capita, measured in purchasing power parity terms, taking into account the real local cost of living, is higher, at $2,330, but still well below

that of a more secure and well connected coastal economy such as Benin ($3,750).

Pressures on the thin base of natural resources and public service provision are accentuated by a high rate of population growth. The fertility rate (the average number of offspring each woman would have if she lived to the end of child-bearing years) is an average 4.9 children per woman. Just 28% of women aged 15–49 now use modern contraceptive methods; some 57% of those who want modern family planning still cannot get access to it.

Burkina has seen development progress disrupted by the spread of insecurity. Jihadist violence had forced the closure of 3,683 schools by March 2022, affecting 590,327 children and 17,309 teachers; however, the dramatic deterioration in security conditions over the subsequent months forced further closures and on 7 September 2022 the UN reported that 4,258 schools had now been shut. Hundreds of health centres have also been closed.

However, average life expectancy has risen to 62 years for men and 64 years for women—a reflection of improvements in basic food security, education and health services. The large majority of births are attended by trained personnel, which helps to explain why, by 2017, the incidence of maternal mortality had sunk to only 320 deaths for every 100,000 live births, far lower than in Niger, Mali, Benin or even a more prosperous economy such as Cameroon. Some 91% of children aged 12–23 months are immunized against diphtheria, whooping cough and tetanus. Even so, serious health problems and service shortcoming do persist: 13.4% of children under five are underweight. The spread of COVID-19 through the community was relatively modest and the Government did manage to expand testing. Yet like most African countries, Burkina struggled to secure adequate supplies of vaccines. Moreover, the deterioration in security conditions over the last three years may well have seriously eroded access to basic healthcare in the northern and eastern rural communities worst affected by the violence.

ECONOMIC POLICY AND PERFORMANCE

The cornerstones of Burkinabè economic policy are membership of UEMOA, with its tight monetary and fiscal stance, close policy co-ordination with the IMF and a long-term focus on basic development, the roots of which extend back to the radical regime of Thomas Sankara in the mid-1980s, although this was somewhat eroded by poor governance during the latter Compaoré years and is now seriously impeded by the spread of jihadist violence. The Kaboré Government sought to reinvigorate growth, poverty reduction and key service provision through its 2016–20 National Economic and Social Development Plan, but officials admit that northern and eastern areas were to some extent neglected, a contributory factor in the violent insecurity that has since developed.

In March 2018 the IMF approved a three year ECF programme for Burkina and the country did manage to meet most of the performance targets set by the Fund, despite the impacts of insecurity and the COVID-19 pandemic, which forced the Government to impose lockdown curbs on urban commerce and social life. In April 2020, to help the country cope with these shocks, the IMF provided an additional US $115.3m. from its Rapid Credit Facility and granted relief on $11.9m. in debt service repayments; furthermore, in October 2020 it granted an extra $14.5m. in debt relief, followed in November 2020 with a fresh disbursement of $51.3m. of ECF funding.

The ECF programme sought to sustain macroeconomic stability and bolster revenues, improve the efficiency of public expenditure and develop a framework for future public-private partnerships (PPPs), while adjusting the fuel price mechanism to ease subsidy costs.

The cost of COVID-19 added to the pressure on state finances, with the public deficit growing from 3.2% of GDP in 2019 to 5.3% in 2020 and an estimated 5.5% of GDP in 2021. Government current revenue, excluding grant aid, was 18.7% of GDP in 2019 but shrank to 16.6% in 2020. In cash terms budget receipts have increased from 1,064,700m. francs CFA in 2014 to 1,747,700m. francs CFA in 2019, before slipping back to 1,659,400m. francs CFA in 2020, the first year of the pandemic.

Current expenditure, measured as a proportion of GDP, rose from 14.5% in 2014 to 16.1% in 2017 and to 17.6% in 2019. In cash terms the Government's current spending in 2020 was 1,724,300m. francs CFA, of which salaries and other forms of staff remuneration accounted for more than one-half, at 897,200m. francs CFA. Total public spending in 2020 was 2,504,300m. francs CFA.

AGRICULTURE

The rural economy of Sahelian countries such as Burkina has always been vulnerable to drought. And now climate appears to be making an impact, with reports of even higher temperatures during the March–June hot season, while heavy rains sometimes fall outside the June–September wet season for which farmers are prepared. The annual climate cycle is the foundation for Sahelian agriculture: cereal crops grown during the wet season are the core of household nutrition over the long dry months that follow, supplemented with *contre-saison* crops (mainly vegetables) watered from wells and local reservoirs. Pressures are at their most intense during the four or five month 'lean season' before the next annual crops can be harvested from September onwards; to supplement villagers's dwindling reserves during the lean months, Burkina operates a network of community and regional cereal banks, managed at national level by the Government's Société Nationale de Gestion du Stock de Sécurité Alimentaire.

Governments have therefore supported projects to restore the environment and strengthen communities' resilience and capacity to cope with crisis, for example, by expanding local irrigation and market gardening schemes. Amid concern that land could be exhausted by overuse and the clearing of natural vegetation for farming and firewood, some pilot schemes now plant hedges and conserve local woodland to foster biodiversity and conserve biomass cover and soil fertility. However, in large parts of the north, the east and even the centre, insecurity now seriously disrupts farmers' access to their fields, and particularly to irrigated market gardening plots, and the local networks of trade and distribution; in September 2022 the Burkinabè military, assisted by French forces, had to deliver emergency stocks to one eastern village by air because landmines had rendered access by road too dangerous.

Cotton, Burkina's main export crop, plays a crucial role, as a source of cash income for farmers; some 3m. people depend on cotton to a substantial degree. As an annual crop, it can be grown in rotation with cereals, which benefiting from the residues of fertilizer remaining from cotton cultivation the previous year; and declines in cotton output are sometimes mirrored by a rise in cereals production, as farmers shift more land over to food crops if demand and prices for these are attractive. Cotton producer prices are market based but fixed annually by the Government to provide farmers with a stable framework to plan their costs and decide how to split their land between cotton and other crops. The price was set at 235 francs CFA per kg for the 2017/18 and 2018/19 seasons, increased sharply to 265 francs CFA for the 2019/20 season as the Government sought to encourage the sector's revival but then pruned back again, to 240 francs CFA for 2020/21.

Sahelian cotton faces competition from cheap Asian production and subsidized output from the USA. There is growing European demand for hand-picked organic African cotton, but Burkina has been poorly placed to exploit this opportunity because the Compaoré regime had promoted the genetically modified (GM) varieties. Introduced in 2008 under an agreement with the US agro-technology group Monsanto, the Coton Bt variety of GM cotton was promoted because of its resistance to drought and worms and whitefly, which means that only two doses of pesticide are required, compared with the six doses used to protect conventional cotton crops. By 2011/12 the Coton Bt variety accounted for 60% of the harvest. However, serious problems began to appear: with short fibres, most of the harvest fell below conventional quality standards, while pests began to build up resistance, forcing farmers to revert to heavy pesticide use, which rendered Coton Bt uneconomic, given that the seed cost 25 times the price of conventional seed. Villagers

in eastern areas reported a sharp decline in bee populations and worsening animal health and there were indications that the crop might also be impacting the mineral composition of the soil. Many farmers switched land to other crops, while many of the workers who used to apply pesticide left, to find work in the booming gold sector.

Compaoré's downfall in 2014 left the three main cotton sector companies, Société Burkinabè des Fibres Textiles (SOFITEX), Société Cotonnière du Gourma (SOCOMA) and Faso Coton, free to reduce reliance on GM seed and the Association Interprofessionnelle du Coton au Burkina (AICB), which represents for the sector, decided to end all use of Monsanto GM seed by 31 December 2018. However, the sector was left with the challenge of selling off unsold poor quality stocks.

SOFITEX, SOCOMA and Faso Coton support research, input supply and technical advice, purchase and gin the crop for onward sale and try to promote local textile manufacture. The western regions that produce 85% of Burkinabè output are entrusted to SOFITEX—a joint venture between Geocoton (a subsidiary of French group Advens) and the state, the cotton producers union (Union Nationale des Producteurs de Coton du Burkina—UNPCB), local private investors and the FBDES, a government investment fund; it has 12 ginning plants. Central areas, producing 5% of the crop, are served by Faso Coton, which is supported by the Aga Khan group and operates one ginning plant. The east, which produces 10% of national output, is the responsibility of SOCOMA, a Geocoton subsidiary in which the UNPCB and local investors have minority stakes; it has three ginning plants.

Although the adoption of Coton Bt sent output surging from 334,000 metric tons in 2010/11 to 768,900 tons in 2015/16, harvests subsequently declined as the sector retreated from GM seed: output fell to 681,300 tons in 2016/17, and then just 458,500 tons in 2019/20. However, the 2020/21 season finally brought a modest recovery, to 472,000 tons.

The main food crops are millet and sorghum, maize and paddy rice. Millet and sorghum are Burkina's most important food crop, able to withstand more arid conditions; yet output still fluctuates markedly. It slipped from 3.00m. metric tons in 2012/13 to 2.38m. tons in 2015/16, rebounded to 2.57m. tons in 2016/17 before sinking to just 2.19m. tons in 2017/18. The 2018/19 agricultural year brought a sharp resurgence, to 3.12m. tons, but in 2019/20 the harvest fell back to 2.84m. tons, before a fresh recovery, to 3.9m. tons in 2020/21. Maize production has also seen fluctuations, within an overall upward trend in production: this rose from 1.56m. tons in 2012/13 to 1.60m. tons in 2016/17, although this was followed by a decline to 1.53m. tons the year after. Output then rebounded to 1.70m. tons in 2018/19, then 1.72m. tons in 2019/20 and 1.88m. tons in 2020/21.

Paddy rice is farmed in low-lying areas that can be irrigated or flooded, with a campaign to bolster production in the Bagré area. Output declined from 384,700 metric tons in 2016/17 to 325,600 tons in 2017/18. However, there has been a recent resurgence, to 350,400 tons in 2018/19, and then to 376,500 tons in 2019/20 and to 390,500 tons in 2020/21.

Other important crops include fonio, cowpeas and groundnuts. Highly nutritious, fonio is well adapted to the tough Sahelian growing conditions, but output plunged from 20,000 metric tons in 2013/14 to just 8,600 tons in 2014/15 and has yet to strongly recover; the 2019/20 harvest, some 11,300 tons, was followed by a decline to 10,200 tons the next year, before a resurgence to 11,800 tons in 2020/21. Groundnut production reached an impressive 519,300 tons in 2016/17, but then fell back to 329,800 tons in 2018/19, before rebounding to 396,100 tons in 2019/20 and to 630,500 tons in 2020/21.

Mangoes, cashew nuts, sesame, vegetables, sugar and sheanuts are also grown for cash sale as well as local use. Burkina is the world's second largest producer of sheanuts, after Nigeria. Annual production is around 400,000 metric tons and shea products are now Burkina's fourth largest export, with sales worth US $61.8m. in 2019. Burkina is the world's leading exporter of shea butter, in demand for the manufacture of natural soaps, skin products and cosmetics. Cashew nuts are also an increasingly important export. There is great potential to expand mango exports, with more investment in quality

132   **www.europaworld.com**

control and processing, and rapid transport to Ouagadougou for export as air freight.

The livestock sector may account for close to 20% of GDP. Most rural households have poultry and often a few goats or sheep. And many people, notably from the Peul (Fulani) and Tuareg communities, live mainly from pastoralism, with herds of cattle, camels, sheep and goats and following local or regional cycles of transhumance. However, amid insecurity and shifting patterns of rainfall there is a risk of disputes with farming communities when resources of water and vegetation are scarce. Herds are also moved, on the hoof, to the large urban markets of coastal West Africa, but restrictions imposed by Benin and Togo because of insecurity and COVID-19 seriously disrupted pastoralists' access to grazing land and livestock markets, limiting animal bodyweights and sales opportunities.

MINING

In recent years there has been a major expansion in the industrial mining of gold, which is Burkina's largest export, generating around 300,000m. francs CFA in annual fiscal revenues for the state; artisanal production of gold has also grown strongly and now contributes 10%–20% of total output. Burkina also has deposits of manganese, zinc, silver, lead, copper, nickel, titanium, vanadium, bauxite, phosphates and limestone. Of these, silver and zinc are produced in substantial quantities. However, the geographical extent of jihadist militant activity is now such that it could pose a serious threat to the continuing operational security of some mines.

In 2008 Burkina had only two major gold mines, producing about 5.5 metric tons per annum, but by 2020 some 17 industrial mines were in operation, with a further three preparing to start production in 2021. Canadian companies are major players in the sector. Output fluctuates—reflecting both the pace of mine construction and the disruptive impact of insecurity—but remains on a broadly upward trend. Total national output reached 52.6 tons in 2018, and although it slipped back to 50.3 tons in 2019, it rebounded to 62.1 tons in 2020 and amounted to 66.9 tons in 2021, despite the worsening national security situation; the sector's turnover in 2020 was over 2,000,000m. francs CFA (more than €3,000m.). Major operators today include Endeavour Mining, which now runs the Mana, Wahngion and Boungou mines, and the new Houndé and Karma mines; Nordgold, with mines at Taparko and Bissa; Avesoro Resources, with the Youga mine and Balogo deposit; Iamgold, which operates the Essakane mine in the far north-east; and Fortuna, which later merged with Roxgold and runs the Yaramoko mine and the new Boussoura mine. Orezone Gold of Canada announced in September 2022 that it had poured first gold at its newly built mine at Bomboré, with the start of commercial production expected in the final quarter of the year. Artisanal gold exploration and production also makes a useful contribution to officially recorded national production; but a significant share of the output from the hundreds of artisanal sites is sold informally, often through neighbouring countries such as Togo.

World prices heavily influence the value of gold exports and the value of exports fell from 1,162,200m. francs CFA in 2012 to just 800,000m. francs CFA in 2014 even though production rose throughout this period. Price conditions have since become more favourable and the value of exports reached 1,492,500m. francs CFA in 2018, before rising to 1,685,800m. francs CFA in the following year and 1,857,900m. francs CFA in 2020.

Burkina's production of silver reached 10 tons in 2020, but slipped back to 8.9 tons in 2021. Canada's Trevali Mining operates a zinc mine and processing mill at Perkoa and in 2020 the country's total output of zinc was 152.5 tons, rising to 166.3 tons in 2021.

The Tambao manganese deposit, in the far north-east, has reserves estimated at 119m. metric tons. However, it sits in the insecure 'tri-border' region where Burkina, Mali and Niger converge, and in which jihadist groups have been active. In 2018 the Burkina Government cancelled development rights that had previously been awarded to Timis Corp subsidiary Pan African Minerals, which unsuccessfully brought an international legal challenge. This cleared the way for the Government to begin the search for a new investor for the project, which would need to be connected to the current terminus of the railway network at Kaya, 300-km to the south. Development of the nearby Tin Hrassan limestone deposits, for cement production, could generate additional freight loads that would enhance the viability of the rail link.

In 2013 Burkina was deemed compliant with the terms of the Extractive Industries Transparency Initiative, a benchmark for improved mine sector governance, while a new mining code, introduced in 2015, seeks to protect the country's interests while encouraging mine development: it allocates 20% of royalties and 1% of the industry's monthly turnover to a fund for provincial development projects.

POWER

Some 19% of the Burkinabè population has access to electricity, but there is a sharp disparity between levels of connection in urban areas and levels in rural areas, where people rely mainly on other sources of energy or on local or household solar installations. The Kaboré Government had set a goal of ensuring that 75% of the urban population and 19% of the rural population would have access to electricity; it aimed to achieve this through an expansion of renewable generating capacity and the import of power from neighbouring countries with lower generation costs. The state fuel company Société Nationale Burkinabè d'Hydrocarbures (SONABHY) charges world market prices for the fuel it sells to the national utility Société Nationale Burkinabè d'Electricité (SONABEL), so the Government subsidizes retail power tariffs, to keep these affordable. However, favourable market conditions have reduced the cost of subsidy to the Government which, in these improved circumstances, was able to agree a settlement of mutual debts in August 2020. The Government abolished SONABEL's generation monopoly in 2017, hoping to stimulate external investment in new power plants.

There is great scope to expand the production of power from renewable sources. Burkina's potential capacity for solar generation has been calculated at a huge 5.5 kWh per sq m per day, owing to the dry Sahelian climate. The 33-MW Zagtouli solar plant, opened in 2017, provides 55 GWh, enough to meet 5% of national demand and a 150-MW solar plant is planned, while France's EREN Renewable Energy was chosen to install a 15-MW solar power plant for the Essakane gold mine. The national agencies for energy efficiency (Agence Nationale des Energies Renouvelables et de l'Efficacité) and rural electrification (Agence Burkinabé de l'Electrification Rurale, ABER) support the development of local rural power networks supplied from small solar plants; ABER regulates and finances these schemes. Burkina also has a surprisingly large capacity for hydro-power generation. Hydro plants on the Kompienga and Bagré rivers have capacities of 43 GWh and 44 GWh, respectively, while more power could also be produced by new hydro projects, including those primarily developed for other purposes. The primary purpose of the 16.8-GWh Samendéni dam, which became operational in late 2019, is to support irrigated agriculture, but it also includes a 3.74-MW power plant.

However, Burkina still remains heavily dependent on thermal generation, which in January 2019 accounted for 287 MW of Burkina's 355 MW installed generating capacity. The largest power station is the 90-MW Komsilga thermal plant, which the Government wants to expand by 50 MW; Burkina also possesses a biogas power plant connected to the grid. At moments of peak consumption the domestic power plants are unable to satisfy demand and the country has to import up to 70 MW from Côte d'Ivoire through a 225 kV transmission link and 40 MW from Ghana through a 330 kV connection opened in 2018.

MANUFACTURING AND SERVICES

With a small home market and limited local supply of resources and components, and high transport costs, Burkina presents difficult conditions for most manufacturing activity other than cotton ginning. Yet there is strong urban demand for French-style bread, baked from imported flour and milled by two companies, La Minoterie du Faso and Minoterie de l'Orient.

Beer is particularly popular and Brakina, an offshoot of the French group Castel, has breweries in Ouagadougou and Bobo-Dioulasso.

The shift away from GM cotton has posed challenges for Burkina's 16 ginning plants, but in January 2020 the cotton sector companies SOFITEX and UNPCB opened Secobio, a joint venture plant in Koudougou designed to gin organic cotton for export to Western markets. Beyond ginning, only 5% of Burkina's cotton undergoes further value-added processing and just one factory makes thread from local cotton. Cheap supplies imported from the People's Republic of China present a daunting competitive challenge for any attempt to revive local textile and garment manufacture. However, artisanal production is widespread and in early 2020 it was confirmed that the Turkish group Ayka Textile planned to build three plants, in Koudougou, Bobo-Dioulasso and Ouagadougou, at a cost of US $336m. creating up to 12,000 direct jobs and many spin-off livelihoods.

The main service and commercial hubs are Ouagadougou and Bobo-Dioulasso. UEMOA strengthened its prudential regulatory standards for the banking sector in 2018 and this obliged Burkinabè banks to tighten up their approach; in 2020 only 7.8% of the sector's loan book was categorized as non-performing and the sector had a provisioning ratio of 71.5% against bad debt, so a mere 2.4% of the sector's loan book was non-performing and not covered by provisions. The Burkina-based Coris banking group has developed into a significant player within the West African region.

FESPACO, Ouagadougou's biennial film festival, remains highly regarded by international critics and the October 2021 edition attracted a wide range of African actors and directors. However, the terrorism attacks of 2016–18 and the COVID-19 pandemic have severely constrained tourism, with consequent painful impacts on hotels, restaurants, craftwork and retailing.

TRANSPORT AND COMMUNICATIONS

Being landlocked, Burkina is critically dependent on road and rail links to the West African coast, while roads from rural areas are fundamental to the close social and economic interdependence of urban and rural communities, particularly the delivery of farm produce to market.

The main west–east highways run from the Mali and Côte d'Ivoire borders to Bobo-Dioulasso and then on to Ouagadougou, and from there eastwards to Fada Ngourma and the border with Niger. Main roads fan out from the capital to key provincial centres, including Pô, the main frontier crossing into Ghana; most are paved, but sometimes in a poor state of repair. Construction of a 125-km dual carriageway ring around Ouagadougou is well advanced and extensive studies have been completed for a motorway from the capital to Bobo-Dioulasso and on to Yamoussoukro in Côte d'Ivoire, where it would connect with the existing Ivorian motorway network. Another route to the coast, at Lomé in Togo, is also being improved.

SITARAIL, an offshoot of French logistics giant Bolloré, operates the rail line from Abidjan (Côte d'Ivoire) to Bobo-Dioulasso, Ouagadougou and Kaya. A revised concession agreement in 2016 entrusted the company with responsibility for infrastructure and maintenance and it has been modernizing the route. Construction of a spur to the manganese deposit at Tambao will depend on the future of that potential mining project. Prospects for a rail connection to Niamey in Niger and potentially on to Cotonou (Benin) remain uncertain because of a legal dispute. However, Burkina and Ghana have agreed to build a 1,100-km line linking Accra and Ghana's main container port at Tema to Ouagadougou via Tenkodogo and Pô. In mid-2021 the two governments agreed a timetable for finalizing procedures for land acquisition, tax and customs, financing and the selection of a main contractor.

Development of the new Donsin airport for Ouagadougou—to replace the current airport lying within the city limits—is well advanced. The first phase includes a 3.5-km runway and a new terminal, both to be expanded in a second phase from 2026 onwards. The facility will be managed by the French group Meridiam under a 30-year concession. Direct flights link Ouagadougou to African cities and to Paris (France). From Bobo-Dioulasso there are flights to Ouagadougou and to Abidjan. Air Burkina—one of several small national carriers owned by the Aga Khan Fund for Economic Development and managed by its offshoot Celestair—services West African routes.

Fixed-line telecoms, largely for business, government and institutional customers, and some private households, are provided by the national operator Moov Africa Burkina, (formerly known as ONATEL). Use of mobiles is almost universal, with 106 subscriptions per 100 people; there are three mobile service providers—Orange, Moov and Télécel-Faso.

FOREIGN TRADE AND PAYMENTS

Burkina's current account balance of payments is structurally in deficit. However, with gold exports rising steadily in value, the deficit has gradually shrunk, from 6.4% of GDP in 2017 to 1.0% to 2020. In financial values, the deficit contracted from 520,400m. francs CFA in 2017 to just 369,300m. francs CFA in 2018 and then 306,900m. francs CFA the year after and finally 101,100m. francs CFA in 2020. The balance of trade in goods is stronger still, and has moved into a substantial surplus: there was a deficit of 142,700m. francs CFA in 2015 but by 2018 the trade balance actually shifted into a surplus of 161,100m. francs CFA in 2018, rising to 214,300m. francs CFA the year after and 436,200m. francs CFA in 2020. Remittances from the Burkina diaspora rose gently from 211,500m. francs CFA in 2015 to 241,700m. francs CFA in 2019; moreover, they held steady, at 242,000m. francs CFA in 2020, despite the impact of COVID-19 in slowing economic activity in countries with a large Burkinabè diaspora, such as France and Côte d'Ivoire. Interest payments on external debt more than doubled to 53,500m. francs CFA in 2018, rising further to 62,100m. francs CFA in 2019, but then in 2020 they fell sharply back to just 21,300m. francs CFA.

Exports have climbed steadily in value from 1,362,300m. francs CFA in 2014 to 2,301,300m. francs CFA in 2019 and to 2,503,500m. francs CFA in 2020. This trend has been driven by the growth in exports of gold from 800,000m. francs CFA in 2014 to 1,492,500m. francs CFA in 2018 and then to 1,857,900m. francs CFA in 2020.

Shipments of the other main export commodities have fluctuated. Cotton exports declined from 237,000m. francs CFA in 2014 to just 198,400m. francs CFA in 2016; a rebound to 253,300m. francs CFA in 2017 has been followed by a steady decline, to 250,400m. francs CFA in 2018 and then just 206,100m. francs CFA in 2019 and a mere 153,700m. francs CFA in 2020. This downward trend may reflect both the difficulty of adjusting away from the failed strategy of promoting GM cotton and perhaps also the disruptive impact of violent insecurity in many rural areas. Cashew nut exports also rose from 21,300m. francs CFA in 2014 to 99,700m. francs CFA in 2017 and 117,100m. francs CFA the year after, but then slumped to just 56,000m. francs CFA in 2019 and a feeble 32,100m. francs CFA in 2020. Exports of zinc exports grew from 43,100m. francs CFA in 2014 to 95,800m. francs CFA in 2017, but have since declined to just 64,100m. francs CFA in 2020. On average in the 2015–19 period some 60.3% of all Burkinabè exports went to Switzerland, a pattern that reflects the flow of gold shipments to this important centre for trading precious metals. India (15.6%) was the second largest market for exports; other Asian and European countries buy cotton, while livestock is sold to coastal West Africa,

Imports have also been rising and increased from 1,770,400m. francs CFA in 2014 to 2,267,100m. francs in 2017 and to 2,491,600m. francs CFA in 2019 before slipping back to 2,474,400m. francs CFA in the pandemic year 2020, when commerce was slowed down by government lockdown controls. The inflow of capital equipment, including for the mines, expanded from 509,000m. francs CFA in 2014 to 907,800m. francs CFA, in 2019, but fell back to 863,400m. francs CFA in 2020. Burkina is reliant on imported supplies of petroleum products, and the cost of these varies as a consequence of fluctuations in world oil prices, peaking at 478,900m. francs CFA in 2017 but sinking to 420,500m. francs CFA the next year, before a rebound to 455,200m. francs CFA in 2019 and then a fresh plunge, to 358,800m. francs CFA, in 2020. Domestic production of food is inevitably affected by rainfall or drought, but there was a steady rise in the value of imports of food from 135,100m. francs CFA in 2014 to 182,500m. francs CFA in 2018, before a decline to 161,700m. francs CFA in 2019 and then a resurgence, to 209,500m. francs CFA in 2020. China and other Asian countries supply information technology, consumer electronics and perhaps also textiles, while capital equipment is imported from Europe and the USA. Long-standing links with France are reflected in imports of certain foods and other niche consumer items, while India and Thailand appear to be major suppliers of rice and Côte d'Ivoire is an important regional source of tropical produce.

With functioning democratic politics and a solid track record of grassroots development, Burkina has a strong partnership with international donors and some provide general budget aid—leaving the Government to decided detailed expenditure priorities—and this rose from 81,200m. francs CFA in 2016 to 92,700m. francs CFA in 2018; a slight fall in donor budget support the next year, to 88,500m. francs CFA, was followed by a dramatic doubling in grant assistance, to some 176,700m.

francs CFA in 2020, as external partners helped Burkina cope with the impact of COVID-19 and protect its underlying long-term development strategy. However, Burkina also receives large volumes of project aid from multilateral partners such as the World Bank, the IMF, the EU, the AfDB and Islamic and Arab institutions. Once a significant partner, Taiwan ceased assistance after President Kaboré switched recognition to China in 2018, and thereafter Beijing stepped up support. Major bilateral donors include Japan, France and the USA. Burkina received an initial US $481m. allocation from the US Government's Millennium Challenge Corporation and a second funding package of similar scale was approved in 2020, focused mainly on electricity supply. The Agence Française de Développement (AFD) funds education and training, water and sanitation, agriculture and energy (including the Zagtouli solar power plant). Donors have stepped up humanitarian support in response to the security crisis and mass displacement of population, while the AFD has launched a programme of basic social and economic development support for the north and east, designed to alleviate the socioeconomic problems that increase the risks of conflict in these regions.

Statistical Survey

Source (except where otherwise stated): Institut National de la Statistique et de la Démographie, Av. Pascal Zagré, 01 BP 374, Ouagadougou 01; tel. 25-49-85-00; e-mail insd@insd.bf; internet www.insd.bf.

Area and Population

AREA, POPULATION AND DENSITY

Area (sq km)	273,187*
Population (census results)	
9–23 December 2006	14,017,262
16 November– 31 December 2019	
Males	9,900,847
Females	10,604,308
Total	20,505,155
Population (UN estimates at mid-year)†	
2020	20,903,278
2021‡	21,497,097
2022‡	22,102,838
Density (per sq km) at mid-2022‡	80.9

* 105,478 sq miles.
† Source: UN, *World Population Prospects: The 2019 Revision*; estimates not revised to take account of results of 2019 census.
‡ Projection.

POPULATION BY AGE AND SEX
(2019 census)

	Males	Females	Total
0–14 years	4,674,839	4,611,424	9,286,263
15–64 years	4,904,369	5,626,848	10,531,217
65 years and over	321,639	366,036	687,675
Total	**9,900,847**	**10,604,308**	**20,505,155**

PROVINCES
(population at 2019 census unless otherwise indicated)

	Population	Capital	Population of capital*
Balé . . .	297,468	Boromo . .	40,229
Bam . . .	476,054	Kongoussi . .	121,595
Banwa . .	346,989	Solenzo . .	158,763
Bazèga . .	280,870	Kombissiri . .	77,756
Bougouriba . .	153,653	Diébougou . .	63,304
Boulgou . .	737,843	Tenkodogo . .	159,105
Boulkiemdé . .	689,709	Koudougou . .	216,830
Comoé . .	633,043	Banfora . .	160,302
Ganzourgou . .	482,763	Zorgho . .	76,431
Gnagna . .	676,476	Bogandé . . .	128,943
Gourma . . .	437,310	Fada N'Gourma .	187,692

—*continued*	Population	Capital	Population of capital*
Houet . . .	1,510,638	Bobo-Dioulasso .	984,603
Ioba . . .	265,956	Dano	64,237
Kadiogo . .	3,030,384	Ouagadougou . .	2,415,266
Kénédougou .	399,949	Orodara . . .	44,679
Komandjari . .	105,604	Gayéri . . .	76,218
Kompienga . .	117,682	Pama	61,722
Kossi . . .	357,089	Nouna . . .	89,742
Koulpélogo . .	362,644	Ouargaye . .	42,626
Kouritenga . .	480,021	Koupéla . . .	91,023
Kourwéogo . .	181,242	Boussé . . .	58,643
Léraba . . .	179,423	Sindou . . .	25,748
Loroum . . .	198,192	Titao	104,977
Mouhoun . .	391,561	Dédougou . .	123,973
Nahouri . .	195,816	Pô	64,609
Namentenga .	513,796	Boulsa . . .	113,416
Nayala . . .	223,151	Toma . . .	39,109
Noumbiel . .	98,915	Batié . . .	44,526
Oubritenga . .	314,609	Ziniaré . . .	88,316
Oudalan . . .	158,206	Gorom-Gorom .	72,454
Passoré . . .	457,930	Yako	117,422
Poni	356,918	Gaoua . . .	78,081
Sanguié . . .	391,617	Réo	75,866
Sanmatenga .	884,819	Kaya	207,740
Séno	404,716	Dori	180,559
Sissili . . .	337,078	Léo	85,574
Soum	363,661	Djibo	83,211
Sourou . . .	285,011	Tougan . . .	89,181
Tapoa . . .	605,733	Diapaga . . .	58,951
Tuy	329,253	Houndé . . .	133,403
Yagha . . .	171,594	Sebba . . .	34,881
Yatenga . . .	825,975	Ouahigouya . .	199,436
Ziro	241,731	Sapouy . . .	86,745
Zondoma . .	240,018	Gourcy . . .	117,761
Zoundwéogo .	312,045	Manga . . .	44,074
Total . . .	**20,505,155**		

* Municipalities.

PRINCIPAL TOWNS
(population at 2019 census)

Ouagadougou (capital) . .	2,415,266	
Bobo-Dioulasso .	904,920	
Koudougou . . .	160,239	
Ouahigouya . . .	124,587	
Kaya	121,970	
Banfora	117,452	

Pouytenga . . .	96,469
Houndé	87,151
Fada N'gourma .	73,200
Dédougou . . .	63,617
Tenkodogo . . .	61,936
Djibo	61,462

BIRTHS AND DEATHS
(annual averages, UN estimates)

	2005–10	2010–15	2015–20
Birth rate (per 1,000)	43.7	40.8	38.2
Death rate (per 1,000)	11.9	9.6	8.3

Source: UN, *World Population Prospects: The 2019 Revision*.

Life expectancy (years at birth, estimates): 62.0 (males 61.1; females 62.7) in 2020 (Source: World Bank, World Development Indicators database).

ECONOMICALLY ACTIVE POPULATION
(2006 census, persons aged 15–64 years)

	Males	Females	Total
Agriculture, hunting, forestry and fishing	2,057,719	1,891,402	3,949,121
Mining and quarrying	17,674	4,550	22,224
Manufacturing	97,751	86,923	184,674
Electricity, gas and water . . .	4,974	540	5,514
Construction	55,632	1,012	56,644
Trade, restaurants and hotels .	218,220	205,707	423,927
Transport, storage and communications	12,866	1,832	14,698
Financial intermediation . . .	3,192	1,966	5,158
Real estate and business services .	6,489	2,100	8,589
Public administration	37,202	7,619	44,821
Education	40,526	17,165	57,691
Health and social work	16,581	11,138	27,719
Community, social and personal services	45,251	31,965	77,216
Private households with employed persons	5,057	14,443	19,500
Extraterritorial organizations and bodies	1,234	545	1,779
Sub-total	2,620,368	2,278,907	4,899,275
Activities not adequately defined .	96,070	40,546	136,616
Total employed	2,716,438	2,319,453	5,035,891
Unemployed	84,180	39,559	123,739
Total labour force	2,800,618	2,359,012	5,159,630

Note: In addition, the 2006 census recorded 1,417,821 children aged between 5 and 14 years engaged in mostly agricultural work within the family, and a further 261,986 employed persons aged 65 years and above.

Mid-2015 ('000, estimates): Agriculture, etc. 7,683; Total labour force 8,354 (Source: FAO).

Health and Welfare

KEY INDICATORS

Total fertility rate (children per woman, 2020)	5.0
Under-5 mortality rate (per 1,000 live births, 2020) . . .	85.0
HIV/AIDS (% of persons aged 15–49, 2020)	0.7
COVID-19: Cumulative confirmed deaths (per 100,000 persons at 31 August 2022)	1.8
COVID-19: Fully vaccinated population (% of total population at 28 August 2022)	11.0
Physicians (per 1,000 head, 2019)	0.09
Hospitals (per 100,000 head, 2013)	0.3
Domestic health expenditure (2019): US $ per head (PPP) .	51.2
Domestic health expenditure (2019): % of GDP	2.3
Domestic health expenditure (2019): public (% of total current expenditure)	41.8
Access to water (% of persons, 2020)	47
Access to sanitation (% of persons, 2020)	22
Total carbon dioxide emissions ('000 metric tons, 2018) . .	4,270
Carbon dioxide emissions per head (metric tons, 2018) . .	0.2
Human Development Index (2021): ranking	184
Human Development Index (2021): value	0.449

Note: For data on COVID-19 vaccinations, 'fully vaccinated' denotes receipt of all doses specified by approved vaccination regime (Sources: Johns Hopkins University and Our World in Data). Data on health expenditure refer to current general government expenditure in each case. For more information on sources and further definitions for all indicators, see Health and Welfare Statistics: Sources and Definitions section (europaworld.com/credits).

Agriculture

PRINCIPAL CROPS
('000 metric tons)

	2018	2019	2020
Bambara beans	63.3	58.4	57.4*
Cashew nuts, with shell* . . .	135.0	142.2	162.1
Cotton lint*	175.7	247.4	—
Cow peas, dry	683.2	656.4*	666.0*
Groundnuts, with shell	329.8	396.1	270.0†
Karité nuts (sheanuts)* . . .	120.0	138.3	140.0
Maize	1,700.1	1,710.9	1,920.0†
Millet	1,189.1	970.2	957.0†
Okra*	22.9	22.7	22.5
Potatoes	63.6	70.5*	66.8*
Rice, paddy	350.4	376.5	395.4*
Seed cotton	482.2	724.2	782.9*
Sesame seed	253.9	374.7	270.0†
Sorghum	1,929.8	1,871.8	1,840.0†
Sugar cane*	497.9	500.7	503.5
Sweet potatoes	64.5	66.4	70.0*
Yams	35.9	50.2	53.1*

* FAO estimate(s).
† Unofficial figure.

Aggregate production ('000 metric tons, may include official, semi-official or estimated data): Total cereals 5,180.7 in 2018, 4,939.6 in 2019, 5,122.8 in 2020; Total fruit (primary) 104.7 in 2018, 104.3 in 2019, 104.4 in 2020; Total oilcrops 1,217.2 in 2018, 1,685.1 in 2019, 1,510.9 in 2020; Total pulses 763.8 in 2018, 723.0 in 2019, 740.6 in 2020; Total roots and tubers 168.3 in 2018, 191.3 in 2019, 194.1 in 2020; Total treenuts 137.2 in 2018, 144.4 in 2019, 164.1 in 2020; Total vegetables (primary) 304.4 in 2018, 304.1 in 2019, 302.9 in 2020.

Source: FAO.

LIVESTOCK
('000 head, year ending September)

	2018	2019*	2020*
Asses	1,230	1,254	1,265
Cattle	9,840	10,000	10,312
Chickens	37,988	38,932	39,847
Goats	15,635	16,060	16,407
Pigs	2,539	2,588	2,506
Sheep	10,442	10,703	10,849

* FAO estimates.

Source: FAO.

LIVESTOCK PRODUCTS
('000 metric tons, FAO estimates)

	2018	2019	2020
Cattle hides, fresh	17.8	17.8	17.8
Cattle meat	108.8	108.7	108.3
Cattle offals, edible	18.7	18.7	18.6
Cows' milk	210.0	220.0	214.1
Chicken meat	42.6	44.1	45.3
Goat meat	29.2	34.9	37.2
Goats' milk	150.0	153.0	161.1
Pig meat	40.2	40.5	40.5
Sheep meat	22.5	23.1	23.4
Sheep's (Ewe's) milk	74.4	75.6	76.3
Hen eggs	51.0	50.3	49.8

Source: FAO.

Forestry

ROUNDWOOD REMOVALS
('000 cubic metres, excluding bark, FAO estimates)

	2017	2018	2019
Sawlogs, veneer logs and logs for sleepers	73	73	73
Other industrial wood	1,098	1,098	1,098
Fuel wood	14,030	14,193	14,359
Total	15,201	15,364	15,530

2020: Production assumed to be unchanged from 2019 (FAO estimates).

Source: FAO.

SAWNWOOD PRODUCTION
('000 cubic metres)

	2018	2019	2020
Total (all broadleaved) . . .	5.2	5.2	5.2

Note: Production assumed to be unchanged from 2007 (FAO estimates).
Source: FAO.

Fishing

(metric tons, live weight)

	2018	2019	2020
Capture	27,299	27,803	29,104
Freshwater fishes	27,299	27,803	29,104
Aquaculture	408	440*	645
Total catch	27,707	28,243*	29,749

* FAO estimate.

Source: FAO.

Mining

('000 metric tons unless otherwise indicated)

	2017	2018	2019
Cement*	300	310	310
Gold (kg)†	46,200	36,000*	45,000*

* Estimate(s).
† Does not include artisanal mining, which was estimated to fluctuate between 1,600 kg and 5,000 kg annually.

Source: US Geological Survey.

Industry

SELECTED PRODUCTS
(metric tons unless otherwise indicated)

	2000	2001	2002
Edible oils	17,888	19,452	19,626
Shea (karité) butter	186	101	21
Flour	12,289	13,686	10,005
Pasta	211	n.a.	n.a.
Sugar	43,412	46,662	47,743
Beer ('000 hl)	494	500	546
Soft drinks ('000 hl)	221	222	250
Cigarettes (million packets) . .	85	78	78
Printed fabric ('000 sq m) . . .	275	n.a.	n.a.
Soap	12,079	9,240	9,923
Matches (cartons)	9,358	4,956	3,009
Bicycles (units)	22,215	17,718	20,849
Mopeds (units)	16,531	19,333	19,702
Tyres ('000)	397	599	670
Inner tubes ('000)	2,655	3,217	2,751
Electrical energy (million kWh) .	390	365	361

Source: mainly IMF, *Burkina Faso: Selected Issues and Statistical Appendix* (September 2005).

Raw sugar ('000 metric tons): 25 in 2014; 25 in 2015; 25 in 2016 (Source: UN Industrial Commodity Statistics Database).

Electrical energy (million kWh): 1,095 in 2017; 1,021 in 2018; 752 in 2019 (Source: UN Energy Statistics Database).

Finance

CURRENCY AND EXCHANGE RATES

Monetary Units
100 centimes = 1 franc de la Communauté Financière Africaine (CFA).

Sterling, Dollar and Euro Equivalents (31 May 2022)
£1 sterling = 770.824 francs CFA;
US $1 = 612.300 francs CFA;
€1 = 655.957 francs CFA;
10,000 francs CFA = £12.97 = $16.33 = €15.24.

Average Exchange Rate (francs CFA per US $)
2019   585.911
2020   575.586
2021   575.531

Note: An exchange rate of 1 French franc = 50 francs CFA, established in 1948, remained in force until January 1994, when the CFA franc was devalued by 50%, with the exchange rate adjusted to 1 French franc = 100 francs CFA. This relationship to French currency remained in effect with the introduction of the euro on 1 January 1999. From that date, accordingly, a fixed exchange rate of €1 = 655.957 francs CFA has been in operation.

BUDGET
('000 million francs CFA)

Revenue*				2019	2020†	2021†
Tax revenue	.	.	. . .	1,425	1,411	1,585
Non-tax revenue	.	.	. .	323	237	221
Royalties from gold	.	.	.	37	77	79
Total	.	.	. . .	**1,748**	**1,648**	**1,805**

Expenditure‡				2019	2020†	2021†
Current expenditure	.	.	. .	1,644	1,669	1,754
Wages and salaries	.	.	.	844	898	950
Goods and services	.	.	.	198	186	199
Interest payments	.	.	.	117	114	174
Current transfers	.	.	.	485	471	431
Capital expenditure	.	.	.	557	884	898
Total	.	.	. . . .	**2,201**	**2,553**	**2,652**

* Excluding grants received ('000 million francs CFA): 134 in 2019; 413 in 2020 (projection); 295 in 2021 (projection).
† Projections.
‡ Excluding net lending ('000 million francs CFA): –24 in 2019; –10 in 2020 (projection); –11 in 2021 (projection).

Source: IMF, *Burkina Faso: Fourth and Fifth Reviews Under the Extended Credit Facility Arrangement, Request for a Waiver of Nonobservance of Performance Criterion & Rephasing of Access—Press Release; Staff Report; and Statement by the Executive Director for Burkina Faso* (November 2020).

INTERNATIONAL RESERVES
(excluding gold, US $ million at 31 December)

			2019	2020	2021
IMF special drawing rights	.	.	46.5	219.8	375.2
Reserve position in IMF	.	. .	31.9	33.3	32.4
Foreign exchange	.	. . .	3.1	4.3	1.0
Total	. . .	. . . .	**81.5**	**257.3**	**408.5**

Source: IMF, *International Financial Statistics*.

MONEY SUPPLY
('000 million francs CFA at 31 December)

		2019	2020	2020
Currency outside depository corporations	. . . . .	662.2	706.4	908.3
Transferable deposits	. . . .	1,578.4	2,010.8	2,482.0
Other deposits	. . . . .	1,571.9	1,781.0	1,967.9
Broad money	. . . . . .	**3,812.5**	**4,498.3**	**5,358.3**

Source: IMF, *International Financial Statistics*.

COST OF LIVING
(Consumer Price Index; base: 2014 = 100)

		2019	2020	2021
Food and non-alcoholic beverages .		102.1	105.9	113.1
Housing, fuel and other utilities .		98.9	97.4	99.4
Clothing and footwear	. . . .	101.3	101.3	101.4
All items (incl. others)	. . .	**102.2**	**104.2**	**108.0**

Source: International Monetary Fund (IMF).

NATIONAL ACCOUNTS
('000 million francs CFA in current prices)

Expenditure on the Gross Domestic Product

	2017	2018	2019
Final consumption expenditure .	6,905	7,299	7,699
Households	5,152	5,369	5,444
Non-profit institutions serving households	300	304	336
General government	1,453	1,626	1,919
Gross fixed capital formation . .	1,711	1,779	2,029
Change in stocks	95	139	75
Total domestic expenditure .	**8,711**	**9,217**	**9,803**
Exports of goods and services .	2,167	2,478	2,618
Less Imports of goods and services	2,688	2,870	2,943
GDP in purchasers' values .	**8,191**	**8,826**	**9,479**

Gross Domestic Product by Economic Activity

	2019	2020	2021
Agriculture, hunting, forestry and fishing	1,742	1,899	1,911
Mining and quarrying . . .	1,183	1,963	1,999
Manufacturing	950	960	1,042
Electricity, gas and water . . .	91	99	107
Construction	349	342	356
Wholesale and retail trade . .	789	678	812
Restaurants and hotels . . .	203	149	175
Transport and communications .	385	395	465
Finance, insurance, real estate and business services	772	760	756
Public administration and defence	2,105	2,233	2,399
Sub-total	**8,568**	**9,478**	**10,022**
Indirect taxes (net)	911	845	923
GDP in purchasers' values .	**9,479**	**10,322**	**10,945**

BALANCE OF PAYMENTS
(US $ million)

	2018	2019	2021
Exports of goods	3,954.2	3,927.8	4,847.0
Imports of goods	–3,664.2	–3,562.0	–3,517.0
Balance on goods	**290.1**	**365.8**	**1,330.0**
Exports of services	557.1	539.9	508.7
Imports of services	–1,502.8	–1,461.2	–1,261.8
Balance on goods and services	**–655.6**	**–555.5**	**576.8**
Primary income received . . .	238.7	214.6	248.3
Primary income paid . . .	–719.3	–725.7	–804.0
Balance on goods, services and primary income	**–1,136.2**	**–1,066.6**	**21.1**
Secondary income received . .	751.6	769.9	964.0
Secondary income paid . . .	–280.1	–227.2	–241.9
Current balance	**–664.8**	**–523.8**	**743.2**
Capital account (net)	316.6	214.9	367.7
Direct investment assets . . .	–67.7	–16.4	7.1
Direct investment liabilities . .	268.4	163.0	–98.8
Portfolio investment assets . .	285.2	–189.9	–789.9
Portfolio investment liabilities .	303.7	289.8	271.8
Other investment assets . . .	–212.1	–777.0	–361.3
Other investment liabilities . .	–158.2	1,008.3	–399.0
Net errors and omissions . . .	–16.7	–6.3	0.7
Reserves and related items .	**54.4**	**162.6**	**–258.5**

Source: IMF, *International Financial Statistics*.

External Trade

PRINCIPAL COMMODITIES
(distribution by HS, US $ million)

Imports f.o.b.	2019	2020	2021
Vegetable and vegetable products	216.0	212.0	212.7
Cereals	158.2	144.1	147.6
Rice	118.2	101.4	71.4
Prepared foodstuffs; beverages, spirits, vinegar, tobacco and articles thereof	180.5	209.0	271.4
Mineral products	1,307.5	1,311.4	1,586.3
Salt, sulphur, earth, stone, plaster, lime and cement	105.3	197.2	222.8
Mineral fuels, lubricants and related materials	1,202.0	1,113.9	1,363.1
Cement, etc.	82.2	167.9	190.8
Petroleum oils	1,010.9	872.3	1075.2
Petroleum gas	74.1	89.1	116.0
Electrical energy	106.8	142.1	146.8
Chemicals and related products	474.5	541.5	549.7
Pharmaceutical products	218.1	242.7	249.1
Medicament mixtures	155.8	199.7	199.6
Iron and steel, other base metals and articles of base metal	346.1	320.0	380.3
Iron and steel	158.8	155.5	176.8
Iron and steel articles	148.1	126.2	157.3
Machinery and mechanical appliances; electrical equipment; parts thereof	792.2	707.8	715.6
Boilers, machinery, etc.	515.4	451.5	436.0
Electrical, electronic equipment	276.8	256.3	279.6
Vehicles, aircraft, vessels and associated transport equipment	440.9	333.8	376.9
Vehicles other than railway, tramway	359.8	318.9	369.4
Total (incl. others)	4,259.3	4,185.1	4,712.4

Exports f.o.b.	2019	2020	2021
Vegetables and vegetable products	273.4	244.1	273.7
Edible fruit and nuts; peel of citrus fruit or melons	119.2	95.8	148.7
Coconuts, Brazil nuts and cashew nuts, fresh or dried, whether or not shelled or peeled	95.6	68.1	116.2
Oil seed, oleagic fruits, grain, seed, fruit, etc.	141.8	116.6	117.5
Oil seeds	137.1	109.8	105.6
Mineral products	28.5	149.3	213.4
Textile and textile articles	356.8	267.8	460.4
Cotton	355.3	265.4	459.3
Cotton, not carded or combed	351.8	262.2	454.7
Pearls, precious stones, metals, coins, etc.	2,271.5	3,574.8	3,926.0
Gold	2,268.5	3,568.2	3,918.7
Iron and steel, other base metals and articles of base metal	172.5	20.3	24.7
Zinc and articles thereof	155.1	1.2	0.0
Total (incl. others)	3,261.1	4,381.1	5,062.6

Source: Trade Map-Trade Competitiveness Map, International Trade Centre, marketanalysis.intracen.org.

PRINCIPAL TRADING PARTNERS
(US $ million)

Imports c.i.f.	2019	2020	2021
Australia	63.4	32.7	29.8
Belgium	86.9	65.0	86.7
Brazil	86.3	22.1	21.8
China, People's Republic	520.7	520.7	655.1
Côte d'Ivoire	451.9	342.1	398.3
Finland	44.4	27.4	21.9
France	312.6	306.8	368.1
Germany	121.9	144.8	131.9
Ghana	293.1	264.3	276.5
India	240.3	229.5	264.5
Italy	86.0	95.6	54.6
Japan	115.8	129.9	130.6
Korea, People's Republic	62.6	100.1	126.5
Mali	18.4	45.0	29.3
Morocco	70.7	51.9	57.6
Netherlands	94.7	127.0	143.2
Niger	21.4	100.8	121.8
Norway	38.0	14.0	5.1
Russian Federation	335.9	289.4	236.4
South Africa	63.9	64.9	69.3
Spain	59.4	88.3	76.2
Sweden	56.5	46.8	52.9
Thailand	54.5	19.4	25.1
Togo	69.9	141.8	131.2
Türkiye	63.6	84.5	136.6
United Kingdom	77.8	80.6	93.4
USA	271.4	298.7	325.8
Total (incl. others)	4,259.3	4,185.1	4,712.4

Exports f.o.b.	2019	2020	2021
Côte d'Ivoire	178.4	125.2	182.4
France	104.7	54.9	40.1
Ghana	88.8	59.2	50.3
India	574.0	296.4	485.3
Niger	30.6	52.6	35.2
Singapore	211.3	120.1	194.8
Switzerland	1,790.2	3,342.9	3,680.4
Togo	27.1	35.2	35.3
Viet Nam	26.6	21.1	2.2
Total (incl. others)	3,261.1	4,381.1	5,062.6

Source: Trade Map-Trade Competitiveness Map, International Trade Centre, marketanalysis.intracen.org.

Transport

RAILWAYS

	2017	2018	2019
Freight carried ('000 metric tons)	806.6	799.7	936.6
Freight ton-km ('000)	784,195	765,848	861,252
Passengers ('000 journeys)	139	n.a.	n.a.

ROAD TRAFFIC
(motor vehicles in use)

	2018	2019	2020
Passenger cars	260,707	284,574	308,542
Vans	45,793	48,354	50,675
Trucks	34,689	37,300	40,125
Tractors, trailers and semi-trailers	47,845	52,076	55,854
Motorbikes and mopeds	2,607,279	2,891,064	3,238,362

CIVIL AVIATION

	2018	2019	2020
Passengers carried ('000) . .	189.5	185.8	70.2
Departures (domestic and international)	3,988	4,105	1,790

Source: World Bank, World Development Indicators database.

Tourism

FOREIGN VISITORS BY COUNTRY OF ORIGIN*

	2018	2019	2020
Belgium	2,292	1,985	378
Benin	7,488	7,163	2,595
Canada	1,969	3,045	833
China, People's Republic . . .	2,765	3,670	155
Côte d'Ivoire	16,715	18,791	6,718
France	20,062	19,367	6,620
Germany	2,499	2,041	1,001
Ghana	6,169	5,639	3,173
Mali	9,203	9,882	3,745
Niger	7,503	7,186	3,873
Senegal	6,013	9,553	2,773
Togo	6,714	6,338	4,489
USA	4,091	5,534	1,776
Total (incl. others)	144,492	143,331	66,878

* Arrivals at hotels and similar establishments.

Tourism receipts (US $ million, excl. passenger transport): 122 in 2016; 117 in 2017; 121 in 2018 (Source: World Tourism Organization).

Communications Media

	2018	2019	2020
Telephones (main lines in use) .	76,760	75,291	75,039
Mobile telephone subscriptions ('000)	19,339.1	20,364.5	22,117.2
Broadband subscriptions, fixed .	13,818	12,015	13,979
Broadband subscriptions, mobile ('000)	5,907.8	6,441.2	10,903.7
Internet users (% of population) .	17.4	18.0	22.0

Source: International Telecommunication Union.

Education

(2019/20 unless otherwise indicated)

	Institutions	Teachers	Students ('000)		
			Males	Females	Total
Pre-primary .	1,597	6,013	62.9	61.1	124.0
Primary . .	15,077*	87,304	1,659.8*	1,629.9*	3,289.7*
Secondary (general) .	3,938	50,896†	635.8	657.7	1,293.5
Secondary (technical and vocational) .	161	4,511†	23.0	13.1	36.1
Tertiary* . .	186	8,758	120.6	69.6	190.2

* 2020/21.
† 2017/18.

Sources: Ministry of National Education and Literacy, Ouagadougou; UNESCO Institute for Statistics.

Pupil-teacher ratio (qualified teaching staff, primary education, UNESCO estimate): 39.0 in 2019/20 (Source: UNESCO Institute for Statistics).

Adult literacy rate (UNESCO estimates): 39.3% (males 49.2%; females 31.0%) in 2018 (Source: UNESCO Institute for Statistics).

Directory

The Constitution

The present Constitution was approved in a national referendum on 2 June 1991, and was formally adopted on 11 June. Following the assumption of power by the military on 24 January 2022, the Constitution was suspended, and the Government and the National Assembly dissolved; the Constitution was restored on 31 January, with an amended text awarding power to the Mouvement Patriotique pour la Sauvegarde et la Restauration (MPSR). A transitional charter, adopted on 1 March, provided for a three-year transitional period prior to elections, and the creation of a new, 71-member legislative body, the Transitional National Assembly. The Constitution was again suspended on 30 September after the transitional President and head of the MPSR, Lt-Col Paul Henri Sandaogo Damiba, was deposed by junior members of the military.

The Government

HEAD OF STATE

Transitional President: Capt. IBRAHIM TRAORÉ (assumed power 30 September 2022).

TRANSITIONAL GOVERNMENT
(October 2022)

Following the removal from the presidency of Lt-Col Paul-Henri Sandaogo Damiba on 30 September 2022, the Transitional Government was dissolved.

Transitional President: Capt. IBRAHIM TRAORÉ.

MINISTRIES

Office of the President: Palais Présidentiel de Kossyam, blvd Muammar Kaddafi, 03 BP 7030, Ouagadougou 03; tel. 25-49-83-00; internet www.presidencedufaso.bf.

Office of the Prime Minister: 03 BP 7027, Ouagadougou 03; tel. 25-32-48-89; internet www.gouvernement.gov.bf.

Ministry of Agriculture and Animal and Fishing Resources: 03 BP 7005, Ouagadougou 03; tel. 25-49-99-00; internet www.agriculture.gov.bf.

Ministry of the Civil Service, Labour and Social Security: Immeuble de la Modernisation, 922 ave Kwamé N'Krumah, 03 BP 7006, Ouagadougou 03; tel. 25-30-19-52; internet www.fonction-publique.gov.bf.

Ministry of Communication, Culture, the Arts and Tourism: 03 BP 7045, Ouagadougou 03; tel. 25-31-45-72; e-mail mcrp.infos@communication.gov.bf; internet www.communication.gov.bf.

Ministry of Defence and War Veterans: ave Blaise Compaoré, 01 BP 496, Ouagadougou 01; tel. 25-40-79-72; e-mail cabinet.mdnac.226@gmail.com; internet www.defense.gov.bf.

Ministry of Digital Transition, Postal Services and Electronic Communications: Ouagadougou; e-mail contact@mdenp.gov.bf; internet www.mdenp.gov.bf.

Ministry of the Environment, Energy, Water and Sanitation: 03 BP 7044, Ouagadougou 03; tel. 25-33-54-84; internet www.environnement.gov.bf.

Ministry of the Economy, Finance and Planning: 395 ave du 11 Décembre, 01 BP 7008, Ouagadougou 01; tel. 25-32-42-11; internet www.finances.gov.bf.

Ministry of Foreign Affairs, Regional Co-operation and Burkinabè Abroad: ave du Burkina, 03 BP 7038, Ouagadougou 03; tel. 50-31-80-17; e-mail mae@diplomatie.gov.bf; internet www.mae.gov .bf.

Ministry of Gender and the Family: 01 BP 303, Ouagadougou 01; tel. 25-50-53-67; e-mail secretariat@mpf.gov.bf; internet www .action-sociale.gov.bf.

Ministry of Health and Public Hygiene: ave du Burkina, 03 BP 7009, Ouagadougou 03; tel. 25-32-63-40; e-mail contact@sante.gov .bf; internet www.sante.gov.bf.

Ministry of Higher Education, Research and Innovation: 03 BP 7047, Ouagadougou 03; tel. 25-33-73-34; internet www.mesrsi .gov.bf/accueil.

Ministry of Industrial Development, Trade, Handicrafts and Small and Medium-sized Enterprises: ave de l'Indépendance, 01 BP 514, Ouagadougou 01; tel. 25-32-48-28; internet www.commerce .gov.bf.

Ministry of Infrastructure and Improving Access to Isolated Regions: 35 Pr Joseph Ki-Zerbo, 03 BP 7011, Ouagadougou 03; tel. 25-32-42-46; internet www.infrastructures.gov.bf.

Ministry of Justice and Human Rights: 01 BP 526, Ouagadougou 01; tel. 25-30-22-13; e-mail info@justice.gov.bf; internet www.justice .gov.bf.

Ministry of Mines and Quarries: ave de l'Indépendance, Ouagadougou 01; internet energie.bf.

Ministry of National Education, Literacy and the Promotion of National Languages: ave de l'Indépendance, 03 BP 7032, Ouagadougou 03; tel. 25-48-09-08; e-mail cpm.edu@education.gov .bf; internet www.mena.gov.bf.

Ministry of National Solidarity and Humanitarian Action: Ouagadougou.

Ministry of Religious and Traditional Affairs: Ouagadougou.

Ministry of Sports, Youth Empowerment and Employment: ave de l'Indépendance, 03 BP 7035, Ouagadougou 03; tel. 25-32-47-86; internet www.sports.gov.bf.

Ministry of Territorial Administration, Decentralization and Security: ave de l'Indépendance, 03 BP 7034, Ouagadougou; tel. 25-31-68-91; internet www.matd.gov.bf.

Ministry of Town Planning, Land Affairs and Housing: 03 BP 7011, Ouagadougou 03; tel. 25-30-57-86; e-mail contact@mhu.gov.bf; internet www.mhu.gov.bf.

Ministry of Transport, Urban Mobility and Road Safety: Immeuble du 15 Octobre, ave de l'Indépendance, Ouagadougou 01; internet www.transports.gov.bf.

President

Presidential Election, 22 November 2020

Candidate	Valid votes	% of valid votes
Roch Marc Christian Kaboré (MPP) .	1,645,229	57.74
Wend-Venem Eddie Constance Hyacinthe Komboigo (CDP) . .	442,693	15.54
Zéphirin Diabré (UPC) . .	354,988	12.46
Kadré Désiré Ouédraogo (AE) . .	95,661	3.36
Tahirou Barry (MCR) . . .	62,231	2.18
Ablassé Ouédraogo (FA) . . .	51,461	1.80
Others*	197,272	6.92
Total	**2,849,535†**	**100.00**

* There were seven other candidates.
† Excluding invalid votes (123,055).

Legislature

Following the removal from the presidency of Roch Marc Christian Kaboré on 24 January 2022 by disaffected members of the military, the National Assembly was dissolved. On 22 March a 71-member Transitional National Assembly (TNA) was installed; 21 members were appointed by the transitional President, Lt-Col Paul-Henri Sandaogo Damiba, while the remainder included 16 representatives of the defence and security forces, 13 representatives of civil society organizations, eight representatives of political parties and 13 representatives of the country's regions. Damiba was, however, deposed on 30 September and the new transitional President, Capt. Ibrahima Touré, announced the dissolution of the TNA.

Transitional National Assembly: 01 BP 6482, Ouagadougou 01; tel. 25-49-19-00; e-mail info@assembleenationale.bf; internet www .assembleenationale.bf.

President: Prof. ABOUBACAR TOGUYENI.

Election Commission

Commission Electorale Nationale Indépendante (CENI): 01 BP 5152, Ouagadougou 01; tel. 25-30-80-44; e-mail ceni@fasonet.bf; internet www.ceni.bf; f. 2001; 15 mems; Pres. ELYSÉE OUÉDRAOGO.

Advisory Council

Economic and Social Council (Conseil Economique et Social): 01 BP 6162, Ouagadougou 01; tel. 25-32-40-91; e-mail ces@ces.gov.bf; internet www.ces.gov.bf; f. 1985; present name adopted in 1992; 90 mems; Pres. BONAVENTURE D. OUÉDRAOGO.

Political Organizations

A total of 61 political parties contested the 2020 legislative elections.

Alliance pour la Démocratie et la Fédération—Rassemblement Démocratique Africain (ADF—RDA): 01 BP 1991, Ouagadougou 01; tel. 25-43-03-69; internet fb.com/AdfRdaOfficiel; f. 1990 as Alliance pour la Démocratie et la Fédération; absorbed faction of Rassemblement Démocratique Africain in 1998; Pres. GILBERT NOËL OUÉDRAOGO; Sec.-Gen. BOUBA YAGUIBOU.

Congrès pour la Démocratie et le Progrès (CDP): 1146 ave Kwamé N'Krumah, 01 BP 1605, Ouagadougou 01; tel. 25-31-50-18; f. 1996; Pres. ACHILLE MARIE JOSEPH TAPSOBA (acting).

Convention Nationale pour le Progrès (CNP): Ouagadougou.

Le Faso Autrement (FA): Ouagadougou; tel. 25-40-76-40; e-mail info@lefasoautrement.org; internet www.lefasoautrement.org; Pres. ABLASSÉ OUÉDRAOGO; Sec.-Gen. WENDPLOUMDÉ ROCH OUÉDRAOGO.

Mouvement Africain des Peuples (MAP): Ouagadougou; internet fb.com/MAP-Mouvement-Africain-des-Peuples -1497825837213680; f. 2011; Pres. VICTORIEN BARNABÉ WENDKOUNI TOUGOUMA.

Mouvement Agir Ensemble pour le Burkina Faso: Ougadougou; tel. 76204294; internet fb.com/Mouvement-AGIR-Ensemble -pour-le-Burkina-Faso-100112618052911; f. 2019; Leader KADRÉ DÉSIRÉ OUÉDRAOGO; Sec.-Gen MATHIEU SANOU.

Mouvement pour le Burkina du Futur (MBF): Ouagadougou; f. 2019; Pres. ASSANE SINARÉ; Sec.-Gen. HALHASSANE SINARÉ.

Mouvement pour la Démocratie en Afrique (MDA): ave Père Joseph, Secteur 52, Ouagadougou; tel. 25-40-75-60; internet fb.com/ Mouvement-pour-La-Democratie-en-Afrique-499035630264743; Pres. AMADOU TALL.

Mouvement du Peuple pour le Progrès (MPP): ave de la Nation, Rue 12, Porte 2, Ouagadougou; tel. 25-40-26-82; e-mail bpn@mpp.bf; internet mpp.bf/fr; f. 2014; Pres. ALASSANE BALA SAKANDÉ.

Nouveau Temps pour la Démocratie (NTD): Ouagadougou; Pres. VINCENT T. DABILGOU.

Nouvelle Alliance du Faso (NAFA): Ouagadougou; internet fb .com/nafaburkina; f. 2015; Pres. MAMADOU DICKO.

Organisation pour la Démocratie et le Travail (ODT): 02 BP 5274, Ouagadougou 02; tel. 25-35-64-61; Pres. MOÏSE SAWADOGO.

Parti pour la Démocratie et le Progrès—Parti Socialiste (PDP—PS): 11 BP 26, Ouagadougou 11; tel. 78-04-12-53; e-mail pdp-ps@fasonet.bf; f. 2001 by merger of the Parti pour la Démocratie et le Progrès and the Parti Socialiste Burkinabè; Nat. Pres. TORO DRABO; Sec.-Gen. TIDJANE OUÉDRAOGO.

Parti pour la Démocratie et le Socialisme/Parti des Bâtisseurs (PDS/METBA): Ouagadougou; tel. 25-34-34-04; Pres. PHILIPPE OUÉDRAOGO.

Parti pour le Développement et le Changement (PDC): Ouagadougou; Pres. ABDEL AZIZ FADEL SÉRÉMÉ.

Parti de la Renaissance Nationale (PAREN): Ouagadougou; tel. 25-43-12-26; f. 2000; social-democratic; Pres. ABDOUL KARIM SANGO.

Rassemblement pour la Démocratie et le Socialisme (RDS): Ouagadougou; Pres. FRANÇOIS OUINDÉLASSIDA OUÉDRAOGO.

Rassemblement pour le Développement du Burkina (RDB): Pres. CÉLESTIN SEYDOU COMPAORÉ.

Rassemblement Patriotique pour l'Intégrité (RPI): Ouagadougou; Pres. RAPHAËL KOUAMA.

Union pour un Burkina Nouveau (UBN): Ouagadougou; tel. 25-38-08-10; internet www.ubn.bf; Pres. YACOUBA OUÉDRAOGO.

Union Nationale pour la Démocratie et le Développement (UNDD): 03 BP 7114, Ouagadougou 03; tel. 25-31-15-15; f. 2003 by fmr mems of the ADF—RDA; liberal; Pres. Me HERMANN YAMÉOGO.

Union pour le Progrès et le Changement (UPC): Secteur 07, rue 07.67, Porte 296, 01 BP 2179, Ouagadougou 01; tel. 25-50-30-71; internet www.upcburkina.org; f. 2010; Pres. ZÉPHIRIN DIABRÉ; Nat. Gen. Sec. RABI YAMÉOGO.

Union pour la Renaissance—Parti Sankariste (UNIR—PS): Ouagadougou; tel. 25-36-30-45; e-mail contact@unirps.org; internet unirps.org; f. 2000 as Union pour la Renaissance—Mouvement Sankariste; renamed as above in 2009; Pres. BÉNÉWÉNDÉ STANISLAS SANKARA.

Diplomatic Representation

EMBASSIES IN BURKINA FASO

Algeria: Secteur 13, Zone du Bois, 295 ave Babanguida, 01 BP 3893, Ouagadougou 01; tel. 25-36-81-81; internet www.ambalgbf.net; Ambassador (vacant).

Belgium: 417 ave Kwamé N'Krumah, 01 BP 1624, Ouagadougou 01; tel. 25-31-21-64; e-mail ouagadougou@diplobel.fed.be; internet burkinafaso.diplomatie.belgium.be; Ambassador JEAN JACQUES QUAIRIAT.

Brazil: Parcele 20, Lot 38, Section F, Zone A, 10 BP 13571, Ouagadougou 10; tel. 25-37-60-30; e-mail brasemb.uagadugu@itamaraty.gov.br; internet www.gov.br/mre/pt-br/embaixada-uagadugu; Ambassador ELLEN OSTHOFF FERREIRA DE BARROS.

Canada: 316 ave du Prof. Joseph Ki Zerbo, 01 BP 548, Ouagadougou 01; tel. 25-49-08-00; e-mail ouaga@international.gc.ca; internet www.canadainternational.gc.ca/burkinafaso; Ambassador LEE-ANNE HERMANN.

Chad: 01 BP 3226, Ouagadougou; tel. 25-50-09-79; e-mail ambassadetchadburkina@yahoo.fr; Ambassador (vacant).

China, People's Republic: Bâtiment 1, Parcelle No. 2, Lot 38, Section F, Zone A, Ouagadougou; tel. 25-37-66-38; internet bf.china-embassy.gov.cn; Ambassador LU CHAN.

Côte d'Ivoire: pl. des Nations Unies, 01 BP 20, Ouagadougou 01; tel. 25-31-82-28; Ambassador LAMINE OUATTARA.

Cuba: 270 rue François Lompo, Secteur 4, Ouagadougou; tel. 25-30-64-91; e-mail embacuba.bf@fasonet.bf; internet misiones.minrex.gob.cu/es/burkina-faso; Ambassador NADIESKA NAVARRO BARRO.

Denmark: 316 ave Pr. Joseph Ki-Zerbo, 01 BP 1760, Ouagadougou 01; tel. 25-32-85-40; e-mail ouaamb@um.dk; internet burkinafaso.um.dk; Ambassador STEEN SONNE ANDERSEN.

Egypt: Zone du Conseil de L'Entente, blvd du Faso, 04 BP 7042, Ouagadougou 04; tel. 25-50-66-39; e-mail embassy.ouagadougou@mfa.gov.eg; internet www.mfa.gov.eg/french/embassies/egyptian_embassy_burkina_faso; Ambassador IBRAHIM ABDELAZIM EL-KHOULI.

France: ave du Trésor, 01 BP 504, Ouagadougou 01; tel. 25-49-66-66; internet bf.ambafrance.org; Ambassador LUC HALLADE.

Germany: 14 rue Kafando Romuald, La Rotonde, 01 BP 600, Ouagadougou 01; tel. 25-50-67-31; e-mail info@ouag.diplo.de; internet ouagadougou.diplo.de; Ambassador Dr ANDREAS MICHAEL PFAFFERNOSCHKE.

Ghana: 22 ave Thomas Sankara, 01 BP 212, Ouagadougou 01; tel. 25-50-76-35; e-mail embagna@fasonet.bf; Ambassador ADAGBILA BONIFACE GAMBILA.

Holy See: rue Pape Benoît XVI, Ouaga 2000, BP 1902, Ouagadougou 01; tel. 25-37-43-58; e-mail na.burkina@diplomat.va; Ambassador MICHAEL FRANCIS CROTTY (Titular Archbishop of Lindisfarna).

India: Parcel 13, Lot 38, Sector 15, 10 BP 13977, Ouagadougou; e-mail 25-37-63-61; internet www.eoiburkinafaso.gov.in; Ambassador (vacant).

Italy: Ouagadougou; e-mail amb.ouagadougou@cert.esteri.it; Ambassador ANDREA ROMUSSI.

Japan: 01 BP 5560, Ouagadougou 01; tel. 25-37-65-06; internet www.bf.emb-japan.go.jp; Ambassador MASAAKI KATO.

Libya: ave Pascal Zagré, 01 BP 1601, Ouagadougou 01; tel. 25-50-67-53; Ambassador (vacant).

Mali: ave Pascal Zagré, Ouaga 2000, 01 BP 1911, Ouagadougou 01; tel. 25-37-46-08; e-mail amba.mali.ouaga@fasonet.bf; internet ambamali-bf.org; Ambassador AMADOU SOULALÉ.

Morocco: ave Pascal Zagré, Ouaga 2000, 01 BP 6467, Ouagadougou 01; tel. 25-37-40-16; e-mail maroc1@fasonet.bf; Ambassador YOUSSEF SLAOUI.

Netherlands: 316 ave du Prof. Joseph Ki Zerbo, 01 BP 5542, Ouagadougou 01; tel. 54755779; e-mail oua@minbuza.nl; internet www.nederlandwereldwijd.nl/landen/burkina-faso; Ambassador ESTHER LOEFFEN.

Nigeria: rue de l'Hôpital Yalgado, 01 BP 132, Ouagadougou 01; tel. 25-36-30-15; Ambassador Hajia MISITURA ABDULRAHEEM.

Saudi Arabia: Villa M05, rue de la Francophonie, 01 BP 2069, Ouagadougou 01; tel. 25-37-42-07; internet embassies.mofa.gov.sa/sites/burkinafaso; Ambassador FAHAD BIN ABDULRAHMAN AL-DOSARI.

Senegal: Immeuble Espace Fadima, ave de la Résistance du 17 Mai, 01 BP 3226, Ouagadougou 01; tel. 25-31-14-18; Ambassador M'BABA COURA N'DIAYE.

South Africa: Villa No. 149, ave Pascal Zagré, rue de Badnogo, Ouaga 2000, BP 12, Ouagadougou; tel. 25-37-60-98; e-mail saemb.ouaga@dirco.gov.za; Ambassador H. S. M. MAJEKE.

Sudan: 01 BP 3226, Ouagadougou; tel. 25-31-01-31; Ambassador MAGDI MOHAMED TAHA.

Sweden: 187 ave de l'Europe, 11 BP 755, CMS, Ouagadougou 11; tel. 25-49-61-70; e-mail ambassaden.ouagadougou@gov.se; internet www.swedenabroad.com/ouagadougou; Ambassador MARIA SARGREN.

Tunisia: BP 2923, Ouagadougou; tel. 25-37-62-37; e-mail at .ouagadougou@diplomatie.gov.tn; internet www.diplomatie.gov.tn/nc/mission/etranger/ambassade-de-tunisie-a-ouagadougou-burkina-faso; Ambassador MOHAMED KAHLOUN.

Türkiye (Turkey): rue El Hadj Goama Ousmane Kienfangue, 01 BP 603, Ouagadougou; tel. 25-37-63-18; internet ugudugu.be.mfa.gov.tr; Ambassador NILGÜN ERDEM ARI.

USA: Secteur 15, Ouaga 2000, ave Ousmane Sembène, rue 15873, 01 BP 35, Ouagadougou 01; tel. 25-49-53-00; e-mail amembouaga@state.gov; internet bf.usembassy.gov; Ambassador SANDRA E. CLARK.

Judicial System

In accordance with constitutional amendments approved by the National Assembly in April 2000, the Supreme Court was abolished; its four permanent chambers were replaced by a Constitutional Council, a Council of State, a Court of Cassation and a National Audit Court, all of which commenced operations in December 2002. Judges are accountable to a Higher Council, under the chairmanship of the President of the Republic, in which capacity he or she is officially responsible for ensuring the independence of the judiciary. A High Court of Justice is competent to try the President and members of the Government in cases of treason, embezzlement of public funds, and other crimes and offences.

Constitutional Council: 40 ave de la Nation, 11 BP 1114, Ouagadougou 11; tel. 25-50-05-53; e-mail conseil@conseil-constitutionnel.gov.bf; internet www.conseil-constitutionnel.gov.bf/accueil; f. 2002 to replace Constitutional Chamber of fmr Supreme Court; Pres. (vacant).

Council of State: 40 ave de la Nation, 01 BP 586, Ouagadougou 01; tel. 25-30-05-53; e-mail conseil@conseil-etat.gov.bf; internet www.conseil-etat.gov.bf/accueil; f. 2002 to replace Administrative Chamber of fmr Supreme Court; comprises 2 chambers: a Consultative Chamber and a Chamber of Litigation; First Pres. JEAN-BAPTISTE OUÉDRAOGO.

Court of Cassation: 01 BP 586, Ouagadougou 01; tel. 25-30-64-16; e-mail courdecassationburkina@yahoo.com; internet www.cour-cassation.gov.bf/accueil; f. 2002 to replace Judicial Chamber of fmr Supreme Court; First Pres. MAZOBÉ JEAN KONDÉ.

High Court of Justice: Ouagadougou; f. 1998; comprises 6 deputies of the National Assembly and 3 magistrates appointed by the President of the Court of Cassation; Pres. KHALIL BARA.

National Audit Court: 01 BP 2534, Ouagadougou 01; tel. 25-50-36-00; e-mail infos@cour-comptes.gov.bf; internet www.cour-comptes.gov.bf/accueil; f. 2002 to replace Audit Chamber of fmr Supreme Court; comprises 3 chambers, concerned with: local government organs; public enterprises; and the operations of the state; First Pres. LATIN PODA.

Religion

The Constitution provides for freedom of religion, and the Government respects this right in practice. The country is a secular state. Islam, Christianity and traditional religions operate freely without government interference. According to the 2019 census, some 63.8% of the population were Muslims, 26.3% were Christians and 9.0%

followed animist beliefs, with the remaining population being adherents of other religions or practising no religion.

ISLAM

Communauté Musulmane du Burkina Faso: 01 BP 368, Ouagadougou 01; tel. 25-31-44-05; Pres. El Hadj ABDOU RASMANÉ SANA.

Fédération des Associations Islamiques du Burkina (FAIB): Ouagadougou; tel. 25-37-47-44; e-mail faib.burkina@gmail.com; internet fb.com/FAIBofficielle; f. ; Pres. El Hadj OUMAROU KOANDA; Exec. Sec. El Hadj ADAMA SAKANDÉ.

CHRISTIANITY

The Roman Catholic Church

Burkina Faso comprises three archdioceses and 12 dioceses.

Bishops' Conference: Conférence des Evêques de Burkina Faso et du Niger, 01 BP 1195, Ouagadougou 01; tel. 25-30-60-26; e-mail cebn@fasonet.bf; internet www.egliseduburkina.org; f. 1966; legally recognized 1978; Pres. Most Rev. LAURENT BIRFUORÉ DABIRÉ (Bishop of Dori).

Archbishop of Bobo-Dioulasso: Most Rev. PAUL YEMBOARO OUÉDRAOGO, Archevêché, Lafiaso, 01 BP 312, Bobo-Dioulasso; tel. 20-97-00-35; e-mail lafiaso@fasonet.bf.

Archbishop of Koupéla: Most Rev. GABRIEL SAYAOGO, Archevêché, BP 51, Koupéla; tel. 24-71-00-30; e-mail ardiokou@fasonet.bf.

Archbishop of Ouagadougou: Cardinal PHILIPPE NAKELLENTUB OUÉDRAOGO, Archevêché, 01 BP 1472, Ouagadougou 01; tel. 25-50-67-04; e-mail untaani@fasonet.bf.

Protestant Churches

Assemblées de Dieu du Burkina Faso: 01 BP 458, Ouagadougou 01; tel. 25-34-35-45; e-mail adlagengo@fasonet.bf; f. 1921; Pres. Pastor ÉTIENNE ZONGO; Sec.-Gen. SALAM PHILÉMON SABA.

Fédération des Eglises et Missions Evangéliques (FEME): BP 108, Ouagadougou; tel. 25-36-14-26; e-mail feme@fasonet.bf; internet www.femebf.org; f. 1961; Pres. HENRI YE.

BAHÁ'Í FAITH

Assemblée Spirituelle Nationale: 01 BP 977, Ouagadougou 01; tel. 25-34-29-95; e-mail asnduburkina@hotmail.com; internet www.bahai.org/national-communities/burkina-faso; Nat. Sec. JEAN-PIERRE SWEDY.

The Press

DAILY NEWSPAPERS (PRINT AND ONLINE)

Aujourd'hui au Faso: 1292 ave Kwamé N'Krumah, 11 BP 529, Ouagadougou; tel. 25-30-27-37; e-mail aujourd8@aujourd8.net; internet www.aujourd8.net; f. 2014; Dir of Publication DIEUDONNÉ ZOUNGRANA.

Bulletin de l'Agence d'Information du Burkina: 01 BP 2507, Ouagadougou 01; tel. 25-33-73-16; e-mail infoaiburkina@gmail.com; internet www.aib.media; f. 1964 as L'Agence Voltaïque de Presse; current name adopted in 1984; Dir ALBAN KINI.

L'Express du Faso: 01 BP 1, Bobo-Dioulasso 01; tel. 20-96-09-87; e-mail contact@lexpressdufaso.com; internet www.lexpressdufaso-bf.com; f. 1998; privately owned; Editor-in-Chief KANI MOUNTAMOU.

L'Observateur Paalga: 01 BP 584, Ouagadougou 01; tel. 25-33-27-05; internet www.lobservateur.bf; f. 1973; privately owned; Dir EDOUARD OUÉDRAOGO.

Le Pays: Cité 1200 logements, 01 BP 4577, Ouagadougou 01; tel. 25-36-20-46; e-mail editionslepays@gmail.com; internet www.lepays.bf; f. 1991; independent; Dir-Gen. BELDH'OR CHEICK SIGUE; Editor-in-Chief BOUNDI OUOBA.

Le Quotidien: Ouagadougou; tel. 25-41-99-71; f. 2010; Dir of Publication SOULEYMANE TRAORÉ.

Sidwaya Quotidien (Daily Truth): rue du Nasser, 01 BP 507, Ouagadougou 01; tel. 25-31-22-89; e-mail contact@sidwaya.info; internet www.sidwaya.bf; f. 1984; state-owned; Dir-Gen. MAHAMADI TIÉGNA; Editor-in-Chief VICTORIEN AIMAR SAWADOGO.

Le Soir: Ouagadougou; tel. 25-50-96-59; e-mail jlesoir@yahoo.com; internet fb.com/LeSoir.bf; f. 2012; privately owned; Dir of Publication EL HADJ LOOKMAN SAWADOGO.

PERIODICALS

Bendré (Drum): 16.38 ave du Yatenga, 01 BP 6020, Ouagadougou 01; tel. 25-33-27-11; e-mail bendrekan@hotmail.com; f. 1990; weekly; current affairs; Dir SY MOUMINA CHERIFF.

Courrier Confidentiel: Paglayiri, Arrondissement 6, Secteur 25, 01 BP 4636, Ouagadougou; tel. 25-41-18-61; e-mail contact@courrierconfidentiel.net; internet www.courrierconfidentiel.net; f. 2011; 3 a month; Dir of Publication HERVÉ TAOKO.

L'Economiste du Faso: Ouagadougou; internet www.leconomistedufaso.bf; f. 2013; Dir of Publication ABDOULAYE TAO.

Evasion: Cité 1200 logements, 01 BP 4577, Ouagadougou 01; tel. 25-36-20-46; e-mail editionslepays@gmail.com; internet evasion.lepays.bf; f. 1996; publ. by Editions le Pays; weekly; current affairs; Dir-Gen. BOUREIMA JÉRÉMIE SIGUE; Editor-in-Chief CHRISTINE SAWADOGO.

L'Evénement: 01 BP 1860, Ouagadougou 01; tel. 25-37-33-03; e-mail jlevenement@gmail.com; internet www.evenement-bf.net; f. 2001; bi-monthly; Dir of Publication GERMAIN BITTIOU NAMA; Editor-in-Chief BASIDOU KINDA.

Fasozine: Ouagadougou; tel. 25-50-76-01; e-mail ecrire@fasozine.com; internet www.fasozine.com; f. 2005; Dir of Publication SERGE MATHIAS TOMONDJI.

L'Indépendant: 01 BP 5663, Ouagadougou 01; tel. 25-33-37-75; e-mail sebgo@fasonet.bf; f. 1993 by Norbert Zongo; weekly, Tuesdays; Dir of Publication BASILE BALOUM.

Le Journal du Jeudi (JJ): 01 BP 3654, Ouagadougou 01; tel. 25-31-41-08; e-mail info@journaldujeudi.com; internet www.journaldujeudi.com; f. 1991; weekly; satirical; Dir BOUBAKAR DIALLO; Editor-in-Chief ANSELME LALSAGA.

Laabaali: Association Tin Tua, BP 167, Fada N'Gourma; tel. 24-77-01-26; e-mail info@tintua.org; internet www.tintua.org/Liens/Laabali.htm; f. 1988; monthly; promotes literacy, agricultural information, cultural affairs; Gourmanche; Dir of Publishing BENOÎT B. OUOBA; Editor-in-Chief SIBIDI DIANOU.

La Lettre du Faso: Immeuble de la Pharmacie Louis Pasteur, 2e étage, rue Guinko, Dapoya, 02 BP 5285, Ouagadougou 02; tel. 70140456; e-mail lalettredufaso@gmail.com; internet lalettredufaso.net; weekly.

L'Opinion: 01 BP 6459, Ouagadougou 01; tel. 25-50-89-49; e-mail zedcom@fasonet.bf; internet www.zedcom.bf; weekly; Dir of Publication ISSAKA LINGANI.

Le Reporter: 158 rue 30.131, 01 BP 4636, Ouagadougou 01; tel. 25-45-62-77; e-mail reporterbf@reporterbf.net; internet www.reporterbf.net; f. 2007; fortnightly; Dir of Publication BOUREIMA OUÉDRAOGO; Editor-in-Chief HERVÉ TAOKO.

Revue des Réflexions Constitutionnelles: 03 BP 7104, Ouagadougou; tel. 25-40-86-05; e-mail associationsbdc@gmail.com; monthly; constitutional law; publ. by Société Burkinabè de Droit Constitutionnel.

Sidwaya Sport: rue du Nasser, 01 BP 507, Ouagadougou 01; tel. 25-31-22-89; e-mail contact@sidwaya.info; internet www.sidwaya.bf; f. 1997; state-owned; weekly.

Votre Santé: Cité 1200 logements, 01 BP 4577, Ouagadougou 01; tel. 25-36-20-46; e-mail lepays91@yahoo.fr; internet www.lepays.fr; f. 1996; publ. by Editions le Pays; monthly; Dir-Gen. BOUREIMA JÉRÉMIE SIGUE; Editor-in-Chief ALEXANDRE LE GRAND ROUAMBA.

NEWS AGENCIES

Agence d'Information du Burkina (AIB): 01 BP 2507, Ouagadougou 01; tel. 25-32-46-39; e-mail infoaiburkina@gmail.com; internet www.aib.media; f. 1964; fmrly Agence Voltaïque de Presse; Dir ALBAN KINI.

PRESS ASSOCIATIONS

Association des Journalistes du Burkina Faso: 04 BP 8524, Ouagadougou 04; tel. 25-34-37-45; e-mail contact@ajb.bf; internet www.ajb.bf; Pres. GUÉZOUMA SANOGO.

Centre National de Presse—Norbert Zongo (CNP—NZ): 04 BP 8524, Ouagadougou 04; tel. 25-34-37-45; e-mail cnpress@cnpress-zongo.org; internet www.cnpress-zongo.org; f. 1998 as Centre National de Presse; centre of information and documentation; provides journalistic training; incorporates Association des Journalistes du Burkina (f. 1988); Dir ABDOULAYE DIALLO.

Société des Éditeurs de la Presse (SEP): Ouagadougou; f. 1992; Pres. BOUREIMA OUÉDRAOGO.

Publishers

Les Editions Harmattan Burkina: ave Mohamar Kadhafi, 12 BP 226, Ouagadougou 12; tel. 25-37-54-36; e-mail harmattanburkina@yahoo.fr; internet harmattan-burkina.com; academic.

Editions Flamme: 04 BP 8921, Ouagadougou 04; tel. 25-34-15-31; e-mail flamme@fasonet.bf; f. 1994; owned by the Assembleés de Dieu du Burkina Faso; literature of Christian interest in French, in Mooré and in Dioula; Editor-in-Chief DANIEL KABORÉ.

Editions Sankofa et Gurli: 01 BP 3811, Ouagadougou 01; tel. 70-24-30-81; e-mail sankogur@hotmail.com; f. 1995; literary fiction, social sciences, African languages, youth and childhood literature; in French and in national languages; Dir JEAN-CLAUDE NABA.

Les Editions Sidwaya: BP 507, Ouagadougou 01; tel. 25-31-22-89; e-mail contact@sidwaya.info; internet www.sidwaya.bf; f. 1998 to replace Société Nationale d'Editions et de Presse; state-owned; transfer to private ownership proposed; general, periodicals; Pres. AUGUSTE MARIE ROMAIN BAMBARA; Dir-Gen. MAHAMADI TIÉGNA.

Broadcasting and Communications

TELECOMMUNICATIONS

IPSyS Telecom: 11 BP 757 Ouagadougou 11; tel. 25-30-55-00; e-mail contact@mail-bf.com; internet www.ipsys-bf.com; internet service provider.

M'data Telecom: Immeuble Élite Voyages, rue François Bouda, Koulouba Ouagadougou; tel. 25-33-52-33; e-mail contact .burkinafaso@afr-ix.com; internet afr-ix.com/mdataburkinafaso; internet service provider.

Moov Africa Burkina: 705 ave de la Nation, 01 BP 10000, Ouagadougou 01; tel. 25-33-40-01; e-mail contact@moov-africa.bf; internet moov-africa.bf/Pages/index.aspx; fmrly Office National des Télécommunications; name changed as above in 2021; fixed-line telephone, mobile and internet services; 61% owned by Maroc Télécom (Morocco, Vivendi); 23% state-owned; Dir-Gen. SIDI MOHAMED NAIMI; 10.5m. mobile subscribers (Dec. 2021).

Orange Burkina Faso: ave du Général Aboubacar Sangoulé Lamizana, 01 BP 6622, Ouagadougou 01; tel. 25-33-14-00; internet www.orange.bf; f. 2001; fmrly Zain and Airtel Burkina Faso; mobile telephone and internet operator; CEO MAMADOU COULIBALY; 10.9m. subscribers (Dec. 2021).

Sky Net Telecom: ave Dimdolossom, 02 BP 5056, Ouagadougou 02; tel. 77074848; e-mail infos@skynet-telecom.net; internet skynet-telecom.net; internet service provider.

Telecel-Faso: 396 ave de la Nation, 08 BP 11059, Ouagadougou 086; tel. 25-33-35-56; e-mail contact@telecelfaso.bf; internet www .telecelfaso.bf; f. 2000; mobile telephone operator in Ouagadougou, Bobo-Dioulasso and 19 other towns; 80% owned by Orascom Telecom (Egypt); Dir-Gen. DIMITRI W. OUÉDRAOGO; 3.3m. subscribers (Dec. 2021).

Regulatory Authority

Autorité de Régulation des Communications Electroniques et des Postes (ARCEP): ave Dimdolobsom, porte 43, rue 3 angle rue 48, 01 BP 6437, Ouagadougou 01; tel. 25-37-53-60; e-mail secretariat@arcep.bf; internet www.arcep.bf; f. 2009 to replace Autorité Nationale de Régulation des Télécommunications (ARTEL); Pres. TONTAMA CHARLES MILLOGO; Sec.-Gen. SIBIRI OUATTARA.

BROADCASTING

Regulatory Authority

Conseil Supérieur de la Communication (Higher Council of Communication): 290 ave Ho Chi Minh, 01 BP 6618, Ouagadougou 01; tel. 25-50-11-24; e-mail infos@csc.bf; internet www.csc.gov.bf/accueil; f. 1995 as Higher Council of Information, present name adopted 2005; Pres. ABDOULAZIZE BAMOGO; Sec.-Gen. MASSADALO YVETTE NACOULM SANOU.

Radio

Radiodiffusion-Télévision du Burkina (RTB): 01 BP 2530, Ouagadougou 01; tel. 25-40-78-71; e-mail dcm@rtb.bf; internet www.rtb.bf; f. 2001; Pres. ZOUMANA TRAORÉ; Dir-Gen. RABANKHI ABOU-BÂKR ZIDA.

Radio Nationale du Burkina (La RNB): 03 BP 7029, Ouagadougou 03; tel. 25-32-43-02; e-mail contact@rtb.bf; f. 1959; state radio service; comprises national broadcaster of informative and discussion programmes, music stations *Canal Arc-En-Ciel* and *Canal Arc-en-Ciel Plus*, and 2 regional stations, broadcasting in local languages, in Bobo-Dioulasso and Gaoua; Dir HAROUNA SANA.

Horizon FM: 01 BP 2714, Ouagadougou 01; tel. 25-33-23-23; f. 1990; private commercial station; broadcasts in French, English and 8 vernacular languages; operates 10 stations nationally; Dir JUDITH IDA SAWADOGO.

Omega FM: Centre Commercial Ouaga 2000, 4e étage, 02 BP 5801, Ouagadougou 02; tel. 25-37-59-67; e-mail ouaga@omegabf.net; internet www.omegamedias.info; Dir-Gen. FIDÈLE TAMINI.

Ouaga FM: blvd France-Afrique, Ouagadougou; tel. 25-37-51-21; e-mail contact@ouagafm.bf; internet www.ouagafm.bf; Pres. JOACHIM BAKY; Dir-Gen. (vacant).

Radio Evangile Développement (RED): 04 BP 8050, Ouagadougou 04; tel. 25-43-51-56; e-mail burkinared@gmail.com; internet www.redburkina.info; f. 1993; broadcasts from Ouagadougou, Bobo-Dioulasso, Ouahigouya, Léo, Houndé, Koudougou, Yako and Fada N'Gourma; evangelical Christian; Dir-Gen. ETIENNE KIEMDE.

Radio Locale-Radio Rurale: 03 BP 7029, Ouagadougou 03; tel. 25-35-59-26; e-mail burkinafaso@farmradio.org; internet fb.com/rriburkina; f. 1969; community broadcaster; local stations at Diapaga, Djibasso Gasson, Kongoussi, Orodara and Poura.

Radio Maria: BP 51, Koupéla; tel. 24-70-00-10; e-mail info.bur@radiomaria.org; internet www.radiomariaburkinafaso.org; f. 1993; Roman Catholic; Dir LAZARE TOUGMA.

Radio Pulsar: blvd des Tansoaba, 01 BP 5976, Ouagadougou 01; tel. 25-37-00-52; e-mail info@monpulsar.com; internet www.monpulsar .com; f. 1996; Dir OUSMANE OUEDRAOGO.

Radio Salankoloto-Association Galian: 01 BP 1095, Ouagadougou 01; tel. 25-31-64-93; f. 1996; community broadcaster; Dir ROGER NIKIÉMA.

Radio Vive le Paysan: BP 75, Saponé; tel. 25-40-56-21; e-mail a2oyigde@yahoo.fr; f. 1995; Dir ADRIEN VITAUX.

Savane FM: 10 BP 500, Ouagadougou 10; tel. 25-43-37-43; e-mail contact@savanemedias.net; Dir-Gen. CHARLEMAGNE ABISSI.

Television

BF1: Ouagadougou; tel. 25-37-63-33; e-mail bf1television@gmail .com; internet bf1.tv; f. 2010; Dir-Gen. ISSOUFOU SARE.

Burkina Info TV: 11 BP 1782, Ouagadouga; tel. 25-40-86-85; e-mail redactionburkinainfo@gmail.com; internet fb.com/burkinainfotv.

Impact TV: 933 rue 28.71 Dassasgho, 01 BP 1474, Ouagadougou 01; tel. 25-36-72-72; e-mail television.impact@gmail.com; internet www .impacttele.tv; f. 2010; Dir-Gen. EDMOND COULIBALY.

La Télévision Nationale du Burkina: 955 blvd de la Révolution, 01 BP 2530, Ouagadougou 01; tel. 25-31-83-53; e-mail rtburkina@gmail.com; internet www.rtb.bf/television-en-direct; branch of Radiodiffusion-Télévision du Burkina; broadcasts 75 hours per week; Dir EVARISTE COMBARY.

TV Canal 3: ave Kwamé N'Krumah, 11 BP 340, Ouagadougou 11; tel. 25-50-06-55; f. 2002.

TV Maria: Ouagadougou; f. 2009; Roman Catholic; Dir PAUL OUÉDRAOGO.

Finance

BANKING

Central Bank

Banque Centrale des Etats de l'Afrique de l'Ouest (BCEAO): ave Gamal Abdel Nasser, BP 356, Ouagadougou; tel. 25-49-05-00; e-mail courrier.cdn@bceao.int; internet www.bceao.int; HQ in Dakar, Senegal; f. 1962; bank of issue for the mem. states of the Union Economique et Monétaire Ouest-Africaine (UEMOA, comprising Benin, Burkina Faso, Côte d'Ivoire, Guinea-Bissau, Mali, Niger, Senegal and Togo); Gov. JEAN-CLAUDE KASSI BROU; Dir in Burkina Faso CHARLES LUANGA KI-ZERBO.

Other Banks

In 2021 there were 15 banks and four financial institutions in Burkina Faso.

Bank of Africa—Burkina Faso (BOA—B): 770 ave du Président Sangoule Lamizana, 01 BP 1319, Ouagadougou 01; tel. 25-50-88-70; e-mail information@boaburkinafaso.com; internet www .boaburkinafaso.com; f. 1998; Dir-Gen. FAUSTIN AMOUSSOU.

Banque Agricole du Faso (BADF): Projet Zaca, Ouagadougou; tel. 25-32-99-00; f. 2019; Pres. MAMADOU SÉRÉMÉ.

Banque Atlantique Burkina Faso (BABF): Immeuble Nouria Holding, rue de l'Hôtel de Ville, 01 BP 3407, Ouagadougou 01; tel. 25-30-49-59; e-mail infobabf@banqueatlantique.net; internet www .banqueatlantique.net/bf; f. 2005; Dir-Gen. DRAMANE CISSÉ.

Banque Commerciale du Burkina (BCB): 653 ave Kwamé N'Krumah, 01 BP 1336, Ouagadougou 01; tel. 25-30-12-66; e-mail bcb@bcb.bf; internet www.bcb.bf; f. 1988; 50% owned by Libyan Arab Foreign Bank, 25% state-owned, 25% owned by Caisse Nationale de Sécurité Sociale; Pres. BRUNO RAYMOND BAMOUNI; Dir-Gen. ALI BACHIR KARWA.

Banque Sahélo-Saharienne pour l'Investissement et le Commerce—Burkina (BSIC—Burkina): ave Kwamé N'Krumah, 10 BP 13701, Ouagadougou 10; tel. 25-32-84-01; internet bsicbank.com/burkina; Pres. AHMAT SENOUSSI HISSÈNE; Dir-Gen. ZEDDAN DREF BUDEEB.

Banque de l'Union (BDU-BF): Immeuble Abdoulaye Traoré, ave Loudun 01, Secteur 05, Projet ZACA, Ouagadougou; tel. 25-49-36-00; e-mail bdu@bdu-bf.com; internet www.bdu-bf.com; f. 2014; subsidiary of Banque de Développement du Mali; Dir-Gen. KARIM BAGAYOKO.

CBAO Groupe Attijariwafa Bank: 479 ave du Président Sangoulé Lamizana Koulouba, Ouagadougou; tel. 25-33-77-77; e-mail cbao@cbaofaso.bf; internet www.attijariwafabank.com/en/international-subsidiaries/CBAO-Burkina-Faso; f. 2014; Dir-Gen. MOHAMED A. WILSON.

Coris Bank International: 1242 ave Kwamé N'Krumah, 01 BP 6585, Ouagadougou 01; tel. 25-49-10-00; e-mail corisbank@coris-bank.com; internet burkina.coris.bank; Pres. and Dir-Gen. IDRISSA NASSA.

Ecobank Burkina: 49 rue de l'Hôtel de Ville, 01 BP 145, Ouagadougou 01; tel. 25-49-64-00; e-mail ecobank.bf@ecobank.com; internet www.ecobank.com; f. 1996; 82% owned by Ecobank Transnational Inc; Chair. AMADOU SANGARÉ; Dir-Gen. MOUKARAMOU CHANOU ALAO.

International Business Bank: 1200 ave Kwamé N'Krumah, 01 BP 5585, Ouagadougou; tel. 25-30-63-35; internet www.ib-bank.com; f. 2005 as Banque de l'Habitat du Burkina Faso; name changed as above in 2018; Dir-Gen. MAHAMADOU BONKOUNGOU.

Orabank Burkina: 1416 ave Kwamé N'Krumah, 01 BP 1305, Ouagadougou 01; tel. 25-49-60-00; e-mail info-bf@orabank.net; internet www.orabank.net/fr/filiale/burkina; Dir-Gen. MARTIAL GOEH-AKUE.

Société Générale Burkina Faso (SGBF): 248 rue de l'Hôtel de Ville, 01 BP 585, Ouagadougou 01; tel. 25-32-32-32; e-mail sgbf.burkina@socgen.com; internet www.societegenerale.bf; f. 1998; 52.6% owned by Groupe Société Générale (France), 15% owned by Groupe Castel, 15% state-owned; Pres. EMILE PARÉ; Dir-Gen. JEAN HAROLD N. ABOYA COFFI.

United Bank for Africa Burkina: 1340 ave Dimdolobsom, 01 BP 362, Ouagadougou 01; tel. 25-30-00-00; e-mail CFCBurkina@ubagroup.com; internet www.ubaburkinafaso.com; f. 1974; 57.28% owned by UBA PLC, 20.16% owned by Holding COFIPA (Mali), 10% state-owned; fmrly Banque Internationale du Burkina; name changed as above in 2012; Pres. DAMO JUSTIN BARRO; Dir-Gen. NOELLIE TIENDREBEOGO.

Vista Bank Burkina: 479 ave Kwamé N'Krumah, 01 BP 08, Ouagadougou 01; tel. 25-32-56-00; internet www.biciab.bf; f. 1973; fmrly Banque Sahélo-Saharienne pour l'Investissement et le Commerce—Burkina; present name adopted 2021; 51% owned by Groupe Vista Holding SA, 22% state-owned; Pres. SEYDOU DIAKITÉ; Dir-Gen. MOHAMED BA.

Wendkuni Bank International: Arrondissement 1, Secteur 2, Quartier Projet ZACA, rue 5.11, 01 BP 10270, Ouagadougou 01; tel. 25-49-16-00; internet wendkunibank.bf; Pres. APPOLINAIRE TIMPIGA COMPAORÉ; Dir-Gen. JEANNE MARIE CHRISTINE TANI.

Financial Institutions

Alios Finance Burkina: 1851 ave Kwame NKrumah, 10 BP 13876, Ouagadougou 10; tel. 25-31-80-04; e-mail burkinafaso@alios-finance.com; internet www.alios-finance.com; f. 2007; Dir SAMBA BEN BOUBAKAR CAMARA.

Fidelis Finance Burkina Faso: 1043 ave Kwamé N'Krumah, Immeuble SODIFA, 01 BP 1913, Ouagadougou 01; tel. 25-30-01-01; e-mail infolease@fidelis-finance.com; internet www.fidelis-finance.com; f. 1998; fmrly Burkina Bail, SA; name changed as above in 2014; 22% owned by Africapitalpartners, 15% owned by BOAD, 15% owned by BIDC, 15% owned by FBDES, 15% owned by FSA, 10% owned by Portage FBDES, 8% owned by others; Dir-Gen. KOUAFILANN ABDOULAYE SORY.

FINEC Burkina SA: Wemtenga, Secteur 23, rue de Jeunesse, Ouagadougou 01; tel. 25-37-01-35; e-mail info@finec-burkina.com; internet www.finec-burkina.com; f. 2019; Dir-Gen. SEYDOU SOUNGALO YAMÉOGO.

Réseau des Caisses Populaires du Burkina (RCPB): 01 BP 5382, Ouagadougou 01; tel. 25-37-42-85; e-mail fcpb@rcpb.bf; internet www.rcpb.bf; f. 1972; Pres. El Hadj INOUSSA SAVADOGO; Dir-Gen. DAOUDA SAWADOGA.

Société Burkinabè de Crédit Automobile (SOBCA): 700 ave de la Nation, 01 BP 83, Ouagadougou 01; tel. 25-30-63-10; Pres. DAMASE A. MYAOUENUH; Dir-Gen. MAMADI NAPON.

Société Financière de Garantie Interbancaire (SOFIGIB): 981 ave Kwamé N'Krumah, 11 BP 1345, Ouagadougou 11; tel. 25-30-03-32; e-mail sofigib@sofigib.bf; internet www.sofigib.com; Dir-Gen. PHILIPPE CONSIGUI.

Bankers' Association

Association Professionnelle des Banques et Etablissements Financiers du Burkina (APBEF-B): Immeuble BARRO Yacouba, ave Kwamé N'Krumah, 01 BP 6215, Ouagadougou 01; tel. 25-31-20-65; e-mail apbef@fasonet.bf; internet apbef-bf.org; f. 1967; Pres. DIAKARYA OUATTARA; Exec. Dir OUMAR KY.

STOCK EXCHANGE

Bourse Régionale des Valeurs Mobilières (BRVM): s/c Chambre de Commerce et d'Industrie du Burkina, 01 BP 502, Ouagadougou 01; tel. 25-50-87-73; e-mail dsoubeiga@brvm.org; internet www.brvm.org; f. 1998; national branch of BRVM (regional stock exchange based in Abidjan, Côte d'Ivoire, serving the member states of UEMOA); Man. DAVY SOUBEIGA.

INSURANCE

CIF Assurances—Vie: 1350 ave France-Afrique, 06 BP 9324, Ouagadougou 06; tel. 25-38-51-59; e-mail contact@cif-vie.bf; internet www.cif-vie.bf; f. 2012; Dir-Gen. DAOUDA SAWADOGO.

Coris Assurances: 1242 ave Kwamé N'Krumah, 01 BP 880, Ouagadougou 01; tel. 25-33-23-30; e-mail coris@coris-assurances.com; internet coris-assurances.com; Dir-Gen. HAIDARAÏ RABO.

Générale des Assurances: ave du Président Aboubacar Sangoulé Lamizana, 01 BP 6275, Ouagadougou 01; tel. 25-31-77-75; e-mail info@ga.bf; internet www.generaledesassurances.com; Dir-Gen. (non-life insurance) AUGUSTIN LOADA.

Globus Re: ave Kwamé N'Krumah, BP 6648, Ouagadougou 01; tel. 25-33-88-88; e-mail h.allou@globus-re.com; internet www.globus-re.com; reinsurance; Dir-Gen. ANTOINE COMPAORÉ.

Jackson Assurances: 01 BP 2545, Ouagadougou 01; tel. 25-33-27-27; e-mail infos@jacksonassurances.com; f. 2013; Dir-Gen. ABDOULAYE TOURÉ.

Sanlam Assurance Burkina Faso: ave Kwamé N'Krumah, 01 BP 6469, Ouagadougou 01; tel. 25-49-17-00; e-mail contact@bf.sanlam.com; internet bf.sanlam.com; f. 2000; fmrly Colina SA, subsequently Saham Assurance; name changed as above in 2021; Dir-Gen. SI SALIFOU TRAORÉ.

Société Nationale d'Assurances et de Réassurances (SONAR): 284 ave de Loudun, 01 BP 406, Ouagadougou 01; tel. 25-49-69-00; e-mail sonar@sonar.bf; internet www.sonar.bf; f. 1974; 42% owned by Burkinabè interests, 33% by French, Ivorian and US cos, 22% state-owned; life and non-life; Dir-Gen. THOMAS ZONGO.

Sunu Assurances IARD Burkina Faso: 99 ave Léo Frobénius, 01 BP 398, Ouagadougou 01; tel. 25-32-82-00; e-mail burkinafaso.iard@sunu-group.com; internet sunu-group.com; fmrly Allianz Burkina, name changed as above in 2020; non-life; Pres. LASSINÉ DIAWARA; Dir-Gen. MONHAMED COMPAORÉ.

Union des Assurances du Burkina (UAB): ave Houari Boumedienne, 08 BP 11041, Ouagadougou 08; tel. 25-30-18-18; e-mail uab@uabassurances.com; internet www.uabassurances.com; f. 1991; 11% owned by AXA Assurances Côte d'Ivoire; life and non-life; Dir-Gen. JEAN DAMASCÈNE NIGNAN.

Insurance Association

Association Professionnelle des Sociétés d'Assurances du Burkina (APSAB): ave Bassawarga, Samandin, 01 BP 3233, Ouagadougou 01; tel. 25-30-69-49; internet apsab.org; Pres. MOHAMED COMPAORÉ.

Trade and Industry

GOVERNMENT AGENCIES

Agence pour la Promotion des Exportations du Burkina (APEX): 30 ave de l'UEMOA, 01 BP 389, Ouagadougou 01; tel. 25-31-13-00; e-mail info@apexb.bf; internet www.apexb.bf; f. 2011 to replace Office National du Commerce Extérieur; promotes and supervises external trade; Pres. JEAN-PIERRE GUINKO; Dir-Gen. GUÉSWENDÉ BOUBAKAR SORÉ.

Agence Burkinabè des Investissements (ABI): Ouaga 2000, Zone A, rue Badnogo, face pl. de l'Union Africaine, 03 BP 7030, Ouagadougou 03; tel. 25-37-44-49; e-mail info@investburkina.com; internet www.investburkina.com; f. 2018 to replace Agence de Promotion des Investissements; Dir-Gen. HUGUETTE RADEGONDE NEBGNIGA BAMA/OUILI.

Bureau des Mines et de la Géologie du Burkina (BUMIGEB): 4186 route de Fada N'Gourma, 01 BP 601, Ouagadougou 01; tel. 25-36-48-02; e-mail bumigeb@bumigeb.bf; internet bumigeb.bf; f. 1978; restructured 1997; research into geological and mineral resources; Pres. MABOURLAYE NOMBRÉ; Dir-Gen. GUESWINDÉ SAMUEL DJIGUEMÉ.

DEVELOPMENT ORGANIZATIONS

Agence de Financement et de Promotion des Petites et Moyennes Entreprises du Burkina Faso (AFP-PME): Immeuble Pharmacie Nouvelle, 2e étage, Zone Commerciale, Kadiogo 01 BP 1777, Ouagadougou; tel. 25-31-83-11; e-mail direction@afppme.bf; internet afppme.bf; f. 2008; supports small and medium-sized enterprises; Dir-Gen. MANDIALI LOMPO.

Agence Française de Développement (AFD): 52 ave de la Nation, 01 BP 529, Ouagadougou 01; tel. 25-50-60-92; e-mail afdouagadougou@afd.fr; internet www.afd.fr; Country Dir (vacant).

Agence Nationale d'Appui au Développement des Collectivités Territoriales (ADCT): Ouagadougou; tel. 25-50-53-78; Dir-Gen. DONBEYITWOR JEANNE MARIE RAÍSSA YAMÉOGO-DABIRÉ.

Autorité de Régulation de la Commande Publique (ARCOP): ave d l'Europe, Ouagadougou 01; tel. 25-33-11-67; e-mail arcop@arcop.bf; internet www.arcop.bf; f. 2014 to replace the Autorité de Régulation des Marchés Publics; Pres. DRAMANE MILLOHO; Permanent Sec. TAHIROU SANOU.

France Volontaires: 755 ave du Président John Kennedy, Koulouba, 01 BP 947, Ouagadougou 01; tel. 25-50-70-43; e-mail ev.burkina@france-volontaires.org; internet www.france-volontaires.org; f. 1973 as Association Française des Volontaires du Progrès; name changed as above in 2009; supports small business; Nat. Rep. ADOLPHE SOMDA.

CHAMBERS OF COMMERCE

Chambre de Commerce et d'Industrie du Burkina Faso (CCI-BF): ave de Lyon, 01 BP 502, Ouagadougou 01; tel. 25-30-61-14; e-mail info@cci.bf; internet www.cci.bf; f. 1948; Pres. MAHAMADI SAVADOGO; Dir-Gen. ISSAKA KARGOUGOU; brs in Bobo-Dioulasso, Koupéla and Ouahigouya.

Chambre des Mines du Burkina (CMB): 01 BP 126, Ouagadougou; tel. 25-36-19-35; e-mail cmb@chambredesmines.bf; internet www.chambredesmines.bf; f. 2011; Pres. ADAMA SORO.

EMPLOYERS' ORGANIZATIONS

Club des Hommes d'Affaires Franco-Burkinabé (CHAFB): 132 ave de Lyon, 01 BP 6890, Ouagadougou 01; tel. 70-21-20-20; e-mail chafb@chafb.org; internet www.chafb.com; f. 1990; represents 65 major enterprises and seeks to develop trading relations between Burkina Faso and France; Pres. ARNAUD BOUHIER.

Comité Interprofessionnel de l'Anacarde du Burkina Faso (CIAB): Ouagadougou; tel. 72-06-70-70; e-mail ciab.interprofession@gmail.com; internet fb.com/interprofession.ciab; f. 2015; Pres. IBRAHIM SANFO.

Conseil National du Patronat Burkinabè (CNPB): 1221 ave Kwamé N'Krumah, 01 BP 1482, Ouagadougou 01; tel. 25-33-03-09; e-mail cnpb@fasonet.bf; internet patronat.bf; f. 1974; comprises 70 professional groupings; Pres. APOLLINAIRE COMPAORÉ; Sec.-Gen. PHILOMÈNE YAMEOGO.

Groupement Professionnel des Industriels (GPI): Appartement A1, Cité Saint Exupéry, ave Bénoît Badoua, 01 BP 5381, Ouagadougou 01; tel. 25-50-11-59; e-mail gpi@fasonet.bf; f. 1974; Pres. MAMADY SANOH.

Jeune Chambre Internationale du Burkina Faso: Immeuble Kanazoe, ave du Travail, 11 BP 136, Ouagadougou; tel. 78-85-40-41; e-mail kroser73@yahoo.fr; f. 1976; org. of entrepreneurs aged 18–40 years; affiliated to Junior Chambers International, Inc; Pres. MIKAËL YAGUIBOU.

Maison de l'Entreprise du Burkina Faso (MEBF): rue 3-1119, porte 132, 11 BP 379, Ouagadougou 11; tel. 25-39-80-60; e-mail info@me.bf; internet www.me.bf; f. 2002; promotes devt of the private sector; Pres. OUMAROU YUGO; Dir-Gen. KARIM OUATTARA.

Union Nationale des Producteurs de Coton du Burkina Faso (UNPCB): 02 BP 1677, Bobo-Dioulasso 02; tel. 20-97-33-10; e-mail unpcb@fasonet.bf; internet unpcb.org; f. 1998; Pres. BAMBOU BIHOUN.

UTILITIES

Electricity

Agence Burkinabè de l'Electrification Rurale (ABER): ave El Hadj Salifou Cissé, 01 BP 545, Ouagadougou 01; tel. 25-37-45-01; e-mail info@aber.bf; internet www.aber.bf; f. 2017; Dir-Gen. SOULEYMANE KONATÉ.

Autorité de Régulation du Sous-secteur de l'Électricité: 10 BP 13153, Ouagadougou 10; tel. 25-32-48-17; e-mail infos@arse.bf; internet www.arse.bf; Pres. SIDBEWINDÉ AHMED YACHINE OUEDRAOGO.

Fonds de Développement de l'Electrification: Ouaga 2000, ave EL Hadj Salifou Cisse, 01 BP 545, Ouagadougou 01; tel. 25-37-45-01; e-mail fde@fasonet.bf; internet www.fde.bf; f. 2003; Dir-Gen. JEAN BAPTISTE KABORE.

Société Générale de Travaux et de Constructions Electriques (SOGETEL): rue Fadoul, Gounghin Secteur 9, 01 BP 429, Ouagadougou 01; tel. 25-34-29-80; internet groupefadoul.com/sogetel; transport and distribution of electricity.

Société Nationale Burkinabè d'Electricité (SONABEL): 55 ave de la Nation, 01 BP 54, Ouagadougou 01; tel. 25-50-61-00; e-mail infos@sonabel.bf; internet sonabel.bf; f. 1984; state-owned; production and distribution of electricity; Dir-Gen. DANIEL SERMÉ.

Water

Office National de l'Eau et de l'Assainissement (ONEA): 01 BP 170, Ouagadougou 01; tel. 25-43-19-00; e-mail onea@fasonet.bf; internet oneabf.com; f. 1977; storage, purification and distribution of water; transferred to private management (by Veolia Water Burkina Faso) in 2001; Dir-Gen. GILBERT BASSOLÉ.

CO-OPERATIVES

Union des Coopératives Agricoles et Maraîchères du Burkina (UCOBAM): 01 BP 277, Ouagadougou 01; tel. 25-50-65-27; e-mail ucobam@zcp.bf; internet www.ucobam.bf; f. 1968; comprises 8 regional co-operative unions (6,500 mems, representing 35,000 producers); production and marketing of fruit, vegetables, jams and conserves; Dir-Gen. YASSIA OUÉDRAOGO.

MAJOR COMPANIES

The following are some of the largest companies in terms of either capital investment or employment.

CFAO Motors Burkina: 2280 blvd Tansoba Kiéma, 01 BP 23, Ouagadougou 01; tel. 25-49-88-00; internet yamaha.cfaomotors-burkinafaso.com; f. 1985; import and distribution of motorcycles and power generators; private co.

Comptoir Burkinabè de Papier (CBP): 907 ave Yennenga, 01 BP 1338, Ouagadougou 01; tel. 25-31-16-21; e-mail cbpburkina@gmail.com; f. 1989; paper producer; private co; Pres. and Dir-Gen. JOSEPH BAAKLINI.

FASOPLAST—Société des Plastiques du Faso: Zone Industrielle de Gounghin, Secteur 9, 01 BP 534, Ouagadougou 01; tel. 25-50-34-28-35; e-mail fasoplast@fasoplast.bf; internet www.fasoplast.net; f. 1986; mfrs of plastics; Man. Dir MAMADY SANOH.

Minoterie du Faso: BP 64, Banfora; f. 2016; flour millers and mfrs of animal feed; Dir-Gen. MADANI HAMADOUM BARRY.

Société Burkinabè des Fibres Textiles (SOFITEX): 2744 ave William Ponty, 01 BP 147, Bobo-Dioulasso 01; tel. 20-97-00-24; e-mail dg@sofitex.bf; internet www.sofitex.bf; f. 1979; 36% state-owned; devt and processing of cotton and other fibrous plants; offers technical and financial support to growers; Dir-Gen. BOBOU BAYOULOU.

Société de Construction et de Gestion Immobilière du Burkina (SOCOGIB): 01 BP 1646, 01 Ouagadougou; tel. 25-50-01-97; internet www.socogib.bf; f. 1961; construction and housing management; Man. Dir EUGÈNE ZAGRÉ.

Société d'Exploitation des Phosphates du Burkina (SEPB): Ouagadougou; tel. 25-30-01-83; internet fb.com/sepbfaso; f. 2012; Pres. MAMOUDOU TRAORÉ; Dir-Gen Dr BOUNDIA ALEXANDRE THIOMBIANO.

Société des Mines de Bélahouro SA (Avocet Mining SMB): rue 22.29, Porte C01, Secteur 22, Zone du Bois, 01 BP 3422, Ouagadougou 01; tel. 25-36-04-60; gold mining; Dir-Gen. SAÏDOU IDÉ.

Société Nationale de l'Aménagement des Terres et de l'Équipement Rural (SONATER): Ouagadougou; Dir-Gen. STANISLAS BIENVENUE GOUNGOUNGA.

Société Nationale Burkinabè d'Hydrocarbures (SONABHY): 01 BP 4394, Ouagadougou 01; tel. 25-43-00-01; e-mail sonabhy.bobo@sonabhy.bf; internet www.sonabhy.bf; f. 1985; import, transport and distribution of refined hydrocarbons; state-owned; privatization proposed; Dir-Gen. ALPHA OUMAR DISSA.

Société Nationale de Gestion du Stock de Sécurité Alimentaire (SONAGESS): 01 BP 354, Ouagadougou; tel. 25-31-28-05; internet sonagess.bf; f. 1994; food security co; Pres. ALASSANE GUIRE; Dir-Gen. BÉNÉDICTA OUÉDRAOGO AKOTIONGA.

Société Nouvelle Huilerie et Savonnerie-Compagnie Industrielle du Textile et du Coton (SN-Citec): 01 BP 1300, Bobo-Dioulasso 01; tel. 20-97-25-50; e-mail sncitec@sncitec.bf; internet www.sncitec.bf; f. 1995; subsidiary of Geocoton (France); production of groundnut oil; mfrs of oil, soap, oil cake and animal feed; Man. Dir ALEXANDRE ZANNA.

Société Nouvelle Sucrière de la Comoé (SN-SOSUCO): BP 13, Banfora; tel. 20-91-81-11; e-mail sn@sn-sosuco.com; internet snsosuco.com; f. 1972; 52% owned by Groupe IPS (Côte d'Ivoire); sugar refining; Man. Dir MOUCTAR KONÉ; c. 800 employees.

TotalEnergies Burkina: 1080 ave Kwamé N'Krumah, 01 BP 21, Ouagadougou 01; tel. 25-50-50-00; e-mail total@total.bf; internet www.total.bf; petroleum distribution; fmrly Elf Oil Burkina, subsequently TotalFinaElf Burkina and Total Burkina; present name adopted 2021; Dir-Gen. JOSEPH KWAMÉ.

Vivo Energy: rond point des Nations Unies, 01 BP 569, Ouagadougou 01; tel. 25-32-76-00; internet www.vivoenergy.com; f. 1976; marketing and distribution of petroleum products; a Shell licensee and a jt venture between Vitol (40%), Helios Investment Partners (40%) and Shell (20%); Dir-Gen. MASSAMBA TOURÉ.

TRADE UNIONS

Confédération Générale du Travail Burkina (CGTB): 01 BP 547, Ouagadougou; tel. 25-31-36-71; e-mail infos@cgtburkina.org; internet cgtburkina.org; f. 1988; confed. of several autonomous trade unions; Sec.-Gen. MOUSSA DIALLO.

Confédération Nationale des Travailleurs Burkinabè (CNTB): 584 ave Kwamé N'Krumah, 01 BP 445, Ouagadougou 01; tel. 25-31-23-95; e-mail cntb@fasonet.bf; internet cntb-bf.com; f. 1945; Sec.-Gen. AUGUSTIN BLAISE HIEN.

Confédération Syndicale Burkinabè (CSB): 36 rue du Travail, 01 BP 1921, Ouagadougou 01; tel. 25-31-83-98; e-mail cosybu2000@yahoo.fr; internet csb-burkina.org; f. 1974; mainly public service unions; Sec.-Gen. GUY OLIVIER OUÉDRAOGO.

Organisation Nationale des Syndicats Libres (ONSL): 01 BP 99, Ouagadougou 01; tel. 25-34-34-69; e-mail onslbf@yahoo.fr; f. 1960; Sec.-Gen. PAUL NOBILA KABORÉ.

Syndicat National des Travailleurs de l'Agriculture (SYNATRAG): Ouagadougou; Sec.-Gen. GISLAIN KONATÉ.

Union Syndicale des Travailleurs Burkinabè (USTB): BP 381, Ouagadougou; tel. 25-33-73-09; e-mail ustb_bf@yahoo.fr; internet www.ustb-bf.com; f. 1958; Sec.-Gen. ABDOULAYE ERNEST OUÉDRAOGO.

Transport

RAILWAY

SITARAIL—Transport Ferroviaire de Personnes et de Marchandises: rue Dioncolo, 01 BP 5699, Ouagadougou 01; tel. 25-31-07-35; 67% owned by Groupe Bolloré, 15% state-owned, 15% owned by Govt of Côte d'Ivoire; national branch of SITARAIL (based in Abidjan, Côte d'Ivoire); responsible for operations on the railway line between Kaya, Ouagadougou and Abidjan; Dir-Gen. JOËL HOUNSINOU.

Société de Gestion du Patrimoine Ferroviaire du Burkina (SOPAFER—B): 97 rue de la Culture, 01 BP 192, Ouagadougou 01; tel. 25-31-35-99; e-mail sopafer-b@outlook.fr; internet fb.com/pg/sopaferb; f. 1995; railway network services; Dir-Gen. MALICK KOUANDA.

ROADS

Conseil Burkinabè des Chargeurs (CBC): Rond-point Bataille du Rail, Ouagadougou; tel. 25-30-62-11; Pres. AL HASSANE SIÉNOU; Dir-Gen. HERVÉ SÉBASTIEN ILBOUDO.

Fonds Spécial Routier du Burkina (FSR-B): 01 BP 2517, Ouagadougou 01; f. 2016 to replace Fonds d'Entretien Routier du Burkina; Dir-Gen. DAOUDA ZONGO.

Office National de la Sécurité Routière (ONASER): Ouagadougou; Dir-Gen. (vacant).

Société de Transport en Commun de Ouagadougou (SOTRACO): 2257 ave du Sanematenga, 01 BP 5665, Ouagadougou 01; tel. 25-35-67-87; internet fb.com/SOTRACOBUS; f. 2003; Dir-Gen. PASCAL TENKODOGO.

CIVIL AVIATION

There are international airports in Ouagadougou and Bobo-Dioulasso, 49 small airfields and 13 private airstrips. Plans were announced in 2006 for the construction of a new international airport at Donsin, 35 km north-east of the capital; the new airport was intended to open in 2024 and replace the existing international airport, which is located near the centre of Ouagadougou.

Air Burkina: 29 ave de la Nation, 01 BP 1459, Ouagadougou 01; tel. 25-49-23-70; e-mail resa@airburkina.bf; internet www.air-burkina .com; f. 1967 as Air Volta; 56% owned by Aga Khan Group, 14% state-owned; operates domestic and regional services; Dir-Gen. (vacant).

Tourism

Office National du Tourisme Burkinabè (ONTB): ave Frobénius, 01 BP 1311, Ouagadougou; tel. 25-31-19-59; e-mail officeburkinabe@gmail.com; internet www.ontb.bf; Dir-Gen. KISWENDSIDA MARIE AIMÉ OUÉDRAOGO.

Defence

National service is voluntary, and lasts for two years on a part-time basis. As assessed at November 2021, the armed forces numbered 11,200 (army 6,400, air force 600, gendarmerie 4,200). There was also a 'security company' of 250 and a part-time people's militia of 45,000.

Defence Budget: 254,000m. francs CFA in 2021.

Chief of the General Staff of the Armed Forces: Col-Maj. DAVID KABRÉ.

Chief of Staff of the Army: Lt-Col ADAM NÉRÉ.

Chief of Staff of the Air Force: Col SOULEYMANE OUÉDRAOGO.

Education

Education is provided free of charge, and is officially compulsory for 10 years between the ages of six and 16. Primary education begins at six years of age and lasts for six years, comprising three cycles of two years each. Secondary education, beginning at the age of 13, lasts for a further seven years, comprising a first cycle of four years and a second of three years. Enrolment levels are among the lowest in the region. According to estimates by the United Nations Educational, Scientific and Cultural Organization (UNESCO), in 2019/20 enrolment at pre-primary level was equivalent to 6% of children in the relevant age-group (males 6%; females 6%). In 2018/19 primary enrolment included 78% of children in the relevant age-group (males 79%; females 78%), while secondary enrolment was equivalent to 41% of children in the appropriate age-group (boys 41%; girls 42%). In 2018 public spending on education was estimated at 22.7% of total budgeted government expenditure.

Bibliography

Asche, H. *Le Burkina Faso contemporain: L'expérience d'un auto-développement*. Paris, L'Harmattan, 2000.

Badolo, C. *Politique et mercatique au Burkina Faso*. Paris, L'Harmattan, 2013.

Balima, S. T. *Medias et démocratie au Burkina Faso*. Dakar, CODESRIA, 2012.

Balima, S. T., and Frère, M.-S. *Médias et Communications sociales au Burkina Faso: Approche socio-économique de la circulation de l'information*. Paris, L'Harmattan, 2003.

Bila Kaboré, R. *Histoire politique du Burkina Faso 1919–2000*. Paris, L'Harmattan, 2002.

Burton, J.-D. *Nabaas: Traditional Chiefs of Burkina Faso*. Leuven, Snoeck-Ducaji & Zoon, 2006.

Dafinger, A. *The Economics of Ethnic Conflict: The Case of Burkina Faso*. Oxford, James Currey, 2013.

Engberg-Pedersen, L., *Endangering Development: Politics, Projects and Environment in Burkina Faso*. Westport, CT, Praeger, 2003.

Korbéogo, G. *Pouvoir et accès aux ressources naturelles au Burkina Faso: la topographie du pouvoir*. Paris, L'Harmattan, 2013.

Guion, J. R. *Blaise Compaoré: Réalisme et intégrité*. Paris, Mondes en devenir, 1991.

Guirma, F. *Comment perdre le pouvoir?: Le cas de Maurice Yaméogo*. Paris, Chaka, 1991.

Guissou, B. *Burkina Faso, un espoir en Afrique*. Paris, L'Harmattan, 1995.

Harsch, E. *Thomas Sankara: An African Revolutionary*. Athens, OH, Ohio University Press, 2014.

     Burkina Faso: A History of Power, Protest, and Revolution. London, Zed Books, 2017.

Kongo, J.-C., and Zeilig, L. *Thomas Sankara: Voices of Liberation*. Pretoria, HSRC Press, 2016.

Kuba, R., Lentz, C., and Nurukyor Somda, C. *Histoire du peuplement et relations interethniques au Burkina Faso.* Paris, Éditions Karthala, 2004.

Madiega, G., and Nao, O. (Eds). *Burkina Faso: Cent ans d'histoire, 1895–1995.* 2 vols, Paris, Editions Karthala, 2003.

Massa, G., and Madiéga, Y. G. (Eds). *La Haute-Volta coloniale: témoignages, recherches.* Paris, Editions Karthala, 1995.

McFarland, D. M., and Rupley, L. A. *Historical Dictionary of Burkina Faso.* 2nd edn. Lanham, MD, Scarecrow Press, 1998.

Obinwa Nnaji, B. *Blaise Compaoré: The Architect of Burkina Faso Revolution.* Ibadan, Spectrum Books, 1989.

Ouédraogo, B. N. *Droit, démocratie et développement en Afrique: Un parfum de jasmin souffle sur le Burkina Faso.* Paris, L'Harmattan, 2014.

Sankara, T. *Thomas Sankara Speaks: The Burkina Faso Revolution 1983–87.* Havana, Editora Politica, 2007.

Savadogo, K., and Wetta, C. *The Impact of Self-Imposed Adjustment: The Case of Burkina Faso 1983–1989.* Florence, Spedale degli Innocenti, 1991.

Sawadogo, A. Y. *Le Président Thomas Sankara, chef de la revolution Burkinabè 1983–1987: portrait.* Paris, L'Harmattan, 2001.

Souyris, B. *Oppression coloniale et résistance en Haute-Volta: L'exemple de la région de la Boucle du Mouhoun, 1885–1935.* Paris, L'Harmattan, 2014.

Zagre, A. *L'Église-famille de Dieu face à la société contemporaine en mutation au Burkina Faso.* Paris, L'Harmattan, 2013.

BURUNDI

Physical and Social Geography

The Republic of Burundi, like its neighbour Rwanda, is exceptionally small in area, comprising 27,834 sq km (10,747 sq miles), but with a relatively large population of an estimated 12,624,845 at mid-2022, according to a projection by the United Nations. The result is a high population density, of an estimated 453.6 persons per sq km at mid-2022. The principal towns are the capital, Bujumbura (with a population of an estimated 1.1m. at mid-2022), and Gitega.

Burundi is bordered by Rwanda to the north, by the Democratic Republic of the Congo (DRC) to the west, and by Tanzania to the south and east. The natural divide between Burundi and the DRC is formed by Lake Tanganyika and the Ruzizi river on the floor of the western rift-valley system. To the east, the land rises sharply to elevations of around 1,800 m above sea level in a range that stretches north into the much higher, and volcanic, mountains of Rwanda. Away from the edge of the rift valley, elevations are lower, and most of Burundi consists of plateaux of 1,400 m–1,800 m. Here the average temperature is 20°C and annual rainfall 1,200 mm. In the valley the temperature averages 23°C, while rainfall is much lower, at an average of 750 mm per year.

Population has concentrated on the fertile, volcanic soils at 1,500 m–1,800 m above sea level, away from the arid and hot floor and margins of the rift valley. The consequent pressure on the land, together with recurrent outbreaks of violent internal unrest, has resulted in extensive migration, mainly to Tanzania, the DRC and Uganda. The ethnic composition of the population is much the same as that of Rwanda: about 85% Hutu, 14% Tutsi and less than 1% Twa, pygmoid hunters. Historically, the kingdoms of Urundi and Ruanda had a strong adversarial tradition, and rivalry between the successor republics remains intense. There are three official languages: Kirundi (the national language, spoken by the vast majority of the population), French and English (which became the third official language in 2014). Swahili is widely spoken in the Great Lakes region and is especially used in commerce. According to the 2008 census, some 86% of the population professed Christianity, with the majority of these being Roman Catholics.

History

DEVON E. A. CURTIS

At the time of its absorption into German East Africa in 1898–99, most of the territory that now comprises Burundi and Rwanda had already been incorporated into two kingdoms. The kingship in Burundi was the focus of popular loyalties and also the site of factional struggles. In 1916 Belgium occupied Ruanda-Urundi (the League of Nations-mandated territory encompassing Rwanda and Burundi) and continued the system of 'indirect rule' operated by the German authorities. The policy had a large impact, as an ethnic minority, the Tutsi (comprising 14% of the population, according to an unreliable colonial census), had by then established dominance over the majority Hutu (85%) and a hunter-gatherer group, the Twa (1%). However, the potential for conflict between Hutu and Tutsi in Burundi was contained by the existence of the *ganwa*, a princely class whose clans comprised both ethnic groups.

Rivalry within the *ganwa* was intense, especially from the mid-19th century between two clans, the Batare (sons of Ntare) and the Bezi (sons of the Mwezi). Reluctantly, in order to meet demands stipulated by a United Nations (UN) Trusteeship Council after 1948, the Belgian administration moved towards democratization. Two main political parties came to the fore. The Union pour le Progrès National (UPRONA), led by Prince Louis Rwagasore (a Bezi *ganwa* and eldest son of the *mwami*—king), was a progressive nationalist movement, with widespread support. The rival Parti Démocrate Chrétien (PDC), dominated by Batare *ganwa*, was more conservative, seeking internal reforms to improve Batare status relative to the Bezi before independence. Concerned about Prince Rwagasore's nationalism, the Belgian administration strongly favoured the PDC.

At legislative elections held in September 1961, prior to the granting of internal self-government in January 1962, UPRONA won 58 of the 64 seats in the new Assemblée Nationale (National Assembly). Rwagasore became Prime Minister, but was assassinated in October 1961 by a Greek agent of the PDC, reportedly with Belgian assistance. Rwagasore's assassination proved a crucial event in the history of Burundi; the absence of his unifying influence led to the division of UPRONA and fostered increased polarization and open conflict between Hutu and Tutsi.

Throughout the colonial period and especially in the lead-up to independence, ethnic identities had become ever more inflexible, and other social identities had become less central. The *ganwa* increasingly came to be seen as part of the Tutsi group.

PRESIDENTS MICOMBERO AND BAGAZA

UPRONA proved unable to contain the ethnic tensions that followed independence on 1 July 1962. The revolution in 1959 in neighbouring Rwanda, where Hutu overthrew the Rwandan monarchy, had a significant impact in Burundi. The Rwandan revolution led to thousands of Rwandan Tutsi refugees fleeing to Burundi and other neighbouring countries, thereby strengthening ethnic identities and animosities. While UPRONA support was ethnically mixed, the party's youth wing, the Jeunesse Nationaliste Rwagasore, was an urban-based, anti-Western, Tutsi movement.

Ethnic tensions worsened when Hutu Prime Minister Pierre Ngendandumwe was assassinated in January 1965 by a Tutsi refugee. Hutu candidates won a decisive victory in parliamentary elections in May, but the *mwami*, Mwambutsa IV, appointed a *ganwa* with Bezi origins as the new Prime Minister. Incensed, in October a faction of the Hutu-dominated gendarmerie attempted a coup. Tutsi armed forces retaliated by arresting and killing a large part of the Hutu political establishment in Bujumbura and thousands of rural Hutu who had supported the revolt. The *mwami* fled to Zaire (now the Democratic Republic of the Congo—DRC).

In July 1966 Mwambutsa's son formally acceded to the throne as Ntare V. He appointed Capt. (later Lt-Gen.) Michel Micombero as Prime Minister, but there were increasing confrontations between the monarchy and the Government, army and bureaucracy. In November Ntare was removed from power by Micombero, who declared Burundi a republic and himself President.

President Micombero attempted to project a revolutionary image, but relied upon his own ethno-regional group—Tutsi from Bururi province—for support. This led to the intensification of Hutu–Tutsi tensions, as Tutsi from Bururi accused Tutsi moderates from the north (especially from Muramvya) of being sympathetic to the monarchy and Hutu interests. Many Hutu officers were purged from the army. In April 1972 Hutu soldiers led an abortive coup, which degenerated into indiscriminate killings of Tutsi in Bujumbura and Cankuzo. Martial law was proclaimed, and the Tutsi military retaliated with genocidal massacres of unprecedented size and brutality. An estimated 100,000–200,000 Hutu were killed, and up to 200,000 fled Burundi. Nearly all Hutu elements were eliminated from the armed forces, government and the country's university.

In November 1976 Col Jean-Baptiste Bagaza, a Tutsi Hima from Bururi, seized power from Micombero in a bloodless coup. Although the army remained the dominant force in Burundi's politics, the first legislative elections under universal adult suffrage were held in October 1982, and in August 1984 Bagaza, the sole candidate, was elected head of state.

However, authoritarian rule and ethnic discrimination continued, with Tutsi controlling political, military and economic structures. By the mid-1980s the Government had imposed several restrictions on Catholic and Protestant churches, including the abolition of catechism schools, which deprived many (mostly Hutu) students of educational opportunities. The crisis in church-state relations resulted in many donor countries withholding development aid. Critics of the Government complained about corruption and arbitrary arrests, and some army officers were forced into early retirement.

THE BUYOYA REGIME, 1987–93

In September 1987 Bagaza was deposed by an army-led coup instigated by Maj. Pierre Buyoya (another Tutsi Hima from Bururi province). Buyoya accused Bagaza of corruption and formed a 31-member ruling Conseil Militaire pour le Salut National (CMSN—Military Committee for National Salvation). UPRONA was dissolved, and the 1981 Constitution was suspended. Buyoya's regime was more tolerant of religious freedom, many of the restrictions on the church were lifted, and there was increased political liberalization.

Hutu–Tutsi Tensions

However, ethnic tensions remained high. In August 1988 groups of Hutu, claiming Tutsi provocation, slaughtered hundreds of Tutsi in the northern communes of Ntega and Marangara. The army retaliated, killing an estimated 15,000–20,000 Hutu. Approximately 60,000 Hutu refugees fled to Rwanda. President Buyoya subsequently introduced a number of political reforms, including bringing several Hutu into his cabinet to achieve an equal number of Hutu and Tutsi in government. He appointed Adrien Sibomana, a Hutu, as Prime Minister.

Hardliners on both sides were alarmed by these reforms. In March 1989 there was an attempted coup by hardline Tutsi activists and Bagaza supporters. Following the publication of the report of the national unity commission in April, Buyoya announced plans to combat discrimination against Hutus. In March 1992 there was another attempted coup against Buyoya and violent disturbances along the border with Rwanda, blamed by the Government on the Parti de Libération du Peuple Hutu (PALIPEHUTU)—a Hutu militant movement, which had been formed in a Tanzanian refugee camp in 1980. In the early 1990s many Hutu refugees, including some PALIPEHUTU activists, returned to Burundi from Tanzania and Rwanda.

Multi-party Democratic Elections

Buyoya pressed on with political reform, with the support of international donors. A draft charter was produced in April 1990, which was submitted to extensive national debate. Public discussion, however, was closely directed and monitored by the re-established UPRONA and failed to satisfy opposition groups. UPRONA dissolved the CMSN in December and transferred its functions to an 80-member central committee of UPRONA, with a Hutu, Nicolas Mayugi, as its Secretary-General. The Charter of Unity was adopted by national referendum in February 1991, giving a mandate to the Government to draft a new constitution.

A referendum held in March 1992 resulted in a vote of 90% in support of the proposed new Constitution, which was

promulgated on 13 March. The Constitution included the principles of the separation of powers, human rights protection and multi-partyism. By October eight political parties had been recognized, including the Front pour la Démocratie au Burundi (FRODEBU).

In the presidential poll, conducted on 1 June 1993, Melchior Ndadaye, the FRODEBU candidate, won with 64.8% of votes cast, supported by the Rassemblement du Peuple Burundien (RPB), the Parti du Peuple (PP) and the Parti Libéral, defeating Buyoya, the UPRONA candidate, with support from the Rassemblement pour la Démocratie et le Développement Economique et Social and the Parti Social Démocrate.

Elections to the new National Assembly were held on 29 June 1993. FRODEBU won 71% of the votes cast and 65 of the 81 seats in the new legislature. UPRONA, with 21.4%, secured the remaining 16 seats. On 10 July Ndadaye became Burundi's first Hutu President. The elections were widely hailed by the international donor community as an example of a successful transition to democracy.

THE NEW GOVERNMENT AND ETHNIC UNREST

Ndadaye appointed an inclusive 23-member cabinet, naming only 13 FRODEBU ministers. The new Prime Minister, Sylvie Kinigi of UPRONA, was one of nine Tutsi. However, many provincial governors and senior civil servants were replaced by Hutu FRODEBU supporters, and some Tutsi military officers were concerned about possible army reform that would diminish Tutsi dominance.

On 21 October 1993 more than 100 army paratroopers occupied the presidential palace and the headquarters of the national broadcasting company. The insurgents detained and killed several prominent Hutu politicians and officials, including President Ndadaye and the parliamentary Speaker, Gilles Bimazubute. An estimated 50,000 people were killed in the ensuing inter-ethnic violence. François Ngeze, one of the only senior Hutu members of UPRONA and a minister in the former Buyoya administration, was proclaimed as head of a Comité National de Salut Public (CNSP—National Committee of Public Salvation). International condemnation of the coup undermined support for the insurgents from within the armed forces and precipitated the collapse of the CNSP, which was disbanded on 25 October. On 28 October the FRODEBU Government regained control. Ngeze and 10 coup leaders were arrested, and at least 40 other insurgents fled. In December a commission of judicial inquiry was established to investigate the insurgency.

The immediate challenge was to restore security and prevent further political and institutional uncertainty. Negotiations took place between a coalition of predominantly Hutu parties led by FRODEBU—the Forces du Changement Democratique (FCD)—and the predominantly Tutsi Coalition des Partis Politiques de l'Opposition (CPPO) led by UPRONA. In January 1994 FRODEBU deputies in the National Assembly approved a draft amendment to the Constitution, enabling the President to be elected by the legislature. The National Assembly duly elected the former Minister of Agriculture, Cyprien Ntaryamira, as President; he assumed office on 5 February. Anatole Kanyenkiko of UPRONA was appointed Prime Minister, and a new multi-party cabinet was formed in mid-February.

In February 1994 an international commission of inquiry, established by several human rights organizations, concluded that some members of the armed forces had been involved in or had supported the October 1993 coup attempt. Clashes between the army and Hutu militias exacerbated divisions between FRODEBU's moderate faction, led by Ntaryamira (who supported the forced disarmament of Hutu and Tutsi militia groups), and Léonard Nyangoma's hardline faction, which opposed further military action against Hutu militias.

POLITICAL MANOEUVRES AND COALITION GOVERNMENT

On 6 April 1994 President Ntaryamira and two of his government ministers were returning from a regional summit meeting in Dar es Salaam, Tanzania, with Rwandan President Juvénal Habyarimana. In an attack on Habyarimana, the plane was shot down by a missile as it approached the airport in Kigali, the Rwandan capital, killing all those on board. Sylvestre Ntibantunganya of FRODEBU was confirmed as interim national President on 8 April for a three-month period, after which a presidential election would be held. The downing of the aircraft precipitated a genocide in Rwanda, in which an estimated 800,000 Tutsi were killed, together with moderate Hutu and political opponents, further enflaming intercommunal fears and tensions in Burundi.

Hardliners in Burundi gained strength and visibility. In May 1994 a former FRODEBU cabinet member, Nyangoma, left the Government and established a new party, the Conseil National pour la Défense de la Démocratie (CNDD), with an armed wing, the Forces pour la Défense de la Démocratie (FDD). The CNDD aimed to take back power through force. Meanwhile, UPRONA elected as its new leader a Hutu hardliner, Charles Mukasi, who was none the less radically opposed to FRODEBU and other Hutu political parties, which he accused of perpetrating genocide.

In June 1994 the major political parties engaged in UN-sponsored negotiations to restore an elected presidency. A new power-sharing agreement, the Convention of Government, was announced in September. It was agreed that a coalition government would be established with 55% of ministers from the FCD (the predominantly Hutu parties) and 45% from the CPPO (the predominantly Tutsi parties). The Convention also provided for the creation of a National Security Council (inaugurated on 10 October) to address the security crisis. Ntibantunganya was sworn in as President on 1 October. Kanyenkiko was reappointed as Prime Minister on 3 October, and two days later a coalition Government was formed.

The Convention of Government did not satisfy all political movements. Nyangoma's CNDD and another Hutu rebel movement, PALIPEHUTU—FNL (Forces Nationales de Libération), began to recruit Hutu fighters. Ethnic tensions in Burundi were aggravated by the arrival of an estimated 200,000 Rwandan Hutu refugees fleeing the advancing Rwandan Patriotic Front in the Rwandan civil war and genocide.

In February 1995 Prime Minister Kanyenkiko was forced out of UPRONA, having failed to support the party's temporary withdrawal from the Government in protest against the appointment of FRODEBU's Jean Minani as Speaker of the National Assembly. Many UPRONA members alleged that Minani had incited genocide against Tutsi in 1993. Kanyenkiko was replaced as Prime Minister on 1 March by Antoine Nduwayo, a hardline UPRONA member.

ETHNIC CONFRONTATION

In February 1996 UN Secretary-General Boutros Boutros-Ghali reiterated a request to the UN Security Council to authorize the intervention of a peacekeeping force in Burundi, following publication of a UN report that concluded that a state of near civil war existed in many areas of the country. However, the Government (and Tutsi political opinion) remained fiercely opposed to a foreign military presence and persuaded the Security Council that a negotiated settlement to the conflict was possible.

At a conference of regional heads of state in Arusha, Tanzania, in June 1996, Nduwayo and President Ntibantunganya (following pressure from former Tanzanian President Julius Nyerere) requested a regional peacekeeping force to calm the situation in Burundi. However, there were fundamental differences regarding the purpose and mandate of the intervention force, with Nduwayo accusing the President of attempting to neutralize the country's military capability. At a mass rally of Tutsi-dominated opposition parties, organized in the capital on 5 July, Nduwayo joined other political leaders in rejecting foreign military intervention and denouncing Ntibantunganya. Some days later, however, member states of the Organization of African Unity (now the African Union, AU) endorsed the Arusha proposal for intervention at a summit meeting in Yaoundé, Cameroon.

Tensions intensified following reports of a massacre of more than 300 Tutsi civilians at Bugendana, allegedly committed by Hutu rebels, including heavily armed Rwandan Hutu refugees. FRODEBU made an urgent appeal for foreign military intervention to contain the increasingly violent civil and military reaction to these events. On 23 July 1996 Ntibantunganya was forced to abandon an attempt to attend the funeral of the victims of the Bugendana massacre, following attacks on his presidential helicopter. The next day, Ntibantunganya sought refuge in the residence of the US ambassador. Several government ministers and the Speaker of the National Assembly took refuge in the German embassy.

THE RETURN OF BUYOYA

With the FRODEBU members of government in hiding, the armed forces seized power on 25 July 1996, declaring Buyoya as the interim President of a 'transitional' republic. Ntibantunganya refused to relinquish office, but Nduwayo immediately resigned. Buyoya announced that a largely civilian, broad-based government of national unity would be installed, and that future negotiations with all Hutu groups would be considered. Echoing his political strategy of the early 1990s, Buyoya appointed Pascal-Firmin Ndimira, a Hutu member of UPRONA, as Prime Minister.

The military coup was condemned internationally. A summit of regional heads of state, convened in Arusha on 31 July 1996, declared its intention to impose economic sanctions against the new regime, with the aim of pushing Buyoya to restore the 1993 constitutional order. The summit also affirmed the support of regional leaders for Nyerere to serve as facilitator for Burundi. Regional leaders specified three conditions for the lifting of sanctions: the unbanning of political parties, the restoration of the suspended National Assembly and the start of unconditional negotiations with all political parties and armed groups. In early August 1996 Buyoya appointed a new multi-ethnic cabinet and, shortly afterwards, an expanded transitional National Assembly with limited powers. However, party political activity remained banned.

In September 1996 some powers of the National Assembly were restored, although not including its authority to dismiss the Government. Exiled deputies were invited to return to Burundi. In the same month the Regional Sanctions Coordinating Committee eased restrictions on the importation of emergency relief supplies. In December discussions were held in Arusha, when Nyerere unsuccessfully sought to bring together the Government, FRODEBU, the CNDD and UPRONA. A meeting of regional heads of state also took place, at which it was agreed to retain economic sanctions until the opening of negotiations between the Government and Hutu rebel movements. In August 1997 at a meeting in Kampala, Uganda, regional foreign ministers decided to maintain the embargo on Burundi; the Government subsequently withdrew from all-party talks organized by Nyerere.

By the end of 1997 national courts had imposed 220 death sentences on Hutu found guilty of committing genocide in 1993. Verdicts in the trial of the Tutsi accused of involvement in the 1993 coup attempt and of assassinating President Ndadaye and six others were delivered in May 1999. Five members of the armed forces were sentenced to death, and several other defendants received prison terms. Hutu political parties complained that all the senior officers implicated in the coup attempt were acquitted.

THE ARUSHA NEGOTIATIONS

On 6 June 1998 the transitional Constitution, which combined elements of the 1992 Constitution and the 1996 decree adopted by Buyoya after the July coup, was promulgated. Under this Constitution, the National Assembly was expanded to include many of the smaller (mainly Tutsi) parties, the size of the Council of Ministers was reduced, and two vice-presidential posts were created. On 11 June 1998 Buyoya was sworn in as head of state, and two days later a new cabinet was announced. Later in that month all-party negotiations began in Arusha.

The launch of comprehensive negotiations represented significant progress, but several major internal divisions among political groupings remained. In October 1998 Mukasi was replaced as UPRONA President by Luc Rukingama, a Buyoya loyalist. Hutu political space was similarly fragmented. There was dissent between supporters of internal FRODEBU leaders and supporters of exiled members such as FRODEBU

Chairman Minani (in Tanzania). There were also divisions between the military and political wings of the Hutu rebel movements. The CNDD had split in May, leaving Nyangoma in charge of one faction (which retained the name CNDD), while the FDD Chief of Staff, Jean-Bosco Ndayikengurukiye, assumed leadership of the larger part of the party, including most of its armed forces, which became known as the CNDD—FDD.

At the onset of the war in the DRC in August 1998, the regional sponsors of the Burundian peace process faced multiple cross-pressures and competing interests. Rwanda and Uganda strongly supported the regional initiative and had previously been critical of Buyoya. However, the Burundian CNDD—FDD rebels joined an alliance of convenience with Laurent-Désiré Kabila's forces, supporting Congolese government troops in Sud-Kivu and Katanga. Rwanda and Uganda were on the other side, against the Rwandan and Burundian Hutu insurgencies in the DRC. Burundi became more directly involved in co-ordinating its military effort in the DRC with Rwanda and Uganda. Meanwhile, the CNDD—FDD and PALIPEHUTU—FNL continued attacks throughout 1998 and early 1999 against camps for the internally displaced in Burundi.

The Arusha negotiations continued intermittently over the next two years, with several impediments. Principally, the two active Hutu rebel movements declined to participate. Nyangoma's faction of the CNDD attended, but Ndayikengurukiye's faction rejected his leadership and continued to fight. PALIPEHUTU—FNL had also split, and those in Arusha had no control over the remaining fighters. Furthermore, Nyerere initially insisted on maintaining the regional sanctions, which contributed to the mistrust of many Tutsi towards Tanzania. The sanctions were suspended in January 1999.

In March 1999 FRODEBU Secretary-General Augustin Nzojibwami suspended former President Ntibantunganya and other senior members from the party's executive committee, for alleged ethnicism and ill-discipline. In response, Minani ordered Nzojibwami's expulsion from the party. However, Nzojibwami refused to recognize his expulsion, and by June two factions had developed within FRODEBU, centred around Minani (the external wing) and Nzojibwami (the internal wing).

Strongly encouraged by Nyerere, in early May 1999 seven predominantly Hutu parties, including the CNDD and the external wing of FRODEBU, met in Moshi, Tanzania, to negotiate a common position. The parties assumed a joint stance on most issues and eventually became known as G7. The predominantly Tutsi parties responded by forming a negotiating bloc (known initially as G8 and later as G10). At the end of May Buyoya proposed a 10-year political transition, including plans for the establishment of an upper legislative chamber, the Sénat (Senate), and the enlargement of the National Assembly. Buyoya proposed that he rule for five years and a FRODEBU representative for the remaining five years. The proposals were rejected by all externally based political forces.

By August 1999 the all-party Arusha negotiations were stalled. Political tensions inside Burundi escalated, owing to the weakening of the internal partnership, an army massacre of Hutu civilians and continued rebel attacks targeting Tutsi. Nyerere's death in October resulted in the suspension of the Arusha process, and fighting intensified.

MANDELA BECOMES MEDIATOR

Buyoya requested in August 1999 that South Africa play an active role in the peace process. In December regional heads of state, meeting in Arusha, unanimously selected former South African President Nelson Mandela as the new mediator for the peace process. Nyerere's facilitation team, led by Tanzanians, would remain to support Mandela.

At the Arusha discussions in February 2000, Mandela spoke of the need to end Tutsi domination but also the need for the majority Hutu to reassure minority groups. On several occasions, Mandela invited the CNDD—FDD and PALIPEHUTU—FNL to South Africa to meet him, but both groups continued to denounce the Arusha negotiations. The CNDD—FDD leader, Ndayikengurukiye, travelled to Arusha in July,

but refused to be associated with the drawing up of an accord. PALIPEHUTU—FNL maintained its boycott. Consequently, the eventual draft accord did not include a ceasefire.

At the July 2000 gathering in Arusha of regional leaders and Burundian delegations, Mandela circulated the draft of the proposed peace agreement prepared by the facilitation team. He announced that the signing ceremony would be held in Arusha in August. However, several power-sharing issues remained contentious, and many details on the reform and integration of the Burundian army were unresolved.

THE ARUSHA AGREEMENT

To increase pressure on the parties, Mandela invited heads of state, including the US President, Bill Clinton, and other senior international politicians to attend a further Arusha negotiating round in August 2000. The round culminated on 28 August with the signing of the accord by the Government and all but three small Tutsi parties (which signed in September). The agreement included arrangements for a pre-transitional, and then transitional, period, which would be followed by democratic elections, the creation of a Senate and changes to the National Assembly, judicial reform, the establishment of an international force to assist during the transition and an independent investigation into alleged crimes of genocide.

The agreement did not, however, resolve the contentious issue of transitional leadership. After pressure from Mandela and direct talks between FRODEBU and UPRONA, it was decided in February 2001 that the transitional period would be divided into two parts. The first part would be under the leadership of a Tutsi President and the second under a Hutu President. However, there was still no agreement on who the President would be. In July Mandela convened a regional summit meeting in Arusha, announcing two days later that Buyoya would remain as President for 18 months and would be replaced by a Hutu head of state for the following 18 months.

The CNDD—FDD and PALIPEHUTU—FNL rejected the Arusha accord, and the war subsequently intensified. Ndayikengurukiye declined to attend a meeting arranged by Mandela in Nairobi, Kenya, in September 2000 between the rebel leadership, the Government and regional heads of state. The PALIPEHUTU—FNL leader, Kossan Kabura, was present, but refused to engage in discussions with Buyoya. South Africa's Deputy President, Jacob Zuma, subsequently assumed responsibility for negotiations between the armed rebel movements and the Burundian Government. Internal divisions within the rebel movements contributed to difficulties in negotiating a ceasefire. In February 2001 a political committee within PALIPEHUTU—FNL announced that it had deposed Kabura and installed Agathon Rwasa in his place. Kabura insisted, however, that he remained the leader of PALIPEHUTU—FNL. In October the CNDD—FDD split, with a new faction led by Pierre Nkurunziza receiving the support of almost all combatants.

THE TRANSITIONAL GOVERNMENT

In October 2001 Mandela announced that a South African protection force would be deployed in Burundi to protect politicians returning from exile so that they could participate in the transitional Government. The 700-member South African protection force was deployed later in October, and, under the terms of the August 2000 agreement, a new 26-member transitional Government was installed in November 2001. Buyoya remained as President, while the Secretary-General of FRODEBU, Domitien Ndayizeye, became Vice-President. The cabinet included members from all the signatory parties to the Arusha agreement but was dominated by UPRONA and FRODEBU.

The new transitional National Assembly was inaugurated on 4 January 2002. In addition to 121 deputies from the previous legislature, 57 new representatives had been nominated, most of them by parties that had signed the Arusha agreement. FRODEBU was the largest party in the National Assembly, and Minani, its Chairman, was elected President (Speaker) on 10 January. In February the transitional Senate commenced operations, with Libère Bararunyeretse, a close associate of Buyoya and a senior UPRONA negotiator in Arusha, as its President.

Progress towards a ceasefire was slow. Peace negotiations, convened in Dar es Salaam in August 2002, were boycotted by Rwasa, but attended for the first time by a newly emerged minority faction of PALIPEHUTU—FNL, led by Alain Mugabarabona. In October Mugabarabona's faction signed a ceasefire agreement with the Government, although it was unclear whether Mugabarabona actually commanded any forces. (PALIPEHUTU—FNL forces under Rwasa's faction continued to fight.) Ndayikengurukiye's faction of the CNDD—FDD signed a memorandum of understanding, which later resulted in a ceasefire agreement. However, there was heavy fighting between government forces and CNDD—FDD combatants. Further discussions between the Government and Nkurunziza, beginning in Dar es Salaam on 26 October, also failed to broker a truce.

In December 2002 Nkurunziza and Buyoya attended a summit of regional heads of state on Burundi, which resulted in the signing of a long-awaited ceasefire agreement with the larger faction of the CNDD—FDD. Buyoya and Nkurunziza met in Pretoria, South Africa, in January 2003 to discuss the implementation of the ceasefire and agreed that CNDD—FDD combatants should assemble in camps in Bubanza and Ruyigi provinces. This agreement immediately exacerbated the conflict in both provinces, however, as the CNDD—FDD intensified its efforts to capture territory, and the armed forces fought to retain it. Regional heads of state, Buyoya and the CNDD—FDD's Secretary-General, Hussein Radjabu, met in Dar es Salaam in March. Buyoya and Radjabu reiterated their commitment to the ceasefire agreement, but the fighting between their forces continued unabated.

NDAYIZEYE SECURES AGREEMENT WITH THE CNDD—FDD

On 30 April 2003, at the transitional period's halfway mark, the presidency was transferred from Buyoya to FRODEBU's Ndayizeye, with UPRONA's Alphonse Kadege serving as Vice-President. In accordance with the December 2002 ceasefire agreement, the African Union Mission in Burundi (AMIB) commenced deployment in May. Meanwhile, in April 2003 the National Assembly adopted a bill providing for the establishment of an international judicial commission of inquiry into war crimes committed since mid-1962.

Ndayizeye and Nkurunziza signed a power-sharing agreement in Pretoria on 8 October 2003. According to the agreement, the CNDD—FDD would abandon hostilities and assemble its combatants into camps, in return for substantial representation in the Government and the armed forces. In late October the CNDD—FDD secured a promise of immunity from prosecution for its combatants. This immunity was extended to members of the armed forces. Tutsi parties and some international human rights groups denounced the granting of immunity for crimes against humanity.

Nkurunziza's CNDD—FDD officially ended hostilities on 10 November 2003, and fighting ceased soon after throughout most of Burundi. On 16 November the Global Ceasefire Agreement was signed at a summit of regional heads of state in Dar es Salaam, and on 23 November Ndayizeye established a new Government of National Unity, incorporating CNDD—FDD representatives. Nkurunziza was appointed to the newly created post of Minister of State for Good Governance and State Inspection.

In January 2004 Ndayizeye appointed a new Joint Military High Command, comprising 21 members selected from the armed forces and 13 from Nkurunziza's faction of the CNDD—FDD, to be followed by the establishment of new and reconstituted armed forces, the Force de Défense Nationale du Burundi (FDNB).

THE ROAD TO ELECTIONS

During February–March 2004 Ndayizeye failed to secure agreement with other parties in the Government on key unresolved issues, including the content of a new draft constitution and electoral code, and pushed for a delay in holding the elections. In April the CNDD—FDD withdrew from the Government, claiming that Ndayizeye was not respecting the agreement.

Ndayizeye presented a new draft electoral timetable in May 2004, postponing for a year the presidential poll, which was originally scheduled for October. The CNDD—FDD rejected the proposed extension, but the predominantly Tutsi parties supported it. A summit of regional heads of state in Dar es Salaam in June ruled that elections must proceed according to the original schedule. Despite renewed contact between PALIPEHUTU—FNL and Zuma just before the summit, the heads of state condemned the rebel movement for remaining outside the peace process and imposed sanctions on its leadership.

In May 2004 the UN Security Council approved the replacement of the AMIB mission with a UN contingent, the UN Operation in Burundi (ONUB), which officially commenced deployment on 1 June for an initial six-month period. ONUB was to have a maximum strength of 5,650 troops.

The main Hutu parties finally signed a draft power-sharing accord on 6 August 2004, but it was rejected by the predominantly Tutsi parties. There was broad agreement that the Government and National Assembly should have 60% Hutu and 40% Tutsi representation. However, the Tutsi parties insisted that the quotas be reserved for Tutsi politicians belonging to predominantly Tutsi parties, whereas the Hutu parties pushed for ethnically inclusive political parties and quotas on the basis of ethnicity (not political parties). The South African Government supported the Hutu position, and in the end this was adopted.

On 13 August 2004 PALIPEHUTU—FNL, allegedly with the support of Rwandan Hutu militia and elements within the DRC's armed forces, massacred 152 Congolese Banyamulenge refugees at the Gatumba refugee camp near Bujumbura, despite a significant military presence nearby. One faction of the DRC Government temporarily suspended its participation in the Congolese political transition, and the Rwandan Government threatened to reinvade the DRC if the perpetrators were not penalized. Many of the Banyamulenge refugees subsequently fled to refugee camps in Rwanda. Talks between PALIPEHUTU—FNL and Ndayizeye were suspended.

Ndayizeye called an extraordinary joint session of the National Assembly and Senate in September 2004 to ratify the draft constitution. Hutu delegates approved the draft document, but Tutsis boycotted the session, owing to disagreements regarding the text. The Constitutional Court declined to conduct a scheduled hearing to endorse the text, declaring that its role was to interpret the Constitution, not rule on its legality. Insisting that this implied the Court's endorsement of the text, Ndayizeye announced that a referendum on the proposed constitution would be conducted on 20 October, which was later postponed. As the interim Constitution was due to expire on 1 November, the regional heads of state decided that the disputed draft constitution would replace the transitional charter. In addition, the regional heads of state recommended that Ndayizeye's mandate, which was also due to expire, be extended until April 2005, which became the new scheduled date for national elections.

NKURUNZIZA, THE CONSTITUTION AND THE CNDD—FDD'S ELECTORAL TRIUMPH

In mid-November 2004 Ndayizeye dismissed Vice-President Kadege, owing to his alleged obstruction of government policy. He was replaced by another Tutsi member of UPRONA, Frédéric Ngenzebuhoro. The long-awaited demobilization programme began in December. Approximately 55,000 combatants from Hutu rebel movements and the mainly Tutsi existing armed forces were to be demobilized within five years, leaving around 30,000 combatants to form the new FDNB, which was formally established on 31 December.

The constitutional referendum finally took place on 28 February 2005, with some 92% of votes cast (on a turnout of around 88% of the electorate) endorsing the new Constitution. Ndayizeye signed the Constitution into law on 19 March, thereby enabling legislative elections to proceed. PALIPEHUTU—FNL observed a truce during the referendum period and in

April declared that it was prepared to negotiate with the Government.

The new Constitution was based upon principles of ethnic power-sharing, as elaborated in the Arusha agreement. The President would be assisted by two Vice-Presidents, belonging to different ethnic groups and different political parties. The Government was to include 60% Hutu and 40% Tutsi, and 30% of its members must be women. Political parties should not be established on the basis of ethnic or regional exclusivity. Parties that obtained at least 5% of the votes in parliamentary elections could participate in a coalition government. According to the Arusha agreement and the new Constitution, the Senate would comprise two delegates from each province of different ethnicities, indirectly elected by the communal councils. The Senate would include three members of the Twa ethnic group, by co-option if necessary.

The Arusha agreement and Constitution also applied power-sharing principles to other levels. Not more than 67% of communal administrators should belong to the same ethnic group. In public administration and diplomatic postings, the Government must take into account ethnic, regional, political and gender balance. Positions in leading state-owned enterprises should be divided on a 60% Hutu, 40% Tutsi basis. The Arusha agreement also stipulated that, for a period of time determined by the Senate, not more than 50% of the national defence force would be drawn from any one ethnic group. According to the electoral schedule, there were to be local elections in June 2005 and legislative elections in July. The new National Assembly and Senate members were jointly to elect the new President in August.

In the July 2005 legislative elections, the CNDD—FDD won 57.8% of the votes, FRODEBU received 21.6% and UPRONA 7.1%. The CNDD—FDD secured 59 seats in the National Assembly, FRODEBU 25 and UPRONA 10. A further 18 deputies were subsequently nominated in accordance with the constitutional requirements of balance of ethnic representation and gender, with the result that representatives from the Twa ethnic group were allocated three seats, while the CNDD—FDD, FRODEBU and UPRONA each received five additional seats, leaving the CNDD—FDD with an absolute majority in the Assembly.

Communal councillors participated in elections to the Senate in July 2005. The CNDD—FDD won 30 of the 34 contested seats, and FRODEBU the remaining four. Four former Presidents were subsequently allocated seats, and Twa representatives were designated three seats. Eight senators (the four political parties with the highest votes each nominated two women) were later added in order to achieve the required minimum representation of women. On 19 August a joint session of the National Assembly and the Senate elected Nkurunziza, the sole candidate, as President, by 151 votes to nine. He was duly sworn into office on 26 August.

CNDD—FDD RULE AND PARTY SPLITS

Nkurunziza appointed a 20-member Government on 30 August 2005, including Martin Nduwimana of UPRONA as First Vice-President, Alice Nzomukunda, a Hutu from the CNDD—FDD, as Second Vice-President, and the Tutsi former Chief of Staff, Maj. Germain Niyoyanka, as Minister of National Defence. The establishment of the new Government was welcomed by international donors, but denounced as illegitimate by PALIPEHUTU—FNL, which increased its military campaign after Nkurunziza's election, leading the new President to intensify counter-insurgency operations in October.

The leader of PALIPEHUTU—FNL, Rwasa, announced in March 2006 that he would accept unconditional negotiations with the Government to end hostilities. Following talks between the Government and PALIPEHUTU—FNL, in September the two parties signed a ceasefire agreement, despite having failed to resolve several key issues, including the future composition of the Government and the armed forces. A ceasefire verification commission was inaugurated in October, but this was boycotted by PALIPEHUTU—FNL, which demanded the release of its leaders from detention before it would cease hostilities.

Meanwhile, in January 2006 President Nkurunziza made new appointments to senior civil service and parastatal positions, almost all of which were awarded to CNDD—FDD supporters. Frustrated by the party's weak representation in the new Government and angered by alleged human rights abuses, in mid-March FRODEBU President Léonce Ngendakumana ordered his party's representatives to withdraw from the Government. The ministers in question, however, refused to do so, and the strategy was denounced by Ngendakumana's rival within FRODEBU, Minani.

In March 2006 Nkurunziza announced that senior members of the armed and security forces had plotted a coup against him. The allegations were dismissed as scaremongering by opposition parties. In August the security forces arrested several prominent opposition politicians, including former President Ndayizeye and former Vice-President Kadege, on suspicion of involvement in the alleged coup plot. Despite protests from donors and human rights organizations, they remained in detention without charge during September–October. On 5 September Second Vice-President Nzomukunda resigned, citing the allegedly divisive role played in the Government by CNDD—FDD Chairman Radjabu. A week later Nzomukunda was replaced by Marina Barampana, a close ally of Radjabu.

The trial of Ndayizeye, Kadege and others charged with involvement in the coup plot began in November 2006, but was immediately adjourned, resuming in December. The prosecution alleged that the accused were part of a regional plot to overthrow the Government, also apparently involving the Chief of Staff of the Rwandan armed forces, Gen. James Kabarebe, Salim Saleh (the half-brother of Ugandan President Yoweri Museveni), former Burundian President Buyoya and renegade Congolese General Laurent Nkunda. In January 2007 the Constitutional Court acquitted Ndayizeye and Kadege, citing lack of evidence.

One week after the Constitutional Court decision, Radjabu took temporary refuge in the South African embassy in Bujumbura, claiming that he feared for his life. In February 2007 an extraordinary congress of the CNDD—FDD was convened by Nkurunziza but boycotted by Radjabu and his supporters. Radjabu was replaced as party Chairman by Col Jérémie Ngendakumana, a Nkurunziza supporter. Shortly afterwards Nkurunziza dismissed other Radjabu supporters from prominent positions in the Government, including Second Vice-President Barampana, who was charged with fraud. In late April the National Assembly voted to strip Radjabu of his immunity from prosecution, and he was immediately arrested and detained.

The President's purge of Radjabu's supporters resulted in a bloc of 22 CNDD—FDD members of the National Assembly withdrawing support for the Government, thus ending its parliamentary majority. Nkurunziza formed a new Government in July 2007, incorporating more FRODEBU and UPRONA ministers and including two Radjabu supporters. However, government legislation remained blocked in parliament. In September Nkurunziza agreed to award FRODEBU five posts in a new administration. He concluded a similar agreement with UPRONA, resulting in the formation of a fragile coalition administration in November.

However, FRODEBU and UPRONA withdrew their parliamentary support for the Government in February 2008. At the end of February 46 members of the National Assembly wrote to the UN Secretary-General, Ban Ki-Moon, alleging that they were under threat and requesting UN protection. In April the Supreme Court convicted Radjabu of plotting against the state and sentenced him to 13 years' imprisonment. Five others accused of the same offence received shorter sentences, including the former Minister of Planning, Jean Bigirimana. Fighting intensified between government forces and PALIPEHUTU—FNL in that month, resulting in hundreds of civilian casualties. On 4 May the Ugandan and Tanzanian foreign affairs ministers demanded that PALIPEHUTU—FNL end the military offensive within 10 days, and that its leadership return to Bujumbura, or face expulsion from Dar es Salaam. Although fighting between the Burundian army and the PALIPEHUTU—FNL continued, in late May the rebel leadership, including Rwasa, returned to Bujumbura, raising hopes that an end to the civil war was near.

In June 2008 the Constitutional Court controversially supported a petition from Nkurunziza, expelling the 22 CNDD—FDD National Assembly members who supported Radjabu and had voted against the Government. They were replaced by Nkurunziza loyalists, despite claims by opposition parties that their replacement was illegal and unconstitutional. At the end of the month the Supreme Court postponed indefinitely Radjabu's appeal against his sentence.

In December 2008 Rwasa agreed to change PALIPEHUTU—FNL's name to the FNL, thereby meeting a government demand that it remove all ethnic references from its name before being allowed to register as a political party. Rwasa symbolically surrendered his weapons at a special ceremony in Bubanza on 18 April 2009, marking the start of the demobilization of FNL combatants. The FNL and the Government had earlier agreed that 3,500 FNL combatants would be integrated into the national army and police force, a further 5,000 would be demobilized, and another 12,500 (later reduced to 10,500) would be returned to civilian life with a small cash payment. The FNL was formally registered as a political party on 21 April. In June the Government agreed to appoint 24 senior FNL members to government posts, although these did not include cabinet and armed force command positions. Rwasa was appointed Director of the Institut National de Sécurité Sociale. The Government also released 385 FNL prisoners.

The FNL transition, however, was not smooth, and the party was fractured. In August 2009 Rwasa expelled several senior FNL members, including its spokesperson, Pasteur Habimana, and Jacques Kenese, the party's head of foreign relations, accusing them of disloyalty. Kenese and Habimana subsequently obtained government permission to hold a congress for the FNL in Bujumbura, which removed Rwasa as leader and replaced him with Kenese. Rwasa rejected the legality of the congress, claiming that it was an attempt by the ruling party to weaken the FNL.

THE 2010 ELECTIONS

An electoral commission was appointed in April 2009, comprising two civil society activists and three political appointees from the CNDD—FDD, FRODEBU and UPRONA. The electoral timetable was released in December, announcing voter registration in January 2010, local elections in May, the presidential poll in June, and elections to the National Assembly and Senate in July.

Relations between the CNDD—FDD and the UN (as well as some donors) were strained. Since the CNDD—FDD's victory in 2005, the Government had accused some international diplomats and donors of being biased towards the opposition parties, particularly FRODEBU and UPRONA, which had liaised closely with the international donor community during the Arusha negotiations. Relations deteriorated further in December 2009, when a UN panel of experts on the DRC claimed that the Government of Burundi was allowing a Rwandan rebel movement, the Forces Démocratiques pour la Libération du Rwanda (FDLR), to use Burundian territory as a base. The panel's report also alleged that gold mined in eastern DRC and taxed by the FDLR was entering Burundi in large quantities, purchased by a dealer close to Gen. Nshimirimana, the Director-General of National Intelligence. The Government denied the allegations.

Voter registration proceeded as planned in January 2010, amid opposition party allegations that the CNDD—FDD had illegally distributed national identity documents to thousands of people who either possessed the documents already or who were ineligible. The FNL selected Rwasa as its presidential candidate, while FRODEBU chose Ndayizeye, and the CNDD—FDD selected Nkurunziza.

As the elections approached there were accusations that the youth wing of the CNDD—FDD, Imbonerakure, and that of the FNL, the Ivyuma—FNL, were becoming increasingly militarized, with the former suspected of receiving weapons from the armed forces. However, the communal elections were peaceful, and, despite some logistical and technical difficulties, the European Union (EU) electoral observer mission reported that they were generally conducted in accordance with international standards. The CNDD—FDD won 64% of the vote, ahead of the FNL with 14%, UPRONA with 6% and FRODEBU with 5%. Many of the opposition groups, except UPRONA, subsequently set up a new alliance, the Alliance des Démocrates pour le Changement (ADC—Ikibiri). They requested the annulment of the communal elections, denouncing them as fraudulent, and the appointment of a new electoral commission.

The presidential election, which was conducted by direct universal suffrage, took place as scheduled on 28 June 2010. Nkurunziza received 91.6% of the votes cast. (The ADC—Ikibiri and UPRONA refused to participate in the poll.) International observers expressed concerns about the worsening political climate, but believed that the election met international standards.

Elections to the National Assembly took place on 23 July 2010. UPRONA participated in these elections, but they were boycotted by many of the parties in the ADC—Ikibiri alliance, including FRODEBU. The CNDD—FDD increased its number of seats to 81, while UPRONA took 17, and FRODEBU-Nyakuri (a small, pro-Government, breakaway faction of FRODEBU) received five. In accordance with constitutional requirements for ethnic representation, three deputies from the Twa ethnic group were subsequently co-opted. On 28 July indirect elections to the Senate were held through provincial electoral colleges composed on the basis of the communal elections. Owing to its success in the communal elections, the CNDD—FDD performed very well in the elections to the Senate, winning 32 seats. UPRONA secured two seats, and a further four seats were allocated to former Presidents and three to the Twa ethnic group, giving a total of 41 senators.

NKURUNZIZA'S SECOND TERM

President Nkurunziza was sworn in on 28 August 2010. As required by the Constitution, he appointed two Vice-Presidents of different ethnic groups and different parties: Térence Sinunguruza from UPRONA and Gervais Rufyikiri from the CNDD—FDD. The other constitutional requirements of ethnic and gender balance were also met. The success of the CNDD—FDD in the elections reduced political pluralism. In the legislature, a two-thirds' majority was required to approve bills, and the CNDD—FDD had obtained this level of representation in both the National Assembly and Senate. Despite the ADC—Ikibiri alliance, the opposition remained fragmented, and many opposition party members were arrested. The independent media was increasingly targeted, and human rights activists also faced constraints on their work.

The leader of the FNL, Rwasa, fled the country in June 2010 and reportedly moved to the DRC's Sud-Kivu province, where he allegedly began recruiting combatants. Nyangoma (of the CNDD) left Burundi in July, following appeals for his arrest from government members. In August a congress of the FNL replaced Rwasa as party Chairman with Emmanuel Miburo, a former presidential adviser. Speaking from exile, Rwasa denounced the congress as illegitimate; however, the Government formally recognized Miburo as the FNL's legal representative.

Low-intensity violence continued during Nkurunziza's second term. The police arrested and detained hundreds of FNL activists in the aftermath of the 2010 elections; many were tortured, and some executed extrajudicially. In December the UN Security Council adopted Resolution 2027, which demanded that the Government halt extrajudicial killings.

In September 2011 armed men killed 36 people in a bar in Gatumba. The FNL was widely accused of having been involved in the attack, but denied responsibility. In October the findings of an inquiry by the national intelligence services into the massacre were released, which blamed the FNL for the attack. The report of the UN panel of experts on the DRC, published in December, found that the FNL had a military leadership based in the Ruzizi Plain, south of Bujumbura, and used at least five unofficial border crossings with Sud-Kivu to join FNL combatants in the Fizi district of this DRC province.

Following the 2010 elections, the international presence in Burundi was reduced. In December the UN Security Council replaced BINUB (the UN Integrated Office in Burundi) with BNUB (the UN Office in Burundi) which had a more restricted mandate. BNUB completed its mandate on 31 December 2014 and transferred its responsibilities to the UN Country Team.

The Burundian armed forces continued to participate in international peacekeeping operations. The country first sent troops to the AU Mission in Somalia (AMISOM) in December 2007. The Burundian contingent was the second largest in AMISOM, with approximately 5,400 troops. By mid-2021 it was estimated that there had been more than 500 Burundian casualties in Somalia. Burundi also contributed to peacekeeping operations in the Central African Republic (CAR).

Media repression increased during Nkurunziza's second term, and progress on justice and human rights was slow. In May 2011 the National Assembly appointed a seven-member national human rights commission, which was welcomed by the UN, but criticized by domestic civil society organizations, which asserted that the commission was dominated by ruling party loyalists. The Government continued to delay setting up a Truth and Reconciliation Commission (TRC) and a special tribunal to prosecute crimes against humanity committed during the country's civil war. Draft legislation on the establishment of the TRC was approved in November 2012, but in the following month President Nkurunziza announced that the creation of the TRC would be postponed further. In April 2014 the CNDD—FDD voted to launch the commission, but UPRONA and FRODEBU boycotted the vote, expressing concerns about its composition. In December the National Assembly elected 11 members to serve on the TRC, but opponents claimed that the delegates were too closely linked to the ruling party.

In February 2011 Manasse Nzobonimpa, the Executive Secretary of the CNDD—FDD's 'council of the wise' and a member of the East African Legislative Assembly, made public accusations of corruption against senior members of the ruling party, including Minister of Finance Clotilde Nizigama, party Chairman Ngendakumana and Minister of Transport, Public Works and Equipment Dr Saidi Kibeya. All of the accused denied any wrongdoing. In June Nzobonimpa was the target of a failed assassination attempt in Kampala.

Nkurunziza reorganized the Government several times, including in November 2011 and February 2012. In October 2013 Vice-President Sinunguruza resigned, and Bernard Busokoza was appointed to replace him. Busokoza was dismissed in February 2014, prompting the resignation of three other UPRONA ministers in protest. A new UPRONA Vice-President, Prosper Bazombanza, was appointed without UPRONA majority support. In November two of President Nkurunziza's closest allies, Alain Guillaume Bunyoni, the head of the Office of the Minister of Civil Affairs in the Office of the President, and Gen. Nshimirimana, were removed from office in a government reorganization.

Meanwhile, tensions over land ownership continued. A number of Tutsi accused the Commission Nationale des Terres et Autres Biens (CNTB—National Commission for Land and Other Properties) of being biased towards Hutu refugees. In May 2013 there were riots in Bujumbura over this issue, and in December the National Assembly approved a law increasing the authority of the CNTB, which its opponents claimed to be unconstitutional.

THE CONTROVERSIAL 2015 ELECTIONS

Preparations for the 2015 elections were highly contentious. In March 2013 the UN organized negotiations whereby the Government and opposition parties were to produce a road map for the polls. Following further discussions, parliament approved a new electoral code in April 2014, and in June the country's political parties adopted a code of good conduct. Meanwhile, in August 2013 FNL leader Rwasa came out of hiding and declared that he would stand in the 2015 presidential election.

In the run-up to the elections, there was increasing violence and intimidation by Imbonerakure. An internal UN report alleging that the CNDD—FDD was arming its youth wing was leaked in April 2014, and the BNUB security chief was expelled from Burundi. The head of a prominent human rights group, Pierre Claver Mbonimpa, was arrested in May after claiming

that Imbonerakure was receiving arms and training in the DRC. He was released in September. In December and January 2015 the Burundian security forces and Imbonerakure staged a brutal crackdown in Cibitoke, including extrajudicial killings, in response to a rebel incursion.

The opposition alleged that voter registration, which began in November 2014, was beset by irregularities. Meanwhile, the private sector media continued to be targeted, with some well-known journalists being arrested. In March 2015 Radjabu, a vociferous opponent of Nkurunziza, escaped from prison and fled the country.

The greatest controversy surrounded the question of the eligibility of President Nkurunziza to run for a third term in office. Citing an ambiguity in the Constitution, supporters of the President claimed that, as he had been elected by parliament in 2005 and not directly elected by the people, he was eligible to stand again. Opponents countered that the Arusha agreement clearly stipulated a maximum of two presidential terms. In March 2014 a proposal to revise the Constitution to clarify the issue was narrowly defeated in the National Assembly. In February 2015 a letter written by the new Director-General of National Intelligence, Godefroid Niyombare, was leaked. The letter outlined what he considered to be the dangers of a third term and stated that it would be unconstitutional. Niyombare was subsequently dismissed. Evariste Ngoyagoye, the Archbishop of Bujumbura and Vice-President of the Conference of Catholic Bishops, also made a clear statement in favour of the two-term limit, as did several senior CNDD—FDD members in March, resulting in their expulsion from the party.

In April 2015 the CNDD—FDD officially announced President Nkurunziza's candidacy in the presidential election. The Constitutional Court validated the party's decision on 4 May, although the Vice-President of the Court fled to Rwanda, claiming that the Court's decision had been made under duress. Following the announcement that the President would run for a third term, mass protests took place in Bujumbura and lasted for several weeks. The protests were met by fierce police repression. Key regional and international figures condemned the violence, and many warned against a third term for the President. The EU and Belgium suspended election aid, and the EU and the AU cancelled their election-monitoring missions. The Conference of Catholic Bishops also withdrew its support for the electoral process.

On 13 May 2015, while President Nkurunziza was in Dar es Salaam attending a regional summit convened to discuss the crisis, Niyombare led an unsuccessful coup attempt. Niyombare then fled the country, and several of those implicated in the coup attempt were arrested. A subsequent East African Community (EAC) summit on 31 May appealed for the postponement of elections, but did not discuss the issue of the third presidential term.

Despite the internal turmoil and external criticism, legislative and local elections were held on 29 June 2015, but were largely boycotted by the opposition parties. The CNDD—FDD won 74.8% of the vote in the legislative poll, equating to 77 of the 100 elected National Assembly seats; however, according to the UN electoral mission, the elections were neither free nor fair. Some high-ranking members of the political and military elite fled Burundi, including Second Vice-President Rufyikiri and the President of the National Assembly, Pie Ntavyohanyuma, highlighting deep divisions within the CNDD—FDD. Following the presidential election on 21 July, which was marred by violence and also boycotted by the opposition, the electoral commission declared a victory for Nkurunziza, who received 73.9% of the valid votes cast.

On 20 August 2015 President Nkurunziza was sworn in for a third term. Gaston Sindimwo of UPRONA was appointed First Vice-President, while Dr Joseph Butore of the CNDD—FDD became Second Vice-President. (Rwasa was appointed First Vice-President of the National Assembly, despite having initially boycotted the elections.) The new Government, which was announced on 24 August, included five pro-Rwasa ministers, and Bunyoni returned as Minister of Public Security.

CONTINUED INSECURITY AND THE CLOSING OF POLITICAL SPACE IN NKURUNZIZA'S THIRD TERM

From the onset of the electoral crisis in 2015 and throughout Nkurunziza's third term in office Burundi was beset by assassinations, human rights abuses, diplomatic tensions with the UN and international donors, security challenges, inconclusive political negotiations and humanitarian and economic challenges.

Several high-profile assassinations were carried out, especially during 2015–16. In May 2015 Zedi Feruzi, the leader of the Union pour la Paix et le Développement (UPD) opposition party, was shot and killed. On 2 August Gen. Nshimirimana, former head of the national intelligence service and one of the highest-ranking officials in Nkurunziza's inner circle, was killed. Two days later, human rights activist Mbonimpa survived an assassination attempt; however, his son was killed in November. Later in August Jean Bikomagu, the former Chief of Staff of the army during the civil war in the 1990s, and Pontien Barutwanayo of the FNL were both shot dead. On 7 September 2015 UPD spokesman Patrice Gahungu was killed, and on 11 September there was an attempted assassination against the army Chief of Staff, Maj.-Gen. Prime Niyongabo. In July 2016 a former journalist and member of the East African Legislative Assembly, Hafsa Mossi, was assassinated, and in January 2017 the Minister of Water and the Environment, Emmanuel Niyonkuru, was killed. Daily violence, arrests, disappearances and other human rights violations continued throughout Nkurunziza's third term.

Relations between international actors and the Burundian Government were strained. The EU imposed sanctions (travel bans and asset freezes) on four Burundians in October 2015, which were extended in October 2018. In December 2015 the US Administration introduced measures against Bunyoni, a police official and two leaders of the May coup attempt. In the same month the AU adopted a resolution that included the possibility of deploying a 5,000-member AU Prevention and Protection Mission. However, the Burundian Government insisted that any AU deployment would be treated as a hostile force. At an AU summit in January 2016, the proposal to deploy a peacekeeping mission without the consent of the Burundian Government was abandoned. Instead, the AU sent a high-level delegation to consult with members of the Government and opposition in February.

The EU suspended direct budgetary support to the Government in March 2016, and the Organisation Internationale de la Francophonie (OIF) suspended co-operation with Burundi in April. In March the EU announced that it would no longer pay Burundian soldiers deployed in AMISOM through the Government. The latter responded by threatening to withdraw its troops from the mission. A compromise involving paying the soldiers through a commercial bank was reached in January 2017. In July 2018 the European Parliament adopted a resolution expressing deep concern about impunity and human rights violations in Burundi and the violence towards and harassment of journalists and opposition supporters, while reaffirming support for the EU's decision to suspend direct financial support to the Burundian Government. It also demanded an end to further payments to Burundian troops involved in UN and AU peacekeeping missions. Relations deteriorated further after legislation regarding foreign non-governmental organizations (NGOs) came into effect in Burundi in January 2017, requiring them to respect ethnic quotas when hiring local staff and stipulating that one-third of their programme budget be deposited in a foreign currency account with the central bank. In September 2018 the operations of almost all foreign NGOs in Burundi were suspended. By March 2019, however, 93 out of the 130 foreign NGOs operating in Burundi had resumed their activities.

The Burundian Government also had poor relations with international human rights organizations, and human rights abuses continued. The Office of the UN High Commissioner for Human Rights (OHCHR) estimated that there were 348 extrajudicial executions targeting opposition and civil society members and 650 cases of torture between April 2015 and April 2016. The International Criminal Court (ICC) announced in April 2016 that it would investigate political violence in Burundi, and in October the Burundian parliament voted to withdraw from the Court; the withdrawal from the ICC took effect in October 2017. In September 2016 the UN Independent Investigation on Burundi reported systematic gross human rights violations committed primarily by state agents and their affiliates. In October the Government banned UN human rights investigators and several human rights and civil society organizations from operating in the country. In September 2017 the UN Commission of Inquiry on Burundi reported that it had reasonable grounds to believe that crimes against humanity had been committed since April 2015 and that perpetrators included senior government and military officials, intelligence and police officers and Imbonerakure. The Burundian Government established a 12-member commission to investigate the claims in the UN report. In October 2017 ICC judges authorized the Office of the Prosecutor of the ICC to open an investigation into crimes allegedly committed between 26 April 2015 and 26 October 2017 (the day before Burundi's withdrawal from the Court). In March 2019 the UN Human Rights Office in Burundi was closed at the Government's request.

Owing to violence and continued repression following Nkurunziza's re-election in 2015, many opposition leaders went into exile. In August several opposition parties formed a grouping, the Conseil National pour le Respect de l'Accord d'Arusha pour la Paix et la Réconciliation au Burundi et de l'Etat de Droit (CNARED). A new rebel movement, the Forces Républicaines du Burundi (FOREBU), was launched in December. In that month there were co-ordinated attacks against three military camps by armed insurgents, followed by heavy government retaliation, in which up to 200 people were killed. During 2015–16 several officers defected from the army, many of whom fled abroad, sometimes joining the rebellion. FOREBU changed its name to the Forces Populaires du Burundi in August 2017 and vowed to escalate its attacks from bases in Sud-Kivu. Another armed opposition group based in eastern DRC, RED-TABARA, launched attacks on Burundian military positions in October 2018, prompting a military response in November. In January 2019 fighting took place in eastern DRC between a coalition of rebels and the Burundian army (and some Imbonerakure). In October and November there were attacks on military and police posts in Bubanza and Cibitoke provinces, causing casualties on both sides. Armed opposition groups, however, remained fractured and did not pose a significant threat to the Government.

The internal and external political opposition was also deeply fractured, with several groups leaving the CNARED umbrella. In February 2019 Rwasa created a new party, the Congrès National pour la Liberté (CNL), which replaced his FNL. There were reports of clashes between CNL members and Imbonerakure, and many of the CNL party offices were vandalized. In May properties belonging to over 30 politicians, activists and journalists living in exile were seized. In September eight former members of CNARED created a new opposition platform, the Coalition des Forces de l'Opposition Burundaise pour le Rétablissement de l'Accord Arusha, although this failed to heal divisions within the opposition.

Throughout Nkurunziza's third term, international and regional organizations tried, unsuccessfully, to promote dialogue to resolve the Burundian crisis. After the 2015 elections, the EAC made a fruitless attempt to promote dialogue between the Government and the opposition. An EAC summit in 2016 in September made little progress, and in December CNARED declared that it no longer recognized former Tanzanian President Benjamin Mkapa as mediator. Talks proceeded in January 2017 without CNARED, while further negotiations in February included CNARED but not the Government. Meetings between the Government and CNARED took place in Finland in July–August, but CNARED boycotted another session of the inter-Burundian dialogue, held in Arusha in November–December. In August 2018 the UN Security Council reiterated its deep concern about the slow progress of the dialogue. In February 2019 Mkapa announced the end of the mediation process, owing to inadequate progress. Relations between the AU and Burundi also deteriorated, and in November 2018 the Burundian Government issued an international arrest warrant for former President Buyoya, who had been appointed as the AU's High Representative for Mali and the Sahel, and several others for their alleged roles in the assassination of President Ndadaye in 1993.

The humanitarian situation in Burundi remained critical throughout Nkurunziza's third term. The Burundian economy entered into recession in 2015, while social services collapsed, unemployment rose and poverty deepened. The People's Republic of China provided the Burundian Government with some budgetary support, but this did not compensate for the reduction in funds from traditional donors. According to the UN Office for the Coordination of Humanitarian Affairs, as of July 2021 an estimated 2.3m. Burundians (about 20% of the population) required humanitarian assistance. The Office of the UN High Commissioner for Refugees (UNHCR) estimated that between April 2015 and May 2019 almost 400,000 Burundians had fled to neighbouring countries, especially to Tanzania (some 186,000), with large numbers also in Rwanda, the DRC and Uganda. In addition, over 100,000 Burundians were internally displaced. Actual numbers of emigrants were estimated to be significantly higher, as not all those who had left the country had registered as refugees. UNHCR and its partners began to assist the voluntary repatriation of Burundian refugees, mainly from Tanzania, in September 2017. According to UNHCR, at the end of July 2021 the number of Burundian refugees in neighbouring states totalled 271,427 (including 131,799 in Tanzania), while more than 169,000 had returned to the country under the voluntary repatriation programme.

On 17 May 2018 a referendum was held on proposed amendments to the Constitution: 73% of those who voted endorsed the changes, with a reported turnout of 96%. The changes increased the powers of the President and of the party that received the largest number of votes in legislative elections. The constitutional amendments included an extension of the presidential mandate from five to seven years (renewable once), a reduction in the number of Vice-Presidents from two to one, the reintroduction of the post of Prime Minister, a review of ethnic quotas in five years and the replacement of the two-thirds' majority requirement for certain types of legislation with a simple majority. Furthermore, whereas the previous Constitution stipulated that any party that secured more than 5% of the legislative vote had the right to a ministerial position, the new charter eliminated this right and specified that the party that won a majority of votes would appoint the cabinet. In the run-up to the referendum, opponents of the Government were imprisoned, and some people were allegedly forced to register to vote. The opposition-in-exile reported violence and intimidation and appealed for a boycott of the poll. In April the Catholic Church criticized the Government for forcing citizens to contribute funding for the referendum. On 4 May the Government controversially suspended British Broadcasting Corporation (BBC) and Voice of America (VoA) broadcasts for six months, and in March 2019 it permanently revoked the BBC's operating licence and maintained the suspension of VoA.

President Nkurunziza enacted the new Constitution in June 2018. Under the new charter, Nkurunziza was allowed to run for two further terms, potentially giving him the chance to remain in the presidency until 2034. However, in a speech at its promulgation, he unexpectedly announced that he would not seek re-election in 2020. The UN and the EU welcomed his declaration, and France resumed bilateral support to Burundi in certain sectors. In early 2019 the national capital was officially moved from Bujumbura to Gitega, although Bujumbura remained the country's commercial centre. In April the National Assembly approved a new electoral code, which, among other changes, stipulated that presidential, parliamentary and communal elections should all be held on the same day.

THE 2020 ELECTIONS, COVID-19 AND THE DEATH OF PRESIDENT NKURUNZIZA

One of the key questions throughout 2019 was whether Nkurunziza would honour his pledge not to stand for re-election in 2020, and, if so, who would replace him. At a party congress in January 2020 the CNDD—FDD selected its

Secretary-General, Evariste Ndayishimiye, as its candidate for the presidential election in May. After he stepped down as head of state, President Nkurunziza was to be accorded the status of 'Supreme Leader' and be granted accommodation and a generous pension.

In the run-up to the elections, CNL members and supporters continued to be harassed, allegedly by Imbonerakure. There were several violent clashes, and in March 2020 the UN Commission of Inquiry on Burundi outlined political, economic and security concerns in its briefing to OHCHR. There was also an increase in extra-judicial killings. In April government soldiers clashed with RED-TABARA in Sud-Kivu. Owing to the spread of the COVID-19 pandemic to East Africa in early 2020, in mid-March the border with Rwanda was closed, and all flights out of Bujumbura international airport were suspended. Just before the elections were due to be held, the Burundian authorities ordered election observers from the EAC to go into quarantine for 14 days, thus preventing them from observing the polls.

Presidential and legislative elections were held as scheduled on 20 May 2020. Ndayishimiye won the presidential poll with 71.5% of the valid votes cast, defeating Rwasa of the CNL, who took 25.2%, and Sindimwo of UPRONA (1.7%). In the legislative elections, the CNDD—FDD received 71.0% of the valid votes cast (86 seats in the National Assembly, including co-opted members), the CNL took 23.4% (32 seats), and UPRONA 2.5% (two seats); Twa representatives were allotted three seats. There were widespread allegations of electoral fraud and other irregularities. Rwasa filed an appeal with the Constitutional Court, which was subsequently rejected.

On 8 June 2020 outgoing President Nkurunziza died suddenly following a reported heart attack, although it was widely believed that he had contracted COVID-19. The Constitutional Court ruled that President-elect Ndayishimiye should be sworn in immediately, and he took office on 18 June.

PRESIDENT NDAYISHIMIYE: A TURNING POINT?

It is debatable whether governance under President Ndayishimiye marked a break from that of his predecessor or whether there was a general continuity. Ndayishimiye has had to balance powerful interests within the party with the desire to lift international sanctions and restrictions on the country. Shortly after taking office Imelde Sabushimike was appointed as Minister of National Solidarity, Social Affairs, Human Rights and Gender Equality—the first female Twa to be appointed to a Burundian Government. Ndayishimiye also named Bunyoni as Prime Minister and Gervais Ndirakobuca as Minister of the Interior, Community Development and Public Security; both men were under international sanctions, owing to their role in repressing protests in 2015. There was domestic and international criticism about the number of hardliners and former army officers included in the new administration. The EU extended its sanctions against Burundi for a further 12 months in October 2020. The predominance of those perceived as hardliners was reinforced in January 2021 when former Senate President Révérien Ndikuriyo was elected as Secretary-General of the CNDD—FDD.

Crackdowns on civil society and the opposition continued under President Ndayishimiye. In September 2020 the UN Commission of Inquiry on Burundi noted several violations of civil liberties, including summary executions and arbitrary arrests. In October former UPRONA legislator Fabien Banciryaniro was arrested and in May 2021 sentenced to one year in prison. Arrests, killings and disappearances, particularly of members of the CNL and of Tutsi, were reported throughout the latter half of 2020.

Buyoya, along with 18 other defendants, was convicted *in absentia* in October 2020 of the murder of President Ndadaye in 1993; however, Buyoya died of COVID-19 in France in December 2020. In February 2021 the Supreme Court issued a ruling convicting 34 individuals for planning the 2015 coup against President Nkurunziza. The following month the TRC presented the National Assembly with a report focusing on the genocidal massacres that took place in 1972. Many members of civil society criticized the report as being biased, as it focused on responsibility for violence against Hutu and failed sufficiently to address violence committed against Tutsi. Forced disappearances and the arbitrary arrest of opposition figures continued, especially targeting the CNL. In May 2022 several key members of the CNL were sentenced to prison terms. In the same month, Human Rights Watch condemned the security forces and youth groups for extra-judicial killings, torture, harassment and arbitrary detention of people suspected of belonging to opposition parties of working with armed opposition groups.

Armed opposition to the Government has continued. RED-TABARA claimed responsibility for attacks on the CNDD—FDD and its youth wing in September and October 2020, and the security forces retaliated. Occasional violence occurred throughout 2021 and 2022, including mortar attacks on Bujumbura airport in September 2021 and clashes between RED-TABARA and the armed forces and Imbonerakure along the border with the DRC. Until August 2022 the Burundian Government denied that its armed forces were in eastern DRC, but there were reports of frequent military operations against RED-TABARA and the FNL in Sud-Kivu province. In August 2022 the Government finally acknowledged that its troops were in the DRC to counter armed group violence.

Ndayishimiye's presidency has shown some signs of breaking away from Nkurunziza's legacy. Four jailed independent journalists from the Burundian news organization IWACU who had been imprisoned for threatening national security received a presidential pardon in December 2020, and during the first half of 2021 bans on a number of NGOs and media outlets (including the BBC and the Burundian news website Ikiriho) were lifted. In March Ndayishimiye granted amnesty to more than 5,250 prisoners. The UN Commission of Inquiry on Burundi commended the steps that had been taken to improve the human rights situation in the country, but questioned whether or not this would last. In October 2021 the UN Human Rights Council voted to appoint a special rapporteur on human rights in Burundi, Fortuné Gaétan Zongo, but the Burundian Government has not co-operated. In September 2022 Zongo stated that despite some commitments and measures taken by the Government, the human rights situation in Burundi had not changed in a substantial way.

There has, however, been an improvement in Burundi's regional and international relations. Burundian refugees started to return from Rwanda in August 2020. Furthermore, Burundi hosted a meeting of heads of intelligence and security from the DRC, Rwanda, Tanzania and Uganda in July 2021, while there were several high-level official visits between Rwanda and Burundi in 2021 and 2022, with the aim of normalizing relations between the two countries. In July 2022 Ndayishimiye was elected as chair of the East African Community for a one-year term.

Burundi was readmitted as a member of the OIF in November 2020, and the UN Security Council removed Burundi from its agenda of countries of concern in December. In that month Ndayishimiye met the EU ambassador to Burundi, Claude Bochu, in what was the first formal bilateral meeting since the EU suspended financial co-operation with Burundi in 2016. In February 2021 the EU formally resumed dialogue with Burundi, and in June the bloc stated that it would resume financial assistance if the Burundian Government agreed to certain reforms. In November 2021 the USA removed sanctions on Bunyoni, Ndirakobuca and other political figures, in response to decreased violence and the pursuit of political reforms. In February 2022 the EU lifted its financial sanctions on Burundi; however, four months later Bochu stated that the Burundian Government would not receive budget support from the EU until it increased financial transparency.

In September 2022, having been warned about a coup plot against him, President Ndayishimiye dismissed Bunyoni as Prime Minister and Gabriel Nizigama as chief of cabinet, along with several ministers. Ndayishimiye may have targeted some of Bunyoni's business activities as part of a larger anti-corruption campaign. Many police provincial commissioners were also replaced. Gervais Ndirakobuca was appointed as the new Prime Minister. Like his predecessor, Ndirakobuca is considered to be a hardline securocrat and remains under EU sanctions for his role during the 2015 political unrest.

Economy

DUNCAN WOODSIDE

INTRODUCTION

Burundi's recent economic history has been afflicted by civil war and political crisis. These factors exacted a particularly severe toll during 1993–2003, and rebel activity subsequently continued in some areas. The country's main rebel group, the Conseil National pour la Défense de la Démocratie—Forces pour la Défense de la Démocratie (CNDD—FDD), signed a power-sharing agreement in late 2003, before winning elections resoundingly in 2005. During 2005–14 the economy grew by an average of 4.5% per year—a creditable, if unspectacular, rate by regional standards. Per capita income rose during this period from US $106 to $285. However, Burundi remained one of the poorest states in the world, with the majority of citizens living on substantially less than $1 per day. For several years from 2015 renewed political conflict sent the country spiralling into renewed economic crisis, marked by donor funds drying up, rising illicit activity and declining productivity. As a tiny landlocked country with few natural resources, prospects for substantial near-term improvement are limited, despite significant political change in mid-2020. Low levels of education and per capita productivity also hamper Burundi's economy. In the 2020 Human Development Index of the United Nations (UN) Development Programme (with figures for 2019), Burundi was ranked 185th out of 189 countries, ahead of only Chad, South Sudan, the Central African Republic and Niger. According to the Index, life expectancy in Burundi fell from 60.1 years in 2016 to 57.6 years in 2019.

In 2015 Burundi suffered its worst political crisis since the end of the main phase of the civil war, which reversed many of the hard-won gains of the previous decade. The selection by the CNDD—FDD of Pierre Nkurunziza, the country's President and leader of the ruling party, to run for a third term in office resulted in street protests in the capital, Bujumbura, from April, with the opposition and many observers viewing the move as unconstitutional. A coup attempt took place in May, which was swiftly suppressed but raised concerns about a potential return to civil war. Over 200,000 people fled the country during the course of 2015, according to the Office of the UN High Commissioner for Refugees (UNHCR). The economy contracted by 3.9% in real terms in that year and by a further 0.6% in 2016, according to the International Monetary Fund (IMF).

After applying sanctions against three key regime figures in October 2015, in March 2016 the European Union (EU) formally suspended direct budgetary support to Burundi's Government. The country had been eligible for US $475m. in financial assistance during 2014–20. Burundi was therefore increasingly isolated, politically and commercially. In November 2015 the US Administration had registered its displeasure with the regime by imposing sanctions on the public security minister, the deputy director of the national police and the two main leaders of the failed May coup (see *History*).

The COVID-19 pandemic, which spread to Africa in early 2020, hit Burundi hard, not least owing to the Government expelling a World Health Organization delegation in May and, bizarrely, instructing people to rely on prayers rather than practical measures to protect themselves from the disease. However, the departure from office of President Nkurunziza, who did not run for a fourth term and died in June, officially as a result of cardiac arrest, ushered in a less isolationist policy agenda, which sought to reverse some of the damage sustained over the previous five years. Incoming President Evariste Ndayishimiye (previously the ruling CNDD—FDD's Secretary-General), declared COVID-19 to be the country's 'biggest enemy', and his new Government lobbied traditional donors to restore the financial support that was lost as a result of his predecessor's highly divisive third mandate. That lobbying paid off in early 2022, when the EU restored funding and the US Agency for International Development (USAID) signed a bilateral five-year development agreement with Burundi valued at US $400m. The restoration of major donor support provided a strong boost, and was expected to spur Burundi's recovery, after the economy grew by just 0.3% in real terms in 2020. In March 2022 the IMF estimated that in 2021 gross domestic product (GDP) grew by 2.4% in real terms, owing to a recovery in both the primary and tertiary sectors facilitated by an easing of social distancing measures and travel restrictions. The Fund also cited an improvement in agricultural productivity, driven by better use of fertilizers and higher-quality crops. Inflation, however, remained stubbornly high; it increased slightly to 8.3% in 2021, from 7.5% in 2020. The IMF forecast that Burundi's GDP would grow by 3.6% in real terms in 2022, thereby continuing the country's rebound in the wake of the pandemic. However, it noted that the impact of the Russian Federation's military invasion of Ukraine on global economic output would constrain the extent of the rebound. The rising price of oil would drive Burundi's fuel import bill higher and put pressure on an already significant trade deficit.

AGRICULTURE

In mid-2015, according to the Food and Agriculture Organization of the UN (FAO), an estimated 88.4% of the labour force were engaged in agriculture (including forestry and fishing), mainly at subsistence level, and the sector provided 37.2% of GDP in 2020. In 2017 the UN Economic Commission for Africa (UNECA) traced a decline in agricultural production per capita of 28% since 1982, owing to erosion, heavy pressure on land, climate change, land conflicts and poor distribution of fertilizers. UNECA estimated agricultural yields to be some 20%–40% lower than in neighbouring nations. According to World Bank estimates, agricultural GDP increased, in real terms, at an average annual rate of 1.4% in 2011–20. It grew by 3.0% in 2018 and by 3.1% in 2019. With the end of the main phase of the civil war in 2003, the path appeared to be open to a shift from subsistence farming to long-term expansion of agricultural production. In a further boost for Burundi's food production potential, the Mines Advisory Group, a British non-governmental organization which undertakes demining in former conflict zones, declared in December 2011 that Burundi was finally 'mine-free' after seven years of clearance activities, mainly in the north-west of the country. However, the economy remained hampered by a lack of state capacity and expertise, together with persistent insecurity.

Burundi's dominant cash crop is coffee, which is also a key employer (accounting for about 800,000 jobs, or 10% of the working population). Coffee production peaked in the 2018/19 financial year (May–April), when output of parchment Arabica coffee reached 32,786 metric tons, according to the Banque de la République du Burundi. In 2019/20 production of parchment Arabica coffee declined to 10,885 tons, before a partial recovery, to 18,868 tons, in 2020/21. The harvest in 2021/22 was again on course to be disappointing, as output of parchment Arabica coffee reached a cumulative 11,360 tons for the eight months to the end of December, which compared unfavourably to 18,580 tons for the same period in 2020/21.

In March 2019 the international news agency Bloomberg reported that the Burundi Coffee Farmers' Confederation (BCFC) had urged the 'government and partners to invest in coffee by supplying enough fertilizers'. In an effort to address the shortfall in fertilizer supply and the high cost of imports, Burundi established an organic mineral fertilizer plant, which began operations in 2019, with the capacity to produce 120,000 metric tons annually. Reported plans to nationalize the coffee sector provoked alarm from the BCFC in October, after the Minister of the Environment, Agriculture and Stockbreeding,

Dr Déo Guide Rurema, claimed that 'the state will rewrite laws to reform the sector and increase revenue for the national treasury'. In an interview with Bloomberg, the President of the BCFC, Joseph Ntirabampa, stated that his organization had not been consulted about the proposed changes and questioned how the authorities would seek to take control of plantations, following significant investment by farmers' platforms since the liberalization of the sector in 1991. According to the International Trade Centre, revenue from exports of coffee totalled US $40.9m. in 2018 (equivalent to 22.7% of total export revenue), before declining to $37.8m. in 2019 (20.9%) and further to $30.8m. in 2020 (19.0%).

Tea is Burundi's second most important crop and accounts for about 300,000 jobs. Production of dried leaves reached 10,701 metric tons in 2018 and 10,823 tons in 2019, according to the central bank. However, although receipts from exports of tea totalled a respectable 46,871m. Burundian francs in 2018, they dipped to 41,710m. Burundian francs in 2019 as prices fell. The harvest was lower in 2020, as production of dried leaves reached 10,763 tons. In December 2020 the Office du Thé du Burundi announced ambitious plans to boost production further, by bringing an additional 500 ha under cultivation each year over a period of 10 years. The decade-long state-led expansion, encompassing some 5,000 ha across three provinces, was to be accompanied by irrigating plantations during dry seasons, with the aim of tripling output. Some 50,000m. Burundian francs (US $25.7m.) was to be invested in the project—an outlay equivalent to just over a year's worth of revenue from tea exports. The harvest in 2021 was moderately better, as Burundi produced 11,097 tons of dried leaves.

Burundi has received foreign assistance for the development of other crops. On the Imbo plain, land is being reclaimed for the cultivation of cotton and rice in an integrated rural development scheme assisted by the UN Development Programme and FAO. In 2020 rice production amounted to 150,000 metric tons, according to FAO. An integrated sugar scheme was established in the south-east of the Mosso region, with finance provided mainly by the African Development Bank (AfDB), the Organization of the Petroleum Exporting Countries Fund for International Development and the Arab Bank for Economic Development in Africa. Plantations of sugar cane have been established on the Mosso plain, near Bujumbura, in association with a refinery. The country has become a net sugar exporter in recent times, albeit an irregular one. Bananas, sweet potatoes, cassava, pulses and maize are other important, but mainly subsistence, crops.

Although Burundi is potentially self-sufficient in food production, civil disturbances and inclement weather have disrupted its infrastructure and prevented supplies from reaching urban centres. The political crisis in 2015 threatened to wreak fresh havoc on the agricultural sector. According to UNHCR, more than 158,000 people fled the country between late April and early July, largely to Tanzania and Rwanda, fearing widespread violence. By March 2018 the UN World Food Programme was assisting more than 590,000 people inside and outside the country, with an estimated 3.6m. Burundians being in need of assistance and protection.

Favourable rains and success in tackling the Fall Armyworm pest that affected much of sub-Saharan Africa led to a forecast for cereal production of about 315,000 metric tons in 2018—8% higher than in 2017. As a consequence, the price of maize in Bujumbura declined by almost 30% between November 2017 and February 2018. Meanwhile, an outbreak of goat and sheep plague hit the country in December 2017, spreading across five provinces, killing 8,500 goats and forcing the Government to shut livestock markets in affected areas. A vaccination programme was launched, with about 3m. animals being treated by June 2018. According to FAO, cereal output increased from 459,300 tons in 2018 to 546.8 tons in 2019, before declining to 466,100 tons in 2020.

MINERALS

Burundi has moderate confirmed mineral resources. The AfDB estimated in 2010 that Burundi's nickel deposits amounted to about 260m. metric tons, containing some 4m. tons of metal, although this resource remains unexploited, owing to the heavy burden that such activity would place on a limited electricity network. The country has estimated reserves of 15m. tons of phosphate rock and reserves of carbonatite near Gatara and produces small quantities of bastnaesite, cassiterite, niobium, tungsten and gold. In July 2019 the Ministry of Water Resources, Energy and Mines reported that in the second quarter of that year the value of mineral exports had surpassed the combined value of coffee and tea exports. According to the ministry, the combined value of exports of gold, rare earth minerals, tantalum, tin and tungsten during that three-month period amounted to some US $12m., accounting for more than one-half of the country's foreign exchange earnings.

Petroleum has been detected beneath Lake Tanganyika and in the Ruzizi valley, for which test drillings were carried out in the late 1980s by US petroleum interests in association with the Burundian Government. However, petroleum experts stated that complete seismic surveys in Lake Tanganyika would also require prospecting in the Democratic Republic of the Congo (DRC) and Tanzanian parts of the lake. Stability in the DRC would consequently be a precondition to relaunching the project. Although known and easily exploitable mineral reserves within Burundi's territory are modest, the country has served as a significant conduit for output mined in eastern DRC, one of the most mineral-rich regions in the world. However, much of the output exported via Burundi has been transported illegally, often from areas under the control of armed groups, according to various sources, including the UN Group of Experts on the DRC.

Burundi is emerging as a potentially significant source of rare earth minerals, including neodymium oxide, praseodymium oxide and lanthanum oxide. In April 2015 German steel firm ThyssenKrupp Metallurgical Products signed an exclusive agreement with Rainbow Rare Earths (RRE) to bring to market 5,000 metric tons of rare earth concentrate and downstream products each year for a 10-year period, from Burundi's Gakara prospect, located 20 km south-east of Bujumbura. RRE had announced in early April that it had secured a US $12m. financing deal with Pala Investments to exploit the deposits. RRE took a 90% stake in the project, with Burundi's Government holding the remaining 10%, according to an initial deal between the two entities signed in 2011. In March 2015 Burundi's Ministry of Energy, Mining and Economic Development granted RRE a 25-year renewable licence, which was ratified by presidential decree in April and June. RRE claimed to have exposed 800 'rare earth occurrences' within the prospecting area, compared with the existence of just 30 or 40 in 1985. Some 520 of the 800 confirmed areas involved veins that were 'in-situ' (exposed at the surface), making the mining process relatively easy.

RRE listed on the London Stock Exchange in January 2017, which raised US $10m. for investment in initial operations at Gakara, including road building, haulage and initial mining. Work at the first site, Gasagwe, began in June, with sales of concentrated rare earths scheduled to begin by the end of the year. Exploration work, which included mapping of geological traverses, had already indicated an average rare earth oxide (REO) occurrence of 58%, according to 150 analysed samples. The REO content of the samples broke down as follows: 46% cerium, 31% lanthanum, 16% neodymium, 5% praseodymium and 2% classified as 'other'. RRE described the Gakara project as one of the highest-grade rare earth projects in the world. Results released in August from laboratory testing returned an average total REO grade of 62.2% in the main vein at Gasagwe. The importance of REOs has risen in part owing to their use in wind turbine motors, electric and hybrid vehicle motors, and cameras. Initial extraction would be based on a time frame of two to four years at Gasagwe, before potential heavier investment at the site and intensification of activity, depending on yields. By the end of December some 270 metric tons had been extracted manually from the site. In the year to March 2019 a total of 1,100 tons of rare earth ore were dug from the site. In September 2019 the chief executive of RRE, George Bennett, told the *Financial Times* daily newspaper that his firm was aiming to ramp up extraction to 10,000 tons per year, before a further eventual boost to 20,000 tons annually. Shares in RRE more than quadrupled in value between late 2020 and early 2021, owing to a surge in international demand for rare earths,

although the share value fell, by over 40%, by August, owing in part to a decision in July by the Burundian Government to suspend the operations of several international mining companies in the country (including those conducting the Gakara project), claiming that the state was not receiving a fair share of income from the country's mineral wealth.

In November 2017 the Government approved a permit for Canadian firm CVMR Energy Minerals Inc to conduct explorations in the Waga-Nyabikere and Mukanda areas. CVMR committed US $40m. to carrying out surveys and feasibility studies. The authorities estimated that Mukanda holds vanadium, titanium and iron reserves covering 144 sq km, with proven reserves of vanadium (an element primarily used as a steel alloy but now increasingly utilized in batteries) of 12m. metric tons and an additional 5m. tons of probable reserves. CVMR, which partnered with South African firm DRA and a local Burundian engineering company, Jacob Mining Engineering, presented its findings from a feasibility study to the Government in August 2018. It planned eventually to build several modular refineries to produce metal powders used in next-generation batteries and electric vehicles.

The World Bank released an evaluation of Burundi's mineral sector in January 2016, which estimated that approximately 34,000 people were employed directly in artisanal mining of cassiterite, tantalum and tungsten, and 14,000–27,000 people were engaged directly in gold mining. Some 160,000 people were dependent on the sector, given that the average miner was estimated to have several dependants. Much of Burundi contains deposits of these commodities, especially the northern provinces of Bubanza, Cibitoke, Kayanza, Kirundo, Muyinga and Ngozi. Ruyigi (in the east) and Gitega (in central Burundi) also offer prospects. In late 2017 a Russian-Burundian venture, Tanganyika Gold, began work on an open pit gold mine in Cibitoke province, with targeted production of 24,000 oz.

Illicit trade accounts for much of the mining activity in Burundi; nearly one-half of all mines operate without a licence, according to the World Bank, while some sources claim that the official level of gold exports represents only about 20% of the total. In the latter half of the 2010s the World Bank warned that the security crisis could result in the country losing its 'conflict-free' mineral status, if the Government remained unable to restore stability. This would make it impossible to export minerals legally, resulting in a decline in output and employment, allowing traffickers or state-aligned mafias to gain control of the sector.

INDUSTRY, UTILITIES, SERVICES AND FOREIGN INVESTMENT

There is little industrial activity in Burundi, apart from the processing of agricultural products such as cotton, coffee, tea and vegetable oil, as well as small-scale wood mills. Industry contributed 18.8% of GDP in 2020, and in 2017 manufactured exports accounted for 12.8% of merchandise trade. According to estimates by the World Bank, during 2011–20 industrial GDP increased at an average annual rate of 0.2%; it increased by 1.8% in 2020.

One of the key problems that has held back the development of industry and manufacturing is the lack of a fully functioning banking sector, which has been hampered by a legacy of bad loans (largely to bankrupt state companies). Without access to credit, very few small and medium-sized private enterprises can establish themselves. The IMF noted in early 2022 that the central bank had undertaken various measures since 2019 to stimulate the banking sector, including increasing domestic liquidity—partly through the introduction of interest rate subsidy schemes—and the establishment of new banks. The new lenders provided credit to women, young people and the housing market.

The manufacturing sector accounted for 13.8% of GDP in 2020. By the mid-1980s several small enterprises, including glass, cement, footwear and insecticide factories, a flour mill and a brewery, had been established. A textile industry was also developed, with aid from the People's Republic of China, which exported fabrics to neighbouring Rwanda. However, a decrease in domestic cotton production forced the main company, Complexe Textile du Bujumbura, to rely heavily on imports.

Burundi has long been affected by power supply issues, resulting in frequent outages. In 2016 only 58.5% of urban households had access to an electricity supply, falling to 1.2% in rural areas, according to AfDB data. A total of 11.1% of Burundi's population had access to electricity in 2019, according to the World Bank, comparing highly unfavourably with 37.8% in Rwanda. However, there has been an improvement in power supply in recent years, according to central bank data. Electricity production in 2020 totalled 262.6m. kWh, up from 232.2m. kWh in 2018. This upward trend over three years represented a marked improvement on the 2014–16 period, when annual output ranged between 166.0m. kWh and 173.8m. kWh. However, electricity production declined in 2021 to 248.7m. kWh, in a context whereby the country consumed around 331.7m. kWh in that year.

A key source of future power supply is being sought through further development of the hydroelectric sector. Regional projects include an 80-MW station at the Rusumo Falls on the Kagera river at the border between Rwanda and Tanzania. In August 2013 the World Bank approved a grant of US $340m. to finance the Rusumo project, which was scheduled for completion in late 2022. An even bigger project is a third Ruzizi facility (Ruzizi III), with a planned generating capacity of 147 MW, for joint exploitation with the DRC and Rwanda. The EU, the AfDB and the European Investment Bank all contributed initial funding to the Ruzizi III project, and in July 2019 Burundi, the DRC and Rwanda signed an agreement with a consortium comprising SN Power and Industrial Promotion Services for a 25-year concession to build, operate and transfer the project. The plant, costing $650m.–$700m., is due to be operational by 2026. Burundi also intends to develop two other dams—Jiji and Mulembwe—with a view to generating a further 50 MW. The World Bank stated in April 2014 that the Jiji and Mulembwe projects had been confirmed, with the provision of a $100m. grant to the Burundian authorities and a completion date set at June 2023. In February 2020 the World Bank approved a $100m. grant to be disbursed through the International Development Association for the development of mini-grids and stand-alone solar power systems. In providing about 17 MW of renewable generation capacity, more than 91,000 families, 4,000 small businesses, 500 schools and 400 health care centres would gain access to electricity, according to the multilateral lender.

The politico-security crisis that started in April 2015 effectively suspended the country's nascent tourism industry, causing many of the lakeside capital's hotels, which were also affected by a collapse in foreign trade, to close or drastically reduce their operations. Bujumbura had undergone a post-war boom during the decade from 2005, but much of the construction had been built on credit, so the onset of the crisis left many borrowers and lenders financially exposed. Foreign direct investment (FDI) fell from US $46m. in 2014 to just $7m. in 2015 as the political situation deteriorated. However, by 2018 the level of FDI had increased substantially to reach $984m.

The crisis had a profound effect on the country's businesses, especially as foreign exchange shortages started to bite. Fuel became increasingly hard to source, to such an extent that in May 2017 the Government imposed rationing of the resource, with obvious implications for the transport business and those who relied on generators for power. In January the central bank had informed exporters that they would be required to lodge repatriated earnings in accounts held at the monetary authority, in a move designed to boost the central bank's waning access to US dollars. However, this requirement threatened to damage affected firms' operations and prevent access to their own earnings at a fair price, especially given that a gulf of nearly 40% existed by that stage between the central bank's exchange rate and the black market rate. Moreover, it would further constrain the dollar liquidity of Burundi's commercial banks, which, similarly to all but the most favoured associates of the regime, were already grappling with the effects of chronic shortages of foreign currency.

In November 2018 the central bank announced that the country planned to establish a securities exchange, in an effort to generate funds for local companies affected by a squeeze in

bank lending. Local companies were reportedly keen to expand their shareholder base to fund purchases of basic materials and increase productivity. The lending squeeze was generated mainly by the Government's heavy demand for credit, which commercial banks were forced to shoulder, leaving little credit for productive private enterprises. AfDB data published in early 2019 showed that domestic credit to the private sector was equivalent to 16.7% of GDP in 2016 and just 13.8% in 2017. The ratio in Rwanda in the latter year stood at 20.9%, and in Kenya it was 31.0%.

Shortages of foreign exchange have been compounded by the Burundian authorities maintaining an overvalued official local exchange rate and by crackdowns on those trading at market-determined rates. The Ministry of the Interior, Community Development and Public Security announced in October 2019 that more than 40 people had been arrested during the previous month for trading the Burundian franc illegally, in a context whereby it was priced at 2,900 Burundian francs = US $1 on the streets of the capital, against the official rate of 1,876 Burundian francs = US $1. By that stage, very few companies—largely limited to those operating in the fuel and fertilizer sectors—were able to buy US dollars at the official rate, leaving many firms struggling to obtain US dollars legally. The dollars available on the limited black market were sourced mainly from the DRC, according to traders. In February 2020 the central bank announced that it was suspending the licences of all the country's foreign exchange bureaux, owing to their selling of dollars at rates beyond the permitted 18% margin of the official rate. However, commercial banks were permitted to continue offering foreign exchange services. As of May 2022 the official exchange rate had weakened to about 2,029 Burundian francs = US $1.

In the months following Ndayishimiye's accession to office, the Government made various efforts to reopen the country and put an end to the international isolation that had characterized the previous five years under Nkurunziza's rule. Burundi was readmitted to the Organisation Internationale de la Francophonie in December 2020, while the UN Security Council noted that the 'improved security' situation in Burundi had allowed it to remove the country from its rolling agenda of countries of concern. Despite the ongoing constraints imposed by the COVID-19 pandemic, from 2020 the Burundian authorities began more assertively to promote the country as a tourist destination. In an interview with the *East African* newspaper in January 2021, Vénant Ngendabanka, the head of Burundi's Office National du Tourisme (ONT), said that the Ministry of Commerce, Transport, Industry and Tourism would soon launch both a local and an international marketing drive—the latter targeting EU citizens by means of an online campaign. In the previous month, Burundi's Government had announced that it would re-establish a national airline (see *Transport and Communications*). As of January 2021 there were 595 hotels in the country, up from only 87 in 2010, according to the ONT. Of these establishments, just under 10% had been awarded stars based on the international hostelry ratings system.

FISCAL POLICY AND DEVELOPMENT AID

In the immediate post-war period of the early 2000s Burundi benefited strongly from foreign assistance, both for capital projects and budgetary support. The country also benefited from significant debt relief, albeit several years later than many of its African peers. The 'Paris Club' of sovereign creditors wrote off all the debt owed to it by Burundi in early 2009, cancelling US $129.5m. of debt, amounting to 96% of the country's sovereign obligations, while bilateral creditors wrote off the remaining $4.8m. However, with the onset of the political crisis in 2015, key donors responded negatively to the growing instability and corruption in Burundi and the repeated allegations of extrajudicial killings.

Aside from the IMF and the World Bank, Burundi found significant favour from the EU, particularly under the auspices of the European Development Fund. International aid accounted for just under one-half of planned 2015 budget revenues, amounting to 679,800m. Burundian francs, compared with total expected government revenues of some

1,500,000m. Burundian francs. The violent suppression of public protests by the police and the regime's refusal to compromise over the issue of Nkurunziza's third mandate resulted in a suspension of aid in May 2015 by key donors, including the EU and Belgium. In late July, shortly after the presidential poll, which was widely regarded as neither free nor fair, the USA announced that it would review its assistance to Burundi, having already suspended support for a number of projects, owing in part to the evacuation of some of the US embassy personnel, following a coup attempt and associated violence in mid-May.

Sanctions were initially imposed against regime and rebel officials alike by the EU in October 2015. In March 2016 the EU Council suspended all remaining financial support to the regime, including direct budgetary support, after concluding that the Government had failed to fulfil its commitments. However, in view of the impact of the political and economic crisis on the country's citizens, the EU stated that it remained committed to ensuring 'access to basic services for the population', including, increasingly, through emergency assistance, while emphasizing that it would avoid 'channelling financial resources through accounts held by the Government of Burundi'. Despite facing calls from leaders in East Africa to lift its sanctions, the EU opted to extend the punitive measures each year between 2016 and 2020, expressing its deep concern about the human rights situation in the country, particularly 'the persistence of extrajudicial executions and arbitrary arrests'.

One month after President Ndayishimiye came to power, the IMF granted Burundi US $7.6m. in debt relief over a period of three months, extending to a potential $25m. over the following 21 months. This leeway was provided under the Catastrophe Containment and Relief Trust (CCRT), in order, according to the Fund, to 'free up resources for public sector health needs ... other emergency spending and [to] help mitigate the balance of payments shock posed by the COVID-19 pandemic'. Burundi had not been among an initial group of 25 countries that benefited in mid-April from the CCRT—an emergency organ mobilized by the IMF to grant relief to impoverished countries most at risk from the negative effects of the pandemic. In a statement accompanying the confirmation of debt relief in July, the IMF stressed that it was 'important to resume Article IV consultations' between the two parties; such policy co-ordination had been in abeyance since the onset of the political crisis in 2015. The IMF identified an improvement in economic data provision by the Burundian Government as a key prerequisite for re-engagement by multilateral and other donors. Nearly one year later, in June 2021, there had not yet been any announcement about a new lending programme for Burundi. However, in October the IMF did approve a disbursement of $76.2m. under a Rapid Credit Facility (RCF), to bolster the country's policy response to the COVID-19 pandemic. The funds were earmarked for fiscal assistance and emergency balance of payments support. The RCF was also viewed by the IMF as a precursor to wider donor support.

Under Ndayishimiye, Burundi repeatedly engaged in dialogue with the EU in a bid to have sanctions lifted and unlock aid funding. In February 2022 the European Council repealed its suspension of direct financial assistance to Burundi's Government and institutions, pointing to 'progress ... with respect to human rights, good governance and the rule of law'. In the same month, the Government and USAID signed a five-year bilateral support programme, thereby completing the restoration of full relations between Burundi and its key donors, almost seven years after Nkurunziza's push for a third term blocked crucial funding streams. Burundi's Minister of Foreign Affairs and Development Co-operation, Albert Shingiro, announced that the aid agreement, worth US $400m., would be funnelled towards agriculture, health, education, good governance, the environment and the private sector.

Meanwhile, the World Bank maintained key programmes in Burundi. In December 2016 the multilateral lender approved US $25m. for the ongoing Agro-Pastoral Productivity and Markets Development project, with the money to be disbursed during 2017–19. The project was conceived to help smallholders via various schemes, including post-harvest technology, irrigation and nutritionally enhanced crops. In February 2020 the World Bank approved two grants to Burundi worth a total of $160m., including $100m. to develop electrification in rural areas. The remaining $60m. was allocated to improve nutrition and access to basic services and economic opportunities for the most vulnerable populations, including refugees.

Burundi has sought new donors since the 2015 crisis. The authorities received an external lifeline in May 2017, following a three-day visit to Burundi by the Vice-President of China, Li Yuanchao. During the visit the two Governments signed an agreement that China would provide US $30m. in budget support; in addition, China donated 5,000 metric tons of rice, according to Burundian news media. The boost to the country's foreign exchange holdings could not have come at a better time for a Government that was struggling to provide its population with basic necessities, including fuel imports. In September 2018 Russian news media reported that Burundi and the Russian Federation were seeking to extend co-operation, including in the gas sector, following the gold mining venture initiated in late 2017. Burundi signed a trade co-operation agreement with Türkiye (Turkey) in 2017 and opened an embassy in Ankara.

Burundi's fiscal deficit rose only marginally in 2019, to 270,521m. Burundian francs, from 264,214m. Burundian francs in 2018, according to central bank data. Tax revenues increased substantially in 2019, to 890,452m. Burundian francs, from 770,878m. Burundian francs in 2018, and overall revenues and grants totalled 1,244,008m. Burundian francs, while overall spending reached 1,514,529m. Burundian francs, up from 1,312,439m. Burundian francs in 2018. Encouragingly, the bulk of increased expenditure in 2019 was accounted for by capital spending, which rose to 585,306m. Burundian francs, from 398,284m. Burundian francs in 2018, while current expenditure increased only moderately, to 929,223m. Burundian francs, from 914,156m. Burundian francs in 2018.

Burundi almost halved its budget deficit in 2021, according to the central bank. The overall deficit, on an accrual basis, stood at 214,077m. Burundian francs in 2021, down from 404,270m. Burundian francs in 2020. Total revenues and grants rose to 1,492,247m. Burundian francs in 2021, up from 1,330,291m. Burundian francs in 2020, owing in large part to a jump in tax revenues, which reached 1,098,872m. Burundian francs in 2021, up from 970,491m. Burundian francs in 2020. Total expenditures, meanwhile, fell slightly in 2021, reaching 1,706,324m. Burundian francs, down from 1,734,561m. Burundian francs in 2020, when public spending peaked due to the initial strains of the COVID-19 pandemic. Encouragingly, the deficit in 2021 was also lower than the 270,521m. Burundian francs recorded in 2019, the last full year before the outbreak of the pandemic. The IMF stated in March 2022 that it anticipated that the improved fiscal performance would spill over into 2022, as a consequence of the continued advances in revenue collection and restraint on the spending side. However, the Fund noted that the deficit was expected to widen afresh later in 2022 and in 2023, due to an increase in public investment.

FOREIGN TRADE

The trade deficit accelerated in 2021, reaching 1,709,017m. Burundian francs, up from 1,430,915m. Burundian francs in 2020, according to the central bank. The widening gap was driven by an increase in imports, which increased from 1,741,908m. Burundian francs to 2,035,264m. Burundian francs, eclipsing a very modest rise in exports from 310,993m. Burundian francs to 326,247m. Burundian francs. The higher import bill was driven in part by a rise in fuel costs, as global oil prices recovered from a multi-year low reached in 2020. Even taking into account balance of payments support provided by the RCF, foreign exchange reserves by the end of 2021 covered little more than two months of imports, according to the IMF. The Fund noted in March 2022 that the conflict in Ukraine—and notably the impact of Russia's invasion of its neighbour on already elevated oil prices—would put further pressure on Burundi's current account deficit. The United Arab Emirates (UAE) was by far the largest recipient of Burundian exports in 2020, taking 32.2% of the total, ahead of the DRC, which received 19.6%, Pakistan (5.5%), Belgium (5.0%) and Switzerland (4.9%). Coffee and tea accounted for 32.2% of Burundi's exports by value in 2020, according to the International Trade Centre; gold accounted for 28.3% of exports, prepared foodstuffs, beverages and tobacco-related products 10.8%, and mineral products 7.5%. The principal imports in 2020 were mineral products (accounting for 20.1% of the total), chemicals and related products (16.2%) and machinery, mechanical appliances and electrical equipment (12.4%). The country's primary export markets in 2020 were the UAE (taking 32.2% of the total) and the DRC (19.6%). The primary sources of imports in that year were China (providing 15.6% of the total), Saudi Arabia (11.8%), India (9.5%), Tanzania (8.6%) and the UAE (6.8%).

In January 2010 a full customs union came into force throughout the East African Community (EAC), comprising Burundi, Kenya, Rwanda, Tanzania and Uganda. This meant that tariffs between member states were eliminated, creating a free trade area, completing an incremental reduction begun in 2005. Burundi (and Rwanda) signed a memorandum of understanding for membership of the EAC in November 2006, but did not sign the full accession treaties until June 2007. As a result, while Tanzania and Uganda were given five years to adjust to full competition with Kenya (the region's most competitive exporter), Rwanda and Burundi were faced with a sharper adjustment. In November 2009 the member states of the EAC signed a common market protocol, seeking to build on the existing customs union. The common market came into force in July 2010, and would, upon completion of its phased implementation, entail the free circulation of services, citizens and capital.

TRANSPORT AND COMMUNICATIONS

The Burundian network of roads is dense, but underdeveloped. In 2016 only about 1,500 km of the 12,300-km network was paved, including the roads connecting Bujumbura with Gitega, Kayanza and Nyanza-Lac. A new development strategy, led by the AfDB in 2010, heralded ambitious new plans for the long-term development of the country's road network. The goal was to pave the entire existing road network and add 1,000 km of new roads to major urban centres by 2020.

Lake Tanganyika (of which Burundi has about 8% sovereignty) is a crucial component in Burundi's transport system, as most of the country's external trade is conducted along the lake between Bujumbura and Tanzania and the DRC. In 2005 the Burundian authorities expressed concern that the falling water levels of Lake Tanganyika (resulting from deforestation and climate change) had severely affected activities at the port of Bujumbura, making large amounts of dock space unusable.

Twelve years after the country's previous flag carrier, Air Burundi, ceased operations, in December 2020 the Government announced that it would launch a new national airline. Burundi Airlines was officially incorporated in February 2021, with the state taking a 92% shareholding, the national insurance company, Société d'Assurances du Burundi, 4% and a Belgian entity 4%. Initial capital for the new company was put at 15,000m. Burundian francs. However, at that stage the airline did not possess a single aircraft. As of mid-2021 only a small number of airlines were operating flights to Bujumbura international airport: Brussels Airlines, Ethiopian Airlines, Kenya Airways and RwandAir. South African Airways, Air Tanzania and Uganda Airlines had temporarily ceased services to the Burundian capital during the COVID-19 pandemic.

Burundi's mobile cellular telephone market has expanded considerably in recent years. By 2020 the number of subscriptions had risen to 6.63m. The largest operator is U-Com (also known as Leo Burundi), a subsidiary of Egypt's Orascom, although the mobile telephone sector has become reasonably competitive, with state-owned ONAMOB, South Africa's Econet Wireless, Nepal's Lacell SU and Africell (a unit of VTEL Holdings based in Dubai, UAE) all operating in Burundi. A sixth operator, Viet Nam's Viettel, entered the market in February 2014 as Lumitel Burundi. Mobile banking is a particularly strong potential growth area for Burundi's cellular sector.

Burundi has sought to develop local internet services. In January 2014 the country launched a US $25m. scheme to develop a fibre-optic cable network, to enhance broadband access. The project, which entailed a joint venture between the Office National des Télécommunications and four private companies, Africell, Cbinet, Econet Wireless and U-Com, was part of an overall plan to ensure total nationwide internet access by 2025. The internet penetration rate in 2017 was just above 5% of the population, but had risen to 9.4% by 2020. In March 2018 Lumitel Burundi announced that it had expanded 4G services across the whole of the country, after launching them in several regions in February 2016. The firm, which by then claimed a market share of some 55%, deployed about 3,300 km of fibre-optic cable and more than 110 4G antennae to bolster its infrastructure.

Statistical Survey

Sources (unless otherwise stated): Institut de Statistiques et d'Etudes Economiques du Burundi, BP 1156, Bujumbura; tel. 22226729; e-mail isteebu@isteebu.bi; internet www.isteebu.bi; Banque de la République du Burundi, BP 705, Bujumbura; tel. 22222744; e-mail brb@brb.bi; internet www.brb.bi.

Area and Population

AREA, POPULATION AND DENSITY

Area (sq km)	27,834*
Population (census results)†	
16–30 August 1990	5,139,073
16–31 August 2008	
Males	3,964,906
Females	4,088,668
Total	8,053,574
Population (UN estimates at mid-year)‡	
2020	11,890,781
2021§	12,255,429
2022§	12,624,845
Density (per sq km) at mid-2022§	453.6

* 10,747 sq miles.
† Excluding adjustment for underenumeration.
‡ Source: UN, *World Population Prospects: The 2019 Revision*.
§ Projection.

POPULATION BY AGE AND SEX
('000, UN projections at mid-2022)

	Males	Females	Total
0–14 years	2,851.9	2,806.9	5,658.8
15–64 years	3,273.1	3,373.2	6,646.3
65 years and over	143.2	176.5	319.7
Total	**6,268.1**	**6,356.7**	**12,624.8**

Note: Totals may not be equal to the sum of components, owing to rounding.

Source: UN, *World Population Prospects: The 2019 Revision*.

PRINCIPAL TOWNS
(excl. suburbs, population at 2008 census)

Bujumbura (capital)	497,166	Cibitoke	. . .	23,885
Gitega . . .	41,944	Kayanza	. .	21,767
Ngozi . . .	39,884	Bubanza	. .	20,031
Rumonge . . .	35,931			

Mid-2022 (urban population, incl. suburbs, UN projection): Bujumbura 1,139,265 (Source: UN, *World Urbanization Prospects: The 2018 Revision*).

BIRTHS AND DEATHS
(UN estimates, annual averages)

	2005–10	2010–15	2015–20
Birth rate (per 1,000)	43.1	42.2	39.3
Death rate (per 1,000)	11.2	9.2	8.0

Source: UN, *World Population Prospects: The 2019 Revision*.

Life expectancy (years at birth, estimates): 61.9 (males 60.1; females 63.7) in 2020 (Source: World Bank, World Development Indicators database).

ECONOMICALLY ACTIVE POPULATION
('000 at mid-year, FAO estimates)

	2013	2014	2015
Agriculture, etc.	4,435	4,536	4,642
Total labour force (incl. others) .	5,000	5,123	5,253

Source: FAO.

Health and Welfare

KEY INDICATORS

Total fertility rate (children per woman, 2020)	5.2
Under-5 mortality rate (per 1,000 live births, 2020) . . .	54.4
HIV/AIDS (% of persons aged 15–49, 2020)	1.0
COVID-19: Cumulative confirmed deaths (per 100,000 persons at 31 August 2022)	0.3
COVID-19: Fully vaccinated population (% of total population at 28 August 2022)	0.1
Physicians (per 1,000 head, 2020)	0.1
Hospital beds (per 1,000 head, 2014)	0.8
Domestic health expenditure (2019): US $ per head (PPP) .	20.6
Domestic health expenditure (2019): % of GDP	2.7
Domestic health expenditure (2019): public (% of total current expenditure)	33.4
Access to improved water resources (% of persons, 2020) .	62
Access to improved sanitation facilities (% of persons, 2020) .	46
Total carbon dioxide emissions ('000 metric tons, 2018) . .	590
Carbon dioxide emissions per head (metric tons, 2018) . .	0.1
Human Development Index (2021): ranking	187
Human Development Index (2021): value	0.426

Note: For data on COVID-19 vaccinations, 'fully vaccinated' denotes receipt of all doses specified by approved vaccination regime (Sources: Johns Hopkins University and Our World in Data). Data on health expenditure refer to current general government expenditure in each case. For more information on sources and further definitions for all indicators, see Health and Welfare Statistics: Sources and Definitions section (europaworld.com/credits).

Agriculture

PRINCIPAL CROPS
('000 metric tons)

	2018	2019	2020
Bananas	1,655.0	1,179.8	1,280.0*
Beans, dry	393.2	619.2	461.2*
Cashew nuts, with shell . . .	266.4	283.3	300.9*
Cassava (Manioc)	2,386.7	2,409.0	2,440.0*
Coffee, green	14.2	14.1	15.9†
Groundnuts, with shell . . .	12.4	10.0*	9.3*
Maize	290.5	270.8	260.0†
Oil palm fruit*	84.3	84.0	84.5
Peas, dry*	10.0	12.4	14.0
Plantains and others	818.0	426.1*	314.9*
Potatoes	302.7	376.4	294.7*
Rice, paddy	89.3	241.2	150.0†
Sorghum	28.5	8.9	25.0†
Sugar cane	178.4	154.1*	196.4*
Sweet potatoes	583.0	1,023.5	950.2*
Taro (Coco yam)	118.2*	217.5	243.3*
Tea	11.4	11.4	16.3*
Wheat	22.8	4.9	8.6*

* FAO estimate(s).
† Unofficial figure.

Aggregate production ('000 metric tons, may include official, semi-official or estimated data): Total cereals 459.5 in 2018, 546.8 in 2019, 466.1 in 2020; Total fruit (primary) 2,602.4 in 2018, 1,734.0 in 2019, 1,723.5 in 2020; Total oilcrops 101.1 in 2018, 98.4 in 2019, 98.1 in 2020; Total pulses 405.7 in 2018, 634.4 in 2019, 478.4 in 2020; Total roots and tubers 3,397.5 in 2018, 4,026.4 in 2019, 3,931.2 in 2020; Total treenuts 266.4 in 2018, 283.3 in 2019, 300.9 in 2020; Total vegetables (primary) 485.3 in 2018, 481.0 in 2019, 482.7 in 2020.

Source: FAO.

LIVESTOCK
('000 head, year ending September)

	2018	2019	2020
Cattle	1,111	756	628*
Chickens*	2,850	2,664	2,569
Goats	3,250	3,228	3,366*
Pigs	775	804	847*
Sheep	549	728	747*

* FAO estimate(s).

Source: FAO.

LIVESTOCK PRODUCTS
('000 metric tons, FAO estimates)

	2018	2019	2020
Cattle hides, fresh	2.7	2.9	2.0
Cattle meat	13.8	15.1	10.5
Cows' milk	74.0	55.0	65.0
Chicken meat	7.1	6.6	6.7
Goat meat	8.9	9.9	7.7
Goats' milk	51.7	51.5	52.9
Goats' skins, fresh	2.1	2.4	1.9
Pig meat	9.3	9.8	10.1
Hen eggs	2.2	2.2	2.4

Source: FAO.

Forestry

ROUNDWOOD REMOVALS
('000 cubic metres, excl. bark, FAO estimates)

	2012	2013	2014
Sawlogs, veneer logs and logs for sleepers	307	307	307
Other industrial wood	310	318	318
Fuel wood	5,743	6,007	5,999
Total	6,360	6,632	6,624

2015–20: Production assumed to be unchanged since 2014 (FAO estimates).

Source: FAO.

SAWNWOOD PRODUCTION
('000 cubic metres, incl. railway sleepers)

	2012	2013	2014
Coniferous (softwood)	18.3*	20.9	20.9*
Broadleaved (hardwood)	19.5	18.8	13.2
Total*	37.8	39.7	34.1

* FAO estimate(s).

2015–20: Production assumed to be unchanged since 2014 (FAO estimates).

Source: FAO.

Fishing

(metric tons, live weight, FAO estimates)

	2018	2019	2020
Capture	20,310	20,372	19,589
Lake Tanganyika sprat	8,330	8,430	8,466
Sleek lates	6,350	6,769	6,709
Dagaas	4,210	3,973	3,450
Aquaculture	1,550	1,555	1,450
Total catch (incl. others)	21,860	21,927	21,039

Source: FAO.

Mining

(metric tons unless otherwise indicated)

	2016	2017	2018
Gold (kg)*	396	953	576
Tin ore*†	14	140	200
Tantalum and niobium (columbium) concentrates‡	31.7	143.4	219.0
Peat	9,541	13,948	14,118

* Figures refer to the metal content of ores.

† Estimates.

‡ The estimated tantalum content (in metric tons) was 6.2 in 2016; 28.0 in 2017; 43.0 in 2018.

Source: US Geological Survey.

Industry

SELECTED PRODUCTS
('000 metric tons unless otherwise indicated)

	2019	2020	2021
Beer ('000 hl)	2,081.9	2,260.3	2,354.2
Soft drinks ('000 hl)	416.0	369.3	429.9
Cottonseed oil ('000 litres)	18.0	17.8	27.4
Sugar	18.6	20.4	15.9
Cigarettes (million)	636.3	980.1	882.6
Paint	0.9	1.0	1.3
Soap (metric tons)	15,014.3	16,338.1	17,654.4
Plastic racks ('000)	194.2	130.2	193.3
Moulds (metric tons)	22.6	30.9	40.3
PVC tubing (metric tons)	116.1	38.7	17.6
Electrical energy (million kWh)	255.8	262.6	248.7

Finance

CURRENCY, EXCHANGE RATES AND FISCAL YEAR

Monetary Units
100 centimes = 1 Burundian franc.

Sterling, Dollar and Euro Equivalents (31 May 2022)
£1 sterling = 2,554.5 francs;
US $1 = 2,029.1 francs;
€1 = 2,173.8 francs;
10,000 Burundian francs = £3.91 = $4.93 = €4.60.

Average Exchange Rate (Burundian francs per US dollar)
2019   1,845.623
2020   1,915.046
2021   1,975.951

Fiscal Year
Although since 2018 officially the fiscal year ends on 30 June, the calendar year is still used widely for financial reporting.

GOVERNMENT FINANCE
(central government operations, '000 million Burundian francs)

Revenue*	2019	2020	2021
Tax revenue	890.5	970.5	1,098.9
Taxes on income, profits and capital gains	218.0	218.5	230.1
Taxes on goods and services	530.9	572.6	658.6
Taxes on international trade	90.8	121.8	130.0
Other tax revenue	50.7	57.6	80.2
Non-tax revenue	99.6	102.8	138.5
Total	990.1	1,073.3	1,237.3

Expenditure	2019	2020	2021
Current expenditure	929.2	1,318.2	1,159.5
Wages and salaries	441.6	532.1	484.3
Goods and services	161.7	196.7	168.4
Transfers and subsidies	289.9	508.9	311.0
Interest payments	28.3	80.4	195.9
Other expenses	7.7	0.0	0.0
Capital expenditure	585.3	416.3	546.8
Total	1,514.5	1,734.6	1,706.3

* Excluding grants received ('000 million Burundian francs): 253.9 in 2019; 257.0 in 2020; 254.9 in 2021.

INTERNATIONAL RESERVES
(US $ million at 31 December)

	2019	2020	2021
Gold (national valuation) . . .	1.47	1.83	1.76
IMF special drawing rights . .	0.26	9.16	215.43
Reserve position in IMF . . .	27.46	14.26	13.86
Foreign exchange	82.18	65.07	35.12
Total	111.37	90.32	266.17

Source: IMF, *International Financial Statistics.*

MONEY SUPPLY
(million Burundian francs at 31 December)

	2018	2019	2020
Currency outside depository corporations	295,599	359,960	433,279
Transferable deposits	1,031,459	1,213,285	1,531,331
Other deposits	454,386	613,503	751,026
Broad money	1,781,443	2,186,748	2,715,636

Source: IMF, *International Financial Statistics.*

COST OF LIVING
(Consumer Price Index for Bujumbura; base: fiscal year ending 30 June 2017 = 100)

	2019	2020	2021
Food and non-alcoholic beverages .	105.2	117.9	130.2
Clothing and footwear	120.2	125.9	133.1
Housing and utilities	122.1	128.2	138.3
All items (incl. others) . . .	110.9	119.0	128.9

NATIONAL ACCOUNTS
('000 million Burundian francs at current prices)

Expenditure on the Gross Domestic Product

	2018	2019	2020
Government final consumption expenditure	1,114	1,263	1,277
Private final consumption expenditure	4,999	5,421	5,737
Gross fixed capital formation . .	841	813	873
Change in inventories	35	42	52
Total domestic expenditure .	6,988	7,540	7,939
Exports of goods and services . .	540	552	520
Less Imports of goods and services	1,614	1,875	1,956
Statistical discrepancy	—	—	7
GDP in purchasers' values .	5,914	6,217	6,510
GDP at constant 2015 prices .	4,985	5,207	5,153

Gross Domestic Product by Economic Activity

	2018	2019	2020
Agriculture, hunting, forestry and fishing	2,091	2,122	2,345
Mining, quarrying and utilities .	65	70	76
Manufacturing	784	792	869
Construction	210	224	243
Wholesale and retail trade; restaurants and hotels . . .	325	321	377
Transport and communications .	234	252	269
Other services	1,862	2,051	2,131
Sub-total	5,572	5,832	6,310
Indirect taxes (net)*	342	385	200
GDP in purchasers' values .	5,914	6,217	6,510

* Figures obtained as residuals.

Source: UN National Accounts Main Aggregates Database.

BALANCE OF PAYMENTS
('000 million Burundian francs)

	2019	2020	2021
Exports of goods	262.6	211.3	214.3
Imports of goods	−945.1	−989.8	−1,360.6
Balance on goods	−682.5	−778.5	−1,146.3
Services (net)	−100.5	−40.1	−69.0
Balance on goods and services	−783.1	−818.6	−1,215.4
Primary income (net)	17.6	31.6	18.7
Balance on goods, services and primary income . . .	−765.5	−787.1	−1,196.6
Secondary income (net) . . .	543.4	707.0	857.8
Current balance	−222.1	−80.0	−338.8
Capital account (net)	250.7	231.5	253.7
Direct investment assets . . .	−1.4	−2.2	−2.2
Direct investment liabilities . .	1.9	16.7	19.6
Other investment assets . . .	−17.3	−5.4	−0.7
Other investment liabilities . .	90.7	41.7	201.9
Overall balance	102.6	202.3	133.4

Source: Banque de la République du Burundi, Bujumbura.

External Trade

PRINCIPAL COMMODITIES
(distribution by HS, US $ million)

Imports c.i.f.	2019	2020	2021
Vegetables and vegetable products	71.0	58.1	62.9
Cereals	52.6	40.7	42.8
Wheat and meslin	30.9	22.9	24.6
Prepared foodstuffs; beverages, spirits, vinegar; tobacco and articles thereof .	54.5	63.0	67.3
Sugars and sugar confectionery .	21.5	25.2	21.1
Mineral products	216.0	182.7	227.5
Mineral fuels, oils, distillation products, etc.	164.9	142.7	178.8
Petroleum oils, not crude . .	160.7	137.4	174.9
Chemicals and related products	131.4	147.1	145.1
Pharmaceutical products . . .	62.6	64.5	69.8
Medicament mixtures put in dosage	44.1	49.7	46.8
Fertilizers	27.5	34.3	19.4
Mineral or chemical phosphatic fertilisers	10.0	34.0	18.5
Mineral or chemical fertilisers .	13.8	0.1	0.4
Miscellaneous chemical products .	10.3	19.9	29.5
Plastics, rubber, and articles thereof	29.8	32.3	46.4
Plastics and articles thereof . .	19.4	22.2	31.7
Pulp of wood, paper and paperboard, ...	26.7	22.1	19.1
Textiles and textile articles .	58.1	41.7	47.8

Imports c.i.f.—*continued*	2019	2020	2021
Other made-up textile articles .	39.8	25.9	30.8
Iron and steel, other base metals and articles of base metal	81.4	96.1	124.9
Iron and steel	55.6	63.9	89.6
Machinery and mechanical appliances; electrical equipment; parts thereof	79.8	112.3	107.9
Machinery, boilers, etc. . . .	41.2	51.7	61.1
Electrical and electronic equipment	38.6	60.6	46.8
Vehicles, aircraft, vessels and associated transport equipment	81.0	88.3	59.4
Vehicles other than railway, tramway	80.6	87.0	59.0
Motor cars and other motor vehicles principally designed for the transport of persons .	36.1	43.3	28.8
Total (incl. others)	887.3	909.1	981.1

Exports f.o.b.	2019	2020	2021
Vegetables and vegetable products	70.9	63.3	57.7
Coffee, tea, mate and spices . .	59.9	52.4	52.2
Coffee	37.8	30.8	28.0
Tea	22.0	21.6	24.1
Milling products, malt, starches, inulin and wheat gluten . .	10.3	9.5	5
Prepared foodstuffs; beverages, spirits, vinegar; tobacco and articles thereof .	9.5	17.5	14.3
Beverages, spirits and vinegar .	4.2	9.1	7.3
Beer made from malt . . .	3.1	4.6	6.5
Tobacco and manufactured tobacco substitutes	4.1	6.9	6.1
Cigars, cheroots, cigarillos and cigarettes of tobacco . . .	4.1	6.9	6.1
Mineral products	18.0	12.1	18.2
Ores, slag and ash	13.2	9.0	15.6
Niobium, tantalum, vanadium .	10.1	6.5	13.7
Mineral fuels, oils, distillation products, etc.	4.8	3.0	2.6
Petroleum oils, not crude . .	4.8	3.0	2.6
Plastics, rubber, and articles thereof	0.6	3.4	3.9
Plastics and articles thereof . .	0.5	3.1	3.8
Articles of stone, plaster, cement, asbestos; ceramic and glass products . . .	1.3	3.3	3.5
Glass and glassware	1.2	3.3	3.5
Pearls, precious or semi-precious stones, precious metals, and articles thereof .	66.8	45.9	0.0
Gold (unwrought or semi-manufactured)	66.8	45.9	0.0
Iron and steel, other base metals and articles of base metal	3.8	9.8	7.1
Iron and steel	3.5	9.1	5.9
Total (incl. others)	180.8	162.3	113.2

Source: Trade Map-Trade Competitiveness Map, International Trade Centre, marketanalysis.intracen.org.

PRINCIPAL TRADING PARTNERS
(US $ million)

Imports c.i.f.	2019	2020	2021
Belgium	36.1	47.8	34.8
China, People's Republic . . .	136.3	141.7	176.8
India	70.1	86.2	80.6
Japan	37.2	37.1	28.4
Kenya	47.1	47.2	53.3
Saudi Arabia	134.6	107.6	131.6
Tanzania	48.8	78.0	89.9
Uganda	37.0	45.7	53.4
United Arab Emirates . . .	61.2	62.2	78.2
Zambia	43.7	32.8	36.7
Total (incl. others)	887.3	909.1	981.1

Exports f.o.b.	2019	2020	2021
Belgium	6.4	8.1	13.8
China, People's Republic . . .	5.6	1.9	1.1
Congo, Democratic Republic . .	19.9	31.8	27.1
Egypt	5.6	4.4	4.9
Germany	6.6	6.1	5.3
Kenya	2.6	5.4	5.9
Oman	3.0	5.8	6.0
Pakistan	11.1	9.0	9.7
Singapore	6.4	1.6	0.8
Sudan	2.9	6.1	5.1
Switzerland (incl. Liechtenstein) .	10.3	8.0	3.2
Tanzania	3.2	8.6	6.5
Uganda	6.3	2.4	2.7
United Arab Emirates . . .	70.5	52.3	4.9
United Kingdom	3.9	2.7	3.7
USA	2.0	1.4	1.1
Total (incl. others)	180.8	162.3	113.2

Source: Trade Map-Trade Competitiveness Map, International Trade Centre, marketanalysis.intracen.org.

Transport

ROAD TRAFFIC
('000 motor vehicles in use, estimates)

	2001	2002	2003
Passenger cars	6.6	6.9	7.0
Commercial vehicles	9.3	9.3	9.3

Source: UN, *Statistical Yearbook*.

LAKE TRAFFIC
(Bujumbura, '000 metric tons)

	2019	2020	2021
Goods:			
arrivals	197.0	214.3	240.2
departures	5.9	14.1	9.1

Tourism

TOURIST ARRIVALS BY REGION
('000)*

	2015	2016	2017
Africa	58.0	85.0	138.0
Americas	26.0	28.0	33.0
East Asia and the Pacific . . .	7.0	21.0	42.0
Europe	1.0	2.0	8.0
Middle East	22.0	25.0	55.0
South Asia	11.0	17.0	15.0
Unspecified	6.0	9.0	8.0
Total	**131.0**	**187.0**	**299.0**

* Including Burundian nationals residing abroad.

Tourism receipts (US $ million, excl. passenger transport): 2.0 in 2016; 3.0 in 2017; 3.9 in 2018.

Source: World Tourism Organization.

Communications Media

	2018	2019	2020
Telephones (main lines in use)	24,810	20,936	18,300
Mobile telephone subscriptions ('000)	6,318.0	6,532.0	6,631.2
Broadband subscriptions, fixed .	3,935	3,891	4,230
Broadband subscriptions, mobile ('000)	1,279.0	1,284.0	1,303.7
Internet users (% of persons) . .	4.1	6.2	9.4

Source: International Telecommunication Union.

Education

(2020/21 unless otherwise indicated)

	Teachers	Students		
		Males	Females	Total
Pre-primary . . .	2,409	62,409	63,258	125,667
Primary	51,921	1,149,938	1,152,342	2,302,280
Secondary:				
Lower	11,041*	173,260	218,340	391,600
Upper	14,049	162,044	187,605	349,649
Higher†	3,456	25,952	15,917	41,869

* 2018/19.
† 2017/18.

Institutions (1988/89): Primary 1,512; Secondary 400.

Source: UNESCO Institute for Statistics.

Pupil-teacher ratio (primary education, qualified teaching staff, UNESCO estimate): 47.4 in 2020/21 (Source: UNESCO Institute for Statistics).

Adult literacy rate (UNESCO estimates): 68.4% (males 76.3%; females 61.2%) in 2017 (Source: UNESCO Institute for Statistics).

Directory

The Constitution

The Constitution of Burundi was endorsed at a national referendum on 17 May 2018 and was promulgated on 7 June (replacing the Constitution of March 2005). The main provisions of the Constitution are summarized below:

FUNDAMENTAL VALUES

The Constitution upholds the rights of the individual, and provides for a multi-party political system. The Government is based on the will of the people, and must be composed in order to represent all citizens. The function of the political system is to unite and reconcile all citizens and to ensure that the established Government serves the people. The Government must recognize the separation of powers, the primacy of the law, and the principles of good governance and transparency in public affairs. All citizens have equal rights and are assured equal protection by the law. The civic obligations of the individual are emphasized.

POLITICAL PARTY SYSTEM

Political parties may be established freely, subject to conformity with the law. Their organization and activities must correspond to democratic principles, and membership must be open to all civilians. They are not permitted to promote violence, discrimination or hate on any basis, including ethnic, regional or religious affiliation, or gender. Members of defence and security bodies, and acting magistrates are prohibited from joining political parties. A seven-member Commission Electorale Nationale Indépendante guarantees the freedom, impartiality and independence of the electoral process.

EXECUTIVE POWER

Executive power is vested in the President, who is the Head of State. The President is elected by universal direct suffrage for a term of seven years, which is renewable once. The President is assisted in the exercise of his powers by a Vice-President, whom he appoints, and presides over the Government. The President, in consultation with the Vice-President and the Prime Minister, who is the head of the Government, appoints the members of the Government.

GOVERNMENT

The Government comprises at most a 60% proportion of Hutu ministers and deputy ministers and a 40% of Tutsi ministers and deputy ministers, and must include a minimum 30% proportion of women.

LEGISLATURE

Legislative power is vested in the bicameral legislature, comprising a lower chamber, the National Assembly, and an upper chamber, the Senate. The National Assembly has a minimum of 100 deputies, with a proportion of 60% Hutu and 40% Tutsi representatives, and including a minimum 30% of women. Deputies are elected by direct universal suffrage for a term of five years, while the Twa ethnic group nominates three representatives. If the election results fail to conform to the stipulated ethnic composition, additional deputies may be appointed in accordance with the electoral code. The Senate comprises a minimum of two senators elected by ethnically balanced colleges from each of the country's provinces, and three Twa representatives, and includes a minimum 30% of women. Both chambers have a President and Vice-Presidents.

JUDICIARY

The President guarantees the independence of the judiciary, with the assistance of the High Council of the Judiciary. The highest judicial power is vested in the Supreme Court. All appointments to these organs are made by the President, on the proposal of the Minister of Justice and in consultation with the High Council of the Judiciary, and are endorsed by the Senate. The Constitutional Court interprets the provisions of the Constitution and ensures the conformity of new legislation. The Constitutional Court comprises seven members, who are appointed by the President, subject to the approval of the Senate, for a non-renewable, eight-year term.

DEFENCE AND SECURITY FORCES

The establishment and operations of defence and security forces must conform to the law. Members of defence and security forces are prohibited from belonging to, participating in the activities of, or demonstrating prejudice towards, any political parties. All citizens are eligible to join the defence and security forces. During a period to be determined by the Senate, defence and security forces are not permitted to comprise more than 50% of one single ethnic group, in order to ensure an ethnic balance and guard against acts of genocide and military coups.

The Government

HEAD OF STATE

President: Maj.-Gen. EVARISTE NDAYISHIMIYE (inaugurated 18 June 2020).

Vice-President: PROSPER BAZOMBANZA.

COUNCIL OF MINISTERS
(October 2022)

The Government comprises members of the Conseil National pour la Défense de la Démocratie—Forces pour la Défense de la Démocratie (CNDD—FDD).

Prime Minister: GERVAIS NDIRAKOBUCA.

Minister of the Interior, Community Development and Public Security: MARTIN NITERETSE.

Minister of National Defence and War Veterans: ALAIN TRIBERT MUTABAZI.

Minister of Justice: DOMINE BANYANKIMBONA.

Minister of Foreign Affairs and Development Co-operation: ALBERT SHINGIRO.

Minister of Finance, the Budget and Economic Planning: AUDACE NIYONZIMA.

Minister of National Education and Scientific Research: Dr FRANÇOIS HAVYARIMANA.

Minister of Public Health and the Fight against AIDS: Dr SYLVIE NZEYIMANA.

Minister of the Environment, Agriculture and Stockbreeding: Dr SANCTUS NIRAGIRA.

Minister of Infrastructure, Equipment and Social Housing: DIUEDONNÉ DUKUNDANE.

Minister of the Civil Service, Labour and Employment: DÉO RUSENGWAMIHIGO.

Minister of Water Resources, Energy and Mining: IBRAHIM UWIZEYE.

Minister of Commerce, Transport, Industry and Tourism: MARIE CHANTAL NIJIMBERE.

Minister of East African Community Affairs, Youth, Sport and Culture: EZÉCHIEL NIBIGIRA.

Minister of National Solidarity, Social Affairs, Human Rights and Gender Equality: IMELDE SABUSHIMIKE.

Minister of Communication, Information Technology and the Media: LÉOCADIE NDACAYISABA.

Secretary-General of the State: PROSPER NTAHORWAMIYE.

MINISTRIES

Office of the President: blvd de l'Indépendance, Bujumbura; tel. 22226063; internet presidence.gov.bi.

Office of the Prime Minister: Bujumbura.

Ministry of the Civil Service, Labour and Employment: Quartier Rohero I, ave de la Révolution, BP 1480, Bujumbura; tel. 22225485; e-mail info@ministerefptss.gov.bi; internet www .ministerefptss.gov.bi.

Ministry of Commerce, Transport, Industry and Tourism: ave des Manguiers 34, 3e et 4e étages, BP 492, Bujumbura; tel. 22226317; internet mincommerce.gov.bi.

Ministry of Communication, Information Technology and the Media: Immeuble l'Orée du Golf, 2e étage, blvd du 1er Novembre, BP 2870, Bujumbura; tel. 22253472; e-mail info@mintic.gov.bi; internet mintic.gov.bi.

Ministry of East African Community Affairs, Youth, Sport and Culture: Bujumbura.

Minister of the Environment, Agriculture and Stockbreeding: Quartier 4, ave Mwambutsa, Ngagara, BP 631, Bujumbura; tel. 22222087; e-mail info@minagrie.gov.bi; internet minagrie.gov.bi.

Ministry of Finance, the Budget and Economic Planning: ave des Non-Aligens, BP 1830, Bujumbura; tel. 22222775; e-mail finances@finances.gov.bi; internet www.finances.gov.bi.

Ministry of Foreign Affairs and Development Co-operation: blvd de la Liberté 15, BP 1840, Bujumbura; tel. 22250678; e-mail info@mae.gov.bi; internet www.mae.gov.bi.

Ministry of Infrastructure, Equipment and Social Housing: Bujumbura.

Ministry of the Interior, Community Development and Public Security: Bujumbura; internet mininterinfos.gov.bi.

Ministry of Justice: Grand Bureau, pl. de la Révolution, ave de la Liberté, Bujumbura; tel. 22253379.

Ministry of National Defence and War Veterans: ave Pierre Ngendandumwe, Bujumbura; tel. 22225566; e-mail contact@mdnac .bi; internet www.mdnac.bi.

Ministry of National Education and Scientific Research: Bujumbura.

Ministry of National Solidarity, Social Affairs, Human Rights and Gender Equality: BP 224, Bujumbura; tel. 22225394; e-mail ministre@miniplan.bi; internet www.cslpminiplan.bi.

Ministry of Public Health and the Fight against AIDS: rue Pierre Ngendandumwe, Bujumbura; tel. 22242542; e-mail info@ minisante.bi; internet minisante.bi.

Ministry of Water Resources, Energy and Mining: Rohero I, ave de la Révolution 7, BP 745, Bujumbura; tel. 22225101; e-mail minergiemine@gmail.com; internet ministere-energie-mines.gov.bi.

President

Presidential Election, 20 May 2020

Candidate	Valid votes	% of valid votes
Evariste Ndayishimiye (CNDD—FDD) .	3,082,210	71.45
Agathon Rwasa (CNL)	1,084,788	25.15
Gaston Sindimwo (UPRONA) . . .	73,353	1.70
Domitien Ndayizeye (CKB)	24,470	0.57
Léonce Ngendakumana (FRODEBU) . .	21,232	0.49
Dieudonné Nahimana (Ind.) . . .	18,709	0.43
Francis Rohero (Ind.)	8,942	0.21
Total	4,313,704*	100.00

* In addition, there were 87,534 blank and 83,690 invalid votes.

Legislature

SENATE

Senate: Gitega; internet www.senat.bi.

President: Rev. EMMANUEL SINZOHAGERA (CNDD—FDD).

First Vice-President: DÉNISE NDADAYE (CNDD—FDD).

Second Vice-President: CYRIAQUE NSHIMIRIMANA (CNDD—FDD).

Elections, 20 July 2020

Party	Seats
CNDD—FDD	34
CNL	1
UPRONA	1
Total	36*

* In accordance with constitutional requirements for balance of ethnic representation and a minimum 30% representation of women, a further three seats were allocated to the Twa ethnic group, increasing the total number of senators to 39.

NATIONAL ASSEMBLY

National Assembly: BP 120, Bujumbura; tel. 22267055; e-mail communication@assemblee.bi; internet assemblee.bi.

President: DANIEL GÉLASE NDABIRABE (CNDD—FDD).

First Vice-President: Dr SABINE NTAKARUTIMA (CNDD—FDD).

Second Vice-President: ABEL GASHATSI (UPRONA).

Elections, 20 May 2020

Party	Valid votes	% of valid votes	Seats*
CNDD—FDD	3,036,286	70.98	72
CNL	1,001,230	23.41	27
UPRONA	108,865	2.54	1
Others	131,273	3.07	—
Total	4,277,654	100.00	100

* In accordance with constitutional requirements for balance of ethnic representation and a minimum 30% representation of women, a further 20 Tutsis (11 women and nine men) were allocated seats, while three seats were allotted to the Twa ethnic group, increasing the total number of deputies to 123. The CNDD—FDD received 14 additional seats, the CNL five and UPRONA one.

Election Commission

Commission Electorale Nationale Indépendante (CENI): Commune Ngagara, Quartier Industriel, blvd de l'OUA, rue Nyankoni, Parcelle N° 690/C, BP 1128, Bujumbura; tel. 22274464; e-mail info@ceniburundi.bi; internet www.ceniburundi.bi; f. 2004; independent; 5 mems; Chair. Dr PIERRE CLAVER KAZIHISE.

Political Organizations

Political parties are required to demonstrate firm commitment to national unity, and impartiality with regard to ethnic or regional origin, gender and religion, in order to receive legal recognition.

Alliance Démocratique pour le Changement au Burundi (ADC—Ikibiri): Bujumbura; f. 2010; coalition of 12 opposition parties, including Front pour la Démocratie au Burundi (FRODEBU); Pres. LÉONCE NGENDAKUMANA.

Congrès National pour la Liberté (CNL): internet fb.com/CNL-Burundi-332115027569968; f. 2019; Pres. AGATHON RWASA.

Conseil National pour la Défense de la Démocratie—Forces pour la Défense de la Démocratie (CNDD—FDD): internet www.cndd-fdd.org; Chair. of the Council of Elders Maj.-Gen. EVARISTE NDAYISHIMIYE; Sec.-Gen. RÉVÉRIEN NDIKURIYO.

Forces Nationales de Libération—Iragi rya Gahutu: f. 2009; Leader JACQUES KENESE.

Front pour la Démocratie au Burundi (FRODEBU): Bujumbura; internet www.frodebu.bi; f. 1992; Hutu; Chair. LÉONCE NGENDAKUMANA.

FRODEBU-Nyakuri: Bujumbura; f. 2008; Leader KEFA NIBIZI.

Mouvement pour la Réhabilitation du Citoyen—Rurenzangemero (MRC—Rurenzangemero): Bujumbura; f. June 2001; regd Nov. 2002; Leader (vacant).

Mouvement pour la Sécurité et la Démocratie (MSD): tel. 29550803; e-mail msdburundi@yahoo.fr; Pres. ALEXIS SINDUHIJE; Sec.-Gen. FRANÇOIS NYAMOYA.

Mouvement Socialiste Panafricaniste—Inkinzo y'Ijambo Ry'abarundi (MSP—Inkinzo) (Guarantor of Freedom of Speech in Burundi): Bujumbura; f. 1993; Tutsi; Chair. TITE BUCUMI.

Parti pour la Réconciliation du Peuple (PRP): Bujumbura; f. 1992; Tutsi; Leader DÉOGRATIAS RUSENGWAMIHIGO.

Parti pour le Redressement National (PARENA): Bujumbura; f. 1994; Leader ZÉNON NIMUBONA.

Rassemblement pour la Démocratie et le Développement Economique et Social (RADDES): Bujumbura; f. 1992; Tutsi; Chair. DISMAS NDITABIRIYE.

Union pour le Progrès National (UPRONA): BP 1810, Bujumbura; tel. 22225028; internet www.uprona.org; f. 1958; Pres. OLIVIER NKURUNZIZA; Sec.-Gen. JEAN DE DIEU NIYONKURU.

Diplomatic Representation

EMBASSIES IN BURUNDI

Algeria: Bujumbura; Ambassador HAMID BOUKRIF.

Belgium: 18 blvd de la Liberté, BP 1920, Bujumbura; tel. 22226176; e-mail bujumbura@diplobel.fed.be; internet burundi.diplomatie .belgium.be; Ambassador ALAIN VAN GUCHT.

China, People's Republic: 8A ave du Lycée, Parcelle 675, BP 2550, Bujumbura; tel. 22224307; e-mail sinoburundi@hotmail.com; internet bi.china-embassy.gov.cn; Ambassador ZHAO JIANGPING.

Congo, Democratic Republic: Rohero II, 2–4 ave de la RDC, BP 872, Bujumbura; tel. 22226916; e-mail ambardcbujumbura@yahoo .fr; Chargé d'affaires a.i. CHRISTOPHE KATANGA WA BANZA.

Egypt: 46 ave Nzero, BP 1520, Bujumbura; tel. 22223161; e-mail embassy.bujmubura@mfa.gov.eg; Ambassador YASSER EL-ATTAWI.

France: 60 blvd de l'UPRONA, BP 1740, Bujumbura; tel. 22203000; e-mail cad.bujumbura-amba@diplomatie.gouv.fr; internet bi .ambafrance.org; Ambassador JÉRÉMIE BLIN.

Germany: 30 ave du 18 Septembre, BP 480, Bujumbura; tel. 22257777; e-mail info@bujumbura.diplo.de; internet bujumbura .diplo.de; Ambassador DIETER REINL.

Holy See: 46 ave des Travailleurs, BP 1068, Bujumbura; tel. 22225415; Apostolic Nuncio DIEUDONNÉ DATONOU (Titular Archbishop of Vico Equense).

Kenya: 52 ave des Travailleurs, off Chaussée du Prince Louis Rwagasore, BP 5138, Mutanga, Bujumbura; tel. 22258160; e-mail bujumbura@mfa.go.ke; internet www.kenyaembassyburundi.com; Ambassador DANIEL WAISIKO WAMBURA.

Libya: ave de la Révolution, Centre-ville, Bujumbura; tel. 22244871.

Morocco: Bujumbura.

Netherlands: Immeuble Old East, pl. de l'Independance, Bujumbura; tel. 22252055; e-mail buj@minbuza.nl; internet www .nederlandwereldwijd.nl/landen/burundi; Ambassador JEROEN STEEGHS.

Nigeria: Quartier Kabondo, 44 ave Gihungwe, BP 822, Bujumbura; tel. 22257076; e-mail nigeria.bujumbura@foreignaffairs.gov.ng; internet www.nigeriaembassyburundi.org; Ambassador ELIJAH ONYEAGBA.

Russian Federation: 43 blvd de l'UPRONA, BP 1034, Bujumbura; tel. 22226098; e-mail ambrusburundi@mid.ru; internet burundi.mid .ru; Ambassador VALERY ALEKSANDROVICH MIKHAYLOV.

Rwanda: 40 ave de la RDC, BP 400, Bujumbura; tel. 22228755; e-mail ambabuja@minaffet.gov.rw; internet www.rwandainburundi .gov.rw; Chargé d'affaires a.i. FIDELE MUNYESHYAKA.

Somalia: 22 blvd du 28 Novembre, Kiriri, Bujumbura; tel. 75677777; Chargé d'affaires a.i. ZAKARIA OSMAN MOHAMED.

South Africa: ave de la Plage, Quartier Asiatique, BP 185, Bujumbura; tel. 22248220; e-mail higap@dirco.gov.za; Ambassador KGOMOTSO NOMI JOLOBE.

Tanzania: Kabondo, Mpotsa Ave, BP 855, Bujumbura; tel. 22248636; e-mail tanzanrep@usan-bu.net; internet www.bi .tzembassy.go.tz; Ambassador Dr JILLY MALIKO.

Türkiye (Turkey): Bujumbura; e-mail embassy.bujumbura@mfa .gov.tr; Ambassador SERAP ATAAY.

Uganda: Parcelle 8467C, Quartier Mirroir, Kiyange, POB 5155, Bujumbura; tel. 75156156; e-mail ugembu@hotmail.com; internet bujumbura.mofa.go.ug; Ambassador Maj.-Gen. MATAYO KYALIGONZA.

USA: 50 ave des Etats-Unis, BP 1720, Bujumbura; tel. 22207000; internet bi.usembassy.gov; Ambassador MELANIE H. HIGGINS.

Judicial System

Constitutional Court: BP 151, Bujumbura; comprises a minimum of 7 judges, who are nominated by the President for a 6-year term; Pres. VALENTIN BAGORIKUNDA.

Supreme Court: BP 1460, Bujumbura; tel. 22213544; court of final instance; 3 divisions: ordinary, cassation and administrative; Pres. EMMANUEL GATERETSE.

Courts of Appeal: Bujumbura, Gitega, Ngozi, Bujumbura Mairie, Makamba, Muha, Ntahangwa and Bururi.

Attorney-General: SYLVESTRE NYANDWI.

Religion

According to the 2008 census, some 86% of the population were Christians, the majority of whom were Roman Catholics, while about 2.5% of the population were Muslims.

Conseil Interconfessionnel du Burundi (CICB): 42 ave de France, BP 1390, Bujumbura; tel. 22259153; f. 2008; Exec. Sec. ISIDORE HAKIZIMANA.

CHRISTIANITY

Conseil National des Eglises Protestantes du Burundi (CNEB): BP 17, Bujumbura; tel. 22224216; f. 1935; 10 mem. churches; Pres. Rev. JUVÉNAL NZOSABA; Gen. Sec. Rev. NOAH NZEYIMANA.

The Anglican Communion

The Church of the Province of Burundi, established in 1992, comprises nine dioceses.

Archbishop of Burundi and Bishop of Buye: Most Rev. SIXBERT MACUMI, BP 447, Bujumbura; tel. 22924595; e-mail anglicanburundinews@gmail.com; internet www.anglicanburundi.org.

Provincial Secretary: FÉLIBIEN NDINTORE, BP 2098, Bujumbura; tel. 22224389; e-mail anglicanburundinews@gmail.com; internet www.anglicanburundi.org.

The Roman Catholic Church

Burundi comprises two archdioceses and six dioceses.

Bishops' Conference: Conférence des Evêques Catholiques du Burundi, 5 blvd de l'UPRONA, BP 1390, Bujumbura; tel. 22223263; internet eglisecatholique.bi; f. 1980; Pres. Rev. JOACHIM NTAHONDEREYE (Bishop of Muyinga).

Archbishop of Bujumbura: Rt Rev. GERVAIS BANSHIMIYUBUSA, BP 690, Bujumbura; tel. 22231476; e-mail dicabu@cni.cbinf.com.

Archbishop of Gitega: Most Rev. BONAVENTURE NAHIMANA, Archevêché, BP 118, Gitega; tel. 22402160; e-mail archigi@bujumbura.ocicnet.net; internet www.archidiocese-gitega.org.

Other Christian Churches

Union of Baptist Churches of Burundi: 29 ave de la Revolution, Bujumbura; tel. 22235764; internet fb.com/Union-des-Eglises-Baptistes-du-Burundi-475643155973108; 87 mem. churches; Pres. JEAN JACQUES MASABO.

Other denominations active in the country include the Evangelical Christian Brotherhood of Burundi, the Free Methodist Church of Burundi and the United Methodist Church of Burundi.

ISLAM

Communauté Islamique du Burundi (COMIBU): BP 2741, Bujumbura; tel. 22215749; e-mail comibu2006@yahoo.fr; Mufti SHEIKH SHABANI ALI.

BAHÁ'Í FAITH

National Spiritual Assembly: BP 1578, Bujumbura; tel. 69472210; e-mail bahaiburundi@yahoo.fr; f. 1973; Sec. TIMOTHEE MIGABOMYIZA.

The Press

Conseil National de la Communication (CNC): Immeuble Nyogozi, blvd de l'UPRONA, Marcoil, BP 1398, Bujumbura; tel. 22259064; e-mail cncburundi@yahoo.fr; internet cnc-burundi.bi; f. 1993; responsible for ensuring press freedom; Pres. VESTINE NAHIMANA; Exec. Sec. CHANEL NSABIMONA.

Observatoire de la Presse Burundaise: Maison de la Presse du Burundi, 1 ave de Mars, BP 6719, Bujumbura; tel. 22218780; e-mail info@maisondelapresse-burundi.org; self-regulatory body; Pres. INNOCENT MUHOZI.

DAILY NEWSPAPERS (PRINT AND ONLINE)

Le Renouveau du Burundi: ave du Luxembourg, BP 2573, Bujumbura; tel. 22225411; e-mail pressequotidienne@yahoo.fr; f. 1978; French; govt-owned; Dir of Publication CHANNEL SABIMBONA; Editor-in-Chief PASCALINE BIDUDA.

PERIODICALS

Burundi Eco: Rohero II, ave Moso, Bujumbura; tel. 22277868; e-mail info@burundi-eco.com; internet www.burundi-eco.com; weekly; Dir of Publication BENJAMIN KURIYO.

Get-It: 32 ave des Paysans (Galerie au Coeur d'Afrique No. 21), BP 2501, Bujumbura; tel. 78099099; monthly; Editor-in-Chief MARCO EBERLEIN.

Gutwara Neza: ave Belvédère, Kiriri, BP 7359, Bujumbura; tel. 22256690; quarterly; Editor-in-Chief TONY NSABIMANA.

Ikiyago c'inama Nshingamateka: Palais de Kigobe, BP 120, Bujumbura; tel. 22238137; internet www.assemblee.bi; bi-monthly; Editor-in-Chief THARCISSE MANIRAKIZA.

Iwacu: Rohero I, Quartier INSS, 18 ave Mwaro, BP 1842, Bujumbura; tel. 22258957; e-mail iwacuweb@iwacu-burundi.org; internet www.iwacu-burundi.org; f. 2008; weekly; publ. by the Union Burundaise des Journalistes; Editor-in-Chief ANTOINE KABURAHE.

Ndongozi Y'uburundi: Catholic Mission, BP 690, Bujumbura; tel. 22222762; fortnightly; Kirundi; Dir of Publication JEAN NOËL NTIRANDEKURA.

Rumurikirangabo: BP 2705, Bujumbura; tel. 22220971; e-mail rumurikirangabo@yahoo.fr; monthly; Dir of Publication FLORIBERT BIYEREKE.

Tribune Libre des Travailleurs (Twungururunani): Quartier Muyaga, 35 ave Kivyeyi, Bujumbura; tel. 22231530; e-mail rhatungimana@yahoo.fr; monthly; Dir of Publication RICHARD HATUNGIMANA.

Ubumwe: ave du Luxemboug, BP 2573, Bujumbura; tel. 22225654; e-mail ubumwebdi@yahoo.fr; weekly; Dir of Publication LONGIN NIYONKURU.

PRESS ASSOCIATIONS

Association des Femmes Journalistes du Burundi (AFJO): 1 ave Mars, blvd du 28 novembre, Maison de la Presse du Burundi, BP 2414, Bujumbura; tel. 79949460; e-mail afjo2005@yahoo.fr; internet afjo.org.bi; Pres. AGATHONIQUE BARAKUKUZA.

Burundian Journalists' Alliance: Bujumbura; e-mail burundianjournalists@gmail.com; internet fb.com/Burundian-JournalistsAlliance-109312767474319; f. 2020; Pres. MELCHIOR NICAYENZI.

Union Burundaise des Journalistes (UBJ): Maison de la Presse, BP 189, Bujumbura; tel. 22218780; e-mail ubjburundi@gmail.com; internet ubjburundi.org; fmrly Association Burundaise des Journalistes (ABJ), present name adopted 2009; Pres. ALEXANDRE NIYUNGEKO; Sec.-Gen. ANNICK NDAYIRAGIJE.

NEWS AGENCIES

Agence Burundaise de Presse (ABP): Quartier Asiatique, 7 ave des Paysans, BP 2870, Bujumbura; tel. 22213083; internet abpinfo.bi; f. 1975; publ. daily bulletin; Dir-Gen. NICOLAS BARAJINGWA.

Publishers

Editions Intore: 19 ave Matana, BP 2524, Bujumbura; tel. 22223499; e-mail anbirabuza@yahoo.fr; f. 1992; philosophy, history, journalism, literature, social sciences; Dir Dr ANDRÉ BIRABUZA.

IMPARUDI: 3 ave du 18 septembre, BP 3010, Bujumbura; tel. 22223125; e-mail imparudi.1982@yahoo.fr; f. 1950; Dir-Gen. THÉONESTE MUTAMBUKA.

GOVERNMENT PUBLISHING HOUSES

Imprimerie Nationale du Burundi (INABU): BP 991, Bujumbura; tel. 22224046; f. 1978; Dir NICOLAS NIJIMBERE.

Publications de Presse Burundaise: BP 2573, Bujumbura; tel. 22226232; e-mail pressequotidienne@yahoo.fr; internet www.ppbdi.com; Dir-Gen. LOUIS KAMWENUBUSA.

Broadcasting and Communications

TELECOMMUNICATIONS

CBINET: 61 chaussée du Prince Louis Rwagasore, BP 2270, Bujumbura; tel. 76181010; e-mail info@cbinet.net; internet www.cbinet.net; f. 1999; internet service provider; Gen. Man. FABRICE BUTOKE.

Econet Leo: 281A, blvd de l'UPRONA, BP 431, Bujumbura; tel. 76222506; e-mail info@econet-leo.bi; internet www.econet.bi; formerly Spacetel; mobile and fixed telecommunications services and products, satellite services, and internet solutions; Pres. HARDY PEMHIWA; CEO NEÉPIAS NJARAVAZA.

Lumitel Burundi: 51 blvd de l'UPRONA, Quartier Rohero II, Bujumbura; tel. 31000009; e-mail contact@lumitel.co.bi; internet lumitel.bi; f. 1999 as Africell; subsidiary of Viettel Group (Viet Nam); mobile telephone service provider; Dir-Gen. SON ANH NGUYEN.

Office National des Télécommunications (ONATEL): 1 ave du Commerce, BP 60, Bujumbura; tel. 22266601; internet www.onatel.bi; f. 1979; Dir-Gen. PRIVAT KABEBA.

ONAMOB: Bujumbura; mobile telephone operator owned by ONATEL.

Smart Mobile: Immeuble White Stone, blvd de l'UPRONA Centre, BP 3150, Bujumbura; internet www.smart.bi/LetsTalk; f. 2010; trade name of Lacell SU; Dir-Gen. BHUPENDRA BHANDARI.

Spidernet: Quartier Asiatique, 6 rue Kirundo, Bujumbura; tel. 22258480; e-mail info@spidernet-bi.com; internet spidernet.bi; f. 2008; internet service provider; CEO SULTAN KALULA.

Regulatory Authority

Agence de Régulation et de Contrôle des Télécommunications (ARCT): 14 ave de France, BP 6702,

Bujumbura; tel. 22255667; e-mail info@arct.gov.bi; internet arct.gov
.bi; Dir-Gen. Télésphore Irambona.

BROADCASTING
Radio

Buja FM (87.6 FM): Bujumbura; tel. 75822622; e-mail ambuhinja@
yahoo.fr; internet bujafm.com; f. 2013 as Radio 10; independent; Dir-
Gen. Alain Michel Buhinja.

Destiny FM (90.5 FM): Bujumbura; tel. 22279393; internet fb.com/
Destiny-FM-494210720977745; f. 2016; Dir Alice Mucowintore.

Radio Isanganiro: 27 ave de l'Amitié, BP 810, Bujumbura; tel.
22246595; e-mail info@isanganiro.org; internet www.isanganiro
.org; f. 2002; controlled by Association Ijambo, f. by Studio Ijambo
(see below); broadcasts on 89.7 FM frequency, in Kirundi, French and
Swahili; services cover Bujumbura area, and were to be extended to
all Great Lakes region; Dir Slyvère Ntakarutimana.

Radio Scolaire Nderagakura: Bujumbura; internet
radionderagakura.com; f. 2000; educational; Dir-Gen. Stany
Nahayo.

Radio Télévision Nationale du Burundi (RTNB): 12 ave du 13
Octobre, BP 1900, Bujumbura; tel. 22216559; e-mail rtnb@rtnb.bi;
internet www.rtnb.bi; f. 1960; govt-controlled; daily radio broadcasts
in Kirundi, Swahili, French and English; Dir-Gen. Eric Nshimirimana; Dir of Radio Jonas Ndikumuremyi.

Rema FM: 29 rue de la Mission, BP 3610, Bujumbura; tel. 69364901;
f. 2008; Dir Jean Claude Nkurunziza.

Television

Héritage TV: Quartier Industriel, ave l'OUA, BP 4251, Bujumbura;
tel. 22212711; e-mail info@heritagetv.bi; internet www.heritagetv
.bi; Christian religious programming; broadcasts in Kirundi, French,
English and Swahili; Dir Libérat Hatungimana.

Radio Télévision Nationale du Burundi (RTNB): 12 ave 13
Octobre, BP 1900, Bujumbura; tel. 22216559; e-mail rtnb@rtnb.bi;
internet www.rtnb.bi; f. 1960; govt-controlled; television service in
Kirundi, Swahili, French and English; Dir-Gen. Eric Nshimirimana;
Dir of Television Faustin Ndayizeye.

Rema TV: 29 rue de la Mission, Bujumbura; tel. 22258402; internet
www.rematelevision.com; Dir Jean Claude Nkurunziza.

Télévision Salama: Bujumbura; tel. 79901986; Dir Josiane
Inamahoro.

Finance

BANKING
Central Bank

Banque de la République du Burundi (BRB): 1 ave du Gouvernement, BP 705, Bujumbura; tel. 22204000; e-mail brb@brb.bi;
internet www.brb.bi; f. 1964 as Banque du Royaume du Burundi;
state-owned; bank of issue; Gov. Jean Ciza; First Vice-Gov. Melchior
Wagara.

Commercial Banks

**Banque Burundaise pour le Commerce et l'Investissement
SARL (BBCI):** blvd du Peuple Murundi, BP 2320, Bujumbura; tel.
22223328; e-mail contact@bbcibank.com; internet www.bbcibank
.com; f. 1988; Pres. Salout Kunzi; Dir-Gen. Côme Gitegetse.

Banque Commerciale du Burundi SM (BANCOBU): 84 chaussée Prince Louis Rwagasore, BP 990, Bujumbura; tel. 22265200;
e-mail info@bancobu.com; internet www.bancobu.com; f. 1960;
19.22% owned by the Société d'Assurance du Burundi, 13.25%
owned by the Institut Nationale de Sécurité Sociale; Pres. Léa
Ngabire; Dir-Gen. Gaspard Sindayigaya.

Banque de Crédit de Bujumbura SM: 5 blvd Patrice Emery
Lumumba, BP 300, Bujumbura; tel. 22201111; e-mail info@bcb.bi;
internet www.bcb.bi; f. 1964; 21.70% owned by SOCABU, 20.25%
owned by Groupe BOA and 17.38% owned by BIO; Dir-Gen.
Tharcisse Rutumo.

Banque de Gestion et de Financement SA (BGF): 1 blvd de la
Liberté, BP 1035, Bujumbura; tel. 22221352; e-mail info@bgf.bi;
internet bgf.bi; f. 1996; Gen. Man. Jean Marie Clair Gashubije.

Diamond Trust Bank (DTB): 14 chaussée Prince Louis Ragasore,
Bujumbura; tel. 22259988; e-mail contactcentre@dtbafrica.com;
internet dtbb.co.bi; f. 2008; Pres. Shafiq Jiwani; Dir-Gen. Ida Marie
Mabushi.

Ecobank Burundi: 6 rue de la Science, BP 270, Bujumbura; tel.
22226351; e-mail ecobankbi@ecobank.com; internet www.ecobank
.com; Chair. Evariste Minani; Man. Dir (vacant).

FinBank SA: 4 blvd de l'Independance, BP 2998, Bujumbura; tel.
22243206; internet www.finbank.co.bi; Dir-Gen. Rukundo Joe
Dassin.

Interbank Burundi SARL: 15 rue de l'Industrie, BP 2970, Bujumbura; tel. 22220629; e-mail info@interbankbdi.com; internet www
.interbankbdi.com; f. 1993; Pres. Georges Coucoulis; Dir-Gen. Eric
Jonckheere.

KCB Bank Burundi: Bujumbura; internet fb.com/
KCBbankBurundiLTD; f. 2012; Dir-Gen. Gloria Adhiambo
Nyambok.

Development Banks

**Banque Nationale pour le Développement Economique SARL
(BNDE):** 3 ave du Marché, BP 1620, Bujumbura; tel. 22222888;
internet bnde.bi; f. 1966; 40% state-owned; Pres. Gervais Ndirakobuca; Dir-Gen. Audace Bukuru.

Financial Institutions

Fonds de Promotion de L'Habitat Urbain (FPHU): ave de la
Liberté, BP 1996, Bujumbura; tel. 22224986; e-mail info@fphu.bi;
internet fphu.bi; f. 1989; Dir-Gen. Didace Ngendakumana.

INSURANCE

Bicor Assurances: 11 ave de Grèce, BP 2377, Bujumbura; tel.
22222820; e-mail bicor@bicor.bi; internet www.bicor.bi.

Jubilee Insurance Company of Burundi Ltd: 8 chaussée Prince
Louis Rwagasore, BP 2290, Bujumbura; tel. 22275820; e-mail jicb@
jubileeburundi.com; internet www.jubileeinsurance.com/bu; f. 2008;
CEO Denis Huyberechts.

Société d'Assurances du Burundi (SOCABU): BP 2440, Bujumbura; tel. 22226520; e-mail socabu@socabu-assurances.com; internet
www.socabu-assurances.com; f. 1977; Dir-Gen. Trinitas
Girukwishaka.

Union Commerciale d'Assurances et de Réassurance (UCAR):
chaussée du Peuple Murundi, BP 3012, Bujumbura; tel. 22223638;
f. 1986; Dir-Gen. Emery Ndikumagenge.

Regulatory Authority

Agence de Régulation et de Contrôle des Assurances (ARCA):
blvd de Japon, Bujumbura; internet arca.bi; f. 2014; Sec.-Gen. Dr
Joseph Butore.

Trade and Industry

GOVERNMENT AGENCIES

Agence de Développement du Burundi (ADB): Immeuble
Asharif, blvd du 28 Novembre, Mutanga Nord, BP 7057, Bujumbura;
tel. 22275996; e-mail contact@investburundi.bi; internet www
.investburundi.bi; f. 2021 to replace the Agence de Promotion
d'Investissement au Burundi (API); Dir-Gen. Didace
Ngendakumana.

Observatoire des Filières Agricoles (OFB): 7 ave Imbo, Quartier
Asiatique, BP 5, Bujumbura; tel. 22251865; Co-ordinator Patrice
Ntahompagaze.

Office Burundais des Mines et Carrières (OBM): Bujumbura;
e-mail info@obm.bi; internet www.obm.bi; f. 2018; Dir-Gen. Didace
Ntirampeba.

Office pour le Développement du Café du Burundi (ODECA):
279 blvd de la Tanzanie, BP 450, Bujumbura; tel. 22225333; e-mail
info@odeca.gov.bi; internet odeca.gov.bi; f. 2020 to replace the
Autorité de Régulation de la Filière Café; contributes to policy
formulation for the coffee sector and supervises coffee plantations
and coffee exports; Pres. Evrard Ndayikeje; Dir-Gen. Emmanuel
Niyungeko.

Office du Thé du Burundi (OTB): 46 blvd de l'UPRONA, Bujumbura; tel. 22224228; e-mail communication@otb.co.bi; internet otb.co
.bi; f. 1979; supervises production and marketing of tea; Dir-Gen.
Déogratias Ndayitwayeko.

DEVELOPMENT ORGANIZATIONS

Agence Française de Développement (AFD): Immeuble Old
East, pl. de l'Indépendance, BP 2740, Bujumbura; tel. 222255931;
internet www.afd.fr; Regional Dir Christian Yoka.

Fonds National d'Investissement Communal (FONIC): blvd du
28 Novembre, BP 2799, Bujumbura; tel. 22284576; e-mail info@
fonicbdi.bi; internet fonicbdi.bi; f. 2007 to replace Fonds de
Développement Communal; Pres. Martin Niteretse; Dir-Gen.
Servelien Nitunga.

Institut des Sciences Agronomiques du Burundi (ISABU): Rohero 1, blvd du Japon, BP 795, Bujumbura; tel. 22227349; e-mail info@isabu.bi; internet isabu.bi; f. 1962 for the scientific development of agriculture and livestock; Pres. Dr MÉLANCE NTUNZWENIMANA; Dir-Gen. Dr ALFRED NIYOKWISHIMIRA.

Office National de la Tourbe (ONATOUR): route de l'Aéroport, BP 2360, Bujumbura; tel. 22226480; e-mail kariyo@yahoo.fr; internet fb.com/Onatour-101251741827923; f. 1977 to promote the exploitation of peat deposits; Dir-Gen. ISIDORE MBAYAHAGA.

INDUSTRIAL AND TRADE ASSOCIATIONS

Association des Commerçants du Burundi (ACOBU): 254 ave du Commerce, Rohero, BP 6373, Bujumbura; tel. 22248663; Pres. ANTOINE MUZANEZA.

Association des Employeurs du Burundi (AEB): 187 rue de la Mission, BP 141, Bujumbura; tel. 22221119; e-mail assosaebbi@yahoo.fr; internet aeb-burundi.com; Pres. THÉODORE KAMWENUBUSA; Sec.-Gen. GASPARD NZISABIRA.

Association des Femmes Entrepreneurs du Burundi (AFAB): 13 ave Kunkiko, Rohero II, BP 1628, Bujumbura; tel. 22242784; e-mail afab.afab2013@gmail.com; f. 1992; Pres. CLAUDETTE NGENDANDUMWE.

Association des Industriels du Burundi (AIB): 187 rue de la Mission, BP 141, Bujumbura; tel. 22278140; e-mail info@aib-burundi.com; internet aib-burundi.org/fr; Pres. OLIVIER SUGURU; Sec.-Gen. MELANCE BUREGEYA.

InterCafé Burundi: Bujumbura; tel. 68968471; asscn of coffee producers, wet and dry millers, roasters and exporters; Exec. Sec. OSCAR BARANYIZIGIYE.

CHAMBERS OF COMMERCE

Chambre Fédérale de Commerce et d'Industrie du Burundi (CFCIB): 1 ave Mpotsa, Rohero I, BP 313, Bujumbura; tel. 22222280; e-mail info@cfcib.bi; internet cfcib.bi; f. 2010 to replace Chambre de Commerce, d'Industrie, d'Agriculture et d'Artisanat du Burundi; Pres. SUGURU OLIVIER.

UTILITIES

Autorité de Régulation des Secteurs de l'Eau Potable et de l'Energie (AREEN): Immeuble le Savonnier, Ground Floor, Commune Mukaza, Zone Rohero, BP 2662, Bujumbura; internet areen.bi; Dir-Gen. BALTHAZAR NGANIKIYE.

Agence Burundaise pour l'Electrification Rurale (ABER): BP 7139, Bujumbura; tel. 22221932; e-mail dgaber@gmail.com; internet www.aber.bi; f. 2011; Dir-Gen. ERIC MPAYIMANA.

Régie de Distribution d'Eau et d'Electricité (REGIDESO): ave de la Révolution, Rohero, BP 660, Bujumbura; tel. 22221218; e-mail info@regideso.bi; internet regideso.bi; state-owned distributor of water and electricity services; Pres. MARTIN NDAYIZEYE; Dir-Gen. Dr JEAN ALBERT MANIGOMBA.

MAJOR COMPANIES

Brarudi: blvd du 1er Novembre, BP 540, Bujumbura; tel. 22288000; e-mail info@brarudi.bi; internet brarudi.bi; f. 1955; production of beer and soft drinks; 60% owned by Heineken; Dir-Gen. CHIDUM AYENI.

Compagnie de Gérance du Coton (COGERCO): BP 2571, Bujumbura; tel. 22222208; f. 1984; development of cotton industry; Dir-Gen. GUSTAVE MAJAMBERE.

Interpetrol Energy SA: 6 pl. de l'Indépendance, BP 15, Bujumbura; tel. 22222848; e-mail info@ipenergy.bi; internet ipenergy.bi; fmrly Fina BP Burundi, subsequently Engen Petroleum Burundi SA; Dir-Gen. FREDDY B. IPOMA.

Société de Deparchage et Conditionnement du Café (SODECO): BP 6000, Bujumbura; tel. 22231830.

Société de Gestion des Stations de Lavage du Café (SOGESTAL): Bujumbura; Pres. SALVATOR SINDAYIHEBURA; Dir-Gen. KAYANZA CLAUDE NZAMBIMANA.

Société Sucrière du Moso (SOSUMO): Gihofi, Rutana, BP 835, Bujumbura; tel. 22507101; e-mail sosumobu@yahoo.fr; internet sosumo-burundi.com; f. 1982 to develop and manage sugar cane plantations; Pres. PASCAL NGENDAKURIYO; Dir-Gen. ALOYS NDAYIKENGURUKIYE.

TRADE UNIONS

Confédération des Syndicats du Burundi (COSYBU): Immeuble Business Plazza B, 2e étage, ave de l'Amitié, Commune Mukaza, BP 2220, Bujumbura; tel. 79147776; e-mail info@cosybu.bi; internet cosybu.bi/fr; Pres. CÉLESTIN NSAVYIMANA; 32 mem. asscns.

Confédération des Syndicats Libres du Burundi (CSLB): BP 1570, Bujumbura; Pres. THARCISSE NIBOGORA; Sec.-Gen. MATHIAS RUVARI.

Transport

RAILWAYS

There are no railways in Burundi. Both Tanzania and Kenya are constructing rail lines that will connect into Rwanda and it was hoped that a subsequent extension into Burundi would eventually be constructed. These rail link would relieve Burundi's isolated trade position.

ROADS

Agence Routière du Burundi: ave Heha, Quartier Kabondo, Bujumbura; tel. 22222940; e-mail info@agenceroutiereduburundi.bi; internet www.agenceroutiereduburundi.bi; Director-General Dr RÉGIS MPAWENAYO.

Office des Transports en Commun (OTRACO): BP 1486, Bujumbura; tel. 22231313; 100% govt-owned; operates public transport; Dir-Gen. DENIS BUKURU.

INLAND WATERWAYS

Bujumbura is the principal port for both passenger and freight traffic on Lake Tanganyika, and the greater part of Burundi's external trade is dependent on the shipping services between Bujumbura and lake ports in Tanzania, Zambia and the Democratic Republic of the Congo.

Autorité Maritime, Portuaire et Ferroviaire: 1 ave de la Tanzanie, Quartier Asiatique, Bujumbura; tel. 22279027; e-mail ampfburundi1@gmail.com; internet www.ampf.bi; f. 2011; Dir-Gen. JACQUES BIGIRIMANA.

Société Concessionnaire de l'Exploitation du Port de Bujumbura (EPB): BP 59, Bujumbura; tel. 22226036; f. 1967; 43% state-owned; controls Bujumbura port; Dir-Gen. MÉTHODE SHIRAMBERE.

CIVIL AVIATION

Autorité de l'Aviation Civile du Burundi (AACB): BP 694, Bujumbura; tel. 22223707; e-mail aacb@aacb.bi; internet www.aacb.bi; f. 2012; Dir-Gen. JOËL NKURABAGAYA.

Burundi Airlines: Bujumbura International Airport, Bujumbura; f. 2021; national carrier; 92% owned by the state, 4% owned by Société d'Assurances du Burundi and 4% by Belgian interests.

Tourism

Office National du Tourisme (ONT): 2 ave des Euphorbes, BP 902, Bujumbura; tel. 22222023; f. 1972; responsible for the promotion and supervision of tourism; Pres. SAMSON NDAYIZEYE; Dir-Gen. VÉNANT NGENDABANKA.

Société Hôtelière et Touristique du Burundi (SHTB): Bujumbura; Dir-Gen. GRÉGOIRE BUNANI.

Defence

Burundi's armed forces, as assessed at November 2021, comprised an army of 30,000, a navy of 50 and a paramilitary force of an estimated 1,000 gendarmes. In 2021 a total of 4,765 Burundian troops were stationed abroad.

Defence Budget: 136,000m. Burundian francs in 2022.

Chief of Staff of the Force de Défense Nationale: Maj.-Gen. PRIME NIYONGABO.

Education

Education is provided free of charge. Primary education, which is officially compulsory, begins at six years of age and lasts for nine years, comprising four cycles. Kirundi is the language of instruction in the first two cycles, while the second two cycles are taught in French or English. Secondary education begins at the age of 15 and lasts for up to six years. Kirundi, French, English and Kiswahili are the languages of instruction. In 2020/21, according to estimates by the United Nations Educational, Scientific and Cultural Organization (UNESCO), enrolment at pre-primary schools included 16% of children in the relevant age-group (males 16%; females 16%). Primary enrolment in 2017/18 included 93% of children in the relevant age-group (males 92%; females 94%), while enrolment at secondary schools in that year included an estimated 28% of children in the relevant age-group (males 24%; females 31%). In 2018 spending on education represented an estimated 18.7% of total budgeted government expenditure.

Bibliography

Brennan, K. *Burundi*. Broomall, PA, Mason Crest Publishers, 2004.

Chrétien, J.-P. *Histoire rurale de l'Afrique des Grands Lacs*. Paris, Editions Karthala, 1983.

    The Great Lakes of Africa: Two Thousand Years of History. New York, Zone Books, 2003.

Chrétien, J.-P., Guichaoua, A., and Le Jeune, G. *La crise d'août 1988 au Burundi*. Paris, Editions Karthala, 1989.

Daley, P. *Gender and Genocide in Burundi: The search for spaces of peace in the Great Lakes Region*. Oxford, James Currey, 2007.

Eggers, E. *Historical Dictionary of Burundi*. 2nd edn. Metuchen, NJ, Scarecrow Press, 1997.

Ewusi, K., and Akwanga, Jr, K. *Burundi's Negative Peace: The Shadow of a Broken Continent in the Era of NEPAD*. Bloomington, IN, Trafford Publishing, 2010.

Gahama, J. *Le Burundi sous administration belge*. Paris, Editions Karthala, 1983.

Guichaoua, A. (Ed.). *Les crises politiques au Burundi et au Rwanda (1993–1994)*. Paris, Editions Karthala, 1995.

Hakizimana, A. *Naissances au Burundi : Entre Tradition et Planification*. Paris, L'Harmattan, 2002.

International Business Publications. *Burundi Foreign Policy and Government Guide*. Washington, DC, 2004.

Krueger, R., and Krueger, K. *From Bloodshed to Hope in Burundi: Our Embassy Years During Genocide*. Austin, TX, University of Texas Press, 2007.

Lambert, M. Y. *Enquête démographique Burundi (1970–1971)*. Bujumbura, Ministère du Plan, 1972.

Lemarchand, R. *Rwanda and Burundi*. London, Pall Mall, 1970.

    Ethnocide as Discourse and Practice. Washington, DC, Woodrow Wilson Center Press and Cambridge, Cambridge University Press, 1994.

    Burundi: Ethnic Conflict and Genocide. Cambridge, Cambridge University Press, 1996.

    The Dynamics of Violence in Central Africa. Philadelphia, PA, University of Pennsylvania Press, 2009.

Longman, T. P. *Burundi—Proxy Target: Civilians in the War on Burundi*. New York, Human Rights Watch, 1998.

Malkii, L. *Purity and Exile: Violence, Memory and National Cosmology among Hutu Refugees in Tanzania*. Chicago, IL, University of Chicago Press, 1995.

Minani Passy, P. *Femmes en politique au Burundi: Leur nombre, leur influence?* Paris, L'Harmattan, 2014.

    Burundi: Les relations interethniques et intra-ethniques. Et la réconciliation? Paris, L'Harmattan, 2019.

Mitchell, S. *Institutional Legacies, Decision Frames and Political Violence in Rwanda and Burundi*. Abingdon, Routledge, 2018.

Mukuri, M., Nduwayo, J., and Bugwabari, N. (Eds). *Un demi-siècle d'histoire du Burundi*. Paris, Editions Karthala, 2017.

Mwakikagile, G. *Civil Wars in Rwanda and Burundi: Conflict Resolution in Africa*. New York, Nova Science Publishers, 2004.

Mworoha, E. *Histoire du Burundi*. Paris, Hatier, 1987.

Nintunze, N. *Burundi 1972: Massacre des Tutsis dans le Sud*. Bujumbura, Editions Iwacu, 2019.

Nsanzé, T. *Le Burundi au carrefour de l'Afrique*. Brussels, Remarques africaines, 1970.

Ntahombaye, P. *Des noms et des hommes. Aspects du nom au Burundi*. Paris, Editions Karthala, 1983.

Ould Abdallah, A. *Burundi on the Brink 1993–95: A UN Special Envoy Reflects on Preventative Diplomacy (Perspectives Series)*. Washington, DC, United States Institute of Peace, 2000.

Reyntjens, F. *Burundi 1972–1988. Continuité et changement*. Brussels, Centre d'étude et de documentation africaines (CEDAF—ASDOC), 1989.

    Again at the Crossroads—Rwanda and Burundi, 2000–2001. Uppsala, Nordiska Afrikainstitutet, 2001.

Russell, A. *Politics and Violence in Burundi: The Language of Truth in an Emerging State*. Cambridge, Cambridge University Press, 2019.

Schraml, C. *The Dilemma of Recognition: Experienced Reality of Ethnicised Politics in Rwanda and Burundi*. Wiesbaden, Springer VS, 2012.

Sommers, M. *Fear in Bongoland: Burundi Refugees in Urban Tanzania (Studies in Forced Migration, Vol. 8)*. New York, Berghahn Books, 2001.

Southall, R., and Bentley, K. *African Peace Process: Mandela, South Africa, and Burundi*. Pretoria, Human Sciences Research Council, 2005.

Timpson, W. M., Ndura, E., and Bangayimbaga, A. *Conflict, Reconciliation, and Peace Education: Moving Burundi Toward a Sustainable Future*. Abingdon, Routledge, 2016.

Tuhabonye, G., and Brozek, G. *This Voice in My Heart: A Genocide Survivor's Story of Escape, Faith, and Forgiveness*. New York, Amistad, 2006.

Uvin, P. *Life After Violence: A People's Story of Burundi*. London, Zed Books, 2008.

Vandeginste, S. *Stones Left Unturned. Law and Transitional Justice in Burundi*. Antwerp, Intersentia, 2010.

Watt, N. *Burundi: The Biography of a Small African Country*. Revised edn. London, C. Hurst & Co, 2016.

Wilén, N. *Justifying Interventions in Africa: (De)stabilizing Sovereignty in Liberia, Burundi and the Congo*. Basingstoke, Palgrave Macmillan, 2012.

CABO VERDE

Physical and Social Geography

RENÉ PÉLISSIER

The island Republic of Cabo Verde, comprising 10 islands, of which nine are inhabited, and five islets, lies in the Atlantic Ocean, about 500 km west of Dakar, Senegal. The archipelago comprises the windward islands of Santo Antão (754 sq km), São Vicente (228 sq km), Santa Luzia (34 sq km), São Nicolau (342 sq km), Boavista (622 sq km) and Sal (215 sq km) to the north, while to the south lie the leeward islands of Maio (267 sq km), Santiago (992 sq km), Fogo (477 sq km) and Brava (65 sq km).

The total area is 4,033 sq km (1,557 sq miles) and the administrative capital is Praia (with a population of some 142,000, according to preliminary results of the 2021 census) on Santiago island. The other main centre of population is Mindelo (São Vicente), which is the principal port and, together with Praia, the economic centre of the archipelago. The 2021 census recorded a total population of 483,628 (giving a density of 119.9 inhabitants per sq km). Santiago is the most populous of the inhabited islands, with an estimated population of 269,370 in 2021, followed by São Vicente (74,016), Santo Antão (36,632) and Fogo (33,519). Santa Luzia has no permanent inhabitants.

Except for the low-lying islands of Sal, Boavista and Maio, the archipelago is mountainous, craggy and deeply indented by erosion and volcanic activity. The highest point is Mt Fogo (2,829 m), an active volcano. Located in the semi-arid belt, the islands have an anaemic hydrography, and suffer from chronic shortages of rainfall, which, combined with high temperatures (yearly average 22°C–26°C at Praia), cause intense periodic droughts.

Ethnically, about 71% of the inhabitants are of mixed descent, except on Santiago, where the majority is of pure African stock. Whites represent about 1% of the population. The two official languages are Portuguese and Crioulo, a creole Portuguese, which is influenced by African vocabulary, syntax and pronunciation. In 2020 the average life expectancy at birth was 69.7 years for men and 76.4 years for women.

Since independence, a significant number of islanders have emigrated, principally to the USA, the Netherlands, Italy and Portugal, where Cabo Verdeans have replaced Portuguese migrants to other countries of the European Union. At least 700,000 Cabo Verdeans live outside the country, and their remittances provide an important source of development capital.

History

GERHARD SEIBERT

The Cabo Verde islands were colonized by Portugal from the 15th century. In the movement for independence from Portuguese rule during the 1960s and 1970s, some Cabo Verdean nationalists aligned themselves with their colleagues in the mainland territory of Portuguese Guinea (now Guinea-Bissau) in a unified nationalist movement, the Partido Africano da Independência do Guiné e Cabo Verde (PAIGC). On 24 September 1973 the PAIGC unilaterally declared the independence of Guinea-Bissau. Although Portugal recognized Guinea Bissau's declaration of independence in September 1974, the PAIGC leadership in Cabo Verde pursued its claims separately, rather than seeking an immediate federation with Guinea-Bissau. In December the Portuguese Government and representatives of the islands' PAIGC formed a transitional administration. Elections to the Assembleia Nacional Popular (National People's Assembly) took place in June 1975, and independence, as the Republic of Cabo Verde, followed on 5 July.

Aristides Pereira, the PAIGC Secretary-General, became the country's first President. Pedro Pires was appointed Prime Minister. In 1980 the PAIGC was constitutionally established as the sole legal party, and in November prospects of unification with Guinea-Bissau receded, when the latter's President was removed in a coup. In 1981 the Cabo Verdean branch of the PAIGC renamed itself the Partido Africano da Independência de Cabo Verde (PAICV). Although Cabo Verde was until September 1990 a one-party state, government policies were generally pragmatic. In the mid-1980s non-PAICV members played an increasingly prominent role in public and political life. Central control of the economy was eased, and in 1989 the Government introduced legislation to encourage Cabo Verdeans abroad to become involved in the development process.

DEMOCRATIC CHANGE

Moves towards a relaxation of the PAICV's political monopoly emerged in early 1990, amid political changes in West Africa and Eastern Europe. In April a newly formed opposition group, the Movimento para a Democracia (MpD), demanded immediate introduction of a multi-party system. Pereira announced that the next presidential election, scheduled for December, would be held, for the first time, on the basis of universal adult suffrage.

In September 1990 the National People's Assembly approved a constitutional amendment abolishing the PAICV's monopoly of power. The MpD duly obtained registration and held its first congress in November, at which Carlos Veiga was elected Chairman. The MpD subsequently declared its support for the candidacy of António Manuel Mascarenhas Gomes Monteiro, a former Supreme Court judge, in the forthcoming presidential election.

At multi-party legislative elections held in January 1991 the MpD secured 56 of the 79 seats in the National People's Assembly. The PAICV took the remaining 23 seats. Veiga was sworn in as Prime Minister at the head of an interim Government, pending the outcome of the presidential election in February. Mascarenhas defeated Pereira, securing 73.5% of the vote. Mascarenhas took office in March, and a new Government was formed in April.

THE SECOND REPUBLIC

A new Constitution, enshrining the democratic basis of the 'Second Republic', took effect in September 1992. At an extraordinary convention of the MpD in February 1994, the party split, and a new opposition group, the Partido da Convergência Democrática (PCD), was formed. At legislative elections held in December 1995 the MpD secured 50 seats in a smaller, 72-seat National Assembly (as the legislature had been renamed). The PAICV obtained 21 seats, and the PCD won the remaining seat. At the presidential election held in February 1996 Mascarenhas was re-elected unopposed. In June 2000 the PAICV elected José Maria Pereira Neves as its new President. At the MpD convention in July António Gualberto do Rosário was elected Chairman. Meanwhile, Veiga resigned from the premiership and declared his intention to contest the forthcoming presidential election. Do Rosário succeeded him as Prime Minister.

The Return of the PAICV

At legislative elections held in January 2001 the PAICV won 40 seats against 30 for the MpD. A new electoral alliance—the Aliança Democrática para a Mudança, formed in October 2000 by the PCD, the Partido de Trabalho e Solidariedade and the União Caboverdiana Independente e Democrática (UCID)—obtained the remaining two seats. Neves was appointed Prime Minister, and his Government was inaugurated in February 2001. The first round of the presidential election, held on 11 February, was inconclusive, and a second round was held on 25 February, in which Pires narrowly defeated Veiga, securing 50.01% of valid votes cast. Official results eventually confirmed that Pires had defeated Veiga by just 17 votes. Appeals against the results by Veiga (citing voting irregularities) were rejected by the Supreme Court in March, which confirmed Pires as the new President.

Do Rosário resigned as MpD leader in August 2001. Agostinho Lopes was elected Chairman in December, and the party became increasingly confrontational towards the Government. It established a newspaper, *Expresso das Ilhas*, to counter the PAICV's perceived dominance of the media and successfully opposed tax changes in the 2002 budget, which the Supreme Court subsequently declared unconstitutional.

In December 2005 Pires announced that he would stand for re-election, and the MpD nominated Veiga as its official candidate for the presidency. Concerns about unemployment and a crime wave on Santiago dominated the election campaign. On 6 February 2006 the Comissão Nacional de Eleições (CNE—National Elections Commission) announced that the PAICV had won the legislative elections held on 22 January, securing 41 seats in the National Assembly. The MpD won 29 seats, and the UCID took the remaining two. Later in that month Pires was re-elected to the presidency after securing 51.0% of the votes cast. Lopes resigned as MpD Chairman and was succeeded by Jorge Santos.

Domestic Developments

In January 2009 the National Assembly created a bipartisan commission to formulate proposals to revise the Constitution. The PAICV and MpD agreed to expand the Supreme Court from five to seven judges, but there was deadlock on several other key proposals. Veiga was elected as MpD leader in October, and Neves was re-elected as leader of the PAICV in November. Meanwhile, in September an outbreak of dengue fever spread across the archipelago, prompting a state of emergency; the Government declared it an epidemic in October. By December the situation had been brought under control, following assistance from the World Health Organization (WHO).

In February 2010 the National Assembly ratified several draft amendments to the Constitution, including reform of the composition of the judiciary and the creation of the Conselho Superior da Magistratura Judicial (Supreme Council of Judiciary) to approve judicial appointments. Other changes included authorization for the police to carry out night raids on properties linked to organized crime, authorization for Cabo Verdean citizens to be extradited for international crimes and recognition of the International Criminal Court. However, there was no agreement about whether Crioulo should be made the country's second official language. In the same month, as part of a wider government reorganization, Neves created a Ministry for Cabo Verdeans Abroad.

The 2011 Elections

Legislative elections took place on 6 February 2011; the PAICV won 38 seats in the National Assembly. The MpD took 32 seats, and the UCID retained its two seats. Prime Minister Neves announced a new Council of Ministers in March. A new Ministry of Youth, Employment and Human Resources Development was created, with a remit to tackle high youth unemployment.

At the first round of the presidential election, held in August 2011, Jorge Carlos Fonseca, a former Minister of Foreign Affairs supported by the MpD, won 37.8% of the vote, while Inocêncio Sousa, a former Minister of Infrastructure backed by the PAICV, took 32.5% and Aristides Lima, an independent candidate, received 27.8%. In the run-off ballot, Fonseca secured 54.2% of votes cast. Turnout averaged only 46% in both rounds, owing partly to heavy rains. Fonseca was inaugurated as President on 7 September, becoming the country's first non-PAICV head of state.

Neves was re-elected unopposed as PAICV President for a third term in March 2013, although he promised to resign in 2015, one year before presidential, legislative and local elections were scheduled. Meanwhile, in June 2013 former Minister of Finance and Mayor of Praia Dr José Ulisses de Pina Correia e Silva was elected unopposed as the MpD Chairman.

The 2016 Elections

In December 2014 Janira Isabel Fonseca Hopffer Almada, the Minister of Youth, Employment and Human Resources Development, won the ruling PAICV's leadership election convincingly, succeeding Neves as party leader and becoming the PAICV's candidate for the premiership in the 2016 legislative elections. In March 2015 a 64% salary increase for the President, government members and parliamentarians, which had been approved by the three parties represented in the National Assembly, provoked widespread protests. In April President Fonseca agreed to veto the salary increases.

At the elections to the National Assembly, which were held on 20 March 2016, the opposition MpD secured an absolute majority of 40 seats (taking 54.5% of the votes), while the PAICV obtained 29 seats (38.2%), and the UCID took three (6.9%). Voter turnout was 65.8%. This represented the third time (after 1991 and 2001) that the opposition had won legislative elections. On 22 April 2016 the new Government, led by Correia e Silva as Prime Minister, took office. At the local elections of 4 September 2016, the ruling MpD strengthened its control of the municipalities. The party won in 18 municipalities (four more than in 2012), while the opposition PAICV lost six of its eight municipalities. Independent groups obtained the majority in the two remaining municipalities. Following the PAICV's second disappointing electoral performance, Hopffer Almada resigned as party leader, although she was re-elected unopposed in January 2017.

Meanwhile, on 2 October 2016 the incumbent Jorge Carlos Fonseca was re-elected to the presidency with 74.1% of votes cast; two independent candidates, Albertino da Graça, dean of the private University of Mindelo, and Joaquim Monteiro, a former independence fighter, obtained 22.5% and 3.4%, respectively. Turnout was just 35.5%—the lowest recorded since 1991. The PAICV did not nominate a candidate to contest the elections.

In December 2017 Correia e Silva reorganized the Council of Ministers, pledging to improve government efficiency and co-ordination. Notably, José Gonçalves became Minister of Tourism and Transport, and of the Maritime Economy. Part of the Ministry was relocated to Mindelo in São Vicente, as several administrative units related to the maritime economy were situated there.

The Government submitted a bill on decentralization and 'regionalization' to the National Assembly in April 2018. This proposed establishing 10 administrative regions—one per island in the archipelago of Cabo Verde, except Santiago, which would constitute two regions—and thereby guarantee more equal socioeconomic development across the different islands. In October the National Assembly adopted the bill at the first reading. However, in April 2019 the final vote to approve the legislation was cancelled, after the Government failed to obtain the PAICV's votes, which were indispensable in securing the requisite two-thirds' majority.

In October 2019 the National Assembly unanimously approved a parity law. The law promotes gender equality in politics and administration, including at least 40% female representation in election lists and decision-making positions in the public administration and state enterprises and institutions. In December Hopffer Almada was re-elected unopposed as PAICV leader. In February 2020 Prime Minister Correia e Silva was re-elected unopposed as MpD leader.

COVID-19 and the 2021 Elections

On 28 March 2020 President Fonseca declared a nationwide state of emergency following the outbreak of coronavirus disease (COVID-19). On 27 April the emergency was lifted on six islands where no infections had been reported, but it was maintained in São Vicente until 3 May, in Boa Vista until 14 May and in Santiago until 29 May. In October the Government reopened the country's international airports and sea ports. Between 20 March 2020 and 27 June 2022 WHO reported 59,265 cases of COVID-19 in Cabo Verde, including 403 deaths.

At local elections held in October 2020, the ruling MpD unexpectedly lost control of Praia to the PAICV. The MpD lost a further four of the 18 municipalities that it won in 2016 to the PAICV, while gaining one that had been held by independents since 2016. The PAICV also won in Boa Vista, hitherto also governed by independents. Altogether the MpD won in 14 municipalities, while the PAICV was victorious in the remaining eight.

In January 2021 Luís Filipe Tavares, the Minister of Foreign Affairs, Communities and Defence, resigned following reports in the Portuguese media that Cabo Verde's honorary consul in Florida, USA, a Portuguese businessman, César do Paço, whom Tavares had appointed, had financed Chega, a right-wing Portuguese party. Tavares was replaced by Rui Alberto de Figueiredo Soares, who had served as foreign minister in 1999–2000; Paço was dismissed from his diplomatic post.

In April 2021 the ruling MpD won an absolute majority of 38 seats (taking 50.4% of the votes) in the legislative elections, while the PAICV obtained 30 seats (39.6%). The UCID took the remaining four seats (9.0%). The voter turnout was 57.5%. Following the result PAICV leader Fonseca Hopffer Almada resigned and was replaced on an interim basis by Rui Semedo. In May the new Government, led by Prime Minister Correia e Silva, took office, and Austelino Correia (MpD) was elected President of the National Assembly.

In October 2021 former Prime Minister Neves of the PAICV won the presidential election with 51.7% of the valid votes. His principal rival, Veiga of the MpD, obtained 42.4% of the votes. Despite partial restrictions as a result of the COVID-19 pandemic, the turnout was 48%. Immediately after the elections, President-elect Neves assured the MpD-led Government of Correia e Silva that he would offer the administration the support necessary jointly to confront the challenges facing the archipelago. In November Neves formally took office as the country's fifth head of state since independence.

Semedo was elected unopposed as the new leader of the PAICV in December 2021. At the party's 17th congress, held in April 2022, the delegates elected the members of the party's National Council and National Committee. Meanwhile, in March, at the UCID's 18th congress, João Santos Luís was elected unopposed as the party's new President, to replace António Monteiro.

EXTERNAL AFFAIRS

During the 1990s the MpD Government expanded Cabo Verde's range of international contacts, with special emphasis on potential new sources of development aid, including Israel, Cuba, the People's Republic of China and states of the Persian (Arabian) Gulf. Cabo Verde has also maintained particularly good relations with the former colonial power, Portugal, and countries with large Cabo Verdean expatriate communities, such as the USA, Luxembourg and the Netherlands. Ties have been developed with the neighbouring autonomous regions of the Canary Islands (Spain), the Azores (Portugal) and Madeira (Portugal), with protocols signed to promote co-operation. In February 2003 Portugal announced its support for Cabo Verde's plan to seek 'special status' within the European Union (EU) and was followed by Spain and Luxembourg. In November 2007 the EU granted Cabo Verde special partnership status, under which the two would co-operate in key areas, including governance, security, information and the knowledge society, technical and normative convergence, regional

integration and poverty reduction. The Government also strengthened co-operation with the EU on preventing illegal immigrants, drugs and criminal funds flowing into the EU via Cabo Verde. In June 2008 a mobility partnership convention was signed, covering 2009–11, aimed at facilitating circular migration to the EU and preventing illegal immigration. In July 2017 the EU extended the scope of the partnership to cover investment, growth and employment; management of the oceans; and institutional reform.

Cabo Verde has maintained good relations with the USA, where some 260,000 expatriate Cabo Verdeans live. In March 2013 Neves made an official visit to the USA and was one of four African leaders chosen to meet US President Barack Obama, who commended Cabo Verde's strong democratic and governance record. In August 2014 President Fonseca emphasized his country's willingness to deepen co-operation with the USA in maritime security and all other areas of common bilateral interest. In April–May 2016 Cabo Verde hosted the US military exercise Epic Guardian in its territorial waters. This is regularly organized with African countries to improve bilateral maritime security co-operation with the USA. The manoeuvres were held in partnership with the Praia-based Centro de Operações e Segurança Marítima and generated revenue of some US $5,000m. for the archipelago.

In recent years Cabo Verde has sought to strengthen bilateral ties with China, which has become an increasingly important trade partner and source of funding. Foreign ministry officials visited China in May 2007 to discuss Cabo Verde's suitability to host one of six special economic zones, which China planned to establish in Africa. In August 2011 the Chinese Vice-Minister of Commerce, Jiang Yaoping, visited Cabo Verde, signing agreements on trade, education, energy, water and health care. According to the Chinese Government, Chinese investment in development projects in Cabo Verde totalled US $211m. in 2000–11. In May 2013 the Chinese Government pledged $50m. in military funding, and in March 2015 China donated several modern patrol boats equipped to Cabo Verde's coastguard in order to improve the surveillance of the archipelago's extensive territorial waters. In December President Fonseca participated in the Forum on China-Africa Co-operation held in Johannesburg, South Africa. Chinese investment in Africa worth $16,000m. was announced at the Forum for 2016–18.

Cabo Verde maintains close relations with Portugal's other former African colonies—Guinea-Bissau, Mozambique and São Tomé and Príncipe, known collectively, with Cabo Verde and Angola, as the Países Africanos de Língua Oficial Portuguesa (PALOP). In July 1996 the Comunidade dos Países de Língua Portuguesa (CPLP), comprising the five PALOP countries, together with Portugal and Brazil, was formed with the intention of benefiting each member state through joint co-operation on technical, cultural and social matters. In December Cabo Verde also became a full member of the Sommet Francophone (a commonwealth comprising the world's French-speaking countries), having been an observer at its annual meetings since 1977. Cabo Verde is a member of the African Union (formerly the Organization of African Unity), the Economic Community of West African States, the African Development Bank and the United Nations (UN) and was a signatory to the Lomé Conventions, which promoted co-operation between the EU and African, Caribbean and Pacific countries. In October 2002 Cabo Verde ratified the successor to the Lomé Conventions, the Cotonou Agreement.

In May 2006 Cabo Verde hosted the first North Atlantic Treaty Organization military exercise in Africa: Steadfast Jaguar 2006. Much of the equipment used in the exercise was subsequently transferred to its military. Since 2007 Cabo Verde has signed accords with Portugal, Spain and the United Kingdom to carry out joint naval exercises and patrols in Cabo Verde's maritime waters, with a focus on intercepting drug traffickers and illegal migrant flows. In May 2010 the US Government donated US $3m. to the country to purchase new maritime surveillance equipment to prevent drug trafficking, and in 2011 the US Africa Command provided $200,000 for the purchase of coastguard patrol ships. In March 2013 a Cabo Verdean patrol ship arrested Adm. José Américo Bubo Na Tchuto, a former Guinea-Bissau Navy Chief of Staff, in an operation mounted by the US Central Intelligence Agency. He was subsequently extradited to the USA and charged with drug trafficking offences.

In September 2014 Cabo Verde submitted a request to the UN Division for Ocean Affairs and the Law of the Sea to extend its continental platform beyond 200 miles, as part of a West African regional initiative that began in 2009 and was co-ordinated by Cabo Verde with Norwegian technical support. The seven West African countries participating in the initiative hoped to benefit from the exploitation of deep-sea natural resources in their extended continental platforms.

At an ECOWAS summit in Abuja, Nigeria in December 2017, Cabo Verde was overlooked in the elections for the rotating presidency of the organization's Commission in favour of Côte d'Ivoire, although, according to ECOWAS statutes, it was Cabo Verde's turn. (ECOWAS justified its decision by claiming that Cabo Verde owed the bloc US $25m. in backdated membership contributions). President Fonseca criticized the election procedure and claimed that the decision was politically motivated.

In June 2018 the MpD adopted the controversial Status of Forces Agreement (SOFA) with the USA, despite the opposition PAICV and UCID abstaining in parliamentary votes. Under this military co-operation agreement, US military personnel are not subject to the local judiciary, irrespective of the gravity of any crime committed. Both countries also mutually renounced compensation claims in the case of property destruction or the death of military or civilian personnel occurring during activities subject to the agreement, and Cabo Verde allowed the US certain logistical support structures. In September, after having confirmed the agreement's constitutionality, Fonseca ratified the SOFA.

Cabo Verde hosted the 12th summit of the nine-member CPLP in July 2018, held under the theme 'Culture, People, Oceans', and which was attended by eight heads of state. The summit encouraged all member states to implement the agreements on improving their people's mobility and free circulation within the community's geographic space. Cabo Verde assumed the CPLP presidency for a two-year term.

In August 2020 Guinea-Bissau opened an embassy in Praia, where hitherto it had maintained only a general consulate. In January 2021 Camilo Leitão da Graça was appointed Cabo Verde's first resident ambassador in Guinea-Bissau. In the same month President Fonseca made the first official visit by a Cabo Verdean head of state to Guinea-Bissau, in a sign of improved bilateral relations.

In March 2021 the Supreme Court approved a request by the USA for the extradition of Columbian businessman Alex Saab, special envoy of Venezuela's President Nicolás Maduro, who had been detained by the local authorities during a stopover at Sal airport in June 2020 en route to Iran. Saab's legal representatives appealed against the decision at the Constitutional Court, but in August the latter rejected the appeal, and in October Saab was deported to the USA. The US authorities accused Saab of money laundering and undermining US sanctions against the Maduro regime, while the Venezuelan Government claimed that Saab held diplomatic immunity from any charges.

Economy

GERHARD SEIBERT

INTRODUCTION

According to the World Bank, in 2020 Cabo Verde's gross national income (GNI) was US $1,700m., equivalent to $3,064 per head. Cabo Verde's GNI per head is the highest of the five former Portuguese African colonies. Cabo Verde remains the only lusophone African nation not to be classified by the World Bank as a least developed country (LDC); it graduated from this category to that of medium development country (MDC) in 2008. Heavy government investment in social sectors has reduced the level of poverty, and by 2019 the unemployment rate had decreased to 11.3% from 16.0% in 2017. However, owing to the economic consequences of the coronavirus (COVID-19) pandemic, in 2020 the unemployment rate rose to 14.5%.

Despite the country's physical disadvantages, the economy has grown fairly steadily since independence in 1975, benefiting from official aid on highly favourable terms, economic reforms since the 1990s and the substantial remittances of Cabo Verdean émigrés, whose number was estimated at 518,000 in 2009, compared with a domestic population of an estimated 483,628 at the census of June 2021. In 2015 Cabo Verde had the highest per capita rate of remittances (US $386) of any African country, and in 2021 total remittances accounted for 25,833.4m. escudos.

In 2011–20 Cabo Verde's gross domestic product (GDP) increased, in real terms, at an average annual rate of 0.6%. In comparison, the population increased by an average of 1.2% per year in 2011–20. The impact of the global economic downturn resulted in a contraction in GDP of 1.3% in 2009, but growth resumed in 2011, buoyed by a rise in tourist arrivals and remittance inflows, reaching 4.0%. Growth slowed to 0.8% in 2014, according to the Banco de Cabo Verde (BCV), the central bank, before rising to 5.7% in 2019. Owing to the pandemic, in 2020 GDP dropped by 14.8%, but increased by 7.1% in 2021, thanks to a gradual recovery of the tourism sector.

According to the Ministry of Finance, public debt totalled 200,013m. escudos in 2015 (compared with 85,340m. escudos in 2009), or 127.8% of GDP; this ratio increased to 128.6% in 2016. In 2018 the International Monetary Fund (IMF) estimated that public debt totalled 127.7% of GDP. In 2021 public debt rose to an estimated at 157.1% of GDP, owing mainly to extraordinary expenditure to support the economy during the pandemic. According to official data, the annual rate of inflation averaged 0.7% in 2011–20. In 2021 the average inflation rate was 1.9%—the highest since 2013.

The Government has improved its fiscal situation by reforming tax collection and public expenditure management. In 2004 the authorities introduced value-added tax (VAT) and reformed the tariff system. Higher VAT and import duty revenues gradually reduced the fiscal deficit to 1.4% of GDP in 2008. According to the African Development Bank (AfDB), the fiscal deficit was 1.8% of GDP in 2019, but this widened to 8.9% in 2020, after public expenditure was raised dramatically in order to protect the economy from the effects of the COVID-19 pandemic. The current account deficit narrowed from 4.6% of GDP in 2015 to a surplus of 0.3% in 2019, but this tipped over into a deficit of 15.6% of GDP in 2020. In 2021 the deficit narrowed to 14.2%, owing mainly to an increase in migrant remittances.

TRANSPORT AND COMMUNICATIONS

Cabo Verde is strategically located between Africa, Europe and the Americas. International maritime and air transport, including transshipment, were identified as an important source of foreign exchange by various governing administrations. Cabo Verde has three international ports—at Porto Grande (São Vicente), Praia (Santiago) and Palmeira (Sal)—and several smaller commercial ports.

Strong growth in trade is being accompanied by large-scale investment to upgrade existing port facilities. In June 2005 the US Millennium Challenge Account (MCA) agreed to fund a US $53m. project further to modernize and expand the port of Praia. Following completion of the first two phases, a third phase of expansion, also financed by the MCA, at a total cost of $114m., commenced in 2011, extending of one of the docks to accommodate container ships and dredging the port, with the aim of increasing its handling capacity to 2m. metric tons of goods by 2030. Meanwhile, in 2010 expansion work commenced at the port of Sal Rei (Boavista), including the construction of a new container port. In 2012 the Government initiated a $65.3m. project to modernize and expand the port of Palmeira. The Government intended to open up the archipelago's port operations to private companies, starting with the three largest ports.

The state ferry company Arca Verde was liquidated in 1999, and since then private maritime transport companies have operated passenger and goods services between the islands. Since December 2010 Cabo Verde Fast Ferry (CVFF) has provided ferry services from Brava to other islands in the archipelago. In 2014 CVFF, which operated two ferries on the inter-island passenger service, recorded total operational losses of some 700m. escudos. The company, which since 2013 has been 53% state-owned, reported total debts of 2,400m. escudos, and its assets were valued at about 1,800m. escudos. In March 2018 the Government suggested that an international tender for the concession of the inter-island shipping service, launched in January, could mean the end of CVFF. In April the Government approved the participation of CVFF, West African Company, Polaris Shipping (South Korea), Palm Shipping (Malta) and the Portuguese groups Sousa and ETE (Transinsular) in the public tender for the inter-island shipping licence.

Meanwhile, in February 2016 the Government permitted the ports authority Empresa Nacional de Administração dos Portos, SA (ENAPOR, SA) to sublet the ports of Praia, Porto Grande, Sal Rei and Palmeira and the CABNAVE shipyards to private investors. In August 2017 the Government cancelled the public tender for the sub-concession of the ports on the grounds that the model would not correspond with the administration's strategy for the sector. The French company Balloré was the only investor that had expressed interest in the sub-concession.

In April 2021, after a public tender, ENAPOR awarded a consortium of Mota-Engil, Engenharia e Construção, SA (both Portugal) and Empreitel Figueiredo, SA (Cabo Verde) the construction of a cruise ship terminal in São Vicente with an annual capacity of 200,000 visitors. The investment was co-financed with loans of €10m. from the Facility for Infrastructure Development ORIO funded by the Dutch Ministry of Foreign Affairs and US $19.5m. from the OPEC Fund for International Development. In January 2022 Prime Minister José Ulisses de Pina Correia e Silva laid the foundation stone of the construction works of the terminal complex.

In 2018 cargo movements in Cabo Verde's ports totalled 2.6m. metric tons (an annual increase of 12.6%), and the number of containers increased by 13.9% to 86,059 twenty-foot equivalent units. In 2021 the ports handled 6,802 ships (an annual increase of 5.7% compared with the previous year), some 1.1m. passengers (43.5%) and cargo of about 2.4m. tons (8.4%).

In February 2019 nine local ship-owners signed an agreement with the Government pledging their combined ownership of 49% of the capital of the future company CV Interilhas, each worth 2,722m. escudos. The majority shareholder (of 51%) was the Portuguese company Transinsular, which in January 2018 had won the public tender for a 25-year concession to provide an inter-island public maritime passenger and cargo transport service. CV Interilhas acquired the *Chiquinho* in 2020, and in November 2021 the company put into operation a 220-passenger ferry, which formerly operated between the Bahamas and Florida, USA and was renamed *Dona Tututa* in homage to a local composer.

At mid-2018 there were 1,650 km of roads in Cabo Verde, 1,113 km of which were national and 537 km were municipal roads. Asphalted roads represented 37% of the total, 57% were gravel roads, 6% were earth roads, and 1% were bitumenized roads.

The Government has pledged to improve air transport infrastructure on the islands, with the objective of turning Cabo Verde into a regional transport hub. The Amílcar Cabral international airport on Sal has an annual throughput capacity of 1m. passengers (it currently handles more than

300,000 passengers annually) and can accommodate aircraft of up to 50 metric tons.

A new international airport in Praia, designed to accommodate large aircraft, became operational in November 2005. In June 2013 the AfDB agreed to fund the construction of new passenger and cargo terminals at the airport (renamed Aeroporto Nelson Mandela in 2012), costing €32.8m. The airport's runway was to be increased from 2,100 m to 2,600 m. A third international airport, on Boavista, became operational in October 2007. In December 2009 a fourth international airport commenced operations, on São Vicente. In May 2013 the airport authority, Empresa Nacional de Aeroportos e Segurança, AEREA (ASA), announced plans to invest €17m. to upgrade the archipelago's airports, including the expansion of the passenger terminal at Amílcar Cabral international airport and the doubling of capacity at Boavista airport.

In May 2022 VINCI Airports (France) established a local subsidiary in Praia, Cabo Verde Airports, SA, to manage the concessions of the country's airports awarded by the Government for 40 years, in exchange for €80m. plus a share of the gross income of 2.5% during 2022–41, 3.5% during 2042–51 and 7% during 2052–61. VINCI promised to invest €619m. during the concession period and expected to integrate up to 382 of the 511 employees of ASA. ANA–Aeroportos de Portugal took a 30% stake in the new company.

The national airline, Transportes Aéreos de Cabo Verde (TACV), which once operated a regular inter-island service and flights to major European cities, Brazil and the USA has been beset by financial problems since April 2009, when it declared 'technical insolvency', owing to the accumulation of losses, and urged the Government to increase assistance while it underwent restructuring. Despite a restructuring of debt owed to ASA, in October 2012 TACV revealed that the company had debts of €50m. A financial restructuring process began in 2013, reducing the company's fleet to two Boeing aircraft for international flights and a single ATR 72 for domestic flights. Numerous financial injections by several banks have been granted to the company since 2015, backed by Government guarantees.

In November 2016 a new Cabo Verdean subsidiary of the Spanish airline Binter, which had since 2012 operated regular flights between the Canary Islands and Cabo Verde, began to offer domestic inter-island services, which by June 2018 connected seven islands across the archipelago and which had replaced the domestic operations of TACV, following a decision reached by the Government in May 2017, whereby the state assumed a 49% stake in Binter (this was to be offered for eventual sale to private investors). Also in May 2017 the Government authorized TACV (which had accumulated debts of about €110m. by that time) to take out loans worth US $5.3m. to meet urgent financial obligations. In August TACV ceased inter-island flights, and Binter assumed the monopoly of domestic flights. In the same month the Government signed a renewable one-year management contract with Icelandair for TACV's international operations. The Government paid Icelandair $100,000 per month for the airline's management services. It was expected that some 260 employees, comprising one-half of TACV's personnel, would lose their jobs following privatization. TACV's operational hub was moved from Praia to Sal International Airport. In October the Government allowed TACV to take out another bank loan, of $16.2m., to finance the redundancy of personnel. In November the airline took delivery of the first two of 11 planes from Icelandair that were due to enter into service by 2022 to operate TACV flights to the USA, Brazil and Europe. In January 2018 the Government authorized TACV to take out a loan of $5.6m. to lease a new Boeing aircraft. In May the carrier was renamed Cabo Verde Airlines (CVA). In March 2019 Loftleidir Cabo Verde (a 70%-owned subsidiary of Loftleidir Icelandic) acquired 51% of CVA. Loftleidir paid the Government €1.3m. and another €6m. for the capitalization of CVA. The airline's total liabilities of €105m. were transferred to a newly created company, Newco, owned 100% by the Cabo Verdean state, which guaranteed 50% of the debts. In April the Government announced plans to sell 10% of its 49% stake in the airline on the stock exchange (5% each to company employees and Cabo Verdeans overseas). In

August 2019 Binter was renamed Transportes Interilhas de Cabo Verde (TICV).

In March 2021 the Government signed a new agreement with Loftleidir Icelandic to safeguard CVA and resume operations interrupted as a result of the pandemic in March 2020. The Government strengthened its position on the airline's executive board, provided additional financing and agreed to a fleet reduction from three leased planes to two. However, in July 2021 the Government unilaterally acquired Loftleidir Cabo Verde's 51% stake in CVA, claiming that the latter had violated its contractual agreements. In December CVA resumed international operations with two flights per week between Praia and Lisbon. In January 2022 CVA suspended for four months the contracts of 132 employees, who had already been laid off with 75% of their wages since April 2020, owing to the pandemic, with the payment of 62.5% of their salaries during this period. In February 2022 the Government approved a 10-month loan of 165.3m. escudos for CVA's current expenditure, including salaries.

In July 2021 Bestfly World Wide (Angola) acquired Binter's 70% stake in TICV, while the Government maintained the remaining 30%. In October TICV announced the redundancy of 60 employees, owing to the pandemic-related reduction of domestic flights. In February 2022 the company began operations with a second, 72-passenger plane.

In 1995 40% of the state telecommunications company, Cabo Verde Telecom (CVT), was sold to Portugal Telecom International for US $20m., and a further 50% of CVT was divested in 1997–98. The network expanded from 21,500 main lines in use in 1995 to 74,500 in 2011, yielding the third highest density of fixed telephone lines in sub-Saharan Africa, at 14.9 per 100 inhabitants, after Mauritius and Seychelles. In 2007 the Government formally ended CVT's monopoly on fixed-line services. In April 2009 CVT and Portugal Telecom launched a $50m. project to install a new undersea cable linking Cabo Verde to the West African Cable System from 2011. In December 2018 CVT and EllaLink signed an agreement to connect Cabo Verde to EllaLink's submarine cable system between Europe and Latin America, which finally became operational in June 2022. In 1998 CVT introduced a mobile telephone network, Telemóvel, and in December 2007 a second mobile telephone operator, T+, launched its services. In October 2012 T+ was acquired by Angola's Unitel Internacional in 2012. According to the International Telecommunication Union (ITU), in 2020 there were an estimated 544,729 mobile telephone users in Cabo Verde and 24,839 broadband subscribers. However, the fixed-line network was in decline, with just 57,668 fixed lines. In May 2019 CVMóvel and Unitel T+ won the public tender for 4G mobile communication systems licences, and the Instituto Nacional da Previdência Social (INPS) and ASA bought a 40% stake in CVT from PT Ventures, a subsidiary of the Brazilian Oi, for $26.3m. The CVT was now owned by the INPS (57.9%), ASA (20%), the Cabo Verdean state (3.4%), Correios de Cabo Verde (0.7%) and 18% by private Cabo Verdean investors. The telecommunications sector contributes about 5% to total GDP.

Internet arrived in Cabo Verde in 1996, and ADSL broadband technology was introduced in 2004. According to the ITU's ICT Development Index 2017, Cabo Verde was ranked fourth in Africa in terms of internet penetration with 48.2%, far higher than Guinea-Bissau's 3.8%, but less than the 53.2% of Mauritius, Africa's ICT leader. According to the ITU, 61.9% of Cabo Verde's population used the internet in 2020.

AGRICULTURE AND FISHERIES

The Cabo Verde archipelago is situated in the Sahelian climatic zone and thus suffers from severe periodic droughts. Less than 10% (39,000 ha) of Cabo Verde's total surface area is cultivable (one-half of this is on Santiago). Lacking the necessary infrastructure to combat the effects of droughts, Cabo Verde has been unable to achieve self-sufficiency in food production. Cereal production covers on average only 15% of Cabo Verde's annual food requirements, and the remainder, varying from 28,000 metric tons to 70,000 tons, is imported. Erratic rains, upon which most agriculture depends, have led to unpredictable harvests. Agriculture (including forestry and fishing) contributed only 5.4% of GDP in 2020, although the

sector is an important source of employment, involving 10.6% of the total labour force, according to estimates from the Food and Agriculture Organization of the United Nations (FAO). About 55% of farms on cultivated land are smaller than 1 ha, and fewer than 3% exceed 5 ha. According to the United Nations (UN), during 2011–20 the average annual GDP of the agricultural sector increased, in real terms, by 4.1%; it decreased by 6.5% in 2020.

Since independence, re-afforestation plans have been put into effect with assistance from FAO. Some 23m., mostly drought-resistant, trees (American acacias) have been planted, in order to reduce soil erosion and increase groundwater levels. In addition, about 7,200 rainwater dykes have been built, new wells have been sunk, and a more efficient system of irrigation has been adopted. About 3,000 ha are currently irrigated. Estimates suggest that the total potentially exploitable groundwater and surface water resources of Cabo Verde are about 150m. cu m per year. In January 2010 Cabo Verde's Government launched a tender for a €100m. project, funded by the Portuguese Government, to construct three new reservoirs on Santiago to capture rainwater. The project also aimed to build new flood-control dykes and 70 bore wells. In March 2011 Portugal granted Cabo Verde a US $72m. credit line to construct the three dams, which were expected to distribute 75m. cu m of water per year, mostly for agriculture and livestock-raising. Portugal also funded the construction of the Canto da Cagarra dam on Santo Antão (the island's first dam), which was to have a capacity to store 418,000 cu m of water and was partly completed in August 2014. In June 2013 the Government contracted a Portuguese company, Monte Adriano, to develop the Flamengos and Principal Water Basins project, financed by the Arab Bank for Economic Development in Africa. The $10m. project included the construction of two new dams (with a combined capacity of 2m. cu m of water).

Santiago is the main agricultural producer (contributing about one-half of total production), followed by Santo Antão and São Nicolau. The main food crops include maize, beans, cassava and sweet potatoes, supplemented (wherever soils, terrain and rainfall permit) with bananas, vegetables, sugar cane and fruits. The principal staples are beans and maize, which are intercropped. Cabo Verde's overall annual cereal requirement is estimated at about 110,000 metric tons. More than one-half of Cabo Verde's total irrigated land is used for sugar cane (production totalled 22,900 tons in 2020), most of which is used in the production of a popular alcoholic beverage, grogue (cane brandy), for local consumption. The Government is seeking to reallocate this land to staple and cash crops by encouraging the manufacture (and future export) of an alternative liquor using imported molasses. The country also produced 12,500 tons of tomatoes and 5,200 tons of coconuts in 2020, all for domestic consumption.

Cash crops, such as bananas, Arabica coffee, groundnuts, castor beans and pineapples, are encouraged, but poor inter-island communications, the shortage of government funds, lack of suitable available land and adverse climatic conditions hinder the development of a thriving agricultural sector. As a result, the islands' only significant export crops are bananas (with production of 5,600 metric tons in 2020) and guavas, mangoes and mangosteens (800 tons). Cabo Verde has a 4,800-ton banana quota with the European Union (EU), and bananas are shipped mainly to Portugal. An exotic commodity, locally known as purgueira (*Jatrophacurcas*), which grows wild, is also exported (for soap-making). A small quantity of coffee and castor beans is produced on Fogo for domestic consumption. In 2012 a coffee-processing operation—Fogo Coffee Spirit—was established in Fogo, with the capacity to process 500 kg of coffee per hour. Wine production, mostly for local consumption in tourist resorts, has been encouraged on Fogo, the volcanic terrain of which is suitable for viniculture. About 50,000 bottles are produced each year, and efforts are being made to market the wine internationally.

Livestock herds have been reduced to one-quarter, or even one-10th, of their pre-drought levels, but are recovering. According to FAO, in 2020 29,500 cattle, 131,700 goats, 18,800 sheep and 70,200 pigs were raised for food and milk. About 18,500 asses, mules and horses provide the main form of transport in mountainous rural areas.

Fishing offers great development potential. Cabo Verde's exclusive economic zone comprises 734,265 sq km and contains one of the last significantly under-used fishing grounds in the world, with a total sustainable yield estimated at about 35,000 metric tons per year. The Government, which privatized the state-owned fishing company, Empresa Caboverdiana de Pescas, has encouraged private entrepreneurs by means of credit facilities, training and research.

Fishing exports consist primarily of tuna. The total catch was about 19,292 metric tons in 2019, according to FAO. In August 2014 the EU renewed its fishing accord with Cabo Verde for a further four years (September 2014–August 2018). Under the new accord, the number of ships would be reduced to 71, the annual quota would remain at 5,000 tons of tuna, and the compensation would be increased to €550,000, in the first two years, before declining to €500,000 in the final two years of the agreement. One-half of the fees was destined to be invested in sustainable fishing management, including the strengthening of surveillance and monitoring capacities, and in local fishing communities, and the other 50% was intended to pay for access to fishing resources. In May 2017 the Cabo Verdean Government announced that the EU had approved Cabo Verde's request for exemption of import taxes on fish exports to the EU's member states. In October 2018 Cabo Verde and the EU renewed the fishing accord for 2019–23. Under the agreement, vessels from Spain, Portugal and France were allowed to catch 8,000 tons of tuna and tuna-like species in Cabo Verdean waters. In return, the EU increased the annual payment from €550,000 to €750,000, of which €350,000 was allocated to promote sustainable fisheries.

In September 2009 the Brazilian organization Serviço de Apoioàs Micro e Pequenas Empresas do Ceará, together with Cabo Verdean businessmen, launched a €1.5m. project to farm prawns in Cabo Verde. The Government signed an agreement with two US companies, Peer Fish and Carlos Seafood, in July 2011 to export fresh and frozen fish from Cabo Verde to the USA, creating 150 local jobs. In June 2015 the fish cannery Frescomar inaugurated a new production line for tuna in São Vicente, which was expected to create more than 300 jobs.

In June 2021 the Government and the Norwegian company Nortuna Holding CV signed a 50-year concession agreement for a maritime area of 236,000 sq m off Praia Flamengo in São Vicente to be used for aquaculture. Under the agreement, the concessionaire of the project, Nortuna Atlantic Bluefin Tuna, pays annual fees to the Government to exploit the zone. The investor expected to create 400 jobs by 2023 and export up to 10,000 metric tons per year of Atlantic bluefin tuna.

MANUFACTURING

The manufacturing sector remains largely undeveloped, although it contributed 23.5% to GDP in 2020 (far higher than in previous years, owing to the sharp relative fall in the services sector as a result of the COVID-19 pandemic). During 2011–20, according to UN estimates, the GDP of the manufacturing sector increased, in real terms, at an average annual rate of 3.4%; the manufacturing sector decreased by 7.5% in 2019. Manufacturing consists primarily of fish canning, clothing, footwear, rum distilling and bottling plants and employed 20.3% of the total labour force in 2020. In order to attract foreign investment and promote the expansion of industrial exports, the Free-zone Enterprise Law was enacted in 1993, permitting enterprises producing goods and services exclusively for export (and new firms specializing in transshipment) to benefit from exemptions on tax and customs duties for 10 years. Legislation enacted in 1999 provided for the transformation of industrial parks at Mindelo and Praia into free trade zones and for the establishment of a further free trade zone on Sal. The free trade zone in Mindelo is being extended with support from Portugal.

EXTRACTIVE INDUSTRIES

Cabo Verde has no known hydrocarbon resources, although the Government has encouraged petroleum companies to prospect in its waters. In 2010 the Brazilian oil company Petróleo Brasileiro signed an accord with the Government to explore for petroleum and gas in Cabo Verde's offshore area. Mining represents less than 1% of GDP, and pozzolana (a volcanic ash used in cement manufacture) and unrefined salt traditionally are the main products. Small quantities of clay, gypsum and limestone are also produced. A pozzolana cement factory in Porto Novo (Santo Antão), which commenced production in late 2005, closed in June 2016 after experiencing financial difficulties. In 2017 the Government began to seek new investors in Asia in an effort to re-open the factory.

POWER

Cabo Verde imports all of its fuel, which keeps costs for transport and electricity high. The country provides refuelling services for ships and aircraft, and re-exports of fuel (bunkering) comprise a significant proportion of the total merchandise exports.

Electricity is generated by the national electricity and water utility, Empresa de Electricidade e Água (Electra), which has struggled to meet rising demand, leading to frequent power and water shortages. In 2012 Electra had an installed capacity of 21.5 MW. In May 2013 a €52m. project was completed to increase power provision on Santiago, funded by the Government, the AfDB, the Economic Community of West African States Bank for Investment and Development and Japan. The project boosted output at the Palmarejo plant to 47 MW and included the construction of a new high-tension power line to the island's interior.

In May 2009 two new desalination units started operations in Palmarejo, increasing the plant's pumping capacity from 5,000 cu m/day to 6,200 cu m/day. In 2011 Electra opened a third desalination plant, with a capacity of 5,000 cu m/day, supplemented by 10,000 cu m/day from bore holes, with the aim of reducing the chronic water shortages affecting Praia. In June 2013 the Japan International Cooperation Agency agreed to fund a €140m. project to construct two more desalination plants in Praia, each with a capacity of 20,000 cu m/day, to boost the provision of fresh drinking water. According to official data, 89% of the population had access to clean drinking water and 79% to sanitation in 2020. In March 2018 Electra announced that it would open two desalination plants, each with a capacity of 10,000 cu m/day in São Vicente and Sal in August, costing €21m.

In December 2010 Electra was saved from bankruptcy by an emergency capital injection worth 525m. escudos from the national pension fund, and in early 2011 the Government started negotiations with Angola's Banco Africano de Investimento to inject 700m. escudos into Electra in return for shares. The company underwent further restructuring in 2012 with the assistance of the World Bank and US $41.4m. in funding from the MCA. In July 2021 the Government finally approved plans for the privatization of Electra, which would result in the division of the entity into two companies and the subsequent sale of up to 75% of the capital.

According to the World Bank, 94.2% of the population had access to electricity in 2020. However, the provision of electricity in rural communities remains poor, and about 40% of the population relies on firewood for fuel. The Government has supported efforts to develop renewable energy by drawing on the archipelago's wind and solar power in order to reduce its dependence on petroleum imports. In December 2009 the Government contracted the Cabeólica consortium to construct four wind farms (on Santiago, São Vicente, Sal and Boavista). The US $84m. project aimed to produce 28 MW of power. In December 2010 the European Investment Bank and the AfDB awarded Cabo Verde a grant of $59m. to finance the project. The first generation started in September 2011, and in the first year of the wind farms' commercial operations 25.5 MW was produced (providing more than 20% of the total electricity requirements of the archipelago's four main islands). In early 2010 a Spanish company, Martifer Solar, began construction of two solar energy plants on Santiago and Sal, at an estimated cost of $36.5m., which would produce 7.5 MW. The Government aimed to meet 25%–50% of the archipelago's energy needs from renewable sources by 2020, compared with just 4% in 2010. In 2021 about one-fifth of energy produced derived from renewable sources.

TOURISM

Cabo Verde benefits from its proximity to the European market, a favourable climate for most of the year, white sandy beaches and spectacular mountain scenery. Tourism has been the sector to benefit most from foreign direct investment (FDI), and consequently the tourism industry's contribution to national GDP increased from 4.0% in 1998 to 21.1% in 2012. The number of tourists also increased dramatically, from about 60,000 in 1998 to 819,308 in 2019. In that year the largest number of tourists came from the United Kingdom (24.0%), Germany (11.3%) and France (10.4%). Sal was the most visited island, with almost half of all visits, followed by Boavista and Santiago. However, the advances in the tourism sector slowed drastically following the onset of the COVID-19 pandemic in early 2020, and tourist arrivals in that year totalled just 207,125. In 2021 arrivals recovered only modestly, to 229,263, and they were expected to return to pre-pandemic levels only in 2023.

Prior to 2020 there was massive foreign investment in luxury hotels and tourism resorts, as well as golf courses, water parks, convention centres, diving facilities, deep-sea fishing operations and eco-tourism (notably on Fogo and Santo Antão). In September 2012 Resort Group of Gibraltar started construction of an €80m. tourism complex, the Llana Beach Hotel and Spa in Santa Maria (Sal). The company planned to build six more tourist resorts on Boavista by the late 2020s. Llana Beach complex opened in December 2016 and eventually employed some 500 people. In 2017 the USA's Viceroy Hotels and Resorts opened a hotel in the Sambala development, north of Praia, and the first Hilton hotel in Cabo Verde, at Sal, adding 240 beds and with five-star spa and casino facilities, opened in early 2018. In February The Resort Group commenced construction of a five-star, 201-room Hilton Hotel in Praia. The investment of €45m. was expected to create 150 jobs. In April the Hotel Ocean View in São Filipe, Fogo reopened after being modernized and extended to 50 rooms, and local private investors inaugurated the 33-room Hotel Ouril Agueda in Sal-Rei, Boa Vista in the same month. In November RIU Hotels & Resorts of Spain opened its fifth hotel in Cabo Verde, the RIU Palace Boa Vista, a 500-room resort with extensive leisure facilities.

Following a delay, owing to the COVID-19 pandemic, in March 2021 RIU Hotels & Resorts inaugurated its sixth hotel in Cabo Verde, the Hotel RIU Palace Santa Maria, on Sal. The €90m. investment comprised 1,001 rooms distributed among six buildings, five swimming pools, an aquatic park, spa, five restaurants and seven bars and was expected to employ 600 people.

The Government introduced legislation in June 2011 permitting gambling and the building of casinos on São Vicente, Santiago and Sal. In April 2013 the Government awarded the country's first gaming and gambling concession to a Cabo Verdean company, Royal Casino, which planned to invest US $66m. in building a casino and luxury hotel on Sal and another casino on Santa Maria.

In July 2015 Cabo Verde and Macau Legend Development signed a 75-year concession agreement, renewable for 30-year periods, for the construction of Cape Verde Integrated Resort and Casino. The luxury tourism project, budgeted at US $250m., including a marina, sports complex and casino, was to be constructed on a total area of 15.3 ha on the islet Santa Maria (Djéu) and on the opposing Gamboa beach in Praia, as well as above the sea between the two locations. Construction began in 2016. In May 2019 the Government accepted Macau Legend Development's proposal to advance only with the first phase of the project with an investment of only $100m. The complex was still under construction in mid-2022.

In May 2018 the Government approved legislation on visa waivers for visits of up to 30 days for European citizens, aimed at increasing the number of European tourists arrivals, who currently account for more than 80% of all foreign visitors. The law became effective in January 2019. In December the Government replaced visa duty for arrivals from 36 European countries with a modest airport security tax.

FINANCIAL SECTOR

In 1993 the islands' first commercial bank was established, the Banco Comercial do Atlântico (BCA), and new legislation provided for the creation of financial institutions to offer credit to small and medium-sized entrepreneurs. Although its capital was raised solely from state funds provided by BCV, BCA enjoyed relative independence from the central bank. The state's shares in BCA were sold in 1999 to a consortium led by the Portuguese Caixa Geral de Depósitos. BCV now functions solely as a central bank.

Cabo Verde's financial sector is well developed by regional standards, and an estimated 89.1% of the population has a bank account (one of the highest rates in sub-Saharan Africa). In March 2010 the Government created a socially focused bank, Novo Banco, to provide credit to low-income households and small and medium-sized enterprises (SME). In March 2017 BCV transferred 1,700m. escudos of the ailing Novo Banco's total liabilities, together with assets worth 2,600m. escudos, to Caixa Económica de Cabo Verde (CECV). Novo Banco retained credits worth 800m. escudos, as well as debts with public shareholders and an African bank, and obligations related to staff contracts. The dissolution of Novo Banco was expected to cost the Cabo Verdean Treasury US $20.2m. BCV announced that the deposits of Novo Banco's 13,200 account holders would be transferred to CECV. At mid-2022 a total of 10 commercial banks were authorized to operate in the country.

Meanwhile, in August 2015 the Government agreed to transfer seven government-owned buildings located in Praia worth 149m. escudos to the Banco Internacional de Cabo Verde (BICV). Inaugurated in 2010, BICV was the local branch of the Portuguese Banco Espírito Santo Group that was declared bankrupt in August 2014 and renamed Novo Banco in Portugal. The buildings were to be sold, with the proceeds used to increase the state's share in the institution's capital stock. If BICV failed to sell the buildings, they would revert to the state. The transaction aimed to strengthen the bank's finances to attract other investors. In March 2017 BCV fined BICV 100m. escudos for ignoring proceedings and rules to prevent money laundering, in reference to its activities before the bankruptcy of Banco Espírito Santo Group in 2014. In May 2018 BCV authorized the Novo Banco in Portugal to sell its 90% stake in BICV to International Business Group of Bahrain (IIBG Holdings). The Portuguese bank retained a 10% stake in BICV.

Concerns that Cabo Verde's financial system had become a target for money laundering led to the introduction of a law in 2008 requiring lawyers and accountants to co-operate with the authorities in identifying criminals suspected of money laundering. Following a scandal involving the transfer of illicit funds through the Cabo Verdean offshore subsidiary of Banco Português de Negócios (BPN) in 2009, the Government abolished its offshore banking sector and regulated banks under a single code based on EU standards. In March 2013 Angola's Banco BIC acquired the Cabo Verdean subsidiary of BPN for €30m. The global economic crisis undermined Cabo Verde's financial sector, forcing BCV to take remedial measures. In June, following the implementation of financial 'stress tests', BCV suspended banks' dividend payments to shareholders in order to boost their capital and reduce the risk of bank failures. In January 2016 the National Assembly unanimously adopted stricter legislation against money laundering.

In February 2017 Cabo Verde was admitted as a full member of the Egmont Group of Financial Intelligence Units, the international organization for information exchange to combat money laundering and financing terrorism. In May a Macanese-based investor, David Chow, who funded construction of Cape Verde Integrated Resort and Casino in Praia, signed a memorandum of understanding with the Cabo Verdean Government to establish a commercial bank, provisionally named Banco Sino-Atlântico (BSA) in Praia. The BSA was expected to manage revenue generated in the casinos under construction and to attract Chinese capital for investments in West Africa.

The IMF reported in April 2018 that between 2015 and 2017 the number of correspondent banks for operations abroad in Cabo Verde fell from 38 to 33, and the volume of payments between such banks dropped by 27% during 2014–16. The fall in activity represented increased vulnerability for Cabo Verde, given its dependence on emigrant remittances. Also in April 2018, the Government signed an agreement with seven local commercial banks to open a credit line for the private sector worth 5,000m. escudos. The state subsidized of the credit and guaranteed up to 50% of the credit amount conceded. In June the Government established a financial institution funded with exclusively public capital, the Sociedade de Garantia Parcial de Crédito (Pró-Garante), to provide financing to micro-enterprises and SMEs. With initial capital of 1,000m. escudos, Pró-Garante intended to provide guarantees to eligible banks (which are supervised by BCV) to grant credit to SMEs.

A stock exchange, the Bolsa de Valores de Cabo Verde (BVC), was founded in 1998 and finally started operations in December 2005. In July 2012 the BVC signed a co-operation deal with Euronext Lisbon, a subsidiary of the USA's NYSE Euronext. In 2012 BVC issued bonds for Electra (1,202m. escudos), Tecnicil (a local real estate firm—750m. escudos) and the ASA (450m. escudos). At June 2022 four companies (BCA, CECV, ENACOL and the Sociedade Cabo-verdiana de Tabacos) were listed on the BVC.

In December 2018 the Government agreed to repurchase financial consolidation securities of about 6,400m. escudos owned by the BCA. The securities were created as part of a financial reform programme in 2008 as credit titles issued by the state, which incorporate the right to receive 90% of the annual net result of the International Support for Cabo Verde Stabilization Trust Fund (ISCVSTF—established in 1998 with the aim of eliminating public debt). The other major holder of these securities was BCV, with some 4,000m. escudos. In May 2019 the National Assembly approved legislation to wind up the ISCVSTF and create the Sovereign Guarantee Fund for Private Investments.

TRADE

Cabo Verde's principal merchandise exports are canned tuna and mackerel, frozen fish and lobster and clothing and footwear. Small amounts of salt and pozzolana are exported. Among cash crops, only bananas are exported in significant quantities. Cabo Verde also resells fuel (bunkering) to passing ships and aircraft. Exports of processed fish and light manufactured goods are expected to increase substantially as new freezing and canning plants come into operation, as well as free trade zones at Praia and Mindelo. Cabo Verde traditionally operates a substantial trade deficit, which stems from the need to import some 85% of its food requirements, as well as manufactured goods, fuel and other essential goods. In 2021 the trade deficit increased by 10.5%, to €642.8m.

In recent years Portugal has increased its trading with Cabo Verde significantly. In 1989 Portugal supplied 32% of imports to Cabo Verde, but by 2020 the proportion had reached 49.9%. Other important sources of imports in 2020 were Spain (10.7%), the People's Republic of China (6.7%) and the Netherlands (6.6%). Spain was the principal market for exports in that year, accounting for 64.6% of the total, followed by Portugal (13.4%). In 2020 exports of goods accounted for US $53.1m., while imports of goods totalled $735.3m. Exports of services amounted to $289.8m. in 2019, while imports of services totalled $218.1m.

In July 2008 Cabo Verde joined the World Trade Organization (WTO)—the first African country successfully to negotiate entry since the WTO's foundation in 1995. Cabo Verde was granted until 2018 to meet all of its WTO convergence targets, which would include introducing new legislation on commercial, customs and copyright law.

In June 2016 the Government created Cabo Verde TradeInvest, as a new government agency (replacing Cabo Verde Investimento) for the promotion of investments and exports. TradeInvest was to deal with projects with a value higher than 50m. escudos.

AID AND INVESTMENT

In January 2008 the UN formally upgraded Cabo Verde's status from an LDC to an MDC, following the country's steady progress in social development, training of the workforce, poverty reduction and economic growth since the mid-1990s. Cabo Verde consequently lost access to the highly preferential loans from multilateral sources that were available to less-developed countries. However, given the Government's strong track record in macroeconomic management, donors pledged to continue to provide funding and budget support for Cabo Verde's development projects.

Historically, total FDI inflows have been low, averaging US $20m. annually in 1999–2004. However, with strong investment in tourism and infrastructure development, FDI inflows rose from $82m. in 2005 to a peak of $209m. in 2008, increasing the total FDI stock to $909m., according to data from the UN Conference on Trade and Development (UNCTAD). Owing to the impact of the global financial crisis and the consequent postponement or cancellation of the more speculative projects, FDI inflows declined to $70m. in 2013 but recovered to $180m. in 2014; however, by 2020 they had fallen again, to $74m., bringing the total FDI stock to some $2,000m. at the end of 2020, according to UNCTAD. The main sources of FDI are the UK, France, Portugal, Italy and the United Arab Emirates.

Cabo Verde receives one of the highest levels of foreign aid per head in the world (US $286 per head in 2015 or 10.1% of the country's GNI, according to the World Bank). According to the Organisation for Economic Co-operation and Development, in 2017 Cabo Verde received net official development assistance worth $123m.; Portugal, the EU, the USA and France were the main contributors.

In January 2015 Portugal ended a credit facility of €200m. that Cabo Verde had used to finance the social housing project Casa para Todos, which the Government had established in 2009. When the credit facility ceased, Cabo Verde had used only €115m. of the total amount but had not yet made available the country's own 10% contribution, as demanded in the credit agreement. Subsequently, the construction works were suspended, and the construction companies involved in the project were not paid on time. In May–June 2015 the Imobiliária Fundiária e Habitat (IFH), the agency in charge of the programme, settled debts of 500m. escudos owed to the construction companies. By October the construction of 2,188 of the 6,010 low-cost houses for disadvantaged citizens had been concluded, scheduled for the programme's first phase. After the Government had, in December, satisfied the contractual conditions, the Portuguese Government endorsed the state-owned Caixa Geral de Depósitos in Lisbon to continue the credit line (of the remaining €85m.) for the housing programme for another two years. In January 2016 IFH announced that the construction works could be resumed. In May, however, the Cabo Verdean Government announced that construction works on one-half of the houses had been suspended, as the project had accumulated debts of €20m. in interest arrears with the construction companies involved in the programme.

The EU announced in May 2016 that it had granted Cabo Verde budget support of €50m. In the same month it was announced that the China-Africa Development Fund, established in 2007, would finance investment projects worth at least $25m. in Cabo Verde, primarily in the tourism sector. In June 2016 Luxembourg pledged budget support of €10m. to finance employment promotion projects worth €45m., which had been agreed with Cabo Verde in 2015. In February 2017 Cabo Verde signed a strategic co-operation agreement with Portugal worth €120m. to cover 2017–21, focusing on assistance in education, culture, science and innovation, security, health care, energy and climate change.

The UN pledged assistance of US $16.6m. to Cabo Verde in March 2017 as part of the annual UN Development Assistance Framework for 2017, focusing on poverty reduction, consolidation of institutions and adaptation to climate change. In April the Government announced that during the following three years the World Bank would grant Cabo Verde an International Development Association loan of $90m. at concessional terms, in support of educational development, the promotion of SMEs and the restructuring of TACV.

The EU announced in May 2017 that Cabo Verde would receive, for the first time, US $10m. from the EU Regional Funds for Economic Community of West African States member states, in order to finance energy, competitiveness and transport projects. This came in addition to the €55m. of EU funding to Cabo Verde's national financial programme for 2016–20.

In June 2017 Prime Minister Correia e Silva laid the foundation stone for a new campus of the Universidade de Cabo Verde, the construction of which was to be financed by China at a cost of €45m. The new campus in Praia opened in October 2021, accommodating 4,890 students and 476 professors and extensive facilities. Also in June 2017, the Government signed agreements with Luxembourg worth €48m. for two projects as part of the Fourth Indicative Co-operation Programme. The first aimed to strengthen renewable energy infrastructure, and the second intended to improve sanitary facilities in schools.

In March 2018 the Government and the World Bank signed an agreement on a credit line of US $15m. to finance SMEs in Cabo Verde. In June the Government signed an agreement with the Netherlands for a grant of €10m. for the construction of a cruise ship terminal in Porto Grande, Mindelo, costing €28m. In April Cabo Verde signed an aid agreement with Belgium for the purchase of medical equipment worth €9.2m., and the UN granted Cabo Verde $21.8m. for 2018 as part of the UN Development Assistance Framework for 2018–22.

In February 2019 the World Bank and the Government agreed a US $10m. loan for the expansion of a social inclusion and poverty reduction programme. In March Hungary and Cabo Verde signed a credit agreement worth €35m. to finance agricultural and irrigation projects. In June the World Bank awarded Cabo Verde direct budget support of $40m. and disbursed $10m. for the country's Sovereign Emergency Fund.

In June 2021 Hungary and Cabo Verde signed an agreement for a €35m. loan to finance the modernization of water treatment stations. In September the AfDB approved the first tranche of €20m. as part of a total loan of €40m. as direct budget support in 2021 and 2022 to finance the modernization of public administration and electronic governance. In December the World Bank approved a US $30m. loan to support Cabo Verde's efforts to strengthen policies for a sustainable recovery from the COVID-19 pandemic.

DEBT

The country's general government gross debt was 230,708m. escudos in 2018, equivalent to 125.6% of GDP. According to the IMF, at the end of 2019 total external debt was US $1,821m., equivalent to just over 95% of GDP. In that year the cost of servicing long-term public and publicly guaranteed debt and repayments to the IMF was equivalent to 5.9% of the value of exports of goods, services and income (excluding workers'

remittances). The World Bank was the largest multilateral creditor in 2017, with $345.8m., and Portugal was the main bilateral creditor, with $168m. Total gross government debt declined from 129.5% of GDP in 2016 to 125.6% in 2018. By December 2021 external public debts amounted to €2,534m. equivalent to 157.1% of GDP.

ECONOMIC POLICY

The IMF's most recent Article IV consultation took place in July 2019, following which the Fund announced that it expected GDP growth of 5.0% in Cabo Verde for 2019. The Fund noted that in 2018 the budget deficit narrowed to 2.8% of GDP from 3.0% in the previous year and encouraged the Government to strengthen economic adjustment efforts through revenue and expenditure measures, to further reduce the high level of public debt. In April 2020 the Fund approved US $32m. of funding under its Rapid Credit Facility to support Cabo Verde's response to the COVID-19 pandemic, the AfDB approved a loan of $30m., and the World Bank approved $5m. of credit. The Fund recorded a contraction of real GDP of 14.8% in 2020 but estimated a rebound in growth of 6.9% in 2021. In June 2022 the Fund approved a $60m. three-year Extended Credit Facility Arrangement for Cabo Verde to mitigate the economic effects of the pandemic and the war in Ukraine. The Fund forecast real GDP growth of 5.2% in 2022.

In July 1998 Cabo Verde and Portugal linked their respective currencies through a fixed exchange rate. This new development transformed the Cabo Verde escudo into a convertible currency and established a firm monetary link to the single European currency, the euro, following its introduction in January 1999. It was also expected to encourage trade with West African countries in the CFA franc zone, which was linked to the euro. Portugal agreed to underwrite the link with some US $50m. to augment Cabo Verde's foreign currency reserves. The IMF advised the Government that stronger reserves were necessary to maintain the country's currency peg with the euro (set at a rate of 110.27 escudos = €1), but some economists were concerned that the cost of maintaining the peg would harm economic competitiveness by preventing devaluation. The Government was nevertheless strongly committed to the peg as part of its efforts to promote closer integration with the EU. In 2001–08 the escudo strengthened against the US dollar, in line with the euro, appreciating from an average of 123.2 escudos = $1 in 2001 to an average of 75.3 escudos = $1 in 2008. However, since 2009 the currency has fluctuated in line with the exchange rate between the euro and the dollar, depreciating to about 105 escudos = $1 as at mid-2022.

Statistical Survey

Sources (unless otherwise stated): Instituto Nacional de Estatística, Rua da Caixa Económica 18, CP 116, Fazenda-Praia, Santiago; tel. 2613827; e-mail inecv@ine.gov.cv; internet www.ine.cv; Statistical Service, Banco de Cabo Verde, Av. Amílcar Cabral 117, CP 101, Praia, Santiago; tel. 2607060; e-mail asemedo@bcv.cv; internet www.bcv.cv.

AREA AND POPULATION

Area: 4,033 sq km (1,557 sq miles).

Population: 491,875 at census of 16–30 June 2010; 483,628 (males 243,047, females 240,581) at census of 16–30 June 2021 (preliminary). *By Island* (2021 census, preliminary): Boavista 12,613; Brava 5,594; Fogo 33,519; Maio 6,298; Sal 33,347; Santo Antão 36,632; São Nicolau 12,239; Santiago 269,370; São Vicente 74,016; Total 483,628.

Density (at 2021 census): 119.9 per sq km.

Population by Age and Sex ('000, UN projections at mid-2022): *0–14 years:* 155.0 (males 78.5, females 76.5); *15–64 years:* 384.0 (males 196.0, females 188.0); *65 years and over:* 28.7 (males 10.5, females 18.2); *Total* 567.7 (males 285.0, females 282.7). Note: UN projections not adjusted to take account of results of 2021 census.

Municipalities ('000, population at 2021 census, preliminary): Boavista 12.6; Brava 5.6; Maio 6.3; Mosteiros 8.1; Paúl 5.7; Porto Novo 15.9; Praia 142.0; Ribeira Brava 7.0; Ribeira Grande 15.0; Ribeira Grande Santiago 7.6; Sal 33.3; Santa Catarina 37.5; Santa Catarina Fogo 4.7; Santa Cruz 25.0; São Domingos 14.0; São Filipe 20.7; São Lourenço Orgaos 6.3; São Miguel 12.9; São Salvador Mundo 7.5; São Vicente 74.0; Tarrafal 16.6; Tarrafal São Nicolau 5.3; *Total* 483.6.

Births, Marriages and Deaths (official estimates, 2020): Live births 8,209 (birth rate 14.7 per 1,000); Deaths 2,959 (death rate 5.3 per 1,000); Marriages 1,511 (marriage rate 2.7 per 1,000).

Life Expectancy (years at birth, estimates): 73.2 (males 69.7; females 76.4) in 2020. Source: World Bank, World Development Indicators database.

Economically Active Population (employment survey, persons aged 15 years and over, 2020): Agriculture, hunting, forestry and fishing 25,617; Mining and quarrying 1,295; Manufacturing 15,064; Electricity, gas and water 1,733; Construction 19,549; Trade, restaurants and hotels 43,063; Transport, storage and communications 11,822; Financial, insurance, real estate and business services 12,242; Public administration and defence; compulsory social security 20,353; Education 13,253; Health and social services 5,222; Community, social and personal services 16,393; *Sub-total* 185,605; Activities not adequately defined 1,021; *Total employed* 186,627; Unemployed 31,724; *Total labour force* 218,351 (males 123,610, females 94,741).

HEALTH AND WELFARE

Total Fertility Rate (children per woman, 2020): 2.2.

Under-5 Mortality Rate (per 1,000 live births, 2020): 14.2.

HIV/AIDS (% of persons aged 15–49, 2020): 0.5.

COVID-19: Cumulative Confirmed Deaths (per 100,000 persons at 31 August 2022): 69.7.

COVID-19: Fully Vaccinated Population (% of total population at 28 August 2022): 52.4.

Physicians (per 1,000 head, 2018): 0.8.

Hospitals (per 100,000 head, 2013): 1.0.

Domestic Health Expenditure (2019): US $ per head (PPP): 243.1.

Domestic Health Expenditure (2019): % of GDP: 3.2.

Domestic Health Expenditure (2019): public (% of total current expenditure): 65.8.

Access to Improved Water Resources (% of persons, 2020): 89.

Access to Improved Sanitation Facilities (% of persons, 2020): 79.

Total Carbon Dioxide Emissions ('000 metric tons, 2018): 620.

Carbon Dioxide Emissions Per Head (metric tons, 2018): 1.1.

Human Development Index (2021): ranking: 128.

Human Development Index (2021): 0.662.

Note: For data on COVID-19 vaccinations, 'fully vaccinated' denotes receipt of all doses specified by approved vaccination regime (Sources: Johns Hopkins University and Our World in Data). Data on health expenditure refer to current general government expenditure in each case. For more information on sources and further definitions for all indicators, see Health and Welfare Statistics: Sources and Definitions section (europaworld.com/credits).

AGRICULTURE, ETC.

Principal Crops ('000 metric tons, 2020): Bananas 5.6; Cabbages 3.8; Coconuts 5.2 (FAO estimate); Cucumbers and gherkins 0.9; Maize 0.4; Mangoes, mangosteens, guavas 0.8; Onions, dry 3.0; Potatoes 2.6; Sugar cane 22.9; Sweet potatoes 3.3; Tomatoes 12.5. *Aggregate Production* ('000 metric tons, may include official, semi-official or estimated data): Total fruit (primary) 8.4; Total pulses 6.0; Total roots and tubers 8.4; Total vegetables (primary) 30.5.

Livestock ('000 head, 2020): Asses 16.0 (FAO estimate); Cattle 29.5; Chickens 1,000 (FAO estimate); Goats 131.7; Horses 0.6 (FAO estimate); Mules 1.9 (FAO estimate); Pigs 70.2; Sheep 18.8.

Livestock Products ('000 metric tons, 2020): Cattle meat 0.7 (FAO estimate); Cows' milk 4.4; Goats' milk 5.2; Pig meat 2.5 (FAO estimate); Hen eggs 2.6 (unofficial figure).

Fishing (metric tons, live weight, 2020): Total catch 19,292 (Demersal percomorphs 1,677; Skipjack tuna 6,155; Yellowfin tuna 6,239; Bigeye tuna 576; Pelagic percomorphs 1,777).

Source: FAO.

MINING

Production (metric tons, 2012): Salt (unrefined) 1,600. Clay, gypsum, limestone and volcanic rock were also produced, at unreported levels. Source: US Geological Survey.

INDUSTRY

Production (metric tons, 2003 unless otherwise indicated): Canned fish 200; Frozen fish 900; Flour 15,901 (1999); Beer 4,104,546 litres (1999); Soft drinks 922,714 litres (1996); Cigarettes and tobacco 77 kg (1999); Paint 628,243 kg (1997); Cement 1,100,000 (2012); Footwear 670,676 pairs (1996); Soap 1,371,045 kg (1999); Electrical energy 513m. kWh (estimate, 2019). Sources: mainly UN Energy Statistics Database, US Geological Survey and IMF, *Cape Verde: Statistical Appendix* (October 2001).

FINANCE

Currency and Exchange Rates: 100 centavos = 1 Cabo Verde escudo; 1,000 escudos are known as a conto. *Sterling, Dollar and Euro Equivalents* (31 May 2022): £1 sterling = 128.960 escudos; US $1 = 102.439 escudos; €1 = 109.743 escudos; 1,000 Cabo Verde escudos = £7.75 = $9.76 = €9.11. *Average Exchange Rate* (escudos per US dollar): 98.495 in 2019; 96.796 in 2020; 93.218 in 2021.

Central Government Budget (million escudos, 2020, preliminary): *Revenue:* Taxation 32,237 (Taxes on income and profits 9,779, Taxes on international trade 6,593, Consumption taxes 15,196, Other tax revenue 669); Non-tax revenue 6,291; Grants 5,224; Total 43,752.

Expenditure: Recurrent 64,537 (Wages and salaries 23,654, Acquisition of goods and services 15,206, Transfers and other subsidies 8,447, Interest payments 4,957, Other recurrent expenditure and social benefits 12,273); Capital 6,907; Total 71,444. *2021* (projections): Total revenue and grants 53,896; Total expenditure 68,229. Source: IMF, *Cabo Verde: Third Review Under the Policy Coordination Instrument—Press Release; and Staff Report* (April 2021).

International Reserves (excluding gold, US $ million at 31 December 2021): IMF special drawing rights 0.05; Reserve position in the IMF 4.96; Foreign exchange 706.40; *Total* 711.41. Source: IMF, *International Financial Statistics*.

Money Supply (million escudos at 31 December 2020): Currency outside depository corporations 11,114.7; Transferable deposits 95,826.2; Other deposits 99,691.4; *Broad money* 206,632.3. Source: IMF, *International Financial Statistics*.

Cost of Living (Consumer Price Index; base: 2018 = 100): All items 101.1 in 2019; 101.7 in 2020; 103.6 in 2021.

Expenditure on the Gross Domestic Product (million escudos at current prices, 2021, preliminary estimates): Government final consumption expenditure 44,165; Private final consumption expenditure 114,299; Gross capital formation 82,294; *Total domestic expenditure* 240,757; Exports of goods and services 44,429; *Less* Imports of goods and services 104,700; *GDP in purchasers' values* 180,486.

Gross Domestic Product by Economic Activity (million escudos at current prices, 2021, preliminary estimates): Agriculture, hunting and forestry 6,779; Fishing 1,180; Mining and quarrying 629; Manufacturing 15,536; Electricity, gas and water supply 5,358; Construction 23,843; Wholesale and retail trade 16,482; Hotels and restaurants 3,287; Transport, storage and communications 19,935; Financial intermediation 9,158; Other services 54,592; *Gross value added in basic prices* 156,779; Indirect taxes (net) 23,708; *GDP at market prices* 180,486.

Balance of Payments (US $ million, 2021): Exports of goods 174.1; Imports of goods −887.8; *Balance on goods* −713.7; Exports of services 299.8; Imports of services −233.5; *Balance on goods and services* −647.4; Primary income received 22.0; Primary income paid −60.1; *Balance on goods, services and primary income* −685.5; Secondary income received 483.5; Secondary income paid −55.3; *Current balance* −257.3; Capital account (net) 28.9; Direct investment assets −7.3; Direct investment liabilities 116.5; Other investment assets −76.5; Other investment liabilities 205.5; Net errors and omissions −10.3; *Reserves and related items* −0.5. Source: IMF, *International Finance Statistics*.

EXTERNAL TRADE

Principal Commodities (distribution by HS, US $ million, 2020): *Imports c.i.f.:* Live animals and animal products 56.3; Vegetables and vegetable products 66.1; Prepared foodstuffs; beverages, spirits, vinegar; tobacco and articles thereof 84.5; Mineral products 95.5; Chemicals and related products 50.1; Plastics, rubber, and articles thereof 37.1; Articles of stone, plaster, cement, asbestos; ceramic and glass products 22.7; Iron and steel, other base metals and articles of base metal 50.7; Machinery and mechanical appliances; electrical equipment; parts thereof 117.1; Vehicles, aircraft, vessels and associated transport equipment 54.3; Total (incl. others) 735.3. *Exports f.o.b.:* Live animals and animal products 9.0; Prepared foodstuffs; beverages, spirits, vinegar; tobacco and articles thereof 36.1; Textiles and textile articles 4.0; Footwear, headgear, umbrellas, walking sticks, etc. 2.7; Total (incl. others) 53.1. Source: Trade Map-Trade Competitiveness Map, International Trade Centre, marketanalysis.intracen.org.

Principal Trading Partners (US $ million, 2020): *Imports c.i.f.:* Argentina 10.0; Belgium 20.5; Brazil 23.9; China, People's Republic 49.1; France 10.6; Germany 8.8; Italy 17.0; Malta 10.9; Netherlands 48.2; Portugal 367.2; Senegal 7.6; Spain 79.0; USA 17.8; Total (incl. others) 735.3 *Exports f.o.b.:* Germany 0.7; Italy 6.9; Morocco 0.6; Portugal 7.1; Spain 34.3; USA 3.0; Total (incl. others) 53.1. Source: Trade Map-Trade Competitiveness Map, International Trade Centre, marketanalysis.intracen.org.

TRANSPORT

Shipping: *Flag Registered Fleet* (at 31 December 2021): Number of vessels 56; Total displacement 60,301 grt (Source: Lloyd's List Intelligence—www.bit.ly/LLintelligence). *International Seaborne Freight Traffic* ('000 metric tons, 2019): Goods loaded 542.4; Goods unloaded 1,786.6.

Civil Aviation (traffic on scheduled services, 2015): Kilometres flown (million) 7; Passengers carried ('000) 567; Passenger-km (million) 711; Total ton-km (million) 2 (Source: UN, *Statistical Yearbook*). **2020** (domestic and international): Departures 5,067; Passengers carried 0.3m. (Source: World Bank, World Development Indicators database).

TOURISM

Tourist Arrivals by Country of Residence (2021): Belgium and Netherlands 11,416; France 10,344; Germany 16,849; Portugal 28,384; United Kingdom 11,126; USA 4,498; Total (incl. others) 169,068.

Tourism Receipts (US $ million, excl. passenger transport): 431 in 2017; 484 in 2018; 502 in 2019 (provisional) (Source: World Tourism Organization).

COMMUNICATIONS MEDIA

Telephones (2020): 57,668 main lines in use.

Mobile Telephone Subscriptions (2020): 544,729.

Broadband Subscriptions, Fixed (2020): 24,839.

Broadband Subscriptions, Mobile (2020): 419,751.

Internet Users (% of population, 2019): 61.9.

Source: International Telecommunication Union.

EDUCATION

Pre-primary (2018/19 unless otherwise indicated): 543 schools (2015/16); 1,459 teachers; 24,140 pupils.

Primary (2018/19 unless otherwise indicated): 413 schools (2015/16); 3,093 teachers; 62,596 pupils.

Total Secondary (2018/19 unless otherwise indicated): 44 schools (2015/16); 3,498 teachers; 53,616 pupils.

Higher (2017/18): 1,461 teachers; 11,659 pupils.

Teacher Training (2003/04): 3 colleges; 52 teachers; 948 pupils.

Pupil-teacher Ratio (qualified teaching staff, primary education, UNESCO estimate): 21.7 in 2018/19.

Adult Literacy Rate (UNESCO estimates): 86.8% (males 91.7%; females 82.0%) in 2015.

Sources (unless otherwise indicated): Comunidade dos Países de Língua Portuguesa; Ministry of Education and Sport, Praia; UNESCO Institute for Statistics.

Directory

The Constitution

A new Constitution of the Republic of Cabo Verde ('the Second Republic') came into force on 25 September 1992. The Constitution defines Cabo Verde as a sovereign, unitary and democratic republic, guaranteeing respect for human dignity and recognizing the inviolable and inalienable rights of man as a fundament of humanity, peace and justice. It recognizes the equality of all citizens before the law, without distinction of social origin, social condition, economic status, race, sex, religion, political convictions or ideologies and promises transparency for all citizens in the practising of fundamental liberties. The Constitution gives assent to popular will, and has a fundamental objective in the realization of economic, political, social and cultural democracy and the construction of a society that is free, just and in solidarity.

The Head of State is the President of the Republic, who is elected by universal adult suffrage and must obtain two-thirds of the votes cast to win in the first round of the election. If no candidate secures the requisite majority, a new election is held within 21 days and contested by the two candidates who received the highest number of votes in the first round. Voting is conducted by secret ballot. Legislative power is vested in the National Assembly, which is also elected by universal adult suffrage. The Prime Minister is nominated by the Assembly, to which he/she is responsible. On the recommendation of the Prime Minister, the President appoints the Council of Ministers, whose members must be elected deputies of the Assembly. There are 22 local government councils, elected by universal suffrage for a period of five years.

A constitutional revision, adopted in July 1999, gave the President the right to dissolve the National Assembly, created a new advisory chamber (the Economic and Social Council), and gave the state the right to adopt Crioulo as the country's second official language.

A series of further amendments to the Constitution were approved by the National Assembly on 9 February 2010.

The Government

HEAD OF STATE

President: JOSÉ MARIA PEREIRA NEVES (took office 9 November 2021).

COUNCIL OF MINISTERS
(October 2022)

The Government is composed of members of the Movimento para a Democracia.

Prime Minister: Dr JOSÉ ULISSES DE PINA CORREIA E SILVA.

Deputy Prime Minister, Minister of Finance and Business Promotion, and of the Digital Economy: Dr OLAVO AVELINO GARCIA CORREIA.

Minister of State for Family, Inclusion and Social Development: Dr FERNANDO ELÍSIO FREIRE.

Minister of State for Defence and Territorial Cohesion: Dr JANINE TATIANA SANTOS LÉLIS.

Minister of Foreign Affairs, International Co-operation and Regional Integration: Dr RUI ALBERTO DE FIGUEIREDO SOARES.

Minister of Communities: JORGE SANTOS.

Minister of Internal Administration: Dr PAULO AUGUSTO COSTA ROCHA.

Minister of Justice: Dr JOANA GOMES ROSA AMADO.

Minister of State Modernization and Public Administration: Dr EDNA MANUELA MIRANDA DE OLIVEIRA.

Minister of the Presidency of the Council of Ministers and of Parliamentary Affairs: Dr FILOMENA MENDES GONÇALVES.

Minister of Education: Dr AMADEU CRUZ.

Minister of Health: Dr ARLINDO NASCIMENTO DO ROSÁRIO.

Minister of Culture, Creative Industries and the Sea: ABRAÃO ANÍBAL BARBOSA VICENTE.

Minister of Tourism and Transport: Dr CARLOS JORGE DUARTE SANTOS.

Minister of Agriculture and the Environment: Dr GILBERTO CORREIA CARVALHO SILVA.

Minister of Industry, Trade and Energy: ALEXANDRE DIAS MONTEIRO.

Minister of Infrastructure, Spatial Planning and Housing: Dr EUNICE ANDRADE DA SILVA SPENCER LOPES.

Deputy Minister to the Prime Minister, responsible for Youth and Sports: Dr CARLOS MONTEIRO.

There were also eight secretaries of state and one deputy secretary of state.

MINISTRIES

Office of the President: Palácio do Plateau, CP 100, Plateau, Praia, Santiago; tel. 2612829; e-mail info@presidencia.cv; internet presidencia.cv.

Office of the Prime Minister: Gabinete do Primeiro Ministro, Palácio do Governo, Várzea, CP 16, Praia, Santiago; tel. 2610411; e-mail gab.imprensa@gpm.gov.cv; internet www.governo.cv.

Ministry of Agriculture and the Environment: CP 115, Praia, Santiago; tel. 3337370; e-mail maa@maa.gov.cv; internet www.maa .gov.cv.

Ministry of Communities: Praia, Santiago.

Ministry of Culture and Creative Industries: Palácio do Governo, Várzea, CP 302, Praia, Santiago; tel. 2610123; e-mail ministeriocultura1@gmail.com; internet fb.com/cultura.caboverde.

Ministry of Defence and Territorial Cohesion: Palácio do Governo, Várzea da Companhia, Praia, Santiago; tel. 2610344; internet fb.com/mdncv.

Ministry of Education: Palácio do Governo, Várzea, CP 111, Praia, Santiago; tel. 2610510; e-mail cci.mees@palgov.gov.cv; internet minedu.gov.cv.

Ministry of Family, Inclusion and Social Development: Achada Santo António, Praia, Santiago; tel. 3336785; internet www.mfis.gov.cv.

Ministry of Finance and Business Promotion: 107 Av. Amílcar Cabral, CP 30, Praia, Santiago; tel. 2607400; e-mail mfgeral@mf.gov .cv; internet www.mf.gov.cv.

Ministry of Foreign Affairs, International Co-operation and Regional Integration: Av. Liberdade e Democracia, Achada de

Santo António, CP 60, Praia, Santiago; tel. 2607853; e-mail mnecomunidades@gmail.com; internet fb.com/MinisteriodosNegociosEstrangeiros.

Ministry of Health: Palácio do Governo, CP 47, Praia, Santiago; tel. 2610116; internet www.minsaude.gov.cv.

Ministry of Industry, Trade and Energy: Rua UCCLA 23, Praia, Santiago; e-mail ministerioice@gmail.com; internet fb.com/mice.cv.

Ministry of Infrastructure, Spatial Planning and Housing: Rua Judice Biker 114, Ponta Belém, Praia, Santiago; tel. 2608300; e-mail info@mioth.gov.cv; internet mioth.gov.cv.

Ministry of Internal Administration: Praia, Santiago; tel. 2604020; e-mail samory.araujo@govcv.gov.cv; internet fb.com/maicaboverde.

Ministry of Justice: Rua Cidade do Funchal, CP 205, Praia, Santiago; tel. 3337371; e-mail minjus@govcv.gov.cv; internet fb.com/oficialministeriojustica.

Ministry of the Presidency of the Council of Ministers and of Parliamentary Affairs: Praia, Santiago.

Ministry of Tourism and Transport: Rua Cidade do Funchal 2, Praia, Santiago; Mindelo, São Vicente; tel. 2604800; e-mail info@mtt.gov.cv; internet mtt.gov.cv.

President

Presidential Election, 17 October 2021

Candidate	Valid votes	% of valid votes
José Maria Pereira Neves	95,803	51.73
Carlos Alberto Wahnon de Carvalho Veiga	78,474	42.37
Casimiro Jeusu Lopes de Pina	3,343	1.81
Fernando Rocha Delgado	2,516	1.36
Hélio de Jesus Pina Sanches	2,119	1.14
Gilson João Santos Alves	1,558	0.84
Joaquim Jaime Monteiro	1,378	0.74
Total	**185,191***	**100.00**

* Excluding 4,266 blank votes and 1,662 spoiled ballots.

Legislature

National Assembly: Achada de Santo António, CP 20A, Praia, Santiago; tel. 2608000; e-mail ancv@parlamento.cv; internet www.parlamento.cv.

Speaker: Dr AUSTELINO TAVARES CORREIA.

General Election, 18 April 2021

Party	Valid votes	% of valid votes	Seats
MpD	110,121	50.03	38
PAICV	87,063	39.55	30
UCID	19,834	9.01	4
PTS	2,088	0.95	—
PP	756	0.34	—
PSD	271	0.12	—
Total	**220,133***	**100.00**	**72**

* Excluding 2,448 blank votes and 3,061 invalid votes.

Election Commission

Comissão Nacional de Eleições (CNE): Bairro da Prainha, Praia, Santiago; tel. 2624323; e-mail cne@cne.cv; internet www.cne.cv; Pres. MARIA DO ROSÁRIO PEREIRA.

Political Organizations

Movimento para a Democracia (MpD): Av. Cidade Lisboa, 4° andar, CP 90A, Praia, Santiago; tel. 2614082; e-mail gabinetecommpd@gmail.com; internet fb.com/MpD.Cabo.Verde; f. 1990; Chair. JOSÉ ULISSES DE PINA CORREIA E SILVA; Sec.-Gen. FILOMENA DELGADO.

Partido Africano da Independência de Cabo Verde (PAICV): Av. Amílcar Cabral, CP 22, Praia, Santiago; tel. 2605430; e-mail info@paicv.cv; internet paicv.cv; f. 1956 as the Partido Africano da

Independência do Guiné e Cabo Verde (PAIGC); name changed in 1981, following the 1980 coup in Guinea-Bissau; sole authorized political party 1975–90; Pres. RUI SEMEDO; Sec.-Gen. JULIÃO VARELA.

Partido Popular de Cabo Verde: Praia, Santiago; tel. 5927070; internet fb.com/partidopopularcaboverde; f. 2015; Leader AMÁNDIO BARBOSA VICENTE.

Partido Socialista Democrático (PSD): Praia, Santiago; f. 1992; Sec.-Gen. JOÃO ALÉM.

Partido do Trabalho e da Solidariedade (PTS): Praia, Santiago; f. 1998; Pres. CARLOS LOPES.

União Caboverdiana Independente e Democrática (UCID): Rua Academia Música Jota-Monte, Monte Sossego, CP 56, Mindelo; tel. 2316259; e-mail ucidcaboverde@gmail.com; internet ucid.cv; Pres. JOÃO SANTOS LUÍS.

Diplomatic Representation

EMBASSIES IN CABO VERDE

Angola: Av. OUA, Achada de Santo António, CP 78A, Praia, Santiago; tel. 2623235; Ambassador JÚLIA CIPRIANO MACHADO.

Brazil: Chã de Areia 2, CP 93, Praia, Santiago; tel. 2615607; e-mail brasemb.praia@itamaraty.gov.br; internet www.gov.br/pt-br/embaixada-praia; Ambassador COLBERT SOARES PINTO, Jr.

China, People's Republic: Achada de Santo António, CP 8, Praia, Santiago; tel. 2623027; e-mail embchinacv@hotmail.com; internet cv.china-embassy.gov.cn; Ambassador XU JIE (designate).

Cuba: Achada de Santo António, CP 251, Praia, Santiago; tel. 2614050; e-mail embajador@cv.embacuba.cu; internet misiones.minrex.gob.cu/es/cabo-verde; Ambassador ROSA OLIVIA WILSON RILL.

France: Quartier du Plateau, 28 Tenente Valadim, CP 192, Praia, Santiago; tel. 2604535; e-mail ad.praia-amba@diplomatie.gouv.fr; internet cv.ambafrance.org; Ambassador OLIVIER SEROT ALMERAS LATOUR.

Guinea-Bissau: rua de UCCLA, Achada Santo António, Praia; Ambassador (vacant).

Portugal: Av. OUA, Achada de Santo António, CP 160, Praia, Santiago; tel. 2623037; e-mail secretariado.praia@mne.pt; internet praia.embaixadaportugal.mne.pt; Ambassador ANTÓNIO MANUEL ALBUQUERQUE DE VILHENA MONIZ.

Russian Federation: Av. OUA 9, Achada de Santo António, Praia, Santiago; tel. 2622739; e-mail embrus@sapo.cv; internet capeverde.mid.ru; Ambassador YURI B. MATERIY (designate).

Senegal: Rua Abílio Macedo, Plateau, CP 269, Praia, Santiago; tel. 2615621; Ambassador ELY SY BEYE.

Spain: Rua de Espanha 1, Achada de Santo António, Praia, Santiago; tel. 2601800; e-mail emb.praia@maec.es; internet www.exteriores.gob.es/embajadas/praia; Ambassador ANA PAREDES PIETRO.

USA: Rua Abílio Macedo 6, Praia, Santiago; tel. 2608900; internet cv.usembassy.gov; Ambassador JOHN JEFFERSON 'JEFF' DAIGLE.

Judicial System

Supreme Court of Justice (Supremo Tribunal de Justiça—STJ): Gabinete do Juiz Presidente, Edif. dos Correios, Rua Cesário de Lacerda, CP 117, Praia, Santiago; tel. 2615808; e-mail stj@supremo.gov.cv; f. 1975; Pres. BENFEITO MOSSO RAMOS (acting).

Attorney-General: Dr LUÍS JOSÉ LANDIM.

Religion

CHRISTIANITY

The Roman Catholic Church

Cabo Verde comprises two dioceses, directly responsible to the Holy See. The Bishops participate in the Episcopal Conference of Senegal, Mauritania, Cabo Verde and Guinea-Bissau, currently based in Senegal.

Bishop of Mindelo: Rt Rev. ILDO AUGUSTO DOS SANTOS LOPES FORTES, CP 447, 2110 Mindelo, São Vicente; tel. 2318870; e-mail diocesemindelo@cvtelecom.cv.

Bishop of Santiago de Cabo Verde: Cardinal ARLINDO GOMES FURTADO, Av. Amílcar Cabral, Largo 5 de Outubro, CP 46, Praia, Santiago; tel. 2611119; e-mail diocesecv@cvtelecom.cv.

The Anglican Communion

Cabo Verde forms part of the diocese of The Gambia, within the Church of the Province of West Africa. The Bishop is resident in Banjul, The Gambia.

Other Christian Churches

Church of the Nazarene: District Office, Av. Amílcar Cabral, Plateau, CP 96, Praia, Santiago; tel. 2613611.

Other churches represented in Cabo Verde include the Church of the Assembly of God, the Church of Jesus Christ of Latter-day Saints, the Evangelical Baptist Church, the Maná Church, the New Apostolic Church, the Seventh-day Adventist Church and the Universal Church of the Kingdom of God.

BAHÁ'Í FAITH

National Spiritual Assembly: Rua Madragoa, Plateau, CP 230, Praia, Santiago; tel. 2617739; f. 1984.

The Press

Expresso das Ilhas: Achada de Santo António, OUA No. 21, R/C, CP 666, Praia, Santiago; tel. 2619807; e-mail jornal@expressodasilhas .publ.cv; internet expressodasilhas.cv; f. 2001 by the MpD; daily; Editor-in-Chief JORGE MONTEZINHO.

Jornal de Cabo Verde: Prédio Gonçalves, 6º piso, Av. Cidade de Lisboa, CP 889, Praia, Santiago; tel. 2601414; print version of online news website O Liberal; Dir DANIEL MEDINA.

A Nação: CP 690, Cidadela, Praia, Santiago; tel. 2628677; e-mail jornalanacaocv@gmail.com; internet www.anacao.cv; f. 2007; weekly; independent; Dir-Gen. FERNANDO RUI ORTET.

A Semana: Rotunda do Palmarejo, Av. Santiago 59, CP 36C, Praia, Santiago; tel. 2629860; e-mail asemana@cvtelecom.cv; internet www .asemana.publ.cv; f. 1991; weekly; independent; Editor FILOMENA SILVA.

Terra Nova: Rua Guiné-Bissau 1, CP 166, Mindelo, São Vicente; tel. 9998026; e-mail jornalterranova@gmail.com; internet terranova.cv; f. 1975; quarterly; Roman Catholic; Editor P. ANTÓNIO FIDALGO BARROS.

NEWS AGENCIES

Inforpress: Achada de Santo António, CP 40A, Praia, Santiago; tel. 2622562; e-mail inforpress_agencia@yahoo.com.br; internet www .inforpress.cv; f. 1988 as Cabopress; Pres. JOSÉ MARIO CORREIA.

PRESS ASSOCIATIONS

Associação de Jornalistas de Cabo Verde (AJOC): Rua João Chapuzet (Travessa do mercado), CP 350A, Praia, Santiago; tel. 2622121; internet www.ajoc.cv; f. 1993; Pres. GEREMIAS FURTADO; 11 media cos and 159 individual mems.

Publishers

GOVERNMENT PUBLISHING HOUSE

Imprensa Nacional: Av. Amílcar Cabral, Calçada Diogo Gomes, CP 113, Praia, Santiago; tel. 2612145; e-mail kioske.incv@govcv.gov.cv; internet kiosk.incv.cv; Pres. LUCÍDIO MOREIRA.

Broadcasting and Communications

TELECOMMUNICATIONS

Cabo Verde Telecom (CVTelecom): Rua Cabo Verde Telecom, Várzea, CP 220, Praia, Santiago; tel. 2609200; e-mail apoiocliente@ cvt.cv; internet www.cvtelecom.cv; f. 1995; 57.9% owned by INPS, 20% owned by ASA and 3.4% state-owned; Chair. JOSÉ LUÍS LIVRAMENTO.

CVMóvel: Chã de Areia, Praia, Santiago 126-A; e-mail marketing@cvt.cv; internet www.cvmovel.cv; wholly owned subsidiary of Cabo Verde Telecom providing mobile telephone services; Exec. Dir FRANCISCO ALMEIDA.

Unitel T+ Telecomunicações: Edifício BAI Center, 4ºe 6º Piso, Av. Cidade Lisboa, CP 346A, Praia, Santiago; tel. 3303030; e-mail 555@ tmais.cv; internet www.uniteltmais.cv; f. 2007; est. as T+ Telecomunicações; acquired by Unitel Internacional of Angola in 2012 and renamed as above; Dir-Gen. INOWEZE DIAS FERREIRA.

Regulatory Authority

Agência Reguladora Multissectorial da Economia (ARME): Prédio ARME, 5º andar, Av. da China, Chã d'Areia, CP 892, Praia, Santiago; tel. 2604400; e-mail info@arme.cv; internet www.arme.cv; f. 2018 following merger of Agência Nacional das Comunicações and Agência de Regulação Económica; regulatory agency for communications, energy, water and urban and interurban passenger transport; Pres. LEONILDE TATIANA DOS SANTOS.

BROADCASTING

Rádiotelevisão Caboverdiana (RTC): Rua 13 de Janeiro, Achada de Santo António, Praia, Santiago; tel. 2605200; e-mail multimedia@ rtc.cv; internet www.rtc.cv; govt-controlled; Pres. POLICARPO DE CARVALHO.

Rádio de Cabo Verde (RCV): Rua 13 de Janeiro, Achada de Santo António, Praia, Santiago; tel. 2605200; internet www.rcv.cv; part of RTC; Dir of Radio NÉLIO SANTOS.

Televisão de Cabo Verde: Rua 13 de Janeiro, Achada de Santo António, Praia, Santiago; tel. 2605200; e-mail tcv@rtc.cv; internet www.tcv.cv; f. 1986; sole television broadcaster; part of RTC; Dir ANTONIO TEIXEIRA.

Praia FM: Rua Visconde de S. Januario 19, 4° andar, CP 276C, Praia, Santiago; tel. 2616356; e-mail atendimento@praiafm.biz; internet praiafm.sapo.cv; f. 1999; Dir GIORDANO CUSTÓDIO.

Rádio Comercial: Av. Liberdade e Democradia 6, Prédio Gomes Irmãos, 3° esq., CP 507, Praia, Santiago; tel. 2623156; e-mail radiocomercial.cv@hotmail.com; f. 1997; Admin. HENRIQUE PIRES; Dir CARLOS FILIPE GONÇALVES.

Rádio Educativa de Cabo Verde: Rua Pedagogo Paulo Freire, Achada de Santo António, Praia, Santiago; tel. 2621075; internet www.radioeducativa.cv; Dir JOSÉ FURTADO.

Rádio Morabeza: Av. Netherlands 38A, Mindelo, São Vicente; tel. 2324431; e-mail geral@radiomorabeza.cv; internet radiomorabeza .cv; f. 1999; Editor-in-Chief NUNO ANDRADE FERREIRA.

Finance

BANKING

Central Bank

Banco de Cabo Verde (BCV): Av. OUA 2, CP 7954-094, Praia, Santiago; tel. 2607000; e-mail fevora@bcv.cv; internet www.bcv.cv; f. 1976; bank of issue; Gov. OSCAR HUMBERTO ÉVORA DOS SANTOS.

Other Banks

Banco BAI Cabo Verde SA (BAI): Edifício BAICENTER, R/C-Chã DAreia, CP 459, Praia, Santiago; tel. 2602300; e-mail bai@bancobai .cv; internet www.bancobai.cv; f. 2008; fmrly Banco Africano de Investimentos Cabo Verde SA; name changed as above in 2012; 71% owned by BAI Angola, 19% owned by Sonangol and 10% owned by SOGEI; Pres. Dr LUÍS FILIPE RODRIGUES LÉLIS; Dir-Gen. Dr CARLOS AUGUSTO BESSA VICTOR CHAVES.

Banco Caboverdiano de Negócios (BCN): Av. Amílcar Cabral 97, CP 593, Praia, Santiago; tel. 2616662; e-mail bcn@bcn.cv; internet www.bcn.cv; f. 1996 as Banco Totta e Açores (Cabo Verde); renamed as above in 2004; 46% owned by Banif (Portugal); Pres. PAULO JORGE FERRO RIBEIRO DE OLIVEIRA LIMA; Dir-Gen. Dr LUÍS MIGUEL ANDRADE VASCONCELOS LOPES.

Banco Comercial do Atlântico (BCA): Praça Alexandre Albuquerque, Av. Amílcar Cabral, CP 474, Praia, Santiago; tel. 2600913; e-mail bca@bca.cv; internet www.bca.cv; f. 1993; privatized in 2000; main commercial bank; Pres. and Gen. Man. FRANCISCO PINTO MACHADO COSTA.

Banco Interatlântico: Av. Cidade de Lisboa, CP 131A, Praia, Santiago; tel. 2603684; e-mail bi@bi.cv; internet www.bi.cv; f. 1999; Chair. JOSÉ JOÃO GUILHERME; Dir-Gen. PEDRO BRUNO CARDOSO BRAGA GOMES SOARES.

Caixa Económica de Cabo Verde, SA (CECV): Av. Cidade de Lisboa, CP 199, Praia, Santiago; tel. 2603600; e-mail caixa@caixa.cv; internet www.caixa.cv; f. 1928; commercial bank; Pres. JAILSON DA CONCEIÇÃO TEIXEIRA DE OLIVEIRA; CEO ANTÓNIO CARLOS MOREIRA SEMEDO.

Ecobank Cabo Verde: Praça Infante Dom Henrique 18, Palmarejo, CP 374C, Praia, Santiago; tel. 2603660; e-mail ecobankcv@ecobank .com; internet www.ecobank.com; f. 2010; Pres. JOSÉ TOMAZ WAHNON DE CARVALHO VEIGA; Man. Dir JOSÉ MANUEL CORREIA MENDES.

International Investment Bank: Av. Cidade de Lisboa-Fazenda, CP 35, Praia, Santiago; tel. 2602626; e-mail infocv@iibanks.com; internet www.iibanks.com/cape-verde; f. 2010 as Banco Espírito

Santo Cabo Verde SA, subsequently Banco Internacional de Cabo Verde SA; present name adopted 2019; Pres. SOHAIL SULTAN AHMAD.

STOCK EXCHANGE

Bolsa de Valores de Cabo Verde, Sarl (BVC): 16 Achada de Santo António, CP 115A, Praia, Santiago; tel. 2603030; e-mail bcv@bvc.cv; internet www.bvc.cv; f. 1998; reopened December 2005; Pres. Dr MANUEL JOAQUIM DE LIMA.

INSURANCE

Companhia Caboverdiana de Seguros (IMPAR): Rua Amílcar Cabral, CP 469, Praia, Santiago; tel. 2603127; e-mail comercial@impar.cv; internet www.impar.cv; f. 1991; Pres. JOSÉ ANTÓNIO DE AREZ ROMÃO.

Garantia Companhia de Seguros: Chã de Areia, CP 138, Praia, Santiago; tel. 2608600; e-mail garantia@garantia.cv; internet www.garantia.cv; f. 1991; privatized in 2000; Pres. Dr EUGÉNIO MANUEL DOS SANTOS RAMOS; Dir-Gen. JORGE FERNANDO GONÇALVES ALVES.

Trade and Industry

GOVERNMENT AGENCIES

Cabo Verde TradeInvest: Rotunda da Cruz do Papa 5, CP 89C, Praia, Santiago; tel. 2604110; e-mail info@cvtradeinvest.cv; internet cvtradeinvest.com; f. 2016; Pres. JOSÉ ALMADA DIAS.

Entidade Reguladora Independente da Saúde (ERIS): Av. Cidade de Lisboa, Várzea, CP 296A, Praia, Santiago; tel. 2626457; e-mail eris@eris.cv; internet www.eris.cv; f. 2019; absorbed Agência de Regulação e Supervisão dos Produtos Farmacêuticos e Alimentares; Pres. EDUARDO JORGE MONTEIRO TAVARES.

CHAMBERS OF COMMERCE

Câmara de Comércio de Barlavento/Agremiação Empresarial (CCB/AE): Rua Boa Vista, CP 728, Mindelo, São Vicente; tel. 2328495; e-mail camara.com@cvtelecom.cv; internet www.camara.cv; f. 1996; Pres. JOÃO GOMES; Sec.-Gen. ADRIANO CRUZ.

Câmara de Comércio, Indústria e Serviços de Sotavento (CCISS): Av. OUA 39, CP 105, Praia, Santiago; tel. 2615352; e-mail ccisspraia@gmail.com; internet www.ccs.org.cv; Pres. MARCOS RODRIGUES.

STATE INDUSTRIAL ENTERPRISES

Empresa Nacional de Avicultura, SARL (ENAVI): Tira Chapéu Zona Industrial, CP 135, Praia, Santiago; tel. 2627268; poultry farming.

Empresa Nacional de Combustíveis, SARL (ENACOL): Largo John Miller, CP 1, Mindelo, São Vicente; tel. 2306060; e-mail energia@enacol.cv; internet www.enacol.cv; f. 1979; supervises import and distribution of petroleum; Pres. Dr VANDA MARIA LIMA ÉVORA; Dir JORGE BORGES CARVALHO.

Empresa Nacional de Produtos Farmacêuticos, SARL (EMPROFAC): Tira Chapéu Zona Industrial, CP 59, Praia, Santiago; tel. 2601510; e-mail geral@emprofac.cv; internet www.emprofac.cv; f. 1979; state monopoly of pharmaceuticals and medical imports; Pres. Dr FERNANDO GIL EVORA.

UTILITIES

Electricity and Water

Agência Nacional de Água e Saneamento: Rotunda Braz, Tira Chapéu, CP 567, Praia, Santiago; tel. 2614214; e-mail anas@anas.gov.cv; internet www.anas.gov.cv; Pres. CLÁUDIO LOPES DOS SANTOS.

Empresa de Electricidade e Agua, SARL (Electra): Av. Baltasar Lopes Silva 10, CP 137, Mindelo, São Vicente; tel. 2303030; e-mail electra@electra.cv; internet www.electra.cv; divided into 3 separate cos: Electra, ELECTRA Norte and ELECTRA-Sul; f. 1982; 51% govt-owned; Chair. LUÍS TEIXEIRA; Dir-Gen. ALEXANDRE DIAS MONTEIRO.

MAJOR COMPANIES

Construções de Cabo Verde, SA (CVC): Achada Grande, CP 242, Praia, Santiago; tel. 2633879; e-mail cvc@cvc.cv; 90% owned by Grupo SOMAGUE (Portugal); construction, mainly on govt infrastructure and building projects; Pres. JOSÉ FERREIRA TEIXEIRA.

Sociedade Caboverdiana de Tabacos, Lda (SCT): Av. 5 de Julho, CP 270, São Vicente; tel. 2323349; e-mail sct@sct.cv; internet www.sct.cv; f. 1996; Pres. EUCLIDES JESUS MARQUES OLIVEIRA.

TRADE UNIONS

Confederação Caboverdiana dos Sindicatos Livres (CCSL): Rua Dr Júlio Abreu, CP 155, Praia, Santiago; tel. 9917279; e-mail ccsl.org.cv@gmail.com; f. 1992; Pres. JOSÉ MANUEL VAZ.

Sindicato dos Transportes, Comunicações e Turismo (STCT): Praia, Santiago; tel. 2616338.

União Nacional dos Trabalhadores de Cabo Verde—Central Sindical (UNTC—CS): Av. Cidade de Lisboa, CP 123, Praia, Santiago; tel. 2614155; internet www.untc-cs.cv; f. 1978; Sec.-Gen. JOAQUINA ALMEIDA.

Transport

ROADS

Estradas de Cabo Verde (ECV): Prédio Ordem dos Engenheiros, 4° andar, Av. Santiago 28, CP343A, Palmarejo, Praia; tel. 2629951; e-mail info@ecv.cv; internet www.estradas.cv; f. 2019 to replace the Instituto de Estradas (created 2003); road maintenance and devt; Pres. EDUARDO LOPES.

SHIPPING

Cargo-passenger ships call regularly at Porto Grande, Mindelo, on São Vicente, and at Praia, on Santiago. The ports at Praia, Sal, São Vicente and Porto Novo (Santo Antão) have all been upgraded in recent years. There are small ports on the other inhabited islands.

CV Interilhas: Av. Cidade de Lisboa, Edif. BAI Center Loja 2, Praia, Santiago; tel. 3500330; e-mail info@cvinterilhas.cv; internet www.cvinterilhas.cv; f. 2019.

Empresa Nacional de Administração dos Portos, SA (ENAPOR, SA): Av. Marginal, CP 82, Mindelo, São Vicente; tel. 2307500; e-mail info@enapor.cv; internet www.enapor.cv; f. 1982; Chair. IRINEU CAMACHO.

CIVIL AVIATION

The Amílcar Cabral international airport, at Espargos, on Sal island, can accommodate aircraft of up to 50 metric tons and 1m. passengers per year. The airport's facilities were expanded during the 1990s. A second international airport, Aeroporto da Praia (renamed Aeroporto Nelson Mandela in 2012) on Santiago, was opened in late 2005, and a third, Rabil International Airport on Boavista, commenced operating in 2007. In addition, following upgrade work, São Pedro Airport, on the island of São Vicente, received its first international arrival in December 2009. There is also a small airport on each of the other inhabited islands.

Agência de Aviação Civil (AAC): 34 Av. Cidade de Lisboa, CP 371, Praia, Santiago; tel. 2603430; e-mail info@acivil.gov.cv; internet www.aac.cv; f. 2005; regulatory agency; Pres. JOÃO DOS REIS MONTEIRO; Exec. Administrator SEILA FERNANDES PIRES.

Cabo Verde Airlines: Av. Amílcar Cabral, CP 1, Praia, Santiago; tel. 2608200; e-mail pferreira@tacv.aero; internet flytacv.com; f. 1958 as Transportes Aéreos de Cabo Verde; operates regional services to Senegal, The Gambia, Angola and Guinea-Bissau, and long-distance services to Europe and the USA; CEO ERLENDUR SVAVARSSON.

Empresa Nacional de Aeroportos e Segurança AEREA, SA (ASA): Aeroporto Amílcar Cabral, CP 58, Ilha do Sal; tel. 2419200; e-mail info@asa.cv; internet www.asa.cv; f. 1984; state-owned; airports and air navigation; Pres. JORGE BENCHIMOL DUARTE.

Transportes Interilhas de Cabo Verde: Praia; tel. 4360060; e-mail reservascv@binter.cv; internet www.binter.cv; fmrly Binter Cabo Verde; present name adopted in 2019; internal services connecting 7 islands; also operates services to the Spanish Canary Islands; Dir-Gen. LUÍS QUINTA.

Tourism

The islands of Santiago, Santo Antão, Fogo and Brava offer attractive mountain scenery. There are extensive beaches on the islands of Santiago, Sal, Boavista and Maio. The sector is undergoing rapid expansion, with development in a number of Zonas de Desenvolvimento Turístico Integral.

Defence

The armed forces numbered about 1,200 (army 1,000, air force of up to 100, coastguard 100), as assessed at November 2021. There is also a police force, the Police for Public Order, which is organized by the local municipal councils. National service of 14 months is by selective conscription.

Defence Budget: 1,120m. escudos in 2021.

Chief of Staff of the Armed Forces: Col ANILDO EMANUEL DA GRAÇA MORAIS.

Education

Compulsory primary education begins at six or seven years of age and lasts for six years. Secondary education, beginning at 13 years of age, is divided into two cycles, the first comprising a three-year general course, the second a two-year pre-university course. There are three teacher training units and two industrial and commercial schools of further education. According to estimates by the UN Educational, Scientific and Cultural Organization (UNESCO), in 2018/19 pre-primary enrolment included 75% of children in the relevant age-group (males 74%; females 76%). Primary enrolment in 2017/18 included 94% of children in the relevant age-group (males 94%; females 93%), while secondary enrolment in that year included 70% of children in the relevant age-group (males 66%; females 74%). In 2002 a private university, the Universidade Jean Piaget de Cabo Verde, opened in Praia. According to UNESCO estimates, in 2021 spending on education represented 15.1% of total budgetary expenditure.

Bibliography

Ascher, F. *Os Rebelados de Cabo Verde. História de uma Revolta.* Paris, L'Harmattan, 2011.

Barcellos, C. *Subsidíos para a história de Cabo Verde e Guiné.* Praia, Instituto da Biblioteca Nacional e do Livro, 2003.

Batalha, L., and Carling, L. (Eds) *Transnational Archipelago: Perspectives on Cape Verdean Migration and Diaspora.* Amsterdam, Amsterdam University Press, 2008.

Bigman, L. *History and Hunger in West Africa: Food Production and Entitlement in Guinea-Bissau and Cape Verde.* Santa Barbara, CA, Greenwood Press, 1993.

Brooks, G. *Western Africa and Cabo Verde 1790s–1830s: Symbiosis of Slave and Legitimate Trades.* Bloomington, IN, Authorhouse, 2010.

Bussotti, L., Ngoenha, S.E. *Capo Verde: Dall'Indipendenza a Oggi: Studi Post-Coloniali.* Udine, Aviani & Aviani, 2011.

Cardoso, P. (Ed.). *Cabo Verde. Atlas da Lusofonia.* Lisbon, Prefácio, 2006.

Chabal, P. *Amílcar Cabral: Revolutionary Leadership and People's War.* Trenton, NJ, Africa World, 2003.

Correia e Silva, A. *Dilemas de Poder na História de Cabo Verde.* Praia, Rosa de Porcelana Editora, 2014.

Davidson, B. *The Fortunate Isles: A Study of Cape Verde.* London, Hutchinson, and Trenton, NJ, World Press, 1989.

dos Santos, D. *Amílcar Cabral. Um outro olhar.* Lisbon, Chiado Editora, 2014.

Fonseca dos Santos, I., da Costa Esteves, J., and Rolland, D. *Les îles du Cap-Vert: Langues, mémoires, histoire.* Paris, L'Harmattan, 2007.

Gomes, C. *Mulher e Poder: O Caso De Cabo Verde.* Praia, Instituto da Biblioteca Nacionale do Livro, 2011.

Green, T. *The Rise of the Trans-Atlantic Slave Trade in Western Africa, 1300–1589.* Cambridge, Cambridge University Press, 2011.

Halter, M. *Between Race and Ethnicity: Cape Verdean American Immigrants, 1860–1965.* Champaign, IL, University of Illinois Press, 1993.

Langworthy, M., and Finan, T. J. *Waiting for Rain: Agriculture and Ecological Imbalance in Cape Verde.* Boulder, CO, Lynne Rienner, 1997.

Lesourd, M. *État et société aux îles du Cap-Vert: Alternatives pour un petit état insulaire.* Paris, Editions Karthala, 1995.

Lobban, R. *Historical Dictionary of Cape Verde.* 4th edn. Metuchen, NJ, Scarecrow Press, 2007.

  Cape Verde: Crioulo Colony to Independent Nation. Boulder, CO, Westview Press, 1998.

Lopes, J. *Cabo Verde. Os Bastidores da Independência.* Praia, Spleen, 2002.

  Aristides Pereira, minha vida, nossa história. Praia, Spleen, 2012.

Pereira, D. A., and Marinho, J. P. *Memória Sobre Cabo Verde do Governador Joaquim Pereira Marinho & Outros Textos.* Praia, Instituto Camões-Centro Cultural Português Praia, 2008.

Rego, M. *The Dialogic Nation of Cape Verde: Slavery, Language and Ideology.* Lanham, MD, Lexington Books, 2015.

Santos, M., Torrão M., and Soares, M. *História Concisa de Cabo Verde.* Lisbon, Instituto de Investigação Científica Tropical and Praia, Instituto da Investigação e do Património Culturais, 2007.

Sousa, J. *Amílcar Cabral (1924–1973). Vida e morte de um revolucionário africano.* Lisbon, Vega, 2011.

Tomás, A. *O Fazedor de Utopias. Uma Biografia de Amílcar Cabral.* Lisbon, Tinta da China, 2007.

CAMEROON

Physical and Social Geography

JOHN I. CLARKE

PHYSICAL FEATURES

The Republic of Cameroon covers an area of 475,650 sq km (183,649 sq miles) and contains exceptionally diverse physical environments. The country occupies a fairly central position within the African continent, with the additional advantage of a 200-km coastline. Its environmental diversity arises from various factors, including the country's position astride the volcanic belt along the hinge between west and central Africa, together with its intermediate location between the great basins of the Congo, the Niger and Lake Chad, its latitudinal extent between 2° and 13°N, its altitudinal range from sea level to more than 4,000 m, and its spread from coastal mangrove swamp to remote continental interior.

In the south and centre of the country a large undulating and broken plateau surface of granites, schists and gneisses rises northwards away from the Congo basin to the Adamawa plateau (900 m–1,520 m above sea level). North of the steep Adamawa escarpment, which effectively divides northern from southern Cameroon, lies the basin of the Benue river, a tributary of the Niger, which is floored by sedimentary rocks, interspersed with inselbergs and buttes. In the west of the country a long line of rounded volcanic mountains and hills extends from Mt Cameroun (4,095 m), the highest mountain in west and central Africa, north-eastwards along the former boundary between East and West Cameroon and then along the Nigerian border. Volcanic soils derived from these mountains are more fertile than most others in the country and have permitted much higher rural population densities than elsewhere.

Cameroon has a marked south–north gradation of climates, from a seasonal equatorial climate in the south (with two rainy seasons and two moderately dry seasons of unequal length), to southern savannah and savannah climates (with one dry and one wet season), to a hotter drier climate of the Sahel type in the far north. Annual rainfall thus varies from more than 5,000 mm in the south-west to around 610 mm near Lake Chad. Corresponding to this climatic zonation is a south–north gradation of vegetal landscapes: dense rainforest, Guinea savannah, Sudan savannah and thorn steppe, while Mt Cameroun incorporates a vertical series of sharply divided vegetation zones.

POPULATION

The population of Cameroon was enumerated at 17,052,134 at the census of November 2005, and at mid-2022 was projected to have risen to 27,911,544, giving an average density of 59.9 inhabitants per sq km. Population growth has been rapid (an average rate of 2.7% per year in 2011–20) and the composition and distribution of the population are extremely diverse. In the southern forest regions Bantu peoples predominate, although there are also pygmy groups in some of the more remote areas. North of the Bantu tribes live many semi-Bantu peoples, including the ubiquitous Bamileke. Further north the diversity increases, with Sudanese, Hamitic Fulani (or Foulbe) and Arab Choa.

The distribution of population is uneven, with concentrations in the west, the south-central region and the Sudan savannah zone of the north. An important religious and social divide lies across the country. While the peoples of the south and west have been profoundly influenced by Christianity and by the European introduction of an externally orientated colonial-type economy, the peoples of the north are either Muslim or animist and have largely retained their traditional modes of life. Consequently, the population of the south and west is much more developed, economically and socially, than that of the north, although the Government has made efforts to reduce this regional disparity.

One aspect of this disparity is the southern location of the capital, Yaoundé (projected population 4.3m. at mid-2022), and the main port of Douala (3.8m.), as well as most of the other towns. Much of their growth results from rural–urban migration; many of the migrants come from overcrowded mountain massifs in the west, and the Bamileke constitute more than one-third of the inhabitants of Douala. Nevertheless, about two-thirds of all Cameroonians remain rural village-dwellers.

One other major contrast in the social geography of Cameroon is between anglophone north-west and south-west Cameroon, accounting for less than one-10th of the country's total area and just over one-fifth of the population, and the much larger, more populous francophone area of former East Cameroon. The contrasting influences of British and French rule remain evident in education, commerce, law and elsewhere, although unification of the civil services since 1972, official bilingualism and the integration of transport networks and economies have helped to reduce some of the disparities between the two zones.

History

HELEN WARE

HISTORICAL CONTEXT

The region which is now Cameroon has a long written history, beginning with Muslim records dating back to the 800s. The Kanem-Borno Empire led by the Kanuri covered much of the north for the period 700 to 1900. In the south of the region the Portuguese established sugar plantations from the 1520s and dealt with the local chiefs to buy slaves for the newly developing international slave trade, which was taken over by the Dutch in the 1600s. The British, French and Germans also became involved in trading both slaves and local produce in the south. In the early 19th century much of the north of the region was taken over by the Muslim Fulani under the Emir of Adamaoua, while the south was covered by a range of small chiefdoms yet to be influenced by Christian missionaries. A number of chiefdoms united under the Douala kingdom. This history retains much contemporary significance as the northern rebels of Boko Haram (a militant Islamist group active in Nigeria), some 85% of whom are Kanuri, still explicitly dream of re-establishing a caliphate across the former Kanem-Borno Empire, and Douala remains the political and cultural capital of highly restive anglophone Cameroon.

One Country, Three Colonial Legacies

The Germans established their colony of Kamerun in 1884. Supplies of quinine had made settlement in malaria-prone areas possible for Europeans who established cash crop plantations growing cocoa, coffee, bananas, palm oil, cotton and rubber and which were highly exploitative of local labour. In 1916, during the First World War, British, French and Belgian troops forced Germany to leave its colony. In their brief three decades of colonization the Germans had established the country's boundaries; introduced a monetary system; set up structures for administration; and laid the foundations for significant infrastructural resources, including the railways and the port of Douala, as well as the cash crop plantation system which still causes severe conflict between locals and outsiders.

In 1919 the London Declaration divided Cameroon into French (80% of the territory) and British (20%) administrative zones, which were subsequently placed under League of Nations mandates. The French administered their territory (French Cameroun) directly from Paris as part of their colonial empire, while the British administered theirs via Lagos (Nigeria). The British zone was divided into Northern (Muslim) and Southern (Christian) Cameroons. After the Second World War these mandated areas became United Nations (UN) Trust Territories destined for eventual independence. French Cameroun became independent on 1 January 1960 as the Republic of Cameroon. At a UN plebiscite in 1961 some 60% of the largely Muslim Northern area voted to join Nigeria with a voter turnout of 84%, while about 70% of the largely Christian Southern area voted to join with the Republic of Cameroon with a voter turnout of 95%. The difference in turnout largely reflected higher education levels in the south, and the choice of destination reflected historical, religious and ethnic differences. Voters in the British territory were not offered the option of independence, which was opposed by the British in the UN Trusteeship Council and by John Ngu Foncha, the southern political leader. This forced two-way choice became highly significant in the 2010s (see below).

The modern state of Cameroon has thus had a unique experience of three colonial rulers. All three allowed exploitation of the people by business interests, especially the plantation owners, but also did a great deal to bring their administrative systems, educational provisions and cultures to influence unity and divisions across the country. Overall, the French had a policy of assimilation which meant that the native Cameroonians who had been educated to French standards, the *évolués*, could receive French citizenship and vote in elections. The British had no such policy.

CONSTITUTIONAL HISTORY

Cameroon has had more Constitutions or significant constitutional amendments (in 1961, 1972, 1996, 2008 and 2016) than it has had heads of state. There have been only two presidents to date, namely Ahmadou Ahidjo, who was in power from 1960 to 1982, and Paul Biya, who has ruled more like a hereditary monarch than a democratically elected leader since 1982.

After the 1961 plebiscite in Southern Cameroons its leaders attempted to negotiate a new constitutional agreement with President Ahidjo based on a relatively loose and decentralized federation in which they hoped to protect their language, culture and legal and educational systems. However, since the commitment to reunification had already been made they were in a very weak negotiating position. What became the 1961 Federal Constitution was no more than a law revising the Republic of Cameroon's 1960 Constitution, which provided for a two-state federation in which most powers were retained by the Federal Government. The threat of the potential elimination of the anglophone identity was reinforced when on 2 June 1972 a new Constitution was introduced by which, without any regard to the 1961 Federal Constitution which forbade this, the federal system was abolished and replaced with a unitary system for the United Republic of Cameroon.

The 1972 Constitution also abolished the position of Vice-President destroying the compromise of a francophone President and an anglophone Vice-President. When in 1984 President Biya renamed the country the Republic of Cameroon this was seen by many anglophones as removing the last symbolic vestige of the 1961 federal reunification.

Following pressure from the international community and the Social Democratic Front (SDF), the party formed in 1990 by anglophone John Fru Nidi, in 1996 President Biya reluctantly followed the post-1989 wave of constitutional renewals across Africa by revising the 1972 Constitution. Many hoped that the 1996 Constitution would enhance democracy, good governance and respect for human rights. Instead, the new basic law did little more than reinforce the underlying philosophy of the 1972 Constitution: centralization and power to the President. The already limited powers of the legislature were further curtailed. The President was awarded the power to dismiss the Prime Minister, government members, judges, army generals, provincial governors, prefects and the heads of parastatals. The President could also approve or veto newly enacted laws, declare a state of emergency and authorize public expenditure. Indeed, it was unclear what the President could not do. The new Constitution did introduce bicameralism, creating the Senate as a second chamber (70 members were to be elected by municipal councillors and 30 appointed by the President), but the Senate and the National Assembly remained subservient to the executive and had minimal power to initiate or influence legislation. The main impact was to give the President new opportunities to dispense patronage positions. Typifying the President's tendency to delay reforms, the Senate did not actually meet until 2013. The Constitutional Council, with some powers of judicial review, has never been appointed. Overall, the 1996 Constitution was technically weaker than that of 1972 and also less liberal and less progressive.

Many Cameroonians believe that it is too easy to change the Constitution but too hard to change the President. The procedures required to amend the Constitution are that either an absolute majority of the members of Parliament pass the amendment or the President can put the question to a public referendum, which requires a simple majority to pass. Discussions of future constitutional reforms talk in terms of returning to a variant of the original federal system, perhaps incorporating lessons from Canada (Québec) and Nigeria. Many ask whether, had Cameroon's oil resources had not been concentrated in the anglophone South-West Region, the francophone elite would have been so keen to destroy a functional federation keeping the country together, but failing to maximizing the wealth flowing to the francophone presidential coterie.

INDEPENDENCE UNDER PRESIDENT AHIDJO: THE CREATION OF A UNITARY CENTRALIZED STATE

French Cameroun gained independence in 1960 as the Republic of Cameroon under the rule of President Ahidjo supported by the French Government. Ahidjo was a northerner, a Muslim Fulani from Garoua, who became Prime Minister at the age of 34. A popular insurrection led by the Bamilike peoples of the Cameroon Highlands and the Union des Populations du Cameroun (UPC, founded in 1947) followed, but was put down with the assistance of French troops in 1970. The Bamilike, who are known for their strong entrepreneurial capabilities, had competed with the French colonists for a range of economic opportunities, and continued to compete with some northerners and the Bulu southerners (Biya is a Bulu). The Vice-President was Ngu Foncha, an anglophone Catholic, who had founded the Kamerun National Democracy Party in 1955.

In 1966 Ahidjo formed the Union Nationale Camerounaise (UNC) and it became the sole legal political party. In the two post-independence decades Ahidjo's policy was 'cultural renewal' to engender a sense of national consciousness within a diverse country of some 250 ethnic groups and languages. It was typical of his style of government that he attracted 'praise-singer' musicians with wages, training and instruments with their songs even being taught in state schools, while at the same time those who sang songs of opposition were censored, barred from state radio and sometimes 'disappeared'.

On the economic front, the country (which was 85% rural) was managed by a succession of five-year plans. The first plan for 1960–65 aimed to double per capita gross domestic product (GDP) by 1980. It emphasized infrastructure and rural development and less dependence on France. The second plan for 1966–71 was known as the 'farmers' plan' for its rural focus. Dominated by French experts, the first two plans largely excluded anglophone areas and took limited account of rural realities.

Ahidjo ruled from independence until 1982; however, his opponents claimed that for much of this time Jean-Pierre Bénard, the French ambassador to Cameroon, was the real power behind the throne. Ahidjo centralized political power in himself and in the capital, Yaoundé, which was the epicentre of francophone politics and patronage. Cameroon became an authoritarian single-party state in the Cold War era when this was an African norm. Ahidjo declared nation building as his major goal, using the fear of ethnic conflict to justify authoritarianism and the lack of human rights.

THE EARLY YEARS OF THE BIYA REGIME

In a most unusual move for an African head of state, Ahidjo resigned in 1982 and was replaced by his Prime Minister Biya. In 1983 Ahidjo went into exile after Biya accused him of attempting to mastermind a coup. In 1984 Biya was elected as President and changed the country's name to the Republic of Cameroon. As Cameroon is a state dominated by one political party, most elections hold limited interest. There have been presidential elections in 1965, 1970, 1980, 1984, 1988, 1997, 2004, 2011 and 2018 with the next due in 2023. Parliamentary elections, in which the ruling party has always been victorious, were held in 1964, 1970, 1973, 1983, 1988, 1992, 1997, 2002, 2013 and 2020. Municipal elections have only been held in 2007, 2015 and 2020.

Economically the first two decades after independence were Cameroon's boom period, owing to the country's unprecedented growth. However, the economy collapsed in the 1980s leading to the impoverishment of the majority of its people. The prices of Cameroon's main exports fell, its debts increased and mismanagement was rampant. In late 1988 the Government was obliged to accept the macroeconomic reforms proposed by the International Monetary Fund (IMF) and the World Bank in exchange for major structural adjustment loans. Trade barriers were removed; the economy was liberalized; subsidies, which had amounted to up to 80% of the total cost of agricultural inputs, were cut or abolished; the role of the state was substantially restricted; and the currency was devalued. Despite many Cameroonians detesting these new policies, the country remained an autocracy where political opposition was largely mute. When commentators blamed the crisis on corruption and mismanagement, Biya maintained that it was due to adverse changes in the terms of trade.

In 1990 Ngu Foncha resigned from the ruling party, the Rassemblement Démocratique du Peuple Camerounais (RDPC, as the UNC had been restyled in 1985), writing to Biya, in French, regretting that the anglophones he had led into the union had been ridiculed and called 'les ennemis dans la maison' (the enemies inside the house). Throughout the early 1990s the closing of political opportunities further exacerbated Cameroon's political marginalization of the anglophones, who constituted about one-fifth of the population.

Although Cameroon's governance was decentralized following an amendment to the Constitution in 1996 and the Orientation of Decentralization Law of 2004, constant administrative bottlenecks and political interference prevent the country's 360 municipal councils from carrying out their responsibility to lead development in areas such as health care and education. Persistent blockages to creating an autonomous functional infrastructure for sub-national governance continue to exacerbate grievances and hinder progress towards a government structure that could maintain Cameroon's territorial integrity while greatly increasing its responsiveness to its citizen's needs. Under President Biya Cameroon has been largely a closed space for civil society and political activists. Rights-based organizations are routinely persecuted for exercising their oversight role and exposing human rights violations committed by the Government.

Cameroon's one truly competitive presidential election was held in October 1992, at which Biya secured re-election with just 39.9% of the votes cast. Fru Ndi was placed second with 35.9% of the vote, and Bello Boubu Maïgari (Cameroon's second Prime Minister) came third with 19.2%. However, because there was no provision for a second round, the majority vote for opposition candidates did not count. The results were much disputed, and since then the influence of opposition parties has steadily declined.

In 1994 fighting erupted between Cameroon and Nigeria over the location of their border and the ownership of the contested oil-rich Bakassi peninsula. In 1996 the two countries agreed to UN mediation, which eventually resulted, in 2002, in the granting of the peninsula to Cameroon by the International Court of Justice (ICJ). Nigeria rejected the ICJ finding but finally agreed to withdraw its troops from the peninsula in 2006, but in 2007 suspected Nigerian militants killed 21 Cameroonian soldiers there. Meanwhile, in 1995 Cameroon joined the Commonwealth, despite failing to meet the commitments to democracy which were theoretically required of members. Cameroon has been a member of the Organization of Islamic Co-operation since 1974 and joined the Organisation Internationale de la Francophonie (OIF) in 1991, despite proclamations at the time of the original union that the country would join neither the OIF nor the Commonwealth.

THE LATER BIYA PERIOD 2000–

In 2005 President Biya named five priorities: (i) to modernize the country's democracy; (ii) to exceed annual GDP growth rates of 5% by improving agriculture, industry and tourism; (iii) to achieve better distribution of the country's wealth; (iv) to better equip the county's forces of law and order to fight crime, terrorism and 'insecurity'; and (v) to improve Cameroon's international image. Little progress has been made. For example, by 2015 only US $4m. out of an alleged $152m. in stolen public funds had been recovered since the launch by Biya of Operation Epervier, an anti-corruption movement, in 2006.

President Biya has pursued his political enemies with particular vigour, and Cameroonian law allows corruption suspects to be detained and have their passports seized while investigations are still ongoing. Between 2009 and 2016 at least two dozen former government figures were arrested, including several former ministers and heads of state-owned corporations. At least four politicians arrested for corruption have died in jail. In 2016 former Minister of Health Urbain Awono published a book entitled *Mensonges d'Etat* (*Lies of the State*) in which he argued that he and other such detainees are 'prisoners of conscience'. Awono, was charged with embezzlement in 2008, when President Biya was changing the Constitution to allow himself to run for two more terms in office, and Awono was rumoured to be planning to oust him.

Regional elections were held for the first time in December 2020. The ruling party, the RDPC, won a decisive majority in nine of the 10 regional councils. Each regional council comprises a chamber of 70 regional councillors (elected by municipal councillors) and a chamber of 20 representatives of traditional rulers (elected by their peers). The President has the power to suspend or dissolve a regional council. The SDF had appealed to citizens to boycott the elections.

The Constitution guarantees President Biya immunity from prosecution after retirement and sometimes he clearly appears tired, yet he does not leave office, perhaps remembering how he drove his predecessor to a death in exile. Competition to be his successor is strongest among the members of his own party since the opposition parties are unpopular and are blamed by the public for the 'politics of njangui' (deals with the enemy). While the francophone public in general might consider Biya to be corrupt, they also credit him with having successfully steered Cameroon through many difficult periods. Since the death of Queen Elizabeth II of the United Kingdom in September 2022, Biya is now the world's oldest head of state (and the second longest-serving executive head of state). As he approaches the age of 90 in 2023, the question of who will succeed him becomes ever more sensitive. In May 2021 the head of news for the government-run television station CRTV was suspended for using a photograph of Biya's publicity-shy son, Franck, to promote, in what the President deemed to be a disrespectful manner, a story about International Labour Day. By that time a movement dedicated to supporting the Biya dynasty, known as the 'Franckists' had attained sizeable influence in the country.

The Anglophone Problem

Depending upon their political backgrounds Cameroonians refer to the country's 'anglophone problem', its 'anglophone crisis' or, in the case of the President, the 'non-existent anglophone crisis', which, as he maintained in a speech in December 2016, has been engineered by the 'acts of a group of manipulated and exploited extremists and rioters'.

In October 2001 tensions increased between the Government and separatists until lobbying on behalf of the country's approximately 5m. anglophones resulted in street clashes, leading to several deaths and arrests. Although it is both convenient and customary to refer to the anglophones as a homogenous group, the reality is more complex. Francophones who learn English and move to the anglophone South-West region do not thereby become anglophones. Being an anglophone is a matter of culture, history, education and ethnicity more than language use. In February 2008 riots erupted in major cities, both anglophone and francophone, sparked by rising food prices and dissatisfaction with the constitutional amendments that removed presidential term limits securing Biya's hold on power.

In October 2016 demonstrations occurred when lawyers in the two anglophone regions (South-West and North-West) protested against the domination of the judiciary by francophones who were alleged to have little or no knowledge of, or training in, the common law. The protests were followed by a strike led by the Confederation of Anglophone Teachers' Trade Unions and the Teachers' Association of Cameroon, which prompted the closure of all schools in the two anglophone regions. The teachers complained that francophone teachers had been deployed to teach in French to children who did not understand the language. Competitive public examinations for entrance to professional schools were claimed to be biased against anglophones. University lecturers objected to the appointment of francophones as lecturers and heads of departments in the regions' two universities. Local public servants were similarly aggrieved by senior appointments of francophones. By December the anglophone regions had come to a virtual halt because of a general strike.

The Government's response was to deploy troops across the two regions. Street demonstrations were suppressed, causing the deaths of a dozen protesters and the arrest of many more. Numerous anglophone leaders, including parliamentarians, were arrested and transferred to detention centres in francophone areas to be tried by military tribunals for treason. International media were barred from entering the country, and telephone and internet access was blocked for nine months. Local commentators began to write of two different countries within one.

By 2017 the violence could be said to have reached the stage of constituting an ongoing civil war, with some anglophones aiming to establish their own state—the Republic of Ambazonia. In 2018 anglophones exercised a new form of strike: the 'ghost town', where, instead of coming out on the street and risking attack by gendarmes and soldiers, the separatist leaders declared 'stay home Mondays', when businesses stayed shut, and the streets were left deserted. The Mayor of Buea (in the South-West Region), declared that businesses taking part would be closed down permanently.

Yet social media still flourished with videos of the atrocities being committed shared widely. In June 2018 the BBC produced a graphic documentary using the video clips entitled 'Cameroon Burning: The Unseen War' which has been viewed 290,000 times. It used Google Earth to confirm videos of villages being torched but could not always prove who was responsible: the Cameroonian Government's soldiers and gendarmes, violent separatists or criminals in search of loot.

The crisis in the anglophone North-West and South-West regions which erupted in 2016 was ongoing by late 2022. It has led to at least 3,500 deaths, some 65,000 refugees fleeing to Nigeria and almost 800,000 internally displaced persons (IDPs) within Cameroon. President Biya instigated a five-day national dialogue to resolve the crisis which met in September–October 2019. However, neither anglophone separatists in the two affected regions nor those in the diaspora were invited to attend. On 3 October President Biya announced the pardoning of 333 anglophone detainees (333 is a popular brand of beer in Cameroon). Local civil society organizations, especially those led by women, religious figures and traditional chiefs, have tried to fill the service delivery vacuums left by ineffective government agencies. They are also 'back-channel' negotiators persuading separatist family and friends to consider non-violent approaches to advertising their grievances.

In March 2021 separatists launched a series of bomb attacks. Another new trend was the kidnapping of Catholic priests for ransom. In August Monseigneur Agbortoko, the Vicar General of the Mamfe diocese, was kidnapped by youths identifying themselves as separatist fighters; he was released in the following month. By late 2022 there was general agreement that measures needed to be taken to quell the violence in anglophone Cameroon, but disagreement among governing officials about whether to aim for military victory over the rebels or a negotiated settlement. The Biya faction believes that it should increase the number of gendarmes and soldiers but hesitates to recruit from ethnic groups other than its own Beti group, owing to fears about a coup attempt. In 2021 a group of gendarmerie officers based in Yaoundé saw their numbers reduced from 210 to just 26, owing to killings during the crisis. Consequently, there were queues for medical certificates excusing soldiers from active service; moreover, scores of the military handed themselves in for six-month prison terms for allegedly disobeying war orders. In 2021 the African Union (AU) estimated that there were at least 120,000 small arms and light weapons in illegal circulation in Cameroon but only 3,800 licences to carry. Many of these weapons are brought in from neighbouring Nigeria.

By late 2022 the Swiss-based news agency *New Humanitarian* concluded that a tipping point has been reached where the spoils of the war in anglophone regions might outweigh the incentives for peace, as the conflict had created a lucrative war economy. Notably, kidnapping had become a regular source of income, as had arbitrary arrests by members of the security forces, who demanded payment of bribes to release their charges from prison. Meanwhile, informal taxes were levied on cultivators of cocoa. Peace initiatives involving the UN, the Catholic Church and foreign governments have all failed as well as the non-governmental organizational-led Swiss Process and negotiations with the imprisoned 'Nera 10' (a group of senior anglophone figures who were abducted and imprisoned in Yaoundé in 2018). The anglophone secessionists were bitterly divided among themselves, while the Government apparently cared little that anglophones were suffering from multiple human rights abuses at the hands of the armed forces and rebels alike and was unwilling even to consider minor political concessions. It was difficult for civil society organizations to work for peace, owing to government restraints on their actions and the violence of state troops (who notably destroyed the village of Missoni village in June 2022), rebels and bandits from across the Nigerian border who continued to carry out random, opportunistic attacks. In July the Government toured the body of a leading separatist, 'Field Marshal' Lekeaka Olive, the fallen leader of the Red Dragon group, on display across the anglophone regions to 'deter recruitment' to rebel factions.

In August 2022 Prime Minister Dr Joseph Dion Ngute optimistically claimed that the separatists' fight for independence had largely been crushed. His statement was made following three days of fighting between government troops and separatist fighters in Batibo, in the North-West Region, in which 17 separatists were killed and 18 captured. In the following month a separatist splinter group of the Ambazonia Liberation Movement attacked a bus in Ekona in the South-West Region, killing six people and injuring nine others. This was allegedly carried out to protest against the reopening the nation's approximately 14,000 government schools and some 8,000 private schools early in September. The presence of multiple uncontrolled splinter groups in Cameroon and among the diaspora, who provide significant funding, makes peace unattainable and has added to the deleterious impact of the COVID-19 pandemic upon the education of the nation's children in many areas. A Catholic think tank based in Germany recorded over 300 killings of anglophones by the Cameroonian army between June and September 2022 alone. It is a measure of the complexity of the situation that Ngute is himself an anglophone with two degrees from British universities and inherited a position as a traditional ruler in the South-West Region.

Boko Haram and Islamic State in West Africa Province

In 2009 Cameroonian authorities first officially became aware of the presence of members of Boko Haram within their borders. In July Nigerian security forces had attacked the militants in Maiduguri (Nigeria), killing the group's Kanuri founder, Mohamed Yusuf, and some 800 followers. Many remaining members then scattered, including into northern Cameroon. Boko Haram's involvement inside Cameroon grew between 2011 and 2013 as it recruited Cameroonians and used the Far North Region as a safe haven and rear base. Here they bought food and infiltrated networks involved in the smuggling of motorbikes, fuel and narcotics. Like Chad, northern-most Cameroon served as a transit point for weapons bought by Boko Haram from Libya and Sudan, passing them on through Fokotol into Nigeria. Cameroonian media generally show Boko Haram as criminals entering the country from Nigeria. However, the movement's origins were in religious objections to high levels of corruption and activities included running microcredit schemes and facilitating young men's marriages, vital in a culture where only married men count as adults.

From February 2013 Boko Haram engaged in the kidnapping of foreigners in Cameroon in order to raise funds. Between 2013 and 2014 the movement raised an estimated US $11m. and freed 40 members of the group in exchange for the release of foreign hostages. In 2014 Boko Haram's strategy changed from kidnapping to full-frontal attacks on police stations and small military bases. From 2014 to 2016 Boko Haram carried out more than 400 attacks in Cameroon, as well as 50 suicide bombings, which killed a combined 92 soldiers and more than 1,350 civilians. Each attack aimed at civilians was relatively small, but their combined effects on the local population were horrendous creating some 300,000 IDPs who fled the violence and abandoned their homes and crops. In 2014 Boko Haram abducted 10 Chinese nationals working for a Chinese construction company in Waza in northern Cameroon, as well as the Deputy Prime Minister's wife; all were ransomed and released in October, but the Chinese-based Yan Chang company ceased its successful mineral exploration near the Chadian border. Attacks alternated between small sorties by some dozen fighters on motorbikes, up to groups of 1,000 or more using armoured vehicles and mortars captured in Nigeria to assault military targets.

In 2014–15 Boko Haram reached its apogee, controlling some 30,000 sq km of north-eastern Nigeria. However, Nigerian troops stepped up their efforts, and the election as Nigerian President in early 2015 of Muhammadu Buhari who, as a former general and a Fulani Muslim from Katsina, brought about positive developments, and he reorganized and re-energized the fight against the terrorists in the north of the country. From 2014 to 2017 popular rumours suggested that the French authorities were manipulating Boko Haram in Cameroon to damage Biya's reputation.

In January 2019 President Biya announced that Boko Haram had been expelled from the country. Yet by November a further 275 people in Cameroon had been killed by Boko Haram, of whom 223 were civilians. Some 270,000 IDPs had fled Boko Haram, and about 50 villages had been abandoned after being burnt down. In June 2021 it was announced that the leader of Boko Haram, Abubakar Shekau, had died by his own hand after being besieged by the Islamic State in West Africa Province (ISWAP). In September Nigeria and Cameroon negotiated the return of over 1,000 former Boko Haram militants from a Disarmament, Demobilization, and Reintegration Centre in Meri, Cameroon, to their homes in Borno State, Nigeria. Following Shekau's death, ISWAP appeared to have largely taken over from Boko Haram as the more successful rebel movement, primarily attacking in Cameroon military and police targets in the north of the country. In June 2022 Cameroon deployed several hundred troops along the border with Nigeria after attacks by militants had forced some 40,000 villagers to flee the area. Local officials complained that troops had been withdrawn to fight anglophone secessionists in the south. The Cameroonian Government, unwilling as ever to accept blame for negative developments, claimed that anti-Boko Haram militias had been infiltrated by Boko Haram and ISWAP. In an indication of the dire state of security in the country, in the 2022 Global Peace Index, Cameroon ranked 142nd out of 163 countries—three places less peaceful than in the previous year. Neighbouring Nigeria, which shared common threats from Boko Haram and ISWAP, was in 143rd place.

For President Biya, the most significant threat might not come from his own people but from the overseas countries upon whose support he relies. The USA has supported Cameroon as a bulwark against Islamist terrorism but has increasing difficulty in justifying its support of a corrupt and dictatorial regime. Between 2015 and 2020 US Africa Command maintained an intelligence and reconnaissance operation in northern Cameroon with some 300 personnel, but this was withdrawn by the Administration of President Donald Trump (2017–21). In 2019 the State Department withheld nearly US $18m. in planned security assistance because of human rights abuses by Cameroonian troops, and in June 2021 US Secretary of State Antony Blinken denounced Cameroon before the US Senate, owing to attacks by its armed forces on the anglophone population and likened it to Uganda as one of two African countries that had held corrupt elections in 2020–21. This negative stance dismayed President Biya who had used his army's attacks on Boko Haram as a bargaining tool with the US Administration to avoid incurring the imposition of sanctions on himself or his officials. Attacks on Muslim rebels speaking African languages in the north of Cameroon are viewed very differently by the US Congress from attacks on Christian rebels fighting for the right to use English in the south.

Reactions to Continuing French Influence

On 28 February 2015 some 10,000 Cameroonians attended a march in Yaoundé, which had been organized by a group of journalists (under the banner 'Uni pour le Cameroun'), some of whom had already been active in attacking French 'imperialism on the black continent'. Several government ministers attended the march, as did the Canadian and French ambassadors, the latter being greeted by anti-French slogans. A flood of anti-French headlines in the local press followed, telling the French to leave in terms implying that colonialism had never ended. In July 2015 French President François Hollande visited Cameroon and met Biya briefly. In January 2016 the French ambassador to Cameroon presented 11 P4 tactical vehicles to the Cameroon Government to assist with the fight against Boko Haram.

Many in the francophone elite share both a strong cultural affinity and a jealous animosity towards France. They resent French meddling in Cameroonian politics and in the economy; however, they spend their holidays in Paris and send their children to university there. Overall, the striking result of popular anti-French rumours has been to bring some otherwise disaffected francophone Cameroonians to see the highly autocratic President Biya as the victim of foreign plots for regime change in Cameroon. More recently, blame for foreign support of terrorists has shifted to the USA, with claims that the Central Intelligence Agency was funding Boko Haram. The Cameroonian authorities worry that animosity towards France and the USA could lead to physical attacks on foreign citizens and their businesses, which would discourage investment. In February 2020 French President Emmanuel Macron attacked Cameroon's human rights record. This enraged many francophone Cameroonians, resulting in demonstrations outside the French embassy in Yaoundé. Members of the diaspora play a significant role in Cameroonian politics, including by funding opposition political parties and secessionist activities. Often, they are more intransigent and unwilling to negotiate than those who live in Cameroon and who must contend with the ongoing violence.

In July 2022 President Macron visited Cameroon as part of an African charm offensive, His first priority for talks was the threat to food security in Africa following the outbreak of war in Ukraine earlier in that year. France's other concerns also included Cameroon's abstentions on UN motions to deplore the Russian Federation's invasion of Ukraine and the military agreement with Russia signed by Cameroon's Minister of

Defence, Joseph Beti Assoma, in April, which was rumoured to include provisions for access to the Russian 'private' Wagner mercenaries with close links to the Russian Government, who were already playing an active role in combating Islamist rebels in Mali. Macron also discussed French investment and governance issues in Cameroon, but there were no reports of concessions by President Biya, whose followers considered that the visit visibly supported the prestige of their leader. The next presidential elections in Cameroon are not due until 2025 (when Biya will be 92 years old), and he refused to tell French journalists accompanying Macron whether he intends to contest another term.

The 2018 Presidential Election and its Aftermath

In October 2018 Biya was re-elected for a seventh presidential term with 70.8% of the vote in an election marred by numerous irregularities and a low 54% turnout (in which just 10% of voters cast their ballots in anglophone areas). Maurice Kamto, the leader of the Mouvement pour la Renaissance du Cameroun (MRC) and distant runner-up (with 14.3% of the vote) in the presidential election, challenged the election results, claiming that he had won. Kamto, a Bamileke lawyer, was a member of the Government from 2004 until 2011 and founded the MRC on leaving his ministerial post. In late January 2019 Kamto and his followers were arrested after holding peaceful demonstrations. Many of the francophone elite regard Kamto and the MRC as domestic accomplices in a Western plot to destabilize Cameroon. Kamto was charged with the crimes of subversion, incitation to insurrection, hatred of the Fatherland (*sic*) and disturbance of public order. Rumours circulated that Kamto had received funding from the US embassy in Yaoundé as part of a US plot to unseat Biya, while the outgoing US ambassador had publicly invited President Biya to think about his historical legacy and to choose to leave power peacefully. Such statements serve to strengthen rather than weaken the President's hold on power, since they deflect attention from the weakness in delivery of public services of a regime designed only to ensure the supremacy of the President and his small clique. In October the President ordered the Military Tribunal to release Kamto and the many followers arrested with him, allegedly following pressure for the release from the French and US Governments.

In January 2019 President Biya appointed Ngute as his eighth Prime Minister. The Prime Minister is frequently described as a powerless figure, as he can be dismissed on the whim of the President. However, Biya, at the age of 89 by late 2022, spends up to one-third of each year outside Cameroon, often in luxury hotels in Europe. He does not govern the country on a day-to-day basis—that is the role of the Prime Minister, so long as he protects the President's interests.

In November 2019 a tripartite mission of the AU, the Commonwealth and the IOF visited Cameroon in an attempt to reduce the violence and to 'increase national cohesion'. However, the AU's Peace and Security Council (AUPSC) has declined, under pressure from Cameroon, to add the country to its agenda. (In April 2020 Cameroon was elected unopposed to the AUPSC, ending hopes of further AU involvement in the anglophone issue).

Events Since 2020

Parliamentary elections were held, concurrently with municipal elections, on 9 February 2020. The RDPC retained its legislative majority, as it has at every election since independence, securing 139 of the 167 seats decided on election day. (Elections in 11 constituencies were postponed or annulled, owing to ongoing violent protests and electoral irregularities.) The remaining seats were divided among seven smaller parties, none of which won more than seven seats. The Parti Camerounais pour la Réconciliation Nationale lost 13 seats and retained only five. Total voter turnout was only 44%.

By the beginning of 2020 the level of violence associated with the anglophone crisis had reached the point where there were significant events, often involving deaths, almost every second day. Some details of what occurred in early 2020 provide an indication of the complexity of the violent interactions and the range of players involved including local traditional authorities; local government officials; villagers on both government and separatist sides; armed fighters, leaders and followers

alike, also on both sides; as well as government gendarmes, some obeying some sort of rules, others totally lawless. On 1 January suspected separatists burnt down the divisional office in Muyuka after clashing with soldiers there. Clashes were also reported in Buea. Significantly, the Ambazonia military forces declared that a lockdown would occur between 7 and 12 February in order to prevent the parliamentary elections from taking place in the anglophone regions. The separatists declared that anyone found outdoors would be considered an enemy and warned people to stock up on food supplies. Villagers in Balikumbat, guarded by government soldiers, demonstrated against the separatists accusing them of raising money by force and bringing insecurity with them. The villagers then raided a nearby separatist camp, seizing weapons and arresting fighters. The Fon of Babungo gave separatist fighters 24 hours to release kidnap victims threatening them with the expulsion of their families from the village and also arguing that villagers should support government troops.

Some 350 government troops were deployed across the South-West Region to protect prospective voters under threat with a further 350 gendarmes deployed across the North-West Region. Villagers attacking separatists' camps become more common and the separatists were obliged to claim that some separatist crimes were actually committed by government forces pretending to be separatists, a claim strongly repudiated by the Government. On 10 January 2020 five soldiers of the much-feared French/US/Israeli-trained Rapid Intervention Battalion were arrested for abducting a man in Buea. On 14 January government troops raided the villages of Bangem and Babubock, burning down dozens of houses. Four days later a gun battle between government soldiers and separatist fighters took place in Mulang, after the separatists had set fire to a refuse truck. On 21 January suspected separatists abducted 24 schoolchildren (the separatists opposed children attending school under a 'foreign' regime). Security forces rescued the children on the same day and killed two of the abductors, and on the following day a government soldier was killed in Ndoh, following which a retaliatory raid inside a market was carried out, in which 16 people were killed, and several more were injured.

In February 2020 the International Crisis Group (ICG) issued its 'Eight Priorities for the African Union in 2020'. The fifth of these was 'Push for Inclusive Dialogue in Cameroon'. The ICG cited UN estimates that the anglophone crisis had claimed some 3,000 lives since 2017, created about 700,000 IDPs and forced around 52,000 people to flee into Nigeria. About one-half of all anglophones were in need of humanitarian assistance—a proportion 15 times greater than had been the case before the conflict started. For the fourth year in a row, schools were forced to close, and some 800,000 children (about 85% of the anglophone school-aged population) had no access to formal education. The ICG believed that without externally mediated talks and shuttle diplomacy between the Government and separatist leaders, conditions would not improve and could even get worse. The Government-controlled national dialogue held in September–October 2019 had achieved very little, although it had proposed the granting of a special status to the North-West and South-West Regions. The President responded by referring the 'rich and varied' recommendations to a raft of committees. The ICG recommended confidence-building measures such as the Government releasing some detainees and the separatists agreeing to a ceasefire. It also suggested that the Government should allow the Anglophone General Conference to meet and discuss achieving a united position, while advocating the involvement of the Catholic Church in mediation and inviting Kamto to discuss with the Government how to reduce ethnic tensions with the Bulu.

February 2020 was no more peaceful than January. Police convoys shielding political campaigners were attacked. On 3 February a raid by security forces in Mukuya killed three civilians, led to the burning down of 45 houses, the detention of some 300 people and resulted in some 3,000 more fleeing the area. The separatist-enforced electoral lockdown came into place, and the electoral turnout in the polls on 9 February in anglophone regions was as low as perhaps 10%, as many civilians had fled a few days earlier. The separatists had abducted at least 120 candidates in the previous two weeks, and about one-half of them were still in captivity on election day. While the separatists claimed that 98% of the local population had boycotted the election, the Government maintained that there had been a massive turnout, and Elections Cameroon stated that there had been 'no major incidents'. While separatists attacked a polling site and a military convoy in Ndop and Ndu, government forces arrested several hundreds of civilians, many of whom were forced to vote in an unique example of Cameroonian democracy. On 14 February at least 22 civilians were killed in an alleged massacre by government soldiers in Ntumbo in the North-West Region. The army dismissed claims of a massacre, providing a complex counter-account, which involved an accidental explosion triggered by stray bullets. The incident was condemned by both the UN and the USA.

By late 2022 Cameroon was under immense pressure from two incipient civil wars with hundreds of deaths in the year to date and hundreds of thousands of its people displaced from their homes in both the South-West and the Far North. The country's armed forces were either frequently out of control when distant from the capital or were under orders to commit human rights abuses. The country has a highly centralized government. The frequently absent 89-year-old President has no official successor. The constitutional changes that Biya has introduced allow him to stay in power at least until 2035. However, Cameroonian politics is now very largely focused on who will succeed Biya, with no shortage of willing contenders. The President's son, Franck, is increasingly viewed as the most likely successor.

As at August 2022 the Office of the UN High Commissioner for Refugees (UNHCR) reported that Cameroon was hosting 2,018,697 persons of interest, of whom 483,409 were refugees, 975,786 were IDPs and 548,206 were IDP returnees. Of the refugees, 347,937 were from the CAR, and 135,472 from Nigeria. These figures have to be balanced alongside an estimated total Cameroonian population of 27.9m., more than one-half of whom live in urban areas. Despite the extensive services provided by UNHCR, the vast numbers of forced migrants inevitably place a severe economic and social burden on Cameroon. Nigeria and Cameroon are in continual negotiations regarding exchanges of refugees in the areas previously affected by Boko Haram raids. Following the alleged death of the Boko Haram leader Shekau in June 2021 (see *Boko Haram and Islamic State in West Africa Province)*, returnees to Nigeria have included former Boko Haram fighters, some of whom were recruited by misrepresentation, and some who joined for ideological reasons. National life expectancy in Cameroon is as low as 60 years. More than two-thirds of the population were born since Biya became President in November 1982, and these citizens have never experienced a different head of state.

The COVID-19 Pandemic

In March 2020 Cameroon recorded its first confirmed case of infection from COVID-19. The authorities implemented a number of measures in an attempt to curb the further spread of the disease. Cameroon's land, sea and air borders were closed, as were its schools and universities, and non-political prisoners were released from gaol. In May six members of the MRC opposition party were arrested for handing out free face coverings, after the Government had made wearing them compulsory. Schools were instructed to reopen by June and universities by October, but as at September 2022 the borders had not been officially reopened, although most airlines had resumed flights in and out of the country. As at 15 September Cameroon had recorded over 120,000 confirmed cases of COVID-19, including nearly 2,000 fatalities. By that time only about 5% of the population had been fully vaccinated against the virus—among the lowest rate of any country in the world. People were more likely to get vaccinated when it was a requirement for international travel. Cameroonians' general lack of trust in their government was reflected in their scepticism towards the national vaccination programme. Rumours that the COVID-19 vaccines could hinder sexual potency and fertility were especially damaging. According to Malachie Manaouda, the Minister of Public Health, the country had

only about 25,000 health care workers instead of the 75,000 that it claimed that it needed.

In May 2021 Cameroon secured US $335m. in financial aid from the IMF to alleviate the negative effects of COVID-19. Allegations of widespread mismanagement and corruption emerged after large amounts of these funds went missing. According to an audit for the Supreme Court there were 'numerous abuses' in the use of the funds. Mediline Medical Cameroon (MMC), based in the Republic of Korea, was awarded a 'quasi monopoly' on government contracts for personal protective equipment and COVID-19 testing kits despite not being active in Cameroon before the pandemic. The MMC then overcharged for its products, delivered defective material and did not provide documentation for transactions. The medical authorities could not account for materials received, including a large number of COVID-19 testing kits.

Only about 20% of Cameroonians have health insurance and 70% of the country's total health care expenditure is met by private households, many of whom prefer cheaper and more helpful traditional healers to the hospitals which generally they only approach as a last resort.

In August 2021, with less than 5% of citizens in the region vaccinated against COVID-19, President Biya hosted an extraordinary summit via video link to co-ordinate a response to the pandemic. The heads of state reported that the pandemic had heightened the problems of conflict, terrorism and scarce resources in the region. The majority of people had been further impoverished following the closure of businesses, while millions of workers had lost their jobs. Unemployment had increased by two-thirds in the region. The communiqué listed 24 standard economic recommendations for peace, security and the stability of the financial system.

In early 2021 two cases of polio were detected in Yaoundé. However, a polio vaccination campaign initiated by UNICEF stalled owing to parents' refusal to take their children to hospital for inoculation for fear of contracting COVID-19 there. Owing to the pandemic, local anti-female genital mutilation (FGM) campaigns were halted, so that in some areas the illegal practice rose from 2% to 20%. This was because female practitioners who had been given funding, of US $200, with which to start small businesses, experienced failure and returned to carrying out FGM procedures in order to earn a living. Meanwhile, incursions by Boko Haram in the north disrupted health care programmes and facilitated the importation of diseases from the poverty-stricken areas of north-east Nigeria.

The Economy Struggles

Cameroon had experienced the beginnings of economic recovery from mid-2021, but by mid-2022 this recovery was increasingly threatened by spillover effects from the war in Ukraine, high inflationary pressures especially from food and fuel prices, and a tightening of global financial conditions. In August 2022 the IMF Board approved the Second Reviews of the Extended Credit Facility and Extended Fund Facility Arrangements for Cameroon allowing access to Special Drawing Rights worth about US $346m. Cameroon's 2021 arrangements with the IMF covered five varied pillars including mitigating the consequences of the pandemic whilst ensuring fiscal stability, reinforcing good governance and strengthening the transparency and anti-corruption frameworks, modernizing the tax system and reforming state-owned enterprises, strengthening debt management, implementing structural reforms across the financial sector and promoting gender equality and a greener economy. The Government is theoretically committed to reducing fuel subsidies, but this is politically highly controversial and will be implemented very slowly if at all. In 2012 the Government created the Special Crime tribunal on Corruption and Economic Crimes. It is reported to have tried 225 cases and recovered $323m. by July 2020. In 2021 Cameroon still ranked 144 out of 180 in the Transparency International Corruption Perceptions Index and 167th on the World Bank's *Ease of Doing Business* index; it takes 14 procedures and 82 days to establish a foreign-owned limited liability company in Douala, the nation's economic capital, with each step offering the possibility of bribe taking and other forms of corruption.

The IMF forecasts for GDP growth in 2022 have been revised downwards from an optimistic 4.5% to 3.8%. Inflation is projected to rise to 4.6% for 2022 but to remain below 3.0% in the medium term. Some 2% of Cameroon's GDP comes from oil but almost 20% of government revenue comes from that source. On the upside Cameroon is likely to benefit from new oil and gas opportunities and the completion of major hydroelectric plants.

Meanwhile, in July 2022 the Government appealed for emergency food supplies for more than 2.4m. people facing hunger along its northern borders with Chad and Nigeria. Devastating migratory caterpillars, crickets and weaver birds had decimated thousands of hectares of farmland especially on the northern borders, an area already severely damaged by floods and elephants. Cameroon relied on Ukraine for 60% of its wheat imports. Owing to the war, a 50-kg bag of wheat had increased in price from US $35 to $50—an amount beyond the means of most of the hungry population.

CAMEROON AND THE PEOPLE'S REPUBLIC OF CHINA

At independence, Cameroon established diplomatic relations with the Republic of China (Taiwan), and it was not until 1971 that the country changed policy and established diplomatic links with the People's Republic of China, which in turn promised to stop supporting the allegedly African-Marxist UPC. The Chinese have built visible infrastructure projects including a new presidential palace, the convention centre in Yaoundé and the Lagdo hydroelectric dam. (In 2012 the dam flooded land across the Nigeria border killing 10 citizens and flooding over 10,000 homes along the Benue River.) It is often said that China needs Cameroon's natural resources, notably oil, cotton and timber, and that Cameroon needs Chinese assistance with the building of infrastructure. This is too simple a summary. China could buy these resources elsewhere, and Cameroon needs to consider the debt and social disadvantages of infrastructure building by Chinese labourers, which is often of inferior quality. An example is the first phase of the Yaoundé–Doula highway. Cheap Chinese imports drive Cameroonian firms out of business and by 2005 a total of 82% of Cameroon's trade deficit was the result of Chinese imports. Chinese-Cameroonian relations are most public in highly visible infrastructure projects and the pomp and ceremony of state visits. The Chinese Prime Minister visited Cameroon in 2003, and President Biya returned the visit soon after.

Chinese contributions to hospital services and combating malaria are appreciated, but Cameroonians have very mixed feelings about the Chinese influence in the country, and there have been anti-Chinese riots in the main cities. Popular concerns relate less to Cameroon's massive debts to China (61% of the country's external debt is owed to Beijing), than to the visible physical presence of Chinese, with Chinese labourers commanding higher wages. In 2011 the sale of two M60s to Cameroon for double the price charged to the Democratic Republic of the Congo provided a very public case of Chinese exploitation of Cameroon to reinforce the image locally of the Chinese as 'predators' and 'imperialists'. However, the Government prefers Chinese loans, which come without the conditionalities imposed by the International Financial Institutions.

China and Cameroon are both strong supporters of non-interference in the affairs of other states, especially on human rights grounds. However, they have both offered qualified support to French interventions in Mali and the Central African Republic (CAR). Some in the elite have even suggested that Chinese military bases should be welcomed as a counterweight in Africa to the former colonial powers and the USA. Cameroon and China maintain close military relations. Chinese arms sales to Cameroon surfaced in 2012 and include extensive support for the Cameroonian navy plus equipment valued at US $25m. for use by the AU's Logistics Hub based in Cameroon. Bilateral trade lies at the core of the relationship. According to the Cameroonian Ministry of the Economy Chinese investment in Cameroon amounted to $2,430m. in 2016. Chinese-backed investment projects include the construction of the Kribi Industrial Port Complex, the Memve'ele

Hydroelectric Dam and football stadia for Africa Cup of Nations tournament. The 1,015- metre navigation channel for the port of Kribi, which forms part of China's Maritime Silk Road, was opened in May 2021, offering an alternative to the clogged, corrupt and inefficient port of Douala which previously handled 95% of Cameroon's maritime trade, as well as much of that for Chad, the CAR and the broader region.

THE MEDIA

The Cameroonian Government tries to restrict the media to government-owned sources or those that are reliant on government advertising. Despite this, Cameroon has more than 200 illegal radio stations and more than 400 newspapers, many of them little more than news sheets. Under 20% of households have access to a television set, and in 2020 only 37.8% of people used the internet. In 2017 the Government shut down access to the internet in anglophone areas in an attempt to prevent the co-ordination of demonstrations and strikes. However, with 22.4m. mobile telephone subscriptions in 2020, almost 75% of households had access to the media via that route. However, in September 2021 the Government banned television debates about the fate of the anglophone areas, after revelations that army officers might have been giving contracts to their relatives. The Government has imprisoned many journalists who have criticized it, charging and convicting them with publishing fake news and detaining them long beyond the legal limit. According to the World Press Freedom Index, in 2021 Cameroon ranked 135th out of 180 countries.

HUMAN DIGNITY AND CORRUPTION

The Penal Code of 2016 Article 347-1 penalizes sexual relations between persons of the same sex with imprisonment for a maximum of five years and a fine of up to 200,000 francs CFA. Cameroon has consistently rejected international calls to decriminalize homosexuality. It is often argued that part of the governance style of the ruling elite is to create a series of moral panics to deflect attention away from the authoritarianism and corruption of the regime. President Biya's statements on the subject have been ambivalent, implying that he personally would allow repeal, but that Cameroonian parliamentarians should be allowed to protect the nation's moral values.

Over 100 trade unions and 12 trade union confederations operate in the country. However, disagreements and fractures within the union movement mean that it is often ineffective in promoting workers' rights, as employers choose to bargain with the more pliant and less militant union leaders. In recent years there have been frequent complaints about breaches of human rights and labour laws by Chinese mining companies. Strikes occur frequently, especially when workers have not been paid for several months, and are often broken up with brutality by the police. In February 2022 the Syndicat National des Employés de l'Eau Potable took strike action about misadministration, corruption and a lack of forward-planning in the water sector, and in the same month teachers launched a national strike over unpaid wages and benefits amounting to the equivalent of several hundred millions of US dollars.

ENVIRONMENTAL ISSUES

Cameroon experiences multiple environmental problems including deforestation, destructive mining practices, poor urban conditions and shortages or excesses of water. Many of these problems are exacerbated in areas of poor security. Embassies in the capital, Yaoundé, advise citizens and visitors alike to avoid areas within 40 km of Cameroon's five international borders, owing to incursions and kidnappings. Displaced people and refugees, trying to avoid the risk of being attacked by rebels, criminal gangs or government forces, move into areas which are often already inhabited by locals who resist sharing their land, water and fuel wood resources with these incomers. Conflict between crop farmers and cattle herders is endemic.

Cameroon exports the largest volume of timber of any country in Africa. In times of economic crises, pressure to overexploit forested areas is facilitated by governmental corruption. Between 2002 and 2020 Cameroon lost an estimated 708,000 ha of humid primary forest, which made up about one-half of its total tree cover loss during the period. China is the largest importer of timber from Cameroon, and there have been a number of scandals involving the illegal sources of this timber. Indigenous communities have complained that the Government does not enforce the laws regulating logging concessions. As the price of beef (among many other commodities) has risen since the outbreak of war in Ukraine, Cameroonians have stepped up their consumption of bush meat sourced from local wildlife as a source of protein, and many households can no longer afford to purchase cooking gas. As a result, the use of wood and biomass to use as fuel to prepare food is altering the country's topography and possibly setting the stage for flooding and other natural disasters in future. Furthermore, changes in the pattern of rainfall, owing to anthropogenic climate change, are posing problems to farmers who no longer know what the best time is to plant their crops. They must also bear in mind that where people cut down

trees for firewood, this can lead to areas of water catchment drying up.

Mining in Cameroon is often a major source of pollution, although about 55% of the country's electricity is generated from hydropower. The high proportion of hydro resources used in the generation of electricity is environmentally friendly, although local gas has to be used as a significant back-up in the dry season. Cameroon has the second highest hydroelectric potential in Africa and the 18th largest in the world. The UN Educational, Scientific and Cultural Organization is assisting with the diffusion of solar and biomass energy production in the extreme north of the country but this is still very small scale. Cameroon's climate mitigation target is to reduce greenhouse emissions by 35% by 2035 through better management of the vast carbon sink provided by its forests, as well as stewardship of its energy, agriculture and waste sectors. The Cameroonian authorities published their first atlas of land coverage in 2021. There are few constraints on the private sector, although all infrastructure projects are expected to undergo environmental and social impact assessments.

Economy

TICKY MONEKOSSO

Revised for this edition by the editorial staff

INTRODUCTION

Cameroon covers an area of 475,650 sq km and is a bridge between West Africa and Central Africa, bordering six other countries. According to United Nations (UN) projections, the population numbered 27.9m. at mid-2022. The country is endowed with rich natural resources, including petroleum and gas, minerals, high-value species of timber and agricultural crops, such as coffee, cotton, cocoa, maize and cassava.

However, poverty in Cameroon is widespread, with an estimated 40% of Cameroonians continuing to live below the poverty line in mid-2022 (see *Socioeconomic Development*). Since the 1980s the country has pursued a variety of programmes under guidance from the International Monetary Fund (IMF) and the World Bank in an attempt to reduce poverty. Numerous industries have been privatized, and the Government has also tried to encourage the growth of tourism in the country.

The Government in 2009 adopted an ambitious economic plan ('Vision 2035') with the aim of developing Cameroon into a middle-income, industrialized economy by 2035. (Cameroon is currently classified as a lower-middle income economy.) In 2017 the World Bank noted that for Cameroon to achieve this objective it needed to develop the potential of the country's private sector and to increase productivity. The country's real gross domestic product (GDP) would need to grow by an average of 8.0% (or 5.7% per capita) per year between 2015 and 2035. During 2011–20 GDP increased, in real terms, at an average annual rate of 4.2%, while GDP per capita grew by an average of 1.5% per year.

In 2019 Cameroon's GDP growth fell to 3.5% from 4.1% in 2018. According to the IMF, this was due mainly to a lower than anticipated performance in the non-oil sector, although this decline was partly offset by a rebound in the oil and gas sector. Following the onset of the COVID-19 pandemic, GDP growth dropped to a minimal 0.5% in 2020. However, GDP growth returned to the pre-pandemic level of 3.5% in 2021 (according to the World Bank), stimulated by a recovery in the agricultural and services sectors.

SOCIOECONOMIC DEVELOPMENT

Cameroon's economic structure and performance do not meet the criteria for a socially responsible market democracy. Despite significant improvements in poverty alleviation and human development since the 1990s, Cameroon still ranks poorly by international standards, and the rate of

improvement has stalled. Cameroon has met only one of the Millennium Development Goals (for net school enrolment). The continuing crises of Islamist insurgency in the Lake Chad Basin from 2018, affecting Cameroon's Far North Region, and armed conflict in the anglophone North-West and South-West Regions from 2016–17 have had a devastating humanitarian impact (see *History*). The UN World Food Programme (WFP) reported in July 2022 that some 40% of the population were living below the poverty line, while 3.9m. people were in need of humanitarian assistance in that year, and more than 955,000 had been internally displaced. The global impact of Russia's invasion of Ukraine in February was expected to result in a further deterioration in food security: in particular, disruptions in supply chains caused a surge of up to 54% in the prices of wheat and fertilizer between February and July (with Cameroon having previously obtained 43% of its fertilizer imports and 46% of its wheat from Russia).

The country's socioeconomic development is strongly shaped by persistent inequalities. Over 40% of the population lives in rural areas, and poverty is heavily concentrated in the rural Far North and East Regions. Cameroon's score for 2021 (in terms of inequality) on the UN Development Programme's Human Development Index (HDI), an indicator of well-being that provides a composite measure of three basic dimensions of human development (health, education and income), was just 0.393, which was below the average for countries with HDI scores in the medium range (0.481). Gender inequality is also an issue, most evident in differences in educational attainment and labour force participation. Cameroon's gender inequality score on the HDI was 0.885, which was about the average for medium HDI countries (0.880). The inequality indicator measured using the Gini coefficient index averaged 46.6 in 2010–21.

With a per-capita GDP of US $1,662 in 2021, Cameroon is a lower-middle income country. Its overall rank on the HDI placed it 151st out of 191 countries (with a score of 0.576) in 2021, which was at the low end of the 'medium human development' spectrum. Life expectancy at birth was 60.3 years in 2021. Average annual HDI growth in 2010–21 was around 1.1%, reflecting only a slight improvement from levels in 2010. In addition to the continued high level of poverty, there have been mixed improvements according to other indicators of development. Between 2010 and 2020, according to the World Bank, infant mortality fell from 69 per 1,000 live births to 48 per 1,000 live births. However, primary school completion rates declined from 72% in 2010 to 65% in 2019. In 2020 66% of the population had access to improved water resources and 45% access to improved sanitation facilities, but in both cases the rates were reported to be far lower in rural areas. The official unemployment rate in the country was only 3.6% in 2020, according to the World Bank, although this did not reflect the number of people reliant on the often insecure and low-paying informal economy for their livelihood.

Nevertheless, because of its influence within the region (largely as a consequence of its strategic location in the Gulf of Guinea compared with its landlocked neighbours) Cameroon has the potential to become one of the most prosperous economies in Central Africa and an attractive destination for foreign investment. Yet entrepreneurship remains limited, and corruption is widespread in the country's public administration, which also suffers from excessive bureaucracy, while poor infrastructure and weak rule of law limit access to some key sectors for foreign investors. It is to be hoped that the growth of non-oil sector of the Cameroonian economy and the resolution of the security crises in the northern and anglophone parts of the country could boost investments in infrastructure and energy projects. However, the closure of Cameroon's borders from mid-March 2020 as a result of the COVID-19 pandemic led to a deterioration in the economy. The country's borders remained officially closed at early October 2022, although some international air services had resumed.

THE INFORMAL ECONOMY

Cameroon is well served in terms of the prevalence of the informal sector in the economy, supported by traditional saving and banking systems (known locally as '*Tontines*'), local and cross-border trade, transport, agriculture and many other activities. The informal sector is estimated to employ some 90% of the economically active population in the country.

According the IMF, the informal sector in Cameroon contributes 20%–30% of the country's GDP (although the International Labour Organization—ILO—estimates that it accounts for as much as 50%) and is as productive as that of countries with bigger economies on the continent, such as South Africa. However, the informal sector in Cameroon is characterized by precarious activities, with little or no formal supervision, which are not covered in the official national accounts.

In general, the informal sector comprises very small, unregistered individual enterprises operating on a small scale outside the agricultural sector. More than 2.5m. enterprises in the informal sector, or informal production units (IPUs), have been estimated on Cameroonian territory, of which around one-half are located in rural areas and 33% in the cities of Yaoundé, the administrative capital, and Douala, the economic capital.

By late 2020 the COVID-19 pandemic presented both challenges and opportunities to Cameroon's informal sector. The slowdown in economic activity was likely to result in a significant loss of income in the informal sector. According to the Institut National de la Statistique du Cameroun (INSC), the average monthly income of those employed in the informal sector was 48,400 francs CFA (about US $85), with the average wage being 58,600 francs CFA in urban areas and 38,200 francs CFA in rural areas. Inevitably, a drop in income would have repercussions on the working conditions and productivity of IPUs—a situation that could affect the quality of the goods and services produced.

The slowdown in economic activity could also push those affected to migrate to the informal sector to compensate for unemployment and pursue livelihood opportunities. As a main consequence, the rate of informal employment in the economy could increase in line with the growth of subsistence activities.

At the national level the COVID-19 pandemic has given rise to various needs. These include hydroalcoholic solutions (for hand sanitizer), protective masks, gloves and other personal protective equipment. The manufacture and marketing of protective masks sold at an average of 500 francs CFA per unit offers a market of at least 13,000m. francs CFA to IPUs in the field of clothing and medical equipment. With this potential revenue, the transition from informal to formal employment would be less difficult for many Cameroonians. Indeed, the development of the activities of IPUs would push stakeholders into formalizing their production processes for goods and services to be able to capture significant shares of income. In this way, the number of activities that were not previously taken into consideration in the national accounts could be reduced. However, if the tax burden remains high for the formal sector of the economy, then a return to, or continuation in, the informal sector is probable for many workers.

According to the IMF, among the factors preventing the development of the formal sector in Cameroon were unduly high taxes and social charges, the small size of the market and the low volume of economic activity, an inefficient judiciary, excessive bureaucracy, difficulties accessing financing to develop and invest in economic activities, a weak business environment, obstacles in the way of development of the digital economy and weaknesses in governance.

AGRICULTURE

The country's climate varies with terrain, from tropical along the coast to semi-arid and hot in the north. Cameroon is well known for its climatic, geographic and ecological diversity, which enables farmers to grow a wide variety of crops. Agriculture has long been the main driver of the Cameroonian economy, but in recent times its contribution to the economy has declined, particularly since the discovery of oil and gas. In 2021 agriculture, including forestry and fishing, contributed just 18.9% of GDP, while industry contributed 25.9% and services 55.2%. However, agriculture remains a major employer, engaging an estimated 41.4% of the labour force at mid-2015, according to estimates by the UN Food and Agriculture Organization (FAO).

Agricultural activities are generally carried out on a subsistence scale using simple implements. The soils and climate along the coastal region lend themselves to the commercial cultivation of crops such as rubber, tea, bananas, oil palms and cocoa. The southern part of the country is largely a plateau, and crops common in this part of the country include sugar, coffee and tobacco. In the Western highlands of Cameroon, the most common cash crop is coffee, while in the southern part of the country the natural conditions favour crops including rice, groundnuts and cotton.

The agricultural sector is characterized by small artisanal exploitations with low productivity and by significant state intervention, mainly in the form of price controls on some products. The majority of farmers in Cameroon are small-scale farmers, who produce about 80% of the country's food crops. These traditional family farm enterprises, which produce through limited mechanized processes, have generally low productivity. However, there are also substantial state-owned production companies in some sub-sectors.

Cameroon's long-term 'Vision 2035' and associated government implementation plans aim to make agriculture the engine of national development and the source of national food security. In 2009 the Cameroon Government adopted the Strategic Document for Growth and Labour and a National Plan for Agriculture Development (2014–20). The Government planned to implement a large development programme to increase agricultural production, not only to satisfy the food needs of the population, but also to develop an agro-industrial sector. According to this strategic plan, investment in agriculture aims to modernize and to enhance the commercial viability of the country's agricultural sector by: i) making factors of production including land, water and agricultural inputs accessible and available; ii) promoting access to technological innovations, particularly by strengthening research/extension links; and iii) developing the competitiveness of production and value chains.

The country's principal agricultural output can be classified into two main groups: i) food crops, mainly rice, cassava, corn, sugar cane and plantains; and ii) cash crops mainly for export, which include cocoa, coffee (Robusta and Arabica), cotton (grain and fibre), rubber, palm oil and bananas.

In Cameroon, there are several organizations that represent operators in the organic sector, most notably the Association de Promotion de l'Agriculture Biologique au Cameroun in francophone areas and the Association of Vegetable Growers in anglophone areas. Both groups focus on promoting the sector and raising public awareness. They provide their members with information services, technical assistance and training in organic agriculture. The most frequently cultivated export crops on Cameroonian organic farms are bananas, pineapples, avocados, mangoes, papayas, coffee and cocoa. Other certified products include herbs, spices, tubers and medical plants. There is a growing emphasis on processing some of the fruit crops through drying, pulping and juicing.

Among the food crops, rice is one of the most important, as it is also an important part of daily consumption. Cameroon's production of rice was 329,000 metric tons in 2020, according to FAO estimates, compared with local demand of around 400,000 tons. Imports of rice cost US $259.6m. in 2018. Rice is produced by independent farmers, by producer organizations, by the Upper Noun Valley Development Authority and by areas served by the Société d'Expansion et de Modernisation de la Riziculture de Yagoua (SEMRY), which accounts for about two-thirds of the country's total production.

Local rice production faces longstanding constraints. These include poor access to fertilizer and pesticides, the poor availability of high-yielding seeds, inadequate organization among producers, high post-harvest losses, outdated processing equipment, the poor availability of financing and challenges resulting from the long distances between the main producing areas in the north and the main consumption centres in the more heavily populated south and centre. Irrigation is a critical component of food security in the rice-producing areas in the Far North Region of Cameroon, which frequently suffers from low rainfall. Furthermore, although locally produced rice is increasingly appreciated for its good quality, its retail price remains about 50% higher than the price of imported rice.

In the early 2020s SEMRY was still providing a package of services to farmers in the areas that it served, comprising seeds, irrigation and ploughing. The company also buys rice from local producers for distribution. However, the state-owned company has not been able to acquire all the rice that is produced. The farmers in the area that SEMRY cover often prefer to sell their products to neighbouring countries, particularly Nigeria, rather than locally. SEMRY's distribution activity is very limited in scope. The company provides transportation of products to Yaoundé and the sale of products through a single distribution point. This offers only limited access to the wider market.

The Cameroon Development Corporation (CDC) has been active since 1947, when it was created to produce tropical crops in the anglophone areas of Cameroon. The CDC grows rubber, bananas and oil palm and produces semi-finished rubber, palm oil, palm kernel oil and high quality bananas for export. It has a total of 42,027 ha under cultivation, of which 22,262 ha are planted with rubber, 15,240 ha with oil palm and 4,525 ha with bananas. With more than 22,000 employees, the CDC is the second largest employer in Cameroon, behind only to the Government. Rubber accounts for about 30% of CDC's sales, and about 90% of rubber is sold to Michelin, a tyre manufacturer based in France.

Annual production of oil palm products is around 21,000 metric tons, accounting for 20% of CDC's sales. 90% of palm oil products are sold to local edible oil refineries. Oil palm prices in Cameroon are controlled at levels that do not allow the CDC to recover its cost of production. Other market players include local companies such as the Société Camerounaise de Palmeraies. Imported oil, with its lower selling price, is a serious competitor for locally produced vegetable oil. On average Cameroon imports around 100,000 metric tons of vegetable oil per year.

Bananas, which account for around 50% of CDC's total sales, are shipped for export to Europe by a French company, Compagnie Fruitière. Production of bananas amounted to 1.2m. metric tons in 2020, according to FAO estimates. The CDC's plantations are old and have lacked sufficient maintenance and new plantings for many years. The financial situation of the CDC has not allowed the company to undertake much-needed investment in crop rehabilitation, and Compagnie Fruitière has made proposals for a partnership with the CDC that would aim to upgrade the existing 3,500 ha in banana production, while developing 1,100 ha of new growing territory in the Mganga region near the production zone operated by Plantations du Haut-Penja, transferring the fruit shipping terminal from Douala to Limbe, pledging investment in upgrading the facilities at Limbe and implementing a package of tax and other incentives aimed at increasing the competitiveness of the banana industry. Until recently the CDC has regularly produced about 35% of Cameroon's bananas for export. However, because of the unrest in the banana-producing areas in the south-west of the country, it is clear that the CDC is facing a deepening crisis. Exports of bananas and plantains accounted for only 1.6% of total export revenue in 2018.

Cameroon is among the world's largest producers of cocoa. About 600,000 rural households in Cameroon depend on cocoa for their income, and most of these cultivate the crop on smallholdings. Some 80% of the cocoa is grown in the South-West and Centre Regions. Annual cocoa bean production remained at about 120,000 metric tons per year between 1990 and 2013 before rising to 280,000 tons by 2019, on a planted area of about 850,000 ha. Around 80% of the volume produced in 2018 was exported, putting the country in fifth position worldwide in terms of cocoa output. In 2018 cocoa and cocoa products accounted for 14.6% of Cameroon's export receipts. Cocoa bean production increased to 290,000 tons in 2020, according to FAO estimates.

The Société de Développement du Cacao (SODECAO) was created by decree in February 1974 as a public establishment reporting to the Ministry of Agriculture and Rural Development. Its main objectives are to support cocoa production by protecting cocoa standards, maintaining agricultural lands and production systems, opening and maintaining feeder roads, distributing planting material and promoting of agricultural diversification in cocoa-producing areas. In addition to maintaining infrastructure and providing advisory services, the organization operates three large seed production units. SODECAO is primarily a public service provider, financed by direct subsidies from the Ministry of Agriculture and Rural Development and the Ministry of Finance and support from donors, and it generates little or no direct income from sales of its services or products.

SODECAO's Strategic Plan for 2020–27 lays out a series of measures intended to put SODECAO in a position to fulfil its mission and to enable the cocoa industry to realize its economic potential. The plan includes three programmes: i) to double cocoa yields by distributing high-quality planting material and training producers; ii) to stimulate increased production activity through incentives to young farmers, partnering with growers' organizations and other partners; and iii) to re-dynamize SODECAO itself through investments in its physical facilities and equipment, the implementation of performance management, improved information, financial and human resources management and improved public information programmes.

SODECAO's size has been reduced over time, and its plant and equipment is eroding. Its operational structure consists of seven regional centres handling devolved management and quality control functions, 25 geographical sectors where the bulk of SODECAO's support services are based and 81 sections, which cover small local areas. There are three seed production facilities: at Mengang in the Centre Region, Abong-Mbang in the East and Nkoemvone in the South.

As the cocoa market in Cameroon is liberalized, with three main private exporters handling most of the trade, price fluctuations are passed on to producers, resulting in uncertainty and frequently a lack of commitment by growers. Cocoa production in Cameroon is adversely affected by a number of factors. The challenges include low yields because of the predominant smallholder production model (sometimes referred to as cocoa farming by default), insufficient investment and planting material and inadequate collaboration between stakeholders.

Cotton is an important crop for the Cameroonian economy, and the crop provided 5.5% of the total value of the country's exports in 2018. Cameroon's production is relatively small compared with other countries, despite an increase in output of seed cotton to 470,000 metric tons in 2019, remaining at 446,000 tons in 2020, according to FAO estimates. There are about 350,000 cotton growers supporting a household population of about 2m.

Cotton growing and processing activities are led by the Société de Développement du Coton (SODECOTON), a vertically integrated entity based in Garoua in the North Region, which dominates the financing, purchasing, processing and marketing of cotton and the supply of agricultural inputs for cotton production, in partnership with the National Confederation of Cotton Producers of Cameroon. Production levels in the early 2020s were about 10 times the level when SODE-COTON was created in 1974. About 90% of the company's output is exported to international markets.

SODECOTON is a limited liability company whose shareholders are the state (59%) and two private companies: Géocoton (30%) and the Société Immobilière d'Investissements du Cameroun (11%). SODECOTON's main objectives are to improve the standard of living of the population in the cotton growing areas by creating jobs and contributing to the modernization of agriculture. It provides farmers with advice on improved techniques as well as seeds, fertilizers and pesticides and engages in cotton ginning and the production of cotton fibre, refined vegetable oil and cotton seed cake. It also supports the production of other crops in rotation with cotton. SODE-COTON has nine ginneries with a combined capacity of about 300,000 metric tons per year, which is equivalent to more than 120,000 tons of fibre. It also has two oil mills with a capacity of crushing some 120,000 tons of seed annually. About 14m.–19m. litres of edible oil and 60,000–70,000 tons of feed are produced annually. The company has about 500 light vehicles as well as heavy machinery and it employs about 5,000 staff.

Agriculture could be a major driver of economic growth in Cameroon if the transition from traditional agriculture towards diversified and commercially viable activity can be achieved. Problems faced by the Cameroonian agriculture sector include security challenges, outdated and depleted assets, shortages of production and planting materials, as well as adverse weather and climate change which affect productivity and the quality of the output. Despite these factors, the Government continues to have ambitious plans to transform agriculture into a modern, commercially viable activity, which can satisfy national food needs and generate agro-industrial activity. The Government's objectives are also to make land, water and inputs accessible to farmers, to promote technical innovations and to improve the competitiveness of production and value chains.

Cameroon has a lack of agricultural research capacity, although it does have a public agency specializing in agricultural research (the Institut de Recherche Agricole pour le Développement—IRAD). Like many public agencies in the agriculture sector, IRAD faces challenges that impede its effectiveness in delivering on its mandate. Furthermore, research outputs are not widely used to support the commercial needs of local companies.

NATURAL RESOURCES

Following aeromagnetic and gravimetic surveys and subsequent geochemical and geological studies as part of a five-year (2014–19) Mining Sector Capacity Building Project sponsored by the World Bank, significant occurrences of diverse minerals including, *inter alia*, gold, cobalt, nickel, manganese, base metals, rare earth elements, uranium and rutile were identified in five regions of the country. Details of this large discovery—the largest since independence, and comprising some 300 new mineral deposits—were made available at the third Cameroon International, Investment Mining and Exhibition Conference in 2019. Cameroon receives royalties from the pipeline linking petroleum reserves at Doba, Chad, to the port of Kribi, which transports some 100,000 barrels per day.

Cameroon is the site of the main part of the Central African iron ore belt that stretches from the Democratic Republic of the Congo through Gabon to Cameroon along which are found world class iron ore deposits, including Mbalam (operated by Sundance of Australia), Nkot (operated by Caminex of Cameroon) and the Mamelles iron ore deposit of Kribi (operated by Sinosteel of China). Cameroon also possesses the largest lateritic cobalt deposit in the world at Lomie (operated by Geovic of the USA) and the rutile deposit of Akonolinga in

Minim Martap, which is the second largest bauxite reserve in Africa. Previously, only about 40% of the country had been explored.

Although in the early 2020s Cameroon's mining sector was still in its infancy, the Government was taking significant steps to develop its considerable potential. In March 2022 Canyon Resources Ltd of Australia announced that its subsidiary, Camalco Cameroon, had obtained extensions for research permits, allowing it to continue mining activities in the Minim Martap area (following conflicting claims by two other international mining companies). Canyon Resources in June released the results of a bankable feasibility study into its planned Minim Martap bauxite project, which confirmed an initial 20-year mine life, with the project expected to produce 6.4m. metric tons of high-grade bauxite annually.

Cameroon's dependence on natural resources exposes the country to global commodity price fluctuations. Mineral products are a principal source of revenue, accounting for 50.5% of the total in 2018, with crude petroleum oils alone providing 40.8%. Production of crude petroleum amounted to 26.0m. barrels in 2019. In 2020 Cameroon's oil revenue fell considerably following a collapse in demand and lower international prices for the commodity as a result of the COVID-19 pandemic. However, oil revenue increased sharply year-on-year during 2022, as a result of the surge in global fuel prices.

TRADE AND FINANCE

Foreign direct investment (FDI) inflows to Cameroon reached US $1,024.8m. in 2019, increasing from $765.1m. in the previous year, but dropped to $675.2m. in 2020 as a result of the COVID-19 pandemic. Total FDI stocks were estimated at $8,400m. in 2019. In terms of attracting FDI, Cameroon was ranked 167th out of 190 countries surveyed by the World Bank in that year. Despite this ranking, the country has made improvements in giving access to credit by establishing a framework through the Communauté Economique et Monétaire de l'Afrique Centrale (CEMAC—Central African Economic and Monetary Community) for the licensing and operation of credit bureaus. However, most FDI has traditionally come from the European Union (EU), particularly France and Germany, and targets the mining industry, including oil extraction.

In recent years the People's Republic of China has become the dominant investor in the country, carrying out large infrastructure projects such as the construction of the Kribi Port and Industrial Complex, the Memve'ele hydroelectric dam in the south and new football stadiums for the 2021 Africa Cup of Nations (which was postponed to January–February 2022, owing to the COVID-19 pandemic). Total Chinese direct and indirect investments amounted to US $2,430m. in 2016. Large French companies are also well-placed in future projects to develop infrastructure and, notably, the exploitation of gas.

Cameroon's trade balance is structurally negative. According to the IMF, in 2020 Cameroon recorded a trade deficit of US $679m., with imports of goods falling to $5,095m. from $6,262m. in 2019, and exports to $4,416m. from $5,526m. in 2019, amid the impact of the COVID-19 pandemic on global trade. A deficit of $1,512m. on the current account of the balance of payments was recorded in 2020. Cameroon's main export commodities are fuel (oil, gas), minerals (coal, aluminium), wood, cocoa, cotton and rubber. Cameroon imports mineral fuels and oil, food (rice, wheat, fish, etc.), medicines and manufactured products (vehicles, machinery, electrical and electronic equipment). In 2018 the principal source of imports was China (providing 18.5% of the total); other major suppliers were France and Nigeria. The principal source of exports in that year was also China, taking 24.8% of the total; other significant purchasers were Italy, the Netherlands, France, Spain and India. Cameroon signed a free trade agreement with the EU in August 2016. For the past two decades Cameroon has been reinforcing its trade ties with Asian countries, especially China, Japan, India, Malaysia and Thailand. Cameroon is part of CEMAC and the Communauté Economique des Etats de l'Afrique Centrale (CEEAC—Economic Community of Central African States), and it is a member of both the Commonwealth and the Franc Zone.

Cameroon's rate of value-added tax (VAT) is 19.25%, comprising 17.5% of the value of the item in question, plus a 10% surcharge on the taxable amount, while corporation tax is charged up to a rate of 33%, comprising 30% corporation tax and a 10% surcharge on the taxable amount. The minimum company tax is 2.2% of annual turnover and up to 5.5% for companies that are subject to a simple tax regime. The social security contributions paid by employers are between 9.65% and 16.2% of an employee's wages.

Cameroon's general government gross debt was 10,511,218m. francs CFA in 2020, equivalent to 45.8% of GDP. The IMF projected that public debt stock would decline from an estimated 45.5% of GDP in 2021 to 44.0% in 2022 and 40.8% in 2023. According to official figures, the annual rate of inflation averaged 1.8% in 2012–20; consumer prices increased by 2.4% in 2020 and 2.3% in 2021. However, following the inflationary pressures ensuing from the war in Ukraine, in August 2022 the INSC reported an overall year-on-year rise in domestic consumer prices of 4.3%, with a year-on-year increase in food prices of 14.9%.

Cameroon secured additional funding totalling about US $382m. in 2020, under the IMF's Rapid Credit Facility (RCF), to help mitigate the effects of the COVID-19 pandemic, while the Government adopted a revised budget for that year, with a larger deficit, to accommodate emergency-related increased expenditure, including a three-year US $600m. COVID-19 Preparedness and Response Plan and the development of a national fund (the COVID Special Account). The budget deficit was estimated at of 749,000m. francs CFA in 2020 and was projected to increase to 822,000m. francs CFA in 2021. In May of that year allegations of official mismanagement and embezzlement of much of the IMF emergency funds emerged (see *History*). Nevertheless, in July the IMF approved three-year Extended Credit Facility (ECF) and Extended Fund Facility (EFF) arrangements totalling some $689.5m. for Cameroon, in support of a government programme that aimed to mitigate the consequences of the pandemic, while strengthening anti-corruption measures, diversifying the economy,

enhancing financial resilience and promoting a greener economy. The second reviews of performance under the ECF and EFF arrangements were completed in July 2022; allowing the disbursement of about $24.3m. under the first arrangement, and purchases of $48.6m. under the second (bringing total access under both to around $346.1m.). The IMF noted delays in the implementation of structural reforms in some of the targeted areas.

CONCLUSION

Cameroon is well endowed with the commodities required for a healthy primary sector; however, in recent years the Cameroonian economy has stagnated as oil production has decreased and the non-extractive sectors have struggled to grow, bogged down by severe infrastructure gaps and a difficult business environment. Cameroon's economic prospects rest largely on the revival of the hydrocarbons sector. In addition to the slight increase in oil output anticipated over the medium term, Cameroon's economic growth will be underpinned by infrastructure programmes, support to the agricultural sector and accelerated growth in the services sector, most notably telecommunications and transport.

Cameroon began to demonstrate recovery from the COVID-19 pandemic in 2021, with a GDP growth rate of 3.5%. However, the IMF in July 2022 revised downwards its projection for Cameroon's growth in that year, to 3.8% from 4.5%, due to new uncertainties ensuing from the war in Ukraine, including high inflationary pressures, further disruptions to supply chains and a deterioration in global financial conditions. In addition, by that time less than 5% of the population had been fully vaccinated against the virus (among the lowest rates in the world), leaving the country vulnerable to further COVID-19 waves. Despite benefits to Cameroon's crude oil export revenue, the elevated global prices had by mid-2022 significantly increased the cost of government fuel subsidies and resulted in sharp rises in domestic prices, especially of food and fertilizers, with expected consequences for the already severe humanitarian situation in many parts of the country.

Statistical Survey

Source (unless otherwise stated): Institut National de la Statistique du Cameroun, BP 134, Yaoundé; tel. 222-22-04-45; internet www.statistics-cameroon.org.

Area and Population

AREA, POPULATION AND DENSITY

Area (sq km)	
Continental	466,050
Maritime	9,600
Total	475,650*
Population (census results)	
9 April 1987	10,493,655
11 November 2005	
Males	8,408,495
Females	8,643,639
Total	17,052,134
Population (UN estimates at mid-year)†	
. . . .	
2020	26,545,864
2021‡	27,224,262
2022‡	27,911,544
Density (per sq km) at mid-2022‡	59.9§

* 183,649 sq miles.
† Source: UN, *World Population Prospects: The 2019 Revision.*
‡ Projection.
§ Continental area only.

POPULATION BY AGE AND SEX
('000, UN projections at mid-2022)

	Males	Females	Total
0–14 years	5,839.1	5,735.6	11,574.7
15–64 years	7,782.4	7,791.2	15,573.6
65 years and over	342.5	420.8	763.3
Total	**13,964.0**	**13,947.5**	**27,911.5**

Note: Totals may not be equal to the sum of components, owing to rounding.

Source: UN, *World Population Prospects: The 2019 Revision.*

REGIONS
(official population projections, 2016)

	Area (sq km)*	Population	Density (per sq km)
Adamaoua	63,701	1,236,148	19.4
Centre	68,953	4,283,260	62.1
East	109,002	841,014	7.7
Far North	34,263	4,089,430	119.4
Littoral	20,248	3,446,388	170.2
North	66,090	2,503,445	37.9
North-West	17,300	2,006,210	116.0
South	47,191	757,739	16.1
South-West	25,410	1,593,728	62.7
West	13,892	1,952,530	140.6
Total	**466,050**	**22,709,892**	**48.7**

* Continental area only.

PRINCIPAL TOWNS
(population at 2005 census)

Douala . . .	1,907,479	Maroua	201,371
Yaoundé (capital) .	1,817,524	Kumba	144,268
Bamenda . . .	269,530	Nkongsamba . .	104,050
Bafoussam . . .	239,287	Limbé	84,223
Garoua	235,996		

Mid-2022 ('000, incl. suburbs, UN projections): Yaoundé (capital) 4,337; Douala 3,927; Bamenda 573; Loum 549; Mbouda 546; Bafoussam 451 (Source: UN, *World Urbanization Prospects: The 2018 Revision*).

BIRTHS AND DEATHS
(annual averages, UN estimates)

	2005–10	2010–15	2015–20
Birth rate (per 1,000)	40.3	38.3	35.6
Death rate (per 1,000)	12.3	10.8	9.4

Source: UN, *World Population Prospects: The 2019 Revision*.

Life expectancy (years at birth, estimates): 59.6 (males 58.4; females 60.9) in 2020 (Source: World Bank, World Development Indicators database).

ECONOMICALLY ACTIVE POPULATION
('000, FAO estimates at mid-year)

	2013	2014	2015
Agriculture, etc.	3,803	3,815	3,824
Total labour force (incl. others) .	8,665	8,949	9,245

Source: FAO.

Health and Welfare

KEY INDICATORS

Total fertility rate (children per woman, 2020)	4.4
Under-5 mortality rate (per 1,000 live births, 2020) . .	72.2
HIV/AIDS (% of persons aged 15–49, 2020)	3.0
COVID-19: Cumulative confirmed deaths (per 100,000 persons at 31 August 2022)	7.1
COVID-19: Fully vaccinated population (% of total population at 24 July 2022)	4.5
Physicians (per 1,000 head, 2018)	1.3
Hospitals (per 100,000 head, 2013)	0.8
Domestic health expenditure (2019): US $ per head (PPP) .	4.6
Domestic health expenditure (2019): % of GDP	0.1
Domestic health expenditure (2019): public (% of total current expenditure)	3.4
Access to improved water resources (% of persons, 2020) .	66
Access to improved sanitation facilities (% of persons, 2020) .	45
Total carbon dioxide emissions ('000 metric tons, 2018) . .	8,620
Carbon dioxide emissions per head (metric tons, 2018) . .	0.3
Human Development Index (2021): ranking	151
Human Development Index (2021): value	0.576

Note: For data on COVID-19 vaccinations, 'fully vaccinated' denotes receipt of all doses specified by approved vaccination regime (Sources: Johns Hopkins University and Our World in Data). Data on health expenditure refer to current general government expenditure in each case. For more information on sources and further definitions for all indicators, see Health and Welfare Statistics: Sources and Definitions section (europaworld.com/credits).

Agriculture

PRINCIPAL CROPS
('000 metric tons)

	2018	2019	2020
Avocados*	75	76	75
Bambara beans*	40	40	40
Bananas*	1,209	1,206	1,210
Beans, dry*	410	413	422
Cabbages and other brassicas* .	64	63	63
Cassava (Manioc)*	4,800	4,800	4,858
Chillies and peppers, dry* . .	38	38	38
Chillies and peppers, green* . .	55	55	54
Cocoa beans†	250	280	290
Coffee, green*	36	368	36
Cotton lint	100†	140†	—
Cow peas, dry*	179	177	178
Cucumbers and gherkins* . .	293	303	315
Ginger*	66	69	65
Groundnuts, with shell† . . .	480	500	500
Kola nuts*	47	47	47
Maize*	2,100	2,109	2,091
Melonseed*	48	47	49
Millet*	97	97	98
Oil palm fruit*	2,500	2,400	2,465
Okra*	83	85	83
Onions, dry*	314	308	310
Pineapples*	311	316	310
Plantains*	4,500	4,500	4,526
Potatoes*	340	365	354
Pumpkins, squash and gourds* .	182	181	181
Rice, paddy*	300	311	329
Rubber, natural†	48	48	47
Seed cotton*	380	470	446
Sesame seed†	70	70	70
Sorghum*	1,200	1,200	1,215
Sugar cane*	1,256	1,247	1,249
Sweet potatoes*	468	496	520
Taro (Coco yams)*	1,799	1,812	1,815
Tomatoes*	1,172	1,207	1,247
Yams*	679	688	708

* FAO estimates.
† Unofficial figure(s).

Aggregate production ('000 metric tons, may include official, semi-official or estimated data): Total cereals 3,697 in 2018, 3,719 in 2019, 3,733 in 2020; Total fruit (primary) 6,381 in 2018, 6,385 in 2019, 6,410 in 2020; Total oilcrops 3,504 in 2018, 3,515 in 2019, 3,558 in 2020; Total roots and tubers 8,129 in 2018, 8,205 in 2019, 8,299 in 2020; Total vegetables (primary) 2,957 in 2018, 3,001 in 2019, 3,052 in 2020.

Source: FAO.

LIVESTOCK
('000 head, year ending September, FAO estimates)

	2018	2019	2020
Cattle	6,018	6,036	6,055
Chickens	52,745	55,405	55,425
Goats	5,556	5,400	5,533
Pigs	1,886	1,921	1,953
Sheep	3,626	3,629	3,633

Source: FAO.

LIVESTOCK PRODUCTS
('000 metric tons, FAO estimates)

	2018	2019	2020
Cattle hides, fresh	12.2	12.0	11.8
Cattle meat	83.8	82.3	80.8
Cattle offals, edible	14.0	13.8	13.5
Cows' milk	178.5	179.0	179.5
Chicken meat	80.5	84.9	85.3
Game meat	72.9	73.0	72.7
Goat meat	18.5	18.6	18.7
Goats' milk	54.9	53.9	54.8
Pig meat	32.4	32.6	32.8
Sheep meat	15.6	15.5	15.4
Sheep's (Ewe's) milk	19.0	19.0	19.0
Hen eggs	15.6	15.6	15.6

Source: FAO.

Forestry

ROUNDWOOD REMOVALS
('000 cubic metres, excl. bark, FAO estimates)

	2017	2018	2019
Sawlogs, veneer logs and logs for sleepers	3,332	3,332	3,332
Other industrial wood	500	500	500
Fuel wood	10,498	10,571	10,646
Total	14,330	14,403	14,478

2020: Annual production assumed to be unchanged from 2019 (FAO estimates).

Source: FAO.

SAWNWOOD PRODUCTION
('000 cubic metres, incl. railway sleepers, FAO estimates)

	2018	2019	2020
Total (all broadleaved) . . .	1,122	1,322	1,022

Source: FAO.

Fishing

('000 metric tons, live weight)

	2018	2019	2020
Capture	281.9	296.9*	281.6*
Freshwater fishes	30.6	31.0*	30.6*
Bonga shad	95.1	100.7	95.1*
Aquaculture*	2.3	3.1	3.6
Total catch*	284.7	300.1	285.2

* FAO estimate(s).

Source: FAO.

Mining

	2017	2018	2019
Crude petroleum (million barrels)	27.7	25.1	26.0
Gold (kg)*	1,000	1,000	n.a.
Pozzolan ('000 metric tons)† . .	300	300	300
Limestone ('000 metric tons) .	114	113†	113†

* From artisanal mining.
† Estimated figure(s).

Source: US Geological Survey.

Industry

SELECTED PRODUCTS
('000 metric tons unless otherwise indicated)

	2017	2018	2019
Palm oil*	290	300	300
Raw sugar*	130	130	130
Veneer sheets ('000 cu m)† . .	56	76	96
Plywood ('000 cu m)†	18	18	18
Jet fuels	87	79	41
Motor spirit (petrol)	240	218	113
Gas-diesel (distillate fuel) oil .	471	427	221
Residual fuel oils	222	201	104
Liquefied petroleum gas . . .	11	10	5
Electrical energy (million kWh) .	8,082	8,581	8,476

* Unofficial figure(s).
† FAO estimates.

2020 ('000 cu m): Plywood 10; Veneer sheets 71.

Sources: FAO; UN Energy Statistics Database.

Finance

CURRENCY AND EXCHANGE RATES

Monetary Units
100 centimes = 1 franc de la Coopération Financière en Afrique Centrale (CFA).

Sterling, Dollar and Euro Equivalents (31 May 2022)
£1 sterling = 770.824 francs CFA;
US $1 = 612.300 francs CFA;
€1 = 655.957 francs CFA;
10,000 francs CFA = £12.97 = $16.33 = €15.24.

Average Exchange Rate (francs CFA per US $)
2019   585.911
2020   575.586
2021   554.531

Note: An exchange rate of 1 French franc = 50 francs CFA, established in 1948, remained in force until January 1994, when the CFA franc was devalued by 50%, with the exchange rate adjusted to 1 French franc = 100 francs CFA. This relationship to French currency remained in effect with the introduction of the euro on 1 January 1999. From that date, accordingly, a fixed exchange rate of €1 = 655.957 francs CFA has been in operation.

BUDGET
('000 million francs CFA)

Revenue*	2019	2020†	2021†
Petroleum revenue	585	428	482
Non-petroleum revenue . . .	2,867	2,682	3,010
Direct taxes	729	732	698
Special tax on petroleum products	129	136	147
Taxes on international trade .	393	349	398
Other taxes on goods and services	1,451	1,277	1,601
Non-tax revenue (excluding privatization proceeds) . .	164	189	167
Total	3,451	3,110	3,492

Expenditure§	2019	2020†	2021†
Current expenditure	2,693	2,530	2,970
Wages and salaries	1,016	1,014	1,074
Other goods and services . .	706	734	963
Interest on public debt . . .	232	198	242
Subsidies and transfers . .	740	585	691
Capital expenditure	1,594	1,161	1,148
Externally financed investment	927	515	511
Domestically financed			
investment	625	630	617
Restructuring	42	16	20
COVID-19 spending	n.a.	161	52
COVID-19 vaccine procurement			
and delivery	n.a.	n.a.	20
Other expenditure	n.a.	n.a.	58
Total	**4,287**	**3,852**	**4,248**

* Excluding grants received ('000 million francs CFA): 133 in 2019; 35 in 2020 (estimate); 67 in 2021 (estimate).
† Estimates.
§ Excluding net lending ('000 million francs CFA): 51 in 2019; 42 in 2020 (estimate); −91 in 2021 (estimate).

Source: IMF, *Cameroon: Second Reviews Under The Extended Credit Facility And The Extended Fund Facility Arrangements, And Requests For Waivers For Performance Criteria Applicability And Modification Of Performance Criterion—Press Release; Staff Report; And Statement By The Executive Director For Cameroon* (August 2022).

INTERNATIONAL RESERVES
(US $ million at 31 December)

	2016	2017	2018
Gold (national valuation) . . .	34.31	38.58	38.30
IMF special drawing rights . .	20.37	21.75	21.25
Reserve position in IMF . . .	1.38	1.51	1.49
Foreign exchange	2,203.95	3,173.53	3,436.59
Total	**2,260.01**	**3,235.37**	**3,497.63**

2019: IMF special drawing rights 21.18; Reserve position in IMF 1.48.
2020: IMF special drawing rights 22.43; Reserve position in IMF 1.55.
2021: IMF special drawing rights 306.01; Reserve position in IMF 1.90.

Source: IMF, *International Financial Statistics*.

MONEY SUPPLY
('000 million francs CFA at 31 December)

	2016	2017	2018
Currency outside depository			
corporations	921.3	989.5	1,078.0
Transferable deposits	1,497.2	1,589.4	1,809.2
Other deposits	1,537.2	1,591.7	1,864.7
Broad money	**3,955.7**	**4,170.6**	**4,751.9**

Source: IMF, *International Financial Statistics*.

COST OF LIVING
(Consumer Price Index; base: 2010 = 100, preliminary)

	2018	2019	2020
Food and non-alcoholic beverages .	112.3	115.6	119.7
Clothing and footwear	108.3	111.4	114.0
Housing, water, electricity, gas and			
other fuels	114.8	116.7	120.3
All items (incl. others) . . .	**112.1**	**114.9**	**117.7**

All items (Consumer Price Index; base: 2010 = 100): 118.7 in 2019; 121.5 in 2020; 124.3 in 2021 (Source: IMF, *International Financial Statistics*).

NATIONAL ACCOUNTS
('000 million francs CFA at current prices)
Expenditure on the Gross Domestic Product

	2019	2020	2021
Government final consumption			
expenditure	2,811.6	2,898.4	3,039.6
Private final consumption			
expenditure	16,885.9	17,170.3	18,365.6
Gross capital formation . .	4,436.9	4,191.9	4,564.5
Change in inventories . . .	−35.8	−24.7	−50.7
Total domestic expenditure .	24,098.6	24,235.9	25,919.0
Exports of goods and services . .	4,613.9	3,531.2	4,371.8
Less Imports of goods and services	5,468.9	4,280.7	5,133.2
GDP in purchasers' values .	**23,243.7**	**23,486.5**	**25,157.8**

Gross Domestic Product by Economic Activity

	2019	2020	2021
Agriculture	3,905.5	4,082.4	4,419.1
Mining and quarrying . . .	915.3	593.7	856.5
Manufacturing	2,981.2	3,121.5	3,321.8
Electricity, gas and water . .	337.9	352.4	359.4
Construction	1,303.8	1,416.3	1,515.9
Wholesale and retail trade;			
repair of vehicles . . .	2,551.9	2,576.4	2,733.1
Finance and insurance . . .	509.2	549.5	587.9
Transportation	2,368.2	2,457.5	2,588.9
Hotels and restaurants . . .	1,257.0	1,227.4	1,355.3
Information and			
telecommunications . . .	483.9	507.2	541.9
Public administration and			
defence	1,290.3	1,377.0	2,540.2
Education, health and social			
services	1,044.8	1,088.1	} 2,531.5
Other services	2,355.3	2,425.8	}
Sub-total	**21,304.2**	**21,775.1**	**23,351.1**
Indirect taxes	1,939.4	1,711.3	1,806.8
GDP in purchasers' values .	**23,243.7**	**23,486.5**	**25,157.8**

Note: Totals may not be equal to the sum of components, owing to rounding.

BALANCE OF PAYMENTS
(US $ million)

	2018	2019	2020
Exports of goods	5,184.3	5,525.6	4,415.8
Imports of goods	−5,717.4	−6,262.4	−5,095.1
Balance on goods	**−533.0**	**−736.8**	**−679.4**
Exports of services	2,116.8	2,205.2	1,708.7
Imports of services	−2,705.2	−2,823.0	−2,117.3
Balance on goods and services	**−1,121.4**	**−1,354.6**	**−1,088.0**
Primary income received . .	210.5	231.5	162.4
Primary income paid	−951.9	−1,075.0	−1,000.9
Balance on goods, services and			
primary income	**−1,862.9**	**−2,198.1**	**−1,926.5**
Secondary income received . .	749.2	780.6	656.6
Secondary income paid . . .	−295.7	−277.6	−242.6
Current balance	**−1,409.3**	**−1,695.1**	**−1,512.4**
Capital account (net)	159.2	230.1	74.0
Direct investment assets . . .	−107.9	−125.9	−84.4
Direct investment liabilities . .	765.1	1,024.8	675.2
Portfolio investment assets . .	−9.8	114.0	47.1
Portfolio investment liabilities .	−25.1	—	−11.3
Financial derivatives and employee			
stock options assets (net) . .	8.9	8.4	8.9
Other investment assets . . .	−703.1	−983.4	−322.8
Other investment liabilities . .	1,761.4	1,735.2	1,024.0
Net errors and omissions . . .	−152.2	−62.9	−443.1
Reserves and related items .	**287.1**	**245.2**	**−544.9**

Source: IMF, *International Financial Statistics*.

External Trade

PRINCIPAL COMMODITIES
(US $ million)

Imports c.i.f.	2016	2017	2018
Live animals and animal products	325.4	250.9	349.4
Fish, crustaceans, molluscs and other aquatic invertebrates .	282.0	198.1	279.4
Frozen and whole fish . . .	281.2	197.0	278.5
Vegetables and vegetable products	493.8	595.8	565.0
Cereals	405.3	515.8	481.7
Wheat and meslin	153.1	178.8	208.8
Rice	242.1	316.7	259.6
Prepared foodstuffs; beverages, spirits, vinegar; tobacco and articles thereof .	243.1	293.8	292.7
Mineral products	703.9	969.2	1,522.9
Salt, sulphur, earths, stone, plastering materials . . .	170.1	226.2	195.9
Cement, incl. cement clinkers .	142.4	190.0	162.1
Mineral fuels, oils, distillation products, etc.	533.7	742.7	1,326.8
Crude petroleum oils . . .	229.2	221.5	311.3
Petroleum oils, not crude . .	216.9	434.3	852.7
Chemicals and related products	549.5	629.7	767.3
Pharmaceutical products . . .	185.4	226.9	239.4
Medicaments consisting of mixed or unmixed products . . .	164.2	194.6	206.6
Plastics, rubber, and articles thereof	243.0	239.5	268.8
Plastics and articles thereof . .	171.6	168.3	190.9
Textiles and textile articles .	152.6	149.7	172.2
Iron and steel, other base metals and articles of base metal	400.1	378.4	434.0
Iron or steel	176.7	167.5	196.6
Machinery and mechanical appliances; electrical equipment; parts thereof .	981.9	846.3	929.0
Machinery and boilers . . .	449.5	496.1	511.2
Electrical and electronic equipment	532.4	350.2	417.9
Telephone sets, incl. telephones for cellular networks . . .	246.2	104.2	109.0
Vehicles, aircraft, vessels and associated transport equipment	382.4	379.9	382.9
Vehicles other than railway, tramway	358.9	346.8	340.0
Total (incl. others)	4,898.9	5,183.6	6,133.6

Exports f.o.b.	2016	2017	2018
Vegetables and vegetable products	130.1	127.8	128.1
Edible fruit, nuts, peel of citrus fruit and melons	66.0	63.5	62.6
Bananas and plantains (fresh, dried)	65.4	62.8	61.6
Prepared foodstuffs; beverages, spirits, vinegar; tobacco and articles thereof .	826.2	580.8	604.5
Cocoa and cocoa products . .	777.4	534.3	555.7
Cocoa beans (whole, broken, raw, roasted)	669.6	403.0	420.5
Mineral products	168.6	1,428.0	1,920.3
Mineral fuels, oils, distillation products, etc.	163.9	1,418.5	1,912.8
Crude petroleum oils . . .	0.0	1,284.4	1,553.2
Non-crude petroleum oils . .	120.4	110.6	95.6
Chemicals and related products	93.2	102.5	72.1
Wood, wood charcoal, cork, and articles thereof	480.2	505.9	553.1

Exports f.o.b.—*continued*	2016	2017	2018
Wood and articles of wood and wood charcoal	480.2	505.9	553.0
Wood in the rough	152.0	196.3	218.3
Wood sawn (chipped lengthwise, sliced or peeled)	286.1	261.8	284.2
Textiles and textile articles .	153.2	171.8	212.8
Cotton	148.5	165.4	211.3
Cotton (non-carded or combed) .	147.3	164.5	210.7
Iron and steel, other base metals and articles of base metal	158.0	180.1	177.5
Aluminium and articles thereof .	122.4	139.7	132.4
Aluminium (unwrought) . .	109.9	130.1	122.0
Total (incl. others)	2,130.5	3,264.2	3,804.8

Source: Trade Map-Trade Competitiveness Map, International Trade Centre, marketanalysis.intracen.org.

PRINCIPAL TRADING PARTNERS
(US $ million)

Imports c.i.f.	2016	2017	2018
Antigua and Barbuda	17.7	59.2	0.0
Argentina	33.4	52.8	51.0
Belgium	95.6	128.0	191.7
Brazil	62.5	98.3	102.4
Canada	51.9	45.7	51.0
China, People's Republic . . .	1,046.8	892.8	1,132.5
Côte d'Ivoire	27.1	41.7	84.5
Egypt	29.3	34.0	63.8
Equatorial Guinea	52.4	23.6	28.2
France (incl. Monaco)	591.6	519.5	517.4
Germany	197.2	196.9	183.7
India	158.7	187.7	207.5
Italy	117.9	135.1	157.5
Japan	156.5	123.0	117.0
Korea, Republic	30.9	27.0	101.2
Malaysia	39.9	67.1	64.9
Mauritania	116.1	46.7	79.9
Morocco	81.8	74.3	80.9
Netherlands	91.6	120.2	296.3
Nigeria	223.0	254.6	342.2
Portugal	27.0	59.0	56.8
Russian Federation	75.9	133.0	173.9
Senegal	61.5	30.4	23.9
South Africa	74.1	68.2	96.8
Spain	192.3	215.5	156.0
Thailand	222.5	297.6	258.8
Togo	130.1	264.7	208.5
Türkiye	83.5	84.2	131.6
United Arab Emirates	46.1	60.7	75.3
United Kingdom	69.1	60.5	131.8
USA	175.4	180.6	239.0
Total (incl. others)	4,898.9	5,183.6	6,133.6

Exports f.o.b.	2016	2017	2018
Bangladesh	49.3	80.1	126.4
Belgium	198.6	175.3	135.5
Central African Republic . . .	37.6	43.7	55.7
Chad	91.8	68.3	99.9
China, People's Republic . . .	150.6	394.5	944.1
Congo, Republic	36.8	35.4	31.7
France (incl. Monaco)	164.1	343.2	265.7
Gabon	41.3	54.5	46.2
Germany	43.1	37.8	76.3
India	24.0	224.7	209.9
Indonesia	37.6	50.1	42.8
Italy	166.4	453.2	521.6
Malaysia	103.7	77.7	115.9
Netherlands	454.9	312.6	369.5

Exports f.o.b.—*continued*	2016	2017	2018
Nigeria	40.8	37.9	32.8
Portugal	12.5	112.8	8.3
Senegal	23.2	32.9	30.9
Spain	67.5	295.0	224.2
Togo	41.3	31.3	12.6
Türkiye	27.8	45.2	32.9
United Kingdom	24.1	24.9	26.3
USA	96.7	72.8	107.1
Viet Nam	83.0	100.0	116.5
Total (incl. others)	2,130.5	3,264.2	3,804.8

Source: Trade Map-Trade Competitiveness Map, International Trade Centre, marketanalysis.intracen.org.

Transport

RAILWAYS
(traffic, year ending 30 June)

	2011	2012	2013
Passengers carried ('000)	1,487.0	1,451.3	1,419.2
Passenger-km (million)	540.4	525.8	473.8
Freight carried ('000 tons)	1,543.8	1,617.2	1,664.0
Freight ton-km (million)	1,001.0	1,094.3	1,086.1

ROAD TRAFFIC
(motor vehicles in use)

	2007	2008	2009
Passenger cars	190,341	197,383	204,292
Buses and coaches	17,287	17,926	18,554
Vans and lorries	51,842	53,790	55,642
Motorcycles and mopeds	72,351	75,029	77,655

SHIPPING

Flag Registered Fleet
(at 31 December)

	2019	2020	2021
Number of vessels	117	165	198
Total displacement ('000 grt)	613.0	1,843.3	2,749.9

Source: Lloyd's List Intelligence (www.bit.ly/LLintelligence).

International Seaborne Freight Traffic
(freight traffic at Douala, '000 metric tons)

	2011	2012	2013
Goods loaded	2,257	2,652	2,550
Goods unloaded	6,385	6,990	7,836

CIVIL AVIATION
(traffic)

	2013	2014	2015
Passengers carried ('000)	287	276	267
Kilometres flown (million)	5	5	5
Passenger-kilometres (million)	293	291	282

Source: UN, *Statistical Yearbook*.

2020 (domestic and international): Departures 1,169; Passengers carried 40,884. (Source: World Bank, World Development Indicators database).

Tourism

FOREIGN VISITORS BY COUNTRY OF ORIGIN*

	2018	2019	2020
Belgium	22,814	14,230	3,052
Canada	10,222	7,574	1,542
France	53,114	53,012	13,627
Germany	14,246	15,304	3,186
Italy	10,473	11,254	1,993
Netherlands	5,992	5,595	1,354
Switzerland	8,263	7,908	1,373
United Kingdom	26,138	15,375	2,304
USA	22,652	17,627	4,191
Total (incl. others)	546,491	460,477	147,093

* Arrivals at hotels and similar establishments.

Receipts from tourism (US $ million, excl. passenger transport): 505 in 2016; 524 in 2017; 581 in 2018.

Source: World Tourism Organization.

Communications Media

	2018	2019	2020
Telephones ('000 main lines in use)	902.3	856.4	964.4
Mobile telephone subscriptions ('000)	18,455.8	21,400.7	22,350.3
Broadband subscriptions, fixed ('000)	395.8	400.9	722.6
Broadband subscriptions, mobile ('000)	4,069.9	4,831.0	10,821.6
Internet users (% of population)	29.7	33.5	37.8

Source: International Telecommunication Union.

Education

(2018/19 unless otherwise indicated)

	Institutions	Teachers	Students ('000)		
			Males	Females	Total
Pre-primary	1,371*	27,822	271.0	271.5	542.5
Primary	9,459*	96,546	2,332.4	2,067.5	4,399.9
Secondary:					
general	700*	84,234†	891.4†	838.3†	1,729.7†
technical/ vocational	324*	30,367†	302.6†	174.6†	477.2†
Universities	6‡	7,568§	154.9§	175.9§	330.8§

* 1997/98.
† 2015/16.
‡ 1996/97.
§ 2017/18.

Source: UNESCO Institute for Statistics.

Pupil-teacher ratio (primary education, UNESCO estimate): 44.8 in 2017/18 (Source: UNESCO Institute for Statistics).

Adult literacy rate (UNESCO estimates): 77.1% (males 82.6%; females 71.6%) in 2018 (Source: UNESCO Institute for Statistics).

Directory

The Constitution

In December 1995 the National Assembly formally adopted amendments to the 1972 Constitution which provided for a democratic system of government, with the establishment of an upper legislative chamber (to be known as the Senate), a Council of Supreme Judiciary Affairs, a Council of State, and a Civil Service High Authority, and restricted the power vested in the President, who was to serve a maximum of two seven-year terms. The restoration of decentralized local government areas was also envisaged. In April 2008 further amendments to the Constitution were adopted, the most notable of which was the abolition of the presidential two-term limit. The Senate was finally established in April 2013 and 10 regional councils in December 2020. The main provisions of the 1972 Constitution, as amended, are summarized below:

The Constitution declares that the human being, without distinction as to race, religion, sex or belief, possesses inalienable and sacred rights. It affirms its attachment to the fundamental freedoms embodied in the Universal Declaration of Human Rights and the United Nations Charter. The state guarantees to all citizens of either sex the rights and freedoms set out in the preamble of the Constitution.

SOVEREIGNTY

The Republic of Cameroon shall be one and indivisible, democratic, secular and dedicated to social service. It shall ensure the equality before the law of all its citizens. Provisions exist that the official languages be French and English, for the motto, flag, national anthem and seal, that the capital be Yaoundé.

Sovereignty shall be vested in the people who shall exercise it either through the President of the Republic and the members returned by it to the National Assembly or by means of referendum. Elections are by universal suffrage, direct or indirect, by every citizen aged 21 years or over in a secret ballot. Political parties or groups may take part in elections subject to the law and the principles of democracy and of national sovereignty and unity.

State authority shall be exercised by the President of the Republic and the National Assembly.

THE PRESIDENT OF THE REPUBLIC

The President of the Republic, as head of state and head of the government, shall be responsible for the conduct of the affairs of the Republic. He or she shall define national policy and may charge the members of the Government with the implementation of this policy in certain spheres.

Candidates for the office of President must hold civic and political rights, be at least 35 years old and have resided in Cameroon for a minimum of 12 consecutive months, and may not hold any other elective office or professional activity. The President is elected for seven years, by a majority of votes cast by the people; there is no limit on the number of terms that may be served. Provisions are made for the continuity of office in the case of the President's resignation.

The Ministers and Vice-Ministers are appointed by the President to whom they are responsible, and they may hold no other appointment. The President is also head of the armed forces, he or she negotiates and ratifies treaties, may exercise clemency after consultation with the Higher Judicial Council, promulgates and is responsible for the enforcement of laws, is responsible for internal and external security, makes civil and military appointments, and provides for necessary administrative services.

The President, by reference to the Supreme Court, ensures that all laws passed are constitutional.

Provisions exist whereby the President may declare a state of emergency or state of siege.

THE NATIONAL ASSEMBLY

The National Assembly shall be renewed every five years, although it may at the instance of the President of the Republic legislate to extend or shorten its term of office. It shall be composed of 180 members elected by universal suffrage.

Laws shall normally be passed by a simple majority of those present, but if a bill is read a second time at the request of the President of the Republic a majority of the National Assembly as a whole is required.

The National Assembly shall meet twice a year, each session to last not more than 30 days; in one session it shall approve the budget. It may be recalled to an extraordinary session of not more than 15 days.

THE SENATE

Senators shall serve a term of five years. Each region shall be represented in the Senate by 10 senators, of whom seven shall be elected by indirect universal suffrage on a regional basis and three appointed by the President of the Republic

Laws shall be passed by a simple majority of the senators. The Senate may amend or reject all or part of a bill submitted to it for consideration.

RELATIONS BETWEEN THE EXECUTIVE AND THE LEGISLATURE

Bills may be introduced either by the President of the Republic or by any member of the National Assembly.

Reserved to the legislature are the fundamental rights and duties of the citizen; the law of persons and property; the political, administrative and judicial system in respect of elections to the National Assembly; general regulation of national defence; authorization of penalties and criminal and civil procedure, etc.; the organization of the local authorities; currency, the budget, dues and taxes, legislation on public property; economic and social policy; and the education system.

The National Assembly may empower the President of the Republic to legislate by way of ordinance for a limited period and for given purposes.

Other matters of procedure include: the right of the President of the Republic to address the Assembly, and of the Ministers and Vice-Ministers to take part in debates; and the right of the National Assembly to inquire into governmental activity and to question the responsibility of the Government through a motion of censure.

The President of the Republic shall promulgate laws passed by the legislature (unless he or she requests a second reading or refers the matter to the Constitutional Council). The promulgated legislation shall then be published in the Official Gazette of the Republic in both English and French.

Provisions exist whereby the President of the Republic, after consultation with the National Assembly, may submit to referendum certain reform bills liable to have profound repercussions on the future of the nation and national institutions.

THE REGIONAL COUNCILS

Each of the country's 10 regions has a bicameral regional council (with limited powers over local economic, educational, social, health, cultural and sports issues), which is elected for a five-year term. Each regional council comprises a chamber of 70 regional councillors (elected by municipal councillors) and a chamber of 20 representatives of traditional rulers (elected by their peers), and elects from among its members a regional president and a regional bureau. The country's President has the power to suspend or dissolve a regional council if deemed necessary.

THE JUDICIARY

Justice is administered in the name of the people. The President of the Republic shall ensure the independence of the judiciary and shall make appointments with the assistance of the Higher Judicial Council.

THE SUPREME COURT

The Supreme Court has powers to uphold the Constitution in such cases as the death or incapacity of the President and the admissibility of laws, to give final judgments on appeals on the Judgment of the Court of Appeal and to decide complaints against administrative acts. It may be assisted by experts appointed by the President of the Republic.

IMPEACHMENT

There shall be a Court of Impeachment with jurisdiction to try the President of the Republic for high treason and the Ministers and Vice-Ministers for conspiracy against the security of the state.

THE ECONOMIC AND SOCIAL COUNCIL

There shall be an Economic and Social Council, regulated by the law.

AMENDMENT OF THE CONSTITUTION

Bills to amend the Constitution may be introduced by either the President of the Republic or the National Assembly. The President may decide to submit any amendment to the people by way of a referendum. No procedure to amend the Constitution may be accepted if it is liable to impair the republican character, unity or territorial integrity of the state, or the democratic principles by which the Republic is governed.

The Government

HEAD OF STATE

President: Paul Biya (took office 6 November 1982; elected 14 January 1984; re-elected 24 April 1988, 11 October 1992, 12 October 1997, 11 October 2004, 9 October 2011 and 7 October 2018).

CABINET

(October 2022)

Prime Minister: Dr Joseph Dion Ngute.

Ministers of State

Minister of State, Minister of Tourism and Leisure: Bello Bouba Maïgari.

Minister of State, Minister of Justice and Keeper of the Seals: Laurent Esso.

Minister of State, Minister of Higher Education: Jacques Fame Ndongo.

Minister of State, Secretary-General at the Presidency: Ferdinand Ngoh Ngoh.

Ministers

Minister of Territorial Administration: Paul Atanga Nji.

Minister of Decentralization and Local Development: Géorges Elanga Obam.

Minister of Social Affairs: Pauline Irène Nguene.

Minister of Agriculture and Rural Development: Gabriel Mbairobe.

Minister of Arts and Culture: Pierre Ismaël Bidoung Kpwatt.

Minister of Trade: Luc Magloire Mbarga Atangana.

Minister of Communication: René Emmanuel Sadi.

Minister of State Property and Land Tenure: Henry Eyebe Ayissi.

Minister of Water and Energy: Gaston Eloundou Essomba.

Minister of the Economy, Planning and Land Settlement: Alamine Ousmane Mey.

Minister of Basic Education: Laurent Serge Etoundi Ngoa.

Minister of Livestock, Fisheries and Animal Industries: Dr Taïga.

Minister of Employment and Vocational Training: Bakary Issa Tchiroma.

Minister of Secondary Education: Pauline Egbe Nalova Lyongha.

Minister of the Environment, the Protection of Nature and Sustainable Development: Pierre Hélé.

Minister of Finance: Louis Paul Motaze.

Minister of Public Service and Administrative Reform: Joseph Le.

Minister of Forests and Wildlife: Jules Doret Ndongo.

Minister of Housing and Urban Development: Célestine Courtes.

Minister of Youth and Civic Education: Mounouna Foutsou.

Minister of Mines, Industry and Technological Development: Gabriel Dodo Ndoke.

Minister of Small and Medium-sized Enterprises, Social Economy and Handicrafts: Achille Bassilekin, III.

Minister of Posts and Telecommunications: Minette Libom Li Likeng.

Minister of Women's Affairs and the Family: Marie Thérése Abena Ondua.

Minister of Scientific Research and Innovation: Madeleine Tchuinte.

Minister of External Relations: Lejeune Mbella Mbella.

Minister of Public Health: Malachie Manaouda.

Minister of Sports and Physical Education: Narcisse Mouelle Kombi.

Minister of Transport: Jean Ernest Massena Ngalle Bibehe.

Minister of Labour and Social Security: Grégoire Owona.

Minister of Public Works: Emmanuel Nganou Djoumessi.

Ministers, Deputy Secretaries-General at the Presidency: Paul Che Elung, Mohamadou Moustapha.

Ministers-delegate

Minister-delegate at the Presidency, in charge of Defence: Joseph Beti Assomo.

Minister-delegate at the Presidency, in charge of the Contrôle Superieur de l'État: Rose Ngwari Mbah Acha.

Minister-delegate at the Presidency, in charge of Public Contracts: Ibrahim Talba Malla.

Minister-delegate at the Presidency, in charge of Relations with Parliament: Bolvine Wakata.

Minister-delegate at the Ministry of Agriculture and Rural Development: Clémentine Antoinette Ananga Messina.

Minister-delegate at the Ministry of the Environment, the Protection of Nature and Sustainable Development: Nana Aboubakar Djalloh.

Minister-delegate at the Ministry of Finance: Yaouba Abdoulaye.

Minister-delegate at the Ministry of Justice: Jean de Dieu Momo.

Minister-delegate at the Ministry of External Relations, in charge of Relations with the Commonwealth: Félix Mbayu.

Minister-delegate at the Ministry of External Relations, in charge of Relations with the Islamic World: Adoum Gargoum.

Minister-delegate at the Ministry of the Economy, Planning and Land Settlement, in charge of Planning: Paul Tasong Njukang.

Minister-delegate at the Ministry of Transport: Njoya Zakariaou.

Secretaries of State

Secretary of State for Defence, in charge of the National Gendarmerie: Galax Yves Landry Etoga.

Secretary of State for Defence, in charge of Former Combatants and War Victims: Koumpa Issa.

Secretary of State for Basic Education: Vivian Asheri Kilo.

Secretary of State for Secondary Education, in charge of Teacher Training: Boniface Bayaola.

Secretary of State for Justice, in charge of Penitentiary Administration: Jérôme Penbaga Dooh.

Secretary of State for Industry, Mines and Technological Development: Calistus Gentry Fuh.

Secretary of State for Public Health, in charge of the Fight against Epidemics and Pandemics: (vacant).

Secretary of State for Public Works, in charge of Roads: Armand Ndjodom.

Secretary of State for Housing and Urban Development: Marie Rose Dibong.

Secretary of State for Forests and Wildlife: Boukar Koulsoumi.

Other Officials with the Rank of Minister

Ministers, Chargés de Mission at the Presidency: Phillippe Mbarga Mboa, Benoît Ndong Soumhet, Paul Mingo Ghoghomu, Hamadou Moustapha, Victor Arrey-Nkongho Mengot.

Secretary-General at the Office of the Prime Minister: Séraphin Magloire Fouda.

Deputy Secretary-General at the Office of the Prime Minister: Pascal Nguihé Kanté.

Deputy Directors of the Civil Cabinet at the Presidency: Samuel Mvondo Ayolo, Oswald Baboke.

Delegate-General for National Security: Martin Mbarga Nguélé.

MINISTRIES

Office of the President: Palais de l'Unité, Yaoundé; tel. 222-23-40-25; e-mail cellcom@prc.cm; internet www.prc.cm.

Office of the Prime Minister: Yaoundé; tel. 222-23-80-05; e-mail spm@spm.gov.cm; internet www.spm.gov.cm.

Ministry of Agriculture and Rural Development: Quartier Administratif, Yaoundé; tel. 222-22-97-02; e-mail sg.celtique@minader.cm; internet www.minader.cm.

Ministry of Arts and Culture: Quartier Hippodrome, BP 1053, Yaoundé; tel. 658922483; e-mail info@minac.cm; internet minac.cm.

Ministry of Basic Education: Quartier Administratif, Yaoundé; tel. 222-23-40-50; internet www.minedub.cm.

Ministry of Communication: Quartier Hippodrome, Yaoundé; tel. 222-23-34-67; internet www.mincom.gov.cm.

Ministry of Decentralization and Local Development: Yaoundé; tel. 222-21-39-92; e-mail contact@minddevel.gov.cm; internet www.minddevel.gov.cm.

Ministry of Defence: Quartier Général, Yaoundé; tel. 222-23-40-55; internet fb.com/mindefcm.

Ministry of the Economy, Planning and Land Settlement: Yaoundé; internet www.minepat.gov.cm/index.php?lang=fr.

Ministry of Employment and Vocational Training: Yaoundé; tel. 222-22-01-86; internet www.minefop.gov.cm.

Ministry of the Environment, the Protection of Nature and Sustainable Development: blvd du 20 Mai, Immeuble Ministériel 2, BP 320, Yaoundé; tel. 222-23-34-23; e-mail celcomminep@yahoo.fr; internet www.minep.gov.cm.

Ministry of External Relations: 703 rue 1025, BP 18, Yaoundé; tel. 222-20-30-27; e-mail contact@diplocam.cm; internet diplocam.cm.

Ministry of Finance: BP 13750, Quartier Administratif, Yaoundé; tel. 677232099; internet www.minfi.gov.cm.

Ministry of Forests and Wildlife: BP 1341, Yaoundé; tel. 222-20-42-58; internet www.minfof.cm.

Ministry of Higher Education: BP 1739, Yaoundé; tel. 222-22-67-16; e-mail contact@minesec.cm; internet www.minesec.gov.cm/en/accueil.

Ministry of Housing and Urban Development: Yaoundé; tel. 222-23-22-82; internet www.minhdu.gov.cm.

Ministry of Justice: Quartier Administratif, Yaoundé; tel. 222-23-42-92; e-mail jpouloumou@yahoo.fr; internet minjustice.gov.cm.

Ministry of Labour and Social Security: Yaoundé; tel. 222-23-00-04; e-mail cabinetmintss@yahoo.fr; internet www.mintss.gov.cm.

Ministry of Livestock, Fisheries and Animal Industries: Yaoundé; tel. 222-23-52-47; e-mail mboudgara@yahoo.fr; tel. www.minepia.gov.cm.

Ministry of Mines, Industry and Technological Development: Quartier Administratif, BP 955, Yaoundé; tel. 222-23-34-04; e-mail infos@minmidt.cm; internet fb.com/minmidt.gov.cm.

Ministry of Posts and Telecommunications: Quartier Administratif, Yaoundé; tel. 222-23-06-15; e-mail contact@minpostel.gov.cm; internet www.minpostel.gov.cm.

Ministry of Public Health: Quartier Administratif, Yaoundé; tel. 222-22-02-33; internet www.minsante.gov.cm.

Ministry of Public Service and Administrative Reform: Yaoundé; tel. 222-22-03-56; e-mail webmaster@minfopra.gov.cm; internet www.minfopra.gov.cm.

Ministry of Public Works: BP15406, Yaoundé; tel. 222-22-19-18; internet www.mintp.cm.

Ministry of Scientific Research and Innovation: Yaoundé; tel. 222-22-13-34; internet www.minresi.net.

Ministry of Secondary Education: BP 16185, Yaoundé; tel. 222-22-67-16; e-mail contact@minesec.cm; internet www.minesec.cm.

Ministry of Small and Medium-sized Enterprises, Social Economy and Handicrafts: BP 6096, Yaoundé; tel. 222-22-45-28; internet www.minpmeesa.gov.cm.

Ministry of Social Affairs: Quartier Administratif, Yaoundé; tel. 222-22-29-58; e-mail infos@minas.cm; internet www.minas.cm.

Ministry of Sports and Physical Education: POB 1016, Yaoundé; tel. 222-23-12-01; e-mail minsepinfos@yahoo.fr; internet www.minsep.cm.

Ministry of State Property and Land Tenure: Yaoundé; internet www.mindaf.gov.cm.

Ministry of Territorial Administration: Quartier Administratif, Yaoundé; tel. 222-23-45-46; e-mail minatdcm@minat.cm; internet www.minat.gov.cm.

Ministry of Tourism and Leisure: BP 266, Yaoundé; tel. 222-22-44-11; e-mail mintour@camnet.cm; internet www.mintour.gov.cm.

Ministry of Trade: Immeuble Rose, BP 27, Yaoundé; tel. 222-23-02-16; internet www.mincommerce.gov.cm.

Ministry of Transport: Quartier Administratif, Yaoundé; tel. 222-22-87-09; e-mail minetatcam@gmail.com; internet www.mint.gov.cm.

Ministry of Water and Energy: Quartier Administratif, BP 70, Yaoundé; tel. 222-22-34-00; e-mail courrierminee@yahoo.fr; internet www.minee.cm.

Ministry of Women's Affairs and the Family: Quartier du Lac, Yaoundé; tel. 222-23-25-50; e-mail cab_minproff@yahoo.fr; internet www.minproff.cm.

Ministry of Youth and Civic Education: rue Albert Ateba Ebe, Yaoundé; tel. 222-20-35-64; internet www.minjec.gov.cm.

President

Election, 7 October 2018

Candidate	Votes	% of votes
Paul Biya (RDPC)	2,461,733	70.75
Maurice Kamto (MRC)	498,536	14.33
Cabral Libii Li Ngué (UNIVERS)	218,834	6.29
Joshua Oshi (SDF)	110,449	3.17
Adamou Ndam Njoya (UDC)	59,884	1.72
Garga Haman Adji (ADD)	55,971	1.61
Serge Espoir Matomba (PURS)	34,106	0.98
Franklin Afanwi Ndifor (MCNC)	23,298	0.67
Akere Tabeng Muna (FPD)	16,753	0.48
Total	**3,479,564***	**100.00**

* In addition, there were 61,553 invalid votes.

Legislature

SENATE

Senate: Immeuble ARMP, Dragage, BP 20, Yaoundé; internet www.senat.cm.

President: Marcel Niat Njifenji.

Election, 25 March 2018

Party	Seats
RDPC	63
SDF	7
Total	**70***

* In addition to the 70 elected senators, a further 30 senators are appointed by the President of the Republic of Cameroon.

NATIONAL ASSEMBLY

National Assembly: Yaoundé; tel. 222-22-04-84; e-mail contact@assnat.cm; internet www.assnat.cm.

President: Cavaye Yéguié Djibril.

General Election, 9 February 2020

Party	Seats
RDPC	139
UNDP	7
SDF	5
PCRN	5
UDC	4
FSNC	3
MDR	2
UMS	2
Total	**167***

* Elections in 11 constituencies, which would have returned 13 deputies, were postponed or annulled, owing to ongoing violent protests and electoral irregularities. These were held on 22 March, and on 7 April the Constitutional Court announced that all 13 seats had been won by the RDPC, bringing that party's total to 152 seats.

Election Commission

Elections Cameroon (ELECAM): BP 13506, Yaoundé; tel. 222-21-25-52; e-mail elecam@elecam.cm; internet www.elecam.cm; f. 2006 to replace Observatoire National des Élections/National Elections Observatory; 12 mems appointed by the head of state in consultation with political parties represented in the National Assembly and civil society; Pres. Abrams Enow Egbe; Dir-Gen. Dr Erik Essousse.

Political Organizations

In 2021 there were some 328 political parties registered with the Ministry of Territorial Administration.

Action for Meritocracy and Equal Opportunity Party (AMEC): BP 20354, Yaoundé; tel. 699919154; e-mail Tabijoachim@yahoo.fr; Leader Joachim Tabi Owono.

Alliance pour la Démocratie et le Développement (ADD): BP 231, Garoua; Sec.-Gen. Garga Haman Adji.

Alliance des Forces Progressistes (AFP): BP 4724, Douala; tel. 661734412; internet www.afpparty.org; f. 2002; Leader ALICE SADIO.

Alliance Nationale pour la Démocratie et le Progrès (ANDP): BP 5019, Yaoundé; tel. 222-20-98-98; Pres. HAMADOU MOUSTAPHA.

Cameroon National Democratic Party (CNDP): Penn Pan Pacific Hotel, Bamenda; f. 2015; Pres. Prof. GEORGE PENN MULUH.

Front pour le Salut National du Cameroun (FSNC): Yaoundé; internet   fb.com/ Front-Pour-Salut-National-Du-Cameroun-422017905301542; f. 2007; Pres. ISSA TCHIROMA BAKARY.

Mouvement Africain pour la Nouvelle Indépendance et la Démocratie (MANIDEM): BP 10298, Douala; tel. 233-42-00-76; f. 1995; fmrly a faction of the UPC; Leader DIEUDONNÉ YEBGA.

Mouvement pour la Défense de la République (MDR): BP 6438, Yaoundé; tel. 222-20-89-82; f. 1991; Leader DAKOLE DAÏSSALA.

Mouvement des Démocrates Camerounais pour la Paix (MDCP): BP 3274, Yaoundé; tel. 222-20-81-73; f. 2000; Leader GAMEL ADAMOU ISSA.

Mouvement pour la Démocratie et le Progrès (MDP): BP 8379, Douala; tel. 222-39-11-74; f. 1992; Pres. ARON MUKURI MAKA; Sec.-Gen. RENÉ MBANDA MANDENGUE.

Mouvement pour la Libération et le Développement du Cameroun (MLDC): BP 886, Edéa; tel. 233-46-44-31; f. 1998 by a breakaway faction of the MLJC; Leader MARCEL YONDO.

Mouvement Patriotique pour le Changement du Cameroun (MPCC): BP 4988, Douala; tel. 698-34-93-56; e-mail jbgwet@yahoo .fr; internet mpcc.be; f. 2008; Pres. JEAN BLAISE GWET.

Mouvement Progressiste (MP): BP 2500, Douala; tel. 699872513; e-mail djombyves@yahoo.fr; f. 1991; Pres. JEAN JACQUES EKINDI.

Mouvement pour la Renaissance du Cameroun (MRC): BP 8704, Yaoundé; tel. 222-19-80-65; internet www.mrcparty.org; Pres. Prof. MAURICE KAMTO.

Nouvelle Force Populaire (NFP): BP 1139, Douala; f. 2002; Leader LÉANDRE DJINO.

Parti Camerounais pour la Réconciliation Nationale (PCRN): Immeuble Bayiga Center, Nkoldongo Carrefour IPTEC, BP 35425, Yaoundé; tel. 678166516; internet www.pcrnparty.org; Pres. CABRAL LIBII.

Parti des Démocrates Camerounais (PDC): Nlongkak, BP 4070, Yaoundé; tel. 699615297; e-mail contact@pdc-cpd.org; internet www .pdc-cpd.org/fr; f. 1991; Leader LOUIS-TOBIE MBIDA; Sec.-Gen. ARNOLD ALBERT MBITI.

Popular Action Party (PAP): Bomaka; tel. 678358029; internet fb .com/popularactionpartyPAP; founded as People's Action Party; adopted present name in 2016; Nat. Pres. AYAH PAUL ABINE.

Rassemblement Démocratique du Peuple Camerounais (RDPC): Palais des Congrès, 2e étage, BP 867, Yaoundé; tel. 222-21-24-17; internet www.rdpcpdm.cm; f. 1966 as Union Nationale Camerounaise by merger of the Union Camerounaise, the Kamerun National Democratic Party and four opposition parties; adopted present name in 1985; sole legal party 1972–90; Pres. PAUL BIYA; Sec.-Gen. JEAN NKUETE.

Social Democratic Front (SDF): BP 490, Mankon, Bamenda; tel. 233-36-39-49; e-mail webmaster@sdfparty.org; internet www .sdfcameroon.org; f. 1990; Chair. NI JOHN FRU NDI; Sec.-Gen. JEAN TSOMELOU.

Southern Cameroons National Council (SCNC): BP 131, Eyumojock; tel. 677964888; f. 1995; supports the establishment of an independent republic in anglophone Cameroon; Chair. PAUL ABINE AYAH.

Union Démocratique du Cameroun (UDC): Immeuble Njoya Arouna, Monté Ane Rouge, 219 ave de l'Indépendance, BP 1638, Yaoundé; tel. 222-22-95-45; e-mail secretary@udc-party.com; internet www.udc-party.com; f. 1991; Leader PATRICIA TOMAÏNO NDAM NJOYA.

Union des Forces Démocratiques du Cameroun (UFDC): BP 7190, Yaoundé; tel. 222-23-16-44; f. 1991; Leader VICTORIN HAMENI BIELEU.

Union des Mouvements Socialistes (UMS): internet fb.com/ UMS-Union-Des-Mouvements-Socialistes-572321423135416; f. 2011; Leader PIERRE KWEMO.

Union Nationale pour la Démocratie et le Progrès (UNDP): BP 656, Douala; tel. 222-20-98-98; f. 1991; split in 1995; Chair. BELLO BOUBA MAÏGARI; Sec.-Gen. PIERRE FLAMBEAU NGAYAP.

Union des Populations du Cameroun (UPC): BP 2860, Yaoundé; tel. 676776794; e-mail akhaneton1@gmail.com; internet fb.com/UPC .Cameroun.Afrique; f. 1948; Sec.-Gen. BAPOOH LIPOT ROBERT.

Diplomatic Representation

EMBASSIES AND HIGH COMMISSIONS IN CAMEROON

Algeria: 433 rue 1828, Quartier Bastos, BP 1619, Yaoundé; tel. 222-21-53-51; e-mail ambalgcmr@gmail.com; internet www .ambassade-algerie-cameroun.org; Ambassador BOUMEDIENE MAHI (designate).

Belgium: Quartier Nouveau Bastos, rue 1792, BP 816, Yaoundé; tel. 222-21-52-91; e-mail yaounde@diplobel.fed.be; internet cameroon .diplomatie.belgium.be; Ambassador ERIC JACQUEMIN.

Brazil: rue 1828, Quartier Bastos, BP 16227, Yaoundé; tel. 222-20-10-85; e-mail brasemb.iaunde@itamaraty.gov.br; internet www.gov .br/mre/pt-br/embaixada-iaunde; Ambassador (vacant).

Canada: Edifice les Colonnades, Nouveau Bastos, rue 1792, BP 572, Yaoundé; tel. 222-50-39-00; e-mail yunde@international.gc.ca; internet   www.canadainternational.gc.ca/cameroon-cameroun; High Commissioner RICHARD BALE.

Central African Republic: 41 rue 1863, Quartier Bastos, Montée du Carrefour de la Vallée Nlongkak, BP 396, Yaoundé; tel. 222-20-51-55; e-mail rcaambassade@yahoo.fr; Ambassador (vacant).

Chad: Quartier Bastos, BP 506, Yaoundé; tel. 222-21-06-24; e-mail ambatchad_yaounde@yahoo.fr;   internet   fb.com/ ambassadedutchadaucameroun; Ambassador DJIDDI BICHARA HASSAN.

China, People's Republic: Nouveau Bastos, BP 1307, Yaoundé; tel. 222-21-00-83; e-mail chinaemb_cm@mfa.gov.cn; internet cm .china-embassy.gov.cn; Ambassador WANG YINGWU.

Congo, Democratic Republic: 540 blvd de l'URSS, BP 632, Yaoundé; tel. 222-20-51-03; e-mail missionrdcyaounde@gmail.com; Chargé d'affaires a.i. FRANÇOIS LUAMBO.

Congo, Republic: 86 rue 1975, Quartier Bastos, BP 1422, Yaoundé; tel. 222-21-17-33; e-mail ambacongo-cameroun@outlook.com; Ambassador DANIEL NGASSIKI.

Côte d'Ivoire: rue 1983, Résidence 140, Quartier Bastos, BP 1715, Yaoundé; tel. 222-21-32-91; e-mail ambacicam@yahoo.fr; internet cameroun.diplomatie.gouv.ci; Ambassador MANLAN NARCISSE AHOUNOU.

Egypt: 718 rue 1828, Quartier Bastos, BP 809, Yaoundé; tel. 222-20-39-22; e-mail egypt.cameroun@yahoo.fr; Ambassador DALIA FAYEZ FARAG GHUBRIAL.

Equatorial Guinea: 82 rue 1851, Quartier Bastos, BP 277, Yaoundé; tel. 222-21-08-04; Ambassador ARMANDO KOTE ECHUACA.

France: Plateau Atémengué, BP 1631, Yaoundé; tel. 222-22-79-00; e-mail chancellerie.yaounde-amba@diplomatie.gouv.fr; internet cm .ambafrance.org; Ambassador THIERRY MARCHAND (designate).

Gabon: Quartier Bastos, Ekoudou, BP 4130, Yaoundé; tel. 222-20-29-66; e-mail ambaga.cameroun@diplomatie.gouv.ga; High Commissioner PAUL PATRICK BIFFOT.

Germany: Nouvelle Route Bastos, Bastos-Usine, BP 1160, Yaoundé; tel. 222-21-00-56; e-mail info@jaun.diplo.de; internet jaunde.diplo .de; Ambassador Dr CORINNA FRICKE.

Holy See: rue du Vatican, BP 210, Yaoundé; tel. 222-20-04-75; e-mail nuntius.cam@gmail.com; Apostolic Nuncio JULIO MURAT (Titular Archbishop of Orange).

India: rue 1813, Mini Prix Bastos, Yaoundé; tel. 672229274; e-mail hoc.yaounde@mea.gov.in; internet hciyaounde.gov.in; High Commissioner ANINDYA BANERJEE (designate).

Israel: 154 rue du Club Olympique à Bastos, Longkak, BP 5934, Yaoundé; tel. 222-20-16-91; e-mail info@yaounde.mfa.gov.il; internet embassies.gov.il/yaounde/Pages/default.aspx; Ambassador ISI YANOUKA.

Italy: ave Rosa Parks, Quartier Golf, BP 827, Yaoundé; tel. 697185585; e-mail ambasciata.yaounde@esteri.it; internet ambyaounde.esteri.it; Ambassador FILIPPO SCAMMACCA DEL MURGO.

Japan: 1513 rue 1828, Quartier Bastos, Ekoudou, BP 6868, Yaoundé; tel. 222-20-62-02; e-mail info@yd.mofa.go.jp; internet www.cmr.emb-japan.go.jp; Ambassador TAKAOKA NOZOMU.

Korea, Democratic People's Republic: BP 735, Yaoundé; tel. 222-23-30-81; Ambassador KIM RYONG YONG.

Korea, Republic: ave Rosa Parks, BP 13286, Yaoundé; tel. 222-20-37-56; e-mail cameroon@mofa.go.kr; internet overseas.mofa.go.kr/ cm-ko/index.do; Ambassador KIM JONG-HAN.

Liberia: Quartier Bastos BP 1185, Yaoundé; e-mail libemyaounde .gov60@yahoo.com; Chargé d'affaires a.i. DAN S. TOBY.

Libya: Quartier Bastos, BP 1980, Yaoundé; tel. 222-20-41-38; e-mail lyecm@yahoo.fr; Chargé d'affaires a.i. IBRAHIM O. AMAMI.

Morocco: 32 rue 1793, Quartier Bastos, BP 1629, Yaoundé; tel. 222-20-50-92; e-mail ambmaroccam@yahoo.fr; Ambassador MUSTAPHA BOUH.

Niger: derrière Usine Bastos, rue 1768, BP 13801, Yaoundé; tel. 222-21-89-67; e-mail ambanigercmr222@yahoo.com; Ambassador ABDOU SALIFOU.

Nigeria: Quartier Bastos, BP 448, Yaoundé; tel. 222-22-34-55; e-mail nhc_yde@yahoo.com; High Commissioner Gen. ABAYOMI GABRIEL OLONISAKIN.

Russian Federation: blvd de l'URSS, Quartier Bastos, BP 488, Yaoundé; tel. 222-20-17-14; e-mail russie.ambassade@mail.ru; internet cameroun.mid.ru; Ambassador ANATOLY G. BASHKIN.

Saudi Arabia: rue 1951, Quartier Bastos, BP 1602, Yaoundé; tel. 222-21-26-75; internet embassies.mofa.gov.sa/sites/cameroon/ar/pages/default.aspx; Ambassador ABDUL ILAH BIN MOHAMMED AL-SHUAIBI.

Senegal: face à l'Hôtel Meumi Palace, Quartier Bastos, BP 4494, Yaoundé; tel. 222-20-90-61; Ambassador KHARE DIOUF.

South Africa: rue 1801, Quartier Bastos, BP 1636, Yaoundé; tel. 222-20-04-38; e-mail yaounde.political@dirco.gov.za; High Commissioner (vacant).

Spain: blvd de l'URSS, Quartier Bastos, BP 877, Yaoundé; tel. 222-20-35-43; e-mail emb.yaunde@maec.es; internet www.exteriores.gob.es/embajadas/yaunde; Ambassador IGNACIO RAFAEL GARCIA LUMBRERAS.

Sudan: rue 6060, Bâtiment 401, derrière Foire Tsinga, BP 15159, Yaoundé; tel. 222-21-93-02; Chargé d'affaires a.i. ABDALLAH ABAKAR SALEH NUBA.

Switzerland: angle rues 1811 et 1814, Quartier Bastos, BP 1169, Yaoundé; tel. 222-20-50-67; e-mail yaounde@eda.admin.ch; internet www.eda.admin.ch/yaounde; Ambassador MARTIN STRUB.

Tunisia: rue de Rotary, Quartier Bastos, BP 6074, Yaoundé; tel. 222-20-33-68; internet www.diplomatie.gov.tn/nc/mission/etranger/ambassade-de-tunisie-a-yaounde-cameroun; Ambassador MOHAMED KARIM BEN BÉCHER.

Türkiye (Turkey): 1782 blvd de l'URSS, Quartier Bastos, BP 35155, Yaoundé; tel. 222-20-67-77; internet yaounde.be.mfa.gov.tr; Ambassador VOLKAN IŞIKÇI.

United Kingdom: ave Winston Churchill, BP 547, Yaoundé; tel. 222-22-07-96; e-mail bhc.yaounde@fco.gov.uk; internet www.gov.uk/world/organisations/british-high-commission-yaounde; High Commissioner Dr CHRISTIAN DENNYS-MCCLURE.

USA: ave Rosa Parks, BP 817, Yaoundé; tel. 222-20-15-00; internet cm.usembassy.gov; Ambassador CHRISTOPHER LAMORA.

Judicial System

The independence of the judiciary is enshrined in the Constitution and judicial power is exercised by the Supreme Court, courts of appeal and tribunals. The President of the Republic guarantees the independence of the judicial power and appoints members of the bench and of the legal department. He or she is assisted in this task by the Higher Judicial Council (HJC), which gives him or her its opinion on all nominations for the bench and on disciplinary action against judicial and legal officers. The HJC is composed of six members who serve five-year terms. Justice is rendered in Cameroon by: courts of first instance; high courts; military courts; courts of appeal and the Supreme Court. In 2012 a Special Criminal Court was established in Yaoundé; the new court was to conduct trials relating to the embezzlement of public funds.

Supreme Court: Yaoundé; tel. 222-22-01-64; consists of a president, 9 titular and substitute judges, a procureur général, an avocat général, deputies to the procureur général, a registrar and clerks; Pres. DANIEL MEKOBE SONE.

Constitutional Council: Yaoundé; f. 2018; 11 mems; Pres. CLÉMENT ATANGANA.

Attorney-General: LUC NDJODO.

Religion

CHRISTIANITY

The Anglican Communion

The diocese (Region Missionaire) of Cameroon, forms part of the Church of the Province of West Africa (CPWA). In September 2012 the CPWA was subdivided into two internal provinces: the Internal Province of Ghana, comprising the 10 (now 11) dioceses in Ghana, and the Internal Province of West Africa, comprising the remaining five (now six) dioceses. The Archbishop of the CPWA is the Bishop of Liberia.

Bishop of Cameroon: Rt Rev. DIBO THOMAS BABYNGTON ELANGO, BP 15705, Douala; tel. 233-07-18-38; e-mail camangdiocese@yahoo.com; internet www.anglicandioceseofcameroon.org.

Other Protestant Churches

Conseil des Eglises Protestantes du Cameroun (CEPCA): BP 491, Yaoundé; tel. 694838334; e-mail generalngandocepca18@gmail.com; internet www.cepca-cpcc.org; f. 1968; name changed as above in 2005; 12 mem. churches; Pres. Rev. SAMUEL FORBA FONKI; Sec.-Gen. Rev. Dr PAUL NGANDO MBENDE.

Church of the Lutheran Brethren of Cameroon: POB 16, Garoua; tel. 622-27-25-73; e-mail eflcsynode@yahoo.fr; Pres. Rev. ALVIUS DEBSIA DABAH.

Eglise Evangélique du Cameroun (Evangelical Church of Cameroon—EEC): 13 rue Alfred Saker, Akwa, Centenaire, BP 89, Douala; tel. 233-42-36-11; f. 1957; 2m. mems; Pres. Rev. ISAAC BATOMEN HENGA; Sec. Rev. JEAN SAMUEL HENDJE TOYA.

Eglise Presbytérienne Camerounaise (Presbyterian Church of Cameroon): BP 519, Yaoundé; tel. 233-32-42-36; e-mail ondjiitoung@yahoo.fr; internet www.eglisepresbyteriennecamerounaise.com; independent since 1957; comprises 8 synods and 38 presbyteries; Moderator Rev. MARC BERTRAND ATANGAN.

Eglise Protestante Africaine (African Protestant Church): BP 26, Lolodorf; e-mail epasecretariat@gmail.com; f. 1934; Pres. Rev. FRANÇOIS PUASSE.

Evangelical Lutheran Church of Cameroon: POB 6, Ngaoundéré-Adamaoua; tel. 222-25-20-66; e-mail evequenational_eelc@yahoo.fr; Pres. Rev. Dr THOMAS NYIWE.

Presbyterian Church in Cameroon: BP 19, Buéa; tel. 233-32-24-87; e-mail pcc_modoffice19@yahoo.com; 1.8m. mems; 302 ministers; Moderator Rt Rev. FONKI SAMUEL FORBA.

Union des Eglises Baptistes du Cameroun (Union of Baptist Churches of Cameroon): New Bell, BP 6007, Douala; tel. 696577740; e-mail r.ziloua@gmail.com; autonomous since 1957; Pres. Dr JEAN PAUL EKOULE MAKA; Gen. Sec. Rev. RAPHAËL ZILOUA.

Other Protestant churches active in Cameroon include the Cameroon Baptist Church, the Cameroon Baptist Convention, the Presbyterian Church in West Cameroon and the Union of Evangelical Churches of North Cameroon. The Eglise Evangélique du Cameroun and the Union des Eglises Baptistes du Cameroun have also formed a Conseil des Eglises Baptistes et Evangéliques du Cameroun.

The Roman Catholic Church

Cameroon comprises five archdioceses and 21 dioceses.

Bishops' Conference: Conférence Episcopale Nationale du Cameroun, BP 1963, Yaoundé; tel. 222-31-15-92; e-mail info@cencp.org; internet www.cenc.cm; f. 1989; Pres. Most Rev. ANDREW NKEA FUANYA (Archbishop of Bamenda); Sec.-Gen. JERVIS BEBEI KEWI.

Archbishop of Bamenda: Most Rev. ANDREW NKEA FUANYA, Archbishop's House, BP 82, Bamenda; tel. 233-36-12-41; e-mail info@bamendaarchdiocese.org; internet bamendaarchdiocese.org.

Archbishop of Bertoua: Most Rev. JOSEPH ATANGA, Archevêché, BP 40, Bertoua; tel. 222-24-17-48; e-mail atangajoseph11@gmail.com; internet www.archidiocesedebertoua.org.

Archbishop of Douala: Most Rev. SAMUEL KLEDA, Archevêché, BP 179, Douala; tel. 233-42-37-14; e-mail mikjp2004@yahoo.fr.

Archbishop of Garoua: Most Rev. FAUSTIN AMBASSA NDJODO, Archevêché, BP 272, Garoua; tel. 222-27-13-53; e-mail archigaroua@yahoo.fr.

Archbishop of Yaoundé: Most Rev. JEAN MBARGA, Archevêché, BP 207, Yaoundé; tel. 222-01-10-48; e-mail simonvita2000@yahoo.fr.

ISLAM

Conseil Supérieur Islamique du Cameroun (CSIC): BP 4171, Yaoundé; tel. 674001072; e-mail csicweb@yahoo.fr; internet conseil-superieur-islamique-du-cameroun.fr.gd; f. 1984; Sec.-Gen. ZOUNEDOU MFONYOUMDI.

BAHÁ'Í FAITH

National Spiritual Assembly: 4230 Yaoundé; tel. 677046614; e-mail nsacameroon@gmail.com; f. 1968; Nat. Sec. SILAS BANOLOK; mems in 1,744 localities.

The Press

DAILY NEWSPAPERS (PRINT AND ONLINE)

Cameroon Tribune: route de l'Aéroport, BP 1218, Yaoundé; tel. 222-30-41-47; internet www.cameroon-tribune.cm; f. 1974; publ. by the Société de Presse et d'Editions du Cameroun (SOPECAM), which also publishes a weekly *Weekend*, a monthly *Nyanga* and a fortnightly *Alter Ego*; govt-controlled; French and English; Publr MARIE CLAIRE NNANA; Editorial Dir MARTIN BADJANG BA NKEN.

Le Jour: BP 14097, Yaoundé; tel. 222-04-01-85; e-mail lejourquotidien@yahoo.fr; Mon.–Fri.; Dir of Publication HAMAN MANA; Editor-in-Chief ROMUALD NKONLA.

Le Messager: BP 5925, Douala; tel. 699989664; f. 1979; independent; Dir of Publication JEAN FRANÇOIS CHANNON; Man. Editor ALAIN NJIPOU.

Mutations: South Media Corporation, 183 rue 1,055, Pl. Repiquet, BP 12348, Yaoundé; tel. 656180264; e-mail quotidienmutations2017@gmail.com; internet quotidienmutations.cm; daily; French; independent; Dir of Publication GEORGES ALAIN BOYOMO.

La Nouvelle Expression: rue Jamot, BP 15333, Douala; tel. 233-43-22-27; internet www.lanouvelleexpression.info; Dir of Publication SEVERIN TCHOUNKEU.

Le Quotidien de l'Économie: Essos Camp Sonel, BP 312, Yaoundé; tel. 242-00-17-31; internet leconomie.cm; f. 2012; Dir of Publication THIERRY EKOUTI.

PERIODICALS

L'Anecdote: rue de Nsam, face Garanti Express, BP 25070, Yaoundé; tel. 242-71-88-13; e-mail journalanecdote@yahoo.fr; internet fb.com/journalanecdote; weekly; conservative; Dir of Publication JEAN PIERRE AMOUGOU BELINGA; Editor-in-Chief FRANÇOIS BIKORO.

Aurore Plus: BP 7042, Douala; tel. 233-42-92-61; e-mail jouraurplus@yahoo.fr; f. 1990; 2 a week; Dir of Publication MICHEL MICHAUT MOUSSALA.

Cameroon Panorama: BP 46, Buéa; tel. 233-32-21-78; e-mail cainsbuea@yahoo.com; f. 1962; monthly; English; Roman Catholic; Editor Rev. Fr WILSON NGEMA.

Cameroon Weekly: Yaoundé; e-mail editorial@cameroonweekly.com; internet cameroonweekly.com; f. 2012; weekly; French and English.

Ecovox: BP 1256, Bafoussam; tel. 233-44-66-68; 2 a year; French; environmental news.

L'Effort Camerounais: BP 15231, Douala; tel. 233-43-27-26; e-mail leffortcamerounais@yahoo.com; internet www.leffortcamerounais.com; bi-monthly; Catholic; f. 1955; Editor-in-Chief IRENEAUS CHIA CHONGWAIN.

Journal Officiel de la République du Cameroun: BP 1603, Yaoundé; tel. 222-20-17-19; weekly; official govt notices; Man. Editor JOSEPH MARCEL.

The Messenger: BP 15043, Douala; English edn of *Le Messager*; Editor HILARY FOKUM.

Nyanga: route de l'Aéroport, BP 1218, Yaoundé; tel. 222-30-41-47; e-mail infos@nyanga.cm; internet nyanga.cm; publ. by the Société de Presse et d'Editions du Cameroun (SOPECAM); Dir EMMANUEL TATAW.

L'Œil du Sahel: Immeuble ancien Fonader, Porte 303, BP 3288, Yaoundé; tel. 699923270; e-mail loeildusahel100@yahoo.fr; internet fb.com/loeildusahelcameroun; f. 1997; 2 a week; Dir of Publication GUIBAÏ GATAMA.

Ouest Echos: BP 767, Bafoussam; tel. 3344-1091; weekly; regional; Dir MICHEL ECLADOR PÉKOUA.

The Post: POB 91, Buéa; tel. 233-32-32-87; bi-weekly; English; Publr (vacant); Editor CHARLY NDI CHIA.

Le Temps des Réalisations: Yaoundé; f. 2012; monthly; publ. by the Office of the President; Dir of Publication SAMUEL MVONDO AYOLO.

Weekly Post: BP 30420, Yaoundé; tel. 699904866; e-mail weeklyp@yahoo.com; internet weeklypost1.tripod.com; English; f. 1992; independent; Editor-in-Chief BISONG ETAHOBEN.

PRESS ASSOCIATIONS

Conseil Camerounais des Médias (CCM): Yaoundé; internet www.ccm-info.org; f. 2005; created by the UJC to strengthen the quality and independence of journalism in Cameroon; 9 mems; Pres. PIERRE ESSAMA ESSOMBA; Sec.-Gen. PIERRE-PAUL TCHINDJI.

Union des Journalistes du Cameroun (UJC): Yaoundé; Pres. CHARLY NDI CHIA.

Publishers

AES Presses Universitaires d'Afrique: 1077 rue Mballa Eloumden, BP 8106, Yaoundé; tel. 2220-2695; e-mail contact@aes-pua.com; internet www.aes-pua.com; f. 1986; literature, social sciences and law; Dir-Gen. SERGE DONTCHUENG KOUAM.

Editions Akoma Mba: Nlongkak-Direction Générale de la Sureté Nationale, BP 14268, Yaoundé; tel. 699888577; e-mail contact@editionsakomamba.com; internet www.editionsakomamba.com; f. 1995; children's books; Gen. Man. ULRICH TALLA WAMBA.

Editions Clé (Centre de Littérature Evangélique): ave Maréchal Foch, BP 1501, Yaoundé; tel. 222-22-35-54; e-mail editionscle@yahoo.fr; internet editionscle.info; f. 1963; African and Christian literature and studies; school textbooks; medicine and science; general non-fiction; Dir Dr MARCELIN VOUNDA ETOA.

Editions Ndzé: BP 647, Bertoua; tel. 699509295; internet www.ndze.com; fiction; Commercial Dir ALEXIS LIMBONA.

Editions Semences Africaines: BP 7171, Yaoundé; tel. 699171439; e-mail renephilombe@yahoo.fr; f. 1974; fiction, history, religion, textbooks; Man. Dir RÉNÉ LÉA PHILOMBE.

Presses de l'Université Catholique d'Afrique Centrale (PUCAC): BP 11628, Yaoundé; tel. 222-30-55-08; e-mail p_ucac@yahoo.fr; Man. GABRIEL TSALA ONANA.

GOVERNMENT PUBLISHING HOUSES

Imprimerie Nationale: BP 1603, Yaoundé; tel. 690-98-95-27; e-mail contact@imprimerienationale.cm; internet imprimerienationale.cm; f. 1906; Chair. ANGELINE FLORENCE NGOMO.

Société de Presse et d'Editions du Cameroun (SOPECAM): route de l'Aéroport, BP 1218, Yaoundé; tel. 222-304-147; e-mail infos@sopecam.com; internet editions.sopecam.cm; f. 1977; under the supervision of the Ministry of Communication; Pres. JOSEPH LE; Dir-Gen. MARIE CLAIRE NNANA.

Broadcasting and Communications

TELECOMMUNICATIONS

Cameroon Telecommunications (CAMTEL): BP 1571, Yaoundé; tel. 222-23-40-65; e-mail contact@camtel.cm; internet www.camtel.cm; f. 1999 by merger of INTELCAM and the Dept of Telecommunications; state-owned; 51% privatization pending; provides fixed-line, mobile telephone and internet services under the Blue brand; Pres. MOHAMADOU SAOUDI; Dir-Gen. JUDITH YAH SUNDAY.

CREOLINK Telecoms: BP 12725, Yaoundé; tel. 69801696; internet www.creolink.com; internet service provider.

Mobile Telephone Networks (MTN) Cameroon Ltd: 360 rue Drouot, Bonamouti, Akwa, BP 15574, Douala; tel. 679009000; internet www.mtncameroon.net; f. 1999 as CAMTEL Mobile; acquired by MTN in 2000; mobile telephone operator; 70% owned by MTN Ltd, 30% owned by Broadband Telecom Ltd; CEO MITWA NG'AMBI.

Nexttel: Immeuble Sci John Lae, face Palais Dika Akwa, BP 990, Douala; tel. 666000789; e-mail care.complaints@nexttel.com.cm; internet www.nexttel.cm; f. 2014; trade name of Viettel Cameroun SA; owned by Viettel Group and Bestinver; Dir-Gen. BENOÎT YAOUSSOU.

Orange: rue Franqueville, BP 864, Douala; tel. 233-41-00-11; e-mail support.internet@orange.cm; internet www.orange.cm; mobile telephone and internet operator; CEO PATRICK BENON.

Ringo SA: Immeuble LMT, rue Djoungolo, Elig-Essono, BP 15283, Yaoundé; tel. 222-50-50-00; e-mail contact@ringo-group.com; internet www.ringo.cm; f. 2008; internet service provider.

Saconets PLC: BP 6064, Yaoundé; tel. 222-23-10-18; e-mail info@saconets.com; internet saconets.com; f. 2008; internet service provider.

Regulatory Authority

Agence de Régulation des Télécommunications (ART): rue Joseph Mballa Eloumdem Bastos, BP 6132, Yaoundé; tel. 222-23-03-80; e-mail art@art.cm; internet www.art.cm; f. 1998; Pres. JUSTINE DIFFO TCHUNKAM; Dir-Gen. PHILÉMON ZO'O ZAME.

BROADCASTING

Regulatory Authority

Conseil National de la Communication (CNC) (National Communication Council): Quartier Bastos, BP 12535, Yaoundé; tel. 222-21-03-09; internet cnc.gov.cm; Pres. PETER ESSOKA.

Radio

Office de Radiodiffusion-Télévision Camerounaise (CRTV): BP 1634, Yaoundé; tel. 222-21-40-77; e-mail infos@crtv.cm; internet www.crtv.cm; f. 1987; broadcasts in French and English; satellite broadcasts commenced in Jan. 2001, reaching some 80% of the national territory; Pres. of Council of Administration RENÉ EMMANUEL SADI (Minister of Communication); Dir-Gen. CHARLES PYTHAGORE NDONGO.

Radio Yaoundé FM 94: BP 1634, Yaoundé; tel. 222-20-20-89; e-mail fm94@crtv.cm; Head of Station SIDONIE SIKOA.

Kalak (94.5 FM): Yaoundé; tel. 222-72-77-27; e-mail contact@kalakfm.com; internet www.kalakfm.com; Dir-Gen. MARCEL AMOKO.

Television

Office de Radiodiffusion-Télévision Camerounaise (CRTV): see Radio.

Canal 2 International: Bonapriso, 877 rue Njo-Njo, BP 15244, Douala; tel. 233-43-21-92; e-mail infodirection@canal2international.net; internet www.canal2international.net; Dir-Gen. ERIC FOTSO.

Equinoxe TV: BP 15333, Douala; tel. 242-64-29-87; e-mail contact@equinoxetv.com; Dir-Gen. SÉVÉRIN TCHOUNKEU.

Spectrum Television: Immeuble Kassap, 4e étage, BP 4883, Douala; tel. 233-43-14-44; e-mail msilla@stvgroup.com; Dir-Gen. COLIN EBARKO MUKETE.

Vision4TV: BP 25070, Yaoundé; tel. 242-71-88-13; internet vision4tv.com; f. 2008; Pres. and Dir-Gen. JEAN PIERRE AMOUGOU BELINGA.

Finance

BANKING

Central Bank

Banque des Etats de l'Afrique Centrale (BEAC): 736 ave Monseigneur Vogt, BP 1917, Yaoundé; tel. 222-23-40-60; e-mail beac@beac.int; internet www.beac.int; f. 1973; bank of issue for mem. states of the Communauté Economique et Monétaire de l'Afrique Centrale (CEMAC, fmrly Union Douanière et Economique de l'Afrique Centrale): Cameroon, the Central African Repub., Chad, the Repub. of the Congo, Equatorial Guinea and Gabon; Gov. ABBAS MAHAMAT TOLLI; Dir in Cameroon PIERRE EMMANUEL NKOA AYISSI.

Commercial Banks

Access Bank: Yaoundé; f. 2022; Dir-Gen. IBUKUN ODEGBAIKE.

Afriland First Bank: 1063 pl. de l'Indépendance, BP 11834, Yaoundé; tel. 222-23-30-68; e-mail firstbank@afrilandfirstbank.com; internet www.afrilandfirstbank.com; formerly Caisse Commune d'Epargne et d'Investissement (CCEI); SBF & Co (36.62%), FMO (19.80%), private shareholders (43.58%); Pres. Dr JEAN-PAULIN FONKOUA KAKE; Gen. Man. CÉLESTIN GUELA SIMO.

Bange Bank Cameroun: Douala; f. 2021; Dir-Gen. PASCAL EMILIO MOYO AVORO.

Banque Internationale du Cameroun pour l'Epargne et le Crédit (BICEC): ave du Général de Gaulle, BP 1925, Douala; tel. 233-43-60-00; e-mail bicec@bicec.banquepopulaire.com; internet www.bicec.com; f. 1962 as Banque Internationale pour le Commerce et l'Industrie du Cameroun; name changed as above in 1997, following restructuring; 68.5% owned by Groupe BPCE (France), 17.5% state-owned; Pres. JEAN-BAPTISTE BOKAM; Dir-Gen. OUTMAN ROQDI.

Citibank N.A. Cameroon: 96 rue Flatters, Bonanjo, BP 4571, Douala; tel. 233-42-42-72; internet www.citigroup.com; f. 1997; Country Officer GORDON ACHA.

Commercial Bank Cameroon SA (CBC): 148 ave du Général de Gaulle, BP 4004, Douala; tel. 233-42-02-02; e-mail cb@commercialbank-cm.com; internet www.commercialbank-cm.com; f. 1997; Pres. ALFRED TIKI; Dir-Gen. LÉANDRE DJUMMO.

Ecobank Cameroun SA: blvd de la Liberté, BP 582, Douala; tel. 233-43-82-51; e-mail ecobankcm@ecobank.com; internet www.ecobank.com; f. 2001; Chair. RICHARD NDOUMBE LOBE; Man. Dir GWENDOLINE ABUNAW.

National Financial Credit Bank SA (NFC): ave Charles de Gaulle, BP 6578, Yaoundé; tel. 222-20-28-23; e-mail info@nfcbanksa.com; internet www.nfcbanksa.com; f. 1989; Gen. Man. JULIUS B. MANJO.

Société Commerciale de Banque Cameroun SA: 530 rue du Roi George, BP 300, Douala; tel. 233-43-53-00; internet www.scbcameroun.net; f. 1989 as Société Commerciale de Banque—Crédit Lyonnais Cameroun; renamed Crédit Lyonnais Cameroun SA in 2002, and as above in 2007; 35% state-owned; Gen. Man. ALEXANDRE BEZIAUD.

Société Générale Cameroun (SGC): 78 rue Joss, BP 4042, Douala; tel. 233-42-70-10; e-mail sgbcdla@camnet.cm; internet www.societegenerale.cm; f. 1963; fmrly Société Générale de Banques au Cameroun; present name adopted 2013; 25.6% state-owned, 58.08% owned by Groupe Société Générale (France) and 16.32% owned by Allianz Assurance Cameroun; Chair. ALAIN MALONG; Dir-Gen. STERGHIOS DASSARECOS.

Standard Chartered Bank Cameroon SA: blvd de la Liberté, BP 1784, Douala; tel. 233-43-52-00; e-mail premierservices_cm@sc.com; internet www.sc.com/cm; f. 1980 as Boston Bank Cameroon; name changed 1986; 100% owned by Standard Chartered Bank (UK); CEO CHUKS UGHA.

Union Bank of Cameroon, Ltd (UBC): NWCA Ltd Bldg, 2nd Floor, Commercial Ave, BP 110, Bamenda, Douala; tel. 233-36-23-14; e-mail ubc@unionbankcameroon.com; internet www.unionbankcameroon.com; f. 2000; 54% state-owned; Pres. NJONG ERIC NJONG; Gen. Man. CHARLOTTE CHEKEP KOUECHEU.

United Bank for Africa Cameroon: blvd de la Liberté-Akwa, BP 2088, Douala; tel. 233-43-36-83; e-mail cfccameroon@ubagroup.com; internet www.ubagroup.com/ubacameroon; CEO JUDE ANELE.

Development Banks

Banque Camerounaise des PME: Carrefour Nlongkak, rue Albert Ateba Ebe, BP 12962, Yaoundé; e-mail contact@bc-pme.cm; internet www.bc-pme.cm; f. 2015; state-owned; Dir-Gen. AGNÈS NDOUMBE.

Banque de Développement des Etats de l'Afrique Centrale: see Franc Zone.

Crédit Foncier du Cameroun (CFC): 484 blvd du 20 mai 1972, BP 1531, Yaoundé; tel. 222-23-52-16; internet www.creditfoncier.cm; f. 1977; 75% state-owned; provides assistance for low-cost housing; Chair. JULES DORET NDONGO; Gen. Man. JEAN PAUL MISSI.

Société Nationale d'Investissement du Cameroun (SNI): pl. Ahmadou Ahidjo, BP 423, Yaoundé; tel. 222-22-44-22; e-mail sni@sni.cm; internet www.sni.cm; f. 1964; state-owned investment and credit agency; Chair. DÉSIRÉ GEOFFROY MBOCK; Dir-Gen. YAOU AISSATOU.

Financial Institutions

Alios Finance Cameroun: 319 rue Alfred Saker, BP 554, Douala; tel. 233-50-23-00; e-mail cameroun@alios-finance.com; internet www.alios-finance.com; fmrly Société Camerounaise de Crédit-Bail; name changed as above in 2006; Dir-Gen. GEORGES FOTSO NDZUTUE.

Caisse Autonome d'Amortissement du Cameroun: blvd du 20 Mai, BP 7167, Yaoundé; tel. 222-22-22-26; internet www.caa.cm; f. 1985; Dir-Gen. RICHARD EVINA OBAM.

Société Camerounaise d'Equipement: ave Giscard d'Estaing, rue 1.022, face boulangerie Calafatas, BP 178, Yaoundé; tel. 693056095; internet www.sce-cameroun.com; f. 1963; Dir-Gen. DOMINIQUE IPPOLITO.

Banking Association

Association Professionnelle des Etablissements de Crédit du Cameroun (APECCAM): Immeuble BECIC, ave Mgr Vogt, BP 133, Yaoundé; tel. 222-23-54-01; e-mail info@apeccam.com; f. 1985; Pres. ALPHONSE NAFACK.

STOCK EXCHANGE

Bourse des Valeurs Mobilières de l'Afrique Centrale (BVMAC): 1450 blvd de la Liberté, BP 442, Douala; tel. 233-43-85-83; e-mail bvmac@bvmac.cm; internet www.bvm-ac.org; absorbed the Douala Stock Exchange in 2019; 47.15% state-owned; Pres. HENRI-CLAUDE OYIMA; Dir-Gen. LOUIS BANGA-NTOLO.

INSURANCE

Acam Vie: ave de l'Indépendance, Bonapriso, BP 2000, Douala; tel. 679453227; e-mail service.clients@acamvie.com; internet acamvie.cm; f. 2016; Pres. and Dir-Gen. AYMRIC KAMEGA.

Activa Assurances: rue du Prince du Galles 1385, BP 12970, Douala; tel. 233-50-13-00; e-mail activa.assur@group-activa.com; internet www.activa-cameroun.com; f. 1999; all branches except life insurance; 66% owned by Cameroonian investors, 33% by Ivorian investors; Pres. and Dir-Gen. RICHARD NZONLIÉ LOWE; also **Activa Vie**, life insurance.

Allianz Cameroun: 1124 rue Manga Bell, BP 105, Douala; tel. 233-50-20-00; e-mail allianz.cameroun@allianz-cm.com; internet www.allianz-africa.com; formerly AGF Cameroun Assurances; all classes of insurance; Dir-Gen. OLIVIER MALÂTRE.

AXA Assurances Cameroun: 309 rue Bebey-Eyidi, BP 4068, Douala; tel. 233-42-67-72; e-mail service.contact@axa.cm; internet www.axa.cm; f. 1974 as Compagnie Camerounaise d'Assurances et de Réassurances; renamed as above in June 2000; Dir-Gen. THIERRY KEPEDEN.

Chanas Assurances: 1 rue du DWARF, BP 109, Douala; tel. 233-42-14-74; e-mail chanas@chanasassurances.com; internet fb.com/chanasassurancessaofficiel; f. 1999; Pres. MATANGA MAURICE; Dir-Gen. AUGOU LEONCE.

Prudential Beneficial Life Insurance SA: 1944 blvd de la République, BP 2328, Douala; tel. 233-42-86-77; e-mail clientele@

prubeneficial.cm; internet www.beneficial-life.cm; f. 1974; fmrly Beneficial Life Insurance SA; name changed as above in 2020; Pres. and Dir-Gen. EDDIE FORD BROWN; also **Prudential Beneficial General** non-life insurance.

Sanlam Assurances Cameroun: 34 rue Dinde, BP 12125, Douala; tel. 233-50-25-01; e-mail contact@cm.sanlam.com; internet cm .sanlam.com; f. 1985 as Compagnie Nationale d'Assurances; fmrly Colina La Citoyenne Cameroun, subsequently Saham Assurances Cameroun; name changed as above in 2021; life and non-life; Dir-Gen. THÉOPHILE GÉRARD MOULONG.

Saham Life Cameroun: blvd de la Liberté, BP 267, Douala; tel. 233-43-09-04; e-mail cameroun@sahamassurance.com; internet www .sahamassurance.cm; f. 1996; fmrly Colina All Life; name changed as above in 2014; life insurance; Dir-Gen. MARTIN FONCHA.

Société Africaine d'Assurances et Réassurances (SAAR): 111 rue de la Pérouse, Quartier Bonanjo, BP 1011, Douala; tel. 233-43-17-65; e-mail contact@saar-assurances.com; internet www .saar-assurances.com; f. 1990; Pres. Dr PAUL K. FOKAM; Dir-Gen. GEORGES LÉOPOLD KAGOU; also **SAAR-Vie**, life insurance; Dir-Gen. FERDINAND MENG.

Sunu Assurances Vie Cameroun: Immeuble Champagne Plaza, 578 rue Tobie Kuoh Bonanjo, BP 2153, Douala; tel. 233-42-12-46; e-mail cameroun.vie@sunu-group.com; internet cameroun.vie .sunu-group.com; Dir-Gen. CHANTAL MOUELLE; also **SUNU Assurances IARD**, non-life insurance.

Insurance Association

Association des Sociétés d'Assurances du Cameroun (ASAC): BP 1136, Douala; tel. 233-42-06-68; e-mail contact@asac-cameroun .org; internet asac-cameroun.org; Pres. THIERRY KEPENDEN; Sec.-Gen. GEORGES MANDENG LIKENG.

Trade and Industry

GOVERNMENT AGENCIES

Economic and Social Council: BP 1058, Yaoundé; tel. 222-23-24-74; advises the Govt on economic and social problems; comprises 150 mems, who serve a five-year term, and a perm. sec.; Pres. LUC AYANG; Sec.-Gen. ZACHARIE NGOUMBÉ.

Agence de Promotion des Investissements (API): Nouvelle Route Bastos, BP 20771, Yaoundé; tel. 222-21-89-70; e-mail info@ investincameroon.net; internet investincameroon.net; Gen. Man. MARTHE ANGELINE MINJA.

Agence de Régulation des Marchés Publics: BP 6604, Yaoundé; tel. 222-20-18-03; e-mail infos@armp.cm; internet armp.cm; f. 2001; Pres. HAMADJODA ADJOUDI; Dir-Gen. JOSEPH NGO.

Mission de Régulation des Approvisionnements des Produits de Grande Consomation: BP 12584, Yaoundé; tel. 222-23-41-45; internet www.mirap.cm; f. 2011; Dir-Gen. CYPRIEN BAMZOK NTOL.

DEVELOPMENT ORGANIZATIONS

Agence Française de Développement (AFD): Plateau Atéméngué, BP 46, Yaoundé; tel. 222-22-00-15; e-mail afdyaounde@afd.fr; internet www.afd.fr; fmrly Caisse Française de Développement; Dir VIRGINIE DAGO.

Cameroon Development Corporation (CDC): Bota Area, Limbé; tel. 233-33-22-51; e-mail info@cdc-cameroon.com; internet cdc-cameroon.net/new2014; f. 1947; reorg. 1982; statutory corpn established to acquire and develop plantations of tropical crops for local and export markets; operates 3 palm oil mills and 5 rubber factories; Chair. BENJAMIN MUTANGA ITOE; Gen. Man. FRANKLIN NGONI IKOME NJIE.

Hévéa-Cameroun (HEVECAM): 44 blvd du Gen. Leclerc, BP 1298, Douala; tel. 233-46-19-19; internet hevecam.com; f. 1975; 10% state-owned, 90% owned by GMG Global Ltd (Singapore); devt of 15,000-ha rubber plantation; Pres. JEAN NKUÉTÉ; Man. Dir R. S. RAJASEGAR.

Institut de Recherche Agricole pour le Développement (IRAD): 62 BP 2123, Yaoundé; tel. 222-23-26-44; e-mail irad@irad .cm; internet irad.cm; Pres. NNANGA NGA; Dir-Gen. NOÉ WOIN.

Institut de Recherche pour le Développement (IRD): 1095 rue Joseph Essono Mballa, Quartier Elig Essono, BP 1857, Yaoundé; tel. 222-20-15-08; e-mail cameroun@ird.fr; internet www.cameroun.ird .fr; f. 1944; Rep. in Cameroon (vacant).

Mission d'Aménagement et d'Equipement des Terrains Urbains et Ruraux (MAETUR): 716 ave Winston Churchill, Quartier Hippodrome, BP 1248, Yaoundé; tel. 222-22-31-13; internet maetur-cameroun.com; f. 1977; Pres. ABOUBAKARY ABDOULAYE; Dir-Gen. LOUIS ROGER MANGA.

Mission d'Aménagement et de Gestion des Zones Industrielles: BP 1431, Yaoundé; tel. 222-31–84-40; e-mail magzicameroun@yahoo.fr; internet www.magzicameroun.com; f. 1971; state-owned industrial land authority; Gen. Man. CHRISTOL GEORGES MANON.

Mission de Développement de la Province du Nord-Ouest (MIDENO): BP 442, Bamenda; Dir-Gen. MATOYA CLETUS ANYE.

Office Céréalier: BP 298, Garoua; tel. 222-27-14-38; f. 1975 to combat effects of drought in northern Cameroon and stabilize cereal prices; Chair. DJIBRILL NANA; Dir-Gen. MOHAMADOU GASSIMOU.

Office National du Cacao et du Café (ONCC): BP 3018, Douala; tel. 243-42-00-02; e-mail oncc2003@yahoo.fr; internet www.oncc.cm; Pres. LUC AYANG; Dir-Gen. MICHAËL NDOPING.

Service de Coopération et d'Action Culturelle: 140 ave du Président Ahmadou Ahidjo, BP 1616, Yaoundé; tel. 222-22-84-25; e-mail scac.yaounde-amba@diplomatie.gouv.fr; administers bilateral aid from France; Dir YANN LORVO.

Société de Développement du Cacao (SODECAO): BP 1651, Yaoundé; tel. 222-30-45-44; internet www.sodecao.cm; f. 1974; reorg. 1980; devt of cocoa, coffee and food crop production in the Littoral, Centre, East and South regions; Chair. ZACHERIE NGBA; Gen. Man. JEAN-CLAUDE EKO'O AKOUAFANE.

Société de Développement du Coton (SODECOTON): BP 302, Garoua; tel. 222-27-15-56; f. 1974; Pres. JEAN ABATE EDI'I; Dir-Gen. BAYERO MOHAMADOU BOUNOU.

Société de Développement et d'Exploitation des Productions Animales (SODEPA): rue Foe, BP 1410, Yaoundé; tel. 222-20-08-10; e-mail infos@sodepa.cm; internet sodepa.cm; f. 1974; devt of livestock and livestock products; Man. Dir DENIS KOULANGNA KOUTOU.

Société d'Expansion et de Modernisation de la Riziculture de Yagoua (SEMRY): BP 46, Yagoua; tel. 222-29-62-13; internet semry-online.com; f. 1971; commercialization of rice products and expansion of rice growing in areas where irrigation is possible; Pres. MIDJIYAWA BAKARY; Dir-Gen. FISSOU KOUMA.

Société Immobilière du Cameroun (SIC): 510 ave de l'Indépendance, BP 387, Yaoundé; tel. 699-80-41-69; e-mail info@sic.cm; internet www.sic.cm; f. 1952; housing construction and devt; Pres. CÉLESTINE KETCHA COURTES; Dir-Gen. AHMADOU SARDAOUNA.

Sud Cameroun Hévéa S.A.: POB 382, Yaoundé; 20% state-owned, 80% owned by GMG Global Ltd (Singapore); rubber plantation and processing; Dir-Gen. ONG CHEE SING.

CHAMBERS OF COMMERCE

Chambre d'Agriculture, des Pêches, de l'Elevage et des Forêts du Cameroun (CAPEF): BP 6620, Yaoundé; tel. 222-22-04-41; e-mail ccfe_cameroun@yahoo.fr; f. 1955; 120 mems; Pres. MARTIN PAUL MINDJOS MOMENY; Sec.-Gen. TANYI JACOB TACHOT; other chambers at Ebolowa, Bertoua, Douala, Ngaoundéré, Garoua, Maroua, Buéa, Bamenda and Bafoussam.

Chambre de Commerce, d'Industrie, des Mines et de l'Artisanat du Cameroun (CCIMA): rue de Chambre de Commerce, BP 4011, Douala; also at BP 36, Yaoundé; BP 211, Limbé; BP 59, Garoua; BP 944, Bafoussam; BP 551, Bamenda; BP 824, Ngaoundéré; BP 86, Bertoua; tel. 233-42-68-55; e-mail siege@ccima.cm; internet www .ccima.cm; f. 1921; 160 mems; Pres. CHRISTOPHE EKEN; Sec.-Gen. HALIDOU BELLO.

EMPLOYERS' ORGANIZATIONS

Groupement des Femmes d'Affaires du Cameroun (GFAC): blvd de la Réunification, BP 17570, Douala; tel. 699884629; e-mail gfacnational@yahoo.fr; internet legfaccameroun.com; f. 1985; Pres. AGNÈS NTUBE NDODE; Exec. Dir HÉLÈNE TIOMA.

Groupement Inter-Patronal du Cameroun (GICAM): rue des Ministres, Bonanjo, BP 829, Douala; tel. 233-42-31-41; e-mail gicam@legicam.cm; internet www.legicam.org; Pres. CÉLESTIN TAWAMBA.

Mouvement des Entrepreneurs du Cameroun (MECAM): BP 12443, Douala; tel. 233-39-50-00; Pres. DANIEL CLAUDE ABATÉ.

Syndicat des Commerçants Importateurs-Exportateurs du Cameroun (SCIEC): 16 rue Quillien, BP 562, Douala; tel. 233-42-03-04; Pres. EMMANUEL UGOLINI; Treas. MICHEL CHUPIN.

Syndicat des Industriels du Cameroun (SYNDUSTRICAM): BP 673, Douala; tel. 233-42-30-58; f. 1953; Pres. ALAIN MALONG; Sec.-Gen. MOÏSE FERDINAND BEKE.

UTILITIES

Electricity

Agence de Régulation du Secteur de l'Électricité (ARSEL): BP 6064, Yaoundé; tel. 222-21-10-12; e-mail contact@arsel.cm; internet arsel-cm.org; f. 1998; regulatory authority; Dir-Gen. JEAN PASCAL NKOU.

Electricity Development Corpn: Immeuble Hibiscus, BP 15111, Yaoundé; tel. 222-23-19-30; e-mail info@edc-cameroon.org; f. 2006; state-owned; Pres. VICTOR MENGOT; Dir-Gen. Dr THÉODORE NSANGOU.

Eneo Cameroon S.A.: 63 ave de Gaulle, BP 4077, Douala; tel. 233-43-00-33; e-mail contact@eneo.cm; internet eneocameroon.cm; f. 1974; fmrly AES-SONEL; name changed as above in 2014; 56% owned by Actis, 44% state-owned; Pres. SÉRAPHIN MAGLOIRE FOUDA; CEO PATRICK EECKELERS.

Gas

Glocalgaz: Akwa Nord, Douala; tel. 233-33-37-05; e-mail info@glocalgaz.com; internet www.glocalgaz.com.

Société Camerounaise de Gaz Liqueries (CAMGAZ): BP 4085, Douala; tel. 233-42-72-49.

Water

Cameroon Water Utilities Corpn (Camwater): BP 524, Douala; tel. 243-42-96-84; internet www.camwater.cm; f. 1967; 73% state-owned; Pres. PATRICK KUM BONG AKWA; Dir-Gen. BLAISE MOUSSA.

MAJOR COMPANIES

The following are some of the largest companies in terms of either capital investment or employment:

Africa Bio: rue Koufrah, 10 BP 1273, Douala; tel. 233-20-29-36; f. 2005; production and export of tropical fruits; Gen. Man. BÉATRICE PICKER.

ALUCAM, Compagnie Camerounaise de l'Aluminium: BP 1090, Douala; tel. 233-42-29-30; internet www.alucam.cm; f. 1984; 39% state-owned; manufacture of aluminium by electrolysis using imported alumina; Pres. and Man. Dir (vacant).

Biotropical SA: BP 12315, Douala; tel. 233-39-32-96; f. 2006; Dir-Gen. JEAN PIERRE IMÉLÉ.

Bofor SA: Magzi, BP 1528, Yaoundé; tel. 222-01-24-09; internet www.boforcameroun.com; f. 2006; Dir-Gen. JEHU SIKEUBAM.

Bolloré Africa Logistics: Vallée Tokoto, Zone des Professions Maritimes, BP 4057, Yaoundé; tel. 233-50-12-12; e-mail bollore.africa-logistics.cm@bollore.com; internet www.bollore-logistics.com/fr/Pages/focus/Cameroon.aspx; f. 2008; group includes, *inter alia*, fmr entities SAGA Cameroon and TRANSINTRA; transport services; Dir-Gen. MOHAMED DIOP.

Buetec Broderie SARL: BP 3461, Douala; tel. 233-47-01-39; e-mail buetec@buetec-broderie.com; internet www.buetec-broderie.com.

Cameroon Oil Transportation Co. (COTCO): 179 rue de la Motte Piquet-Bonanjo, BP 3738, Douala; tel. 670741439; Dir-Gen. XAVIER FOLCH.

Cameroon Tea Estates SA (CTE): BP 605, Limbé; tel. 233-37-57-34; e-mail cte@ctetea.com; f. 2007; Dir-Gen. JEAN PIERRE CROZE.

Camlait SA: rue des Industries, BP 1838 Douala; tel. 233-37-44-60; e-mail direction.marketing@camlait.com; internet www.camlait.com; dairy products; Pres. and Dir-Gen. PAULIN L. TOUKAM ZUKO.

Chantier Naval et Industriel du Cameroun (CNIC): BP 2389, Douala; tel. 233-40-34-88; e-mail enquiries@cnicyard.com; internet cnicyard.com; ship repair and oil rig rehabilitation; Pres. LOUIS-CLAUDE NYASSA; Dir-Gen. ROLAND MAXIME AKA'A NDI'I.

Cimenteries du Cameroun (CIMENCAM): BP 1323, Douala; tel. 654-90-00-00; e-mail serviceclient.cimencam@lafargeholcim.com; internet www.cimencam.com; f. 1963; cement works at Figuil, clinker-crushing plant at Douala-Bonabéri, factory at Garoua; a subsidiary of Groupe LafargeHolcim; Dir-Gen. XAVIER PIERRE JEAN LEGRAND.

Coton Hydrophile du Cameroun (COFIL): BP 1254, Garoua; tel. 655859772; e-mail cofil_cam@yahoo.fr; internet cofilcameroun.com; f. 2007; 61.24% owned by Soficoton (Cameroon), 38.76% owned by Coton Invest Group (Belgium); Pres. and Man. Dir BILKISSOU KINGUI.

Cotonnière Industrielle du Cameroun (CICAM): BP 7012, Douala-Bassa; tel. 233-40-62-15; e-mail cicam@groupecicam.com; internet cicam.cm; f. 1967; 100% owned by Société Nationale d'Investissement du Cameroun; factory for bleaching, printing and dyeing of cotton at Douala; Pres. YAOU AÏSSATOU; Dir-Gen. EDOUARD EBAH ABADA.

GIC Le Moineau: BP 154, Yaoundé; tel. 677510808; e-mail regine@giclemoineau.com; internet www.giclemoineau.com; agro-based.

Groupe BOCOM: 1460 blvd de la République, Akwam, BP 9546, Douala; tel. 233-43-48-44; e-mail contact@groupebocom.com; internet groupebocom.com/bnb; f. 2002; petroleum products, mining, logistics, transport; Pres. and Dir-Gen. DIEUDONNÉ BOUGNE.

Guinness Cameroun SA: BP 1213, Douala; tel. 233-40-70-00; f. 1967; production and marketing of beers; Man. Dir ANDREW ROSS.

Ndawara Highland Tea Estate: BP BP 5538, Yaoundé; tel. 233-37-57-34; f. 2006.

Perenco Cameroun: Immeuble Saticam-Bata, blvd du President Ahidjo, BP 1225, Douala; tel. 233-42-32-91; internet www.perenco.com/cameroon; f. 1993; Dir-Gen. ARMEL SIMONDIN.

Plasticam: Zone Industrielle de Bassa, 2060 rue 3W854, BP 4071, Douala; tel. 233-37-50-57; e-mail secretariat.com@plasticam.net; internet plasticam.net; f. 1961; plastic packaging producers; Chair. DANIEL FORGET; Gen. Man. RAOUL NGUEDEU NGNEPI.

Proleg S.A.: BP 1916, Douala; tel. 233-44-60-00; internet www.proleg-sa.net; vegetable production; Pres. (vacant).

Société Anonyme des Brasseries du Cameroun (SABC): 77 rue Prince Bell, BP 4036, Douala; tel. 233-42-91-33; e-mail siege@sabc-cm.com; internet www.lesbrasseriesducameroun.com; f. 1948; production of beer and soft drinks; Dir-Gen. STÉPHANE DESCAZEAUD.

Société Camerounaise des Dépôts Pétroliers (SCDP): rue de la Cité Chardy, BP 2272, Douala; tel. 233-40-54-45; e-mail courrier@scdp.cm; internet www.scdp.cm; f. 1978; 51% state-owned; storage and distribution of petroleum; Pres. JEAN-FABIEN MONKAM NITCHEU; Dir-Gen. VÉRONIQUE MANZOUA.

Société Camerounaise de Fabrication de Piles Electriques (PILCAM): BP 1916, Douala; tel. 233-42-26-28; f. 1970; Pres. (vacant); Dir ANDRÉ FONTANA.

Société Camerounaise de Palmeraies (SOCAPALM): rue de la Motte Piquet Bonanjo, BP 691, Douala; tel. 233-43-77-83; e-mail socapalm@socapalm.org; internet socapalm.com; f. 1968; 67.46% owned by Socfinaf; management of palm plantations and production of palm oil and manufactured products; Chair. MICHEL NOULOWE; Gen. Man. DOMINIQUE CORNET; 2,244 employees (2019).

Société Camerounaise de Verrerie (SOCAVER): rue de Ndogbong Bassa, BP 1456, Douala; tel. 233-40-05-06; f. 1966; 52.9% owned by SABC; mfrs of glassware; Pres. MICHEL PALU; Gen. Man. JEAN PIERRE KAMGNA.

Société des Eaux Minérales du Cameroun (SEMC): 77 rue du Prince Bell, BP 4036, Douala; tel. 233-42-79-19; subsidiary of the Société Anonyme des Brasseries du Cameroun (SABC); producer of mineral water; Dir-Gen. PIERRE PROUVEU.

Société Industrielle Camerounaise des Cacaos (SIC CACAOS): route de Deido, BP 570, Douala; tel. 233-40-37-95; f. 1949; production of cocoa and cocoa butter; Pres. BENOIT VILLERS; Man. Dir LOÏC BIARDEAU.

Société Industrielle des Tabacs du Cameroun (SITABAC): BP 1105, Douala; tel. 233-42-49-19; manufacture and sale of cigarettes; Pres. and Dir-Gen. JAMES ONOBIONO.

Société Nationale des Hydrocarbures (SNH): BP 955, Yaoundé; tel. 222-20-19-10; e-mail info@snh.cm; internet www.snh.cm; f. 1980; national petroleum co; Pres. FERDINAND NGOH NGOH; Dir-Gen. ADOLPHE MOUDIKI.

Société Nationale des Mines (SONAMINES): Yaoundé; e-mail infos@sonamines.cm; internet sonamines.cm; f. 2020; Pres. (vacant); Dir-Gen. SERGE HERVÉ BOYOGUENO.

Société Nationale de Raffinage (SONARA): BP 365, Cap Limboh, Limbé; tel. 233-33-22-38; e-mail contact@sonara.cm; internet sonara-cm.cm; f. 1976; 66% state-owned; establishment and operation of petroleum refinery at Cap Limboh; Chair. NDOAH BERTHA BAKATA; Dir-Gen. JEAN PAUL SIMO NJONOU.

Société des Plantations du Haut Penja: BP 05, Nyombé; tel. 677731121; e-mail j.tchoumba@phpcam.com; Dir-Gen. FRANÇOIS ARMEL.

Société des Plantations de Mbanga: Immeuble TMC, 1871 blvd de la Liberté, BP 711, Douala; tel. 233-43-40-78; e-mail douala_spm@hotmail.com; Pres. and Dir-Gen. JEAN-YVES BRETHES.

Société Sucrière du Cameroun (SOSUCAM): BP 875, Yaoundé; tel. 222-23-05-85; f. 1965; 24% state-owned, 72.72% owned by SOMDIAA group of France; sugar refineries at Nkoteng and M'bandjock; produces 130,000 metric tons of sugar per year; Dir-Gen. ALEXANDRE VILGRAIN.

TotalEnergies Cameroun: 589 blvd de la Liberté, Akwa, BP 4048, Douala-Bassa; tel. 233-42-63-41; e-mail serviceclient@total.cm; internet totalenergies.cm; f. 1977; 75.8% owned by Total (France); 20% owned by Société Nationale des Hydrocarbures; exploration for, exploitation and distribution of petroleum reserves; Dir-Gen. ADRIEN BÉCHONNET.

PRINCIPAL CO-OPERATIVE ORGANIZATION

Union Centrale des Coopératives Agricoles de l'Ouest (UCCAO): ave Samuel Wanko, BP 1002, Bafoussam; tel. 233-44-42-96; f. 1958; marketing of cocoa and coffee; Pres. PLACIDE NGUEFACK; Gen. Man. FRANÇOIS MEFINJA FOKA.

TRADE UNION FEDERATIONS

Confederation of Cameroon Trade Unions (CCTU): BP 1610, Yaoundé; tel. 222-22-33-15; f. 1985; fmrly the Union Nationale des

Travailleurs du Cameroun (UNTC); Pres. JEAN-MARIE ZAMBO AMOUGOU.

Confédération des Syndicats Autonomes du Cameroun (CSAC): Yaoundé; Pres. JEAN MARIE NDI; Sec.-Gen. PIERRE LOUIS MOUANGUE.

Union des Syndicats Libres du Cameroun (USLC): BP 13306, Yaoundé; tel. 2223-4196; Pres. ANDRÉ SEME SEME.

Other trade union federations include the Union Générale des Travailleurs du Cameroun (UGTC), the Confédération Camerounaise du Travail (CCT), the Confédération Générale du Travail-Liberté du Cameroun (CGT-L), the Confédération des Syndicats Indépendants du Cameroun (CSIC) and the Confédération des Travailleurs Unis du Cameroun (CTUC).

Transport

RAILWAYS

The Trans-Cameroon railway runs from Douala to Ngaoundéré, with a branch line from Ngoumou to Mbalmayo and there were plans for the construction of a 510-km railway linking the iron ore-producing area of Mbalam, in the east of the country, with the new deep-water seaport at Kribi. Ambitious further expansion plans sought to increase the total rail network to over 6,000 km by 2035.

CAMRAIL: Gare Centrale de Bessengué, blvd de la Réunification, BP 766, Douala; tel. 233-50-26-02; e-mail service.voyageurs@camrail .net; internet www.camrail.net; f. 1999; passenger and freight transport; Pres. HAMADOU SALI; Dir-Gen. PASCAL MINY.

ROADS

Fonds Routier du Cameroun: Immeuble SNI, rue Many Ewondo, BP 6221, Yaoundé; tel. 222-22-47-52; internet www .fondsroutiercameroun.org; f. 1996; Dir-Gen. PIERRE TITTI; Administrator JEAN CLAUDE ATANGA BIKOE.

Société Camerounaise de Transport Urbain (SOCATUR): BP 1347, Douala; tel. 233-40-12-97; e-mail socatur@hotmail.fr; f. 2000; bus operator in Douala; Dir-Gen. LYDIENNE MOULOBY NGALLE BIBEHE.

SHIPPING

There are seaports at Kribi and Limbé-Tiko, a river port at Garoua, and an estuary port at Douala-Bonabéri, the principal port and main outlet, which has 2,510 m of quays and a minimum depth of 5.8 m in the channels and 8.5 m at the quays.

Autorité Portuaire Nationale (APN): Immeuble CAA, blvd du 20 Mai, BP 11538 Yaoundé; tel. 222-23-73-16; e-mail infos@apn.cm; internet www.apn.cm; Dir-Gen. SIMON PIERRE EDIBA (acting).

Port Autonome de Douala (PAD): 5 blvd Leclerc, BP 4020, Douala; tel. 233-42-01-33; e-mail pad@pad.cm; internet www.pad .cm; Chair. SHEY JONES YEMBE; Dir-Gen. CYRUS NGO'O.

Port Autonome de Kribi: BP 203, Kribi; tel. 222-46-21-00; e-mail contact@pak.cm; internet www.pak.cm; Dir-Gen. PATRICE MELOM.

Camtainer: Para-maritime Area, Douala Port, BP 4993, Douala; tel. 233-42-77-04; f. 1984; Chair. JOSEPH TSANGA ABANDA; Man. ZACHARIE KUATE.

Conseil National des Chargeurs du Cameroun (CNCC): BP 1588, Douala; tel. 233-43-67-67; e-mail info@cncc.cm; internet www .cncc.cm; f. 1975; promotion of the maritime sector; Gen. Man. AUGUSTE MBAPPE PENDA.

Consignation et Logistique du Golfe de Guinée (CLGG): Centre des Affaires Maritimes, BP 4054, Douala; tel. 233-42-00-

64; e-mail agencies@clgg-cm.com; internet www.clgg-cm.com; f. 1975; privatized Feb. 1997; 6 vessels trading with Western Europe, the USA, Far East and Africa; Chair. RENÉ MBAYEN; Man. Dir BERNARD ANDRÉ NDENGUE.

CIVIL AVIATION

There are international airports at Douala, Garoua and Yaoundé.

Cameroon Civil Aviation Authority (CCAA): BP 6998 Yaoundé; tel. 222-30-30-90; e-mail contact@ccaa.aero; internet www.ccaa .aero; f. 1999; Chair. MAXIMIN PAUL NKOUE NKONGO; Dir-Gen. PAULE ASSOUMOU KOKI.

Aéroports du Cameroun (ADC): Nsimalen, BP 13615, Yaoundé; tel. 222-23-36-02; e-mail adc@adcsa.aero; internet www.adcsa.aero; f. 1999; manages major airports; 63% state-owned; Pres. JOSEPH DIPITA; Dir-Gen. THOMAS DIEUDONNÉ OWONA ASSOUMOU.

Cameroon Airlines Corpn (CAMAIRCO): Immeuble La Rotonde, blvd de la liberté, BP 4852, Douala; tel. 233-50-55-55; internet www .camair-co.cm; f. 2008 to replace Cameroon Airlines; commenced operations in 2011; Chair. JEAN CLAUDE MAUGER AYEM; Dir-Gen. Col JEAN CHRISTOPHE ELA NGUEMA.

Tourism

Ministry of Tourism and Leisure: see Ministries.

Defence

As assessed at November 2021, Cameroon's armed forces were estimated to total 25,400 men (army 23,500, navy 1,500, air force 400). There was also a 9,000-strong paramilitary force.

Defence Budget: 246,000m. francs CFA in 2021.

Commander-in-Chief of the Armed Forces: PAUL BIYA.

Chief of Staff of the Armed Forces: Lt-Gen. RENÉ CLAUDE MEKA.

Chief of Staff of the Army: Maj.-Gen. BABA SOULEY.

Chief of Staff of the Air Force: Brig.-Gen. JEAN CALVIN MOMHA.

Chief of Staff of the Navy: Rear-Adm. JEAN MENDOUA.

Education

Since independence, Cameroon has achieved one of the highest rates of school attendance in Africa, but provision of educational facilities varies according to region. Education, which is bilingual, is provided by the Government, missionary societies and private concerns. Primary education in state schools is available free of charge, and the Government provides financial assistance for other schools. It begins at six years of age, and lasts for six years. Secondary education, beginning at the age of 12, lasts for a further seven years, comprising two cycles: four years and three years in the francophone sub-system; and five years and two years in the anglophone sub-system. In 2018/19, according to estimates by the United Nations Educational, Scientific and Cultural Organization (UNESCO), enrolment at pre-primary institutions was equivalent to 36% of children in the relevant age-group (males 35%; females 36%). In 2018/19 92% of children in the relevant age-group (96% boys; 87% girls) were enrolled at primary schools, while in 2015/16 secondary enrolment included only 46% of children in the appropriate age-group (boys 49%; girls 43%). Spending on education constituted 14.8% of total government expenditure in 2021.

Bibliography

Bieleu, V. *Politique de défense et sécurité nationale du Cameroun*. Paris, L'Harmattan, 2012.

Biyong, M. I. N. *Cameroun: combats pour l'independance*. Paris, L'Harmattan, 2009.

Chem-Langhëë, B. *The Paradoxes of Self-Determination in the Cameroons under United Kingdom Administration: The Search for Identity, Well-Being and Continuity*. Lanham, MD, University Press of America, 2004.

Chiabi, E. M. *The Making of Modern Cameroon*. Lanham, MD, University Press of America, 1997.

De Lancey, M. W., and Schrader, P. J. *Cameroon*. Oxford, Clio, 1986.

Deltombe, T., Domergue, M., and Tatsitsa, J. *Kamerun! Une guerre cachée aux origines de la Françafrique (1948–1971)* Paris, Editions la Découverte, 2011.

   La guerre du Cameroun: L'invention de la Françafrique. Paris, Editions la Découverte, 2016.

Enonchong, L. E. *The Constitution and Governance in Cameroon*. Abingdon, Routledge, 2020.

Fon, L., and Balgah, S. N. *The Urbanisation Process in Cameroon: Patterns, Implications and Prospects*. New York, Nova Publishers, 2010.

Fonge, F. *Modernization Without Development: Patterns of Change and Continuity in Post-independence Cameroonian Public Service*. Trenton, NJ, Africa World Press, 1998.

Fonjong, L. (Ed.) *Natural Resource Endowment and the Fallacy of Development in Cameroon*. Bamenda, Langaa RPCIG, 2019.

Fossungu, P. A-A. *Democracy and Human Rights in Africa: The Politics of Collective Participation and Governance in Cameroon*. Bamenda, Langaa RPCIG, 2013.

   Understanding Confusion in Africa: The Politics of Multiculturalism and Nation-Building in Cameroon. Oxford, Langaa RPCIG, 2013.

Goheen, M. *Men Own the Fields, Women Own the Crops: Gender and Power in the Cameroon Grassfields*. Madison, WI, University of Wisconsin Press, 1996.

Gros, J.-G. *Cameroon: Politics and Society in Critical Perspective*. Lanham, MD, University Press of America, 2003.

Ignatowski, C. *Journey of Song: Public Life and Morality in Cameroon*. Bloomington, IN, Indiana University Press, 2006.

Kamé, B. *The Anglophone Crisis in Cameroon*. Paris, L'Harmattan, 2018.

Kengne-Pokam, E. *La France et les Etats-Unis au Cameroun: le processus démocratique national en question*. Paris, L'Harmattan, 2009.

Konings, P. J. J. *The Politics of Neoliberal Reforms in Africa: State and Civil Society in Cameroon*. Bamenda, Langaa RPCIG, 2011.

Krieger, Milton. *Cameroon's Contemporary Culture and Politics: Prospects and Problems*. Bamenda, Langaa RPCIG, 2014.

Manga, E. J. *The African Economic Dilemma: The Case of Cameroon*. Lanham, MD, University Press of America, 1998.

Mbaku, J. M., and Takougang, J. (Eds). *The Leadership Challenge in Africa: Cameroon Under Paul Biya*. Trenton, NJ, Africa World Press, 2004.

Mehler, A. *Kamerun in der Ära Biya: Bedingungen, erste Schritte und Blockaden einer demokratischen Transition*. Hamburg, Institut für Afrika-Kunde, 1993. (Hamburger Beiträge zur Afrika-Kunde; 42).

Mougoué. J.-B. *Gender, Separatist Politics, and Embodied Nationalism in Cameroon*. Ann Arbor, MI, University of Michigan Press, 2019

Muñoz, J.-M. *Doing Business in Cameroon: An Anatomy of Economic Governance*. Cambridge, Cambridge University Press, 2018.

Neba-Fuh, E. *The Unrefined History of Southern Cameroons*. Kansas City, MO, Miraclaire Publishing, 2018.

Ngoh, V. J. *Cameroon 1884–1985: A Hundred Years of History*. Yaoundé, Imprimerie Nationale, 1988.

   Southern Cameroons 1922–1961: A Constitutional History. Farnham, Ashgate Publishing Ltd, 2001.

Nyamnjoh, F. B. *Mass Media & Democratisation in Cameroon in the Early 1990s*. Bamenda, Langaa RPCIG, 2011.

Olinga, A. D. *Cameroun:la crise anglophone sur le prisme du droit international*. Paris, L'Harmattan, 2019.

Owona, A. *La naissance du cameroun 1884–1914*. Paris, L'Harmattan, 2003.

Pingeaud, F. *Au Cameroun de Paul Biya*. Paris, Editions Karthala, 2011.

Sindjoun, L. *Comment Peut-On Etre Opposant au Cameroun?: Politique Parlementaire et Politique Autoritaire*. Dakar, Council for the Development of Social Science Research in Africa, 2005.

Takougang, J., and Krieger, M. H. *African State and Society in the 1990s: Cameroon's Political Crossroads*. Boulder, CO, Westview Press, 1998.

Takougang, J., and Amin, J. (Eds). *Post-Colonial Cameroon: Politics, Economy, and Society*. Lanham, MD, Lexington Books, 2018.

Tamuedjon, J-C. *La colonisation et le Cameroun contemporain: Cinquante ans après l'indépendance et la réunification*. Paris, L'Harmattan, 2012.

Terretta, M. *Nation of Outlaws, State of Violence: Nationalism, Grassfields Tradition, and State Building in Cameroon*. Athens, OH, Ohio University Press, 2013.

   Petitioning for our Rights, Fighting for our Nation: The History of the Democratic Union of Cameroonian Women, 1949–1960. Oxford, Langaa RPCIG, 2013.

Torrent, M. *Diplomacy and Nation-Building in Africa: Franco-British Relations and Cameroon at the End of Empire*. London, I.B. Tauris, 2012.

Yenshu, E. *State of a Union: The Half Century of Cameroon's Bicultural Experience*. Bamenda, Langaa RPCIG, 2012.

THE CENTRAL AFRICAN REPUBLIC

Physical and Social Geography

DAVID HILLING

Bordered to the north by Chad, to the east by Sudan and South Sudan, to the south by the Republic of the Congo and the Democratic Republic of the Congo, and to the west by Cameroon, the Central African Republic forms a geographic link between the Sudano-Sahelian zone and the Congo basin. The country consists mainly of plateau surfaces at 600 m–900 m above sea level, which provide the watershed between drainage northwards to Lake Chad and southwards to the Oubangui-Congo river system. There are numerous rivers, and during the main rainy season (July–October) much of the south-east of the country becomes inaccessible as a result of extensive inundation. The Oubangui river to the south of Bangui provides near-year-round commercial navigation and is the main outlet for external trade. However, development of the country is inhibited by its landlocked location and the great distance (1,815 km) to the sea by way of the fluvial route from Bangui to Brazzaville, in the Republic of the Congo, and thence by rail to Pointe-Noire.

The Central African Republic covers an area of 622,984 sq km (240,535 sq miles). At the census of December 2003 the population was 3,151,072. According to United Nations estimates, the population numbered 5,016,678 at mid-2022, giving an average density of 8.1 inhabitants per sq km. The greatest concentration of population is in the western part of the country; large areas in the east are virtually uninhabited. Of the country's numerous ethnic groups, the Gbaya and Banda jointly comprise around 60% of the population. Sango, an inter-ethnic lingua franca, was adopted as the national language in 1963 and became an official language, alongside French (the official administrative language), in 1991.

Only in the south-west of the country is the rainfall sufficient (1,250 mm) to sustain a forest vegetation. The south-western Lobaye region is a source of coffee (traditionally one of the main cash crops), cocoa, rubber, palm produce and timber. Cotton, also an important cash crop, is cultivated in a belt beyond the forest. This area could benefit substantially from a proposed rail link with the TransCameroon railway.

Alluvial deposits of diamonds occur widely and are exploited, but uranium is potentially of much greater economic importance. The exploitation of ore-rich uranium deposits at Bakouma, 480 km east of Bangui, which had previously been inhibited by inadequate access routes and by technical problems, commenced in the late 2000s but were suspended indefinitely in 2011.

History

JUAN FANDOS-RIUS

INTRODUCTION

In 1958 the French-administered territory of Oubangui-Chari was granted internal self-government and became the Central African Republic (CAR). David Dacko became the republic's first President at independence on 13 August 1960. In January 1966 Col (later Marshal) Jean-Bédel Bokassa, the Commander-in-Chief of the Armed Forces, seized power in a coup. Bokassa's regime became increasingly despotic, corrupt and brutal. Several external opposition groups were formed, including the Mouvement pour la Libération du Peuple Centrafricain (MLPC), led from exile in France by a former Prime Minister, Ange-Félix Patassé. In September 1979 Bokassa, while in Libya, was deposed in a bloodless coup carried out by French troops, who returned Dacko to power. A multi-party system was restored in February 1981, and in September Army Chief of Staff Gen. André Kolingba took power in a bloodless coup.

Patassé, who had returned to the country in 1992, won the presidential election held in 1993. The Government's repeated failure to pay the salaries of public sector employees and members of the armed forces provoked frequent strikes and mounting political unrest during the mid-1990s. In February 1997 Gen. François Bozizé Yangouvonda was appointed Chief of Staff of the Armed Forces.

In May 2001 rebel soldiers attacked Patassé's official residence in an attempted coup. However, the insurgency was quickly suppressed by troops loyal to Patassé. Gen. Bozizé was dismissed from the post of Chief of Staff of the Armed Forces in October, and in the following month, after attempts were made to arrest him, violence erupted in Bangui between his supporters and the presidential guard, the latter supported by forces from Libya. Bozizé fled to southern Chad with his armed supporters.

BOZIZÉ ASSUMES POWER

Armed supporters of Bozizé and mercenaries from Chad converged on Bangui in March 2003, encountering little resistance from government troops. Bozizé declared himself head of state, dissolved the Assemblée Nationale (National Assembly) and suspended the Constitution. From mid-2006 Bozizé's administration was increasingly confronted by rebel activity in the north of the country. In June the Government signed a comprehensive peace agreement in Libreville, Gabon, with two rebel groups, including the Union des Forces Démocratiques pour le Rassemblement (UFDR), which provided for an amnesty for rebel fighters and their integration into either the national Forces Armées Centrafricaines (FACA) or civilian life.

In August 2012 a coalition ('Seleka' in Sango) of rebels was formed by factions of the UFDR, the Convention des Patriotes pour la Justice et la Paix (CPJP), the Convention Patriotique pour le Salut du Wa Kodro and the Union des Forces Républicaines (UFR). In December, after Seleka rebels had occupied several strategically important towns in central and northern areas of the CAR, Chadian troops were despatched to support the FACA.

President Bozizé dismissed Prime Minister Faustin Archange Touadéra on 12 January 2013, and on 15 January Seleka selected a prominent opposition figure, Nicolas Tiangaye, to be the new premier. Bozizé named the new Government in February, including representatives of the groups that had signed the Libreville accord. Tiangaye also assumed the finance portfolio, while Michel Am Nondroko Djotodia of the UFDR was appointed first Deputy Prime Minister and Minister of National Defence. However, President Bozizé also appointed several personal advisers who functioned independently of Tiangaye's Government, which weakened or nullified the power of the Seleka ministers. Some dissatisfied Seleka leaders reportedly left Bangui to join their troops in the countryside.

DJOTODIA: THE NEW STRONGMAN

On 20 March 2013 Seleka forces launched an offensive against Bangui and by 24 March had taken control of the capital. Bozizé fled the country into exile, while Djotodia declared himself head of state, dissolved the National Assembly and suspended the Constitution, stating that he would abide by the Libreville accord. In July 2013 the Conseil National de Transition (CNT—National Transitional Council) approved a provisional Constitution. Djotodia was inaugurated as transitional head of state on 18 August for a period of 18 months. In Bangui—where the majority Christian population had suffered months of looting by Seleka's predominantly Muslim soldiers—and at various locations around the country, angry anti-Balaka ('anti-machete') groups began attacking Seleka soldiers and unarmed Muslim civilians.

On 5 December 2013 the United Nations (UN) Security Council approved an African Union (AU) Peace and Security Council proposal to send an African-led Mission Internationale de Soutien à la Centrafrique (MISCA—International Support Mission) to the CAR. On the same day France launched Operation Sangaris, and its troops imposed a curfew that lasted for three months. Anti-Balaka attacks on Muslims nevertheless continued in Bangui and other locations around the country.

PRESIDENT SAMBA-PANZA: A HOPE FOR TRANSITION

After the transitional authorities' efforts to organize democratic elections failed, on 10 January 2014 the CNT voted to terminate Djotodia's rule. Prime Minister Tiangaye resigned on the same day, and on 11 January Djotodia left for exile in Benin. On 20 January the CNT elected Catherine Samba-Panza (the mayor of Bangui and a former business executive) to the role of interim President, thus making her the CAR's first female head of state. Samba-Panza was elected from a reduced field of only eight candidates, following a controversial decision by the CNT to eliminate party leaders from the contest.

In April 2014 the UN Security Council authorized the dispatch, by 15 September, of 12,000 peacekeeping troops to the CAR to replace the contingents of both MISCA and the Bureau Intégré de l'Organisation des Nations Unies en Centrafrique (BINUCA). This Mission Multidimensionnelle Intégrée des Nations Unies pour la Stabilisation en République Centrafricaine (MINUSCA—UN Multidimensional Integrated Stabilization Mission in the Central African Republic) was mandated 'to devise, facilitate and provide technical assistance' for elections to be held in 2015, with support from French troops under Operation Sangaris.

In July 2014 former Seleka officers met in Birao and established the Front Populaire pour la Renaissance de Centrafrique (FPRC); Djotodia was appointed as President of the new organization, while Noureddine Adam (the leader of the CPJP and former deputy head of Seleka) was named as a Vice-President.

THE BANGUI NATIONAL FORUM: AN OPPORTUNITY FOR RECONCILIATION

During August–December 2014 the humanitarian situation remained critical throughout the CAR, with attacks on civilians and violent confrontations between former Seleka and anti-Balaka groups frequently reported in Bangui and elsewhere. On 15 September MINUSCA troops duly replaced the MISCA and BINUCA contingents. Later in that month the International Criminal Court (ICC), in The Hague, Netherlands, opened an inquiry into the crimes that had been committed in the CAR since August 2012.

The defection of several former Seleka leaders led to the creation in October 2014 of a new politico-military group, the Union pour la Paix en Centrafrique (UPC) led by Gen. Ali Darassa. Negotiations were launched in late December by Congolese President Denis Sassou Nguesso, supported by President Uhuru Kenyatta of Kenya, between former Seleka members (the pro-Djotodia FPRC) and anti-Balaka (pro-Bozizé) representatives. An initial agreement was signed in Nairobi, Kenya, in January 2015, but this was rejected by the CAR Government on the grounds that it would involve the installation of new transitional authorities in the CAR, the revision of the provisional Constitution of 2013 and a general amnesty, thus granting impunity for serious crimes.

Following popular consultations in early 2015, the Government announced that the Forum National de Bangui (FNB), comprising delegates from across CAR society, was to be convened in early May to discuss and compile plans for the process of reconciliation. It was agreed that the armed groups would participate in the event. On 23 April, in Bangui, Prime Minister Mahamat Kamoun and 10 armed groups signed a binding agreement, which included acceptance of a peace deal signed in July 2014 in Brazzaville, Republic of the Congo, and a pledge by the groups to release all captive children and to participate actively in the forthcoming FNB.

Also in April 2015, *The Guardian*, a British newspaper, revealed details of French and UN inquiries into the alleged sexual abuse of women and children by international peace-keepers in Bangui between December 2013 and June 2014. These revelations caused widespread outrage, and the Governments of the CAR and France announced that an investigation would be conducted. In May 2015 the French public prosecutor opened an inquiry into the allegations, and the French Government denied reports that it was suppressing coverage of the scandal. In June UN Secretary-General Ban Ki-Moon announced the establishment of an independent inquiry into the allegations of sexual abuse. The inquiry's report, which was published in December, confirmed the credibility of the allegations and condemned the failure of the UN peacekeeping mission to take any retaliatory action.

The FNB was convened in Bangui on 4 May 2015: it was attended by some 600 representatives, including former Seleka and anti-Balaka members. After a week of discussions, the FNB adopted recommendations on a national strategy for peacebuilding, including measures to end impunity for crimes against humanity and war crimes, to make certain leaders (both past and present) ineligible to hold power during the transitional period, to extend the mandate of Samba-Panza's Government and to postpone the elections. Samba-Panza declared that the elections would be held by the end of 2015. On the sidelines of the FNB, several key agreements were also concluded. On 5 May the UN Children's Fund (UNICEF) brokered an agreement with 10 armed groups, which pledged to release, and end the recruitment of, child soldiers. Nine days later some 350 children were freed by armed groups in Bambari, and it was envisaged that the agreement would ultimately result in the release of up to 10,000 children who had been used as soldiers or slaves. On 10 May a Republican Pact for Peace, National Reconciliation and Reconstruction and an Agreement on Disarmament, Demobilization, Reintegration and Repatriation (DDRR) was signed by the Government and nine armed groups. On 23 May Samba-Panza appointed an FNB monitoring committee, led by Prime Minister Kamoun. The Government, the UN, the AU, the European Union (EU), the Organization of Islamic Cooperation (OIC) and the CAR's other international partners considered the FNB to have been a success, as it had brought all of the opposing parties together. However, there were subsequent concerns that some rebel leaders, including Adam of the FPRC and Abakar Sabone of the Mouvement des Libérateurs Centrafricains pour la Justice (MLCJ), had disavowed their FNB representatives, rejected the signed agreements or even threatened to declare war against the Government.

In late August 2015 the electoral law was revised in order to allow refugees to take part in the forthcoming constitutional referendum and elections, and the country was divided into 140 electoral districts, each of which would elect one representative to the National Assembly. On 28 August the Transitional Constitutional Court (TCC) confirmed that provisional Presidents, Prime Ministers and government members who had held power in the CAR between 18 August 2013 and 30 December 2015 could not run for office, once the transition period ended. On 30 August the CNT approved a revised constitutional draft.

During a visit to the CAR in early September 2015, UN High Commissioner for Human Rights Zeid Ra'ad Zeid al-Hussein commended the progress made by MINUSCA through its arrest of former Seleka and anti-Balaka leaders, but noted the lack of a functioning national justice system to investigate and prosecute the detainees. The continuing instability was highlighted in late September when four days of violence and confrontations reportedly left 60 people dead and more than 300 injured.

In early October 2015 the President of the Autorité Nationale des Élections (ANE—National Electoral Authority), Dieudonne Kombo Yaya, resigned, citing difficulties over establishing a timetable for the electoral process. He was replaced by Marie-Madeleine Nkouet-Hoornaert, who, on 9 November, announced that the constitutional referendum would take place on 13 December, followed by the first round of concurrent presidential and legislative elections on 27 December, and—if no candidate received a majority—by a run-off presidential poll on 31 January 2016. The transitional period was extended from 31 December 2015 to 31 March 2016.

TOUADÉRA: CENTRAL AFRICANS' CHOICE FOR PEACE

On 8 December 2015 the TCC published a list of 30 approved candidates for the presidential election. These included former Prime Ministers Anicet-Georges Dologuélé of the Union pour le Renouveau Centrafricain (URCA), Martin Ziguélé of the MLPC and Touadéra (standing as an independent); other prominent candidates included Désiré Kolingba of the Rassemblement Démocratique Centrafricain (RDC) and the non-affiliated Jean-Serge Bokassa (son of the former President) and Charles-Armel Doubane. Among the rejected candidates were Bozizé, who did not appear on the electoral roll, and anti-Balaka leader Patrice Edouard Ngaïssona, who was reported to have unpaid debts to the Treasury.

Violence aimed at destabilizing the democratic process was reported during the referendum on the draft Constitution, which was held as scheduled on 13–14 December 2015 and attracted a turnout of just 38%. Nevertheless, the Constitution was approved by an overwhelming majority, of 93% of the vote. On 14 December Adam proclaimed an autonomous republic in Kaga-Bandoro, but one week later, following mediation by the OIC, he recanted and publicly acknowledged that he would henceforth support the election process.

The first round of elections to the presidency and to the National Assembly took place on 30 December 2015, contested by 30 candidates. At the first ballot, in which voter turnout was a reported 65.6%, Dologuélé obtained 23.7% of the votes, and Touadéra 19.1%; the two thus proceeded to a second round of voting. On 25 January the TCC annulled the results of the concurrent National Assembly elections on the grounds of irregularities. President Samba-Panza announced that the second round of voting in the presidential election would take place, concurrently with a rerun of the first round of legislative elections, on 14 February. Touadéra, who garnered support from the MLPC and other minor parties, obtained 62.7% of the vote against Dologuélé's 37.3%. Touadéra was inaugurated as President on 30 March, following which the CAR's two-year suspension from the AU was lifted (see *External Relations*).

The second round of the legislative elections, for 85 seats, was conducted on 31 March 2016, following the first round in February, in which 46 deputies were elected. Results were annulled in 12 constituencies, where polls were subsequently rerun. Independent candidates secured 60 seats, while the Union Nationale pour la Démocratie et le Progrès took 16 seats, the URCA 11 seats, the MLPC 10, the RDC eight and the Kwa na Kwa coalition (KNK—'Work and Only Work' in Sango) seven.

President Touadéra appointed the head of his electoral campaign, Mathieu Simplice Sarandji, as the new Prime Minister in early April 2016. Doubane was appointed as Minister of Foreign Affairs, African Integration and Central Africans Abroad, and Jean-Serge Bokassa as Minister of the Interior, Public Security and Territorial Administration. The new administration prioritized peace, security, social inclusion and cohesion, and post-crisis economic recovery.

In mid-April 2016 national and international human rights organizations, including the Observatoire Centrafricain des Droits de l'Homme, Human Rights Watch and Amnesty International, sent an open letter to President Touadéra urging the CAR Government to effect the establishment of the Special Criminal Court (SCC). Later that month Touadéra resumed talks with armed groups on the DDRR process. In April and July the UN Security Council agreed successive extensions to the mandate of MINUSCA until 15 November 2017, in order that the latter could complete post-conflict priority activities, including supporting the political process and national reconciliation and establishing state authority nationwide.

Adama Dieng, the UN Secretary-General's Special Adviser on the Prevention of Genocide, visited Bangui in May 2016 to attend the launch of the CAR's National Committee for the Prevention and Punishment of the Crime of Genocide, Crimes against Humanity and all Forms of Discrimination. In August President Touadéra announced appointments to a 41-member national DDRR consultative and monitoring committee, which was to serve as a formal framework for the DDRR process and included representatives of 11 armed groups from both anti-Balaka and Seleka factions. The inaugural meeting of the committee was held in October. Also in August, Jean-Francis Bozizé, a former cabinet minister and the son of the former President, was detained after handing himself in at the MINUSCA mission headquarters, on historical charges of torture, extra-judicial killings and the misappropriation of public funds; he was subsequently released by court order and placed on probation.

THE DDRR PROCESS AND EFFORTS TOWARDS RECOVERY

Violence escalated across the country during September 2016, threatening to derail the nascent DDRR process and resulting in about 50 deaths and the displacement of a further 3,500 people. The situation worsened after the assassination in Bangui on 4 October of Marcel Mombeka, a senior military officer and former member of Samba-Panza's security staff. Renewed violence ensued, lasting for several days, between Seleka and anti-Balaka factions in the capital.

On 18–19 October 2016 several former Seleka factions assembled in the central town of Bria and confirmed their amalgamation into the FPRC (of which Adam remained a key leader) together with the Bambari-based Rassemblement Patriotique pour la Renaissance en Centrafrique (RPRC), led by Gen. Joseph Zindeko. The assembly produced the 'Bria Declaration', which called for the partition of the country and the resumption of dialogue between former Seleka rebels, anti-Balaka groups and the Government.

At the end of October 2016 Operation Sangaris was formally ended; a 'tactical reserve force' of 350 French troops was to remain in the country in support of MINUSCA.

Also in October 2016, with support from the EU and the World Bank, the CAR Government approved the Plan National de Relèvement et de Consolidation de la Paix (National Recovery and Peacebuilding Plan) to cover the period 2017–21, articulated around three priority pillars: to reinforce peace, security and reconciliation (with support from the UN); renew the social contract between the state and the population (supported by the EU); and promote economic recovery and boost productive sectors (supported by the World Bank), at the considerable total cost of US $3,161m. The Plan was presented and discussed at an international donor conference held in Brussels, Belgium, in November 2016, with donors pledging aid to the CAR Government totalling $2,268m. over three years.

FURTHER ESCALATIONS OF VIOLENCE IN 2017

Further confrontations between FPRC and UPC factions in Bria in November 2016 resulted in the deaths of 48 people, with some 5,000 being displaced. Tensions escalated in early 2017. Nine people died, and more than 9,000 were displaced following violent attacks in Bocaranga in early February, with further clashes occurring in Ndassima (near Bambari) and in Bangui in the ensuing days, resulting in at least 24 further deaths. The MINUSCA unit in Bocaranga was heavily criticized for failing to intervene to protect civilians in the attacks there. On 11 February Gen. Zindeko, the military chief of the FPRC, was killed near Ippy, in central CAR, reportedly in a MINUSCA strike aiming to prevent the movement of troops belonging to the FPRC and to another former Seleka faction, the Mouvement Patriotique pour la Centrafrique (MPC), towards Bambari, where they were seeking to dislodge the authority of the UPC and its military leader, Gen. Darassa. Following negotiations with, and an ultimatum given by, MINUSCA, Darassa left Bambari on 21 February before open confrontation occurred between the two sides. The country was wracked by further violent confrontations in March and April.

Meanwhile, in December 2016 the UN announced that it had completed an internal investigation into allegations of the sexual abuse of 139 women and children in the CAR in 2014 and 2015 by Burundian and Gabonese peacekeepers and had identified 41 suspects.

The World Bank agreed in March 2017 to provide US $10.5m. in aid to rebuild 23 health centres in the Bambari region, which had been destroyed during the recent fighting. In mid-April the CAR was awarded a $30m. grant by the International Development Association (the World Bank's development finance arm), which was to finance the reintegration of 5,000 former combatants under the DDRR process. The fourth meeting of the DDRR monitoring committee, on 20–21 April, was for the first time attended by all 14 of the country's armed militia groups, although not all had yet formally engaged with the DDRR process.

On 8 May 2017 a confrontation between MINUSCA soldiers and anti-Balaka fighters near the eastern diamond-mining town of Bangassou resulted in 13 deaths and was followed by prolonged violent clashes between the UPC and anti-Balaka groups in Alindao, in south-central CAR, in which at least 37 people were killed, and some 3,000 were displaced. These events escalated into several days of fighting in late May in and around Bangassou, following which Red Cross workers confirmed that some 115 people had died, with some 7,200 inhabitants having fled the city. Meanwhile, FPRC troops engaged with anti-Balaka forces in Bria, with at least 37 lives being lost. On 18 May President Touadéra met representatives of 14 political parties, including the URCA, the RDC, the Convention Républicaine pour le Progrès Social (CRPS, represented by Tiangaye), the KNK and the MLPC to discuss the spiralling violence; all parties attending the meeting signed a declaration exhorting their members to work towards the restoration of peace.

In June 2017 Gen. Abdoulaye Miskine signed the DDRR Agreement on behalf of his faction of the former Seleka group, the Front Démocratique du Peuple Centrafricain (FDPC), at a meeting with CAR government officials in Brazzaville. Reconciliation talks brokered by the Catholic Church's Sant'Egidio Community culminated in Rome, Italy, on 19 June, in the CAR Government and representatives of 13 armed groups signing a political agreement, including an immediate ceasefire: this was soon broken, however, when fighting resumed in Bria.

Meanwhile, in May 2017 the Office of the UN High Commissioner for Human Rights published a report mapping human rights violations in the CAR from 2003 to 2015. This was to serve as a working document for future investigations by the SCC. Six of the SCC's 25 members and a prosecutor (from the Democratic Republic of the Congo—DRC) were sworn in on 30 June 2017.

In July 2017 Human Rights Watch published *Killing Without Consequence*, an extensive report which ascribed blame for the war crimes and atrocities against humanity that had occurred in central CAR during 2014–17 to Seleka and anti-Balaka forces alike, and criticized MINUSCA for frequently failing to protect civilians.

A 'ROADMAP' FOR PEACE AND NATIONAL RECONCILIATION

Delegates to a regional round-table meeting held under the auspices of the African Union Initiative for Peace and Reconciliation in Libreville on 17 July 2017 approved a new 'roadmap' for peace and national reconciliation. The AU document integrated the Sant'Egidio Community's peace agreement, the

CAR National Assembly's initiative for peace, adopted in May, and recommendations made by the FNB in May 2015, and envisaged the creation of a facilitation panel to mediate between the different parties in the peace process. Managed by the International Support Group for the CAR (ISG-CAR, see *External Relations*) the facilitation panel met for the first time in September 2017.

Violent confrontations continued during the second half of 2017. In mid-July the UN Office for the Coordination of Humanitarian Affairs warned that a new humanitarian crisis was emerging in the CAR after an escalation of violence in the east of the country, which resulted in an increase of more than 100,000 in the number of IDPs. On 26 July the UN Panel of Experts on the CAR submitted a mid-term report to the UN Security Council in which it acknowledged that, more than a year after the election of President Touadéra, little progress had been made in addressing the root causes of the crisis in the CAR. Moreover, the panel stated that the prospects for disarmament remained distant, as most CAR territory continued to be under the control of armed groups, despite the nationwide presence of MINUSCA. For its part, MINUSCA pointed to the establishment of new armed groups such as the Rassemblement des Républicains (RDR), led by Gaëtan Boade and reported to be based around Ippy, as being in direct contravention of the mission's aims of ensuring sustainable peace in the country. In early September, following violence in the southern prefecture of Basse-Kotto, Amnesty International criticized MINUSCA for failing effectively to protect the civilian population amid a deteriorating security situation. Meanwhile, in August the CAR Government and the UN Development Programme (UNDP) signed the UN Development Assistance Framework for 2018–21.

In early November 2017 representatives of several former rebel groups, including the UFDR, the MLCJ, anti-Balaka groups, the FDPC and Révolution et Justice (RJ, led by a former minister, Armel Sayo), founded a new alliance, Coalition Siriri ('peace' in Sango), which aimed to work towards achieving sustainable peace and national reconciliation. Meanwhile, the UN Panel of Experts on the CAR submitted the final report on its work to the UN Security Council Committee. The report, which the Security Council considered in December, stated that the actions of self-proclaimed self-defence groups in several parts of the country were contributing to the deterioration of the humanitarian and human rights situations, and that economic and trafficking interests lay behind the violence.

In mid-November 2017 the UN Security Council extended the mandate of MINUSCA for a further year, increasing the mission's maximum authorized strength by 900 personnel. Clashes between the RDR and a joint force of the FPRC and the UPC erupted at Ndassima on 10 December, in which Boade was reportedly killed. Further violent confrontations took place on 27 December between former Seleka and anti-Balaka groups at Paoua, in the north-west of the country. Two days later it was reported that Abdoulaye Hissène of the CPJP was among three rebel leaders who had been driven out of Bria in an operation led by French forces.

On 11 January 2018 the High Court of Paris in France dismissed a case concerning the alleged sexual abuse of children by French forces in the CAR (based on the inquiry opened by the French public prosecutor in 2015), citing a lack of sufficient evidence against the alleged perpetrators. Meanwhile, on 10 January 2018, following confrontations in Paoua between Ahamat Bahar's Mouvement National pour la Libération de la Centrafrique and the RJ, which resulted in the displacement of more than 65,000 people, Sayo announced the dissolution of the RJ, in accordance with the national DDRR programme. A total of 158 former combatants joined the FACA in February and May under a programme launched by President Touadéra in August 2017 to enable the rehabilitation into the armed forces of 560 former rebel fighters.

Fatou Bensouda, the Chief Prosecutor of the ICC, visited Bangui in March 2018 with the aim of strengthening co-operation between the ICC and the CAR court system, including the SCC, on war crimes and crimes against humanity. There was a resurgence of violence in Bangui during 8–10 April, when a joint MINUSCA–FACA operation to arrest the leader of a local armed group in the capital's largest Muslim neighbourhood, Pointe Kilométrique 5 (PK5), resulted in the deaths of at least 32 people (including a Rwandan peace-keeper). Against this backdrop, on 11 April the first meeting of the ISG-CAR was held in Bangui, and on 13 April Prime Minister Sarandji convened the inaugural meeting of a steering group charged with establishing a national Truth, Justice, Reparation and Reconciliation Commission.

President Touadéra dismissed Jean-Serge Bokassa from his ministerial post on 14 April 2018, after a dispute reportedly arose between the two over a decision to put Bokassa's late father's estate at the disposal of Russian soldiers. Clashes in mid-May led to open confrontation between MINUSCA forces and an armed group reported to be linked to Gen. Darassa's UPC, after the latter attacked Bambari. MINUSCA regained control of the town after two days' fighting. Further attacks on MINUSCA units by different militia groups took place in early June. On 8 June the Appeals Chamber of the ICC overturned the 2016 conviction on charges of war crimes and crimes against humanity of Jean-Pierre Bemba Gombo, the former commander-in-chief of the Mouvement de Libération du Congo, a rebel group based in the DRC, whose troops were found to have committed crimes including murder, rape and pillaging in the CAR during 2002–03.

Meanwhile, an attempt by the Government of the Russian Federation in July 2018 to convene peace talks in Khartoum, Sudan, between the CAR Government and several armed groups foundered, when the former refused to enter into direct negotiations, which, it claimed, could compromise its efforts to reach a peace deal under AU mediation. Instead, following separate Russian-convened negotiations in Khartoum in August, five of the principal CAR armed groups (including the FPRC and the UPC) signed a preliminary agreement envisaging the establishment of a joint negotiating platform, to be known as the Rassemblement Centrafricain. Concurrently, the AU panel of facilitators held a series of consultations with all 14 armed groups in Bouar, in north-western CAR, in preparation for the staging of a national conference between the CAR Government and the rebels. The latter drew up a list of nearly 90 demands, including a general amnesty for armed combatants.

On 26 October 2018 the President of the National Assembly, Abdou-Karim Meckassoua, was dismissed by a majority vote in the legislature after a petition was filed against him alleging financial malpractice. The vote to elect Meckassoua's replacement on 29 October was marred first by the abstention of 20 of the 140 deputies in protest against the dismissal, and second when the debate escalated into a violent exchange between two deputies, one of whom, Alfred Yekatom (known as Rombhot), was a former anti-Balaka leader. Eventually, Laurent Ngon Baba, a former minister, was elected as the new President of the legislature. In mid-November the ICC issued an arrest warrant against Rombhot for crimes against humanity and war crimes committed in western CAR during 2013–14. He was subsequently extradited to face charges at the ICC, as was Ngaïssona, who was arrested on an ICC warrant in France in December and was to face the same charges as Rombhot. Also in mid-November, the UPC launched an attack on Alindao, killing some 40 people.

In November 2018, at a constitutive assembly in Bangui, a new political movement, known as the Mouvement Coeurs Unis (MCU—United Hearts Movement), was launched in support of President Touadéra, who had been elected as an independent candidate in December 2015. Prime Minister Sarandji was appointed as the movement's Executive Secretary. On 14 December 2018 President Touadéra dismissed the Minister of Foreign Affairs and Central Africans Abroad, Doubane, replacing him with Sylvie Baïpo-Témon. Doubane was reported to have opposed Russia's increasing presence in the CAR. His dismissal occurred two days after the National Assembly ratified a new security co-operation agreement between the CAR and Russia.

Meanwhile, on 13 December 2018 the UN Security Council adopted a resolution extending the mandate of MINUSCA for a further 12 months. On 17 December President Touadéra officially launched the national DDRR programme in Paoua, at a ceremony attended by representatives of MINUSCA and of most of the CAR's armed groups. The programme, which had received World Bank funding totalling US $78m., was expected to support the reintegration of some 7,000 former combatants nationwide.

THE KHARTOUM CONFERENCE AND THE POLITICAL AGREEMENT FOR PEACE AND RECONCILIATION

A fresh round of peace talks began in Khartoum in January 2019, following preparatory negotiations mediated by the AU and the UN. The discussions were attended by representatives of the Government, political parties and all 14 armed rebel groups. The armed groups' initial demands included: the appointment of a Prime Minister from the ranks of the former rebel groups; a general amnesty for all former rebels; special legal status for rebel leaders; and the transformation of rebel groups into paramilitary units, which would co-operate with and support the FACA. On 5 February the participants at the talks initialled an accord, the Political Agreement for Peace and Reconciliation (PAPR), which was signed in Bangui on the following day by President Touadéra and representatives of the 14 armed groups.

Described by Touadéra as a landmark achievement in the history of the CAR, the accord provided for the appointment by the President of an inclusive national government, but the rebels' demands for a Prime Minister to be appointed from their ranks remained unmet. Although a general amnesty was denied, the accord did provide for a transitional justice mechanism, under which crimes committed by members of the armed groups would be considered as individual cases; an amnesty could be granted for less serious crimes. The PAPR also envisaged the establishment of a national Truth, Justice, Reparation and Reconciliation Commission and the MINUSCA-monitored formation of mixed brigades of rebel and national forces to disarm, demobilize and reintegrate former rebels. On 9 February 2019 the AU's Peace and Security Council adopted a decision on the situation in the CAR, welcoming the achievement of a political agreement while urging the UN Security Council to take the necessary measures to adapt MINUSCA's mandate to the provisions of the PAPR to realize 'adequate' post-conflict national reconstruction and development.

INCLUSIVE GOVERNMENT IN THE POST-AGREEMENT PERIOD

In accordance with the provisions of the peace accord regarding the formation of an inclusive government, Prime Minister Sarandji resigned on 22 February 2019. On 25 February President Touadéra appointed Firmin Ngrébada, his former private secretary, as Prime Minister. On 3 March Ngrébada presented a new Government, which included Maxime Mokom, a former anti-Balaka group leader, as Minister for Disarmament, Demobilization, Reintegration and Repatriation, as well as representatives of the FPRC, the UPC, the MPC and the KNK. However, shortly afterwards several participants in the peace process, including the FPRC and other rebel groups, as well as the KNK, withdrew from the Government, criticizing their representation as inadequate.

Following AU-mediated talks in Addis Ababa, Ethiopia, President Touadéra appointed an expanded Government on 22 March 2019, which included an additional 12 representatives of the armed groups. Further positions were created of civilian and military special advisers to the Presidency, and regional leaders were appointed in areas under the control of armed groups; these latter posts were filled by leading members of the armed groups. The National Assembly approved the policy programme of the Ngrébada Government, largely predicated on the provisions of the PAPR, in April.

To direct the implementation of the PAPR, an Executive Monitoring Committee, co-chaired by the CAR Government and the AU, and including all the signatory parties to the agreement and other stakeholders, was launched on 15 May 2019. The committee was to meet at least once a month. At a meeting in Bangui on 17 May, 10 of the 14 former rebel groups (excepting the FPRC, the FDPC, the MLCJ and the anti-

Balaka group led by Mokom) submitted an initial list of 1,000 former combatants to be supported under the DDRR programme. A 106-member FACA unit was deployed in mid-May at Kaga-Bandoro, in central CAR, in accordance with the PAPR's aim of creating joint security units.

The new arrangements came under pressure on several occasions in the ensuing weeks. In the worst incident, on 21 May 2019, members of the armed group known as 3R (Réclamations, Réhabilitation et Retour—Reclamation, Rehabilitation and Return), attacked several villages around Paoua, killing at least 34 people. The 3R leadership later acceded to government and MINUSCA demands and handed over three suspected perpetrators of the attack to the authorities. On 28 May the establishment of two new political groupings was announced: the Parti du Rassemblement de la Nation Centrafricaine (PRNC), which was led by Nourd Gregaza and was a splinter group of the RPRC; and E Zingo Biani ('Wake Up Earnestly' in Sango), an association formed by several Bangui-based civil society groups and political parties, under the leadership of Gervais Lakosso, a civil society activist. On 6 June former Prime Minister Kamoun launched his own party, Béafrika ti é Kwè ('Central Africa for All of Us' in Sango).

On 14 June 2019 the Ministry of the Interior banned a demonstration that E Zingo Biani planned for the following day, on security grounds. The demonstration nevertheless took place, prompting the security forces to disperse the participants and arrest Joseph Bendounga, the leader of the Mouvement Démocratique pour la Renaissance et l'Evolution de Centrafrique (MDREC) and two French journalists. Bendounga was released four days later. On the same day the ANE published the schedule for the forthcoming elections: the first rounds of the presidential and legislative elections were to be held jointly on 27 December 2020, followed by a second round on 14 February 2021. The elections were expected to cost some €30m., one-half of which was to be funded by the EU.

Violence between traders and residents in the PK5 neighbourhood of Bangui reportedly left four people dead and more than 25 injured on 10–11 July 2019. On 17 July the deputy head of MINUSCA stated that more than 450 former armed rebels had laid down their weapons, including the FDPC, which had been disbanded, and some former members of the RJ, the UFR and 3R. On 26 July the leader of the FPRC, Adam, announced that his group would abide by the PAPR and therefore disarm with immediate effect.

BOZOUMGATE AND THE GRADUAL IMPLEMENTATION OF THE PEACE PROCESS

The so-called Bozoumgate scandal made national headlines in late July 2019, after reports were published by, *inter alia*, the National Assembly and the Government, revealing that gold-mining operations by four Chinese companies in the Ouham river near Bozoum in western CAR were causing extensive environmental damage, including dangerous levels of mercury in the water. The Ministry of Mining and Geology nevertheless allowed the mining operations to continue. In April 2020 Amnesty International published a report on the Bozoumgate scandal, demanding that President Touadéra launch an independent inquiry into the situation, especially in relation to access to clean water and the health of the local population, and urging the Government to suspend the local gold-mining activities. In December 2019 the National Assembly had ordered that the Chinese companies halt mining in the Bozoum area, owing to concerns about environmental degradation. In July 2020 Amnesty International reported that the Chinese companies had left the area in April.

Meanwhile, several new political parties were formed in mid-2019, in preparation for the forthcoming elections: in July the Alliance pour la Renaissance et l'Emergence de la Centrafrique was founded, led by Bertrand Kemba and supported by other prominent politicians such as Emile Gros Raymond Nakombo, the mayor of Bangui; and in August the Cohésion Centrafricaine pour la Reconstruction, led by Sébastien Wénézoui, a former environment minister and leader of an anti-Balaka group, and Lawa Amadou, the head of a Muslim youth association, was launched in Bangui. In August the KNK voted to leave the coalition of parties that supported President Touadéra and join the opposition. The KNK also voted to expel Touadéra, owing to the recent foundation of his own party, the MCU. In October the RDC also decided to leave the pro-Touadéra coalition of parties and join the opposition, but did not withdraw its sole minister from the cabinet.

Meanwhile, in late August 2019 the CAR Government issued an arrest warrant against the FDPC leader, Gen. Miskine, who had contravened the terms of the PAPR by repeatedly threatening to ignore certain of its provisions. The following day the leader of the MPC, Mahamat al-Khatim, resigned as the Government's military adviser for the Unité Spéciale Mixte de Sécurité (USMS—Special Mixed Security Unit) in north-central CAR, claiming that his duties were inconsequential. Under the PAPR, it was envisaged that some the units would be established across the country and incorporate members of both the national military and former armed groups. Meanwhile, the murder of the son of a local leader in Birao at the end of August provoked violent confrontations in the first half of September between the FPRC and the MLCJ; at least 58 people died in the violence, and about 13,000 were displaced. In late September, owing to persistent illegal activity by 3R in western CAR, MINUSCA troops attacked and destroyed three of the armed group's operational bases in the region. On the following day clashes between two armed groups erupted at Bangao, in central-southern CAR. Despite MINUSCA's intervention to quash the violence, at least 12 people were killed in further confrontations the next day.

In mid-October 2019 the Global Hunger Index report highlighted alarming levels of hunger in the CAR, ranking it the lowest out of the 117 countries reviewed for food availability. In late October a delegation of MINUSCA, AU and Communauté Economique des Etats de l'Afrique Centrale (CEEAC) representatives held a meeting in Bouar with Gen. Sidiki Abass, the leader of 3R, who agreed that the group would be disarmed and demobilized and that its former members would then join the USMS in north-western CAR. In November Prime Minister Ngrébada established an electoral advisory committee, which was criticized by some opposition parties, including the MDREC, whose leader, Bendounga, claimed that the new body would infringe on the remit of the ANE. In the same month four leaders of CAR armed groups, including Gen. Miskine, were arrested by the Chadian authorities near the Chadian-CAR border. The detainees were transferred to N'Djamena, the Chadian capital, prompting the CAR Government to demand their extradition. Also in November the UN Security Council extended the mandate of MINUSCA for a further year, maintaining its previous troop levels of 11,650 military personnel and 2,080 police personnel.

THE RETURN OF BOZIZÉ AND DJOTODIA

Following several months of rumours and despite a UN Security Council travel ban against former President Bozizé, he returned to Bangui on 15 December 2019. Bozizé's immediate focus was on standing for the presidential election scheduled for December 2020, as all candidates were legally required to reside in the country for at least one year prior to contesting an election. Several days later, Ngaïssona, the leader of the Parti Centrafricain pour l'Unité et le Développement, announced that the party was ending its support for President Touadéra and joining the ranks of the opposition. In late December 2019 violence erupted again between traders and members of a self-defence group in the PK5 neighbourhood of Bangui, which reportedly left at least 47 people dead and 70 injured. The violence was suppressed by the deployment of MINUSCA troops.

On 10 January 2020 former President Djotodia also returned to the CAR and was formally received by President Touadéra. Later that month, as part of the PAPR reconciliation process, Touadéra also received former President Samba-Panza, former President Bozizé and several former prime ministers and other high-ranking politicians.

Simmering tensions between the FPRC and the MLCJ turned violent in Birao during 19–21 January 2020, leaving 20 people dead. A few days later ethnically based violence between two opposing factions of the FPRC—the Runga on the one side and the Gula and Kara on the other—erupted in Bria, resulting in at least 35 deaths.

In early February 2020 the Court of Appeal in Bangui sentenced 28 members of anti-Balaka self-defence groups who had attacked and killed at least 72 people in a Muslim area of Bangassou and 10 MINUSCA soldiers in May 2017. This was the first time in the CAR's history that a national court had tried individuals on charges of war crimes and crimes against humanity; five of those convicted received sentences of 10–15 years' imprisonment, life imprisonment and forced labour.

In February 2020 16 opposition parties, including the URCA, the KNK, the CRPS, the Parti Africain pour une Transformation Radicale et l'Intégration des Etats (PATRIE) and the MDREC, formed the Coalition de l'Opposition Démocratique 2020 (COD-2020) to contest the forthcoming elections under the leadership of Dologuélé. In the same month 12 rebel fighters were killed in clashes between the FPRC and the MLCJ near Birao, before MINUSCA intervened to halt the violence. In early March the MLPC nominated Ziguélé as its candidate for the presidential election. A few days later at least 13 people were killed in renewed clashes between opposing factions of the FPRC in Ndélé in northern CAR. In mid-March, following mediation by the UPC's military commander, Gen. Darassa, the two warring factions of the FPRC based in Bria that had been in conflict since January signed an agreement to effect an immediate ceasefire.

THE COVID-19 PANDEMIC AND THE IMPENDING ELECTIONS

On 14 March 2020, three days after the outbreak of the coronavirus disease (COVID-19) had been declared a global pandemic by the World Health Organization (WHO), the Government announced the first reported case of the disease in the CAR. On 19 March President Touadéra urged Central Africans to adopt basic protective measures including social distancing and proper hygiene, and on 26 March he introduced formal measures to prevent the spread of COVID-19 in the CAR. Restrictions were placed on entry at Bangui international airport and cross-border access to and from the DRC, a ban was imposed on gatherings of more than 15 people, and attendance at weddings and funerals was restricted. Furthermore, schools, bars and restaurants were closed, and individuals who had been infected were obliged to self-isolate. In April several Western countries, non-governmental organizations and UN agencies provided funds and material to the CAR to fight the pandemic, and in late April the International Monetary Fund (IMF) granted the country US $38m. in emergency assistance. On 23 May the CAR recorded its first COVID-19 fatality. As at 4 July 2022, according to WHO data, 14,371 confirmed cases of COVID-19 had been reported in the CAR, with 113 fatalities.

In mid-April 2020 draft legislation was presented to the National Assembly which would allow the Constitution to be amended in order to revise the President's and the deputies' terms, in the event that the pandemic disrupted the electoral timetable, prompting criticism from the opposition. At the end of April the ANE nevertheless confirmed that, as scheduled, the first rounds of the presidential and legislative elections would be held on 27 December. Furthermore, in June the Constitutional Court ruled any potential extension of the National Assembly's term in office as unconstitutional.

Meanwhile, in mid-April 2020 the UN Security Council added Gen. Miskine, the FDPC leader, who remained in prison in Chad, to its sanctions list, which involved the imposition of a travel ban and a freeze on his assets. On 12 May President Touadéra attended the inauguration ceremony of the USMS for the north-west in Bouar. The unit comprised more than 600 troops, including some 200 former combatants, as provided for under the PAPR. Later that month Touadéra's MCU joined with 34 other parties and political associations, including the Parti Centrafricain pour le Développement Intégré, the Parti pour la Renaissance de Centrafrique and the Front Patriotique pour le Progrès, to found the Be Oko ('One Heart' in Sango) alliance to contest the forthcoming legislative elections; the alliance supported another presidential term for Touadéra. In

June 3R suspended its participation in the PAPR process, after MINUSCA warned it about the consequences of violating the agreement if the group sought to expand the territory over which it had control.

On 10 July 2020 the CAR lifted partial pandemic-related restrictions on air traffic at Bangui international airport. On 25 July the KNK nominated former President Bozizé as its candidate for the forthcoming presidential election. Meanwhile, on 23 July, at the invitation of President Touadéra, UPC leader Darassa and MPC leader al-Khatim arrived in Bangui for negotiations. Several days later, the CAR Government and the UPC signed an agreement, under which the UPC committed not to oppose the establishment of state authority in the areas under its control, to withdraw from the eastern region of Bambouti and to end its alliance with 3R; in exchange, the UPC was permitted to return to central Bambari. However, on 24 July members of the PRNC attacked a village near Bria, where they killed at least 11 people and caused the displacement of over 400 others. In August the UN Security Council added 3R leader Gen. Abass to its sanctions list.

By early September 2020 some 2,000 former militiamen—accounting for about 90% of the estimated total eligible—most of them from the MLCJ and the FPRC, had been identified for the DDRR programme in the northern Vakaga and Haute-Kotto prefectures. A convention of the Rassemblement pour la République, held on 11–12 September, elected its leader, former head of the CNT Alexandre-Ferdinand N'Guendet, as its candidate for the forthcoming presidential elections. On 26 September the MCU nominated President Touadéra, and Béafrika ti é Kwè nominated Kamoun. Meanwhile, on 23 September the National Assembly adopted amendments to the electoral law aimed at facilitating the ANE's work by extending deadlines to ensure the registration of eligible voters.

The registration of two armed group leaders—Darassa of the UPC and Abass of 3R—on the voters' lists was widely criticized by some civil society groups, including the Groupe de Travail de la Société Civile, on the grounds that they were both foreigners and mercenaries. In October 2020 a report published by The Sentry, a US-based independent investigative organization, denounced President Touadéra, accusing him of having 'turned the country into a breeding ground for transnational criminal networks', with the support of his foreign allies. The Sentry recommended an end to the provision of financial support for the implementation of the PAPR agreement, claiming that this only served to encourage government corruption, organized crime and impunity. The Sentry urged supporting an innovative process based on dialogue.

On 7 November 2020 three armed group leaders—Gen. Darassa, Hissène of the CPJP and al-Khatim of the MPC—met in Bangui at the invitation of the CAR Government, with MINUSCA support, to negotiate a truce for the forthcoming elections. These discussions led to the signature on 10 November of a reconciliation pact among warring ethnic communities in the north-east: the Gula and Kara ethnic groups (which were linked to the MLCJ) on the one side, and the Runga and Sara (linked to the FPRC) on the other. Tensions nevertheless remained high among these communities.

On 27 November 2020 the Constitutional Court confirmed 1,502 candidates (and rejected 78) to contest the legislative elections. On 3 December the Constitutional Court upheld the registration of 17 candidates for the presidential election, including President Touadéra (of the MCU), Dologuélé (the URCA), Ziguélé (the MLPC), Kamoun (Béafrika ti é Kwè), Samba-Panza (non-affiliated), Meckassoua (Chemin de l'Espérance) and Tiangaye (the CRPS), but rejected former President Bozizé's application, citing the national and international charges and sanctions against him. Following the court's decision on Bozizé, tensions mounted in Bangui and several western cities. Later that month Bozizé announced that he accepted the Constitutional Court's decision.

The leaders of six armed groups, the MPC, 3R, the UPC, the FPRC, Mokom's anti-Balaka group and Ngaïssona's anti-Balaka group, met on 15 December 2020 in the north-western village of Kamba Kota and signed a joint declaration reiterating demands for the organization of a national political conference before the elections. They also created an alliance, the Coalition des Patriotes pour le Changement (CPC), against the

Government. Shortly afterwards, URCA leader Dologuélé met Bozizé in Bossangoa, where they signed an agreement under which Bozizé's KNK would officially support Dologuélé's presidential candidacy. On 18 December fighting erupted in the western town of Bossembélé, while Bozoum and Yaloké were seized by CPC forces, as part of the rebel strategy of besieging the Bangui-Douala corridor—the key route for supplies to the capital. On the following day heavy clashes were reported in Mbaiki, near Bangui, between rebel forces and the FACA, which was supported by Russian mercenaries reported to be personnel from the Wagner Group, a Russian private military company. Prior to the elections, further armed confrontation also took place at a Béloko border post in western CAR and in central Bambari.

The membership of the ANE was renewed on 24 December 2020, and Mathias-Barthélémy Morouba was elected as its President. Owing to the climate of violence, several presidential candidates, including Dologuélé, Tiangaye and Kamoun, requested that the Constitutional Court postpone the elections to allow for an improvement in the security situation, but on 26 December the Court rejected these appeals. The first round of the concurrent presidential and legislative elections consequently proceeded on 27 December. However, owing to the ongoing violence, polling did not take place in 29 of the 71 districts (and only partly in six). Thus, only a reported 35% of the total electorate voted. The COD-2020 promptly demanded that the elections be declared invalid, while other political groups, including the MLPC, urged that polls be carried out in the districts affected by violence. At the end of December Abass (representing 3R), al-Khatim (the MPC), Darassa (the UPC) and Mokom (anti-Balaka) were dismissed from their government positions by President Touadéra, owing to their suspected involvement in the recent unrest. On 4 January 2021 the Public Prosecutor opened a judicial inquiry against Bozizé over his alleged involvement in the violence and disruption of the election process.

TOUADÉRA'S DISPUTED RE-ELECTION AND POST-ELECTORAL VIOLENCE

Meanwhile, according to provisional results announced by the ANE on 4 January 2021, President Touadéra had been re-elected outright in the first round. Despite the Government's imposition of a nationwide night-time curfew on 7 January, in an attempt to halt the violence, clashes between rebel groups and the FACA were reported over the following days in several cities. On 13 January CPC forces launched an attack on the outskirts of Bangui, which was repelled by MINUSCA; one peacekeeper and 37 rebels were killed in the fighting. Former Chief of Staff of the Armed Forces Gen. Ludovic Ngaïfeï was subsequently arrested for alleged involvement in the attack, which was regarded by the Government as an attempted coup. On 18 January amid allegations by the opposition of malpractice, and despite the very low voter turnout and poor organization of the polls, the Constitutional Court confirmed Touadéra's re-election as President, with 53.2% of the votes cast. On the same day two MINUSCA peacekeepers were killed during fighting over control of south-eastern Bangassou. On 21 January a 15-day nationwide state of emergency was imposed by President Touadéra to facilitate arrests during ongoing investigations by the authorities. Shortly afterwards, Mahamat Said-Abdel-Kani, a former Seleka commander, was arrested and on 24 January transferred to the ICC by the CAR army. On the following day the judiciary issued an arrest warrant against rebel leader Sabone (who was reportedly a CPC spokesperson) for inciting disobedience and refusing to pay taxes.

On 1 February 2021 the Constitutional Court confirmed the election of candidates to only 22 of the 140 seats in the National Assembly, including seven MCU representatives. On the following day the COD-2020 opposition coalition again demanded the annulment of the elections, and its members suspended further participation in both the second round and re-run polls, with the exception of Dologuélé's URCA, which distanced itself from the coalition's stance. On 5 February the National Assembly approved the extension of the nationwide state of emergency for six months in a stated attempt to improve the security

situation. During early February the FACA made progress in clearing the Bangui-Douala corridor in the west and regained control over five towns, including Bossembélé and Yaloké, thereby allowing a humanitarian aid convoy to reach Bangui, after a 50-day blockade. The CAR Government accused several political figures of having instigated the CPC's insurrection, including former President Bozizé, two of his sons and Mokom. On 19 February President Touadéra barred nearly all leaders and representatives of armed groups from the Government. Meanwhile, during the second half of February, following armed confrontations, the FACA expelled rebel forces from central Bambari and Ippy, followed by Bossangoa and Bozoum.

The second round of the legislative elections was held on 14 March 2021 in 118 districts, together with first-round voting in the areas previously affected by violence (however, the holding of polls remained impossible in three districts, owing to continuing rebel action). According to provisional results, of the approximately 90 deputies elected to the National Assembly, the MCU obtained 25 seats, the MLPC seven, the KNK and the RDC six each, and the URCA and the Mouvement National des Indépendants five each. On 19 March President Touadéra announced plans to organize a national conference between all parties involved in the ongoing crisis. On 23 March it was reported that Bozizé had resigned as head of the KNK to become leader of the CPC. The Russian ambassador to Bangui, Vladimir Titorenko, subsequently warned Bozizé about the consequences of his decision and accused Dologuélé of supporting Bozizé and his forces against the CAR Government. Titorenko also accused Chad of being unwilling to help the CAR in protecting their common border to prevent arms trafficking and the passage of armed groups. Titorenko's remarks drew widespread criticism for violating diplomatic norms, as well as public protestations from Dologuélé and the Chadian Government. Later in March Dologuélé and Ziguélé were prevented from leaving the country at Bangui airport, on the grounds that under the state of emergency all departures should be made only upon request. In late March it was confirmed that Gen. Abass had died from injuries reportedly sustained during fighting in Bossembélé in December 2020. On 30 March 2021 President Touadéra was sworn in for a second five-year term, although some opposition parties, including the KNK, boycotted the ceremony, continuing to reject the election results on the grounds of widespread irregularities.

On 5 April 2021, in a statement apparently issued by UPC leader Gen. Darassa, he pledged to withdraw from the CPC alliance, owing to the suffering of the population. Meanwhile, during April ongoing hostilities between the FACA and Russian mercenaries on one side and the rebel groups on the other continued in some parts of the country. On 2 April rebels attacked central Bria but were repelled by the FACA and its allies, which recaptured the towns of Bakala and Morouba on 10 April. In the west of the country, the FACA regained control of Batangafo on 12 April and Kabo on 15 April. In the east, government and allied forces recaptured Yalinga on 22 April, Mobaye on 4 May and Bakouma on 10 May.

Meanwhile, at the inaugural session of the new National Assembly on 5 May 2021, MCU Secretary-General and former Prime Minister Sarandji was elected as its President. On 14 May, following an exchange of information between MINUSCA and the CAR Government regarding alleged crimes and abuses perpetrated by the FACA and its allies (including Russian mercenaries) during the recent offensives against armed groups, the CAR authorities established a 19-member inquiry mission, charged with investigating the allegations over the following three months.

A third round of legislative elections, at which the remaining 50 seats in the National Assembly were contested, took place on 23 May 2021. Following the release of provisional results at the end of May, the representation of Touadéra's MCU in the National Assembly now stood at 36 seats, far short of a majority. However, six seats remained undeclared, and on 29 June the Constitutional Court invalidated the result in one constituency. A further round of elections, for the outstanding seven seats, was scheduled to take place on 25 July. On 11 June, following the resignation of Prime Minister Ngrébada the previous day, President Touadéra appointed Henri Marie Dondra, hitherto the Minister of Finance, as the new head of government. Meanwhile, the local population of the western town of Koui reported that its mayor and local leader and his deputy had been killed on 12 June by Russian mercenaries. A communiqué by the CAR military stated that the mayor and his deputy had died in a landmine explosion. However, on 21 June COD-2020 issued a statement attributing responsibility for the death of the two men to Russian mercenaries and demanding the immediate withdrawal of the Wagner Group's military personnel from the CAR. Furthermore, a joint report released by the US CNN television channel and The Sentry on 14 June implicated Russian mercenaries in the torture and killing of civilians in the CAR in recent months. Evariste Ngamana, the National Assembly's First Vice-President, accused CNN and The Sentry of conspiring against the CAR. On 23 June a new, 32-member Government was appointed by President Touadéra; among the six women in the administration, Baïpo-Témo retained the post of Minister of Foreign Affairs, the Francophonie and Central Africans Abroad; Claude Rameaux Bireau, previously an economic adviser to Touadéra, was appointed Minister of National Defence and Restructuring of the Army. A few days later the Government rejected as slanderous a UN report that denounced 'violations of international humanitarian law' by the CAR military and Russian mercenaries operating in the country.

On 1 July 2021 the Russian Ministry of Foreign Affairs acknowledged the arrival in Bangui of an additional contingent of Russian 'military advisers' bringing the total in the CAR to 1,135. On 2 July in Bangui the 11 members of the Truth, Justice, Reparation and Reconciliation Commission were sworn in, and Marie Edith Douzima-Lawson was appointed its Chairwoman. On 5 July, following the publication of President Touadéra's decree on the organizing committee for the 'republican dialogue' national conference in late June, several opposition leaders, including Ziguélé, criticized the unrepresentative membership of the committee and demanded that the Government revise its composition before they would participate in it. On 21 July at least 12 civilians were killed near Bossangoa, for which Russian mercenaries, UN peacekeepers and CPC rebels were all variously blamed, amid persisting uncertainty over responsibility for the assault. On 25 July legislative elections were held in the remaining seven constituencies of the 140-seat National Assembly, with a voter turnout of some 60%. Final results of the elections were published in August: the ruling MCU occupied 41 seats, independent candidates, many of whom supported the MCU, held 35, the KNK won 10, and representatives of 22 small opposition parties accounted for the remaining 54 seats.

Meanwhile, in north-western CAR heavy clashes between Russian mercenaries and 3R rebels took place near Koui in early August 2021, and in Sabewa, Bozou and other villages and the town of Beïna later in the month. On 10 August the Constitutional Court annulled the election of Meckassoua as a member of the National Assembly, prompting criticism from the COD-2020. On 18 August The Sentry published a report claiming that a CAR subsidiary company of Castel Group, a French beverage company, had funded and provided support to UPC rebels responsible for mass killings, abductions and torture in the CAR.

In early September 2021, in an offensive against the FACA and its allies, 3R rebels attacked a convoy on the Beloko–Baboua road in north-western CAR and seized the village of Zoukombo. Shortly afterwards, Russian mercenaries launched an offensive against UPC rebels in the central town of Maloum. On 4 September Capt. Eugène Ngaïkosset (known colloquially as the 'Butcher of Paoua') of the Presidential Guard was arrested on the orders of the SCC; he was officially charged in court with crimes against humanity in the following week. In mid-September UPC leader Gen. Darassa reaffirmed his group's withdrawal from the CPC, and Hamadou Tanga, the leader of a dissident faction of the UPC, requested that the Government integrate his approximately 300 soldiers under the DDRR programme. In late September a conference sponsored by the Sant'Egidio Community, held in the Italian capital, Rome, brought together representatives from parties including the MCU, the MLPC, PATRIE, the URCA, the KNK and the Parti National pour la Nouvelle Afrique Central (PNCN), as well as religious leaders, who at the conclusion of the gathering signed the Rome Declaration, aimed at facilitating a forthcoming 'republican dialogue'.

Following the release of a UN report in June 2021 detailing crimes and abuses both by rebel groups and by FACA soldiers and Russian mercenaries, President Touadéra ordered the creation of a special commission of inquiry. In the report of its findings issued in early October, the CAR Government acknowledged some of the accusations made by the UN about war crimes and acts of torture committed mainly by rebel groups, but also by FACA soldiers and their Russian allies, since a broad counter-offensive had started in December 2020.

On 15 October 2021, following the recommendations made by the International Conference on the Great Lakes Region (ICGLR) held in mid-September in Luanda, Angola, President Touadéra declared a nationwide unilateral ceasefire in order to pave the way for the implementation of the roadmap approved by the other ICGLR member states. The CAR Government acknowledged the contents of the roadmap, including the CPC coalition's pledge to suspend its armed struggle against the CAR state and to embrace the DDRR programme. Meanwhile, the President of the National Assembly, Sarandji, thanked the Russian contingent for its support to the FACA in restoring state authority in many parts of the country. On 27 October the Minister of State and Chief of Staff at the Presidency, and Chairman of the organizing committee of the 'republican dialogue', Obed Namsio, announced that armed group representatives would not be invited to the forthcoming conference. At the end of the month, following disagreements about membership of the organizing committee and the National Assembly's intention to remove the parliamentary immunity of several high-ranking members, including Dologuélé and Ziguélé, the COD-2020 announced its withdrawal from the 'republican dialogue' process.

On 10 November 2021 the Criminal Court in Bangui issued a list of some 30 people to be put on trial for crimes linked to unrest across the country in recent years, including former President Bozizé, former President of National Assembly Meckassoua, and former ministers and senior members of armed groups. On 19 November Ali Hassan Bouba, the Minister in charge of Stockbreeding and Animal Health, was arrested in his office on the orders of the SCC on charges of war crimes and crimes against humanity as a former leader of the UPC, after his followers threatened to resume hostilities. However, at Bouba's initial appearance before the SCC on 26 November, he was unexpectedly released, to public dismay and criticism from the MLPC. At the end of the month Gen. Darassa of the UPC accused government forces and their Russian allies of repeatedly flouting the ceasefire and announced his group's withdrawal from the PAPR agreement and its return to the rebel CPC (later becoming the coalition's Chief of General Staff).

In early December 2021 Amnesty International expressed criticism that current legal proceedings to prosecute human rights crimes were falling far short of addressing the needs for justice in the CAR, as most SCC arrest warrants were not being executed, claiming that despite the Government's promises, very few individuals suspected of war crimes or crimes against humanity had been arrested, prosecuted or tried. Later in the month the UN Security Council voted to add Gen. Darassa to its list of individuals under sanctions.

In early January 2022 the FACA and CPC rebels clashed in Kamba Kota, and four civilians were killed by Russian mercenaries in central Bria. Later that month some 65 civilians died during an armed confrontation between Russian mercenaries and UPC rebels in Aïgbado village near Bria. Alarmed by the large number of casualties, several political leaders, including Ziguélé of the MLPC, called for an inquiry into the incident. Meanwhile, local elections were scheduled by the ANE to place on 11 September, only to be postponed in March to an unspecified date, owing to lack of funding to organize the polls.

A NEW PRIME MINISTER

Meanwhile, in early February 2022, after the National Assembly voted against removing parliamentary immunity from several senior deputies, including Dologuélé and Ziguélé, the

COD-2020 opposition coalition announced that it would participate in the organizing committee of the 'republican dialogue' national conference. On 4 February the pro-French Prime Minister Dondra resigned, amid factional tensions in the legislature, and was replaced by Félix Moloua, hitherto Minister of the Economy, Planning and International Co-operation. On 12 February Russian mercenaries, in a dispute over local diamond control, attacked Ouadda in north-eastern CAR and killed RPRC leader Zakaria Damane and about 20 of his soldiers. Later in the month four armed French soldiers serving in MINUSCA were arrested by FACA forces on suspicion of planning to assassinate President Touadéra. On the following day the UN appealed to Touadéra for the immediate release of the soldiers; they were released from custody two days later.

In mid-March 2022 a clash between Russian mercenaries and FPRC rebels in Gounda, near Ndélé, resulted in four Russians, six rebels and two civilians being killed. Further clashes and killings took place in Gordile, Tiringoulou and Sikikédé, in the northern Vakaga prefecture, in which at least 20 people were killed. On 14 March anti-Balaka group leader Mokom, who had been arrested in southern Chad, near the border with the CAR, by the Chadian army in February, was transferred to the ICC.

THE 'REPUBLICAN DIALOGUE'

On 21 March 2022 the highly anticipated 'republican dialogue' national conference commenced in Bangui, but the main opposition groups, including COD-2020, the MLPC and PATRIE refused to attend, on the grounds that armed groups had been excluded from the talks. Over the next week some 450 participants organized into five committees, including foreign affairs and international co-operation, peace and security, the rule of law, and economic and social development, produced some 600 recommendations. A particular point of contention among the opposition and civil society groups was the conference's discussion about amending the Constitution to allow the re-election of President Touadéra for a further term, but in order to avert the risk of public protests the issue was finally discharged from the proceedings, on the grounds that the conference was not competent to hear and produce such a recommendation, and the issue was sent to the National Assembly for debate. The conference's recommendations included, *inter alia*, asking for a complete removal of the arms embargo imposed against the CAR, the reopening of the Ecole Militaire des Enfants de Troupe military academy and the compulsory training of former combatants at the Jeunesse Pionnière Nationale youth organization for civic education, as well as property restitution and compensation for victims of violence.

Michelle Bachelet, the UN High Commissioner for Human Rights, at the end of March 2022 condemned persistent serious human rights violations in the CAR, including murders and sexual violence against civilians by all parties. On 1 April Prime Minister Moloua proposed a four-pillar strategy for national development, based on peace, security, justice and the development of foreign relations, which was approved by a majority of members of the National Assembly. In mid-April an anti-Balaka militia attacked ethnic Fulani in the village of Békadili, near Yaloké in western CAR, killing at least 13 people, and Russian mercenaries reportedly killed more than 10 people in the northern Vakaga prefecture. In the following days MINUSCA opened an investigation into the latter attack.

BITCOIN: A NEW OFFICIAL CURRENCY

In late April 2022 the National Assembly unanimously adopted Bitcoin as an official national currency alongside the franc CFA, thus making the CAR the second country in the world to adopt a cryptocurrency as legal tender (after El Salvador, which did so in 2021). At the same time, the Agence Nationale de Régulation de Transactions Electroniques was established to regulate cryptocurrency transactions and automated teller machines nationwide. In response to this decision, the IMF warned the CAR Government that cryptocurrencies were not a quick remedy for the nation's financial problems. Following strong opposition from the Banque des Etats de l'Afrique Centrale (BEAC), in July the CAR Government froze the application of its law adopting Bitcoin as an official currency until the BEAC issued regulations for cryptocurrency throughout the CFA franc monetary zone.

Régis Lionel Dounda, the former Minister of Youth, Sport and Civic Education, was convicted of misappropriation of public funds by the Criminal Court in Bangui in early May 2022 and sentenced to 10 years' imprisonment with hard labour and a fine of 3m. francs CFA; he planned to appeal against the Court's judgement. In the following week MINUSCA claimed that the UPC had killed 10 civilians in an attack in the village of Bokolobo near Bambari. Later in May the Government announced a plan to launch a national cryptocurrency hub called Sango, using a US $35m. grant from the World Bank for the digitalization of public services. For its part, the World Bank advised against using the funding for this purpose and expressed concerns about the CAR's adoption of Bitcoin. On 26 May, despite past recommendations to the contrary by the Constitutional Court, the National Assembly State Institutions Commission presented proposals to the legislature for a debate to amend the Constitution and allow the re-election of President Touadéra for another term, prompting criticism from the opposition and civil society organizations. Meanwhile, the National Assembly passed a law at the end of the month to abolish the death penalty.

Unrest continued across the CAR in June 2022: the FACA and Russian mercenaries gained control of Dimbi village, near the southern town of Kembé, after fighting with the CPC, while the town of Ouanda-Djallé in the north-east of the country was seized by the FPRC and the UPC following clashes with FACA forces.

EXTERNAL RELATIONS

Following his confirmation as President-elect in February 2016, Touadéra undertook a month-long round of diplomatic meetings in Africa and France. President Touadéra was received in Paris by his French counterpart, President François Hollande, in April; the French Government subsequently reaffirmed its commitment to supporting the CAR economy through the Agence Française de Développement and the EU.

The CAR's relations with Russia deepened from 2017. In October, during a private visit to Russia, President Touadéra met Russian Minister of Foreign Affairs Sergei Lavrov in the Black Sea resort of Sochi; it was reported that Touadéra had primarily requested military assistance from Russia, but that both countries had also agreed to enhance their economic partnership. In December the UN granted Russia permission to supply the FACA with light arms, anti-aircraft weapons and ammunition. In May 2018 Touadéra attended the 22nd International Economic Forum in St Petersburg, meeting Russian President Vladimir Putin for discussions about bilateral humanitarian and economic cooperation. In July three Russian journalists under contract to a private company to film a documentary about mercenaries were killed by unidentified gunmen near Bangui. The Russian Government launched an inquiry into the murders, as did several international newspapers and the Russian democracy activist and former oil tycoon Mikhail Khodorkovskii, who alleged that the Russian authorities were involved. The Russian Government denied Khodorkovskii's claims. In August the CAR and Russia signed a military co-operation agreement.

In January 2018 the Chinese Government cancelled US $30.2m. of debt arising from loans granted by the People's Republic of China to the CAR between 2001 and 2005. Relations with China were enhanced in September 2018, when President Touadéra visited the Chinese capital, Beijing, to attend the summit meeting of the Forum on China-Africa Cooperation. During his visit, Touadéra signed agreements with the Chinese Government, which were expected to lead to several infrastructure development projects in the CAR, notably the construction of schools and roads. Touadéra also held a meeting with Chinese President Xi Jinping, during which he expressed his support for the Chinese Government's 'one China' policy, calling for the reunification of mainland China with the Republic of China (Taiwan).

In June 2019 an agreement on the conditions of the voluntary repatriation of some 285,000 Central Africans living in Cameroon was signed in Bangui by the UN Refugee Agency (UNHCR) and the CAR and Cameroon. Similarly, in July UNHCR and the CAR and DRC Governments concluded an agreement on facilitating the voluntary repatriation of more than 172,000 Central Africans living in the DRC. A third such agreement was signed in August by UNHCR and the Governments of the CAR and Republic of the Congo regarding the conditions of the voluntary repatriation of more than 31,000 Central African refugees living in the Republic of the Congo.

In mid-September 2019 the UN Security Council announced a partial revision of the arms embargo on the CAR, allowing, *inter alia*, supplies of small arms for security patrols in several wildlife national parks and supplies of several types of weapons and ammunition to CAR security forces. Later that month President Touadéra attended the UN General Assembly in New York, where he called for the complete lifting of the arms embargo on the CAR, claiming that it deprived the armed forces of the means to protect civilians. On the following day, at a high-level meeting on the CAR at the UN headquarters, the EU announced a new assistance package worth €60m. to support the implementation of the PAPR. On the same day, Sudan closed its border with the CAR, claiming that instability in the CAR posed a threat to Sudan's economy and security.

In mid-October 2019 President Kagame of Rwanda made an official visit to Bangui, where he and President Touadéra signed five bilateral agreements, including one concerning military co-operation. During the inaugural Russian-African summit held in late October in Sochi, Touadéra requested that President Putin authorize new shipments of weapons for the FACA and urged him to work to overturn the UN arms embargo on the CAR.

On 15 November 2019 the UN Security Council extended MINUSCA's mandate for a further 12 months and assigned it the task of assisting the CAR Government in preparations for the presidential, legislative and local elections in 2020 and 2021. Later in November 2019, as part of its Common Security and Defence Policy (CSDP), the Council of the EU announced that a new civilian mission, the CSDP Advisory Mission in the CAR, would be established to support reform of the CAR's security forces.

MINUSCA launched the 2020 Humanitarian Response Plan for the CAR in January 2020 and stated that US $401m. was required to meet the basic necessities of some 1.6m. extremely vulnerable Central Africans. At the end of that month President Touadéra made an official visit to Luanda, where he asked President João Lourenço for support in the implementation of the PAPR and in his bid to persuade the UN to lift the arms embargo on the CAR. Touadéra made similar requests to President Cyril Ramaphosa during an official visit to Pretoria, South Africa, in March.

In April 2020 President Touadéra and the Russian ambassador to the CAR, Titorenko, discussed strengthening bilateral co-operation in the fields of trade and investment, including the extraction of mineral resources, crude oil, railway construction and agriculture. Titorenko announced the continuation of military co-operation between Russia and the CAR, including the delivery of Russian weapons to the FACA and the training of the CAR security forces by Russian military personnel.

In May 2020 the CAR was the first African country to benefit from a major airlift operation by the EU to help the most vulnerable African countries to combat the COVID-19 pandemic. Some 70 humanitarian workers and 8 metric tons of medical equipment were dispatched from France to Bangui.

ICC Chief Prosecutor Bensouda arrived in Bangui on 29 September 2020 on a two-day official working visit to inform the Government of the progress made in the ICC's investigations on war crimes and crimes against humanity in the country. On the same day the EU signed an agreement with the CAR Government, the UNDP and the CAR's Special Criminal Court (see above) on a €2.5m. fund to support the operations of the court.

Prime Minister Ngrébada made a working visit to Russia on 25 October 2020, meeting Russian Minister of Industry and Trade Denis Manturov, who stated that his country was open to increased co-operation and exchanges with the CAR in sectors including transportation, mining, natural resources and medical equipment. In November the UN Security Council renewed MINUSCA's mandate until November 2021; one of the mission's priority tasks was to assist the CAR Government in the preparation and conduct of peaceful elections.

Following heavy clashes near Bangui between rebel forces and the FACA, which was supported by Russian mercenaries (see above), on 22 December 2020 Russian ambassador Titorenko denied that his country had sent any military personnel to assist the FACA, but claimed that the CAR Government had engaged Russian private security companies. On 24 December a 300-member peacekeeping contingent temporarily transferred from the UN Mission in South Sudan arrived in Bangui, as part of reinforcements for the FACA and MINUSCA prior to the elections.

The passport of former President Samba-Panza was withdrawn on 17 January 2021, and she was prevented from leaving the country at Bangui airport to attend a meeting in Dubai, United Arab Emirates. International pressure over the issue forced the Government reverse its decision, and her passport was returned to her a few days later. On 29 January President Touadéra arrived in Luanda to attend an ICGLR meeting; the participants expressed their support for the election results in the CAR and warned all rebel forces about the consequences of failing to observe an immediate ceasefire and to withdraw from around Bangui and the Bangui-Douala corridor in order to allow the free movement of supplies.

On 4 February 2021 the CAR Government and the Chinese ambassador to Bangui signed a €19.2m. trade and financial agreement aimed at assisting the reconstruction of the country. On 15 February, after a meeting with President Touadéra, Titorenko firmly ruled out negotiating with former President Bozizé or with any of the CPC armed groups fighting against the central Government in Bangui.

On 12 March 2021 the UN Security Council approved an increase in the size of MINUSCA, then comprising 13,838 personnel, by a further 3,690, in order to enable the mission to focus on protecting civilians and facilitating humanitarian access nationwide. On 20 April a second meeting on the political and security situation in the CAR took place in Luanda, among several ICGLR leaders, including President Touadéra. The ICGLR instructed the CAR Government to implement a nationwide ceasefire and charged ICGLR ministers of foreign affairs with monitoring a follow-up working group on the CAR.

On 6 May 2021 Dominic Ongwen, a commander of the Ugandan-based Lord's Resistance Army, was found guilty of crimes against humanity and war crimes in the CAR and sentenced to 25 years' imprisonment by the ICC. On 26 May President Touadéra met Angolan President Lourenço in Luanda during a working visit that was intended to strengthen diplomatic and co-operative relations between the two countries. On 30 May, following an attack launched from the CAR, allegedly by the FACA and Russian mercenaries, against a border post in southern Chad, killing six Chadian soldiers, tensions between the two countries intensified. In an effort to resolve the dispute, the two Governments agreed on an international inquiry mission into the attack, comprising representatives of the UN, the AU and the CEEAC. In early June the mission visited Bangui and met the main groups involved in the crisis. The mission urged President Touadéra to focus on the rapid and effective implementation of the PAPR agreement through dialogue rather than military action. On 7 June France suspended financial aid and military co-operation to the CAR, accusing it of complicity in an anti-French disinformation and denigration campaign by Russia.

On 23 June 2021 President Lourenço of Angola reported on the general situation in the CAR at the UN General Assembly in New York and met António Guterres, the UN Secretary-General, informing him that Central African states were in favour of lifting the arms embargo on the CAR Government. On 28 June a four-day observation mission by the AU arrived in Bangui in order to assess the implementation of the PAPR agreement. Following the publication of a UN report on the CAR on 25 June, in which the Panel of Experts on the CAR documented abuses against civilians that allegedly involved Russian mercenaries, the Russian Permanent Representative to the UN, Vassily Nebenzia, denied the accusations against Russian military instructors.

A delegation by the Libyan Government arrived in Bangui at the start of September 2021 in order to strengthen co-operation with the CAR, holding meetings with Prime Minister Dondra and President Touadéra. In mid-September Touadéra participated in an ICGLR summit in Luanda on the persistence of the security crisis in the CAR, where heads of state, including Denis Sassou Nguesso of the Republic of the Congo, Mahamat Deby of Chad and Lourenço of Angola, approved the Luanda joint roadmap for peace in the CAR, which was signed by the CPC coalition groups except for Adam's FPRC and Gen. Darassa's UPC. In the following week Touadéra arrived in New York to participate in the UN General Assembly, where he met Russian Minister of Foreign Affairs Sergei Lavrov and UN Secretary-General Guterres for working meetings.

On 16 October 2021 the ceasefire declared by the CAR Government was welcomed by the ICGLR, which called for armed groups to observe it. At a session of the UN Security Council on 18 October, Russia denied that Russian military instructors were participating in hostilities in the CAR and insisted that they were present in the country only to improve the professional capacity of the FACA; the Russian delegation expressed its readiness to study reports of reported violations committed by its instructors, if the CAR Government presented any such evidence.

In November 2021 the UN Security Council extended MINUSCA's mission term for 12 months. Later in the month the European Parliament urged EU member states to impose a travel ban and asset freeze sanctions on the Russian paramilitary Wagner Group, urged the CAR not to use the company's services and appealed to the European Commission not to allocate funds to countries employing Russian mercenaries.

President Touadéra met several senior EU representatives in Brussels on 10 December, who informed him that the EU was expecting significant progress on the Luanda joint roadmap from the CAR Government. On 13 December the EU approved sanctions, including a travel ban and asset freeze, on the Wagner Group and individuals and entities connected to it, notably Valerii Zakharov, a security adviser to Touadéra, for committing serious human rights abuses in the CAR and other countries. On 17 December the US Treasury's Office of Foreign Assets Control added UPC leader Gen. Darassa to its list of individuals whose assets were frozen in the USA, owing to his alleged involvement in human rights abuses, including murder, torture, rape, kidnapping and violence against children.

A strategic review meeting on the political process in the CAR was held in Bangui in June 2022, led by President Touadéra and attended by representatives from, *inter alia*, the ICGLR, the AU, MINUSCA, the EU and the World Bank. The meeting assessed progress in the implementation of the Luanda joint roadmap and noted with concern the non-compliance on the part of the FPRC and the UPC, as well as the cross-border threats to peace and stability in the CAR.

Economy

DUNCAN WOODSIDE

INTRODUCTION

The Central African Republic (CAR) has, since independence in 1960, been one of the most politically unstable countries in the world. Repeated coups, ethnic violence and a lack of central government authority have prevented the creation and growth of viable national institutions, so the rule of law remains weak. The economy is woefully underdeveloped, despite an abundance of natural resources, including timber, uranium and diamonds, which, under the scenario of a functioning nation-state, would make the country's citizens wealthier than most of the world's population. Instead, the majority of Central Africans languish in poverty, including the approximately one in four citizens who are displaced by conflict, according to the United Nations (UN) Food and Agriculture Organization (FAO). The Institute for Economics and Peace estimated in its Global Peace Index for 2018 that years of conflict have cost the CAR 38% of its gross domestic product (GDP), putting it sixth in the world in terms of nations most undermined economically by repeated cycles of violence.

The descent into severe conflict following a coup in March 2013—characterized by sectarian violence and the displacement of close to 1m. people, prompting greater French military intervention and warnings by the UN of a potential genocide (see *History*)—had a predictably catastrophic effect on the economy, as crops rotted in untended fields and businesses fell prey to looting. The International Monetary Fund (IMF) recorded a contraction of real GDP of 36.4% in 2013.

Relatively peaceful elections in late 2015 and early 2016 led to the installation of a permanent Government under the presidency of Faustin Archange Touadéra. However, a renewed deterioration of the security situation from late 2016 put further pressure on economic indicators. In August 2018 Central African groups signed a peace agreement in the Sudanese capital of Khartoum, in an initiative sponsored by Sudan and the Russian Federation, reflecting an increasing engagement by the latter in the CAR's affairs. However, this involvement, which included the donation of hundreds of Russian weapons and the deployment of a military training force, provoked concerns in France. These indications of rivalry between a key Western power and Russia—in a resource-rich country where France itself retained troops—fuelled fears that heightened external intervention in the CAR risked exacerbating, rather than dismantling, competition among unaccountable armed factions for control over mineral wealth and entrenching these groups' hold over the economy and population as a whole. Such fears accelerated through the remainder of the decade and into the 2020s, in a context where tensions between Russia and Western powers rose to levels unseen since the end of the Cold War, following the Russian invasion of Ukraine in February 2022.

In February 2019 the CAR Government reached a peace deal, under the auspices of the African Union and the UN, with 14 armed groups. However, there was a reversion to large-scale conflict during a presidential election in December 2020. The rebel advance at one stage endangered the capital, Bangui. Touadéra, who was elected for a second term in a poll that was marred both by allegations of irregularities and by a low turnout stemming from the renewed violence, imposed a state of emergency in late January 2021. With the help of Russian and Rwandan forces, the army expelled the rebel forces—which were aligned with former President François Bozizé under the Coalition des Patriotes pour le Changement—from a number of towns during the first quarter of the year, amid substantial new displacement of the population away from their livelihoods (see *Agriculture and Food Crises*) and major disruption to cross-border trade.

The renewed deterioration in security came after the global coronavirus disease (COVID-19) pandemic—and, more particularly, policy responses around the world to contain the disease—had already wrought significant damage on CAR's economy. However, a recession was at least avoided, as real GDP in 2020 grew by 1.0%, despite trade, tourism, hospitality and mining all being hit by the pandemic. However, while most countries' economies performed better in 2021 than in 2020, the CAR's economy again generated annual real growth of only 1.0%, according to the IMF, owing to the renewed insecurity, especially early in the year. GDP per capita fell for a second consecutive year, as a result of the country's rising population.

In April 2022 the IMF forecast a moderate economic rebound in real GDP of 3.7% in that year and an annual average of 4.0% in 2023–25—enough for GDP per capita to resume an upward trend. The Fund based those forecasts on a reopening of the trade corridor between Bangui and the Atlantic port of Douala in Cameroon, after the earlier disruption caused by the security shock that intensified from the end of 2020 and into 2021. The Fund also factored in improvements in mining and agricultural production, alongside higher demand in the services sector, all driven by security gains in the provinces. However, the multilateral lender emphasized numerous downside risks to its forecasts, driven mostly by the potential for a reversal in security gains and the related possibility of reduced donor support stemming from any protracted delay in concluding peace negotiations. The Fund also pointed to the risk of slow implementation of fiscal and other structural reforms, persistent global supply chain congestions and high international oil prices, which surpassed US $100 per barrel in the wake of Russia's invasion of Ukraine. By May 2022 at least some of those downside risks were becoming realized as the Ministry of the Economy, Planning and International Cooperation warned of an 'alarming' financing outlook that would leave it unable to execute its budget in the absence of further foreign funding.

AGRICULTURE AND FOOD CRISES

Agriculture, hunting, forestry and fishing dominate the economy, contributing 33.4% of GDP in 2020, according to UN estimates, while 74% of people made a living out of agriculture in 2016, according to the African Development Bank, which also estimated that women constituted 83% of the agricultural workforce. According to the World Bank, agricultural GDP decreased at an average annual rate of 4.8% during 2011–20; the sector's GDP declined by 1.0% in 2020. Agriculture is concentrated in the tropical rainforest area of the south-west and the savannah lands in the central region and north-west.

FAO estimates the country's total agricultural area at just under 5.1m. ha, with 80% of the population living in rural areas. According to FAO, in 2021 about one in four of the country's citizens were displaced, owing to repeated cycles of violence, notably related to the sectarian conflict that followed the 2013 coup and attacks by multiple armed groups, including Uganda's Lord's Resistance Army. In mid-2022 FAO estimated that some 2.4m. people in the CAR (43% of the population) were suffering from 'acute food insecurity' and forecast that more than 300,000 people were or would be 'acutely malnourished' between September 2021 and August 2022.

Output of the major food crops (cassava, maize, millet, sorghum, groundnuts and rice) increased in the late 1990s as the Government placed greater emphasis on this sector in its regional development programmes. As a result, for a time the CAR reached near self-sufficiency in staple foods, primarily cassava, sorghum and millet. Agricultural diversification was also promoted, mainly to substitute imports. This notably involved the establishment of a palm oil complex at Bossongo, with an annual capacity of 7,500 metric tons, servicing 2,500 ha of plantations, and a sugar refinery at Ouaka, supplied from 1,300 ha of new plantations. The Government also encouraged the cultivation of vegetables (particularly peppers and green beans) for export to the European market.

The country's descent into sectarian strife in 2013 devastated the agricultural sector, as nearly 1m. people were displaced. Consequently, several hundred thousand people became dependent on food aid. In March 2020 the UN's World Food Programme reported that it had distributed 2,492 metric tons of food in the CAR and assisted over 504,000 people; it estimated that it would need US $88.7m. in funding for the period April–September to meet local food requirements. In late January 2021 the UN High Commissioner for Refugees reported that over 200,000 people had fled fighting in the country since the disputed December election, including 92,000 across the southern border into the Democratic Republic of the Congo, adding to the CAR's already substantial displaced population. This new wave of displacement further interrupted farming activity, which was already under significant strain from a range of other factors. In its 2021 Humanitarian Response Plan for the CAR, FAO noted that the 'effects

of the urgent and essential restrictive measures related to COVID-19 have hampered farmers' access to agricultural land and inputs across the country'. It also noted that excessive rainfall had triggered floods in the north of the country, damaging crops, while output of the staple cassava had been adversely affected by cassava mosaic disease.

For several decades efforts have been made to develop the livestock industry. Until the security crisis that blighted the country from 2013, the number of cattle had increased substantially, despite problems caused by droughts, limited available fodder and the prevalence of the tsetse fly. Efforts were made to improve marketing and to encourage the sedentary raising of cattle to allow for treatment against disease. The herd also grew as a result of migration from Chad and Sudan. FAO estimated a total of 20.1m. head of livestock in 2020, compared with 17.9m. in 2011. However, domestic meat production fails to satisfy demand, and even before the security crisis the development of the sector had been hindered by widespread land disputes between livestock producers and crop producers.

The CAR's large forest resources (an estimated 102,000 sq km of tropical rainforest) have remained largely unexploited commercially, mainly as a result of a lack of adequate roads and low-cost means of transportation to the coast. Only about 10% of the forest area is accessible to river transport. In addition, large areas are held as private hunting reserves. However, timber exploitation expanded considerably from the late 1960s, following the formation of new companies geared towards export and the establishment of new sawmills. The forestry sector continues to suffer from major constraints, including smuggling and low water levels on the traditional transport route along the Congo river. Between 1990 and 2010 the CAR lost approximately 598,000 ha of woodland, equivalent to 2.6% of its forest cover. In December 2018 the IMF noted that the CAR had commenced issuing forestry and mining permits in January. Wood product exports amounted to an estimated 58,000m. francs CFA in 2019 and 50,600m. francs CFA in 2020, according to data from the IMF in its report published in February 2022, following the country's request for a staff-monitored programme.

An outline Responsible Procurement Programme (RPP) was approved by the multilateral Forest Carbon Partnership Facility (FCPF) for the CAR in Berlin, Germany, in October 2011. The CAR Government requested that it work in partnership with the UN Development Programme (UNDP) to establish the RPP. The World Bank, as the principal trustee of the FCPF, was therefore reportedly preparing for a transfer of the CAR's RPP mandate to the UNDP. The European Union (EU) was designated as a potential funder of this forestry initiative in the CAR, although other funding avenues were also being pursued. In 2012 the Government made a crucial move towards tackling illegal logging by signing a Voluntary Partnership Agreement with the EU for the timber trade. The deal offered favourable trading terms to encourage the country to implement more stringent forestry laws, but the outbreak of fresh fighting from 2013 set back the accord's implementation. However, there appeared to be renewed commitment after elections in 2016.

MINING

The contribution of mining and quarrying to GDP was likely to be much greater than the UN estimate of 0.8% in 2020, as an estimated one-half of the output of diamonds—the leading mineral—is thought to be smuggled out of the country, eluding the official record. The diamond industry in the CAR employs about 80,000 artisanal miners, providing a source of income for some 600,000 people, according to the World Trade Organization. Diamonds are found in widely scattered alluvial deposits (mainly in the south-west and west of the country), rather than kimberlite deposits, which are concentrated and thus more easily exploited and policed. Data from the US Geological Survey (USGS) indicated that official diamond production rose from 13,600 carats in 2018 to 23,600 carats in 2019, although the long-term trend showed a steep decline, from 609,000 carats in 1968 and 416,400 carats in 2002, in part probably reflecting increasing levels of smuggling.

From 2003 the CAR was a signatory to the Kimberley Process—an international initiative that seeks to keep 'conflict diamonds' (i.e. diamonds that have been traded for arms by rebel movements in conflict zones) out of the global supply chain. However, its status as a member of this organization came under threat in 2013, owing to the seizure of power by Seleka, a rebel group originating from the diamond-rich north of the country. Although the CAR's new regime lobbied against its exclusion, there was mounting pressure for action, with human rights organizations pointing to the many abuses that had been committed by Seleka forces during their march on Bangui, and following their seizure of power. Among those calling for a suspension of Seleka's membership of the Kimberley Process was the US State Department, which claimed in May that 'the conflict in the Central African Republic shows that the Kimberley Process isn't living up to its mandate'. Later that month the CAR's membership of the Kimberley Process was temporarily suspended. However, there were concerns that, as the CAR's suspension had the unavoidable side effect of making the country's diamond industry entirely illegitimate, the only export option open to the regime would be to ship gemstones onto the global black market.

In June 2016 the Touadéra Government announced that it would resume the export of diamonds, initially from Berbérati, in southern CAR, after overseers of the Kimberley Process agreed in 2015 to allow a partial resumption of rough diamond exports, on condition that the CAR implement a process to guarantee the traceability of stones. In a bid to re-energize the sector, the Government reduced the cost of licences for collectors by 30%, to some US $1,200. The authorities described the lifting of the ban in five regions as very important, amid estimates that some 60,000 people in western regions earned a living from diamonds at that time. In November 2017 the IMF stated that official diamond exports were among several key goods from government-controlled areas to have 'increased significantly', with the Kimberley process estimating 2016 shipments to have reached 10,957 carats. In the 2018 budget, the Government sought to boost income from the sector by increasing export duties on diamonds, as well as on timber and gold.

Despite the partial lifting of the export ban, major concerns persisted regarding the flow of diamonds from areas under rebel control. The fighting that erupted in mid-2017 between remnants of sectarian militias was linked to the diamond trade and highlighted once more the disconnect between internationally brokered peace initiatives and the resource-driven realities of militia rivalries on the ground.

In its report to the UN Security Council in December 2019, the UN Panel of Experts on the Central African Republic stated that the country exported 18,171 carats of rough diamonds through official channels between 1 January and 15 October, compared with 9,228 carats during the same period in 2018. However, the Panel described such exports as negligible, on the basis of estimated annual countrywide production of 330,000 carats, and concluded that almost all of the CAR's diamond production continued to be smuggled through neighbouring countries. While indicating areas outside of government control in the north and east as being key areas of illicit diamond trading, the Panel of Experts claimed that trafficking was also 'rampant in the western part of the country, including in Kimberley Process-compliant zones'. The Kimberley Process reported that total legal production of diamonds in the CAR in 2018 amounted to 13,571 carats. This compared with legal production of 365,917 carats, valued at US $62.1m., in 2012—the last full year before the ban was imposed. These data further indicated how the vast majority of the country's diamond industry remained outside the Government's control. In November 2019 the Kimberley Process had agreed to allow the CAR's authorities to begin issuing certificates for exports of rough diamonds from 'conflict free' areas under its control, rather than through approvals by the multilateral body's monitoring team. In January 2020 Russia assumed the rotating chair of the Kimberley Process, and announced in February that it would work to remove the remaining Kimberley restrictions on diamond exports from the CAR, claiming that they were not having any impact on the country's output of diamonds, but merely increasing the volume sold illegally, to the benefit of illicit traders rather than local communities. Lobaye Invest, a Russian company operating as part of a conglomerate owned by Yevgeny Prigozhin—a close associate of the Russian President, Vladimir Putin—secured a licence in April 2019 to mine diamonds in Bangassou, Bria, Ouadah and Sam Ouandja. In order to help the CAR Government and the country's armed forces to extend their authority and to eliminate the illegal exploitation and taxation of minerals, Russia, backed by the People's Republic of China, lobbied hard at the UN Security Council in early 2020 to have the remaining elements of the UN arms embargo on the CAR lifted. However, this campaign was resisted by a number of European states, which claimed that the CAR authorities were still too weak to prevent arms from falling into the hands of illegitimate actors. Moreover, the EU stated that it would not support the termination of restrictions on diamond exports from the CAR without firm evidence that all shipments were originating from conflict-free areas. Further demonstrating the UN Security Council divide on the CAR between Western powers and Russia, the US Treasury Department in September 2020 imposed sanctions on the Internet Research Agency (based in St Petersburg, Russia), on the grounds that the organization was being used by Prigozhin—himself subject to US sanctions—to 'advance Russia's influence' in the country. The extent to which the diamond trade continued largely to evade government control was again illustrated by data for 2020, published in the IMF's February 2022 report. Officially registered diamond exports were estimated at some 3,800m. francs CFA ($7.2m., based on the exchange rate at the end of 2020). However, the Fund projected that as the security situation improved more output would be routed through the Kimberley Process. It forecast that official diamond exports would rise to 6,900m. francs CFA in 2021, to 9,600m. francs CFA in 2022 and 13,800m. francs CFA in 2023.

Gold is also mined in the CAR, although official production levels have fluctuated sharply, from a peak of 538 kg in 1980 to as low as 43 kg in 2008. According to the USGS, annual production totalled an average of 60 kg in 2014–16. The signing of a first 25-year gold mining convention in January 2006 with Aurafrique—a subsidiary of the Canadian company Axmin—was expected to increase long-term gold production. However, in January 2013 Axmin announced that the firm had postponed further development of its Passendro Gold Project, after Seleka rebels overran the site, which lies about 280 km northeast of the capital. By that time Axmin had invested US $96m. in the project, which, when it eventually gets under way, is expected to yield more than 200,000 oz of gold in its first year. However, all operations at the mining project remained officially suspended at mid-2021, although the USGS reported that artisanal miners had mined illegally for gold at the site since the shutdown. In late 2019 a UN Panel of Experts reported that the CAR exported 194.5 kg of gold through official channels during 1 January–15 October, building on a steady rise in exports of the commodity since 2016. However, in a context where the Panel estimated that total gold output in the country stood at about 2 metric tons annually, it was evident that the vast majority of gold continued to be smuggled out of the CAR. The Panel reported that it had confirmed the continued existence of parallel taxation structures, despite the 2019 peace agreement requiring reversion to state authority. The Front Populaire pour la Renaissance de la Centrafrique (FPRC), a former Seleka militia, was reportedly orchestrating such parallel taxation in Ndélé. The Panel claimed that the FPRC forced miners and associated businesses to pay annual fees of between 2,000 francs CFA and 300,000 francs CFA.

Uranium deposits exist near Bakouma, 480 km east of Bangui. Reserves are estimated at about 20,000 metric tons, with a concentration ratio of some 50%. Rising uranium prices and declining global stock resulted in renewed interest from foreign companies in the Bakouma site, and a licence to mine uranium was eventually awarded to South Africa's Uramin in 2006. The Bakouma uranium mining project was officially inaugurated in October, with the state owning a 10% interest. Reserves of iron ore, copper, tin, lignite and limestone have also been located, although the inadequacy of the country's transport infrastructure has deterred mining companies from attempting their commercial exploitation. Despite potentially drillable petroleum prospects along the CAR's border with Chad, energy requirements are currently satisfied through imports.

The mining sector suffered a significant reverse in late 2011, when Areva halted uranium extraction at the Bakouma plant. The company reportedly suspended operations in response to reduced demand for the commodity in global markets, sparked by the Fukushima disaster in Japan in March, when a tsunami caused the overheating of a nuclear reactor and a consequent fuel leak. The shutdown of Japan's nuclear facilities, together with a rise in nuclear risk-aversion elsewhere in the world, led to a 30% fall in the global price of uranium during March–November. As a result, Areva announced that it was suspending extraction at the Bakouma facilities for one to two years, although it reassured investors and concerned local parties that it had no intention of abandoning the project entirely, having reportedly invested US $147m. in the plant. However, insecurity in the area increased following the 2013 coup and continued periodically over subsequent years, preventing Areva's return.

MANUFACTURING AND POWER

Manufacturing is based on the processing of primary products and is relatively undeveloped, contributing an estimated 19.2% of GDP in 2020, according to UN estimates. In the mid-1990s the major activities were the processing of foods, beverages and tobacco, furniture, fixtures, and paper and textiles. Out of 250 enterprises that were in operation before the 1996 mutiny, only a dozen or so, often involving foreign participation, have survived: these include the Société Centrafricaine de Cigarettes (SOCACIG—tobacco, reopened in 2000), the Société de Gestion des Sucreries Centrafricaines (SOGESCA—sugar, privatized in 2003), MOCAF (beverages), Centrafricaine des Palmiers (CENTRAPALM—palm oil, mooted for privatization) and a number of sawmills. In July 2019 the National Assembly created the Office National du Coton to help restructure the cotton sector, which is the primary source of earnings for nearly 1m. Central Africans. SOGESCA, which was renamed Sucrerie Africaine de Centrafrique (SUCAF) upon its privatization, announced in early 2020 that it was processing 450 metric tons of sugar cane daily and producing 12,000 tons of white sugar annually. Manufacturing activities suffered greatly from the political and civil disruption in 2002 and 2003, notably ginning activities, as the partly state-owned Société Centrafricaine de Développement des Textiles suspended operations, and several ginneries were destroyed. The sector was decimated again by the security crisis that commenced in 2013. According to the World Bank, in real terms, the GDP of the manufacturing sector increased by 4.2% in 2020.

The main source of power supply is hydroelectric, from the two stations at the Boali Falls. Access to electricity is low, at only 15.5% of the total population in 2020, according to World Bank estimates. Plans have been under way for several years to construct a new hydroelectric plant at Kembe, but no progress has been made, owing to lack of funding. The Government has proposed several projects to increase the country's hydroelectric capacity and reduce electricity shortages, but their implementation will depend on the Government's ability to secure sufficient funding.

TRANSPORT AND TELECOMMUNICATIONS

The transport infrastructure is underdeveloped and is a major constraint on the country's economic development. In 2018 there was an extensive road network, with a total estimated length of 24,000 km. However, only about 700 km of the network was paved, down from an estimate of nearly 1,400 km less than a decade earlier, owing to lack of maintenance. There is no railway network, but there are longstanding plans to extend the Trans-Cameroon line to Bangui and also to link the CAR with the rail systems in Sudan and Gabon. A large volume of freight is carried by river; of a total of about 7,000 km of inland waterways, some 2,800 km are navigable, most importantly the Oubangui river south of Bangui, which is the country's main outlet for external trade, and the Sangha

and Lobaye rivers. Port facilities are being improved, with assistance from France and the EU.

The principal route for the import and export trade has traditionally been the trans-equatorial route, which involves 1,800 km by river from Bangui to Brazzaville, in the Republic of the Congo, and then rail from Brazzaville to Pointe-Noire. There is an international airport at Bangui-M'Poko, and there are also around 37 small airports for internal services. However, internal services are irregular, underserviced and dependent on the availability of fuel.

The telecommunications sector has grown rapidly in recent years, driven by mobile cellular telephone services. The Société Centrafricaine de Télécommunications (SOCATEL) is 60% owned by the state and the remainder by France Câbles et Radio (France Télécoms). Four mobile telephone companies— Orange Centrafrique (with a total of around 700,000 subscribers in early 2020), Telecel, Azur RCA (formerly known as NationLink Telecom RCA) and Atlantique Telecom Centrafrique—operate in the country. Orange launched a 3G (third generation) network in the CAR in March 2013. The service was initially centred on Bangui, boasting a maximum downlink speed of 21 Mbps (megabytes per second). The CAR had a total of 2.3m. cellular connections at the beginning of 2020, representing an increase of 11% year-on-year and a penetration rate of 48% of the country's population.

MACROECONOMIC POLICY AND THE EXTERNAL ACCOUNTS

The CAR's fiscal position remains precarious—a situation compounded by continued political instability. The narrow tax base is vulnerable to adverse trends in international prices for coffee and cotton and prone to erosion as a result of tax evasion and smuggling, while losses incurred by the parastatal organizations and personnel expenditure for the cumbersome civil service have put constant pressure on public spending. The country's collapse into chaos and plunder during 2013–14 destroyed the modest progress with fiscal reform that had been achieved earlier in the decade. However, in May 2014 the IMF, having cancelled a three-year Extended Credit Facility (ECF) arrangement as a result of the country's descent into political turmoil, approved funding under a new Rapid Credit Facility (RCF). The CAR maintained funding from the IMF during the first half of 2021, but made little progress in mobilizing tax revenue to support government expenditure, despite its programmes with the Fund having consistently prioritized this policy area. In 2019 domestic revenue, at 116,100m. francs CFA, was equivalent to just 8.7% of GDP, according to estimates by the IMF in its ECF review of February 2021. This compared unfavourably with 2012—the last full year before the coup against Bozizé, when tax revenue had reached nearly 10.0% of GDP. The ECF had targeted an increase in tax revenue to 9.7% of GDP for 2020, but the onset of the COVID-19 crisis made that unachievable. The IMF estimated in February 2021 that domestic revenue in 2020 had fallen slightly, to 115,700m. francs CFA, representing just 8.5% of GDP, an indicator that was itself stagnant in real terms during the year. In early 2021 the IMF projected that domestic revenue over the year as a whole would rise to 133,900m. francs CFA, equivalent to 9.3% of GDP. The Fund identified the following as crucial to boosting domestic revenue sustainably: a significant increase in the number of corporate taxpayers; the digitalization of companies' tax payments (and declarations); and the exertion of control over imports arriving through Cameroon's border. Reflecting the challenges relating to the latter, commercial traffic on the road between Bangui and Cameroon's principal economic city, Douala, tentatively resumed in mid-January on the CAR side, but in convoy and under the protection of the UN, after the route had been closed for more than a month due to repeated rebel attacks close to the border.

The deficit in the overall fiscal balance, excluding grants, rose dramatically, from an estimated 109,700m. francs CFA (8.2% of GDP) in 2019 to an estimated 219,100m. francs CFA (16.0% of GDP) in 2020, according to a revised estimate provided by the IMF in its February 2022 country report. This was far above the 9.3% of GDP initially forecast under the country's

ECF and above even the 13.1% of GDP projected under its RCF—a programme that was utilized to help the country to respond to the enormous challenges generated by the COVID-19 crisis. The negative overall fiscal balance, excluding grants, was projected to fall to 157,300m. francs CFA (11.0% of GDP) in 2021, owing largely to a significant retrenchment in government spending, which was expected to fall from an estimated 344,700m. francs CFA in 2020 to 281,300m. francs CFA in 2021. Reflecting substantially increased assistance under the emergency RCF, the fiscal deficit was contained at an estimated 46,100m. francs CFA (3.4% of GDP) in 2020, once grants were included in the balance. However, this measure of the fiscal deficit (i.e. inclusive of grants) rose significantly in 2021, to 87,700m. francs CFA (6.1% of GDP), according to IMF projections published in February 2022. This reflected a decline in grants from a peak of 172,900m. francs CFA in 2020, at the height of the pandemic, to a much more modest 69,600m. francs CFA in 2021. The IMF cautioned that the fiscal outlook for 2022 would remain under pressure, owing in part to a decline in budgetary support from the EU, which was due to fall from an annual €30m. in 2020 and 2021 to €17m. annually during 2022–24. A statement by the CAR's Ministry of the Economy, Planning and International Co-operation in May 2022 described the country's fiscal situation as 'alarming'. It warned that in the absence of further foreign funding it would be impossible to implement the initial budget fully and that some ministries faced spending cuts of between 40% and 60%.

The CAR is a member of the Banque des Etats de l'Afrique Centrale (BEAC), together with Cameroon, Chad, the Republic of the Congo, Equatorial Guinea and Gabon. It is also a member of the Communauté Economique des Etats de l'Afrique Centrale, which forms part of the CFA zone. The currency area also encompasses all eight countries operating under the auspices of the Banque Centrale des Etats de l'Afrique de l'Ouest (BCEAO). As at July 2022 the exchange rate remained fixed at €1 = 655.957 francs CFA. The inability of national central banks to manipulate the value of the franc CFA (monetary policy is set by the BEAC and the BCEAO, which focus on maintaining the fixed exchange rate against the euro) has acted as a powerful disciplinary force on member states. This has been particularly important for the CAR, where democratic accountability has often been undermined by a tendency towards military rule, corruption and coups. The inability of governments to fund spending by printing money has thus helped to restrain inflation and enabled trade to be conducted at stable rates of exchange. However, in a move that raised questions about the CAR's commitment to the CFA franc monetary zone, the President's Office announced in April 2022 that Touadéra had signed into law a bill making the Bitcoin cryptocurrency legal tender alongside the franc CFA. The CAR was only the second country in the world, after El Salvador, to endorse Bitcoin in this way. The legislation also legalized the use of other cryptocurrencies, with the President's Chief of Staff, Obed Namsio, claiming that the move made the CAR one of the world's 'boldest and most visionary countries'. However, financial market analysts suggested that the measure would undermine efforts to enhance fiscal transparency. The policy announcement came as Russia, an increasingly important player in the CAR militarily and financially (see *Development Aid and Debt Relief*), was increasingly cut off from mainstream international payments mechanisms, as a result of EU and US sanctions imposed in the wake of the invasion of Ukraine. The Commission Bancaire de l'Afrique Centrale (the regulator of the CFA franc zone) reiterated in a letter sent to member states in May that cryptocurrencies were banned in the zone. Despite this warning, the CAR's Presidency declared that the country was also ready to launch a cryptocurrency investment hub, although details remained scant, and analysts expressed scepticism about how usage of digital currencies would gain traction in a country beset by electricity shortages and poor internet coverage. However, on 26 July the CAR Government froze the application of its law adopting Bitcoin as an official currency until the BEAC issued regulations for cryptocurrency throughout the zone.

The CAR's foreign trade balance turned from small surpluses from the mid-1990s to deficits from 2003. Structural weaknesses (especially in transport), political instability, power shortages and fluctuations in the international prices for diamonds, coffee, timber and cotton have prevented the CAR's exports from reaching their full potential. In addition, a large proportion of diamond and wood exports are believed to be unrecorded. The CAR has traditionally recorded a large net outflow on the services account. As a result, the country's current account balance has remained in deficit, and the shortfall has become more pronounced in recent years, owing in part to the emergence of the structural trade deficit. The country's current account deficit widened further as the COVID-19 pandemic took hold. After a strong performance in 2019, when the current account deficit was recorded at an estimated 65,700m. francs CFA (4.9% of GDP)—lower than the 76,500m. (5.6% of GDP) envisaged under the ECF—the deficit reached 116,100m. francs CFA (8.5% of GDP) in 2020, according to estimates by the IMF in April 2022. Exports of goods underperformed significantly, totalling an estimated 82,700m. francs CFA in 2020, compared with an estimated 94,100m. francs CFA in 2019. Imports of goods, meanwhile, rose to an estimated 313,100m. francs CFA in 2020, up from the 300,100m. estimated for 2019. This resulted in an estimated goods trade deficit of 230,400m. francs CFA (16.8% of GDP) in 2020, compared with an estimated 206,000m. francs CFA in 2019. The capital account rose from a surplus of 48,500m. francs CFA in 2019 to a surplus of 102,800m. francs CFA in 2020, owing entirely to grants increasing year-on-year by 54,300m. francs CFA. The IMF's estimates for 2021, provided in its April 2022 report, showed a further projected significant widening of the current account deficit, to 152,100m. francs CFA (10.6% of GDP). The Fund estimated that the trade deficit in goods narrowed slightly, to 215,300m. francs CFA (15.0% of GDP), owing to exports rising slightly, to 84,800m. francs CFA, and imports falling modestly, to 300,100m. francs CFA. However, other components of the current account were projected to more than offset the modest improvement in the trade deficit in 2021, most notably a decline in official net transfers, from 93,100m. francs CFA in 2020 to just 26,900m. francs CFA in 2021.

DEVELOPMENT AID AND DEBT RELIEF

The CAR has traditionally received moderate inflows of aid in grant form. However, the country has not proved particularly attractive to foreign private investors (other than in the diamond, timber and telecommunications sectors). The CAR has repeatedly received IMF loans and benefited from significant World Bank funding.

The IMF in January 2021 completed its first and second reviews of the CAR's progress under an ECF programme agreed in December 2019. It announced that these successful reviews had allowed the disbursement of US $34.4m., bringing total disbursements under the ECF arrangement to $51.6m. These disbursements were in addition to emergency assistance of $38m. extended to the CAR in April 2020, under an RCF which was designed to help poorer developing countries to address the enormous economic repercussions of the pandemic crisis. In the same month the IMF provided the CAR with about $4m. in debt relief from interest payments due over the following six months, under a third initiative, the Catastrophe Containment and Relief Trust. The Fund noted in its February 2021 report that it had approved the 'authorities' request for waiver of non-observance of performance criteria', acknowledging that the ECF had been 'adversely affected by the pandemic', although it also highlighted initial 'policy and reform shortfalls'. However, it stated that programme implementation had improved in recent months and that the CAR authorities had also 'focused on ensuring that emergency donor financing is efficiently and transparently used' to forestall the pandemic and support the most vulnerable, despite the substantial renewed deterioration in the security situation in late 2020 and early 2021. In April 2022 the IMF approved a first review of the CAR's Staff Monitored Programme—an initiative designed to improve 'policy implementation and unlock budget support from donors'. It described the CAR's performance under the programme in 2021 as satisfactory, noting that all quantitative benchmarks for the year had been met, citing in particular improved revenue mobilization.

Beyond continued reliance on multilateral loans, the Government has also sought increased bilateral assistance, and at an international donor conference in Brussels, Belgium in November 2016, a total of US $2,280m. was pledged to the CAR by various bodies. The conference, attended by delegations from more than 80 countries and international agencies, was convened to cement funding pledges for the Government's National Recovery and Peacebuilding Plan, due to be implemented over the period 2017–21. The European Commission pledged $450m., and bilateral contributions from EU member states totalled an additional $328m. Much of the EU funding was to be channelled through the Bêkou Trust Fund. This EU body, led by France, Germany and the Netherlands, was established in July 2014 to disburse funds for the CAR more efficiently and to ensure better accountability for donors at each stage of the process. The permanent secretariat co-ordinating the investment programme began operations in October 2017, its main task being to direct the aid pledges into approved projects. A list was drawn up of some 150 projects ready for implementation, 15 of which were included in the 2018 budget.

The EU has provided the CAR with more than €233m. in humanitarian funding alone since 2014. For 2022 the EU pledged €17m. in humanitarian aid to the country. However, budgetary support from the EU, which has amounted to around €30m. annually, is expected to nearly halve from 2022 onwards, amid increasing concerns about the Government's ties with Russia and notably its reliance on Wagner, a Kremlin-linked private military company. In June 2021 the French Government suspended €10m. in budgetary support for the CAR, as well as military co-operation. Both France and the USA decried the CAR's continued use of Wagner operatives at a meeting of the UN Security Council in February 2022, accusing the group of committing atrocities against CAR civilians.

The CAR has increasingly sought to benefit from Russian support, extending beyond military assistance, as Russia has aimed to gain influence in the resource-rich country. Pascal Bida Koyagbélé, a CAR government official, told Russian state media in April 2021 that his Government planned to secure up to US $11,000m. in investment from Russia, including $6,000m. for roads, $3,000m. for a railway and funding for a new commercial city projected to cost $2,000m. He declared that the CAR was engaged 'in discussions with the Russian state … (and) public and private banks', noting that the investments could be backed by 'plenty of guarantees', including stakes in the CAR's mining sector. However, Russia's costly invasion of Ukraine in early 2022 was likely to limit its capacity to advance these infrastructure plans.

Statistical Survey

Source (unless otherwise stated): Division des Statistiques et des Etudes Economiques, Ministère de l'Economie, du Plan et de la Coopération Internationale, BP 696, Bangui; tel. 21-61-72-61; e-mail dsees_rca@yahoo.fr; internet www.stat-centrafrique.com.

Area and Population

AREA, POPULATION AND DENSITY

Area (sq km)	622,984*
Population (census results)	
8 December 1988	2,463,616
8 December 2003†	
Males	1,569,446
Females	1,581,626
Total	3,151,072
Population (UN estimates at mid-year)‡	
2020	4,829,764
2021§	4,919,987
2022§	5,016,678
Density (per sq km) at mid-2022§	8.1

* 240,535 sq miles.
† Source: UN, *Population and Vital Statistics Report*.
‡ Source: UN, *World Population Prospects: The 2019 Revision*.
§ Projection.

POPULATION BY AGE AND SEX
('000, UN projections at mid-2022)

	Males	Females	Total
0–14 years	1,073.6	1,060.9	2,134.5
15–64 years	1,357.1	1,383.1	2,740.2
65 years and over	56.5	85.5	142.0
Total	2,487.2	2,529.5	5,016.7

Source: UN, *World Population Prospects: The 2019 Revision*.

PREFECTURES
('000, official population projections, 2020)

Bamingui-Bangoran	59.7		Nana-Gribizi . .	162.6
Bangui	947.8		Nana-Mambéré .	322.5
Basse-Kotto . .	343.9		Ombella-Mpoko .	492.4
Haut-Mbomou . .	79.5		Ouaka	382.0
Haute-Kotto . .	124.7		Ouham	509.7
Kémo	163.5		Ouham-Pendé . .	594.3
Lobaye	340.8		Sangha-Mbaéré .	139.5
Mambéré-Kadéi .	503.5		Vakaga	72.1
Mbomou	226.4		**Total**	5,464.9

PRINCIPAL TOWNS
(population at 2003 census)

Bangui (capital) .	622,771		Carnot	45,421
Bimbo	124,176		Bambari	41,356
Berbérati . . .	76,918		Bouar	40,353

Mid-2022 (incl. suburbs, UN projection): Bangui 933,176 (Source: UN, *World Urbanization Prospects: The 2018 Revision*).

BIRTHS AND DEATHS
(annual averages, UN estimates)

	2005–10	2010–15	2015–20
Birth rate (per 1,000)	40.0	37.7	35.4
Death rate (per 1,000)	17.4	15.1	12.4

Source: UN, *World Population Prospects: The 2019 Revision*.

Life expectancy (years at birth, estimates): 53.7 (males 51.5; females 55.9) in 2020 (Source: World Bank, World Development Indicators database).

ECONOMICALLY ACTIVE POPULATION
('000 at mid-year, FAO estimates)

	2013	2014	2015
Agriculture, etc.	1,272	1,282	1,292
Total labour force (incl. others) .	2,113	2,168	2,224

Source: FAO.

Health and Welfare

KEY INDICATORS

Total fertility rate (children per woman, 2020)	4.6
Under-5 mortality rate (per 1,000 live births, 2020) . . .	103.0
HIV/AIDS (% of persons aged 15–49, 2020)	2.9
COVID-19: Cumulative confirmed deaths (per 100,000 persons at 31 August 2022)	2.1
COVID-19: Fully vaccinated population (% of total population at 28 August 2022)	23.6
Physicians (per 1,000 head, 2018)	0.07
Hospitals (per 100,000 head, 2013)	0.5
Domestic health expenditure (2019): US $ per head (PPP) .	8.3
Domestic health expenditure (2019): % of GDP . . .	0.8
Domestic health expenditure (2019): public (% of total current expenditure)	10.6
Access to improved water resources (% of persons, 2020) .	37
Access to improved sanitation facilities (% of persons, 2020).	14
Total carbon dioxide emissions ('000 metric tons, 2018) . .	330
Carbon dioxide emissions per head (metric tons, 2018) . .	0.1
Human Development Index (2021): ranking	188
Human Development Index (2021): value	0.404

Note: For data on COVID-19 vaccinations, 'fully vaccinated' denotes receipt of all doses specified by approved vaccination regime (Sources: Johns Hopkins University and Our World in Data). Data on health expenditure refer to current general government expenditure in each case. For more information on sources and further definitions for all indicators, see Health and Welfare Statistics: Sources and Definitions section (europaworld.com/credits).

Agriculture

PRINCIPAL CROPS
('000 metric tons)

	2018	2019	2020
Bananas*	140.0	139.8	139.8
Cassava (Manioc)*	719.0	723.9	728.8
Coffee, green*	9.4	10.1	10.4
Groundnuts, with shell* . . .	154.1	141.0	138.7
Maize†	90.0	90.0	90.0
Mangoes, mangosteens and guavas*	13.3	12.9	13.1
Melonseed*	38.5	38.2	38.3
Millet†	10.0	10.0	10.0
Oil palm fruit*	5.5	3.6	3.7
Oranges*	34.7	35.3	34.7
Pineapples*	16.9	17.1	16.9
Plantains and others*	87.5	87.8	88.1
Pumpkins, squash and gourds* .	21.7	21.6	21.8
Rice, paddy	12.0	10.2*	6.1*
Seed cotton*	16.5	17.4	15.7
Sesame seed*	10.6	7.5	6.7
Sorghum†	30.0	30.0	30.0
Sugar cane*	115.0	125.0	127.9
Taro (Coco yam)*	133.5	133.9	133.5
Yams*	487.2	489.8	492.0

* FAO estimate(s).
† Unofficial figures.

Aggregate production ('000 metric tons, may include official, semi-official or estimated data): Total cereals 142.0 in 2018, 140.2 in 2019, 136.1 in 2020; Total fruit (primary) 309.5 in 2018, 310.6 in 2019, 310.8 in 2020; Total pulses 45.0 in 2018, 44.6 in 2019, 48.7 in 2020; Total oilcrops 243.5 in 2018, 226.3 in 2019, 221.4 in 2020; Total roots and tubers 1,341.1 in 2018, 1,348.9 in 2019, 1,355.6 in 2020; Total vegetables (primary) 94.7 in 2018, 95.0 in 2019, 95.2 in 2020.

Source: FAO.

LIVESTOCK
('000 head, year ending September, FAO estimates)

	2018	2019	2020
Cattle	4,521	4,601	4,679
Chickens	6,957	7,112	7,287
Goats	6,226	6,434	6,658
Pigs	1,045	1,063	1,082
Sheep	420	430	440

Source: FAO.

LIVESTOCK PRODUCTS
('000 metric tons, FAO estimates)

	2018	2019	2020
Cattle hides, fresh	11.8	12.0	12.2
Cattle meat	95.8	97.5	99.2
Cattle offals, edible	13.5	13.7	13.9
Cows' milk	79.5	80.5	81.5
Chicken meat	6.6	6.7	6.9
Game meat	22.3	22.5	22.4
Goat meat	23.7	24.3	25.0
Pig meat	19.1	19.4	19.7
Sheep meat	2.5	2.6	2.6
Hen eggs	2.0	2.4	2.4
Honey (natural)	16.2	16.2	16.7

Source: FAO.

Forestry

ROUNDWOOD REMOVALS
('000 cubic metres, excluding bark)

	2015	2016	2017
Sawlogs, veneer logs and logs for sleepers	315	418	537
Other industrial wood* . . .	308	308	308
Fuel wood*	2,000	2,000	2,000
Total*	2,623	2,726	2,845

* FAO estimates.

2018–20: Figures assumed to be unchanged from 2017 (FAO estimates).

Source: FAO.

SAWNWOOD PRODUCTION
('000 cubic metres, including railway sleepers, FAO estimates)

	2018	2019	2020
Total (all broadleaved) . . .	41	43	41

Source: FAO.

Fishing

('000 metric tons, live weight of capture, FAO estimates)

	2018	2019	2020
Total catch (freshwater fishes) .	29.2	29.2	29.2

Source: FAO.

Mining

	2016	2017	2018
Gold (kg)*	60	n.a.	n.a.
Diamonds ('000 carats)† . . .	10.7	47.6	13.6

* Estimates.
† Production is approximately 70% to 80% gem quality.

Diamonds ('000 carats): 23.6 in 2019.

Source: US Geological Survey.

Industry

SELECTED PRODUCTS
('000 metric tons unless otherwise indicated)

	2017	2018	2019
Sugar (raw, centrifugal)* . . .	10.6	10.6	11.6
Palm oil*	0.7	0.4	0.2
Groundnut oil†	28.0	28.0	28.0
Electrical energy (million kWh) .	145	147	149

* FAO estimates.
† Unofficial figures.

Electrical energy (million kWh): 150 in 2020.

Sources: FAO; UN, Energy Statistics Database.

Beer ('000 hectolitres): 118.7 in 2004; 118.9 in 2005; 123.1 in 2006 (Source: IMF, *Central African Republic: Selected Issues and Statistical Appendix*—January 2008).
Soft drinks ('000 hectolitres): 41.4 in 2004; 46.7 in 2005; 51.8 in 2006 (Source: IMF, *Central African Republic: Selected Issues and Statistical Appendix*—January 2008).
Cigarettes (million packets): 16.0 in 2004 (Source: IMF, *Central African Republic: Selected Issues and Statistical Appendix*—January 2008).

Finance

CURRENCY AND EXCHANGE RATES

Monetary Units
100 centimes = 1 franc de la Coopération Financière en Afrique Centrale (CFA).

Sterling, Dollar and Euro Equivalents (31 May 2022)
£1 sterling = 770.824 francs CFA;
US $1 = 612.300 francs CFA;
€1 = 655.957 francs CFA;
10,000 francs CFA = £12.97 = $16.33 = €15.24.

Average Exchange Rate (francs CFA per US $)
2019   585.911
2020   575.586
2021   554.531

Note: An exchange rate of 1 French franc = 50 francs CFA, established in 1948, remained in force until January 1994, when the CFA franc was devalued by 50%, with the exchange rate adjusted to 1 French franc = 100 francs CFA. This relationship to French currency remained in effect with the introduction of the euro on 1 January 1999. From that date, accordingly, a fixed exchange rate of €1 = 655.957 francs CFA has been in operation.

BUDGET
('000 million francs CFA)

Revenue*	2019†	2020†	2021‡
Tax revenue	104.1	103.3	101.1
Income and property tax . .	23.5	28.0	28.7
Taxes on goods and services .	54.3	48.5	46.1
Taxes on international trade .	26.2	26.8	26.3
Non-tax revenue	12.0	22.4	24.8
Total	116.1	125.7	125.9

Expenditure	2019†	2020†	2021‡
Current primary expenditure .	146.1	184.8	171.6
Wages and salaries	65.1	80.1	81.2
Goods and services	42.2	51.7	49.7
Transfers and subsidies . .	38.9	53.0	40.7
Interest payments	4.6	4.2	4.0
Capital expenditure	75.0	155.7	106.3
Domestically financed . . .	17.1	31.0	27.7
Externally financed	58.0	124.7	78.6
Total	225.8	344.7	281.9

* Excluding grants received ('000 million francs CFA): 128.7 in 2019 (estimate); 172.9 in 2020 (estimate); 69.8 in 2021 (projection).
† Estimates.
‡ Projections.

Source: IMF, *Central African Republic: First Review Under the Staff-Monitored Program* (April 2022).

INTERNATIONAL RESERVES
(US $ million at 31 December)

	2017	2018	2019
Gold (national valuation) . .	14.33	14.23	16.86
IMF special drawing rights . .	4.46	4.93	1.39
Reserve position in IMF . . .	0.74	0.72	0.71
Foreign exchange	357.52	356.15	348.20
Total	377.05	376.03	367.16

2020: IMF special drawing rights 0.73; Reserve position in IMF 0.74.
2021: IMF special drawing rights 87.9; Reserve position in IMF 0.72.

Source: IMF, *International Financial Statistics*.

MONEY SUPPLY
('000 million francs CFA at 31 December)

	2017	2018	2019
Currency outside depository corporations	162.12	183.65	192.57
Transferable deposits	79.86	97.80	118.51
Other deposits	58.74	61.51	62.46
Broad money	300.72	342.96	373.54

Source: IMF, *International Financial Statistics*.

COST OF LIVING
(Consumer Price Index for Bangui; base: 2000 = 100)

	2011	2012	2013
Food*	273.7	293.8	298.3
All items (incl. others) . . .	139.8	148.0	150.2

* Base: 2009 = 100.
Source: ILO.

All items (base: 2010 = 100): 151.8 in 2019; 154.4 in 2020; 161.0 in 2021 (Source: IMF, *International Financial Statistics*).

NATIONAL ACCOUNTS
(million francs CFA at current prices)
Expenditure on the Gross Domestic Product

	2018	2019	2020
Government final consumption expenditure	175,210	193,382	192,200
Private final consumption expenditure	1,085,501	1,154,687	1,156,840
Gross capital formation . . .	319,531	190,727	252,661
Total domestic expenditure .	1,580,242	1,538,796	1,601,700
Exports of goods and services . .	232,955	204,853	180,885
Less Imports of goods and services	579,562	443,398	445,385
GDP in purchasers' values .	1,233,635	1,300,251	1,337,200
GDP at constant 2015 prices .	1,139,364	1,173,206	1,184,581

Gross Domestic Product by Economic Activity

	2018	2019	2020
Agriculture, hunting, forestry and fishing	385,404	415,866	427,971
Mining, quarrying and utilities	8,534	10,040	10,047
Manufacturing	223,677	242,827	246,256
Construction	21,372	19,888	21,255
Wholesale and retail trade, restaurants and hotels	229,880	238,006	247,027
Transport, storage and communication	21,622	29,732	28,645
Other services	279,067	290,129	298,687
GDP at factor cost	1,169,556	1,246,487	1,279,888
Indirect taxes (net)*	64,079	53,764	57,312
GDP in purchasers' values	1,233,635	1,300,251	1,337,200

* Figures obtained as a residual.

Source: UN National Accounts Main Aggregates Database.

BALANCE OF PAYMENTS
('000 million francs CFA)

	2018*	2019*	2020†
Exports of goods	91.1	94.1	82.7
Imports of goods	−279.6	−300.1	−313.1
Trade balance	−188.5	−206.0	−230.4
Services (net)	−36.6	−38.7	−39.3
Balance on goods and services	−225.1	−244.7	−269.7
Income (net)	−1.6	−1.9	−1.6
Balance on goods, services and income	−226.7	−246.6	−271.3
Current transfers (net)	125.9	180.9	155.1
Current balance	−100.8	−65.7	−116.2
Capital account (net)	60.6	48.5	102.8
Direct investment (net)	10.0	15.0	1.0
Portfolio investment (net)	0.2	0.0	0.0
Other investment (net)	27.4	8.8	−3.5
Errors and omissions	−19.4	−21.2	0.0
Overall balance	−22.0	−14.7	−15.8

* Estimates.
† Projections.

Source: IMF, *Central African Republic: First Review Under the Staff-Monitored Program* (April 2022).

External Trade

PRINCIPAL COMMODITIES
(distribution by HS, US $ million)

Imports c.i.f.	2018	2019	2020
Live animals and animal products	16.8	22.3	21.7
Vegetable products	22.5	27.0	25.5
Prepared foodstuffs, beverages and tobacco	35.3	42.8	39.0
Miscellaneous edible preparations	16.2	19.1	14.5
Mineral products	26.6	87.7	80.9
Mineral fuels, mineral oils and products of their distillation; bituminous substances, etc.	22.4	80.7	70.7
Petroleum oils and oils obtained from bituminous minerals (excluding crude)	22.0	79.8	68.1
Chemical and related products	26.3	88.1	66.0
Pharmaceutical products	18.8	74.8	52.6
Medicament mixtures in dosage	16.5	66.3	31.6
Textiles and textile articles	9.9	19.9	24.8
Base metals and articles	13.0	21.1	16.9
Machinery and electrical equipment	55.6	85.0	92.1

Imports c.i.f.—*continued*	2018	2019	2020
Machinery, boilers, etc.	23.7	33.6	37.4
Electrical, electronic equipment	31.9	51.5	54.7
Vehicles, aircraft, vessels and transport equipment	131.0	111.8	103.7
Vehicles other than railway, tramway	110.3	21.8	99.3
Cars (incl. station wagons)	24.9	9.0	43.5
Trucks and goods motor vehicles	15.6	2.6	20.6
Tanks and other armoured fighting vehicles	50.5	0.8	16.1
Aircraft, spacecraft, and parts thereof	18.2	87.5	3.8
Powered aircraft (helicopters and aeroplanes), spacecraft, incl. satellites	18.2	86.5	0.0
Total (incl. others)	384.4	567.8	544.9

Exports f.o.b.	2018	2019	2020
Wood and articles of wood	15.0	15.2	7.5
Pearls, precious or semi-precious stones, precious metals, and articles thereof	10.5	16.4	17.1
Machinery and electrical equipment	11.9	0.4	4.1
Machinery and boilers, etc.	2.5	0.3	3.8
Electrical, electronic equipment	9.5	0.1	0.3
Vehicles, aircraft, vessels and transport equipment	15.3	91.7	10.8
Vehicles other than railway, tramway	13.6	3.9	10.2
Aircraft, spacecraft and parts thereof	0.0	87.7	0.0
Total (incl. others)	54.9	125.2	41.0

Source: Trade Map-Trade Competitiveness Map, International Trade Centre, marketanalysis.intracen.org.

PRINCIPAL TRADING PARTNERS
(US $ million)

Imports c.i.f.	2018	2019	2020
Belgium	8.4	22.1	38.4
Cameroon	31.0	107.8	143.0
Chad	0.3	0.4	15.5
China, People's Republic	45.4	103.2	93.4
Congo, Republic	6.3	4.4	3.2
Denmark	8.0	7.4	14.8
France (incl. Monaco)	66.0	67.2	76.5
Germany	10.7	4.5	3.0
India	27.3	17.1	18.3
Italy	13.9	6.8	27.6
Japan	19.5	4.9	13.2
Nepal	30.0	0.0	0.1
Netherlands	8.8	10.8	9.2
Portugal	0.6	0.5	14.6
Senegal	4.3	2.4	3.0
South Africa	6.4	0.9	0.1
Spain	5.8	2.7	4.2
Switzerland and Liechtenstein	4.7	2.5	3.1
Tanzania	6.9	0.0	0.0
Uganda	3.1	9.3	1.2
United Arab Emirates	9.4	8.8	8.3
United Kingdom	12.2	12.3	1.5
USA	13.3	136.4	19.6
Total (incl. others)	384.4	567.8	544.9

Exports f.o.b.	2018	2019	2020
Belgium	0.8	0.2	0.3
Burkina Faso	0.0	0.0	1.1
Cameroon	7.2	2.8	1.7
Chad	0.1	0.0	1.2
China, People's Republic	7.0	7.4	2.8
France (incl. Monaco)	18.1	6.5	4.2
Germany	1.8	1.7	1.0
Morocco	1.9	—	—
Niger	2.5	—	0.1
Senegal	0.3	87.8	0.0
Sweden	—	—	6.2
Switzerland	0.8	3.0	3.3
Uganda	—	—	2.9
United Arab Emirates	9.0	9.4	10.0
Viet Nam	2.3	2.1	1.1
Total (incl. others)	54.9	125.2	41.0

Source: Trade Map-Trade Competitiveness Map, International Trade Centre, marketanalysis.intracen.org.

Transport

CIVIL AVIATION
(traffic on scheduled services)

	2014	2015	2016
Aircraft movements	7,865	13,520	14,500
Passengers carried ('000)	178.4	218.4	228.8
Freight handled (metric tons)	23,454	4,389	3,585

Tourism

FOREIGN VISITORS BY NATIONALITY*

	2017	2018	2019
Belgium	3,055	4,033	3,722
Cameroon	7,953	8,025	8,913
China, People's Republic	3,015	3,543	1,212
Congo, Democratic Republic	6,855	5,375	4,831
Congo, Republic	5,894	6,135	5,030
France	14,302	16,394	14,504
Germany	5,407	6,511	3,041
Italy	1,905	2,108	1,551
Lebanon	6,078	5,845	3,588
Rwanda	2,001	3,201	3,547
Total (incl. others)	106,669	109,193	87,263

* Arrivals at hotels and similar establishments.

Receipts from tourism (US $ million, incl. passenger transport): 15.0 in 2011; 15.0 in 2012; 16.0 in 2013.

Source: World Tourism Organization.

Communications Media

	2018	2019	2020
Telephones (main lines in use)	2,193	2,000	2,000
Mobile telephone subscriptions ('000)	1,279.3	1,595.3	1,831.0
Broadband subscriptions, fixed ('000)	608	499	n.a.
Broadband subscriptions, mobile ('000)	248	239	285
Internet users (% of population)	5.1.	8.3	10.4

Source: International Telecommunication Union.

Education

(2016/17 unless otherwise indicated)

	Institutions*	Teachers	Students Males	Students Females	Students Total
Pre-primary	162	338†	6,152	6,337	12,489
Primary	930	9,756†	458,857†	354,910†	813,767†
Secondary:					
general	46	4,052	79,548	53,147	132,695
vocational	n.a.	305	2,979	2,170	5,149
Tertiary	n.a.	384‡	9,153§	3,369§	12,522§

* 1990/91 figures.
† 2015/16 figure.
‡ 2010/11 figure.
§ 2011/12 figure.

Source: UNESCO Institute for Statistics.

Pupil-teacher ratio (qualified teaching staff, primary education, UNESCO estimate): 83.4 in 2015/16 (Source: UNESCO Institute for Statistics).

Adult literacy rate (UNESCO estimates): 37.4% (males 49.5%; females 25.8%) in 2018 (Source: UNESCO Institute for Statistics).

Directory

The Constitution

The Constitution of the Central African Republic, approved by 93.0% of those who voted at a referendum held on 13–14 December 2015 and promulgated on 30 March 2016, provides for a presidential term of five years, renewable only once. Executive authority is held by the President, who is elected by direct popular vote and who, in turn, appoints a Council of Ministers (upon the advice of a Prime Minister, who is head of government). The legislature comprises a directly elected 140-member National Assembly, which remains in office for a five-year term, and a Senate, whose members also serve five-year terms.

The Government

HEAD OF STATE

President: Faustin Archange Touadéra (inaugurated 30 March 2016; re-elected 27 December 2020).

COUNCIL OF MINISTERS
(October 2022)

Prime Minister and Minister of State, in charge of the Economy, Planning and International Co-operation: Félix Moloua.

Minister of State, in charge of Justice, the Promotion of Human Rights and Good Governance, Keeper of the Seals: Arnaud Djoubaye-Abazene.

Minister of State, in charge of Disarmament, Demobilization, Reintegration, Repatriation and Implementation of the Political Accord on Peace and Reconciliation: Jean Willybiro-Sako.

Minister in charge of Transport and Civil Aviation: Gontran Ndjono-Ahaba.

Minister of National Defence and Restructuring of the Army: Claude Rameaux Bireau.

Minister of Foreign Affairs, the Francophonie and Central Africans Abroad: Sylvie Valérie Baïpo-Témo.

Minister of the Interior and Public Security: MICHEL NICAISE NASSIN.

Minister in charge of Finance and the Budget: HERVÉ NDOBA.

Minister in charge of the Digital Economy, Postal Services and Telecommunications: JUSTIN GOURNA-ZACKO.

Minister in charge of National Education: MOUKADAS NOURÉ.

Minister in charge of Humanitarian Action, Solidarity and National Reconciliation: VIRGINIE BAÏKOUA.

Minister in charge of the Environment and Sustainable Development: THIERRY KAMACH.

Minister in charge of Health and Population: PIERRE SOMSÉ.

Minister in charge of Communication and the Media, Government Spokesperson: SERGE GHISLAIN DJORIE.

Minister in charge of the Promotion of Youth, Sport and Civic Education: ARISTIDE BRIAND REBOAS.

Minister in charge of the Civil Service and Administrative Reform: MARCEL DJIMASSE.

Minister in charge of the Secretariat-General of the Government and Relations with the Institutions of the Republic: MAXIME BALALOU.

Minister in charge of Equipment and Public Works: GUISMALA AMZA.

Minister in charge of Trade and Industry: LÉA KOVASSOUM-DOUMTA MBOUA.

Minister in charge of the Development of Energy and Water Resources: ARTHUR BERTRAND PIRI.

Minister in charge of Water, Forests, Hunting and Fishing: AMIT IDRISS.

Minister in charge of Stockbreeding and Animal Health: HASSAN BOUBA.

Minister in charge of Territorial Administration, Decentralization and Local Development: BRUNO YAPANDÉ.

Minister in charge of Higher Education, Scientific Research and Technological Innovation: JEAN-LAURENT SYSSA-MAGALÉ.

Minister in charge of the Promotion of Gender Equality and the Welfare of Women, Families and Children: MARGUERITTE RAMADAN.

Minister in charge of Mining and Geology: RUFIN BENAM-BELTOUNGOU.

Minister in charge of Agriculture and Rural Development: MATHIEU ERIC REKOSSÉ-KAMOT.

Minister in charge of Small and Medium-sized Enterprises and the Promotion of the Private Sector: MOHAMED LAWAN.

Minister in charge of the Arts, Culture and Tourism: VINCENTE MARIE LIONELE JENNIFER SARAÏVA-YANZÉRÉ.

Minister in charge of Town Planning, Land Reform and Housing: NICOLE NKOUÉ.

Minister in charge of Labour, Employment, Social Security and Professional Training: ANNIE MICHELLE LYVIA MOUANGA GAMBOR.

Minister-delegate to the Minister of State, in charge of Disarmament, Demobilization, Reintegration, Repatriation and Implementation of the Political Accord on Peace and Reconciliation: GILBERT TOUMOU DÉYA.

MINISTRIES

Office of the President: Palais présidentiel, Bangui; tel. 21-61-46-63.

Office of the Prime Minister: BP 932, Bangui; tel. 21-61-59-23.

Ministry of Agriculture and Rural Development: BP 786, Bangui; tel. 21-61-03-92; e-mail infos@madr-rca.com; internet www.agriculture.gouv.cf.

Ministry of the Arts, Culture and Tourism: Bangui; tel. 21-61-04-16; internet fb.com/tourismeRCA/.

Ministry of the Civil Service and Administrative Reform: Bangui; internet www.fonction-publique.gouv.cf.

Ministry of Communication and the Media: BP 940, Bangui; tel. 21-61-05-27; internet communication.gouv.cf.

Ministry of the Development of Energy and Water Resources: Bangui.

Ministry of the Digital Economy, Postal Services and Telecommunications: Bangui; tel. 21-61-29-66.

Ministry of the Economy, Planning and International Cooperation: rue Martin Luther King, BP 696, Bangui; tel. 75535898; internet www.mepc-rca.org.

Ministry of the Environment and Sustainable Development: Bangui; tel. 21-61-79-21.

Ministry of Equipment and Public Works: Bangui.

Ministry of Finance and the Budget: ave Abdel Gamal Nasser, BP 912, Bangui; tel. 21-61-38-28; internet www.finances.gouv.cf.

Ministry of Foreign Affairs, the Francophonie and Central Africans Abroad: ave des Martyrs, Bangui; internet www.diplomatie.gouv.cf.

Ministry of Health and Population: BP 883, Bangui; tel. 21-61-16-35; e-mail contact@msp-centrafrique.net; internet www.msp-centrafrique.net.

Ministry of Higher Education, Scientific Research and Technological Innovation: BP 791, Bangui; tel. 21-61-08-38.

Ministry of Humanitarian Action, Solidarity and National Reconciliation: ave Nasser, Bangui; tel. 21-61-55-65; internet www.reconciliation.gouv.cf.

Ministry of the Interior and Public Security: Bangui.

Ministry of Justice, the Promotion of Human Rights and Good Governance: Bangui; tel. 21-61-52-11; internet fb.com/ministerejusticeetdroisdelhommecentrafrique.

Ministry of Labour, Employment, Social Security and Professional Training: Bangui.

Ministry of Mining and Geology: BP 26, Bangui; internet www.mines.gouv.cf.

Ministry of National Defence and Restructuring of the Army: Bangui; tel. 21-61-00-25.

Ministry of National Education: Bangui.

Ministry of the Promotion of Gender Equality and the Welfare of Women, Families and Children: Bangui.

Ministry of the Promotion of Youth, Sport and Civic Education: Bangui; tel. 21-61-39-69.

Ministry of Small and Medium-sized Enterprises and the Promotion of the Private Sector: Bangui.

Ministry of Stockbreeding and Animal Health: Bangui.

Ministry of Territorial Administration, Decentralization and Local Development: Bangui; e-mail aristide@sokambi.com.

Ministry of Town Planning, Land Reform and Housing: Bangui.

Ministry of Trade and Industry: Bangui; tel. 21-61-10-69.

Ministry of Transport and Civil Aviation: Bangui.

Ministry of Water, Forests, Hunting and Fishing: BP 941, Bangui.

President

Presidential Election, 27 December 2020

Candidate	Valid votes	% of valid votes
Faustin Archange Touadéra (MCU) . .	318,626	53.23
Anicet Georges Dologuélé (URCA) . . .	130,017	21.72
Martin Ziguélé (MLPC)	45,206	7.55
Désiré Nzanga-Bilal-Kolingba (RDC) . .	22,157	3.70
Crépin Mboli-Ngoumba-Béndéré (PATRIE)	19,231	3.21
Sylvain-Eugène Ngakoutou-Patassé (CANE)	8,760	1.46
Augustin Agou (RDD)	8,436	1.41
Others*	46,137	7.71
Total	**598,570†**	**100.00**

* There were 10 other candidates.
† In addition, there were 19,284 blank ballots and 22,046 spoiled ballots.

Legislature

National Assembly: BP 1003, Bangui.

President: SIMPLICE MATHIEU SARANDJI.

General Election, 27 December 2020, and 14 March and 23 May 2021

Party	Seats
Mouvement Cœurs Unis (MCU)	40
Kwa na Kwa (KNK)	9
Mouvement pour la Libération du Peuple Centrafricain (MLPC)	7
Mouvement National des Indépendants (MNI)	7
Union pour le Renouveau Centrafricain (URC)	7
Rassemblement Démocratique Centrafricain (RDC)	6
Chemin de l'Espérance (CE)	3
Parti Africain pour une Transformation Radicale et l'Intégration des Etats (PATRIE)	3
Others	9
Independents	32
Total	133*

*Following the third round of voting, seven seats remained undeclared. A further round of elections for those seats took place on 25 July 2021. According to results released by the Autorité Nationale des Elections on 30 July, four seats were won by independent candidates, while KNK, the MCU and the MLPC each took one seat.

Election Commission

Autorité Nationale des Elections (ANE): 207 rue de Lakouanga, 1er Arrondissement, Bangui; tel. 72505039; e-mail contact@anerca.cf; internet anerca.cf; f. 2012; Pres. Dr MATHIAS-BARTHÉLÉMY MOROUBA.

Political Organizations

Alliance pour la Démocratie et le Progrès (ADP): Bangui; internet alliance-democratie-progres.over-blog.com; f. 1991; progressive; Pres. CLÉMENT BELIBANGA.

Convention Républicaine pour le Progrès Social (CRPS): Bangui; Leader NICOLAS TIANGAYE.

Forum Démocratique pour la Modernité (FODEM): ave Dejean, Sicai, Bangui; tel. 21-61-29-54; f. 1997; Pres. STÉPHANE PENTCHOAKI.

Front Démocratique de Libération du Peuple Centrafricain (FDPC): e-mail miskinedardar@yahoo.fr; Leader Gen. ABDOULAYE MISKINE.

Front Patriotique pour le Progrès (FPP): BP 259, Bangui; tel. 21-61-52-23; f. 1972; aims to promote political education and debate; Leader ALEXANDRE GOUMBA.

Kwa na Kwa (KNK): Bangui; internet fb.com/Kwa-Na-Kwa-103890177647115; f. 2004; formally constituted as a political party in 2009; Acting Pres. CHRISTIAN OLIVIER GUÉNÉBEM DÉDIZOUM.

Mouvement Cœurs Unis (MCU): Bangui; f. 2018; Exec. Sec. SIMPLICE MATHIEU SARANDJI.

Mouvement pour la Démocratie et le Développement (MDD): Bangui; f. 1993; aims to safeguard national unity and the equitable distribution of national wealth; Leader LOUIS PAPENIAH.

Mouvement pour la Démocratie, l'Indépendance et le Progrès Social (MDI-PS): BP 1404, Bangui; tel. 21-61-18-21; Sec.-Gen. DANIEL NDITIFEI BOYSEMBE.

Mouvement pour la Libération du Peuple Centrafricain (MLPC): Bangui; f. 1979; leading party in govt Oct. 1993–March 2003; Pres. MARTIN ZIGUÉLÉ; Sec.-Gen. JEAN-MICHEL MANDABA.

Mouvement National pour le Renouveau: Bangui; Leader PAUL BELLET.

Mouvement National de Solidarité (MNS): Bangui; tel. 70450061; Pres. ERIC SORONGOPÉ ZOUMANDJI.

Parti d'Action pour le Développement (PAD): Bangui; tel. 70966913; Pres. LAURENT NGON-BABA.

Parti Africain pour une Transformation Radicale et l'Intégration des Etats (PATRIE): Bangui; tel. 70021212; Pres. CRÉPIN MBOLI GOUMBA.

Parti pour la Gouvernance Démocratique (PGD): Bangui; Pres. JEAN-MICHEL MANDABA.

Parti pour la Renaissance Centrafricaine (PARC): Bangui; Pres. GASTON MANDATA NGUÉRÉKATA.

Parti de l'Unité Nationale (PUN): Bangui; Pres. LÉA MBOUA DOUMTA.

Parti Social-Démocrate (PSD): BP 543, Bangui; tel. 21-61-59-02; Leader ENOCH DERANT LAKOUÉ.

Rassemblement Démocratique Centrafricain (RDC): BP 503, Bangui; tel. 21-61-53-75; f. 1987; sole legal political party 1987–91; Interim Pres. HENRI PIERRE ASSANGOU.

Rassemblement pour la Republique (RPR): Bangui; Pres. ALEXANDRE-FERDINAND N'GUENDET.

Union Nationale des Démocrates Républicains (UNADER): Bangui; tel. 75504242; Pres. LAURENT GOMINA PAMPALI.

Union Nationale pour la Démocratie et le Progrès (UNDP): Bangui; e-mail info@balad.com; internet www.undp-rca.com; Pres. AMINE MICHEL.

Union pour le Renouveau Centrafricain (URCA): ave Conjugo, SICA II, BP 1817, Bangui; Pres. ANICET GEORGES DOLOGUÉLÉ.

Diplomatic Representation

EMBASSIES IN THE CENTRAL AFRICAN REPUBLIC

Cameroon: rue du Languedoc, BP 935, Bangui; tel. 72717070; e-mail ambacambangui@yahoo.fr; Ambassador NICOLAS NZOYOUM.

Chad: ave Valéry Giscard d'Estaing, BP 461, Bangui; tel. 21-61-46-77; e-mail tchadambassade_bangui@yahoo.fr; Ambassador NOH TAMOUR ALEJIDEYE.

China, People's Republic: ave des Martyrs, BP 1430, Bangui; tel. 21-61-27-60; e-mail chinaemb_cf@mfa.gov.cn; internet cf.china-embassy.gov.cn; Ambassador (vacant).

Congo, Democratic Republic: BP 989, Bangui; tel. 21-61-33-44; Ambassador ESDRAS KAMBALE BAHEKWA.

Congo, Republic: ave Barthélemy Boganda, BP 1414, Bangui; tel. 21-61-03-09; e-mail diplobrazzabangui@yahoo.fr; Ambassador DELPHIN EMBODZA.

Egypt: angle ave Léopold Sédar Senghor et rue Emile Gentil, BP 1422, Bangui; tel. 21-61-46-88; e-mail embassy.bangui@mfa.gov.eg; Ambassador MEDHAT MOHAMED KAMAL EL-MELIGY.

Equatorial Guinea: ave Abdel Nasser, Bangui; tel. 21-61-83-15; e-mail emolamu@gmail.com; Ambassador NARCISO EDU NSUE.

France: blvd du Général de Gaulle, BP 884, Bangui; tel. 21-61-30-05; internet cf.ambafrance.org; Ambassador JEAN-MARC GROSGURIN.

Holy See: ave Boganda, BP 1447, Bangui; tel. 75041492; Apostolic Nuncio (vacant).

Libya: Bangui; tel. 21-61-46-62; Chargé d'affaires ABDOUL-MAJED ALBAHLOUL.

Morocco: ave de l'Indépendance, BP 1609, Bangui; tel. 21-61-39-51; Ambassador MUSTAPHA EL-HALFAOUI.

Nigeria: ave des Martyrs, BP 1010, Bangui; tel. 21-61-07-44; e-mail jimgom7@yahoo.com; Ambassador ROLAND OZAWUMI OMOWA.

Qatar: Ledger Plaza, Bangui; tel. 21-61-72-67; Ambassador AHMAD ABDUL RAHMAN MOHAMMED AL-SUNAIDI.

Russian Federation: ave du Président Gamal Abdel Nasser, BP 1405, Bangui; tel. 21-61-03-11; e-mail rusconsrca@yandex.ru; internet rca.mid.ru; Ambassador ALEXANDER BIKANTOV.

South Africa: 5686 ave de l'Indépendance, Ndakala Anne, Bangui; tel. 75081684; e-mail bangui.general@dirco.gov.za; Ambassador (vacant).

Sudan: ave de France, BP 1351, Bangui; tel. 21-61-38-21; e-mail sudanibangui@gmail.com; Ambassador ABDUL-RAOUF AMER ALI AMER.

USA: ave David Dacko, BP 924, Bangui; tel. 21-61-02-00; e-mail BanguiConsular@state.gov; internet cf.usembassy.gov; Ambassador PATRICIA MAHONEY.

Judicial System

The independence of the judiciary is enshrined in the Constitution of 2016 and judicial power is exercised by the nine-member Constitutional Court, the Court of Cassation, the Audit Court and the High Court of Justice.

In October 2018 the Special Criminal Court, which had been appointed in June 2017, held its inaugural session in Bangui, with a five-year mandate to prosecute crimes against humanity and war crimes. The Court comprised the Special Prosecutor, Toussaint Muntazini Mukimapa (a former military prosecutor in the Democratic Republic of the Congo), and five national magistrates.

Constitutional Court: BP 2104, Bangui; tel. 21-61-99-58; f. 1995; 9 mems; Pres. DANIÈLE DARLAN.

High Court of Justice: Bangui; Pres. CHRISTIAN LONDOUMON.

Religion

CHRISTIANITY

Alliance des Evangéliques en Centrafrique (AEC): Bangui; Pres. CLOTAIRE-RODONNE SIRIBI.

The Roman Catholic Church

The Central African Republic comprises one archdiocese and eight dioceses.

Bishops' Conference: Conférence Episcopale Centrafricaine (CECA), BP 1518, Bangui; tel. 75114102; e-mail ceca_rca@yahoo .fr; f. 1982; Pres. NESTOR-DÉSIRÉ NONGO-AZIAGBIA (Bishop of Bossangoa).

Archbishop of Bangui: Cardinal DIEUDONNÉ NZAPALAINGA, Archevêché, BP 1518, Bangui; tel. 75199176; e-mail archbangui@yahoo.fr.

Protestant Church

Eglise Evangélique Luthérienne de la République Centrafricaine: BP 100, Bouar; tel. 70807336; Pres. Rev. ANDRÉ GOLIKE.

Eglise Protestante du Christ Roi: rue des Missions, BP 608, Bangui; tel. 21-61-14-35; f. 1968.

ISLAM

Communauté Islamique de RCA: Bangui; Pres. (vacant).

The Press

The independent press is highly regulated. Independent publications must hold a trading licence and prove their status as a commercial enterprise. They must also have proof that they fulfil taxation requirements. There is little press activity outside Bangui.

DAILY NEWSPAPERS (PRINT AND ONLINE)

Le Citoyen: BP 974, Bangui; tel. 21-61-89-16; e-mail ltdc@yahoo.fr; independent; Dir MAKA GBOSSOKOTTO.

Corbeau News Centrafrique: BP 1500, Bangui; e-mail corbeaunewscentrafrique@gmail.com; internet corbeaunews-centrafrique.com; f. 2014; Editor-in-Chief ALAIN NZILO.

Le Démocrate: BP 427, Bangui; Dir of Publication FERDINAND SAMBA.

L'Hirondelle: Bangui; independent; Editor-in-Chief JULES YANGANDA.

PERIODICALS

Centrafrique-Presse: BP 1058, Bangui; tel. 21-61-39-57; e-mail contact@centrafrique-presse.info; internet www .centrafrique-presse.info; weekly; Publr PROSPER N'DOUBA.

Journal Officiel de la République Centrafricaine: BP 739, Bangui; f. 1974; fortnightly; economic data; Dir-Gen. GABRIEL AGBA.

Le Patriote: Bangui; Dir of Publ. AMBROISE YALIMA.

PRESS ASSOCIATIONS

Groupement des Editeurs de la Presse Privée Indépendante de Centrafrique (GEPPIC): Bangui; Pres. PATRICK AGOUNDOU.

Observatoire des Médias Centrafricains (OMCA): Bangui; Pres. PIERRE DÉBATO, II.

Union des Journalistes de Centrafrique (UJCA): Bangui; tel. 72725943; Pres. TITA SAMBA SOLÉ.

NEWS AGENCIES

Agence Centrafrique Presse (ACAP): BP 40, Bangui; tel. 75030656; e-mail acapnews@gmail.com; internet www.acap.cf; f. 1960; Dir SIMON-PIERRE NDOUBA.

Publishers

GOVERNMENT PUBLISHING HOUSE

Imprimerie Centrafricaine: ave David Dacko, BP 329, Bangui; tel. 21-61-72-24; f. 1974; Dir-Gen. SERGE BOZANGA.

Broadcasting and Communications

TELECOMMUNICATIONS

Atlantique Telecom Centrafrique SA: Immeuble Moov, ave du Président Mobutu, BP 2439 Bangui; tel. 21-61-23-85; internet www .moov-rca.com; operates mobile telephone services under Moov network; Dir-Gen. KHAIRI ABDELAHIKIM.

Azur RCA: ave de l'Indépendance, Ex FNUAP, BP 1418, Bangui; tel. 21-61-33-97; internet www.azur-rca.com; f. 2004; established as NationLink Telecom RCA; mobile telephone operator; Dir-Gen. GEORGE AKOURY.

Orange Centrafrique: Immeuble SODIAM, ave Barthélemy Boganda, BP 863, Bangui; tel. 72270800; internet www.orangerca .com; f. 2007; mobile telephone operator; Dir-Gen. RÉGIS DELIÈRE.

Société Centrafricaine de Télécommunications (SOCATEL): BP 939, Bangui; tel. 21-61-42-68; f. 1990; 60% state-owned, 40% owned by France Câbles et Radio (France Télécoms); Dir-Gen. SATURNIN CYRIAQUE SEM.

Telecel: rue Monseigneur Grandin, BP 849, Bangui; tel. 21-61-19-30; internet www.telecel-rca.com; f. 1996; mobile telephone operator; Dir-Gen. AIMABLE MPORÉ.

Regulatory Authority

Autorité de Régulation des Communications Electroniques et de la Poste (ARCEP): Immeuble de la Poste, BP 1046, Bangui; tel. 21-61-56-51; internet www.arcep.cf; f. 2017 to replace the Agence de Régulation des Télécommunications; Dir-Gen. BENJAMIN PANZE-SEBAS.

BROADCASTING

Radiodiffusion-Télévision Centrafricaine: BP 940, Bangui; tel. 21-61-25-88; f. 1958 as Radiodiffusion Nationale Centrafricaine; govt-controlled; broadcasts in French and Sango.

Lego Ti La Ouaka: Bambari; tel. 779964; f. 2015; community radio station.

Radio Centrafrique: Bangui; tel. 75503632; e-mail yakanet.rca@ gmail.com; Dir-Gen JÉSUS TARCIL BOMONGO JUNIOR.

Radio Ndeke Luka: Concession du PNUD, BP 558, ave de l'Indépendance, Bangui; tel. 72295252; e-mail s.panika@radiondekeluka .org; internet www.radiondekeluka.org; f. 2000; Dir SYLVIE PANIKA.

TELEVISION

Télévision Centrafricaine (TVCA): Bangui; tel. 21-61-61-02; Dir-Gen. ALFRED NGOE-BENGUE.

REGULATORY AUTHORITY

Haut Conseil de la Communication (HCC): Bâtiment Annexe du Ministère des Affaires Etrangères, BP 1997, Bangui; tel. 21-61-63-20; e-mail info@hcc-rca.org; internet www.hcc-rca.org; f. 2004; Pres. JOSÉ RICHARD POUAMBI.

Finance

BANKING

Central Bank

Banque des Etats de l'Afrique Centrale (BEAC): BP 851, Bangui; tel. 21-61-24-00; internet www .beac.int; headquarters in Yaoundé, Cameroon; f. 1973; bank of issue for mem. states of the Communauté Economique et Monétaire de l'Afrique Centrale (CEMAC, fmrly Union Douanière et Economique de l'Afrique Centrale), comprising Cameroon, the CAR, Chad, the Repub. of the Congo, Equatorial Guinea and Gabon; Gov. ABBAS MAHAMAT TOLLI; Dir in CAR ALI CHAÏBOU.

Commercial Banks

Banque Populaire Maroco-Centrafricaine (BPMC): rue Guérillot, BP 844, Bangui; tel. 21-61-31-90; f. 1991; 57.5% owned by Groupe Banque Populaire (Morocco); Gen. Man. ALEXIS LOUEKE.

Banque Sahélo-Saharienne pour l'Investissement et le Commerce Centrafrique (BSIC): ave du Tchad, angle ave du Président Mobutu, PK 0, BP 864, Bangui; tel. 21-61-27-48; e-mail bsic .centralafrica@bsicbank.com; internet www.bsicbank.com/ centralafrica; f. 2008; Dir-Gen. SAFIROU ZOUMAROU WALLIS.

Commercial Bank Centrafrique (CBCA): rue de Brazza, BP 59, Bangui; tel. 21-61-29-90; f. 1999; 54.5% owned by Groupe Fotso, 40.5% owned by CAR private shareholders, 5% owned by Commercial Bank Cameroon SA; Dir-Gen. HERVÉ KOGBOMA YOGO.

Ecobank Centrafrique: pl. de la République, BP 910, Bangui; tel. 21-61-00-42; e-mail ecobankcf@ecobank.com; internet www.ecobank.com; f. 1946 as BAO; Man. Dir CHRISTIAN ASSOSSOU.

Development Bank

Banque de Développement des Etats de l'Afrique Centrale: see Franc Zone.

INSURANCE

Ascoma Centrafrique: ave Barthélemy Boganda, BP 743, Bangui; tel. 21-61-19-33; e-mail centrafrique@ascoma.com; f. 1968; owned by Ascoma (Monaco); Dir-Gen. ABAKAR BOUTOU.

Sunu Assurances IARD Centrafrique: rue de la Victoire, BP 896, Bangui; tel. 21-61-31-02; e-mail centrafrique.iard@sunu-group.com; internet www.sunu-group.com; f. 1999; fmrly Union des Assurances Centrafricaine; name changed as above in 2015; non-life insurance; Pres. PATHÉ DIONE; Dir-Gen. MARTIAL SOUKÉ.

Trade and Industry

DEVELOPMENT ORGANIZATIONS

Agence Centrafricaine de Développement Agricole (ACDA): ave David Dacko, BP 997, Bangui; tel. 21-61-54-85; e-mail acda_2010@yahoo.fr; internet fb.com/ACDA.RCA; f. 1993; purchasing, transport and marketing of cotton, cotton ginning, production of cottonseed oil and groundnut oil; Dir-Gen. RODRIGUE YAKENDÉ.

Agence Française de Développement: route de la Moyenne Corniche, BP 817, Bangui; tel. 21-61-03-06; e-mail afdbangui@afd.fr; internet www.afd.fr; administers economic aid and finances specific development projects; Man. DENIS VASSEUR.

Service de Coopération et d'Action Culturelle: BP 934, Bangui; tel. 21-61-30-30; administers bilateral aid from France; Sec.-Gen. LOUIS ESTIENNE.

INDUSTRIAL AND TRADE ASSOCIATIONS

Agence Nationale pour le Développement de l'Elevage (ANDE): BP 1509, Bangui; tel. 21-61-69-60; assists with development of livestock; Dir-Gen. FIDÈLE DIEUDONNÉ KOYANONGO.

Caisse de Stabilisation et de Péréquation des Produits Agricoles (CAISTAB): BP 76, Bangui; tel. 21-61-08-00; supervises marketing and pricing of agricultural produce; Dir-Gen. M. BOUNANDELE-KOUMBA.

Fédération Nationale des Eleveurs Centrafricains (FNEC): ave des Martyrs, BP 588, Bangui; tel. 21-61-23-97; Pres. BI AMADOU SOUAIBOU; Sec.-Gen. YOUSSOUFA MANDJO.

Groupement des Industries Centrafricaines (GICA): rue des Missions, BP 804, Bangui; e-mail cotact@gica.cf; internet gica.cf; umbrella group representing 12 principal companies of various industries; Pres. LAURENCE NASSIF.

Office National des Forêts (ONF): BP 915, Bangui; tel. 21-61-38-27; f. 1969; afforestation, development of forest resources; Dir-Gen. C. D. SONGUET.

CHAMBERS OF COMMERCE

Chambre d'Agriculture, d'Elevage, des Eaux, Forêts, Chasses, Pêches et du Tourisme: 200 Villas Arrière plan BARC, BP 850, Bangui; tel. 21-61-06-38; e-mail chagri_rca@hotmail.com; f. 1964; Sec.-Gen. HENRI OUIKON.

Chambre de Commerce, d'Industrie, des Mines et de l'Artisanat (CCIMA): blvd Charles de Gaulle, BP 823, Bangui; tel. 21-61-16-68; f. 1935; Pres. ROBERT NGOKI; Treas. THÉODORE LAWSON.

EMPLOYERS' ORGANIZATIONS

Union Nationale du Patronat Centrafricain (UNPC): Immeuble Tropicana, 1°, BP 2180, Bangui; tel. 21-61-16-79; Pres. GILLES GILBERT GRESENGUET.

UTILITIES

Electricity

Société Energie de Centrafrique (ENERCA): ave de l'Indépendance, BP 880, Bangui; tel. 21-61-00-00; e-mail contact@enerca-rca.com; internet enerca-rca.com; f. 1967; state-owned; production and distribution of electric energy; Dir-Gen. THIERRY PATIENT BENDIMA.

Water

Société de Distribution d'Eau en Centrafrique (SODECA): BP 1838, Bangui; tel. 21-61-59-66; f. 1975 as the Société Nationale des Eaux; state-owned co responsible for supply, treatment and distribution of water; Dir-Gen. JUSTINE SOW OUAKARA.

MAJOR COMPANIES

The following are among the largest companies in terms of either capital investment or employment.

COLALU: rue Chavannes, BP 1326, Bangui; tel. 75-50-34-83; e-mail info.ct@colalu.com; f. 1969; owned by Yeshi Group (Côte d'Ivoire); mfrs of household articles and sheet aluminium.

Huilerie Savonnerie Centrafricaine (HUSACA): BP 1020, Bangui; tel. 75-17-28-95; e-mail infos.snhusaca@gmail.com; internet snhusaca.com; mfrs of soap, edible oil and animal feed; Dir RAED HARIRI.

K GROUP: ave David Dacko, BP 804, Bangui; tel. 21-61-18-05; internet kamachgroup.com; mining and forest products; Pres. and Dir-Gen. YVON KAMACH.

Motte-Cordonnier-Afrique (MOCAF): PK 9, route de M'Baiki, Bimbo, BP 806, Bangui; tel. 21-61-18-13; internet mocafrca.com; f. 1951; production of beer, soft drinks and ice; Dir-Gen. ALAIN HERAIBI.

Société Centrafricaine de Cigarette (SOCACI): BP 681, Bangui; Dir-Gen. PATRICK DE JEAN.

Société Centrafricaine des Gaz Industriels (SOCAGI): blvd Bouganda, BP 905, Bangui; tel. 21-61-16-42; e-mail socagi@yahoo.fr; f. 1965; manufacture and sale of industrial and medical gases; Pres. and Dir-Gen. PAUL LALAGUE.

Société Centrafricaine des Palmiers (CENTRAPALM): BP 1355, Bangui; tel. 21-61-49-40; f. 1975; state-owned; production and marketing of palm oil; operates the Bossongo agro-industrial complex.

Société d'Exploitation Forestière Centrafricaine (SEFCA): 260 rue Valéry Giscard d'Estaing, BP 391, Bangui; tel. 21-61-66-12; e-mail info@sefca-rca.com; internet www.sefca-rca.com; f. 1988; Pres. and Dir-Gen. JAMAL EL-SAHELY.

Société des Fibres Centrafricaines (SOFICA): BP 154, Bangui-Lakouanga; tel. 21-61-76-23; f. 2007 to replace the Société Centrafricaine de Développement des Textiles (SOCADETEX); cotton producer.

Sucrière en Afrique (SUCAF-RCA): ave Boganda, km 4, BP 1572, Bangui; tel. 21-61-32-88; acquired in 2003 by the SOMDIAA (France); sugar producer; annual production of 12,000 metric tons of brown sugar; factory at Ouaka; Dir-Gen. STÉPHANE JAFFRET.

TotalEnergies Centrafrique: ave de l'Indépendance, BP 3295, Bangui; tel. 21-61-26-07; e-mail carte.ngoutidada@total-rca.com; internet totalenergies.com/central-african-republic; f. 2000; storage and retailing petroleum products; Dir-Gen. FABRICE MOUSSA-KEMBE.

TRADE UNIONS

Confédération Syndicale des Travailleurs de Centrafrique (CSTC): BP 386, km 5, Bangui; tel. 21-61-38-69; Sec.-Gen. SABIN KPOKOLO.

Organisation des Syndicats Libres du Secteur Public, Parapublic et Privé (OSLP): BP 1450, Bangui; tel. 21-61-20-00; Sec.-Gen. MICHEL LOUDÉGUÉ.

Union Générale des Travailleurs de Centrafrique (UGTC): BP 346, Bangui; tel. 21-61-05-86; Sec.-Gen. JEAN-MARIE AGOUTOCO.

Union Syndicale des Travailleurs de Centrafrique (USTC): BP 1390, Bangui; tel. 21-61-60-15; e-mail vvesfon@yahoo.fr; Sec.-Gen. NOËL RAMADAN.

Transport

RAILWAYS

There are no railways at present. There are long-term plans to connect Bangui to the Trans-Cameroon railway. A line linking Sudan's Darfur region with the CAR's Vakaga province has also been proposed.

ROADS

Eight main routes serve Bangui, and those that are surfaced are toll roads. Both the total road length and the condition of the roads are inadequate for current requirements. The CAR is linked with Cameroon by the TransAfrican Lagos–Mombasa highway. Roads are frequently impassable in the rainy season (July–October).

Fonds d'Entretien Routier (FER): BP 962, Bangui; tel. 21-61-62-95; f. 1981; Dir-Gen. MARIE-CLAIRE BITOUANGA.

INLAND WATERWAYS

There are some 2,800 km of navigable waterways along two main water courses. The first, formed by the Congo river and its tributary the Oubangui, can accommodate convoys of barges (of up to 800 metric tons load) between Bangui and Brazzaville and Pointe-Noire in the Republic of the Congo, except during the dry season, when the route is impassable. The second is the Sangha river, also a tributary of the Congo, on which traffic is again seasonal. There are two ports, at Bangui and Salo, on the rivers Oubangui and Sangha, respectively. Bangui port has a handling capacity of 350,000 tons, with 350 m of wharfs and 24,000 sq m of warehousing. Efforts are being made to develop the Sangha upstream from Salo, to increase the transportation of timber from this area and to develop Nola as a timber port.

Société Centrafricaine de Transports Fluviaux (SOCA-TRAF): rue Parent, BP 1445, Bangui; tel. 21-61-43-15; f. 1980; Man. Dir FRANÇOIS TOUSSAINT.

CIVIL AVIATION

The international airport is at Bangui-M'Poko. There are also some 37 small airports providing internal services.

Autorité National de l'Aviation Civile de la République Centrafricaine (ANAC—Centrafrique): BP 134, Bangui; tel. 21-61-34-00; f. 2009; Dir-Gen. Col FRANÇOIS EDLY FOLLOT.

Tourism

Office National Centrafricain du Tourisme (OCATOUR): rue Roger Guérillot, BP 645, Bangui; tel. 21-61-45-66.

Defence

As assessed at November 2021, the armed forces numbered about 9,150 men (army 9,000 and air force 150). Military service is selective and lasts for two years. There was also a paramilitary gendarmerie with 1,000 members. At mid-2021 the UN Multidimensional Integrated Stabilization Mission in the Central African Republic (MINUSCA) had a maximum authorized strength of 11,650 military personnel and 2,080 police personnel. MINUSCA has a mandate to remain in the country until 15 November 2022.

Defence Expenditure: Estimated at 24,000m. francs CFA in 2021.

Commander-in-Chief of the Armed Forces: FAUSTIN ARCHANGE TOUADÉRA.

Chief of Staff of the Armed Forces: Maj.-Gen. ZÉPHIRIN MAMADOU.

Education

Education is officially compulsory for eight years between six and 14 years of age. Primary education begins at the age of six and lasts for six years. Secondary education begins at the age of 12 and lasts for up to seven years, comprising a first cycle of four years and a second of three years. In 2016/17, according to estimates by the United Nations Educational, Scientific and Cultural Organization (UNESCO), enrolment at pre-primary level was equivalent to 3% of children in the relevant age-group (males 3%; females 3%). In that year enrolment at secondary schools enrolment was equivalent to 17% (20% of boys; 14% of girls). According to the World Bank, in 2021 public spending on education was equivalent to 9.0% of total government expenditure.

Bibliography

Baxter, P. *France In Centrafrique: From Bokassa and Operation Barracude to the days of EUFOR.* Solihull, Helion and Company, 2011.

Bevarrah, L. *Centrafrique: mon combat politique. Vers une nouvelle République.* Paris, L'Harmattan, 2010.

Bradshaw, R., and Fandos-Rius, J. *Historical Dictionary of the Central African Republic.* Lanham, MD, Rowman & Littlefield, 2016.

Carayannis, T., and Lombard, L. (Eds). *Making Sense of the Central African Republic.* London, Zed Books, 2015.

Dangabo Moussa, A. *Centrafrique: Invention de la démocratie et du citoyen, ou, les expériences locales d'invention démocratique en Centrafrique.* Paris, Menaibuc, 2014.

Doubane, C. A. *Ma vie, ma vision pour le Centrafrique.* Paris, L'Harmattan, 2015.

Doui-Wawaye, A. *L'insécurité en République Centrafricaine.* Paris, L'Harmattan, 2015.

Flichy de la Neuville, T., et al. *Centrafrique, pourquoi la guerre?* Panazol, Lavauzelle Graphic, 2014.

Germain, E. *Centrafrique et Bokassa 1965–1979: Force et déclin d'un pouvoir personnel.* Paris, L'Harmattan, 2001.

Goumba, A. *Les Mémoires & les Réflexions politiques du Résistant anti-colonial, démocrate et militant Panafricaniste, Abel Goumba. De la Loi-Cadre à la mort de Barthélemy Boganda, Vol. 1.* Paris, CINIA Communication, 2006.

Les Mémoires & les Réflexions politiques du Résistant anti-colonial, démocrate et militant Panafricaniste, Abel Goumba. De la succession du Président B. Boganda au procès de la honte du Militant Abel Goumba, Vol. 2. Paris, CCINIA Communication, 2009.

Lachèse, M.-C. *De l'Oubangui à la Centrafrique: La construction d'un espace national.* Paris, L'Harmattan, 2015.

Lasserre Yakite, C. *Le désarmement des groupes armés en Centrafrique.* Paris, Les Impliqués Editeur, 2018.

Lombard, L. *State of Rebellion: Violence and Intervention in the Central African Republic.* London, Zed Books, 2016.

Hunting Game: Raiding Politics in the Central African Republic. Cambridge, Cambridge University Press, 2020.

Mété-Nguemeu, Y. *Femmes de Centrafrique.* Besançon, Editions Centrafrique Sans Frontières, 2008.

Mossoa, L. *Où va la Centrafrique?* Paris, L'Harmattan, 2015.

N'Douba, P. *L'otage du général rebelle centrafricain François Bozizé: Journal d'un Captif des 'Libérateurs'.* Paris, L'Harmattan, 2006.

Ndoutingaï, S. *Au coeur des pouvoirs en Centrafrique.* Paris, Jean Picollec, 2017.

Ngoupandé, J.-P. *Chronique de la crise centrafricaine 1996–1997: le syndrome barracuda.* Paris, L'Harmattan, 1997.

Parse, R.-B. *Centrafrique, un vrai-faux départ: Cas atypique d'un mal africain.* Paris, L'Harmattan, 2017.

Reboas, A. B. *Pour une politique de paix en Centrafrique.* Paris, L'Harmattan, 2016.

Reyntjens, F., and Lanotte, P. *La grande guerre Africaine: Instabilité, violence et déclin de l'etat en Afrique Centrale, 1996–2006.* Paris, les Belles lettres, 2012.

Saulet-Surungba, C. *Centrafrique, 1993–2003: La Politique du Changement d'Ange Félix Patassé.* Paris, L'Harmattan, 2012.

Serre, J. *David Dacko Premier Président de la République Centrafricaine 1930–2003.* Paris, L'Harmattan, 2007.

Serre, J., and Fandos-Rius, J. *Répertoire de l'administration territorial de la République Centrafricaine.* Paris, L'Harmattan, 2014.

Wagon, J.-B. *L'économie centrafricaine: pour rompre avec la logique de rente.* Paris, L'Harmattan, 1998.

Woodfork, J. *Culture and Customs of the Central African Republic.* Westport, CT, Greenwood Press, 2006.

Yele, R., and Doko, P. *Les Defis de la Centrafrique: Gouvernance et Stabilisation du Systeme Economique.* Dakar, CODESRIA, 2011.

Yepoussa, F. *Plaidoyer pour la paix en Centrafrique.* Paris, L'Harmattan, 2016.

Zoctizoum, Y. *Histoire de la République Centrafricaine,* 2 vols. Paris, L'Harmattan, 1984.

CHAD

Physical and Social Geography

DAVID HILLING

The Republic of Chad is bordered to the north by Libya, to the south by the Central African Republic, to the west by Niger and Cameroon, and to the east by Sudan. The northernmost of the four independent states that emerged from French Equatorial Africa, Chad is, with an area of 1,284,000 sq km (495,800 sq miles), the largest in terms of size and population (some 17.4m. at mid-2022, according to United Nations projections). Traditionally a focal point for equatorial and Saharan trade routes, the country's vast size, landlocked location and great distance from the coast create problems for economic development. The only large city is the capital, N'Djamena (known as Fort-Lamy during the colonial period), which had an estimated population of 1.5m. in 2021.

The relief is relatively simple. From 240 m in the Lake Chad depression in the south-west, the land rises northwards through the Guéra massif at 1,800 m to the mountainous Saharan region of Tibesti at 3,350 m. Eastwards, heights of 1,500 m are attained in the Ouaddaï massif. In the south the watershed area between the Chari and Congo rivers is of subdued relief and only slight elevation. The only rivers of importance, both for irrigation and seasonal navigation, are the Chari and Logone, which traverse the south-west of the country and join at N'Djamena, before flowing into Lake Chad.

Extending across more than 16° of latitude, Chad has three well-defined zones of climate, natural vegetation and associated economic activity. The southern third of the country has annual rainfall in excess of 744 mm (increasing to 1,200 mm in the extreme south), and has a savannah woodland vegetation. This is the country's principal agricultural zone, providing the two main cash crops, cotton and groundnuts, and a variety of local food crops (especially rice). Northwards, with rainfall of 250–500 mm per year, there is a more open grassland, where there is emphasis on pastoral activity, limited cultivation of groundnuts and local grains, and some collection of gum arabic. This marginal Sahel zone was adversely affected by drought during most of the 1970s and 1980s, when the cattle herds were greatly reduced in number. The northern third of the country has negligible rainfall and a sparse scrub vegetation, which grades north into pure desert with little apparent economic potential, although the 'Aozou strip', a region of 114,000 sq km in the extreme north, is believed to contain significant reserves of uranium and other minerals. The development of substantial petroleum reserves in the Doba Basin, in the south of the country, and also at Sedigi commenced in the late 1990s, and production of petroleum at Doba began in 2003. There is also believed to be considerable potential for the commercial exploitation of gold, particularly in the Mayo-Kebbi Ouest region, in the south-west of the country.

Chad's total population is relatively small in relation to its large area, and is markedly concentrated in the southern half of the country. Religious and ethnic tensions between the people of the north and south have traditionally dominated the history of Chad. The population of the north is predominantly Islamic, of a nomadic or semi-nomadic character, and is largely engaged in farming and in breeding livestock. Rivalry between the various ethnic groups in the north is strong. By contrast, the inhabitants of the south are settled farmers, the majority of whom traditionally followed animist beliefs. The Sara tribes, some 10 ethnic groups with related languages and cultural links, comprise a large section of the population of the south. Since the end of the Second World War, the population of the south has inclined towards a more Westernized culture; the rate of literacy has increased rapidly, and Christianity has attracted a growing number of adherents. The population of the north, however, forms a traditional, Islamic society, and is largely unaffected by modern education. The state is secular and exercises neutrality in relation to religious affiliations. Some 52% of the population are Muslims (mainly living in the north), about 44% are Christians, and most of the remainder follow animist beliefs. French and Arabic are the official languages. Karembou, Ouadi, Teda, Daza and Djonkor are the principal vernaculars.

History

MOUDWE DAGA

INTRODUCTION

A former French colony, Chad became independent on 11 August 1960 under President François (later Ngarta) Tombalbaye. Shortly after assuming the presidency, he introduced a policy restricting public liberties and campaigned for a cultural transformation that would provoke strong political hostilities against his regime, ultimately leading to his demise. More than 60 years after independence, yet another head of state, Idriss Deby Itno, was killed on the battlefield fighting against a rebellion seeking to topple him from power. The history of Chad is one of political violence interrupted by failed attempts to build democratic institutions. The structure of this essay will reflect on this ongoing cycle of political violence fed by political exclusion and failed democratic processes.

CHAD UNDER TOMBALBAYE

A teacher by profession, Tombalbaye made his first political appearance under the Parti Progressiste Tchadien (PPT), which was founded by Gabriel Lisette in 1946, and represented Chad in the French Assemblée Nationale (National Assembly). The PPT was affiliated with the Rassemblement Democratique Africain (RDA), the federation of African political parties created in Bamako, Mali, in 1946 under the leadership of Dr Félix Houphouët-Boigny (the first President of Côte d'Ivoire) and which claimed an anti-colonial ideology. It was under the colours of the PPT/RDA that Lisette became Prime Minister on 1 January 1959, after Chad was declared an autonomous republic on 28 November 1958.

Tombalbaye succeeded in ousting Lisette from the leadership of the PTT, and became President of the Council of Ministers in March 1959. Shortly after full independence was achieved, Tombalbaye sought to consolidate his authority within the party. In August 1960 he removed Lisette from his position as Deputy Prime Minister while the latter was overseas, and Lisette was subsequently banned from returning to Chad. Following the PPT/RDA victory in the general election, Tombalbaye signed the ordinance of 19 January 1962 dissolving and banning all political parties, with the exception of the PPT/RDA. Chad thus entered into a one-party system in which dissenting voices had no choice but to submit or resist through violence. In September 1963 a demonstration at the residence of Djibrine Kerallah, an opposition leader, was brutally suppressed, causing the deaths of at least 30 people and leading to the arrest of all political opponents.

Beyond the brutal repression against opposition leaders, Tombalbaye also implemented a stringent cultural policy in order to consolidate his power. As he sought to destroy the legacy of Lisette, who had the support of the majority of liberals, and Ahmed Koulamallah, the first politician to introduce ethnic based politics, Tombalbaye soon realized that his consolidation of power could only be achieved with the support of his ethnic base, the Sara, who were also the most represented ethnic group in the colonial administration and army.

The Mangalme Revolt and the Creation of FROLINAT

In October 1965 a violent peasant revolt shook the town of Mangalme, in the region of Guéra. The origin of the revolt was popular dissatisfaction with the national borrowing programme and the increasing rates of tax. The peasants felt that they were victims of an extortion campaign led by local officials. During the unrest, local representatives of the administration were killed, and, in reprisal, the national army razed several villages. The revolt took place in a particular political context where the mainly Muslim populations of the northern regions accused the civil servants, the majority of whom were from the south and mostly Christians and animists, of practising on them a policy of humiliation and extortion. In 1966, citing his humiliations at the hands of government officials, Kinimi Weddey, the traditional leader of the Tubu (and father of Goukouni Weddey), a northern Muslim population, fled to Libya.

In June 1966 delegates at a congress in Nyala, Sudan, used the pretext of the humiliations suffered by the Muslim communities at the hands of Christian and animist civil servants to found the Front de Libération Nationale du Tchad (FROLINAT). Under the leadership of Ibrahim Abatcha, the movement waged an armed resistance against the regime of President Tombalbaye, which FROLINAT accused of persecuting the northern Muslim populations.

The Claustre Affair

In April 1974 archaeologist Françoise Claustre and aid worker Marc Combe, both French nationals, and Christophe Staewen, a German doctor, were abducted in Bardai by FROLINAT fighters. Following negotiations, Staewen was quickly released, but the French hostages were kept in captivity. In April 1975, one year after the hostage-taking, Commdr Pierre Galopin was sent as a mediator to secure the release of the two Frenchmen. However, he was in turn arrested and executed. Combe succeeded in defying the vigilance of his guards and escaped captivity, while Claustre was not released until February 1977, after 33 months of detention. The ransom obtained from this liberation, especially in the form of military aid paid on behalf of France from Libya, which was at that time attempting a rapprochement with France, changed the course of the conflict. With their new armaments, the rebels occupied the military garrisons of Bardai and Zouar, while increasing the pressure on government forces and stoking tensions in the already conflictual relationship between Tombalbaye and the army. On 13 April 1975 Tombalbaye was assassinated by officers of the regular army. Officially, they were stated to have revolted against the President's iron-handed policy towards southern civilian and military cadres, including the arrest, in 1973, and arbitrary detention of Gen. Félix Malloum, who had served as army Chief of Staff since independence. Malloum succeeded Tombalbaye as President of Chad.

THE CIVIL WAR AND THE NATIONAL UNITY GOVERNMENT

Despite the military taking charge of the country, it was unable to restore peace and security in the face of the persistence of the FROLINAT fighters led by Goukouni Weddey and Hissène Habré. Thus Malloum's regime attempted to negotiate with a faction of the rebellion led by Habré. On 17 September 1977 the two sides signed an accord in Khartoum, Sudan, which provided for a power-sharing settlement that would result in Malloum retaining the post of President of the Republic and Habré becoming Prime Minister. The Khartoum Agreement

allowed Habré to return to the Chadian capital, N'Djamena, in April 1978.

Upon his return, Habré was accompanied by about 500 fighters of the Forces Armées du Nord (FAN) and several rebel factions, who found their path to the capital without being integrated into the regular army.

On 29 August 1978 Habré was installed as Prime Minister of a unity Government. However, the power-sharing arrangement was to be short-lived. In February 1979 the FAN fighters called for a general strike to protest against what they perceived as the Government's ill-will in implementing the Khartoum Agreement. In February 1979 students supportive of the strike broke up a protest at the Félix Eboué High School. The police intervened and, in the confusion, attacked Habré's residence, which was located in the vicinity. The ensuing clashes between the regular army and the FAN led to the first battle of N'Djamena, plunging Chad into a civil war. It was in this context that Chadian stakeholders were invited to the Conference of Kano, Nigeria, in early March 1979. The Conference culminated in an agreement that provided for the formation of a Gouvernement d'Union Nationale de Transition (GUNT), the demilitarization of N'Djamena and the withdrawal of fighters from all factions. The GUNT thus replaced the alliance between Malloum and Habré, and was to be led by Weddey as President. A second Kano Conference and a further meeting in Lagos, Nigeria, failed to silence the rivalries between the warlords that paralysed the first and second GUNT. The second battle of N'Djamena broke out on 20 March 1980 and did not end until 15 December, when Habré and the FAN fighters were expelled from the capital following the intervention of Libyan forces.

THE DICTATORSHIP UNDER HABRÉ

On 7 June 1982 Habré led a coup which ousted the administration of President Weddey. After seizing power, Habré abolished the position of Prime Minister and conducted a policy of repression against his political opponents. The internal secret service, the Direction de la Documentation et de la Sécurité (DDS), was believed to have been responsible for the abduction, sequestration, torture and murder of more than 40,000 opponents. During his trial by the Extraordinary African Chambers (EAC) in Dakar, Senegal, in the mid 2010s, Habré was found guilty of these crimes and sentenced to life in prison (see *The Trial of Hissène Habré*).

The DDS and its Political Crimes

Habré's regime was swiftly confronted with pockets of resistance, especially in the south and centre of the country. Indeed, following the civil war of 1979, a significant part of the regular Chadian army had fallen under the leadership of Lt-Col (later Gen.) Wadal Abdelkader Kamougué. The Chadian armed forces retreated to the southern areas of the country, where they formed the Permanent Committee, an autonomous government that administered the south. From 1979 to 1982 the Chadian territories were in effect divided in two, and when Habré came to power in 1982, he had the difficult mission of reuniting the southern part of the country to its new regime. He attempted the *coup de force* against the Permanent Committee and managed to take Moundou, the largest southern city, in September 1982. With their commander, Kamougué, on the run, the remaining fighters of Chad's armed forces formed the movements of the Codos. The Codos rebels (a diminutive of commandos) were particularly active in southern Chad and their resistance against Habré provoked a brutal period of repression by the regime known as 'Black September'. During this month in 1984 hundreds of people (civil administrators, religious leaders, peasants, etc.) were killed on the basis of mere suspicion of their involvement in insurrectional activities against the Habré regime.

This brutal repression also happened in the centre of the country, where people suspected of collusion with a rebel organization, the Mouvement du Salut National du Tchad, in Guéra were assassinated. The policy of terror would be extended throughout Chad, facilitated by the logistical and institutional support of the DDS, which had been created by Habré in October 1982 and placed officially in charge of espionage and counterespionage. In fact, the service acted as the political police that took its orders directly from the President 'because of the confidential nature of its activities'.

However, on 1 December 1990 the dictatorial regime of President Habré was overthrown by a rebellion led by Idriss Deby, who was a close military aid to the President and the army Chief of Staff.

The Trial of Hissène Habré

Habré, who sought refuge in Senegal after he was ousted from power in December 1990, has been the subject of several attempts by human rights organizations to prosecute him on behalf of the victims of his policy of repression. In Senegal, a first procedure was launched against Habré in February 2000, accusing him of crimes against humanity, torture and barbarism. The procedure, which followed a complaint filed by a group of his victims within the Association for the Victims of Crimes and Political Repression in Chad, was rejected by the judge of the Dakar Court of Appeal, who ruled himself incompetent to judge on the case in July 2000. This decision was confirmed by the Court of Cassation in September 2001.

In September 2005 a Belgian judge issued an arrest warrant against Habré, seeking his extradition from Senegal. This followed an initial case brought to justice in November 2000 by a group of Habré's victims living in Belgium. The judge at the Dakar Appeal Court denied the Belgian request and Habré, who was arrested in November 2005 pending the request, was released from bail. At the same time, the victims of Habré who lost their case in Dakar referred the issue to the United Nations (UN) Committee against Torture, on the grounds that Senegal's refusal to prosecute Habré was a violation of the International Convention against Torture. In May 2006 the Committee agreed with the querants and concluded that the state of Senegal must implement the legislative measures necessary to prosecute the crimes alleged against Habré. Following these conclusions, the African Union (AU) encouraged Senegal to proceed with the legislative and institutional reforms required to facilitate Habré's prosecution.

After these measures were adopted by Senegal, Habré in turn referred the matter to the Court of the Economic Community of West African States (ECOWAS) in October 2008, challenging the application of the new legislative measures on the grounds that the crimes had taken place prior to the law being in place, in effect claiming the principle of non-retroactivity of the penal law. The ECOWAS Court ruled in his favour in November 2010 and, in order to remedy the violation of the principle of non-retroactivity, recommended that Senegal establish a special ad hoc jurisdiction with an international character. In 2012 the AU and Senegal signed an agreement to create the EAC within the Senegalese judicial system. A law to this effect was adopted by the Senegalese National Assembly in December 2012, and the Chambers were inaugurated on 8 February 2013. Habré was arrested and taken into custody on 30 June and charged with war crimes, crimes against humanity and torture. On 30 May 2016 the EAC sentenced him to life imprisonment for war crimes, crimes against humanity, torture and rape. In July 2016 the same Chambers ordered him to pay compensation worth 20m. francs CFA to each of his victims. This judgment was confirmed on 27 April 2017 following an appeal trial, and the EAC was dissolved on 30 June. Even if this judicial saga finally provides justice for the 40,000 victims of Habré's regime, the survivors of these atrocities are still waiting for the financial compensation they were promised at the end of the trial. After testing positive for COVID-19 Habré died in Dakar on 24 August 2021.

CHAD UNDER IDRISS DEBY

On 1 December 1990 Idriss Deby toppled Habré's regime after a successful rebellion swept from Darfur, Sudan, to N'Djamena. On his first address to the nation, Deby promised nothing but freedom and democracy. However, after more than 30 years in power, the promise faded away, and on 20 April 2021 Idriss Deby Itno (as he was renamed in 2006) was killed by yet another rebellion supported by people who felt disenchanted by his regime.

The National Sovereign Conference and its Democratic Achievements

The sessions of the National Sovereign Conference began on 15 January 1993 and lasted until 4 April. For three months participants from political parties, civil society and religious organizations debated issues concerning the structure of the state, the political regime and public liberties. At the end of the Conference, mechanisms for a new constitution were adopted and a transitional Government was put in place.

The Conference was in charge of designating the three personalities to lead the transition to Chad's first democratic elections since the establishment of single party rule under President Tombalbaye. Idriss Deby would remain President during the transition, while Dr Fidèle Abdelkérim Moungar was designated as Prime Minister and Lol Mahamat Choua as President of the Conseil Supérieur de la Transition (CST), a legislative body. However, repeated confrontations between Prime Minister Moungar and President Deby led to a motion of no confidence against his Government, which was adopted by the CST in October 1993. In early November the Government resigned and Moungar was replaced as Prime Minister by Nourredine Delwa Kassiré Koumakoye.

Perhaps the Conference's greatest resolution remains the adoption of the Transitional Charter, which paved the way for the introduction of a new constitution which would later be adopted by referendum and promulgated on 31 March 1996. The new Constitution re-established the post of Prime Minister, which was abolished during the Habré era. Individual and collective public liberties were also enshrined in the new Constitution, which additionally ushered in the return of multi-party rule, and thus allowed for the holding of free and transparent elections, which took place later in 1996 and in 1997.

The Transitional Elections and Hopes for a Multi-party System

On 2 and 23 June 1996 Chadians took part in the most democratic and competitive elections in the country's history. The plethora of registered presidential candidates, with 20 overall applications but only 15 authorized to compete, was testimony to the popular appeal of the event. During the campaign, candidates were prohibited from using state resources or religious slogans and from campaigning in places of worship. In a sign that the election was genuinely contested, a second round was required to decide the winner between the two candidates, Deby and Abdelkader Kamougué, who came first and second, respectively, according to the results of the first round. Deby was declared the winner of the second round and he thus began the first ever presidential term of the democratic era in Chad.

The competitive character of this first democratic presidential election was also confirmed in the legislative elections of January and February 1997. A total of 656 candidates, drawn from more than 30 political parties, contested the 125 seats in the National Assembly. President Deby's Mouvement Patriotique du Salut (MPS) won only 65 of the 125 seats, with the rest being won by various parties, including 29 seats by Kamougué's Union pour le Renouveau et la Démocratie.

The popular enthusiasm surrounding the elections, the number of registered candidates, the peaceful campaigns and the more or less balanced results between the ruling party and opposition groups gave hope for a nascent democratic process, in a state whose contemporary history has been marked by 30 years of conflict and armed violence. These presidential and legislative elections thus closed the transition and opened a new chapter designed to usher in the normalization and pacification of political life in Chad. However, the process of state decentralization announced in the 1996 Constitution was yet to be achieved, and the establishment of regional councils elected by universal suffrage was postponed *sine die*.

The Disenchanted Hopes for Democracy

Despite the holding of a National Sovereign Conference, which was intended as a forum in which Chadians could iron out their differences, a fresh rebellion was brewing in the northern parts of the country, in the Borkou-Ennedi-Tibesti region. This revolt was originally led by members of the Tubu ethnic group, who were protesting against the preponderant role of the Zaghawa, President Deby's ethnic group, in Chad's various administrative and economic levers. In October 1998 the Minister of the Interior, Youssouf Togoimi, fled the capital to join the insurgency. Himself a member of the Tubu ethnic group, he had been briefly arrested on suspicion of complicity with the rebellion. Togoimi organized the insurgents into a group called the Mouvement pour la Démocratie et la Justice au Tchad (MDJT).

For more than three years the MDJT undertook successful military offensives against government positions in the north of Chad, but after the mediation of the Libyan leader, Col Muammar al-Qaddafi, the Government reached a ceasefire agreement with the rebel movement in January 2002. In August of that year Togoimi was seriously injured after his car ran over a mine and exploded. Having been transferred to Libya for medical care, he died in Tripoli on 24 September. Togoimi's movement then faced a crisis of succession that would pit different factions against each other, including a wing led by Adoum Togoi. The latter signed a peace agreement with the Chadian Government in September 2003, which was contested by the military command of the movement led by Youssouf Barkai and Hassan Abdallah Mardigue. However, they eventually signed a separate peace agreement with the Government in August 2005.

It was in the evolution of this security context that the presidential election of 2001 was held, but with the hopes raised by the 1996 process dissipating. Seven candidates took part in the election, including four from the 1996 campaign (Deby, Kamougué, Saleh Kebzabo and Dr Jean Bawoyeu Alingué). The list was completed by Ngarlejy Yorongar, Koumakoye and Ibni Oumar Mahamat Saleh. The official results proclaimed Deby as the winner in the first round, with more than 63% of the votes cast, while Yorongar was placed second, with over 16%. The results were contested by the remaining six candidates.

On 28 May 2001, when the unsuccessful candidates met at the residence of Kebzabo, who came third, the police opened fire on demonstrators, killing a young opposition activist. On 30 May the leaders of the protest were arrested, along with some 30 trade unionists and civil society figures. Chad's political climate was thus darkening, in addition to a security context that was already deleterious.

The 2005 Constitutional Amendment and the Breakdown of Political Dialogue

On 6 June 2005 Chadian voters were asked to vote on a proposal to amend the Constitution, adopted by the National Assembly in May 2004. These amendments heralded important reforms, including the abolition of the Senate and its replacement by the Economic, Social and Cultural Council. However, the most contested reform concerned Article 61 of the 1996 Constitution, which limited to two the number of five-year terms that the President of the Republic could serve. Indeed, after securing a first mandate in 1996 and a second in 2001, President Deby was no longer constitutionally permitted to contest the 2006 presidential election. The opposition accused the President of clinging to power by all means, and thus appealed for a boycott of the electoral process, including the electoral census and referendum of June 2005, and also the 2006 presidential election, (at which Deby was decisively re-elected). The main parties of the democratic opposition also formed a broad political coalition, the Coordination des Partis Politiques pour la Défense de la Constitution (CPDC). The political dialogue between the main actors at the national level was quickly degrading, leading to a climate of mistrust between the democratic opposition and the ruling regime.

At the request of the Government of Chad, in April–August 2007 the European Union (EU) engaged in talks with the two sides, which finally led to a political agreement on 13 August. This made provision for two important changes in the transparency of future elections. The first point of agreement was regarding the control of the electoral registers. To this end, the Government committed to a new general population census, on the basis of which a digital electoral register would be established containing the biometric information of all voters. Second, the ruling party also committed to demilitarize the

territorial administration, including the positions of governors which were mostly held by military officials. Other major advances included the establishment of a 31-member joint election commission, the Commission Electorale Nationale Indépendante (CENI). All parties agreed that the President of the CENI should be drawn from civil society and the other 30 members split equally between the Government and opposition political parties. Subsequently, a joint committee to monitor the political agreement was also set up.

Despite these major agreements, Yorongar decided to boycott the signing of the accord as he believed that the votes of members of the military would be more susceptible to fraud in favour of the regime. Nevertheless, on 16 April 2008, two months after the rebel offensive on the Chadian capital (see *The Return of Violence and the Battles of N'Djamena in 2006 and 2008*), Youssouf Saleh Abbas was appointed Prime Minister. On 23 April 2008, in accordance with the terms of the 13 April 2007 agreement, the Government was reshuffled and four opposition figures from the CPDC were promoted to ministerial positions. Kamougué was appointed to head the Ministry of Defence, Alingué became the Attorney-General, Naimbaye Lossimian became the Minister of Agriculture, while Hamit Mahamat Dahalob was placed in charge of the Ministry of Land Development, Urbanism and Housing.

The Return of Violence and the Battles of N'Djamena in 2006 and 2008

President Deby's will to cling on to power at all costs pushed the country to reconnect with the old demons of political violence, a dark page in the history of Chad that the 1993 National Sovereign Conference had sought to turn definitively. Since the request by the MPS Congress of November 2003 for a constitutional amendment to allow the President to remain in power, armed movements had begun to emerge in the north and east of the country. In December 2005 Mahamat Nour Abdelkérim succeeded in establishing the Front Uni pour le Changement (FUC), a rebel coalition composed of elements of the Rassemblement pour la Démocratie et les Libertés (RDL), the Socle pour le Changement, l'Unité et la Démocratie (SCUD) and the Conseil National pour le Redressement. The RDL was a rebel movement operating from Darfur in Sudan. Formed in August 2005 and led by Mahamat Nour Abdelkérim, it was made up of deserters from the Chadian army and mainly those from the Tama ethnic group. The SCUD was also composed of deserters from the Chadian national army who took part in the failed coup of May 2004, a military mutiny which sought increased pay and better conditions but which was subdued by factions loyal to Deby. Under the leadership of Yaya Dillo Djerou, the movement had more than 600 armed men. After over-running several government military positions in the east and centre of the country, the FUC launched a military offensive on N'Djamena during 12–13 April 2006. This was met with fierce resistance from forces supporting the Government and the Chadian national army was declared victorious in the battle, while numerous rebels were captured or killed. On 24 December 2006 in Tripoli, Abdelkérim signed a peace agreement with the Government. He was appointed Minister of Defence in March 2007, and was joined in government by two other FUC members: Laona Gong Raul and Ismael Idriss Ismael.

However, the Government's triumph against the FUC did not seal Chad's return to peace. In early February 2008 N'Djamena was the subject of a second assault by a rebel coalition launched from the east of the country. On 2 February 2008 a column of more than 2,000 rebel elements entered N'Djamena and organized a siege of the capital. The assault was launched by a coalition of three rebel groups: the Union des Forces pour la Démocratie et le Développement (UFDD) of Mahamat Nouri, the Rassemblement des Forces pour le Changement of the twin brothers Tom and Timan Erdimi, and the UFDD-Fondamental led by Abdelwahid Aboud Makaye and Acheikh Ibn Oumar. Departing from Sudan at the end of January 2008, the heavily armed rebels had crossed the border between the two states inflicting military defeats on government positions throughout the eastern front before organizing the military siege of N'Djamena. After three days of battle, the rebels ran out of ammunition and the army regained control largely as a result of its air superiority and to the logistical and intelligence support of the French forces stationed in N'Djamena.

Thus, since coming to power in 1990 President Deby had on several occasions narrowly escaped dangerous challenges to his rule. This most recent attempt to remove him was all the more significant because it was orchestrated by individuals who for a long time had made a career under the Deby regime. Nouri, the leader of the UFDD, the coalition's largest rebel movement, and which had provided more than one-half of the combatants, had held numerous ministerial posts under President Deby, including Minister of Defence and Minister of the Interior. He had then served as Chad's ambassador to Saudi Arabia, a position he abandoned in protest against Deby's re-election in May 2006, and in October he founded the UFDD.

In late October 2007 the UFDD and a number of other rebel movements signed the Sirte (Libya) agreements, but the alliance was short-lived. In addition to their political proximity to Deby, the Erdimi twins were also the President's nephews and from the same ethnic group as him. Timan had held important positions including Chief of Staff to the President and Director-General of CotonTchad, the country's largest company. The Erdimi brothers broke ranks with the Government in 2005 and founded the SCUD in the same year.

The Disappearance of Mahamat Saleh

On 3 February 2008, during the Battle of N'Djamena, the opposition leader Mahamat Saleh was abducted from his home by unidentified armed men, although his party, the Parti pour les Libertés et le Développement, indicated that it had been carried out by elements of the presidential guard. Since then, he has remained missing. In March Yorongar, who was abducted on the same day, claimed that Mahamat Saleh had died in detention in a cell adjacent to his own.

In April 2008, under international pressure, including from the French Parlement, a national commission of inquiry was set up to bring light to the events of 28 January–8 February, including crimes committed by government forces and the rebellion. The commission's final report blamed the Chadian army for the disappearance of Mahamat Saleh, while indicating that the capture of the opposition leaders was the result of an operation co-ordinated by Chad's highest authorities. Despite the findings, the Chadian justice system has never formally identified or prosecuted those responsible for Mahamat Saleh's disappearance. During 2016–17 the Government attempted to reconcile with Mahamat Saleh's family by appointing his sons to lead two national companies: CotonTchad and the Banque de l'Habitat du Tchad. Their passage at the helm of these two institutions was only short-lived, but was sufficient to reduce international pressure on the Chadian authorities. Since then, the disappearance of Mahamat Saleh has remained a political mystery.

THE CENTRALITY OF SECURITY ISSUES IN CHADIAN INTERNATIONAL RELATIONS

Security issues remain the cornerstone of Chadian international relations. However, in 60 years there has been a remarkable shift from a country which was the theatre of international interventions by neighbouring states and France, to a country that is driving the international war on terrorism in the Sahel region. Chad has gone from a recipient of intervention to the status of troop provider in the major coalition against terrorism in Mali and the wider Sahel.

The Tumultuous Relationship with Neighbouring Sudan

During the two rebel offensives that led to the battles of N'Djamena in April 2006 and February 2008, the Government of Chad repeatedly accused Sudan of colluding with the rebels. After the attack by FUC rebels on the Adre garrison in December 2005, Chad officially declared itself in a state of belligerence with Sudan. This episode marked the lowest point in the deterioration of official relations between the two states.

However, to understand how the two states reached this level of such execrable relations, it is necessary to go back to the beginning of the Darfur conflict in 2003. When the war began in

February 2003, the Justice and Equality Movement (JEM) was allied with the Sudan Liberation Movement (SLM) as two armed groups that were fighting the forces of the Sudanese Government, which they accused of oppressing the non-Arab black communities of Darfur. The JEM was predominantly made up of Zaghawa fighters, an ethnic group whose communities live on horseback between the two states and to which President Deby belonged. Furthermore, the JEM was led by Khalil Ibrahim, a nephew of the Chadian President. Sudan accused the Chadian authorities of supporting the rebel movement and JEM fighters took part in the 2008 Battle of N'Djamena on the side of the government forces. The Chadian authorities accused the Sudanese of giving carte blanche to Chadian rebel movements that were using Sudanese territory as back bases to launch offensives against Chadian government positions. Thus, on 18 December 2005, when the rebel forces of SCUD and the RDL violently attacked the town of Adre, near the Sudanese border, damaging one helicopter and destroying another of the Chadian army, the Chadian Government saw the logistical and material support that Sudan was providing to rebel forces. Chad declared a state of belligerence with Sudan.

In April 2007 Chadian armed forces entered Sudanese territory in pursuit of a rebel column of more than 200 vehicles that had just carried out attacks on Chadian territory. Sudan declared the loss of more than 17 members of its defence forces during the pursuit and pledged to retaliate, while the Government of Chad claimed an international right to pursue its aggressors on Sudanese territory. However, in early May President Deby and his Sudanese counterpart, Omar Hassan Ahmad al-Bashir, both seeking to enhance the co-operation between their countries, reached an agreement in Riyadh, Saudi Arabia. According to the text both sides agreed 'to work with the African Union and the UN to end the conflict in Darfur and eastern Chad, in order to achieve stability and peace for all'. Yet this agreement had little effect, since in February 2008 the Government of Chad once again accused Sudan of supporting the rebels.

In March 2008, one month after the rebels' incursion into N'Djamena, Presidents Deby and al-Bashir signed a new agreement in Dakar, in which the two states pledged not to support rebel groups against each other. On 3 May 2009 the two men signed another agreement in Doha, Qatar, in which they pledged to abide by the terms of the previous agreements. Finally, on 15 January 2010 the two states signed the Agreement on the Normalization of Relations between Chad and Sudan in N'Djamena. This aimed to end hostilities between the two countries and to restore a climate of mutual trust. In particular, it created the Force Mixte Tchado-Soudanaise, a military detachment of 3,000 men supplied equally by the two states and stationed along the border with a right of pursuit for 100 km inside the territory of each state. To show good faith in the outcome of this agreement, in mid-May Chadian authorities arrested and expelled JEM leader Ibrahim. In a sign of reciprocity, in July the Sudanese authorities arrested the three leaders of the Chadian rebellion, Timan Erdimi, Mahamat Nouri and Adouma Hassaballah, who were also expelled from Sudan. The following day President al-Bashir made an official visit to N'Djamena, after a similar visit by President Deby to Khartoum in February. Relations between the two states were thus gradually normalized after several years of high tensions at the borders.

The Humanitarian Crisis in Darfur, Central African Refugees and International Forces

The diplomatic and security conflict between Chad and Sudan has also played out against a background of humanitarian crisis. Since the Darfur conflict in 2003, more than 240,000 Sudanese refugees have found refuge in camps run by the office of the UN High Commissioner for Refugees (UNHCR) in eastern Chad, mainly in the Ouaddaï, Wadi Fira and Ennedi regions. In an area where environmental degradation makes it difficult to access survival resources, the presence of these Sudanese refugees brings to nearly 1m. the number of people in need of humanitarian assistance, of whom at least one-third live in a state of severe food insecurity. This massive influx of refugees also leads to tensions with local populations, who find themselves competing for scarce resources while they are also excluded from the international aid. Repeated incursions by the *Janjaweed*, the Sudanese pro-Government militia, as well as the activities of the Chadian and Sudanese rebels in this region, have contributed to the deterioration of the security climate at the tri-border area of Chad, Sudan and the Central African Republic (CAR).

It was in this context that on 25 September 2007 the UN Security Council addressed the situation by adopting Resolution 1778, which established the UN Mission in the CAR and Chad (MINURCAT). The peacekeeping mission's mandate included the protection of civilians, the promotion of regional peace, the facilitation of the delivery of humanitarian aid and the movement of humanitarian personnel. Initially, it was anticipated that more than 5,200 military personnel and 300 police officers would be deployed to carry out the mission's mandate, but this goal was never to be achieved. In February 2010 the Government of Chad referred the matter to the Security Council, asking it not to renew the mandate of MINURCAT. Chadian President Deby denounced the operation as having failed in providing protection for refugees and displaced persons in the east of the country. The Government was committed to ensuring the safety of these people on its territory. It should be noted that this assurance from the Chadian Government came in a context of diplomatic rapprochement between Chad and Sudan. On 31 December 2010 the mandate of MINURCAT ended at Chad's request and in accordance with Security Council Resolution 1923.

Meanwhile, on 15 October 2007 the EU Council decided on a joint military operation in Chad (EUFOR Tchad/RCA). The force's objective was to ensure the safety of refugee camps and humanitarian personnel in the eastern areas of Chad. The operational force was not deployed until 2008. On 15 March 2009 the military component of MINURCAT succeeded EUFOR.

Since 2013, and mainly in the south of the country, Chad has received a new influx of refugees fleeing conflict in the CAR. The International Organization for Migration estimated that 113,000 people fleeing to Chad are Central African refugees and Chadian returnees. Although this new influx has less serious security consequences than those observed in the eastern regions, the risk of conflict with local communities, induced by a new competition for access to natural resources, has been pointed out by humanitarian organizations. By highlighting the humanitarian consequences of the Central African crisis in this section, it allows us to better understand the role played by the Chadian Government in the political instability affecting the CAR since 2003.

Terrorism and Military Interventions

Since January 2013 Chad has embarked on a series of costly military interventions against terrorism in the Sahel. On 16 January a message from President Deby was read to the National Assembly, informing people that Chadian armed forces were being sent to Mali as the Forces Armees Tchadiennes d'Intervention au Mali (FATIM). This decision, which followed an official request by the Malian transitional Government and at the insistence of France, came shortly after France had launched Operation Serval. (On 11 January the French Government had decided to deploy a military operation in Mali with the aim of stemming the advance of the Islamist fighters of al-Qa'ida in the Islamic Maghreb—AQIM—who were advancing towards Bamako.)

The context of the intervention in Mali can be traced back to January 2012 when northern Mali was confronted by two rebellions: one led by Ansar Dine, a Salafist armed group, and another by the Mouvement National pour la Libération de l'Azawad (MNLA), an independent group. The repeated offensives of these two rebellions, also known as the Fifth Tuareg rebellion, allowed them to take the towns of Aguel'hoc, Menaka and Tessalit. The repeated failures in the face of the rebels' advance caused dissatisfaction within the Malian army. These dissensions inside the Malian army culminated in the coup of 21–22 March 2012, which toppled President Amadou Toumani Touré. On 6 April the MNLA declared the independence of the Azawad region, after taking the cities of Kidal, Timbuktu and Gao. However, there were also major discordances between the

independentists and Salafists, the latter turning their guns against the MNLA and chasing them out from the cities of Gao and Timbuktu.

In January 2013, joined by AQIM and other terrorist movements, the jihadists of Ansar Dine launched an offensive on Segou and Mopti. It was at this point that the French Government decided to carry out Operation Serval, with the stated mission of preventing the progress of the terrorist movements. Just one week after the start of operations, 1,400 Chadian soldiers were present in Mali after entering through Niger, as Chad responded to a promise to deploy a contingent of 2,000 men. (The Chadian army is admired and valued for the effectiveness of its actions against terrorist groups in desert battlegrounds.) With the support of the French army, the FATIM managed to regain control of the Malian cities that had fallen into the hands of terrorist groups. In March 2013 Chadian soldiers in Mali joined the African-led International Support Mission in Mali (MISMA), the operational force of ECOWAS, authorized on 20 December 2012 by the UN Security Council. MISMA was later replaced by the UN Multidimensional Integrated Stabilization Mission in Mali (MINUSMA), a peacekeeping operation created in April 2013, of which the Chadian contingent was to represent one of the main military components.

On another front, in January 2015, more than 2,500 Chadian soldiers were deployed to Cameroon at the request of the Cameroonian Government in the fight against Boko Haram. Repeated attacks by the Nigerian Islamist sect on the Nigerian Government and its excursions into Cameroonian territory led to a massive influx of about 8,000 Nigerian refugees onto Chadian soil. In addition, the activities of this sect threatened the main access routes to the sea of Chad, an landlocked country, through the ports of Douala (Cameroon), Port Harcourt (Nigeria) and others in West Africa. This intervention first allowed the recapture of the Cameroonian town of Fotokol, which had been seized by the jihadists. In February the Chadian army was stationed in Nigerian territory from Cameroon, where it took over the town of Gambaru, which had been in the hands of Boko Haram for several weeks. The recapture of these two cities allowed the armies of Chad, Cameroon and Nigeria to regain control over a conflict that was in severe danger of spiralling out of control.

However, Chadian civilians would also have to pay the price for these military excursions of the national army outside the country. In June 2015 several concerted suicide bombings by Boko Haram elements were carried out in N'Djamena. The central police station and the National Police Academy were the targets of explosions detonated by Boko Haram suicide bombers, with the death toll reaching 38, while a further 101 people were wounded. On 11 July another suicide bombing hit the central market in N'Djamena, killing 15 people and injuring 80 others.

Outside the capital Boko Haram's attacks on Chadian soldiers and civilians were repeated mainly in the Lake Chad region in the central-western part of the country and at the border of the three neighbouring states of Niger, Nigeria and Cameroon. The deadliest of these attacks occurred on 23 March 2020, when 92 soldiers of the Chadian army were massacred by Boko Haram elements in an attack on Bohoma, a town in the islands of Lake Chad. Following this incident, President Deby moved to the province of Lake Chad, where he launched the military operation 'Bohoma's Anger' on 31 March and which he personally led for more than two weeks. At least 6,000 Chadian soldiers were deployed on the ground along the border with Niger and Nigeria, and operations were carried out far inside the territories of these two countries. On 4 April Deby declared that the area had been completely cleared of terrorists. At the end of the operations, the Chadian army declared the loss of 52 soldiers and claimed the deaths of more than 1,000 jihadists. In recognition of his actions, on 26 June Chadian parliamentarians adopted a resolution to elevate the President to the rank of Field Marshal (Marechal) during a session boycotted by Saleh Kebzabo and other members of the opposition. On 11 August Deby officially received the attributes of his new title at a ceremony that eclipsed the traditional celebration of Independence Day.

The French Military Presence in Chad

In August 1960, along with the CAR and the Republic of the Congo, Chad signed the four-party defence agreements with France that allowed for the mutual military assistance and the stationing of France's defence forces in those countries. Since then, France has continued to maintain a significant armed presence in Chad, at the request of successive Chadian regimes. The region of Borkou-Ennedi-Tibesti, in the far north of the country, remained under French military administration until 1965.

The presence of units of the French army in Chad began in 1965 with the transfer to Fort Lamy (as N'Djamena was then known) of the 6th Overseas Interarms Regiment, which was until then based in Bouar in the CAR. In March 1968 elements of the Garde Nationale et Nomade du Tchad organized a mutiny and seized the garrison of Aouzou, in the Tibesti region. The post was taken over by the national army. In July 1968 a convoy of the Armées Nationales Tchadiennes (ANT) attempted to recapture the garrison, but was attacked by rebels, who seized its armaments. In August two ANT companies that left to carry out the same mission were also attacked and suffered significant losses that forced them to withdraw. Later that month President Tombalbaye asked for French military assistance to help the ANT restore order and security in the Tibesti region, in the face of the threat posed by the FROLINAT rebellion. This first intervention by the French army in Chad lasted until November.

In March 1969 the French President, Gen. Charles de Gaulle, ordered the sending of French troops to Chad following a new request from President Tombalbaye. This was the very first military operation by the French army since the Algerian war of 1954–62. Operation Limousin began in April 1969, a direct intervention led by the command of French soldiers and which carried out combat actions in place of the Chadian national army. The operation ended in August 1972 with the departure of the Military Delegate in Chad and the cessation of the French army's direct involvement in the conflict.

However, France's withdrawal from the Chadian conflicts would be short-lived. From February 1978 until May 1980 a new operation of the French army was carried out: Operation Tacaud. This followed the capture of the town of Faya-Largeau in February 1978 by elements of the FROLINAT rebellion. It was important because it allowed the rebellion to open and control several axes towards N'Djamena. Operation Tacaud was later followed by Operation Manta (1983–84).

In June 1983 the rebel elements of the GUNT, supported by units of the Libyan army, invaded the regions of the far north of Chad, and succeeded in seizing Faya-Largeau at the end of that month. The air bombings by the Libyan army paved the way for GUNT elements to capture the towns of Koro Toro and Oum Chalouba. In July Abéché, the main city in the east of Chad, also fell to the rebels, giving them control over two main offensive routes to N'Djamena. With the help of Zaire's soldiers and the military assistance of the USA, the Chadian armed forces managed to regain control of Abéché later in July. In early August President Habré requested the humanitarian assistance of France, which responded days later with the deployment of a force that would reach almost 3,500 fighters, the largest external commitment of the French army since the Algerian war. The presence of the French army thus allowed the establishment of a 'red zone' corresponding to the 15th parallel and which prevented the advance of the rebels further south to N'Djamena. Following a meeting between French President François Mitterrand and Libyan leader al-Qaddafi in September 1984, the two sides agreed on a gradual withdrawal of their respective weapons, which began in that month and was scheduled to be finalized in November. After the effective withdrawal from France, however, Mitterand was informed that Qaddafi had concealed about 3,000 of his soldiers in the northern regions of Chad.

In February 1986 the Libyan army, which supported Goukouni Weddey's forces against Hissène Habré, bombed N'Djamena. The Chadian Government asked for assistance from France, which responded by deploying Operation Epervier. With military numbers growing rapidly (by 1,300) to reach 2,800 men, the presence of the French allowed the Chadian army to retake the towns of Borkou, Ennedi and Tibesti in March 1987. Despite the end of the Libyan threat, the Epervier force remained in Chad, where it intervened to provide logistical and intelligence support to the Chadian army, particularly against the incursions of rebel groups in 2008 and more recently in 2021. The force has also intervened to ensure the protection of French interests and the safety of French nationals residing in Chad.

In August 2014 Operation Epervier was merged with Operation Serval, France's military force in Mali since 2013, to create the Barkhane force, the joint command post of which remains in N'Djamena. With the help of the armies of Chad, Niger, Burkina Faso, Mali and Mauritania, the Barkhane force is a reconfiguration of French troops already present in the Sahel region in order to ensure France's military strategy against armed Salafist jihadist groups.

THE FAILED POLITICAL DIALOGUE AND THE DEMISE OF PRESIDENT DEBY

Could the cycle of political violence possibly break without an inclusive dialogue? In 2018 and 2019 President Deby missed the opportunity to organize such discussions which would have brought the major political stakeholders into the same room. Instead, he chose to rely on his political allies and to exclude both the civil and military oppositions. This radical position would trigger yet another cycle of political violence, ultimately leading to Deby's death. He was killed as he ruled the country: countering a violent attempt to remove him from power.

The First and Second National Inclusive Forum

In late March 2018 about 1,000 participants gathered in N'Djamena to discuss institutional reforms concerning the structure of the state and major institutions such as the legislature and the judiciary. The aim of this first National Inclusive Forum was to lay down the structures for peace and political stability through institutional reforms.

While the Government saw the Forum as an opportunity to bring Chadians together, the main opposition parties decided to boycott the process. Indeed, the opposition had been contesting the validity of the 2016 presidential election, which they considered to have been rigged to allow President Deby to win a fifth term in power. For the opposition, the Forum should have been a real opportunity for political dialogue but, instead, they perceived it as denying them any voice, as they believed that the agenda had been set in advance by the Deby regime.

Following the debate, the Forum instituted a new Constitution, which laid the ground for the Fourth Republic. The most significant change was the suppression of the post of Prime Minister, reinforcing the power of the President, whose term was increased from five to six years. Another major novelty was the introduction of a confessional oath for people serving in high public office. This point was controversial and contested, especially by the Chadian Bishops' Conference, because it breached the existing constitutional principle of laicity.

The Forum created additional political frustrations rather than solving the existing ones. This state of affairs led to a second National Forum, which took place between 29 October and 1 November 2020. However, this was also boycotted by the major opposition parties. Further amendments were made to the Constitution, most notably the creation of the office of the Vice-President. The new constitutional amendments also introduced a Senate and a Court of Auditors. Finally, the major controversy raised in 2018 was now solved, with the suppression of the confessional oath. However, held just six months prior to the 11 April 2021 presidential election, this national forum also failed to provide the foundations for peaceful and inclusive political participation in Chad.

A Last Chance for Democracy? Deby's Death and the Military Transition

On 20 April 2021 Chadians were stunned to learn of the death of President Deby, who was killed on the battlefield while leading a military offensive against the Front pour l'Alternance et la Concorde au Tchad (FACT) rebels. Through a declaration read on national television, a group of high-ranking officers, subsequently known as the Conseil Militaire de Transition (CMT), took control of the state, promising an 18-

month transition before returning power to a civilian authority. While news of the demise of the country's longest-serving President came unexpectedly, during the last months of his rule there were major confrontations between his regime and both the civilian and military opposition.

Civil unrest had erupted in N'Djamena in early February 2021 following appeals from opposition parties and civil society organizations aimed at preventing President Deby from seeking a sixth term in the April presidential election. The movement progressively gained momentum, with protesters facing police tear gas in the streets of the capital every weekend. On 28 February events took a dramatic turn when military tanks raided the home of Yaya Dillo, an outspoken opposition leader from the same ethnicity as Deby, killing his mother and sparking further public anger. Following this event, a number of leading opposition candidates—namely Saleh Kebzabo, who came second in the 2016 presidential election, Ngarlejy Yorongar and Theophile Bongoro—decided to withdraw from the presidential election, citing security concerns.

President Deby thus ran almost unchallenged against low-key candidates in the April 2021 election, and on the night of 19 April the CENI declared him the victor with more than 77% of the votes. However, Deby was already dead at the point in time when he was declared the winner and when his supporters were celebrating the prospect of many more years in power.

On the day of the presidential election Chadian rebels from the FACT movement, who were trained and stationed in Libya, crossed the border and launched offensives against military targets in the Tibesti region. During the following week the rebels eschewed any confrontation with governmental forces, choosing instead to rally along the border with Niger towards N'Djamena. With intelligence being gathered by the French army, the presence of the rebels was detected in the region of Kanem, leading to intense fighting on 18 April, led by President Deby himself. Seriously wounded during the battle, he would not survive yet another attempt to remove him from power by force.

On 20 April 2021 the CMT suspended the Constitution, dissolved the National Assembly and declared an 18-month transition period. During the funeral of the late President on 23 April, Emmanuel Macron, the French President, provoked controversy by pledging support to the junta. He was further accused of neo-colonialism by promising that France would not allow any person or group to attack the sovereignty and stability of Chad.

In the following days, the appointment of Gen. Mahamat Idriss Deby Itno, a son of the late President, as head of the CMT sparked further protest against what the public perceived as a dynastic succession within a republic. On 27 April more than a dozen protesters were killed across the country when a coalition of political parties and civil society organizations appealed to people to demonstrate against the military junta.

Meanwhile, on 26 April 2021 Albert Pahimi Padacké, an ally of the late President, was appointed as Prime Minister to lead a civilian transitional Government. While the major opposition leaders decided to join the newly formed civilian Government, another wing of the opposition supported by civil society organizations decided to continue the fight to remove the CMT from power. Chad appeared braced for an uncertain future as the politicians and their supporters remained divided over the next course of action and what steps to take against the junta. However, there was a general consensus that a further national dialogue should take place, which would decide on a new constitution and the democratic future of the nation. For the first time in more than three decades, Chad had a real opportunity to chart its path towards a democratic transition without the shadow of Idriss Deby Itno.

THE DOHA PEACE AGREEMENT AND THE NATIONAL DIALOGUE

The military junta's first attempt to end the long cycle of political violence in Chad came through the creation of two separate bodies endowed with the responsibility to conduct peace negotiations and to organize a national dialogue. On 13 August 2021 the CMT signed a decree setting up a structure in charge of planning and preparing a national dialogue (the Comité d'Organisation de Dialogue Nationale Inclusive—CODNI). Saleh Kebzabo was among the major personalities appointed to oversee the planning of the dialogue. At the same time, the junta appointed former President Goukouni Weddeye to supervise peace negotiations with past and active rebel organizations. However, Weddeye subsequently resigned and was replaced by Cherif Mahamat Zene, the foreign minister, and the latter represented the Government during the four months of peace negotiations in Qatar.

On 8 August 2022 the Chadian Government and more than 30 past and active rebel organizations signed the Doha peace agreement in the Qatari capital. The accord made provision for a general ceasefire between all the belligerents, along with guarantees for the disarmament and reinsertion of active combatants. More importantly, the signatory rebels agreed to return to Chad and participate in the national dialogue, while the Government guaranteed their security once back in the country. Notably, Mahamat Nouri and Tom and Timan Erdimi returned to Chad. (All of them had been living in exile since their military attack on N'Djamena in February 2008.) However, among the more than 18 rebel groups that withdrew or refused to take part in the peace negotiations was FACT, the rebel group that had launched the offensive that ultimately led to the death of Idriss Deby in April 2021. The FACT rebels expressed their dissatisfaction with the continued imprisonment of their combatants since the offensive, and also wanted the peace agreement to include a provision barring members of the junta and the transitional Government from contesting the next elections, a claim that the Chadian Government refused to discuss or endorse.

On 17 August 2022 Mahamat Idriss Deby Itno signed a decree granting sovereignty to the forthcoming national dialogue. The terms of the decree implied that the resolutions decided during the conference would be fully enforced by the Government. On 20 August the national dialogue effectively commenced in N'Djamena with the participation of the major political parties, civil society organizations and the rebel groups that had signed the Doha Agreement. The inaugural speech of Moussa Faki Mahamat (a former Chadian Prime Minister and currently the AU Chairperson) made the headlines of local newspapers for several days, as journalists interpreted it as a warning against the junta trying to cling onto power. As soon as the debates started, many organizations, including the National Association of Lawyers, withdrew from the process. They claimed that the junta had predetermined the major resolutions before the national dialogue had even begun. They also contested the mandate of the CODNI to preside over the adoption of the rules of procedure and the designation of members of the presidium. Shortly afterwards the Roman Catholic Church and the Entente des Eglises et Missions Evangéliques au Tchad also followed suit, albeit the latter subsequently rejoined the conference. A group of Catholic elders had previously failed to facilitate negotiations between the Government and various coalitions of opposition political parties and civil society organizations, including Wakit Tamma and Les Transformateurs, which had been contesting the legitimacy of the junta since April 2021, and refused to join the national dialogue. On 2 September 2022 a meeting at the headquarters of Les Transformateurs was violently broken up by the police.

Despite these various setbacks, the conference proceeded under the leadership of Gali Ngotte Gata, a former ally of Idriss Deby Itno who had since become a significant opposition figure. The questions of whether members of the transitional Government would be eligible to participate in the future elections, and whether to adopt a federal state or maintain the unitary state, were the two most contentious issues under discussion. On the first point, an ad hoc committee proposed allowing anyone who served in the transitional Government, including the head of the CMT, to run for the future election while extending the transition for a further 24-month period. This recommendation contradicted the AU's appeal to the transitional authorities to respect the 18-month period for the completion of the transition and that no member of the transitional Government should run for the future elections. Many diplomatic missions in Chad, including those of the USA, Canada and the United Kingdom, expressed their disapproval of the recommendation from the ad hoc committee, which was, none the less, adopted by the dialogue's plenary. On the second point concerning the transition from a unitary to a federal state, the participants decided that the question should be put to a referendum.

The national dialogue was scheduled to conclude on 8 October 2022, at which point a new period of transition was supposed to commence, extending beyond the initial 18-month timeframe. However, two major uncertainties still loomed ahead. First, would the AU impose sanctions on the country because the transitional authorities could now stand in the future elections following the recommendations of the dialogue? In April 2021 the AU chose not to impose any sanctions on Chad, arguing that the military took power under exceptional circumstances. However, that body made its position explicit that the transitional period should not exceed 18 months and that the transitional authorities should not contest the post-transition elections. Second, could the provisions of the Doha Agreement successfully uphold peace and stability in Chad while many active rebel organizations remained outside the framework of the agreement?

Economy

PAUL MELLY

INTRODUCTION

Extending from the Tropic of Cancer in the Sahara desert deep into the tropical bush of central Africa, and bordering six countries, the contours of the modern Chadian state encompass a broad range of climatic zones and areas of social and economic activity, often closely connected to adjacent communities in neighbouring states. However, Chad's landlocked location has been a constraint on economic progress and diversification, imposing heavy transport costs on export and import trading sectors and capital project investment. Prospects have also been complicated by the recurrent and widespread insecurity of recent decades. The far east has close ethnic and economic ties with the Darfur region of Sudan, periodically disrupted by political differences with Governments in Khartoum, although relations are better now. Since 2011 the disintegration of Libya as a coherent sovereign state, unable to prevent Chadian insurgents using its territory as a safe haven, was a source of concern for the regime of the late President Idriss Deby Itno (in power from 1990 to 2021), hampering any hope of developing a coherent bilateral strategy for managing cross-Sahara trade and security. Meanwhile, the pattern of economic activity and connections with the other neighbouring states of the Lake Chad basin, and particularly the important trade axis between N'Djamena, the capital, and Maiduguri, in north-east Nigeria, remain vulnerable to disruptive attacks and harassment by the jihadist militants of Boko Haram and Islamic State West Africa Province (ISWAP), despite the partial success of military campaigns to curb their activities. Negotiations with insurgents in 2022 have begun to create some conditions for a more stable economic environment.

However, continuing uncertainties about the evolution of the current transition and the eventual political and governance landscape leave Chad trapped under a sometimes heavy-handed 'caretaker management' and hinder the state's capacity to draft a coherent longer term development strategy and vision for addressing deep-seated economic, social and environmental challenges and to reinvigorate its engagement with international development partners. This also impedes any prospect of resolving the grievances of populations in the Tibesti massif in the Sahara and in the tropical south, who for years have felt marginalized and discriminated against by the central Government.

However, the transitional Government is internationally recognized as legitimate and this has enabled the International Monetary Fund (IMF) to fully engage with Chad. In December 2021 the Fund approved a three-year Extended Credit Facility (ECF) programme for the country, worth US $570.75m. This provides a medium term strategic framework for government economic development policy; by the time that Chad's political transition is completed, the ECF programme will be well advanced and established—and the post-transition government, of whatever form, will therefore have a powerful incentive to continue with it.

N'Djamena is the sole major city in this vast country, which has a population of just 17.4m., scattered from oasis settlements in the Sahara to pastoral and farming communities in the Sahelian belt (with agriculture particularly productive around the shores of Lakes Chad and Fikri and the lower reaches of the Chari and Logone rivers) and the cotton farming communities of the south.

Although Chad is a petroleum producing country, it remains one of the world's least developed nations, with average per capita gross domestic product (GDP) of just US $696.4 in 2021, well below Mali and Burkina Faso, although still ahead of Niger, the Central African Republic (CAR) and the Democratic Republic of Congo. In purchasing power parity terms that reflect the real cost of living, GDP per capita is $1,590.6, but that is still weak compared with many sub-Saharan African countries.

Economic development and diversification is hamstrung by the small size and low purchasing power of the domestic market, by security impediments to trade with Nigeria, and by Chad's landlocked location, far from ports in Cameroon and Nigeria, which imposes heavy transport costs. The country attracts little interest from international investors. As a consequence of internal insecurity and conflict and tensions in neighbouring states, more than 400,000 Chadians were still internally displaced in March 2021, while the country was also hosting 105,000 refugees from the CAR and 16,000 from Nigeria. There is also a long history of refugee movements across the eastern frontier with Sudan, from where 374,000 refugees have arrived since 2003, including 20,000 since late 2019. The combined impact of violent instability, COVID-19 and floods left 5.1m. Chadians facing insecurity during the most severe phases of the 2021 lean season. Moreover, the 2022 rainy season brought devastating floods, affecting at least 340,000 people across 11 of the 23 provinces and damaging homes, farmland, livestock and infrastructure. In mid-August the United Nations (UN) Office for the Coordination of Humanitarian Affairs reported that Chad had received only US $171m. of the $510m. in needed humanitarian assistance.

Meanwhile, Chad is struggling to reconsolidate state finances badly affected by the fall in income resulting from the 2014 petroleum market collapse and subsequent fluctuations in world energy prices and demand. The health and economic impacts of the COVID-19 pandemic compounded these pressures. Moreover, the state has tried to sustain high levels of expenditure on the military, both for reasons of national security and as the foundation of the power of the late President Idriss Deby Itno, who was killed in April 2021, and the army-led transitional regime that succeeded him. These spending choices have left Chad seriously lagging behind neighbouring Niger in terms of food security and basic education, health and social development.

FUNDAMENTALS OF THE ECONOMY

Chad is in some respects a typical Sahelian economy, with the majority rural population living from pastoralism and agriculture, producing both food crops and cotton, while oasis agriculture and artisanal gold mining are key activities in the thinly populated desert north. However, Chad's territory extends relatively far south, well into the tropical savannah zone, where farmers can benefit from a longer rainy season. Meanwhile, Chad is a significant oil producer. The fertile surroundings of Lake Chad and the basins of the Logone and Chari rivers that feed into it are part of a potentially prosperous regional rural economy, servicing the urban markets of N'Djamena and Maiduguri (Nigeria). However, the activities of the Boko Haram and ISWAP jihadist groups, of Nigerian origin, are a serious disruption to the full realization of this potential and are a factor in social destabilization for communities around the shores of the Lake and on its islands.

The development of manufacturing in Chad has been hampered by high transport costs, the paucity of local sources of component supply and decades of authoritarian rule that has constrained transparent economic governance. Cotton ginning and the production of oil, which is sent by pipeline from the Doba field to an export terminal at Kribi on the Cameroonian coast, are the main industrial activities. The N'Djamena city economy is largely fuelled by public administration employment and expenditure, trade and service activity. However, the distribution of resources and opportunities through the patronage networks that have flowed from the Deby regime and its clan and military base also have been a significant factor and has alienated some communities; for example, southern farming communities feel that their longstanding local land rights have been eroded by major livestock owning interests supported by the regime in N'Djamena. The future of these networks of economic interest, and whether they are willing to countenance a broader sharing of power and economic opportunity, has remained a significant factor in the playing out of politics since Deby's sudden death in April 2021, during a transition presided over by the late ruler's son, Mahamat Deby.

Although oil money has enabled the Government to invest heavily in the development of central N'Djamena, erecting many new public buildings, Chad remains an overwhelmingly rural society, with most households reliant on agriculture, livestock husbandry, artisanal craft production and informal activities, including gold mining in Tibesti province.

Looking ahead at longer term development prospects, there could be marked regional differences in rates of economic growth or enhanced household wellbeing. The rural south should benefit from the recovery of the cotton sector, but more arid Sahelian regions in the centre are exposed to the potential impacts of climate change. Prospects for the far north will be influenced by the expansion of gold mining and progress, or the lack of it, and increased stability in Libya, with which the area has trade and migration ties. Hopes of development in the areas fringing Lake Chad will depend on the state's capacity to curb the activities of Boko Haram and ISWAP militants. Internally, social and economic progress both in Tibesti and in the far south will be influenced by the extent to which the central Government adopts a more conciliatory approach towards local grievances, such as the encroachments on southern agricultural areas by livestock interests hitherto protected by the circles of power in N'Djamena. Nationwide, the weakness of governance institutions and development strategy further limits the prospects for any rise in living standards for most people.

Chad belongs to the six-strong Communauté Economique des Etats de l'Afrique Centrale (CEMAC), along with Cameroon, Gabon, Equatorial Guinea, the CAR and the Republic of the Congo. The bloc has a common currency, the CFA franc, and central bank, the Banque des Etats de l'Afrique Centrale (BEAC), based in Yaoundé, Cameroon. Under an arrangement with roots in the colonial era, the value of the CFA franc is fixed against the euro, under a French treasury guarantee, which means that the BEAC aligns its monetary policy broadly with the conservative stance of the European Central Bank. The peg to the euro is underpinned by an agreement that Chad and other member countries will deposit one-half of their foreign exchange reserves in a special Operations Account at the French treasury, while France has had seats on the governing boards of the CEMAC core institutions. The bloc also operates a common system of bank regulation and arrangements for close policy co-ordination between member governments.

A sister eight-country West African CFA franc bloc, the Union Economique et Monétaire Ouest-Africaine (UEMOA),

has negotiated reforms with France that will abolish the foreign exchange deposit rule in France; CEMAC has been exploring the scope to follow suit. However, UEMOA's reforms are the first stage of a strategy preparing for eventual merger into an all-West African single currency that will be free floating or based on a multi-currency basket valuation. No such prospect of a wider-reaching central African common currency is available for the CEMAC countries; in their region general progress towards economic integration is much more limited. Moreover, with Chad and several other members heavily reliant on oil exports and severely indebted, CEMAC is more vulnerable than the much more diversified and resilient UEMOA bloc and therefore it has to take a more cautious approach to reform.

Like many francophone African states, Chad is a member of a harmonized framework of business law (the Organisation pour l'Harmonisation en Afrique du Droit des Affaires), which has a supranational disputes tribunal.

The country also belongs to the Communauté Economique des Etats de l'Afrique Centrale (CEEAC), which encompasses all of CEMAC, together with Rwanda, Burundi, the Democratic Republic of the Congo, São Tomé and Príncipe and Angola. The bloc co-ordinates action to help manage some of the region's security crises, notably in the CAR. However, although it is committed to the principle of forging a common regional market, progress towards economic integration has been limited and trade relationships and transport links between some members are patchy. Possibilities for progress are complicated by the fact that some members also belong to other regional groups that are much further advanced in implementing their own economic integration strategies, while for Chad the relationships with Nigeria and Sudan are probably more important than any links with CEEAC states outside CEMAC.

Together with Mauritania, Mali, Burkina Faso and Niger, Chad is a member of the G5 Sahel, formed in 2014 to address regional security. Donors are funding 40 development projects across the G5, largely in areas close to national frontiers, to tackle the economic marginalization that nudges some disenchanted young men into joining criminal or terrorist groups. Mali withdrew from the group in 2022, but the other member states remain keen to maintain it.

SOCIETY

The Human Development Index published by the UN Development Programme (UNDP) ranks Chad 190th out of 191 countries assessed in 2021, a reflection of the deep social and economic challenges that it faces. Many social indicators are moving in a positive direction, but progress is only gradual and starting out from a weak base.

Average life expectancy is steadily increasing, but is still only 57 years for women and 54 years for men, compared with 65 years and 62 years in neighbouring Niger, and is also below the averages for western and central Africa. This low rating reflects the poor state of health services, particularly for women: trained personnel are present to assist at only 24% of births (compared with 40% in Niger) and the rate of maternal mortality, at 1,140 deaths for every 100,000 live births, is the second highest in the world. Only in South Sudan do pregnant women face greater risks.

These grim indicators of maternal health are in part a consequence of premature marriage and pregnancies: 61% of Chadian girls are married before the age of 18, a figure that is declining and is admittedly well below Niger's 76%, but remains dauntingly high. Only 7% of women aged 15–49 use modern contraception, while 75% of those who want to do so cannot access it. When so many young teenagers give birth without the support of a trained midwife there is a high risk of suffering damaging conditions such as fistula, or worse. Early marriage also drives the high fertility rate although in decline, this still averages 5.4 children per woman.

However, infant health is improving: some 58% of children aged 12–23 months are now immunized against diphtheria, whooping cough and tetanus, although Chad still lags far behind Mali (77%) and Burkina Faso (91%). The proportions of children under five suffering from anaemia (66%) or stunting

(31%) are in decline, albeit still higher than in many other Sub-Saharan countries.

The predominance of teenage marriage also has an impact on education: some 34% of girls and 47% of boys complete primary school and the majority of those who do so then move on to secondary education.

ECONOMIC POLICY AND PERFORMANCE

With an economy founded on smallholder agriculture, pastoralism, commerce and oil, Chad has struggled to diversify its base of production and employment or develop a model of growth that is more socially inclusive and can benefit the population as a whole.

Rates of growth in Chad have stabilized since the strong performances of 2012–14 (which were driven by favourable conditions in the oil sector) and the subsequent brutal plunge that followed amid a tough world hydrocarbons market, that sent real GDP plunging by 5.6% in 2016. Gradual recovery followed, with real GDP increasing by 3.4% in 2019; within this headline total, output in the non-oil sectors upon which most Chadians depend grew by 2.0%, as a result of an accelerating recovery for cotton, public investment, and progress in the clearing of government arrears to local creditors. Consumer prices actually shrank slightly, easing the pressure on household budgets.

However, the advent of the COVID-19 pandemic in 2020, impacting both on domestic economic activity and world demand for Chad's oil exports, came as a fresh blow. The IMF was quick to respond, disbursing US $183.6m. in emergency financing from its Rapid Credit Facility in two tranches, but the slowdown derailed Chad's hopes of meeting the final performance targets set under its existing Extended Credit Facility (ECF) arrangement with the Fund, which therefore agreed to terminate the programme in July 2020, two months early. The IMF also indicated a readiness to provide debt relief on the repayments it was due to receive from Chad until April 2022.

Compared with the 2016 recession, the impact of COVID-19 was modest, with real GDP shrinking by 2.2% in 2020, as non-oil activity contracted by 1.7%, while oil output rose by 2.4%. Yet while a severe crisis was averted, inflation rebounded by 4.5% in 2020, putting further pressure on consumers, particularly those in urban areas who must buy their food and fuel. Initially, Chad appeared on course to return to growth in 2021, but in fact oil output fell by 3% and as a consequence oil sector GDP actually contracted for a second successive year, albeit by only 0.3%; non-oil sectors managed only the most anaemic growth, with non-oil GDP increasing by just 0.2%. In such a feeble environment, demand pressures were low and annual inflation was actually negative, with consumer prices contracting by 0.8%.

The IMF remained strongly supportive, agreeing a new three-year ECF programme in December 2021. This backing has been critical at a time when recovery is fragile. Concluding a mission to N'Djamena in March 2022, the IMF projected real GDP growth for the year at 2.3%, with inflation at 4.1%. The Fund warned that Chad's prospects remained exposed to the risks of any resurgence in COVID-19, security issues, obstacles to the rollover of domestic debt or possible delays in implementing reform, although it did note that progress had been made with some structural reforms. Questions about reform are clearly linked to the potential evolution of the political transition, although the IMF tactfully refrained from stating this; clearly, a post-transition Government with stronger political legitimacy would be in a better position to implement difficult measures that were unpopular or that challenged vested interests. The Fund and the Government, however, did discuss measures to raise more revenue, improve the management of public finances and enhance transparency.

Government revenues have fluctuated in recent years (mainly reflecting shifts in oil income). They declined to 576,000m. francs CFA in 2016, before recovering in 2016–20 to reach 915,800m. francs CFA in 2020. Within these totals, oil revenues sank to just 171,000m. francs CFA in 2016, but recovered to 401,100m. francs CFA by 2020 in local currency terms. The Government established a mechanism to smooth

the impact of fluctuations in the oil price by setting oil revenues aside until they reach the equivalent of 0.8% of non-oil GDP.

Chad's current expenditure was 595,000m. francs CFA in 2018, before rebounding to 639,800m. francs CFA in 2019 and 694,700m. francs CFA in 2020. Within that year's current spending total, public sector salaries accounted for 424,400m. francs CFA, while interest payments on domestic debt were 27,000m. francs CFA and interest payments on external debt were 25,000m. francs CFA. Capital expenditure fell to just 180,000m. francs CFA in 2016 as the oil slump curbed the state's spending power, but then recovered in every year thereafter, to reach a hefty 394,000m. francs CFA in 2020.

The Deby regime did recognize the need to further diversify the economy, producing a development plan for 2017–21 that prioritized the agriculture and livestock, fisheries and mining sectors and also aimed to broaden financial inclusion. In 2020 it reached agreement with the African Development Bank (AfDB) on measures to promote business, particularly small enterprises and women entrepreneurs.

External debt totalling US $3,000m. has been a major challenge for Chad but, supported by the IMF programme, the Government gradually managed to reduce public debt from 50.3% of GDP in 2017 to 44.3% in 2020. In January 2021 Chad became the first country to seek restructuring under the new Common Framework developed by the Paris Club of official creditors and the G20 group of major economies. In June 2021 it reached agreement with government creditors, but it proved more difficult to come to an arrangement with private creditors, such as the commodities trading giant Glencore, to whom it owed $1,000m.; however, negotiations were continuing in late 2022.

AGRICULTURE

While oil is the dominant export, traditional rural activities (farming and livestock husbandry, fisheries, hunting and forestry) remain the foundation of domestic economic life, accounting for an average 31.9% of GDP in 2016–20 and providing the main source of livelihood for at least 80% of the population. Agriculture is already feeling the effects of climate change, besides the permanent risk of drought that is always a factor of life in the Sahel. Yet there is considerable scope to boost productivity and total output volumes, through improved cultivation techniques and the judicious use of fertilizer and better seed varieties. Improved, if still simple, crop storage techniques and more added value processing, even using simple manually powered machinery, could also bolster rural incomes. However, compared with some other Sahelian countries, well placed to supply the populous cities of the West African coast, Chadian agriculture and pastoralism is disadvantaged by its distance from major markets.

Northern Chad, almost one-half of the country's sprawling territory, is desert, but includes the Tibesti massif and a number of oases—with fruit, vegetables and cereals grown on irrigated plots and a combined total 6,000–7,000 ha of date palm plantations. Starch is also produced. Nomadic camel herding is an important activity and many households have goats, sheep or chickens.

Gradually the Sahara transitions into the Sahel, where annual rainfall ranges from 100mm–700mm, increasing steadily towards the south and concentrated between late June and early September, the season for cultivation of the main annual cereal crop and when grazing vegetation regenerates. Sorghum, maize, wheat and millet are the principal cereal crops, but farmers also grow sesame, groundnuts and, in areas of higher rainfall, root crops such as sweet potatoes and cassava. Rice and vegetables are produced on low lying plots that can be irrigated. The Ouaddaï region in the east is noted for its onion and garlic crops, while fruit and vegetables are grown in the fringes of urban areas for local sale. Gum arabic, a resin collected from acacia trees for use as a stabilizer in the industrial production of food and soft drinks, and in the printing and textile industries, is a major cash crop.

The islands and shoreline fringes of Lake Chad—where seasonal fluctuations in water levels expose rich farming and grazing land at certain times of year—and the surrounds of the smaller Lake Fitri in central Chad are particularly fertile and productive. The annual grain harvest must sustain Sahelian households throughout the following 10–12 months, albeit supplemented with *contre-saison* crops (mainly vegetables) watered from local reservoirs and village wells or boreholes. Pressures on dwindling household food supplies are intense during the 'lean season' (*la soudure*), the final dry months and subsequent rainy period until the new crops are ready for harvest, in September–November. Serious drought or even total rainfall failure is a fact of Sahelian life. Since the severe droughts of the 1970s, countries across the region, from Chad to Mauritania, have developed early warning systems for monitoring weather, vegetation growth and farming and livestock data, collected at local level and then collated and analysed nationally, to identify areas threatened with food crisis, so that emergency stocks can be released or food aid mobilized from donors. The national monitoring systems use a harmonized set of data criteria overseen by the Ouagadougou-based Permanent Interstate Committee for Drought Control in the Sahel. Chad's national strategy is organized through the national food security and nutrition programme, co-ordinated by the Ministry of the Economy, Development Planning and International Co-operation. The Office National de Sécurité Alimentaire manages national reserve food stocks.

Moving southwards, the Sahel phases into the savannah—or *soudanien*—zone, covering about 10% of Chad's territory, where higher levels of precipitation provide more diverse agricultural options and sustain the farming of cotton, a key cash crop. Annual rainfall is highest in the far south-west, at more than 1,200mm, where tree cover is particularly extensive. Savannah crops include cereals, legumes (such as beans), groundnuts and tropical root crops such as yam, cassava and taro. Cotton is an important source of cash income for many households and, as an annual crop, it can be grown in rotation with cereals, which benefit from fertilizer residues left in the ground where cotton was planted the previous year. With the commercial viability of cotton under pressure from cheap Asian and subsidized US competition, some families have switched more of their land to food crops for sale to urban consumers. Fruit trees are also a growing source of income. Most households have some small livestock, while oxen are often kept for ploughing. There are also populations that live mainly from cattle herding, traditionally nomadic, but increasingly settled year round in fixed locations; occasionally, as so often across western and central Africa, there are disputes over land rights with local farming communities. However, in recent years social and economic tensions in the south—a region unsympathetic to the Deby regime and significantly neglected by central government—have been exacerbated by the expanding depredations of large livestock investors from outside the region; well-connected with elite circles in N'Djamena, these have benefited from the supportive protection of the military as they encroach on the land used by indigenous agricultural populations.

The Government has estimated that Chad has 39m. ha of cultivable land (30% of its land area), of which 5.6m. ha could be irrigated. Yet as recently as 2012 only 335,000 ha (two-thirds of which lay in the Sahel and one-third in the savannah) was actually under cultivation and so there is potential to further expand the area that is farmed. However, soils in much of the Sahel are sandy, with low levels of fertility, even where animals are allowed to graze on the stubble and enrich the ground with their droppings. Crop rotation is more feasible in the savannah, but this region's laterite and clay soils are easily eroded, increasing the importance of tree cover as a protective measure. The Government encourages crop rotation and agroforestry (the planting of trees and bushes alongside cultivated land); even so, yields for both cotton and food crops are low by sub-Saharan standards. Significant areas are suitable for irrigated cultivation or benefit from either seasonal flooding that renews fertility or from rainfall run-off: 90,000 ha around Lake Chad; 80,000 ha in the Chari-Logone river basin; 10,000 ha in *wadis* (dry valleys) in the Kanem and Lac regions; 15,000 ha around Lake Fitri; 20,000 ha in the Chari river valley; and 115,000 ha in the Logone valley.

The leading cereal crops are sorghum and millet, which can withstand fairly arid conditions: harvests have fluctuated from 1.61m. metric tons in 2017 to 1.74m. tons in 2018 before falling to 1.69m. tons in 2019 and just 1.66m. tons in 2020. Production of cassava was 290,600 tons in 2017, falling to 284,300 tons in 2018, before recovering to 297,000 tons in 2019 and then to 293,900m. tons in 2020. Groundnut output increased from 870,100 tons in 2017 to 893,900 tons in 2018 before sinking back to 873,200 tons in 2019 and 840,000 tons in 2020.

Chad also produces sugar cane. Output accelerated from just 280,300 metric tons in 2014 to 347,900 tons in 2020. Production of gum arabic, a crucial earner for communities in the Sahelian belt, has gradually expanded, from 45,500 tons in 2014 to 50,800 tons in 2020.

Until the commercial development of oil reserves, cotton was Chad's main export earner, and the crop is hugely important to the social and economic fabric of the south, providing a major source of cash income that supports perhaps 4m. people. It has struggled to cope with competition from low priced Asia and the USA, but at the farm level a range of factors influence how much land is planted to cotton and the resulting harvests—the cost of fertilizer, seed and other inputs, the timing and geographical distribution of rainfall, the official producer price paid to cotton farmers, and the speed with which they are paid. Set at 240 francs CFA per kg in 2014–16, the producer price was then held at just 220 francs CFA per kg over the following four years. Discouraged by the lower price and delays in payment, many farmers decided to grow other annual crops instead and the area planted with cotton fell from 118,533 ha in 2017 to just 60,092 ha in 2018, with output plunging to just 15,500 metric tons in 2019 before rebounding to 113,500 tons in 2020.

This sharp recovery appears to have been driven by the ambitious recovery drive launched by the Singapore-based trading and business group Olam, to whom the Government in 2018 sold a 60% interest in CotonTchad, the national company that supplyies farmers with tools, seeds and fertilizer and then buys the crop. Olam consolidated CotonTchad's finances, cleared payment arrears to growers and reinvigorated the technical support provided to them, distributing 10,000 ploughs in 2021; it raised the producer price to 227.5 francs CFA for the 2021/22 season. Farmers quickly responded to Olam's rapid injection of support, planting 288,540 ha with cotton for the 2019/20 season, and producing a recovery in output, with 150,000 metric tons projected for 2020/21 and 200,000 tons targeted for 2021/22.

In the long term, under Olam's ownership, CotonTchad aims to boost the planted area to some 400,000 ha and to sustain harvests at around 280,000 metric tons, higher even than the strong performances of the late 1990s. It is upgrading rural roads to improve farmers' access to supplies and markets, and connecting the main CotonTchad processing plant to the national gas supply grid. Furthermore, it is also encouraging complementary diversification, notably the commercialization of the cashew nuts already widely grown in the southern cotton belt, which until recently have been mostly consumed locally.

Livestock is also a sector of massive importance, a key source of livelihood and store of personal wealth for large populations in the Sahelian belt, extending from the areas just north of Lake Chad right across the centre of the country to the eastern border. The Zaghawa communities from whom the Deby regime drew much of its support have deep roots in the eastern pastoralist economy. There are also large pastoralist communities in southern Chad, but pressure on resources of land and grazing in this region have increased in recent years, with the growth of herds owned by large commercial livestock investors new to the area but connected to influential circles in Niger. The livestock herd has risen steadily, from 22.7m. in 2014 to 27.6m. head in 2020. For pastoralist communities animals are not only a source of income, but also a critical store of value and social status; however, the growth in the south of large herds owned by absentee investors is fuelling tensions with local farmers and eroding their land rights.

Chad is the world's second largest producer of gum arabic, which is tapped from the trunks of acacia trees. It is a major source of income for 300,000 families and the collection and processing of this resin may provide as many as 500,000 livelihoods. Gum arabic is mainly produced in central regions of the country, but, with global demand on the rise for this product that can be used in so many industrial processes, there is huge growth potential. Chad has the capacity to produce 230,000 metric tons per year of the highest grade hard gum (known locally as *kitir*) and 324,000 tons per year of the lower grade *seyal* gum. Yet commercialized output is currently a small fraction of these figures, although development organizations are trying to promote the sector.

Fishing on Lake Chad and other places such as Lake Fitri and in the Logone-Chari river system is an important economic activity and source of nutrition, even attracting migrant fishermen from outside Chad. Much of the fish is smoked for preservation while it is transported and sold. Historic data highlights the importance of this sector: the national catch was 70,000 metric tons in 2003, while in 2002 the sector's output was estimated at $112m. and it provided livelihoods for some 300,000 people. However, the resources of Lake Chad in particular are under strain, potentially vulnerable to climate change or overuse, and fishermen report catching fewer species than previously. Moreover, the lake is now heavily affected by the activities of Boko Haram and ISWAP jihadist militants, who often base themselves on its islands and raid shoreline communities. Fish remains a highly valuable commodity, particularly because it can be quickly dried and sold on for cash.

EXTRACTIVES AND ENERGY

Oil makes a crucial contribution to the Chadian economy and state finances. In 2017–20 the sector accounted for 10% of GDP, 41% of budgeted government revenues and 91.7% of the country's exports. International companies began to search for oil in the 1960s; however, the early discoveries were small or of poor quality and an effort to develop the Sédigui field, north of Lake Chad, and connect it by pipeline to a refinery in N'Djamena broke down. The industry's key breakthrough was the discovery and development of the Doba basin fields—Bolobo, Komé and Miandoum—in the south-west, with reserves of 900m. barrels. Crude oil destined for export is transported through the 1,070-km Chad–Cameroon pipeline to Kribi, on the Atlantic coast of Cameroon. The Djermaya refinery, opened in 2011, processes crude for the domestic market. The base of production has gradually broadened, although output is far below previous levels. In 2020 the Chad-Cameroon pipeline transported an average of 129,200 barrels per day (b/d) of crude; however, in 2021 Doba produced only an average of 33,000 b/d.

Doba was for many years operated by Esso Exploration and Production Chad Inc (EEPCI), a joint venture between Exxon-Mobil subsidiary Esso (40%), Petronas (35%) and Chevron (25%). However, in December 2021 the UK-based independent Savannah Energy signed a US $626m. deal to acquire all the upstream and midstream assets of ExxonMobil and Petronas in both Chad and Cameroon, including their 75% stake in the Doba field and a roughly 70% stake in the pipeline and export infrastructure. Savannah has set out ambitious plans for further drilling and believes that reserves will allow continuing production for about 25 more years. Meanwhile, in 2017 Chinese investors including Blue Ocean Clean Energy relaunch a project to develop the Sédigui field (which holds 15m.–21m. barrels of oil and 7,000m. cu m of natural gas) and operate a gas purification plant and oil refinery, to serve local demand. Further, in June 2019 the China National Petroleum Company began production from the Daniela field, near Bousso, in the south, producing 15,000 b/d. The Chadian Government has been cautious about revealing comprehensive data, but official sources confirmed in mid-2021 that seven fields—Komé, Miandoum, Bolobo, Moundouli, Maikeri, Nya and Timbré—are producing oil solely for export, while the Rônier and Mimosa fields, in the Bongo basin, supply the domestic market.

Oil's contribution to state revenues is inevitably heavily shaped by world market demand and prices and has fluctuated between just 18% and a dominant 70% of fiscal revenues. In 2015 Chadian crude fetched an average of US $43 per barrel, but the following year prices slipped to an average of $37, before recovering to reach $65 in 2018; prices then slipped to an average $58 per barrel in 2019 and to just $40 in 2020. The COVID-19 pandemic in 2020 initially triggered a fall in world

oil markets, but they gradually recovered and government oil revenue was equal to 5.1% of GDP in 2020 (compared with 5.3% of GDP in 2019). Nevertheless, the state's oil income has consistently been outpaced revenues from non-oil sources. Oil revenue surged to 335,000m. francs CFA in 2018, then fell back slightly to 326,000m. francs CFA in 2019, before rebounding to 401,100m. francs CFA in 2020. Non-oil revenues were 402,500m. francs CFA in 2018 before recovering to 480,000m. francs CFA in 2019 and to 514,700m. francs CFA in 2020. At various times the Government has borrowed heavily against future oil shipments, a high risk practice that has been a major contributor to the debt trap in which Chad has been caught in recent years.

Although Chad is thought to have deposits of silver, platinum, copper, lead, zinc, chrome, nickel, iron ore, titanium, manganese, tungsten, bauxite, marble and diamonds, there has been little serious prospecting and the commercial viability of industrial-scale development is mostly untested. The country does produce natron (sodium carbonate). Gold is also now produced on a substantial scale, but largely at artisanal sites around the Tibesti massif in the Sahara that are effectively beyond official oversight; data is necessarily piecemeal, but exports are thought to have been worth US $137m. in 2018, mostly shipped to Dubai. Government attempts to exert more control over the northern gold mining sites have been a cause of friction with local Tibesti communities.

The country has just 125 MW of installed electricity generating capacity, all of it diesel-fuelled—a costly and polluting option. Overall, just 11.1% of Chadians have access to electricity, but beneath this headline figure there are huge disparities between urban areas, where about one-third of the population have access to power, and rural areas, where few households are connected to the network, although some do receive electricity from solar panels at household or community level. Donors are supporting an initiative to help Chad make far greater use of its huge potential for generating solar power. Local projects will often be the most cost-effective means of serving scattered rural communities; however, commercial investors have signed an agreement with the national power utility Société Nationale d'Electricité to build a 60-MW solar power plant at Djermaya, 30 km south of N'Djamena, which will be connected to the national transmission grid. In mid-2022 Savannah Energy signed a deal with the Government to develop 500 MW in renewable generating capacity: a 300 MW solar plant and battery storage facility at Komé, to supply both the Doba oilfield and N'Djamena and the towns of Moundou and Doba, as well as a 100 MW wind farm and a 100 MW solar plant to provide extra power supply to the capital.

MANUFACTURING AND SERVICES

Besides Chad's nine cotton ginning plants, there is little industry. Operations to produce soap from cotton oil were privatized in 2003 and there are a few small import substitution operations.

By contrast, the country has a diverse range of service sector and trading activity, including much informal business. There are eight commercial banks and around 200 micro-credit institutions; the fluctuating performance of the economy and fragile state of public finances have impacted on the banks and in 2020 some 13.1% of the banking sector's loan book was categorized as non-performing.

TRANSPORT AND COMMUNICATIONS

The key transport corridors serving Chad's landlocked economy are the main roads to Maiduguri in north-east Nigeria and southwards to the main cities and ports of Cameroon. Both start from Kousseri, the Cameroonian town that faces N'Djamena across the Logone river, which is traversed by two bridges. Although trade in the Lake Chad basin is impacted by the activities of ISWAP and Boko Haram, the city of Maiduguri remains a major regional economic hub and it is also the north-eastern terminus of the Nigerian railway network. Northern Cameroon is also affected by insecurity, but the roads through this region do connect to the railhead at Ngaoundéré, from where trains continue south to Yaoundé and to the port city of Douala; substantial volumes of cargo also travel through Cameroon by road. In February 2020 work started on construction of a 620 m bridge over the Logone river between Bongor in Chad and the road to Yagoua in Cameroon, financed by the AfDB and the European Union (EU) at a cost of US $178.5m; once open, potentially in 2023, this will open up a second major corridor into Cameroon that avoids the most insecure areas further north. Cross-border routes also link Chad to Libya, Niger, the CAR and Sudan's Darfur region, an area where there are dense local social and economic connections.

There are no railways in Chad. As recently as 2006 only 840 km of the 40,000 km road network was tarmac and during the rainy season many routes were usable only with difficulty, seriously impeding the movement of people and goods between the countryside and urban markets. However, over the past 15 years the Islamic Development Bank and other donors have funded a programme of improvements and Chad now has at least 3,200 km of all-weather tarmac highways. Key priorities were roads serving agricultural areas and two corridors for export/import trade: the route around the north of Lake Chad to Niger to open up an extra all-weather connection to West African markets and ports; and the main west–east highway from N'Djamena to Abéché and on to the border with Sudan and the corridor to the Red Sea coast.

Air transport could play a valuable role in a country where the main towns are so widely scattered. However, Air Tchad and its successor, Toumaï Air Tchad, both failed. Therefore, in 2018 the Government launched Tchadia Airlines, a joint venture with Ethiopian Airlines, one of Africa's largest and most resilient operators. The new carrier launched domestic routes from N'Djamena to Moundou, Sarh, Abéché and Faya Largeau, and international routes to Bangui (CAR), Douala (Cameroon), Kano (Nigeria), Khartoum (Sudan) and Niamey (Niger). N'Djamena airport is served by various African carriers and by Air France, Egyptair and Turkish Airlines. In January 2020 Chad became the first country to operate an upgraded airspace control system introduced by the Agence pour la Sécurité de la Navigation Aérienne en Afrique et à Madagascar, the organization that oversees technical air traffic issues in francophone African airspace.

National telecommunications company SOTELTCHAD provides fixed-line phone and internet connections and there are two mobile telephone operators, Moov Africa (formerly Tigo) and Airtel; however, levels of mobile use are well below the norm for sub-Saharan Africa, at only 53 mobile cellular subscriptions for every 100 people. A 2020 agreement with the People's Republic of China provided for the Huawei group to build a 1,200-km fibre-optic link from Doba in the south-west to Iriba in the north-east, a 50-km fibre-optic loop around N'Djamena and 200 hub sites with 2G, 3G or 4G capacity.

FOREIGN TRADE, AID AND PAYMENTS

Fluctuations in the current account balance of payments are caused by shifts in the value of both export and import flows and in the balance of the services account, almost all elements of which have seen sharp year to year variations. In 2017 there was a current account surplus of 667,500m. francs CFA (equivalent to 10.3% of GDP), but a deficit of 422,200m. francs CFA (7.4% of GDP) was recorded in 2018; the deficit then deepened, to 574,800m. francs CFA (9.7% of GDP) in 2019 and further, to 815,100m. francs CFA (13.7% of GDP), in 2020.

The balance of trade in goods recorded a surplus of 921,900m. francs CFA in 2017. However, the surplus fell to 274,700m. francs CFA in 2018, recovering to 291,300m. francs CFA in 2019. In 2020 the goods trade balance slipped back into a deficit of 170,900m. francs CFA.

The services balance is structurally in deficit, but to a fluctuating extent: a deficit of 367,800m. francs CFA in 2017 widened to 757,000m. francs CFA in 2018 before shrinking to 727,500m. francs CFA in 2019 and to 684,800m. francs CFA in 2020. Remittances from the Chadian diaspora reached 18,100m. francs CFA in 2017, but slumped to just 2,500m. francs CFA the following year and then 2,400m. francs CFA in both 2019 and 2020.

Chad's exports totalled 1,494,900m. francs CFA in 2017, 1,483,200m. francs CFA in 2018 and 1,605,500m. francs CFA in 2019, but slumped to just 1,097,000m. francs CFA in 2020 as the COVID-19 pandemic impacted on global oil demand and prices. Despite fluctuations in the value of shipments, oil has continued to dominate the picture, with exports valued at 1,050,200m. francs CFA in 2017, 1,505,200m. francs CFA in 2018 and 1,605,300m. francs CFA in 2019; however, then came a sharp decline, to 1,047,200m. francs CFA, in 2020. Livestock and gum arabic have overtaken cotton as exports, at least temporarily until the recovery strategy for the cotton sector begins to bear fruit. Exports of livestock rose from just 85,200m. francs CFA in 2016 to 136,400m. francs CFA in 2020, while sales of gum arabic had edged up from 85,200m. francs CFA in 2016 to 87,700m. francs CFA in 2020. Cotton exports rose to 83,700m. francs CFA in 2017, slumped to 31,500m. francs CFA in 2018 and to a mere 8,500m. francs CFA in 2019, but recovered, to 56,500m. francs CFA, in 2020.

As the oil price collapse dramatically curbed Chad's spending power, total imports declined 807,800m. francs CFA in 2017, then rebounded to 1,762,600m. francs CFA in 2018, before settling back at 1,578,40m. francs CFA the following year and to 1,522,700m. francs CFA in 2020.

Debt interest payments to external creditors reached 59,000m. francs CFA in 2017, but sank to 38,000m. francs CFA in 2018; they rose back to 43,000m. francs CFA in 2019, but then fell to just 25,000m. francs CFA in 2020.

The importance of oil is reflected in the geographical spread of Chadian exports. In 2015–19 on average some 41% of exports were shipped to the USA, with other notable markets being in Asia and the Far East.

Although relations with the international financial organizations were strained by the late President Deby's abandonment of commitments made to the World Bank on the oversight of oil financed public expenditure, Chad has since rebuilt a close policy partnership with the IMF and with the Bank, which funds initiatives in a range of sectors. The AfDB is also a key partner.

The EU is also a key source of support, both through long-term development funding under multi-year agreements and emergency humanitarian assistance. The UNDP and other UN agencies and some Islamic and Arab donors are also active. The Agence Française de Développement funds urban development, health care and rural programmes, including irrigation.

Statistical Survey

Source (unless otherwise stated): Institut National de la Statistique, des Etudes Economiques et Démographiques, BP 453, N'Djamena; tel. 22-52-31-54; e-mail info@inseed.td; internet www.inseed.td.

Area and Population

AREA, POPULATION AND DENSITY

Area (sq km)	
Land	1,259,200
Inland waters	24,800
Total	1,284,000*
Population (census results)	
8 April 1993	6,279,931
20 May–30 June 2009	
Males	5,452,483
Females	5,587,390
Total	11,039,873
Population (UN estimates at mid-year)†	
2020	16,425,859
2021‡	16,914,985
2022‡	17,413,574
Density (per sq km) at mid-2022‡	13.6

* 495,800 sq miles.
† Source: UN, *World Population Prospects: The 2019 Revision.*
‡ Projection.

POPULATION BY AGE AND SEX
('000, UN projections at mid-2022)

	Males	Females	Total
0–14 years	4,018.8	3,980.0	7,998.8
15–64 years	4,476.3	4,499.4	8,975.7
65 years and over	199.1	240.0	439.1
Total	8,694.1	8,719.4	17,413.6

Note: Totals may not be equal to the sum of components, owing to rounding.

Source: UN, *World Population Prospects: The 2019 Revision.*

REGIONS
(population at 2009 census)

Barh El Gazel . .	257,267	Mayo-Kebbi Est .	774,782
Batha	488,458	Mayo-Kebbi Ouest .	564,470
Borkou	93,584	Moyen-Chari . .	588,008
Chari-Baguirmi .	578,425	N'Djamena . . .	951,418
Ennedi	167,919	Ouaddaï	721,166
Guéra	538,359	Salamat	302,301
Hadjer-Lamis .	566,858	Sila	387,461
Kanem	333,387	Tandjilé	661,906
Lac	433,790	Tibesti	25,483
Logone Occidental .	689,044	Wadi Fira . . .	508,383
Logone Oriental .	779,339	**Total**	11,039,873
Mandoul . . .	628,065		

PRINCIPAL TOWNS
(population at 2009 census)

N'Djamena (capital)	951,418	Sarh	97,224
Moundou . . .	137,251	Kélo	57,859
Abéché	97,963	Am-Timan . . .	52,270

Mid-2021 (incl. suburbs, UN projection): N'Djamena 1,476,115 (Source: UN, *World Urbanization Prospects: The 2018 Revision*).

BIRTHS AND DEATHS
(annual averages, UN estimates)

	2005–10	2010–15	2010–20
Birth rate (per 1,000)	48.0	45.1	42.4
Death rate (per 1,000)	15.7	13.5	12.2

2001 (preliminary): Live births 397,896; Deaths 138,025.

Sources: UN, *World Population Prospects: The 2019 Revision* and *Population and Vital Statistics Report.*

2014: Birth rate 48.9 per 1,000; Death rate 14.3 per 1,000.

Life expectancy (years at birth, estimates): 54.5 (males 53.1; females 55.9) in 2020 (Source: World Bank, World Development Indicators database).

ECONOMICALLY ACTIVE POPULATION
('000, FAO estimates at mid-year)

	2013	2014	2015
Agriculture, etc.	3,234	3,280	3,326
Total labour force (incl. others) .	5,204	5,381	5,565

Source: FAO.

Health and Welfare

KEY INDICATORS

Total fertility rate (children per woman, 2020)	5.6
Under-5 mortality rate (per 1,000 live births, 2020) . . .	110.0
HIV/AIDS (% of persons aged 15–49, 2020)	1.1
COVID-19: Cumulative confirmed deaths (per 100,000 persons at 31 August 2022)	1.1
COVID-19: Fully vaccinated population (% of total population at 28 August 2022)	21.0
Physicians (per 1,000 head, 2020)	0.06
Hospitals (per 100,000 head, 2013)	0.65
Domestic health expenditure (2019): US $ per head (PPP) .	12.0
Domestic health expenditure (2019): % of GDP	0.8
Domestic health expenditure (2019): public (% of total current expenditure)	17.3
Access to improved water resources (% of persons, 2020) .	46
Access to improved sanitation facilities (% of persons, 2020) .	12
Total carbon dioxide emissions ('000 metric tons, 2018) . .	1,070
Carbon dioxide emissions per head (metric tons, 2018) . .	0.1
Human Development Index (2021): ranking	190
Human Development Index (2021): value	0.394

Note: For data on COVID-19 vaccinations, 'fully vaccinated' denotes receipt of all doses specified by approved vaccination regime (Sources: Johns Hopkins University and Our World in Data). Data on health expenditure refer to current general government expenditure in each case. For more information on sources and further definitions for all indicators, see Health and Welfare Statistics: Sources and Definitions section (europaworld.com/credits).

Agriculture

PRINCIPAL CROPS
('000 metric tons)

	2018	2019	2020
Beans, dry	152	153	155
Cassava (Manioc)	284	297	294
Dates*	21	21	21
Groundnuts, with shell . . .	894	873	840
Mangoes, mangosteens and guavas*	35	36	36
Maize	438	415	407
Melonseed*	24	24	24
Millet	757	718	687
Onions, dry*	22	22	22
Potatoes*	42	40	40
Rice, paddy	260	291	278
Seed cotton†	36	182	145
Sesame seed	173	218	202
Sorghum	988	973	970
Sugar cane*	456	457	456
Sweet potatoes	255	217	206
Taro (Coco yam)	21	25	25
Yams*	461	456	458

* FAO estimates.
† Unofficial figures.

Aggregate production ('000 metric tons, may include official, semi-official or estimated data): Total cereals 3,022 in 2018, 2,925 in 2019, 2,882 in 2020; Total fruit (primary) 125 in 2018; 125 in 2019, 126 in 2020; Total oilcrops 1,127 in 2018, 1,296 in 2019, 1,296 in 2020; Total pulses 196 in 2018, 196 in 2019, 199 in 2020; Total roots and tubers 1,064 in 2018, 1,036 in 2019, 1,023 in 2020; Total vegetables (primary) 110 in 2018, 110 in 2019, 111 in 2020.

Source: FAO.

LIVESTOCK
('000 head, year ending September)

	2018	2019	2020
Asses	3,397	3,621	3,860
Camels	7,765	8,276	8,821
Cattle	29,070	30,612	32,237
Chickens*	6,219	6,285	6,171
Goats	36,535	38,793	41,190
Horses	1,217	1,269	1,323
Pigs*	112	113	112
Sheep	33,231	35,864	38,705

* FAO estimates.
Source: FAO.

LIVESTOCK PRODUCTS
('000 metric tons, FAO estimates)

	2018	2019	2020
Cattle hides, fresh	68.2	70.9	73.8
Cattle meat	437.0	454.5	472.9
Cattle offals, edible . . .	74.3	77.3	80.4
Cows' milk	200.6	200.6	200.5
Goat meat	119.1	125.4	132.3
Goats' milk	108.7	112.8	117.0
Goats' skins, fresh . . .	21.9	23.1	24.3
Sheep meat	164.1	177.0	190.9
Sheep's (Ewe's) milk . . .	42.0	43.9	45.8
Sheepskins, fresh . . .	27.4	29.5	31.8
Hen eggs	4.1	4.1	4.1

Source: FAO.

Forestry

ROUNDWOOD REMOVALS
('000 cubic metres, excl. bark, FAO estimates)

	2018	2019	2020
Sawlogs, veneer logs and logs for sleepers*	14	14	14
Other industrial wood† . . .	747	747	747
Fuel wood	7,982	8,092	8,204
Total	8,743	8,853	8,965

* Output assumed to be unchanged since 1993.
† Output assumed to be unchanged since 1999.
Source: FAO.

SAWNWOOD PRODUCTION
('000 cubic metres, incl. railway sleepers, FAO estimates)

	2017	2018	2019
Total (all broadleaved)	2.9	3.4	3.4

2020: Production assumed to be unchanged from 2019 (FAO estimates).
Source: FAO.

Fishing

('000 metric tons, live weight, FAO estimates)

	2018	2019	2020
Total catch (freshwater fishes) .	107.1	107.1	107.1

Source: FAO.

Mining

	2019	2020	2021
Crude petroleum ('000 metric tons)	6,663	6,649	6,118

Source: BP, *Statistical Review of World Energy*.

Industry

SELECTED PRODUCTS
('000 metric tons unless otherwise indicated)

	2017	2018	2019
Oil of groundnuts*	64.0	64.0	64.0
Electrical energy (million kWh) .	299	303	308

* Unofficial figures.

Raw sugar: 35.0 in 2016.

Sources: FAO; UN Industrial Commodities Statistics Database; UN Energy Statistics Database.

Finance

CURRENCY AND EXCHANGE RATES

Monetary Units
100 centimes = 1 franc de la Coopération Financière en Afrique Centrale (CFA).

Sterling, Dollar and Euro Equivalents (31 May 2022)
£1 sterling = 770.824 francs CFA;
US $1 = 612.300 francs CFA;
€1 = 655.957 francs CFA;
10,000 francs CFA = £12.97 = $16.33 = €15.24.

Average Exchange Rate (francs CFA per US $)
2019   585.911
2020   575.586
2021   554.531

Note: An exchange rate of 1 French franc = 50 francs CFA, established in 1948, remained in force until January 1994, when the CFA franc was devalued by 50%, with the exchange rate adjusted to 1 French franc = 100 francs CFA. This relationship to French currency remained in effect with the introduction of the euro on 1 January 1999. From that date, accordingly, a fixed exchange rate of €1 = 655.957 francs CFA has been in operation.

BUDGET
('000 million francs CFA)

Revenue*	2018†	2019†	2020‡
Petroleum revenue	335	326	562
Non-petroleum revenue . . .	403	480	481
Tax revenue	372	461	452
Non-tax revenue	31	19	29
Total	737	806	1,043

Expenditure	2018†	2019†	2020‡
Current expenditure	595	639	800
Wages and salaries	319	360	431
Goods and services	100	83	115
Transfers	109	133	194
Interest	67	64	60
External	38	21	26
Investment expenditure . . .	223	285	377
Domestically financed . . .	84	153	170
Foreign financed	138	132	207
Total	818	924	1,177

* Excluding grants received ('000 million francs CFA): 173 in 2018 (preliminary); 79 in 2019 (preliminary); 236 in 2020 (estimate).
† Preliminary.
‡ Estimates.

Source: IMF, *Chad: Request for a Three-Year Arrangement under the Extended Credit Facility—Press Release; Staff Report; and Statement by the Executive Director for Chad* (December 2021).

INTERNATIONAL RESERVES
(US $ million at 31 December)

	2017	2018	2019
Gold (national valuation) . . .	14.33	14.23	16.86
IMF special drawing rights . .	0.13	0.14	0.22
Reserve position in IMF . . .	4.49	4.51	4.48
Foreign exchange	8.58	147.75	310.03
Total	27.53	166.63	331.59

2020: IMF special drawing rights 0.17; Reserve position in IMF 4.67.

2021: IMF special drawing rights 0.11; Reserve position in IMF 4.54.

Source: IMF, *International Financial Statistics.*

MONEY SUPPLY
('000 million francs CFA at 31 December)

	2017	2018	2019
Currency outside depository corporations	406.52	415.18	471.93
Transferable deposits	403.97	397.39	550.31
Other deposits	97.21	100.88	99.03
Broad money	907.70	913.45	1,121.26

Source: IMF, *International Financial Statistics.*

COST OF LIVING
(Consumer Price Index for five cities*; base: 2014 = 100)

	2019	2020	2021
Food and non-alcoholic beverages .	89.3	97.8	96.4
Clothing and footwear	91.3	94.9	95.4
Housing, water, gas, electricity and other fuels	134.0	133.2	130.8
All items (incl. others) . . .	105.3	110.0	109.1

* N'Djamena, Moundou, Abéché, Sarh and Doba.

NATIONAL ACCOUNTS
('000 million francs CFA)

Expenditure on the Gross Domestic Product

	2018	2019	2020
Government final consumption expenditure	551	578	604
Private final consumption expenditure	4,648	4,645	4,908
Gross fixed capital formation . .	810	1,043	1,011
Change in inventories	368	474	459
Total domestic expenditure .	6,377	6,739	6,981
Exports of goods and services . .	1,721	1,877	1,496
Less Imports of goods and services	1,827	2,015	2,005
Statistical discrepancy . . .	46	3	−52
GDP in purchasers' values .	6,317	6,604	6,420

Gross Domestic Product by Economic Activity

	2018	2019	2020
Agriculture, forestry and fishing .	2,049	2,055	2,018
Mining and utilities	458	488	498
Manufacturing	758	800	832
Construction	67	66	78
Trade, restaurants and hotels .	1,423	1,657	1,685
Transport, storage and communication	529	583	585
Other services	1,379	1,575	1,601
Gross value added	6,664	7,224	7,298
Net of taxes on products . . .	−347	−620	−878
GDP in purchasers' values .	6,317	6,604	6,420

Source: UN National Accounts Main Aggregates Database.

BALANCE OF PAYMENTS
('000 million francs CFA)

	2017	2018	2019
Exports of goods f.o.b.	1,436	1,931	2,064
Imports of goods f.o.b.	−1,256	−1,346	−1,381
Trade balance	180	585	683
Services (net)	−1,037	−1,191	−1,295
Balance on goods and services	−857	−606	−612
Factor income (net)	−78	−145	−170
Balance on goods, services and income	−935	−751	−782
Private unrequited transfers (net).	344	317	358
Official unrequited transfers (net).	149	108	111
Current balance	−442	−327	−313
Capital transfers	100	49	69
Foreign direct investment . . .	211	256	277
Other medium- and long-term investments	−71	−30	−38
Short-term capital	−9	22	−15
Errors and omissions	0	0	0
Overall balance	−211	−30	−19

Source: IMF, *Chad: Request for a Three-Year Arrangement under the Extended Credit Facility—Press Release; Staff Report; and Statement by the Executive Director for Chad* (December 2021).

External Trade

PRINCIPAL COMMODITIES
(US $ million)

Imports	2014	2015	2016
Iron and steel bars, rods, angles, shapes & sections . . .	88	69	176
Tobacco, manufactured . . .	89	88	74
Petroleum oils or bituminous minerals	187	154	113
Civil engineering and contractors' plant and equipment . . .	316	227	180
Aircraft and associated equipment, etc.	273	157	131
Total (incl. others)	3,100	2,600	2,200

Exports	2014	2015	2016
Crude vegetable materials . .	35	33	21
Gold, non-monetary (excluding gold ores and concentrates) .	241	100	197
Cotton	90	84	108
Crude petroleum	3,289	2,248	1,190
Total (incl. others)	3,800	2,600	1,600

Source: African Development Bank.

PRINCIPAL TRADING PARTNERS
(US $ million)

Imports	2014	2015	2016
Cameroon	295	285	246
China, People's Republic . . .	283	138	105
France	654	615	509
Portugal	179	167	138
USA	365	340	269
Total (incl. others)	3,100	2,600	2,200

Exports	2014	2015	2016
China, People's Republic . . .	138	104	100
India	18	382	123
Japan	338	256	58
United Arab Emirates	242	101	199
USA	2,687	1,395	821
Total (incl. others)	3,800	2,600	1,600

Source: African Development Bank.

Transport

ROAD TRAFFIC
(new vehicles registered)

	2012	2013	2014
Tourist vehicles	2,872	3,265	3,681
Light vehicles	5,090	6,310	6,420
Heavy vehicles	797	705	809
Public transport vehicles . . .	1,513	1,480	1,058
Total	10,272	11,760	11,968

CIVIL AVIATION
(traffic on scheduled services)

	2013	2014
Aircraft movements	3,774	5,243
Passengers carried ('000)	449.8	478.6
Freight handled (metric tons)	8,827	15,799

Tourism

FOREIGN VISITORS BY NATIONALITY*

	2012	2013	2014
Belgium	496	593	900
Canada	537	1,115	2,658
China, People's Republic . . .	535	393	1,492
France	6,865	7,066	9,750
Germany	625	302	617
Italy	563	516	1,182
United Kingdom	355	668	592
USA	2,936	1,674	3,353
Total (incl. others)	30,054	32,126	42,833

* Arrivals at hotels and similar establishments.

Total arrivals: 62,539 in 2018; 81,458 in 2019; 10,499 in 2020.

Tourism receipts (US $ million, incl. passenger transport): 14 in 2000; 23 in 2001; 25 in 2002.

Source: World Tourism Organization.

Communications Media

	2018	2019	2020
Telephones (main lines in use) .	9,036	6,524	5,340
Mobile telephone subscriptions ('000)	6,984.1	7,664.8	8,687.2
Broadband subscriptions, fixed .	334	68	n.a.
Broadband subscriptions, mobile .	612,175	475,818	480,262
Internet users (% of population)* .	8.0	9.8	10.4

* Estimates.

Source: International Telecommunication Union.

Education

(2018/19 unless otherwise indicated)

			Students		
	Institutions	Teachers	Males	Females	Total
Pre-primary .	24*	664	8,926	8,500	17,426
Primary . . .	2,660†	44,691	1,391,643	1,077,141	2,468,784
Secondary . .	n.a.	22,927	351,101	186,287	537,388
Tertiary‡ . .	n.a.	1,585	32,467	9,354	41,821

* 1994/95 figure; public institutions only.
† 1995/96.
‡ 2014/15.

Source: mainly UNESCO Institute for Statistics.

Pupil-teacher ratio (qualified teaching staff, primary education, UNESCO estimate): 68.9 in 2018/19 (Source: UNESCO Institute for Statistics).

Adult literacy rate (UNESCO estimates): 22.3% (males 31.3%; females 14.0%) in 2016 (Source: UNESCO Institute for Statistics).

Directory

The Constitution

The Constitution of the Republic of Chad, which was adopted on 4 May 2018 (replacing that of 1996), enshrines a sovereign, independent, unitary state. The President is elected for a term of six years (renewable once) by direct universal adult suffrage and appoints, and presides over, the Council of Ministers. The legislature comprises a National Assembly, which is elected by direct universal adult suffrage for a term of five years. The Constitution provides for an independent judicial system, with a Supreme Court. There is also an Economic, Social and Cultural Council, which is consulted on any project of an economic, social or cultural nature.

Constitutional amendments promulgated by President Idriss Deby on 14 December 2020 provided for the creation of an upper parliamentary chamber (Senate) and the post of Vice-President, whose incumbent would be directly appointed (and could be dismissed) by the President. The upper chamber would be indirectly elected by an electoral college composed of provincial and municipal councillors. In addition, the minimum age for presidential candidates was to be lowered from 45 to 40 years. The changes were to come into effect from the elections scheduled to be held in 2021—the presidential election on 10 April and the legislative elections on 24 October. However, following the death of Deby on 20 April, and the assumption of power by the Conseil Militaire de Transition (Transitional Military Council) led by his son, Gen. Mahamat Idriss Deby, it was confirmed that the Constitution would be suspended. The legislative elections were postponed until 2023 and the timeline regarding the introduction of the Senate remained unclear. In late September 2021 the 93-member Conseil National de Transition, which was to serve as an interim legislative body, was appointed.

The Government

HEAD OF STATE

Transitional President: Gen. MAHAMAT IDRISS DEBY (inaugurated 10 October 2022).

TRANSITIONAL GOVERNMENT
(October 2022)

Prime Minister: SALEH KEBZABO.

Minister of State, Minister of Foreign Affairs, Chadians Abroad and International Co-operation: MAHAMAT SALEH ANNADIF.

Minister of State, Minister of Agricultural Production and Transformation: LAOUKEIN KOURAYO MEDARD.

Minister of State, Minister of Higher Education, Scientific Research and Innovation: Dr TOM ERDIMI.

Minister of State, Minister of Telecommunications and the Digital Economy: MAHAMAT ALLAHOU TAHER.

Minister of Territorial Administration, Decentralization and Good Governance: LIMANE MAHAMAT.

Minister of the Armed Forces, War Veterans and War Victims: DAOUD YAYA BRAHIM.

Minister of Public Security and Immigration: Gen. IDRISS DOKONY ADIKER.

Minister of Justice, Keeper of the Seals, in charge of Human Rights: MAHAMAT AHMAT ALHABO.

Minister of Finance, the Budget and Public Accounts: TAHIR HAMID NGUILIN.

Minister of National Education and Civic Promotion: MOUSSA KADAM.

Minister of Communication, Government Spokesperson: AZIZ MAHAMAT SALEH.

Minister of Petroleum and Energy: DJERASSEM LE BEMADJIEL.

Minister of Gender and National Solidarity: AMINA PRISCILLE LONGOH.

Minister of Infrastructure and Improving Access to Isolated Regions: Dr IDRISS SALEH BACHAR.

Minister of National Reconciliation and Social Cohesion: ABDRAMAN KOULAMALLAH.

Minister of Economic Forecasting and International Partnership: MOUSSA BATRAKI.

Minister of Stockbreeding and Animal Production: Dr ABDERAHIM AWAT ATTEIB.

Minister of Sport and Leisure: PATALET GEO.

Minister of the Civil Service and Social Dialogue: ABDOULAYE MBODOU MBAMI.

Minister of Water and Sanitation: ALIO ABDOULAYE IBRAHIM.

Minister of Civil Aviation and National Meteorology: HISSEIN TAHIR SOUGOUMI.

Minister of Transport and Road Security: FATIMÉ GOUKOUNI WEDEYE.

Minister of Mining and Geology: ABDELKERIM MAHAMAT ABDELKERIM.

Minister of the Environment, Fisheries and Sustainable Development: MAHAMAT HANNO.

Minister of Cultural Affairs, Historical Heritage and Tourism: ABAKAR ROZI TEGUIL.

Minister of Public Health and Prevention: Dr ABDOULMADJID ABDERAHIM.

Minister of Professional Training, Trades and Microfinance: OUSMANE MOUSSA MAHAMAT.

Minister of Land Management, Housing and Town Planning: MAHAMAT ASSILECK HALATA.

Minister of Trade and Industry: WANLEDOM ROBERTINE.

Minister of Youth and Entrepreneurial Leadership: MAHAMAT AHMAT LAZINA.

Minister Secretary-General of the Government and the Promotion of Bilingualism in Administration, in charge of Relations with the Major Institutions: HALIKI CHOUA MAHAMAT.

Minister-delegate to the Minister of Territorial Administration, Decentralization and Good Governance, in charge of Decentralization: HISSEIN IBRAHIM ACYL.

Minister-delegate to the Minister of the Armed Forces, War Veterans and War Victims: IDRISS ABDRAMAN DICKO.

Minister-delegate to the Minister of Petroleum and Energy, in charge of Energy Independence: Dr RAMATOU MAHAMAT HOUTOUIN.

Secretary of State for Foreign Affairs, Chadians Abroad and International Co-operation: IZABELLE HOUSNA KASSIRÉ.

Secretary of State for Agricultural Production and Transformation: ABAKAR RAMADAN.

Secretary of State for Higher Education, Scientific Research and Innovation: BAIRRA ASSANE.

Secretary of State for Justice and Human Rights: BOURKOU LOUISE NGARADOUMRI.

Secretary of State for Finance and Public Accounts: RONEL BAIONG MALLOUM DOUBANGAR.

Secretary of State for National Education and Civic Promotion: GUELDJE LILIANE.

Secretary of State for Economic Forecasting and International Partnership: MADELEINE ALINGUÉ.

Secretary of State for Stockbreeding and Animal Production: FATIMÉ KODBÉ.

Secretary of State for Public Health and Prevention: ZENABE BECHIR MOUSSA.

Deputy Secretary-General of the Government: ADJINE MAHAMAT GARFA.

Minister of State, Secretary-General at the Presidency: GALI NGOTHÉ GATTA.

Deputy Secretary-General at the Presidency: Dr MAHAMAT BORGOU HASSAN.

MINISTRIES

Office of the President: BP 74, N'Djamena; tel. 22-51-44-37; e-mail contact@presidence.td; internet www.presidence.td.

Office of the Prime Minister: BP 463, N'Djamena; tel. 22-52-63-39.

Ministry of Agricultural Production and Transformation: BP 441, N'Djamena; tel. 22-52-65-66; internet agriculture.gouv.td.

Ministry of the Armed Forces, War Veterans and War Victims: BP 916, N'Djamena; tel. 22-52-35-13.

Ministry of Civil Aviation and National Meteorology: BP 846, N'Djamena; internet macmn.gouv.td; tel. 22-52-51-51.

Ministry of the Civil Service and Social Dialogue: BP 637, N'Djamena; tel. 22-52-21-98.

Ministry of Communication: N'Djamena; internet communication.gouv.td.

Ministry of Cultural Affairs, Historical Heritage and Tourism: N'Djamena.

Ministry of Economic Forecasting and International Partnership: N'Djamena; tel. 22-51-45-87; e-mail contact@mepd.gouv.td; internet mepdci.gouv.td.

Ministry of the Environment, Fisheries and Sustainable Development: BP 905, N'Djamena; tel. 22-52-60-12; internet environnement.gouv.td.

Ministry of Finance, the Budget and Public Accounts: BP 144, N'Djamena; tel. 98639818; e-mail contact@finances.gouv.td; internet finances.gouv.td.

Ministry of Foreign Affairs, Chadians Abroad and International Co-operation: BP 746, N'Djamena; tel. 22-51-80-50; e-mail tchaddiplomatie@gmail.com; internet diplomatie.gouv.td.

Ministry of Gender and National Solidarity: N'Djamena; internet femme.gouv.td.

Ministry of Higher Education, Scientific Research and Innovation: BP 743, N'Djamena; tel. 66300954; e-mail matnajoel@gmail.com.

Ministry of Infrastructure and Improving Access to Isolated Regions: route de Farcha, Chari Baguirmi, N'Djamena; tel. 22-52-20-96.

Ministry of Justice: BP 426, N'Djamena; tel. 22-52-21-72; e-mail contact@minjustchad.org; internet www.minjustchad.org.

Ministry of Land Management, Housing and Town Planning: N'Djamena; internet amenagement.gouv.td.

Ministry of Mining and Geology: N'Djamena.

Ministry of National Education and Civic Promotion: N'Djamena; internet education.gouv.td.

Ministry of National Reconciliation and Social Cohesion: N'Djamena.

Ministry of Petroleum and Energy: BP 816, N'Djamena; tel. 22-52-56-03; internet petrole.gouv.td.

Ministry of Professional Training, Trades and Microfinance: N'Djamena.

Ministry of Public Health and Prevention: BP 440, N'Djamena; tel. 22-51-51-14; internet www.sante-tchad.org.

Ministry of Public Security and Immigration: N'Djamena.

Ministry of Sport and Leisure: N'Djamena.

Ministry of Stockbreeding and Animal Production: N'Djamena.

Ministry of Telecommunications and the Digital Economy: BP 154, N'Djamena; tel. 22-52-15-56; e-mail contact@mpntic.gouv.td; internet fb.com/MpenTchad.

Ministry of Territorial Administration, Decentralization and Good Governance: N'Djamena; internet interieur.gouv.td.

Ministry of Trade and Industry: N'Djamena.

Ministry of Transport and Road Security: N'Djamena.

Ministry of Water and Sanitation: N'Djamena.

Ministry of Youth and Entrepreneurial Leadership: BP 519, N'Djamena; tel. 22-52-26-58; internet jeunesse.gouv.td.

President

Presidential Election, 11 April 2021, provisional results

Candidate	Valid votes	% of valid votes
Idriss Deby Itno	3,663,431	79.32
Albert Pahimi Padacké	476,464	10.31
Lydie Beassemda	145,867	3.16
Félix Nialbé Romadoumngar	87,722	1.90
Brice Mbaïmon Guedmbaye	64,540	1.40
Alladoum Djarma Balthazar	59,965	1.30
Saleh Kebzabo	47,518	1.03
Théophile Bongoro	34,610	0.75
Théophile Yombombé Madjitoloum	19,923	0.43
Ngarlejy Yorongar	18,693	0.40
Total	**4,618,733***	**100.00**

* In addition, there were 104,507 invalid votes.

Legislature

National Assembly: Palais du 15 janvier, BP 01, N'Djamena; tel. 22-53-08-25.

General Election, 13 February 2011

Party	Seats
Alliance pour la Renaissance du Tchad (ART)*	132
Union Nationale pour le Développement et le Renouveau (UNDR)	11
Rassemblement National pour la Démocratie au Tchad—le Réveil	8
Union pour le Renouveau et la Démocratie-Parti pour la Liberté et le Développement (URD-PLD)	8
Fédération Action pour la République-Parti Fédération (FAR-PF)	4
Convention Tchadienne pour la Paix et le Développement (CTPD)	2
Parti Démocratique et Socialiste pour l'Alternance (PDSA)	2
Union pour la Démocratie et la République (UDR)	2
Others†	15
Total	**184‡**

* Comprising the Mouvement Patriotique du Salut, the Rassemblement pour la Démocratie et le Progrès and VIVA—Rassemblement National pour la Démocratie et le Progrès.

† A total of 15 other parties all secured one seat each.

‡ Results in the Mayo-Boneye constituency, which was to return four deputies, were not declared by the Commission Electorale Nationale Indépendante.

A constitutional amendment promulgated by President Idriss Deby on 14 December 2020 provided for the creation (following the legislative elections scheduled for 24 October 2021) of an upper parliamentary chamber (Senate), which would be indirectly elected by an electoral college composed of provincial and municipal councillors. However, following the assumption of power by the Conseil Militaire de Transition in May 2021, the legislative elections were postponed until 2023 and the timeline regarding the introduction of the Senate remained unclear. In late September 2021 the 93-member Conseil National de Transition (CNT), which was to serve as an interim legislative body, was appointed. Dr Haroun Kabadi, who had served as President of the National Assembly until its dissolution, was elected as President of the CNT in early October.

Election Commission

Commission Electorale Nationale Indépendante (CENI): N'Djamena; tel. 96997617; internet fb.com/CENI.TCHAD; f. 2000; 31 mems; Pres. Dr KODI MAHAMAT BAM.

Political Organizations

Action Socialiste Tchadienne pour le Renouveau (ASTRE): N'Djamena; Pres. ALLADOUM DJARMA BALTHAZAR.

Action Tchadienne pour l'Unité et le Socialisme/Parti Révolutionnaire Populaire et Ecologique (ACTUS/PRPE): N'Djamena; e-mail actus_pr@yahoo.com; f. 1981; Marxist-Leninist; Sec.-Gen. Dr DJIMADOUM LEY-NGARDIGAL.

Alliance Socialiste pour un Renouveau Intégral (ASRI): tel. 66287410; e-mail info@asritchad.org; Pres. NADJI MADOU.

Alliance Tchadienne pour la Démocratie et le Développement (ATD): N'Djamena; Leader ABDERAMAN DJASNABAILLE.

Convention pour la Démocratie et le Fédéralisme: N'Djamena; f. 2002; socialist; supports the establishment of a federal state; Leader ALI GOLHOR.

Convention Tchadienne pour la Paix et le Développement (CTPD): internet www.fb.com/Convention-Tchadienne-pour -la-Paix-et-le-Développement-CTPD-207944972917634/; Pres. LAOKEIN KOURAYO MÉDARD.

Coordination des Partis Politiques pour la Défense de la Constitution (CPDC): f. 2004; mems include the URD and the UNDR (qq.v.).

Fédération Action pour la République-Parti Fédération (FAR-PF): BP 4197, N'Djamena; tel. 66268967; e-mail yorongar@ gmail.com; supports the establishment of a federal republic; Leader NGARLEDJY YORONGAR.

Front pour le Salut de la République (FSR): f. 2007 to unite opposition groups in attempt to oust Pres. Deby Itno; member of the Mouvement National Coalition; Pres. Col AHMAT HASSABALLAH SOUBIANE.

Mouvement Patriotique du Salut (MPS): Assemblée Nationale, Palais du 15 janvier, BP 01, N'Djamena; f. 1990 as a coalition of several opposition movements; other opposition groups joined during the Nov. 1990 offensive against the regime of Hissène Habré, and following the movement's accession to power in Dec. 1990; Sec.-Gen. Dr HAROUN KABADI.

Parti Démocratique et Socialiste pour l'Alternance (PDSA): Pres. MALLOUM YOBOÏDE DJEKARI.

Parti pour les Libertés et le Développement (PLD): N'Djamena; f. 1993; Sec.-Gen. JEAN BAPTISTE LAOKOLÉ.

Parti Pour le Rassemblement et l'Equité au Tchad: BP 1786, N'Djamena; tel. 66292680; internet fb.com/Parti-Pour-le -Rassemblement-et-lEquité-au-Tchad-751100638622785/; Pres. THÉOPHILE BONGORO.

Rassemblement pour la Démocratie et le Progrès (RDP): N'Djamena; internet fb.com/ali.abdoulaye.koulaye; f. 1992; seeks to create a secure political environment by the establishment of a reformed national army; Pres. MAHAMAT ALLAHOU TAHER.

Rassemblement Pour la Justice et l'Environnement (RPJE): N'Djamena; tel. 65588199; e-mail partirpje@gmail.com; internet fb .com/rpje.tchad; f. 2022; Nat. Pres. BOLOUMI OUARDOUDOUGOU.

Rassemblement National pour la Démocratie au Tchad—le Réveil: Leader ALBERT PAHIMI PADACKÉ.

Union Nationale pour le Développement et le Renouveau (UNDR): BP 1064, N'Djamena; tel. 66253205; e-mail partiundr@ yahoo.com; internet fb.com/Union-Nationale-pour-le -Développement-et-le-Renouveau-UNDR-878000605620592; supports greater decentralization and increased limitations on the power of the state; Pres. SALEH KEBZABO; Sec.-Gen. Admin. Dr BOUZABO PATCHILI.

Union pour le Renouveau et la Démocratie (URD): BP 92, N'Djamena; tel. 22-51-44-23; f. 1992; Pres. FÉLIX ROMADOUMNGAR NIALBÉ.

Union des Travailleurs Progressistes pour la Cohésion (UTPC): N'Djamena; Leader THÉOPHILE YOMBOMBÉ MADJITOLOUM; Sec.-Gen. LOTODINGAO GAETAN.

VIVA—Rassemblement National pour la Démocratie et le Progrès (VIVA—RNDP): N'Djamena; f. 1992; supports a unitary, democratic republic; Pres. KASSIRÉ DELWA COUMAKOYE.

A number of unregistered dissident groups (some based abroad) are also active. These organizations, largely 'politico-military', included the following:

Front Uni pour la Démocratie et la Paix (FUDP): f. 2003 in Benin; seeks by all possible means to establish a new constitution and a transitional govt in advance of free and transparent elections; faction of MDJT led by Adoum Togoi Abbo claims membership, but this is rejected by principal faction of MDJT; Pres. Brig.-Gen. ADOUM TOGOI ABBO.

Front National du Tchad Renové (FNTR): Dabo, France; e-mail yasaid2001@yahoo.fr; f. 1996; publishes monthly bulletin, *Al-Widha*, in French and Arabic; Hon. Pres. MAHAMAT CHARFA-DINE; Sec.-Gen. SALAHADINE MAHADI.

Mouvement Nationale des Rénovateurs Tchadiens (MNRT): democratic opposition in exile; Sec.-Gen. ALI MUHAMMAD DIALLO.

Rassemblement des Forces pour le Changement (RFC): f. 2006 as Rassemblement des Forces Démocratiques; Pres. TIMANE ERDIMI.

Union des Forces pour le Changement (UFC): f. 2004; National Co-ordinator ACHEIKH IBN OUMAR.

Conseil Démocratique Révolutionnaire (CDR): Leader ACHEIKH IBN OUMAR.

Front Démocratique Populaire (FDP): Leader Dr MAHAMOUT NAHOR.

Mouvement pour la Démocratie et le Développement (MDD): comprises two factions, led respectively by ISSA FAKI MAHAMAT and BRAHIM MALLAH.

Mouvement pour la Démocratie et la Justice au Tchad (MDJT): based in Tibesti, northern Chad.

Mouvement pour l'Unité et la République (MUR): f. 2000 by faction of the MDD; Pres. HASSAN DADJOULA.

Union des Forces pour la Démocratie et le Développement (UFDD): f. 2006; Leader Gen. MAHAMAT NOURI.

Union des Forces pour la Démocratie et le Développement— Fondamentale (UFDD—F): Leader ABDELWAHID ABOUD MAKAYE.

Diplomatic Representation

EMBASSIES IN CHAD

Algeria: BP 178, rue de Paris, N'Djamena; tel. 22-52-38-15; e-mail amb.algerie@intnet.td; Ambassador AMOR FRITAH.

Burkina Faso: rue de 40 M, N'Djamena; tel. 65383515; e-mail infos@ambabf-td.com; Ambassador (vacant).

Cameroon: rue des Poids Lourds, BP 58, N'Djamena; tel. 22-52-28-94; e-mail ambacamtchad@yahoo.com; Ambassador MOHAMAN SANI TANIMOU.

Central African Republic: rue 1036, près du Rond-Point de la Garde, BP 115, N'Djamena; tel. 22-52-32-06; e-mail ambarcatchad@ gmail.com; Ambassador JEAN-BERTRAND L. BIAMBA.

China, People's Republic: rue 1021, 1er arrondissement, BP 735, N'Djamena; tel. 22-52-29-49; e-mail chinaemb_td@mfa.gov.cn; internet td.china-embassy.gov.cn; Ambassador (vacant).

Congo, Democratic Republic: ave du 20 août, BP 910, N'Djamena; tel. 22-52-21-83; Ambassador XAVIER-HONORÉ TATY.

Congo, Republic: Quartier Hille Rouge, Secteur 1, Lot 43, Lot 12 rond-point de la SONASUT, N'Djamena; e-mail ambacobtchad@ yahoo.fr; Ambassador Dr VALENTIN OLLESSONGO.

Côte d'Ivoire: BP 1943, N'Djamena; tel. 22-51-00-60; Ambassador ZOUINGNAN RICHOLO.

Egypt: Quartier Clemat, ave Georges Pompidou, auprès rond-point de la SONASUT, BP 1094, N'Djamena; tel. 22-51-09-72; e-mail embassy.ndjamena@mfa.gov.eg; internet www.mfa.gov.eg/ NDjamena_emb; Ambassador AMROU ROUFAI.

Equatorial Guinea: rue Parcha Millezi 2, Section 2, N'Djamena; tel. 22-52-14-98; Ambassador (vacant).

France: rue de l'Adjudant Chef Zouala Agoyna, BP 431, N'Djamena; tel. 22-52-25-75; e-mail admin-francais.ndjamena-amba@diplomatie .gouv.fr; internet td.ambafrance.org; Ambassador BERTRAND COCHERY.

Germany: ave Félix Eboué, Quartier Sabangali, BP 893, N'Djamena; tel. 22-51-62-02; e-mail info@ndjamena.diplo.de; internet ndjamena.diplo.de; Ambassador GORDON KRICKE.

Holy See: rue de Béguinage, BP 490, N'Djamena; tel. 62333218; e-mail nonciature.tchad@yahoo.fr; Apostolic Nuncio (vacant).

Korea, Democratic People's Republic: N'Djamena; Ambassador JONG YONG CHOL.

Libya: rue de Mazieras, BP 1096, N'Djamena; tel. 22-51-92-89; Ambassador SALAH ALI ABU REINA.

Morocco: Quartier Cuvette, Saint Martin (Clement), rue 3256, N'Djamena; tel. 22-52-20-33; e-mail ambamarndj.sercons@gmail.com; Ambassador ABDELLATIF ERROUJA.

Niger: N'Djamena; Ambassador ABOUBACAR HASSANE DAN SOKOTO.

Nigeria: 35 ave Charles de Gaulle, BP 752, N'Djamena; tel. 22-52-24-98; e-mail nigeria.ndjamena@foreignaffairs.gov.ng; Ambassador SADIQUE ABUBAKAR BABA.

Qatar: Villas Ledger Plaza, Quartier Diguel Est, rue 6632, BP 2375, N'Djamena; tel. 22-52-41-41; e-mail ndjamena@mofa.gov.qa; Ambassador HAMAD ABDULHADI SAEED AL-HAJRI.

Russian Federation: 2 rue Adjutant Collin, BP 891, N'Djamena; tel. 98-20-94-17; e-mail amrustd@yandex.ru; internet tchad.mid.ru; Ambassador ALEKSANDR MIKHAILOVITCH TCHVYKOV.

Saudi Arabia: Airport Quarter, Jander Miry St, BP 974, N'Djamena; tel. 22-52-36-96; e-mail tdemb@mofa.gov.sa; internet embassies.mofa.gov.sa/sites/chad; Ambassador AMER BIN ALI AL SHEHRY.

South Africa: Quartier Mardjan Daffac, 1124 rue 3035, ave Gaourang, BP 1243, N'Djamena; tel. 22-52-22-09; e-mail ndjamena@foreign.gov.za; Ambassador JOSEPH MUZI KHEHLA NKOSI.

Sudan: rue de la Gendarmerie, BP 45, N'Djamena; tel. 22-52-43-59; e-mail sudanindj@hotmail.com; Ambassador (vacant).

Türkiye (Turkey): Quartier Béguinage, rue de Marseille, BP 5629, N'Djamena; tel. 22-52-43-77; e-mail ambassade.ndjamena@mfa.gov.tr; internet encemine.be.mfa.gov.tr; Ambassador VOLKAN ISIKÇI.

United Arab Emirates: Sabangali Cornich Rd, nr Hilton N'Djamena, N'Djamena; tel. 22-51-99-83; e-mail ndjamenaemb@mofaic.gov.ae; Ambassador RASHID SAID AL-SHAMSI.

United Kingdom: 150 ave Gen. Kérim Nassour, N'Djamena; e-mail ukinchad@gmail.com; internet www.gov.uk/world/organisations/british-embassy-ndjamena; Ambassador JON MARK DEAN.

USA: Rond-Point Chagoua, ave Félix Eboué, BP 413, N'Djamena; tel. 22-51-50-17; e-mail publicaffairs-ndjamena@state.gov; internet td.usembassy.gov; Chargé d'affaires a.i. ELLEN THORBURN.

Judicial System

The highest judicial authority is the Supreme Court, which comprises a Judicial Chamber, an Administrative Chamber, a Constitutional Chamber, an Audit Chamber and a Non-permanent Chamber.

Supreme Court: rue 0221, Quartier Résidentiel, 1er arrondissement, BP 5495, N'Djamena; tel. 22-52-01-99; Pres. SAMIR ADAM ANNOUR.

Religion

It is estimated that some 52% of the population are Muslims and about 44% Christians. Most of the remainder follow animist beliefs.

ISLAM

Conseil Supérieur des Affaires Islamiques: POB 1101, N'Djamena; tel. 22-51-81-80; Pres. CHEIKH MAHAMAT HATTIR ISSA; Sec.-Gen. CHEICK ABDOUDAIM ABDOULAYE.

CHRISTIANITY

The Roman Catholic Church

Chad comprises one archdiocese, six dioceses and one apostolic vicariate. Approximately 20% of the total population are Roman Catholics, most of whom reside in the south of the country and in N'Djamena.

Bishops' Conference: Conférence Episcopale du Tchad, BP 456, N'Djamena; tel. 22-51-74-44; e-mail cetchad@yahoo.fr; f. 1991; Pres. Most Rev. GOETBÉ EDMOND DJITANGAR (Archbishop of N'Djamena).

Archbishop of N'Djamena: Most Rev. GOETBÉ EDMOND DJITANGAR, Archevêché, BP 456, N'Djamena; tel. 22-51-74-44; e-mail archnja@intnet.td.

The Anglican Communion

Within the Episcopal/Anglican Province of Alexandria (which was inaugurated in June 2020), Chad lies within the jurisdiction of the Bishop of the North Africa.

Other Protestant Churches

Approximately 24% of the total population are Protestants.

Entente des Eglises et Missions Evangéliques au Tchad (EEMET): BP 2006, N'Djamena; tel. 66734097; f. 1964; asscn of churches and missions working in Chad; includes Assemblées Chrétiennes au Tchad (ACT), Assemblées de Dieu au Tchad (ADT), Eglise Evangélique des Frères au Tchad (EEFT), Eglise Evangélique au Tchad (EET), Eglise Fraternelle Luthérienne au Tchad (EFLT), Eglise Evangélique en Afrique Centrale au Tchad (EEACT), Eglise Evangélique Missionnaire au Tchad (EEMT); also 5 assoc. mems: Union des Jeunes Chrétiens (UJC), Groupe Biblique des Hôpitaux au Tchad (GBHT), Mission Evangélique contre la Lèpre (MECL), Croix Bleue du Tchad (CBT); Sec.-Gen. BATEIN KALIGUE.

BAHÁ'Í FAITH

National Spiritual Assembly: BP 181, N'Djamena; tel. 22-51-47-05; e-mail nsabfchad@yahoo.fr.

The Press

Abba Garde: N'Djamena; fortnightly; Dir of Publication AVENIR DOUMLAH MOUSSAYE.

Alwihda: 5 rue Fianga, N'Djamena; tel. 63627588; e-mail alwihda@aol.com; internet www.alwihdainfo.com; weekly; Dir of Publication DJIMET WICHE WAHILI; Editor AHMAT BRAHIM OUSMAN.

Le Baromètre: N'Djamena; tel. 66462545; e-mail journalbarometre@yahoo.fr; internet fb.com/JournalBarometre; Dir of Publication ONGNAYE MODÉ ISRAEL.

Carrefour: Centre al-Mouna, BP 456, N'Djamena; tel. 22-51-42-54; f. 2000; every 2 months; Dir NADIA KARAKI.

N'Djamena Hebdo: BP 4498, N'Djamena; tel. 66271557; e-mail info@ndjamenahebdo.net; internet ndjamenahebdo.net; f. 1989; 2 a week; Arabic and French; Dir of Publication (vacant).

L'Observateur: BP 2031, N'Djamena; tel. 22-51-80-05; f. 1997; weekly; Dir NGARADOUMBE SAMBORY.

Le Pays: ave Mathias Ngarteri, BP 4306, N'Djamena; tel. 66297954; e-mail contact@lepaystchad.com; internet www.lepaystchad.com; weekly.

Le Progrès: 1976 ave Charles de Gaulle, BP 3055, N'Djamena; tel. 22-51-55-86; f. 1993; daily; Dir MAHAMAT HISSÈNE.

Le Sahel: pl. de la Nation, BP 1325, N'Djamena; tel. 66290719; internet lesahel.td; daily; Dir of Publication FRANCK MBAIDJE MBAIDIGOTAR.

Le Temps: face Ecole Belle-vue, Moursal, BP 1333, N'Djamena; tel. 22-51-70-28; f. 1995; weekly; Publishing Dir MICHAËL N. DIDAMA.

Le Visionnaire: Quartier Atrone, ave Jacques Nadingar, N'Djamena; tel. 65485047; e-mail pressevisionnaire@gmail.com; internet levisionnairetchad.com; weekly; Dir JUDA ALLAHODOUM.

La Voix: N'Djamena; tel. 66484799; e-mail lavoix.tchad@gmail.com; internet fb.com/Journal-La-Voix-213150099027862; weekly.

PRESS ASSOCIATIONS

Maison des Médias du Tchad: N'Djamena; tel. 66254959; internet maison-des-medias.org; Exec. Sec. ANDRÉ KODMADJINGAR.

Union des Journalistes Tchadiens: N'Djamena; Pres. BELNGAR LARMÉ.

NEWS AGENCY

Agence Tchadienne de Presse et d'Edition (ATPE): BP 670, N'Djamena; tel. 22-52-30-09; f. 2012 to replace Agence Tchadienne de Presse; Pres. AICHA KHALIL; Dir-Gen. HADJÉ BINTOU KACHALLAH KASSER.

Publishers

Imprimerie AGB: ave Ornano, BP 2052, N'Djamena; tel. 22-51-21-67.

Imprimerie du Tchad (IDT): BP 456, N'Djamena; tel. 22-52-44-40; Gen. Dir D. E. MAURIN.

Broadcasting and Communications

TELECOMMUNICATIONS

Société des Télécommunications du Tchad (SOTEL TCHAD): BP 1132, N'Djamena; tel. 22-52-16-40; internet fb.com/Groupe-Sotel-Tchad-124122862323598; f. 2000 by merger of telecommunications services of fmr Office National des Postes et des Télécommunications and the Société des Télécommunications Internationales du Tchad; state-owned; 80% to be privatized; Pres. YAMTA NOËL; Dir-Gen. ELYSE GOLDOM.

Salam: N'Djamena; wholly owned subsidiary of SOTEL TCHAD providing mobile telephone services; 18,567 subscribers (Dec. 2020).

Airtel Tchad: ave Charles de Gaulle, BP 5665, N'Djamena; tel. 22-52-04-18; e-mail serviceclient@td.airtel.com; internet www.airtel.td; f. 2000; acquired by Bharti Airtel (India) in 2010; fmrly Celtel-Tchad, subsequently Zain au Tchad, present name adopted in 2010; Dir-Gen. DJIBRIL TOBE; 4.1m. subscribers (Dec. 2020).

Moov Africa Tchad: ave Charles de Gaulle, BP 6505, N'Djamena; tel. 99900100; internet moovafrica.td; f. 2005; fmrly Tigo Tchad; present name adopted 2020; a subsidiary of Maroc Telecom; Dir-Gen. MOHAMED DKHISSI; 4.6m. subscribers (Dec. 2020).

Regulatory Authority

Agence de Développement des Technologies de l'Information et de la Communication (ADETIC): N'Djamena; tel. 66200071; e-mail info@adetic.td; internet adetic.td; f. 2014; Pres. MAHAMAT AWARE; Dir-Gen. YVE KOLDJIMADJI.

Autorité de Régulation des Communications Electroniques et des Postes (ARCEP): ave Gen. Daoud Soumaïne, BP 5808, N'Djamena; tel. 22-52-15-16; e-mail info@arcep.td; internet arcep.td; Pres. EMMANUEL NADINGAR; Dir-Gen. SADICK BASSI LOUGOUMA.

BROADCASTING

Regulatory Authority

Haute Autorité des Médias et de l'Audiovisuel (HAMA): BP 1316, N'Djamena; tel. 22-52-52-65; e-mail arseneradingaye53@gmail.com; internet www.hamatchad.org; f. 2018 to replace Haut Conseil de la Communication; 9 mems; responsible for registration and regulation of radio and television stations, in addition to the printed press; funds independent radio stations; Pres. ABDERAMANE BARKA DONINGAR.

Radio

Office National des Médias Audiovisuels (ONAMA): ave Mobotu, N'Djamena; tel. 22-52-15-13; e-mail contact@onama.td; internet onama.td; f. 2018 to replace Office National de Radiodiffusion et de Télévision du Tchad; Pres. ABDOULAYE NGARDIGUINA; Dir-Gen. BOUKAR SANDA.

Radiodiffusion Nationale Tchadienne (RNT): BP 4589, N'Djamena; tel. 22-51-60-71; f. 1955; state-controlled; programmes in French, Arabic and 11 vernacular languages; 5 regional stations; Dir ROSALIE BAGUEPENG GANGUÉ.

Union des Radios Privées du Tchad (URPT): N'Djamena; f. 2002 as a federation of 9 private and community radio stations; Pres. MÉKONDO SONY; includes the following:

DJA FM: BP 1312, N'Djamena; tel. 62101010; e-mail contact@djafm.com; internet djafm.com; f. 1999; music, cultural and informative programmes in French, Arabic and Sara; Dir ZARA MAHAMAT YACOUB.

Ngato FM: Marché Central, rue de la Friperie, N'Djamena; tel. 63931393; e-mail radiongato@gmail.com; internet fb.com/ngato.fm.

Radio Brakoss (Radio de l'Agriculture): Moïssala, Mandoul; f. 1996; community radio station.

Radio FM Liberté: BP 892, N'Djamena; tel. 22-51-42-53; f. 2000; financed by 9 civil society orgs; broadcasts in French, Arabic and Sara; Dir DJEKOURNINGA KAOUTAR LAZAR.

Television

Electron TV: BP 4588, N'Djamena; tel. 22-53-31-96; e-mail contacts@electrontv.tv; internet fb.com/ChaineCitoyenne; f. 2013; Pres. and Dir-Gen. DJÉRAKOR GAMBAYE.

Télévision Nationale Tchadienne (Télé Tchad): BP 274, N'Djamena; tel. 22-52-26-79; e-mail contact@onama.td; internet onama.td; state-controlled; broadcasts c. 38 hours per week in French and Arabic; Dir SOULEYMAN DJABO.

Finance

BANKING

Central Bank

Banque des Etats de l'Afrique Centrale (BEAC): ave Charles de Gaulle, BP 50, N'Djamena; tel. 22-52-41-76; e-mail beacndj@beac.int; internet www.beac.int; HQ in Yaoundé, Cameroon; f. 1973; bank of issue for mem. states of the Communauté Economique et Monétaire de l'Afrique Centrale (CEMAC, fmrly Union Douanière et Economique de l'Afrique Centrale), comprising Cameroon, the Central African Repub., Chad, the Repub. of the Congo, Equatorial Guinea and Gabon; Gov. ABBAS MAHAMAT TOLLI; Dir in Chad IDRISS AHMED IDRISS.

Other Banks

Attijari bank Tchad: ave Charles de Gaulle, N'Djamena; tel. 95358014; f. 2020.

Banque Agricole et Commerciale (BAC): ave Charles de Gaulle, BP 1727, N'Djamena; tel. 22-51-90-41; e-mail bac_bank@bactchad.com; internet bactchad.com; f. 1997; 50% state-owned, 50% owned by the Government of Sudan; Pres. MOUHAMED OUSMAN AWAD; Dir-Gen. ABDELKADER OUSMAN HASSAN MOHAMED.

Banque Commerciale du Chari (BCC): ave Charles de Gaulle, BP 757, N'Djamena; tel. 22-51-89-58; e-mail info@bcc-bank.com; internet fb.com/banquecommercialechari1; f. 1981 as Banque Tchad-Arabe Libyenne; present name adopted in 1995; 50% state-owned, 50% owned by Libya Arab Foreign Bank (Libya); Pres. BIDJERE BINDJAKI; Dir-Gen. HAMED EL MISTIRI.

Banque Sahélo-Saharienne pour l'Investissement et le Commerce (BSIC): ave Charles de Gaulle, BP 81, N'Djamena; tel. 22-52-26-92; e-mail bsic-chad@bsicbank.com; internet www.bsicbank.com/tchad; f. 2004; Pres. and Dir-Gen. ALHADJI MOHAMED ALWARFALLI; Dir BASHIR ALI KARWA.

Commercial Bank Tchad (CBT): rue du Capitaine Ohrel, BP 19, N'Djamena; tel. 22-52-28-29; internet www.cbc-bank.com; f. 1962; 62% state-owned, 18% owned by Groupe FOTSO (Cameroon), 9% owned by CNPS, 4% owned by Star Nationale, 2% owned by BDEAC, 2% owned by Commercial Bank (Cameroon); fmrly Banque de Développement du Tchad; Pres. BARADINE HAROUN; Dir-Gen. ISSA BATIL.

Ecobank Tchad: ave Charles de Gaulle, BP 87, N'Djamena; tel. 22-52-43-14; e-mail ecobanktd@ecobank.com; internet www.ecobank.com; f. 2006 following acquisition of the former Banque Internationale pour l'Afrique au Tchad (BIAT); Pres. MAHAMAT ALAMINE MAOULOUD; Dir-Gen. ALASSANE SORGO.

Orabank Tchad: ave Charles de Gaulle, BP 804, N'Djamena; tel. 22-52-26-60; e-mail info-td@orabank.net; internet www.orabank.net; f. 1992; fmrly Financial Bank Tchad, present name adopted in 2012; 100% owned by Oragroup SA (Togo); Pres. FERDINAND NGON KEMOUM; Dir-Gen. MAMADOU BASS.

Société Générale Tchad (SGT): 2–6 rue Cdt Galyam Negal, BP 461, N'Djamena; tel. 22-52-28-01; e-mail contact.qualitesgtchad@socgen.com; internet societegenerale.td; f. 1963; 40% owned by Groupe Société Générale, 26.16% by Société Générale de Banque au Cameroun, 20% state-owned; Dir-Gen. (vacant).

United Bank for Africa—Tchad: ave Charles de Gaulle, BP 1148, N'Djamena; tel. 62821717; e-mail cfctchad@ubagroup.com; internet www.ubachad.com; f. 2009; Pres. TIDJANI BADAOUI; Dir-Gen. NOUBASRA NATOLBAN.

Bankers' Organization

Association Professionnelle des Etablissements de Crédits du Tchad (APEC): BP 1914, N'Djamena; tel. 22-52-32-36; Pres. BICHARA BRAHIM KOSSI.

INSURANCE

Gras Savoye Tchad: rue Idriss Miskine, BP 5620, N'Djamena; tel. 22-52-00-72; affiliated to Willis Towers Watson; Man. DOMKRÉO DJAMON.

SAAR Assurances SA: ave Ngarta Tombalbaye, BP 6089, N'Djamena; tel. 22-52-09-80; e-mail difosso@yahoo.fr; internet www.saar-assurances.com/fr/tchad; Dir FOSSO DIFFO EVARISTE.

Société Tchadienne d'Assurances et de Réassurances (La STAR Nationale): ave Charles de Gaulle, BP 914, N'Djamena; tel. 22-52-56-77; e-mail star@lastarnationalesa.com; internet lastarnationalesa.com; f. 1977; privatized in 1996; brs in N'Djamena, Moundou and Abéché; Dir-Gen. ABDELKERIM BATIL TOGOÏ.

STAR Vie: BP 2639, N'Djamena; tel. 22-52-59-62; e-mail starvie.nouvelle@yahoo.fr.

Trade and Industry

GOVERNMENT AGENCIES

Agence Nationale d'Appui au Développement Rural (ANADER): ave Poids Lourd, BP 896, N'Djamena; tel. 22-52-23-20; e-mail contact@anader-tchad.com; internet anader-tchad.com; f. 2016; Pres. MAHAMAT TOGOI TEKILIO; Dir-Gen. MAHAMAT EL-MAHADI SOULEYMAN.

Agence Nationale des Investissements et des Exportations (ANIE): rue de Béguinage, BP 424, N'Djamena; tel. 22-52-52-35; e-mail info@anie.td; internet anie.td; f. 2007; Pres. ABDELKERIM IDRISS DÉBY; Dir-Gen. NASSOUR MAHAMAT DELIO.

Autorité de Régulation du Secteur Pétrolier Aval du Tchad (ARSAT): Quartier Jambal Barh, rue Behagle, N'Djamena; e-mail info@arsat.td; internet www.arsat.td; f. 2012; Chair. IBRAHIM MAHAMAT DJAMOUS; Dir-Gen. ADOUM DJIMET SABOUN.

Conseil Economique, Social et Culturel (CESC): blvd Ngarta Tombalbaye, rue 6.405, BP 5038, N'Djamena; tel. 22-53-03-30; e-mail cesc_tchad@yahoo.fr; internet www.cesc.td; f. 2006; 31 mems; Pres. ABDELKERIM AHMADYE BAKIT; Sec.-Gen. KOMONDI PATRIT.

Conseil Présidentiel pour l'Amélioration du Climat des Affaires au Tchad (CPACAT): N'Djamena; f. 2021; aims to improve Chad's business and investment climate.

Initiative pour la Transparence dans les Industries Extractives au Tchad (ITIE-Tchad): BP 816, N'Djamena; tel. 66801842; e-mail itie.tchad@gmail.com; internet itie-chad.org; Pres. DJERASSEM LE BÉMADJIEL.

Office National pour la Promotion de l'Emploi (ONAPE): BP 721, N'Djamena; tel. 22-52-20-42; internet onapetchad.com; Dir-Gen. SADICK BRAHIM DICKO.

DEVELOPMENT ORGANIZATIONS

Agence Française de Développement (AFD): route de Farcha, BP 478, N'Djamena; tel. 22-52-70-71; e-mail afdndjamena@afd.fr; internet www.afd.fr; Country Dir OLIVIER CADOR.

France Volontaires: Quartier Béguinage, rue Joseph Brahim Seïd, BP 448, N'Djamena; tel. 66119857; e-mail ev.tchad@france-volontaires.org; internet www.france-volontaires.org; f. 1965; name changed as above in 2009; Nat. Rep. DARO N'DIAYE.

Service de Coopération et d'Action Culturelle: BP 898, N'Djamena; tel. 22-52-42-87; administers bilateral aid from France; Advisor JUDIKAËL REGNAUT.

Société de Développement du Lac (SODELAC): BP 782, N'Djamena; tel. 22-52-35-03; f. 1967; Pres. HASSANTY OUMAR CHAIB; Dir-Gen. ABBO YOUSSOUF.

CHAMBER OF COMMERCE

Chambre de Commerce, d'Industrie, d'Agriculture, des Mines et d'Artisanat (CCIAMA): 13 rue du Col Moll, BP 458, N'Djamena; tel. 22-52-52-64; e-mail cciama_tchad@yahoo.fr; internet cciama-tchad.com; f. 1935; brs at Sarh, Moundou, Bol and Abéché; Pres. ALI ADJI MAHAMAT SEID; Dir-Gen. AL-HASSANA IDRISS OUTMAN.

TRADE ASSOCIATION

Office National de Sécurité Alimentaire (ONASA): BP 21, N'Djamena; tel. 22-52-20-18; e-mail info@onasa.td; internet onasa.td; f. 2001; Pres. GAYANG SOUARÉ; Dir-Gen. IBRAHIM ALKHALIL HILEOU.

EMPLOYERS' ORGANIZATION

Conseil National du Patronat Tchadien (CNPT): rue Bazelaire, angle ave Charles de Gaulle, BP 134, N'Djamena; tel. 22-52-25-71; internet cnpt-tchad.org; Pres. BICHARA DOUDOUA; Sec.-Gen. RENAUD DINGUEMNAIAL.

UTILITIES

Agence pour le Développement de l'Électricité Rurale et de la Maitrise de l'Energie (ADERM): N'Djamena; Pres. MAHAMAT BÉCHIR OKORMI; Dir-Gen. TAHER CHEMI KOGRIMI.

Société Nationale d'Electricité (SNE): 11 rue du Col Largeau, BP 44, N'Djamena; tel. 22-52-23-42; e-mail info@sne.td; internet fb.com/tchadsne; f. 2010; state-owned; created following the dissolution of the Société Tchadienne d'Eau et d'Electricité (STEE, f. 1968); production and distribution of electricity; Pres. KOREY DJIMI; Dir-Gen. NATHANIEL DOLMIA.

Société Tchadienne des Eaux (STE): N'Djamena; f. 2010; state-owned; created following the dissolution of the Société Tchadienne d'Eau et d'Electricité (STEE, f. 1968); Pres. MARCELIN KANABÉ PASSALÉ; Dir-Gen. KOUBRA HISSEINE ITNO.

MAJOR COMPANIES

The following are some of the largest private and state-owned companies in terms of capital investment or employment.

Al-Mahry Groupe Tchad: BP 3061, N'Djamena; tel. 22-51-00-76; e-mail aaabhs@yahoo.fr; internet www.almahrigroup.com; export of gum arabic, import of food products, textiles and building and construction materials, printing and gas distribution; Dir-Gen. ALI A. ANNADIF.

Aubaine Graphic: BP 1180, N'Djaména; tel. 22-52-77-06; e-mail contact@aubaine-graphic.com; internet aubaine-graphic.com; f. 1999; printing; Dir-Gen. MAHAMAT ABDERAMANE.

Les Brasseries du Tchad (BDT): route d'Abéché, BP 63, N'Djamena; tel. 22-52-81-87; e-mail cdc@bdt-td.com; internet bdt-td.com; f. 2004 following merger of Les Brasseries du Logone and Les Boissons et Glacières du Tchad; production of mineral water, beer, soft drinks and wine; Dir-Gen. JEAN-MARIE CASTRO.

CFAO Motors Tchad: 340 ave Félix Eboue, BP 474, N'Djamena; tel. 22-51-92-81; e-mail hmannerie@cfao.com; internet toyota.cfaomotors-tchad.com; milling of flour; distributor of Toyota vehicles; Dir-Gen. VINCENT COLLIGNON.

Compagnie Sucrière du Tchad (CST): BP 5763, N'Djamena; tel. 22-52-32-70; e-mail contact@cst.somdiaa.com; internet www.somdiaa.com/groupe/filiales/cst; f. 1976; fmrly Société Nationale Sucrière du Tchad (SONASUT); affiliated to Groupe Somdiaa (France); refining of sugar; mfrs of lump sugar and confectionery; Dir-Gen. BENOIT COQUELET.

Computer Golfe Tchad (CGT): BP 49, N'Djamena; tel. 22-52-48-63; e-mail contact@cgt-tchad.com; internet www.cgt-tchad.com; IT services; Dir-Gen. MAHAMAT ZENE IBRAHIM.

Esso Exploration & Production Chad: 1206 rue de Bordeaux, BP 694, N'Djamena; 40% owned by Esso, 35% owned by Petronas and 25% owned by Chevron; prospecting for petroleum; Gen. Man. CHRISTIAN LENOBLE.

Geyser: 184 rue Beck Cecaldi Beguinage, BP 41, N'Djaména; tel. 22-52-53-00; e-mail geyser@geyser-sa.com; internet geyser-sa.com; f. 1998; construction; Dir-Gen. OUSMANE HAMIDOU.

Groupe Almanna: Quartier Djambal Bahr, ave Charles de Gaulle, BP 1410, N'Djamena; tel. 22-52-17-17; internet www.groupealmanna.com; construction, transport, petroleum products and general trade; Pres. and Dir-Gen. ABAKAR TAHIR MOUSSA.

Nouvelle Société Textile du Tchad: Sarh; Pres. ALBADOUR ACYL AHMAT.

Société de Commerce Général de Construction et de Transport (SOGECT): ave Mobutu, BP 1658, N'Djamena; tel. 22-52-37-29; internet sogect-tchad.com; f. 2003; Pres. and Dir-Gen. ABDERAMAN HASSAN MAHAMAT ITNO.

Société Cotonnière du Tchad, Société Nouvelle (CotonTchad SN): BP 151, Moundou, Logone Occidental; tel. 22-69-12-10; f. 1971; 60% owned by Olam (Singapore); buying, ginning and marketing of cotton; owns 11 cotton gins; Pres. ROUTOUANG MOHAMED NDONGA CHRISTIAN.

Société des Hydrocarbures du Tchad (SHT): BP 6179, N'Djamena; tel. 22-52-06-30; e-mail info@sht-tchad.com; f. 2006; state-owned petroleum company; Dir-Gen. ÉRIC NDOASSAL.

Société Industrielle de Matériels Agricoles et d'Assemblage de Tracteurs (SIMATRAC): N'Djamena; Pres. ABDOULAYE AFFADINE; Dir-Gen. JEAN MICHEL DJERANE.

Société Moderne des Abattoirs—Abattoir Frigorifique de Farcha (AFF): BP 177, Farcha; tel. 22-52-98-61; privatized 1998; industrial slaughterhouse for meat industry; Dir-Gen. DOUMDÉ GOSMADINGAR.

Société Nationale de Ciment (SONACIM): N'Djamena; tel. 22-53-00-80; e-mail sonacim@sonacim.com; Dir-Gen. ELHADJ BINEYE EMMA.

Société Nationale des Mines et de la Géologie (SONAMIG): N'Djamena; f. 2018; Pres. HASSAN SYLLA BAKARI; Dir-Gen. ADOUM NOUCKI CHARFADINE.

Société des Produits Pétrolier: route de Mara, BP 75, N'Djaména; tel. 22-52-89-55.

Société de Raffinage de N'Djaména: BP 6550, rue 1031, ave Brazza, N'Djamena; tel. 22-52-00-32; f. 2008; 60% owned by CNPCI Chad, 40% state-owned; Dir-Gen. XU ZHIHONG.

Tchad Oil Transportation Co (TOTCO): 3223 rue d'Abéché, BP 6321, N'Djamena; subsidiary of ExxonMobil Corpn (USA); Gen. Man. JOHNNY MALEC.

TotalEnergies Tchad: Zone Industrielle de Farcha, route de Mara, BP 75, N'Djamena; tel. 22-52-77-27; internet www.totalenergies.com/fr/au-tchad; distribution of petroleum; Dir-Gen. RAPHAEL BOUTEILLER.

TRADE UNIONS

Confédération Libre des Travailleurs du Tchad (CLTT): ave Charles de Gaulle, BP 553, N'Djamena; tel. 22-51-76-11; e-mail confederationlibre@yahoo.fr; Pres. BRAHIM BEN SAID.

Union des Syndicats du Tchad (UST): BP 1143, N'Djamena; tel. 22-51-42-75; e-mail ustchad@yahoo.fr; f. 1988; federation of trade unions; Pres. MICHEL BARKA; Sec.-Gen. GOUNOUG GAN-FARE.

Transport

RAILWAYS

There are no operational railways in Chad. However, in December 2011 the Government signed an agreement with the China Civil Engineering Construction Corporation to build over 1,300 km of standard gauge railway line (primarily for freight but also for passengers) in Chad. It was planned that two lines would be constructed—one from N'Djamena to Moundou and Koutéré on the border with Cameroon, and the other from the capital to the Sudanese border via Abéché and Adré. This latter line would then be extended to Nyala in western Sudan, from where the existing line runs via Sudan's capital Khartoum to Port Sudan on the Red Sea. Building work commenced in 2016. The project was to cost US $5,600m. and was to be partially funded by the Export-Import Bank of China.

Office National des Chemins de Fer (ONCF): N'Djamena; Dir-Gen. BRAHIM TAHIR ABDERAMANE.

ROADS

Agence d'Entretien Routier: BP 6055, N'Djamena; tel. 22-51-68-48; f. 2000; Pres. YOUSSOUF HAMAT MOUSSA.

Bureau National de Fret Terrestre (BNFT): N'Djamena; f. 2008; effective management of the transport sector; Dir-Gen. RAYHANNA ADAM SALEH.

Conseil des Chargeurs (CC): N'Djamena; Dir-Gen. MAHAMAT ABDELKERIM BAGARI.

Société Tchadienne d'Affrètement et de Transit (STAT): 21 ave Félix Eboué, BP 100, N'Djamena; tel. 22-51-88-72; affiliated to Groupe Saga (France); road haulage.

INLAND WATERWAYS

The Chari and Logone rivers, which converge to the south of N'Djamena, are navigable. These waterways connect Sarh with N'Djamena on the Chari, and Bongor and Moundou with N'Djamena on the Logone.

CIVIL AVIATION

There is an international airport at N'Djamena. There are also more than 40 smaller airfields. In 2011 the China CAMC Engineering Co secured a contract of about US $1,060m. to construct a new international airport in Djarmaya, some 40 km to the north of N'Djamena.

Autorité de l'Aviation Civile (ADAC): blvd Mahamat Khamiss Djongos, BP 96, N'Djamena; tel. 22-52-54-14; e-mail assistante.dg@ adac-td.org; internet adac-tchad.org; Pres. HAOUA ACYL A. AKHA-BACHE; Dir-Gen. ALLADJIM NAORGUE.

Tchadia Airlines: N'Djamena; tel. 22-52-30-07; e-mail reservations@tchadianairlines.com; internet www.tchadianairlines.com; f. 2018; 51% state owned, 49% owned by Ethiopian Airlines; internal flights.

Tourism

Office National de Promotion du Tourisme, de l'Artisanat et des Arts (ONPTA): N'Djamena; tel. 22-52-44-20; internet www.destinationtchad.com; f. 2016 following merger of Office Tchadien du Tourisme, Fonds National d'Appui aux Artistes and Agence National pour le Développement de l'Artisanat; Dir-Gen. ABAKAR ROZZI TEGUIL.

Société de Voyages Sahariens (SVS Tchad): Farcha, Carrè 4, BP 272, N'Djamena; tel. 66297174; e-mail info@svstchad.com; internet www.svstchad.com.

Defence

As assessed at November 2021, the Armée Nationale Tchadienne was estimated to number 33,250 (army approximately 27,500, air force 350, Republican Guard 5,400). In addition, there was a 4,500-strong gendarmerie. Military service is by conscription. Under defence agreements with France, the army receives technical and other aid: in 2021 there were some 1,500 French troops deployed in Chad. At November 2021 1,451 Chadian troops were deployed as part of the UN Multidimensional Integrated Stabilization Mission in Mali, while some 600 Chadian troops were part of the G5 Sahel.

Defence Budget: 159,000m. francs CFA in 2021.

Chief of Defence Staff: Gen. ABAKAR ABDELKERIM DAOUD.

Chief of Staff of the Army: Gen. ABDALLAH AHMAT ABDALLAH.

Chief of Staff of the Air Force: Brig.-Gen. IDRISS AMINE.

Education

Education is officially compulsory for 10 years between six and 16 years of age and is provided free of charge in public institutions. Primary education begins at the age of six and lasts for six years. Secondary education, from the age of 12, lasts for seven years, comprising a first cycle of four years and a second of three years. In 2018/19 enrolment in primary education was equivalent to 89% of students in the relevant age-group (males 100%; females 78%), while secondary enrolment was equivalent to only 21% of children in the appropriate age-group (males 27%; females 14%). The Université de N'Djamena was opened in 1971. In addition, there are several technical colleges. According to estimates by the United Nations Educational, Scientific and Cultural Organization (UNESCO), in 2021 spending on education represented 15.1% of total government expenditure.

Bibliography

Abakar, M. *Chronique d'une enquête criminelle nationale. Le cas du régime de Hissein Habré, 1982–1990.* Paris, L'Harmattan, 2007.

Azevedo, M. J. *Roots of Violence: A History of War in Chad.* Amsterdam, Gordon and Breach, 1997.

Azevedo, M. J., and Naadozie, E. U. *Chad: A Nation in Search of its Future.* Boulder, CO, Westview Press, 1998.

Bangoura, M. T. *Violence politique et conflits en Afrique: le cas du Tchad.* Paris, L'Harmattan, 2005.

Bangui-Rombaye, A. *Tchad: élections sous contrôle, 1996–1997.* Paris, L'Harmattan, 1999.

Baou, L. *Quel changement pour le Tchad?* N'Djamena, Editions SAO, 2010.

Bouquet, C. *Tchad: Genèse d'un conflit.* Paris, L'Harmattan, 2000.

Britsch, J. *La mission Foureau-Lamy et l'arrivée des français au Tchad 1898–1990.* Paris, L'Harmattan, 1995.

Buijtenhuijs, R. *Transition et élections au Tchad, 1993–1997: restauration autoritaire et recomposition politique.* Paris, Editions Karthala, 1999.

Burr, M., and Collins, R. O. *Africa's Thirty Years' War: Libya, Chad and the Sudan 1963–1993.* Boulder, CO, Westview Press, 1999.

Chapelle, J. *Le peuple tchadien, ses racines et sa vie quotidienne.* Paris, L'Harmattan, 1986.

Dalal, A. *La sécurité alimentaire au Tchad.* Paris, L'Harmattan, 2017.

Debos, M. *Le métier des armes au Tchad: Le gouvernement de l'entreguerres.* Paris, Editions Karthala, 2013.

Decalo, S. *Historical Dictionary of Chad.* 3rd Edn. Metuchen, NJ, Scarecrow Press, 1997.

Dingammadji, A. *Ngarta Tombalbaye: Parcours et rôle dans la vie politique du Tchad.* Paris, L'Harmattan, 2007.

    Les gouvernements du Tchad: De Gabriel Lisette à Idriss Déby Itno (1957-2010). Paris, L'Harmattan, 2011.

Haggar, B. *Tchad: Les partis politiques et les mouvements d'opposition armés de 1990 à 2012.* Paris, L'Harmattan, 2015.

Harvey, D. *Peace Enforcers: The EU Military Intervention in Chad.* Dunboyne, Book Republic, 2010.

Hicks, C. *The Trial of Hissène Habré: How the People of Chad Brought a Tyrant to Justice*. London, Zed Books, 2018.

Hoinathy, R. *Pétrole et changement social au Tchad: Rente pétrolière et monétisation des relations économiques et sociales dans la zone pétrolière de Doba*. Paris, Editions Karthala, 2013.

Kovana, V. *Précis des guerres et conflits au Tchad*. Paris, L'Harmattan, 2000.

Ladiba, G. *L'émergence des organisations islamiques au Tchad: Enjeux, acteurs et territoires*. Paris, L'Harmattan, 2012.

Lanne, B. *Tchad-Libye. La querelle des frontières*. Paris, Editions Karthala, 1982.

   Histoire politique du Tchad de 1945 à 1958. Paris, Editions Karthala, 1999.

Le Cornec, J. *Histoire politique du Tchad de 1900 à 1962*. Paris, Librairie générale de Droit et Jurisprudence, 1963.

Lemoalle, J., and Magrin, G. *Le développement du Lac Tchad: Situation actuelle et futurs possibles*. Marseille, IRD, 2014.

Lemoine, T. *Tchad, 1960–1990: trente années d'indépendance*. Paris, Lettres du monde, 1997.

Lisette, Y. *Le RDA et le Tchad: Histoire d'une décolonisation*. Paris, Présence africaine, 2000.

Mays, T. M. *Africa's first peacekeeping operation: the OAU in Chad, 1981–1982*. Westport, CT, Praeger, 2002.

Nadji, O. *La guerre de N'Djamena. Tchad, 1979–2006. Un survivant raconte*. Paris, L'Harmattan, 2009.

Nebardoum, D. *Le labyrinthe de l'instabilité politique au Tchad*. Paris, L'Harmattan, 1998.

   Contribution à une pensée politique de développement pour le Tchad. Paris, L'Harmattan, 2001.

Nolutshungu, S. C. *Limits of Anarchy: Intervention and State Formation in Chad*. Charlottesville, VA, University Press of Virginia, 1996.

Petry, M., Bambe, N., and Liebermann, M. *Le pétrole du Tchad: Rêve ou cauchemar pour les populations?* Paris, Editions Karthala, 2005.

Powell, N. K. *France's Wars in Chad: Military Intervention and Decolonization in Africa*. Cambridge, Cambridge University Press, 2020.

Ramadji, A. *Partis, pouvoir et opposition au Tchad: la démocratie à l'épreuve*. Paris, L'Harmattan, 2017.

Samy, P. *Tchad: Déby vers una fin fatale*. Paris, Publibook, 2009.

Sikes, S. K. *Lake Chad versus the Sahara Desert: A Great African Lake in Crisis*. Newbury, Mirage, 2003.

Tétémadi Bangoura, M. *Violence politique et conflits en Afrique: le cas du Tchad*. Paris, L'Harmattan, 2006.

Toingar, E. *A Teenager in the Chad Civil War: A Memoir of Survival, 1982–1986*. Jefferson, NC, McFarland, 2006.

Triaud, J.-I. *Tchad 1900–1902: Une guerre franco-libyenne oubliée?—Une confrérie musulmane: La Sanusiyya face à la France*. Paris, L'Harmattan, 2001.

Tubiana, J., Arditi, C., and Pairault, C. (Eds). *L'identité tchadienne: L'héritage des peuples et les apports extérieurs*. Paris, L'Harmattan, 1994.

Wright, J. *Libya, Chad and the Central Sahara*. London, Hurst & Co., 1989.

Yorongar, N. *Tchad, le procès d'Idriss Déby: Témoignage à charge*. Paris, L'Harmattan, 2003.

THE COMOROS*

Physical and Social Geography

R. J. HARRISON CHURCH

The Comoro Islands, an archipelago of four small islands, together with numerous islets and coral reefs, lie between the east coast of the African mainland and the north-western coast of the island of Madagascar. The four islands cover a total land area of 2,236 sq km (863 sq miles) and are scattered along a NW–SE axis, a distance of 300 km separating the towns of Moroni in the west and Dzaoudzi in the east. The French names for the islands, Grande-Comore (on which the capital, Moroni, is situated), Anjouan, Mohéli and Mayotte were changed in May 1977 to Ngazidja, Nzwani, Mwali and Mahoré, respectively, although the former names are still widely used. The islands are volcanic in structure, and Mt Karthala (rising to 2,440 m above sea level) on Ngazidja is still active; it erupted in April 2005, forcing an estimated 10,000 people to leave their homes, although no deaths were reported. Climate, rainfall and vegetation all vary greatly from island to island. There are similar divergences in soil characteristics, although in this instance natural causes have been reinforced by human actions, notably through deforestation and exhaustion of the soil.

The combined population of Ngazidja, Nzwani and Mwali totalled 907,411 at mid-2022, according to United Nations projections, giving a population density of 487.3 per sq km.

Moroni had an estimated population of 62,351 (including the suburbs) at mid-2018. The ethnic composition of the population is complex. The first settlers were probably Melano-Polynesian peoples who came to the islands from the Far East by the sixth century CE. Immigrants from the coast of Africa, Indonesia, Madagascar and Persia, as well as Arabs, had all arrived by about 1600, when the Comoros were becoming established as a port of call on European trade routes to India and the Indonesian archipelago. The Portuguese, the Dutch and the French further enriched the ethnic pattern, the latter introducing into the islands Chinese (who have since left) and Indians. In Mayotte and Mwali Arabic features are less evident, mainly because the two islands were settled by immigrants from Madagascar and the coast of the African mainland. In fact, while Arab characteristics are strong in the islands generally, in particular in the coastal towns, African characteristics are predominant in the territory as a whole. Islam is the prevalent religion (and state religion) of the islands. The official languages are Comorian (a mixture of Swahili and Arabic), French and Arabic. In Mayotte, Shimaore (a Mahorian dialect of Comorian) and Shibushi are spoken; French—the official language—is little used outside of the administration and education systems.

History

PAUL MELLY

SWAHILI, MALAGASY AND ARAB INFLUENCES

The islands that comprise the modern Union of the Comoros were not permanently inhabited until the arrival in 600–800 CE of Swahili-speaking Bantu from mainland Africa, who settled on the largest island, Ngazidja (known to the French as Grande-Comore), and Mwali (Mohéli). Malagasy populations from the East, particularly concentrated on Nzwani (Anjouan) and Maouti (Mayotte) islands. Thus, the archipelago became the merging point of the quite distinct cultures of Swahili eastern coastal Africa and the Malagasy culture of Madagascar, which had been settled by peoples from what is now Indonesia. The islands were ruled mainly by Fani chieftains.

Islam arrived through the region's maritime trading links with Arabia and the Gulf. Shirazi sultans of Persian origin began to establish their authority from about 1470 onwards, while the Sunni Shafi'i school of Islam became the predominant religious influence, as it remains in the present day. Portuguese navigators then brought the first contact with Europe and a few even settled on the islands, which became a source of supplies for European ships and even the new Portuguese settlements in Mozambique.

Political authority was divided among rival local sultans, leaving the archipelago vulnerable to Malagasy slave raiders, which by the early 19th century had pushed the smaller islands into economic decay; for a time, Nzwani and Mwali fell under Malagasy control and the islands were never a collective political entity.

During the 19th century the sultans were also impacted by the spread of the competing British and French colonial powers. Andriantsoly, the Malagasy ruler of Maouti/Mayotte, fearing attack by other island rulers or the mainland Madagascar monarchy—at that stage allied with the British—sold his island into French control in 1841; for a time Paris ruled it as part of a single colonial territory with the islands of Nosy Be and Sainte Marie, off the coast of Madagascar.

Because of the archipelago's strategic location on the key shipping route around Africa's southern tip and up its eastern coast towards Arabia and the Indian subcontinent, French and US interests also developed influence over the other islands, which were eventually brought under a French protectorate through an agreement with the sultan of Ngazidja in 1886. They were overseen by resident officials posted to each island, under the authority of the French Governor in Mayotte. French was imposed as the official language of administration and formal education, although the local Kiswahili dialects remained the currency of everyday life and commerce. Attempts at French colonial settlement proved temporary, leaving space for a local elite to re-emerge.

In 1904 the islands were legally linked together and then treated as an offshoot of the much more important French colony of Madagascar for more than 40 years, before becoming a united and distinct French overseas territory in 1946.

MAYOTTE AT ISSUE AS FRENCH RULE ENDS

Most mainland French territories in Africa were granted independence in 1960 but at first the Comoros archipelago only secured local autonomy. Under pressure France finally conceded the principle of independence in 1973, promising a referendum for the following year. That vote delivered vote in favour of independence in Grande Comore, Anjouan and Mohéli, but this was strongly opposed by the Mahorais (the

---

*Some of the information contained in this chapter refers to the whole Comoros archipelago, which the independent Comoran state claims as its national territory. However, the island of Mayotte (Mahoré) is, in fact, administered by France. Separate information can be found in the chapter on Mayotte.

residents of Mayotte), who had been under French rule for much longer.

Indeed, each island had a distinct history. The archipelago had never been a united political entity until the early 20th century, and this history is important in understanding the frequent tensions and disagreements between all the islands over the past 50 years.

The Mahorais pressed for their island to be accorded the status of a full French Overseas Department (Département d'Outre-Mer), like Réunion. Concerned for the heavy development and public service costs this would impose, France had tried to persuade the Comoran Government to draft a highly decentralized constitution that it hoped the Mahorais would ultimately accept. However, the Comoran Chamber of Deputies opted instead for a unilateral declaration of independence on 6 July 1975, reconstituted itself as a sovereign legislative Assemblée Nationale (National Assembly) and named the archipelago's President of the Government Council, Ahmed Abdallah Abderamane, as head of state of a new republic. France recognized the new state later that year, but retained control of Mayotte.

The French island eventually secured full status as an Overseas Department in 2009, combined from 2011 with regional prerogatives, and in 2014 it was confirmed as fully part of the European Union (EU). The presence of this EU territory just a short journey from the rest of the archipelago has been a powerful social and economic draw, attracting a constant flow of informal migrants from the Comoros. Mayotte's status remains a source of grievance for the Comoros in its relationship with France, even as the latter remains a key international partner and the guarantor of its currency.

SOILIH AND ABDALLAH

Only weeks after Abdallah had taken office he was deposed on 3 August 1975 in a mercenary coup led by Col Robert ('Bob') Denard, a French military veteran who had seen service in many African conflicts. Paris was widely seen as having tacitly favoured the putsch, which installed Prince Saïd Mohammed Jaffar as head of state and the radical progressive Ali Soilih as head of defence. Social reforms to emancipate women and create more opportunities for the country's youth were introduced and Soilih, shaped by both Maoist and Islamic philosophies, himself took over as head of state in January 1976, going on to assume the role of Mongozi ('guide') of the National Executive Council, which had replaced the National Assembly, in October 1977. However, his rule became increasingly reliant on radical youth militias, forced labour and sporadic repression, and it alienated traditional voices.

This created the conditions for Abdallah himself to instigate a Denard-led mercenary coup, on 13 May 1978, to regain power; two weeks later Soilih was murdered. Many Comorians now look back on him as a radical reformist icon—often forgetting the repressive dimensions of his regime—and a contrast to Abdallah, who then steered the Comoros onto a more conventional path, restoring good relations with Paris, and thus securing French economic, cultural and military support. Arab donors and the European Community (EC, now the EU) also became key sources of assistance.

Abdallah transformed the Comoros into a Federal Islamic Republic. A new Constitution, approved almost unanimously by referendum provided for an elected president and an Assemblée Fédérale (Federal Assembly), and Abdallah was elected head of state for a six-year term. However, he became increasingly authoritarian: although unofficial opposition groups were in practise tolerated, from January 1979 the President's ruling Union Comorienne pour le Progrès (Udzima), formed in 1982, was the sole legal party. Central power was increasingly asserted over the individual islands and their economic resources, potentially antagonizing local island sentiment. Denard was installed as commander of a 500-strong presidential guard, funded largely by the apartheid regime in South Africa, which was allowed to use the Comoros as a channel for evading sanctions.

Amid corruption and the harsh treatment of political detainees, Abdallah secured a further six-year term in the September 1984 presidential election, in which he was the sole candidate;

the following January he abolished the post of premier and took full personal control of government. He did come under growing pressure to allow for a widening of political expression and in the 1987 Federal Assembly elections he allowed opposition candidates to stand for seats on Ngazidja island, where they won more than 35% of the vote. However, Udzima remained dominant and in November 1989 Abdallah, ignoring widespread discontent and some violent protests, proposed a constitutional amendment to permit him to seek a third six-year presidential term, which was approved by an officially claimed 92.5% of voters in a referendum.

ABDALLAH KILLED IN DENARD PUTSCH

On the night of 26–27 November 1989 Abdallah and his personal bodyguard were shot dead while in a meeting with Denard, whose mercenaries then took control, killing a reported 27 members of the Comoran security forces and preventing the constitutionally mandated installation of the Supreme Court President, Saïd Mohamed Djohar, as interim head of state. However Denard had failed to appreciate the deep personal loyalty to Abdallah felt by the French President, François Mitterand, who in the 1950s had escaped a scandal thanks to the supportive stance of the Comorian, then a fellow politician in the French system. Mitterand ordered a French military intervention, which forced Denard to surrender in December 1989 and depart into exile in South Africa with 25 other mercenaries. (A decade later he was tried in France for the killing of Abdallah but was acquitted owing to a lack of clear evidence.)

The country's main political groups formed a provisional unity government, freed all political prisoners and organized a genuine multi-candidate presidential election on 4 and 11 March 1990. Djohar, supported by Udzima, won 55.3% of the vote in the second round, defeating Mohamed Taki Abdulkarim, of the Union Nationale pour la Démocratie aux Comores (UNDC). However, Djohar did try to broaden his base by awarding government posts to two minor opponents—Prince Saïd Ali Kemal, a grandson of the Comoros' last sultan and the founder of the opposition Islands' Fraternity and Unity Party (CHUMA), and Ali Mroudjae, a former Prime Minister and the leader of the Parti Comorien pour la Démocratie et le Progrès (PCDP).

Yet less than two years into his term, on 3 August 1991, Djohar was challenged by his successor as Supreme Court President, Ibrahim Ahmed Halidi, who dismissed him on grounds of alleged negligence and declared himself interim head of state in a move backed by opposition leaders. The President hit back, imposing a state of emergency, ordering the arrest of Halidi and several other Supreme Court members and banning public demonstrations, although he did then try to reach out by bringing in to the Government two members of the Front Démocratique (FD) and two opposition figures from Mwali, where locals were demanding more autonomy. However, this upset his core support in Udzima and the PCDP, both of which left the Government and joined opponents in pressing for the formation of a national unity government and the dissolution of the Federal Assembly.

Confusion persisted until November 1991 when Djohar reached an understanding with Taki and the other opposition leaders to launch a national reconciliation process, form a unity government and organize a constitutional review conference, while keeping President Djohar in place. The next step in this compromise route forward was the appointment of Taki at the head of a transitional Government of National Unity and the drafting of constitutional reform proposals, to limit the presidential tenure to two five-year terms and set up a bicameral legislature—a Federal Assembly elected for four years and a 15-member Sénat (Senate), to which each island council would appoint five members, for six-year terms. This new framework secured the approval of 74.3% of voters in a referendum.

DJOHAR ABANDONS COMPROMISE

However, Djohar soon dismissed Taki and the legislative elections in November 1992 were marred by violence and irregularities and boycotted by Udzima and the UNDC.

Candidates supporting the President secured a narrow Federal Assembly majority and Ibrahim Abdérémane Halidi, the leader of the Nzwani-based Union des Démocrates pour le Développement (UDD), was appointed Prime Minister.

The absence of elected representatives from Udzima and the UNDC, two of the largest political groups, rendered the situation fundamentally unstable, while the April 1993 conviction of nine people—including two sons of former President Abdallah and two prominent members of Udzima—for complicity in the September 1992 putsch attempt engendered further mistrust; they were condemned to death, although the sentences were later commuted, after domestic and international pressure. By May 1993 the Government had been voted down, forcing Djohar to dissolve the Assembly and opponents demanded fresh legislative elections within 40 days, as the Constitution required. Djohar procrastinated as he tried to construct a fresh political base for his administration, setting up his own party, the Rassemblement pour la Démocratie et le Renouveau (RDR).

Finally staged in December 1993 amid controversy and allegations of manipulation, the elections resulted in a narrow victory for the RDR, with 22 seats, and Djohar named the party's Secretary-General, Mohamed Abdou Madi, as his new premier. A dozen opposition parties responded by forming the Forum pour le Redressement National (FRN) alliance, led by Abbas Djoussouf, from the Mouvement pour la Démocratie et le Progrès. Djohar, unable to provide stable leadership, soon dismissed Abdou Madi and then his successor, before appointing former finance minister Mohamed Caabi el-Yachroutu as premier in April 1995.

However, just five months later, in September 1995, Denard intervened again, leading a mercenary takeover of Ngazidja and detaining Djohar. With the support of 300 Comoran troops, the putschists installed former Denard associate Capt. (later Lt-Col) Ayouba Combo, as interim leader. Taki and the CHUMA leader, Saïd Ali Kemal, had welcomed the coup and were appointed as joint civilian Presidents.

The FRN opposed the coup and reached out to el-Yachroutu who, as the deposed official premier, was able to invoke a 1978 bilateral defence accord calling for intervention by France, which despatched 900 troops. The mercenaries and Comoran mutineers quickly yielded, enabling el-Yachroutu to declare himself interim President, as the Constitution provided, and form a Government of National Unity, including FRN member parties. Confirmed in post by a National Reconciliation Conference, el-Yachroutu granted an amnesty to all the Comoran putschists and included some figures from the UNDC and Udzima in the Government, despite these parties' support for the takeover. Djohar abortively sought to form a rival administration. On the smaller islands, Mwali and Nzwani, exasperation at the instability on Ngazidja fuelled demands for more autonomy. (In 2006 a French court imposed a five-year suspended jail term on Denard for his role but he died the following year.)

THE TAKI PRESIDENCY, 1996–98

Defeating Djoussouf, Taki comfortably won the March 1996 presidential election and named Tadjidine Ben Saïd Massoundi as premier. However, the new head of state also soon sought to concentrate his personal hold on power, dissolving the Federal Assembly and postponing fresh legislative elections, and appointing members of his own UNDC party as new Governors for each of the three islands; he also awarded himself unconstitutional absolute powers and created a cross-party consultative committee to advise on drafting of a new constitution based on a strong presidency, with six-year presidential terms and the two-term limit abolished. Understandably, the committee was boycotted by the FRN and other opponents, but in an increasingly hegemonic climate an October 1996 referendum produced an unsurprising 85% endorsement of the new framework.

Taki merged the UNDC, the RDR, Udzima and 20 other pro-Government parties into a dominant single force, the Rassemblement National pour le Développement (RND), while seeking to marginalize critics as new rules dissolved all parties that failed to secure two parliamentary deputies from each island,

while empowering the head of state to appoint island governors who could then initiate their own constitutional amendments.

Djoussouf and other opponents formed the Collectif de l'Opposition and boycotted the December 1996 legislative elections. Consequently, these polls saw the ruling RND gain 36 of the 43 seats in an expanded Federal Assembly, while three were won by the Islamist Front National pour la Justice (FNJ) and four by independents. Taki appointed Ahmed Abdou, an Abdallah era veteran, as Prime Minister.

Taki Faces Separatist Movements

The President's strong centralizing tendencies, perceived on Nzwani and on Mwali as a drive to impose the political and administrative supremacy of Ngazidja, fuelled growing separatism movements on the smaller islands.

This was not just about politics: Nzwani faced serious development problems, particularly the erosion of soil fertility as land use intensified with the growth of population; and being the island closest to Mayotte it had become the departure point for a steady trickle of informal migration to the much more prosperous French territory, just 80 km away. Against this pressured socioeconomic context, Nzwani saw the emergence of a co-ordinated separatist campaign and demands for a return to French sovereignty, culminating in a unilateral declaration of secession from the Comoros on 3 August 1997. Abdallah Ibrahim, leader of the Mouvement Populaire Anjouanais, was proclaimed as head of a 13-member 'politico-administrative co-ordination', with former Prime Minister Mohamed Abdou Madi as spokesperson. Even Mwali—the smallest Comoros island—witnessed, on 11 August 1997, a declaration of secession, announcement of an island government and an appeal for re-attachment to France. However, the former colonial power refused to countenance resuming sovereignty over the dissident islands.

Taki took a hard line, despatching 300 troops to Nzwani in September 1997 to suppress the separatist movement. However, the force was repulsed, although some 40 Comoran soldiers and 16 local civilians died in fighting in the island capital, Mutsamudu. It was only at this late stage that Taki dismissed the Abdou Government, declared a temporary state of emergency and set up a transitional commission including representatives from Nzwani and Mwali and excluding those associated with the failed invasion strategy. Envoys from the League of Arab States (Arab League) and the Organization of African Unity (OAU, now the African Union—AU) convened negotiations. Nevertheless, the prospects for a compromise settlement were set back when the Nzwani separatist leader Ibrahim pressed ahead with a referendum on self-determination which, on 26 October, produced a massive vote in favour of independence, thus limiting local leaders' room to negotiate; Ibrahim continued with plans for an independent constitution and a presidential election.

Taki responded by cutting telephone and transport links, but his own support on Ngazidja was dwindling, which created space for the OAU to promise a reconciliation conference and broker conciliatory measures, including the restoration of air and maritime links and the release of federal soldiers still detained on Nzwani. Although Nzwani separatists secured significant approval for a new Constitution in a referendum, their movement was weakened by a rift between advocates of re-attachment to France and Ibrahim's camp favouring outright independence within an association of the Comoran islands. Meanwhile, Taki persuaded Abdou Madi, a Nzwani moderate, to become federal Prime Minister once more.

President Taki died unexpectedly on 6 November 1998, reportedly from a heart attack, although some officials expressed serious doubts about the circumstances of his death. The President of the High Council of the Republic, the Nzwani native Tadjidine Ben Saïd Massoundi, was designated acting head of state, in accordance with the Constitution; he immediately lifted the travel and trade blockade of his native island and pressed forward with plans Taki had drawn up for a government of public salvation, led by the opposition leader, Djoussouf, and with ministers drawn from both Taki's RND and the opposition FRN.

Continuing rifts within the Nzwani separatist movement created space for compromise at an OAU-sponsored inter-island conference, held in Antananarivo, Madagascar, on 19–23 April 1999. This produced an understanding on substantial autonomy for Nzwani and Mwali, and the rotation of the presidency among natives of the three islands, although the Nzwani delegation insisted they had to secure approval at home before actually signing the deal.

AZALI IN POWER (1999–2006)

However, as so often in the Comoros' modern history, progress towards compromise was suddenly derailed: on 30 April 1999 the armed forces Chief of Staff, Col Assoumani Azali, seized power in a bloodless coup and dissolved all constitutional institutions. He declared himself head of state and of government, and assumed all legislative functions, promising that he would remain in power for just one year, to establish the arrangements envisaged in the Antananarivo Accord. He formed a State Committee comprising six members from Ngazidja, four from Mwali and two from Nzwani, overseen by a State Council of eight civilians and 11 army officers. Many politicians were angered by Azali's intervention and the OAU condemned the coup and called on the international community to refuse to recognize the new regime.

Nzwani's 'national mediator', Lt-Col Saïd Abeid Abdérémane, formed a local 'unity government' and joined inter-island talks, but his room to compromise was eroded by a hardline secessionist victory at elections for the Nzwani assembly; the island's executive council stated that it would not sign the Antananarivo Accord. Meanwhile, Azali missed the chance to cultivate goodwill when he appointed only one minister from Nzwani to his Government, whereas Mwali was well represented.

The OAU's threat of sanctions pressured Abeid into organizing a local referendum on 23 January 2000, which the separatist administration claimed had delivered a 94.5% vote for independence. However, amid reports of hardline intimidation against voters favouring compromise, the OAU refused to recognize the result, imposing sanctions and then a maritime blockade; the Comoros Government cut transport and telecommunications links.

These pressures finally induced a compromise deal, agreed at talks between Azali and Abeid in Fomboni, on Mwali, in August 2000 and signed by the federal and Nzwani administrations, opposition parties and civil society, with the OAU, the Organisation Internationale de la Francophonie and the EU as guarantors. This devolved wide powers to each island and provided for a referendum on a new constitution, to be drafted by an independent commission comprised of delegates from the three islands and all the signatory groups.

Yet senior Nzwani advocates of the Fomboni compromise deal struggled to secure its acceptance at home: Abeid was deposed in a bloodless 8–9 August 2001 putsch and his successors reaffirmed acceptance of the deal only to find themselves facing further coup attempts.

Presidential Elections Under the New Constitution

Finally, on 23 December 2001 a nationwide referendum produced a 76.4% vote in favour of the proposed settlement, transforming the country into the Union of the Comoros, with a President heading a governing Council of the Union, and legislative power vested in a 33-member Assemblée de l'Union (Assembly of the Union). The Presidency would rotate between natives of the islands—with the first incumbent coming from Ngazidja—and the other two islands represented through two Vice-Presidents, who would also be members of the Council. Each island would enjoy financial autonomy, with its own local government and institutions. The Union was to be responsible for religion, nationality, currency, foreign affairs and external defence. On 20 January 2002 a transitional National Unity Government was installed to oversee the establishment of the new structure.

However, the Government was soon weakened by disputes, while Azali resigned as transitional head of state, so that he could contest the new presidential election, in which he comfortably topped the 17 March 2002 first round with 39.8%, ahead of the Shawiri party's Mahamoud Mradabi (15.7%) and CHUMA's Saïd Ali Kemal (10.7%); they both boycotted the 14 April run-off, leaving Azali victorious. (He was officially declared to have gained more than 75% of the votes cast.) When the electoral commission insisted the vote had not been free and fair, it was replaced with a more compliant body that was willing to declare Azali the new Federal President. The post of Prime Minister was abolished. Meanwhile, voters on all three islands had approved their local constitutions, opening the way for the election of their local presidents—Abdou Soule Elbak on Ngazidja, Mohamed Bacar on Nzwani and Mohamed Saïd Fazul on Mwali.

Elections to the Assembly of the Union were repeatedly postponed until April 2004, when Azali's Convention pour le Renouveau des Comores (CRC) won only six of the 18 directly elected seats, and CHUMA just one seat, whereas 11 were gained by a coalition supporting the three island Presidents, and the remaining 15 allocated to allocated to island nominees (five seats each). Recognizing the strength of local island identities, Azali awarded the Vice-Presidents from Nzwani and Mwali government roles overseeing Union affairs on their own islands; other posts went to a member of CHUMA and to representatives of the Ngazidja and Mwali Presidents; however, Nzwani's President Bacar spurned the invitation to name a member of the new administration.

Legislation adopted in November 2004 to allocate responsibilities between national and island administrations, giving the latter control over the local police and the island Presidents, sparked complaints from the security forces and the island Presidents, while the Union's new Constitutional Court declared the law invalid and sent it back for reconsideration. In mid-2005 the Assembly of the Union rejected proposals that would allow a head of state to seek a second consecutive term, confirming the rotating presidency, which would next pass to a resident of Nzwani. It also granted expatriate Comorans the right to vote—a reform particularly significant for the 200,000 living in France.

With international observers present, a 400-strong AU security force deployed and national troops confined to barracks, the 2006 presidential election was unusually credible. As stipulated by the new Constitution, only Nzwani voters took part in the first ballot, on 16 April, and three of the 13 candidates then qualified for the second, nationwide ballot, on 14 May. That produced a victory for Ahmed Abdallah Sambi, a businessman and the founder of the FNJ, who gained 58% of the vote, in a poll praised by international observers as 'free and fair'. Azali's favoured candidate, former Prime Minister Ibrahim Halidi, received only 28.3%, with Mohamed Djaanfari trailing on 13.7%. In the first ever peaceful and constitutional handover of power in the Comoros, Sambi was sworn in as federal head of state on 26 May. In forming his Government he placed the defence portfolio under his own office and reunified the security forces under unified command—hinting at concern that elements of the military might still sympathize with Azali, their former Chief of Staff.

SAMBI ASSERTIVE ON NZWANI

In June 2007 elections were held to elect a local president for each island, with straightforward victories for Mohamed Abdouloihabi on Ngazidja and Mohamed Ali Said on Mwali. The run up to the vote on Nzwani was marred by violence and allegations of corruption and intimidation as the island leader, Bacar, brushed aside requests from both President Sambi and the AU for a delay; he stuck to the original 10 June polling date and then claimed to have secured outright victory with 73.2% of the vote. The AU and the Union Government disputed the validity of the contest, but Bacar ignored them and proclaimed himself President of Nzwani for a second term.

The AU responded firmly, imposing a travel ban and asset freeze on Bacar and his supporters and then, in February 2008, mandated the deployment of a 1,500-strong military force, the Mission d'Assistance Electorale et Sécuritaire (MAES), to restore the authority of the Union government over Nzwani; this was the first time that the AU had approved military peace enforcement intervention in a member state. On 25 March some 450 Sudanese, Tanzanian and Comoran troops landed on the island and took control, while Bacar fled to Mayotte. Although the Union government demanded his extradition, the French flew him to Réunion and then persuaded Benin to accept him as an exile resident. With Bacar removed, the

President of Nzwani's Court of Appeal, Laili Zamane Abdou, was sworn in as interim island President on 31 March. Three months later fresh elections were held, with Moussa Toybou, President Sambi's preferred candidate, securing a 52.4% victory in the run-off; however, with turnout having sunk below 50% as many disenchanted voters stayed away from the polls, his personal mandate was weak.

By early 2009 Sambi was following his predecessors as head of state, Taki and Azali, in seeking to reinforce central authority at the expense of the individual islands, announcing a referendum to approve measures supposedly to 'harmonize' the Constitution by extending the Union President's term of office, while downgrading island Presidents to the status of Governors and shortening their terms; he proposed reducing the number of island nominees in the Assembly of the Union to nine (from 15), while increasing the number of members directly elected—a move that would increase the relative political clout of Ngazidja. He also proposed curbs on public expenditure structures and, as a moderate Islamist, advocated the designation of Islam as the 'religion of the state', while continuing to keep state and religion separate. With opposition campaigners inhibited by the security forces, the Government claimed that 93.9% of voters had endorsed the plans in a referendum held on 17 May and the reforms were implemented just one week later.

Legislative elections, twice delayed, eventually took place in December 2009, with opposition candidates gaining only four seats, while Sambi's Mouvance Présidentielle and its allies won 20—a sufficient majority to allow them to legislate a postponement of the presidential election until November 2011, extending the head of state's tenure by 18 months and jeopardizing the scheduled rotation of the presidency to a candidate from Mwali. Opposition leaders appealed to the AU, but in April 2010 Libya deployed troops to bolster the Government's position. Sambi's term was due to expire the next month; however, the Constitutional Court prolonged his term until the election of his successor could be organized.

THE DHOININE PRESIDENCY (2011–16)

Although delayed, this next round of elections took place smoothly, opening a rare period of political calm and orderly constitutional process for a nation that had endured years of political disputes, instability and occasional violence. This time around it was up to Mwali's residents to vote in the first ballot, on 7 November 2010, to select finalists to go through to the nationwide run-off on 26 December. Three contenders qualified: Union Vice-President Ikililou Dhoinine, former President of Mwali Fazul and Dr Abdou Djabir, and it was Dhoinine who finally emerged triumphant with 60.9% of the vote, with turnout reported by the Commission Electorale Nationale Indépendante (CENI) at 52.8%. Gubernatorial polls held concurrently saw Ali Said re-elected in Mwali, while Anissi Chamsidine and Mouigni Baraka Saïd Soilihi became Governors of Nzwani and Ngazidja, respectively. All these results were confirmed by the Constitutional Court and the three island Governors took office on 23 May 2011, with Dhoinine, a pharmacist by training, sworn in as head of state three days later. Forming his new Government, he included a Vice-President from each of the three islands, rather than just the two Vice-Presidents stipulated in the 2001 Constitution.

That Basic Law was further amended in March 2014 to complete the 'harmonization' process begun in 2009, with Assembly of the Union members henceforth serving terms of five years, like the President, the Governors and the members of the three island legislatures. The mandate of the incumbent federal legislature was extended to December, before elections on 25 January and 22 February 2015, which saw Dhoinine's Union pour le Développement des Comores (UPDC) gain eight of the 24 elective seats, while Sambi's Juwa (Sun) took seven seats and independents three; Azali's CRC and the Rassemblement Démocratique des Comores (RDC) each won two seats, while the Parti pour l'Entente Comorienne and the Rassemblement pour une Alternative de Développement Harmonisé et Intégré won just one seat each. Turnout was above 70% in both rounds. In April 2015 the President's UPDC party reached a

deal with four legislators from smaller parties to establish an overall majority in the Assembly.

AZALI RETURNS TO POWER

The next presidential and gubernatorial elections were set by the CENI for February and April 2016, with Ngazidja scheduled to provide the new head of state. Sambi sought to stand but as a native of Nzwani, the Constitutional Court rejected his candidature. In the first round Ngazidja's voters selected Ali Soilihi of the UPDC, island Governor Saïd Soilihi (representing the RDC) and former President Azali (of the CRC) to go forward to the national run-off, at which Azali secured 41.0% to narrowly defeat Soilihi (39.9%), with Saïd Soilihi trailing on 19.2%. As some 6,000 people on Nzwani had been prevented from voting, the Constitutional Court ordered a partial re-run on 11 May; however, this left the final outcome almost unchanged, with Azali on 41.4%, Ali Soilihi on 39.7% and Saïd Soilihi on 18.9%. Gubernatorial polls saw Mohamed Saïd Fazul return to office in Mwali, while Adbou Salami Abdou and Hassane Hamadi became Governors of Nzwani and Ngazidja, respectively.

Azali was inaugurated as Federal President, for a third time, on 26 May, naming his new Government a few days later. Probes into alleged past governance failings soon followed: the CENI President, Ahmed Mohamed Djaza, was arrested over the alleged diversion of €300,000 of public funds, while Ali Soilihi and Nourdine Bourhane were accused of bypassing proper tender procedures in the award of public contracts during their term as Vice-Presidents from 2011 to 2016. (Djaza was later released and reinstated.) The Supreme Court and the Assembly of the Union also investigated a 2008 government scheme to sell Comoran citizenship to stateless persons from the Middle East; senior figures in the Sambi and Dhoinine administrations were accused of corrupt involvement as even diplomatic passports were sold to foreigners, supposedly including criminals from Iran. More than 170 irregularly issued passports were revoked and in March 2018 a legislative commission claimed that US $100m. in passport sales revenue was missing and accused former Presidents Sambi and Dhoinine of embezzlement; the former was placed under house arrest and charged with corruption, embezzlement and forgery. However, critics claimed this was a politically motivated move by the Azali administration to neutralize a potential opponent.

2018 CONSTITUTIONAL REFERENDUM

With the anti-graft probe forcing his two immediate predecessors and several other opponents on to the defensive, Azali now seized the chance to reinforce his own power—and with little regard for democratic norms.

In April 2018 he suspended the Constitutional Court, transferring its powers to the Supreme Court. His Government set out plans for constitutional amendments to increase the presidential term limit from one to two consecutive terms, scrap the automatic rotation of the presidency between the three islands, empower the President to abolish the vice-presidencies and replace the Constitutional Court with a Supreme Court Constitutional Chamber, whose members the President himself would appoint, and abolish the legal separation of religion and state, proclaiming Sunni Islam as the state religion.

Sambi and other opponents organized protests against this power grab, while Vice-President Djaffar Ahmed Said Hassani urged Comorans to vote against this 'dangerous abuse of power'; even the army's Deputy Chief of General Staff, Col Ibrahim Salim Abdoulmadjid, criticized the proposals. Azali responded with a ban on demonstrations, the placing of Sambi under house arrest and the detention of the Juwa party's Secretary-General, Ahmed el-Barwane. Hassani was accused of conspiracy to destabilize the Government, but managed to escape to Tanzania, while Abdoulmadjid was arrested on conspiracy and terrorism charges and el-Barwane was sentenced to six months' imprisonment. The Vice-President from Nzwani, Moustadroine Abdou, survived an assassination attempt by unidentified assailants.

The CENI declared that in a referendum on 30 July 2018 some 92.4% of voters had approved the constitutional changes, with a turnout of 62.7%. Azali announced that the next presidential election would be brought forward by two years, to 2019, to take place concurrently with gubernatorial elections. There followed a fresh wave of arrests, with some detainees accused of coup plotting. At least three people died in violent protests on Nzwani in October 2018. An agreement between the Government and the Juwa-controlled Nzwani island administration appeared to offer a respite from confrontation, but this proved temporary. The authorities detained Nzwani's elected Governor, Abdou Salami Abdou, and installed an Administrator in his place; heavy jail terms were imposed on Abdoulmadjid and various opponents, including the exiled Hassani.

THE 2019 PRESIDENTIAL AND GUBERNATORIAL ELECTIONS

It was therefore no surprise when Azali was among the 13 candidates confirmed by the Supreme Court as qualified for the 24 March 2019 presidential election; the candidacy of Ngazidja's Governor, Hassane Hamadi, was also accepted. However, the Court rejected seven would-be contenders, including Ali Soilihi of the UPDC and the Juwa party's Ibrahim Mohamed Soule, leaving Azali to claim an easy victory with 60.8% of the valid votes cast. Second place went to Ahamada Mahamoudou on 14.6%, while former Ngadzidja Governor Saïd Soilihi was placed third with 5.6%. Observers from the AU and the Common Market for Eastern and Southern Africa (COMESA) dismissed the polls as lacking credibility and transparency. However, ignoring opposition complaints and public protests, the Supreme Court predictably confirmed Azali's victory, albeit trimming his vote tally to 59.1%, ahead of Mahamoudou (15.7%) and Saïd Soilihi (5.5%), on a turnout of 53.0%. In the gubernatorial elections Anissi Chamsidine was elected in Nzwani and Mhoudine Sitti Farouata in Ngazidja, while Mohammed Saïd Fazul was re-elected as Governor of Mwali.

The Vice-Presidential posts were abolished as planned, thus further centralizing power in the hands of Azali, who was sworn in for his fourth Federal Presidential term. From this dominant position he felt able to pardon 17 jailed opponents, including el-Barwane, and four political prisoners. He may have been nudged into taking this more magnanimous stance during a July 2019 official visit to France, at which he secured a package of €130m.–€150m. in development aid in return for promising tougher action to curb informal migration by boat to Mayotte.

However, no mercy was shown to Sambi, who was still regarded as a potent political threat and kept under house arrest, despite deteriorating health. In June 2020 the courts rejected an appeal by the former President and in December the justice minister stated that there was no limit to the period he could be detained, even though he had still not faced trial.

In this climate, where genuine political freedoms had become so severely constrained, the opposition had decided to boycott legislative elections in January–February 2020 and was angered that the AU sent observers to watch a contest that they believed would be rigged. Facing little serious challenge, Azali's CRC party won 16 of the 24 Assembly seats in the first round and a further four seats in the second ballot on 24 February. Its dominance was further protected by a powerful legal defence against dissidence and breakaways—a clause of Azali's 2018 constitutional package that automatically deprived a deputy of their seat if they left the party under whose banner they were elected.

COVID-19 EXERTS PRESSURE

The COVID-19 pandemic was slow to make an impact, with the first officially confirmed case not announced until 30 April 2020. However, frustration at lockdown controls and the ongoing resentments of opposition sympathizers gradually made themselves more strongly felt, and the sour mood was intensified in May 2020 when the Government claimed to have uncovered a bomb plot and launched a fresh wave of arrests. The authorities cracked down on opponents' attempt to organize their own independence day events on 6 July in Ntsudjini,

the Ngazidja home town of Saïd Soilihi, as an alternative to the official ceremony that Azali organized on Nzwani.

By January 2021 the Government was under growing pressure, as COVID-19 claimed 67 lives in just one month (compared with just seven in the entire first wave of the pandemic). Azali tightened curfew rules, closed places of worship and imposed the compulsory wearing of masks, blaming the South African originating (subsequently Beta) variant for the crisis, although he did concede there had been errors in the official response. In March the People's Republic of China sent a medical team to the Comoros with 100,000 doses of vaccine.

Azali was also under pressure from the United Nations (UN) over human rights failings. There was concern over the case of Inssa Mohamed ('Bobocha'), who had fled to Madagascar after being accused of an assassination attempt on Azali in April 2020, but had then been unlawfully extradited back to the Comoros in January 2021 and detained in secret. In April the Government came under scrutiny over the death in custody of a retired soldier, detained over an alleged 'destabilization' attempt.

Moreover, external partners discreetly sympathized with a call from Ulezi, an opposition party, for a national dialogue to discuss the approaching 26 May 2021 deadline for swearing in a new President. Most opponents, united in a Front Commun de l'Opposition, disputed Azali's claim that his 2019 election was legitimate and entitled him to a further term and the right to stay in office until 2024. Ulezi argued that a dialogue would provide him with a dignified route to climb down. The President sent mixed messages, pardoning the exiled former Vice-President Djaffar but dismissing opposition complaints and deploying the security forces to curb protests, a tough message reaffirmed in June 2021 when seven people were sentenced to jail terms of up to five years for participating in the January 2020 protests.

In November 2021 President Azali finally acceded to the appeal from the opposition party Ulezi for the creation of a structure for national dialogue; two weeks later Djaffar returned from exile. On 28 February 2022 the dialogue meeting finally began, but its potential effectiveness was undermined when several main opposition parties, forming the COMRED alliance, decided to boycott the talks after the Government had refused to release political detainees, their key precondition for taking part. The dialogue drew up proposals for redrawing electoral boundaries, increasing the number of parliamentarians and re-establishing the anti-corruption commission, which Azali had abolished. Ulezi did take part in the talks and felt they had proved worthwhile.

However, the COMRED parties dismissed the process as neither inclusive nor sincere; the group pointed out that while residents of Mwali enjoyed freedom of association, those on Nwazi remained subject to much more repressive controls. In March 2022 the former Nwazi Governor, Abdou Salami Abdou, was sentenced by a specially convened session of the State Security Court to a 12-year jail term for his alleged role in the island's separatist actions. Furthermore, in August former President Sambi remained under house arrest, deprived of contact even with his close family, four years after he was originally detained. He had still not been put on trial and his family stated that he was also denied medical treatment, despite deteriorating health.

EXTERNAL RELATIONS

The Comoros maintains a range of significant external relationships, although the country's small size means that only about 22 partners have a permanent diplomatic presence in Moroni. About one-half of these are consulates, reflecting local travel and family connections—as in the case of Madagascar—or dealing with the welfare of the crew of foreign fishing vessels operating in Comoran waters.

France and the EU are the most significant Western actors permanently represented. The USA maintained an embassy in Moroni from 1985 until 1993, but has no permanent presence today, although it has sometimes operated military education and training programmes, as has France. Most other states with a diplomatic presence are African, Arab or Asian, including China, Saudi Arabia, the United Arab Emirates, Libya and

Sudan, which all maintain full embassies in Moroni. The Comoros joined the Arab League in 1993.

France is a crucial partner, even though the Comoros continues to claim Mayotte, disputing the legitimacy of the electoral processes through which its inhabitants have repeatedly reaffirmed their wish to remain under French rule. In an African context, where decolonization remained a key issue for decades, the issue did not fade away. The UN General Assembly repeatedly voted to affirm Comoran sovereignty over the French island and diplomatic relations with France were suspended for three years from 1975. However, in November 1978 the two countries signed agreements on economic and military co-operation. The relationship with Paris is sensitive and often impacted by the bumpy and frequently contentious evolution of Comoran domestic politics, which can sometimes find an echo among the diaspora in France, particularly among the 100,000-strong Comoran community in Marseille, many of whom staged regular demonstrations in 2019 in protest at the circumstances in which Azali secured re-election.

A visit to France by Azali in 2005 resulted in the restoration of the two countries' bilateral commission (after a decade-long hiatus) and the next year Paris approved a €88m. five-year aid package. However, relations deteriorated again in 2008 after the French allowed the Nzwani separatist leader Bacar, who had fled to Mayotte, to move to safe exile in Benin. This created an already strained context for the 29 March 2009 referendum in which the Mahorais voted—by a hefty 95.2% on a turnout of 61%—to become an Overseas Department within the French Republic. The Comoros predictably denounced the vote as 'null, void and without effect', but France honoured the result and conferred full departmental status on Mayotte on 31 March 2011.

Relations have since continued on contrasting parallel tracks of co-operation and fundamental disagreement. The two countries signed a defence partnership in 2010, including co-operation on maritime security—a serious concern at a time when Somalian pirates had extended their activities southwards. In 2013 President Dhoinine and his French counterpart François Hollande signed an accord providing for the creation of a bilateral high joint council. Agreements on judicial and police co-operation soon followed and France and the EU jointly budgeted for a €135m. development programme for 2015–20. Nevertheless, Mayotte remained an issue of contention: at the UN General Assembly in September 2012 Dhoinine argued that the imposition by France in 1995 of visa requirements on Comorans visiting the French island was partly to blame for the fact that some had drowned while trying to circumvent the controls by crossing to Mayotte by small boat. Exact casualty numbers are unknown, but in 2017 the Comoran authorities suggested that at least 10,000 had died since 1995 while trying to make the crossing. However, Paris has continued to insist the visa regime is an essential control on the influx of Comorans seeking a share of the relative prosperity on Mayotte—where housing and public services are under already pressure and locals have been fiercely resistant to any suggestion that the visa requirement might be suspended in an effort to improve overall Franco-Comoran relations.

Bilateral relations thus remain stuck in a pattern where neither government feels able to give ground over the issue. French President Emmanuel Macron has sought to defuse longstanding grievances in the Overseas Departments, where living standards are generally lower than in mainland France; visiting Mayotte in October 2019 he was confronted with locals' insistence that tight migration controls should remain. Yet he has also sought to cultivate Comoran goodwill, despite concerns over the Azali regime's poor human rights record. Notably, Azali was Macron's guest at the 14 July celebration in the French capital in 2022.

Economy

PAUL MELLY

INTRODUCTION

Extending across three small islands, with a fragile environment and a population of less than 1m., the Comoros faces distinctive development challenges. The post-independence track record of political instability and sporadic if small-scale violent change, and the recent intensification of political repression, are deterrents to potential investors. The archipelago is a competitive producer of only a few specialist tropical crops and with such a small local market, the range of specialist service and support providers is limited. Regional neighbours, similarly reliant on agricultural exports, are more competitors than natural trade partners.

The spectacular lush coastal and mountainous scenery of the archipelago offers great potential for tourism development, but in practical terms the industry's growth is constrained by the limited range of travel links. The Comoros is densely populated and the supply of agricultural land is under pressure, particularly on Nzwani (Anjouan) island, where soil erosion is a serious problem. Intense socioeconomic strains fuel a steady flow of informal migration to the nearby French island of Mayotte. The large expatriate Comoran populations in Mayotte and in Marseille, in mainland France, are an indication of the limited economic opportunities at home.

Technical data indicators classify the Comoros as a lower-middle income country, with average per capita gross domestic product (GDP) of US $1,494.7 in 2021. Yet it suffers from many of the problems of poorer states and is ranked 156th out of the 191 countries assessed by the Human Development Index produced by the United Nations (UN) Development Programme. With a narrow economic base, high logistical costs and limited options for diversification, the Comoros faces a profound challenge in trying to improve standards of living and public service provision for a population in which 40% still live below the national poverty line.

However, there is economic potential. The offshore economic zone extending to the 200-mile limit harbours rich fisheries and may offer scope for oil and gas exploration. Modern telecommunications and a substantial young workforce well educated in French, and the supportive proximity of offshore finance hubs in Mauritius and Seychelles, could facilitate the development of niche digital or technology sector activities. The rich land and marine biodiversity may offer scope for developing 'blue economy' environmentally-sensitive activities. And there is evident potential to expand high value tourism, drawn by the Comoros' natural beauty and distinctive culture, perhaps combined with other nearby destinations such as Madagascar, Mauritius, Réunion or Seychelles that have better long haul travel links. Yet the current increasingly authoritarian political model hampers professional policymaking and will deter many investors and foreign donors. If repression persists this may constrain the growth of some specialist service businesses and deter Western development support, leaving the country increasingly reliant on authoritarian partners and cronyist investors who do not prioritize transparency, socially inclusive growth or the protection of the environment.

COVID-19 impacted the islands when they were already struggling to repair the economic damage wrought by Cyclone Kenneth in April 2019. Real GDP growth fell from 3.6% in 2018 to just 1.9% in 2019. The pandemic further slowed local business activity, paralysed tourism and threatened a serious fall in remittances from the Comorian diaspora in France and Madagascar (whose economies had also been impacted by COVID-19). Yet the Comoros' real GDP contracted by only

0.3% in 2020 and it grew by 2.2% in 2021, the International Monetary Fund (IMF) estimates.

The Comoros franc provides an anchor of monetary stability, even through periods of political tension, because it is pegged to the euro at rate guaranteed by the French Treasury. This arrangement means that the central bank (Banque Centrale des Comores—BCC) follows a relatively conservative monetary stance, loosely aligned with that of the eurozone. In mainland West and Central Africa similar systems operate and reforms are under way or planned, in response to growing criticism of the currency link to France; but the status of the Comoros franc has not been a major political or policy issue. The Comoros is a member of the Indian Ocean Commission, but this is not a structure of substantial economic standing.

MACROECONOMIC AND FISCAL SITUATION

The Comoros experienced recession in 2006 but then enjoyed continual growth in real GDP—albeit at fluctuating rates—until the pandemic struck, with a peak of 4.2% in 2017. In the aftermath of the 2019 cyclone the IMF provided US $12.3m. in rapid financial assistance and, as COVID-19 began it make itself felt, the Fund stepped in with a further $12m. in emergency support in April 2020. These IMF interventions injected much-needed funding to meet urgent short-term needs. Poorer households risked suffering a fall in remittances from expatriate family members, while the slump in trade and tourism hurt employment, business turnover and government revenue. While the IMF funding cushioned the pandemic blow to public finances, the impact of COVID-19 on the wider economy, family incomes and business viability was much harder to palliate. In August 2020 the World Bank warned that the money transfer service operated by the state-owned postal bank Société Nationale des Postes et Services Financiers (SNPSF) was in a vulnerable position. Despite the tight monetary stance resulting from the Comoros franc's peg to the euro, inflation rose from 1.7% in 2018 to 3.7% in 2019, probably fuelled by cyclone damage to agricultural production; it fell back to 0.8% in 2020 as the pandemic cooled economic activity, but rebounded to 1.5% in 2021 and was on course to reach 5% in 2022. As a small island economy with limited local production and heavily reliant on imports, the Comoros is always vulnerable to the sort of surge in global prices of core food and fuel commodities that was seen in 2022 in the aftermath of the Russian Federation's invasion of Ukraine in February.

In October 2021 the IMF agreed a Staff Monitored Programme (SMP) for the Comoros, under which the Fund monitors performance towards key targets but provides no financial support; successful completion of an SMP can help a country qualify for a full IMF programme with funding.

The Fund and other partners have also been working on longer term strategies to tackle the fundamental fragility of the Comorian economy and develop more inclusive growth. There has been concern about the weakness of some state owned enterprises such as Comoros Télécom, while the difficult operating climate for banks hampers the flow of credit to business. The IMF had pressed the Government to curb tax exemptions and bolster fiscal revenue collection, spend more on social priorities and strengthen governance and the judicial system; however, in reality, the latter has actually been weakened by the subjugation of the highest court to political control.

The Government had also drawn up a longer term development strategy for the period 2020–30, the 'Emerging Comoros Plan', presented to donors in the French capital, Paris, in December 2019. This aims to stimulate more inclusive growth, around five priority themes: tourism and crafts, fishing and port activities, establishing the Comoros as a western Indian Ocean hub for financial and logistical services, agriculture—for example, improving farmers' access to markets—and manufacturing. To support progress in these areas it envisages reformed and stable politics and institutions, measures to strengthen infrastructure and human capital, structural reform and digital development. This ambitious reform strategy hinted at an implicit recognition of the need to address the socioeconomic pressures and separatist frustrations in individual islands, especially Nzwani. However, it was unclear whether the personalized, centralizing and sporadically authoritarian Azali regime really had the will to tackle such deep-seated problems in a genuinely inclusive and open-minded way.

Donors pledged more than US $4,300m. in support for the programme. The World Bank, an important partner, designed a framework for the Comoros for 2021–24 that focuses on the business environment, opportunities for women, government revenue collection and a more equitable allocation of state resources across all three islands (Ngazidja, Nzwani and Mwali). It has supported vaccination, the strengthening of health and social protection, financial inclusion and solar energy. Other key members of the Comoros' small circle of regular financial partners are France, the European Union (EU), the African Development Bank (AfDB) and UN agencies.

The Comoros' public finances are heavily dependent on donor support, with a chronic deficit if grant aid is excluded from the total. The volume of budget receipts has fluctuated wildly, compounding the challenge of planning fiscal strategy and expenditure. Receipts surged from 39,600m. Comoros francs in 2016 to 56,600m. Comoros francs in 2017 and 57,300m. Comoros francs the next year, before sliding back to just 50,000m. Comoros francs in 2019 and 49,500m. Comoros francs in 2020. Public expenditure rose to 110,200m. Comoros francs in 2017, before slipping back to 94,800m. Comoros francs in 2018, then rebounding to 102,100m. Comoros francs the year after and then sinking back to 99,400m. Comoros francs in 2020. Within this overall total, current expenditure climbed from 49,600m. Comoros francs in 2016 to 70,200m. Comoros francs in both the following year and again in 2018, but then slumped back to only 58,100m. Comoros francs in 2019 and 58,500m. Comoros francs in 2020. In that year, salaries and other remuneration for public service personnel accounted for almost half of all current expenditure, at 27,500m. Comoros francs. Capital spending sank from 40,100m. Comoros francs in 2017 to just 24,600m. Comoros francs the following year, but then rebounded to 44,000m. Comoros francs in 2019 and 40,900m. Comoros francs in 2020. Grant aid—or the grant equivalent element of soft loans—from external partners remains critical in providing support for state finances and funding development. Such aid reached 52,600m. Comoros francs in 2017, slipped to 35,500m. Comoros francs the next year and to 39,000m. Comoros francs in 2018, but then rose again to 51,500m. Comoros francs in 2020.

POPULATION AND SOCIAL CONTEXT

The Comoros' population has almost doubled since 1994 to exceed 900,000 in 2022, according to estimates by the UN Population Fund; however, the rate of growth (at a projected average rate of 2.1% per year over 2020–25) is gently slowing. With 454 people per sq km, the archipelago is densely inhabited, exerting severe pressure on the limited resources of land. Deforestation and soil erosion are serious problems, particularly on Nzwani. Located in a tropical zone prone to both drought and cyclones, and with a hilly topography vulnerable to soil erosion in heavy rainfall, the Comoros is heavily exposed to climate change shocks, and the World Bank estimates that 54.2% of the country's inhabitants live in areas at risk.

The impact of Cyclone Kenneth and COVID-19 compounded already severe social pressures. The World Bank calculates that almost one-quarter of the population is 'extremely poor' and lacks the reliable means to buy food adequate to meet basic human nutritional requirements of 2,200 kilocalories per person per day, and 31% of children under five are stunted. Only 16% of women aged 15–49 years use modern contraception, less than one-half of the number who would like access to it, and the rate of teenage pregnancy is particularly high.

Nevertheless, health indicators have been slowly improving and the UN Population Fund estimates average life expectancy at 63 years for men and 67 years for women, while the rate of maternal mortality fell from 576 deaths per 100,000 live births in 1994 to 273 deaths in 2017, while 85% of children aged 12–23 months are immunized against diphtheria, tetanus and pertussis (whooping cough). Some 77% of girls and 76% of boys complete primary school and around 50% of children enrol in secondary school. Until the University of Comoros opened in

2003 young people had to travel abroad for higher education; the institution offers a broad range of courses, including many with direct practical relevance to the economy and development, and it has a faculty of medicine and public health.

AGRICULTURE, FORESTRY AND FISHERIES

Slash and burn land clearance and the use of fertilizer in ways that actually damage the soil and vegetation cover contribute to a high rates of deforestation; further threats come from rising temperatures, droughts and cyclones, which damage both crops and the roads serving agricultural communities, and the arrival of new pests. Yet the UN's Food and Agriculture Organization (FAO) believes farming could produce much better results, through improved but still affordable technology, better irrigation and the upgrading of local roads. It has been advising villagers on 'climate smart' production and processing techniques, and cooking highly nutritional local crops. There is also a need for better control of pests that damage vanilla—an important export crop. The UN's International Fund for Agricultural Development is helping to improve productivity while conserving a landscape already degraded by serious erosion.

The primary sector of the economy accounts for more than 30% of GDP. Farmers grow both food crops for the local market and vanilla, cloves and ylang-ylang, the cash crops that accounted for around 90% of exports in 2020. These are niche, high value crops and the Comoros is established in this specialist international market; however, the scope for overall demand growth is limited, which can leave the islands open to severe competitive pressures if new suppliers enter the field. Moreover, production of these important cash crops is highly vulnerable to the weather and other natural factors. In 2018 output of cloves reached about 4,300 metric tons, its peak for more than a decade at least, but in 2019 Cyclone Kenneth hit plantations and output slipped back to 3,500 tons. Vanilla was also severely affected, with the harvest falling to only about 900 tons in both 2019 and 2020, from the 1,400 tons collected in 2018, far below the almost 4,000 tons harvested in 2012 and almost 4,500 tons produced in 2013. Ylang-ylang (grown for its flowers and their essential oil, used in aromatherapy and perfume) enjoyed a marked recovery from 2017 onwards, with output in 2019 reaching around 2,700 tons, the highest level for more than a decade; but in 2020 the harvest plunged back to about 1,300 tons, comparable with the production trough of five years earlier.

Fishing is a significant sector, employing around 11,400 people. Most of the catch caught by local artisanal boats—estimated at 5,800 in number in 2012 by FAO—is consumed locally. With annual consumption averaging some 25 kg per capita, this is an important contribution to nutrition, especially as the scope for livestock husbandry is limited. Waters up to 10 miles offshore are reserved for Comorian boats. Beyond, and up to the Comoros' 200 mile limit, foreign vessels catching tuna predominate. The locally registered catch has fluctuated between around 20,000 metric tons and almost 55,000 tons. However, this does not include what is caught by the foreign vessels operating under framework agreements with international partners landing their catches outside the country. In 2018 the EU pulled out of its accord with the Comoros, complaining that tuna stocks were subject to poaching by local vessels operating in breach of the accord.

POWER AND HYDROCARBONS

Electricity is at present produced almost entirely by small diesel generation plants and the power infrastructure has become run down. In 2019 it was reported that only five of the 15 diesel units on Ngazidja were operational, while all three of the Comoros' hydro-generation plants were out of working order. By mid-2021 the reliability of power supply had been further undermined by delays in fuel deliveries, which forced the power utility SONELEC to impose frequent outages, with power only provided during the evening in certain districts. Therefore, although Ngazidja has an installed generating capacity of 28 MW—double the normal level of demand—output has often been as low as 7.4 MW. The situation is no better on Nzwani, where for much of the time only 2.6 MW of

the 7 MW installed capacity has been operational. Only on Mwali, the smallest island, has power supply been sufficient to satisfy demand.

President Azali has prioritized tackling this problem. The Abu Dhabi Fund for Development has helped finance the provision of 6.4 MW in extra capacity for Ngazidja and 3.6 MW for Nzwani. The AfDB has a programme initially to revamp the diesel plants and power distribution links and then to return the three existing hydroelectric plants to operation and build a fourth. Thermal power, particularly using small generation units, is costly and the case for restoring and expanding renewable generation capacity is therefore strong. A 3-MW solar power station, backed up with battery storage, was installed by the French company Innovent on a lava field at Fombouni in the south of Ngazidja and began production in January 2021, and the company has been building a 4-MW plant at Mitsamiouli, at the northern tip of the island. A consortium of Engie (France), Vigor (Tanzania) and EPS (Italy) has built a 6.6-MW solar plant on Nzwani that should generate sufficient power to meet more than 85% of the island's needs.

The Comoros produces no oil and gas and it was only in 2012 that the then President, Ikililou Dhoinine, awarded the first offshore exploration blocs. UK-based Tullow was briefly active in exploration but later withdrew. Western Energy has also been engaged in a 3D seismic programme, set to run until 2022.

MANUFACTURING AND SERVICES

There are some small craft and light manufacturing businesses. However, instability, weak governance and high costs are a deterrent to the emergence of export industries of the kind long established in nearby Madagascar and Mauritius. The central bank believes that there is scope to develop the processing of cloves and vanilla, the import substitution manufacture of furniture and household fittings and the processing of locally caught fish, some of which is currently landed and processed in neighbouring countries. Such diversification and growth of value-added activities could create more livelihoods for young people, some 22.5% of whom were unemployed in 2019.

The service sector accounts for around one-half of the Comoros' GDP. Key activities include financial, business and technical services catering for the local market and the tourism sector, which was of course severely impacted by the curbs on international leisure travel during COVID-19.

The banking sector market leader is the mutual and savings network Union des Mutuelles d'Epargne et de Credit des Comores, with a 29% share of all deposits and a 30% share of all lending. It is followed by the largest of the four private sector banks, Exim Bank Comores (18%), then the national postal bank SNPSF (13%) and the Banque pour l'Industrie et le Commerce (BIC—12%). In 2020 France's BNP Paribas sold control of BIC to Atlantic Financial Group, based in Côte d'Ivoire, another franc zone market with a currency peg to the euro; the state remains the minority shareholder. The other private sector banks are the Banque Fédérale de Commerce (BFC) and the Banque de Développement des Comores (BDC), which in 2019 was taken over by Finafrica. Also significant is the Sanduk microfinance network, present on Mwali, Nzwani and, since 2018, Ngazidja.

Unsurprisingly, the economic slowdown caused by COVID-19 was reflected in borrowers' more limited capacity to service their debts, although only to a small extent. The proportion of bank loans that were non-performing nudged up to 22% in 2020, from 21% the previous year, and banks sensibly raised their level of provisions against doubtful credits to 71% (from 69% in 2019).

The Comoros' scenery, distinct ecology and cultural heritage could be a major draw for tourists and the islands attracted 35,900 visitors in 2018, some 28% up on the previous year, with a further rise, to 50,000, in 2019. Numbers slumped to just 7,000 in 2000, owing to the pandemic. However, around 90% of those who visit the islands are members of the Comorian diaspora, most staying with family and spending relatively little on excursions, meals and souvenirs. By late 2019 the Galawa hotel on Ngazidja, which used to attract a regular flow of visitors from South Africa, had shut.

The major obstacle to the revival of a more diverse tourism industry, with higher-spending visitors without family connections to the islands, is the limited range and high cost of international flight connections; the Comoros' best hope of overcoming that obstacle may lie in developing more upscale or specialist leisure facilities and in partnerships with other destinations in the region, for the high-spending 'two-centre' holiday market.

TRANSPORT INFRASTRUCTURE

The Comoros attracts only a limited range of international shipping. The French group CMA CGM operates a feeder connection from its major deep sea routes to Mutsamudu port on Nzwani and to Moroni's small container terminal, modernized and operated by the French logistics group Bolloré. There are local shipping links between the three Comoros islands, while Mayotte-based SGTM operates passenger services to Mutsamudu and Moroni.

Moroni airport is serviced by routes to regional destinations and by Kenya Airways, Ethiopian Airlines and Turkish Airlines, which have extensive African and international networks. Réunion-based Air Austral and Air Madagascar offer onward connections to France. The AfDB is funding improvements to the road network.

FOREIGN TRADE AND PAYMENTS

Exports slumped by roughly half in 2020 – a reflection both of lingering cyclone damage and the disruptive impact of the pandemic, as well as the poor harvests for vanilla, cloves and ylang-ylang. From a very low base of just 7,500m. Comoros francs in 2015, export shipments had surged to 13,700m. Comoros francs the next year and then to 17,300m. in 2017 and 18,200m. Comoros francs in 2018. However, they slipped back to 17,900m. Comoros francs in 2019, before slumping to just 9,600m. Comoros francs in 2020. Cloves have remained the largest export commodity, with shipments of 8,200m. Comoros francs in 2016, 9,400m. Comoros francs in 2017 and 9,600m. Comoros francs in 2018, before recording a sharp drop to just 6,300m. Comoros francs in 2019, the year of Cyclone Kenneth, and a mere 3,900m. Comoros francs in 2020. Vanilla exports, after a steady climb from 1,300m. Comoros francs in 2016 to 3,600m. Comoros francs in 2017 and to 4,500m. Comoros francs the following year, fell back to 3,100m. Comoros francs in 2019 and just 2,000m. Comoros francs in 2020. However, exports of ylang-ylang followed a different trend: from 1,300m. Comoros francs in 2016 they edged up to 1,800m. Comoros francs the next year, slipped to 1,700m. Comoros francs in 2017, but then rebounded strongly in 2019 to reach 5,400m. Comoros francs, before sharply falling to just 1,900m. Comoros francs in 2020.

However, exports are massively outweighed by the flow of import shipments into the Comoros: these surged from 81,800m. Comoros francs in 2016 to 91,700m. Comoros francs in 2017 and then to 103,000m. Comoros francs in 2018 and to 105,700m. Comoros francs the next year, before settling back to 103,000m. Comoros francs in 2020. The increase value of fuel product imports, from just 16,300m. Comoros francs in 2016 to 29,700m. Comoros francs in 2020 has been a major contributing factor. Other major imports are meat and fish (totalling 17,500m. Comoros francs in 2020) and rice (12,700m. Comoros francs in 2020, vehicles and spare parts (11,000m. Comoros francs in the same year). With almost no industry, the Comoros is reliant on imports of cement (10,400m. Comoros francs in 2020) and iron, castings and steel (8,400m. Comoros francs in the same year).

The structural deficit in merchandise trade has been rising steadily, from 68,200m. Comoros francs in 2016 to 93,500m. Comoros francs by 2020. Yet the overall current account deficit is smaller, contracting from 19,600m. Comoros francs in 2016 to little more than one-half of that amount in 2017, before gradually expanding again, to 16,400m. Comoros francs (equivalent to 3.2% of GDP), in 2019 and then contracting once more, to just 10,300m. Comoros francs in 2020. This is mainly explained by the huge inflow of remittances from the 400,000 or so diaspora residents, including 130,000 Comorians in Mayotte and the 80,000-strong Comorian community in Marseille. In 2020 net private transfers to the Comoros amounted to 88,000m. Comoros francs. Remittance funds mainly finance family needs, food, education, health treatment, religious and family events and pilgrimages and home improvements. The BCC hopes that structures might be devised to encourage some of this funding to flow into purposes that are economically productive.

Statistical Survey

Source (unless otherwise stated): Banque Centrale des Comores, place de France, BP 405, Moroni; tel. 7731814; e-mail gdir-etudes@ banque-comores.km; internet www.banque-comores.km.

Note: Unless otherwise indicated, figures in this Statistical Survey exclude data for Mayotte.

AREA AND POPULATION

Area: 1,862 sq km (719 sq miles). *By Island:* Ngazidja (Grande-Comore) 1,146 sq km, Nzwani (Anjouan) 424 sq km, Mwali (Mohéli) 290 sq km.

Population: 575,660 at census of 1 September 2003; 758,316 (males 381,812, females 376,503) at census of 15 December 2017. *Mid-2022* (UN projection): 907,411 (Source: UN, *World Population Prospects: The 2019 Revision*). *By Island* (2017 census): Ngazidja (Grande-Comore) 379,367; Nzwani (Anjouan) 327,382; Mwali (Mohéli) 51,567.

Density (UN projection at mid-2022): 487.3 per sq km.

Population by Age and Sex ('000, UN projections at mid-2022): *0–14 years:* 349.0 (males 177.6, females 171.4); *15–64 years:* 528.9 (males 266.6, females 262.3); *65 years and over:* 29.5 (males 13.5, females 16.0); *Total* 907.4 (males 457.7, females 449.7). Source: UN, *World Population Prospects: The 2019 Revision.*

Principal Town (incl. suburbs, mid-2018, UN estimate): Moroni (capital) 62,351. Source: UN, *World Urbanization Prospects: The 2018 Revision.*

Births and Deaths (UN estimates, 2015–20): Average annual birth rate 32.1 per 1,000; Average annual death rate 7.3 per 1,000 (Source: UN, *World Population Prospects: The 2019 Revision*). *2017:* Crude birth rate 33.5; Crude death rate 6.1 (Source: African Development Bank).

Life Expectancy (years at birth, including Mayotte, estimates): 64.5 (males 62.8; females 66.3) in 2020. Source: World Bank, World Development Indicators database.

Economically Active Population ('000, FAO estimates at mid-2015): Agriculture, etc. 234; Total labour force 348. Source: FAO.

HEALTH AND WELFARE

Total Fertility Rate (children per woman, 2020): 4.1.

Under-5 Mortality Rate (per 1,000 live births, 2020): 61.3.

HIV/AIDS (% of persons aged 15–49, 2020): < 0.1.

COVID-19: Cumulative Confirmed Deaths (per 100,000 persons at 31 August 2022): 19.6.

COVID-19: Fully Vaccinated Population (% of total population at 26 July 2022): 46.5.

Physicians (per 1,000 head, 2016): 0.27.

Hospitals (per 100,000 head, 2013): 0.68.

Domestic Health Expenditure (2019): US $ per head (PPP): 27.1.

Domestic Health Expenditure (2019): % of GDP: 0.8.

Domestic Health Expenditure (2019): public (% of total current expenditure): 16.1.

Access to Improved Water Resources (% of persons, 2019): 80.

Access to Improved Sanitation Facilities (% of persons, 2019): 36.

Total Carbon Dioxide Emissions ('000 metric tons, 2018): 260.

Carbon Dioxide Emissions Per Head (metric tons, 2018): 0.3.

Human Development Index (2021): ranking: 156.

Human Development Index (2021): value: 0.558.

Note: For data on COVID-19 vaccinations, 'fully vaccinated' denotes receipt of all doses specified by approved vaccination regime (Sources: Johns Hopkins University and Our World in Data). Data on health expenditure refer to current general government expenditure in each case. For more information on sources and further definitions for all indicators, see Health and Welfare Statistics: Sources and Definitions section (europaworld.com/credits).

AGRICULTURE, ETC.

Principal Crops ('000 metric tons, 2020, FAO estimates): Bananas 46.6; Cassava (Manioc) 65.6; Cloves 6.8; Coconuts 84.9; Groundnuts, with shell 1.0; Maize 6.3; Potatoes 0.7; Rice, paddy 30.5; Sweet potatoes 7.2; Taro 11.0; Tomatoes 0.7; Yams 4.7. *Aggregate Production* ('000 metric tons, may include official, semi-official or estimated data, 2020): Total fruit (primary) 50.5; Total pulses 15.1; Total vegetables (primary) 5.3.

Livestock ('000 head, year ending September 2020, FAO estimates): Asses 5.6; Cattle 51.0; Chickens 545; Goats 121.2; Sheep 25.0.

Livestock Products (metric tons, 2020, FAO estimates): Cattle meat 1,216; Cows' milk 13,429; Chicken meat 585; Sheep and goat meat 475; Hen eggs 1,108.

Fishing ('000 metric tons, live weight of capture, 2020): Total catch 20.8 (Skipjack tuna 6.2; Yellowfin tuna 6.7).

Source: FAO.

INDUSTRY

Electrical Energy (production, million kWh, estimates): 98 in 2018; 108 in 2019; 130 in 2020 (Source: UN Energy Statistics Database).

FINANCE

Currency and Exchange Rates: 100 centimes = 1 Comoros franc. *Sterling, Dollar and Euro Equivalents* (31 May 2022): £1 sterling = 578.118 Comoros francs; US $1 = 459.225 Comoros francs; €1 = 491.968 Comoros francs; 1,000 Comoros francs = £1.73 = $2.18 = €2.03. *Average Exchange Rate* (Comoros francs per US $): 439.463 in 2019; 430.721 in 2020; 415.956 in 2021. Note: The Comoros franc was introduced in 1981, replacing (at par) the CFA franc. The fixed link to French currency was retained, with the exchange rate set at 1 French franc = 50 Comoros francs. This remained in effect until January 1994, when the Comoros franc was devalued by 33.3%, with the exchange rate adjusted to 1 French franc = 75 Comoros francs. This relationship to French currency remained in effect with the introduction of the euro on 1 January 1999. From that date, accordingly, a fixed exchange rate of €1 = 491.968 Comoros francs has been in operation.

Budget (million Comoros francs, 2021): *Revenue:* Tax revenue 45,695; Non-tax revenue 7,522; Other revenue 1,766; Total 54,983 (excluding grants received 36,353). *Expenditure:* Current expenditure 66,068 (Wages and salaries 29,115); Capital expenditure 37,920; Total 103,988.

International Reserves (US $ million at 31 December 2021): IMF special drawing rights 12.67; Gold (national valuation) 0.70; Reserve position in IMF 4.27; Foreign exchange 311.68; Total 329.32. Source: IMF, *International Financial Statistics*.

Money Supply (million Comoros francs at 31 December 2020): Currency outside depository corporations 41,592; Transferable deposits 69,277; Other deposits 52,678; *Broad money* 163,547. Source: IMF, *International Financial Statistics*.

Cost of Living (Consumer Price Index; base: 2010 = 100): All items 106.0 in 2013; 106.6 in 2014; 97.9 in 2015. Source: IMF, *International Financial Statistics*.

Gross Domestic Product (million Comoros francs at constant 2015 prices): 483,765 in 2018; 501,293 in 2019, 520,674 in 2020. Source: UN National Accounts Main Aggregates database.

Expenditure on the Gross Domestic Product (million Comoros francs at current prices, 2020): Government final consumption expenditure 53,008; Private final consumption expenditure 530,533; Gross fixed capital formation 66,984; Changes in inventories 0; *Total domestic expenditure* 650,525; Exports of goods and services 29,664; *Less* Imports of goods and services 148,077; *GDP in purchasers' values* 532,113. Source: UN National Accounts Main Aggregates database.

Gross Domestic Product by Economic Activity (million Comoros francs at current prices, 2020): Agriculture, hunting, forestry and fishing 195,289; Mining, manufacturing and utilities 40,168 (Manufacturing 34,110); Construction 4,375; Wholesale and retail trade, restaurants and hotels 101,379; Transport, storage and communications 33,540; Other activities 137,805; *Total gross value added* 512,556; Net taxes on products 19,557 (figure obtained as a residual); *GDP in purchasers' values* 532,113. Source: UN National Accounts Main Aggregates database.

Balance of Payments (million Comoros francs, 2020): Exports of goods f.o.b. 9,553; Imports of goods f.o.b. −103,035; *Trade balance* −93,482; Services (net) −24,931; *Balance on goods and services* −118,413; Income (net) 2,546; *Balance on goods, services and income* −115,867; Current transfers (net) 105,586; *Current balance* −10,281; Capital account (net) 14,979; Direct investment (net) 1,668; Other investment (net) 21,712; Reserve assets −29,539; *Overall balance* 1,460.

EXTERNAL TRADE

Principal Commodities (distribution by HS, US $ million, 2021): *Imports c.i.f.:* Live animals and animal products 48.2 (Meat and edible meat offal 37.5); Vegetables and vegetable products 44.1 (Cereals 34.1); Mineral products 174.3 (Mineral fuels, mineral oils and products of their distillation 148.7); Chemicals and related products 12.0; Iron and steel, other base metals and articles of base metal 18.5 (Iron and steel 12.4); Machinery and mechanical appliances; electrical equipment; parts thereof 35.8 (Electrical machinery and equipment and parts thereof 25.2); Vehicles, aircraft, vessels and associated transport equipment 36.4 (Vehicles other than railway or tramway rolling stock, and parts and accessories thereof 36.2); Miscellaneous manufactured articles 10.3; Total (incl. others) 442.9. *Exports f.o.b.:* Vegetables and vegetable products 18.5; Chemicals and related products 6.4; Iron and steel, other base metals and articles of base metal 3.3; Vehicles, aircraft, vessels and associated transport equipment 3.6 (Ships, boats and floating structures 3.0); Total (incl. others) 35.0 (Source: Trade Map-Trade Competitiveness Map, International Trade Centre, marketanalysis.intracen.org).

Principal Trading Partners (distribution by HS, US $ million, 2021): *Imports:* Belgium 8.8; China, People's Republic 28.3; France (incl. Monaco) 46.6; Hong Kong 6.9; India 19.1; Japan 7.7; Mauritius 6.5; Pakistan 31.8; Poland 9.1; Spain 4.7; Tanzania 7.2; Türkiye 12.5; United Arab Emirates 192.4; Viet Nam 12.8; Total (incl. others) 442.9. *Exports:* France (incl. Monaco) 7.0; Germany 1.7; India 8.6; Madagascar 1.6; Tanzania 7.5; USA 2.0; Total (incl. others) 35.0 (Source: Trade Map-Trade Competitiveness Map, International Trade Centre, marketanalysis.intracen.org).

TRANSPORT

Shipping: *Flag Registered Fleet* (at 31 December 2021): Number of vessels 335; Total displacement (grt) 1,303,749. Source: Lloyd's List Intelligence (www.bit.ly/LLintelligence).

Civil Aviation (traffic at Prince Said Ibrahim international airport, 1999): Passengers carried ('000) 130.4; Freight handled 1,183 metric tons.

TOURISM

Tourist Arrivals by Nationality (2020): France 5,041; Madagascar 119; Réunion 113; Tanzania 187; Total (incl. others) 6,959.

Receipts from Tourism (US $ million, excl. passenger transport): 50 in 2015; 60 in 2017; 76 in 2018.

Source: World Tourism Organization.

COMMUNICATIONS MEDIA

Telephones (2020): 7,573 main lines in use.

Mobile Telephone Subscriptions ('000, 2020): 472.8.

Broadband Subscriptions, Fixed ('000, 2020): 0.9.

Broadband Subscriptions, Mobile ('000, 2020): 279.8.

Internet Users (% of population, 2017, estimate): 8.5.

Source: International Telecommunication Union.

EDUCATION

Pre-primary (2017/18): 534 teachers; 15,175 pupils (males 7,607, females 7,568). Source: UNESCO Institute for Statistics.

Primary (2017/18 unless otherwise indicated): 348 schools (1998); 4,428 teachers; 124,240 pupils (males 63,265; females 60,975). Sources: UNESCO Institute for Statistics and IMF, *Comoros: Statistical Appendix* (August 2005).

Secondary (2017/18 unless otherwise indicated): *Teachers:* General education 8,870; Teacher-training 11 (1991/92); Vocational 20 (2004/05). *Pupils:* 73,695 (males 36,269, females 37,426). Sources: UNESCO Institute for Statistics and IMF, *Comoros: Statistical Appendix* (August 2005).

Post-secondary Vocational (2004/05): 51 teachers (males 41, females 10); 734 pupils (males 399, females 335). Source: UNESCO Institute for Statistics.

Tertiary (2013/14): 247 teachers; 6,499 pupils (males 3,635, females 2,864). Source: UNESCO Institute for Statistics.

Pupil-teacher Ratio (primary education, UNESCO estimate): 28.1 in 2017/18. Source: UNESCO Institute for Statistics.

Adult Literacy Rate: 58.8% (males 64.6%; females 53.0%) in 2018. Source: UNESCO Institute for Statistics.

Directory

The Constitution

In accordance with an agreement on national reconciliation, signed on 17 February 2001 by representatives of the Government, the separatist administration on Nzwani, opposition parties and civil society, a new Constitution was presented in August and approved by referendum on 23 December. Under the terms of the new Constitution, the country was renamed the Union of the Comoros, and each of the three islands, Ngazidja, Nzwani and Mwali, was to be granted partial autonomy and headed by a local government. The Union, governed by a central government, was to be headed by the President. The main provisions of the Constitution are summarized below.

PREAMBLE

The preamble affirms the will of the Comoran people to derive from the state religion, Islam, inspiration for the principles and laws that the state and its institutions govern; to guarantee the pursuit of a common future; to establish new institutions based on the rule of law, democracy and good governance, which guarantee an equal division of power between the Union and those islands that compose it; to adhere to the principles laid down by the Charters of the United Nations (UN), the Organization of African Unity (now the African Union) and the Organization of the Islamic Conference and by the Treaty of the League of Arab States; and to guarantee the rights of all citizens, without discrimination, in accordance with the UN Declaration of Human Rights and the African Charter of Human Rights.

The preamble guarantees solidarity between the Union and the islands, as well as between the islands themselves; equality among the islands and their inhabitants, regardless of race, origin, or religion; the right to freedom of expression, education, health and justice; the freedom and security of individuals; the inviolability of an individual's home or property; and the right of children to be protected against abandonment, exploitation and violence.

THE UNION OF THE COMOROS

The Comoros archipelago constitutes a republic. Sovereignty belongs to the people, and is exercised through their elected representatives or by the process of referendum. There is universal secret suffrage, which can be direct or indirect, for all citizens who are over the age of 18 years and in full possession of their civil and political rights. Political parties and groups operate freely, respecting national sovereignty, democracy and territorial integrity.

COMPETENCIES OF THE UNION AND THE ISLANDS

Each island freely administers its own affairs, while respecting the unity of the Union and its territorial integrity. Each island establishes its own fundamental laws, which must respect the Constitution. All Comorans within the Union have equal rights, freedoms and duties. All the islands are headed by an elected executive and assembly. The Union has ultimate authority over the individual islands and legislates on matters of religion, nationality, currency, foreign affairs, external defence and national identity. As regards those competencies shared by both the Union and the islands, the Union has ultimate jurisdiction only if the issue concerned affects more than one island, if the matter cannot be resolved by one island alone, or if the judicial, economic or social integrity of the Union may be compromised. The islands are responsible for those matters not covered by the Union, or by shared responsibility. The islands are financially autonomous.

THE UNION'S INSTITUTIONS

Executive Power

The President of the Union is the symbol of national unity. He or she is the guarantor of national independence, the unity of the Republic, the autonomy of the islands, territorial integrity and adherence to international agreements. He or she is the head of state and is responsible for external defence and security, foreign affairs, and negotiating and ratifying treaties.

The President appoints the members of the Government (ministers of the Union) and determines their respective portfolios. The composition of the Government must represent all of the islands equally.

Legislative Power

Legislative power is vested in the Assembly of the Union, which is composed of 33 deputies, elected for a period of five years. Nine of the deputies are selected by the islands' local assemblies (three deputies per island) and 24 are directly elected by universal suffrage. The Assembly of the Union sits for two sessions each year and, if necessary, for extraordinary sessions.

Judicial Power

Judicial power is independent of executive and legislative power. The President of the Union is the guarantor of the independence of the judicial system and is assisted by the Higher Council of the Magistracy. The Supreme Court is the highest ruling authority in judicial, administrative and fiscal matters, and its rulings are final and binding. An eight-member Constitutional Court was created in 2004.

THE HIGH COUNCIL

The High Council considers constitutional matters, oversees the results of elections and referendums, and guarantees basic human rights and civil liberties. Moreover, the High Council is responsible for ruling on any conflicts regarding the separate competencies of the Union and the islands. The President of the Union, the Vice-Presidents, the President of the Assembly of the Union, and the three island Governors each appoint one member to the High Council. Members are elected for a six-year mandate, renewable once; the President of the High Council is appointed by the members for a six-year term.

REVISION OF THE CONSTITUTION

The power to initiate constitutional revision is jointly vested in the President of the Union and the members of the Assembly of the Union. Constitutional revision must be approved by a majority of two-thirds of the deputies in the Assembly of the Union and by two-thirds of the members of the islands' local assemblies. However, the organizational structure of the Union cannot be revised, and any revision that may affect the unity and territorial boundaries of the Union is not permitted.

AMENDMENTS OF MAY 2009

At a referendum held on 16 May 2009 93.9% of those who voted approved changes to the Constitution, which took effect on 23 May. Most notably the presidential mandate was extended from four to five years, while the powers of the regional Governors (formerly Presidents) were significantly reduced.

AMENDMENTS OF JULY 2018

At a referendum held on 30 July 2018 92.7% of those who voted approved changes to the Constitution. The amendments included: ending the single-term limit for the presidency and allowing an individual to run for a maximum of two consecutive terms; rescinding the requirement for the presidency to rotate between the three main islands; giving the President the authority to abolish the vice-presidencies and the Constitutional Court, and to replace the latter body with a new Constitutional Chamber within the Supreme Court (the members of the Chamber would all be appointed by the President); and effectively abandoning the country's secularism by removing the clause specifying the separation of religion and state and explicitly proclaiming Sunni Islam as the state religion.

The Government

HEAD OF STATE

Federal President: Col Assoumani Azali (inaugurated 26 May 2016; re-elected 24 March 2019, took office 26 May).

REGIONAL GOVERNORS
(October 2022)

Mwali: Mohammed Saïd Fazul.
Ngazidja: Mhoudine Sitti Farouata.
Nzwani: Anissi Chamsidine.

GOVERNMENT OF THE UNION OF THE COMOROS
(October 2022)

Federal President: Col Assoumani Azali.

Minister of Maritime and Air Transport: Bianrifi Tharmidhi.

Minister of Agriculture, Fishing and the Environment, and of Tourism and Handicrafts, Government Spokesperson: Houmed M'Saidié.

Minister of Health, Solidarity, Social Protection and the Promotion of Gender: Loub Yacout Zaidou.

Minister of Foreign Affairs and International Co-operation, with responsibility for the Diaspora and the Francophonie: Dhoihir Dhoulkamal.

Minister of Justice, Islamic Affairs and the Civil Service, with responsibility for Human Rights, Transparency and Public Administration: Djae Ahamada Chanfi.

Minister of Finance, the Budget and the Banking Sector: Mze Abdou Mohamed Chanfiou.

Minister of the Economy, Industry and Investment, with responsibility for Economic Integration: Ahmed Ali Bazi.

Minister of Postal Services, Telecommunications and the Digital Economy: Kamalidini Souef.

Minister of the Interior, Information, Decentralization and Territorial Administration: Mahamoud Fakridine.

Minister of National Education, Teaching, Scientific Research and Professional Training and Integration: Dr Takiddine Youssouf.

Minister of Youth, Employment, Labour, Sport, the Arts and Culture: Dr Takiddine Youssouf.

Minister of Territorial Management and Urban Planning, with responsibility for Land Affairs and Land Transport: Afretane Yssoufa.

Minister of Energy, Water and Hydrocarbons: Ali Ibouroi.

Secretary-General of the Government: Dr Daniel Ali Bandar.

There were also two secretaries of state.

MINISTRIES

Office of the Head of State: Palais de Beit Salam, BP 521, Moroni; tel. 7744808; e-mail presidence@comorestelecom.km; internet www.beit-salam.km.

Ministry of Agriculture, Fishing and the Environment, and of Tourism and Handicrafts: Moroni.

Ministry of the Economy, Industry and Investment: Moroni.

Ministry of Energy, Water and Hydrocarbons.

Ministry of Finance, the Budget and the Banking Sector: 7 ave de l'Indépendance, BP 324, Moroni; tel. 7744140; e-mail contact@finances.gov.km; internet www.finances.gouv.km.

Ministry of Foreign Affairs and International Co-operation: rue de la Corniche, BP 428, Moroni; tel. 7644500; internet diplomatie-comores.org.

Ministry of Health, Solidarity, Social Protection and the Promotion of Gender: Moroni; internet fb.com/Ministère-de-la-Santé-Union-des-Comores-320950001695355.

Ministry of the Interior, Information, Decentralization and Territorial Administration: Moroni; internet fb.com/Miidiofficiel.

Ministry of Justice, Islamic Affairs and the Civil Service: BP 2028, Moroni; tel. 7744040; e-mail ministre@ministerejustice.gouv.km; internet www.ministerejustice.gouv.km.

Ministry of Maritime and Air Transport: Moroni.

Ministry of National Education, Teaching, Scientific Research and Professional Training and Integration: BP 73, Moroni; tel. 3444359; e-mail ministereeducation18@gmail.com.

Ministry of Postal Services, Telecommunications and the Digital Economy: BP 1315, Moroni; tel. 7734266.

Ministry of Youth, Employment, Labour, Sport, the Arts and Culture: Moroni; tel. 4554716; e-mail minijeunesportcom@gmail.com; internet fb.com/Min.JeunesseEmploiTravailSportArtCulture.

Ministry of Territorial Management and Urban Planning: Moroni.

President

Presidential Election, 24 March 2019

Candidate	Valid votes	% of valid votes
Col Assoumani Azali	83,078	59.05
Ahamada Mahamoudou	22,099	15.71
Mouigni Baraka Saïd Soilihi . . .	7,777	5.53
Soilihi Mohamed	5,023	3.57
Hamidou Karihla	3,944	2.80
Saïd Ibrahim Fahmi	3,677	2.61
Larifou Saïd	3,551	2.52
Hassane Hamadi Mgomri	3,093	2.20
Saïd Mohamed Achmet	3,013	2.14
Ibrahim Ali Mzimba	1,940	1.38
Saïd Jaffar El-Macelie	1,194	0.85
Saadi Salim	1,167	0.83
Ali Mhadji	1,140	0.81
Total	**140,696***	**100.00**

* Excluding 6,502 invalid votes.

Legislature

Assembly of the Union: BP 447, Moroni; tel. 7739252; e-mail secretariatpauc@gmail.com; internet assemblee-comores.com.

President: Moustadroine Abdou.

Elections, 19 January and 23 February 2020

Party	Seats
Convention pour le Renouveau des Comores . .	20
Parti Orange	2
Independents	2
Total	**24***

* A further nine seats were filled by nominees from the islands' local assemblies, each of which selected three members.

Election Commission

Commission Electorale Nationale Indépendante aux Comores (CENI): BP 385, Moroni; tel. 7636481; e-mail commissionelectoralecomores@gmail.com; internet fb.com/cenicomores; f. 2007 to succeed the Commission Nationale des Elections aux Comores; 13 mems; each island has a Commission Electorale Insulaire, consisting of 9 mems; Pres. (vacant).

Political Organizations

CHUMA (Islands' Fraternity and Unity Party): Moroni; f. 1985; Leader Saïd Ali Kemal.

Convention pour le Renouveau des Comores (CRC): f. 2002; Leader Col Assoumani Azali; Sec.-Gen. Yahya Mohamed Illiassa.

Faliki: Pres. Kaambi Roubani.

Front Démocratique (FD): BP 758, Moroni; tel. 7733603; internet fb.com/Front-Démocratique-des-Comores-268550343659117; f. 1982; Chair. Moustoifa Saïd Cheikh; Sec.-Gen. Mohamed Issimaila.

Front National pour la Justice (FNJ): Islamist fundamentalist orientation; Leader Ahmed Rachid.

Juwa (Sun): Immeuble Barwan, Quartier Oasis, Moroni; f. 2013; Leader Ahmed Abdallah Mohamed Sambi; Sec.-Gen. Ahmed El-Barwane.

Mouvement pour la République, l'Ouverture et l'Unité de l'Archipel des Comores (Mouroua) (Movement for the Republic, Openness and Unity of the Comoran Archipelago): Moroni; internet fb.com/hassani.mouroua; f. 2005; advocates institutional reform; Pres. Saïd Abbas Dahalani.

Parti Orange: Moroni; Pres. MOHAMED DAOUDOU.

Parti Social Démocrate des Comores (PSDC-Dudja): Ngazidja; f. 2008; Leader ABDOU SOULÉ ELBAK; Sec.-Gen. Dr SOULE AHAMADA.

Rassemblement pour une Alternative de Développement Harmonisé et Intégré (RADHI): Sec.-Gen. HOUMEDI M'SAIDIE.

Rassemblement Démocratique des Comores (RDC): Moroni; e-mail rdc@live.fr; internet fb.com/rdemocratiquecomores; Sec.-Gen. DJAÉ AHAMADA CHANFI.

Rassemblement pour une Initiative de Développement avec une Jeunesse Avertie (RIDJA): BP 1905, Moroni; tel. 7733356; f. 1999; Leader LARIFOU SAÏD; Sec.-Gen. ME BACO.

Union pour le Développement des Comores (UPDC): Moroni; Leader IKILILOU DHOININE.

Diplomatic Representation

EMBASSIES IN THE COMOROS

China, People's Republic: Coulée de Lave, C109, BP 442, Moroni; tel. 7632038; e-mail chinaemb_km@mfa.gov.cn; internet km .china-embassy.gov.cn; Ambassador HE YANJUN.

France: blvd de Strasbourg, BP 465, Moroni; tel. 7730615; e-mail cad .moroni-ambassade@diplomatie.gouv.fr; internet km.ambafrance .org; Ambassador SYLVAIN RIQUIER.

Libya: BP 1787, Moroni; tel. 7732910; Ambassador ABUBAKER ELFARAWI.

Saudi Arabia: Hotel Retaj, ave Ali Soilih, Moroni; tel. 7735261; e-mail coemb@mofa.gov.sa; internet embassies.mofa.gov.sa/sites/ Comoros; Ambassador ATALLAH BIN ZAYED BIN ZAYED.

South Africa: Voidjou, BP 2589, Moroni; tel. 7734783; e-mail moroni@dirco.gov.za; internet www.dirco.gov.za/comoros; Ambassador ANESHWAREN MAISTRY.

Sudan: Moroni; tel. 7739917; Ambassador (vacant).

Tanzania: Oasis, BP 8141, Moroni; tel. 7737859; e-mail moroni@nje .go.tz; internet www.km.tzembassy.go.tz; Ambassador PEREIRA AME SILIMA.

United Arab Emirates: Hotel Golden Tulip, Voidjou, Moroni; tel. 7733333; Ambassador SAEED MOHAMED MURSHID AL-MUQBALI.

Judicial System

Under the terms of the Constitution, the President is the guarantor of the independence of the judicial system, and is assisted by the Higher Council of the Magistracy. The highest ruling authority in judicial, administrative and fiscal matters is the Supreme Court, which comprises a President, a Vice-President, an Attorney-General, at least nine councillors, at least one law commissioner, a general advocate, a chief clerk and other clerks. The High Council considers constitutional matters. A Constitutional Court, comprising eight members was established in 2004. In April 2018, in view of the fact that the number of Constitutional Court judges had been reduced to just three, President Assoumani Azali suspended the Constitutional Court and transferred its competencies to the Supreme Court. Under the constitutional amendments endorsed by a referendum in July 2018, the President was given the authority to abolish the Constitutional Court, and to replace it with a new Constitutional Chamber within the Supreme Court (with the members of the Chamber all being appointed by the President).

Supreme Court: Route Coulée, Moroni; tel. 7744113; e-mail contact@coursupremecomores.km; internet www .coursupremecomores.km; f. 2011; Pres. CHEIKH SALIM SAÏD ATTOUMANI.

Religion

The majority of the population are Muslims, mostly Sunni.

ISLAM

Organisation Islamique des Comores: BP 596, Coulée, Moroni; tel. 7732071.

CHRISTIANITY

The Roman Catholic Church

Adherents comprise just 1% of the total population.

Office of Vicariate Apostolic of the Comoros: Mission Catholique, BP 46, Moroni; tel. 7631996; e-mail mcatholique@ comorestelecom.km; f. 1975; Vicar Apostolic Bishop CHARLES MAHUZA YAVA.

The Press

Al-Fajr: Moroni; tel. 7735859; e-mail laredaction@al-fajrquotidien .com; internet www.al-fajrquotidien.com; daily; privately owned; Editor-in-Chief KAMAL DINE BACAR ALI.

Al Watwan: Nagoudjou, BP 984, Moroni; tel. 3494448; e-mail contact@alwatwan.net; internet www.alwatwan.net; f. 1985; weekly; state-owned; Editor-in-Chief ABDALLAH MZEMBABA.

La Gazette des Comores: BP 2216, Moroni; tel. 7739121; e-mail contact@lagazettedescomores.com; internet www .lagazettedescomores.com; f. 1999; daily; Dir of Publication EL-HAD SAÏD OMAR.

Masiwa: Moroni; tel. 4271528; e-mail journal.masiwa@gmail.com; internet masiwa-comores.com; weekly; French; privately owned.

NEWS AGENCY

Agence Comorienne de Presse (HZK-Presse): BP 2216, Moroni; tel. 7739121; e-mail hzk_presse2@yahoo.fr; f. 2004; Dir EL-HAD SAÏD OMAR.

PRESS ASSOCIATION

Organisation Comorienne de la Presse Ecrite (OCPE): Moroni; f. 2004; Pres. ABOUBACAR MCHANGAMA.

Publishers

KomEdit: BP 535, Moroni; tel. 7738178; e-mail edition@komedit .com; internet www.komedit.net; f. 2000; general.

Broadcasting and Communications

TELECOMMUNICATIONS

Autorité Nationale de Régulation des TIC (ANRTIC): BP 6540, Moroni; tel. 7738761; e-mail contact@anrtic.km; internet www .anrtic.km; f. 2009; Dir-Gen. SAÏD MOUINOU AHAMADA.

Comores Télécom (Comtel): BP 7000, Moroni; tel. 7734469; e-mail directeur.general@comorestelecom.km; internet www .comorestelecom.km; formerly Société Nationale des Postes et des Télécommunications; post and telecommunications operations separated in 2004; also operates mobile telephone network (HURI); Dir-Gen. M'SA MLADJAWO.

Telma Comores: Oasis, BP 06, Moroni; tel. 4110277; internet www .telma.km; owned by Télécom Malagasy (Telma) of Madagascar; awarded Comoros' second telecommunications licence Oct. 2015, commenced operations Dec. 2016; Dir-Gen. CHRISTOPHE OLIVIER.

BROADCASTING

Office de la Radio Télévision des Comores (ORTC): Moroni; tel. 7732531; e-mail ortcvoidjou@yahoo.fr; internet www.ortc.fr; Comoran state broadcasting company; broadcasts Radio Comoros (f. 1960) and Télévision Nationale Comorienne (TNC, f. 2006); Dir-Gen. MOHAMED ABDOU MHADJI.

Radio-Télévision Anjouanaise (RTA): Mbouyoujou-Ouani, Nzwani; tel. 7710124; e-mail contact@rtanjouan.org; internet www .rtanjouan.org; f. 1997; television station f. 2003; owned by the Nzwani regional government; Dir (Radio) FAHARDINE ABDOULBAY; Dir (Television) AMIR ABDALLAH.

Radio

Radio Ocean Indien: Mkazi, BP 2398, Ngazidja; tel. 7731291; e-mail mroiviliy@rcm13.fr; internet www.radioceanindien.fr; govt-controlled; Dir-Gen. SAID YOUSSOUFALIBOUROI MROIVILI.

Television

Djabal TV: Iconi, BP 675, Moroni; tel. 7736767; e-mail contact@ djabaltv.com; internet www.djabaltv.com; f. 1993.

TV—SHA: Shashagnogo; tel. 7733636.

Finance

BANKING

Central Bank

Banque Centrale des Comores: pl. de France, BP 405, Moroni; tel. 7731814; e-mail secretariat@banque-comores.km; internet www

.banque-comores.km; f. 1981; bank of issue; Gov. Dr IMANI YOUNOUSSA.

Commercial Banks

Banque Fédérale de Commerce (BFC): pl. de France, BP 6274, Moroni; tel. 7738880; e-mail carte@bfcbanque.com; internet www .bfcbanque.com; f. 2009; Pres. SHEIKH SABAH JABER AL-MUBARAK AL-SABAH.

Banque pour l'Industrie et le Commerce—Comores (BIC): pl. de France, BP 175, Moroni; tel. 7730243; e-mail bic@bnpparibas.com; f. 1990; 51% owned by BNP Paribas-BDDI Participations (France); 34% state-owned; Dir-Gen. ANTOINE GANGA.

Exim Bank Comores: pl. de France, BP 03, Moroni; tel. 7739401; internet fb.com/eximbankKm; f. 2007; Dir GANESH S. KUMAR.

Savings Bank

Société Nationale des Postes et Services Financiers (SNPSF): BP 5000, Moroni; tel. 7734343; e-mail commercial@snpsf.com; internet www.snpsf.com; f. 2005; Pres. and Dir-Gen. NADJIB DHAKOINE.

Development Bank

Banque de Développement des Comores (BDC): pl. de France, BP 298, Moroni; tel. 7730818; e-mail info@bdevcom.net; internet www.bdevcom.net; f. 1982; provides loans, guarantees and equity participation for small- and medium-scale projects; Dir-Gen. GERVAIS ATTA; Sec.-Gen. NADHOIRI SAID ALI.

Trade and Industry

GOVERNMENT AGENCIES

Agence Nationale pour la Promotion des Investissements (ANPI): BP 8393, Moroni; tel. 7738569; e-mail contact@ investcomoros.net; internet investcomoros.net; f. 2009; Dir-Gen. NADJATI SODIKI.

Office National d'Importation et de Commercialisation du Riz (ONICOR): en face du Stade Baumer, Itsambouni, Moroni; tel. 7636117; internet fb.com/Onicor-Officiel; f. 1982; Dir-Gen. ABOUDOU MIROIDI.

Société de Développement de la Pêche Artisanale des Comores (SODEPAC): Moroni; state-operated agency overseeing fisheries development programme.

DEVELOPMENT ORGANIZATION

Institut National de Recherche pour l'Agriculture, la Pêche et l'Environnement (INRAPE): BP 289, Moroni; tel. 756005; e-mail contact@inrape.org; internet inrape.org; f. 1995; agricultural, fishing and environmental research.

CHAMBER OF COMMERCE

Union des Chambres de Commerce, d'Industrie et d'Agriculture des Comores: BP 763, Moroni; tel. 7730958; e-mail secretariat-sg@uccia-comores.com; internet www.uccia-comores .com; privatized in 1995; Pres. CHAMSOUDINE AHMED; Sec.-Gen. SAÏD ALI SAÏD ATTOUMAN.

EMPLOYERS' ORGANIZATION

Mouvement des Entreprises Comoriennes (MODEC): Rond-Point Salimamoud, derrière Immeuble ANPI, Moroni; tel. 3593161; e-mail contact@modec-km.com; internet www.modec-km.com; f. 2014 to replace the Fédération du Secteur Privé Comorien (FSPC) and the Organisation Patronale des Comores; represents the private sector; Pres. IRCHAD ABDALLAH.

UTILITIES

Société Nationale de l'Electricité des Comores (SONELEC): Volvolo, Moroni; tel. 3342148; internet fb.com/ Sonelec-328439231333758; f. 2019; Dir-Gen. SOILIHI MOHAMED DJOUNEID.

Société Nationale d'Exploitation et de Distribution des Eaux (SONEDE): BP 1762, Moroni; tel. 7732442; internet fb.com/profile .php?id=100057043826413; f. 2019; Dir-Gen. GOULAM SOUNDI.

Société d'Electricité d'Anjouan (EDA): BP 54, 98113 Mutsamudu, Nzwani; tel. 3321318; f. 2002; Dir-Gen. SAINDOU MALINDÉ.

STATE-OWNED ENTERPRISE

Société Comorienne des Hydrocarbures (SCH): blvd de Strasbourg, BP 28, Moroni; tel. 7730971; e-mail info@ comoreshydrocarbures.km; internet www.comoreshydrocarbures .km; imports petroleum products; Dir-Gen. OUMARA MGOMRI.

MAJOR COMPANIES

Cementis Comores: BP 196, Moroni; tel. 7732197; e-mail contact@ cementis.io; internet cementis.io/km; Dir-Gen. LOUIS MALIKITÉ.

Entreprise Générale de Terrassement (EGT): BP 576, Moroni; tel. 3332499; e-mail contact@egt-comores.com; internet www .egt-comores.com; earthworks; Man. SOIDIKI MOHAMED.

Komocash: rue du Port, Moroni; tel. 7632016; supermarket; Gen. Man. DOUDOU TAINAMOR.

Smartview Web Solutions: Batiment Mohamed Ahmed, rue de la Corniche, Moroni; tel. 7730027; e-mail infos@sv-websolutions.com; web development and design; Man. TOIMIMOU IBRAHIM.

Société d'Economie et de Développement de l'Archipel des Comores (SEDACO): BP 8066, Moroni; tel. 3527114; e-mail advisdijoux@hotmail.com.

Société de Production de Matériaux and de Construction (SCPMC): Moroni; tel. 3331814; e-mail scpmc@comorestelecom.km; Man. BEN DAROUECHE NAGUIB.

Vaniacom: BP 981, Moroni; tel. 7734424; e-mail contact.vaniacom@ gmail.com; internet vaniacom.com; f. 1999; cultivates and exports vanilla; Man. SITTI DJAOUHARIA CHIHABIDDIN.

TRADE UNIONS

Confédération des Travailleurs Comoriens (CTC): BP 1199, Moroni; tel. 7633439; e-mail syndicatctcomores@yahoo.fr; f. 1996; Sec.-Gen. SALIM SOULAIMANE; 5,000 mems.

Transport

SHIPPING

The port of Mutsamudu, on Nzwani, can accommodate vessels of up to 11 m draught. Goods from Europe are routed via Madagascar, and coastal vessels connect the Comoros with the east coast of Africa.

Agence Nationale des Affaires Maritimes (ANAM): BP 97, Moroni; tel. 7739779; e-mail info@comorosmaritime.org; internet www.comorosmaritime.org; Dir-Gen. SAID SALIM.

Autorité Portuaire des Comores (APC): Moroni; internet fb.com/ DE-LAUTORITE-PORTUAIRE-DES-CO-MORES-241021926045711; f. 2001; Pres. and Dir-Gen. MIRADJI ABDOU SAHER.

CIVIL AVIATION

The international airport is at Moroni-Hahaya on Ngazidja. Each of the other islands has a small airfield. International services are operated by Air Austral (Réunion), Air Mayotte, Air Tanzania, Sudan Airways, Kenya Airways, Precision Air (Tanzania) and Yemenia.

Agence Nationale de l'Aviation Civile et de la Météorologie (ANACM): Moroni; tel. 7730948; e-mail direction@anacm-comores .com; internet www.anacm-comores.com; f. 2008; Dir-Gen. NASSUR BEN ALI.

AB Aviation: Hadoudja, Moroni; tel. 7739570; e-mail contact@ flyabaviation.com; internet www.flyabaviation.com; f. 2013; provides domestic, inter-island services; Dir-Gen. AYAD BOURHANE.

Comores Aviation International: route Corniche, Moroni; tel. 7733400; e-mail contact@comorosaviation.com; f. 1999; twice-weekly charter flights between Moroni and Mayotte; Dir JEAN-MARC HEINTZ.

Tourism

Office National du Tourisme: blvd de Strasbourg, Moroni; tel. 7737816; e-mail communication.ontc@gmail.com; internet comorosdiscover.com; Dir RACHID MOHAMED.

Defence

The national army, the Armée Nationale de Développement, comprised about 1,100 men in the late 2010s. In December 1996 an agreement was ratified with France, which provided for the permanent presence of a French military contingent in the Comoros.

Chief of Staff of the Armée Nationale de Développement: Col YOUSSOUF IDJIHADI.

Education

Education is officially compulsory for 10 years between six and 16 years of age. Primary education begins at the age of six and lasts for six years. Secondary education, beginning at 12 years of age, lasts for seven years, comprising a first cycle of four years and a second of three years. According to estimates by the United Nations Educational, Scientific and Cultural Organization (UNESCO), enrolment at pre-primary level in 2017/18 was equivalent to 22% of children in the relevant age-group (males 21%; females 22%). In that year enrolment at primary schools included 82% of children in the relevant age-group (males 82%; females 82%), while enrolment at secondary schools was equivalent to 59% of children in the relevant age-group (males 58%; females 61%). Children may also receive a basic education through traditional Koranic schools, which are staffed by Comoran teachers. The Comoros' first university opened in Mkazi, on Ngazidja, in 2003. In 2015 public spending on education was equivalent to 13.3% of total government expenditure.

Bibliography

Abdelaziz, M. R. *Comores: Les institutions d'un état mort-né*. Paris, L'Harmattan, 2001.

Assoumani, S. *Comores: Chroniques des Rendez-vous Manqués*. Moissy-Cramayel, Coelacanthe, 2012.

Caminade, P. *Comores-Mayotte, une histoire néocoloniale*. Marseille, Agone, 2004.

Chamoussidine, M. *Comores: L'enclos ou une existence en dérive*. Moroni, KomÉdit, 2002.

Djohar, S. M. *Mémoires du président des Comores: quelques vérité's qui ne sauraient mourir*. Paris, L'Harmattan, 2012.

Mattoir, N. *Les Comores de 1975 à 1990: Une histoire politique mouvementée*. Paris, L'Harmattan, 2004.

Mmadi, A. *Pourquoi les Comores s'enfoncent-elles?* Grenoble, Thot, 2003.

Nassor Halifa, F. *Le séparatisme aux Comores: enjeux géopolitiques*. Moroni, Coelacanthe, 2010.

Newitt, M. *The Comoros Islands: Struggle against Dependency in the Indian Ocean*. Aldershot, Gower, 1985.

Saïd Abdillah, S. A. *Les Comores: Pour une indépendance financière et monétaire de l'archipel*, Paris, L'Harmattan, 2014.

Souef, M. *Les Comores en mouvement*. Levallois-Perret, De la lune, 2008.

Vérin, E., and P. *Histoire de la révolution comorienne: Décolonisation, idéologie et séisme social*. Paris, L'Harmattan, 1999.

Vermay, L. *Les Comores, un peuple bafoué: un archipel aux avatars coloniaux*. Paris, L'Harmattan, 2014.

THE DEMOCRATIC REPUBLIC OF THE CONGO

Physical and Social Geography

PIERRE GOUROU

PHYSICAL FEATURES

Covering an area of 2,344,885 sq km (905,365 sq miles), the Democratic Republic of the Congo (DRC, formerly Zaire) is bordered by the Republic of the Congo to the north-west, by the Central African Republic and South Sudan to the north, by Uganda, Rwanda, Burundi and Tanzania to the east, and by Zambia and Angola to the south. There is a short coastline at the outlet of the River Congo. The DRC is the largest country of sub-Saharan Africa. Despite its vast size, it lacks any particularly noteworthy points of relief, affording it a considerable natural advantage. Lying across the equator, the DRC has an equatorial climate in the whole of the central region. Average temperatures range from 26°C in the coastal and basin areas to 18°C in the mountainous regions. Rainfall is plentiful in all seasons. In the north the winter of the northern hemisphere is a dry season; in Katanga in the south, the winter of the southern hemisphere is dry. The only arid region (less than 800 mm of rain per annum) is an extremely small area on the bank of the lower Congo.

The basin of the River Congo forms the country's dominant geographical feature. This basin had a deep tectonic origin; the continental shelf of Africa had given way to form an immense hollow, which drew towards it the waters from the north (Ubangi), from the east (Uele, Arruwimi), and from the south (Lualaba—that is the upper branch of the River Congo, Kasaï, Kwango). The crystalline continental shelf levels out at the periphery into plateaux in Katanga and the Congo-Nile ridge. The most broken-up parts of this periphery can be found in the west, in Bas-Congo, where the river cuts the folds of a Pre-Cambrian chain by a 'powerful breach', and above all in the east. Here, as a result of the volcanic overflow from the Virunga, they are varied by an upheaval of the rift valleys (where Lakes Tanganyika, Kivu, Edward and Albert are located).

The climate is generally conducive to agriculture and forestry. Evergreen equatorial forest covers approximately 1m. sq km in the equatorial and sub-equatorial regions. In the north as in the south of this evergreen forest, tropical vegetation appears. Vast stretches from the north to the south are, probably as a result of frequent fires, covered by sparse forest land, where trees grow alongside grasses (*biombo* from east Africa), and savannah dotted with shrubs.

The natural resources of the DRC are immense: its climate is favourable to profitable agriculture; the forests, if rationally exploited, could yield excellent results; the abundance of water is useful to industry and agriculture; and finally, there is considerable mineral wealth. The network of waterways is naturally navigable. The Congo carries the second largest volume of water of any river in the world. With the average flow to the mouth being 40,000 cu m per second, there are enormous possibilities for hydroelectric power generation, some of which are being realized at Inga. Indeed, the potential hydroelectric resources are considerable in the whole of the Congo basin. The DRC's energy requirements are now met almost exclusively by hydroelectric power.

The major exports of the DRC derive from the exploitation of its mineral resources. Copper is mined in upper Katanga, as are other metals—tin, silver, uranium, cobalt, manganese and tungsten. Diamonds are found in Kasaï, and tin, columbite, etc., in the east, around Maniema. In addition, many other mineral resources await exploitation.

POPULATION

The DRC's population comprises numerous ethnic groups, which the external boundaries separate. The Kongo people are divided between the DRC, the Republic of the Congo and Angola; the Zande between the DRC and South Sudan; the Chokwe between the DRC and Angola; the Bemba between the DRC and Zambia; and the Alur between the DRC and Uganda. Even within its frontiers, the ethnic and linguistic geography of the DRC is highly diverse. The most numerous people are: the Kongo; the people of Kwangu-Kwilu, who are related to the Kongo; the Mongo, with their many subdivisions, who inhabit the Great Forest; the Luba, with their related groups the Lulua and Songe; the Bwaka; and the Zande. The majority speak Bantu languages, of which there are a great diversity. However, the north of the DRC belongs linguistically to South Sudan. The extreme linguistic variety of the DRC is maintained to some extent by the ability of the people to speak several languages, by the existence of 'intermediary' languages (a Kongo dialect, a Luba dialect, Swahili and Lingala) and by the use of French.

According to United Nations (UN) projections, the country's population was estimated at 95,240,782 at mid-2022. The average density of population is low (estimated by the UN to be 40.6 per sq km at mid-2022), and the population is unevenly distributed. The capital, Kinshasa, had 15,628,085 inhabitants at mid-2022, according to UN estimates, and is the principal urban centre. The second most important town, Mbuji-Mayi, had an estimated 2,765,002 inhabitants at mid-2022, while other major centres of population were Lubumbashi (2,695,331), Kananga (1,592,924) and Kisangani (1,366,342).

History

DUNCAN WOODSIDE

INTRODUCTION

The modern history of the Democratic Republic of the Congo (DRC) is one that has been consistently plagued by extraordinarily abusive elites, both nationally and at local levels. The atrocities and wholesale plunder committed during Belgian colonial rule resulted in the deaths of millions of people, and have increasingly been acknowledged by modern-day Belgium; King Philippe expressed his country's regret over the historic 'abuse and humiliation' when he visited the DRC in June 2022, although he stopped short of issuing an apology.

The vast size and ethnic diversity of the DRC, along with continued external manipulation by foreign powers attracted by the country's vast mineral wealth, exacerbated turmoil in the immediate post-colonial era, driven in part by Cold War competition between the USA and the Russian Federation. Viable post-colonial institutions therefore failed to take root and were quickly succeeded by a kleptocracy that continued for three decades and eventually collapsed under assault by insurgents backed by eastern neighbours Rwanda and Uganda.

The consequences of that external military intervention—which include subsequent damaging incursions of varying length, most notably during the Second Congo War (1998–2003), which has been dubbed 'Africa's World War'—are still playing out today in the resource-rich east of the country, where central government authority has never durably returned and multiple insurgent groups continue to vie for ascendancy. The consistent failure to consolidate central government authority has ensured that the DRC's vast mineral wealth—historically predicated largely on rubber, timber and copper, and subsequently extending to include cassiterite, lithium, gold and oil—has remained more of a curse than a blessing for most of the population in the vast east, with many people repeatedly displaced by violence and remaining dependent on humanitarian aid.

COLONIAL ERA AND INDEPENDENCE

In 1879 the Association Internationale du Congo, nominally a philanthropic venture under the control of King Léopold II of Belgium, began to establish a chain of trading stations along the River Congo. Increasing international demand for rubber led to a brutal economic exploitation of the territory now comprising the DRC, with atrocities inflicted on the indigenous population, and by 1908 millions of people, perhaps as many as one-third of the population, had been killed, mutilated or displaced. In that year, following sustained pressure from civil society groupings and churches, responsibility for the administration of the territory was transferred from the King to the Belgian Government, and the Congo became a Belgian colony, known as the Belgian Congo. The territory was covered with dense forest, and most major towns were built at mining installations, or at the geographical periphery, to facilitate the export of natural resources. The River Congo allowed for transport from the east of the country, and the sea port on the 37-km stretch of coast onto the Atlantic at Matadi provided a crucial exit point for resources to be taken to Europe. Under Belgian rule, African political activity in the Congo was forbidden, but following a violent demonstration in January 1959 organized by the Alliance des Ba-Kongo (ABAKO), under the leadership of Joseph Kasavubu, the Belgian Government, alarmed at the prospect of a prolonged colonial war, greatly accelerated the independence process for the territory. The country gained independence as the Republic of the Congo on 30 June 1960 with Kasavubu as head of state. Five days later the armed forces mutinied, and the United Nations (UN) subsequently dispatched troops to the region to maintain order. In September Kasavubu dismissed the Prime Minister, Patrice Lumumba, and later in that month government was assumed temporarily by Col (subsequently Marshal) Joseph-Désiré Mobutu. Mobutu returned power to Kasavubu in February 1961. A few days later Lumumba, who was suspected by

several Western governments of having pro-Communist influences, was murdered. In July 1964 Kasavubu appointed Moïse Tshombe, the former leader of a group supporting the secession of the Katangan region, as interim Prime Minister, pending elections, and in August the country was renamed the Democratic Republic of the Congo.

MOBUTU'S KLEPTOCRACY

Following elections held in March and April 1965, a power struggle developed between Tshombe and Kasavubu and in November Mobutu intervened again seizing power and proclaiming himself head of the 'Second Republic'. In 1970 Mobutu was elected unopposed as President. (From January 1972, as part of a national policy of 'authenticity', he became known as Mobutu Sese Seko.) In November 1970 elections to a new National Assembly (subsequently renamed the National Legislative Council, NLC) took place. In October 1971 the Democratic Republic of the Congo was renamed the Republic of Zaire, and one year later the Government of Zaire and the Executive Committee of the Mouvement Populaire de la Révolution (MPR), the sole legal political party, merged into the National Executive Council (NEC). Mobutu's prohibition of other political parties ensured that there were very few official avenues through which to challenge his rule or hold the leadership to account. Furthermore, Mobutu's system of governance ensured that resource distribution was commanded through the dual mechanism of favours and threats. Patrimonialism quickly became entrenched, while protection was afforded to those who supported his regime.

In March 1977, and again in May 1978, Katangan separatists invaded Zaire from Angola, taking much of Shaba (formerly Katanga) region; however, the separatists were repulsed on both occasions by the Zairean army, with armed support from a number of Western governments. The invasion of 1977 prompted Mobutu to introduce a series of political reforms. Nevertheless, he was the sole candidate at a presidential election in December, at which he was re-elected for a further seven-year term, while in August 1980 he assumed the new post of Chairman of the MPR.

During the 1980s Mobutu retreated to his palace at Gbadolité in the north-west of the country, while the national economy was essentially only sustained by wide-scale smuggling along trade routes that linked agricultural produce and mineral resources into regional and international sales. Mobutu's hitherto charismatic power waned as the security forces operated increasingly through violent force. Although Mobutu appointed some reconciled opponents of the Government to senior posts in state-owned enterprises, in the early 1990s a series of pillages, led by the army but involving civilian participation, destroyed what remained of the country's agricultural, industrial and commercial infrastructure. The violence was widely believed to have been orchestrated by the President, and the economy was left almost completely in ruins.

Under increasing domestic and international pressure, in April 1990 Mobutu announced that a plural political system would be introduced after a one-year transitional period; the Union pour la Démocratie et le Progrès Social (UDPS, formed in 1982 by opponents of the country's one-party system of government) was immediately granted legal status. At the same time Mobutu declared the inauguration of the 'Third Republic' and relinquished the post of Chairman of the MPR. In May 1990 Mobutu announced the imminent 'depoliticization' of the security forces and of the administration in general. In the following month he relinquished presidential control of the NEC and of foreign policy. However, in October the USA announced that it was to suspend military and economic aid to Zaire, following renewed allegations of human rights abuses by the Mobutu regime (and continued speculation that Mobutu had personally misappropriated funds).

In April 1991 Mobutu announced that a National Conference of government and opposition representatives would be convened at the end of that month to draft a new constitution, but the Conference was postponed, owing to widespread disturbances and anti-Government demonstrations in several parts of the country. Later that month Mobutu resumed the chairmanship of the MPR. The National Conference was convened in August, but was repeatedly suspended prompting renewed civil unrest and the dispatch of French and Belgian troops to Zaire to evacuate nationals of those countries. Despite the expiry of his mandate as President in December, Mobutu remained in office.

In April 1992 the National Conference reopened and declared its status to be sovereign and its decisions to be binding, although Mobutu reacted with cautious opposition to the erosion of his powers. In August the Conference elected Etienne Tshisekedi Wa Mulumba, the leader of the UDPS, as First State Commissioner. A 'transition act' adopted by the Conference afforded Tshisekedi a mandate to govern for 24 months, pending the promulgation of a new constitution that would curtail the powers of the President. Later that month Tshisekedi appointed a transitional 'Government of National Union', which included opponents of Mobutu.

The political interests of Tshisekedi and Mobutu clashed almost immediately when the President declared his intention to promote the adoption of a 'semi-presidential constitution', in opposition to the parliamentary system favoured by the Conference. In November 1992 the National Conference (without the participation of Mobutu's supporters) adopted a draft Constitution, which was vigorously opposed by Mobutu, who unsuccessfully attempted in early December to remove the Tshisekedi Government. In the same month the National Conference dissolved itself and was succeeded by a 453-member High Council of the Republic (HCR), headed by Archbishop Laurent Monsengwo Pasinya, which, as the supreme interim executive and legislative authority, was empowered to amend and adopt the new Constitution and to organize legislative and presidential elections.

At the same time Monsengwo declared that the report of a special commission, established by the Conference in order to examine allegations of corruption brought against Mobutu and his associates, would be considered by the HCR. Mobutu responded by ordering the suspension of both the HCR and the Government. Attempts by the presidential guard to obstruct the convening of the HCR ended, following the organization of a public rally in Kinshasa by Monsengwo and other members of the HCR. With support from the USA, Belgium and France, Monsengwo reiterated the HCR's recognition of Tshisekedi as head of Zaire's Government. In January 1993 the HCR declared Mobutu to be guilty of treason, on account of his mismanagement of state affairs, and threatened impeachment proceedings unless he recognized the legitimacy of the 'Government of National Union'. Later that month several Kinshasa-based units of the army rioted in protest against an attempt by the President to pay them with discredited banknotes. Order was eventually restored, but only after the deaths of some 65 people, and the intervention of French troops.

In early March 1993, in an attempt to reassert his political authority, Mobutu convened a special 'conclave' of political forces to debate the country's future. In mid-March the 'conclave' appointed Faustin Birindwa, a former UDPS member and adviser to Tshisekedi, as Prime Minister, charged with the formation of a 'Government of National Salvation'. The NLC was also revived to rival the HCR. While the Birindwa administration was denied widespread official international recognition, Tshisekedi became increasingly frustrated at the impotence of his own Government (the armed forces recommenced blocking access to the HCR) and the deteriorating stability of the country.

At the end of September 1993 an agreement was tentatively concluded between representatives of President Mobutu and of the principal opposition groups, providing for the adoption of a single constitutional text for the transitional period, which would be subject to approval by a national referendum. However, the opposing positions of the principal political parties became more firmly entrenched during November and December, and Mobutu was widely deemed to be fostering such

divisions within the political opposition through the extensive use of his personal patronage, since, despite the reduction of his formal political powers, he retained access to much of the country's capital and assets.

An ultimatum, issued to all political parties by President Mobutu in early January 1994, in an attempt to end the political impasse, resulted in the conclusion of an agreement to form a government of national reconciliation. Encouraged by the unexpected level of political support for the initiative, in mid-January Mobutu announced the dissolution of the HCR and the NLC, the dismissal of the Birindwa administration and the formation of a transitional legislature (to be known as the Haut Conseil de la République—Parlement de Transition, HCR—PT).

On 8 April 1994 the HCR—PT endorsed a new Transitional Constitution Act, reiterating the provisions of previous accords for the organization of a constitutional referendum and presidential and legislative elections, and defining the functions of transitional institutions during a 15-month period. The Government, to be accountable to the HCR—PT, was to assume some former powers of the President, including the control of the Central Bank and the security forces, while a new Prime Minister was to be appointed from opposition candidates.

n mid-June 1994 it was reported that Léon Kengo Wa Dondo had been elected Prime Minister by 322 votes to 133 in the HCR—PT. However, Kengo Wa Dondo's election was immediately denounced as illegitimate by the opposition and by the Speaker of the HCR—PT, Monsengwo Pasinya (who refused to endorse the actions of the legislature). A new transitional Government, announced on 6 July, was similarly rejected by the radical opposition.

By mid-1995 opposition frustration at the Government's failure to publish an electoral timetable had intensified. In July an anti-Government demonstration in the capital, organized by the Parti Lumumbiste Unifié (a group supporting the aims of the murdered former Prime Minister, Patrice Lumumba), led to violent clashes. A subsequent anti-Government protest in Kinshasa in August decried international endorsement of Kengo Wa Dondo as Prime Minister and urged his removal. In December opposition groups unanimously rejected a government offer to participate in a national coalition government and reiterated their demands for the prompt announcement of a timetable for multi-party elections.

THE 1996–97 WAR AND MOBUTU'S FALL

In the mid-1990s existing ethnic tensions in eastern Zaire were heightened by the inflow of an estimated 1m. Hutu refugees from Rwanda. The plight of the region's Zairean Tutsis (Banyamulenge) aroused international concern in late 1996, following reports of the organized persecution of Banyamulenge communities by elements of the Zairean security forces and by extremist Hutu refugees. In October Banyamulenge rebels launched a violent counter-offensive, allegedly supported by the Tutsi-dominated authorities in Rwanda and Burundi. Support for the rebels from dissidents of diverse ethnic origin increased during the month, and later in October the rebels announced the formation of the Alliance des Forces Démocratiques pour la Libération du Congo-Zaïre (AFDL), under the leadership of Laurent-Désiré Kabila (a known opponent of the Mobutu regime since the 1960s). AFDL forces made rapid territorial gains, and the movement soon gathered momentum, emerging as a national rebellion aimed at overthrowing Mobutu. In March 1997 the AFDL entered the strategically important northern town of Kisangani (which had served as the centre of military operations for the Government), and AFDL troops entering Lubumbashi on 9 April were welcomed as liberators, while government troops withdrew from the city. The Zairean Government continued to allege that the AFDL offensive was being supported by government troops from Rwanda, Uganda, Burundi and Angola, while the AFDL counter-claimed that the Zairean army was being augmented by white mercenary soldiers and by forces of the União Nacional para a Independência Total de Angola (UNITA).

Meanwhile, in August 1996 Mobutu had travelled to Switzerland to receive treatment for cancer. His absence contributed to the poor co-ordination of the Zairean Government's response to the AFDL, which by the end of November was in control of most of Kivu. In December Mobutu returned to Zaire, and reorganized the Government, but retained Kengo Wa Dondo as Prime Minister.

On 8 April 1997 Mobutu declared a national state of emergency, dissolving the Government and ordering the deployment of security forces throughout Kinshasa. Gen. Likulia Bolongo was appointed Prime Minister at the head of a new 28-member 'Government of National Salvation'. An arrest warrant was subsequently issued for Kengo Wa Dondo, who was alleged to have fled to Switzerland with funds from the national treasury.

After peace talks between Mobutu and Kabila ended in failure in May 1997, Kabila reiterated his intention to take the capital by force. On 16 May Mobutu left Kinshasa (travelling to Morocco, where he died in September), while many of his supporters and family fled across the border to Brazzaville. On 17 May AFDL troops entered Kinshasa, and Kabila declared himself President of the Democratic Republic of the Congo (the name in use during 1964–71), which swiftly gained international recognition. On 23 May Kabila formed a transitional Government dominated by members of the AFDL. Political parties were indefinitely banned, as were public demonstrations. On 28 May Kabila issued a constitutional decree (which was to remain in force pending the adoption of a new constitution), investing the President with virtually absolute legislative and executive power, as well as control over the armed forces and the treasury. On the following day Kabila was sworn in as President of the DRC, assuming full executive, legislative and military powers. Despite concern regarding the new administration's treatment of refugees, Kabila's assumption of power was well received internationally.

'AFRICA'S WORLD WAR' (1998–2003)

The Rwandan Patriotic Front (RPF) had been a pivotal actor in the AFDL's ousting of Mobutu, and after Kabila's accession to power the RPF's chief military strategist, Gen. James Kabarebe, became the DRC Army Chief of Staff. While initially extremely grateful for the military guidance provided by Kabarebe, Kabila's relations with his RPF supporters soured quickly. Kabila issued a decree expelling Rwandan troops from the country in July 1998, amid concerns that his initial popularity was being destroyed by the perception that the RPF was attempting to run the country as a client state and plundering its natural resources. This order precipitated a catastrophe; an anti-Kabila rebellion was launched in the east of the DRC, and Western governments advised their citizens to leave the country. The rebels advanced quickly and gained control of the Inga Dam, which supplies both electricity and water to Kinshasa and the Katanga mining region, enabling the rebels to interrupt power supplies. They also seized control of a number of towns in the west of the country. At that time the rebel forces announced that they had formed a political organization, the Rassemblement Congolais Démocratique (RCD), with the aim of introducing political democracy in the DRC. While Rwanda had initially denied accusations that it was supporting the rebels, it quickly became evident that the anti-Kabila insurgents had the support of both Rwanda and Uganda, and that Kabila was receiving support from Angola, Namibia and Zimbabwe.

In mid-August 1998, following a meeting of Ministers of Defence of the Southern African Development Community (SADC, which the DRC had joined in September 1997), Zimbabwean troops arrived in Kinshasa and secured the international airport. Although the Rwandan Government believed that it had confirmed the agreement of the Angolan administration in its plan to overthrow Kabila, Angolan troops had by the end of August 1998 defeated the RCD in the west of the country. The RCD, however, assisted by Rwandan and Ugandan troops, consolidated its control in the east, capturing Kisangani in late August and a series of smaller towns during September.

In the first major government counter-attack in eastern DRC, hundreds of Mai-Mai fighters and Rwandan Interahamwe (Hutu militia, who had become allied with DRC government forces, after participating in the genocide in Rwanda

in 1994) attacked Goma in September 1998, but were defeated by the RCD and Rwandan forces. Rwanda subsequently accused Kabila of rearming the Interahamwe (a claim later endorsed by the UN commission of inquiry into illicit trade in armaments in the Great Lakes region). Meanwhile, Kabila continued his efforts to enlist further support for his Government, which resulted in Chad temporarily deploying 2,000 troops in the DRC. The RCD continued its military offensive and in mid-October captured the strategic town of Kindu, which allowed RCD forces to advance into Kasaï and Katanga. Concerned at developments, the Presidents of Angola, Namibia and Zimbabwe increased their military deployment in the DRC. In November a new rebel group emerged called the Mouvement de Libération du Congo (MLC), led by Jean-Pierre Bemba Gombo. The MLC soon developed close ties with the Ugandan Government, while Rwanda remained committed to the RCD. In November 1998 the Rwandan Vice-President, Maj.-Gen. Paul Kagame, finally admitted publicly that Rwandan troops were fighting alongside the RCD.

Despite a number of regional initiatives to end the conflict in late 1998 and early 1999, no lasting ceasefire agreement was negotiated. However, some progress was made at a summit held in June 1999 in Lusaka, Zambia, after the rebels were accorded a place at the negotiations. Following this meeting, a ceasefire agreement was signed by the heads of state of the DRC, Angola, Namibia, Rwanda, Uganda and Zimbabwe on 10 July, by Bemba on 1 August and, following the resolution of a dispute, by the founding members of the RCD on 31 August. (Divisions had emerged within the RCD, which had split into several factions and had been engaged in serious fighting alongside their respective Rwandan and Ugandan supporters in Kisangani in mid-August, signalling the final collapse of Rwanda and Uganda's increasingly precarious relationship in the DRC, and the increased significance of control of the country's mineral and other resources for the combatant factions.) The agreement provided for an immediate ceasefire, the establishment of a Joint Military Commission (JMC), which was to investigate ceasefire violations and monitor the withdrawal of foreign troops, and the deployment of a UN peacekeeping force. In July a general amnesty for rebels within the DRC was announced, and in that month the JMC was formed, comprising representatives of the rebel groups and the six Lusaka accord signatories.

At the end of November 1999 the UN Security Council established the UN Mission in the Democratic Republic of the Congo (MONUC) to comprise some 5,000 troops, together with up to 500 military observers and liaison and technical assessment officers, with an initial mandate until March 2000. At a meeting of the UN Security Council in January 2000, regional heads of state expressed support for the rapid deployment of MONUC forces to assist with implementation of the Lusaka peace accord. In February the Security Council authorized the expansion of MONUC to number 5,537 personnel and the extension of its mandate to the end of August.

Recognizing that the 1999 ceasefire agreement had been widely ignored, participants at a meeting of the JMC in early April 2000 agreed to a new three-month ceasefire, which came into effect on 14 April. In early May, however, Ugandan and Rwandan forces again clashed in Kisangani, in violation of the ceasefire. After meeting a UN Security Council delegation, the Rwandan and Ugandan contingents agreed to the demilitarization of the town, and its transfer to the control of MONUC. In late June UN military personnel confirmed that Rwandan and Ugandan forces had withdrawn from the town, although some RCD members remained.

Meanwhile, in May 2000 Kabila announced the formation of a 300-member transitional Parliament, the delegates of which were selected by a committee supervised by the Ministry of the Interior and subsequently approved by presidential decree. In August Kabila inaugurated the new Parliament in Lubumbashi, and on the following day unilaterally declared the Lusaka Accord invalid.

DRC government forces captured the town of Pepa in October 2000 after launching an unexpected attack, at the same time as a regional summit on the DRC conflict convened in Maputo, Mozambique, where it was agreed that all combative forces should withdraw 15 km from their current positions. The

15-km withdrawal plan was taken up by another summit in Maputo later in the month, chaired by the South African President, Thabo Mbeki, who eventually secured agreement from all rebel forces. Strongly assisted by Rwandan troops, a major faction of the RCD (known as RCD—Goma) recaptured Pepa in mid-November, and then continued its counter-offensive, seizing Pweto on the Zambian border in early December. Thousands of DRC and Zimbabwean government forces were forced to abandon the town, with most fleeing to Zambia, together with at least 60,000 civilian refugees.

On 16 January 2001 Kabila was fatally injured by one of his bodyguards at his private residence in Kinshasa. (The circumstances of his death were initially unclear, but in May 2001 a report by the DRC state prosecutor claimed that the RCD factions and Rwandan and Ugandan troops had conspired to assassinate Kabila, with the aim of seizing power.) The transitional Parliament approved the nomination by the political leadership of Kabila's son, Joseph (hitherto Chief of Staff), as interim President.

Following his inauguration on 26 January 2001, Maj.-Gen. Joseph Kabila immediately engaged in international diplomatic efforts to resolve the conflict and urged rebel leaders to attend peace discussions with him. Following a meeting with Kabila in early February, Kagame (now President of Rwanda) announced that Rwandan troops would be withdrawn from Pweto on condition that control of the town was transferred to MONUC. However, the UN Security Council continued to demand that the DRC Government demonstrate its commitment to peace prior to the deployment of MONUC troops and insisted that the implementation of the disengagement plan agreed in December 2000 was essential to this end. At a meeting of the UN Security Council in February 2001, attended by representatives of the six countries and three rebel factions involved in the conflict, it was agreed that the 15-km withdrawal of forces was to commence by mid-March.

The withdrawal from positions of military engagement duly commenced in mid-March 2001, with the retreat from Pweto of the RCD—Goma faction and allied Rwandan troops. The first contingents of MONUC troops duly arrived in the DRC, and by the end of the month were stationed in the north-east of the country. At the beginning of April, however, the Ugandan-supported Forces pour la Libération du Congo (FLC), which had been formed earlier that year by breakaway members of the MLC and the RCD—Mouvement de Libération (RCD—ML), refused to proceed with the withdrawal from military positions near Kisangani until MONUC guaranteed security in the region. The deployment of MONUC troops in the east of the country was delayed, after the peacekeeping forces were prevented from entering Kisangani. In mid-April Kabila appointed a new, enlarged Cabinet, which included only four members of the previous administration; it was reported that he had removed all ministers opposed to negotiating a settlement with the rebels.

In April 2001 a UN Panel of Experts issued a report that accused Rwandan and Ugandan troops of systematic illegal exploitation of the DRC's mineral resources, and urged the Security Council to impose a trade embargo against the two countries. The Ugandan Government pledged to investigate the allegations of corruption (which implicated close members of the Ugandan President's family) and to complete the withdrawal of its forces from the DRC. In early May representatives of the DRC Government and the rebel factions, meeting in Lusaka under the aegis of the Organization of African Unity (OAU, now the African Union—AU), SADC and the UN, signed a declaration establishing the principles for an 'Inter-Congolese National Dialogue' (a formal process of national consultation, with the aim of reaching a permanent peace settlement). Later in May Kabila ended restrictions on political activity (thereby removing a major impediment to conducting the Inter-Congolese National Dialogue) and ordered the release of a number of detained human rights activists. In June the UN Security Council approved a resolution extending the mandate of MONUC until mid-2002; the Council welcomed the progress towards negotiating a peace settlement, but reiterated demands that all foreign forces complete their withdrawal from the country.

The Inter-Congolese National Dialogue commenced in the Ethiopian capital, Addis Ababa, in October 2001, and was reconvened in Sun City, South Africa, in February 2002. At the end of July a peace agreement was signed by Kabila and Kagame of Rwanda in Pretoria, South Africa. Under the accord, Kabila pledged to arrest and disarm the Interahamwe, while the Rwandan Government was to withdraw all troops from the country (thereby also providing for the integration of RCD—Goma into the peace process). President Robert Mugabe of Zimbabwe subsequently announced his intention to withdraw the remaining Zimbabwean troops supporting the DRC Government. In early September the DRC and Uganda reached an accord in the Angolan capital, Luanda, providing for the normalization of relations between the two countries, and the full withdrawal of Ugandan troops in the DRC. The Ugandan and Zimbabwean Governments then commenced the withdrawal of forces from the DRC (although the UN permitted some Ugandan troops provisionally to remain near Bunia to assist in the maintenance of security). Donors linked continued assistance to Rwanda to its troops leaving the DRC; at the end of September the withdrawal of Rwandan forces commenced, and in the following month it was announced that all 23,400 Rwandan troops had left the DRC.

After the convening of a peace conference in December 2002 in Pretoria, the DRC Government and rebels signed an extensive power-sharing agreement. Under the terms of this accord, Kabila was to remain as President, while four vice-presidential posts were to be allocated, respectively, to the incumbent Government, opposition parties, RCD—Goma and the MLC. The new transitional administration, to remain in power for a two-year period, was to comprise representatives of the Government, all three RCD factions, the MLC, the opposition and civil society.

In early 2003 further discussions regarding the transitional arrangements were conducted in Pretoria, following which agreement was reached on the adoption of a new constitution and the deployment of a neutral international force in the country, pending the establishment of a new national army (which would include former rebel combatants). The official adoption of the Constitution on 4 April was followed by Kabila's inauguration as interim head of state on 7 April. Despite the deployment of some 700 MONUC troops at Bunia to compensate for the Ugandan withdrawal, militia forces recaptured the town following intensive fighting. On 30 May the UN Security Council authorized the establishment of a 1,500-member Interim Emergency Multinational Force (IEMF), with a three-month mandate to restore order.

POST-WAR TRANSITION (2003–06)

On 29 June 2003 all former combatant groups finally signed an agreement on power-sharing in the future integrated transitional armed forces. This final stage in the peace process allowed Kabila on the following day to nominate a transitional Government, in which portfolios were divided between representatives of the former rebel factions, the incumbent administration, political opposition and civil society organizations. The four Vice-Presidents, who included Bemba and the new leader of RCD—Goma, Azarias Ruberwa, were inaugurated on 17 July and the new transitional Government was installed on 24 July. On 22 August the inaugural session of the new bicameral transitional Parliament was conducted; representation in the 500-member National Assembly and 120-member Senate was likewise divided between the former rebel groups, the Mai-Mai, the incumbent Government, political opposition and civil society. Meanwhile, in late July the UN Security Council approved a one-year extension of MONUC's mandate, and significantly increased the contingent's military strength. At the beginning of September the IEMF officially transferred control of the Ituri region to MONUC reinforcements.

In November 2003, following a final report by the Panel of Experts, the UN Security Council issued a statement condemning the widespread illicit exploitation of the DRC's natural resources, which had financed the activities of former combatant groups, and urged the imposition of state authority throughout the country. Some 85 companies, including many large multi-nationals, were cited as having contravened

Organisation for Economic Co-operation and Development regulations through their involvement in mining operations in the country.

At the end of May 2004 some 2,000 dissident troops, led by two former RCD—Goma commanders who had been integrated into the national army, attacked forces loyal to the Government deployed in Bukavu, and by 2 June the rebels had seized control of the town. The failure of MONUC troops to prevent the capture of Bukavu caused protest riots in Kinshasa and several other towns, in which 12 civilians were killed. The Rwandan Government denied accusations by Kabila that Rwandan troops had been redeployed on DRC territory, and troops loyal to Kabila succeeded in regaining control of the town by 9 June. Kabila subsequently dispatched some 10,000 troop reinforcements to the eastern border with Rwanda, prompting Kagame to warn that Rwanda would take any necessary measures to protect national security.

In August 2004 some 160 people who had fled from Bukavu in June to take refuge in Burundi, were massacred at a refugee camp at Gatumba, near the border with the DRC. A Burundian Hutu rebel faction, Forces Nationales de Libération, admitted responsibility for the atrocity; however, the Governments of Rwanda and Burundi believed that the Interahamwe militia operating within the DRC were also implicated and threatened to resume military engagement in the country. Ruberwa announced that RCD—Goma, in view of the collapse of the peace process, was to suspend participation in the transitional Government. At the end of August the Governments of the DRC, Uganda and Rwanda agreed to co-operate in the disarmament of the militia continuing to operate in the country, and at the beginning of September, following a visit by Mbeki to Kinshasa for mediation, Ruberwa announced that RCD—Goma had rejoined the Government.

At the beginning of December 2004, after MONUC troops confirmed the presence of Rwandan forces in the DRC, Kabila requested that the UN Security Council impose sanctions against Rwanda. MONUC announced that its troops were to establish a temporary 'buffer zone' between the factions engaged in conflict. A US-based humanitarian organization, the International Rescue Committee, estimated that some 3.8m. people had been killed in the DRC since August 1998. Elections due to be conducted by the end of June were postponed until later that year, prompting opposition protests (which were violently dispersed by the security forces), while Bemba threatened again to withdraw from the transitional administration in response to lack of progress in the peace process.

In early 2005 hopes rose of significant advances in tackling the root causes of insecurity that continued to plague the eastern provinces of Nord-Kivu, Sud-Kivu and Ituri. On 31 March Ignace Murwanashyaka, the leader of the Forces Démocratiques de Libération du Rwanda (FDLR), which comprised the Interahamwe and remnants of the national army that had been defeated in Rwanda's 1990–94 civil war, declared that his exiled Hutu rebel group was ready to 'abandon armed struggle' in favour of a 'political process'. The UN estimated that this group maintained 10,000 personnel in DRC in 2005 and it remained at the epicentre of insecurity in mineral-rich Kivu provinces. The insurgency not only threatened Congolese Tutsis, but also gave the post-genocide Rwandan regime a cloak of legitimacy for its own deeply destabilizing episodes of cross-border interference.

The FDLR's announcement followed talks facilitated by Sant'Egidio, a Christian community based in Italy. In what appeared to be a major step forward, Murwanashyaka also condemned Rwanda's 1994 genocide of Tutsis and moderate Hutus. His declaration was hailed as a 'turning point' for the region by the DRC Minister of Foreign Affairs and International Co-operation, Raymond Ramazani Baya. It was also welcomed by MONUC and by Richard Sezibera, Rwanda's presidential envoy to the Great Lakes region, albeit cautiously in the latter's case. In the following month MONUC announced that the number of militia fighters disarmed in Ituri province—a separate crucible of conflict to the Kivu provinces, largely centred on fighting between the Hema and Lendu ethnic groups—had exceeded 10,000, leaving only 3,000 further combatants to be disarmed therein.

However, while further progress was indeed made in Ituri, with Matata Wanaloki, the last of that region's warlords, signing a disarmament deal in November 2006, conflicts in other parts of the east remained intractable. Demobilization of the FDLR, which only signed up for 'voluntary disarmament' under the terms of the Sant'Egidio agreement, proved slow. In late June 2005, under pressure from Rwanda, Kabila announced that his Government had 'decided to implement immediately the forcible disarmament of foreign armed groups . . . particularly in the east'. However, the FDLR would remain a disruptive presence for many years, a presence that Kigali would consistently denounce as an unacceptable threat. This would set the stage for further Rwandan military interference in the DRC through Rwanda's support of Congolese Tutsi militia, repeatedly leaving Kigali and Kinshasa at loggerheads. Hundreds of Congolese Tutsis deserted from the national army in August 2005, and in the following month it emerged that international arrest warrants had been issued for Laurent Nkunda and Jules Mutebutsi, the renegade RCD—Goma commanders who had seized Bukavu briefly in 2004. UN helicopters and troops fired on Nkunda's men in the town of Sake, close to Goma, in late November 2006, as he began to step up a renewed Tutsi-led insurgency that would cast a shadow over daily lives in Nord-Kivu for much of the remainder of the decade.

Another insurgency, close to the town of Beni in Nord Kivu, to the north of both the FDLR's and Nkunda's rival spheres, also persisted—that of the ADF-Nalu, an Islamist group exiled from western Uganda since 1995. While MONUC in April 2005 disputed assertions by the Ugandan military that an aerial survey showed evidence of new field bases established by the ADF, by December of that year UN troops were engaged in a joint military offensive with the DRC's army against this outfit. Moreover, the presence of Joseph Kony's Lord's Resistance Army (LRA), another rebel group that originated in Uganda, which was infamous for forcing abducted boys into 'combat' that heavily involved atrocities against civilians, and forcing girls into sexual slavery, was detected in the DRC in September. Two months later the Congolese military alleged that a band of LRA rebels had again penetrated the country's borders, to operate in the north-eastern reaches of Garamba National Park. These intrusions came against a backdrop of peace talks between the rebels and the Ugandan Government in Southern Sudan. In the ensuing years marauding LRA bands resulted in significant displacement of the local population in the DRC's Kasaï Oriental province, following a collapse of peace efforts.

However, military activity by the FDLR, Congolese Tutsi rebels, the ADF and the LRA was relatively light throughout 2005 and most of 2006, and thus did not jeopardize the completion of the political transition. The National Assembly approved a draft of the new Constitution on 13 May 2005 by a margin of 348 to five. This legislation set a minimum age of 30 for presidential hopefuls and a maximum of two terms for any individual. The transitional authorities oversaw a referendum across several days in late December, at which the Constitution was approved by more than four-fifths of those who voted. Turnout was especially high in the Kivu provinces, although enthusiasm was less marked in Kinshasa and particularly Kasaï Occidental, where ex-Prime Minister and opposition heavyweight Tshisekedi had strong support. Tshisekedi had urged a boycott of the referendum, and his UDPS, sceptical of the post-war transition as an undue political platform for warlords, announced in April 2006 that it would boycott the forthcoming elections as well.

After repeated delays, the presidential poll eventually took place on 30 July 2006. Some 33 candidates contested the election, although Kabila and one of his transitional Vice-Presidents, Bemba, were always seen as the most serious contenders. Full preliminary results published by the Commission Electorale Indépendante on 20 August indicated that Kabila had secured 44.8% of the votes cast, well ahead of the 20.0% received by Bemba, but necessitating a run-off poll. Kabila fared extremely well in the east of the country, where he garnered over 90% of the vote, but was much less popular in the west.

The announcement of the preliminary results sparked clashes in Kinshasa between armed elements loyal to Kabila and Bemba, respectively. Military tanks fired on Bemba's residence on 21 August 2006 as he met with foreign diplomats, prompting MONUC to deploy a protective force to that location. A European Union (EU) peacekeeping force, created to help safeguard the electoral process, was also called into action on that day for the first time since its deployment. The clashes abated on 22 August, as Kabila ordered all soldiers to return to their barracks, after his own meeting with diplomats.

The new 500-seat parliament convened for the first time on 22 September 2006, with the distribution of seats reflecting the results of the first round of the presidential poll. Kabila's Alliance pour la Majorité Présidentielle (AMP) took more than 200 seats, falling short of an outright majority; however, Kabila was able to count on a majority in the legislature thanks to backing from defeated candidates and their blocs, notably Antoine Gizenga, who had served as Deputy Prime Minister during the Lumumba premiership, and Nzanga Mobutu, son of the erstwhile dictator.

In the run-off presidential poll, held on 29 November 2006, Kabila officially won 58.1% of the vote, while Bemba took 42.0%. Bemba initially rejected the results, but the Supreme Court formally declared Kabila the victor on 27 November, dismissing an MLC court challenge as 'unfounded'. Kabila's victory was widely hailed by members of the international community, including UN Secretary-General Kofi Annan, the US Government and the European Commission, and Bemba quickly accepted his defeat.

KABILA'S FIRST ELECTED TERM

Kabila was sworn in for his first elected presidential term on 6 December 2006. Nine days later he signed a security and development agreement in Nairobi, Kenya, along with 10 other regional leaders, underpinned by US $2,000m. in donor funding for the Great Lakes. Kabila declared that the 'crisis in the Congo ... is a page that we have turned', and identified 'consolidation of peace and stability' as the key priority for the DRC. He selected the 80-year-old Gizenga as Prime Minister.

However, a renewed deterioration in the security situation was evident during 2007–08, again mainly in the east of the country. The capital was also hit by a bout of intense, albeit very temporary, violence in late March 2007, when fighters loyal to Bemba clashed with the military, after the former Vice-President refused to integrate his men within the army. Several days of clashes left up to 500 people dead, according to the German embassy in Kinshasa, before Bemba announced that his troops would integrate after all. In July MONUC reported a worrying presence of soldiers dressed in badge-less Rwandan army uniforms among 'mixed brigades' of the national army—i.e. units comprising loyalists mixed with supposedly reintegrated members of Nkunda's militia—indicating a failure by the latter to integrate genuinely. Renewed armed clashes between Government loyalists and Nkunda's Congrès Nationale pour la Défense du Peuple (CNDP) intensified to the point where, in September, the DRC's foreign minister declared that the Government was facing 'a full-fledged situation of war' in Nord-Kivu. Desertions accelerated over the following year, and in October 2008 Nkunda's renegades closed in on the provincial capital, Goma. A collapse in the national army's ranks meant that MONUC was left as the last line of defence. Holland and Sweden suspended aid to the Rwandan Government, after the UN Panel of Experts accused Kigali of providing senior officers and arms to Nkunda's rebels.

Meanwhile, in the north-east of the DRC, the threat posed by the LRA increased. In December the Government, under pressure from Uganda, agreed to a short tripartite military offensive that included the Ugandan army and South Sudanese troops. That initiative prompted Human Rights Watch to warn of a 'history of grave abuses by every belligerent force operating in eastern Congo, including foreign armies'. The start of that offensive was quickly followed by LRA massacres during late 2008, which killed more than 400 people in the town of Faradje and a string of other settlements, according to the Christian charity Caritas Internationalis. Kony's fighters provoked enormous waves of displacement during 2009, and at least 290 people died in further massacres in December 2009, according to the UN.

In a highly surprising and risky bid to unwind the conflict dynamics in Nord-Kivu and Sud-Kivu, Kabila came to an agreement with Kagame that allowed the Rwanda Defence Force (RDF) across the border for a joint offensive against the FDLR, which commenced in late January 2009. In effect, Rwanda was given a green light to rout the Hutu extremists, in exchange for removing Nkunda from the battlefield and reining in the Congolese Tutsi insurgency. Rwanda captured Nkunda, who, according to analysts, had increasingly sought to enhance his status in Nord-Kivu independently of Kigali, almost immediately, and subsequently withdrew its troops in late February, in line with the bilateral agreement. On 23 March, a date that would assume major significance early in Kabila's second term, the DRC Government concluded a peace deal with the CNDP. However, while the RDF ensured that the fight was very much taken to the FDLR, the goal of eliminating it as a military force (which would have substantially reduced any future justification for Congolese Tutsi military units to operate independently of the DRC's army, let alone for Rwanda to support such units) was not achieved. The UN Panel of Experts stated in a draft report in late 2009 that attempts militarily to disarm the FDLR, which continued after Rwanda's withdrawal, had failed and action was needed to stem the Hutu extremists' transnational funding.

Kabila's extraordinary rapprochement with Rwanda also had repercussions for him in Kinshasa, notably including the loss of support of long-term ally Vital Kamerhe. The AMP heavyweight had reacted with public shock to Kabila inviting Rwandan troops across the border, and resigned as parliamentary Speaker in late March 2009, ahead of a bid for the presidency in 2011. Having boycotted the previous election in 2006, Tshisekedi also ran in the 2011 presidential poll, which was held on 28 November. According to the official results, Kabila won 49.0% of the vote, ahead of Tshisekedi with 32.3%. While the election proceedings were less volatile than in 2006, international observers were far more dubious about the integrity of the 2011 election, which even Kabila conceded was accompanied by 'mistakes' and 'errors'. The EU's observer mission and the US Government heavily criticized the conduct of the poll, while the Archbishop of Kinshasa, Cardinal Laurent Monsengwo, attested that the credibility of the poll was under 'serious question'. Although Kabila had fared very strongly in the east in the 2006 election, his popularity even there in 2011 was deeply undermined by the 2009 rapprochement with Rwanda, a neighbour regarded very unfavourably by much of the DRC's population, in view of the Second Congo War in particular.

However, while Tshisekedi contested the results, going so far as to organize a ceremony at which he was 'sworn in' by his allies, there was no descent into post-election violence. In early February 2012 the reconstituted Commission Electorale Nationale Indépendante (CENI) announced the parliamentary breakdown: Kabila's bloc secured a narrow majority, winning 260 out of the 500 seats, in a result that was 'compromised', according to US-based non-governmental organization The Carter Center.

KABILA'S PROTRACTED SECOND TERM

In a significant step forward for victims of militia violence, Thomas Lubanga, the leader of the Front Patriotique pour la Libération du Congo (FPLC—a Hema militia), was convicted by the International Criminal Court (ICC) on 14 March 2012 on charges of the war crimes of abducting children and forcing them to fight for the FPLC in Ituri between 1998 and 2003. He received a 14-year jail term in July 2012. In May 2014 Germain Katanga was convicted by the ICC on four counts of war crimes and one count of crimes against humanity for atrocities carried out in 2003 when leading the Force de Résistance Patriotique de l'Ituri, a Lendu militia. Both men were transferred by the ICC to Kinshasa in December 2015 to serve the remainder of their sentences.

Meanwhile, a further unravelling of the security situation took place in Nord-Kivu during 2012. In April Congolese Tutsi officers, this time led by Bosco Ntaganda, once again began to desert from the national army, setting in motion yet another incarnation of their insurgency in Nord-Kivu. The Mouvement du 23 Mars (commonly known as M23) was officially formed in early May, following the emergence of RCD—Goma and Nkunda's CNDP. (Ntaganda was also wanted by the ICC for war crimes allegedly committed during his membership of the FPLC.)

Once again, as military clashes between the insurgents and DRC Government loyalists escalated, the UN Panel of Experts repeatedly identified the Rwandan Government as the guiding force behind the insurgency, identifying Kabarebe, by then Rwanda's Minister of Defence, as playing a pivotal role. Despite donor pressure on the Rwandan Government steadily mounting, with the USA suspending military aid and the Netherlands part of its development aid in July, and the EU freezing new funding in September, the M23 insurgency claimed more and more territory, culminating in the rebels entering Goma on 20 November, helped by yet another collapse in the national army's defensive line. On the following day rebel spokesperson Vianney Kazarama declared that M23 would advance on Kinshasa. The insurgents, whom Rwanda consistently denied that it was supporting, occupied Goma until 29 November, and only withdrew following intensive international diplomacy. The threat posed by M23 subsequently petered out, aided in part by a split in its leadership, but also as a result of intense international pressure exerted on Rwanda by its traditional allies. Ntaganda entered the US embassy building in March 2013 and requested that he be transferred to The Hague, Netherlands, to face charges at the ICC. In November military pressure by the DRC army and a UN Intervention Brigade (which operated as part of the UN Organization Stabilization Mission in the Democratic Republic of Congo—MONUSCO—as MONUC had been renamed in July 2010) forced M23 to announce that it was ending its rebellion, following fighting that included shells landing on the Rwandan side of the border. Rwanda quickly voiced concern that the FDLR was moving into positions vacated by the vanquished M23. In December the Intervention Brigade and the DRC army launched yet another offensive against the FDLR in Nord-Kivu, focusing on the Masisi region.

In September 2016 a new rebellion emerged in the DRC, following the killing by security forces of a local chief, Jean-Prince Mpandi, at his residence in Kasa Central in August. Fighting between Mpandi's followers and forces aligned with the Government quickly spread to Kasa Oriental and Kasa Occidental, and killed more than 3,380 people, according to the Roman Catholic Church, while the UN estimated that around 1.4m. people were displaced.

In May 2016 the Constitutional Court voted to allow Kabila to stay in office beyond his constitutionally mandated two elected five-year terms and in October, a month after a crackdown by the security forces resulted in the deaths of dozens of protesters in the capital, his parliamentary bloc reached an agreement with minority factions that would keep him in office beyond his mandate. More than 50 people were killed during clashes in the capital in December, and the EU imposed sanctions on several Kabila loyalists, while the US expanded a list of individuals whom it had sanctioned in September. Human Rights Watch later alleged that former M23 personnel were drafted by the Government to suppress the protests. Kabila's mandate expired on 20 December. It would be two full years before the country eventually went to the polls, on 30 December 2018.

Under substantial international pressure to step down, in August 2018 Kabila finally named Emmanuel Ramazani Shadary—a former Minister of the Interior and Security, and a Kabila loyalist—as his preferred successor. In the same month the CENI announced that six candidates were prohibited from running, most notably including Bemba, who had been acquitted by the ICC on appeal in June 2018 of war crimes and crimes against humanity in the Central African Republic, and Moise Katumbi, a former Governor of Katanga province. Félix Tshisekedi, son of veteran opposition leader Etienne (who had died in 2017), was among the candidates approved by the CENI. Both Bemba and Katumbi declared their support for a common candidate, Martin Fayulu, a low-profile legislator, who emerged as the favourite according to

opinion polls in the run-up to the vote. Shortly prior to the election, in mid-December 2018, members of the Batende community killed at least 535 ethnic Banunu and caused widespread damage in Yumbi and two other settlements, following a dispute over the recent burial of a Banunu customary chief on land that was claimed by the Batende. The UN decried oversight by the authorities, and on the first anniversary of the massacre Human Rights Watch criticized the lack of progress made in holding the perpetrators accountable.

THE POST-KABILA ERA

The presidential election was held as scheduled on 30 December 2018. The CENI declared in early January 2019 that Tshisekedi had secured election with 38.6% of the vote, marginally ahead of Fayulu, who garnered 34.8%, while Shadary attracted 23.8%. However, Fayulu alleged an 'electoral coup', claiming that a secret deal had been brokered between Kabila and Tshisekedi. Fayulu's claim appeared to be corroborated by an investigation conducted by the Reuters news agency, which found that as initial results came in showing favoured successor Shadary trailing Fayulu by some margin, Kabila's camp had switched to a strategy of damage limitation. Calculating that a Tshisekedi presidency would erode his power base far less substantially than a Fayulu presidency, the Kabila camp established contacts with Tshisekedi, according to foreign diplomats and Congolese political sources who spoke to Reuters on condition of anonymity. The Catholic Church, drawing on data from its 40,000 observers, declared that the official result did not reflect the real outcome. Although it did not explicitly name Fayulu as the real winner, an internal report corroborated Fayulu's claim to have won around 60% of the vote, with most of the remainder shared relatively equally between Tshisekedi and Shadary. The *Financial Times* also reported that it was privy to data showing a clear win for Fayulu. However, both Kabila and Tshisekedi strenuously denied that they had colluded to cheat Fayulu out of victory.

Tshisekedi's elevated share of the presidential vote was also inconsistent with a weak legislative performance by his UDPS, which won only 32 out of 500 seats. Meanwhile, the legislative result for the pro-Kabila electoral coalition, which took more than 360 seats, was difficult to reconcile with what all stakeholders, including the CENI, acknowledged to be a weak performance by Shadary. Traditional donors initially held back from congratulating Tshisekedi, and the AU called on the DRC's Constitutional Court to suspend a declaration of the final results. However, the court certified the results on 20 January 2019, after dismissing Fayulu's calls for a recount. SADC quickly congratulated Tshisekedi on his confirmed victory, despite initially having supported calls for a recount, and most East African Presidents also conveyed their congratulations. However, others remained more guarded. The French Government stated that it had 'taken note' of the result, while the US Department of State urged the establishment of a broad-based government and urged electoral 'irregularities' to be addressed.

State television named Sylvestre Ilunga Ilunkamba, who had previously served as an economic adviser to Kabila, as Prime Minister in May 2019, but it was not until August that the composition of a coalition Government was finally announced by the new premier. The enduring influence of Kabila was again underscored; Kabila allies headed a number of ministries, including Aimé Ngoy Mukena as Minister of National Defence and War Veterans and José Sele Yalaghuli as Minister of Finance. Tshisekedi identified corruption, judicial reform and human rights issues as key priorities for his administration, but he was hampered initially by the need to maintain the favour of the old regime's loyalists.

The country's omnipresent security challenges also largely dictated the agenda. Even prior to his formation of the Government, Tshisekedi quickly sought to bolster relations with Rwandan President Kagame, despite the latter having been instrumental, as AU Chairman at that time, in the Union's decision to urge the DRC's Constitutional Court to suspend validation of the presidential results. In a deeply symbolic move in late March 2019, days ahead of the 25th anniversary of Rwanda's descent into genocide, Tshisekedi laid a wreath at the Kigali memorial, a move that predictably elicited significant domestic criticism. In September the DRC's military announced that it had killed FDLR military commander Sylvestre Mudacumara—who had been wanted by the ICC since 2012—during an operation in Rutshuru, Nord-Kivu. The news was warmly welcomed by Rwanda.

However, while it was clear that the FDLR's threat had waned considerably after two decades of intermittent military pressure, other armed groups gained in strength. North of the FDLR's sphere of operations in Nord-Kivu, the ADF had become the most lethal ongoing insurgency in the Kivu provinces, repeatedly perpetrating massacres around Beni territory. Meanwhile, clashes between Hema and Lendu in Ituri again escalated and on 30 June 2019 Tshisekedi announced a large-scale operation in Ituri, after 160 civilians were killed during the preceding three weeks.

Despite the security crises, Tshisekedi increasingly sought to emerge from Kabila's shadow. In July 2020 he reshuffled the leadership of the country's security apparatus, dismissing John Numbi as head of the military; however, he appointed Numbi's deputy, Gen. Gabriel Amisi Kumba (another Kabila appointee), as Numbi's successor. Later in the year Tshisekedi paved the way for a bigger reorganization, appointing three new judges to the Constitutional Court in October and preparing key political constituencies for a major onslaught against Kabila's influence. His carefully orchestrated campaign forced out the parliamentary Speaker, Jeanine Mabunda, in December and culminated in the overwhelming approval by the National Assembly of a vote of no confidence in Ilunga and his Government, by 367 votes to seven, in January 2020, facilitated in both cases by a substantial number of defections from Kabila's previously dominant legislative bloc. Following Ilunga's constitutionally mandated resignation, on 29 January, in February Tshisekedi selected one of his own allies, Jean-Michel Sama Lukonde Kyenge, a trained engineer who had served as Director-General of the state mining company La Générale des Carrières et des Mines (Gécamines) since June 2019, as the new Prime Minister.

Tshisekedi's successful extension of his authority in Kinshasa came even as the security situation in the east deteriorated even further. The militant Islamic State organization claimed responsibility for a pre-dawn prison break in Beni in which hundreds of prisoners escaped in October 2020. Islamic State had been claiming responsibility for attacks that the authorities attributed to the ADF from April 2019. In March 2021 the US Department of State designated the Islamic State of Iraq and Syria-Democratic Republic of the Congo (ISIS-DRC), which it identified as being synonymous with the ADF, as a foreign terrorist organization. In August the USA sent special forces at the DRC Government's request to bolster the national army's efforts to counter these insurgents, who by that time had dispersed out of Nord-Kivu and into Ituri. Tshisekedi had in May imposed a state of siege, effectively equating to martial law, in both Nord-Kivu and Ituri. However, the situation in Nord-Kivu continued to deteriorate, as M23 once again re-emerged as a destabilizing force, attacking army positions in November 2021 and in January 2022; more than 20 loyalist soldiers were killed during the latter assault, according to media reports citing civil society and security sources.

Clashes persisted throughout the first half of 2022, resulting in a significant re-escalation of tensions between the DRC and Rwanda. The DRC military accused its neighbour in June of dispatching 500 special forces personnel across the border to aid the rebels' campaign, during which the insurgents also launched an offensive against the town of Bunagana in the same month. A draft report by the UN Panel of Experts on the DRC leaked to media in August 2022 accused Rwanda of being illegitimately militarily active in the east from November 2021, including by sending 'troop reinforcements' for M23 missions. US Secretary of State Antony Blinken stated during a visit to Kigali that month that such support 'must cease', but in an address to the UN General Assembly the following month, Tshisekedi again accused Rwanda of providing 'massive support' to the rebels.

Economy

DUNCAN WOODSIDE

INTRODUCTION

The Democratic Republic of the Congo (DRC, formerly Zaire) is potentially one of the richest countries in the world, owing to extraordinary mineral wealth, which includes copper, cobalt, gold, cassiterite (a tin ore) and columbo-tantalite (coltan), spread across a country that is roughly equivalent in size to Western Europe. However, since independence from Belgium in 1960, economic performance has repeatedly flattered to deceive, owing mainly to high levels of corruption, institutional deficiencies and, perhaps above all, authoritarian traits displayed by consecutive leaders, which in turn have provoked several cycles of insurgency and collapses in formal economic activity.

Development was severely hindered by three decades of rule by Mobutu Sese Seko (formerly Joseph-Désiré Mobutu), who came to power in a coup in 1965 and established a kleptocracy, before being ousted by an insurgency that gathered pace in 1996 and overran the capital, Kinshasa, in 1997. His replacement, rebel leader Laurent-Désiré Kabila, had been propelled to power in large part thanks to military backing by an aggressively expansionist new regime in neighbouring Rwanda, but the new President quickly fell out with his erstwhile sponsors. This set in motion an even more damaging six-year conflict, the Second Congo War (1998–2003), which involved at least six countries in a scramble for the DRC's mineral resources. Kabila was assassinated by a bodyguard in January 2001 and succeeded by his son, Joseph, who concluded a peace deal with regional powers but continued to grapple with multiple insurgencies and oversaw little real

improvement in governance or socioeconomic indicators during a near 20-year tenure. The majority of the population continues to subsist in abject poverty, largely as a result of the failure on the part of the country's post-war leadership to build viable and respected institutions. Control of extractive wealth may have been wrested from the direct hands of neighbouring regimes, but it has been concentrated in the hands of a tiny domestic elite and in some resource-rich areas militias have continued to prevail, especially in the Kivu provinces, often allegedly with significant links to neighbouring countries. Alongside a re-escalation of fighting in the perennially unstable Kivu provinces, the Kasaï region emerged as a major crucible of conflict, with more than 1m. people displaced between August 2016 and May 2017 in a crisis triggered by the military assassinating a revered local leader.

The commercial elite under Joseph Kabila was increasingly centred around his family circle and favoured companies, according to an extensive investigation conducted by the media organization Bloomberg, which was published in December 2016. His refusal to step down from office when a second five-year electoral mandate expired that month was accompanied by a flurry of sanctions against senior military and civilian figures, imposed by the European Union (EU) and the USA, two erstwhile key donors. Kabila's hold on power beyond the expiry of his mandate in late 2016 increased tensions and provoked militancy to the extent that a new period of civil war, dwarfing the localized but highly damaging rebellions that had been largely neutralized during 2006–13, had appeared to be a very real risk. The presidential poll, which eventually took place two years after Kabila's second term had been due to expire, resulted in an official victory for Félix Tshisekedi, the son of a former Prime Minister (under President Mobutu) and later a longstanding opponent of the Kabila dynasty, Etienne Tshisekedi Wa Mulumba. A wide range of independent bodies, including the Catholic Church, which was able to call on a local network of around 40,000 election observers, were adamant that another opposition candidate, Martin Fayulu, was the true victor and there were widespread allegations that Kabila's entourage had engineered a clandestine deal with Tshisekedi involving guarantees that their vast business network would remain unimpeded. However, Tshisekedi asserted his independence from Kabila's legislative bloc as his term progressed, allowing the country to rebuild bridges with Western donors. Emblematic of the shifting politico-commercial winds, the Congolese Business Federation, the principal private business lobby, replaced its Chairman in December 2020. Albert Yuma, a Kabila loyalist who had held the position for 15 years and also held the chairmanship of the state mining company Générale des Carrières et des Mines (Gécamines), made way for Dieudonne Kasembo, a logistics executive.

During 2020 the DRC benefited from multilateral support arranged for a host of developing countries to help cope with the novel coronavirus disease (COVID-19) pandemic and associated lockdowns, in a context where the International Monetary Fund (IMF) had just months earlier—in December 2019—restored bilateral relations for the first time in seven years. On top of an existing US \$368m. credit facility that came into force in late 2019, the IMF Executive Board in April 2020 approved a \$363.3m. disbursement to the DRC from a Rapid Credit Facility (RCF) in direct response to the pandemic, in order to help the country cope with the 'severe economic shock' and 'urgent' balance of payments needs.

The DRC's overall macroeconomic performance was less severely affected by the pandemic in 2020 than that of many countries, especially fellow developing nations with high debt burdens, even if the country's external accounts remained highly precarious. The economy managed to maintain positive gross domestic product (GDP) growth in 2020, expanding at a rate of 1.7% in real terms, according to the IMF. Crucial support came during the second half of the year from rising commodity prices as well as increased production, notably of copper and cobalt, a highly supportive trend that also continued into 2021, as copper prices traded at record highs, above US \$10,000 dollars per metric ton in May of that year. By December the IMF was noting a strong economic recovery, an assessment that gained further traction after the Fund sent a team to Kinshasa in March 2022 to discuss policy priorities with officials at the Banque Centrale du Congo (BCC) and the Ministry of Finance. Real GDP growth of 5.7% was recorded in 2021, driven by mining and the service sector. According to the IMF, the current account deficit as a percentage of GDP more than halved in 2021 year-on-year, while the rate of inflation stood at 5.3% at the end of the year, a dramatic fall from 15.8% in December 2020. Equally notably, the country's gross foreign exchange reserves recovered from just \$800m. at the end of 2020 to \$3,300m. in October 2021. The significant easing in inflation and the improved external position gave the BCC latitude to reduce the cost of borrowing and it duly reduced the discount rate, its principal interest rate, by a total of 10 percentage points during 2021, from 18.5% to 8.5%, in three separate rate cuts, and further reduced the rate to 7.5% with effect from January 2022. The IMF forecast real GDP growth of 6.1% and a modest current account surplus for 2022. However, it warned of downside risks stemming from the Russian invasion of Ukraine in February, notably the impact of that conflict on already elevated global food and oil prices, with the latter of particular concern for the DRC's fiscal position owing to fuel subsidies.

There were several important regional developments in 2022. In February the International Court of Justice (ICJ) ordered Uganda to pay US \$325m. in reparations to the DRC, with five instalments of \$65m., for its military occupation and exploitation of parts of Ituri province during the Second Congo War of 1998–2003. While the amount of reparations was substantially below the \$11,000m. sought by the DRC, and came some 17 years after the ICJ had first adjudged Uganda to have violated international law, the ruling was still opposed by

the Ugandan Ministry of Foreign Affairs, which denounced it as 'unfair and wrong'. On 29 March the East African Community (EAC) admitted the DRC as its seventh partner state, despite rising tensions between the DRC and Rwanda, an existing member of the regional common market. Those tensions centred on the resurgence of the Tutsi-led Mouvement du 23 Mars (M23) rebel group, which had wrought havoc in mineral-rich Nord-Kivu in 2012, when it was, according to UN experts, heavily backed by the Rwandan Government. The re-emergence of the group was symptomatic of the DRC Government's consistent failure to exert its authority over the Kivu provinces, whose extraordinary riches not only remained largely beyond the reach of the public purse, but also continued significantly to finance forces that stifled any hope of the national economy and its beleaguered population achieving its full potential.

MINERAL CERTIFICATION AND REGULATION

The illegal trade in minerals, particularly in the restive Nord-Kivu and Sud-Kivu provinces, began in earnest in 1996, initially when the armies of neighbouring Rwanda (and later Uganda) invaded. Although the Rwandan and Ugandan armies withdrew in 2002, their exit created a vacuum in terms of control over much of eastern DRC's mineral trade. This enabled a number of foreign and domestic rebel groups to extend their own influence over mining activity.

Although the Kimberley Process Certification Scheme (initiated by a United Nations—UN—General Assembly resolution in 2000, before a number of Southern African producing states began to enforce the scheme in 2003) represented an attempt to scrutinize and halt the trade in 'conflict diamonds', definitive progress in confronting the trade in other conflict-tarnished minerals has been much slower. However, major international powers eventually agreed that substantive action was required to break the link between conflict and (non-diamond) mineral resources in eastern DRC. An initial key development was a UN Security Council resolution adopted in 2005, which made companies buying minerals sourced from illegal armed groups in the DRC liable to sanctions. A UN Panel of Experts was commissioned to report on the activity of armed groups in eastern DRC and the dynamics of the illicit mineral trade (and remained in operation in the 2020s). It presented evidence in 2008–09 that European entities had been buying produce either mined or traded by one or more of the various armed groups. This resulted in two European companies withdrawing from activity in the DRC.

In August 2012 the USA's financial regulator, the Securities and Exchange Commission (SEC), adopted a regulatory policy on conflict minerals. The policy obliged companies listed in the USA that use gold, tantalum, tin or tungsten to undertake a 'reasonable country of origin inquiry', in order to ascertain whether the mineral content was derived from the DRC or its neighbours, with a requirement that the findings be publicly disclosed. If a company found that it was sourcing minerals from the DRC or a neighbouring nation, it would then be obliged to carry out an evaluation of its supply chain, with the findings conveyed in a Conflict Minerals Report to the SEC. However, pressure from manufacturing lobbyists ensured that there were caveats to these requirements, including the scheme being restricted to manufacturers (with retailers and miners exempted) and an initial two-year stay of execution on reporting obligations.

Also in August 2012—as a rebellion by M23 in Nord-Kivu gained momentum—the DRC Government addressed a letter to the SEC asking for an outright ban by the USA on the import of minerals from Rwanda, owing to the latter's alleged involvement in the smuggling of minerals through rebel-controlled parts of the Kivu provinces. However, the SEC did not possess the mandate to impose a trade embargo. Tagging exercises were then undertaken in Nord-Kivu, facilitated by the national army's apparently comprehensive defeat of M23 in late 2013, in a context where the USA and the United Kingdom, traditionally two staunch allies of the Rwandan Government, exerted huge pressure on Rwanda to withdraw cross-border support for the rebels. By April 2014 a total of 17 mining locations in the province had been validated by the International Tin Research

Institute, the country's tin regulator, on the basis of a 'traffic light' code: red for output sourced from war-affected, or militia-controlled, areas; yellow for produce of indeterminate origin; and green for supplies deemed conflict free. The latter category is tagged with barcodes denoting the exact origin. However, the efficacy of this initiative has been questioned by campaign groups, which again raised concerns that the initiative did not take account of illegal groups taxing supplies en route from the point of extraction to the point of export.

US-listed companies were required to comply by 2 June 2014 with the disclosure requirements under Section 1502 of the Dodd-Frank Act—i.e. whether they used conflict minerals sourced from the DRC or adjacent countries. Despite the generous nature of the disclosure requirements (for the first two years firms were able to state merely that they were unable to determine whether their products originated from conflict-affected areas), industry lobbyists were buoyed by a ruling by a US appellate court in April 2014 that the obligation for companies to state whether their products were 'conflict free' violated their rights to free speech.

The election of Donald Trump as US President in November 2016 brought the prospect of a reversal of 'conflict minerals' legislation, as part of a broader rollback of regulations governing the conduct and responsibilities of the US Government and firms from that country. The Responsible Sourcing Network (RSN), an organization that seeks to rate listed companies' compliance with disclosures set out under Section 1502 of the Dodd-Frank Act (on a scale of one to 100), noted in its 2017 report an average 7.0 drop year-on-year in adherence by a sample of companies. 'Some of the shortfall may be attributed to uncertainty since the Trump administration and other legislators have alluded to deregulating Section 1502 of the Dodd-Frank Act', RSN concluded. The organization identified another fall in 2019, to an average score among its sample of 40.1, from 40.3 in 2018.

Meanwhile, the EU has continued to advocate a more interventionist policy. In April 2017 the European Council formally adopted the European Parliament's regulatory policy on conflict minerals, which would apply to direct importers of gold, tantalum, tin and tungsten (as well as products containing these minerals) and oblige such parties to conduct supply chain due diligence in order to prove that they were not funding armed conflict. The legislation, applying across the EU and extending to smelters and refiners, came into effect from 1 January 2021.

In a letter dated 5 December 2018, a coalition of 13 non-governmental organizations (NGOs), including Global Witness and Amnesty International, welcomed an initiative announced by the London Metals Exchange (LME) in October 2018 that would expand listing criteria to incorporate responsible sourcing of minerals, but took issue with a number of elements of the bourse's proposals. The NGOs' letter proposed that risk assessments be consistent across the mining of all metals, and that the LME fully adopt the Organisation for Economic Co-operation and Development's (OECD) Guidelines for Multinational Enterprises on due diligence for supply chains, together with the UN Guiding Principles on Business and Human Rights, neither of which were referenced in the exchange's initial proposals. An article in the *Financial Times* in April 2019 reported that the LME would require producers to take a 'red flag' test, which would allow the LME to designate which brands posed a risk, with those deemed most high risk then being compelled to adopt OECD-aligned sourcing standards by the end of 2022. However, despite the urgings of NGOs and extended consultations, the LME chose not to fully adopt the OECD Guidelines and UN Guiding Principles for all producers listing on its exchange. In September 2019 the Reuters news agency reported that the LME had pushed back its deadline from 2022 to 2025 for barring metal trading on its exchange that failed to meet corruption and labour standards. Some sources pointed to a lack of Chinese legislation, experience and knowledge in sourcing conflict-free minerals as a key factor behind slippage on introducing guidelines, in a context where the People's Republic of China remained a key buyer but without the existing framework of the EU (in place since 2017).

Copper and Cobalt

Copper production has traditionally been of great significance to the DRC economy through the state-run Gécamines. The DRC accounted for 70.6% of global cobalt output in 2021. The US Geological Survey (USGS) estimated that the DRC's total cobalt reserves totalled 3.5m. metric tons in 2021—representing just over 46% of the world's identified reserves. China is the principal buyer of cobalt, with global demand fluctuating in line with the performance of the Chinese economy. Demand for cobalt in the late 2010s was boosted by its use in lithium-cobalt batteries, which are used to power electric vehicles, an increasingly popular alternative to purely petrol- or diesel-powered cars, especially in the developed world. According to the IMF, copper and cobalt accounted for 72% and 16%, respectively, of the DRC's total goods exports in 2021.

Copper output in the DRC in 2020 reached 1.6m. metric tons, a rise of 11.8% compared with the previous year, according to the central bank, while cobalt production rose 10% year-on-year to 85,855 tons. The rise in output came despite Glencore recording a decline in production across the year. Although Glencore announced in September that it was scaling up output at 75%-owned subsidiary Kamoto Copper Company (KCC) to 270,000 tons for 2020 as a whole, its overall output was affected by the continued closure of the Mutanda mine since November 2019. Output by other operators in the DRC buoyed overall production in 2020, helped by a recovery of prices over the course of the year. Copper production rose further in 2021, to an estimated 1.8m. tons, while cobalt output reached an estimated 120,000 tons, with a further rise forecast for 2022, to be bolstered by anticipated production of 10,000 tons at Mutanda.

Since the official withdrawal of foreign armies from the DRC in 2002, Western companies and Chinese businesses have engaged significantly in the copper and cobalt sector. One of the most important developments has been China's decision to invest some US $9,000m. in exchange for enhanced access to the mining sector. In May 2008 the DRC's Assemblée Nationale (National Assembly) gave preliminary approval to an agreement that provided for a $3,000m. loan to revive the mining industry and a $6,000m. facility to develop other infrastructure, including 9,000 km of new roads and railway tracks, hospitals, housing, two dams and numerous schools. A further condition of the agreement was that 80% of the labour for the projects would be provided by Congolese nationals. In exchange, China would receive a 68% share in a venture between Gécamines and the China Railway Engineering Company and Sinohydro Corporation. China would therefore gain access to the rights for more than 10m. metric tons of copper and 600,000 tons of cobalt.

In May 2016 Freeport-McMoRan announced that it had reached a US $2,650m. agreement with China Molybdenum Co (CMOC) to sell its 56% stake in the Tenke Fungurume mine, which reportedly holds the world's largest reserves of unexploited copper and cobalt. In 2019 CMOC increased its stake in Tenke Fungurume to 80% and in December 2020 the Chinese firm announced that it had purchased a 95% stake in the Kisanfu copper-cobalt mine, just over 30 km from Tenke Fungurume. The deal, again with Freeport, gave CMOC control over the vast bulk of the mine's estimated 6.28m. metric tons of copper and 3.1m. tons of cobalt, for a price of $550m., with the DRC Government holding the remaining 5%.

Frontier Services Group, a company run by Erik Prince, the founder of controversial private security firm Blackwater, was reported to have registered a subsidiary in the DRC in August 2018. The subsidiary, Frontier Services Group Congo, aimed to focus on activities, including 'the exploration, exploitation and commercialisation of minerals', according to a report by Reuters in June 2019. In January the *Financial Times* had reported that Prince aimed to raise as much as US $500m. to invest in the exploitation of minerals including cobalt, copper and lithium, in order to feed what he predicted would be 'enormously high' demand for these base materials among manufacturers of electric vehicles and automotive batteries. Prince told the *Financial Times* that it would not be possible to 'build those vehicles without minerals that come from generally weird, hard-to-access places', and that his new fund would seek out upstream, unexplored deposits, which could then be sold to larger mining firms.

Global commodities trader Trafigura in November 2020 agreed a five-year deal to source cobalt from Enterprise Générale du Cobalt (ECG), a state buyer established by the DRC in late 2019 to manage and regulate the in-country artisanal supply of the commodity. A subsidiary of Gécamines, ECG would have a monopoly on artisanal cobalt produced in the country. The deal involved Trafigura purchasing an initial US $10m. per month of cobalt, with a view to increasing that amount five-fold over time. However, the Minister of Mining, Antoinette Nsamba Kalambayi, told Reuters in May 2022 that her ministry was seeking to cancel ECG's monopoly, in a context where it had not yet purchased any artisanal cobalt, in part owing to the introduction of stringent safety standards that banned tunnelling and severely limited the depth of mines. Tensions between government departments and the appointment of new management at Gécamines were also cited as an obstacle to ECG initiating cobalt purchases. Kalambayi described the monopoly as a violation of DRC law.

Diamonds and Gold

The DRC has moderately high levels of diamond reserves, which are largely located in the Kasaï provinces. However, output has been experiencing a generally declining trend in recent years. In 2021 the country produced only 5.9m. carats compared with 15.4m. carats in 2017. (In 2004 the country exported 33m. carats.) Despite this long-term decline, the DRC still accounted for over 5% of global gemstone output in 2012, according to the USGS. In 2014 gold output increased to 31 metric tons, more than seven times that of the previous year, owing in large part to the opening of new mines by Randgold Resources and AngloGold Ashanti's Kibali mine in the northeast of the country.

AngloGold and the Office des Mines d'Or de Kilo-Moto (OKIMO) reached a joint venture agreement in March 2010 to develop the Ashanti Goldfields Kilo (AGK) project, which includes the Mongbwalu concession. By that stage mineral resources of 3m. troy oz had been identified at Mongbwalu. Under the terms of the agreement, AngloGold would take an 86.2% majority share in the AGK venture, with OKIMO taking the remaining 13.8%. AGK would pay OKIMO US $10.5m. and the DRC Government a further $1.25m. AngloGold granted final approval to the project—together with a second development, at Kibali, in Orientale—during 2012. For the Kibali project, which had gold reserves of more than 10m. oz, Anglo-Gold and Randgold Resources each took a 45% share, with OKIMO taking the remaining 10%. The Kibali mine became operational in mid-2014, with a targeted production volume of 400,000 oz per year. A processing plant was also to be constructed, with a processing capacity of 4m.–6m. metric tons per year. Randgold announced in July 2012 that it had begun open-pit mining at Kibali. In 2013 the Kibali concession generated 88,200 oz of gold, according to Randgold. This output was extracted from a vast open pit called KCD, which was estimated to contain 12m. oz of gold ore.

In its June 2020 report to the UN Security Council, the Panel of Experts reported that the vast majority of gold output from mines in the east of the DRC continued to be exported through clandestine channels, to the detriment of the national coffers. It cited official provincial data from Nord-Kivu, Sud-Kivu and Ituri as showing that a combined total of just over 73 kg of gold was exported from these three provinces in 2019. Yet, based in part on an assessment of quantities of gold lodged with eight gold-buying houses in Bunia, it calculated that 1,100 kg was smuggled out of the DRC from Ituri alone that year, dwarfing the quantities exported legally.

A September 2020 report by IMPACT, a Canadian NGO that has repeatedly examined in detail the DRC's gold mining sector, exposed the difficulties in encouraging the gold trade to move through official, rather than clandestine, channels. The investigation behind the report found that the cost of legally exporting just under 250 g of gold from Ituri province amounted to 15% of the commodity's US dollar value. As a result, smugglers were able to tempt local producers into selling to them by purchasing at a premium of between just over 3% and just over 5% above the level legitimate exporters

were prepared to pay in the city of Bunia. The US Department of the Treasury's Office of Foreign Assets Control in March 2022 imposed sanctions on Belgian businessman Alain Goetz and the African Gold Refinery (AGR), a venture operated by Goetz in Uganda that maintains an annual refining capacity of 219 metric tons. The Treasury also sanctioned eight other businesses or subsidiaries that were reported to be owned or controlled by Goetz, including three gold refining or trading companies based in the United Arab Emirates (UAE). AGR and two of the UAE-based entities were accused by the Treasury of sourcing 'illicit' gold from mines in regions of the DRC controlled by armed groups, including Mai-Mai Yakatumba and Raia Mutomboki, two militias reported to be involved in 'destabilizing activities' in Sud-Kivu.

Cassiterite and Lithium

Cassiterite mining is a major industry in the DRC. The country accounts for around 6% of global output and is the largest exporter of cassiterite in Africa, according to the USGS. However, much of the cassiterite mining industry has long been outside central government control, with various armed groups exploiting the mineral. In 2012 Mauritius-based Alphamin Resources established a base camp and began exploration at the crucial Bisie mine, which accounts for about 70% of Nord-Kivu province's cassiterite output. After a tumultuous few years during which Alphamin's fledgling set up was attacked by local artisanal miners and caught up in the M23 rebellion, the drive to establish the first modern mining operation in perennially unstable Nord-Kivu gathered momentum later in the decade. The Bisie deposit was described by Alphamin as 'one of the largest and most significant tin deposits in the world' and the company had hoped to begin production in the first quarter of 2019 and to reach a steady level of output by the end of that year. The launch of a major project supplying conflict-free minerals from what has historically been one of the DRC's most war-torn areas was considered as potentially transformative for the troubled region. The new mining code of March 2018, which shook confidence in the industry, reportedly also jeopardized Alphamin's chances of completing construction work, as the financing for the project had been agreed under the earlier mining legislation. However, *Mining Review* reported in September 2019 that Alphamin Resources had continued with its commissioning work at the Bisie mine, and added that a move into full-scale production was 'imminent'. By that stage the mine was expected to generate 152,300 metric tons of high-grade tin over a 12-year lifespan. In March 2022 Alphamin announced results for several drill holes at the Mpama South section of the Bisie mine, which left management 'optimistic' about the project's future prospects. Unlike the Mpama North section of the mine, Mpama South was not yet operational at that stage.

AVZ Minerals announced in early 2021 that it had struck high-grade lithium after drilling beneath an old pit at southern DRC's Manono Project, an old site where the Australia-listed firm was conducting renewed work owing to what it described as 'potentially one of the world's largest lithium-rich LCT (lithium, caesium, tantalum) pegmatite deposits'. Tests in Canada confirmed that primary lithium sulphate from the Manono mine could be used in the production of lithium-ion batteries.

Petroleum

Zaire became a producer of offshore petroleum in 1975, operating from fields on the Atlantic coast and at the mouth of the River Congo. Output was estimated at 10.0m. barrels in 2005 (and amounted to between 8.4m. and 9.4m. barrels per year in 2008–10). Lake Albert, which borders Uganda (and the surrounding area), is one of the most oil-rich areas in sub-Saharan Africa and has been estimated to contain reserves of up to 1,000m. barrels. In August 2014 Oil of DRCongo declared that it had discovered an estimated 3,000m. barrels of oil in the DRC around Lake Albert. The announcement was based on analysis of seismic survey data. Nearby blocks in Uganda are being developed by Tullow, Total and China National Offshore Oil Corporation. Oil of DRCongo said that it was preparing to drill two exploration wells on the site, which would require the relocation of local communities. However, the figures quoted by the company were no more than an early assessment, and the difficulty of exporting oil from eastern Congo would be a factor in the commercial viability of the find. Political tensions between the DRC and Uganda were also a complicating factor in any possible deal to export the oil via Uganda.

In early 2013 the DRC Government drafted legislation that would allow exploitation of oil in the country's national parks, including Virunga, although this plan was opposed by donors, particularly the British Government and the World Bank. SOCO International, a hydrocarbons company based in the UK, announced in April 2014 that it was beginning seismic testing on Lake Edward, but then pledged in June that it would not commence exploration unless the DRC Government and the UN Educational, Scientific and Cultural Organization (UNESCO) both agreed that extraction would not endanger Virunga's status as a World Heritage Site. The announcement followed a complaint about SOCO's activities filed by the World Wildlife Fund for Nature (WWF) with the OECD in October 2013. The environmental lobby group had in August declared that the Virunga National Park had the potential to generate US $1,100m. annually in revenues and 45,000 jobs from the development of fisheries, hydropower and tourism, in the absence of oil production. SOCO insisted that it could operate in the park using environmentally sensitive drilling techniques; however, the company has also come in for criticism for a reported payment of $42,250 to an army major in the DRC to provide security for its personnel, accompanied by allegations that men under his command tortured an activist opposed to oil extraction. In June 2018 the DRC Government declared that it had approved the establishment of inter-ministerial commissions to prepare plans to declassify sections of the Virunga and Salonga National Parks, in order to permit drilling in these areas. The plans included declassifying 1,720 sq km, or 21.5%, of the Virunga National Park, according to a government statement. One of Kabila's final acts as President was to sign an oil-drilling licence for an area extending across Salonga National Park. The agreement, one of three with South Africa's DIG Oil, was signed by Kabila and Tshibala in December. Kabila had also awarded a contract allowing drilling in part of Salonga to another oil firm, COMICO, in that year. The Salonga National Park spreads across 33,350 sq km of the Congo basin; in February the Government had also approved a production sharing agreement with Compagnie Minière Congolaise for three blocks in an area that covers part of the park, which is also a World Heritage Site. The agreement was criticized by the WWF (the park's co-manager), which warned that any exploration there posed a 'real danger for the exceptional flora and fauna'.

AGRICULTURE AND FORESTRY

The DRC's varying geography and climate produces a wide range of both food and cash crops. Agriculture extends across 32.0m. ha and employs about 70% of the country's workforce, according to a 2016 estimate by the Food and Agriculture Organization (FAO) of the UN. Land under cultivation thus stands at only around 40% of the 80m. ha of arable land cited by the Ministry of Agriculture, which acknowledges that 'a large part of Congo's population suffers from food and nutrition insecurity'. The agricultural sector (including forestry, live-stock, hunting and fishing) contributed 21.6% of GDP in 2020, according to UN data. The principal food crops are cassava, plantains, maize, groundnuts and rice, grown mainly by small-scale subsistence farmers. Cash crops include coffee, palm oil and palm kernels, rubber, cotton, sugar, tea and cocoa, many of which are grown on large plantations. The DRC has the potential to be not only self-sufficient in food but also to be a net exporter, given high levels of rainfall and rich soils across vast expanses of the country; however, production has been severely curtailed by the repeated cycles of armed conflict and massive population displacements over the last 25 years, especially in the fertile east of the country bordering Uganda, Rwanda and Burundi. In a State of the Nation address in December 2019, President Tshisekedi stated that the sustain-able economic development model that he had devised 'enshrines the primacy of agriculture over mining'. In the following year the Ministry of Agriculture formulated a

sectoral recovery plan, which aimed to enhance the supervision of and assistance towards households engaged in agriculture. It envisaged initial investment of US $4,400m., which, along-side boosting the productivity of existing agricultural house-holds, aimed to create a (very specific) 28,109,157 new jobs, although it was not immediately clear from where the invest-ment would come. The IMF disclosed in January 2022 that it was making available funding of around $15m. (equivalent to 0.03% of GDP) for investment in the agriculture sector in that year, alongside investment in other sectors. However, it made clear that any significant improvement in agricultural prod-uctivity would require the fostering of private investment in the sector.

In 1980 coffee had been the DRC's second biggest export earner, thanks to exports by volume of 100,000–120,000 metric tons per year; however, the industry was decimated by the two conflicts of 1996–97 and 1998–2002, and by subsequent sub-stantial episodes of military turmoil. The nation's annual coffee exports reached a nadir of 8,000 tons in 2008 and still only registered 11,000 tons in 2020, according to Virunga Coffee, a firm active in the DRC since 2011. More favourable tax regimes in neighbouring countries and the effect of dis-eases such as tracheomycosis, which affected Robusta coffee fields in Ituri and Beni, have also been cited as factors hin-dering a stronger recovery in coffee output. A decades-old but increasingly destructive rebellion by the Allied Democratic Forces was also causing severe disruption in the Beni area, displacing an estimated 40,000 people in less than three months in early 2021, according to the UN High Commissioner for Refugees, cutting yet more people off from their fields. However, in a potentially significant boost, Nespresso, owned by food behemoth Nestle, announced in August 2020 that it had launched a new range of coffees grown in volcanic soils on the edge of Lake Kivu, as part of a programme that began the previous year and aimed to boost participation by eastern Congolese farmers from 450 to more than 5,000 individuals by 2024.

Forested areas cover 152.6m. ha of the DRC's total landmass of 234.5m. ha, according to FAO. The Government formally ceased issuing new industrial logging licences in 2002, in an apparent effort to slow the rate of deforestation. However, this legislation has had little effect. Global Witness warned in 2015 that major logging companies were still maintaining large-scale operations in the DRC. In April 2016 the Government signed a US $200m. agreement under the auspices of the Central African Forest Initiative (CAFI)—supported by the UK, the EU, France, Germany and Norway—to protect the country's forests and reduce carbon emissions. Forests in the Congo basin were being cut down at a rate of 5,600 sq km per year, in a context where around 2m. sq km remained. The funding would be made available to counter illegal logging and burning, although it remained difficult to envisage how this would be enforced, given the continued prevalence of militia groups and poor discipline within the national army.

In February 2018 Greenpeace alleged that the DRC's Min-ister of the Environment and Sustainable Development, Amy Ambatobe Nyongolo, had reinstated three illegal concessions, covering 6,500 sq km of forested land, which had been cancelled in August 2016. The three concessions were allegedly given to Chinese-owned logging companies Forestière pour le Dével-oppement du Congo and Société La Millénaire Forestière. This action prompted CAFI to suspend payments to the DRC. A number of aid donors, including Norway, stated that the reinstatement of the logging concessions breached the Gov-ernment's obligations to conserve forests in return for inter-national assistance.

An escalation of the security crisis in the Kasaï provinces and increasing pressure points in the ever-restive Kivu provinces led to a surge in the number of displaced people in the DRC in 2016. The UN World Food Programme reported in December 2018 that some 13m. people across the country were suffering from severe food insecurity, with over one-third of those located in the Kasaï region. In its 2020 Humanitarian Response Plan, FAO's estimate of the number of people in severe acute food insecurity in the DRC was 15.6m., while 1.1m. people were suffering from severe acute malnutrition. Large swathes of Kasaï Central, Kasaï and Tanganyika fell into the 'Emergency

Category' (fourth on FAO's five-point scale, in a context where the fifth category amounts to 'Famine'). Meanwhile, the northern reaches of Sud-Kivu and easternmost areas of Ituri province also fell into the 'Emergency Category'. Armed conflict and displacement remained the key factors behind the worst instances of food insecurity, but FAO also pointed to the adverse impact of floods, insufficient rainfall in some parts of the country, epidemics and armyworm. Further stoking the emergency situation in Ituri, a desert locust outbreak that had already ravaged much of East Africa arrived in the province in late February 2020. It was the first such invasion of the DRC by desert locusts in 75 years, with 'a small group' of the insects arriving on the western shore of Lake Albert near Bunia on 21 February, according to FAO.

UTILITIES AND INFRASTRUCTURE

The DRC produced 10,561m. kWh of electricity in 2018, but electricity reached only 17.1% of the population, leaving 69m. people without a power supply. In rural areas electrification was a pitiful 0.4%, while even in urban areas the proportion of people able to access the electricity supply was only 47.2%. Upon assuming office, President Tshisekedi pledged to ensure that 30% of the country's population received electricity by 2023.

The country's shortfall in power production has hampered the development of its mining sector. The shortfall reached 950 MW in 2015, prompting complaints from the Chamber of Mines. A renovation programme is under way, but additional generation capacity is required.

The DRC's potential for producing hydroelectric power is matched on the African continent only by that of Cameroon. The country's most ambitious infrastructure project (which is estimated to account for a substantial proportion of the DRC's foreign indebtedness) is the Inga hydroelectric power project, based near the port of Matadi, at the mouth of the River Congo. Despite the debt already incurred by the project, there have long been plans to expand the existing Inga hydropower facilities.

In April 2008 African politicians and financiers met in London, UK, under the auspices of the World Energy Council to discuss ways of funding the Grand Inga project, which was scheduled to begin supplying power to countries across the continent by 2025. The project, which would see power distributed to Saharan Africa, West Africa and South Africa, involved the creation of a continent-wide distribution network, a 15-km-long reservoir and a 200-m dam. The new facility would be in addition to Inga's two existing hydroelectric dams and would produce an estimated 320m. kWh of electricity annually. The total cost of the project was estimated at US $80,000m.

The Inga plant also supplies some power to the Republic of the Congo. In addition, the state electricity board, the Société Nationale d'Electricité, is linked to the grid of the Zambia Electricity Supply Corporation, and the South African Electricity Supply Commission has carried out joint studies to optimize the connection with those companies and the Zimbabwe Electricity Supply Authority.

In late 2011, as Kabila's first elected term in office came to an end, overall progress in developing the DRC's power sector remained slow. The authorities were still seeking a developer for a 4,800-MW Inga-3, and plans to construct the 39,000-MW Grand Inga project had stalled. In June 2017 the Government requested that two rival potential developers of Inga-3—China Three Gorges Corporation and a consortium led by Spain's Actividades de Construccion y Servicios—join forces to submit a single bid. The request came in the same month as work on the dam (according to earlier scheduling) had originally been due to begin. Estimates for the cost of the project by that stage stood at US $14,000m., according to Reuters. In July 2016 the World Bank announced that it was suspending funding for Inga-3, as control of the project had been transferred from the Prime Minister's Office to the Office of the President. This had followed approval of grants by the multilateral lender totalling $73.1m. in March 2014, although the African Development Bank stepped in bridge the gap in June 2019. In the mean time, the Office for the Development and Promotion of the Grand

Inga Project concluded a number of power export agreements to supply electricity from the Inga-3 project. A deal between the DRC and South Africa had stipulated that power exports would start flowing from Inga-3 by 2020, but that deadline passed without any progress. Of Inga-3's total planned capacity of 4,800 MW, 1,300 MW was to be reserved for the mining sector, 2,500 MW was to be sold to South Africa and 1,000 MW was to be sold on the domestic market. Actividades de Construccion y Servicios pulled out of the project in January 2020, but an updated consortium was put together in August that year, led by China Three Gorges Corporation, and including Spain's AEE Power Holdings and Brazil's Andrade Gutierrez, as the Tshisekedi administration sought to push the stalled project forwards.

Separately, in late 2014 plans emerged in which Glencore and its then local partner, the Fleurette Group, would invest US $360m. in the rehabilitation of two turbines at the Inga-2 power plant and upgrade about 2,000 km of transmission lines to transport the electricity to Katanga. The aim was to bring on production of 450 MW, 380 MW of which would be reserved for the Mutanda Mining copper project and another mine at Kamoto, projects in which Glencore and the Fleurette Group have a controlling stake. Mutanda's operations reportedly suffered more than 860 hours of power interruptions between May and September 2014.

The Government announced in June 2016 that it had concluded a US $660m. deal with China Railway Group and Sinohydro to build a 240-MW hydropower plant in Katanga province, following a six-year negotiating process. The deal was tied to the Busanga mineral deposit, where there were copper reserves of 6.8m. metric tons; 170 MW of electricity from the plant would be delivered to power this mining operation, which was to be overseen by Gécamines.

In an effort to reduce the large national energy deficit, in June 2018 the DRC Government signed a deal with British-based utility firm BBOXX to provide 2.5m. people with access to solar-powered electricity by 2020, by means of off-grid solar kits and mini-grids. The partnership came under the Government's 'Energie pour Tous' initiative, which sought ways to reach the approximately 62m. people in the country who were still living beyond the reach of the central power grid. Under the agreement, the Government offered an exemption from import tax for solar technology.

TRANSPORT AND COMMUNICATIONS

Poor transport and communications infrastructure has proved a major handicap to the DRC's economic development. With a small strip of coastline of just 40 km, the DRC depends on the port of Matadi, which is situated close to the mouth of the River Congo and is able to accommodate up to 10 deep-water vessels, for its maritime traffic. In January 2022 construction work began on the DRC's first deep-water port, Banana Port, located at the mouth of the River Congo. The facility, which was to be built at a projected cost of US $1,200m. by Dubai's DP World, was to have an annual capacity of more than 320,000 containers. However, the project elicited criticism from environmentalists, owing to its proximity to the Mangrove Marine Park, a nature reserve for a variety of vulnerable and endangered species of plants and animals.

A US $9,000m. arrangement made between the DRC and China in the late 2000s, which offered the latter significant access to copper and cobalt (see *Copper and Cobalt*, above), was heavily tied to investment in Congolese infrastructure and an important part of the agreement involved Chinese modernization of the rail network. In the west, rail links were to be upgraded between Kinshasa, Matadi and also Muambe; in the east, between Kindu, Kalemie and Lubumbashi (in the southeast); and also from Lubumbashi to Ilebo and back to Kinshasa.

In March 2018 the rail connection between the DRC and Angola began operating again for the first time since the early 1980s, opening up a key route for mineral exports. The 1,344-km rail line from Dilolo in the far south of the DRC to the Angolan port of Lobito had closed down during the civil war in Angola during 1975–2002, with the track falling into disrepair. After a decade of work by the Chinese Railway Construction Corporation, the Angolan part of the line was inaugurated in

February 2015. The reopened cross-border route was considered crucial for reducing the high cost of transporting cobalt and copper exports from the DRC's southern mining belt, replacing the previous cumbersome journey by truck via Zambia.

Transport to the north and north-east is possible along the River Congo, and historically river traffic has probably been the single most important means of transport in the country. The Société Commerciale des Transports et des Ports is responsible for almost 14,000 km of waterways. However, the road network is wholly inadequate for a country of the DRC's size: of the estimated 152,373 km of roads in 2015, only 3,047 km were paved—little changed from the 2,800 km of paved roads in 2004. Modernization of the road infrastructure was foreseen under the investment agreement with China, including the construction of a major roadway linking Katanga to the Kisangani river port. Additionally, 250 km of roads were to be rebuilt around Kinshasa, and a new ring road around the city was to be constructed.

The DRC maintained 26 airports with paved runways in 2017, of which three had runways that extended over 3,047 m. A new national airline, Congo Airways, was launched in October 2015. The airline was to service eight Congolese airports, including Kinshasa, Goma and Lubumbashi. It expected to increase its network to 54 domestic airports and overseas destinations, with the acquisition of additional planes over the next two to three years. Congo Airways is entirely state-owned, although there are plans to open up the company to private investment in the future. In early 2018 the national carrier added two new international routes to its existing domestic services: to Johannesburg, South Africa, and Douala, Cameroon.

In July 2000 the Chinese company ZTE signed an agreement with the Congolese Government providing for the creation of the Congo Chine Télécom (CCT) corporation. The sale of a 49% stake in mobile operator CCT to France Télécom was approved by the DRC Government in September 2011. At that time CCT had 1.5m. subscribers and was the DRC's fourth largest cellular telecommunications company. In October France Télécom announced that it had completed the purchase of the remaining 51% stake in CCT, which was held by ZTE. The DRC Minister of Posts, Telecommunications and New Information and Communication Technologies, Emery Okundji, informed Reuters in June 2019 that Vodacom Congo, a unit of Vodacom Group, had filed a lawsuit challenging a revocation of its 2G licence, which had been suspended two months earlier. The operator's 3G and 4G licences remained valid, but the ministry contended at the time of the 2G revocation that Vodacom Congo had underpaid for the renewal of its licence in 2015, paying only US $15m., when it should have paid $65m. The number of mobile phone subscriptions per 100 people in the DRC rose to 46 in 2020, up from 43 in 2018, according to World Bank data. According to the International Telecommunication Union, just 13.6% of the population had regular access to the internet in 2020, compared with 11.7% in 2018.

EXTERNAL ACCOUNTS, DEBT AND DONOR SUPPORT

The DRC became the EAC's seventh partner state in 2022, its membership having been approved at an EAC Heads of State Summit held virtually in March. President Tshisekedi immediately told his fellow EAC heads of state that he was keen to establish a new Kinshasa-based instrument of the EAC that would be 'solely focused on mining, natural resources and energy'. The DRC's membership of the EAC created a trade zone stretching from the Atlantic Ocean to the Indian Ocean coastlines of Kenya and Tanzania. The DRC's trade outlook had received an earlier boost in December 2020, when the country rejoined the USA's African Growth and Opportunity Act (AGOA), after a suspension of nearly a decade. Tshisekedi's office described the DRC's readmittance, allowing duty-free access to US markets, as a 'great economic advance', which came amid efforts by the US Administration to rebuild ties with the DRC in the post-Kabila era.

Meanwhile, the DRC benefited from debt forgiveness early in the 21st century. In July 2003 the IMF and the World Bank

announced that the DRC had qualified for debt reduction, amounting to about US $10,000m. in total, under the enhanced initiatives for heavily indebted poor countries. The World Bank's International Development Association (IDA) was to provide a total of $1,031m. in nominal debt-servicing relief, which was to be delivered in part through a 90% reduction in debt servicing on IDA credit during 2003–26.

Yet in more recent years the DRC Government fell out of favour with major donors, to the point where it was increasingly isolated by Western powers as Kabila's second five-year term officially expired. The Government's progressively more hardline response to protests and opposition during 2015 and 2016 (against the backdrop of Kabila seeking to remain in power) led to both the US Administration and the EU imposing targeted sanctions on several individuals close to Kabila.

In March 2019 newly elected President Tshisekedi, who had emphasized the importance of combating corruption and reducing poverty during the electoral campaign, presented an economic recovery plan to a forum of international investors and business leaders in Rwanda. However, the DRC continued to face growing pressure on its external position through much of 2019, despite Kabila finally relinquishing the presidency in the wake of the December 2018 election. Gross international reserves fell to just US $302m. by the end of October 2019, down from $657m. at the end of December 2018. This was equivalent to only a week of imports, according to the IMF, which described the reserve position as 'critically low'. However, after a break of seven years the IMF restored financial support to the DRC on 16 December 2019, by approving disbursement of $368.4m. under the terms of a newly agreed RCF. The IMF's Managing Director approved a Staff-Monitored Programme (SMP) running to May 2020. The IMF declared that the RCF and the SMP were 'intended to guide policy implementation [and] provide authorities with more time to identify, prioritise and implement reforms aimed at boosting revenue, tackling corruption and improving governance'.

The IMF responded quickly to the emergency funding needs provoked by the COVID-19 pandemic. The DRC was among 25 countries that qualified for immediate debt service relief under the IMF's Catastrophe Containment and Relief Trust in April 2020, as the initial global economic effects of pandemic lockdowns took hold, ahead of the much more significant boost of US $363.3m. approved for disbursement under the RCF later that month. However, by the end of July foreign exchange reserves totalled just $836m., equating to just over three weeks of imports, according to the BCC. That month the Government moved to suspend an exemption of VAT on imports enjoyed by mining companies since 2016, a move that had been designed to encourage such firms to continue importing equipment and materials needed for development of mining capacity amid a commodity downturn. The suspension of the measure was aimed at bringing in hard currency over the short term. The Fund pointed in May 2021 to a number of other factors that fed into a stabilization of macroeconomic indicators during the second half of 2020 and early 2021, including a Stability Pact agreed between the BCC and the Government—which promised to give the central bank's board greater autonomy—and additional support by other development partners. China, for example, provided debt relief amid the pandemic, covering all interest-free loans that had been due for repayment to the end of 2020. Furthermore, in late May 2021 the IMF approved a $1,500m. three-year programme under an Extended Credit Facility (ECF). The IMF in December completed its first review under the ECF, enabling the DRC immediately to draw $212.3m., which was to be used to meet balance of payments needs. Although a strong rebound in the mining industry had led to more robust economic performance than the IMF and the DRC Government had anticipated when formulating the lending programme, the Fund cautioned that 'downside risks to the domestic and global economic outlook and recovery' persisted. Funding from the IMF was also to be invested during 2022 in health care, education, infrastructure, agriculture, rural development, transport and hydropower projects.

The World Bank announced in June 2020 that it had approved US $1,000m. in funds for the DRC's health care and education systems, with $800m. allocated to a government programme to provide free primary school education—a policy priority announced by President Tshisekedi upon taking office in January 2019—and \$200m. for maternal and paediatric health care. The two sectors would receive a combined total of \$435m in grants, with the remainder constituting loans. In a further boost in May 2021 the World Bank signed an agreement regarding a \$500m. infrastructure project to develop Kinshasa, comprising a \$250m. grant and a \$250m. loan.

Preliminary IMF estimates, released in a report attached to its first review of the ECF in January 2022, indicated a substantial improvement in revenue collection in the DRC in 2021 compared with 2020, but this was due more to the economic boost provided by the swift recovery in global commodity prices from the pandemic-induced nadir than to fiscal reform. The recovery contributed to an increase in government revenue from a preliminary figure of 7,889,000m. new Congolese francs in 2020 to an estimated 11,951,000m. new Congolese francs in 2021, which included a rise in tax revenue from 5,634,000m. to 8,594,000m. However, there was also a substantial increase in expenditure, from a preliminary 9,096,000m. new Congolese francs in 2020 to an estimated 15,322,000m. in 2021, although much of this rise was due to a surge in capital spending from just 308,000m. new Congolese francs in 2020 to an estimated 4,387,000m. in 2021. Factoring in other elements, including grants, the overall fiscal deficit

was estimated to have nearly doubled on a commitment basis, from a preliminary 1,024,000m. new Congolese francs in 2020 to an estimated 2,006,000m. new Congolese francs in 2021.

However, the DRC's current account deficit more than halved in 2021, according to preliminary estimates provided by the IMF. After an estimated deficit of US \$1,095m. in 2020, the Fund estimated the 2021 current account deficit, inclusive of grants, at \$308m., amid a substantial increase in the goods trade surplus, which was estimated to have risen from \$1,923m. in 2020 to \$3,810m. in 2021. The goods trade surplus was buoyed by resurgent commodity prices and by rising output in some key mining sectors, which propelled the value of the country's exports from an estimated \$13,789m. in 2020 to an estimated \$21,910m. in 2021, more than offsetting an increase in estimated imports from \$11,865m. to \$18,100m. However, the services and primary income components of the current account continued to exert a drag, and were the main factors responsible for keeping the overall balance in deficit. The estimated services deficit rose from \$2,548m. in 2020 to \$3,683m. in 2021, while the estimated primary income deficit rose from \$1,274m. to \$1,802m. In its January 2022 report, the IMF forecast that the current account deficit in that year would remain largely unchanged, at \$319m. However, in May the Fund announced that it now expected a small current account surplus.

Statistical Survey

Sources (unless otherwise stated): Département de l'Economie Nationale, Kinshasa; Institut National de la Statistique, Bâtiment de la Fonction Publique, Aile droite, Rez-de-chaussée, BP 20, Kinshasa; internet www.ins.cd; Banque Centrale du Congo, 563 blvd Colonel Tshatshi au nord, BP 2627, Kinshasa; e-mail info@bcc.cd; internet www.bcc.cd.

Area and Population

AREA, POPULATION AND DENSITY

Area (sq km)	2,344,885*
Population (census result)	
1 July 1984	
Males	14,543,800
Females	15,373,000
Total	29,916,800
Population (UN estimates at mid-year)†	
2020	89,561,404
2021‡	92,377,986
2022‡	95,240,782
Density (per sq km) at mid-2022‡	40.6

* 905,365 sq miles.
† Source: UN, *World Population Prospects: The 2019 Revision.*
‡ Projection.

POPULATION BY AGE AND SEX
(UN projections at mid-2022)

	Males	Females	Total
0–14 years	21,806.0	21,422.9	43,228.9
15–64 years	24,436.5	24,683.8	49,120.3
65 years and over	1,317.5	1,574.0	2,891.6
Total	**47,560.0**	**47,680.8**	**95,240.8**

Note: Totals may not be equal to the sum of components, owing to rounding.

Source: UN, *World Population Prospects: The 2019 Revision.*

REGIONS*

	Area (sq km)	Population (31 Dec. 1985)†
Bandundu	295,658	4,644,758
Bas-Zaïre	53,920	2,158,595
Equateur	403,293	3,960,187
Haut-Zaïre	503,239	5,119,750
Kasaï Occidental	156,967	3,465,756
Kasaï Oriental	168,216	2,859,220
Kivu	256,662	5,232,442
Shaba (formerly Katanga) . . .	496,965	4,452,618
Kinshasa (city)‡	9,965	2,778,281
Total	**2,344,885**	**34,671,607**

* In October 1997 a statutory order redesignated the regions as provinces. Kivu was divided into three separate provinces, and several of the other provinces were renamed. The Constitution of February 2006 increased the existing 11 provinces to 26: Bas-Uele, Equateur, Haut-Katanga, Haut-Lomami, Haut-Uele, Ituri, Kasaï Central, Kasaï Occidental, Kasaï Oriental, Kongo Central, Kwango, Kwilu, Lomami, Lualaba, Mai-Ndombe, Maniema, Mongala, Nord-Kivu, Nord-Ubangi, Sankuru, Sud-Kivu, Sud-Ubangi, Tanganyika, Tshopo, Tshuapa and Kinshasa (city).
† Provisional.
‡ Including the commune of Maluku.

Source: Département de l'Administration du Territoire.

PRINCIPAL TOWNS
(urban agglomerations, UN estimates at mid-2022)

Kinshasa (capital) .	15,628,085	Goma	706,978
Mbuji-Mayi . .	2,765,002	Uvira	656,701
Lubumbashi .	2,695,331	Likasi	605,313
Kananga . .	1,592,924	Kikwit	546,313
Kisangani . .	1,366,342	Kabinda . . .	536,653
Bukavu . . .	1,190,367	Kolwezi . . .	510,648
Tshikapa . .	1,023,575	Mbandaka . .	475,913
Bunia	767,645	Matadi . . .	416,310

Source: UN, *World Urbanization Prospects: The 2018 Revision.*

BIRTHS AND DEATHS
(annual averages, UN estimates)

	2005–10	2010–15	2015–20
Birth rate (per 1,000)	45.4	44.0	41.4
Death rate (per 1,000)	12.5	10.9	9.6

Source: UN, *World Population Prospects: The 2019 Revision.*

Births (official figures): 712,537 in 2012; 1,433,702 in 2013; 1,040,594 in 2014.

Deaths (official figures): 125,198 in 2012; 104,443 in 2013; 141,916 in 2014.

Marriages (official figures): 17,671 in 2012; 22,367 in 2013; 13,466 in 2014.

Life expectancy (years at birth, estimates): 61.0 (males 59.4; females 62.5) in 2020 (Source: World Bank, World Development Indicators database).

Economically Active Population ('000, estimates, mid-2015): Agriculture, etc. 14,646; Total labour force 26,745 (Source: FAO).

Health and Welfare

KEY INDICATORS

Total fertility rate (children per woman, 2020)	5.7
Under-5 mortality rate (per 1,000 live births, 2020) . . .	81.2
HIV/AIDS (% of persons aged 15–49, 2020) . . .	0.7
COVID-19: Cumulative confirmed deaths (per 100,000 persons at 31 August 2022)	1.5
COVID-19: Fully vaccinated population (% of total population at 28 August 2022)	3.0
Physicians (per 1,000 head, 2018)	3.8
Hospitals (per 100,000 head, 2013)	0.5
Domestic health expenditure (2019): US $ per head (PPP) .	6.4
Domestic health expenditure (2019): % of GDP . . .	0.6
Domestic health expenditure (2019): public (% of total current expenditure)	15.8
Access to improved water resources (% of persons, 2020) .	46
Access to improved sanitation facilities (% of persons, 2020) .	15
Total carbon dioxide emissions ('000 metric tons, 2018) . .	2,200
Carbon dioxide emissions per head (metric tons, 2018) . .	0.0
Human Development Index (2021): ranking	179
Human Development Index (2021): value	0.479

Note: For data on COVID-19 vaccinations, 'fully vaccinated' denotes receipt of all doses specified by approved vaccination regime (Sources: Johns Hopkins University and Our World in Data). Data on health expenditure refer to current general government expenditure in each case. For more information on sources and further definitions for all indicators, see Health and Welfare Statistics: Sources and Definitions section (europaworld.com/credits).

Agriculture

PRINCIPAL CROPS
('000 metric tons)

	2018	2019	2020
Avocados*	63	63	63
Bambara beans*	11	11	11
Bananas	803	805	822*
Beans, dry	256	260	265*
Cassava (Manioc)	38,873	40,050	41,014*
Chillies and peppers, dry* .	37	37	37
Cocoa beans†	15	10	12
Coffee, green*	30	30	30
Cow peas, dry*	71	71	71
Groundnuts, with shell . .	445	455	315†
Maize	2,186	2,139	2,112*
Mangoes, mangosteens and guavas*	298	300	299
Melonseed*	63	63	63
Millet*	45	45	45
Oil palm fruit*	1,890	2,020	2,149
Onions, dry*	56	56	56
Oranges*	168	167	166
Papayas*	211	211	210

—continued	2018	2019	2020
Pineapples*	192	192	191
Plantains and others	4,832	4,856	4,892*
Potatoes	102	103	104*
Pumpkins, squash and gourds* .	31	32	31
Rice, paddy	1,287	1,379	1,379†
Rubber, natural	14	10	13†
Seed cotton*	29	29	29
Soybeans (Soya beans) . . .	24	25	26†
Sugar cane*	2,123	2,118	2,136
Sweet potatoes	514	543	555*
Taro (Cocoyam)*	69	69	70
Tomatoes*	50	50	50
Yams	109	112	109*

* FAO estimate(s).
† Unofficial figure(s).

Aggregate production ('000 metric tons, may include official, semi-official or estimated data): Total cereals 3,536 in 2018, 3,579 in 2019, 3,551 in 2020; Total fruit (primary) 6,674 in 2018, 6,699 in 2019, 6,748 in 2020; Total oilcrops 2,507 in 2018, 2,647 in 2019, 2,639 in 2020; Total roots and tubers 40,586 in 2018, 41,782 in 2019, 42,761 in 2020; Total vegetables (primary) 589 in 2018, 591 in 2019, 592 in 2020.

Source: FAO.

LIVESTOCK
('000 head, year ending September)

	2018	2019	2020
Cattle	1,145	1,212	1,268
Chickens	18,443	18,558	18,668
Goats	4,105	4,112	4,113
Pigs	992	996	998
Sheep	911	913	914

Source: FAO.

LIVESTOCK PRODUCTS
('000 metric tons)

	2018	2019	2020
Cattle hides, fresh*	3.1	3.3	3.4
Cattle meat*	19.1	20.4	21.0
Cattle offals, edible* . . .	2.5	2.7	2.8
Cows' milk*	7.7	8.0	8.2
Chicken meat	10.3	10.4	10.4*
Game meat*	89.1	89.1	89.1
Goat meat	18.6	16.6	17.0*
Goat offals, edible* . . .	3.3	3.0	3.0
Goats' skins, fresh* . . .	3.3	3.0	3.0
Pig fat*	2.6	2.6	2.6
Pig meat*	26.0	26.1	25.6
Pig offals, edible*	2.6	2.6	2.6
Sheep meat	2.8	2.8	2.8*
Hen eggs*	8.9	8.8	8.9

* FAO estimate(s).

Source: FAO.

Forestry

ROUNDWOOD REMOVALS
('000 cubic metres, excl. bark, FAO estimates)

	2018	2019	2020
Sawlogs, veneer logs and logs for sleepers	329	329	329
Other industrial wood . . .	4,282	4,282	4,282
Fuel wood	85,625	86,702	87,801
Total	**90,236**	**91,313**	**92,412**

Source: FAO.

SAWNWOOD PRODUCTION
('000 cubic metres, incl. railway sleepers, FAO estimates)

	2018	2019	2020
Total (all broadleaved) . . .	150	150	101

Source: FAO.

Fishing

('000 metric tons, live weight, FAO estimates)

	2018	2019	2020
Capture	238.0	238.0	217.8
Aquaculture	3.3	3.4	3.6
Total catch	241.3	241.4	221.4

Source: FAO.

Mining

(metric tons unless otherwise indicated, provisional)

	2019	2020	2021
Crude petroleum ('000 barrels) .	8,162	8,737	8,578
Copper ore	1,506,461	1,601,208	1,797,423
Tantalum and niobium (columbium) concentrates . .	1,256	1,712	2,422
Cobalt concentrates . . .	79,295	86,591	93,144
Diamonds ('000 carats) . . .	15,404	10,076	5,923

Hard coal: 120,000 in 2010.

Silver (kg): 835 in 2016.

Gold (kg): 46,000 in 2018.

Germanium (kg): 1,000 in 2018.

Source: partly US Geological Survey.

Industry

SELECTED PRODUCTS
('000 metric tons unless otherwise indicated)

	2018	2019	2020*
Maize flour	20	21	21
Wheat flour	213	203	195
Sugar	122	123	128
Beer (million litres) . . .	425	480	540
Soft drinks (million litres) . .	209	289	259
Soaps	11	12	12
Acetylene	18	31	30
Cement	1,048	1,382	1,285
Explosives	5	10	11
Bottles ('000 units)	24	27	26
Cotton fabrics ('000 sq m) . .	146	147	148
Printed fabrics ('000 sq m) . .	3	1	1
Footwear ('000 pairs) . . .	124	74	76
Electrical energy (million kWh) .	10,561	11,448	12,397

* Provisional.

Cigarettes (million units): 639 in 2014.

2016: Tyres ('000 units) 125; Steel 123,000 metric tons.

2021 ('000 metric tons unless otherwise indicated, provisional): Wheat flour 189; Beer (million litres) 607; Soft drinks (million litres) 262; Cement 1,560; Electrical energy (million kWh) 13,149.

Finance

CURRENCY AND EXCHANGE RATES

Monetary Units
100 centimes = 1 new Congolese franc.

Sterling, Dollar and Euro Equivalents (31 May 2022)
£1 sterling = 2,523.8 new Congolese francs;
US $1 = 2,004.8 new Congolese francs;
€1 = 2,147.7 new Congolese francs;
10,000 new Congolese francs = £3.96 = $4.99 = €4.66.

Average Exchange Rate (new Congolese francs per US $)
2019	1,647.760
2020	1,851.122
2021	1,989.391

Note: In June 1967 the zaire was introduced, replacing the Congolese franc (CF) at an exchange rate of 1 zaire = CF 1,000. In October 1993 the zaire was replaced by the new zaire (NZ), equivalent to 3m. old zaires. On 30 June 1998 a new Congolese franc, equivalent to NZ 100,000, was introduced. The NZ was withdrawn from circulation on 30 June 1999.

BUDGET
('000 million new Congolese francs)*

Revenue†	2018	2019	2020
Tax revenue	5,599.6	5,723.5	5,738.6
Income tax	2,594.3	2,442.5	2,192.9
Value-added tax (VAT) . . .	1,561.4	1,661.8	1,905.7
International trade . . .	1,352.2	1,498.0	1,447.5
Other taxes on goods . . .	91.7	121.2	192.5
Non-tax revenue	1,486.9	1,450.9	1,285.7
Exceptional taxes	850.5	207.7	1,609.9
Total	7,937.1	7,382.1	8,634.3

Expenditure	2018	2019	2020
Current expenditure	6,888.7	7,217.2	7,556.3
Wages and salaries	2,694.1	3,616.2	4,758.3
Purchase of goods and services .	1,613.7	1,242.9	982.3
Transfers and subsidies . . .	1,954.1	2,044.9	1,469.5
Interest due	140.2	175.3	22.7
Capital expenditure	2,955.4	1,737.5	1,867.7
Foreign	1,279.9	839.8	1,286.4
Domestic	1,675.4	897.7	581.3
Total	9,844.0	8,954.7	9,424.0

* Figures refer to the accounts of central government.
† Excluding grants received ('000 million new Congolese francs): 1,766.5 in 2018; 977.8 in 2019; 1,609.9 in 2020.

2021 ('000 million new Congolese francs, projections): *Revenue:* Tax revenue 8,594 (Income tax 3,936, Taxes on goods and services 3,648, Taxes on international trade 1,010); Non-tax revenue 3,357; Total 11,951 (excluding grants received 1,365). *Expenditure:* Current expenditure 10,772 (Wages and salaries 5,277, Interest due 189, Goods and services 2,385, Transfers and subsidies 2,922); Capital expenditure 4,387 (Foreign-financed 3,361, Domestically-financed 1,026); Exceptional expenditure 164; Total 15,322 (Source: IMF—see below).

2022 ('000 million new Congolese francs, projections): *Revenue:* Tax revenue 10,371 (Income tax 4,695, Taxes on goods and services 4,595, Taxes on international trade 1,081); Non-tax revenue 3,455; Total 13,826 (excluding grants received 1,451). *Expenditure:* Current expenditure 12,429 (Wages and salaries 6,176, Interest due 338, Goods and services 2,659, Transfers and subsidies 3,256); Capital expenditure 4,792 (Foreign-financed 2,879, Domestically-financed 1,913); Exceptional expenditure 404; Total 17,625 (Source: IMF, *Democratic Republic of the Congo: First Review under the Extended Credit Facility Arrangement, Request for Modification of Performance Criteria, and Financing Assurances Review—Press Release; Staff Report; and Statement by the Executive Director for the Democratic Republic of the Congo*—January 2022).

INTERNATIONAL RESERVES
(excluding gold, US $ million at 31 December)

	2019	2020	2021
IMF special drawing rights . .	53.03	38.77	1,467.22
Foreign exchange	1,141.34	708.89	1,999.90
Total	1,194.37	747.66	3,467.12

Source: IMF, *International Financial Statistics*.

MONEY SUPPLY
(million new Congolese francs at 31 December)

	2018	2019	2020
Currency outside depository corporations	1,551,281	1,766,512	2,217,050
Transferable deposits . . .	4,816,606	6,366,625	10,745,011
Other deposits	3,213,886	4,772,153	5,835,022
Broad money	9,581,773	12,905,290	18,797,083

Source: IMF, *International Financial Statistics.*

COST OF LIVING
(Consumer Price Index for Kinshasa at 31 December; base: August 1995 = 100)

	2005	2006	2007
Food	546,165	697,790	762,946
Rent	622,109	736,670	817,241
Clothing	930,811	1,077,902	1,128,393
All items (incl. others) . . .	644,137	798,297	877,842

Source: IMF, *Democratic Republic of the Congo: Statistical Appendix* (January 2010).

Cost of living (Consumer Price Index; base: 2010 = 100): 129.1 in 2014; 130.1 in 2015; 133.9 in 2016 (Source: IMF, *International Financial Statistics*).

NATIONAL ACCOUNTS
('000 million new Congolese francs at current prices)

Expenditure on the Gross Domestic Product

	2018	2019	2020
Government final consumption expenditure	4,796.3	5,435.5	6,831.8
Private final consumption expenditure	58,544.1	55,241.5	64,966.5
Gross fixed capital formation . .	15,739.0	19,538.1	17,629.3
Change in inventories	160.9	217.3	293.6
Total domestic expenditure .	79,240.3	80,432.4	89,721.3
Exports of goods and services . .	26,094.6	25,001.9	21,071.1
Less Imports of goods and services	28,839.4	27,462.9	26,922.4
GDP in purchasers' values .	76,495.5	77,971.4	83,870.0
GDP at constant 2015 prices .	39,441.0	41,194.8	41,909.7

Gross Domestic Product by Economic Activity

	2018	2019	2020
Agriculture, hunting, forestry, fishing	14,657.9	15,567.2	17,681.6
Mining and utilities	18,982.4	15,063.5	16,123.9
Manufacturing	13,648.3	15,601.6	16,079.5
Construction	1,088.9	1,095.5	1,186.3
Wholesale, retail trade, restaurants and hotels . . .	8,914.4	9,698.9	11,566.5
Transport, storage and communication	6,238.3	6,692.4	7,589.6
Other activities	9,847.1	11,187.2	11,784.0
Gross value added	73,377.3	74,906.4	82,011.3
Indirect taxes (net)*	3,118.2	3,065.0	1,858.8
GDP at market prices . . .	76,495.5	77,971.4	83,870.0

*Figures obtained as residuals.

Source: UN National Accounts Main Aggregates Database.

BALANCE OF PAYMENTS
(US $ million)

	2018	2019	2020
Exports of goods	15,966.8	15,031.3	13,788.7
Imports of goods	−14,972.7	−14,631.7	−11,865.3
Balance on goods	994.2	399.6	1,923.4
Exports of services	114.8	141.9	143.6
Imports of services	−2,801.7	−2,260.0	−2,691.4
Balance on goods and services	−1,692.8	−1,718.5	−624.3
Primary income received . . .	72.7	72.9	193.0
Primary income paid	−1,781.4	−1,511.9	−1,467.3
Balance on goods, services and primary income	−3,401.5	−3,157.5	−1,898.7
Secondary income received . .	2,853.1	2,599.5	1,791.8
Secondary income paid . . .	−1,123.9	−1,135.2	−987.8
Current balance	−1,672.3	−1,693.2	−1,094.7
Capital account (net)	437.1	146.9	626.5
Direct investment liabilities . .	1,407.6	1,351.0	1,498.1
Portfolio investment assets . .	−30.9	−40.7	−33.9
Portfolio investment liabilities .	−7.4	−29.6	−5.6
Other investment assets . . .	52.3	−624.1	−2,599.7
Other investment liabilities . .	76.9	637.9	1,098.7
Net errors and omissions . . .	−113.0	568.6	24.0
Reserves and related items .	150.3	316.8	−486.5

Source: IMF, *International Financial Statistics.*

External Trade

PRINCIPAL COMMODITIES
(US $ million)

Imports c.i.f.	2018	2019	2020*
Consumer goods	3,555	3,043	2,899
Food and drink	1,919	1,645	1,608
Tobacco, textiles and clothing .	1,636	1,397	1,291
Energy	1,109	1,134	1,121
Raw materials and semi-products	3,188	2,901	2,644
Agriculture, building materials and metals	2,011	1,755	1,597
Leather, Rubber and articles thereof	884	839	757
Capital goods	7,121	5,865	5,201
Transport equipment . . .	1,028	1,100	998
Machines for specialized industries	5,288	4,091	3,599
Total (incl. others)	14,973	12,943	11,865

Exports f.o.b.	2018	2019	2020*
Mining products and hydrocarbons	15,827	13,072	13,638
Cobalt	6,351	2,562	2,245
Copper	7,436	8,227	9,412
Gold	1,101	1,387	1,202
Crude petroleum	597	509	387
Agricultural products and timber .	124	101	140
Cocoa	25	26	27
Coffee	25	24	61
Industrial products	16	11	11
Total (incl. others)	15,967	13,184	13,789

*Preliminary.

SELECTED TRADING PARTNERS
(US $ million)

Imports c.i.f.	2018	2019	2020*
Belgium and Luxembourg . .	614	548	338
China, People's Republic . . .	1,774	2,098	2,013
France	365	329	207
Germany	124	134	69
Netherlands	192	259	151
South Africa†	1,621	1,843	1,580
United Kingdom	124	100	102
Total (incl. others)	14,973	12,943	11,865

Exports f.o.b.	2018	2019	2020*
Belgium and Luxembourg . .	353	360	106
China, People's Republic . . .	5,661	4,429	7,031
Germany	28	12	7
Netherlands	11	6	9
South Africa†	3,212	3,491	1,967
United Kingdom	70	80	11
Total (incl. others)	15,967	13,184	13,789

* Preliminary.

† Figures estimated on the basis of reciprocal data.

Transport

SHIPPING

Flag Registered Fleet
(at 31 December)

	2019	2020	2021
Number of vessels	31	33	33
Total displacement ('000 grt) . .	38.7	40.2	42.7

Source: Lloyd's List Intelligence (www.bit.ly/LLintelligence).

CIVIL AVIATION
(domestic and international)

	2018	2019	2020
Departures	8,271	7,532	3,788
Passengers carried ('000) . . .	588	550	278
Freight carried (million ton-km) .	1	1	1

Source: World Bank, World Development Indicators database.

Tourism

FOREIGN TOURIST ARRIVALS BY COUNTRY OF RESIDENCE

	2015	2016	2017
Angola	20,085	14,689	5,933
Belgium	29,898	25,063	20,647
China, People's Republic . . .	18,647	16,748	16,979
Congo, Republic	14,202	35,085	22,429
Eswatini	15 184	13,757	13,603
France	26,225	23,145	17,407
India	16,618	15,794	15,399
Lesotho	18 521	15,973	13,078
Nigeria	4,306	16,258	15,464
Rwanda	657	64,119	40,785
Seychelles	15 683	15,177	13,896
South Africa	34,202	14,954	9,748
Tanzania	15,184	13,757	13,603
Zambia	18,521	15,973	13,078
Zimbabwe	15,683	15,177	13,896
Total (incl. others)	353,639	351,106	346,975

Tourism receipts (US $ million): 6.0 in 2017; 60.5 in 2018; 99.7 in 2019 (provisional).

Source: World Tourism Organization.

Communications Media

	2018	2019	2020
Mobile telephone subscriptions ('000)	36,470.6	37,123.2	40,798.4
Broadband subscriptions, fixed ('000)	4.6	11.9	31.0
Broadband subscriptions, mobile ('000)	13,360.1	16,950.0	20,878.2
Internet users (% of population) .	11.7	12.5	13.6

Telephones ('000 main lines in use): 59.5 in 2012.

Source: International Telecommunication Union.

Education

(2017/18 unless otherwise indicated)

	Teachers	Students Males	Students Females	Students Total
Pre-primary . .	18,222	233,133	240,601	473,734
Primary	544,039	8,735,117	8,071,897	16,807,014
General secondary*	} 324,324	2,263,673	1,484,261	3,747,934
Technical and vocational* . .		563,048	307,913	870,961
Tertiary	28,877†	298,646‡	166,032‡	464,678‡

* 2014/15.

† 2012/13.

‡ 2015/16.

Institutions (1998/99): Primary 17,585; Secondary 6,007.

Source: UNESCO Institute for Statistics.

Pupil-teacher ratio (qualified teaching staff, primary education, UNESCO estimate): 30.9 in 2017/18 (Source: UNESCO Institute for Statistics).

Adult literacy rate (UNESCO estimates): 77.0% (males 88.5%; females 66.5%) in 2016 (Source: UNESCO Institute for Statistics).

Directory

The Constitution

A new Constitution was approved by the transitional legislature in May 2005, and endorsed by a national referendum in December. The Constitution officially entered into effect on 18 February 2006 and was amended on 15 January 2011; its main provisions are summarized below:

GENERAL PROVISIONS

The state of the Democratic Republic of the Congo is divided for the purposes of administration into 25 provinces and the capital of Kinshasa (which has the status of a province). The provinces are granted autonomous powers for managing local resources, and also powers that are exercised in conjunction with the central Government, including control of between 40% and 60% of public funds. Each province has a Government and an Assembly. The Constitution reaffirms the principle of democracy, guarantees political pluralism, and protects fundamental human rights and freedoms. The establishment of a one-party system is prohibited and punishable by law as an act of treason.

PRESIDENT

The President is the head of state and Commander-in-Chief of the armed forces. He or she is elected by direct universal suffrage for a term of five years, which is renewable once. Presidential candidates must be of Congolese nationality and a minimum of 30 years of age. The President nominates a Prime Minister from the political party that commands a majority in the legislature and other members of the Government on the proposal of the Prime Minister. He or she exercises executive powers in conjunction with the Government and subject to the approval of the legislature. The areas of defence, security and foreign affairs are conducted jointly by the President and the Government.

GOVERNMENT

The Government comprises the Prime Minister and a number of ministers and deputy ministers. The Government is responsible for conducting national politics, which it determines in conjunction with the President. The Government is accountable to the National Assembly, which is empowered to adopt a motion of censure against it.

LEGISLATURE

Legislative power is vested in a bicameral Parliament, comprising a lower chamber, the National Assembly, and an upper chamber, the Senate. Members of the National Assembly are elected by direct universal suffrage for a renewable term of five years. The number of deputies is determined by electoral law. Members of the Senate are indirectly elected by the Assemblies of each of the country's provinces for a renewable term of five years. Both chambers have a President and two Vice-Presidents.

JUDICIARY

The Constitution guarantees the independence of the judicial system. Members of the judiciary are under the authority of the High Council of the Judiciary. The Court of Cassation has jurisdiction over legal decisions and the Council of State over administrative decisions. The Constitutional Court interprets the provisions of the Constitution and ensures the conformity of new legislation. The system also comprises a Military High Court, and lower civil and military courts and tribunals. The High Council of the Judiciary has 18 members, including the Presidents and Chief Prosecutors of the main courts. The Constitutional Court comprises nine members, who are appointed by the President (including three nominated by Parliament and three by the High Council of the Judiciary) for a term of nine years. The head of state appoints and dismisses magistrates, on the proposal of the High Council of the Judiciary.

The Government

HEAD OF STATE

President: FÉLIX ANTOINE TSHISEKEDI TSHILOMBO (inaugurated 24 January 2019).

CABINET
(October 2022)

Prime Minister: JEAN-MICHEL SAMA LUKONDE KYENGE.

Deputy Prime Minister, Minister of the Interior, Security, Decentralization and Traditional Affairs: DANIEL ASSELO OKITO WA NKOY.

Deputy Prime Minister, Minister of the Environment and Sustainable Development: EVE BAZAIBA MASUDI.

Deputy Prime Minister, Minister of Foreign Affairs: CHRISTOPHE LUTUNDULA APALA.

Deputy Prime Minister, Minister of the Civil Service, Administrative Modernization and Innovation in Public Services: JEAN-PIERRE LIHAU EBUA.

Minister of State, Minister of Justice, Keeper of the Seals: ROSE MUTOMBO KIESE.

Minister of State, Minister of Infrastructure and Public Works: ALEXIS GIZARO MUVUNI.

Minister of State, Minister of Portfolio: ADÈLE KAHINDA MAYINA.

Minister of State, Minister of Planning: CHRISTIAN MWANDO NSIMBA KABULO.

Minister of State, Minister of the Budget: AIMÉ BOJI SANGARA BAMANYIRUE.

Minister of State, Minister of Town Planning and Housing: PIUS MUABILU MBAYU MUKALA.

Minister of State, Minister of Rural Development: FRANÇOIS RUBOTA MASUMBUKO.

Minister of State, Minister of Entrepreneurship and Small and Medium-sized Enterprises: EUSTACHE MUHANZI MUBEMBE.

Minister of State, Minister of Land Management: GUY LOANDO MBOYO.

Minister of National Defence and War Veterans: GILBERT KABANDA RUKEMBA.

Minister of Primary, Secondary and Technical Education: TONY MWABA KAZADI.

Minister of Public Health, Hygiene and Disease Prevention: JEAN-JACQUES BUNGANI MBANDA.

Minister of Finance: NICOLAS SERGE KAZADI KADIMA NZUJI.

Minister of Transport, Communication Routes and Improving Access to Isolated Regions: CHÉRUBIN OKENDE SENGA.

Minister of Agriculture: DÉSIRÉ NZINGA BILIHANZE.

Minister of Fishing and Stockbreeding: ADRIEN BOKELE DJEMA.

Minister of the National Economy: (vacant).

Minister of Industry: JULIEN PALUKU KAHONGYA.

Minister of Regional Integration: DIDIER MAZENGA MUKANZU.

Minister of Higher and University Education: BUTONDO MUHINDO NZANGI.

Minister of Scientific Research and Technological Innovation: JOSÉ MPANDA KABANGU.

Minister of Hydrocarbons: DIDIER BUDIMBU NTUBUANGA.

Minister of Postal Services, Telecommunications and New Information and Communication Technologies: AUGUSTIN KIBASSA MALIBA LUBALALA.

Minister of Digital Technology: DÉSIRÉ-CASHMIR KOLONGELE EBERANDE.

Minister of Employment, Labour and Social Security: NTEMBE NDUSI.

Minister of Properties and Real Estate Affairs: AIMÉ SAKOMBI MOLENDO.

Minister of Water Resources and Electricity: OLIVIER MWENZE MUKALENG.

Minister of Human Rights: ALBERT FABRICE PUELA.

Minister of Gender, Families and Children: GISÈLE NDAYA LUSEBA.

Minister of External Trade: JEAN LUCIEN BUSSA TONGBA.

Minister of Mining: ANTOINETTE NSAMBA KALAMBAYI.

Minister of Communication and the Media, Government Spokesperson: PATRICK MUYAYA KATEMBWE.

Minister of Social Affairs, Humanitarian Actions and National Solidarity: MODESTE MUTINGA MUTUSHAYI.

Minister of Professional Training and Crafts: ANTOINETTE KIPULU KABENGA.

Minister of Youth, Initiation of New Citizenship and National Cohesion: YVES BUNKULU ZOLA.

Minister of Sport and Leisure: SERGE TSHEMBO NKONDE.

Minister of Tourism: MODERO NSIMBA MATONDO.

Minister of Culture, the Arts and Heritage: Cathérine Katumbu Furaha.

Minister of Relations with Parliament: Anne-Marie Karume Bakaneme.

Minister to the President of the Republic: Nana Manuanina Kihimba.

Minister-delegate to the Minister of Social Affairs, in charge of the Disabled and Other Vulnerable Persons: Irène Esambo Diata.

In addition, there were 11 deputy ministers.

MINISTRIES

Office of the President: Hôtel du Conseil Exécutif, ave de Lemera, Kinshasa-Gombe; tel. 852740563; internet www.presidence.cd.

Office of the Prime Minister: 5 ave du Roi Baudouin, BP 8931, Kinshasa-Gombe; tel. 815555667; e-mail cabinet@primature.cd; internet www.primature.cd.

Ministry of Agriculture: Croissement blvd du 30 Juin et ave Batetela, Kinshasa; tel. 998900675; e-mail info@minagri.gouv.cd; internet minagri.gouv.cd.

Ministry of the Budget: Immeuble du Gouvernement, pl. Ex-Royale, blvd du 30 Juin, Kinshasa; tel. 824668908; e-mail budget@budget.gouv.cd; internet budget.gouv.cd.

Ministry of the Civil Service, Administrative Modernization and Innovation in Public Services: blvd du Palais de la Nation/blvd de l'Office des Routes, Kinshasa-Gombe; tel. 825008115; e-mail info@fonctionpublique.gouv.cd; internet fb.com/FonctionPubliqueRdc.

Ministry of Communication and the Media: Immeuble RATELESCO, 83 ave Tabu Ley, Kinshasa; tel. 814175139; e-mail info@communication.gouv.cd; internet fb.com/MinComMediasRDC.

Ministry of Culture, the Arts and Heritage: Kinshasa-Gombe.

Ministry of Digital Technology: 6 et 8 Tshatshi, Kinshasa; tel. 850682868; e-mail info@numerique.gouv.cd; internet numerique.gouv.cd.

Ministry of Employment, Labour, and Social Security: blvd du 30 Juin, BP 3840, Kinshasa-Gombe; internet www.mintravail.gouv.cd.

Ministry of Entrepreneurship and Small and Medium-sized Enterprises: Kinshasa; tel. 810520121; internet fb.com/MinPME.

Ministry of the Environment and Sustainable Development: 15 ave Papa Ileo, Kinshasa-Gombe; tel. 816500333; e-mail info@medd.gouv.cd; internet medd.gouv.cd.

Ministry of External Trade: Bâtiment Administratif du Gouvernement, 4e Etage, Aile C, blvd Triomphal, Lingwala, Kinshasa; tel. 821419414; e-mail ministereducommercerdc@gmail.com; internet fb.com/CommerceExterieurRdc.

Ministry of Finance: blvd du 30 Juin, BP 12998 KIN I, Kinshasa-Gombe; tel. 810867623; e-mail cabfinances@minfinrdc.com; internet minfinrdc.com.

Ministry of Fishing and Stockbreeding: Kinshasa.

Ministry of Foreign Affairs: pl. de l'Indépendance 1, Kinshasa; tel. 990561665; e-mail cabinet@diplomatie.gouv.cd; internet diplomatie.gouv.cd.

Ministry of Gender, Families and Children: 27 blvd Colonel Tshatshi, Kinshasa-Gombe; tel. 810140714; internet fb.com/Ministère-du-GenreEnfant-et-Famille-449981422044361.

Ministry of Higher and University Education: blvd Tshatshi 67, Kinshasa; e-mail contact@minesu.gouv.cd; internet minesu.gouv.cd.

Ministry of Hydrocarbons: Kinshasa; e-mail info@hydrocabures.gouv.cd; internet hydrocarbures.gouv.cd.

Ministry of Human Rights: Kinshasa-Gombe.

Ministry of Industry: Bâtiment Paul Panda Farnana, 2e Niveau, Commune Lingwala, blvd Triomphal, Kinshasa; tel. 811810712; internet minindustrie.gouv.cd.

Ministry of Infrastructure and Public Works: Kinshasa; e-mail ministereitp@gmail.com.

Ministry of the Interior, Security, Decentralization and Traditional Affairs: Immeuble du Gouvernement, blvd Triomphal, Kinshasa-Gombe; tel. 822431066; e-mail info@mininterieur.gouv.cd; internet interieur.gouv.cd.

Ministry of Justice: pl. de l'Indépendance, BP 3137, Kinshasa-Gombe; tel. 814943082; e-mail contact@justice.gouv.cd; internet justice.gouv.cd.

Ministry of Land Management: Hôtel du Gouvernement, 6e Niveau, pl. Royal, blvd du 30 Juin, Kinshasa; tel. 825777499; e-mail info@amenagement.gouv.cd; internet amenagement.gouv.cd.

Ministry of Mining: Hôtel du Gouvernement, 3e étage, blvd du 30 Juin, Kinshasa-Gombe; tel. 972246923; e-mail info@mines-rdc.cd; internet mines-rdc.cd.

Ministry of National Defence and War Veterans: BP 4111, Kinshasa-Gombe.

Ministry of the National Economy: Immeuble du Gouvernement, blvd du 30 Juin, Kinshasa; tel. 813638160; e-mail contact@economie.gouv.cd; internet economie.gouv.cd.

Ministry of Planning: 4155 rue des Côteaux, Quartier Petit Pont, BP 9378, Kinshasa-Gombe 1; tel. 824191329; e-mail sg.minplanrdc@gmail.com; internet plan.gouv.cd.

Ministry of Postal Services, Telecommunications and New Information and Communication Technologies: Immeuble intelligent, 3e Niveau, Kinshasa-Gombe; tel. 8403523027; e-mail info@ptntic.gouv.cd; internet ptntic.gouv.cd.

Ministry of Primary, Secondary and Technical Education: 2 ave des Ambassadeurs, Kinshasa-Gombe; tel. 840018006; e-mail sgc@eduquepsp.education; internet www.eduquepsp.education/v1.

Ministry of Professional Training and Crafts: Kinshasa.

Ministry of Properties and Real Estate Affairs: 27 Croisement des ave de la Gombe et ave de Batetela, Kinshasa; tel. 815999570; e-mail contact@cadastre.gouv.cd; internet cadastre.gouv.cd.

Ministry of Public Health, Hygiene and Disease Prevention: blvd du 30 Juin, BP 3088 KIN I, Kinshasa-Gombe; tel. 817005479; e-mail secretariat.dep@sante.gouv.cd; internet sante.gouv.cd.

Ministry of Regional Integration: Kinshasa.

Ministry of Relations with Parliament: Kinshasa.

Ministry of Rural Development: Kinshasa.

Ministry of Scientific Research and Technological Innovation: Immeuble Semois, 3e et 6e Niveaux, pl. Royale, blvd du 30 Juin, Kinshasa; e-mail cabmin.rsc.rdc@gmail.com; internet fb.com/MinistereRsit.

Ministry of Social Affairs, Humanitarian Actions and National Solidarity: Kinshasa.

Ministry of Sport and Leisure: ave de la Libération 34, Kinshasa; tel. 816065688; e-mail cabinet@jeunessesportsloisirs.cd; internet minjsl.gouv.cd.

Ministry of Tourism: Immeuble Mongala, 2e et 6e étages, Kinshasa-Gombe; tel. 845084479; e-mail cabinet@tourisme.gouv.cd; internet tourisme.gouv.cd.

Ministry of Town Planning and Housing: Immeuble Paul Panda, 2e Niveau, Croisement ave Kutu et blvd Triomphal, Lingwala, Kinshasa; tel. 815080472; e-mail sg@urbanisme-habitat.cd; internet urbanisme-habitat.cd.

Ministry of Transport, Communication Routes and Improving Access to Isolated Regions: pl. Royale, 117 blvd du 30 Juin, Kinshasa-Gombe; tel. 820000002; e-mail contact@transports.gouv.cd; internet transports.gouv.cd.

Ministry of Water Resources and Electricity: Immeuble SNEL, 239 ave de la Justice, BP 5137 KIN I, Kinshasa-Gombe; tel. 994922800; internet www.energie.gouv.cd.

Ministry of Youth, Initiation of New Citizenship and National Cohesion: 34 ave de la Libération, Kinshasa-Gombe; tel. 993434596.

President

A presidential election took place on 30 December 2018, and on 9 January 2019 the Commission Electorale Nationale Indépendante released provisional, partial results of the poll. These were confirmed by the Constitutional Court on 20 January and indicated that a total of 18,329,318 votes had been cast. Of these, 7,051,013 were attributed to Félix Tshisekedi, 6,366,732 were received by Martin Fayulu, while Emmanuel Shadary took 4,357,359 votes. However, no figures were released for the number of votes secured by the 18 other candidates and the total number of valid votes cast was also not declared.

Legislature

The bicameral Parliament (Parlement) of the Democratic Republic of the Congo comprises a lower chamber, or National Assembly (Assemblée Nationale), and an upper chamber, or Senate (Sénat), members of which are elected by the deputies of the provincial Assemblies.

NATIONAL ASSEMBLY

National Assembly: Palais du Peuple, cnr ave des Huileries et blvd Triomphale, Lingwala I, Kinshasa; e-mail contact@assemblee-nationale.cd; internet www.assemblee-nationale.cd.

President: CHRISTOPHE MBOSO N'KODIA PWANGA.

General Election, 30 December 2018

Party	Seats
Parti du Peuple pour la Reconstruction et la Démocratie	49
Alliance des Forces Démocratiques du Congo . . .	41
Union pour la Démocratie et le Progrès Social . . .	32
Action Alternative pour le Bien-être et le Changement	30
Parti du Peuple pour la Paix et la Démocratie . . .	25
Mouvement Social	23
Alliance des Acteurs pour la Bonne Gouvernance du Congo	22
Alliance pour l'Avenir	22
Mouvement de Libération du Congo	22
Alliance des Démocrates pour le Renouveau et le Progrès	21
Alliance des Mouvements du Kongo	20
Parti Lumumbiste Unifié	17
Union pour la Nation Congolaise	15
Others*	136
Total	**485†**

* Comprising political parties that won fewer than 15 seats.

† Elections in four districts (for a total of 15 seats) were postponed owing to an outbreak of Ebola Virus Disease, and finally took place on 31 March 2019.

SENATE

Senate: Palais du Peuple, Kinshasa; e-mail senatrdcongo@senat.cd; internet www.senat.cd.

President: MODESTE BAHATI LUKWEBO.

Election, 15 March 2019

Party	Seats
Parti du Peuple pour la Paix et la Démocratie . . .	10
Parti du Peuple pour la Reconstruction et la Démocratie	9
Action Alternative pour le Bien-être et le Changement	7
L'Avenir du Congo	6
Alliance des Forces Démocratiques du Congo . . .	6
G7	4
Mouvement de Libération du Congo	4
Alliance pour l'Avenir	2
Alliance des Démocrates pour le Renouveau et le Progrès	2
Alliance des Travaillistes Congolais pour le Développement	2
Action des Alliés pour l'Amélioration des Conditions de Vie des Congolais	2
Mouvement pour l'Intégrité du Peuple	2
Others*	19
Independents	33
Total	**108†**

* Comprising 19 political parties that each won one seat.

† There is also provision for the election of a senator for life, taking the total number of senators to 109.

Election Commission

Commission Electorale Nationale Indépendante (CENI): 4471 blvd du 30 juin, Kinshasa; tel. 813543857; e-mail info@ceni.cd; internet www.ceni.cd; f. 2010 to replace the Commission Electorale Indépendante; 7 mems; Pres. DENIS KADIMA.

Political Organizations

Action Alternative pour le Bien-être et le Changement (AAB): Quartier Babylone, 121 ave Bolemba, Kintambo; Pres. ÉLYSÉE MUNEMBWE TAMUKUMWE.

Alliance des Forces Démocratiques du Congo (AFDC): 54 blvd du 30 Juin, C/Gombe, Kinshasa; internet www.afdcrdc.cd; officially registered as a political party in 2010; Pres. PLACIDE TSHISUMPA TSHIAKATUMBA; Sec.-Gen. PASCAL RUKENGWA.

Alliance pour le Renouveau du Congo (ARC): 1165–1175 ave Tombalbaye, C/Gombe, Kinshasa; tel. 998911096; e-mail arc_secgen@yahoo.fr; internet fb.com/ARC-Alliance-pour-le-renouveau-du-Congo-422323627959671; f. 2006; Leader OLIVIER KAMITATU ETSU.

L'Avenir du Congo: 2 ave Poids Lourds, C/Gombe, Kinshasa; Leader DANNY BANZA.

Congrès National pour la Défense du Peuple (CNDP): Goma, Nord-Kivu; officially registered as a political party in 2009; Pres. DÉSIRÉ KAMANZI.

Convention des Démocrates Chrétiens: 6 ave Boma, Lisala, C/Kintambo, Kinshasa; tel. 818107754; internet fb.com/Convention-des-Démocrates-Chrétiens-CDC-125217304246685; officially registered as a political party in 2010; Leader FLORENTIN MOKONDA BONZA.

Démocratie Chrétienne Féderaliste—Convention des Fédéralistes pour la Démocratie Chrétienne (DCF—COFEDEC): Quartier Industriel, 19 9e rue, C/ Limete, Kinshasa; officially registered as a political party in 2005; Leader VENANT TSHIPASA VANGI.

Eveil de la Conscience pour le Travail et le Développement (ECT): 77A ave de la Justice, C/Gombe, Kinshasa; officially registered as a political party in 2011; Pres. SHADRAC BAITSURA MUSOWA.

Forces Novatrices pour l'Union et la Solidarité (FONUS): 130 ave de l'Enseignement, Kasa-Vubu, Kinshasa; f. 2004; advocates political pluralism; Pres. JOSEPH OLENGHANKOY; Sec.-Gen. EMERY OKUNDJI.

Mouvement pour l'Intégrité du Peuple (MIP): 48 ave Tulundi, C/Bandalungwa, Kinshasa; officially registered as a political party in 2011; Pres. COLETTE TSHOMBA.

Mouvement de Libération du Congo (MLC): 6 ave du Port, C/Gombe, Kinshasa; e-mail contact@mlc-rdc.org; internet www.mlc-rdc.org; f. 1998; Leader JEAN-PIERRE BEMBA GOMBO; Sec.-Gen. EVE BAZAIBA.

Mouvement Social pour le Renouveau (MSR): ave de la Libération, Kinshasa; internet www.lemsr.com; Pres. FRANÇOIS RUBOTA MASUMBOKO.

Parti Démocrate Chrétien (PDC): 345 petit blvd Industrie, Limete; Leader JOSÉ ENDUNDO BONONGE.

Parti Démocrate et Social Chrétien (PDSC): 18 ave de l'Enseignement, Kasavubu; tel. (12) 21211; f. 1990; centrist; Pres. ANDRÉ BOBOLIKO; Sec.-Gen. TUYABA LEWULA.

Parti Lumumbiste Unifié (PALU): blvd Lumumba Pont-Matete, C/Matete, Kinshasa; e-mail partilumumbiste.rdc@gmail.com; internet fb.com/PALUofficiel; Gen. Sec. SYLVAIN NGABU.

Parti du Peuple pour la Paix et la Démocratie (PPPD): L13, Plateau des Professeurs, Kinshasa; f. officially registered as a political party in 2011; Pres. CÉLESTIN MBUYU KABANGO.

Parti du Peuple pour la Reconstruction et la Démocratie (PPRD): 3915 Croisement des aves Pumbu et Batetela, C/Gombe, Kinshasa; tel. 850379458; e-mail contact@pprd.cd; f. March 2002 by Pres. Joseph Kabila; Sec.-Gen. HENRI MOVA SAKANYI.

Rassemblement Congolais pour la Démocratie (RCD—Goma): 26 ave Lukusa, C/Gombe, Kinshasa; f. 1998; rebel movement until Dec. 2002 peace agreement; Leader AZARIAS RUBERWA; Sec.-Gen. FRANCIS BEDY MAKHUBU MABELE.

Rassemblement des Congolais Démocrates et Nationalistes (RCDN): blvd du 30 juin, S.V./64 Haut-Uélé (Isiro); fmrly Rassemblement Congolais pour la Démocratie—National; Leader ROGER LUMBALA.

Rassemblement des Forces Sociales et Fédéralistes (RSF): 98 rue Poto-poto, Kimbanseke; officially registered as a political party in 1992; Leader VINCENT DE PAUL LUNDA BULULU.

Rassemblement pour une Nouvelle Société (RNS): 632 ave Begonias, C/Limete, Kinshasa; registered as a political party in 2006; Leader Dr ALAFUELE M. KALALA.

Rassemblement pour la Reconstruction du Congo (RRC): 8 ave Mweneditu, C/Gombe, Kinshasa; officially registered as a political party in 2011; Leader JEAN MARIE ELESSE BOKOKOMA.

Union des Démocrates Mobutistes (UDEMO): f. by son of fmr Pres. Mobutu; officially registered as a political party in 2007; Leader FRANÇOIS JOSEPH MOBUTU NZANGA NGBANGAWE.

Union des Forces du Changement (UFC): 13 ave Lubefu, Royal, C/Gombe, Kinshasa; internet www.ufcrdc.com; officially registered as a political party in 2005; Pres. LÉON KENGO WA DONDO.

Union Nationale des Démocrates Féderalistes (UNADEF): A1/D ave Tshikapa, Matonge, C/Kalamu, Kinshasa; internet fb.com/unadefnationale; Leader CHRISTIAN MWANDO NSIMBA KABULO.

Union des Nationalistes Féderalistes du Congo (UNAFEC): A1 ave Mpozo, Loc 5Q, Matonge, C/Kalamu, Kinshasa; officially registered as a political party 2001; Leader (vacant).

Union des Patriotes Congolais (UPC): 25 blvd de la Libération, Bunia; rebel group of Hema ethnic group, fmrly in conflict with Lendu in north-east; registered as political org. 2004, after peace agreement with Govt; Leader THOMAS LUBANGA.

Union pour la Démocratie et le Progrès Social (UDPS): 521 ave Pétunias, Quartier Résidentiel, C/Limete, Kinshasa; tel. 813140685; f. 1982; Pres. FÉLIX TSHISEKEDI.

Union pour le Développement du Congo (UDCO): 5 ave Ongunda, C/Gombe, Kinshasa; internet fb.com/ unionpourledeveloppementdelardc; officially registered as a political party in 2007; Pres. EDMOND KABONGO NGOY.

Union pour la Nation Congolaise (UNC): ave Croix-Rouge 3, C/ Barumbu, Kinshasa; tel. 999915385; internet unc-rdcongo.com; officially registered as a political party in 2010; Sec.-Gen. BILLY KAMBALE; Pres. VITAL KAMERHE LWA-KANYIGINYI.

Union pour la Reconstruction du Congo (UREC): 3 ave Tulipis, C/Goma, Nord-Kivu; Leader OSCAR LUKUMWENA KASHALA.

Union pour la République—Mouvement National (UNIR— MN): Immeuble VeVe center, 2 rue de Bongandanga, C/Kasa-Vubu, Kinshasa; tel. 812431078; e-mail contact@unir-mn.com; internet www.unir-mn.com; f. 2001; officially registered as a political party in 2005; Pres. FRÉDÉRIC BOYENGA-BOFALA; Sec.-Gen. OLIVIER MESKENS NTAMBU KUFUANGA.

Diplomatic Representation

EMBASSIES IN THE DEMOCRATIC REPUBLIC OF THE CONGO

Algeria: 50–52 ave Col Ebeya, C/Gombe, Kinshasa; tel. 818803717; e-mail kinambalg@yahoo.fr; Ambassador DJOUAMA TOUFIK.

Angola: 4413–4429 blvd du 30 juin, BP 8625, Kinshasa; tel. 810093543; e-mail contact@ambassadeangolardc.org; internet ambassadeangolardc.org; Ambassador MIGUEL DA COSTA.

Belgium: 133 blvd du 30 Juin, Kinshasa-Gombe; tel. 996022100; e-mail kinshasa@diplobel.fed.be; internet diplomatie.belgium.be/ rd_congo; Ambassador JOHAN INDEKEU.

Benin: 3990 ave des Cliniques, BP 3265, Kinshasa-Gombe; tel. 98128659; Ambassador GISELLE BALLEY MEDEGAN.

Brazil: ave Batetela 3098, 14e étage, Kinshasa-Gombe; tel. 817009471; e-mail brasemb.kinshasa@itamaraty.gov.br; internet www.gov.br/mre/pt-br/embaixada-kinshasa; Ambassador ROBERTO PARENTE.

Burundi: 22 ave Lubefu, Kinshasa; tel. 992551927; e-mail ambabukinshasa@yahoo.fr; internet ambabukinshasa.com/accueil; Ambassador MWAMBA NTIRAMPEBA AGRICOLE.

Cameroon: 171 blvd du 30 juin, BP 10998, Kinshasa; tel. 99952628; e-mail ambacamkinshasa@yahoo.fr; Ambassador (vacant).

Canada: 17 ave Pumbu, C/Gombe, BP 8341, Kinshasa 1; tel. 996021500; e-mail knsha@international.gc.ca; internet www .canadainternational.gc.ca/congo; Ambassador BENOÎT-PIERRE LAMARÉE.

Central African Republic: 11 ave Pumbu, BP 7769, Kinshasa; tel. 815906996; e-mail rdc.rcaembassy@gmail.com; Ambassador (vacant).

Chad: 67–69 ave du Cercle, BP 9097, Kinshasa; tel. 993802772; e-mail tchadrdc@gmail.com; Ambassador MAHADJIR OUSMAN IBRAHIM.

China, People's Republic: No. 447, ave des Aviateurs, BP 9098, Kinshasa-Gombe; tel. 848470801; e-mail chinaemb_cd@mfa.gov.cn; internet cd.china-embassy.gov.cn; Ambassador ZHU JING.

Congo, Republic: 179 blvd du 30 juin, BP 9516, Kinshasa; tel. (12) 34028; e-mail ambacokin@yahoo.fr; Ambassador CYPRIEN SYLVESTRE MAMINA.

Côte d'Ivoire: 68 ave de la Justice, C/Gombe, BP 9197, Kinshasa; tel. 812900354; e-mail ambacirdcongo@yahoo.fr; internet rdcongo .diplomatie.gouv.ci; Ambassador SILAS ADJÉ METCH.

Cuba: ave Uvira 40A, BP 10699, Kinshasa; tel. 816603995; e-mail embacubardc@gbs.cd; internet misiones.minrex.gob.cu/es/ republica-democratica-del-congo; Ambassador JESUS DEL AMO FERNANDEZ.

Egypt: 519 ave de l'Ouganda, BP 8838, Kinshasa; tel. 813680440; e-mail embassy.kinshasa@mfa.gov.eg; Ambassador HAMDY SHAABAN ABDELHALIM MOHAMED.

Ethiopia: BP 8435, Kinshasa; Ambassador WOINSHET TADESSE WOLDEGIORGIS.

France: 1 ave du Col Mondjiba, BP 3093, Kinshasa; tel. 815559999; e-mail cad.kinshasa-amba@diplomatie.gouv.fr; internet cd .ambafrance.org; Ambassador BRUNO AUBERT.

Gabon: 167 ave Col Mondjiba, BP 9592, Kinshasa; tel. 999931689; e-mail ambagabrdc@yahoo.fr; Ambassador MICHEL XAVIER BIANG.

Germany: 82 ave Roi Baudouin, BP 8400, Kinshasa-Gombe; tel. 815561380; internet www.kinshasa.diplo.de; Ambassador Dr OLIVER SCHNAKENBERG.

Ghana: 206 ave Pierre Mulele, BP 7955, Kinshasa; tel. 999994109; e-mail ghanaemkin@yahoo.com; internet ghanaembassy-drc.com; Ambassador KWAKU DOMFEH (designate).

Greece: Immeuble de la Communauté Hellénique, 87 blvd du 30 juin, BP 478, Kinshasa; tel. 815554941; e-mail gremb.kin@mfa.gr; internet www.mfa.gr/congo; Ambassador CALLIOPE PENNY DOUTI.

Guinea: ave Lubefi 7/9, Kinshasa-Gombe; tel. 847499950; e-mail ambaguikinshasa@mae.gov.gn; Chargé d'affaires a.i. ALY DOUMBOUYA.

Holy See: 81 ave Goma, BP 3091, Kinshasa; tel. 813330124; Apostolic Nuncio Most Rev. ETTORE BALESTRERO (Titular Archbishop of Victoriana).

India: 18B, ave Batetela, Kinshasa-Gombe; tel. 815559770; e-mail amb.indembkin@gbs.cd; internet eoi.gov.in/kinshasa; Ambassador RAM KARAN VERMA.

Iran: 78 blvd du 30 juin, BP 16599, Kinshasa; tel. 817005298; e-mail iranemb.fih@mfa.gov.ir; internet congo.mfa.gov.ir; Ambassador MOHAMMAD JAVAD SHARIATI.

Italy: 8 ave de la Mongala, Kinshasa; tel. 815553651; e-mail ambkinshasa.mail@esteri.it; internet www.ambkinshasa.esteri.it; Ambassador ALBERTO PETRANGELI.

Japan: 372 ave Col Mondjiba, Concession Immotex, BP 1810, Kinshasa; tel. 815554731; e-mail ambjaponrdc@yahoo.fr; internet www.rdc.emb-japan.go.jp; Ambassador MINAMI HIROYUKI.

Kenya: 4002 ave de l'Ouganda, BP 9667, Kinshasa; tel. 815565935; internet kinshasa.mfa.go.ke; Ambassador GEORGE S. MASAFU.

Korea, Democratic People's Republic: 168 ave de l'Ouganda, BP 16597, Kinshasa; tel. 8801443; Ambassador KIM MYONG-SIK.

Korea, Republic: 63 ave de la Justice, Kinshasa; tel. 150350014; e-mail amb-congo@mofa.go.kr; internet overseas.mofa.go.kr/cd-ko/ index.do; Ambassador CHO JAI-CHEL.

Lebanon: 3 ave de l'Ouganda, Kinshasa; tel. 90022111; e-mail libancongodrc@gmail.com; Chargé d'affaires a.i. HAYTHAM IBRAHIM.

Liberia: 3 ave de l'Okapi, BP 8940, Kinshasa; tel. (12) 82289; Ambassador JALLA D. LANSANAH.

Libya: ave du Fleuve, Gombe, Kinshasa 1; tel. (12) 34766; Chargé d'affaires a.i. ALI MANSOUR ETHINI.

Morocco: POB 912, ave Corteaux et Vallée No. 40, Kinshasa 1; tel. (12) 34794; e-mail ambamarocongo@yahoo.fr; Ambassador RACHID AGASSIM.

Namibia: 138 blvd du 30 juin, BP 8934, Kinshasa; tel. 815559840; Ambassador SIMEON UULENGA.

Netherlands: 133 blvd du 30 Juin, BP 10299, Kinshasa; tel. 996050600; e-mail kss@minbuza.nl; internet www .nederlandwereldwijd.nl/landen/congo-democratische-republiek; Ambassador JOLKE OPPEWAL.

Nigeria: 141 blvd du 30 juin, BP 1700, Kinshasa-Gombe; tel. 817000538; e-mail nigeria.kinshasa@foreignaffairs.gov.ng; internet nigeriaembassydrc.org; Ambassador OMAR SULAIMAN.

Norway: Kinshasa; Ambassador JON-ÅGE ØYSLEBØ.

Portugal: 270 ave des Aviateurs, BP 7775, Kinshasa-Gombe; tel. 811922520; e-mail sconsular.kinshasa@mne.pt; internet kinshasa .embaixadaportugal.mne.pt; Chargé d'affaires a.i. FRANCISCO-XAVIER GRAÇA MOURA DE MEIRELES.

Russian Federation: 80 ave de la Justice, BP 1143, Kinshasa; tel. 858271983; e-mail ambrus_drc@mail.ru; internet drc.mid.ru; Ambassador ALEKSEI SENTEBOV.

Rwanda: POB 967, Kinshasa; tel. 812756969; e-mail ambakinshasa@minaffet.gov.rw; internet www.rwandaindrc.gov .rw; Ambassador VINCENT KAREGA.

Senegal: Kinshasa; Ambassador PAPA TALAM DIAO.

Serbia: 112 ave de l'Etoile, Kinshasa-Gombe; tel. 971594988; e-mail serbambakin@gmail.com; internet kinshasa.mfa.gov.rs; Ambassador MIROLJUB JEVTIĆ.

South Africa: 77 ave Ngongo Lutete, BP 7829, Kinshasa-Gombe; tel. 815566586; e-mail rsaembassydrc@gmail.com; internet www .dirco.gov.za/kinshasa; Ambassador ABEL MXOLISI SHILUBANE.

South Sudan: Kinshasa; tel. 971100286; e-mail rsskinshasa@yahoo .fr; Ambassador MAYEN MAJAK MALOU ATHIAN.

Spain: Immeuble Communauté Hellénique, 37 blvd Col Tshatshi, BP 8036, Kinshasa-Gombe; tel. 818843195; e-mail emb.kinshasa@ maec.es; internet www.exteriores.gob.es/embajadas/kinshasa; Ambassador CARLOS ROBLES FRAGA.

Sudan: 24 ave de l'Ouganda, Kinshasa; tel. 999937396; e-mail sudembkinsh@yahoo.com; Ambassador HUSSEIN ELAMIN ELFADIL.

Sweden: 93 ave Roi Baudouin, BP 11096, Kinshasa-Gombe; tel. 999301102; e-mail ambassaden.kinshasa@gov.se; internet www .swedenabroad.se/sv/utlandsmyndigheter/d.r.-kongo-kinshasa; Ambassador HENRIC RÅSBRANT.

Switzerland: 654 blvd Col Tshatshi, BP 8724, Kinshasa-Gombe; tel. 898946800; e-mail kin.vertretung@eda.admin.ch; internet www.eda .admin.ch/kinshasa; Ambassador CHASPER SARROT.

Tanzania: 142 blvd du 30 juin, BP 1612, Kinshasa; tel. 815565850; e-mail tanzanrepkinshasa@yahoo.com; Ambassador SAID JUMA MSHANA.

Togo: 3 ave de la Vallée, BP 10117, Kinshasa; tel. (12) 30666; e-mail ambatogo_kinyahoo.fr; Ambassador YAWO ADOMAYAKPOR.

Tunisia: 67–69 ave du Cercle, BP 1498, Kinshasa; tel. 818803901; e-mail atkinshasa@yahoo.fr; Ambassador ADEL BOUZEKRI REMILI.

Türkiye (Turkey): 18 ave Pumbu, BP 7817, Kinshasa; tel. 817007500; e-mail embassy.kinshasa@mfa.gov.tr; internet kinsasa .be.mfa.gov.tr; Ambassador HUSNU MURAT ULKU.

Uganda: 12 ave de l'Ouganda, BP 8804, Kinshasa-Gombe; tel. 810507179; e-mail kinshasa@mofa.go.ug; internet kinshasa.mofa .go.ug; Ambassador JAMES MBAHIMBA.

United Kingdom: 83 ave Roi Baudouin, BP 8049, Kinshasa; tel. 81556620; e-mail ambassade.britannique@fco.gov.uk; internet www .gov.uk/world/organisations/british-embassy-kinshasa; Ambassador EMILY MALTMAN.

USA: 310 ave des Aviateurs, BP 697, Kinshasa; tel. 815560151; e-mail USEmbassyKinshasa@state.gov; internet cd.usembassy.gov; Ambassador MICHAEL A. HAMMER.

Zambia: 54–58 ave de l'Ecole, BP 1144, Kinshasa; tel. 819999437; Ambassador KOSITA PAULU.

Zimbabwe: Immeuble Ogedep, 2nd Floor, East Wing, 4 ave de la Justice, Kinshasa-Gombe; tel. 813602073; e-mail zimkinshasa@ zimfa.gov.zw; Ambassador JOHANNES TOMANA.

Judicial System

Under the Constitution that entered into effect in February 2006, the judicial system is independent. Members of the judiciary are under the authority of the High Council of the Judiciary. The Court of Cassation has jurisdiction over legal decisions and the Council of State over administrative decisions. The Constitutional Court interprets the provisions of the Constitution and ensures the conformity of new legislation. The judicial system also comprises an Audit Court, a Military High Court, and lower civil and military courts and tribunals. The High Council of the Judiciary has 18 members, including the Presidents and Chief Prosecutors of the main courts. The Constitutional Court comprises nine members, who are appointed by the President (including three nominated by the legislature and three by the High Council of the Judiciary) for a term of nine years. The head of state appoints and dismisses magistrates, on the proposal of the High Council of the Judiciary.

Court of Cassation (Cour de Cassation): cnr ave de la Justice and ave de Lemera, BP 3382, Kinshasa-Gombe; tel. (12) 25104; First Pres. DAVID-CHRISTOPHE MUKENDI MUSANGA.

Council of State (Conseil d'Etat): 7639 Croisement des aves Pumbu et des Bâtonniers, Kinshasa-Gombe; e-mail contact@conseil-etat.cd; internet www.conseil-etat.cd; f. 2018; First Pres. Prof. FÉLIX VUNDUAWE TE PEMAKO.

Constitutional Court (Cour Constitutionnelle): Nouveau Palais de Justice, ave des Batoniers, Kinshasa-Gombe; e-mail info@ cour-constitutionnelle.cd; internet www.cour-constitutionnelle.cd; f. 2015; 9 mems; Pres. DIEUDONNÉ KAMULETA BADIBANGA.

Audit Court (Cour des Comptes): 13 rue Comité Urbain, Kinshasa; tel. 891111119; e-mail contact@courdescomptes.cd; internet www .courdescomptes.cd; Pres. ERNEST IZEMENGIA NSAA-NSAA.

Military High Court (Haute Cour Militaire): Kinshasa; First Pres. JOSEPH MUTOMBO KATALAY.

Attorney-General of the Republic: JEAN-PAUL MUKOLA NKOKESHA.

Religion

Many of the country's inhabitants follow traditional beliefs, which are mostly animistic. A large proportion of the population is Christian, predominantly Roman Catholic, and there are small Muslim, Jewish and Greek Orthodox communities.

CHRISTIANITY

The Roman Catholic Church

The Democratic Republic of the Congo comprises six archdioceses and 42 dioceses.

Bishops' Conference: Conférence Episcopale Nationale du Congo, 59 ave Monts Virunga, BP 3258, Kinshasa-Gombe; tel. 818542268; e-mail cecoscenco@gmail.com; internet www.cenco.cd; Pres. Most Rev. MARCEL UTEMBI TAPA (Archbishop of Kisangani).

Archbishop of Bukavu: FRANÇOIS-XAVIER MAROY RUSENGO, Archevêché, ave Mbaki 18, BP 3324, Bukavu; tel. 813180621; e-mail archevechebk@yahoo.fr; internet www.archidiocesebukavu.com.

Archbishop of Kananga: Most Rev. MARCEL MADILA BASANGUKA, Archevêché, BP 70, Kananga; tel. 815013942; e-mail archidiocesekananga@yahoo.fr; internet www.archi-kananga.org.

Archbishop of Kinshasa: Cardinal FRIDOLIN AMBONGO BESUNGU, Archevêché, ave de l'Université, BP 8431, Kinshasa; tel. 822992036; e-mail archikin.tv@gmail.com; internet www.archikin.net.

Archbishop of Kisangani: Most Rev. MARCEL UTEMBI TAPA, Archevêché, ave Mpolo 6, BP 505, Kisangani; tel. 853572553; e-mail archidiocesekisangani@gmail.com.

Archbishop of Lubumbashi: Most Rev. FULGENCE MUTEBA MUGALU, Archevêché, BP 72, Lubumbashi; tel. 997031991; e-mail archidiolub@mwangaza.cd.

Archbishop of Mbandaka-Bikoro: ERNEST NGBOKO NGOMBE, Archevêché, BP 1064, Mbandaka; tel. 810408691; e-mail mbandakabikoro@yahoo.fr.

The Anglican Communion

The Church of the Province of the Congo comprises 12 dioceses (one of which, Brazzaville, is in the Republic of the Congo).

Archbishop of the Province of the Congo and Bishop of Aru: Most Rev. Dr GEORGE TITRE ANDE, 11 ave Basalakala, Quartier Immocongo, Commune de Kalamu, BP 16482, Kinshasa; tel. 998611180; e-mail peac_isingoma@yahoo.fr.

Bishop of Aru: Rt Rev. Dr GEORGE TITRE ANDE, POB 226, Aru, Uganda; tel. 810393071; e-mail revdande@yahoo.co.uk.

Bishop of Boga: Rt Rev. MUGENYI WILLIAM BAHEMUKA, CAC-Boga, Congo Liaison Office, POB 25586, Kampala, Uganda; e-mail mugenywiliam@yahoo.com.

Bishop of Bukavu: Rt Rev. SYLVESTRE BALI-BUSANE BAHATI, ave Pagni 2, Quartier Nyalukemba, Ibanda, Bukavu; tel. 994013647; e-mail bahati_bali@yahoo.fr.

Bishop of Goma: (vacant), Goma; tel. 997046544.

Bishop of Kamango: Rt Rev. SABITI TIBAFA DANIEL, PO Box 25586, Kampala, Uganda; tel. 997791013; e-mail sabititibafa@gmail.com.

Bishop of Kasaï: (vacant), 5 ave Makenga, Bonzola, Mbuji-Mayi; tel. 816061423; e-mail anglicanekasai2@gmail.com.

Bishop of Katanga: Rt Rev. BERTIN SUBI, c/o UMM, POB 22037, Kitwe, Zambia; tel. 97047173; e-mail peac_isingoma@yahoo.fr.

Bishop of Kindu: Most Rev. ZACHARIE MASIMANGO KATANDAe-mail angkindu@yahoo.fr.

Bishop of Kinshasa: Rt Rev. ACHILLE MUTSHINDU, POB 16482, Kinshasa 1; tel. 810176596; e-mail anglikin100@gmail.com.

Bishop of Kisangani: Rt Rev. LAMBERT FUNGA BOTOLOME, 10 rue Bowane, Quartier des Musiciens, BP 861, Kisangani; tel. 997252868; e-mail botolome@gmail.com.

Bishop of Nord-Kivu: Rt Rev. MUHINDO ISESOMO, CAZ-Butembo, POB 506, Bwera-Kasese, Uganda; e-mail bishopisesomo@hotmail .com.

Kimbanguist

Eglise de Jésus Christ sur la Terre par le Prophète Simon Kimbangu: BP 7069, Kinshasa; tel. (12) 68944; f. 1921; officially est. 1959; Spiritual Head HE SIMON KIMBANGU KIANGANI.

Protestant Churches

Eglise du Christ au Congo (ECC): ave de la Justice 75, BP 4938, Kinshasa-Gombe; tel. 9929348; e-mail eccm@ic.cd; internet ecc .faithweb.com; f. 1902; a co-ordinating agency for all the Protestant churches, with the exception of the Kimbanguist Church; 62 mem. communities and a provincial org. in each province; Pres. Rev. Dr ANDRÉ BOKUNDOA BO-LIKABE.

Evangelical Lutheran Church in Congo: 150 ave Kasaï, BP 525, Lubumbashi; tel. 995360559; e-mail secretgeneral.eelco@gmail.com; Pres. Bishop RENÉ MWAMBA SUMAILI.

The Press

DAILIES

L'Avenir: Immeuble Ruzizi, 873 ave du Bas-Congo, Kinshasa-Gombe; tel. 998410588; internet groupelavenir.org; owned by Groupe de l'Avenir; Chair. PIUS MUABILU.

Elima: 1 ave de la Révolution, BP 11498, Kinshasa; tel. (12) 77332; f. 1928; evening.

Le Forum des As: 15/C, 11e rue Limete, Kinshasa; tel. 998461089; e-mail forumdesas2001@gmail.com; internet www.forumdesas.net; f. 1990; Editor JOSÉ NAWEJ.

L'Observateur: 4722A, ave Col Ebeya, Kinshasa-Gombe; tel. 810350611; e-mail observateur.mavo@laposte.net; f. 1990; Dir of Publication VALERY MANKENDA; Editor LUC-ROGER MBALA.

Le Phare: BImmeuble Interfina, 2e et 4e Niveau, 9 blvd du 30 Juin, BP 2481, Kinshasa; tel. 813330195; e-mail contact@lephareonline.net; internet lephareonline.net; f. 1983; Editor (vacant).

Le Potentiel: Immeuble Ruzizi, 873 ave du Bas-Congo, BP 11338, Kinshasa; tel. 999999546; e-mail lepotentiel@yahoo.com; internet lepotentiel.cd; f. 1982; Editorial Dir BEN-CLET KANKONDE DAMBU.

La Prospérité: Kinshasa; tel. 818135157; e-mail ngoyimarcel@ymail.com; internet laprosperiteonline.net; f. 2001; Dir-Gen. MARCEL NGOYI.

La Référence Plus: Kasongolunda 290B, Lingwala, BP 12520, Kinshasa; tel. 999923379; e-mail contact@mareferenceplus.cd; internet lareferenceplus.cd; f. 1991; Dir ANDRÉ IPAKALA.

La Tempête des Tropiques: Kinshasa; Pres. and Dir-Gen. ALEXI MUTANDA.

PERIODICALS

Allo Kinshasa: 3 rue Kayange, BP 20271, Kinshasa-Lemba; monthly; Editor MBUYU WA KABILA.

Cahiers des Religions Africaines: Faculté de Théologie Catholique de Kinshasa, BP 712, Kinshasa-Limete; tel. (12) 78476; f. 1967; English and French; religion; 2 a year.

Congo-Afrique: Centre d'Etudes pour l'Action Sociale, 9 ave Père Boka, BP 3375, Kinshasa-Gombe; tel. 898912981; e-mail congoafrique@yahoo.fr; f. 1961; economic, social and cultural; monthly; Editors FRANCIS KIKASSA MWANALESSA, RENÉ BEECKMANS.

La Cruche: Mbuji-Mayi; f. 2016; monthly; Publr and Editor ESTHER NDALAFINA KAPINGA.

Etudes d'Histoire Africaine: National University of the Congo, BP 1825, Lubumbashi; f. 1970; French and English; history; annually.

Mutaani Magazine: Goma; tel. 995652115; f. 2012.

NResources: Immeuble Concem 226, ave Kalembelembe, Commune de Lingwala, Kinshasa; tel. 998758532; e-mail info@nresources.cd; internet www.nresources.cd; French; natural resources and environment; Publr MARCEL MUBENGA; Editor-in-Chief GABY KUBA BEKANGA.

La Percée: Kinshasa; Editor SYLVANIE KIAKU; weekly.

Post: Immeuble Linzadi, 1538 ave de la Douane, Kinshasa-Gombe; e-mail thepostrdc@yahoo.com; 2 a week; Editor-in-Chief MUKEBAYI NKOSO.

Telema: Faculté Canisius, Kimwenza, BP 3724, Kinshasa-Gombe; f. 1974; religious; quarterly; edited by the Central Africa Jesuits.

La Voix du Paysan Congolais: 1150 ave Tabora, C/Barumbu, BP 14582, Kinshasa; tel. 999982097; e-mail lavoixdupaysan_rdc@yahoo.fr; f. 2008; agricultural issues; 4 a year; Dir of Publication JEAN BAPTISTE LUBAMBA.

NEWS AGENCIES

Agence Congolaise de Presse (ACP): 44–48 ave Tombalbaye, BP 1595, Kinshasa-Gombe; tel. 814516656; e-mail info@acpcongo.com; internet acpcongo.com; f. 1957; state-controlled; Pres. KASONGO MWEMA YAMBA-YAMBA; Dir-Gen. BIENVENU-MARIE BAKUMUANYA.

Digital Congo: 21 ave Kabasele Tshiamala, Kinshasa-Gombe; tel. 999045687; e-mail info@digitalcongo.net; internet www.digitalcongo.net; news service owned by Multimedia Congo.

Publishers

Editions Elondja: 22 7ème rue, Quartier Industriel, C/Limete, Kinshasa; tel. 898975868; f. 1987.

Éditions Nzoi: Kinshasa; internet www.editions-nzoi.org.

Broadcasting and Communications

TELECOMMUNICATIONS

Africell RDC: 25 ave de la Justice, Kinshasa; internet www.africell.cd; f. 2012; CEO ZIAD DALLOUL; 4.0m. subscribers (March 2020).

Airtel Congo: croisement des aves Tchad et Bas-Congo, Kinshasa; tel. 996000121; e-mail infos@cd.airtel.com; internet www.airtel.cd; acquired by Bharti Airtel (India) in 2010; mobile telephone network; fmrly Celtel Congo, subsequently Zain Congo, present name adopted in 2010; Man. Dir EMMANUEL HAMEZ; 9.8m. subscribers (March 2020).

Orange RDC: ave du Port, Kinshasa; tel. 840001777; internet www.orange.cd; fmrly Congo Chine Telecom, present name adopted 2012; mobile telephone network; covers Kinshasa and Bas-Congo, Kasaï, Katanga and Oriental provinces; 100% owned by France Télécom; Dir-Gen. BENCHEICK HAIDARA; 10.5m. subscribers (March 2020).

Vodacom Congo: Immeuble Mobil–Oil, 2ème étage, 3157 blvd du 30 juin, BP 797, Kinshasa; tel. 813131000; e-mail vodacom@vodacom.cd; internet www.vodacom.cd; 51% owned by Vodacom (South Africa); Dir-Gen. (vacant); 13.8m. subscribers (March 2020).

Regulatory Authority

Autorité de Régulation de la Poste et des Télécommunications du Congo (ARPTC): blvd du 30 juin, BP 3000, Kinshasa; tel. 821918814; e-mail secretariat@arptc.gouv.cd; internet www.arptc.gouv.cd; Pres. ODON KASINDI (acting).

BROADCASTING

Radio-Télévision Nationale Congolaise (RTNC): ave Kabinda, Lingwala, Kinshasa; tel. 840168733; e-mail rtnc@rtnc.cd; internet rtnc.cd; state radio, terrestrial and satellite television broadcasts; Dir-Gen. (vacant).

Radio

Several private radio broadcasters operate in Kinshasa. Radio France Internationale broadcasts via FM in nine localities.

Digital Congo FM (106.5 FM): ave Kabasele Tshiamala 21, Kinshasa; tel. 999936373; e-mail info@digitalcongo.net; internet www.digitalcongo.net; owned by Multimedia Congo; broadcasts in French and Swahili; relay stations at Lubumbashi, Mbandaka, Mbuji-Mayi, Kikwit, Matadi, Kindu, Kisangani and Goma.

Mutaani FM: Goma; tel. 995652115; f. 2011.

Radio Okapi: 12 ave des Aviateurs, Kinshasa-Gombe; tel. 818906747; e-mail contact@radiookapi.net; internet www.radiookapi.net; f. 2002; owned by the United Nations; Public Information Chief CHARLES BAMBARA.

Radio 7: ave Col Ebeya, Kinshasa; tel. 997406485; Lingala and French.

Radio Télévision Kimbanguiste (RATELKI): Centre d'Accueil Kimbanguiste, ave Saïo, Kinshasa; e-mail contact@ratelki.net; internet www.ratelki.net; f. 2003; religious; owned by Kimbanguist Church.

Raga FM: 22 ave des Aviateurs, Kinshasa; tel. 999929922; broadcasts in Kinshasa, Goma, Lubumbashi, Kisangani, Matadi, Kindu, Kikwit and Mbuji-Mayi; also relays programmes from the BBC and Voice of America.

RTGA Radio FM 88.1: Immeuble Ruzizi, ave Bas-Congo 873, Kinshasa-Gombe; tel. 998410588; French and Lingala.

Top Congo FM: ave Col Mondjiba, Complexe UTEX, Ngaliema, Kinshasa; tel. 818120812.

Television

Several private television broadcasters operate in Kinshasa.

Digital Congo TV: ave Kabasele Tshiamala 21, Kinshasa; tel. 999936373; e-mail info@digitalcongo.net; internet www.digitalcongo.net; owned by Multimedia Congo; broadcasts in French, Lingala and Swahili.

RTGA TV: Immeuble Ruzizi, ave Bas-Congo 873, Gombe, Kinshasa; tel. 998410588; broadcasts in French and Lingala.

Télévision Congolaise: ave Kabinda, Lingwala, Kinshasa; tel. 840168733; internet rtnc.cd; govt commercial station; operated by RTNC; broadcasts 2 channels.

Regulatory Authority

Conseil Supérieur de l'Audiovisuel et de la Communication: Immeuble Likasi, 2e niveau, blvd du 30 Juin, pl. Royal, Kinshasa-Gombe; tel. 816452767; e-mail csac.contact@gmail.com; internet www.csac.cd; f. 2011; Pres. TITO NDOMBI.

Finance

BANKING

Central Bank

Banque Centrale du Congo: 563 blvd Colonel Tshatshi au nord, BP 2697, Kinshasa; tel. 992320001; e-mail info@bcc.cd; internet www.bcc.cd; f. 1964; Gov. MARIE-FRANCE MALANGU KABEDI-MBUYI.

Commercial Banks

Access Bank DRCongo SA: 158 ave de la Démocratie, Kinshasa-Gombe; tel. 812222160; e-mail info.drcongo@accessbankplc.com; internet congo.accessbankplc.com; Pres. IGNACE MABANZA METI; Dir-Gen. IFEANYI NJOKU.

Advans Banque Congo: ave du Bas Congo 4, Kinshasa-Gombe; tel. 817111140; e-mail contact@advansbanquecongo.com; internet www.advansbanquecongo.com; f. 2008; 50.06% owned by Advans, 23.59% owned by KfW, 13.77% owned by IFC and 12.58% owned by AfDB; Dir-Gen. ZINE EL ABIDINE OTMANI.

Afriland First Bank: 767 blvd du 30 juin, BP 10470, Kinshasa-Gombe; tel. 990901111; e-mail firstbankcd@afrilandfirstbankcd.com; internet afrilandfirstbankcd.com; f. 2004; Pres. JOSEPH TOUBI; Dir-Gen. SOUAIBOU ABARY.

Bank of Africa: 22 ave des Aviateurs, BP 7119, Kinshasa-Gombe; tel. 993004600; e-mail infos@boa-rdc.com; internet www.boa-rdc.com; f. 2010; Pres. GUY-ROBERT LUKAMA; Dir-Gen. JAMAL AMEZIANE.

BGFIBank RDC: 128 blvd du 30 juin, BP 7891, Kinshasa-Gombe; tel. 995809999; e-mail eqc.rdc@bgfi.com; internet rdc.groupebgfibank.com; f. 2010; Dir-Gen. FRANCESCO DE MUSSO.

Byblos Bank RDC SA: 4 ave du Marché, BP 7613, Kinshasa-Gombe; tel. 817070701; e-mail byblosbankrdc@byblosbank.com; f. 1983; fmrly Solidaire Banque Internationale SARL; 66.67% owned by Byblos Bank SAL (Lebanon); Dir-Gen. BOUTROS ABI AAD.

Citigroup (Congo) SARL Congo: 657 Immeuble Citibank Congo, angle aves Col Lukusa et Ngongo Lutete, BP 9999, Kinshasa; tel. 815554808; f. 1971; Dir-Gen. WILLY MULAMBA.

Ecobank DRC: 47 ave Ngongo Lutete, BP 7515, Kinshasa; tel. 996016000; e-mail ecobankcd@ecobank.com; internet www.ecobank.com.

EquityBCDC: 4B ave des Aviateurs, Kinshasa-Gombe; tel. 818302700; e-mail mail@equitybcdc.cd; internet equitygroupholdings.com/cd; f. 2020 following the merger of Equity Bank Congo and Banque Commerciale du Congo SARL; Pres. NESTOR ANKIBA; Dir-Gen. CÉLESTIN MUKEBA MUNTUABU.

FBNBank DRC (BIC): 191 ave de l'Équateur, BP 1299, Kinshasa; tel. 815558858; e-mail contact@fbnbankrdc.com; internet www.fbnbankrdc.com; f. 1994; fmrly Banque Internationale de Crédit SARL; present name adopted in 2014; Pres. OLAYINKA OLUMIDE AKINKUGBE; Dir-Gen. AKEEM BABATUNDE AJIBOLA OLADELE.

Rawbank Sarl: Immeuble Atrium, 66 ave Col Lukusa, BP 2499, Kinshasa-Gombe; tel. 996016300; e-mail contact@rawbank.cd; internet www.rawbank.com; f. 2002; CEO MUSTAFA RAWJI.

Sofibanque SA: 4258 ave Kabasele Tshamala, Kinshasa-Gombe; tel. 817300200; e-mail contact@sofibanque.com; internet www.sofibanque.com; Pres. ABDALLAH WAZNI; Dir-Gen. HENRY YOAN WAZNI.

Standard Bank RDC: 12 ave de Mongala, BP 16297, Kinshasa; tel. 996060060; e-mail serviceclient.drc@standardbank.cd; internet www.standardbank.cd; f. 1973; subsidiary of Standard Bank Investment Corpn (South Africa); CEO AMEDEO ANNICIELLO.

Trust Merchant Bank SA (TMB): 1223 ave Lumumba, Centre Ville, Lubumbashi; tel. 997023000; e-mail tmb@tmb.cd; internet www.trustmerchantbank.com; f. 2004; Pres. ROBERT LEVY; Dir-Gen. OLIVER MEISENBERG.

United Bank for Africa RDC SARL: 1853 ave de la Libération, BP 7351, Kinshasa-Gombe; tel. 996020064; e-mail cfccongodr@ubagroup.com; internet www.ubardc.com; Dir-Gen. PATRICK FITA KABISI.

Specialized Financial Institutions

Fonds pour l'Inclusion Financière en République Démocratique du Congo (FPM SA): 17 ave Kauka, Quartier Batetela, Commune de Gombe, Kinshasa; tel. 992006139; e-mail contact@fpm.cd; internet fpm.cd; f. 2007; Pres. PIERRE DAUBERT.

Fonds National de la Microfinance: 10 Nioki, Kinshasa-Gombe; tel. 999917188; e-mail ngoy_thierry@yahoo.fr; internet www.fonami.org; f. 2011; Co-ordinator-Gen. THIERRY NGOY KASUMBA.

Fonds de Promotion de l'Industrie (FPI): ave Lukusa 16, en face du cercle Elaeis, Kinshasa; tel. 816905362; e-mail dgkinshasa@fpi-rdc.cd; internet www.fpi-rdc.cd; Dir-Gen. JEAN-CLAUDE KALENGA (acting).

Société Financière de Développement SARL (SOFIDE): Immeuble SOFIDE, 9–11 angle aves Ngabu et Kisangani, BP 1148, Kinshasa; tel. 990102513; e-mail sofide@sofide-cd.com; internet www.sofide-cd.com; f. 1970; partly state-owned; provides tech. and financial aid, primarily for agricultural devt; Pres. JACQUES MASANGU-A-MWANZA; Dir-Gen. LOUIS-JOSÉ LISASILI BOOTO.

Banking Association

Association Congolaise des Banques: 1 pl. du Marché, Kinshasa; tel. 817562771; f. 1952; Pres. YVES CUYPERS; 18 mems.

INSURANCE

Activa Assurance RDC: 4 ave Pumbu, Kinshasa-Gombe; tel. 858586382; e-mail contact.rdc@group-activa.com; internet www.group-activa.com/rdc; f. 2019; Dir-Gen. DENIS OUEDRAOGO.

Rawsur RDC: 90 blvd du 30 Juin, Kinshasa-Gombe; tel. 81558686; e-mail contact@rawsur.com; internet rawsur.com; f. 2019; Dir-Gen. TARIK LEFRIYEKH; also **Rawsur Life**.

Société Nationale d'Assurances (SONAS): 6664 blvd du 30 juin, Immeuble Sankuru, Kinshasa-Gombe; tel. 999914956; e-mail communication@sonas.cd; internet www.sonas.cd; f. 1966; state-owned; Dir-Gen. LUCIEN EKOFO BONYEM.

Regulatory Authority

Autorité de Régulation et de Contrôle des Assurances (ARCA): 16 ave Pumbu, Kinshasa-Gombe; tel. 821920174; e-mail info@arca.cd; internet arca.cd; f. 2016; Pres. DEOGRATIAS MUTOMBO NYEMBO; Dir-Gen. ALAIN KANYINDA NGALULA.

Trade and Industry

GOVERNMENT AGENCIES

Agence Nationale de Développement de l'Entrepreneuriat Congolais (ANADEC): Immeuble Royal Entrée C, blvd du 30 Juin, BP 16799, Kinshasa; tel. 815101420; e-mail contact@anadec.cd; internet anadec.cd; f. 2009 as Office de Promotion des Petites et Moyennes Entreprises Congolais; name changed as above in 2021; Dir-Gen. EZÉCHIEL BIDUAYA MUSUMBU.

Agence Nationale de Promotion des Exportations (ANAPEX): 01 ave de l'OUA, Concession Procoki, Kinshasa-Ngaliema; e-mail info@anapex.cd; internet fb.com/anapexRDC; f. 2020; Dir-Gen. MIKE TAMBWE LUBEMBA.

Agence Nationale pour la Promotion des Investissements (ANAPI): 33C blvd du 30 Juin, BP 1797, Kinshasa-Gombe; tel. 999925026; e-mail anapi@investindrc.cd; internet www.investindrc.cd; Pres. HUGUES NTOTO; Dir-Gen. ANTHONY KINZOKAMOLE.

Bureau Central de Coordination (BCECO): ave Colonel Mondjiba 372, Complexe Utex Africa, Kinshasa; tel. 815096430; e-mail bceco@bceco.cd; internet www.bceco.cd; f. 2001; manages projects funded by the African Development Bank and the World Bank; Dir-Gen. JEAN MABI MULUMBA.

Guichet Unique de Création d'Entreprise: 482 ave de la Science, Kinshasa-Gombe; tel. 822284008; e-mail guce@guichetunique.cd; internet guichetunique.cd; single-window trade facilitation; Dir-Gen. Prof. AMISI HERADY.

Office Congolais de Contrôle (OCC): 98 ave du Port, Kinshasa-Gombe; tel. 852935143; e-mail infos@occ.cd; internet occ.cd; f. 1974 as Office Zaïrois de Contrôle; Pres. FORTUNAT NDAMBO; Dir-Gen. MUTOMBO TSHIMANGA.

DEVELOPMENT ORGANIZATIONS

Agence Congolaise des Grands Travaux: 1 ave de l'OUA, Kinshasa-Ngaliema; tel. 990783779; e-mail contact@acgt.cd; internet acgt.cd; f. 2008; Dir-Gen. CHARLES MÉDARD ILUNGA MWAMBA.

Centre National d'Appui au Développement et à la Participation Populaire (CENADEP): 1150 ave Tabora, Barumbu, BP 14582, Kinshasa; tel. 998311827; e-mail info@cenadepasbl.org; internet www.cenadepasbl.org; f. 1999; Pres. BAUDOUIN HAMULI; Dir-Gen. DANNI SYNGOMA.

Fonds de Promotion de l'Industrie (FPI): Kinshasa; internet www.fpi-rdc.cd; Pres. MUKALAYI KATUMBWA; Dir-Gen. BERTIN MULIMU TSHISEKEDI.

La Générale des Carrières et des Mines (Gécamines): 419 blvd Kamanyola, BP 450, Lubumbashi; tel. 997031931; e-mail info@gecamines.cd; internet www.gecamines.cd; f. 1967 to acquire assets of Union Minière du Haut-Katanga; engaged in mining and marketing of copper, cobalt, zinc and coal; also has interests in agriculture; Pres. ALPHONSE KAPUTO; Dir-Gen. DESTIN HILAIRE NTAMBWE NGOYI KABONGO.

Institut National pour l'Etude et la Recherche Agronomiques (INERA): 13 ave des Cliniques, BP 2037, Kisangani; tel. 818504779; e-mail ineradev@gmail.com; internet fb.com/inerardc; f. 1933; agricultural research.

Office National des Produits Agricoles du Congo (ONAPAC): ave Gen. Bobozo 1082, BP 8931, Kinshasa; tel. (12) 77144; f. 1979; fmrly Office National du Café; present name adopted 2018; state agency for coffee and also cocoa, tea, quinquina and pyrethrum; Dir-Gen. NICODÈME MULUMBA WA KASONGO.

CHAMBERS OF COMMERCE

Chambre de Commerce, d'Industrie et d'Agriculture du Congo: 10 ave des Aviateurs, BP 7247, Kinshasa; tel. (12) 22286; Pres. ILUNGA KONYA.

Chambre de Commerce et d'Industrie Franco-Congolaise (CCIFC): 407 ave Roi Baudouin 1er, Kinshasa-Gombe; tel. 843771582; e-mail direction@ccife-rdcongo.org; internet www.ccife-rdcongo.org; f. 1987; Pres. BERTRAND BISENGIMANA.

EMPLOYERS' ASSOCIATIONS

Fédération des Entreprises du Congo: 10 ave des Aviateurs, BP 7247, Kinshasa; tel. 812488909; e-mail fec@fec–rdc.com; internet www.fec-rdc.com; f. 1972 as the Association Nationale des Entreprises du Zaïre; name changed as above in 1997; represents business interests for both domestic and foreign institutions; Pres. ALBERT YUMA MULIMBI.

Fédération des Industriels du Bois (FIB): 2165 ave des Poids Lourds, BP 552, Kinshasa; tel. 810753021; e-mail gabrielmola58@yahoo.fr; f. 2006; Pres. GABRIEL MOLA MOTIYA.

Confédération Nationale de Producteurs Agricoles du Congo (CONAPAC): 28 ave Essandja, Quartier Bon Marché, Commune de Barumbu, Kinshasa; tel. 998286456; e-mail conapac_rdc@conapacrdc.org; internet www.conapacrdc.org; f. 2011; Pres. PALUKU MIVIMBA; 16 fed. mems.

UTILITIES

Electricity

Autorité de Régulation du Secteur de l'Électricité (ARE): Immeuble Royal, 3e et 4e étages, Entrée D, blvd du 30 Juin, Kinshasa/Gombe; tel. 970099291; e-mail contact@are.gouv.cd; internet are.gouv.cd; regulatory authority for electricity; Dir-Gen. SANDRINE NGALULA MUBENGA.

Société Nationale d'Électricité (SNEL): 2831 ave de la Justice, BP 500, Kinshasa; tel. 816076254; e-mail info@snel.cd; internet www.snel.cd; f. 1970; state-owned; Pres. ANDRÉ-ALAIN ATUNDU LIONGO; Dir-Gen. FABRICE LUSINDE.

Water

Régie de Distribution d'Eau (REGIDESO): 59–63 blvd du 30 juin, BP 12599, Kinshasa; e-mail courrier@regidesordc.com; internet www.regidesordc.com; f. 1978; water supply admin; Pres. THOMAS MAKETA LUTETE; Dir-Gen. DAVID TSHILUMBA MUTOMBO.

MAJOR COMPANIES

The following are some of the largest companies in terms either of capital investment or employment.

Manufacturing and Trading

Bio Agro Business SAS (BAB): Immeuble Quantum, 8e Niveau, 8177 blvd du 30 Juin, Kinshasa; tel. 898051579; e-mail info@bab-rdc.com; internet bab-rdc.com; f. 2018.

Les Brasseries du Congo (BRACONGO): 7666 ave des Brasseries, Quartier Kingabwa, BP 7600, Kinshasa; tel. 815586874; e-mail secdg@bracongo.cd; internet bracongo.cd; Dir-Gen. CYRIL SEGONDS.

Brasseries, Limonaderies et Malteries du Congo (BRALIMA): 1 ave du Flambeau, BP 7246, Kinshasa; tel. 998946910; internet bralima.net; f. 1923; production of beer, soft drinks and ice; Gen. Man. VICTOR MADIELA.

Compagnie des Margarines, Savons et Cosmétiques au Congo SARL (MARSAVCO CONGO): 1 ave Kalemie, BP 8914, Kinshasa; e-mail info@marsavco.com; internet www.marsavco.com; f. 1922; subsidiary of Unilever NV; mfrs of detergents, foods and cosmetics; Pres. C. GODDE.

Compagnie Sucrière: blvd du 30 juin, bldg BCDC, BP 8816, Kinshasa; tel. 818946387; internet www.finasucre.com; f. 1925; 40% state-owned; mfrs of sugar, alcohol, acetylene, oxygen and carbon dioxide; Dir-Gen. JEAN ARTHUR PILOT LAGESSE.

Feronia: Route des Poids, Lourds 1963, Gombe, Kinshasa; internet feronia.com; f. 1911; oil palm plantations.

Groupe Blattner Elwyn: Route des Poids, Lourds 2, Kingabwa, Kinshasa; tel. 851303685; e-mail contact@gbedrc.com; internet www.gbedrc.com; agro-based industries; Pres. ELWYN BLATTNER.

Groupe Orgaman: 4354 Lt Col Lukusa, BP 1598, Kinshasa; tel. 8821899; conglomerate with interests in food distribution, coffee, animal rearing, transport, real estate and mining, etc.; Gen. Man. JEAN-CLAUDE DAMSEAUX.

Société Commerciale d'Import-Export Sprl (SOCIMEX): 952 ave Métallurgie, Quartier Industriel de Kingabwa, Kinshasa-Limete; tel. 999928866; e-mail contact@group-socimex.com; internet www.group-socimex.com; foodstuff distribution.

Société de Développement des Forêts: 2165 ave des Poids Lourds, Kinshasa-Gombe; tel. 851272991; e-mail mail@sodefor.net; internet sodefor.net; f. 1994; Dir JOSÉ ALBANO TRINDADE.

Minerals

Engen RDC: ave du Port 14/16, BP 2799, Kinshasa-Gombe; tel. 817005590; e-mail info@engen.cd; internet www.engenoil.com; f. 1978; marketing of petroleum products; Dir-Gen. CHARLES NIKOBASA.

Perenco: 11ème étage, Immeuble BCDC, blvd du 30 juin, BP 15596, Kinshasa; tel. 817008002; f. 2000; producer of petroleum; Dir-Gen. PEREZE BRETON.

Société Aurifère du Kivu et Maniema (SAKIMA): 316 ave Lt-Col Lukusa, Kinshasa-Gombe; tel. 993462002; e-mail sakimardc@sakima.cd; internet sakima.cd; f. 1997 as successor to Société Minière du Kivu; 93% owned by Banro Resources Corpn, 7% by DRC Government; exploitation of gold; Man. Dir FIDÈLE BASEMENANE KASONGO (acting).

Société Congolaise des Industries de Raffinage: Immeuble BCDC, 10e niveau, blvd du 30 juin, BP 1478, Kinshasa-Gombe; tel. 999933240; fmrly Société Congo-Italienne de Raffinage; petroleum refinery.

Société de Développement Industriel et Minière du Congo (SODIMICO): 4219 ave de l'Ouganda, BP 7064, Kinshasa; tel. (12) 32511; subsidiary of Gécamines; see Development Organizations; copper mining consortium exploiting mines of Musoshi and Kinsenda in Katanga.

Société Minière de Bakwanga (MIBA): 4 pl. de la Coopération, BP 377, Mbuji-Mayi; tel. 816081406; e-mail sdgmiba@mibardc.net; internet www.mibardc.net; f. 1961; 80% state-owned; industrial diamond mining; Pres. DIEUDONNÉ MBAYA TSHAKANI TSHABANTU; Dir-Gen. (vacant).

Société Minière de Kilo-Moto (SOKIMO): 15 avenue des Sénégalais, BP 8498, Kinshasa; e-mail info@sokimo.cd; internet sokimo.cd; state-owned; operates gold mines; Pres. CHRISITINE FEZA; Man. Dir BONONGE TOKOLE.

Tenke Fungurume Mining: Luano City, Route de l'Aéroport, Lubumbashi, Katanga; tel. 991005218; e-mail tfmcommunications@fmi.com; f. 1996 to take over the operations of Société Minière du Tenké-Fungurume; copper and cobalt mining.

TRADE UNIONS

Confédération Démocratique du Travail (CDT): ave de la Presse, BP 10897, Quartier Industriel, Kinshasa-Limete; tel. 990519482; e-mail cdtcongo@yahoo.fr; internet cdtrdcongo.org; Pres. GUY KUKU GEDILA.

Confédération Syndicale du Congo: 461 ave Kasa-Vubu, Kinshasa-Gombe; tel. 971971851; e-mail csc_congo@hotmail.com; f. 1991; Pres. GUY KOLELA TSHIBANGU.

Syndicat des Enseignants du Congo (SYECO): Kinshasa; Sec.-Gen. CÉCILE TSHIYOMBO.

Union Nationale des Travailleurs du Congo: 5 ave Mutombo Katshi, BP 8814, Kinshasa-Gombe; tel. 998616193; e-mail untcrdc@yahoo.fr; f. 1967; comprises 14 unions; Pres. MODESTE AMÉDÉE NDONGALA N'SIBU.

Transport

Office de Gestion du Fret Multimodal (OGEFREM): 9 ave TSF, Kinshasa-Gombe; e-mail admin@ogefrem.org; internet ogefrem.org; f. 1980 as Office de Gestion du Fret Maritime; present name adopted 2009; Pres. AMISI MAKUTANO; Dir-Gen. WILLIAM KAZUMBA.

Société Commerciale des Transports et des Ports (SCTP): BP 98, Kinshasa; tel. 812316707; e-mail contact@sctp.com; internet www.sctp-sa.com; f. 1935; fmrly Office National des Transports; present name adopted 2011; operates 12,674 km of waterways, 366 km of railways, and road and air transport; administers ports of Matadi, Boma and Banana; Pres. JOSÉ MAKILA SUMANDA; Dir-Gen. FRANKLIN MABAYA BONGILA.

RAILWAYS

The main line runs from Lubumbashi to Ilebo. International services run to Dar es Salaam (Tanzania) and Lobito (Angola), and also connect with the Zambian, Zimbabwean, Mozambican and South African systems. Under a major investment programme agreed with the People's Republic of China in the late 2000s, the rail network was to be extensively modernized.

Société Nationale des Chemins de Fer du Congo (SNCC): 115 pl. de la Gare, BP 297, Lubumbashi; tel. (2) 346306; internet snccsa.com; f. 1974; administers all internal railway sections as well as river transport and transport on Lakes Tanganyika and Kivu; Pres. GABRIEL KYUNGU; CEO FABIEN MUTOMB.

ROADS

Under a major investment programme agreed with the People's Republic of China in the late 2000s, modernization of the road network (which remained in a very poor state of repair) was to be undertaken, including the construction of a major highway linking Katanga to the Kisangani river port and the building of a new ring road around Kinshasa.

Fonds d'Entretien Routier (FONER): 6 ave Kwango, Kinshasa-Gombe; tel. 990287400; f. 2008; raises and manages funds for the maintenance of road networks; Dir-Gen. PIERRE BUNDOKI NDONGALA.

Office des Routes: 1 ave Office des Routes, BP 10899, Kinshasa-Gombe; tel. 971870091; e-mail contact@officedesroutes.cd; internet www.officedesroutes.cd; construction and maintenance of roads; Pres. KONGOLO TSHINGOMBE (acting); Man. Dir JEANNOT KIKANGALA NGOYU.

INLAND WATERWAYS

The River Congo is navigable for more than 1,600 km. Above the Stanley Falls the Congo becomes the Lualaba, and is navigable along a 965-km stretch from Ubundu to Kindu and Kongolo to Bukama. The River Kasaï, a tributary of the River Congo, is navigable by shipping as far as Ilebo, at which the line from Lubumbashi terminates. The total length of inland waterways is 14,935 km.

Congolaise des Voies Maritimes (CVM): rue du Kasai, Kinshasa; Pres. MARIE-MADELEINE MIENZE KIAKU; Dir-Gen. CHRISTINE TUSE DAHOMBO.

Régie des Voies Fluviales: 109 ave Lumpungu, BP 11697, Kinshasa-Gombe; f. 1971; administers river navigation; Pres. BENJAMIN MUKULUNGU; Dir-Gen. RUFFIN NGOMPER ILUNGA.

Société de Transports du Congo (TRANSCO): Kinshasa-Gombe; f. 2013; Pres. LAURENT BOYI BOYOMBE (acting); Dir-Gen. CHIEF TSHIPAMBA NGAMBAMALU (acting).

SHIPPING

The principal seaports are Matadi, Boma and Banana on the lower Congo. The port of Matadi has more than 1.6 km of quays and can accommodate up to 10 deep-water vessels. Matadi is linked by rail with Kinshasa.

Lignes Maritimes Congolaises SA: Immeuble LMC-AMICONGO, 6ème étage, 13 ave des Aviateurs, BP 9496, Kinshasa-Gombe; tel. 815682447; e-mail info@lmc.cd; internet lmc.cd; f. 1974; fmrly Compagnie Maritime du Congo, name changed as above in 2009; services (monthly): Anvers–Boma–Matadi–Viana do Castelo–Caen–Anvers; Pres. LAMBERT MENDE OMALENGA; Dir-Gen. JEAN-CLAUDE MUKENDI MBIYA.

CIVIL AVIATION

International airports are located at Ndjili (for Kinshasa), Luano (for Lubumbashi), Bukavu, Goma and Kisangani. There are smaller airports and airstrips dispersed throughout the country.

Autorité de l'Aviation Civile (AAC/RDC): Immeuble SCTP, 117 blvd du 30 Juin, Kinshasa; tel. 812237602; e-mail info@aacrdc.org;

internet www.aacrdc.org; f. 2011; Pres. SÉBASTIEN LESENJINA; Man. JEAN TSHIUMBA MPUNGA.

Compagnie Africaine d'Aviation (CAA): Route des Poids Lourd n° 1, Limete, Kinshasa-Gombe; tel. 820002601; e-mail info@caacongo.com; internet www.caacongo.com; Pres. and Dir-Gen. DAVID BLATTNER.

Congo Airways: Futur Tower, 3642 blvd du 30 Juin, Kinshasa-Gombe; tel. 829781921; internet www.congoairways.com; f. 2014; Pres. LOUISE MAYUMA KASENDE; Man. Dir PASCAL KASONGO MWEMA (acting).

Régie des Voies Aériennes: ave Aérodrome 548, C/Barumbu, BP 6574, Kinshasa; e-mail rva.dg@rva.cd; internet www.rva.cd; Dir-Gen. ALPHONSE SHUNGU MAHUNGU.

Tourism

Office National du Tourisme: 1148A ave Tombalbaye, BP 2502, Kinshasa-Gombe; tel. 998319053; e-mail info@visit-rdcongo.com; internet www.visit-rdcongo.com; f. 1959; Dir-Gen. ROSETTE SAÏBA LWANZO.

Defence

The total strength of the armed forces of the Democratic Republic of the Congo, as assessed at November 2021, was estimated at 134,250 (central staff 14,000; army 103,000; Republican Guard 8,000; navy 6,700; air force 2,550). The United Nations (UN) Organization Stabilization Mission in the Democratic Republic of the Congo (MONUSCO) has a maximum authorized strength of 13,500 military personnel, 660 military observers and staff officers, 591 police officers and 1,050 members of the formed police units. MONUSCO has a mandate to remain in the country until 20 December 2022, and in March 2013 was the first ever UN peacekeeping mission to be authorized to carry out 'offensive combat operations'. To this end, a specialized 'intervention brigade' was created within the operation's existing force.

Defence Budget: CF 580,000m. in 2021.

Commander-in-Chief: FÉLIX ANTOINE TSHISEKEDI TSHILOMBO.

Chief of General Staff of the Armed Forces: Gen. CHRISTIAN TSHIWEWE SONGESHA.

Chief of Staff of the Army: Gen. SUKABWE ASINDA FALL.

Chief of Staff of the Navy: Vice-Adm. JEAN-MARIE VALENTIN MATALINGUMA.

Chief of Staff of the Air Force: Gen. RENÉ DIASUKA.

Education

Primary education, beginning at six years of age and lasting for six years, is officially compulsory and is available free of charge in public institutions. Secondary education, which is not compulsory, begins at 12 years of age and lasts for up to six years, comprising a first cycle of two years and a second of four years. In 2017/18, according to estimates by the United Nations Educational, Scientific and Cultural Organization (UNESCO), pre-primary enrolment was equivalent to 6% of pupils (6% of boys; 6% of girls) in the appropriate age-group. There are four universities, located at Kinshasa, Kinshasa/Limete, Kisangani and Lubumbashi. According to estimates by the United Nations Educational, Scientific and Cultural Organization (UNESCO), in 2017 spending on education represented 14% of total government expenditure.

Bibliography

Abdulai, N. *Zaire: Background to the Civil War*. London, ARIB, 1997.

Afoaku, O. G. *Explaining the Failure of Democracy in the Democratic Republic of the Congo: Autocracy and Dissent in an Ambivalent World*. New York, Edwin Mellen Press, 2005.

Autesserre, S. *The Trouble with the Congo: Local Violence And The Failure Of International Peacebuilding*. Cambridge, Cambridge University Press, 2010.

Ayoub, K. *L'ONU face à l'irrationnel en RDC*. Paris, L'Harmattan, 2011.

Berwouts, K. *Congo's Violent Peace: Conflict and Struggle Since the Great African War*. London, Zed Books, 2017.

Bugandwa Mungu Akonkwa, D. *Province du Sud-Kivu, RD Congo: Enjeux economiques et financiers*. Paris, L'Harmattan, 2013.

Clark, J. *The African Stakes of the Congo War*. London, Palgrave, 2002.

Deibert, M. *The Democratic Republic of Congo: Between Hope and Despair*. London, Zed Books, 2013.

Dunn, K. *Imagining the Congo: The International Relations of Identity*. New York, Palgrave Macmillan, 2003.

Edgerton, R. *The Troubled Heart of Africa: A History of the Congo*. New York, St Martin's Press, 2002.

Ekpebu, L. B. *Zaire and the African Revolution*. Ibadan, Ibadan University Press, 1989.

Ewans, M. *European Atrocity, African Catastrophe: Leopold II, the Congo Free State and its Aftermath*. London, Curzon Press, 2001.

Freedman, J. *Gender, Violence and Politics in the Democratic Republic of Congo*. Farnham, Ashgate, 2015.

Gondola, D. *The History of Congo*. Westport, CT, Greenwood Press, 2002.

Hedlund, A. *Hutu Rebels: Exile Warriors in the Eastern Congo*. Philadelphia. PA, Pennsylvania University Press, 2019.

Hochschild, A. *King Leopold's Ghost*. London, Macmillan, 1999.

Institute for Global Dialogue. *The Transition in the Democratic Republic of the Congo: Problems and Prospects*. Midrand, 2006.

Kabatusuila, P. *Les Frontières Internationales de la République Démocratique du Congo: Impacts Ecologiques, Economiques et Stratégiques en Afrique Centrale*. Saint-Denis, Edilivre, 2013.

Kadima, D., Kabemba, C., and Sharpe, K. *Whither Regional Peace and Security: The Democratic Republic of Congo After the War*. Pretoria, Africa Institute of South Africa, 2003.

Kisangani, E. F. *Guerres Civiles dans la République Démocratique du Congo: 1960-2010*. Paris, L'Harmattan, 2015.

Kisangani, E. F., and Scott, B. *Historical Dictionary of the Democratic Republic of the Congo*. (3rd ed). Lanham, MD., Scarecrow Press, 2010.

Kitenge bin Kitoko, E. T., and Makosso, A.-C. *RDCongo, les élections et après: intellectuels et politiques posent les enjeux de l'après-transition*. Paris, L'Harmattan, 2006.

Langellier, J.-P. *Mobutu*. Paris, Perrin, 2017.

Makengo Nkutu, A. *Les institutions politiques de la RDC: de la République du Zaïre à la République Démocratique Du Congo (1990–à Nos Jours)*. Paris, L'Harmattan, 2010.

Makungu Masudi, N. M. *Economie Mondialisée, Coopératives Délaissées: Sociologie Du Développement et de la Coopération en République Démocratique du Congo*. Paris, L'Harmattan, 2014.

Malu-Malu, J.-J. A. *Le Congo Kinshasa*. (2nd edn). Paris, Karthala, 2014.

Mapendo, C. *Développement Durable et Politique de Zones Economiques Spéciales en République démocratique du Congo*. Paris, L'Harmattan, 2017.

Marriage, Z. *Formal Peace and Informal War. Security and Development in Congo*. Abingdon, Routledge, 2013.

Marysse, S. *La libération du Congo dans le contexte de la mondialisation*. Antwerp, UFSIA, 1997.

Mbaya, K. (Ed.). *Zaire: What Destiny?* Dakar, CODESRIA, 1993.

Mokoli, M. M. *State Against Development: The Experience of Post-1965 Zaire*. Westport, CT, Greenwood Press, 1992.

Mukenge, T. *Culture and Customs of the Congo (Culture and Customs of Africa)*. Westport, CT, Greenwood Publishing Group, 2001.

Mungal, A. S. *Le consensus politique et la renaissance de la République démocratique du Congo*. Paris, Editions du Cerdaf, 2002.

Ndaywel è Nziem, I. *Nouvelle histoire du Congo: Des origines à la République Démocratique*. Brussels, Editions Le Cri, 2009.

Nest, M., Grignon, F., and Kisangani, E. F. (Eds.). *Democratic Republic of Congo: Economic Dimensions of War and Peace*. Boulder, CO, Lynne Rienner Publishers, 2006.

Nzongola-Ntalaja, G. *The Congo from Leopold to Kabila: A People's History*. London, Zed Books, 2002.

Okende Senga, C. *Leadership et jeu politique en Rd-Congo: l'audace d'une révolution substantielle!* Paris, Edilivre, 2015.

Prunier, G. *Africa's World War: Congo, the Rwandan Genocide, and the Making of a Continental Catastrophe*. New York, Oxford University Press, 2008.

Quick, I. D. *Follies in Fragile States: How International Stabilisation Failed in the Congo*. London, Double Loop, 2015.

Sanqmpam, S. N. *Pseudo-capitalism and the Overpolitical State: Reconciling Politics and Anthropology in Zaire*. Brookfield, VT, Ashgate Press, 1994.

Stanard, M. G. *Selling the Congo: A History of European Pro-Empire Propaganda and the Making of Belgian Imperialism*. Lincoln, NE, University of Nebraska Press, 2011.

Stearns, J. *Dancing in the Glory of Monsters: The Collapse of the Congo and the Great War of Africa*. New York, Public Affairs, 2011.

The War That Doesn't Say Its Name: The Unending Conflict in the Congo. Princeton, NJ, Princeton University Press, 2022

Trefon, T. (Ed.). *Reinventing Order in the Congo: How People Respond to State Failure in Kinshasa*. London, Zed Books, 2004.

Van Reybrouck, D. *Congo*. London, Fourth Estate, 2014.

Vellut, J.-L., Loriaux, F., and Morimont, F. *Bibliographies historiques du Zaïre à l'époque coloniale (1880–1960)*. Louvain-la-Neuve, Tervuren, 1996.

Willame, J. C. *Patrice Lumumba—La crise congolaise revisitée*. Paris, Editions Karthala, 1990.

Wondo, Jean-Jacques. *Les armées au Congo-Kinshasa: Radioscopie de la force publique aux FARDC*. Saint-Légier, Editions Monde Nouveau/Afrique Nouvelle, 2013.

Wrong, M. *In the Footsteps of Mr. Kurtz: Living on the Brink of Disaster in Mobutu's Congo*. London, Harper Collins, 2001.

Young, M. C., and Turner, T. *The Rise and Decline of the Zairean State*. Madison, WI, University of Wisconsin Press, 1985.

Zeilig, L. *Lumumba: Africa's Lost Leader*. London, Haus, 2017.

THE REPUBLIC OF THE CONGO

Physical and Social Geography

DAVID HILLING

AREA AND POPULATION

The Congo river forms approximately 1,000 km of the eastern boundary of the Republic of the Congo, the remainder of which is provided by the Oubangui river from just south of the point at which the Equator bisects the country. Across these rivers lies the Democratic Republic of the Congo. To the north, the republic is bounded by the Central African Republic and Cameroon. Gabon lies to the west, and the Cabinda exclave of Angola to the south, adjoining the short Atlantic coastline. Covering an area of 342,000 sq km (132,047 sq miles) the country supported a population of 3,697,490 at the census of 28 April 2007. The population was projected by the United Nations (UN) to have increased to 5,797,801 by mid-2022, giving an average density of 17.0 inhabitants per sq km. The main ethnic groups are the Vili on the coast, the Kongo (centred on Brazzaville), and the Téké, Mbochi and Sanga of the plateaux in the centre and north of the country. The principal centres of urban population are the capital, Brazzaville (with an projected population of 2,469,630 at mid-2021, according to the UN), and the main port of Pointe-Noire (1,253,939).

PHYSICAL FEATURES AND RESOURCES

The exploitation of substantial offshore petroleum deposits represents a major sector of the economy. The immediate coastal zone is sandy in the north, more swampy south of Kouilou, and in the vicinity of Pointe-Indienne yields small amounts of petroleum. A narrow coastal plain does not rise above 100 m, and the cool coastal waters modify the climate, giving low rainfall and a grassland vegetation. Rising abruptly from the coastal plain are the high-rainfall forested ridges of the Mayombé range, parallel to the coast and reaching a height of 800 m, in which gorges, incised by rivers such as the Kouilou, provide potential hydroelectric power sites. At Hollé, near the Congo-Océan railway and at the western foot of the range, there are considerable phosphate deposits. Mayombé also provides an important export commodity, timber, of which the main commercial species are okoumé, limba and sapele.

Inland, the south-western Niari valley has lower elevation, soils that are good by tropical African standards and a grassland vegetation, which facilitates agricultural development. A variety of agricultural products (such as groundnuts, maize, vegetables, palm oil, coffee, cocoa, sugar and tobacco) are obtained from large plantations, smaller commercial farms and also peasant holdings. These products provide the support for a more concentrated rural population and the basis for some industrial development.

A further forested mountainous region, the Chaillu massif, is the Congo basin's western watershed, and this gives way north-eastwards to a series of drier plateaux, the Batéké region and, east of the Likouala river, a zone of Congo riverine land. Here are numerous watercourses, with seasonal inundation, and dense forest vegetation, which supports some output of forest products, although the full potential has yet to be realized. The rivers Congo and Oubangui, with tributaries, provide more than 6,500 km of navigable waterway, which are particularly important, owing to the lack of a developed network of roads.

History

KATHARINE MURISON

Revised for this edition by the editorial staff

The Republic of the Congo became autonomous within the French Community in November 1958, with Abbé Fulbert Youlou as Prime Minister. Full independence followed on 15 August 1960. Youlou was elected President in March 1961, transferring power in 1963 to a provisional Government led by Alphonse Massamba-Débat, who was elected President in December. In 1964 the Marxist-Leninist Mouvement National de la Révolution (MNR) was formed as the sole political party. In August 1968 Capt. (later Maj.) Marien Ngouabi deposed Massamba-Débat in a coup. A new Marxist-Leninist party, the Parti Congolais du Travail (PCT), replaced the MNR, and in January 1970 the country was renamed the People's Republic of the Congo.

In March 1977 Ngouabi was assassinated during an attempted coup by supporters of Massamba-Débat, who was subsequently executed. In April Col (later Brig.-Gen.) Jacques-Joachim Yhombi-Opango, a former Chief of Staff of the armed forces, was appointed head of state. In February 1979 Yhombi-Opango surrendered his powers to a Provisional Committee appointed by the PCT. In March the President of the Committee, Col (later Gen.) Denis Sassou Nguesso, was appointed President of the Republic and Chairman of the Central Committee of the PCT.

At a PCT congress in July 1989, Sassou Nguesso was re-elected Chairman of the party and President of the Republic for a further five-year term. At legislative elections, held in September, the single list of 133 candidates, including, for the first time, candidates who were not members of the PCT, was approved by 99.2% of those who voted.

POLITICAL TRANSITION

Several political prisoners were released in August 1990, including Yhombi-Opango, who had been imprisoned for alleged complicity in a coup plot in 1987. In December 1990 the PCT abandoned Marxism-Leninism as its official ideology, and formulated constitutional amendments legalizing a multiparty system, which took effect in January 1991. Gen. Louis Sylvain Goma, Prime Minister in 1975–84, returned to that position, leading an interim Government.

A national conference, including opposition representatives, was convened in February 1991. In April the conference announced the abrogation of the Constitution and the dissolution of the legislature. In June a 153-member legislative Haut Conseil de la République (HCR) was established. The Prime Minister replaced Sassou Nguesso as head of government, and the country reverted to the name Republic of the Congo. André Milongo, a former World Bank official, succeeded Goma as Prime Minister.

ELECTORAL DISCORD

A new Constitution, which vested legislative power in an elected Assemblée Nationale (National Assembly) and Sénat

(Senate) and executive power in an elected President, was approved by 96.3% of voters at a referendum in March 1992. At elections to the National Assembly in June and July, the Union Panafricaine pour la Démocratie Sociale (UPADS) became the largest party, winning 39 of the 125 contested seats, followed by the Mouvement Congolais pour la Démocratie et le Développement Intégral (MCDDI), with 29 seats, and the PCT (18). At elections to the Senate in July, the UPADS also became the largest party, with 23 of the 60 contested seats. At the presidential election in August, Pascal Lissouba, the leader of the UPADS and a former Prime Minister, defeated Bernard Kolélas, the leader of the MCDDI, winning 61.3% of the votes cast in the second round; Sassou Nguesso and Milongo were among 14 other candidates eliminated in the first round. In October, however, a recently formed alliance between the PCT and the Union pour le Renouveau Démocratique (URD), a seven-party grouping including the MCDDI, won a vote of no confidence in the Government, and Lissouba dissolved the National Assembly.

At the first round of legislative elections, held in May 1993, the Mouvance Présidentielle (MP), comprising the UPADS and its allies, won 62 of the 125 seats in the National Assembly, while the URD-PCT coalition, led by Kolélas, secured 49. Alleging electoral irregularities, the URD-PCT refused to contest the second round in June, after which the MP held 69 seats. Lissouba appointed a new Council of Ministers, under Yhombi-Opango's premiership. Kolélas nominated a rival government. Violent conflict ensued between armed militias, representing political and ethnic interests, and the security forces. In late June the Supreme Court ruled that electoral irregularities had occurred at the first round of elections. In August the Government and the opposition agreed to restage the second round. Following the repeated second round of elections in October, the MP held 65 seats and the URD-PCT 57. Confrontations between armed militias and the security forces erupted again in November, with some 2,000 deaths reported during the second half of 1993. A ceasefire was agreed by the MP and the opposition in January 1994, although sporadic fighting continued.

SASSOU NGUESSO RESUMES POWER

In June 1997 a government attempt to disarm the militia group associated with Sassou Nguesso's Forces Démocratiques et Patriotiques (FDP) developed into a fierce conflict. Brazzaville was effectively split into three zones, controlled by supporters of Sassou Nguesso, Lissouba and Kolélas, respectively. The conflict soon became polarized between troops loyal to Lissouba and the 'Cobra' forces of Sassou Nguesso. Despite mediation, none of numerous ceasefires signed during mid-1997 endured. French troops assisted in the evacuation of foreign residents from Brazzaville in June before departing themselves. In September Lissouba appointed a Government of National Unity, under the premiership of Kolélas.

In October 1997 the 'Cobra' forces, assisted by Angolan government troops, won control of Brazzaville and the strategically important port of Pointe-Noire. Lissouba and Kolélas fled Congo. Sassou Nguesso was inaugurated as President, and appointed a transitional Government. It was reported that some 10,000 people had been killed during the civil war and about 800,000 displaced. Sassou Nguesso decreed that party militias would be disarmed and outlawed.

In January 1998 a Forum sur l'Unité et la Reconstruction, comprising some 1,420 delegates, approved a three-year transitional period, during which a 75-member Conseil National de Transition (CNT) was to act as a legislative body.

Clashes continued throughout 1998 in the Pool region, south of Brazzaville, a stronghold of the 'Ninja' militia loyal to Kolélas (who remained in exile). In December a battle for control of Brazzaville broke out between 'Ninja' forces, allegedly supported by Angolan dissident groups, and Congolese government forces, augmented by Sassou Nguesso's militia and Angolan government troops, and government forces launched offensives against 'Ninja' forces in the south and west of Congo. By early March 1999 the rebel militias had withdrawn to Pool. In May the army secured Kinkala, the

capital of the Pool region, and captured the main rebel base in the south-west of Congo.

In September 1999 it was reported that some 600 militiamen loyal to Kolélas had surrendered. In October the authorities announced that the armed forces had regained control of all towns in the Pool region. In November the Government declared that it had reached an agreement with the militias loyal to Lissouba and Kolélas, which included provision for a ceasefire and a general amnesty. In December representatives of the armed forces and of the rebel militias signed a second peace agreement, which provided for the integration of militiamen into the armed forces and measures to facilitate the return of displaced persons. By February 2000 around one-half of the estimated 810,000 people displaced by the conflict had returned to their homes. In May Kolélas was convicted, *in absentia*, of operating personal prisons in Brazzaville and of mistreating prisoners and causing their deaths during the 1997 civil war. He was sentenced to death. In December 2000 Lissouba was sentenced, *in absentia*, to 20 years' imprisonment with hard labour for the mismanagement of public funds.

In November 2000 the Government adopted a draft Constitution, which provided for a presidential system of government, with a bicameral legislature. The head of state would be elected for a term of seven years, renewable once. The new Constitution was approved on 20 January 2002 by 84.5% of votes cast, with a participation rate of 77.5% of the electorate.

SASSOU NGUESSO AND THE PCT CONSOLIDATE POWER

In February 2002 10 presidential candidates were approved by the Supreme Court. However, in early March Milongo, who was regarded as the sole credible challenger to Sassou Nguesso, and two others withdrew their candidacies. Milongo urged his supporters to boycott the poll, citing concerns about the impartiality of the Commission Nationale d'Organisation des Elections (CONEL). Sassou Nguesso won an overwhelming victory in the presidential election on 10 March, securing 89.4% of the votes cast. A turnout of 69.4% was recorded.

Renewed violence erupted in the Pool department in March 2002, apparently instigated by members of a 'Ninja' militia group led by Rev. Frédéric Bitsangou (also known as Ntumi). Government forces regained control of the Congo-Océan railway (linking Brazzaville to Pointe-Noire) in late April and the rebel stronghold of Vindza in late May.

The first round of elections to the 137-member National Assembly was held on 26 May 2002. As a result of continued unrest in Pool, voting was indefinitely postponed in eight constituencies, while disruption caused by protesters and administrative irregularities necessitated a re-run of polling in a further 12 constituencies on 28–29 May. Turnout was around 65%. In mid-June, prior to the second round, 'Ninja' militiamen attacked Brazzaville's main military base; 72 rebels, three army officers and five civilians were killed in the fighting. The second round took place on 23 June, although the rate of participation was only an estimated 30%. Following the polls, supporters of Sassou Nguesso held an absolute majority in the new Assembly, the PCT with 53 seats and its allies in the 29-party Forces Démocratiques Unies (FDU) with 30. Milongo's party, the Union pour la Démocratie et la République—Mwinda (UDR—Mwinda), secured only six seats and the UPADS four. The 66-member Senate, elected on 7 July, included 44 members of the PCT and 12 from the FDU. Sassou Nguesso was inaugurated as President on 14 August.

In March 2003 the Government and Ntumi's 'Ninja' militia group signed an agreement aimed at restoring peace to Pool. The rebels agreed to end hostilities and disarm, while the Government was to guarantee an amnesty for the rebels and integrate former combatants into the national armed forces. In August the National Assembly approved an amnesty for former 'Ninja' fighters, to cover the period from January 2000.

The rail service linking Brazzaville to the Pool department resumed operations in May 2004, but was suspended in October following numerous attacks on trains in Pool. Ntumi denied claims that the attacks had been perpetrated by his 'Ninja' rebel group, also known as the Conseil National de la Résistance (CNR).

A reorganization of the Council of Ministers in January 2005 included the reintroduction of the post of Prime Minister, which was allocated to Isidore Mvouba, hitherto Minister of State, Minister of Transport and Privatization, responsible for the Co-ordination of Government Action. The PCT's representation in the Senate was reduced to 39 seats in partial elections held on 2 October.

In July 2005 the trial commenced in Brazzaville of Gen. Norbert Dabira (also sought in France, see *Foreign Relations*) and 14 other senior army and police officers suspected of involvement in what had become known as the 'Beach affair', in which some 353 Congolese citizens, former refugees from the civil war in the southern regions who had sought asylum in the Democratic Republic of the Congo (DRC), had disappeared from the Beach area of Brazzaville following their voluntary repatriation to Congo in 1999. All 15 defendants were acquitted in August 2005 of charges of murder, genocide, crimes against humanity and war crimes. However, the court ordered the Government to pay compensation to the families of 86 acknowledged victims, in recognition of the state's civil responsibility for the safety of its citizens.

Following the return of Kolélas to Congo in October 2005, at least six people were killed in heavy fighting between 'Ninja' rebels and government troops in southern Brazzaville. In December the legislature granted amnesty to Kolélas, overturning his death sentence in the interests of national reconciliation. Kolélas died in November 2009 in Paris, France. In the following month the legislature granted former President Lissouba, who was living in exile in France, amnesty from the 20-year prison sentence imposed on him in 2000. Lissouba died in France in August 2020.

Sassou Nguesso resigned from the leadership of the PCT in January 2007, as the Constitution stated that the role of President of the Republic was incompatible with holding office within a political party. Meanwhile, Ntumi announced that the CNR was to be transformed into a political party, the Conseil National des Républicains (retaining the acronym CNR), and would participate in forthcoming elections to the National Assembly. In April the Government and the CNR signed an agreement providing for the destruction of weapons held by members of the movement, the integration of 250 former combatants into the national armed forces and the appointment of Ntumi to the Government. In May Sassou Nguesso designated Ntumi as Delegate-General to the President, in charge of promoting peace and reconciliation.

ELECTIONS OF 2007 AND 2009

Some 40 smaller opposition parties boycotted the first round of the elections to the National Assembly on 24 June 2007, citing concerns over the independence of the electoral commission. Irregularities, mainly related to voter registration, led to the repetition of polling in 19 constituencies on 8 and 15 July. Following the second round of the elections, which was postponed until 5 August, the PCT remained the largest party in the National Assembly, with 46 of the 137 seats, while the MCDDI (which had formed an alliance with the PCT in April) held 11 seats and parties belonging to the pro-presidential FDU 31. In addition, most of the 37 independent deputies were reported to be close to the President. Of the opposition parties, the UPADS increased its representation to 11 seats, but the UDR—Mwinda secured only one and the CNR failed to win a seat.

In June 2008 a ceremony was held in Kinkala to initiate a World Bank-funded programme for the demobilization, disarmament and reintegration of 30,000 former combatants (comprising 5,000 followers of Ntumi, 6,000 government forces and 19,000 former militias who had already disbanded). Attending the event, Ntumi, who still remained based in Pool, proclaimed the dissolution of the armed 'Ninja' wing of the CNR.

At local elections held in June 2008, the recently formed Rassemblement de la Majorité Présidentielle (RMP), an alliance of around 100 political parties and associations loyal to the President, secured 364 of the 864 seats contested; more than 200 seats were won by parties or independent candidates considered close to the RMP, and a further 43 were taken by the

MCDDI (still allied to the PCT). The UPADS obtained 76 seats. At elections to fill 42 of the 72 seats in the expanded Senate on 5 August, the RMP secured 33 seats, while independent candidates took seven and the UPADS two.

A presidential election took place on 12 July 2009, contested by 13 candidates. Sassou Nguesso secured a decisive victory, with 78.6% of the votes cast. In second place, with 7.5% of the votes, was Joseph Kignoumbi Kia Mbougou (standing as an independent). Observers from the African Union (AU) and the Communauté Economique des Etats de l'Afrique Centrale (CEEAC) concluded that the poll had been conducted transparently, although a national human rights organization, the Observatoire Congolais des Droits Humains (OCDH), alleged fraud and irregularities, claiming that the number of voters registered (some 2.1m.) was far in excess of what could be expected. Sassou Nguesso was inaugurated on 14 August. Mvouba remained the most senior member of a new Government appointed in September, but was no longer afforded the title of Prime Minister, instead being designated Minister of State, Co-ordinator of Basic Infrastructures, and Minister of Civil Aviation and of Maritime Trade.

In December 2009 Ntumi finally assumed the government post to which he had been appointed in May 2007. However, his return to Brazzaville followed reports of increased violence in Pool. Ntumi failed in his attempt to secure a seat in the National Assembly in a by-election held in the Pool constituency of Minduli in July 2010. A military and police operation to restore full law and order to Pool commenced in October.

LEGISLATIVE ELECTIONS, 2011–12

At partial elections to the Senate held on 9 October 2011, the PCT, the RMP and allies secured a total of 33 of the 36 seats contested, the PCT winning 12 and the RMP 11.

A series of explosions caused by a fire in a munitions depot at an army barracks in Brazzaville in March 2012 resulted in 282 deaths and the displacement of more than 14,000 people. The Congolese Government promised to pay compensation to those affected. The Chinese Government was to provide substantial funding for reconstruction in accordance with bilateral agreements signed in September.

Elections to an enlarged, 139-member National Assembly took place on 15 July and 5 August 2012. Polling was postponed in three Brazzaville constituencies affected by the March explosions. The PCT secured 89 of the 136 seats contested, followed by its ally, the MCDDI, and the opposition UPADS, which each won seven seats. The PCT and its allies took a total of 117 seats in the Assembly. Two of the President's children, Denis Christel Sassou Nguesso and Claudia Lembouma Sassou Nguesso, notably secured election. Observers from the CEEAC and the AU criticized some aspects of the organization of the elections.

As part of a government reorganization in September 2012, Charles Richard Mondjo, hitherto Chief of General Staff of the armed forces, replaced Charles Zacharie Bowao as Minister at the Presidency, responsible for National Defence. Bowao was subsequently charged with negligence and other offences in connection with the explosions at the arms depot in March, but claimed that the charges were politically motivated. In September 2013 six soldiers were found guilty of charges related to the explosions, receiving sentences ranging from two years to 15 years' hard labour.

Local elections took place on 28 September 2014; the PCT and allied parties and individuals reportedly secured 820 of the 860 seats contested, with the UPADS winning the remainder. At partial elections to fill 38 seats in the 72-member Senate held on 12 October, the PCT took 30 seats, increasing its overall representation in the Senate to 42 seats.

CONSTITUTIONAL REFORM

In December 2014 the PCT proposed revising the Constitution, provoking concern among opposition parties and Congo's Roman Catholic archbishops that the PCT's aim was to allow Sassou Nguesso to seek a further term of presidential office. (Provisions stipulating that the presidential term was renewable only once and imposing an age limit of between 40 and 70 years for presidential candidates would prevent Sassou

Nguesso from standing in the election due in 2016.) The 45 signatories to a memorandum released in January 2015 opposing any amendment also included representatives of civil society organizations and two parties allied to the PCT. In April the PCT-allied MCDDI elected its Interim President, the Minister of the Civil Service and State Reform, Guy Brice Parfait Kolélas (the son of the late Bernard Kolélas), as its presidential candidate for the 2016 poll.

President Sassou Nguesso hosted meetings on institutional reform with political parties and civil society groups in May 2015, although the UPADS and the recently formed opposition coalition Front Républicain pour le Respect de l'Ordre Constitutionnel et l'Alternance Démocratique (FROCAD) refused to participate. FROCAD also boycotted a national dialogue conducted in the south-western town of Sibiti in July and attended by some 500 political, civil society and religious representatives, at which, according to a communiqué released at its conclusion, a 'large majority' favoured amending the Constitution to remove the limits on the maximum age of presidential candidates and on the number of presidential terms. Later in July opposition leaders held a counter-dialogue, in which some 600 delegates participated, following which they urged Sassou Nguesso not to revise the Constitution. A government reorganization in August included the dismissal of two ministers who had participated in the counter-dialogue, Guy Brice Parfait Kolélas and the Minister of Trade and Supplies, Claudine Munari. A mass demonstration against constitutional reform was organized in September by FROCAD and the Initiative pour la Démocratie au Congo (IDC), which largely comprised former allies of the President. None the less, on 5 October it was announced that a constitutional referendum would proceed on 25 October. The new draft constitution included a reduction in the presidential term from seven to five years but an increase in the number of times the mandate could be renewed from once to twice, while the minimum age of a presidential candidate would be 30 years (instead of 40) with no upper age limit, and provision was made for the post of Prime Minister. Civil disobedience by those opposed to the referendum subsequently escalated, and at least four protesters were killed on 20 October, when police used live ammunition to disperse prohibited demonstrations in Brazzaville and Pointe-Noire. The opposition claimed that 17 people had died in the unrest and urged a boycott of the referendum.

At the referendum, which took place peacefully on 25 October 2015, the draft Constitution was approved by 92.3% of the votes cast, according to official results announced two days later, with a turnout of 72.4%. Alleging fraud, the opposition disputed the participation rate in particular. Sassou Nguesso officially promulgated the new Constitution on 6 November, after the Constitutional Court released revised official results, according to which 94.3% of voters endorsed the charter, with a turnout of 71.2%.

SASSOU NGUESSO RE-ELECTED, 2016

A Commission Nationale Electorale Indépendante (CNEI), comprising representatives of the ruling party, opposition parties and civil society, was appointed in February 2016 to replace the CONEL; the creation of an independent election commission was a principal condition of FROCAD and the IDC for their participation in a presidential election to be held in March. However, the EU announced that it would not be dispatching observers to monitor the election on the grounds that insufficient measures had been taken to ensure a transparent vote. Moreover, in mid-March the establishment of a parallel election commission was announced by five of Sassou Nguesso's eight challengers for the presidency: former government ministers Guy Brice Parfait Kolélas, Claudine Munari and André Okombi Salissa; UPADS Secretary-General Pascal Tsaty Mabiala; and Gen. Jean-Marie Michel Mokoko, who had served as armed forces chief of staff in 1987–93 and as the President's adviser on security matters from 2005 until his resignation in February 2016.

With opposition support divided, Sassou Nguesso was re-elected in a first round of voting in the presidential election on 20 March 2016, securing 60.2% of the votes cast. Kolélas was placed second, with 15.0%, followed by Mokoko (13.7%), Mabiala (4.7%) and Salissa (4.1%). A turnout of 68.9% was recorded. The Government blocked telecommunications links during the election for 'reasons of national security and safety' and to prevent the publication by the opposition of 'illegal results'. Both Kolélas and Mokoko rejected the results as fraudulent, and several violent incidents followed the election. Attacks on government buildings in southern Brazzaville on 4 April were attributed by the Government to former 'Ninja' militiamen. The Government subsequently announced that 17 people had died in security operations against those deemed responsible for the incursion, while thousands of civilians in the Pool department were displaced, amid reports of military air strikes on residential areas. A warrant was issued for the arrest of former rebel leader Ntumi, and he was dismissed as Delegate-General to the President. Later in April the Government ordered the closure of the national and departmental headquarters of the CNR.

Sassou Nguesso was sworn in as President on 16 April 2016. On 23 April the President appointed as Prime Minister Clément Mouamba, who had served as Minister of Finance in 1992–93 and had been a leading figure in the UPADS until 2015, when he had been excluded from the party for participating in the national dialogue on constitutional reform.

In May 2016 the UN Secretary-General, Ban Ki-Moon, expressed concern to Sassou Nguesso about the Government's ongoing security operation in Pool and its impact on the civilian population. Meanwhile, the Congolese Government requested that the EU recall its ambassador to Brazzaville, after the EU criticized the presidential poll and post-election period, noting that the latter had been marked by human rights violations, arrests and intimidation of the opposition and the media.

POLITICAL TENSIONS AND VIOLENCE IN POOL

Several prominent opposition leaders were arrested and imprisoned in the months following the presidential election. In June 2016 third-placed candidate Mokoko, who had come under investigation during the election campaign over a video that appeared to implicate him in a coup attempt, was arrested and charged with threatening internal security and possession of weapons; his supporters insisted that the video was a forgery. Mokoko was further charged in August with inciting public disorder, apparently owing to his calls for civil disobedience after the results of the election were announced. In July Paulin Makaya, the leader of the minor opposition Unis Pour le Congo (UPC), was sentenced to two years' imprisonment and fined 2.5m. francs CFA, having been convicted of inciting public disorder in connection with a demonstration organized in protest against the 2015 constitutional referendum. Additional charges were brought against Makaya in January 2017, following a shooting that had occurred the previous month at the main prison in Brazzaville during a visit by six UPC members; he was convicted and sentenced to a further year in prison in September 2018, but released a few days later, having already served this additional time. Meanwhile, also in January 2017, unsuccessful presidential candidate André Okombi Salissa was arrested and charged with possession of illegal weapons and threatening the security of the state.

Meanwhile, violence in the Pool department continued. The Government claimed that the rebels were seeking to destabilize the Sassou Nguesso administration by mounting attacks, while Ntumi, who remained at large, asserted that the confrontations were provoked by the Government's security operation against militants in the department, including aerial bombardments. The death of two soldiers in September in a reported 'Ninja' attack on an ambulance on the Brazzaville–Kinkala road and a further two at a construction site prompted several thousand more residents to flee Pool. Police sources claimed that at least 14 people had been killed in an attack by former rebel fighters on a train in the town of Mindouli at the end of September, although Ntumi denied 'Ninja' involvement, maintaining that the train had simply derailed. Further soldiers were killed in October during attacks on the Brazzaville–Kinkala and Brazzaville–Pointe Noire roads. In March 2017 the security forces announced that they had killed some 15 'Ninja' fighters during an operation against a group believed to be led by Ntumi's military chief, Daniel Bayidikila Malonga. Several soldiers (reported unofficially to number at least 18) were killed in clashes with militants loyal to Ntumi in April in the Pool district of Kindamba. The Government refused to consider negotiating with the 'Ninja' rebels, whom it regarded as terrorists. By June almost 81,000 people had been displaced in Pool since mid-2016, according to the UN.

Political tensions persisted during 2016–17, with opposition parties in September 2016 rejecting government attempts at dialogue and urging the international community to exert pressure on the Government to release those imprisoned following the presidential election. The leaders of the IDC and FROCAD boycotted political discussions held in Ouesso in March 2017 with the aim of preparing for elections due to be held that year, although the 300 delegates included representatives of the UPADS. Also that month Guy Brice Parfait Kolélas, Sassou Nguesso's closest challenger in the presidential vote, formed a new opposition party, the Union des Démocrates Humanistes-Yuki (UDH-Yuki).

2017 LEGISLATIVE ELECTIONS AND CEASEFIRE ACCORD

Elections to an enlarged National Assembly (comprising 151 seats) were held on 16 and 30 July 2017, together with local elections to fill 1,158 municipal council seats. The PCT retained its absolute majority in the Assembly, securing 91 of the 142 seats contested, voting having been postponed indefinitely in nine of the 14 Pool constituencies owing to ongoing violence. Three of the President's children won seats, with Denis Christel Sassou Nguesso and Claudia Lembouma Sassou Nguesso being re-elected and Stella Sassou Nguesso obtaining a seat for the first time. The UPADS became the second largest party in the legislature, taking eight seats, while eight members of the UDH-Yuki also reportedly secured representation, formally standing as independents; 11 other independents were elected. The elections were boycotted by an opposition alliance comprising the IDC, FROCAD and the Composante Jean-Marie Michel Mokoko and by the Mouvement pour l'Unité, la Solidarité et le Travail, led by Claudine Munari. The official participation rate was 44.4%. In the local polls, the PCT was also dominant, securing 450 of the seats, followed by the UPADS, with 54.

Mouamba was reappointed as Prime Minister on 21 August 2017. At indirect elections to the 72-member Senate held on 31 August, the PCT secured 44 of the 66 seats contested (the six incumbent senators representing Pool were to remain in office until voting could take place in the department).

On 23 December 2017 the Government signed a ceasefire accord in Kinkala with Ntumi's rebel group, represented by Jean-Gustave Ntondo, the Secretary-General of the CNR, who had been one of 25 leading members of the party released from prison in the previous month as part of efforts to end hostilities in Pool. Under the agreement, the rebels were to disarm and allow the free movement of trade between Brazzaville and Pointe-Noire. A joint commission formed by the two sides to implement the peace accord held its first meeting in January 2018. The improved security situation allowed the main road through the Pool department to be reopened in March.

In January 2018 Gen. Norbert Dabira, the former Inspector-General of the Congolese armed forces and a close associate of Sassou Nguesso, and Gen. Nianga Ngatsé Mbouala, who had been dismissed as commander of the Republican Guard, were accused of plotting to overthrow the President in 2017. Following his trial in May 2018 (at which Mbouala appeared as a witness), Dabira was convicted of undermining state security and sentenced to five years' imprisonment. Earlier in May Gen. Jean-Marie Michel Mokoko, the third-placed candidate in the 2016 presidential election, was sentenced to a 20-year prison term, also for threatening state security (see *Political Tensions and Violence in Pool*); seven co-defendants (six of whom were French) received the same sentence, having been tried *in absentia*. In June 2018 a former justice minister, Jean-Martin Mbemba, was sentenced *in absentia* to 10 years' imprisonment, again for threatening state security, having been found guilty of plotting to overthrow Sassou Nguesso in 2003. In August 2018 the UN Working Group on Arbitrary Detention urged the

Congolese authorities to release Mokoko immediately, in an advisory opinion that the Congolese Government rejected. In March 2019 André Okombi Salissa, the fifth-placed candidate in the 2016 presidential election, and three co-defendants were found guilty of possession of illegal weapons and threatening the security of the state (see *Political Tensions and Violence in Pool*) and all sentenced to 20 years' hard labour.

Meanwhile, in March 2018 the UN requested international donor funding of US $70.7m. to provide humanitarian assistance and to stimulate recovery for around 114,000 people in Pool (64,086 displaced people, some 25,000 members of host families and 25,000 people who had remained in affected areas). In accordance with the ceasefire accord, around 80 associates of Ntumi were released from prison in June, and the arrest warrant for Ntumi was withdrawn in July. The disarmament of former combatants commenced in August. At the end of the operation, on 5 October, the joint commission responsible for implementing the peace accord between the Government and the rebels in Pool reported that it had collected 8,007 weapons and explosives from more than 5,600 former combatants. Meanwhile, at the end of August the Congolese Government and the UN signed a financing agreement, estimated at 8,300m. francs CFA, to implement the demobilization, disarmament and reintegration programme, which was to involve at least 7,500 former fighters, as well as returning displaced people. The Congo-Océan rail service between Brazzaville and Pointe-Noire resumed operations in November, having been suspended since mid-2016, partly owing to the destruction of three bridges during the conflict in Pool. In April 2019 the Congolese Government removed the suspension on the activities of the CNR imposed some three years earlier. Meanwhile, in January a UN-supported initiative to provide forums for dialogue in Pool commenced. A departmental-level forum for dialogue took place in Kinkala in June and discussed recommendations resulting from 15 local intra-community dialogues. Proposals made by the participants included a gradual reduction in the military presence in Pool and the restoration of state authority, and clarification of the status of Ntumi. Former combatants urged the Congolese authorities to organize an inclusive national dialogue aimed at definitively consolidating peace in Pool.

CORRUPTION CONCERNS AND COVID-19

President Sassou Nguesso promulgated legislation on the creation of an anti-corruption body, the Haute Autorité de Lutte contre la Corruption (HALC), in February 2019 and on the establishment of an institution to ensure the sound management of public funds, the Commission Nationale de Transparence et de Responsabilité dans la Gestion des Finances Publiques, in May. These measures to improve governance, together with a deal to restructure the bilateral debt owed to the People's Republic of China (see *Foreign Relations*), facilitated the approval by the International Monetary Fund (IMF) in July of a three-year credit facility for Congo in support of a programme aimed at restoring macroeconomic stability. (Congo had been experiencing a severe financial and economic crisis, resulting partly from a decline in the international price of petroleum, the country's principal export.) The 35 members of the HALC were sworn into office in July 2020.

Allegations of corruption were made against two of the President's children in 2019 by the non-governmental organization (NGO) Global Witness, which accused Claudia Sassou Nguesso (in April) and Denis Christel Sassou Nguesso (in August) of misappropriating state funds amounting to around US $20m. and $50m., respectively. The claims prompted a group of civil society movements, led by the OCDH, to demand the removal of the two deputies' immunity from prosecution and the initiation of parliamentary and judicial inquiries. In October, furthermore, the group appealed to the Prosecutor of the Republic to investigate the allegations. These demands were renewed in July 2020, after it emerged that US federal prosecutors had initiated civil proceedings to confiscate a property in the US city of Miami, Florida, allegedly acquired by Denis Christel Sassou Nguesso in 2011 with funds misappropriated from the Société Nationale des Pétroles du Congo (of which he was a Deputy Director-General). The Mayor of

Brazzaville, Christian Roger Okemba, was suspended from office in February 2020 on suspicion of misappropriating some 1,250m. francs CFA in public funds; following Okemba's detention in March and dismissal in April, Dieudonné Bantsimba, a member of the PCT central committee, was elected unopposed as the new Mayor in May. Okemba was convicted and sentenced to five years' imprisonment in July.

Congo recorded its first case of coronavirus disease (COVID-19) in mid-March 2020, a few days after the World Health Organization (WHO) declared the global outbreak to be a pandemic. The Congolese Government implemented various measures aimed at curbing the spread of the disease, including social distancing, the closure of schools and the suspension of flights. On 28 March President Sassou Nguesso declared a state of health emergency, and a nationwide lockdown, in which most people were confined to home, and a night curfew took effect at the end of that month. Although specific measures were gradually eased from mid-May, the state of emergency was regularly extended. Flights resumed fully from 24 August 2020, and schools reopened on 12 October. A vaccination programme against COVID-19 commenced in March 2021.

THE 2021 PRESIDENTIAL ELECTION

Preparations for the presidential election due to be held in March 2021 began in December 2019, when UPADS Secretary-General Mabiala proposed that the election be postponed until 2023—with Sassou Nguesso retaining office until then, but precluded from contesting a further term—on the grounds that conditions would not be in place by 2021 to hold a fair ballot, citing a need to introduce biometric identification of voters and restructure the CNEI, among other issues. A few days later, however, a congress of the PCT unanimously selected Sassou Nguesso as the party's candidate. (The 2015 Constitution allowed him to stand in both the 2021 and 2026 presidential polls.) In early 2020 several opposition parties called for the organization of an inclusive political dialogue before the election and demanded the release of Mokoko and Salissa. In February, however, the PCT rejected any delay in the 2021 election, noting that this would be unconstitutional, and maintained that dialogue took place on a continuous basis within state institutions. In mid-July 2020, citing the risk of spreading COVID-19, the authorities banned a march planned by civil society organizations to demand the release and medical evacuation of Mokoko, whose health had deteriorated in prison.

Opposition parties and civil society groups denounced amendments to the electoral law adopted in August 2020 which allowed the security forces to vote in elections several days ahead of the rest of the electorate. UPADS deputies boycotted the vote, while Guy Brice Parfait Kolélas, the leader of the UDH-Yuki, expressed concern that the change could lead to electoral fraud. Later that month former Minister of Finance Mathias Dzon, the President of the Alliance pour la République et la Démocratie, was selected as his party's presidential candidate. In late October the Ministry of the Interior officially recognized 45 (of some 200) political parties; those not securing accreditation included the UPC, which denounced the process as being arbitrary. A two-day political consultation, convened by the Government and involving around 150 representatives of political and civil society movements, took place in Madingou, in south-western Congo, in November to discuss the organization of the presidential election. Participants agreed on a revision of the electoral register and the introduction of a mechanism to avoid duplication between the special list of members of the security forces and the general list of voters. However, opposition representatives expressed dissatisfaction, with Mabiala suggesting that the decisions apparently made at the consultation had in fact been largely imposed by the Government.

In January 2021 the PCT's central committee confirmed Sassou Nguesso as the presidential candidate of the party and 16 allied groups. At the end of that month the UPADS announced that it would not contest the poll, claiming that the Government had failed to improve the electoral system to guarantee the credibility of the results. Kolélas was officially designated as the UDH-Yuki candidate in February. On the following day the Bishops' Conference expressed serious reservations about the organization and transparency of the forthcoming election, citing concerns regarding the electoral system and the impact of restrictions related to COVID-19, notably the curfew.

Polling was largely peaceful in the presidential election, which took place on 17 March 2021 for the security forces and 21 March for the general electorate, although AU observers noted some organizational deficiencies, and, as in the 2016 ballot, telecommunications links were blocked. Sassou Nguesso was re-elected with an overwhelming 88.4% of the valid votes cast, according to final results released on 6 April by the Constitutional Court, which dismissed three challenges. His closest rival, Kolélas, who received 8.0% of the votes, died on 21 March while being transported to France for treatment for COVID-19. Despite the boycott, a turnout of 67.2% was recorded. Meanwhile, the OCDH and other human rights groups denounced as arbitrary the detentions of human rights activist Dr Alexandre Ibacka Dzabana on 11 March and Christ Dongui of the citizen movement Ras-Le-Bol (Enough is Enough) on 25 March, demanding their release; in April both men were accused of endangering state security, and they were provisionally released in mid-July.

Sassou Nguesso was sworn in as President on 16 April 2021. After Prime Minister Mouamba tendered his Government's resignation on 5 May, Anatole Collinet Makosso, the outgoing Minister of Primary and Secondary Education and Literacy, was appointed as the new Prime Minister on 12 May, and the 36 other members of the Council of Ministers were named on 15 May. Notable among the 11 new appointees were Denis Christel Sassou Nguesso as Minister of International Co-operation and the Promotion of Public-Private Partnership, Honoré Ntsayi, hitherto President of the UPADS parliamentary group, as Minister of Energy and Water Resources, and Roger Rigobert Andely as Minister of Finance, the Budget and the Public Portfolio, a post that he had occupied in 2002–05. (Ntsayi was subsequently suspended from his party's governing bodies.) One of many challenges confronting the new Government was a demand for the payment of more than 33 months of pension arrears by some 40,000 retired civil servants, who had staged a sit-in protest in front of the Office of the Prime Minister earlier in May. Makosso met representatives of pensions organizations in July to discuss clearance of the arrears; the state budget for the following year, adopted in December, included provisions for the payment of 12 months of pensions.

Following a government acknowledgement that six people had died while in detention at the central police station in Brazzaville on 5 November 2021, relatives of the dead prisoners and several human rights organizations demanded an independent investigation, citing suspicions of torture. In February 2022 a local human rights group, Observatoire Congolais des Droits de l'Homme, urged the Government to adopt a new penal code. Meanwhile, in January the Senate approved legislation establishing procedures for a planned revision of the 2015 Constitution. Opposition leaders, including Dzon, dismissed as inadequate a government invitation to participate in a political dialogue in March prior to local and legislative elections, which were scheduled to take place in July.

After further surges in cases of COVID-19 during late 2021 had stabilized, at the end of February 2022 the Congolese authorities substantially eased pandemic-related domestic and international restrictions, lifting the night curfew in Brazzaville and Pointe-Noire, and fully reopening the country's land borders. Nevertheless, on 20 July the nationwide state of health emergency was again extended, to 19 October. According to Johns Hopkins University and Our World in Data, 24,837 confirmed cases of COVID-19 had been reported in Congo at late August (the number having remained constant since early July), with 386 fatalities, equivalent to a rate of 6.6 deaths per 100,000 persons; by the end of July 11.9% of the total population had received at least one dose of vaccine.

THE 2022 LEGISLATIVE ELECTIONS

In June 2022 campaigning began for the forthcoming elections to the National Assembly. The UDH-Yuki, led by Pascal Ngouanou since the death of Kolélas, had registered 32 candidates to contest the polls, and the UPADS 45, while a reconstituted opposition platform comprising the IDC, FRO-CAD and the Composante Jean-Marie Michel Mokoko, the Fédération de l'Opposition Congolaise, again announced an electoral boycott, as did the Collectif des Partis de l'Opposition Congolaise, led by Dzon. The PCT secured a substantial victory of 102 seats in the first round of voting on 10 July, while opposition groups in the country denounced the results as fraudulent. A participation rate of 59.8% of the registered electorate was officially reported, although the voter turnout was as low as 36.7% in Brazzaville. Following a second round on 31 July, the PCT had increased its majority to 112 of the 151 seats (a gain of 16 seats), while the UDH-Yuki won seven seats, equalling the representation of UPADS; the pro-presidential Mouvement Action et Renouveau obtained four seats and the remainder were taken by 13 small parties and four independent candidates. The PCT was also reported to have secured 559 of the 1,154 contested seats in the concurrent elections to local councils. The Constitutional Court endorsed the election results on 15 August, dismissing some 30 appeals by unsuccessful candidates. Two days later, Isidore Mvouba, an ally of Sassou Nguesso, was re-elected as President of the National Assembly with 142 of the 145 votes cast. A new Government was appointed in September, again headed by Makosso.

FOREIGN RELATIONS

After the 1997 civil war the principal aim of Congolese foreign policy was to gain international recognition of the legitimacy of the Sassou Nguesso Government, and to ensure the continued support of Congo's bilateral and multilateral donors. These efforts were largely successful, particularly following Sassou Nguesso's election to the presidency in March 2002.

Relations between Congo and France, the former colonial power, were strained from mid-2002, however, as a result of an investigation by a French court into several Congolese officials, including President Sassou Nguesso, in connection with the reported disappearance of some 353 Congolese citizens, following their return from asylum in the DRC to Congo in 1999. In December 2002 Congo filed a case against France at the International Court of Justice (ICJ) at The Hague, Netherlands, claiming that the investigations violated Congolese sovereignty and disregarded Sassou Nguesso's immunity as a head of state. In June 2003 the ICJ ruled that investigations into the Inspector-General of the Congolese armed forces, Gen. Norbert Dabira, could continue, while noting that no action that warranted the intervention of the ICJ had yet been undertaken against Sassou Nguesso or other government ministers. In November 2004 the Court of Appeal in Paris ruled that all French legal proceedings relating to the so-called 'Beach affair' should be halted, as the French judiciary did not have legitimate jurisdiction in the case. In January 2007 the French Court of Cassation overturned this ruling, prompting Sassou Nguesso to accuse France of interfering in Congolese affairs. In June, however, the Court of Appeal in Versailles, France, formally dismissed the case against the head of Congo's national police force, Col (later Gen.) Jean-François Ndenguet, in relation to the disappearances, a ruling that was upheld by the Court of Cassation in April 2008. In November 2010 Congo withdrew its complaint against France at the ICJ, and proceedings at the Court were discontinued. Gen. Dabira was briefly detained in France in August 2013 and placed under formal investigation in connection with the 1999 disappearances.

Sassou Nguesso was again threatened with legal proceedings in France in December 2008, when the French wing of the anti-corruption NGO Transparency International, together with a Gabonese citizen, filed a lawsuit against the President and his Equato-Guinean and Gabonese counterparts, accusing them of using misappropriated public funds to purchase properties and other assets in France. In November 2010 the French Court of Cassation ruled Transparency International's complaint to be 'admissible', thus allowing a judicial investigation to be opened into the case. In April 2013, following a meeting with his French counterpart, François Hollande, Sassou Nguesso asserted that the French judiciary had no right to investigate his finances, citing the principle of non-interference in internal affairs. In February and August 2015, respectively, the judges in charge of the French investigation ordered the seizure of some 15 luxury vehicles at Neuilly-sur-Seine, near Paris, from members of Sassou Nguesso's family and of two French properties believed to be owned by Sassou Nguesso's nephew, Wilfried Nguesso. Several members of Sassou Nguesso's family were placed under formal investigation in France in 2017 on suspicion of money laundering and misuse of public funds. Meanwhile, the French Government continued to provide considerable financial assistance to Congo. In April 2019 Congo's Minister of National Defence and the French ambassador to Congo signed three agreements aimed principally at facilitating the resumption of the Congolese armed forces' participation in African defence and peacekeeping operations. President Sassou Nguesso visited Paris in September 2019, holding talks with Hollande's successor, Emmanuel Macron, and signing agreements on education and an initiative to protect the rainforest in the Congo Basin. In August 2021 Prime Minister Makosso headed a large visiting delegation to Paris, which met French government officials and representatives of the business community. President Sassou Nguesso made a working visit to Paris in November, when he attended an international conference for Libya. Makosso again visited Paris in April 2022, after which he made a four-day visit to Washington, DC. However, at the end of June 2022 the French authorities seized a mansion in Neuilly-sur-Seine that was believed to be the property of Denis Christel Sassou Nguesso, who was under suspicion of having laundered funds of some €19m. through real estate purchases in France.

Relations between Congo and the DRC improved from the late 1990s. In May 2001 some 19 DRC nationals suspected of involvement in the assassination of President Laurent-Désiré Kabila in January of that year were extradited from Congo to the DRC. In May 2004 Congo and the DRC reached agreement on the urgent need to repatriate and reintegrate former combatants who had taken refuge in their respective countries; the presence of these former soldiers and militiamen had often created tensions between the two countries. In April 2005 the repatriation of some 57,000 refugees from Congo to the DRC's Equateur province commenced. However, inter-ethnic violence in Equateur province led to a renewed influx of DRC refugees to Congo from October 2009, with 131,648 registered with the office of the UN High Commissioner for Refugees (UNHCR) by the end of 2011. Around 119,000 refugees returned to the DRC from Congo under a voluntary repatriation programme conducted between May 2012 and June 2014. Bilateral relations were strained by Congo's expulsion of thousands of DRC citizens between April and September 2014 in a police operation to deport migrants suspected of criminality. Amid allegations that some of those expelled had held valid residency permits, in May the UN peacekeeping mission in the DRC urged Congo to halt the mass deportations and investigate claims of abuses. By late June, according to the Congolese police force, more than 300,000 DRC nationals had returned to their country from Congo since the operation began. However, after intensified militant violence in eastern regions of the DRC from early 2021 caused mass displacements, the number of DRC refugees and asylum seekers in Congo had increased to 22,138 at the end of July 2022, according to UNHCR.

In November 2018 the Congolese and DRC Governments signed an agreement to construct a 1,757-km bridge linking Brazzaville and the capital of the DRC, Kinshasa, across the Congo river. Estimated to cost US $550m. (part of which was to be financed by the African Development Bank—AfDB), the new bridge was to incorporate a four-lane highway, a rail track and a pedestrian walkway; construction was initially scheduled to commence in August 2020, but later delayed until 2021. Following his election in December 2018, the new DRC President, Félix Tshisekedi, was warmly welcomed by Sassou Nguesso during a state visit to Congo in February 2019. Tshisekedi made further visits to Congo in August that year, in July and October 2020, and in January and April 2021, attending Sassou Nguesso's presidential inauguration during this sixth trip. Later in April the DRC's former Minister of Primary, Secondary and Technical Education, Willy Bakonga Wilima, was arrested in Brazzaville and extradited to the DRC, where he was convicted of illegally transferring funds abroad. Tshisekedi and Sassou Nguesso met again the following month, in Kinshasa.

In May 2013 President Sassou Nguesso announced the enlargement of the Congolese component of a CEEAC-led peacekeeping force in the Central African Republic (CAR), whose President had been forced to flee the country in March, from some 150 troops to 350. In December a 6,000-strong AU mission, the International Support Mission in the Central African Republic (MISCA), was authorized to succeed existing regional forces in the country. MISCA, to which Congo contributed more than 800 troops, was, in turn, replaced by a UN-led force, the UN Multidimensional Integrated Stabilization Mission in the Central African Republic (MINUSCA), in September 2014. Congo withdrew its military (but not police) contingent from MINUSCA (the only UN peacekeeping force to which it was contributing) in mid-2017, after a review into allegations of sexual abuse found 'systemic problems in command and control'. Meanwhile, Sassou Nguesso hosted a reconciliation forum in Brazzaville in July 2014, at which the main protagonists in the CAR conflict signed a ceasefire agreement. However, there was renewed fierce fighting between armed groups in the CAR from May 2017. In April 2018, despite ongoing clashes, the voluntary repatriation of refugees from Congo to the CAR commenced, with UNHCR assistance. However, following a renewed rebel insurgency in the CAR associated with elections in December 2020, at the end of July 2022, according to UNHCR, the number of refugees and asylum seekers from the CAR in Congo had risen to 29,168. At the end of May Congo contributed 190 police personnel to MINUSCA.

At an extraordinary AU summit held in March 2018, Congo was among 44 of the 55 member states to sign an agreement on the establishment of an African Continental Free Trade Area (AfCFTA), and also signed, together with 26 other member states, an accord on the free movement of people across borders. The AfCFTA agreement entered into force on 30 May 2019, and trading under the AfCFTA commenced on 1 January 2021, by which time the accord had been signed by 54 states and ratified by 34 (including Congo).

Congo's relations with its largest export market, China, have expanded substantially in recent years, particularly following a visit to Congo by Chinese Premier Minister Wen Jiabao in 2006, when a strategic co-operation accord was signed. A visit to Congo by Xi Jinping in March 2013 was the first by a Chinese President since the establishment of diplomatic relations between the two countries in 1964. Several bilateral agreements were signed, including on the construction of a river port in Oyo and a seaport in Pointe-Noire. In December 2013, moreover, the Congolese Government and the China Railway Construction Corporation concluded an accord on the rehabilitation of the Congo-Océan railway. Bilateral relations were further strengthened during state visits by President Sassou Nguesso to China in June 2014 and July 2016; during the latter visit Sassou Nguesso and Xi elevated bilateral relations to a comprehensive strategic co-operative partnership. In April 2019, following two years of negotiations, an agreement was signed on the restructuring of the debt owed to China by Congo, which reportedly amounted to some US $3,150m., or 35% of Congo's total public debt. In June, furthermore, China announced the cancellation of some $20m. of Congo's debt. A new, Chinese-funded parliament building in Brazzaville, constructed at a cost of more than 34,400m. francs CFA, was inaugurated in March 2021. Chinese President Xi agreed to a further restructuring of Congo's debt in June.

During a visit to the Russian Federation in May 2019, President Sassou Nguesso met his Russian counterpart, Vladimir Putin, and signed an agreement providing for Russian training of Congolese troops and the repair of previously purchased Russian military equipment. A further bilateral military co-operation accord was signed in October. Russia's Minister of Foreign Affairs, Sergei Lavrov, made his first visit to Congo in July 2022, meeting Sassou Nguesso in Oyo, as part of a tour of four African nations to gain support following the imposition of Western sanctions against Russia in response to its invasion of Ukraine in February.

Economy

TICKY MONEKOSSO

Revised for this edition by the editorial staff

INTRODUCTION

The economy of the Republic of the Congo is largely dominated by petroleum production, which accounts for around 50% of gross domestic product (GDP), some 80% of exports and 70% of budget revenue. The country holds significant hydrocarbons reserves, with an estimated 2,900m. barrels of oil reserves and 284,000m. cu m of natural gas in 2021. In addition, Congo has abundant mining resources.

According to World Bank estimates, Congo's gross domestic product (GDP) per head decreased, in real terms, by an average of 4.3% per year during 2011–20, and amounted to US $2,214 (at current prices) in 2021. Overall GDP also contracted after 2014 (when the international price of petroleum fell sharply, at rates of 3.6% in 2015, 10.8% in 2016, 4.4% in 2017, 4.8% in 2018 and 0.1% in 2019. The onset of the COVID-19 global pandemic in early 2020, precipitating a collapse in the international prices of petroleum and mineral commodities, led to a large economic contraction, of 6.2%, in that year. In addition to lockdown restrictions, due to the drop in global demand an agreement was reached in April by the Organization of Petroleum Exporting Countries (OPEC), of which Congo was a member, and other countries to cut output of crude petroleum. An expected post-pandemic recovery was undermined by weak petroleum production in 2021 (see *Natural Resources*), and GDP fell by a further 3.5% in that year, according to the World Bank.

In recent years Congo has attracted foreign direct investment (FDI) on a regular basis. Like many countries in the region, Congo is a country rich in oil and other raw materials, and its economy is seriously affected by any falls in global prices of these commodities and the resulting macroeconomic consequences. According to the World Bank, net FDI inflows into Congo amounted to US $4,315m. in 2018, but became negative, at a value of $1,428m., in 2019 (amid unsustainable levels of public debt—see *Banking and Finance*), remaining negative, at $1,983m., in 2020. Oil and timber are the main sectors that attract FDI.

The oil sector attracts the greatest investment, resulting in insufficient economic diversification, and although the Congolese Government has adopted some reforms, such as reducing property transfer fees and establishing rules to settle conflicts arising from contract execution, the economy is still not particularly favourable to foreign investors. They are discouraged by a variety of factors, including the country's political instability, inadequate infrastructure, high cost of labour and raw materials, as well as low productivity.

In order to compensate for a decrease in Congo's oil production in recent years, emphasis has been placed on the mining sector, which is attracting a growing number of investors.

Moreover, the country is expected to play an important role in the Central African region owing to the ongoing modernization of transport links between its capital, Brazzaville, and Pointe-Noire, its second largest city and hub of economic and commercial activities (being the location of the Gulf of Guinea's only deep-water port). The People's Republic of China has played a leading role in the reconstruction of Congo's ports, roads, rail and electricity infrastructure.

Although some progress has been made in translating its natural resources into economic growth, Congo has not fully succeeded in leveraging them to achieve robust socioeconomic outcomes. According to the World Bank, the economic contraction in the country resulted in an increase in extreme poverty from 51.9% of the population in 2020 to 53.9% in 2021. With little progress in the areas of health and education, infant mortality remained high, at a rate of 36 deaths per 1,000 live births in 2020. Access to electricity in urban areas was 66%, compared with just 13% in rural areas. Only 74% of households had access to improved water resources in 2020. The rate of unemployment in 2021 was estimated to be 23.0% by the World Bank. Congo ranked 153rd out of 191 countries on the 2021 Human Development Index of the United Nations Development Programme (UNDP). Although the rate of inflation was low, at 1.8% in 2020 and 1.7% in 2021, the International Monetary Fund (IMF) projected a rise to 3.5% in 2022, as the country became affected by global inflationary pressures (see *Agriculture*).

TRADE AND TAXATION

Congo's foreign trade policy promotes a favourable social and economic environment. Customs duties are harmonized by the Union Douanière et Economique de l'Afrique Centrale (UDEAC) and fluctuate between 5% and 30%. Congo is a member of the Communauté Economique et Monetaire de l'Afrique Centrale (CEMAC) and of the Communauté Economique des Etats de l'Afrique Centrale (CEEAC). According to IMF estimates, the merchandise trade surplus fell to 1,500,000m. francs CFA in 2020, due to the effects of the COVID-19 pandemic, but rose strongly to 2,631,000m. francs CFA in 2021, as a recovery in global oil prices compensated for lower petroleum production in that year. The balance on the current account, meanwhile, improved from a deficit of 5,000m. francs CFA (0.1% of GDP) to a surplus of 885,000m. francs CFA (12.6% of GDP).

According to figures from the International Trade Centre, in 2010 the principal source of imports (contributing 19.6% of the total) was China; other major import providers were France, Belgium, the Russian Federation and the USA. In that year China was also the principal market for exports (accounting for 45.8% of the total); Côte d'Ivoire and Togo were other important purchasers. The principal imports in 2021 were live animals and animal products, vehicles, aircraft, vessels and associated transport equipment, chemicals and related products, and machinery and mechanical appliances, and electrical equipment. The principal exports in that year were mineral products, vehicles, aircraft, vessels and associated transport equipment, and wood and wood charcoal.

As a member of the UDEAC, Congo adopts the common external tariff (CET), of which most the favoured nation simple average is estimated at 18.1% by the World Trade Organization. However, the CET is difficult to apply because members invoke country-specific exceptions and 'safeguard' measures. Congo applies the exceptions to a varied range of products, but its average tariff rate is lower than the CET, at 11.6%, according to the Heritage Foundation.

Products imported from outside the CEMAC region are subject to customs duties according to four tariff rate categories: products of first necessity (e.g. flour and rice) at 5%; primary materials and equipment at 10%; intermediate goods (e.g. tools and tyres) at 20%; and consumer goods (e.g. canned foods and electronic goods) at 30%.

Trade between Congo and its other neighbours, including Angola, but particularly the Democratic Republic of the Congo (DRC), is intensive. Thanks to a co-operation agreement and trade treaties, Congo and the DRC trade goods worth more than 50,000m. francs CFA every month. The bulk of trade is conducted from the deep-water port in Pointe-Noire via Brazzaville to Kinshasa, the capital of the DRC. Congo trades with Angola primarily from the district of Tchiamba-Nzassi in the far south of the country. Many products are subject to Congolese customs duties, and, in accordance with CEEAC-recognized indices, they enter Congo via Pointe-Noire. A direct connection has been established between Congo and Rwanda. Agricultural and livestock products, particularly from the Rwandan capital, Kigali, arrive in Brazzaville three times a week on flights operated by RwandAir, the national carrier of that country.

Under the Central African Backbone (CAB) project that primarily aimed to expand the capacity of the digital link between the 11 CEMAC countries, a first phase in Congo was launched in July 2011, with US $30m. in joint financing from the Government and the World Bank. Its completion was announced in December 2017, with the construction by Chinese telecommunications company Huawei of a 504-km fibre-optic network from Pointe-Noire to the border city of Lekoko, where it connected to the Gabonese network. A second phase, co-financed by the African Development Bank and the Government, began in August 2020 to connect the Congolese network to those of Cameroon and the Central African Republic (CAR), undertaken by Huawei and telecommunications operator China Communications Services International. A 347-km connection with Cameroon became operational in mid-2022. Construction of a 285-km connection between Brazzaville and the CAR capital, Bangui, began in January that year.

The rate of value added tax (VAT) in Congo is up to 18.9% (with a 5% surcharge that applies to certain consumer goods). Company tax consists of standard corporate income tax of up to 30% and an alternative minimum tax of 1% of turnover or 2% for companies recording losses in two consecutive fiscal years on the sum of gross turnover, products and benefits realized by the company in the latest year in which it earned a profit. Mining and real estate companies pay 30%, while microfinance companies and private schools organized as companies are taxed at 25%. Agricultural, agro-pastoral, poultry and fisheries activities are exempt from tax. Furthermore, for micro-sized and small enterprises whose turnover does not exceed 100m. francs CFA, a flat rate of 5% of annual turnover applies for operators selling products with unregulated profit margins, or 8% of the annual margin for operators selling products at regulated prices and with controlled margins.

FORESTRY

The Republic of the Congo, which straddles the Equator, comprises an area of 342,000 sq km; about 69%, or 23.5m. ha, is covered by forest, of which some 18.4m. ha is commercially exploitable. The ecosystems of Congo's forests provide subsistence goods (food, drinking water, etc.) and services (traditional pharmaceutical products, recreational activities, etc.). This vast landscape is a key factor in slowing anthropogenic global warming, in view of the forests' ability to absorb carbon.

Forestry is the main private sector employer in Congo. The sector is also an important source of export revenue (with wood and wood articles contributing 14.5% of the total in 2021), and both production and exports of forestry products have grown significantly in recent years.

Congo's forests are located in three mountainous areas: the Kouilou-Mayombe mountains (about 1.5m. ha) and the Chaillu-Niari mountains (some 3.5m. ha) in the south of Congo, and the Nord-Congo mountains (about 7.5m. ha) in the north. Congo also has 70,000–83,000 ha of limba and eucalyptus plantations in the Pointe-Noire department. According to the Congolese authorities, the country's protected areas cover more than 3.7m. ha, divided into three national parks, six reserves, three hunting areas and three sanctuaries.

In July 2020 Congo adopted new legislation introducing into the country's Forestry Code concepts such as certification, the verification of legality, the consideration of riverside communities, deforestation and reforestation, the fight against climate change and carbon credits. Sustainable management and certification of forest concessions have become major priorities in the exploitation of Congo's forestry resources to all stakeholders, including the public sector, the private sector, civil society, and local communities and indigenous groups. Congo signed a letter of intent with the Central African Forest Initiative in September 2019. The implementation of the following measures have had a significant impact on the forestry sector: the obligation for forestry companies to certify the management of their managed concessions or the legality of their exploited and processed products therefrom (Article 72 of the Forestry Code); recognition of certification for the verification of legality (Article 65) and the establishment of a national forest certification system (Article 70); the introduction of simplified management for medium-sized forest management units (Article 77); the obligation mainly to process forest products on national territory, leading to a ban on the export of logs, with the exception of logs of heavy and hardwood species whose machining requires specific technology (Article 97); the introduction of the plantation timber valuation agreement (Article 118); and the introduction of two new taxes: the occupancy tax and the residue tax (Article 110). The regulatory framework provides the basis for sustainable forestry management and is being implemented in Congo, which is one of the first countries in the world to do so. The forests in the Congo Basin are covered by the Treaty on the Conservation and Sustainable Management of Forest Ecosystems in Central Africa.

Forests are classified as either state forests, national public forests or private forests. State forests are divided into forest management units (Unités Forestières d'Aménagement—UFAs), of which there are 34, ranging from about 200,000 ha to 1m. ha. In the mountains in the south of the country (where logging dates back to the French colonial era), the UFAs are of medium size, but are much larger in the north (where logging started only recently) with a view to attracting investors capable of exploiting the timber on a large scale (at least 100,000 cu m annually) by building roads and setting up facilities for primary processing *in situ*. Owing to the proximity of the Pointe-Noire port, it is easier to ship timber from the south of the country than from the north, which involves the timber having to be transported over 1,200 km on rural roads to the port of Douala in Cameroon.

UFAs are exploited for commercial purposes by various concession holders. The concessions comprise industrial processing agreements (for a maximum period of 15 years); management and processing agreements (for a maximum period of 25 years); permits for the harvesting of plantations; and special permits (restricted to Congolese nationals, non-governmental organizations and associations established under Congolese law). Industrial processing and management and processing agreements are awarded following a tendering process. Under the Forestry Code, the UFAs are monitored by officials from the water resources and forestry administration. Concession holders draw up management plans (for 25 to 35 years) in collaboration with foreign or Congolese business consultants and forestry administration offices.

TOURISM AND BIODIVERSITY

In 2018 Congo recorded a total of 319,410 tourist arrivals and earned about US $42.9m. in revenue from the tourism sector (equivalent to around 0.4% of GDP). Congo is renowned for its biodiversity, including its native flora and fauna, which attract many visitors.

The north of Congo is home to natural parks, including Odzala-Kokoua in the Cuvette Ouest department and Nouabalé-Ndoki in Sangha department, which have the potential to create a mass tourism industry. In Pointe-Noire, Loango Bay on the Atlantic coast opens onto the Conkouati-Douli National Park and the Tchimpounga chimpanzee sanctuary. There is the potential for hotels and restaurants to be opened along the length of the coast, which is highly popular with employees in the oil industry who live in Pointe-Noire. In the area around Brazzaville, M'Bamou island is awaiting the establishment of hotel and tourism infrastructure to fulfil its potential. As noted above, forests cover almost 70% of national territory. These areas are home to a diverse range of rare and endangered large mammals, including forest elephants, chimpanzees, western

lowland gorillas, leopards and bongo antelope. In addition, Congo boasts ancient forests containing enormous mahogany trees and other species which are many hundreds of years old, particularly in the forestry concessions in the north of the country. The forests include protected areas, wildlife reserves and hunting areas that encompass a range of ecosystems. Congo is positioning itself as a primary destination for tourists who wish to visit tropical forests and view their iconic species, such as the lowland gorilla. Congo has a modest number of hotels, including several luxury establishments. Tourism infrastructure mainly comprises hotels owned by private investors; the Congolese state owns a single hotel, in Brazzaville.

The Congolese authorities have put in place a number of projects and institutions to develop the tourism industry, including an office to promote tourism whose responsibilities include attracting tour operators to invest in the country and seeking funding from multilateral and foreign institutions (including the World Bank, the UNDP and the African Development Bank—AfDB) to support Congo's tourism development programme, and a national tourism agency to develop sites and areas of tourist interest that it will either operate itself or lease to private promoters. Although tourism in Congo is disadvantaged in certain ways that seriously undermine its development, it should also be noted that the geopolitical situation in recent years has encouraged a much-anticipated burgeoning of the industry. Nevertheless, the tourism sector in Congo remains severely underdeveloped and its share of GDP is still negligible. However, efforts are now under way to make the country a destination for tourism on a par with its neighbours.

An estimated 11% of Congo's total territory is currently under protected area status, according to the Map of Protected Areas of Congo drawn up in 1990. Congo established the Nouabalé-Ndoki National Park (NNNP) in 1993 and the park was extended in 2001 when part of a neighbouring logging concession known as the Gouloago triangle was annexed. The Nouabalé-Ndoki Buffer Zone Project, a collaborative project between the Wildlife Conservation Society, the Congolese Government, the timber company Congolaise Industrielle du Bois (CIB) and the local community, was launched in 1999 to reduce the negative effects of logging on the national park. In 2018 the Government opened the country's fifth national park, the Ogooué-Leketi National Park, in the Batéké plateau area in the south-west of the country, and has implemented a programme (covering 2019–21) to improve the management of the Odzala-Kokoua National Park. The Government seeks to conserve biodiversity in Congo by establishing and maintaining a network of well-managed protected areas, to ensure that there is high-quality habitat in protected areas. The NNNP, covering an area of just over 4,000 sq km, is home to more than 300 bird species and some 1,000 plant and tree species. The park is located in the Congolese sector of the Sangha Trinational Zone and provides integral protection to wildlife through a collaborative management programme with the Congolese Ministry of the Forest Economy. In recent years mechanized logging has developed in the region, and active logging concessions threaten local wildlife. In response, the Ministry of the Environment, Sustainable Development and the Congo Basin has implemented an adaptive management approach, putting in place structures and personnel to respond quickly and effectively to emergent threats in the landscape. This includes effective systems and strategies for protection, research and monitoring and administration. National park staff have developed an ecotourism programme that focuses on the viewing of gorillas at Mbeli Bai, a large forest clearing in the NNNP, which has led to an increase in tourist arrivals.

The Congolese Government has pioneered an experimental approach in its work with the private sector. The Ministry of the Environment, Sustainable Development and the Congo Basin realized that the increase in logging activities around the NNNP meant that it was no longer sufficient to restrict wildlife management activities to within the park's boundaries. The resulting discussions led to the establishment of collaborative projects between the Government, the CIB and the local community to protect critical habitat, minimize commercial hunting and provide safe passage for wildlife in logging areas. The Ministry of the Environment, Sustainable

Development and the Congo Basin advises logging companies about reducing the negative impact of logging on wildlife, while working with the local population to manage activities such as hunting within the logging concessions. The Government is also working to develop community-based management of the Lac Télé Community Reserve (LTCR). The reserve is located in northern Congo, between the Sangha and Oubangui rivers, and covers an area of 4,400 sq km, making it the second largest protected area in the country. The LTCR hosts an undisturbed and unique wetland ecosystem containing flooded forest and one of the highest densities of western lowland gorillas in the region. The local villagers depend heavily on the natural resources within the LTCR for food, construction materials, canoes and medicines and they play an important role in managing these resources. However, the growing local demand for bushmeat poses a threat to the many wildlife species in the reserve, while unrestricted access to fisheries is reducing the density of stocks of fish. In an attempt to mitigate these problems, the Government is helping the local villagers to develop sustainable resource-use programmes in the community management of traditional hunting and fishing territories. Created in 1999, the Conkouati-Douli National Park (CDNP) is the second largest of Congo's national parks. Situated in the south-west of the country, on the Atlantic coast, the CDNP is the most ecologically diverse habitat in Congo. The protected area extends from a beach and coastal habitat to the mountainous zones of the Mayombian forest and the Niari savannah. The area is home to an extraordinarily diverse range of fauna, with marine species such as manatees, turtles, dolphins and whales, as well as many terrestrial threatened species, such as forest elephants, gorillas, chimpanzees, mandrills and forest buffalo. As a result, there is great potential for eco-tourism development. A significant human population is also based in the zone, many of whom rely on these natural resources for their livelihoods. In addition to these management interventions in well-established sites across Congo, the Government regularly carries out surveys with the goal of creating new protected areas.

FISHERIES

Congo has a coastline that stretches 170 km along the Atlantic Ocean and an exclusive economic zone of some 60,000 sq km, the waters of which are well stocked with fish. The potential annual catch is estimated at 180,000 metric tons, including 100,000 tons for inland fisheries. However, according to estimates by the UN Food and Agriculture Organization (FAO), the total catch amounted to 71,500 tons in 2020. Marine and coastal fishing in Congo is mainly small-scale or industrial (conducted out of Pointe-Noire port), while inland waters support only small-scale fishing. Fisheries development is none the less hampered by several obstacles, such as the instability of institutions, the obsolescence and inappropriateness of the means of production and a lack of infrastructure. The Congolese authorities are seeking to establish fishing and aquaculture as a modern, industrialized sector that will play an important role in providing food and employment. They envisage providing fisheries and aquaculture workers with viable equipment and infrastructure (such as fishing ports, fish markets, microbiological and chemical analysis laboratories, modern landing points and international-class facilities for preserving and curing fish in order to enable fishermen and aquaculture operatives to work in conditions that meet the necessary hygiene standards).

An analysis of the legal and regulatory framework governing the Congolese maritime sector shows that much remains to be done to improve, streamline and optimize regulations so that they correspond better with the Government's objectives for the sector. Fishing at sea requires an annual fishing licence granted by the Ministry of Agriculture, Stockbreeding and Fisheries. The licences are subject to the payment of a fee, depending on the type of vessel. Foreign vessels may be authorized to fish in Congo's territorial waters; because of a lack of resources on the part of the Congolese authorities, such activities are not closely monitored. Since June 2010 Congo has legally defined the conditions governing the exploitation, conservation and management of biological resources in the coastal waters under its jurisdiction, together with any associated activities. The legislation specifies the various taxes that apply to coastal fishing and aquaculture operations and imposes penalties for violations. In addition, a number of orders and decrees have bolstered the drive for organizational improvements to operations in the sector.

The principal obstacle to the development of the fisheries industry in Congo, aside from the limited appeal to foreign vessels of the Congolese flag, is excessive taxation. The result is that the profit margins of fisheries companies are squeezed, making it difficult for them to pursue other investment and almost impossible for them to create new jobs. In order to revive the sector Congo has adopted several regulatory texts on sustainable fishing, including, in 2009, laying down provisions on the mesh-sizes of nets and maritime fishing gear; in 2011 laying down the conditions for the pursuit of professional small-scale marine fishing and establishing procedures for the conduct of technical visits to fishing vessels in waters under Congolese jurisdiction; and in 2012 on the status of observers on board a fishing vessel. Since 2001 Congo has been included on the list of countries that are deemed to satisfy the conditions for recognition of equivalence with the health requirements determined by the European Union, and the country regularly exports about 1,000 metric tons of crustaceans annually to Spain. Congo has established a laboratory in Pointe-Noire to conduct the necessary microbiological and chemical analyses for these exports. Congo has signed agreements with other countries on fisheries matters. Under these agreements, Congolese legislation provides that industrial fishing in waters under Congolese jurisdiction is reserved for the following: vessels registered in the Republic of the Congo; vessels of states that have concluded a fisheries agreement with the Republic of the Congo; vessels of foreign operators who have concluded a contract with the marine fisheries authority authorizing them to fish in waters under Congolese jurisdiction; and fishing vessels chartered by a Congolese operator. In addition, any purchase or charter of a fishing vessel is subject to prior authorization by the marine fisheries authority. The conditions governing the chartering of foreign fishing vessels are also subject to local regulations.

AGRICULTURE

Congo benefits from a privileged geographical location, good climatic conditions (high rainfall and heat) and soil quality that is favourable to the development of a thriving and diverse agricultural sector. The country has more than 10m. ha of arable land, which is still largely unexploited. The obstacles to agricultural development are numerous, but they can be overcome. In an already highly urbanized country, with 68% of residents living in urban areas in 2020, the rural exodus of young people is alarming. This problem is exacerbated by difficult access to inputs and production plots, a lack of organization in production and the low involvement of the private sector. Middle Congo was one of the main agricultural regions of French Equatorial Africa. In the north, agro-industrial production of palm oil, coffee and cocoa was established in colonial times, while the south produced mostly sugar cane and peanuts, of which Congo was the second largest African producer during the 1980s. The years of civil conflict that followed curtailed an already weakened agricultural sector. The destruction and deterioration of infrastructure during this period undermined the country's agricultural economy, and agro-industrial production collapsed. Food crops (notably cassava, rice, plantains, potatoes, beans and yams) continue to be cultivated, but have never been the subject of an export strategy or industrial processing and, above all, are not produced in sufficient quantities to meet local demand and ensure Congo's food security. Although the number of undernourished citizens has fallen sharply since the late 1990s, the level of malnourishment remains high. Remedying this situation is a government priority.

A national food security programme was implemented during 2008–12 to guide production targets toward food self-sufficiency. This has helped to increase production and initiate agricultural partnerships for training and equipment. At the same time, the Government launched, with the support of the

World Bank, the Project for Agricultural Development and Rehabilitation of Rural Access Roads (PDARP). In areas covered by this project, farmers' average income increased between 2010 and 2013. The rehabilitation of infrastructure has reduced transportation costs and, by extension, average commodity prices. A report on the project concluded that 'the actions of the PDARP in targeted areas have been very beneficial for small producers and PDARP objectives have largely been achieved'. However, they were still not sufficient to enable the agricultural sector to contribute significantly to the national objectives, 'Path of the Future' (as outlined operationally in the 2012–16 National Development Plan—NDP), and they continue to be featured in the new 'March Toward Development' social project. Although the agricultural sector accounted for 24% of GDP at the time of independence and 10% in 1998, it represented only 7.5% in 2020, according to UN estimates—a figure that fell short of the 10.5% target specified in the 2012–16 NDP. Most of the current output still consists of food crops for domestic consumption, and the agricultural production deficit forces Congo to import a significant volume of food supplies every year.

For many years the Government has drawn up plans to make agriculture a pillar of the country's modernization and industrialization, and the sector lies at the centre of Congo's efforts in this regard. Notably, a new position, that of Minister of State responsible to the Minister of Agriculture, Stockbreeding and Fisheries was created in April 2016. In its 2016–21 social project, Congo expressed interest in 'fostering the emergence of private production initiatives by organizing and supporting small business incubators', particularly in the primary sector. The country has undertaken many sustainable projects. In collaboration with the UN World Food Programme and International Fund for Agricultural Development, the Ministry of Agriculture, Stockbreeding and Fisheries launched the Support of Small Bean Producers Project in the department of Bouenza in September 2016. As part of this project, 200 producers were to be trained in technical and economic management and business planning. These initiatives were considered as a first step toward reducing food imports (which are necessary to supply about 70% of Congo's needs) and consequently the high cost of living. However, the IMF reported that more than one-fifth of children were malnourished and that there were 700,000 food insecure people in Brazzaville and Pointe-Noire in 2021, following a pandemic-related increase in poverty and the adverse impact of climate change on food insecurity. Sharp increases in global food prices and supply shortages resulting from Russia's invasion of Ukraine in February 2022 were expected to exacerbate the situation further. The rising price of fertilizer (of which Congo was a net importer) was also likely to damage agricultural activity. In terms of social protection, an emergency cash transfer programme for affected households, which had been introduced in response to the pandemic, was extended by the authorities; its coverage was to increase from 230,000 beneficiaries to 300,000 by the end of 2022.

NATURAL RESOURCES

Congo's future depends to a large extent on its rich reserves of assets below the ground. However, this does not mean that the country should live off its oil and mining income and overlook subcontracting development opportunities that generate employment. Congo is demonstrating its ambition by creating oil refining and oil-processing industries and is not content to settle for the role of being only an exporter of crude oil.

Any inventory of the investment opportunities in Congo would have to begin with hydrocarbons, which represent some 70% of the state's revenue. In 2016 the Government adopted a new Hydrocarbons Code. The new Code took its main provisions from the previous Code, adopted in 1994, to which it added substantial innovations, notably by setting out: the exclusive licensing of mining titles to the Société Nationale des Pétroles du Congo (SNPC), with the possibility of joining forces with national or foreign partners; the strengthening of sanctions in cases of oil companies' non-compliance with legal and contractual provisions; the establishment of a tax and customs regime, which was applicable to all oil companies; a

minimum share for the state of 35% of oil profits; a definitive ban on gas-flaring in Congo; the establishment of a minimum stake of 15% for private national companies in production-sharing contracts; and the establishment of a national environmental risk prevention fund, capable of dealing with emergency situations resulting from serious accidents or industrial catastrophes. One of the reasons behind drafting of the Hydrocarbons Code was the progress being made in exploitation. Moho-Bilondo, a field 80 km off the coast of Pointe-Noire and more than 500 m deep, operated by TotalEnergies of France, began production in 2015. The Moho Nord extension, located in the northern part of the same area, followed in 2017. Both developments had 30-year lifespans and a reported production volume of 140,000 barrels per day (b/d). The Nene Marine offshore development, located in the Marine XII block and operated by Italian multinational energy company Eni, began producing in 2014, with an estimated peak production of 50,000 b/d. The Lianzi offshore area at the border with Angola, the country's first cross-border development, was operated by Chevron of the USA from 2015 and had an estimated peak production of 40,000 b/d.

The production cuts agreed by OPEC in April 2020, following the onset of the COVID-19 pandemic, reduced Congo's crude extraction to an estimated 275,000 b/d from 328,000 b/d in 2019. In addition, despite some recovery in global oil prices, oil production in 2021 unexpectedly fell further, by 11%, largely owing to the impact of the pandemic on production-related investments in 2020. Crude petroleum output fell to 14.0m. metric tons in 2021, from 15.8m. tons in 2020 and 17.2m. tons in 2019. Output levels were expected to recover gradually from 2022 with a resumption of investment, and reach pre-pandemic annual levels of 125m. barrels by 2024 (according to IMF projections), with new fields beginning production, but decline thereafter owing to the depletion of reserves.

The 2016 Hydrocarbons Code aimed to strengthen the hygiene, safety and environment elements of the Congo's hydrocarbons projects, and to consider the impact of oil activities by the major companies on local small and medium-sized enterprises (SMEs) and small and medium-sized industries (SMIs). Finally, the Hydrocarbons Code was to enable the state to increase income, develop national expertise and improve the downstream hydrocarbons sector, through the construction of a new refinery near Pointe-Noire; construction of the country's second refinery, the US $600m. Atlantic Petrochemical Refinery (with a capacity of 2.5m. metric tons per year), commenced in February 2021. The Government has planned to undertake two other projects in order not to restrict itself to exporting crude oil: the modernization of the existing Pointe-Noire refinery to increase production capacity for refined products and the construction of a north–south pipeline. Under five memorandums of understanding signed between Congo and Russia in September 2022, Russian company Zaknefte-gazstroy Prometey was to construct a 1,000-km oil-pipeline traversing Brazzaville.

The other core asset of the energy sector is natural gas, where the investment and exploitation prospects are good. The Centrale Electrique du Djéno (CED) gas power plant first began operating in 2002 and was upgraded to a capacity of 50 MW in 2008. In January 2021 Turkey's Aksa Enerji Üretim signed a concession agreement with the Congolese Government under which its subsidiary, Aksa Energy Company Congo, obtained 30-year operating rights of the CED power plant, and undertook rehabilitation of the plant to expand its capacity by at least 100 MW. Some of Djéno's output was to be sold directly to the DRC, under bilateral export contracts involving state utility Société Energie Electrique du Congo. Eni Congo (80% of which is owned by the Congolese state and 20% by Eni) has a significant presence in the country, particularly in Pointe-Noire, where it initiated and carried out the construction of the Centrale Electrique du Congo (CEC) gas power plant, which entered into operation in 2010. The capacity of the CEC plant was increased from 314 MW to 484 MW in early 2020 through the construction of a third gas turbine, after which it supplied 70% of the country's electricity requirements. In April 2022 the Government signed an agreement with Eni to increase Congo's gas production and exports, primarily through the development of a liquefied natural gas project, which was scheduled to become operational in 2023 with a capacity of over 4,500m. cu m per year.

The Government has long planned the construction of dams in Sounda (with a capacity of 1,000 MW) and in Chollet (600 MW), to be operated jointly with Cameroon. In April 2021 China Gezhouba Group Company secured an international tender (launched by the Congolese and Cameroonian Governments in December 2019) for construction of the Chollet dam, hydroelectric plant and associated infrastructure, after undertaking an environmental and social assessment. The project required an investment of an estimated US $700m. The Government also announced that it had accepted a proposal by the China Railways 20 Bureau Group Corporation to construct the Sounda dam, near Pointe-Noire. At that time Congo had four existing hydroelectric dams—Djoué, Moukoukoulou, Imboulou (the largest, with a capacity of 120 MW) and Liouesso—and an estimated hydropower potential of 3,942 MW.

Mineral Resources

Gold, diamonds, iron, potash, magnesium, phosphate, uranium, colombo-tantalite (coltan), polymetals (copper, zinc, lead), bauxite, rare soils (granite, clay), cassiterite: the mineral resources of the Republic of the Congo are vast and require significant investment. Apart from hydrocarbons, the exploitation of iron is the most developed, and major mining projects are aimed first and foremost at this sector. In April 2019 the country shipped its first iron ore exports. Congo's priority is none the less to become the leading producer of potash in Africa and one of the 13 largest producers in the world. In December 2008 MagMinerals Potasses Congo, a subsidiary of Canada's MagIndustries, signed a 25-year potash investment agreement with the Government to exploit potash reserves in Mengo, in the province of Kouilou. In 2011 Evergreen Holding Group, a private Chinese company, purchased a majority stake in MagIndustries. However, continued development of the project became uncertain after MagIndustries was subject to numerous allegations of corruption, including the bribing of officials in Congo, and was delisted from the Toronto Stock Exchange in 2015, while the financial position of Evergreen deteriorated severely. China's Zhengwei Technique Congo, established in Brazzaville in 2001, aimed to exploit potash salts in Mboukoumasi, as well as in Kouilou, within the framework of a strategic partnership agreement concluded between Congo and China in 2016, encouraging Chinese businesses to invest in the country. In 2014 another Chinese company, Lulu, signed an agreement with the Congolese Government to mine copper, zinc and lead in Mindouli, in the Mpassa region. For polymetals, a licence to exploit mineral deposits in Boko Songo and Yanga Koubanza (in the department of Bouenza) was granted to Soremi Investments Ltd, a subsidiary of America's Gerald Metals, for an investment of more than US $50m. Under Congo's Mining Code, the state's share is limited to 10%, the mining royalty fluctuates between 3% and 7%, and licensing procedures have been simplified.

A decision by the Congolese Government to withdraw several iron ore mining permits in late 2020 caused the launch of arbitration proceedings involving at least US $40,000m, against Congo by several companies, including Australia's Sundance Resources and Equatorial Resources, Avima Iron Ore, based in Saint Kitts and Nevis, which had mined the high-grade Avima iron ore deposits in the north-west, and Midus Holdings of the United Kingdom. In July 2022 Kanga Potash, a subsidiary of SARMIN Mining Inc. of Canada, was granted a mining and production licence (subject to approval by the Congolese legislature) for the Kanga potash project, 32 km north of Pointe Noire. The Kanga asset contained resources of 12,000m. metric tons (with an additional 13,000m. tons located in the adjacent Loango permit area owned by the company). According to a feasibility study, the Kanga project was to be developed at an estimated cost of $457m., and was expected to produce 600,000 tons of muriate of potash annually for more than 30 years, with potential to become the world's lowest-cost muriate of potash producer.

BANKING AND FINANCE

At December 2020 the Congo's financial sector comprised 10 commercial banks, 24 microfinance institutions, eight insurance companies and two pension funds. Of the 10 banks in the Congo, two were subsidiaries of international banking groups, five subsidiaries of African groups, two controlled by Congolese capital and one a subsidiary of a Chinese group. Over the past few years, the development of the banking sector has accelerated, as a result of liberalization measures taken by the Government. In various announcements, the Conseil National du Crédit (CNC) has expressed its satisfaction with regard to the consolidation of the financial and prudential situation of the majority of Congolese banks in accordance with Central African Banking Commission standards. The Council noted that the equity held by the six main banks complies with the regulatory provisions stating that net equity must be positive. In terms of their 'solvency', they have a risk-adjusted coverage ratio greater than 45% of net equity. At the end of December 2020 the total equity of the financial sector stood at 275,000m. francs CFA and accounted for 4.4% of GDP, with 73.5% coming from the banking sector, 19.1% from the microfinance sector and 7.3% from the insurance sector.

Over the past five years Congolese banks have undertaken efforts to implement programmes to modernize their management tools and operations, by introducing new payment systems. Automated teller machines are flourishing all over the country's main cities. Brazzaville's financial centre is making up for lost time with respect to its Gabonese and Cameroonian neighbours, and the CNC has invited lending institutions to set up operations throughout the country. It is important to proceed with a closely integrated national network in this field, in order to accelerate access to deposits and loans. The financial benefit resulting from the restructuring of the banking system has the potential to last a long time, but this staying power is mainly influenced by the diversification of the economy. The public authorities must engage with certain measures, for example to direct excess liquidity toward investment, so that it benefits the national economy, and to diversify the latter using savings generated by establishing other structures that are able to create wealth (such as in mineral ore exploitation and SME and SMI creation) or from oil boom revenues by reinvesting them in the industry.

The restructuring of the banking sector that began in the mid-2000s resulted in the privatization of the three principal institutions and the resumption of foreign investment. The sector experienced a resurgence and attracted new providers, and the banking landscape was rebuilt under the influence of foreign banks. Although the importance of the informal sector (which represents nearly two-thirds of GDP) could in theory dissuade financial institutions from investing in Congo, in practice this is not the case. Alongside French banks and insurance companies, financial companies from other nations are now entering the market. Ecobank (pan-African), United Bank for Africa (United Kingdom), Banque Congolaise de l'Habitat, Banque Postale du Congo, Banque Espirito Santo Congo and Société Générale Congo have all set up operations in the country, in addition to Banque Sino-Congolaise pour l'Afrique, which is the most recent entrant. The modernization of banking services can be seen in the introduction of voice servers and SWIFT international electronic money transfers. All of the commercial banks have Western Union sales outlets for the receipt of remittances payments from Congolese migrant workers living abroad.

However, individual customers face difficulties accessing the banking system. BGFI Bank Congo, which is considered to be the largest in the country in terms of capital, lends more than 80% of its money to large corporations. As a deposit of 50,000 francs CFA is needed to open an account, very few average Congolese citizens are willing to take the risk with investing their money with this bank. With its vision of a new community bank, BGFI, which locally is considered to be an elitist institution, wants to put personal loans back at the centre of its operations. Meanwhile, Ecobank and LCB Bank are placing particular emphasis on treasury credit, specifically aimed at average consumers. For small customers, obtaining credit is subject to the presentation of a large number of documents and an array of required guarantees. Banking sector analysts are calling for the creation of an SME support fund. In 2015 the Development Bank of the Central African States increased its line of credit to SMEs from 10,000m. francs CFA to 60,000m. francs CFA. The Government, for its part, established a fund of about 180,000m. francs CFA, and about 30 SMEs have taken advantage of loans.

In 2019 Congo succeeded in reducing its public debt stocks, to 78.5% of GDP compared with 87.8% one year earlier, following the signature of a debt restructuring agreement with China in April. Meanwhile, the adoption of reform measures, including the creation of a new institution to regulate the management of public funds, helped to fulfil IMF preconditions for improving governance. Consequently, in July 2019 the IMF approved a US $448.6m. Extended Credit Facility (ECF) arrangement to support the authorities' structural reform programme. Following the impact of the COVID-19 pandemic, however, public debt reached an estimated $12,555m., or 114.0% of GDP, in 2020 (with external public debt of $7,307m., equivalent to 66.3% of GDP), and Congo was unable to access further funds from the IMF. In June 2020 the Paris Club of major creditor countries approved Congo's participation in the Group of 20 Debt Service Suspension Initiative, allowing it to temporarily suspend its debt service repayments for one year. The Government engaged in debt restructuring negotiations with external creditors, and in June 2021 announced that China had agreed to a further rescheduling of Congo's debt (believed to amount to $2,400m.). Following lengthy negotiations, in January 2022 the IMF approved a new, three-year ECF arrangement, amounting to about $455m., for Congo, with an immediate disbursement of some $90m. It was announced that Congo's debt restructuring discussions with its largest external commercial creditors have all been concluded by the end of January, with agreements in principle reached on arrears to Brazil and Russia. The level of public debt was reduced to an estimated 103.4% of GDP in 2021 and was projected to decline to 84.4% in 2022. The IMF also welcomed the adoption of a new, more comprehensive anti-corruption law in January. In June the IMF completed the first review of performance under the ECF-supported programme, which was deemed satisfactory, and disbursed a further tranche of $87m.

CONCLUSION

The economy of Congo remains extremely vulnerable to shifts in the international prices of some commodities, as evidenced particularly in the early years of the 2020s during the COVID-19 pandemic. However, the World Bank considered that, due to debt restructuring agreements, higher oil prices and improved debt management, Congo had made significant progress in restoring the sustainability of public debt by the end of 2021, and was classified as being in 'debt distress'. The post-pandemic recovery was constrained by lower petroleum production in 2021 but gained momentum during 2022, as sharp increases in global oil prices resulting from the war in Ukraine increased revenue. Despite the concomitant adverse effects of inflationary pressures on the non-oil sector, in its report of July 2022 the IMF expected that the higher oil prices would raise oil revenues by 12.6% of GDP in that year, more than offsetting an increase in the cost of fuel and food imports equivalent to 1.9% of GDP. The IMF forecast the resumption of GDP growth at a rate of 2.4% in 2022.

Statistical Survey

Source (unless otherwise stated): Direction Générale, Centre National de la Statistique et des Etudes Economiques, Immeuble du Plan, Rond point du Centre Culturel Français, BP 2031, Brazzaville; tel. 22-281-59-09; e-mail cnsee@hotmail.fr; internet www.cnsee.org.

Area and Population

AREA, POPULATION AND DENSITY

Area (sq km)	342,000*
Population (census results)	
30 July 1996	2,591,271
28 April 2007	
Males	1,821,357
Females	1,876,133
Total	3,697,490
Population (UN estimates at mid-year)†	
2020	5,518,092
2021‡	5,657,017
2022‡	5,797,801
Density (per sq km) at mid-2022‡	17.0

* 132,047 sq miles.
† Source: UN, *World Population Prospects: The 2019 Revision*.
‡ Projection.

POPULATION BY AGE AND SEX
('000, UN projections at mid-2022)

	Males	Females	Total
0–14 years	1,188.7	1,166.5	2,355.2
15–64 years	1,636.6	1,640.0	3,276.6
65 years and over	72.2	93.9	166.0
Total	**2,897.5**	**2,900.3**	**5,797.8**

Note: Totals may not be equal to the sum of components, owing to rounding.

Source: UN, *World Population Prospects: The 2019 Revision*.

DEPARTMENTS
(official population estimates at 2018)

	Area (sq km)	Population	Capital
Bouenza . . .	12,265	434,925	Madingou
Brazzaville . .	100	1,932,610	Brazzaville
Cuvette . . .	} 74,850 {	219,584	Owando
Cuvette Ouest .		102,724	Ewo
Kouilou . . .	13,650	129,398	Hinda
Lékoumou . . .	20,950	135,643	Sibiti
Likouala . . .	66,044	216,869	Impfondo
Niari . . .	25,942	325,442	Loubomo (Dolisie)
Plateaux . . .	38,400	245,683	Djambala
Pointe-Noire .	44	1,006,611	Pointe-Noire
Pool . . .	33,955	332,934	Kinkala
Sangha . . .	55,800	120,650	Ouesso
Total	342,000	5,203,073	

PRINCIPAL TOWNS
(official population estimates at 2018)

Brazzaville (capital)	1,932,610	Loubomo (Dolisie) .	117,920
Pointe-Noire . .	1,006,611	Nkayi	100,783

Mid-2021 (incl. suburbs, UN projections): Brazzaville 2,469,630; Pointe-Noire 1,253,939 (Source: UN, *World Urbanization Prospects: The 2018 Revision*).

BIRTHS AND DEATHS
(annual averages, UN estimates)

	2005–10	2010–15	2015–20
Birth rate (per 1,000)	37.9	36.0	33.0
Death rate (per 1,000)	9.6	7.8	6.8

Source: UN, *World Population Prospects: The 2019 Revision.*

Life expectancy (years at birth, estimates): 64.8 (males 63.3; females 66.3) in 2020 (Source: World Bank, World Development Indicators database).

ECONOMICALLY ACTIVE POPULATION
('000, FAO estimates at mid-year)

	2013	2014	2015
Agriculture, etc.	544	547	550
Total labour force (incl. others) .	1,834	1,892	1,953

Source: FAO.

Health and Welfare

KEY INDICATORS

Total fertility rate (children per woman, 2020)	4.3
Under-5 mortality rate (per 1,000 live births, 2020) . . .	44.6
HIV/AIDS (% of persons aged 15–49, 2020	3.3
COVID-19: Cumulative confirmed deaths (per 100,000 persons at 31 August 2022)	6.6
COVID-19: Fully vaccinated population (% of total population at 31 July 2022)	11.2
Physicians (per 1,000 head, 2018)	0.1
Hospital beds (per 1,000 head, 2005)	1.6
Domestic health expenditure (2019): US $ per head (PPP) .	30.7
Domestic health expenditure (2019): % of GDP . . .	0.8
Domestic health expenditure (2019): public (% of total current expenditure)	37.6
Access to improved water resources (% of persons, 2020) .	74
Access to improved sanitation facilities (% of persons, 2020) .	20
Total carbon dioxide emissions ('000 metric tons, 2018) . .	3,220
Carbon dioxide emissions per head (metric tons, 2018) . .	0.6
Human Development Index (2021): ranking	153
Human Development Index (2021): value	0.571

Note: For data on COVID-19 vaccinations, 'fully vaccinated' denotes receipt of all doses specified by approved vaccination regime (Sources: Johns Hopkins University and Our World in Data). Data on health expenditure refer to current general government expenditure in each case. For more information on sources and further definitions for all indicators, see Health and Welfare Statistics: Sources and Definitions section (europaworld.com/credits).

Agriculture

PRINCIPAL CROPS
('000 metric tons, FAO estimates unless otherwise indicated)

	2018	2019	2020
Avocados	9.2	9.1	9.1
Bananas	85.5	85.7	86.0
Cassava (Manioc)	1,584.4	1,570.4	1,584.7
Cocoa beans*	4.5	5.0	7.0
Coffee, green	3.0	3.0	3.0
Grapefruits and pomelos . . .	5.2	5.2	5.2
Groundnuts, with shell . . .	26.0	26.2	26.1
Maize	12.8	14.0*	13.0*
Mangoes, mangosteens and guavas	34.6	34.3	34.6
Millet	13.4	13.5	13.6
Oil palm fruit	149.9	149.9	149.4

—continued	2018	2019	2020
Peas, dry	6.9	6.8	6.8
Plantains and others	88.2	89.0	88.1
Rubber, natural	2.4	2.3	2.3
Sugar cane	645.1	648.5	644.7
Sweet potatoes	8.8	8.8	8.8
Yams	15.4	15.5	15.5

* Unofficial figure(s).

Aggregate production ('000 metric tons, may include official, semi-official or estimated data): Total cereals 30.0 in 2018, 31.3 in 2019, 30.3 in 2020; Total fruit (primary) 269.5 in 2018, 270.3 in 2019, 270.0 in 2020; Total oilcrops 182.2 in 2018, 182.9 in 2019, 182.4 in 2020; Total roots and tubers 1,674.8 in 2018, 1,660.9 in 2019, 1,675.2 in 2020; Total vegetables (primary) 142.7 in 2018, 142.0 in 2019, 142.5 in 2020.

Source: FAO.

LIVESTOCK
('000 head, year ending September, FAO estimates)

	2018	2019	2020
Cattle	348	350	352
Chickens	2,981	2,937	2,977
Goats	328	330	331
Pigs	100	103	106
Sheep	123	124	124

Source: FAO.

LIVESTOCK PRODUCTS
('000 metric tons, FAO estimates)

	2018	2019	2020
Cattle meat	5.8	5.8	5.8
Cows' milk	4.0	4.1	4.1
Chicken meat	6.7	6.8	6.8
Game meat	43.8	42.8	43.1
Pig meat	1.8	1.8	1.8
Sheep and goat meat	1.5	1.5	1.4
Hen eggs	1.5	1.5	1.5

Source: FAO.

Forestry

ROUNDWOOD REMOVALS
('000 cubic metres, excluding bark, FAO estimates)

	2018	2019	2020
Sawlogs, veneer logs and logs for sleepers	1,812	1,812	1,812
Pulpwood	237	237	237
Other industrial wood	370	370	370
Fuel wood	1,508	1,529	1,551
Total	3,927	3,948	3,970

Source: FAO.

SAWNWOOD PRODUCTION
('000 cubic metres, including railway sleepers)

	2018	2019	2020
Total (all broadleaved) . . .	403	403	303

Source: FAO.

Fishing

('000 metric tons, live weight)

	2018	2019	2020
Capture	98.7	70.4	70.6
Freshwater fishes . . .	41.0	38.9	39.1
Largehead hairtail . . .	7.6	2.5	2.4
Round sardinella . . .	20.7	11.1	10.2
Madeiran sardinella . . .	5.1	2.1	2.1
Other marine fishes . . .	23.4	15.0	16.8
Aquaculture	0.6*	0.7	0.9
Total catch	99.4*	71.1	71.5

* FAO estimate.

Source: FAO.

Mining

	2019	2020	2021
Crude petroleum ('000 metric tons)	17,227	15,755	14,020

Gold (kg, estimated metal content of ore): 150 in 2016.

Sources: US Geological Survey; BP, *Statistical Review of World Energy*.

Industry

SELECTED PRODUCTS

('000 metric tons unless otherwise indicated)

	2017	2018	2019
Jet fuels	37	38	38
Motor gasoline (petrol) . . .	64	65	65
Kerosene	7	7	7
Distillate fuel oils	214	214	n.a.
Residual fuel oils	358	358	368
Electrical energy (million kWh) .	2,965	3,096	3,655

Sources: UN Industrial Commodity Statistics Database; UN Energy Statistics Database.

Veneer sheets ('000 cubic metres, FAO estimates): 34 in 2018; 34 in 2019; 29 in 2020 (Source: FAO).

Finance

CURRENCY AND EXCHANGE RATES

Monetary Units
100 centimes = 1 franc de la Coopération Financière en Afrique Centrale (CFA).

Sterling, Dollar and Euro Equivalents (31 May 2022)
£1 sterling = 770.825 francs CFA;
US $1 = 612.300 francs CFA;
€1 = 655.957 francs CFA;
10,000 francs CFA = £12.97 = $16.33 = €15.24.

Average Exchange Rate (francs CFA per US $)
2019   585.911
2020   575.586
2021   554.531

Note: The exchange rate of 1 French franc = 50 francs CFA, established in 1948, remained in force until January 1994, when the CFA franc was devalued by 50%, with the exchange rate adjusted to 1 French franc = 100 francs CFA. The relationship to French currency remained in effect with the introduction of the euro on 1 January 1999. From that date, accordingly, a fixed exchange rate of €1 = 655.957 francs CFA has been in operation.

BUDGET

(central government operations, '000 million francs CFA)

Revenue*	2019†	2020‡	2021§
Oil revenue	1,317	651	950
Non-oil revenue	629	570	617
Total	1,946	1,221	1,567

Expenditure	2019†	2020‡	2021§
Current expenditure	1,374	1,179	1,179
Wages and salaries . . .	349	352	370
Other current expenditure . .	782	748	679
Interest payments . . .	243	80	130
Capital expenditure	277	214	272
Domestically financed . . .	97	119	147
Externally financed . . .	180	95	124
Total	1,650	1,393	1,451

* Excluding grants received ('000 million francs CFA): 57 in 2019 (estimate); 100 in 2020 (preliminary estimate); 15 in 2021 (revised budget figure).
† Estimates.
‡ Preliminary estimates.
§ Revised budget figures.

Source: IMF, *Republic of Congo: 2021 Article IV Consultation—Press Release; Staff Report; and Statement by the Executive Director for the Republic of Congo* (October 2021).

INTERNATIONAL RESERVES

(US $ million at 31 December)

	2017	2018	2019
Gold (national valuation) . . .	14.33	14.23	16.86
IMF special drawing rights . .	72.19	70.55	70.23
Reserve position in IMF . .	28.40	27.77	27.61
Foreign exchange	279.39	325.30	890.47
Total	394.31	437.85	1,005.17

2020: IMF special drawing rights 73.04; Reserve position in IMF 28.76.
2021: IMF special drawing rights 10.28; Reserve position in IMF 27.95.
Source: IMF, *International Financial Statistics*.

MONEY SUPPLY

('000 million francs CFA at 31 December)

	2017	2018	2019
Currency outside depository			
corporations	471.56	447.02	517.45
Transferable deposits	893.70	844.95	832.36
Other deposits	318.62	290.72	355.05
Broad money	1,683.88	1,582.68	1,704.86

Source: IMF, *International Financial Statistics*.

COST OF LIVING

(Consumer Price Index; base: 2005 = 100)

	2015	2016	2017
Food and non-alcoholic beverages .	159.1	159.9	158.0
Clothing and footwear	121.8	125.7	123.1
Housing, utilities and fuels . .	143.6	153.9	152.5
All items (incl. others) . . .	140.1	144.5	145.2

All items (Consumer Price Index; base: 2010 = 100): 124.7 in 2019; 127.0 in 2020; 129.2 in 2021.

Source: International Monetary Fund (IMF).

NATIONAL ACCOUNTS
('000 million francs CFA at current prices)

Expenditure on the Gross Domestic Product

	2018	2019	2020
Government final consumption expenditure	1,108	1,279	1,067
Private final consumption expenditure	2,900	2,802	2,442
Gross capital formation . . .	1,740	1,531	1,233
Total domestic expenditure .	5,749	5,612	4,743
Exports of goods and services . .	5,393	5,128	3,262
Less Imports of goods and services	3,721	3,445	2,343
Statistical discrepancy	—	45	152
GDP at purchasers' values .	7,421	7,339	5,814
GDP at constant 2015 prices .	5,585	5,561	5,107

Gross Domestic Product by Economic Activity

	2018	2019	2020
Agriculture, hunting, forestry and fishing	522	527	420
Mining, quarrying and utilities .	3,151	2,030	1,851
Manufacturing	563	718	552
Construction	88	430	257
Trade, restaurants and hotels .	1,011	1,069	801
Transport and communications .	421	479	367
Other activities	1,487	1,801	1,383
Sub-total	7,242	7,054	5,630
Indirect taxes (net)*	178	285	184
GDP in purchasers' values .	7,421	7,339	5,814

* Figures obtained as residuals.

Source: UN National Accounts Main Aggregates Database.

BALANCE OF PAYMENTS
(US $ million)

	2014	2015	2016
Exports of goods	8,866.8	4,678.3	4,355.7
Imports of goods	−5,402.6	−5,787.3	−5,071.0
Balance on goods	3,464.2	−1,108.9	−715.4
Exports of services	641.7	400.1	240.7
Imports of services	−3,735.5	−3,717.0	−2,215.0
Balance on goods and services	370.4	−4,425.8	−2,689.7
Primary income received . . .	43.8	58.7	13.8
Primary income paid	218.7	−124.5	−404.3
Balance on goods, services and income	632.9	−4,491.6	−3,080.2
Secondary income received . .	106.8	76.4	27.3
Secondary income paid . . .	−60.8	−213.5	−540.6
Current balance	678.9	−4,628.7	−3,593.6
Capital account (net) . . .	7.3	70.0	68.2
Direct investment assets . .	−1,249.3	−549.2	−1,196.9
Direct investment liabilities .	2,887.8	4,278.4	−36.6
Portfolio investment assets . .	−42.3	−22.5	−0.8
Portfolio investment liabilities .	1.2	—	35.8
Other investment assets . .	−3,071.4	−3,182.6	−1,610.5
Other investment liabilities .	1,366.8	1,394.5	1,592.5
Net errors and omissions . .	−199.6	411.7	3,105.1
Reserves and related items .	379.4	−2,228.4	−1,646.8

Source: IMF, *International Financial Statistics*.

External Trade

PRINCIPAL COMMODITIES
(distribution by HS, US $ million)

Imports c.i.f.	2019	2020	2021
Live animals and animal products	273.7	296.2	386.1
Meat and edible meat offal . .	171.8	187.6	254.6
Meat and edible offal of fowls, ducks, geese, turkeys, etc. .	110.4	119.8	162.1
Fish and crustaceans, molluscs and other aquatic invertebrates .	76.3	72.8	94.2
Vegetables and vegetable products	122.0	121.4	170.1
Cereals	91.0	94.3	138.5
Prepared foodstuffs; beverages, spirits, vinegar; tobacco and articles thereof .	123.8	125.9	148.4
Mineral products	96.9	84.2	113.2
Mineral fuels, mineral oils and products of their distillation .	82.0	69.4	100.2
Petroleum oils and oils obtained from bituminous minerals (excluding crude)	75.5	54.8	91.2
Chemicals and related products	220.5	208.6	353.8
Pharmaceutical products . .	67.1	69.3	80.9
Iron and steel, other base metals and articles of base metal	179.8	113.8	120.6
Articles of iron or steel . . .	129.6	77.9	79.3
Machinery and mechanical appliances; electrical equipment; parts thereof .	456.0	308.7	296.3
Machinery, boilers, etc. . . .	316.1	208.2	199.4
Taps, cocks, valves and similar appliances for pipes, boiler shells, tanks, vats, etc. . .	44.0	33.1	20.9
Electrical machinery and equipment and parts thereof; sound recorders and reproducers, television . . .	139.9	100.5	96.8
Vehicles, aircraft, vessels and associated transport equipment	517.2	363.0	359.3
Vehicles other than railway, tramway	73.2	78.2	113.7
Ships, boats and other floating structures	428.1	262.5	229.3
Cruise ships, cargo ships, barges	344.3	131.1	94.6
Light vessels, dredgers; floating docks; floating/submersible drill platforms	25.6	84.9	118.7
Total (incl. others)	2,302.1	1,912.6	2,351.5

Exports f.o.b.	2019	2020	2021
Mineral products	4,689.7	3,744.9	1,308.9
Mineral fuels, oils, distillation products, etc.	4,680.5	3,738.7	1,301.4
Crude petroleum oils . . .	4,409.5	3,508.2	1,072.0
Petroleum oils and oils obtained from bituminous minerals (excluding crude) . . .	243.1	176.1	216.6
Wood, wood charcoal, cork, and articles thereof	335.7	339.8	343.6
Wood and articles of wood; wood charcoal	335.6	339.8	343.6
Wood in the rough, whether or not stripped of bark or sapwood, or roughly squared .	192.0	183.8	168.4
Iron and steel, other base metals and articles of base metal	104.5	60.2	128.3
Vehicles, aircraft, vessels and associated transport equipment	312.8	741.9	475.8
Ships, boats and other floating structures	286.8	711.6	337.0
Cruise ships, cargo ships, barges	153.0	166.5	147.0
Light vessels, dredgers; floating docks; floating/submersible drill platforms	128.7	514.1	170.1
Total (incl. others)	5,577.7	4,977.5	2,362.2

Source: Trade Map-Trade Competitiveness Map, International Trade Centre, marketanalysis.intracen.org.

PRINCIPAL TRADING PARTNERS
(US $ million)

Imports c.i.f.	2019	2020	2021
Angola	137.6	30.0	29.7
Argentina	16.4	16.4	29.5
Belgium	230.8	141.3	211.3
Brazil	25.3	33.1	76.4
Cameroon	80.3	21.9	27.8
China, People's Republic . . .	256.3	358.0	460.3
Côte d'Ivoire	5.3	40.0	12.7
Congo, Democratic Republic . .	61.3	4.7	59.9
France (incl. Monaco)	336.8	278.1	293.0
Gabon	51.0	18.4	51.7
Germany	30.2	28.4	42.3
Ghana	33.8	2.2	2.1
India	44.8	52.3	77.1
Indonesia	39.2	65.1	49.1
Italy	91.4	49.4	51.7
Malaysia	25.2	24.3	20.1
Namibia	78.6	19.3	86.6
Netherlands	29.2	22.1	39.8
Nigeria	19.0	22.9	24.4
Norway	24.7	18.2	19.9
Russian Federation	37.8	54.5	104.5
Senegal	32.5	15.4	18.2
Singapore	17.1	44.1	9.5
South Africa	36.2	34.1	39.2
Spain	40.9	76.2	24.1
Thailand	29.6	13.4	14.3
Togo	57.5	25.6	19.4
Türkiye	48.7	42.3	55.4
United Arab Emirates . . .	73.0	38.4	66.9
United Kingdom	24.3	16.8	19.1
USA	109.6	127.3	97.6
Total (incl. others)	2,302.1	1,912.6	2,351.5

Exports f.o.b.	2019	2020	2021
Angola	70.6	67.6	50.8
Australia	118.8	16.0	68.9
Belgium	33.9	29.4	44.4
Cameroon	67.3	24.9	127.0
China, People's Republic . . .	3,333.7	3,173.4	1,081.1
Côte d'Ivoire	13.0	1.9	202.2
France (incl. Monaco)	37.1	41.9	40.1
Gabon	67.8	230.7	94.2
India	736.0	114.4	74.0
Israel	64.3	0.1	0.1
Italy	75.2	20.0	21.8
Malaysia	61.7	28.3	15.6
Namibia	24.2	62.5	3.2
Netherlands	229.1	31.3	16.2
Peru	0.0	108.9	0.0
Portugal	60.2	77.2	3.4
Singapore	33.3	25.6	54.1
Spain	144.9	429.3	10.7
Togo	7.4	93.9	177.8
United Kingdom	70.9	90.7	33.4
USA	183.4	145.1	15.2
Total (incl. others)	5,577.7	4,977.5	2,362.2

Source: Trade Map-Trade Competitiveness Map, International Trade Centre, marketanalysis.intracen.org.

Transport

RAILWAYS
(traffic)

	2008	2009	2010
Passengers carried ('000) . . .	770	592	576
Passenger-km (million) . . .	233	207	196
Freight carried ('000 metric tons) .	630	593	770
Freight ton-km (million) . . .	253	257	331

SHIPPING

Flag Registered Fleet
(at 31 December)

	2019	2020	2021
Number of vessels	13	13	13
Total displacement ('000 grt) . .	2,319	2,319	2,319

Source: Lloyd's List Intelligence (www.bit.ly/LLintelligence).

Freight Traffic
(ports of Brazzaville and Pointe-Noire, '000 metric tons)

	2008	2009	2010
Goods loaded	12,941.8	15,566.3	16,656.2
Goods unloaded	3,889.3	4,525.3	3,640.9

CIVIL AVIATION
(traffic)

	2018	2019	2020
Departures	4,976	4,991	2,047
Passengers carried ('000) . . .	509.0	541.8	226.4
Freight carried (million ton-km) .	5	4	1

Source: World Bank, World Development Indicators database.

Tourism

FOREIGN VISITORS BY COUNTRY OF RESIDENCE*

	2016	2017	2018
Angola	43,350	14,171	13,701
Cameroon	23,248	17,916	29,752
China, People's Republic . . .	9,879	3,687	11,646
Congo, Democratic Republic . .	27,653	29,506	38,092
Côte d'Ivoire	11,042	5,573	6,719
France	197,200	56,964	67,323
Gabon	13,497	38,092	1,863
India	8,100	2,801	3,116
Italy	24,380	4,953	9,831
United Kingdom	14,882	3,326	5,199
USA	28,184	3,927	5,415
Total (incl. others)	724,397	229,562	319,410

* Arrivals at hotels and similar establishments.

Tourism receipts (US $ million, excl. passenger transport): 38 in 2013.

Source: World Tourism Organization.

Communications Media

	2015	2016	2017
Telephones ('000 main lines in use)	17.0	17.0	17.0
Mobile telephone subscriptions ('000)	5,216.0	5,424.0	5,056.0
Broadband subscriptions, mobile ('000)	n.a.	n.a.	309
Internet users (% of population)* .	7.6	8.1	8.7

* Estimates.

2018: Mobile telephone subscriptions ('000): 5,000.0.

Broadband subscriptions, fixed: 500 in 2014.

Source: International Telecommunication Union.

Education

(2017/18 unless otherwise indicated)

			Students		
	Institutions	Teachers	Males	Females	Total
Pre-primary .	199	3,813	32,143	34,413	66,556
Primary . . .	4,020	27,845	400,276	383,172	783,448
Secondary . .	2,252	25,847	182,429*	156,821*	339,250*
Tertiary† . .	n.a.	4,493	32,933	21,888	54,821

* 2011/12.
† 2016/17.

Sources: mostly UNESCO Institute for Statistics.

Pupil-teacher ratio (primary education, UNESCO estimate): 44.4 in 2011/12 (Source: UNESCO Institute for Statistics).

Adult literacy rate (UNESCO estimates): 80.3% (males 86.1%; females 74.6%) in 2018 (Source: UNESCO Institute for Statistics).

Directory

The Constitution

A new Constitution, which was endorsed by a public referendum on 25 October 2015, took effect on 6 November. Its main provisions are summarized below:

PREAMBLE

The Congolese people, having chosen a pluralist democracy as the basis for the development of the country, condemn the tyrannical use of power and political violence and declare that the fundamental principles proclaimed and guaranteed by the UN Charter, the Universal Declaration of Human Rights and other international treaties form an integral part of the present Constitution.

I. THE STATE AND SOVEREIGNTY

Articles 1–7: The Republic of the Congo is a sovereign, unitary and indivisible, decentralized, secular and democratic state. The principle of the Republic is government of the people, by the people and for the people. National sovereignty belongs to the people, who exercise it through universal suffrage by their elected representatives or by referendum. The official language of the Republic is French. The national languages of communication are Lingala and Kituba.

II. RIGHTS, LIBERTIES AND DUTIES OF THE CITIZENS

Articles 8–56: All citizens are equal before the law. Arbitrary arrest and all degrading forms of punishment are prohibited, and all accused are presumed innocent until proven guilty. Incitement to ethnic hatred, violence or civil war and the use of religion to political ends are forbidden. Equal access to education, which is compulsory until the age of 16 years, is guaranteed to all. The state is obliged to create conditions that enable all citizens to enjoy the right to work. All citizens, excluding members of the police and military forces, may participate in trade union activity. Slavery is forbidden, and forced labour permitted only as a judicial punishment.

All citizens have duties towards their family, society, the state and other legally recognized authorities. All citizens are obliged to conform to the Constitution, the laws of the Republic and to fulfil their obligations towards the state and society.

III. POLITICAL PARTIES AND THE STATUS OF THE OPPOSITION

Articles 57–63: Political parties may not be identified with an ethnic group, a region, a religion or a sect. They must protect and promote fundamental human rights, the rule of law, democracy, individual and collective freedoms, national territorial integrity and sovereignty, proscribe intolerance, ethnically based extremism, and any recourse to violence, and respect the secular form of the state.

IV. EXECUTIVE POWER

Articles 64–106: The President of the Republic is the head of state. The President is directly elected by an absolute majority of votes cast, for a term of five years, renewable twice. Presidential candidates must be of Congolese nationality and origin, of at least 30 years of age. If required, a second round of voting takes place between the two highest-placed candidates in the first ballot. In the event of the death, resignation, or long-term incapacity of the President of the Republic, the President of the Senate assumes limited executive functions for up to 90 days, pending an election, which he or she may not contest.

The President appoints the Prime Minister, who proposes the members of the Government. The President appoints senior civil servants, military staff and ambassadors. The President of the Republic is the Supreme Head of the armed forces and the President of the Higher Council of Magistrates, and possesses the right of pardon. The President of the Republic chairs the Council of Ministers.

The Prime Minister is the head of government.

V. LEGISLATIVE POWER

Articles 107–137: The Parliament is bicameral. Deputies are directly elected to the National Assembly for a renewable term of five years. Senators are elected indirectly to the Senate by local councils for a term of six years. Deputies and senators must be Congolese nationals, aged over 18 years in the case of deputies, or over 45 years in the case of senators, residing in national territory. A deputy or senator elected as a member of a political grouping may not resign from the grouping without simultaneously resigning his or her parliamentary position.

VI. RELATIONS BETWEEN THE LEGISLATIVE AND EXECUTIVE INSTITUTIONS

Articles 138–165: The President of the Republic may dissolve the National Assembly. The National Assembly may remove the Government. The legislative chambers consider proposed legislation in succession, with a view to adopting an identical text. If necessary, the Prime Minister may convene a joint commission to present a revised text to the two chambers. The Prime Minister may then call the National Assembly to make a final decision. Special conditions apply to the passage of certain laws, including the national budget, and to a declaration of war or state of emergency.

VII. JUDICIAL POWER

Articles 166–174: Judicial power is exercised by the Supreme Court, the appeal courts and other national courts of law, which are independent of the legislature. The President of the Republic chairs a Higher Council of Magistrates, which guarantees the independence of the judiciary. The President of the Republic nominates judges to the Supreme Court and to the other courts of law, at the suggestion of the Higher Council of Magistrates. Judges of the Supreme Court may not be removed from office.

VIII. CONSTITUTIONAL COURT

Articles 175–188: The Constitutional Court consists of nine members, each with a mandate of four years renewable twice. The President of the Republic nominates three members of the Constitutional Court independently, and the others at the suggestion of the President of each legislative chamber and of the Bureau of the Supreme Court. The President of the Republic nominates the President of the Constitutional Court. The Court ensures that laws, treaties and international agreements conform to the Constitution and oversees presidential elections.

IX. AUDIT COURT

Articles 189–190: The establishment of an Audit Court is provided for.

X. HIGH COURT OF JUSTICE

Articles 191–195: The High Court of Justice is composed of an equal number of deputies and senators elected by their peers, and of members of the Supreme Court elected by their peers. It is chaired by the First President of the Supreme Court and is competent to try the President of the Republic in case of high treason. Members of the legislature, the Supreme Court and the Constitutional Court and government ministers are accountable to the High Court of Justice for crimes or offences committed in the execution of their duties, subject to a two-thirds' majority in a secret vote at a joint session of Parliament.

XI. ECONOMIC AND SOCIAL COUNCIL

Articles 196–199: The Economic and Social Council is a consultative assembly, which may become involved in any economic or social problem concerning the Republic, either of its own will or at the request of the President of the Republic or the President of either legislative chamber.

XII. MEDIATOR OF THE REPUBLIC

Articles 200–203: The Mediator of the Republic is an independent authority responsible for simplifying and humanizing relations between government and citizens, and may be addressed by any person dissatisfied with the workings of any public organization.

XIII. POLICE AND MILITARY FORCES

Articles 204–207: The police and military bodies consist of the national police force, the national gendarmerie and the Congolese armed forces. These bodies are apolitical and subordinate to the civil authority. The creation of militia groups is prohibited.

XIV. LOCAL AUTHORITIES

Articles 208–211: The local administrative bodies of the Republic of the Congo are the department and the commune, and any others created by law.

XV. HIGHER COUNCIL FOR THE FREEDOM OF COMMUNICATION

Articles 212–213: The Higher Council for the Freedom of Communication ensures freedom of information and communication, formulating recommendations on applicable issues.

XVI. NATIONAL COMMISSION FOR HUMAN RIGHTS

Articles 214–216: The National Commission for Human Rights seeks to promote and protect human rights.

XVII. INTERNATIONAL TREATIES AND AGREEMENTS

Articles 217–223: The President of the Republic negotiates, signs and, with the approval of Parliament, ratifies international treaties and agreements. Any proposed change to the territorial boundaries of the Republic must be submitted to popular referendum.

XVIII. STATUS OF FORMER LEADERS

Articles 224–226: The former Presidents of the Republic receive, upon completion of their mandate, state protection of both their assets and their persons.

XIX. NATIONAL CONSULTATIVE COUNCILS

Articles 227–239: A total of six councils exist and are responsible for issuing opinions from various sections of society.

XX. ON REVISION

Articles 240–242: The Constitution may be revised at the initiative of the President of the Republic or members of Parliament. The territorial integrity of the Republic, the republican form of government and the secular nature of the state, may not be the subject of any revision. Any constitutional amendments proposed by the President of the Republic are submitted directly to a referendum. Any constitutional changes proposed by Parliament must be approved by three-quarters of the members of both legislative chambers convened in congress. In both cases the Constitutional Court must have declared the acceptability of the proposals.

XXI. TRANSITIONAL AND FINAL PROVISIONS

Articles 243–246: International treaties and agreements, laws, ordinances and regulations currently in force remain applicable as long as they are not expressly modified or repealed.

The Government

HEAD OF STATE

President: Gen. DENIS SASSOU NGUESSO (assumed power 15 October 1997; inaugurated 25 October 1997; elected 10 March 2002; re-elected 12 July 2009, 20 March 2016 and 21 March 2021).

COUNCIL OF MINISTERS
(October 2022)

Prime Minister: ANATOLE COLLINET MAKOSSO.

Minister of State, Minister of the Civil Service, Labour and Social Security: FIRMIN AYESSA.

Minister of State, Minister of Trade, Food Supplies and Consumer Affairs: ALPHONSE CLAUDE NSILOU.

Minister of State, Minister of the Mining Industry and Geology: PIERRE OBA.

Minister of State, Minister of Land Affairs and the Public Domain, in charge of Relations with the Parliament: PIERRE MABIALA.

Minister of State, Minister of Land Management, Infrastructure and Road Maintenance: JEAN-JACQUES BOUYA.

Minister of National Defence: CHARLES RICHARD MONDJO.

Minister of the Interior, Decentralization and Local Development: RAYMOND ZÉPHIRIN MBOULOU.

Minister of State Control, Quality of Public Service and the Fight against Corruption in Public Administration: JEAN ROSAIRE IBARA.

Minister of Foreign Affairs, Francophone Affairs and Congolese Nationals Abroad: JEAN-CLAUDE GAKOSSO.

Minister of Agriculture, Stockbreeding and Fisheries: PAUL VALENTIN NGOBO.

Minister of the Economy and Finance: JEAN BAPTISTE ONDAYE.

Minister of Hydrocarbons: BRUNO JEAN RICHARD ITOUA.

Minister of Communication and Media, Government Spokesperson: THIERRY LÉZIN MOUNGALLA.

Minister of Special Economic Zones and Economic Diversification: JEAN-MARC THYSTÈRE TCHICAYA.

Minister of Transport, Civil Aviation and the Merchant Navy: HONORÉ SAYI.

Keeper of the Seals, Minister of Justice, Human Rights and the Promotion of Indigenous Peoples: AIMÉ ANGE WILFRID BININGA.

Minister of Planning, Statistics and Regional Integration: GHISLAINE INGRID OLGA EBOUKA-BABACKAS.

Minister of the River Economy and Waterways: GUY GEORGES MBAKA.

Minister of Construction, Town Planning and Housing: JOSUÉ RODRIGUE NGOUONIMBA.

Minister of the Environment, Sustainable Development and the Congo Basin: ARLETTE SOUDAN-NONAULT.

Minister of the Forest Economy: ROSALIE MATONDO.

Minister of Health and Population: GILBERT MOKOKI.

Minister of International Co-operation and the Promotion of Public-Private Partnership: DENIS CHRISTEL SASSOU NGUESSO.

Minister of Energy and Water Resources: ÉMILE OUOSSO.

Minister of Youth and Sport, and of Civic Education, Vocational Training and Employment: HUGUES NGOUÉLONDÉLÉ.

Minister of Industrial Development and the Promotion of the Private Sector: ANTOINE THOMAS NICÉPHORE FYLLA SAINT-EUDES.

Minister of Small and Medium-sized Enterprises and Handicrafts: JACQUELINE LYDIA MIKOLO.

Minister of Higher Education, Scientific Research and Technological Innovation: EDITH DELPHINE EMMANUELLE ADOUKI.

Minister of Pre-primary, Primary and Secondary Education and Literacy: JEAN LUC MOUTOU.

Minister of Technical and Professional Education: GHISLAIN THIERRY MANGUESSA EBOME.

Minister of Postal Services, Telecommunications and the Digital Economy: LÉON JUSTE IBOMBO.

Minister of the Promotion of Women, the Integration of Women into Development and the Informal Economy: INÈS NEFERT BERTILLE INGANI.

Minister of the Budget, Public Accounts and the Public Portfolio: LUDOVIC NGATSÉ.

Minister of Social Affairs, Solidarity and Humanitarian Action: IRÈNE MARIE CÉCILE MBOUKOU KIMBATSA GOMA.

Minister of the Culture, Tourism and Arts Industries and Leisure: LYDIE PONGAULT.

Minister-delegate to the Prime Minister, in charge of State Reform: JOSEPH LUC OKIO.

Minister-delegate to the Minister of the Interior, Decentralization and Local Development, in charge of Decentralization and Local Development: JUSTE DÉSIRÉ MONDELÉ.

MINISTRIES

Office of the President: Palais du Peuple, Brazzaville; tel. 22-281-17-11; internet www.presidence.cg.

Office of the Prime Minister: blvd Denis Sassou N'guesso, Centre Ville, Brazzaville; tel. 05-626-95-35; e-mail patrice.passy@primature.gouv.cg; internet www.primature.gouv.cg.

Ministry of Agriculture, Stockbreeding and Fisheries: BP 2453, Brazzaville; tel. 22-281-41-31.

Ministry of the Budget, Public Accounts and the Public Portfolio: Brazzaville.

Ministry of the Civil Service, Labour and Social Security: BP 12151, Brazzaville; tel. 06-783-17-18; internet fonction-publique.gouv.cg.

Ministry of Communication and Media: BP 114, Brazzaville; tel. 22-281-41-29; internet fb.com/MinistereComMCG.

Ministry of Construction, Town Planning and Housing: Immeuble MANGRITE, 5e étage, BP 1580, Brazzaville; tel. 22-281-34-48; e-mail contact@construction.gouv.cg; internet www.construction.gouv.cg.

Ministry of the Culture, Tourism and Arts Industries and Leisure: BP 20480, Brazzaville; tel. 22-281-02-35; internet fb.com/cultureetarts.

Ministry of the Economy and Finance: BP993, Brazzaville; tel. 22-613-40-13; e-mail contact@economie.gouv.cg; internet economie.gouv.cg.

Ministry of Energy and Water Resources: Brazzaville; tel. 22-281-02-61; e-mail mehcab@yahoo.fr.

Ministry of the Environment, Sustainable Development and the Congo Basin: 11e étage, Tour Nabemba, Brazzaville; tel. 222-81-54-36; e-mail secretariatministre@ministere-tourisme.gouv.cg; internet ministere-tourisme.gouv.cg.

Ministry of Foreign Affairs, Francophone Affairs and Congolese Nationals Abroad: BP 2070, Brazzaville; tel. 22-281-10-89.

Ministry of the Forest Economy: blvd Denis Sassou Nguesso, Brazzaville; tel. 22-281-41-37; internet www.mefdd.cg.

Ministry of Health and Population: BP 20101, Brazzaville; tel. 22-281-30-75; internet www.sante.gouv.cg.

Ministry of Higher Education, Scientific Research and Technological Innovation: Ancien Immeuble de la Radio, BP 169, Brazzaville; tel. 22-281-08-15.

Ministry of Hydrocarbons: BP 2120, Brazzaville; tel. 22-281-10-86; internet www.mhc.cg.

Ministry of Industrial Development and the Promotion of the Private Sector: Brazzaville.

Ministry of the Interior, Decentralization and Local Development: Brazzaville.

Ministry of International Co-operation and the Promotion of Public–Private Partnership: Brazzaville.

Ministry of Justice, Human Rights and the Promotion of Indigenous Peoples: BP 2497, Brazzaville; tel. 22-281-41-49.

Ministry of Land Affairs and the Public Domain: Brazzaville; tel. 22-281-34-48.

Ministry of Land Management, Infrastructure and Road Maintenance: Brazzaville; tel. 05-536-01-93; internet www.grandstravaux.org.

Ministry of the Mining Industry and Geology: BP 2124, Brazzaville; tel. 22-281-02-64.

Ministry of National Defence: Brazzaville; tel. 22-281-22-31.

Ministry of Planning, Statistics and Regional Integration: Brazzaville.

Ministry of Postal Services, Telecommunications and the Digital Economy: BP 44, Brazzaville; tel. 22-613-40-99; e-mail contact@postetelecom.gouv.cg; internet postetelecom.gouv.cg.

Ministry of Pre-primary, Primary and Secondary Education and Literacy: BP 5253, Brazzaville; tel. 22-281-24-52; e-mail contact@enseignement-general.gouv.cg; internet www.enseignement-general.gouv.cg.

Ministry of the Promotion of Women, the Integration of Women into Development and the Informal Economy: Brazzaville; tel. 22-281-19-29.

Ministry of the River Economy and Waterways: Brazzaville.

Ministry of Small and Medium-sized Enterprises and Handicrafts: Brazzaville; tel. 22-281-41-58.

Ministry of Social Affairs, Solidarity and Humanitarian Action: rue Lucien Fournier, Brazzaville; tel. 01-223-00-39; internet www.masahs-gouv.net.

Ministry of Special Economic Zones and Economic Diversification: BP 866, Brazzaville; tel. 222-81-01-58; e-mail contact@zes.gouv.cg; internet zes.gouv.cg.

Ministry of State Control, Quality of Public Service and the Fight against Corruption in Public Administration: Brazzaville.

Ministry of Technical and Professional Education: BP 2076, Brazzaville; tel. 22-281-17-27; e-mail metp_cab@yahoo.fr.

Ministry of Trade, Food Supplies and Consumer Affairs: BP 2965, Brazzaville; tel. 22-281-41-16; e-mail mougany@yahoo.fr; internet www.ministere-commerce.cg.

Ministry of Transport, Civil Aviation and the Merchant Navy: Immeuble Mafoua Virgile, BP 2066, Brazzaville; tel. 22-281-53-39.

Ministry of Youth and Sport, and of Civic Education, Vocational Training and Employment: 26e étage, Tour Nabemba, Brazzaville; tel. 06-950-46-03; internet www.mjeciv.net.

President

Presidential Election, 21 March 2021

Candidate	Valid votes	% of valid votes
Denis Sassou Nguesso	1,539,725	88.40
Guy Brice Parfait Kolélas	138,561	7.96
Mathias Dzon	33,497	1.92
Joseph Kignoumbi Kia Mboungou	10,718	0.62
Dave Uphrem Mafoula	9,143	0.52
Albert Oniangué	6,977	0.40
Anguios Nganguia Engambé	3,157	0.18
Total	1,741,778*	100.00

* The figure for invalid votes was not included in the official results released by the Constitutional Court on 6 April.

Legislature

The legislature, Parliament, comprises two chambers: a directly elected lower house, the National Assembly; and an indirectly elected upper house, the Senate.

NATIONAL ASSEMBLY

National Assembly: Palais du Parlement, blvd Alfred Raoul, BP 2106, Brazzaville; tel. 22-281-11-12; e-mail contact@assemblee-nationale.cg; internet www.assemblee-nationale.cg.

President: ISIDORE MVOUBA.

General Election, 10 and 31 July 2022

Party	Seats
Parti Congolais du Travail (PCT)	112
Union des Démocrates Humanistes-Yuki (UDH-Yuki)	7
Union Panafricaine pour la Démocratie Sociale (UPADS)	7
Mouvement d'Action et pour le Renouveau (MAR)	4
Club 2002	2
Dynamique Républicaine pour le Développement (DRD)	2
Parti Républicain et Libéral (PRL)	2
Rassemblement pour la Démocratie et le Progrès Social (RDPS)	2
Action pour le Congo (AC)	1
La Chaine	1
Club Perspectives et Réalité (CPR)	1
Mouvement Congolais pour la Démocratie et le Développement Intégral (MCDDI)	1
Mouvement pour la Démocratie et le Progrès (MDP)	1
Mouvement pour l'Unité, la Solidarité et le Travail (MUST)	1
Rassemblement Citoyen (RC)	1
Union Patriotique pour la Démocratie et le Progrès (UPDP)	1
Union pour la Reconstruction et le Développement du Congo (URDC)	1
Independents	4
Total	**151**

SENATE

Senate: Palais du Parlement, BP 2642, Brazzaville; tel. 06-668-94-53; e-mail foutysoungou@yahoo.fr; internet www.senat.cg.

President: PIERRE NGOLO.

The upper chamber comprises 72 members, elected by representatives of local, regional and municipal authorities for a six-year term. After elections to the Senate held on 31 August 2017 the strength of the parties was as follows:

Party	Seats
Parti Congolais du Travail (PCT)	44
Mouvement d'Action et pour le Renouveau (MAR)	2
Rassemblement pour la Démocratie et le Progrès Social (RDPS)	2
Union Panafricaine pour la Démocratie Sociale (UPADS)	2
Club 2002-Parti pour l'Unité et la République	1
Front Patriotique (FP)	1
Parti Républicain et Libéral (PRL)	1
Parti pour l'Unité, la Liberté et le Progrès (PULP)	1
Independents	12
Total	**66***

* Elections in the département of Pool did not take place owing to security reasons.

Election Commission

Commission Nationale Electorale Indépendante (CNEI): Brazzaville; f. 2016 to replace the Commission Nationale d'Organisation des Elections; Pres. HENRI BOUKA.

Advisory Council

Economic and Social Council (Conseil Economique et Social): Bâtiment Ex Trésor, blvd Denis Sassou Nguesso, BP 1064, Brazzaville; tel. 06-983-17-27; e-mail infos@cesecongo.com; internet cesecongo.com; f. 2003; 75 mems, appointed by the President of the Republic; Pres. EMILIENNE RAOUL.

Political Organizations

The following were among the most important political organizations believed to be active in 2021:

Action pour le Congo (AC): Brazzaville.

Alliance pour la Démocratie et le Développement National (ADDN): Brazzaville; f. 2005; supports Govt of Pres. Sassou Nguesso; Pres. BRUNO MAZONGA.

Alliance pour la République et la Démocratie (ARD): Brazzaville; f. 2007

Union Patriotique pour le Renouveau National (UPRN): 1333 rue Mouleke bis Ouenze 242, Brazzaville; internet fb.com/UPRN.congo; Leader MATHIAS DZON.

La Chaine: Brazzaville.

Club 2002-Parti pour l'Unité et la République (Club 2002 PUR): Brazzaville; f. 2002; Pres. WILFRID NGUESSO.

Club Perspectives et Réalité (CPR): Brazzaville; Pres. AIMÉ HYDVERT MOUAGNI.

Congrès Africain pour le Progrès (CAP): Brazzaville; f. 2014 as breakaway faction of Union Panafricaine pour la Démocratie Sociale; Pres. JEAN ITADI.

Conseil National des Républicains (CNR): formed as political wing of 'Ninja' rebel group, the Conseil National de la Résistance; Leader Rev. FRÉDÉRIC BITSANGOU (NTUMI).

Dynamique Républicaine pour le Développement (DRD): Brazzaville; tel. 05-560-14-59; internet fb.com/President.quartier49; f. 2013; Pres. HELLOT MATSON MAMPOUYA.

Mouvement Action et Renouveau (MAR): BP 1287, Pointe-Noire; Pres. ROLAND BOUITI VIAUDO.

Mouvement Congolais pour la Démocratie et le Développement Intégral (MCDDI): 744 route de Djoué, Brazzaville; internet www.mcddi-cg.com; f. 1990; Pres. EULOGE LANDRY KOLÉLAS.

Mouvement pour la Démocratie et le Progrès (MDP): Brazzaville; f. 2007; Leader JEAN-CLAUDE IBOVI.

Mouvement pour la Solidarité et la Démocratie (MSD): Brazzaville; Leader RENÉ SERGE BLANCHARD OBA.

Mouvement pour l'Unité, la Solidarité et le Travail (MUST): Brazzaville; Pres. CLAUDINE MUNARI.

Parti Congolais du Travail (PCT): Immeuble PCT, Quartier Mpila, 5 rue Léon Jacob, BP 59, Brazzaville; e-mail info@particongolaisdutravail.org; internet www.particongolaisdutravail.org; f. 1969; sole legal political party 1969–90; Pres. DENIS SASSOU NGUESSO; Sec.-Gen. PIERRE NGOLO.

Parti Républicain et Libéral (PRL): Brazzaville; Pres. NICÉPHORE FYLLA DE SAINT-EUDES.

Parti Social-Démocrate Congolais (PSDC): Brazzaville; internet fb.com/partisocialdemocrate.congolais; Pres. CLÉMENT MIÉRASSA.

Rassemblement Citoyen (RC): route du Djoué, face Centre Sportif de Bacongo, Brazzaville; Pres. CLAUDE ALPHONSE NSILOU.

Rassemblement pour la Démocratie et le Progrès Social (RDPS): Pointe-Noire; f. 1990; Pres. BERNARD MBATCHI.

Rassemblement de la Majorité Présidentielle (RMP): Brazzaville; f. 2007; org. of some 100 political parties and associations supporting Pres. Sassou Nguesso; Pres. PIERRE NGOLO.

Union des Démocrates Humanistes-Yuki (UDH-Yuki): Brazzaville; f. 2017; Leader GUY BRICE PARFAIT KOLÉLAS.

Union pour la Démocratie et la République—Mwinda (UDR-Mwinda): Brazzaville; f. 1992; Leader GUY ROMAIN KIMFOUSSIA.

Union des Forces Démocratiques (UFD): Brazzaville; supports Govt; Pres. (vacant).

Union pour le Mouvement Populaire (UMP): Brazzaville; internet fb.com/Union-pour-le-Mouvement-Populaire-Congo-Brazza-275136092673180/; Pres. DIGNE ELVIS GIREL OKOMBI TSALISSAN.

Union Panafricaine pour la Démocratie Sociale (UPADS): BP 1370, Brazzaville; Pres. (vacant); Sec.-Gen. PASCAL TSATY MABIALA.

Union Patriotique pour la Démocratie et le Progrès (UPDP): 112 rue Lamothe, Brazzaville; Pres. AUGUSTE-CÉLESTIN GONGARAD-NKOUA.

Union pour le Progrès (UP): 64 rue Ewo, Brazzaville; tel. 05-551-68-32; Pres. JEAN-MARTIN MBEMBA; Sec.-Gen. OMER DEFOUNDOUX.

Union pour la Reconstruction et le Développement du Congo (URDC): Brazzaville; Pres. LUC ADAMO MATETA.

Diplomatic Representation

EMBASSIES IN THE REPUBLIC OF THE CONGO

Algeria: rue Col Brisset, BP 2100, Brazzaville; tel. 22-281-17-37; e-mail ambalgbzv@gmail.com; Ambassador LARBI EL-HADJ ALI.

Angola: ave Fourneau, BP 388, Brazzaville; tel. 22-281-47-21; e-mail miranotom@yahoo.fr; Ambassador VICENTE MUANDA.

Belgium: 4 Impasse ave Auxence Ickonga, Poto Poto, Brazzaville; tel. 05-200-13-13; e-mail brazzaville@diplobel.fed.be; internet congo-brazzaville.diplomatie.belgium.be; Chargé d'affaires e.p. JEAN-PAUL CHARLIER.

Brazil: rue Mfoa, angle ave Nelson Mandela, 1er étage, BP 2476, Brazzaville; tel. 06-896-95-50; e-mail brasemb.brazzaville@itamaraty.gov.br; internet www.gov.br/mre/pt-br/embaixada-brazzaville; Ambassador RENATO SOARES MENEZES.

Cameroon: ave Bayardelles, BP 2136, Brazzaville; tel. 06-675-57-26; e-mail ambacambrazza@yahoo.fr; Ambassador LOUIS-MARIE MAGLOIRE NKOUM-ME-NTSENY (designate).

Central African Republic: rue Fournier, face Paroisse St François, BP 10, Brazzaville; tel. 05-526-75-55; e-mail mcfayanga@yahoo.fr; Ambassador (vacant).

Chad: rue des Ecoles, BP 386, Brazzaville; tel. 05-558-92-06; e-mail madjikalzeubeta@yahoo.fr; Ambassador MBAÏDICKOYE SOMMEL YABAO.

China, People's Republic: ave Auxence Ickonga, BP 213, Brazzaville; tel. 05-566-98-98; e-mail chinaemb_cg@mfa.gov.cn; internet cg.china-embassy.gov.cn; Ambassador MA FULIN.

Congo, Democratic Republic: 130 ave de l'Indépendance, BP 2457, Brazzaville; tel. 22-281-30-52; e-mail ambardcbrazza1@yahoo.fr; Ambassador CHRISTOPHE MUZUNGU.

Cuba: rue de Reims, face Ecole de la Poste, BP 80, Brazzaville; tel. 22-281-04-91; e-mail embacuba@congob.embacuba.cu; internet misiones.minrex.gob.cu/es/republica-del-congo; Ambassador JOSÉ ANTONIO GARCÍA GONZÁLEZ.

Egypt: 7 bis ave Bayardelle, BP 917, Brazzaville; tel. 06-617-39-23; e-mail embassy.brazzaville@mfa.gov.eg; internet www.mfa.gov.eg/brazzaville_emb; Ambassador HATEM KANDIL.

Equatorial Guinea: Messe des Officiers, Brazzaville; tel. 06-688-72-90; e-mail embaregecongo@gmail.com; internet ambassade-guinee-equatoriale.cg/es; Ambassador SAMUEL ATEBA OWONO IYANGA.

France: rue Alfassa, BP 2089, Brazzaville; tel. 05-361-24-06; e-mail admin-francais.brazzaville-amba@diplomatie.gouv.fr; internet cg.ambafrance.org; Ambassador FRANÇOIS BARATEAU.

Gabon: 40 ave du Maréchal Lyautey, BP 20336, Brazzaville; tel. 22-281-56-20; e-mail ambagaboncongo@diplomatie.gouv.ga; Ambassador RENÉ MAKONGO.

Germany: rue Alfassa, BP 2051, Brazzaville; tel. 06-510-01-48; internet brazzaville.diplo.de; Ambassador Dr WOLFGANG KLAPPER.

Holy See: rue Col Brisset, BP 1168, Brazzaville; tel. 06-950-56-66; e-mail nonapcg@yahoo.com; Apostolic Nuncio JAVIER HERRERA CORONA (Titular Archbishop of Vulturaria).

Italy: 2 ave Auxence Ickonga, BP 2484, Brazzaville; tel. 04-444-00-60; e-mail amb.brazzaville@esteri.it; internet ambbrazzaville.esteri.it; Ambassador LUIGI DODATI.

Libya: BP 920, Brazzaville; tel. 22-281-56-35; e-mail ambalibyabz@yahoo.com; Chargé d'affaires a.i. IBRAHIM TAHAR EL-HAMALI.

Mali: 17 blvd Maréchal Lyautey, BP 2607, Brazzaville; tel. 06-664-72-16; internet ambamali-brazza.com; Ambassador AGUIBOU DIALLO.

Namibia: 255 Prosper Gandzion, Centre-Ville, Brazzaville; tel. 06-466-74-23; e-mail vhifindaka@gmail.com; Ambassador SIPAPELA CLETIUS SIPAPELA.

Nigeria: 11 blvd Lyauté, BP 790, Brazzaville; tel. 22-613-16-52; e-mail nigeria.brazzaville@foreignaffairs.gov.ng; internet nigerianembassy-congobrazza.org; Ambassador MAMAN KONÉ TOURÉ (designate).

Russian Federation: ave Félix Eboué, BP 2132, Brazzaville; tel. 22-281-19-23; e-mail amrussie@yandex.ru; internet congo.mid.ru; Ambassador GEORGY Y. CHEPIK.

Rwanda: 353 ave Prosper Gandzion, Centre Ville, Brazzaville; tel. 22-613-30-39; e-mail ambabrazza@minaffet.gov.rw; internet www.rwandaincongo.gov.rw; Ambassador THÉONESTE MUTSINDASHYAKA.

Senegal: Brazzaville; tel. 06-499-02-02; e-mail ambassencongo@gmail.com; Ambassador ABOU LO.

South Africa: 82 ave Maréchal Lyautey, Brazzaville; tel. 22-281-08-49; e-mail morenat@dirco.gov.za; Ambassador JOHNNY SEXWALE.

Türkiye (Turkey): Hôtel Mbamou Palace, Radisson Blu Business Center, ave Amílcar Cabral, BP 1054, Brazzaville; tel. 05-603-72-12; e-mail turquie.brazzaville@mfa.gov.tr; internet brazavil.be.mfa.gov.tr/Mission; Ambassador SERHAN ALI YIĞIT.

USA: blvd Maya-Maya, BP 1015, Brazzaville; tel. 06-612-20-00; e-mail BrazzavilleHR@state.gov; internet cg.usembassy.gov; Ambassador EUGENE S. YOUNG.

Venezuela: Villa 6, rue Albert Bassaanza, Brazzaville; tel. 06-604-40-40; internet congo.embajada.gob.ve; Ambassador ANIBAL JOSÉ MARQUEZ MUNOZ.

Judicial System

The 2015 Constitution provides for the independence of the judiciary from the legislature. Judges are accountable to the Higher Council of Magistrates, under the chairmanship of the President of the Republic. The constituent bodies of the judiciary are the Supreme Court, the Constitutional Court, the Revenue and Budgetary Discipline Court, the appeal courts, tribunals of grand instance and tribunals of first instance. The High Court of Justice is chaired by the First President of the Supreme Court and is competent to try the President of the Republic in case of high treason, and to try members of the legislature, the Supreme Court, the Constitutional Court and government ministers for crimes or offences committed in the execution of their duties.

Supreme Court: Palais de Justice, BP 597, Brazzaville; tel. 22-283-01-32; e-mail ndallaa@yahoo.fr; First Pres. HENRI BOUKA.

High Court of Justice: BP 595, Brazzaville; tel. 22-281-45-17; f. 2003.

Constitutional Court: blvd Alfred Raoul (ex blvd des Armées), BP 543, Brazzaville; tel. 06-508-09-99; e-mail contact@cour-constitutionnelle.cg; internet cour-constitutionnelle.cg; 9 mems; Pres. AUGUSTE ILOKI; Vice-Pres. PIERRE PASSI.

Revenue and Budgetary Discipline Court: rue Lastour, BP 131, Brazzaville; tel. 06-551-35-62; e-mail ccdb@courdescomptes.cg; internet courdescomptes.cg; Pres. CHARLES ÉMILE APESSE.

Courts of Appeal: located at Brazzaville, Pointe-Noire, Dolisie and Owando; First Pres. CHRISTIAN OBA (Brazzaville); First Pres. ANTOINE MICHAEL CÉSAR MBOU (Pointe-Noire).

Religion

CHRISTIANITY

The Roman Catholic Church

Congo comprises three archdioceses and six dioceses.

Bishops' Conference: Conférence Episcopale du Congo, BP 200, Brazzaville; tel. 04-100-94-26; e-mail conepiscongo71@hotmail.fr; internet www.cecongo.net; f. 1992; Pres. Most Rev. DANIEL MIZONZO (Bishop of Nkayi); Sec.-Gen. BRICE ARMAND IBOMBO.

Archbishop of Brazzaville: Most Rev. MANAMIKA BAFOUAKOUA-HOU, Archevêché, BP 2301, Brazzaville; tel. 06-662-95-76; e-mail archibrazza@yahoo.fr.

Archbishop of Owando: Most Rev. VICTOR ABAGNA MOSSA, BP 06, Owando; tel. 06-857-27-04.

Archbishop of Pointe-Noire: Most Rev. MIGUEL ÁNGEL OLAVERRI ARRONIZ, 82 rue Moe Vangoula, Pointe-Noire; tel. 05-559-30-70.

Protestant Church

Eglise Evangélique du Congo: BP 3205, Brazzaville; tel. 06-640-05-52; f. 1909; Presbyterian; autonomous since 1961; Pres. Rev. JUSTE GONARD ALAIN BAKOUA.

Eglise Evangélique Luthérienne du Congo: 137 rue Ossélé-Mougali, BP 1456, 00242 Brazzaville; tel. 05-557-15-00; e-mail evlcongo@yahoo.fr; Pres. Rev. JOSEPH TCHIBINDA MAVOUNGOU.

ISLAM

Conseil Supérieur Islamique du Congo (CSIC): 5 bis rue Paul Kamba, Poto-Poto, BP 55, Brazzaville; tel. 06-624-38-11; e-mail csicbureauexecutifnational@gmail.com; f. 1988; Pres. El Hadj DJIBRIL ABDOULAYE BOPAKA.

BAHÁ'Í FAITH

Assemblée Spirituelle Nationale: BP 2094, Brazzaville; tel. 22-281-36-93.

The Press

DAILY NEWSPAPERS (PRINT AND ONLINE)

ACI Actualité: BP 2144, Brazzaville; tel. 22-281-01-98; publ. by Agence Congolaise d'Information; Dir-Gen. THÉODORE KIAMOSSI.

Les Dépêches de Brazzaville: 84 ave Denis Sassou Nguesso, Immeuble Les Manguiers (Mpila), Brazzaville; tel. 05-532-01-09; internet www.adiac-congo.com; Dir of Publication JEAN-PAUL PIGASSE.

PERIODICALS

L'Autre Vision: 48 rue Assiéné-Mikalou, BP 5255, Brazzaville; tel. 05-551-57-06; e-mail lautrevision@yahoo.fr; 2 a month; Dir JEAN PAULIN ITOUA.

Capital: 3 ave Charles de Gaulle, Plateau Centre-Ville, BP 541, Brazzaville; tel. 05-558-95-10; e-mail capital@hotmail.com; 2 a month; economics and business; Dir SERGE-DENIS MATONDO; Editor-in-Chief HERVÉ SAMPA.

Le Choc: BP 1314, Brazzaville; tel. 06-666-42-96; e-mail groupejustinfo@yahoo.fr; internet www.lechoc.info; weekly; Dir-Gen. and Publr ASIE DOMINIQUE DE MARSEILLE; Dir of Publication MARIEN NGAPILI.

Les Echos du Congo: Immeubles Fédéraux 036, Centre-Ville, Brazzaville; tel. 05-551-57-09; e-mail contact@lesechos-congobrazza.com; internet lesechos-congobrazza.com; weekly; pro-govt; Dir-Gen. ADRIEN WAYI-LEWY; Editor-in-Chief INNOCENT OLIVIER TATY.

Le Flambeau: BP 1198, Brazzaville; tel. 06-666-35-23; e-mail congolink1@aol.com; weekly; independent; supports Govt of Pres. Sassou Nguesso; Dir and Man. Editor PRINCE-RICHARD NSANA.

La Lettre de Brazzaville: Résidence Méridien, BP 15457, Brazzaville; tel. 22-281-28-13; f. 2000; weekly; publ. by Agence d'Information d'Afrique Centrale; Man. Dir JEAN-PAUL PIGASSE; Editor-in-Chief BELINDA AYESSA.

La Nouvelle République: 3 ave des Ambassadeurs, BP 991, Brazzaville; tel. 22-281-00-20; state-owned; weekly; Dir-Gen. GASPARD NWAN; Editorial Dir HENRI BOUKOULOU.

L'Observateur: 165 ave de l'Amitié, BP 13370, Brazzaville; tel. 06-666-33-37; e-mail lobservateur_2001@yahoo.fr; f. 1999; weekly; independent; opposes Govt of Pres. Sassou Nguesso; Dir GISLIN SIMPLICE ONGOUYA.

La Référence: BP 13778, Brazzaville; tel. 05-556-11-37; 2 a month; supports Govt of Pres. Sassou Nguesso; Dir PHILIPPE RICHET; Editor-in-Chief R. ASSEBAKO AMAIDJORE.

La Semaine Africaine: blvd Lyautey, face Chu, BP 2080, Brazzaville; tel. 06-543-23-95; e-mail lasemaineafricaine@yahoo.fr; internet www.lasemaineafricaine.net; f. 1952; 2 a week; Roman Catholic; general news and social comment; circulates widely in francophone equatorial Africa; Editor-in-Chief ALBERT MIANZOUKOUTA.

NEWS AGENCIES

Agence Congolaise d'Information (ACI): blvd Denis Sassou Nguesso, BP 2144, Brazzaville; tel. 22-281-17-96; e-mail agencecongoinfo@yahoo.fr; internet www.agencecongoinfo.net; f. 1961; Gen. Man. WILFRID ANASTH MBOSSA.

Agence d'Information d'Afrique Centrale (ADIAC): 84 blvd Denis Sassou Nguesso, Brazzaville; tel. 05-532-01-09; e-mail redaction@lesdepechesdebrazzaville.fr; internet www.adiac-congo.com; f. 1997; Dirs JEAN-PAUL PIGASSE, BELINDA AYESSA.

Publishers

Editions ADIAC—Agence d'Information d'Afrique Centrale: 84 blvd Denis Sassou Nguesso, BP 15457, Brazzaville; tel. 05-532-01-09; e-mail redaction@lesdepechesdebrazzaville.fr; internet www.adiac-congo.com; f. 1997; publishes chronicles of current affairs; Dir JEAN-PAUL PIGASSE.

Editions Lemba: 20 ave des Emetteurs, Sangolo-OMS, Malékélé, BP 2351, Brazzaville; tel. 06-667-65-58; e-mail editions_lemba@yahoo.fr; literature; Dir APOLLINAIRE SINGOU-BASSEHA.

GOVERNMENT PUBLISHING HOUSE

Imprimerie Nationale du Congo (INC): BP 58, Brazzaville; Dir-Gen. JEAN-PAUL MAKHOKO.

Broadcasting and Communications

TELECOMMUNICATIONS

In February 2022 there were 5.6m. mobile telephone subscribers in Congo.

Airtel Congo: blvd Charles de Gaulle, angle allée Makimba, BP 1267, Pointe-Noire; tel. 05-000-01-21; e-mail serviceclients@cg.airtel

.com; internet www.airtel.cg; f. 1999 as Celtel Congo and fmrly Zain Congo; acquired by Bharti Airtel (India) in 2010; mobile telephone operator; network covers Brazzaville, Pointe-Noire, Loubomo (Dolisie), Ouesso, Owando and other urban areas; Man. Dir ALAIN KAHASHA NTUMWA; 2.3m. subscribers (Feb. 2022).

AMC Telecom: Immeuble CNSS, ave Alphonse, Brazzaville; tel. 05-545-07-60; e-mail amc@amc-telecom.com; internet service provider.

MTN Congo: 36 ave Amílcar Cabral, 1150 Brazzaville; tel. 06-700-01-23; e-mail sos.client.cg@mtn.com; internet fb.com/MTNCONGO; f. 2000; mobile telephone operator; Dir-Gen. AYHAM MOUSSA; 3.3m. subscribers (Feb. 2022).

Regulatory Authority

Agence de Régulation des Postes et des Communications Electroniques (ARPCE): Immeuble ARPCE, 91 bis ave de l'Amitié, BP 2490, Mpila, Brazzaville; tel. 05-510-72-72; e-mail contact@arpce.cg; internet www.arpce.cg; f. 2009; Dir-Gen. LOUIS-MARC SAKALA.

RADIO AND TELEVISION

Radiodiffusion-Télévision Congolaise (RTC): BP 2241, Brazzaville; tel. 22-281-24-73; state-owned; Pres. JEAN-GILBERT FOUTOU; Dir-Gen. GILBERT-DAVID MUTAKALA.

> **Radio Congo:** BP 2241, Brazzaville; tel. 22-281-50-60; radio programmes in French, Lingala, Kikongo, Subia, English and Portuguese; transmitters at Brazzaville and Pointe-Noire; Dir-Gen. EMÉRY GODEFROY YOMBI.

Radio Magnificat: Centre Interdiocésain des Oeuvres (CIO), Brazzaville; tel. 06-628-93-69; e-mail radiomagnificat93.5@gmail.com; internet fb.com/RadioMagnificat93.5FM; f. 2006; Roman Catholic; Man. Fr BENOÎT NZIÉ.

Radio Maria Congo: Brazzaville; tel. 05-535-50-95; e-mail radiomariacongo@yahoo.fr; internet www.radiomaria.cg; religious, social, economic and cultural.

Yakala FM: Brazzaville; e-mail www.yakalafm.net.

Regulatory Authority

Conseil Supérieur de la Liberté de la Communication (Higher Council for the Freedom of Communication): Immeuble Ministère de la Justice et des Droits Humains, 2e étage, Brazzaville; tel. 06-668-93-49; f. 2003; 11 mems, nominated by the President of the Republic; Pres. PHILIPPE MVOUO.

Finance

BANKING

Central Bank

Banque des Etats de l'Afrique Centrale (BEAC): BP 126, Brazzaville; tel. 22-281-10-73; e-mail beacbzv@beac.int; internet www.beac.int; HQ in Yaoundé, Cameroon; f. 1973; bank of issue for mem. states of the Communauté Economique et Monétaire de l'Afrique Centrale (CEMAC, fmrly Union Douanière et Economique de l'Afrique Centrale) comprising Cameroon, the Central African Repub., Chad, the Repub. of the Congo, Equatorial Guinea and Gabon; Gov. ABBAS MAHAMAT TOLLI; Dir in Repub. of the Congo SERGE DANIEL GASSACKYS.

Commercial Banks

Banque Commerciale Internationale (BCI): ave Amílcar Cabral, BP 147, Brazzaville; tel. 22-281-58-34; internet www.bci.banquepopulaire.com; f. 2001 on privatization of Union Congolaise de Banques; renamed as above in 2006; acquired by BCP International in 2019; Dir-Gen. ANDRÉ COLLET.

Banque Congolaise de l'Habitat (BCH): ave Amílcar Cabral, BP 987, Brazzaville; tel. 22-281-25-88; e-mail audriche.elenga@bch.cg; f. 2008; Pres. JEAN ALFRED ONANGA; Dir-Gen. FADHEL GUIZANI.

BGFI Bank Congo: angle rue Reims, face à paierie de France, BP 14579, Brazzaville; tel. 06-632-65-05; e-mail eqccongo@bgfi.com; internet congo.groupebgfibank.com; subsidiary of BGFIBANK Group (Gabon); Dir-Gen. NARCISSE OBIANG ONDO.

La Congolaise de Banque (LCB): ave Amílcar Cabral, BP 2889, Brazzaville; tel. 05-310-11-57; e-mail contact@lcb-bank.com; internet lcb-bank.com; f. 2004 on privatization of Crédit pour l'Agriculture, l'Industrie et le Commerce (CAIC); Dir-Gen. MOHAMED ESSAID BENJELLOUN TOUIMI.

Crédit du Congo (CDCo): ave Amilcar Cabral, BP 2470, Brazzaville; tel. 05-530-06-49; internet www.attijariwafabank.com/fr/filiale-internationale/credit-du-congo; f. 2002 to replace Banque Internationale du Congo; fmrly Crédit Lyonnais Congo; name changed as above in 2007; 91% owned by Attijariwafa bank (Morocco), 9% state-owned; Dir-Gen. BRAHIM AHABBANE.

Ecobank Congo: Immeuble de l'ARC, 3e étage, ave du Camp, BP 2485, Brazzaville; tel. 05-802-01-00; e-mail ecobankcg@ecobank .com; internet www.ecobank.com; Pres. AISSATA MOUSSA; Dir-Gen. IBRAHIM ABOUBACAR BAGARAMA.

Société Générale Congo (SGC): ave Amílcar Cabral, Centre-Ville, BP 598, Brazzaville; tel. 06-504-22-22; e-mail sgc.qualite@socgen .com; internet www.societegenerale.cg; f. 2012; Dir-Gen. ALAIN CALMELS.

Co-operative Banking Institution

Mutuelle Congolaise d'Epargne et de Crédit (MUCODEC): blvd Sassou Nguesso, BP 13237, Brazzaville; tel. 06-987-90-00; e-mail contact@mucodec.com; internet www.mucodec.com; f. 1994; Pres. FLORIAN MOUGNENGUE; Dir-Gen. DIEUDONNÉ NDINGA.

Development Bank

Banque de Développement des Etats de l'Afrique Centrale (BDEAC): blvd Sassou Nguesso, BP 1177, Brazzaville; tel. 04-426-83-00; e-mail bdeac@bdeac.org; internet www.bdeac.org; Pres. DIEUDONNÉ EVOU MEKOU.

Financial Institution

Caisse Congolaise d'Amortissement (CCA): ave Foch, BP 2090, Brazzaville; tel. 22-281-57-35; f. 1971; management of state funds; Dir-Gen. THÉODORE IKÉMO.

INSURANCE

Allianz Congo Assurances: ave Linguissi Pembellot, BP 340, Pointe-Noire; tel. 05-601-12-00; e-mail allianz.congo@allianz-cg .com; internet www.allianz-africa.com; f. 2011; general insurance; Dir-Gen. JOSEPH EYOK.

Assurances Générales du Congo: ave Sergent Malamine, BP 1110, Brazzaville; tel. 22-281-50-94; e-mail agccongo@yahoo.fr; internet agccongo.com; f. 1999; Pres. and Dir-Gen. RAYMOND IBATA.

Assurances et Réassurances du Congo (ARC): ave Amílcar Cabral, BP 14524, Brazzaville; tel. 22-281-35-08; e-mail gaston .akobo@arc.cg; internet www.arc.cg; f. 1973; Dir-Gen. MARC GASTON AKOBO.

Willis Towers Watson Congo: 13 rue Germain Bikouma, angle route de la Radio, Immeuble Guenin, BP 1901, Pointe-Noire; tel. 22-294-79-72; fmrly Gras Savoye Congo; name changed as above in 2018; insurance brokers and risk managers.

Nouvelle Société Interafricaine d'Assurances (NSIA): 1 ave Foch, angle rue Sergent Malamine, face Hôtel de Ville, BP 1151, Brazzaville; tel. 23-350-27-00; e-mail info@groupensia.com; internet nsiassurancescongo.com; f. 2004; life and non-life; acquired Sanlam Non-vie Congo in 2022; Dir-Gen. ALFRED YAMEOGO.

Trade and Industry

GOVERNMENT AGENCIES

Comité des Privatisations et de Renforcement des Capacités Locales: Immeuble ex-SCBO, 7ème étage, BP 1176, Brazzaville; tel. 22-281-46-21; e-mail privat@aol.com; oversees and co-ordinates transfer of state-owned enterprises to the private sector.

Agence de Régulation de l'Aval Pétrolier (ARAP): Brazzaville; f. 2006; Dir-Gen. ERNEST DENIS SOUAMY.

DEVELOPMENT ORGANIZATIONS

Agence Française de Développement (AFD): 1 rue Béhagle, BP 96, Brazzaville; tel. 05-602-56-56; e-mail afdbrazzaville@afd.fr; internet www.afd.fr; French fund for economic co-operation; Country Dir MAURIZIO CASCIOLI.

Service de Coopération et d'Action Culturelle: BP 2175, Brazzaville; tel. 22-283-15-03; f. 1959; administers bilateral aid from France; Dir MICHEL PRE.

CHAMBERS OF COMMERCE

Chambre de Commerce, d'Industrie, d'Agriculture et des Métiers de Brazzaville (CCIAMB): ave Amílcar Cabral, Centre-Ville, BP 92, Brazzaville; tel. 05-521-70-04; internet cciambrazzaville .com; f. 1935; Pres. PAUL OBAMBI; Sec.-Gen. ALPHONSE MFOURGA.

Chambre de Commerce, d'Industrie, d'Agriculture et des Métiers de Pointe-Noire: 35 blvd Général Charles de Gaulle, BP 665, Pointe-Noire; tel. 05-584-82-31; e-mail info@cciampnr .com; internet www.cciampnr.com; f. 1947; Chair. SYLVESTRE DIDIER MAVOUENZELA; Sec.-Gen. EVELYNE TCHICHELLE.

EMPLOYERS' ORGANIZATIONS

Confédération Générale du Patronat Congolais (COGE-PACO): Brazzaville; f. 1998; Pres. JEAN GALESSAMY-IBOMBOT.

Forum des Jeunes Entreprises du Congo (FJEC): Quartier Milice, Villa 43B, ave de l'OUA, BP 13700, Makélékélé, Brazzaville; tel. 06-666-26-06; internet fjec-congo.com; f. 1990; Sec.-Gen. PAUL KAMPAKOL.

Union Nationale des Opérateurs Economiques du Congo (UNOC): Immeuble ELBO-Suites, 2e étage, Centre-ville, BP 5187, Brazzaville; tel. 05-526-22-04; e-mail contact@patronat-unoc.cg; internet patronat-unoc.cg; f. 1985; operates a professional training centre; Pres. JEAN DANIEL OVAGA.

Union Patronale et Interprofessionnelle du Congo (UNI-CONGO): Immeuble CAPINFO, 1er étage, blvd Denis Sassou Nguesso, Mpila, BP 42, Brazzaville; tel. 06-841-04-07; internet unicongo.org; f. 1958; Nat. Pres. ALPHONSE MISSENGUI; Sec.-Gen. JEAN-JACQUES SAMBA.

UTILITIES
Electricity

Agence Nationale d'Électrification Rurale du Congo (ANER): BP 2120, Brazzaville; tel. 05-570-19-52; e-mail aner_congo@yahoo.fr; f. 2003.

Société Energie Electrique du Congo (E2C): blvd Denis Sassou Nguesso, Centre Ville, BP 95, Brazzaville; tel. 22-281-05-62; internet www.sne.cg; f. 2018 to replace Société Nationale d'Electricité; operates hydroelectric plants at Djoué, Imboulou, Liouesso and Moukoukoulou; Dir-Gen. JEAN BRUNO ADOU DANGA.

Water

La Congolaise des Eaux (LCDE): rue du Sergent Malamine, BP 229, Brazzaville; tel. 22-294-22-16; internet www.sndecongo.com; f. 2018 to replace Société Nationale de Distribution d'Eau; water supply and sewerage; Dir-Gen. PARFAIT CHRISOSTHOME MAKITA.

Organe de Régulation du Secteur de l'Eau (ORSE): Immeuble du 5 Février 1979, Appartement Q 54/S, 3e étage, Centre Ville, BP 13059, Brazzaville; tel. 22-281-00-16; internet www.orse.cg; f. 2003; regulatory authority for water.

MAJOR COMPANIES

The following are some of the largest companies in terms of either capital investment or employment.

Alucongo: POB 1105, Pointe-Noire; tel. 22-294-04-12; e-mail commercial-cng@bernabeafrique.com; internet www .bernabeafrique.com; owned by Yeshi Group (Côte d'Ivoire); Dir ALUS TABOLA.

Brasseries du Congo (BRASCO): ave Edith Bongo Odimba, Mpila, POB 105, Brazzaville; tel. 06-673-80-80; internet www .brasseriesducongo.com; mfrs of beer, soft drinks, ice and carbon dioxide; 50% owned by Toyota Tsusho Corpn (Japan), 50% by Heineken (Netherlands); Man. Dir FRANÇOIS GAZANIA.

Compagnie Bio Petro Chimie (CBPC): BP 242, Brazzaville; tel. 06-663-43-43.

Congo Mining Ltd: 3 ave de Loango, 2e étage, Ndjinji Arrondissement 1, EP Lumumba, Pointe-Noire; internet www .congomininglimited.com; a subsidiary of Midus Global Ltd; Dir-Gen. JOHN WELBORN.

Congolaise Industrielle des Bois (CIB): BP 41, Ouesso; tel. 06-900-14-30; e-mail rcongo@olamnet.com; f. 1968; acquired by Olam International (Singapore) in 2011; logs and timber production; Pres. Dr HEINRICH LÜDER STOLL; Dir-Gen. CHRISTIAN SCHWARZ.

La Congolaise de Raffinage (CORAF): Quartier Mbota Raffinerie, BP 755, Pointe-Noire; tel. 22-294-80-00; e-mail contact@coraf .cg; f. 1982; state-owned; subsidiary of SNPC; production of petroleum and petroleum products; Dir-Gen. DENIS AUGUSTE MARIE GOKANA.

ENI Congo: ave Charles de Gaulle, BP 706, Pointe-Noire; tel. 22-294-03-08; f. 1968; wholly owned by Eni (Italy); fmrly Agip Congo, present name adopted 2010; exploration and exploitation of petroleum resources; Chair. PIETRO CAVANNA; Man. Dir LORENZO FIORILLO.

Eucalyptus Fibre Congo (EFC): BP 1227, Pointe-Noire; tel. 22-294-04-17; f. 2005 to replace Eucalyptus du Congo (ECO); subsidiary of MagIndustries Corpn (Canada); production of wood pulp and other products for export from eucalyptus plantations; Dir-Gen. HUANG FENG.

Groupe Africa Oil and Gas Corpn—Congo: blvd Denis Sassou Nguesso, BP 15073, Brazzaville; tel. 06-654-54-63; e-mail direction@ aogc.cg; internet aogc.cg; f. 2003; comprises Phenix SA, GPL SA and Afric; exploration, production and distribution of petroleum; Pres. ANDRÉ ERNEST NGANGUIA; Dir-Gen. JEAN CHRISTOPHE DA SILVA.

Industrie Forestière d'Ouesso (IFO): BP 135, Ouesso; tel. 22-291-02-04; f. 1964; timber mills; fmrly Société Congolaise des Bois; owned by Danzer Group (Germany); Dir JOSÉ QUARESMA.

Minoterie du Congo (MINOCO): Immeuble Eric Junior, BP 871, Pointe-Noire; tel. 22-294-37-07; e-mail direction@minoco.cg; internet www.seaboardoverseas.com/location/minoco; f. 2000; affiliated with Seaboard Corpn (USA); fmrly Minoterie et Aliments du Bétail; production of flour and animal feed; Dir-Gen. RICHARD PRINCE.

Perenco Congo: Concession Liliane, Quartier Ndjinji, Pointe-Noire; tel. 05-553-66-67; internet www.perenco.com/fr/filiales/congo; f. 2001; Dir-Gen. CHRISTOPHE BLANC.

Société Agricole et de Raffinage Industriel du Sucre (SARIS-Congo): BP 71, Nkayi; sugar production; Dir-Gen. GUILLAUME RANSON.

Société Commune de Logistique Petrolière (SCLOG): BP 14522, Pointe-Noire; f. 2002; 25% state-owned, privately managed; distribution of petroleum products; Dir-Gen. MICHEL DJOMBO.

Société Nationale d'Exploitation des Bois (SNEB): Pointe-Noire; tel. 22-294-02-09; f. 1970; state-owned; production of timber; Chair. BRUNO ITOU.

Société Nationale des Pétroles du Congo (SNPC): Tour SNPC, blvd Denis Sassou Nguesso, BP 188, Brazzaville; tel. 06-555-21-00; e-mail contact@snpc-group.com; internet snpc-group.com; f. 1998; petroleum research and exploration; owns refinery at Pointe-Noire; Dir-Gen. MAIXENT RAOUL OMINGA.

Société Nouvelle des Ciments du Congo (SONOCC): BP 72, Loutété; tel. 22-292-61-26; f. 2002 to replace Les Ciments du Congo; 56% owned by China Road and Bridge Corpn (People's Republic of China), 44% state-owned; Dir-Gen. II XINGTAO.

Société Nouvelle des Plastiques du Congo (SN PLASCO): route de l'Aéroport, BP Pointe-Noire; tel. 06-667-17-17; e-mail dg-pnr@sourcemayo.net; internet www.sourcemayo.net; f. 1974 as PLASCO; present name adopted 1990; mineral water.

SOCOFRAN CDE: ave de l'Emeraude, BP 1148, Pointe-Noire; tel. 06-626-33-33; e-mail info@socofran.com; internet www.socofran.com; f. 1944; building, construction, public works; Pres. HUBERT PANDINO; Dir-Gen. DAVID BOURION.

TotalEnergies Congo: rue de la Corniche, BP 1037, Brazzaville; tel. 22-281-11-12; internet totalenergies.cg; f. 1969; fmrly Elf Congo, subsequently renamed TotalFinaElf Congo; present name adopted 2003; wholly owned by Total (France); exploration and exploitation of petroleum resources.

TRADE UNION FEDERATIONS

Independent trade unions were legalized in 1991.

Confédération Syndicale Congolaise (CSC): BP 2311, Brazzaville; tel. 22-283-19-23; f. 1964; 80,000 mems; Sec.-Gen. DANIEL MONGO.

Confédération Syndicale des Travailleurs du Congo (CSTC): BP 14743, Brazzaville; tel. 06-661-47-35; f. 1993; fed. of 13 trade unions; Chair. ELAULT BELLO BELLARD.

Confédération des Syndicats Libres Autonomes du Congo (COSYLAC): BP 14861, Brazzaville; tel. 22-282-42-65; Sec.-Gen. JEAN BERNARD MALOUKA.

Transport

RAILWAYS

Chemin de Fer Congo-Océan (CFCO): ave Charles de Gaulle, BP 651, Pointe-Noire; tel. 05-559-91-24; internet www.cfco.cg; f. 1969; entered partnership with Rail Afrique International in 1998; transfer to private management proposed; Dir-Gen. JEAN FRANÇOIS COUTIN.

ROADS

The principal routes link Brazzaville with Pointe-Noire, in the south, and with Ouesso, in the north. A number of major construction projects initiated by President Sassou Nguesso have involved the highways from Brazzaville to Kinkala, and from Brazzaville to the Pool department.

INLAND WATERWAYS

The Congo and Oubangui rivers form two axes of a highly developed inland waterway system. The Congo river and seven tributaries in the Congo basin provide 2,300 km of navigable river, and the Oubangui river, developed in co-operation with the Central African Republic, an additional 2,085 km.

Coordination Nationale des Transports Fluviaux: BP 2048, Brazzaville; tel. 22-283-06-27; Dir MÉDARD OKOUMOU.

SHIPPING

The deep-water Atlantic seaport at Pointe-Noire is the most important port in Central Africa, and Brazzaville is one of the principal ports on the Congo river. A major rehabilitation programme began in 1999, with the aim of establishing Pointe-Noire as a regional centre for container traffic and as a logistics centre for offshore petroleum exploration.

Port Autonome de Brazzaville et des Ports Secondaires (PABPS): BP 2048, Brazzaville; tel. 22-283-00-42; f. 2000; port authority; Pres. JEAN LOUIS OSSO; Dir-Gen. PIERRE BOSSOTO.

Port Autonome de Pointe-Noire (PAPN): BP 711, Pointe-Noire; tel. 22-294-00-13; e-mail info@papn-cg.org; internet www.papn-cg.org; f. 2000; port authority; Dir-Gen. SÉRAPHIN BALHAT.

SAGA Congo: 18 rue du Prophète Lasse Zephirin, BP 674, Pointe-Noire; tel. 22-294-10-16; e-mail emmanuelle.peillon@bollore.com; acquired by Bolloré Africa Logistics au Congo in Oct. 2013; Dir-Gen. PIERRE BELLEROSE.

Société Congolaise de Transports Maritimes (SOCOTRAM): BP 4922, Pointe-Noire; tel. 22-294-49-21; e-mail info@socotram.com; internet www.socotram.fr; f. 1990; Dir JUSTE MONDELE.

CIVIL AVIATION

There are international airports at Brazzaville (Maya-Maya), Oyo (Oyo Ollombo) and Pointe-Noire (Agostinho Neto). There are also five regional airports, at Loubomo (Dolisie, Ngot-Nzounzoungou), Nkayi, Owando, Ouesso and Impfondo, as well as 12 smaller airfields.

Agence Nationale de l'Aviation Civile: rue de la Libération de Paris, Camp Clairon, BP 128, Brazzaville; tel. 22-281-02-27; e-mail contact@anaccongo.org; internet anaccongo.org; Dir-Gen. SERGE FLORENT DZOTA.

Aéro-Service: ave Charles de Gaulle, BP 1138, Pointe-Noire; tel. 05-556-41-41; f. 1967; scheduled and charter passenger and freight services; operates nationally and to regional destinations; Pres. and Dir-Gen. R. GRIESBAUM.

Equatorial Congo Airlines SA (ECAir): 1604 ave des Trois Martyrs, Quartier Batignolles, Brazzaville; tel. 06-509-05-09; e-mail info@flyecair.com; f. 2011; operates flights between Brazzaville and Pointe-Noire; operations suspended since 2016; Dir-Gen. FATIMA BEYNA MOUSSA.

Trans Air Congo: Immeuble City Center, ave Amílcar Cabral, BP 2422, Brazzaville; tel. 06-626-26-05; e-mail info@flytransaircongo.com; internet www.flytransaircongo.com; f. 1994; private airline operating internal scheduled and international charter flights; Pres. and Dir-Gen. MUSTAPHA ELHAGE.

Tourism

Office National du Tourisme: BP 456, Brazzaville; tel. 22-613-69-06; e-mail contact@officedutourisme.gouv.cg; internet www.officedutourisme.gouv.cg; f. 1980; Dir-Gen. ANTOINE KOUNKOU-KIBOUILOU.

Defence

As assessed at November 2021, the army numbered 8,000, the navy about 800 and the air force 1,200. In addition, there was a 2,000-strong gendarmerie. National service is voluntary for men and women, and lasts for two years.

Defence Budget: 164,000m. francs CFA in 2022.

Supreme Commander of the Armed Forces: Gen. DENIS SASSOU NGUESSO.

Chief of General Staff of the Congolese Armed Forces: Gen. GUY BLANCHARD OKOÏ.

Chief of Staff of the Air Force: Col JEAN-BAPTISTE PHILIPPE TCHIKAYA.

Chief of Staff of the Navy: Capt. RENÉ NGANONG.

Sec.-Gen. of the National Security Council: Vice-Adm. JEAN-DOMINIQUE OKEMBA.

Education

Education is officially compulsory for 10 years between six and 16 years of age and is provided free of charge in public institutions. Primary education begins at the age of six and lasts for six years. Secondary education, from 12 years of age, lasts for seven years, comprising a first cycle of four years and a second of three years. According to estimates by the United Nations Educational, Scientific and Cultural Organization (UNESCO), in 2017/18 enrolment at pre-primary institutions was equivalent to 14% of children in the relevant age-group (boys 14%; girls 15%), while in 2011/12 primary schools included 89% of children in the relevant age-group (boys 85%; girls 93%). In that year secondary enrolment was equivalent to 53% of children in the relevant age-group (boys 56%; girls 49%). In 2021 spending on education represented an estimated 16.5% of total budgetary expenditure.

Bibliography

Amin, S., and Coquery-Vidrovitch, C. *Histoire économique du Congo 1880–1968*. Paris, Anthropos, 1969.

Babu-Zale, R., et al. *Le Congo de Pascal Lissouba*. Paris, L'Harmattan, 1996.

Baniafouma, C. *Congo démocratie*. 5 vols. Paris, L'Harmattan, 1995–2003.

Batota-Mpeho, R. *From Political Monolithism to Multiparty Autocracy: The Collapse of the Democratic Dream in Congo-Brazzaville*. Lulu Publishing, 2015.

Clark, J. F. *The Failure of Democracy in the Republic of Congo*. Boulder, CO, Lynne Rienner Publishers, 2008.

Dabira, N. *Brazzaville à feu et à sang: 5 juin–15 octobre 1997*. Paris, L'Harmattan, 1998.

Dandou, W. *Un nouveau cadre constitutionnel pour le Congo-Brazzaville*. Paris, L'Harmattan, 2006.

Decalo, S., Thompson, V., and Adloff, R. *Historical Dictionary of Congo*. 3rd edn. Lanham, MD, Scarecrow Press, 1996.

Dzaba, L. *Pour un Congo-Brazzaville Libre et Prospère! Le temps d'agir*. Paris, L'Harmattan, 2014.

Dzon, C. M. M. *Pour relancer le Congo: la politique du possible*. Paris, L'Harmattan, 2007.

Gankama, E. *Oua / Ua: les deux mandats de Denis Sassou N'Guesso*. Paris, L'Harmattan, 2013.

Gouemo, R. *Le Congo-Brazzaville: de l'état postcolonial à l'état multinational*. Paris, L'Harmattan, 2004.

Idourah, S. N. *Justice et pouvoir au Congo-Brazzaville 1958–92: La confusion des rôles*. Paris, L'Harmattan, 2002.

Ikiemi, S. *Le systeme bancaire du Congo-Brazzaville: organisation et perspectives*. Paris, L'Harmattan, 2006.

Kinata, C. *Les ethnochefferies dans le Bas-Congo français: collaboration et résistance: 1896-1960*. Paris, L'Harmattan, 2001.

Kouvibidila, G.-J. *Histoire du multipartisme au Congo-Brazzaville. Volume 1: La marche à rebours 1940–1991*. Paris, L'Harmattan, 2001.

Histoire du multipartisme au Congo-Brazzaville. Volume 2: Les débuts d'une crise attendue 1992–1993. Paris, L'Harmattan, 2001.

Histoire du multipartisme au Congo-Brazzaville. Volume 3: La République en otage mai–octobre 1993. Paris, L'Harmattan, 2003.

Likaka, O. *Naming Colonialism: History and Collective Memory in the Congo, 1870–1960*. Madison, WI., University of Wisconsin Press, 2009.

Mabeko-Tali, J.-M. *Barbares et citoyens, l'identité nationale à l'épreuve des transitions africaines: Congo-Brazzaville, Angola*. Paris, L'Harmattan, 2005.

MacGaffrey, J., and Bazenguissa-Ganga, R. *Congo-Paris: Transnational Traders on the Margins of the Law*. Oxford, James Currey Publishers, 2000.

Makaya, J. *Pour une nouvelle gouvernance du Congo-Brazzaville*. Paris, L'Harmattan, 2016

Mbéri, M. *Congo-Brazzaville: Regard sur 50 ans d'indépendance nationale 1960-2010*. Paris, L'Harmattan, 2011.

M'Kaloulou, B. *Dynamique paysanne et développement rural au Congo*. Paris, L'Harmattan, 1984.

M'paka, A. *Démocratie et vie politique au Congo-Brazzaville: Enjeux et recompositions politiques*. Paris, L'Harmattan, 2007.

Ndaki, G. *Crises, mutations et conflits politiques au Congo-Brazzaville*. Paris, L'Harmattan, 1998.

Ndinga Mbo, A. C. *Introduction a l'histoire des migrations au Congo-Brazzaville*. Paris, L'Harmattan, 2006.

Nkaya, M. (Ed.). *Le Congo-Brazzaville à l'aube du XXIe siècle: Plaidoyer pour l'avenir*. Paris, L'Harmattan, 2004.

Nsafou, G. *Congo: de la démocratie à la démocrature*. Paris, L'Harmattan, 1996.

Obenga, T. *L'Histoire sanglante du Congo-Brazzaville (1959–1997)*. Paris, Présence Africaine, 1998.

Pigasse, J.-P. *Congo: Chronique d'une guerre annoncée (5 juin–15 octobre 1997)*. Brazzaville, Editions ADIAC, 1998.

Rabut, E. *Brazza, commissaire général. Le Congo français (1886–1897)*. Paris, Editions de l'école des hautes études en sciences sociales, 1989.

Sassou Nguesso, D. *Le Manguier, le fleuve et la souris*. France, Jean-Claude Lattes, 1997.

Whitehouse, B. *Migrants and Strangers in an African City: Exile, Dignity, Belonging*. Bloomington, IN., Indiana University Press, 2012.

Yengo, P. *La guerre civile du Congo-Brazzaville (1993–2002)*. Paris, Karthala, 2006.

Zika, J.-R. *Démocratisme et misère politique en afrique: Le cas du Congo-Brazzaville*. Paris, L'Harmattan, 2002.

CÔTE D'IVOIRE

Physical and Social Geography

R. J. HARRISON CHURCH

The Republic of Côte d'Ivoire is situated on the west coast of Africa, between Ghana to the east and Liberia to the west, with Guinea, Mali and Burkina Faso to the north. The country has an area of 322,462 sq km (124,503 sq miles) and, according to United Nations estimates, at mid-2022 the population was 27,742,301 (giving an average population density of 86.0 inhabitants per sq km). There is a diversity of peoples, with the Agni and Baoulé having cultural and other affinities with the Ashanti of Ghana. At the time of the 2014 census 24.2% of the population of the country were nationals of other states. According to the 2014 census, some 42% of the total population were Muslims, 34% of the population were Christians (mainly Roman Catholics), 4% followed traditional indigenous beliefs, 1% practised other religions, while 19% had no religious affiliation. The official language is French, and many African languages are also spoken. The largest city is the former capital, Abidjan, which remains the principal commercial centre in Côte d'Ivoire, and which had a population of 4,395,243 (including suburbs) at the time of the 2014 census. The official capital, the central city of Yamoussoukro, had a population of 286,071 in 2014, while Bouaké, the largest city in the north, had a population of 608,138.

From the border with Liberia eastwards to Fresco, the coast has cliffs, rocky promontories and sandy bays. East of Fresco, the rest of the coast is a straight sandbar, backed, as in Benin, by lagoons.

Although Tertiary sands and clays fringe the northern edge of the lagoons, they give way almost immediately to Archaean and Pre-Cambrian rocks, which underlie the rest of the country. Diamonds are obtained from gravels south of Korhogo, and near Séguéla, while gold is mined at Ity, in the west. The Man mountains and the Guinea highlands on the border with Liberia and Guinea are the only areas of vigorous relief in the country. There are plans to develop substantial deposits of haematite iron ore near Man for export through the country's second deep-water port of San-Pédro. There is considerable commercial potential for large offshore deposits of petroleum and also of natural gas, exploitation of which began in 1995; Côte d'Ivoire aims to become self-sufficient in (and, in the medium term, a net exporter of) hydrocarbons. Plans for the development of nickel reserves are proceeding.

Except for the north-western fifth of Côte d'Ivoire, the country has an equatorial climate. This occurs most typically in the south, which receives annual rainfall of 1,250 mm–2,400 mm, with two maxima, and where the relative humidity is high. Much valuable rainforest survives in the south-west, but elsewhere it has been extensively planted with coffee, cocoa, bananas, pineapples, rubber and oil palm. Tropical climatic conditions prevail in the north-west, with a single rainy season of five to seven months, and 1,250 mm–1,500 mm of rain annually. Guinea savannah occurs here, as well as in the centre of the country, and projects southwards around Bouaké.

History

MARIE GIBERT

THE HOUPHOUËT-BOIGNY ERA, 1960–93

From independence from French rule in August 1960 until his death in 1993, political life in Côte d'Ivoire was dominated by Dr Félix Houphouët-Boigny; he was the sole candidate for the presidency at every election until 1990, and his Parti Démocratique de la Côte d'Ivoire—Rassemblement Démocratique Africain (PDCI—RDA) the only legal political party. President Houphouët-Boigny guided the economic and political evolution of the country without any effective challenge to his rule. From the late 1960s efforts were made to 'Ivorianize' public administration and the economy. None the less, French financial backing, together with membership of the Franc Zone, were of major influence in Côte d'Ivoire's economic development.

Persistent unrest against government austerity policies led to the deployment of troops in Abidjan in 1990. In response, Houphouët-Boigny appointed Alassane Ouattara, the Governor of the Banque Centrale des Etats de l'Afrique de l'Ouest (BCEAO, the regional central bank), to head a commission to formulate alternative adjustment measures; a less stringent programme of austerity measures was announced in late May. Also in May Houphouët-Boigny agreed to the establishment of a multi-party political system.

Côte d'Ivoire's first contested presidential election took place in October 1990. Houphouët-Boigny, who was challenged by Laurent Gbagbo, the candidate of the Front Populaire Ivoirien (FPI), was elected for a seventh term by 81.7% of those who voted (69.2% of the electorate). In November the Assemblée Nationale (National Assembly) approved two constitutional amendments allowing, respectively, the President of the Assembly to assume the functions of the President of the Republic, should this office become vacant, and the appointment of a Prime Minister, a post subsequently awarded to Ouattara.

At parliamentary elections held in November 1990, the PDCI—RDA secured 163 seats in the new 175-member legislature, while the FPI won nine.

The political and social climate deteriorated following the publication, in January 1992, of the findings of a commission of inquiry into the security forces' suppression of a student gathering at the University of Abidjan in May 1991. Although the commission found the Chief of the General Staff of the armed forces, Brig.-Gen. Robert Guëi, directly responsible for acts of violence committed by his troops, Houphouët-Boigny declined to subject him to disciplinary proceedings.

THE BÉDIÉ PRESIDENCY

President Houphouët-Boigny died in December 1993. Later on the same day Henri Konan Bédié, the President of the National Assembly, assumed the duties of President of the Republic, with immediate effect, in accordance with the Constitution. Ouattara initially refused to recognize Bédié's right of succession, but resigned two days later, after France had acknowledged Bédié's legitimacy as President. Daniel Kablan Duncan, hitherto Minister-delegate, responsible for the Economy, Finance and Planning, was appointed Prime Minister. Bédié subsequently conducted an effective purge of Ouattara sympathizers, appointing his own supporters to positions of influence throughout the public sphere.

Bédié was elected Chairman of the PDCI—RDA in April 1994. In June a group of Ouattara loyalists left the PDCI—

RDA and founded the Rassemblement des Républicains (RDR). By the end of the year the new party had supplanted the FPI as the principal parliamentary opposition. Ouattara, who in July had taken up the post of Deputy Managing Director of the International Monetary Fund, officially announced his membership of the RDR in early 1995.

A new electoral code was adopted in December 1994. Opposition parties denounced clauses imposing restrictions on eligibility for public office, in particular requirements that candidates be of direct Ivorian descent and have been continuously resident in Côte d'Ivoire for five years prior to seeking election, both of which were interpreted as being directly aimed at preventing Ouattara from contesting the presidency. An FPI congress formally adopted Gbagbo as its candidate for the presidency, while Bédié was likewise adopted as the candidate of the PDCI—RDA.

The presidential election took place in October 1995, following a week of violent incidents. According to the official results, Bédié secured an overwhelming victory with 95.2% of the valid votes cast. At the legislative elections held in November, voting was reported to have proceeded largely without incident. The PDCI—RDA secured 146 seats in the National Assembly, with the RDR winning 14 and the FPI nine.

Wide-ranging constitutional amendments were approved by the National Assembly in June 1998. The RDR and the FPI objected to provisions conferring wider powers on the head of state—specifically a clause allowing the President to delay elections or the proclamation of election results, on the grounds of 'events, serious troubles or *force majeure*'. The presidential mandate was to be extended to seven years, with no limit on the number of times an incumbent might seek re-election. Conditions of eligibility for public office were written into the Constitution: candidates would be required to be Ivorian by birth, of direct Ivorian descent and to have been continuously resident in Côte d'Ivoire for 10 years.

In August 1999 Ouattara was selected as the RDR's presidential candidate. However, Bédié regarded Ouattara as a Burkinabè citizen and warned that he would suppress any protests on his behalf. When Ouattara's claim to citizenship was subjected to a new inquiry by judicial police, clashes occurred in September in Abidjan between security forces and supporters of Ouattara. In October a court in Dimbokro, Ouattara's birthplace, cancelled his nationality certificate, prompting further violent demonstrations, during which a number of senior RDR figures were arrested.

BRIG.-GEN. GUEÏ ASSUMES POWER

With Bédié's authority and his personal popularity rapidly declining, a mutiny among soldiers in late December 1999 quickly escalated into a national crisis. The President initially sought to appease the soldiers, who seized most public buildings in Abidjan, with the promise of improved pay and conditions; however, the troops subsequently demanded the reinstatement of Brig.-Gen. Gueï as Chief of Staff of the Ivorian armed forces. (Gueï had been dismissed from the army in January 1997.) Gueï then announced that he had assumed power, at the head of a Comité National de Salut Public (CNSP). Meanwhile, Bédié fled to the French embassy, and eventually into exile in France. The unexpected coup was apparently widely welcomed within Côte d'Ivoire, with both the RDR and FPI leaders promptly returning to the country from abroad, and France soon established a dialogue with the new administration.

Order and calm were restored rapidly, and an all-party Government was formed in January 2000. However, the publication of a draft Constitution in May provoked a renewed political crisis, as the articles restricting the eligibility of candidates for the presidency were retained. In response to RDR protests, Gueï dismissed most of that party's ministers in a government reorganization. Gueï also appointed a Prime Minister, Seydou Elimane Diarra, an experienced civil servant and diplomat. In the same month the authorities issued an international warrant for the arrest of Bédié, on charges of embezzlement. At a referendum conducted in July, voters approved the new Constitution, which, *inter alia*, granted immunity from prosecution to members of the CNSP and to all those involved in the coup.

THE EARLY YEARS OF THE GBAGBO PRESIDENCY, 2000–02

In August 2000 Gueï announced that the country's four main political parties had agreed in advance to form a government of national unity following the forthcoming legislative elections. The Supreme Court upheld the disqualification of both Ouattara and Bédié from the presidential election, which had been postponed from September until late October, leaving the field clear for the two main contenders, Gueï and Gbagbo. Following a further minor government reorganization, at the end of September, the FPI became the sole political party to be represented in the transitional Government.

After the presidential election, with preliminary results indicating a victory for Gbagbo, Gueï suspended the electoral commission and proclaimed himself the winner. Gbagbo's supporters protested in Abidjan, and key units of the army and gendarmerie proclaimed their support for Gbagbo. Gueï fled the country, while Gbagbo reinstated the electoral commission, which published official results showing that he had received 59.4% of the vote to Gueï's 32.7%. Although a low rate of participation (an estimated 33.2%) cast doubt on the legitimacy of his victory, Gbagbo was sworn in as the new President on 26 October 2000. On the following day Pascal Affi N'Guessan, Minister of Industry and Tourism in the outgoing Government, was appointed as Prime Minister.

In protest against Ouattara's continued exclusion from the political process, the RDR boycotted the legislative elections held in December 2000 and in a number of northern constituencies (where unrest had led to a postponement) in January 2001. The FPI won 96 seats in the National Assembly, ahead of the PDCI—RDA with 94 seats. N'Guessan remained at the head of a new Government appointed in late January, which included, in addition to members of the FPI, ministers from the PDCI—RDA, the Parti Ivoirien des Travailleurs, and two independents.

In July 2001 N'Guessan was elected to replace Gbagbo as leader of the FPI. Negotiations between Gbagbo, Bédié, Gueï and Ouattara took place in Yamoussoukro during January 2002. Thereafter, it appeared that Gueï had decided to support Ouattara's case for Ivorian nationality. Ouattara's Ivorian citizenship was finally restored in June, although he remained barred from contesting the presidency, as a result of having held Burkinabè citizenship. A further attempt at reconciliation was evident in the appointment of four RDR ministers to a government of national unity in August. However, opposition parties withdrew their support from the Government.

THE FIRST IVORIAN CIVIL WAR, 2002–07

In September 2002, while Gbagbo was on a state visit to Italy, groups of soldiers (who were mainly supporters of Gueï) staged a mutiny that rapidly split the armed forces throughout the country. In Abidjan dissidents killed the Minister of State, Minister of the Interior and Decentralization, Emile Boga Doudou, a close ally of Gbagbo. Gueï was also killed, apparently by soldiers loyal to Gbagbo. On his return, Gbagbo implied that Burkina Faso was implicated in the insurgency. Amid renewed inter-ethnic tension and an upsurge in violence directed against northern Muslims and citizens of neighbouring states, the USA deployed some 200 special forces to Korhogo, to airlift foreigners from the rebel-held town. An emergency summit of the Economic Community of West African States (ECOWAS), convened in Accra, Ghana, in late September, resolved to dispatch a peacekeeping force to act as a 'buffer' between government and rebel troops, and mandated the Presidents of five member nations, in addition to the South African President, Thabo Mbeki, in his capacity as Chairman of the African Union (AU), to form a 'contact group' to undertake negotiations between Gbagbo and the insurgents.

The rebels identified themselves as the Mouvement Patriotique de la Côte d'Ivoire (MPCI) and stated as their principal demand the removal of Gbagbo from the presidency and the holding of fresh presidential and legislative elections.

Negotiations between the MPCI and ECOWAS mediators took place in early October 2002. The signature of a ceasefire accord by the Government was cancelled after repeated delays, precipitating the departure of the ECOWAS contact group from Côte d'Ivoire. Thereafter, the Government's forces consistently failed to make any advances in rebel-held areas, especially around Bouaké, which had become the main rebel stronghold. Across the south, which remained under government control, homes of suspected rebel supporters (often ethnic Dioula in addition to people of Burkinabè, Malian or Guinean origin) were destroyed, resulting in both large-scale migration of foreign citizens away from the south and further loss of life.

At the end of October 2002 the Government and the MPCI entered into their first substantive negotiations, in Lomé, Togo, under the aegis of ECOWAS. However, the negotiations broke down following the apparently politically motivated assassination of the brother of an MPCI negotiator. Meanwhile, the rebellion had spread to western regions of Côte d'Ivoire, bordering Guinea and Liberia. As clashes continued in the west, France steadily increased its overall presence to some 3,000 troops in January 2003, and the first contingent of ECOWAS forces arrived.

In French-hosted talks at Marcoussis, near Paris, France, in January 2003, it was agreed by all parties that a government of national reconciliation would be formed, led by Diarra. The Marcoussis Accords were signed on 24 January, but immediately provoked a violent reaction among government supporters, who attacked the French embassy and other French-associated institutions in Abidjan, amid more assaults on immigrants.

Further rounds of negotiations and diplomacy took place throughout February 2003. Although the proposed government of national reconciliation remained in abeyance, Diarra was officially inaugurated as Prime Minister. A new agreement was signed by the main parties and rebel movements in Accra in early March. The agreement provided for a six-month peace process, involving the deployment of more than 4,000 French and ECOWAS peacekeeping personnel and the creation of an international monitoring group by the United Nations (UN), ECOWAS and the AU.

By April 2003, amid a humanitarian crisis, a 1,260-strong ECOWAS military mission had been deployed to take over a section of the 'front line' near Yamoussoukro from French troops. On 1 May the Chief of Staff of the armed forces, Gen. Mathias Doué, and the military leader of the MPCI, Col Michel Gueu, signed a ceasefire agreement, which was intended to apply to all rebel groups operating in Côte d'Ivoire. Later in May Guillaume Kigbafori Soro, the Secretary-General of the political wing of the MPCI, confirmed that the MPCI's military activities had ceased. In mid-June the national army and rebel forces agreed to the eventual confinement of troops, and at the end of the month the Government announced that all former rebels would be disarmed by mid-September. Also in late June, the UN Mission in Côte d'Ivoire, authorized by the UN Security Council in May and charged with overseeing the implementation of the Marcoussis Accords, commenced operations in Abidjan. In early July, in a ceremony held at the presidential palace, MPCI leaders formally announced the end of the conflict. Although tensions persisted, in August the National Assembly approved legislation providing for an amnesty for those involved in political unrest (excluding abuses of human rights or violations of international humanitarian law) between mid-September 2000 and mid-September 2002. Meanwhile, the MPCI effectively absorbed smaller rebel groups based in western regions, and announced that the organization was henceforth to be known as the Forces Nouvelles (FN).

In February 2004 the UN Security Council established the UN Operation in Côte d'Ivoire (UNOCI) with an authorized military strength of 6,240. None the less, the process of national reconciliation appeared to be stalling, with Soro's announcement, at the end of February, that former rebel fighters would not disarm prior to legislative and presidential elections scheduled for 2005. In March 2004 the PDCI—RDA announced that its ministers were to suspend their participation in the Government, in response to what it termed acts of humiliation and aggression against the party by supporters of Gbagbo. A few days later the disarmament process was indefinitely postponed.

A protest march in Abidjan in March 2004, organized by seven of the 10 signatory parties of the Marcoussis Accords (known collectively as the G7), in defiance of a temporary ban on demonstrations announced by Gbagbo earlier that month, prompted clashes between protesters and members of the security forces. According to official figures, 37 were killed, although the G7, comprising the PDCI—RDA, the RDR, the Union pour la Démocratie et pour la Paix de la Côte d'Ivoire (UDPCI, formed in early 2001 by followers of Gueï), the Mouvement des Forces d'Avenir (MFA) and the three former rebel movements now united in the FN, estimated the number of deaths at more than 300. An inquiry conducted by the Office of the UN High Commissioner for Human Rights later reported that at least 120 civilians had been killed by the security forces in a 'carefully planned operation' organized by 'the highest authorities of the state'. The RDR, the FN and the MFA subsequently suspended their participation in the Government. The first contingent of UNOCI forces arrived in Côte d'Ivoire in early April; the mission's initial mandate was for a 12-month period and was periodically extended thereafter.

In mid-April 2004 President Gbagbo acceded to the opposition G7's principal demands in an attempt to restore stability, agreeing to respect the right to demonstrate, to ensure the security of the people and to allow equal access to the state media by all political organizations. The peace process remained stalled, however, and in mid-May Gbagbo dismissed three opposition ministers, including Soro.

In July 2004 all parties to the conflict attended a meeting of West African heads of state in Accra and signed an agreement on the implementation of the Marcoussis Accords. Under the agreement, which was to be monitored by UNOCI, ECOWAS and the AU, disarmament of the FN troops was to commence by mid-October. In August, in accordance with the agreement, Gbagbo reinstated the three government ministers dismissed in May, and all ministers from opposition parties and the former rebel groups resumed participation in the Government. Shortly afterwards, the President delegated some of his powers to the Prime Minister, pending a presidential election. However, the October disarmament deadline was not observed by the rebels, who declared that insufficient progress had been made towards the realization of the proposed political reforms.

In early November 2004 the 18-month ceasefire was broken when the Ivorian air force launched bombing raids on Bouaké and other targets in the north of the country, reportedly resulting in the deaths of more than 80 civilians and nine French peacekeeping troops. In retaliation, French forces, acting on the direct orders of French President Jacques Chirac, destroyed the entire fleet of the Ivorian air force on the ground. This precipitated several days of violence, with thousands of Ivorians rioting, looting and attacking French and other foreign targets. In mid-November the UN Security Council voted unanimously in favour of imposing an arms embargo on Côte d'Ivoire. Meanwhile, Soro and eight other opposition ministers announced that they would not attend meetings of the Government, citing personal security concerns.

In mid-December 2004 the National Assembly voted in favour of amending the Constitution to permit persons with only one, rather than two, Ivorian parents to contest the presidency (thus allowing Ouattara to contest the election scheduled for October 2005). Gbagbo, however, insisted that any constitutional change would require ratification by referendum.

In early April 2005 President Mbeki hosted a summit in Pretoria, South Africa, attended by Bédié, Diarra, Gbagbo, Ouattara and Soro. An agreement was signed committing all parties to the disbandment of militia groups and the disarmament of former rebel troops. In mid-April Mbeki issued a statement ruling that the Ivorian Constitutional Council should confirm the presidential candidates of those parties that had signed the Marcoussis Accords. Following this statement, which was interpreted as permitting Ouattara's eventual candidacy, two of the FN ministers resumed participation in the Government, while Gbagbo declared that he would accept Ouattara as a legitimate candidate.

In July 2005 Gbagbo signed legislation on nationality and on the establishment of an independent electoral commission. In August the FN declared that its members were not ready to begin disarming, stating that the terms of the legislation recently decreed by Gbagbo differed from those that had been agreed in Pretoria. In early September UN Secretary-General Kofi Annan announced that the presidential election would be delayed indefinitely, owing to the failure of the country's political parties to implement the peace accords. In early October the AU announced proposals for the extension of Gbagbo's mandate as President by up to 12 months and for the appointment of a new Prime Minister acceptable to all parties. Meanwhile, mediation efforts were to continue. In mid-October the UN Security Council adopted Resolution 1633, endorsing the AU's recommendations and previous peace agreements. In early December the AU mediation team nominated Charles Konan Banny, Governor of the BCEAO, as the new Prime Minister. In mid-December the Security Council adopted a resolution to ban imports of diamonds from Côte d'Ivoire and to renew the arms embargo for a further year (both of these sanctions were renewed annually thereafter until the ban was lifted in April 2014—see *Economy*).

In late December 2005 Prime Minister Banny announced his new Government of National Unity, comprising members of the FPI, the FN, the PDCI—RDA and the RDR. However, in January 2006 the new Government faced its first crisis, when the UN-mandated International Working Group (IWG) issued a statement rejecting the extension of the mandate of the National Assembly, which had expired in December 2005. Interpreting the statement as a formal dissolution of the legislature, militias loyal to President Gbagbo seized control of main roads and government buildings in Abidjan and the south-west of the country, and clashed with UN troops. In late January 2006 Banny issued a decree that prolonged the mandate of the National Assembly.

In March 2006 Banny announced his intention to initiate a new identification campaign for the registration of voters. Although this was strongly contested by Gbagbo, the opposition supported Banny's initiative. In July the two-month identification process was officially launched, only to be severely delayed by procedural challenges and claims of electoral fraud by both the FPI and the FN. The latter withdrew from disarmament talks in August, after Gbagbo pledged to issue a decree naming new magistrates to oversee the identification process. Given the political deadlock, at a meeting in early September the UN-mandated IWG agreed that the elections scheduled for October should be postponed.

In November 2006 the UN Security Council adopted Resolution 1721, which renewed the transitional period established by Resolution 1633 for a maximum of 12 months, and appealed for presidential and legislative elections to be held by 31 October 2007. The resolution extended the mandates of Gbagbo and Banny for the duration of the transitional period, and increased Banny's powers to enable him to issue decrees without the consent of the National Assembly. Gbagbo made a televised address, accepting Resolution 1721 in principle, but implicitly rejecting Banny's authority over the armed forces. The opposition parties, led by the FN, were also cautious in their acceptance of Resolution 1721, expressing doubts that it could be successfully implemented.

THE OUAGADOUGOU ACCORD AND TRANSITION, 2007–10

In February 2007 talks began in the Burkinabè capital, Ouagadougou, between representatives of the Government and the FN, under the mediation of President of Burkina Faso Blaise Compaoré. On 4 March Gbagbo and Soro signed the Ouagadougou Accord providing for the resumption of *audiences foraines* (localized courts to register citizens); the drawing up of a new electoral register under the supervision of the Commission Electorale Indépendante (CEI); the resumption of the demobilization process and the integration of the FN into the national army; and the dissolution of the 'buffer zone', to be followed by the deployment of joint army and FN patrols in the area and the extension of the Government's control across the whole country. Two new bodies were also to be established: the

Cadre Permanent de Concertation (CPC), comprising Gbagbo, Soro, Bédié, Ouattara and Compaoré; and the Comité d'Evaluation et d'Accompagnement, comprising representatives appointed by Gbagbo, Soro and Compaoré.

In mid-March 2007 Gbagbo signed a decree setting up an integrated central command for the armed forces (the Centre de Commandement Integré—CCI), which would be jointly headed by army Chief of Staff Gen. Philippe Mangou and the FN Chief of Staff, Gen. Soumaïla Bakayoko. The CCI was tasked with completing the disarmament and demobilization process, and ensuring security during the identification campaign and elections. In further talks in Ouagadougou, Gbagbo nominated Soro as Prime Minister; he took office in early April. A new transitional Government, dominated by FPI and FN figures but retaining several members of the previous administration, was announced. In mid-April Gbagbo issued an amnesty for crimes committed during the extended conflict, and the 'buffer zone' was officially abolished.

Under the demobilization programme, 36,000 FN troops were to be demobilized in four stages by the end of October 2008. In addition, 12,000 militia troops loyal to Gbagbo were to be demobilized. However, the process caused renewed tensions within the FN, and in June FN troops staged a series of mutinies in Bouaké, partly in response to the Government's failure to pay demobilization allowances. In July the CCI began demobilization talks with pro-Government militias in western Côte d'Ivoire.

In December 2008 Gbagbo and Soro signed a fourth complementary peace agreement to the Ouagadougou Accord, known as 'Ouaga IV', under Compaoré's mediation. The agreement created the framework for demobilizing 36,000 FN troops and an unspecified number of militia forces, integrating 9,000 of them into a new national army and police force, and extending the central government administration into rebel-held areas.

In April 2009 the CCI announced that a mixed force of 8,000 troops would be redeployed into the north of the country under Ouaga IV, with a mandate to re-establish the Government's authority across the national territory and provide security for the electoral process. The first contingents of this force were deployed to Bouaké in May, and late that month control was formally transferred from the FN's 10 regional commanders to central government *préfets*. By September, according to the Government, more than 7,700 rebel fighters had been demobilized. However, at least a further 18,000 had failed to do so, in addition to other militia forces believed to total over 20,000. This contravened the October deadline established in the Ouagadougou Accord.

Meanwhile, from September 2007 the *audiences foraines* were gradually extended across the country. In April 2008 Gbagbo issued a decree stating that the presidential election would take place on 30 November, to be followed by legislative elections at a later date. The Government subsequently signed an agreement with French company Sagem Sécurité to revise the electoral register. In mid-May the *audiences foraines* formally ended, having held a total of 7,400 public hearings and issued 660,000 new birth certificates. The second phase of the revision of the national birth register commenced shortly thereafter.

In September 2008 the voter registration process finally began. However, industrial action disrupted registration in October, and late that month the CEI announced that only 300,000 out of an estimated 8m. voters had been registered. Soro conceded that the presidential election would not be conducted as planned in November.

The CPC met for the fifth time in November 2008 and unanimously agreed to postpone the election, requesting that the CEI draw up a new timetable. However, the registration process continued to be delayed by logistical problems and allegations of fraud. In May 2009 Soro announced that the first round of the presidential election would take place on 29 November. The identification and registration of voters was finally completed by the end of June, following four extensions. However, the CEI estimated that at least 2m. eligible Ivorians had not registered. In August the CEI formally began the registration of candidates for the presidential election. The provisional electoral register was released in

October. However, more than 2.7m. voters had no previous official record, encouraging suspicions of electoral fraud.

When the final voter registrations were not released as scheduled in early November 2009, an emergency meeting was held between the Government and the main bodies involved in preparing the register. Personal details collected during the registration process were cross-referenced with existing data—1.7m. voters had their identities confirmed, reducing the number of unregistered voters to just over 1m., or 16.2% of the electorate. Gbagbo then accused Robert Beugré Mambé, the President of the CEI, of fraudulently including 429,000 suspect voters on the electoral roll. A criminal investigation was ordered by the Ministry of the Interior, which found evidence of misappropriation of electoral funds by Mambé and four senior CEI staff. In response, Soro convened the electoral authorities for a series of meetings. The registration of the suspect voters was subsequently annulled, and a new authenticating procedure devised. The opposition claimed that supporters of Gbagbo had resorted to law to disqualify voters in the north of the country—where Gbagbo's popularity was low—from the register.

In mid-February 2010 Gbagbo dissolved the CEI and the Government, citing Article 48 of the Constitution, which allowed the President to take 'exceptional measures' if confronted by a serious and immediate threat to national institutions. Gbagbo stated that the electoral process had broken down and that a free and fair election could no longer be guaranteed. The peace process stalled as opposition parties questioned the legality of President Gbagbo's move—Alphonse Djédjé Mady, leader of the Rassemblement des Houphouétistes pour la Démocratie et la Paix (RHDP, a coalition of four opposition parties founded in 2005), denounced the move as a coup. Shortly afterwards, clashes with the police erupted in Bouaké, Gagnoa, Korhogo and Daloa, and in opposition strongholds in Abidjan; at least 10 protesters were killed.

Soro attempted to broker an emergency deal between the FPI and the opposition. After further mediation by Compaoré, Soro announced the formation of a new Government in late February 2010, with 11 of the 27 portfolios awarded to the opposition and 16 to the FPI. A compromise saw the President and four Vice-Presidents of the CEI replaced. Youssouf Bakayoko, former Minister of Foreign Affairs and member of the PDCI—RDA, was named CEI President, and the opposition ended its protests.

THE SECOND IVORIAN CIVIL WAR, 2010–11

A revised electoral list was published in mid-July 2010 and was confirmed in August. The Government subsequently announced a new date for the presidential election, of 31 October. After five years of delays, the first round of the presidential election accordingly took place on that date. More than 5.7m. Ivorians were registered to vote. UNOCI provided logistical assistance to the Government and the CEI. A total of 14 candidates contested the poll, the most prominent being Gbagbo (representing the FPI), Ouattara (the RDR) and Bédié (the PDCI—RDA).

Gbagbo secured the highest number of votes cast in the first round of the presidential election, with 38.0%, while Ouattara was placed second, with 32.0% of the vote (followed by Bédié, who received 25.2%). Gbagbo and Ouattara contested a second ballot on 28 November 2010. On 2 December the CEI declared Ouattara as the victor, with 54.1% of the votes cast. On the following day, however, the President of the Constitutional Council, Paul Yao N'Dré (an ally of Gbagbo), announced that Gbagbo had won the election, after rejecting the second-round results. Citing voting irregularities, electoral violence, and a failure by the CEI formally to announce poll results within the legally mandated three-day period, the Constitutional Council annulled poll results in seven northern departments and proclaimed Gbagbo as President, ruling that he had received 51.5% of the votes cast. This outcome prompted a post-election confrontation between the two opposing sides that was to continue for four months.

Both Gbagbo and Ouattara claimed to have won the second round of the election, were sworn in to the presidency in separate ceremonies, and appointed cabinets, forming parallel administrations. Both claimed to exercise national executive authority over state institutions and took steps to consolidate their control. Ouattara established his Government in the Golf Hotel in Abidjan, where he resided under the protection of a reported 800 UNOCI troops.

The Constitutional Council's decision was widely viewed with scepticism, since it involved the invalidation of almost 600,000 votes, equivalent to 10.4% of the total registered electorate, or a highly unlikely 13% of all votes cast during the second round. Furthermore, all the annulled districts were located in northern regions that were considered Ouattara electoral strongholds and were largely controlled by the FN. The Special Representative of the UN Secretary-General for Côte d'Ivoire, Choi Young-Jin, endorsed Ouattara as the legitimate President, based on an independent tally process carried out entirely separately to that undertaken by the CEI. The UN, African regional organizations, including the AU and ECO-WAS, as well as most international governments, rejected Gbagbo as the elected leader of the country. Gbagbo, however, asserted that the international community's repudiation of the Constitutional Council's decision and its efforts to force him to concede the presidency infringed upon Ivorian national sovereignty and the constitutional rule of law.

On 2 December 2010 Gbagbo sealed the country's air, land and sea borders, without giving any reason for doing so. In mid-December pro-Ouattara demonstrators attempted to take control of the state-owned Radiodiffusion Télévision Ivorienne, which had been broadcasting pro-Gbagbo messages since the election. The action was violently suppressed by the security forces, which opened fire on the demonstrators, killing an estimated 20 and injuring many more. There were also raids on numerous opposition-affiliated newspapers and printing presses, and at least nine foreign journalists were detained during the post-electoral period. Clashes broke out between the two sides' military forces. Extrajudicial killings and other human rights abuses by state security forces during operations to suppress Ouattara's supporters were also reported. Furthermore, there were attacks on, and abductions of, Ouattara and Gbagbo partisans by groups of unidentified armed men, described as 'death squads'. In late January 2011 UNOCI comprised 9,024 troops and police, after being temporarily supplemented by several hundred additional troops from the neighbouring UN Mission in Liberia (UNMIL).

A new pro-Gbagbo militia, the Force de Résistance et de Libération de la Côte d'Ivoire, was formed, while in March 2011 Ouattara merged the military forces that had supported him into a new army under his control, the Forces Républicaines de Côte d'Ivoire (FRCI), with Soro as its commander. Police and other state security forces, in co-operation with youth groups, reportedly looted the homes and property of a number of Ouattara government officials in early March. Reports indicated that pro-Ouattara youth groups were carrying out similar actions against pro-Gbagbo officials. In some cases, militant supporters of both presidential claimants perpetrated attacks on individuals and communities based on their presumed ethnicity and supposed political affiliation. According to the human rights organization Amnesty International, from late March the members of the FRCI stepped up the level of violence in a campaign involving the systematic killing of hundreds of people in western Côte d'Ivoire.

OUATTARA'S FIRST PRESIDENTIAL MANDATE, 2011–15

On 11 April 2011 President Gbagbo was captured by pro-Ouattara forces, which had launched intensive military assaults on his residence in Abidjan since late March. Ouattara's forces were assisted by UNOCI personnel and by French troops. UNOCI confirmed that Gbagbo had 'surrendered' to the forces loyal to Ouattara. Heavy fighting, in which up to 3,000 people were believed to have been killed, had been waged in Abidjan for 11 days preceding Gbagbo's capture and arrest.

On 6 May 2011 Ouattara was officially sworn in as President. An inauguration ceremony attended by many heads of state, including French President Nicolas Sarkozy, followed two weeks later in Yamoussoukro. Ouattara subsequently requested that the International Criminal Court (ICC) investigate allegations of serious human rights crimes committed during the recent fighting. In June Ouattara appointed a new Government; Soro was retained as Prime Minister. It was subsequently announced that legislative elections would be held in December. In September Ouattara created a national Commission Dialogue, Vérité et Réconciliation (CDVR—Commission for Dialogue, Truth and Reconciliation), which had a two-year mandate.

In July 2011 Mamadou Koulibaly resigned as interim President of the FPI and established his own party, Liberté et Démocratie pour la République (LIDER). Later that month the FPI appointed Sylvain Miaka Oureto as its new interim President and demanded that the Government release Gbagbo and his associates from detention as a condition for national reconciliation and for FPI participation in the legislative elections. (The former President and his son, Michel Gbagbo, had been held under house arrest since April.) None the less, Laurent Gbagbo was transferred to the ICC in The Hague, Netherlands, in November to face four charges of crimes against humanity—murder, rape and other forms of sexual violence, persecution, and 'other inhuman acts'. (In March 2014 the Côte d'Ivoire authorities also transferred Charles Blé Goudé, a former FPI militia leader and Minister of Youth under Gbagbo, to face trial at the ICC.)

Côte d'Ivoire held its first legislative elections in more than a decade in December 2011. These polls ushered in the first democratically elected parliament since the expiry of the previous National Assembly's mandate in 2005. Despite an initial agreement between the RDR and the PDCI—RDA to submit candidates under the umbrella of the RHDP, both parties registered candidates separately in most of the 205 electoral districts. The FN fielded the majority of its candidates, including Soro, under the RDR banner. The FPI boycotted the vote.

Following the election, the CEI announced that the RDR had won 127 of the 255 parliamentary seats, while the PDCI—RDA secured 77, the UDPCI seven, the RHDP four, the MFA three and the Union pour la Côte d'Ivoire one; independent candidates gained control of 35 seats (several later joined the RDR-led alliance). According to the CEI, voter turnout was higher than in the 2000 parliamentary elections, with 2.7m. people casting their votes out of a registered electorate of 5.6m. Following the annulment of the results in 12 constituencies owing to alleged irregularities, polls for those seats were held again in late February 2012. According to final results published by the CEI in early March, the RDR held 138 of the 253 declared seats (the results remaining undeclared in two constituencies), the PDCI—RDA 86, independent candidates 17 and the UDPCI eight seats.

In early March 2012 Soro announced his resignation and that of his Government. Soro was elected President of the National Assembly in mid-March, following which Jeannot Ahoussou-Kouadio of the PDCI—RDA, and hitherto Minister of Justice, was appointed Prime Minister, while retaining the justice portfolio. All other members of the outgoing administration were reappointed to the posts that they had held under Soro.

Ouattara dissolved the Government in mid-November 2012 following a dispute among its members regarding legislation giving women equal rights with men within the family: members of the PDCI—RDA opposed to the measure had attempted to block the introduction of the new law in the National Assembly. Ahoussou was replaced as Prime Minister by Daniel Kablan Duncan, the premier in 1993–99, who had latterly held the post of Minister of Foreign Affairs. Duncan also assumed responsibility for the economy and finance in the new Council of Ministers, while Charles Koffi Diby was assigned the foreign affairs portfolio.

By mid-2013 the CDVR was facing severe criticism, although the Commission itself complained about a lack of financial resources and argued that its task had been complicated by political and legal interference. Furthermore, the Government had achieved little success in disarming and reintegrating former combatants from both sides. This resulted in persistent trafficking of weapons and light arms throughout the country, while the security forces themselves often acted with impunity. These elements all contributed to an enduring climate of instability and division along political and ethnic lines.

Following an announcement in November 2013 that the presidential election would be conducted in October 2015, there was increasing concern about the levels of political partisanship in the country and the lack of genuine reconciliation. The CDVR's mandate was extended in February 2014, but the Commission continued to attract criticism.

At the end of April 2014 the UN Security Council adopted a resolution that lifted the longstanding ban on the import of diamonds from Côte d'Ivoire, after the authorities were deemed to have complied with the requirements of the Kimberley Process, and also relaxed the arms embargo (differentiating between lethal and non-lethal arms). In June the Security Council authorized a further reduction in the size of UNOCI (which had already been reduced to 6,437 over the previous 18 months), stipulating a maximum of 5,437 personnel. The deployment of French forces in support of UNOCI was also authorized for a further year.

A new, 17-member CEI was inaugurated in August 2014. The trial of Gbagbo's wife, Simone, and 82 other supporters and officials, in relation to the events of 2010–11, began in Abidjan in December 2014. In March 2015 Simone Gbagbo, together with former commander of the Republic Guard Bruno Dogbo Blé and former head of the navy Adm. Vagba Faussignaux, were each sentenced to 20 years' imprisonment on the charge of undermining state security; 15 of the defendants were acquitted, and the others received lesser sentences. In March 2017 Simone Gbagbo was acquitted on charges of committing crimes against humanity by a court in Abidjan (after Ivorian authorities had refused to extradite her to the ICC in The Hague). Human rights groups criticized the verdict and questioned the impartiality of the judiciary. President Ouattara granted her an amnesty in August 2018 (one of 800 individuals he pardoned) and she was duly released from prison.

In April 2015 a rally of the ruling coalition nominated Ouattara as its presidential candidate in the forthcoming election. An opposition alliance, the Coalition Nationale pour le Changement (CNC), which was formed in May by Mamadou Koulibaly, the President of the National Assembly under Gbagbo, and which included leaders such as former premier Banny, organized a protest against Ouattara in Abidjan in June. The FPI designated former Prime Minister N'Guessan as its presidential candidate, causing a further rift within the main opposition party, with hardliners contesting his leadership and calling for a boycott of the election.

The election campaign was marked by tensions, notably among the FPI hardliners who used the CNC to voice their demands. In early September 2015 the CNC presented a series of grievances, including security issues linked to the country's political transition, and threatened to prevent the vote being held. In addition, clashes broke out in mid-September between opposition and government supporters, with some sections of the opposition reviving the theory that Ouattara was not eligible to stand. Ouattara, meanwhile, conducted a nationwide campaign, making full use of the tools of incumbency, including state visits, state media coverage, and strict security to suppress unauthorized opposition gatherings.

The election took place on 25 October 2015 in the absence of violence or major incidents. The CEI declared a turnout of 56.4%, although some opposition strongholds registered a turnout below 40% following calls for a boycott. Ouattara was re-elected for a second term, winning an overwhelming majority with 83.7% of the vote, while his main rival N'Guessan garnered only 9.3%.

OUATTARA'S SECOND PRESIDENTIAL MANDATE, 2015–20

In January 2016 Ouattara reappointed Duncan as Prime Minister and a new Government was named the following week. While being expanded to include more women (10 compared with the previous five) and to improve the regional and ethnic balances, the key faces of the previous Government remained.

The first months of Ouattara's second mandate were marked by ongoing post-conflict concerns. In early December 2015 an attack on the south-western town of Olodio raised concerns about security in that part of the country. In February 2016 the trial of former President Gbagbo and former militia leader Blé Goudé opened before the ICC in The Hague. In April a report by the UN Group of Experts on Côte d'Ivoire expressed serious concerns about the stockpiling of unregistered weapons in 2011 in breach of UN sanctions. The report alleged that Soro had played an orchestrating role in their importation. Soro had also been accused in January 2016 of having been involved in a coup against Burkina Faso's transitional regime in September 2015.

In April 2016 the UN Security Council renewed the mandate of UNOCI for a final period, until 30 June 2017 (when the mission was terminated), and lifted all arms, travel and financial sanctions against Côte d'Ivoire, with immediate effect, citing the progress that the country had made in terms of disarmament, demobilization and national reconciliation. In July 2016, in a further sign of the normalization of the political situation, four prominent supporters of former President Gbagbo, including former Minister of Defence, Kadet Bertin, returned from self-imposed exile in Ghana.

In October 2016 Ouattara presented a new Constitution, in accordance with his presidential campaign pledge. The draft was overwhelmingly approved by the National Assembly, with 239 votes in favour. Key institutional changes included the creation of a vice-presidency and an upper legislative chamber, the Senate. The Vice-President would be elected alongside the President and complete the President's term if required. The Senate would be elected indirectly through the regions, with the President appointing one-third of its members. Eligibility was also to be amended so that a potential presidential candidate need only have one documented Ivorian parent, thus closing the national identity debate that had fuelled Côte d'Ivoire's crisis in the 2000s.

The Constitution was submitted to a referendum in October 2016. Opposition calls for a boycott were fragmented and ineffective, though turnout at the referendum was low, at 42.4%, according to official figures. The new Constitution was none the less approved by 93.4% of votes cast and signed into law on 8 November.

The legislative elections took place peacefully on 18 December 2016. As with the referendum, turnout was low, at just 34.1%. The ruling RHDP coalition won an outright majority, securing 167 of the 255 National Assembly seats and increasing its representation by 30 seats; the UDPCI obtained six seats, the FPI only three and the Union pour la Côte d'Ivoire (previously part of the RHDP alliance) also three; independent candidates secured the remaining 75 seats. In early January 2017 Ouattara appointed Duncan, the outgoing Prime Minister, to the newly created post of Vice-President. Two days later Duncan and Amadou Gon Coulibaly, a former Secretary-General of the Presidency who had been named as Duncan's successor as premier, formed a new Government in which most of the previous ministers retained their portfolios. Preparations subsequently began for the organization of polls to elect a Senate.

The first half of 2017 was dominated by a series of public sector strikes and military revolts. The latter started with an ultimately unsuccessful uprising by low-ranking soldiers on 6–7 January in Bouaké over unpaid bonuses promised to 8,400 former rebel soldiers. Ouattara subsequently ordered that the heads of the police, the gendarmerie and the army be replaced by their deputies. Unrest flared up again on 13–14 January. Following tense negotiations, the Government agreed to pay part of the overdue bonuses immediately and the remainder in instalments. Another revolt, by special forces stationed in Adiaké on the Ghanaian border, erupted in early February over unpaid bonuses but was rapidly quelled following negotiations and an undisclosed settlement. Yet another uprising among demobilized members of the FN demanding jobs and the payment of the same bonus promised to active soldiers was quelled in Bouaké at the beginning of May before spreading to several other cities including Abidjan. This time, the Government dispatched loyalist troops to Bouaké before negotiating once again and agreeing to the payment of bonuses.

Following weeks of unrest, in July 2017 President Ouattara carried out a reorganization of the Council of Ministers: among notable changes was the replacement of Alain-Richard Donwahi as Minister of Defence by the erstwhile Minister of the Interior and Security, Hamed Bakayoko, who, on taking office, stated that the army needed to be reformed. The vacated interior and security portfolio was assigned to Sidiki Diakité, while Prime Minister Coulibaly took charge of the Ministry of the Budget and the State Portfolio.

In February 2018 President Ouattara published a decree setting the date of the country's first senatorial election as 24 March. There were to be 99 senators, with 66 to be elected by local elected representatives (two per region) and 33 to be appointed by the President. Opposition parties organized a demonstration in Abidjan to protest against the decree, which it considered as a further attempt at concentrating power by the ruling coalition. The new Senate was inaugurated on 12 April, with 50 of the 66 elected Senators coming from the ruling coalition, and the other 16 being independents. Ahoussou-Kouadio of the PDCI—RDA was elected as President of the new chamber.

The following months were marked by tensions between the ruling coalition partners (the PDCI—RDA and President Ouattara's RDR), with both parties attempting to nominate the coalition's candidate for the next presidential election in 2020 from their own ranks. President Ouattara did not rule out seeking a further term in office, suggesting that his election victories in 2010 and 2015 did not count towards the two-term limit set in the 2016 Constitution. Furthermore, in April 2018 President Ouattara announced the reformation of the umbrella RHDP, which included his own RDR, the PDCI—RDA, the UDPCI and elements from the smaller parties of the UPCI, the MFA and the PIT. In July the PDCI—RDA voted to appoint its leader, Bédié, as its presidential candidate, thus breaking the coalition agreement. In response, Ouattara dissolved premier Coulibaly's Government on 4 July, although he immediately reappointed him as Prime Minister. A new Government was formed on 10 July, again comprising the RDR and the PDCI—RDA, though in early August Bédié announced that the PDCI—RDA was to leave the coalition. This led to tensions and reshuffles within the PDCI—RDA, with Bédié removing several pro-RHDP executives and replacing them with others loyal to him.

Ahead of the municipal and regional elections of October 2018, opposition parties called for a boycott in the absence of reforms of the electoral commission that Ouattara had promised. The polls were marred by violence between opposing activists, and five people were reportedly killed. The RHDP won a majority, taking control of 92 municipalities—including most municipalities in Abidjan—and 18 regional councils.

On 15 January 2019 the ICC acquitted Gbagbo and Blé Goudé of crimes against humanity, after deeming the burden of proof brought by the prosecution 'exceptionally weak'. Gbagbo was released on 1 February, but was ordered to reside in Belgium pending an appeal by the prosecutors. (The appeal was rejected on 31 March 2021 by the Appeals Chamber of the ICC and Gbagbo was allowed to return to Côte d'Ivoire in June 2021.)

In January 2019 talks on the reform of the CEI began between the Government and 17 political parties, ahead of the 2020 presidential election. The opposition sought a restructuring, including guarantees of independent supervision of the commission's funding and membership and a redrawing of electoral boundaries. In early February Soro resigned from his position as President of the National Assembly, after refusing to join Ouattara's RHDP. Amadou Soumahoro, the RHDP's candidate, was elected to replace him in March, in a vote largely boycotted by the opposition members of the legislature. In April Soro left the country amid reports of intensifying disputes with Ouattara. In July the National Assembly voted to approve a reduction in the membership of the CEI from 17 to 15 members. The new commission was appointed in October.

In September 2019 the Government was reshuffled and expanded, in a move interpreted by many observers as an attempt by President Ouattara to strengthen his grip over the ruling RHDP. In December the Public Prosecutor issued an international arrest warrant against Soro, who in October had declared his intention to stand as an independent candidate in the 2020 presidential election, accusing him of endangering state security, embezzlement of public funds and money laundering. Both moves were widely interpreted as attempts by

Ouattara to undermine potential rivals ahead of the election. Ouattara himself announced unexpectedly on 5 March 2020 that he would not seek a third presidential term. One week later, Prime Minister Coulibaly was designated as the RHDP's presidential candidate.

On 11 March 2020 Côte d'Ivoire reported its first confirmed case of COVID-19, amid the escalating pandemic. On 23 March, when Côte d'Ivoire had reported 25 cases, a national state of emergency was declared: the land, sea and air borders were closed; a night curfew was implemented; and unauthorized travel between Abidjan and the interior of the country was prohibited. Domestic flights resumed at the end of June and international flights on 1 July, while hospitality outlets, mostly closed since March, were authorized to reopen.

Meanwhile, on 22 April 2020 the AU's African Court on Human and Peoples' Rights ordered Côte d'Ivoire to suspend its arrest warrant against Soro and to release those of his relatives who had been imprisoned. Instead, a court convicted Soro *in absentia* of embezzlement of public funds and sentenced him to 20 years' imprisonment. In May–June he was tried, again *in absentia*, on separate charges relating to a December 2019 plot to overthrow the government and sentenced to life imprisonment, together with the seizure of his assets.

On 20 June 2020 former President Henri Konan Bédié, the leader of the PDCI—RDA, confirmed his candidacy for the presidential election to be held on 31 October. Voter registration was completed by the CEI by early July. On 8 July, however, Prime Minister Coulibaly, the candidate of the ruling RHDP, died (he had previously travelled to France for medical treatment in May); Vice-President Duncan resigned his post just five days later, ostensibly for personal reasons. Tensions within the ruling party were further highlighted when former Minister of Foreign Affairs Marcel Amon-Tanoh, who had resigned from the Government in March following the announcement of Coulibaly's candidacy, presented his own candidacy, thus breaking ranks with the RHDP. Tanoh's announcement prompted RHDP deputies to call on President Ouattara to reverse his earlier decision and stand for re-election. On 29 July Ouattara was designated by all structures of the RHDP as the party's official candidate; he accepted the nomination one week later. The announcement of Ouattara's candidacy was immediately followed by widespread protests across the country, in which at least six people were killed. The Government banned protests on 14 August.

On 14 September 2020 the Constitutional Council approved the registration of only four of the 45 prospective presidential candidates: Ouattara; former President Bédié; FPI leader N'Guessan (representing a joint PDCI-FPI ticket); and Kouadio Konan Bertin, a former PDCI—RDA dissident. The Council thus confirmed that the Constitution adopted in 2016 allowed Ouattara to seek a third mandate. The candidacies of both Soro and former President Gbagbo, on the other hand, were rejected, on grounds of their previous criminal convictions. Following the Council's decision, riots were reported in urban centres across the country. Later in September both Bédié and N'Guessan urged opposition parties to form a coalition, demanding that Ouattara stand down and that the Constitutional Council and the CEI be reformed. Two of the CEI's four opposition members also withdrew from the body, while a third had refused to take the inaugural oath. In October the opposition organized a large gathering in Abidjan despite the ban on public protests, and called for civil disobedience and a boycott of the poll; Bédié and N'Guessan did not campaign. Violence, often fomented on social media, escalated ahead of the poll, notably in the country's south and east.

OUATTARA'S THIRD PRESIDENTIAL MANDATE, 2020–

The presidential election took place on 31 October 2020, amid widespread violence that prevented voting from proceeding in about one-fifth of polling stations. The CEI announced provisional results on 3 November, awarding Ouattara 94% of the votes cast, with a 53.9% turnout.

The result was immediately contested by the opposition, which announced the creation of the Conseil National de la Transition (CNT), a National Transitional Council, headed by Bédié, with N'Guessan as its spokesperson. The aim of the council was to form a transitional government that would organize new elections in the following months. On 7 November 2020 21 opposition leaders, including N'Guessan, were arrested, while Bédié was placed under house arrest; 12 of them were later charged with acts of terrorism and conspiracy against the authority of the state, murder, robbery with violence, theft and destruction of property, and with organizing and participating in an insurrectionary movement. Clashes in towns across the country caused an estimated 85 deaths and the displacement of several thousand Ivorians to neighbouring countries. On 9 November the Constitutional Court confirmed that Ouattara had been elected to a further term with 95.3% of votes cast. On 11 November Ouattara and Bédié met in order to initiate talks and resolve tensions. The following day the opposition issued statements welcoming the talks but also demanding the release of opposition leaders and further discussions on reform of the electoral registers, the CEI and the Constitutional Council. Further talks ensued and on 9 December Bédié disbanded the CNT. Ouattara was officially reinstalled as President on 14 December. N'Guessan was released from prison under judicial supervision on 31 December.

In January 2021 the deadline for the submission of candidates to contest the 6 March legislative elections was extended by two days in order to allow all parties to present their lists. The main opposition parties confirmed their participation, while seven smaller parties, including Soro's newly founded Générations et Peuples Solidaires, announced that they would boycott the election. The elections on 6 March took place peacefully and, notably, with the participation of the FPI for the first time in a decade. Voter turnout was low, at 51.4%, owing to fears of violence. President Ouattara's RHDP won 137 of the 254 contested seats, while a coalition of the PDCI—RDA and the Ensemble pour la Démocratie et la Souveraineté, a grouping of organizations supporting Gbagbo (including the FPI), won 50 seats.

On 18 February 2021 Prime Minister Hamed Bakayoko, who had succeeded Coulibaly in July 2020, was evacuated to France for health reasons. He was then flown to Germany, where he died on 10 March. On 8 March Patrick Achi, the Secretary-General at the Presidency, was named interim Prime Minister, and Téné Birahima Ouattara, a brother of the President, was named interim Minister of State, Minister of Defence. Following the legislative elections, Achi was confirmed as Prime Minister on 26 March and his Government appointed on 6 April; Téné Birahima Ouattara was confirmed in his post, while Vagondo Diomandé became Minister of the Interior and Security, and Kandia Kamissoko Camara was appointed as the new Minister of State, Minister of Foreign Affairs, African Integration and the Diaspora.

In late July 2021 President Ouattara, pursuing his reconciliation and peace strategy, met his predecessor Laurent Gbagbo, who had been allowed to return to Côte d'Ivoire the previous month, following the dismissal of the appeal against his acquittal by the ICC. At a leadership meeting of the FPI in August, Gbagbo announced that he was leaving the party, where he retained some factional popularity. He launched a new party, the Parti des Peuples Africains—Côte d'Ivoire (PPACI) in October.

In November 2021 Prime Minister Achi announced that the political dialogue between the ruling party and the opposition would resume in December. On 27 December the Government released a report into the unrest that had surrounded the 2020 presidential election. The report blamed opposition activists and politicians for stoking instability during this period, and the public prosecutor, Richard Adou, stated that charges would be brought against those who organized the unrest. None the less, the political dialogue between the Government and the opposition continued until March 2022, with agreement being reached on the need to reform the CEI, redraw some constituency boundaries, establish a process of compensation for the victims of the political violence that followed the 2020 presidential election and strengthen the role of local chiefs, religious leaders and civil society organizations in conflict resolution.

On 13 April 2022 Prime Minister Achi submitted his resignation and that of this Government—President Ouattara reappointed him six days later, together with a cabinet of 32 members, reduced from 41. President Ouattara also appointed Tiémoko Meyliet Koné, the former Governor of the BCEAO, to the position of Vice-President, which had been vacant since July 2020. In July President Ouattara met with former presidents Gbagbo and Bédié, in a further effort to promote reconciliation.

By mid-July 2022 Côte d'Ivoire had recorded a total of 84,347 cases of COVID-19, with 806 deaths. The state of health emergency, which had been lifted at the end of August 2020, was reinstated in late January 2021, and regularly extended thereafter, with the latest extension announced in early July 2022. Côte d'Ivoire was among the first sub-Saharan African countries to receive a shipment of vaccine under the World Health Organization's COVAX Facility, the global scheme established to provide vaccines to low-income nations, receiving some 500,000 doses in late February 2021. The vaccination programme proceeded slowly at first, but by the end of May this initial stock had nearly been exhausted. By mid-July 2022 Côte d'Ivoire had administered 14.4m. vaccine doses and by late August 31.6% of its population was fully vaccinated.

FOREIGN RELATIONS AND REGIONAL CONCERNS

Throughout his presidency Houphouët-Boigny tended to favour the maintenance of close links with the West. Relations with France remained cordial following Bédié's accession to the presidency. However, in 1999 the deterioration in the political situation in Côte d'Ivoire attracted considerable concern among the country's regional and international allies. The coup in December, which brought Brig.-Gen. Robert Gueï to power, was widely condemned by France, the USA and the Organization of African Unity (OAU, now the AU), although intervention to reinstate Bédié was ruled out. In January 2000 the OAU ordered the military regime to announce a schedule for democratic elections or face exclusion from the July OAU summit.

International Relations in the 2000s

Despite expressing disapproval at the exclusion of Ouattara from the elections in 2000, France recommended limited co-operation with Côte d'Ivoire in January 2001, with bilateral aid resuming from May. From late 2002 France dispatched 3,500 additional troops to Côte d'Ivoire, under a mission codenamed Operation Licorne, to supplement the 550 already stationed in the country, and the French Government took an active role in the diplomatic efforts that led to the signature of the Marcoussis Accords in January 2003 (see above). None the less, there was widespread anti-French feeling, particularly in Abidjan, following the conclusion of the Accords. After the destruction of the Ivorian air force by the French military in early November 2004, in retaliation for an Ivorian bombing raid that had resulted in the deaths of nine French peacekeeping troops (see above), numerous French targets in Abidjan, including schools, businesses and homes, were attacked. French troops entered Abidjan to secure the international airport and to protect French citizens, airlifting many of them out of the city. Some 600 troops were dispatched to reinforce France's military presence in Côte d'Ivoire, while diplomatic relations between the two countries remained tense. The French military contingent in Côte d'Ivoire remained the target of anti-colonial sentiment among Gbagbo's supporters, and in January 2009 the French Government announced that Operation Licorne would be reduced from 2,000 to 900 troops.

After the rebellion of September 2002 and the effective division of Côte d'Ivoire, at least 1m. immigrants living and working in the south were forced to flee, losing their jobs and property. Many Burkinabè businesses were destroyed. As stability appeared to return to Côte d'Ivoire, the border with Burkina Faso, closed since the onset of the rebellion, was reopened in September 2003. In July 2004 representatives of the two countries pledged to combat 'destabilizing acts' against their respective countries and agreed to increase co-operation in security and defence matters. In late 2006 relations with the Burkinabè Government began to improve, after President Blaise Compaoré offered to mediate in the crisis; he subsequently became involved in peace negotiations and presided over the signature of the Ouagadougou Accord (see above). In

July 2008, on his first state visit to Burkina Faso, Gbagbo signed a treaty of friendship and co-operation with Compaoré. In early 2010 the Ivorian Minister of Economy and Finance pledged to pay an outstanding debt to the Burkinabè Post Office of 3,200m. francs CFA, non-payment of which had caused the suspension of transactions between the two countries since 2000 and had adversely affected the 3m. Burkinabè citizens working in Ivorian cocoa plantations.

In August 2006 a Panamanian-registered ship, *Probo Koala*, illegally unloaded toxic waste, including petroleum residue, sulphur and caustic soda, at several locations around Abidjan. The ship had been in the custody of Trafigura, a Dutch company linked with Nigerian and Ivorian business interests. In February 2007 Gbagbo signed an agreement with Trafigura, under which the company agreed to pay €152m. towards a clean-up operation, the construction of a local waste processing factory (and in compensation to the victims), in return for immunity from prosecution. In 2008 a British law firm representing Ivorians affected by the toxic waste launched a class action against Trafigura in the British courts. In September 2009 the British High Court approved a £30m. payout. Trafigura would pay 750,000 francs CFA to each of the 31,000 victims in the suit. In March 2010 the Dutch Supreme Court ruled that the Dutch city of Amsterdam would face full responsibility for failing to supervise the ship.

International Response during the Political Crisis and Transition

The conflict over the results of the 2010 presidential election (see above) prompted wide-ranging international political, financial, and threatened military pressure, which was aimed at forcing Gbagbo to concede the outcome and relinquish state power to Ouattara. In early December former President of South Africa Thabo Mbeki attempted to mediate the issue on behalf of the AU, but with no success. The USA, the UN, the EU and ECOWAS, as well as former colonial power France, affirmed support for Ouattara. In late December Presidents Yayi Boni of Benin, Ernest Bai Koroma of Sierra Leone and Pedro Pires of Cabo Verde were dispatched by ECOWAS to attempt to convince Gbagbo to resign and go into exile, in order to avert the deployment of military force against him. In February 2011, in response to the continued political impasse, Operation Licorne was strengthened to 1,100 troops (and subsequently to 1,600). French forces played an important role in the capture of Gbagbo in April, and French advisers supported the country's economic reconstruction once Ouattara had taken office. In January 2012 Ouattara made his first state visit to France, where he signed a new security agreement with President Nicolas Sarkozy; by that time the French military contingent in Côte d'Ivoire had been reduced to around 500.

The role of France as intermediator in the post-election crisis also received considerable international attention. The complete withdrawal of French troops was considered by many to be essential in order not to taint President Ouattara's chances to achieve national reconciliation. The Chairman of the AU declared that foreign military intervention was unjustified.

In May 2014 French Minister of Defence Jean-Yves Le Drian, during a visit to Côte d'Ivoire, announced that, with effect from January 2015, Operation Licorne was to be restructured as a logistical hub and advance operational military presence for a new French mechanism mandated to combat terrorism in the Sahel region. Legislation governing future defence co-operation between Côte d'Ivoire and France was endorsed by President Ouattara in July 2014. In January 2015 Operation Licorne was officially reconstituted as Forces Françaises en Côte d'Ivoire, comprising around 800 French troops stationed in Abidjan.

Post-election Regional Concerns

After taking office in May 2011, Ouattara voiced concerns for the security of the wider West African region due to activities involving mercenaries loyal to former President Gbagbo who had fled to neighbouring countries. The UN substantiated reports that in the immediate post-electoral period, pro-Gbagbo troops had been assisted by mercenaries from Liberia, and possibly from other countries. Since December 2010, more than 100,000 people had fled Côte d'Ivoire, amid continued unrest in the west of the country, mainly to Liberia, Ghana, Guinea and Togo. A spokesman for the UN High Commissioner for Refugees (UNHCR) accused mercenaries from neighbouring Liberia of taking advantage of the lawlessness to loot, rape and kill in the Guiglo region, close to the Liberian border. In August 2011 UNHCR signed an accord with the Governments of Côte d'Ivoire and Liberia to facilitate the voluntary repatriation of Ivorian refugees from Liberia.

In early June 2012 a militia group allegedly crossed from Liberia into western Côte d'Ivoire, where it ambushed and killed seven UN peacekeepers and 10 civilians near the Ivorian border town of Tai; the UN described the incident as the worst attack against peacekeepers in Côte d'Ivoire since 2004. The Ivorian authorities attributed the ambush to Liberian mercenaries and Ivorian militants loyal to former President Gbagbo. Senior Ivorian officials held discussions with their Liberian counterparts and representatives of UNOCI and UNMIL later in June 2012. The talks ended with a joint communiqué pledging to stabilize territory on both sides of the border, improve information exchanges, tighten extradition procedures and increase consultation with community leaders. The two countries also expressed a wish to reactivate their bilateral commission, which had been established in the 1970s but subsequently rendered inactive by the civil war in Liberia. Renewed attacks on military positions close to the Liberian border in 2014–15 led to new talks between the Liberian President, Ellen Johnson Sirleaf, and Ouatarra. The two Presidents met in Abidjan in January 2016, before travelling together to Guiglo, to meet traditional rulers from border areas of both countries. In September Côte d'Ivoire officially reopened its borders with Liberia and Guinea, two years after closing them during the 2014 Ebola epidemic that had struck both of these neighbouring countries. In April 2021 Liberian militants attacked the military camp of Abobo, near Abidjan. The Governments of Côte d'Ivoire and Liberia subsequently committed to strengthening joint border surveillance.

In August 2013 a request made by the Government of Côte d'Ivoire for the extradition of a former spokesman and minister for the budget under Gbagbo, Justin Koné Katinan, was rejected by a Ghanaian judge on the grounds that charges against him were politically motivated. In December a UN expert panel report noted claims by Ghanaian officials that Côte d'Ivoire had sent 'hit squads' to abduct or kill pro-Gbagbo exiles and that the authorities had thwarted two such attempts. In September 2014, following a longstanding dispute between Côte d'Ivoire and Ghana concerning the delineation of their territorial waters, Ghana sought international arbitration. In April 2015 the International Tribunal for the Law of the Sea (ITLOS) ruled that Ghana should not begin any new offshore drilling, but was allowed to continue developing current oilfields in the area disputed with Côte d'Ivoire (which had requested the suspension of all drilling), pending a ruling on the maritime border. In September 2017 ITLOS ruled in favour of Ghana. In a sign that relations between the two countries were warming, a strategic partnership was pledged by their heads of state during an official visit to Côte d'Ivoire by the Ghanaian President, Nana Akufo-Addo, in May 2017.

Relations with Burkina Faso were threatened by the fall in late 2015 of the Burkinabè President, Compaoré, a close ally of Ouatarra who found asylum in Abidjan, prompting accusations that Côte d'Ivoire was protecting him. These were exacerbated by suspicions of Ivorian involvement—notably by the President of the National Assembly and former rebel leader, Guillaume Soro—in a failed coup against Burkina Faso's transitional Government in September.

In 2017 Burkina Faso, Benin, Côte d'Ivoire, Ghana and Togo began the Accra Initiative, a joint effort to prevent insecurity in the Sahel region from spilling over through intelligence sharing, training and joint operations. In May 2018 Mali, Burkina Faso and Côte d'Ivoire announced that they were to establish a special economic zone (SEZ) across their border area, encompassing the regions of Sikasso (in Mali), Bobo-Dioulasso (Burkina Faso) and Korhogo (Côte d'Ivoire), with the intention of signalling a normalization of trilateral relations and taking a further step towards economic integration in the region. While plans for an SEZ were confirmed in 2019–20, their implementation in the near term was threatened by the remilitarization of borders, in response to a growing threat of extremist activity in the border region, and by the global economic crisis brought about by the COVID-19 pandemic. This threat became more tangible during 2020–21, as the military post of Kafolo, near the northern border with Burkina Faso, was attacked on two occasions. In July 2020 the Government announced the creation of a special military zone in northern Côte d'Ivoire, in order to prevent the infiltration of armed jihadist groups from neighbouring Mali or Burkina Faso. In March-June 2021 four attacks against Ivorian security forces were reported in the border area, each claiming several lives. In late November President Ouattara announced plans for the recruitment of 3,000 new soldiers in 2022 and a total of 10,000 by 2024 in order to bolster counter-insurgency capabilities. That same month, Côte d'Ivoire, along with Burkina Faso, Ghana and Togo conducted a joint cross-border military operation as part of the Accra Initiative, in which weapons, ammunition, bomb-making material, vehicles and drugs were seized and up to 300 suspected jihadis were arrested.

Relations with Mali soured in 2022 as Mali experienced two successive military coups and Côte d'Ivoire supported economic and financial sanctions against Mali's military authorities. In July Mali arrested 49 Ivorian soldiers, who were on a rotation in support of the United Nations Multidimensional Integrated Stabilisation Mission (MINUSMA) at the international airport in Bamako. The Malian authorities described them as 'mercenaries', while the Ivorian Government demanded their immediate release.

Economy

MARIE GIBERT

INTRODUCTION

For some 20 years following independence, Côte d'Ivoire was remarkable for its very high rate of economic growth. Gross domestic product (GDP) increased, in real terms, at an average annual rate of 11% in 1960–70 and 6%–7% in 1970–80, bringing it into the ranks of middle-income developing countries. During the 1980s the economy entered a period of overall decline. By late 1994, however, a marked recovery was in progress, with annual GDP growth reaching an average of 6.3% per year in 1995–98. A stimulus for this recovery was the 50% devaluation of the CFA franc in January 1994, which improved the competitiveness of Côte d'Ivoire's timber and non-traditional exports, such as fish and rubber, at a time when a boom in international prices for coffee was coming to an end. The economy's promising performance was interrupted by Henri Konan Bédié's Government's loss of policy control in 1998 and 1999, and the suspension of disbursements by the European Union (EU) and the International Monetary Fund (IMF, see below). The military overthrow of the Bédié Government in December 1999, and the subsequent political instability that persisted after 2000 severely limited new foreign investment.

Following the outbreak of civil conflict in November 2002, which severely disrupted cocoa and cotton output, real GDP contracted by 1.7% in 2002 and 1.4% in 2003. The political crisis had a serious effect on economic activity, with a sharp decline in agro-processing and manufacturing. A modest recovery followed, although economic growth was erratic as a result of persistent political uncertainty. Economic activity came to a practical halt during the fighting that followed the political impasse from November 2010 until the end of April 2011 (see *History*). As a result of the political crisis, real GDP contracted by 4.4% in 2011. None the less, with an improvement in the security situation, the lifting of sanctions, a resumption of international co-operation, greater public investment, more diversified economic development (beyond natural resources and agriculture), and a recovery in final consumption, real GDP grew at an average annual rate of 8.9% in 2012–16, according to the World Bank. The growth rate remained strong, if slightly lower, at an average of 7.1% in 2016–19. Prior to the global outbreak of COVID-19 in early 2020, growth was initially predicted to fall only slightly, to 7.0%, over the following years. Côte d'Ivoire, however, was deeply affected by the pandemic and the consequent global lockdown: GDP growth of only 2.3% was recorded in 2020. The rate rose again, to 7.0%, in 2021, but was projected to fall slightly to 6.0% (later amended to 5.7% amid challenging global economic conditions) in 2022. The main long-term concern is the country's dependence on cocoa, which renders the economy vulnerable to price fluctuations on international markets.

Inflation remained low in 2003–07, averaging an annual 2.9%, but rose sharply in 2008, reaching 6.3%, as the authorities were forced to introduce emergency measures to alleviate high international prices for oil and food. From late 2008, however, inflationary pressures moderated. According to figures from the IMF, annual average inflation reached 4.9% in 2011, before declining to reach 0.4% in 2014, following a decrease in food prices, then varying between 1.2% and 0.4% annually over the next five years. Average annual inflation increased to 2.5% in 2020 and 4.1% in 2021, as a result of the pandemic-induced crisis.

The census of 2021 enumerated the total population at 29,389,150. According to official figures, population growth averaged about 3.3% per year between 1988 and 1998, falling to an average annual rate of 2.4% in 1998–2021. Although mounting political instability and inter-ethnic tensions in the early 2000s prompted a significant proportion of the immigrant population to leave Côte d'Ivoire, at the 2021 census non-Ivorian nationals still constituted 22% of the population. The rate of urban growth has been rapid (at around 150% of the overall rate of population growth) and, according to the World Bank, 52% of the total population resided in urban areas in 2021. Abidjan's population was measured at 5.4m. in the 2021 census (compared with 2.9m. in the 1998 census). Population pressure on Abidjan was a significant factor in the designation of Yamoussoukro as the country's political capital from 1983, although Abidjan remains the principal centre for economic activity.

The country's demographic patterns were drastically altered by the upheavals that commenced in 2002, with over 1m. people estimated to have been internally displaced; according to the Office of the United Nations (UN) High Commissioner for Refugees, this figure had declined to some 300,000 by February 2015. Pending detailed results of the 2021 census, the country's second largest city, Bouaké, had an estimated population of 705,000 that same year and Yamoussoukro, the capital, 300,000.

In terms of Côte d'Ivoire's performance on the UN's Human Development Index (HDI), a composite measure of three basic dimensions of human development (health, education and income), the country has shown steady progress. Between 1980 and 2021 Côte d'Ivoire's HDI rose at an average annual rate of 1.1%, from 0.348 to 0.550, giving the country a ranking in 2021 of 159th out of 191 countries with comparable data, and remaining just above the threshold for a ranking of medium human development, first reached in 2019. Since the HDI of sub-Saharan Africa as a region increased from 0.366 in 1980 to 0.547 in 2021, Côte d'Ivoire performed slightly better than the regional average, and it now outranks all of its neighbours, with the exception of Ghana. According to the World Bank, life expectancy in 2021 was estimated at 58.6 years.

AGRICULTURE, FORESTRY AND FISHING

The Ivorian economy is strongly dependent on agriculture, which, together with forestry and fishing, contributed 21.4% of GDP in 2020, according to provisional official figures. Agriculture employed 40% of the labour force in 2019. The sector provides about three-quarters of export earnings, and its rapid growth was the basis for the economic expansion of the 1960s and 1970s. In 2010–20, according to World Bank estimates, agricultural GDP increased at an average annual rate of 3.1%. During the late 2010s the rate of growth fluctuated between a high of 16.2% in 2014 and a contraction of 4.0% in 2016.

Cocoa has become the mainstay of the Ivorian economy and currently contributes approximately 15% of GDP. In 2018 an estimated 600,000 smallholder farmers were growing cocoa, and an estimated 6m. people depended on the wages drawn from cocoa production. The country became the world's largest cocoa producer after 1977, when its level of production overtook that of Ghana. Overall output continued to rise and in the main crop season of 1999/2000 (October–September) it reached 1.4m. metric tons. This increase owed much to a major replanting programme implemented by the Government in the 1980s. The outbreak of the civil conflict in 2002 cut off cocoa growing areas from the government-held coast and caused the flight of thousands of immigrant workers from the plantations, stifling growth. The political impasse of late 2010 to mid-2011 (see *History*) most severely affected the cocoa sector, where international sanctions had the greatest impact. However, following the restoration of some stability in the country, production recovered. The country's first industrial-scale chocolate factory, with an annual production capacity of 10,000 tons, opened in May 2015. Others followed and by 2019 Côte d'Ivoire processed about 20% of its own cocoa. In September 2020 Côte d'Ivoire's Coffee and Cocoa Council (CCC), the industry regulatory body, announced plans to increase its cocoa processing capacity, which stood at 710,000 tons, by 110,000 tons, and to strengthen storage capacity, with the establishment of two new processing plants, one in Abidjan and the other in San-Pédro, by 2022. Construction of the sites was to be financed by Chinese investment amounting to 216,000m. francs CFA ($389m.), and undertaken by China Light Industry Design Engineering Company. About 40% of processed output would be designated for the People's Republic of China. Cocoa output reached a record 2.2m. tons in 2020.

Under pressure from the World Bank and the IMF, Côte d'Ivoire initiated a series of reforms in the cocoa sector in early 2012, establishing a new regulatory body for coffee and cocoa, the Conseil du Café-Cacao (CCC). The principal change was the introduction of a minimum reference price for cocoa, replacing the indicative price used in previous seasons, which was routinely flouted by local buyers at the farm gate. The overriding aim was to ensure that farmers received at least 60%–70% of the international price throughout the season. In June 2018 Ghana and Côte d'Ivoire announced that they had reached an agreement jointly to manage the production, marketing and transformation of their cocoa crops from the 2018/19 season in order to avoid crops being trafficked across borders. In June 2019 both countries announced that they would apply a living income differential for cocoa farmers if global market prices fell below $2,600 per ton of exported cocoa. In August it was announced that they would set a price floor of $2,600 from 1 October, and in September 2019 the introduction of a ceiling on production was proposed. In August 2020 Ghana and Côte d'Ivoire announced the creation of a joint body, the Ivory Coast-Ghana Cocoa Initiative (ICCIG), to improve co-ordination across their cocoa sectors in research, price-setting and the fight against child labour in the sector. On 30 November Côte d'Ivoire and Ghana announced that they had withdrawn from membership of a US cocoa industry association, the Cocoa Merchants' Association of America, accusing the body of helping US chocolate companies to avoid paying the living income differential.

In January 2021 the effects of the COVID-19 pandemic were becoming apparent, as the CCC reported that several metric tons of cocoa beans remained undelivered at the port of Abidjan and that it was obliged to suspend the registration of new stocks from rural areas. In reaction to this, but also to attempts by buyers to undercut prices and the non-payment of arrears by the Government from the 2017/18 season, the cocoa-growers' unions announced a strike. The strike was cancelled, however, after the Government convened an urgent meeting and reassured the unions that it would support the sector in the pandemic-induced crisis. In mid-February the CCC announced that it had reduced the high-quality premium that cocoa exporters pay by \$443 per ton, in an effort to revive weak sales. In October a new 'farm gate' price (i.e. the market price less selling costs) of 825 francs CFA/kg was announced for the 2021/22 season, thus raising sales prospects but limiting the capacity of farmers to offset the increase in fertilizer prices resulting from the Russian Federation's 2022 invasion of Ukraine. As a result of these higher production costs and poor weather in mid-year, national cocoa production was expected to decrease to 2.15m. tons, in 2021/22. In May 2022 Côte d'Ivoire and Ghana announced that they would jointly publish the price paid by chocolate-makers and cocoa merchants for cacao on a monthly basis.

Production levels of coffee (green) have varied widely since the early 2000s. Output recovered from three years of decline in 2014 and remained above the 100,000-metric ton mark annually thereafter, according to the Food and Agriculture Organization of the UN (FAO), before declining to 59,400 tons in 2020.

From the 1960s Côte d'Ivoire became a major producer of palm oil, and local processing of palm products developed. A series of replanting programmes was supported by the World Bank, the European Community (now the EU), France and the United Kingdom. After collapsing during the civil war, palm oil output rose sharply to reach 360,000 metric tons in 2010, according to FAO figures. Following further increases, to a peak of 418,000 tons in 2012, production fell in 2013–14, to reach 370,000 tons in 2014, before recovering steadily to 510,000 tons in 2019. Côte d'Ivoire is the main producer of palm oil within the Union Economique et Monétaire Ouest-Africaine (UEMOA), accounting for 90% of total palm oil volume, and is Africa's largest exporter. According to the African Palm Oil Congress, an estimated 2m. people in Côte d'Ivoire, just under 10% of the overall population, depend on the oil palm for the majority of their revenues. Production, processing and transportation of palm products together currently generate some 200,000 stable jobs and contribute about 2% of GDP.

Cotton cultivation has become established in the north of the country. In the 1990s output of seed cotton averaged more than 300,000 metric tons per year, with a record crop of 399,933 tons achieved in the 1999 season. A new ginning plant, reportedly the largest in West Africa, was opened in M'bengue in May 2001, with planned output of more than 200,000 tons per year. The political upheavals from 2002 directly affected national cotton production, with cotton output collapsing from 396,100 tons in 2002/03 to just 125,000 tons in 2007/08, as a result of low cotton prices (forcing many farmers to switch to other cash crops), lack of fertilizers and political uncertainty. Cotton continued to perform poorly in subsequent years, due to the destruction of quality seeds in research centres in the former rebel zones, difficulties in financing the sector and continued low world market prices. However, according to FAO estimates, output of cottonseed and cotton lint recovered from 2011 following government initiatives to improve productivity through the provision of pesticides and fertilizer, market access, a guaranteed minimum price, assistance to co-operatives and a farm gate price guaranteed to cotton producers. Cottonseed production amounted to 490,400 tons in 2020. According to the US Department of Agriculture, 80% of Côte d'Ivoire's cotton production is exported, mostly to South and South-East Asia. There are six ginning companies in Côte d'Ivoire, with a total combined capacity of over 600,000 tons.

The rubber industry underwent strong growth from the mid-1980s, registering an average output of 70,825 metric tons per year in 1989–91, and an average of 115,874 tons in 1998–2000, as the Government pursued plans for Côte d'Ivoire to become Africa's leading rubber producer. Exports were estimated to be somewhat higher than local production, on account of the smuggling of rubber produced in Liberia. In 2011 a privatization programme led to the sale of state holdings in the three major companies involved in rubber production—the Compagnie des Caoutchoucs du Pakidie, the Société Africaine de Plantations d'Hévéas and the Société des Caoutchoucs de Grand-Béréby. The 2010–11 political crisis precipitated a large refugee outflow from the country's southern rubber regions, thus restricting the sectoral labour market. None the less, according to FAO data, rubber output totalled 238,700 tons in 2011, rising steadily over the following years to reach a record 936,100 tons in 2020, notably because of cocoa farmers diversifying into rubber in the face of unstable cocoa incomes. By 2020 about 50% of the country's rubber production was processed before shipment; in September 2021 the Parliament approved a law that established tax incentives for processing rubber in a bid to support the sector.

Côte d'Ivoire is a significant producer of bananas and pineapples (historically the world's second largest producer after Costa Rica), with exports directed principally at the European market. According to FAO figures, pineapple production increased steadily to a peak of 72,000 metric tons in 2013, before decreasing over the following years. According to FAO estimates, pineapple output reached an estimated 50,900 tons in 2020. Banana output rose steadily from 302,500 tons in 2011 to 626,000 tons in 2020.

The country is normally self-sufficient in maize, cassava, yams and plantains, and the Government has encouraged the production of rice, large quantities of which are imported. Two of the country's sugar mills have been converted to rice processing. By the mid-1980s the rice development programme was proving successful, and output of paddy rice averaged 1.2m. metric tons per year in 1996–2000. However, output had declined to 606,300 tons by 2007, meeting less than 40% of domestic demand, which had increased rapidly as the population moving from rural areas to towns tended to switch its grain preference to rice. According to FAO figures, the output of paddy rice rose significantly from 722,600 tons in 2010 to a peak 1.9m. tons in 2019, before declining to an estimated 1.0m. in 2020.

Following the implementation of a sugar development programme by the Government, two complexes were in operation by 1980, but were producing sugar at twice the cost on the world market. This situation led to the cancellation of six more planned complexes and the reduction of sugar cane plantations, resulting in a decline in sugar cane production from the 1.8m. tons recorded in 1983 to an average of 1.2m. tons per year in 1997–2000. The industry witnessed a gradual recovery from 2000, with production increasing from 1.8m. tons in 2010 to a peak of 2.0m. tons in 2015 before falling again in subsequent years. According to FAO estimates, sugar cane output reached 2.1m. tons in 2020.

Côte d'Ivoire is the largest producer of cashew nuts in Africa. In 2013 the Government pledged that cashew nut farmers would receive a minimum price for their produce as the administration sought to increase sectoral earnings and expand domestic processing of the crop. Although output rose by 20% year on year in 2013, to 450,000 metric tons, less than 5% of the harvest was processed locally. In July 2019 the Government issued an order granting new tax incentives to entrepreneurs to process cashew nuts, in an attempt to increase local processing capacity from 10% to 50%. In March 2021 the Government announced the creation of three new industrial zones in Bondoukou, Korhogo and Bouaké, respectively, in the north of the country, which were to be entirely designated for cashew nut processing, with the aim of increasing domestic processing by 50% by 2023. In November 2021 the country's Conseil du Coton et de l'Anacarde (CCA—Cotton and Cashew Council) announced that three new cashew processing facilities would be operational in 2022. Output of cashew nuts (with shells) was estimated at 848,700 tons in 2020.

Forestry has long been a significant source of export earnings, from both logs and sawn timber. Most production is carried out by large integrated firms, many of which are foreign-owned. The breakdown of law and order during Côte d'Ivoire's conflict years contributed to forest degradation by allowing indiscriminate illegal logging in hitherto protected government forests. In the 1960s Côte d'Ivoire had 16m. ha of forest, but the country is believed to have lost up to 90% of its forested area since independence, including 17% between 2001 and 2017, because of inadequate reforestation and encroachment on forest areas by expanding cocoa plantations. According to UN figures, revenue from wood exports peaked at US \$448m. in 2005 before falling steadily over the following years, to $98.1m. in 2019. Deforestation remains a serious concern.

Livestock herds are small—in 2020, according to FAO, there were some 1.8m. head of cattle, 2.3m. sheep, 3.7m. goats and an estimated 84.4m. poultry—and meat production satisfies only around one-third of national demand. In 2014 it was reported that a funding agreement had been reached between the Fonds pour l'Accélération du Développement Agricole and the Société Ivoirienne de Productions Animales for the construction of livestock farms and feed mills to meet domestic demand.

Fishing is a significant activity, with industrial fishing accounting for about two-thirds of the annual catch, which averaged 55,000–70,000 metric tons in the 1990s. Although production declined in the following year, FAO estimated the total fish catch to have risen from 45,500 tons in 2009 to 113,700 tons in 2019. Most traditional fishing is undertaken by non-Ivorians. Domestic production currently meets only about one-third of local demand, and in 2019 the country's imports of fish cost US $525.5m. (5.0% of total imports), according to the International Trade Centre (ITC). In March 2018 the Government signed a six-year fishing accord with the EU (which came into effect on 1 July), giving access to Ivorian waters to 36 EU-registered ships. In addition to shipowner contributions, the EU would pay Côte d'Ivoire annual compensation of €682,000. Since 2006 the tuna export industry has seen rapid growth. There are three Ivorian canneries, and in 2012 the EU imported about 192m. cans of tuna from Côte d'Ivoire, making the country one of its main canned tuna suppliers.

MANUFACTURING AND MINING

The manufacturing sector, which, according to UN estimates, expanded by 4.8% in 2019, has been dominated by agro-industrial activities—such as the processing of cocoa, coffee, cotton, oil palm, pineapples and fish. However, there are challenges to processing and exporting higher-value finished agro-industrial products. The high tariffs frequently imposed on finished chocolate products, for example, mean that Côte d'Ivoire has remained low on the value chain as a mere commodities exporter. Industrial GDP (including mining, construction and utilities, in addition to manufacturing) declined significantly following the political crisis of 2002. Much of the industrial sector, which had been developing new export capacities, was forced to curtail or suspend production, and further new investment was placed on hold. During 2010–19 industrial GDP increased at an average annual rate of 7.8%; following a growth peak of 15.4% in 2017, industrial GDP grew by 10.7% in 2018, 10.4% in 2019 and 1.9% in 2020. Industry (including mining, manufacturing, construction and power) contributed 20.9% of GDP in 2020, according to provisional official figures.

The mining sector is expanding rapidly, notably due to its diversification beyond the diamond and gold sectors. Mining accounted for 3.2% of GDP, according to provisional official figures, and a total of 50,000 direct and indirect jobs in 2019. Two diamond mines, at Tortiya and Séguéla, are in operation, but much larger quantities are produced in illicit operations. Most production of diamonds is by artisanal methods in the north of the country. In December 2005 the UN Security Council imposed a ban on imports of rough diamonds from Côte d'Ivoire, which was subsequently extended. However, despite the UN ban, in June 2009 the Kimberley Process reported that diamond production was continuing to increase in Côte d'Ivoire. According to the US Geological Survey (USGS), 210,000 carats were produced in 2008. The UN embargo on the export of rough diamonds was lifted in April 2014, shortly after Côte d'Ivoire was declared compliant with the Kimberley Process Certification Scheme. Meanwhile, a new mining code adopted in February aimed to attract investment to the mining sector, and to double gold output within a year. Côte d'Ivoire legally exported 14,000 carats of diamonds in 2015 and 20,235 carats in 2016. Production fell over the following years to reach 4,015 carats in 2020 as existing deposits neared exhaustion.

There are five industrial gold mines. The exploitation of deposits of gold-bearing rock at Ity began in 1991, in a joint venture with the Compagnie Française des Mines. The Ity mine is now operated by Endeavour Mining, which has an 85%

stake in the project, while the Government holds 10% and the state-owned mining operator Société pour le Développement Minier de la Côte d'Ivoire (SODEMI) the remaining 5%. Production increased substantially in the late 2000s, partly owing to the significant rise in the price of gold on the world market; it fluctuated between 4,500 kg and 8,000 kg in the early 2020s. A second gold mine, at Yaouré, which had ceased operations in 1993, resumed production in late 2009, when it was brought back into commission by British firm Cluff Gold. Australian firm Perseus Mining Ltd acquired control of the Yaouré mine, with a 90% stake, in 2016 and, following development work, declared the commencement of commercial production in March 2021. Production increased rapidly from 1,058 kg in the second term to 1,830 kg in the third term of 2021. Perseus had begun production at its Sissingué mine in Tengrela in the north of the country in January 2018. The smaller mine's output reached 455 kg in the third term of 2021. Following a US $280m. investment, the Tongon mine operated by Australian company Randgold, located 375 km north of Abidjan, was officially opened in October 2011. Owned by Canada-based Barrick Gold following its merger with Randgold, Tongon produced a record 9.1 metric tons of gold (30% of the national total) in 2020. The Agbaou gold mine, located approximately 200 km north of Abidjan, which was owned 85% by the Endeavour Mining Corporation of Canada and 15% by the state, began commercial production in January 2014 and reported production of 7,556 kg in 2015. By early 2021, with declining reserves, the mine was acquired by Australia-based Allied Gold Corporation. A sixth mine, at Bonikro in southern Côte d'Ivoire, was acquired by Afrique Gold from Australian firm Newcrest in 2018 and has been undergoing development works since 2020. In November 2021 Australia-based Tietto Minerals announced that it had secured $140m. in to develop the Abujar gold mine in Côte d'Ivoire; it expected production from the mine to start by the end of 2022 and to average 200,000 oz over the first six years of operation. Nevertheless, the Government has had to contend with illegal gold mines, notably as a remnant of the civil war. By late 2015 the Government had shut down a total of 304 small-scale gold mining sites as well as the larger Gamina illegal gold mine. The Ministry of Mining, Petroleum and Energy also announced in late 2018 the creation of a special police force to counter illegal mining, and of learning centres to encourage informal miners to move into the formal sector. According to the Government, the country's total gold production amounted to 25.4 tons in 2017; it declined slightly, to 24.5 tons, in 2018, before reaching 32.5 tons in 2019 and 38.9 tons in 2020.

Nickel production began in 2017 and reached an estimated 889,585 metric tons in 2018, before falling to 660,144 tons in 2019. Local firm Compagnie Minière du Bafing operates several nickel production sites in the Biankouma and Touba regions in western Côte d'Ivoire. Canadian company Sama Resources is also developing a nickel-copper mine in Samapleu, in the west, which it plans to operate in a joint venture with SODEMI; positive preliminary exploration and economic assessment results were announced in 2020 and early 2021.

In addition, there are substantial manganese and bauxite reserves. Manganese production has increased rapidly in recent years, reaching 1.2m. metric tons in 2019. Côte d'Ivoire's Shiloh Manganese (a subsidiary of India's Shiloh Industries) signed an agreement in September 2016 to exploit manganese deposits in Korhogo and Kikodougou in the north of the country, while Taurian Manganese and Ferro Alloy CI of India announced in April 2017 that it would relaunch production at its deposit at Kaniasso in the north-west.

Bauxite production commenced in April 2018, at a site situated in the central Moronou region which was operated by Lagune Exploitation de Bongouanou. Production was, however, suspended in 2020, due to election-related civil unrest.

ENERGY

Rapid urbanization and industrialization in recent years have greatly increased demand for electricity. As a result of greater demand, power cuts have become more frequent. The Compagnie Ivoirienne d'Electricité (CIE) manages the state-owned generation facilities, as well as electricity transmission and distribution, and has a monopoly on the supply of electricity.

Electricity generating capacity rose very rapidly in the early 1980s, as a result of the development of hydroelectric plants. However, the focus of development changed after the 1982–84 drought severely reduced the contribution of hydroelectric power, and policy switched to the development of thermal capacity. Plans for a thermal plant in the Vridi port area of Abidjan, utilizing offshore reserves of natural gas, were realized in 1994. A consortium led by United Meridian of the USA developed the Panthère gasfield to supply a 100-MW plant at Vridi, which became fully operational in 1997. Plans were developed to use Panthère's resources to expand Côte d'Ivoire's exports of electricity. A gas-fired complex at Azito, close to Abidjan, opened in January 1999; by 2008 output at the complex had more than doubled to 300 MW. In that year the Government signed an agreement with Energie Electrique Ivoirienne (EEI) to build a 120-MW gas-fired power station at Vridi, at an estimated cost of US $134m., to be financed by EEI's main shareholder, the Libyan African Investment Corporation.

During 2010 Côte d'Ivoire suffered from a power crisis, with severe shortages provoking angry demonstrations and attacks on the CIE's offices in Abidjan. Temporary power generation company Aggreko (of the UK) secured a three-year contract extension to a 200-MW, gas-fuelled power facility in Abidjan in January 2015, which had been installed by late 2010. In 2015 the expansion and renovation of the Azito gas-fired plant was completed. Meanwhile, in February of that year the CIPREL IV independent power plant was expanded with the addition of a 111-MW steam turbine and two 111-MW gas turbines. In September the Government signed an agreement with Eranove, the parent company of CIPREL, to build 350–400 MW of new capacity. In May 2017 the Government announced that it had signed an agreement with Korhogo Solaire, a subsidiary of Morocco's Nova Power, to build a 25-MW solar power plant in Benguébougou, in the north of the country.

In addition to gas and solar power generation, a new 274-MW hydroelectric power dam at Soubré on the Sassandra river was inaugurated in November 2017, while at the same time the first stone of the 1,112-MW Gribo Popoli dam, some 7 km along the river from Soubré, was being laid. Gribo Popoli, mostly financed by the Export-Import Bank of China (Eximbank), was scheduled to be completed by late 2020. In December 2017 the African Development Bank (AfDB) agreed to provide a €50m. (US $59m.) loan to finance the construction of a 44-MW hydropower plant called Singobo-Ahouaty, north of Abidjan. In December 2018 the Government announced that it had entered into a public-private partnership with Ciprel, a subsidiary of French investment group Eranove, to build and operate the 390-MW Atinkou gas-to-power plant at Jacqueville near Abidjan. In the same month the independently owned Azito plant was given approval to expand its planned capacity from 430 MW to 710 MW; the expansion was complete and operational by the end of June 2022. In January 2020 BIOVEA Energie, a joint venture of the utility Electricité de France (EDF), the global investment company Meridiam and the agribusiness company SIFCA Group, and signed a contract with the Government of Côte d'Ivoire to build a 46-MW biomass power facility, to be financed by the three construction companies as well as the Agence Française de Développement. Côte d'Ivoire's overall electricity production had reached 2,229 MW by 2019, and 94% of the population were connected to the power grid. However, a series of major power outages across Côte d'Ivoire's cities in April 2021, due to low water levels at hydroelectric dams, lack of supplies for the two thermal power plants, and breakdowns at the Azito plant demonstrated some ongoing weaknesses and forced the Government to impose electricity rationing from late April to early July.

As part of the West African Power Pool, Côte d'Ivoire's power grid is connected to Ghana, Togo, Benin, Burkina Faso and Mali. In July 2009 the European Investment Bank agreed to finance the construction of a new power line between Riviera (Côte d'Ivoire) and Prestea (Ghana), at an estimated cost of €1,750m., as part of a project to improve power supplies in West Africa. Plans to connect the Ivorian power grid to Guinea and Sierra Leone were confirmed in 2019. The Interconnection

Côte d'Ivoire-Liberia-Sierra Leone-Guinea project aims to boost reconstruction efforts in those countries, which possess only limited transmission capabilities. In November 2021 the Government agreed to export 11 MW of electricity annually to neighbouring Guinea until 2023. Côte d'Ivoire's electricity exports already represented 10% of its total production by the end of 2019.

Petroleum and Gas

Côte d'Ivoire became a new player in the petroleum and gas sector in the 2000s although production remained modest in the following two decades. New interest and exploration results in the early 2020s, however, led President Alassane Ouattara to announce that the country would be a major petroleum producer by 2023. Although offshore exploration for petroleum had virtually ceased by 1984, a new round of exploration undertaken in the early 1990s proved successful, with a major discovery of offshore petroleum, near Jacqueville and Grand-Lahou, in 1994. A joint venture by United Meridian of the USA and the state-owned Société Nationale d'Opérations Pétrolières de la Côte d'Ivoire (PETROCI) began production at the Lion field in April 1995. After production-sharing arrangements were renegotiated, Canadian Natural Resources (CNR), with Tullow Oil as a partner, developed the East Espoir field, and production resumed in 2002, averaging 35,000 barrels per day (b/d). CNR also operates the West Espoir field, which started production in mid-2006, and the Baobab field, which began operations from 11 wells in mid-2005 and—following the drilling of four new wells in 2009—is currently Côte d'Ivoire's largest single source of crude petroleum. CNR reported an increase in crude petroleum production of 54% in 2015, mainly due to new wells coming onstream at both fields during the year. The Italian energy company Eni announced in March 2017 that it had acquired a 90% stake in two offshore blocks (CI-101 and CI-205) situated 50 km from Côte d'Ivoire's coastline. At the end of August 2021 Eni announced that it had discovered a major oil deposit, nicknamed Baleine, with reserves estimated at 1,500m. to 2,000m. barrels of oil and 51m. to 68m. cu m of natural gas, in its CI-101 block. A development plan was approved by the Government in December, with production expected to start in 2023 and to progressively increase to between 75,000 and 100,000 barrels of oil and 17.5m. cu ft of gas a day by 2026. A discovery in an adjacent block announced in July 2022 increased Baleine's stated reserves to an estimated 2,500m. barrels of oil and 93m. cu m of gas. In November 2017 Tullow Oil announced that it had been awarded a 90% stake (with the remaining 10% owned by PETROCI) in four new onshore blocks (CI-301, CI-302, CI-518 and CI-519) located to the west of Abidjan. In May 2020 Qatar Petroleum announced that it would take half of the French company Total's 90% operating stake in two blocks in the Ivorian Tano Basin.

Total national petroleum production rose from just 2.1m. barrels in 2001 to 22.2m. barrels in 2006. However, production decreased thereafter, due to maturing fields, the silting of wells in the main oilfields, and technical delays in new fields starting production. Although production recovered slightly as a result of new discoveries in the Baobab field and investment to reduce silting, according to the USGS, output of crude petroleum declined from 14.6m. barrels in 2010 to an average of 12.4m. barrels in 2012–15 and 10.9m. barrels in 2016. Production further decreased in 2017–18, before recovering in 2019 to an estimated 36,000 b/d. A decrease in production in two offshore blocks (CI-26 and CI-40), combined with the effects of the COVID-19 pandemic, accounted for a decline in overall output in 2020 and 2021. Output reached some 24,000 b/d in the first half of 2021.

The principal oil refinery, owned by Société Ivoirienne de Raffinage (SIR), currently has a capacity of around 76,000 b/d. It receives oil directly by pipeline from the Lion field, and it also processes crude petroleum shipped from Nigeria. PETROCI owns a 48% stake in the company, and in December 2007 it signed an agreement with two US companies to build a second refinery in Abidjan, with a capacity of 60,000 b/d, at an estimated cost of US $1,400m. However, construction of the refinery was subsequently delayed. In March 2009 Angola's national oil company, SONANGOL, purchased a 22% stake in

SIR from the Ivorian Government for $45m. Financial difficulties suffered by both SIR and PETROCI, compounded by large arrears owed by the Government, were exacerbated by the impact of sharply falling international oil prices and the appreciation of the US dollar in 2014. Agreement was subsequently reached with the authorities on the settlement of arrears between the Government and PETROCI, and an increase in electricity subsidies in 2015. However, PETROCI's problems persisted into 2016 and 2017 with its main trade union organizing several strikes in protest against the dismissal of employees (to reduce costs in response to persistently subdued international prices). In May 2017 the Government announced that it would seek to privatize the liquefied petroleum gas distribution branch of PETROCI in an attempt to reduce the company's losses. In February 2018, in a further move to restructure the company, the Government authorized the sale of PETROCI's 37 petrol stations to Puma Energy Côte d'Ivoire, owned by the Singaporean commodity trading company, Trafigura. In January 2019 SIR obtained a loan of €577m. from various international banks, and in June 2019 the Minister of Petroleum and the Development of Renewable Energy, Abdourahmane Cissé, announced that the company had recovered from past financial difficulties and had recorded 20,000m. francs CFA in benefits in 2018. In September 2021 SIR announced that it had increased its oil storage capacities to some 150,000 cu m.

Natural gas has primarily been used to generate electricity. In 2015 PETROCI forecast that demand for gas would increase more than 17-fold from its existing level to reach 850m. standard cu ft per day by 2023, mainly owing to the expansion of gas-fired power stations. In 1999 a US, French and Ivorian consortium began production at the Foxtrot offshore gasfield in Block CI-27. Further gas wells were discovered in the 2000s and by 2013 the country's natural gas output totalled some 170m. cu ft per day. Block CI-27 also includes the Marlin and Manta fields. Devon Energy has been operating the Panthère field, with production of around 70m. cu ft per day, and CNR announced the start of natural gas production from its West Espoir field in mid-2006. In response to a demand by donors that improvements be made to transparency in the energy sector as a precondition for resuming full funding, the Government pledged to carry out audits of the oil, gas, refinery and electricity sectors, and to implement an automatic price adjustment system. In May 2013 Côte d'Ivoire was designated a compliant country by the international Extractive Industries Transparency Initiative programme, a step seen by donor countries as important to winning debt relief. Total gas production was officially 202,166m. BTU (British Thermal Units) in 2019.

During the 2000s Côte d'Ivoire's hydrocarbons sector continued to grow strongly, increasing its contribution to real GDP growth. Crude petroleum represented 3.2% of total exports (in terms of value) in 2021, down from 7.0% in 2019. According to the ITC, exports of mineral fuels, oils, distillation products, etc. reached a peak of US $3,159.9m. in 2012 (29.1% of total exports), but declined steadily over the following years as oil prices fell on the world market to reach $1,878m. in 2018. They rebounded in 2019, to $2,226m. (17.2% of total exports), due to increases in petroleum and gas production, before declining again to $1,280m. in 2020 and $716m. in 2021 as a result of a decrease in production and the COVID-19 pandemic.

TRANSPORT AND TELECOMMUNICATIONS

The most important transport facilities are the deep-water ports of Abidjan and San-Pédro, which handle freight not only for Côte d'Ivoire but also for its landlocked neighbours Burkina Faso, Mali and Niger. Abidjan's port is operated by Société d'Exploitation du Terminal de Vridi, a subsidiary of France's Bolloré. San-Pédro is the main export point for cocoa beans, rubber and timber. Both Ivorian ports have sought to increase container traffic, but face competition from the ports of Conakry (Guinea) and Lomé (Togo). In April 2018 Bolloré and the Danish shipping company Maersk announced that they were investing €400m. (US $490m.) in the development of a new container terminal which was expected to increase the port's capacity by 15%. The construction of the new terminal followed

work on the Vridi Canal to enlarge and deepen it, thus allowing for the docking of larger container ships. In December 2014 it was announced that China's Eximbank had provided a loan of $875m. for the construction of a second container terminal at Abidjan port by a Bolloré-led consortium, which was scheduled for completion in 2021. In September 2016 the Government announced that Bilal General Transport of the United Arab Emirates (UAE) and Swiss-based Mediterranean Shipping Co were to invest a total of 308,000m. francs CFA ($517m.) to extend and upgrade San-Pédro's container terminal. In 2020 Abidjan port handled freight totalling 25.3m. tons, while the volume of freight handled in San-Pédro reached 4.8m. tons in that year.

Côte d'Ivoire has about 82,000 km of classified roads, only 8.1% of which are paved, according to the World Bank. Repair and extension of the road network has received funding from both multilateral agencies and donor governments (notably France, Germany and Japan). A new motorway between Abidjan and Yamoussoukro, constructed with finance from four Middle Eastern development funds, was inaugurated in December 2013. In December 2014 a new 1.5 km-long toll bridge in Abidjan, constructed at a cost of US $330m., was officially opened. In 2012 a project to build a highway between Nigeria's commercial capital, Lagos, and Abidjan, by 2040 was endorsed by West African heads of state. Côte d'Ivoire and Burkina Faso have for many years planned to build a motorway linking Abidjan, Yamoussoukro and Ouagadougou, Burkina Faso's capital city. Some 50 km of new road—the extension of the existing Abidjan–Yamoussoukro motorway—had been completed by mid-2018, but progress was slower on the Burkinabé side.

A railway line links Abidjan to Ouagadougou with 660 km of line in Côte d'Ivoire. Management responsibility for the railway lies with the Société Internationale de Transport Africain par Rail (SITARAIL), now a subsidiary of the Bolloré Group. SITARAIL's total freight traffic amounted to 800,000–900,000 metric tons in 2014–17. The number of passengers transported by the railway increased from 164,000 in 2004 to an estimated 200,000 in 2017. In September 2015 the Bolloré Group announced investment of 262,000m. francs CFA (US $455m.) over the following five years, to modernize the rail infrastructure, increase the network's capacities to 5m. tons a year and improve passenger comfort. Works to this effect began in late 2017. The Government signed a concession agreement in July 2015 with Groupe Bouygues and Keolis of France and South Korean companies Hyundai Rotem and Dongsan Engineering to build and operate a 37-km urban rail line in Abidjan, to traverse the city centre from Abidjan's northern suburbs to the international airport in the south of the city. This was confirmed through a formal agreement signed in October 2019. The first stage of the rail line was expected to be completed in 2023.

In April 2014 a project was initiated for the construction of an extensive rail network along the West African coast from Abidjan to Lomé in Togo, which was to improve rail infrastructure and increase trade in the region. The initial section was to link Niamey, the capital of landlocked Niger, and the seaport of Cotonou (Benin). The line would subsequently be extended to Badagry (Nigeria), Accra (Ghana) and Ouagadougou. By early 2022, however, despite ministerial declarations reiterating the associated Governments' interest in the network, major work had not yet started.

Côte d'Ivoire has international airports at Abidjan, Bouaké and Yamoussoukro, and there are some 25 domestic and regional airports. The management of Abidjan airport was ceded to a French consortium, Aeria, in 1996 and its capacity now stands at 2m. passengers per year. Passenger movements declined from a level of 1.4m. in 2000 to only 700,000 in 2003, showing no significant growth in the following two years as many long-haul carriers suspended their services. Passenger movements at Abidjan airport reportedly increased to reach nearly 2.3m. in 2019. Due to the COVID-19 pandemic the international airport remained shut from late March until 1 July 2020 and the total number of passenger movements fell to 839,000 that year, before rebounding to 1.5m. in 2021. In April 2021 French group Bouygues began expansion work at Abidjan's international airport. The work was expected to be completed in 2023 and to raise the airport's capacity to 5m. passengers. Air Côte d'Ivoire, which is 58% state-owned and has never recorded an operating profit, was also deeply affected by the pandemic-related lockdown. In July 2020 the airline was granted a US $14m. rescue package by the Government and Air Côte d'Ivoire's revenues increased by 52% as the recovery provided for better trading conditions in 2021.

The fixed-line telephone network is operated by the national telecommunications company, Côte d'Ivoire-Télécom (CI-Télécom), which was sold to France Télécom in 1997, the Government retaining a 49% share. In 2007 CI-Télécom launched a programme to modernize and expand the national network, at a cost of 7,500m. francs CFA (US $16.7m.), resulting in an increase in the number of fixed lines to 356,500 in 2008. In 2017 CI-Télécom merged with Orange Côte d'Ivoire (85% owned by France Télécom), which thereafter became one of the sub-region's leading telecommunication providers with more than 26m. customers by mid-2022, and operations in Liberia and Burkina Faso as well as Côte d'Ivoire. According to the International Telecommunications Union (ITU), the total number of fixed lines in Côte d'Ivoire increased slightly from 276,200 in 2012 to 305,563 in 2017, but had declined to 264,073 by 2020.

Mobile telecommunications have developed significantly since 2002. Orange Côte d'Ivoire and MTN Côte d'Ivoire (formerly Télécel) initially dominated the market and were joined in 2005 by Acell, which launched services under the name Moov Télécom. In June 2007 a fourth mobile telephone operator, consisting of Comium (owned by Etisalat) and KoZ (operated by the Lebanese Comium Group), was established. In January 2009 a fifth operator, Green Network (also referred to as GreenN), was launched by Libya's LAP GreenN, under the name of Oricel, with the result that by 2012 there were seven licensed mobile telephone operators and five active operators. Additional operators have acquired licences since then. By the end of 2020 these smaller operators had been bought by the three larger operating companies: in early 2022 Orange had a 44% share of the market, MTN 32.7% and Moov (owned by Maroc Telecom) 23%. The three companies were also in competition to attract an increasing number of mobile money clients, especially after California-based Wave entered the Ivorian market in April 2021.

In October 2011 Nigerian telecommunications operator Globacom announced that, in partnership with French operator Alcatel-Lucent, it planned to land its Glo-1 international submarine fibre optic-cable in Côte d'Ivoire, which would help to lower the cost of international bandwidth. In addition, several other cables were scheduled to reach the country in the coming years. The Ivorian internet and broadband market has remained underdeveloped due to the high cost of international bandwidth, caused by a monopolization of access to the sole international connection currently serving the country. Despite these obstacles, Côte d'Ivoire has become West Africa's third largest internet market after Nigeria and Ghana, with services superior to those in many other African countries. In September 2018 Côte d'Ivoire launched its first satellite broadband service, YahClick, in a partnership between Ivorian CEE-NET Technologies and the UAE-based Yahsat.

According to the ITU, by 2020 the number of mobile telephone subscribers had risen to 40.1m., meaning that there were 152 mobile telephone subscriptions per 100 inhabitants. According to the same source, internet penetration increased from 2.7% of the population in 2010 to 36.5% in 2019. The number of broadband subscribers rose from 49,500 in 2011 to 260,097 in 2020.

ECONOMIC POLICY

Following the visit to Abidjan of an IMF mission in May 2007, in July the Fund awarded Côte d'Ivoire an emergency post-conflict assistance programme (EPCA), worth US $62.2m. The EPCA was designed to support the Government's efforts to strengthen administrative capacity, and was considered a first step towards a Poverty Reduction and Growth Facility (PRGF), which would enable Côte d'Ivoire to work towards securing debt relief under the initiative for heavily indebted poor countries (HIPC) and the Multilateral Debt Relief Initiative (MDRI). Although the budget deficit was reduced to 1.2% of

GDP in 2007, the Fund noted above-target discretionary spending, which forced the Government to cut some priority sector projects. The main aim of the EPCA in 2008 was fiscal consolidation, through the re-establishment of the tax administration in rebel-held areas and the capping of public sector wages.

In January 2009 the Government presented its Poverty Reduction Strategy Paper (PRSP) to the IMF, which aimed to reduce the level of poverty from 49.0% in 2008 to 16.2% in 2015, with a focus on boosting rural development where poverty levels were twice as high as in urban areas. The cost of the PRSP, estimated at 17,650,000m. francs CFA over 2009–15, was expected to be funded by donors. Following a joint mission to Abidjan in February 2009, the IMF, the World Bank and the AfDB reported strong revenue growth, due to higher international commodity prices, and commended the Government for incorporating off-budget spending on presidential projects into the revised 2008 budget. Consequently, the IMF awarded Côte d'Ivoire a new PRGF arrangement, worth US $566m., covering the period 2009–11, for the expansion of the tax revenue base, the completion of the unification of state finances and improvements in public expenditure management.

From late 2010 to May 2011 the country faced a growing range of economic sanctions, as a consequence of the post-election impasse between President Laurent Gbagbo and Alassane Ouattara (see *History*). Economic sanctions were used as part of a strategy to isolate Gbagbo and his Government financially. In April 2011 the Ouattara administration initiated a programme of recovery, with the assistance of the international community, and business activity rapidly normalized. In June the UN removed the remaining sanctions against Ivorian enterprises. In October the USA announced that Côte d'Ivoire, excluded since 2005, was again eligible to benefit from the African Growth and Opportunity Act, which granted preferential access to the US market. The AfDB also resumed assistance from 2011, particularly in relation to strengthening social services, the capacity of the administration and infrastructure investment projects. In addition, the European Commission announced a US $260m. grant-based 'recovery package' to support basic social spending in the country, and the IMF approved a three-year Extended Credit Facility (ECF) arrangement totalling SDR 390.2m. to support the Government's national development plan for 2012–15, with interim assistance equivalent to some $8m. under the enhanced HIPC initiative.

In August 2013 the International Development Association approved a US $50m. credit to support Côte d'Ivoire's long-term efforts to strengthen its government institutions, improve the business climate, and encourage private sector growth and job creation (especially for cocoa, cotton and cashew nut farmers in rural communities). The funds were designed to support the First Poverty Reduction Support Credit (PRSC-1), the first of a series of three policy operations designed to help Côte d'Ivoire become an emerging market by 2020.

At the end of 2015, in its eighth and final assessment under the ECF, the IMF commended Côte d'Ivoire's continued strong performance; growth in real GDP per head had reached 20% in 2012–15. The IMF urged the Government to pursue further ambitious reforms to strengthen the financial sector, improve the business climate, foster private sector activity and economic diversification, and maintain levels of social spending. In May 2016 the IMF Executive Board concluded its annual Article IV consultation with Côte d'Ivoire, confirming previous positive assessments and approving a 2016–20 national development plan, aimed at halving poverty and fostering structural transformation.

In December 2016, following negotiations with the Government, the IMF approved two new three-year arrangements under the ECF and the Extended Fund Facility (EFF) for Côte d'Ivoire for a combined total of US $658.9m., to support the country's economic and financial reform programme. In its reviews of the programmes, the IMF considered Côte d'Ivoire's performance satisfactory, noting that the Government had contained the budget deficit and was on track to reduce the fiscal deficit and meet the UEMOA convergence criterion of 3% of GDP in 2019; that growth prospects remained good; and that structural reforms were on track. By the end of 2019 total disbursements under the two IMF programmes amounted to $896.7m. and the IMF Executive Board had agreed to an extension of the two programmes by one year, in order to support financial stability through the 2020 presidential election. In April 2020, in the context of the COVID-19 pandemic, the IMF approved the disbursement of $886.2m. to Côte d'Ivoire, to be drawn under the Rapid Credit Facility and the Rapid Financing Instrument, to help the country meet urgent balance-of-payment needs stemming from the outbreak. In December the IMF Executive Board completed the final reviews under the ECF/EFF arrangements, noting performance had been satisfactory and that Côte d'Ivoire had weathered the economic consequences of the COVID-19 pandemic reasonably well. A final tranche of $278.2m. was disbursed. The IMF recommended that Côte d'Ivoire return to the standard 12-month cycle for Article IV consultations and engage in post-programme monitoring, as outstanding credit to the Fund exceeded 200% of its quota, making the country ineligible for a new programme. This was implemented and in the 2022 Article IV consultation, the IMF noted that the country's economy had proven its resilience amid the COVID-19 pandemic, recovering strongly in 2021. Nevertheless, the deterioration in the external environment linked to the war in Ukraine and regional security challenges were expected to negatively impact the macroeconomic outlook in 2022.

PUBLIC FINANCE

The political crises of 2000 and 2001 severely worsened the Government's overall financial position. By the end of 2001 there was an accumulated stock of domestic payment arrears of 361,000m. francs CFA, estimated at 4.7% of GDP. In response, in 2002 the Government introduced a 5% tax on new project-related imports, an increase in the tax on cocoa exports, the reform of customs clearing procedures and the computerization of import management systems. Moreover, in 2004 a new tax on incomes to provide for the war effort was announced. The Government's domestic arrears were estimated at 3% of GDP, and there was an ongoing crisis in the banking sector. The accumulation of arrears, both foreign and domestic, amounted to 26% of GDP at the end of 2005. The fiscal deficit (excluding grants) was estimated at 2.4% of GDP in 2006, financed largely by further domestic borrowing. Total external and domestic debt was estimated at 85.7% of GDP in that year.

In January 2009 the Government started the process of unifying state finances by deploying tax and customs officials to the rebel-controlled north of the country, and in April revised the budget for that year to incorporate the targets agreed in the new PRGF awarded the previous month. Spending was to rise to 2,525,000m. francs CFA, most of which related to new capital investments, increased poverty reduction expenditure and higher debt repayment. Revenue was to rise to 1,840,000m. francs CFA, reflecting higher customs revenue, increased donor aid and the withdrawal of the emergency measures introduced in 2008. In June 2009 the Government paid arrears worth 128,900m. francs CFA to domestic suppliers, in an operation funded by the IMF and the World Bank.

The ban on coffee and cocoa exports during the first four months of 2011, combined with the cessation of business activities and the closure of commercial banks, all contributed to a decline in state revenues in that year. The overall fiscal deficit narrowed from 5.7% of GDP in 2011 to 4.5% in 2017, to 4.0% in 2018 and to 2.3% in 2019, essentially as a result of lower expenditures and improved tax collection over the period. However, it widened to 5.6% of GDP in 2020 and 2021, as a result of the COVID-19 pandemic.

The draft budget for 2022 totalled 9,901,100m. francs CFA—a 17.9% increase compared with the 2021 budget. The draft budget was based on projected GDP growth of 7.1% for 2022, and aimed to reduce the fiscal deficit to 4.7% of GDP. The draft budget included measures to revitalize the economy following the COVID-19 pandemic, as well as the pursuit of long-term development plans, together with the implementation of the 2021–25 national development plan, to improve livelihoods. However, by mid-2022 a widened fiscal deficit was expected as

a result of the economic and social measures (such as price caps on food products and oil subsidies) adopted to offset the impact of the war in Ukraine.

Côte d'Ivoire's external debt stock represented 27.2% of GDP at the end of 2019 and had grown to an estimated 31.6% of GDP by 2021 as a result of the COVID-19 pandemic. Despite heavy borrowing and spending, the country's public debt stock was estimated to have decreased from some 44% of GDP at the end of 2013 to around 41% of GDP at the end of 2019. It increased to some 47% of GDP in 2020 and reached 51.4% of GDP in 2021, as a result of pandemic-related expenditure.

FOREIGN TRADE AND PAYMENTS

Côte d'Ivoire's balance of trade has regularly been in surplus, owing to the level of export earnings from sales of coffee and cocoa. In addition, the surge in the value of crude petroleum exports from 2005 helped to stimulate both the trade payments surplus and foreign exchange reserves.

On the capital account, inflows of foreign direct investment (FDI) had risen steadily since the end of the civil war, from just US $283m. in 2004 to $427m. in 2007 and $402m. in 2008, comparable to the highest levels of the late 1990s. This investment was channelled towards oil, gas and telecommunications. Although FDI totalled only $302m. in 2011, according to the UN Conference on Trade and Development, it subsequently recovered to reach $936m. in 2019, assisted by measures to improve the business climate, including the simplification of business start-up procedures, and the introduction of tax incentives contained in a new investment code. FDI totalled $509m. in 2020 as a result of the pandemic-induced economic slowdown.

With the suspension of an IMF credit facility and new uncertainties generated by the military coup of December 1999, the implementation of a HIPC debt relief programme was inevitably postponed and debt stocks increased significantly over the following years. Debt repayments to most international financial institutions ceased during the course of 2004. The country's arrears to the World Bank had increased to US $422m. by the time agreement was reached in April 2007 on a plan to repay part of them, as well as part of the arrears owed to the AfDB. In January 2009 the World Bank indicated that Côte d'Ivoire was eligible in principle for HIPC assistance, and following the award of the new PRGF, on 31 March US $3,000m. of the country's external debt was written off, out of an estimated total of $14,300m. at the end of 2007. Côte d'Ivoire reached completion point in June 2012, at which time the country became eligible for an additional $1,300m. of MDRI debt relief.

Meanwhile, a debt rescheduling arrangement was signed with the 'Paris Club' of bilateral creditors in May 2009 (to write off US $845m. of the country's debt and to defer repayment of $1,200m. arrears, $2,600m. of debt falling due and $179m. of moratorium interest until April 2012). As Côte d'Ivoire's main external creditor, France held an estimated 60% of the country's 'Paris Club' debt. In December 2009 France agreed to write off, reschedule or defer total external debt worth more than $3,400m., which would reduce debt-service repayments to France by 90% for the duration of the 2009–12 IMF programme. In September the Government also reached a preliminary agreement with the 'London Club' of commercial creditors to restructure the equivalent of 18.6% of the country's external debt at the end of 2008. Implemented in April 2010, this was seen as a further step towards regaining access to international capital markets.

In April 2011 France agreed a US $400m. assistance package for the country, in response to the political and economic strife that had taken place from late 2010 (see *History*). However, in July 2011 Côte d'Ivoire sought a complete reassessment of $2,300m. of Eurobonds, after suspending debt payments for that year due to the damage caused to the economy by post-election conflict. Repayments resumed in June 2012 and in November an agreement was reached with creditors to clear arrears and cancel penalties.

Côte d'Ivoire returned to the bond market in July 2014 with the issuance of a US $750m. Eurobond, the proceeds of which were allocated to budgetary support, extending average debt maturities, and the repayment of some domestic debt. By the end of April 2016 Côte d'Ivoire had issued 11 regional bonds totalling 996,200m. francs CFA ($1,720m.). The funds were intended to finance the national development plan for 2016–20. A further eight-year Eurobond, worth $624m., and a 16-year US dollar-denominated bond worth $1,250m. were issued in June 2017, in order to refinance a portion of previous Eurobonds issued in 2014–15, and to cover the Government's cash flow problems, following a drop in cocoa prices and higher international oil prices. In 2018 Côte d'Ivoire sold Eurobonds totalling €1,700m. ($1,900m.) to finance its fiscal deficit, and in October 2019 the Government raised a further $1,800m.

Côte d'Ivoire also turned to so-called Southern lenders, such as the Islamic financial market, by issuing *sukuks*, an Islamic finance instrument similar to a bond, in 2015 and 2016, to raise a total of 300,000m. francs CFA (US $511.3m.) to support its 2016–20 national development plan. The first such *sukuk* attracted 56% of funds from the UEMOA market, 6% from North Africa and 38% from the Middle East. Likewise, Côte d'Ivoire has sought investments, but also loans, from China. By mid-2019 Chinese investments in the country were estimated to total more than $6,000m., and China had agreed to write off debt worth 20,000 francs CFA ($34.6m.).

In 2020, in response to the global economic crisis triggered by the COVID-19 pandemic, international lenders announced a series of measures in support of indebted countries. In addition to the relief offered by the IMF (see *Economic Policy*), in June 2020 the Paris Club of creditor nations agreed to grant Côte d'Ivoire debt service relief, suspending repayments from 1 May to 31 December. The suspension was then extended until the end of 2021. In November 2020 Côte d'Ivoire raised US $1,000m. through a Eurobond issuance, which was allocated to financing the 2020 budget deficit. In January 2021 the Government obtained $61.1m. on the regional financial market of the West African Economic and Monetary Union in order to cover its supplemental budgetary resources over that year. It raised a further $1,000m. from a Eurobond sale in February. In all three cases the bonds were heavily oversubscribed. In February the World Bank announced a $300m. loan for Côte d'Ivoire to help mitigate the impact of the COVID-19 pandemic. Côte d'Ivoire secured a further $100m. from the World Bank in May to support its ongoing COVID-19 vaccination programme.

In October 2021 Côte d'Ivoire signed a debt reduction and development contract with France, which converted more than $1,000m. of its bilateral debt into grants administered by the French development agency to finance development projects in the country.

Statistical Survey

Source (unless otherwise stated): Institut National de la Statistique, BP V55, Abidjan; tel. 27-20-33-88-60; e-mail ins.rci.diffusion@gmail.com; internet www.ins.ci.

Area and Population

AREA, POPULATION AND DENSITY

Area (sq km)	322,462*
Population (census results)	
20 December 1998	15,366,671
15 May 2014	
Males	11,708,244
Females	10,963,087
Total	22,671,331
Population (UN estimates at mid-year)†	
2020	26,378,275
2021‡	27,053,629
2022‡	27,742,301
Density (per sq km) at mid-2022‡	86.0

* 124,503 sq miles.
† Source: UN, *World Population Prospects: The 2019 Revision*.
‡ Projection.

POPULATION BY AGE AND SEX
('000, UN projections at mid-2022)

	Males	Females	Total
0–14 years	5,744.7	5,683.6	11,428.3
15–64 years	7,800.8	7,699.4	15,500.2
65 years and over	427.2	386.6	813.8
Total	13,972.7	13,769.6	27,742.3

Source: UN, *World Population Prospects: The 2019 Revision*.

POPULATION BY DISTRICT
(at 2014 census)

	Population
Abidjan (Autonomous District)	4,707,404
Bas-Sassandra	2,280,548
Comoé	1,203,052
Denguélé	289,779
Gôh-Djiboua	1,605,286
Lacs	1,258,604
Lagunes	1,478,047
Montagnes	2,371,920
Sassandra-Marahoué	2,293,304
Savanes	1,607,497
La Vallée du Bandama	1,440,826
Woroba	845,139
Yamoussoukro (Autonomous District)	355,573
Zanzan	934,352
Total	22,671,331

PRINCIPAL TOWNS
(population at 2014 census)

Abidjan (incl. suburbs)* . . .	4,395,243	Korhogo . . .	281,735
		San-Pédro . . .	261,616
Bouaké	608,138	Gagnoa . . .	213,918
Daloa	319,427	Man	188,704
Yamoussoukro* .	286,071		

* The process of transferring the official capital from Abidjan to Yamoussoukro began in 1983.

BIRTHS AND DEATHS
(annual averages, official estimates)

	2007	2008	2009
Birth rate (per 1,000)	37.5	37.1	36.7
Death rate (per 1,000)	13.8	13.6	13.3

2016: Birth rate 36.3 per 1,000; Death rate 10.5 per 1,000 (Source: African Development Bank).

Life expectancy (years at birth, estimates): 58.1 (males 56.9; females 59.5) in 2020 (Source: World Bank, World Development Indicators database).

ECONOMICALLY ACTIVE POPULATION
('000, FAO estimates at mid-year)

	2013	2014	2015
Agriculture, etc.	2,715	2,719	2,720
Total labour force (incl. others) .	7,802	8,047	8,296

Source: FAO.

Health and Welfare

KEY INDICATORS

Total fertility rate (children per woman, 2020)	4.5
Under-5 mortality rate (per 1,000 live births, 2020) . . .	77.9
HIV/AIDS (% of persons aged 15–49, 2020)	2.1
COVID-19: Cumulative confirmed deaths (per 100,000 persons at 31 August 2022)	3.0
COVID-19: Fully vaccinated population (% of total population at 21 August 2022)	31.6
Physicians (per 1,000 head, 2019)	0.16
Hospitals (per 100,000 head, 2013)	1.7
Domestic health expenditure (2019): US $ per head (PPP) .	52.2
Domestic health expenditure (2019): % of GDP . . .	1.0
Domestic health expenditure (2019): public (% of total current expenditure)	29.1
Access to improved water resources (% of persons, 2020) .	71
Access to improved sanitation facilities (% of persons, 2020) .	35
Total carbon dioxide emissions ('000 metric tons, 2018) . .	9,910
Carbon dioxide emissions per head (metric tons, 2018) . .	0.4
Human Development Index (2021): ranking	159
Human Development Index (2021): value	0.550

Note: For data on COVID-19 vaccinations, 'fully vaccinated' denotes receipt of all doses specified by approved vaccination regime (Sources: Johns Hopkins University and Our World in Data). Data on health expenditure refer to current general government expenditure in each case. For more information on sources and further definitions for all indicators, see Health and Welfare Statistics: Sources and Definitions section (europaworld.com/credits).

Agriculture

PRINCIPAL CROPS
('000 metric tons)

	2018	2019	2020
Aubergines (Eggplants) . . .	103.0	106.1	109.1
Avocados*	35.4	35.5	35.4
Bananas	270.0	499.6	626.0
Beans, dry*	38.0	37.7	37.8
Cashew nuts, with shell . . .	761.3	634.6	848.7
Cassava (Manioc)	5,608.0	5,877.2	6,443.6
Cocoa beans	2,113.2	2,235.0	2,200.0
Coconuts	108.8†	106.6*	105.7*
Coffee, green*	41.4	65.0	59.4
Chillies and peppers, dry* . .	130.1	126.6	127.6
Groundnuts, with shell . . .	209.5	217.6	227.6
Karité nuts (Sheanuts)* . . .	31.4	31.5	31.6
Kolanuts*	56.6	58.3	57.9
Maize	1,055.0	1,102.4	1,175.7
Maize, green*	194.4	193.7	193.9
Mangoes, mangosteens and guavas*	97.4	98.9	103.4
Millet	63.8	66.2	69.5
Oil palm fruit	2,130.8	2,486.7	2,346.7
Okra	176.1	181.3	188.7
Oranges*	40.4	40.3	40.6
Plantains and others*	1,854.5	1,857.2	1,882.8

—*continued*	2018	2019	2020
Pineapples	32.5	49.1	50.9*
Rice, paddy*	1,338.6	1,256.6	987.9
Rubber, natural	624.1	780.1	936.1
Seed cotton	412.6	469.0	490.4
Sorghum	65.7	68.1	72.2
Sugar cane*	2,026.3	2,098.5	2,134.3
Sweet potatoes	55.6	57.2	58.0
Taro (Cocoyam)	85.3	87.9	89.2
Tomatoes	44.1	45.4	47.3
Yams	7,391.1	7,450.5	7,654.6

* FAO estimate(s).
† Unofficial figure.

Aggregate production ('000 metric tons, may include official, semi-official or estimated data): Total cereals 3,214.1 in 2018, 3,139.2 in 2019, 2,817.2 in 2020; Total fruit (primary) 2,482.3 in 2018, 2,732.8 in 2019, 2,891.1 in 2020; Total oilcrops 2,902.8 in 2018, 3,321.2 in 2019, 3,211.7 in 2020; Total roots and tubers 13,180.1 in 2018, 13,513.3 in 2019, 14,286.3 in 2020; Total treenuts 770.6 in 2018, 643.8 in 2019, 857.9 in 2020; Total vegetables (primary) 749.6 in 2018, 758.0 in 2019, 770.6 in 2020.

Source: FAO.

LIVESTOCK
('000 head, year ending September)

	2018	2019	2020
Cattle	1,695	1,723	1,756
Goats	2,990	3,324	3,657
Pigs	421	479	439
Poultry	76,397	80,814	84,375*
Sheep	2,101	2,182	2,263

* FAO estimate.

Source: FAO.

LIVESTOCK PRODUCTS
('000 metric tons)

	2018	2019	2020
Cattle hides, fresh*	4.4	4.4	4.5
Cattle meat	33.0	33.6	34.1
Cattle offals, edible* . . .	7.3	7.4	7.5
Cows' milk	33.6	34.1	34.8
Chicken meat	71.1	74.1	72.8*
Game meat*	153.8	152.0	152.6
Goat meat*	6.8	7.6	8.5
Pig meat	11.3	11.6	11.9
Sheep meat*	8.2	8.5	8.7
Hen eggs	66.4	66.0	66.0

* FAO estimate(s).

Source: FAO.

Forestry

ROUNDWOOD REMOVALS
('000 cubic metres, excluding bark)

	2018	2019	2020
Sawlogs, veneer logs and logs for sleepers*	2,400	2,400	2,400
Fuel wood*	9,225	9,241	9,259
Total	11,625	11,641	11,659

* FAO estimates.

Source: FAO.

SAWNWOOD PRODUCTION
('000 cubic metres, including railway sleepers, FAO estimates)

	2018	2019	2020
Total (all broadleaved) . . .	874	874	753

Source: FAO.

Fishing

('000 metric tons, live weight)

	2018	2019*	2020*
Capture	109.1	109.0	103.4
Freshwater fishes	11.9	11.9	11.9
Bigeye grunt	6.5	6.5	6.5
Round sardinella	10.3	10.3	10.3
Skipjack tuna	0.0	3.2	3.2
Aquaculture	4.5*	4.6	4.6
Total catch	113.6*	113.7	108.0

* FAO estimate(s).

Source: FAO.

Mining

	2016	2017	2018
Gold (kg)	20,827	20,318	20,000*
Natural gas (million cu m) . .	2,300	2,300	2,300*
Crude petroleum ('000 barrels) .	17,885	19,710	18,980
Manganese ore (metric tons) . .	211,000	470,000	864,000

* Estimate.

Source: US Geological Survey.

Industry

SELECTED PRODUCTS
('000 metric tons unless otherwise indicated)

	2017	2018	2019
Plywood ('000 cu m)*	106	106	106
Jet fuel	327†	359	552
Motor gasoline (petrol) . . .	888†	771	844
Gas-diesel (distillate fuel) oils .	1,222†	1,241	1,411
Residual fuel oils	313†	652	704
Cement‡	3,500	4,000	n.a.
Electrical energy (million kWh) .	10,121	10,058	10,697

2014 ('000 metric tons): Beer of barley 330 (FAO estimate); Palm oil—unrefined (unofficial figure) 370.

2016 ('000 metric tons): Raw sugar 200; Kerosene 13.

* Data from FAO.
† Estimated figure.
‡ Data from the US Geological Survey.

Source: mainly UN Energy Statistics Database.

Finance

CURRENCY AND EXCHANGE RATES

Monetary Units
100 centimes = 1 franc de la Communauté Financière Africaine (CFA).

Sterling, Dollar and Euro Equivalents (31 May 2022)
£1 sterling = 770.824 francs CFA;
US $1 = 612.300 francs CFA;
€1 = 655.957 francs CFA;
10,000 francs CFA = £12.97 = $16.33 = €15.24.

Average Exchange Rate (francs CFA per US $)
2019   585.911
2020   575.586
2021   554.531

Note: An exchange rate of 1 French franc = 50 francs CFA, established in 1948, remained in force until January 1994, when the CFA franc was devalued by 50%, with the exchange rate adjusted to 1 French franc = 100 francs CFA. This relationship to French currency remained in effect with the introduction of the euro on 1 January 1999. From that date, accordingly, a fixed exchange rate of €1 = 655.957 francs CFA has been in operation.

BUDGET
('000 million francs CFA)

Revenue*	2019	2020†	2021‡
Tax revenue	4,205.4	4,356.1	4,622.3
Direct taxes	1,139.7	1,184.9	1,285.4
Indirect taxes§	2,832.6	2,964.3	3,100.1
Earmarked taxes . . .	233.1	206.9	236.8
Non-tax revenue	678.2	739.9	697.6
Total	4,883.6	5,095.9	5,319.9

Expenditure	2019	2020†	2021‡
Current expenditure . . .	4,444.6	5,340.6	5,580.1
Wages and salaries . . .	1,703.0	1,828.1	1,831.4
Subsidies and other current transfers	431.1	666.4	832.1
Crisis-related expenditure . .	54.7	181.7	148.1
Other current expenditure . .	1,170.3	1,440.8	1,398.1
Interest due	521.0	663.8	767.3
Internal	221.7	273.6	296.5
External	299.3	390.3	470.8
Capital expenditure	1,499.2	1,914.4	2,049.6
Domestically funded . . .	977.3	1,239.1	1,092.6
Funded from abroad . . .	521.9	675.3	957.0
Total	5,943.8	7,255.1	7,629.7

* Excluding grants received ('000 million francs CFA): 107.4 in 2019; 101.4 in 2020 (estimate); 146.2 in 2021 (projection).
† Estimates.
‡ Projections.
§ Excluding taxes on petroleum products.

Source: IMF, *Côte d'Ivoire: 2021 Article IV Consultation—Press Release; Staff Report; Informational Annex; Debt Sustainability Analysis; Selected Issues; and Statement by the Executive Director for Côte d'Ivoire* (August 2021).

INTERNATIONAL RESERVES
(excluding gold, US $ million at 31 December)

	2019	2020	2021
IMF special drawing rights . .	603.2	1,667.0	2,291.8
Reserve position in IMF . . .	115.3	120.1	116.7
Foreign exchange	4.0	3.4	5.1
Total	722.5	1,790.5	2,413.6

Source: IMF, *International Financial Statistics*.

MONEY SUPPLY
('000 million francs CFA at 31 December)

	2019	2020	2021
Currency outside depository corporations	2,694.52	3,291.32	3,671.21
Transferable deposits	4,612.47	5,843.45	7,192.00
Other deposits	3,465.30	3,910.02	4,574.31
Broad money	10,772.30	13,044.79	15,437.52

Source: IMF, *International Financial Statistics*.

COST OF LIVING
(Consumer Price Index for African households; base: 2014 = 100)

	2019	2020	2021
Food and non-alcoholic beverages .	107.8	112.4	121.0
Clothing and footwear	104.1	106.0	107.5
Housing, water, electricity, gas and other fuels	105.1	108.3	112.6
All items (incl. others) . . .	103.8	106.4	110.8

NATIONAL ACCOUNTS
('000 million francs CFA at current prices)

Expenditure on the Gross Domestic Product

	2018	2019	2020
Government final consumption expenditure	3,423	3,598	3,674
Private final consumption expenditure	22,218	23,426	23,825
Change in inventories . . .	468	−360	−368
Gross fixed capital formation . .	6,368	7,240	8,170
Total domestic expenditure .	32,477	33,904	35,300
Exports of goods and services . .	7,295	8,155	7,483
Less Imports of goods and services	7,549	7,760	7,374
Statistical discrepancy	—	—	−216
GDP in purchasers' values .	32,222	34,299	35,193
GDP at constant 2015 prices .	33,315	35,391	36,097

Gross Domestic Product by Economic Activity

	2018	2019	2020
Agriculture, forestry and fishing .	6,621	7,090	7,027
Mining, quarrying and utilities .	1,742	1,957	2,066
Manufacturing	3,854	4,042	3,961
Construction	1,177	1,268	1,295
Wholesale and retail trade, restaurants and hotels . . .	4,215	4,513	4,648
Transport and communications .	3,161	3,236	3,490
Other services	9,302	9,958	10,246
Sub-total	30,072	32,064	32,731
Indirect taxes (net)*	2,151	2,235	2,462
GDP in purchasers' values .	32,222	34,299	35,193

*Figures obtained as residuals.

Source: UN National Accounts Main Aggregates Database.

BALANCE OF PAYMENTS
('000 million francs CFA)

	2018	2019	2020*
Exports of goods f.o.b.	6,142	7,399	7,061
Imports of goods f.o.b.	−5,007	−5,553	−5,547
Balance on goods	1,135	1,846	1,514
Services (net)	−1,186	−1,313	−1,408
Balance on goods and services	−51	533	106
Income (net)	−840	−986	−1,017
Balance on goods, services and primary income	−891	−453	−911
Current transfers (net) . . .	−287	−338	−311
Current balance	−1,177	−790	−1,222
Capital account (net)	79	105	101
Foreign direct investments . .	245	433	352
Portfolio investment (net) . .	825	−173	535
Other investment (net) . . .	273	1,118	1,114
Errors and omissions	−45	14	—
Reserves and related items .	198	706	880

* Estimates.

Source: IMF, *Côte d'Ivoire: 2021 Article IV Consultation—Press Release; Staff Report; Informational Annex; Debt Sustainability Analysis; Selected Issues; and Statement by the Executive Director for Côte d'Ivoire* (August 2021).

External Trade

PRINCIPAL COMMODITIES
(distribution by HS, US $ million)

Imports c.i.f.	2018	2019	2020
Live animals and animal products	719.2	754.9	793.5
Fish, crustaceans and molluscs, and preparations thereof . .	531.4	570.9	577.6
Fish, frozen, whole	528.0	565.9	572.8
Vegetables and vegetable products	1,038.0	951.9	939.3
Cereals	881.4	793.5	758.9
Rice	693.5	604.5	550.3
Prepared foodstuffs; beverages, spirits, vinegar; tobacco and articles thereof .	500.3	557.7	539.9
Mineral products	2,633.8	2,548.9	2,298.6
Mineral fuels, oils, distillation products, etc.	2,387.1	2,308.0	2,040.6
Crude petroleum oils . . .	1,548.8	1,485.6	1,436.7
Chemicals and related products	1,170.6	1,241.5	1,257.1
Pharmaceutical products . . .	385.8	370.5	399.6
Plastics, rubber, and articles thereof	553.0	573.1	615.3
Plastics and articles thereof . .	462.2	472.0	513.9
Iron and steel, other base metals and articles of base metal	798.6	757.2	697.9
Articles of iron and steel . . .	310.3	330.3	245.4
Machinery and mechanical appliances; electrical equipment and parts thereof	1,671.8	1,690.6	1,689.4
Machinery, nuclear reactors, boilers, etc.	1,028.9	1,021.2	1,028.6
Electrical, electronic equipment .	642.9	669.4	660.8
Vehicles, aircraft, vessels and associated transport equipment	962.4	675.4	717.3
Vehicles other than railway, tramway	720.3	637.5	700.2
Cars (incl. station wagon) . .	303.4	245.9	259.5
Total (incl. others)	10,999.9	10,692.6	10,532.2

Exports f.o.b.	2018	2019	2020
Vegetables and vegetable products	1,597.5	1,263.1	1,305.3
Edible fruit, nuts, peel of citrus fruit, melons	1,380.2	1,015.5	1,121.8
Brazil nuts, cashew nuts and coconuts	1,164.7	807.8	924.5
Prepared foodstuffs; beverages, spirits, vinegar; tobacco and articles thereof	4,843.7	5,328.7	5,478.5
Cocoa and cocoa preparations	4,560.5	4,949.0	5,169.8
Cocoa beans, raw, roasted	3,245.3	3,575.4	3,628.6
Cocoa paste	561.0	623.0	710.5
Mineral products	2,006.9	2,406.9	1,459.0
Mineral fuels, oils, distillation products, etc.	1,878.1	2,225.7	1,279.9
Crude petroleum oils	706.7	901.8	446.2
Petroleum oils, not crude	938.7	1,077.4	1,465.3
Chemicals and related products	442.8	404.1	446.4
Plastics, rubber, and articles thereof	907.8	1,042.0	1,170.9
Rubber and articles thereof	756.2	908.0	1,040.6
Natural rubber, balata, etc.	753.5	906.3	1,039.2
Textiles and textile articles	363.6	436.5	356.5
Pearls, precious or semi-precious stones, precious metals, and articles thereof	801.4	1,078.6	1,465.6
Total (incl. others)	11,793.2	12,935.3	12,454.0

Source: Trade Map-Trade Competitiveness Map, International Trade Centre, marketanalysis.intracen.org.

PRINCIPAL TRADING PARTNERS
(US $ million)

Imports c.i.f.	2018	2019	2020
Belgium	236.0	157.2	215.1
China, People's Republic	1,645.9	1,815.1	1,577.3
Colombia	263.6	139.2	72.3
France (incl. Monaco)	1,134.9	1,155.0	1,142.3
Germany	324.5	280.7	313.2
Ghana	93.7	116.0	159.5
India	500.4	453.0	539.5
Italy	248.4	234.6	281.3
Japan	237.6	162.1	187.3
Korea, Republic	298.3	90.5	124.4
Malaysia	111.1	55.9	63.4
Mauritania	165.1	150.7	130.2
Morocco	171.5	211.7	250.7
Netherlands	401.4	290.9	289.1
Nigeria	1,353.1	1,410.7	1,375.0
Russian Federation	134.2	154.6	116.6
Saudi Arabia	117.7	109.4	104.7
Senegal	134.4	172.2	211.4
South Africa	124.7	105.4	107.7
Spain	330.3	254.3	265.1
Thailand	253.8	121.1	117.9
Togo	164.7	23.5	124.7
Türkiye	186.4	297.4	329.0
United Kingdom	203.3	148.5	168.1
USA	372.1	539.9	423.4
Viet Nam	181.9	283.3	306.0
Total (incl. others)	10,999.9	10,692.6	10,532.2

Exports f.o.b.	2018	2019	2020
Australia	8.8	6.9	155.5
Belgium	439.8	581.7	678.1
Brazil	88.3	131.0	65.0
Burkina Faso	613.8	598.1	506.9
Canada	261.6	356.1	227.0
China, People's Republic	177.7	371.2	457.2
Estonia	112.7	175.3	143.2
France (incl. Monaco)	637.8	814.2	635.0
Germany	752.4	592.0	550.7
Ghana	352.9	235.9	236.2
India	524.0	470.0	258.4
Indonesia	207.4	173.0	151.9

Exports f.o.b.—*continued*	2018	2019	2020
Italy	181.3	224.2	187.0
Malaysia	457.2	634.1	653.8
Mali	569.8	621.5	662.5
Netherlands	1,348.9	1,358.6	1,244.5
Nigeria	199.7	218.6	122.9
Poland	111.7	125.5	129.4
Senegal	117.9	130.5	147.0
South Africa	345.9	402.7	538.5
Spain	284.6	617.2	351.2
Switzerland-Liechtenstein	427.8	598.4	805.0
Togo	114.2	212.4	153.6
Türkiye	162.3	160.8	268.9
United Kingdom	281.3	336.0	392.3
USA	1,079.0	770.4	834.8
Viet Nam	800.1	621.3	800.6
Total (incl. others)	11,793.2	12,935.3	12,454.0

Source: Trade Map-Trade Competitiveness Map, International Trade Centre, marketanalysis.intracen.org.

Transport

RAILWAYS
(traffic)

	2001	2002	2003
Passengers ('000)	399.5	320.0	87.5
Freight carried ('000 metric tons)	1,016.3	900.7	149.7

Passenger-km (million): 93.1 in 1999 (Source: SITARAIL—Transport Ferroviaire de Personnel et de Marchandises, Abidjan).

Freight ton-km (million): 537.6 in 1999 (Source: SITARAIL—Transport Ferroviaire de Personnel et de Marchandises, Abidjan).

Freight carried ('000 metric tons): 883.6 in 2012; 868.0 in 2013; 910.0 in 2014.

SHIPPING

Flag Registered Fleet
(at 31 December)

	2019	2020	2021
Number of vessels	19	19	20
Total displacement ('000 grt)	3.3	3.3	3.5

Source: Lloyd's List Intelligence (www.bit.ly/LLintelligence).

CIVIL AVIATION
(domestic and international)

	2018	2019	2020
Departures	14,666	16,616	8,030
Passengers carried ('000)	825.3	748.5	322.8
Freight carried (ton-km)	4	9	4

Source: World Bank, World Development Indicators database.

Tourism

VISITOR ARRIVALS BY REGION/COUNTRY OF RESIDENCE
('000)

	2018	2019	2020
Africa	1,697,500	1,788,617	577,292
North America	n.a.	18,424	5,947
Other Americas	21,808	4,554	1,470
Asia Pacific	106,291	111,996	36,147
China, People's Republic . .	n.a.	35,814	11,559
Europe	129,277	136,216	43,966
France	n.a.	65,831	21,248
Switzerland	n.a.	4,554	1,470
Middle East	9,823	10,351	3,341
Lebanon	n.a.	10,351	3,341
Total	1,964,699	2,070,158	668,163

Tourism receipts (US $ million, excl. passenger transport): 379 in 2016; 396 in 2017; 443 in 2018.

Source: World Tourism Organization.

Communications Media

	2018	2019	2020
Telephones ('000 main lines in use)	302.4	271.7	264.1
Mobile telephone subscriptions ('000)	33,807.9	37,376.6	40,095.2
Broadband subscriptions, fixed ('000)	175.9	216.7	260.1
Broadband subscriptions, mobile ('000)	15,442.0	17,021.2	19,651.4
Internet users (% of population) .	46.8	36.5	n.a.

Source: International Telecommunication Union.

Education

(2019/20 unless otherwise indicated)

		Students		
	Teachers	Males	Females	Total
Pre-primary . . .	10,236	118,921	125,436	244,357
Primary	101,085	2,119,318	1,982,112	4,101,430
Secondary . . .	87,795	1,307,408	1,078,105	2,385,513
Tertiary*	20,142	140,704	105,827	246,531

* 2018/19 figures.

Institutions: 207 pre-primary in 1995/96; 7,599 primary in 1996/97.

Source: mostly UNESCO Institute for Statistics.

Pupil-teacher ratio (qualified teaching staff, primary education, UNESCO estimate): 40.6 in 2019/20 (Source: UNESCO Institute for Statistics).

Adult literacy rate (UNESCO estimates): 89.9% (males 93.1%; females 86.7%) in 2019 (Source: UNESCO Institute for Statistics).

Directory

The Constitution

On 30 October 2016 the Constitution of the Third Republic of Côte d'Ivoire was approved at a national referendum by some 94% of those who voted. The Constitution entered into force on 8 November. The main provisions of the Constitution, including amendments adopted in March 2020, are summarized below:

PREAMBLE

The people of Côte d'Ivoire recognize their diverse ethnic, cultural and religious backgrounds, and desire to build a fraternal, unified, peaceful and prosperous nation based on constitutional legality and democratic institutions, the rights of the individual, cultural and spiritual values, transparency in public affairs, and the promotion of regional and subregional integration, and of African unity.

RIGHTS, FREEDOMS AND DUTIES

Articles 1–47: The state guarantees the implementation of the Constitution and guarantees to protect the rights of each citizen. The state guarantees its citizens equal access to health, education, culture, information, professional training, employment and justice. Freedom of thought and expression are guaranteed to all, although the encouragement of social, ethnic and religious discord is not permitted. Freedom of association and peaceful demonstration are guaranteed. Political parties may act freely within the law; however, parties must not be created on a regional, religious, tribal, ethnic, or racial basis. The rights of free enterprise, the right to join a trade union and the right to strike are guaranteed.

NATIONAL SOVEREIGNTY

Articles 48–52: Côte d'Ivoire is an independent and sovereign republic. The official language is French. The Republic of Côte d'Ivoire is indivisible, secular, democratic and social. Sovereignty belongs to the people, and is exercised through referendums and the election of

representatives. The right to vote freely and in secret is guaranteed to all citizens over 18 years of age.

EXECUTIVE POWER

Articles 53–84: The President of the Republic is the head of state. The President is elected for a five-year mandate (renewable once only) by direct universal suffrage. Candidates must be at least 35 years of age, hold only Ivorian nationality and have one Ivorian parent. If one candidate does not receive a simple majority of votes cast, a second round of voting takes place between the two most successful candidates.

If the presidency falls vacant by death, resignation or impeachment of the President, the Vice-President assumes the presidency.

The President holds executive power, and appoints a Prime Minister to co-ordinate government action. The President appoints the Government on the recommendation of the Prime Minister. The President presides over the Council of Ministers, is the head of the civil service and the supreme head of the armed forces. The President may initiate legislation and call referendums. The President may not hold any parliamentary mandate or other public office.

LEGISLATIVE POWER

Articles 85–100: Legislative power is exercised by Parliament, which is composed of the National Assembly and the Senate. Members of the National Assembly are elected for periods of five years by direct universal suffrage. Members of the Senate serve for five years, with two-thirds of the members elected by indirect universal suffrage and one-third appointed by the President.

RELATIONS BETWEEN THE EXECUTIVE AND THE LEGISLATURE

Articles 101–118: The President communicates with the National Assembly and the Senate either directly or by messages which are read by the Vice-President in each of the chambers of Parliament. These communications do not give rise to any debate.

INTERNATIONAL AGREEMENTS

Articles 119–123: The President negotiates and ratifies treaties and international agreements. International agreements that modify internal legislation must be ratified by further legislation. The Constitution must be amended prior to the ratification of certain agreements if the Constitutional Council deems this necessary.

ASSOCIATION, CO-OPERATION AND INTEGRATION AMONG AFRICAN STATES

Articles 124–125: Côte d'Ivoire may conclude association or integration agreements with other African states, including partial surrender of sovereignty, in order to achieve African unity.

CONSTITUTIONAL COUNCIL

Articles 126–138: The Constitutional Council rules on the constitutionality of legislation. It also regulates the functioning of government. It is composed of a President, the former Presidents of Côte d'Ivoire and six councillors (three named by the President, two by the President of the National Assembly and one by the President of the Senate) for mandates of six years. The Council supervises referendums and announces referendum and election results. It also examines the eligibility of candidates to the presidency and the legislature. There is no appeal against the Council's decisions.

JUDICIAL POWER

Articles 139–155: The judiciary is independent, and is composed of the Court of Cassation, the Council of State, the Audit Court, courts of appeal, courts of first instance, administrative tribunals and regional audit chambers. The Higher Council of Magistrates examines questions relating to judicial independence and nominates and disciplines senior magistrates.

THE HIGH COURT OF JUSTICE

Articles 156–162: The High Court of Justice judges the President, the Vice-President and the members of the Government in cases relating to the execution of their duties. The High Court of Justice is composed of members elected by the National Assembly and the Senate and is presided over by the President of the Court of Cassation.

THE ECONOMIC, SOCIAL, ENVIRONMENTAL AND CULTURAL COUNCIL

Articles 163–164: The Economic, Social, Environmental and Cultural gives its opinion on proposed legislation or decrees relating to its sphere of competence. The President may consult the Council on any economic, social, environmental or cultural matter.

THE MEDIATOR OF THE REPUBLIC

Articles 165–169: The Mediator is an independent mediating figure, appointed for a non-renewable six-year mandate by the President, in consultation with the President of the National Assembly and the President of the Senate. The Mediator, who may not hold any other political or public office or professional position, receives immunity from prosecution during the term of office.

LOCAL AUTHORITIES

Articles 170–174: The local authorities are the regions and communes. These are represented by a prefect.

TRADITIONAL LEADERS

Articles 175–176: Traditional chiefs are represented by the National Chamber of Kings and Traditional Leaders. The Chamber is charged with the protection of traditional customs, the promotion of peace and social cohesion, and the non-judicial settlement of conflicts in villages and between communities.

REVISION OF THE CONSTITUTION

Articles 177–178: Only the President or Parliament may propose amendments to the Constitution. Proposed amendments to the Constitution must be submitted simultaneously to the National Assembly and the Senate and must be approved by an absolute majority of members. The revision of the Constitution must be approved by referendum by an absolute majority of the votes cast. However, the proposed revision is not submitted to referendum where the President submits it to Parliament. In this case, the proposed revision is adopted if it is approved by a two-thirds' majority of the members of Parliament. The republican form of government and the secular nature of the state may not be the subject of any revision.

TRANSITIONAL AND FINAL PROVISIONS

Articles 179–184: The President of the Republic in office at the date of the promulgation of this Constitution appoints the Vice-President of the Republic.

The Government

HEAD OF STATE

President of the Republic: ALASSANE DRAMANE OUATTARA (elected 28 November 2010; sworn in 6 May 2011; re-elected 25 October 2015 and 31 October 2020).

Vice-President: TIÉMOKO MEYLIET KONÉ.

COUNCIL OF MINISTERS
(October 2022)

Prime Minister: PATRICK JÉRÔME ACHI.

Minister of State, Minister of Foreign Affairs, African Integration and the Diaspora: KANDIA KAMISSOKO CAMARA.

Minister of State, Minister of Defence: TÉNÉ BIRAHIMA OUATTARA.

Minister of State, Minister of Agriculture and Rural Development: KOBENAN KOUASSI ADJOUMANI.

Keeper of the Seals, Minister of Justice and Human Rights: JEAN SANSAN KAMBILÉ.

Minister of the Interior and Security: Gen. VAGONDO DIOMANDÉ.

Minister of Planning and Development: NIALÉ KABA.

Minister of Mining, Petroleum and Energy: MAMADOU SANGAFOWA COULIBALY.

Minister of the Civil Service: ANNE DÉSIRÉE OULOTO.

Minister of Transport: AMADOU KONÉ.

Minister of the Economy and Finance: ADAMA COULIBALY.

Minister of Construction, Housing and Town Planning: BRUNO NABAGNÉ KONÉ.

Minister of the Budget and the State Portfolio: MOUSSA SANOGO.

Minister of Water and Forests: LAURENT TCHAGBA.

Minister of Equipment and Road Maintenance: AMEDÉ KOFFI KOUAKOU.

Minister of National Education and Literacy: MARIATOU KONÉ.

Minister of Trade, Industry and the Promotion of Small and Medium-sized Enterprises: SOULEYMANE DIARRASSOUBA.

Minister of National Reconciliation and Cohesion: BERTIN KOUADIO KONAN.

Minister of Sport: PAULIN CLAUDE DANHO.

Minister of Animal and Fishing Resources: SIDI TIÉMOKO TOURÉ.

Minister of Communication and the Digital Economy, Government Spokesperson: AMADOU COULIBALY.

Minister of the Promotion of Youth, Professional Integration and Civic Services, Deputy Government Spokesperson: MAMADOU TOURÉ.

Minister of Tourism: SIANDOU FOFANA.

Minister of Higher Education and Scientific Research: ADAMA DIAWARA.

Minister of Health, Public Hygiene and Universal Health Coverage: PIERRE DIMBA.

Minister of Water Resources, Sanitation and Wellbeing: BOUAKÉ FOFANA.

Minister of the Promotion of Good Governance and the Fight against Corruption: EPIPHANE ZORO BI BALLO.

Minister of Solidarity and Poverty Alleviation: LOGBOH MYSS BELMONDE DOGO.

Minister of Employment and Social Protection: ADAMA KAMARA.

Minister of Women, the Family and Children: NASSENEBA TOURÉ.

Minister of Technical Education, Professional Training and Apprenticeships: KOFFI N'GUESSAN.

Minister of Culture and Francophone Affairs: FRANÇOISE REMARCK.

Minister of the Environment and Sustainable Development: JEAN-LUC ASSI.

MINISTRIES

Office of the President: 01 BP 1354, Abidjan 01; tel. 27-20-22-02-22; internet www.presidence.ci.

Office of the Prime Minister: blvd Angoulvant, 01 BP 1533, Abidjan 01; tel. 27-20-31-50-00; internet www.gouv.ci.

Ministry of Agriculture and Rural Development: Immeuble Caisse de Stabilisation, 25e étage, 01 BP 12243, Abidjan; tel. 27-20-21-43-03; e-mail minagri.cabinet@agriculture.gouv.ci; internet www.agriculture.gouv.ci.

Ministry of Animal and Fishing Resources: Immeuble Caisse de Stabilisation, 11e étage, Plateau, Abidjan; tel. 27-20-21-33-94; internet ressourcesanimales.gouv.ci/accueil.

Ministry of the Budget and the State Portfolio: Immeuble SCIAM, 10e–11e étages, 01 BP 12666, Abidjan 01; tel. 27-20-21-59-95; e-mail infos@budget.gouv.ci; internet www.budget.gouv.ci.

Ministry of the Civil Service: Immeuble Fonction Public, blvd Angoulvant, BP V93, Abidjan; tel. 27-20-25-90-00; e-mail info@fonctionpublique.ci; internet www.fonctionpublique.gouv.ci.

Ministry of Communication and the Digital Economy: Tour C, 22e étage, Tours Administratives, Plateau, BP V138, Abidjan; tel. 27-20-24-47-34; e-mail communication@communication.gouv.ci; internet www.communication.gouv.ci.

Ministry of Construction, Housing and Town Planning: Tour A, 16e–17e étages, Cité Administrative, Plateau, BP V153, Abidjan; tel. 27-20-23-90-70; internet construction.gouv.ci.

Ministry of Culture and Francophone Affairs: Tour E, 22e étage, Cité Administrative, BP V39, Abidjan; tel. 27-20-21-83-94; e-mail cellulecommunication@gmail.com; internet culture.gouv.ci.

Ministry of Defence: 01 BP 12243, Abidjan; tel. 27-20-21-07-84; e-mail info@defense.gouv.ci; internet www.defense.gouv.ci.

Ministry of the Economy and Finance: Immeuble SCIAM, 16e étage, ave Marchand, BP V163, Abidjan; tel. 27-20-20-08-42; internet finances.gouv.ci.

Ministry of Employment and Social Protection: 20 BP 1027, Abidjan; tel. 27-20-31-85-41; e-mail infos@emploi.gouv.ci; internet emploi.gouv.ci.

Ministry of the Environment and Sustainable Development: Tour D, 10e étage, Tours Administratives, BP V06, Abidjan; tel. 27-20-22-61-35; internet www.environnement.gouv.ci.

Ministry of Equipment and Road Maintenance: Immeuble POSTEL 2001, 14e et 20e étages, Plateau, Abidjan; tel. 27-20-34-73-15; e-mail info@entretienroutier.gouv.ci; internet www.entretienroutier.gouv.ci.

Ministry of Foreign Affairs, African Integration and the Diaspora: Bloc Ministériel, blvd Angoulvant, BP V109, Abidjan; tel. 27-20-22-71-50; e-mail diplomatie@gouv.ci; internet diplomatie.gouv.ci.

Ministry of Health, Public Hygiene and Universal Health Coverage: Tour C, 16e étage, Cité Administrative, Plateau, Abidjan; tel. 27-20-21-08-71; e-mail ministere.sante@egouv.ci; internet www.sante.gouv.ci.

Ministry of Higher Education and Scientific Research: Cité Administrative, Tour C, 20e étage, BP V120, Abidjan; tel. 27-20-21-02-75; internet www.enseignement.gouv.ci.

Ministry of the Interior and Security: Immeuble SETU, en face de la préfecture, BP V241, Abidjan; tel. 27-20-22-38-16; internet www.interieur.gouv.ci.

Ministry of Justice and Human Rights: Immeuble Symphonie, rue du Commerce, 01 BP 2020, Plateau, Abidjan; tel. 27-20-32-07-58; internet www.justice.gouv.ci.

Ministry of Mining, Petroleum and Energy: Immeuble Postel 2001, 01 BP V65, Abidjan; tel. 27-20-21-30-89; e-mail mines@mines.gouv.ci; internet mines.gouv.ci.

Ministry of National Education and Literacy: 28e étage, Tour D, Tours Administratives, BP V120, Abidjan; tel. 27-20-21-02-75; e-mail infoline@menci.org; internet www.education.gouv.ci.

Ministry of National Reconciliation and Cohesion: Abidjan.

Ministry of Planning and Development: Immeuble SCIAM, 16e étage, Plateau, BP V165, Abidjan; tel. 27-20-20-08-96; internet www.plan.gouv.ci.

Ministry of the Promotion of Good Governance and the Fight against Corruption: Tour A, 6e étage, Plateau, Abidjan; tel. 27-20-21-94-77; e-mail info.mp@investissement.gouv.ci; internet www.investissementprive.gouv.ci.

Ministry for the Promotion of Youth, Professional Integration and Civic Services: Immeuble CNPS, 5e étage, Plateau, BP V136, Abidjan; tel. 27-20-21-41-41; internet jeunesse.gouv.ci.

Ministry of Solidarity and Poverty Alleviation: Abidjan; internet solidaritecohesion.ci.

Ministry of Sport: Tour B, 8e étage, Tours Administratives, BP V136, Abidjan; tel. 27-20-21-21-96; internet fb.com/MSLCI.

Ministry of Technical Education, Professional Training and Apprenticeships: Abidjan.

Ministry of Tourism: Immeuble Postel 2001, 19e étage, BP V184, Abidjan 01; tel. 27-20-24-26-59; e-mail infos@tourisme.gouv.ci; internet www.tourisme.gouv.ci.

Ministry of Trade, Industry and the Promotion of Small and Medium-sized Enterprises: Immeuble Postel 2001, 18e étage, BP V142, Abidjan; tel. 27-20-22-95-28; e-mail info@commerce.gouv.ci; internet www.commerce.gouv.ci.

Ministry of Transport: Immeuble Postel 2001, 15e et 21e étage, 01 BP 739, Abidjan; tel. 27-20-34-48-58; e-mail infos@transport.gouv.ci; internet www.transports.gouv.ci.

Ministry of Women, the Family and Children: Tour E, Tours Administratives, BP V200, Abidjan; tel. 27-20-21-76-26; e-mail ministere@famille.gouv.ci; internet www.famille.gouv.ci.

Ministry of Water and Forests: Tour A, 14e étage, Cité Adminsitrative, BP 650, Abidjan; tel. 27-20-23-95-30; e-mail contact@eauxetforets.gouv.ci; internet www.eauxetforets.gouv.ci.

Ministry of Water Resources, Sanitation and Wellbeing: Immeuble POSTEL 2001, 11e étage, 17 BP 150, Abidjan 17; e-mail infoline@hydraulique.gouv.ci; internet hydraulique.gouv.ci.

President

Presidential Election, 31 October 2020

Candidate	Valid votes	% of valid votes
Alassane Dramane Ouattara (RHDP) .	3,031,483	95.31
Kouadio Konan Bertin (Ind.) . . .	64,011	2.01
Aimé Henri Konan Bédié (PDCI—RDA)	53,330	1.68
Pascal Affi N'Guessan (FPI) . . .	31,986	1.01
Total	3,180,810*	100.00

* In addition, there were 53,904 invalid votes and 35,099 blank votes.

Legislature

SENATE

Senate: Abidjan; tel. 27-22-51-07-40; e-mail contact@senat.ci; internet senat.ci.

First President: Jeannot Ahoussou-Kouadio.

Election, 24 March 2018

Party	Seats
Rassemblement des Houphouëtistes pour la Démocratie et la Paix (RHDP)*	50
Independents	16
Total	66†

* A coalition of the Rassemblement des Républicains and the Parti Démocratique de la Côte d'Ivoire—Rassemblement Démocratique Africain.

† In addition to the 66 members elected by an electoral college, the President of the Republic appoints 33 senators.

NATIONAL ASSEMBLY

National Assembly: blvd Angolvant, 01 BP 1381, Abidjan 01; tel. 27-20-20-96-48; e-mail info@assnat.ci; internet www.assnat.ci.

President: Adama Bictogo.

General Election, 6 March 2021

Party	Seats
Rassemblement des Houphouëtistes pour la Démocratie et la Paix (RHDP)	137
PDCI—RDA/EDS*	50
Parti Démocratique de la Côte d'Ivoire— Rassemblement Démocratique Africain (PDCI— RDA)	23
Ensemble pour Bâtir (EPB)	8
Ensemble pour la Démocratie et la Souveraineté (EDS)	8
Front Populaire Ivoirien (FPI)	2
Independents	26
Total	254†

* Candidates representing a coalition of the Parti Démocratique de la Côte d'Ivoire—Rassemblement Démocratique Africain and the Ensemble pour la Démocratie et la Souveraineté.

† Excluding one constituency where voting did not take place due to the death of a candidate. The election took place there on 24 April and the seat was won by the RHDP candidate. Voting was repeated for six further legislative seats on 12 June.

Election Commission

Commission Electorale Indépendante (CEI): blvd Latrille, Résidence Angoua, Cocody II Plateaux, 08 BP 2648, Abidjan; tel. 27-22-52-86-10; e-mail info@cei.ci; internet www.cei.ci; f. 2001; 15 mems; Pres. IBRAHIME COULIBALY-KUIBIERT.

Advisory Councils

Constitutional Council (Conseil Constitutionnel): 22 blvd Card, BP 4642, Abidjan 01; tel. 27-20-25-38-50; e-mail info@ conseil-constitutionnel.ci; internet www.conseil-constitutionnel.ci; f. 2000; Pres. Prof. MAMADOU KONÉ.

Economic, Social, Environmental and Cultural Council (Conseil Economique, Social, Environnemental et Culturel): blvd Card, angle ave Terrasson de Fougère, 04 BP 301, Abidjan 04; tel. 27-20-25-02-00; internet ces.ci; f. 1961; Pres. Dr EUGÈNE AKA AOUÉLÉ; 120 mems.

Political Organizations

Alliance pour le Changement (APC): Abidjan; f. 2019; est. in 2009 as a civil society movement; Pres. ALPHONSE TIORNAN SORO.

Congrès Panafricain pour la Justice et l'Egalité des Peuples (COJEP): ; f. 2001; Pres. CHARLES BLÉ GOUDÉ.

Ensemble Pour Bâtir (EPB): Abidjan.

Ensemble pour la Démocratie et la Souveraineté (EDS): Abidjan; e-mail presidium.eds@gmail.com; internet fb.com/ presidiumEDS; a coalition of political parties and organizations in support of former Pres. Gbagbo; Pres. Prof. GEORGES-ARMAND OUEGNIN; Sec.-Gen. ETIENNE M'PONON.

Front Populaire Ivoirien (FPI): Marcory Zone 4C, 22 BP 302, Abidjan 22; tel. 0707908690; e-mail info@fpi-ci.com; internet fpi-ci .com; f. 1990; socialist; Pres. PASCAL AFFI N'GUESSAN; Sec.-Gen. ISSIAKA SANGARÉ.

Liberté et Démocratie pour la République (LIDER): LIDER House, rue D07 des Jardins de la Riviera Golf, Cocody, 22 BP 836, Abidjan 22; tel. 27-22-00-33-33; e-mail info@lider.ci; internet liderci .com; f. 2011; Pres. Dr ROCHE OMER KRAIDY.

Mouvement des Générations Capables (MGC): Abidjan; f. 2022; Pres. SIMONE GBAGBO.

Parti Démocratique de la Côte d'Ivoire—Rassemblement Démocratique Africain (PDCI—RDA): 20 BP 1081, Abidjan 20; tel. 27-22-48-05-14; e-mail info@pdcirda.ci; internet pdcirda.ci; f. 1946; Pres. HENRI KONAN BÉDIÉ; Exec. Sec MAURICE KAKOU GUIKAHUÉ.

Parti des Peuples Africains—Côte d'Ivoire (PPA—CI): Abidjan; f. 2021; Leader LAURENT GBAGBO.

Rassemblement pour la Côte d'Ivoire (RACI): Abidjan; tel. 0546431919; e-mail abidamankone@gmail.com; internet www .raci-ci.com; f. 2019; Pres. MAMADOU SORO.

Rassemblement des Houphouëtistes pour la Démocratie et la Paix (RHDP): Abidjan; internet rhdp.ci; Pres. ALASSANE DRAMANE OUATTARA.

Mouvement des Forces d'Avenir (MFA): 15 BP 794, Abidjan 15; tel. 27-21-24-42-02; e-mail contact@mfa-ci.com; f. 1995; Pres. SIAKA OUATTARA; Sec.-Gen. KONAN DJAHA.

Parti Ivoirien des Travailleurs (PIT): Adjamé 220 logements, face Cinéma Liberté, Immeuble Mistral Appartement 602, 20 BP 43, Abidjan 20; tel. 27-20-39-04-76; e-mail pit.ci@aviso.ci; social-democratic; f. 1990; Pres. JOSEPH SÉKA SÉKA; Sec.-Gen. MERMOZ KOUADIO KOUASSI.

Rassemblement des Républicains (RDR): 8 rue Lepic, Cocody, 06 BP 111, Abidjan 06; tel. 27-22-44-33-51; e-mail rdr@rdr.ci; internet www.rdr.ci; f. 1994 following split from PDCI—RDA; Pres. HENRIETTE DAGRI DIABATÉ; Sec.-Gen. KANDIA KAMISSOKO CAMARA.

Union Pour la Côte d'Ivoire (UPCI): Abidjan; tel. 0707410000; e-mail info@upci.ci; internet www.upci.ci; Pres. SIDIBÉ YACOUBA; Sec.-Gen. FADIGA MAMADOU.

Union pour la Démocratie et pour la Paix de la Côte d'Ivoire (UDPCI): 06 BP 1481, Abidjan 06; tel. 27-22-41-60-94; e-mail info@udpci.org; internet fb.com/udpci; f. 2001 following split from PDCI—RDA by supporters of fmr head of state Gen. Robert Gueï; Pres. ALBERT TOIKESSE MABRI; Sec.-Gen. LAURENT TCHAGBA.

Rassemblement du Peuple de Côte d'Ivoire (RPCI): Abidjan; internet www.rpci-ci.org; f. 2012; Pres. MORIFERÉ BAMBA.

Parti pour le Progrès et le Socialisme (PPS): Abidjan; f. 1993; Pres. KAKOU MATHIAS.

Union des Sociaux-Démocrates (USD): 08 BP 1866, Abidjan 08; tel. 27-22-44-06-70; Sec.-Gen. Me JÉRÔME CLIMANLO COULIBALY.

Renouveau pour la Paix et la Concorde (RPC): Cocody II Plateaux, Sideci, 06 BP 6710, Abidjan 06; tel. 27-22-41-49-77; e-mail rpc_ctedivoire@yahoo.com; Pres. ADJOUA HENRIETTE LAGOU.

Union Démocratique Citoyenne (UDCY): 37 bis rue de la Canebière—PISAM, 01 BP 1410, Abidjan 01; tel. 27-22-47-12-94; f. 2000 following split from PDCI—RDA; Pres. THÉODORE MEL-EG.

Diplomatic Representation

EMBASSIES IN CÔTE D'IVOIRE

Algeria: 53 blvd Clozel, 01 BP 1015, Abidjan 01; tel. 27-20-21-23-40; e-mail ambalgci2020@gmail.com; internet ambalg.ci; Ambassador (vacant).

Angola: Lot 2461, rue des Jardins, Cocody II Plateaux, 01 BP 1734, Abidjan 01; tel. 27-22-44-45-91; e-mail ambafcon@aviso.ci; Ambassador DOMINGOS BERNADO FELICIANO PACHECO.

Belgium: Cocody Ambassades, angle rue de Bélier et rue A56, 01 BP 1800, Abidjan 01; tel. 27-22-48-33-60; e-mail abidjan@diplobel.fed .be; internet cotedivoire.diplomatie.belgium.be; Ambassador MICHAEL WIMMER.

Benin: rue des Jardins, Lot 1610, Cocody II Plateaux, 09 BP 283, Abidjan 09; tel. 27-22-41-44-13; e-mail ambabenin@aviso.ci; internet ambassadebeninci.com; Ambassador ADJOUAVI MARTINE-FRANÇOISE DOSSA.

Brazil: Immeuble Alpha 2000, 22ème étage, 01 BP 3820, Abidjan; tel. 27-20-22-74-83; e-mail brasemb.abidja@itamaraty.gov.br; internet www.gov.br/mre/pt-br/embaixada-abidja; Ambassador JOSE CARLOS DE ARAUJO LEITAO.

Burkina Faso: Immeuble SIDAM, 5e étage, 34 ave Houdaille, 01 BP 908, Plateau, Abidjan 01; tel. 27-20-21-15-01; e-mail ambassadebfaso@aviso.ci; Ambassador MAHAMADOU ZONGO.

Cameroon: Immeuble le Général, 3ème étage, blvd Botreau Roussel, 06 BP 326, Abidjan 06; tel. 27-20-21-33-31; e-mail ambacamci@ yahoo.fr; Ambassador MARIE-YVETTE KOLOKO ASSENE NKOU.

Canada: Immeuble Trade Center, 23 ave Noguès, 01 BP 4104, Abidjan 01; tel. 27-20-30-07-00; e-mail abdjn@international.gc.ca; internet www.canadainternational.gc.ca/cotedivoire; Ambassador ANDERSON BLANC.

Central African Republic: 9 rue des Jasmins, Cocody Danga Nord, 01 BP 3387, Abidjan 01; tel. 27-20-21-36-46; e-mail ambasrca.rci@ gmail.com; Ambassador (vacant).

Chad: Cocody, Riviera Golf, rue D36, Abidjan; tel. 27-22-43-63-13; e-mail ambtchadci@gmail.com; Ambassador MAHAMAT ABDERAHIM ACYL.

China, People's Republic: Lot 45, ave Jacques Aka, Cocody, 01 BP 3691, Abidjan 01; tel. 27-22-44-59-00; e-mail ambchine@aviso.ci; internet ci.china-embassy.gov.cn; Ambassador WAN LI.

Congo, Democratic Republic: Carrefour France-Amérique, RAN Treichville, ave 21, 01 BP 541, Abidjan 01; tel. 27-21-24-69-06; Ambassador GILBERT MAYA NABINA.

Congo, Republic: Ilot 14, ave Beverly Hills, 08 BP 3578, Abidjan 08; tel. 27-22-47-29-00; e-mail info@ambacongo-ci.org; internet www .ambacongo-ci.org; Ambassador VÉRONIQUE OKOUMOU.

Egypt: Immeuble El Nasr, 17e étage, rue du Commerce, 01 BP 2104, Abidjan 01; tel. 27-20-22-62-31; e-mail egypte.ambassade@aviso.ci; Ambassador WAEL IBRAHIM ALI BADAWI EL-SHEIKH.

Equatorial Guinea: Angré 7ème tranche, rue L169, Abidjan; tel. 27-22-54-45-26; e-mail embajadageabidjan@gmail.com; Ambassador BERNARDINO MBA ONDO MIKUE.

Ethiopia: Cocody Danga Nord, blvd de l'Université, SODEMI, rue B49, Lot No. 5, 01 BP 3712, Abidjan 01; tel. 27-22-44-03-90; e-mail ambethio@gmail.com; internet www.ethiopiaembassyabidjan.org; Ambassador SHITAYE MINALE (designate).

France: 17 rue Lecoeur, 17 BP 175, Abidjan 17; tel. 27-20-20-74-00; e-mail scac.abidjan-amba@diplomatie.gouv.fr; internet ci .ambafrance.org; Ambassador JEAN-CHRISTOPHE BELLIARD.

Gabon: Immeuble Les Heveas, blvd Carde, 01 BP 3765, Abidjan 01; tel. 27-22-44-51-54; e-mail ambga.cotedivoire@diplomatie.gouv.ga; Ambassador FAUSTIN MOUNGUENGUI NZIGOU.

Germany: 39 blvd Hassan II, Cocody, 01 BP 1900, Abidjan 01; tel. 27-22-44-20-30; e-mail info@abidjan.diplo.de; internet abidjan.diplo .de; Ambassador INGO HERBERT.

Ghana: Lot 2393, rue J 95, Cocody II Plateaux, 01 BP 1871, Abidjan 01; tel. 27-20-33-11-24; e-mail ghanaemb.abj@aviso.ci; internet www .ghanaembassy-ci.org; Ambassador FREDERICK DANIEL LARYEA.

Guinea: Immeuble Duplessis, 08 BP 2280, Abidjan 08; tel. 27-20-22-25-20; e-mail ambaguiabidjan@mae.gov.gn; Ambassador ABDOULRAMANE SINKOUN CAMARA.

Holy See: rue Mgr. René Kouassi 18, 08 BP 1347, Abidjan 08; tel. 27-22-40-17-70; e-mail nuntius.ci@gmail.com; Apostolic Nuncio (vacant).

India: Riviera IV Golf, Îlot No. 2, Lot No. 29, 06 BP 318, Abidjan 06; tel. 27-22-47-95-80; e-mail amb.office@eoiabidjan.org; internet www.eoiabidjan.gov.in; Ambassador Y. K. SAILAS THANGAL.

Iran: blvd de France, en face de Campus Université de Cocody, rue Belier, Villa No. 1, 08 BP 44, Abidjan 08; tel. 27-22-48-75-48; e-mail iranemb.abj@mfa.gov.ir; internet cotedivoire.mfa.gov.ir; Ambassador AMIR HOSSEIN NIKBIN.

Israel: Immeuble Nour Al-Hayat, ave Chardy, 01 BP 1877, Abidjan 01; tel. 27-20-21-31-78; e-mail info@abidjan.mfa.gov.il; internet embassies.gov.il/abidjan; Ambassador RONY YEDIDIA-CLEIN.

Italy: 16 rue de la Canebière, Cocody, 01 BP 1905, Abidjan 01; tel. 27-22-44-61-70; e-mail ambasciata.abidjan@esteri.it; internet ambabidjan.esteri.it; Ambassador ARTURO LUZZI.

Japan: Immeuble La Prévoyance, Bâtiment B, 2ème étage, ave Noguès, 01 BP 1329, Abidjan 01; tel. 27-20-21-28-63; e-mail administratif@aj.mofa.go.jp; internet www.ci.emb-japan.go.jp; Ambassador KATSUYA IKKATAI.

Korea, Republic: rue Saint Marie, Lot 18–19, Cocody Sud, 01 BP 3950, Abidjan 01; tel. 27-22-48-67-01; e-mail ambcoabj@mofa.go.kr; internet overseas.mofa.go.kr/ci-fr/index.do; Ambassador LEE SANG RYUL.

Lebanon: Immeuble Trade Center, ave Noguès, 01 BP 2227, Abidjan 01; tel. 27-20-33-28-24; e-mail ambliban@hotmail.com; internet www.abidjan.mfa.gov.lb/abidjan/arabic/home; Ambassador NAJEM HASSAN.

Liberia: Villa No. 23, rue Monseigneur Kouassi, Cocody, 01 BP 2514, Abidjan 01; tel. 27-24-32-81-31; e-mail libemabidjan@gmail.com; Ambassador WILLYE MAI TOLBERT KING.

Libya: Immeuble Shell, 01 BP 5725, Abidjan 01; tel. 27-20-22-01-27; Ambassador OMAR IBRAHIM MOHAMED AL-DADAH.

Mali: 46 blvd Lagunaire, 01 BP 2746, Abidjan 01; tel. 27-20-32-31-47; e-mail houleynette@yahoo.fr; Ambassador OUSMAN AG RHISSA.

Mauritania: rue Pierre et Marie Curie, 01 BP 2275, Abidjan 01; tel. 27-22-41-16-43; Ambassador MOHAMED ABDALLAHI KHATTRA.

Morocco: 24 rue de la Canebière, 01 BP 146, Cocody, Abidjan 01; tel. 27-22-44-58-73; e-mail sifmaabj@aviso.ci; Ambassador ABDELMALEK KETTANI.

Netherlands: Immeuble Union Européenne (rez de chaussée), ave Terrasson de Fougères, Plateau, 08 BP 3824 Abidjan 08; tel. 27-20-20-40-00; e-mail abi@minbuza.nl; internet www.netherlandsworldwide.nl/countries/cote-divoire; Ambassador YVETTE DAOUD.

Niger: 23 ave Angoulvant, 01 BP 2743, Abidjan 01; tel. 27-21-26-28-14; Ambassador ABOUKAR ABDOULAYE DIORI.

Nigeria: Immeuble Maison du Nigéria, 35 blvd de la République, 01 BP 1906, Abidjan 01; tel. 27-20-22-30-82; e-mail info@nigeriaembassyci.org; internet www.nigeriaembassyci.org; Ambassador MARTIN ADAMU.

Portugal: Abidjan; Ambassador MARIA DA CONCEIÇÃO DE SOUSA PILAR.

Qatar: Lot 1, rue D30, Riviera Golf 1, 08 BP 3424, Abidjan 08; tel. 27-22-43-12-12; e-mail abidjan@mofa.gov.qa; Ambassador JABER JARALLAH MASOUD AL-GHAFRANI AL-MERI.

Russian Federation: BP 583, Riviera, Abidjan 01; tel. 27-22-43-09-59; e-mail ambrci@mid.ru; internet cotedivoire.mid.ru; Ambassador ALEXEI E. SALTYKOV.

Saudi Arabia: Villa No. 15, rue Victor Scheolcher, BP 2664, Abidjan 08; tel. 27-22-44-24-80; internet embassies.mofa.gov.sa/sites/IvoryCoast; Ambassador ABDULLAH BIN HAMAD AL-SUBAI'I.

Senegal: Immeuble Nabil Choucair, 6 rue du Commerce, 08 BP 2165, Abidjan 08; tel. 27-20-33-28-76; Ambassador ABDOU KHADIR AGNE.

South Africa: Villa Marc André, rue Mgr René Kouassi, Cocody, 08 BP 1806, Abidjan 08; tel. 27-22-44-59-63; e-mail abidjan@dirco.gov.za; internet www.dirco.gov.za/abidjan; Ambassador ZOLANI MTSHOTSHISA.

Spain: Impasse Abla Pokou, Cocody Danga Nord, 08 BP 876, Abidjan 08; tel. 27-22-44-48-50; e-mail emb.abidjan@maec.es; internet www.exteriores.gob.es/embajadas/abidjan; Ambassador RAFAEL SORIANO ORTIZ.

Sudan: Abidjan; Ambassador IDRIS ISMAIL FARAGALLA HASSAN.

Switzerland: Cocody Ambassades, rue du Bélier, 01 BP 1914, Abidjan 01; tel. 27-22-44-79-89; e-mail abidjan@eda.admin.ch; internet www.eda.admin.ch/abidjan; Ambassador ANNE LUGON-MOULIN.

Tunisia: Immeuble Shell, ave Lamblin, 01 BP 3906, Abidjan 01; tel. 27-20-22-61-23; e-mail ambtunisie.abj@aviso.ci; Ambassador (vacant).

Türkiye (Turkey): Immeuble N'Zarama, 3ème étage, blvd Lagunaire Charles de Gaulle, Plateau, 01 BP 5137, Abidjan 01; tel. 27-20-25-51-10; internet abidjan.be.mfa.gov.tr; Ambassador HAVVA YONCA GÜNDÜZ ÖZÇERI.

United Kingdom: Cocody Quartier Ambassades, rue l'Impasse du Belier, 01 BP 2581, Abidjan 01; tel. 27-22-44-26-69; e-mail British.Embassy.Abidjan@fco.gov.uk; internet www.gov.uk/government/world/organisations/british-embassy-abidjan; Ambassador CATHARINE BROOKER.

USA: 03 BP 730, Abidjan 03; tel. 27-22-49-40-00; e-mail abidjanpas@state.gov; internet ci.usembassy.gov; Ambassador RICHARD K. BELL.

Judicial System

The judiciary is independent, and is composed of the Supreme Court (the Court of Cassation and the Council of State), the Audit Court, courts of appeal, courts of first instance, administrative tribunals and regional audit chambers. The Higher Council of Magistrates examines questions relating to judicial independence and nominates and disciplines senior magistrates.

Supreme Court: rue Gourgas, Cocody, BP V30, Abidjan; tel. 27-20-22-73-72; internet www.coursupreme.ci; comprises 3 chambers: judicial, administrative and auditing; Pres. RENÉ APHING KOUASSI; Pres. of the Judicial Chamber CHANTAL NANABA CAMARA; Pres. of the Administrative Chamber PIERRE CLAVER KOBO.

Courts of Appeal: Abidjan: First Pres. ALY YÉO; Bouaké: First Pres. DEMBÉLÉ TAHIROU; Daloa: First Pres. AUGUSTIN KOUAMÉ.

Courts of First Instance: Abengourou: Pres. SORO DRISSA; Abidjan: Pres. AHMED SOULEYMANE COULIBALY; Bouaké: Pres. DEMBÉLÉ TAHIROU; Daloa: Pres. KOUAMÉ AUGUSTIN YAO; Korhogo: Vice-Pres. HERMANN KOUA KADJO; Gagnoa: Pres. KOUAMÉ TÉHUA; Yopougon: Pres. KOUADIO KOFFI BERNARD; Man: Pres. CISSOKO AMOUROULAYE; there are a further 25 courts in the principal centres.

Revenue Court (Cour des Comptes): Cocody Angré, 7e Tranche, Cité Cascade, 17 BP 131, Abidjan 17; tel. 27-22-52-21-93; e-mail chambredescomptesci@aviso.ci; internet www.courdescomptes.ci; f. 2018; Pres. KANVALY DIOMANDE.

Tribunal de Commerce d'Abidjan: Cocody II Plateaux, derrière la Fondation Donwahi, Abidjan; tel. 27-22-51-03-41; e-mail infos@tribunalcommerceabidjan.org; internet tribunalcommerceabidjan.org; f. 2012; Pres. AMINATA TOURÉ.

High Court of Justice: judges the President, the Vice-President and the members of the Government in cases relating to the execution of their dutiescomposed of members elected by the National Assembly and the Senate and presided over by the President of the Supreme Court.

Constitutional Council: 22 blvd Card, 01 BP 4642, Abidjan 01; tel. 27-20-25-38-50; e-mail info@conseil-constitutionnel.ci; internet www.conseil-constitutionnel.ci; f. 2000 to replace certain functions of the fmr Constitutional Chamber of the Supreme Court; Pres. Prof. MAMADOU KONÉ.

Religion

The Constitution guarantees religious freedom, and this right is generally respected. Religious groups are required to register with the authorities, although no penalties are imposed on a group that fails to register. At the 2014 census it was estimated that about 42% of the total population were Muslims, 34% of the population were Christians (mainly Roman Catholics), 4% followed traditional indigenous beliefs, 1% practised other religions, while 19% had no religious affiliation. It was, however, recorded that the proportion of Muslims was much greater among the non-Ivorian population, where they represented 72% of the 5.49m non-nationals. Thus, Christians comprised 39% of the Ivorian population, while 34% of the Ivorian population were Muslims. Muslims are found in greatest numbers in the north of the country, while Christians are found mostly in the southern, central, western and eastern regions. Traditional indigenous beliefs are generally prevalent in rural areas.

ISLAM

Conseil National Islamique (CNI): Mosquée d'Aghien les deux Plateaux, BP 174 Cédex 03, Abidjan 08; tel. 27-22-42-67-79; f. 1993; groups more than 5,000 local communities organized in 13 regional and 78 local organizations; Chair. Imam El Hadj IDRISS KOUDOUSS KONÉ.

Conseil Supérieur des Imams (COSIM): 05 BP 2092, Abidjan 08; tel. 27-21-35-87-51; e-mail contact@cosim-ci.org; internet www.cosim-ci.org; Pres. OUSMANE DIAKITÉ.

Conseil Supérieur Islamique (CSI): 11 BP 71, Abidjan 11; tel. 27-21-25-24-70; f. 1978; Pres. ALMAMY MAMADOU CISSÉ.

Other Islamic organizations include the Association des Musulmans Sunnites, Conseil des Imams Sunnites, Front de la Oummat Islamique and Haut Conseil des Imamats et Oulémas.

CHRISTIANITY

The Roman Catholic Church

Côte d'Ivoire comprises four archdioceses and 11 dioceses.

Bishops' Conference: Conférence des Evêques Catholiques de Côte d'Ivoire, BP 713 Cédex 03, Abidjan-Riviera; tel. 27-22-47-20-00; e-mail contact@eglisecatholique.ci; internet fb.com/ceccivoire; Pres. Rev. IGNACE BESSY DOGBO (Archbishop of Korhogo).

Archbishop of Abidjan: Cardinal JEAN-PIERRE KUTWA, Archevêché, ave Jean-Paul II, 01 BP 1287, Abidjan 01; tel. 27-20-21-23-08.

Archbishop of Bouaké: Most Rev. PAUL-SIMÉON AHOUANAN DJRO, Archevêché, 01 BP 649, Bouaké 01; tel. 27-31-63-24-59; e-mail archevbke@gmail.com; internet fb.com/archeveche.bouake.

Archbishop of Gagnoa: Most Rev. JOSEPH YAPO AKÉ, Archevêché, BP 527, Gagnoa; tel. 27-32-77-25-68; e-mail evechegagnoa@aviso.ci.

Archbishop of Korhogo: IGNACE BESSI DOGBO, BP 1581, Yamoussoukro; tel. 25-36-86-01-18; e-mail dieulesauve@yahoo.fr.

Protestant Churches

Conseil National des Eglises Protestantes et Evangéliques de Côte d'Ivoire (CNEPECI): Abidjan; Pres. Rev. BERNARD KPANGUI.

Eglise Evangélique des Assemblées de Dieu de Côte d'Ivoire: 26 BP 1396, Abidjan 26; tel. 27-21-35-55-48; e-mail daplexhonore@yahoo.fr; internet www.eeadci.org; f. 1960; Pres. DAPLEX HONORÉ OUENTCHIST; Sec.-Gen. JEAN MARIE TIACOH.

Eglise Harriste: 01 BP 3620, Abidjan 01; tel. 27-22-42-31-03; internet egliseharriste.org; f. 1913 by William Wadé Harris; affiliated to World Council of Churches 1998; allows polygamous new converts; 100,000 mems, 1,400 preachers, 7,000 apostles; Sec.-Gen. DOGBO JULES.

Eglise Méthodiste Unie de Côte d'Ivoire: 41 blvd de la République, 01 BP 1282, Abidjan 01; tel. 27-20-21-17-97; e-mail infoconf@emu.ci; internet emu.ci; f. 1924; publ. *Le Méthodiste* (monthly); autonomous since 1985; c. 800,000 mems; Pres. BENJAMIN BONI.

Eglise du Nazaréen (Church of the Nazarene): 22 BP 623, Abidjan 22; tel. 27-22-41-07-80; e-mail awfcon@compuserve.com; f. 1987; active in evangelism, ministerial training and medical work.

Eglise Protestante Baptiste Oeuvres et Mission Internationale: 03 BP 1032, Abidjan 03; tel. 27-23-45-20-18; e-mail epbomi2018@gmail.com; internet epbomi-officiel.org; f. 1975; active in evangelism, teaching and social work; medical centre, 6,000 places of worship, 400 missionaries and 193,000 mems; Pres. Rev. Dr YAYE ROBERT DION.

Eglise Protestante Evangélique CMA de Côte d'Ivoire: Plateaux Vallon, BP 685, Abidjan 2; tel. 27-22-41-79-26; e-mail infos@eglisecma.ci; internet www.eglisecma.ci; f. 1930; 350,000 mems; Nat. Pres. Dr NOËL N'GUESSAN KOUADIO; Sec.-Gen KOUAKOU JEAN DIBY.

Union des Eglises Evangéliques, Services et Œuvres de Côte d'Ivoire: 08 BP 20, Abidjan 08; tel. 0140227500; e-mail ueesoci63@yahoo.fr; f. 1927; c. 250 places of worship; Pres. GILBERT GOUENTOUEU; Sec.-Gen. MICHEL LOH.

The Press

Autorité Nationale de la Presse (ANP): Cocody II Plateaux, 7ème tranche, BP V 106, Abidjan; tel. 27-22-52-04-52; e-mail contact@anp.ci; internet www.anp.ci; f. 1991; fmrly Conseil National de la Presse; present name adopted 2018; Pres. SAMBA KONÉ.

Agence de Soutien et de Développement des Médias (ASDM): Abidjan; f. 2022 to replace Fonds de Soutien et de Développement de la Presse; MEÏTÉ SINDOU.

DAILY NEWSPAPERS (PRINT AND ONLINE)

L'Expression: Cocody Angré, 7e Tranche, 13 BP 712, Abidjan 13; tel. 27-22-42-37-98; e-mail contact@lexpressionci.com; internet www.lexpressionci.com; Dir of Publication MARIMA TOURÉ; Editor-in-Chief ABDOUL KARIM OUATTARA.

Fraternité Matin: blvd du Général de Gaulle, 01 BP 1807, Abidjan 01; tel. 27-20-37-06-66; e-mail contact@fratmat.info; internet www.fratmat.info; f. 1964; official newspaper; state-owned; Dir-Gen. ABDEL SERGE OLIVIER NOUHO.

L'Intelligent d'Abidjan: 28 BP 1475 Abidjan 28; tel. 27-22-45-85-25; e-mail redaction@lintelligentdabidjan.info; internet www.lintelligentdabidjan.info; f. 2003; Dir-Gen. ALAFÉ WAKILI.

L'Inter: rue Louis Lumière, Zone 4C, 10 BP 2462, Abidjan 10; tel. 27-21-21-28-00; e-mail linfodrome@gmail.com; internet www.linfodrome.com; f. 1998; publ. by Editions Olympe; national and international politics and economics; Dir of Publication VAMARA COULIBALY; Editor-in-Chief HAMADOU ZIAO.

Le Jour Plus: 26 Cocody II Plateaux, 25 BP 1082, Abidjan 25; tel. 27-20-21-95-78; f. 1994; publ. by Editions Le Nere; independent; Dir of Publication COULIBALY SEYDOU; Editor-in-Chief FRÉDÉRIC KOFFI.

Le Point d'Abidjan: Plateaux, 7e Tranche, 11 BP 1035, Abidjan 11; tel. 0506061559; e-mail lepoindabidjan@yahoo.fr; Dir of Publication ELIAS ELIE HALLASSOU; Editor-in-Chief MARCEL TIM.

Nord-Sud: Abidjan; internet nordsudquotidien.net; f. 2005; Dir TOURÉ MOUSSA.

Le Nouveau Courrier: Abidjan; tel. 27-22-49-53-47; e-mail bahi_stephane@yahoo.fr; f. 2010; Dir of Publication STÉPHANE BAHI GUÉDÉ; Editor-in-Chief SAINT-CLAVER OULA.

Le Nouveau Réveil: Cocody II Plateaux, Lot 458, Îlot 51, près de l'Eglise St Jacques, 01 BP 10684, Abidjan 01; tel. 27-22-41-29-15; e-mail lenouveaureveil@yahoo.fr; internet www.lenouveaureveil.com; f. 2001 to replace weekly *Le Réveil-Hebdo*; supports PDCI—RDA; Dir-Gen. DENIS KAH ZION; Dir of Publication PATRICE YAO; circ. 18,000.

Le Patriote: 23 rue du Canal, Biétry, 22 BP 509, Abidjan 22; tel. 27-21-75-45-45; e-mail lepatriote99@yahoo.fr; internet www.lepatriote.ci; organ of the RDR; Dir of Publication CHARLES SANGA; Editor-in-Chief KORÉ EMMANUEL.

Le Quotidien d'Abidjan: Cocody, 8e Tranche, Abidjan; tel. 27-22-42-14-41; e-mail votrequotidien@yahoo.fr; Dir-Gen. and Dir of Publication ALLAN ALIALI; Editor-in-Chief BOHUI WILFRIED.

Soir Info: rue Louis Lumière, Zone 4C, 10 BP 2462, Abidjan 10; tel. 27-21-21-28-00; e-mail quotidiensoirinfo@yahoo.fr; internet www.linfodrome.com; f. 1994; publ. by Editions Olympe; independent; Dir of Publication VAMARA COULIBALY; Editor-in-Chief NAZAIRE KIKIÉ.

Le Sport: Cocody Attoban, face au Groupe Scolaire Jules Ferry, 09 BP 3685, Abidjan 09; tel. 27-22-43-92-54; internet www.lesport.ci; Dir of Publication ASSI ADON AMÉDÉE.

Supersport: rue du Commerce, près d'Hotel de Ville, Plateau, 28 BP 1362, Abidjan 28; tel. 27-20-32-07-75; e-mail supersport_2006@yahoo.fr; internet www.supersportci.net/fr; f. 2006; Dir-Gen. HAMIDOU FOMBA.

Le Sursaut: Cocody Centre, SICOGI Nord Est, Villa N° 22, 08 BP 3809, Abidjan 08; tel. 27-22-44-10-32; e-mail infoslesursaut@yahoo.com; internet sursautdafrique.info/category/cote-divoire; f. 2015.

Le Temps: Abidjan; tel. 27-22-40-99-55; e-mail cyletemps@yahoo.fr.

BI-WEEKLY AND WEEKLY NEWSPAPERS (PRINT AND ONLINE)

Abidjan Sport: Abidjan; weekly.

Allo Police: 10 BP 399, Abidjan 10; tel. 27-21-56-47-20; e-mail info@allopolice.ci; internet allopolice.ci; weekly.

Eléphant Déchaîné: Cocody Angré, les Oscars, Abidjan; tel. 27-22-52-47-68; e-mail elephantdechaine@gmail.com; internet lelephant-dechaine.ci; satirical; 2 a week; Dir-Gen. ANTOINE ASSALÉ TIÉMOKO.

Gbich!: Koumassi Remblais, IST la Colombe, Lot 1619, Îlot 109, 10 BP 11111, Abidjan 10; tel. 27-21-56-47-20; e-mail info@gbich.net; internet gbich.net; weekly; satirical; Editor-in-Chief SIMPLICE ILLARY.

Go Magazine: 10 BP 399, Abidjan 10; tel. 27-21-56-47-20; e-mail info@gomagazine.ci; internet www.gomagazineci.com; f. 2004; Dir of Publication LASSANE ZOHORE; Editor-in-Chief KOUASSI KOUAMÉ NARCIS.

Select: Villa 12S, Bâtiment Star 4, 19 BP 1534, Abidjan 19; tel. 27-22-42-71-61.

Star Magazine: Abidjan; tel. 27-21-21-28-00; internet fb.com/starmagazine.ci; weekly; circ. 15,000.

Top-Visages: 119 rue Lotus, Abri 2000, Cité Emeraude, Attoban, 06 BP 6808, Abidjan 06; tel. 01-01-16-90-90; e-mail info@topvisages.net; internet topvisages.net; weekly; Editor-in-Chief E. TONGA BÉHI.

SELECTED PERIODICALS

Cordon Bleu: 2 Plateaux, Las Palmas, 01 BP 11607, Abidjan 01; tel. 27-22-42-09-07; internet cordonbleu.ci; gastronomy.

Côte d'Ivoire Economie: Cocody II Plateaux, rue K24, 28 BP 1473, Abidjan 28; tel. 27-21-75-16-10; f. 2010; monthly; Dir of Publication and Editor-in-Chief IBRAHIM OUATTARA.

Life: Riviera Bonoumin, 06 BP 2095, Abidjan 06; tel. 27-22-43-75-50; e-mail redactionlife@voodoo-media.net; internet lifemag-ci.com.

News&Co: Cocody II Plateaux, Vallons, 28 BP 580, Abidjan 28; tel. 27-22-51-04-72; monthly; financial and economic affairs; publ. by Publi Services Editions; Dir of Publication MARION N'GOUAN EZZE-DINE; Editor-in-Chief ÉLODIE VERMEIL.

PME Magazine: Abidjan; tel. 27-22-48-80-76; e-mail info@pmemag.ci; internet www.pmemag.ci; economics.

NEWS AGENCY

Agence Ivoirienne de Presse (AIP): ave Chardy, 04 BP 312, Abidjan 04; tel. 27-20-22-64-13; e-mail aip@aip.ci; internet www.aip.ci; f. 1961; Dir OUMOU BARRY-SANA.

PRESS ASSOCIATIONS

Organisation des Journalistes Professionnels de Côte d'Ivoire (OJPCI): Abidjan; Pres. ARMAND HUÉ BI GOORÉ.

Réseau des Femmes Journalistes de Côte d'Ivoire: Abidjan; Pres. AGNÈS KRAIDY.

Syndicat National des Agents de la Presse Privée de Côte d'Ivoire (SYNAPPCI): Adjamé 220 Logements, Abidjan; Sec.-Gen. GUILLAUME GBATO.

Union Nationale des Journalistes de Côte d'Ivoire (UNJCI): 06 BP 1675, Plateau, Abidjan 06; tel. 27-20-33-10-82; e-mail info@unjci.net; internet www.unjci.net; f. 1991; Pres. JEAN-CLAUDE COULIBALY.

Publishers

Centre d'Edition et de Diffusion Africaines (CEDA): 17 rue des Carrossiers, 04 BP 541, Abidjan 04; tel. 27-20-24-65-10; internet www.ceda-ci.com; f. 1961; 20% state-owned; general non-fiction, school and children's books, literary fiction; Pres. and Dir-Gen. VENANCE KACOU.

Centre de Publications Evangéliques: 08 BP 900, Abidjan 08; tel. 27-22-44-48-05; e-mail cpe@aviso.ci; internet www.editionscpe.com; f. 1967; evangelical Christian; Dir JULES OUOBA.

Nouvelles Editions Ivoiriennes: 1 blvd de Marseille, 01 BP 1818, Abidjan 01; tel. 27-21-21-64-70; internet neiceda.com; f. 1972; literature, criticism, essays, drama, social sciences, history, in French and English; Dir GUY LAMBIN.

Presses Universitaires et Scolaires d'Afrique (PUSAF—Editions Cissé): 08 BP 177, Abidjan 08; tel. 27-22-41-12-71; mathematics, economics, medicine.

GOVERNMENT PUBLISHING HOUSE

Imprimerie Nationale: Externat Saint Paul du Plateau, 7 ave Marchand, blvd Angoulvant, BP V87, Abidjan; tel. 27-20-30-08-06; e-mail info@imprimerienationale.ci; internet www.imprimerienationale.ci; Dir-Gen. EMILE BOY KOUASSI.

Broadcasting and Communications

TELECOMMUNICATIONS

Atlantique Telecom—Moov (Moov): Immeuble Karrat, rue du Commerce, 01 BP 2347, Abidjan 01; tel. 27-20-25-01-01; e-mail moovcontact@moov.com; internet www.moov-africa.ci; f. 2005 as jt venture by Atlantique Télécom (Côte d'Ivoire) and Etisalat (United Arab Emirates); subsidiary of Maroc Telecom Group; CEO LHOUS-SAINE OUSSALAH.

MTN Côte d'Ivoire: Immeuble Loteny, 12 rue Crossons Duplessis, 01 BP 3685, Abidjan 01; tel. 27-20-31-63-16; e-mail mtnbusiness.ci@mtn.com; internet www.mtn.ci; f. 1996 as Loteny Télécom-Télécel; present name adopted 2005; 58.8% owned by Mobile Telephone Network International (South Africa); Dir-Gen. DJIBRIL OUATTARA.

Orange Côte d'Ivoire: Immeuble Le Quartz, blvd Valéry Giscard d'Estaing, Marcory, 11 BP 202, Abidjan 11; tel. 27-21-23-07-07; e-mail orangebusiness.oci@orange.com; internet www.orange.ci; f. 1996 as Ivoiris, present name adopted 2002; merged with Côte d'Ivoire-Télécom in 2017; 69% owned by Orange (France), 31% state-owned; Man. Dir MAMADOU BAMBA.

Regulatory Authority

Autorité de Régulation des Télécommunications/TIC de Côte d'Ivoire (ARTCI): Immeuble Postel 2001, 4e étage, rue Lecoeur, 18 BP 2203, Abidjan 18; tel. 27-20-34-43-74; e-mail courrier@artci.ci; internet www.artci.ci; f. 2015 following the merger of Agence des Télécommunications de Côte d'Ivoire (ATCI) and Conseil des Télécommunications de Côte d'Ivoire (CTCI); Pres. SOULEYMANE DIAKITÉ; Dir-Gen. NAMAHOUA TOURÉ BAMBA.

BROADCASTING
Regulatory Authority

Haute Autorité de la Communication Audiovisuelle (HACA): Cocody Angré, 7e Tranche, Lot No 3769, Ilot No 307, 05 BP 56, Abidjan; tel. 27-22-41-96-64; e-mail infos@haca.ci; internet www.haca.ci; f. 2011 to replace Conseil National de la Communication Audiovisuelle (CNCA); Pres. RENÉ BOURGOUIN; Dir-Gen. YACOUBA DEMBÉLÉ.

Radio

Radiodiffusion-Télévision Ivoirienne (RTI): blvd des Martyrs, Cocody, 08 BP 883, Abidjan 08; tel. 27-22-40-12-50; e-mail digital@rti.ci; internet www.rti.ci; f. 1962; state-owned; 2 national TV channels, La Première and TV2, and 2 national radio channels, La Nationale and Fréquence II; Dir-Gen. FOUSSENY DEMBÉLÉ.

Frequence Vie 89.4 FM: 08 BP 886, Abidjan 08; tel. 27-20-21-10-67; e-mail frequencevie@gmail.com; internet www.radiofrequencevie.com; f. 1999; Dir DIEUDONNÉ NGUMBI.

Ivoire FM 103.4: 09 BP 112, Abidjan; tel. 27-20-22-07-63.

Radio Al Bayane 95.7 FM: 03 BP 174, Abidjan 08; tel. 27-22-40-59-99; e-mail contact@radio-albayane.info; internet albayane.ci; f. 2001; broadcasts from Yamoussoukro, San Pedro and Korhogo; Dir-Gen. IMAM CISSÉ DJIGUIBA ABDALLAH.

Radio Amitié 100.1 FM: Yopougon, Abidjan; tel. 0707676730.

Radio Espoir: Paroisse Sainte Anne de Port-Bouët, 12 BP 27, Abidjan 12; tel. 27-21-75-68-01; e-mail info@radioespoir.ci; internet www.radioespoir.ci; f. 1991; Roman Catholic; broadcasts in French, local and subregional languages; Dir PIERRE S. KIENÉ.

Radio JAM: Abidjan; tel. 25-21-01-78-00; e-mail radiojam993@gmail.com; internet www.radiojam.biz.

Radio Nationale Catholique: Paroisse St Joseph de la Gare Abidjan-Yopougon, Abidjan; tel. 0759004837; e-mail info@rnc-ci.net; internet www.rnc-ci.net; f. 2001; broadcasts in Abidjan, Gagnoa, Abengourou and Bondoukou.

Radio Nostalgie: Immeuble Le Paris, ave Chardy, 01 BP 157, Abidjan 01; tel. 27-20-21-10-52; e-mail contact@nostalgie.ci; internet www.nostalgie.ci; f. 1993.

Radio Notre Dame: BP 1555, Yamoussoukro; tel. 27-30-64-41-55; broadcasts religious programmes; Dir-Gen. JEAN-CLAUDE ATSAIN.

Trace FM: II Plateaux, 08 BP 4180, Abidjan; tel. 27-22-50-82-00; e-mail assistantepub@trace.fm; internet trace.ci; f. 2015; CEO NADEIGE TUBIANA.

Vibe Radio (94.6 FM): Immeuble Botreau Roussel, 1er étage, 28 ave Delafosse, Plateau, Abidjan; tel. 27-20-24-20-51; internet www.viberadio.ci; f. 2015; subsidiary of Lagardère Active Radio International.

Television

Radiodiffusion-Télévision Ivoirienne (RTI): see Radio section.

A+ IVOIRE: Abidjan; internet www.aplusivoire.ci; f. 2001; Chair. FRANÇOISE REMARCK; Dir-Gen. MICHEL MUTOMBO CARTIER.

Canal+ Côte d'Ivoire: Immeuble Alpha 2000, 01 BP 1132, Abidjan 01; tel. 27-20-31-99-97; internet www.canalplus-afrique.com/ci; broadcasts commenced 1994; subsidiary of Canal Plus (France); Dir-Gen. AZIZ AZIZ DIALLO.

LIFE TV: Abidjan; e-mail info@lifetv.ci; internet lifetv.ci/home; f. 2017; Chair. and CEO FABRICE SAWEGNON.

Nouvelle Chaine Ivoirienne (NCI): Treichville, rue des Thoniers, 15 BP 726, Abidjan 15; tel. 27-21-59-87-00; e-mail info@nci.ci; internet www.nci.ci; f. 2019.

Télévision Al Bayane: Abidjan; tel. 27-22-40-59-99; internet fb.com/tvalbayane; religious; Dir-Gen. IMAM CISSÉ DJIGUIBA ABDALLAH.

Finance

BANKING
Central Bank

Banque Centrale des Etats de l'Afrique de l'Ouest (BCEAO): ave Abdoulaye Fadiga, angle blvd Botreau Roussel, 01 BP 1769, Abidjan 01; tel. 27-20-20-85-00; e-mail webmaster@bceao.int; internet www.bceao.int; f. 1962; HQ in Dakar, Senegal; bank of issue for the mem. states of the Union Economique et Monétaire

Ouest-Africaine (UEMOA, comprising Benin, Burkina Faso, Côte d'Ivoire, Guinea-Bissau, Mali, Niger, Senegal and Togo); Gov. JEAN-CLAUDE KASSI BROU; Dir in Côte d'Ivoire CHALOUHO COULIBALY.

Commercial Banks

Afriland First Bank Côte d'Ivoire: Immeuble Woodin Center, ave Noguès, 01 BP 6928, Abidjan 01; tel. 27-20-31-58-30; internet www.afrilandfirstbankci.com; f. 1996; fmrly Access Bank Côte d'Ivoire; name changed as above in 2013; Pres. GUY M'BENGUE; Dir-Gen. OLIVIER DADJEU.

Bank of Africa-Côte d'Ivoire (BOA-CI): ave Terrasson de Fougères, angle rue Gourgas, 01 BP 4132, Abidjan 01; tel. 27-20-30-34-00; e-mail information@boacoteivoire.com; internet www.boacoteivoire.com; f. 1996; 69.18% owned by BOA West Africa; Pres. LALA MOULAYE; Dir-Gen. REDOUANE TOUBI.

Banque Atlantique Côte d'Ivoire (BACI): Immeuble Atlantique, ave Noguès, Plateau, 04 BP 1036, Abidjan 04; tel. 27-20-31-59-50; f. 1979; merged with Compagnie Bancaire de l'Atlantique Côte d'Ivoire in 2009; Dir-Gen. ARSÈNE COULIBALY.

Banque de l'Habitat de Côte d'Ivoire (BHCI): 22 ave Joseph Anoma, 01 BP 2325, Abidjan 01; tel. 27-20-22-60-00; e-mail info@bhci.ci; internet www.bhci.ci; f. 1993; Dir-Gen. ABOU TOURÉ.

Banque Internationale pour le Commerce et l'Industrie de la Côte d'Ivoire SA (BICI-CI): ave Franchet d'Espérey, 01 BP 1298, Abidjan 01; tel. 27-20-20-16-00; e-mail michel.lafont@africa.bnpparibas.com; internet www.bicici.com; f. 1962; 67.5% owned by BNP Paribas (France); absorbed BICI Bail de Côte d'Ivoire in 2003 and Compagnie Financière de la Côte d'Ivoire in 2004; Dir-Gen. YAO KOUASSI.

Banque Nationale d'Investissement (BNI): Immeuble SCIAM, ave Marchand, Plateau, 01 BP 670, Abidjan 01; tel. 27-20-20-98-00; e-mail info@bni.ci; internet www.bni.ci; f. 1959 as Caisse Autonome d'Amortissement de Côte d'Ivoire (CAA); name and operations changed as above in 2004; Dir-Gen. YOUSSOUF FADIGA.

Banque Populaire de Côte d'Ivoire: 11 ave Joseph Anoma, 01 BP 6889, Abidjan 01; tel. 27-20-25-43-43; internet www.banquepopulaire.ci; f. 1998; fmrly La Caisse d'Epargne de Côte d'Ivoire; name changed as above in 2019; Pres. JEAN BAPTISTE AMAN AYAYE; Dir-Gen. ISSA TANOU FADIGA.

Banque Sahélo-Saharienne pour l'Investissement et le Commerce de Côte d'Ivoire (BSIC—CI): ave Noguès, Plateau, 01 BP 10 323, Abidjan 01; tel. 27-20-30-99-99; internet bsicbank.com/cotedivoire; f. 2009; Pres. ADAMA DIOP; Administrator MAMADOU PONA.

Banque de l'Union—Côte d'Ivoire: Immeuble JECEDA, blvd de la République, Plateau, 01 BP 5294, Abidjan 01; tel. 27-20-20-30-50; internet bduci.com; f. 2015; 70% owned by Banque de Développement du Mali (70%), 20% owned by Banque Ouest Africaine de Développement and 10% owned by Chambre de Commerce et d'Industrie du Mali; Dir-Gen. IDRISSA WÉLÉ DIALLO.

BGFIBank Côte d'Ivoire: blvd Valery Giscard d'Estaing, Marcory, Abidjan 01; tel. 27-20-32-62-92; internet fb.com/BGFIBankCI; Dir-Gen. MALICK N'DIAYE.

Bridge Bank Group Côte d'Ivoire: Immeuble TEYLIOM, ave du Général de Gaulle, Plateau, 01 BP 13002, Abidjan 1; tel. 27-20-25-85-85; e-mail info@bridgebankgroup.com; internet www.bridgebankgroup.com/index.php; Pres. AMADOU KOUYATÉ; Dir-Gen. KASSI EHOUMAN MARTIAL KOUADIO.

Citibank Côte d'Ivoire: Immeuble Botreau Roussel, 28 ave Delafosse, 01 BP 3698, Abidjan 01; tel. 27-20-20-90-00; f. 1976; Dir VIVIANE BAKAYOKO.

Coris Bank International: 23 blvd de la République, angle ave Marchand, 01 BP 4690, Abidjan 01; tel. 27-20-20-94-50; e-mail corisbank-ci@coris-bank.com; internet corisbank.ci; Pres. MAMADOU SANON.

Ecobank Côte d'Ivoire: Immeuble Alliance, 1 ave Terrasson de Fougères, 01 BP 4107, Abidjan 01; tel. 27-20-31-92-00; e-mail ecobankci@ecobank.com; internet www.ecobank.com; f. 1989; 94% owned by Ecobank Transnational Inc (Togo); Chair. MICHEL AKA ANGHUI; Dir-Gen. PAUL-HARRY AITHNARD.

Guaranty Trust Bank Côte d'Ivoire SA: 11 ave du Senateur Lagarosse, Plateau, 01 BP 13141, Abidjan 01; tel. 27-20-31-15-00; e-mail contact.ci@gtbank.com; internet www.gtbankci.com; f. 2012; Dir-Gen. DAN IBRAHIM SHUAIB.

NSIA Banque: 8–10 ave Joseph Anoma, 01 BP 1274, Abidjan 01; tel. 27-20-20-07-20; e-mail nsiabanque.ci@groupensia.com; internet www.nsiabanque.ci; f. 1980; fmrly Banque Internationale pour l'Afrique de l'Ouest—Côte d'Ivoire; name changed as above in 2015; Pres. JEAN KACOU DIAGOU; Dir-Gen. LÉONCE DANIEL DJEKET YACE.

Orabank Côte d'Ivoire: rue des Banques, angle blvd de la République, BP 312, Abidjan; tel. 27-20-25-55-55; internet www.orabank.net; fmrly Banque Régionale de Solidarité Côte d'Ivoire; name

changed as above in 2014; owned by Oragroup SA (Togo); Pres. M'BAYE THIAM; Dir-Gen. MAMOUDOU KANÉ.

Société Générale Côte d'Ivoire: 5–7 ave Joseph Anoma, 01 BP 1355, Abidjan 01; tel. 27-20-20-12-34; e-mail cotedivoire.societe-generale@socgen.com; internet www.societegenerale.ci; f. 1962; present name adopted in 2019; 66.8% owned by Société Générale (France); Dir-Gen. AYMERIC VILLEBRUN.

Société Ivoirienne de Banque (SIB): Immeuble Alpha 2000, 34 blvd de la République, 01 BP 1300, Abidjan 01; tel. 27-20-20-00-00; e-mail info@sib.ci; internet www.sib.ci; f. 1962; 51% owned by Attijariwafa Bank (Morocco), 49% state-owned; reduction of state holding to 19% proposed; Pres. N'DIA GEORGES COFFI; Dir-Gen. MOHAMED EL GHAZI.

Stanbic Bank: Immeuble Stanbic Bank, blvd Valery Giscard d'Estaing, 26 BP 701, Abidjan 26; tel. 27-21-22-34-23; e-mail clienteleentreprises@stanbicbank.com.ci; internet www.stanbicbank.com.ci; f. 2018; Dir-Gen. JOËL TOURÉ.

Standard Chartered Bank Côte d'Ivoire (SCBCI): 23 blvd de la République, face Commissariat du 1er arrondissement, 17 BP 1141, Abidjan 17; tel. 27-20-30-32-00; internet www.sc.com/ci; f. 2001; subsidiary of Standard Chartered Bank (UK); Chair. MATHIEU MANDENG; CEO JOHN MOKOM.

United Bank for Africa Côte d'Ivoire: blvd Botreau Roussel, Plateau, 17 BP 808, Abidjan; tel. 27-20-31-22-92; e-mail cfccotedivoire@ubagroup.com; internet www.ubacotedivoire.com; f. 2008; Pres. KOUAMÉ KOUASSI; Dir-Gen. SARATA KONÉ THIAM.

Versus Bank: Immeuble CRAAE-UMOA, blvd Botreau Roussel, angle ave Joseph Anoma, 01 BP 1874, Abidjan 01; tel. 27-20-25-60-60; e-mail infos@versusbank.com; internet www.versusbank.ci; f. 2004; Dir-Gen. JERÔME EHUI.

Credit Institution

Société Africaine de Crédit Automobilier (SAFCA): 1 rue des Carrossiers, Zone 3, 04 BP 27, Abidjan 04; tel. 27-21-21-07-07; e-mail cotedivoire@alios-finance.com; internet www.alios-finance.com; f. 1956; also known as Alios Finance Côte d'Ivoire; Dir-Gen. ERIC LECLERE.

Bankers' Association

Association Professionnelle des Banques et Etablissements Financiers de Côte d'Ivoire (APBEFCI): Immeuble Aniaman, ave Lamblin, 01 BP 3810, Abidjan 01; tel. 27-20-32-20-08; internet www.apbef-ci.net; affiliated to Confédération Générale des Entreprises de Côte d'Ivoire; Pres. JERÔME EHUI; Exec. Dir SERGE KOUAMELAN.

STOCK EXCHANGE

Bourse Régionale des Valeurs Mobilières (BRVM): 18 ave Joseph Anoma, 01 BP 3802, Abidjan 01; tel. 27-20-32-66-85; e-mail brvm@brvm.org; internet www.brvm.org; f. 1998 to succeed Bourse des Valeurs d'Abidjan; regional stock exchange serving mem. states of UEMOA; Pres. Dr PARFAIT KOUASSI; Dir-Gen. Dr EDOH KOSSI AMENOUNVÉ.

INSURANCE

Allianz Côte d'Ivoire: 2 blvd Roume, 01 BP 1741, Abidjan 01; tel. 27-20-30-40-00; e-mail azci-infos@allianz.com; internet www.allianz.ci; comprises Allianz Côte d'Ivoire Assurances Vie (life) and Allianz Côte d'Ivoire Assurances Non-Vie (general); Dir-Gen. MAMADOU KONÉ.

AMSA Assurances: 19 ave Delafosse, 01 BP 1333, Abidjan 01; tel. 27-20-30-05-00; e-mail amsa-ci@amsaassurances.com; internet www.amsaassurances.com; f. 1972; fmrly Compagnie Nationale d'Assurances; insurance and reinsurance; Dir-Gen. SOULEYMANE CISSÉ.

Atlantique Assurances Côte d'Ivoire: Immeuble AMCI, 15 ave Joseph Anoma, Plateau, 01 BP 1841, Abidjan 01; tel. 27-20-31-78-00; e-mail aaci@atlantique-assurances.net; internet www.atlantique-assurances.net; f. 1956; Dir-Gen. ROSALIE LOGON.

Atlantique Assurances Vie Côte d'Ivoire: Maison de la Mutualité, 4e et 5e étages, 15 ave Joseph Anoma, 01 BP 1337, Abidjan 01; tel. 27-21-31-21-41; internet www.aavie.net; Dir-Gen. ESTELLE TAGNONGOH TRAORÉ.

AXA Assurances Côte d'Ivoire: ave Lamine Fadiga Prolongée, 01 BP 378, Abidjan 01; tel. 27-20-31-88-88; internet corporate.axa.ci; f. 1981; fmrly l'Union Africaine-IARD; insurance and reinsurance; Dir-Gen. ROGER EUGENE BOA JOHNSON.

Génération Nouvelle d'Assurances Côte d'Ivoire (GNA-CI): Ground Floor, Immeuble l'Ebrien, rue du commerce, 01 BP 12182 Abidjan 01; tel. 27-20-25-98-00; e-mail gnassurances@aviso.ci; internet www.gna-assurances.com; f. 2006; Dir-Gen. ROMUALD KOUASSI (acting).

Leadway Vie: Immeuble SUNU, 6e étage, blvd Botreau Roussel, 01 BP 11944, Abidjan 01; tel. 27-20-01-31-00; e-mail rc@leadway.com; internet ci.leadway.com; a subsidiary of Leadway Assurance Co. Ltd (Nigeria); fmrly Alliance Africaine d'Assurances (3A); present name adopted 2018; Dir-Gen. TIORNAN COULIBALY.

Nouvelle Société Africaine d'Assurances (NSIA—CI): Immeuble Manci, rue A43, 01 BP 4092, Abidjan 01; tel. 27-20-22-76-21; e-mail info@groupensia.com; f. 1995; Pres. and Dir-Gen. JANINE DIAGOU WODIÉ.

NSIA-Vie: Immeuble Zandaman, ave Noguès, 01 BP 4092, Abidjan 01; tel. 27-20-31-98-00; e-mail nsiavi_eassurances.ci@groupensia .com; f. 1988; fmrly Assurances Générales de Côte d'Ivoire-Vie (AGCI-Vie); life; Pres. and Dir-Gen. JEAN KACOU DIAGOU.

Sanlam Assurance Côte d'Ivoire: blvd Roume 3, 01 BP 3832, Abidjan 01; tel. 27-20-25-36-00; e-mail contact@sanlam.co.ci; internet ci.sanlam.com; f. 1980; fmrly Colina, subsequently Saham Assurance Côte d'Ivoire; present name adopted 2020; life and non-life; Chair. MOULAY HAFID ELALAMY; Dir-Gen. (non-life) ROLAND ZWEWENDPAOGRE OUEDRAOGO; Dir-Gen. (life) PHILIPPE ATTOBRA.

Serenity SA: Immeuble AMIRAL, 2e et 5e étages, Plateau, Rue du Commerce, 01 BP 10244, Abidjan 01; tel. 27-20-32-16-52; e-mail serenity@serenity-sa.com; internet www.serenity-sa.com; f. 2009; Pres. and Dir-Gen. MAURICE KIPRÉ DIGBEU.

Sunu Assurances IARD Côte d'Ivoire: Immeuble SUNU, Plateau, 01 BP 3803, Abidjan 01; tel. 27-20-25-18-18; e-mail cotedivoire .iard@sunu-group.com; internet www.sunu-group.com; Pres. ALEXANDRE AHUI ATTÉ; Dir-Gen. FAUSTIN ATEBI-ZIRIGA.

Sunu Assurances Vie Côte d'Ivoire: 9 ave Houdaille, 01 BP 2016, Abidjan 01; tel. 27-20-31-04-00; e-mail cotedivoire.vie@sunu-group .com; internet cotedivoire.vie.sunu-group.com; f. 1985; fmrly Union Africaine Vie, subsequently AXA Vie Côte d'Ivoire and Union des Assurances de Côte d'Ivoire; present name adopted 2015; life assurance and capitalization; Pres. PATHÉ DIONE; Dir-Gen. SALIOU BAKAYOKO.

Willis Towers Watson Côte d'Ivoire: Immeuble Trade Center, ave Noguès, 01 BP 5675, Abidjan 01; tel. 27-20-25-25-00; e-mail grassavoyeci@ci.grassavoye.com; internet www.willistowerswatson .com/fr-CI; fmrly Gras Savoye; name changed as above in 2018.

Insurance Association

Association des Sociétés d'Assurances de Côte d'Ivoire (ASA-CI): 8 blvd de France, Cocody, 01 BP 3873, Abidjan 01; tel. 27-22-45-18-45; e-mail secretariat@asaci.net; internet www.asaci.net; f. 1966; Pres. MAMADOU KONÉ; 40 mem cos.

Trade and Industry

GOVERNMENT AGENCIES

Agence Nationale d'Appui au Développement Rural (ANADER): blvd de la Paix, BP V183, Abidjan; tel. 27-20-21-67-00; e-mail anader@anader.ci; internet www.anader.ci; f. 1993 to replace CIDV, SATMACI and SODEPRA; Pres. ADAMA COULIBALY (acting); Man. Dir SIDIKI CISSÉ.

Agence Nationale de l'Habitat (ANAH): Immeuble le Mirador, blvd Général de Gaulle, Adjamé, Abidjan; tel. 25-20-01-09-05; f. 2021 to replace Société Ivoirienne de Construction et de Gestion Immobilière.

Autorité Nationale de Régulation des Marchés Publics: Abidjan; tel. 27-22-40-00-40; e-mail info@anrmp.ci; internet www.anrmp .ci; Pres. YACOUBA PÉNAGNABA COULIBALY.

Autorité pour la Régulation du Café et du Cacao (ARCC): blvd Botreau Roussel, Immeuble Caistab 17ème–19ème étages, Plateau, 25 BP 1501, Abidjan 25; tel. 27-20-20-29-87; internet www.arcc.ci; f. 2000; implements regulatory framework for coffee and cocoa trade; Pres. GILBERT N'GUESSAN.

Bureau National d'Etudes Techniques et de Développement (BNETD): blvd Hassan II, Cocody, 04 BP 945, Abidjan 04; tel. 27-22-48-34-00; e-mail contact@bnetd.ci; internet www.bnetd.ci; f. 1978 as Direction et Contrôle des Grands Travaux; management and supervision of major public works projects; Dir-Gen. KINAPARA COULIBALY.

Comité de Privatisation: Immeuble 55, Plateau, rue de commerce, 09 BP 1518, Abidjan 03; tel. 27-21-21-52-25; internet privatisation .gouv.ci; f. 1990; state privatization authority; Pres. AHOUTOU EMMANUEL KOFFI.

Conseil de Régulation, de Stabilisation et de Développement de la Filière Café-Cacao (Conseil du Café-Cacao): Immeuble Caistab, 23e étage, 17 BP 797, Abidjan 17; tel. 27-20-25-69-69; e-mail info@conseilcafecacao.ci; internet www.conseilcafecacao.ci; f. 2012 to replace the Comité de Gestion de la Filière Café-Cacao; comprises the Autorité pour la Régulation du Café et du Cacao

(ARCC), the Bourse du Café et du Cacao (BCC), the Fonds de Régulation et de Contrôle du Café et du Cacao (FRCC) and the Fonds de Développement et de Promotion des Activités des Producteurs de Café et de Cacao (FDPCC); Pres. MINAYA SIAKA COULIBALY; Dir-Gen. BRAHIMA YVES KONÉ.

Fonds de Régulation et de Contrôle du Café et du Cacao (FRC): Immeuble Caistab, 17 BP 797, Abidjan 17; tel. 27-20-20-27-11; e-mail frc@frc.ci; internet www.frc.ci; f. 2002; assists small-scale producers and exporters of coffee and cocoa; administrative bd comprises 5 representatives of producers, 2 of exporters, 3 of banks and insurance cos, 20 of the state.

Initiative pour la Transparence dans les Industries Extractives: Cocody II Plateaux, Lot 490, rue K61, 06 BP 1340, Abidjan 06; tel. 27-22-41-15-36; internet www.cn-itie.ci; f. 2008; Pres. of the National Council ANTOINE KOCOUNSEU MIMBA.

PETROCI: Immeuble les Hévéas, 14 blvd Carde, BP V194, Abidjan 01; tel. 27-20-20-25-00; e-mail info@petroci.ci; internet www.petroci .ci; f. 1975 as Société Nationale d'Opérations Pétrolières de la Côte d'Ivoire (PETROCI); restructured 2000 to comprise 3 companies—Petroci Exploration Production, SA, Petroci Gaz and Petroci Industries Services; Dir-Gen. VAMISSA BAMBA.

Société de Développement des Forêts (SODEFOR): blvd François Mitterrand, 01 BP 3770, Abidjan 01; tel. 27-22-48-30-00; e-mail info@sodefor.ci; internet sitesodefortest.e-bordereaux.ci; f. 1966; establishment and management of tree plantations, sustainable management of state forests, marketing of timber products; Pres. KONÉ OUSMANE; Dir-Gen. MAMADOU SANGARÉ.

Société pour le Développement Minier de la Côte d'Ivoire (SODEMI): 31 blvd des Martyrs, 01 BP 2816, Abidjan 01; tel. 27-22-44-29-94; e-mail infos@sodemi.ci; internet sodemi.ci; f. 1962; geological and mineral research; Pres. IBRAHIM KALIL KONATÉ; Man. Dir MOUSSA KONÉ.

Société de Gestion et de Développement des Infrastructures Industrielles (SOGEDI): Abidjan; f. 2022; responsible for planning, promotion and financing of industrial infrastructure.

DEVELOPMENT AGENCIES

Agence Française de Développement (AFD): blvd François Mitterrand, 01 BP 1814, Abidjan 01; tel. 27-22-40-70-40; e-mail afdabidjan@afd.fr; internet www.afd.fr; Country Dir ADRIEN HAYE.

Association pour la Promotion des Exportations de Côte d'Ivoire (Apex-CI): Immeuble Tropique 3, Mezzanine 1 et 2, blvd de la République, 01 BP 3485, Abidjan 01; tel. 27-20-30-25-30; internet www.apex-ci.net; Dir-Gen. GUY M'BENGUE.

Centre de Promotion des Investissements en Côte d'Ivoire (CEPICI): Immeuble Memanou, 2e étage, blvd Clozel, Plateau, BP V152, Abidjan 01; tel. 27-20-31-14-00; e-mail infos.cepici@cepici.ci; internet www.cepici.gouv.ci; f. 1993; investment promotion authority; Dir-Gen. SOLANGE AMICHIA.

Fonds de Développement des Infrastructures Industrielles: Cocody, 06 BP 2552, Abidjan 06; tel. 27-22-41-26-63; e-mail info@fodi .ci; internet www.fodi.ci; f. 2015; Pres. HIEN PHILIPPE; Dir-Gen. FELIX BLEY.

France Volontaires: 17 BP 1089, Abidjan 17; tel. 27-20-22-85-09; e-mail ev.ci@france-volontaires.org; internet www .france-volontaires.org; f. 1965; name changed as above in 2009; Nat. Rep. ALEXIS K. SOUNGALO.

Institut de Recherche pour le Développement: Université Félix Houphouët Boigny, Commune de Cocody, 08 BP 3800, Abidjan 08; tel. 27-22-48-50-00; e-mail cote-ivoire@ird.fr; internet cote-ivoire.ird .fr; Rep. JEAN-MARC HOUGARD.

CHAMBERS OF COMMERCE

Chambre de Commerce et d'Industrie de Côte d'Ivoire (CCI-CI): 6 ave Joseph Anoma, 01 BP 1399, Abidjan 01; tel. 27-20-33-16-00; e-mail info@cci.ci; internet www.cci.ci; f. 1992; Pres. FAMAN TOURÉ; Sec.-Gen. SERGE KOFFI-OURA.

Chambre Nationale d'Agriculture: 11 ave Lamblin, 01 BP 1291, Abidjan 01; tel. 27-20-32-92-13; internet www.chambragri.ci; Pres. BAMBA SINDOU.

TRADE ASSOCIATIONS

Association Nationale des Organisations Professionnelles Agricoles de Côte d'Ivoire (ANOPACI): Cocody Cité des Arts, derrière la Cité BAD, rue C7, 20 BP 937, Abidjan 20; tel. 27-22-44-11-76; e-mail anopaci@yahoo.fr; f. 1998; Pres. CLOVIS BONY (acting).

Bourse du Café et du Cacao (BCC): blvd Botreau Roussel, 04 BP 2576, Abidjan 04; tel. 27-20-20-27-20; e-mail info@bcc.ci; internet www.bcc.ci; f. 2001 to replace marketing, purchasing and certain other functions of La Nouvelle Caistab (Caisse de Stabilisation et de Soutien des Prix des Productions Agricoles).

Fédération Ivoirienne des Producteurs de Café-Cacao de Côte d'Ivoire (FIPCC): 05 BP 3405, Abidjan 05; tel. 27-22-42-83-99; f. 2000; coffee and cocoa growers' asscn; Pres. FAMO DIOMANDÉ; c. 230,000 individual and 264 co-operative mems.

Mouvement des Petites et Moyennes Entreprises (MPME): Immeuble MPME, Marcory, 141 blvd de Marseille, 18 BP 32, Abidjan 18; tel. 27-21-35-32-06; e-mail permanence@mpme-ci.org; internet mpme-ci.org; Pres. PATRICIA ZOUNDI YAO.

Organisation de Commercialisation de l'Ananas et de la Banane (OCAB): Abidjan; pineapple and banana growers' asscn; Pres. MICHEL GNUI; Exec. Sec. EMMANUEL DOLI.

EMPLOYERS' ORGANIZATIONS

Association Nationale des Paysans de Côte d'Ivoire (ANAPA-CI): Bouaké; Pres. KONÉ WAYARAGA.

Association Nationale des Producteurs de Café-Cacao de Côte d'Ivoire (ANAPROCI): BP 840, San-Pédro; tel. 27-34-71-20-98; Pres. KANGA KOFFI; Sec.-Gen. YAO KOUADIO HUBERT EYIMIN.

Association Nationale des Riziculteurs de Côte d'Ivoire (ANARIZ-CI): BP 2546, Abidjan 04; tel. 27-22-48-00-02; internet www.anariz-ci.org; f. 2001; 40 mem. co-operatives; Pres. THOMAS KOUADIO TIACOH.

Confédération Générale des Entreprises de Côte d'Ivoire (CGECI): 01 BP 8666, Abidjan 01; tel. 27-20-30-02-00; e-mail cgeci@cgeci.ci; internet www.cgeci.com; f. 1993 as Conseil National du Patronat Ivoirien; current name adopted 2005; Pres. JEAN-MARIE ACKAH; Dir-Gen. STÉPHANE AKA-ANGHUI; 19 affiliated federations, including the following:

> **Fédération Nationale des Industries et Services de Côte d'Ivoire (FNISCI):** Immeuble Les Harmonies, 1er étage, Plateau, 01 BP 1340, Abidjan 01; tel. 27-20-31-90-70; internet www.fnisci.net; f. 1993; Pres. JOSEPH-DESIRÉ BILEY; Dir-Gen. LOUIS S. AMÉDÉ; 180 mems.

> **Groupement Ivoirien du Bâtiment et des Travaux Publics (GIBTP):** 25 rue des Carrossiers, Concession SIDELAF, zone 3, 01 BP 464, Abidjan 01; tel. 27-22-43-77-91; e-mail gibtp@gibtp.org; internet gibtp.ci; f. 1934 as Syndicat des Entrepreneurs et des Industriels de la Côte d'Ivoire; present name adopted 1997; Pres. PHILIPPE EPONON; 80 mem cos.

Syndicat Autonome des Producteurs de Café-Cacao de Côte d'Ivoire (SYNAPROCI): 16 BP 165, Abidjan 16; f. 2003; Pres. BANNY KOFFI GERMAIN (acting).

Syndicat des Exportateurs et Négociants en Bois de Côte d'Ivoire (SENBCI): route du Lycée Technique, Cocody Danga, Villa No. 4, 01 BP 1979, Abidjan 01; tel. 27-22-44-44-80; f. 1960; Pres. SOULEYMANE COULIBALY.

Syndicat des Producteurs Industriels du Bois (SPIB): route du Lycée Technique, Cocody Danga, Villa No. 4, 01 BP 318, Abidjan; tel. 27-22-44-44-80; e-mail spib1943@gmail.com; internet spib-ci.org; f. 1943; Pres. BOUBARCAR BEN SALAH.

Union des Entreprises Agricoles et Forestières: route du Lycée Technique, Cocody Danga, Villa No. 4, 01 BP 2300, Abidjan 01; tel. 27-22-44-44-80; e-mail unemaf@aviso.ci; internet www.unemaf.org; f. 1952; Pres. YORO BI TRAZIÉ.

UTILITIES

Electricity

Autorité Nationale de Régulation du Secteur de l'Electricité (ANARE): Immeuble EECI, ave Houdaille, Plateau 9, 16 BP 1106, Abidjan 16; tel. 27-20-20-60-10; e-mail info@anare.ci; internet www.anare.ci; f. 1998; Pres. YOUSSOUF FOFANA; Dir-Gen. AMIDOU TRAORÉ.

Compagnie Ivoirienne d'Electricité (CIE): 1 ave Christiani, 01 BP 6932, Abidjan 01; tel. 27-21-23-33-00; e-mail info@cie.ci; internet www.cie.ci; f. 1990; 71% controlled by Groupe Bouygues (France); Pres. DOMINIQUE KAKOU; Dir-Gen. AHMADOU BAKAYOKO.

Compagnie Ivoirienne de Production d'Electricité (CIPREL): Tour Sidom, 12e étage, ave Houdaille, 01 BP 4039, Abidjan 01; tel. 27-21-23-63-62; e-mail info@ciprel.ci; internet ciprel.ci; independent power production; Dir-Gen. DIALLO KADIDJATOU.

Société des Energies de Côte d'Ivoire (CI-ENERGIES): Immeuble EECI, 01 BP 1345, Abidjan 01; tel. 27-20-20-62-01; e-mail secretariatdg@cinergies.ci; internet www.cinergies.ci; f. 2011; management of state assets in the electricity sector; Dir-Gen. SIDIBÉ NOUMOURY.

Water

Office National de l'Eau Potable (ONEP): II Plateaux Vallons, rue J93, Ilot 212, Lot 2470, Abidjan; tel. 27-22-51-43-00; internet onepci.net; f. 2006; Pres. LOUIS KOUAKOU-HABONOUAN; Dir IBRAHIMAN BERTÉ.

Société de Distribution d'Eau de la Côte d'Ivoire (SODECI): 1 ave Christiani, Treichville, 01 BP 1843, Abidjan 01; tel. 27-21-23-33-00; e-mail sodeci@sodeci.ci; internet www.sodeci.ci; f. 1959; production, treatment and distribution of drinking water; 46.07% owned by ERANOVE (France), 3.25% state-owned; Pres. FIRMIN AHOUNÉ; Dir-Gen. AHMADOU BAKAYOKO.

MAJOR COMPANIES

The following are among the largest companies in terms of either capital investment or employment.

AirGaz Côte d'Ivoire: 15 BP 619, Abidjan 15; tel. 27-21-27-44-44; e-mail direction@airgazci.com; internet www.airgazci.com/index.php; mfrs of industrial and medical gases; Gen. Man. MOUSSA KLEIT.

Air Liquide-Société Ivoirienne d'Oxygène et d'Acetylène (SIVOA): Zone Industrielle Vridi, rue Sylvestre L14, 01 BP 1753, Abidjan 01; tel. 27-21-21-04-00; internet www.ci.airliquide.com; f. 1962; 20% state-owned, 72% owned by Air Liquide (France); mfrs of industrial and medical gases; Pres. GÉRARD PRIET; Man. Dir ALEXANDRE DUFOUR.

Filatures, Tissage, Sacs–Côte d'Ivoire (FILTISAC): Km 8, route d'Adzopé, 01 BP 3962, Abidjan 01; tel. 27-20-30-46-00; e-mail info@filtisac.com; f. 1965; mfrs of jute bags and other packaging; Pres. MAHMOUD RAJAN; Man. Dir CHARLES AMADOU.

Globale Protection: blvd des Martyrs ENA, Cocody II Plateaux, 30 BP 561, Abidjan 30; tel. 27-22-51-47-60; e-mail info@globaleprotection.com; internet www.globaleprotection.com; f. 1996; mfrs of protection and surveillance systems; Dir-Gen. CHRISTIAN LEJOSNE.

LafargeHolcim Côte d'Ivoire: blvd du Port, 01 BP 887, Abidjan 01; tel. 27-21-75-51-22; e-mail serviceclients-civ@lafargeholcim.com; internet lafargeholcim.ci; f. 1952 as Société Ivoirienne de Ciments et Matériaux; name changed as above in 2016; clinker crushing plant; Man. Dir SERGE GBOTTA.

Libya Oil Côte d'Ivoire: route de Petit Bassam, 15 BP 900, Abidjan 15; tel. 27-21-75-37-00; f. 1974; distribution of petroleum products; Chair. MICHEL BONNET; Dir J. LABAUNE.

Nestlé Côte d'Ivoire: rue du Lycée Technique, 01 BP 1840, Abidjan 01; tel. 27-22-40-45-45; f. 1959; subsidiary of Nestlé (Switzerland); production of coffee and cocoa products, manufacture and sale of food products; Chair. DANIEL YAPOBI; Dir-Gen. THOMAS JEFFREY CASO.

Olheol Industries Côte d'Ivoire: Zone Industrielle, route de Béoumi, 01 BP 2000, Bouaké 01; tel. 27-31-63-60-60; e-mail admin@olheol.com; internet www.olheol.com; f. 1973; fmrly TRITURAF; production of vegetable oils; Dir-Gen. SÉKOU KEITA.

PALMCI: blvd de Vridi, 18 BP 3321, Abidjan 18; tel. 27-21-21-09-00; internet groupesifca.com/palmci.php; f. 1997; owned by SIFCA; Pres. ALASSANE DOUMBIA; Dir-Gen. CHRISTOPHE KOREKI.

Puma Energy Côte d'Ivoire SA: rue de Canal de Vridi 15, 15 BP 522, Abidjan 15; tel. 27-21-27-00-72; e-mail enquiries@pumaenergy.com; internet www.pumaenergy.com; petroleum; Dir-Gen. PIERRE SOW.

Sania cie: Zone Industrielle de Vridi, rue du Textile, 01 BP 2949, Abidjan 01; tel. 27-21-75-77-57; e-mail infos@sania.ci; internet www.sania.ci; f. 2008; refined palm oil, margarine and other related products; Dir-Gen. JEAN-LOUIS KODO.

SIFCA: blvd du Havre, 01 BP 1289, Abidjan 01; tel. 27-21-75-75-75; e-mail communication@sifca.ci; internet www.groupesifca.com; f. 1964; export of cocoa and coffee; Pres. ALASSANE DOUMBIA; Dir-Gen. PIERRE BILLON.

Société Africaine de Cacao (SACO): Zone 4, site 6, rue Pierre et Marie Curie, 01 BP 1045, Abidjan 01; tel. 27-21-75-02-00; f. 1956; a subsidiary of Groupe Barry Callebaut (Switzerland); mfrs of cocoa powder, chocolate products, cocoa butter and oil-cake; Man. Dir LOÏC BIARDEAU.

Société Africaine de Pétrole et d'Hydrocarbures Raffinés (Saphyr): Riviera Palmeraie, Immeuble Labogem, Abidjan 01; tel. 27-22-49-13-17; e-mail info@saphyr-sa.com; internet www.saphyr-sa.com; f. 2015; Dir-Gen. JEAN-PAUL KAKOU-MARCEAU.

Société Africaine de Plantations d'Hévéas (SAPH): Immeuble EX-SIT, rue des Galions, 01 BP 1322, Abidjan 01; tel. 27-21-75-76-76; e-mail communication@sifca.ci; f. 1956; owned by Groupe SIFCA; production of rubber on 24,440 ha of plantations; Pres. JEAN-LOUIS BILLON; Dir-Gen. MARC GÉNOT; c. 5,400 employees.

Société des Caoutchoucs de Grand-Béréby (SOGB): 01 BP 365, San Pedro; tel. 27-34-71-23-16; e-mail msorho@sogbci.com; internet www.sogbci.com; f. 1979; 15% state-owned; rubber plantations and processing; Pres. FULGENCE KOFFI; Gen. Man. JEAN-CHRISTOPHE DIENST.

Société de Gestion des Stocks Pétroliers de Côte d'Ivoire (GESTOCI): blvd de Vridi, 15 BP 89, Abidjan 15; tel. 27-21-75-98-00; e-mail infos@gestoci.ci; internet www.gestoci.ci; f. 1983; management of petroleum stocks; Man. Dir DOUMBIA IBRAHIMA.

Société Ivoirienne de Béton Manufacturé (SIBM): 12 rue Thomas Edison, 01 BP 902, Abidjan 01; tel. 27-21-35-52-71; e-mail sibm@aviso.ci; internet www.sibmci.com; f. 1978; mem. of Société Africaine de Béton Manufacturé group; mfrs of concrete; Man. Dir SERGE AIMÉ AMON BENOÎT BILE.

Société Ivoirienne de Câbles (SICABLE): Zone Industrielle de Vridi, rue du Textile, 15 BP 35, Abidjan 15; tel. 27-21-21-35-35; e-mail contact@sicable.ci; internet www.sicable.ci; f. 1975; 51% owned by Pirelli SpA (Italy); mfrs of electricity cables; Chair. LAURENT TARDIF; Man. Dir FRÉDÉRIC TAILHEURET.

Société Ivoirienne de Raffinage (SIR): blvd de Petit-Bassam, Vridi, 01 BP 1269, Abidjan 01; tel. 27-21-23-70-70; e-mail info@sir.ci; internet www.sir.ci; f. 1962; 45.74% owned by PETROCI; operates petroleum refinery at Abidjan; Pres. SOUMAÏLA BAKAYOKO; Dir-Gen. SORO TIOTIOHO.

Société Ivoirienne des Tabacs (SITAB): Quartier Gendarmerie TF 5937, Cocody Nord, 01 BP 724, Abidjan 01; tel. 27-22-48-98-03; f. 1956; mfrs of cigarettes; Pres. and Dir-Gen. PIERRE MAGNE.

Société de Limonaderies et Brasseries d'Afrique (SOLIBRA): 35 rue des Brasseurs, 01 BP 1304, Abidjan; tel. 27-21-21-12-00; internet www.solibra.ci; f. 1955; mfrs of beer, lemonade and ice at Abidjan and Bouaflé; Pres. JEAN-CLAUDE PALU; Dir-Gen. ERIC SAMSON.

Société des Mines d'Ity (SMI): ave Joseph Blohorn, Impasse des Chevaliers de Malte, Cocody, 08 BP 872, Abidjan 08; tel. 27-22-44-63-63; e-mail smiphp@aviso.ci; f. 1989; 85% owned by Endeavour Mining, 10% state-owned and 5% by SODEMI; mining of gold reserves (2.0 metric tons per year) at Ity; Man. Dir RIAAN VAN DER WALT.

Société Multinationale de Bitumes (SMB): blvd de Petit-Bassam, Zone Industrielle de Vridi, 12 BP 622, Abidjan 12; tel. 27-21-23-70-70; e-mail infosmb@sir.ci; internet www.smbci.ci; f. 1978; 72% owned by SIR; Pres. AMINATA DRAMANE TRAORÉ; Dir-Gen. MARIE JOSEPHINE SIDIBÉ.

Société Nationale Ivoirienne de Travaux (SONITRA): Abobo, route d'Anyama, 01 BP 2609, Abidjan 01; tel. 27-20-30-58-58; f. 1963; 55% state-owned; building and construction; Gen. Man. SHAUL LAHAT.

Société Nouvelle Abidjanaise de Carton Ondulé (SONACO): Zone Industrielle de Yopougon, 01 BP 1119, Abidjan; tel. 27-23-51-52-00; e-mail directiongenerale@sonaco.com.ci; internet www .rossmann.com/fr/implantations/international/sonaco.html; f. 1964; mfrs of paper goods and corrugated cardboard; owned by Groupe Rossman (France); Dir-Gen. JÉRÔME MEPLON.

Société de Tubes d'Acier et Aluminium en Côte d'Ivoire (SOTACI): Zone Industrielle de Yopougon, 01 BP 2747, Abidjan 01; tel. 27-23-51-54-54; e-mail sotaci@sotaci.com; internet www .sotaci.com; f. 1977; mfrs of steel and aluminium tubing and pipes; Pres. and Dir-Gen. ADHAM EL-KHALIL.

TotalEnergies Côte d'Ivoire: Immeuble Rive Gauche, 100 rue des Brasseurs, 01 BP 336, Abidjan 01; tel. 27-21-22-22-23; e-mail service .clients@totalenergies.ci; internet totalenergies.ci; f. 1967; petroleum marketing and distribution; fmrly Elf Oil-CI, subsequently renamed TotalFinaElf Côte d'Ivoire and Total Côte d'Ivoire; present name adopted 2021; subsidiary of TotalEnergies (France); Dir-Gen. FABIEN VOISIN.

Unilever Côte d'Ivoire: blvd de Vridi, 01 BP 1751, Abidjan 01; tel. 27-21-24-90-60; f. 1932; 90% owned by Unilever Group (Netherlands/UK); fmrly Blohorn Huilerie-Savonnerie-Lipochimie (Blohorn HSL); production and marketing of edible oils, incl. margarine, and of palm oil products, incl. soap; Pres. and Dir-Gen. MANON KARAMOKO.

Union Ivoirienne de Traitement de Cacao (UNICAO): Zone Industrielle de Vridi, 15 BP 406, Abidjan 15; tel. 27-21-27-14-49; e-mail unicao@globeaccess.net; f. 1989; owned by Olam Group; processing of cocoa beans; Country Head PARTHEEBAN THEDORE.

Uniwax: Zone Industrielle de Yopougon, 01 BP 3994, Abidjan 01; tel. 27-23-53-54-54; internet www.uniwax.com; f. 1967; mfrs of batik fabrics; owned by Vlisco Group (Netherlands); Pres. and Dir-Gen. JEAN-LOUIS MENUDIER.

Vivo Energy Côte d'Ivoire: rue des Pétroliers, Zone Industrielle de Vridi, 15 BP 378, Abidjan 15; tel. 27-21-75-27-27; internet www .vivoenergy.com; f. 1974; a Shell licensee; jt venture between Vitol (40%), Helios (40%) and Shell (20%); distribution of petroleum products; Dir-Gen. MOHAMED CHAABOUNI.

TRADE UNIONS

Dignité: 03 BP 2031, Abidjan 03; tel. 27-21-37-74-89; e-mail dignite@aviso.ci; Sec.-Gen. BOGA DAGO ELIE.

Fédération des Syndicats Autonomes de la Côte d'Ivoire—Confédération Générale (FESACI—CG): Abidjan; tel. 27-20-32-01-88; e-mail centralefesaci@gmail.com; internet fesaci.org;

breakaway group from the Union Générale des Travailleurs de Côte d'Ivoire; Sec.-Gen. DOHIA MAMADOU TRAORÉ.

Union Générale des Travailleurs de Côte d'Ivoire (UGTCI): Bourse du Travail de Treichville, 05 BP 1203, Abidjan 05; tel. 27-21-24-09-78; e-mail ugtcisg@yahoo.fr; internet www.ugtci.org; f. 1962; Sec.-Gen. JOSEPH LÉON EBAGNERIN; 108,000 individual mems; 157 affiliated unions.

Transport

RAILWAYS

SITARAIL—Transport Ferroviaire de Personnel et de Marchandises: Résidence Memanou, blvd Clozel, Plateau, 16 BP 1216, Abidjan 16; tel. 27-20-20-80-00; f. 1995 to operate services on Abidjan–Ouagadougou–Kaya (Burkina Faso) line; subsidiary of the Bolloré Group (France); Man. Dir (vacant).

ROADS

Agence de Gestion des Routes (AGEROUTE): ave Terrasson de Fougères, 08 BP 2604, Abidjan; tel. 27-20-25-10-00; e-mail ageroute@ ageroute.ci; internet www.ageroute.ci; Dir-Gen. FABRICE COULIBALY (acting).

Fonds d'Entretien Routier (FER): Immeuble FER, ave Chardy, Plateau, 04 BP 3089, Abidjan 04; tel. 27-20-31-13-05; e-mail contact@ fer-ci.org; internet fer-ci.org; f. 2001; Dir-Gen. LANCINÉ DIABY.

Société des Transports Abidjanais (SOTRA): 01 BP 2009, Abidjan 01; tel. 27-21-24-90-80; e-mail infos@sotra.ci; internet www.sotra.ci; f. 1960; 60% state-owned; urban transport; Dir-Gen. BOUAKÉ MÉITÉ.

SHIPPING

Côte d'Ivoire has two major ports, Abidjan and San-Pédro, both of which are industrial and commercial establishments with financial autonomy. Abidjan is the largest container and trading port in West Africa. Access to the port is via the 2.7-km Vridi Canal. The port at San-Pédro remains the main gateway to the south-western region of Côte d'Ivoire.

Port Autonome d'Abidjan (PAA): A22 rue des Piroguiers, blvd du Port, BP V85, Abidjan; tel. 27-21-23-80-00; e-mail info@paa-ci.org; internet www.portabidjan.ci; f. 1992; transferred to private ownership in 1999; Dir-Gen. HIEN SIÉ.

Port Autonome de San-Pédro (PASP): BP 339/340, San-Pédro; tel. 27-34-71-72-00; e-mail pasp@pasp.ci; internet www .sanpedro-portci.com; f. 1971; Pres. YAYA DEMBÉLÉ; Man. Dir HILAIRE MARCEL LAMIZANA.

CIVIL AVIATION

There are three international airports: Abidjan–Félix Houphouët-Boigny, Bouaké and Yamoussoukro. In addition, there are 25 domestic and regional airports, including those at Bouna, Korhogo, Man, Odienné and San-Pédro.

Autorité Nationale de l'Aviation Civile (ANAC): blvd de l'Aéroport, 07 BP 148, Abidjan 07; tel. 27-21-58-69-00; e-mail info@anac.ci; internet www.anac.ci; Dir SINALY SILUÉ.

Air Côte d'Ivoire: Immeuble République, pl. de la République, 01 BP 7782, Abidjan 01; tel. 27-20-25-15-61; e-mail reservation@ aircotedivoire.com; internet www.aircotedivoire.com; f. 2012 to replace Air Ivoire (f. 1960); 50% state-owned; 20% owned by Air France; Pres. ABDOULAYE COULIBALY; Dir-Gen. LAURENT LOUKOU.

Tourism

Office National du Tourisme (Côte d'Ivoire Tourisme): Immeuble ex-EECI, pl. de la République, 01 BP 8538, Abidjan 01; tel. 27-20-25-16-00; e-mail infos@cotedivoiretourisme.ci; internet www .cotedivoiretourisme.ci; f. 1992; Dir-Gen. MALÉKAH MOURAD-CONDÉ.

Defence

As assessed at November 2021, Côte d'Ivoire's active armed forces comprised an army of an estimated 23,000 troops, a navy of about 1,000 and an air force of 1,400. There were also some 2,000 troops in the Special Forces. Military service is by selective conscription and lasts for 18 months.

Defence Budget: 354,000m. francs CFA in 2021.

Commander-in-Chief of the Armed Forces: ALASSANE DRAMANE OUATTARA.

Chief of Staff of the Armed Forces: Gen. LASSINA DOUMBIA.

Chief of Staff of Land-based Forces: Col-Maj. JUSTIN ALY DEM.

Chief of Staff of the Navy: Capt.-Maj. KOUAMÉ CÉLÉSTIN N'GUESSAN.

Chief of Staff of the Air Force: Col-Maj. N'GUESSAN ALFRED KOFFI.

Commander of the Special Forces: Col TIBÉ-BI LOPOUA TOUSSAINT.

Education

Education at all levels is available free of charge. Primary education is officially compulsory for six years between the ages of seven and 13 years. Secondary education, from the age of 12, lasts for up to seven years, comprising a first cycle of four years and a second cycle of three years. According to estimates by the United Nations Educational, Scientific and Cultural Organization (UNESCO), enrolment at pre-primary institutions in 2019/20 was equivalent to 10% of children in the relevant age-group (males 10%; females 11%). In 2018/19 enrolment at primary schools included 95% of children in the relevant age-group (males 98%; females 92%), while enrolment at secondary schools was equivalent to 55% (males 61%; females 48%). The Université Félix Houphouët-Boigny (as the Université de Cocody was renamed in 2012), in Abidjan, has 13 faculties and a research centre. There are two other universities, at Abodo-Adjamé (also in Abidjan) and at Bouaké. In 2006 there were 18 private universities and 120 private grandes écoles in the country. The country's first Islamic university, Université Musulmane de Côte d'Ivoire (UMCI), was opened in 2009. According to the World Bank, in 2021 spending on education represented 14.9% of total government expenditure.

Bibliography

Abo, F. K. *Pour un véritable réflexe patriotique en afrique: Le cas ivoirien*. Paris, L'Harmattan, 2002.

Akindès, F. *The Roots of the Military-political Crises in Côte D'Ivoire*. Uppsala, Nordic African Institute, 2004.

Côte d'Ivoire: la réinvention de soi dans la violence. Dakar, CODESRIA, 2011.

Baulin, J. *La succession d'Houphouët-Boigny*. Paris, Editions Karthala, 2000.

Bédié, H. Konan. *Les chemins de ma vie: Entretiens avec Eric Laurent*. Paris, Plon, 1999.

Bla, A.-M. K. K. *La Côte d'Ivoire en crise face au droit international*. Paris, L'Harmattan, 2013.

Boa-Thiémélé, R. L. *L'Ivoirité entre culture et politique*. Paris, L'Harmattan, 2003.

Boni, T. (Ed.). *Africulture 56: Côte d'Ivoire: le pari de la diversité*. Paris, L'Harmattan, 2003.

Charvin, R. *Côte d'Ivoire 2011: La bataille de la seconde indépendance*. Paris, L'Harmattan, 2011.

Contamin, B., and Fauré, Y.-A. *La bataille des entreprises publiques en Côte d'Ivoire: L'histoire d'un ajustement interne*. Paris, Editions Karthala, 1990.

Coulibaly, L. G. *Côte-d'Ivoire: Au coeur du bois sacré*. Paris, L'Harmattan, 2004.

Daniels, M. *Côte d'Ivoire*. Santa Barbara, CA, ABC Clio, 1996.

Diabaté, I., Dembele, O., and Akindes, F. (Eds). *Intellectuels ivoiriens face à la crise*. Paris, Editions Karthala, 2005.

Doh-Djanhoundy, T. *Autopsie de la crise ivoirienne: la nation au coeur du conflit*. Paris, L'Harmattan, 2006.

Eder, K. *Voting for Disorder: Post-conflict Elections as a Challenge in Peace Processes—the Case of Côte d'Ivoire*. München, Akademische Verlagsgemeinschaft München, 2012.

Ellenbogen, A. *Succession d'Houphouët-Boigny: Entre tribalisme et démocratie*. Paris, L'Harmattan, 2003.

Gbagbo, L. *Côte d'Ivoire: Fonder une nation africaine démocratique et socialiste en Côte d'Ivoire*. Paris, L'Harmattan, 1999.

Gombeaud, J.-L., Moutout, C., and Smith, S. *La Guerre du cacao, histoire secrète d'un embargo*. Paris, Calmann-Lévy, 1990.

Harrison Church, R. J. *West Africa*. 8th edn. London, Longman, 1979.

Hilaire, G. G. *Le rempart: attaque terroriste contre la Côte d'Ivoire*. Paris, L'Harmattan, 2004.

Jarret, M. F., and Mahieu, F.-R. *La Côte d'Ivoire de la destabilisation à la refondation*. Paris, L'Harmattan, 2002.

Katinan, J. K. *Côte d'Ivoire: l'audace de la rupture*. Paris, L'Harmattan, 2013.

Kokora, P. D. *Le Front populaire ivoirien: de la clandestinité à la légalité: le vécu d'un fondateur*. Paris, L'Harmattan, 1999.

Koné, A. *Houphouët Boigny et la Crise ivoirienne*. Paris, Editions Karthala, 2003.

Koulibaly, M. *La Responsabilité Politique: le Cas de la Côte d'Ivoire*. Paris, L'Harmattan, 2011.

Kouyate, M. D. *Le Budget de l'Etat Ivoirien: Financer le Développement*. Paris, L'Harmattan, 2014.

Le Pape, M., and Vital, C. (Eds). *Côte d'Ivoire: l'année terrible, 1999–2000*. Paris, Editions Karthala, 2002.

Lisette, G. *Le Combat du Rassemblement Démocratique Africain*. Paris, Présence Africaine, 1983.

McGovern, M. *Making War in Côte D'Ivoire*. London, C. Hurst & Co, 2011.

Miran, M. *Islam, histoire et modernité en Côte d'Ivoire*. Paris, Editions Karthala, 2006.

Guerres Mystiques en Côte d'Ivoire: Religion, Patriotisme, Violence (2002–2013). Paris, Karthala, 2015.

Nandjui, P. *Houphouët-Boigny: l'homme de la France en Afrique*. Paris, L'Harmattan, 1995.

La prééminence constitutionnelle du Président de la République en Côte d'Ivoire. Paris, L'Harmattan, 2004.

Navarro, R. *Côte d'Ivoire: Le culte du blanc: Les territoires culturels et leurs frontières*. Paris, L'Harmattan, 2003.

Notin, J.-C. *Le crocodile et le scorpion: la France et la Côte d'Ivoire (1999–2013)*. Monaco, Ed. du Rocher, 2013.

Ouedraogo, J.-B., and Sall, E. (Eds). *Frontières de la Citoyenneté et Violence Politique en Côte D'Ivoire*. Dakar, CODESRIA, 2008.

Rapley, J. *Ivorien Capitalism: African Entrepreneurs in Côte d'Ivoire*. London, Lynne Rienner Publishers, 1993.

Viti, F. *La Côte d'Ivoire, d'une crise à l'autre*. Paris, L'Harmattan, 2014.

Zoumana, D. *Côte d'Ivoire: Alassane Ouattara ou la renaissance pour un développement durable* Paris, L'Harmattan, 2019.

DJIBOUTI

Physical and Social Geography

I. M. LEWIS

The Republic of Djibouti is situated at the southern entrance to the Red Sea. It is bounded on the far north by Eritrea, on the west and south by Ethiopia, and on the south-east by Somalia. Djibouti covers an area of 23,200 sq km (8,958 sq miles), consisting mostly of volcanic rock-strewn desert wastes, with little arable land and spectacular salt lakes and pans. The climate is torrid, with high tropical temperatures and humidity during the monsoon season. The average annual rainfall is less than 260 mm. Only in the upper part of the basaltic range north of the Gulf of Tadjoura, where the altitude exceeds 1,200 m above sea level, is there continuous annual vegetation.

At the census of May 2009 the population was officially estimated at 818,159. According to United Nations (UN) projections, the population was 1,016,098 at mid-2022. The capital city, Djibouti (whose port and railhead dominate the country's economy), was projected by the UN to have a population of 591,469 at mid-2022. There are two main indigenous ethnic groups, the Issa, who are of Somali origin and comprise more than 50% of the population (predominating in the south-east and Djibouti city), and the Afar, who comprise around 35% of

the population and are of Ethiopian origin. Both groups are Muslims, and their Cushitic languages (Somali and Afar) are related. Both have a traditionally nomadic economy and close cultural affinities, despite frequent local rivalry, and both span the artificial frontiers separating the Republic of Djibouti from Ethiopia, Eritrea and Somalia.

Since the development of the port of Djibouti in the early 1900s, the indigenous Issas have been joined by immigrants from the adjoining regions of Somalia. The Afar generally follow more restricted patterns of nomadic movement than the Issa, and a more hierarchical traditional political organization. While they formed a number of small polities, these were linked by the pervasive division running throughout the Afar population between the 'noble' Asaimara (or 'red') clans and the less prestigious Asdoimara (or 'white') clans. There is also a long-established Arab trading community, most of whom have ancestral ties to Yemen. European expatriates are mainly French, mostly in government employment, commerce and the armed forces. Djibouti's official languages are Arabic and French.

History

DAVID STYAN

INTRODUCTION

The Republic of Djibouti is one of Africa's smallest states, in both demographic and economic terms. It achieved independence from France only in 1977. In recent decades the country's small ruling elite has skilfully used its strategic location to forge close ties with both the USA and the People's Republic of China. Chinese foreign direct investment has transformed port and rail infrastructure. This both enhanced Djibouti's status as an economic gateway to Ethiopia and reinforced its economic dependence on that country. Djibouti hosts the principal African military bases of both the USA and France. In 2011 it became host to Japan's first contemporary overseas military facility; in 2016 China deepened the trend, constructing its first overseas naval base in the Gulf of Tadjoura. In addition, the European Union (EU) and Japan station anti-piracy forces in the port of Djibouti, which is now the principal port at the gateway between the Red Sea and the Indian Ocean. Foreign military and naval presences all generate significant economic rents for the Government, while growing ties with Ethiopia have prompted the expansion of free trade zones in addition to the improved infrastructure.

Increased investment has boosted economic growth, yet the benefits of this accrue almost exclusively to an elite for whom business and politics are closely aligned. Government policies have made little impact on what remain some of the worst indices of poverty and deprivation in the region. Change is impeded by a sclerotic political system, power being channelled primarily via presidential patronage. The incumbent President, Ismaïl Omar Guelleh, has ruled since 1999; he was re-elected in April 2021 for a fifth presidential term. While tentative political reforms since 2012 have raised expectations, to date they have failed to deliver either greater accountability, significant job creation or income redistribution.

A COLONIAL MARITIME HUB

Often perceived of as a city-state, in reality Djibouti has a large, yet sparsely populated, hinterland covering an area of more

than 23,000 sq km. However, with an estimated population of 1,018,000 in 2021, it remains the least populous state on the African mainland.

The population comprises two principal groups, the Afar and the Issa, a Somali sub-clan. Both groups are present in larger numbers in neighbouring Ethiopia. Other significant groups in Djibouti include the Gadabursi and Isaaq Somali sub-clans, and a smaller number of Arabs, most with ancestral ties to Yemen. Since independence, the state has had two official languages, French and Arabic. Notwithstanding extensive urbanization and intermarriage, the Afar–Somali divide remains of social, economic and political significance.

Djibouti owes its existence to geography and imperial rivalries. Its strategic importance to foreign navies stems from its location. Its ports lie at the intersection of maritime trade routes between the southern mouth of the Red Sea and the north-western reaches of the Indian Ocean. For centuries the ports of Obock and Zeila linked highland Abyssinia to Arabia and the Indian Ocean; trade included slaves and the world's first ever coffee exports.

The opening of the Suez Canal in 1869, and Britain's subsequent closure of facilities at Aden to French military vessels during France's Indo-Chinese conflicts, enhanced the utility of a permanent French presence, first established with the signing of a treaty over Obock in 1862. France opened a coaling station at Obock, on the northern coast of the Gulf of Tadjoura, in 1883. This served the French fleet during its campaigns in both Indo-China and Madagascar. Frontiers were delineated in the 1880s with British Somaliland to the south and Italian Eritrea to the north.

In 1888 the settlement of Djibouti was established on the southern coast of the Gulf of Tadjoura. It offered better anchorages and a more efficient location for caravans to begin the arduous trek to the highlands of southern Ethiopia. In 1892 the French administration was transferred from Obock to Djibouti, at that time a minuscule trading post on isolated marshy islands. Léonce Lagarde became Governor of the colony, which was renamed the Côte Française des Somalis, the name by which the French colony was known until 1967, although it was often referred to as French Somaliland.

Lagarde's expansion of the French colony not only defined the frontiers and economy of what was to become the modern state of Djibouti, but also advanced French interests in Ethiopia. In 1894 Emperor Menelik II of Ethiopia concluded a contract with the French to build a railway between Djibouti and Dire Dawa (in Ethiopia) and on to the new Ethiopian capital, Addis Ababa. Lagarde secured Menelik's signature to a treaty in 1897, defining the border between the colony and Ethiopia, and stipulating that the port of Djibouti would handle Ethiopia's foreign trade. Work on the narrow-gauge railway began in that year and in 1917 it reached Addis Ababa. Of the 781 km of track, 97 km lie within Djibouti. Having fallen into disrepair in the late 20th century, the railway was completely rebuilt by Chinese companies; inaugurated in late 2016, it opened for passengers and freight in early 2018. The project is the centrepiece of several large rail and port developments in Djibouti aimed at enhancing trade access to and from Ethiopia's rapidly growing economy (see *Economy*).

MODERN POLITICS AND STATEHOOD

While the majority of colonial subjects in Central and West Africa gained their political independence in 1960, Djibouti's political trajectory was to be halting and protracted. Neighbouring northern British Somaliland gained independence on 26 June 1960, and the southern Italian United Nations (UN) Trust Territory of Somalia followed on 1 July. The two immediately merged to form the Somali Republic, bolstering nationalist sentiment among Djibouti's Somalis. Notwithstanding rising pan-Somali and pan-African sentiment, in 1958 a referendum on independence had resulted in 75% of Djibouti's 12,000-strong electorate voting to retain full links with France. As an overseas territory, Djiboutian representatives, including the young Somali Issa leader Hassan Gouled Aptidon, sat in the French legislature in Paris. The subsequent decades witnessed a complex series of highly personalized struggles among a narrow, largely urban political elite. In the 1960s the French Government's alarm at the rise of pan-Somali sentiment hastened shifts in its policy of alliances in the territory. Officials in Paris and Djibouti switched local political allegiances increasingly towards Afar notables, at the expense of Somali Issas.

In August 1966 a visit by French President Charles de Gaulle to Djibouti was marred by the violent repression of pro-independence protests. De Gaulle later declared that the Djibouti people would be given the opportunity to effect change. A referendum was held on 19 March 1967, ostensibly to provide the inhabitants of French Somaliland with a choice of remaining within the French Republic or gaining full independence. Amid allegations of vote rigging, those in favour of continued ties to France won with 60% of the votes. On 5 July 1967 the French Government renamed French Somaliland the French Territory of the Afars and the Issas. New elections to the local government were held on 29 July 1967, and Ali Aref Bourhan, an Afar, was elected President.

Using funds provided by the Somali Government, Aptidon and his ally, a nationalist Afar leader, Ahmed Dini Ahmed, visited African countries to raise the profile of the territory and to strengthen their campaign for independence. Within one year of its establishment, their Ligue Populaire Africaine pour l'Indépendance was recognized as the dominant political party by most potential voters and by the French Government. On 17 July 1976 Ali Aref resigned as head of government and was replaced by another Afar, Abdallah Mohamed Kamil, one of Djibouti's first university graduates and a notary.

Independence, Aptidon and the Single-party State

In February 1977 the French Government sponsored a round-table conference in Paris, on the future of the French Territory of the Afars and the Issas. Dates for a referendum on self-determination and eventual independence were set; however, sharp differences became apparent between Aptidon and Ahmed Dini on the distribution of seats in the future legislature between Somalis, Afars and Arabs. Ahmed Dini and Abdallah Kamil wanted the distribution to be fixed in Paris, while Aptidon wished to wait until after independence and

make those decisions within Djibouti. Ahmed Dini's position prevailed, with 33 seats reserved for Somalis and 30 for Afars. Elections for the independent Assemblée Nationale (National Assembly) took place on 8 May. Aptidon was elected as a representative of Djibouti city, and on 16 May he was selected by the National Assembly as President of the Government Council; Aptidon was sworn in at midnight on 26 June 1977, the eve of Djibouti's independence, as President of Djibouti.

At independence there was still no document determining the responsibilities of the presidency or members of the eventual government. On 8 July 1977 President Aptidon declared that the President would also serve as head of government. He then named Ahmed Dini as Prime Minister. Ahmed Dini accepted the nomination without enthusiasm, noting that the post of Prime Minister without power or responsibility was an empty gesture, and in December he, along with four other Afar ministers, resigned. The resignations disrupted Aptidon's ethnic template for Issa-Afar political ties, and he did not make the departures publicly known for several weeks. Nevertheless, the principle that the Prime Minister should be an Afar prevailed. This has resulted in a succession of, largely quiescent, Afar premierships; a tradition which persists today.

Aptidon's Governments relied heavily on French technocrats. The French expanded their military presence in the territory, and their expenditure accounted for a significant share of the nascent state's gross domestic product. Meanwhile, growing numbers of Djiboutians began to receive higher education in Paris and in francophone African capitals. Politically, Aptidon established legitimacy largely via financial largesse and state patronage. Constitutional change in 1981 created a single-party state, in keeping with broader trends throughout Africa. Thus, the Rassemblement Populaire pour le Progrès (RPP) became the sole formal channel for political and economic patronage. This largely benefited a narrow, mostly southern elite, closely allied to extensive French commercial and military interests.

AFAR DISCONTENT AND INSURGENCY

Economic marginalization of the north fed broader frustrations among Afars. This fuelled sympathy for an armed rebellion during the late 1980s and early 1990s, spearheaded by the Front pour la Restauration de l'Unité et de la Démocratie (FRUD). This was led by Ahmed Dini and attracted significant support from Afars both in the sparsely populated north and west, as well as the largely French-based diaspora.

Amid a broader regional military upheaval, prompting a change of government in Ethiopia, and the creation of breakaway states in Eritrea and 'Somaliland', in late 1991 FRUD guerrillas overran a number of villages and military posts in the north and west of Djibouti. (French troops had contained a large influx of defeated Ethiopian troops who fled via northern Djibouti when the Ethiopian Government fell in May.) However, Djibouti's mutual defence treaty with France, signed at independence, could only be invoked in the event of a foreign invasion. Yet while the French Government officially considered the FRUD's Afar insurgency to be a domestic matter, tacit French military support was forthcoming. Although fighting remained small-scale, the costs of war on Djibouti were considerable. The Government lost full control of the northern and western provinces, while the army expanded to more than 16,000, and by 1994 the war was consuming 35% of the national budget. France pushed for political negotiations between the rebels and Aptidon, who astutely wielded both political and financial incentives in order to splinter the FRUD. The tactic of deploying (usually financial) incentives to split opposition movements, effectively a 'divide-and-rule' strategy, has become a central characteristic of Djibouti's domestic political life. Thus a 'legalist' wing of the FRUD signed a deal and was permitted to register as a party, on the condition that it allied to the ruling RPP, in March 1996. A 'rejectionist', wing, led by Ahmed Dini, pledged to continue the uprising. While never fully defeated, an aging Ahmed Dini abandoned armed struggle in 2000 and the Government gradually re-established control over Obock and Tadjoura.

THE GUELLEH PRESIDENCY: CONSTITUTIONAL CHANGE, PARTIES AND PATRONAGE

The FRUD's threat coincided with post-Cold War pressures for political pluralism from France. Djibouti thus followed other francophone African states in adopting a new Constitution in March 1992. This provided, at least on paper, for a multi-party legislature within a presidential republic. The Constitution initially provided for up to four parties to contest both the presidency and seats in the National Assembly, which was to be re-elected every five years. Crucially for subsequent developments, the new Constitution limited the President to two six-year terms of office. Elections to the National Assembly were held on 18 December, and all 65 seats were won by the RPP. Five candidates then contested the presidential election on 7 May 1993; Aptidon received about 61% of the 70,000 votes cast, on a turnout of around one-half of the electorate.

Aptidon announced in February 1999 that he was to step down as President and he was succeeded by Guelleh following the presidential election in April. Guelleh, like his predecessor an Issa Somali from the Mamassan sub-clan, was a close family member of Aptidon. He had served as his predecessor's *Chef de Cabinet* as well as head of intelligence. It was this latter role that had embroiled him in the 1995 death of Bernard Borrel, a French judge serving in Djibouti. The protracted fallout from the death of Borrel, and legal challenges pursued by his wife, partially clouded Guelleh's ties with France in subsequent years.

Multi-party legislative elections were held in January 2003, with the ruling RPP creating a broad coalition, the Union pour la Majorité Présidentielle (UMP). This comprised the RPP and the legal wing of FRUD, plus two smaller formations, the Parti National Démocratique (PND) and the Parti Populaire Social Démocrate. While the UMP only secured 63% of votes cast, it still retained all 65 legislative seats. Opposition forces were subsequently regrouped under the banner of the Union pour l'Alternance Démocratique coalition. However, the opposition boycotted both the April 2005 presidential poll and the 2008 legislative elections. These were duly won by Guelleh and the UMP, which reinforced its principal function as an instrument for the distribution of patronage and political favour. During the first decade of the 21st century, allegations of widespread corruption and lack of political pluralism exacerbated discontentment stemming from a stagnant economy, recurrent drought and widespread unemployment among young Djiboutians.

THE THIRD TERM DEBATE AND THE POLLS OF 2011 AND 2013: TOWARDS A PRESIDENT FOR LIFE?

In 2008–09 political tensions were heightened due to the fact that following his re-election in the 2005 presidential poll Guelleh had stated publicly that he would not seek a third term in office. In early 2008 he reneged on this commitment. Considerable friction was generated by the need for constitutional amendments in order for Guelleh to be eligible for re-election after his second six-year term lapsed in early 2011; the amendments met with widespread opposition, including from within the presidential entourage, the governing UMP and the media. Guelleh pre-emptively removed the President of the Constitutional Court, Mohamed Warsame Ragueh, and replaced him with a close kinsman. In a move that was to have far-reaching implications for Djibouti's relations with Dubai and the United Arab Emirates (UAE)—and thence its broader international reputation—Guelleh also broke with Abdourahman Boreh, a close friend and business associate. Boreh had played a key role in securing the Dubai Ports World (DPW) container terminal at Doraleh (see *Economy*). Faced with allegations of corruption, he promptly fled into exile, having declared his ambition to replace Guelleh. Boreh went on to fund diaspora opposition groups. He was pursued, at considerable expense, by the Djiboutian authorities on corruption charges linked to the DPW agreement in a series of court cases. After four years of litigation, in March 2016 Boreh was acquitted of all charges in the Commercial Court in London (United Kingdom).

Meanwhile, in April 2010 the National Assembly amended the Constitution, abolishing term-limits. It also imposed a 75-year age limit for presidential candidates and reduced the presidential mandate from six years to five. The subsequent presidential elections, in April 2011, were marred by sporadic violence but—contrary to opposition reports at the time—this was not linked to the 'Arab Spring' uprisings elsewhere.

Opposition party candidates withdrew the poll, initially scheduled for 18 February 2011, protesting against state harassment and denial of access to media. Public meetings were banned and the presidential election was held amid tight security on 8 April. According to the official results, published on the following day, Guelleh was decisively re-elected, winning 80% of the 112,000 votes cast, with a turnout of an estimated 70%. He was sworn in for a third term in office on 8 May, at a ceremony attended by many regional leaders and representatives.

Prior to the 2011 poll, Guelleh had stated that if re-elected he would not contest a further, fourth term in office. Despite this, a political system, which since 1977 had been based essentially on patronage and highly personalized, clan-based support for an ageing political elite, was clearly under pressure. As a consequence, in early 2012 the Government appeared to have encouraged younger, independent-minded candidates to participate in regional and municipal elections. This resulted in the election in March of Abdourahman Mohamed Guelleh, known as 'TX', of the Rassemblement pour l'Action, le Développement et la Démocratie, an apparently autonomous, youth-based grouping, as the new mayor of Djibouti city.

Furthermore, on 28 November 2012 the National Assembly approved a mixed electoral system, combining the single-list system that had been in place since independence with a limited proportional representation system applicable to 20% of the seats. Potential opposition gains in the legislative elections scheduled for February 2013 would accordingly be limited to a maximum of 20% of the contested seats, or 13 of the 65 seats.

In Djibouti's tiny, patronage-based polity the myriad political parties invariably represent little more than heavily personalized, sub-clan groupings. This is as true of government allies as it is of the fragmented opposition groupings. In 2013 the UMP governing coalition principally comprised the RPP, the legalized faction of FRUD and three smaller groupings. Elements of the PND, which had split from the opposition, also joined the UMP to contest the 2013 legislative elections. The opposition, whose perennial boycott of elections reflected divided leadership and disorganization, decided to participate in the polls. Thus, an opposition formation comprising three main groups—the Alliance Républicaine pour le Développement, the Parti Djiboutien pour le Développement (PDD) and the Mouvement pour le Renouveau Démocratique et le Développement—was established in early January; it rapidly gained new members, and by mid-January was refashioned into an opposition coalition known as the Union pour le Salut National (USN). To widespread surprise, this grouping retained a semblance of cohesion between the 2013 legislative elections and the April 2016 presidential poll.

A longstanding opposition leader, author and activist, Daher Ahmed Farah, returned to the country on 13 January 2013, after a nine-year exile in Belgium, to take on the responsibility of acting as co-ordinator and spokesman for the USN. Reinforcing the appeal of the opposition coalition, the head of the USN list for Djibouti city was Ismaïl Guedi Hared, former confidant of President Aptidon (who had died in 2006) and longstanding rival of Guelleh.

The candidates for both the governing and the opposition coalition were permitted to begin their campaigns on 8 February 2013, two weeks prior to the elections. The opening USN public meeting was joined by 'TX' and many of his supporters. Despite the fact that the Government was in control of the national press, radio and television, the USN's primary vehicles for access to the public were open meetings and the internet. During relatively free campaigning there appeared to be a considerable groundswell of support for the younger, more dynamic USN grouping.

USN OPPOSITION ALLIANCE THWARTED, AND GUELLEH'S FOURTH AND FIFTH PRESIDENTIAL TERMS

The 2013 legislative elections were held on 22 February, in an atmosphere of relative calm. However, a strong showing by opposition forces, and the harsh repression of ensuing protests against alleged vote-rigging, proved a watershed in domestic political life. Subsequent patronage-based elections have been very tightly controlled, with the President's UMP tolerating no serious criticism.

According to the preliminary official results of the February 2013 poll, announced by the Minister of the Interior on the following day, the UMP had won 49 of the 65 seats in the National Assembly. The Government's voting figures indicated a near statistical tie in the results for Djibouti city. However, significant irregularities were alleged during the counting and collation of results, with the opposition obtaining and releasing earlier versions of the preliminary results for Djibouti city that indicated the victory of opposition candidates, and accusing the Government of falsifying the outcome.

Opposition supporters responded to the controversy surrounding the close vote in Djibouti city with angry protests. These escalated into riots that began on 27 February 2013 and continued for about seven days. Over 600 protesters, most of them university and high school students, were subsequently detained. Live ammunition was used in some cases to suppress the riots, with several fatalities reported. While compliant international electoral observers generally upheld the election results, reporting free and fair polling, considerable contradictions and doubts remained over the outcome.

According to final official results released on 12 March 2013, the UMP had secured 61.5% of the votes cast and 55 seats, while the USN had obtained 35.7% of the votes and the remaining 10 seats (seven of a total of 35 in Djibouti city, and one seat in each of the principal towns of Ali Sabieh, Arta and Tadjoura); a minor centrist party, the Centre des Démocrates Unifiés (CDU), won just 2.8% of the votes. To much consternation, the Government claimed to have taken 90% of the votes in the historic Afar town of Obock—a traditional stronghold of Afar insurgency and opposition activity.

The new National Assembly held its first session on 18 March 2013, which was boycotted by the newly elected USN deputies. Against a backdrop of simmering civil strife, particularly in the suburb of Arhiba, on 1 April President Guelleh announced his new Government. The most notable appointment was that of Abdoulkader Kamil Mohamed, hitherto Minister of Defence, as Prime Minister, replacing Dileita Mohamed Dileita, who had held the position since 2001.

The Government continued to resort to arrests and punitive raids on suspected opposition meetings for much of 2013–14, while seeking to split the USN by enticing individuals back to the UMP. With the Government's formal legitimacy still undermined by the refusal of USN deputies to take their seats in the National Assembly, in December 2014 a preliminary accord was finally signed, formally opening talks between the USN and the Government. The objectives of the accord included the investigation of human rights violations, ensuring the independence of the Commission Electorale Nationale Indépendante and securing the release of activists, in exchange for the USN accepting just eight National Assembly seats.

By late 2014, however, the political accord had been sidelined by the President. Despite harassment and frequent arrests of its leaders, the USN managed to maintain a united opposition against Guelleh throughout 2015 until December, when government forces violently dispersed a religious gathering by members of the Issa Yonis Moussa sub-clan at Bouldhoqo in the capital's suburb of Balbala, killing at least nine and injuring many others. The political impact of the incident was intensified by a government raid on a meeting of the USN leadership a few hours later. A number of USN parliamentary deputies and lawyers were injured and two key leaders were arrested. The USN subsequently splintered, with several of its component parties calling for an electoral boycott. Dissent and resurgent factionalism resulted in two rival opposition candidates, Omar Elmi Khaireh and Mohamed Daoud Chehem, contesting the presidential poll in April 2016, while three nominally 'independent' loyalists further enhanced the impression of pluralism. Following extensive campaigning and a well-organized and costly public relations campaign, Guelleh was duly elected for a fourth term on 8 April, winning 87% of the 135,000 votes cast. Guelleh's victory was welcomed by all of Djibouti's main foreign allies.

Guelleh won a fifth presidential term in an uneventful poll on 9 April 2021, securing 97.3% of the 172,000 votes cast (on a 79% turnout), according to official results. Despite the Government's ban on the holding of public gatherings of more than 10 people (imposed in 2020 in an attempt to curb the spread of the novel coronavirus disease COVID-19), large rallies in support of Guelleh's candidacy took place during the electoral campaign. No credible opposition figures were willing or able to stand for election; a little-known businessman, Zakaria Ismail Farah, eventually being brought in as a candidate to lend the poll legitimacy Patronage and public relations allow the Djiboutian elite to maintain its self-image as an oasis of political stability in the conflict-prone Horn of Africa. However, local politics is studded with sporadic inter-communal violence, while government surveillance and repression are extensive. In August 2021 Afar–Issa clashes in neighbouring Ethiopia triggered arson attacks and at least three deaths in suburbs of the capital.

The next National Assembly elections are scheduled for 2023. Low-key legislative elections were held on 23 February 2018, at which the UMP took 57 of the 65 seats. A coalition of the Union pour la Démocratie et la Justice (UDJ) and the PDD secured seven seats and the CDU the remaining seat. (In January the Government had introduced a requirement that 25% of those elected to the legislature be female.) The reported rate of voter participation was 67.1%. Both domestically and internationally, the 2018 elections were entirely overshadowed by the announcement on the eve of the polling of the nationalization of the Doraleh container terminal (see *Economy*).

REGIONAL AND FOREIGN AFFAIRS

Since taking office in 1999 President Guelleh has reinforced the state's activist regional policy, bolstering its political capital in both Africa and the Arab world. The scope and status of the foreign ministry has been enhanced and in 2014 an ambitious, Chinese-funded Institute of Diplomatic Studies was opened. Djibouti hosts the headquarters of the Horn of Africa's regional body, the Intergovernmental Authority on Development (IGAD). The organization, which is largely dependent on donor funding, has its origins in an Ethio-Djiboutian initiative in the late 1980s. It now encompasses eight states of the greater Horn, including, since 2012, South Sudan. Djibouti has limited influence in IGAD, which since 1998 has been partly paralysed by the Ethio–Eritrean conflict, but derives political capital from hosting the body. Djibouti is also an active member of the Arab League and has close ties to Saudi Arabia and member states of the Gulf Co-operation Council (GCC), although Djibouti's ties with the fractious GCC states are far from straightforward (see *Economy*). Since the latest phase of Yemen's civil war in 2015, Djibouti has been a key conduit for humanitarian assistance to Yemenis, from both Arab and Organisation for Economic Co-operation and Development donors. It also hosts several thousand Yemeni refugees, both in the capital and in a camp near Obock. Military aircraft of the Saudi-led coalition participating in the Yemen campaign have used Djiboutian facilities. In April 2015 a disagreement over landing rights for a UAE jet degenerated into a major diplomatic dispute, prompting the UAE Government to suspend all ties with Djibouti. Following the rupture of GCC members' links with Qatar in June 2017, Djibouti's ties with the Qatari authorities, which had acted as a diplomatic broker between Djibouti and Eritrea, cooled (see below).

Djibouti generally maintains cordial relations with the neighbouring autonomous territory of Somaliland, but these relations are periodically subject to strains due both to transborder clan dynamics and Djibouti's ongoing role in endeavours to reconstruct a central Somali state. President Guelleh attempted to adopt a central role in Somali reconciliation, hosting protracted negotiations during 2000 in Arta, 30 km from Djibouti's capital. The Arta Conference ultimately failed to facilitate clan-based reconciliation, and brought few benefits to Djibouti. Since then, much of Djibouti's diplomacy towards Somali issues has been conducted through regional and multilateral fora. Djibouti reopened its embassy in the Somalian capital, Mogadishu, in 2018. President Guelleh hosted his Somalian counterpart, Mohamed Abdullahi Mohamed, in August 2019, and in June 2020 chaired talks in Djibouti aimed at reconciliation between the authorities of Somalia and 'Somaliland'.

Djibouti participates in the African Union Mission in Somalia (AMISOM) operation that was established in 2007, deploying about 960 troops in central Somalia. French and US troops based in Djibouti also contribute to training both Djiboutian and AMISOM troops. Djibouti's hosting of US military facilities and support for AMISOM have prompted threats from Somali militants from the Islamist group Al-Shabaab. A café frequented by Westerners in Djibouti was the target of a suicide bomb attack on 24 May 2014, a rare exception to the general belief that Djibouti and the military bases that it hosts are insulated from Islamist violence.

Djibouti's relations with neighbouring Eritrea, which gained independence from Ethiopia in 1993, are strained. They reached a new low when Eritrea deployed troops into Djibouti territory at Ras Doumeira, in the far north-east of the country, in April 2008, prompting a tense stand-off. The Eritrean incursion comprised as many as 4,000 Eritrean soldiers and Djibouti committed some 8,000 military personnel to the area, around two-thirds of its total armed forces at that time. Fighting between the opposing forces broke out on 10 June. The Eritrean advances into Djibouti were strongly condemned by the UN Security Council, the Arab League, the African Union (AU) and IGAD. Following months of negotiations, mediation efforts led by the Government of Qatar succeeded in securing the withdrawal of Eritrean forces from Djibouti territory in June 2010. In June 2017 Qatari troops, which had been monitoring the border between Eritrea and Djibouti, were abruptly withdrawn in the wake of the rupture between Qatar and other Arabian Gulf states. Djibouti protested to IGAD, the AU and the UN that Eritrean troops had immediately seized the disputed territory, on the headland and the island of Doumeira. Following the Ethiopian-Eritrean rapprochement which began in mid-2018, in July Djibouti opposed the lifting of UN sanctions against Eritrea, requesting that the UN first facilitate the resolution of its own border dispute with Eritrea. While this was finally agreed in principle via Security Council Resolution 2444 of 14 November 2018, the border remains closed. Djibouti's bitter stand-off with the UAE (see below) complicates ties with Eritrea, particularly given the UAE's maintenance of a naval base at Assab, adjacent to Ras Doumeira.

Relations with Ethiopia have become closer since 1998, when Ethiopia became almost entirely dependent upon Djibouti as a conduit for its foreign trade. Significant new infrastructure developments have facilitated the upsurge in trade. These include the Doraleh container port and oil terminals, as well as a Chinese-funded and -constructed Multi-Purpose Port, the reconstruction of the railway linking to the two capitals, as well as a new road link between Ethiopia and the northern port of Tadjourah (see *Economy*). Politically, the two states' policies are closely aligned over a series of bilateral issues, notably border security across Afar and Issa areas. Close bilateral ties reflect both mutual geostrategic and economic interests and have been further tightened by Ethiopia's recent supply of both hydroelectric power and drinking water to Djibouti, as well as co-ordinated border closures due to the COVID-19 pandemic.

Foreign Military Presence

Since the mid-2000s Djibouti's external military links have evolved rapidly. In 2016 China transferred troops to Djibouti as construction began on a Chinese naval facility in the Gulf of Tadjoura (China's first overseas military installation). The facility lies adjacent to the Chinese-built Multi-Purpose Port in Doraleh, which was formally opened in May 2017. While historically Djibouti's primary military role was as a French military base, by 2017 Djibouti was hosting an unparalleled

array of US, Asian and Arab naval and air forces. Since 2005, anti-piracy forces operating in the region have used Djibouti as a logistical and administrative hub. The 2015 Saudi-led attacks on Yemen also resulted in an increase in military traffic. The USA, France, Japan and the EU all have de facto permanent military presences in Djibouti.

At independence in 1977 there were approximately 4,000 French military personnel in the country. Between independence and 2010 France maintained troops under a mutual defence agreement signed in 1977; the agreement was renewed most recently in 2011. Djibouti remained an essential part of French military projection in both Africa and the Indian Ocean, and the garrison, which included large numbers of dependants, provided a crucial source of income for Djibouti. Forces were reconfigured in the 1990s and the numbers of troops declined with the transfer of the 13th Demi-Brigade of the French Foreign Legion from Djibouti to the UAE in June 2011. However, Djibouti still remains France's largest military garrison in Africa, with 1,400 permanent troops, and an additional 500 on rotation, and France pays the Government of Djibouti around €30m. annually for the right to maintain military facilities in the country. French forces also play a significant role in the EU's anti-piracy mission, EU NAVFOR (see below), and conduct frequent joint training missions with US forces in the region.

Following the creation of US Africa Command (AFRICOM) in 2008, Djibouti became the USA's sole permanent military base in Africa, at the heart of which is the Combined Joint Task Force-Horn of Africa (CJTF-HOA). By 2015 there were around 3,200 US personnel assigned to CJTF-HOA. In addition to its various military responsibilities, CJTF-HOA acts as a staging post for US missions in the Indian Ocean and Middle East, and has a civilian outreach programme. The US base is also the headquarters for counter-terrorism efforts. These include drone flights throughout East Africa and the eastern portion of the Arabian Peninsula. Drone flights are now conducted principally from a second base at Chebelley, away from the built-up areas of Camp Lemonnier (the former French Foreign Legion complex). In May 2014 Guelleh and US President Barack Obama met in Washington, DC, USA, and announced a 10-year extension to the US military facilities in Djibouti. Under the new lease, the USA agreed to pay Djibouti US $63m. per year. The 2014 agreement contains an option to renew the facility for a further 10 years. Since 2017 US strategists have argued that there is a need to counter China's growing presence in the region, as well as continued Islamist activity in Yemen and Somalia.

Djibouti has become a major staging area for international air and naval forces that have joined efforts to oppose sea piracy in the Gulf of Aden and the Indian Ocean. Djibouti port also supplies fuel and provisions to the many naval ships involved in anti-piracy patrols. In January 2009 Djibouti hosted a meeting of 17 countries from the Western Indian Ocean, the Gulf of Aden and the Red Sea. Convened by the International Maritime Organization, the states agreed on a document termed the Djibouti Code of Conduct, in which they declared themselves ready to co-operate to the fullest extent possible under international law to interdict, arrest and prosecute persons who had committed piracy. In 2009 Djibouti became the base for EU NAVFOR, the mandate of which was renewed in January 2021 for a further two years, to the end of 2022.

In July 2011 the Japanese Maritime Self-Defense Force established a base in Djibouti; significantly, this was Japan's first overseas military base since the end of the Second World War. Japan is an important aid donor to Djibouti, and has also constructed an anti-piracy centre to the west of Doraleh port.

Between 2015 and 2017 China progressively expanded its civil and military presence in Djibouti. What began as limited training and medical assistance for Djibouti's armed forces has grown as Chinese vessels have increasingly participated in anti-piracy convoys. During 2012–17 China funded and constructed several major infrastructure projects, as Djibouti became an evermore prominent node in China's 'Maritime Silk Road' (MSR) economic initiative.

In August 2017 China's Ministry of Defence formally opened what it termed a 'naval support facility' in Djibouti. Both the opening ceremony, and the first live-fire exercises by Chinese troops operating from the base the following month, were publicized widely in both Western and Chinese media, with the coverage in China emphasizing Djibouti's pivotal role in China's MSR initiative. Although the naval base was constructed adjacent to the quays of the Chinese-built commercial Multi-Purpose Port at Doraleh (which was formally opened in May 2017), by 2021 the Chinese Navy had also constructed a bespoke, 400-m deep-water jetty from their base.

Despite often alarmist Western reporting, the close proximity of Chinese and NATO-member military facilities in practice have necessitated discreet co-operation between ostensibly rival forces, a fact acknowledged by the outgoing head of the US base in mid-2022. The Chinese naval support facility not only abuts the Multi-Purpose Port, but also complements China's substantial investment in civil construction and infrastructure projects in Djibouti and neighbouring Ethiopia. These include the Ethiopia–Djibouti railway, the new Doraleh port and associated free trade zone, and the Ghoubet salt export facility, formally opened in June 2017, as well as a Sino-Djiboutian liquefied natural gas terminal at Damerjog. The financial dimensions of China's civil and military presence remain opaque, although substantial debt-rescheduling was agreed with China in mid-2019. Nevertheless, acute concern continues to be raised by Western allies about unsustainable non-concessional debt levels. In December 2018 the US National Security Advisor, John Bolton, placed allegations about Chinese 'debt-diplomacy' in Djibouti at the centre of a review of US policy in Africa. However, he offered no evidence to substantiate his claim that China was intent on seizing control of the Doraleh container terminal (see *Economy*).

Economy

DAVID STYAN

INTRODUCTION

Despite sustained growth, improving infrastructure and sharp increases in inward foreign direct investment (FDI) in recent years, Djibouti's economy retains severe structural weaknesses. According to World Bank indicators, Djibouti's economy is officially classed as 'lower middle-income', with a gross national income estimated at US $3,300 per head in 2021. Yet income distribution is extremely uneven, malnutrition and acute poverty remain widespread, and Djibouti scores poorly on most indices of development, ranking 171st out of 191 states in the 2021 United Nations (UN) Development Programme's Human Development Index.

The Republic of Djibouti has an official population of just over 1m. people. The 2009 census recorded a population of 818,159, while the UN estimate for mid-2022 was 1,018,000. However, many observers believe that, even allowing for regional migrants, the total may be smaller. Around 680,000 people—over 70% of the country's population—live in the sprawling suburbs of Djibouti city. After war closed Ethiopia's access to Eritrean ports in 1998, Djibouti became the primary conduit for Ethiopia's foreign trade flows, which have increased steadily over the past two decades. With its population now over 115m. and annual gross domestic product (GDP) growth of around 10% to 2020, Ethiopia's growing transit trade boosted Djibouti's service sector. In addition to being a gateway for trade, highland Ethiopia also supplies hydroelectric power and drinking water to Djibouti. Substantial investments in port facilities, notably by Dubai Ports World (DPW) prior to 2018 and by China Merchants Group (CMG) since 2013, and an improving transport system, financed initially by DPW and subsequently by Chinese companies, have further boosted trade links with Ethiopia. Alongside the rents from foreign military bases, transit trade to Ethiopia represents Djibouti's principal source of income. While both have generated considerable revenues for the country's minuscule political and business elite, they have generated only meagre benefits for the bulk of the population.

As a small but pivotal state in the region, Djibouti has in the past decade secured significant inwards FDI. In 2013 the People's Republic of China overtook Dubai as the country's leading investor, providing inflows of well over US $1,000m. into port, rail and water infrastructure in 2013–18. This has consolidated a shift evident since 2000, whereby hitherto dominant French financial capital has been largely displaced by Asian, Arab and Somali funds.

Virtually all of Djibouti's food supplies are imported, and food and energy prices are particularly high. Coupled with widespread unemployment, levels of inequality and deprivation are among the highest in the region, despite Djibouti having a considerably higher average per head income than Ethiopia, Eritrea or the self-declared 'Republic of Somaliland'. This reflects particularly flagrant income inequalities in what is a highly dualistic economy. A small, relatively well-educated and salaried middle class maintains economic links with Ethiopia, France, Canada and Arab Gulf states, with remittances growing in economic importance. The Djibouti franc is pegged to the US dollar.

Most of the country physically presents either moon-like rocky desert or broad, dry plains with little vegetation. There are isolated forested areas in the north, most notably the Forêt du Daï. There are no significant surface fresh water sources anywhere in Djibouti except during rare rains. These occur infrequently, often triggering flash floods. The country endures very high daily temperatures, commonly exceeding 40°C, during at least 10 months of the year.

ECONOMIC GROWTH, DONORS AND DEBT

In recent years Djiboutian economic growth has been largely tied to expanding trade ties with Ethiopia, in part linked to its prominent position on China's 'Maritime Silk Road'. Both roles underpin increases in inward FDI, primarily from China. Economic management is improving, yet remains fragile and largely beholden to both a patronage-based political system and a limited pool of qualified personnel. The rapid rise of Chinese interests in the economy have prompted questions over the sustainability of current levels of economic growth and sharply rising levels of external indebtedness, as well as the country's externally dependent economic governance.

Djibouti has traditionally received extensive economic assistance from both Arab donors and those of the Organisation for Economic Co-operation and Development, and retains close ties with the European Union (EU), France and the Bretton Woods institutions. However, economic data collection and reporting is weak and the country has a poor history of debt management. As of mid-2022 the most recent substantive economic update remained the October 2019 publication of the International Monetary Fund (IMF) Article IV consultation with Djibouti. At that point FDI had increased markedly, inflation was stable at around 3%, while annual GDP growth had averaged around 7.0% in 2014–19. The impact of both COVID-19 and conflict in Ethiopia in 2020–21 slashed trade and growth; the IMF estimated GDP growth at 0.5% in 2020, recovering to 4–5% in 2021–22.

Djibouti received an emergency IMF Catastrophe Containment and Relief Trust disbursement in May 2020, with a further US $43.4m. in temporary IMF balance-of-payments funding and the option of a further $8m. in debt relief. The World Bank claimed that this funding, coupled with buoyant re-exports from Djibouti's free trade zone, had helped stabilize growth in 2020. Although by mid-August 2022 a total of only 15,690 cases of COVID-19 had been reported in Djibouti, with 189 deaths, the economic impact of the global pandemic remained significant for the country, largely due to trade effects.

An IMF staff mission in June 2022 repeated longstanding donors' concerns in over ongoing widespread household poverty as well as Djibouti's rapidly rising debt ratios. The Fund noted that rising global commodity prices exacerbated Djibouti's acute budgetary pressures. Debt service costs tripled in 2022, to 5% of GDP, as the G20's exceptional Debt Service Suspension Initiative (DSSI) expired in December 2021.

According to IMF statistics, 41% of Djibouti's population lives in extreme poverty, while just under one-half of the labour force is unemployed. The unemployment rate rises to 70% for those under the age of 30 years. The majority of employment is informal. According to the World Bank, in 2012 only 44,000 formal sector jobs existed, almost one-half of them in the civil service. These figures also highlight the extremely narrow nature of Djibouti's tax base. Beyond the fiscal windfall, the economic benefits of hosting foreign bases, including the USA's principal military facility in Africa, and China's naval installation, are meagre. The bases generate relatively little private sector business or employment for Djiboutian companies and employees. Under the renewed US facility lease agreement signed in May 2014 (see *History*), covering the period 2014–24, the major share of sub-contracting will remain in US hands. Several hundred Djiboutian personnel are employed, primarily in menial activities, around the base. Similar employment patterns prevail at the Japanese and Chinese facilities. China's large civil construction projects, the Ethiopia–Djibouti railway and the multi-purpose port at Doraleh, are staffed mostly by Chinese engineers and labourers.

As noted above, for the past decade the IMF has consistently underscored the dangers of Djibouti's steadily rising external debts. The 2019 Article IV consultation again stressed that debt-financed public capital spending was considerably increasing both fiscal and external debt burdens. World Bank and IMF estimates in late 2021 suggested that even under relatively optimistic scenarios, Djibouti faced a financing gap arising from COVID-19 and Ethiopia's ongoing civil strife of US $70.7m. in 2022 and $52.1m. in 2023. While Djibouti's macroeconomic management and transparency appears to have improved in recent years, with the media largely under state control, there is little public awareness or debate of macroeconomic issues.

Hong Kong-based conglomerate China Merchants Group (CMG) is a central player in Djibouti. It purchased a 23.5% equity stake in the Port of Djibouti in 2013 and in May 2016 established a strategic partnership, linking Djibouti with the port of Qingdao, where CMG has a strong presence. In July 2018 CMG inaugurated a 240-ha pilot phase of the Djibouti International Free Trade Zone (DIFTZ), adjacent to its new multi-purpose port at Doraleh. If and when fully completed, the DIFTZ would encompass 4,800 ha, making it the largest free trade zone in Africa.

With multiple outstanding debts to China a matter of concern, an initial debt rescheduling package regarding China's loan for the construction of the railway was negotiated between September 2018 and July 2019; the roll-over period for repayment was extended from 10 to 30 years, with interest rates lowered to 2.1% above the London Interbank Offered Rate.

While the Government of Djibouti maintains a generally co-operative relationship with the major international financial institutions, there is perennial scepticism as to the Djiboutian authorities' capability and willingness to address deep-seated structural problems and mounting debts, particularly since US $813m. was incurred to China for rail, port and water pipeline projects in 2013. In 2012 the World Bank assisted in the drawing up of a new growth strategy for Djibouti, which comprised two main strands: acceptance that existing economic models were unsustainable; and recognition that economic governance had to improve. This new growth model became the basis for Djibouti's 'Vision 2035' statement (see below), which in turn largely framed the 2014–17 World Bank Country Partnership Strategy.

By 2021–22 the World Bank's portfolio in Djibouti consisted of 14 projects funded by the International Development Association, valued at US $240m. However, as of mid-2022 analysts were still awaiting the publication of a revamped Country Partnership Framework between the World Bank and Djibouti; the five-year hiatus since the 2017 strategy lapsed accurately reflecting the ad-hoc nature of Djibouti's development.

Ongoing World Bank projects in the country focus in particular on education, social infrastructure and attempts to ameliorate acute poverty. In May 2020 the Bank announced a further US $25m. in project funding, focusing on the improvement of Djibouti's statistical service, and boosting support for migrants from neighbouring states.

DJIBOUTI 'VISION 2035'

Since 2012 Djibouti has vigorously promoted a new economic development strategy, which aims to capitalize on its location and plans to upgrade infrastructure in tandem with Ethiopia. Named 'Vision 2035', this is largely the work of the office of the Minister of the Economy and Finance, Ilyas Moussa Dawaleh, a technocrat with a private-sector background. Dawaleh was first appointed to the post in 2011 (retaining the portfolio after the presidential election of 2016). In 2012 he also became the Secretary-General of the ruling party—he is viewed by many outsiders as a potential presidential successor. The 'Vision 2035' strategy aims to create sustained economic growth via synergies generated by the ongoing upgrade of both rail and port links with Ethiopia. A core aspect of the new policy framework is job creation, within a framework of medium-term policy interventions over the next 20 years aimed at boosting private-sector growth. 'Vision 2035' was relaunched, with World Bank and UN backing, at a high-profile conference in June 2014, which aimed to draw comparative lessons from the growth successes of other micro-states. Among the attendees were delegations from Mauritius, the United Arab Emirates (UAE—prior to the recent rupture, a key supporter of Djibouti—see below) and Singapore. 'Vision 2035' in theory corresponds with the Djiboutian Government's sectorial five-year national 'Strategy for Accelerated Growth and Promotion of Employment' for 2015–19 (known by its French acronym 'SCAPE'). In the five years since its adoption, Djibouti's growth plans have expanded to incorporate ambitious Chinese project financing.

THE PRIVATE SECTOR, FDI, PORTS AND INFRASTRUCTURE

In principle, the Government is mindful of external criticism of the difficulties in doing business in Djibouti, although in practice reforms to improve the private sector have been piecemeal. In 2012 a National Committee on Doing Business in Djibouti was established, with a steering committee on business environment formed to monitor future progress. Officials from the World Bank, the EU and the Common Market for Eastern and Southern Africa have all been involved in such initiatives. While in May 2013 the United Kingdom hosted a major conference designed to showcase Djibouti's private sector investment opportunities, and in June 2014 the World Bank announced a US $4m. programme to support private sector development in the country, over the past decade the reality is that the overwhelming majority of FDI has been Chinese, primarily in infrastructure.

The private sector remains stymied by both the limited size and rentier characteristics of the economy. Political patronage remains central to accessing the private sector, for both local and foreign investors. Small-scale start-ups are rare, and bank credit for younger entrepreneurs is extremely scarce. The members of the presidential entourage tend to have extensive roles in private industry, especially in construction and trading. Opportunities for profitable business are often made available to loyal supporters.

Nevertheless, FDI has soared in recent years. In March 2015 Dawaleh claimed that US $1,800m. worth of funds was invested in the country at that time (primarily in ports, railway and construction). A hugely ambitious projected investment plan sought to attract a further $6,000m. by 2020. China's integrated investments include the renovation of the Ethiopia–Djibouti railway, as well as several new port developments in Djibouti and associated free zones.

On 22 February 2018 Djibouti unilaterally terminated DPW's management contract for the country's principal economic asset, the Doraleh Container Terminal (DCT), seizing DPW's 33% stake in the port. Lying 12 km to the west of the capital city and its congested old port facilities, the terminal was among several high-profile investments undertaken by the Gulf Emirates in Djibouti in the 2000s. The February 2018 seizure was the culmination of five years of strained ties, and was linked to Abdourahman Boreh, a close business associate of President Ismaïl Omar Guelleh, who brokered DPW's construction and management of the DCT. Relations between Boreh and Guelleh broke down in 2009, amid corruption allegations and political rivalry. Boreh fled into exile and was subsequently convicted of both tax and terrorism charges in Djibouti. Between 2012 and 2016 the Government pursued a protracted series of legal actions against Boreh, but in March 2016 the latter was acquitted of all charges in the Commercial Court in London, UK, in a judgment that was highly critical of the Government's case. Meanwhile, in a separate legal case in London, in July 2014 Djibouti's Ports and Free Zone Authority (DPFZA) sought to nullify its existing management contract with DPW, alleging malpractice by Boreh. After protracted hearings, this too was rejected in a February 2017 ruling. In both cases, the Djiboutian authorities were ordered to pay full costs. Following the 2018 seizure and nationalization of the DCT, further court decisions in London ordered the Djiboutian Government to pay DPW full compensation of around US $385m., plus legal costs. The litigation remained unresolved as of mid-2022, although the COVID-19 pandemic and Ethiopia's ongoing civil strife both served to deflect international criticism from Djibouti.

As the dispute over the DCT intensified, in May 2016 DPW announced a US $440m. deal to upgrade the port of Berbera, in neighbouring Somaliland. While the head of the DPFZA stated that he welcomed such competition, some analysts viewed DPW's decision to invest in Berbera as having been influenced by the recent tensions between Djibouti and the UAE.

A Chinese-built and -managed replacement for the anti-quated 781-km railway from Djibouti city to Dire Dawa and Addis Ababa (Ethiopia) was fully opened to both cargo and passengers in early 2018. The rail link was realigned, widened to standard gauge and converted to run on electrical power. Work on the Djibouti tranche began in 2014, with 95% of the US $550m. cost being met via loans from China's Export-Import Bank. Within Djibouti the rail project included the construction of a new terminus located just outside the capital city. Branch lines also link the main line to both the DCT and the new, Chinese-constructed multi-purpose port at Doraleh. This port is the centrepiece of a considerable expansion of the DPFZA's free zone programme, including the construction of extensive special economic and free trade zones. Originally involving the Turkish, Chinese and Djiboutian authorities, these zones now appear to be entirely Chinese-led. The Djiboutians hope that the railway will accelerate Ethiopia's current policy of export-led industrialization, and enable some associated warehousing, processing and assembly activities to be located in Djibouti.

In 2012 Ethiopia also signed preliminary contracts with China (valued at US $1,500m.) and Turkey ($1,700m.) to build a railway from Mekele (in the Ethiopian region of Tigray) through Ethiopia. Draft plans included a link to northern Djibouti and the new port at Tadjoura, on the north coast of the Gulf of Tadjoura; the link's primary function would be the export of potash, traversing the Afar Triangle, connecting Tigray to Tadjoura. Work on Tadjoura port was inaugurated by President Guelleh and Ethiopia's Prime Minister Haile-mariam Desalegn in 2013 and the port was formally opened in June 2017. Constructed by a Chinese company, the $120m. project was financed by Saudi Arabian and other Arab development funds. In July 2020 a road link between Tadjourah port and Balho, near the Ethiopian border, was inaugurated.

However, the road link from Tadjoura remains precarious, and railway plans have been sidelined. This appears primarily due to issues of project management and the arid terrain and hostile climate—the Afar depression being one of the world's hottest places. However, Afars in Tadjoura and Obock also criticized the investments for failing to provide local employment. In 2018 the possibility that Ethiopia would regain access to the Eritrean port of Assab, following the Ethiopian-Eritrean rapprochement in mid-2018 (see below), further cast doubts on the future of the putative Ethiopia–Tadjourah rail link.

In November 2017 Djibouti signed an initial agreement with China's POLY-GCL Petroleum Group Holdings Ltd for a natural gas project. The project was to comprise a pipeline, a liquefaction plant and an export terminal, to be located at the southern port of Damerjog, near the border with Somaliland. The proposed facility would be the terminus of a 700-km pipeline from the Kalub and Hilala gasfields in south-eastern Ethiopia, which were to be developed by an Ethiopian-Chinese joint venture. Two further ports were completed in 2017: the first at Goubet (Ghoubbet-el-Kharab), a collapsed volcanic cone in the centre of Djibouti, connected by an inlet to the Gulf of Tadjoura. The port is intended to facilitate the export of salt from Lake Assal; the deposits are reportedly the most extensive in the world. The other port is a livestock facility, also located at Damerjog. In addition, in June 2016 the President inaugurated two new airport construction sites, both of which were reported dependent upon Chinese finance and construction companies. The first, located at Bicidley, 25 km south-west of the capital, is the proposed site of the new international airport. This is expected to replace the current, small Ambouli airport on the outskirts of Djibouti city, and is to be named after the country's first President, Hassan Gouled Aptidon. The site of the second airport is at Ras Syan, close to Obock and Djibouti's prime tourist sites, and will bear the name of Ahmed Dini, the country's first Prime Minister.

INTERDEPENDENCE WITH ETHIOPIA

Prior to 1998 most of Ethiopia's foreign trade was shared between the Eritrean port of Assab and Djibouti, for whom Ethiopia represented by far its most important customer. However, the border war between Ethiopia and Eritrea (fought during 1998–2000) dramatically increased Ethiopian use of Djibouti overnight, engendering a near total dependence on the Red Sea port's facilities. The opening of Djibouti's DCT in 2009, and the adjacent Emirates National Oil Company petroleum terminal, were largely premised on the growing needs of Ethiopian trade. Volumes of trade rose further from 2017 due to the opening of the Djibouti–Addis Ababa railway, accelerating Ethiopia's plans to become a global manufacturing hub.

Nevertheless, Djibouti has been historically wary of allowing total Ethiopian economic dominance. The Government continues to resist Ethiopian overtures to establish direct equity stakes in the port facilities. Ethiopia's Prime Minister, Dr Abiy Ahmed Ali, visited Djibouti immediately after his inauguration in April 2018. While Abiy Ahmed surprised analysts, and his Djiboutian hosts, by announcing that he would like to see the two states have joint equity stakes in ports, telecommunications and airlines, the reality has been closer technical co-operation, rather than joint investments.

Economic interdependency has been accentuated by Ethiopia growing trade flows as well as supplies of electricity and water to Djibouti. From 2011 Ethiopia began to supply hydro-electric power to Djibouti, whose electricity was hitherto expensively produced by ageing and unreliable oil-fired generators. In a climate where air conditioning is crucial for offices, housing and industry, electricity costs have been a major barrier to growth. Following Djibouti's connection to Ethiopia's electricity grid in 2012, retail and industrial domestic electricity tariffs were significantly reduced, easing pressure on both household and business budgets. The 283-km transmission line between the two countries was 90% financed by loans and grants from the African Development Bank (AfDB). Maximum power flow between the two countries using current facilities is estimated to peak at 35 MW, with a second line now being prepared to boost capacity to 50 MW. An AfDB feasibility study indicates that, with additional investment, capacity could rise to 100 MW, an amount that would consume only 0.05% of Ethiopia's present power potential.

While hydroelectric imports clearly increase Djibouti's economic and political dependency on its vast neighbour, this appears a price worth paying. For Ethiopia it is also the first stage in what is envisaged as a major regional export strategy of abundant hydroelectric power. A further element of bilateral infrastructure integration was added in January 2013, through the construction of a Chinese-financed water pipeline, supplying 100,000 cu m of drinking water per day free of charge to Djibouti city from a source 70 km within Ethiopia.

POWER GENERATION

Geologically, Djibouti lies at the junction of three tectonic plates. These spreading cleavages in the earth's mantle are forcing Africa away from Arabia, and thus generate often violent seismic activity in and around Djibouti. With huge amounts of energy so close to the surface, it has long been the aim of power experts to discover some economic means of harnessing Djibouti's volcanic foundation. Work began in 1986 on a major geothermal exploration project, funded by the World Bank and foreign aid, but the project was not completed. However, the arrival of cheaper power from Ethiopia has not diminished Djibouti's enthusiasm to develop its geothermal potential. In July 2012 in the Chinese capital, Beijing, President Guelleh and the Chairman of the China Petroleum & Chemical Corporation (Sinopec) witnessed the signing of an agreement for Chinese support to develop geothermal power from the Lake Assal rift.

DROUGHT, HUMANITARIAN CRISES AND MIGRATION

Life in Djibouti for its people and livestock remains precarious due to recurrent drought emergencies. According to estimates by the UN Office for the Coordination of Humanitarian Affairs (OCHA), Djibouti's urban and rural populations are both severely affected by food shortages. OCHA's 2018–22 Chronic Food Insecurity assessment indicated that 98% of people living in rural areas of Djibouti had an inadequate and insufficiently varied diet, while around one-third of the country's total population (280,000) were in a chronic food insecurity situation.

In February 2022 the Government of Djibouti issued a drought alert. Low groundwater levels and the failure of rains throughout the Horn of Africa further exacerbated deteriorating pasture conditions by mid-2022. The World Food Programme (WFP) reported declining pasture, prompting families to run down assets and hastening rural–urban migration into the suburbs of the capital. Due to drought and high urban food prices, WFP estimated that by mid-2022 almost 200,000 Djiboutians—over 15% of the total population—would face dire food shortages.

Such stark data is reflected in numerous other UN agency reports produced on Djibouti. Despite sustained and repeated emergency interventions by a plethora of UN and local agencies, the percentage of children without basic rights to water and sanitation, information, nutrition, education and health care remains stubbornly high.

OCHA has regularly estimated that Djibouti's global acute malnutrition rate is at least 20%, with far higher rates in provincial settlements, particularly Obock and Tadjoura. The UN's inter-agency plans for the country in recent years have estimated that over 250,000 people, around one-quarter of the total population, require some form of external assistance.

In addition to its own internally displaced population caused by drought and poverty, the bulk of whom have settled informally around the capital city, by mid-2022, according to the Office of the UN High Commissioner for Refugees (UNHCR), Djibouti was also hosting some 31,300 Somali, Ethiopian, Eritrean and Yemeni refugees, with a small influx of refugees having recently arrived from Ethiopia's war-torn province of Tigray. The longstanding Somali refugee populations are housed in refugee camps at Ali Addeh and Hol-hol, 130 km south of Djibouti city near Ali Sabieh. When the camp at Ali Addeh was established in 1991, it was designed to accommodate about 7,000 refugees. In 2020 the camp housed almost 10,800, many of whom had been in exile from Somalia for many years.

From early 2015 Djibouti hosted growing numbers of Yemeni refugees, with the total number estimated at 38,000 in December 2017, although this had fallen to less than 5,000 by 2020. Yemeni migrants comprise two distinct groups: those arriving on Djibouti's northern coast—who have been temporarily settled in a refugee camp near Obock; and those seeking refuge with relatives and extended families in the capital city.

In addition to those formally identified as refugees, Djibouti is a conduit for migrants from neighbouring states, namely Ethiopia, Eritrea and Somalia. While data is sparse, UNHCR estimated that in recent years up to 10,000 such migrants attempted to transit the country annually, although many are believed to transit briefly and are unrecorded. Despite the current phase of Yemen's civil war, large numbers of young Eritreans and Ethiopians continue to seek passage to Yemen and thence Saudi Arabia, using traffickers transiting Djibouti. Confusingly, since early 2015 there has been two-way traffic; some migrants have returned, while others continue to pay traffickers for passage to Yemen. In May 2020 the World Bank launched a US $10m. project to assist Djibouti with the management of migrant flows, as part of a wider Horn of Africa strategy.

EDUCATION, HEALTH AND QAT

The UN Children's Fund (UNICEF) estimates that there are approximately 130,000 children in Djibouti who are of primary school age, yet barely one-half actually attend school. For those able to receive education, the overwhelming majority of their schools and classrooms are in very poor condition. Since 2006, donors have contributed some US $12m. within the multilateral Global Partnership for Education framework in order to improve classroom conditions and the quality of teaching, to promote greater access to schools, and to increase the number of female students in the school system. In June 2021 the World Bank announced a new $28m. multi-year facility to boost primary education in Djibouti. Again working within the Global Partnership for Education framework, the Bank's partner in the project is the Education Above All Foundation.

Djibouti has improved access and coverage in the education sector, with the World Bank claiming a 44% increase in the number of primary schools built and functioning since 2003, although the quality of education is frequently poor and uneven. The Government also continues to insist on French-language education within the formal education sector, which many experts perceive as a barrier to improved literacy. While the elite francophone *lycées* of the capital have largely retained their standards, and continue to funnel a small number of students into francophone universities, both in France and elsewhere in Africa, overall secondary education standards are low.

The University of Djibouti was founded by decree in January 2006. Through an ambitious effort by the Government, with the assistance of donor states and some private funding, the aim has been to establish a university with full capacities. By 2014 the university had 7,000 students enrolled, across five faculties and two technical institutes.

In principle, Djibouti provides universal health care to its population. However, there are significant disparities between health care in urban and rural areas, and there are signs that overall health services in the country are in decline. During 2010–19, it was estimated, the population increased at an average annual rate of 1.7%, fuelled by high fertility rates and immigration. Despite being ranked as a lower middle-income country, Djibouti continues to have some of the poorest social indicators in the world. None the less, in 2019 life expectancy at birth was 67 years, representing a significant improvement on a decade earlier; infant and child mortality rates have also improved in recent years, although significant regional disparities persist. Female genital mutilation remains a major public health problem.

Widespread daily consumption of qat is a major feature in both household expenditures and Djibouti's national economy. Qat, also spelt chat or khat, is picked from a shrub—*Catha edulis*—which grows at altitudes above 1,000 m in neighbouring Ethiopia, Kenya and Yemen. Supplies are imported daily by plane, then swiftly distributed across the country; qat must be consumed within 48 hours of being harvested in order to be considered fresh. Normally chewed fresh, qat produces a mild hallucinogenic high that its users claim both facilitates conversation and eases hunger and thirst. However, many blame the habit for lethargy and low labour productivity. Government and donor agency reports regularly highlight qat consumption as a major contributor to national poverty levels. Research carried out in Djibouti by UNICEF found that despite extreme poverty affecting significant portions of the population, households continued to devote considerable resources to the purchase of qat. UNICEF also found that 13% of children aged 15–19 years chew qat. In discussions with government officials, it was agreed that UNICEF would work with the Government to develop programmes to respond to the use of the amphetamine-like stimulant among young people.

Statistical Survey

Source (unless otherwise stated): National Institute of Statistics of Djibouti, Saharion Heron Bldg, Djibouti; tel. 21351825; internet www.instad.dj.

Area and Population

AREA, POPULATION AND DENSITY

Area (sq km)	23,200*
Population (census result)	
29 May 2009	818,159
Population (UN estimates at mid-year)†	
2020	988,002
2021‡	1,002,197
2022‡	
Males	532,524
Females	483,574
Total	1,016,098
Density (per sq km) at mid-2022‡	43.8

* 8,958 sq miles.
† Source: UN, *World Population Prospects: The 2019 Revision.*
‡ Projection(s).

POPULATION BY AGE AND SEX
('000, UN projections at mid-2022)

	Males	Females	Total
0–14 years	148.2	140.1	288.3
15–64 years	360.0	317.4	677.4
65 years and over	24.3	26.1	50.3
Total	532.5	483.6	1,016.1

Totals may not be equal to the sum of components, owing to rounding.

Source: UN, *World Population Prospects: The 2019 Revision.*

REGIONS
(population at 2009 census)

	Population
Ali-Sabieh	86,949
Arta	42,380
Dikhil	88,948
Djibouti (ville)	475,322
Obock	37,856
Tadjoura	86,704
Total	818,159

PRINCIPAL TOWNS
(population at 2009 census)

Djibouti (capital)	475,322	Tadjourah		14,820
Ali Sabieh	37,939	Arta		13,260
Dikhil	24,886	Obock		11,706

2022 (UN projection at mid-year): Djibouti (capital) 591,469 (Source: UN, *World Urbanization Prospects: The 2018 Revision*).

BIRTHS AND DEATHS
(annual averages, UN estimates)

	2005–10	2010–15	2015–20
Birth rate (per 1,000)	26.5	24.2	21.7
Death rate (per 1,000)	9.5	8.7	7.1

Source: UN, *World Population Prospects: The 2019 Revision.*

2020 (capital district only): Births 13,115; Deaths 1,548.

Marriages (capital district only): 3,599 in 2020.

Life expectancy (years at birth, estimates): 67.5 (males 65.5; females 69.8) in 2020 (Source: World Bank, World Development Indicators database).

Economically Active Population ('000, FAO estimates at mid-2015): Agriculture, etc. 291; Total labour force 407. Source: FAO.

Health and Welfare

KEY INDICATORS

Total fertility rate (children per woman, 2020)	2.6
Under-5 mortality rate (per 1,000 live births, 2020)	55.9
HIV/AIDS (% of persons aged 15–49, 2020)	0.8
COVID-19: Cumulative confirmed deaths (per 100,000 persons at 31 August 2022)	17.1
COVID-19: Fully vaccinated population (% of total population at 29 August 2022)	18.6
Physicians (per 1,000 head, 2014)	0.2
Hospital beds (per 1000 head, 2017)	1.4
Domestic health expenditure (2019): US $ per head (PPP)	55.9
Domestic health expenditure (2019): % of GDP	1.0
Domestic health expenditure (2019): public (% of total current expenditure)	53.7
Access to improved water resources (% of persons, 2020)	76
Access to improved sanitation facilities (% of persons, 2020)	67
Total carbon dioxide emissions ('000 metric tons, 2018)	490
Carbon dioxide emissions per head (metric tons, 2018)	0.5
Human Development Index (2021): ranking	171
Human Development Index (2021): value	0.509

Note: For data on COVID-19 vaccinations, 'fully vaccinated' denotes receipt of all doses specified by approved vaccination regime (Sources: Johns Hopkins University and Our World in Data). Data on health expenditure refer to current general government expenditure in each case. For more information on sources and further definitions for all indicators, see Health and Welfare Statistics: Sources and Definitions section (europaworld.com/credits).

Agriculture

PRINCIPAL CROPS

('000 metric tons, FAO estimates)

	2018	2019	2020
Beans, dry	2.2	2.2	2.3
Chillies and peppers, dry . . .	0.5	0.5	0.5
Lemons and limes	2.7	2.7	2.8
Mangoes, mangosteens and guavas	0.6	0.6	0.6
Tomatoes	1.8	1.8	1.8

Aggregate production ('000 metric tons, may include official, semi-official or estimated data): Total fruit (primary) 4.7 in 2018, 4.8 in 2019, 4.9 in 2020; Total vegetables (primary) 33.4 in 2018, 33.2 in 2019, 33.3 in 2020.

Source: FAO.

LIVESTOCK

('000 head, year ending September, FAO estimates)

	2018	2019	2020
Asses	8.4	8.4	8.4
Camels	72.2	72.4	72.6
Cattle	298.9	299.0	299.0
Goats	516.3	516.7	517.2
Sheep	469.4	469.7	469.9

Source: FAO.

LIVESTOCK PRODUCTS

('000 metric tons, FAO estimates)

	2018	2019	2020
Cattle hides, fresh	1.1	1.1	1.1
Cattle meat	6.0	6.0	6.1
Cattle offals, edible	1.1	1.1	1.1
Cows' milk	8.8	8.8	8.8
Goat meat	2.3	2.3	2.3
Goat offals, edible	0.5	0.5	0.5
Goats' skins, fresh	0.5	0.5	0.5
Sheep meat	2.2	2.2	2.2

Source: FAO.

Forestry

ROUNDWOOD REMOVALS

('000 cubic metres, excluding bark, FAO estimates)

	2017	2018	2019
Total (all fuel wood)	394.6	399.6	404.6

2020: Production assumed to be unchanged from 2019.

Source: FAO.

Fishing

(metric tons, live weight, capture only)

	2018	2019	2020
Groupers	223	35	49
Narrow-barred Spanish mackerel .	n.a.	320	292
Kawakawa	n.a.	184	230
Longtail tuna	n.a.	116	291
Barracudas	260	87	44
Carangids	264	29	20
Seerfishes	279	n.a.	n.a.
Tuna-like fishes	175	63	26
Cobia	121	57	70
Bigeye trevally	n.a.	245	183
Orangespotted trevally . . .	n.a.	136	153
Talang queenfish	n.a.	78	108
Pickhandle barracuda	n.a.	96	75
Other marine fishes	n.a.	822	782
Total catch	2,102	2,270	2,323

Source: FAO.

Mining

('000 metric tons*)

	2017	2018	2019
Common clay	38.0	38.0	38.0
Salt	830.0	2,500.0	3,800.0
Stone, crushed, limestone . . .	290.0	290.0	290.0

* Estimates.

Source: US Geological Survey.

Industry

SELECTED PRODUCTS

	2017	2018	2019
Cement (metric tons)*† . . .	190,000	190,000	190,000
Electrical energy (million kWh)‡ .	566.9	580.9	605.2

* Source: US Geological Survey.
† Estimates.
‡ Source: Banque Centrale de Djibouti *Rapport Annuel 2020*.

Electrical energy (million kWh): 627.1 in 2020.

Finance

CURRENCY AND EXCHANGE RATES

Monetary Units
     100 centimes = 1 Djibouti franc.

Sterling, Dollar and Euro Equivalents (31 May 2022)
     £1 sterling = 223.733 Djibouti francs;
     US \$1 = 177.721 Djibouti francs;
     €1 = 190.393 Djibouti francs;
     1,000 Djibouti francs= £4.47 = \$5.63 = €5.25.

Exchange Rate: Fixed at US \$1 = 177.720 Djibouti francs since February 1973.

BUDGET
(million Djibouti francs)

Revenue*	2018	2019	2020
Tax revenue	70,900	74,981	64,943
Direct taxes	29,350	31,204	27,410
Indirect taxes	36,012	37,748	34,019
Other taxes	5,538	6,029	3,514
Non-tax revenue	39,660	39,239	40,252
Total	**110,560**	**114,220**	**105,195**

Expenditure	2018	2019	2020
Current expenditure	88,846	91,476	103,903
Salaries and wages	35,122	35,509	36,420
Goods and services . . .	27,187	27,493	27,734
Maintenance	1,418	1,410	1,221
Transfers	17,697	18,426	18,800
Interest	6,559	7,157	6,806
Foreign-financed current spending	863	1,481	500
Capital expenditure	35,974	47,750	34,990
Total	**124,820**	**139,227**	**138,893**

* Excluding grants received (million Djibouti francs): 10,573 in 2018; 23,342 in 2019; 23,270 in 2020.

INTERNATIONAL RESERVES
(excl. gold, US $ million at 31 December)

	2019	2020	2021
IMF special drawing rights . .	1.78	4.02	3.90
Reserve position in IMF . . .	7.13	7.42	7.21
Foreign exchange	492.95	674.90	577.31
Total	**501.86**	**686.34**	**588.42**

Source: IMF, *International Financial Statistics.*

MONEY SUPPLY
(million Djibouti francs at 31 December)

	2017	2018	2019
Currency outside depository corporations	35,542	36,626	37,667
Transferable deposits	230,450	214,520	230,768
Other deposits	104,572	98,733	112,167
Broad money	**370,565**	**349,879**	**380,601**

Source: IMF, *International Financial Statistics.*

COST OF LIVING
(Consumer Price Index; base: 2013 = 100)

	2019	2020	2021
Food and non-alcoholic beverages .	121.2	127.0	129.2
Clothing and footwear	103.0	104.8	105.2
Housing and utilities	102.1	100.2	101.4
All items (incl. others) . . .	**108.5**	**110.4**	**111.7**

NATIONAL ACCOUNTS
(million Djibouti francs at current prices)

Expenditure on the Gross Domestic Product

	2018	2019	2020
Government final consumption expenditure	106,345	116,082	127,392
Private final consumption expenditure	315,262	344,060	372,624
Gross fixed capital formation . .	141,128	155,242	167,506
Change in inventories	10,882	106,892	101,957
Total domestic expenditure .	**573,618**	**722,276**	**769,480**
Exports of goods and services . .	798,766	845,094	916,927
Less Imports of goods and services	852,844	1,004,650	1,077,990
GDP at purchasers' values .	**519,540**	**562,720**	**608,417**
GDP at constant 2015 prices .	**529,646**	**570,482**	**570,984**

Gross Domestic Product by Economic Activity

	2018	2019	2020
Agriculture, hunting, forestry and fishing	6,568	7,161	7,799
Mining, quarrying and utilities .	22,842	24,544	26,842
Manufacturing	13,940	15,793	17,112
Construction	20,100	21,243	23,770
Wholesale and retail trade; restaurants and hotels . . .	154,100	168,027	181,287
Transport and communications .	122,228	130,206	139,561
Other services	143,528	156,362	169,223
Sub-total	**483,307**	**523,336**	**565,593**
Indirect taxes (net)*	36,233	39,384	42,824
GDP at purchasers' values .	**519,540**	**562,720**	**608,417**

* Figures obtained as residuals.

Source: UN National Accounts Main Aggregates Database.

BALANCE OF PAYMENTS
(US $ million)

	2018	2019	2020
Exports of goods	3,522.0	3,996.2	2,784.6
Imports of goods	−3,602.8	−4,138.1	−2,911.2
Balance on goods	**−80.8**	**−142.0**	**−126.6**
Exports of services	1,041.1	1,153.5	910.2
Imports of services	−586.2	−625.5	−513.5
Balance on goods and services	**374.1**	**386.0**	**270.1**
Primary income received . . .	59.9	79.5	64.1
Primary income paid	−202.0	−173.3	−162.6
Balance on goods, services and primary income	**231.9**	**292.2**	**171.5**
Secondary income received . .	216.5	284.9	210.9
Secondary income paid . . .	−19.8	−13.1	−16.1
Current balance	**428.6**	**564.0**	**366.4**
Capital account (net)	73.5	44.1	36.6
Direct investment liabilities . .	170.0	175.0	158.2
Portfolio investment assets . .	−0.2	−11.5	−9.8
Portfolio investment liabilities .	0.0	0.0	219.5
Other investment assets . . .	81.6	−82.3	−346.0
Other investment liabilities . .	14.1	276.2	140.2
Net errors and omissions . . .	−872.3	−920.5	−418.4
Reserves and related items .	**−104.6**	**44.9**	**146.9**

Source: IMF, *International Financial Statistics.*

External Trade

SELECTED COMMODITIES
(US $ million)

Imports c.i.f.	2017	2018	2019
Animal or vegetable fats and oils .	203	121	280
Cereals	143	153	285
Iron and steel	214	1,135	673
Mineral fuels, mineral oils and products of their distillation .	273	305	404
Vehicles other than railway or tramway	1,518	768	746
Total (incl. others)	4,125	3,928	4,530

Exports f.o.b.	2017	2018	2019
Animal or vegetable fats and oils .	139	212	465
Cereals	154	212	364
Iron and steel	106	192	702
Plastics and articles thereof . .	453	117	267
Vehicles other than railway or tramway	721	1,323	1,219
Total (incl. others)	2,858	3,343	4,546

Source: African Development Bank.

SELECTED TRADING PARTNERS
(US $ million)

Imports c.i.f.	2017	2018	2019
China, People's Republic . . .	791	459	819
India	302	480	399
Saudi Arabia	337	379	434
United Arab Emirates	439	346	899
Total (incl. others)	4,125	3,928	4,530

Exports f.o.b.	2017	2018	2019
China, People's Republic . . .	594	393	1,070
India	231	368	432
Saudi Arabia	447	1,101	581
Türkiye	37	48	363
United Arab Emirates	609	331	653
Total (incl. others)	2,858	3,343	4,546

Source: African Development Bank.

Transport

ROAD TRAFFIC
(registered motor vehicles)

	2018	2019	2020
Passenger cars	3,650	2,604	2,630
Trucks	317	181	176
Trailers	232	59	86
Motorcycles	104	329	2,775

SHIPPING

Flag Registered Fleet
(at 31 December)

	2019	2020	2021
Number of vessels	16	31	37
Total displacement ('000 grt) . .	9.6	1,038.0	1,689.2

Source: Lloyd's List Intelligence (www.bit.ly/LLintelligence).

Freight Traffic ('000 metric tons, 2019): Goods 5,986.3; Fuels 4,435.5 (Source: Banque Centrale de Djibouti, *Rapport Annuel 2019*).

CIVIL AVIATION
(international traffic, 2018)

	2017	2018
Passengers	173,532	208,730
Freight (metric tons)	35,271	5,669

Source: Banque Centrale de Djibouti, *Rapport Annuel 2018*.

Tourism

	2011	2012	2013
Total tourist arrivals ('000) . .	51	60	63

Tourism receipts (excl. passenger transport, US $ million): 33 in 2016; 35 in 2017; 57 in 2018.

Source: World Tourism Organization.

Communications Media

	2018	2019	2020
Telephones ('000 main lines in use)	36.9	37.1	38.9
Mobile telephone subscriptions ('000)	395.0	413.9	434.0
Broadband subscriptions, fixed ('000)	25.5	24.4	25.1
Broadband subscriptions, mobile ('000)	197.5	230.0	241.2
Internet users (% of population) .	58.0	59.0	59.0

Source: International Telecommunication Union.

Education

(2020/21 unless otherwise indicated)

	Institutions	Teachers	Students Males	Females	Total
Pre-primary . .	18*	179	2,539	2,175	4,714
Primary . . .	165*	2,437	37,607	32,717	70,324
Secondary . .	93*	3,278	37,748	30,986	68,734
Higher† . .	n.a.	245	2,828	1,877	4,705

* 2014/15.
† 2010/11.

Sources: UNESCO Institute for Statistics; Ministère de l'éducation nationale et de l'enseignement supérieur; Université de Djibouti.

Pupil-teacher Ratio (qualified teaching staff, primary education, UNESCO estimate): 28.9 in 2020/21 (Source: UNESCO Institute for Statistics).

Adult Literacy Rate (UNESCO estimate): 65.5% in 2003 (Source: UN Development Programme, *Human Development Report*).

Directory

The Constitution

A new Constitution was approved by national referendum on 4 September 1992 and entered into force on 15 September. It was amended in February 2006, January 2008 and April 2010.

The Constitution of Djibouti guarantees the basic rights and freedoms of citizens; the functions of the principal organs of state are delineated therein.

The President of the Republic, who is head of state and h of government, is directly elected, by universal adult suffrage, for a period of five years and must be between the ages of 40 and 75 years at the time of the announcement of his or her candidature. The President nominates the Prime Minister and, following consultation with the latter, appoints the Council of Ministers. The legislature is the 65-member National Assembly, which is elected, also by direct universal suffrage, for a period of five years.

The 1992 Constitution provided for the establishment of a maximum of four political parties. On 4 September 2002, however, this limit on the number of political parties was revoked.

The Government

HEAD OF STATE

President and Commander-in-Chief of the Armed Forces: ISMAÏL OMAR GUELLEH (inaugurated 7 May 1999; re-elected 8 April 2005, 8 April 2011, 8 April 2016 and 9 April 2021).

COUNCIL OF MINISTERS
(October 2022)

The Government is formed by the Union pour la Majorité Présidentielle.

Prime Minister: ABDOULKADER KAMIL MOHAMED.

Minister of Justice and Penal Affairs, in charge of Human Rights: ALI HASSAN BAHDON.

Minister of the Economy and Finance, in charge of Industry: ILYAS MOUSSA DAWALEH.

Minister of Foreign Affairs and International Co-operation, Government Spokesperson: MAHAMOUD ALI YOUSSOUF.

Minister of Defence, in charge of Relations with Parliament: HASSAN OMAR MOHAMED BOURHAN.

Minister of the Interior: SAID NOU HASSAN.

Minister of the Budget: ISMAN IBRAHIM ROBLEH.

Minister of Health: Dr AHMED ROBLEH ABDILLEH.

Minister of National Education and Professional Training: MOUSTAPHA MOHAMED MAHAMOUD.

Minister of Higher Education and Research: Dr NABIL MOHAMMED AHMED.

Minister of Women and Families: MOUNA OSMAN ADEN.

Minister of Agriculture, Water, Fishing, Stockbreeding and Fishing Resources: MOHAMED AHMED AWALEH.

Minister of Infrastructure and Equipment: HASSAN HOUMED IBRAHIM.

Minister of Muslim Affairs, Culture and Endowments: MOUMIN HASSAN BARREH.

Minister of Social Affairs and Solidarity: OULOUFA ISMAIL ABDO.

Minister of Energy, in charge of Natural Resources: YONIS ALI GUEDI.

Minister of Labour, in charge of Formalization and Social Protection: OMAR ABDI SAID.

Minister of the Environment and Sustainable Development: MOHAMED ABDOULKADER MOUSSA HELEM.

Minister of Cities, Town Planning and Housing: AMINA ABDI ADEN.

Minister of Communication, in charge of Post and Telecommunications: RADWAN ABDILLAHI BAHDON.

Minister of Trade and Tourism: MOHAMED WARSAMA DIRIEH.

Minister of Youth and Culture: Dr HIBO MOUMIN ASSOWEH.

Minister-delegate in charge of Decentralization: KASSIM HAROUN ALI.

Secretary of State in charge of Investment and the Development of the Private Sector: SAFIA MOHAMED ALI GADILEH.

Secretary of State in charge of Sport: HASSAN MOHAMED KAMIL.

MINISTRIES

Office of the President: Djibouti; e-mail sggpr@intnet.dj; internet www.presidence.dj.

Office of the Prime Minister: BP 2086, Djibouti; tel. 21325214; e-mail contact@primature.gouv.dj; internet primature.gouv.dj.

Ministry of Agriculture, Water, Fishing, Stockbreeding and Fishing Resources: BP 453, Djibouti; tel. 21351297; internet www.maem.dj.

Ministry of the Budget: BP 470, Djibouti; tel. 21325301; internet www.ministerebudget.gouv.dj.

Ministry of Cities, Town Planning and Housing: Zone Industrielle Sud Boulaos, Djibouti; tel. 21327230; e-mail contact@logement.gouv.dj; internet logement.gouv.dj.

Ministry of Communication: blvd Georges Pompidou, BP 32, Djibouti; tel. 21353928; e-mail contact@communication.gouv.dj; internet communication.gouv.dj.

Ministry of Defence: BP 42, Djibouti; tel. 21352062; e-mail info@defense.gouv.dj; internet www.defense.gouv.dj.

Ministry of the Economy and Finance: BP 13, Djibouti; tel. 21325105; e-mail cabinet@economie.gouv.dj; internet economie.gouv.dj.

Ministry of Energy: 47 blvd de la République, BP 175, Djibouti; tel. 21350341; e-mail cabinet@energie.gouv.dj; internet www.mern.dj.

Ministry of the Environment and Sustainable Development: Zone Industrielle Sud, Djibouti; tel. 21351020; e-mail info@environnement.dj; internet www.environnement.dj.

Ministry of Foreign Affairs and International Co-operation: blvd Cheik Osman, BP 1863, Djibouti; tel. 21352471; e-mail contact@diplomatie.gouv.dj; internet diplomatie.gouv.dj.

Ministry of Health: BP 1974, Djibouti; tel. 21353331; e-mail contact@sante.gouv.dj; internet sante.gouv.dj.

Ministry of Higher Education and Research: Djibouti; tel. 21327302; e-mail sgmensur@gmail.com; internet www.mensur.gov.dj.

Ministry of Infrastructure and Equipment: Djibouti.

Ministry of the Interior: BP 33, Djibouti; tel. 21352542; e-mail contact@interieur.gouv.dj; internet fb.com/mininterieurdjib.

Ministry of Justice and Penal Affairs: BP 12, Djibouti; tel. 21333333; e-mail contact@justice.gouv.dj; internet justice.gouv.dj.

Ministry of Labour: Cité Ministérielle, Djibouti; tel. 21325243; e-mail contact@min-travail.dj; internet mtra-djibouti.net.

Ministry of Muslim Affairs, Culture and Endowments: Djibouti; internet www.mamcbw.dj.

Ministry of National Education and Professional Training: BP 16, Cité Ministérielle, Djibouti; tel. 21350997; e-mail education.gov@intnet.dj; internet www.education.gov.dj.

Ministry of Social Affairs and Solidarity: Cité Ministerielle, Djibouti; tel. 21325481; e-mail affairessociales@intnet.dj; internet sociales.gouv.dj.

Ministry of Trade and Tourism: Djibouti.

Ministry of Women and Families: blvd Hassan Gouled, BP 458, Djibouti; tel. 21353409; e-mail contact@famille.gouv.dj; internet famille.gouv.dj.

Ministry of Youth and Culture: Djibouti; tel. 21339918; e-mail mjcdjibouti@gmail.com.

President

Presidential Election, 9 April 2021

Candidate	Valid votes	% of valid votes
Ismaïl Omar Guelleh (UMP)	155,291	97.30
Zakaria Ismaèl Farah (Ind.)	4,314	2.70
Total	159,605*	100.00

* Excluding 5,261 invalid votes.

Legislature

National Assembly (Assemblée Nationale): 138 blvd Gen. de Gaulle, Djibouti; tel. 21330003; internet www.assemblee-nationale.dj.

Speaker: MOHAMED ALI HOUMED.
General Election, 23 February 2018

Party	Valid votes	% of valid votes	Seats
Union pour la Majorité Présidentielle (UMP)* . .	105,278	87.83	57
Union pour la Démocratie et la Justice (UDJ)/Parti Djiboutien pour le Développement (PDD) . .	13,088	10.92	7
Centre des Démocrates Unifiés (CDU)	811	0.68	1
Alliance Républicaine pour le Développement (ARD) . .	684	0.57	—
Total	119,861	100.00	65

* A coalition comprising the FRUD, the PND, the PSD and the RPP.

Election Commission

Commission Electorale Nationale Indépendante: ave Maréchal Lyautey, Djibouti; tel. 21353654; e-mail ceni@intnet.dj; f. 2002; reconstituted in 2015; Pres. FARAH ABDILLAHI WALIEH.

Political Organizations

Centre des Démocrates Unifiés (CDU): Quartier 7, ave Nasser, Djibouti; tel. 77821033; internet centredemocrateunifie.weebly.com; f. 2012; Pres. OMAR ELMI KHAIREH.

Union pour la Majorité Présidentielle (UMP): Siège de l'UMP, Djibouti; tel. 21340056; internet fb.com/ump.dj; coalition of major parties in support of Pres. Guelleh; Pres. ABDOULKADER KAMIL MOHAMED.

Front pour la Restauration de l'Unité et de la Démocratie (FRUD): Djibouti; tel. 21250279; e-mail frud_djibouti@hotmail .com; internet fb.com/Frud-Djibouti-114964753208166; f. 1991 by merger of 3 militant Afar groups; advocates fair representation in govt for all ethnic groups; commenced armed insurgency in Nov. 1991; split into 2 factions in March 1994; the dissident group, which negotiated a settlement with the Govt, obtained legal recognition in March 1996.

Parti National Démocratique (PND): BP 10204, Djibouti; tel. 21342194; internet fb.com/PND-529013120613950; f. 1992; Pres. ABDOURAHMAN MOHAMED ALLALEH.

Parti Social Démocrate (PSD): BP 434, route Nelson Mandela, Djibouti; f. 2002; Pres. HASNA MOUMIN BAHDON; Sec.-Gen. HASSAN IDRISS AHMED.

Rassemblement Populaire pour le Progrès (RPP): Djibouti; e-mail rpp@intnet.dj; internet www.rpp.dj; f. 1979; sole legal party 1981–92; Pres. ISMAÏL OMAR GUELLEH; Sec.-Gen. ILYAS MOUSSA DAWALEH.

Union pour le Salut National (USN): Quartier 4, ave 16, Maison 10, BP 892, Djibouti; tel. 21341822; e-mail realite_djibouti@yahoo.fr; internet fb.com/USNDJIBOUTI; f. 2013; coalition of major opposition parties; Pres. MOHAMED DAOUD CHEHEM.

Alliance Républicaine pour le Développement (ARD): BP 1074, Marabout, Djibouti; tel. 21341822; e-mail realite_djibouti@ yahoo.fr; internet www.ard-djibouti.org; f. 2002; Leader ADAN MOHAMED ABDOU.

Mouvement pour le Renouveau Démocratique et le Développement (MRD): BP 3570, ave Nasser, Djibouti; internet www .mrd-djibouti.com/mrd; f. 1992 as the Parti du Renouveau Démocratique; renamed as above in 2002; Pres. DAHER AHMED FARAH; Sec.-Gen. SOULEIMAN HASSAN FAIDAL.

Parti Djiboutien pour le Développement (PDD): BP 892, Djibouti; tel. 77822860; f. 2002; Pres. MOHAMED DAOUD CHEHEM; Sec.-Gen. ABDOULFATAH HASSAN IBRAHIM.

Union pour la Démocratie et la Justice (UDJ): ave Nasser, BP 752, Djibouti; tel. 77829999; tel. info@udj-djibouti.com.

Diplomatic Representation

EMBASSIES IN DJIBOUTI

Algeria: Djibouti; Ambassador MOHAMED IRKI.

China, People's Republic: rue Addis Ababa, Lotissement Heron, BP 2021, Djibouti; tel. 21352247; e-mail chinaemb_dj@mfa.gov.cn; internet dj.china-embassy.gov.cn; Ambassador HU BIN.

Cuba: Lotissement Haramouss, Lot 383, Djibouti; tel. 21340671; e-mail secretaire.cuba@intnet.dj; internet misiones.minrex.gob.cu/ es/djibouti; Ambassador MARCELO DE LA CARIDAD CABALLERO TORRES.

Egypt: Cité du Heron, Djibouti; tel. 21351231; e-mail embassy .djibouti@mfa.gov.eg; Ambassador HOSSAM ELDINE EFAT REDA.

Eritrea: BP 1944, Djibouti; tel. 21354961; Chargé d'affaires a.i. ALI MOHAMED SAID.

Ethiopia: rue Clochette, BP 230, Djibouti; tel. 21350718; e-mail ethemb@intnet.dj; Ambassador BERHANU TSEGAYE.

France: blvd Omar Guelleh, BP 2039, Djibouti; tel. 21350963; e-mail internet.djibouti-amba@diplomatie.gouv.fr; internet dj.ambafrance .org; Ambassador DANA PURCARESCU (designate).

Germany: Lotissement Haramous, BP 2082, Djibouti; tel. 21344024; e-mail info@dschi.diplo.de; internet djibouti.diplo.de; Ambasador Dr HEIKE FULLER.

India: HB2, Lootah Village Complex, Haramous, Djibouti; tel. 21349246; e-mail com.djibouti@mea.gov.in; internet www .eoidjibouti.gov.in; Ambassador RAMACHANDRAN CHANDRAMOULI.

Japan: rue de l'Imam Hassan Abdallah Mohamed, BP 2051 Héron, Djibouti; tel. 21354981; e-mail japanembassydjibouti@do.mofa.go.jp; internet www.dj.emb-japan.go.jp; Ambassador UMIO OTSUKA.

Kenya: Djibouti; Ambassador SALIM SALIM.

Kuwait: Haramous Villa 353, Djibouti; tel. 21320770; Ambassador SAUD HADDAD AL-SAEEDI.

Libya: BP 2073, Djibouti; tel. 21350202; Chargé d'affaires a.i. Dr AL AHADI MOHAMED AL WAHICHI.

Qatar: Extension du Héron, Lot 52, BP 1900, Djibouti; tel. 21322408; internet djibouti.embassy.qa; Ambassador JASSIM JABER JASSIM SOROUR.

Russian Federation: Plateau du Marabout, BP 1913, Djibouti; tel. 21350740; e-mail embdjibouti@mid.ru; internet djibouti.mid.ru; Ambassador MIKHAIL A. GOLOVANOV.

Saudi Arabia: BP 1921, Djibouti; tel. 21351898; internet embassies .mofa.gov.sa/sites/djibouti; Ambassador FAISAL BIN SULTAN AL-QABBANI AL-SIHALI.

Somalia: BP 549, Djibouti; tel. 21353521; Ambassador SALAD ALI JELE.

Sudan: BP 4259, Djibouti; tel. 21356404; Ambassador RAHMA SALEH AL-OBAID.

Türkiye (Turkey): Duplex Grandstanding No. 1, Haramous, Djibouti; tel. 21351290; internet cibuti.be.mfa.gov.tr; Ambassador SALIM LEVENT ŞAHINKAYA.

United Kingdom: rue de Djibouti, Djibouti; Ambassador JO MCPHAIL.

USA: Lot No. 350B, Haramous, Djibouti; tel. 21453000; internet dj .usembassy.gov; Ambassador JONATHAN GOODALE PRATT.

Yemen: BP 194, Djibouti; tel. 21352975; e-mail yemb-djibouti@mofa .gov.ye; Ambassador ABDULLA MOSSLEM KASSEM AL-SOCOTY.

Judicial System

Supreme Court: blvd de la République, Djibouti; tel. 21357027; f. 1979; Pres. ABDOURAHMAN CHEICK MOHAMED.

Court of Appeal: Djibouti; Pres. NIMA ALI WARSAMA.

Constitutional Council: Plateau du Serpent, blvd Foch, BP 4081, Djibouti; tel. 21358662; e-mail conseil@intnet.dj; f. 1992; Pres. ABDI ISMAÈL HERSI; 6 mems.

Religion

ISLAM

Almost the entire population are Muslims.

Qadi of Djibouti: MOGUE HASSAN DIRIR, BP 168, Djibouti; tel. 21352669.

High Islamic Council (Haut Conseil Islamique): Djibouti; f. 2004; 7 mems; Exec. Sec. ABDOU SALAM FARAH MAGARREH.

CHRISTIANITY

The Roman Catholic Church

Djibouti comprises a single diocese, directly responsible to the Holy See.

Bishop of Djibouti: GIORGIO BERTIN, Evêché, blvd de la République, BP 94, Djibouti; tel. 21354831; e-mail evechcat@intnet.dj.

The Anglican Communion

Within the Episcopal/Anglican Province of Alexandria (which was inaugurated in June 2020), Djibouti lies within the jurisdiction of the Bishop of the Horn of Africa.

Other Christian Churches

Eglise Protestante: blvd de la République, BP 416, Djibouti; tel. 21359924; internet eglises-protestantes-francophones.org/djibouti; f. 1957.

The Greek and Ethiopian Orthodox Churches are also active in Djibouti.

The Press

Al Qarn: blvd Georges Pompidou, BP 32, Djibouti; tel. 21355193; e-mail alqarn@intnet.dj; internet www.alqarn.dj; biweekly; Arabic; Dir YASSIN ABDULLAH BOUH.

La Nation de Djibouti: blvd Bonhoure, près de l'IGAD, BP 32, Djibouti; tel. 21352201; e-mail lanation@intnet.dj; internet www.lanation.dj; daily; Dir MOHAMED GASS BARKHADLEH.

Le Renouveau: BP 3570, ave Nasser, Djibouti; tel. 21351474; weekly; independent; publ. by the MRD; Editor-in-Chief DAHER AHMED FARAH.

NEWS AGENCIES

Agence Djiboutienne d'Information (ADI): 1 rue de Moscou, BP 32, Djibouti; tel. 21354013; internet www.adi.dj; f. 1978; Dir YASSER HASSAN BOULLO.

Broadcasting and Communications

TELECOMMUNICATIONS

Djibouti Télécom: 3 blvd Georges Pompidou, BP 2105, Djibouti; tel. 21321316; e-mail djibouti_telecom@intnet.dj; internet www.djiboutitelecom.dj; f. 1999 to replace Société des Télécommunications Internationales; 100% state-owned; Dir-Gen. MOHAMED ASSOWEH BOUH.

BROADCASTING

Radio and Television

Radiodiffusion-Télévision de Djibouti (RTD): BP 97, 21 ave St Laurent du Var, Djibouti; tel. 21350484; e-mail rtd.djibouti@gmail.com; internet www.rtdd.dj; f. 1967; state-controlled; programmes in French, Afar, Somali and Arabic; Dir-Gen. ADEN ABDI DJAMEH.

Telesat Djibouti: rue Ras-Makonen, BP 2240, Djibouti; tel. 21355290; e-mail telesat@gmail.com; internet fb.com/telesatdjibouti.

Finance

BANKING

In 2022 there were 13 banks operating in Djibouti, of which three were Islamic banks.

Central Bank

Banque Centrale de Djibouti: BP 2118, ave St Laurent du Var, Djibouti; tel. 21352751; e-mail bndj@intnet.dj; internet www.banque-centrale.dj; f. 1977 as Banque Nationale de Djibouti; present name adopted 2002; bank of issue; Gov. AHMED OSMAN ALI.

Banks

Bank of Africa—Mer Rouge (BOA—MR): 10 pl. Lagarde, BP 88, Djibouti; tel. 21353016; e-mail information@boamerrouge.com; internet www.boamerrouge.com; f. 1908 as Banque de l'Indochine; present name adopted in 2010; 80% owned by BOA Group SA; Dir-Gen. FARID BOURI.

Banque pour le Commerce et l'Industrie—Mer Rouge (BCI—MR): 11 pl. Lagarde, BP 2122, Djibouti; tel. 21350857; e-mail contact@bcimr.dj; internet www.bcimr.dj; f. 1977; 51% owned by BRED Banque Populaire (France); Pres. ERIC MONTAGNE; Dir-Gen. YAHYA OULD AMAR.

Banque de Dépôt et Crédit de Djibouti: pl. Lagarde, BP 1929, Djibouti; tel. 21353534; e-mail contact@bdcdjibouti.com; internet bdcdjibouti.com; f. 2008; Dir-Gen WALID RIZK.

Commercial Bank of Djibouti: Plateau du Serpent, 2nd Floor, rue Jean Jaurés, Nouveau Batiment, BP 2086, Djibouti; tel. 21-33-03-00; internet www.cbdji.com; f. 2015; CEO RAJAT MITTAL.

CAC International Bank: Immeuble Dar al Karaam, Quartier Commercial, rue de Marsile, BP 1868, Djibouti; tel. 21356363; e-mail info@cacintbank.com; internet cacintbank.com; f. 2009; Dir-Gen AHMED HAMEED ALDEIB.

Exim Bank of Djibouti: 13 pl. Lagarde, BP 4455, Djibouti; tel. 21351514; e-mail info-dj@eximbank.co.tz; internet www.eximbank-dj.com; f. 2011; Dir-Gen. KAYITESHONGA JACKY.

International Investment Bank (Djibouti) SA: Immeuble 15, pl. du 27 juin, rue d'Ethiopie, pl. Ménélik, BP 2032, Djibouti; tel. 21355006; e-mail infos-dj@eximbank.co.tz; internet www.iibanks.com/djibouti; f. 2007; Dir-Gen. RAJ DUSSOYE.

Silk Road International Bank: Haramous 1, Lot No. 2, BP 1877, Djibouti; tel. 21341266; e-mail info@silkroadibank.com; internet www.silkroadibank.com; f. 2015.

Development Bank

Fonds de Développement Economique de Djibouti (FDED): angle ave Georges Clemenceau et rue Pierre Curie, BP 520, Djibouti; tel. 21353391; internet www.fdeddjibouti.com; f. 2004; Dir-Gen. ALI DAOUD HOUMED.

Islamic Banks

East Africa Bank: rue de Athenes, BP 2022, Djibouti; tel. 21311900; e-mail info@eastafricabank.com; internet eastafricabank.com; f. 2010; Dir-Gen. IBRAHIM RASHID JAFFAR.

Saba Islamic Bank (SIB): Salines Ouest, BP 1972, Djibouti; tel. 21355777; internet www.sabafrican.com; f. 2006; Dir-Gen. ABDUL-RAEEB FAREE SALEM.

Salaam African Bank (SAB): Salaam Tower, Route Mohamed Kamil, Cité Saline Ouest, BP 2550, Djibouti; tel. 21351544; e-mail info@banksalaam.com; internet www.banksalaam.com; f. 2008.

Banking Association

Association Professionnelle des Banques: c/o Banque pour le Commerce et l'Industrie—Mer Rouge, pl. Lagarde, BP 2122, Djibouti; tel. 21350857; Pres. YAHYA OULD AMAR.

INSURANCE

Les Assureurs de la Mer Rouge et du Golfe Arabe (AMERGA): 8 rue Marchand, BP 2653, Djibouti; tel. 21352510; e-mail direction.m@amerga.com; internet www.amerga.com; f. 2000; Dirs THIERRY MARILL, LUC MARILL, ABDOURAHMAN BARKAT ABDILLAHI, MOHAMED ADEN ABOUBAKER.

GXA Assurances: BP 200, Djibouti; tel. 21353636; e-mail accueil@gxaonline.com; internet www.gxaonline.com; Country Man. CHRISTIAN BOUCHER.

Trade and Industry

CHAMBER OF COMMERCE

Chambre de Commerce de Djibouti: pl. Lagarde, BP 84, Djibouti; tel. 21351070; e-mail ccd@ccd.dj; internet www.ccd.dj; f. 1906; 44 mems, 22 assoc. mems; Pres. YOUSSOUF MOUSSA DAWALEH; Sec.-Gen. HIBO OSMAN AHMED.

UTILITIES

Electricity

Electricité de Djibouti (EdD): 47 blvd de la République, BP 175, Djibouti; tel. 21352851; e-mail directionedd.68@gmail.com; internet www.edd.dj; Dir-Gen. DJAMA ALI GUELLEH.

TRADE UNIONS

Union Djiboutienne pour les Droits Economiques Sociaux et Culturels et Civils et Politiques: rue Pierre Pascal, BP 2767, Djibouti; tel. 77823979; e-mail uddesc@yahoo.fr; internet www.uddesc.org; f. 2005; confed. of 21 trade unions; Sec.-Gen. HASSAN CHER HARED.

Union Générale des Travailleurs Djiboutiens (UGTD): 489 rue Pierre Pascal, Djibouti; tel. 77822816; internet fb.com/UnionGeneraleTravailleursDjiboutiens; Sec.-Gen. SAÏD YONIS WABERI.

Transport

RAILWAYS

The construction of a new 756-km railway line connecting Addis Ababa, Ethiopia, with Djibouti city and port (of which 100 km was in Djibouti) was completed in late 2016.

Ethio-Djibouti Railway (EDR): POB 41100, Addis Ababa, Ethiopia; tel. +251 (11) 8721234; e-mail admin@edr.gov.et; internet edr.gov.et; f. 2017; jtly owned by govts of Djibouti and Ethiopia; Dir-Gen. TILAHUN SARKA.

SHIPPING

Djibouti Ports and Free Zones Authority (DPFZA): POB 198, Djibouti; tel. 21359070; internet dpfza.gov.dj; Chair. ABOUBAKER OMAR HADI.

Port de Djibouti: BP 2107, Djibouti; tel. 21357372; e-mail customer .care@port.dj; internet www.portdedjibouti.com; Gen. Man. SAAD OMAR GUELLEH.

Principal Shipping Agents

Cie Maritime et de Manutention de Djibouti (COMAD): ave des Messageries Maritimes, BP 89, Djibouti; tel. 21351028; e-mail hettam@intnet.dj; f. 1990; stevedoring; Man. Dir ALI A. HETTAM.

Inchcape Shipping Services & Co (Djibouti) SA: 9–11 rue de Genève, BP 81, Djibouti; tel. 21353844; e-mail portagencydjibouti@ iss-shipping.com; internet www.iss-shipping.com; f. 1942; Man. Dir AHMED OSMAN GELLEH.

J. J. Kothari & Co Ltd: Amerga Bldg, 2nd Floor, ave Georges Clemenceau, BP 171, Djibouti; tel. 21350219; e-mail nalin@kothari .dj; internet www.kotharishipping.net; f. 1957; shipping agents; also ship managers, stevedores, freight forwarders, project cargo movers; Man. Dir NALIN KOTHARI; Dep. Man. Dir PIERRE VINCIGUERRA.

Smart Logistic Services: BP 1579, Djibouti; tel. 21343950; e-mail sls@intnet.dj; internet www.smartforwarders.com; f. 2010; Man. Dir FAHMI A. HETTAM.

Société Maritime L. Savon et Ries: blvd Cheik Osman, BP 2125, Djibouti; tel. 21352352; e-mail smsr@riesgroup.dj; Gen. Man. JEAN-PHILIPPE DELARUE.

CIVIL AVIATION

The international airport is at Ambouli, 6 km from Djibouti city. There are six other airports providing domestic services. In 2016 construction began on two new airports with a proposed combined capacity of 2.3m. passengers per year.

Air Djibouti: 9–11 rue de Genève, Djibouti; tel. 21343737; e-mail reservations@air-djibouti.com; internet www.air-djibouti.com; f. 2015; CEO ABDOURAHMAN ALI ABDILLAHI.

Daallo Airlines: BP 2565, Djibouti; tel. 21353401; e-mail daallo@ intnet.dj; internet www.daallo.com; f. 1991; operates services to Somalia, Saudi Arabia, the United Arab Emirates, Kenya and Ethiopia; CEO MOHAMED IBRAHIM YASSIN.

Tourism

Office National du Tourisme de Djibouti (ONTD): pl. du 27 juin, BP 1938, Djibouti; tel. 21352800; e-mail infotourisme@visitdjibouti .dj; internet guide.visitdjibouti.dj; Dir-Gen. OSMAN ABDI MOHAMED.

Defence

Arrangements for military co-operation exist between Djibouti and France, and in November 2021 there were about 1,450 French military personnel stationed in Djibouti. There were also 240 Chinese military personnel and 180 Japanese military personnel stationed in the country. The US-led Combined Joint Task Force-Horn of Africa has its headquarters in Djibouti; around 4,000 US military, naval and air force personnel are stationed there. Djibouti currently contributes some 1,800 troops to the African Union Mission in Somalia (AMISOM). As assessed at November 2021, the total armed forces of Djibouti itself, in which all services form part of the army, numbered some 10,450 (including 200 naval and 250 air force personnel). There were also paramilitary forces numbering 2,650 personnel including a coast guard of 150, as well as an estimated 2,000-strong gendarmerie. Conscription of all men between 18 and 25 years of age was introduced in 1992.

Defence Budget: 1,720m. Djibouti francs in 2014.

Commander-in-Chief of the Armed Forces: Pres. ISMAÏL OMAR GUELLEH.

Chief of Staff of the Armed Forces: Gen. ZAKARIA CHEIK IBRAHIM.

Education

The Government has overall responsibility for education. Primary education generally begins at six years of age and lasts for six years. Secondary education, usually starting at the age of 12, lasts for seven years, comprising a first cycle of four years and a second of three years. According to estimates by the United Nations Educational, Scientific and Cultural Organization (UNESCO), in 2020/21 enrolment at pre-primary institutions was equivalent to 11% of children in the relevant age-group (boys 12%; girls 10%). In 2019/20 primary enrolment included 67% of pupils in the relevant age-group (boys 68%; girls 65%), while the comparable ratio for secondary enrolment was equivalent to 55% (54% of boys; 56% of girls). Djibouti's sole university, the Université de Djibouti, was established in January 2006 as a replacement for the Pôle Universitaire de Djibouti. In 2018 spending on education represented 14.0% of total budgeted government expenditure.

Bibliography

Aden, M. *Ourrou-Djibouti 1991–1994: Du Maquis Afar à la Paix des Braves*. Paris, L'Harmattan, 2002.

Alwan, D. A., and Mibrathu, Y. *Historical Dictionary of Djibouti*. Lanham, MD, Scarecrow Press, 2001.

Belbéoch, O., Charbit, Y. and Houssein, S. (Eds) *La population de Djibouti: Recherches sociodémographiques*. Paris, L'Harmattan, 2008.

Bezabeh, S. *Djibouti: The Politics of a Strategic State*. London, Hurst, 2021.

Chiré, A. *Le nomade et la ville à Djibouti: Stratégies d'insertion urbain et production de territoire*. Paris, Karthala, 2012.

Chiré, A. (Ed.). *Djibouti contemporaine*. Paris, Karthala, 2013.

Chiré, A. and Ndagano, B. (Eds) *Traversées, histoires et mythes de Djibouti*. Paris, Karthala, 2011.

Coubba, A. *Djibouti: Une nation en otage*. Paris, L'Harmattan, 1993.

Dubois, C. *Djibouti 1888–1967: Héritage ou frustration?* Paris, L'Harmattan, 1997.

L'or blanc de Djibouti: Salines et sauniers (XIXe–XXe siècles). Paris, Editions Karthala, 2003.

Dubois, C., and Soumille, P. *Des chrétiens à Djibouti en terre d'Islam: XIXe–XXe siècles*. Paris, Karthala, 2004.

Fontaine, H. *Un train en Afrique; Djibouti-Ethiopie*. Addis Ababa, CFEE & Shama Books, 2012.

Fontrier, M. *Abou-Bakr Ibrahim, Pacha de Zeyla–Marchand d'Esclaves: Commerce et Diplomatie dans le Golfe de Tadjoura 1840–1885*. Paris, L'Harmattan, 2003.

Imbert-Vier, S. *Tracer des frontières à Djibouti: Des territoires et des hommes aux XIXe et XXe siècles*. Paris, Karthala, 2011.

Koburger, C. W. *Naval Strategy East of Suez: The Role of Djibouti*. New York, Praeger, 1992.

Labrousse, H. *Récits de la Mer Rouge et de l'Océan Indien*. Paris, Commission Française d'Histoire Maritime, 1992.

Laudouze, A. *Djibouti, Nation carrefour*. Paris, Karthala, 1982.

Mesfin. B. *Elections, politics and external involvement in Djibouti*. ISS Situation Report, April 2011.

Morin, D. *Dictionnaire historique afar (1288–1982)*. Paris, Karthala, 2004.

Oberle, P., and Hugot, P. *Histoire de Djibouti: des origines à la république*. Paris, Editions Présence Africaine, 1985.

Prijac, L. *Lagarde L'Éthiopien: Le fondateur de Djibouti (1860–1936)*. Paris, L'Harmattan, 2012.

Schrader, P. J. *Djibouti*. Oxford, Clio Press, 1991.

'Ethnic Politics in Djibouti: From the "Eye of the Hurricane" to "Boiling Cauldron"', in *African Affairs*, Vol. 92, No. 367 (April 1993), pp. 203–221.

Styan, D. *Djibouti: changing influence in the Horn's strategic hub*. Briefing Paper, Chatham House, Royal Institute for International Affairs, 2013.

Tholomier, R. *Djibouti: Pawn of the Horn of Africa*. Metuchen, NJ, Scarecrow Press, 1981.

Thompson, V., and Adloff, R. *Djibouti and the Horn of Africa*. London, Oxford University Press, 1968.

Tramport, J. *Djibouti Hier: de 1887 à 1939*. Paris, Hatier, 1990.

Woodward, P. *The Horn of Africa: State Politics and International Relations*. London, I. B. Tauris, 1996.

EQUATORIAL GUINEA

Physical and Social Geography

RENÉ PÉLISSIER

The Republic of Equatorial Guinea occupies an area of 28,051 sq km (10,831 sq miles). Geographically, the main components of the republic are the islands of Bioko (formerly known as Fernando Póo and subsequently renamed Macías Nguema Biyogo under the regime of President Francisco Macías Nguema), covering 2,017 sq km, and Annobón (previously known also as Pagalu), 17 sq km; and, on the African mainland, bordered to the north by Cameroon, to the south and east by Gabon and westwards by the Gulf of Guinea, lies the province of Río Muni (formerly known also as Mbini), comprising 26,017 sq km, including three coastal islets, Corisco (15 sq km) and the Great and Little Elobeys (2.5 sq km).

Bioko is a parallelogram-shaped island, 72 km by 35 km, formed from three extinct volcanoes. To the north lies the Pico de Basilé (rising to 3,007 m above sea level), with an easy access. In the centre of the island are the Moka Heights, while, further south, the Gran Caldera forms the remotest and least developed part of the island. The coast is steep to the south. Malabo (formerly Santa Isabel) is the only natural harbour. Crop fertility is high, owing to the combination of volcanic soils and plentiful rainfall. At the southern extremity of the Guinean archipelago lies the remote island of Annobón, south of the island of São Tomé.

Mainland Río Muni is a jungle enclave, from which a coastal plain rises steeply toward the Gabonese frontier. Its main orographic complexes are the spurs of the Monts de Cristal of Gabon. The highest peaks are Piedra de Nzas, Monte Mitra and Monte Chime, all rising to 1,200 m. The main river is the Mbini (formerly known as the Río Benito), non-navigable except for a 20-km stretch, which bisects the mainland province. On the Cameroon border is the Río Campo; its tributary, the Kye, constitutes the de facto eastern border with Gabon. The coast is a long beach, with low cliffs towards Cogo. There is no natural harbour.

The country has an equatorial climate with heavy rainfall, especially in Bioko. The annual average temperature of Malabo is 25°C and the average yearly rainfall is in excess of 2,000 mm. Humidity is high throughout the island, except on the Moka Heights. Río Muni has less debilitating climatic conditions.

According to the final results of the June 2015 census, the population totalled 1,225,377, giving an average population density of 43.7 persons per sq km. By mid-2022, according to United Nations (UN) projections, the population had risen to 1,496,673 (53.4 persons per sq km). The main city is Malabo (with 296,770 inhabitants, including the suburbs, at mid-2018, according to UN estimates), the capital of Bioko and of the republic, as well as the principal economic, educational and religious centre. The other town of note on Bioko is Luba, which had a population of an estimated 7,739 in 2012. Bubi villages are scattered in the eastern and western parts of the island. On the mainland the only urban centre is the port of Bata, which had a population of 454,940 at mid-2022, according to UN projections. Other ports include Mbini and Cogo. Inland are located the small market and administrative centres of Mikomeseng, Nkumekie, Ebebiyín and Evinayong. The country is divided into eight administrative provinces: Bioko Norte, Bioko Sur and Annobón for the two main islands; Centro-Sur, Djibloho, Kié-Ntem, Litoral and Wele-Nzas for the mainland and its adjacent islets. Legislation creating the eighth province, Djibloho, located in Río Muni, was promulgated in June 2017. In January of that year the Government transferred its operations for a three-month period from Malabo to the capital of the new province, Ciudad de la Paz (originally known as Oyala). Ciudad de la Paz is envisaged eventually to replace Malabo as the national capital.

The ethnic composition of Equatorial Guinea is unusually complex for so small a political unit. The Fang are the dominant group in Río Muni, where they are believed to comprise 80%–90% of the population. North of the Mbini river are the Ntumu Fang, and to the south of it the Okak Fang. Coastal tribes—notably the Kombe, Balengue and Bujeba—have been pushed towards the sea by Fang pressure. Both Fang and coastal peoples are of Bantu origin. Since independence in 1968, many inhabitants of Río Muni have emigrated to Bioko, where they have come to dominate the civil and military services and now outnumber the Bubi, the indigenous inhabitants of the island. The Fernandino, of whom there are a few thousand on Bioko, are the descendants of former slaves liberated by the British, mingled with long-settled immigrants from coastal west Africa. The working population of Annobón comprises mainly seafarers and fishermen.

The official languages are Spanish, French and, since 2010, Portuguese. In Río Muni the Fang language is spoken, as well as those of coastal tribes. Bubi is the indigenous language on Bioko, although Fang is also widely used in Malabo, and Ibo is spoken by the resident Nigerian population. Around 90% of the population are Christian, predominantly adherents of the Roman Catholic Church, although traditional forms of worship are also followed and there is a small Muslim minority.

History

MARISÉ CASTRO

INTRODUCTION

The Republic of Equatorial Guinea comprises the region of Río Muni, on the West African mainland, and the islands of Bioko, Annobón, Corisco and the Elobeys. It was granted independence on 12 October 1968, after 190 years of Spanish colonial rule. Francisco Macías Nguema, a mainland Fang from the Esangui clan, took office as President of the new republic, after multi-party elections in which he received the support of a moderate coalition grouping. Once in office, he moved swiftly to suppress opposition (outlawing all existing political parties) and to assert absolute power through a 'reign of terror', in which his nephew Lt-Col Obiang Nguema Mbasogo played a major role. The brutal nature of the regime, which killed tens of thousands of people, led to the flight of as many as one-third of the total population, including nearly all of the skilled and educated elements of Equato-Guinean society. Macías Nguema obtained much of his economic and military aid from Eastern bloc countries; relations with Spain deteriorated, and serious regional disputes arose with Gabon and Nigeria. The country's economy, centred on cocoa plantations on Bioko and reliance on imported African labour, was devastated by the excesses of Macías Nguema's regime.

THE EARLY YEARS OF OBIANG NGUEMA'S PRESIDENCY

In August 1979 Macías Nguema was overthrown in a coup led by his nephew Obiang Nguema. Having fled the capital, Malabo, Macías Nguema was captured, tried and executed in September. Obiang Nguema announced the restoration of the rule of law, but banned all political parties and ruled through a Supreme Military Council (SMC).

In December 1981 the first civilians were appointed to the SMC, and in August 1982 a new Constitution was approved by 95% of voters in a referendum. Obiang Nguema was appointed to a seven-year term as President. As the sole candidate in the first presidential election since independence, he was elected in June 1989 with 99% of the votes cast. Meanwhile, the first legislative elections since 1968 were held in August 1983. All candidates were nominated by the President and were elected to serve a five-year term, albeit with no legislative powers. In October 1987 Obiang Nguema created a 'governmental party', the Partido Democrático de Guinea Ecuatorial (PDGE), which, together with the higher ranks of the civil service and armed forces, remained predominantly the preserve of the President's Esangui clan.

Although the atrocities of the Macías period abated, Obiang Nguema failed to honour his pledge to restore democracy, and the country remained a one-party state until 1991. He maintained his uncle's authoritarian style of rule and extended the family's control over the country's economic and political life, including the justice system, fuelling a culture of fear through military purges and the ruthless repression of any potential opposition. The human rights organization Amnesty International has consistently denounced the Government's systematic harassment, detention and mistreatment of political opponents.

OPPOSITION PRESSURES

No political parties other than the PDGE were permitted until 1992, although some parties established by exiles abroad have played an important role in bringing about what little political change has occurred.

Prior to 2000 the most influential exiled opposition party was the Alianza Nacional para la Restauración Democrática de Guinea Ecuatorial, based in Geneva, Switzerland. However, the Gabonese capital, Libreville, later took over as the preferred base for many Equato-Guinean opposition groups in exile, the most important being the Unión para la Democracia y el Desarrollo Social. Opposition groups and coalitions continued to emerge outside the country, primarily in Spain; however, with the exception of the Partido del Progreso de Guinea-Ecuatorial (PPGE), these proved short-lived, with negligible impact within Equatorial Guinea itself. Even the PPGE has since been largely marginalized. In 2014 the Coalición para la Restauración de un Estado Democrático (CORED) emerged in France, claiming the allegiance of 12 political parties in exile. However, the coalition failed to attract support from long-established opposition parties both in exile and within Equatorial Guinea.

Under growing internal and international pressure, Obiang Nguema eventually conceded the principle of political plurality in 1991, when a new Constitution was approved by referendum. However, the few human rights safeguards enshrined in the 1982 Constitution were not incorporated in the new charter. Furthermore, the new Constitution exempted Obiang Nguema from any judicial proceedings arising from his presidential tenure, while Equato-Guinean citizens who held foreign passports or who had not been continuously resident in Equatorial Guinea for 10 years (subsequently reduced to five) were barred from standing as election candidates, thereby excluding virtually all exiled political opponents from participation. New laws promulgated in 1992 included legislation on political parties and freedom of assembly and association. A new transitional Government was formed (comprising only PDGE members), and a general amnesty was offered to all political exiles. Although some opposition parties began moving back to prepare for the first multi-party legislative elections in 1993, most Equato-Guinean exiles reacted cautiously to Obiang Nguema's efforts to encourage their return. The

monopoly on power held by Obiang Nguema's family, persistent human rights abuses and corruption, together with economic factors, continue to discourage the return of many émigrés.

The first two opposition parties, the Unión Popular (UP) and the Partido Liberal, were legalized in June 1992, and in September an alliance of opposition parties, the Plataforma de Oposición Conjunta (POC), was formed. The legalization of the Convergencia para la Democracia Social (CPDS) in March 1993 brought the total number of legalized political parties to 14, which included a few still operating in exile. However, these opposition parties found themselves under constant threat, and few survived beyond the mid-2000s. The POC itself was dissolved in 1996.

In May 1997 the Angolan authorities arrested the PPGE leader, Severo Moto Nsá, on board a boat carrying a consignment of arms reportedly intended for use in a coup in Equatorial Guinea. He eventually received political asylum in Spain, where he had previously resided. After it was banned, the PPGE split into various factions: the only one to survive, albeit with reduced influence, was Moto Nsá's, based in Spain, while other party members defected to the PDGE. In August Moto Nsá was sentenced to 101 years' imprisonment, having been convicted *in absentia* (along with 11 others) of treason. In June 2005 the Equato-Guinean embassy in Madrid, Spain, was occupied and damaged by opposition activists who blamed the Obiang Nguema regime for the attempted murder in that city of the exiled brother of a leading figure in the Fuerza Demócrata Republicana (FDR). Following the attack, Equatorial Guinea temporarily closed the embassy. In April 2006 several people were convicted in Spain in connection with the murder attempt, although the court failed to find any evidence implicating the Equato-Guinean Government. Meanwhile, Spain revoked Moto Nsá's refugee status in December 2005, but this was restored on appeal in March 2008 by the Spanish Supreme Court. In August 2020 Moto Nsá resigned as leader of the PPGE, and was replaced by Armengol Engonga Ondó, hitherto the party's Vice-President.

Contagion from the political unrest in North Africa and the Middle East from early 2011 was viewed by Obiang Nguema as a serious potential threat to his prestige and authority in the run-up to the African Union (AU) summit in Malabo, held in June of that year. In March he banned all marches and demonstrations, and imposed a complete blackout on media coverage of events of the so-called 'Arab Spring'. Requests by the UP and the CPDS to hold meetings and demonstrations were rejected; in order to pre-empt any clandestine preparations for a May Day rally, several of the parties' leading members were briefly detained at the end of April, together with some 100 students.

In March 2011 Obiang Nguema announced his intention to implement political reforms, to be submitted for popular approval by referendum. He proposed the revision of the Constitution to limit the presidential mandate to two five-year terms; the creation of a Senado (Senate); and the establishment of an Audit Court to counter corruption. The CPDS and the UP issued a joint statement proposing the creation of a working group comprising all political parties to negotiate the reforms, and the revision of the electoral law, the law regulating local entities and the organic law of the Superior Judicial Council. They also demanded that legislative and municipal mandates be reduced to four years, and appealed for the adoption of measures to guarantee the exercise of fundamental freedoms, a general amnesty for all political prisoners allowing for the return of political exiles, and the legalization of all political parties, trade unions and other civic associations.

In April 2011 the Comisión de Vigilancia y Seguimiento del Pacto Nacional (Commission for the Monitoring and Follow-up of the National Pact—originally established in 1997) met in Malabo for the first time since September 2008 to discuss the political reform proposals and the creation of a joint commission to liaise between the Government and the political parties. Then in May, Obiang Nguema announced a loose timetable for his programme of reforms, and issued a decree establishing the Comisión Nacional para el Estudio de la Reforma de la Ley Fundamental de Guinea Ecuatorial (National Commission for the Study of the Reform of the Equatorial Guinean

Constitution); he then proceeded to appoint all its members, with the majority drawn from the PDGE. The CPDS, the UP and the Acción Popular de Guinea Ecuatorial (APGE) declined an invitation to participate, on the grounds that none of their proposals had been included and that the timetable did not allow for meaningful discussions. However, the APGE subsequently agreed to join the Commission, which presented its draft reforms to parliament in July.

The referendum on the proposed reforms was held on 13 November 2011. It was beset with numerous irregularities, including voter harassment and intimidation by police and soldiers deployed at polling stations, who also expelled opposition observers. The proposals were reportedly approved by 97.7% of the votes cast, and the revised Constitution was promulgated on 16 February 2012. The new Constitution limited the President's tenure of office to two consecutive seven-year terms, but this restriction was not to apply retroactively, effectively extending Obiang Nguema's mandate, which was further facilitated by the removal of the upper age limit for presidential candidates, previously set at 75 years. The Constitution also provided for the creation of a 70-member Senate, an Audit Court, a State Council, an Economic and Social Council, and a Council for the Defence of the People, as well as the posts of Ombudsman and Vice-President, with the latter reserved exclusively for a PDGE party member. The President was granted the power to appoint all senior officials, as well as 15 senators (the remaining 55 would be elected). In April a 28-member commission, 12 of whom represented opposition parties (including the CPDS), was created to draft the internal regulations of the newly created state bodies, revise electoral legislation and harmonize existing laws with the new Constitution.

In December 2013, at the party's fifth ordinary congress, the CPDS adopted a resolution urging Obiang Nguema to organize a national dialogue to discuss the restoration of harmonious relations among all political groupings. The party also elected a new leadership, with Andrés Esono Ondo as Secretary-General. In February 2014 CPDS leaders met with Obiang Nguema, who recognized that the previous national pact (negotiated in 1997) was obsolete, and agreed to organize the proposed round-table dialogue. This was followed in March by a meeting of opposition parties in Madrid, convened by the CPDS to discuss its proposals and the framework for the round-table talks. The resulting 'Madrid Manifesto', signed by various exiled individuals and representatives of political parties and civil society groups, sought a general amnesty for all political prisoners, the right of return for political exiles, and the legalization of all political parties, trade unions and other civic associations. The round table, intended 'to facilitate national reconciliation and solve the political problems of the country', was finally held in November 2014.

Seventeen parties participated in the round table, including the ruling PDGE and its allies, and four others yet to be legalized. The parties, however, had not been given the opportunity to contribute to the round-table agenda. This, together with the Government's refusal to countenance even their minimum demands, prompted the withdrawal of all parties grouped under the Madrid Manifesto banner. Although the smaller parties subsequently returned to the negotiations, the CPDS, the FDR and the UP maintained their boycott, and the round table was widely deemed a failure. The next round table, in which 16 parties participated, was not held until July 2018, when, again, no agreement was reached. The CPDS and the Unión de Centro Derecha de Guinea Ecuatorial (UCD) refused to sign the minutes, on the grounds that their longstanding demands for the release of all political prisoners and the legalization of all political parties had yet to be met.

In March 2015 the CPDS, the FDR and the UP formed the Frente de Oposición Democrática (FOD) in Malabo (subsequently being joined by the Movimiento para la Autodeterminación de la Isla de Bioko in November). The day before the formal launch of the FOD, FDR spokesperson Guillermo Nguema Ela was arrested and banished to his native village. In June the UCD was granted legal status as a political party, as was Ciudadanos por la Innovación (CI—previously known as Candidatura Independiente) in November. However, the latter party was banned in February 2018 following the

shambolic trial of 146 of its members for alleged sedition, undermining state authority and public disorder; 36 of the defendants were convicted and sentenced to 26 years' imprisonment each. The authorities continued to deny the FDR legal recognition. Meanwhile, in May 2015 a series of laws agreed during the November 2014 round table were promulgated with minor amendments. They included legislation governing political parties; freedom of assembly and association; and presidential and senate elections. Nevertheless, independent political parties continue to suffer harassment, with members facing arrest, imprisonment and severe constraints on the exercise of their legitimate political activities.

ELECTIONS SINCE 1993

Since the establishment of a formal multi-party political system in 1993, the activities of opposition political parties have been curtailed: elections are manipulated and consistently won by Obiang Nguema and the PDGE with unrealistically overwhelming majorities. They invariably involve harassment of political opponents before and during polling, and numerous irregularities and violations of electoral law. Opposition complaints and demands for fresh elections have been persistently dismissed by the courts, the President and his supporters thus consolidating power while maintaining a democratic façade.

The first multi-party legislative elections took place in November 1993. They were boycotted by most of the parties in the POC alliance, in protest against Obiang Nguema's refusal to review contentious clauses of the electoral law. Although representatives of the Organization of African Unity (now the African Union—AU) attended as observers, the United Nations (UN) declined a request to send monitors, on the grounds that electoral procedures were being flagrantly disregarded. Following a turnout variously estimated at between 30% and 50%, the PDGE won 68 of the 80 seats in the legislative Cámara de Representantes del Pueblo (House of Representatives).

Subsequent legislative elections followed the same pattern of harassment and irregularities. In March 1999 the PDGE won 75 of the 80 parliamentary seats, with, according to official figures, more than 90% of the votes cast. The UP and the CPDS secured four seats and one seat, respectively, but rejected the results and demanded that the elections be annulled. As expected, the PDGE won the 2004 elections, obtaining 68 of the 100 seats in the newly enlarged parliament. A coalition of eight parties allied to Obiang Nguema secured a further 30 seats, while the CPDS, which contested the results, won the remaining two. In the 2008 elections, held concurrently with municipal polls, the PDGE won 90 of the 100 seats in the House of Representatives. The PDGE-allied coalition won nine seats and the CPDS just one.

Meanwhile, local elections scheduled for November 1994 were postponed until September 1995. Contested by 14 parties, these were the first—and to date the only—truly representative multi-party elections to take place in Equatorial Guinea since independence and be monitored by international observers. Despite early indications that opposition parties had won an overwhelming victory, the official results credited the PDGE with a majority of the votes cast in two-thirds of local administrations. Judicial appeals by the opposition, supported by international observers, were rejected. In all subsequent polls, Obiang Nguema's regime made sure to exercise much tighter control over the electoral process. Threats, coercion, harassment and imprisonment of opposition party members all increased. At the local elections held in May 2008, the PDGE and its allies secured control of all councils, winning 96% of the seats.

The next parliamentary and municipal elections took place in May 2013, when, for the first time, voters also elected 55 of the 70 members of the new Senate (the remaining 15 being directly appointed by Obiang Nguema). The CPDS and the APGE presented their own candidates, while the 10 other 'opposition' parties allied themselves with the PDGE. Although the campaign period and election day proceeded peacefully, the CPDS alleged numerous irregularities. The elections were duly won by the PDGE, which claimed 99 of the 100 seats in the Cámara de los Diputados (Chamber of

Deputies—as the House of Representatives had been renamed), 329 of the 334 municipalities, and 54 of the 55 elective seats in the Senate. The CPDS was allocated the remaining legislative seats and municipalities. The outcome provoked strong criticism from Spain and the USA, while a demonstration organized by the CPDS to protest against the results was banned by the authorities.

Parliamentary, municipal and senate elections were unexpectedly held on 12 November 2017 and were, unsurprisingly, boycotted by some independent opposition parties. The CPDS and the UCD formed an electoral coalition, Juntos Podemos (Together We Can), while the CI stood on its own. As on previous occasions, throughout the election process numerous irregularities took place. A total of 146 CI members were arrested before and after the elections and were tried in February 2018 on charges of sedition, undermining state authority and public disorder. Access to the internet and social media was blocked for about one month. Official figures put electoral turnout at 84%, while independent sources estimated it at around 30%. As in previous polls, the PDGE claimed to have received 99% of the votes, securing all but one seat in the Chamber of Deputies and all of the seats in the Senate, and retaining control of all of the councils. The newly elected legislators took office in January 2018, except for the sole opposition representative (a member of the CI), who was by then in prison awaiting trial. Although he was released from prison in October following an amnesty decreed in July, he was not allowed to take up his parliamentary seat.

The first presidential election under the multi-party system was held in February 1996. Obiang Nguema was returned to office with more than 90% of the votes cast, a percentage that progressively increased at each successive election. The election was boycotted by the main opposition parties, in protest against widespread electoral irregularities and official intimidation. The electoral roll drawn up by the UN in 1995 was discarded in favour of a government-compiled list, widely viewed as fraudulent, and the conduct of the election was roundly criticized by foreign observers.

President Obiang Nguema was again returned to office in December 2002 with an overwhelming majority. Four opposition candidates withdrew on the day of voting in protest against egregious irregularities, including the presence of military personnel in some voting booths, intimidation of voters and threats to opposition parties' electoral monitors. Obiang Nguema again secured re-election in November 2009, defeating four other candidates. The next presidential election, scheduled for late 2016, was brought forward to 24 April of that year, and was duly won by Obiang Nguema. Seven candidates, including three independents, contested the election. The FOD boycotted the poll, denouncing it as unconstitutional; the opposition front also expressed concern over the holding of a disputed electoral census in January and the appointment by Obiang Nguema of the members of the Junta Electoral Nacional (National Electoral Board). Although the opposition calculated voter abstention in excess of 65%, the Government claimed a turnout of over 90%.

In April 2022 an electoral census was compiled in preparation for parliamentary and municipal elections later that year, and a presidential election due to be held in 2023. Under a decree issued by Obiang Nguema in September 2022, the presidential election was brought forward to take place concurrently with the legislative and municipal elections on 20 November; the decision had received parliamentary approval shortly beforehand on grounds of economic constraints.

OBIANG NGUEMA'S DOMINANCE OF THE POLITICAL SPHERE

With each new election and government enlargement, the Obiang Nguema family further consolidated its hold on power in the country. The President also made frequent use of government reorganizations to include more family members. It was not until 2003 that non-PDGE members were finally brought into government.

After the 2004 legislative elections a new Government was formed, led by Prime Minister Miguel Abia Biteo Boricó. In August 2006 he resigned, together with his Government, following accusations of corruption and incompetence. Obiang Nguema then appointed a new Government led by Ricardo Mangue Obama Nfubea, a member of the Fang majority, thus breaking with the tradition of appointing a Prime Minister drawn from the minority Bubi tribe. Like his predecessor, Obama Nfubea resigned in July 2008 amid accusations of corruption and economic mismanagement. Most members of his Council of Ministers were reinstated in the new administration headed by Ignacio Milam Tang.

In January 2010 Milam Tang was reappointed to lead a 68-member Government, notable for its promotion of Obiang Nguema's eldest son, Teodoro (Teodorín) Nguema Obiang Mangue, from Minister-delegate of Agriculture and Forestry to Minister of State. Further government reorganizations in January and in April 2011 included the appointment of a niece of the President, Montserrat Afang Ondo, as Minister-delegate in charge of the Treasury, and further extended the allocation of cabinet posts to family members, mainly at the level of secretary of state. Another niece, Mariola Bibang Obiang, was appointed as the country's permanent representative to the United Nations Educational, Scientific and Cultural Organization (UNESCO).

Then, in August 2011, Obiang Nguema announced his intention to lead the nation for as long as it continued to vote for him. The main purpose of the constitutional amendments promulgated in February 2012 (see *Opposition Pressures*) was to prolong his leadership and secure his eldest son's succession. Teodorín Nguema Obiang was widely expected to be appointed as Vice-President, a post newly provided for in the revised Constitution. With the maximum age for presidential candidates abolished, Obiang Nguema was able to stand in the 2016 presidential election, and seek a further elective term thereafter, despite new term limits. Crucially, the new Constitution greatly increased Obiang Nguema's power by granting him full legal control of the executive. In the event of his death occurring before completion of his term in office, he would be replaced by the Vice-President.

In April 2012 a PDGE congress appointed Obiang Nguema as President for life, and confirmed his son, Teodorín Nguema Obiang, as leader of the party's youth movement; the President's wife, Constancia Mangue Nsue, was designated honorary President of the PDGE's women's organization. In accordance with the amended Constitution, whereby the President became head of government as well as head of state, Obiang Nguema dissolved the Government in May and appointed a new, 60-member administration which included an even greater number of his close relatives. Unexpectedly, former Prime Minister Milam Tang was named as Vice-President, while Teodorín Nguema was appointed as Second Vice-President, in charge of Defence and State Security, a post not envisaged in the Constitution. The post of Prime Minister reverted to a member of the Bubi ethnic group, but now became a purely administrative, co-ordinating role. Two Deputy Prime Ministers (also new roles not mentioned in the Constitution) were appointed. A new, 62-member Government was appointed under this new structure in September 2013. This reincorporated most members of the outgoing administration, while a third Deputy Prime Minister post was created. In April 2015 President Obiang Nguema dismissed the entire Government, apparently in order to reduce its size. However, most of the ministers were reappointed within two days.

Following the presidential election in April 2016, in June President Obiang Nguema appointed a Government that remained largely unchanged, but which included Teodorín Nguema Obiang as the sole Vice-President, with continued responsibility for state security and defence, paving the way for him to succeed his father as the future head of state. Milam Tang was appointed President of the State Council. The November 2017 legislative elections had no major impact on the allocation of government posts. With a few notable exceptions, including the appointment of Simeón Oyono Esono Angue as the new Minister of Foreign Affairs and Co-operation and that of the former Governor of the Bank of Central Africa States, Lucas Abaga Nchama, as the Minister of Finance, the Economy and Planning, most of the cabinet members were returned to office in February 2018. In an unexpected government reorganization in April 2019, Clemente Engonga Nguema Onguene was moved from the post of Minister of the Interior and Local Government to head the Ministry of Education, Universities and Sport, but retained his position as First Deputy Prime Minister, while Abaga Nchama was replaced by César-Augusto Mba Abogo.

With the country's economy suffering the combined impact of the ongoing COVID-19 pandemic and another sharp decrease in global oil prices, on 14 August 2020 Prime Minister Francisco-Pascual Obama Asué (who had been appointed to the premiership in June 2016) and his Government were obliged to resign for mismanagement of the economic downturn. Five days later, however, the President reappointed Obama Asué as Prime Minister, and a new Council of Ministers, in which the incumbents of the most senior posts remained largely unchanged, was subsequently installed. In October the Minister of Finance, the Economy and Planning, Mba Abogo, was replaced by his deputy, Valentín Ela Maye.

Surprisingly, a PDGE congress held in the city of Bata in November 2021 did not nominate a candidate for the forthcoming presidential election. Moreover, during a subsequent press conference President Obiang Nguema declined to discuss his succession, stating that 'there would be a normal democratic handover'.

ATTEMPTED COUPS

Since independence, numerous rumours of coup plots and conspiracies to kill President Obiang Nguema have rarely been substantiated. The President has long made systematic use of such rumours to justify the arbitrary arrest of rivals and opponents, with some eventually being released uncharged and others sentenced to long prison terms. With the advent of regular elections, alleged coup plots would typically be announced in the run-up to polling as grounds for the repression of opposition parties.

The authorities claimed to have prevented at least three coups in 2004. In the first of these, in March, 14 South African and Armenian nationals resident in the country were arrested following intelligence allegedly received from South Africa. Together with Severo Moto Nsá and the members of his government-in-exile, who were tried *in absentia*, 11 of the foreign nationals were convicted in November of a plot to overthrow the Government and assassinate President Obiang Nguema. They received prison terms ranging from 14 to (in Moto Nsá's case) 63 years. The authorities also accused some Western governments, businessmen and multinational companies of involvement in the alleged plot.

The March 2004 arrests followed those of 70 South Africans at Zimbabwe's Harare international airport. In August these detainees were convicted by a Zimbabwean court of immigration offences; two were also convicted of contravening aviation laws, while the suspected operational leader of the alleged coup plot, British national Simon Mann, was convicted of attempting to purchase weapons. On completion of his four-year prison sentence, Mann was extradited secretly to Equatorial Guinea in February 2008, where, in July, he was found guilty of attempting to overthrow President Obiang Nguema and sentenced to 34 years' imprisonment. Mann and the four South African nationals who were still in prison were pardoned by the President in November 2009.

In August 2004, meanwhile, Sir Mark Thatcher (a businessman and the son of former British Prime Minister Margaret Thatcher) was arrested in South Africa on suspicion of having financed the alleged coup plot uncovered in March. In January 2005 Thatcher admitted having contravened South African anti-mercenary legislation by agreeing to finance the use of a helicopter. He was fined R 3m. (more than US $500,000) and received a four-year suspended sentence. In June the six Armenian nationals convicted of involvement in the coup plot were pardoned by Obiang Nguema and released from prison. In June 2006 one of the South African prisoners was pardoned on humanitarian grounds and released from prison, together with dozens of other political prisoners and detainees—including those convicted in June 2002 and in September 2005 of involvement in alleged coup attempts. A further 25

prisoners convicted in those trials were released following a presidential pardon in June 2008.

In February 2009 it was alleged that there had been an attack on the presidential palace in Malabo, attributed to the Nigerian Movement for the Emancipation of the Niger Delta (which denied any involvement in the incident). The authorities subsequently accused the Equato-Guinean opposition of organizing, financing and participating in the assault, which, it was alleged, was intended to assassinate Obiang Nguema. A number of foreign nationals were arrested and expelled from the country, while 10 members of the UP were detained and subsequently charged with offences relating to the attack. The charges against eight of the detainees were dismissed at the beginning of their trial in March 2010. However, former UP leader Faustino Ondo Ebang—exiled in Spain since 2007 and tried *in absentia*—together with two other UP members and seven Nigerian nationals (believed to be fishermen and traders who were arrested at sea on the day of the alleged attack) were tried on charges of attempting to assassinate the President. The Nigerians were convicted and received prison sentences of 12 years each, although they were released under a presidential pardon in October 2010. The two Equato-Guineans were acquitted, but after a retrial in August were both sentenced to 12 years' imprisonment. They, too, were pardoned and released in October. On trial with them at the same military court were four Equato-Guineans previously exiled in Benin, who had been abducted in January and secretly transferred to Equatorial Guinea by members of the country's security personnel. All four were sentenced to death in August for organizing and taking part in the alleged attack on the palace and, to international outrage, were executed immediately afterwards.

In December 2017 the Equato-Guinean authorities announced that they had foiled a coup attempt after Cameroonian security services claimed to have arrested some 30 armed men attempting to enter Equatorial Guinea at the Kye-Ossi border crossing. The Equato-Guinean authorities subsequently asserted, without producing any evidence, that the group of men comprised Equato-Guineans and mercenaries from Chad, the Central African Republic and Sudan, led by a former Chadian general who had been contracted by 'radical opposition political parties' and assisted by unnamed foreign powers. They further claimed that the plot had been planned and financed by Equato-Guineans in France. Large numbers of people were reported to have been arrested in Equatorial Guinea, including Chadian nationals, many of whom were later released and expelled from the country. Relatives of President Obiang Nguema and PDGE members, as well as former military and security officers, were also reportedly arrested. The lack of reliable information and the numerous contradictions led some national and international commentators to express doubts regarding the veracity of the coup attempt claim. Over 150 people were subsequently charged with treason, rebellion, possession of arms and ammunition, and terrorism. Seventy-nine of the accused, including 24 foreign nationals, were present at their trial, which commenced in March 2019, while the remainder were tried *in absentia*. In May, 130 of the defendants, including a number of the foreign nationals and those tried *in absentia*, were convicted and sentenced to prison terms ranging from three to 96 years, while 21 of the defendants were acquitted. In November three of those tried *in absentia* and one other man, all of whom were residents of Spain (two of them also holding Spanish citizenship), were abducted in South Sudan and subsequently imprisoned in Equatorial Guinea, where they were summarily tried in March 2020. They were convicted of the charges and received prison sentences ranging from 30 to 90 years.

POLITICS AFTER THE OIL BOOM

The discovery of significant oil and gas reserves in the mid-1990s transformed Equatorial Guinea from one of the poorest countries in Africa to one of its richest in terms of average income per head. The vast majority of the population, however, derived minimal benefit from the exploitation of these resources, and the country's infant mortality and life expectancy rates continued to rank among the world's worst.

From the early 2000s President Obiang Nguema came under increasing pressure from Western governments and international organizations to improve human rights and transparency, and to establish the rule of law and democracy. However, any incentive to allow the emergence of civil society and political diversity diminished as the President's control over government became increasingly lucrative as a result of Equatorial Guinea's oil wealth. With Western oil companies operating in the country also under pressure to demonstrate good governance, the Government was persuaded in 2004 to seek participation in the Extractive Industries Transparency Initiative (EITI). In February 2008 Equatorial Guinea was accepted as a candidate country, but its candidacy was rejected in 2010, mainly on the grounds of the Equato-Guinean authorities' failure to allow genuine civil society participation in transparency initiatives. In 2012 the country announced its intention to reapply for EITI membership; however, in February 2020 its application was rejected, again for failure to provide evidence of civil society involvement in the process. Shortly before a scheduled re-evaluation of Equatorial Guinea's candidacy in October, the Government, concerned about another embarrassing rejection, considered withdrawing its application, opting finally in September to seek formal postponement instead. In view of these 'mixed messages', however, the EITI declared that the country's application had been 'withdrawn'.

In March 2021 the Equato-Guinean regime's carefully projected image as a capable, modernizing state was tarnished following a catastrophic explosion at a military barracks negligently sited in the populous centre of the burgeoning city of Bata. The explosion reportedly killed 107 people and injured over 600 others, and damaged or destroyed scores of homes and other buildings. This incident not only exposed the ineptitude of the Government, but also the dearth of public facilities in the country despite the implementation of various grandiose infrastructure projects. Basic medical and emergency materials and services were found to be sorely lacking, with notable deficiencies in human resources and organizational capacity, highlighting the Government's persistent failure to use the country's enormous oil wealth to improve the wellbeing of the population. Cameroon, the Republic of the Congo, France, Spain and Israel, among others, provided emergency assistance in the form of field hospitals and medical supplies, as well as medical personnel and debris-removal experts and machinery. President Obiang Nguema blamed the accident on the 'irresponsibility' of those who had lit fires and stored natural gas cylinders near the barracks. In June the commanding officer and another soldier were tried and convicted of negligence and manslaughter, and were sentenced to 32 and 50 years' imprisonment, respectively.

CORRUPTION

Corruption has been a widespread and persistent problem in Equatorial Guinea, but since the discovery and exploitation of oil in the mid-1990s its place at the heart of the regime has been highlighted by a succession of serious accusations of corruption made against President Obiang Nguema and his family. Allegations have included money laundering and the squandering and misappropriation of state revenues for personal gain. Transparency International has consistently ranked the Equato-Guinean Government as one of the most corrupt in the world, placing it among the bottom 10 countries in its Corruption Perceptions Index.

Internally, President Obiang Nguema has often levelled charges of corruption against his ministers, and has announced measures to combat this, including the creation by presidential decree in February 2007 of a national agency to counter money laundering and the financing of terrorism. However, the announcement of such measures appears to have been aimed more towards placating international criticism and diverting attention away from allegations of corruption involving the President's own family, and has had no lasting impact on the persistence of corrupt practices within the Government and state institutions.

Obiang Nguema and his family have been the subject of two inquiries by the US Senate's Permanent Subcommittee on Investigations. In 2004 the subcommittee, reporting on its investigation into alleged money-laundering practices by the former Riggs Bank, found that the bank held US $700m. in state funds deposited by US oil companies in personal accounts belonging to Obiang Nguema, members of his family and several ministers, and revealed that between 2000 and 2003 they had unduly transferred large amounts of money from the state oil revenue account into shell corporations and bank accounts in other countries. The investigation had also uncovered several luxury housing purchases by the President and close relatives in Maryland, USA.

The focus subsequently turned to the President's eldest son, Teodorín Nguema Obiang. In September 2007 the US Department of Justice reported that since 2005 Teodorín Nguema had funnelled some US $75m. through European banks to banks in the USA. The report also stated that the family's assets came largely from 'extortion and theft of public funds or other corrupt conduct'. In February 2010 the same Senate subcommittee that had earlier investigated Riggs Bank published a report on money laundering, leading to a criminal investigation into Teodorín Nguema. This revealed that during the mid-2000s, using suspect funds, he had acquired immense assets, including a mansion in California, USA, an aircraft and a fleet of luxury motorcycles and cars.

In October 2011 the US Department of Justice started legal proceedings to seize Teodorín Nguema's US assets, then valued at US $71m. In October 2014, in exchange for having all charges against him dropped, Teodorín Nguema reached an agreement with the Department of Justice to forfeit his property in the USA. It was estimated that the sale would generate some $30m., most of which was to be earmarked for donation to a charitable organization for the benefit of the people of Equatorial Guinea, with a further $10.3m. to be forfeited to the USA for a similar purpose. In September 2021 the US Administration announced that over $26m. obtained from the sale of the confiscated property was being used to purchase COVID-19 vaccines for the population of Equatorial Guinea through the UN and to fund other medical programmes.

In September 2008 the Spanish human rights group Asociación pro Derechos Humanos de España filed a complaint with the Audiencia Nacional (Spain's central investigation court) against 11 people, including President Obiang Nguema, several of his relatives and members of the Equato-Guinean Government, who were accused of misappropriating some US $26m. from the Equato-Guinean state oil company to buy properties in Spain. The money had allegedly been transferred from the account held at Riggs Bank in the USA and paid into branches of the Spanish bank Santander. After a two-year investigation, the Banco de España and the Unidad de Delitos Económicos y Fiscales de la Policía Judicial (Judicial Police Unit for Economic and Fiscal Crimes) in Las Palmas, on Spain's Canary Islands, concluded that there was evidence of money laundering by Obiang Nguema's family and members of the Equato-Guinean Government. The police report, released in April 2012, stated that two Russian nationals in Las Palmas had laundered misappropriated funds for the Obiang family and government ministers, using several offshore companies registered in tax havens. Transactions included the transfer of $26.4m. from the Riggs Bank account to Santander between 2000 and 2003, as well as the purchase in 2006 of 25 apartments in Lanzarote for €4.8m. In September 2015 Russian national Vladimir Kokorev, along with his wife and son, was arrested in Panama and extradited to Spain to face charges of money laundering on behalf of Obiang Nguema and his family. Police investigators revealed in January 2018 that between 2001 and 2007 Kokorev had carried out several corrupt arms deals between Equatorial Guinea and Ukraine, which involved the payment of millions of US dollars in bribes to Obiang Nguema's family and Equato-Guinean government officials. In March 2021 the Spanish Public Prosecutor authorized trial proceedings against the Kokorev family for money laundering and arms trafficking.

In late 2010 a French court ruled that a corruption case brought by non-governmental organizations against President Obiang Nguema's family could proceed. Meanwhile, it was alleged that in November 2009 Teodorín Nguema Obiang had bought 26 luxury cars and six motorcycles at a cost of some

€12m., and that in March 2010 he had purchased works of art valued at €18m., which were paid for by a state forestry company over which he presided. As part of the investigation, in September 2011 French police confiscated 11 of Teodorín Nguema's vehicles and in February 2012 they searched his mansion in Paris, seizing luxury goods and artworks worth an estimated €40m. The Equato-Guinean Government accused France of violating diplomatic immunity and insisted that the mansion was for diplomatic use and not a private residence; it subsequently emerged that Teodorín Nguema had bought the residence in 2004 but had sold it to his country in November 2011, after the police investigation in France had begun. In April 2012 an international warrant was issued for his arrest on suspicion of using public funds to buy property in France. In July the French Minister of Justice approved the request, and an international warrant for Teodorín Nguema's arrest was issued for failure to appear in court to answer money-laundering and embezzlement charges. Later that month police raided and seized his mansion in central Paris. In response, in September Teodorín Nguema formally lodged a libel action in Malabo against the head of the French chapter of Transparency International, who, in an article published in February, had accused him of embezzling public money. At the same time, the Equato-Guinean authorities filed a complaint against France at the International Court of Justice (ICJ) in The Hague, Netherlands, seeking a ruling for France to end the investigation of Teodorín Nguema, cancel the arrest warrant against him and return seized property. In March 2014 the French judicial authorities indicted Teodorín Nguema for embezzlement of public funds.

In January 2015 police investigators in France concluded that Teodorín Nguema had laundered 'several hundred million euros' from public funds and the proceeds of illegal commissions charged to foreign enterprises. They highlighted the key role played by the French bank Société Générale, which in the late 1990s had created a subsidiary bank of which the Equato-Guinean state held 30% of the capital and President Obiang Nguema 7%. A search of the bank's registry had allowed investigators to trace the source of the money. The investigation was completed in August 2015. In December a French court rejected Teodorín Nguema's demand for immunity and the dismissal of the case against him. Then, in May 2016 prosecutors requested that he stand trial on charges including embezzlement of public funds and money laundering. The trial, scheduled to start in October, was postponed following the Equato-Guinean Government's request for precautionary measures to the ICJ in The Hague. In December the ICJ ruled that Teodorín Nguema's mansion in Paris formed part of a diplomatic mission and was therefore protected under the Vienna Convention, but it declared itself incompetent to rule on France's investigation of Teodorín Nguema. His trial eventually commenced in June 2017 in his absence, and in October he was found guilty and given a three-year suspended prison sentence and a €30m. fine, also suspended, while the property was confiscated. In June 2018 the ICJ further ruled that Teodorín Nguema's diplomatic immunity did not exempt him from the ongoing legal proceedings. Teodorín Nguema's appeal against the sentence was rejected, with the ruling confirmed in July 2021. Once again, the Equato-Guinean Government rejected the verdict, threatening to close the embassy in Paris if it was confiscated, and retaliated a few days later by briefly detaining a French helicopter crew when it landed in Bata to refuel. Meanwhile, in December 2020 the ICJ rejected Equatorial Guinea's claims to diplomatic status for the Paris mansion, allowing the confiscation of Teodorín Nguema's property in France, valued at an estimated €150m., and the eventual restitution of this wealth to the Equato-Guinean people. A bill providing for this action was formally adopted in July 2021. However, at the end of September 2022 the ICJ announced that Equatorial Guinea had lodged a new case against France, alleging that France had violated its obligations under the UN Convention against Corruption and requesting that the sale of the Paris mansion be blocked.

In a separate legal wrangle, on 1 October 2016, at the request of the French telecommunications company Orange, the French authorities temporarily confiscated an Equato-Guinean aircraft, used by President Obiang Nguema, at Lyon airport. The Equato-Guinean Government and Orange had been in dispute since 2010 over the sale of the latter's shares in the parastatal telecommunications company Orange Guinée Equatoriale (GETESA). In November 2014 the International Arbitration Chamber of Paris had ruled in favour of Orange and ordered the Equato-Guinean Government to pay Orange the sum of €150m.

In September 2018 Brazilian customs officials at São Paulo's Viracopos International Airport detained Teodorín Nguema and searched his luggage when he failed to declare its contents. These consisted of large sums of Brazilian currency as well as US $1.5m. and 20 watches valued at a total of $15m., which were duly confiscated. Teodorín Nguema claimed that the money was to finance his medical treatment in Brazil. The Equato-Guinean Government accused the Brazilian authorities of acting in bad faith and demanded the return of the property. However, in January 2019 Brazil's Federal Supreme Court rejected the Equato-Guinean Government's claim that the search had been illegal. Meanwhile, in December 2018 the Brazilian federal police ordered the Equato-Guinean embassy in Brasília to hand over Teodorín Nguema's luxury cars, which had been concealed there to avoid confiscation.

In October 2016 the Geneva Public Prosecution Office also opened a criminal investigation into possible money laundering by Teodorín Nguema and confiscated 11 luxury cars at Geneva airport. According to Swiss airport authorities, both President Obiang Nguema and his son had made frequent visits to Switzerland in recent years, especially after the US and French authorities constrained their movements. The Equato-Guinean Government denied that the cars belonged to Teodorín Nguema, claiming they belonged to a company that had sent the cars to Switzerland for repair. Meanwhile, at the behest of the Swiss judicial authorities, in December Dutch authorities embargoed two luxury yachts belonging to Teodorín Nguema. In March 2017 the Equato-Guinean authorities initiated legal proceedings in The Hague to recover the yachts, claiming that they belonged to the Government by virtue of Teodorín Nguema's position as Vice-President. In February 2019 the Geneva Public Prosecutor closed the case against him, after he agreed to pay 1.3m. Swiss francs for the cost of the investigation and maintenance of the yachts. He agreed to forfeit the confiscated cars, which were sold on condition that the proceeds were designated for a social project in Equatorial Guinea.

In July 2020, as part of an agreement for financial assistance signed in December 2019 with the International Monetary Fund, the Government published an anti-corruption bill, which was presented for legislative debate. The draft legislation notably exempted President Obiang Nguema and Vice-President Teodorín Nguema from declaring their assets. The anti-corruption law was approved by the parliament on 28 April and officially adopted by the President on 10 May.

FOREIGN RELATIONS

Spain, the former colonial power, has traditionally provided substantial economic aid, but relations have been consistently strained by allegations of corruption, the misuse of aid funds and human rights abuses in Equatorial Guinea, and by the frequent detention and expulsion of Spanish citizens.

Spain's repeated refusals to extradite Severo Moto Nsá, whom the Obiang Nguema regime accused of involvement in an alleged coup plot in March 2004, caused further tensions, as did the 2005 attack on the Equato-Guinean embassy in Spain by opposition activists. Following a two-day visit by Obiang Nguema to Spain in November 2006, there was a degree of rapprochement between the two countries, with frequent visits by Spanish government and trade delegations to Equatorial Guinea, during which important commercial and co-operation agreements were signed. In June 2014 the attendance by the Spanish Prime Minister at the AU summit in Malabo was widely condemned in Spain and by the Equato-Guinean opposition. However, following a change of government in Spain in mid-2018, relations again cooled. The abduction in South Sudan of four Equato-Guineans (two of whom had Spanish citizenship) and their subsequent imprisonment in Equatorial Guinea further strained relations (see *Attempted Coups*).

From the early 1980s Obiang Nguema attempted to move Equatorial Guinea away from Spanish influence and into France's economic sphere. In December 1983 the country became a member of the Union Douanière et Economique de l'Afrique Centrale (which was succeeded by the Communauté Economique et Monétaire de l'Afrique Centrale—CEMAC—in 1999), and in August 1984 it joined the Banque des Etats de l'Afrique Centrale (BEAC). Full entry to the Franc Zone followed in January 1985, and in February 1998 French became Equatorial Guinea's second official language. However, legal proceedings in France against President Obiang Nguema and his family in 2011 resulted in growing tension between the two countries (see *Corruption*), and relations deteriorated further as the court cases against Teodorín Nguema proceeded.

Since 2000 Equatorial Guinea has also sought to establish relations with other European countries, particularly the United Kingdom, where it opened an embassy in May 2005. However, the embassy was closed permanently in January 2022, following the British Government's imposition of sanctions on Teodorín Nguema for corruption in July 2021. Relations with the Russian Federation have been strengthened, with Russia becoming a major supplier of arms and other military equipment by the late 2000s. In July 2015 Equatorial Guinea and Russia signed a naval defence agreement, which facilitated access by the Russian navy to Equato-Guinean ports. Equatorial Guinea was absent at a UN General Assembly vote in March 2022 that was overwhelmingly in favour of condemning Russia's invasion of Ukraine in February. Germany opened an embassy in Malabo in July 2011, but closed it 10 years later.

Relations with the European Union (EU) have long been fraught. The EU has repeatedly demanded the release of political prisoners, and has urged the Government to begin the process of democratization without delay—at times suspending aid and cancelling agreements.

From 2006 Equatorial Guinea sought membership of the Comunidade de Países de Língua Oficial Portuguesa (CPLP). To that end, throughout 2009 it formed strong ties with CPLP member states, particularly Brazil, which opened an embassy in Malabo and became a major investor in the country, and Portugal. Several trade agreements were signed in March 2010 during a visit by a delegation of Portuguese government officials and business leaders. It was expected that Equatorial Guinea would be admitted to the CPLP as a full member later that year, in anticipation of which the Government announced legislation to adopt Portuguese as a third official language. However, it was not until March 2014, at the CPLP heads of government meeting in Maputo, Mozambique, that Equatorial Guinea's membership was finally accepted; this was formalized in July at the CPLP summit in Dili, Timor-Leste. In order to ensure admission to the CPLP, in February Equatorial Guinea had decreed a temporary moratorium on the death penalty—one of the prerequisites for membership of the organization—but not before executing nine convicted prisoners at the end of January. However, Equatorial Guinea has yet to fulfil all the requirements for CPLP membership, including the abolition of the death penalty, despite repeated pledges to do so.

Equatorial Guinea's relationship with the USA has also been fraught at times. Following the closure of the US embassy in Malabo in 1996 amid increasing tension between the two states, improving relations and pressure from US oil companies led to its reopening in 2003, and a resident ambassador was appointed in 2006. Since then, US investment in the country, estimated at US $5,000m. in 2002, has increased. In the wake of the suicide attacks on the US mainland on 11 September 2001, the US Administration had approved further military aid to train a coastguard service to protect petroleum installations in Equatorial Guinea. Relations were somewhat strained in February 2010 after a US Senate subcommittee report named Teodorín Nguema Obiang as a main suspect in money laundering (see *Corruption*). Uncertain relations with Europe and the USA meanwhile encouraged President Obiang Nguema to diversify his alliances, and relations were established, or strengthened, elsewhere. In particular, the People's Republic of China and the Democratic

People's Republic of Korea (North Korea) have become major economic partners. In the case of China, widening co-operation has been facilitated by regular reciprocal visits by senior government officials. During a visit to China in October 2005, when agreements on infrastructure and housing, natural resource exploitation, agriculture, forestry and fishing were signed, President Obiang Nguema stated that thenceforth Equatorial Guinea's main development partner was to be China. In exchange for a share in Equatorial Guinea's petroleum exploitation, China then cancelled a reportedly large but undisclosed part of the debt owed by Equatorial Guinea. In August 2006 an agreement was signed in Malabo whereby some 15 Chinese companies were contracted to build thousands of social housing units, around 2,000 km of roads, a hydroelectric terminal to supply electricity to 23 mainland towns, and another hydroelectric terminal on Bioko. In February 2020 President Obiang Nguema donated US $2m. to China to support efforts to suppress the country's escalating COVID-19 epidemic. Exactly one year later, Equatorial Guinea became the first African nation to receive COVID-19 vaccines from China, which donated 100,000 doses.

Co-operation has also been promoted with Latin American countries, notably Cuba. In February 2008 a government delegation led by President Obiang Nguema embarked on a tour of several Latin American countries. His visit to Argentina provoked public demonstrations and protests against human rights abuses in Equatorial Guinea, a cause also taken up by Argentine parliamentarians and government officials, who boycotted a number of state ceremonies. The tour was cut short, with the visit to Uruguay postponed indefinitely. Good relations with Venezuela were formalized with the opening in April 2010 of an Equato-Guinean embassy in Caracas. Relations with other Latin American countries were further developed following an Africa-South America summit held in Malabo in February 2013. An Equato-Guinean embassy was opened in the Bolivian capital of La Paz at the end of that year.

Strong links with Israel have been cultivated since 2005, when a major programme for improving health care provision in Equatorial Guinea was initiated. Israel has become an important supplier of military equipment, and provides military advisers and training to the Equato-Guinean armed forces and presidential guard. The first Equato-Guinean resident ambassador to Israel presented his credentials in August 2019. In February 2021 the Equato-Guinean Government announced that it was moving its embassy from Tel Aviv to Jerusalem, thereby effectively recognizing the disputed city as Israel's capital.

After months of intense campaigning for support, particularly among African countries, in June 2017 Equatorial Guinea was elected as a non-permanent member of the UN Security Council for the 2018–19 period, prompting widespread criticism from both inside and outside the country. In November 2017 Equatorial Guinea was elected as a member of UNESCO's Executive Board for the period 2017–21, and in November 2019 former foreign affairs minister Agapito Mba Mokuy was elected as its President.

REGIONAL STANDING

Since 2000 President Obiang Nguema has sought to play a more prominent role in regional African affairs, to reflect his country's improved economic standing. He has established economic and diplomatic ties with most countries in Africa. Despite sporadic setbacks over territorial disputes, relations with neighbouring countries have gradually improved.

Already strong, relations with Morocco were further consolidated by the visit of King Muhammad VI of Morocco to Equatorial Guinea in April 2009. Morocco's military aid after 1979 had been crucial in maintaining Obiang Nguema's regime until 1994, when most troops were withdrawn except for a small number of guards overseeing the President's security. These guards were recalled in April 2012 and replaced with Israeli guards and Equato-Guinean forces trained by Israel. In October 2020 Equatorial Guinea opened a consulate to Morocco in Dakhla, Western Sahara, thereby reaffirming the country's unequivocal support for Morocco's occupation of Western Sahara.

In mid-1994 Nigeria and Equatorial Guinea agreed to establish an international commission to demarcate maritime borders in the Gulf of Guinea, although negotiations were complicated by the presence of substantial petroleum reserves in the disputed offshore areas. Bilateral relations improved with the signing of several agreements, including one on defence co-operation in 2000, and were further enhanced in 2002 when Equatorial Guinea supported Nigeria in its dispute with Cameroon over the Bakassi peninsula. In April 2008 Equatorial Guinea and Nigeria held talks aimed at improving security in the Gulf of Guinea, where pirates and smugglers were threatening offshore and coastal facilities. To counter increasing sea piracy, joint patrols by the two countries and Cameroon commenced in November 2009. In March 2022 the two countries signed an agreement under which Nigerian offshore gas would be processed in Equatorial Guinea.

Relations with Cameroon have been intermittently strained, exacerbated by frequent action by the Equato-Guinean authorities against undocumented migrants, often involving the forcible expulsion of hundreds of Cameroonian nationals from the country. One such mass expulsion took place in 2008–09 in the aftermath of a seaborne raid in December 2007 on a number of banks in Bata and the alleged attack on the presidential palace in Malabo in February 2009. Over the years Equatorial Guinea has frequently closed its border with Cameroon at Kye-Ossi for various reasons and varying lengths of time. Confrontations at the border between Cameroonians and Equato-Guineans continue to be a regular occurrence. In March 2012, just two weeks after the Joint Cameroon-Equatorial Guinea Commission had met in the Cameroonian capital, Yaoundé, supposedly to improve bilateral relations, the Equato-Guinean authorities unilaterally closed the border for two days following an incident in which five Cameroonians were injured. The border was closed in December 2017 following the arrest of alleged mercenaries (see *Attempted Coups*) and was not reopened until January 2019. The border was subsequently closed on several further occasions.

Unresolved territorial disputes between Equatorial Guinea and Gabon, revived by petroleum exploration activity in southern Río Muni, have affected bilateral relations. In March 2003 Gabonese forces occupied the small island of Mbañé, over which both countries have long claimed ownership. (Sovereignty over the islands of Cocoteros and Conga is also disputed.) In June Equatorial Guinea rejected a Gabonese proposal to share petroleum revenues from Mbañé, but a year later, in an attempt to settle the dispute amicably, Obiang Nguema proposed joint exploitation of the petroleum in the area. Both countries had meanwhile agreed in January 2004 to seek UN mediation, although this failed to resolve the dispute. A step towards an agreement was taken during a meeting between Obiang Nguema and the Gabonese President, Ali Bongo Ondimba, in New York, USA, in February 2012, when the two leaders agreed to draft a legal document to be submitted to the ICJ for consideration. In November 2016 the two parties signed an agreement referring the resolution of the dispute to the ICJ, where proceedings began in March 2021.

Equatorial Guinea and South Africa established diplomatic relations in 1993. Ties between the two countries improved markedly after South Africa provided intelligence pertaining to the alleged coup plot in March 2004 (see *Attempted Coups*) and opened an embassy in Malabo. Numerous bilateral commercial and security agreements have since been signed, including an agreement in March 2011 for the deployment of 28 South African soldiers to help guarantee security during the AU summit in June. Under the terms of the agreement, South Africa was also to equip and train the Equato-Guinean police.

Closer links were also forged with Zimbabwe following the arrest in March 2004 at Harare's international airport of 70 alleged mercenaries accused of planning to overthrow the Government of Equatorial Guinea. In June the two Governments agreed to open reciprocal diplomatic missions, and in November the President of Zimbabwe, Robert Mugabe, visited Equatorial Guinea, where he was acclaimed as the 'saviour of the nation'. The two countries signed several trade agreements during a visit to Zimbabwe by Obiang Nguema in April 2006 and, following a visit by President Mugabe in March 2007, Equatorial Guinea began to supply petroleum to Zimbabwe on favourable terms.

In April 2017, during official visits by President Obiang Nguema, co-operation agreements were signed with South Sudan, Mozambique and Uganda, primarily in the oil, agriculture, health, communications and education sectors. Uganda reportedly dispatched some 4,000 troops to Equatorial Guinea in the aftermath of the alleged coup attempt in December.

In recent years Equatorial Guinea has come to assume a prominent regional role. In January 2010 an Equato-Guinean, Lucas Abaga Nchama, was appointed as governor of the BEAC, and in the following month Equatorial Guinea was elected to the AU's 15-member Peace and Security Council for a three-year term. In April the CEMAC parliament was inaugurated in Malabo. However, in November 2013 the Government of Equatorial Guinea announced that it would not implement the CEMAC's agreement on the free movement of people within the bloc, which came into force on 1 January 2014, citing fears of a mass influx of immigrants.

In January 2011 Obiang Nguema was formally elected as rotating chairperson of the AU, Malabo having been chosen as the venue of the organization's summit in June of that year. The summit represented the culmination of years of intense lobbying by Obiang Nguema for prestigious regional roles commensurate with his growing economic influence. A new city, Sipopo, was purpose-built outside Malabo to accommodate the attending dignitaries. In 2013 Obiang Nguema agreed to host the 2014 AU summit in Malabo, in view of organizational difficulties in Malawi, where the meeting had been scheduled to take place. In May 2022 Malabo was again the venue of an AU extraordinary summit, which was convened to discuss terrorism and the recent series of coups in African countries.

Economy

MARISÉ CASTRO

INTRODUCTION

The economy of Equatorial Guinea was traditionally based on agriculture and forestry, the principal products being timber, cocoa, coffee, palm oil, bananas and cassava. At independence in 1968, the country had a flourishing industrial sector based primarily on processing agricultural derivatives and timber, and the highest per head income in Africa. However, under Equatorial Guinea's first President, Francisco Macías Nguema, the economy was devastated by years of economic and political chaos, and both industrial and commercial agricultural production were effectively eliminated. By the time Macías Nguema was deposed by his nephew, Lt-Col Obiang

Nguema Mbasogo, in August 1979, Equatorial Guinea had become one of the poorest and most heavily indebted countries in Africa.

The discovery of significant petroleum and natural gas reserves in the mid-1990s transformed Equatorial Guinea, placing it among the richest nations in Africa in terms of income per head and on a par with some of the most developed countries in the world. As the petroleum sector became increasingly important, bringing unprecedented levels of economic growth, the agricultural sector contracted sharply. By 2002 oil had become the country's most valuable asset, responsible for turning Equatorial Guinea into the fastest growing economy in the world. Massive foreign investments in the oil and gas sector, together with a sharp rise in oil exports and favourable terms of trade, contributed to the country's impressive gross domestic product (GDP) expansion, with average annual real growth reaching 26.2% between 2001 and 2005. Since 2005 some 90% of the country's total revenue has been generated from its non-renewable natural resources. According to the International Monetary Fund (IMF), exports of crude petroleum accounted for 63.9% of total export revenue by 2012; sales of petroleum and petroleum derivatives (including liquefied natural gas—LNG—and methanol) together amounted to 93.4% of overall export revenue in that year. However, owing to a worldwide reduction in oil prices, the share of crude petroleum exports fell to 68.8% of total export revenue in 2015. According to the African Development Bank (AfDB), the contribution of the extractive sector to overall GDP decreased from 85.9% in 2014 to 78.3% in 2015. The decline in oil prices had a wide-ranging impact on the economy, particularly with regard to state expenditure, forcing the Government to delay payments to the public sector, small local businesses and international enterprises operating in the country. The accumulation of debts has hindered economic growth, job creation and the development of a robust financial sector. In 2020 the coronavirus disease (COVID-19) pandemic, together with another sharp decline in international oil prices, further exacerbated the situation.

An IMF report published in April 2013 ranked Equatorial Guinea's per capita income as the highest in sub-Saharan Africa, comparable with countries of Central Europe. In 2020 the World Bank estimated the country's gross national income (GNI), measured at average 2018–20 prices, at US $8,145m., equivalent to $5,810 per head (or $13,350 per head on an international purchasing-power parity basis). Real GDP per head was estimated by the World Bank at $8,462 in 2021, having decreased, in real terms, at an average annual rate of 7.8% during 2011–20. Over the same period, the population was estimated to have increased by an average of 4.0% per year. According to the World Bank, real GDP increased by 8.3% in 2012, before contracting by 4.1% in 2013 and—apart from a small increase in 2014—continuing to decline in the succeeding years, decreasing by 5.5% in 2019. GDP contracted by a further 4.2% in 2020. In April 2021 the Government forecast that GDP would register positive growth of 2.8% in that year, based on an anticipated increase in gas production. By June, however, even government estimates conceded that GDP had decreased by 7.5% in the first quarter, owing primarily to reduced crude oil and condensate production caused by the COVID-19 pandemic and the ageing of oil fields. In April 2022 the IMF estimated a fall in GDP of 3.5% in that year, and forecast growth of 6.1% in 2022, followed by a further contraction in 2023. According to the World Bank, GDP declined by 0.9% in 2021. Only a small elite has benefited from the oil-derived wealth. It is estimated that 80% of the national revenue is still concentrated in the hands of the ruling oligarchy. The vast majority of the population, which totalled 1,496,673 at mid-2022, according to UN projections, have derived minimal benefit and remain impoverished, depending largely on subsistence agriculture and small family enterprises. Despite high levels of expenditure on massive construction projects, the country remains largely underdeveloped, and government expenditure on social services has not increased in line with revenue growth. This situation was vividly highlighted in March 2021 when an explosion at a military barracks in the centre of the city of Bata killed over 100 people and injured more than 600 others (see *History*). Infant mortality and life expectancy rates, together with other human development indicators, continue to rank among the world's worst. Nepotism, corruption, financial mismanagement, a lack of transparency and accountability, and weak state institutions are regularly cited as the most serious obstacles hindering the development of the country and a more equitable distribution of its wealth.

ECONOMIC POLICY

Following independence, President Macías Nguema imposed a centralized economy, whereby private entrepreneurial activity was forbidden and all the significant economic sectors were taken over—and mismanaged—by the state, which became the main employer. After Obiang Nguema's seizure of power, the process of nationalization was reversed, and state enterprises, especially in agriculture and timber, were gradually privatized or granted as fixed-term concessions, mostly to foreign companies. The state, however, continued to be the country's main employer.

The domestic private sector remains negligible, and is still largely monopolized by Obiang Nguema's family and associates. According to the IMF, in July 2017 the informal sector still represented 50% of the country's economy. Limited financing for small and medium-sized businesses, insufficient skilled labour and the prohibitive cost of imported goods have also deterred private sector development. The state continues to dominate domestic investment, concentrated predominantly in the hydrocarbons and construction sectors. The latter accounted for about 50% of public investment in 2011. By contrast, investment in health and education accounted for just 3% of total capital expenditure over the same period. The business environment remains difficult, with corrupt bureaucracy and poor governance hindering foreign investment outside the oil and gas industry, thus impeding economic diversification. Equatorial Guinea's ranking in the World Bank's Ease of Doing Business Index dropped from 155th out of 183 countries in the 2012 index to 178th out of 190 countries in the 2020 index (the last before the index was withdrawn). Concerned at increasing constraints on its ability to implement economic development plans and diversification, in September 2019 the Government created the National Technical Committee for Improving the Business Climate and Competitiveness of Equatorial Guinea's Economy. The anti-corruption organization Transparency International has consistently ranked Equatorial Guinea as one of the most corrupt countries in the world, placing it 172nd out of 180 countries in 2021. Since 2004, 35% of the share capital of all foreign companies established in Equatorial Guinea must be held by Equato-Guinean citizens or by companies belonging to Equato-Guineans. In addition, foreign companies operating in Equatorial Guinea are obliged to have at least three national partners, and one-third of the board members must also be nationals.

The economy has become almost totally reliant on hydrocarbon revenues. However, as a result of the worldwide decline in petroleum prices from the latter half of 2014, in 2015 revenue from exports of petroleum and petroleum products decreased by nearly one-half year-on-year, resulting in a 9.1% contraction in real annual GDP. Nevertheless, Equatorial Guinea remained highly dependent on oil revenue, which accounted for around 85% of public revenue at April 2020. Agriculture has yet to recover from the near-total destruction of the sector under President Macías Nguema: still only a few agricultural products are currently marketed. Fishing remains limited, and there is little manufacturing activity.

The importance of the hydrocarbons sector has been formalized by a number of government measures. In 2001 the Government created Guinea Ecuatorial de Petróleo (GEPetrol), a mixed venture with predominantly Equato-Guinean capital, to safeguard the country's interests against the foreign petroleum companies operating there. In the same year President Obiang Nguema renegotiated hydrocarbons contracts to increase the country's participation in petroleum licences to 15% from around 5%, following the granting of the first new licence. Legislation adopted in 2002 formalized state control of all oilfields. A new hydrocarbons law approved in 2006 aimed to increase royalties due to the state, hitherto set at a minimum of 10% of production, and to extend state involvement in oil projects overall. At late 2008 the percentage of state royalties stood at 25%. The Sociedad Nacional de Gas de Guinea (SONAGAS) was created in 2005 to oversee gas exploration and development. Since the rejection in 2010 of its candidacy to join the Extractive Industries Transparency Initiative (EITI), Equatorial Guinea has made no progress on reform; consequently, a further attempt to join the initiative in 2020 was again rejected (see *History*). Its failure, to date, to attain membership of the EITI has discouraged some international engagement with the country. In May 2017

Equatorial Guinea became a member of the Organization of the Petroleum Exporting Countries (OPEC).

The oil boom has manifestly failed to improve human development outcomes, which remain poor, as evidenced by the country's low ranking in the United Nations Development Programme (UNDP) Human Development Index (HDI). Despite Equatorial Guinea's abundant petroleum revenues, the standard of living of the majority of the population has not been significantly improved, and poverty remains widespread. In the UNDP's 2021 *Human Development Report* Equatorial Guinea was ranked 145th out of the 189 countries assessed in 2020 (although its HDI value of 0.596 remained higher than the average for sub-Saharan Africa). Life expectancy followed an overall upward trajectory during the early 21st century, rising from 49.1 years in 2001 to an estimated 59.1 years in 2020, although notable decreases were recorded in several years over this period. According to a World Health Organization (WHO) report published in 2015, the maternal mortality rate had been reduced by 74%, compared with levels observed in 1990, and this decline was attributed to health services becoming more accessible. UN data showed that the incidence of mortality of the under-fives population had been reduced from 184 per 1,000 births in 1990 to 78.5 per 1,000 by 2020. Nevertheless, health and education remain underfunded, despite increased budget allocations to these sectors since 2006. In 2019 health expenditure comprised 21.3% of total public expenditure and represented only 0.7% of GDP.

In November 2007 the Government asserted that it had the necessary resources to eradicate poverty and achieve full development by 2020, and announced a five-year plan to diversify the economy away from petroleum and gas. Infrastructural investment of more than US $12,000m. was envisaged. In February 2008 the Cámara de Representantes del Pueblo (House of Representatives) approved the Plan Nacional de Desarrollo Económico y Social: Horizonte 2020 (National Economic and Social Development Plan: Horizon 2020), ostensibly aimed at eradicating poverty within 12 years, but seen by many as a delaying tactic. Progress in both economic diversification and poverty eradication has remained slow, partly reflecting the difficult business environment—the bureaucracy and the corruption—which has constrained private sector investment and has not been conducive to job creation, and also because of the lack of a comprehensive policy addressing social needs and the development of human capital. Despite the Government's declared commitment to economic diversification and investment in strategic sectors such as fisheries, agriculture and eco-tourism, investment remains concentrated on infrastructural development and other capital projects. Diversification efforts in recent years have been largely limited to staging conferences on the topic, with negligible results. In February 2014 the Government announced the creation of a Fondo de Co-Inversión (FCI—Co-investment Fund), with a pledged allocation of some $1,000m. to finance economic diversification. Three months later the Council of Ministers approved a draft bill to establish the FCI, which was to provide investment over the next three years in key economic sectors. However, the Government failed to convince international partners to invest in such diversification initiatives in the country, while the drastic decline in oil revenues from mid-2014 significantly curtailed Equatorial Guinea's own ability to invest in major diversification and infrastructure projects. In 2017 public investment represented 17.2% of GDP, compared with 24.6% in 2013. In December 2019 the Government reported that it would need as much as $2,000m. to diversify the economy. In March 2021 the Government declared that it was ready to resume its economic diversification efforts, with a focus on promoting fishing, agriculture and tourism to reduce dependency on oil revenues.

Together with oil, construction has dominated economic activity since the mid-2000s, propelled by ambitious projects under the aegis of the Government's Programa de Inversiones Públicas (Public Investment Programme) to rebuild derelict infrastructure. However, some of the more grandiose prestige projects have failed to attract significant numbers of paying customers or to contribute in any tangible way to the socio-economic development of the country. Examples include the construction of new ministry buildings as well as a motorway linking Malabo airport to the Ela Nguema district (the Malabo II project); the building of a marina and a ring road in Bata (the Bata II project), as well as numerous hotels and luxury housing; the creation of the new city of Sipopo, a luxury tourism complex which cost the Government over €580m.; and the construction of the stadia that enabled Equatorial Guinea to host the Africa Cup of Nations football tournament in 2012 and 2015. Most ambitious of all was the founding of a new administrative capital, Oyala —modelled on Brazil's federal capital, Brasília—in the newly created province of Djibloho, in the centre of the continental region. Although it remained unfinished at mid-2022, the new capital was formally inaugurated in August 2015, with the Government moving there from Malabo for a three-month period in January 2017, when it was formally renamed Ciudad de la Paz (City of Peace).

MONETARY POLICY

Equatorial Guinea entered the Franc Zone in 1985, having been admitted to the Union Douanière et Economique de l'Afrique Centrale (now the Communauté Economique et Monétaire de l'Afrique Centrale—CEMAC) in 1983. The issuing bank for the six Central African member countries is the Banque des Etats de l'Afrique Centrale (BEAC), which Equatorial Guinea joined in 1984. The BEAC determines monetary policy for all CEMAC members. With admission to the Franc Zone, Equatorial Guinea's epkwele, which had been linked to the Spanish peseta, was replaced by the franc CFA at a rate of 4 bipkwele = 1 franc CFA. By entering the monetary union, Equatorial Guinea accepted monetary and fiscal rules on the yearly inflation rate and total government debt.

Admission to the BEAC was instrumental in keeping Equatorial Guinea's monetary and fiscal policy under control, and immediately brought exchange rate stability to the country. Since 1999 the franc CFA has been pegged to the euro at a rate of €1 = 655.957 francs CFA, and its exchange rate *vis-à-vis* other currencies fluctuates through the euro. Other advantages accrued included the guaranteed issuing of money, access to a fully functional banking system, and the establishment of a clear and consistent monetary policy. During the early 21st century, Equatorial Guinea's massive oil wealth enabled it to play a major role in the affairs of the BEAC.

The high levels of fiscal spending that began in 2009 with the Government's ambitious public investment programme, combined with a decline in oil prices in the same year, led to the country's first fiscal deficit in a generation, equivalent to 3.5% of GDP. The deficit was reportedly funded by borrowing more than US $500m. from the People's Republic of China, resulting in a threefold total debt stock increase from 2008.

Official budgets are seldom reliable indicators of government revenue and expenditure, the latter consistently being much higher than budget projections. According to the IMF, general government total expenditure was equivalent to 41.6% of GDP in 2015, before declining to 27.8% in 2016, 19.9% in 2017 and an estimated 18.5% in 2018. The overall fiscal deficit (after grants and on a cash basis) widened from 2.9% of GDP in 2015 to 7.9% in 2016, before narrowing again to 4.9% in 2017; an estimated overall fiscal surplus of 1.2% of GDP was recorded in 2018. General government revenue was equivalent to 26.5% of GDP in 2015 (with hydrocarbons contributing 22.2%), but fell to 16.9% in 2016, before recovering slightly to 17.3% in 2017 and an estimated 19.0% in 2018.

Since the early 2000s Equatorial Guinea's levels of public and external debt have been among the lowest in the world, both in real terms and as a percentage of GDP. Total external debt was equivalent to 8.6% of GDP in 2017, with debt service equivalent to 3.3% of the value of exports in that year. In 2018 the country's outstanding public debt (including domestic arrears) was equivalent to an estimated 43.0% of its GDP, falling to 39.9% in 2021, according to the IMF, which in April 2022 forecast a further drop in public debt to 27.8% of GDP in that year. In May 2019 the Government securitized part of the country's debt with the Caisse Commune d'Epargne et d'Investissement Bank Guinea Ecuatorial by issuing bonds to the value of 291,000m. francs CFA. In June the AfDB granted a €26,453m. loan to Equatorial Guinea for its Public Finances

Modernization Project (2019–23), which was intended to improve financial management and governance.

The rate of inflation has usually been higher in Equatorial Guinea than in the other CEMAC member states. The inflation rate rose to 4.8% in 2020 from 1.3% in 2019. According to the BEAC, inflation decreased to 2.9% in 2021, but was expected to reach a rate of around 5% in 2022.

AGRICULTURE, FORESTRY AND FISHING

Equatorial Guinea has a fertile terrain capable of sustaining intensive cultivation of fruit and vegetables, which, in turn, could stimulate the development of a food-processing industry. However, the potential for a revival of an important economic role for agriculture has diminished with decades of neglect by successive governments. Repeated government pledges to diversify the economy and promote agricultural development have come to little, as have programmes to improve food security, and basic foodstuffs still have to be imported. In addition to the wide range of crops already produced, there are opportunities for investing in areas such as the production and processing of cocoa and coffee, fruit and vegetables, palm oil, coconut, sugar, soap and fertilizer. Major obstacles continue to be the lack of material and financial support for farmers, and the poor road infrastructure outside the main cities.

Agriculture and timber, previously the main drivers of Equatorial Guinea's economy, became secondary contributors to GDP once oil production started in the mid-1990s. Since 2000 the area of land devoted to agriculture and forestry has continued to shrink. The agriculture sector, which suffers from chronic underfunding, accounted for just 2.6% of GDP in 2021, according to official figures. An investment guide published by the Government in 2014 put total arable land at 880,000 ha, equivalent to 32% of the country's area, with only 26% of this land under cultivation. In mid-2015 the Food and Agriculture Organization (FAO) of the United Nations (UN) estimated that agriculture, mainly subsistence-based, employed 61.5% of the labour force, thus constituting the main source of income for Equato-Guineans, but still satisfying less than 30% of the country's needs. In October of that year FAO and the Government signed an agreement to promote agricultural development in the country over the next seven years. The programme, which was to be funded by Equatorial Guinea at a cost of US $31.5m., would focus on the priorities contained in the country's National Plan for Food Security, including increasing production, diversifying food supplies and managing natural resources; marketing, processing, conservation and rural finance; and strengthening human and institutional capacities. In September 2018 the AfDB pledged to support Equatorial Guinea's economic diversification through a programme centred on agricultural transformation and development. The main areas earmarked for diversification in the next 10 years were: agriculture, which was expected to grow by 12% over that period; industrial fishing, by 18%; maritime transport, by 16%; and electricity, by 15%. As part of this programme, in July 2019 the AfDB provided a loan of €55.5m. towards the implementation of a project to support the development of value chains in the fishing and aquaculture industry. The project was expected to increase fishing production through sustainable development of industrial and artisanal fishing, as well as aquaculture, to improve the provision of fish to the local market, and to reduce fish imports. Ultimately, it was hoped that the project would increase revenue and improve employment opportunities in the sector, thereby contributing to diversification.

Cocoa was the main hard currency earner until the industry was destroyed under Macías Nguema. Nevertheless, it remains the primary export crop. Cocoa is the main crop of Bioko, where its cultivation still accounts for about 90% of the country's total output, and it continues to employ the highest proportion of Equatorial Guinea's workforce. Most cocoa plantations are owned by members of the presidential entourage and are managed by two Spanish companies. They are worked on a share-cropping basis by small-scale local farmers. Only about one-third of the land that was cultivated before independence is now exploited, and most of the trees are old and poorly tended. The cocoa sector has also been undermined by the rising costs of inputs, the scarcity of skilled labour and,

most damagingly, the instability of producer prices. As part of the Government's plan to diversify the economy, and following IMF recommendations made in April 2010, Equatorial Guinea sought to revitalize the cocoa industry, and signed an agreement to this end with Ghana in September of that year. The programme was expected to result in annual production of 2,000–4,000 metric tons of cocoa over the next 10 years. However, according to FAO estimates, cocoa bean output amounted to just 1,000 tons annually during 2017–20.

Coffee was traditionally the second most important export crop after cocoa, and the sector began to recover slightly after 2006, owing to a relative increase in purchases from planters, although its contribution to GDP remained negligible. As part of the economic diversification programme, the Government intended to prioritize coffee production in the mainland region of Río Muni and to develop local varieties. However, there has been little evidence of real progress in such efforts.

Cassava, coco yam, sweet potatoes, plantain, bananas, rice, maize, palm oil and eggs are all produced for the domestic market. The Government is promoting the production of spices (vanilla, pepper and coriander) for export, and in November 2012 it signed an agreement with FAO for the development of poultry-rearing projects in rural areas.

Timber, primarily from Río Muni, is the second largest revenue earner after petroleum. It accounted for 25.8% of export revenue in 1996, but by 2009 its contribution had fallen to a mere 0.8%. In that year the value of timber exports was reported to be 129.5m. francs CFA. Exports of wood, charcoal and articles of wood generated 52m. francs CFA in 2020, representing 2.9% of the country's total export revenue. Government figures estimated the total area of forest in 2012 at 2.2m. ha, of which only 625,000 ha were suitable for lumbering operations. The devaluation in 1994 of the franc CFA stimulated timber exploration and output to such an extent that its sustainability was questioned; the environmental impact on easily accessible areas close to the coast or to navigable waterways was devastating. It was estimated that during 1990–2000 Equatorial Guinea lost 0.6% of its forest annually. To preserve its forestry resources, the Government set limits on what land could be exploited and on the number of enterprises permitted to operate. This reduced the area of exploited forests from 1.2m. ha in 1994 to 400,000 ha in 2009, and the number of enterprises from 52 (mainly of European origin) to about 15. In 2018, according to FAO figures, some 87.9% of the country's land area was covered by forest, compared with 96.2% in 1990. In September 2020 the Government issued a decree forbidding tree felling and timber exploitation activities. However, just one month later another decree was issued authorizing exports of roundwood 'owing to the economic crisis'. Since 1999 the sector has been dominated by Asian firms, and China has become the main importer of Equato-Guinean timber. The principal exploited species of wood are okoumé (most of which is exported, with only 3% processed locally) and akoga. According to FAO, estimated total annual roundwood removals increased from 1,437,000 cu m in 2016 to 1,747,000 cu m in 2018 (remaining at that level in 2019–20:). Nevertheless, the timber sector's contribution to GDP remains modest. The sector's potential has not been fully exploited, and there remain untapped opportunities for investment and development in the areas of industrial wood processing, and pulp and paper production.

Fishing constitutes one of the most abundant resources of Equatorial Guinea, but has been seriously neglected. The country has an exclusive economic zone of 314,000 sq km and a potential minimum catch of 50,000 metric tons per year, which is under-exploited. Artisanal fishing predominates, but along with small-scale industrial fishing remains insufficient to satisfy local demand. Under Macías Nguema, the domestic fishing industry collapsed and the Union of Soviet Socialist Republics (USSR) was granted a fishing monopoly. Following the termination of this arrangement in 1980, a major fisheries agreement was concluded with the European Community (now the European Union—EU) in 1984, which has since been renewed at three-yearly intervals. By 2017 annual EU financial compensation for Equatorial Guinea had risen to €1.11m. (in addition to shipowners' fees) for a catch of 9,000 tons by 59 permitted European vessels. The EU has also financed research and training schemes to improve Equatorial Guinea's own artisanal fishing operations. Given the importance of the primary sector, particularly with regard to employment, the Government has repeatedly pledged commitment to the diversification and development of agro-fisheries production. A processing plant was built in the coastal town of Mbini, Río Muni, in 2007 and was expected to lead to an increase in total fish output. In April 2016 the Banque de Développement des Etats de l'Afrique Centrale (BDEAC) agreed to invest some 9,000m. francs CFA (approximately €13.7m.) to build a fish-processing factory in Annobón (Pagalu). It was anticipated that under the agricultural development programme Equatorial Guinea would eventually produce a surplus for the export market, particularly from the fishing industry. In the 2000s Equatorial Guinea also signed fishing agreements with Nigeria, Ghana, Morocco, Benin and Angola, and established a new state agency, the Sociedad Nacional de Pesca Marítima de Guinea Ecuatorial (SONAPESCA), to promote commercialization of the fisheries sector. The total catch (including foreign fleets) amounted to an estimated 6,057 tons in 2020, according to FAO.

INDUSTRY

There was a diversified and flourishing light industrial sector at independence, centred in Malabo and Bata; this infrastructure was effectively destroyed by Macías Nguema and has yet to be restored. According to official figures, the industrial sector provided 53.1% of GDP in 2021, with manufacturing alone contributing 25.9%. Two sawmills in Bata currently account for most of the country's industrial activity. There is also a small cement works and a bleach factory. Food processing and soap production are carried out on a small scale. Cocoa fermenting and drying is the only significant manufacturing industry on Bioko.

Industrial activity is concentrated almost entirely within the oil and gas sector. This gave rise to the rapid expansion of the construction sector, as revenue from the hydrocarbons industry was spent on large-scale public infrastructure projects such as the rehabilitation of ports and airports, urban regeneration, and the development of the new districts of Malabo II, Bata II, Sipopo and Oyala/Ciudad de la Paz. The construction sector accounted for 3.5% of GDP in 2021, according to official figures. As with the oil industry, the growth of the construction sector has had a negligible impact on the living standards of the majority of the population and has not contributed to sustainable diversification. Most, if not all, of the inputs needed by the industry have to be imported. Furthermore, although labour intensive, the industry is dominated by Chinese, French and North African companies and has not created domestic employment opportunities, as most companies import their own labour. Plans for industrial diversification are limited to the oil and gas industries. Proposals in the early 2010s, however, by the US firm KBR to construct an oil refinery in Mbini, at a cost of US $422m. and with the capacity to refine 20,000 barrels per day (b/d), appeared by 2014 to have been shelved. Meanwhile, in August 2011 the Government signed an exclusive rights agreement with the US company Energy Allied International Corporation to develop the petrochemical industry, in which it was investing about $150m. In 2015 the Government established Riaba Fertilizers Ltd, which was to oversee the development of a petrochemical complex in Riaba, Bioko, to include a plant to produce ammonia and urea derivatives. In February 2016 the East China Engineering Science and Technology Co Ltd was awarded the engineering, procurement and construction contract for the project.

Oil and Gas

Mining and quarrying contributed 22.8% of GDP in 2021, according to official figures. Petroleum and gas production is by far the main source of revenue in the country. Hydrocarbons continue to account for more than 90% of government revenue. Oil is produced mainly in three fields: Zafiro, Alba (off Bioko) and Ceiba-Okume (off Río Muni). The Aseng and Alen fields began to make substantial contributions by the mid-2010s. Overall petroleum output peaked in 2008 at around 450,000 b/d, and began to decline the following year. In May 2010 the Government announced that oil production stood at 295,000 b/

d but insisted that it would maintain oil production at around 300,000 b/d throughout 2011 and increase it in 2012 as new wells came into production. However, there was no notable increase in oil production, partly attributable to the ageing of the Zafiro field, which was not offset by output from the new wells. According to government figures, oil output decreased progressively from an estimated 282,000 b/d in 2013 to 120,000 b/d in 2019. In March 2018 the International Energy Agency predicted that oil production would decline to 110,000 b/d by 2023. During 2020 oil production ranged between 90,000 b/d and 118,000 b/d, while output remained below 110,000 b/d in the first half of 2022. According to the AfDB, revenue from exports of crude petroleum and petroleum products nearly halved from 8,593m. francs CFA in 2014 to 4,341m. francs CFA in 2015, and decreased further, to 3,255m. francs CFA, in 2016, as production declined and world oil prices remained subdued. Revenue from exports of crude petroleum and petroleum products amounted to 2,306m. francs CFA in 2018 and fell to 1,617m. francs CFA in 2020, amid the COVID-19 pandemic. Although oil prices increased sharply in the first half of 2022 as a consequence of the Russian Federation's invasion of Ukraine in February, Equatorial Guinea was not expected to benefit from the rise, with its oil production stagnating due to ageing wells and lack of investment. According to multinational oil and gas company BP, proven oil reserves stood at 1,100m. barrels at the end of 2020. The fact that this figure represented only 0.1% of the global total was attributed by one report to a lack of geological studies, which, if undertaken, might confirm suspicions that the country's reserves actually account for as much as 10% of total global reserves. Some forecasts suggest that Equatorial Guinea's oil reserves will be depleted by 2030, while other industry sources suggest that this projection is overly pessimistic. The IMF estimates that Equatorial Guinea has 4.3% of the world's reserves of crude petroleum. Recoverable reserves have been put at approximately 88m. barrels of condensate.

Petroleum production greatly increased from 1995, when the Zafiro field of ExxonMobil (Mobil Oil Corporation until 1999) came on stream; output at Zafiro rose from 40,000 b/d in 1996 to 280,000 b/d by 2004. Although the Zafiro field has peaked (annual production having fallen to around 90,000 b/d by 2019 and to 30,000 b/d by the first quarter of 2022), it remains Equatorial Guinea's largest producer, accounting for about 70% of all Equatorial Guinea's oil. Over the last 20 years the field has produced more than 1,000m. barrels and currently has an estimated 600m. barrels in crude petroleum reserves. In December 2017 ExxonMobil announced the discovery of a new oilfield in the Avestruz–1 well, in Block B of EG-06; the importance of the field has yet to be assessed. Nevertheless, the company announced its intention to sell all its assets in Equatorial Guinea, including the Zafiro field. In January 2019 ExxonMobil entered into negotiations with the United Kingdom-based Trident Energy for the sale of 70% of its share in the Zafiro field. However, this was blocked by the Equato-Guinean Government, apparently owing to the fact that Trident Energy's management was French. Negotiations with other companies, including Marathon Oil of the USA and Russian companies Lukoil and Gazprom Neft, which had been initiated in 2020, were also blocked by the Government. Some analysts believed that the Government was deliberately prolonging the process until 2025, when the Zafiro licence was due to expire, so that control of the oilfield would automatically revert to the Equato-Guinean state.

Important oil discoveries off Río Muni led to a territorial dispute with neighbouring Gabon in 2003 (see *History*). In early 2001 the US company Triton Energy (now owned by Hess Corporation), in partnership with the South African oil and gas exploration group Energy Africa, began production at the Ceiba oilfield in the Río Muni basin off the Mbini coast, the second most important field after Zafiro. New discoveries increased the field's estimated proven reserves to 450,000m. barrels by 2008. Output from the field totalled an estimated 80,000 b/d in 2009. In 2003 Energy Africa acquired a 20% stake in ChevronTexaco's production in Block L, immediately north of Ceiba. Production in the Okume field, next to Ceiba, started in December 2006. The field reached peak production in 2010, at 86,000 b/d, declining to an average daily output in 2012 of

59,000 b/d. In November 2017 Hess Corporation sold all of its gas and oil interests in the Ceiba and Okume fields to US-based Kosmos Energy.

The offshore Alba gas and condensate field, discovered in 1984, began production in late 1991, at a rate of 1,200 b/d. By 2006 Alba's production of condensate had reached 40,000 b/d. Original estimates of reserves in the Alba field stood at 69m. barrels of oil equivalent (boe), but new discoveries have since increased the assessment to almost 1,000m. boe. In November 2011 the Aseng field, operated by the US company Noble Energy (which was acquired by Chevron in July 2020), began production. The field's initial output of 51,000 b/d rose to an average daily production of 60,000 b/d during 2012. The Alen field, located in Block O some 24 km from the Aseng field, is also owned by Noble Energy, which developed the field at a cost of US $1,600m. The projected oil output of the Alen field was set at 37,500 b/d, and gas production of 440m. cu ft per day was envisaged. Noble Energy developed a gas pipeline linking the Alen field to a LNG plant in Bioko operated by EG LNG; the connection was successfully tested in March 2021 and became fully operational that year. In December the Ministry of Mines, Industry and Energy announced that it had signed a production-sharing contract with Chevron Corporation for Block 09 in the Doula Basin, in which Chevron would hold 80% of the shares and GePetrol the remaining 20%. However, reports in February 2022 suggested that Chevron was planning to sell most of its assets in Equatorial Guinea, including the Alen and Aseng fields. Although the oil industry is dominated by US companies, since 2010 contracts have also increasingly been signed with companies from other countries, including operators from other emerging economies, as well as China and Russia. In February 2010 a new production-sharing agreement for an offshore block near Bioko was signed between the Government of Equatorial Guinea, GEPetrol, Marathon Oil EG Production Ltd (a subsidiary of Marathon Oil of the USA) and SK Innovation Co Ltd of the Republic of Korea (South Korea). Marathon Oil was to hold 70.6% of the participating interest, while GEPetrol would hold 20% and SK Innovation Co Ltd the remainder. In August 2011 an agreement was reached with the Dutch firm Vopak to build a crude petroleum storage terminal in Malabo. This terminal would also enable the processing and distribution of oil on Bioko. After the Ministry of Mines, Industry and Energy took over responsibility for granting licences from GEPetrol in 2012, there was a rush to award new contracts. Nine new contracts were signed in that year alone, including with the multinationals Glencore and Ophir Energy, compared with eight in 2006–11. In March 2015 the Government ratified the production-sharing agreement signed two months earlier with ExxonMobil Exploration, Production Equatorial Guinea (Offshore) Ltd and GEPetrol for offshore Block EG-06, north of Bioko. In April 2021 UK-based Tullow Oil completed the sale of its assets in Equatorial Guinea, namely its share in the Ceiba-Okume fields, estimated to contain 25m. barrels of oil reserves, to Panoro Energy ASA of Norway for US $88.8m. In May 2022 Panoro Energy and its partners and the Government of Equatorial Guinea agreed to extend the production-sharing agreement until 2040. Production in Block G06 increased from 29,904 b/d in 2021 to 42,000 b/d by May 2022.

Equatorial Guinea's oilfields also contain considerable reserves of natural gas. The main gasfields are Alba, Aseng and Alen, with some gas also produced by the Zafiro field. Gas production increased from 28.3m. cu m in 2001 to 6,286.3m. cu m in 2013. According to government figures, natural gas production in 2018 totalled an estimated 13,000m. cu m, of which 45% was sent to the LNG plant for liquefaction and export, and 13% to the Alba Compression plant (see below). The natural gas is processed as condensate, liquefied petroleum gas, methanol and LNG. Annual production of LNG was projected to rise from 6,200m. cu m to 8,500m. cu m during 2016–20. The Government regards gas as key to its programme of economic diversification, and has announced plans to focus on the gas industry as oil production stagnates. According to OPEC, in 2019 proven natural gas reserves in Equatorial Guinea amounted to 39,000m. cu m. Plans to build a second LNG plant have been under way for more than a decade, but progress in the construction of the Train 2 plant has proved

slow. A memorandum of understanding (MOU) was signed in May 2011 by the Government, SONAGAS and several companies operating on different blocks—including Noble Energy, Glencore and Atlas Petroleum (operating Blocks I and O), the shareholders of 3G Holding Ltd (Spain's Unión Fenosa Gas, Portugal's Galp Energia and Ophir—operating Block R) and the partners of EG LNG Holdings Ltd—to develop LNG Train 2, construction of which started in 2012. Gas production was expected to increase further following the discovery of gas in September 2014 by Ophir Energy in the Silenus East-1 well of Block R. According to the company, the well included renewable gas reserves of some 11,500m. of cu m equivalent, which represented about one-quarter of all Equato-Guinean proven gas reserves. Ophir Energy estimated that total renewable resources in Block R amounted to 3,400,000m. cu ft (96,277m. cu m).

Natural gas resources have been extracted by the US-based Atlantic Methanol Production Company (AMPCO) since 2001. A US $400m. methanol plant, completed on Bioko that year, was designated to process most of the natural gas that was previously being flared. In 2006 it was estimated that 1,982m. cu m of gas was flared every year. The condensate output of the Alba field, in particular, rose substantially, and was generating as much as $300,000 per day within a few years. A new condensate plant, with an annual capacity of 3.4m. metric tons, constructed by Marathon Oil at a cost of $1,500m., loaded its first cargo in May 2007. Equatorial Guinea thus became the 14th country in the world to export LNG. Marathon Oil also constructed the Alba B3 Compression complex, inaugurated in August 2016, which was to process gas, liquid petroleum propane and butane. By 2018 the plant was producing just over 37,000 b/d of condensate, as well as nearly 7,000 b/d of butane and just under 12,000 b/d of propane. In 2016 the country exported 4,304m. of cu m equivalent of LNG, the majority of which went to Asia (with India taking some 32% of the total). LNG exports generated 487m. francs CFA in 2019. Gas exports were temporarily halted in September 2021 following a fire in the AMPCO plant, which processes gas from the Alba field. Exports reportedly resumed in late November.

In May 2006 Nigeria and Equatorial Guinea signed an agreement whereby Nigeria would provide 600m.–800m. cu ft (17m.–23m. cu m) of gas per day, to be processed in the LNG plant in Bioko. A co-operation agreement to establish a joint venture for gas infrastructure projects and LNG production was signed in October 2008 between Gazprom and EG LNG, in which Marathon Oil controlled a 60% stake and SONAGAS 25%, with the remaining shares split between Mitsui (8.5%) and Marubeni (6.5%) of Japan. Earlier that year, in February, an agreement had been signed with the Spanish company Unión Fenosa Gas whereby the company, jointly with EON, formed a consortium with SONAGAS, Marathon Oil, Mitsui and Marubeni, to carry out the largest integrated energy project in the Gulf of Guinea. This included the construction of a second LNG liquefaction and purification facility on Bioko, as well as three gas pipes that would join Nigerian, Cameroonian and Equato-Guinean oilfields with the Punta Europa LNG plant in Malabo. In April 2011 EON withdrew from the consortium and sold its holdings to Unión Fenosa Gas and Galp Energia. In February 2014 the Ministry of Mines, Industry and Energy, together with Ophir Energy, signed letters of intent with Bumi Armada of Malaysia and with the US Excelerate Energy for the development, implementation and commercialization of Block R, following the construction of a floating LNG platform. Bumi Armada and Excelerate were to be responsible for the design, construction, operation and maintenance of the facility.

In November 2016 Ophir Energy and OneLNGSM (a joint venture between units of the Bermuda-registered Golar LNG and the US oil company Schlumberger) signed a letter of intent to create a joint venture company to develop the floating LNG installation in the Fortuna field in Block R, the first such deepwater installation in Africa, with an estimated annual production capacity of 2.2m. metric tons. The facility, with a production capacity of 67,000 b/d of oil equivalent, was initially expected to come into service in 2020, but was subsequently delayed until 2022 while Ophir Energy sought financing for the project. It was reported in May 2017 that Ophir Energy was seeking a loan of US $1,200m. from Chinese banks. In January 2018 the Industrial and Commercial Bank of China reportedly agreed to finance the project, at a cost of US $2,000m. Although production had not yet started, in August 2017 it was reported that a Swiss-based trading company, Gunvor, had already bought the facility's entire output. However, in January 2019 Ophir Energy had its licence rescinded owing to its failure to secure financing.

Other Minerals

Reserves of gold, iron ore, manganese, tantalum, uranium, bauxite and diamonds have also been discovered on the mainland, but these have yet to be exploited, apart from some activity by artisanal miners, notably for alluvial gold, which over the course of the 1970s produced an estimated total of 2,300 kg of gold. In March 2009 the Government announced that it was cancelling all mining contracts signed before 27 February of that year, and gave exploration companies two months to renegotiate new agreements. The Government stated that this formed part of a range of measures designed to safeguard the interests of the country's mining sector. In December 2018 the Government announced a national plan for the development of the mining sector, and in February 2019 it launched the country's first-ever licensing round for the exploration, prospection and production of minerals, in Río Muni. Five companies (Manhattan Mining Investment, Blue Magnolia, Shefa Minerals SA, Oro Sac Corp, and Akoga Resources) were granted licences to mine gold, silver, copper, lead, nickel, zinc, cobalt, and platinum and platinum group elements. In May 2020 the Government signed five contracts with the first three of the five companies listed to commence mining exploration in Río Muni.

Power

Equatorial Guinea has an estimated 2,600 MW of hydroelectric potential. The Government is making efforts to diversify its energy resources and improve electrification nationwide. Electricity is still provided only to the main towns on Bioko and in Río Muni; supply remains erratic and blackouts are common, despite recent improvements. Since 1989 a 3.6-MW hydroelectric power station built on the Riaba river has provided most of the power on Bioko. During the dry season the Malabo diesel plant supplements output from Riaba. A new thermal power station to supply Malabo came on stream in 2000. Another, 3.6-MW thermal power station, constructed with aid from China, at Bikomo, near Bata, supplies 90% of Río Muni's energy requirements. Construction by a Chinese firm of the 120-MW Djibloho hydroelectric power station in Añisok, Río Muni, began in 2008. The first phase was inaugurated in October 2012. The plant was expected to provide electricity to the whole of the continental region and also to export surplus output to neighbouring countries. A 220-kV substation was also being built in conjunction with the power station to supply electricity to the mainland region. Completion of the 200-MW Sendje hydroelectric plant, on the Wele river, initiated in 2012 by the Ukrainian company Duglas Alliance, was originally scheduled for 2017 but was subsequently delayed. In June 2020 the BDEAC approved a loan of 80,000m. francs CFA to allow the Equato-Guinean Government to complete the construction of the Sendje plant. In July 2012 China Eximbank signed a US $174m. agreement with the Equato-Guinean Government to finance the completion of the electrification of Malabo. This credit was in addition to a $2,000m. credit granted in 2011, also intended to improve power supply throughout the country. In April 2015 the Government signed agreements with two Chinese companies—one to build a new hydroelectric plant on the Wele river, and the other to carry out a feasibility study of building a power plant in Río Muni's coastal town of Cogo (or Kogo) and electricity supply connections with neighbouring countries. Following the commencement of operations at the Djibloho power station in 2012, Equatorial Guinea's output of hydroelectricity increased from just 18 GWh in 2013 to 393 GWh in 2015. Accordingly, over the same period total electricity production (including output from thermal power plants) rose from 414 GWh in 2015 to 1,043 GWh in 2019. In 2019 the rate of access to electricity in the country was estimated at 66.6%, according to World Bank data.

TRANSPORT AND COMMUNICATIONS

The entire road network fell into disrepair after independence. In the late 1990s Equatorial Guinea embarked on a programme of nationwide road repairs, together with the rehabilitation of buildings and infrastructure in the main cities. International donors provided assistance for the upgrading of road access from the town of Mbini to Cogo, on the Gabonese border, much of which was impassable in the rainy season. Government-financed urban regeneration and infrastructure building intensified in the second half of the 2000s. In August 2006 an agreement was signed with China to build 2,000 km of roads throughout the country. By 2015 Equatorial Guinea had one of the best road networks in Africa, with 2,500 km of paved roads. Since 2010 a six-lane motorway has linked Malabo and the international airport to the new city of Sipopo, 16 km from Malabo. Sipopo was inaugurated in June 2011, in time to accommodate dignitaries attending that year's African Union summit. A bridge joining Mbini with Bolondo, south of Bata, was inaugurated in August 2012. Built by the Chinese firm China Road, and financed entirely by the Government of Equatorial Guinea, the bridge is reportedly the largest in Central Africa, at some 1,057 m in length. China financed a road linking Mongomo to Bata, while the EU supported an inter-state road linking Equatorial Guinea to Gabon and Cameroon. In addition, 'food for work' programmes have been introduced, in order to maintain the network of feeder roads. In December 2018 Equatorial Guinea and Cameroon agreed to build an 800-m bridge over the river Ntem, to be partially financed by the AfDB. The bridge would enable road links between the two countries, thereby facilitating an increase in trade. However, disagreements persist between the two countries as to the exact location of the bridge. In February 2022 the AfDB and the Equato-Guinean Government signed an agreement whereby the AfDB would finance the building of a road between the town of Acurenam and Minang, in Gabon, at a cost of US $150.7m. Equatorial Guinea has no railways.

Equatorial Guinea has two of the deepest seaports in the region, at Bata and Malabo. Bata, which is used by the timber companies, handles by far the largest volume of exports. Malabo has an excellent natural harbour, formed by a sunken volcanic crater. There are regular shipping services to Europe, but maritime communications between Malabo, Bata and Annobón remain erratic, and there is little maritime traffic with neighbouring countries. A new port to service the oil industry was built in Malabo in 2008 by the Dutch firm Pils. Also in 2008 a major new free port at Luba, on the south-west coast of Bioko, was inaugurated. The port was to handle much of Equatorial Guinea's petroleum production, and many of the petroleum companies operating in the country subsequently relocated there. The port also provides logistics and services to oil vessels. A new deep-water dock, capable of simultaneously handling several large cargo ships, was inaugurated in February 2009. In that year the Government announced its intention to double the capacity of the ports at Malabo and Bata. Work on the Malabo project was completed in 2011, at an estimated cost of US $2,000m.; the port was further expanded in 2015 to increase storage facilities and berths for additional vessels.

Malabo and Bata international airports have both been considerably expanded and improved since the 1990s, as part of the national infrastructure programme. In October 2012 the country's third international airport was inaugurated at Mongomo, in eastern Río Muni, the tribal stronghold of the Obiang clan. However, apart from serving the President's own family and entourage, it remains barely used. Another international airport was inaugurated at Oyala/Ciudad de la Paz in 2017, but this is also under-used. There are also five domestic airports. An airport and a seaport were inaugurated on Annobón in October 2010, built by the Moroccan company Somagec, at a cost of some €100m. The new seaport allowed access for larger cargo ships and passenger ferries, and it was hoped that it would open the island to trade.

Attempts to form a national airline have been beset by mismanagement and alleged corruption. Aerolíneas Guinea Ecuatorial, founded in 1982, had collapsed by 1985. Its successor, Ecuato Guineana de Aviación, established in 1986 as a partnership between the Government and Air Inter-Gabon, went into liquidation in 1990 after incurring heavy losses. Although the company continued to operate limited regional and domestic services, by 2021 it appeared to be defunct. There were some 20 small airlines in 2006, most operating domestic flights. In 2007 Ceiba Intercontinental Airlines was created as the national airline. It expanded its network of destinations to include 10 international routes, mostly in the region, but also to Madrid, Spain, in partnership with Iberia. However, in January 2018 Iberia ceased its flights to Equatorial Guinea, declaring them to be unprofitable. Air traffic has risen markedly since the mid-1990s as a result of the growth in the petroleum industry, with an increasing number of international airlines flying to the country.

Information and communications networks remain underdeveloped. Telephone lines, fixed and mobile, as well as internet services, are provided principally by Guinea Ecuatorial de Telecomunicaciones, jointly, until 2010, with Orange (formerly France Télécom), when Orange sold its shares and entered into a dispute with the Government of Equatorial Guinea (see *History*). Mobile telephone usage has continued to expand: by 2020, according to the UN's International Telecommunication Union, mobile subscribers numbered 645,000, while the number of fixed-line telephones was only 11,000. However, rates of internet access are among the lowest in the world.

In 2010 Equatorial Guinea signed a construction and maintenance agreement with the submarine cable consortium Africa Coast to Europe for a 7,000-km fibre-optic cable extending from France to South Africa. The cable, which was the first international submarine cable to reach Equatorial Guinea, became operational in December 2012 and has reportedly greatly improved the connectivity of the country to global telecommunications networks, as well as between its major cities, with consequent reductions in connection costs. The project was carried out by France Télécom Orange.

AID AND TRADE

Until the development of the petroleum sector, Equatorial Guinea's economy relied heavily on Spanish aid. In April 2004 Spain cancelled one-half of Equatorial Guinea's debt, estimated at €70m., and in December it waived a further US $17m. In February 2005 a Spanish aid package for Equatorial Guinea worth €24m. was announced. Since then, with the improvement in bilateral relations, Spanish commercial interests in Equatorial Guinea have increased considerably, and Spain continues to be a major donor—with annual funding of approximately €12m., primarily for education and health care. France (the second main provider of aid until the end of the 1990s), China, Cuba and the EU continue to provide varying levels of financial support, and have become more significant as trade partners.

The IMF supported several programmes in Equatorial Guinea in the 1980s and 1990s. However, there had been no formal agreement between the IMF and the Government of Equatorial Guinea between 1996 and 2019, although there were periodic consultations. In August 2001 the Government sought assistance from the IMF to restructure the economy, but negotiations broke down when the Government refused to comply with IMF demands for greater fiscal transparency, full disclosure of government bank accounts and external audits of the petroleum sector, on the grounds that the information was a state secret. The IMF has repeatedly emphasized the need for Equatorial Guinea to diversify its economy and establish greater fiscal discipline, accountability and transparency in the management of public sector resources, particularly regarding revenue from the energy sector. In June 2018 the IMF approved a Staff-Monitored Programme for Equatorial Guinea, and in December 2019 agreement was reached on a three-year credit arrangement of US $282.8m. to support the Government's efforts in economic diversification and sustainable growth. The main objectives of the programme were to reduce macroeconomic and fiscal imbalances, promote the development of human capital, and increase social protection, as well as to improve governance and the fight against corruption. The agreement was conditional on three key areas that the IMF considered essential for economic growth and

development: improved governance and transparency, thereby qualifying the country for EITI membership (however, the country's candidacy was cancelled in October 2020—see *History*), and effective measures against corruption. The Fund disbursed $40m. immediately on approval of the programme, with release of the remaining funds subject to six-month reviews and the implementation of reforms agreed with the IMF. No further tranches of funds were released, following the Government's lack of progress in combating corruption and improving transparency. The COVID-19 pandemic inevitably hindered progress in 2020, also delaying the first review of the programme. However, the programme has since been suspended pending reassessment, owing to the worsening economic outlook. At the Government's request, in September 2021 the IMF approved emergency aid to Equatorial Guinea of $67.3m. to address the aftermath of the military barracks explosion in Bata and the COVID-19 pandemic. Owing to endemic government corruption, the funds were transferred to a BEAC account from which they would only be disbursed on fulfilment of rigorous prerequisites in accordance with strict internal financial regulations.

Oil production has changed Equatorial Guinea's trade relations, and in recent years the country has forged strong commercial links with emerging economies such as Brazil, Russia and South Africa. In addition, Brazilian engineering companies have signed contracts worth $5m. for road building and services. Equatorial Guinea has also greatly strengthened its ties with China, which is increasingly involved in the oil and construction industries. In 2020 China constituted Equatorial Guinea's largest export market (accounting for 37.1% of the total) and also an important source of imports.

The role of China as an economic partner and provider of development aid has increased significantly during the early 21st century: by 2015 China had become the third largest investor in Equatorial Guinea. In 2001 China waived some of the country's debt and provided interest-free loans. In 2005 Equatorial Guinea declared China to be its main development partner; in that year China again cancelled a large part of the debt owed to it by Equatorial Guinea in exchange for a share in Equatorial Guinea's oil and construction industries. China remains very active in the construction industry, particularly in public works and infrastructure, and supplies most of the inputs and labour force required by the industry. Major projects have included the construction of the new city of Oyala/Ciudad de la Paz, at a cost of some US $14,400m. In 2016, according to the AfDB, bilateral trade between Equatorial Guinea and China amounted to 1,042m. francs CFA. China is also a major credit provider, and in 2006 it extended a $2,000m. non-concessional credit line to Equatorial Guinea to fund electrification projects and improvements to Bata harbour. By 2008 Equato-Guinean exports of oil to China had increased to 16% of the country's total petroleum exports. Thereafter China became the main market for Equatorial Guinea's crude petroleum and gas. During a state visit to China in April 2015, President Obiang Nguema signed agreements covering the areas of technology and telecommunications, infrastructure, and for the construction of hospitals and teacher-training facilities. An import/export credit line of $500m. was agreed, as well as bank credits worth $2,000m. to support Equatorial Guinea's construction projects. The President also signed agreements with China Machinery Engineering Corporation to carry out a feasibility study for a power plant in Cogo and electricity supply connections with neighbouring countries, and with Sinohydro to build a new hydroelectric plant on the Wele river.

After China, Equatorial Guinea's largest export markets in 2020 were Spain, Portugal and India. In that year the main sources of imports were Nigeria, Togo, Spain and the USA. Equatorial Guinea's exports consist predominantly of oil and gas, together with small quantities of cocoa and timber. The country is dependent upon imports, particularly of food (which represents about 10% of total imports), but also of agricultural inputs, machinery and other goods.

Within Africa, trade links are particularly strong with Morocco and Egypt, which are very active in the construction sector, and with Ghana. In May 2010 an agreement was signed with Ghana whereby Equatorial Guinea would provide 2m.

barrels of crude petroleum annually to the new refinery in the Ghanaian capital, Accra; the first consignment was exported in July of that year. Ghana was also to assist with revitalizing Equatorial Guinea's cocoa industry. Terms were revised in August 2013, when the two Governments agreed to co-operate in hydrocarbons exploration and in the maintenance of oil equipment, as well as in the production, storage, transport and commercialization of hydrocarbons. In addition, Equatorial Guinea was to provide technical assistance to the Ghana National Gas Company to enable the development of its gas resources. Equatorial Guinea has also sought to expand its commercial relations with West African countries, notably with Côte d'Ivoire, with which relations had been poor for some years. In November 2013 the two countries signed an agreement under which GEPetrol would supply oil to Côte d'Ivoire, replacing the Angolan state oil company, Sonangol. In May 2014 Equatorial Guinea signed an MOU with Côte d'Ivoire and Ghana to initiate discussions concerning the creation of a regional gas company.

Statistical Survey

Source (unless otherwise stated): Instituto Nacional de Estadística de Guinea Ecuatorial, 4th Floor, Edificio Anayak, Malabo II; tel. 222196724; internet www.inege.gq.

Area and Population

AREA, POPULATION AND DENSITY

Area (sq km)	28,051*
Río Muni	26,017
Bioko	2,017
Annobón	17
Population (census results)	
4 July 2001	1,014,999
20 June 2015 (preliminary)†	
Males	651,820
Females	570,622
Total	1,222,442
Population (UN estimates at mid-year)‡	
2020	1,402,985
2021§	1,449,891
2022§	1,496,673
Density (per sq km) at mid-2022§	53.4

* 10,831 sq miles.
† The final total population count was 1,225,377, but figures for males and females were not available.
‡ Source: UN, *World Population Prospects: The 2019 Revision*.
§ Projection.

POPULATION BY AGE AND SEX
('000, UN projections at mid-2022)

	Males	Females	Total
0–14 years	278.6	271.2	549.8
15–64 years	537.3	374.4	911.7
65 years and over	16.7	18.5	35.1
Total	832.6	664.0	1,496.7

Note: Totals may not be equal to the sum of components, owing to rounding.

Source: UN, *World Population Prospects: The 2019 Revision*.

PROVINCES
(population at census of 20 June 2015, preliminary)

	Area (sq km)	Population	Density (per sq km)
Annobón	17	5,232	307.8
Bioko Norte	776	299,836	386.4
Bioko Sur	1,241	34,627	27.9
Centro-Sur	9,931	141,903	14.3
Kié-Ntem	3,943	183,331	46.5
Litoral	6,665	366,130	54.9
Wele-Nzas	5,478	191,383	34.9
Total	28,051	1,222,442	43.6

Note: A law to create an eighth province, Djibloho (with an area of 453 sq km, formerly part of Wele-Nzas), was promulgated in June 2017.

Principal Towns (incl. suburbs, UN figures): Bata 454,940 at mid-2022 (projection); Malabo (capital) 296,770 at mid-2018 (estimate). Source: UN, *World Urbanization Prospects: The 2018 Revision*.

BIRTHS AND DEATHS
(annual averages, UN estimates)

	2005–10	2010–15	2015–20
Birth rate (per 1,000)	38.9	36.2	33.5
Death rate (per 1,000)	11.9	10.6	9.4

Source: UN, *World Population Prospects: The 2019 Revision*.

Live births (registrations): 8,673 in 2018; 7,477 in 2019; 9,918 in 2020.

Life expectancy (years at birth, estimates): 59.1 (males 58.1; females 60.3) in 2020 (Source: World Bank, World Development Indicators database).

ECONOMICALLY ACTIVE POPULATION
('000)

	2012	2013	2014
Agriculture, etc.	184	188	192
Total labour force (incl. others) .	380	392	404

Source: African Development Bank.

Mid-2015 ('000 persons, estimates): Agriculture, etc. 195; Total labour force 317 (Source: FAO).

Health and Welfare

KEY INDICATORS

Total fertility rate (children per woman, 2020)	4.3
Under-5 mortality rate (per 1,000 live births, 2020) . . .	78.5
HIV/AIDS (% of persons aged 15–49, 2020)	7.3
COVID-19: Cumulative confirmed deaths (per 100,000 persons at 31 August 2022)	11.2
COVID-19: Fully vaccinated population (% of total population at 24 July 2022)	13.1
Physicians (per 1,000 head, 2017)	0.4
Hospital beds (per 1,000 head, 2010)	2.1
Domestic health expenditure (2019): US $ per head (PPP) .	129.1
Domestic health expenditure (2019): % of GDP	0.7
Domestic health expenditure (2019): public (% of total current expenditure)	21.3
Access to improved water resources (% of persons, 2017) .	65
Access to improved sanitation facilities (% of persons, 2017) .	66
Total carbon dioxide emissions ('000 metric tons, 2018) . .	6,670
Carbon dioxide emissions per head (metric tons, 2018) . .	5.1
Human Development Index (2021): ranking	145
Human Development Index (2021): value	0.596

Note: For data on COVID-19 vaccinations, 'fully vaccinated' denotes receipt of all doses specified by approved vaccination regime (Sources: Johns Hopkins University and Our World in Data). Data on health expenditure refer to current general government expenditure in each case. For more information on sources and further definitions for all indicators, see Health and Welfare Statistics: Sources and Definitions section (europaworld.com/credits).

Agriculture

PRINCIPAL CROPS
('000 metric tons, FAO estimates)

	2018	2019	2020
Bananas	29.8	29.9	29.8
Cassava (Manioc)	73.0	73.1	73.0
Cocoa beans	1.0	1.0	1.0
Coconuts	7.7	7.8	7.7
Coffee, green	4.2	4.2	4.2
Oil palm fruit	36.3	36.4	36.5
Plantains and others . . .	40.8	40.3	40.5
Sweet potatoes	100.3	98.2	98.8

Aggregate production ('000 metric tons, may include official, semi-official or estimated data): Total fruit (primary) 70.6 in 2018, 70.2 in 2019, 70.3 in 2020; Total oilcrops 44.0 in 2018, 44.2 in 2019, 44.2 in 2020; Total roots and tubers 211.3 in 2018, 208.9 in 2019, 209.5 in 2020.

Source: FAO.

LIVESTOCK
('000 head, year ending September, FAO estimates)

	2018	2019	2020
Cattle	5.4	5.4	5.5
Chickens	374	378	374
Ducks	39	38	38
Goats	9.7	9.8	9.9
Pigs	7.1	7.1	7.1
Sheep	41.0	41.2	41.5

Source: FAO.

LIVESTOCK PRODUCTS
('000 metric tons, FAO estimates)

	2018	2019	2020
Chicken meat	0.3	0.3	0.3
Pig meat	0.2	0.2	0.2
Sheep meat	0.1	0.1	0.1
Hen eggs	0.2	0.2	0.3

Source: FAO.

Forestry

ROUNDWOOD REMOVALS
('000 cubic metres, FAO estimates)

	2016	2017	2018
Sawlogs, veneer logs and logs for sleepers	990	1,200	1,300
Fuel wood	447	447	447
Total	1,437	1,647	1,747

2019–20: Production assumed to be unchanged from 2018 (FAO estimates).

Source: FAO.

SAWNWOOD PRODUCTION
('000 cubic metres, FAO estimates)

	2018	2019	2020
Total (all broadleaved) . . .	15	45	45

Source: FAO.

Fishing

(metric tons, live weight, FAO estimates)

	2018	2019	2020
Capture	6,410	6,421	6,042
Freshwater fishes	1,000	1,000	900
Clupeoids	4,000	4,000	3,700
Marine fishes	453	453	453
Aquaculture	15	15	15
Total catch (incl. others) . . .	6,425	6,436	6,057

Source: FAO.

Mining

(estimates)

	2019	2020	2021
Crude petroleum ('000 metric tons)	7,395	7,382	6,432

2013 (million cu m): Natural gas 8,000.

Source: BP, *Statistical Review of World Energy*.

Industry

	2018	2019	2020
Veneer sheets ('000 cu m)*† . .	31.0	41.0	41.0
Palm oil*†	5.5	5.5	n.a.
Electrical energy (million kWh) .	1,024	1,043	1,081

* Source: FAO.
† Estimates.

Finance

CURRENCY AND EXCHANGE RATES

Monetary Units
100 centimes = 1 franc de la Communauté Financière Africaine (CFA).

Sterling, Dollar and Euro Equivalents (31 May 2022)
£1 sterling = 770.824 francs CFA;
US $1 = 612.300 francs CFA;
€1 = 655.957 francs CFA;
10,000 francs CFA = £12.97 = $16.33 = €15.24.

Average Exchange Rate (francs CFA per US $)
2019   585.911
2020   575.586
2021   554.531

Note: An exchange rate of 1 French franc = 50 francs CFA, established in 1948, remained in force until January 1994, when the CFA franc was devalued by 50%, with the exchange rate adjusted to 1 French franc = 100 francs CFA. This relationship to the French currency remained in effect with the introduction of the euro on 1 January 1999. From that date, accordingly, a fixed exchange rate of €1 = 655.957 francs CFA has been in operation.

BUDGET
('000 million francs CFA)

Revenue	2018	2019*	2020*
Resource revenue	1,178	984	611
Tax revenue	155	177	131
Other revenue	114	80	78
Total	1,447	1,240	820

Expenditure	2018	2019*	2020*
Current expenditure	761	771	726
Compensation of employees .	176	190	195
Purchase of goods and services .	346	370	322
Interest	48	57	76
Subsidies	192	154	133
Capital expenditure	647	347	194
Total	1,408	1,119	921

* Estimates.

Source: IMF, *Republic of Equatorial Guinea: Request for Purchase Under the Rapid Financing Instrument—Press Release; Staff Report; and Statement by the Executive Director* (September 2021).

2021 ('000 million francs CFA, budget projections): Total revenue 860 (Petroleum 612); Total expenditure 1,086.

2022 ('000 million francs CFA, budget projections): Total revenue 915 (Petroleum 647); Total expenditure 1,091.

INTERNATIONAL RESERVES
(excluding gold, US $ million at 31 December)

	2017	2018	2019
IMF special drawing rights . .	30.11	29.38	28.85
Reserve position in IMF . . .	7.01	6.85	6.83
Foreign exchange	8.38	12.70	5.13
Total	45.50	48.93	40.82

2020: IMF special drawing rights 29.91; Reserve position in IMF 7.11.

2021: IMF special drawing rights 28.61; Reserve position in IMF 6.91.

Source: IMF, *International Financial Statistics*.

MONEY SUPPLY
('000 million francs CFA at 31 December)

	2017	2018	2019
Currency outside depository corporations	175.58	171.96	183.27
Transferable deposits	527.05	512.70	444.77
Other deposits	199.01	210.60	202.32
Total money (incl. others) . .	901.64	895.25	830.36

Source: IMF, *International Financial Statistics*.

COST OF LIVING
(Consumer Price Index; base: 2006 = 100)

	2018	2019	2020
Food and non-alcoholic beverages .	142.4	143.0	149.6
Clothing and footwear	122.4	123.2	132.7
Housing, water, electricity, gas and other fuels	149.3	150.4	153.5
All items (incl. others) . . .	136.7	138.5	145.1

NATIONAL ACCOUNTS
(000' million francs CFA in current prices, preliminary)
Expenditure on the Gross Domestic Product

	2019	2020	2021
Government final consumption expenditure	1,683.5	1,688.8	1,718.3
Private final consumption expenditure	3,747.1	3,955.9	4,106.6
Gross fixed capital formation . .	523.2	310.3	261.0
Change in inventories	−7.4	−5.2	−3.6
Total domestic expenditure .	5,946.4	5,949.7	6,089.6
Exports of goods and services . .	3,532.5	2,499.2	3,757.7
Less Imports of goods and services	2,789.4	2,679.5	2,954.0
GDP in purchasers' values .	6,689.5	5,769.4	6,893.3

Gross Domestic Product by Economic Activity

	2019	2020	2021
Agriculture	162.6	172.8	179.1
Mining and quarrying	1,628.8	1,107.3	1,566.1
Manufacturing	1,554.4	1,191.7	1,779.0
Electricity, gas and water . . .	59.7	56.1	57.4
Construction	305.0	252.9	240.6
Trade, restaurants and hotels .	507.6	526.4	536.1
Finance, insurance and real estate	244.5	250.5	254.7
Transport and communication .	516.8	423.7	422.4
Public administration	1,550.9	1,623.2	1,660.9
Other services	146.5	159.0	166.6
Sub-total	6,676.8	5,763.6	6,862.9
Less Imputed bank service charge.	66.3	63.6	62.7
Indirect taxes	79.1	68.6	93.1
GDP in purchasers' values .	6,689.5	5,769.4	6,893.3

BALANCE OF PAYMENTS
('000 million francs CFA)

	2018	2019*	2020†
Exports of goods f.o.b.	3,046	2,477	1,605
Imports of goods f.o.b.	−1,284	−1,083	−820
Trade balance	1,762	1,394	785
Services (net)	−912	−737	−434
Balance on goods and services	850	657	351
Income (net)	−999	−866	−538
Balance on goods, services and income	−149	−209	−187
Current transfers (net) . . .	−233	−196	−178
Current balance	−382	−405	−365
Direct investment (net) . . .	310	240	155
Portfolio investment (net) . . .	−1	−1	−1
Other investment (net) . . .	99	−20	39
Net errors and omissions . . .	0	0	0
Overall balance	25	−186	−172

* Estimates.
† Projections.

Source: IMF, *Republic of Equatorial Guinea: Request for Purchase Under the Rapid Financing Instrument—Press Release; Staff Report; and Statement by the Executive Director* (September 2021).

External Trade

PRINCIPAL COMMODITIES
(million francs CFA)

Imports c.i.f.	2018	2019	2020
Meat and edible offal	28	29	25
Beverages, spirits and vinegar .	42	44	38
Mineral fuels, mineral oils . .	144	169	128
Articles of cast iron, iron or steel .	29	39	39
Machines, appliances and electrical equipment, ...	48	44	28
Machines, apparatus and mechanical devices, boilers; parts	86	147	74
Motor vehicles, tractors, cycles and other land vehicles, their parts and accessories	33	25	17
Ships and other floating artifacts .	63	31	214
Total (incl. others)	707	759	801

Exports f.o.b.	2018	2019	2020
Crude petroleum or bituminous mineral oils	2,306	2,065	1,617
Liquefied natural gas	756	487	n.a.
Methanol	239	198	n.a.
Wood, charcoal and articles of wood	187	108	52
Total (incl. others)	3,634	2,988	1,791

PRINCIPAL TRADING PARTNERS
(million francs CFA)

Imports c.i.f.	2018	2019	2020
China, People's Republic . . .	81	66	70
France	30	22	15
Italy	18	22	34
Netherlands	23	25	26
Nigeria	0	19	206
Singapore	47	3	2
Spain	116	111	109
Togo	137	162	126
Türkiye	17	12	22
United Kingdom	20	32	24
USA	77	126	84
Total (incl. others)	707	759	801

Exports f.o.b.	2018	2019	2020
Chile	107	28	55
China, People's Republic . . .	1,185	1,010	664
India	349	556	205
Italy	142	34	34
Korea, Republic	148	92	84
Netherlands	114	88	48
Portugal	356	116	225
Singapore	247	126	37
Spain	271	329	237
USA	337	205	84
Total (incl. others)	3,634	2,988	1,791

Transport

SHIPPING
(at 31 December)

	2019	2020	2021
Number of vessels	46	48	54
Total displacement (grt) . . .	51,350	52,902	65,016

Source: Lloyd's List Intelligence (www.bit.ly/LLintelligence).

CIVIL AVIATION
(domestic and international)

	2018	2019	2020
Departures	7,930	7,423	3,051
Passengers carried ('000) . . .	404	425	139
Freight carried ('000 ton-km) . .	0	0	3

Source: World Bank, World Development Indicators database.

Communications Media

	2018	2019	2020
Telephones ('000 main lines in use)	10.8	11.0	11.0
Mobile telephone subscriptions ('000)	591.2	617.0	645.0
Broadband subscriptions, fixed ('000)	1.6	1.0	1.0
Broadband subscriptions, mobile ('000)	1.8	8.0	8.0

Internet users (% of population): 23.8 in 2016; 26.2 in 2017.

Source: International Telecommunication Union.

Education

(2018/19)

	Institutions	Teachers	Students ('000)		
			Males	Females	Total
Pre-primary . .	984	2,904	26,001	25,806	51,807
Primary . . .	936	5,222	60,253	57,751	118,004
Secondary . .	232	3,215	26,734	26,917	53,651
Higher . . .	70	845	2,226	3,868	6,094

Pupil-teacher Ratio (qualified teaching staff, primary education, UNESCO estimate): 38.0 in 2014/15 (Source: UNESCO Institute for Statistics).

Adult Literacy Rate (UNESCO estimates): 95.2% (males 97.3%; females 92.9%) in 2015 (Source: UNESCO Institute for Statistics).

Directory

The Constitution

The present Constitution was approved by a national referendum on 16 November 1991 and amended in January 1995. It provided for the introduction of a plural political system. Further amendments to the Constitution were endorsed at a national referendum held on 13 November 2011. These included the limitation of the President's tenure of office to two seven-year terms, while the upper age limit for presidential candidates, previously set at 75 years, was withdrawn. The amendments also established the post of Vice-President, who was to be appointed by the President and who was required to be a member of the ruling Partido Democrático de Guinea Ecuatorial, and five other institutions—the Senate, the Audit Court, the State Council, the Economic and Social Council and the Council for the Defence of the People. The amended Constitution was promulgated on 16 February 2012. The President is immune from prosecution for offences committed before, during or after his or her tenure of the post. The bicameral legislature—comprising the 100-member Chamber of Deputies (known until 2013 as the House of Representatives) and the 70-member Senate—serves for a term of five years. Both the President and the Chamber of Deputies are directly elected by universal adult suffrage. The Senate is composed of 55 directly elected senators and 15 senators nominated by the President. The President appoints a Council of Ministers from among the members of the Chamber of Deputies, and heads the Government.

The Government

HEAD OF STATE

President and Supreme Commander of the Armed Forces: Gen. (retd) OBIANG NGUEMA MBASOGO (assumed office 25 August 1979; elected President 25 June 1989; re-elected 25 February 1996, 15 December 2002, 29 November 2009 and 24 April 2016).

COUNCIL OF MINISTERS
(October 2022)

President: Gen. (retd) OBIANG NGUEMA MBASOGO.

Vice-President: Col TEODORO (TEODORÍN) NGUEMA OBIANG MANGUE.

Prime Minister, in charge of Administrative Co-ordination: FRANCISCO-PASCUAL OBAMA ASUE.

First Deputy Prime Minister and Minister of Education, Universities and Sport: CLEMENTE ENGONGA NGUEMA ONGUENE.

Second Deputy Prime Minister, in charge of Relations with Parliament and Legal Affairs: ANGEL MESIE MIBUY.

Third Deputy Prime Minister, in charge of Human Rights: ALFONSO NSUY MOKUY.

Minister of State at the Presidency of the Republic, in charge of Missions: ALEJANDRO EVUNA OWONO ASANGONO.

Minister of State at the Presidency of the Republic, in charge of Regional Integration: BALTASAR ENGONGA EDJO.

Minister of State, in charge of National Security: NICOLÁS OBAMA NCHAMA.

Minister of State of the Interior and Local Government: FAUSTINO NDONG ESONO AYANG.

Minister at the Presidency of the Republic, in charge of External Security: JUAN ANTONIO BIBANG NCHUCHUMA.

Minister and Secretary-General of the Government: BALTASAR ESONO OWORO NFONO.

Minister of Health and Social Wellbeing: DIOSDADO VICENTE NSUE MILANG.

Minister of Foreign Affairs and Co-operation: SIMEÓN OYONO ESONO ANGUE.

Minister of Justice, Religion and Penitentiary Institutions: SALVADOR ONDO NCUMU.

Minister of National Defence: VICTORIANO BIBANG NSUE OKOMO.

Minister of Finance, the Economy and Planning: VALENTÍN ELA MAYE.

Minister of Public Works, Housing and Town Planning: CLEMENTE FERREIRO VILLARINO.

Minister of Labour, the Promotion of Employment and Social Security: ALFREDO MITOGO MITOGO ADA.

Minister of Agriculture, Livestock, Forests and Environment: FRANCISCA ENEME EFUA.

Minister of Fisheries and Water Resources: ADORACIÓN SALAS CHONCO.

Minister of Mines and Hydrocarbons: GABRIEL MBEGA OBIANG LIMA.

Minister of Industry and Energy: MIGUEL EKUA ONDO.

Minister of Information, the Press and Radio: VIRGILIO SERICHE RILOHA.

Minister of Social Affairs and Gender Equality: MARIA CONSUELO NGUEMA OYANA.

Minister of Transport, Postal Services and Telecommunications: RUFINO OVONO ONDO.

Minister of the Civil Service and Administrative Reform: EUCARIO BACALE ANGUE.

Minister of Trade and the Promotion of Small and Medium-sized Enterprises: PASTOR MICHA ONDO BILE.

Minister of Civil Aviation: NORBERTO-BARTOLOME MENSUY MAÑE ANDEME.

Minister of Culture, Tourism and the Promotion of Handicrafts: RUFINO NDONG ESONO NCHAMA.

In addition, there were seven ministers-delegate, 16 deputy ministers and 18 secretaries of state.

MINISTRIES

Office of the President: Malabo.

Ministry of Agriculture, Livestock, Forests and Environment: Apdo 504, Malabo.

Minister of Civil Aviation: Malabo.

Ministry of the Civil Service and Administrative Reform: Malabo; e-mail info.funcion_publica@gob.gq; internet minfuncionpublica.gob.gq.

Ministry of Culture, Tourism and the Promotion of Handicrafts: Malabo; e-mail infocultur@gob.gq; internet mincultur.gob.gq.

Ministry of Education, Universities and Sport: Malabo.

Ministry of Finance, the Economy and Planning: Malabo; tel. 333333333; e-mail info@minhacienda-gob.com; internet minhacienda-gob.com.

Ministry of Fisheries and Water Resources: Malabo.

Ministry of Foreign Affairs and Co-operation: Zona Ministerial, Malabo; tel. 222501405; e-mail info.maec@gob.gq; internet minexteriores.gob.gq.

Ministry of Health and Social Wellbeing: Malabo; internet guineasalud.org.

Ministry of Industry and Energy: Zona Ministerial, Malabo; e-mail info@minindustria.gob.gq; internet minindustria.gob.gq.

Ministry of Information, the Press and Radio: Malabo.

Ministry of the Interior and Local Government: Malabo.

Ministry of Justice, Religion and Penitentiary Institutions: Apdo 459, Malabo.

Ministry of Labour, the Promotion of Employment and Social Security: Malabo; tel. 333092979; e-mail info@mtfessge.com; internet mtfess.gob.gq.

Ministry of Mines and Hydrocarbons: Calle 12 de Octubre s/n, Malabo; tel. 222271741; internet mmie.gob.gq.

Ministry of National Defence: Malabo; tel. 333092794.

Ministry of National Security: Malabo; tel. 333093469.

Ministry of Public Works, Housing and Town Planning: Malabo.

Ministry of Social Affairs and Gender Equality: Malabo; tel. 333000000; e-mail info@minasig.gob.gq; internet minasig.gob.gq.

Ministry of Trade and the Promotion of Small and Medium-sized Enterprises: Apdo 404, Malabo; tel. 333093105.

Ministry of Transport, Postal Services and Telecommunications: Carretera de Aeropuerto, Malabo; e-mail mintct@gob.gq; internet mintct.gob.gq.

President

Presidential Election, 24 April 2016

Candidate	Votes	% of votes
Obiang Nguema Mbasogo (PDGE) .	271,177	93.53
Avelino Mocache Benga (UCD) . .	4,556	1.57
Bonaventura Monsuy Asumu (PCSD)	4,417	1.52
Benedicto Obiang Mangue (Ind.) .	2,802	0.97
Carmelo Mba Bacale (APGE) . .	2,415	0.83
Agustín Masoko Abegue (Ind.) . .	2,412	0.83
Tomás Mba Monabang (Ind.) . .	2,154	0.74
Total	**289,933***	**100.00**

* Excluding 7,032 invalid votes and 4,832 blank votes.

Legislature

CHAMBER OF DEPUTIES
(Cámara de los Diputados)

Chamber of Deputies: Malabo.

President: GAUDENCIO MOHABA MESU.

General Election, 12 November 2017

Party	Seats
Partido Democrático de Guinea Ecuatorial (PDGE) .	99
Ciudadanos por la Innovación (CI)	1
Total	**100**

SENATE
(Senado)

Senate: Malabo.

President: TERESA EFUA ASANGONO.

General Election, 12 November 2017

Party	Seats
Partido Democrático de Guinea Ecuatorial (PDGE) .	55
Total	**55***

* An additional 15 senators are nominated by the President of the Republic.

Election Commission

Junta Electoral Nacional: Malabo; Pres. CLEMENTE ENGONGA NGUEMA ONGUENE.

Political Organizations

Acción Popular de Guinea Ecuatorial (APGE): pro-Govt party; Pres. EDUARDO MBA BACALE; Sec.-Gen. MIGUEL ESONO.

Alianza Nacional para la Restauración Democrática de Guinea Ecuatorial (ANRD): 95 Ruperto Chapi, 28100 Madrid, Spain; tel. (91) 623-88-64; f. 1974; Sec.-Gen. LUIS ONDO AYANG.

Ciudadanos por la Innovación (CI): Malabo; e-mail ci@candidaturaindependiente-guineaecuatorial.com; internet candidaturaindependiente-guineaecuatorial.com; fmrly known as

Candidatura Independiente; legalized in 2015, banned in 2018; Leader GABRIEL NSÉ OBIANG OBONO.

Convención Liberal Democrática (CLD): pro-Govt party; Pres. ALFONSO NSUE MOKUY.

Convención Socialdemocrática Popular (CSDP): pro-Govt party; Leader DEOGRACIAS KUNG NSUE.

Convergencia para la Democracia Social (CPDS): Calle Tres de Agosto 72, 2°, 1 Malabo; tel. 333092013; e-mail cpdsge@hotmail.com; internet www.cpdsge.org; f. 1990; Pres. SANTIAGO OBAMA NDONG; Sec.-Gen. ANDRÉS ESONO ONDO.

Movimiento para la Autodeterminación de la Isla de Bioko (MAIB): f. 1993 by Bubi interests seeking independence of Bioko; clandestine; Gen. Co-ordinator WEJA CHICAMPO.

Partido de la Convergencia Social Demócrata (PCSD): pro-Govt party; Pres. BUENAVENTURA MONSUY ASUMU.

Partido Democrático de Guinea Ecuatorial (PDGE): Malabo; e-mail prensapdge@gmail.com; internet www.pdge -guineaecuatorial.com; f. 1987; sole legal party 1987–92; Chair. Gen. (retd) OBIANG NGUEMA MBASOGO; Sec.-Gen. JERÓNIMO OSA OSA ECORO.

Partido del Progreso de Guinea Ecuatorial (PPGE): Madrid, Spain; internet www.partidodelprogreso.org; f. 1983; Pres. ARMENGOL ENGONGA ONDÓ (acting); Sec. GABRIEL MOTO NSÁ.

Partido Socialista de Guinea Ecuatorial (PSGE): pro-Govt party; Sec.-Gen. TOMÁS MECHEBA FERNÁNDEZ-GALILEA.

Unión de Centro Derecha (UCD): f. 2001; legalized 2015; Pres. AVELINO MOKACHE MEHENGA.

Unión para la Democracia y el Desarrollo Social (UDDS): e-mail uddsguineaecuatorial@yahoo.es; f. 1990; Sec.-Gen. AQUILINO NGUEMA ONA NCHAMA; in Cameroon.

Unión Democrática Nacional (UDENA): Leader DEOGRACIAS BUERIBERI EDU NSANG.

Unión Democrática y Social de Guinea Ecuatorial (UDS): pro-Govt party; Sec.-Gen. MIGUEL MBA NSANG.

Unión Popular (UP): f. 1988; conservative; Pres. CELESTINO NVO OKENVE NDO; Sec.-Gen ALFREDO MITOGO MITOGO ADA.

Diplomatic Representation

EMBASSIES IN EQUATORIAL GUINEA

Angola: Malabo; Ambassador ANTÓNIO MANUEL LUVUALU DE CARVALHO.

Benin: 300 Calle de Enrique Nvó, Malabo; tel. 222575766; Ambassador COLLETE ADJOVI.

Brazil: Parque de las Avenidas de Africa, Caracolas, Malabo; tel. 333099986; e-mail brasemb.malabo@itamaraty.gov.br; internet www.gov.br/mre/pt-br/embaixada-malabo; Ambassador EVALDO FREIRE.

Cameroon: 37 Calle Rey Boncoro, Apdo 292, Malabo; tel. 333002263; e-mail lamebala@hotmail.fr; Ambassador DÉSIRÉ JEAN CLAUDE OWONO MENGUELE.

Central African Republic: Santa Marie 2, Malabo; tel. 555958818; internet ambarca-malabo.org; Ambassador CHRISTELLE SAPPOT.

Chad: Caracolas, Malabo; tel. 222586870; Ambassador OUTMAN DJIDDA MOUSSA.

China, People's Republic: Carretera del Aeropuerto, Apdo 44, Malabo; tel. 333093505; e-mail chinaemb_gq@mfa.gov.cn; internet gq.china-embassy.gov.cn; Ambassador QI MEI.

Congo, Republic: Carretera Paraiso, BP 110, Malabo; e-mail ambacomalabo1803@gmail.com; Ambassador MARTINE RENÈE GALLOY.

Côte d'Ivoire: Av. Hassan II, N°1353, Apdo 221, Malabo; tel. 666597679; e-mail dorotheeackah@yahoo.fr; Ambassador (vacant).

Cuba: Barrio Paraiso, Malabo; tel. 333090975; e-mail consul@gq .embacuba.cu; internet misiones.minrex.gob.cu/es/guinea -ecuatorial; Ambassador ZAID MALLULY DÍAZ MEDINA.

Egypt: Caracolas, in front of Bahiaa II Hotel, Malabo; tel. 555537742; e-mail embassy.malabo@mfa.gov.eg; Ambassador HADAD ABDELGOHARY.

France: Carretera del Aeropuerto, Apdo 326, Malabo; tel. 333092005; e-mail chancellerie.malabo-amba@diplomatie.gouv.fr; internet gq.ambafrance.org; Ambassador LAURENT POLONCEAUX (designate).

Gabon: Carretera Paraiso, Calle de Argelia, Apdo 18, Malabo; tel. 333093180; e-mail ambagabonmalabo@yahoo.fr; Ambassador (vacant).

Germany: Edificio Venus, 4° Piso, Carretera del Aeropuerto, Km 4, Apdo 321, Malabo; tel. 333093117; e-mail info@malabo.diplo.de; internet malabo.diplo.de; Ambassador RALPH TIMMERMANN.

Ghana: BP 289, Caracolas, Malabo; tel. 33398909; Ambassador PERPETUA JOYCE NAANA DONTOH.

Guinea: Parque de las Avenidas de Africa, Caracolas, Malabo; tel. 333099242; e-mail ambaguimalabo@mae.gov.gn; Ambassador AMADOU TIANY DOUMBOUYA.

India: Villa Bico, Malabo; e-mail 222410618; internet www .eoimalabo.gov.in; Ambassador (vacant).

Korea, Democratic People's Republic: Malabo; tel. 333092047; Ambassador TONG CHOL HO.

Korea, Republic: Villa 14, Hotel 3 de Agosto, Avda Hassan II, Malabo; tel. 333090775; e-mail malabo@mofa.go.kr; internet overseas.mofa.go.kr/gq-ko/index.do; Ambassador RYU CHANG-SOO.

Mali: Calle Rey Malabo Vivienda 16, Caydasa, BP 567, Malabo; tel. 222272584; e-mail consmalimalabo@yahoo.fr; Ambassador FIDELE DIARRA.

Morocco: Avda Enrique Nvo, Apdo 329, Malabo; tel. 333092650; Ambassador GHALLAM MICHANE.

Nigeria: 4 Paseo de los Cocoteros, Apdo 78, Malabo; tel. 333093385; e-mail nigeria.malabo@foreignaffairs.gov.ng; Ambassador STEVE AGBANA EKPEBIKE.

São Tomé and Príncipe: Parque de las Avenidas de Africa, Malabo; tel. 333095717; e-mail embrdstpmalabo@hotmail.com; Ambassador ÁNGELA DOS SANTOS RAMOS JOSÉ DA COSTA PINHEIRO.

South Africa: Parque de las Avenidas de Africa s/n, Apdo 5, Malabo; tel. 333099522; e-mail malabo@dirco.gov.za; internet www.dirco.gov .za/malabo; Ambassador EPHRAIM LUNGILE DANTJIE.

Spain: Carretera del Aeropuerto s/n, Malabo; tel. 333092020; e-mail emb.malabo@maec.es; internet www.exteriores.gob.es/embajadas/ malabo; Ambassador ALFONSO BARNUEVO SEBASTIÁN DE ERICE.

Türkiye (Turkey): KM 5, Malabo II; tel. 555114494; e-mail embajada.malabo@mfa.gov.tr; internet malabo.be.mfa.gov.tr; Ambassador ADNAN KEÇECI (designate).

USA: K-3, Carretera del Aeropuerto, Malabo; tel. 333095741; e-mail malabopublic@state.gov; internet gq.usembassy.gov; Ambassador DAVID R. GILMOUR.

Venezuela: Santa María III, A500 Metros de la Nueva Sede de RTVGE, Malabo; tel. 333040090; e-mail embavenezuelage@yahoo .com; Ambassador NELSON JAVIER ORTEGA BONILLA.

Judicial System

The Supreme Court of Justice and the Constitutional Court sit in Malabo. The Supreme Court has four chambers (Civil and Social, Penal, Administrative and Common) and consists of a President and 12 magistrates, from whom the President of each chamber is selected. Provincial courts have been created in all provinces to replace the former courts of appeal. At present they are functional only in Malabo and Bata. Courts of first instance sit in Malabo and Bata, and may be convened in the other provincial capitals. Local courts may be convened when necessary.

Supreme Court of Justice (Corte Suprema de Justicia): Malabo; Pres. FRANCISCO EVUY NGUEMA MIKUE.

Constitutional Court (Tribunal Constitucional): Malabo; Pres. FERMÍN NGUEMA ESONO.

Attorney-General: ANATOLIO NZANG NGUEMA.

Religion

More than 90% of the population are Christian, predominantly adherents of the Roman Catholic Church, although traditional forms of worship are also followed and there is a small Muslim minority.

CHRISTIANITY

The Roman Catholic Church

Equatorial Guinea comprises one archdiocese and four dioceses.

Bishops' Conference: Arzobispado, Apdo 106, Malabo; tel. 333092909; e-mail arzobispadomalabo@hotmail.com; f. 1984; Pres. Most Rev. JUAN NSUE EDJANG MAYÉ (Archbishop of Malabo).

Archbishop of Malabo: Most Rev. JUAN NSUE EDJANG MAYÉ, Arzobispado, Apdo 106, Malabo; tel. 333092660; e-mail arzobispadomalabo@hotmail.com.

Protestant Church

Iglesia Reformada Evangélica de Guinea Ecuatorial (Evangelical Reformed Church of Equatorial Guinea): Apdo 195, Malabo; f. 1960; c. 8,000 mems; Sec.-Gen. Pastor JUAN EBANG ELA.

The Press

Atanga: Carretera del Aeropuerto, Km 0, Malabo; tel. 333092186; e-mail info.cc.malabo@aecid.es; 6 a year; Spanish; cultural review; publ. by the Centro Cultural de España en Malabo; Dir ÁLVARO ORTEGA SANTOS.

Ebano: Malabo; f. 1940; weekly; govt-controlled.

El Correo Deportivo: Malabo; tel. 222259223; e-mail lagacetademalabo@gmail.com; monthly; Dir ROBERTO MARTÍN PRIETO.

El Lector: Malabo; f. 2011; fortnightly; Dir ANTONIO NSUE ADÁ.

La Gaceta: Malabo; tel. 222259223; e-mail info@lagacetadeguinea.com; f. 1996; monthly; Dir YAMILA IZQUIERDO BRETONES.

La Verdad: Talleres Gráficos de Convergencia para la Democracia Social, Calle Tres de Agosto 72, Apdo 441, Malabo; 5 per year; publ. by the Convergencia para la Democracia Social; Editor PLÁCIDO MICÓ ABOGO.

Poto-poto: Bata; f. 1940; weekly; govt-controlled.

Voz del Pueblo: Malabo; publ. by the Partido Democrático de Guinea Ecuatorial.

PRESS ASSOCIATIONS

Asociación para la Libertad de Prensa y de Expresión en Guinea Ecuatorial (ASOLPEGE Libre): Calle Isla Cabrera 3, 5°, 46026 Valencia, Spain; tel. (660) 930629; f. 2006; Pres. PEDRO NOLASCO NDONG OBAMA.

Asociación de Periodistas Profesionales de Guinea Ecuatorial: Malabo; f. 2007 by former Secretary of State for Information, Santiago Ngua.

Publisher

Centro Cultural de España en Malabo: Carretera del Aeropuerto, Km 0, Malabo; tel. 333092186; e-mail info.cc.malabo@aecid.es; internet ccemalabo.es; f. 2003; owned by the Agencia Española de Cooperación Internacional para el Desarrollo; Dir ALVARO ORTEGA SANTOS.

Broadcasting and Communications

TELECOMMUNICATIONS

Guinea Ecuatorial de Comunicación Sociedad Anónima (GECOMSA): Edif. Torres Gemelas, Caracolas, Malabo; tel. 666800961; e-mail info@gecomsa.net; internet fb.com/GECOMSA; f. 2011; Dir-Gen. MARÍA DEL MAR BINDANG.

Guinea Ecuatorial de Telecomunicaciones, SA (GETESA): Calle Rey Boncoro 219, Apdo 494, Malabo; tel. 333099975; internet getesa.gq; f. 1987; Dir-Gen. CARLOS ESONO MIKO NSING.

MUNI SA: Malabo; tel. 350090999; e-mail info@muni-eg.com; internet www.muni-eg.com; subsidiary of Aan Digital Services (Kuwait); mobile telecommunications.

Regulatory Authority

Oficina Reguladora de las Telecomunicaciones (ORTEL): Malabo; tel. 555797404; e-mail info@ortelge.gq; internet fb.com/ortelguineaecuatorial; Dir-Gen. CÁNDIDO MUATETEMA BAITA.

RADIO

Radio Nacional de Guinea Ecuatorial: Apdo 749, Barrio Comandachina, Bata; Apdo 195, Avda 30 de Agosto 90, Malabo; tel. 333092260; govt-controlled; commercial station; programmes in Spanish, French and vernacular languages; Dir (Bata) SEBASTIÁN ELÓ ASEKO; Dir (Malabo) JUAN EYENE OPKUA NGUEMA.

Radio Televisión Asonga: Bata and Malabo; private; owned by Teodorín Nguema Obiang Mangue.

TELEVISION

Televisión de Guinea Ecuatorial (TVGE): Malabo; internet tvgelive.gq; Dir ERNESTO MFUMU MIKO.

Finance

BANKING

Central Bank

Banque des Etats de l'Afrique Centrale (BEAC): POB 501, Malabo; tel. 333092010; e-mail beacmal@beac.int; internet www.beac.int; HQ in Yaoundé, Cameroon; agency also in Bata; f. 1973; bank of issue for mem. states of the Communauté Economique et Monétaire de l'Afrique Centrale (CEMAC, fmrly Union Douanière et Economique de l'Afrique Centrale), comprising Cameroon, the Central African Repub., Chad, the Repub. of the Congo, Equatorial Guinea and Gabon; Gov. ABBAS MAHAMAT TOLLI; Dir in Equatorial Guinea GENEVOVA ANDEME OBIANG.

Commercial Banks

Banco Nacional de Guinea Ecuatorial (BANGE): Avda de la Independencia, Apdo 430, Malabo; tel. 222318011; e-mail atencionalcliente@bannge.com; internet www.bannge.com; f. 2005; Dir-Gen. MANUEL OSA NSUE.

BGFIBANK Guinea Ecuatorial: Carretera de Luba, Apdo 749, Malabo; tel. 333096352; e-mail Eqc.ge@bgfi.com; internet guineeequatoriale.groupebgfibank.com; 55% owned by BGFIBANK, 35% owned by private shareholders, 10% state-owned; Chair. HENRI CLAUDE OYIMA; Dir-Gen. CHRISTOPHE MOUNGUENGUI.

Caisse Commune d'Epargne et d'Investissement Bank Guinea Ecuatorial (CCEI-GE): Calle del Presidente Nasser, Apdo 428, Malabo; tel. 333092203; e-mail contact@cceibank.com; internet www.cceibankge.com; 51% owned by Afriland First Bank (Cameroon); f. 1995; Pres. BÁLTASAR ENGONGA EDJO'O; Dir-Gen. JOSEPH CÉLESTIN TINDJOU DJAMENI.

Ecobank: Avda de la Independencia, Apdo 268, Malabo; tel. 333098271; e-mail ecobankenquiries@ecobank.com; internet www.ecobank.com; Pres. EVELYNE TALL; Dir-Gen. ADAMA SENE CISSE.

Société Générale de Banques en Guinée Equatoriale (SGBGE): Avda de la Independencia, Apdo 686, Malabo; tel. 333093337; internet societegenerale.gq; f. 1986; present name adopted 1998; 57.24% owned by Société Générale SA (France), 31.80% state-owned, 10.96% owned by local investors; Man. Dir JOSE REBOLLAR.

Development Bank

Banque de Développement des Etats de l'Afrique Centrale: see Franc Zone.

INSURANCE

Equatorial Guinean Insurance Company, SA (EGICO): Avda de la Libertad, Apdo 272, Malabo; tel. 333093578; state-owned.

Trade and Industry

GOVERNMENT AGENCIES

Cámaras Oficiales Agrícolas de Guinea: Bioko and Bata; purchase of cocoa and coffee from indigenous planters, who are partially grouped in co-operatives.

Empresa General de Industria y Comercio (EGISCA): Malabo; f. 1986; parastatal body jtly operated with the French Société pour l'Organisation, l'Aménagement et le Développement des Industries Alimentaires et Agricoles (SOMDIA); import-export agency.

DEVELOPMENT ORGANIZATIONS

Agencia Española de Cooperación Internacional para el Desarrollo (AECID): Carretera del Aeropuerto, Malabo; tel. 333091621; internet www.aecid.es.

Asociación Hijos de Lommbe (A Vonna va Lommbe): Malabo; f. 2000; agricultural devt org.

Camasa: Finca Sampaka, Km 7 Camino a Luba, Malabo; tel. 333098692; e-mail casamallo@hotmail.com; internet www.fincasampaka.com; f. 1906; agricultural devt on Bioko island; operates projects for the cultivation and export of cocoa, pineapple, coffee, vanilla, nutmeg, peppers and tropical flowers.

Centro de Estudios e Iniciativas para el Desarrollo de Guinea Ecuatorial (CEIDIGE): Malabo; internet www.eurosur.org/CEIDGE; umbrella group of devt NGOs; Pres. JOSÉ ANTONIO NSANG ANDEME.

Family Care Guinea Ecuatorial (FGCE): Malabo; f. 2000; health and education devt; Dir LAUREN TAYLOR STEVENSON.

Instituto Nacional de Promoción Agropecuaria (INPAGE): Malabo; govt agricultural devt agency; reorg. 2000; Nat. Dir BENJAMÍN CAEFA MALABO.

Sociedad Anónima de Desarrollo del Comercio (SOADECO–Guinée): Malabo; f. 1986; parastatal body jtly operated with the French Société pour l'Organisation, l'Aménagement et le Développement des Industries Alimentaires et Agricoles (SOMDIA); devt of commerce.

Sociedad Nacional de Pesca Marítima de Guinea Ecuatorial (SONAPESCA): Apdo 295, Malabo; tel. 666178088; internet www .sonapesca.com; established to promote commercialization of the fisheries sector; under Ministry of Fisheries and Water Resources; office in Bata; Pres. GABRIEL MBA BELA; Dir-Gen. ELÍAS ONDO EDJO.

CHAMBER OF COMMERCE

Cámara Oficial de Comercio, Agrícola y Forestal de Bioko: Avda de la Independencia 43, Apdo 51, Malabo; tel. 333094576; internet www.camarabioko.com; Pres. ÁNGEL NOKONOKO NIKOSO.

INDUSTRIAL AND TRADE ASSOCIATIONS

INPROCAO: Malabo; production, marketing and distribution of cocoa.

Unión General de Empresas Privadas de la República de Guinea Ecuatorial (UGEPRIGE): Apdo 138, Malabo; tel. 222278326.

UTILITIES

Electricity

Sociedad de Electricidad de Guinea Ecuatorial (SEGESA): Carretera de Luba, Apdo 139, Malabo; tel. 333093466; holding co; owns SEGESA Commercial, SEGESA Transmisión and SEGESA Generación; Dir-Gen. JUAN LUPERCIO NSIBI OMOGO.

MAJOR COMPANIES

Atlantic Methanol Production Co (AMPCO): Malabo; tel. 333090166; internet www.atlanticmethanol.com; f. 2001; methanol production; Chair. NATHANIAL SCOTT; Pres. and Gen. Man. PAUL MOSCHELL.

ECOCSA: Avda Asonga, Ngolo s/n, Bata, Litoral; e-mail office@ecocsa-ge.com; internet ecocsa-ge.com; construction.

Ecuatoguineana Trading Co (EGTC): EGTC Groupe, BP 269, Bata; tel. 333082956; e-mail egtc@egtc.com; internet egtc.com; multi-line importer and retailer of fast-moving consumer products.

Efusilia: Malabo; owned by Armengol Ondo Nguema, President Obiang Nguema's brother.

Equatorial Guinea LNG Holdings Ltd: Malabo; internet www .eglng.com; Man. Dir CURTIS RYLAND.

Expertos Asociados S.L.: Malabo; tel. 222248488; e-mail sales@expertosasociados.com; internet www.expertosasociados.com.

Grupo Abayak: Km 3, Carretera al Aeropuerto Internacional, Malabo; tel. 222230907; owned by President Obiang Nguema's family.

Guinea Ecuatorial de Petróleo (GEPetrol): Calle Acacio Mane 39, BP 965, Malabo; tel. 333096769; e-mail laamaye@hotmail.com; internet equatorialoil-lng.com; f. 2001; state-owned petroleum company; Dir-Gen. ANTONIO OBURU ONDO.

Mobil Equatorial Guinea Inc (MEGI): Complejo Residencial Abajak, Malabo; oil producer; majority owned by ExxonMobil.

Ortrun Equatorial Guinea: Malabo; tel. 333096098; consultancy and translation services; Man. Dir MARIA NCHANA.

Shimmer International: Bata; controls 90% of wood production in Río Muni.

Sociedad Equatoguineana de Bebidas (SOEGUIBE): Apdo 554, Bata; tel. 222954220; e-mail soeguibe@soeguibe.com; internet soeguibe.com; production and bottling of various brands of beer, water and soft drinks; Dir-Gen. (vacant).

Sociedad Nacional de Gas de Guinea Ecuatorial (SONAGAS, G.E.): Autovia Malabo II, Malabo; tel. 222132282; e-mail contacto@sonagas-ge.com; internet sonagas-ge.com; f. 2005; oversees gas exploration and devt; Dir-Gen. JUAN ANTONIO NDONG.

Sociedad Nacional de Vigilancia (SONAVI): Malabo; owned by Armengol Ondó Nguema.

Steel Proyect: Malabo; tel. 555404893; e-mail info@steelproyectsl .com; internet steelproyectsl.com; Dir-Gen. DIAMANTINO ASUMU.

TotalEnergies Guinea Ecuatorial: Apdo 647, Malabo; internet totalenergies.gq; f. 1984; fmrly GE—Total, subsequently Total Guinea Ecuatorial; name changed as above in 2021; owned by Total (France); petroleum marketing and distribution; Dir-Gen. PHILIPPE PRUDENT.

TRADE UNIONS

A law permitting the establishment of trade unions was introduced in 1992. However, trade unions have not been granted authorization to operate.

Transport

RAILWAYS

There are no railways in Equatorial Guinea.

ROADS

Bioko: a semi-circular tarred road serves the northern part of the island from Malabo down to Batete in the west and from Malabo to Basacato Grande in the east, with a feeder road from Luba to Moka and Bahía de la Concepción. Since 2010 a six-lane motorway has linked Malabo and the international airport to the new city of Sipopo, 16 km from the capital.

Río Muni: a tarred road links Bata with the nearby town of Mbini in the south; another tarred road links Bata with the frontier post of Ebebiyín in the east and then continues into Gabon; previously earth roads joining Acurenam, Mongomo and Anisok are now tarred. A new road links Bata to Mongomo.

SHIPPING

The main ports are Bata (general cargo and most of the country's export timber), Malabo (general), Luba (bananas, timber and petroleum), Mbini and Cogo (timber). There are regular shipping services to Europe from Bata and Malabo; however, communications between Bata, Malabo and Annobón remain erratic, and there is little maritime traffic with neighbouring mainland states.

CIVIL AVIATION

There are four international airports; those in Malabo and Bata have both been expanded in recent years (including the construction of a new, asphalt-surfaced runway at Bata). A third international airport, in Mengomeyén (serving Mongomo), in eastern Río Muni (the tribal stronghold of the Obiang clan), was opened in 2012. A fourth international airport was inaugurated at Oyala ('Ciudad de la Paz') in 2017. There are, in addition, five domestic airports. All flights operated by carriers based in Equatorial Guinea are prohibited from flying in European Union airspace. SONAGESA, jointly operated by GEPetrol and SONAIR of Angola, offers direct connections between Malabo and Houston, USA. Other international carriers regularly link Malabo to Madrid (Spain), Paris (France), Doula (Cameroon), Zürich (Switzerland), Amsterdam (Netherlands) and Frankfurt (Germany).

Autoridad Aeronotica de Guinea Ecuatorial: Autopista Malabo II, Zona Aeropuerto, Malabo; tel. 333093999; e-mail info@aage-gob .gq; internet www.aage-gob.gq; civil aviation authority; Pres. NORBERTO-BARTOLOME MENSUY MAÑE ANDEME; Dir-Gen. SANTIAGO OYONO AFUGU EYANGA.

Ceiba Intercontinental Airlines: Calle del Presidente Nasser, Apdo 916, Malabo; internet ceiba.irc-conseil.com; f. 2007; state-owned national carrier; provides domestic and regional services; CEO SANTIAGO NSOBEYA EFUMAN NCHAMA; Dir-Gen. LUCIANO ESONO BITEGUE.

Cronos Airlines: Malabo International Airport, Malabo; tel. 551008659; e-mail info@cronosair.com; internet cronosair.com; f. 2007; provides domestic and regional services; CEO ANDREAS KAÏAFAS.

Tourism

Tourism remains undeveloped. Future interest in this sector would be likely to focus on the unspoilt beaches of Río Muni and Bioko's scenic mountain terrain.

Defence

As assessed at November 2021, there were 1,100 men in the army, an estimated 250 in the navy and 100 in the air force. Paramilitary forces include a Civil Guard and a Coast Guard. Military service is voluntary.

Defence Expenditure: Estimated at 3,800m. francs CFA in 2013.

Supreme Commander of the Armed Forces: Gen. (retd) OBIANG NGUEMA MBASOGO.

Chief of Staff of the Armed Forces: Gen. LUCAS OBAMA NDONG MIKUE.

Inspector-Gen. of the Armed Forces in the Continental Region: EZEQUIEL ANDA ASUMU.

Inspector-Gen. of the Armed Forces and State Security Bodies in the Insular Region: JUAN NSUE ESONO NCHAMA.

Education

Education is officially compulsory and free for five years between the ages of six and 11. Primary education starts at six years of age and normally lasts for five years. Secondary education, beginning at the age of 12, spans a seven-year period, comprising a first cycle of four years and a second cycle of three years. According to estimates by the United Nations Educational, Scientific and Cultural Organization (UNESCO), enrolment at pre-primary institutions in 2014/15 was equivalent to 43% children in the relevant age-group (males 43%; females 44%). In that year total enrolment at primary schools included 45% of children in the relevant age-group (males 44%; females 45%). Since 1979 assistance in the development of the educational system has been provided by Spain. Two higher education centres, at Bata and Malabo, are administered by the Spanish Universidad Nacional de Educación a Distancia. There is also a university, Universidad Nacional de Guinea Ecuatorial, founded in 1995, at Malabo and Bata, as well as the Escuela Universitaria de Estudios Agropecuarios, Pesca y Forestal, a vocational college established (as the Escuela Nacional de Agricultura) in 1987 in Malabo with funding from the African Development Bank.

Bibliography

Agencia Española de Cooperación Internacional. *Segundo plano marco de cooperación entre el Reino de España y la República de Guinea Ecuatorial*. Madrid, AECI, 1990.

Boneke, J. B. *La transición de Guinea Ecuatorial: Historia de un fracaso*. Madrid, Labrys 54 Ediciones, 1998.

Castro, A., Mariano, and de la Calle Muñoz, M. L. *Geografía de Guinea Ecuatorial*. Madrid, Programa de Colaboración Educativa con Guinea Ecuatorial, 1985.

Castroviejo Bolívar, J., Juste Balleste, J., and Castelo Alvarez, R. *Investigación y conservación de la naturaleza en Guinea Ecuatorial*. Madrid, Oficina de Cooperación con Guinea Ecuatorial, 1986.

Cohen, R. (Ed.). *African Islands and Enclaves*. London, Sage Publications, 1983.

Cronj, S. *Equatorial Guinea: The Forgotten Dictatorship*. London, 1976.

Cusack, I. *Equatorial Guinea: The Inculcation and Maintenance of Hispanic Culture*. Bristol, University of Bristol, 1999.

Equatorial Guinea Research Group. *Executive Report on Strategies in Equatorial Guinea*. San Diego, CA, Icon Group International, annual.

Fegley, R. *Equatorial Guinea: An African Tragedy*. New York, Peter Lang, 1989.

González-Echegaray, C. *Estudios Guineos: Filología*. Madrid, IDEA, 1964.

Estudios Guineos: Etnología. Madrid, IDEA, 1964.

Jakobeit, C. 'Äquatorialguinea' in Hanisch, R., and Jakobeit, C. (Eds). *Der Kakaoweltmarkt*. Vol. 2. Hamburg, Deutsches Übersee-institut, 1991.

Klitgaard, R. *Tropical Gangsters*. London, I. B. Tauris, 1990.

Liniger-Goumaz, M. *Guinea Ecuatorial: Bibliografía General*. 5 vols. Bern and Geneva, 1976–85.

Statistics of Nguemist Equatorial Guinea. Geneva, Editions du Temps, 1986.

Small is not always Beautiful: The Story of Equatorial Guinea. London, Hurst, 1988.

Mann, S. *Cry Havoc*. London, John Blake Publishing, *Equatorial Guinea: An African Historical Dictionary*. Metuchen, NJ, Scarecrow Press, 2000.2011.

Martín de Molino, A. *Los Bubis, ritos y creencias*. Malabo, Centro Cultural Hispano-Guineano, 1989.

La ciudad de Clarence: Primeros años de la actual ciudad de Malabo, capital de Guinea Ecuatorial, 1827–1859. Malabo, Centro Cultural Hispano-Guineano, 1993.

Ndongo Bidyogo, D. *Historia y Tragedia de Guinea Ecuatorial*. Madrid, Cambio, 1977.

Nerín, G. *Guinea Ecuatorial: Historia en Blanco y Negro*. Barcelona, Atalaya Península, 1997.

Nfumu, A. N. *Macías: ¿Verdugo o Víctima?* Madrid, Herrero y asociados, Pool de Servicios Editoriales, S.L., 2004.

Nguema-Obam, P. *Aspects de la religion fang*. Paris, Editions Karthala, 1984.

Obiang Nguema, T. *Guinea Ecuatorial, País Joven: Testimonios Políticos*. Malabo, Ediciones Guinea, 1985.

Roberts, A. *The Wonga Coup*. London, Profile Books, 2006.

Sundiata, I. K. *Equatorial Guinea*. Boulder, CO, Westview Press, 1990.

From Slaving to Neoslavery. Madison, WI, University of Wisconsin, 1996.

Ugarte, M. *Africans in Europe: The Culture of Exile and Emigration from Equatorial Guinea to Spain*. Champaign, IL, University of Illinois Press, 2013.

ERITREA

Physical and Social Geography

MILES SMITH-MORRIS

The State of Eritrea, which formally acceded to independence on 24 May 1993, covers an area of 121,144 sq km (46,774 sq miles). Its territory includes the Dahlak islands, a low-lying coralline archipelago offshore from Massawa. Eritrea, which has a coastline on the Red Sea extending for almost 1,000 km, is bounded to the north-west by Sudan, to the south and west by Ethiopia, and to the south-east by Djibouti. The terrain comprises the northern end of the Ethiopian plateau (rising to more than 2,000 m above sea level), where most cultivation takes place, and a low-lying semi-desert coastal strip, much of which supports only pastoralism. Lowland areas have less than 500 mm of rainfall per year, compared with 1,000 mm in the highlands. Annual average temperatures range from 17°C in the highlands to 30°C in Massawa. The Danakil (Dallol) depression in the south-east descends to more than 130 m below sea level and experiences some of the highest temperatures recorded on Earth, frequently exceeding 50°C. Much of the coniferous forest that formerly covered the slopes of the highlands has been destroyed by settlement and cultivation; soil erosion is a severe problem.

The extent of Eritrea's natural resources awaits fuller exploration and evaluation. Copper ores and gold were mined from the Eritrean plateau in prehistoric times and there has been some extraction of iron ore. The Danakil depression is known to have valuable potash deposits. The world's first open-pit potash mine, at Colluli, was anticipated to go into production in the early 2020s as a joint venture between the Eritrean National Mining Corpn and an Australian mining company. Some exploration for petroleum has taken place in Red Sea coastal areas; oil seepages and offshore natural gas discoveries have been reported.

The population of Eritrea was enumerated at around 2.75m. in the Ethiopian census of 1984, but the war of independence resulted in large-scale population movements. Some 500,000 refugees fled to neighbouring Sudan and a significant, but unquantified, number of Eritreans have remained in Ethiopia. At mid-2022, according to United Nations estimates, Eritrea's population totalled 3,662,248, giving an average density of 30.2 inhabitants per sq km. The population is fairly evenly divided between Tigrinya-speaking Christians (mainly Orthodox), the traditional inhabitants of the highlands, and the Muslim communities of the western lowlands, northern highlands and east coast.

History

WARKA SOLOMON KAHSAY

Revised for this edition by the editorial staff

Modern Eritrea dates from the establishment of an Italian colony in the late 19th century. From a small concession gained near Assab in 1869, the Italians extended their control to Massawa in 1885 and to most of Eritrea by 1889. In the same year, the Ethiopian emperor, Menelik II, and the Italian Government signed the Treaty of Ucciali, which in effect recognized Italian control over Eritrea (and from which Italy derived its subsequent claim to a protectorate over Ethiopia). The period of Italian rule (1889–1941) and the subsequent years under British military administration (1941–52) created a society, economy and polity more advanced than in the semi-feudal Ethiopian empire. Following the Second World War, Ethiopia, which historically regarded Eritrea as an integral part of its territory, intensified its claims to sovereignty. The strategic interests of the USA and its influence in the newly founded United Nations (UN) resulted in a compromise, in the form of a federation between Eritrea and Ethiopia from 1952. However, no federal institutions were established, and Eritrean autonomy was systematically stifled. In 1962 Eritrea was forcibly and—in the eyes of the Eritrean people—illegally reconstituted as a province of Ethiopia.

THE LIBERATION STRUGGLE AND INDEPENDENCE

The dissolution of the federation brought forth a more militant Eritrean nationalism. The Eritrean Liberation Movement, founded in 1958, was succeeded by the Eritrean Liberation Front (ELF), which launched an armed struggle in 1961 after its repeated calls for independence were ignored by the international community. Organizational and ideological differences erupted into violence within the ELF in the mid-1960s, as a result of demands for reform from the increasing numbers of educated revolutionary fighters. Meanwhile, a reformist group separated from the ELF and established the Popular Liberation Forces (renamed the Eritrean People's Liberation Front—EPLF—in 1977). The EPLF, led by Issaias Afewerki, became the dominant armed organization engaged in fighting for the independence of Eritrea from Ethiopia.

After a prolonged and bloody 30-year war, on 24 May 1991 the EPLF defeated the colonial regime and Eritrea was constituted as a de facto independent country. Following independence, the EPLF immediately established an interim administration in Asmara. Strong commercial and diplomatic relations were subsequently established between the newly installed Governments of Eritrea and Ethiopia. In April 1993 a UN-supervised referendum took place in an atmosphere of national celebration. Of the 1.1m. Eritreans who voted, 99.8% endorsed national independence and in May the country attained international recognition as a sovereign state. Afewerki was subsequently elected by the National Assembly as head of state, by a margin of 99 votes to five.

Following the referendum, the EPLF formally transformed itself from a military front into a mass political movement (the People's Front for Democracy and Justice—PFDJ). Although the party congress confirmed its support for a plural political system, the PFDJ has been the only legitimate political party in existence in Eritrea since that time, and although a new Constitution was ratified in May 1997, President Afewerki failed to implement it. In an interview in 2014 the President stated that he did not recognize the existence of the Constitution and announced that a process to draft a new document would be launched. However, some seven years after this announcement, the Government has not initiated a process to draft a new constitution.

CONFLICT WITH ETHIOPIA

Owing to strong relations between Eritrea and Ethiopia in the early 1990s, border contentions and ideological disputes raised during the struggle were not settled immediately after independence. Relations deteriorated in late 1997 as disagreements arose following Eritrea's introduction of a new currency, the nakfa (see *Economy*). In May 1998 fighting erupted between Eritrean and Ethiopian troops after both laid claim to several border regions, including Badme, Zalambessa and Bure. Despite a series of peace initiatives by various regional and international parties, large-scale conflict between the two countries continued intermittently over a two-year period.

After concerted diplomatic efforts, in September 2000 the UN Security Council approved the deployment of a 4,200-strong UN Mission in Ethiopia and Eritrea (UNMEE) peacekeeping force, which established a Temporary Security Zone in the 25-km area between the two countries' troops. A definitive peace agreement, formally bringing the war to an end, was signed in Algiers, Algeria, in December. Both sides agreed to a permanent cessation of hostilities and the repatriation of all prisoners of war. However, both countries disagreed on implementation of the border demarcation, as the village of Badme, where the war had begun, did not appear on any of the published maps. After the initial confusion, the Boundary Commission announced in March 2003 that Badme was indeed in Eritrean territory. Border demarcation was scheduled to begin in that year, but Ethiopia's rejection of the border ruling put demarcation on hold. In November 2006 the Boundary Commission announced that it would demarcate the Ethiopian–Eritrean border on maps using high-resolution aerial photography to identify points where pillars should be placed to mark the boundary. The Eritrean Government continued to reject any initiative short of enforcing the border ruling. After an eight-year peacekeeping presence, the UN Security Council terminated UNMEE's mandate on 30 July 2008. In June 2016 there was a heavy exchange of artillery lasting for one day, which represented the culmination of longstanding border skirmishes between Eritrea and Ethiopia. It was the first serious attack involving the two nations' militaries since the end of the 1998–2000 border conflict.

The conflict in Somalia also continued to exacerbate tensions between Eritrea and Ethiopia. In 2007 the Eritrean Government vehemently opposed the UN authorization of a regional force comprising troops from the Intergovernmental Authority on Development (IGAD) and the African Union (AU) to protect the Transitional Federal Government (TFG) in Somalia and replace withdrawing Ethiopian forces. In December 2009, in response to allegations that Eritrea was supporting the al-Shabaab Islamist militant insurgency in Somalia, the UN Security Council placed an arms embargo on Eritrea, and imposed travel restrictions and asset freezes on Eritrean political and military leaders. The UN Security Council in December 2011 imposed additional sanctions against Eritrea's mining sector, after the country's East African neighbours accused it of continuing to provide support to al-Shabaab forces in Somalia. In July 2013 the UN Security Council adopted a resolution authorizing Secretary-General Ban Ki-Moon to extend the mandate of the Monitoring Group on Eritrea and Somalia (which, *inter alia*, monitored compliance with sanctions against Eritrea) until 25 November 2014. Following a 2016 report by the Monitoring Group, in November 2017 a UN panel of experts found there to be no conclusive evidence that Eritrea was supporting al-Shabaab, recommending that the sanctions should be lifted. None the less, the UN Security Council renewed its sanctions regime against Eritrea in that month. (Following the normalization of relations between Eritrea and Ethiopia (see *The Peace Agreement of July 2018*), the UN finally lifted the sanctions in November 2018.)

POST-WAR POLITICS

Eritrea is a single-party country, with Afewerki being the sole President for over two decades. His leadership is widely perceived as a dictatorship where political opposition parties, legislature and independent judiciary are prohibited in the country. There have been no elections since 1993. The creation

of a well-organized and effective opposition outside Eritrea remains elusive, due to factionalism and infighting. For many Eritreans and neutral observers, the never-ending proliferation of parties and movements, and their permutations only creates confusion within Eritrea among those longing for political change. The parties and civic organizations lack defined political ideology, structure and strategy.

Eritrea, with its smaller population, fared worse in the conflict with Ethiopia, resulting in growing challenges to President Afewerki and a rift in the ruling front. Although internal party conflicts had been experienced in the period before the war with Ethiopia, the war intensified these divisions. During the conflict, a number of key military strategists of the liberation struggle and senior government officials were subjected to *mdskal* (work suspension with pay). Tensions escalated in January 2000. Afewerki's overruling of the army hierarchy was blamed for the crisis within the army command structure and the collapse of Eritrean positions in the third round of fighting in May. Divisions between the President and senior PFDJ officials also emerged at a meeting of the party's Executive Committee in August, when Afewerki was criticized for failing to convene the Central Committee, the party's core leadership, and the National Assembly. Although the unratified Constitution stipulated that the National Assembly should convene every six months and the Central Committee every four months, the President refused to convene both bodies in the period prior to and immediately after the outbreak of the conflict. In response to threats by senior party and government officials that they would call the National Assembly to session themselves, the President agreed to convene the Assembly in September and reluctantly accepted the decision to establish a commission to define rules for multi-party elections, scheduled for December 2001, which were subsequently rescinded.

A number of exiled fragmented Eritrean opposition groups largely formed by dissident members of the PFDJ and former members of the ELF had emerged. Among efforts to consolidate opposition to the PFDJ regime, the Alliance of Eritrean National Forces, formed in 1999, was reconstituted in 2002 as an umbrella organization, the Eritrean National Alliance, which in 2004 was renamed the Eritrean Democratic Alliance (EDA). Although the EDA pledged to overthrow the Eritrean Government by military means and to unite the political and military wings of the various opposition groups, it remained beset by ethnic and ideological divisions, and underwent frequent splits and mergers. In August 2010 the EDA's then 11 member organizations held a National Conference for Democratic Change in the Ethiopian capital, Addis Ababa, during which plans were reportedly discussed to overthrow the Eritrean Government. The Eritrean Government refused to confirm claims by the EDA that it had staged co-ordinated military attacks against government troops inside Eritrea in early 2010. Other Eritrean opposition in exile initiatives were similarly hampered by fragmentation and lack of a consistent political agenda.

In September 2001 a major political crackdown intensified in the country, when the Government detained without charge 11 prominent politicians, members of the G-15 (15 high-ranking government officials who opposed Afewerki), as the signatories of the letter had become known, including three former cabinet ministers. The Government also arrested nine journalists and two Eritreans employed at the US embassy in Asmara. Afewerki insisted that his former allies had become threats to national security and described their questioning of his conduct during the war as treasonous. In 2016 Eritrea's Minister of Foreign Affairs, Osman Salih Muhammad, denied reports indicating that nine members of the G-15 group had died in detention. However, in the same year the President's head of political affairs and adviser, Yemane Ghebreab, said that the Government would not disclose any information regarding the G-15 for 'reasons of national security'. (No reliable information about the health or whereabouts of the G-15 members has subsequently been made available.) Reports by Amnesty International and other human rights organizations have estimated that there are at least 10,000 prisoners of conscience and political prisoners in Eritrea.

On 21 January 2013 social and international media reported an attempted coup in Asmara. A group of young Eritrean soldiers, backed by two tanks, had laid siege to the Ministry of Information (ERI-TV) building and held staff captive for several hours, including the daughter of President Afewerki. They allegedly ordered the Director-General of ERI-TV, Asmelash Abraha, to announce demands for the release of political prisoners and the implementation of the 1997 Constitution. Eritreans were largely unaware of this incident, and the only indication of something being amiss came when the signal of the sole state-owned media was suspended. Finally, on 14 February 2013 the Eritrean Government claimed that it was a minor non-planned event arranged by a few individuals, stating that the '21 January 2013 incident was, and is, no cause at all for apprehension'. None the less, the Government subsequently imprisoned 187 people without charge or trial.

In early 2015 the government spokesman, Yemane Gebremeskel, was reported to have been appointed as the new Minister of Information. Subsequently, in 2016, a British Broadcasting Corporation news team was allowed into Eritrea for the first time since 2004.

POST-WAR STATE AND SOCIETY

The state's relations with churches, non-governmental organizations (NGOs) and other potential interest groups intensified in the post-war period. The EPLF's experiences in the liberation war had made it intensely committed to secularism, with strong control over societal groups. The major faiths in Eritrea include the Orthodox Church, Islam, the Evangelical Lutheran Church and the Roman Catholic Church. In September 1994 the first bishops of the Eritrean Orthodox Church were consecrated at a ceremony conducted in Cairo, Egypt. These consecrations signified the formal separation of the Eritrean Orthodox Church from the Ethiopian Orthodox Church as an independent body. The third Eritrean Patriarch, Abune Antonios, was elected after the death of Abune Yakob. In January 2006, however, the authorities arrested Antonios, and in 2007 a new, pro-Government Patriarch was appointed. In January 2015 Pope Francis announced the separation of the four Eritrean eparchies (dioceses) from the Ethiopian Catholic Church and created a new metropolitan *sui iuris* church for Eritrea. Menghisteab Tesfamariam, one of the four bishops who had signed the controversial letter, was appointed as the head of the Eritrean Catholic Church in his new capacity as metropolitan Archbishop of Asmara.

The secular state respects Islamic holidays and traditions. However, there is some concern among Muslim communities, which comprise around one-half of the country's population, that language policies discriminate against Arabic (the mother tongue of less than 3% of the population) in favour of Tigrinya. Officially, Arabic and Tigrinya are both recognized as state languages, but in practice it is Tigrinya that functions as the official language of government and the military. Following longstanding tensions between the Al-Diaa Islamic School and the local authorities in Asmara, student protests erupted in October 2017 after an elderly member of the school board, Hajji Musa Muhammad Nur, was arrested for condemning the closure of the school. The military police forcibly dispersed the crowds and arrested several demonstrators. Nur died while in police custody in Asmara in March 2018. A second elder who had been arrested with Nur died in January 2019 while in prison, in unclear circumstances.

Although Jehovah's Witnesses form only a small group, their post-independence history has been marked by conflicts with the state, as has been, to a lesser extent, the experience of Evangelical and Pentecostal churches. Other 'new' churches grew rapidly in the 1990s, as Eritreans returned from the diaspora. A revival movement within the Orthodox Church also emerged at this time, demanding liturgical and institutional change. In April 2002 all churches with less than 40 years' presence in Eritrea were ordered to close. Church leaders were told that they could 'reapply' for licences to operate, but permits were not issued thereafter. The state currently recognizes only three Christian churches—the Roman Catholic Church, the Lutheran Church and the Orthodox Church—together with Islam. The others are classified as unregistered religious groups and are not allowed to exercise their beliefs publicly.

Meanwhile, a high-profile Ethiopian Pentecostal pastor, Surafel Demissie, a self-proclaimed prophet and healer, was among the passengers arriving on the first flight from Ethiopia to Eritrea when Ethiopian Airlines resumed flights to Eritrea on 18 July 2018. He subsequently held a rally and preached an informal sermon on the streets of Asmara. Several hundred followers of the Pentecostal faith welcomed the pastor at Asmara airport, hoping to practise their faith openly. However, in August the security forces arrested several people suspected of having met the pastor. In early 2019 USCIRF maintained its appraisal of Eritrea as a 'Country of Particular Concern' (CPC) with regard to religious freedom, owing to the high number of detentions, the level of persecution and the incidence of torture being reported inside prisons. The report claimed that there were around 1,200–3,000 religious prisoners in Eritrea and noted that the Government continued to impose severe restrictions on the religious activities of the state-approved churches as well as requiring them to provide twice-yearly reports. The country has been on the CPC list since 2014.

Eritrean law criminalizes consensual same-sex sexual activity. These minority groups face severe societal discrimination, and there have been reports that known homosexuals in the armed forces have been subjected to severe abuse. There is a widespread rejection of homosexuality in the country, where religion is central to people's lives. According to the colonial penal code of 1957, homosexuality is punishable by rigorous imprisonment in Eritrea, and it is still a culturally taboo topic. Foreign citizens face deportation for their sexual orientation. There are no known lesbian, gay, bisexual or transgender organizations in the country.

In September 2001 all eight of Eritrea's independent newspapers (including those that were pro-Government) were forcibly closed and a number of journalists were arrested, accused of accepting foreign funding and of violating the 1996 press proclamation. Government sources insisted that newspapers could re-apply for permission to operate, if they agreed to abide by the law, but no permits have since been issued. The journalists arrested in 2001 remain in detention, and none of them has been heard from since.

The Military, National Service and Migration

The military and national service dominates the lives of most adult Eritreans and is compulsory for all able-bodied Eritreans between 18 and 40 years of age, often for years beyond the obligatory 18-month period, including six months of military training. Students are required to complete mandatory military or public service for a minimum of 18 months upon graduation. Following the conclusion of the border conflict with Ethiopia at the end of 2000, reports of youths evading national service multiplied, due to the indefinite postponement of demobilization and release from national service. Several thousand young Eritreans, including high school and university students, serve the Government in different sectors controlled by the Ministry of Defence, and can be deployed at short notice at any time during school terms. In June 2016 the Government increased the stipends for national service from 450 nakfa to 1,500 nakfa. Starting salaries for new college graduates undertaking national service was increased to 2,000 nakfa (US $100), and for graduates it was raised to 3,500 nakfa, which placed them on a par with other wages in the country.

The Eritrean authorities continued to conduct intensified and unregulated *gffas* ('round-ups') of those avoiding conscription at least four or five times a year. In April 2016 a total of 29 conscripts were shot and either killed or injured in Asmara while trying to escape from a truck that was transporting them from training camps in western Eritrea to the port of Assab. Although the details of what transpired remained unclear, it was none the less a signal that extrajudicial execution by security forces occurs inside the reclusive country. Even Eritreans not in active national service are required to carry identity cards. The Government does not issue travel documents or exit visas to Eritreans who are fit for mobilization. Those aged between five and 50 years are not permitted to leave the country. Citizens are also prevented from holding a passport unless they can prove that they have completed national service.

Men aged up to 67 years are also forcibly mobilized in different capacities and conscripted into a People's Army, described as a 'neighbourhood watch' programme. Dispirited youth continue to seek to avoid conscription by evading the military police and fleeing across the border, but there is a 'shoot to kill' policy in place applied against any Eritrean found attempting to do so. A shipwreck in the Mediterranean sea off the coast of the Italian island of Lampedusa in October 2013 led to an estimated 350 migrants drowning, the majority of them Eritrean nationals. The incident drew international attention to the country's human rights record and fuelled a divisive political debate in Eritrea over the increasing numbers fleeing the country. The presidential adviser, Ghebreab, deflected blame on to the USA and the UN, accusing them of aiding people traffickers in Eritrea.

Despite the alarmingly high rate of deaths of migrants during their attempt to reach Europe, the number of refugees fleeing Eritrea continues to rise. Activists claim that even if illegal immigrants successfully flee the country, their relatives remaining in Eritrea are liable to be fined up to 50,000 nakfa. In addition, refugees run the risk of abduction and kidnapping by criminal gangs. Videos circulating on social media reveal that Eritrean refugees hoping to reach Europe have been detained in appalling conditions in Libya and sold into slavery. Armed violence has even been used against detainees who were registered as refugees with the office of the High Commissioner for Refugees (UNHCR). That body raised concerns over the treatment of detainees, and in February 2019 UNHCR and the International Organization for Migration (IOM) evacuated 159 Eritreans from Tripoli airport via the emergency transit mechanism to Niamey, Niger, from where they would join other migrants and start the resettlement process to be placed in other countries. Eritreans have also sought to flee to the Americas.

A commission of inquiry (COI), established in June 2014 by the UN Human Rights Council to investigate the allegations of human rights violations, was denied access to Eritrea. Although government co-operation was not forthcoming, the commission none the less succeeded in collecting testimonies from more than 400 Eritreans in diaspora and refugee camps in 2015, and from another 800 in 2016. Eritrean Minister of Foreign Affairs Osman Salih, in an interview with Radio France International in June 2016, claimed that the COI was a 'foreign motivated political panel'.

The COI's report, published in June 2017, claimed widespread and serious abuses, including detention and indefinite military conscription. The commission asserted that the Eritrean Government had yet to make any progress on addressing the serious human rights violations identified over the preceding years. The COI appealed to the International Criminal Court in The Hague, Netherlands, to put Eritrean officials on trial. Michael Smith, the Chairman of the commission, reported similar findings to an investigation carried out in 2017, including the enslavement of up to 400,000 people under the guise of 'national service', detention for indefinite periods, murder, rape, enforced disappearances and general persecution. An estimated 30,000 Eritreans from all over Europe gathered in front of the Office of the UN High Commissioner for Human Rights in Geneva, Switzerland, and UN offices in Tel Aviv, Israel, and Addis Ababa, to show their support for the COI's report. A pro-Government counter-protest by a similar number of Eritreans also rallied in front of the Office of the UN High Commissioner for Human Rights in Geneva to demonstrate against the COI, condemning the report as a 'total fabrication' and claiming to have submitted a petition with over 200,000 signatures to UNHCR. The commission reported that the Eritrean Government had neither shown any willingness to improve the human rights situation identified by the inquiry, nor accepted accountability for past violations. President Afewerki repeatedly acknowledged that Eritrean youth were fleeing to neighbouring countries in significant numbers, but denied allegations that they were fleeing from political persecution, claiming instead that they were merely leaving in search of economic opportunities.

Eritrean refugees in Israel have been met with riots and a government policy that does not provide adequate protection in line with international refugee legislation. In June 2013 Israel was reported to have reached an agreement with Rwanda and Uganda for the relocation of thousands of Eritrean immigrants living in Israel, in exchange for a payment to each migrant who left voluntarily, and also to the state receiving them—a practice that is banned under international law. Although most of the asylum seekers in Israel had apparently been given renewable permits to live in that country, intense pressure on them to leave Israel continued. From the end of 2013 many Eritrean and Sudanese asylum seekers were placed in detention facilities in southern Israel, under a new indefinite detention policy by the Israeli authorities.

REGIONAL AND INTERNATIONAL RELATIONS

Following its formal accession to independence in 1993, Eritrea gradually increased its international contacts, establishing diplomatic ties with Sudan, Ethiopia, Israel, Australia and Pakistan, as well as several international organizations.

Eritrea's relations with Sudan have been marked by a series of cross-border disputes. In the mid-2000s bilateral relations appeared to improve, following several years of tension, despite accusations made by the Sudanese Government that Eritrea was supporting rebel factions from Darfur, Sudan. In June 2006 Eritrea and Sudan agreed to restore full diplomatic relations. In January 2018 the Sudanese President, Lt-Gen. Omar Hassan Ahmad al-Bashir, having declared a state of emergency in nearby areas, closed Sudan's border with Eritrea, again accusing its Government of supporting militant opposition groupings active on Sudanese territory; it was reopened one year later. After al-Bashir was ousted in a military coup in April 2019, President Afewerki met the head of Sudan's new transitional Sovereign Council in September (representing his first official visit to Sudan since 2014), when a comprehensive agreement was adopted to enhance co-operation in a number of areas.

In 2008 Eritrea accused Djibouti of allowing Ethiopia to deploy long-range artillery weapons on the strategic peak of Mount Musa Ali, where the borders of Djibouti, Eritrea and Ethiopia intersect. Djibouti accused Eritrea of deploying troops and military equipment to Ras Doumeira Mountain and Doumeira Island in March and reported military confrontations between the two countries on two separate occasions in June, following weeks of military build-up and mounting bilateral tensions, with at least 35 people killed. Eritrea denied claims of military aggression against Djibouti, and rejected the conclusions of a UN fact-finding mission—which had contended that the dispute had the potential to destabilize the entire region—protesting that the UN Security Council had already censured Eritrea for attacking Djibouti without independently ascertaining facts on the ground. The UN Security Council adopted a resolution in January 2009, ordering Eritrea to withdraw to positions held before fighting broke out.

On 6 June 2010 by President Afewerki and President Ismaïl Omar Guelleh of Djibouti signed an agreement aimed at resolving the border conflict. The agreement entrusted Qatar with creating a mechanism to facilitate boundary demarcation, monitoring the border, facilitating the exchange of prisoners of war, and normalizing relations between the two countries. However, Qatar pulled its peacekeepers out on 13 June 2017, after both Eritrea and Djibouti expressed support for Saudi Arabia and its allies in a major diplomatic standoff with Qatar. In the wake of Qatar's withdrawal, tension emerged between both countries. Djibouti accused Eritrea of deploying its troops to the buffer zone along the border, and proposed that the AU take over the disputed region. In September 2018 Eritrea and Djibouti signed a new peace agreement and agreed to normalize relations. In February 2019 the two countries announced the resumption of direct flights between Asmara and Djibouti.

In the mid-1990s there was a dispute between Yemen and Eritrea over sovereignty of the islands of Greater Hanish, Lesser Hanish and Zuqar in the Red Sea, which were claimed by both countries. After a series of talks mediated by France, and amid growing military tension between the two countries, in October 1996 Eritrea and Yemen confirmed that they would submit the dispute to an international tribunal, which subsequently ruled that the Hanish islands belonged to Yemen and had been illegally occupied by Eritrea. Both countries accepted the ruling, and shortly afterwards they agreed to establish a joint committee to strengthen bilateral co-operation. In early 2013 new direct flights between Eritrea and Yemen were launched by the privately owned airline Nasair Eritrea.

Eritrea established diplomatic relations with the USA in 1993, following independence. Relations became complicated in 2001, with the arrest of Eritrean nationals working in the US embassy in Asmara. None the less, at the same time Eritrea made great efforts to ingratiate itself with the USA, pledging its support for the 'war on terror'. Subsequently, however, and increasingly vitriolic in tone, the Eritrean Government repeatedly accused the USA of favouring Ethiopia in the border dispute, and of interfering in the Somalia conflict on the pretext of fighting terrorism. The USA accused Eritrea of aiding rebel groups trying to destabilize Ethiopia—the USA's main counter-terrorism ally in the region. In early 2007 the USA suspended visa services for Eritreans until diplomatic delegations were allowed unimpeded entry into Eritrea. In 2010 Eritrean media conducted a sustained campaign of accusations against the USA. In February the US embassy in Asmara suspended its consular services and issued a warning to US nationals against travel to Eritrea, citing a rise in anti-US sentiment. A message posted subsequently on the website of the US embassy accused the Eritrean Government of destabilizing the Horn region. However, Eritrea, together with 33 other Arab, Asian and African countries, joined the Saudi Arabian-led Islamic Military Alliance to Fight Terrorism in December 2015 to combat terrorism, specifically the threat posed by Islamic State and its affiliates. The USA supported Eritrea's role in the bloc and hoped that it would help to normalize relations between the two countries. In May 2017 the USA recertified Eritrea as not co-operating fully with the US counter-terrorism efforts. However, after the normalization of relations with Ethiopia in July 2018, Eritrea was removed from the list in May 2019. A US congressional delegation had visited Eritrea in March of that year (the first such visit since 2005) to support regional peace and security in the Horn of Africa. The delegation urged that human rights and civil liberties must be at the centre of future reforms. In January 2020 the USA extended a travel ban in force for certain states to Eritrea, restricting the visas available to Eritrean citizens and removing their eligibility to obtain permanent residency. The grounds for this decision was that Eritrea had failed to meet US security standards in maintaining a list of suspected terrorists, providing information on criminals and issuing more secure passports.

After Eritrea gained independence, its relations with Italy expanded considerably, although some tensions remained with regard to Eritrean human rights issues. Continuing the long-standing bilateral relationship, in December 2018 the Italian Deputy Minister of Foreign Affairs and International Co-operation, Emanuela Del Re, and a group of Italian entrepreneurs met senior officials in Asmara to draft an ambitious roadmap for mutually beneficial economic and commercial opportunities.

Eritrean-Chinese ties were strengthened in mid-2005, with trade and aid agreements signed in the areas of infrastructure, trade and investment, and agriculture. In June 2011 Eritrea and the People's Republic of China signed a number of economic and technical co-operation agreements. As part of one of these agreements, a new building for the Erafaile Elementary School in Asmara was inaugurated in June 2014. In January 2015 Eritrea and China signed an accord on mutual visa exemption for government officials. China has become increasingly important in supporting projects in the construction, health care and oil sectors in Eritrea. Furthermore, to support its own rapid economic growth, China has an economic interest in Eritrea's emergent mining sector. On 25 November 2021 Eritrea's Minister of Foreign Affairs, Osman Salih, signed a memorandum of understanding with the Chinese ambassador to join China's Belt and Road Initiative of global infrastructure development. Visiting Eritrea as part of a tour of Africa in January 2022, China's Minister of Foreign Affairs, Wang Yi, met President Afewerki and Osman Salih, and was reported to have voiced Chinese opposition to new US sanctions imposed against Eritrea (see *Eritrean Engagement in Ethiopia's Civil Conflict*). During his subsequent visit to Kenya, Wang

announced that China would appoint a special envoy to the Horn of Africa region.

Eritrea's regional and foreign relations with other countries and organizations appear to have slightly improved in recent years. In May 2014 President Afewerki met Pekka Haavisto, the Finnish Minister of International Development, for discussions on developmental programmes between the two countries. In April 2016 Eritrea's Permanent Representative at the UN, Girma Asmerom, signed the Paris Agreement on climate change during a ceremony at the UN headquarters in New York, USA. This was one of several measures that Eritrea has taken to mitigate the adverse effects of climate change, biodiversity loss, deforestation and desertification in the country. The Russian Minister of Foreign Affairs, Sergei Lavrov, and his Eritrean counterpart, Osman Salih, held a joint press conference in Moscow, the capital of the Russian Federation, in February 2014, when Eritrea signed its first-ever agreement with Russia, boosting their co-operation in politics, trade and the economy. In September 2018 Russia indicated its plans to build a naval logistics centre at one of Eritrea's Red Sea ports. In January 2020 Russian news agency Sputnik reported that the Russian Government had signed an agreement to deliver military equipment and helicopters to Eritrea. Following Russia's invasion of Ukraine in February 2022, Eritrea was one of only five states (including Russia) and the only African country to vote against a UN General Assembly resolution on 2 March that demanded the withdrawal of Russia's military forces from Ukraine. A senior Eritrean delegation, led by Osman Salih, made a working visit to Russia in late April.

Canada has repeatedly expressed concerns about human rights issues in Eritrea: in mid-2013 Canada's Minister of Foreign Affairs, John Baird, expelled the head of Eritrea's consulate in Toronto, Canada, for continuing to solicit and collect a 2% tax on Eritreans resident in Canada after he had been ordered to cease doing so. The Eritrean Government responded by accusing the Canadian Government of 'bullying' Eritreans in Canada. Eritrea claimed that the diaspora tax levied on expatriate communities at 2% of their income was voluntary, and was only incurred if they sought to recover property. However, the 2% tax was in reality a requirement for Eritreans abroad in order to receive any services from Eritrean embassies.

THE PEACE AGREEMENT OF JULY 2018

Since the end of active conflict with Ethiopia in 2000, the circumstances of political and social repression under the 'no peace, no war' stalemate had become the norm, with little apparent hope of improvement. In May 2018, for example, Eritrea accused Ethiopia and Sudan of conspiring to destabilize the country by providing support to Eritrean armed opposition groups. However, in the following weeks, Eritrean-Ethiopian relations took a turn for the better. In a move that surprised domestic and international observers, the newly appointed Prime Minister of Ethiopia, Abiy, announced in early June that his Government would accept the terms of the Algiers Agreement of 2000 and the UN ruling of 2002 on the demarcation of the contested 1,000-km border with Eritrea, and hand back to Eritrea disputed border territory, including the flashpoint town of Badme, without any preconditions (Ethiopian residents of Badme subsequently staged protests against the decision, in mid-June). Initially, the Eritrean Government did not react, but in a speech given in Asmara on Martyrs' Day on 20 June 2018, President Afewerki indicated the Government's intention to send a high-level delegation led by Minister of Foreign Affairs Osman Salih to Addis Ababa to hold peace talks. Marking a historic détente in relations, Prime Minister Abiy arrived in Asmara on 8 July to meet Afewerki, where he received a jubilant public welcome. The two leaders signed a declaration of peace on the following day, formally ending the state of war which had persisted since the end of active conflict in 2000. This included accepting demarcation of the joint border (under the UN ruling of 2002), including awarding Badme to Eritrea, resuming diplomatic relations, promoting political, economic and trade collaboration, and restoring transportation telecommunications links, as well as collaboration on regional affairs. Furthermore, Abiy officially asked the Secretary-General of the UN, António Guterres, to lift the sanctions against Eritrea. The Asmara summit had, in the course of 48 hours, apparently resolved one of the most protracted military disputes in Africa.

On 14 July 2018, less than one week after the landmark visit by the Ethiopian premier to Eritrea, and as a continuation of the peace process, President Afewerki made a reciprocal visit to Ethiopia. Afewerki and Abiy immediately embarked on implementing some of the most profound changes either country had experienced in several decades. On 16 July Eritrea reopened its embassy in Addis Ababa; Ethiopia named its ambassador to Eritrea later that week, and one month later Ethiopia reopened its embassy in Asmara. The two countries also restored telephone services with each other—the first time Eritrean and Ethiopian citizens were able to make calls to each other since 1998. In another significant development, on 18 July 2018 Ethiopian Airlines resumed daily flights to Asmara for the first time in 20 years. Among the passengers on the historic first flight were former Ethiopian Prime Minister Hailemariam Desalegn and the popular Ethiopian Pentecostal priest, Surafel Demissie (see above), as well as renowned singers and artists. On 11 September Eritrean–Ethiopian border crossings were officially reopened, providing Ethiopia with a direct route to Eritrean ports. Following the relaxation of border security, some 20,000 Eritreans reportedly sought asylum in Ethiopia. Ethiopian forces remained in control of the town of Badme and the surrounding territory. On 16 September, in Jeddah, Saudi Arabia, Afewerki and Abiy signed the Agreement on Peace, Friendship and Comprehensive Cooperation, ending the state of war between Eritrea and Ethiopia, and initiating comprehensive co-operation. In November the UN Security Council lifted the sanctions which had been in force against Eritrea since 2009.

THE COVID-19 PANDEMIC

The global pandemic of COVID-19 reached Eritrea in March 2020, with 15 confirmed cases. On 2 April the Government implemented plans for a full lockdown of 21 days, which was subsequently extended to 11 May, from which date restrictions were gradually eased. In order to prevent the spread of the virus, passengers arriving from abroad were placed in restrictive quarantine in a hotel outside the capital. However, the lockdown was imposed without the introduction of measures to mitigate the socioeconomic impact on citizens.

Nationally, many citizens were confined to their homes while trying to sustain their existence, with the price of basic food supplies in the shops rising dramatically and leading to acute shortages. In a petition addressed to the UN, an association of NGOs, Eritrea Focus, described that much of the population faced a crisis of hunger and malnutrition, which the Government appeared to be doing little to resolve, while at the same time even deterring medical aid. The broadcaster Voice of America reported that Eritrea did not accept supplies donated by a Chinese technology company, Alibaba Group, to combat the pandemic. Many Eritrean human rights activists reacted on social media networks by asserting that the Government's disregard of the dire need for medical supplies posed an absolute threat to public health.

Lockdown measures were reinstated by the Eritrean authorities with effect from 22 December 2020, after COVID-19 cases had begun to increase in all regions. Some restrictions were lifted in March–April 2021: public transport links resumed on 23 March and the internal travel ban was lifted, and schools were reopened on 1 April. However, a number of measures, including a night-time curfew, were subsequently reported to remain in force. After a further wave of the pandemic during 2021 and January 2022, a total of 10,169 COVID-19 cases, with 103 related deaths, had been confirmed in Eritrea at the end of September. At that time Eritrea remained the only country in the African continent not to have launched a national vaccination programme.

RELEASE OF RELIGIOUS PRISONERS

On 8 October 2020 the European Parliament adopted a further in a series of resolutions condemning the human rights situation in Eritrea, and demanded the immediate and unconditional release of all prisoners of conscience, drawing particular attention to the case of Dawit Isaak, a Swedish-Eritrean journalist who had been detained during the 2001 campaign against the media; since that time, the Eritrean authorities had not confirmed Isaak's whereabouts or provided any evidence about the state of his health. The resolution also emphasized that the overcrowded and unsanitary conditions in Eritrean detention centres endangered prisoners in the context of the COVID-19 health crisis. On 4 December Eritrea released 28 Jehovah's Witnesses who had been detained for between five and 26 years without trial (many for practising their religion, and several for conscientiously objecting on religious grounds to compulsory military service). The cases of three high-profile conscientious objectors who had been held for 26 years had been highlighted by the outgoing UN Special Rapporteur on the situation of human rights in Eritrea the previous October. A further four Jehovah's Witnesses were released at the beginning of February 2021 (while 20 remained incarcerated). Also in early February, the human rights organization Christian Solidarity Worldwide was informed that 70 Christians from evangelical and Orthodox backgrounds had been released from three prisons in Eritrea. In early April a total of 36 Christian prisoners, some of whom had reportedly been arrested in 2017, were freed; by that time a total of 171 Christians had been released since the previous August (with at least 129 Christian prisoners remaining incarcerated). While the releases were widely welcomed, there was speculation that they reflected efforts by the Eritrean regime to distract international attention from the country's involvement in the ongoing conflict in Ethiopia's Tigray region (see below). A number of re-arrests were reported during 2021, including of two elderly pastors in July, and in September the number of Christian prisoners in Eritrea was estimated at about 160.

ERITREAN ENGAGEMENT IN ETHIOPIA'S CIVIL CONFLICT

Following escalating tensions between the Ethiopian Government of Abiy and the former paramilitary Tigray People's Liberation Front (TPLF) in the Tigray region bordering Eritrea, a military offensive by Ethiopia's federal armed forces to suppress the movement and restore central authority in Tigray began in early November 2020, with the support of Eritrean forces. Several rockets were launched from Tigray at Asmara International Airport; the TPLF admitted responsibility for the attack, claiming that the airport was being used by Ethiopian federal forces (under, it later emerged, a security pact between Afewerki and Abiy, following the rapprochement between the two leaders). Although Eritrea repeatedly denied any involvement in the conflict, it was widely reported that Eritrean troops were deployed in the Tigray region, where they were perpetrating numerous abuses, including extrajudicial killings, sexual violence, and the looting and destruction of property and infrastructure such as hospitals and health centres. The Ethiopian federal forces captured Mekelle, the capital of the Tigray region, on 28 November, after which Abiy declared victory in the conflict. However, further rocket attacks were reportedly launched against Asmara from Tigray shortly afterwards. In early December the US Department of State described the reports of the Eritrean presence in Ethiopia as 'credible', despite the continued denials by both Governments, and called for a full withdrawal. Meanwhile, UNHCR expressed concerns over the nearly 100,000 Eritrean refugees who had been registered at four camps in the Tigray region. In January 2021 satellite images showed that two of the refugee camps, the Hitsats and Shimelba shelters, had been destroyed during the intensive fighting. UNHCR announced that around 20,000 Eritreans who had fled from the two camps were unaccounted for, also reporting that refugees had been abducted and forced to return to Eritrea by Eritrean personnel involved in the conflict.

On 23 March 2021 Abiy finally admitted the deployment of Eritrean troops in Ethiopia's border areas, declaring to the Ethiopian parliament that the 'Eritrean people and government did a lasting favour to our soldiers'; after meeting Afewerki in Asmara, he subsequently announced that the

Eritrean Government had agreed to withdraw its forces. However, in mid-April the UN Emergency Relief Coordinator informed the UN Security Council that agencies in the region had observed no evidence of Eritrean withdrawal, also citing reports of Eritrean soldiers wearing Ethiopian uniforms. In a letter to the UN Security Council shortly afterwards, Eritrea stated that it would begin withdrawing its troops from Tigray, acknowledging publicly for the first time its involvement in the conflict. In late May US Secretary of State Antony Blinken announced the imposition of targeted visa restrictions against Ethiopian and Eritrean officials who were accused of perpetuating the conflict. Meanwhile, in late January the Tigray Defence Forces (TDF), comprising special forces of the Tigray regional government, members of the TPLF and of other local militia groups, had renewed its insurgency, and, following advances, regained control of Mekelle on 28 June. The Ethiopian Government announced a unilateral ceasefire and at the end of June claimed that all Eritrean forces had been withdrawn from the region.

On 21 June 2021 a new UN Special Rapporteur on the situation of human rights in Eritrea informed the UN Human Rights Council that there had been no improvements in the internal situation in the country, and that the regime had in addition extended its human rights violations beyond its borders, citing the numerous reports of violations committed by Eritrean troops in the conflict in Tigray. In particular, human rights organizations had reported, based on witness testimony, that Eritrean forces had massacred 720–800 civilians, including children, in the town of Axum in Tigray on 28–29 November 2020. In March 2021 the European Union (EU) listed Eritrea's National Security Office as being subject to sanctions, on the grounds that it was responsible for serious human rights violations in Eritrea, including arbitrary arrests, extrajudicial killings, enforced disappearances and torture. On 23 August the US Treasury Department announced the imposition of sanctions (constituting the freezing of assets and a ban on entering the USA) against the Chief of Staff of the Eritrean Defence Forces, Maj.-Gen. Filipos Woldeyohannes, stating that forces under his command were responsible for serious human rights abuses in Tigray. The Eritrean Ministry of Foreign Affairs immediately rejected the allegations. Shortly afterwards, US Secretary of State Blinken expressed concerns that large numbers of Eritrean troops had returned to Tigray, while a leaked internal memorandum by EU diplomats reported that reinforcements had been redeployed around towns in the western part of the region. In November the US sanctions were expanded to target four entities: the Eritrean Defence Forces, the PFDJ, the Hidri Trust (the holding company of all PFDJ business enterprises) and the Red Sea Trading Corporation, which managed the property and financial interests of the PFDJ. Sanctions were also introduced against a further two government officials, the head of the National Security Office and the economic advisor to the PFDJ. The Eritrean Government denounced the 'illicit and immoral sanctions' and demanded that they be rescinded.

In late March 2022 the Ethiopian Government unexpectedly declared a unilateral truce in the conflict to allow humanitarian access to the blockaded Tigray region, and the TPLF agreed to the cessation of hostilities. However, the TPLF subsequently accused the Government of reneging on its commitments, and following disagreement over the format of negotiations towards a peace settlement, intensive fighting resumed in southern Tigray on 24 August. Following numerous reports that Eritrea was mobilizing its armed forces, on 20 September the TPLF announced that Eritrean troops had launched a full-scale offensive and that heavy fighting was ongoing in several areas along the border. It was reported that Eritrean and Ethiopian forces had seized the town of Sheraro in north-western Tigray, with hostilities there continuing after an ensuing rebel counter-attack, and that Eritrean troops had been deployed in the Afar region of Ethiopia, east of Tigray. Both the Eritrean and Ethiopian Governments failed to confirm the participation of the Eritrean military in the conflict. The US Administration of President Joe Biden extended the sanctions in force against Eritrea for a further year in early September, and subsequently issued demands for the withdrawal of Eritrean forces from Tigray.

Economy

WARKA SOLOMON KAHSAY

Revised for this edition by the editorial staff

INTRODUCTION

The economic realities of Eritrea are dominated by the legacies of war, drought and the continued mobilization of its productive labour force. Unlike any other African country, the economy is highly dependent on taxes paid by members of the diaspora and has few dynamic export sectors, although high hopes have been placed on the mining sector. Restrictions on the activities of the United Nations (UN) and other international non-governmental organizations (NGOs) make assessment of Eritrea's economic health difficult. President Issaias Afewerki has dismissed international organizations' unfavourable reports of Eritrea's economic indicators as fabricated statistics, emphasizing that most such organizations did not have a presence in the country. In addition to its ambitious mining projects, the Government has been actively engaged in the agricultural sector, with the aim of improving water access and food security.

According to the African Development Bank (AfDB), Eritrea's gross national income (GNI), at current prices, was US $3,121m. (equivalent to $880m. per head) in 2020. The population was estimated by the UN at 3,662,248 in mid-2022. Eritrea's long-established diaspora, which helped to fund the independence war and is found mainly in Europe, the USA and the Middle East, continues to contribute to economic growth. Remittances in 2017 accounted for 32% of gross domestic product (GDP). Eritrea's economy is one of the least free, according to the Heritage Foundation's 2021 Index of Economic Freedom, where it is ranked 173rd out of 178 countries worldwide.

According to UN estimates, overall GDP increased at an average annual rate of 0.7 in 2011–20. Large fluctuations in the country's growth levels have been reported, due to the effects of climate conditions on agricultural production, notably a contraction of 10.0% in 2017, followed by growth of 13.0% in 2018. According to the AfDB, real GDP contracted by 0.6% in 2020, after growth of 3.8% in 2019, owing to the regional impact of the COVID-19 pandemic, particularly on remittances, together with other adverse factors including infestations of desert locusts and increased insecurity relating to civil conflict in a border region of Ethiopia (see below). However, the AfDB estimated a recovery in real GDP to growth of 2.9% in 2021, following a rebound in global demand and commodity prices, and forecast growth rates of 4.7% in 2022 and 3.6% in 2023, largely based on expectations of high international prices for the country's metal exports.

The Government has implemented measures intended to stabilize the rate of inflation, including the strict regulation of exchange rates, limitations on imports and the imposition of fixed prices. According to the AfDB, the annual rate of inflation averaged 20.1% in 2004–13; however, significant fluctuations were reported, and average consumer prices decreased by 16.4% in 2019. Consumer prices rose by 4.8% in 2020, according to the AfDB, in part due to pandemic-related disruptions in regional and global supply chains, easing to 4.5% in 2021. However, the inflation rate was projected to increase to 6.2% in 2022, due to the global impact of the Russian Federation's invasion of Ukraine in February.

Shortly after reporting the first case of COVID-19, the Government imposed a national lockdown with effect from 2 April 2020, which was extended to 11 May. The restrictions were then progressively eased, but stringent measures were reinstated from 22 December, in response to an increase in cases in all regions. Some measures were lifted in March–April 2021, with the resumption of public and private transport operations and the reopening of the majority of businesses (although the country remained closed to tourism). Following the onset of the pandemic, the Eritrean authorities rapidly mobilized donations from citizens and expatriate remittances for a National Fund to meet urgent health needs and assist the poorest households. However, recovery from the crisis was slowed by the Government's refusal of vaccine aid, and Eritrea remained the only country in the African continent not to launch a national vaccination programme for its citizens.

ECONOMIC IMPACT OF WAR

The war with Ethiopia (1998–2000) severely damaged the economy of Eritrea, affecting agricultural production, labour, exports and governmental expenditure in a profound and long-lasting way. In addition, trade with Ethiopia, which previously accounted for two-thirds of Eritrean exports and most of Eritrean imports, virtually ceased. Furthermore, since its independence in 1993, Eritrea had been an essential gateway to Red Sea trade for Ethiopia (which had been rendered landlocked when Eritrea seceded), before the commencement of the border war in 1998, but this was severely affected during the war and in its aftermath. However, in a significant development between Eritrea and Ethiopia, the two countries signed a peace agreement in July 2018, which included related agreements to develop mutual trade, and improve transportation and communications ties. It was widely hoped that the peace deal with Ethiopia, the agreement to reopen the borders and the subsequent lifting of sanctions that had been in place for nine years would be followed by economic rehabilitation. However, the four border crossings between the two countries were closed again by Eritrea in April 2019, without explanation, although observers suggested that the closure was related to unresolved tax, customs and visa issues. Further normalization in economic activity was hampered by conflict between Ethiopia's federal armed forces and the rebel Tigray People's Liberation Front (TPLF) in its border Tigray region from late 2020. Reports of substantial Eritrean troop deployments in Tigray in support of the Ethiopian federal forces were subsequently confirmed (despite Eritrea's initial denials). In March 2021 Ethiopian Prime Minister Dr Abiy Ahmed Ali made a visit to Eritrea, during which it was agreed to reopen the border crossings and to expand political and economic relations between the two countries. However, Eritrea's military involvement in the conflict in Tigray undermined development and, following reported human rights violations by Eritrean forces against the local population there, resulted in the imposition of targeted sanctions by the USA during 2021 (see *History*).

Eritrea maintains among the highest proportion of its population in the army of any country in the world. Despite the landmark peace agreement with Ethiopia, the Eritrean Government has made no meaningful change to end the system of indefinite conscription, which has diverted members of the labour force away from economically productive employment. In 2020, according to UN estimates, public administration and defence represented 27.7% of GDP.

ECONOMIC POLICY, AID AND INVESTMENT

Eritrea's economic policy is to reject major loans and foreign food aid, in accordance with the aim for the country to become self-sufficient. This radical policy strategy to end dependency on foreign aid presents a great challenge, and in practice self-reliance means economic activities being under total government control. Import restrictions on private sector companies were imposed in 2003, and domestic entrepreneurs have

complained that only firms closely affiliated to the ruling People's Front for Democracy and Justice (PFDJ) have been able to expand their operations or purchase privatized businesses. The PFDJ and, to a lesser extent, the National Union of Eritrean Youths and Students (NUEYS), are also increasingly active in the manufacturing, service and construction sectors. Relatively little is known about the wide range of ventures owned wholly or partially by the PFDJ, but they include businesses in the construction, information technology and tourism sectors, as well as a major cement factory that commenced production in late 2011. The NUEYS's most financially successful ventures have been in the distribution of liquid petroleum gas for home cooking and the distribution of filtered and bottled water for domestic consumption. Many private businessmen have migrated to South Sudan, Kenya, Uganda, Angola and Zambia, and those who remain in Eritrea face stringent foreign currency regulations, harsh penalties for 'black market' exchanges and a strong market disadvantage *vis-à-vis* the PFDJ enterprises.

In May 2015 the AfDB signed an agreement with the Eritrean Government to provide the country with US $41m. towards the development of the agricultural and educational sectors. Some 50% of the funding was to be in the form of aid, and the remainder was an interest-free loan. In November 2017 the AfDB approved an intervention strategy aimed at promoting agricultural and infrastructural development in Eritrea during 2017–19, in an effort to support economic growth. Net official development assistance amounted to $61m. in 2020.

Eritrea's national development strategies, as presented in its Vision 2030, were to develop human capital, open up the private sector with a conducive regulatory environment for domestic businesses, diversify Eritrea's economy with an emphasis on environmental protection, and invest in infrastructure. Vision 2020 was to be implemented through medium-term National Development Plans (NDPs). The main objectives of Eritrea's interim NDP for 2014–19 were to develop modern irrigation-based commercial agriculture, export-oriented manufacturing and efficient tertiary services. The preparation of the next NDP has been delayed due to the COVID-19 crisis.

Foreign direct investment inflows increased from US $52m. in 2017 to $74m. in 2020, with most investment focused on mining activities. The People's Republic of China is the country's largest investor, creditor and trading partner. Chinese companies have been involved in major infrastructure projects, such as the renovation of the Hirgigo power station in 2016, and the expansion of the port of Massawa (see *Transport and Communications*). On 25 November 2021 Eritrea became the 50th African country to sign a memorandum of understanding to join the China Belt and Road Initiative (BRI). In terms of overall business environment, the World Bank's 2020 *Doing Business* report ranked Eritrea 189th (ahead only of Somalia) out of 190 countries surveyed in terms of ease of doing business, and indicated that starting a business, obtaining construction permits, registering property and securing credit were all extremely difficult in Eritrea. Despite the new era of relative co-operation with Ethiopia, the risk of macroeconomic instability and the use of price controls, regulations and rationing, particularly of foreign exchange, have created an unfavourable business environment in Eritrea. According to the 2020 Corruption Perceptions Index published by Transparency International, Eritrea ranked 160th out of 180 countries in terms of corruption.

FOREIGN TRADE AND FINANCE

With a significant number of Eritreans living outside the country, taxes paid directly to the Government by expatriates (accounting for 2% of their annual income) and remittances to families play a key role in the economy. However, remittance flows to Eritrea have declined as some countries, such as Canada, have taken steps to cease illicit means of collecting taxes from Eritreans in the diaspora. Furthermore, some Eritreans in the diaspora are now sending money to pay people traffickers to transport their family members from Africa to

Europe and even to fund a complex migration route to the USA, rather than supporting relatives financially in Eritrea itself.

Owing to growth in gold and copper production, the volume of merchandise exports increased by 30.5% in 2017. However, this was more than counterbalanced by growth in imported goods for the mining sector. The result was a trade deficit, of 2,230m. nakfa in 2017 and amounting to 9.5% of GDP in 2018. In addition to gold and copper, exported commodities included raw hides, cotton, vegetables and crustaceans, while the principal imports were wheat, sugar, molasses and honey, motor vehicles and petroleum products. However, Eritrea has recorded large surpluses on the current account, recorded at 617m. nakfa in 2017, supported by remittances from abroad. According to the AfDB, the current account surplus fell to 11.4% of GDP in 2020 from 12.1% in 2019, amid subdued economic activity resulting from the pandemic. However, the current account surplus widened to 13.5% of GDP in 2021, reflecting the rise in global metal prices.

Eritrea's membership of the Common Market for Eastern and Southern Africa (COMESA) reduces the intra-COMESA trade tariff by some 80%. Despite this, trade exchanges with other COMESA members have been virtually non-existent. According to the AfDB, Eritrea's main sources of imports are the USA, China, Saudi Arabia, Egypt and Italy, while the main export destinations are China, the Republic of Korea (South Korea), India, the United Arab Emirates (UAE) and Singapore. Eritrea is not a member of the World Trade Organization; this status allows it to pursue an export-orientated strategy without the reciprocal opening of its domestic economy. Eritrea remains the only member state of the African Union not to have signed the 2018 African Continental Free Trade Agreement, the Government having cited the country's long-held stance in advocating regional integration over continental aspirations.

Foreign officials maintain that fiscal and debt sustainability remain the key challenges facing the Eritrean Government. Tight government monetary policy continues to accommodate the budget deficit, but reliance on monetary financing of the budget has hindered the private sector and prompted heavy government borrowing from the banking sector. The foreign exchange shortage has been addressed through foreign currency controls. The use of foreign currency was declared illegal in April 2005, in an attempt to curb the growing 'black market' in foreign exchange. Persons involved in such transactions faced prison sentences of up to two years and fines of more than 2m. nakfa. Inflation was addressed through price controls imposed on 16 'declared goods', including basic foodstuffs, textiles and building materials. In November 2015, in order to stabilize the official currency the parallel currency, while controlling the trafficking of both goods and people, the Bank of Eritrea announced the introduction of new banknotes to replace those already in circulation. All citizens were advised to deposit their existing banknotes in the six-week transition period. As so much money in circulation was illegally accrued, only around 40% of the old notes were handed in, leading to a reduction of some 60% in the money supply. Many business people have reported that their income has halved since the introduction of the new currency, and strict controls on currency withdrawals and import restrictions have hampered the ability to trade. There is a monthly limit of 5,000 nakfa for withdrawal from bank accounts. There are no Automated Teller Machines and payment cards; people can only use cash and occasionally cheques for daily transactions. More positively, although the fixed exchange rate has remained at US $1 = 15 nafka since the dual exchange rate was unified into a single rate in 2005, the parallel rate in the 'black market' has fallen significantly from nearly 50 nafka to the US dollar before the currency reforms of 2015.

In May 2005 the Government issued coupons, which could be obtained at state-owned 'fair-price' shops, for a limited number of 'priority goods' such as bread, sugar, sorghum, wheat, teff, coffee, tea powder, lentils, cooking oil and kerosene. These coupons were still in use in the late 2010s, although the issuance of them was dependent on the recipients' participation in national service and attendance at various public meetings. Permits for most private imports have been in effect denied to all but priority goods since February 2005. Although the controls appear to have been relaxed, the impact on the

private trader and retail sectors has been severe. Strict controls on the transfer of hard currencies remain in place, and the PFDJ-owned Red Sea Corpn controls import-export trade.

There has been an increase in social spending, primarily in the pension and war victims' funds. The Government's budgetary planning framework contains two key elements: the containment of domestic capital expenditure; and a projected decrease in expenditure on grants to follow an improvement in the food security situation (although multilateral agencies predict a long-term decline in agricultural production). After successive fiscal deficits were registered until 2015, the overall balance moved to a surplus in 2016, which then rose from 2.1% of GDP in 2017 to 4.2% in 2018, according to the AfDB, indicating improvements in the country's fiscal policy management. However, the AfDB reported that the fiscal balance returned to a deficit of 1.6% of GDP in 2019; this widened to 4.4% of GDP in 2020, as a result of increased government expenditure to mitigate the effects of the pandemic, in addition to reduced revenue. The fiscal deficit narrowed slightly to 4.0% in 2021, reflecting a gradual recovery in public revenues following the pandemic. Eritrea's large fiscal deficits have contributed to a highly unsustainable debt burden. General government gross debt was 56,119m. nakfa in 2018, equivalent to 185.6% of GDP; according to the AfDB, gross public debt reached 189.2% of GDP in 2019, declining to 175.6% in 2021. External debt at the end of 2019 totalled US $772m., of which $718m. was public and publicly guaranteed debt. The Government has expressed an interest in pursuing Eritrea's eligibility for debt relief under the Heavily Indebted Poor Countries initiative (HIPC). As of February 2020 Eritrea was estimated to be potentially eligible for debt relief, although it was one of only three countries, together with Somalia and Sudan, that had hitherto not met the decision point qualifications and were yet to start the process of qualifying for debt relief under the HIPC initiative; the International Monetary Fund (IMF) had included Eritrea on a list of six African countries judged to be in 'debt distress' at the end of 2019.

In 2021 the Qatar National Bank (QNB) continued to seek the payment of nearly US $300m. in outstanding debt from Eritrea, based on loans totalling $200m. to Afewerki's Government in 2009 and 2010. QNB claimed that the Government had reneged on the debt in May 2012, following the repayment of about $45m. Under the commercial loan agreement. QNB referred its complaint to a court in the United Kingdom, which in 2019 ordered Eritrea to pay the bank $253m. plus interest. QNB in February 2021 requested a judgment by default from a federal court in Washington, DC, USA, to enforce the ruling, after Eritrea had failed to participate in the lawsuits or respond to the bank's claim.

AGRICULTURE

Eritrea's arable land constitutes only 12% of the country's total land area, while approximately 80% of the population subsist in the rural sector. The agricultural sector can support more than 60% of the population with a good harvest, but average production usually does not exceed 30% of cereal requirements, owing to a lack of institution-building in rural communities, water shortages, limited grazing resources for livestock and erratic rainfall patterns, caused by climate change, which has left around 60%–80% of the population vulnerable to food insecurity.

The agricultural sector contributed 17.3% of GDP in 2020, according to UN estimates, but accounted for 63.1% of employment in 2019. Most sedentary agriculture is practised in the highlands, where good *azmera* (early season) and *kremti* (June to October) rainfall is sufficient to cultivate the main crops: teff, sorghum, millet, barley and wheat. According to estimates by the Food and Agriculture Organization (FAO) of the UN, total cereal production amounted to 304,900 metric tons in 2020 (including 140,000 tons of sorghum, 65,000 tons of barley, 25,000 tons of millet and 25,000 tons of wheat). In addition to smallholder agriculture, the Government also allocates land concessions to investors to enable crop production over relatively large areas, primarily vegetables, fruits, and cereal and oilseed crops. The contribution of concessions to the country's food economy remains mediocre. Pastoralists and livestock production predominate in the lowlands, with herding patterns, both within the lowlands and between the lowlands and highlands, in search of grazing areas. The main animals are sheep and goats, followed by cattle, camels, donkeys and horses. According to FAO estimates, in 2020 total livestock in Eritrea included 2.4m. sheep, 2.1m. cattle, 1.8m. goats and 387,000 camels. Most livestock are reared on an extensive system that relies on natural pasture and crop residues. As a result, there is a marked annual fluctuation in stock condition, which reflects the availability of fodder and water. According to UN estimates, the GDP of the agricultural sector increased at an average annual rate of 1.5% in 2011–20; agricultural GDP expanded by 4.1% in 2019, but contracted by 1.1% in 2020.

Eritrea has been beset by erratic production patterns, negatively affected by droughts. As a result, food aid and food imports have been required to supplement harvests. In March 2018 some US $5m. had been allocated from the Central Emergency Response Fund (CERF) to assist 464,115 people in Eritrea whose humanitarian needs were not met by locally available resources. In a report on Eritrea in July 2019 FAO warned of an outbreak of desert locusts that could pose a serious threat to agricultural production and food security. As the infestation (the worst for many years) spread in the Horn countries, in early 2020 Eritrea's Ministry of Agriculture announced that it had effectively controlled the outbreak, following a concerted operation involving more than 11,000 farmers and military personnel. However, smaller locust invasions from neighbouring Ethiopia persisted later that year and in early 2021.

The Government maintains ownership of all land, but farmers are allowed a life-long lease on currently held land. In addition, every Eritrean citizen qualifies for the right to use a specific plot throughout their life in their home village upon finishing their military and national service. Eritreans in the diaspora are also eligible if they had fulfil their obligations to pay the 2% tax on their income. The implications of this policy for pastoralist communities are unclear, although there is little evidence of land tenure change. There are cases where fertile agricultural land is expropriated by the Government from villages located around urban centres, particularly the capital Asmara, without any compensation being given to the village members. Most of the expropriated land is then sold by the Government for the purpose of residential developments and investment.

The Government has invested heavily in the construction of dams in order to alleviate water shortages for local people and livestock. A 30m. cu m dam in Adi Halo, where President Afewerki's office is located, was completed in 2017, and was expected to supply water to Asmara.

Fisheries are a potential growth area for the Eritrean economy. Sardines, anchovies, tuna, breams, jacks, emperors, lizardfish, shark and mackerel are fished in the Red Sea. The fishing industry is largely dominated by traditional small-scale fishermen. Fishermen complain of a lack of resources, including refrigeration facilities, power and food subsidies when fishing, and an underdeveloped transportation infrastructure. As a result, most local fishermen sell their catch at the bigger and closer market in Yemen. In January 2016 the Ministry of Marine Resources offered a training programme to traditional fishermen from Gela'lo, Shieb, Dahlak, Foro and Massawa, aimed at improving their fishing techniques and increasing their yield; it also involved educating them about how to conserve natural fishery reserves and aquatic species. A total catch of only 5,565 metric tons was estimated by FAO in 2020, although, according to the UN, sustainable yields of as much as 80,000 tons per year may be possible.

INDUSTRY

Eritrea's industrial base was traditionally centred on the production of glass, cement, footwear and canned goods. According to UN estimates, the industrial sector (including mining and quarrying, manufacturing, construction and power) contributed 31.3% of GDP in 2020, a share that had increased from 12.0% in 1992, following growth in the construction sector, which contributed 15.7% of GDP in 2020, and in mining. All public enterprises in the sector were scheduled

for divestment or liquidation, following the initiation of a programme of privatization in 1995. Since independence, several small manufacturing companies have been established, including an innovative high-quality surgical intra-ocular lens laboratory which exports to countries in Europe, Africa and Asia. This laboratory produces 200,000 lenses annually. There are some small-scale factories, such as the Dekemhare Wheat Factory, the Alebu Tomato and Banana Factory, the Dekemhare DMK-Pasta Factory, the Massawa PVC Plastic Factory and the Asmara Red-Sea Wheat Factory. Although they are designed to meet demand from the local market, they still need to boost productivity in order to meet the high demand and to go beyond this market. There is also an Italian-operated garment factory employing mainly Eritrean workers who make designer shirts for export and clothes for the local market. The Government has not published any official data on the economic condition of these factories. Industrial GDP increased, in real terms, at an average annual rate of 1.0% in 2011–20; the GDP of the sector grew by 4.1% in 2019, but fell by 1.0% in 2020.

By preventing international investors from entering the country and having a very rigid investment code for the private sector, the Government's trade and industry development agenda does not promise to offer a significant boost to growth. In a small-scale but positive move, however, in 2015 Asmara Brewery began producing canned beer for export to East African countries, mainly South Sudan, and to Sweden in 2018, although it has been reported that production at the brewery is periodically affected by water shortages.

According to a government website, in Massawa 17 hangers of different sizes have been built at a cost of 58m. nakfa, together with a modern international airport. The construction of a multi-million US dollar industrial park complex by a Chinese company was reported to have been completed in late 2018.

MINING AND POWER

The mining, quarrying and utilities sector contributed 9.6% of GDP in 2020. Eritrea's mineral resources are believed to be of significant potential value. Gold-bearing seams exist in many of the igneous rocks forming the highlands of Eritrea. There are reportedly at least 15 gold mines and a large number of prospects close to Asmara, according to the Director-General of the Eritrean Mining Department. There are two regions of widespread gold mineralization in the western lowlands, at Tokombia and Barentu. Other mineral resources include potash, zinc, magnesium, copper, iron ore and marble. In April 1995 a new mining law was promulgated, which declared all mineral resources to be state assets, but recognized an extensive role for private investors in their exploitation. Investor companies would enjoy a concessionary tax regime, pay royalties of 2%–5% and encounter no restriction on repatriating profits. The Government retained the right to acquire a 10% share in any mining undertaking, with an option to buy a further 30%. According to UN estimates, the GDP of the mining sector (combined with utilities) increased at an average annual rate of 1.1% in 2011–20; it increased by 4.1% in 2019, but decreased by 1.0% in 2020.

There are currently only two mines in operation: Bisha mine, with a 60% share held by Nevsun Resources of Canada and a gold mine known as Zara, which is 60% owned by Sichuan Road & Bridge Mining Investment Development Corp (SRBM) of China. Bisha Mining Share Company began commercial gold-silver production in February 2011. Nevsun was the first company to launch commercial production operations in Eritrea, commencing with gold, followed by zinc and copper. The mine was expected to produce in excess of 1.14m. oz of gold, 11.9m. oz of silver, 821m. lb of copper and more than 1,000m. lb of zinc during its initially estimated 13-year life. In 2011 a total of 11,800 kg of gold was produced, with an average realized gold price per oz of US $1,500. Nevsun would receive payments for the Government's 30% purchased interest through the projected revenue from Bisha. In June, by which time the second phase of the copper plant had started, the company's operational cash flow increased to $186m. In 2013 a total of 887,000 metric tons of gold were milled, with 79.4% of gold recovered.

The company transformed its business from gold to copper production, and the copper flotation plant began commercial production in December 2013. Total revenue earned in 2014 amounted to $555.0m., and net income was $166.6m., of which $73.2m. went to the Eritrean National Mining Corporation (ENAMCO) and the remainder to Nevsun Resources shareholders. The company succeeded in processing pyrite sands by flotation, prior to copper ore flotation. The *US Geological Survey* estimated total gold production at 3,700 kg in 2018.

In June 2016 a new zinc flotation plant was completed at the Bisha mine, at a cost of some US $77m. Nevsun was acquired by the Zijin Mining Group Ltd of China in 2018. In 2019 ENAMCO agreed to buy an additional 5% equity interest in Bisha Mining Share Company from Nevsun, henceforth owning a 45% stake. Three Eritrean refugees in Canada brought a lawsuit again Nevsun claiming that more than 1,000 Eritreans had been forcibly conscripted by sub-contractors at the Bisha mine, breaching international law. In February 2020 the British Columbia Supreme Court in Canada (where Nevsun is headquartered) rejected Nevsun's motion to dismiss the lawsuit on the grounds that Canadian courts should not rule on the actions of the Eritrean Government. During the proceedings Nevsun denied that the company or any subsidiaries had enlisted the Eritrean military to build the mine or supply labour, and maintained that the three refugees had not been mistreated. In October human rights organization Amnesty International reported that the lawsuit alleging slavery and torture has been settled out of court by Nevsun for an undisclosed amount.

Meanwhile, in 2017 Nevsun and ENAMCO reduced the primary reserve life of the Bisha mine by 50%, to four years, in order to alleviate processing difficulties related to the more deeply located ore. However, in mid-2018 Nevsun announced an extension of the mine's life to the end of 2022, due to a planned open-pit extension that would access an additional 3.3m. metric tons of high-grade ore. Zijin Mining reported production at the mine in 2021 at 129,641 tons of zinc and 20,224 tons of copper.

Investments in Eritrea's potentially rich mining sector remain dominated by Western companies, despite efforts to attract investors from Asian countries. Sunridge Gold Corpn has four advanced deposits in central Eritrea (Emba Derho, Adi Nefas, Gupo Gold and Debarwa) and another new Kodadu deposit, which are collectively known as the Asmara Project. Sunridge, which has 4,861 metric tons of proven and 51,723 tons of probable mineral reserves, reached an agreement with the Eritrean Government similar to that of Nevsun Resources (whereby Sunridge holds a 60% share and ENAMCO 40%), with the aim of bringing the project to production in 2015. However, Sunridge had not yet received the mining permit required to begin extraction and production activities. In 2016, after 11 years of mining activity in the country, the company announced the sale of the majority of its assets in Asmara Mining Share Company to SRBM for a purchase price of US $65m. Commercial production at the Koka gold mining project, located within the Zara project, began in January 2016, operated by the Zara Mining Share Company, a joint venture between China's Shanghai Corporation for Foreign Economic and Technological Co-operation (60%) and ENAMCO (40%). Australian-based Alpha Exploration, which had been granted a prospecting licence in the southern Kerkasha region of Eritrea in January 2018, announced a significant discovery of gold and copper deposits in 2020.

In view of Eritrea's acute energy shortage, the possibility of large reserves of petroleum and natural gas beneath the Red Sea is of particular importance. In May 2017 the Australian mining company Danakali Ltd reported that there were over 6,000m. metric tons of potash reserves in the Colluli region, on the edge of the Red Sea coast, with the highest amount of sulphate of potash of all 'greenfield projects'. The 1,100m.-ton Colluli Potash Project is owned by the Colluli Mining Share Company, which was a 50-50 joint venture between Danakali Ltd and ENAMCO. After approval by the Ministry of Energy and Mines, Danakali announced in May 2020 that the company was nearing the final stages of completing the second phase of the project's development. In May 2021 Danakali secured further investment financing of A$20.3m. to support

its early works programme at the Colluli Potash Project, with the funds allocated to site road development, geotechnical optimization, reverse osmosis plant completion and installation, and mine camp installation. Danakali, which aimed to become the world's first zero-carbon sulphate of potash producer, released a report outlining the ongoing and planned contributions of the Colluli Potash Project to sustainable development in Eritrea. The company envisaged that production would commence in 2022.

According to the AfDB, in 2021 only 52.2% of the population had access to electricity (compared with 39.9% in 2010). Alternative and renewable energy resources are anticipated eventually to meet 30% of the country's energy requirements. Investments have been made in solar energy, especially in the western lowlands. In November 2014 the state media announced that Tesseney and adjacent development projects in the western lowlands of Eritrea had begun to receive 24-hour electricity supply. In March 2019 Solarcentury of the UK, one of the world's leading solar energy companies, completed two mini-grids in two rural communities in Eritrea to bring reliable power supply to some 40,000 people. Despite ongoing rural electrification, the country is still largely served by small diesel generators, which are environmentally damaging, costly to run, burdensome to maintain and constantly affected by power outages. According to reports from inside Asmara, the capital city suffers from frequent power outages that last for as long as a couple of weeks at a time, impeding several service sectors, including government offices and hospitals, and resulting in economic setbacks. The authorities claim that the high cost of oil imports is to blame. In early 2018, as part of an Egyptian initiative to develop the countries of the Nile Basin, the Egyptian Government approved plans for the construction of three electric power plants in Eritrea. Each power plant was to add electricity generation capacity of 4 MW; the construction of the plants was to be implemented by the Arab Organization for Industrialization, and the Authority for Development and Use of Renewable Energy, at a total cost of $7m.

TRANSPORT AND COMMUNICATIONS

In 2020 51.4% of GDP was provided by services, according to UN estimates, with the transport and communications subsector contributing 12.3%. In 1993 the Government announced plans for the rehabilitation of the Asmara–Massawa railway line, the only train system in the country, which had been severely damaged during the war of independence. Construction work was completed in February 2003. There is only one train that runs through that railway, and it does so infrequently and can only be chartered for events and group visits. As of August 2018 local sources reported that the train did not go as far as Arberobu'e, which is just outside of Asmara. The total length of the railway network between Asmara and Massawa is 118 km, with 30 tunnels and 65 viaducts. Comparatively speaking, Eritrea has a long road network for its land base, totalling 18,540 km. The GDP of the services sector increased, in real terms, at an average annual rate of 1.4% in 2011–20; the GDP of the sector expanded by 3.9% in 2019, but decreased by 1.0% in 2020.

At the end of 2021 the flag registered fleet of Eritrea comprised 17 vessels, with a total displacement of some 14,000 grt. Significant progress has been made in rehabilitating the port of Massawa, which was heavily bombed by Ethiopia during the 1998–2000 war. Priority was given to the dredging of the harbour and the extension of the docks; in Assab the main objective was to accelerate the transfer of cargo through the purchase of cargo handling equipment. Both ports were virtually closed to Ethiopian trade with the outbreak of hostilities in May 1998. Massawa port has a harbour length of 1,000 m with six docks, where the largest is 208.6 m long and 12 m deep. The port also has a 204,057 sq m storage area with a holding capacity of 150,000 metric tons, including 79,000 sq m of heavy duty blocks for container loading, with a computerized container terminal management system. Assab has one more dock than Massawa, which at its deepest is 11 m deep with a length of 210 m. Under the peace agreement signed between Eritrea and Ethiopia in July 2018, landlocked Ethiopia was permitted to use the ports of Assab and Massawa once again. The road from Bure in Ethiopia to Assab was officially opened by the leaders of both countries in September (four bus services across the border were expected to serve this route). However, the main border crossings were closed again in April 2019. None the less, later that year the European Union (EU) provided funds of US $90m. for road works which would allow Ethiopian access to Eritrea's ports. After the disruption surrounding the COVID-19 pandemic further delayed progress, in March 2021, during a visit by Ethiopian Prime Minister Abiy to Eritrea, it was agreed to reopen the border, and it was reported that Eritrea had begun to renovate port facilities to handle Ethiopia's shipments. In the same month a government development programme was announced for the construction and expansion of strategic roads linking the south-western Gash-Barka region with other parts of Eritrea, and of transnational roads linking the country with Ethiopia and Sudan.

In 2017 there were 1,793 buses (the principal means of passenger transport) used for public transportation in rural areas. Despite a significant increase in bus capacity in Asmara, only 60 fully deployed buses serve the city, which had a population of an estimated 963,000 in 2020. There are 30 transport routes in the Anseba region, 63 in the Southern region, 83 in Gash-Barka and 28 in the Northern Red Sea. An unregulated fleet of taxis serve Asmara, although fares are prohibitively expensive for ordinary Eritreans. In response to the COVID-19 pandemic, all travel, with the exception of a few government and business vehicles, was restricted. From April 2020 public transport was suspended, even in Asmara. The use of personal vehicles and taxis was banned and citizens were forced to travel on foot, with these movements also being restricted. The authorities finally reopened public transport on 23 March 2021, and the internal travel ban was lifted.

At July 2015 the national carrier, Eritrean Airlines (EA), offered international flights to Egypt, Saudi Arabia, the UAE and Italy (Milan). In August 2014 Turkish Airlines began services from Istanbul to Asmara, and in December Qatar Airways, operating an Airbus A320, also commenced flights to the Eritrean capital. Two years after launching this flight, however, Qatar Airways suspended all its flights to Eritrea. In July 2018 Ethiopian Airlines operated its first flight to Eritrea since before the war broke out, and commenced a daily service between the Ethiopian capital, Addis Ababa, and Asmara, operating a Boeing 787. By 2020 EA had scheduled services to Egypt, Ethiopia, Sudan and Saudi Arabia. However, international flights were suspended as part of the restrictions adopted in response to the COVID-19 crisis. Asmara International Airport was reopened to international flights to and from Ethiopia and the UAE from mid-April 2021.

The telecommunications sector in Eritrea is under the control of the Eritrea Telecommunication Services Corporation (EriTel), which is the sole provider of landline, mobile and internet services. In January 2013 the Government gave all Eritreans—both those residing inside the country and abroad—the opportunity to buy shares in EriTel. Shares worth US $4.5m. were made available for sale, at a subscription price of $50 per share. For individual buyers, 50,000 shares was the maximum limit, whereas business and institutions could buy up to 500,000 shares. Following the adoption of the company's present name upon the restructuring of the former Telecommunication Service of Eritrea in October 2003, the number of EriTel's customers increased from 38,000 to 674,900 mobile and landline users by 2019. None the less, in January 2019 the mobile subscription rate was equivalent to only 13% of the population. According to the International Telecommunication Union, mobile telephone subscriptions totalled 1.8m. and landlines in use 66,000 in 2020. Poor access to the internet due to severe power shortages was reported to be among the obstacles to efficient project implementation. There is only one state-owned television station and one radio station with two networks, although many people in the country use satellite dishes and can access international television channels.

TOURISM

The country's architecture (Eritrea possesses a number of fine Italian modernist colonial-era buildings), archaeology (pre-Axumite discoveries), the panoramic beauty of landscapes from Asmara to Massawa, and its clean and unpolluted coastal areas are major attractions, yet the number of foreign visitors is severely limited. After 15 years of lobbying, in July 2017 Asmara was recognized as a UNESCO World Heritage site. This recognition has the potential to promote tourism. According to World Bank data, 4.3% of the total Eritrean land area is nationally protected. Moreover, travel restrictions within the country, strict visa requirements, and a 2017 UN report which stated that there are widespread human rights violations in Eritrea, have had a harmful effect on the tourism industry. Nevertheless, tens of thousands of Eritreans from the diaspora, and a number of foreign nationals, visited the country in May 2016 to celebrate the anniversary marking 25 years of independence. Tourist arrivals totalled 114,000 in 2015, rising to 142,000 in 2016, when receipts from tourism amounted to US $48m. Following the signing of a peace agreement between Eritrea and Ethiopia in July 2018 and the resumption of direct flights between the two countries, the number of tourist arrivals from Ethiopia (and beyond) was expected to increase significantly. However, foreign visitors are required to secure a permit from the Ministry of Tourism to travel to tourist sites. Tourism activity was suspended in March 2020, under the travel restrictions relating to the COVID-19 pandemic and had not resumed by September 2022 (despite the resumption of international flights in April 2021).

In collaboration with the NUEYS, the country seeks to attract young Eritreans from the diaspora, also known as Zura N'Hagerka, every year by promoting festivals, seminars and tours to sites of historical importance, thereby contributing significantly to tourism revenue. The national festival dubbed 'Expo' is the largest and longest-running ethno-cultural celebration of its kind in Eritrea. It is held annually for two weeks, mostly in August, and showcases the different traditions and way of life of Eritrea's nine ethnic groups. Expo features lively entertainment and cultural displays and attracts many Eritreans from the diaspora.

THE SOCIAL SECTOR

In recent years, according to the UN Development Programme (UNDP), Eritrea has made progress in health-related developments and notably achieved the UN Millennium Development Goal of halving the proportion of people living in extreme poverty by 2015—five years ahead of schedule. The country has also demonstrated success in preventing the spread of HIV/AIDS and has sustained immunization and vaccination programmes. However, Eritrea's health care infrastructure does not meet the standard of developed countries. Domestic health expenditure represented only 17.6% of total public expenditure and 0.8% of GDP in 2019. Although residents have access to free medical treatment at public hospitals and clinics, many patients with serious illness are referred abroad for treatment which is not available in Eritrea. Recently, it has become a common phenomenon on social media for people to raise money through 'crowdfunding' campaigns to help them in seeking medical care in other countries. In the 2020 UNDP Human Development Index Eritrea was ranked 180th out of 189 countries—an indication of the fundamental improvements that the country needed to make in public services.

According to UNESCO estimates, the adult literacy rate (for those aged 15 and above) stood at 73.7% (males 82.4%; females 65.5%) in 2019. In that year the overall youth (15–24 years old) literacy rate was 93.3%. Education is officially compulsory for children between seven and 13 years of age, and is provided free of charge in government schools and at the seven government colleges of higher education. According to UNESCO, in 2017/18 enrolment at primary schools included 53% of children in the relevant age-group (boys 55%; girls 50%), while the comparable ratio for secondary enrolment was 42% (boys 43%; girls 40%). In 2018 some 7,500 children from pastoralist communities were provided with access to basic education. Technical and vocational education and training as a proportion of total enrolment in secondary education was estimated at only 3.3% in 2018. All schools from pre-primary to secondary level were closed from March 2020 due to pandemic-related restrictions, reopening on 1 April 2021.

Access to safe drinking water remains a significant challenge. In 2016 only around 52% of the population had access to safe water and 12% to improved sanitation facilities. In March 2019 Japan donated US $2.4m. to the UN Children's Fund (UNICEF)'s Expanded Programme on Immunization to benefit 850,000 people in Eritrea, including children and pregnant women. In addition, Japan provided $500,000 for child health care, nutrition, sustainable water, hygiene and sanitation. The supply of piped water, even in large cities such as Asmara, is often interrupted for lengthy periods; water rationing has been reported, with local residents collecting limited supplies from water tankers in exchange for coupons issued by the local municipality.

The average life expectancy at birth in Eritrea increased to an estimated 66.7 years in 2020, according to the World Bank. In 2013 the World Health Organization (WHO) reported that the rate of children dying under the age of five was 50 per 1,000; by 2020 this had improved to 39.3 per 1,000. The country's fertility rate decreased from 4.7 children per woman in 2013 to 3.9 in 2020.

With respect to the major causes of morbidity in the country, government reports have found a decreased prevalence of cases of tuberculosis (TB), diarrhoea and malaria, although TB remains a major public health problem. According to WHO, the estimated TB incidence was reduced from 108 cases per 100,000 people in 2016 to 89 per 100,000 in 2018, while the death rate fell from 19 to 16 per 100,000 in the same period. The Government actively distributes mosquito nets, provides malaria medication in most primary health stations, endeavours to raise public awareness of preventive mechanisms and encourages regular check-ups for people living in high-risk areas. Between 1998 and 2019, according to WHO, the incidence rate for malaria was reduced from 157 cases per 1,000 people annually to 25.6.

Following the onset of the COVID-19 pandemic, the humanitarian situation in Eritrea worsened. Supply disruptions resulting from the restrictions caused food shortages and price rises so that many people were unable to afford basic commodities. Despite further 'crowdfunding' campaigns by Eritreans in the diaspora to support the efforts of the Ministry of Health in combating the pandemic, hardship increased, and there was a lack of transparency and accountability in the distribution of the donated funds. UNICEF reported a continued deterioration in the nutrition situation during the 2021, due to the combined effects of the economic impact of the pandemic, price increases for basic commodities, desert locust infestations and adverse weather conditions. In 2021 77% of the total population were classified as living in extreme poverty. Compounding this situation was the sharp rise in food and oil prices resulting from the global impact of the war in Ukraine that began in February 2022.

CONCLUSION

The historic breakthrough in Eritrea's relationship with Ethiopia when the two countries signed a peace agreement in July 2018 promised a peace 'dividend' and considerable economic opportunities for Eritrea. Hopes were high in Eritrea that the restoration of peace and cordial relations would catalyze the process of economic transformation, including reform of the national conscription service. Military demobilization would reverse the exodus of young Eritreans from their country, which has fuelled outward migration since independence. However, progress in significant economic development soon stalled, while the COVID-19 crisis caused a severe regression in Eritrea's development gains. The pandemic-related lockdown measures imposed by the Government, together with the disruption in global supply chains, contributed to a decline in real GDP of 0.6% in 2020. In addition to the delays in the implementation of the July 2018 agreement and anticipated reforms, Eritrea's engagement in civil conflict in Ethiopia in support of the Ethiopian Government from late 2020 ended the prospect of demobilization and increased investor uncertainties. Nevertheless, real GDP growth resumed at an estimated rate of 2.9% in 2021 and was projected to increase to 4.7% in 2022, following a rebound in global demand and in the prices of Eritrea's metal exports. The war in Ukraine from February 2022, as well as precipitating dramatic increases in global food and oil prices, was likely to exacerbate food shortages since Russia and Ukraine had accounted for almost 100% of Eritrea's wheat imports, and to affect energy generation due to the country's dependence on fuel imports. In the longer term, a return to debt sustainability was considered by the AfDB to be a priority for Eritrea, with reforms, including commitment to an IMF staff-monitored programme, necessary to advance the country's access to debt relief under the HIPC initiative.

Statistical Survey

Source (unless otherwise stated): Ministry of Trade and Industry, POB 1844, Asmara; tel. (1) 126155.

Area and Population

AREA, POPULATION AND DENSITY*

Area (sq km)	121,144†
Population (census results)	
9 May 1984	
Males	1,374,452
Females	1,373,852
Total	2,748,304
Population (UN estimates at mid-year)‡	
2020	3,546,427
2021§	3,601,462
2022§	3,662,248
Density (per sq km) at mid-2022§	30.2

* Including the Assab district.
† 46,774 sq miles.
‡ Source: UN, *World Population Prospects: The 2019 Revision*.
§ Projection.

POPULATION BY AGE AND SEX
('000, UN projections at mid-2022)

	Males	Females	Total
0–14 years	748.0	717.2	1,465.2
15–64 years	1,016.3	1,017.8	2,034.1
65 years and over	71.6	91.3	162.9
Total	**1,835.9**	**1,826.4**	**3,662.2**

Note: Totals may not be equal to the sum of components, owing to rounding.

Source: UN, *World Population Prospects: The 2019 Revision*.

PRINCIPAL TOWNS
(estimated population at January 2013)

Asmara (capital) .	712,882		Keren	84,512
Assab . . .	104,075		Mitsiwa (Massawa) .	54,715

BIRTHS AND DEATHS
(averages per year, UN estimates)

	2005–10	2010–15	2015–20
Birth rate (per 1,000)	37.6	33.9	30.6
Death rate (per 1,000)	9.4	8.2	7.2

Source: UN, *World Population Prospects: The 2019 Revision.*

Life expectancy (years at birth, estimates): 66.7 (males 64.5; females 68.9) in 2020 (Source: World Bank, World Development Indicators database).

ECONOMICALLY ACTIVE POPULATION
('000, FAO estimates at mid-year)

	2013	2014	2015
Agriculture, etc.	1,853	1,910	1,968
Total labour force (incl. others) .	2,550	2,641	2,735

Source: FAO.

Health and Welfare

KEY INDICATORS

Total fertility rate (children per woman, 2020)	3.9
Under-5 mortality rate (per 1,000 live births, 2020) . . .	39.3
HIV/AIDS (% of persons aged 15–49, 2020)	0.5
COVID-19: Cumulative confirmed deaths (per 100,000 persons at 31 August 2022)	2.8
Hospitals (per 100,000 head, 2013)	0.4
Physicians (per 1,000 head, 2016)	0.06
Domestic health expenditure (2019): US $ per head (PPP) .	14.4
Domestic health expenditure (2019): % of GDP	0.8
Domestic health expenditure (2019): public (% of total current expenditure)	17.6
Access to improved water resources (% of persons, 2016) .	52
Access to improved sanitation facilities (% of persons, 2016) .	12
Total carbon dioxide emissions ('000 metric tons, 2018) . .	800
Carbon dioxide emissions per head (metric tons, 2018) . .	0.2
Human Development Index (2021): ranking	176
Human Development Index (2021): value	0.492

Note: For data on COVID-19 vaccinations, 'fully vaccinated' denotes receipt of all doses specified by approved vaccination regime (Sources: Johns Hopkins University and Our World in Data). Data on health expenditure refer to current general government expenditure in each case. For more information on sources and further definitions for all indicators, see Health and Welfare Statistics: Sources and Definitions section. (europaworld.com/credits).

Agriculture

PRINCIPAL CROPS
('000 metric tons, FAO estimates unless otherwise indicated)

	2018	2019	2020
Barley*	65.0	65.0	65.0
Broad beans, dry	0.3	0.3	0.3
Chick peas	3.7	3.7	3.7
Groundnuts, with shell . . .	2.2	2.2	2.2
Lentils	0.2	0.2	0.1
Maize*	20.0	20.0	20.0
Millet*	25.0	25.0	25.0
Peas, dry	0.6	0.5	0.7
Potatoes	0.1	0.1	0.1
Sesame seed	5.2	5.1	5.1
Sorghum*	140.0	140.0	140.0
Wheat*	25.0	25.0	25.0

* Unofficial figures.

Aggregate production ('000 metric tons, may include official, semi-official or estimated data): Total cereals 305.2 in 2018, 304.6 in 2019, 304.9 in 2020; Total fruit (primary) 4.8 in 2018, 4.8 in 2019, 4.9 in 2020; Total oilcrops 22.7 in 2018, 22.7 in 2019, 22.7 in 2020; Total roots and tubers 53.4 in 2018, 55.5 in 2019, 54.8 in 2020; Total vegetables (primary) 55.2 in 2018, 54.6 in 2019, 54.9 in 2020.

Source: FAO.

LIVESTOCK
('000 head, year ending September, FAO estimates)

	2018	2019	2020
Camels	387	382	387
Cattle	2,125	2,129	2,134
Chickens	1,239	1,197	1,184
Goats	1,813	1,814	1,815
Sheep	2,355	2,384	2,413

Source: FAO.

LIVESTOCK PRODUCTS
('000 metric tons, FAO estimates)

	2018	2019	2020
Camel meat	3.1	3.2	3.3
Camels' milk	12.1	12.0	12.1
Cattle hides, fresh	4.5	4.6	4.6
Cattle meat	22.7	22.9	23.1
Cattle offals, edible	4.6	4.7	4.7
Cows' milk	120.0	120.0	120.0
Goat meat	6.1	6.1	6.1
Goats' milk	8.7	8.7	8.7
Sheep meat	6.7	6.7	6.7
Sheep's (Ewes') milk	5.3	5.4	5.4
Hen eggs	2.2	2.2	2.2

Source: FAO.

Fishing

(metric tons, live weight of capture)

	2018	2019	2020*
Requiem sharks	183	247	245
Sea catfishes	266	323	320
Threadfin breams	750	709	705
Lizardfishes	2,404	1,438	1,435
Narrow-barred Spanish mackerel .	250	315	315
Tuna-like fishes	195	203	200
Barracudas	235	399	395
Carangids	186	317	315
Queenfishes	118	161	160
Penaeus shrimps	407	397	395
Total catch (incl. others)* . .	5,798	5,640	5,565

* FAO estimates.

Source: FAO.

Mining

('000 metric tons unless otherwise indicated)

	2016	2017	2018
Gold (kilograms)*	1,400	2,700	3,700
Clay*	88	91	100
Limestone	340	350	460
Salt	310	320	320
Granite	49	49	49

* Estimates.

Source: US Geological Survey.

Industry

SELECTED PRODUCTS
('000 metric tons unless otherwise indicated)

	2016	2017	2018
Cement*	200.0	210.0	280.0
Basalt	36.0	36.0	36.0
Electrical energy (million kWh) .	363	391	495

* Estimates.

2019: Electrical energy (million kWh) 467.

Sources: US Geological Survey; UN Energy Statistics Database.

Finance

CURRENCY AND EXCHANGE RATES

Monetary Units
100 cents = 1 nakfa.

Sterling, Dollar and Euro Equivalents (31 May 2022)
£1 sterling = 18.978 nakfa;
US $1 = 15.075 nakfa;
€1 = 16.150 nakfa;
1,000 nakfa = £52.69 = $66.33 = €61.92.

Note: Following its secession from Ethiopia in May 1993, Eritrea retained the Ethiopian currency, the birr. An exchange rate of US $1 = 5.000 birr was introduced in October 1992 and remained in force until April 1994, when it was adjusted to $1 = 5.130 birr. Further adjustments were made subsequently. In November 1997 the Government introduced a separate national currency, the nakfa, replacing (and initially at par with) the Ethiopian birr. The exchange rate in relation to the US dollar was initially set at the prevailing unified rate, but from 1 May 1998 a mechanism to provide a market-related exchange rate was established. However, since 2005 the exchange rate has been pegged to the dollar at a rate around 15 nakfa per US dollar.

BUDGET
(million nakfa)

Revenue*	2014	2015	2016
Tax revenue	5,112	5,780	6,606
Direct taxes	3,464	3,989	4,575
Indirect domestic taxes . . .	950	1,087	1,241
Import duties and taxes . .	698	704	790
Non-tax revenue	3,652	4,206	4,824
Total	8,764	9,986	11,430

Expenditure	2014	2015	2016
Current expenditure	13,674	15,920	18,034
Wages, salaries and allowances .	5,048	5,896	6,740
Materials and services . . .	4,883	5,668	6,500
Subsidies and transfers . . .	1,835	1,904	1,987
Interest	1,602	2,138	2,476
Others	306	314	331
Capital expenditure	3,795	4,523	5,170
Total	17,469	20,444	23,204

* Excluding grants received (million nakfa): 256 in 2014–16.

Source: African Development Bank.

INTERNATIONAL RESERVES
(US $ million at 31 December)

	2017	2018	2019
IMF special drawing rights . .	5.2	4.9	4.7
Reserve position in IMF . . .	0.0	0.0	0.0
Foreign exchange	138.2	158.1	187.0
Total	143.4	163.0	191.7

2020: IMF special drawing rights 4.9.

2021: IMF special drawing rights 26.1.

Source: IMF, *International Financial Statistics*.

MONEY SUPPLY
(million nakfa at 31 December)

	2012	2013	2014
Currency outside depository corporations	12,301	14,785	17,413
Transferable deposits	13,833	16,173	17,986
Other deposits	26,444	30,279	33,741
Broad money	52,579	61,237	69,140

Source: IMF, *International Financial Statistics*.

COST OF LIVING
(Consumer Price Index; base: 2005 = 100)

	2011	2012	2013
All items	256.3	287.7	323.0

Source: African Development Bank.

NATIONAL ACCOUNTS
(million nakfa at current prices)

Expenditure on the Gross Domestic Product

	2018	2019	2020
Government final consumption expenditure	21,158	21,288	21,521
Private final consumption expenditure	6,902	6,714	7,247
Gross capital formation . . .	885	1,205	2,187
Total domestic expenditure .	28,945	29,208	30,955
Exports of goods and services . .	9,917	9,421	8,910
Less Imports of goods and services	8,627	8,752	8,450
GDP in purchasers' values .	30,235	29,876	31,415
GDP at constant 2015 prices .	33,810	35,107	34,887

Gross Domestic Product by Economic Activity

	2018	2019	2020
Agriculture, hunting, forestry and fishing	5,330	5,280	5,525
Mining, quarrying and utilities .	2,950	2,921	3,060
Manufacturing	1,860	1,842	1,930
Construction	4,852	4,805	5,034
Trade, restaurants and hotels .	3,520	3,479	3,647
Transport and communications .	3,795	3,754	3,934
Public administration and defence	8,564	8,472	8,878
Sub-total	30,870	30,554	32,008
Indirect taxes (net)*	−635	−678	2,879
GDP in purchasers' values .	30,235	29,876	34,887

* Figures obtained as residuals.

Source: UN National Accounts Main Aggregates Database.

BALANCE OF PAYMENTS
(US $ million)

	2000	2001*	2002†
Exports of goods f.o.b.	36.7	19.9	51.8
Imports of goods c.i.f.	−470.3	−536.7	−533.4
Trade balance	−433.5	−516.7	−481.7
Exports of services	60.7	127.5	132.6
Imports of services	−28.3	−33.4	−30.3
Balance on goods and services	−401.1	−422.6	−379.4
Other income (net)	−1.4	−4.6	−6.1
Balance on goods, services and income	−402.5	−427.2	−385.5
Private unrequited transfers (net)	195.7	175.0	205.6
Official unrequited transfers (net)	102.4	120.8	80.3
Current balance	−104.5	−131.4	−99.6
Capital account (net)	—	7.3	3.6
Financial account	98.7	94.8	64.6
Short-term capital (net) . .	−14.7	18.7	15.9
Net errors and omissions . . .	−9.5	36.5	−7.6
Overall balance	−15.2	7.2	−39.0

* Preliminary figures.
† Estimates.

Source: IMF, *Eritrea: Selected Issues and Statistical Appendix* (June 2003).

2017 (nakfa million): Trade balance −2,230; Services (net) −208; Income (net) −245; Current transfers (net) 3,300; *Current account* 617 (Source: African Development Bank).

External Trade

PRINCIPAL COMMODITIES
(US $ '000)

Imports c.i.f.	2014	2015	2016
Sugar, molasses and honey . .	52	48	49
Meal and flour of wheat and flour of meslin	36	28	31
Rubber tyres, tyre treads or flaps and inner tubes	32	28	29
Wheat (including spelt) and meslin, unmilled	65	63	63
Motor vehicles for transport of persons	50	42	45
Total (incl. others)	1,111	1,003	1,037

Exports f.o.b.	2014	2015	2016
Vegetables	34	25	18
Cotton	46	30	23
Raw hides and skins	48	30	24
Gold, non-monetary (excluding gold ores and concentrates) .	7	72	24
Copper ores and concentrates; copper matte; cement . . .	291	172	140
Total (incl. others)	626	485	335

Source: African Development Bank.

PRINCIPAL TRADING PARTNERS
(US $ '000)

Imports c.i.f.	2014	2015	2016
China, People's Republic . . .	163	158	158
Italy	102	93	96
Saudi Arabia	107	94	99
Sudan	38	46	41
United Arab Emirates	195	172	180
Total (incl. others)	1,111	1,003	1,037

Exports f.o.b.	2014	2015	2016
Canada	—	56	17
China, People's Republic . . .	270	165	132
India	211	125	102
Korea, Republic	20	20	12
Switzerland	—	4	1
Total (incl. others)	626	485	335

Source: African Development Bank.

Transport

SHIPPING

Flag Registered Fleet
(at 31 December)

	2019	2020	2021
Number of vessels	17	17	17
Total displacement ('000 grt) . .	14	14	14

Source: Lloyd's List Intelligence (www.bit.ly/LLintelligence).

Tourism

ARRIVALS BY COUNTRY OF ORIGIN

	2009	2010	2011
Germany	775	880	1,004
India	718	730	577
Italy	1,944	1,754	1,694
Japan	151	60	78
Kenya	234	247	343
Sudan	5,866	6,220	19,653
United Kingdom	843	703	968
USA	511	738	831
Total (incl. others)	79,334	83,947	107,090

Total arrivals ('000): 119 in 2014; 114 in 2015; 142 in 2016.

Tourism receipts (US $ million, excl. passenger transport): 48 in 2016.

Source: World Tourism Organization.

Communications Media

(estimates)

	2017	2019	2020
Telephones ('000 main lines in use)	66.2	66.0	66.0
Mobile telephone subscriptions ('000)	695.0	1,311	1,801
Broadband subscriptons, fixed	1,000	3,000	5,000
Internet users (% of population)	1.3	n.a.	n.a.

Note: Data for 2018 were not available.

Source: International Telecommunication Union.

Education

(2017/18 unless otherwise indicated)

	Institutions*	Teachers	Pupils
Pre-primary	95	1,603	47,047
Primary	695	9,028	349,753
Secondary: General	44	7,436	260,421
Secondary: Teacher-training	2	47*	922*
Secondary: Vocational	n.a.	304	2,822
University and equivalent level	n.a.	726†	10,231†

* 2001/02 figure(s).
† 2015/16 figure.

Sources: UNESCO Institute for Statistics; Ministry of Education, Asmara.

Pupil-teacher ratio (qualified teaching staff, primary education, UNESCO estimate): 45.9 in 2017/18 (Source: UNESCO Institute for Statistics).

Adult literacy rate (UNESCO estimates): 76.6% (males 84.4%; females 68.9%) in 2018 (Source: UNESCO Institute for Statistics).

Directory

The Constitution

On 23 May 1997 the Constituent Assembly unanimously adopted the Eritrean Constitution. A presidential regime was instituted, with the President to be elected for a maximum of two five-year terms. The President, as head of state, has extensive powers and appoints, with the approval of the National Assembly (the legislature), the ministers, the commissioners, the Auditor-General, the President of the central bank and the judges of the Supreme Court. The President's mandate can be revoked if two-thirds of the members of the National Assembly so demand. 'Conditional' political pluralism is authorized. Pending the election of a new National Assembly, legislative power was to be held by a Transitional National Assembly, comprising the 75 members of the People's Front for Democracy and Justice (PFDJ) Central Committee, 60 members of the former Constituent Assembly and 15 representatives of Eritreans residing abroad.

The Government

HEAD OF STATE

President: ISSAIAS AFEWERKI (assumed power May 1991; elected President by the National Assembly 8 June 1993).

CABINET
(October 2022)

The Government is formed by the People's Front for Democracy and Justice.

President: ISSAIAS AFEWERKI.

Minister of Justice: FAWZIA HASHIM.

Minister of Foreign Affairs: OSMAN SALIH MUHAMMAD.

Minister of Information: YEMENE GEBREMESKEL.

Minister of Trade and Industry: NESREDIN BEKIT.

Minister of Agriculture: AREFAINE BERHE.

Minister of Labour and Human Welfare: KAHSAY GEBREHIWET.

Minister of Marine Resources: TEWOLDE KELATI.

Minister of Public Works: ABRAHA ASFAHA.

Minister of Energy and Mines: Gen. SEBHAT EPHREM.

Minister of Education: SEMERE RUSSOM.

Minister of Health: AMINA NURHUSSEIN.

Minister of Local Government: WOLDEMIKAEL ABRAHA.

Minister of Tourism: ASKALU MENKERIOS.

Minister of Land, Water and the Environment: TESFAI GHEB-RESELASSIE SEBHATU.

Minister of Transport and Communications: TESFASELASIE BERHANE.

Minister of National Development: Dr GIORGIS TEKLEMICHAEL.

MINISTRIES

Office of the President: POB 257, Asmara; tel. (1) 122132.

Ministry of Agriculture: POB 1048, Asmara; tel. (1) 181499.

Ministry of Defence: POB 629, Asmara; tel. (1) 165952.

Ministry of Education: POB 5610, Asmara; tel. (1) 113044; internet www.erimoe.gov.er.

Ministry of Energy and Mines: POB 5285, Asmara; tel. (1) 116872; internet www.moem.gov.er.

Ministry of Finance: POB 896, Asmara; tel. (1) 118131.

Ministry of Foreign Affairs: POB 190, Asmara; tel. (1) 127838.

Ministry of Health: POB 212, Asmara; tel. (1) 117549.

Ministry of Information: POB 872, Asmara; tel. (1) 120478; internet www.shabait.com.

Ministry of Justice: POB 241, Asmara; tel. (1) 127739.

Ministry of Labour and Human Welfare: POB 5252, Asmara; tel. (1) 181846.

Ministry of Land, Water and the Environment: POB 976, Asmara; tel. (1) 118021.

Ministry of Local Government: POB 225, Asmara; tel. (1) 114254.

Ministry of Marine Resources: POB 923, Asmara; tel. (1) 120400; f. 1994.

Ministry of National Development: Asmara.

Ministry of Public Works: POB 841, Asmara; tel. (1) 120302.

Ministry of Tourism: POB 1010, Warsay Ave, Dembe Sembel (Green Building), Asmara; tel. (1) 154100; e-mail eritreantourism@tse.com.er.

Ministry of Trade and Industry: POB 1844, Asmara; tel. (1) 120080; e-mail berhanem69@yahoo.co.uk.

Ministry of Transport and Communications: POB 1840, Asmara; tel. (1) 114222.

Provincial Governors

There are six administrative regions in Eritrea, each with regional, subregional and village administrations.

Anseba Province: ABDELLA MUSA.

Debub Province: HABTEAB TESFATSION.

Debubawi Keyih Bahri Province: MOHAMMED-SEID MANTAI.

Gash-Barka Province: MAHMUD ALI HIRUY.

Maakel Province: FESEHAYE HAILE.

Semenawi Keyih Bahri Province: ASMERET ABRAHA.

Legislature

NATIONAL ASSEMBLY

The National Assembly comprises the 75 members of the Central Committee of the People's Front for Democracy and Justice (PFDJ) and 75 directly elected members. In May 1997, following the adoption of the Constitution, the Constituent Assembly empowered a Transitional National Assembly (comprising the 75 members of the PFDJ, 60 members of the former Constituent Assembly and 15 representatives of Eritreans residing abroad) to act as the legislature until elections were held for a new National Assembly. As of April 2022, no such elections had taken place. In his role as Head of the Government and Commander-in-Chief of the Army, the President nominates individuals to head the various government departments. These nominations are ratified by the legislative body.

Chairman of the Transitional National Assembly: Issaias Afewerki.

Election Commission

Election Commission: Asmara; f. 2002; five mems appointed by the President; Commissioner Ramadan Mohammed Nur.

Political Organizations

Afar Federal Alliance: e-mail afa_f@hotmail.com; f. 2003.

Democratic Movement for the Liberation of Eritrean Kunama (DMLEK): Postfach 620 124, 50694, Köln, Germany; e-mail kcs@baden-kunama.com; based in Germany; represents the Kunama minority ethnic group.

Eritrean Democratic Alliance (EDA): f. 1999 as the Alliance of Eritrean National Forces, became Eritrean National Alliance in 2002, adopted present name in 2004; broad alliance of 13 parties opposed to PFDJ regime; Chair. Berhane Yemane 'Hanjema'; Sec.-Gen. Husayn Khalifa.

Eritrean Islamic Jihad (EIJ): radical opposition group; in Aug. 1993 split into a military wing and a political wing.

Eritrean Islamic Party for Justice and Development (EIPJD) (Al-Hizb Al-Islami Al-Eritree Liladalah Wetenmiya): f. 1988 as Eritrean Islamic Jihad Movement; changed name to al-Khalas in 1998; political wing of EIJ; Leader Khalil Muhammad Amer.

Eritrean Liberation Front (ELF): f. 1958; commenced armed struggle against Ethiopia in 1961; subsequently split into numerous factions (see below); mainly Muslim support; opposes the PFDJ; principal factions:

> **Eritrean Liberation Front—Central Command (ELF—CC):** f. 1982; Chair. Abdallah Idriss.

> **Eritrean Liberation Front—National Council (ELF—NC):** Leader Dr Beyene Kidane.

> **Eritrean Liberation Front—Revolutionary Council (ELF—RC):** Chair. Ahmed Woldeyesus Ammar.

Eritrean People's Democratic Front (EPDF): internet www.democrasia.org; f. 2004 by merger of People's Democratic Front for the Liberation of Eritrea and a faction of ERDF; Leader Tewolde Gebreselassie.

Eritrean People's Democratic Party (EPDP): Asmara; e-mail webmaster@harnnet.org; internet www.harnnet.org; f. 2010 by merger of the Eritrean Democratic Party, the Eritrean Popular Movement and the Eritrean People's Party; Chair. Menghesteab Asmerom.

Eritrean Revolutionary Democratic Front (ERDF): e-mail webmaster@eritreana.com; internet www.eritreana.com; f. 1997 following merger of Democratic Movement for the Liberation of Eritrea and a faction of People's Democratic Front for the Liberation of Eritrea; Leader Berhane Yemane 'Hanjema'.

Gash Setit Organization: Leader Ismail Nada.

People's Front for Democracy and Justice (PFDJ): POB 1081, Asmara; tel. (1) 121399; f. 1970 as the Eritrean Popular Liberation Forces, following a split in the Eritrean Liberation Front; renamed the Eritrean People's Liberation Front in 1977; adopted present name in Feb. 1994; Christian and Muslim support; in May 1991 took control of Eritrea and formed provisional Govt; formed transitional Govt in May 1993; Chair. Issaias Afewerki.

Red Sea Afar Democratic Organization (RSADO): Afar opposition group; Sec.-Gen. Ibrahim Haroun.

Diplomatic Representation

EMBASSIES IN ERITREA

China, People's Republic: 16 Abo St, Zone 3, Administration 2, POB 204, Asmara; tel. (1) 185271; e-mail chinaemb_er@mfa.gov.cn; internet er.china-embassy.gov.cn; Ambassador Cai Ge.

Djibouti: 38 Zeri Yacob St, POB 7702, Asmara; tel. (1) 111620; e-mail adenalimahamade@yahoo.fr; Chargé d'affaires a.i. Aden Ali Mahamadé.

Egypt: 5 Moursi Fatma St, POB 5570, Asmara; tel. (1) 124935; internet www.mfa.gov.eg/asmara_emb; Ambassador Yasser Ali.

Ethiopia: Franklin D. Roosevelt St, POB 5688, Asmara; tel. (1) 116365; internet fb.com/EthEmbAsmara; Ambassador Fikadu Beyene (designate).

France: SABA Bldg, 8th Floor, Warsay St, POB 209, Asmara; tel. (1) 182875; e-mail cad.asmara@diplomatie.gouv.fr; internet er.ambafrance.org; Ambassador Muriel Soret.

Germany: Sertzu Gebremeskel Bldg, 8th Floor, Warsay St, POB 4974, Asmara; tel. (1) 186670; e-mail info@asmara.diplo.de; internet asmara.diplo.de; Ambassador Gerald Wolf.

India: 6 City Centre St, Asmara; tel. (1) 111103; e-mail hoc.asmara@mea.gov.in; internet www.eoiasmara.gov.in; Ambassador Prakash Chand.

Israel: 32 Abo St, POB 5600, Asmara; tel. (1) 188521; e-mail info@asmara.mfa.gov.il; Ambassador Ishmael Khaldi.

Italy: 11 171–1 St, POB 220, Asmara; tel. (1) 120160; e-mail ambasciata.asmara@esteri.it; internet ambasmara.esteri.it; Ambassador Marco Mancini.

Kuwait: Asmara; e-mail asmara@mofa.gov.kw; Ambassador Faad Saad Almeilih.

Libya: 9 Shelalo St, POB 2153, Asmara; tel. (1) 127514; Ambassador Dr Mohammed R. H. Dukali.

Nigeria: Ras Dashan St, House No. 10, Zonel ADM 09, POB 1241, Asmara; tel. (1) 125606.

Russian Federation: 21 Zobel St, POB 5667, Asmara; tel. (1) 127172; e-mail asmear@yandex.ru; internet eritrea.mid.ru; Ambassador Igor N. Mozgo.

Saudi Arabia: 748 Ras Demaira St, POB 5599, Asmara; tel. (1) 154318; internet embassies.mofa.gov.sa/sites/eritrea; Ambassador Saqr bin Sulaiman al-Qurashi.

South Africa: 51–53 Hitseito St 245, Tiravalo, POB 11447, Asmara; tel. (1) 152517; e-mail franciss@dirco.gov.za; Ambassador T. J. Majokweni-Sipamla.

South Sudan: Ruba-Hadas St, House No. 17, Cambobolo, POB 9335, Asmara; tel. (1) 180612; Ambassador Mary Babodo Francis.

Sudan: 246 Hitseito St, Asmara; tel. (1) 202072; Ambassador Majid Yusuf Yahiya.

Türkiye (Turkey): Bihat St 14, Asmara; tel. (1) 110850; e-mail embassy.asmara@mfa.gov.tr; internet asmara.be.mfa.gov.tr/Mission; Ambassador Ahmet Demirok.

United Kingdom: 66–68 Mariam Gimby St, POB 5584, Asmara; tel. (1) 120145; e-mail asmara.enquiries@fco.gov.uk; internet www.gov.uk/world/organisations/british-embassy-asmara; Ambassador Alisdair Walker.

USA: 179 Ala St, POB 211, Asmara; tel. (1) 120004; e-mail usembassyasmara@state.gov; internet er.usembassy.gov; Chargé d'affaires Steven C. Walker.

Yemen: 27 Areza/Agamat St, POB 5566, Asmara; tel. (1) 181399; e-mail yemb-asmara@mofa.gov.ye; Ambassador Dr Abdelkadir Mohammed Hadi.

Judicial System

The judicial system operates on the basis of transitional laws, which incorporate pre-independence laws of the Eritrean People's Liberation Front, revised Ethiopian laws, customary laws and post-independence enacted laws. The independence of the judiciary in the discharge of its functions is unequivocally stated in Decree No. 37, which defines the powers and duties of the Government. It is subject only to the law and to no other authority. The court structure is composed of first instance sub-zonal courts, appellate and first instance zonal courts, appellate and first instance high courts, a panel of high court judges, presided over by the President of the High Court, and a Supreme Court presided over by the Chief Justice, as a court of last resort. The judges of the Supreme Court are appointed by the President of the State, subject to confirmation by the National Assembly.

Supreme Court: Asmara.

High Court: POB 241, Asmara; tel. (1) 127739.

Religion

Eritrea is almost equally divided between Muslims and Christians. Most Christians are adherents of the Orthodox Church, although there are Protestant and Roman Catholic communities. A small number of the population follow traditional beliefs.

CHRISTIANITY

The Eritrean Orthodox Church

In September 1993 the separation of the Eritrean Orthodox Church from the Ethiopian Orthodox Church was agreed by the respective church leaderships. The Eritrean Orthodox Church announced that it was to create a diocese of each of the country's then 10 provinces. The first five bishops of the Eritrean Orthodox Church were consecrated in Cairo, Egypt, in September 1994. In May 1998 Eritrea's first Patriarch (Abune) was consecrated in Alexandria, Egypt.

Patriarch (Abune): QERLOS, POB 728, Asmara; tel. (1) 184290; e-mail info@lisantewahdo.org; internet www.lisantewahdo.org.

The Roman Catholic Church

In January 2015 Pope Francis announced the separation of the four Eritrean eparchies (dioceses) from the Ethiopian Catholic Church and created a new metropolitan *sui iuris* church for Eritrea. The metropolitan Archbishop of Asmara is the head of the Eritrean Catholic Church. An estimated 3% of the total population are Roman Catholics.

Archbishop of Asmara: Archbishop MENGHISTEAB TESFAMARIAM, 19 Gonder St, POB 244, Asmara; tel. (1) 120206; e-mail catholicasmara@gmail.com; internet www.catholicasmara.com.

The Anglican Communion

Within the Episcopal/Anglican Province of Alexandria (which was inaugurated in June 2020), Eritrea lies within the jurisdiction of the Bishop of the Horn of Africa.

ISLAM

Eritrea's main Muslim communities are concentrated in the western lowlands, the northern highlands and the eastern coastal region.

Mufti: Sheikh SALEM IBRAHIM AL-MUKHTAR.

The Press

There is no independent press in Eritrea.

Chamber News: POB 856, Asmara; tel. (1) 120045; monthly; Tigrinya, Arabic and English; publ. by Asmara Chamber of Commerce.

Eritrea Alhaditha: Asmara; tel. (1) 117099; e-mail alhadisa@zena .gov.er; internet shabait.com/eritrea-alhaditha; Arabic; publ. by the Ministry of Information; Editor-in-Chief MOHAMMEDNUR YAHYA.

Eritrea Haddas: POB 247, Asmara; tel. (1) 201820; e-mail tigreit@ zena.gov.er; internet www.shabait.com/eritrea-haddas; Tigrinya; govt publ; Editor-in-Chief MOHAMMED IDRIS MOHAMMED.

Eritrea Profile: POB 247, Asmara; tel. (1) 114114; e-mail eritreaprofilenews@gmail.com; internet shabait.com/category/ newspapers/eritrea-profile; f. 1994; twice-weekly; English; publ. by the Ministry of Information; Editor AMANUEL MESFUN.

Haddas Ertra (New Eritrea): Asmara; tel. (1) 116266; e-mail hadas@zena.gov.er; internet www.shabait.com/haddas-ertra; f. 1991; six times a week; Tigrinya; govt publ; Editor ASIFIHA TEHILEMARIYAMI.

Newsletter: POB 856, Asmara; tel. (1) 121589; monthly; Tigrinya, Arabic and English; publ. by Eritrean National Chamber of Commerce; Editor MOHAMMED-SFAF HAMMED.

Broadcasting and Communications

TELECOMMUNICATIONS

Eritrea Telecommunication Services Corpn (EriTel): 11 Semaetat Ave, POB 234, Asmara; tel. (1) 127800; e-mail useritel@ tse.com.er; internet www.eritel.com.er; f. 1991; est. as Telecommunications Services of Eritrea; present name adopted in 2003 following restructuring; public enterprise; operates fixed-line and mobile networks and internet services.

TFanus: 46 Daniel Comboni Street, POB 724, Asmara; tel. (1) 202590; internet www.tfanus.com.er; f. 1996; internet service provider.

Regulatory Authority

Ministry of Transport and Communications (Communications Department): POB 6465, Asmara; tel. (1) 189193; Dir-Gen. MEKONNEN FISSEHAZION.

BROADCASTING

Radio

Voice of the Broad Masses of Eritrea (Dimtsi Hafash): POB 242, Asmara; tel. (1) 120426; f. 1979; govt-controlled; programmes in Arabic, Tigrinya, Tigre, Saho, Oromo, Amharic, Afar, Bilien, Nara, Hedareb and Kunama; Dir-Gen. GHIRMAY BERHE.

Voice of Liberty: Asmara; internet selfi-democracy.net; radio programme of the EDP; broadcasts for one hour twice a week.

Television

ERI-TV: Asmara; tel. (1) 116033; internet www.eri.tv; f. 1992; govt station providing educational, tech., entertainment and information services through three channels; broadcasting began in 1993; programming in Arabic, English, Tigre and Tigrinya; Dir-Gen. ASMELASH ABRAHA.

Finance

BANKING

Central Bank

Bank of Eritrea: 21 Nakfa St 175, POB 849, Asmara; tel. (1) 123033; e-mail kibreabw@boe.gov.er; internet www.boe.gov.er; f. 1993; bank of issue; Gov. KIBREAB WELDEMARIAM.

Other Banks

Commercial Bank of Eritrea: 208 Liberty Ave, POB 219, Asmara; tel. (1) 121844; f. 1991.

Eritrean Development and Investment Bank: 29 Bedho St, POB 1266, Asmara; tel. (1) 126777; f. 1996; provides medium- to long-term credit.

Housing and Commerce Bank of Eritrea: POB 235, Bahti Meskerem Sq., Asmara; tel. (1) 120350; e-mail hcbe.compliance@ erhcb.com; internet erhcb.com; f. 1994; finances residential and commercial construction projects and commercial loans; Chair. HAGOS GHEBREHIWET; Gen. Man. BERHANE GHEBREHIWET.

INSURANCE

National Insurance Corporation of Eritrea Share Co (NICE): NICE Bldg, 171 Bidho Ave, POB 881, Asmara; tel. (1) 123000; e-mail nice@niceeritrea.com; internet niceeritrea.com; f. 1992; partially privatized in 2004 and 2013; 60% govt-owned; general and life; Chair. GHIRMAI GHEBREMESKEL; Gen. Man. (vacant).

Trade and Industry

DEVELOPMENT ORGANIZATIONS

Eritrea Free Zones Authority: POB 9150, Asmara; f. 2001; CEO ARAIA TSEGGAI.

CHAMBERS OF COMMERCE

Eritrean National Chamber of Commerce: 46 Abiot Ave, POB 856, Asmara; tel. (1) 121589; e-mail encc@gemel.com.er.

TRADE ASSOCIATIONS

Red Sea Trading Corporation: 29/31 Ras Alula St, POB 332, Asmara; tel. (1) 127846; f. 1983; import and export services; operated by the PFDJ; Gen. Man. NEGASH AFWORKI.

UTILITIES

Electricity

Eritrean Electricity Corporation (EEC): POB 911, Asmara; e-mail awmicael@eeahrg.com.er; Gen. Man. ABRAHAM WOLDEMICHAEL.

Water

Dept of Water Resources: POB 1488, Asmara; tel. (1) 119636; f. 1992; Dir-Gen. MEBRAHTU EYASSU.

MAJOR COMPANIES

Exploration activities have identified reserves of base and precious metals. About 20 mining companies were involved in mineral exploration in different areas in the early 2020s.

Assab Salt Works: POB 6, Assab Debub Keih, Bahri; f. 1922; salt.

Bisha Mining Co.: 1 Mariam Gimby, POB 4276, Asmara; tel. (1) 124941; internet www.bishamining.com; gold and silver; Gen. Man. KEVIN MOXHAM.

Gedem Cement Factory: Massawa; cement.

Margran PLC: POB 1105, Bahti Meskerem; tel. (1) 125004; granite.

TRADE UNIONS

National Confederation of Eritrean Workers (NCEW): POB 1188, Asmara; tel. (1) 116187; e-mail ncew@ncew-er.org; internet www.ncew-er.org; f. 1994; consists of 5 federations; Gen. Sec. TEKESTE BAIRE.

Transport

RAILWAYS

Eritrean Railway: POB 6081, Asmara; tel. (1) 123365.

SHIPPING

Eritrea has two major seaports: Massawa and Assab.

BC Marine Services: 189 Warsay St, POB 5638, Asmara; tel. (1) 202672; e-mail info@bc-marine.com; internet www.bc-marine.com; f. 2000; services include marine consultancy, marine survey and ship management; brs in Assab and Massawa; Dir Capt. NAOD GEBREAM-LAK HAILE.

Eritrean Shipping Lines: 80 Semaetat Ave, POB 1110, Asmara; tel. (1) 120359; f. 1992; provides shipping services in Red Sea and Persian (Arabian) Gulf areas and owns and operates four cargo ships; Gen. Man. TEWELDE TEKESTE.

Maritime Ship Agency Services Corpn (MSASC): POB 99, Massawa; tel. (1) 552483; e-mail mssegm@tse.com.er; f. 1991 as Maritime Ship Services Enterprise; est. as a corpn 2006; state-owned; shipping agents; Gen. Man. EFREM MAKONNEN.

CIVIL AVIATION

There are three international airports: at Asmara, Assab and Massawa. There are also eight domestic airports.

Civil Aviation Department: POB 252, Asmara; tel. (1) 124335; handles freight and passenger traffic for eight scheduled carriers which use Asmara airport; Dir-Gen. PAULOS KAHSAY.

Eritrean Airlines: 101 Harnet Ave, POB 222, Asmara; tel. (1) 125500; internet www.eritrean.aero; state-owned; CEO NASREDDIN IBRAHIM.

Tourism

Eritrean Tourism Service Corpn: Asmara; operates govt-owned hotels.

Defence

As assessed at November 2021, Eritrea's active armed forces included an army of about 200,000, a navy of 1,400 and an air force of some 350; reserve forces numbered around 120,000. Conscription is compulsory for all Eritreans between 18 and 40 years of age (with certain exceptions), for an 18-month period, including four months of military training.

Defence Expenditure: US $78m. in 2014.

Chief of Staff of the Eritrean Defence Forces and Commander of the Eritrean Army: Maj.-Gen. FILIPOS WOLDEYOHANNES.

Commander of the Eritrean Naval Force: Maj.-Gen HOUMED MOHAMED AHMED KARIKARE.

Commander of the Eritrean Air Force: Maj.-Gen. TEKLAI HABTESELASIE.

Education

Education is provided free of charge in government schools and at the seven government colleges of higher education. There are also some fee-paying private schools. Education is officially compulsory for children between seven and 13 years of age. Primary education begins at the age of seven and lasts for five years. Secondary education, beginning at 12 years of age, lasts for as much as six years, comprising a first cycle of two years and a second of four years. According to estimates by the United Nations Educational, Scientific and Cultural Organization (UNESCO), in 2017/18 enrolment at the pre-primary level included 21% of children in the relevant age-group (males 21%; females 21%). In that year primary enrolment included 53% of children in the relevant age-group (boys 55%; girls 50%), while the comparable ratio for secondary enrolment was 42% (boys 43%; girls 40%). The University of Asmara was officially closed in September 2006. Higher education was henceforth to be provided by newly established colleges of higher education, each associated with a relevant government ministry.

Bibliography

Abbay, A. *Identity Jilted or Re-imagining Identity? The Divergent Paths of the Eritrean and Tigrayan Nationalist Struggles.* Lawrenceville, NJ, Red Sea Press, 1998.

Bairu, H. T. *Eritrea And Ethiopia: A Front Row Look At Issues Of Conflict.* Trenton, NJ, Africa World Press, 2017.

Bariagaber, A. *Conflict and the Refugee Experience: Flight, Exile, and Repatriation in the Horn of Africa.* Aldershot, Ashgate, 2006.

Bekoe, D. A. (Ed.). *East Africa and the Horn: Confronting Challenges to Good Governance.* Boulder, CO, Lynne Rienner Publishers, 2006.

Belloni, M. *The Big Gamble: The Migration of Eritreans to Europe.* Oakland, CA, University of California Press, 2019.

Bereketeab, R. *Eritrea: The Making of a Nation.* Trenton, NJ, Red Sea Press, 2007.

Bovo, F. *Eritrea, avanguardia di un'Africa nuova: storia, attualità ed avvenire di una giovane nazione.* Cavriago, Anteo edizioni, 2015.

Connell, D. *Against All Odds: A Chronicle of the Eritrean Revolution.* Trenton, NJ, Red Sea Press, 1993.

  Building a New Nation: Collected Articles on the Eritrean Revolution (1983–2002), Vol. 2. Trenton, NJ, Red Sea Press, 2004.

  Conversations with Eritrean Political Prisoners. Trenton, NJ, Red Sea Press, 2004.

  Historical Dictionary of Eritrea. (2nd Edn). Lanham, MD, Scarecrow Press, 2010.

Denison, E., Ren Yu, G., and Begremedhin, N. *Asmara.* London, Merrell Publishers, 2003.

Doornbos, M., and Tesfai, A. (Eds). *Post-conflict Eritrea: Prospects for Reconstruction and Development.* Lawrenceville, NJ, Red Sea Press, 1999.

Duffield, M., and Prendergast, J. *Without Troops and Tanks: Humanitarian Intervention in Ethiopia and Eritrea.* Lawrenceville, NJ, Red Sea Press, 1995.

Ellingson, L. *The Emergence of Eritrea, 1958–1992.* London, James Currey, 1993.

Fegley, R. *Eritrea.* Oxford, Clio Press, 1995.

Fekadu, T. *The Roads to Asmara 1984–1991.* Asmara, Hdri Publishers, 2016.

Fukui, K., and Markakis, J. (Eds) *Ethnicity and Conflict in the Horn of Africa.* London, James Currey, 1994.

Gaim, K. *Critical Reflections on the Eritrean War of Independence: Social Capital, Associational Life, Religion, Ethnicity, and Sowing Seeds of Dictatorship.* Trenton, NJ, Red Sea Press, 2008.

Gebremedhin, Y. *The Challenges of a Society in Transition: Legal Development in Eritrea.* Trenton, NJ, Red Sea Press, 2004.

Habteselassie, B. *Wounded Nation: How a Once Promising Eritrea was Betrayed and its Future Compromised.* Trenton, NJ, Red Sea Press, 2010.

  Deliverance: A Tale of Colliding Passions and the Muse of Forgiveness. Trenton, NJ, Red Sea Press, 2017.

Habtu, G-A. *Massacre at Wekidiba: The Tragic Story of A Village in Eritrea.* Trenton, NJ, Red Sea Press, 2013.

Henze, P. B. *Eritrea's War: Confrontation, International Response, Outcome, Prospects.* Addis Ababa, Shama Books, 2001.

Iyob, R. *The Eritrean Struggle for Independence: Domination, Resistance, Nationalism 1941–93.* Cambridge, Cambridge University Press, 1995.

Jacquin-Berdal, D., and Plaut, M. (Eds). *Unfinished Business: Ethiopia and Eritrea at War.* Trenton, NJ, Red Sea Press, 2005.

Johan, K., and Ezra, G. *Kenisha: The Roots and Development of the Evangelical Church of Eritrea, 1866-1935.* Trenton, NJ, Red Sea Press, 2011.

Kibreab, G. *Critical Reflections on the Eritrean War of Independence: Social Capital, Associational Life, Religion, Ethnicity and Sowing Seeds of Dictatorship.* Trenton, NJ, Red Sea Press, 2008.

Eritrea: A Dream Deferred. Woodbridge, James Currey, 2009.

The Eritrean National Service: Servitude for 'The Common Good' & The Youth Exodus. Martlesham, Boydell & Brewer, 2017.

Maundi, M. O., Zartman, I. W., Khadiagala, G. M., and Nuamah, K. *Getting In: Mediators' Entry into the Settlement of African Conflicts.* Washington, DC, United States Institute of Peace Press, 2006.

Mehreteab, A. *Wake Up, Hanna! Reintegration and Reconstruction Challenges for Post-War Eritrea.* Lawrenceville, NJ, Red Sea Press, 2004.

Mengisteab, K., and Yohannes, O. *Anatomy of an African Tragedy: Political, Economic and Foreign Policy Crisis in Post-Independence Eritrea.* Trenton, NJ, Red Sea Press, 2005.

Mesfin, D. *Woldeab Woldemariam: A Visionary Eritrean Patriot, a Biography.* Trenton, NJ, Africa World Press, 2017.

Miran, J. *Red Sea Citizens: Cosmopolitan Society and Cultural Change in Massawa.* Bloomington, IN, Indiana University Press, 2009.

Müller, T. *Making of Elite Women: Revolution and Nation Building in Eritrea.* Leiden, Brill Academic Publishers, 2005.

Murphy, S., Kidane, W., and Snider, T. *Litigating War: Mass Civil Injury and the Eritrea-Ethiopia Claims Commission.* OUP, New York, 2013.

Negash, T. *Italian Colonialism in Eritrea, 1882–1941: Policies, Praxis and Impact.* Uppsala, Almqvist and Wiksell International, 1987.

No Medicine for the Bite of a White Snake: Notes on Nationalism and Resistance in Eritrea 1890–1940. Uppsala, University Press, 1987.

Eritrea and Ethiopia: The Federal Experience. New Brunswick, NJ, Transaction Publishers, 1997.

Eritrea: Revolution at Dusk. Lawrenceville, NJ, Red Sea Press, 2001.

O'Kane, D., and Redeker Hepner, T. (Eds). *Biopolitics, Militarism, and Development: Eritrea in the Twenty-First Century.* New York, Berghahn Books, 2011.

Plaut, M. *Understanding Eritrea: Inside Africa's Most Repressive State.* New York, NY, Oxford University Press, 2017.

Pool, D. *From Guerrillas to Government.* Oxford, James Currey Publishers, 2000.

Rena, R. *A Handbook on the Eritrean Economy: Problems and Prospects for Development.* Dar es Salaam, New Africa Press, 2006.

Riggan, J. *The Struggling State: Nationalism, Mass Militarization, and the Education of Eritrea.* Philadelphia, PA, Temple University Press, 2016.

Tekle, A. (Ed.). *Eritrea and Ethiopia: From Conflict to Co-operation.* Lawrenceville, NJ, Red Sea Press, 1994.

Tesfagiorgis, M. *Eritrea (Africa in Focus).* Santa Barbara, CA, ABC-CLIO, 2010.

Tronvoll, K., and Mekonnen, D. *The African Garrison State: Human Rights and Political Development in Eritrea.* (Revised Edn). Woodbridge, James Currey, 2017.

van Reisen, M., and Mawere, M. (Eds). Human Trafficking and Trauma in the Digital Era : The Ongoing Tragedy of the Trade in Refugees from Eritrea. Mankon, Langaa Research & Publishing Common Initiative Group, 2017.

Venosa, J. L. *Paths Toward the Nation: Islam, Community, and Early Nationalist Mobilization in Eritrea, 1941-1961.* Athens, OH, Ohio University Press, 2014.

Welde Giorgis, A. *Eritrea at a Crossroads: A Narrative of Triumph, Betrayal and Hope.* Houston, TX, Strategic Book Publishing and Rights Co., 2014.

Wrong, M. *I Didn't Do It for You: How the World Betrayed a Small African Nation.* London, HarperCollins, 2005.

ESWATINI (SWAZILAND)

Physical and Social Geography

A. MacGREGOR HUTCHESON

The Kingdom of Eswatini (formerly known as the Kingdom of Swaziland) is one of the smallest political entities of continental Africa. Covering an area of only 17,363 sq km (6,704 sq miles), it straddles the broken and dissected edge of the South African plateau, surrounded by South Africa on the north, west and south, and separated from the Indian Ocean on the east by the Mozambique coastal plain.

PHYSICAL FEATURES

From the Highveld on the west, averaging 1,050 m to 1,200 m in altitude, there is a step-like descent eastwards through the Middleveld (450 m to 600 m) to the Lowveld (150 m to 300 m). To the east of the Lowveld, the Lebombo mountain range, an undulating plateau at 450 m–825 m, presents an impressive westward-facing scarp and forms the fourth of Eswatini's north–south aligned regions. Drainage is by four main systems flowing eastwards across these regions: the Komati and Umbeluzi rivers in the north, the Great Usutu river in the centre, and the Ngwavuma river in the south. The eastward descent is accompanied by a rise in temperature and by a decrease in mean annual rainfall from a range of 1,150 mm–1,900 mm in the Highveld to one of 500 mm–750 mm in the Lowveld, but increasing again to about 850 mm in the Lebombo mountain range. The higher parts, receiving 1,000 mm, support temperate grassland, while dry woodland savannah is characteristic of the lower areas.

RESOURCES AND POPULATION

Eswatini's potential for economic development in terms of its natural resources is disproportionate to its size. The country's perennial rivers represent a high hydroelectric potential and their exploitation for irrigation in the drier Middleveld and Lowveld has greatly increased and diversified agricultural production. Sugar, however, is the dominant industry and has traditionally been the principal export commodity. Other major crops include cotton (in terms of the number of producers, this is the most important cash crop), maize, tobacco, rice, vegetables, citrus fruits and pineapples. The well-watered Highveld is particularly suitable for afforestation and over 120,000 ha (more than 100 plantations) have been planted with conifers and eucalyptus since the 1940s, creating the largest man-made forests in Africa. In 2013 there were some 161,000 ha of planted forest in the country (equivalent to about 9% of the total land area).

Eswatini is also rich in mineral wealth. Once a major exporter of iron ore, this industry was substantially diminished with the exhaustion of high-grade ores, although considerable quantities of lower-grade ore remain and continue to be mined. Coal is currently mined at Maloma, mostly for export, and further recoverable reserves have been identified at the long-defunct coal mine at Lubhuku. Other minerals of note are cassiterite (a tin-bearing ore), kaolin, talc, pyrophyllite and silica.

Nearly one-half of the population live in the Middleveld, which contains some of the best soils in the country. This is Eswatini's most densely peopled region, with an average of 50 inhabitants per sq km, rising to more than 200 per sq km in some rural and in more developed areas. The total population of Eswatini (excluding absentee workers) was enumerated at 1,093,238, according to preliminary results, at the census of November 2017, giving an overall density of 63.0 inhabitants per sq km. According to United Nations estimates, the population at mid-2022 was projected at 1,184,821, giving a population density of 68.2 per sq km.

A complex system of land ownership, with Swazi and European holdings intricately interwoven throughout the country, is partly responsible for considerable variations in the distribution and density of the population. Only about 40% of the country was under Swazi control at the time of independence in 1968, but this proportion steadily increased in subsequent years, as non-Swazi land and mineral concessions were acquired through negotiation and purchase. The Swazi Nation, to which most of the African population belongs, has now regained all mineral concessions.

History

HUGH MACMILLAN

KING SOBHUZA II AND INDEPENDENCE

Swaziland, which began to emerge as a nation in the early 19th century, became a British protectorate in 1903 following the Anglo-Boer War, and in 1907 became one of the High Commission Territories. King Sobhuza II's 61-year reign, from 1921, spanned the transition between British territory and independent nation. Moves towards the restoration of independence in the early 1960s were accompanied by increased political activity. The Ngwane National Liberatory Congress (NNLC), an African nationalist party formed in 1962, advocated independence based on universal adult suffrage and a constitutional monarchy. Royalist interests formed the rival Imbokodvo National Movement, which won all the seats in the new House of Assembly in the pre-independence elections of April 1967. The independence Constitution vested legislative authority in a bicameral parliament, with a proportion of its membership nominated by the King. Formal independence followed on 6 September 1968.

The post-independence rule of Sobhuza was characterized by stability and economic expansion as investment flowed in, much of it from South Africa. Growing reliance on South African capital, along with Swaziland's membership of the Southern African Customs Union (SACU), restricted the country's economic and political choices. During this period the royal authorities acquired a significant material base in the economy through their control of Tibiyo Taka Ngwane and Tisuka Taka Ngwane, royal corporations which managed the investment of mineral royalties. Politically, the King extended his influence through his indirect control of the Tinkhundla (singular: Inkhundla) local authorities, each grouping together a small number of chieftaincies. In 1973, following a resolution of the House of Assembly, Sobhuza suspended the Constitution and banned political parties. Parliament effectively voted itself out of existence. By the time of the King's diamond jubilee in 1981, his authority was unchallenged. Sobhuza's death in August 1982 precipitated a prolonged and complex power struggle both within the royal family and among contending factions of the Liqoqo, a traditional advisory body. By early 1985, however, supporters of the Regent, Queen Ntombi Latfwala, mother of the 14-year-old heir apparent, Prince Makhosetive, had emerged as the group most likely to ensure an orderly succession.

ACCESSION OF MSWATI III

Prince Makhosetive was installed as King Mswati III in April 1986. To assert his authority, the Liqoqo was disbanded in May and the Cabinet was reorganized. In October Sotsha Dlamini, a former assistant commissioner of police, was appointed Prime Minister. In September 1987 the indirectly elected legislature was dissolved, and elections were held one year early, in November, when an electoral college duly appointed 40 completely new members of the House of Assembly. The new legislature and King Mswati each appointed 10 members of the Senate. The low turnout at the polls to elect the electoral college appeared to indicate dissatisfaction with the Tinkhundla system.

RE-EMERGENCE OF PUDEMO

In July 1989 the King dismissed Sotsha Dlamini for 'disobedience' and replaced him as Prime Minister with Obed Dlamini, a founder member and former Secretary-General of the Swaziland Federation of Trade Unions (SFTU). This appointment was viewed as an attempt to curb widespread labour unrest. Until late 1989 open criticism of Mswati's maintenance of autocratic rule had been restricted to sporadic appearances of anti-Liqoqo pamphlets linked to the People's United Democratic Movement (PUDEMO), an organization formed in 1983 during the regency. PUDEMO returned to prominence in 1990 with the distribution of new pamphlets advocating a constitutional monarchy.

By mid-1991 PUDEMO apparently had widespread public support, and the organization began to establish civic structures to advance its objectives through legal bodies. The most prominent of these was the Swaziland Youth Congress (SWAYOCO). The King finally agreed to review the Tinkhundla system and established a commission, which became known as the Vusela ('Greeting') committee, to test opinion on political reforms. PUDEMO rejected the Vusela process and set out five demands, including the establishment of a constituent assembly to draw up a new constitution. In February 1992 the King created a second commission (Vusela 2), which included a member of PUDEMO.

PRESSURE FOR REFORM

In October 1992 the King approved a number of proposals that had been submitted by Vusela 2. The House of Assembly (to be renamed the National Assembly) was to be expanded to 65 deputies and the Senate to 30 members. In addition, detention without trial was to cease, and a new constitution, confirming the monarchy, the fundamental rights of the individual and the independence of the judiciary, was to be drafted. King Mswati subsequently dissolved parliament and began to rule by decree, with the assistance of the Council of Ministers (as the Cabinet had been restyled), pending the adoption of the new constitution and the holding of parliamentary elections.

Voting to the expanded National Assembly took place in September and October 1993. In early November the former Minister of Works and Construction, Prince Jameson Mbilini Dlamini, was appointed Prime Minister, and a new Council of Ministers was formed.

In January 1996 PUDEMO announced a campaign of civil disobedience; later that month the SFTU initiated an indefinite general strike and there were clashes with the police. The SFTU suspended its industrial action to hold negotiations with the Government, and in July King Mswati appointed a Constitutional Review Commission, comprising chiefs, political activists and trade unionists, to draft proposals for a new constitution. Dr Barnabas Sibusiso Dlamini, a former Minister of Finance, was appointed Prime Minister.

The draft of the new Constitution was finally published in August 2001. It recommended extending the King's powers, strengthening the Tinkhundla, and continuing the ban on political parties. In December the King appointed a 15-member body, the Constitution Drafting Committee (CDC); he named his brother, Prince David Dlamini, as chairman in February 2002.

In October 2000 the Government announced a ban on trade union meetings, prompting the unions to gather their members in Nelspruit (now Mbombela), South Africa. The resulting 'Nelspruit Declaration' appealed for the establishment of an interim government outside Swaziland, for strike action in mid-November and for a three-day closure of the Swazi borders at the end of the month. The border blockade received the support of the Congress of South African Trade Unions (COSATU) and was partially successful.

PRESS RELATIONS

The press was another major focus of opposition and bore the brunt of government pressure in 1999–2001. A royal decree issued in June 2001 allowed the Minister of Broadcasting and Information, acting on behalf of the King, to ban newspapers and deny them the right of appeal to the courts. The Government revoked the decree in July, in response to international diplomatic pressure and the renewed threat of economic sanctions from the USA, but issued a new decree shortly afterwards, which retained parts of the original text.

In December 2017 the independent *Swaziland Shopping* newspaper was closed down after it published a report suggesting that King Mswati had interfered in the mobile telephone market in support of a company in which he had a personal interest. The paper's editor, Zweli Martin Dlamini, fled to South Africa, claiming that his life had been threatened. In January 2018 Victor Gamedze, the chairman of Swazi Mobile, one of the companies involved in the controversy, was shot dead in an apparent assassination in Ezulwini.

JUDICIAL CRISIS AND GENERAL ELECTION

Meanwhile, it was reported in November 2002 that the six South African judges of the Swaziland Court of Appeal had resigned in protest against a declaration by Prime Minister Barnabas Sibusiso Dlamini that the Government would not enforce two of the Court's rulings. The judges of the High Court subsequently refused to sit or set dates for hearings, and a strike by members of the legal profession ensued.

On 31 May 2003 King Mswati dissolved the National Assembly and pledged to hold elections. The first stage of the general election proceeded on 20 September. Prior to the second round of voting, Mswati dismissed the Council of Ministers and removed Prime Minister Barnabas Sibusiso Dlamini from office, replacing him with Absolom Themba ('AT') Dlamini, the long-serving managing director of Tibiyo Taka Ngwane.

INTRODUCTION OF THE NEW CONSTITUTION

Constitutional legislation was presented for approval to a joint sitting of the Senate and the National Assembly in June 2005. The King signed an amended version of the Constitution on 26 July. This concentrated executive power in the King and preserved the Tinkhundla as the basis of the parliamentary system. The King would have the power to appoint the Prime Minister and the Council of Ministers, the principal secretaries and the judges, although in the case of the last group, the appointments were to be on the advice of public and judicial service commissions. Political parties were not banned, but there was no provision for their recognition or participation in elections. The bill of rights guaranteed freedoms of speech and assembly, while giving the King the right to abrogate these in the public interest. It granted the King the right to veto parliamentary legislation, but guaranteed the independence of the judiciary and obliged the King to respect the Constitution, which included a clause allowing for his removal and replacement by the Queen Mother under certain conditions. The King and the Queen Mother were both immune from prosecution by the courts and were exempt from paying tax on their private incomes.

On 10 February 2006 King Mswati announced to a gathering of 5,000 people at the Ludzidzini royal residence that the new Constitution had come into force. The opposition was divided on how to respond. The NNLC leader, Obed Dlamini, suggested that his party would seek registration to test the legal position. The PUDEMO President, Mario Bongani Masuku, indicated that his party rejected the document outright and would refuse to participate in any elections organized under the terms of the 'royal Constitution'.

THE 2008 ELECTIONS

In June 2008 the King announced that parliament would be dissolved at the end of the month in preparation for a general election later in the year—the first to be held under the new Constitution. Following the second round of the elections, held on 19 September, police officers blocked the road to the Oshoek border post, where COSATU had organized a demonstration on the South African side of the border. On 21 September there was a bomb explosion at Lozitha bridge, near the King's main palace, in which two men were killed and a third seriously injured. The injured man, Amos Mbedzi, a South African citizen and former member of the armed wing of the African National Congress (ANC—see *External Relations*), was detained. He was sentenced in August 2012 to 85 years in prison after being convicted of murder, attempted murder and sedition.

In November 2008 Mario Masuku was detained and charged with treason and terrorism under the new Suppression of Terrorism Act, which had been promulgated in August. The Prime Minister, Barnabas Sibusiso Dlamini, who had been reappointed following the elections after five years out of office, had earlier named PUDEMO, SWAYOCO and the Swaziland Solidarity Network as 'specified entities' under the terms of the Act. Anyone found guilty of aiding and abetting such organizations was liable to up to 25 years' imprisonment. In an apparent response to Masuku's detention, Swaziland's rival trade union federations and its banned political parties came together to form the Swaziland United Democratic Front (SUDF). Masuku was finally brought to court in September 2009, when the case against him was dismissed.

Pressure on the Government increased in August 2009 with the establishment of the Swaziland Action Campaign. This became the Swaziland Democracy Campaign (SDC) in February 2010, when a conference bringing together representatives of banned Swazi political organizations such as PUDEMO and the NNLC, as well as labour organizations such as the SFTU and the Swaziland Federation of Labour, was held in Johannesburg, South Africa, under the chairmanship of the Council of Swaziland Churches. The declared objectives of the SDC included the democratic election of a national constitutional forum to draft a new constitution; the removal of laws inhibiting free political activity; the release of political prisoners; and guarantees of freedom of the press and of the judiciary.

ROYAL EXTRAVAGANCE

In January 2004 the United Nations (UN) World Food Programme (WFP) reported that it was feeding 250,000 people in Swaziland—about one-quarter of the population—and in February the King spoke of a humanitarian disaster in the country as a result of famine and HIV/AIDS. Nevertheless, it was reported in January that the Government was planning to spend US $14m. on the construction of a palace for each of the King's 11 wives.

There were widespread protests over extravagant plans for the joint celebration in September 2008 of the King's 40th birthday and the 40th anniversary of Swazi independence, which were estimated to cost at least E100m. By mid-2019 King Mswati was believed to have been married 18 times, and, as of that date, to have 14 wives and 25 children.

In April 2012 it was reported that King Mswati had acquired a DC-9 airliner for his personal use—it was later impounded in Canada and was only released on payment of US $3.5m. in May 2015. In April 2018 Mswati took delivery of a wide-bodied A340-300 Airbus, which was purchased from China Airways (a Taiwanese airline) for $13.2m. In March 2014 the King had opened a new airport at Sikhuphe, in eastern Swaziland. The airport was believed to have cost around $300m. Widely seen as a royal 'vanity project', King Mswati III International Airport became Eswatini's sole international airport in 2018.

In November 2019 the Government confirmed reports that 15 Rolls-Royce saloons, one for each of the King's wives, had been imported, as well as a Rolls-Royce Cullinan SUV for the King's personal use. A further 79 BMW saloons and SUVs were also imported for government use at an estimated cost of US $15m.

The King's personal wealth was estimated at US $50m.–$100m., but he also controls the $100m. Tibiyo Taka Ngwane Fund, which does not publish accounts. In May 2019 Goodwill Sibiya, who had sought to challenge in the courts royal ownership and control of this fund, was arrested and charged under the Suppression of Terrorism Act as a member of the banned opposition party PUDEMO. In the 2022/23 budget the expenses of the monarchy, including the Queen Mother and the King's 14 wives, was about $100m.

50TH ANNIVERSARY OF INDEPENDENCE

The joint celebration of the 50th anniversary of Swaziland's independence and King Mswati's birthday—the '50/50' celebrations—took place on 19 April 2018. The guest of honour was Taiwan's President Tsai Ing-wen, but no Commonwealth heads of state attended. King Mswati marked the occasion by announcing that the country was to be renamed Eswatini. The change of name, which had been mooted for several years, was officially gazetted in May. The constitutional legitimacy of the King's decision, which was made without prior consultation with elected politicians or members of civil society, was challenged in the courts in mid-2019 by Thulani Maseko, a prominent human rights lawyer. It was reported that the Government planned to spend at least US $125m. on the construction of a hotel and conference centre to host the 2020 African Union (AU) summit, which was originally scheduled to be held in Ezulwini, south of Mbabane, but which, in the event, took place in the Ethiopian capital, Addis Ababa. By March 2021 the estimated cost of this project had grown to $380m.

FURTHER JUDICIAL CONTROVERSY

In April 2015 a warrant was issued for the arrest of Chief Justice Michael Mathealira Ramodibedi (a Lesotho citizen) on 23 counts relating to corruption and abuse of power. In June King Mswati dismissed Ramodibedi, who was allowed to leave the country. His successor as Chief Justice, Bheki Maphalala, who was confirmed in office in November, became the first Swazi to hold the position. Meanwhile, in late June the Supreme Court upheld the appeals of a journalist and a lawyer imprisoned in July 2014 for contempt of court for publishing articles critical of Ramodibedi.

In September 2016 Justice Jacobus Annandale ruled in the High Court that some provisions of the Suppression of Terrorism Act and the Sedition and Subversive Activities Act were illegal as they contravened the Constitution. Questions have also been raised about women's rights and lesbian, gay, bisexual, transgender and intersex (LGBTI) rights. In June 2017 the Senate rejected a proposal for a review of access to the country's health facilities by LGBTI persons.

THE HIV/AIDS CRISIS

The UN estimated in 2005 that 33.4% of the country's adult population (aged 15–49 years) was living with HIV/AIDS. In August 2002 the Government had announced that antiretroviral drugs (ARVs) would be made available to pregnant women in order to prevent the transmission of HIV to their children, and that universal provision would be made when sufficient medical and financial resources became available. In June 2003 the King established the Royal Initiative to Combat AIDS.

A report on the 2007 census indicated that the death rate had increased to 18.3 per 1,000 from 7.6 per 1,000 in 1997. It was also reported that the mortality rate for children under five years of age was 167 per 1,000. However, outcomes improved thereafter. In 2011 95% of pregnant women living with HIV had access to ARVs. Overall ARV coverage stood at around 87% in 2012, which compared favourably with the universal coverage threshold of 80% specified by the World Health

Organization (WHO). In that year the rate of new HIV infections was reported to be declining, or at least stabilizing. In 2017 some 164,000 people were receiving ARV therapy. In 2019 it was estimated that HIV prevalence among adults was 27%. By 2020 Eswatini was one of the few countries in the world that had achieved the goal of 95-95-95, meaning that 95% of the adult population know their HIV status, 95% of the infected are receiving ARVs, and 95% of those people have a reduced viral load and are not infectious.

RECENT POLITICAL DEVELOPMENTS

Democracy campaigners in Swaziland were inspired in 2011 by events in Tunisia and Egypt, where popular protests unseated autocratic rulers, and the Government began to fear contagion. Plans for an 'April 12 Uprising'—coinciding with the 38th anniversary of King Sobhuza's suspension of the democratic Constitution in 1973—first appeared as an anonymous internet campaign. The authorities allowed a demonstration of about 8,000 teachers, students and workers to take place in Mbabane, in March 2011, but they tried to prevent further protest actions. In July 2012 there was a wave of strikes by public service workers.

In October 2012 the House of Assembly, in an unprecedented, but ultimately futile, display of independence, passed a vote of no confidence in Prime Minister Barnabas Sibusiso Dlamini and his Council of Ministers. However, the Prime Minister refused to resign, and the King declined to remove him. As the 40th anniversary of the suspension of the independence Constitution and the outlawing of political parties approached, in February 2013 police officers raided a prayer meeting at the Roman Catholic Cathedral in Manzini, which had been organized by the SUDF and the SDC. In March a group of trade unions and other organizations, including the SUDF and PUDEMO, appealed for a boycott of the forthcoming general election. Voting took place on 24 August and 20 September. Only nine of the incumbent members of the House of Assembly were returned to office, and just one woman was elected. Barnabas Sibusiso Dlamini was reappointed as Prime Minister in October, and a new Council of Ministers was inaugurated in November.

In April 2013 Maxwell Dlamini, the Secretary-General of SWAYOCO, was arrested and charged with two counts of sedition. The President of SWAYOCO, Bheki Dlamini, who had been in prison since June 2010, having been accused of planting explosives in the houses of police officers and public servants, was acquitted in February 2014.

Mario Masuku, the veteran leader of PUDEMO, was arrested on 1 May 2014, together with Maxwell Dlamini, who was rearrested while on bail. The two men were released in July 2015, following an international campaign, although the charges against them remained and they were banned from attending meetings.

Addressing the Southern African Development Community (SADC)'s parliamentary forum in June 2016, King Mswati sought to rebrand Swaziland as 'a monarchical democracy'. He chaired a meeting of SADC in Mbabane in August, but the Government was criticized for spending US $2m. on the event at a time when the country was in the grip of a serious drought. A state of emergency had been declared earlier in the year and many people were receiving food aid from WFP.

In early 2018 it was announced that elections would again be held in two rounds in August/September. The Swaziland Democratic Party petitioned the High Court in May to demand that political parties be allowed to participate in the polls. However, the application was rejected in July, and the elections proceeded without political parties. The turnout, with less than one-third of the 500,000 registered voters taking part in the first round, was very low. A constitutional provision for the co-option of four additional female members of parliament (one from each region) in the event that the number of women elected falls below 30% of the total number of legislators, was implemented for the first time.

The long-serving Prime Minister (1996–2003, 2008–18), Barnabas Sibusiso Dlamini, resigned owing to ill health in August 2018 and died the following month. He was succeeded by another member of the royal clan, Mandvulo Ambrose

Dlamini, who had previously served as managing director of MTN Swaziland, a mobile telephone company in which King Mswati has a personal stake. Neal Rijkenberg, a prominent local businessman of Dutch descent, who had founded the timber company Montigny (which now controlled most of Eswatini's extensive commercial forests), was appointed as Minister of Finance. In his first budget speech, delivered in March 2019, Rijkenberg highlighted Eswatini's difficult economic and fiscal position, as a result of declining sugar prices, and the threat of reduced income from SACU, which provides about one-half of the country's total revenue.

Meanwhile, in May 2018 Mario Masuku and other members or supporters of PUDEMO were barred from leaving Eswatini at the Oshoek border post, despite possessing valid travel documents. They had intended to participate in a protest with 300 South African trade unionists in support of political prisoners in Eswatini, including Amos Mbedzi. In September Masuku stood down as PUDEMO President on the grounds of ill health and was replaced by the party's erstwhile Secretary-General, Mlungisi Makhanya. Masuku died in January 2021.

Protests in 2021

In May–June 2021 there were widespread protests organized by the Swaziland National Union of Students (the union, led by Colani Maseko, has not accepted the country's name change), following the disappearance and alleged murder by police of a 25-year-old law student, Thabani Nkomonye. Students demanding an end to police brutality, and constitutional reform, presented a petition to parliament and lobbied members of the House of Assembly in their constituencies. They supported the unprecedented demand by three 'pro-democracy' members of parliament, Mduduzi Bacede Mabuza, Mduduzi 'Magawugawu' Simelane and Mthandeni Dube, for the Prime Minister to be elected, not appointed. 'Justice for Thabani' demonstrations spread to schools in mid-June. Widespread protests, accompanied by attacks on businesses associated with the royal family, reached a peak on 29 June and continued into July. The Government responded by suspending the internet and imposing a night-time curfew, and there were violent responses to the demonstrations by the police. According to official estimates, 30 people were killed in the disturbances—opposition sources put the number at 80. Many more were injured and at least 600 people were detained.

King Mswati blamed the protests on 'marijuana-smokers', and in a pointed repudiation of 'pro-democracy' demands, on 16 July 2021 appointed a new Prime Minister, Cleopas Sipho Dlamini, formerly CEO of the Public Service Pension Fund. On 25 July Mabuza and Dube were arrested and charged under the Suppression of Terrorism Act. They were denied bail and remained in detention as of July 2022 following a judge's rejection of a motion to dismiss the cases against them, which included incitement to riot and murder. Meanwhile, 'Magu-wagwu' Simelane had taken refuge in South Africa and in November 2021 he announced in Johannesburg the formation of a new political party, the Swaziland Liberation Movement (SWALIMO).

There was a further upsurge of protests in October 2021 when the internet was again shut down and all schools were closed. An attempt by health and public service workers to present a petition to the legislature was opposed by armed police—a bystander was killed and 30 people injured in the resultant clashes; the presentation of petitions was banned in response. A delegation from SADC visited Eswatini in October and South African President Cyril Ramaphosa, chairperson of its Troika security organ, met King Mswati in November. The King agreed to proposals for a national dialogue, but insisted that this should take place through 'traditional' structures, such as public meetings at the Tinkhundla, preventing further progress.

In the first half of 2022 there were several arson attacks on the homes and businesses of people associated with the monarchy—some in the name of a newly established underground organization, the Swaziland International Solidarity Forces. Tension increased in the weeks before 29 June, which was declared by the opposition Multi-Stakeholders Forum, led by Thulani Maseko, as a national stay-away day to commemorate the anniversary of the 2021 protests. Police reported that between April and June two officers were killed and three others injured in shooting incidents. An estimated E2m. damage was done to police residences and infrastructure at police posts. In addition, one of the two military helicopters used in riot control was petrol-bombed. The sabotage of road-building machinery belonging to a company in which King Mswati is alleged to have a personal stake, compelled it to cease operations temporarily. The stay-away on 29 June 2022, seen as an unofficial national holiday, passed without major incident. Whether by accident or design, King Mswati was not in the country at the time. Further protests and clashes with police took place at the University of Eswatini in early July.

On 11 July 2022 it was announced that SADC troika would hold an extraordinary summit on 21 July under the chairmanship of President Ramaphosa and that King Mswati would attend. However, the summit was postponed two days before it was scheduled to take place—South African media reported that the Eswatini Government had said it was unavailable, although the Government disputed this.

THE COVID-19 PANDEMIC

Following the global outbreak of COVID-19 in early 2020, a partial lockdown of Eswatini was introduced on 27 March, the day after a lockdown was imposed in neighbouring South Africa. The regulations prohibited non-essential travel and prescribed working from home wherever possible. A partial relaxation in June included the reopening of schools. In early April 2020 Prime Minister Ambrose Dlamini had announced that by 5 May 300,000 individuals, who would be identified by the National Disaster Management Agency as being in special need, would each be given E700 to purchase food.

On 23 March 2020 it was revealed in *Swaziland News*, an online newspaper published on Facebook and the country's most widely read news source, that King Mswati was in self-isolation following a meeting with a Taiwanese delegation. In mid-April the same source reported that the King was critically ill and had been hospitalized. These reports received some international coverage, but were officially dismissed as being false. The editor of *Swaziland News*, Zweli Martin Dlamini, was briefly detained by the police and informed that he was being investigated for sedition and spreading false reports about the COVID-19 pandemic. Dlamini subsequently fled across the border into South Africa, as he had previously done in December 2017 after receiving alleged death threats. In July 2022 *Swaziland News* and Dlamini, who had remained in hiding in South Africa since April 2020, were both declared 'affected entities' under the terms of Eswatini's controversial Suppression of Terrorism Act. The Government also pursued action against the newspaper and its editor at the High Court in Mpumalanga, South Africa, in an attempt to shut down the publication, although it has continued to appear.

Eugene Dube, the editor of another online newspaper, *The Swati Newsweek*, also fled to South Africa in May 2020. Dube, who had published two articles criticizing the Eswatini Government's response to COVID-19, claimed that he had been detained by police, that his personal computer had been confiscated and that he had been threatened with sedition charges.

In November 2020 Prime Minister Ambrose Dlamini became ill with COVID-19. He was transferred to hospital in Johannesburg and died on 13 December at the age of 52, after only two years in office. He was reported to be the first head of government to die from the illness. Dlamini was succeeded as acting Prime Minister by his deputy, Themba Masuku. In mid-July 2021 Cleopas Sipho Dlamini (see *Recent Political Developments*) was appointed as the new Prime Minister.

Meanwhile, in January 2021 two other members of the Council of Ministers—Makhosi Vilakati, Minister of Labour and Social Security, and Christian Tshangase, Minister of Public Service—died of COVID-19. Mario Masuku, leader of the banned opposition party PUDEMO, also died in Mbabane in that month, apparently from COVID-19.

In February 2021 it was announced that King Mswati had been ill with COVID-19 in early January and had recovered. He attributed his recovery to Taiwanese antiviral medication.

A four-member medical team from Taiwan had arrived in Eswatini in May 2020 and stayed for several months.

King Mswati's sister, Queen Mantfombi Dlamini-Zulu, of the Zulu, died in April 2021. The cause of her death was not announced. She was acting as Queen Regent of the Zulu following the death of her husband, King Zwelethini, in March. Dlamini-Zulu was succeeded by her son, King Misuzulu, who visited his uncle, King Mswati, in Eswatini in May.

In March 2021 a team from an Israeli non-governmental organization, IsraAID, sponsored by the Nathan Kirsh Foundation arrived in the country and vaccinated 35,000 people against COVID-19. In June it was reported that a further 30,000 doses of the AstraZeneca vaccine were due to arrive in Eswatini. By July 2022 official statistics from the Ministry of Health indicated that there had been 73,227 COVID-19 cases and 1,417 deaths in the country. However, it was probable that the officially declared number of cases and fatalities was an underestimate. As of late May 2022 28.7% of the population had been fully vaccinated.

The COVID-19 pandemic has also had serious economic repercussions for Eswatini (see *Economy*). In November 2020 the IMF agreed to a grant of US $110,000m. to help the country through the crisis.

EXTERNAL RELATIONS

After achieving independence in 1968, Swaziland joined a number of international organizations, including the Commonwealth, the UN and the Organization of African Unity (now the AU). It subsequently also became a member of SADC. In view of Swaziland's record on human rights, there was some domestic and international criticism when, in 2008, King Mswati was elected as Chairman of SADC troika on politics, defence and security co-operation.

In May 2014 it was announced that the USA would suspend Swaziland from benefits under the African Growth and Opportunity Act (AGOA), which offers preferential trade terms, as a result of the country's failure to amend the Industrial Relations Act and the Suppression of Terrorism Act. This suspension came into force in January 2015. It was reported in early 2017 that the Government's failure to make the necessary changes to the legislation that would permit the restoration of AGOA trade terms had resulted in a loss of jobs. However, US President Donald Trump announced the restoration of AGOA trade benefits to Swaziland in December of that year.

In February 2018 Lisa Peterson, the US ambassador to Swaziland from 2016, spoke out strongly in support of the party-political system, noting that the European Union and the Commonwealth had frequently found that elections in the country were not 'free and fair' as political parties were banned. In an extraordinary intervention on 23 July 2020, which must have been approved by the US Department of State, Peterson, who was soon to leave the country, called for constitutional changes to curb royal extravagance. Speaking at an online press conference in which she answered questions from three Swazi journalists, she called for the revision of Article 9 of the 2005 Constitution, which prohibits the reduction of the King's remuneration. Peterson also stated that there should be legal provision for the declaration of gifts to all officials, including the King. She maintained that she had been angered by the acquisition in 2019 of 15 Rolls Royces for the royal wives and implied that these luxury vehicles had not been purchased but received as gifts or bribes. The ambassador also cited other egregious examples of royal extravagance, including the King's children being sent to a theme park in Florida, USA, at a time of drought, when many children were starving and the country was receiving food aid. Peterson referred to Eswatini's low scores for political freedom and civil liberties on the annual Freedom House indices and was especially critical of the 2008 Suppression of Terrorism Act. She did, however, claim that US pressure had achieved some moderation of the 2017 Public Order Act.

In what was seen as a major setback to Swaziland's international status, the British Government announced in December 2004 that it was to close its high commission in Mbabane at the end of 2006. It appointed an honorary consul and proceeded to conduct its relations with Swaziland from the high commission in Pretoria, South Africa. In May 2019 the British Government reversed its policy by announcing the reopening of the high commission in Mbabane and the appointment of a new high commissioner, who was to be resident in the country.

At mid-2021 Eswatini was the sole country in the African continent to maintain diplomatic relations with Taiwan and was a recipient of substantial Taiwanese aid and investment. In February 2020 it was reported in *Swaziland News* that the People's Republic of China had threatened to sever business ties with Eswatini if that country retained diplomatic relations with Taiwan. Referring to Eswatini's refusal to recognize the Chinese Government's policy of 'One China', the report was attributed to China's ambassador to South Africa, Lin Songtiang, who in a speech in December 2019 had blamed King Mswati personally for Eswatini's policy on Taiwan. The online newspaper reported that henceforth the visa applications of Eswatini citizens wishing to travel to mainland China would be processed only by the Chinese embassy in Pretoria. In September 2020 Eswatini's ambassador to the UN spoke in favour of Taiwanese membership of the organization.

In October 2019 King Mswati attended the inaugural Russia-Africa Summit, which was held in Sochi, the Russian Federation, and was co-hosted by the Russian President, Vladimir Putin, and the Egyptian President, Abd al-Fatah al-Sisi. In June 2022 he attended the Commonwealth Heads of Government Conference in Kigali, Rwanda. This was the first time that he had left the country in more than two years.

As a small and landlocked country, Eswatini's most important bilateral relationships have been with its two neighbours, South Africa and Mozambique. King Sobhuza II harboured the ambition of reclaiming from South Africa areas in the eastern Transvaal and northern Natal that were separated from the Swazi kingdom in the 19th century. The achievement of independence by Mozambique in 1975 created a situation in which the exiled ANC of South Africa was able to use Swaziland as a corridor for the movement of recruits from South Africa and for the infiltration of guerrilla fighters. South Africa offered to transfer to Swaziland the KaNgwane 'Bantustan' ('homeland') in the Transvaal and the Ingwavuma district in northern Natal (the acquisition of the latter area would have afforded Swaziland direct access to the sea) in exchange for the imposition of more stringent restrictions on the activities of the ANC. However, the proposals for the land transfer were finally abandoned in 1984 due to legal obstacles and strong opposition in South Africa.

In 1984, within days of the signing of the Nkomati Accord between South Africa and Mozambique, the Swazi Government revealed the existence of a security agreement with South Africa that had been concluded in February 1982. The systematic suppression of ANC activities in Swaziland, which had begun in 1982, intensified, and open collaboration between the two countries led to gun battles in Manzini. Conflict escalated in 1986, and armed raids by South African security personnel resulted in a number of ANC deaths in border areas and in Manzini. Growing public outrage at such activities led the Swazi Prime Minister publicly to accuse South Africa of responsibility and to condemn a raid in August as an 'illegal act of aggression'. The release from prison of the South African activist Nelson Mandela in February 1990 led to an improvement in bilateral relations, and in late 1993 formal diplomatic relations were established.

In February 2001 King Mswati restated his determination that parts of the Mpumalanga and KwaZulu/Natal provinces should be reincorporated into Swaziland. In June 2003 Prince Khuzulwandle, Chairman of the Swaziland Border Adjustment Committee, criticized South African President Thabo Mbeki for refusing to discuss the realignment of the border. In November 2006 the Swazi Government announced that it intended to take the border dispute to the International Court of Justice (ICJ) in The Hague, Netherlands. In March 2017 the new chairman of the Border Adjustment Committee, Prince Guduza, claimed that large areas of South Africa, including Pretoria, Limpopo, Mpumalanga and KwaZulu/Natal, belonged to Swaziland.

In 2014 a COSATU spokesperson described Swaziland as 'the forgotten wound of the region' and spoke of the 'deafening silence' of SADC on the affairs of the country. In April 2016 South African President Jacob Zuma attended King Mswati's birthday celebrations and reportedly engaged in talks with him about changes to SACU. His successor, President Cyril Ramaphosa, made an official visit to Eswatini in March 2019, accompanied by his Minister of International Relations and Co-operation, Lindiwe Sisulu. In the following month, both former President Zuma and Sisulu rejected South African press allegations that Zuma had transferred gold bullion worth several million US dollars, which had reportedly belonged to the late Libyan leader Col Muammar al-Qaddafi, from his residence at Nkandla in KwaZulu/Natal, to Eswatini.

In April 2021 South African journalist Peter Bruce, writing in the *Financial Mail*, reported that 'master plans' announced by President Ramaphosa and South Africa's Minister of Trade and Industry, Ebrahim Patel, for the 'localization' of manufacturing threatened Eswatini's sugar, textile and clothing industries, as well as the interests of other SACU members. They were expected to raise these issues at a SACU meeting in June.

In recent years one area of conflict, and co-operation, between Eswatini, South Africa and Mozambique has been the use of the water resources of the Komati (also transliterated as Inkomati, Incomati or Nkomati) river. The apparently excessive use of the river for hydroelectric projects and irrigation schemes in South Africa and Eswatini has severely reduced the flow of water into Mozambique and led that country to present a claim for compensation to the ICJ. In 1995 the Swedish Government provided funds, through the Swedish International Development Agency, for the establishment of the Inkomati Shared River Basin Initiative (ISRBI). This resulted in the presentation by the three involved countries to the Second World Water Forum in The Hague in March 2000 of a proposed scheme for fair and equal access to the water of the river. Mozambique's representative on the ISRBI stated that this plan might encourage the country to withdraw its claim for compensation. Mozambique did not, however, become a signatory to the related Nkomati River Basin Accord until 2002. In the same year Swaziland's Maguga Dam, the water from which was shared by South Africa and Swaziland on a 60:40 basis, commenced operations. In April 2019, following a meeting between King Mswati and President Filipe Nyusi of Mozambique, Eswatini reportedly agreed to release 18m. cu m of water from the Maguga Dam, which would flow down the Umbuluzi river into Mozambique and thereby alleviate a long-term water shortage in Maputo province.

Economy

DONALD L. SPARKS

Revised for this edition by the editorial staff

INTRODUCTION AND RECENT ECONOMIC DEVELOPMENTS

Eswatini (formerly known as Swaziland), with a land area of only 17,363 sq km, is the second smallest state in mainland Africa and had a population of 1,184,821 at mid-2022, according to United Nations (UN) estimates. The World Bank placed the kingdom among 50 of the world's 'lower-middle income' group of countries, with a gross domestic product (GDP) per head of US $3,424 in 2020. Furthermore, some 59% of its population live below the national poverty line. Eswatini scored poorly on the UN Development Programme's 2019 Human Development Index (HDI), ranking (jointly with Ghana) 138th out of 189 countries, placing it in the 'medium human development' category. The HDI is a composite index measuring average achievement in three basic dimensions of human development—a long and healthy life, knowledge and a decent standard of living.

Eswatini is a small, open economy, and the country's recent period of lower rates of growth has been due to a variety of domestic and global factors. A slump in global demand has resulted in the closure of the Sappi Usutu pulp mill (see *Agriculture and Forestry*), as well as the loss of perhaps 3,000 jobs in the textile industry. Demand has also fallen for Eswatini's only mineral export, coal. Other factors contributing to the deceleration in growth include problems associated with the HIV/AIDS pandemic (with an adult HIV/AIDS prevalence rate of 26.8% in 2020, the world's highest rate) and competition from Asian textile producers. Eswatini remains in what could be classified as an economic crisis: education and health care services are severely constrained, as the economy is not growing fast enough to fund such services. Increasing frustration at the population's poor living standards—as well as the lack of political and social change—led to months of civil unrest during 2021. Real GDP grew by 2.4% in 2018 and 2.2% in 2019, but declined by 5.6% in 2020, according to UN estimates, resulting in an average annual growth rate of 2.0% in 2011–20. Despite earlier forecasts of increased growth for 2020, the international health crisis (see below) had a profound impact on Eswatini's principal economic sectors—in particular, manufacturing, construction, trade and tourism. A fiscal deficit of 8.7% of GDP was recorded in 2020/21, due to lower receipts from the Southern African Customs Union (SACU) and higher government spending to tackle the crisis; inflation rose to 3.9% in 2020, and remained at 3.7% in 2021. Nevertheless, amid a modest economic recovery, the International Monetary Fund (IMF) estimated GDP growth of 3.1% in 2021, and forecast growth of 2.1% for 2022. Moreover, the fiscal deficit was expected to fall steadily to reach an estimated 4.8% of GDP in 2022/23.

The first case of COVID-19, which had emerged in December 2019 in the People's Republic of China and was designated as a global pandemic by the World Health Organization (WHO) on 11 March 2020, was confirmed in Eswatini on 13 March. According to Johns Hopkins University and Our World in Data, 73,185 confirmed cases of COVID-19 had been reported in Eswatini by 7 July 2022, with 1,417 fatalities; by 29 May 2022 28.7% of the total population had been fully vaccinated. By early July COVID-19 had caused an estimated 6.3m. deaths worldwide and massive social and economic disruption, prompting a widespread recession in 2020. In an effort to contain the spread of the virus, on 27 March 2020 the Government had ordered a partial lockdown of Eswatini, including border closures and the shutdown of non-essential businesses. Although a gradual easing of these measures was initiated on 8 May, from late 2020 the country experienced a renewed rise in infections (with the Prime Minister and two cabinet ministers themselves dying from the disease—see *History*). The rapid increase in cases of COVID-19 prompted the Government to order a second partial lockdown on 8 January 2021, and this was extended in March.

Since independence there has been noteworthy diversification of the economy away from agriculture and mining. In 2020, according to UN figures, services and industry (including mining, quarrying, utilities, manufacturing and construction) contributed the largest shares of GDP, with an estimated 55.6% and 35.5%, respectively; agriculture, hunting, forestry and fishing contributed an estimated 8.9%. Despite its relatively diverse economy and its wealth, Eswatini has not escaped the extremes of income distribution familiar elsewhere in Africa. The bottom 10% of households receive only 1.6% of total income, and in 2019 around 58.9% of the population were living below the poverty line (but 70% in rural areas). More than two-thirds of the resident population comprises families earning generally poor incomes from smallholder cash cropping or subsistence agriculture on Swazi Nation Land (SNL). Moreover, the living standards of the rural poor have been largely unimproved by periods of rapid growth since independence. In 2007 the Government approved the Poverty Reduction Strategy and Action Programme, with the ambitious goals of reducing poverty by one-half by 2015 and eliminating poverty by 2022. The 2015 goal was not met, and the 2022 goal appears very unlikely to be achieved either.

With skills failing to adapt to the new demands of the productive economy, Eswatini faces both skill shortages and a mismatch between the skills possessed by its workforce and those demanded by employers. This has a particularly negative effect on employment, with the International Labour Organization (ILO) reporting an unemployment rate of 23.7% in 2021. However, the level of disguised or discouraged workers means that the actual rate is much higher. Large numbers are not registered as unemployed or are not actively seeking work, so they are not included in official figures. In addition, Eswatini's private sector is burdened by significant regulatory barriers. The ILO reported youth unemployment of 46.2% in 2019, and the situation has since been exacerbated by the COVID-19 pandemic.

Eswatini's development has been dominated in many ways by its large neighbour, South Africa, the principal regional economic power. For example, in 2020 Swaziland received 71.4% of its imports from, and sold 65.0% of its exports to South Africa. South African capital and imports, the Southern African Customs Union (SACU), the South African labour market and the Common Monetary Area (CMA) have all shaped the economy and restricted the scope for an independent economic policy. However, a consistent determination to maintain an investment climate attractive to foreign business and a policy of accepting the dominance of its powerful neighbour brought Swaziland a rate of post-independence capital formation not achieved in most African states. In the late 1980s the kingdom benefited as foreign and South African companies relocated to Swaziland, often to escape anti-apartheid sanctions. In the early 1990s, however, Swaziland experienced the negative repercussions of political instability and economic recession in South Africa. Since the mid-1990s, political uncertainty, a poor business climate and lack of skilled manpower have been Swaziland's largest economic problems, leading business to favour South Africa. Swaziland traditionally supplied the South African mines with labour, and those miners' remittances back to Swaziland provided a substantial income base. However, since the end of the 20th century the number of Swazi miners has declined considerably, along with their remittances. This has been partially offset by an increase in the number of Swazi professionals moving to South Africa and the United Kingdom.

AGRICULTURE AND FORESTRY

The agricultural sector (including hunting, forestry and fishing) accounted for 8.9% of GDP in 2020, compared with 14.3% in 2004. However, despite this decline, in many ways it remains the backbone of the economy. The sector accounts for around 12% of the formal labour force.

Agro-industry continues to contribute the majority of manufacturing value added; it also provides 70% of employment. Over one-half of the total land area is SNL, where traditional subsistence farming is conducted on land held by the monarchy, access to which is managed by the Swazi aristocracy and local chiefs. However, lack of title ownership prevents farmers from accumulating the necessary collateral to acquire loans, and limits their entry into the productive sector. More than one-half of all SNL is designated as Rural Development Areas, and cash cropping of rain-watered crops, particularly maize and cotton, contributes significantly to total agricultural production when climatic conditions are favourable. The remainder of the land, the Title Deed Land, comprises individual tenure farms, owned by commercial companies, wealthy Swazis and white settlers. The principal agricultural commodities are sugar, maize, citrus fruits, pineapples, potatoes and cotton. Livestock farming is an important sub-sector of the economy, particularly on SNL, where cattle serve as a store of value and a unit of account, and are also used for various cultural purposes (for example, bride price).

Eswatini has traditionally been the third largest sugar producer in sub-Saharan Africa. According to the Swaziland Sugar Association (SSA—renamed the Eswatini Sugar Association—ESA—in 2018), sugar accounts for about 9% of GDP, 60% of agricultural output, 7% of total export earnings, 10% of formal sector employment and 58% of total Swazi exports to the European Union (EU). In 2020/21 some 62% of Swazi sugar was sold to the SACU market (mostly to South Africa), 25% to the EU and world market, 10% to other regional countries and 3% to the USA. The EU has ended its sugar beet quota, which has led to a significant rise of competitively priced sugar into Europe and reduced Eswatini's share. Eswatini's new quota of 60,000 metric tons will not be enough to compensate for lower European demand. Many sugar farmers are still recovering from the 2015–16 drought and can ill afford the new EU measures. Nevertheless, Eswatini is likely to benefit from the new Common Market for Eastern and Southern Africa (COMESA) scheme that will allow for more sugar exports to Kenya.

The sugar industry consists of four components: miller planters and estates (77%), large growers (17%), medium-sized growers (5%) and small growers (1%). There are three sugar mills in the country (Simunye, Mhlume and Ubombo mills), all with approximately the same annual output, at around 200,000 metric tons each. The Swazi Nation has substantial shareholdings in all three mills. Eswatini is vulnerable to world fluctuations in the price of sugar. The SSA reported that sugar production reached 746,983 tons in 2018/19, but decreased to 673,369 in 2019/20, largely due to adverse weather conditions. However, output subsequently increased, to 684,562 tons in 2020/21 and an estimated 696,908 tons in 2021/22.

In the early 21st century cereal harvests have to date failed to meet domestic requirements. Maize production has been on a generally downward trend, owing to erratic weather conditions, high fuel and other input costs, a decline in advanced agricultural practices and the impact of HIV/AIDS. Maize output increased from 84,000 tons in 2017 to some 113,000 tons in 2018, owing to better weather conditions. However, the harvest declined in 2019 and 2020, to 95,000 tons and 87,000 tons, respectively, as a result of disease, pests and adverse weather. This, together with the ongoing impact of COVID-19 and the sharp rise in global food prices, led Eswatini's Vulnerability Assessment Committee to predict that some 336,000 people (about 29% of the population) would suffer from severe food insecurity between December 2021 and March 2022.

The agricultural sector has benefited from the Lower Usuthu Smallholder Irrigation Project (LUSIP), which was launched in 2004 in one of the poorest areas in the country. The climate is semi-arid, droughts are frequent and crop yields are unreliable. Most households have access to less than 2 ha of land and can barely grow enough to feed themselves. Land tenure and access to water for irrigation are key means to improve rural livelihoods and reduce poverty. The long-term objective of the project was to create favourable conditions so that farmers in the Lower Usuthu Basin would be able to commercialize their activities and develop sustainable, high-value crop production. The project involved investing in a large-scale irrigation system for the area, with the construction of three dams to form a reservoir to store water diverted from wet-season flood flows in the Lower Usuthu river. The first phase involved construction of the main infrastructure and the development of an irrigation system spanning more than 6,500 ha. A second phase was to extend the irrigation system and develop a further 5,000 ha. It was evident by 2014 that the LUSIP project was starting to yield results, with increased access to both land and water for the local population and a consequent rise in average household incomes.

More than one-half of Eswatini's planted forest area (conifers and eucalyptus) was traditionally devoted to supplying the kingdom's main forestry industry, the Sappi Usutu pulp mill, which produced unbleached wood pulp. The mill, which closed in 2010, was Swaziland's third largest source of export earnings. The mill's closure (with a loss of 600 jobs) was a result of major forest fires in the area in 2008 and, subsequently, reduced global demand. By 2013 the total area of planted forest totalled 161,000 ha (around 9% of total land area). The development of these large-scale plantations has had a serious negative impact on both the environment and people over the years.

MINING, MANUFACTURING AND TOURISM

Although the kingdom is relatively rich in mineral resources, the contribution of mining and quarrying to GDP has registered an overall decline since independence. From around 10% in the 1960s, the sector's contribution to GDP (including utilities) had decreased to just 1.5% by 2020. The sector's poor performance can be attributed to reduced output at the Maloma colliery, the phasing-out of the country's diamond mine, which closed in 1996, and the cessation of asbestos mining in 2001. Asbestos was the first mineral product to be exploited in Eswatini on a large scale. The Havelock mine was developed in the 1930s, and it was only overtaken by the sugar industry as the territory's leading source of export revenue in 1962. The identification of health problems associated with asbestos and the depletion of reserves resulted in the decline of the sub-sector. The mining sector received a boost in 2011/12 with the reopening of the iron ore mine at Ngwenya (considered to be one of the world's oldest mines). The sector contracted in 2014 due to weakened demand (especially from the People's Republic of China), lower prices for coal and iron ore, and the closing of the Ngwenya mine, but recorded a slight expansion in 2015/16 with the opening of the small Lufafa goldfield. However, the Lufafa mine closed in 2017, owing to mismanagement. According to reports in June 2022, the Ngwenya mine was again expected to reopen, despite the concerns of local residents regarding the lack of maintenance at the site and the likely increase in environmental pollution.

Coal holds the country's most important mineral potential, with reserves estimated at over 2,000m. metric tons. According to figures from the Central Bank of Swaziland (CBS—renamed the Central Bank of Eswatini—CBE—in mid-2018), output totalled 144,375 tons in 2018, before decreasing to 109,926 tons in 2019. Although the CBS registered coal output of 161,768 tons in 2020, production declined to just 62,681 tons in 2021. A lack of adequate investment inhibits meaningful exploitation of Eswatini's mineral resources, and the mining sector is likely to stagnate in the short term.

Since the late 1980s there has been encouraging diversification of the manufacturing sector (which accounted for 31.0% of GDP in 2020, according to the UN), and Eswatini now ranks among some of the most industrialized African economies. Several small factories, producing knitwear, footwear, gloves, refrigerators, office equipment, beverages, confectionery, pine furniture, safety glass and bricks were established during the investment boom of the 1990s, creating many new jobs.

Eswatini's textile industry has been in decline during the past decade, owing to international competition and a lack of new investment in technology. Swaziland was granted provisions under the USA's African Growth and Opportunity Act (AGOA) in 2001 which benefited the local textile industry; under the terms of the Act, Swaziland enjoyed unrestricted, tariff-free access to the US market for the export of textiles and clothes. Consequently, the garment industry enjoyed rapid growth. However, in early 2015 Swaziland was formally excluded from AGOA, because the US Administration held that the Government had failed adequately to address human rights violations in the country. Specifically, there was deemed to be a lack of progress on, *inter alia*, regulation of trade unions and freedom of assembly, speech and organization. As 90% of Swazi textile exports were destined for the USA (textiles being the largest source of export earnings after sugar and soft drink concentrates), such a loss had severe negative consequences. In 2017 the USA restored Swaziland's eligibility after ruling that the Government had made some progress in working conditions and political rights.

During the period of Swaziland's exclusion from AGOA, South Africa became a prime destination for Swazi textile exports, although that country's struggling economy has restricted the growth of exports to the South African market. Moreover, in late 2015 the EU also considered imposing trade sanctions, unless Swaziland granted basic political rights and increased democratic freedom in the country. None the less, in 2016 the EU signed an Economic Partnership Agreement (EPA) with Swaziland which offered similar levels of access to those provided under AGOA.

Eswatini is a relatively high-cost producer. The average wage in the textile industry is about US $200 per month, compared with about $40 per month in the countries of southern and eastern Asia, the major competitors. In addition, the World Trade Organization agreement on textiles and clothing expired in 2004, and import quotas from other major producers (principally China and Bangladesh) were reduced. Two major textile firms (GMS Textiles and First Garments) ceased operating in Swaziland in 2003. During 2004–05 a total of 14 textile factories closed, and the Swaziland Textile Exporters' Association estimated that the number of people employed in the industry had fallen from 30,000 to 15,000. In 2014, before the loss of the AGOA benefits, employment in the textile sector was estimated at 17,300.

Eswatini is blessed with an abundance of natural beauty and a fairly well-developed tourism infrastructure (by regional standards). According to the Eswatini Tourism Authority (ETA), visitor numbers totalled around 1.3m. each year during 2013–18, falling to about 1.2m. in 2019. Tourism receipts amounted to US $16m. in 2018, but fell to a provisional $14m. in 2019, according to the UN World Tourism Organization. Since then, the COVID-19 pandemic has had a severe impact on tourism in Eswatini: the ETA registered a decline to just 345,348 visitor arrivals in 2020, resulting in significant job losses, and the country only received 210,705 tourists in 2021. In that year South Africans and Mozambicans constituted some 71% of tourists, followed by Europeans (particularly Portuguese and British nationals). The tourism sector and related services employed about 5.7% of the total workforce and contributed around 4.6% of GDP in 2021.

POWER, TRANSPORT AND COMMUNICATIONS

The country has a comparatively well-developed and well-maintained physical infrastructure, but the Eswatini Electricity Company still imports approximately 70% of its requirements (770m. kWh) from South Africa. In 2019, however, the Swazi Government began issuing tenders to local companies to increase the production of solar energy and biomass, with the aim that renewable sources would account for 50% of Eswatini's electricity supply by 2030. In 2012 Swaziland signed an agreement with Equatorial Guinea for a guaranteed supply of crude petroleum at preferred rates. Eswatini consumes some 20m. litres of petrol and diesel each month, almost all of which is imported from South Africa. After much public discourse, the Government admitted that it had no plans to establish a refinery and that all of the Equato-Guinean crude would be

refined in South Africa. According to World Bank data, 79.7% of the Swazi population had access to electricity in 2020, with the proportion rising to 92.2% in urban areas.

Eswatini's rail network totalled 466 km in 2017. The kingdom's first railway line was built during 1962–64 to connect the Ngwenya iron ore mine in the far west of the country, via the then railhead across the eastern border at Goma, Mozambique, to the port of Maputo and thence to its Japanese customers. Long disused west of the Matsapha industrial estate, the line was finally taken up in 1995. A southern link via Lavumisa and connecting to the South African port of Richards Bay was completed in 1978, and a northern link, crossing the border near Mananga and running to the South African town of Komatipoort, was opened in 1986. These lines established a direct link between the eastern Transvaal and the Natal ports, integrating the Swazi lines into the South African network. Eswatini is also studying the feasibility of linking its rail network to Mpumalanga province in South Africa. This route could compete with existing lines between South Africa and Mozambique and add alternatives to Durban, South Africa. In 1993 an inland container depot was established in the central Swazi town of Matsapha, which witnessed rapid growth. The inland port receives imports and moves exports that are transported by rail from Durban.

The kingdom's road network is comparatively well developed. In 2004 there were an estimated 4,875 km of roads, of which only 1,111 km were paved. Road projects have dominated the capital expenditure programmes of development plans in recent decades, and in 1991 work began on the rebuilding of the kingdom's main road artery connecting the capital, Mbabane, to Manzini, via Matsapha. The highway was completed in 1999, behind schedule and well over budget. The Ministry of Public Works and Transport has suggested introducing toll roads (as in South Africa) and establishing a roads authority. These plans were still in progress in mid-2022.

The fastest-growing service in the telecommunications sector has been the monopoly mobile cellular telephone operator MTN Swaziland. By the end of 2002 the number of mobile telephone subscribers exceeded the number of fixed-line telephones and by 2017 the number of mobile telephone subscribers had risen to 1.05m., while the number of landlines in use had declined to 41,000. In 2016 there were 414,724 internet users (up from 90,100 in 2012); an estimated 47.0% of the population used the internet in 2017.

TRADE AND BALANCE OF PAYMENTS

SACU—the world's oldest currency union, which celebrated its 100th anniversary in 2010—was renegotiated in 2002 and the new agreement guaranteed a duty rate of 17% between Namibia, Botswana, Lesotho and Swaziland (NBLS), reducing the previous annual fluctuations. In addition, each SACU member would now receive customs revenues based on its relative contribution to SACU GDP, of which Swaziland accounted for just 0.9%. Receipts from SACU played an even more important role from 2007. By 2009 SACU receipts amounted to 55.8% of Swaziland's total fiscal revenue. However South Africa has argued that the revenue-sharing formula means that it subsidizes the other SACU members. In March 2015 the South African Minister of Finance testified that transfers to SACU increased from some R43,000m. in the 2013/14 financial year to R52,000m. in 2014/15, the latter figure being equal to 5.4% of South Africa's total revenue. This sum includes customs revenue from the formula and a development subsidy (based on each member's per capita income level). The 2014/15 allocations involved about two-thirds of the total customs duties collected going to the NBLS countries, despite the fact that South Africa is responsible for the overwhelming majority of trade. The Minister also noted that taxes were lower in other SACU member countries (except for Namibia), placing South Africa at a disadvantage. After a marked decline in 2015/16, Swaziland's SACU receipts recovered in 2017/18, although not enough to balance the Government's budget. Given the volatility of the receipts, in 2018/19 the Government reduced spending and increased some taxes, including value-added tax (VAT). Eswatini's SACU receipts increased from 5,800m. in that year to

E6,300m. in 2019/20 and E8,300m. in 2020/21. However, following the drastic reduction in regional economic activity during the COVID-19 outbreak, they decreased to E6,300m. in 2021/22; a further decline, to E5,800m., was estimated for 2022/23.

From 2004 Swaziland (in partnership with the Southern African Development Community—SADC) held negotiations with the EU regarding the drawing up of an EPA. An interim agreement was signed in 2007 and included the elimination of duties/quotas for imports to the EU from Botswana, Lesotho, Namibia, Swaziland and Mozambique, as well as the elimination of duties/quotas on EU exports to those countries. The agreement enabled all participating countries to reintroduce duties/quotas to help safeguard local economies; it resulted in improved access to EU markets, although Eswatini's economy now faced increased competition from European imports. After 10 years' duration, the EPA negotiations were successfully concluded in South Africa in July 2014. The EPA took effect in 2015, under the Trade, Development and Cooperation Agreement between the EU and South Africa. In December 2018 Eswatini and the Republic of China (Taiwan) signed an economic co-operation agreement that was expected to increase bilateral trade. (At mid-2022 Eswatini was the only African country officially to recognize Taiwan as a sovereign entity, despite coming under growing pressure from the Chinese Government to reverse this policy.)

In 2020, according to figures from the International Trade Centre, the country's merchandise exports amounted to US $1,752.1m. (compared with $2,001.8m. in 2019), while imports totalled $1,605.3m. ($1,841.9m. in 2019), resulting in a visible trade surplus of $169.2m. In 2020 the principal source of imports was South Africa (providing 71.4% of total imports), which was also the principal market for exports (taking 65.0% of the total); Kenya, Mozambique, Nigeria, the USA, China and India were other important markets in that year. According to the IMF, the current account on the balance of payments recorded a surplus of $60.7m. in 2018, $195.7m. in 2019 and $254.9m. in 2020.

Besides being a member of SACU, Swaziland is also a member of SADC and COMESA, but, in common with other CMA members, has not elected to join COMESA's free trade area. However, in 2008 SACU members gave Swaziland permission to negotiate with COMESA on a range of issues. In March 2018 Swaziland signed the African Continental Free Trade Area Agreement (AfCFTA)—a pact between AU member states, with the goal of creating a single market and eventually free movement and a single currency union. AfCFTA entered into force in May 2019, with Nigeria being the last major African economy to sign the agreement in July.

PUBLIC FINANCE, DEBT, INFLATION, FOREIGN AID AND INVESTMENT

The 2019/20 budget forecast a rise in revenue—primarily from increased SACU receipts, an increase of one percentage point in VAT and the sale of government assets. The ratio of the fiscal deficit to GDP was predicted to narrow to 3.1% in 2020/21. However, owing to the financial implications of tackling the COVID-19 outbreak from March 2020, and lower SACU receipts, a deficit of 8.7% of GDP was in fact registered. A smaller fiscal deficit, of 6.5% of GDP, was estimated in 2021/22, and the budget presented by the Minister of Finance in February 2022 anticipated a further reduction, to 4.8% of GDP, for 2022/23.

The national currency is the lilangeni (plural: emalangeni—E), introduced in 1974. The terms of the Trilateral Monetary Agreement, concluded with South Africa and Lesotho to form the CMA in 1986, allowed the Swazi authorities the option of determining the lilangeni's exchange rate independently. Under the amended Multilateral Monetary Agreement (signed in 1992 to formalize Namibia's de facto membership), this freedom was maintained, but the currency has remained pegged at par to the South African rand. In line with the South African rand, in December 2021 the Swazi exchange rate was US $1 = E15.91 (up from E17.49 in May 2020). Although it is generally agreed that this system has served Eswatini well, because the lilangeni is linked to the rand, events in South

Africa have a direct effect on the Swazi currency. For example, when the respected South African Minister of Finance, Pravin Gordhan, was dismissed in March 2017, the rand's value declined almost overnight, and Standard & Poor's downgraded South Africa's credit rating to junk status. Swaziland's foreign currency reserves grew to $842m. at the end of 2013, a rise of 13.6% over the previous year (owing principally to an increase in SACU receipts); however, by 2016 they had fallen to $603.9m. In May 2022 the CBE reported that Eswatini's foreign reserves were sufficient to cover 3.4 months of imports of goods and services (just above the three-month level which is generally considered to be safe).

Eswatini's monetary policy closely aligns with that of South Africa. The South African Reserve Bank (SARB) increased its 'repo' rate by 25 basis points to 5.75% in mid-2014 and the CBE in turn raised its rate to 5.25%. In early 2016 the CBS raised the discount rate by 50 basis points to 6.25% and at mid-year raised it further to 6.5% (50 basis points below that of South Africa). In early 2017 the repo rate in Swaziland stood at 7.25%, the highest since 2009 and above the rate in South Africa. In early 2018, however, the CBS lowered the rate twice, leaving it to stand at 6.75%; in July 2019 it was reduced further, to 6.5%. By late May 2020 the SARB had lowered its repo rate to 3.75%, following the emergence of COVID-19 and, consequently, the drastic downgrading of its economic forecasts for 2020. This, in turn, led the CBE to reduce its rate four times between March and July; it stood at a record low of 3.75% in mid-August, but in January 2022 was raised to 4.0% amid rising inflation.

At the end of 2020 Swaziland's external debt totalled US $766m. (up from $630m. in 2019.) The country received some $148m. in official development assistance (ODA) in 2016 and 2017; however, ODA was recorded at $121m. in 2018 and just $73m. in 2019. The vast majority of ODA is directed to the health care sector. The major donors in 2014/15 were the USA (providing 23% of total ODA) and EU institutions (18%). The debt service ratio remains modest, although it has risen in recent years; it was recorded at 2.3% in 2018, 2.7% in 2019 and 3.3% in 2020.

Eswatini's inflation rate moves almost in tandem with that of South Africa (which is the country's major supplier of imports, see above). In line with declining fuel and basic food prices, year-on-year inflation stood at 5.7% in 2014, but, owing to drought and marked increases in food prices (particularly maize) and electricity tariffs, inflation surged to 8.8% in 2016. In 2017 the inflation rate, at 6.2%, was above that of South Africa (5.2%). However, inflation slowed to 4.9% in 2018, owing to continued downward pressures on food prices, lower global oil prices and reduced government spending; this downward trend continued in 2019, as economic growth stagnated, with inflation averaging 2.6%. Despite the economic downturn in 2020, inflation rose to 3.9%, as the Government raised spending in order to mitigate the worst effects of the COVID-19 pandemic. The inflation rate was 3.7% in 2021. Net foreign direct investment (FDI) has been erratic since the 1990s. Swaziland attracted a record US $135.7m. in FDI in 2010 and, following another period of fluctuations, FDI reached $128.0m. in 2019 before declining to $44.1m. in 2020.

The Eswatini Stock Exchange (ESE)—one of the world's smallest—was established as the Swaziland Stock Market in 1990 and renamed the Swaziland Stock Exchange in 1998. It is a member of the Committee of SADC Stock Exchanges and of the African Securities Exchanges Association. There were seven companies listed on the ESE in May 2022.

ECONOMIC PROSPECTS

Limited economic dynamism, due mainly to lack of new investment in the productive sectors, has contributed to Eswatini's sluggish growth. Private sector investment had been largely subdued, despite a general growing confidence in the economy. Equally important, linkages in mature industries (textiles, sugar and concentrates) require further diversification of the product ranges to create new investment opportunities, which would have significant growth implications for the rest of the economy. In addition, the share of government activity in GDP remains high, with the recovery in SACU revenue receipts critical to recent growth.

Eswatini faces serious economic and social challenges in both the near and long term. It is currently ranked as the country with the highest percentage of its population infected with HIV/AIDS. Nearly 60% of the population lives below the official poverty line, and an estimated one-third of the population is undernourished. The country's political system—the sole absolute monarchy remaining in sub-Saharan Africa—is almost at breaking point. Labour relations are particularly strained, and there is general political instability. The leading political organization, the banned People's United Democratic Movement, has urged the international community to isolate and ostracize King Mswati. In late 2019 the Industrial Court (which has jurisdiction over industrial relations) declared protests by public sector workers in support of their demand for a 7.8% cost of living adjustment to be illegal, pending a judicial decision. The national development strategy, which runs until 2022, will likely be hampered by inadequate funding.

Compounding the numerous constraints discussed above, Eswatini is generally considered as being corrupt and a difficult place in which to do business. For example, it was listed 121st (out of 190 countries) in the 2020 World Bank's Ease of Doing Business Index. The Economist Intelligence Unit's Democracy Index 2021 ranked Eswatini joint 128th (together with Kazakhstan) out of 167 countries, placing it in the 'authoritarian' category. In addition, Eswatini was ranked 36th out of 54 countries in the 2020 Mo Ibrahim Foundation's Index of African Governance. Transparency International ranked Eswatini joint 122nd (together with Ukraine) out of 180 countries in its 2021 Corruption Perceptions Index, while Freedom House's 2022 Index of Economic Freedom classified Eswatini as 'not free'. The lack of political inclusiveness and transparency in Eswatini has had profound and lasting negative effects on the country's economic growth and development, as well as on its near-term prospects.

Eswatini is vulnerable to numerous internal and external shocks, including the weather, the erosion of trade preferences, potential declining terms of trade and an economy that is still not sufficiently diversified or developed, a poorly skilled workforce, insufficient physical infrastructure, a growing youth bulge (with high youth unemployment), a weak financial sector, and continued fluctuations and uncertainty in the SACU revenue stream.

None the less, Eswatini has substantial long-term economic potential. The country has ample natural resources, although it has, to date, managed them poorly. Indeed, most observers believe that with reformed, competent leadership Eswatini would have one of the brightest futures in the region. The country's economy has undergone many changes during recent years, the most important being in its relationship with its economically powerful neighbour South Africa, with which Eswatini's economic future is in many ways linked. There are a number of social, political and economic areas in which Eswatini will have to make changes independently of that relationship. For example, the traditional and inefficient land tenure system is important in Swazi culture and seems unlikely to be reformed soon. The unconducive investment climate and poor business environment (the kingdom ranked 121st out of 141 countries in the World Economic Forum's Global Competitiveness Index 2019) pose challenges to growth. Most importantly, Eswatini will have to find ways of accommodating a strong and growing desire for political reform and inclusiveness—with numerous popular protests again taking place in 2021—in order to establish the domestic and international confidence needed for economic growth and poverty reduction. At mid-2022, unfortunately, the chances of the kingdom achieving such success appeared faint.

Statistical Survey

Source (unless otherwise stated): Central Statistical Office, POB 456, Mbabane; internet www.gov.sz.

Area and Population

AREA, POPULATION AND DENSITY

Area (sq km)	17,363*
Population (census results)†	
11 May 2007 (provisional)‡§	953,524
9 November 2017 (preliminary)	
Males	531,111
Females	562,127
Total	1,093,238
Population (UN estimates at mid-year)‖	
2020	1,160,164
2021¶	1,172,369
2022¶	1,184,821
Density (per sq km) at mid-2022¶	68.2

* 6,704 sq miles.
† Excluding absentee workers.
‡ Source: UN, *Population and Vital Statistics Report*.
§ Population total is *de jure*, although the figure was the subject of some dispute on publication; in early 2009 the Ministry of Economic Planning and Development published the State of Swaziland Population Report, which contained a revised population estimate of 1,018,449 for 2007.
‖ Source: UN, *World Population Prospects: The 2019 Revision*.
¶ Projection.

POPULATION BY AGE AND SEX
('000, UN projections at mid-2022)

	Males	Females	Total
0–14 years	216.9	213.6	430.6
15–64 years	349.5	357.2	706.7
65 years and over	17.7	29.8	47.5
Total	**584.2**	**600.6**	**1,184.8**

Note: Totals may not be equal to the sum of components, owing to rounding.

Source: UN, *World Population Prospects: The 2019 Revision*.

REGIONS
(population at 2017 census, preliminary figures)

	Area (sq km)	Population	Density (per sq km)
Hhohho	3,569	320,651	89.8
Lebombo	3,779	212,531	56.2
Manzini	5,945	355,945	59.9
Shiselweni	4,070	204,111	50.2
Total	**17,363**	**1,093,238**	**63.0**

PRINCIPAL TOWNS
(population at census of May 1997)

Mbabane (capital) .	57,992	Manzini	25,571

Mid-2018 (incl. suburbs, UN estimate): Mbabane 68,010 (Source: UN, *World Urbanization Prospects: The 2018 Revision*).

BIRTHS AND DEATHS
(annual averages, UN estimates)

	2005–10	2010–15	2015–20
Birth rate (per 1,000) . . .	31.9	28.6	26.7
Death rate (per 1,000) . . .	18.1	13.6	9.4

Source: UN, *World Population Prospects: The 2019 Revision*.

Life expectancy (years at birth, estimates): 60.7 (males 56.5; females 65.4) in 2020 (Source: World Bank, World Development Indicators database).

EMPLOYMENT
(persons in paid employment at June)

	2003	2004	2005
Agriculture, hunting, forestry and fishing	21,491	20,804	19,955
Mining and quarrying . . .	1,153	1,407	1,283
Manufacturing	19,485	19,874	20,272
Electricity, gas and water . . .	1,418	1,389	859
Construction	4,824	5,293	5,115
Distribution	9,021	9,988	11,454
Transportation	2,491	2,265	3,007
Finance	6,422	5,202	6,430
Social services	26,758	27,247	27,228
Total employed	93,063	93,469	95,603

Source: IMF, *Kingdom of Swaziland: Selected Issues and Statistical Appendix* (March 2008).

Mid-2015 (estimates in '000): Agriculture, etc. 137; Total labour force 532 (Source: FAO).

Health and Welfare

KEY INDICATORS

Total fertility rate (children per woman, 2020)	2.9
Under-5 mortality rate (per 1,000 live births, 2020) . . .	46.6
HIV/AIDS (% of persons aged 15–49, 2020)	26.8
COVID-19: Cumulative confirmed deaths (per 100,000 persons at 31 August 2022)	119.3
COVID-19: Fully vaccinated population (% of total population at 21 August 2022)	28.7
Physicians (per 1,000 head, 2020)	0.1
Hospitals (per 100,000 head, 2013)	0.8
Domestic health expenditure (2019): US $ per head (PPP) .	309.7
Domestic health expenditure (2019): % of GDP . . .	3.4
Domestic health expenditure (2019): public (% of total current expenditure)	50.7
Access to improved water resources (% of persons, 2020) .	71
Access to improved sanitation facilities (% of persons, 2020) .	64
Total carbon dioxide emissions ('000 metric tons, 2018) . .	1,090
Carbon dioxide emissions per head (metric tons, 2018) . .	1.0
Human Development Index (2021): ranking	144
Human Development Index (2021): value	0.597

Note: For data on COVID-19 vaccinations, 'fully vaccinated' denotes receipt of all doses specified by approved vaccination regime (Sources: Johns Hopkins University and Our World in Data). Data on health expenditure refer to current general government expenditure in each case. For more information on sources and further definitions for all indicators, see Health and Welfare Statistics: Sources and Definitions section (europaworld.com/credits).

Agriculture

PRINCIPAL CROPS
('000 metric tons, FAO estimates unless otherwise indicated)

	2018	2019	2020
Almonds, with shell	1.0	1.0	1.0
Bananas	6.6	6.5	6.5
Grapefruit and pomelos . . .	49.3	49.9	50.4
Groundnuts, with shell . . .	2.2	2.3	2.3
Maize*	113.0	95.0	87.0
Oranges	44.3	44.7	44.4
Pineapples	36.0	38.0	36.3
Plums and sloes	1.4	1.5	1.5
Potatoes	8.2	8.3	8.3
Sugar cane	5,685.5	5,737.0	5,699.5
Sweet potatoes	2.5	2.5	2.5
Tomatoes	5.5	5.5	5.5

* Unofficial figures.

Aggregate production ('000 metric tons, may include official, semi-official or estimated data): Total cereals 115.7 in 2018, 97.7 in 2019, 89.7 in 2020; Total fruit (primary) 144.9 in 2018, 147.8 in 2019, 146.4 in 2020; Total oilcrops 1.5 in 2018; 1.7 in 2019, 1.2 in 2020; Total roots and tubers 73.4 in 2018, 73.6 in 2019, 73.4 in 2020; Total vegetables (primary) 13.2 in 2018, 13.1 in 2019, 13.2 in 2020.

Source: FAO.

LIVESTOCK
('000 head, year ending September, FAO estimates)

	2018	2019	2020
Asses	16	16	16
Cattle	617	619	621
Chickens	3,822	3,846	3,871
Goats	258	261	258
Pigs	36	36	36
Sheep	38	37	37

Source: FAO.

LIVESTOCK PRODUCTS
('000 metric tons, FAO estimates)

	2018	2019	2020
Cattle hides, fresh	1.9	2.0	2.0
Cattle meat	16.3	16.5	16.6
Cattle offals, edible	1.9	2.0	2.0
Cows' milk	40.0	40.1	40.2
Chicken meat	6.1	6.1	6.0
Goat meat	1.7	1.6	1.6
Pig meat	1.4	1.4	1.4
Hen eggs	1.3	1.3	1.3

Source: FAO.

Forestry

ROUNDWOOD REMOVALS
('000 cubic metres, excl. bark, FAO estimates)

	2017	2018	2019
Sawlogs, veneer logs and logs for sleepers	260	260	260
Pulpwood	604	604	604
Other industrial wood	70	70	70
Fuel wood	1,754	1,820	1,939
Total	2,688	2,754	2,873

2020: Production assumed to be unchanged from 2019 (FAO estimates).

Source: FAO.

SAWNWOOD PRODUCTION
('000 cubic metres, incl. railway sleepers, FAO estimates)

	2018	2019	2020
Coniferous (softwood) . . .	102	160	30
Broadleaved (hardwood) . . .	20	20	20
Total	122	180	50

Source: FAO.

Fishing

(metric tons, live weight, FAO estimates)

	2013	2014	2015
Capture	60	65	65
Aquaculture	100	100	100
Total catch	160	165	165

2017–20: Figures are assumed to be unchanged from 2015 (FAO estimates).
Source: FAO.

Mining

(metric tons unless otherwise indicated)

	2019	2020	2021
Coal	109,926	161,768	62,681
Quarrystone ('000 cu m) . . .	277	210	258

Iron ore: 603,251 in 2014.
Source: Central Bank of Eswatini, Mbabane.

Industry

SELECTED PRODUCTS

	2014	2015	2016
Raw sugar ('000 metric tons) . .	689	699	586
Electrical energy (million kWh) .	567	496	388

Electrical energy (million kWh): 414 in 2017; 519 in 2018; 584 in 2019.

Sources: UN Industrial Commodity Statistics Database; UN Energy Statistics Database.

Wood pulp ('000 metric tons, FAO estimates): 102.0 in 2009; 15.0 in 2010; 0.0 in 2011–20 (Source: FAO).

Finance

CURRENCY, EXCHANGE RATES AND FISCAL YEAR

Monetary Units
100 cents = 1 lilangeni (plural: emalangeni).

Sterling, Dollar and Euro Equivalents (31 May 2022)
£1 sterling = 19.686 emalangeni;
US $1 = 15.638 emalangeni;
€1 = 16.753 emalangeni;
100 emalangeni= £5.08 = $6.39 = €5.97.

Average Exchange Rate (emalangeni per US $)
2019   14.452
2020   16.470
2021   14.783

Note: The lilangeni is at par with the South African rand.

Fiscal Year
The fiscal year ends on 31 March.

BUDGET
(central government operations, million emalangeni, fiscal year)

Revenue*	2020/21	2021/22†	2022/23‡
Tax revenue	18,467	17,606	18,294
Taxes on net income and profits	5,592	6,147	6,956
Taxes on property	30	22	24
Taxes on goods and services .	12,846	11,436	11,314
Customs Union receipts . .	8,358	6,388	5,832
Value-added tax	2,996	3,526	3,831
Non-tax revenue	443	363	392
Total	18,910	17,968	18,686

Expenditure (incl. net lending)	2020/21	2021/22†	2022/23‡
Current expenditure	17,753	18,886	17,801
Salaries and wages	7,007	7,211	n.a.
Capital expenditure	4,852	3,794	5,362
Total	22,605	22,680	23,163

* Excluding grants received (million emalangeni): 455 in 2020/21; 552 in 2021/22 (preliminary); 553 in 2022/23 (budget forecast).
† Preliminary.
‡ Budget forecasts.

Source: Central Bank of Eswatini, Mbabane.

INTERNATIONAL RESERVES
(excl. gold, US $ million at 31 December)

	2019	2020	2021
IMF special drawing rights . .	67.56	69.70	172.86
Reserve position in IMF . . .	9.07	9.45	9.18
Foreign exchange	363.68	466.41	390.24
Total	440.31	545.56	572.28

Source: IMF, *International Financial Statistics*.

MONEY SUPPLY
(million emalangeni at 31 December)

	2019	2020	2021
Currency outside depository corporations	714.97	897.23	768.45
Transferable deposits . . .	6,303.09	6,318.09	7,811.45
Other deposits	11,350.54	13,990.46	12,683.86
Broad money	18,368.61	21,205.79	21,263.76

Source: IMF, *International Financial Statistics*.

COST OF LIVING
(Consumer Price Index; June 2020 = 100)

	2017	2018	2019
Food and non-alcoholic beverages .	94.0	93.9	96.0
Clothing and footwear	98.9	97.6	98.5
Housing and utilities	81.8	92.0	95.2
All items (incl. others) . . .	89.6	94.0	96.4

NATIONAL ACCOUNTS
(million emalangeni at current prices)

Expenditure on the Gross Domestic Product

	2018	2019	2020
Government final consumption expenditure	14,217	13,388	13,828
Private final consumption expenditure	40,534	41,471	39,291
Gross capital formation	8,184	8,705	8,297
Total domestic expenditure	62,935	63,563	61,415
Exports of goods and services	24,981	29,655	28,392
Less Imports of goods and services	27,381	27,912	26,640
Statistical discrepancy	1,236	−692	—
GDP at purchasers' values	61,771	64,615	63,167
GDP at constant 2015 prices	54,682	55,909	52,788

Gross Domestic Product by Economic Activity

	2018	2019	2020
Agriculture, hunting, forestry and fishing	5,263	5,463	5,349
Mining, quarrying and utilities	812	1,106	886
Manufacturing	17,938	19,168	18,638
Construction	1,784	1,756	1,788
Wholesale and retail trade; restaurants and hotels	9,565	9,639	9,575
Transport and communications	2,868	3,044	2,936
Other services	20,513	20,968	20,859
Sub-total	58,743	61,143	60,030
Indirect taxes (net)*	3,028	3,471	3,137
GDP at purchasers' values	61,771	64,615	63,167

* Figures obtained as residuals.

Source: UN National Accounts Main Aggregates Database.

BALANCE OF PAYMENTS
(US $ million)

	2018	2019	2020
Exports of goods	1,828.3	1,981.0	1,739.3
Imports of goods	−1,808.1	−1,723.3	−1,498.5
Balance on goods	20.2	257.7	240.8
Exports of services	71.1	88.8	68.5
Imports of services	−258.8	−203.1	−196.9
Balance on goods and services	−167.6	143.4	112.4
Primary income received	144.7	124.3	103.2
Primary income paid	−460.5	−575.3	−513.7
Balance on goods, services and primary income	−483.4	−307.6	−298.1
Secondary income received	581.0	532.9	592.8
Secondary income paid	−36.9	−29.7	−39.9
Current balance	60.7	195.7	254.9
Capital account (net)	−2.4	−1.0	0.9
Direct investment assets	8.1	−20.9	14.1
Direct investment liabilities	31.1	128.0	44.1
Portfolio investment assets	89.0	−85.3	−42.8
Financial derivatives and employee stock options (net)	−7.3	−0.7	−0.2
Other investment assets	−273.8	−134.3	−236.7
Other investment liabilities	91.0	−25.4	101.6
Net errors and omissions	−56.4	−69.3	−153.8
Reserves and related items	−59.9	−13.3	−18.1

Source: IMF, *International Financial Statistics*.

External Trade

PRINCIPAL COMMODITIES
(US $ million)

Imports c.i.f.	2018	2019	2020
Vegetables and vegetable products	140.1	117.4	133.6
Cereals	84.0	63.6	75.9
Prepared foodstuffs; beverages, spirits, vinegar; tobacco and articles thereof	160.3	173.3	154.9
Mineral products	302.4	338.5	273.8
Mineral fuels, oils and distillation products	267.5	304.9	240.4
Petroleum oils, not crude	205.8	210.5	145.9
Chemicals and chemical products	241.3	236.1	241.1
Pharmaceutical products	48.3	44.0	56.3
Essential oils, perfumes, cosmetics and toiletries	57.0	56.9	51.6
Plastics, rubber, and articles thereof	94.8	89.7	80.9
Plastics and articles thereof	75.1	69.9	63.1
Textiles and textile articles	171.8	167.8	148.2
Cotton	70.8	69.5	63.1
Iron and steel, other base metals and articles of base metal	116.5	102.7	88.4
Articles of iron or steel	58.8	48.1	40.7
Machinery and mechanical appliances; electrical equipment; parts thereof	220.9	209.3	168.0
Machinery, boilers, etc.	130.1	119.7	95.9
Electrical, electronic equipment	90.8	89.7	72.1
Vehicles, aircraft, vessels and associated transport equipment	126.9	131.8	93.5
Vehicles other than railway, tramway	124.8	128.5	92.8
Total (incl. others)	1,869.2	1,841.9	1,605.3

Exports f.o.b.	2018	2019	2020
Prepared foodstuffs; beverages, spirits, vinegar; tobacco and articles thereof	475.8	582.2	552.8
Sugars and sugar confectionery	374.7	474.4	440.1
Cane or beet sugar and chemically pure sucrose, in solid form	309.5	421.8	393.1
Chemicals and related products	891.6	941.9	791.8
Essential oils, perfumes, cosmetics and toiletries	628.5	639.3	529.7
Odoriferous mixtures as raw materials for industry	625.5	636.4	527.4
Miscellaneous chemical products	233.1	242.5	207.9
Other chemical industry products and residuals	233.0	242.5	207.5
Plastics, rubber, and articles thereof	94.8	89.7	80.9
Wood, wood charcoal, cork, and articles thereof	105.9	108.3	95.3
Wood and articles of wood, wood charcoal	105.3	107.8	95.0
Textiles and textile articles	233.6	241.6	199.5
Articles of apparel, accessories, not knit or crochet	151.3	157.2	117.3
Total (incl. others)	1,851.1	2,001.8	1,752.1

Source: Trade Map-Trade Competitiveness Map, International Trade Centre, marketanalysis.intracen.org.

PRINCIPAL TRADING PARTNERS
(US $ million)

Imports c.i.f.	2018	2019	2020
China, People's Republic . . .	115.9	131.2	118.0
India	66.9	38.0	54.3
Ireland	19.6	17.5	17.9
Japan	31.2	22.8	23.4
Singapore	21.2	15.3	9.2
South Africa	1,383.4	1,343.1	1,146.5
United Arab Emirates	3.2	26.2	16.7
USA	23.6	29.3	31.2
Total (incl. others)	1,869.2	1,841.9	1,605.3

Exports f.o.b.	2018	2019	2020
Angola	30.8	21.0	3.4
Botswana	18.1	27.5	19.7
China, People's Republic . . .	25.2	0.3	0.0
Italy	21.1	21.5	13.6
Kenya	94.4	126.6	125.5
Mozambique	61.5	70.9	69.2
Namibia	17.7	22.4	19.9
Nigeria	79.6	99.7	102.6
Portugal	10.5	26.9	13.1
South Africa	1,269.6	1,333.0	1,138.0
Spain	0.0	33.4	2.3
Tanzania	35.0	37.7	28.0
Uganda	25.8	24.1	29.5
United Kingdom	20.4	10.8	45.7
USA	11.2	22.3	25.9
Zambia	14.1	20.1	10.7
Zimbabwe	27.2	17.1	26.2
Total (incl. others)	1,851.1	2,001.8	1,752.1

Source: Trade Map-Trade Competitiveness Map, International Trade Centre, marketanalysis.intracen.org.

Transport

RAILWAYS
(traffic)

	2002	2003	2004
Net total ton-km (million) . . .	728	726	710

Source: UN, *Statistical Yearbook*.

2020/21 (Swaziland Railway operations, fiscal year ending 31 March): Goods transported 6.4m. metric tons (Transit traffic 6.0m. metric tons) (Source: Eswatini Railways, Mbabane).

Tourism

TOURIST ARRIVALS BY NATIONALITY
(arrivals of non-resident tourists at national borders)

Country of residence	2019	2020	2021
France	21,091	4,371	692
Germany	16,400	3,261	585
Mozambique	146,421	51,273	28,468
Netherlands	16,389	2,526	298
South Africa	856,095	238,324	147,737
United Kingdom	11,285	2,772	1,473
USA	15,048	2,788	1,702
Zimbabwe	42,956	14,089	10,486
Total (incl. others)	1,225,520	345,348	210,705

Source: Eswatini Tourism Authority, Mbabane.

Tourism receipts (US $ million, excl. passenger transport): 13 in 2017; 16 in 2018; 14 in 2019 (provisional) (Source: World Tourism Organization).

Communications Media

	2015	2016	2017
Telephones ('000 main lines in use)	43.0	42.0	41.0
Mobile telephone subscriptions ('000)	941.0	995.0	1,052.0
Broadband subscriptions, fixed ('000)	6.0	7.0	8.0
Broadband subscriptions, mobile ('000)	160.0	169.2	179.0
Internet users (% of population)* .	25.6	28.6	47.0

* Estimates.

Source: International Telecommunication Union.

Education

(2018/19 unless otherwise indicated)

	Institutions	Teachers	Students
Pre-primary	n.a.	1,935[1]	24,139[1]
Primary	541[2]	9,139	236,002
Secondary	182[2]	6,966[3]	108,288[3]
University[4]	1[5]	712[6]	8,057[7]

[1] 2010/11 figure.
[2] 2001/02 figure.
[3] 2015/16 figure.
[4] Figures exclude vocational, technical and teacher-training colleges. In 2000 there were 1,822 students enrolled at these institutions, which numbered 10 in 2003.
[5] 2000 figure.
[6] 2014/15 figure.
[7] 2012/13 figure.

Source: mainly UNESCO Institute for Statistics.

Pupil-teacher ratio (qualified teaching staff, primary education, UNESCO estimate): 28.5 in 2017/18 (Source: UNESCO Institute for Statistics).

Adult literacy rate (UNESCO estimates): 88.4% (males 88.3%; females 88.5%) in 2018 (Source: UNESCO Institute for Statistics).

Directory

The Constitution

A new Constitution entered into force on 7 February 2006, replacing that of October 1978. It vests supreme executive power in the hereditary King (iNgwenyama—the Lion) and succession is governed by traditional law and custom. In the event of the death of the King, the powers of head of state are transferred to the constitutional dual monarch, the Queen Mother (Ndlovukazi—Great She Elephant), who is authorized to act as Regent until the designated successor, the Crown Prince (Umntfwana), attains the age of 21 years.

The Parliament of Eswatini consists of the Senate, comprising not more than 31 members, of whom 20 are appointed by the King—at least eight of these are women—and 10 elected by the House of Assembly, one-half of whom are women, and the House of Assembly, which comprises not more than 76 members. Of these, not more than 60 are directly elected from candidates nominated by traditional local councils, known as Tinkhundla, and not more than 10 are appointed by the King, one-half of whom are women. The Attorney-General is also an ex officio member of the House of Assembly and the Constitution provides for the co-option of four additional female members of parliament (one each from each of the country's regions) in the event that their number falls below 30% of the total number of legislators).

The King appoints the Prime Minister and the Cabinet and has the power to dissolve the bicameral legislature. The Swazi National Council (Sibaya) constitutes the highest policy and advisory council of the nation and functions as the annual general meeting of the nation. A Council of Chiefs, composed of 12 chiefs drawn from the four regions of Eswatini, advises the King on customary issues and any matter relating to chieftancy.

The Constitution affirms the fundamental human rights and freedoms of the individual.

The Government

HEAD OF STATE

King: HM King Mswati III (succeeded to the throne 25 April 1986).

COUNCIL OF MINISTERS
(October 2022)

Prime Minister: Cleopas Sipho Dlamini.
Deputy Prime Minister: Themba Masuku.
Minister of Finance: Neal Rijkenberg.
Minister of Commerce, Industry and Trade: Manqoba Khumalo.
Minister of Justice and Constitutional Affairs: Pholile Dlamini-Shakantu.
Minister of Information, Communication and Technology: Princess Sikhanyiso.
Minister of Home Affairs: Princess Lindiwe.
Minister of Public Works and Transport: Chief Ndlaluhlaza Ndwandwe.
Minister of Housing and Urban Development: Prince Simelane.
Minister of Foreign Affairs and International Co-operation: Thuli Dladla.
Minister of Health: Lizzy Nkosi.
Minister of Sports, Culture and Youth Affairs: Harries Madze Bulunga.
Minister of Tourism and Environmental Affairs: Moses Vilakati.
Minister of Agriculture and Acting Minister of Natural Resources and Energy: Jabulani Mabuza.
Minister of Tinkhundla Administration and Development: David Ngcamphalala.
Minister of Education and Training: Howard Mabuza.
Minister of Economic Planning and Development: Tambo Gina.
Minister of Public Service: Mabulala Maseko.
Minister of Labour and Social Security: Phila Buthelezi.

MINISTRIES

Office of the Prime Minister: Cabinet Offices, Hospital Hill, Swazi Plaza, POB 395, Mbabane; tel. 24042251; internet www.gov.sz.
Office of the Deputy Prime Minister: Secretarial Bldg, Gwamile St, POB A33, Swazi Plaza, Mbabane H101; tel. 24042723.

Ministry of Agriculture: Hospital Hill, opp. Fire and Emergency Services, POB 162, Mbabane H100; tel. 24042731; internet fb.com/agriceswatini.
Ministry of Commerce, Industry and Trade: Interministerial Bldg, Blk 8, 1st Floor, Mhlambanyatsi Rd, POB 451, Mbabane; tel. 24043201; e-mail mcit@gov.sz.
Ministry of Economic Planning and Development: Finance Bldg, 4th Floor, Lusutfu Rd, POB 602, Mbabane; tel. 24043765.
Ministry of Education and Training: Hospital Hill Rd, POB 39, Mbabane; tel. 24042491; e-mail ps_education@gov.sz.
Ministry of Finance: Mhlambanyatsi Rd, POB 443, Mbabane; tel. 24048145.
Ministry of Foreign Affairs and International Co-operation: Interministerial Bldg, Blk 8, Level 3, Mhlambanyatsi Rd, POB 518, Mbabane; tel. 24042661; e-mail psforeignaffairs@realnet.co.sz.
Ministry of Health: Mhlambanyatsi Rd, POB 5, Mbabane; tel. 24042431; e-mail infohealth@gov.sz.
Ministry of Home Affairs: Home Affairs and Justice Bldg, Mhlambanyatsi Usuthu Link Rd, POB 432, Mbabane; tel. 24042941.
Ministry of Housing and Urban Development: Income Tax Bldg, 5th Floor, Mhlambanyatsi Rd, POB 1832, Mbabane; tel. 24046049; e-mail ps_housing@gov.sz.
Ministry of Information, Communication and Technology: Inter-ministerial Complex, Blk 8, 3rd Floor, Mhlambanyatsi Rd, POB 642, Mbabane; tel. 24054000; e-mail ps_mict@gov.sz.
Ministry of Justice and Constitutional Affairs: Ministry of Justice Bldg, 5th Floor, cnr Mhlambanyatsi and Usuthu Link Rds, POB 924, Mbabane; tel. 24046010.
Ministry of Labour and Social Security: Interministerial Office Block, Mhlambanyatsi Rd, POB 198, Mbabane; tel. 24041971; e-mail min_labour@gov.sz.
Ministry of Natural Resources and Energy: Income Tax Bldg, 4th Floor, Mhlambanyatsi Rd, POB 57, Mbabane; tel. 24046244; e-mail mnre@swazi.net.
Ministry of Public Service: Finance Bldg, 2nd and 3rd Floors, Mhlambanyatsi Rd, POB 170, Mbabane; tel. 24043521; e-mail ps_mops@gov.sz.
Ministry of Public Works and Transport: Mhlambanyatsi Rd, POB 58, Mbabane; tel. 24099000.
Ministry of Sports, Culture and Youth Affairs: Swazi Bank Bldg, 4th Floor, Gwamile St, POB 4843, Mbabane; tel. 24045053.
Ministry of Tinkhundla Administration and Development: Post and Telecom Bldg, Ground, 1st and 2nd Floors, Sheffield Rd, Mbabane; tel. 24041244.
Ministry of Tourism and Environmental Affairs: Income Tax Bldg, 2nd Floor, Mhlambanyatsi Rd, POB 2652, Mbabane H100; tel. 24046162; e-mail ps_tourism@gov.sz.

Legislature

HOUSE OF ASSEMBLY

The House of Assembly comprises not more than 76 members. Of these, not more than 60 are directly elected from candidates nominated by traditional local councils, known as Tinkhundla, and not more than 10 are appointed by the King, one-half of whom are women. Additionally, one woman is selected from each of the four regions of Eswatini (in the event that following an election women constitute less than 30% of the total number of legislators) and the Attorney-General is also an ex officio member. The most recent elections to the House of Assembly took place on 21 September 2018.
House of Assembly: Parliament Bldg, POB 37, Lobamba; tel. 4161286; e-mail adminiparl@swazi.net.
Speaker: Petros Mavimbela.

SENATE

The Senate comprises not more than 31 members, of whom 20 are appointed by the King—at least eight of these are women—and 10 elected by the House of Assembly, one-half of whom are women.
President: Lindiwe Dlamini.

Election Commission

Elections and Boundaries Commission: POB 6358, Mbabane; tel. 24162504; e-mail info@elections.org.sz; internet www.elections.org.sz; 5 mems; Chair. Prince Mhlabuhlangene Dlamini.

Political Organizations

Party political activity was banned by royal proclamation in April 1973, and formally prohibited under the 1978 Constitution. Since 1991, following indications that the Constitution was to be revised, a number of political associations have re-emerged. After the introduction of the new Constitution in February 2006, the legal status of party political activity remained unclear.

African United Democratic Party (AUDP): POB 2999, Manzini M200; tel. 76283926; e-mail audpsd@gmail.com; f. 2005; Pres. STANLEY MALINDZISA.

Communist Party of Swaziland (CPS): internet fb.com/CPSwaziland; f. 2011; Nat. Chair. DUMSANI FAKUDZE; Gen. Sec. KENNETH KUNENE.

Ngwane National Liberatory Congress (NNLC): Ilanga Centre, Martin St, Manzini; tel. 25053935; f. 1962 by fmr mems of Swaziland Progressive Party (SPP); advocates democratic freedom and universal suffrage, and seeks abolition of the Tinkhundla electoral system; Pres. SIBONGILE MAZIBUKO; Sec.-Gen. DUMISA DLAMINI.

People's United Democratic Movement (PUDEMO): POB 4588, Manzini; tel. 25054181; e-mail pudemoinfo@gmail.com; internet pudemo.org; f. 1983; seeks constitutional limitation of the powers of the monarchy; affiliated orgs include the Human Rights Asscn of Swaziland and the Swaziland Youth Congress (SWAYOCO); Pres. MLUNGISI MAKHANYA; Sec.-Gen. WANDILE DLUDLU.

Swaziland Democratic Party (SWADEPA): Hatzin Centre, Office No. S4, POB 7011, Manzini; tel. 35423613; e-mail swaziparty2011@gmail.com; internet www.swadepa.com; f. 2011; Pres. (vacant).

Diplomatic Representation

EMBASSIES IN ESWATINI

India: UN House, Quadrant B & C, 5th Floor, Somhlolo Rd, Mbabane; tel. 24101621; e-mail hoc.mbabane@mea.gov.in; internet www.hcimbabane.gov.in; High Commissioner (vacant).

Mozambique: Highlands View, Princess Dr., POB 1212, Mbabane; tel. 24041296; e-mail moz.high@swazi.net; High Commissioner JORGE HENRIQUE DA COSTA KHALAU.

Qatar: 20 Royal Villas, POB 420, Ezulwini; tel. 24161580; e-mail mbabane@mofa.gov.qa; internet mbabane.embassy.qa; Chargé d'affaires RACHID ALKHELAIFA.

South Africa: The New Mall, 2nd Floor, Dr Sishayi Rd, POB 2507, Mbabane; tel. 24044651; e-mail sahc@africaonline.co.sz; High Commissioner THOKOZILE JOY SIPAMLA.

Taiwan (Republic of China): Makhosikhosi St, Mbabane; tel. 24044739; e-mail rocembassy@africaonline.co.sz; internet www.taiwanembassy.org/sz; Ambassador JEREMY LIANG.

United Kingdom: Mbabane; internet www.gov.uk/world/organisations/british-high-commission-mbabane; High Commissioner SIMON BOYDEN.

USA: cnr MR 103 and Cultural Center Dr., Ezulwini; tel. 24179000; e-mail usembassymbabane@state.gov; internet sz.usembassy.gov; Ambassador JEANNE MARIE MALONEY.

Judicial System

The judicial system is centred around common law (which is based on Roman Dutch law) and customary law (based on Swazi law). The Superior Court of Judicature comprises the Supreme Court, and the High Court. The Supreme Court is headed by the Chief Justice and is the final Court of Appeal. The High Court consists of the Chief Justice and has unlimited original jurisdiction in civil and criminal matters. There are, in addition, the Industrial Court and the Industrial Court of Appeal, which have jurisdiction limited to labour disputes.

Chief Justice of the High Court: BHEKI MAPHALALA.

Attorney-General: Chief SIFISO 'MASHAMPU' KHUMALO.

Religion

About 60% of the adult Swazi population profess Christianity. Under the Constitution, which came into effect on 7 February 2006, Christianity ceased to be recognized as the country's official religion. There is a growing Muslim population, reported to number some 10,000 adherents. Most of the remainder of the population hold traditional beliefs.

CHRISTIANITY

Council of Swaziland Churches: Mandlenkosi Ecumenical House, 142 Esser St, Manzini; POB 1095, Manzini M200; tel. 25053628; f. 1976; Chair. Dean A. DLAMINI; Gen. Sec. BONGINKOSI V. MALAZA; 9 mem. churches incl. Roman Catholic, Anglican, Kukhany'okusha Zion Church and Lutheran.

Eswatini Conference of Churches: 175 Ngwane St, POB 1157, Manzini; tel. 25055253; e-mail thembangozo@yahoo.com; internet fb.com/EswatiniConferenceOfChurches; f. 1929; Pres. Bishop STEPHEN MASILELA; CEO and Gen. Sec. Rev. S. F. DLAMINI.

League of African Churches: POB 230, Lobamba; asscn of 48 independent churches; Pres. SAMSON HLATJWAKO.

The Anglican Communion

Eswatini comprises a single diocese within the Anglican Church of Southern Africa (formerly the Church of the Province of Southern Africa). The Metropolitan of the Province is the Archbishop of Cape Town, South Africa.

Bishop of Eswatini: Very Rev. Dr DALCY BADELI DLAMINI, POB 118, Mbabane; tel. 24043624; e-mail info@swazilanddiocese.org.sz; internet www.swazilanddiocese.org.sz.

The Roman Catholic Church

The Roman Catholic Church was established in Eswatini (then known as Swaziland) in 1913. For ecclesiastical purposes, Eswatini comprises the single diocese of Manzini, suffragan to the archdiocese of Johannesburg, South Africa. The Bishop participates in the Southern African Catholic Bishops' Conference (based in Pretoria, South Africa).

Bishop of Manzini: JOSÉ LUÍS GERARDO PONCE DE LEÓN, Bishop's House, Sandlane St, POB 19, Manzini; tel. 25056900; e-mail media@dioceseofmanzini.org; internet dioceseofmanzini.org.

Other Christian Churches

Church of the Nazarene: POB 832, Manzini; tel. 25054732; f. 1910.

The Evangelical Lutheran Church in Southern Africa: POB 117, Mbabane; tel. 24043411; f. 1902; Head Bishop JEREMIAH BHEKI MAGAGULA.

BAHÁ'Í FAITH

National Spiritual Assembly: POB 298, Mbabane; tel. 24043457; e-mail bahaiswd@gmail.com; f. 1960; mems resident in 153 localities.

ISLAM

Mbabane Islamic Centre: POB 877, Swazi Plaza, Mbabane; tel. 24050209.

The Press

NEWSPAPERS (PRINT AND ONLINE)

Eswatini Observer: Betfusile St, nr Picadilly, POB A385, Swazi Plaza, Mbabane; tel. 24049600; e-mail info@observer.org.sz; internet new.observer.org.sz; f. 1981; Mon.–Fri.; also *Saturday Observer* and *Sunday Observer*; owned by Tibiyo Taka Ngwane; Man. Editor MBONGENI MBINGO.

Independent News Eswatini: Mbabane Golf Course, Suit Offices, Portion 104, Farm 2, Mahleka St, Mbabne; tel. 24041114; e-mail info@independentnews.co.sz; internet independentnews.co.sz; f. 2007; weekly; owned by Mveleza Publishers Pty Ltd.

The Swati Newsweek: tel. 78710099; e-mail eunewsweek@gmail.com; internet fb.com/TheSwatiNewsweek; online; Editor EUGENE DUBE.

The Swazi News: Sheffield Rd, POB 156, Mbabane; tel. 24041550; e-mail swazinews@times.co.sz; internet www.times.co.sz; f. 1897; weekly; English; owned by The Times of Swaziland; Publr PAUL LOFFLER; Editor THOBEKA MANYATHELA.

Swaziland News: tel. 76067236; internet www.swazilandnews.co.za; online; publ. by Swaziland News (Pty) Ltd; Editor ZWELI MARTIN DLAMINI.

The Times of Swaziland: Sheffield Rd, POB 156, Mbabane; tel. 24042211; e-mail editor@times.co.sz; internet www.times.co.sz; f. 1968; Mon.–Fri., Sun.; also monthly edn; English; other publs incl. *What's Happening* (tourist interest).

PERIODICALS

The Nation: Mbabane House, 3rd Floor, Mahlokohla St, POB 4547, Mbabane; tel. 24041480; e-mail thenation@realnet.co.sz; internet fb.com/TheNationMag; f. 1997; monthly; Editor BHEKI MAKHUBU.

Publishers

Macmillan Education Eswatini: Plot 230/231, 1st Ave, Matsapha, Industrial Site, POB 1235, Manzini; tel. 25184533; e-mail marketing@macmillan.co.sz; internet www.macmillan.co.sz; f. 1978; textbooks and general; Man. Dir BONGANI MOTSA.

Broadcasting and Communications

REGULATORY AUTHORITY

Eswatini Communications Commission (ESCCOM): Sibekelo Bldg, 4th Floor, North Wing, POB 7811, Mbabane; tel. 24067000; e-mail info@esccom.org.sz; internet www.esccom.org.sz; f. 2013; licences all systems and services in the communications industry (telecommunications, postal, courier and broadcasting); Chair. THEMBA KHUMALO; CEO MVILAWEMPHI DLAMINI.

TELECOMMUNICATIONS

Eswatini Mobile: Sibekelo Bldg, 2nd Floor, Mhlambanyatsi Rd, POB 2150, Mbabane; tel. 79790101; e-mail info@eswatinimobile.co.sz; internet eswatinimobile.co.sz; f. 2016; Chair. MICHELO SHAKANTU; CEO JEFF PENBERTON.

Eswatini Posts and Telecommunications Corpn (EPTC): Phutfumani Bldg, Mahlokohla St, POB 125, Mbabane H100; tel. 24052000; internet www.sptc.co.sz; f. 1983; Chair. MTITI FAKUDZE; Man. Dir THEMBA KHUMALO.

> **EswatiniTelecom:** Phutfumani Bldg, Mahlokohla St, POB 125, Mbabane; tel. 24052000; internet www.sptc.co.sz; registered as co in July 2017; telecommunications division of EPTC.

MTN Eswatini: Mahlalekhukhwini House, cnr MR103 and Nshakabili Rds, Ezulwini, POB 5050, Mbabane H100; tel. 24060000; e-mail feedback.sz@mtn.com; internet www.mtn.co.sz; f. 1998; jt venture between MTN Group, South Africa, and Swaziland Posts and Telecommunications Corpn; operates mobile telephone network; Chair. DAVID DLAMINI; CEO WANDILE MTSHALI.

BROADCASTING

Radio

Swaziland Broadcasting and Information Service (SBIS): SBIS Bldg, cnr Gwamile and Dzeliwe Sts, POB 338, Mbabane; tel. 24061002; e-mail dlaminimart@gov.sz; f. 1966; broadcasts in English and siSwati; Dir MARTIN DLAMINI.

Voice of the Church (VOC) (Transworld Radio Swaziland): cnr Tenbergen and Martin Sts, POB 4544, Manzini; tel. 25054772; e-mail info@voc.org.sz; internet vocfm.org; f. 1995; religious broadcasts from 5 transmitters in 30 languages to Southern, Central and Eastern Africa and to the Far East; Dir ZACHARIAH MTHETWA.

Television

Eswatini Television Authority (Swazi TV): Hospital Hill, POB A146, Swazi Plaza, Mbabane H100; tel. 24119600; e-mail info@swazitv.co.sz; internet www.swazitv.co.sz; f. 1978; state-owned; broadcasts 7 hours daily in English; Chair. CAROL NGCOBO; CEO ANDREAS DLAMINI.

Finance

BANKING

Central Bank

Central Bank of Eswatini (CBE): Mahlokohla St, POB 546, Mbabane; tel. 24082000; e-mail info@centralbank.org.sz; internet www.centralbank.org.sz; f. 1974; bank of issue; Gov. PHILEMON MFANA MNISI.

Commercial Banks

First National Bank of Swaziland Ltd: Sales House Bldg, 2nd Floor, Swazi Plaza, POB 261, Mbabane H100; tel. 25184637; e-mail callcentreswz@fnb.co.za; internet www.fnbswaziland.co.sz; f. 1988; fmrly Meridien Bank Swaziland Ltd; wholly owned by FirstRand Bank Ltd, Johannesburg; Chair. J. V. NDLANGAMANDLA; CEO DENNIS TIKHALO MBINGO.

Nedbank (Swaziland) Ltd: Nedbank Centre, 3rd Floor, cnr Sozia and Dr Sishayi Rd, Mbabane; tel. 24081000; e-mail info@nedbank.co.sz; internet www.nedbank.co.sz; f. 1974; fmrly Standard Chartered Bank Swaziland Ltd; wholly owned subsidiary of Nedbank Group (South Africa); Chair. NKONZO HLATSHWAYO; Man. Dir FIKILE NKOSI.

Development Banks

Eswatini Development & Savings Bank (Eswatini Bank): Engungwini Bldg, Gwamile St, POB 336, Mbabane; tel. 24095000; e-mail swazibank@swazibank.co.sz; internet www.swazibank.co.sz; f. 1965 as Swaziland Credit and Savings Bank; Chair. SIBONGILE MDLULI; Man. Dir NOZIZWE MULELA.

Standard Bank Eswatini Ltd: 4th and 5th Floors, Corporate Place Bldg, Swazi Plaza, POB A294, Mbabane; tel. 25175300; e-mail swazilandccc@stanbic.com; internet www.standardbank.co.sz; f. 1988; fmrly Stanbic Bank Swaziland; merged with Barclays Bank of Swaziland in Jan. 1998; Chair. JOSEPH SHILUBANE; Chief Exec. MVUSELELO FAKUDZE.

Financial Institution

Eswatini National Provident Fund (ENPF): Lidlelantfongeni Bldg, cnr Ngwane and Martin Sts, POB 1857, Manzini M200; tel. 25082000; e-mail info@snpf.co.sz; internet www.snpf.co.sz; f. 1974; provides retirement benefits schemes; employers are required by law to pay a contribution for every eligible staff member; Chair. MASHUMI SHONGWE; CEO PRINCE LONKHOKHELA.

STOCK EXCHANGE

Eswatini Stock Exchange: Ingcamu (PSPF) Bldg, 2nd Floor, Mhlambanyatsi Rd, POB A636, Mbabane H101; tel. 24068114; e-mail info@ese.co.sz; internet www.ese.co.sz; f. 1990 as Swaziland Stock Market (SSM); state-owned; eight listed cos (2021); Man. JOYCE MHLOBISO DLAMINI.

REGULATORY AUTHORITIES

Financial Services Regulatory Authority (FSRA): Ingcamu Bldg, 5th Floor, Mhlambanyatsi Rd, POB 3365, Mbabane H100; tel. 24068000; e-mail info@fsra.co.sz; internet www.fsra.co.sz; f. 2010; regulates and supervises financial services providers in Eswatini; CEO NCAMISO NTSHALINTSHALI.

INSURANCE

Between 1974 and 1999 the state-controlled Swaziland Royal Insurance Corpn (SRIC) operated as the country's sole authorized insurance company, although cover in a number of areas not served by SRIC was available from several specialized insurers. In 1999 it was proposed that legislation would be enacted to end SRIC's monopoly and provide for the company's transfer to private sector ownership. The legislation was adopted as the Insurance Act in 2005.

Insurance Companies

Eswatini Royal Insurance Corpn (ERIC): Insika House, Somhlolo Rd, POB 917, Mbabane H100; tel. 24081600; e-mail info@sric.sz; internet www.sric.sz; f. 1973; Chair. MUHAWU MAZIYA; Gen. Man. ZAMA NGCOBO.

Lidwala Insurance Co: Sivuno Bldg, Nkoseluhlaza St, POB 1552, Manzini; tel. 25085600; e-mail info@lidwalainsurance.com; internet www.lidwalainsurance.com; f. 2009; Chair Dr GERRIT SANDROCK; CEO SANDILE DLAMINI.

Oracle Insurance: Lot 219, Somhlolo Rd, Eveni, POB 142, Mbabane H103; tel. 24041369; e-mail eswatiniinfo@oraclesz.com; internet oracleinsurance.co; f. 2008; fmrly Metropolitan Swaziland; present name adopted 2020; a member of MMI Holdings Ltd since 2010; CEO DAVID TAKIS.

Trade and Industry

GOVERNMENT AGENCIES

Eswatini Investment Promotion Authority (EIPA): Sibekelo Bldg 1, 1st Floor, Mhlambanyatsi Rd, POB 4194, Mbabane; tel. 24040472; e-mail info@sipa.org.sz; internet investeswatini.org.sz; f. 1998; Chair. THEO HLOPHE; CEO SIBANI MNGOMEZULU.

Eswatini Public Procurement Regulatory Agency (ESPPRA): RHUS Office Park, Karl Grant St, POB 9665, Mbabane; tel. 24047527; e-mail info@sppra.co.sz; internet www.sppra.co.sz; f. 2013; responsible for public procurement regulation; Chair. HARRY NXUMALO.

Eswatini Revenue Service (ERS): Portion 419, Farm 50, Ezulwini MR103; tel. 24064000; e-mail info@ers.org.sz; internet www.ers.org.sz; f. 2011; Commr-Gen. BRIGHTWELL NKAMBULE.

Small Enterprise Development Co (SEDCO): Govt Stores Rd, POB A186, Mbabane; tel. 24042811; e-mail business@sedco.co.sz; internet www.sedco.co.sz; f. 1970; devt agency; supplies workshop space, training and expertise for 165 local entrepreneurs at 8 sites throughout the country; Chair. NELSIWE MABUZA; CEO KHETHIWE MHLANGA.

DEVELOPMENT ORGANIZATIONS

Coordinating Assembly of Non-Governmental Organisations (CANGO): Plot 419, J. S. M. Matsebula St, Mbabane; tel. 24044721; e-mail communications@cango.org.sz; internet cango.org.sz; f. 1983; Chair. DUMISANI MNISI; Exec. Dir EMMANUEL NDLANGAMANDLA; over 70 mem. orgs.

Eswatini Environment Authority: RHUS Office Park, Karl Grant St, POB 2602, Mbabane H100; tel. 24046960; e-mail reception@sea.org.sz; internet eea.org.sz; Chair. Rev. MFANALENI MKHATSHWA; CEO STEPHEN ZUKE.

Eswatini Housing Board (EHB): POB 798, Mbabane; tel. 24055000; e-mail postbox@snhb.co.sz; internet ehb.co.sz; f. 1988; Chair. JINNOH NKAMBULE; CEO MDUDUZI DLAMINI.

Eswatini National Industrial Development Corpn (ENIDC): Sibekelo Bldg, North West Wing, 3rd Floor, Office Park, Mhlambanyatsi Rd, POB 9458, Mbabane H100; tel. 24043846; e-mail info@nidcs.org.sz; internet www.nidcs.org.sz; f. 1971; became dormant in 1985; revived in 2012; state-owned; Chair. BONGILE SIMELANE; Man. Dir MUZIKAYISE DUBE.

Eswatini Water and Agricultural Development Enterprise (ESWADE): MVA Bldg, 3rd Floor, Mbilibhi St, POB 5836, Mbabane; tel. 24047950; e-mail swade@swade.co.sz; internet www.swade.co.sz; f. 1999; fmrly Swaziland Komati Project Enterprise; Chair. ZAKHELE LUKHELE; CEO SAMSON SITHOLE.

Industrial Development Company of Eswatini (IDCE): Dlan'ubeka House, cnr Mdada and Lalufadlana Sts, POB 866, Mbabane; tel. 24044010; e-mail info@idce.co.sz; internet www.idce.co.sz; f. 1987; present name adopted in 2018; state-owned; finances private sector projects and promotes local and foreign investment; Chair. DUMISANI KUNENE; CEO FAIRLIE MABUZA.

Swaziland Solidarity Network (SSN): c/o COSATU House, 3rd Floor, 1–5 Leyds St, Braamfontein, South Africa; POB 1027, Johannesburg 2000, South Africa; tel. (11) 23393621; internet fb.com/SwaziSolidarity; f. 1997; umbrella org. promoting democracy; incorporates mems from Eswatini and abroad incl. PUDEMO, SWAYOCO, and the Swaziland Democratic Alliance (f. 1999); also incl. the African National Congress of South Africa, South African Communist Party and Congress of South African Trade Unions; Chair. CHRIS MATLHAKO; Spokesperson LUCKY LUKHELE.

Tibiyo Taka Ngwane (Bowels of the Swazi Nation): Lomawa House, Lozithehlezi, POB 181, Kwaluseni, Manzini M201; tel. 25101390; e-mail info@tibiyo.com; internet www.tibiyo.com; f. 1968; national devt agency, with investment interests in all sectors of the economy; participates in domestic and foreign jt investment ventures; Chair. PRINCE FIPHA; Man. Dir Dr ABSALOM THEMBA DLAMINI.

INDUSTRIAL AND TRADE ASSOCIATIONS

Eswatini Cotton Board: Mancishane St, POB 230, Manzini; tel. 25052775; e-mail cottonboard@swazi.net; internet www.cottonboard.co.sz; f. 1967; CEO DANIEL KHUMALO.

Eswatini Dairy Development Board: Enguleni House, 3rd Floor, 287 Mahleka St, POB 2975, Manzini; tel. 25058262; e-mail info@dairyboard.co.sz; internet www.dairyboard.co.sz; f. 1971; Chair. PATRICK MYENI; CEO Dr TONY DLAMINI.

Eswatini Sugar Association: Nkotfotjeni Bldg, 4th Floor, cnr Dzeliwe and Msakato Sts, POB 445, Mbabane H100; tel. 24117600; e-mail info@esa.co.sz; internet www.esa.co.sz; f. 1967; CEO PHIL MNISI.

National Agricultural Marketing Board (NAMBoard): Plot 1A, Lot 165, cnr Masalesikhundleni and Bhabha Sts, POB 4261, Manzini; tel. 25055314; e-mail info@namboard.co.sz; internet namboard.co.sz; Chair. JOSEPH NDLANGAMANDLA; CEO BHEKIZWE C. MAZIYA.

National Maize Corpn (NMC): Industrial Site, 11th St, POB 1775, Matsapha; tel. 25187432; e-mail info@nmc.co.sz; internet www.nmc.co.sz; f. 1985; Chair. DUMISANI DLAMINI; CEO RECHI DLAMINI.

United Plantations (Swaziland Citrus Board): Lot 1/649, Henwood Bldg, Ben Dunn St, POB 343, Mbabane H100; tel. 24044266; e-mail scb@upswazi.com; f. 1969; Chair. P. S. NODDEBOE.

EMPLOYERS' ORGANIZATIONS

Business Eswatini: Malagwane Hill, POB 72, Mbabane H100; tel. 24047631; e-mail info@business-eswatini.co.sz; internet business-eswatini.co.sz; f. 2003 by merger of Fed. of Swaziland Employers (f. 1964) and Swaziland Chamber of Commerce & Industry (f. 1916); CEO NATHI DLAMINI.

UTILITIES

Regulatory Authority

Eswatini Energy Regulatory Authority (ESERA): RHUS Office Park, 1st Floor, Karl Grant St, POB 7137, Mbabane H100; tel. 24042103; e-mail info@sera.org.sz; internet www.sera.org.sz; f. 2007; responsible for regulation of electricity tariffs, and quality of supply and services; Chair. LUNGILE DLAMINI; CEO SIKHUMBUZO TSABEDZE.

Electricity

Eswatini Electricity Co: Eluvatsini House, Mhlambanyatsi Rd, POB 258, Mbabane; tel. 24094000; e-mail info@eec.co.sz; internet www.eec.co.sz; f. 1963; statutory body; responsible for generation, transmission and distribution of electricity; Chair. Dr PHILEMON MNISI; Man. Dir ERNEST MKHONTA.

Oil

Eswatini National Petroleum Co (ENPC): Lilunga House, Ground Floor, POB 8307, Mbabane; tel. 34401231; e-mail info@enpc.co.sz; internet www.enpc.co.sz; f. 2021; state-owned; Chair. MUZIWANDILE DLAMINI; CEO NHLANHLA DLAMINI.

Water

Eswatini Water Services Corpn (EWSC): Emtfonjeni Bldg, cnr MR103 and Cultural Village Dr., Ezulwini; POB 20, Mbabane; tel. 24169000; e-mail customercare@swsc.co.sz; internet www.swsc.co.sz; f. 1992; state-owned; Chair. BENEDICT XABA; Man. Dir JABULILE MASHWAMA.

MAJOR COMPANIES

Maloma Colliery Ltd: POB 103, Matata; tel. 22079194; e-mail info@maloma.org; internet maloma.org; f. 1992; coal mining; Chair. D. Z. MNGOMEZULU.

Montigny Investments Ltd: Bhunya, Mbabane H100; tel. 24525000; e-mail info@montigny.co.sz; internet www.montigny.co.sz; f. 1997; diversified timber co; CEO ANDREW LE ROUX.

Palfridge Ltd (The Fridge Factory): Plot 444, King Mswati III Ave, Matsapha Industrial Sites, POB 424, Matsapha M202; tel. 25184104; e-mail info@palfridge.com; internet www.palfridge.com; f. 2001; mfrs of domestic, commercial, medical and camping refrigerators and freezers; Chair. COLIN FOSTER; CEO PETER MCCULLOUGH.

Royal Eswatini Sugar Corpn: King's Rd, off MR3 Rd, POB 1, Simunye L301; tel. 23134000; e-mail info@res.co.sz; internet www.res.co.sz; f. 1977; 53% owned by Tibiyo Taka Ngwane, 29% owned by RCL Foods, 10% owned by the Govt of Nigeria, 6.5% owned by the Govt of Eswatini; mfrs of sugar and potable alcohol (80% for export); estates at Mhlume and Simunye; incorporates Royal Swazi Distillers (RSD); Chair. Dr ABSALOM THEMBA DLAMINI; Man. Dir NICK JACKSON.

Swaziland Meat Industries Ltd (Embiveni): First Ave, Industrial Sites, Matsapha, POB 446, Manzini M200; tel. 25184165; e-mail comms@smi.co.sz; internet fb.com/Embiveni; f. 1965; operates an abattoir and deboning plant at Matsapha to process beef for local and export markets; Gen. Man. JONATHAN C. WILLIAMS.

Ubombo Sugar Ltd: Old Main Rd, POB 23, Big Bend L311; tel. 23638000; e-mail communications@illovo.co.za; internet www.illovosugar.co.za; f. 1958; 60% owned by Illovo Sugar Group (South Africa), 40% owned by Tibiyo Taka Ngwane; produces raw and refined sugar; Man. Dir MUZI SIYAYA.

YKK Zippers (Swaziland) (Pty) Ltd: King Sobhuza II Ave, Matsapha Industrial Area, POB 1425, Manzini; tel. 25186188; internet www.ykkfastening.com; f. 1977; mfrs of zip fasteners; part of YKK Group, Japan; Chair. MASAYUKI SARUMARU; Pres. HIROAKI OTANI.

TRADE UNIONS

Amalgamated Trade Union of Swaziland (ATUSWA): Office No. 2, Luis Bldg, 1st Floor, Trelawny Park, POB 1158, Manzini; tel. 25053477; e-mail admin@atuswa.com; internet www.atuswa.com; f. 2013 by merger of 10 unions incl. the Swaziland Amalgamated Trade Unions (f. 2003) and the Swaziland Processing, Refinery and Allied Workers' Union; Sec.-Gen. WONDER MKHONZA; represents 9,000 workers of textile and apparel industry.

Federation of Swaziland Trade Unions (FESWATU): Plot 162, River Edges Bldg, cnr King Sobhuza II Ave, 2nd St, Matsapha; POB 1356, Nhlangano; tel. 25188367; e-mail feswatu@yahoo.com; internet fb.com/feswatu; f. 2015; affiliates include: Swaziland Property Development Workers' Union, Swazi Economic Improvement Workers' Union, Swaziland Caregivers and Allied Workers Unions, Swaziland Protection Workers' Union; Pres. MASHUMI SHONGWE.

Trade Union Congress of Swaziland (TUCOSWA): POB 1158, Manzini; tel. 25059514; e-mail tucoswa@swazi.net; f. 2012 following merger of the Swaziland Federation of Labour and the Swaziland Federation of Trade Unions (f. 1983); subsequently joined by the Swaziland National Association of Teachers; Pres. BHEKI MAMBA;

Sec.-Gen. MDUDUZI GINA; represents 40,000 workers from 16 affiliated unions; important affiliates include:

National Public Services and Allied Workers' Union (NAP-SAWU): Portion 25, Farm 868, Trelawney Park, POB 2811, Manzini M200; tel. 25058287; e-mail napsawu@napsawu.org.sz; internet www.napsawu.org.sz; f. 1980 as Swaziland National Association of Civil Service; Pres. OSCAR NKAMBULE; Gen. Sec. THULANI HLATSHWAKO.

Swaziland National Association of Teachers (SNAT): opp. William Pitcher, POB 1575, Manzini M200; tel. 25052603; e-mail snatcentre@snat.org.sz; internet www.snat.org.sz; f. 1928; Pres. MBONGWA DLAMINI; Sec.-Gen. SIKELELA DLAMINI.

Swaziland Union of Financial Institutions and Allied Workers (SUFIAW): Swazi Plaza, POB A101, Mbabane; tel. 24044261; e-mail sufiaw@realnet.co.sz; Pres. MPHIKELELI DLAMINI; Sec.-Gen. JABU SHIBA.

Transport

Buses are the principal means of transport for many Swazis. Bus services are provided by private operators; these are required to obtain annual permits for each route from the Road Transportation Board, which also regulates fares.

RAILWAYS

The rail network provides a major transport link for imports and exports. Railway lines connect with the dry port at Matsapha, the South African ports of Richards Bay and Durban in the south, the South African town of Komatipoort in the north and the Mozambican port of Maputo in the east. Goods traffic is mainly in wood pulp, sugar, molasses, coal, citrus fruit and canned fruit. In the late 2010s Eswatini Railways and Transnet of South Africa were collaborating on a project which entailed the construction of a new 150-km railway line from Lothair in South Africa to Sidvokodvo in Eswatini, while restoring two existing lines (Ermelo–Lothair and Sidvokodvo–Richards Bay).

Eswatini Railways: Eswatini Railways Bldg, Dzeliwe St, POB 475, Mbabane; tel. 24117400; e-mail info@eswatinirail.co.sz; internet www.eswatinirail.co.sz; f. 1964; Chair. ALEX MNGOMEZULU; CEO NIXON DLAMINI.

ROADS

Roads Department: Ministry of Public Works and Transport, Mhlambanyatsi Rd, POB 58, Mbabane; tel. 24099105; e-mail dlaminivin@gov.sz; Chief Roads Engineer VINCENT B. DLAMINI.

CIVIL AVIATION

There is an airport at Matsapha, near Manzini, about 40 km from Mbabane, and in March 2014 King Mswati III International Airport at Sikhuphe, in eastern Eswatini, was inaugurated. The airport was constructed at a cost of some US $300m. and has the capacity to handle 360,000 passengers per year. In 2018 the airport at Matsapha was closed to scheduled flights.

Eswatini Civil Aviation Authority (ESWACAA): Matsapha International Airport, POB D361, Matsapha; tel. 23335370; e-mail info@eswacaa.co.sz; internet www.eswacaa.co.sz; 2009; Chair. BONGINKHOSI MAGAGULA; Dir-Gen. SOLOMON DUBE.

Royal Eswatini National Airways Corpn (RENAC): POB 939, Manzini; tel. 25181500; e-mail info@renac.co.sz; internet www.renac.co.sz; f. 1978; Chair. MNDENI MAZIBUKO; CEO Capt. QINISO DHLAMINI.

Tourism

Eswatini National Trust Commission (ENTC): POB 100, Parliament Rd, Lobamba H107; tel. 24161489; e-mail info@sntc.org.sz; internet www.sntc.org.sz; f. 1972; parastatal org. responsible for conservation of nature and cultural heritage (national parks, museums and monuments); CEO (vacant).

Eswatini Tourism Authority (ETA): POB A1030, Swazi Plaza, Mbabane H101; tel. 24049693; e-mail info@thekingdomofeswatini.com; internet www.thekingdomofeswatini.com; f. 2001; CEO LINDA L. NXUMALO.

Hospitality and Tourism Association of Eswatini (HOTAES): Oribi Court, 1st Floor, Gwamile St, POB 462, Mbabane; tel. 24042218; e-mail info@hotaes.com; internet www.hotaes.com; f. 1972; private sector tourism promotion org.; Chair. MARC WARD.

Defence

The Umbutfo Swaziland Defence Force was created in 1973; it was renamed the Umbutfo Eswatini Defence Force in 2018. Compulsory military service of two years was introduced in 1983.

Commander of the Umbutfo Eswatini Defence Force: Lt-Gen. MASHIKILISANA MOSES FAKUDZE.

Education

Education is not compulsory in Eswatini. Primary education begins at six years of age and lasts for seven years. Secondary education begins at 13 years of age and lasts for up to five years, comprising a first cycle of three years and a second of two years. According to estimates by the United Nations Educational, Scientific and Cultural Organization (UNESCO), in 2010/11 enrolment at pre-primary institutions included 19% of children (males 19%; females 19%) in the relevant age-group. In 2017/18, 84% of children (males 85%; females 83%) in the relevant age-group were enrolled at primary schools, while in 2015/16 secondary enrolment was equivalent to 82% of children (males 83%; females 82%). Expenditure on education in 2021/22 was budgeted at E4,050m., representing some 16.0% of the total national budget.

Bibliography

Bischoff, P.-H. *Swaziland's International Relations and Foreign Policy: A Study of a Small African State in International Relations.* Berne, P. Lang, 1990.

Booth, A. R. *Historical Dictionary of Swaziland.* Metuchen, NJ, Scarecrow Press, 1975.

Swaziland: Tradition and Change in a Southern African Kingdom. Boulder, CO, Westview Press, 1983; London, Gower Publishers, 1984.

Booth, M. Z. *Culture and Education: The Social Consequences of Western Schooling in Contemporary Swaziland.* Lanham, MD, University Press of America, 2004.

Daniel, J., and Stephen, M. F. (Eds). *Historical Perspectives on the Political Economy of Swaziland.* Kwaluseni, University of Swaziland, 1986.

Davies, R. H., et al. (Eds). *The Kingdom of Swaziland: A Profile.* London, Zed Press, 1985.

Dlamini, S. *Swaziland Ruling System, The Monarchy, A History: The other side of Democracy.* 2017.

Forster, S., and Nsibande, B. S. (Eds). *Swaziland: Contemporary Social and Economic Issues.* Aldershot, Ashgate Publishing Ltd, 2000.

Funnell, D. C. *Under the Shadow of Apartheid: Agrarian Transformation in Swaziland.* Aldershot, Avebury, 1991.

Gillis, D. H. *The Kingdom of Swaziland.* Westport, CT, Greenwood Publishing Group, 1999.

Konczacki, Z. A., et al. (Eds). *Studies in the Economic History of Southern Africa.* Vol. II. London, Cass, 1991.

Matsebula, J. S. *A History of Swaziland.* 2nd edn. Cape Town, Maskew Miller, Longmans, 1988.

Matsebula, M. S. *The Informal Sector: A Historical and Structural Analysis With Special Reference To Swaziland.* Harare, SAPES Books, 1996.

Msibi, N. *The Delayed Revolution: Swaziland in the Twenty-First Century.* 2014.

Okpalmba, Chuks, et al. (Eds). *Human Rights in Swaziland: The Legal Response.* Kwaluseni, University of Swaziland, 1997.

Rose, L. L. *The Politics of Harmony: Land Dispute Strategies in Swaziland.* Cambridge, Cambridge University Press, 1992.

Schwager, D. *Swaziland.* Mbabane, Websters, 1984.

Simelane, H. S. *Colonialism and Economic Change in Swaziland 1940–1960.* Manzini, Jan Publishing Centre, 2003.

Simelane, N. C. (Ed.). *Social Transformation: The Swaziland Case.* Dakar, CODESRIA, 1995.

ETHIOPIA

Physical and Social Geography

G. C. LAST

The Federal Democratic Republic of Ethiopia is a landlocked country in the Horn of Africa, covering an area of 1,133,380 sq km (437,600 sq miles). Ethiopia's western neighbours are Sudan and South Sudan; to the south it has a common border with Kenya; and to the east and south-east lie Djibouti and Somalia. To the north and north-east lies Eritrea.

PHYSICAL FEATURES

Elevations range from around 100 m below sea level in the Danakil (Dallol) Depression (Kobar Sink), on the north-eastern border with Eritrea, to a number of mountain peaks in excess of 4,000 m above sea level, which dominate the plateaux and of which the highest is Ras Dashen, rising to 4,620 m.

The southern half of Ethiopia is bisected by the Great Rift Valley, ranging between 40 km and 60 km in width and containing a number of lakes. In the latitude of Addis Ababa, the western wall of the rift turns north and runs parallel to the west coast of Arabia, leaving a wide plain between the escarpment and the Red Sea coast of Eritrea. The eastern wall of the rift turns to the east in the latitude of Addis Ababa, forming an escarpment looking north over the Afar plains. The escarpments are nearly always abrupt, and are broken at only one point near Addis Ababa where the Awash river descends from the rim of the plateau.

The plateaux to the west of the rift system dip gently towards the west and are drained by right-bank tributaries of the Nile system, which have carved deep and spectacular gorges. The plateaux to the north of Lake Tana are drained by the Tekeze and Angareb rivers, headwaters of the Atbara. The central plateaux are drained by the Abbai (Blue Nile) river and its tributaries. The Abbai rises in Lake Tana and is known as the Blue Nile in Sudan. Much of the flood water in the Blue Nile system comes from the left-bank tributaries, which rise in the high rainfall region of south-west Ethiopia. This southern region is also drained by the Akobo, Gilo and Baro rivers, which form the headwaters of the Sobat river. The only river of significance to the west of the Rift Valley that is not part of the Nile system is the Omo, which drains southwards into Lake Turkana and is known in its upper course as the Gibie. In the 1960s and 1970s a number of important archaeological discoveries of early human occupation, pre-dating the early remains at Olduvai Gorge in Tanzania, were made in the lower trough of the Omo. The Rift Valley itself contains a number of closed river basins, including the largest, the Awash, which flows north from the Rift Valley proper into the Afar plain and terminates in Lake Abe. It is in the middle and lower Awash regions of the Rift Valley that even earlier remains of man have been discovered, in the locality of Hadow, below the escarpment to the east of Dessie. The highlands to the east of the Rift are drained south-eastwards by the headstreams of the Webi-Shebelli and Juba river systems.

The location of Ethiopia across a series of major fault lines and its association with earth movements, particularly in the Afar plains, which are related to the continuing drift of the African continent away from the Asian blocks, makes it highly susceptible to minor earth tremors.

CLIMATE, VEGETATION AND NATURAL RESOURCES

Ethiopia lies within the tropics but the wide range of altitude produces considerable variations in temperature conditions, which are reflected in the traditional zones of the *dega* (the temperate plateaux), the *kolla* (hot lowlands) and the intermediate frost-free zone of the *woina dega*. The boundaries between these three zones lie at approximately 2,400 m and 1,700 m above sea level. The annual average temperature in the *dega* is about 16°C, in the *woina dega* about 22°C and in the *kolla* at least 26°C. A main rainy season covers most of the country during June–August, when moist equatorial air is drawn in from the south and west.

Ethiopia is extremely vulnerable to drought conditions, particularly in the low-lying pastoral areas, and along the eastern escarpment where there is a widespread dependence upon the spring rains (*belg*). The development of cultivation in areas of marginal rainfall has accentuated this problem.

Despite the significant variations in local climates and in the distribution of rainfall, Ethiopia's climatic conditions can be described generally in terms of well-watered highlands and uplands, mostly receiving at least 1,000 mm of rain a year, with the exception of the Tigraian plateau, and dry lowlands, which usually have less than 500 mm of rain (with the significant exception of the Baro and Akobo river plains in the south-west, which lie in the path of summer rain-bearing winds).

The natural vegetation of the plateaux and highlands above 1,800 m is coniferous forest (notably *zigba* and *tid*), but these forests have now largely disappeared, existing only in the more inaccessible regions of the country. In the south-west, higher rainfall, with lower elevations and higher temperatures, has produced extensive broadleaf rainforests with a variety of species, including abundant *karraro*. Previously densely forested areas in the south-west have now, with the extension of all-weather road systems, been subject to extensive commercial exploitation and the activities of a growing population of traditional cultivators, with devastating impact on the natural vegetation.

Above the treeline on the plateaux are wide expanses of mountain grassland. The highlands are the site of settled agriculture in which some 4m. farmers produce a variety of grain crops. The growth of population and the depletion of resources in forest cover and soil have led to the practice of farming in areas that are very marginal and unreliable in rainfall, notably along the eastern escarpment. This has exacerbated drought and famine conditions. The most important traditional grain crop, teff, used in the highlands for the production of the staple food, injera, has been most seriously affected. This has had a notable impact, as the populations there do not adapt easily to replacement crops (and relief supplies) of maize and rice.

In the lowlands, dependent on rainfall conditions, there is a range of dry-zone vegetation. Extensive natural range-lands, particularly in the Borena and Ogaden plains in the south, are an important resource in Ethiopia and support large numbers of cattle.

Drought conditions, which began in 1972–73, in association with abnormal conditions affecting the whole Sahel region of Africa, have completely disrupted the pastoral economy in many areas, resulting in a high mortality rate both of humans and livestock and severely depleting vegetation cover.

To add to Ethiopia's problems is the frequent invasion by the so-called 'desert' locust. There are breeding grounds of this insect in the drier regions of the country, but much of the damage is inflicted by large swarms of adults, which can contain more than 25m. locusts, each eating its own weight in vegetation daily, and which originate in the semi-desert areas of Sudan, South Sudan, Saudi Arabia, Somalia and Kenya.

Exploration for petroleum was carried out for some years in the Ogaden region without success. More recently, attention has been diverted to the southern borders of Ethiopia. Petroleum reserves have reportedly been identified in the south-east of the country, between the rivers Web and Webi-Shebelli. The geothermal power potential of extensive sources in the regional state of Afar is being evaluated. In 2000 a US company discovered large petroleum and natural gas deposits in the west of the country. However, at mid-2022, despite continuing exploration projects being undertaken by local and foreign hydrocarbons companies, no commercial production of petroleum or natural gas had yet commenced.

Ethiopia commands excellent potential for the generation of hydroelectric power. A number of plants are in operation along the course of the Awash river and along the Blue Nile river basin (where power production is coupled with irrigation schemes), while numerous other possible sites have been identified (some of which are now being developed).

POPULATION

According to a census conducted in May 2007, the total population was 73,750,932 (37,217,130 males, 36,533,802 females). At July 2022, according to official figures, the population of Ethiopia was projected to total 105,166,000, giving an average population density of 92.8 persons per sq km. However, this average conceals a very wide variation among the regions, as might be expected from the multiplicity of natural environments. At July 20202, according to official projections, the population of the capital, Addis Ababa, stood at 3.86m., while a further 13 towns each had more than 150,000 inhabitants. The growth rates in these larger urban settlements are high.

The distribution of population generally reflects the pattern of relief. The highlands, having a plentiful rainfall, are the home of settled agriculture and contain nearly all the major settlements. Land more than 2,000 m above sea level was, in the past, free of the malarial mosquito, a factor contributing to the non-occupation of lowlands that are suitable for farming. However, recent evidence shows that this traditional limit is being breached as average temperatures rise and the mosquito adapts to higher elevations. It would not be unreasonable to assume that 10% of the population live below 1,000 m, 20% at 1,000 m–1,800 m and 70% above the 1,800-m contour line. The distribution of population has been affected by recurrent droughts, which have forced many people to leave their traditional areas in search of emergency aid, and by the erstwhile government policy of resettling famine victims from the former Tigray and Wollo provinces in newly established villages in the lowlands of the south-west; additionally, the civil war, which intensified in 1989–91, caused the displacement of large numbers of the population.

The implementation in 1994 of new administrative regions ('regional states'), which are based on ethnic distributions, resulted in movement of minority groups. Furthermore, the massive recruitment of young men for the war with Eritrea (1998–2000) was believed to have had long-term implications for population growth and distribution.

History

SOLOMON M. GOFIE

INTRODUCTION: THE FORMATION OF THE MODERN STATE OF ETHIOPIA

The emergence of the modern state in Ethiopia towards the end of the 19th century can be viewed against the backdrop of a long history of state-like formations in different parts of the country. Such formations existed at various times and regions in the country's history. Examples of these were: the Axumite and the Zagwe in the northern part of the country, which formed part of the ancient and medieval political history preceding the modern period in Ethiopia; the Muslim sultanates in the south-central region and the east; the egalitarian Oromo Gadaa formations in the south, south-east and central regions and the 'Gibe States' in the west; and the various principalities and small kingdoms of what is now the southern region of Ethiopia. The Nilotic in the north-west and the Omotic societies in the south-west inhabited the land long before the emergence of the modern state in Ethiopia towards the end of the 19th century. Most of the diverse people of the historic southern part of the country were brought into what some called the Ethiopian 'empire state' towards the end of the 19th century.

However, Ethiopia's historiography overlooks the intense scope of migration of people from one place to another within what constitutes Ethiopia today and in the wider regional context. Some of the communities in what now constitutes Ethiopia are recognized to be among those who embraced Christianity and Islam much earlier. The Ethiopian Orthodox Church was an ideological arm of the state before the 1974 revolution. Islam has millions of followers inhabiting the different parts of the country. Equally important are the non-Christian, non-Islam belief systems and sociopolitical systems of the various groups of the population, some of which remained among the most resilient forms of traditional social, economic and political institutions. Of these, the Gadaa, which is widely practised among the Oromo, is one of the most widely known, integrating cosmological and politico-social systems of thought mediating relations within the Oromo communities and beyond their social boundaries.

The political instability that marked the second half of the 19th century in Ethiopia was due largely to the power struggles for supremacy between ambitious local rulers at that time, such as Kassa Hailu of Gondar (who reigned as Emperor Tewodros in 1855–68) and later Kassa Mircha of Tigrai (Emperor Yohannes IV, 1872–89) and Menelik II of Shoa. During this period externally instigated attempts were made to subdue the population in parts of northern and eastern Ethiopia. The Egyptians, the Mahdists of the Sudan and later the Italians were among the major intruders making such attempts.

As stated, the formation of the modern state in Ethiopia is traced back to the last decades of the 19th century, following the conquest of the historic southern part of the country by Menelik II. This prompted a considerable expansion in the country's geographic boundaries. Ethiopia's victory over the Italians at the battle of Adwa in 1896 and the subsequent recognition accorded to it by the major European powers of the time served as the basis for the country's capacity to enter into relations with other states, notably European powers in the international system of the early 20th century. Menelik ruled from 1889 until 1913. His immediate successors, Iyasu (1913–16) and Zewditu (1917–29), more or less continued with a strong sense of allegiance to Menelik. Haile Selassie's rule (1930–74) was different from those of his predecessors. His reign witnessed the quest for centralization, as well as the modernization of the state. The first Constitution, a parliament, the creation of the country's bureaucratic institutions, the building of a professional army, modern education, etc., were taken up more seriously during his rule. Although this process was interrupted by the Italian invasion and occupation of 1935–41, Haile Selassie's imperial Government continued with its policy of centralization after the total liberation of the country in 1941. Ethiopia's political system under Haile Selassie, however, remained essentially a feudal system wherein land was controlled fully by the monarchical family and the feudal lords. The Amharic language was perceived to be the instrument of homogenization of the more than 80 different language and cultural groups in Ethiopia. Rudimentary forms of manufacturing industries and modern agriculture were established in the aftermath of liberation. Modern education supplied a relatively skilled manpower and represented the face of the modernizing monarchy.

The restoration of the monarchy after the removal of the Italian invading army in 1941 paved the way for Eritrea's federation with Ethiopia in 1951, ending the British mandate or protectorate over the former, which lasted for about 10 years. Addis Ababa, the Ethiopian capital, became the headquarters of the United Nations (UN) Economic Commission for Africa in 1958 and of the Organization of African Unity (OAU, now the African Union—AU) in 1963. Haile Selassie's Government maintained strong relations with the USA in the aftermath of Italian invasion and was the main recipient of US aid in Africa during the 1950s and 1960s. The Imperial Government, in turn, served its US counterpart as a regional ally that hosted the latter's communications base in Asmara, Eritrea, in the 1960s.

The land issue, the exploitation of the peasantry and pervasive inequality and the lack of recognition of the languages of the diverse population of the country, interpreted by some as the 'national question', were the sources of contradictions of the Ethiopian 'empire state' and were among the major sources of grievances raised against the feudal autocracy. The attempted coup of 1960, a rebellion in various provinces (including in Bale, Wolo and Gojam) and drought and famine in Wolo province, especially during 1972–74, fuelled the grievances of the various sections of the society—the peasantry, the army, workers, teachers and students. A series of student protests, mutinies within the army and strikes by teachers and workers exerted pressure on the monarchical rule. The monarchy's attempts to reform by appointing Western-educated officials did not change the underlying discontent. The monarchy finally lost control, and in June 1974 a 'co-ordinating committee of the armed forces' arrested and later executed the leading officials of the imperial order. The abolition of the monarchy was officially proclaimed in March 1975.

THE DERG MILITARY-SOCIALIST PERIOD, 1974–91

The Provisional Military Administrative Council known as the *Derg* (Committee), adopted socialism as its ideology in the aftermath of the revolution. As part of the reforms introduced by the *Derg* under a revolutionary slogan known as *Ethiopia Tikdem* (Ethiopia First), land, corporate enterprises and private properties were nationalized; trade unions were restructured; and the lower units of local government (*kebeles*) were established in rural and urban areas. Revolutionary groups such as the All-Ethiopia Socialist Movement (known by its acronym, MEISON, in Amharic) helped the formulation of the 'national democratic revolution programme' in 1976. The Ethiopian People's Revolutionary Party (EPRP)—another popular political grouping—demanded the formation of a civilian government. In February 1977 the Chairman of the *Derg*, Lt-Col Mengistu Haile Mariam, seized power after the elimination of senior *Derg* officials—Teferi Benti, Atnafu Abate and Aman Andom, among others. Mengistu led the 'red terror' campaign aimed at eliminating the EPRP and other groups branded as counter-revolutionaries. Tens of thousands were killed, tortured or went into exile. By 1978 political organizations such as MEISON, the EPRP and members of political organizations perceived as opponents of the *Derg* regime had been eliminated from the domestic political scene.

However, instability spread across the country starting from the second half of the 1970s manifesting in rebellion in Eritrea (which had been annexed by Ethiopia with the status of a province in November 1962) and incursions of Somali irredentist insurgents, supported by forces of the Somali Government that claimed the Ogaden region of Ethiopia. With massive mobilization of the population by the *Derg*, military support from Cuba and supplies of armaments from the Union of Soviet Socialist Republics, Ethiopian forces effectively repulsed Somalia's invading army in 1978 and carried out an offensive against the Eritrean People's Liberation Front (EPLF), its ally, the Tigrian Peoples Liberation Front (TPLF) and other armed groups attempting to wage armed resistance in the northern regions of Ethiopia at that time.

The Commission for Organizing the Workers' People of Ethiopia was established in 1979. Peasant, trade union, youth and women associations were formed and served as the instruments of centralized control of society and were platforms of a repressive military-socialist one-party state. The Workers' Party of Ethiopia was officially inaugurated in September 1984. The Constitution of 1987 provided for a unicameral elected legislature, the National Shengo (Assembly). The Constitution also provided for the reorganization of Ethiopia's internal administrative regions that led to the recognition of regions such as Tigray, Eritrea, Ogaden, Assab and Dire Dawa as autonomous regions. By the late 1980s the various groups advocating for secession or autonomy gained strength by mobilizing the population along 'ethnic' identity lines. At the beginning of the 1990s the EPLF and the TPLF advanced towards the central regions of the country, and other groupings such as the Oromo Liberation Front (OLF) joined the offensive against the *Derg*. On 21 May 1991 Mengistu fled to Zimbabwe, and in the following days the Ethiopian People's Revolutionary Democratic Front (EPRDF) arrived in Addis Ababa and declared its seizure of state power.

THE EPRDF REGIME, 1991–2017

The EPRDF's takeover of power in 1991 heralded one of the most consequential periods in Ethiopia's recent political history. The rhetoric of self-determination and 'revolutionary democracy' raised expectations among various groups in different parts of the country, some of whom were vying for autonomy or independence. A TPLF-led conference in July proclaimed a Transitional Charter that provided for the formation of the Council of Representatives to govern during the subsequent two-year period. The EPRDF Chairman, Meles Zenawi, was elected President and Tamirat Layine of the Amhara National Democratic Movement was appointed Prime Minister, although Meles and the TPLF's core group remained in control of the Government and the country. While the TPLF remained the dominant element in the EPRDF until 2018, the three other groups of the EPRDF controlled three of the post-1991 regional states in Ethiopia (Amhara, Oromia and the Southern Nations, Nationalities and Peoples' Region—SNNPR).

The EPRDF Government supported unconditionally Eritrean independence and emphasized self-determination for Ethiopia's 'nations, nationalities and peoples', arguably in an attempt to address the 'national question', which in its view the 1974 revolution had failed to resolve. The Constitution of 1995 created the nine regional states (*kellil*)—of Tigray, Afar, Amhara, Oromia, Benishangul-Gumuz, Harari, Somali, Gambela and the SNNPR—and Addis Ababa and Dire Dawa remained centrally controlled cities. The underlying basis for the reorganization of the country has largely been 'ethnic' identity and linguistic boundaries, which have often been contested.

In the post-1991 period, however, armed opposition against EPRDF rule occurred frequently in different regions of the country, most notably in the states of Afar, Gambela, Oromia, Somali, Tigray and Amhara. The EPRDF regime accused the OLF and the Ogaden National Liberation Front (ONLF), in particular, of instigating unrest in the Oromia and Somali regions, respectively. The EPRDF used the names of these organizations as an instrument of political repression against the wider sections of the population in these regions, by accusing dissenters of being members of these groups, which were later designated by the TPLF-led EPRDF Government as terrorist organizations.

DEMOCRATIZATION AND ELECTORAL POLITICS, 1995–2015

One of the first electoral events in Ethiopia after the EPRDF takeover was the organization of an election for the formation of a Constituent Assembly, held in June 1994 under a tightly controlled process. In December the Assembly ratified a new Constitution, with its provisions including controversial articles such as on the right to self-determination including secession. In May 1995 what were considered multi-party elections for the lower chamber of parliament (the House of People's Representatives) and for the regional state assemblies were held. Under the Constitution, executive power was vested in a Prime Minister selected by the political organizations holding a majority of seats in the House of Peoples Representatives. The EPRDF and its allies claimed an overwhelming victory in the elections and Meles became Prime Minister. In Tigray regional state the TPLF took all the seats in the federal and state assemblies; other EPRDF member organizations retained control of the assemblies in Amhara, Oromia and the SNNPR. In Addis Ababa the EPRDF secured all 92 local assembly seats; independent candidates won only two of the city's 23 federal parliamentary seats. Some opposition groups boycotted the elections, in protest at a lack of access to the media, arrests and harassment of their representatives and closure of their offices. The new Constitution and official designation of the Federal Democratic Republic of Ethiopia entered into force in August 1995, and Dr Negasso Gidada of the Oromo People's Democratic Organization (OPDO) was elected by the new legislature to the largely ceremonial post of President.

The EPRDF exercised strict control in the conduct of the May 2000 elections. Opposition organizations claimed numerous irregularities, including physical abuse, intimidation of monitors and malpractice. International observers maintained that although the elections represented some progress, they were not free or fair. In the elections to the House of People's Representatives, opposition parties won a small number of seats, although the EPRDF and political organizations allied to it remained in control of the other regional states, which they won by huge margins in their respective regions, where there were further allegations of extensive voting irregularities. In October 2001 Girma Wolde Giorgis replaced Negasso Gidada as President.

The EPRDF totally controlled the political process and political space before the elections of May 2005, although new political organizations and coalitions were beginning to emerge in the run-up to those polls, such as the United Ethiopian Democratic Forces and Rainbow Ethiopia: Movement for Democracy and Social Justice in 2003 and 2004, respectively. By October 2005 Rainbow Ethiopia, together with the All Ethiopian Unity Party, the Ethiopian Democratic Unity Party and the Ethiopian Democratic League, formed the Coalition for Unity and Democracy (CUD). Appearing to open up the political space prior to the elections, the EPRDF regime allowed the conduct of live televised debates during the pre-election period, allowing the participation of opposition groups in discussions about the major aspects of governance, economic and social policy issues. While the pre-election period and the polling were generally peaceful, the aftermath was beset by tensions and conflicts. The situation gradually deteriorated into violence, and protests were held in June and November, which were dispersed by state security forces, resulting in the death of several hundred people, injuries and the detention of thousands of opposition members and supporters, particularly of the CUD. Further protests were organized, mainly by students in western and eastern Oromia, in Addis Ababa and in the Gojam areas of the Amhara region. By early 2006 state security forces had brought the protests under control. Several opposition leaders, including the head of the CUD, were arrested, some of whom were released in July, following a period of international condemnation and diplomatic pressure on the Government.

The ruling EPRDF claimed a total victory in the May 2010 elections, taking 499 of the 547 seats in the House of People's Representatives, and its allied organizations secured a further 46 seats. From among the opposition groups, the Ethiopia Federal Democratic Unity Forum (known as FORUM), which included the Unity for Democracy and Justice Party (UDJ, commonly known by its Amharic name *Andinet*) and the Oromo People's Congress (OPC), obtained just one seat in the legislature. In August 2012 Meles died while receiving medical treatment in Belgium. Hailemariam Desalegn was sworn in as acting Prime Minister and was appointed to replace Meles as Chairman of the EPRDF in September.

The legislative elections of May 2015 took place amid pressure from regime functionaries, forcing people to vote for the EPRDF and its allied parties, with the continued harassment of members and supporters of opposition political groups. In most polling stations, the elections were conducted without observers from opposition parties, and in the absence of

international observers. Nevertheless, the AU endorsed the elections, despite its observers' claims of widespread irregularities based on reports from polling stations that they visited. According to the official results of the elections announced in late June, the EPRDF claimed total victory, securing 501 of the 547 elective seats in the House of People's Representatives, while political organizations allied to it and in control of the Afar, Benishangul-Gumuz, Gambela and Somali regions took the remaining seats. The Semayawi (Blue) Party rejected the election results as an 'undemocratic disgrace'. Other opposition groups reported the killing of some of their members and supporters in the Hadiya, Gojjam and Tigray regions during the electoral period.

Following the 2015 elections, journalists, political activists and academics who criticized the EPRDF regime were subject to considerable pressure. Merera Gudina, the leader of the Oromo Federalist Congress (OFC) and a political science professor at Addis Ababa University (AAU), was dismissed from the University, together with some other senior academics. Their dismissal took place in a context where state functionaries, including members of the AAU authorities, placed tremendous pressure on academics, students and administrative staff to join what was termed a 'one to five' grouping or network. This was a centrally controlled mechanism installed by EPRDF functionaries, requiring all Ethiopian nationals in public institutions, schools, work places and residential quarters to be organized into a group of five people-an ambitious totalitarian political structure. The mechanism has been ridiculed by the political oppositions, human rights organizations and the public at large as a political instrument of the EPRDF, used to intimidate the population and force them to vote for the EPRDF and its allies.

HUMAN RIGHTS, DEMOCRACY AND PROTESTS, 2014–17

While in power, the EPRDF had ratified some of the major international human rights conventions, and in the 1995 Constitution it incorporated civil, political, economic, social and development rights. The Constitution provided for the establishment of the Ethiopian Human Rights Commission (EHRC) and the Institution of the Ombudsman. However, human rights violations were the central feature of EPRDF rule. From the early 1990s international and local human rights organizations frequently expressed concerns about, and extensively reported on, the human rights situation in Ethiopia. In the 1990s various reports published by the EHRC detailed reports of extrajudicial killings, disappearances and widespread arbitrary arrest and imprisonment. Among the many serious allegations of human rights violations, extrajudicial killings, torture and disappearances in the Oromia, Ogaden and Gambela regions featured significantly in the reports of local and international human rights organizations. Non-governmental organizations such as Human Rights Watch criticized some of the laws that the EPRDF Government had passed, especially the 2009 Anti-Terrorism Proclamation, on the grounds that such legislation permitted the EPRDF regime to label anybody expressing dissent a terrorist. In 2009 the International Committee of the Red Cross was ordered to leave the Somali region by the EPRDF regime, which accused the organization of 'collaborating with the enemy'. A regional armed police force known as the *Liyu* ('Special') Police, formed in 2007, was at the centre of accusations of gross human rights violations in the Somali region of Ethiopia until 2018 changes.

In July 2014 several leading members of the Semayawi Party, the UDJ and the Arena Tigray Party were detained. Applications by opposition parties to hold demonstrations were denied and the organizers were arrested repeatedly. Reports by human rights groups indicated that the state authorities consistently harassed, threatened and detained the leaders and supporters of opposition political organizations. In June Ethiopian state security forces at an airport in the Yemeni capital, San'a, apprehended Andargachew Tsige, a naturalized British citizen of Ethiopian origin, who was one of the leaders of Ginbot 7, an armed opposition group operating from Eritrea at that time. Held incommunicado for several months, Andargachew was later transferred to the Kaliti prison in Addis Ababa.

The EPRDF Government announced in April 2014 a policy of urban expansion—the Addis Ababa and Oromia Special Zone Integrated Development Master Plan, AAOSZIDMP—which proposed to expand the capital into parts of the surrounding Oromia region. The proposal prompted demonstrations by students and members of the public in several towns across the Oromia region in the same month. The protesters were particularly opposed to the Plan on the grounds that it would serve as an instrument to evict local farmers from their land. The authorities responded with the disproportionate use of force, and up to 50 demonstrators (including students) had been killed in the town of Ambo in early May, according to local media reports.

Further protests in the Oromia region erupted in November 2015 following rumours about the impending implementation of the AAOSZIDMP. More widespread protests across several regions continued during January–March 2016, resulting in the deaths of hundreds of people; thousands more were injured, and tens of thousands were detained. Various human rights organizations condemned the actions of the security forces and urged the state authorities to investigate the killings. Members of the affected communities were reported to have taken up arms in some of the localities, resulting in deaths of members of several members of the state security forces. Although the Government announced the cancellation of the Master Plan in January 2016, this did not halt the protests, and the regime continued to use repressive measures. Almost all the senior officials of the OFC were arrested around this time, in addition to the thousands of protesters who remained in custody.

There were reports of other conflicts in the southern, western and south-eastern regions of the country while the protests continued. The unrest in the south arose when members of the Konso community demanded autonomy within the SNNPR, holding large protests in the Konso zone in April. Clashes between government forces and members of local communities in the South Omo district were also reported. The major source of the tensions was the displacement of residents owing to the establishment of large-scale sugar plantations sponsored by the Government. In April 2016 it was reported that armed organized groups from the Murle community in South Sudan attacked Nuer communities in the Gambela region of Ethiopia, killing several people, abducting more than 100 children and looting a large number of cattle.

Protests erupted in the North Gondar zone in the Amhara region in July 2016. The status of a number of administrative districts which were brought under the Tigray region when the TPLF-led regime was restructuring of the country in 1991, has long been disputed. Members of communities in these districts, notably in the Wolkait and Tsegede areas, continued to express their grievances about the imposition of 'Tigrayan identity' on them. Consequently, a committee established to represent the rights of these communities and seeking to protect the 'Wolkait Amhara identity' has been in conflict with the authorities, accusing them of intimidation and repression.

Widespread protests broke out in the Oromia and Amhara regions again in August 2016. The protests in the Oromia region were largely viewed as a continuation of the campaign against the AAOSZIDMP, while activists from among the Oromo community were appealing for countrywide action. The Government warned that the organization of demonstrations without authorization would have 'dire consequences'. In North Gondar demonstrators demanded the release of the 'Wolkait Amhara identity' committee members who had been detained during the clashes with state security forces in July 2016. They demanded an end to the continuing killings in Oromia and the release of all political prisoners. Following the demonstrations in North Gondar, social media activists appealed for countrywide demonstration. Repeated threats by the authorities failed to prevent demonstrations in many towns in Oromia, and in Bahir Dar and other parts of the Amhara region. Human rights organizations reported that about 100 people were killed by the state security or police forces in August.

Foreign governments closely following events during those periods issued warnings to their citizens in Ethiopia. In August 2016 the Qatari-based broadcaster Al Jazeera reported that

the Ethiopian Government was rejecting demands by the office of the UN High Commissioner for Human Rights for an independent inquiry into the death of protesters. The death of several people in the town of Bishoftu during the public holiday of *Irrecha*, in Oromia, in September provoked riots in many parts of the region, in which private business and government properties and vehicles were destroyed by protesters. The Government declared a state of emergency in October, which included restrictions on movement, a ban on social media and the prohibition of contact with groups or individuals that it designated as terrorists. A 'Command Post', chaired by Prime Minister Halilemariam was established to implement the state of emergency, and tens of thousands of people were apprehended and sent to so-called 'training camps' at military bases around the country. In November state authorities reported that more than 11,000 people had been arrested since the state of emergency was declared, reportedly for attacking security forces, killing civilians and disrupting public services. Some opposition figures and activists urged the imposition of economic sanctions on the regime in response to the crackdown. In January 2017 the state media announced that about 10,000 detainees in Oromia had been pardoned, while about 70,000 people were still in prisons and detention centres across the region. Although observers believed that the declaration of a state of emergency had helped to restore relative calm and stability in most parts of the country, members of the Oromo population at the borders of the Oromia and the Somali regions in particular continued to demonstrate their grievances, often demanding protection from the attacks of the *Liyu* police and other paramilitary forces of the Somali region, who stood accused of having been abetted by TPLF members within the Ethiopian defence and security forces stationed in the region at that time.

ETHIOPIA'S CONTEMPORARY INTERNATIONAL AND REGIONAL RELATIONS

The EPRDF Government maintained cordial relations with successive US administrations and the governments of several European countries, despite occasional tensions following periods of domestic political unrest in Ethiopia, such as the 2005 electoral crisis. The EPRDF regime was, like its predecessors, dependent on donor assistance. Ethiopia remained one of the major beneficiaries of the European Union's (EU) partnership support programmes, and under the EU's 11th European Development Fund (2014–20) Ethiopia was allocated some €745m. Donor governments, especially those of the USA and the United Kingdom, were reluctant to criticize repression in Ethiopia openly, despite widespread allegations of state security forces involvement in serious forms of human rights violations, as reported by Amnesty International, Human Rights Watch, the EHRC and many other human rights bodies. The US Administration, in particular, viewed the TPLF-led EPRDF Government in Ethiopia before 2018 as its ally in the 'war on terror' in the Horn of Africa. Moreover, in the post-1990 period the People's Republic of China, India and Turkey (now known as Türkiye) emerged as major economic partners in the EPRDF-led Ethiopian Government's state-led development, augmented by external investment and financing from these countries and others.

At the regional level, relations between Ethiopia and Sudan reached a low level in the mid-1990s, following the Sudanese regime's complicity in the attempted assassination of President Hosni Mubarak of Egypt in Addis Ababa in June 1995. Nevertheless, bilateral relations were cordial in the following years. A series of development and security agreements between the Sudanese and Ethiopian Governments were forged prior to the signing of the Comprehensive Peace Agreement of 2005 that ended Sudan's civil war. A road connecting the two countries was upgraded to allow Ethiopia's use of Port Sudan, in eastern Sudan. Ethiopia was a major importer of petroleum from Sudan. The latter also initially extended its support for the construction of the 6,000-MW Grand Ethiopian Renaissance Dam (GERD) on the Blue Nile River, which began in 2011. In August 2014, during the 11th Ethiopian-Sudanese joint meeting of defence ministers held in Addis Ababa, the two countries agreed to establish a joint military force.

With regards to the GERD, the heads of state of Ethiopia, Egypt and Sudan signed a co-operation agreement in the Sudanese capital, Khartoum, in March 2005. As part of the agreement, four foreign consultancy firms were mandated to conduct studies on the potential environmental impact of the Dam. Ethiopian Prime Minister Hailemariam promised that the GERD would not cause harm to the downstream countries of Sudan and Egypt. Although some of the principles incorporated in the agreement were unclear, it included provisions safeguarding Egypt's and Sudanese use of the waters of the Nile. Despite this, Egyptian and Sudanese officials have continued to be suspicious about the project, raising strong concerns about the Dam's impact on its share of the waters. Relations between Egypt and Sudan on one side and Ethiopia on the other have notably worsened since the latter started to fill the Dam in July 2020. Egyptian officials have continued to protest, including following the announcement by Ethiopian state officials of the third filling of the dam, in August 2022.

In the case of South Sudan, the outcome of the referendum in that territory in January 2011, which resulted in its formal secession from Sudan later in that year, was cautiously welcomed by Ethiopia. In the post-2011 period Ethiopia maintained a pragmatic approach in its relations with both South Sudan and Sudan. Under an accord signed between Sudan and South Sudan in Addis Ababa in June 2011, Ethiopia agreed to deploy over 4,200 peacekeeping forces in the contested border region of Abyei. Ethiopian peacekeepers were already stationed in western Sudan, as part of a joint AU-UN Hybrid Operation in Darfur. Ethiopia's involvement in peace efforts continued after the eruption of conflict in South Sudan in December 2013, following an alleged coup attempt by its former Vice-President, Riek Machar Teny-Dhurgon. In May 2014 the UN Security Council approved the deployment of a regional Intergovernmental Authority on Development peacekeeping mission to South Sudan, under the command of an Ethiopian peacekeeping force. Ethiopian government officials also assisted in mediation efforts to resolve the crisis in South Sudan and supported the signing of a peace agreement between the warring factions in August 2015 and have continued to do so since then.

Tensions continue to surface between Sudanese state authorities and army officers on one side and their Ethiopian counterparts on the other. The ongoing conflict in Ethiopia, following an attack by the TPLF on the Northern Command of the Ethiopian army in Tigray in November 2020, was largely responsible for the poor relations, exacerbated by skirmishes in the Al-Fashqa 'triangle'—a contested region along the northern part of the two countries' joint border. Meanwhile, the controversy surrounding the GERD continues to add to the hostilities. Ethiopian state authorities have on occasions accused their Sudanese counterparts of serving as an intermediary in Egypt's attempts to oppose the filling of the dam. Tensions between the Governments of Sudan and Ethiopia were exacerbated in June 2022, when Sudan blamed the Ethiopian armed forces for abducting seven Sudanese soldiers and a civilian from the disputed region and executing them on Ethiopian territory, which was denied by Ethiopian state officials, and fierce clashes between the two sides ensued. During the 39th Extraordinary Summit of the Heads of States and Government of the Intergovernmental Authority on Development (IGAD—a bloc of eight East African countries) held in Nairobi, Kenya, in July, it was reported that Ethiopian Prime Minister Dr Abiy Ahmed Ali and Gen. Abdel Fattah al-Burhan Abdelrahman, the head of the Sudanese junta, had held discussions and agreed to settle their disputes, after which tensions subsided, although relations remained far from cordial.

Relations with Djibouti remained cordial after Djibouti port replaced Assab (Eritrea) as Ethiopia's main outlet to the sea in the post-1991 period, particularly following the war between Ethiopia and Eritrea during 1998–2000. However, bilateral relations have been tense on occasions, for instance after the Dubai Port Authority took over the management of Djibouti port in 2000. In February 2019 Ethiopia and Djibouti signed an agreement for the construction of a cross-border natural gas pipeline. The pipeline was to run from Djibouti port through Dire Dawa and to Awash, in central Ethiopia, from where it was supposed to distribute fuel across the country. In December Ethiopia's House of People's Representatives approved the construction of the 767-km pipeline, which was to be undertaken by Chinese company Poly-GCL, although the status of this project since remained unclear. Djibouti continues to serve as Ethiopia's sole outlet to the sea, although there have been reports of disruption to highways and the railway between the two countries, owing to sporadic clashes between the Issa and Afar ethnic groups in both Ethiopia and Djibouti since mid-2021.

Ethiopia's relations with Kenya have remained cordial, and the Ethiopian Government has explored the possibility of using Kenyan ports, such as Mombasa, as additional outlets to the sea. In March 2012 the large-scale Lamu transportation corridor project was launched as part of a move to boost cross-border trade and transportation throughout the region. Officials from both countries have been reiterating their willingness to collaborate in addressing many other issues, including climate change, terrorism, corruption and cross-border crimes. In the past, however, cross-border activities of Ethiopian rebel groups such as the OLF led to clashes between Ethiopian and Kenyan security forces, particularly in 2000. Border clashes have been a recurring phenomenon between the Ethiopian and Kenyan pastoral communities, sometimes exacerbated by the dynamics of environmental change and impact on the livelihood of the communities. Ethiopian Prime Minister Hailemariam's visit to Kenya in May 2016 attracted wide media coverage. The two countries agreed to cease hosting armed opposition groups in their respective countries, and in July 2017 they signed a military co-operation agreement, having signed several other co-operation agreements in February. The Kenyan President, Uhuru Kenyatta, and Ethiopian Prime Minister Abiy officially launched the 'One-stop Border Post' in Moyale, Marsabit County in December 2020. During the inauguration the two heads of governments noted that the project was evidence of major progress in their bilateral relations and would facilitate the movement of goods and services across the border enhance interaction between the two populations and contribute to an increase in the volume of trade between the two countries. Since the eruption of conflict in Ethiopia following the TPLF's attack on the Northern Command of the Ethiopian army in November 2020, Kenya has played an important role in mediating between the parties, while Ethiopian state officials have emphasized the importance of an AU-led peace process. The attempts by outside bodies to try to bring an end to the conflict was the source of controversy after the two sides signed a ceasefire in early 2022, which was subsequently broken in late August, when the TPLF reportedly launched an offensive towards southern Tigray.

With regards to Somalia, the defeat of the Islamic Courts Union (ICU) militias with the help of Ethiopian forces in December 2006 brought a semblance of peace. The training of some Ethiopian troops by US forces was viewed as tacit acknowledgement of US support for Ethiopian intervention in Somalia at that time. In June 2008 an agreement was signed in Djibouti between the Somali Transitional Federal Government and the Alliance for the Re-liberation of Somalia (a coalition of former members of the ICU established in Asmara, the Eritrean capital) encouraging the withdrawal of Ethiopian troops from Somalia within three months of the signing of the agreement. In July 2013 the Ethiopian Government announced that it had begun to pull troops out of the Somali town of Baidoa, citing the return of relative stability to the former rebel stronghold. Subsequently, it was reported that suicide bombers originating from Somalia were planning to target a football match in Addis Ababa, which was perceived to be a revenge attack for the continuing presence of Ethiopian troops in Somalia. In February 2014 the approximately 4,400 Ethiopian troops who remained in Somalia officially joined the AU Mission in Somalia. In June the same year the Ethiopian security forces detained 25 people who were allegedly associated with the al-Shabaab militant Islamist group (formerly the armed wing of the ICU), accusing them of plotting attacks in Ethiopia. Following the 2018 political changes in Ethiopia (see below), the Ethiopian state authorities continued to engage in cordial relations with the new Federal Government in Somalia that was formed in February 2017. Prime Minister Abiy moved quickly to maintain cordial relations by attending in May 2022 the inauguration ceremony in Mogadishu, the Somali capital, together with other heads of governments of countries in the region, of Hassan Sheikh Mohamud, when he replaced Mohamed Abdullahi Mohamed 'Farmajo', as Somali President following his election to the post earlier in that month.

Despite close links between Prime Minister Meles and Eritrean President Issaias Afewerki of Eritrea in the immediate post-*Derg* period in Ethiopia, a border dispute between the two countries escalated into a full-scale war in May 1998. The conflict was disastrous for both countries, and an estimated 70,000–80,000 people were killed during the war until a cessation of hostilities was agreed in June 2000 in Algeria. In September the UN Security Council approved the deployment of a 4,200-member UN Mission (UNMEE) on both sides of the borders to police a Temporary Security Zone. The Eritrea-Ethiopia Boundary Commission was established in May 2001 and issued decisions on the delineation of the border in April 2002. Based on a boundary line that had been defined in 1908, in March 2003 the Boundary Commission ruled the Ethiopian-held town of Badme to be Eritrean territory. While Eritrea accepted the ruling, the Ethiopian Government rejected a significant part of the Commission's decision, which it described as 'illegal', while insisting on Ethiopia's commitment to the framework of the peace agreement. In December 2005 a Claims Commission ruled that Eritrea was 'liable to compensate Ethiopia' for an attack in May 1998 and that Ethiopia also compensate Eritrea for causing the loss of property during the conflict. Tensions along the disputed border escalated in 2005. In October Meles announced that Ethiopia was willing to accept the Boundary Commission's ruling 'in principle' and urged Eritrea to engage in dialogue about the peace process. Eritrea was accused of imposing restrictions upon UNMEE activities and by mid-2006 UNMEE personnel remained only on the Ethiopian side of the border. In May 2006 the UN Security Council reduced the size of UNMEE's peacekeeping force to 2,300, citing the impasse in the demarcation of the borders. In January 2007 the UN Security Council further reduced the number of UNMEE personnel to 1,700. While Ethiopia in effect refused to recognize the new demarcation of the border, Eritrea vowed to implement it unilaterally and pressurized UNMEE peacekeepers to leave the country by blocking fuel supplies (although the Eritrean Government officially denied having taken this action). Eritrea announced in January 2010 that an Ethiopian raid had been repelled in the Zalambessa border region and that about 10 Ethiopian troops had been killed—a claim that was denied by the Ethiopian Government. In March 2011 Ethiopia warned that it would take all measures necessary against Eritrea, accusing it of planning attacks targeting an AU summit meeting in Addis Ababa. Furthermore, the Ethiopian Government openly declared its support for Eritrean opposition groups working for regime change in Eritrea. Ethiopia also maintained that the al-Shabaab militant group in Somalia continued to receive weapons and assistance from Eritrea. In December of that year the UN Security Council imposed additional sanctions on Eritrea for supporting armed groups in Somalia. Subsequent accusations (particularly Kenya) that Eritrea was continuing to arm al-Shabaab militants were judged to be untrue by the UN monitoring group on Somalia and Eritrea. Ethiopia offered peace talks in an attempt to alleviate tensions in the wake of an incursion into Eritrean territory in March 2012, when Ethiopian troops reportedly killed at least 50 alleged members of the Afar Revolutionary Democratic Unity Front. However, Eritrea rejected Ethiopia's proposal. Subsequent US diplomatic attempts to bring the two sides to the negotiating table ended without success. In December 2014 reports indicated three members of the Ethiopian air force defected to Eritrea in a military helicopter. It was widely reported in March 2015 that the Ethiopian air force had launched attacks on the Bisha gold mine in Eritrea, some 150 km west of Asmara, and on the Eritrean military depot at Mai Edaga, reportedly causing minor damage. In February President Ismaïl Omar Guelleh of Djibouti and Ethiopian Prime Minister Hailemariam held a joint press conference

during which they accused Eritrea of undermining regional stability. In June 2016 there were reports of skirmishes between Ethiopian and Eritrean government forces along the border, resulting in casualties on both sides. Ethiopian state authorities at that time claimed Eritrean provocation as part of its destabilization efforts, while Eritrea accused the Ethiopian authorities of aiming to stage an invasion with the aim of achieving regime change in Asmara. According to the UN High Commissioner for Refugees, about 155,000 Eritrean refugees were sheltering in Ethiopia in 2016. In 2017 Ethiopian state authorities blamed the Eritrean regime for serving as a base for various rebel movements from Ethiopia, including the OLF and the ONLF, which it accused of working to destabilize the country.

THE DEMISE OF HAILEMARIAM AND DEVELOPMENTS UNDER THE ABIY PREMIERSHIP

The domestic protests that continued for about three years until early 2018 affected the country politically, economically and socially. The former EPRDF regime's repressive measures led to the death of hundreds and the detention of tens of thousands; many suffered beating and torture, and thousands of young people were forced to migrate. State repression was met with fierce resistance from the population, including during the state of emergency in force between October 2016 and August 2017. The inability on the part of the TPLF-EPRDF regime to address the longstanding grievances of the population brought it to a standstill towards the end of 2017. Mass displacements of the population in the Somali regions in late 2017, together with spontaneous uprisings in different parts of the country, were indicative of growing uncertainties about the ability of the regime to maintain law and order, undermining the legitimacy of its actions and practices against protesters. The protests ultimately forced the resignation of Hailemariam in February 2018. In his speech, he indicated that the purpose of his resignation was to pave the way for a tangible response to public demands for change. After what appeared to be a power struggle within the EPRDF, Abiy, from the OPDO wing of the regime, emerged as Prime Minister on 2 April. He set about expressing his intentions for political reform and managing a transition to democratic rule. His political rhetoric abandoned much of the EPRDF's language of antagonism. One of the first changes in the rhetoric was the use of the word *tefokakari* ('competitors') in characterizing political organizations outside state power, which were regarded as 'opposition', connoting adversarial relations. He persistently used the word *medemer*, interpreted as 'synergy' or 'unity' in galvanizing support.

In late 2017 tens of thousands of detainees, including high-profile political prisoners, were released from federal as well as regional detention centres, followed by scenes of jubilation among their supporters. Prominent figures such as Merea Gudina were released towards the end of 2017. The subsequent release of opposition politicians and activists, including Eskinder Nega, Andualem Arage, Bekele Gerba and Dejene Tafa, as well as Andargachew of Ginbot 7 and Muslim community leaders, attracted large crowds in Addis Ababa and other towns across the country.

Judges were appointed to the Federal Supreme Court in 2018, and some of the former police; intelligence and security officials who had been accused of human rights violations and involvement in corruption were arraigned. Major reshuffles of some of the key positions in the armed forces were undertaken. A former CUD official, Birtukan Mideksa, was persuaded to return from the USA and was appointed head of the newly reconstituted National Electoral Board of Ethiopia (NEBE). Some individuals who were not directly affiliated with the former EPRDF were appointed to various ministerial positions. Women comprised about one-half of the newly appointed state officials. Development projects in Addis Ababa, campaigns to plant billions of trees and other similar projects created an optimistic mood about the reform initiative. Media groups that were operating from abroad returned, following the promised observance of press freedom. Ethiopian emigrant communities' social media networks, which were previously blocked, have been allowed to operate, and some have opened offices in Addis Ababa. The use of social media for political and other forms of activism has proliferated in a relatively short period of time.

However, from late 2017 the eviction of hundreds of thousands of people from different regions in Ethiopia, which started with the eviction of members of the Oromo community from the Somali region by the regional government, following intercommununal violence, and similar patterns of displacements, accompanied by the looting and burning of properties in North Gondar, the southern Gedeo area and the Benishangul-Gumuz, Wellega and Southern regions undermined the reform process. While the intervention of state security forces helped to stop the evictions and atrocities, state authorities have often been accused of failing to prevent similar attacks or for being late in their response. At times state security forces have also been criticized by human rights organizations for the disproportionate use of force. Politically motivated abductions and killings of students in public universities in some regions and other similar incidents around the country led to frequent demands from the public that the Government uphold its pledges and commitment to the rule of law. The murder of Hachalu Hundessa, a renowned singer and activist, in Addis Ababa in June 2020 precipitated violent anti-Government demonstrations and unrest across the Oromia region and in Addis Ababa. Hundreds of people were killed and property looted and destroyed during the widespread rioting, particularly in the Arsi and Bale zones of the Oromia region, and in and around Addis Ababa. Prominent activists and politicians including Bekele, Nega and Jawar Mohammed were detained following the assassination of Hachalu, and thousands of people were arrested in the Oromia region in connection with the unrest. Protests were held by members of the Oromo communities both inside and outside the country against the detentions and the killing of protesters by the state security forces, which drew some criticism from international and local human rights organizations.

As far as Ethiopia's relations in the Horn of Africa region are concerned since the EPRDF relinquished power in 2018, the most dramatic event was the rapprochement with Eritrea. This followed Prime Minister Abiy's inaugural speech in April 2018, when he indicated his intention for a policy shift towards the normalization of relations with Eritrea and called on its Government to make efforts to this end. President Issaias Afewerki responded favourably, declaring his readiness to send government delegations to Ethiopia for bilateral discussions. A high-level Eritrean delegation arrived and was warmly received in Addis Ababa in June. This was followed by a visit by Abiy to Eritrea on 9 July, where he was received by large crowds in Asmara and signed the Joint Declaration on Peace and Friendship with Afewerki, which restored official bilateral relations that had been severed for about two decades. Afewerki made a reciprocal visit to Ethiopia on 14 July. Direct flights between Addis Ababa and Asmara resumed in the following weeks, after the closure of the border and air spaces since the late 1990s. These rapid and unexpected developments allowed several Eritrean families who had been living in Ethiopia to travel to Eritrea, while some Ethiopians civilians who had been confined to Eritrea returned home. Abiy and Afewerki met again officially in Asmara to mark the Ethiopian New Year in September 2018, visiting the Eritrean ports of Assab and Massawa and officially reopening two principal border crossings between the two countries; many citizens, including members of the Ethiopian and Eritrean armed forces, celebrated together at the border, heralding a new chapter in bilateral relations between the two after some 20 years of impasse. Further meetings between Abiy and Afewerki in Addis Ababa and Asmara since late 2018 have been regarded as particularly significant in the continuation of the cordial relations that were re-established in the middle of that year. The trajectory of the relations between the two looked unclear for much of the second half of 2021. As at September 2022 it appeared that the two Governments were co-ordinating their response to the TPLF's renewed assault, in August, on Tigray province. For its part, the TPLF claimed that Eritrean and Ethiopian forces were attacking its positions from Eritrean territory bordering Tigray, from the north-west.

In the wider regional context, controversies surrounding the GERD (see *Ethiopia's Contemporary International and Regional Relations*) have continued to strain Ethiopia's relations with Egypt and Sudan. The Ethiopian Government appeared to have initially accepted the proposal for negotiations over the GERD to be led by the US Administration under President Donald Trump. The US Secretary of State, Mike Pompeo, had visited Sudan in August 2020 to discuss the GERD, followed which reports suggested that the Trump Administration intended to suspend some financial aid to Ethiopia, for proceeding with the first filling of the GERD, in July, without first reaching an agreement with Egypt and Sudan. By late 2021 Ethiopian state officials and negotiators appeared to have succeeded in pushing for preference of any mediation to take place under the aegis of AU officials. Initially South African President Cyril Ramaphosa led the negotiations process between the three countries from mid-2020, as the rotating Chairman of the AU, although the talks failed to produce an agreement (Egypt withdrew from the talks in August). President Félix Tsikeshedi of the Democratic Republic of the Congo assumed the chairmanship of the AU in early 2021 and proposed a new initiative to resolve the GERD dispute in May, but it was not accepted by all parties. Tensions in the relations between Ethiopia on one side and Egypt and Sudan on the other have continued since that time, notably following the second filling of the Dam in June–July and again, after the third and final filling, in August 2022. The new US Administration led by President Joe Biden appears to have eased direct pressure on Ethiopia as far as the GERD dispute is concerned and has supported AU-led negotiations, in line with Ethiopian demands, which have been notably supported by China and the Russian Federation.

The period since the dramatic political developments of 2018 has contained challenges and uncertainties. While the current Government has been attempting to introduce reform, on occasions it has been accused of a lack of determination to transform the politics of the country. Nevertheless, in 2019 what has since been named the Prosperity Party (PP), led by Abiy, was formed following the merger of three of the former member organizations of the EPRDF. Notably, the TPLF, which had constituted the core of the EPRDF since early 1991, left the bloc, opposing much of the reform agenda set by Abiy. Many former TPLF officials retreated to Mekelle, the capital of the Tigray region, and continued vehemently to oppose almost all aspects of the reform initiatives led by Abiy and eventually attacked the Northern Command of the Ethiopian armed forces in October 2020.

Following the TPLF assault on the army, Abiy ordered the remaining sections of the armed forces to respond militarily, and conflict began in early November 2020. The TPLF refused to take responsibility for the assault, although its officials occasionally mentioned that they had carried out what they called a 'pre-emptive attack'. The conflict started after the TPLF held an election in Tigray in September that had not been approved by the NEBE, which had postponed all elections (these had been due in August) in March, owing to the COVID-19 pandemic. Prior to the conflict, the TPLF had defied the Government by declining calls to participate in a dialogue with various actors, including Ethiopia's Ministry of Peace.

As the fighting intensified in mid-November 2020 TPLF forces fired rockets towards Gondar and other locations in Amhara in northern Ethiopia, as well as towards Asmara. During the first few days of the fighting, TPLF militia were accused of massacring hundreds of people in the town of Humera, close to the Ethiopian border with Sudan. Thousands of refugees fled across the border to Sudan, complicating the relations between Ethiopia and Sudan, which were already in dispute over the GERD, in addition to the long-running border dispute between the two.

On 28 November 2020 Ethiopian armed forces advanced on Mekelle and brought it under their control. The conflict also witnessed the involvement of Eritrean forces, which faced accusations of human rights violations by the authorities in Tigray, which were denied by the Eritrean Government. Accusations of human rights violations have also been levelled against members of the Ethiopian defence forces and allied militias and were investigated by the EHRC and the Office of the Prosecutor. Following the expulsion of the TPLF from Mekelle and its seizure by the national armed forces, the

Ethiopian Government appointed an interim administration in Tigray. Ethiopian state authorities reported the restoration of services such as electricity, banking and health care services in the following two months of the conflict and provided humanitarian support to hundreds of thousands of people in Tigray. However, in a bid to exert pressure on Ethiopian state authorities, global media outlets generally reported the situation in Tigray in a manner that damaged the reputation of the Ethiopian Government and the image of the country in general. In March 2021 the US Secretary of State Antony Blinken urged Eritrea to withdraw from the region and demanded that Amhara regional militias that allied with the Ethiopian armed forces during the early days of the conflict evacuate certain parts of Tigray. The Ethiopian state authorities, while promising that Eritrean forces would withdraw from Tigray, vehemently opposed US and EU diplomats' calls for 'unfettered humanitarian access' in Tigray and criticized their 'interference in the domestic affairs of the country'. In May the US Department of State announced the imposition of economic and security sanctions on Ethiopia, as well as visa restrictions on a number of (unnamed) senior Ethiopian and Eritrean government officials. The visa restrictions apply to members of the Amhara regional armed forces and the TPLF, who were believed to have been 'responsible for, or complicit in, undermining resolution of the crisis in Tigray'.

In June 2021 the Ethiopian Government announced a unilateral ceasefire, which was not recognized by the TPLF. A few days later, the TPLF returned to Mekelle and claimed victory against the Ethiopian and Eritrean forces that were already withdrawing from Tigray, including from Mekelle, and seized back control of the city and eventually the whole region. Subsequently TPLF forces carried out widespread incursions into the Gondar, Wollo and Afar regions, outside Tigray. TPLF operatives and fighters claimed that their aim was to attack and take control of the highway linking Ethiopia with Djibouti through Afar. The TPLF raided several sites and towns in northern Amhara and western Afar, prompting several hundreds of thousands of people to flee, adding to the already dire humanitarian situation in northern Ethiopia. Accounts of TPLF atrocities and human suffering in Gonder, Wolo and Afar proliferated. TPLF forces made considerable inroads into central Ethiopia and reached the Northern Shoa district of the Amhara region in September–October 2021. This prompted international media outlets, including Al Jazeera, to report mistakenly that rebel forces had 'reached near the capital', Addis Ababa. Ethiopian government forces subsequently staged an offensive, making major gains and pushing TPLF troops back to Tigray by the end of the year. The Ethiopian Government declared a ceasefire in March 2022, which was heeded by the TPLF and observed until a resumption of a major armed confrontation in southern Tigray in August.

A rebel group known as Oromo Liberation Army, often referred to as *Shene* ('Five') by the Ethiopian Government and its allies, has continued to wreak havoc in across Oromia state. Members of the national defence forces and regional paramilitary forces have continued to fight back amid allegations by the Government of massacres and other atrocities directed against the civilian population by armed rebel Oromo groups. Meanwhile, it was reported that al-Shabaab, a jihadi group based in Somalia, made a major incursion into Ethiopian territory in July 2022 (the latest of several such assaults by the group over the past two decades). By early August the forces of the Somali region of Ethiopia and the national armed forces had reportedly repulsed the al-Shabaab rebels who threatened further to destabilize the region.

The postponement of the 2020 elections announced in March of that year served as a point of contention that created animosity between the Government in Addis Ababa and the TPLF. In June 2019 the NEBE was reconstituted as part of the political reform initiative of the Abiy administration. It was given the mandate to organize and conduct elections both at the federal and state level, to register and regulate political parties, to conduct civic and voter education on elections and to register and deploy election observers, among other things. NEBE's management board comprises a chairperson, deputy chairperson and three members appointed by the House of Peoples Representatives, upon recommendation by the Prime Minister, in consultation with opposition political organizations. Ethiopia has a first-past-the post electoral system, despite occasional calls for a system based on proportional representation. General elections are held every five years to elect members of the federal House of People's Representatives and the regional State Councils. A political organization or coalition that wins a simple majority forms the Government in both cases. There are 547 seats in the House of People's Representatives. A total of 51 political organizations registered to contest the general elections, which were rescheduled to be held in June. However, a controversial new electoral rule has been introduced which requires that a political organization contesting seats in the legislature must have at least 10,000 registered members, of whom 40% are required to be permanent residents of a specific region, and the remaining 60% in total must reside in at least four Regional States of the country. Political organizations that field candidates for regional State Councils need at least 4,000 registered members, of whom at least 60% are required to be permanent residents of those States. Political organizations can generate financial resources from government, private financial support, membership fees and fundraising activities. It has been reported that the NEBE cancelled the licences of 58 political organizations that were unable to fulfil the aforementioned and other related requirements, as stipulated by the electoral law. The electoral code requires candidates and political organizations, employees, their members and supporters to conduct campaigns peacefully, respect the rights of competing candidates and political parties, co-operate with election officials and observers recognize and accept elections as expressions of the free will of the electorate. The NEBE extended the deadline for registration of voters in the legislative elections, in an effort to increase participation. However, some opposition political organizations alleged that the Government was forcing certain people to register. The NEBE accused 'low-level government officials' in some parts of the country of intervening at polling stations, and registration was cancelled in certain constituencies as a result. Some political organizations, such as the Oromo National Congress, pledged to boycott the 2021 elections, citing the intimidation and detention of their members and supporters.

The COVID-19 pandemic, a sense of insecurity, political constraints and the conflict in Tigray cast a shadow during the electoral campaign period. The majority of the political organizations that took part in the June 2021 elections did not campaign actively. The Ethiopian Citizens for Social Justice party (ECSJ) complained that its campaign was obstructed in a number of locations, and the National Movement of the Amhara reported attacks on its personnel by alleged supporters of the Government. The recently formed Enat party, the ONLF and other organizations accused PP officials of interfering in voter registration, intimidation and, in some cases, the detention of their members.

The elections, which were subject to a further postponement from their original date of 5 June 2021, owing to logistical and security-related problems, finally took place on 21 June. Polls were not held in the Harari and Somali Regional States. Issues of voter eligibility had arisen in Harari, prompting court proceedings brought against the NEBE, forcing it to postpone the elections. Related problems and delays in registration in constituencies halted the process in the Somali region. In Afar and Benishangul-Gumuz people voted in only a limited number of constituencies, owing to errors in ballot printing—a problem that also beset the voting process in Sidama and Gambela regions, among others. Therefore, voting did not take place in about 100 of the 547 constituencies, although polls were expected to take place by the end of September. A referendum on a proposed South West Regional State (comprising Kaffa, Sheka, Bench Sheko, Dawro and West Omo and Konta) was conducted and a new regional state was officially proclaimed on 23 November 2021. From mid-2022 there have been reports indicating the proposal of further new regional states, which might in effect bring about the end of the existence of the SNNPR.

The PP, led by Prime Minister Abiy, took the overwhelming majority of the votes, after the results were announced on 10 July 2021, although voting was delayed in the Regional

States of Harari and Somali and in parts of Benishangul-Gumuz. From the perspective of the post-2018 Government, the elections are a milestone in the context of its political reform initiatives, despite the challenges and uncertainties regarding political instability, conflict-induced insecurity within the population and the fragmentation and polarization of political organizations. A new Government was formed in September 2021, including several cabinet members from the few opposition groups that took part in the elections.

The reconstituted NEBE has been enhancing its image as an independent and impartial institution. In its handling of the electoral process in June 2021, the NEBE received and investigated hundreds of complaints relating to activities before, during and after the polls. It served as the outlet for pronouncements about the various aspects of the process and sponsored a large number of groups and organizations in conducting voter education, election observation and a host of related activities. It has also testified in court cases brought by political organizations regarding the conduct of the polls and held a series of press briefings before, during and after the elections. The NEBE and the Government consider this to be positive progress and an expression of the reform process. However, the NEBE has also been bogged down by myriad logistical problems, causing delays whereby elections have been postponed in certain parts of Ethiopia, prompting several hundreds of complaints to be made, notably by the ECSJ and other organizations.

The EU has often been at the centre of the electoral process in Ethiopia, providing financial assistance and fielding election observation missions, although it declined to observe the elections of June 2021, owing to disagreements with the Ethiopian Government over certain aspects of its conduct. Despite the fears of many domestic and international election observers, post-electoral violence did not occur in the aftermath of the June 2021 elections. Under the EU's 12th European Development Fund (2021–27) Ethiopia was allocated some €1,000m. However, the European Commission stated that it would not resume direct funding to the Government in Addis Ababa, having cut off budget support in December 2020, after condemning the conflict in the Tigray region. The resumption of direct funding to the administration of Prime Minister Abiy was conditional on the cessation of hostilities, improved access to the country by humanitarian organizations and accountability for human rights violations.

Finally, the COVID-19 pandemic, which spread to Ethiopia in March 2020, has had a negative impact on economic, social and political dynamics in the country. Coronavirus-related measures, such as the closure of schools, reductions in the workforce at public institutions and new regulations were introduced, while the authorities undertook an information campaign to create awareness among the public. Various economic sectors, such as the hospitality and tourism industries, have been severely affected by the impact of the pandemic. Meanwhile, daily reports from the Ethiopian Ministry of Health indicated a sharp increase in the rate of infections from mid-2020. According to the World Health Organization, the total number of infections in Ethiopia from COVID-19 stood at 493,278 as at 10 September 2022, including 7,572 deaths. By that time only about 31.9% of the population had been fully vaccinated against the virus, although the number of new infections had fallen to a negligible level, and all restrictions on movement and social and economic activity had been lifted.

By September 2022 the hostilities between the TPLF and government forces were concentrated in Afar, Wolo, Gonder and Tigray. Meanwhile skirmishes across the Ethiopian–Sudanese border were reported amid tensions between the Ethiopian and Sudanese authorities as TPLF forces based in the border area had reportedly opened a new front after the conflict resumed following the ceasefire. Complex political, security and economic challenges, rising inflation, conflict-induced displacement of the civilian population and uncertainties in external relations continued to pose enormous challenges to the Ethiopian Government.

Economy

ROBERT E. LOONEY

INTRODUCTION

Ethiopia has the fourth largest economy in sub-Saharan Africa at market exchange rates after Nigeria, South Africa and Kenya. With a population estimated at 120.8m. at mid-2021, it is the second most populous country in the region, after Nigeria (219.5m.) and ahead of the Democratic Republic of the Congo (105.0m.), giving investors and producers the advantage of a large, dynamic domestic market. With its large population and low levels of income, Ethiopia is one of the few African countries that can compete with Asian economies as a potential production hub. It is also a country of great potential for hydroelectricity, mining (phosphate, hydrocarbons) and tourism. Ethiopia's power and transport infrastructures have improved significantly in recent years.

However, the Ethiopian economy faces several impediments. The agricultural sector, which employed 66% of the country's labour force in 2019, but accounted for just 32% of gross domestic product (GDP), is not very productive. Agriculture is also vulnerable to increasingly adverse weather, infestations of locusts and changes in world commodity prices. The country's manufacturing sector is underdeveloped, with value added accounting for just over 5% of GDP in 2021. Ethiopia is landlocked, with 95% of the country's exports passing through neighbouring Djibouti. Businesses face many challenges stemming from institutional weaknesses and limited governance. The banking system is underdeveloped, and the country's power supply is insufficient. The regional environment is unstable, and high ethno-political tensions risk all-out civil war.

Since 1980 (the date after which most Ethiopian macroeconomic data became available), the Ethiopian economy has registered accelerating growth, with GDP increasing at an average annual rate of 2.5% during the 1980s, 2.8% in the 1990s, 8.6% in the 2000s and 9.0% in 2010–21. By splitting economic growth between 1980 and 2020 into two segments, contrasting patterns become apparent: from 1980–2003 there was a period of low, relatively stagnant growth when the economy expanded by an average of 2.7% per annum, followed by a period of robust and dynamic growth from 2004–21 when average annual growth soared to 9.9%. The share of the urban population among the general population expanded from 6.4% in 1960 to 10.4% by 1980. By 2000 the urban population accounted for 14.7% of the total, reaching 21.7% by 2020. During the 2000s the urban population grew at an average annual rate of 4.3%, before increasing to 5.0% from 2010–20.

Over the past 17 years GDP per capita has grown substantially in Ethiopia, increasing from US $138.3 in 2004 to $995.7 in 2021. In purchasing power parity terms (in 2017 international dollars) per capita income decreased from $863 in 1980 to $737 in 2003. However, by 2021 per capita income had increased to $2,855.

Whether or not the Ethiopian economy took off after 2003 is a matter of considerable debate. According to US economist and political theorist Walt Whitman Rostow, once countries have achieved growth rates in the range of Ethiopia's post-2003 economic expansion over a period of 15–20 years, a new stage—the drive to maturity—sets in with new leading sectors propelling per capita incomes to the levels enjoyed by the advanced industrial countries. Once they do take off, such nations are unlikely to fall back to a lower income level.

472

In Ethiopia's case, there are growing concerns that it may be an exception, a failed take-off stemming from factors that Rostow did not anticipate. Ethiopia's political system is currently in turmoil, and the longstanding developmental state model introduced in the late 1990s by Prime Minister Meles Zenawi (in office from 1995–2012) shows diminishing effectiveness. That state-centred model hindered the much needed private sector investment and growth. Prime Minister Dr Abiy Ahmed Ali, who came to power in 2018, intends to take the economy in a different direction through the privatization of state enterprises and the development of a more open and democratic regime. However, this transition is far from complete, and a number of problems threaten to dampen economic growth. In particular, tensions among Ethiopia's various ethnic groups remain a crucial source of instability. Since Prime Minister Abiy took office, a degree of political liberalization has increased inter-communal violence over disputed land and has emboldened local governments' demands for greater autonomy, thereby weakening the federal state. Fighting between the Government and the Tigray People's Liberation Front (TPLF) resulted in widespread violence in late 2020 and 2021, which has hardened ethnic divisions and damaged relations with Western donors. The humanitarian crisis in Tigray has slowed progress on debt negotiations with bilateral lenders. As a consequence of the ongoing crisis the USA removed Ethiopia from the African Growth and Opportunity Act (AGOA) trade preference programme in January 2022, which is likely to have a detrimental effect on Ethiopian exports to the USA. However, in late June Prime Minister Abiy appeared to be willing to begin negotiations to end the conflict in Tigray.

Much will also depend on the way in which the COVID-19 pandemic evolves. The pandemic reached Ethiopia in March 2020, and by July there were 5,846 confirmed cases of COVID-19. Subsequently, there was a sharp increase in infections, reaching 53,304 confirmed cases by September. After levelling off slightly, the number of infections rose rapidly from March 2021, by which time there were 159,971 confirmed cases, before climbing to 258,062 cases by May. However, several more waves of COVID-19 hit the country, with the total number of confirmed cases reaching 424,340 by 1 January 2022. As of 11 June the number of confirmed cases had levelled off somewhat to a total of 478,544.

ETHIOPIA'S DEVELOPMENT MODELS

Following independence in 1974, Ethiopia was governed by a military-socialist regime, the Provisional Military Administrative Council, known as the *Derg* (Committee), until 1991. The *Derg*'s economic policies reflected the regime's incompetence and were ruinous. The *Derg* nationalized nearly all of the country's private sector firms. It also nationalized all of its land, with peasants forced to work on collective farms, where many starved. Between 1983 and 1985 over 500,000 Ethiopians died owing to drought, crop failure and brutal civil war. Under the *Derg*, from 1980 until the fall of the regime in 1991, per capita GDP contracted at an average annual rate of 1.8%. In stark contrast, during the Zenawi period (1995–2012) and the post-Zenawi period (2013–20) per capita income grew by 5.1% and 6.8%, respectively.

The rapid shift in the country's economic fortunes was utterly unanticipated. To many observers, the Ethiopian experience warrants comparison with the East Asian Economic Miracle achieved by the four 'tigers' (the economies of Singapore, Hong Kong, Taiwan and the Republic of Korea—South Korea). Driven by exports and rapid industrialization for several decades from the 1960s onwards, the 'tigers' have joined the ranks of the wealthiest countries in the world. Under Zenawi, and his political party, the Ethiopian People's Revolutionary Democratic Front (EPRDF), Ethiopia's political and economic system followed the Asian developmental state model, which in the Ethiopian context became a version of what might be termed 'authoritarian developmentalism'. While Zenawi attempted to create permanent encompassing institutions capable of eventually supporting democracy in Ethiopia, he believed, as did Lee Kuan Yew, Prime Minister of Singapore from 1959–1990, that causation was from growth to

democracy rather than the reverse. He concluded that in the Ethiopian setting, a period of state-directed economic growth and the establishment of state-directed political institutions would be necessary preliminaries to an eventual transition to a 'developmental democracy'.

Until recently, Ethiopia's authoritarian developmentalism appeared to have paid off. The country's poverty rate fell from 45.5% in 1995 to 24.5% in 2021. While much of the decline in poverty stemmed from the rapid expansion of the economy, the Government's direct focus on poverty alleviation was also a significant factor.

Ethiopia owes much of its recent economic progress to the ERPDF's decision under Zenawi's leadership to undertake selective governance and economic reforms as a means of increasing the effectiveness of government programmes to achieve higher rates of economic growth. According to the World Bank, government effectiveness during Zenawi's time in office improved sharply, rising from the seventh percentile in 1996 to the 41st percentile in 2012. Regulatory quality improved from the 10th percentile in 1996 to the 15th percentile in 2012. The rule of law also improved, increasing from the 19th percentile in 1996 to the 31st percentile in 2012. Finally, corruption improved from the 19th percentile in 1996 to the 32nd percentile in 2012.

In the post-Zenawi era, there were improvements in regulatory quality (rising from the 13th percentile in 2012 to the 14th percentile in 2020), the rule of law (up from the 32nd percentile in 2012 to the 38th percentile in 2020) and control of corruption (improving from the 32nd percentile to the 41st percentile in 2020). However, these gains are small compared to those recorded during Zenawi's time in office. Perhaps more than offsetting these gains, government effectiveness declined from the 41st percentile in 2012 to the 31st percentile in 2020.

According to the Heritage Foundation's Index of Economic Freedom, in 1995 Ethiopia's economic freedom score of 42.6 placed the country in the 'repressed' economic grouping. By 2004 the country had shown significant improvement, moving into the 'mostly unfree' grouping until Zenawi's death in 2012. Much of this improvement stemmed from greater business freedom, which began in 2006. Subsequently, the Heritage Foundation upgraded the country from the 'moderately unfree' grouping to the 'moderately free' grouping in 2009.

However, by 2022 overall freedom had fallen into the 'repressed' grouping. Business freedom declined rapidly from the top of the 'moderately free' grouping in 2011 to close to the bottom of the 'repressed' grouping in 2018. By 2022 Ethiopia was the 150th freest country in the Heritage Foundation's Index, ranking 35th among 47 sub-Saharan African countries. Trade freedom improved significantly under Zenawi, when the country advanced from the 'repressed' grouping in 1995 to the 'moderately free' grouping by 2007. It has stayed in this range subsequently. Despite the gains in governance and economic freedom made during the Zenawi era, there has been only a slight improvement since then, but growth has accelerated markedly in the post-Zenawi era.

The extent and timing of the governance and economic reforms and their associated patterns of growth or decline suggest that there have been three phases in Ethiopia's development since 1980: the *Derg* and transition (1980–94); the Zenawi era (1995–2012) and the post-Zenawi era (2013–21). Per capita income declined at an average rate of 1.8% per year under the *Derg*, increased at an average annual rate of 5.1% during the Zenawi era, and accelerated to an average annual rate of 6.8% in the post-Zenawi era.

As noted earlier, economic gains in the post-Zenawi era did not stem from improved governance or economic freedom. Instead, increased levels of investment appear to have been the driving force. Investment as a share of GDP increased from 15.8% under the *Derg* to 21.8% under Zenawi and to 35.9% in the post-Zenawi era. However, the financing of this investment, namely domestic savings as a share of GDP, expanded at a slower rate: by 6.8% in the latter *Derg* years, by 18.3% under Zenawi, and by 35.1% in the post-Zenawi era. Subsequently, savings have dwindled somewhat accounting for 6.6%, 17.5% and 29.5% of GDP in the each of the respective three periods. In turn, the financing gaps underlie the growing current account deficits (see *External Trade*) of 1.9%, 3.8% and 7.1% in the three periods, respectively.

SOCIOECONOMIC DEVELOPMENT

Unfortunately, Ethiopia's exceptional growth since 2002 has not resulted in broader-based, improved standards of living for the country's inhabitants. According to the United Nations (UN) Development Programme's Human Development Index (HDI) for 2020, Ethiopia ranked 173rd out of 185 countries, placing the country in the low human development category. The country's HDI score has fluctuated; it rose by 3.7% during 2000–10, before declining by 1.6% from 2010–19.

The Legatum Prosperity Index 2021 presents a similar picture. The Index provides an annual assessment of the 12 'pillars' of economic and social well-being. In 2021 Ethiopia ranked 145th out of 167 countries, just below Sierra Leone but higher than Eritrea, which was ranked 162nd. Ethiopia's ranking on the various components of prosperity was uniformly low. The country ranked 151st for education, followed by living conditions (149th), investment environment (148th), infrastructure and market access (148th), safety and security (144th), health (128th), personal freedom (126th), governance (117th), economic quality (108th), natural environment (113th) and social capital (80th).

With a Gini coefficient of 35 (2010–18), the country's income distribution does not appear to be overly concentrated in a few hands. However, the wealthiest 1% of the population have a 14.3% share of the total income, whereas the lowest 40% have 19.4% and the highest 10% have 28.5%.

AGRICULTURE

Agriculture is a crucial industry in Ethiopia, and the expansion of the sector is key to poverty reduction, employment, improved health of the population and increased volumes of exports. Agricultural growth has always been an essential driver of poverty reduction in Ethiopia. According to the World Bank, each percentage increase in agricultural growth reduces poverty by 0.9% compared with a 0.55% reduction for each per cent of overall GDP growth.

Ethiopia's agricultural sector has several advantages. Given the country's large geographic area, varied terrain and different types of climate, many crops can be cultivated simultaneously. The rural population is continuing to expand, and labour shortages are unlikely to constrain production. Rising incomes stemming from the country's rapid GDP growth in recent years have led to strong demand and, for some farmers, increased profits.

Threatening to offset these advantages are several factors that limit output and productivity. First, most of the country's crops are rain-fed. However, the agricultural sector is negatively affected by climatic conditions exacerbated by the La Niña and El Niño weather phenomena. Droughts and flooding pose an increasing threat to the production and distribution of farm products. Drought is a recurring phenomenon in the country, notably occurring in 2011, 2015, 2016, 2017 and 2022. The 2015 drought was particularly severe and affected over 10.2m. people, mainly those living in the eastern part of the country. The 2022 drought may prove to be equally disastrous.

Second, the agricultural sector is largely fragmented, and most producers are subsistence farmers living in the Ethiopian highlands at elevations of between 1,500 m and 3,000 m. In addition to water shortages, many of these farms are affected by increasing infestations of disease-causing insects and must cope with poor infrastructure and limited assistance from the Government. Third, ongoing political disputes are likely to exacerbate food security issues in affected regions such as Tigray, where famine is rife. The degradation of the country's agricultural land owing to soil erosion, acidity and salinity poses a severe threat to long-term production. Finally, the sector depends on state-owned farms and government subsidies that keep prices for some essential commodities artificially high and are a disincentive to the adoption of more efficient practices.

So far, the forces tending to expand agricultural production appear to be prevailing over the dampening elements. The sector grew at an average annual rate of 1.4% in the 1980s,

increasing to 2.7% in the 1990s and to 6.5% in the 2000s, before dipping to 5.1% from 2010–21. In 1981 the sector accounted for over one-half of Ethiopia's GDP (54.7%), but by 2000 this had declined to 44.7% of GDP and in 2021 it had fallen to just 32.5% of GDP. Nevertheless, the sector is by far the largest employer in Ethiopia; it accounted for 76.9% of the country's labour force in 1991, and, while it has declined since then, it accounted for 66% of the country's labour force in 2019.

Most of the agricultural sub-sectors have maintained reasonable rates of growth in recent years. From 2017–21 crop production grew by an annual average of 5.2%, followed by livestock rearing and hunting (4.0%). Forestry and fishing both expanded by 3.7%. Crop production grew considerably faster than the total area of land under cultivation, suggesting improved productivity levels.

The Ethiopian economy historically has depended heavily on a single export crop—coffee. In 2011 coffee production reached 376,823 metric tons, up from 126,188 tons in 2003. After declining to 275,530 tons in 2012, production expanded rapidly to 584,790 tons in 2020. In 2018 Ethiopia earned US $839.0m. from coffee exports, $764.1m. in 2019 and $855.9m. in 2020. Earnings from coffee provided 29.6% of total export revenue in 2018, 28.7% in 2019 and 28.6% in 2020.

Cereal production has also expanded rapidly in recent years. In 1993 production of cereals totalled 5,304,824 metric tons; however, it had doubled to 10,140,082 tons by 2004. Production increased to 28,763,752 tons in 2017, before declining slightly, by 1.4%, in 2018. Production then recovered, expanding by 4.6% in 2019 and by 1.9% in 2020.

Production of another important crop, sugar, totalled 1,200,000 metric tons in 1995. By 2006 production had reached 2,750,000 tons before falling to 1,851,890 tons in 2007. From 2007 output continued to decrease reaching 1,556,942 tons in 2014. Thereafter, production has fluctuated widely with rates of –11.6% in 2015, 2.3% in 2016, –19.3% in 2017, 13.9% in 2018, 15.9% in 2019 and –10.3% in 2020.

Agricultural products continued to dominate exports in 2020, with 14.1% of Ethiopia's agricultural export earnings derived from cut flowers, 11.5% from oil seeds, 10.9% from qat (also spelt chat or khat, a mildly narcotic plant, which grows at altitudes above 1,000 m) and 7.9% from pulses.

Despite agriculture's healthy growth rates, the country still scored low on the Economist Intelligence Unit's Global Food Security Index for 2020. Overall, Ethiopia ranked 108th out of 113 countries. In that year Ethiopia ranked 109th for affordability, 101st for availability, and 101st for quality and safety. Nearly 20% of Ethiopia's population is undernourished.

In order to address the country's food challenges, the Government plans to provide a better supply of inputs for farmers and to invest in irrigation projects and improvements to infrastructure. The intention is to improve yields and ease transport difficulties over the long term. In recent years the Government has sought to boost the country's capacity to produce sugar. It envisages that the country will become one of the world's leading 10 sugar exporters, and this will require significant investment following the privatization of its sugar mills. The Government also has high ambitions for the coffee sector and hopes to expand production to increase foreign exchange reserves through coffee exports.

MANUFACTURING

Ethiopia's industrial sector expanded by 1.8% in the 1990s, by 8.6% in the 2000s and by 16.0% from 2010–21. By 2020 the sector accounted for around 23% of Ethiopia's GDP. However, only 6.6% of the labour force was employed in the industrial sector in the 1990s, 7.2% in the 2000s and 8.7% from 2010–19. In 2021 construction accounted for 72.2% of the industrial sector, followed by manufacturing (23.4%), electricity and water (2.7%), and mining (1.8%).

Like many developing countries, Ethiopia's manufacturing sector consists primarily of food processing, beverages, textiles, hides and skins, and leather goods. The sector expanded by an average annual rate of 1.1% in the 1990s, by 7.2% in the 2000s and by 13.1% in 2010–21. Despite high growth rates in recent years, the sector still accounted for only 5.3% of GDP in 2020.

Ethiopia's manufacturing sector, particularly textiles, has become an increasingly important driver of growth for the country. Higher Chinese wages and the ongoing US–People's Republic of China trade war convinced many firms operating in China to relocate their labour-intensive operations to Ethiopia. Ethiopia's large population ensures a sizeable supply of relatively cheap labour, and the limited presence of labour unions reduces the risk of widespread industrial strikes (although political protests are likely to increase the risk of disruptions) and work stoppages.

Ethiopia is also a potentially attractive destination for import substitution manufacturing industries, particularly for intermediate consumer goods to serve the large domestic consumer base. As part of efforts to boost the manufacturing sector, the Government of Ethiopia has constructed several new industrial parks through the Growth and Transformation Plan (2015–20). It offers generous incentives for businesses, including tax relief and the privilege of importing duty-free goods.

As of 2020 Ethiopia had 13 operational industrial parks, nine of which were located along the railway line between the capital, Addis Ababa, and the port of Djibouti. According to statistics released by the Ethiopian Industrial Park Development Corporation, Ethiopia's export earnings from the existing parks exceeded US $610m. in the first nine months of the 2020/21 financial year (which runs from July to June). The industrial parks have also created about 89,000 jobs for younger workers in Ethiopia's labour force. It is envisaged that the parks will help to accelerate the country's economic transformation by attracting foreign and domestic investors, and positioning the country as a light manufacturing hub. The Government is prioritizing job creation by attracting firms operating in labour-intensive sectors such as textiles, leather goods and agro-processing.

A significant impediment to this plan is the low competitiveness of firms operating in Ethiopia. In 2019 the *Global Competitiveness Report* published by the World Economic Forum (WEF) ranked Ethiopia 126th out of 141 countries. According to the WEF's 12 pillars of global competitiveness, Ethiopia scored 126th for institutions, 123rd for infrastructure, 137th for ICT adoption, 127th for macroeconomic stability, 108th for health, 137th for skills, 135th for competitive product markets, 124th for the labour market, 107th for financial systems, 131st for business dynamism and 118th for innovative capability. Areas of specific concern include organized crime (124th), property rights (130th), the skill set of graduates (128th), trade tariffs (131st), co-operation in labour-employer relations (137th), the cost of starting a business (131st) and the time it takes to start a business (120th).

While disaggregated data are not available, special economic zones do not appear to have produced a surge of foreign direct investment (FDI). In recent years FDI has been adversely affected by instability in certain parts of the country, including regions where industrial parks have been constructed.

In late 2020 the Government launched a new 10-year transformative industrial strategy plan which will run from 2020/21 to 2029/30. The goal of the plan is to sustain the economic growth achieved under the previous Growth and Transformation Plan (2015–20) while putting greater emphasis on the private sector. Ethiopia aims to reach lower-middle-income status by 2025. The plan will focus on modernizing the manufacturing sector to help Ethiopia to make the transition into a major manufacturing centre. A critical facilitator in this regard is the recently launched African Continental Free Trade Area. The plan also envisions an increase in export earnings, to US $20,000m. annually, through the development of export-oriented products. Finally, the plan envisages the creation of 5m. job opportunities and a sharp increase in the number of small- and medium-scale manufacturing units from about 2,000 to 11,000.

Although some progress is apparent, given manufacturing's currently small share of GDP, the low education levels of workers, the ongoing insurgency in Tigray relating to tensions between the Government and the TPLF (see *History*), and the lingering effects of the COVID-19 pandemic, it is unlikely that the Government will achieve such ambitious goals in the near future.

Reports of companies leaving Ethiopia owing to the suspension of AGOA (see *External Trade*) have emerged. In November 2021 the US apparel company PVH Corporation (the owner of the Calvin Klein and Tommy Hilfiger brands) announced the closure of its facility in Ethiopia's flagship Hawassa Industrial Park.

CONSTRUCTION AND INFRASTRUCTURE

Since the 1990s there has been significant growth in the construction industry. Expansion accelerated from an average annual rate of 14.9% from 2007–12 to 22.6% from 2013–21. As in most countries, the growth of the construction sector is highly volatile. The rate of construction has also slowed in recent years; in 2017 it increased by 20.7% before decreasing to 15.7% in 2018, to 15.0% in 2019, to 9.9% in 2020 and to 6.6% in 2021.

Expanding the country's stock of infrastructure presents significant challenges. Ethiopia lacks a skilled workforce and trained construction professionals in areas such as design and engineering, thus raising labour costs. The Government's reliance on international sources of capital means that many projects are awarded to companies from the financing source nation, resulting in China dominating the competitive landscape.

Companies attach high risk to Ethiopian infrastructure projects. The country's over-reliance on hydropower exposes the economy and infrastructure investment plans to weather fluctuations. Security, especially in regions near Somalia and Eritrea, remains an issue. Continued dependence on Djibouti port for the majority of the country's trade flows puts Ethiopia in a vulnerable negotiating position should the costs of using this channel rise. Social unrest—stemming from the displacement of local farmers without adequate compensation and growing ethnic tensions—poses a growing risk, with foreign firms often becoming the target of this rising discontent.

As Ethiopia's government debt increases, driven by public investment in infrastructure and the cost of tackling the socioeconomic impact of COVID-19, the available funding for public infrastructure spending is likely to diminish. This revenue shortage will compel the Government to turn to the private sector for some of the country's infrastructure expansion. However, revenue and financing risks are likely to limit private sector involvement in this area.

OIL AND GAS

Although the Government strongly supports oil and gas exploration, the country has small proven reserves of petroleum and natural gas but no commercial production of either. The sector has several limitations. The oil and gas infrastructure is underdeveloped. As Ethiopia is landlocked, it is dependent on neighbouring countries such as Djibouti for imports of refined petroleum products. None the less, several international oil companies are carrying out exploration activities. Prospective drilling has revealed that the East African Rift Valley may hold large reserves of hydrocarbons.

Several exploration licences are currently in force, but many of these have been idle. There is little reason to expect a significant increase in exploration activity over the coming years. Companies curtailed exploration spending globally in the wake of the oil price collapse in 2014, with sub-Saharan Africa among the regions worst affected by the downturn. From 2017 prices rose and investment flowed to higher risk and more frontier markets globally. However, competition for capital remained fierce, and Ethiopia struggled to compete. In 2020 prices again collapsed, following the breakdown of the agreement by the Organization of the Petroleum Exporting Countries (OPEC) and its non-OPEC allies (OPEC+) to cut production, aggressive production increases by Saudi Arabia, and a sharp decline in demand stemming from the outbreak of COVID-19. Although prices rebounded in 2021 and in early 2022 following the Russian Federation's military invasion of Ukraine, Ethiopia's risk factors continue to limit interest in exploration and development.

POWER

Access to electricity in Ethiopia has proliferated in recent years. In 2000 only 12.7% of the Ethiopian population had access to electricity, with just 1.7% of the rural population having access compared to 76.2% of those living in urban areas. By 2010 25.4% of the population had access to electricity, with the share of the rural population having access increasing to 12.8% and that of the urban population to 85.6%. As of 2020 51.1% of the Ethiopian population had access to electricity, with 39.4% of the rural population having access compared to 93.2% of the urban population.

After averaging growth of 9.8% per annum from 2007–12, the growth of the electricity sector slowed to 4.9% in 2017, to 3.3% in 2018 and to 4.0% in 2019, before accelerating again, to 7.2%, in 2020 and to 8.9% in 2021. In 2021 the country generated approximately 16.4 TWh of electricity.

The country relies on hydropower for over 90% of its generated electricity, making the country vulnerable to climate change and perennial droughts. Nevertheless, Ethiopia has extensive hydropower resources that it plans to exploit to a greater extent in the future, which should help it to remain a self-sufficient power consumer and increase its revenues from power exports. The country also has plans to install significant amounts of wind, solar and geothermal capacity.

Ethiopia's ambitious development plans have since the early 2000s seen hydropower as the central electricity solution to drive rapid industrialization. Several mega-dam projects are underway, but none rival the Grand Ethiopian Renaissance Dam (GERD—also known as the Hidase Dam) on the Blue Nile river in the regional state of Benishangul-Gumuz; once completed, it is likely to be the largest hydroelectric power plant in Africa.

The US $4,800m. GERD has become a highly symbolic flagship project—not only for the Government's industrialization ambitions but also for Ethiopian modernity. Even bitter opponents of the ruling party broadly support the concept. The Government has entrenched the GERD's nationalist spirit by insisting on financing the entire project domestically, including through citizens' 'donations' or purchases of government 'GERD bonds'.

However, the project has repeatedly missed completion targets and hit cost over-runs amid corruption allegations. Completion was initially planned for 2016. Finally, on 20 February 2022 Prime Minister Abiy activated the first electricity-generating turbine at the GERD. Upon completion, the GERD is expected to have an installed production capacity of more than 5,000 MW, thus doubling Ethiopia's current output, and bringing electricity to the roughly 60m. Ethiopians who lack access. It is also a source of enormous national pride and a rare unifying issue amid serious domestic divisions. However, the project has caused frictions with Ethiopia's downstream neighbours Sudan and Egypt. Their concerns about the impact that the dam will have on their water supply have arisen from Ethiopia's unilateral filling of the reservoir without a water-sharing agreement.

Hydropower will remain the dominant source of electricity generation in Ethiopia for the foreseeable future as the Government pursues ambitious plans to build a series of hydropower mega-projects. Through the Government's second Growth and Transformation Plan (2015–20), the authorities plan to mobilize US $20,000m. of investment to build 10–12 new power generation facilities to account for around 95% of Ethiopia's total electricity by 2030. Ethiopia plans to use its vast hydropower resources to establish itself as an East African electricity export hub.

TRANSPORT AND COMMUNICATIONS

Ethiopia's transport and communications sector has experienced volatile growth in recent years, expanding by 15.1% in 2017 before decelerating by 6.4% in 2018. In 2019 the sector grew by 21.0%; however, in 2020 growth of just 1.2% was recorded following the outbreak of the COVID-19 pandemic in that year. With the economic recovery under way in 2021, the sector expanded by 7.0% in that year.

Ethiopia has the second longest road network after Kenya in sub-Saharan Africa and has tripled its length over the past decade. However, only 13.0% of the country's roads are paved. With financial support from the World Bank, the Government plans to construct an additional 16,000 km of paved roads. In 2022 several significant projects were under way. In June 2021 construction started on the first section of the Adama-Awash Expressway. The US $154m. project includes the construction of a four-lane 60-km road that will link Adama with Nura Era and Wolenchiti. A joint venture between India-based JMC Projects and China-based LRBCL is executing the project. The African Development Bank has committed a $98m. grant for the project, which will also be financed by the Government of Ethiopia.

In March 2021 Xinjiang Communications Construction Group commenced two road projects worth US $123.9m. in the Ethiopian state of Amhara. The Government of Ethiopia will provide funds for the 261-km Durbete-Kunzila-Shagura-Fenjit and Gelago-Gendeweha road projects. On completion the roads will connect to three zones and will serve as a corridor between Ethiopia and Sudan.

Ethiopia has a minimal rail network, which renders supply chains reliant on the country's road network and inhibits the efficient flow of high bulk trade. However, with most large businesses located in Addis Ababa, the recent modernization of the railway line connecting Addis Ababa with Djibouti is expected to reduce transport costs significantly.

As a landlocked country, Ethiopia has no seaports and relies mainly on the port of Djibouti for almost 95% of its trade. Ethiopia does not have any vital river ports as most of the country's rivers are non-navigable, except for the Bardo, which is only navigable during specific periods depending on water levels. Djibouti serves as Ethiopia's main export-import route. Ethiopia faces high risks associated with its dependence on the port of Djibouti, including delays due to congestion and strikes and increased costs due to the lack of competition. However, the country has taken steps to diversify its options for trade, with plans to use the port of Mombasa in Kenya, the port of Berbera in the self-declared 'Republic of Somaliland', and Sudan's commercial seaport, Port Sudan, on the Red Sea.

Ethiopia started using the port of Berbera in February 2015, which has a storage capacity of 1m. metric tons, accommodates more than 1,000 ships per year, and is likely to be increasingly used for trade with the Middle East and Saudi Arabia. The port of Mombasa will serve as an outlet for goods from the southern part of Ethiopia, connecting the country to markets in the East African Community. The construction of newly paved roads to the port is expected to facilitate trade in the medium term. Finally, Ethiopia plans to increase the capacity of its dry ports, which should reduce congestion at the port of Djibouti, thus easing some of the difficulties of trading. In June 2021 China Civil Engineering Construction Corporation started work on the expansion of the Modjo dry port. The US $110m. project includes the construction of six warehouses, road and pavement works, multipurpose buildings, and operating facilities. The project receives funding from the World Bank.

Ethiopia's air transport is a key strategic sector for the economy as it is relatively efficient and well developed by regional standards, compensating somewhat for the country's landlocked status. Airport infrastructure across the country is a crucial focus of Ethiopia's development, with the Government committed to expanding the number of airports over the coming years from 21 to 25.

In 2020 the Government announced that state-owned Ethiopian Airlines was to begin construction of a new mega-hub airport at Bishoftu, near Addis Ababa, with an annual capacity of 120m. passengers. Construction was expected to take 10 years to complete. Provided that the project is realized, the country will receive a significant boost from this new hub, which will include hotels, shopping malls, office buildings and apartments.

Ethiopia's telecommunications market offers significant long-term potential as one of the three remaining African markets with a state telecoms monopoly and having 44m. existing mobile subscribers among a still rapidly expanding population of over 117m. State-owned Ethio Telecom, the country's only mobile telecommunications and internet provider, dominates the market, and the partial privatization of that company is a cornerstone of the new Homegrown

Economic Reform Plan launched in December 2019. The Government subsequently announced plans to raise US $7,500m. from selling state assets, including the Ethiopian Sugar Corporation, rail track of the Ethiopian Railway Corporation, and a minority stake of up to 49% in Ethio Telecom. Two telecommunications licences were also to be granted to private companies.

The first significant milestone in the Government's privatization programme was an auction of the telecommunications spectrum in May 2021, with two licences on offer. However, given the ongoing conflict in Tigray, the outcomes disappointed the Government. A consortium led by the Kenya-based telecommunications provider Safaricom secured one licence, but the other bids fell below the Government's minimum acceptable threshold. In December the Government planned the second telecommunications licensing round but ultimately postponed it, owing to 'concerns' from several prospective bidders. Although the authorities did not specify these concerns, they almost certainly related to the conflict in Tigray.

BANKING AND FINANCIAL SERVICES

Despite allowing the establishment of private banks and insurance companies in 1994, the Ethiopian Government does not yet permit foreign ownership in the banking sector. Full banking operations, including direct lending and deposit-taking by foreign creditors, remain prohibited. To date, Ethiopia has allowed only a few foreign banks (from China, Germany, Kenya, Turkey and South Africa) to open liaison offices to facilitate credit to companies from their countries of origin. Ethiopia has only 18 commercial lenders, two of which are state-owned.

While banking and insurance have excellent growth opportunities, they continue to be limited relative to their potential, given large, underbanked and underinsured groups. The Ethiopian Government plans to liberalize the sector and develop domestic capital markets in order to serve the private sector's financing needs better.

In 2016 the country relaxed restrictions on foreign bank operations, permitting foreign banks to open liaison offices in the country to facilitate credit lines to foreign businesses operating in Ethiopia and to advise them on cross-border trade. These reforms improved the situation, and several foreign banks now have representative offices in Ethiopia, including South Africa-based Standard Bank Group and Kenya-based KCB Group. In July 2019 parliament approved a bill to open the banking sector to foreign nationals of Ethiopian origin, allowing the Ethiopian-born diaspora to invest in local banks and businesses. At the time, foreign ownership of local banks was strictly prohibited. However, on 22 February 2022 Prime Minister Abiy announced plans to open up the banking sector to foreign investors as soon as parliament passes the legal framework permitting this to take place.

In 2022 Ethiopia was in the process of establishing a capital market authority. This action is a prerequisite for setting up a stock exchange, which Prime Minister Abiy put forward in 2018 as a key plank in his promised pivot towards the private sector. A capital market bill passed by parliament in early 2021 has provided for public and private (including foreign) ownership of the stock market, with the Government's share not exceeding 25%.

The impending banking reform presents an opportunity for some of Africa's biggest banks, including the Kenyan-headquartered Equity Group and KCB Group, which have already expressed an interest in running fully fledged operations in Ethiopia. A new Financial Service Code will outline the engagement modalities for foreign creditors planning to invest in the country's financial services sector.

In late April 2022 the National Bank of Ethiopia (the central bank) drafted a bill amending the national payment law to allow foreign investors to offer mobile money services in Ethiopia's telecommunications market. If passed, the bill will open the mobile money services sector to foreign operators, notably allowing Kenya-based Safaricom to introduce its product, M-Pesa, to a new and rapidly growing market in one of Africa's most populous countries.

The proposed amendment is a significant step in Ethiopia's efforts to liberalize the telecommunications sector. Ethio Telecom, a state-owned company, is currently the only mobile money service provider allowed to operate. Nevertheless, the emerging sector should expand in line with expected growth in the country's telecommunications sector. Ethio Telecom reported that there were 58.7m. mobile telephone subscriptions in 2021, with a 49.8% mobile telephone penetration rate, in comparison to an internet penetration rate of just 24.8%. The mobile money sector is significant in increasing financial inclusion, which remains low in Ethiopia. Despite government efforts to extend financial services, only about 20% of the country's adult population have bank accounts, according to World Bank estimates. Thus, the expansion of mobile money services will allow more people to access digital financial instruments.

EXTERNAL TRADE

The country's recent export performance has been poor by historical standards. Exports of goods and services contracted at an average annual rate of −5.5% in the 1980s. Subsequently, exports increased to an average annual rate of 10.2% in the 1990s and to 12.3% in the 2000s. However, from 2010–21 exports declined by an average annual rate of 6.3%. Imports of goods and services followed a somewhat unique pattern, expanding at an average annual rate of 6.2% in the 1980s before contracting by 1.1% in the 1990s. Imports rose to 13.9% in the 2000s, dropping to 7.3% from 2010–21. This pattern resulted in a widening deficit in the current account, equivalent to 0.9% in the 1990s, which increased to 5.2% in the 2000s, and further to 6.3% from 2010–21. However, the deficit has been declining in recent years, falling from 11.5% in 2016 to 8.5% in 2017, to 5.3% in 2019 and to 3.2% in 2020.

The country's recent current account deficits have not been financed by large inflows of FDI. According to the World Bank, net annual inflows of FDI increased from 0.4% of GDP in 2008 to a record high of 5.6% in 2016. However, since then, flows have declined to 4.9% in 2017, 4.0% in 2018, 2.7% in 2019 and 2.2% in 2020. According to the UN Conference on Trade and Development, China was the largest investor in 2019, accounting for 60% of newly approved FDI projects.

In 2020 coffee accounted for 32.1% of Ethiopia's exports. Horticulture was next (21.9%), followed by oil seeds (17.4%), trees and plants (8.6%) and clothing and textiles (3.5%). Machinery comprised the largest group of imports (13%), followed by mineral fuels (12.2%), electrical equipment (7.7%), vehicles (7.3%) and animal or vegetable fats (6.4%).

A small number of countries account for most of Ethiopia's imports and exports. In 2019 China was Ethiopia's largest export destination at 17%, followed by the USA at 16%. In that year Ethiopia received 27% of its imports from China, followed by India (9%), the UAE (9%), France (9%) and the United Kingdom (7%).

On 1 January 2022 the US Administration confirmed the termination of Ethiopia's duty-free trade access to US markets under AGOA owing to allegations of serious human rights violations committed during the conflict in Tigray, in northern Ethiopia, which constitute a violation of the agreement's conditions. The decision was made despite intense lobbying by the Ethiopian Government and diaspora to avert the exclusion.

This action represents a significant loss for Ethiopia. US Department of Commerce data show that, in 2020, exports under the aegis of AGOA accounted for 45% of Ethiopia's total exports to the USA, Ethiopia's second most important trade partner after China. The textiles sector will suffer the worst effects. In 2020 Ethiopian exports to the USA amounted to US $238m., of which $222m., or 93.2% of the total, comprised textiles and apparel.

MONETARY POLICY

The stated objective of the National Bank of Ethiopia (NBE) is to maintain price and exchange rate stability and to support the Government's efforts towards achieving a sustainable economic growth path for the country. Authorities at the bank view price stability as a proxy for macroeconomic stability. The NBE regards exchange rate stability as a policy objective in order for the country to be competitive in international trade. The bank also uses exchange rate intervention as a policy tool to affect both the foreign reserve position and the domestic money supply.

The rate of inflation has accelerated in recent years, increasing from 6.6% in 2016 to 10.7% in 2017, 13.8% in 2018, 15.8% in 2019, 20.4% in 2020 and 26.8% in 2021; the International Monetary Fund (IMF) forecast that it would reach 34.5% in 2022. Since 2013 inflation rates in Ethiopia have been slightly higher than those for the region overall and considerably higher than those of the country's principal trading partners—China, the USA, the UAE, Saudi Arabia, South Korea and Germany. The result has been a continuous devaluation of the birr, with the currency falling from US \$1 = 20.58 birr in 2015 to US \$1 = 23.9 birr in 2017, to US \$1 = 29.1 birr in 2019, to US \$1 = 34.9 birr in 2020 and to US \$1 = 48.2 birr at the end of 2021. By mid-June 2022 the birr had dropped in value to US \$1 = 52.0 birr. The pattern of a depreciating birr and spiralling inflation may be difficult for the monetary authorities to halt due to supply chain disruptions caused by the conflict in Tigray, alongside rising global fuel and food prices stemming from Russia's invasion of Ukraine.

In September 2020 the NBE issued a new set of bank notes to curb counterfeiting, currency hoarding, illegal trade activities and illicit financial flows, while bolstering banking sector liquidity, which suffers from large amounts of cash being held outside banks. The NBE ordered banks to issue the new currency immediately, while Ethiopians had three months to exchange their old bank notes for the new ones. According to the Ethiopian Bankers Association, in that year approximately 113,000m. birr (US \$3,600m.) was circulating in cash outside the banking system—equivalent to 4% of GDP at 2019 levels. In August the NBE issued a directive banning individuals or companies from holding more than 1.5m. birr in cash.

The Ethiopian Government hopes that demonetization could help to contain inflation and currency depreciation. However, this is likely to prove profoundly political and aimed at weakening key opposition groups and former officials—most notably Tigrayan elites—who are believed to hold large cash reserves. Such a rapid and sudden move is risky and could create chaos for the considerable proportion of individuals and businesses who operate in the cash economy.

Several critical financial reforms took place in 2020/21. These included the formulation of a treasury bill market to reduce monetary financing of government deficits and the private sector as well as the implementation of monetary reforms to enable a gradual transition to a market-clearing exchange rate.

FISCAL POLICY

Government revenues and expenditures are not high by international standards. Government revenue as a share of GDP fell from 14.8% in the 1980s to 13.8% in the 1990s. Revenues increased to 18.3% in the 2000s before dropping to 14.5% from 2010–21. Government expenditures were around 18.6% of GDP in the 1980s and 1990s, increasing to 22.4% in the 2000s before dipping to 16.8% from 2010–21. The pattern of revenues and expenditures produced chronic budgetary deficits, averaging 4.0% of GDP in the 1980s. However, after reaching 4.8% of GDP in the 1990s, deficits fell to 4.2% in the 2000s and to 2.7% from 2010–21.

However, the Government urgently needs to address its fiscal and balance of payments problems. Ethiopia's currently high growth rates stem from an infrastructure-driven strategy financed partly by China. One estimate of the country's debt suggests that about 50% of Ethiopia's external debt—or about US \$14,000m.—is owed to China. Ethiopia has already requested China for debt restructuring to address its massive bilateral debt, indicating early signs of debt distress in the context of the COVID-19 pandemic, the ongoing conflict in Tigray, and the legislative elections, which were held on 21 June 2021, having been postponed in 2020.

Although the country's external debt-to-GDP ratio is not high by international standards, it has mushroomed in recent years, from 38.9% in 2010 to 53.0% of GDP by 2021. There has been a sharp increase in funding required to service the debt-to-exports ratio, which rose from 1.5% in 2008 to 45.0% in 2017 before accelerating to 67.8% by 2020.

In April 2020 the IMF extended US \$411m. in emergency funding to assist Ethiopia in combating the COVID-19 pandemic. In July the country began to benefit from debt relief under the Debt Service Suspension Initiative (DSSI) of the Group of Twenty (G20). The G20 created the DSSI in May 2020, after it became clear that the pandemic would pressure government finances worldwide. Under the scheme, eligible economies can defer debt repayments to bilateral lenders in G20 member countries. However, those debts must be repaid in full over a maximum of six years once the suspension expires.

In February 2021 the credit rating agency Fitch downgraded the country's rating to CCC. Fitch cited Ethiopia's announcement in January that it would seek debt restructuring under the G20's Common Framework for Debt Treatments beyond the DSSI as the main reason for the downgrade. Although the agency reported that Ethiopia's fundamentals remained stable, it noted that the risk that bondholders could be negatively affected by the restructuring underpinned the downgrade, even though the Ethiopian authorities stated it was 'very unlikely' that they would seek relief from private creditors. Meanwhile, in May Moody's also downgraded Ethiopia's credit rating, to B2 from B1, as a result of the Government's decision to join the DSSI.

Downgrades into 'junk' bond territory will increase the Government's borrowing costs. The conflict in Tigray also costs the country another essential source of revenue: international aid. In late 2020 the European Union and the USA—two of Ethiopia's most important donors—suspended budgetary support disbursements owing to concerns about the lack of humanitarian access and human rights violations in the conflict zone.

PROSPECTS

The Ethiopian Government's policy agenda for the remainder of 2022 and into 2023 is likely to focus on economic liberalization and the need to attract FDI in critical sectors such as finance and telecommunications. The economy was showing signs of recovery in 2022, but real GDP growth is unlikely to return to pre-pandemic levels for several years. Ethiopia's various regions, particularly Tigray, Afar, Amhara and Oromo, will probably experience frequent outbreaks of politically charged ethnic clashes. The critical risk area remains Tigray, where conflict broke out in November 2020, causing severe damage to infrastructure, human displacement and loss of life. That Prime Minister Abiy appeared to be willing at the end of June 2022 to begin negotiations to end the conflict in Tigray may be the first step in restoring stability and high rates of economic growth.

Statistical Survey

Source (unless otherwise stated): Central Statistics Agency (CSA), POB 1143, Addis Ababa; tel. (11) 553112; internet www.statsethiopia.gov.et.

Area and Population

AREA, POPULATION AND DENSITY

Area (sq km)	1,133,380*
Population (census results)	
11 October 1994	53,477,265
28 May 2007	
Males	37,217,130
Females	36,533,802
Total	73,750,932
Population (official projections at July)†	
2020	100,829,000
2021	102,998,000
2022	105,166,000
Density (per sq km) at July 2022	92.8

* 437,600 sq miles.

† Figures are rounded to nearest 1,000 persons.

Mid-2022 (UN projection): 120,812,698 (Source: UN, *World Population Prospects: The 2019 Revision*).

POPULATION BY AGE AND SEX
('000, UN projections at mid-2022)

	Males	Females	Total
0–14 years	24,003.7	23,382.6	47,386.3
15–64 years	34,459.6	34,624.3	69,083.9
65 years and over	1,984.8	2,357.6	4,342.5
Total	60,448.2	60,364.5	120,812.7

Note: Totals may not be equal to the sum of components, owing to rounding.

Source: UN, *World Population Prospects: The 2019 Revision*.

ADMINISTRATIVE DIVISIONS
('000, official population projections at July 2022)

	Population		
	Males	Females	Total
Regional States			
1 Tigray	2,834	2,905	5,739
2 Afar	1,105	928	2,033
3 Amhara	11,463	11,414	22,877
4 Oromia	20,033	19,948	39,981
5 Somali	3,455	3,052	6,506
6 Benishangul-Gumuz	618	601	1,219
7 Southern Nations, Nationalities			
and Peoples*	10,645	10,848	21,493
8 Gambela	265	244	509
9 Harari	140	137	276
Chartered Cities			
1 Dire Dawa	270	266	536
2 Addis Ababa	1,822	2,038	3,860
Total†	52,724	52,442	105,166

* Sidama and South West, two new regional states created from territory formerly part of the Southern Nations, Nationalities and Peoples Region (SNNPR), were formally inaugurated in February and November 2021 respectively, following endorsement by referendum. Detailed demographic data for the new entities were not available at mid-2022.

† Including 137,000 (males 74,000, females 63,000) persons, detailed as 'special enumeration', not allocated to administrative divisions.

PRINCIPAL TOWNS
(official population projections at July 2022)

Addis Ababà		Dessie . . .	270,366
(capital) . . .	3,860,000	Jimma	250,909
Gondar	567,918	Shashemene . .	208,368
Mekele	457,917	Bishoftu	207,383
Adama (Nazret) .	456,868	Sodo	204,121
Awasa	422,202	Arba Minch . . .	201,049
Bahir Dar . . .	349,995	Jijiga	197,966
Dire Dawa . . .	343,000		

Mid-2021 (incl. suburbs, UN projections): Addis Ababa 5,227,794; Mekele 564,756; Dire Dawa 445,050; Nazret 411,137; Gondar 395,138 (Source: UN, *World Urbanization Prospects: The 2018 Revision*).

BIRTHS AND DEATHS
(annual averages, UN estimates)

	2005–10	2010–15	2015–20
Birth rate (per 1,000)	37.3	34.7	32.6
Death rate (per 1,000)	9.6	7.6	6.7

Source: UN, *World Population Prospects: The 2019 Revision*.

Life expectancy (years at birth, estimates): 67.0 (males 65.0; females 68.9) in 2020 (Source: World Bank, World Development Indicators database).

ECONOMICALLY ACTIVE POPULATION
(labour force survey, '000 persons aged 10 years and over, 2013)*

	Males	Females	Total
Agriculture, hunting, forestry and			
fishing	18,195.8	12,621.3	30,817.1
Mining and quarrying	116.2	63.5	179.7
Manufacturing	739.0	1,163.2	1,902.2
Electricity, gas and water . . .	70.0	157.4	227.3
Construction	650.6	174.2	824.8
Wholesale and retail trade; repair			
of motor vehicles, motorcycles			
and personal and household			
goods	860.1	1,445.2	2,305.4
Hotels and restaurants . . .	135.1	347.2	482.3
Transport, storage and			
communications	352.7	60.1	412.8
Financial intermediation . . .	84.4	49.3	133.7
Real estate, renting and business			
services	191.1	94.0	285.1
Public administration and defence;			
compulsory social security . .	204.1	83.3	287.4
Education	425.5	257.4	682.9
Social work	110.8	140.7	251.5
Community, social and personal			
services	303.8	194.8	498.6
Households with employed persons	433.9	2,657.3	3,091.1
Extraterritorial organizations and			
bodies	13.6	8.4	22.0
Total employed	22,886.6	19,517.3	42,403.9
Unemployed	629.7	1,351.4	1,981.1
Total labour force	23,516.3	20,868.7	44,385.0

* Excluding armed forces.

Mid-2015 (FAO estimates in '000): Agriculture, etc. 37,957; Total labour force 50,906 (Source: FAO).

Health and Welfare

KEY INDICATORS

Total fertility rate (children per woman, 2020)	4.0
Under-5 mortality rate (per 1,000 live births, 2020) . . .	48.7
HIV/AIDS (% of persons aged 15–49, 2020)	0.9
COVID-19: Cumulative confirmed deaths (per 100,000 persons at 31 August 2022)	6.3
COVID-19: Fully vaccinated population (% of total population at 31 July 2022)	30.5
Physicians (per 1,000 head, 2020)	1.1
Hospital beds (per 1,000 head, 2016)	0.3
Domestic health expenditure (2019): US $ per head (PPP) .	17.1
Domestic health expenditure (2019): % of GDP . . .	0.7
Domestic health expenditure (2019): public (% of total current expenditure)	22.7
Access to improved water resources (% of persons, 2020) .	50
Access to improved sanitation facilities (% of persons, 2020).	9
Total carbon dioxide emissions ('000 metric tons, 2018) . .	16,280
Carbon dioxide emissions per head (metric tons, 2018) . .	0.1
Human Development Index (2021): ranking	175
Human Development Index (2021): value	0.498

Note: For data on COVID-19 vaccinations, 'fully vaccinated' denotes receipt of all doses specified by approved vaccination regime (Sources: Johns Hopkins University and Our World in Data). Data on health expenditure refer to current general government expenditure in each case. For more information on sources and further definitions for all indicators, see Health and Welfare Statistics: Sources and Definitions section (europaworld.com/credits).

Agriculture

PRINCIPAL CROPS
('000 metric tons)

	2018	2019	2020
Avocados	85	104	245
Bananas	502	539	898
Barley	1,749	2,378	2,261
Beans, dry	564	486	553
Broad beans, dry	1,042	1,007	1,071
Cabbages and other brassicas .	463	436	433
Castor oil seed (beans)* . . .	11	11	11
Chick peas	459	435	457
Chillies and peppers, dry . . .	307	313	296
Chillies and peppers, green . .	62	67	74
Coffee, green	495	483	585
Cow peas, dry	367	391	376
Garlic	196	153	115
Ginger*	11	10	10
Groundnuts, with shell . . .	144	157	205
Hops	49	42	47
Lentils	141	119	113
Linseed	97	80	80
Maize	10,120	9,636	10,022
Mangoes, mangosteens and guavas	137	109	109
Millet (Dagusa)	1,036	1,126	1,219
Oats	22	46	40
Onions and shallots, green* . .	37	36	36
Onions, dry	262	274	346
Oranges	41	30	40
Papayas	59	52	72
Peas, dry	361	391	376
Potatoes	933	925	1,142
Rapeseed	38	42	13
Rice, paddy	172	171	190
Safflower seed	8	10	9
Seed cotton*	140	155	188
Sesame seed	202	263	260

—continued	2018	2019	2020
Sorghum	5,024	5,266	5,058
Soybeans (Soya beans)	149	126	209
Sugar cane	1,294	1,499	1,345
Sweet potatoes	1,512	1,756	1,599
Tea*	10	10	10
Tomatoes	24	35	42
Wheat	4,838	5,315	5,479
Yams	37	49	46

* FAO estimates.

Aggregate production ('000 metric tons, may include official, semi-official or estimated data): Total cereals 28,364 in 2018, 29,673 in 2019, 30,249 in 2020; Total fruit (primary) 1,018 in 2018, 1,030 in 2019, 1,558 in 2020; Total oilcrops 1,101 in 2018, 1,144 in 2019, 1,197 in 2020; Total pulses 2,944 in 2018, 2,880 in 2019, 2,991 in 2020; Total roots and tubers 4,071 in 2018, 4,182 in 2019, 5,114 in 2020; Total vegetables (primary) 1,601 in 2018, 1,569 in 2019, 1,622 in 2020.

Source: FAO.

LIVESTOCK
('000 head, year ending September)

	2018	2019	2020
Asses	9,655	9,988	10,792
Camels	1,761	1,827	1,637
Cattle	61,510	65,354	70,292
Chickens	59,420	48,956	56,993
Goats	38,964	50,502	52,464
Horses	1,931	2,111	2,148
Mules	371	358	383
Pigs*	35	36	36
Sheep	33,020	39,894	42,915

* FAO estimates.

Source: FAO.

LIVESTOCK PRODUCTS
('000 metric tons, FAO estimates)

	2018	2019	2020
Camel meat	35.5	36.2	39.8
Cattle hides, fresh	56.7	59.4	63.0
Cattle meat	390.1	408.5	433.0
Cattle offals, edible	78.0	81.7	86.6
Cows' milk	3,284.5	3,895.3	4,693.0
Chicken meat	71.3	58.5	67.8
Game meat	89.0	89.6	90.3
Goat meat	110.2	142.5	147.7
Goats' milk	51.2	59.3	60.6
Sheep meat	105.9	128.0	137.8
Sheep's milk	53.1	59.2	61.8
Hen eggs	50.9	53.1	49.8
Honey (natural)	58.6	15.0	12.9

Source: FAO.

Forestry

ROUNDWOOD REMOVALS
('000 cubic metres, excl. bark, FAO estimates)

	2018	2019	2020
Sawlogs, veneer logs and logs for sleepers	11	11	11
Pulpwood	7	7	7
Other industrial wood	2,917	2,917	2,917
Fuel wood	111,875	113,147	114,439
Total	114,810	116,082	117,374

Source: FAO.

SAWNWOOD PRODUCTION
('000 cubic metres, incl. railway sleepers)

	2001	2002	2003
Coniferous (softwood)	25*	1	1
Broadleaved (hardwood) . . .	35*	13	17
Total	60	14	18

* FAO estimate.

2004–20: Figures assumed to be unchanged from 2003 (FAO estimates).

Source: FAO.

Fishing

(metric tons, live weight of capture)

	2018	2019	2020
Capture	57,166	59,002	60,002
Common carp	267	6,153	4,039
Crucian carp	19	2,739	931
Cyprinids	256	8,245	8,236
Tilapias	30,396	17,658	22,725
North African catfish . . .	23,000	17,644	17,889
Nile perch	2,840	3,763	3,035
Aquaculture	165	430	534
Total catch	57,331	59,432	60,536

Source: FAO.

Mining

('000 metric tons unless otherwise indicated, fiscal year)

	2016/17	2017/18	2018/19
Gold (kilograms)	5,390	3,495	3,480
Limestone	4,335	10,896	6,755
Gypsum and anhydrite . . .	85	253	56
Pumice	959	2,436	506
Sandstone	36*	64	64*

* Estimated production.

Source: US Geological Survey.

Industry

SELECTED PRODUCTS
('000 metric tons, fiscal year)

	2010/11	2011/12	2012/13
Wheat flour	351	578	1,384
Macaroni and pasta	50	43	50
Raw sugar	333	333	1,032
Wine ('000 hectolitres) . . .	64	70	1
Beer ('000 hectolitres) . . .	4,106	4,553	4,130
Mineral waters ('000 hectolitres) .	1,344	1,513	4,001
Cigarettes (million)	6,217	6,217	4,112
Cotton yarn	9.8	7.6	15.5
Cotton fabrics ('000 sq m) . .	11,711	19,076	12,856
Nylon fabrics ('000 sq m) . . .	722	732	883
Footwear (including rubber, '000 pairs)	24,149	24,810	12,294
Soap	214.3	70.9	86.9
Tyres ('000)	267	176	265
Clay building bricks ('000) . .	18	14	1
Quicklime	2	6	302
Cement	2,082	3,548	1,908

Electrical energy (million kWh, fiscal year): 13,839.6 in 2018/19; 15,192.2 in 2019/20; 15,532.1 in 2020/21 (Source: National Bank of Ethiopia, Addis Ababa).

Raw sugar ('000 metric tons): 395 in 2014; 350 in 2015; 133 in 2016 (Source: UN Industrial Commodity Statistics Database).

Beer of millet ('000 metric tons): 445.8 in 2011; 457.9 in 2012; 522.4 in 2013 (Source: FAO).

Beer of barley ('000 metric tons, unofficial figures): 994.7 in 2016; 1,161.5 in 2017; 1,426.3 in 2018 (Source: FAO).

Finance

CURRENCY, EXCHANGE RATES AND FISCAL YEAR

Monetary Units
  100 cents = 1 birr.

Sterling, Dollar and Euro Equivalents (31 May 2021)
  £1 sterling = 60.858 birr;
  US \$1 = 43.085 birr;
  €1 = 52.568 birr;
  100 birr = £1.64 = \$2.32 = €1.90.

Average Exchange Rate (birr per US \$)
  2018   27.429
  2019   29.070
  2020   34.927

Fiscal Year
  The fiscal year ends on 7 July.

GENERAL BUDGET
(million birr, fiscal year)

Revenue	2018/19*	2019/20*	2020/21†
Taxation	268,457.4	311,476.5	380,653.3
Direct taxes	115,857.8	132,214.5	144,457.3
Taxes on income and profits .	112,798.6	129,479.3	140,363.6
Tax on personal income .	41,202.5	49,869.6	56,706.7
Tax on business profits .	59,406.6	64,664.1	59,532.0
Land use and lease fee . .	3,059.3	2,735.3	4,093.8
Domestic indirect taxes . .	77,774.0	78,886.5	114,816.5
Sales tax	35,541.9	35,454.8	62,852.4
Service tax	39,400.5	40,264.6	47,857.9
Import duties	74,825.6	100,375.4	121,379.5
Non-tax revenue	42,860.0	42,836.3	67,650.1
Sales of goods and services .	6,872.8	5,794.2	6,358.5
Residual surplus, capital charge, state dividends, etc. . . .	15,821.6	17,488.9	23,083.0
Total‡	311,317.4	354,312.8	448,303.4

Expenditure	2018/19*	2019/20*	2020/21†
Current expenditure	238,156.6	275,967.0	336,179.0
General services	74,660.4	89,920.2	93,221.9
Economic services	31,233.4	36,323.1	44,369.6
Social services	112,516.0	130,356.0	152,838.3
Interest and charges . . .	13,525.8	13,481.1	19,765.1
Miscellaneous	6,221.0	5,886.6	25,984.1
Capital expenditure	174,949.1	204,176.1	263,378.5
Economic development . . .	106,518.0	132,629.1	171,547.6
Social development . . .	47,891.4	51,316.1	61,925.8
General development . . .	20,539.8	20,231.0	29,905.2
Total§	413,105.7	480,143.2	599,557.5

* Preliminary.

† Budget figures.

‡ Excluding grants received from abroad (million birr): 33,619.1 in 2018/19 (preliminary); 40,653.0 in 2019/20 (preliminary); 45,458.7 in 2020/21 (budget figure).

§ Excluding external assistance (million birr): 15,972.9 in 2018/19 (preliminary); 17,855.1 in 2019/20 (preliminary); 24,798.3 in 2020/21 (budget figure).

Source: National Bank of Ethiopia, Addis Ababa.

INTERNATIONAL RESERVES
(US \$ million at 31 December, excluding gold)

	2018	2019	2020
IMF special drawing rights . .	9.0	5.4	13.6
Reserve position in IMF . . .	10.4	10.4	10.8
Foreign exchange	3,957.7	2,964.7	3,021.7
Total	3,977.2	2,980.5	3,046.1

2021: IMF special drawing rights 6.8; Reserve position in IMF 10.5.

Source: IMF, *International Financial Statistics*.

MONEY SUPPLY
(million birr at 30 June)

	2019	2020	2021
Currency outside banks . . .	92,017.0	109,071.8	133,621.3
Demand deposits (net)	216,920.2	251,513.7	303,770.7
Savings deposits	487,302.1	589,174.1	816,380.3
Time deposits	90,513.3	87,886.8	94,493.8
Broad money	886,752.5	1,037,646.3	1,348,266.1

Source: National Bank of Ethiopia, Addis Ababa.

COST OF LIVING
(Consumer Price Index, fiscal year; base: December 2016 = 100)

	2018/19	2019/20	2020/21
Food (incl. non-alcoholic beverages)	133.5	164.7	202.9
Clothing and footwear	147.0	160.5	183.1
Housing, water, electricity, gas and other fuels	132.9	158.6	181.2
All items (incl. others) . . .	132.1	158.4	190.4

Source: National Bank of Ethiopia, Addis Ababa.

NATIONAL ACCOUNTS
(million birr at current prices, year ending 7 July)

Expenditure on the Gross Domestic Product

	2018/19	2019/20	2020/21
Government final consumption expenditure	247,362	307,769	383,565
Private final consumption expenditure	1,848,070	2,360,896	3,134,994
Gross fixed capital formation . .	948,866	1,037,685	1,216,585
Total domestic expenditure .	3,044,298	3,706,350	4,735,144
Exports of goods and services . .	213,437	239,229	329,635
Less Imports of goods and services	561,512	571,230	723,391
GDP in purchasers' values .	2,696,223	3,374,349	4,341,387
GDP at constant 2015/16 prices	1,987,157	2,109,122	2,228,081

Gross Domestic Product by Economic Activity

	2017/18	2018/19	2019/20
Agriculture, hunting, forestry and fishing	686,995	913,610	1,199,974
Mining and quarrying	4,054	3,368	9,643
Manufacturing	128,200	150,531	178,972
Electricity and water	15,026	18,726	23,827
Construction	452,978	495,283	567,201
Trade, hotels and restaurants .	328,954	427,253	523,810
Finance, insurance and real estate	148,912	191,201	257,230
Transport and communications .	82,947	99,884	140,237
Public administration and defence	94,614	103,262	120,236
Education	75,776	85,739	94,199
Health and social work . . .	24,101	27,328	34,928
Other services	49,062	59,322	71,570
Sub-total	2,091,618	2,575,507	3,221,829
Less Imputed bank service charge.	26,829	31,884	38,830
Indirect taxes (net)	137,584	152,600	191,351
GDP in purchasers' values .	2,202,373	2,696,223	3,374,349

Source: National Bank of Ethiopia, Addis Ababa.

BALANCE OF PAYMENTS
(US $ million)

	2018	2019	2020
Exports of goods	2,705.0	2,745.9	3,252.8
Imports of goods	−13,725.8	−13,056.3	−11,762.0
Balance on goods	−11,020.8	−10,310.4	−8,509.2
Exports of services	4,919.3	4,842.3	4,461.8
Imports of services	−6,203.1	−6,170.9	−5,407.6
Balance on goods and services	−12,304.6	−11,639.0	−9,455.1
Primary income received . . .	66.5	66.6	12.9
Primary income paid	−400.3	−665.8	−673.6
Balance on goods, services and primary income	−12,638.4	−12,238.3	−10,115.8
Secondary income received . .	8,088.1	7,335.4	7,512.6
Secondary income paid . . .	−61.0	−122.2	−115.6
Current balance	−4,611.3	−5,025.1	−2,718.8
Direct investment liabilities . .	3,360.4	2,548.7	2,395.8
Other investment assets . . .	171.8	−202.1	909.4
Other investment liabilities . .	2,247.6	1,428.7	29.1
Net errors and omissions . . .	−2,143.3	1,770.2	−1,905.3
Reserves and related items .	−974.8	520.4	−1,289.9

Source: IMF, *International Financial Statistics*.

External Trade

PRINCIPAL COMMODITIES
(distribution by HS, US $ million)

Imports c.i.f.	2019	2020	2021
Vegetables and vegetable products	1,002.3	1,106.1	2,031.1
Cereals	780.5	863.7	1,683.1
Wheat and meslin	459.7	431.2	938.6
Animal, vegetable fats and oils, cleavage products, etc. . .	432.4	898.9	1,397.6
Palm oil and its fractions, whether or not refined	265.6	424.1	883.1
Prepared foodstuffs; beverages, spirits, vinegar; tobacco and articles thereof .	447.2	568.7	857.2
Mineral products	2,651.0	1,735.0	1,101.5
Mineral fuels, oils, distillation products, etc.	2,641.5	1,723.4	1,089.6
Refined petroleum oils . . .	2,433.0	1,582.1	949.1
Chemicals and related products	1,932.5	1,762.1	2,159.9
Pharmaceutical products . . .	638.4	580.5	812.1
Medicaments consisting of mixed or unmixed products for therapeutic or prophylactic uses	557.4	469.1	502.4
Fertilizers	504.1	507.4	590.9
Plastics, rubber, and articles thereof	935.1	872.2	867.9
Plastics and articles thereof . .	697.8	638.8	675.4

Imports c.i.f.—*continued*	2019	2020	2021
Textiles and textile articles .	543.5	658.3	566.4
Iron and steel, other base metals and articles of base metal	1,730.5	1,498.4	1,152.5
Iron and steel	1,017.0	707.1	564.0
Articles of iron and steel . .	411.2	478.8	324.1
Machinery and mechanical appliances; electrical equipment; parts thereof	3,397.6	2,925.2	2,746.0
Boilers, machinery, etc. . . .	2,287.4	1,833.3	1,737.1
Electrical and electronic equipment	1,110.2	1,091.9	1,008.8
Vehicles, aircraft, vessels and associated transport equipment	1,294.9	1,103.6	1,384.7
Vehicles other than railway, tramway	1,177.2	1,036.3	1,196.5
Total (incl. others)	15,575.9	14,134.4	15,290.0

Exports f.o.b.	2019	2020	2021
Live animals and animal products	139.2	111.4	131.1
Meat and edible meat offal . .	77.7	66.6	94.1
Meat of sheep or goats, fresh, chilled or frozen . . .	72.5	64.1	90.5
Vegetables and vegetable products	2,024.5	2,044.0	2,587.8
Live trees, plants, bulbs, roots, cut flowers, etc.	226.4	216.7	290.2
Cut flowers and flower buds for bouquets, fresh or dried . .	200.0	190.2	254.5
Edible vegetables and roots and tubers	547.8	553.3	648.6
Vegetables, fresh or chilled . .	280.7	258.7	270.7
Dried vegetables, shelled . .	188.6	177.0	188.4
Coffee, tea, mate and spices . .	812.5	812.0	1,209.5
Coffee	795.6	795.8	1,189.2
Oil seed, oleagic fruits, grain, seed, fruit, etc.	419.5	439.4	407.2
Oil seeds	341.8	388.4	325.0
Textiles and textile articles .	182.4	155.6	175.6
Machinery and mechanical appliances; electrical equipment; parts thereof .	111.2	63.8	30.8
Total (incl. others)	2,678.5	2,526.2	3,057.6

Source: Trade Map-Trade Competitiveness Map, International Trade Centre, marketanalysis.intracen.org.

PRINCIPAL TRADING PARTNERS
(US $ million)

Imports c.i.f.	2019	2020	2021
Belgium	287.5	147.5	197.9
China, People's Republic . . .	4,283.7	4,169.6	4,035.1
Egypt	201.2	212.8	241.9
France (incl. Monaco) . . .	146.2	226.5	170.8
Germany	318.2	243.4	177.8
India	1,339.5	1,489.1	2,404.0
Indonesia	262.4	322.7	235.6
Italy	298.8	313.9	274.7
Japan	676.7	510.5	358.3
Korea, Republic	184.1	207.9	255.2
Kuwait	1,880.4	585.9	511.1
Malaysia	203.0	266.0	631.2
Morocco	305.4	288.9	364.8
Netherlands	243.0	83.5	139.1

Imports c.i.f.—*continued*	2019	2020	2021
Russia	104.4	53.1	199.8
Saudi Arabia	460.0	362.0	357.4
South Africa	184.1	162.9	126.4
Thailand	140.3	178.3	137.7
Türkiye	713.3	803.2	764.6
Ukraine	315.8	270.1	578.8
United Arab Emirates	454.3	671.5	513.2
United Kingdom	325.6	251.9	206.1
USA	846.2	720.5	1,168.3
Total (incl. others)	15,575.9	14,134.4	15,290.0

Exports f.o.b.	2019	2020	2021
Belgium	66.7	82.9	131.0
China, People's Republic . . .	124.4	91.2	84.5
Djibouti	128.2	108.9	102.9
France (incl. Monaco) . . .	26.2	23.9	35.1
Germany	152.2	138.8	243.9
India	109.3	50.3	101.2
Indonesia	26.8	28.5	32.8
Israel	109.1	98.8	105.9
Italy	60.1	48.9	61.1
Japan	121.6	94.9	106.2
Korea, Republic	49.1	61.1	85.7
Netherlands	190.7	189.7	229.3
Saudi Arabia	177.1	186.9	215.5
Singapore	32.5	56.8	48.1
Somalia	271.9	293.7	360.8
Sudan	46.1	45.5	36.4
Türkiye	49.7	38.8	41.2
United Arab Emirates	154.8	168.9	189.8
United Kingdom	38.2	28.5	37.3
USA	293.4	258.7	330.2
Viet Nam	45.3	70.1	67.5
Yemen	59.1	33.0	31.0
Total (incl. others)	2,678.5	2,526.2	3,057.6

Source: Trade Map-Trade Competitiveness Map, International Trade Centre, \marketanalysis.intracen.org.

Transport

RAILWAYS
(traffic on the Addis Ababa–Djibouti line, fiscal year)*

	2008/09	2009/10
Passengers carried ('000)	55	35
Passenger-km (million)	14	5
Freight carried ('000 tons)	20	2
Freight (million net ton-km)	7	1

* Including traffic on the section of the line that runs through the Republic of Djibouti; data pertaining to freight include service traffic.

2013/14: Passengers carried ('000) 50; Passenger-km (million) 15.

SHIPPING

Flag Registered Fleet
(at 31 December)

	2019	2020	2021
Number of vessels	11	11	11
Displacement ('000 grt) . . .	241.9	241.9	241.9

Source: Lloyd's List Intelligence (www.bit.ly/LLintelligence).

CIVIL AVIATION
(traffic on scheduled services)

	2013	2014	2015
Kilometres flown (million) . .	150	156	179
Passengers carried ('000) . . .	5,672	6,275	7,075
Passenger-km (million) . . .	19,970	22,301	25,118
Total ton-km (million)	791	950	1,229

Source: UN, *Statistical Yearbook*.

2020 (domestic and international): Departures 72,194; Passengers carried 4.9m.; Freight carried 2,897m. ton-km (Source: World Bank, World Development Indicators database).

Tourism

TOURIST ARRIVALS BY COUNTRY OF RESIDENCE

	2018	2019	2020
Canada	21,214	20,278	7,253
China, People's Republic . . .	50,626	41,837	16,569
France	26,804	25,623	6,698
Germany	36,847	36,858	5,311
India	25,066	26,171	13,410
Italy	31,021	29,647	3,194
Kenya	23,380	27,258	18,322
Nigeria	27,422	22,938	59,660
Saudi Arabia	21,054	24,221	1,640
South Africa	17,145	17,171	14,131
Sudan	21,106	23,455	47,656
United Kingdom	42,725	43,295	9,379
USA	147,600	132,884	48,981
Total (incl. others)*	849,122	811,604	518,199

* Including Ethiopian nationals residing abroad.

Tourism receipts (US $ million, excl. passenger transport): 435 in 2017; 969 in 2018; 778 in 2019 (provisional).

Source: World Tourism Organization.

Communications Media

	2016	2017	2018
Telephones ('000 main lines in use)	1,147.0	1,181.0	1,140.0
Mobile telephone subscriptions ('000)	51,224.0	39,600.0	39,540.0
Internet users (% of population) .	15.4	18.6	22.0

2017: Broadband subscriptions, fixed 62,950; Broadband subscriptions, mobile 14,788,000.

2019 (% of population): Internet users 25.0.

Source: International Telecommunication Union.

Education

(2019/20 unless otherwise indicated)

	Institutions	Teachers	Students
Pre-primary	4,117*	35,501	3,599,596
Primary	37,750	537,596	20,419,152
Secondary: grades 9–12 . . .	3,688	12,7741	3,466,972
Secondary: teacher training . .	37*	2,712†	257,247†
Secondary: technical and vocational	919*	27,992†	302,083†
Higher education†	136	32,734	788,033
Government†	38	30,631	679,299
Non-government†	98	2,103	108,734

* 2014/15.
† 2016/17.

Source: Ministry of Education, Addis Ababa.

Pupil-teacher ratio (qualified teaching staff, primary education, UNESCO estimate): 42.2 in 2019/20 (Source: UNESCO Institute for Statistics).

Adult literacy rate (UNESCO estimates): 51.8% (males 59.2%; females 44.4%) in 2017 (Source: UNESCO Institute for Statistics).

Directory

The Constitution

The Constitution of the Federal Democratic Republic of Ethiopia was adopted by the transitional Government on 8 December 1994. The following is a summary of the main provisions of the Constitution, which came into force on 22 August 1995.

GENERAL PROVISIONS

The Constitution establishes a federal and democratic state structure and all sovereign power resides in the nations, nationalities and peoples of Ethiopia. The Constitution is the supreme law of the land. Human rights and freedoms, emanating from the nature of mankind, are inviolable and inalienable. State and religion are separate and there shall be no state religion. The State shall not interfere in religious matters and vice versa. All Ethiopian languages shall enjoy equal state recognition; Amharic shall be the working language of the Federal Government.

FUNDAMENTAL RIGHTS AND FREEDOMS

All persons are equal before the law and are guaranteed equal and effective protection, without discrimination on grounds of race, nation, nationality, or other social origin, colour, sex, language, religion, political or other opinion, property, birth or other status. Everyone has the right to freedom of thought, conscience and religion and the freedom, either individually or in community with others, and in public or private, to manifest his religion or belief in worship, observance, practice and teaching. Every person has the inviolable and inalienable right to life, privacy, and the security of person and liberty.

DEMOCRATIC RIGHTS

Every Ethiopian national, without discrimination based on colour, race, nation, nationality, sex, language, religion, political or other

opinion, or other status, has the following rights: on the attainment of 18 years of age, to vote in accordance with the law; to be elected to any office at any level of government; to freely express oneself without interference; to hold opinions without interference; to engage in economic activity and to pursue a livelihood anywhere within the national territory; to choose his or her means of livelihood, occupation and profession; and to own private property.

Every nation, nationality and people in Ethiopia has the following rights: an unconditional right to self-determination, including the right to secession; the right to speak, to write and to develop its own language; the right to express, to develop and to promote its culture, and to preserve its history; the right to a full measure of self-government which includes the right to establish institutions of government in the territory that it inhabits. Women shall, in the enjoyment of rights and protections provided for by this Constitution, have equal rights with men.

STATE STRUCTURE

The Federal Democratic Republic of Ethiopia shall have a parliamentarian form of government. The Federal Democratic Republic shall comprise nine States. Addis Ababa shall be the capital city of the Federal State.

STRUCTURE AND DIVISION OF POWERS

The Federal Democratic Republic of Ethiopia comprises the Federal Government and the member States. The Federal Government and the States shall have legislative, executive and judicial powers. The House of People's Representatives is the highest authority of the Federal Government. The House is responsible to the people. The State Council is the highest organ of state authority. It is responsible to the people of the State. State government shall be established at state and other administrative levels deemed necessary. Adequate power shall be granted to the lowest units of government to enable the people to participate directly in the administration of such units. The State Council has legislative power on matters falling under state jurisdiction. Consistent with the provisions of this Constitution, the Council has the power to draft, adopt and amend the state constitution. The state administration constitutes the highest organ of executive power. State judicial power is vested in its courts. The States shall respect the powers of the Federal Government. The Federal Government shall likewise respect the powers of the States. The Federal Government may, when necessary, delegate to the States powers and functions granted to it by the Constitution.

THE FEDERAL HOUSES
There shall be two Federal Houses: the House of People's Representatives and the House of the Federation.

Members of the House of People's Representatives shall be elected by the people for a term of five years on the basis of universal suffrage and by direct, free and fair elections held by secret ballot. The House of People's Representatives shall have legislative power in all matters assigned by this Constitution to federal jurisdiction. The political party or coalition of political parties that has the greatest number of seats in the House of People's Representatives shall form and lead the Executive. Elections for a new House shall be concluded one month prior to the expiry of the House's term.

The House of the Federation is composed of representatives of nations, nationalities and peoples. Each nation, nationality and people shall be represented in the House of the Federation by at least one member. Each nation or nationality shall be represented by one additional representative for each one million of its population. Members of the House of the Federation shall be elected by the State Councils. The State Councils may themselves elect representatives to the House of the Federation, or they may hold elections to have the representatives elected by the people directly. The House of the Federation shall hold at least two sessions annually. The term of mandate of the House of the Federation shall be five years. No one may be a member of the House of People's Representatives and of the House of the Federation simultaneously.

PRESIDENT OF THE REPUBLIC
The President of the Federal Democratic Republic of Ethiopia is the Head of State. The House of People's Representatives shall nominate the candidate for President. The nominee shall be elected President if a joint session of the House of People's Representatives and the House of the Federation approves his candidacy by a two-thirds' majority vote. The term of office of the President shall be six years. No person shall be elected President for more than two terms. The President's duties include the opening of the Federal Houses; appointing ambassadors and other envoys to represent the country abroad; granting, upon recommendation by the Prime Minister and in accordance with law, high military titles; and granting pardons.

THE EXECUTIVE
The highest executive powers of the Federal Government are vested in the Prime Minister and in the Council of Ministers. The Prime Minister and the Council of Ministers are responsible to the House of People's Representatives. In the exercise of state functions, members of the Council of Ministers are collectively responsible for all decisions they make as a body. Unless otherwise provided in this Constitution, the term of office of the Prime Minister is the duration of the mandate of the House of People's Representatives. The Prime Minister is the Chief Executive, the Chairman of the Council of Ministers, and the Commander-in-Chief of the national armed forces. The Prime Minister shall submit for approval to the House of People's Representatives nominees for ministerial posts from among members of the two Houses or from among persons who are not members of either House and possess the required qualifications. The Council of Ministers is responsible to the Prime Minister and, in all its decisions, is responsible to the House of People's Representatives. The Council of Ministers ensures the implementation of laws and decisions adopted by the House of People's Representatives.

STRUCTURE AND POWERS OF THE COURTS
Supreme Federal judicial authority is vested in the Federal Supreme Court. The House of People's Representatives may, by a two-thirds' majority vote, establish nationwide, or in some parts of the country only, the Federal High Court and First-Instance Courts it deems necessary. Unless decided in this manner, the jurisdictions of the Federal High Court and of the First-Instance Courts are hereby delegated to the state courts. States shall establish State Supreme, High and First-Instance Courts. Judicial powers, both at federal and state levels, are vested in the courts. Courts of any level shall be free from any interference or influence of any governmental body, governmental official or from any other source. Judges shall exercise their functions in full independence and shall be directed solely by the law. The Federal Supreme Court shall have the highest and final judicial power over federal matters. State Supreme Courts shall have the

highest and final judicial power over state matters. They shall also exercise the jurisdiction of the Federal High Court.

MISCELLANEOUS PROVISIONS
The Council of Ministers of the Federal Government shall have the power to decree a state of emergency in the event of an external invasion, a breakdown of law and order that endangers the constitutional order and cannot be controlled by the regular law enforcement agencies and personnel, a natural disaster or an epidemic. State executives can decree a statewide state of emergency should a natural disaster or an epidemic occur.

A National Election Board independent of any influence shall be established, to conduct free and fair elections in federal and state constituencies in an impartial manner.

The Government

HEAD OF STATE
President: SAHLE-WORK ZEWDE (took office 25 October 2018).

COUNCIL OF MINISTERS
(October 2022)

The Government is formed by members of the Prosperity Party (PP), Ethiopian Citizens for Social Justice (Ezema), the National Movement of Amhara (NaMA) and the Oromo Liberation Front (OLF).

Prime Minister: Dr ABIY AHMED ALI (PP).

Deputy Prime Minister and Minister of Foreign Affairs: DEMEKE MEKONNEN (PP).

Minister of Peace: BINALF ANDUALEM (PP).

Minister of National Defence: Dr ABRAHAM BELAY (PP).

Minister of Trade and Regional Integration: GEBREMESKEL CHALA (PP).

Minister of Finance: AHMED SHIDE (PP).

Minister of Justice: Dr GIDEON TIMOTHEOS (PP).

Minister of Agriculture: OMER HUSEN (PP).

Minister of Industry: MELAKU ALEBEL (PP).

Minister of Innovation and Technology: BELETE MOLLA (NAMA).

Minister of Transport and Logistics: DAGMAWIT MOGES (PP).

Minister of Urban and Infrastructure Development: CHALTU SANI (PP).

Minister of Water and Energy: Dr HABTAMU ITAFA (PP).

Minister of Irrigation and Lowlands Development: AISHA MOHAMMED MUSSA (PP).

Minister of Mines: Dr TAKELE UMA (PP).

Minister of Education: Prof. BERHANU NEGA (Ezema).

Minister of Health: Dr LIYA TADESSE (PP).

Minister of Women and Social Affairs: Dr ERGOGIE TESFAYE (PP).

Minister of Labour and Skills: MUFERIAT KAMIL (PP).

Minister of Culture and Sport: KEJELA MERDASA (OLF).

Minister of Tourism: NASISE CHALI (PP).

Minister of Revenues: LA'QE AYALEW (PP).

Minister of Planning and Development: Dr FITSUM ASSEFA (PP).

MINISTRIES

Office of the President: POB 1031, Addis Ababa; tel. (11) 1551000; e-mail info@thepresidency.gov.et; internet www.thepresidency.gov.et.

Office of the Prime Minister: POB 1031, Addis Ababa; tel. (11) 1400740; e-mail info@pmo.gov.et; internet pmo.gov.et.

Office of the Attorney-General: Bambis, Jomo Kenyatta Ave, POB 1370, Addis Ababa; tel. (11) 5541868; e-mail info@fag.gov.et; internet www.eag.gov.et/am-et.

Ministry of Agriculture: POB 62347, Addis Ababa; tel. (11) 6461971; internet www.moa.gov.et.

Ministry of Culture and Sport: POB 2183, Addis Ababa; tel. (11) 5512310; internet www.moct.gov.et.

Ministry of Education: Arada Sub-City, POB 1367, Addis Ababa; tel. (11) 1553133; e-mail info@moe.gov.et; internet moe.gov.et.

Ministry of Finance: POB 1037, Addis Ababa; tel. (11) 1552400; e-mail infopr@mofed.gov.et; internet www.mofed.gov.et.

Ministry of Foreign Affairs: POB 393, Addis Ababa; tel. (11) 5518928; e-mail spokesperson@mfa.gov.et; internet www.mfa.gov.et.

Ministry of Health: Sudan St, POB 1234, Addis Ababa; tel. (11) 5517011; internet www.moh.gov.et.

Ministry of Industry: Addis Ababa.

Ministry of Innovation and Technology: Alta Bldg, 6th Floor, Mexico Sq., POB 1028, Addis Ababa; tel. (11) 5500191; internet www .mcit.gov.et.

Ministry of Irrigation and Lowlands: Addis Ababa; internet fb .com/MILLsEthiopia.

Ministry of Labour and Skills: Kirkos Kifle Ketema, Wereda 8, Kazanchis, POB 2056, Addis Ababa; tel. (11) 5517080; e-mail molsa@ molsa.gov.et; internet www.molsa.gov.et.

Ministry of Mines: POB 486, Addis Ababa; tel. (11) 5153689; e-mail info@mom.gov.et; internet www.mom.gov.et.

Ministry of National Defence: POB 1373, Addis Ababa; tel. (11) 5551777; internet www.fdredefenceforce.gov.et.

Ministry of Planning and Development: Addis Ababa.

Ministry of Peace: POB 5608, Addis Ababa; tel. (11) 5539719; internet www.mop.gov.et.

Ministry of Revenues: Addis Ababa; tel. (11) 6629843; e-mail nebiyous@revenue.gov.et; internet www.erca.gov.et.

Ministry of Science and Higher Education: Old ERPA Bldg, Arada Sub-City, Churchill Rd, POB 2490, Addis Ababa; tel. (11) 1553133; e-mail moshe@ethernet.edu.et; internet www.moshe.gov .et.

Ministry of Tourism: Addis Ababa.

Ministry of Trade and Regional Integration: Joseph Tito St, Kirikose Sub-City, Woreda 08, POB 704, Addis Ababa; tel. (11) 5518025; e-mail henok_fekadu@yahoo.com; internet www.mot.gov .et.

Ministry of Transport and Logistics: Addis Ababa; tel. (11) 5516166; internet motr.gov.et.

Ministry of Urban and Infrastructure Development: opp. National Bank of Ethiopia, POB 24134/1000, Addis Ababa; tel. (11) 5531688; e-mail mekuria.2000@gmail.com; internet www .mwud.gov.et.

Ministry of Water and Energy: Haile G/Silassie Rd, POB 5744 and 5673, Addis Ababa; tel. (11) 6611111; internet mowie.gov.et.

Ministry of Women and Social Affairs: Kassanchis, POB 1293, Addis Ababa; tel. (11) 8625869; e-mail info@mowsa.gov.et; internet www.mowsa.gov.et.

Regional Governments

Ethiopia comprises 11 regional governments and two chartered cities (Addis Ababa and Dire Dawa), all of which are vested with the authority for self-administration. The executive bodies are respectively headed by Presidents (regional states) and Chairmen (Addis Ababa and Dire Dawa).

PRESIDENTS
(October 2022)

Tigray: Dr ABRAHAM BELAY.
Afar: AWEL ARBA.
Amhara: Dr YILKAL KEFALE.
Oromia: SHIMELIS ABDISSA.
Somali: MUSTAFA MOHAMED OMAR.
Benishangul-Gumuz: ASHADLI HASSEN.
Southern Nations, Nationalities and Peoples: RISTU YIRDAW.
Gambela: OMOT OJULU OBUP.
Harari: ORDIN BEDRI.
Sidama: DESTA LEDAMO.
South West: NEGASH WAGESHO.

CHAIRMEN
(October 2022)

Dire Dawa: AHMED BUH.
Addis Ababa: ADANECH ABIEBIE.

Legislature

FEDERAL PARLIAMENTARY ASSEMBLY

The legislature comprises an upper house, the House of the Federation (Yefedereshn Mekir Bet), with 153 seats (members are selected by state assemblies and serve for a period of five years), and a lower house, the House of People's Representatives (Yehizbtewekayoch Mekir Bet), of no more than 550 directly elected members, who are also elected for a five-year term.

House of the Federation

House of the Federation: Addis Ababa; tel. (11) 1242309; internet www.hofethiopia.gov.et.

Speaker: AGENGEW TESHAGER.

House of People's Representatives

House of People's Representatives: POB 80001, Addis Ababa; tel. (11) 1241000; e-mail info@hopr.gov.et; internet www.hopr.gov .et.

Speaker: TAGESSE CHAFO.

General Election, 21 June 2021, provisional results

Party	Seats
Prosperity Party	410
National Movement of Amhara	5
Ethiopian Citizens for Social Justice	4
Gedeo People's Democratic Organization	2
Independents	4
Total	425*

* No voting took place in three regional states (Harari, Somali and Tigray) and in constituencies in several other regional states. Further elections were held on 30 September 2021 in the regional states of Harari, Somali and the Southern Nations, Nationalities and Peoples.

Election Commission

National Electoral Board of Ethiopia (NEBE): Africa St, Addis Ababa; tel. (11) 5153468; e-mail contact@nebe.org.et; internet nebe .org.et; f. 1993; Chair. BIRTUKAN MIDEKSA.

Political Organizations

A number of new political organizations were formed in 2019–20, following the mergers of several formerly significant parties.

Ethiopian Citizens for Social Justice (Ezema): e-mail ethzema@ gmail.com; internet ethzema.org; f. 2019 following the merger of Patriotic Ginbot 7, the Unity for Democracy and Justice Party, the United Ethiopian Democratic Party, the All Ethiopian Democratic Party, Semayawi, the New Generation Party, and the Gambela Regional Movement; Chair. YESHIWAS ASEFA; Leader Prof. BERHANU NEGA.

Freedom and Equality Party: Adot Multiplex, 4th Floor, House No 606, Wereda 06, Nifas Silk-Lafto Sub-City, Addis Ababa; tel. 953440303; e-mail freedomandequality.et@gmail.com; internet www.fepethiopia.com; Chair. ABDULKADIR ADAM.

Hibr Ethiopia Democratic Party: internet fb.com/ HibirEthiopiaDemocraticParty; f. 2019 following the merger of the Ethiopian Public Movement, the Ethiopian National Transitional Council, the Tusa Ethiopian Renaissance Democratic Organization, the OMO People's Democratic Union and the South Ethiopia Green Stars Coalition.

National Movement of Amhara (NAMA): Chair. BELLETE MOLLA.

Ogaden National Liberation Front (ONLF): Dulqabow D-5, Jijiga; tel. 952456437; e-mail foreign@onlf.org; internet www.onlf .org; f. 1984; seeks self-determination for the Ogaden region; Chair. ABDIRAHMAN MOHAMED SH MAHDI.

Oromo Liberation Front (OLF): POB 73247, Washington, DC 20056, USA; tel. (202) 462-5477; e-mail info@oromoliberationfront .org; internet www.oromoliberationfront.org; f. 1973; seeks self-determination for the Oromo people; participated in the Ethiopian transitional Govt until June 1992; Chair. DAWUD IBSA AYANA; Vice-Chair. ABDULFATTAH A. MOUSSA BIYYO.

Prosperity Party (PP): Addis Ababa; internet prosperity.org.et; f. 1989 as the Ethiopian People's Revolutionary Democratic Front; renamed as above in 2019 following the merger of 8 parties incl. the Amhara Democratic Party, the Oromo Democratic Party and the South Ethiopian People's Democratic Movement; Pres. Dr ABIY AHMED ALI; Vice-Pres ADEM FARAH, DEMEKE MEKONNEN.

Somali People's Democratic Party (SPDP): St Jijiga Somali Regional 365; internet www.spdp.org.et; f. 1998; Chair. AHMED SHIDE; Sec.-Gen. AHMED ARAB ADEN.

Tigray People's Liberation Front (TPLF): internet tplfofficial .org; f. 1975; Chair. Dr DEBRETSION GEBREMICHAEL; Vice-Chair. FETLEWORK GEBRE-EGZIABHER.

Diplomatic Representation

EMBASSIES IN ETHIOPIA

Algeria: Nefas Silk Lafto, Woreda 3, House No. 1348, POB 5740, Addis Ababa; tel. (11) 3719666; e-mail algemb.addis@gmail.com; Ambassador SALAH FRANCIS ELHAMDI.

Angola: Woreda 18, Kebele 26, House No. 6, POB 2962, Addis Ababa; tel. (11) 6180771; Ambassador FRANCISCO JOSÉ DA CRUZ.

Armenia: Sub-city Nifas Silk Lafto, Woreda 03, House No. 2754, POB 18314, Addis Ababa; tel. (11) 3692095; e-mail armembethiopia@mfa.am; Chargé d'affaires a.i. ARTEM AZNAURIAN.

Australia: Turkish Compound, off Cape Verde St, POB 3715, Addis Ababa; tel. (11) 6672678; e-mail adba.info@dfat.gov.au; internet ethiopia.embassy.gov.au; Ambassador JULIA NIBLETT.

Austria: Nifas Silk Lafto, Kifle Ketema 04, House No. 535, Old Airport Area, South Africa Rd, POB 1219, Addis Ababa; tel. (11) 3712144; e-mail addis-abeba-ob@bmeia.gv.at; internet www.bmeia.gv.at/oeb-addis-abeba; Ambassador SIMONE KNAPP.

Azerbaijan: House No. 2467, Kolfe Keranio Sub-City, Woreda, Addis Ababa; tel. (11) 3691586; e-mail azembassy.addis@gmail.com; internet addisababa.mfa.gov.az; Ambassador (vacant).

Bangladesh: Woreda 3, Bole Atlas, POB 5234, Addis Ababa; e-mail mission.addisababa@mofa.gov.bd; internet fb.com/bdembassyaddisababa; Ambassador MD NAZRUL ISLAM.

Belgium: Comoros St, Kebele 8, POB 1239, Addis Ababa; tel. (11) 6611813; e-mail addisababa@diplobel.fed.be; internet ethiopia.diplomatie.belgium.be; Ambassador STEFAAN THIJS.

Benin: Nifas Silk Sub-City, Kebele 04, House No. 990, POB 200084, Addis Ababa; tel. (11) 3722605; e-mail ambaben_addis@yahoo.fr; Ambassador HERVÉ D. DJOKPÉ.

Botswana: Nifas Silk Sub-City, Kebele 04, House No. 1230, POB 22282, Addis Ababa; tel. (11) 715422; e-mail botetho@gov.bw; Ambassador ZENENI SINOMBE.

Brazil: Bole Sub-City, Kebele 2, House No. 2830, POB 2458, Addis Ababa; tel. (11) 6620401; e-mail brasemb.adisabeba@itamaraty.gov.br; internet www.gov.br/mre/pt-br/embaixada-adis-abeba; Ambassador JANDYR FERREIRA DOS SANTOS (designate).

Bulgaria: Bole Kifle Ketema, Kebele 06, Haile Gabreselassie Rd, POB 987, Addis Ababa; tel. (11) 6610032; e-mail bul.addis@gmail.com; internet www.mfa.bg/embassies/ethiopia; Chargé d'affaires e.p. TODOR VASILEV VITEV.

Burkina Faso: Bole Sub-City, Kebele 03, House No. 138, POB 19685, Addis Ababa; tel. (11) 3716972; e-mail ambfet@ethionet.et; Ambassador (vacant).

Burundi: Kirkos Sub-City, Kebele 03, House No. 047, POB 3641, Addis Ababa; tel. (11) 4651300; e-mail burundi.addis@gmail.com; internet burundiembassyethiopia.org; Ambassador WILLY NYAMITWE.

Cabo Verde: Bole Rd, Higher 17, Kebele 19, House No. 107, POB 200093, Addis Ababa; tel. (11) 6610665; Chargé d'affaires a.i. CUSTODIA LIMA.

Cameroon: Bole Rd, Woreda 18, Kebele 26, House No. 168, POB 1026, Addis Ababa; tel. (11) 5504488; e-mail ambcamaa@ethionet.et; Ambassador EWUMBUE MONONO CHURCHILL.

Canada: Nefas Silk Lafto, Kifle Ketema 3, Kebele 4, House No. 122, POB 1130, Addis Ababa; tel. (11) 3170000; e-mail addis@international.gc.ca; internet www.canadainternational.gc.ca/ethiopia-ethiopie/index.aspx; Ambassador STÉPHANE JOBIN.

Chad: Nifas Silk Sub-City, Kebele 01, POB 5119, Addis Ababa; tel. (11) 4180000; e-mail ambatchadaddis@gmail.com; Ambassador MAHAMAT ALI HASSAN.

Chile: Bole Sub-City, Woreda 05, House No. 950/46, POB 46286, Addis Ababa; tel. (11) 6441684; e-mail echile.etiopia@minrel.gob.cl; internet chile.gob.cl/etiopia; Ambassador FERNANDO ZALAQUETT SEPÚLVEDA.

China, People's Republic: Jimma Rd, Woreda 24, Kebele 13, House No. 792, POB 5643, Addis Ababa; tel. (11) 3710010; e-mail chinaemb_et@mfa.gov.cn; internet et.china-embassy.gov.cn; Ambassador ZHAO ZHIYUAN.

Congo, Democratic Republic: Makanisa Rd, Woreda 23, Kebele 13, House No. 1779, POB 2723, Addis Ababa; tel. (11) 3710111; Ambassador JEAN LAON NGANDU.

Congo, Republic: Woreda 3, Kebele 51, House No. 378, POB 5639, Addis Ababa; tel. (11) 5514188; e-mail ambacoaddis@gmail.com; Ambassador DANIEL OWASSA.

Côte d'Ivoire: Woreda 23, Kebele 13, House No. 1308, POB 3668, Addis Ababa; tel. (11) 3712658; e-mail secretariat.addisabeba@diplomatie.gouv.ci; internet ethiopie.diplomatie.gouv.ci; Ambassador ENNIO MAES.

Cuba: Woreda 18, Kebele 35, House No. 192, Kirkos Subcity, POB 90546, Addis Ababa; tel. (11) 4702855; e-mail embacuba@et.embacuba.cu; internet misiones.minrex.gob.cu/es/etiopia; Ambassador JORGE FERNANDO LEFEBRE NICOLÁS.

Czech Republic: Kebele 15, House No. 289, Kirkos Kifle Ketema Rd, POB 3108, Addis Ababa; tel. (11) 5516132; internet www.mzv.cz/addisababa; Ambassador PAVEL MIKEŠ.

Denmark: Bole Subcity, Woreda 03, 629 St, House No. 99/11, POB 12955, Addis Ababa; tel. 911255587; e-mail addamb@um.dk; internet etiopien.um.dk; Ambassador KIRA SMITH SINBERG.

Djibouti: Bole Sub-City, Kebele 03, House No. 003, POB 1022, Addis Ababa; tel. (11) 6613200; e-mail info@ambassadedjibouti-eth.net; internet www.ambassadedjibouti-eth.net; Ambassador ABDI MAHAMOUD AYBEH.

Egypt: Gullele Sub-City, Kebele 02, Madgascar St, POB 1611, Addis Ababa; tel. (11) 1226422; Ambassador MOHAMED OMAR GAD.

Equatorial Guinea: Bole Sub-City, Kebele 03, House No. 2162, POB 246, Addis Ababa; tel. (11) 6626278; e-mail embarge@gmail.com; Ambassador CRISANTOS OBAMA ONDO.

Eritrea: POB 2571, Addis Ababa; tel. (11) 5512844; Chargé d'affaires e.p. BINIAM BERHE.

Eswatini: Bole Kifle Ketema, Kebele 13, House No. 1185, POB 416, Addis Ababa; tel. (11) 6263703; e-mail swaziaddis@ethionet.et; Ambassador (vacant).

Fiji: Addis Ababa; Ambassador Brig.-Gen. MOSESE TIKOITOGA.

Finland: Fitawrari Damtew St, Kirkos Sub-City, Kebele 10, House No. 436, POB 1017, Addis Ababa; tel. (11) 4704390; e-mail sanomat.add@formin.fi; internet finlandabroad.fi/web/eth; Ambassador OUTI HOLOPAINEN.

France: Kabana, POB 1464, Addis Ababa; tel. (11) 1236022; e-mail scacamb@ethionet.et; internet et.ambafrance.org; Ambassador RÉMI MARECHAUX.

Gabon: Woreda 17, Kebele 18, House No. 1026, POB 1256, Addis Ababa; tel. (11) 6611075; e-mail gabonembassy@ethionet.et; Ambassador HERMANN IMMONGAULT.

The Gambia: Kebele 3, House No. 79, POB 60083, Addis Ababa; tel. (11) 8959258; e-mail gambiaembassy.addis@gmail.com; Ambassador JAINABA JAGNE.

Georgia: Kirkos Sub-City, House No. 717, Kebele 02/03, POB 21093/1000, Addis Ababa; tel. (11) 4671999; e-mail addisababa.emb@mfa.gov.ge; internet ethiopia.mfa.gov.ge; Ambassador ZURAB DHAVALISHVILI.

Germany: Yeka Kifle Ketema (Khebena), Woreda 03, POB 660, Addis Ababa; tel. (11) 1235139; e-mail info@addis-abeba.diplo.de; internet addis-abeba.diplo.de; Ambassador STEPHAN AUER.

Ghana: Jimma Rd, Woreda 24, Kebele 13, House No. 108, POB 3173, Addis Ababa; tel. (11) 3711402; e-mail addisababa@mfa.gov.gh; internet addisababa.mfa.gov.gh; Ambassador AMMA ADOMAA TWUM-AMOAH.

Greece: off Debre Zeit Rd, POB 1168, Addis Ababa; tel. (11) 4654911; internet www.telecom.net.et/~greekemb; Ambassador ANNA FARROU.

Guinea: Debre Zeit Rd, Woreda 18, Kebele 14, House No. 58, POB 1190, Addis Ababa; tel. (11) 4669562; e-mail ambaguiaddis@mae.gov.gn; Ambassador GAOUSSOU TOURÉ.

Guinea-Bissau: Addis Ababa; Ambassador (vacant).

Holy See: Makanissa Rd, POB 588, Addis Ababa; tel. (11) 3712100; Apostolic Nuncio ANTOINE CAMILLERI (Titular Archbishop of Skálholt).

India: Arada District, Kebele 13/14, House No. 224, POB 528, Addis Ababa; tel. (11) 6362034; e-mail amb.addisababa@mea.gov.in; internet eoiaddisababa.gov.in; Ambassador ROBERT SHETKINTONG.

Indonesia: Egypt St (Mekanissa Rd), Woreda 05, Kebele 03, House No. 1816, POB 1004, Addis Ababa; tel. (11) 3710121; e-mail addisababa.kbri@kemlu.go.id; internet kemlu.go.id/addisababa; Ambassador AL-BUSYRA BASNU.

Iran: Nifas Silk Sub-City, Kebele 05, POB 1144, Addis Ababa; tel. (11) 3727600; e-mail iranemb.add@mfa.gov.ir; internet ethiopia.mfa.gov.ir; Ambassador SAMAD ALI LAKIZADEH.

Ireland: Kazanches, Guinea Conakry St, POB 9585, Addis Ababa; tel. (11) 5180500; e-mail addisababaembassy@dfa.ie; internet www.dfa.ie/irish-embassy/ethiopia; Ambassador NICOLA BRENNAN.

Israel: Woreda 16, Kebele 22, House No. 283, POB 1266, Addis Ababa; tel. (11) 6460999; e-mail embassy@addisababa.mfa.gov.il; internet embassies.gov.il/addis_ababa; Ambassador ALELIGNE ADMASU.

Italy: Villa Italia, POB 1105, Addis Ababa; tel. (11) 1235684; e-mail ambasciata.addisabeba@esteri.it; internet www.ambaddisabeba.esteri.it; Ambassador AGOSTINO PALESE.

Japan: House No. 431, Bole Sub-City, Woreda 6, POB 5650, Addis Ababa; tel. (11) 6671166; e-mail japan-embassy@ad.mofa.go.jp; internet www.et.emb-japan.go.jp; Ambassador TAKATO ITO.

Jordan: Addis Ababa; Ambassador ZUHAIR AL-NSOUR.

Kazakhstan: Rwanda St, House No. 1185, Kebele 01, Bole City, Addis Ababa; e-mail kazembethiopia@mfa.kz; internet mfa.gov.kz/kz/addis-ababa; Ambassador BARLYBAY K. SADYKOV.

Kenya: Woreda 16, Kebele 1, Comoros St, POB 3301, Addis Ababa; tel. (11) 6610033; e-mail info@kenyaembassyaddis.org; internet addisababa.mfa.go.ke; Ambassador JEAN NJERI KAMAU.

Korea, Democratic People's Republic: Bole Sub-City, Kebele 03, House No. 198, POB 2378, Addis Ababa; tel. (11) 6637430; Ambassador SIM TONG GUK.

Korea, Republic: Jimma Rd, Old Airport Area, POB 2047, Addis Ababa; tel. (11) 3728111; e-mail ethiopia@mofa.go.kr; internet overseas.mofa.go.kr/et-ko/index.do; Ambassador KANG SEOK-HEE.

Kuwait: Woreda 17, Kebele 20, House No. 128, POB 19898, Addis Ababa; tel. (11) 6615411; e-mail kuwait@ethionet.et; Ambassador SHAMLAN AL-ROOMI.

Lesotho: Bole Sub-City, Kebele 03, House No. 2118, Addis Ababa; tel. (11) 6614368; internet lesothoaddis.org; Ambassador MAFA M. SEJANAMANE.

Liberia: Roosevelt St, Woreda 21, Kebele 4, House No. 237, POB 3116, Addis Ababa; tel. (11) 5513655; e-mail liberianembassyethiopia@yahoo.com; Ambassador (vacant).

Libya: Ras Tessema Sefer, Woreda 3, Kebele 53, House No. 585, POB 5728, Addis Ababa; tel. (11) 5511077; Ambassador MAHFUD RAJAB RAHIAM.

Madagascar: Woreda 17, Kebele 19, House No. 629, POB 60004, Addis Ababa; tel. (11) 612555; e-mail emb.mad@ethionet.et; Ambassador (vacant).

Malawi: Cameroon St, POB 2316, Addis Ababa; tel. (11) 6620295; e-mail addis.malawimission@foreignaffairs.gov.mw; internet addismwembassy.gov.mw; Ambassador (vacant).

Mali: Kebele 03, House No. 418, POB 4561, Addis Ababa; tel. (25) 84528589; Ambassador FAFRÉ CAMARA.

Mauritania: Lidete Kifle Ketema, Kebele 2, House No. 431A, POB 200015, Addis Ababa; tel. (11) 3729165; e-mail rimambassade@yahoo.com; Ambassador KHADJETOU M'BAREK FALL.

Mauritius: Kebele 03, House No. 750, POB 200222, Kifle Ketema, Addis Ababa; tel. (11) 6615997; internet addisababa.mauritius .govmu.org; Ambassador DHARMRAJ BUSGEETH.

Mexico: Bole Sub-City, Woreda 05, House No. 950/46, POB 21021, Code 1000, Addis Ababa; tel. (11) 6461479; e-mail embetiopia@sre .gob.mx; internet embamex.sre.gob.mx/etiopia; Ambassador VICTOR MANUEL TREVIÑO ESCUDERO.

Morocco: 210 Bole Rd, POB 60033, Addis Ababa; tel. (11) 5508440; e-mail morocco.emb@ethionet.et; Ambassador NEZHA MHAMMEDI ALAOUI.

Mozambique: Bole Sub-City, Kebele 05, House No. 477, POB 5671, Addis Ababa; tel. (11) 6633811; e-mail embamoc-add@ethionet.et; Ambassador ALFREDO FABIÃO NUVUNGA.

Namibia: Bole Sub-City, Kebele 19, House No. 575, POB 1443, Addis Ababa; tel. (11) 6611966; e-mail nam.emb@ethionet.et; Ambassador EMILIA MKUSA.

Netherlands: Old Airport Zone, Kifle Ketema, Lideta, Kebele 02/03, POB 1241, Addis Ababa; tel. (11) 3711100; e-mail add@minbuza.nl; internet www.netherlandsworldwide.nl/countries/ethiopia; Ambassador HENK JAN BAKKER.

New Zealand: House No. 111, Bole Sub-City, Woreda 09, Addis Ababa; tel. (11) 5151269; e-mail aue@mfat.govt.nz; internet mfat .govt.nz/ethiopia; Ambassador MICHAEL UPTON.

Niger: Woreda 9, Kebele 23, POB 5791, Addis Ababa; tel. (11) 4651175; e-mail ambnigeraddis@yahoo.fr; Ambassador AMADOU HASSANE MAÏ DAWA.

Nigeria: Gulele KK, Kebele 06, House No. 001, POB 1019, Addis Ababa; tel. (11) 1550644; e-mail addis_nigeria@yahoo.com; internet nigerianaddis.org; Ambassador VICTOR ADEKUNLE ADELEKE.

Norway: Nifas Silk Lafto Sub-City, House No. 744, Woreda 4, POB 8383, Addis Ababa; tel. (11) 3170420; e-mail emb.addisabeba@mfa .no; internet www.norway.no/ethiopia; Ambassador STIAN CHRISTENSEN.

Pakistan: Bole Kifle Ketema, Kebele 03, House No. 2038, POB 19795, Addis Ababa; tel. (11) 6188392; e-mail parepaddisababa@gmail.com; internet www.mofa.gov.pk/ethiopia; Ambassador SHOZAB ABBAS.

Poland: Guelele Sub-City, Dej Belay Zeleke Rd, Kebele 08, House No. 583, POB 27207/1000, Addis Ababa; tel. (11) 1574189; e-mail addisabeba.amb.sekretariat@msz.gov.pl; internet www.gov.pl/web/ethiopia/embassy; Ambassador PRZEMYSŁAW BOBAK.

Portugal: Yeshi Bldg, Bole Rd, Addis Ababa; tel. (11) 5575806; e-mail embportaddis@gmail.com; internet adisabeba .embaixadaportugal.mne.gov.pt; Ambassador LUISA FRAGOSO.

Qatar: Bole Rwanda, House No. 928, Woreda 02, Addis Ababa; tel. (11) 6663526; e-mail addisababa@mofa.gov.qa; internet addisababa .embassy.qa; Ambassador HAMAD MOHAMMED ABDULLAH AL-DOSARI.

Romania: Bole Kifle Ketema, Kebele 03, House Nos 9–10, POB 2478, Addis Ababa; tel. (11) 6610156; e-mail roembaddis@ethionet.et; internet addisabeba.mae.ro; Ambassador MARIUS NICOLESCU.

Russian Federation: Kebele 08, Comoros St, POB 1500, Addis Ababa; tel. (11) 6612060; e-mail ethiopia@mid.ru; internet ethiopia .mid.ru; Ambassador YEVGENY TEREKHIN.

Rwanda: Bole Kifle Ketema, Kebele 02, House No. 001, POB 5618, Addis Ababa; tel. (11) 6610300; e-mail ambaddis@minaffet.gov.rw; internet www.rwandainethiopia.gov.rw; Ambassador HOPE TUMUKUNDE GASATURA.

Saudi Arabia: Kirkos Sub-City, Kebele 4, House No. 179B, POB 1104, Addis Ababa; tel. (11) 4425643; internet embassies.mofa.gov .sa/sites/ethiopia; Ambassador Dr FAHAD OBAYDALLAH AL-HUMAYDANI AL-MOTAIRI.

Senegal: Africa Ave, POB 2581, Addis Ababa; tel. (11) 6611376; e-mail ambassene-addis@ethionet.et; Ambassador MOHAMED LAMINE THIAW.

Serbia: Woreda 15, Kebele 26, House No. 923, POB 1341, Addis Ababa; tel. (11) 5517804; e-mail serbambadis@yahoo.com; internet addisababa.mfa.gov.rs; Ambassador ALEKSANDAR RISTIĆ.

Seychelles: Bole Sub-City, Woreda 13, Addis Ababa; tel. (11) 6297721; e-mail sezethiopia@gmail.com; internet fb.com/seychellesembassyaddis; Ambassador CONARD VINCENT MEDRERIC.

Sierra Leone: Bole Sub-City, Woreda 03, POB 5619, Addis Ababa; tel. (11) 6358047; e-mail info@slembassyaddisababa.org; internet slemet.com; Ambassador ADEKUNLE JOLIFF MILTON KING.

Slovakia: Yeka Sub-City, Kebele 2, Woreda 7, POB 6627, Addis Ababa; tel. (11) 6450849; e-mail emb.addisababa@mzv.sk; internet www.mzv.sk/addisabeba; Ambassador DRAHOMIR STOS.

Somalia: Bole Kifle Ketema, Kebele 20, House No. 588, POB 1643, Addis Ababa; tel. (11) 6180673; internet www.ethiopia.somaligov .net; Ambassador ABDULLAHI AHMED JAMA.

South Africa: Nifa Silk Lafto, Kebele 03, South Africa Ave, Old Airport Area, POB 1091, Addis Ababa; tel. (11) 3711002; e-mail admin.addis@dirco.gov.za; internet www .southafricanembassyethiopia.com; Ambassador EDWARD XOLISA MAKAYA.

South Sudan: Bole Olympia, POB 3140/1250, Addis Ababa; tel. (11) 5522636; e-mail embassysouthsudan@yahoo.com; Ambassador JAMES PITIA MORGA.

Spain: Gulele Sub-City, Kebele 19, House No. 036, POB 2312, Addis Ababa; tel. (11) 1230083; e-mail emb.addisabeba@maec.es; internet www.exteriores.gob.es/embajadas/addisabeba; Ambassador MANUEL SALAZAR PALMA.

Sri Lanka: Bole Sub City, POB 5738, Addis Ababa; tel. (11) 6154681; e-mail slemb.ethiopia@gmail.com; internet slembassyethiopia.lk; Ambassador (vacant).

Sudan: Kirkos Sub-City, Kebele 10, House No. 543, POB 1110, Addis Ababa; tel. (11) 5516477; Ambassador JAMAL EL-SHEIKH (recalled in Feb. 2021).

Sweden: Lideta Sub-city, Woreda 09, House No. 891, POB 1142, Addis Ababa; tel. (11) 5180000; e-mail ambassaden.addis-abeba@gov .se; internet www.swedenabroad.se/sv/utlandsmyndigheter/etiopien-addis-abeba; Ambassador HANS LUNDQUIST.

Switzerland: Kolfe Keranyo, Woreda 09, Jimma Rd, Old Airport Area, POB 1106, Addis Ababa; tel. (11) 3711107; e-mail addisababa@eda.admin.ch; internet www.eda.admin.ch/countries/ethiopia/de/home.html; Ambassador TAMARA MONA.

Tanzania: Bole Kifle Ketema, Kebele 03/05, House. No. 2213, POB 1077, Addis Ababa; tel. (11) 6634353; e-mail addisababa@nje.go.tz; internet et.tzembassy.go.tz; Ambassador INNOCENT EUGENE SHIO.

Togo: Nifas Silk Lafto, Kebele 13, House No. 2234, POB 25523, Addis Ababa; tel. (11) 3206515; e-mail togo.emb@ethionet.et; internet ambatogoaddis.com; Ambassador SÉBADÉ TOBA.

Tunisia: Bole Kifle Ketema, Kebele 03, House No 08, POB 100069, Addis Ababa; tel. (11) 6612063; e-mail at.addis@diplomatie.gov.tn; Ambassador ABDELHAMID GHARBI.

Türkiye (Turkey): Bole Sub-City, Kebele 03, House No. 018, POB 1506, Addis Ababa; tel. (11) 6612321; e-mail turk.emb@ethionet.et; internet addisababa.emb.mfa.gov.tr; Ambassador YAPRAK ALP.

Uganda: Kirkos Sub-city, Woreda 02, House No. 383, Meskel Flower, POB 5644, Addis Ababa; tel. (11) 5513088; e-mail addis@mofa.go.ug; internet addisababa.mofa.go.ug; Ambassador REBECCA AMUGE OTENGO.

Ukraine: Woreda 5, Kebele 7, Block 8, House No. 0825, Yeka sub-city, Addis Ababa, POB 18368, Addis Ababa; tel. (11) 6611698; e-mail emb_et@mfa.gov.ua; internet ethiopia.mfa.gov.ua; Chargé d'affaires a.i. OLEKSANDR ZUB.

United Arab Emirates: Nifas Silk Lafto, Kebele 13, House No. 1826, POB 22055, Addis Ababa; tel. (11) 3203680; e-mail addis

.ababa@mofa.gov.ae; Ambassador MOHAMMED SALEM AHMED MUSED AL-RASHIDI.

United Kingdom: Comoros St, POB 858, Addis Ababa; tel. (11) 6170100; e-mail britishembassy.addisababa@fco.gov.uk; internet www.gov.uk/government/world/ethiopia; Ambassador Dr ALASTAIR MCPHAIL.

Uruguay: Woreda 03, St B40-9, House No. 538, Bole Sub-City, Addis Ababa; tel. (11) 6672351; e-mail uruetiopia@mrree.gub.uy; Ambassador NÉSTOR ALEJANDRO ROSA NAVARRO.

USA: Entoto St, POB 1014, Addis Ababa; tel. (11) 1306000; e-mail pasaddis@state.gov; internet et.usembassy.gov; Chargé d'affaires a.i. TRACEY ANN JACOBSON.

Venezuela: Bole K. K., House No. 314–6, POB 15816, Addis Ababa; tel. (11) 6467440; e-mail embavenet@yahoo.es; internet etiopia .embajada.gob.ve; Ambassador MODESTO ANTONIO RUIZ ESPINOZA.

Yemen: Old Airport Rd, Kebele 12, POB 664, Addis Ababa; tel. (11) 3712204; e-mail yemb-addisababa@mofa.gov.ye; Chargé d'affaires a.i. YAHYA AL-IRYANI.

Zambia: Nifas Silk Lafto, Kebele 04, POB 1909, Addis Ababa; tel. (11) 3711302; e-mail zam.emb@ethionet.et; Ambassador (vacant).

Zimbabwe: Bole Sub-City, Kebele 19, House No. 007, POB 5624, Addis Ababa; tel. (11) 6613877; Ambassador Dr TAONGA MUSHAYAVANHU.

Judicial System

The 1994 Constitution stipulates the establishment of an independent judiciary in Ethiopia. Judicial powers are vested in the courts, both at federal and regional state level. The supreme federal judicial authority is the Federal Supreme Court. This court has the highest and final power of jurisdiction over federal matters. The regional states of the Federal Democratic Republic of Ethiopia can establish Supreme, High and First-Instance Courts. The Supreme Courts of the regional states have the highest and the final power of jurisdiction over state matters. They also exercise the jurisdiction of the Federal High Court. According to the Constitution, courts of any level are free from any interference or influence from government bodies, government officials or any other source. In addition, judges exercise their duties independently and are directed solely by the law.

Federal Supreme Court: POB 6166, Addis Ababa; tel. (11) 1553400; e-mail fscpublicrelation@gmail.com; internet www.fsc .gov.et; f. 1995; comprises civil, criminal and military sections; its jurisdiction extends to the supervision of all judicial proceedings throughout the country; the Supreme Court is also empowered to review cases upon which final rulings have been made by the courts (including the Supreme Court) where judicial errors have occurred; Pres. MEAZA ASHENAFI.

Federal High Court: POB 3483, Addis Ababa; tel. (11) 2751911; internet www.fsc.gov.et; hears appeals from the state courts; has original jurisdiction; Pres. BELACHEW ANSHESO.

Religion

About 45% of the population are Muslims and about 40% belong to the Ethiopian Orthodox (Tewahido) Church. There are also significant Evangelical Protestant and Roman Catholic communities. The Pentecostal Church and the Society of International Missionaries carry out mission work in Ethiopia. There are also Hindu and Sikh religious institutions. It has been estimated that 5%–15% of the population follow animist rites and beliefs.

CHRISTIANITY

Ethiopian Orthodox (Tewahido) Church

The Ethiopian Orthodox (Tewahido) Church is one of the five oriental orthodox churches. It was founded in 328 CE. The Supreme Body is the Holy Synod and the National Council, under the chairmanship of the Patriarch (Abune).

Patriarchate Head Office: POB 1283, Addis Ababa; tel. (11) 1116507; e-mail webmaster@ethiopianorthodox.org; internet www .ethiopianorthodox.org; Patriarch (Abune) Archbishop MATHIAS; Gen. Sec. L. M. DEMTSE GEBRE MEDHIN.

The Roman Catholic Church

Bishops' Conference: Ethiopian Episcopal Conference, POB 2454, Addis Ababa; tel. (11) 1550300; e-mail info@cbce-gs.org; f. 1966; Pres. Cardinal BERHANEYESUS DEMEREW SOURAPHIEL (Metropolitan Archbishop of Addis Ababa).

Alexandrian-Ethiopian Rite

Adherents are served by one archdiocese (Addis Ababa) and three dioceses (Adigrat, Bahir Dar-Dessie and Emdeber).

Archbishop of Addis Ababa: Cardinal BERHANEYESUS DEMEREW SOURAPHIEL, Catholic Archbishop's House, POB 21903, Addis Ababa; tel. (11) 1111667; e-mail ecs@telecom.net.et.

Latin Rite

Adherents are served by the eight Apostolic Vicariates of Awasa, Gambela, Harar, Hosanna, Jimma-Bonga, Meki, Nekemte and Soddo, and the Apostolic Prefecture of Robe.

Other Christian Churches

The Anglican Communion: In June 2020 the Episcopal/Anglican Province of Alexandria was inaugurated. This comprises four dioceses, and serves 10 countries across North and East Africa, including Ethiopia. The Archbishop of the Province is the Bishop of Egypt.

Armenian Orthodox Church: St George's Armenian Church, POB 116, Addis Ababa; f. 1923; Deacon VARTKES NALBANDIAN.

Ethiopian Evangelical Church (Mekane Yesus): POB 2087, Jomo Kenyatta Rd, Addis Ababa; tel. (11) 5533293; e-mail eecmyco@ eecmy.org; Pres. Rev. Dr YONAS YIGEZU; f. 1959; affiliated to Lutheran World Fed., All Africa Confed. of Churches and World Council of Churches.

Greek Orthodox Church: POB 571, Addis Ababa; tel. (11) 1226459; Metropolitan of Axum Most Rev. PETROS YIAKOUMELOS.

Seventh-day Adventist Church: POB 145, Addis Ababa; tel. (11) 5511319; e-mail info@ecd.adventist.org; internet www.ecd.adventist .org; f. 1907; Pres. ALEMU HAILE.

ISLAM

Ethiopian Islamic Affairs Supreme Council: Addis Ababa; tel. (11) 3725965; internet fb.com/eiasc; Chair. SHEIKH KIYAR MOHAMED AMAN.

JUDAISM

A phased emigration to Israel of about 27,000 members of the 'Beta Israel' Jewish ethnic group in Ethiopia took place during 1984–91. In February 2003 the Israeli Government ruled that Falashmura (Ethiopian Christians whose forefathers had converted from Judaism) had been forced to convert to Christianity to avoid religious persecution and that they had the right to settle in Israel. In January 2004 Ethiopia and Israel agreed to allow the Falashmura to be flown to Israel; some 17,000 had arrived in Israel by May 2008. The transportation of Falashmura to Israel continued intermittently during 2010–19. An Israeli Government decision made in 2015 stated that all remaining Falashmura were to be evacuated from Ethiopia by the end of 2020; however, this deadline was not met. It was reported in early 2021 that around 7,000 Falashmura remained in Ethiopia, many in camps, awaiting transit to Israel.

The Press

DAILY NEWSPAPERS (PRINT AND ONLINE)

Addis Zemen: POB 30145, Addis Ababa; internet www.ethpress .gov.et/addiszemen; f. 1941; Amharic.

The Daily Monitor: POB 22588, Addis Ababa; tel. (11) 1560788; f. 1993; English; Editor-in-Chief NAMRUD BERHANE TSAHAY.

Ethiopian Herald: POB 30701, Addis Ababa; tel. (11) 6625466; internet www.ethpress.gov.et/herald; f. 1943; English; Editor-in-Chief DAGNE BIAZEN.

Ethiopian Monitor: POB 100057, Addis Abeba; tel. 910927245; e-mail editor@ethiopianmonitor.com; internet ethiopianmonitor .com.

PERIODICALS

Addis Fortune: Tegene Bldg, 7th Floor, House No. 542, Ginbot Haya Ave, Kebele 03, POB 259, Addis Ababa; tel. (11) 4163020; e-mail addisfortune@hotmail.com; internet addisfortune.news; weekly; English; Man. Editor TAMRAT G. GIORGIS; Editor-in-Chief FASIKA TADESSE.

Al-Alem: POB 30232, Addis Ababa; tel. (11) 6625936; f. 1941; publ. by the Ethiopian Press Agency; weekly; Arabic; Editor-in-Chief EYOB GIDEY.

Birritu: National Bank of Ethiopia, POB 5550, Addis Ababa; tel. (11) 5530040; e-mail nbeinfo@nbe.gov.et; internet nbebank.com/ birritu-magazine; f. 1982; quarterly; Amharic and English; banking, insurance and macroeconomic news; owned by National Bank of Ethiopia; Chair. GEBREYESUS GUNTE; Editor-in-Chief ELIAS SALAH.

Capital: Wereda 1, House No. 2, Bole Sub City, POB 95, Addis Ababa; tel. 911226900; e-mail info@capitalethiopia.com; internet www.capitalethiopia.com; f. 1998; weekly; Sunday; business and economics; Man. Editor TEGUEST YILMA; Editor-in-Chief GROUM ABATE.

Ethiopian Reporter: Kebele 03, House No. 2347, POB 7023, Addis Ababa; tel. (11) 6616185; internet www.ethiopianreporter.com; f. 1987; weekly; English and Amharic; Editor-in-Chief ASRAT SEYOUM.

Satenaw: Addis Ababa; e-mail admin@etzena.com; internet www.etzena.com; Chief Editor HENOK ALEMAYEHU; Man. Editor ALYOU TEBEJE.

NEWS AGENCIES

Ethiopian News Agency (ENA): nr Semen Hotel, POB 530, Addis Ababa; tel. (11) 1550011; e-mail info@ena.et; internet www.ena.gov.et; f. 1942; Chair. BEKELE MULETA.

PRESS ASSOCIATIONS

Ethiopian Journalists' Association: POB 30288, Addis Ababa; tel. (11) 1117852; Pres. KEFALE MAMMO.

Ethiopian National Journalists Union: Addis Ababa; e-mail info@enju.org; f. 2003; Pres. ANTENEH ABRAHAM; Vice-Pres. ESHETU GELETU.

Publishers

Addis Ababa University Press: POB 1176, Addis Ababa; tel. (11) 1239746; e-mail yacob.arsano@aau.edu.et; internet www.aau.edu.et/services/university-press; f. 1968; educational and reference works in English and Amharic, general books in English and Amharic; Dir Dr YACOB ARSANO.

Berhanena Selam Printing Enterprise: POB 980, Addis Ababa; tel. (11) 1553233; e-mail bspe@ethbspe.com; internet ethbspe.com; f. 1921; fmrly Govt Printing Press; publishes and prints newspapers, periodicals, books, security prints and other miscellaneous commercial prints; Gen. Man. TEKA ABADI.

Educational Materials Production and Distribution Enterprise (EMPDE): Gured Sholla, POB 5549, Addis Ababa; tel. (11) 6463481; f. 1999; textbook publishers.

Mega Publishing: POB 423, Addis Ababa; tel. (11) 1247839; e-mail info@megabooksplc.com; internet www.megabooksplc.com; f. 2007; general publishers.

Broadcasting and Communications

TELECOMMUNICATIONS

Ethiopian Communications Authority (ECA): New Robel Plaza Bldg, Bole Sub-City, Woreda 03, House No. 2483, POB 9991, Addis Ababa; tel. (11) 6928043; e-mail contact@eca-ethiopia.com; internet eca.et; f. 2019 to replace the Communication and Information Technology Standardization and Regulation Directorate; regulatory authority; aims to promote the devt of high quality, efficient, reliable and affordable telecommunication services in Ethiopia; Dir-Gen. BALCHA REBA.

Ethio Telecom (ETC): POB 1047, Addis Ababa; tel. (11) 5510500; e-mail etcweb@ethionet.et; internet www.ethiotelecom.et; f. 1894; under the management of France Telecom since 2010; Chair. DEBRE TSION GEBRE MICHAEL; CEO FREHIWOT TAMIRU; 57.34m. subscribers.

BROADCASTING

Radio

Afro FM: Addis Ababa; tel. (94) 4335252; e-mail afronewsroom@yahoo.com; internet fb.com/105.3afrofm; f. 2009; broadcasts in English and other foreign languages; Gen. Man. HASIET FISSHA.

Amhara Radio: POB 955, Bahir Dar; tel. 583207207; e-mail ammainfo@amharaweb.com; internet www.amharaweb.com; also operates a local FM radio station, Bahir Dar 96.9 FM; music and light entertainment, news and phone-in programmes; Amharic.

Dire Dawa 106.1 FM: Dire Dawa; f. 2005; govt-owned; Amharic, Oromo and Somali.

Oromia Radio: POB 2919, Adama; f. 2008; govt-owned; regional; broadcasts in Oromo.

Finfine 92.3 FM: POB 2919, Adama; govt-owned.

Harari 101.4 FM: Jinela Woreda, Kebele 14, Harar; f. 2008; state-owned, regional; Amharic and Oromo.

Mekele 104.4 FM: Kedamay Woyane Sub-City, Kebele 16, Mekele; tel. (34) 4406058; e-mail mekellefm@yahoo.com; internet fb.com/104.4FMMekelle; state-owned.

Radio Ethiopia: POB 1020/5544, Addis Ababa; tel. (11) 15156647; f. 1941; Amharic, English, French, Arabic, Afar, Oromifa, Tigre, Tigrinya and Somali; Gen. Man. SOLOMON TESFAYE.

FM Addis 97.1: POB 1020/5544, Addis Ababa; tel. (11) 5157574; e-mail fmaddis97.1@yahoo.com; internet fb.com/FMaddis; music and light entertainment station for Addis Ababa.

Radio Fana: POB 30702, Addis Ababa; tel. (11) 5516777; internet www.fanabc.com; f. 1994; Amharic, Oromo, Somali and Afar; operated by the EPRDF.

Sheger 102.1 FM: Gulele Sub-City, Semien Mazegaja, Addis Ababa; tel. 911208075; e-mail info@shegerfm.com; internet www.shegerfm.com; music and light entertainment; Amharic and English; f. 2000; Gen. Man. TEFERI ALEMU.

Voice of the Revolution of Tigray (Dimtsi Woyane Tigray): POB 450, Mekele; tel. (34) 4410544; e-mail dimtsiweyane@gmail.com; internet dimtsiweyane.com; f. 1985; Tigrinya and Afargna; supports Tigray People's Liberation Front.

Zami 90.7 FM: Lideta Sub-City, Kebele 04/07, Ambassador Theatre Bldg, House No. 904/13A and B, Addis Ababa; tel. (11) 5543319; internet fb.com/Zami90.7; Amharic; current affairs, music and light entertainment.

Television

Dire Dawa Television: Dire Dawa; f. 2005; govt-owned; Amharic, Oromo and Somali; f. 2009.

Ethiopian Broadcasting Corpn (EBC): Churchill Rd, POB 5544, Addis Ababa; tel. (11) 5172539; e-mail ebc@ebc.et; internet ebc.et; f. 2014 to replace the Ethiopian Radio and Television Agency; semi-autonomous station; accepts commercial advertising; programmes transmitted from Addis Ababa to 26 regional stations; CEO FISSEHA YITAGESU.

Kana Television: Zimbabwe St, Addis Ababa; e-mail workhere@kanatelevision.com; internet kanatelevision.com; f. 2016; Exec. Chair. ELIAS SCHULZE.

Oromia Radio and Television Organization: POB, 2919, Adama; internet www.orto.gov.et; f. 2006; govt-owned; regional; part of Oromia Mass Media Agency.

Regulatory Authority

Ethiopia Media Authority (EMA): Haile-Alem Bldg, nr Urael Church, Haile Gebrselassie Rd, Kazanchiz, POB 43142, Addis Ababa; tel. (11) 5538759; e-mail info@ema.gov.et; internet www.ema.gov.et; fmrly Ethiopia Broadcasting Authority; present name adopted in 2021; Dir-Gen. MOHAMED IDRIS MOHAMED.

Finance

BANKING

In 2021 there were 19 banks (of which two were state-owned) and 41 microfinance institutions operating in Ethiopia.

Central Bank

National Bank of Ethiopia: Sudan Ave, POB 5550, Addis Ababa; tel. (11) 5517430; e-mail nbe.edpc@ethionet.et; internet www.nbe.gov.et; f. 1964; bank of issue; Chair. GIRMA BIRRU; Gov. Dr YINAGER DESSIE.

Other Banks

Abay Bank SC: Zequala Complex, Jomo Kenyatta St, City-Kirkos Kebele-17/18, POB 5887, Addis Ababa; tel. (11) 5549731; e-mail info@abaybank.com.et; internet www.abaybank.com.et; f. 2010; Chair. ETHIOPIA TADESSE AKANA; Pres. YEHUALA GESSESSE.

Addis International Bank SC (AdIB): Zequala Complex, Jomo Kenyatta St, POB 2455, Addis Ababa; tel. (11) 5549800; e-mail info@addisbanksc.com; internet www.addisbanksc.com; f. 2011; Chair. KASSAHUN BEKELE; Pres. HAILU ALEMU.

Awash International Bank SC: Awash Towers, Right Side, Africa Ave, Bole Rd, POB 12638, Addis Ababa; tel. (11) 5570167; e-mail contactcenter@awashbank.com; internet www.awashbank.com; f. 1994; Chair. TABOR WAMI; Pres. TSEHAY SHIFERAW.

Bank of Abyssinia SC: Red Cross Bldg, Ras Desta Damtew Ave, POB 12947, Addis Ababa; tel. (11) 5514130; e-mail info@bankofabyssinia.com; internet www.bankofabyssinia.com; f. 1905; closed 1935, reopened 1996; commercial banking services; Chair. MESERET TAYE; CEO BEKALU ZELEKE.

Berhan International Bank SC: POB 387, Addis Ababa; tel. (11) 6185732; e-mail info@berhanbanksc.com; internet www .berhanbanksc.com; f. 2009; Chair. GUMACHEW KUSSE; Pres. ABRAHAM ALARO.

Bunna International Bank SC: Wollo Sefer, Addis Ababa; tel. (11) 1580825; e-mail info@bunnabanksc.com; internet bunnabanksc .com; f. 2009; Chair. Dr SEWALE ABATE; Pres. MULUGETA ALEMAYEHU.

Commercial Bank of Ethiopia (CBE): Gambia St, POB 255, Addis Ababa; tel. (11) 1228755; e-mail cbe@combanketh.et; internet combanketh.et; f. 1943; reorg. 1996; state-owned; Chair. TEKLEWOLD ATNAFU; Pres. ABIE SANO.

Dashen Bank: Beklobet, Garad Bldg, Debre Zeit Rd, POB 12752, Addis Ababa; tel. (11) 5183091; e-mail info@dashenbanksc.com; internet www.dashenbanksc.com; f. 1995; Chair. (vacant); Pres. ASFAW ALEMU.

Debub Global Bank SC: National Tower, Woreda 07, Kirkose Sub-City, POB 100743, Addis Ababa; tel. (11) 5581245; e-mail info@ debubglobalbank.com; internet www.debubglobalbank.com; f. 2012; Chair. NUREDIN AWOL YISHAK; Pres. Dr TESFAYE BORU LELISSA.

Development Bank of Ethiopia (DBE): Josef Tito St, POB 1900, Addis Ababa; tel. (11) 5511188; e-mail dbe@ethionet.et; internet www.dbe.com.et; f. 1909; provides devt finance for industry and agriculture, technical advice and assistance in project evaluation; state-owned; Chair. TEGEGNEWORK GETTU; Pres. HAILEYESUS BEKELE.

Enat Bank: Kirkos Sub-City, Woreda 8, Jomo Kenyatta Ave, POB 18401, Addis Ababa; tel. (11) 5507074; e-mail enat@enatbanksc.com; internet www.enatbanksc.com; f. 2012; Chair. HANNA TILAHUN; Pres. ERMIAS ANDARGE.

Lion International Bank SC (LIB): Lex Plaza Bldg, Haile G/ Selassie Ave, Addis Ababa; tel. (11) 6626000; e-mail info@ anbesabank.com; internet www.anbesabank.com; f. 2006; Chair. Prof. TASSEW WOLDEHANNA KAHSAY; Pres. GETACHEW SOLOMON.

NIB International Bank SC: Africa Ave, Dembel City Centre, 6th Floor, POB 2439, Addis Ababa; tel. (11) 5503304; e-mail nibcontact@ nibbanksc.com; internet www.nibbanksc.com; f. 1999; Chair. WOLDETENSAIE W/GIORGIS; Pres. GENENE RUGA.

Oromia International Bank SC: Bole Rd, POB 27530, Addis Ababa; tel. (11) 5572113; e-mail info@orointbank.com; internet www.orointbank.com; f. 2008; Chair. OBBO ASEGID REGASSA; Pres. OBBO TEFERI MEKONNEN.

United Bank SC: Beklobet, Mekwor Plaza Bldg, Debe Zeit Rd, Kirkos District, Kebele 06, POB 19963, Addis Ababa; tel. (11) 4655222; e-mail hibretbank@ethionet.et; internet www .unitedbank.com.et; f. 1998; commercial banking services; Chair. ZAFU EYESSUSWERK ZAFU; Pres. TAYE DIBEKULU.

Wegagen Bank SC: Wegagen Tower, Ras Mekonen St, POB 1018, Addis Ababa; tel. (11) 8787921; e-mail info@wegagen.com; internet www.wegagenbanksc.com; f. 1997; commercial banking services; Chair. ABDISHU HUSSIEN; Pres. and CEO AKILILU WUBET.

Zemen Bank: Josef Tito St, POB 1212, Addis Ababa; tel. (11) 5501111; e-mail customerservice@zemenbank.com; internet www .zemenbank.com; f. 2008; Chair. ABEBE DINKU; Pres. and CEO DEREJE ZEBENE.

Bankers' Associations

Ethiopian Bankers' Association: Lion Bldg 2, 3rd Floor, Meakel Sq., POB 23850, Addis Ababa; tel. (11) 5533874; e-mail ethbankers@ yahoo.com; internet ethiopianbankers.com; f. 2001; Pres. ADDISU HABA; Sec.-Gen. TEGENE SISAY.

INSURANCE

In 2021 there were 18 insurance companies Ethiopia.

Abay Insurance SC: Bambis Enat Tower, 2nd Floor, Addis Ababa; tel. (11) 5536333; internet www.abayinsurancesharecompany.com; f. 2010; Chair. MITIKU BEYENE; CEO ALEMNEW TEGEN.

Africa Insurance Co: Africa Ave, POB 12941, Addis Ababa; tel. (11) 6637716; e-mail info@africainsurancesc.com; internet africainsurancesc.com; f. 1994; Man. Dir and CEO KIROS JIRANIE.

Awash Insurance Co: Awash Tower, Sengatera, Ras Abebe Aregay St, POB 12637, Addis Ababa; tel. (11) 5570001; e-mail aic@ethionet .et; internet www.awashinsurance.com; f. 1994; Chair. HAMBISSA WAKWAYA; CEO TSEGAYE KEMSI.

Berhan Insurance SC: Yeshitam Bldg, Debrezeit Rd, POB 9266, Addis Ababa; tel. (11) 4674431; e-mail berhaninsurance@yahoo.com; internet berhaninsurance.com; f. 2010; general insurance; Chair. TEWODROS MEHERET; Man. Dir ALEMAYEHU TEFERA.

Ethio Life and General Insurance SC: Kirkos Sub-City, Keble 17/ 18, Ziquala Complex, Jomo Kenyatta St, POB 170791, Addis Ababa; tel. (11) 5549650; e-mail elig.insurance@ethionet.et; internet www .ethiolifeandgeneralinsurance.com; Chair. YOSEPH ENDESHAW; Gen. Man. SHIMELES G/GIORGIS.

Ethiopian Insurance Corpn: POB 2545, Addis Ababa; tel. (11) 5512400; e-mail eic.md@ethionet.et; internet www.eic.com.et; f. 1976; life, property and legal liabilities insurance cover; Man. Dir NETSANET LEMESSA.

Global Insurance Co SC: Gobena Aba Tigu St, Somale Tera, POB 180112, Addis Ababa; tel. (11) 1567400; e-mail info@ globalinsurancesc.com; internet globalinsurancesc.com; f. 1997; Chair. AHMED A. SHERIEF; CEO YAHYA MOHAMMED AFFAN.

Lion Insurance Co SC: Haile G/Selasie Ave, Comet Bldg, POB 26281/1000, Addis Ababa; tel. (11) 6187000; e-mail lioninsurance@ ethionet.et; internet www.anbessainsurance.com; f. 2007.

National Insurance Co of Ethiopia: Kirkos Sub-City, ZEFCO Bldg, Debre Zeit Rd, K05/06/07, House No. 894, POB 12645, Addis Ababa; tel. (11) 4661129; e-mail info@niceinsurance-et.com; internet www.niceinsurance-et.com; Chair. GEBEYEHU BEKELE; Man. Dir and CEO TESFAYE DEBELLA.

NIB Insurance Co: Dembel City Center, 2nd, 3rd and 11th Floors, Africa Ave, Bole Rd, POB 285, Addis Ababa; tel. (11) 5528195; e-mail nibinsgm@ethionet.et; internet www.nibinsurancethiopia.com; f. 2002; Chair. ABERA SHIRE; Gen. Man. ZUFAN ABEBE.

Nile Insurance Co: Nile Insurance Bldg, Nations and Nationalities Sq., POB 12836, Addis Ababa; tel. (11) 4426000; e-mail info@ nileinsurancesc.com; internet nileinsurancesc.com; f. 1995; Chair. MEKEDES AKLILU; CEO NIGUSU ANTENEH.

Nyala Insurance SC: Protection House, Mickey Leland St, POB 12753, Addis Ababa; tel. (11) 6626667; e-mail nisco@ethionet.et; internet www.nyalainsurance.com; Chair. KEMAL MOHAMMED; CEO YARED MOLA.

Oromia Insurance Co SC (OIC): Oromia International Bank Bldg, Africa Ave, Olympia Area, POB 10090, Addis Ababa; tel. (11) 5572121; e-mail oromiainsurance@ethionet.et; internet www .oromiainsurancecompany.com.et; f. 2009; Chair. ABERRA BEKELE; CEO ASFAW BENTI.

United Insurance Co SC: Kirkos Sub-City, Alpaulo Bldg, Debrezeit Rd, Woreda 06, POB 1156, Addis Ababa; tel. (11) 5515656; e-mail united.insurance@unic-ethiopia.com; internet www.unicportal.com .et; Chair. MULUALEM BIRHANE; Man. Dir MESERET BEZABEH.

Trade and Industry

GOVERNMENT AGENCIES

Agricultural Transformation Agency: off Meskal Flower Rd, Addis Ababa; tel. (11) 5570678; e-mail info@ata.gov.et; internet www .ata.gov.et; f. 2010; secretariat of the Agricultural Transformation Council chaired by the Prime Minister; CEO Dr MANDEFRO NIGUSSIE.

Ethiopian Investment Commission (EIC): POB 2313, Addis Ababa; tel. (11) 5510033; e-mail info@eic.gov.et; internet www .investethiopia.gov.et; f. 1992 as Ethiopian Investment Agency; present name adopted in 2014; Commr LELISE NEME.

Public Enterprises Holding and Administration Agency: POB 11835, Addis Ababa; tel. (11) 6610641; internet www.pehaa.gov.et; f. 2018.

DEVELOPMENT ORGANIZATIONS

Entrepreneurship Development Center: Nega City Mall Bldg, 3rd Floor, Kazanchis, Addis Ababa; tel. (11) 5571150; e-mail info@ edcethiopia.org; internet edcethiopia.org; f. 2013 by the Ministry of Urban Development, Housing and Construction in partnership with the United Nations Development Programme; CEO Dr HASSEN HUSSEIN.

Ethiopian Institute of Agricultural Research (EIAR): POB 2003, Addis Ababa; tel. (11) 6454452; e-mail eiar@eiar.gov.et; internet www.eiar.gov.et; f. 1966; Dir-Gen. Dr FETO ESIMO.

CHAMBERS OF COMMERCE

Ethiopian Chamber of Commerce and Sectorial Associations: Mexico Sq., POB 517, Addis Ababa; tel. (11) 5514005; e-mail info@ ethiopianchamber.com; internet ethiopianchamber.com; f. 1947; regional chambers in 18 regions; Pres. MELAKU EZEZEW; Sec.-Gen. YESUF ADEMNUR.

Addis Ababa Chamber of Commerce and Sectoral Associations: POB 2458, Addis Ababa; tel. (11) 5518055; e-mail info@ addischamber.com; internet addischamber.com; f. 1947; Pres. MESENBET SHENKUTE; Sec.-Gen. GETACHEW REGASSA.

INDUSTRIAL AND TRADE ASSOCIATIONS

Coffee Plantation Development Enterprise (CPDE): Deber Zeit Rd, POB 4363, Addis Ababa; tel. (11) 4670688; f. 1993; Dir-Gen. EPHREM MERSIHE HAZEN.

Ethiopia Commodity Exchange (ECX): Al-Sam Tower 2, 3rd Floor, Lideta, POB 17341, Addis Ababa; tel. (11) 5547001; internet www.ecx.com.et; f. 2008; trading of agricultural produce; Chair. Dr YINAGER DESSIE; CEO WONDIMAGEGNEHU NEGERA.

Ethiopian Association of Basic Metal and Engineering Industries: Bole Sub-City, House No. 0377, Addis Ababa; tel. (11) 6293429; e-mail eabmei@ethionet.et; internet www.eabmei.org; Pres. ASEGED MAMMO; Gen. Man. SOLOMON MULUGETA.

Ethiopian Fruit and Vegetable Marketing Share Co (Etfruit): POB 2374, Addis Ababa; tel. (11) 4163665; e-mail etfruit@ethionet .et; internet www.etfruit.et; f. 1980; sole wholesale domestic distributor and exporter of fresh and processed fruit and vegetables, and floricultural products; CEO MENGISTU KEBEDE.

Ethiopian Grain Trade Enterprise (EGTE): Kirkos Sub-City, Debrezit Rd, POB 3321, Addis Ababa; tel. (11) 4652436; e-mail info@ egte-ethiopia.com; internet www.egte-ethiopia.com; f. 1949 as Grain Board; Gen. Man. BERHANE HAILU.

Ethiopian Horticulture Producer Exporters Association (EHPEA): NB Business Center, Rm 603, 6th Floor, Micky Leyland Ave, POB 22241, Addis Ababa; tel. (11) 6636750; e-mail info@ehpea .org; internet www.ehpea.org; f. 2002; Chair. ZELALEM MESSELE; Exec. Dir TEWODROS ZEWDIE.

Ethiopian Industrial Inputs Development Enterprise: Addis Ababa; f. 2015; CEO WONDALE HABTAMU.

Ethiopian Petroleum Supply Enterprise (EPSE): POB 3375, Addis Ababa; tel. (11) 5512938; e-mail eth-petroleum@ethionet.et; internet www.epse.gov.et; f. 2012 following merger of the Ethiopian Petroleum Supplier Enterprise and the National Petroleum Depot Administration; CEO TADESSE HAILEMARIAM.

Ethiopian Pharmaceuticals Supply Agency (EPSA): POB 21904, Addis Ababa; tel. (11) 2763276; e-mail info@epsa.gov.et; internet epsa.gov.et; fmrly Pharmaceuticals Fund and Supply Agency; present name adopted 2019; Dir-Gen. Dr ABDULKEDIR GELGELO.

Ethiopian Pulses, Oilseeds and Spices Processors Exporters' Association (EPOSPEA): Rebeqa Bldg, Haile Gebrselassie Rd, POB 8686, Addis Ababa; tel. (11) 6623545; e-mail epospea@gmail .com; internet www.epospeaeth.org; f. 1975; Pres. SISAY ASMARE.

Ethiopian Sugar Corpn: Genete Limate Bldg, Office No. 755/29-3, Africa Ave, Woreda 3, Bole Sub-City, POB 20034, Code 1000, Addis Ababa; tel. (11) 5526653; e-mail info@ethiosugar.com; internet etsugar.com; f. 2010 to replace Ethiopian Sugar Development Agency; CEO WEYO ROBA.

Merchandise Wholesale and Import Trade Enterprise (MEWIT): Addis Ababa; tel. (11) 1114566; f. 1993 following merger of the Ethiopian Domestic Distribution Corpn and the Ethiopian Import Export Corpn; import of building materials, general merchandise, foodstuffs, medicine, automobiles, etc.; Gen. Man. GEMEDA ALEME.

Metals and Engineering Corpn (METEC): POB 21431, 1000 Addis Ababa; tel. (11) 5541572; internet www.metec.gov.et; f. 2010; comprises 15 semi-autonomous cos; Dir-Gen Brig.-Gen. AHMED HAMZA.

Natural Gum Processing and Marketing Enterprise: POB 62322, Addis Ababa; tel. (11) 5527082; e-mail natgum@ethionet.et; internet naturalgum.diytrade.com; f. 1976; state-owned; Gen. Man. TEKLEHAIMANOT NIGATU BEYENE.

Oromia Seed Enterprise: Balker Tower, 3rd and 4th Floors, POB 312, Addis Ababa; tel. (11) 4662512; e-mail oromiyaseed2007@gmail .com; internet www.oromiaseedenterprise.com; f. 2008; state-owned; Gen. Man. ASHINIE BOGALE GONFA.

EMPLOYERS' ORGANIZATION

Ethiopian Employers' Federation: Kirkos Sub-City, Wereda 01, Bambis, POB 2536, Addis Ababa; tel. (11) 5500248; e-mail info@ eef-ethiopia.org; internet www.eef-ethiopia.org; f. 1997; Pres. DAWIT MOGES; Exec. Dir ASMERA DEFA.

UTILITIES

Electricity

Ethiopian Energy Authority: Addis Ababa; tel. (11) 507735; e-mail energyauthority2012@gmail.com; internet www.eea.gov.et; regulatory authority; Exec. Dir GETAHUN MOGES.

Ethiopian Electric Power (EEP): Kirkos Sub-City, Meba Bldg, POB 15881, Addis Ababa; tel. (11) 5580607; internet www.eep.gov.et; f. 2013 as a successor co to Ethiopian Electric Power Corpn; CEO ASHEBER BALCHA.

Ethiopian Electric Utility (EEU): POB 1233, Addis Ababa; tel. (11) 1550811; e-mail eeucommunication@gmail.com; internet www .eeu.gov.et; f. 2013 following division of the Ethiopian Electric Power Corpn; CEO SHIFERAW TELILA.

Water

Addis Ababa Water and Sewerage Authority: POB 1505; Addis Ababa; tel. (11) 6674036; e-mail aawsa.ha@ethionet.et; internet aawsa.gov.et; f. 1971; CEO ZERIHUN ABATE.

MAJOR COMPANIES

Abyssinia Cements PLC: POB 122014, Addis Ababa; tel. (11) 6639755; f. 2007.

Addis Ababa Tannery Share Co.: Kolfe Keranio Sub-City, Woreda 14, ASCO Area, POB 22498, Addis Ababa; tel. (11) 5547186; e-mail aat@ethionet.et; Gen. Man. ENDRIS IBRAHIM.

Ambo Mineral Water Factory: POB 1805, Addis Ababa; tel. (11) 4713199; e-mail info@ambowater.com; internet fb.com/ ambomineralwater.

Amibara Business Group: Gotera Beside Shell Depot, Addis Ababa; tel. (11) 4407503; e-mail info@amibara.com; internet www .amibara.com; Man. Dir SHEIK YUSUF OMAR.

Anbessa Shoe Share Co: Woreda 2, House No. 202, Akaki Kality Sub-City, Addis Ababa; tel. (11) 4715454; e-mail marketing@ anbessashoesc.com; internet www.anbessashoesc.com; f. 1935; nationalized in 1975; returned to private ownership in 2011; Gen. Man. BAMLAKU DEMISSIE.

Avon Industries PLC: Woreda 7, Avon Blk, Akaki Kality Sub City, Kality Industrial Area, POB 120544, Addis Ababa; tel. 944747037; e-mail gm.avonplc@gmail.com; f. 2003; plastic manufactures.

Belayneh Kindie Import, Export and Transport Enterprise: M. K. Business Center, 6th Floor, Mahatama Ghandi St, POB 29118, Addis Ababa; tel. (11) 1118740; e-mail belaynehkindie@gmail.com; internet www.belaynehkindie.com; CEO BELAYNEH KINDIE.

Bedele Brewery: POB 75, Addis Ababa; tel. 474450147; f. 1993; subsidiary of Heineken NV (Netherlands) since 2011.

BGI Ethiopia PLC: Mexico Area, POB 737, Addis Ababa; tel. (11) 5515196; e-mail info@bgiethiopia.com; internet www.bgiethiopia .com; f. 1997; operates three breweries, at Addis Ababab, Awasa and Kombolcha, and one winery at Zeway; CEO LAURENT LESCUYER.

Dalol Oil Share Co: S. C. Bldg, 2nd Floor, POB 8049, Addis Ababa; tel. (11) 6672501; e-mail info@daloloil.com; internet www.daloloil .com; CEO TADESSE GIRMA.

Ethiopia Plastic Share Co: POB 2340, Addis Ababa; tel. (11) 5512666; e-mail ethplast@ethionet.et; internet www.ethioplastic .com.et; state-owned.

Ethiopia Tannery Share Co: Addis Ababa; f. 1975; privatized in 2010; Gen. Man. JASON PERRY.

Ethiopian Minerals Development Share Co (EMDSC): Addis Ababa; tel. (11) 6632290; e-mail eemindvt@ethionet.et; internet www.emdsc.org.et; f. 1995; present name adopted in 2000; Gen. Man. Dr ZERIHUN DESTA.

Ethiopian Steel PLC: Akaki Kaliti, Debrazid Rd, POB 8692, Addis Ababa; tel. (11) 4342719; e-mail esplc.enquiries@safalgroup.com; internet www.ethiopiansteelplc.com; f. 1996.

The Ghions: Addis Ababa; tel. (11) 2793360; e-mail ghiongas@ ethionet.et; internet www.ghions.com.et; conglomerate comprising Ghion Industrial and Commercial PLC, Ghion Industrial and Chemical PLC, Ghion Gas PLC, Ghion Transport PLC, etc.

Great Abyssinia PLC: POB 33136, Addis Ababa; tel. (11) 8605266; e-mail info@greatabyssiniaplc.com; internet greatabyssinia.com; beverages and printing.

Habesha Brewery: Yeka Sub-City, Waryt Bldg, 5th Floor, House No. 934/01, Kebele 12/08, POB 197, Addis Ababa; tel. (11) 6625655; e-mail info@habeshabreweries.com; internet www .habeshabreweries.com; f. 1960; CEO ZEWDU NEGATE.

Habesha Cement Share Co: POB 3317, Addis Ababa; tel. (11) 8601314; e-mail info@hagbes.com; internet www.habeshacement .com.et; Chair. MESFIN ABI.

Hagbes PLC: Airport Rd, POB 1044, Addis Ababa; tel. (11) 6639191; e-mail info@hagbes.com; internet www.hagbes.com; f. 1957; importation and distribution of machinery.

Medtech Ethiopia PLC: Bole Sub-City, Kebele 11, House No. 304, POB 12528, Addis Ababa; tel. (11) 6299915; e-mail info@ medtechethiopiaplc.com; internet www.medtechethiopiaplc.com; manufacturer and supplier of medicine and medical equipment; Man. Dir MOHAMMED NURI.

MIDROC Ethiopia PLC: POB 8677, Addis Ababa; tel. (11) 5549969; e-mail mid.pr@ethionet.et; internet www.midroc-ethiopia .com.et; Chair. SHEIKH MOHAMMED HUSSEIN ALI AL-AMOUDI; CEO ABENNET GEBRE-MESKEL.

Derba MIDROC Cement PLC: Nani Bldg, 9th–12th Floor, Ras Desta Damitew St, POB 23202, Addis Ababa; tel. (11) 5549888; e-mail info@derbacement.com; internet www.derbacement.com; f. 2012; mnfrs of cement; CEO HAILE ASSEGDIE.

Ethio Agri-CEFT: Nefas Silk Lafto, Woreda 03, House No. 1009, Lasetho Ave, Addis Ababa; tel. (11) 3690379; e-mail esake21@ yahoo.com; internet www.ethioagriceft.com; f. 1998; Gen. Man. ESAYAS KEBEDE.

Ethio-Leather Industry PLC (ELICO): House No. 138, Akaki Kality Sub-City, Woreda 6, POB 9281, Addis Ababa; tel. (11) 4400773; e-mail elicogm@elicoplc.com.et; internet www.elicoplc .com.et; f. 1997; Gen. Man. Ambassador BIRUK DEBEBE.

Star Soap and Detergent Industries Co: POB 5521, Addis Ababa; tel. (11) 4392036; internet www.star-soap.com.

Moplaco Trading PLC: Bole Kifle Ketema, K. 14, POB 3035, Addis Ababa; tel. (11) 6455999; e-mail info@moplaco.com; internet www .moplaco.com; f. 1971; coffee exporter; Gen. Man. HELEANNA GEORGALIS.

Mugher Cement Enterprise: POB 5782, Addis Ababa; tel. (11) 4420688; e-mail info@mughercement.com.et; internet www .mughercement.com.et; f. 1999, following amalgamation of the Mugher Cement Factory and the Addis Ababa Cement Factory; state-owned; Dir-Gen. FEKADU DEME.

National Cement Share Co: POB 94, Dire Dawa; tel. (25) 1113440; e-mail sales@nationalcementsc.com; internet nationalcementsc .com; f. 2005; owned by East African Mining Corpn; cement; CEO EGZIAEL BUZUAYEHU.

National Oil Ethiopia PLC (NOC): Airport Rd, POB 951, Addis Ababa; tel. (11) 6639494; e-mail info@noc.com.et; internet www .nocethiopia.com; f. 2004; CEO TADESSE TILAHUN.

SUR Construction PLC: Gabon St, POB 34360, Addis Ababa; tel. (11) 4668650; internet www.sur.com.et; f. 1992; Gen. Man. TADESSE YEMANE.

TotalEnergies Ethiopia Share Co: Mullege Bldg, 7th Floor, POB 1462, Addis Ababa; tel. (11) 4668327; e-mail contact@total.com.et; internet totalenergies.et; fmrly Total Ethiopia Share Co; present name adopted 2021; Man. Dir THIBAULT LESUEUR.

TRADE UNIONS

Confederation of Ethiopian Trade Unions (CETU): POB 3653, Addis Ababa; tel. (11) 5155473; internet www.cetu.org.et; f. 1975; Pres. KASSAHUN FOLLO; Sec.-Gen. BERHANU DERIBA.

The National Federation of Farm, Plantation, Fishery and Agro Industry Trade Unions: POB 100637, Addis Ababa; tel. (11) 5155965; e-mail abyotta@gmail.com; Pres. GEBEYEHU ADUGNA.

Ethiopian Teachers Asscn (ETA): Lideta Sub-City, Kebele 53, Sudan Ave, POB 13205, Addis Ababa; tel. (11) 5524235; e-mail eta@ ethionet.et; internet www.ethiopianteachers.org; f. 1949; Pres. YOHANNES BENTI; Gen. Sec. TILAHUN TAREKEGN.

Transport

RAILWAYS

Railway construction was a central component of Ethiopia's 2010–15 five-year plan to boost economic growth. In 2010 construction of a 5,000-km railway network to link Addis Ababa with various parts of the country was started. Phase one of the five-year project included the construction of a new 2,000-km line to the border with Djibouti. Under phase two, work commenced in late 2011 on a 34.3-km light railway network in Addis Ababa; the construction of the network was completed in January 2015 and it commenced operating in September.

Ethio-Djibouti Railway (EDR): POB 41100, Addis Ababa; tel. (11) 8721234; e-mail admin@edr.gov.et; internet edr.gov.et; f. 2017; jtly owned by Govts of Ethiopia and Djibouti; Dir-Gen. TILAHUN SARKA.

Ethiopian Railways Corporation (ERC): POB 27558/1000, Addis Ababa; tel. (11) 6189060; internet www.fb.com/ Ethiopian-Railways-Corporation-1383526198555601; f. 2007; CEO Dr SINTAYEHU WOLDEMICHAE.

ROADS

A highway links Addis Ababa with Nairobi in Kenya, forming part of the Trans-East Africa Highway.

Ethiopian Road Transport Authority: POB 2504, Addis Ababa; tel. (11) 5510244; e-mail kasahun_khmariam@yahoo.com; internet www.rta.gov.et; enforces road transport regulations, promotes road safety, registers vehicles and issues driving licences; Gen. Man. KASAHUN H. MARIAM.

Ethiopian Roads Authority: POB 1770, Addis Ababa; tel. (11) 5517170; internet www.era.gov.et; f. 1951; construction and maintenance of roads, bridges and airports; Dir-Gen. AREYA GIRMAY.

Sky Bus Transport System SC: Addis Ababa; tel. (11) 4673331; internet www.skybusethiopia.com; f. 2007; intercity coach service to 8 destinations within Ethiopia; Chief Exec. SOLOMON GAREDEW BEKELE.

SHIPPING

The formerly Ethiopian-controlled ports of Massawa and Assab now lie within the boundaries of the State of Eritrea. Although an agreement exists between the two Governments allowing Ethiopian access to the two ports, which can handle more than 1m. metric tons of merchandise annually, in mid-1998 Ethiopia ceased using the ports, owing to the outbreak of hostilities. Ethiopia's maritime trade subsequently passed through Djibouti (in the Republic of Djibouti), and also through the Kenyan port of Mombasa. An agreement was also signed in July 2003 to allow Ethiopia to use Port Sudan (in Sudan). However, following the rapprochement between Ethiopia and Eritrea in 2018, it was envisaged that Ethiopia would regain access to Eritrean seaports.

Ethiopian Maritime Affairs Authority: Tadesse Tefera Bldg, 5th Floor, opp. Hotel d'Afrique, POB 1861, Addis Ababa; tel. (11) 5503638; e-mail maritime@ethionet.et; internet etmaritime.com; f. 2007; regulates maritime transport services; Dir-Gen. MEKONNEN ABERA.

Ethiopian Shipping and Logistics Services Enterprise (ESLSE): Ras Mekonen St, Addis Ababa; tel. (11) 5518280; e-mail esl@ethionet.et; internet eslse.et; f. 2011 following merger of the Ethiopian Shipping Lines Corpn, the Maritime and Transit Services Enterprise and the Dry Port Services Enterprise; serves Red Sea, Europe, Mediterranean, Gulf and Far East with its own fleet and chartered vessels; CEO ROBA MEGERSA.

CIVIL AVIATION

Ethiopia has two international airports (at Addis Ababa and Dire Dawa) and around 40 smaller airports and airfields. Bole International Airport in the capital handles 95% of the country's international air traffic and 85% of domestic flights.

Ethiopian Airlines: Bole International Airport, POB 1755, Addis Ababa; tel. (11) 5178165; internet www.ethiopianairlines.com; f. 1945; operates regular services to 18 domestic destinations and 82 international destinations; Chair. GIRMA WAKE; CEO MESFIN TASEW.

Ethiopian Civil Aviation Authority (ECAA): POB 978, Addis Ababa; tel. (11) 6650200; e-mail civil.aviation@ethionet.et; internet www.ecaa.gov.et; regulatory authority; provides air navigational facilities; Dir-Gen. Col WOSENYELEH HUNEGNAW.

Tourism

Ethiopian Tourism Transformation Council: Addis Ababa; f. 2014.

Ethiopian Tourism Organization: Addis Ababa; tel. (11) 5545678; e-mail infote@ethiopia.travel; internet www.ethiopia .travel; f. 2013; CEO SELESHI GIRMA.

Defence

As assessed at November 2021, Ethiopia's active armed forces numbered an estimated 138,000, including an air force of some 3,000. A total of 8,830 soldiers were stationed abroad.

Defence Budget: 16,500m. birr in 2021.

Chief of Staff of the Ethiopian National Defence Forces: Gen. BIRHANU JULA GELALCHA.

Education

Education in Ethiopia is available free of charge, and, after a rapid growth in the number of schools, it became compulsory between the ages of seven and 13 years. Since 1976 most primary and secondary schools have been controlled by local peasant associations and urban dwellers' associations. Primary education begins at seven years of age and lasts for eight years. Secondary education, beginning at 15 years of age, lasts for a further four years, comprising two cycles of two years, the second of which provides preparatory education for entry to the tertiary level. According to estimates by the United Nations Educational, Scientific and Cultural Organization (UNESCO), in 2019/20 enrolment at pre-primary institutions was equivalent to 33% of children in the corresponding age-group (34% of boys; 32% of girls). In 2014/15 total enrolment at primary schools included 86% of children in the appropriate age-group (89% of boys; 82% of girls), while secondary enrolment in that year was equivalent to 35% of children in the appropriate age-group (36% of boys; 34% of girls). In 2018 expenditure on education constituted 24.0% of total government expenditure.

Bibliography

Aalen, L. *The Politics of Ethnicity in Ethiopia*. Leiden, Brill, 2011.

Abraham, K. *Ethiopia: from Bullets to the Ballot Box: The Bumpy Road to Democracy and the Political Economy of Transition*. Lawrenceville, NJ, Red Sea Press, 1994.

Appleyard, D., Bausi, A. Hahn, W., Kaplan, S., and Uhlig, S. (Eds) *Ethiopia: History, Culture and Challenges*. East Lansing, MI, Michigan Sate University Press, 2018.

Attilo, A., Berhanu, K., and Ketsella, Y. *Ethiopia: Politics, Policy Making and Rural Development*. Addis Ababa, Addis Ababa University Press, 2006.

Bairu, H. T. *Eritrea And Ethiopia: A Front Row Look At Issues Of Conflict*. Trenton, NJ, Africa World Press, 2017.

Bariagaber, A. *Conflict and the Refugee Experience: Flight, Exile, and Repatriation in the Horn of Africa*. Aldershot, Ashgate, 2006.

Bekele, G. *Ploughing New Ground: Food, Farming & Environmental Change in Ethiopia*. Woodbridge, James Currey, 2017.

Bekoe, D. A. (Ed). *East Africa and the Horn: Confronting Challenges to Good Governance*. Boulder, CO, Lynne Rienner Publishers, 2006.

Benti, G. *Addis Ababa: Migration and the Making of a Multiethnic Metropolis, 1941–1974*. Lawrenceville, NJ, Red Sea Press, 2007.

Berhanu, K., Olika, T., Kefale, A., and Erega, J. *Electoral Politics, Decentralized Governance and Constitutionalism in Ethiopia*. Addis Ababa, Addis Ababa University Press, 2007.

Berhe, A. *A Political History of the Tigray People's Liberation Front*. Tsehai Publishers, Los Angeles, CA, 2009.

Berhe, M. G. *Laying the Past to Rest: The EPRDF and the Challenges of Ethiopian State-Building*. London, C. Hurst & Co., 2019.

Binns, J. *The Orthodox Church of Ethiopia: A History*. London, I. B. Tauris, 2018.

Breines, M. R. *Becoming Middle Class: Young People's Migration between Urban Centres in Ethiopia* Singapore, Palgrave Macmillan, 2021.

Campbell, I. *The Addis Ababa Massacre: Italy's National Shame*. London, C. Hurst & Co., 2017.

Cheru, F., Cramer, C., and Oqubay, A. (Eds) *The Oxford Handbook of the Ethiopian Economy*. Oxford, Oxford University Press, 2019.

Chinigò, D. *Everyday Practices of State Building in Ethiopia: Power, Scale, Performativity*. Oxford, Oxford University Press, 2022.

Clapham, C. *Transformation and Continuity in Revolutionary Ethiopia*. Cambridge, Cambridge University Press, 1988.

Desplat, P., and Østebø, T. *Muslim Ethiopia: the Christian Legacy, Identity Politics, and Islamic Reformism*. Basingstoke, Palgrave Macmillan, 2013.

Freeman, D. and Pankhurst, A. *Peripheral People: The Excluded Minorities of Ethiopia*. Lawrenceville, NJ, Red Sea Press, 2003.

Gebreselassie, S. E. *The Ethiopian People's Revolutionary Party: Between a Rock and a Hard Place, 1975–2008*. Lawrenceville, NJ, Red Sea Press, 2016.

Getachew, M. *Ethiopia and the United States: history, diplomacy and analysis*. New York, Algora Publishing, 2009.

Ghebre-Ab, H. (Ed.). *Ethiopia and Eritrea: A Documentary Study*. Trenton, NJ, Red Sea Press, 1993.

Gudina, M. *Ethiopia: From Autocracy to Revolutionary Democracy, 1960–2011*. Addis Ababa, Chamber Printing House, 2011.

Haile Selassie I. *The Autobiography of Emperor Haile Selassie I. 'My Life and Ethiopia's Progress'*. Oxford, Oxford University Press, 1976.

Haile-Selassie, T. *The Ethiopian Revolution, 1974–1991: From a Monarchical Autocracy to a Military Oligarchy*. London, Kegan Paul International, 1997.

Hameso, S.Y., and Hassen, M. (Eds). *Arrested Development in Ethiopia: Essays on Underdevelopment, Democracy, and Self-Determination*. Lawrenceville, NJ, Red Sea Press, 2006.

Hammond, J. *Fire from the Ashes: A Chronicle of the Revolution in Tigray, Ethiopia, 1975–1991*. Lawrenceville, NJ, Red Sea Press, 1999.

Hammond, L. *This Place Will Become Home: Refugee Repatriation to Ethiopia*. Ithaca, NY, Cornell University Press, 2004.

Hassan, M. *The Oromo and the Christian Kingdom of Ethiopia, 1300–1700*. Woodbridge, James Currey, 2015.

Henze, P. *Layers of Time: A History of Ethiopia*. London, Hurst, 2000.

Jacquin-Berdal, D. and Plaut, M. (Eds). *Unfinished Business: Ethiopia and Eritrea at War*. Lawrenceville, NJ, Red Sea Press, 2006.

Jalata, A. *Oromia and Ethiopia: State Formation and Ethnonational Conflict, 1868–2000*. Piscataway, NJ, Transaction Publishers, 2005.

Cultural Capital and Prospects for Democracy in Botswana and Ethiopia. Abingdon, Routledge, 2021.

Kebbede, G. *Environment and Society in Ethiopia*. Abingdon, Routledge, 2018.

Kefale, A. *Federalism and Ethnic Conflict in Ethiopia: A Comparative Regional Study*. Abingdon, Routledge, 2012.

Lockot, H. W. *Haile Selassie I: The Formative Years 1892–1936*. Berkeley, CA, University of California Press, 1987.

The Mission: The Life, Reign and Character of Haile Selassie I. London, Hurst, 1992.

A History of Ethiopia. Berkeley, CA, University of California Press, 2001.

McVety, A. K. *Enlightened Aid: U.S. Development as Foreign Policy in Ethiopia*. New York, Oxford University Press, 2015.

Markakis, J. *Ethiopia: Anatomy of a Traditional Polity*. Addis Ababa, Shama Books, 2006.

Ethiopia: The Last Two Frontiers. London, James Currey, 2011.

Markakis, J. and Ayele, N. *Class and Revolution in Ethiopia*. Addis Ababa, Shama Publishers, 2006.

Negash, T., and Tronvoll, K. *Brothers at War*. London, James Currey, 2000.

Østebø, T. *Islam, Ethnicity, and Conflict in Ethiopia: The Bale Insurgency, 1963-1970*. Cambridge, Cambridge University Press, 2020.

Ofcansky, T. P., and Shinn, D. H. (Eds). *Historical Dictionary of Ethiopia*. Lanham, MD, Scarecrow Press, 2004.

Ottaway, M. *Soviet and American Influence in the Horn of Africa*. New York, Praeger, 1982.

(Ed.). *The Political Economy of Ethiopia*. New York, Praeger, 1990.

Pankhurst, A., van Uffelen, J. G., and Rahmato, D. *Food Security, Safety Nets and Social Protection in Ethiopia*. Addis Ababa, Forum for Social Studies, 2013.

Pankhurst, R. *Economic History of Ethiopia, 1880–1935*. Addis Ababa, 1968.

The Ethiopians. Oxford, Blackwell, 1999.

Pausewang, S. *Ethiopia Since the Derg: A Decade of Democratic Pretension and Performance*. London, Zed Books, 2003.

Praeg, B. *Ethiopia and Political Renaissance in Africa*. New York, Nova Science Publishers, 2006.

Prunier, G., and Ficquet, E. *Understanding Contemporary Ethiopia*. London, C. Hurst & Co., 2012.

Schwarz, T. *Ethiopian Jewish Immigrants in Israel*. Curzon Press, 2000.

Sharomo, R., and Mesfin, B. *Regional Security in the Post Cold War Horn of Africa*. Pretoria, The Institute of Security Studies, 2011.

Sishagne, S. *Unionists and Separatists: The Vagaries of Ethio-Eritrean Relation, 1941–1991*. Tsehai Publishers, Los Angeles, CA, 2007.

Smith, L. *Making Citizens in Africa: Ethnicity, Gender, and National Identity in Ethiopia*. Cambridge, Cambridge University Press, 2013.

Tareke, G. *The Ethiopian Revolution: War in the Horn of Africa*. New Haven, CT, Yale University Press, 2013.

Tesfaye, A. *State and Economic Development in Africa: The Case of Ethiopia*. London, Palgrave Macmillan, 2017.

Teferra, D. *Economic Development and Nation Building in Ethiopia*. Lanham, MD, University Press of America, 2005.

Tibebu, T. *The Making of Modern Ethiopia, 1896–1974*. Lawrenceville, NJ, Red Sea Press, 1995.

Tiruneh, A. *The Ethiopian Revolution, A Transformation from an Aristocratic to a Totalitarian Autocracy, 1974-1987*. Cambridge, Cambridge University Press, 1993.

Tronvoll, K. *War and the Politics of Identity in Ethiopia: Making Enemies and Allies in the Horn of Africa*. Woodbridge, James Curry, 2009.

Tronvoll, K., and Hagmann, T. *Contested Power in Ethiopia: Traditional Authorities and Multi-Party Elections*. Leiden, Brill, 2012.

Turton, D. *Ethnic Federalism: The Ethiopian Experience in Comparative Perspective*. Oxford, James Currey, 2006.

Young, J. *Peasant Revolution in Ethiopia: The Tigray People's Liberation Front, 1975–91*. Cambridge, Cambridge University Press, 1997.

GABON

Physical and Social Geography

DAVID HILLING

Lying along the equator, on the west coast of Africa, the Gabonese Republic covers an area of 267,667 sq km (103,347 sq miles) and comprises the entire drainage basin of the westward-flowing Ogooué river, together with the basins of several smaller coastal rivers such as the Nyanga and Como.

The low-lying coastal zone is narrow in the north and south but broader in the estuary regions of the Ogooué and of Gabon. South of the Ogooué numerous lagoons, such as the N'Dogo, M'Goze and M'Komi, back the coast, and the whole area is floored with cretaceous sedimentary rocks, which at shallow depth yield oil. The main producing oilfields are in a narrow zone stretching southwards from Port-Gentil, both on and off shore. The interior consists of Pre-Cambrian rocks, eroded into a series of plateau surfaces at heights of 450 m–600 m and dissected by the river system into a number of distinct blocks, such as the Crystal mountains, the Moabi uplands and the Chaillu massif. This area is one of Africa's most mineralized zones, with the large-scale exploitation of manganese and uranium contributing significantly to Gabon's economy. There are also deposits of high-grade iron ore, gold and diamonds.

Gabon has an equatorial climate, with uniformly high temperatures, high relative humidities and mean annual rainfalls of 1,500 mm–3,000 mm. More than 80% of the country's area is covered with rainforest, one of the highest national proportions in the world, and wood from the okoumé tree provided the basis for the country's economy until superseded by minerals in the 1960s. Grassland vegetation is restricted to the coastal sand zone south of Port-Gentil and parts of the valleys of the Nyanga, upper N'Gounié and upper Ogooué.

Agricultural development in the potentially rich forest zone has been limited by the small size of the country's population. According to the October 2013 census the population was enumerated at 1,811,079; however, at mid-2022, according to United Nations projections, it totalled 2,331,532, giving an average density of 8.7 inhabitants per sq km. As the population is small in relation to national income, Gabon has one of the highest levels of income per head in mainland sub-Saharan Africa, although many of the country's enterprises depend on labour imported from neighbouring countries. The three main urban concentrations may now account for more than one-half of the population; in 2013 Libreville, the capital, had 703,940 inhabitants; Port-Gentil, the centre of the petroleum industry, 136,462; and Franceville, a mining centre, had 110,685. The major rural concentrations are found in Woleu N'Tem, where coffee and cocoa are the main cash crops, and around Lambaréné, where palm oil and coffee are important. The country's principal ethnic groups are the Fang (30%) and the Eshira (25%).

History

DOUGLAS A. YATES

FRENCH NEOCOLONIALISM AND LÉON MBA (1960–1967)

Gabon's independence was recognized on 17 August 1960, after the signing of a series of 'co-operation accords' that ensured the former colony would remain within the French sphere of influence. Gabon is a territory which was first given shape geographically by the French, colonized by the French, forested by the French, mined by the French and was led by a francophone assimilated elite who received a French education, learned French ideas, read French books and papers, listened to French radio, watched French television, practised French law and worked for French businesses. At independence the country adopted a French Fifth Republic semi-presidential system of government that was dominated by France through the co-operation accords (bilateral military, economic, and diplomatic agreements), and adopted a French currency (the CFA franc) and thus a monetary policy also run by France. Gabon's dependent relationship with France did not end with decolonization, but simply became more complex.

Gabon's first President Léon Mba (1960–67) was brought to power with the financial assistance of French foresters as well as the support of voters from his own Fang ethnicity. However, he also collaborated with Jacques Foccart, Charles de Gaulle's advisor for African affairs, who was developing Gabon's uranium and petroleum for French strategic energy independence. After four years of increasingly authoritarian presidentialism, an attempted coup in February 1964 was averted by French paratroopers who protected the Gabonese President thereafter.

Shortly afterwards Mba was diagnosed with cancer and flown to France for treatment, where Foccart visited him regularly and, in the interests of stability, convinced him to change the Gabonese Constitution to create the position of vice-president who could succeed him in the event of his death. Foccart persuaded Mba to name Albert Bernard (later El Hadj Omar) Bongo (Ondimba) as Gabon's Vice-President. Born in Gabon, but educated in what became the Republic of the Congo, Bongo had worked for French military intelligence in that country's capital, Brazzaville, before being scouted by Foccart's network upon his arrival in Libreville (after Gabon's independence black soldiers were forced to return to 'their' country of origin). In order to prevent any opposition leader from taking power and adopting anti-French policies, presidential elections were hurriedly organized by Foccart's men, who flew the young and as yet unknown Bongo around the country (there were few roads for his opponents to do likewise) where he campaigned on behalf of the absent Mba, downplaying the President's grave medical condition. Voters thus believed they were only re-electing Mba, not bringing into power a new president. In this way the Mba/Bongo ticket won the 1967 presidential elections, and, following Mba's death in November, Bongo became President.

THE DYNASTIC RULE AND RENTIER STATE OF OMAR BONGO (1967–2009)

Upon assuming power Bongo dissolved all existing political parties and on 12 March 1968 established a new single party regime under the Parti Démocratique Gabonais (PDG) of which he was the Secretary-General. The PDG was the only legal forum for political discussion or activity. In addition to being President of the Republic and Secretary-General of the sole and ruling party, Bongo also headed the Government (as the position of Prime Minister had been abolished) and several ministries. Among the portfolios he assumed responsibility for were those of defence, information, planning and development (which he held in 1969–81), territorial management (1972–81), national guidance (1974–81), and postal services and telecommunications (1975–81), and at times, he was also Minister of Foreign Affairs.

His style of authoritarian 'personal rule' came under criticism, and therefore in 1981 he acceded to the reinstatement of the position of Prime Minister. In an informal compact that he made with the Fang, who were the largest ethnic group and thus the critically important electoral base in the country, Bongo agreed that the premier would always be a Fang from the Estuaire region (as Mba had been) with the first person appointed to the post being Léon Mebiame. However, in practice the Prime Minister was extremely limited in their role.

Omar Bongo's regime lasted for over four decades. On the death of Togo's Etienne (Gnassingbé) Eyadéma in 2005, Bongo became sub-Saharan Africa's longest-serving head of state, and following the resignation of Cuba's Fidel Castro Ruz in 2008, he became the world's longest serving non-royal head of state. Much is made about this virtue of political stability; however, Bongo's six re-elections (in 1973, 1979, 1986, 1993, 1998 and 2005), first via one-party plebiscites, then through disputed multi-party elections, aborted any democratic political culture from emerging in the country. Having excluded, eliminated, exiled or co-opted all of his potential presidential challengers, the problem of his succession became acute. Bongo ruled with dynastic style, but Gabon was still legally a republic and therefore there were no rules of legitimate hereditary succession. Nor had he designated a clear heir apparent.

According to information made public in his will in 2010 (following his death in 2009), Bongo had 52 legitimately recognized children. (Although by some estimates his children totalled over 100 if you include illegitimate offspring of extramarital affairs.) Among these, and perhaps the most visible members of the ruling clan, were his eldest daughter and Chief of Staff Pascaline Bongo (born in 1956), his eldest son and Minister of Defence in 1999–2009 Ali Bongo Ondimba (born in 1959), Arthur Bongo, who flew his father's private jet, Christian Bongo, director of the prestigious Transgabonais Railway, Fabrice Bongo, director of the budget, and Frédéric Bongo, head of intelligence and national security. Two other noteworthy younger offspring—Yacine 'Queenie' Bongo and Omar Denis 'Junior' Bongo Ondimba—born of his late-life marriage to Edith Bongo (the daughter of the Congolese head of state Denis Sassou Nguesso) were closer to the patriarch in his last days, and were protected after their father's sudden demise by their maternal grandfather Sassou Nguesso. 'Junior' Bongo Ondimba was educated at Harvard University and currently represents something of a dynastic rival to his half-brother Ali Bongo Ondimba.

Oil, Forests and Tourism

Gabon is considered to be a rich country by African standards. In the early years of the 21st century Gabon doubled its gross domestic product (GDP) in just four years, largely as a result of high petroleum prices, from US $4,900m. in 2000 to $9,100m. in 2004. It was sub-Saharan Africa's fifth largest oil producer in the latter year, and the high average price of oil ($39 per barrel) was positive in the short term for the Bongo dynasty, with Gabon's small population creating a statistically high per capita income of $5,500 (on an international purchasing-power parity basis), four times that of most African nations. Gabon was often described as an 'African Kuwait'; however, the long-term effects of oil-rent dependency caused Gabon more problems than it solved, and by the turn of the century, as Gabon's oil production declined below 300,000 barrels per day (b/d), although new oil discoveries were regularly made, none was large enough to offset the larger reserve depletion.

Gabonese oil production had already 'peaked' in 1997 (at 364,000 b/d) and lacking any new major discoveries, the economy entered thereafter into a long, slow and ineluctable period of post-boom decline. The traditional multinational oil companies who had originally developed the Gabonese oil sector in the 20th century like Elf Aquitaine (now Total) and Royal Dutch Shell became reluctant to make any major new investments in research and development for new oilfields. Geological factors tended to make Gabonese oilfields small and therefore not very profitable, and thus these foreign firms made smaller, more targeted investments in horizontal

drilling, or they used cheaper techniques such as sub-surface mineral injection of existing fields, in order to increase crude oil extraction from fields they had discovered previously. This reticence on the part of French, British and US oil companies resulted in new actors, particularly from Asia, entering Gabon's oil sector in the early 2000s. Omar Bongo courted Chinese investors in particular during his last years in office, signing a series of agreements in the oil, manganese, iron, and forestry sectors.

Although Gabon has been an 'oil-rentier state' since independence (highly dependent on oil and natural gas rents) the leading employer in the country remained the forestry sector. It was believed that around 30% of the rainforest in Gabon was pristine primary (also known as 'virgin') forest. Around 90% of this forest is original species, and so-called 'frontier forest' (a large, relatively undisturbed ecosystem) accounts for around 32%. However, the share of this virgin rainforest continued to decrease with the extension of timber concessions and then subsequent planting of oil palms by Olam, the Singapore agribusiness company. During the first oil price boom in the 1970s when clear-cutting of timber could have been supplanted by windfall oil rents, the annual deforestation rate was 27,000 ha per year. By 1990 that rate had more than quadrupled and at the turn of the century Gabon remained Africa's chief exporter of plywood and its fourth most important producer of tropical woods.

In 2002, however, influenced by an environmental activist J. Michael Fay who had traversed Gabon's rainforests on foot in 1999, Omar Bongo consented to transform around 11% of his country into protected national forestland, decreeing an 11,294-sq-mile system of national parks so large that *National Geographic* magazine, who had sponsored Fay's 'mega transect', described Bongo's act as 'roughly equivalent to the Queen of England putting a fence around Wales'. The 13 national parks are managed by the Agence Nationale des Parcs Nationaux (ANPN), which is committed to rainforest and wildlife conservation based on scientific research. During Ali Bongo's first presidential term Lee White, a British-born zoologist, had started serving as a consultant for the Government on how to manage the country's new national parks. White had first arrived in Gabon in 1989 to undertake his doctoral research, joined the Wildlife Conservation Society (WCS) to create a research and conservation programme in the country, and then expanded this to an organization with 200 employees. In 2008 he joined the Gabonese Ministry of the Environment, and in 2009 he became the ANPN's Director of National Parks. In June 2019 he was named Minister of Water, Forestry and the Environment.

'GABON EMERGENT': ALI BONGO'S FIRST TERM (2009–2016)

A landmark year in the political history of Gabon came in 2009 when Omar Bongo died. As noted above, no member of the Bongo family had been officially designated as heir apparent and no government official was prepared to assume power and continue his mandate. Instead of preparing for his succession, Omar Bongo had spent his last decades in office consolidating and prolonging his own personal power. He amended the Constitution in March 1991 to change the rules for presidential elections from a French-style two-round ballot (where he had to face a single opponent in a run-off) to a single round contest (where he only needed to win a plurality instead of a majority); he amended the Constitution again in 29 July 2003 to remove any term limits from the presidential office, thereby enabling himself to remain in power until his death. In the final presidential election that he contested, held in November 2005, he secured a seventh term with 79.2% of the vote against a weakened opposition represented by Pierre Mamboundou (13.6%) and Zacharie Myboto (6.6%).

In early May 2009 he withdrew from his official duties, ostensibly to recover from the death in March of Edith Bongo. However, it soon became apparent that this sudden withdrawal from all public life was really due to his own grave health problems. In May he was admitted to a private clinic in Barcelona, Spain, where he died from a heart attack on 8 June 2009. The actual cause of death is still something of a controversy, and presidential staff and regime insiders all denied that he was dead for almost one week while they scrambled to solve the pressing political problem of his succession.

Temporarily, power was transferred on 10 June 2009 to Senate President Rose Francine Rogombé, who subsequently appointed a Fang, Paul Biyoghé Mba, as the interim premier. Rogombé was also responsible for organizing a presidential election within 40 days and this was duly scheduled for 30 August. The election campaign divided powerful barons of the old regime into two camps: those who supported the former President's eldest son (Ali Bongo Ondimba); and those who opposed him, mostly former prime ministers of Fang ethnicity, which remained the country's largest ethnic group. The ruling party's selection of Ali Bongo Ondimba as the PDG candidate proved divisive leading three senior Fang politicians to challenge him as independents: Jean Eyéghé Ndong (who had resigned as Prime Minister earlier in June), Casimir Oyé Mba (the oil minister and a former premier), and André Mba Obame (the Minister of the Interior). Each had to resign their office in order to present themselves in the presidential contest, but Rogombé did not require Ali Bongo Ondimba to do the same.

In total 23 candidates stood against Bongo Ondimba, yet despite his supposed unpopularity he managed to win, in part because of a low turnout (44.2%) and in part because his opponents had failed to rally around a single candidate. When results were announced, disturbances erupted in Libreville and Port-Gentil. Following a ballot recount, the Constitutional Court (presided over by another of his relatives) confirmed that Bongo Ondimba had won the election with 141,665 votes (41.8%), while Mamboundou had received 86,875 votes (25.6%) and Mba Obame 85,814 (25.3%).

Once in power Bongo Ondimba pursued a policy programme he denoted 'Gabon Emergent', a catchphrase that had first served as his election campaign slogan before becoming his Government's official policy programme in 2010. 'Emergence' represented Bongo Ondimba's economic objective of elevating Gabon to the status of an 'emerging country' by the year 2025. (This is an International Monetary Fund—IMF—concept defined as a country with low-to-middle-per-capita income that has undertaken economic development and reform programmes and has begun to emerge as a significant player in the global economy). The Plan Stratégique Gabon Emergent (PSGE), as 'Gabon Emergent' was formally designated, codified some 28 policies aimed at developing four key 'factors of competitiveness': (1) sustainable development; (2) good governance; (3) human capital; and (4) infrastructure. Each of these four factors was pursued through massive public spending programmes, including Gabon Vert (Green Gabon) policies protecting rainforests, animal species and the national parks system, and banning the export of unprocessed logs while promoting the export of processed tropical woods. Other policies introduced included: increasing funding for schools and vocational training; building a free trade zone in Nkok; refurbishing the port of Owendo; building roads linking the north and south of the country; and reinvesting in the oil, gas and mining sectors.

The first Bongo Ondimba Government under Prime Minister Biyoghé Mba (2009–2012) presented a strategic five-year plan (2011–2016) that had the ambition of constructing 2,000 km of newly paved roads, a 524-m bridge over the Banio Lagoon, a new international airport at Andeme outside Libreville, and a hydroelectric dam at Grand Poubara, which would, once constructed, be the largest power generator in the country. One of Bongo Ondimba's most controversial measures was a ban on the export of unprocessed lumber, setting a target for three-quarters of total timber exports to be processed locally, and imposing a total moratorium on the export of unstripped raw timber, in order to stimulate the development of local timber processing. In 2010 he created a Special Economic Zone at Nkok to serve as Gabon's timber processing centre.

Resource Nationalism, Commodities Boom and Bust

In a stroke of good fortune, petroleum prices increased to record highs during Ali Bongo's first presidency, averaging over US $100 per barrel in 2011 during a short-lived commodity boom. Consequently, even with declining oil production Bongo Ondimba was able to purchase development, that is, pursue massive government spending of external oil and mineral rents to pay for his 'Gabon Emergent' development strategy, not only by spending windfall oil revenues, but also by using future oil revenues as collateral for borrowing money from the People's Republic of China, European states and institutions and private financial markets. Petroleum's contribution rebounded to 58% of government revenues in 2012, which qualified Gabon statistically as an 'oil-rentier' state: that is, a country which depends substantially upon its oil revenues. One of the dangers facing such oil-dependent economies is that whenever oil prices fall (a regular cyclical occurrence) the administration faces difficulties servicing its debt. Oil-backed-collateral loans, paradoxically, put oil-rich Gabon deeper in debt, even as it increased its oil revenues during the commodities boom.

World oil prices plummeted in mid-2014, falling from US $100 per barrel to under $50. Ignoring this price collapse, and relying on oil-backed loans, Bongo Ondimba stubbornly continued to increase deficit budgetary spending in his trademark 'Gabon Emergent' plan. Meanwhile, still acting as though it were a seller's market, Bongo Ondimba's Government presented a new oil code that came into effect in September. This new code was much more demanding on oil companies, allowing the state to take a 20% share in all the Gabonese affiliates of foreign oil companies, adding to the 15% reserved for the state-owned Gabon Oil Company, so that 35% of any new permit would be controlled by the Government. The new oil code also gave the state a 55% share of production at the well. Few new oil blocks were thereafter acquired by foreign oil firms and Total and Shell divested themselves almost entirely of their Gabonese portfolios.

In the PSGE's first phase (2010–14) high oil revenues helped propel economic growth to 6%, led by the construction and service sectors. However, declining oil prices and production caused a doubling of the national debt with Gabon's issuing of Eurobonds of US $1,500m. in 2013 and of $500m. in 2015 also playing a role in this development. Previously, Gabon's public debt had reached its all-time high in 1993 at 87% of GDP before Omar Bongo had consecrated his last two decades in power rigorously paying down that debt burden with painful austerity. When Bongo Ondimba came to power payments on debt had occupied less than one-half (42%) of the Government's budget. However, his unbridled spending on PSGE programmes led to a doubling of national debt in just a decade.

To offset deficit spending, Bongo Ondimba needed more foreign investments. New York Forum, founded in 2010 by Richard Attias (and sponsored by the *New York Times*) was a US organization whose main purpose was to run conferences debating economic models. The New York Forum had interested Bongo Ondimba during his many stays in New York and in 2012 he began hosting a spin-off in Libreville called the New York Forum Africa, inviting foreign leaders and international businessmen to make new investments in Gabon's oil refinement and tourism sectors. Over four sessions of these annual summits Bongo Ondimba also became ostentatiously involved in highly mediatized climate change accords. He was the first African head of state (through his PSGE/Gabon Vert policies) to publish a commitment to the emissions reduction targets and climate resilience goals of the Paris Agreement, adopted in 2015 at the 21st United Nations (UN) Framework Convention on Climate Change Conference of the Parties.

Political Opposition: Mba Obame, Jean Ping

During his first presidential term Bongo Ondimba's main political opponent was Mba Obamé, a long-serving politician and moderate reformer, and a political theoretician of 'reform from within', who had worked with the President's son in the 1990s on attempts to reform the ruling PDG. His drive to incorporate talented opponents into the regime and replace older, poorly educated, incompetent PDG stalwarts, had brought Mba Obame into conflict with many members of Omar Bongo's old guard, the regime's so-called 'barons'. Mba Obame had served in Omar Bongo's administrations in various ministerial positions in the 2000s and became a close confident of both Omar Bongo and Bongo Ondimba, until Omar's death in

2009. At that point Mba Obame made the political miscalculation of challenging Bongo Ondimba in the 2009 presidential election.

In early 2010 Mba Obame, along with a number of the other defeated opposition candidates, created a united opposition party, the Union Nationale, and became Bongo Ondimba's most outspoken critic. In December 2010 a French television documentary showed a former senior French official declaring that Mba Obame had actually won the presidential election. Returning to Libreville, Mba Obame staged a presidential oath taking ceremony, broadcast on his own private television channel. On 25 January 2011 he declared himself the true president of Gabon. Hoping for an African version of the 'Arab Spring', Mba Obame had once more miscalculated the balance of forces in the country. The people did not rise up against Bongo Ondimba. After he moved his 19-member shadow 'government' to the UN Development Programme (UNDP) offices, the legitimate Government accused him of 'high treason' and prohibited the Union Nationale. Only with the assistance of UN Secretary-General Ban Ki-Moon were Mba Obame and his team able to leave UNDP offices safely on 27 February. After the Assemblée Nationale (National Assembly) revoked his parliamentary immunity in May, he fled Gabon for South Africa to receive medical treatment before moving to France to live in exile.

The opposition suffered a further serious blow when Pierre Mamboundou died in October 2011. With Mba Obame's Union Nationale by this point having been officially dissolved, and all Fang dissenters in the Government having been dismissed, there was no longer any effective democratic opposition to Bongo Ondimba nor his ruling PDG. Legislative elections held on 17 December were boycotted by the banned opposition, therefore enabling the ruling PDG to take 114 of the 120 seats. Turnout was extremely low, at only 34.3%. In February 2012 Raymond Ndong Sima, a Fang politician from Woleu-N'Tem region (in the north of the country), became the new Prime Minister. Sima's appointment represented a break with a longstanding Bongo family tradition of appointing a Fang from the Estuaire region.

Mba Obame died in Yaoundé, Cameroon, in 2015. In an effort to appease the mourning opposition, Bongo Ondimba allowed the Union Nationale party to be reauthorized. However, in 2016 its party congress voted against nominating any candidate for presidential elections because it believed Bongo Ondimba was preparing for massive electoral fraud. Eventually the Union Nationale threw its support behind former Bongo Ondimba loyalist and diplomat Jean Ping, who had been one of Omar Bongo's closest and longest serving ministers (notably serving as Minister of Foreign Affairs in the 2000s) before being excluded from the inner circle of power by Bongo Ondimba in 2009. (This circle was by the mid-2010s increasingly comprised of foreigners like the Beninois courtier Maixent Accrombessi—see below.)

Ping, who was one of the most prominent politicians in Gabon, had also served as the African Union (AU) Commission Chairman in (2008–12) and resigned from the ruling PDG in 2014 to join the growing opposition to Bongo Ondimba. Following his departure from the AU, Ping had tried to stay out of politics altogether, going into private consulting; however, over time he became increasingly discontented with the gross mismanagement of government affairs, and began participating in anti-Bongo demonstrations. At one such gathering in December 2014, which the Government had deemed illegal, Ping and other participants were tear-gassed and beaten by the security forces. This was a turning point. Styling himself thereafter as Bongo's main challenger, Ping stood as the candidate of the reauthorized Union Nationale in the 2016 presidential election. Learning from their errors in 2009, opposition leaders created a 'Front de l'Opposition pour l'Alternance and endorsed Ping as their sole candidate.

During the election campaign accusations that Bongo Ondimba was not the natural son of Omar Bongo gained credibility. Pascaline Bongo, Bongo Ondimbas elder half-sister, alleged that his birth certificate had been forged, an accusation supported by facsimiles of the fraudulent document in French investigative journalist Pierre Pean's 2014 best-selling book *Nouvelles affaires africaines*, which brought a

defamation lawsuit against its author (although this was subsequently dismissed owing to lack of evidence). In this dirty campaign the pro-government newspaper *L'Union* made negative references to Ping's Chinese heritage and insulted his presidential campaign as cheap 'Chinese junk'. The official electoral commission, which was solely composed of members of the ruling party, declared Bongo Ondimba the winner of the election (held on 27 August 2016) with 49.8% of the vote, with a scarcely credible turnout rate of over 99% reported in the Bongo clan fief of Haut-Ogooué, where some 95.5% of electors were reported as voting for Bongo Ondimba. Ping secured 48.2% of the votes cast. Bongo Ondimba was re-elected by just 5,594 votes out of 627,805 registered voters and the high turnout was crucial to this.

In response to the announcement of the results, violence broke out in the major cities, the National Assembly building was set on fire, and over 100 protesters were killed by the police and/or 'disappeared'. Ping demanded the publication of results for Haut-Ogooué's polling stations, a demand supported by the European Union's (EU) observer team, as well as by France and the USA. The AU also offered to send a conciliation team of African heads of state to calm tensions. Divisions within the Government were exposed by the resignation of the justice minister, who also resigned from the ruling party, and then fled to France. Although Ping challenged the official results at the Constitutional Court, these were ultimately upheld, albeit with some slight amendments. International criticism came quickly after media reports of these irregularities. On 25 September 2016 the French Minister of Foreign Affairs, Jean-Marc Ayrault, stated that he 'regretted' that the court's judgment had not 'removed all doubts,' indicating that he did not believe them himself. The UN, the AU and the USA simply 'noted' the judgment, avoiding weighing in on the side of the opposition, and in that way becoming complicit to the electoral fraud.

Ping was warned of his imminent arrest if any of his inflammatory speeches caused further disturbances. It was also becoming evident that, without external support, public appetite for resistance had eroded. Ping received a short-lived boost in October 2016 when the International Criminal Court (ICC) in The Hague, Netherlands, announced that it would conduct a preliminary inquiry into the matter of electoral fraud. Therefore Ping spent a month abroad, testing the ground for international sanctions. By late September, however, the AU was signalling that Gabon's leaders should find their own solution, a message that the French Prime Minister, Manuel Valls, repeated publicly in November. Nevertheless, after the EU observer team's highly critical report was published in December, EU officials arrived in Libreville to press the Government over the reforms that it recommended. In February 2017 the European Parliament adopted a critical resolution, but the European Council declined to press further, while the ICC mission to Libreville in June failed to lead to a formal inquiry. At Bongo Ondimba's re-investiture on 27 September 2016 he invited opponents to join him in a 'national dialogue' to restore calm. He then named a career diplomat and former foreign minister, Emmanuel Issoze Ngondet, as his new Prime Minister.

BONGO ONDIMBA'S SECOND TERM (2016–)

In his second term Bongo Ondimba has tried to centralized all power inside the presidential palace. He reduced the size of his Council of Ministers, combining several ministries in the hands of single loyal servants, such as Magloire Ngambia, who became responsible for investment, transport, public works, housing, tourism and territorial planning—six of the most strategic portfolios in the 'Gabon Emergent' programme—and who opaquely oversaw large part of the new major investments coming into the country from international partners like Olam. Bongo Ondimba also set up new governmental agencies that were answerable only to himself, not to his ministers. These were parallel agencies with large opaque budgets. Most notably, however, presidential Chief of Staff, Accrombessi, who had been born in Benin to a voodoo priest father, became Bongo Ondima's *eminence grise* in his second term. He had befriended Bongo Ondimba during his time a

Minister of Defence in the 2000s, and reportedly invited him to Benin to participate in voodoo rituals. Accrombessi, who was granted Gabonese citizenship in 1996, established himself as a luxury real estate agent representing Gabonese state enterprises that owned Bongo family properties in France.

Accrombessi was also a businessman for the family group Marck, which sold military uniforms and anti-riot equipment to Gabon, all the while serving as an advisor to Bongo Ondimba who was by then diversifying into offshore banking in Panama, Cyprus and Monaco. In 2011 Bongo Ondimba appointed Accrombessi as his presidential Chief of Staff, a title that included diverse functions such as strategic political intelligence, communication, and management of sensible business and judicial dossiers including the disputed inheritance of the late Omar Bongo. At the same time Accrombessi's wife Evelyne had become the director of communications for Bongo Ondimba's wife, Sylvia Bongo. This close personal relationship between the Bongos and Accrombessi only came to an end in Bongo Ondimba's second term once investigators from the US Justice Department and their counterpart French investigatory judges began revealing embarrassing acts of alleged corruption and money laundering. The triggering event occurred in 2013 when one of Bongo Ondimba's hairdressers was arrested carrying US $150,000 in a suitcase through Los Angeles International Airport but could not explain its origin.

In 2015 Maixent Accrombessi was arrested by French police at Charles de Gaulle Airport (Paris) under suspicion of corruption and money laundering. Although he was later released, he had become the epicentre of a mediatized French investigation into scandals surrounding the Bongo offshore banking empire. However, a few days after Bongo's 2016 re-election Accrombessi suffered a cerebral vascular attack and had to be evacuated to the United Kingdom for convalescence. Bongo Ondimba, in response to mounting scandals, distanced himself from his Chief of Staff, whose corrupt patron-client system had become something of an embarrassment. In 2017 Bongo launched a new anti-corruption campaign, named 'Operation Scorpion' (see below), which led to the arrest of 90 individuals, mostly from Accrombessi's inner circle, including Ngambia.

Responding to the lack of new investments in Gabon's oil sector, caused by diminished world demand as well as his previously aggressive resource nationalism, Bongo Ondimba decided, in 2018, to once again rewrite the oil code. The corporate income tax rate for oil companies was reduced to 0%, and the state's share of profit in oil was reduced from 55% to 50% in conventional zones and from 50% to 45% in deep water concessions.

Stroke, Attempted Coup and Noureddin Bongo

Just when it appeared that Bongo Ondimba was extracting himself from difficulties, on 23 October 2018, while visiting Saudi Arabia for an investor's conference, the President suffered a stroke. This was officially denied for two weeks by government officials, who declared that he had only been admitted to hospital because of 'fatigue'.

The whole spectacle was reminiscent of official denials of his father's demise in 2009, briefly leading to wild speculation about whether or not Bongo Ondimba was still alive. Having been initially hospitalized in the Saudi capital, Riyadh, Bongo Ondimba stayed there for more than one month before being transferred by air on 29 November 2018 to Rabat, Morocco, first to a royal military hospital, and then to a private residence for convalescence and rehabilitation. Pierre-Claver Maganga Moussavou, the Vice-President, had not been written into the Constitution as the President's successor in the event of a temporary vacancy of the presidential office. Article 13 had only determined that if the President was permanently incapacitated then the President of the Senate was to assume the position of President *pro tempore* until new elections could be organized. No constitutional article addressed the problem of a temporary vacancy. Therefore, on 14 November 2009 the President of the Constitutional Court, Marie-Madeleine Mborantsuo, herself a member of the Bongo clan, simply 'announced' in an unprecedented act a new constitutional amendment to accommodate her son-in-law's temporary absence, allowing

Bongo Ondimba's half-brother Frédéric Bongo, head of the state intelligence services, to take charge.

On 7 January 2019, while such irregular legal procedures were being proffered by the ruling clan to a tired and cynical public, a handful of idealistic green berets from the Republican Guard took over the tower of Radio Télévision Gabonais (RTG) in Libreville. Their leader, Lt Kelly Ondo Obiang, announced the establishment of a Conseil National de la Restoration, dismissing all government institutions as 'illegitimate and illegal', and asked his fellow citizens 'to rise up like one single man and take control of the streets'. But no crowds descended onto the streets. He and his fellow junior officers had miscalculated the courage of the Gabonese people, and they were quickly neutralized by better-armed red berets from the loyalist National Guard. Two mutineers were killed, three were arrested, and one escaped. It was the first attempted coup in the 52-year-long reign of the Bongo dynasty.

As Bongo Ondimba was still convalescing in Morocco when the coup attempt occurred, a struggle between powerful factions in the ruling family was revived. (Cabinet meetings for example legally required his presence.) Initially, Bongo Ondimba's stroke followed by the failed putsch appeared to have played into the hands of the regime's 'securocrats' led by Frédéric Bongo, with the support of Mborantsuo, who from her position had constitutionalized such government prerogatives. However, Bongo Ondimba soon perceived Frédéric as a potential rival, and therefore in an act of sibling rivalry deprived him of the armed wing of his intelligence service in July 2019 and placed men personally loyal to himself at the head of every intelligence and security agency. Frédéric, thus disempowered, was sent to South Africa, where he quietly served as a military attaché in the Gabonese embassy there.

The real influencer behind the scenes in the presidential palace was now the First Lady, Sylvia Bongo, daughter of powerful French businessman Edouard Pierre Valentin, who had been raised in Gabon. She was Bongo Ondimba's second wife, and the mother of two children with the President, including his eldest son Nourredin Edouard Bongo. It was in the absence of Bongo Ondimba, during his convalescence in Morocco, when his future as President was in doubt and his half-brother Frédéric seemed to be taking the reins of power, that Sylvia Bongo began to step out of the shadows and take an active role promoting her son's future in government. Her goal became to assure her son's succession to supreme presidential power. Nourredin Bongo had not been educated in France, as his father before him, nor groomed by French *coopérants*, as his grandfather had been, but instead had been sent to the prestigious British public school Eton College, and had studied political science and international relations at the School of Oriental and African Studies at the University of London, and completed a masters' degree in finance and accounting at the London Business School. Nourredin was a pure product of elite British public school education, not an assimilated Franco-Gabonese, and his only real contact with ordinary Gabonese realities appeared to have been living in the presidential palace.

In 2014 Bongo Ondimba had named Nourredin deputy general manager of Olam International in Libreville, without him having had any experience of working for that company or for that matter in its palm oil business. The Singapore based agro-industrial firm had invested €2,000m. in Gabon between 2010 and 2019, so this was seen as the best place for a dynastic head of state to place his eldest son to 'supervise' the development of palm oil plantations and acquire information about other capital-intensive projects in Gabon's Special Economic Zone and the deep-water port at Owendo, near Libreville. In 2019 his father also conferred upon Nourredin a mission of fighting corruption, in particular focusing on monitoring the Chief of Staff Brice Laccruche Alihanga. Bongo Ondimba's nepotistic anti-corruption campaign, 'Operation Scorpion', led to the arrest of Alihanga and his associates, thereby eliminating potential obstacles to the rise to power of the President's son.

In early December 2019 Nourredin was appointed to the newly created position of Co-ordinator of Presidential Affairs, described by observers as a 'super chief of staff' and more aptly as the 'regime number two'. This appointment by his father was widely seen as preparatory for another Bongo dynastic succession. For the next two years while his father convalesced Noureddin acquired considerable influence in Gabon, involving himself during the COVID-19 pandemic in major public works, public health matters, and annulling two-thirds of the domestic public debt. Since 2021 Nourredin has collaborated with Rose Christiane Ossouka Raponda (who was appointed as Gabon's first female Prime Minister in July 2020) on a three-year Plan d'Accélération de la Transformation (PAT, Transformation Acceleration Plan) with 20 new projects aimed at diversifying the economy away from raw material exports to the local production of consumer goods. Having demonstrated his prowess at managing the well-oiled machinery of government administration, the next step in his preparation for dynastic succession was to teach him how to manipulate the entangling ropes of the ruling party. In March 2020 Nourredin was named to the PDG's political bureau, and in September 2021 he was named by his father as a strategic advisor to the party's President (i.e. Bongo Ondimba). From this post he was expected to occupy himself not with his country's development or rapid transformation into an emerging economy, but with securing his ailing father's re-election in 2023.

After briefly rebounding, oil prices collapsed once again in 2020, following the outbreak of the COVID-19 pandemic; oil prices reached as low as US $25 per barrel in May. Meanwhile, Gabon's oil output fell over the course of that year from 200,000 b/d to 150,000 b/d because of the lack of new investments and a decline in production caused by Bongo Ondimba's aggressive resource nationalism in his first presidential term. As the Government had continued to borrow on future oil production as collateral for debt, Gabon was now the 10th most indebted country in sub-Saharan Africa. An IMF report concluded that the Bongo regime had spent over $5,000m. on 'Gabon Emergent' and that vast sums had been wasted on the multiplication of strategic and operational bodies (agencies, general directions, etc.) with unclear management roles.

On 26 June 2021 Bongo Ondimba addressed deputies and senators gathered in a joint session of the National Assembly, his first live public speech since his stroke in 2018. He expressed his satisfaction following the modification of the Constitution in late 2020, in particular with regard to controversial changes in 'the event of impediment, temporary or permanent, of the President of the Republic, and vacancy of power'. With the position of Vice-President having been abolished in 2019, the revised Constitution now provided for a different line of succession in the event of another vacancy,

ensuring that power would remain in the hands of the ruling PDG. A core change to Article 13 instituted an 'interim presidency' triumvirate composed jointly of the speakers of the Senate and the National Assembly and the Minister of National Defence (all three currently PDG members). The triumvirate will make it possible to manage the transition while excluding these three individuals from running in subsequent presidential elections, thereby paving the way, despite Bongo Ondimba's protestations to the contrary, for a quasi-dynastic succession.

In March 2021 President Bongo Ondimba broke his long-standing practice of avoiding direct questions from the press and granted an interview to *The Africa Report* at his official residence in which he denied that he had been preparing his eldest son Noureddin as his successor. In September it was announced that Noureddin would no longer hold the post of Co-ordinator of Presidential Affairs. This decision came a few days after the appointment of Noureddin to the PDG advisory role (see above).

In April 2021 it was revealed that the five gendarmes who had stood guard at the RTG property in Libreville stormed by the putschists who had carried out the short-lived coup of 18 January 2019, and a civilian prosecuted in this case, were still being held in prison. In early July 2021 a special military court sentenced coup leader Lt Ondo Obiang to 15 years in prison; two other members of the Republican Guard were also convicted for their role in the failed 2019 coup.

Since his accession to power Bongo Ondimba has repeatedly expressed his desire to expand the country's partnerships away from France, Gabon's privileged economic partner. Since the majority of Gabonese still speak French, to change the situation fundamentally, Bongo officially introduced English as a second language in Gabon, modelled upon the official bilingualism in Rwanda, a member of both La Francophonie and the Commonwealth. In April 2021 Prime Minister Raponda met with Luis Franceschi, the Commonwealth's Senior Director of the Governance and Peace Directorate. Raponda declared that it was the will of Bongo Ondimba to open Gabon up to new partnerships. On 23 October, during a second visit of Commonwealth experts, Gabon was submitted to an inspection of the state of its democracy, in particular with regard to the organization of elections and the role of the interior ministry and the police in these. On 25 June 2022 Gabon was admitted to the Commonwealth as its 55th member, turning a page in its dominance-dependence relationship with France.

Economy

MEDARD MENGUE BIDZO

INTRODUCTION

This essay takes the form of a presentation and analysis of the facts and figures relevant to the Gabonese economy. It is specifically focused on examining the performance, over the past 10 years or so, of the main sectors and sub-sectors of activity that support this economy in the early 2020s.

THE PRIMARY SECTOR

This section will focus on the evolution of the main export products, in particular petroleum, manganese and timber, which are the three dominant resources of the primary sector in Gabon.

Petroleum

Petroleum contribution to the Gabonese economy has fluctuated sharply over time, although in recent years the general trend has been downwards. In 2017 national oil production of 10.5m. metric tons was recorded, compared with 12.1m. tons in 2011. The natural decline of mature fields, trade union-led strikes, as well as the technical problems encountered by operators, can all be presented as explanations for this

situation. Exports have also generally been falling, and declined from 11.1m. tons in 2012 to 10.1m. tons in 2013 and to just 8.7m. tons in 2018. Asia remains the main buyer of Gabonese crude, traditionally taking more than 50% of exports.

In 2020 oil activity was marked by the suspension and/or postponement of well appraisal and exploration projects by certain operators as a result of the COVID-19 pandemic. It has thus been severely impacted by the preventative measures taken by the Government to counter the spread of the disease. Therefore, after the strong performance of 2019, crude oil production fell by 1.2% to 10.8m. metric tons in 2020. (A further decline, to 10.4m. tons was recorded in 2021.) This decline in performance is mainly explained by the application of OPEC+ (the members of the Organization of the Petroleum Exporting Countries and 11 non-member oil producing nations) quotas aimed at reducing the global supply of oil. On the export side in 2020 there was also a decline, of 6.4% compared with the previous year, to 9.9m. metric tons, due to the drop in global demand due to the enduring health crisis. Asia remained the main destination for Gabonese crude, receiving 79% of the exported volume in 2020.

Manganese

Manganese remains one of Gabon's most important resources and since 2011 output and exports have generally trended on a positive growth path.

In 2013 total national production of manganese ore and sinter amounted to some 4m. metric tons, an increase of 27.7% compared with the previous year, and included 3.7m. tons produced by the Compagnie Minière de l'Ogooué (COMILOG). The better availability of wagons to transport the commodity and the resolution of technical problems allowed this improvement. In terms of exports and sales, world steel production rose by 3.5% in 2013, driven by the People's Republic of China's steel industry which rose by 7.5%. (Manganese is an essential alloy that helps convert iron into steel.) In this context in 2013 exports of Gabonese manganese ore and sinter increased by 29.3%, to reach 3.9m. tons.

In 2017 the manganese ore mining business posted further impressive results, in a favourable international context, marked by an increase in steel industry activity worldwide. Thus, Gabonese production of manganese ore and sinter expanded by 42.5% from 3.6m. metric tons in 2016 to 5.1m. tons in 2017. This increase was linked to an improvement in output from COMILOG and the contribution of the two other operators, namely Nouvelle Gabon Mining, which entered the production phase at the beginning of the year, and Compagnie Industrielle et Commerciale des Mines de Huazhou, which relaunched its activities in 2017 after a suspension of around 18 months. Exports grew by 48.3%, due to firm global demand driven by China, Europe and India. The increase in the level of exports was linked to the disposal of stocks built up in 2016 following the collapse of world manganese prices.

In 2020 manganese mining activity was adversely affected by the global COVID-19 pandemic, with a 1.5% drop in global carbon steel production—the main outlet for manganese—recorded. While production in Europe declined by 14.4% and that in North America by 18.1%, production in China (which accounts for approximately 57% of world production) actually rose by 5.4%, after a strong rebound observed from the second quarter onwards. At the same time, the world supply of manganese ore fell by 2.7% in 2020 due to the decline in production, following the temporary closure of South African mines. The normal resumption of activities for these mines in the second half of the year led to a surplus in the supply/demand balance, with stocks of more than 7m. metric tons at the end of 2020 in Chinese ports compared with 4.7m. tons a year before.

Despite this unfavourable context, the manganese sector consolidated its performance in 2020, supported by the normal operation of the facilities, after taking measures to adapt to the COVID-19 crisis, and production increased by 25.1% to 8.4m. metric tons. The Bangombé mine expansion programme, the commissioning of the Lebaye deposit in Okondja, combined with the opening of the new Okouma plateau in October have made it possible to reach this level of production. It should be noted, however, that this increase was mitigated by the drop in production at the Ndjolé site, which experienced technical problems during the last quarter of 2020 on one of its production lines. On the commercial front, despite the train derailments recorded during the year, exports of manganese increased by 28.7% compared with 2019, to reach 7.9m. tons, benefiting from the rebound in Chinese demand for steel.

Timber

Timber is Gabon's second most significant source of wealth, after oil. The timber sector (or more broadly, the forestry activities sector) has undergone significant changes in recent years, with a revival linked to the exploitation of new forest areas, the firmness of demand from local industries and the relaxation of legislation on the conditions of exploitation of kevazingo (a rare and high-value hardwood) and ozigo trees. Production reached 1.6m. cu m in 2017, representing an increase of 13.5% compared with the previous year. However, log sales to local industries that do not have forestry permits or use appropriate species also increased from 444,099 cu m in 2016 to 497,979 cu m in 2017.

In 2018 timber production increased further with output reaching 2.0m. cu m, before falling back to 1.8m. cu m in 2020. The increase in 2018, mainly supported by rising okoumé output, was explained by the exploitation of new forest areas. Over the same period log sales to local industries rose from 882,838 cu m to 976,925 cu m, an increase of 8.6%.

THE SECONDARY SECTOR

This section will largely focus on agricultural, livestock and fishing activities, on the one hand, and industrial activities, on the other.

Agricultural Activity, Fishing and Stockbreeding

Vegetable Crops

Market gardening, and the production of short-cycle vegetables (and some fruits) in greenhouses, have been recent success stories in Gabon. Tomatoes, peppers, cucumbers and aubergines are among the highest yielding items. In 2017 agricultural activity was characterized by a good performance, due to the contribution of the first harvests from the plantations of the Gabonaise des Réalisations Agricoles et des Initiatives des Nationaux Engagés (GRAINE) programme, success in the fight against parasites, as well as the firmness of the order book, in particular from local catering service providers. Thus, the production of market garden crops increased by 9.6% to reach 296 metric tons in 2017, while food production improved (by a remarkable 339.9%) to stand at 1,566 tons in 2017 compared with 356 tons in the previous year.

In 2020 the market gardening and food crop industry performed well. Indeed, market gardening production consolidated to stand at 772 metric tons, while overall food production also increased. This situation is explained by increasing yields from cultivated areas (appropriation of new cultivation techniques) and good management of diseases, in particular the 'tutaabsoluta' disease which affects tomatoes. Following the same trend, overall turnover in the food production industry increased sharply to stand at 4,100m. francs CFA, driven by the good performance of the trade in market gardening products. The total workforce increased by 6.3% compared to 2019.

Fishing

The fishing sector was the subject of a restructuring plan in December 2012. Indeed, with a view to organizing the sector, the Government implemented legal texts relating in particular to respect for fishing zones, landing sites and the small-scale fishing production tax. Similarly, the 'Gabon Bleu' reform has made it possible to specify the fishing equipment to be used (the authorized nets) in order to ensure the regeneration of the various species found off the Gabonese coast. This reform has been credited with an increase in the number of fishing licences granted. However, fishing output has generally been on a declining trend and totalled around 29,000 tons in 2020. Fishing agreements with the European Union (EU) have existed since 1998, allowing EU trawlers to operate in Gabonese waters; the latest renewal, in February 2021, permitted a European fleet of 27 tuna seiners, 6 pole-and-line tuna vessels and 4 trawlers to fish in Gabonese waters, with Gabon receiving nearly €1.6m. annually.

Stockbreeding

In 2017 the cattle breeding sector experienced contrasting developments. Although the total herd increased by 8.8% to 5,832 head of cattle, overall turnover fell by 4.7% to 303m. francs CFA. A herd reconstitution strategy had been put in place, which aimed to reduce the mortality rate of the animals and the frequency of slaughter, while also introducing young animals suitable for reproduction. A total volume of 68,450 kg of meat was produced, down 4.2% on the previous year, and largely explained by the decrease in the number and frequency of animals to be culled.

Between 2019 and 2020 cattle breeding activity was generally sluggish, with a virtual stagnation in the number of animals, while meat sales fell by 56.4% to just 38.6 metric tons in 2020, compared with 88.6 tons the previous year. Regarding poultry farming, the number of eggs produced in 2020 fell by 4.2% to 3.0m. units, although the number of laying hens remained largely the same.

Industry

Sugar Production

Sugar production amounted to 24,337 metric tons in 2013, virtually unchanged from the previous year. However, in order to meet demand from households and breweries, the industry operator Sucrerie Africaine du Gabon (SUCAF) had to again resort to imports of sugar cubes from Cameroon (around 1,500 tons) and almost 6,000 tons from the EU and Brazil.

In that year the quantity of sugar processed into cubes and pods reached 11,220 metric tons, an increase of 37.5%. However, the transport of sugar to the capital, Libreville, encountered difficulties due to the defective state of the railway. This situation caused a drop in sales of around 6.9%. As a result, turnover fell by 2.1% to stand at 18,179m. francs CFA.

Furthermore, in 2017 the country's sugar refinery experienced sluggish activity both agronomically and industrially, due to unfavourable weather conditions. Thus, the production of granulated sugar fell by 1.0% compared with the previous year, to 24,376 metric tons. Similarly, the quantity of sugar processed into lumps and other qualities fell by 2.3% to 20,173 tons, following the technical problems encountered (including the temporary shut down of the condenser). On the commercial front, volumes sold fell by 5.3% in connection with the weakness of domestic demand. As a result, turnover fell by 5.2% to 19,200m. francs CFA.

In 2020 the sugar refinery again recorded a poor performance both agronomically and industrially. From an agronomic point of view, production fell by 15.3% from the previous year, settling at 22,372 metric tons, due to unfavourable climatic conditions (for example, the poor maturation of sugar cane) and technical problems at the level of cane harvesters, as well as the effects of preventative measures to combat the spread of COVID-19. However, at the industrial level, sugar processing experienced virtual stability at 14,633 tons, with production of sugar cubes up by 3.7%. At the same time, in order to satisfy local demand, sugar imports increased by 51.7% to 10,179 tons. Commercially, the COVID-19 pandemic has had a negative impact on sugar sales, with a 3% drop in the quantities sold, i.e. 30,588 tons in 2020, following the contraction in demand from the main industrial customer (Société des Brasseries du Gabon—SOBRAGA), as a consequence of the closure of bars, restaurants and hotels. Added to this are the difficulties in transporting products as a result of the poor state of the country's transport infrastructure. Despite these impediments, turnover at the refinery rose by 1.3% to 21,600m. francs CFA compared with 21,300m. in 2019, due to the rise in sugar prices at the start of 2020.

Investment totalling 2,300m. francs CFA was mobilized by SUCAF in 2020, mainly for the purchase of equipment. The company's workforce fell by 6.2% to 241 permanent staff, while 333 people were in temporary employment.

Beer and Soft Drinks

In 2013 total production in the carbonated and alcoholic beverages sector was 2.5m. hl, up 4.8% on the previous year. This improvement was mainly due to modernization work on the brewing equipment carried out at the start of the year. Beer production rose by 7.2% compared with 2012 to reach 1.4m. hl and soft drinks by 3.0% to stand at 1.0m. hl. Consequently, with an increase of 9.3%, the turnover amounted to 149,400m. francs CFA in 2013.

Production volumes and sector turnover were similar in 2017, although this was a slowdown compared with the previous year, following a contraction in domestic demand. Thus, total production fell by 6.3% for a volume of 2.6m. hl. In 2020 beer output reached 1.7m. hl although soft drinks output totalled just 933,300 hl. In the following year production increased to 1.9m. hl and 996,300 hl, respectively.

Mineral Water

Mineral water production increased by 16.3% between 2011 and 2015, standing at 466,969 hl in the latter year, with turnover in the sector increasing by 5.4% to 9,800m. francs CFA. The commissioning of a new production line contributed to this performance. This trend continued in the mid-2010s as in 2017 mineral water production increased by 18% compared with the previous year, reaching 920,782 hl. This development

was supported by the strong performance from the SOBRAGA brands (Akewa and Aning'eau). In addition, the interruptions recorded in the Société d'Energie et d'Eau du Gabon drinking water distribution network have had the effect of consolidating local demand for mineral water. Turnover from the sub-sector amounted to approximately 15,000m. francs CFA in 2017. The production of mineral water increased by 1.9% in 2020, for a total volume of 1.11m. hl, following growth in demand from customers for the ranges offered by the leading distributors. Turnover amounted to 21,300m. francs CFA in that year. (A slight increase in output, to 1.14m. hl was recorded in 2021.)

Wood Industries

Wood processing can be broken down into three levels of transformation, namely: a) sawing and peeling; b) mouldings, profiles, parquet and plywood; and c) carpentry and cabinet making. In 2013 the wood processing industries recorded a total output volume of 658,342 cu m, which represented a decline from the previous year of 6.9%. This situation is explained by the difficulties in supplying logs, following the withdrawal of permits from operators who did not apply the regulations on sustainable forest management. Exports in 2013 fell by 7.1% to 536,101 cu m due to port congestion and weak orders. However, local sales increased by 7.3% to reach 82,282 cu m.

In 2014 the wood processing industries recorded a solid production and commercial performance. Thus, the consolidated production of all segments increased by 11.1%, reaching a volume of 720,654 cu m, attributable, *inter alia*, to the better supply of log processing units and increased processing capacity at a number of newly installed factories. On the commercial side, exports increased by 19.9% to 448,869 cu m, in connection with the firmness of external orders. Likewise, local sales continued their upward trend (increasing by 4.9%).

The positive trend continued in 2017, as a result of a better supply of logs to factories, the strengthening of the industrial fabric and the ramp-up of newly installed factories. Thus, total production, combining output across all three segments, increased by 10.3% to 824,072 cu m. On the commercial side, local sales and exports increased by 54.6% and 2.5%, respectively, to post 79,150 cu m and 645,298 cu m, and total turnover rose by 7.6% to 245,200m. francs CFA.

SERVICES

Transportation

The transport sector includes four branches of activity: land transport; rail transport; transportation by air; and maritime transport. In addition to the operators in these branches, there are also transport auxiliaries.

Land transport encompasses both the transport of people and goods in peri-urban and inter-urban areas.

In 2013 rail activity was characterized by a significant decline in the number of passengers on the network and an increase in the overall volume of goods. Indeed, the overall volume of goods evacuated by rail increased by 18.7% due to the increase in the quantity of manganese ore transported. However, log and clinker volumes fell by 15.1% and 35.9%, respectively, following technical difficulties on the railway. The number of passengers fell by 3.1%, attributable to the reduction in the frequency of trains due to maintenance work on the track.

The rail business performed well in 2017 in view of the upward trend in the main indicators. Indeed, the overall volume of goods transported by rail increased by 38.2%, i.e. 5.9m. metric tons compared with 4.2m. in 2016. This development was attributable to the strong performance of the main sectors using this means of transport, in particular the increase in activity recorded in mining and timber. At the same time, the number of passengers transported reached 321,705, up 15.6% on the previous year, due to the improved regularity and reliability of passenger trains.

By the end of 2020 rail transport had consolidated its performance with regard to the evolution of the main indicators. Indeed, a 24.4% increase in the overall volume of goods transported by rail (8.9m. metric tons against 7.2.m. tons in 2019) was recorded. This result was attributable to a significant rise in the evacuations of manganese (up 29%, compared with 2019), the transportation of petroleum products (up 11%) and movements of containerized lumber (up 9.8%). However, the number of passengers transported fell by 49.3% to 163,113, due to the temporary ban on the movement of people between Greater Libreville and the rest of Gabon, as part of lockdown measures and associated attempts to prevent the spread of COVID-19.

Air transport is provided by a number of national and international companies. Although Libreville's Léon M'Ba International Airport has an annual capacity of 1.5m. passengers, the construction of a new airport with capacity for 2m. began in August 2017. Meanwhile, in 2013, there was a significant increase in commercial aircraft movements (up 10.5% compared with the previous year), freight volumes (up 17%) and the number of passengers (which increased by 13.6%). The improvement observed in the air transport sector was confirmed at the level of its turnover, which increased by 12% to nearly 76,000m. francs CFA.

However, in 2017 the activity of the air transport branch declined. Indeed, commercial movements of aircraft fell by 9.6% compared with the previous year, with a reduction in both the domestic network (down 18.7%) and international flights. The number of passengers and freight also fell by 4.6% and 11.1%, respectively.

All air transport indicators fell in 2020, due to the COVID-19 pandemic which paralysed transport. This branch has been severely impacted by the measures taken internationally and the arrangements put in place locally to reduce the flow of passengers. Thus, the commercial movements of aircraft fell by 52.4% to just 7,281 flights, while the number of passengers collapsed by 62.4%, resulting in the number of people transported declining to just 298,629, while the total volume of cargo moved fell by 9.3%. However, it is to be noted that a trend reversal began in towards the end of the third quarter of 2020, following the Government decision to increase the frequency of passenger transport flights, both domestically and internationally.

The activity of the main shipping companies was sluggish in 2013, due to the loss of some contracts with the oil producing enterprises and the weakness of orders. This poor performance continued in 2017 with a general slowdown in global economic activity negatively affecting the sector, and performance was even worse in 2020 when turnover in this branch declined by 25.1% compared with the previous year to reach just 49,200m. francs CFA. National maritime borders were closed in order to try to prevent the spread of COVID-19, which led to a slowdown in foreign trade flows (imports and exports), while the workforce employed in the sector declined by 19%.

Trade

In 2013 activity in this sector resulted in a consolidated turnover of 1,298,300m. francs CFA. However, understandably, activity in the trading sector slowed down in 2020, with overall turnover declining by 10.2% to stand at 862,000m. francs CFA. The strategy to combat COVID-19 has resulted in the reduction of working hours, and the confinement and the closure of certain structures which have weakened the sector. At the same time, investments contracted by 15.6%, due to the completion of major projects undertaken by companies in recent years and the cash flow pressures that many companies are facing.

General trade consists of companies specializing in the sale of miscellaneous goods (hardware, food, clothing, cosmetics, etc.). In 2017 structured general trade (which includes a wider range of products) recorded a 9% drop in turnover, and totalled 466,600m. francs CFA. The branch continued to suffer from the effects of the economic downturn which affected domestic demand. In 2020 the turnover of structured general trade fell by 2.6% to 463,000m. francs CFA, in a context of reduced domestic demand. This drop in activity was induced by the measures taken to combat the spread of COVID-19.

CONCLUSION

As has been depicted in the sections above, the COVID-19 pandemic had a significant and immediate economic impact in Gabon, and affected all sectors of the economy. Most significantly, the collapse in the international prices of petroleum and mineral commodities resulting from a drop in global demand weakened financial inflows. Gabon was obliged to seek emergency funding from the International Monetary Fund in April 2020, and secured US $147m. under its Rapid Financing Instrument (RFI); in July the Fund approved the disbursement of a further $152.6m. under the RFI to meet Gabon's immediate financing and balance-of-payments requirements, while in July 2021 a three-year Extended Fund Facility (EFF) arrangement totalling $553.2m. for was agreed, which included an immediate disbursement of $115.3m. towards budgetary support. GDP contracted by 1.3% in 2020, but a modest recovery followed, with estimated GDP growth of 1.6% in 2021, supported by higher international oil prices. In March 2022 the Government ended longstanding domestic COVID-19 containment measures, including restrictions on movement. However, the economy's fragility will continue while Gabon depends on the export of a limited range of raw materials.

Statistical Survey

Sources (unless otherwise stated): Direction Générale de la Statistique (DGS), BP 2119, Libreville; tel. 01-72-04-55; e-mail infodgstat@gmail.com; internet www .statgabon.ga; Direction Générale de l'Economie et de la Politique Fiscale (DGEPF), Ministry of the Economy and Economic Revival, Immeuble Arambo, BP 747, Libreville; tel. 01-76-34-35; internet www.dgepf.ga.

Area and Population

AREA, POPULATION AND DENSITY

Area (sq km)	267,667*
Population (census results)	
1 December 2003	1,269,732†
5 October 2013	
Males	933,711
Females	877,368
Total	1,811,079
Population (UN estimates at mid-year)‡	
2020	2,225,728
2021§	2,278,829
2022§	2,331,532
Density (per sq km) at mid-2022§	8.7

* 103,347 sq miles.
† Source: UN, *Population and Vital Statistics Report*.
‡ Source: UN, *World Population Prospects: The 2019 Revision*.
§ Projection.

POPULATION BY AGE AND SEX
('000, UN projections at mid-2022)

	Males	Females	Total
0–14 years	439.5	431.3	870.8
15–64 years	709.4	668.8	1,378.2
65 years and over	36.9	45.7	82.6
Total	**1,185.8**	**1,145.8**	**2,331.5**

Note: Totals may not be equal to the sum of components, owing to rounding.
Source: UN, *World Population Prospects: The 2019 Revision*.

REGIONS
(population at 2013 census)

Region	Area (sq km)	Population	Density (per sq km)	Chief town
Estuaire . .	20,740	895,689	43.2	Libreville
Haut-Ogooué .	36,547	250,799	6.9	Franceville
Moyen-Ogooué .	18,535	69,287	3.7	Lambaréné
N'Gounié . .	37,750	100,838	2.7	Mouila
Nyanga . .	21,285	52,854	2.5	Tchibanga
Ogooué-Ivindo .	46,075	63,293	1.4	Makokou
Ogooué-Lolo .	25,380	65,771	2.6	Koulamoutou
Ogooué-Maritime .	22,890	157,562	6.9	Port-Gentil
Woleu-N'Tem .	38,465	154,986	4.0	Oyem
Total . . .	**267,667**	**1,811,079**	**6.8**	

PRINCIPAL TOWNS
(population at 2013 census)

Libreville (capital) .	703,940	Ntoum	51,954
Port-Gentil . . .	136,462	Lambaréné . . .	38,775
Franceville . . .	110,568	Mouila	36,061
Owendo	79,300	Akanda	34,548
Oyem	60,685	Tchibanga . . .	30,042
Moanda	59,154		

Mid-2022 (incl. suburbs, UN projections): Libreville (capital) 856,854 (Source: UN, *World Urbanization Prospects: The 2018 Revision*).

BIRTHS AND DEATHS
(annual averages, UN estimates)

	2005–10	2010–15	2015–20
Birth rate (per 1,000)	32.9	33.2	32.0
Death rate (per 1,000)	10.4	8.2	6.9

Source: UN, *World Population Prospects: The 2019 Revision*.

Life expectancy (years at birth, estimates): 66.7 (males 64.4; females 68.9) in 2020 (Source: World Bank, World Development Indicators database).

ECONOMICALLY ACTIVE POPULATION
(FAO estimates, '000 persons at mid-year)

	2013	2014	2015
Agriculture, etc.	196	198	200
Total labour force (incl. others) .	807	831	857

Source: FAO.

2005 (persons aged 15 years and over): Total employed 639,180; Unemployed 115,499; Total labour force 664,117.

Health and Welfare

KEY INDICATORS

Total fertility rate (children per woman, 2020) . . .	3.9
Under-5 mortality rate (per 1,000 live births, 2020) . . .	41.7
HIV/AIDS (% of persons aged 15–49, 2020)	3.0
COVID-19: Cumulative confirmed deaths (per 100,000 persons at 31 August 2022)	13.1
COVID-19: Fully vaccinated population (% of total population at 14 August 2022)	11.0
Physicians (per 1,000 head, 2017)	0.7
Hospitals (per 100,000 head, 2013)	3.5
Domestic health expenditure (2019): US $ per head (PPP) .	260.7
Domestic health expenditure (2019): % of GDP . . .	1.7
Domestic health expenditure (2019): public (% of total current expenditure)	60.3
Access to improved water resources (% of persons, 2020) .	85
Access to improved sanitation facilities (% of persons, 2020) .	50
Total carbon dioxide emissions ('000 metric tons, 2020) . .	4,610
Carbon dioxide emissions per head (metric tons, 2020) . .	2.2
Human Development Index (2021): ranking	112
Human Development Index (2021): value	0.706

Note: For data on COVID-19 vaccinations, 'fully vaccinated' denotes receipt of all doses specified by approved vaccination regime (Sources: Johns Hopkins University and Our World in Data). Data on health expenditure refer to current general government expenditure in each case. For more information on sources and further definitions for all indicators, see Health and Welfare Statistics: Sources and Definitions section (europaworld.com/ credits).

Agriculture

PRINCIPAL CROPS
('000 metric tons, FAO estimates)

	2018	2019	2020
Bananas	18	18	18
Cassava (Manioc)	311	312	316
Groundnuts, with shell . . .	32	34	36
Maize	44	45	45
Oil palm fruit	21	20	20
Plantains and others	350	347	346
Rubber, natural	24	24	24
Sugar cane	285	288	292
Taro (Cocoyam)	87	87	87
Yams	218	218	218

Aggregate production ('000 metric tons, may include official, semi-official or estimated data): Total cereals 46 in 2018, 46 in 2019, 46 in 2020; Total fruit (primary) 391 in 2018, 388 in 2019, 387 in 2020; Total oilcrops 57 in 2018, 58 in 2019, 60 in 2020; Total roots and tubers 619 in 2018, 621 in 2019, 624 in 2020; Total vegetables (primary) 50 in 2018, 50 in 2019, 50 in 2020.

Source: FAO.

LIVESTOCK
('000 head, year ending September, FAO estimates)

	2018	2019	2020
Cattle	39	39	39
Chickens	3,221	3,232	3,244
Goats	115	113	115
Pigs	222	223	224
Sheep	220	221	222

Source: FAO.

LIVESTOCK PRODUCTS
('000 metric tons, FAO estimates)

	2018	2019	2020
Cattle meat	1.0	1.0	1.0
Cows' milk	14.0	14.0	14.0
Chicken meat	4.0	4.0	4.0
Game meat	27.7	27.8	27.9
Pig meat	3.5	3.6	3.6
Rabbit meat	2.0	2.1	2.1
Hen eggs	2.2	2.5	2.5

Source: FAO.

Forestry

ROUNDWOOD REMOVALS
('000 cubic metres, FAO estimates)

	2018	2019	2020
Sawlogs, veneer logs and logs for sleepers	2,034	2,139	2,919
Fuel wood	1,070	1,070	1,070
Total	3,104	3,209	3,989

Source: FAO.

SAWNWOOD PRODUCTION
('000 cubic metres, incl. railway sleepers, FAO estimates)

	2018	2019	2020
Total	951	952	765

Source: FAO.

Fishing

('000 metric tons, live weight, FAO estimates)

	2015	2016	2017
Capture	33.0	31.0	29.0
Tilapias	0.5	0.5	0.5
Sampa	7.3	7.3	7.3
African obscure snakehead . .	1.3	1.3	1.3
Other freshwater fishes . . .	0.3	0.3	0.3
West African croakers . . .	2.4	2.2	2.0
Giant African threadfin . . .	1.3	1.1	1.0
Mullets	2.5	2.3	2.1
Bonga shad	7.5	6.8	6.1
Dentex	1.4	1.3	1.1
Aquaculture	0.0	0.1	0.1
Total catch	33.0	31.1	29.1

2018–20: Figures are assumed to be unchanged from 2017 (FAO estimates).

Source: FAO.

Mining

	2019	2020	2021
Crude petroleum ('000 metric tons)	10,901	10,766	10,040
Natural gas ('000 cu m)* . . .	n.a.	464,434	444,497
Manganese ('000 metric tons)† .	6,749	8,443	9,522
Gold (kg)‡	100	400	100

* Marketed production.
† Figures refer to gross weight rather than metal content of ore, which was estimated at ('000 metric tons) 2,759 in 2019, 3,314 in 2020 and 3,600 in 2021, by the US Geological Survey.
‡ Figures refer to the metal content of ore.

Industry

PETROLEUM PRODUCTS
('000 metric tons)

	2017	2018	2019
Motor spirit (petrol)	32	29	30
Kerosene	22	20	19
Distillate fuel oils	254	233	189
Residual fuel oils and asphalt .	396	362	308

Source: UN Energy Statistics Database.

SELECTED OTHER PRODUCTS
(metric tons unless otherwise indicated)

	2020	2021
Palm oil, raw	70,340	107,336
Refined oils and soaps, etc.	31,688	33,330
Timber production ('000 cu m)	1,173.1	1,577.9
Veneer sheets ('000 cu m)	421.6	624.8
Plywood ('000 cu m)	49.7	80.7
Raw sugar	22,641	26,004
Rubber (processed)	7,324	5,496
Beer ('000 hl)	1,702	1,892
Wine ('000 hl)	42.0	39.3
Soft drinks ('000 hl)	933.3	996.3
Mineral water ('000 hl)	1,116	1,147
Paints	3,147	3,729
Electrical energy (million kWh)	2,396	2,404

Hydraulic cement (metric tons, estimates): 350,000 in 2016, 340,000 in 2017, 490,000 in 2018–19 (Source: US Geological Survey).

Finance

CURRENCY AND EXCHANGE RATES

Monetary Units
100 centimes = 1 franc de la Coopération Financière en Afrique Centrale (CFA).

Sterling, Dollar and Euro Equivalents (31 May 2022)
£1 sterling = 770.824 francs CFA;
US $1 = 612.300 francs CFA;
€1 = 655.957 francs CFA;
10,000 francs CFA = £12.97 = $16.33 = €15.24.

Average Exchange Rate (francs CFA per US $)
2019   585.91
2020   575.59
2021   554.53

Note: An exchange rate of 1 French franc = 50 francs CFA, established in 1948, remained in force until January 1994, when the CFA franc was devalued by 50%, with the exchange rate adjusted to 1 French franc = 100 francs CFA. This relationship to French currency remained in effect with the introduction of the euro on 1 January 1999. From that date, accordingly, a fixed exchange rate of €1 = 655.957 francs CFA has been in operation.

BUDGET
('000 million francs CFA)

Revenue*	2020	2021†	2022‡
Petroleum revenue	596	595	981
Taxes	874	970	1,137
Taxes on income, profits and capital gains	303	321	397
Taxes on goods and services	134	214	283
Value-added tax	63	134	194
Other	71	79	89
Taxes on international trade and transactions	310	323	338
Other taxes	127	113	118
Non-tax revenue	79	75	84
Total	**1,549**	**1,641**	**2,202**

Expenditure§	2020	2021†	2022‡
Current expenditure	1,431	1,491	1,563
Wages and salaries	683	682	684
Goods and services	202	232	213
Interest payments	297	309	330
Capital expenditure	241	273	320
Domestically financed investment	152	199	180
Externally financed investment	89	74	140
Special funds (incl. road funds)	74	96	192
Total	**1,746**	**1,860**	**2,075**

* Excluding grants ('000 million francs CFA): 4 in 2020; 12 in 2021 (preliminary); 54 in 2022 (projection).
† Preliminary.
‡ Projections.
§ Excluding net lending ('000 million francs CFA): 4 in 2020; 0 in 2021 (preliminary); 0 in 2022 (projection).

Source: IMF, *Gabon: First and Second Reviews of the Extended Arrangement under the Extended Fund Facility, Requests for Waivers for Nonobservance of Performance Criteria, Establishment of Performance Criteria, and Financing Assurances Review—Press Release; Staff Report; Staff Supplement; and Statement by the Executive Director* (July 2022).

INTERNATIONAL RESERVES
(US $ million at 31 December)

	2017	2018	2019
Gold*	16.53	16.42	19.45
IMF special drawing rights	167.22	163.46	162.07
Reserve position in IMF	23.75	23.63	23.76
Foreign exchange	774.09	1,133.97	1,186.15
Total	**981.59**	**1,337.48**	**1,391.43**

* Valued at market-related prices.

2020: IMF special drawing rights 167.79; Reserve position in IMF 25.05.
2021: IMF special drawing rights 454.91; Reserve position in IMF 24.66.
Source: IMF, *International Financial Statistics*.

MONEY SUPPLY
('000 million francs CFA at 31 December)

	2017	2018	2019
Currency outside depository corporations	384.95	426.15	416.66
Transferable deposits	728.38	1,027.77	1,195.50
Other deposits	565.19	782.41	654.67
Total money	**1,678.51**	**2,236.33**	**2,266.83**

Source: IMF, *International Financial Statistics*.

COST OF LIVING
(Consumer Price Index; base: 2004 = 100)

	2016	2017	2018
Food and non-alcoholic beverages	139.7	138.7	143.8
Clothing and footwear	135.9	137.7	140.1
Rent, water, electricity, gas and other fuels	127.5	140.1	145.9
All items (incl. others)	130.1	133.5	139.9

All items (Consumer Price Index; base: 2010 = 100): 119.7 in 2018; 122.6 in 2019; 124.1 in 2020 (Source: IMF, *International Financial Statistics*).

NATIONAL ACCOUNTS
('000 million francs CFA at current prices)

Expenditure on the Gross Domestic Product

	2019	2020	2021*
Government final consumption expenditure	1,086.9	1,161.0	1,274.2
Private final consumption expenditure	3,724.8	3,700.5	3,687.3
Gross fixed capital formation	2,165.1	1,754.1	1,882.3
Total domestic expenditure	**6,976.8**	**6,615.6**	**6,843.8**
Exports of goods and services	5,084.9	4,187.5	6,255.6
Less Imports of goods and services	2,174.8	1,988.2	1,888.6
GDP at purchasers' values	**9,886.9**	**8,814.9**	**11,210.9**
GDP in constant 2001 prices	**5,747.5**	**5,641.9**	**5,724.4**

Gross Domestic Product by Economic Activity

	2019	2020	2021*
Agriculture, livestock, hunting, forestry and fishing	549.2	584.3	674.6
Mining and quarrying	3,515.5	2,523.1	4,352.9
Manufacturing	754.4	729.3	869.6
Electricity, gas and water . .	116.6	115.4	117.9
Construction	327.8	298.2	367.7
Wholesale, retail trade, restaurants and hotels . . .	526.9	498.5	515.4
Finance, insurance and real estate	279.3	285.9	306.1
Transport, storage and communication	1,028.7	1,134.2	1,252.7
Education and health	264.3	266.3	268.9
Other activities	1,901.7	1,772.7	1,990.5
Sub-total	**9,264.4**	**8,207.9**	**10,716.3**
Indirect taxes (net) . . .	622.5	607.0	494.6
GDP at purchasers' values .	**9,886.9**	**8,814.9**	**11,210.9**

* Preliminary.

BALANCE OF PAYMENTS
('000 million francs CFA)

	2018*	2019†
Exports of goods f.o.b.	3,446	3,706
Imports of goods f.o.b.	−1,761	−1,832
Trade balance	**1,685**	**1,874**
Services (net)	−964	−1,085
Balance on goods and services	**722**	**789**
Other income (net)	−861	−820
Balance on goods, services and income .	**−139**	**−31**
Current transfers (net)	−57	−59
Current balance	**−196**	**−89**
Direct investment (net)	477	735
Portfolio investment (net)	166	176
Other investment assets and liabilities (net) .	−660	−1,159
Errors and omissions	−4	0
Overall balance	**−217**	**−336**

* Estimates.
† Preliminary.

Source: IMF, *Gabon: Request for a Three-Year Extended Arrangement under the Extended Fund Facility—Press Release; Staff Report; Supplementary Information, and Statement by the Executive Director for Gabon* (August 2021).

External Trade

PRINCIPAL COMMODITIES
(distribution by SITC, US $ million)

Imports c.i.f.	2016	2017	2018
Mineral fuels, mineral oils and products of their distillation; bituminous substances; mineral waxes	3,872	1,631	1,284
Boilers, machinery and mechanical appliances; parts thereof . .	537	837	904
Vehicles other than railway or tramway rolling-stock, and parts	189	135	173
Electrical machinery and equipment and parts thereof; sound recorders and reproducers	193	165	161
Total (incl. others)	**6,534**	**4,401**	**4,224**

Exports f.o.b.	2016	2017	2018
Mineral fuels, mineral oils and products of their distillation; bituminous substances; mineral waxes	2,946	3,545	4,574
Ships, boats and floating structures	5,869	1,630	1,856
Boilers, machinery and mechanical appliances; parts thereof . .	221	70	1,029
Wood and articles of wood; wood charcoal	438	489	473
Ores, slag and ash	130	186	229
Total (incl. others)	**9,981**	**6,149**	**8,443**

Source: African Development Bank.

PRINCIPAL TRADING PARTNERS
(US $ million)

Imports c.i.f.	2016	2017	2018
Belgium	295	278	279
China, People's Republic . . .	623	295	336
Congo, Republic	798	305	339
France	679	730	664
Spain	46	485	553
Total (incl. others)	**6,534**	**4,401**	**4,224**

Exports f.o.b.	2016	2017	2018
China, People's Republic . . .	950	1,576	1,810
Congo, Republic	2,435	609	427
India	36	222	405
Netherlands	249	290	785
Spain	624	98	571
Total (incl. others)	**9,981**	**6,149**	**8,443**

Source: African Development Bank.

Transport

RAILWAYS
(traffic)

	2019	2020	2021
Passengers carried ('000) . . .	321.6	163.1	227.0
Freight carried ('000 metric tons) .	7,165.1	9,117.5	10,012.2

SHIPPING

Flag Registered Fleet
(at 31 December)

	2019	2020	2021
Number of vessels	82	103	115
Total displacement ('000 grt) . .	397.2	680.4	940.1

Source: Lloyd's List Intelligence (www.bit.ly/LLintelligence).

International Seaborne Freight Traffic

	2019	2020	2021
Vessels entered	3,065	3,608	3,884
Goods handled ('000 metric tons) .	9,072.8	10,960.1	12,710.3

CIVIL AVIATION
(traffic on scheduled services)

	2019	2020	2021
Flights (number)	15,311	10,068	11,960
Passengers carried ('000) . . .	793.5	298.6	516.4
Freight carried (metric tons) . .	13,506	12,247	11,726

Tourism

	2015	2016	2017
Tourist arrivals ('000) . . .	624	664	586
Tourism receipts (US $ million) .	10	11	11

Source: African Development Bank.

Communications Media

	2018	2019	2020
Telephones ('000 main lines in use)	21.8	22.3	25.4
Mobile telephone subscriptions ('000)	2,930.6	2,992.8	3,088.7
Broadband subscriptions, fixed ('000)	21.1	20.6	44.6
Broadband subscriptions, mobile ('000)	1,945.8	2,048.7	2,071.5
Internet users (% of population) .	59.6	61.0	n.a.

Source: International Telecommunication Union.

Education

(2010/11 unless otherwise indicated, estimates)

			Pupils		
	Institutions	Teachers	Males	Females	Total
Pre-primary .	232*	515†	22,416	22,809	45,225
Primary . .	1,563‡	12,961	162,708	155,238	317,946
Secondary:					
General .	} 107* {	5,062	70,623	75,457	146,080
Technical and vocational		394†	5,025§	2,562§	7,587§
Tertiary . .	5*	585§	6,414‖	3,662‖	10,076‖

* 2008/09 figure.
† 2000/01 figure.
‡ 2005/06 figure.
§ 1998/99 figure.
‖ 2002/03 figure.

Source: mostly UNESCO Institute for Statistics.

Pupil-teacher ratio (qualified teaching staff, primary education, UNESCO estimate): 35.0 in 2018/19 (Source: UNESCO Institute for Statistics).

Adult literacy rate (UNESCO estimates): 84.7% (males 85.9%; females 83.4%) in 2018 (Source: UNESCO Institute for Statistics).

Directory

Note: The telephone numbers listed in this Directory are those used when dialling from within Gabon. In order successfully to dial from abroad, it is necessary to omit the initial 0.

The Constitution

The Constitution of the Gabonese Republic was adopted on 14 March 1991 and amended in March 1994, September 1995, April 1997, October 2000, August 2003, January 2011, November 2018 and December 2020. The main provisions are summarized below.

PREAMBLE

Upholds the rights of the individual, liberty of conscience and of the person, religious freedom and freedom of education. Sovereignty is vested in the people, who exercise it through their representatives or by means of referendums. There is direct, universal and secret suffrage.

HEAD OF STATE

The President is elected by direct universal suffrage for a seven-year term. There is no limit on the number of terms that may be served. The President is head of state and of the armed forces. The President may, after consultation with his or her ministers and leaders of the National Assembly, order a referendum to be held. The President appoints the Prime Minister, who is head of government and who is accountable to the President. The President is the guarantor of national independence and territorial sovereignty.

EXECUTIVE POWER

Executive power is vested in the President and the Council of Ministers, who are appointed by the Prime Minister, in consultation with the President.

LEGISLATIVE POWER

The National Assembly is elected by direct universal suffrage for a five-year term. It may be dissolved or prorogued for up to 18 months by the President, after consultation with the Council of Ministers and President of the National Assembly. The President may return a bill to the National Assembly for a second reading, when it must be passed by a majority of two-thirds of the members. If the President dissolves the National Assembly, elections must take place within 40 days.

The Senate comprises 67 members, who serve six–year terms, 52 of whom are directly elected and 15 are elected by the President of the Republic.

POLITICAL ORGANIZATIONS

Article 2 of the Constitution states that 'political parties and associations contribute to the expression of universal suffrage. They are formed and exercise their activities freely, within the limits delineated by the laws and regulations. They must respect the principles of democracy, national sovereignty, public order and national unity'.

JUDICIAL POWER

The President guarantees the independence of the judiciary. Supreme judicial power is vested in the Supreme Court.

The Government

HEAD OF STATE

President: ALI BONGO ONDIMBA (inaugurated 16 October 2009; re-elected 27 August 2016).

COUNCIL OF MINISTERS
(October 2022)

Prime Minister and Head of Government: ROSE CHRISTIANE OSSOUKA RAPONDA.

Deputy Prime Minister, Minister of Energy and Water Resources, Government Spokesperson: ALAIN CLAUDE BILIE BY NZE.

Minister of State, Minister of Relations with the Constitutional Institutions and the Independent Administrative Authorities: DENISE MEKAM'NE EDZIDZIE TATY.

Minister of State, Minister of the Interior: LAMBERT NOËL MATHA.

Minister of Foreign Affairs: MICHAEL MOUSSA ADAMO.

Minister of Employment, the Civil Service and Labour: MADELEINE BERRE.

Minister of the Promotion of Good Governance and the Fight against Corruption: FRANCIS NKEA NDZIGUE.

Minister of National Defence: FÉLICITÉ ONGOUORI NGOUBILI.

Minister of the Decentralization, Cohesion and Development of Territories: MICHEL MENGA M'ESSONE.

Minister of Justice, Keeper of the Seals, in charge of Human Rights and Equality: ERLYNE ANTONELLA NDEMBET DAMAS.

Minister of Communication: PASCAL HOUANGNI AMBOUROUET.

Minister of Professional Training: RAPHAËL NGAZOUZE.

Minister of Water, Forestry, the Sea and the Environment, in charge of Planning for Climate Change and Planning for Land Allocation: Prof. LEE WHITE.

Minister of Tourism: JEAN-NORBERT DIRAMBA.

Minister of the Economy and Economic Revival: NICOLE JEANINE LYDIE ROBOTY-MBOU.

Minister of Higher Education, Scientific Research, Technology Transfer, Culture and Arts: PATRICK DAOUDA MOUGUIAMA.

Minister of the Digital Economy: JEAN-PIERRE DOUKAGA KASSA.

Minister of the Promotion of Investment and Public-Private Partnerships, in charge of the Improvement of the Business Environment: HUGUES MBADINGA MADIYA.

Minister of Health and Social Affairs: GUY PATRICK OBIANG NDONG.

Minister of Housing and Town Planning: OLIVIER NANG EKOMIE.

Minister of Trade and Small and Medium-sized Enterprises: YVES FERNAND MAMFOUMBI.

Minister of Youth and Sport: FRANCK NGUEMA.

Minister of Petroleum and Gas: VINCENT DE PAUL MASSASSA.

Minister of National Education, in charge of Civic Education: CAMELIA NTOUTOUME-LECLERCQ.

Minister of the Budget and Public Accounts: EDITH EKIRI MOUNOMBI OYOUOMI.

Minister of Agriculture and Food: CHARLES MVE ELLA.

Minister of Transport: BRICE CONSTANT PAILLAT.

Minister of Fisheries and the Maritime Economy: SÉVERIN MAYOUNOU.

Minister of Mining: ELVIS OSSINDJI.

Minister of Public Works, Equipment and Infrastructure: TOUSSAINT KOUMA EMANA.

Minister-delegate to the Minister of Foreign Affairs: YOLANDE NYONDA.

Minister-delegate to the Minister of Foreign Affairs, in charge of Relations with the Commonwealth: HERMANN IMMONGAULT.

Minister-delegate to the Minister of Water, Forestry, the Sea and the Environment, in charge of Planning for Climate Change and Planning for Land Allocation: STÉPHANE BONDA.

Minister-delegate to the Minister of National Education, in charge of Civic Education: AUBIERGE SYLVINE NGOMA.

Minister-delegate to the Minister of the Digital Economy: HUGUETTE ABODO YOMBIYENI.

Minister-delegate to the Minister of Health and Social Affairs: JUSTINE LEMBIMBI MIHINDOU.

Minister-delegate to the Minister of State, Minister of Energy and Water Resources: SIDONIE MOUSSIROU.

Minister-delegate to the Minister of Higher Education, Scientific Research, Technology Transfer and National Education, in charge of Civic Education: MAX-SAMUEL OBOUMADJOGO.

MINISTRIES

Office of the President: BP 546, Libreville; tel. 011-72-76-00; internet presidence-gabon.ga.

Office of the Prime Minister: Immeuble du 2 Décembre, ave Jean Paul II, BP 95, Libreville; tel. 011-77-56-24; internet www.primature .gouv.ga.

Ministry of Agriculture and Food: Immeuble de l'Ancienne Primature, ave Cornut Gentille, BP 551, Libreville; tel. 011-74-00-43; internet www.agriculture.gouv.ga.

Ministry of the Budget and Public Accounts: Libreville; internet www.budget.gouv.ga.

Ministry of Communication: blvd de l'Indépendance, BP 2280, Libreville; tel. 011-76-34-35; e-mail info-mencp@gouv.ga; internet www.economie-numerique.gouv.ga.

Ministry of the Decentralization, Cohesion and Development of Territories: Libreville.

Ministry of the Digital Economy: Libreville.

Ministry of the Economy and Economic Revival: Immeuble Arambo, BP 747, Libreville; tel. 011-79-55-27; internet www .economie.gouv.ga.

Ministry of Employment, the Civil Service and Labour: BP 496, Libreville; tel. 011-76-06-72; internet fonction-publique.gouv .ga.

Ministry of Energy and Water Resources: Libreville; internet www.energie.gouv.ga.

Ministry of Fisheries and the Maritime Economy: Libreville.

Ministry of Foreign Affairs: blvd du Bord de Mer, Libreville; tel. 011-74-23-71; e-mail mae@diplomatie.gouv.ga; internet www .affaires-etrangeres.gouv.ga.

Ministry of Health and Social Affairs: BP 50, Libreville; tel. 011-72-26-61; internet www.sante.gouv.ga.

Ministry of Higher Education, Scientific Research, Technology Transfer, Culture and Arts: Libreville.

Ministry of Housing and Town Planning: Libreville.

Ministry of the Interior: ave de Cointet, BP 2110, Libreville; tel. 011-76-20-64; internet www.interieur.gouv.ga.

Ministry of Justice: BP 547, Libreville; tel. 011-72-18-30; internet www.justice.gouv.ga.

Ministry of Mining: Libreville.

Ministry of National Defence: BP 13493, Libreville; tel. 011-76-35-79; internet www.defense-nationale.gouv.ga.

Ministry of National Education: BP 6, Libreville; tel. 011-76-42-65; internet www.education-nationale.gouv.ga.

Ministry of Petroleum, Gas and Mining: Immeuble du 2 Décembre, 852 blvd Triomphal Bâtiment B, 3e étage, BP 874, Libreville; tel. 011-77-86-54; e-mail sg@mines.gouv.ga; internet www.petrole.gouv .ga.

Ministry of the Promotion of Good Governance and the Fight against Corruption: Libreville.

Ministry of the Promotion of Investment and Public-Private Partnerships: Libreville; internet fb.com/ PromotionInvestissementGOUVGA.

Ministry of Professional Training: Libreville.

Ministry of Relations with the Constitutional Institutions and the Independent Administrative Authorities: Libreville; internet www.relations-institutions.gouv.ga.

Ministry of Tourism: Libreville; internet www.pme.gouv.ga.

Ministry of Trade and Small and Medium-sized Enterprises: Libreville.

Ministry of Transport: BP 47, Libreville; tel. 011-72-03-96; internet www.equipement.gouv.ga.

Ministry of Water, Forestry, the Sea and the Environment: blvd Triomphal Omar Bongo Ondimba, BP 199, Libreville; tel. 011-76-13-81; internet www.eaux-forets.gouv.ga.

Ministry of Youth and Sport: Libreville.

President

Presidential Election, 27 August 2016

Candidate	Valid votes	% of valid votes
Ali Bongo Ondimba (PDG)	172,990	50.66
Jean Ping (FUOA)	161,287	47.24
Bruno Ben Moubamba (UPG) . .	2,010	0.59
Raymond Ndong Sima (Ind.) . .	1,432	0.42
Pierre Claver Maganga Moussavou (PSD)	1,173	0.34
Others*	2,557	0.75
Total	341,449†	100.00

* There were five other candidates.
† The figure declared by the Constitutional Court for the number of valid votes was 341,447.

Legislature

NATIONAL ASSEMBLY

National Assembly: Palais Léon Mba, blvd Triomphal Omar Bongo Ondimba, BP 29, Libreville; tel. 011-74-90-21; internet www .assemblee-nationale.ga.

President: FAUSTIN BOUKOUBI.

General Election, 6 and 27 October 2018

Party	Seats
Parti Démocratique Gabonais (PDG)	95
Les Démocrates (LD)	9
Restauration des Valeurs Républicaines (RV)	6
Sociaux Démocrates Gabonais (SDG)	5
Rassemblement Héritage et Modernité (RHM)	4
Parti Social-Démocrate (PSD)	2
Cercle des Libéraux Réformateurs (CLR)	1
Démocratie Nouvelle (DN)	1
Front d'Egalité Républicaine (FER)	1
RV/PDG	1
Union pour la Démocratie et l'Intégration Sociale/PDG	1
Union Nationale (UN)	1
Union pour la Nouvelle République (UPNR)	1
Independents	6
Total	**134***

* The result in one constituency was not immediately declared, and, following investigations by the Constitutional Court, in December 2018 the results in a further eight constituencies were annulled.

SENATE

Senate: Palais Omar Bongo Ondimba, 3 blvd Triomphal, BP 7513, Libreville; tel. 011-76-20-53; internet fb.com/senatgabon.

President: LUCIE MILEBOU AUBUSSON.

Election, 30 January and 6 February 2021

Party	Seats
Parti Démocratique Gabonais (PDG)	46
Les Démocrates (LD)	3
Sociaux Démocrates Gabonais (SDG)	2
Parti Social-Démocrate (PSD)	1
Total	**52***

*A further 15 senators are appointed by the President of the Republic.

Election Commission

Centre Gabonais des Elections (CGE): Libreville; f. 2018; 10 mems; Pres. MOÏSE BIBALOU KOUMBA.

Political Organizations

Alliance Démocratique et Républicaine (ADERE): Pres. DIDJOB DIVUNGUI-DI-N'DINGUE.

Cercle des Libéraux Réformateurs (CLR): f. 1993 by breakaway faction of the PDG; Leader JEAN-BONIFACE ASSELE.

Coalition pour la Nouvelle République: Pres. JEAN PING.

Congrès pour la Démocratie et la Justice (CDJ): tel. 011-70-00-00; Pres. JULES BOURDÈS OGOULIGUENDE.

Démocratie Nouvelle: f. 2016; Pres. RENÉ NDEMEZO'O OBIANG.

Ensemble pour la République: f. 2017; Pres. DIEUDONNÉ MINLAMA MINTOGO.

Les Démocrates (LD): Pres. GUY NZOUBA-NDAMA.

Parti Démocratique Gabonais (PDG): Immeuble PETROGAB, BP 268, Libreville; tel. 011-70-31-21; e-mail pdg.partidemocratiquegabonais@gmail.com; internet fb.com/pdggabon; f. 1968; sole legal party 1968–90; Leader ALI BONGO ONDIMBA; Sec.-Gen. STEEVE NZEGHO DIEKO.

Parti Gabonais du Centre Indépendant (PGCI): allied to the PDG; Leader LUCCHERI GAHILA.

Parti Gabonais du Progrès (PGP): f. 1990; Pres. BENOÎT MOUITY NZAMBA.

Parti Social-Démocrate (PSD): f. 1991; Leader PIERRE-CLAVER MAGANGA MOUSSAVOU.

Rassemblement pour la Démocratie et le Progrès (RDP): Pres. PÉPIN MOUNGOKODJI.

Rassemblement pour le Gabon (RPG): BP 6740, Libreville; internet fb.com/Rassemblement-Pour-le-Gabon-519741498170935; f. 1990 as MORENA des Bûcherons; renamed Rassemblement National des Bûcherons in 1991, present name adopted in 2000; allied to the PDG; Pres. LAURENT ANGUÉ MEZUI.

Rassemblement Héritage et Modernité (RHM): Port Gentil; f. 2016; Pres. ALEXANDRE BARRO CHAMBRIER.

Rassemblement National des Bûcherons—Démocratique (RNB): Libreville; f. 1991; Leader PIERRE ANDRÉ KOMBILA.

Rassemblement pour la Patrie et la Modernité (RPM): Pres. ALEXANDRE BARRO CHAMBRIER.

Sociaux Démocrates Gabonais (SDG): Libreville; Pres. JUSTE LOUANGOU BOUYOMEKA.

Union Démocratique et Sociale (UDS): f. 1996; Leader HERVÉ OSSAMANÉ ONOUVIÉ.

Union Nationale (UN): f. 2010 through the merger of the Union Gabonaise pour la Démocratie et le Développement (UGDD), the Mouvement Africain de Développement (MAD) and the Rassemblement National des Républicains (RNR); forcibly banned by the Government in Jan. 2011; ban revoked in Jan. 2015; Pres. PAULETTE MISSAMBO.

Union pour la Nouvelle République (UPNR): Immeuble Score, 657 ave du Col Parant, BP 4049, Libreville; tel. 011-77-40-13; e-mail info@louisgastonmayila.com; internet www.louisgastonmayila.com; f. 2007 following the merger of the Front pour l'Unité Nationale (FUNDU) and the Rassemblement des Républicains Indépendants (RRI); Leader LOUIS-GASTON MAYILA.

Union du Peuple Gabonais (UPG): BP 6048, Awendjé, Libreville; tel. 077-14-61-61; internet upg-ga.com; f. 1989 in Paris, France; Pres. BRUNO BEN MOUBAMBA; Sec.-Gen. JEAN OLIVIER KOUMBA MBOUMBA.

Union pour le Progrès National (UPN): Leader DANIEL TENGUE NZOUNDO.

Diplomatic Representation

EMBASSIES IN GABON

Algeria: blvd du Bord de Mer, BP 4008, Libreville; tel. 011-44-34-80; internet ambalglibreville.com; Ambassador ABDELHAK AISSAOUI.

Angola: Trois Quartiers, avant Eglise St André, BP 4884, Libreville; tel. 011-73-04-26; e-mail ncosmefr@yahoo.fr; Ambassador LIZETH NAWANGA SATUMBO PENA.

Brazil: blvd du Bord de Mer, Pont de Gué, BP 3899, Libreville; tel. 011-44-22-63; e-mail brasemb.libreville@itamaraty.gov.br; internet libreville.itamaraty.gov.br; Ambassador JOSÉ MARCOS NOGUEIRA VIANA.

Burkina Faso: allée Iguindi, Haut de Gué Gué, BP 7763, Libreville; tel. 011-44-11-48; e-mail contacts@ambaburkina-ga.org; internet ambaburkina-ga.org; Ambassador SAÏDOU ZONGO.

Cameroon: blvd Léon Mba, BP 14001, Libreville; tel. 011-73-28-00; e-mail ambacamgabon@yahoo.fr; High Commissioner EDITH FÉLICIE NOËLLE NGAETO ZAM.

Chad: Libreville; Ambassador ALI ALIFEI MOUSTAPHA.

China, People's Republic: blvd Triomphale Omar Bongo Ondimba, BP 3914, Libreville; tel. 011-74-32-07; e-mail chinaemb_ga@mfa.gov.cn; internet ga.china-embassy.gov.cn; Ambassador JINJIN LI.

Congo, Democratic Republic: Batterie IV, BP 2257, Libreville; tel. 011-73-11-61; e-mail ambardcgabon@yahoo.fr; Ambassador FRANÇOIS LWAMBO SIONGO.

Congo, Republic: Batterie IV, BP 269, Libreville; tel. 011-73-29-06; e-mail ambacobrazzalibreville@yahoo.fr; internet ambacongogabon.wordpress.com; Ambassador FRANÇOIS IBOVI.

Côte d'Ivoire: Quartier Louis, rue Pierre Barrot, BP 3861, Libreville; tel. 011-73-82-70; e-mail ambacigabon@hotmail.com; internet gabon.diplomatie.gouv.ci; Ambassador NICOLAS KOUAKOU KOUADIO.

Cuba: 290 rue Abdulaye Moctar Mbigith, Libreville; tel. 011-73-33-74; e-mail embacuba.gabon@gmail.com; internet misiones.minrex.gob.cu/fr/gabon/ambassade-de-cuba-au-gabon; Ambassador LLUSIF SADIN TASSÉ.

Egypt: Immeuble Floria, 3e étage, 1 blvd de la Mer, Quartier Batterie IV, BP 4240, Libreville; tel. 011-73-25-38; e-mail embassy.libreville@mfa.gov.eg; Ambassador AHMED HAMDI BAKR MOHAMED.

Equatorial Guinea: centre de Tris Postaux des Charbonnages, BP 14262, Libreville; tel. 011-73-25-23; e-mail embargega@yahoo.fr; Ambassador ANTONIO EBALE AYINGONO.

France: 185 rue du Pont Pirah, BP 2125, Libreville; tel. 011-79-70-00; e-mail presse@ambafrance-ga.org; internet ga.ambafrance.org; Ambassador ALEXIS LAMEK.

Germany: Immeuble les Frangipaniers, 329 blvd de la Nation, Centre-Ville, BP 299, Libreville; tel. 011-76-01-88; e-mail info@libreville.diplo.de; internet libreville.diplo.de; Ambassador PASCAL RICHTER.

Guinea: blvd Triomphal, BP 4046, Libreville; tel. 011-73-40-09; e-mail ambaguinéegabon@yahoo.fr; Ambassador Elhadji ABDOULAYE BALDE.

Holy See: blvd Monseigneur Bessieux, BP 1322, Libreville; tel. 74-45-41; e-mail nonapcg@yahoo.com; Apostolic Nuncio Fr JAVIER HERRERA CORONA (Titular Archbishop of Vulturaria; designate) (resident in Brazzaville, Republic of Congo).

Italy: ave Paul Moukambi 967, Haut de Gué, BP 23731, Libreville; tel. 011-74-28-92; e-mail ambasciata.libreville@esteri.it; internet amblibreville.esteri.it; Ambassador GABRIELE DI MUZIO.

Japan: blvd du Bord de Mer, BP 2259, Libreville; tel. 011-73-22-97; e-mail japon@lv.mofa.go.jp; internet www.ga.emb-japan.go.jp; Ambassador SHUJI NOGUCHI.

Korea, Republic: BP 2620, Libreville; tel. 011-73-40-00; e-mail gabon-ambcoree@mofa.go.kr; internet overseas.mofa.go.kr/ga-ko/index.do; Ambassador RYU CHANG-SOO.

Kuwait: BP 4884, Libreville; tel. 011-44-33-94; e-mail kwt-lbv@outlook.com; Ambassador ASAD ABDELAZIZ ALBAHR.

Lebanon: blvd Triomphal Omar Bongo Ondimba, BP 3341, Libreville; tel. 011-74-24-91; e-mail amblib241@yahoo.fr; internet www.amblibgabon.org; Ambassador ALINE YOUNES.

Libya: Sablière, BP 13483, Libreville; tel. 011-44-36-23; Chargé d'affaires a.i. KHALED S. O. SWESSI.

Mali: Batterie IV, BP 4007, Libreville; tel. 011-73-82-73; e-mail ambamaga@yahoo.fr; Ambassador MAMADOU MANDJOU BERTHE.

Mauritania: BP 3917, Libreville; tel. 011-74-31-65; Ambassador ABDARRAHMANE BA.

Morocco: blvd de Léon M'Ba, BP 3983, Libreville; tel. 011-44-48-92; e-mail ambmaroc@yahoo.fr; Ambassador ABDALLAH MASSIHI.

Nigeria: 1081 ave Paul Marie Ymbit, BP 1191, Libreville; tel. 011-73-22-03; e-mail nigeria.libreville@foreignaffairs.gov.ng; internet nigeriaembassylibreville.org; High Commissioner RAYMOND UDOFFE BROWN.

Russian Federation: blvd Triomphal Omar Bongo Ondimba, BP 3963, Libreville; tel. 011-72-48-68; e-mail ambrusga@mail.ru; internet gabon.mid.ru; Ambassador ILYAS ISKANDEROV.

São Tomé and Príncipe: blvd de l'Indépendance, BP 489, Libreville; tel. 011-72-09-94; Ambassador URBINO JOSÉ GONHALVES BOTELÇO.

Saudi Arabia: Haut de Gué-Gué, derrière l'Hotel Park Inn, Libreville; tel. 011-73-17-19; internet embassies.mofa.gov.sa/sites/gabon; Ambassador ABDULRAHMAN BIN SALEM AL-DAHHAS.

Senegal: Quartier Sobraga, BP 3856, Libreville; tel. 011-77-42-67; e-mail ambasengab@yahoo.fr; Ambassador MARNE OUMAR TIAW.

South Africa: Immeuble les Arcades, 142 rue des Chavannes, BP 4063, Libreville; tel. 011-77-45-30; e-mail saelbv@gmail.com; internet www.dirco.gov.za/gabon; High Commissioner NCUMISA PAMELLA NOTUTELA.

Spain: Immeuble Diamant, 2ème étage, blvd de l'Indépendance, BP 1157, Libreville; tel. 011-72-12-64; e-mail emb.libreville@maec.es; internet www.exteriores.gob.es/embajadas/libreville; Ambassador RAMÓN MOLINA LLADÓ.

Togo: Batterie IV, 398 ave Mihindou Minzamba, BP 14160, Libreville; tel. 011-44-43-97; e-mail ambatogolbv@ymail.com; internet ambatogogabon.com; High Commissioner (vacant).

Türkiye (Turkey): Bas de Gué-Gué, en face de l'Immeuble Samira, Libreville; tel. 011-73-00-12; internet librevil.be.mfa.gov.tr; Ambassador NILÜFER ERDEM KAYGISIZ.

USA: Avorbam, La Sablière, BP 4000, Libreville; tel. 011-45-71-00; e-mail usembassylibreville@state.gov; internet ga.usembassy.gov; Chargé d'affaires a.i. SAMUEL R. WATSON.

Judicial System

Justice is dispensed on behalf of the Gabonese people by the three autonomous chambers of the Supreme Court (judicial, administrative and accounting), the Constitutional Court, the Council of State, the Courts of Appeal, the Audit Court, the Provincial Courts, the High Court and the other special courts of law.

Supreme Court (Cour de Cassation): Palais de Justice, BP 1043, Libreville; tel. 011-72-17-00; 3 chambers: judicial, administrative and accounting; First Pres. JULIENNE OLGA N'ZAMBA MASSOUNGA TCHIKAYA.

Constitutional Court: BP 4025, Libreville; tel. 011-76-62-88; has jurisdiction on: the control of the constitutionality of laws before promulgation; all electoral litigations; all matters concerning individual fundamental rights and public liberties; the interpretation of the Constitution; and arbitration of conflicts of jurisdiction arising among the state's institutions; Pres. MARIE-MADELEINE MBORANTSUO.

Council of State: BP 547, Libreville; tel. 011-72-17-00; Pres. BASILE MOUTELET NGUELE.

Courts of Appeal: Libreville, Franceville, Port-Gentil, Mouila and Oyem.

Audit Court (Cour des Comptes): BP 752, Libreville; tel. 011-70-54-15; e-mail contact@ccomptes.ga; internet www.ccomptes.ga; Pres. RENÉ ABOGHE ELLA.

Religion

About 60% of Gabon's population are Christians, mainly adherents of the Roman Catholic Church, although many people practice elements of both Christianity and traditional indigenous religious beliefs. Some 12% of the population practice Islam; of these people around 80%–90% are foreigners.

CHRISTIANITY

The Roman Catholic Church

Gabon comprises one archdiocese, four dioceses and one apostolic vicariate.

Bishops' Conference: Conférence Episcopale du Gabon, BP 2146, Libreville; tel. 011-72-20-73; internet fb.com/eglisecatholiqueaugabon; f. 1989; Pres. Most Rev. MATHIEU MADÉGA LÉBOUAKÉHAN (Bishop of Mouila).

Archbishop of Libreville: Most Rev. JEAN-PATRICK IBA-BA, Archevêché, Sainte-Marie, BP 2146, Libreville; tel. 066-26-27-78; e-mail basilemve@yahoo.fr.

Protestant Churches

Christian and Missionary Alliance: BP 13021, Libreville; tel. 011-73-24-39; e-mail fdgabon@gmail.com; active in the south of the country; Dir Dr DAVID THOMPSON.

Eglise Evangélique du Gabon: BP 10080, Libreville; tel. 011-72-41-92; f. 1842; independent since 1961; Pres. Rev. LOUIS-SYLVAIN ALLOGHO ENGO; Sec. Rev. BASILE NGUEMA OLLOGHO.

The Evangelical Church of South Gabon and the Evangelical Pentecostal Church are also active in Gabon.

ISLAM

Conseil Supérieur des Affaires Islamiques du Gabon (CSAIG): blvd Triomphal Omar Bongo Ondimba, en face de l'Institut Français (ex-CCF), BP 358, Libreville; tel. 011-76-06-80; internet www.csaig.ga; Pres. ISMAËL OCENI OSSA.

BAHÁ'Í FAITH

National Spiritual Assembly: BP 5455, Libreville; e-mail aspirituellenationalegabon@yahoo.com; internet www.bahai.org/national-communities/gabon.

The Press

L'Aube: BP 1343, Libreville; tel. 077-95-44-86; weekly.

Echos du Nord: Libreville; internet echosdunord.com; weekly; satirical.

Economie Gabon +: Immeuble BICP, BP 4562, Libreville; tel. 011-44-11-62; e-mail neltoh.nargo@gmail.com; internet economie-gabon.ga; quarterly; Dir of Publication PHILIPPE CHANDEZON; Editor Dr NELTOH NARGONGAR.

Gabon-Matin: BP 168, Libreville; internet gabonmatin.com; daily; publ. by Agence Gabonaise de Presse; Dir of Publication JEAN ROBERT EL MUT MOUTSINGA.

La Griffe: Libreville; weekly; satirical.

La Loupe: Libreville; weekly.

Le Mbandja: Libreville; tel. 077-77-65-30; e-mail journal.lembandja@gmail.com; biweekly; Dir of Publication GUY PIERRE BITÉGHÉ.

La Nation: Libreville; fortnightly.

La Nouvelle République: Libreville; fortnightly.

L'Union: Sonapresse, BP 3849, Libreville; tel. 011-73-58-61; e-mail union.sonapresse@gmail.com; internet www.union.sonapresse.com; f. 1974; 75% state-owned; daily; official govt publ; Dir-Gen. ALBERT YANAGRI.

Zoom Hebdo: Carrefour London, BP 352, Libreville; tel. 011-76-44-54; e-mail zoomhebdo@assala.net; internet www.zoomhebdo.com; Friday; f. 1991; Dir-Gen. HANS RAYMOND KWAAITAAL.

NEWS AGENCIES

Agence Gabonaise de Presse (AGP): BP 168, Libreville; tel. 011-44-35-07; e-mail contact@agpgabon.ga; internet fb.com/AgencepresseAGP; f. 1960; Pres. PASCAL ASSIAMI; Dir-Gen. SÉBASTIEN NTOUTOUM BEKALÉ.

BERP International: BP 8483, Libreville; tel. 066-06-62-91; e-mail berp8483@hotmail.com; internet www1.infosplusgabon.com/berp.php3; f. 1995; Dir ANTOINE LAWSON.

Publishers

Multipress Gabon: blvd Léon-M'Ba, BP 3875, Libreville; tel. 011-73-22-33; e-mail secretariat@multipress-gabon.com; internet multipress-gabon.com; f. 1973; monopoly distributors of magazines and newspapers; Dir-Gen. JEAN-LUC PHALEMPIN.

Société Nationale de Presse et d'Edition (SONAPRESSE): BP 3849, Libreville; tel. 011-73-58-60; internet union.sonapresse.com; f. 1975; Man. Dir ALBERT YANGARI.

Broadcasting and Communications

TELECOMMUNICATIONS

In 2022 Airtel Gabon and Moov Africa Gabon Telecom provided mobile telephone services in Gabon, while the latter was the sole provider of fixed-line services.

Airtel Gabon SA: 124 ave Bouët, Montagne Sainte, BP 9259, Libreville; tel. 074-74-00-00; e-mail info.africa@ga.airtel.com; internet www.airtel.ga; f. 2000; fmrly Zain Gabon, present name adopted 2010; Man. Dir KAMAL OKBA; 1.47m. subscribers (Sept. 2021).

Moov Africa Gabon Telecom: Immeuble du Delta Postal, BP 40000, Libreville; tel. 011-79-22-00; e-mail contact@gabontelecom.ga; internet www.moov-africa.ga; f. 2001; fmrly Gabon Télécom; present name adopted 2021; provider of telecommunications, incl. satellite, internet, fixed-line and mobile systems; 51% owned by Maroc Telecom; Dir-Gen. ABDERRAHIM KOUMAA; 1.60m. subscribers (Sept. 2021).

Regulatory Authorities

Agence de Régulation des Communications Electroniques et des Postes (ARCEP): Quartier Haut de Gué-Gué, face Bureau de la Francophonie, BP 50000, Libreville; tel. 011-44-68-11; e-mail arcep@arcep.ga; internet www.arcep.ga; f. 2012 following merger of the Agence de Régulation des Télécommunications (f. 2001) and the Agence de Régulation des Postes (f. 2001); Pres. LIN MOMBO; Exec. Sec. SERGE ESSONGUÉ EWAMPONGO.

Agence Nationale des Infrastructures Numériques et des Fréquences: Cours Pasteur, Immeuble de la Solde, BP 798, Libreville; tel. 011-76-32-49; e-mail info@aninf.ga; internet www.aninf.ga; f. 2011; Dir-Gen. DANIEL ROGOMBE.

BROADCASTING

Haute Autorité de la Communication (HAC): BP 6437, Libreville; tel. 011-72-82-60; f. 2018 to replace Conseil National de la Communication (f. 1991); Pres. GERMAIN NGOYO MOUSSAVOU.

Radio

Africa Radio: BP 1, Libreville; tel. 011-74-07-34; e-mail africaradio1@yahoo.fr; internet www.africaradio.com; f. 1981; fmrly Africa No. 1; present name adopted 2019; 35% state-controlled; int. commercial radio station; daily programmes in French and English; Pres. ELMAHJOUR AMMAR GOMAA; Sec.-Gen. LOUIS BARTHÉLEMY MAPANGOU.

Radio Télévision Gabonaise (RTG): blvd Triomphal, BP 150, Libreville; tel. 011-73-20-25; internet gabontelevisions.ga; f. 1959; state-controlled; broadcasts 2 channels, RTG1 and RTG2; Dir-Gen. ALI REYNALD RADJOUMBA; Dir of Radio BERTRAND EBIAGHÉ ANGOUÉ.

Radio Nour: Batavea, Libreville; f. 2014; Islamic.

Television

Radio Télévision Gabonaise (RTG): see Radio.

Radio Télévision Nazareth (RTN): Okala Carrière, BP 9563, Libreville; tel. 066-12-50-05; e-mail rtntv@yahoo.fr; internet fb.com/rtngabon; f. 2003; Pres. and Dir-Gen. GEORGES BRUNO NGOUSSI.

TV+: Immeuble Dumez, blvd du Bord de Mer, BP 8344, Libreville; Co-founder and CEO FRANCK NGUEMA.

Finance

BANKING

Central Bank

Banque des Etats de l'Afrique Centrale (BEAC): BP 112, Libreville; tel. 011-76-13-52; e-mail beaclbv@beac.int; internet www.beac.int; f. 1973; HQ in Yaoundé, Cameroon; bank of issue for mem. states of the Communauté Economique et Monétaire de l'Afrique Centrale (CEMAC, fmrly Union Douanière et Economique de l'Afrique Centrale), comprising Cameroon, the Central African Repub., Chad, the Repub. of the Congo, Equatorial Guinea and Gabon; Gov. ABBAS MAHAMAT TOLLI; Dir in Gabon PATRICK ROMUALD ALILI.

Commercial Banks

Banque Internationale pour le Commerce et l'Industrie du Gabon, SA (BICIG): ave du Colonel Parant, BP 2241, Libreville; tel. 011-76-26-13; e-mail bicignet@bnpparibas.com; internet bicig-gabon.com; f. 1973; 26.30% state-owned, 46.67% owned by BNP Paribas SA; Pres. MARIE-ANGE N'DOUNGOU; Dir-Gen. BENE SAMMARIE.

BGFI Bank: 1295 blvd de l'Indépendance, BP 2253, Libreville; tel. 011-79-63-88; e-mail contactbgfi@bgfi.com; internet gab.groupebgfibank.com; f. 1972 as Banque Gabonaise et Française Internationale (BGFI); name changed as above in March 2000; Pres. HENRI-CLAUDE OYIMA; Dir-Gen. LOUKOUMANOU WAÏDI.

Citibank: 810 blvd Quaben, rue Kringer, BP 3940, Libreville; tel. 011-73-19-16; Dir-Gen. JULIETTE WEISFLOG.

Ecobank Gabon: 214 ave Bouet, 9ème étage, Montagne Sainte, BP 12111, Libreville; tel. 011-76-20-71; e-mail ecobankga@ecobank.com; internet www.ecobank.com; Chair. JOSEPH BERRE OWONDAULT; Dir-Gen. GAËLLE BITEGHE.

Orabank Gabon: Immeuble des Frangipaniers, blvd de l'Indépendance, BP 20333, Libreville; tel. 011-79-15-00; e-mail info-ga@orabank.net; internet www.orabank.net; f. 2002; 85.47% owned by Oragroup SA (Togo); Pres. RENÉ-HILAIRE ADIAHENO; Dir-Gen. KAYI ROSE MIVEDOR.

Union Gabonaise de Banque, SA (UGB): ave du Colonel Parant, BP 315, Libreville; tel. 011-77-70-00; e-mail contactugb@ugb-banque.com; internet www.ugb-banque.com; f. 1962; a subsidiary of Groupe Attijariwafa Bank; Dir-Gen. ABDELOUAHED EL-KIRAM.

Development Banks

Banque Gabonaise de Développement (BGD): rue Alfred Marche, BP 5, Libreville; tel. 011-77-41-50; internet www.bgd-gabon.com; f. 1960; 51% state-owned, 18.01% owned by Caisse des Dépôts et Consignations du Gabon, 11.40% owned by Agence Française de Développement; Dir-Gen. (vacant).

Financial Institutions

Alios Finance Gabon (AFG): Immeuble SOGACA, BP 63, Libreville; tel. 011-76-08-46; e-mail gabon@alios-finance.com; internet www.alios-finance.com; f. 1966; car finance; 71.9% owned by Groupe Alios Finance.

BICI-Bail Gabon: Immeuble BICIG, 5ème étage, ave du Colonel Parant, BP 2241, Libreville; tel. 011-77-75-52; BNP Paribas-owned.

Société Financière Transafricaine (FINATRA): Immeuble Concorde, blvd de l'Indépendance, BP 8645, Libreville; tel. 011-77-40-82; e-mail eqcfinatra@bgfi.com; internet finatra.groupebgfibank.com; f. 1997; 50% owned by BGFI Bank; Dir-Gen. HYGIN ANKAMA.

INSURANCE

Assinco: Immeuble Odyssee, blvd de l'Indépendance, BP 7812, Libreville; tel. 011-72-19-25; e-mail assinco@assinco-sa.com; internet assinco-sa.com; Pres. RICHARD AUGUSTE ONOUVIET; Dir STEPHEN MOUSSIROU.

Axa Gabon: 1935 blvd de l'Indépendance, BP 4047, Libreville; tel. 074-04-04-41; e-mail axa-assurances@axa.ga; internet www.fb.com/axagabon; f. 1985; Dir THÉOPHILE JOCELYN MBORO ASSOGHO.

Gras Savoye Gabon: ave du Colonel Parant, BP 2148, Libreville; tel. 011-74-31-53; e-mail contact@ga.grassavoye.com; internet www.willistowerswatson.com; insurance broker; acquired by Willis Towers Watson in 2018; Dir CEDRIC CHEVALY.

NSIA Gabon: Résidence les Frangipaniers, blvd de l'Indépendance, BP 2221–2225, Libreville; tel. 011-72-13-90; e-mail ecoute.clientga@groupensia.com; internet nsiassurancesgabon.com/fr; f. 2000 by acquisition of Assurances Mutuelles du Gabon; name changed as above in 2006; non-life insurance; owned by NSIA Participations S.A. Holding (Côte d'Ivoire); Dir-Gen. CÉSAR EKOMIE-AFENE.

NSIA Vie Gabon: BP 2221, Libreville; tel. 011-72-13-90; e-mail nsiaviegabon@groupensia.com; acquired Sanlam Assurances Vie Gabon 2022; Dir-Gen. CÉSAR EKOMIE-AFENE.

OGAR Gabon: 1881 blvd de l'Indépendance, BP 201, Libreville; tel. 011-76-15-96; e-mail contact@groupeogar.com; internet www.groupeogar.com; f. 1976; non-life insurance; Pres. WILFRID MIDONGO; also OGAR Vie for life insurance.

Sanlam Assurances Gabon: Immeuble Rénovation, ave du Colonel Parant, BP 6239, Libreville; tel. 011-76-06-51; e-mail contact@ga.sanlam.com; internet ga.sanlam.com; fmrly Colina Assurances Gabon, subsequently Saham Assurances Gabon; name changed as above in 2021; non-life; Dir-Gen. YOUSSEF BENABDALLAH.

SUNU Assurances IARD Gabon: ave du Colonel Parant, BP 915, Libreville; tel. 011-74-36-92; e-mail gabon.sunuiard@sunu-group.com; internet www.sunu-group.com; f. 2015; 53.8% owned by SUNU Participations Gabon and 44.0% owned by SUNU Assurances Vie Gabon; Pres. PATHÉ DIONE; Dir-Gen. IDRISSA FALL.

Sunu Assurances Vie Gabon: ave du Colonel Parant, BP 2137, Libreville; tel. 011-74-34-34; e-mail gabon.sunuvie@sunu-group.com; internet www.sunu-group.com; fmrly Union des Assurances du Gabon-Vie; present name adopted 2015; life insurance; 80.64% owned by Groupe SUNU; Pres. APOLLINAIRE EVA ESSANGONE; Dir-Gen. JEAN CONSTANT ASSI.

Insurance Associations

Fédération Gabonaise des Sociétés d'Assurances (FEGASA): rue Ange M'ba, BP 4005, Libreville; tel. 011-74-45-29; e-mail fegasa_gabon@yahoo.fr; internet fegasagabon.wixsite.com/gabon; Pres. Dr ANDREW CRÉPIN GWODOG.

Trade and Industry

GOVERNMENT AGENCIES

Agence Gabonaise de Sécurité Alimentaire (AGASA): Immeuble Bel Espace 2, Batterie IV, BP 2735, Libreville; tel. 011-44-21-33; e-mail info@agasa.site; internet agasa.site; Pres. SAMUEL ABEIGNE NGUEMA; Dir-Gen. ALIA MAEVA BONGO ONDIMBA.

Centre de Développement des Entreprises (CDE): Quartier Okala, BP 13740, Libreville; tel. 011-76-87-65; f. 2010 to replace the Agence pour la Promotion des Investissements Privés du Gabon (APIP); promotes private investment; Pres. ANICETTE NANDA OVIGA; Dir-Gen. ALFRED NGUIA BANDA.

Conseil Economique et Social: BP 1075, Libreville; tel. 011-73-19-47; internet www.cesgabon.ga; comprises representatives from salaried workers, employers and Govt; commissions on economic, financial and social affairs, and forestry and agriculture; Pres. RENÉ N'DEMEZOO OBIANG.

Fonds Gabonais d'Investissement Stratégique (FGIS): blvd du Bord de Mer, BP 3873, Libreville; tel. 01-74-22-46; e-mail contact@fgis-gabon.com; f. 2010; Pres. CLAUDE AYO INGUENDA; Dir SERGE THIERRY MICKOTO CHAVAGNE.

Haut Conseil pour l'Investissement (HCI): Libreville; f. 2017; Pres. ALI BONGO ONDIMBA.

DEVELOPMENT ORGANIZATIONS

Agence Française de Développement (AFD): blvd de l'Indépendance, BP 64, Libreville; tel. 011-74-33-74; e-mail afdlibreville@afd.fr; internet www.afd.fr; Dir MARIE SENNEQUIER.

Agence Nationale de l'Urbanisme, des Travaux Topographiques et du Cadastre (ANUTTC): BP 23792, Libreville; e-mail info@anuttc.ga; internet www.anuttc.ga; f. 2013; Dir-Gen. DEXTER ILBERT MEYE M'OBIANG.

Bureau International de Conseil et de Promotion (BICP): Immeuble BICP, Bord de Mer, 1474 ave Georges Pompidou, BP 4562, Libreville; tel. 011-73-18-80; e-mail pchandezon@gmail.com; internet bicpgabon.com; f. 1984; real estate development; Dir-Gen. PHILIPPE CHANDEZON.

Groupes d'Etudes et de Recherches sur la Démocratie et le Développement Economique et Social au Gabon (GERDDES-Gabon): BP 13114, Libreville; tel. 066-25-14-38; e-mail gerddesgabon@yahoo.fr; f. 1991; Pres. MYNNA MARYVONNE C. NTSAME NDONG.

Institut Gabonais d'Appui au Développement (IGAD): BP 20423, Libreville; tel. 065-72-19-19; e-mail contact@igad-gabon.com; internet igad-gabon.com; f. 1992; Dir-Gen. SÉBASTIEN KOUMBA.

Société de Transformation Agricole et de Développement Rural (SOTRADER): Libreville; 51% state-owned, 49% owned by Olam Gabon; Dir-Gen. AHMED BONGO ONDIMBA.

Société Equatoriale des Mines (SEM): Immeuble du Bord de Mer, 5th Floor, blvd de l'Indépendance, Libreville; tel. 011-72-20-88; e-mail genevieve.gnali@gabonmining.com; internet gabonmining.com; f. 2011; established by presidential decree to facilitate the development of Gabon's mineral resources; Dir-Gen. WESBERT MOUSSOUNDA NGOUMBA.

Société d'Investissement pour l'Agriculture Tropicale (SIAT): BP 3928, Libreville; tel. 011-72-22-16; e-mail gabon@siat-group.com; internet www.siatgabon.com; f. 2004; 99.9% state-owned; Pres. PIERRE VANDEBEECK; Dir-Gen. GERT VANDERSMISSEN.

CHAMBER OF COMMERCE

Chambre de Commerce, d'Agriculture, d'Industrie, des Mines et de l'Artisanat du Gabon (CCAIMAG): BP 2234, Libreville; tel. 011-72-20-64; f. 1935; regional offices at Port-Gentil and Franceville; Pres. JEAN BAPTISTE BIKALOU.

EMPLOYERS' ORGANIZATION

Fédération des Entreprises du Gabon (FEG): Immeuble Odyssée, blvd de l'Indépendance, BP 410, Libreville; tel. 011-44-44-45; e-mail infocpg@lacpg.org; internet www.lacpg.org; f. 1959 as Union interprofessionnelle du Gabon; renamed Confédération Patronale Gabonaise in 1978; name changed as above in 2022; represents industrial, mining, petroleum, public works, forestry, banking, insurance, commercial and shipping interests; Pres. HENRI CLAUDE OYIMA.

UTILITIES

Agence de Régulation du Secteur de l'Eau Potable et de l'Energie Electrique (ARSEE): BP 1215, Libreville; tel. 011-72-16-90; internet www.arsee-gabon.com; f. 2010; Dir-Gen. EMMANUEL BERRE.

Société d'Electricité, de Téléphone, et d'Eau du Gabon (SETEG): BP. 4386, Libreville; tel. 011-76-55-63; e-mail seteggabon@yahoo.fr; internet www.seteggabon.com; f. 2011; Pres. MARCELLIN MASSILA; Dir-Gen. MARCELLIN SIMBA NGABI.

Société d'Energie et d'Eau du Gabon (SEEG): BP 2187, Libreville; tel. 011-76-12-82; e-mail communication@seeg-gabon.com; internet www.seeg-gabon.com; f. 1950; state-owned; controls 35 electricity generation and distribution centres and 32 water production and distribution centres; Pres. MARCELLIN MASSILA AKENDENGUE; Dir-Gen. GUSTAVE AIMÉ MAYI.

MAJOR COMPANIES

The following are some of the largest private and state-owned companies in terms of either capital investment or employment.

Addax Petroleum Gabon: BP 452, Port-Gentil; tel. 011-56-48-27; internet www.addaxpetroleum.com; fmrly PanOcean Energy Corpn Ltd; oil exploration and distribution; Dir-Gen. THIERRY NORMAND.

Assala Gabon SA: rue Roger Butin, BP 146, Port-Gentil; tel. 011-55-26-62; internet www.assalaenergy.com/assalagabon; f. 1960; fmrly Shell-Gabon; owned 75% by Assala Energy, 25% state-owned; exploration and production of hydrocarbons; Dir-Gen. JEAN-YVES GRAIL; c. 500 employees.

CIMGABON: BP 477, Libreville; tel. 011-70-20-23; f. 1976; privatized in Jan. 2001, 75% owned by Ciment de l'Afrique (Morocco); Man. Dir SALIM KADDOURI.

Compagnie Minière de l'Ogooué (COMILOG): BP 2728, Moanda; tel. 011-66-40-15; internet www.eramet-comilog.com; f. 1953; 63.7% owned by Eramet (France), 28.9% state-owned; manganese mining at Moanda; Man. Dr LÉOD-PAUL BATOLO.

Corà Wood Gabon: BP 521, Port-Gentil; tel. 011-55-20-45; e-mail info@corawood.com; internet www.coralegnami.it/en/cora-wood-gabon; f. 1945; fmrly Compagnie Forestière du Gabon; name changed as above in 2000; production of okoumé plywood and veneered quality plywoods; Chair. MICHEL ESSONGHÉ.

Gabon Oil Company: blvd Georges Rawiri, POB 635, Libreville; tel. 01-48-41-00; e-mail contact@gabonoil.com; internet www.gabonoil.com; Pres. CLAUDE AHAVI; CEO FRANÇOIS NTOMBO TSIBAH.

Gabon Oil Marketing: Libreville; f. 2016.

Gabon Service Matériel Pétrolier (GSMP): BP 1067, Port-Gentil; tel. 011-56-09-98; e-mail information@gsmp-ga.com; internet www.gsmp-gabon.com.

Gabonaise de Chimie (GCIAE): BP 20375, Z. I. d'Ouloumi, Libreville; tel. 011-72-06-56; e-mail gciae@ymail.com; internet www.gciae.com; f. 1990; wholesalers of pharmaceuticals and agricultural chemicals; Pres. and Dir-Gen. DOMINIQUE GRIMALDI.

Maurel & Prom: Zone Portuaire de l'Oprag, BP 2862, Port-Gentil; tel. 011-56-46-91; internet www.maureletprom.fr; f. 2004.

Olam Gabon: Galeries Tsika, 2e étage, BP 1024, Libreville; tel. 062-12-31-31; f. 1999; palm oil, rubber and fertilizer; Pres. and Country Head GAGAN GUPTA.

Perenco Gabon: BP 780, Port-Gentil; tel. 011-55-06-41; internet www.perenco.com/fr/filiales/gabon; f. 1982; Dir-Gen. GHISLAIN BOUKOUBI.

Petro Gabon: rue Nomba Domaine, Owendo, BP 20132, Libreville; tel. 011-70-46-76; e-mail petrogabon@petrogabon.com; distributor of petroleum products; Dir-Gen. JEAN-BAPTISTE BIKALOU.

Société Bernabé Gabon: BP 2084, Libreville; tel. 011-74-34-32; e-mail info.gb@bernabeafrique.com; internet www.bernabeafrique .com; f. 1961; 90% owned by Yeshi Group, 10% state-owned; metallurgical products, construction materials, hardware.

Société des Brasseries du Gabon (SOBRAGA): Zone Industrielle Owendo, BP 487, Libreville; tel. 011-70-19-69; e-mail info@ sobraga.com; internet www.sobraga.net; f. 1966; mfrs of beer and soft drinks; Chair. and Dir-Gen. FABRICE BONATTI.

Société Gabonaise Industrielle (SOGI): BP 837, Libreville; tel. 077-17-01-70; f. 1975; industrial construction, metal-smelting; Dir-Gen. CHRISTIAN RENOUX.

Société Gabonaise de Raffinage (SOGARA): BP 530, Port-Gentil; tel. 011-56-30-00; f. 1965; 25% state-owned; refines locally produced crude petroleum; Chair. JEAN RICHARD SYLONG; Man. Dir KEVIN MOUNGALA.

Société Meunière et Avicole du Gabon (SMAG): BP 462, Z. I. d'Oloumi, Libreville; tel. 011-70-18-76; internet www.somdiaa.com/ groupe/filiales/smag-gabon; f. 1968; 30% state-owned; production of eggs, cattle feed, flour, bread; Dir-Gen. BRUNO LARDIT.

Société Nationale des Bois du Gabon (SNBG): BP 67, Libreville; tel. 011-79-98-71; e-mail direction.commerciale@snbg-gabon.com; f. 1944; 51% state-owned; has a monopoly of marketing all okoumé production; Pres. EDMOND OKEMVELE; Dir-Gen. SERGE RUFIN OKANA.

Société Nationale Immobilière (SNI): BP 515, Libreville; tel. 011-76-05-81; e-mail snigabon@sni.ga; internet sni-gabon.com; f. 1976; 77% state-owned; housing management and development; Pres. CHRISTOPHE EYI; Dir-Gen. HERMANN KAMONOMONO.

Société Pizo de Formulation de Lubrifiants (PIZOLUB): BP 699, Port-Gentil; tel. 011-55-28-40; f. 1978; mfrs of lubricating materials; Dir-Gen. JOËL PONO OPAPÉ.

Société de Transformation de l'Aluminium au Gabon (SOTRALGA): POB 3880, Libreville; tel. 011-70-32-69; e-mail info.gb@sotralga.com; owned by Yeshi Group (Côte d'Ivoire); Dir-Gen. TABOULA ALUS.

Sucreries d'Afrique Gabon (SUCAF Gabon): BP 610, Franceville; tel. 011-67-03-61; f. 1974; 53% state-owned; sugar production and agro-industrial complex at Ouélé; Chair. SAMUEL MBAYE; Dir-Gen. CHRISTIAN NOËL RENARDET.

Total Gabon: blvd Hourcq, BP 525, Port-Gentil; tel. 011-77-62-10; e-mail martin.amegasse-efoe@total.com; internet www.total.ga; f. 1934; 25% state-owned, 58.28% owned by Total group (France); petroleum exploration and extraction; Pres. NICOLAS TERRAZ; Dir-Gen. STÉPHANE BASSENE.

Tullow Oil Gabon: rue Louise Charron Fortin, Batterie IV, BP 9773, Libreville; e-mail info@tullowoil.com; tel. 011-73-27-34; exploration and exploitation of petroleum; Dir-Gen. NICOLAS MARTIN.

Vivo Energy Gabon: 234 blvd Bessieux, BP 224, Libreville; tel. 01-74-01-01; e-mail info@engen.ga; internet www.vivoenergy.com/ fr-FR/Nos-Sites/Gabon; f. 1987; fmrly PIZO Shell, subsequently Engen Gabon; name changed as above in 2019; Man. Dir ISSA ISSA.

TRADE UNIONS

Confédération Gabonaise des Syndicats Libres (CGSL): BP 8067, Libreville; tel. 066-03-97-73; e-mail cgsl_2012@yahoo.fr; f. 1991; Sec.-Gen. JEAN CLAUDE BEKALÉ.

Confédération Syndicale Gabonaise (COSYGA): BP 14017, Libreville; tel. 066-68-07-26; e-mail mintsacosyga@yahoo.fr; f. 1969 by the Govt, as a specialized organ of the PDG, to organize and educate workers, to contribute to social peace and economic devt, and to protect the rights of trade unions.

Organisation Nationale des Employés du Pétrole (ONEP): Libreville; Sec.-Gen. SYLVAIN MAYABI BINET.

Transport

RAILWAYS

The Transgabonais railway comprises a section running from Owendo (the port of Libreville) to Booué and a second section from Booué to Franceville.

Agence des Régulation des Transports Ferroviaires (ARTF): Libreville; internet fb.com/ARTFGabon; adviser, controller and arbiter in the devt of the railways; Pres. CÉLESTIN NDOLIA-NHAUD; Exec. Sec. PROSPER EKOMESSE NGUEMA.

Société d'Exploitation du Transgabonais (SETRAG): BP 578, Libreville; tel. 011-70-24-78; e-mail c.communication@setrag.com; internet setrag.ga; operates Transgabonais railway under a 30-year

concession awarded in 2005; 84% owned by COMILOG; Chair. HENRI JOBIN.

ROADS

Action Rapide Transit (ART): BP 9391, Libreville; tel. 011-73-79-40; e-mail contactlbv@artgabon.com; internet artgabon.com; f. 1993; freight; Dir-Gen. PHILIPPE BERGON.

AGS Frasers: BP 9161, Libreville; tel. 011-70-23-16; e-mail manager-gabon@agsmovers.com; internet www.agsfrasers.com; Man. BERNARD DURET.

Fonds Autonome National d'Entretien Routier (FANER): Libreville; f. 2021; Dir-Gen. PATRICE MEZUI.

Société Gabonaise de Transport (SOGATRA): Quartier Camp de Police, BP 8575, Libreville; tel. 011-76-85-46; internet sogatra.ga; Dir-Gen. BRUNO MINKO MI NGOUA.

INLAND WATERWAYS

The principal river is the Ogooué, navigable from Port-Gentil to Ndjolé (310 km) and serving the towns of Lambaréné, Ndjolé and Sindara.

Compagnie Nationale de Navigation Intérieure et Internationale (CNNII): BP 3982, Libreville; tel. 011-72-39-28; internet fb.com/CNNIIGABON; f. 1978; fmrly Compagnie de Navigation Intérieure; name changed as above in 2013; responsible for inland waterway transport; agencies at Port-Gentil, Mayumba and Lambaréné; Pres. OUMAROU BABA TOUKOUR; Dir-Gen. FRANÇOIS OYABI.

SHIPPING

The principal deepwater ports are Port-Gentil, which handles mainly petroleum exports, Owendo, 15 km from Libreville, which services mainly barge traffic, and Mayumba. The principal ports for timber are at Owendo, Mayumba and Nyanga, and there is a fishing port at Libreville.

Bolloré Transport and Logistics Gabon: Zone Portuaire d'Owendo, BP 77, Libreville; tel. 011-79-41-00; e-mail customerservice.kinshasa@bollore.com; internet www.bollore -transport-logistics.com/en/about-us/our-locations/bollore-transport -logistics-gabon.html; Dir-Gen. PATRICK GERENTHON.

Conseil Gabonais des Chargeurs (CGC): Libreville; internet www.cgcworld.com; f. 1971; Pres. LUCCHERIE NGAYILA; Dir-Gen. LILIANE NADÈGE NGARI.

Office des Ports et Rades du Gabon (OPRAG): Owendo, BP 1051, Libreville; tel. 011-70-01-04; e-mail communication.oprag@ yahoo.fr; internet www.opraggabon.com; f. 1974; 25-year management concession acquired in April 2004 by the Spanish PIP group; national port authority; Pres. PIERRE RETENO NDIAYE; Dir-Gen. Col APOLLINAIRE ALASSA.

CIVIL AVIATION

There are international airports at Libreville, Port-Gentil and Franceville, and 65 other public and 50 private airfields, linked mostly with the forestry and petroleum industries.

Agence Nationale de l'Aviation Civile (ANAC): BP 2212, Libreville; tel. 011-44-54-00; e-mail anac@anac-gabon.com; internet www .anacgabon.org; f. 2008; Dir-Gen. NADINE NATHALIE ANOTO.

Nouvelle Air Affaires Gabon: BP 3962, Libreville; tel. 011-73-25-13; f. 1975; domestic passenger chartered and scheduled flights, and medical evacuation; Chair. HERMINE BONGO ONDIMBA.

Tropical Air Gabon: BP 1717, Libreville; tel. 01-44-33-21; internet tropicalair-gabon.com; Dir-Gen. BERNARD BEN NDEMA.

Tourism

Agence Gabonaise de Développement et de Promotion du Tourisme et de l'Hôtellerie (AGATOUR): BP 3964, Libreville; tel. 011-45-23-24; e-mail contacts@tourisme-gabon.org; internet www .tourisme-gabon.org; f. 2014; Dir-Gen. GABRIEL AWORE MAYINDO.

Agence Nationale des Parcs Nationaux du Gabon (ANPN): Libreville; internet www.anpn.ga; f. 2007; Exec. Sec. Prof. LEE WHITE.

Defence

As assessed at November 2021, the army consisted of 3,200 men, the air force of 1,000 men and the navy of an estimated 500 men. Paramilitary forces (gendarmerie) numbered 2,000. Military service is voluntary. France maintains a detachment of 350 troops in Gabon.

Defence Budget: 173,000m. francs CFA in 2021.

Chief of Staff of the Armed Forces: Gen. JEAN MARTIN OSSIMA NDONG.

Education

Education is officially compulsory and free of charge for 10 years between six and 16 years of age. According to estimates by the United Nations Educational, Scientific and Cultural Organization (UNESCO), in 2018/19 enrolment at pre-primary level was equivalent to 43% of children in the relevant age-group (males 42%; females 44%). Primary education begins at the age of six and lasts for five years. Secondary education, beginning at 12 years of age, lasts for up to seven years, comprising a first cycle of four years and a second of three years. The Université Omar Bongo is based at Libreville and the Université des Sciences et Techniques de Masuku at Franceville. Many students go to France for university and technical training. In 2021 expenditure on education constituted 15.1% of total government spending, according to World Bank figures.

Bibliography

Aicardi de Saint-Paul, M. *Le Gabon du roi Denis à Omar Bongo.* Paris, Editions Albatros, 1987. Trans. by Palmer, A. F., and Palmer, T., as *Gabon: The Development of a Nation.* New York and London, Routledge, 1989.

Allogho-Nkoghe, F. *Décentralisation et développement local au Gabon: une mise en perspective.* Paris, Publibook, 2013.

Allogho-Nkoghe, F., and Mambani, J. *Les politiques d'aménagement du territoire au Gabon: Problèmes et perspectives.* Paris, L'Harmattan, 2018.

Ambouroué-Avaro, J. *Un peuple gabonais à l'aube de la colonisation.* Paris, Editions Karthala, 1983.

Barnes, J. F. *Gabon: Beyond the Colonial Legacy.* Boulder, CO, Westview Press, 1992.

    Culture, Ecology and Politics in Gabon's Rainforest (African Studies). New York, Edwin Mellen Press, 2003.

Bongo, O. *El Hadj Omar Bongo par lui-même.* Libreville, Multipress Gabon, 1988.

Eyene Essono, A. *Le Gabon, un pays en crise.* Paris, L'Harmattan, 2016.

Fernandez, J. W. *Bwiti.* Princeton, NJ, Princeton University Press, 1982.

Garandeau, V. *La décentralisation au Gabon: Une réforme inachevée.* Paris, L'Harmattan, 2010.

Gardinier, D. E. *Historical Dictionary of Gabon.* Lanham, MD, Scarecrow Press, 1994.

Gaulme, F. *Le Gabon et son ombre.* Paris, Editions Karthala, 1988.

Ghazvinian, J. *Untapped: The Scramble for Africa's Oil.* Orlando, FL, Harcourt, 2007.

Gray, C. *Colonial Rule and Crisis in Equatorial Africa: Southern Gabon, 1880–1940.* Rochester, NY, University of Rochester Press, 2002.

Institut de Recherche en Sciences Humaines (IRSH). *L'histoire de l'Assemblée Nationale.* Libreville, 2012.

    Les Pouvoirs de l'Assemblée Nationale. Libreville, 2012.

    Lexique du Parlementaire Gabonais. Libreville, 2012.

Kombila-Koumba, P. *Une Autre Vision du Gabon.* Paris, L'Harmattan, 2014.

Loungou, S. *Les enjeux et défis du Gabon au XXIe siècle: réflexions critiques et prospectives des géographes.* Paris, Connaissances et Savoirs, 2014.

Matsiegui Mboula, F. *Les élections politiques au Gabon: de 1990 à 2011.* Paris, L'Harmattan, 2015.

Mbah, J. *La construction de l'etat au Gabon: 1957–2009.* Paris, L'Harmattan, 2015.

Mbem, A. J. *Jean Ping: Le diplomate et l'homme d'Etat.* Paris, L'Harmattan, 2016.

Ndzigue, F. N. *Les droits de la défense en matière pénale au Gabon.*Paris, L'Harmattan, 2009.

    La procédure pénale au Gabon. Paris, L'Harmattan, 2012.

    Le contentieux électoral au Gabon. Paris, L'Harmattan, 2015.

Ndong Sima, R. *Quel renouveau pour le Gabon? Essai.* Paris, Pierre-Guillaume de Roux, 2015.

Nguema Minko, E. *Gabon: l'unité nationale ou la rancune comme mode de gouvernance.* Paris, L'Harmattan, 2010.

Ndombet, W.-A. *Processus électoraux et immobilisme politique au Gabon (1990–2009).* Paris, L'Harmattan, 2015.

Obiang, J.-F. *France-Gabon: pratiques clientélaires et logiques d'état dans les relations franco-africaines.* Paris, Editions Karthala, 2007.

Pa, M. *Transition Politique et Enjeux Post Electoraux au Gabon.* Paris, L'Harmattan, 2011.

Péan, P. *Nouvelles affaires Africaines: mensonges et pillage au Gabon.* Paris, Fayard, 2014.

Raponda-Walker, A. *Notes d'histoire du Gabon.* Montpellier, Imprimerie Charité, 1960.

Rich, J. *A Workman is Worthy of His Meat: Food and Colonialism in the Gabon Estuary.* Lincoln, NE, University of Nebraska Press, 2007.

Shaxson, N. *Les Plans de Développement des Pays d'Afrique Noire.* 4th edn. Paris, Ediafric, 1977.

Tinasti, K. *Le Gabon, Entre Démocratie et Régime Autoritaire.* Paris, L'Harmattan, 2014.

Toung N.J., and Minko Mve, B. *Elites et compromissions en Afrique: légitimation d'un système et sous-développement eu Gabon.* Paris, L'Harmattan, 2013.

Yates, D. *The Rentier State in Africa: Oil Dependency and Neo-colonialism in the Republic of Gabon.* Trenton, NJ, Africa World Press, 1996.

THE GAMBIA

Physical and Social Geography

R. J. HARRISON CHURCH

The Republic of The Gambia occupies an area of 11,295 sq km (4,361 sq miles). Apart from a very short coastline, The Gambia is a semi-enclave in Senegal, with which it shares some physical and social phenomena, but differs in history, colonial experience and certain economic affiliations. Its population (enumerated at 1,857,181 in April 2013, according to census results) was one of the fastest growing of mainland Africa during the early 21st century. At mid-2022, according to United Nations projections, the country's total population was 2,558,493, giving a density of 226.5 inhabitants per sq km.

The Gambia essentially comprises the valley of the navigable Gambia river. Around the estuary (3 km wide at its narrowest point) and the lower river, the state is 50 km wide, and extends eastward either side of the navigable river for 470 km. In most places the country is only 24 km wide with but one or two villages within it on either bank, away from mangrove or marsh. The former extends about 150 km upstream, the limit of the tide in the rainy season, although in the dry season and in drought years the tide penetrates further upstream. Annual rainfall averages 1,150 mm.

Small ocean-going vessels can reach Kaur, 190 km upstream, throughout the year; Georgetown, 283 km upstream, is accessible to some small craft. River vessels regularly call at Fatoto, 464 km upstream, the last of 33 wharf towns served by schooners or river boats. Unfortunately, this fine waterway is under-utilized because it is separated from most of its natural hinterland by the nearby frontier with Senegal.

Some mangrove on the landward sides has been removed for swamp rice cultivation. Behind are seasonally flooded marshes with freshwater grasses, and then on the upper slopes of Tertiary sandstone there is woodland with fallow bush and areas cultivated mainly with groundnuts and millet.

The Gambia has few viable mineral resources, although offshore deposits of petroleum have been identified, and in 2008 the discovery of commercially exploitable quantities of uranium was announced.

The principal ethnic groups are the Mandinka, Fula, Wolof, Jola, Serahule, Serere, Manjago and Bambara. There is also a small but influential Creole (Aku) community. Each ethnic group has its own vernacular language, although the official language is English. About 95% of the inhabitants are Muslims; most of the remainder are Christians, and there are a small number of animists.

History

ISMAILA CEESAY and ESSA NJIE

INTRODUCTION

The Gambia, a small country in West Africa, is located on the mouth of the Atlantic Ocean and surrounded by the former French colony of Senegal to the east, north and south. This essay examines the political history of The Gambia, from independence to post-dictatorship and focuses on *inter alia* how The Gambia was able to defy the odds to survive post-independence status, as well as key events such as the tragic abortive 1981 coup, the formation and collapse of a political union between The Gambia and Senegal (the Senegambia Confederation), and the 1994 military takeover, which ended the 30-year civilian leadership of Sir Dawda Kairaba Jawara, and established a military-turned-civilian dictatorship. This essay argues that the advent of the 1994 coup only derailed the Gambia's democratic trajectory through state-sanctioned violations of fundamental rights and freedoms. The essay also argues that the 2016 presidential election, which saw, for the first time, a change of government through the ballot, marked the moment of democratic restoration in The Gambia. In a post-dictatorship The Gambia, the essay surveys a key transitional justice programme—the Truth, Reconciliation and Reparations Commission, TRRC—which remains a crucial component of The Gambia's democratic trajectory. Finally, the 2021 and 2022 presidential and parliamentary elections and their aftermath are also examined in this essay.

THE ROAD TO INDEPENDENCE: AN ERA OF SCEPTICISM

The Gambia gained political independence from the United Kingdom on 18 February 1965. With a population at the time of about 300,000, a weak economy, poor infrastructural conditions in both rural and urban communities, and few educated political elites, scholars and observers doubted if the country could survive as a viable independent nation-state. Berkeley Rice was among the sceptics who argued in his seminal book, *Enter The Gambia: The Birth of an Improbable Nation*, that the country could not survive as an independent state. In fact there were earlier suggestions of integrating the country with Senegal which was not considered 'a matter of if, but when'.

However, for very obvious reasons, an integration of the two countries with different colonial experiences was not overly appealing, especially from the side of The Gambia. Although, the two countries shared the same ethnic composition, divergences in administrative, cultural and economic patterns served as severe obstacles to any form of closer association. Despite these clear indications, efforts towards a merger were put forward.

To this end the United Nations (UN) sent a team of experts to look into the possibility of the integration option. However, despite the recommendation by the experts of a merger, political leaders in Banjul (the Gambian capital) fought for the independence of the country which began with official negotiations with the colonial authorities. The first of a series of negotiations was held in London in 1964. This eventually culminated in the granting of political independence to the country. Yet it seemed to be just a question of time as to when the seemingly unviable entity would lose that status. Jawara, a native of Barajali Tenda in the country's Central River Region, who had studied in the UK, served as the Prime Minister at independence in 1965. Five years later in 1970 The Gambia attained republican status and Jawara became the first President of the First Republic.

It is noteworthy that the country has been praised for having been one of the longest surviving multi-party democracies in Africa (originating in the 1950s), alongside Botswana and Mauritius, at a time when most African leaders, including Dr Kwame Nkrumah in Ghana, built one-party states. The Gambia Democratic Party and the Gambia Muslim Congress were formed in June 1951 and January 1952 and led by John Colley Faye and Ibrahim Garba Jahumpa, respectively. The formation of these two political parties would later render a snowball effect on the formation of other political parties as the United Party (UP) was formed in April 1954, led by a lawyer by profession, Pierre Sarr Njie, while in February 1959 the Protectorate Peoples' Party (PPP) was formed.

As per its nomenclature the PPP was akin to the plight of the people living in the protectorate part of The Gambia by fighting for the extension of franchise to the protectorate populace. However, for strategic political reasons—namely to assist in attracting support from urban electorates—the party's name was changed to the People's Progressive Party (PPP) with Jawara as its leader. The PPP would dominate The Gambia's political landscape from independence until July 1994 when a group of disaffected army officers overthrew the Jawara Government.

Jawara's widely-known reputation as a protector and promoter of democratic values and principles, human rights and a free-market economy is acknowledged in literature on Gambian studies without any major misgivings. Consequently, The Gambia became a continental beacon of democratic governance and human rights, justifying the decisions to establish the offices of African Commission on Human and People's Rights in Banjul and the African Centre for Democracy and Human Rights Studies as well as the African Society for International and Comparative Law. These were proceeded by the drafting of the African Charter on Human and Peoples' Rights, known as the Banjul Charter. Yet despite its outright dominance of the political landscape, the PPP did not constitute a one-party system.

Fully committed to parliamentary democracy, the first Gambian legislature, the House of Representatives, was established in 1960 with 27 members, 19 of whom were elected directly and eight were indirectly elected by Protectorate chiefs. In 1962 the number of elected deputies was increased to 32 and in 1977 this figure was increased to 35. The election of representatives was a reflection of popular participation by Gambians in the country's democratic dispensation. With a unique voting style of 'drum and marble', multiple voting was prevented which improved the credibility of Gambian elections.

Nevertheless, the PPP dominated the political scene. In the 1960 legislative elections the party secured nine seats, and had increased its representation to 28 seats by those held in 1977. It won 27 seats in 1982, 31 seats in 1987, and 25 seats in 1992. The country experienced its first direct presidential elections in 1982 at which Jawara took 72.5%, while Sheriff Mustapha Dibba (of the National Convention Party, NCP) won 27.5%. The 1987 presidential election witnessed the addition of Assan Musa Camara of the Gambia People's Party (GPP), Jawara's one-time Vice-President, to the list of candidates. With a third person in the race, Jawara recorded a significant reduction in the percentage of votes 59.2%.

Interestingly, Dibba maintained his vote share of 27.5% which meant that Jawara's 13.3% went to Camara. The addition of Dr Lamin Bolonding Bojang of the newly formed People's Democratic Party (PDP) and Sidia Jatta of the People's Democratic Organization for Independence and Socialism (PDOIS—formed by young graduates as the country's first political party with a socialist orientation) in the 1992 presidential election meant that Jawara's dominance could be threatened once more. However, his share of the vote was only reduced to 58.5%, compared to Dibba's significant drop from 27.5% to 22.2%. It has been argued that Jawara's political ploy to include members of minority ethnic groups within the ranks of the party, cabinet and civil service had paid dividends by winning him support, even though this move was resented by ethnic Mandinkas (Jawara's own tribe).

THE ABORTIVE COUP OF 1981

Since independence The Gambia had enjoyed relative peace and stability. However, on 30 July 1981 a mixed group of civilians and members of The Gambia's paramilitary Field Force took advantage of the fact that Jawara was in the UK and launched a coup against his Government. Led by Kukoi Samba Sanyang, a civilian, a 12-man National Revolutionary Council announced the overthrow of the Government and proclaimed the establishment of a 'dictatorship of the proletariat'. There

was, however, division in the Field Force. While some joined the bandwagon of the coup which was described as a rebellion, others remained loyal to the Government. The arrival of Senegalese forces to help restore Jawara to power (after Jawara had issued a personal plea to his counterpart, President Abdou Diouf, who was only seven months into his term of office as Senegal's second President) led to intense fighting in the capital and its outskirts, culminating into civilian casualties, but also the complete surrender of the rebels. Diouf had invoked the 1965 defence and external representation agreements signed between the two countries. However, opposition figures, including Abdoulaye Wade (who became President of Senegal in 2000) strongly opposed the intervention.

It is noteworthy that Sanyang was a politician who had failed in his attempt to win a seat in the 1977 legislative elections, which he contested as a candidate for the opposition NCP. While observers argued that the failed coup was the outcome of Sanyang's failed political ambition, for him, he was only interested in radically transforming The Gambia's socioeconomic trajectory. Equally, it has been observed that there was an ethnic element of motivation for the coup. As a Jola, Sanyang felt that the Jolas had been marginalized in the country, prompting his description of Jawara, in his coup announcement speech on Radio Gambia, as 'corrupt and tribalist'. With a Marxist orientation, suspicion grew that Libya's leader, Col Muammar al-Qaddafi, had been involved in the coup.

Without an iota of doubt, the coup precipitated a crisis of image for Gambian democracy, which the Government had to cautiously deal with, especially in the context of the rights of those accused of having taken part in what was described by many as a week of rebellion/banditry, and not a coup. In the context of Jawara's foreign policy, relations with Senegal had improved overnight which led to the creation of the long-awaited Senegambia Confederation. For obvious reasons, Jawara was obliged to do Senegal's bidding in return for their assistance in restoring him to power. However, the confederation was only built on the condition of a 'marriage of convenience'. The essay now turns to look at the confederation, the formation of which had both domestic and external impacts on The Gambia.

THE SENEGAMBIA CONFEDERATION

A decision reached in November 1981 during a post-coup tour of The Gambia's interior, in Kaur, came to be known as the 'Kaur Declaration', according to which the national legislatures of both The Gambia and Senegal agreed to the formation of a confederation between their two countries. However, it was only in February 1982 that the Senegambia Confederation formally came into effect. Key among the objectives of the confederation were security in a sub-regional context (namely relating to the Casamance conflict), a political union, economic and monetary union, and an attempt to promote the idea of pan-African unity. While this could be described as a genuine attempt to promote political integration between the two countries for sustainable economic growth and productivity, critics, especially in Banjul, only portrayed it as a 'sell-out' move by the Jawara Government.

While it can be argued that the idea of political integration between The Gambia and Senegal was not necessarily an immediate product of the 1981 coup, one could also strongly argue that the events of 30 July 1981 were decisive in the finalization of the persistent efforts on the side of Dakar to see such a body being created. It is not misleading to claim that Jawara's immediate decision to agree to the idea of the confederation was a return of the goodwill gesture initially rendered by Senegal, which secured his restoration to political power after the failed coup.

However, the confederation would only last for seven years and it came to an abrupt end in October 1989. Various reasons accounted for the collapse of the confederation, including The Gambia's perceived refusal to agree to a customs union, which would have opened the doors for a total economic integration, and the demand by Jawara for the presidency and vice-presidency to be rotational. Considered by Dakar as a delaying tactic for the integration objectives of the confederation, Diouf swiftly acted by dissolving the body. This move was equally reciprocated in Banjul as Jawara did not make any effort to restore the 'marriage of convenience'.

THE 1994 MILITARY TAKEOVER: THE U-TURN IN GAMBIAN POLITICS

In the early morning of 22 July 1994 a group of soldiers overthrew Jawara's Government. The five-man team was led by Lt (later Col) Yahya Jammeh who took over key installations, including the country's only airport and Radio Gambia. The 'soldiers with a difference', as they described themselves, hijacked the country's democracy by suspending the Constitution, banning political parties, muzzling the institutions of governance and stifling the media. The coup disrupted one of Africa's longest surviving multi-party democracies and paved way for a military regime that later transformed itself into a civilian government but presided over a dictatorship for 22 years.

Jawara's appeal for the soldiers to return to their barracks was unsurprisingly met with an outright rejection from both the putschists and the US Administration. For the deposed President's own safety, a US warship, which was on the coast ahead of a joint military training exercise, transported Jawara to Dakar before his final departure to the UK for a life in exile. As was often the case in an African military takeover, the soldiers arrested government ministers, including Omar Jallow, one of Jawara's closest allies, and subjected them to torture. This would mark the beginning of terror and dictatorship in a country previously credited with sustaining one of the longest surviving multi-party democracies in Africa and known for its relative peace and stability.

CAUSES OF THE COUP

What may have accounted for the coup is a subject of debate. However, one factor was the appointment of Nigerian military personnel to senior command positions, and which was responsible for the growing grievances within the Gambia National Army, especially among junior officers. It was also reported that Jammeh had a personal gripe against Jawara following his removal as commander of presidential guard. In his testimony at TRRC, founded in 2018, Sanna Sabally, the former Vice-Chairman of the military junta, affirmed that the appointment of Nigerian officers to key positions in the military ignited the urge in them to stage the coup as a means to take ownership of the army and defend the territorial integrity of The Gambia.

In addition, the 'rampant corruption' present in the Jawara Government has been widely acknowledged as a motivating factor for the coup, with the military considering themselves to have had a moral obligation to 'rescue' the state from a corrupt and an inept civilian government. Sabally equally affirmed that, on the junta's part, it was a moral duty to salvage the country from the widespread corruption and nepotism that the Jawara Government was known for. Arguably, Jawara did little to address corruption in the country which pushed the population into poverty and prevented the attainment of any meaningful sustainable socioeconomic development.

Following the takeover, Jammeh received the general support of the public, with little resentment either within the country or externally. Reportedly, even some supporters of the PPP welcomed the coup, coupled with some sections of the opposition parties, including the NCP and the GPP, which hailed the coup as the only way to end the self-perpetuating rule of Jawara. It was only the leaders of the PDOIS, Halifa Sallah and Sedia Jatta, who opposed the coup and were arrested and charged for illegal publication of their *Foroyaa* newspaper.

In contrast with the 1981 abortive coup, Jawara did not receive any support from strategic allies such as Senegal, Nigeria or the USA. In fact, relations with Senegal were already poor following the collapse of the Senegambia Confederation, and with the existing acrimonious relations between Jawara and Diouf, it was obvious that Senegal would not come to Jawara's aid. Furthermore, Senegal was very much aware that any attempt to crush a successful coup would be met with stiff resistance from the Gambian army as the country already had by now an established military as opposed to the situation of 1981 when there was no standing army at the time.

Having succeeded in winning the support of the public, the Armed Forces Provisional Ruling Council (AFPRC), established by the junta to govern the country, had the task of maintaining that support, amid the poor socioeconomic situation in The Gambia. In light of this, the Council made promises to embark on reforms and set up commissions of inquiry to recover stolen public assets and hold public officials accountable for their financial activities. The AFPRC announced a four-year transitional period before a return to civilian rule. However, internal and external pressures, including a recommendation by the National Consultative Committee, subsequently obliged Jammeh to agree to a two-year transition period.

Jammeh resigned from the army and formed the Alliance for Patriotic, Reorientation and Construction (APRC) in order to contest the 1996 presidential election. Prior to this, a referendum approving a new Constitution had taken place—this was introduced in 1997 ushering in the Second Republic, of which Jammeh became the first President after 29 years of both independence and Jawara's reign. Jammeh had used the politics of infrastructure as campaign rhetoric to win the hearts of the electorate.

HUMAN RIGHTS AND GOVERNANCE UNDER JAMMEH

Upon retiring from the army to contest the 1996 presidential election, Jammeh had vowed to respect the constitutionally guaranteed right of every Gambian. In the APRC's manifesto, the party claimed that it sought to build a 'New Gambia', anchored on a people-centered democracy and government, in a free society that encouraged the right and freedom of Gambians to choose the Government of their choice and share 'ideas in a spirit of tolerance and mutual respect'.

However, these rights would be consistently and brazenly violated by the Jammeh regime. In fact, under Jammeh The Gambia gained a reputation for its terrible human rights records, especially in regards to civil and political rights. Arbitrary arrests and detentions of political opponents, journalists and activists became the orders of the day. An environment marked by fear and terror forced several journalists and citizens critical of the regime into exile. Journalists were particularly threatened with Jammeh quoted as stating that 'journalists are less than one percent of the population and, if anybody expects me to allow less than one percent of the population to destroy 99 percent of the population, you are in the wrong place'.

In his seminal work *The Paradox of Third Wave Democratization in Africa: The Gambia Under AFPRC-APRC (1994–2008)*, Prof. Abdoulaye Saine argued that there was a total absence of democratic accountability, transparency, the rule of law, judicial independence as well as parliamentary and civilian management and control of the country's security apparatus. The combination of these posed great challenges to good governance. To create what Andrew Heywood termed 'Political Soldiers' in his book *Politics*, Jammeh politicized and personalized the security sector which was transformed to protect the regime, and thus regime security was prioritized over public security. This led to the widespread human right violations committed by security forces with impunity.

The constant rights violations of citizens attracted international attention. Organizations such as Amnesty International and Human Rights Watch (HRW) were reporting annually on The Gambia's human rights situation—with the country being described by observers as a pariah state. As a military-turned-civilian dictator, Jammeh ruled The Gambia with an iron fist and once vowed to rule the country 'for one billion years'. Testimonies at the TRRC revealed that Jammeh's rights violations began immediately after the coup when former Jawara ministers, including Omar Jallow, were arrested and tortured at the State Central Prison (Mile II). This was followed by violations meted out on civilians in the streets.

However, of all the right violations witnessed in the immediate aftermath of the coup, the gruesome events of 11 November 1994 (in which dozens of soldiers at Fajara barracks were executed in cold blood for their role in suspected coup plot) revealed to Gambians that the 'soldiers with a difference' mantra was only an illusion. Edward Singhateh (a former Junta member) stated during his testimony before TRRC Commissioners in October 2019 that, acting on Jammeh's orders of 'take no prisoners', the coup plot ring leaders (Lt Basirou Barrow, Lt Gibril Saye, Lt Abdoulie Dot Faal, Sgt Ebrima Ceesay, Sgt Fafa Nyang and Cpl Landing Bojang) had been executed in a vicious manner and buried in mass graves. While both Singhateh and Sabally claimed that Barrow's group had planned to stage a coup and execute all AFPRC members and their families, other testimonies suggested that the 'planned coup' was a mere rumour, not based on any evidence at the junta's disposal.

It was only a matter of time before Sabally would become a victim of Jammeh's suspicions. His arrest and that of another senior AFPRC member, Sadibou Hydara, in January 1995 marked the moment of estrangement in the junta. While Jammeh claimed that Sabally and Hydara planned to stage a counter-coup, Sabally's version of events was that he and Hydara had merely requested AFPRC members to respect the six months internal agreement they had concluded to return to barracks and handover the country to civilian rule. Another high profile victim in 1995 of Jammeh's purges was the finance minister of the junta regime, Ousman Koro Ceesay, who had taken a principled stance in blocking financial mismanagement by the regime. Koro's murder was widely believed to have resulted from the his discovery of dubious financial dealings by members of the AFPRC. This would appear to confirm the considerable level of corruption in the AFPRC, which was outrightly contradictory to their claims of countering graft. In July 2021 a former member of the AFPRC, Yankuba Touray, was found guilty and sentenced to death for the murder of Koro.

Regarding the human rights violations, several common themes were reported including the detention incommunicado for weeks and months, and the targeting of political opponents, journalists, human rights defenders, students and religious leaders, while even civil servants were reported to have disappeared or had been summarily executed. That body reported that detainees were subjected to torture with wooden clubs, guns, electric wires, metal pipes and a traditional whip made of dried animal skin. In some instances plastic bags were tied over the heads of detainees in order to suffocate them. Despite these inhumane treatments, the regime failed to hold to account any member of the security agencies, neither those from the National Intelligence Agency (NIA), notorious for its brutality, or the Serious Crime Unit of the police force, for their actions. In fact, several testimonies at the TRRC revealed that these were state sanctioned systematic rights violations; as such, impunity became the order of the day.

The largest opposition party, the UDP, arguably suffered the most under Jammeh. Shortly before the presidential election of September 1996, Jammeh's security forces attacked the party's convoy at the Denton Bridge, a few miles from Banjul. It was reported that 150 people were injured while numerous others were detained and tortured, with three people killed. Several death threats forced UDP leader Ousainou Darboe to seek refuge at the Senegalese High Commission in Banjul. This event would mark the beginning of the continued targeting of political opponents.

In mid-April 2000 more than a dozen students were shot and killed in the streets of Serrekunda, on the outskirts of Banjul, by the paramilitary armed wing of the police force. This event marked the beginning of this unit's use of firearms in dispersing demonstrators. To shield security forces involved in the brutal shooting from any criminal liability, the APRC-dominated National Assembly passed into law, under Jammeh's orchestration, an 'Indemnity Bill' in total disregard of national and international outrage. Jammeh went on to secure victory in the 2001 presidential election, and human rights violations became more gruesome.

As if the rights violations meted on Gambians was not enough, the Jammeh regime also victimized other nationals. In July 2005 a reported 58 migrants (although the exact number is disputed) from various West African countries (including 44 Ghanaians and others from *inter alia* Nigeria, Togo, Liberia, Sierra Leone and Senegal), were massacred by Jammeh's *junglars* (death squad) after being falsely accused of being mercenaries and planning to attack and dislodge the Jammeh Government.

However, journalists remained Jammeh's prime target in his attempts to curtail freedom of expression. Most notably Deyda Hydara, proprietor of *The Point* newspaper, was killed December 2004, while Ebrima Manneh of *The Daily Observer* was killed in July 2006. While it took many years for the facts surrounding the Manneh case to become public (as the Government failed to launch any form of investigation into his disappearance/death), it was widely known that Hydara was killed by Jammeh's death squad. Ousman Sonko, who served as interior minister from 2006 is presently standing trial in Switzerland for his role in numerous crimes under the Jammeh regime, including the killing of Hydara. A large number of other journalists also suffered attacks under the Jammeh regime and the President intensified his attacks on the media during the later stages of his rule by creating an unfriendly environment for journalists through weaponization of legal frameworks such as the 'false news' law that was considered by HRW as detrimental to the proper functioning of civil society and the media.

As Jammeh exercised unchecked powers, human rights violations increased in their frequency and volume. However, the combination of consistent and barefaced violations of the fundamental rights and freedoms of Gambians, coupled with several other factors, resulted in Jammeh being defeated in the December 2016 presidential election, bringing to an end the era of a man who had vowed to rule the country 'for one billion years'.

THE DECEMBER 2016 PRESIDENTIAL ELECTION: JAMMEH'S SURPRISE DEFEAT

The December 2016 presidential election in The Gambia defied the theory that incumbents like Jammeh cannot be defeated at the polls. This is premised on the notion that popular uprising, as was evident in the 'Arab Spring', has become the only viable means of removing longstanding dictators in Africa, in addition to the resurfacing of military coups. As noted earlier in this essay, The Gambia under Jammeh had become a pariah state, marked by rights violations that were akin to the days of Maj.-Gen. Idi Amin Dada in Uganda, Marshal Jean-Bédel Bokassa in the Central African Republic and Francisco Macías Nguema in Equatorial Guinea. As an impoverished, tiny West African country, with limited opportunities for young people, the 2016 election presented two options for The Gambia: change; or continuity of political leadership.

Several factors accounted for Jammeh's electoral defeat. The consistent and massive rights violations did not spare any Gambian. A survey conducted by Afrobarometer revealed that 'more than one in four Gambians say they or a member of their family suffered at least one form of human-rights abuse under the Jammeh regime'. Such violations alone were sufficient justification for the electorates to vote out Jammeh.

In addition, as noted by Niklas Hultin, Baba Jallow, Benjamin N. Lawrance and Assan Sarr in theor article for *African Affairs* entitled 'Autocracy, migration, and The Gambia's 'unprecedented' 2016 election' 'widespread poverty, an economic blockade by Senegal, increasing migration of young Gambians, and hints of dissatisfaction among the military' all contributed to Jammeh's defeat. They argued that the emergence of Dr Isatou Touray as the country's first female presidential aspirant since independence was partly informed by the increase in the mass movement of young people to Europe in search of better economic opportunities. An awful economic situation, coupled with escaping politically motivated prosecutions, gender-based violence, ethnic persecution and state-sanctioned homophobia against lesbian, gay, bisexual, transgender and queer people as revealed in horrifying testimonies by asylum seekers all accounted for Jammeh's defeat.

Furthermore, Jammeh's outrageous public remark against the Mandinka ethnic group, the largest in the country, was considered by many observers as politically suicidal in an election year.

At the election, which took place on 1 December 2016, the UDP candidate, Adama Barrow, under the banner of Coalition 2016, and supported by a number of the smaller opposition parties, secured 43.3% of the votes cast, compared with 39.6% for Jammeh and 17.1% for Mammah Kandeh of the recently founded Gambia Democratic Congress (GDC). Voter turnout was 59.3%.

THE TRRC: THE 'NEVER AGAIN' MANTRA

In fulfilment of an electoral campaign promise to the electorate, anchored on the need to embark on a broader transitional justice programme geared towards correcting the wrongs of the past and to ensure that they were not repeated, but to also strengthen The Gambia's democratic future, the Barrow administration, through domestic legislation, and with financial and technical support from international development partners such as the UN Development Programme and the Office of UN High Commissioner for Human Rights, established the TRRC. It was mandated to set out a historical record of the human rights violations committed between 22 July 1994 and 21 January 2017, with the objectives of healing the nation and addressing the needs of victims in the country, with a strong emphasis on preventing the reoccurrence of those violations through legal and institutional reforms.

Divided into 14 themes, the TRRC started with 'Soldiers with a Difference' which centred on the events of July 22 1994 and its aftermath, when the junta took over the Government and forced Jawara into exile. Thirteen witnesses testified and revealed how the junta took power under the mantra of promoting transparency, accountability and probity, only to blatantly violate the fundamental rights and freedoms of Gambians with impunity. A report commissioned by Saine summarized that 'these young soldiers, and mostly inexperienced junior officers, were motivated to stage the 1994 coup primarily by personal economic gain and improvement and, certainly, their quest for political power'. The remaining 13 themes covered, but were not limited to, enforced disappearances, sexual and gender-based violence, attacks on religious freedoms, the media and political opponents, student demonstrations, the unproven HIV/AIDS treatment and the killing of West African migrants.

It is noteworthy that the formation of the TRRC had attracted controversy among Gambians. While, arguably, a majority of Gambians appreciated the historic decision of the Government to set up such a commission, many Jammeh sympathizers described the commission as a witch hunt against Jammeh. The interim leader of the APRC (following Jammeh's ousting), who became Speaker of the National Assembly, Fabakary Tombong Jatta, had cast doubt on the credibility of the commission, questioning the appointment of the Director of Research and Investigations, Alagie Barrow, who was involved in an attempt to overthrow the Jammeh regime in December 2014. Jatta continued to express reservations with the commission when he led the handing over of a petition to the Ministry of Justice, requesting that the TRRC's report be treated like 'tissue paper', while lashing out at the its Chairperson, Dr Lamin J. Sise, and Executive Secretary, Dr Baba Galleh Jallow.

However, the work of the TRRC, especially the public hearings, attracted undivided attention from large numbers of Gambians, and most notably from the victims of atrocities and their families. In 2018 the inaugural national survey conducted by Afrobarometer, led by the Centre for Policy, Research and Strategic Studies, revealed that 68% of Gambians expected the TRRC to heal the nation but wanted perpetrators of human rights violations to face prosecution. Among the key findings of the survey was that 51% of Gambians sought Jammeh's prosecution for crimes and right abuses under his regime.

The work of the TRRC has been hailed as unprecedented in the political history of The Gambia, attracting both national and international attention. Following the submission of its report in December 2021 (shortly after the presidential election, see below), as mandated by law, the Government had six months to produce a White Paper on the implementation of the TRRC's recommendations. In a historic move, the White Paper, which was released in May 2022, accepted 95% of the recommendations contained in the report, and was earmarked for implementation by the Government. The recommendations ranged from the prosecution of individuals and bans on holding public office, to institutional reforms and the strengthening of social ties as part of efforts to heal the nation and foster reconciliation for a peaceful co-existence. While the White Paper remains a commitment on the part of the Government, action towards implementation remains the biggest concern for Gambians and the international community.

THE DECEMBER 2021 PRESIDENTIAL ELECTION

On 4 December 2021 Gambians voted in the country's first post-dictatorship presidential election, and prior to this there were some significant changes in the country's political dynamics. Nevertheless, with little political experience and considered an underdog in the political arena, the incumbent Adama Barrow led his newly formed National People's Party (NPP) to electoral success, defeating his 'political Godfather' and closest contender, Ousainou Darboe, a veteran lawyer, and the much-admired Halifa Sallah, who had been instrumental in the formation of Coalition 2016, and had contributed significantly to creating political awareness and education among Gambians through his political messaging. During his first term Barrow had developed a degree of mistrust with Darboe and the UDP, which led to the dismissal of all UDP members of the Government, including Darboe who was removed as Vice-President in March 2019. However, what actually led to the surprising development of an acrimonious relationship between the two remains a subject of debate and speculation.

In the liberalized political space, and for the country's first presidential election since the electoral defeat of Jammeh, a total of 21 presidential aspirants submitted nomination forms to the Independent Electoral Commission (IEC). Darboe had resided in exile after the overthrow of Jawara and only returned to The Gambia following the defeat of Jammeh, but showed interest in reviving the PPP, which was struggling under the leadership of Omar Jallow, another veteran politician. This wrangle over the leadership of the party between Darboe and Jallow led to an eventual rupture, and in its first elective congress since 1992, which was dominated by controversy, the party eventually elected Mohamadou Papa Njie as its leader.

However, Njie's subsequent appointment as Gambian High Commissioner to Nigeria caused a leadership vacuum within the party, while Darboe had already proceeded to break away from the PPP and formed Gambia For All (GFA). Kebba Jallow took over as PPP leader, leading to another controversy, with Banjul South legislator, Fatoumata Touma Njie describing the election of Jallow as fraudulent.

The IEC rejected a number of candidatures, including many filed by independent aspirants and, most notably, those of Mai Ahmed Fatty of the Gambia Moral Congress (GMC) and Dr Ismaila Ceesay of the Citizen's Alliance (CA). Both Fatty and Ceesay challenged their rejections in court and won against the IEC but had their nominations rejected by the electoral body for the second time and could not contest in the election. Those permitted to contest the election included newcomers, Abdoulie Ebrima Jammeh of the National Unity Party (NUP) and the independent Essa Mbye Faal, an internationally known lawyer who had represented the former Kenyan President, Uhuru Kenyatta, and his then deputy, and successor as President, William Ruto, during their trial at the International Criminal Court (ICC), and was the lead counsel of the TRRC. Mammah Kandeh, a former APRC parliamentarian contested under the GDC ticket for the second time, while veteran politician Sallah contested as the candidate of the PDOIS for the first time.

According to the official results, Barrow secured 53.2% of the votes and thus a second term, while Darboe, who contested the election on behalf of the UDP, trailed with 27.7%. In protest at the 'unfair' nature of the election, the UDP filed a petition at the Supreme Court, contesting the outcome; however, the Supreme Court struck out the petition on grounds of technicality.

FACTORS FOR BARROW'S SECOND ELECTORAL SUCCESS

Overwhelming Political Backing

What accounted for Barrow's resounding victory remains the subject of analysis. Securing the backing of 11 political forces was unprecedented in the election history of The Gambia. While the UDP, the PDOIS and the GMC were members of the Coalition 2016 who fielded their own candidates in 2021, the National Reconciliation Party (NRP), the Gambia Party for Democracy and Progress (GPDP), the PPP and the NCP maintained loyalty to Barrow. However, the 'marriage of convenience' that was built on grounds of survival between the NPP and APRC is arguably a greater factor for Barrow's electoral success. An alliance of the two parties remained a controversial issue, leading to the formation of a breakaway APRC grouping, known as the No To Alliance Movement (NAM).

While the Jatta-led APRC, the legally recognized camp, claimed that Jammeh, who still retained significant influence, had endorsed a merger with the NPP, the NAM camp refuted this, with Jammeh making a surprise telephone call in denouncement of any form of political marriage between his party and the NPP. While many considered Jammeh's pronouncement as detrimental to Barrow's chances of electoral success, it was seen by some as a blessing in disguise for the incumbent. Barrow had earlier received criticism for embracing the APRC, a party that presided over a 22-year dictatorship, with many considering it a mockery to the victims of Jammeh's brutality. Therefore, a denouncement of such cooperation by Jammeh had saved Barrow's image, at least, prior to the election. However, critics still describe Barrow's move to embrace the Jatta-led APRC as an insensitive one to the plight of victims.

Rejection of the UDP

The 2021 presidential election was arguably a referendum between the NPP and the UDP. Anecdotal evidence revealed that some of the electorate would prefer an NPP victory to the UDP, on the grounds that the latter posed a survival threat to other political parties. The APRC deputy leader, Ousman Rambo Jatta, remarked shortly before the December polls 'God forbid for the UDP to take leadership of this country', claiming that the APRC and many other political parties would not want a UDP government in The Gambia, especially under the leadership of Darboe.

The Ethnic Card

It has been argued that, from the time of independence, incumbent parties in Gambian politics have always embraced almost all the ethnic groups in the country, with growing weakness on the side of the opposition to pose any serious challenge to the incumbent. In fact, in his study on local elections in The Gambia, John Wiseman argued that, compared with most West African states, 'ethnicity and religion enjoy a low political salience in The Gambia'. This trend of incumbent domination and acceptance by almost all ethnic groups continued in the Jammeh era until the point when he decided to play the ethnic card. Jammeh's derogatory remarks against ethnic Mandinkas, which has been highlighted above as a major factor for his electoral loss, was a manifestation of the influence of ethnicity in Gambian politics under Jammeh. In the lead up to the December 2021 presidential poll, politicians, especially Barrow and Darboe, were engaged in war of words with tribal rhetoric becoming more widespread. In a meeting in a rural Serahule community, Darboe attacked members of the tribe for claiming ownership of Barrow and his party, when they 'did not even vote for him in 2016'. These remarks received widespread condemnation from the Serahule community. Meanwhile, also prior to the election, President Barrow was set on inviting members of different ethnic groups to the State House for political gains, while the National

President of the NPP, Dembo Bojang, in a meeting in Bakau, appealed to members of other tribes, especially the Fulas, Jolas and Wollofs to vote for Barrow, because a UDP victory, in his words, would pose a 'threat to the survival and security of all other tribes in the country'. There is little doubt that the ethnic card was used, especially by the incumbent, to lure support, and which can be seen to have had successful results.

THE 2022 PARLIAMENTARY ELECTIONS

The second parliamentary elections in a transitional Gambia demonstrated, once again, the fluidity of Gambia's political dynamics. After Barrow had secured a comfortable majority in the presidential election, and with his party heading with the advantage of incumbency, many observers had predicted an outright majority for the NPP. However, past performances have proven in The Gambia that outcomes of presidential elections do not necessarily reflect on parliamentary polls as electorates are motivated by different factors. While the voter turnout for presidential and parliamentary elections fluctuated considerably during the First Republic, in the Second Republic, voter turnout has consistently been significantly higher in presidential elections than in parliamentary polls.

This trend continued in 2022 when a turnout of just 51% was recorded for the legislative elections, compared with the 89% of the electorate who participated in the presidential poll the year before. Of the 53 elected seats the NPP secured 18, the UDP 15, the NRP four seats and the APRC and the PDOIS each took two. Five candidates of the pro-Jammeh NAM faction of the APRC, who contested constituencies as independent candidates in Jammeh's birth region of Foni, were successful. The results in Foni are manifestations of Jammeh's modicum of influence in the region. The remaining seven seats went to independent candidates.

Arguably, the NPP was not able to secure a comfortable majority for several reasons, the most significant of which was perhaps its poor performance in changing the economic conditions of Gambians and providing employment opportunities in a country with high unemployment rate among young people. One could argue that the calibre of candidates selected by the NPP in some constituencies was another factor. It is noteworthy that the outcome of the parliamentary polls surprised many observers, and even the opposition, since it was assumed to be a forgone conclusion that the NPP would secure most seats by a significant margin. However, the results proved otherwise and once again, provided an example of the changing dynamics of Gambian politics.

CONCLUSION

From independence to the present day, The Gambia has had only three presidents, as opposed to many other countries on the African continent that have had four and more. As noted earlier in this essay, the country was initially a beacon of hope for democratic governance and stability. However, the 1994 military takeover disrupted that democracy and stability, with human rights violations and disregard for the rule of law and liberal democratic principles being the hallmark of the military-turned-civilian Government of Yahya Jammeh. This essay has examined important moments in The Gambia's political history, and recent political events, such as the December 2016 presidential election, which marked a watershed moment, namely the restoration of democracy in The Gambia, provide hope that the country is once again on a path which will benefit the majority of its people. The essay has also examined an important post-dictatorship transition programme and its relevance in the new democratic dispensation. Of importance in this essay are also the 2021 and 2022 presidential and parliamentary elections, and our examination of possible explanations for their outcomes and their meanings for The Gambia's democratic trajectory.

Economy

ROBERT E. LOONEY

INTRODUCTION

The Gambia has a small, open economy, exposing the country to external shocks over which it has little or no control. Droughts are increasingly frequent and can, as in 2011, trigger a severe economic contraction through poor harvests. The country's tourism sector relies on visitors from Europe, notably the United Kingdom. Therefore, recessions in Europe or disruptions caused by events such as the UK's decision to leave the European Union (EU) and the lockdowns associated with the COVID-19 pandemic can significantly affect The Gambia's economy. The country is also in the early stages of recovery from years of mismanagement under the administration of Yahya Jammeh. It now faces the long-term challenge of restoring institutions while, in the short term, attempting to provide impetus to the economy.

The country's current President, Adama Barrow, elected in 2017, has successfully negotiated a resumption in aid flows from donors such as the EU. Donors had curtailed some aid flows because of The Gambia's poor human rights record under Jammeh; however, external budgetary support has gained momentum with political repression easing under Barrow's presidency. Another growth-boosting factor following Jammeh's departure was the return of some skilled workers from the Gambian diaspora, with many having fled the country during Jammeh's time in power. Remittances from the diaspora amounted to 20.6% of gross domestic product (GDP) in 2020. Unfortunately, the country was unprepared to deal with the collapse in September 2019 of a major British tour operator, which, along with the COVID-19 pandemic, caused the economy to contract by 0.2% in 2020. However, the economy recovered to grow by 5.6% in 2021, with the International Monetary Fund (IMF) predicting a similar growth rate in 2022. In 2021 the country's per capita income was US $2,210 (on an international purchasing-power parity—PPP—basis), down from $2,271 in 2000 and $2,347 in 2010.

GROWTH AND DEVELOPMENT

The Gambia's economic growth declined under the 22-year rule of Jammeh (1994–2016). Under his regime, GDP growth decelerated to an average annual rate of 2.7% in 1994–2016 (falling from 3.6% in 1994–2005 to 2.0% in 1995–2016), compared with average growth of 3.3% per year in 1980–93. In the post-Jammeh era (2017–20), economic growth increased to an average of 4.7% per year, despite the onset of the COVID-19 pandemic in 2020.

The deceleration in growth under Jammeh coincided with a deterioration in the country's governance structures, as documented by the World Bank Governance Indices. In 1996, in terms of political stability, the World Bank ranked The Gambia in the 65th percentile of countries; however, by 2016 (the final year of the Jammeh regime), the country's ranking had declined to the 13th percentile. Similarly, over the same period, the country's government effectiveness ranking fell from the 32nd percentile to the 19th, its rule of law ranking from the 52nd percentile to the 24th, and its control of corruption ranking from the 44th percentile to the 22nd. Under Barrow's presidency, by 2020 (the latest year for which data is available), The Gambia's political stability ranking had risen to the 55th percentile, government effectiveness to the 26th, the rule of law to the 31st, and control of corruption to the 43rd percentile. The country's ranking in terms of voice and accountability rose from the 13th percentile in 2016 to the 39th by 2020.

The 2022 Index of Economic Freedom, compiled by the US-based Heritage Foundation, ranked The Gambia 14th among sub-Saharan African countries and thus above the regional average. However, The Gambia still ranks considerably below the world average despite recent improvements. While still classified as 'mostly unfree', the Barrow administration has actively been improving and streamlining regulatory structures and reducing corporate taxes to improve the business environment.

The economy has undergone several significant structural changes in recent years, with agriculture's contribution falling from 30.2% of GDP in 1970 to 25.5% in 2000 and 21.0% in 2020. Consistent with the pattern usually found in low-income countries, manufacturing has declined in recent years. After increasing from 3.0% of GDP in 1970 to 6.8% in 2000, the sector's share of GDP fell back to 2.9% in 2020. Contrary to the pattern found in most sub-Saharan African countries, the percentage of services has also declined. In 1970 services accounted for 61.5% of GDP, decreasing to 60.6% in 2000 and 52.2% in 2020. However, several sub-components of the services sector have increased in recent years, with financial and insurance activities averaging 6.7% growth per year in 2005–20. Other service sectors that registered high rates of growth during this period include human health and social work activities (6.6%), transport and storage (3.4%), education (6.6%), and real estate activities (3.0%).

Sectoral employment in The Gambia has not followed the usual patterns experienced by other countries in the same income group. Despite several distinct structural shifts in recent years, employment patterns have been remarkably stable. Agriculture employed nearly 37.6% of the country's workforce in 1991, falling to 31.0% in 2000 and 27.0% in 2019. Given the drop in its GDP share over the past few decades, the sector is likely experiencing declining productivity. Industry employed 17.9% of the country's workforce in 1991, decreasing to 17.3% in 2000 and 15.0% in 2019. In sharp contrast to the decline in its contribution to GDP, employment in the services sector increased from 44.1% of the labour force in 1991 to 47.3% in 2000 and 58.0% in 2019. The expansion in service employment as a share of the workforce and its contraction as a share of GDP suggests that the sector is experiencing lower productivity by absorbing many people leaving agriculture.

Several macroeconomic trends appear entrenched, leading to severe external imbalances. The country's saving rate is meagre, averaging just 6.5% of GDP in 2000–09 and 8.9% in 2010–21. These rates are less than one-half of that in sub-Saharan Africa as a whole, which averaged 16.6% of GDP in the first period and 16.7% in the second. The Gambia's insufficient savings rates have, given higher rates of investment (at 11.3% of GDP in the first period and 16.5% in the second), led to a severe increase in the country's balance of payments on the current account, the deficit on which increased from an annual average of 4.9% of GDP in 2000–09 to 7.6% in 2010–21.

Under the new Barrow administration, government policy focused primarily on several problems negatively affecting the economy. The first involved, as noted above, the balance of payments difficulties stemming from low savings; however, there were also several severe shocks arising from volatility in the price of oil on the world market and a decline in tourism during the period of uncertainty before transferring power to Barrow.

The second problem involves the Jammeh Government's systemic mismanagement and misappropriation, which led to a series of fiscal crises. From mid-2014, mass embezzlement from the country's state-owned enterprises (SOEs) may have reached the equivalent of 4% of GDP and resulted in unbudgeted bailouts and additional borrowing, which significantly increased public debt in 2016.

Third, the rapid rise in external debt from 43.0% of GDP in 2010 to 87.0% by 2017 was unsustainable and impeded the Government's ability to release funds to implement essential infrastructure investments. The financial resources required for debt servicing crowded out the private sector, delaying that sector's ability to channel investments towards profitable commercial activities and job creation.

The fourth problem involves the frequent power outages arising from the inability of the electricity sector to keep pace with expanded economic activity. The fifth issue is that agriculture, as noted above, is experiencing declining productivity and remains primarily based on subsistence farming. The sixth problem is that there will be no significant growth in the tourism sector without a series of investments in supporting infrastructures.

The seventh problem is that the country's imports exceed its exports. This situation is critical in contributing to a persistent current account deficit since 1990. The eighth issue is the state of the country's education system. While females now have improved access to education, the system still suffers from inferior quality and relevance. Finally, The Gambia's health system has deteriorated to where it can no longer adequately perform many essential services for an expanding population.

The Government hopes to address these nine major issues and related matters in the coming years. First, however, most of its attention is currently focused on combating the COVID-19 pandemic, with limited resources at its disposal. Since the pandemic broke out in March 2020, the country has experienced three periods of rapid increase. Cases increased from 49 on 1 July 2020, to 3,474 by 17 September 17. From 1 July 2021 cases increased from 6,079 to 9,698 by 31 August, and from 26 December cases increased to 11,863 by 3 February 2022.

SOCIOECONOMIC PROGRESS

In The Gambia, the benefits of economic growth have failed to trickle down to the masses. Official figures show that growth in recent years has had little impact on reducing poverty or other standard measures of socioeconomic progress. According to the United Nations (UN) Development Programme's *Human Development Report 2020*, The Gambia's Human Development Index (HDI) ranking was in the 'low human development' group at 172nd out of 189 countries (and 39th in Africa), slightly above its ranking on a gross national income (GNI) per capita basis. In 2019 the mean years of schooling in the country was 3.9, and life expectancy was 62.1 years. The Gambia's rate of improvement in its HDI has slowed from 1.45% per year in 1990–2000 to 1.31% in 2000–2010 and 0.89% in 2010–19. As a result, the country's HDI ranking rose by only one place between 2014 and 2019.

In 2022 The Gambia's population totalled 2.6m. and was growing at 2.9% per year. By 2030 it should reach 3.0m. The average annual growth rate decreased slightly from 3.2% in 2005–10 to 3.0% in 2015–20. With these high rates of growth, the median age of the population is low, at 17 years, with a high youth dependency rate—there are 86.6 people aged 14 years and under for every 100 people aged 15–64, and only 4.5 people aged 65 and older for every 100 people of working age. Urbanization has increased steadily, rising from 54.9% of the population in 2009 to 61.9% in 2019.

Overall unemployment stood at 11.1% in 2020, up from 9.5% in 2019. In 2019 youth unemployment (those aged 15–24 years) was 12.4%. By a broader measure of inactivity (youths not in school or employment), the rate reached 34%. Stubbornly high unemployment and weak human rights protection drove many Gambians to emigrate during the Jammeh years. In 2016 alone, before Jammeh's electoral defeat, and despite the country's relatively small population, refugees from The Gambia represented some 3% of those crossing the Mediterranean. Only Syria, Afghanistan, Iraq, and Nigeria, all affected by conflict, and Eritrea, with its abysmal human rights record, accounted for more of the total number of migrants who attempted the perilous crossing in that year. The Government hoped that improved human rights and an enhanced economy would induce many to return.

Contrary to the country's lack of progress in many areas affecting the quality of life, its income distribution has shown steady progress towards greater equality (albeit from high initial levels of inequality). The Gini index (with higher numbers signifying greater inequality) fell from 48.5 in 1998 to 43.6 in 2010 and 35.9 in 2015 (the latest year for which data is available). Similarly, the income share of the upper 10% of the population fell from 37.7% in 1998 to 34.9% in 2010 and 28.7% in 2015. The income share received by the lowest 10% of the population steadily increased from 1.5% in 1998 to 3.0% by 2015. The poverty rate in The Gambia remains high. The rate in 2021 was only 8.5% with poverty defined as US $1.9 per day in 2011 PPP. However, at $3.2 (PPP) the rate rises to 33.6%, and at $5.5 (PPP) the rate increases to 69.3%.

AGRICULTURE

Agriculture in The Gambia remains predominantly organized through small-scale units, and much production is subsistence-based. Although accurate statistics are scant, only approximately 23% of The Gambia's arable land is suitable for crops. Cultivated land is less than 3%, with most small-scale farmers not using improved seeds and fertilizers. There is limited mechanization, with modern equipment unaffordable for most farmers, who have only limited access to finance and support from the Government. Nevertheless, the country is a significant exporter of groundnuts and cashews, and nut production alone accounts for around 10% of GDP.

Although agriculture is a critical sector in the Gambian economy, its contribution to GDP has declined, falling from 31.5% of GDP in 2004 to 21.0% in 2020; over this period the sector grew at an average annual rate of only 0.8%. Within the sector, the contribution of crops fell from 21.1% of GDP in 2004 to 7.6% in 2020, while forestry's share of GDP decreased from 1.5% to 0.6%. Fishing was the only agricultural sub-grouping to record growth in its contribution to GDP, increasing from 4.4% in 2004 to 9.3% in 2020.

The most crucial factor affecting agricultural output, particularly crops, is the rainfall level. Since the mid-1960s, the country has experienced severe droughts, reducing production and causing significant environmental degradation. During the 2011/12 growing season, insufficient rainfall had a devastating impact on all crops, with output decreasing by 40.4% in 2011 (livestock, forestry and fishing each increased by around 3.5%). Similarly, during the 2014/15 season, late rains reduced crop production by about 20%, while livestock, forestry and fishing grew by 4.6%, 3.0%, and 6.4%, respectively.

Cereal production rose from 37,900 metric tons in 1976 to 223,852 tons in 2004 and to a high of 363,549 tons in 2010. Since then, production has fallen fairly steadily, to 112,365 tons in 2018. The 2018 agricultural season suffered from late rains, periodic dry spells, and an infestation of caterpillars. As a result, cereal production reached just 112,365 tons. The most notable declines involved rice (down 18% compared with 2017), millet (–29%), and maize (–15%). The UN's Food and Agriculture Organization (FAO) estimated that about 99,000 people needed food assistance in October–December 2018, a significant increase from the 45,000 classified as food insecure in March-May. Crop production fell further to 104,778 tons in 2019. However, with improved weather, crop production expanded to 173,776 tons in 2020.

The Gambia's principal cash crop is groundnuts (peanuts), first introduced from Brazil in the 18th century. As with other crops, the output of groundnuts varies considerably according to weather conditions. Data from FAO showed production in the drought year of 2011 of 83,858 metric tons, down from 137,631 tons in 2010. Although production rebounded to 119,614 tons in 2012, it dropped to 80,650 tons in 2014. Subsequently, output recovered to reach 108,933 tons in 2017 and increased further to some 110,000 tons in 2020. Around 20% of groundnut production is for domestic consumption, while the country exports the rest, notably in processed forms (groundnut processing makes up the country's leading manufacturing activity).

Rice is the more critical crop in terms of subsistence. Farmers and their families consume most of the production while selling some of the crops in local markets; the country remains a net importer of rice (mainly from South-East Asia). Traditionally, rice farming took place in the swamplands along the edge of the Gambia river, but since independence, pump-irrigated rice acreage has increased. Production, however, has been variable. A record crop of 99,890 metric tons was produced in 2010, up from 11,395 tons in 2007, but output tumbled to 51,136 tons in 2011 and to just 22,000 tons in 2019. Production then rose slightly to 28,000 tons in 2020. In 2013, to encourage local production, the Government announced it would ban all rice imports in the future. However, the country could not meet the shortfall between local output and import requirements. Despite the ban, rice imports have remained buoyant in recent years, totalling 225,000 tons in 2017, 160,000 tons in 2018, 260,000 tons in 2019 and 250,000 tons in 2020.

Other important subsistence crops include millet, maize, sorghum, and cassava. In recent years there has been some expansion in the domestic market of fruit cultivation (notably bananas, mangoes, papayas and oranges) and horticulture.

Livestock activities (cattle, sheep, goats and other farm animals) contribute notably to the rural economy. However, while the sector expanded at an average annual rate of 3.2% in 2005–12, it contracted at an average annual rate of 4.7% in 2012–20. The fisheries sub-sector grew at a healthy average yearly rate of 4.7% in 2005–12, increasing to 13.0% in 2013–20, making it the fastest growing agricultural sub-sector during this period. Fishermen continue to use primarily traditional methods of catching fish, which are a vital source of local food. Currently, fishing faces several problems, the most significant being overfishing by Senegalese and Chinese boats. In 2015 the non-governmental environmental organization Greenpeace accused Chinese fishing companies of persistent 'illegal, unreported and unregulated fishing activities and gross tonnage fraud' in West Africa. There have also been reports of European vessels operating unlawfully in the exclusive economic zones of Equatorial Guinea and The Gambia.

Forests have played a significant role in the country's development. At the turn of the last century, pristine forests covered much of The Gambia; however, deforestation began as the population expanded. While some 43% of the country's entire land area (505,000 ha) is still under forest cover, managed woodland makes up only 10%. The rest primarily comprises savanna and mangroves along the Gambia river. Forestry activities grew at an average annual rate of 2.6% in 2005–11, but this growth rate proved unsustainable. An average yearly contraction of 9.0% was recorded in the sub-sector in 2013–20 because of climate change and deforestation. With financial and technical help from FAO, The Gambia is currently implementing a programme designed to halt environmental degradation and deforestation.

Yields far below global averages characterize The Gambia's agricultural sector, with insufficient irrigation, poor soil management, and inefficient farming methods all acting as significant impediments. The Government recognizes the importance of increasing investment to modernize the sector. Growth in agricultural output would make The Gambia less reliant on food imports, which represent about 50% of consumption. It would help to create employment for the country's unemployed youth. However, given the Government's limited ability effectively to fund programmes, progress along these lines is likely to be slow.

Hoping to speed up the process, in April 2019 President Barrow instructed the Gambian National Army to begin large-scale agricultural production. The army was to work in partnership with the US agricultural machinery manufacturer AGCO Corporation, which had established similar alliances with the Egyptian armed forces and other African militaries.

TOURISM

The Gambia's tourism industry began in 1965, but it was not until 2001 that the Gambian Tourist Authority began operations and 2003 before the introduction of the Tourism Development Master Plan. Traditionally, the industry focused on coastline package holidays, but activities are increasingly expanding into other areas, such as eco and adventure tourism. As with agriculture, the tourism sector is vulnerable to external shocks. Most of The Gambia's tourists come from Europe, and in times of economic crisis (for example, 2008), the Gambian economy is adversely affected. Tourist arrivals totalled 91,000 in 2010, and the sector expanded by 16.5% in 2011 and by a further 48.1% in 2012. The increase in tourist arrivals decelerated to 8.9% in 2013, and the total declined by 8.8%, to 156,000, in 2014. There was a subsequent surge in tourist numbers, reaching 522,000 by 2017 and 620,000 in 2019. However, with the outbreak of COVID-19 and associated lockdowns and suspension of air flights, tourist arrivals fell by 60.1% in 2020 to 246,000.

In 2019 tourism was the second largest industry in The Gambia, contributing around 15.5% of GDP, 17.1% of total employment, and 50.5% of total exports. However, with the onset of the COVID-19 pandemic in 2020, the sector's contribution to GDP dropped to just 8.4%. Similarly, employment declined by 30.5% to 12.6% of employment, and the sector's contribution to exports fell by 67.0% to 21.6%. The industry is gradually recovering from the pandemic, but it may be several years before it operates at levels approaching those in 2019. Much will depend on the country's vaccination rates and the economic conditions in Europe. In 2019 12% of inbound arrivals were from the UK, 6% from the Netherlands, 3% from Sweden, 2% from Spain, and 2% from Belgium.

TRADE AND EXTERNAL FINANCIAL FLOWS

The Gambia's principal exports in 2019 were mineral products, wood, wood charcoal, cork, and articles thereof, vegetable products, animal, vegetable fats and oils, and prepared foodstuffs. The principal imports in that year were mineral products (primarily mineral fuels and oils), machinery and mechanical appliances, vegetable products, prepared foods, vehicles, aircraft and transport equipment, and animal, vegetable fats and oils. The country's pattern of trade altered considerably between 2000 and 2019. In 2000 33.8% of the country's exports went to the advanced economies, with 24.4% going to the eurozone and 66.2% going to emerging and developing economies, with sub-Saharan Africa receiving 64.2%. By 2019 the advanced economies received only 14.6% of the country's exports, with the eurozone accounting for 9.0%. In that year, 85.4% of the country's exports went to emerging and developing economies, with sub-Saharan African countries accounting for 29.2%.

Imports also experienced a shift in trading patterns. In 2000 63.2% of the country's imports came from the advanced economies, with the eurozone accounting for 44.3%. Emerging and developing countries accounted for 36.8% of The Gambia's imports, with 15.4% coming from sub-Saharan African countries. By 2019 the advanced countries accounted for only 22.0% of the country's imports, with 14.4% coming from the eurozone, while the share of imports from sub-Saharan African countries had increased to 40%. In 2000 12.7% of The Gambia's imports came from emerging and developing Asia, but by 2019 this had risen to 23.4%.

In recent years a significant change has taken place in the area of re-exports. At one stage, 90% of the country's exports consisted of importing goods into the country under low import tariffs and then re-exporting them (not always legally) to neighbouring countries, principally Senegal, but also Guinea, Guinea-Bissau, and Mali. This practice ultimately led to border disputes with Senegal. The profitability of the re-export trade has since eroded with the harmonization of import and sales taxes among members of the Economic Community of West African States (ECOWAS) and improvements in ports and customs operations in Senegal. Although re-export earnings had historically accounted for around one-third of GDP, they had declined to just 1% of GDP by 2012.

Exports of goods and services grew at an average annual rate of 0.8% in 2000–09, increasing to 1.2% in 2010–21. Over the same period, however, the average yearly growth rate of imports of goods and services increased from 0.3% to 7.7%. Owing to these growth patterns and the widening gap between savings and investment noted earlier, the deficit on the country's current balance of payments account increased from an average of 4.9% of GDP in 2000–09 to 7.6% in 2010–21.

Foreign direct investment (FDI) has increased in recent years, but not by enough to finance the current account deficits. Inflows averaged 3.5% of GDP from 2010–16, increasing to 5.8% from 2017–20 with Barrow's election to the presidency.

An essential source of external finance has been the remittances of the estimated 500,000 Gambians working abroad, mainly in the UK, other parts of Western Europe and the USA. The level of remittances received increased from 7.5% of GDP in 2010 to 11.2% in 2014. After falling to 9.8% of GDP in 2016, remittances rose to 10.6% of GDP in 2017, to 12.7% in 2018, to 15.2% in 2019, and to 22.3% in 2020.

With insufficient FDI likely available to finance the current account deficit and with a possible fall in remittances as many of those who left the country during the era of Jammeh's rule return home, development assistance is likely to be the most important means of funding the country's chronic current account deficits in the near term. Official development assistance (ODA) was equivalent to 6.6% of the country's GNI in

2000, rising to 8.0% in 2010 and 10.0% in 2012. However, it flattened out due to concerns over human rights violations witnessed under the Jammeh regime. ODA fell to 8.3% of GNI in 2013 and 6.3% in 2016. Following Barrow's assumption of the presidency in 2017, ODA rose to 19.3% of GNI before decreasing to 14.3% in 2018 and 10.8% in 2019. While the country remains highly vulnerable to shifts in foreign assistance, the end of Jammeh's authoritarian rule has considerably reduced the risk of severe shortfalls.

The Gambia is a member of ECOWAS and the World Trade Organization. In 2019 the country joined the new African Continental Free Trade Area (AfCFTA), a trading block encompassing 54 countries launched in January 2021.

MONETARY POLICY AND THE BANKING SYSTEM

The Gambian financial system is relatively free from restrictions or controls. Nevertheless, the country's banking system lags in several vital areas. The World Economic Forum's 2019 *Global Competitiveness Report* ranked The Gambia's financial system at 113th out of 141 countries assessed in terms of competitiveness. Regarding domestic credit to the private sector as a percentage of GDP, the country ranked 136th, while regarding the financing of small and medium-sized enterprises, it ranked 101st. To non-performing loans as a percentage of total gross loans, it ranked 85th. Reforms introduced under Barrow's administration have reduced lending risk and, combined with lower interest rates, have revived credit to the private sector. Private sector loan year-on-year growth reached an eight-year high of 29.7% in September 2018, following annual contractions between 2015 and 2017. Further improvements in the financial system will be critical if the country is to achieve a relatively high sustained rate of growth in the years ahead.

The Central Bank of The Gambia pursues an orthodox monetary policy that uses a monetary targeting framework to focus on its inflation objectives. However, this policy has not been entirely successful, with the country experiencing inflation rates averaging 8.0% in 2017, 6.5% in 2019, 7.1% in 2019, 5.9% in 2020, and 7.4% in 2021, with the IMF forecasting 8.0% for 2022.

The central bank responded to the economic downturn arising from the pandemic with an accommodative set of policies involving lowering its benchmark policy rate. However, monetary policy remains constrained by concerns of excessive selling pressure on the country's currency, the dalasi.

FISCAL POLICY

Both government expenditure and revenue as a share of GDP are low compared with other sub-Saharan African countries. None the less, both have improved in recent years, with government revenue increasing from an average annual of 9.9% of GDP in 2000–09 to 16.0% in 2010–21. However, government expenditure rose at a higher rate over the same period, increasing from an average annual rate of 11.3% of GDP to 20.0%. As a result, the budget deficit widened and averaged 1.4% of GDP in 2000–09, before expanding to an average of 4.1% in 2010–21.

There has been a marked improvement in revenue performance under the Barrow administration, with revenue increasing from 13.1% of GDP in 2016 to 19.3% in 2017. While revenue fell to 15.1% of GDP in 2018, it recovered to reach 21.1% in 2019 and a high of 22.8% in 2020 before falling back to 17.2% in 2021. However, the IMF expected an increase to 19.9% in 2022. The increase in expenditure was less dramatic, from 19.3% of GDP in 2016 to 24.9% in 2020, before falling to 21.6% in 2021. Thus, while the budget deficit reached a dangerous level of 6.2% of GDP in 2016, it had narrowed to a manageable level of 2.5% by 2019 and 2.2% in 2020 before increasing to 4.4% in 2021. Financing the deficit has led to government debt as a share of GDP increasing from 42.9% in 2010 to the dangerous level of 83.0% in 2021. However, this was lower than the 87% registered in 2017.

In its April 2019 assessment of The Gambia's fiscal situation, the IMF noted that 'improved revenue mobilization and expenditure restraint were essential to ensure fiscal discipline and create fiscal space for much-needed public investment and social spending'. The Fund stressed the need for a comprehensive reform of the country's SOEs to address budgetary risks and improve public service delivery. Finally, the Fund cautioned that restoring debt sustainability would require prudent fiscal policy, limiting external borrowing, and restructuring existing external debt. At that time, the IMF reached an agreement with The Gambia on a Staff-Monitored Programme, with assistance from other sources also forthcoming. An international conference held by the EU and the Gambian authorities in May 2018 resulted in foreign donors pledging US $1,700m. to support the Government's 2018–21 National Development Plan. The plan's goals involved expanded infrastructure and an improved business climate. The plan also focused on agricultural and tourism development.

In late March 2020 the IMF approved a US $75.4m. Extended Credit Facility (ECF) for The Gambia to help alleviate the impact of the COVID-19 pandemic. On 9 April 2022 IMF staff concluded the fourth review of The Gambia's ECF programme and found that the Government had met most of the conditional indicators, qualifying the country for additional funding under the ongoing ECF arrangement.

As noted above, fiscal indicators worsened in 2021, with the deficit widening, mainly due to electoral spending during the presidential and parliamentary elections held in 2021 and 2022, respectively. The IMF sees the fiscal deficit narrowing to 4.3% of GDP in 2022 before shrinking further to 2.3% of GDP in 2023 as government expenditure declines, owing to enhanced control of arrears and adherence to expenditure guidelines under the ECF arrangement. These include parastatal reforms, which will relieve pressure on the national purse, and cuts to the wage bill. The Gambia's 2022 national budget had a fiscal deficit target of 2% of GDP, but this is likely to prove unrealistic. Before the presidential election, the Government promised a 50% salary increase to civil servants, with effect from June 2022. Failure to fulfil this promise would be politically costly. This commitment could undermine attempts to meet the core benchmark ECF target of reducing the wage bill.

ASSESSMENT

Barrow announced that the priorities for his second term (2022–26) would centre on infrastructure, energy and technology as ways to achieve economic development. The Government is currently implementing many programmes, some of which were attempted by the Jammeh regime but proved unsuccessful owing to a lack of funding and political will. That same lack of funding may undermine many of the Government's current development initiatives.

The IMF's ECF will probably continue to urge the authorities towards fiscal discipline. The Government will pursue the privatization of parastatals, which will eventually help to reduce wasteful expenditure. However, cuts to the wage bill remain politically challenging and are unlikely materialize. Instead, revenue enhancement mechanisms, such as new taxes, can be expected in 2022 to counter the rising wage bill. Debt repayments due in 2022 will weigh heavily on the fiscal space, producing a wide but narrowing budgetary deficit.

Statistical Survey

Sources (unless otherwise stated): Gambia Bureau of Statistics, Kanifing Institutional Layout, PO Box 3504, Serrekunda; tel. 4377847; e-mail statgeneral@gbos.gov.gm; internet www.gbosdata.org; Central Bank of The Gambia, 1/2 Ecowas Ave, Banjul; tel. 4228103; e-mail info@cbg.gm; internet www.cbg.gm.

Area and Population

AREA, POPULATION AND DENSITY

Area (sq km)	11,295*
Population (census results)	
15 April 2003	1,360,681
8 April 2013	
Males	913,755
Females	943,426
Total	1,857,181
Population (UN estimates at mid-year)†	
2020	2,416,664
2021‡	2,486,937
2022‡	2,558,493
Density (per sq km) at mid-2022‡	226.5

* 4,361 sq miles.
† Source: UN, *World Population Prospects: The 2019 Revision.*
‡ Projection.

POPULATION BY AGE AND SEX
('000, UN projections at mid-2022)

	Males	Females	Total
0–14 years	563.4	553.1	1,116.5
15–64 years	674.4	703.7	1,378.1
65 years and over	31.0	32.8	63.9
Total	1,268.9	1,289.6	2,558.5

Note: Totals may not be equal to the sum of components, owing to rounding.

Source: UN, *World Population Prospects: The 2019 Revision.*

ADMINISTRATIVE DIVISIONS
(population at 2013 census)

Banjul . . .	31,054		Kerewan . . .	220,080
Basse . . .	237,220		Kuntaur . . .	96,703
Brikama . .	688,744		Mansakonko . .	81,042
Janjanbureh* . .	125,204		**Total**	1,857,181
Kanifing . . .	377,134			

* Formerly Georgetown.

PRINCIPAL TOWNS
(population at 1993 census)

Serrekunda . . .	151,450		Lamin	10,668
Brikama . . .	42,480		Gunjur	9,983
Banjul (capital) .	42,407		Basse	9,265
Bakau	38,062		Soma	7,925
Farafenni . . .	21,142		Bansang . . .	5,405
Sukuta	16,667			

Mid-2022 (incl. suburbs, UN projection): Banjul 469,534 (Source: UN, *World Urbanization Prospects: The 2018 Revision*).

BIRTHS AND DEATHS
(annual averages, UN estimates)

	2005–10	2010–15	2015–20
Birth rate (per 1,000) . . .	41.2	40.4	38.8
Death rate (per 1,000) . . .	9.4	8.7	8.0

Source: UN, *World Population Prospects: The 2019 Revision.*

Life expectancy (years at birth, estimates): 62.4 (males 61.0; females 63.8) in 2020 (Source: World Bank, World Development Indicators database).

ECONOMICALLY ACTIVE POPULATION
('000, FAO estimates at mid-year)

	2013	2014	2015
Agriculture, etc.	649	677	694
Total labour force (incl. others) .	865	899	934

Source: FAO.

Health and Welfare

KEY INDICATORS

Total fertility rate (children per woman, 2020)	5.1
Under-5 mortality rate (per 1,000 live births, 2020) . .	49.4
HIV/AIDS (% of persons aged 15–49, 2020)	1.8
COVID-19: Cumulative confirmed deaths (per 100,000 persons at 31 August 2022)	14.1
COVID-19: Fully vaccinated population (% of total population at 7 August 2022)	13.5
Physicians (per 1,000 head, 2020)	0.1
Hospitals (per 100,000 head, 2013)	0.7
Domestic health expenditure (2019): US $ per head (PPP) .	24.2
Domestic health expenditure (2019): % of GDP	1.0
Domestic health expenditure (2019): public (% of total current expenditure)	27.2
Access to improved water resources (% of persons, 2020) .	81
Access to improved sanitation facilities (% of persons, 2020) .	47
Total carbon dioxide emissions ('000 metric tons, 2018) . .	570
Carbon dioxide emissions per head (metric tons, 2018) . .	0.2
Human Development Index (2021): ranking	174
Human Development Index (2021): value	0.500

Note: For data on COVID-19 vaccinations, 'fully vaccinated' denotes receipt of all doses specified by approved vaccination regime (Sources: Johns Hopkins University and Our World in Data). Data on health expenditure refer to current general government expenditure in each case. For more information on sources and further definitions for all indicators, see Health and Welfare Statistics: Sources and Definitions section (europaworld.com/credits).

Agriculture

PRINCIPAL CROPS
('000 metric tons)

	2018	2019	2020
Cassava (Manioc)*	11.8	11.8	11.8
Groundnuts, with shell . . .	109.7*	110.0†	110.0†
Guavas, mangoes and mangosteens*	1.4	1.4	1.4
Maize†	18.0	17.0	35.0
Millet†	38.0	35.0	80.0
Oil palm fruit*	35.1	35.1	35.1
Rice, paddy	26.0	22.0	28.0†
Sesame seed*	1.0	0.9	1.0
Sorghum	29.6*	30.0†	30.0†

* FAO estimate(s).
† Unofficial figure(s).

Aggregate production ('000 metric tons, may include official, semi-official or estimated data): Total cereals 112.4 in 2018, 104.8 in 2019, 173.8 in 2020; Total fruit (primary) 9.5 in 2018, 9.5 in 2019, 9.5 in 2020; Total oilcrops 146.3 in 2018, 146.5 in 2019, 146.6 in 2020; Total pulses 2.5 in 2018, 2.5 in 2019, 2.5 in 2020; Total vegetables (primary) 12.8 in 2018, 12.9 in 2019, 12.8 in 2020.

Source: FAO.

LIVESTOCK

('000 head, year ending September, FAO estimates)

	2018	2019	2020
Asses	62	62	62
Cattle	479	483	487
Chickens	1,380	1,445	1,485
Goats	364	362	359
Horses	6	5	5
Pigs	14	15	13
Sheep	65	65	65

Source: FAO.

LIVESTOCK PRODUCTS

('000 metric tons, FAO estimates)

	2018	2019	2020
Cattle hides, fresh	0.5	0.5	0.5
Cattle meat	4.2	4.2	4.2
Cattle offals, edible	0.8	0.8	0.8
Cows' milk	77.4	77.9	78.4
Chicken meat	1.6	1.6	1.6
Game meat	1.4	1.4	1.4
Goat meat	0.9	0.9	0.9
Pig meat	0.5	0.6	0.5
Sheep meat	0.3	0.3	0.3
Hen eggs	1.0	1.0	1.0

Source: FAO.

Forestry

ROUNDWOOD REMOVALS

('000 cubic metres, excluding bark, FAO estimates)

	2018	2019	2020
Sawlogs, veneer logs and logs for sleepers	60	110	110
Other industrial wood* . . .	8	8	8
Fuel wood	766	774	783
Total	834	892	900

* Assumed to be unchanged since 1993.

Source: FAO.

Fishing

('000 metric tons, live weight of capture)

	2018	2019	2020
Tilapias	1.3	1.8	1.7
Sea catfishes	3.2	2.4	2.2
Cassava croaker	1.7	1.2	1.1
Bonga shad	17.7	18.8	17.0
Sardinellas	9.7	8.2	7.4
Sharks, rays, skates	0.0	0.5	1.3
Total catch (incl. others) . . .	49.5*	56.2	51.0

* FAO estimate.

Source: FAO.

Mining

	2010	2011	2012
Laterites ('000 metric tons) . .	226	1,035	2,386
Silica sand ('000 metric tons) . .	1,121	n.a.	n.a.

2007 (metric tons): Clay 6,713; Zircon 355.

Source: US Geological Survey.

Industry

SELECTED PRODUCTS

('000 metric tons unless otherwise stated)

	2017	2018	2019
Beer of barley*	3.1	3.0	3.1
Palm oil—unrefined†	4.2	4.2	n.a.
Groundnut oil	12.0*	18.0†	18.0†
Electrical energy (million kWh) .	317	321	325

* Unofficial figure(s).
† FAO estimate(s).

Sources: FAO; UN Energy Statistics Database.

Finance

CURRENCY AND EXCHANGE RATES

Monetary Units
100 butut = 1 dalasi (D).

Sterling, Dollar and Euro Equivalents (29 April 2022)
£1 sterling = 67.234 dalasi;
US $1 = 53.490 dalasi;
€1 = 56.378 dalasi;
1,000 dalasi = £14.87 = $18.70 = €17.74.

Average Exchange Rate (dalasi per US $)
2019   50.062
2020   51.502
2021   51.484

BUDGET

(million dalasi)

Revenue*	2020	2021†	2022‡
Tax revenue	10,326	10,833	11,838
Direct taxes	2,803	3,254	3,421
Domestic taxes on goods and services	4,934	4,776	5,142
Taxes on international trade .	2,588	2,803	3,276
Other taxes	1	0	0
Non-tax revenue	3,213	4,168	5,469
Total	13,539	15,001	17,307

Expenditure§	2020	2021†	2022‡
Current expenditure . . .	16,877	15,959	17,073
Wages and salaries . . .	4,049	4,593	5,063
Other goods and services . .	3,850	3,985	3,945
Interest payments	2,967	3,180	3,126
Internal	2,419	2,470	2,533
External	548	709	593
Subsidies	6,011	4,201	4,938
Capital expenditure	6,600	6,537	10,935
Gambia Local Fund . . .	1,763	3,174	3,050
Foreign financed . . .	4,837	3,363	7,885
Total	23,477	22,496	28,008

* Excluding grants received (million dalasi): 7,907 in 2020; 2,648 in 2021 (preliminary); 5,774 in 2022 (projection).
† Preliminary.
‡ Projections.
§ Excluding lending minus repayments (million dalasi): –2,031 in 2020; –4,848 in 2021 (preliminary); –4,928 in 2022 (projection).

Source: IMF, *The Gambia: Fourth Review Under the Extended Credit Facility Arrangement—Press Release; and Staff Report* (June 2022).

INTERNATIONAL RESERVES
(US $ million at 31 December)

	2019	2020	2021
IMF special drawing rights . .	1.12	3.33	86.66
Reserve position in IMF . . .	12.93	13.46	13.08
Foreign exchange	242.91	370.25	552.93
Total	256.96	387.04	652.67

Source: IMF, *International Financial Statistics.*

MONEY SUPPLY
(million dalasi at 31 December)

	2019	2020	2021
Currency outside depository corporations	7,843.54	10,071.74	11,486.82
Transferable deposits . . .	14,721.32	17,427.64	23,063.10
Other deposits	17,765.73	21,908.83	25,599.62
Broad money	40,330.59	49,408.21	60,149.55

Source: IMF, *International Financial Statistics.*

COST OF LIVING
(Consumer Price Index; base: January 2020 = 100)

	2019	2020	2021
Food and non-alcoholic beverages .	95.9	102.2	110.0
Housing, fuel and utilities . .	96.7	99.6	104.9
Clothing, textiles and footwear .	97.2	101.7	105.9
All items (incl. others) . . .	96.7	102.4	112.0

NATIONAL ACCOUNTS
(million dalasi at current prices)

Expenditure on the Gross Domestic Product

	2019	2020	2021*
Government final consumption expenditure	7,484	8,392	10,293
Private final consumption expenditure	78,452	81,889	92,401
Gross capital formation . . .	22,384	30,185	34,147
Total domestic expenditure .	108,320	120,466	136,841
Exports of goods and services .	18,309	8,967	6,980
Less Imports of goods and services	32,533	35,267	37,427
Statistical discrepancy (incl. changes in inventories) . . .	–3,302	–835	–1,448
GDP in purchasers' values .	90,794	93,330	104,947
GDP at constant 2013 prices .	61,769	62,134	64,785

Gross Domestic Product by Economic Activity

	2019	2020	2021*
Agriculture, hunting, forestry and fishing	18,162	19,827	23,528
Mining and quarrying	460	499	545
Manufacturing	3,439	2,439	1,963
Electricity, gas and water . .	1,911	2,117	2,196
Construction	9,882	10,674	13,229
Wholesale and retail trade . .	30,303	30,616	33,915
Hotels and restaurants . . .	1,870	695	883
Finance and insurance . . .	2,760	3,344	3,918
Transport and communications .	5,872	6,114	6,332
Real estate, renting and business activities	2,575	2,616	2,767
Public administration and defence	2,570	2,935	3,341
Education	1,757	2,061	2,513
Health and social work . . .	623	817	968
Other services	1,401	1,156	1,361
GDP at factor cost	83,586	85,911	97,459
Indirect taxes, *less* subsidies . .	7,208	7,418	7,487
GDP in purchasers' values . .	90,794	93,330	104,947

* Provisional.

BALANCE OF PAYMENTS
(US $ million)

	2019	2020	2021
Exports of goods	154.5	70.1	31.7
Imports of goods	–532.5	–581.8	–607.4
Balance on goods	–378.0	–511.8	–575.7
Exports of services	205.7	105.6	103.8
Imports of services	–108.1	–109.2	–118.9
Balance on goods and services	–280.3	–515.3	–590.8
Primary income received . .	12.4	7.7	5.1
Primary income paid	–27.7	–34.0	–55.6
Balance on goods, services and primary income	–295.7	–541.5	–641.2
Secondary income received . .	268.1	410.0	543.5
Secondary income paid . . .	–9.5	–9.9	–13.9
Current balance	–37.1	–141.4	–111.6
Capital account (net)	69.4	95.2	22.2
Direct investment assets . .	1.6	3.5	3.4
Direct investment liabilities . .	71.1	189.6	251.8
Other investment assets . .	–26.1	–19.1	–47.3
Other investment liabilities . .	–25.5	–35.5	75.0
Net errors and omissions . .	–36.3	–99.7	61.9
Reserves and related items .	17.1	–7.5	255.3

Source: IMF, *International Financial Statistics.*

External Trade

PRINCIPAL COMMODITIES
(distribution by HS, US $ million)

Imports c.i.f.	2018	2019	2020
Live animals and animal products	16.4	17.9	16.5
Vegetable products	72.7	57.7	72.5
Cereals	55.3	40.7	44.7
Rice	49.5	40.3	44.5
Milling products; malt, starches, insulin; wheat gluten . .	8.6	10.5	21.4
Wheat or meslin flour . . .	7.8	7.8	20.9
Animal, vegetable fats and oils	21.0	34.3	23.6
Fixed vegetable fats, oils and their fractions	21.0	34.3	23.6
Prepared foodstuffs; beverages and spirits; tobacco, etc.	44.9	53.8	46.4
Sugars and sugar confectionery .	30.2	37.1	26.6
Cane or beet sugar and chemically pure sucrose, in solid form	29.6	36.1	25.6

Imports c.i.f.—*continued*	2018	2019	2020
Mineral products	304.3	97.5	115.3
Salt, sulphur, earth, stone, plaster, lime and cement	21.6	21.6	34.0
Granite, porphyry, basalt, sandstone and other monumental or building stone	6.1	0.4	0.0
Cements, portland, aluminous, slag, and similar hydraulic materials	14.2	19.4	29.6
Mineral fuels, oils, etc.	282.7	75.9	81.3
Petroleum oils, not crude . .	281.9	73.1	77.4
Chemicals and related products	17.2	16.1	14.7
Textiles and textile articles .	12.4	17.9	15.0
Iron and steel, other base metals and articles of base metal	13.6	32.2	24.7
Articles of iron or steel . . .	5.6	15.0	9.0
Machinery and mechanical appliances	35.8	76.5	38.9
Machinery, boilers, etc. . . .	16.5	42.1	21.3
Electrical and electronic equipment	19.3	34.4	17.5
Vehicles, aircraft and transport equipment . . .	27.6	40.1	125.2
Vehicles other than railway, tramway	27.1	40.0	49.7
Cars (incl. station wagons) . .	22.5	28.7	44.8
Total (incl. others)	601.9	494.0	553.1

Exports f.o.b.	2018	2019	2020
Live animals and animal products	2.8	0.8	0.8
Fish and crustaceans	2.8	0.8	0.6
Vegetable products . . .	1.2	2.1	2.5
Edible fruit, nuts, peel of citrus fruit, melons	0.7	1.6	1.1
Brazil nuts, cashew nuts and coconuts	0.7	1.5	1.0
Oil seed, oleagic fruits, grain, seed, fruit, etc.	0.3	0.1	0.7
Groundnuts, whether or not shelled or broken	0.3	0.0	0.0
Animal, vegetable fats and oils, products, etc.	0.1	1.6	1.1
Prepared foodstuffs; beverages and spirits; tobacco, etc. .	0.8	1.5	1.3
Sugars and sugar confectionery .	0.0	0.5	0.4
Miscellaneous edible preparations	0.0	0.3	0.3
Mineral products	0.0	11.9	5.7
Mineral fuels, oils, etc. . . .	0.0	11.5	0.1
Petroleum oils, not crude . .	0.0	11.5	0.1
Wood, wood charcoal, cork, and articles thereof	0.0	2.7	0.0
Wood and articles of wood, wood charcoal	0.0	2.7	0.0
Fuel wood, in logs, billets, twigs, faggots; wood in chips or particles; sawdust	0.0	2.4	0.0
Pulp of wood, paper and paperboard, and articles thereof	0.4	0.1	0.0

Exports f.o.b.—*continued*	2018	2019	2020
Paper and paperboard	0.4	0.0	0.0
Textiles and textile articles .	3.2	1.2	1.0
Man-made filaments	2.6	0.8	0.6
Woven fabrics of synthetic filament yarn	2.6	0.8	0.6
Footwear, headgear, umbrellas, walking sticks, etc.	0.4	0.3	0.4
Footwear, gaiters, etc.	0.4	0.3	0.4
Machinery and mechanical appliances; electrical equipment; parts thereof .	0.0	0.7	12.5
Vehicles, aircraft, vessels and associated transport equipment	0.1	1.0	0.3
Vehicles other than railway, tramway	0.1	1.0	0.3
Total (incl. others)	9.2	24.6	25.9

Source: Trade Map-Trade Competitiveness Map, International Trade Centre, marketanalysis.intracen.org.

PRINCIPAL TRADING PARTNERS
(US $ million)

Imports c.i.f.	2018	2019	2020
Algeria	4.4	8.6	4.3
Belgium	10.2	16.9	8.3
Brazil	48.4	52.0	42.7
China, People's Republic . . .	40.1	52.3	57.6
Côte d'Ivoire	279.5	71.4	50.9
France (incl. Monaco)	3.6	5.2	9.5
Germany	8.0	9.2	9.2
India	30.7	59.7	25.1
Indonesia	4.1	8.2	6.5
Japan	0.4	0.5	21.9
Malaysia	15.7	20.0	14.8
Netherlands	15.4	21.5	14.4
Norway	0.6	0.8	75.2
Pakistan	6.6	7.2	10.3
Paraguay	6.4	2.1	1.5
Russian Federation	2.2	3.7	8.6
Senegal	15.3	12.6	18.3
Singapore	1.8	5.2	3.6
Spain	17.3	28.5	17.1
Switzerland	1.0	0.8	5.6
Togo	0.3	0.2	24.9
Türkiye	16.8	16.1	42.1
United Arab Emirates	7.1	12.5	14.6
United Kingdom	12.3	13.0	14.6
USA	12.7	13.4	11.0
Total (incl. others)	601.9	494.0	553.1

Exports f.o.b.	2018	2019	2020
Chile	0.0	0.3	0.1
China, People's Republic . . .	0.0	3.3	1.0
Guinea	0.1	0.2	0.0
Guinea-Bissau	0.2	4.7	2.3
India	0.7	1.4	1.2
Italy	0.1	0.0	0.0
Korea, Republic	1.2	0.6	0.3
Mali	4.3	11.9	6.6
Netherlands	0.5	0.0	0.0
Senegal	0.2	0.5	13.1
South Africa	0.1	0.0	0.0
Spain	0.5	0.1	0.1
Tunisia	0.1	0.1	0.0
United Kingdom	0.2	0.1	0.1
USA	0.1	0.1	0.0
Viet Nam	0.5	0.3	0.3
Total (incl. others)	9.2	24.6	25.9

Source: Trade Map-Trade Competitiveness Map, International Trade Centre, marketanalysis.intracen.org.

Transport

SHIPPING

Flag Registered Fleet
(at 31 December)

	2019	2020	2021
Number of vessels	9	12	14
Total displacement (grt) . . .	30,907	31,611	33,595

Source: Lloyd's List Intelligence (www.bit.ly/LLintelligence).

International Seaborne Freight Traffic
(at Banjula sea port, '000 metric tons)

	2018	2019	2020
Goods loaded	324.1	381.3	357.9
Goods unloaded	3,163.9	2,428.8	2,143.8

Tourism

FOREIGN VISITORS BY COUNTRY OF ORIGIN*

	2018	2019	2020
Belgium	8,533	8,864	3,669
Denmark	2,675	4,547	2,155
Finland	4,287	4,674	1,723
Germany	5,397	22,611	7,636
Netherlands	31,509	34,723	14,909
Norway	2,365	2,498	878
Spain	7,587	8,077	2,515
Sweden	17,569	15,700	6,160
United Kingdom	52,102	43,839	13,554
Total (incl. others)	209,134	235,788	89,232

* Air charter tourist arrivals.

Tourism receipts (US $ million, excl. passenger transport): 116 in 2016; 103 in 2017; 154 in 2018 (Source: World Tourism Organization).

Communications Media

	2018	2019	2020
Telephones ('000 main lines in use)	44.0	60.0	60.0
Mobile telephone subscriptions ('000)	3,181.4	2,254.7	2,678.0
Broadband subscriptions, fixed ('000)	4,433	5,000	5,000
Broadband subscriptions, mobile ('000)	838.2	976.7	1,327.0
Internet users (% of population) .	40.0	51.0	36.5

Sources: International Telecommunication Union.

Education

(2021/22)

	Institutions	Teachers	Students		
			Males	Females	Total
Pre-primary . .	1,497	4,305	63,336	67,616	130,952
Primary . . .	1,260	12,786	195,599	218,878	414,477
Junior secondary	539	6,212	55,111	67,970	123,081
Senior secondary	222	3,486	34,456	44,250	78,706

Source: Ministry of Basic and Secondary Education, Banjul.

Pupil-teacher ratio (qualified teaching staff, primary education, UNESCO estimate): 37.8 in 2020/21 (Source: UNESCO Institute for Statistics).

Adult literacy rate (UNESCO estimates): 50.8% (males 61.8%; females 41.6%) in 2015 (Source: UNESCO Institute for Statistics).

Directory

The Constitution

The Constitution of the Second Republic of The Gambia entered into full effect on 16 January 1997.

The Constitution provides for the separation of the powers of the executive, legislative and judicial organs of state. The head of state is the President of the Republic, who is directly elected by universal adult suffrage for a five-year term. No restriction is placed on the number of times a President may seek re-election. Legislative authority is vested in the 58-member National Assembly, comprising 53 members elected by direct universal suffrage and five members nominated by the President of the Republic. The Speaker and Deputy Speaker of the Assembly are elected, by the members of the legislature, from among the President's nominees. The Constitution upholds the principle of executive accountability to parliament. Thus, the head of state appoints government members, but these are responsible both to the President and to the National Assembly. Committees of the Assembly have powers to inquire into the activities of ministers and of government departments, and into all matters of public importance.

In judicial affairs, the final court of appeal is the Supreme Court. Provision is made for a special criminal court to hear and determine all cases relating to the theft and misappropriation of public funds.

The Constitution provides for an Independent Electoral Commission, an Independent National Audit Office, an Office of the Ombudsman, a Lands Commission and a Public Service Commission, all of which are intended to ensure transparency, accountability and probity in public affairs.

The Constitution guarantees the rights of women, of children and of the disabled. Tribalism and other forms of sectarianism in politics are forbidden. Political activity may be suspended in the event of a state of national insecurity.

The Government

HEAD OF STATE

President: ADAMA BARROW (sworn in 19 January 2017; re-elected 4 December 2021; sworn in 19 January 2022).

Vice-President: ALIEU BADARA JOOF.

THE CABINET
(October 2022)

President and Commander-in-Chief of the Armed Forces: ADAMA BARROW.

Vice-President: ALIEU BADARA JOOF.

Minister of Justice and Attorney-General: DAWDA JALLOW.

Minister of Foreign Affairs: Dr MAMADOU TANGARA.

Minister of Finance and Economic Affairs: SEEDY KEITA.

Minister of Defence: SERING MODOU NJIE.

Minister of the Interior: SIAKA SONKO.

Minister of Tourism: HAMAT N. K. BAH.

Minister of Trade, Industry, Regional Integration and Employment: BABOUCARR OUSMAILA JOOF.

Minister of Lands, Regional Government and Religious Affairs: ABBA SANYANG.

Minister of Agriculture: Dr DEMBA SABALLY.

Minister of Transport, Works and Infrastructure: EBRIMA SILLAH.

Minister of Communication and the Digital Economy: OUSMAN A. BAH.

Minister of Health: Dr AHMADOU LAMIN SAMATEH.

Minister of Basic and Secondary Education: CLAUDIANA A. COLE.

Minister of Gender, Children and Social Welfare: FATOU KINTEH.

Minister of Petroleum and Energy: ABDOULIE JOBE.

Minister of Fisheries and Water Resources: MUSA S. DRAMMEH.

Minister of Higher Education, Research, Science and Technology: Prof. PIERRE GOMEZ.

Minister of the Environment, Climate Change and Natural Resources: ROHEY JONE MANJANG.

Minister of Youth and Sports: BAKARY BADJIE.

MINISTRIES

Office of the President: State House, Banjul; tel. 9957592; e-mail info@op.gm; internet op.gov.gm.

Office of the Vice-President: State House, Banjul; tel. 4227605; e-mail info@ovp.gov.gm; internet www.ovp.gov.gm.

Attorney General's Chambers and Ministry of Justice: Marina Parade, Banjul; tel. 4225352; e-mail info@moj.gov.gm; internet www.moj.gov.gm.

Ministry of Agriculture: The Quadrangle, Banjul; tel. 4228270; e-mail info@moa.gov.gm; internet www.moa.gov.gm.

Ministry of Basic and Secondary Education: Willy Thorpe Bldg, Banjul; tel. 4228232; e-mail info@mobse.gov.gm; internet www.mobse.gov.gm.

Ministry of Defence: Banjul; internet fb.com/gambiadefence.

Ministry of the Environment, Climate Change and Natural Resources: 48 Kairaba Ave, Serekunda; tel. 4399447; e-mail info@meccnar.gov.gm; internet meccnar.gm.

Ministry of Finance and Economic Affairs: The Quadrangle, POB 9686, Banjul; tel. 4227221; e-mail info@mof.gov.gm; internet www.mof.gov.gm.

Ministry of Fisheries and Water Resources: Marina Parade, Banjul; tel. 4227773; e-mail info@mofwr.gm; internet www.mofwr.gm.

Ministry of Foreign Affairs: 4 Marina Parade, Banjul; tel. 4223577; e-mail info@mofa.gov.gm; internet mofa.gov.gm.

Ministry of Gender, Children, and Social Welfare: Banjul.

Ministry of Health: The Quadrangle, Banjul; tel. 4228624; e-mail info@moh.gov.gm; internet www.moh.gov.gm.

Ministry of Higher Education, Research, Science and Technology: Senegambia Highway, Bijilo, West Coast Region; tel. 4466752; e-mail info@moherst.gov.gm; internet www.moherst.gov.gm.

Ministry of Information and Communication: GRTS Bldg, MDI Rd, Kanifing, Banjul; tel. 4378028; e-mail info@moici.gov.gm; internet www.moici.gov.gm.

Ministry of the Interior: 5 J. R. Forster St, Banjul; tel. 4223277; e-mail info@moi.gov.gm; internet www.moi.gov.gm.

Ministry of Lands, Regional Government and Religious Affairs: Banjul; e-mail info@molgl.gov.gm; internet www.molgl.gov.gm.

Ministry of Petroleum and Energy: Futurelec Bldg, Bertil Harding Highway, Kotu, Banjul; tel. 8905105; internet fb.com/mope.gov.gm.

Ministry of Tourism: New Administrative Bldg, The Quadrangle, Banjul; tel. 4229563; e-mail info@motc.gov.gm; internet www.motc.gov.gm.

Ministry of Trade, Industry, Regional Integration and Employment: Central Bank Bldg, Independence Dr., Banjul; tel. 4228868; e-mail info@motie.gov.gm; internet www.motie.gov.gm.

Ministry of Transport, Works and Infrastructure: MDI Rd, Kanifing, Banjul; tel. 4375761; internet fb.com/Ministry-of-Transport-Works-and-Infrastructure-Gambia-MOTWI-2299022560172528.

Ministry of Youth and Sports: The Quadrangle, Banjul; tel. 4225264; e-mail info@moys.gov.gm; internet www.moys.gov.gm.

President

Presidential Election, 4 December 2021

Candidate	Votes	% of votes
Adama Barrow (NPP)	457,519	53.23
Ousainou Darboe (UDP)	238,253	27.72
Mammah Kandeh (GDC)	105,902	12.32
Halifa Baboucar Sallah (PDOIS)	32,435	3.77
Essa Mbye Faal (Ind.)	17,206	2.00
Abdoulie Ebrima Jammeh (NUP)	8,252	0.96
Total	859,567	100.00

Legislature

National Assembly: Assembly Bldg, Reverend Pye Lane, Banjul; tel. 4228305; e-mail assembly.clerk@yahoo.co.uk; internet www.assembly.gm.

Speaker: FABAKARY TOMBONG JATTA.

General Election, 9 April 2022

Party	Seats
National People's Party (NPP)	18
United Democratic Party (UDP)	15
National Reconciliation Party (NRP)	4
Alliance for Patriotic Reorientation and Construction (APRC)	2
People's Democratic Organization for Independence and Socialism (PDOIS)	2
Independent	12
Total	53*

* The President of the Republic is empowered by the Constitution to nominate five additional members of the legislature. The total number of legislators is thus 58.

Election Commission

Independent Electoral Commission (IEC): Election House, Bertil Harding Highway, Kanifing East Layout, POB 793 Banjul; tel. 4373804; e-mail admin@iec.gm; internet iec.gm; f. 1997; Chair. ALIEU MOMARR NJAI.

Political Organizations

Alliance for National Re-orientation and Development: Brufut; f. 2021; Sec.-Gen. LAMIN SATU BOJANG.

Alliance for Patriotic Reorientation and Construction (APRC): Sankung Sillah Bldg, Kairaba Ave, Banjul; tel. 7996176; e-mail aprcradio@gmail.com; internet fb.com/NewAPRCGambia; f. 1996; governing party; Chair. FABAKARY TOMBONG JATTA.

Democratic Party (DP): Brikama; f. 2021; Sec.-Gen. YUSUPHA DUMBUYA.

Gambia Democratic Congress (GDC): Latrikunda Sabiji, Kanifing; tel. 7272951; e-mail pro@gdc.gm; internet www.gdc.gm; f. 2016; Leader MAMMA KANDEH; Chair. OMAR CEESAY.

Gambia Moral Congress (GMC): Kerr Serign, Brikama; tel. 7882226; internet fb.com/Gambiamoralcongress; f. 2008; Exec. Chair. MAI AHMAD FATTY.

The Gambia Party for Democracy and Progress (GPDP): IPAM Bldg, Churchills Town, 68 Kombo Sillah Dr., KMC; tel. 3575944; e-mail gpdpgambia@gmail.com; internet fb.com/GPDPGambia-Party-For-Democracy-Progress-190148364665037; f. 2004; Sec.-Gen. HENRY GOMEZ.

National Convention Party (NCP): Bojang Kunda, opp. Old Market, Brikama; tel. 9836565; e-mail nationalconventionparty@gmail.com; f. 1977; left-wing; Leader EBRIMA JANKO SANYANG.

National People's Party (NPP): Churchill's Town, Banjul; tel. 7664408; e-mail nppgam220@gmail.com; internet fb.com/nppgambia; f. 2019; Leader ADAMA BARROW.

National Reconciliation Party (NRP): 3 Kairaba Ave, 1st Floor, opp. St Therese's Lower Basic School, KMC; tel. 4375537; f. 1996; formed an alliance with the UDP in 2006; Leader HAMAT N. K. BAH.

People's Democratic Organization for Independence and Socialism (PDOIS): 1 Sambou St, Churchill, POB 2306, Serrekunda; tel. 4393177; f. 1986; socialist; Leader HALIFA SALLAH.

People's Progressive Party (PPP): Ninth St East, Fajara M Section, POB 365, Banjul; tel. 3299988; e-mail info@pppthegambia.com; internet pppthegambia.com; f. 1959; fmr ruling party in 1962–94; centrist; Leader and Sec.-Gen. KEBBA E. JALLOW.

United Democratic Party (UDP): 1 Rene Blain St, Banjul; tel. 9911588; e-mail udpgambia@info.org; f. 1996; formed an alliance with the NRP in 2006 and with the GMC in 2011; reformist; Leader and Sec.-Gen. OUSAINOU DARBOE; Nat. Pres. Alhaji DEMBO BYFORCE BOJANG.

Diplomatic Representation

EMBASSIES IN THE GAMBIA

China, People's Republic: 66 Atlantic Rd, POB 4001, Banjul; tel. 4498005; e-mail chinaemb_gm@mfa.gov.cn; internet gm.china-embassy.gov.cn; Ambassador LIU JIN.

Cuba: Bijilo Layout, Kombo North District, Banjul; tel. 9960087; e-mail embajador@gm.embacuba.cu; internet misiones.minrex.gob.cu/es/gambia; Ambassador RUBÉN GARCÍA ABELENDA.

Guinea-Bissau: 78 Atlantic Rd, Fajara (Bakau), Banjul; tel. 4226862; e-mail bmalaca2012@yahoo.com; Ambassador LUIS DOMINGO CAMARA DE BARROS.

Libya: Independence Dr., Banjul; tel. 4223213; e-mail libyanembassy.gambia@gmail.com; Ambassador MUNSEF MOHAMMED HAWEEL NASEEB.

Mauritania: Fajara A Section, POB 2592, Serrekunda, Banjul; tel. 4491153; e-mail ambarimbanjul@hotmail.fr; Ambassador SIDI MOHAMED MOHAMED MAHMOUD MOHAMED RADHI.

Nigeria: 52 Garba Jalumpa Ave, Bakau, POB 630, Banjul; tel. 4495803; e-mail nighcgambia@yahoo.com; High Commissioner MOHAMMED MANU.

Qatar: POB 3311, Banjul; tel. 4466874; internet banjul.embassy.qa; Ambassador FAISAL FAHAD AL-MANA.

Senegal: 59 Kairaba Ave, POB 385, Banjul; tel. 4373752; e-mail ambasen.banjul@yahoo.fr; Ambassador BACHIROU SENE.

Sierra Leone: 67 Daniel Goddard St, Banjul; tel. 4228206; e-mail mfodayyumkella@yahoo.co.uk; High Commissioner LUCRETIA MARIAN SHEREEF.

Spain: Bertil Harding Highway, Deloitte/Brussels Airlines Bldg, Kololi, Banjul; tel. 4466101; e-mail ant.banjul@maec.es; internet fb.com/emb.banjul; Chargé d'affaires a.i. ANA GRACIA GALLEGO.

Türkiye (Turkey): 29 Kaira Ave, 4th St, Brufut Gardens, Banjul; tel. 4410650; internet banjul.be.mfa.gov.tr; Ambassador TOLGA BERMEK.

United Kingdom: 48 Atlantic Rd, Fajara, POB 507, Banjul; tel. 4495134; e-mail UKinTheGambia@fcdo.gov.uk; internet www.gov.uk/world/organisations/british-high-commission-banjul; High Commissioner DAVID BELGROVE.

USA: Kairaba Ave, Fajara, PMB 19, Banjul; tel. 4392856; e-mail consularbanjul@state.gov; internet gm.usembassy.gov; Ambassador SHARON L. CROMER.

Judicial System

The judicial system of The Gambia is based on English Common Law and legislative enactments of the Republic's parliament, which include an Islamic Law Recognition Ordinance whereby an Islamic Court exercises jurisdiction in certain cases between, or exclusively affecting, Muslims.

The Constitution of the Second Republic guarantees the independence of the judiciary. The Supreme Court is defined as the final court of appeal. Provision is made for a special criminal court to hear and determine all cases relating to theft and misappropriation of public funds.

Supreme Court of The Gambia: Law Courts, Independence Dr., Banjul; tel. 4227380; consists of the Chief Justice and up to 6 other judges; Chief Justice HASSAN BOUBACARR JALLOW.

Court of Appeal: Banjul; Pres. OMAR MUSA NJIE.

High Court: Banjul; consists of the Chief Justice and up to 7 other judges.

The **Banjul Magistrates Court**, the **Kanifing Magistrates Court** and the **Divisional Courts** are courts of summary jurisdiction presided over by a magistrate or in his or her absence by two or more lay justices of the peace. There are resident magistrates in all divisions. The magistrates have limited civil and criminal jurisdiction, and appeal from these courts lies with the Supreme Court.

Islamic Courts have jurisdiction in matters between, or exclusively affecting, Muslim Gambians and relating to civil status, marriage, succession, donations, testaments and guardianship. The Courts administer Islamic *Shari'a* law. A cadi, or a cadi and two assessors, preside over and constitute an Islamic Court. Assessors of the Islamic Courts are Justices of the Peace of Islamic faith. **District Tribunals** have appellate jurisdiction in cases involving customs and traditions. Each court consists of three district tribunal members, one of whom is selected as president, and other court members from the area over which it has jurisdiction.

Attorney-General: DAWDA JALLOW.

Solicitor-General: CHERNO MARENAH.

Religion

About 95% of the population are Muslims. The remainder are mainly Christians, and there are small numbers of animists, mostly of the Diola and Karoninka ethnic groups.

ISLAM

The Gambia Supreme Islamic Council: MDI Rd, Kanifing, POB 1894, Banjul; tel. 3876310; e-mail info@gsic.gm; internet fb.com/thegsic; f. 1962; Pres. ESSA FODAY DARBOE.

CHRISTIANITY

The Gambia Christian Council: MDI Rd, Kanifing, POB 27, Banjul; tel. 4392092; f. 1966; 7 mems (churches and other Christian bodies); Chair. Rt Rev. ROBERT P. ELLISON (Roman Catholic Bishop of Banjul); Sec.-Gen. Rev. PRISCILLA JOHNSON.

The Anglican Communion

The diocese of The Gambia, which includes Senegal and Cabo Verde, forms part of the Church of the Province of West Africa (CPWA). In September 2012 the CPWA was subdivided into two internal provinces: the Internal Province of Ghana, comprising the 10 (now 11) dioceses in Ghana, and the Internal Province of West Africa, comprising the remaining five (now six) dioceses. The Archbishop of the CPWA is the Bishop of Liberia.

Bishop of The Gambia: Rt Rev. JAMES ALLEN YAW ODICO, Bishopscourt, POB 51, Banjul; tel. 4228405; e-mail anglican@qanet.gm.

The Roman Catholic Church

The Gambia comprises a single diocese (Banjul), directly responsible to the Holy See. The Gambia participates in the Inter-territorial Catholic Bishops' Conference of The Gambia and Sierra Leone (based in Freetown, Sierra Leone).

Bishop of Banjul: Rt Rev. GABRIEL MENDY, Bishop's House, POB 165, Banjul; tel. 4391957; e-mail rpel202@yahoo.co.uk.

Protestant Churches

Abiding Word Ministries (AWM): 156 Mosque Rd, PMB 207, Serrekunda Post Office, Serrekunda; tel. 7640126; f. 1988; Senior Pastor Rev. FRANCIS FORBES.

Evangelical Lutheran Church in The Gambia: POB 5275, Brikama West Coast Region; tel. 9083755; e-mail leadership@elctg.org; internet www.elctg.org.

Methodist Church: 1 Macoumba Jallow St, POB 288, Banjul; tel. 4227506; f. 1821; Chair. and Gen. Supt Rev. WILLIAM PETER STEPHENS.

BAHÁ'Í FAITH

National Spiritual Assembly: POB 2532, Serrekunda; tel. 4229015.

The Press

The Daily News: 65 Kombo Sillah Dr., Churchill's Town, POB 2849, Serrekunda; tel. 8905629; e-mail dailynews.gm@gmail.com; internet dailynewsgm.com; f. 2009; 3 a week; Dir MADI M. K. CEESAY; Editor-in-Chief SAIKOU JAMMEH.

The Daily Observer: Gacem Rd, Kanifing Industrial Area, Bakau, POB 131, Banjul; tel. 4399801; internet www.observer.gm; f. 1992; daily; Deputy Editor-in-Chief ALHAGIE JOBE.

Foroyaa (Freedom): 1 Sambou St, Churchill's Town, POB 2306, Serrekunda; tel. 4393177; e-mail foroyaamarketing@gmail.com; internet foroyaa.net; f. 1987; daily; publ. by the PDOIS; Editors HALIFA SALLAH, SAM SARR, SIDIA JATTA.

Gainako: Banjul; internet gainako.com; online-only.

The Point: 2 Garba Jahumpa Rd, Fajara, POB 66, Bakau, New Town, Banjul; tel. 4497441; e-mail thepoint13@yahoo.com; internet www.thepoint.gm; f. 1991; 3 a week; Co-Publrs PAP SAINE, BABA HYDARA; Editor-in-Chief BEKAI NJIE.

The Standard: Sait Matty Rd, POB 4566, Bakau; tel. 4496481; e-mail info@standard.gm; internet www.standard.gm; f. 2010; daily; Editor LAMIN CHAM.

PRESS ASSOCIATION

The Gambia Press Union (GPU): New Allotment Area, Fajara, POB 1440, Banjul; tel. 7660179; e-mail pressuniongambia@gmail.com; internet gpu.gm; f. 1979; affiliated to the International Federation of Journalists, Federation of African Journalists and West African Journalists' Association; Pres. MUHAMMED S. BAH; Sec.-Gen. MODOU S. JOOF.

Publishers

Observer Company: Bakau New Town Rd, Kanifing, PMB 131, Banjul; tel. 4496087; internet www.observer.gm; f. 1995; indigenous languages and non-fiction; Man. OUSMAN RAMBO JATTA.

Sunrise Publishers: POB 955, Banjul; tel. 4393538; e-mail sunrise@qanet.gm; internet www.sunrisepublishers.20m.com; f. 1985; regional history, politics and culture; Man. PATIENCE SONKO-GODWIN.

Broadcasting and Communications

TELECOMMUNICATIONS

Africell (Gambia): 43 Kairaba Ave, POB 2140, Banjul; tel. 4376022; e-mail mmakkaoui@africell.gm; internet www.africell.gm; f. 2001; provider of mobile telecommunications; CEO ALIEU BADARA MBYE.

Comium Gambia: 27 Kairaba Ave, Pipeline, KSMD, Banjul; tel. 6601601; e-mail info@comium.gm; internet www.comium.gm; f. 2007; operates mobile telephone network under the Nakam brand; Man. Dir ABDALLAH ABOU DAYA.

The Gambia Telecommunications Co Ltd (GAMTEL): Gamtel House, 3 Nelson Mandela St, POB 387, Banjul; tel. 4229999; e-mail info@gamtel.gm; internet www.gamtel.gm; f. 1984; state-owned; Chair. SHOLA MAHONEY; Man. Dir SULAYMAN SUSO.

Gamcel: 59 Franklin D. Roosevelt Ave, Kanifing Industrial Estate, Banjul; tel. 4398169; internet www.gamcel.gm; f. 2000; wholly owned subsidiary of GAMTEL providing mobile telephone services; CEO ELIZABETH JOHNSON.

QCell Gambia: QCell House, Kairaba Ave, Serrekunda; tel. 3333111; e-mail support@qcell.gm; internet www.qcell.gm; f. 2008; mobile services; CEO MUHAMMED JAH.

BROADCASTING

Radio

The Gambia Radio and Television Services (GRTS): GRTV Headquarters, MDI Rd, Kanifing, POB 158, Banjul; tel. 4373913; e-mail info@grts.gm; internet www.grts.gm; f. 1962; state-funded, non-commercial broadcaster; radio broadcasts in English, Mandinka, Wolof, Fula, Diola, Serer and Serahuli; Dir-Gen. MALICK JENG.

Brikama Community Radio Station: Brikama; tel. 7718923; e-mail brikamacommunityradio@yahoo.co.uk; f. 1998; Admin. Man. BAKARY K. TOURAY.

Capital FM 100.4: FIB Bldg, 2 Kaairaba Ave, Banjul; tel. 3979395; e-mail info@capitalfmgm.com; internet www.capitalfm.gm.

Kora FM: 10 Kanifing, Banjul; tel. 4399756; independent commercial broadcaster; Man. PAP MBAYE.

Paradise FM: Banjul; e-mail info@paradisefm.gm; internet www.paradisefm.gm; operates from 3 stations.

Radio 1 FM: 44 Kairaba Ave, POB 2700, Serrekunda; tel. 4396076; e-mail george.radio1@qanet.gm; f. 1990; private station broadcasting FM music programmes to the Greater Banjul area; Dir GEORGE CHRISTENSEN.

Unique FM: Garba Jahumpa Rd, Bakau; tel. 7555777; internet www.uniquefm.gm; f. 2007; Man. LAMIN MANGA.

West Coast Radio: Manjai Kunda, POB 2687, Serrekunda; tel. 4461195; e-mail info@westcoast.gm; internet westcoast.gm; Man. Dir PETER GOMEZ.

Television

The Gambia Radio and Television Services (GRTS): see Radio; television broadcasts commenced in 1995.

QTV: Serrekunda; tel. 3244444; e-mail info@qtv.gm; internet www.qtv.gm; f. 2017; privately-owned television station; CEO MUHAMMED JAH.

Finance

BANKING

Central Bank

Central Bank of The Gambia: 1–2 ECOWAS Ave, Banjul; tel. 4229025; e-mail info@cbg.gm; internet www.cbg.gm; f. 1971; bank of issue; monetary authority; Gov. BUAH SAIDY.

Other Banks

Access Bank (Gambia) Ltd: 47 Kairaba Ave, Fajara, POB 3177, Serrekunda; tel. 6611996; e-mail contactcenter.gm@accessbankplc.com; internet gambia.accessbankplc.com; f. 2007; Man. Dir AYONKUNLE ABRAHAM OLAJUBU.

Arab-Gambian Islamic Bank: Becca Plaza, 5/6 Liberation Ave, POB 1415, Banjul; tel. 4222222; e-mail agib@qanet.gm; internet www.agib.gm; f. 1996; 21.1% owned by The Gambia National Insurance Co Ltd, 20.0% owned by Islamic Development Bank (Saudi Arabia); Chair. MUHAMMED JAH; Man. Dir NUHA MARENAH.

Banque Sahelo-Saherienne pour l'Investissement et Commerce Gambie Ltd: 52 Kairaba Ave, PMB 204, KMC; tel. 4498078; internet www.bsicgambia.gm; f. 2008; Gen. Man. AKRAM AYAD SAID DAHAIM.

Ecobank Gambia Ltd: 42 Kairaba Ave, POB 3466, Serrekunda; tel. 4399033; e-mail ecobankega@ecobank.com; internet www.ecobank.com; Chair. BERNARD MENDY; Man. Dir CARL ASSEM.

FBNBank Gambia: GIPFZA House, Ground Floor, 48 Kairaba Ave, Serrekunda, KMC, POB 1600, Banjul; tel. 4377878; internet www.fbnbankgambia.com; f. 2005; fmrly International Commercial Bank (Gambia) Ltd; name changed as above in 2015; CEO ADEFISAYO ADEFARAKAN.

First International Bank Ltd: 2 Kairaba Ave, Serrekunda; tel. 4396580; internet www.fibankgm.com; f. 1999; 61.9% owned by Slok Ltd (Nigeria); Man. Dir and CEO BINTA JANNEH.

Guaranty Trust Bank (Gambia): 56 Kairaba Ave, Fajara, POB 1958, Banjul; tel. 4376371; e-mail corpaffgm@gtbank.com; internet gtbankgambia.com; f. 2002; subsidiary of Guaranty Trust Bank PLC (Nigeria); Chair. Dr AMADOU SAMBA; Man. Dir ADESINA ADEBESIN.

Mega Bank Gambia: 11A Liberation Ave, POB 211, Banjul; tel. 4227944; e-mail info@megabankgambia.gm; internet megabankgambia.gm; f. 1968; fmrly International Bank for Commerce (Gambia) Ltd, subsequently Bank PHB; name changed to Keystone Bank Gambia 2013; present name adopted in 2015; Chair. SEEKU A. K. JABBIE; Man. Dir OMAR S. JATTA.

Skye Bank Gambia: 70 Kairaba Ave, Fajara, KSMD; tel. 4414370; e-mail info@skyebankgm.com; internet www.skyebankgm.com; subsidiary of Skye Bank PLC (Nigeria); Man. Dir SONI ANWALIMHOBOR.

Standard Chartered Bank (Gambia) Ltd: 8/10 ECOWAS Ave, POB 259, Banjul; tel. 4202929; e-mail gambia.contactus@sc.com; internet www.sc.com/gm; f. 1894; 75% owned by Standard Chartered Holdings BV, The Netherlands; Chair. ALPHA A. BARRY; CEO CHUKS UGHA.

Trust Bank Ltd (TBL): 3–4 ECOWAS Ave, POB 1018, Banjul; tel. 4225777; e-mail info@tblgambia.com; internet www.tblgambia.com; f. 1997; fmrly Meridien BIAO Bank Gambia Ltd; 22.12% owned by Data Bank, 36.97% by Social Security and Housing Finance Corpn; Chair. FRANKLIN HAYFORD; Man. Dir IBRAHIMA SALLA.

Zenith Bank (Gambia) Ltd: 49 Kairaba Ave, Fajara, POB 2823, Serrekunda; tel. 4399471; e-mail enquiry@zenithbank.gm; internet www.zenithbank.gm; f. 2008; subsidiary of Zenith Bank PLC; Chair. Prof. MUHAMMADOU M. O. KAH; Man. Dir NNAMDI ANOZIE.

INSURANCE

Capital Express Assurance (Gambia) Ltd: 19 Kairaba Ave, POB 268, Banjul; tel. 4373034; e-mail info@capitalexpressassurancegm.com; internet www.capitalexpressassurancegm.com; f. 2008; subsidiary of Capital Express Group (Nigeria); Man. Dir and CEO FESTUS AHAOTU.

The Gambia National Insurance Co Ltd (GNIC): 19 Kairaba Ave, Fajara, KSMD, POB 750, Banjul; tel. 4395725; e-mail info@gnic.gm; internet www.gnic.gm; f. 1974; privately owned; Man. Dir FYE K. CEESAY.

Global Security Insurance Co Ltd: 73A Independence Dr., POB 1400, Banjul; tel. 4223716; e-mail info@gsicgambia.com; internet gsicgambia.com; f. 1996; Exec. Chair. MAJA SONKO; Man. Dir EBOU LAMINE BITTAYE.

IGI Gamstar Insurance Co Ltd: 79 Daniel Goddard St, POB 1276, Banjul; tel. 4226021; e-mail fabian.akaneme@igi-gamstar.gm; f. 1991; Man. Dir TAYO OLOWUDE.

New Vision Insurance Co Ltd: 52 Kairaba Ave, POB 239, Banjul; tel. 4223045; Dir BIRAN BAH.

Prime Insurance Co Ltd: 10c Nelson Mandela St, POB 277, Banjul; tel. 4222476; e-mail info@prime.gm; internet www.prime.gm; f. 1997; Alhaji ABDOU A. B. NJIE; Man. Dir DAWDA SARGE.

Royal Insurance Gambia Ltd: Royal House, Kairaba Ave, POB 2605, Serrekunda; tel. 4498736; e-mail info@royalinsurancegm.com; internet royalinsurancegm.com; Man. Dir MAKAIREH BADJAN.

Sunshine Insurance Company Ltd: 7/8 Nelson Mandela St, Banjul; tel. 4202645; Man. Dir ALMAMY B. JOBARTEH.

Takaful Gambia Ltd: Kairaba Ave, POB 978, Banjul; tel. 4380158; internet www.takafulinsurance.gm; Chair. AMIE BENSOUDA; Man. Dir SAINABOU JALLOW GAYE.

Insurance Association

Insurance Association of The Gambia (IAG): IAG Secretariat, 10c Nelson Mandela St, POB 277, Banjul; tel. 4229952; f. 1987; Pres. MAKAIREH BADJAN; Sec.-Gen. MOLIFA SANNEH.

Trade and Industry

GOVERNMENT AGENCIES

The Gambia Investment and Export Promotion Agency (GIEPA): GIEPA House, 48A Kairaba Ave, Serrekunda, KMC, POB 757, Banjul; tel. 4377377; e-mail info@giepa.gm; internet www.giepa.gm; f. 2001; fmrly The Gambia Investment Promotion and Free Zones Agency (f. 2001); the implementing agency of the Gateway Project, funded by the World Bank and the Gambian Government, responsible for fostering local and foreign direct investment; name changed as above in 2010; Chair. YANKUBA DIBBA; CEO OUSAINOU SENGHORE.

Gambia Public Procurement Authority (GPPA): 9 Kairaba Ave, POB 4032, Bakau; tel. 4378502; e-mail info@gppa.gm; internet gppa.gm; f. 2003; Chair. HABIB A. O. JENG; Dir-Gen. PHODAY M. JAITEH.

DEVELOPMENT AGENCY

The Gambia Rural Development Agency (GARDA): Soma Village, Jarra West, PMB 452, Serrekunda; tel. 4496676; internet gardagm.org; f. 1990; Exec. Dir KEBBA BAH.

CHAMBER OF COMMERCE

The Gambia Chamber of Commerce, Industry, Agriculture and Employer's Association: Kerr Jula, Bertil Harding Highway, Bijilo, POB 3382, Serrekunda; tel. 4463452; e-mail info@gcci.gm; internet gcci.gm; f. 1967; Pres. EDRISSA M. JOBE; CEO ALIEU SECKA.

INDUSTRIAL AND TRADE ASSOCIATION

The Gambia Cotton Growers Association: Banjul; Pres. ALPHA BAH; Sec.-Gen. OMAR SUMPO CEESAY.

UTILITIES

Public Utilities Regulatory Authority (PURA): 94 Kairaba Ave, POB 4230, Bakau; tel. 4399601; e-mail info@pura.gm; internet www.pura.gm; f. 2001; monitors and enforces standards of performance by public utilities; Dir-Gen. YUSUPHA M. JOBE.

National Water and Electricity Co Ltd (NAWEC): 53 Mamady Manjang Highway, Kanifing, POB 609, Banjul; tel. 4376607; e-mail info@nawec.gm; internet www.nawec.gm; f. 1996; in 1999 control was transferred to the Bassau Development Corpn, Côte d'Ivoire, under a 15-year contract; electricity and water supply, sewerage services; Chair. MUSTAPHA COLLEY; Man. Dir NANI JUWARA.

MAJOR COMPANIES

Boule & Co Ltd: NTC Complex, 3/4 Liberation Ave, POB 602, Banjul; tel. 22484676; e-mail info@bouleco.com; internet bouleco.com; f. 1976; general merchants; Chair. and Man. Dir CHARBEL N. ELHAJJ.

CFAO Motors Gambia: Mamadi Maniyang Hwy, 14 Liberation Ave, POB 297, Banjul; tel. 4396906; internet suzuki.cfaomotors-gambia.com; f. 1887; fmrly Compagnie Française de l'Afrique Occidental; distributor of Toyota, Suzuki, Yamaha, Bridgestone and FG Wilson; Man. Dir PHILIP HUART.

K. Chellaram & Sons (Gambia) Ltd: Kanifing Industrial Estate, POB 275, Banjul; tel. 4392912; e-mail kchellarams@gmail.com;

internet www.chellaramsgambia.com; f. 1958; importers and general merchants; Man. Dir NITIN R. CHELLARAM.

Elton Oil Gambia: 78 Atlantic Rd, Fajara, POB 4043, Bakau; tel. 4496690; Chair. CHEIKH SADIBOU DIOP.

FAM Engineering: Julbrew Rd, Kanifing, POB 1813 Banjul; tel. 4390200; e-mail famengineering@hotmail.com; internet www.famengineering.gm; civil engineering; Man. Dir FODAY JUWARA.

GALP Gambia Ltd: Independence Dr., POB 263, Banjul; tel. 4228028; marketing and sale of petroleum products; Man. Dir PAULO LOPES.

Gambia Horticultural Enterprises (GHE): 16 Mamadi Manjang Highway, Old Jeshwang, POB 2425, Serrekunda; tel. 4394819; e-mail gamhort@qanet.gm; internet gamhort.com; agro-based; Dir-Gen. MOMODOU CEESAY.

Gamwater: 1 Gacem Rd, Kanifing Industrial Estate, POB 1880, Banjul; tel. 4378947; Man. Dir AMADOU SAMBA.

National Food Security Processing and Marketing Corpn: Banjul; f. 2015 to replace The Gambia Groundnut Corpn; Man. Dir ANTHONY CARLVALHO.

Shyben A. Madi & Sons Ltd: 6 Ecowas Ave, POB 184, Banjul; tel. 4226666; e-mail secretary@shybenmadi.com; internet www.shybenmadi.com; general merchants; Man. Dir GEORGE S. MADI.

TAF Holding Co Ltd: 17–19 Kaira Ave, Madiba Mall, Brufut Gardens Estate, POB 121, Banjul; tel. 7762333; e-mail information.services@tafgambia.com; internet tafgambia.com; f. 1990; has subsidiaries in construction, real estate and tourism; Dir MUSTAPHA NJIE.

TRADE UNIONS

Association of Gambian Sailors (AGS): c/o 31 OAU Blvd, POB 698, Banjul; tel. 4223080; Sec.-Gen. ABDOU SANYANG.

The Gambia Dock and Maritime Workers' Union: Albert Market, POB 852, Banjul; tel. 4229448; Pres. AMADOU TOURAY; Sec.-Gen. MALICK SECKA.

The Gambia National Trades Union Congress (GNTUC): Trade Union House, 31 OAU Blvd, POB 698, Banjul; Pres. MUSTAPHA WADA; Sec.-Gen. EBRIMA GARBA CHAM.

Gambia Teachers' Union (GTU): MDI Rd, Kanifing, POB 133, Banjul; tel. 4392075; e-mail gtu@gtu.gm; internet www.gtu.gm; f. 1937; Sec.-Gen. ANTOINETTE CORR-JACK.

The Gambia Workers' Confederation: Trade Union House, 72 OAU Blvd, POB 698, Banjul; tel. 4222754; f. 1958 as The Gambia Workers' Union; present name adopted in 1985; Sec.-Gen. PA MOMODOU FAAL.

Transport

Gambia Transport Service Co: Factory St, Kanifing Housing Estate, POB 801, Kanifing; tel. 4380006; e-mail info@gtsc.gm; internet www.gtsc.gm; f. 2013 to replace The Gambia Public Transport Corpn; operates road transport and ferry services; Chair. EDWARD GRAHAM; Gen. Man. SEEDY KANYI.

RAILWAYS

There are no railways in The Gambia.

ROADS

National Roads Authority: Banjul; tel. 4375784; e-mail info@nra.gm; internet nra.gm; Chair. BAI IBRAHIM CHAN; Man. Dir MOMODOU SENGHORE.

SHIPPING

The River Gambia is well suited to navigation. A weekly river service is maintained between Banjul and Basse, 390 km above Banjul, and a ferry connects Banjul with Barra. Small ocean-going vessels can reach Kaur, 190 km above Banjul, throughout the year.

The Gambia Ports Authority: 34 Liberation Ave, POB 617, Banjul; tel. 4229940; f. 1972; Man. Dir OUSMAN JOBARTEH.

Maersk Gambia Ltd: 10 Marina Parade, Banjul; tel. 4224450; e-mail gamsalimp@maersk.com; f. 1993; owned by Maersk Line.

CIVIL AVIATION

Banjul International Airport is situated at Yundum, 27 km from the capital.

The Gambia Civil Aviation Authority (GCAA): Banjul International Airport, POB 285, Yundum; tel. 4472831; e-mail dg@gcaa.aero; internet www.gcaa.aero; f. 1991; Chair. EBRIMA N. F. BOJANG; Dir-Gen. ABDOULIE EBRIMA JAMMEH.

Tourism

The Gambia Hotel Association: Djembe Resort, Duplex Rd, Kololi; tel. 7725379; e-mail info@gambiahotels.gm; internet www .gambiahotels.gm; Chair. BUNA NJIE.

The Gambia Tourism Board: POB 4085, Kotu; tel. 4462496; e-mail info@gtboard.gm; internet www.visitthegambia.gm; f. 2001 as The Gambia Tourist Authority; name changed as above in 2011; Dir-Gen. ABDOULIE HYDARA.

Defence

As assessed at November 2021, the Gambian National Army comprised 3,500 men and included an air wing. The Gambian Navy comprised 300 men and there was also a 300-strong Republican National Guard. Military service has been mainly voluntary; however, the Constitution of the Second Republic, which entered into full effect in January 1997, makes provision for conscription.

Defence Budget: D757.5m. in 2021.

Chief of Defence Staff: Lt-Gen. YAKUBA A. DRAMMEH.

Education

Primary education, beginning at seven years of age, is free but not compulsory and lasts for nine years. It is divided into two cycles of six and three years. Secondary education, from 16 years of age, lasts for a further three years. According to estimates by the United Nations Educational, Scientific and Cultural Organization (UNESCO), in 2018/19 total enrolment at pre-primary institutions was equivalent to 43% of children in the relevant age-group (boys 42%; girls 45%), while primary schools included 85% of children in the relevant age-group (boys 81%; girls 90%). Secondary enrolment in 2014/2015 was equivalent to 86% of the appropriate age-group (boys 84%; girls 88%). Post-secondary education is available in teacher training, agriculture, health and technical subjects. The University of The Gambia, at Banjul, was officially opened in 2000. In the 2021 budget the Ministry of Basic and Secondary Education was allocated D2,881.7m. (representing 8.2% of total projected expenditure), while the Ministry of Higher Education, Research, Science and Technology was allocated D274.2m. (0.8%).

Bibliography

Gray, J. M. *A History of the Gambia* (new edn). Cambridge, Cambridge University Press, 2015.

Hughes, A., and Gailey, A. *Historical Dictionary of The Gambia*. 4th edn. Lanham, MD, Scarecrow Press, 2008.

Hughes, A., and Perfect, D. *Political History of The Gambia, 1816–1994*. Woodbridge, James Currey, 2008.

Janson, M. *Islam, Youth and Modernity in The Gambia*. New York, Cambridge University Press, 2014.

Kanyongolo, E., and Norris, C. *The Gambia: Freedom of Expression Still Under Threat: The Case of Citizen FM*. London, Article 19, 1999.

Luom, M. *An Analysis of the Gambian Coup of 1994*. Ottawa, ON, Carleton University Press, 2001.

M'Bai, P. N. *Gambia: The Untold Dictator Yahya Jammeh's Story*. Bloomington, IN, iUniverse, 2012.

People's Progressive Party Special Editorial Commission. *The Voice of the People, the Story of the PPP, 1959–1989*. Banjul, The Gambia Communications Agency and Barou-Ueli Enterprises, 1992.

Rice, B. *Enter Gambia: The Birth of an Improbable Nation*. London, Angus & Robertson, 1968.

Saine, A. S. *The Paradox of Third-wave Democratization in Africa: The Gambia Under AFPRC-APRC Rule, 1994–2008*. Lanham, MD, Lexington Books, 2010.

Culture and Customs of Gambia. Santa Barbara, CA, Greenwood, 2012.

Saine, A., Ceesay, E. J., and Sall, E (Eds). *State and Society in the Gambia since Independence*. Trenton, NJ, Africa World Press, 2012.

Schroeder, R. A. *Shady Practices: Agroforestry and Gender Politics in The Gambia*. Berkeley, CA, University of California Press, 1999.

Senghor, J. (Ed.). *Profiles of Gambian Political Leaders in the Decolonisation Era*. Leicester, Global Hands Publishing, 2017.

Tomkinson, M. *Gambia*. 2nd edn. London, Michael Tomkinson Publishing, 2001.

Touray, O. *The Gambia and the World: A History of the Foreign Policy of Africa's Smallest State, 1965–1995*. Hamburg, Hamburg Institute of African Affairs, 2000.

Wiseman, J. A. *Democracy in Black Africa: Survival and Revival*. New York, Paragon House, 1990.

Wiseman, J. A., and Chongan, E. I. *Military Rule and the Abuse of Human Rights in The Gambia: The View from Mile 2 Prison*. Trenton, NJ, Africa World Press, 2000.

Wright, D. R. *The World and a Very Small Place in Africa*. 4th edn. Abingdon, Routledge, 2018.

GHANA

Physical and Social Geography

E. A. BOATENG

PHYSICAL FEATURES

Structurally and geologically, the Republic of Ghana exhibits many of the characteristics of sub-Saharan Africa, with its ancient rocks and extensive plateau surfaces marked by prolonged sub-aerial erosion. About one-half of the surface area is composed of Pre-Cambrian metamorphic and igneous rocks, most of the remainder consisting of a platform of Palaeozoic sediments believed to be resting on the older rocks. These sediments occupy a substantial area in the north-central part of the country and form the Voltaic basin. Surrounding this basin on all sides, except along the east, is a highly dissected peneplain of Pre-Cambrian rocks at an average of 150 m–300 m above sea level but containing several distinct ranges of up to 600 m. Along the eastern edge of the Voltaic basin and extending right down to the sea near Accra is a narrow zone of highly folded Pre-Cambrian rocks forming the Akwapim-Togo ranges. These ranges rise to 300 m–900 m above sea level, and contain the highest points in Ghana. Continuing northwards across Togo and Benin, they form one of west Africa's major relief features, the Togo-Atakora range.

The south-east corner of the country is occupied by the Accra-Ho-Keta plains, which are underlain by the oldest of the Pre-Cambrian series (known as the Dahomeyan) and contain extensive areas of gneiss, of which the basic varieties weather to form agriculturally useful soils. Extensive areas of young rocks, formed between the Tertiary and Recent ages, are found only in the broad delta of the Volta in the eastern part of the Accra plains, and in the extreme south-west corner of the country along the Axim coast; while in the intervening littoral zone patches of Devonian sediments combine with the rocks of the Pre-Cambrian peneplain to produce a coastline of sandy bays and rocky promontories.

Most of the country's considerable mineral wealth, consisting mainly of gold, diamonds, manganese and bauxite, is associated with the older Pre-Cambrian rocks, although petroleum has been discovered in commercial quantities in some of the younger sedimentaries.

The drainage is dominated by the Volta system, which occupies the Voltaic basin and includes the vast artificial lake of 8,502 sq km formed behind the hydroelectric dam at Akosombo. A second dam is sited at Kpong, 8 km downstream from Akosombo. Most of the other rivers in Ghana, such as the Pra, Birim, Densu, Ayensu and Ankobra, flow between the southern Voltaic or Kwahu plateau and the sea.

CLIMATE AND VEGETATION

Climatic conditions are determined by the interaction of two principal airstreams: the hot, dry, tropical, continental air mass or harmattan from the north-east, and the moist, relatively cool, maritime air mass or monsoon from the south-west across the Atlantic. In the southern part of the country, where the highest average annual rainfall (of 1,270 mm–2,100 mm) occurs, there are two rainy seasons (April–July and September–November), while in the north, with averages per year of 1,100 mm–1,270 mm, rainfall occurs in only a single season between April and September, followed by a long dry season dominated by the harmattan. There is much greater uniformity as regards mean temperatures, which average 26°C–29°C. These temperatures, coupled with the equally high relative humidities, which fall significantly only during the harmattan, tend to produce oppressive conditions, relieved only by the relative drop in temperature at night, especially in the north, and the local incidence of land and sea breezes near the coast.

Vegetation in Ghana is determined mainly by climate and soil conditions. The area of heavy annual rainfall broken by one or two relatively short dry seasons, to be found in the south-west portion of the country and along the Akwapim-Togo ranges, is covered with evergreen forest in the wetter portions and semi-deciduous forest in the drier portions, while the area of rather lower rainfall, occurring in a single peak in the northern two-thirds of the country and the anomalously dry area around Accra, is covered with savannah and scrub. Prolonged farming activities and timber exploitation have reduced the original closed forest vegetation, while in the savannah areas extensive cultivation and bush burning have also caused serious environmental degradation.

POPULATION

Ghana covers an area of 238,533 sq km (92,098 sq miles). The June 2021 census recorded a population of 30,832,019, giving an approximate density of 135.8 inhabitants per sq km. The highest densities occur in the urban and cocoa-farming areas in the southern part of the country, and also in the extreme north-eastern corner, where intensive, compound farming is practised.

There are no fewer than 75 spoken languages and dialects in Ghana, each more or less associated with a distinct ethnic group. The largest of these groups are the Akan (comprising about one-half of Ghana's population), Mossi, Ewe and the Ga-Adangme. Any divisive tendencies that might have arisen from this situation have been absent, largely as a result of government policies; however, a distinction can be made between the southern peoples, who have come most directly and longest under the recent influence of European life and the Christian religion, and the northern peoples, whose traditional modes of life and religion have undergone relatively little change, owing mainly to their remoteness from the coast. One of the most potent unifying forces has been the adoption of English as the official language, although it is augmented by 11 major national languages.

History

GEORGE M. BOB-MILLIAR

Revised for this edition by the editorial staff

INTRODUCTION

'And help us to resist oppressors' rule with all our will and might for evermore.' These words found in the Ghanaian national anthem encapsulate the character of the people who make up the modern state of Ghana. State building in Ghana is an ongoing project that has been partially accomplished through resistance and consensus. Indeed, the political history of modern Ghana revolves around resistance to foreign domination and internal dictatorships, while the 'love for liberty' is ingrained in the DNA of the peoples of Ghana. In the pre-colonial period organizations such as the Fante Confederacy and the Aborigines Right Protection Society emerged in order to resist the policies of the British. Ghana was born out of the merger of three different geographical zones—coastal, forest, and savannah—and over 100 ethnic groups and languages inhabit the territory. Traditional authorities embedded in some pre-colonial centralized states are still very relevant in the body politics of the country, and contestations over access to power and how that power was exercised have dominated Ghana's contemporary political development.

Ghana's troubled history of state building was characterized by short-lived civilian regimes and a heavy dose of authoritarianism, especially during the period of military rule. The first three decades of its founding saw the country experimenting with liberalism, socialism, and militarism. However, since the early 1990s, when the country embraced constitutionalism and inaugurated its Fourth Republic, it has pursued a path of economic development. Ghana is considered as one of the most mature democracies in sub-Saharan Africa.

The country's most recognizable achievement has been the progressive improvement of its electoral politics. The management of elections and the increasing acceptance of poll results as 'free and fair' by the main stakeholders have ensured stability. The state is endowed with a more open political system and several independent democratic institutions. Between 1992 and 2020 eight successive multi-party elections were held, although, while embracing a multi-party framework, two major political parties (the National Democratic Congress—NDC—and the New Patriotic Party—NPP) are the only ones to have governed in this period. Consequently, a de facto two-party system and a highly competitive electoral system is what sets Ghana apart from its neighbours.

THE BIRTH OF GHANA

Formal partisanship started with the formation of the United Gold Coast Convention (UGCC) on 4 August 1947. The political elites joined by traditional leaders, women and youth demanded to be part of the governance of the country. Therefore, partisanship was introduced to enable Ghanaians to play a role in shaping the future of their country. A rival political movement emerged out of the UGCC as a result of disagreements over the strategies to use to demand for self government. The birth of the Convention People's Party (CPP) in June 1949, led by Dr Kwame Nkrumah, added urgency to the independence movement. Ghanaian historian Prof. Albert Adu Boahen argued that bipolarization has characterized Ghanaian political culture, with a 'linear progression' between two political cleavages—right-leaning and left-leaning tendencies, be it civilian or military.

The two leading groupings of the early 1950s advocated a politics of accommodation and a politics that opposed the status quo. Yet both groups were pro-independence. Besides the UGCC and the CPP, other political parties emerged during the era of decolonization. As a mass-based and progressive party, the CPP mobilized across all segments of the Ghanaian society. It was one of the first political parties to acknowledge the critical role that Ghanaian women played in the struggle against British imperialism. The CPP women activists popularized the party's agenda in the market centre. The UGCC, on the other hand, was seen as the party of the elites and conservative forces.

The CPP victory over the conservative forces triggered demands for certain safeguards before independence was granted to Ghana. The opposition to Nkrumah's forward march saw the emergence of several ethno-regional groups, and these groups challenged the terms on which independence was to be granted to Ghana. In April 1954 the Northern People's Party (NoPP) was formed by elites and traditional authorities to champion the cause of the Northern Territories, and in September, in the forest zone, Asante nationalists launched the National Liberation Movement (NLM). However, the combined forces of the NoPP and NLM failed to secure any meaningful electoral victory. The CPP emerged victorious in the June 1956 general elections and on 6 March 1957 the British granted independence to Ghana.

The resistance to officialdom that characterized the birth of Ghana would repeat itself at several points in the 20th century. Massive transformational developments across the political, economic and social landscapes characterized the initial years of the CPP administration under Prime Minister Nkrumah. The first significant political development that paved the way for some form of dictatorship was the passage of the Avoidance of Discrimination Act in October 1957. Opponents of the regime criticized the law, which was aimed at addressing the sectional and ethnic interests that dominated politics in the lead up to political independence. Consequently the legislation banned religious, ethnic and regional political groupings, thereby narrowing the political space and inadvertently creating a de facto two-party system and eventually a one-party dictatorship. All the small opposition parties banded together under the name of the United Party (UP).

On the economic front, the CPP administration embarked on the expansion of agriculture, and the cocoa industry, the leading cash crop of the economy, registered significant growth. To place the country on the path to sustainable development, many factories were established, and an import substitution industrialization policy was pursued. The provision of education, health care and social housing was a key government policy. President Nkrumah's foreign policy was pan-African in orientation, and Ghana provided support to nationalist movements struggling to end Western imperialism on the continent.

Nkrumah's progressive development agenda alienated sections of the 'reactionary' elites and traditional authorities. In the bipolar world of the 1960s the opponents of the regime did not lack allies, and the Nkrumah Government was ousted in a military coup by the National Liberation Council (NLC) on 24 February 1966, thus setting the stage for further coups.

DISAGREEMENTS IN THE POLITICAL COMMUNITY: CIVILIAN/MILITARY ALTERNATIONS

The NLC military administration was ill-suited for governing Ghana. Nevertheless, the regime carefully managed a transition that ensured that all pro-Nkrumahist forces were disadvantaged. Commissions of inquiry findings against leading members of the Nkrumah political tradition made it difficult for many politicians to seek elective office. The leadership of the NLC secured the creation of the Second Republic and partisan politics was unbanned on 1 May 1969. Several political parties were formed in anticipation of the general elections. The new political parties that emerged included, *inter alia*, the Black Power Party, the All People's Party, the People's Popular Party, the All People's Congress, the Progress Party (PP), the National Reconstruction Party, the National Alliance of Liberals (NAL), the Ghana Democratic Party and the People's Action Party. Yet only nine parties were issued with certificates of registration and only five parties presented themselves to the electorate. The impact of the Nkrumah policies affected the fortunes of the NAL, the party that took its inspiration from the outlawed CPP. The election was won by the Dr Kofi Busia's PP, which was backed by the NLC leadership.

The Busia Administration, 1969–72

The PP administration was centre-right and pro-market, and Busia headed the Government as Prime Minister. The 1969 Constitution also created the position of a non-executive Head of State, and this ceremonial role was occupied by Edward Akufo-Addo, a former Chief Justice. The PP administration set about reversing many of the gains chalked up under the Nkrumah regime. Continuing from where the NLC left off, the PP attempted to erase Nkrumah and all that he stood for from the popular imagination. However, Nkrumah had left a bankrupt economy, and the PP struggled to engineer growth and create employment opportunities. There were widespread shortages of 'essential commodities' and corruption in governmental circles compounded the problems. Consequently, resistance to the Government's policies began to mount across the country.

The Acheampong Regime, 1972–78

On 13 January 1972 Ghana's experiment with constitutional rule was abrogated. The Ghana army, under the leadership of Lt-Col (later Gen.) Ignatius Kutu Acheampong, toppled the PP administration. For the second time in this young nation's history the citizens welcomed the military. The wild jubilations in urban centres across the country and the public display of support by traditional authorities showed that the National Redemption Council (NRC) Government was expected to deliver on its promises to run a transparent administration.

The early years of the NRC Government were remarkable for the number of policies that the regime implemented. The regime preached self-sufficiency with two flagship programmes: Operation Feed Yourself and Operation Feed your Industries. It also repudiated Ghana's foreign debt and undertook one of the most significant social housing projects that benefited the public and civil servants. However, the global economic challenges of the 1970s confronted the regime and ignited legitimacy questions. With declining foreign exchange and the country suffering from a lack of creditworthiness, shortages of goods were widespread. Ghanaians began disengaging from the state, and skilled and unskilled labour started an emigration that has continued to this date.

The economic challenges triggered resistance to the regime's other policies. The Government became increasingly repressive and corrupt. Consequently, it attempted a rebranding exercise, changing its name to the Supreme Military Council (SMC I) in 1975. Facing pressure from career politicians to open up space for civilian participation in the governance of the country, Acheampong proposed a Union Government framework in 1977. The proposals were put to a referendum, which the Government rigged in favour of a yes vote. The professional associations and students organizations continued to protest against the administration's management of the economy. The regime was seen to be illegitimate, and to save itself from collapse the Chief of Staff, Lt-Gen. Fredrick Akuffo, removed Acheampong and installed himself as the head of the short-lived administration that became known as the SMC II. However, this cosmetic leadership change did not save the regime from being overthrown.

Rawlings and the AFRC Interregnum

On 4 June 1979 junior ranks within the military staged a successful counter-coup against the moribund SMC II administration. The Armed Forces Revolutionary Council (AFRC) chapter in Ghana's political development has been noted for its brutality and bloodiness. The popular uprising led by 31-year-old Flight-Lt Jerry Rawlings undertook what the junta described as a 'house-cleaning exercise'. Senior military leaders, together with their civilian collaborators, were held accountable for their abuse of public authority, and three former heads of state and numerous other high-ranking military officers were executed by firing squad. The AFRC followed through with the transitional timetable that had been agreed with the political parties and organized general elections.

With the lifting of the ban on civilian politics, the political elites regrouped under the old Danquah-Dombo-Busia and Nkrumah labels. The Danquah-Dombo-Busia group was represented in two political parties: the Popular Front Party (PFP) and the United National Convention (UNC), while the leading Nkrumahist group was the People's National Party (PNP). Other parties included the Action Congress Party, the Third Force and the Social Democratic Front.

The Third Republic and Limann's Presidency, 1979–81

On 18 June 1979 Ghanaians voted to elect a President to inaugurate the Third Republic. The first round of voting was inconclusive, as the two leading contenders, the PNP's Dr Hilla Limann and the PFP's Victor Owusu, failed to gain the necessary 50% of the valid votes cast to secure victory. Consequently, a run-off election was organized at which Limann was declared the winner, thus making him the first elected leader from the northern savannah zone.

In September 1979 the PNP Government inherited a broken and bankrupt economy. Ghana was facing international sanctions and with very few Western allies willing to provide assistance. The first challenge of the Limann administration was to stabilize the post-revolutionary economy. The country's internal and external indebtedness was unsustainable. In June 1979 Ghana's external debt had stood at US $1,330m., while the inflation rate in that year was 54.4%, although it increased to 116.5% in 1981 when the PNP Government was toppled. The economy was shrinking in size, and the world price for cocoa and gold was declining. In contrast, the prices of petroleum products were increasing, unemployment was widespread and manufacturing had declined.

In addition to these challenges, the administration faced internal squabbling between the Nkrumahist 'young Turks' and the old guard, and Limann's leadership was called into question by the opposition. After 27 months in power the political conflict between the civilians allowed the military to exploit the situation and stage a coup.

Rawlings' PNDC Administration, 1981–92

Rawlings led another successful coup on 31 December 1981, which he styled as a 'revolution' and installed himself as the head of the Provisional National Defence Council (PNDC), a quasi-military apparatus that ruled for 11 years. The PNDC launched a sociocultural revolution that sought to eliminate corruption and remodel Ghana's governance structure. It declared 'holy war' on graft and indiscipline, and aimed to decentralize political power. The organs of the 'revolution' penetrated all segments of the Ghanaian society and parallel structures to the existing state institutions were created. Nevertheless, the implementation of probity and accountability principles infringed on the rights of many citizens.

The 'roaring 1980s' did not spare Ghana. The PNDC faced more significant challenges than the previous military administrations. By 1981 the economy had virtually collapsed; natural disasters compounded the already precarious situation. Nevertheless, the regime initially pursued a radical Marxist approach to restructure the economy, with 'power to the people' the regime's slogan. The citizens were told that power would henceforth emanate from the periphery and not the centre. The call for an 'all hands on deck' approach saw university students leaving the lecture halls to join in the national reconstruction effort. Students went to the hinterlands and assisted with the charting of cocoa beans to the buying centres. However, the answer to reviving the economy did not lie with correcting the perceived wrongs of the past through revolutionary justice, and abstract 'power to the people' without the corresponding economic power triggered resistance to the regime's policies.

The PNDC's legitimacy was soon questioned by the professional associations, student organizations and the military, some members of which attempted to overthrow the Government. In November 1982 and June 1983 internal and external opposition led to coup attempts. Furthermore, violent clashes occurred between the regime loyalists and opponents. In the ensuing confusion, there was a temporary breakdown of command. In June 1982 some members of the Government kidnapped three high court judges and a director of the Ghana Industrial Holdings Corporation, who were murdered and their bodies set on fire. The administration investigated the murders and executed a low-ranked official for his role. Sensing that the regime's power base was being eroded, Rawlings changed course, jettisoning socialism and embracing pragmatism. Zaya Yeebo, an original member of the PNDC, described the shift as one 'of the most dramatic "U-turns" of any government in all post-independent African history'. The PNDC 'turned its back on its origins, initial objectives, and social base, and invalidated all possibilities of a genuine revolutionary transformation'.

In early 1983 over 1.2m. Ghanaian immigrants were expelled from Nigeria. The impact of the returnees on an already distressed economy was severe. Above all, however, it was the forces of nature that exacerbated the economic crisis. The country experienced its worst drought in a generation, which resulted in bushfires destroying farmlands, while low levels of water at the Akosombo dam affected electricity generation and supply in the country. Therefore, nature partially played a role in the direction the country took after 1983, and the cumulative effect of food shortages was widespread hunger, with 'Rawlings chains' becoming a euphemism for the malnourishment that threatened the social fabric of the nation-state.

The Government approached its ideological allies in the Eastern bloc for help but very little came. Therefore, the Bretton Woods institutions were asked for technical/financial assistance for the restructuring of the economy. An Economic Recovery Programme was agreed upon, which injected capital and technical expertise into the economy. Ghana's enduring relationship with the World Bank and the International Monetary Fund (IMF) was cemented during this period. Funds provided by the two institutions resuscitated the economy but caused a great deal of hardship to ordinary Ghanaians. The PNDC administration deepened free market capitalism and neoliberalism. State-owned industries and factories were privatized, and a liberal foreign exchange regime was instituted. The PNDC reforms were resisted but forcibly implemented. The legacy was a reconstructed national economy that had become dependent on foreign development aid and expertise for survival.

Meanwhile, a committee was tasked to collate the views of Ghanaians on the appropriate governance model that would be suitable for the country going forward. The National Commission for Democracy reported that Ghanaians preferred a multiparty system.

RETURN TO CIVILIAN POLITICS

The early 1990s has been described by Emmanuel Gyimah-Boadi as the 'rebirth of African liberalism'. Rightly so because military dictatorships and one-party state models were discredited at the end of the Cold War. In 1991 the military, for the third time, agreed to return to civilian politics.

The PNDC administration banned all civilian party activities when it toppled the Limann regime. As a result, politicians used informal associations to mobilize and organized secretly in anticipation of the return to civilian politics. In the early 1990s economic liberalization was matched with political liberalization. As the country opened its political space, informal associations served as the bases for party rejuvenation. The political elites regrouped under the Nkrumahist and the Danquah-Dombo-Busia traditions, neither of which Rawlings belonged to. Consequently, he would engineer the creation of the populist and progressive 'Rawlingsist' tradition, which has come to represent the third political tradition in Ghana.

Prior to 1992, any time military regimes relinquished power, political parties emerged around what were termed the 'founding mythologies' of the Danquah-Dombo-Busia and Nkrumah traditions. Upon the lifting of the ban on party activity, new political parties were registered. The NPP was the vehicle of the Danquah-Dombo-Busia group; the Nkrumahists splintered into several parties, while Rawlings and his supporters founded the NDC.

THE RAWLINGS PRESIDENCY (NDC I), 1993–2001

The return to electoral politics in Ghana was carefully planned, rather than accidental. The PNDC administration engineered the transition to ensure that the political party it founded won

the elections. Nevertheless, the return to constitutionalism brought to the fore factionalism within the junta as to the ideological position of the new party. The PNDC that had given birth to the NDC did not profess any ideological belief. When the radical Marxist group departed in 1983, the administration poached members from the two historical political traditions. The NDC was thus registered as a political party without clearly articulating any formal political ideology. In contrast, the NPP and People's National Convention (PNC) articulated centre-right and centre-left doctrines, respectively.

The PNDC incumbency affected the Nkrumahist group. It was thought that a return to the pre-1981 old party politics was ill-suited for a modernizing Ghana. In that context, the supporters of the PNDC were mindful of the threat that a party formed based on the Nkrumahist ideology would pose for the electoral chances of the NDC. Therefore, the new party that was formed out of the PNDC styled itself as a congress. Consequently, it welcomed all political persuasions.

The newly constituted Interim National Electoral Commission supervised thepresidential and parliamentary elections of 1992. Rawlings, who was the presidential candidate of the NDC, had his nationality challenged in court, but this was dismissed and he was permitted to campaign. The NDC entered into an electoral alliance with one of the newly formed Nkrumahist parties, the National Convention Party (NCP). As a result, the vice-presidential slot was held by Ekow Nkensen Arkaah of that party. The NPP was led by Prof. Boahen, while his running mate was Roland Issifu Alhassan. Former President Limann led the PNC. Rawlings campaigned on his record of transformational developments and while wearing his military fatigues, despite having officially retired from the armed forces three months before the commencement of formal campaigning. His strongman antics were used by the opposition to remind the electorate of the NDC's past. All competing parties emphasized the provisions of quality and affordable health care, education and housing. Improving civil liberties for Ghanaians was emphasized by the NPP, a liberal party.

On 3 November 1992 the first presidential election that ushered in the Fourth Republic was held. Rawlings was declared the winner and his victory was not surprising. Having been in power since 1981, Rawlings was the most recognizable face among the pack of presidential candidates, but his popularity was attributed to the fact that he could identify with ordinary Ghanaians. The NDC won in nine out of the 10 regions, with only the Ashanti region voting for the NPP. Nevertheless, the opposition parties, especially the NPP, claimed that the election had been rigged. Supporters of the NPP staged demonstrations in its stronghold, Kumasi.

The NPP and some of the opposition parties proceeded to boycott the parliamentary elections in December 1992. Yet, independent observers reported the polls as being 'free and fair'. The electoral victories of the NDC and Rawlings gave them a democratic base to continue the work they had started in the PNDC administration. In the end, the opposition parties' attempts to discredit the civilian government of Rawlings were counterproductive, as the NDC and its allies dominated the first parliament. The Constitution of the Fourth Republic came into effect on 7 January 1993 when Rawlings and the elected members of parliament were sworn into office.

The opposition parties took their oversight role to the streets of Ghana and the institutionalization of free media allowed the opposition to criticize government policies. During this period the relationship between the Government and the opposition was generally hostile. In 1995 the Government proposed the introduction of a value-added tax (VAT, at a rate of 17%) in order to mobilize revenue. However, the so-called Kume Perko ('you may as well kill me') demonstrations that were organized in opposition to the VAT legislation forced the Government to cancel the unpopular policy. Furthermore, the political opposition demanded specific electoral reforms before the next presidential polls.

President Rawlings struggled to transition to the civilian administration. He fell out with Vice-President Arkaah in December 1995. Consequently, in the run-up to the December 1996 elections the NDC recruited Prof. John Evans Atta Mills to be the party's vice-presidential candidate. The opposition parties changed leadership and formed electoral alliances in an attempt to unseat Rawlings. The NPP was led by John Kufuor, who choose Arkaah as his running mate, while Dr Edward Mahama led the PNC. Rawlings was re-elected with 57.2% of the votes, and the NDC remained the largest party in the legislature; however, the NPP also had strong representation.

Rawlings continued with the restructuring of the economy. The second administration of the Fourth Republic produced Ghana-Vision 2020, a significant policy document aimed at lifting the economy to upper-middle-income level by 2020. During the late 1990s the political climate between the Government and the opposition slowly improved. Rawlings' international profile was also boosted when in March 1998 US President Bill Clinton paid a visit to Ghana.

By the late 1990s the popularity of the NDC had begun to fade as the opposition successfully exposed corruption within the administration. Rawlings was serving his final term in accordance with constitutional stipulations, and, unlike others elsewhere in Africa, he did not seek to contravene these and extend his presidency. However, the search for a replacement presidential candidate divided the NDC. The so-called Swedru Declaration, named after the town in the Central region where Rawlings made known his intentions to support his Vice-President, threatened party unity. Using his popularity within the party, Rawlings unilaterally declared Mills as the party's candidate. The 'young Turks' within the NDC who favoured internal democracy questioned the mode of selection of the presidential candidate. They split from the NDC and launched the National Reform Party.

Ghana's economic performance during this period was not impressive. Sluggish growth was manifest in all critical sectors of the economy. Above all, corruption in governmental circles had become rampant. A criminal element never before seen in Ghanaian political developments was introduced in the lead-up to the 2000 elections. At least 34 women were murdered in the nation's capital and this became a major campaign issue, with the NPP pledging to commit more resources to improve public security. In the December 2000 presidential election Mills and his running mate, Martin Amidu, faced off against Kufuor and his vice-presidential candidate, Alhaji Aliu Mahama. In the first round of voting no candidate secured a majority and a second round was organized at which Kufuor triumphed, thereby ending the NPP's extended stay in opposition. In the legislative elections the NPP won 100 of the 200 seats, while the NDC obtained 92 seats. The NPP thus became the largest parliamentary party for the first time.

THE KUFUOR PRESIDENCY (NPP I), 2001–09

The December 2000 elections were historic for three important reasons. First, an incumbent party was rejected at the polls, and it accepted the verdict of the electorate. Second, the elections marked the first democratic alternation of power in Ghana's history. Third, the electoral outcome placed the country's democratization project on a sound footing. However, the NPP inherited an economy that was in great distress. Having acknowledged the critical roles that foreign remittances played in the development of Ghana, President Kufuor invited Ghanaians in the diaspora to channel their skills and finance to the productive sectors of the economy. The administration organized a 'homecoming summit' in Accra to tap into the resources of Ghanaians living abroad, allowing for the return of people and capital to boost the country's economy. To attract foreign direct investment (FDI) into the country, the centre-right, pro-business NPP and President Kufuor declared their term in office to be the 'Golden Age of Business'. Yet without the necessary domestic capital to grow the economy, the Government approached the IMF and the World Bank for debt relief. Successive Ghana Poverty Reduction Strategy programmes (GPRS I, 2003–05, and GPRS II, 2006–09) guided the NPP's economic policy direction.

The Kufuor administration established the National Reconciliation Commission to investigate human rights abuses during past military interventions into the civilian domains. The NDC opposed the establishment of the Commission, with leading members of the party arguing that the NPP was undertaking a witch hunt. Nevertheless, findings of the Commission brought closure on a number of troubling issues in Ghana's past.

President Kufuor's management of the economy in his first term was generally rated highly. There was an increase in gross domestic product (GDP), and inflation was under control. However, unemployment was still widespread, and wages were very low. The Kufuor administration implemented many pro-poor social intervention programmes. For example, a mass public transportation system was re-introduced, and the unpopular 'cash and carry' system of health care was abolished in favour of a new health insurance scheme.

The Government's foreign policy was anchored on good neighbourliness. Ghanaians nicknamed President Kufuor the 'gentle giant' because of his unique leadership style. As a lawyer by training he respected the rule of law and due process. His administration investigated some of the major corruption scandals that occurred during the NDC administration and several former government officials were prosecuted and sentenced to jail.

Kufuor was re-elected to the presidency in December 2004, while the NPP won 128 of the 230 seats in the enlarged Parliament. By the time Ghanaians returned to the polls for the fourth consecutive time, a certain pattern had emerged and the de facto and competitive two-party system, between the NDC and the NPP, had been nurtured.

President Kufuor continued his development agenda during his second term. The building of roads, hospitals and schools were high on his administration's agenda, while investments in the petroleum sector led to Ghana discovering oil in commercial quantities. The NPP increased its membership and recruited more members outside its traditional heartlands, with incumbency clearly strengthening the party organization. The number of activists contesting the NPP's internal elections also increased; the 2007 presidential primaries saw 17 candidates competing to replace Kufuor. Meanwhile, Ghana's 50th anniversary of independence was celebrated by the administration in 2007 with much fanfare.

THE MILLS/MAHAMA PRESIDENCY (NDC II), 2009–17

Having reached his constitutional term limits in December 2008, President Kufuor relinquished the NPP presidential slot to Nana Addo Dankwa Akufo-Addo. The NDC was led for the third consecutive time by Mills, who selected John Dramani Mahama as his running mate. In the first round of the presidential election, on 7 December, Akufo-Addo won 49.1% of the votes cast while Mills secured 47.9%. Mills and Akufo-Addo contested a second round of voting, on 28 December, at which Mills emerged victorious with some 50.2% of votes cast. Mills formed the fifth administration of the Fourth Republic. However, his Government had been in power for less than two years when cracks began to appear among the NDC's hierarchy, with Mills struggling to maintain party unity.

The NDC's founder, Rawlings, was unimpressed with the leadership style of his successor. He became the most vociferous critic of the Mills administration, accusing the leadership of incompetence. The opposition, especially the NPP, capitalized on and sought to exploit the NDC internal disagreements. While intra-party unity proved elusive, the NDC's economic modernization programme was producing results. The country continued to attract substantial FDI, with the stability that Ghana enjoyed from constitutional rule explaining its attractiveness to foreign investors. In 2011, for example, US $6,820m. accrued to the Ghana Investment Promotion Centre from the registration of some 514 projects, with the bulk of the investments coming from Asia.

Backed by Chinese and Indian loan facilities, the Mills administration expanded infrastructure throughout the country. An additional US $3,000m. was negotiated for the development of a gas processing plant in the Western region. The impact of oil production was immediately felt in the calculation of the country's GDP. Primarily as a result of oil revenue, the economy grew by 14.4% in 2011, and prudent fiscal management resulted in single-digit inflation for two consecutive years (compared with an annual rate of 19.9%, according to the

Ghana Statistical Service, at the start of the Mills presidency in 2009).

However, the health of President Mills, a source of vexation since 2007, continued to be a concern. Although the President and the party downplayed the seriousness of his health problems, on 24 July 2012, five months before national elections were to be held, the President's death was announced. Fortunately, a seamless transition saw Vice-President Mahama being sworn into office as President, further evidence that Ghana's democracy had consolidated. The National Executive Council of the NDC endorsed Mahama as its presidential candidate in the forthcoming election. Initially, the NPP campaign team continued on the same path as before, arguing that Mahama could not absolve himself of the many failings of the Mills administration. However, unlike Mills, Mahama was a savvy professional politician with some 12 years of grassroots experience, injecting new dynamics into the electoral contest.

While oil and gas resources had been discovered in commercial quantities under the NPP administration in 2007, it was the Mills administration that had turned the tap on for the oil to flow to the export market in December 2010. With oil in the political equation, the 2012 elections became effectively a contest about which elite group would get to exercise ultimate control over Ghana's oil and gas revenue. Thus, it was envisaged that any new administration would preside over a state with significantly improved finances, and, with more resources, the party in government would be able to expand the distribution of patronage and jobs, and also bring infrastructural development to the citizens, enabling it to consolidate its hold on power for the foreseeable future.

Consequently, the elections, held on 7 December 2012, were the most closely contested polls in Ghana's history. Mahama secured a first round victory in the presidential ballot, winning 50.7% of the vote, compared with 47.7% for Akufo-Addo of the NPP.

As well as being the first Ghanaian President to secure election on his first attempt, John Mahama was also the first President to be born in independent Ghana. His election was therefore seen as evidence of a generational shift. The postcolonial Ghanaian generation was expected to inspire confidence and craft a development vision fit for the 21st century. Furthermore, in terms of regional politics, Mahama was only the second person to be sworn into office who did not come from the southern zone of the country.

The Mahama administration appointed people who were not party members to key government posts, in order to broaden the party's appeal to technocrats and professionals. However, party activists resisted these appointments, claiming that the appointees were strangers to the party, and the inexperience of many of the young new appointees was soon exposed.

Managing the economy also proved challenging. The growth recorded in the Mills/Mahama administration dissipated during the electioneering period. Indeed, the NDC overspent its way into government and therefore started off with weak economic fundamentals and high inflation. Additional economic challenges included high interest rates and an irregular electric power supply, due to a load shedding programme implemented by the Government in 2016, which brought manufacturing to a standstill and led to the collapse of many local companies. Meanwhile, in the middle of Mahama's term, several corruption scandals came to public attention.

THE AKUFO-ADDO PRESIDENCY (NPP II), 2017–

The December 2016 election campaign began on 29 August 2013 when the NPP petition against the NDC's 2012 election victory was dismissed. The NPP presidential candidate in the 2012 elections, Akufo-Addo, had challenged the NDC's victory and proceeded to the Supreme Court to have disputed results set aside. However, the nine-member panel of Supreme Court justices dismissed the petition by five votes to four, with one of the justices stating that 'after this case, elections in Ghana will not be the same'. There were two winners in the court ruling. On the political front the NDC and President Mahama instantly enjoyed the legitimacy that the ruling conferred. Yet, in terms of electoral reforms and future political capital,

the NPP was to reap the most significant benefits of its challenge. Akufo-Addo issued a statement in which he noted that he disagreed with the Court's decision but accepted it; he congratulated Mahama on being elected President; and firmly asserted that the NPP would not be appealing the verdict 'so we can all move on in the interest of our nation'. The graciousness of his response enhanced his reputation as a statesman.

At the presidential election, held concurrently with legislative elections on 7 December 2016, Akufo-Addo, running as the NPP presidential candidate for the third time, attracted 53.9% of the valid votes cast, thereby defeating the incumbent Mahama of the NDC, who took 44.4%. Since 1992 a certain political culture has emerged whereby the electorate will reject the incumbent party after two terms in favour of the opposition party.

Ghanaians expected much from Akufo-Addo's first term, and, being the second NPP administration to govern in the Fourth Republic, comparisons were made with the Kufuor regime. The administration wasted little time in implementing the promises that won it power. On the micro- and macroeconomic front, there was a reduction in inflation from 15.4% in 2016 to 10.4% at the end of 2020, and a reduction of the average lending rates from 32% in 2016 to 21% in 2020. The administration's industrial policy saw it implement its flagship programme; One District, One Factory (1D1F), as well as the One District, One Warehouse initiative. At the end of 2020 a total of 76 companies were stated to be operating under 1D1F. The administration also introduced a new automotive policy, which attracted foreign companies, including Volkswagen, Sinotruk and Nissan, to establish vehicle assembling plants in Ghana. The Ghana Integrated Aluminium Development Corporation (GIADEC) and the Ghana Integrated Iron and Steel Development Corporation (GIISDEC) were also established as part of the NPP industrialization agenda. In agriculture, the Government's Planting for Food and Jobs initiative increased food production; maize and paddy rice production increased by 71% and 34%, respectively.

Arguably, it was in the social rather than the governance sectors that the administration derived maximum political capital. The free senior high school policy was rolled out across the country, and proved very popular despite several implementation challenges. Furthermore, the administration strengthened several anti-corruption institutions and established the Office of the Special Prosecutor (OSP) with the powers to investigate and prosecute offenders (although the first occupant of the OSP achieved little and resigned amid claims that the President was interfering in his work). Overall though, the dividends of many of the NPP programmes did not extend to the poor. Youth unemployment remained at an all-time high and urban dwellers paid a high price. Corruption and mismanagement of public resources re-entered the national discourse. The emergence of the COVID-19 pandemic in 2020, an election year, threatened many of the gains made by the administration.

The 7 December 2020 presidential election was a reprise of the 2016 contest, with the NPP led by incumbent President Akufo-Addo and the NDC led by Mahama. The NDC launched scathing attacks on the NPP's numerous unfulfilled promises; however, incumbency allowed the NPP to embark on distributive politics. Several new projects were initiated and funds for the COVID-19 relief programme allowed the administration to outspend the NDC. In the event, Akufo-Addo retained the presidency with 51.3% of the votes, compared to 47.4% for Mahama. At the concurrently held legislative elections the NDC and the NPP each secured 137 seats, with the one remaining seat won by an independent candidate. The NDC won the speaker position in the hung Parliament, a significant achievement by an opposition party in Ghana. Nevertheless, the NDC disputed the presidential outcome and petitioned the Supreme Court to order, among other things, a re-run of the presidential poll. However, in March 2021 the Supreme Court upheld the NPP's victory.

Following the dismissal of the NDC's challenge, anti-Government sentiment gained traction from mid-2021, led by social media activists campaigning under the 'Fix the Country' slogan. Supporters of the movement staged a series of rallies decrying worsening socioeconomic conditions and an apparent increase in lawlessness since Akufo-Addo assumed the presidency in 2017. The movement called for, *inter alia*, improved education, health care and potable water supplies; increased employment opportunities; and better road infrastructure, with many road traffic accidents in Ghana attributed to the parlous state of the roads. In June 2021 Fix the Country activist Ibrahim Muhammed was beaten to death by unidentified assailants in Ejura, in Ashanti region; two people were shot dead and four others injured by security officers at a rally held a few days later to protest against the killing.

Oliver Barker-Vormawor, a lawyer and prominent Fix the Country activist, was arrested and charged with treason in February 2022, in connection with social media posts in which he had appeared to joke about staging a coup if Parliament approved controversial draft legislation providing for the introduction of a new tax on electronic transactions. Disagreements over the bill between legislators had degenerated into physical fighting in Parliament in December 2021. Nevertheless, the controversial legislation received parliamentary approval in March 2022, and the so-called e-levy was implemented, at a rate of 1.5%, in May.

The Ghanaian authorities came under renewed scrutiny in June 2022, when at least 38 people were reported to have been injured during clashes between police officers and students protesting against the frequency of road traffic accidents outside the Islamic High School in Kumasi. Tear gas and warning shots were used to disperse the protesters. A deputy police commander and two other officers were suspended pending further investigations into the police response.

With inflation soaring as the local currency, the cedi, depreciated, further protests were staged in Accra in early July 2022. A few days later the Government announced that it was to commence formal talks with the IMF with a view to securing assistance, and attributed the deteriorating economic situation to external factors, including the COVID-19 pandemic and the Russian invasion of Ukraine. The Minister of Finance, Ken Ofori-Atta, who had previously stated that there was no need to seek IMF assistance, faced numerous calls to resign (including from former President Mahama). Members of the NDC filed a parliamentary motion of censure against Ofori-Atta, but fell short of the 182 votes required to secure his removal from office. In a bid to stem inflation—which had increased for the 14th consecutive month in July, to 31.7% (although some observers suggested that this was a massive underestimate)—in October the Bank of Ghana's Monetary Policy Committee increased the monetary policy rate from 22.0% to 24.5%.

Meanwhile, in June 2021 Ghana was elected to a fourth two-year term on the UN Security Council, having secured 185 of the 190 votes cast by members of the UN General Assembly. It formally assumed its non-permanent seat, along with Albania, Brazil, Gabon and the United Arab Emirates, in January 2022.

A renewed surge of COVID-19 infections in mid-2021 was fuelled by the Delta variant of the virus, while a further surge from mid-December was attributable to the Omicron variant. The daily number of new confirmed cases peaked at 1,691 on 31 December; however, the rate of transmission declined rapidly thereafter, allowing restrictions on movement and assembly to be eased from March 2022. Nevertheless, the poor rate of vaccination uptake in Ghana remained a source of concern, with only 27.3% of the population having been fully vaccinated by early October, leaving the country vulnerable to potential new virulent strains of the virus.

CONCLUSION

Since its founding as a modern state, Ghana's political development has been characterized by resistance. The last major resistance that laid the foundation blocks for the Fourth Republic was the coup of 31 December 1981 (the so-called 31st December Revolution). The return to constitutional rule in 1992 has brought about the consolidation of liberal democracy in the country. Eight administrations have led the country to address its development challenges. Yet, democratization remains an ongoing project in Ghana. At late 2022, ahead of presidential and legislative elections scheduled to be held in 2024, anti-Government sentiment was mounting.

Economy

ROBERT E. LOONEY

INTRODUCTION

Ghana is a rare West African economic success story. The country's vibrant democracy and robust governance structures have facilitated a strong expansion of the economy. Following an average annual rate of growth of 2.2% in the 1980s, Ghana's economy gradually accelerated at an average rate of 4.5% per year in the 1990s, 5.3% in the 2000s and 5.9% in 2010–21, despite the growth rate falling to 0.4% in the COVID-19 pandemic year of 2020.

On a per capita basis, the corresponding rates of growth were –0.5% (1980s), 2.0% (1990s), 2.4% (2000s) and 3.4% (2010–21). In 2010 Ghana's economic progress enabled it to move into the World Bank's group of lower-middle-income countries. In 2020 Ghana, with a GDP of US $68,500m., was the fifth largest economy in Africa, smaller than Ethiopia ($96,600m.) but larger than Tanzania ($64,400m.). In 2021 per capita income in Ghana (expressed in purchasing-power parity 2017 international US dollars) was $5,638, up from $2,609 in 1980.

However, economic growth has not resulted in broad-based improvements in living standards. Ghana ranked 133rd out of 191 countries in the 2021 United Nations (UN) Development Programme's Human Development Index (HDI). Significantly, the average annual growth in the country's HDI score decelerated from 1.4% in 2000–10 to 0.9% in 2010–19. Still, Ghana falls in the 'medium human development' group and ranks considerably above the sub-Saharan average.

Another worrying sign has been the growing inequality in income. The Gini index (where higher numbers signify greater inequality) rose steadily from 0.353 in 1987 to 0.435 in 2016 (the latest year for income data). The UN *Human Development Report* for 2020 showed that the wealthiest 10% of Ghanaians had an income share of 32.2%, with the wealthiest 1% controlling 15.1%, while the share of the poorest 40% amounted to only 14.3%.

Oil presents the ongoing challenge of avoiding the toxic effects of the so-called 'oil curse', which has plagued Angola, Equatorial Guinea, Nigeria, and many other resource-rich developing countries. Increased corruption is one sign of the oil curse. Ghana had experienced steady improvements in the World Bank's control of corruption governance measure, improving from the 46th percentile in 1996 to the 57th by 2011. However, there has been a deterioration since then, with the country falling to the 50th percentile in 2020. Other areas of governance slippage since oil production commenced include government effectiveness, which fell from the 54th percentile in 2011 to the 47th by 2020, and regulatory quality (a proxy for the business environment), which dropped from the 55th percentile in 2011 to the 52nd in 2020. However, the rule of law declined only slightly, falling from the 55th in 2011 to the 54th in 2020.

Unemployment is another area of concern. The rate dropped from 10.4% in 2000 to 4.6% in 2006; however, the global financial crisis and the consequent slower growth in many of Ghana's trading partners resulted in unemployment increasing to 6.8% in 2015. Unemployment then fell to 4.2% by 2018, only to rise again to 4.5% in 2020 with the onset of the pandemic. By 2021, according to census figures, around

13.4% of the labour force was unemployed. Youth unemployment is considerably higher than the national average. Youth unemployment reached 16.3% in 2000 before falling to 9.3% in 2006. The global financial crisis and aftermath saw youth unemployment increasing to 14.1% by 2015, but this had fallen back to 8.8% in 2018. However, with the disruptive effects of the COVID-19 pandemic, youth unemployment increased to 9.2% in 2020.

As found throughout sub-Saharan Africa, Ghana's transformation has not shifted production from agriculture to manufacturing, as occurred in East Asia in the 1960 and 1970s. Instead, it has shifted from agriculture to services. In 1990 agriculture accounted for 44.8% of GDP, with industry at 16.8% and services at 37.9%. Agriculture's share had dropped considerably by 2010, falling to 28.0%, while industry had risen to 24.4% and services to 48.2%. By 2021 agriculture's share had declined to merely 21.0%, with industry increasing to 30.1% and services at 48.9%. During this period manufacturing (a sub-component of industry) rose only slightly, increasing from 9.8% of GDP in 1990 to 11.4% in 2021. Sectoral employment patterns reflect these production shifts, with agricultural employment falling from 57.1% of the labour force in 1991 to 50.1% in 2010 and a provisional 33.0% in 2021. The corresponding numbers for industry are 14.0% (1991), 13.9% (2000) and 13.7% (2021). During this period there was a dramatic increase in service employment, with the share of the workforce in services increasing from 28.9% in 1991 to 36.0% in 2010 and 53.3% by 2021.

Since assuming office in January 2017 and up to the COVID-19 pandemic in early 2020, the Government of President Nana Akufo-Addo maintained high economic growth rates and sharply declining inflation rates. Nevertheless, a late 2019 Afrobarometer poll revealed that Ghanaians were unimpressed. Barely 30% deemed economic conditions to be satisfactory, and 66% believed that the Government had failed to narrow inequality. Finally, 54% sensed that not enough jobs were being created, with 59% concluding that the country was heading 'in the wrong direction'.

To compound matters, Ghana has been one of the hardest-hit countries by the COVID-19 pandemic. After a lockdown that began on 30 March 2020 and continued until 19 April, the case curve of infections flattened. However, infections continued, and, as of 1 May, there were 2,072 cases. Around that time a second wave started, and by 10 August the total number of cases had reached 41,212. A third wave of infections resulted in recorded cases reaching 127,016 by 28 September 2021. A fourth wave began on 22 December, when cases reached 133,555. By 1 October 2022 cases totalled 169,385. The economic effects of slowing growth, tightening financial conditions and a weakening cedi persisted throughout 2020 and 2021. In 2022 the focus is on the national vaccination drive, with only 27.3% of the population fully vaccinated by early October. Mass vaccination will probably not occur before mid-2023 because of the lack of cold-storage facilities and widespread vaccine hesitancy.

AGRICULTURE

Ghana's agricultural sector spans various products, from fruits and vegetables to grains and livestock. The country has approximately 13.6m. ha of usable farmland, with 70% used for that purpose. However, the sector remains underdeveloped and is dominated by small-scale inefficient farms. Many of the country's farmers are old, with few young people attracted to the industry. Cocoa diseases are an ever-present threat, and this vital export sector has faced falling prices in recent years.

Despite a sizeable domestic agriculture sector, Ghana imports much of its food. Most farmers grow some food crops, but much of their output is cash crops (primarily cocoa, cashews nuts, rubber, shea nuts, and mangoes) for export. To reduce the need for imported foodstuffs, successive governments have encouraged and supported attempts at crop diversification. These efforts have paid high dividends. Ghanaian farmers now grow crops such as cashew nuts, brazil nuts, oranges, lemons, limes, apples, melons, papayas, mangoes, avocados, tomatoes, cucumbers, onions, green beans,

aubergines (eggplants), chillies, okra, peppercorns, ginger and raspberries.

In recent years, variable weather resulted in volatile agricultural growth rates, with the sector expanding by 2.1% (2015), 2.7% (2016), 6.2% (2017), 4.9% (2018), 4.7% (2019), 7.3% (2020) and 8.4% (2021). The agriculture sector has also seen variable growth rates among its principal components. While the sector's average annual growth rate in 2014–21 was 4.6%, growth during this period saw the livestock sub-category expanding at an average rate of 5.4%. Fishing expanded by an average of only 1.2%. In 2014–21 the critical cocoa sub-category grew by only 2.4% per year, while forestry and logging contracted at an average annual rate of 0.4%.

Cocoa has traditionally been an important export crop, although its value fell from US $2,437m. in 2018 to $1,852m. in 2019 and $1,312m. in 2020. The crop continues to be a significant contributor to rural incomes. The livelihoods of approximately 800,000 families are based, at least in part, on cocoa farming, with up to 3m. people in Ghana directly or indirectly employed by the cocoa industry. Ghana remains the world's second largest cocoa producer after Côte d'Ivoire.

In recent years, the country has produced around 20% of the world's cocoa, although output has fluctuated with weather conditions. In 2012/13 Ghana produced 835,000 metric tons of cocoa beans, increasing to 897,000 tons in 2013/14, only to fall to 740,000 tons in 2014/15. After rising to 778,000 tons in 2015/16 and further, to 969,000 tons, in 2016/17, cocoa bean output dipped to 905,000 tons in 2017/18, 812,000 tons in 2018/19 and 771,000 tons in 2019/20. Production increased to 1,047,000 tons in 2020/21 before falling to 822,000 tons in 2021/22. The contribution of cocoa to GDP fell from 2.2% in 2013 to 1.7% in 2020.

The decline in cocoa production during the 2018/19 and 2019/20 seasons stemmed primarily from reduced prices. However, the surge in production in 2020/21 stemmed from strong government backing, recovering prices, and farmer incentives that supported yields. Weather conditions were also favourable. The drop in output in 2021/22 resulted from less than ideal weather and reduced yields stemming from the cocoa swollen shoot virus. Since October 2021 the Government has maintained the cocoa price to farmers at 10,560 cedis.

Several factors have constrained cocoa production in recent years, including dry weather, an outbreak of black pod disease, and the fiscal crisis, which led to reductions in the Government's subsidized fertilizers and insecticides programme. Despite budgetary constraints, the upturn in the late 2010s has stemmed from the restoration of some government programmes, particularly those increasing soil fertility through the distribution of free fertilizers (besides pesticide spray) to farmers.

The surge in cocoa production in 2016/17 led to a sharp drop in price. From a high of over US $3,100 per metric ton in mid-2016, the price of cocoa fell to $2,080 per ton in 2018. In their efforts to regulate worldwide cocoa production output to increase returns to local producers, Ghana and Côte d'Ivoire agreed to harmonize cocoa prices and other marketing and industry activities. Their efforts have not been successful. For example, in June 2019 Côte d'Ivoire and Ghana agreed to set a price floor of $2,600 per ton for cocoa, a price higher than both spot London cocoa prices and futures prices until 2021. However, in early 2020 the price fell significantly into the $2,200 per ton range, with falling demand brought on by the pandemic-driven global recession.

In a related development, in October 2020 Ghana and Côte d'Ivoire introduced a Living Income Differential (LID) for cocoa farmers of US $400 per metric ton for the 2020/21 season. However, because of the COVID-19 pandemic, traders began looking for alternative suppliers. This action forced both countries to cut their country premiums on cocoa sales to offset the added LID cost.

The cocoa sector will probably continue expanding, with production benefiting from ongoing investment in the industry and government efforts to boost yields. However, ongoing structural issues, including the spread of disease, ageing tree stock, and land lost to gold mining, will constrain the sector's growth potential.

Livestock remains an important activity, particularly in the northern part of the country. However, the sector is declining, accounting for 1.6% of GDP in 2021, down from 2.6% in 2013. Since 2010 poultry industry output has increased by 50%. The sector hopes to pass a new Livestock and Animal Production Bill to improve industry regulation, reduce imports and increase local food production.

The main commercial varieties of fish in the country include tilapia, mackerel and tuna. Traditionally, most of the catch was sun-dried or smoked and consumed locally. However, a higher percentage has been refrigerated in recent years and sold in export markets. Commercial farming should take on even more importance in the coming years because of the Government's promotion of the sector.

However, recent growth rates of the fishing sector have been irregular, with a decline of 23.3% recorded in 2014, before the growth of 8.5% in 2015 and 3.1% in 2016. The sector contracted by 1.4% in 2017 and by a further 6.8% in 2018, before expanding by 1.7% in 2019, 14.1% in 2020 and 13.4% in 2021. However, there is increased concern over the rapid depletion of fish stocks and a sharp increase in the number of Chinese fishing vessels operating in West African waters. The Government has become increasingly concerned that the country's fisheries might collapse without proper measures to reverse the situation.

Timber has traditionally been a significant source of income, but its importance has declined in recent years. In 2013 forestry accounted for 1.7% of GDP but only 1.2% by 2021. The European Union is Ghana's largest market for timber, buying, on average, 33% by volume and 43% by value. However, exports have declined in recent years because of regulatory limitations on exporting. As a result, there has been a general deceleration of the growth rate within the forestry and logging sector. The sector contracted by 1.5% in 2014 and by a further 3.9% in 2015. A return to expansion occurred in 2016 (2.9%), 2017 (3.4%) and 2018 (2.4%), before contraction set in again in 2019, with the sector declining by 1.7%, followed by a further decline of 9.4% in 2020. Production recovered in 2021, with the industry growing by 4.7%.

Arresting the decline of agriculture is a crucial priority for President Akufo-Addo. The Government's Planting for Food and Jobs programme, launched in April 2017, focuses on creating a more attractive environment for private sector investment while improving efficiency and the quality of the country's food supply. The Government hopes that an agricultural expansion will create jobs for many of the country's unemployed youth.

MINING

Ghana's mines produce gold, manganese, bauxite and diamonds. Gold dominates the sector, accounting for around 90% of the total mining revenues. Gold typically contributes one-third of Ghana's export earnings. Ghana was consistently among the world's leading 10 gold producers, but since 2015 has dropped out of that ranking. However, the country is still Africa's second largest gold producer.

Gold production increased from 82,598 kg metal content in 2011 to 90,754 kg metal content in 2015. Production then dipped to 79,196 kg metal content in 2016, before rising to 142,000 kg metal content in 2019. Production declined in 2020, to 125,000 kg metal content, because of the COVID-19 pandemic. However, it recovered to 130,000 kg metal content in 2021.

Over the last decade Ghana's gold sector has attracted interest from global mining companies seeking alternatives to South Africa, where gold reserves are dwindling, labour disputes are debilitating, and rising costs prevail. In December 2018 the Ghanaian Government lifted the ban on small-scale gold mining imposed in 2017.

President Akufo-Addo has also prioritized the development of Ghana's bauxite sector. A memorandum of understanding (MoU) signed with the People's Republic of China in July 2017 should lead to investment of around US $10,000m. in the bauxite sector, with the potential for significant future growth opportunities.

In recent years, the mineral taxation regime has been receiving increased attention. The Government believes that Ghana has not benefited sufficiently from its mining activities. Changes to tax laws in 2012 included raising the sector's income tax rate to 35% (from 25%). Other actions included a new windfall tax of 10% to be paid by mining companies, and a decrease in the capital allowance rate for mining and hydrocarbons companies to 20%, down from the previous deduction of 80%. Ghana's mineral taxes are higher than those in other countries in the region, and mining companies, particularly those involved in gold mining, are facing growing resentment from local communities because of the sector's limited job creation. The industry also faces the ever-present risk of increased resource nationalism. In 2019 President Akufo-Addo stated that foreign mining companies should not expect to make monumental profits from Africa's resources.

HYDROCARBONS

Ghana started petroleum production in 1978, when a US company began extracting oil from the continental shelf near Saltpond, in the Central region. Geologists estimated reserves at Saltpond at 7m. barrels, but the average output during the early 1980s was only 1,250 barrels per day (b/d). The 2006/07 budget promised a review of the Petroleum Exploration Law to increase Ghana's attractiveness to oil prospectors. Subsequently, in June 2007 US-based Kosmos Energy announced a 'significant oil accumulation' at its Mahogany-1 well, 63 km offshore, which was later renamed the Jubilee Field. Production began in December 2010. The World Bank has estimated total petroleum reserves in the Jubilee Field at 683m. barrels and forecasts that oil production would average around 140,000 b/d between 2013 and 2023. (Production of natural gas reached around 100m. cu ft per day in 2015.)

The Tweneboa-Enyenra-Ntomme (TEN) oilfield is another offshore project with good potential. A third offshore site is the Sankofa well in the Offshore Cape Three Points block. This site also contains Ghana's first source of non-associated gas. Since production at the Jubilee Field began, Ghana's oil output has soared, from 7,081 b/d in 2009 to 200,000 b/d in 2019, dipping slightly to 199,470 b/d in 2020 and to 179,890 b/d in 2021, owing to supply and demand effects stemming from the COVID-19 pandemic.

Crude oil production started to contribute to Ghana's overall GDP in 2010, when its value reached 178m. cedis. The value of the oil sector's output increased to 3,746m. cedis in 2011 and to 6,649m. cedis in 2013. Despite a fall in oil prices and technical and infrastructural difficulties in 2014, output value reached 9,556m. cedis in that year. By 2019 oil's contribution amounted to 21,335m. cedis, before dipping slightly, to 21,156m. cedis, in 2021.

Weak oil prices stemming from the 2014–16 global price decline adversely affected investment. Before the fall in prices, the Ghana National Petroleum Corporation (GNPC) had announced plans to take out a US $700m. loan to finance its expansion, including increasing oil reserves and developing local content. However, by March 2015 the GNPC was forced to scale back its investment and financing plans. In August 2016 the Government revised the country's regulatory framework for exploration and production to attract additional investment into the sector.

One of Ghana's most critical issues is how best to divide and use the influx of oil money. Currently, oil revenue allocations conform to the 2011 Petroleum Revenue Management Act guidelines. The Act requires that all hydrocarbons revenue goes into a single entity, the Petroleum Holding Fund. Of the Fund's benchmark revenue (the estimate of petroleum revenue forecast for the following year), 70% goes to the annual state budget. The GNPC receives a portion to cover operating and investment costs. The rest goes into the Ghana Petroleum Funds, composed of a Ghana Heritage Fund and a Ghana Stabilization Fund.

Ghana's efforts to ensure that the oil sector had a more significant impact on the domestic economy included the enactment in November 2013 of the Petroleum (Local Content and Local Participation) Regulations. Under this legislation, all international oil companies operating in Ghana must subcontract only to vendors and organizations with a 5% indigenous Ghanaian equity stake. After 10 years, firms must buy 90% of all goods and services from domestic companies regardless of cost; and employ Ghanaians in 70%–80% of all managerial and technical posts and 100% of all mid- to junior-level jobs by 2023.

Even before the dramatic drop in oil prices in early 2020, future expansion faced constraints, with major infrastructure projects encountering frequent technical issues and delays. The lack of onshore infrastructure threatens liquefied natural gas (LNG) import projects. Lower than expected production at the Jubilee and TEN fields may cause a short-to-medium term oil production decline. In early 2022 oil reserves stood at approximately 700m. barrels and natural gas reserves at 21,000m. cu m. However, some significant oil and gas discoveries over the last few years offer the potential for reserves and output to grow in the future.

Ghana announced in November 2019 that it planned to revise its laws on oil and gas licences to spur production. Implementing Ghana's new law is essential to encourage exploration after the disappointing outcome of Ghana's first licensing round. However, progress regarding this new legislation appeared stalled in mid-2022. The proposed new law would allow companies to continue exploration after their licences have expired, provided that they meet the criteria stated within their licence contract. This concession is essential for incumbent firms to continue exploring Ghanaian waters. The new law would also allow the revocation of licences from firms that do not meet the minimum exploration commitments. This amendment should motivate licensed firms to increase expenditure and drill more wells.

Current forecasts are for Ghana's crude oil, NGL and other liquids production to decline to 165,700 b/d in 2022. Tullow Oil is spearheading a multi-year, multi-well drilling campaign at its Jubilee and TEN fields to offset production declines and improve field performance. However, natural declines in these maturing assets will continue to weigh on output growth in the short term. The expected final investment decision in 2022 to develop the 110,000 b/d Pecan field holds the key to the country's oil future.

ELECTRICITY

In 2010 Ghana generated 6,750m. kilowatt hours (kWh) of electricity. Production increased to 12,870m. kWh in 2017, and reached 20,170m. kWh in 2020. Ghana's electricity sector has experienced high, albeit irregular, growth in recent years. In 2009 the sector grew by 7.5%, and it expanded by 12.3% in 2010 before declining by 0.8% in 2011. The sector grew by 11.1% in 2012 and 16.3% in 2013, but the expansion rate decelerated considerably to just 1.3% in 2014. The sector expanded by 17.7% in 2015 before contracting by 5.8% in 2016. Subsequently, growth jumped to 19.4% in 2017 before levelling off at 5.5% in 2018, 6.0% in 2019, 7.9% in 2020 and 7.4% in 2021. As a result of this variable growth pattern, the sector has witnessed only a slight expansion in its contribution to GDP, rising from 0.8% in 2006 to 1.2% in 2021. In 2020 94% of the country's urban population had access to electricity, but only 74% of the population in rural areas had access.

As the sector's erratic growth figures suggest, Ghana has experienced difficulties meeting the steady increase in demand for power of around 10% per year. Deficient electricity supplies have caused several power crises in recent years, and power shortages remain a constraint on growth, especially in the manufacturing sector. Power disruptions reached a peak in mid-April 2021. At that time Ghana's transmission company, GRIDCo, announced that it expected power disruptions to continue in parts of the country until September 2021, owing to system upgrades and maintenance projects. GRIDCo has struggled to maintain the infrastructure because of financial constraints caused by the inability of distributors—the Electricity Company of Ghana and the Northern Electricity Distribution Company—to collect revenue from consumers.

The 2019 *Global Competitiveness Report* published by the World Economic Forum ranked Ghana 106th out of 141 countries in electricity access and 120th for electricity supply quality. To alleviate the situation, the Government plans to more than double the country's power capacity over the next five years. The hope is that offshore production of natural gas will be enough to meet the expected demand for power in the longer term. Given its financial and technical capability constraints, the Government has turned to the private sector in a series of joint participation (Private Sector Participation) projects. By March 2018 many companies, including Siemens, Rotan Power, the Shapoorji Pallonji Group and Yam Pro Energy, had begun construction or signed MoUs for additions to the country's power system. However, power disruptions over much of 2021 compounded a challenging recovery from the ongoing pandemic.

In 2019 about 41.9% of the country's generating capacity was hydro and 57.7% thermal, of which 39.7% of the country's generating capacity came from natural gas and 18.0% from oil. Currently, the thermal plants use either light crude imports or gas supplies from Nigeria via the West African Gas Pipeline. Several factors have adversely affected output in recent years, including low rainfall, which has limited hydroelectric generation, erratic gas supplies from Nigeria, and irregular maintenance. However, the development of the domestic natural gas sector will provide future supply to gas-fired power plants, thereby reducing the country's vulnerability to supply interruptions.

Hydropower will undoubtedly remain a significant source of electricity over the medium term, but the steady growth in thermal capacity will reduce Ghana's reliance on hydroelectricity. Growth in renewables will come from several planned wind farms. Investments in the country's grid and the use of a 470-MW power ship, and imports from neighbouring countries such as Côte d'Ivoire, should provide increased stability to Ghana's power supply.

TRANSPORT

Ghana's transport system covers every region of the country, with a heavy concentration in the most economically developed areas, including around the capital, Accra. Rapid economic and demographic growth has increased pressure on the transport sector over the last decade, and some costly bottlenecks have developed. The Government approved an Energy Sector Levies Amendment Bill in January 2016, increasing gas, diesel, and LNG prices by between 18% and 28%, thereby exerting pressure for sharp increases in most transport fees. Analysis by the World Bank suggests that the current transport system suffers from inadequate facilities, insufficient funds for maintenance, upgrading and rehabilitation, and poor co-ordination among the relevant regulatory institutions. Fortunately, the Government is responding with several initiatives to address these issues.

The transport sector accounted for 7.4% of GDP in 2021, down from 13.2% in 2006. As in the electricity sector, transport experienced irregular growth in recent years, averaging 4.4% per year in 2014–21, the same as that for GDP growth overall during the same period.

Ghana's transport sector remains dominated by road activity, facilitating 98% of freight and 95% of passenger traffic. The road network is satisfactory. It comprises three divisions: trunk, feeder and urban. Ongoing major road projects in Ghana intend to strengthen linkages between resource-rich regions in the eastern and western parts of the country with urban centres in the south.

The country has a relatively small railway network of some 977 km, with parts falling into neglect and causing operations to be well below potential. Currently, the rail network handles less than 2% of all passenger and freight traffic. Under its expansive Ghana Railways Master Plan, the Government proposes to begin a series of rehabilitation projects, upgrades, and new construction works to improve access across the country and link up with international rail networks in surrounding nations. As part of this, the Government is moving forward to develop a US $7,800m. countrywide rail upgrade and expansion project. This project will involve constructing a new 595-km line from Kumasi to Paga connecting to the border with Burkina Faso, a 300-km Eastern line from Accra to Kumasi, and a 339-km Western line from Takoradi to Kumasi.

In July 2018 the Government signed an MoU with China Civil Engineering Construction Corporation to construct a section of the Kumasi–Paga railway line funded by a loan from the Export-Import Bank of China. According to government estimates, the benefits of an improved rail network would be enormous; lines in the Western region could absorb 17% of highway traffic, while this figure could reach 40% in the Eastern region.

The country has two major ports: Takoradi, built in the 1920s, and Tema, which opened in 1961. Both are artificial and together handle over 90% of Ghana's foreign trade volume. Both ports are undergoing significant development to improve their capacity and efficiency. Economic growth and rising trade with Asian countries strain West Africa's commercial port capacities. Ghana is in direct competition with Côte d'Ivoire and Nigeria to become the shipping gateway for the region. To this end, in November 2014 the Government approved the construction of a new container terminal at Tema, which was to be operated by a consortium led by APM Terminals and Bolloré Africa Logistics. With four deep-water berths, the new terminal could become the most significant container facility in West Africa.

Ghana still ranks low in most areas, despite recent improvements in its transport system. The 2019 *Global Competitiveness Report* ranked Ghana's road quality 110th out of 141 countries. While it ranked the efficiency of its train services 97th, the efficiency of its air transport services was placed 110th, and that of its seaport services, 114th.

Ghana will need to expand its existing transport system to improve its global competitiveness, particularly as high transport costs continue to erode profitability in all sectors, with mining being the worst affected by the inadequate rail network and high road congestion. Over the medium term, growth in economic activity will also put significant pressure Ghana's ports. The Government is aware of the problems and has outlined some plans to rectify the situation. However, with high levels of public debt, which strain the public sector's capacity to invest more aggressively in critical transport infrastructure, many of the current bottlenecks are unlikely to be eased soon.

MANUFACTURING

Ghana's manufacturing sector has expanded in recent years, but at an irregular rate. There were two years of rapid growth in 2010 and 2011, with rates of 7.6% and 17.0%, respectively, then expansion of just 2.0% in 2012, followed by contractions of 0.5% in 2013 and 2.6% in 2014. Growth has been positive since, with rates of 3.7% in 2015, 7.9% in 2016, 9.5% in 2017, 4.1% in 2018 and 6.3% in 2019. Growth declined to 1.9% in the pandemic year of 2020, but recovered quickly to reach 7.8% in 2021. The sector's contribution to GDP was 11.4% in 2021, up from 9.0% in 2000 and 6.4% in 2010.

Small and medium-sized firms predominate in the manufacturing sector, accounting for around 90% of all businesses and providing 85% of manufacturing employment. Besides traditional industries such as food processing, Ghana has several larger enterprises, including a petroleum refinery. Other larger firms produce textiles, vehicles, cement, paper, chemicals and footwear, while export-orientated firms are involved in cocoa and wood processing.

Manufacturing industries have traditionally been underutilized, high-cost, and dependent on imported equipment and materials. Their expansion lags due to low levels of investment, transport congestion, and persistent shortages of imported materials and spare parts. The consistent over-valuation of the cedi and the irregular supply of raw materials increased the attractiveness of imports relative to home-produced goods. Ghana's once vibrant textile industry has declined due to the influx of cheaper imports, with production capacity decreasing by about 60% because of competition from Asian imports. The textile industry employed only around 3,000 Ghanaians in 2012, down from a peak of some 25,000 in the 1970s.

In a significant initiative, in 2017 the Government launched the One District, One Factory (1D1F) programme, pledging to establish at least one factory in each of Ghana's 216 districts by 2020 (following the creation of six new regions in December 2018, the number of districts increased to around 230). The plan's goal is to speed up the development of the manufacturing sector and reduce the unemployment rate. While it has made some progress, Ghana will have to overcome several obstacles before it can support a robust expansion in manufacturing.

The country's manufacturing firms are generally uncompetitive because of their deficiencies in several key areas. The 2019 *Global Competitiveness Report* ranked Ghana 111th out of 140 countries, compared with 103rd in 2012–13. Ghana is severely deficient in some significant elements of importance to manufacturing, ranking 118th in infrastructure, 116th in its financial system, 102nd in skills, 93rd in labour markets, 102nd in business dynamism and 89th in innovation capacity. While Ghana's manufacturers enjoy comparative advantages in locally available raw materials and growing domestic markets, the country will have to make significant strides in improving governance, infrastructure, macroeconomic environment and primary education before the sector becomes genuinely competitive.

FINANCE AND INSURANCE

Ghana has a growing number of financial and insurance companies, with government policy specified in the Financial Sector Strategic Plan of 2003. The intent has been to broaden and deepen the sector while maintaining oversight and striving for improved governance in the financial markets. The sector's rapid growth reflects the country's full spectrum of financial institutions. Also, microfinance is increasing in popularity.

Until recently, the finance and insurance sector had been one of the country's more rapidly growing areas of the economy, expanding by 21.9% in 2012, 23.2% in 2013 and 21.4% in 2014. Subsequently, the sector faced a challenging environment, including a devaluating currency, rapidly rising government debt, low commodity prices, and a persistent fiscal deficit. Growth decelerated to 12.9% in 2015 and 8.0% in 2016, before contracting by 17.7% in 2017 and by a further 8.2% in 2018. Growth recovered to 1.6% in 2019, 9.3% in 2020 and 2.4% in 2021. As a result, the sector's contribution to GDP fell from 5.0% in 2013 to 3.7% in 2021.

The slowdown and contraction in growth in recent years stem partly from the banking system's high levels of non-performing loans (NPLs) and the central bank's tightening of minimal capital requirements. The more than tripling of minimum capital requirements should increase merger and acquisition activity within the sector. A review of the financial services industry by the central bank in 2016 showed a significant decline in banking asset quality. Some 211 of the more than 500 licensed microfinance companies operating in 2018 had either become non-operational or distressed. NPLs as a proportion of total loans are now falling because of government and central bank efforts to clear NPL stocks. However, NPLs remained relatively high in Ghana, at 13.9% in December 2019. The cost of bailing out the financial sector is accelerating, with the 2020 budget allocating 16,400m. cedis (US $2,800m.) for that effort.

The banking sector faces higher loan loss provisions and subdued lending growth because of the COVID-19 pandemic, although the overall increase in NPLs in 2020 was modest. However, questions arise over the central bank's powers to intervene in the banking sector to close and liquidate banks, with concerns regarding transparency and the antitrust issues that emerge from consolidation.

The 2019 *Global Competitiveness Report* identified some deficiencies within the banking sector. Ghana ranked 116th of 141 countries in overall financial development, 133rd in NPLs, 76th in market capitalization, and 113th in the soundness of banks. The International Monetary Fund (IMF) has expressed concern about the dominant position held by state banks, warning that this situation could cause added bank risk, especially if the Government continues to turn to these banks to finance its budgetary deficits. The proper conduct of monetary policy will be vital in revitalizing the banking system.

The insurance industry in Ghana is still at a relatively early stage of development, with low coverage rates in the life and non-life sectors. However, Ghana is a country where micro-insurance should flourish; the life segment (and in the non-life segment, personal accident insurance) should be a significant beneficiary. Of course, many potential customers are currently unbanked, particularly in remote rural areas. Some insurers should have success distributing micro-insurance products via mobile phones. Also, over the coming years an improving economy and higher employment rates will spur growth across the insurance industry as more households can afford cover and demand for group-based cover rises.

MACROECONOMIC CONDITIONS

As noted above, Ghana's economic growth has gradually accelerated each decade since 1980. However, the current period beginning in 2010 has witnessed significant volatility, with high average annual rates of growth proving challenging to sustain. After averaging 8.0% growth during 2010–14, GDP expanded by only 4.4% in 2015–21. The corresponding per capita growth rates were 5.0% in the first period, dropping to 2.3% in the second. Even though growth declined, inflation picked up from an average of 9.7% in the first period to 12.0% in the second.

The GDP slowdown did not represent a fundamental change in Ghana's growth potential. Instead, it stemmed from severe macroeconomic imbalances caused by excessive public spending even after oil prices declined in 2014. Government revenue averaged 4.5% of GDP per year in the 1980s, increasing to 6.7% in the 1990s and 11.2% in the 2000s. With the onset of oil production, revenue increased to an average of 13.6% of GDP per year in 2010–21. Government expenditure rose from an average of 6.3% of GDP in the 1980s to 11.6% in the 1990s, 15.0% in the 2000s and 21.4% in 2010–21. Rapidly rising spending resulted in the Government's fiscal deficit widening from an average of 3.7% of GDP per year in the 2000s to 7.9% in 2010–21, with the deficit increasing from 4.1% of GDP in 2015 to 15.5% in 2020, before dropping to the still dangerous level of 11.6% in 2021.

The added borrowing requirement arising from the growing fiscal deficit led to the Government's gross debt increasing from 31.3% of GDP in 2011 to 51.9% by 2015 and 81.8% by 2021, with the IMF projecting a further increase to 82.6% in 2022 and 88.4% by 2026. Continued spending over-runs reflect the Government's poor fiscal discipline. Substantial increases in public sector wages ahead of the 2012 elections were a significant factor in expanding the deficit. The deteriorating macroeconomic situation placed the Government under severe pressure to stabilize the economy and resume Ghana's rapid economic development. The political opposition argued that the Government's growing indebtedness was unsustainable and undermined both the country's currency and the private sector's expansion. Disproportionate government borrowing from the domestic sector (25% of total lending by commercial banks) has been the primary cause of the rise in interest rates in recent years.

The other macroeconomic imbalance involved developments in the country's savings and investment pattern, with investment increasingly outrunning domestic savings, thus requiring substantial capital inflows to carry out capital expenditures. While the country's savings rate increased from an average of 20.0% of GDP in the 1990s to 32.8% in the 2000s, it fell back to 20.3% in 2010–21. During these periods, investment outran savings, increasing from 23.5% of GDP in the 1990s to 36.9% in the 2000s, before falling to 25.6% in 2010–21. The massive gaps between savings and investment translated into chronic and increasing deficits in the current account of the balance of payments. The country's

current account deficit increased from an average of 3.7% per year in the 2000s to 7.9% in 2010–21.

Historically, inflows of foreign direct investment (FDI) have funded Ghana's current account deficits. However, FDI has fluctuated considerably in recent years, especially with the decline in commodity prices. The implementation in 2013 of the Ghana Investment Promotion Centre Act brought greater stability. The Act has proven partially effective, with FDI as a percentage of GDP increasing from 5.1% in 2013 to 6.5% in 2015, before declining to 4.4% in 2018. It increased to 5.7% in 2019, before falling again to 2.7% in 2020.

High inflation rates and current account deficits placed considerable pressure on the cedi. During 2014 and 2015 the currency lost over 40% of its value, and over the first quarter of 2017 the cedi's value against the US dollar fell from an average of 3.9 cedis to 4.4 cedis. The cedi kept falling, to reach 5.9 per US dollar in 2021, with forecasts expecting an average of 6.4 per US dollar in 2022.

Starting in 2013, the Government responded to the country's macroeconomic imbalances with a series of initiatives that included increased tariffs on selected imports to reduce the current account deficit and the budget deficit. The authorities also eliminated fuel subsidies, introduced sharp rises in electricity and water tariffs, and reduced non-essential spending. Increases in value-added tax (VAT) occurred in 2014, and the VAT was expanded. The Government also increased its efforts to control public sector wages.

However, when it became apparent that its programme would not stabilize the economy, the Government agreed (in February 2015) to a three-year IMF Extended Credit Facility (ECF) financial support package amounting to US $918m. The programme countered the adverse effects of weak commodity prices and aid in developing reforms to bring down fiscal deficits to sustainable levels. During the ECF period, the economy experienced a solid rebound, with the strong expansion of GDP and, as noted above, falling rates of inflation.

On successfully completing the ECF in April 2019, the IMF praised the country's progress in improving macroeconomic management. An increase in hard currency revenue from the oil and gas sector and the Government's adherence to the IMF programme helped to reduce the current account deficit from 9.0% of GDP in 2013 to 2.7%, while inflation dropped from 17.5% in 2016 to 7.1% in 2019. However, just as conditions improved, the onset of the COVID-19 pandemic occurred. While the economy did not contract in 2020, macroeconomic aggregates such as the fiscal and current account deficits, inflation and foreign reserves all worsened. With a weak recovery and provisional growth of only 5.4% in 2021, much of the progress made under the IMF programme was lost.

PROSPECTS

President Akufo-Addo and his administration will most likely remain focused on limiting the fallout from the COVID-19 pandemic while attempting to restore the high rates of economic growth most Ghanaians began taking for granted. Growth restoration will be complex, considering the country's high debt level, 60% of which is commercial. Other constraints include: a private sector crowded out of the local credit market by the Government's increased borrowing in recent years; public revenue that averages only around 13% of GDP; infrastructure gaps, especially in energy and transport; a weak banking sector impeded by NPLs and high credit costs. However, while the gradually dissipating impact of the pandemic will offer the prospect of more robust growth, elevated global food and fuel prices—particularly following the Russian Federation's invasion of Ukraine in February 2022—will undermine a more significant recovery.

Statistical Survey

Source (except where otherwise stated): Ghana Statistical Service, POB GP1098, Accra; tel. (30) 2671732; internet www.statsghana.gov.gh.

Area and Population

AREA, POPULATION AND DENSITY

Area (sq km)	238,533*
Population (census results)	
26 September 2010	24,658,823
27 June 2021	
Males	15,200,440
Females	15,631,579
Total	30,832,019
Density (per sq km) at 2021 census	135.8

* 92,098 sq miles.

Mid-2022 (UN projection): Total population 32,395,454 (Source: UN, *World Population Prospects: The 2019 Revision*). Note: Figure not adjusted to take account of 2021 census results.

POPULATION BY AGE AND SEX
('000, UN projections at mid-2022)

	Males	Females	Total
0–14 years	6,063.2	5,811.1	11,874.3
15–64 years	9,869.9	9,586.7	19,456.6
65 years and over	490.5	574.0	1,064.5
Total	16,423.6	15,971.8	32,395.5

Note: Totals may not be equal to the sum of components, owing to rounding.

Source: UN, *World Population Prospects: The 2019 Revision*.

REGIONS
(population at 2021 census)

Region	Area (sq km)	Population	Density (per sq km)	Capital
Ahafo	5,196	564,668	108.7	Goaso
Ashanti . . .	24,389	5,440,463	233.1	Kumasi
Bono	11,113	1,208,649	108.8	Sunyani
Bono East . .	23,248	1,203,400	51.8	Techiman
Central . . .	9,826	2,859,821	291.0	Cape Coast
Eastern . . .	19,323	2,925,653	151.4	Koforidua
Greater Accra . .	3,245	5,455,692	1,681.3	Accra
North East . .	9,070	658,946	72.7	Nalerigu
Northern . . .	26,524	2,310,939	87.1	Tamale
Oti	11,066	747,248	67.5	Dambai
Savannah . . .	34,790	653,266	18.8	Damango
Upper East . .	8,842	1,301,226	147.2	Bolgatanga
Upper West . .	18,476	901,502	48.8	Wa
Volta . . .	9,504	1,659,040	174.6	Ho
Western . . .	13,842	2,060,585	148.9	Sefwi Wiawso
Western North . .	10,079	880,921	87.4	Sekondi Takoradi
Total	238,533	30,832,019	129.3	—

PRINCIPAL TOWNS
(population at 2021 census)

Kumasi . . .	443,981		Sunyani . . .	193,595
Tamale . . .	374,744		Cape Coast . .	189,925
Accra (capital) .	284,124		Ho	180,420
Sekondi-Takoradi .	245,382		Tema . . .	177,924
Techiman . .	243,335		Sefwi Wiawso .	151,220
Wa	200,672		Bolgatanga . .	139,864

BIRTHS AND DEATHS
(annual averages, UN estimates)

	2005–10	2010–15	2015–20
Birth rate (per 1,000)	32.9	31.8	29.6
Death rate (per 1,000)	8.8	8.0	7.3

Source: UN, *World Population Prospects: The 2019 Revision*.

Life expectancy (years at birth, estimates): 64.3 (males 63.2; females 65.5) in 2020 (Source: World Bank, World Development Indicators database).

ECONOMICALLY ACTIVE POPULATION
(persons aged 15 years and over at 2021 census)

	Males	Females	Total
Agriculture, hunting, forestry and fishing	1,979,432	1,317,563	3,296,995
Mining and quarrying	100,410	11,092	111,502
Manufacturing	317,271	351,215	668,486
Electricity, gas and water . . .	61,245	6,573	67,818
Construction	491,405	29,866	521,271
Trade, restaurants and hotels .	626,738	1,763,786	2,390,524
Transport, storage and communications	552,290	18,746	571,036
Financing, insurance, real estate and business services . . .	186,755	107,941	294,696
Public administration and defence	175,913	74,850	250,763
Education	332,451	260,156	592,607
Health and social services . .	104,705	156,371	261,076
Household activities	16,420	29,112	45,532
Activities of extraterritorial organizations	2,368	1,149	3,517
Other services	462,273	452,141	914,414
Total employed	5,409,676	4,580,561	9,990,237
Unemployed	707,720	843,398	1,551,118
Total labour force	6,117,396	5,423,959	11,541,355

Health and Welfare

KEY INDICATORS

Total fertility rate (children per woman, 2020)	3.8
Under-5 mortality rate (per 1,000 live births, 2020) . . .	44.7
HIV/AIDS (% of persons aged 15–49, 2020)	1.7
COVID-19: Cumulative confirmed deaths (per 100,000 persons at 31 August 2022)	4.4
COVID-19: Fully vaccinated population (% of total population at 28 August 2022)	25.1
Physicians (per 1,000 head, 2020)	0.2
Hospitals (per 100,000 head, 2013)	1.4
Domestic health expenditure (2019): US $ per head (PPP) .	77.8
Domestic health expenditure (2019): % of GDP	1.4
Domestic health expenditure (2019): public (% of total current expenditure)	40.2
Access to improved water resources (% of persons, 2020) .	86
Access to improved sanitation facilities (% of persons, 2020) .	24
Total carbon dioxide emissions ('000 metric tons, 2018) . .	16,110
Carbon dioxide emissions per head (metric tons, 2018) . .	0.5
Human Development Index (2021): ranking	133
Human Development Index (2021): value	0.632

Note: For data on COVID-19 vaccinations, 'fully vaccinated' denotes receipt of all doses specified by approved vaccination regime (Sources: Johns Hopkins University and Our World in Data). Data on health expenditure refer to current general government expenditure in each case. For more information on sources and further definitions for all indicators, see Health and Welfare Statistics: Sources and Definitions section (europaworld.com/credits).

Agriculture

PRINCIPAL CROPS
('000 metric tons)

	2018	2019	2020
Bananas*	87.9	87.8	87.8
Beans, dry	176.7	188.7*	193.6*
Beans, green*	25.1	25.3	25.5
Cashew nuts, with shell . . .	102.5	86.0	82.4*
Cassava (Manioc)	20,846.0	19,367.9*	21,811.7*
Chillies and peppers, dry* . .	108.5	107.9	108.2
Chillies and peppers, green* . .	120.7	120.2	119.4
Cocoa beans†	904.7	811.7	800.0
Coconuts	395.0†	404.2*	412.5*
Cow peas, dry*	215.4	202.7	204.6
Groundnuts, with shell . . .	521.0	450.0†	450.0†
Lemons and limes*	46.7	46.8	46.7
Maize	2,306.4	2,900.0†	3,071.0†
Millet	181.6	190.0†	170.0†
Oil palm fruit*	2,459.1	2,464.5	2,471.6
Okra*	66.6	67.3	67.6
Onions, dry*	144.2	144.2	144.3
Oranges*	694.4	695.8	697.6
Pineapples*	665.7	667.1	668.9
Plantains and others . . .	4,688.3	4,767.9*	4,668.0*
Rice, paddy	769.4	925.0	973.0†
Rubber, natural†	41.3	34.7	50.4
Sorghum	316.2	345.0†	356.0†
Soybeans (Soya beans) . .	176.7	184.7*	177.0*
Sugar cane*	153.0	153.7	154.4
Sweet potatoes*	139.8	139.2	139.4
Taro (Cocoyam) . . .	1,460.9	1,517.6*	1,252.0*
Tomatoes*	368.0	368.4	368.9
Yams	7,858.2	8,086.3*	8,532.7*

* FAO estimate(s).
† Unofficial figure(s).

Aggregate production ('000 metric tons, may include official, semi-official or estimated data): Total cereals 3,573.6 in 2018; 4,360.0 in 2019, 4,570.0 in 2020; Total fruit (primary) 6,364.3 in 2018, 6,446.9 in 2019, 6,350.7 in 2020; Total oilcrops 3,609.1 in 2018, 3,565.4 in 2019, 3,573.1 in 2020; Total roots and tubers 30,305.1 in 2018, 29,111.2 in 2019, 31,736.0 in 2020; Total vegetables (primary) 787.2 in 2018, 788.0 in 2019, 788.4 in 2020.

Source: FAO.

LIVESTOCK
('000 head, year ending September)

	2018	2019	2020
Cattle	1,922	1,943	1,922
Chickens	81,955	89,210	95,455
Goats	7,509	7,884	8,203
Pigs	792	768	759
Sheep	5,137	5,302	5,458

Source: FAO.

LIVESTOCK PRODUCTS
('000 metric tons, FAO estimates)

	2018	2019	2020
Cattle meat	28.8	29.7	30.7
Cows' milk	45.8	46.2	45.9
Chicken meat	63.1	68.0	72.1
Game meat	74.9	74.6	75.2
Goat meat	27.6	28.9	30.3
Pig meat	26.5	25.7	25.4
Sheep meat	22.2	23.1	24.1
Hen eggs	46.8	46.9	46.8

Source: FAO.

Forestry

ROUNDWOOD REMOVALS
('000 cubic metres, excl. bark)

	2018	2019	2020
Sawlogs, veneer logs and logs for sleepers	1,938	1,464	1,464*
Other industrial roundwood* .	750	750	750
Fuel wood*	47,639	47,639	50,166
Total *	50,327	49,853	52,379

* FAO estimate(s).

Source: FAO.

SAWNWOOD PRODUCTION
('000 cubic metres, incl. railway sleepers)

	2013	2014	2015
Total (all broadleaved) . . .	511*	521*	534†

* Unofficial figure.
† FAO estimate.

2016–20: Production assumed to be unchanged from 2015 (FAO estimates).

Source: FAO.

Fishing

('000 metric tons, live weight)

	2018	2019	2020
Capture	373.2	318.0	356.4
Freshwater fishes	73.6	81.2	80.9
Bigeye grunt	16.6	2.7	11.8
Round sardinella	29.3	6.4	27.4
European anchovy	61.0	41.7	44.7
Skipjack tuna	69.4	63.6	59.9
Yellowfin tuna	24.3	26.2	25.1
Atlantic bumper	11.9	13.6	8.7
Aquaculture*	76.6	52.4	64.0
Nile tilapia*	70.6	45.8	59.5
Total catch *	449.8	370.4	420.4

* FAO estimates.

Source: FAO.

Mining

('000 metric tons unless otherwise indicated)

	2016	2017	2018
Bauxite	1,144	1,477	1,011
Manganese ore: gross weight . .	1,967	3,004	4,552
Manganese ore: metal content .	553	810	1,364
Silver (kg)*†	2,300	1,800	1,800
Gold (kg)‡	79,196	87,352	87,336
Salt (unrefined)*	250	250	250
Crude petroleum ('000 barrels) .	35,770	58,660	62,771
Diamonds ('000 carats) . . .	142	82	54

* Estimated figures.
† Silver content of exported doré.
‡ Gold content of ores and concentrates, excluding smuggled or undocumented output.

Source: US Geological Survey.

Industry

SELECTED PRODUCTS
('000 metric tons unless otherwise indicated)

	2018	2019	2020
Beer of barley	285.0*	285.0*	n.a.
Groundnut oil	70.2†	72.4	n.a.
Coconut oil	6.0*	6.0*	n.a.
Palm oil	312.5†	257.3†	n.a.
Palm kernel oil	58.5*	60.3*	n.a.
Gasoline (petrol)	102	125	66
Jet fuel	21.5	79.7	28.0
Kerosene	33.1	12.1	35.0
Distillate fuel oil . . .	113.0	198.1	150.0
Residual fuel oil	31.5	203.8	216.0
Electrical energy (million kWh) .	16,246	18,188	20,170

* Unofficial figure.
† FAO estimate.

Cement ('000 metric tons, estimate): 4,000 in 2018.

Sources: FAO; US Geological Survey; Energy Commission of Ghana.

Finance

CURRENCY AND EXCHANGE RATES

Monetary Units
100 Ghana pesewas = 1 Ghana cedi.

Sterling, Dollar and Euro Equivalents (31 May 2022)
£1 sterling = 8.994 Ghana cedis;
US $1 = 7.144 Ghana cedis;
€1 = 7.653 Ghana cedis;
10 Ghana cedis = £1.11 = $1.40 = €1.31.

Average Exchange Rate (Ghana cedis per US $)
2019   5.217
2020   5.596
2021   5.806

Note: A new currency, the Ghana cedi, equivalent to 10,000 new cedis (the former legal tender), was introduced over a six-month period beginning in July 2007.

GENERAL BUDGET
(million Ghana cedis, provisional)

Revenue*	2019	2020	2021
Tax revenue	42,774.6	44,447.8	56,533.1
Income and property . . .	22,683.1	23,728.6	27,971.4
Personal (PAYE)	7,313.1	7,507.1	9,250.3
Company tax	10,567.4	11,425.7	13,065.6
Domestic goods and services .	3,919.2	4,403.8	5,958.1
Petroleum tax	3,532.0	3,988.6	5,414.8
International trade	5,410.0	5,513.8	6,944.9
Value added tax	9,330.1	9,207.5	12,480.1
Communication service tax . .	412.3	559.4	528.4
National health insurance levy .	1,745.2	1,804.5	2,494.7
COVID-19 health levy . . .	—	—	775.9
Other levies	1,744.8	1,816.8	2,496.4
Tax refunds	−2,470.2	−2,586.7	−3,116.7
Social contributions	153.3	45.7	448.4
Non-tax revenue	7,567.6	6,667.3	7,908.9
Other revenue	1,898.1	2,738.9	4,023.9
Total	52,393.5	53,899.7	68,914.3

Expenditure	2019	2020	2021
General government expense . .	61,704.3	84,317.5	92,308.7
Compensation of employees .	22,219.0	28,268.9	31,663.3
Wages and salaries . . .	19,479.1	25,047.4	29,310.6
Goods and services	6,169.6	7,388.3	7,160.8
Intergovernmental transfers .	11,423.6	11,882.0	13,511.7
Subsidies	124.2	168.1	135.9
Interest payments	19,769.3	24,599.3	33,522.6
Domestic (accrual) . . .	15,209.5	18,352.1	26,422.0
External (accrual)	4,559.8	6,247.2	7,100.6
Other expenditure	1,998.6	12,010.9	6,314.4
Net acquisition of non-financial			
assets	6,151.8	12,082.9	16,967.1
Domestic	2,528.5	4,811.2	5,330.2
External	3,623.3	7,271.7	11,636.9
Total	67,856.1	96,400.4	109,275.9

* Excluding grants received (million Ghana cedis, provisional): 986.1 in 2019; 1,228.7 in 2020; 1,182.2 in 2021.

Source: Ministry of Finance, Accra.

INTERNATIONAL RESERVES
(US $ million at 31 December)

	2019	2020	2021
Gold (national valuation) . .	301.7	299.2	375.7
IMF special drawing rights . .	27.5	27.8	979.6
Reserve position in IMF . . .	127.9	133.2	129.4
Foreign exchange	6,979.9	7,191.7	8,193.9
Total	7,437.0	7,651.9	9,678.6

Source: IMF, *International Financial Statistics*.

MONEY SUPPLY
(million Ghana cedis at 31 December)

	2019	2020	2021
Currency outside depository			
corporations	14,107.7	20,572.0	21,816.2
Transferable deposits	50,309.2	63,276.5	73,023.0
Other deposits	37,421.1	46,918.4	40,971.5
Broad money	101,838.0	130,766.9	135,810.7

Source: IMF, *International Financial Statistics*.

COST OF LIVING
(Consumer Price Index; base: 2012 = 100)

	2016	2017	2018
Food and non-alcoholic beverages .	133.8	143.6	154.8
Clothing and footwear	204.8	240.0	276.7
Housing, water, electricity and			
other fuels	288.7	309.2	322.6
All items (incl. others) . . .	177.4	199.3	219.0

All items (Consumer Price Index; base: 2018 = 100): 117.8 in 2020; 129.6 in 2021.

Source: Bank of Ghana, Accra.

NATIONAL ACCOUNTS
(million Ghana cedis at current prices)

Expenditure on the Gross Domestic Product

	2019	2020	2021*
Government final consumption expenditure	25,112.1	30,702.3	45,681.4
Private final consumption expenditure	268,185.4	275,022.0	321,908.7
Increase in stocks	5,798.2	5,531.5	7,830.1
Gross fixed capital formation .	64,314.1	69,219.7	77,350.8
Total domestic expenditure .	363,409.9	380,475.6	452,770.9
Exports of goods and services .	133,524.4	81,214.2	137,315.1
Less Imports of goods and services	140,390.0	69,749.1	130,955.1
GDP in purchasers' values .	356,544.3	391,940.7	459,130.9
GDP in constant 2013 prices .	165,307.6	166,157.2	175,057.3

Gross Domestic Product by Economic Activity

	2019	2020	2021*
Agriculture and livestock . . .	54,579.2	65,949.8	81,021.8
Forestry and logging	4,257.0	4,394.9	4,998.5
Fishing	2,928.8	3,551.0	4,468.8
Mining and quarrying	47,459.8	41,714.7	42,716.8
Manufacturing	36,229.2	42,929.5	49,127.7
Electricity and water	6,671.3	7,347.2	8,620.4
Construction	20,552.5	25,107.7	29,306.2
Wholesale and retail trade, restaurants and hotels . . .	66,239.0	70,916.9	82,308.9
Transport, storage and communications	33,706.2	40,374.1	51,821.8
Finance, insurance, real estate and business services	26,659.4	29,619.2	34,664.9
Public administration and defence	11,642.6	14,237.2	18,697.2
Education	12,155.1	11,254.8	11,001.1
Health and social work . . .	7,233.7	7,703.8	8,846.4
Other community, social and personal services	3,312.1	3,004.8	3,541.9
Sub-total	333,626.0	368,105.7	431,142.3
Indirect taxes, less subsidies . .	22,918.3	23,835.0	27,988.6
GDP at market prices . . .	356,544.3	391,940.7	459,130.9

* Provisional.

BALANCE OF PAYMENTS
(US $ million)

	2018	2019	2020
Exports of goods	14,942.7	15,667.5	14,471.5
Imports of goods	−13,134.1	−13,410.7	−12,428.6
Balance on goods	1,808.6	2,256.8	2,043.0
Exports of services	7,572.0	9,924.8	7,605.5
Imports of services	−10,086.5	−13,497.6	−12,116.8
Balance on goods and services	−705.8	−1,315.9	−2,468.3
Primary income received . . .	598.3	482.9	738.5
Primary income paid	−4,520.1	−4,435.1	−4,137.0
Balance on goods, services and primary income	−4,627.6	−5,268.1	−5,866.8
Secondary income received . .	3,539.3	4,071.3	4,460.1
Secondary income paid . . .	−956.2	−667.3	−727.2
Current balance	−2,044.6	−1,864.0	−2,134.0
Capital account (net)	257.8	257.1	250.1
Direct investment assets . . .	−80.9	−587.8	−542.4
Direct investment liabilities .	2,989.0	3,879.8	1,875.8
Portfolio investment liabilities .	929.0	2,297.7	1,561.2
Other investment assets . . .	−564.0	−1,305.7	−930.1
Other investment liabilities . .	−1,997.0	−1,473.6	672.6
Net errors and omissions . .	−304.4	47.4	−1,303.2
Reserves and related items .	−815.2	1,251.1	−550.0

Source: IMF, *International Financial Statistics.*

External Trade

PRINCIPAL COMMODITIES
(distribution by HS, US $ million)

Imports c.i.f.	2017	2018	2019
Live animals and animal products	513.4	512.3	436.7
Vegetables and vegetable products	824.8	894.0	710.8
Cereals	716.2	653.8	522.9
Rice	401.9	451.9	374.9
Prepared foodstuffs; beverages, spirits, vinegar; tobacco and articles thereof .	716.8	774.0	596.8
Mineral products	1,302.1	661.7	682.4
Salt, sulphur, earth, stone, plaster, lime and cement	980.2	384.9	373.8
Cement, incl. cement clinkers, whether or not coloured . .	915.4	323.4	319.7
Chemicals and related products	1,220.2	1,247.4	1,092.6
Plastics, rubber, and articles thereof	647.9	780.2	680.5
Plastics and articles thereof . .	468.5	584.6	499.9
Pulp of wood, paper and paperboard, and articles thereof	808.6	320.9	219.3
Paper and paperboard	524.2	268.0	177.4
Iron and steel, other base metals and articles of base metal	1,281.7	1,179.0	999.6
Iron and steel	412.4	433.4	359.2
Articles of iron or steel . . .	517.5	492.0	391.5
Machinery and mechanical appliances; electrical equipment; parts thereof .	2,178.3	2,273.6	2,045.3
Machinery, boilers, etc. . . .	1,392.8	1,538.5	1,360.3
Electrical, electronic equipment .	785.5	735.1	685.0
Vehicles, aircraft, vessels and associated transport equipment	1,907.2	1,869.0	1,713.2
Vehicles other than railway, tramway	1,872.5	1,854.1	1,691.8
Cars (incl. station wagons) . .	998.6	956.1	881.8
Trucks, motor vehicles for the transport of goods	544.0	476.8	441.9
Total (incl. others)	12,718.1	11,880.5	10,439.8

Exports f.o.b.	2017	2018	2019
Vegetables and vegetable products	474.3	682.2	478.9
Edible fruit, nuts, peel of citrus fruit, melons	409.4	595.3	367.2
Brazil nuts, cashew nuts and coconuts	298.1	460.2	246.1
Prepared foodstuffs; beverages, spirits, vinegar; tobacco and articles thereof .	2,690.3	3,521.4	2,958.8
Cocoa and cocoa preparations .	2,433.7	3,249.9	2,714.5
Cocoa beans, raw, roasted . .	1,642.1	2,437.2	1,852.0
Mineral products	3,917.4	5,604.1	5,740.7
Mineral fuels, oils, distillation products, etc.	3,639.3	5,233.4	5,315.9
Crude petroleum oils . . .	3,619.7	5,195.0	5,251.7
Plastics, rubber, and articles thereof	448.0	264.2	291.5
Pearls, precious stones, metals, coins, etc.	5,861.5	6,094.8	6,199.7
Gold, unwrought or in semi-manufactured forms . . .	5,858.3	6,092.6	6,198.9
Total (incl. others)	14,358.5	17,099.6	16,768.3

Source: Trade Map-Trade Competitiveness Map, International Trade Centre, marketanalysis.intracen.org.

PRINCIPAL TRADING PARTNERS
(US $ million)

Imports c.i.f.	2017	2018	2019
Belgium	718.8	691.2	532.9
Brazil	217.8	158.0	138.7
Canada	363.5	333.0	266.5
China, People's Republic	2,134.2	2,272.6	1,895.9
Côte d'Ivoire	102.0	119.2	93.2
France (incl. Monaco)	192.9	282.6	158.3
Germany	341.5	305.8	246.3
Hong Kong	78.7	71.3	110.4
India	633.3	673.8	582.2
Italy (incl. San Marino)	289.8	302.0	226.8
Japan	200.6	202.9	186.4
Korea, Republic	307.2	302.8	254.5
Malaysia	303.5	230.8	131.1
Netherlands	237.0	259.6	231.5
Nigeria	149.0	159.4	112.3
Russian Federation	135.1	177.9	142.3
South Africa	410.9	406.2	357.6
Spain	754.6	199.2	139.1
Thailand	248.1	212.4	139.5
Türkiye	325.1	332.2	466.8
United Arab Emirates	307.5	303.2	275.8
United Kingdom	1,099.1	604.1	685.6
USA	1,200.1	953.7	976.2
Viet Nam	292.0	342.6	316.5
Total (incl. others)	12,718.1	11,880.5	10,439.8

Exports f.o.b.	2017	2018	2019
Belgium	155.8	162.2	203.3
Brazil	193.9	150.8	17.2
Burkina Faso	490.7	272.8	277.7
Canada	287.4	121.2	266.3
China, People's Republic	2,381.4	2,032.3	2,808.6
France (incl. Monaco)	261.8	358.0	377.0
Germany	233.1	213.5	213.3
Hong Kong	107.2	105.7	216.2
India	2,689.4	3,670.4	2,380.1
Italy (incl. San Marino)	180.3	304.2	308.8
Japan	123.1	166.3	303.1
Malaysia	454.3	1,109.5	267.6
Netherlands	884.6	1,228.6	966.3
South Africa	910.3	1,742.5	1,971.0
Spain	213.2	584.5	171.7
Switzerland-Liechtenstein	1,660.1	1,631.7	2,465.9
Togo	194.5	139.4	159.9
United Arab Emirates	800.8	590.7	899.2
United Kingdom	329.5	491.5	415.1
USA	408.0	613.8	704.3
Viet Nam	223.7	197.7	102.8
Total (incl. others)	14,358.5	17,099.6	16,768.3

Source: Trade Map-Trade Competitiveness Map, International Trade Centre, marketanalysis.intracen.org.

Transport

RAILWAYS
(traffic)

	2002	2003	2004
Passenger-km (million)	61	86	80
Net ton-km (million)	244	242	216

Source: UN, *Statistical Yearbook*.

SHIPPING

Flag Registered Fleet
(at 31 December)

	2019	2020	2021
Number of vessels	143	146	143
Total displacement ('000 grt)	117.6	120.0	115.1

Source: Lloyd's List Intelligence (www.bit.ly/LLintelligence).

CIVIL AVIATION
(traffic on scheduled services)

	2013	2014	2015
Kilometres flown (million)	4	4	5
Passengers carried ('000)	396	408	390
Passenger-km (million)	196	201	229
Total ton-km (million)	1	1	1

Source: UN, *Statistical Yearbook*.

2020 (domestic and international): Departures 8,941; Passengers carried 0.3m. (Source: World Bank, World Development Indicators database).

Tourism

ARRIVALS BY NATIONALITY

	2012	2013	2014
Canada	20.2	27.6	29.4
Côte d'Ivoire	47.1	44.5	55.6
France	21.6	21.9	23.8
Germany	31.1	36.9	41.3
Netherlands	26.7	31.0	33.8
Nigeria	102.3	112.5	123.7
Togo	25.3	29.1	34.4
United Kingdom	66.9	85.4	91.0
USA	114.1	130.3	135.9
Total (incl. others)*	903.3	993.6	1,093.0

* Includes Ghanaian nationals resident abroad: 121.7 in 2012; 117.2 in 2013; 124.6 in 2014.

Total tourist arrivals ('000): 972 in 2017; 1,029 in 2018; 1,088 in 2019 (provisional) (Source: World Tourism Organization).

Tourism receipts (US $ million, excl. passenger transport): 846 in 2016; 850 in 2017; 944 in 2018 (Source: World Tourism Organization).

Communications Media

	2018	2019	2020
Telephones (main lines in use)	278,379	288,531	307,668
Mobile telephone subscriptions ('000)	40,934.9	40,857.1	40,461.6
Broadband subscriptions, fixed*	61,268	58,518	78,371
Broadband subscriptions, mobile ('000)*	27,312.7	30,387.3	26,512.2
Internet users (% of population)*†	43.0	53.0	58.0

* Source: International Telecommunication Union.
† Persons aged 18 years and over.

Source (unless otherwise indicated): National Communications Authority, Accra.

Education

(2019/20 unless otherwise indicated)

	Institutions	Teachers	Students ('000)		
			Males	Females	Total
Pre-primary	36,471	47,317	656.6	635.4	1,292.0
Primary	26,274	125,094	1,640.2	1,578.6	3,218.8
Junior secondary	18,353	111,019	691.4	674.5	1,366.0
Senior secondary	968	52,573	557.7	545.6	1,103.3
Technical and vocational	175	4,623	64.1	22.4	86.5
Tertiary	215*	17,892†	268.5*	211.3*	479.8*

* 2018/19 figure.
† 2015/16 figure.

2018/19: *Teacher-training* 52 institutions; *Universities* 81 institutions.

Sources: UNESCO; Ministry of Education, Accra.

Pupil-teacher ratio (primary education, qualified teaching staff, UNESCO estimate): 36.7 in 2019/20 (Source: UNESCO Institute for Statistics).

Adult literacy rate (UNESCO estimates): 79.0% (males 83.5%; females 74.5%) in 2018 (Source: UNESCO Institute for Statistics).

Directory

The Constitution

Under the terms of the Constitution of the Fourth Republic, which was approved by national referendum on 28 April 1992, Ghana has a multi-party political system. Executive power is vested in the President, who is head of state and Commander-in-Chief of the Armed Forces. The President is elected by universal adult suffrage for a term of four years, and designates a Vice-President (prior to election). The duration of the President's tenure of office is limited to two four-year terms. It is also stipulated that, in the event that no presidential candidate receives more than 50% of votes cast, a new election between the two candidates with the highest number of votes is to take place within 21 days. Legislative power is vested in a 275-member unicameral Parliament (membership increased from 230 in October 2012), which is elected by direct adult suffrage for a four-year term. The Cabinet is appointed by the President, subject to approval by the Parliament. The Constitution also provides for a 25-member Council of State, principally comprising presidential nominees and regional representatives, and a 20-member National Security Council (chaired by the Vice-President), both of which act as advisory bodies to the President.

The Government

HEAD OF STATE

President and Commander-in-Chief of the Armed Forces: NANA AKUFO-ADDO (took office 7 January 2017; re-elected 7 December 2020).

Vice-President: MAHAMUDU BAWUMIA.

CABINET
(October 2022)

President: NANA AKUFO-ADDO.

Minister of Finance: KEN OFORI-ATTA.

Minister of Trade and Industry: ALAN KYEREMATEN.

Minister of Defence: DOMINIC NITIWUL.

Minister of the Interior: AMBROSE DERY.

Minister of Foreign Affairs and Regional Integration: SHIRLEY AYORKOR BOTCHWEY.

Attorney-General and Minister of Justice: GODFRED DAME.

Minister of Local Government, Decentralization and Rural Development: DANIEL BOTWE.

Minister of Parliamentary Affairs: OSEI KYEI MENSAH BONSU.

Minister of Food and Agriculture: Dr OWUSU AFRIYIE AKOTO.

Minister of Energy: Dr MATHEW OPOKU PREMPEH.

Minister of Education: Dr YAW OSEI ADUTWUM.

Minister of Health: KWAKU AGYEMANG MANU.

Minister of Lands and Natural Resources: SAMUEL ABDULAI JINAPOR.

Minister of Works and Housing: FRANCIS ASENSO BOAKYE.

Ministry of Fisheries and Aquaculture Development: MAVIS HAWA KOOMSON.

Minister of Railways Development: JOHN PETER AMEWU.

Minister of Sanitation and Water Resources: CECILIA ABENA DAPAAH.

Minister of Tourism, Arts and Culture: Dr MOHAMMED AWAL.

Minister of Employment and Labour Relations: IGNATIUS BAFFOUR AWUAH.

OTHER GOVERNMENT MINISTERS
(October 2022)

Minister of National Security: ALBERT KAN DAPAAH.

Minister of Communications and Digitalization: URSULA OWUSU-EKUFUL.

Minister of Roads and Highways: KWASI AMOAKO-ATTA.

Minister of Transport: KWAKU OFORI ASIAMAH.

Minister of Gender, Children and Social Protection: LARIBA ZUWEIRA ABUDU (designate).

Minister of Chieftaincy and Religious Affairs: EBENEZER KOJO KUM.

Minister of Environment, Science, Technology and Innovation: Dr KWAKU AFRIYIE.

Minister of Information: KOJO OPPONG NKRUMAH.

Minister of Youth and Sports: MUSTAPHA YUSSIF.

Minister of Public Enterprises: JOSEPH CUDJOE.

Minister of State for Works and Housing: FREDA PREMPEH.

Minister of State at the Ministry of Finance: CHARLES ADU-BOAHEN.

There were also 39 deputy ministers.

REGIONAL MINISTERS
(October 2022)

Ahafo: GEORGE BOAKYE.

Ashanti: SIMON OSEI-MENSAH.

Bono: JUSTINA OWUSU-BANAHENE.

Bono East: AKWASI ADU GYAN.

Central: JUSTINA MARIGOLD ASSAN.

Eastern: SETH KWAME ACHEAMPONG.

Greater Accra: HENRY QUARTEY.

North East: YIDANA ZAKARIA.

Northern: SHANI ALHASSAN SAIBU.

Oti: JOSPEH MAKUBU.

Savannah: SAEED MUHAZU JIBRIL.

Upper East: STEPHEN YAKUBU.

Upper West: Dr HAFIZ BIN SALIH.

Volta: Dr ARCHIBALD YAO LETSA.

Western: KWABENA OKYERE DARKO MENSAH.

Western North: RICHARD OBENG.

MINISTRIES

Office of the President: Jubilee House, Kanda, Accra; tel. (30) 2210000; e-mail info@presidency.gov.gh; internet www.presidency.gov.gh.

Ministry of Business Development: 32 Gamel Abdul Nasser Rd, Ridge, Accra; tel. (30) 2665447; e-mail mobd@mobd.gov.gh; internet mobd.gov.gh.

Ministry of Chieftaincy and Religious Affairs: State House, POB 1627, Accra; tel. (30) 2903306; e-mail info.christianpilgrimage@mcra.gov.gh; internet www.mcta.gov.gh.

Ministry of Communications and Digitalization: POB M38, Accra; tel. (30) 2666465; e-mail info@moc.gov.gh; internet www.moc.gov.gh.

Ministry of Defence: POB CT139, Cantonments, Accra; tel. (30) 2742474; internet mod.gov.gh.

Ministry of Education: POB M45, Accra; tel. (30) 2683627; e-mail pro@moe.gov.gh; internet www.moe.gov.gh.

Ministry of Employment and Labour Relations: POB MB84, Accra; tel. 577701808; e-mail info@melr.gov.gh; internet www.melr.gov.gh.

Ministry of Energy: POB SD40 (Stadium Post Office), Accra; tel. (30) 2683961; e-mail info@petromin.gov.gh; internet www.energymin.gov.gh.

Ministry of Environment, Science, Technology and Innovation: POB M232, Accra; tel. (30) 2666049; e-mail contact@mesti.gov.gh; internet mesti.gov.gh.

Ministry of Finance: POB M40, Accra; tel. (30) 2665587; e-mail minister2009@mofep.gov.gh; internet www.mofep.gov.gh.

Ministry of Fisheries and Aquaculture Development: POB GP630, Accra; internet www.mofad.gov.gh.

Ministry of Food and Agriculture: Accra; tel. (50) 9163727; e-mail info@mofa.gov.gh; internet mofa.gov.gh.

Ministry of Foreign Affairs and Regional Integration: Flat 5, Agostinho Neto Rd, POB M53, Accra; tel. (30) 2999604; e-mail info@mfa.gov.gh; internet www.mfa.gov.gh.

Ministry of Gender, Children and Social Protection: POB MBO186, Accra; tel. (30) 2688187; e-mail info@mogcsp.gov.gh; internet mogcsp.gov.gh.

Ministry of Health: Sekou Toure Ave, North Ridge, POB M44, Accra; tel. (30) 2665651; e-mail info@moh.gov.gh; internet www.moh.gov.gh.

Ministry of Information: Information Dr., Education Close, off Barnes Rd, Adabraka, Accra; tel. (30) 2909609; e-mail info.moi@moi.gov.gh; internet moi.gov.gh.

Ministry of the Interior: POB M42, Accra; tel. (30) 2684421; e-mail info@mint.gov.gh; internet www.mint.gov.gh.

Ministry of Justice and Attorney-General's Department: POB M60, Accra; tel. (30) 2665051; internet www.mojagd.gov.gh.

Ministry of Lands and Natural Resources: POB M212, Accra; tel. (30) 2672336; e-mail mlnrinfo@mlnr.gov.gh; internet www.mlnr .gov.gh.

Ministry of Local Government, Decentralization and Rural Development: POB M50, Accra; tel. (30) 2664763; e-mail info@ mlgrd.gov.gh; internet www.mlgrd.gov.gh.

Ministry of National Security: Accra.

Ministry of Parliamentary Affairs: State House, POB 1627, Accra; tel. (50) 1577987; e-mail info@mopa.gov.gh; internet mopa .gov.gh.

Ministry of Railways Development: POB MB 453, Accra; tel. (30) 2904840; e-mail development@mrd.gov.gh; internet www.mrd.gov .gh.

Ministry of Roads and Highways: POB M57, Accra; tel. (30) 2661575; e-mail info@mrh.gov.gh; internet www.mrh.gov.gh.

Ministry of Sanitation and Water Resources: POB M43, Accra; tel. (30) 2665940; internet mswr.gov.gh.

Ministry of Tourism, Arts and Culture: POB 4386, Accra; e-mail info@motac.gov.gh; internet motac.gov.gh.

Ministry of Trade and Industry: POB M47, Accra; tel. (30) 2686528; e-mail info@moti.gov.gh; internet www.moti.gov.gh.

Ministry of Transport: POB M57, Accra; tel. (30) 2955792; e-mail info@mot.gov.gh; internet mot.gov.gh.

Ministry of Works and Housing: POB M43, Accra; tel. 577902988; e-mail info@mwh.gov.gh; internet www.mwh.gov.gh.

Ministry of Youth and Sports: POB M252, Accra; tel. (30) 2664716; e-mail info@moys.gov.gh; internet moys.gov.gh.

President

Presidential Election, 7 December 2020, provisional results

Candidate	Valid votes	% of valid votes
Nana Akufo-Addo (NPP)	6,730,587	51.30
John Dramani Mahama (NDC) . . .	6,213,182	47.36
Christian Kwabena Andrews (GUM) . .	105,548	0.80
Ivor Kobina Greenstreet (CPP) . . .	12,200	0.09
David Apasera (PNC)	10,882	0.08
Others*	47,061	0.36
Total	13,119,460†	100.00

* There were seven other candidates.

† Excluding results from the Techiman South constituency which were being contested by the NPP and the NDC. There were also 313,397 rejected ballots.

Legislature

PARLIAMENT

Parliament: Parliament House, Accra; tel. (30) 2664042; e-mail info@parliament.gh; internet www.parliament.gh.

Speaker: Alban Sumana Bagbin.

General Election, 7 December 2020

Party	Seats
New Patriotic Party (NPP)	137
National Democratic Congress (NDC)	137
Independents	1
Total	275

COUNCIL OF STATE

The Council of State (the current embodiment of which was inaugurated in February 2021) is a 31-member advisory body to the President of the Republic. It consists of a former Chief Justice, a former Chief of Defence Staff of the Armed Forces, a former Inspector-General of Police, the President of the National House of Chiefs, 16 elected members (one from each of Ghana's 16 regions) and 11 members appointed by the President. The Chairman is elected by members from among their number.

Chairman: Nana Otuo Siriboe, II.

Election Commission

Electoral Commission (EC): POB M214, Accra; tel. (30) 3968750; e-mail info@ec.gov.gh; internet ec.gov.gh; f. 1993; appointed by the President; Chair. Jean Adukwei Mensa.

Political Organizations

In 2022 there were 27 political parties registered in Ghana.

Convention People's Party (CPP): 64 Mango Tree Ave, Asylum Down, POB 104, Accra-North; tel. (30) 2227763; e-mail info@ conventionpeoplesparty.org; internet conventionpeoplesparty.org; f. 1998 as Convention Party by merger of the National Convention Party (f. 1992) and the People's Convention Party (f. 1993); present name adopted in 2000; Nkrumahist; Chair. Prof. Edmund Delle; Gen. Sec. Nana Yaa Akyempim Jantuah.

Democratic People's Party (DPP): POB 373, Madina, Accra; tel. (30) 2500717; f. 1992; Chair. Thomas N. Ward-Brew; Gen. Sec. Lawrence Hornu.

Great Consolidated Popular Party (GCPP): Citadel House, POB 3077, Accra; tel. (30) 2311498; internet greatconsolidatedpopularparty.org; f. 1996; Nkrumahist; Chair. Dr Henry Herbert Lartey; Gen. Sec. Frederick Ato Dadzie.

National Democratic Congress (NDC): 641/4 Ringway Close, POB 5825, Kokomlemle, Accra-North; tel. (30) 2223195; e-mail info@ ndc.org.gh; internet officialndc.com; f. 1992; Chair. Samuel Ofosu-Ampofo; Gen. Sec. Johnson Asiedu Nketiah.

National Democratic Party (NDP): POB 3038, Accra; tel. (27) 7513842; f. 2012 by breakaway faction of NDC; Chair. Nana Konadu Agyeman-Rawlings; Gen. Sec. Mohammed Frimpong.

New Patriotic Party (NPP): C912/2 Duade St, Kokomlemle, POB 3456, Accra-North; tel. (30) 2264288; e-mail info@newpatrioticparty .org; internet newpatrioticparty.org; f. 1992; Chair. Stephen Ayensu Ntim; Gen. Sec. Justin Frimpong Koduah.

People's National Convention (PNC): POB AC120, Arts Centre, Accra; tel. (30) 2226528; internet pncghana.org; f. 1992; Nkrumahist; Chair. (vacant); Gen. Sec. Janet Asana Nabla.

Progressive People's Party (PPP): Asylum Down, POB GP17187, Accra; tel. (30) 3976622; internet www.pppghana.org; f. 2011; Chair. Nana Ofori Owusu; Nat. Sec. Paa Kow Ackon.

Reformed Patriotic Democrats (RPD): POB 13274, Kumasi; f. 2007 by former mems of the NPP; Founding Leader Kwabena Agyei; Gen. Sec. Charles Boateng.

United Front Party (UFP): 14 Blohum St, Kumasi; tel. (540) 379242; internet www.unitedfrontparty.org; f. 2012; Leader Nana Agyenim Boateng; Sec.-Gen. Samuel Bekoe Owusu.

United Renaissance Party (URP): Nima Hwy, POB 104, Accra-North; tel. (30) 28914411; internet www.urpgh.com; f. 2006; Chair. Eric Charles Kofi Wayo; Gen. Sec. Alhassan Saeed.

Diplomatic Representation

EMBASSIES AND HIGH COMMISSIONS IN GHANA

Algeria: 22 Josif Tito Ave, POB 2747, Cantonments, Accra; tel. (30) 2776719; e-mail embdzacc@africaonline.com.gh; Ambassador Ali Redjel.

Angola: 5 Agbaamo St, Airport West Residential Area, Accra; tel. (30) 2766477; e-mail sec@angolaembassyghana.org; internet www .angolaembassyghana.org; Ambassador João Baptista Domingos Quiosa.

Australia: 2 Second Rangoon Close (cnr Josef Tito Ave), Cantonments, Accra; tel. (30) 2216400; e-mail Accrahc.Enquiries@dfat.gov .au; internet ghana.embassy.gov.au; High Commissioner Berenice Owen-Jones.

Benin: 129A North Airport Rd, Accra; tel. (30) 2774860; e-mail ambab.accra@yahoo.fr; Ambassador (vacant).

Brazil: 1 Templesi Lane, Airport Residential Area, POB CT 3859, Accra; tel. (30) 2774908; e-mail brasemb.acra@itamaraty.gov.br; internet www.gov.br/mre/pt-br/embaixada-acra; Ambassador Maria Elisa Teófilo de Luna.

Burkina Faso: 772 Asylum Down, off Farrar Ave, POB 651, Accra; tel. (30) 2221988; e-mail secretariat@ambafaso-gh.org; internet ambaburkina-gh.org; Ambassador Pingrenoma Zagré.

Canada: 42 Independence Ave, Sankara Interchange, POB 1639, Accra; tel. (30) 2211521; e-mail accra@international.gc.ca; internet www.canadainternational.gc.ca/ghana; High Commissioner (vacant).

Chile: 25 Sir Arku Korsah Rd, Airport Residential Area, Accra; tel. (30) 2797942; e-mail echile.ghana@minrel.gob.cl; internet chile.gob.cl/ghana; Chargé d'affaires a.i. MARIO LUIS SILVA VIDAURRE.

China, People's Republic: 6 Agostino Neto Rd, Airport Residential Area, POB 3356, Accra; tel. (30) 2797437; e-mail chinaemb_gh@mfa.gov.cn; internet gh.china-embassy.gov.cn; Ambassador LU KUN.

Colombia: Plot 16, 1st Circular Rd, Cantonments, Accra; tel. (30) 2798701; e-mail eghana@cancilleria.gov.co; internet ghana.embajada.gov.co; Ambassador (vacant).

Côte d'Ivoire: 9 18th Lane, off Cantonments Rd, POB 3445, Christiansborg, Accra; tel. (30) 2774611; internet ghana.diplomatie.gouv.ci; Ambassador TIÉMOKO MORIKO.

Cuba: 22A Akosombo Rd, Airport Residential Area, POB 9163 Airport, Accra; tel. (30) 2775868; e-mail embajada@gh.embacuba.cu; internet misiones.minrex.gob.cu/en/ghana; Ambassador ANETTE CHAO GARCIA.

Czech Republic: C260/5, 2 Hilla Limann Highway, POB 5226, Accra-North; tel. (30) 2223540; internet www.mzv.cz/accra; Ambassador JÁN FÚRY.

Denmark: 67 Dr Isert Rd, North Ridge, POB CT 596, Accra; tel. (30) 2208730; e-mail accamb@um.dk; internet ghana.um.dk; Ambassador TOM HELGE NØRRING.

Egypt: No. 73, 15 Nime Lane, Airport Residential Area, POB 2508, Accra; tel. (30) 2776854; e-mail emb.eg.accra@gmail.com; internet fb.com/egyptembassy.accra; Ambassador ALDESOUKY MAHMOUD YOUSSEF.

Equatorial Guinea: North Airport Rd No. 70 (Kufour Lane), Accra; tel. (30) 2766357; e-mail embaregeghana@hotmail.com; Ambassador MAURICIO-MAURO EPKUA OBAMA BINDANG.

Ethiopia: 2 Milne Close, Airport Residential Area, POB 1646, Accra; tel. (30) 2775928; e-mail ethiopianemb@gmail.com; internet fb.com/Embassy-of-Ethiopia-Accra-793109967496601; Ambassador HADERA ABERA ADMASSU.

France: 12th Rd, off Liberation Ave, POB 187, Accra; tel. (30) 2214550; e-mail info@ambafrance-gh.org; internet gh.ambafrance.org; Ambassador ANNE-SOPHIE AVÉ.

Germany: 6 Kenneth Kaunda Rd, North Ridge, POB 1757, Accra; tel. (30) 2211000; e-mail info@accra.diplo.de; internet accra.diplo.de; Ambassador DANIEL KRULL.

Guinea: 125 Roman Ridge, opp. Accra Girls Senior High School, POB 5497, Accra-North; tel. (30) 2777921; e-mail ambassadeguineaaccra@yahoo.com; internet fb.com/ambassadeguinee.aughana; Ambassador OLGA SYRADIN.

Holy See: 8 Drake Ave, Airport Residential Area, POB 9675, Accra; tel. (30) 2777759; Apostolic Nuncio HENRYK MIECZYSŁAW JAGODZIŃSKI (Titular Archbishop of Limosano).

Hungary: Plot No. 44, Sixth Circular Rd, Cantonments, Accra; tel. 556488650; internet accra.mfa.gov.hu; Ambassador TAMÁS ENDRE FEHER.

India: 9 Ridge Rd, Roman Ridge, POB CT 5708, Cantonments, Accra; tel. (30) 2775601; e-mail info.accra@mea.gov.in; internet www.hciaccra.gov.in; Ambassador C. SUGANDH RAJARAM.

Iran: 3 Nme Lane, Airport Residential Area, POB 12673, Accra-North; tel. 552569802; e-mail iranemb.acc@mfa.gov.ir; internet ghana.mfa.gov.ir; Ambassador Dr BIJAN GERAMI NAZOKSARA.

Israel: 2 First Circular Rd, Unit 1, Josni Residence Cantonments, POB CN 91, Accra; tel. (30) 2743838; e-mail amb-sec@accra.mfa.gov.il; internet embassies.gov.il/accra; Ambassador SHLOMIT SUFA.

Italy: Jawaharlal Nehru Rd, POB CT 885, Accra; tel. (30) 2775621; e-mail ambasciata.accra@esteri.it; internet ambaccra.esteri.it/ambasciata_accra/it; Ambassador DANIELA D'ORLANDI.

Japan: Fifth Ave, POB 1637, West Cantonments, Accra; tel. (30) 2765060; internet www.gh.emb-japan.go.jp; Ambassador MOCHIZUKI HISANOBU.

Kenya: KADTD 10026 Airport Residential Area, Accra; tel. (30) 2961044; e-mail accra@mfa.gov.ke; High Commissioner ELIPHAS M. BARINE.

Korea, Democratic People's Republic: 139 Nortei Ababio Loop, Ambassadorial Estate, Roman Ridge, POB 13874, Accra; tel. (30) 2777825; Ambassador JON TONG CHOL.

Korea, Republic: 10 5th Ave Extension, Cantonments, POB GP 13700, Accra-North; tel. (30) 2776157; e-mail ghana@mofa.go.kr; internet overseas.mofa.go.kr/gh-en/index.do; Ambassador LIM JUNG-TAEK.

Kuwait: North Ring Rd Extension, Vogel House No. 6, Labone, Accra; tel. (30) 2787896; e-mail kwtembassy.gh2015@gmail.com; Ambassador MOHAMMED ABDULLAH AL-KHALIDI.

Lebanon: F864/1, off Cantonments Rd, Osu, POB 562, Accra; tel. (30) 2776727; internet www.accra.mfa.gov.lb; Ambassador MAHER KHEIR.

Liberia: 10 Odoi Kwao St, Airport Residential Area, POB 895, Accra; tel. (30) 2775641; e-mail accramissionlib@gmail.com; Chargé d'affaires a.i. ALIEU M. MASSAQUOI.

Libya: 59 Fourth Circular Rd, Cantonments, POB CT 8212, Accra; tel. (30) 2774819; e-mail libyaem.accra@gmail.com; Ambassador KHAMEES B. A. HASAN.

Malaysia: 5 Nii Amaah Ollenu St, Airport West, POB 16033, Accra; tel. (30) 2763691; e-mail mwaccra@kln.gov.my; internet www.kln.gov.my/web/gha_accra/home; Chargé d'affaires a.i. MOHD FARHAN MOHD AREFFIN.

Mali: 1st Bungalow, Liberia Rd, Airport Residential Area, POB 1121, Accra; tel. (30) 2663276; e-mail ambamaliaccra@yahoo.fr; internet ambamalighana.com; Ambassador ABDOUL KADER TOURÉ.

Malta: 88B, Tabon Loop, North Ridge, Accra; tel. (24) 2420804; e-mail maltahighcommission.accra@gov.mt; internet foreignandeu.gov.mt/en/Embassies/HC_Accra/Pages/The-High-Commission.aspx; High Commissioner JEAN CLAUDE GALEA MALLIA.

Mexico: House No. 25, Sir Arku Korsah Rd, Airport Residential Area, Accra; tel. (30) 2789320; e-mail infoembamexgha@sre.gob.mx; internet embamex.sre.gob.mx/ghana; Ambassador ENRIQUE ERNESTO ESCORZA ZAMUDIO.

Morocco: 1 Switchback Lane, PMB 117, Accra; tel. (30) 2775669; e-mail ambassade.maroc.ghana@gmail.com; Ambassador IMANE OUAADIL.

Namibia: 21 Nortei-Ababio St, Airport Residential Area, Accra; tel. (30) 2799764; e-mail accra@mirco.gov.na; internet www.namibiahc-ghana.org; High Commissioner SELMA ASHIPALA-MUSAVYI.

Netherlands: 89 Liberation Rd, Ako Adjei Interchange, POB CT 1647, Accra; tel. (30) 2214350; e-mail acc@minbuza.nl; internet www.netherlandsworldwide.nl/countries/ghana; Ambassador JEROEN VERHEUL.

Niger: E104/3 Independence Ave, POB 2685, Accra; tel. (30) 2224962; e-mail ambaniggh@yahoo.com; Ambassador LAMIDOSA LAMATOU BALA GOGA.

Nigeria: 20/21 Onyasia Cres., Roman Ridge Residential Area, Accra; tel. (30) 2776158; e-mail info@nigerianhcaccra.org; internet nigerianhcaccra.org; High Commissioner IBOK-ETE EKWE IBAS.

Norway: 89 Liberation Rd, Ako Adjei Interchange, Accra; tel. (30) 2744300; e-mail emb.accra@mfa.no; internet www.norway.no/ghana; Ambassador INGRID MOLLESTAD.

Peru: 25 Sir Arku Korsah Rd, POB 10452, Accra; tel. (30) 3938177; e-mail embaperu-acra@rree.gob.pe; internet www.gob.pe/embajada-del-peru-en-ghana; Ambassador (vacant).

Qatar: c/o Kempinski Hotel, Gamel Abdul Nasser Ave, PMB 66 Ministries Ridge, Accra; e-mail accra@mofa.gov.qa; Ambassador MOHAMMED BIN AHMED AL-HAMID.

Russian Federation: Jawaharlal Nehru Rd, Switchback Lane, POB 1634, Accra; tel. (30) 2775611; e-mail embrus.ghana@mid.ru; internet ghana.mid.ru; Ambassador SERGEI BERDNIKOV.

Rwanda: 129C Nii Nortei Nyanchi St, Accra; tel. (30) 2795270; e-mail ambaaccra@minaffet.gov.rw; internet www.rwandainghana.gov.rw; High Commissioner Dr AISSA KIRABO KACYIRA.

Saudi Arabia: 10 Noi Fetreke St, Roman Ridge Ambassadorial Estate Ext., Airport Residential Area, POB 670, Accra; tel. (30) 2774311; internet embassies.mofa.gov.sa/sites/ghana; Ambassador MISHAAL BIN HAMDAN AL-ROGI.

Senegal: 8F Odoi Kwao St, Airport Residential Area, PMB CT 342, Cantonments, Accra; tel. (30) 2785422; e-mail infos@senegal-embassy-gh.com; internet senegal-embassy-gh.com; Ambassador ABOUBACAR SADIKH BARRY.

Sierra Leone: 83A Senchi St, Airport Residential Area, POB 55, Cantonments, Accra; tel. (30) 2769190; High Commissioner FRANCES VIRGINIA ANDERSON.

South Africa: Speed House, Plot No. A69, Orphan Cres., Labone North, POB 298, Accra; tel. (30) 2740451; e-mail sahcgh@africaonline.com.gh; internet www.dirco.gov.za/Accra; High Commissioner GRACE JEANET MASON.

South Sudan: Plot No. 8616, Second Close, Accra; tel. (30) 2733069; Ambassador (vacant).

Spain: Drake Ave Extension, Airport Residential Area, PMB KA 44, Accra; tel. (30) 2774004; e-mail emb.accra@maec.es; internet www.exteriores.gob.es/embajadas/accra; Ambassador JAVIER GUTIÉRREZ BLANCO-NAVARRETE.

Sudan: House No. 21A, Senchi St, nr former DSTV Airport, East Dzorwulu Residential Area, Accra; tel. (30) 2733027; Ambassador MOHAMMED ABDELRAHMAN YASIN MOHAMED.

Suriname: 21A Akosombo Rd, Airport Residential Area, Accra; tel. (30) 2786864; e-mail amb.accra@gov.sr; Ambassador FIDELIA GRAAND-GALON.

Switzerland: Kanda Highway, North Ridge, POB 359, Accra; tel. (30) 2228125; e-mail accra@eda.admin.ch; internet www.eda.admin.ch/accra; Ambassador SIMONE GIGER.

Togo: Togo House, near Cantonments Circle, POB C 120, Accra; tel. (30) 2777950; High Commissioner Col AWOKI PANASSA.

Türkiye (Turkey): L8 Block 1, Section 17B, Labone Abafum Cres., POB CT149, Cantonments, Accra; tel. (30) 2218180; internet akra.be.mfa.gov.tr; Ambassador ÖZLEM GÜLSÜN ERGÜN ULUEREN.

United Arab Emirates: 4 Obenesu Cres., Accra; tel. (30) 2215555; e-mail accraemb@mofaic.gov.ae; Ambassador KHALIFA YOUSIF AL-ZAABI.

United Kingdom: Julius Nyerere Link, off Gamel Abdul Nasser Ave, POB 296, Accra; tel. (30) 2213200; e-mail high.commission.accra@fco.gov.uk; internet www.gov.uk/world/organisations/british-high-commission-accra; High Commissioner HARRIET CLARE THOMPSON.

USA: 24 Fourth Circular Rd, POB GP 2288, Cantonments, Accra; tel. (30) 2741000; e-mail pressaccra@state.gov; internet gh.usembassy.gov; Ambassador VIRGINA E. PALMER (designate).

Zambia: 6 Agostino Neto Rd, Airport Residential Area, Accra; tel. (30) 2767689; e-mail info@zamhighghana.org; High Commissioner RICHARD MWANZA.

Zimbabwe: 16 Akosombo Rd, PMB CT 88, Cantonments, Accra; tel. (30) 2780956; e-mail zimaccra@ghana.com; Ambassador KUFA EDWARD CHINOZA.

Judicial System

The civil law in force in Ghana is based on the Common Law, doctrines of equity and general statutes that were in force in England in 1874, as modified by subsequent Ordinances. Ghanaian customary law is, however, the basis of most personal, domestic and contractual relationships. Criminal Law is based on the Criminal Procedure Code, 1960, derived from English Criminal Law, and since amended. The Superior Court of Judicature comprises a Supreme Court, a Court of Appeal, a High Court and a Regional Tribunal; Inferior Courts include Circuit Courts, Circuit Tribunals, Community Tribunals and such other Courts as may be designated by law. In 2001 'fast track' court procedures were established to accelerate the delivery of justice.

Supreme Court: Accra; consists of the Chief Justice and not fewer than nine other Justices; is the final court of appeal in Ghana and has jurisdiction in matters relating to the enforcement or interpretation of the Constitution; Chief Justice KWASI ANIN YEBOAH.

Court of Appeal: Consists of the Chief Justice and not fewer than 10 Judges of the Court of Appeal. It has jurisdiction to hear and determine appeals from any judgment, decree or order of the High Court.

High Court: Comprises the Chief Justice and not fewer than 12 Justices of the High Court. It exercises original jurisdiction in all matters, civil and criminal, other than those for offences involving treason. Trial by jury is practised in criminal cases in Ghana and the Criminal Procedure Code, 1960, provides that all trials on indictment shall be by a jury or with the aid of Assessors.

Circuit Courts: Exercise original jurisdiction in civil matters where the amount involved does not exceed 10 Ghana cedis. They also have jurisdiction with regard to the guardianship and custody of infants, and original jurisdiction in all criminal cases, except offences where the maximum punishment is death or the offence of treason. They have appellate jurisdiction from decisions of any District Court situated within their respective circuits.

District Courts: To each magisterial district is assigned at least one District Magistrate who has original jurisdiction to try civil suits in which the amount involved does not exceed five Ghana cedis. District Magistrates also have jurisdiction to deal with all criminal cases, except first-degree felonies, and commit cases of a more serious nature to either the Circuit Court or the High Court. A Grade I District Court can impose fines and sentences of imprisonment of up to two years, and a Grade II District Court may impose fines and a sentence of imprisonment of up to 12 months. A District Court has no appellate jurisdiction, except in rent matters under the Rent Act.

Juvenile Courts: Jurisdiction in cases involving persons under 17 years of age, except where the juvenile is charged jointly with an adult. The Courts comprise a Chairman, who must be either the District Magistrate or a lawyer, and not fewer than two other members appointed by the Chief Justice in consultation with the Judicial Council. The Juvenile Courts can make orders as to the protection and supervision of a neglected child and can negotiate with parents to secure the good behaviour of a child.

National Public Tribunal: Considers appeals from the Regional Public Tribunals. Its decisions are final and are not subject to any

further appeal. The Tribunal consists of at least three members and not more than five, one of whom acts as Chairman.

Regional Public Tribunals: Hear criminal cases relating to prices, rent or exchange control, theft, fraud, forgery, corruption or any offence that may be referred to them by the Provisional National Defence Council.

Special Military Tribunal: Hears criminal cases involving members of the armed forces. It consists of between five and seven members.

Attorney-General: GODFRED YEBOAH DAME.

Religion

According to the 2010 census, 71.2% of the population were Christians and 17.6% were Muslims, while 5.2% followed indigenous beliefs and 5.3% did not profess any religion.

CHRISTIANITY

Christian Council of Ghana: Awula Kpakpa St, Osu, POB GP 919, Accra; tel. (30) 2776678; e-mail info@christiancouncilofghana.org; internet www.christiancouncilofghana.org; f. 1929; advisory body comprising 16 mem. churches and 2 affiliate Christian orgs (2005); Chair. Rev. Dr ERNEST ADU-GYAMFI; Gen. Sec. Rev. Dr CYRIL FAYOSE.

Ghana Pentecostal and Charismatic Council: Otenshie, East Legon, POB CT 483, Accra; tel. (30) 2522226; e-mail info@gpccghana.org; internet www.gpccghana.org; f. 1969; Pres. Rev. Prof. PAUL FRIMPONG–MANSO; Gen. Sec. Rev. EMMANUEL T. BARRIGAH.

The Anglican Communion

Anglicans in Ghana are adherents of the Church of the Province of West Africa, comprising 16 dioceses and a missionary region, of which 11 are in Ghana. In 2012 two internal provinces were created within the Province of West Africa, one for Ghana and the other for West Africa. The Archbishop of the Anglican Church of Ghana is the Bishop of Asante-Mampong.

Primate of the Church of the Province of West Africa and Bishop of Liberia: Rt Rev. Dr JONATHAN BAU-BAU BONAPARTE HART, POB 10-0277, 1000 Monrovia 10; tel. 886516343; e-mail bishop@liberia.net.

Bishop of Accra: Rt Rev. Dr DANIEL SYLVANUS MENSAH TORTO, Bishopscourt, POB 8, Accra; tel. (30) 2662292; e-mail dantorto@yahoo.com.

Bishop of Asante-Mampong and Archbishop of the Anglican Church of Ghana: Rt Revd Dr CYRIL BEN-SMITH, Bishopscourt, St Michael's Ave, POB 220, Mampong; tel. (24) 4774308; e-mail bishop.mampong@yahoo.co.uk; internet dioceseofmampong.weebly.com.

Bishop of Cape Coast: Rt Rev. Dr VICTOR ATTA-BAFFOE, Bishopscourt, POB A233, Adisadel Estates, Cape Coast; tel. (33) 2132502; e-mail victorattabaffoe@yahoo.com; internet capecoast.anglican.org.

Bishop of Dunkwa-on-Offin: Rt Rev. PAUL APPIAH SEKYERE, POB DW 42, Dunkwa-on-Offin; tel. (24) 4464764.

Bishop of Ho: Rt Rev. MATTHIAS MEDADUES-BADOHU, Bishopslodge, POB MA 300, Ho; tel. (20) 8162246; e-mail matthiaskwab@gmail.com.

Bishop of Koforidua: Rt Rev. FELIX ODEI ANNANCY, POB 980, Koforidua; tel. (26) 6819414; e-mail angdiokof@koforiduaanglicandioce.org.

Bishop of Kumasi: Rt Rev. OSCAR CHRISTIAN AMOAH, Bishop's Office, 1987 St Cyprian St, Kumasi; tel. (20) 8318003; e-mail info@kumasianglican.org.

Bishop of Sekondi: Rt Rev. ALEXANDER KOBINA ASMAH, POB 85, Sekondi; tel. (20) 8378295; e-mail alexasmah@yahoo.com; internet anglicandioceseofsekondi.org.

Bishop of Sunyani: Rt Rev. Dr FESTUS YEBOAH-ASUAMAH, Bishop's House, POB 23, Sunyani, BA; tel. (20) 8124378; e-mail fyasuamah@yahoo.com.

Bishop of Tamale: Rt Rev. DENNIS TONG, POB 110, Tamale NR; tel. (24) 4179092; e-mail revtong@gmail.com.

Bishop of Wiawso: Rt Rev. ABRAHAM KOBINA ACKAH, POB 4, Sefwi, Wiawso; tel. (20) 8161826; e-mail bishopackah@yahoo.com.

The Roman Catholic Church

Ghana comprises four archdioceses, 15 dioceses and one apostolic vicariate. Some 13% of the total population are Roman Catholics.

Ghana Catholic Bishops' Conference: National Catholic Secretariat, POB 9712, Airport, Accra; tel. (30) 2500491; e-mail dscncs@africaonline.com.gh; internet www.cbcgha.org; f. 1960; Pres. Most Rev. PHILIP NAAMEH (Archbishop of Tamale).

Archbishop of Accra: Most Rev. JOHN BONAVENTURE KWOFIE, Chancery Office, POB 247, Accra; tel. (30) 2222728; e-mail accrachancery@gmail.com; internet accracatholic.org.

Archbishop of Cape Coast: Most Rev. GABRIEL CHARLES PALMER-BUCKLE, Archbishop's House, POB 112, Cape Coast; tel. (33) 2133471; e-mail archcape@ghanacbc.com.

Archbishop of Kumasi: Most Rev. GABRIEL JUSTICE YAW ANOKYE, POB 99, Kumasi; tel. (32) 2024012; e-mail cadiokum@ghana.com.

Archbishop of Tamale: Most Rev. PHILIP NAAMEH, Archbishop's House, Gumbehini Rd, POB 42, Tamale; tel. (37) 2022425; e-mail tamdio2@yahoo.co.uk.

Other Christian Churches

African Methodist Episcopal Zion Church: POB MP 522, Mamprobi, Accra; tel. (30) 2669200; f. 1898; Pres. Rt Rev. SETH O. LARTEY.

Christian Methodist Episcopal Church: POB AN 7639, Accra; tel. 244630267; Pres. KENNETH W. CARTER; Mission Supervisor Rev. ADJEI K. LAWSON.

Church of Pentecost: Gbeshigon St, POB 2194, Accra; tel. (30) 2777611; e-mail info@thecophq.org; internet www.thecophq.org; Chair. Apostle ERIC NYAMEKE; Gen. Sec. Apostle ALEXANDER NANA YAW KUMI-LARBI.

Evangelical-Lutheran Church of Ghana: POB KN197, Kaneshie, Accra; tel. 240676041; e-mail elcga@africaonline.com.gh; Pres. Rev. JOHN SHADRACK DONKOH.

Evangelical-Presbyterian Church of Ghana: 19 Main St, Tesano, PMB, Accra-North; tel. (30) 2220381; e-mail epchurch@ghana.com; f. 1847; Moderator Rt Rev. Dr Lt-Col BLISS DIVINE KOFI AGBEKO.

Ghana Baptist Convention: The Baptist House, 11 Yiyiwa Dr., Abelenkpe, POB AN 19909, Accra-North; tel. (30) 2769417; e-mail info@gbconvention.com; internet gbconvention.com; f. 1963; Exec. Pres. Rev. Dr ERNEST ADU-GYAMFI.

Ghana Mennonite Church: POB 5485, Accra; f. 1957; Moderator Rev. EMMANUEL GALBAH-NUSETOR; Sec. JOHN ADETA.

Methodist Church of Ghana: Wesley House, E252/2, Liberia Rd, POB 403, Accra; tel. (30) 2670355; e-mail mcghqs@ucomgh.com; Presiding Bishop Most Rev. Dr PAUL KWABENA BOAFO.

Presbyterian Church of Ghana: Osu-Kuku Hill, POB 1800, Accra; tel. (30) 2664761; e-mail info@pcgonline.org; internet www.pcgonline.org; f. 1828; Moderator Rt. Rev. Prof. JOSEPH OBIRI YEBOAH MANTE; Clerk Rev. Dr GODWIN NII NOI ODONKOR.

Southern Ghana Union Conference of Seventh-day Adventists: Gamel Abdul Nasser Ave, POB GP 1016, Accra; tel. (30) 2223720; e-mail info@adventistgh.org; internet www.adventistgh.org; f. 1943; Pres. Pastor THOMAS TECHIE OCRAN; Sec. Pastor CHRIS ANNAN-NUNOO.

The African Methodist Episcopal Church, the Christ Reformed Church, the F'Eden Church, the Gospel Revival Church of God, the Religious Society of Friends (Quakers) and the Society of the Divine Word are also active in Ghana.

ISLAM

According to the 2010 census, Muslims had a particularly large concentration in the Northern region, comprising some 60% of its population. The majority are Malikees.

Coalition of Muslim Organizations (COMOG): Accra; Pres. Dr HUSSEIN ZAKARIAH; Gen. Sec. Hajj ABDEL MANAN ABDEL RAHMAN.

Ghana Muslims Representative Council: 31/1 Columbia Rd, POB 1180, Sekondi-Takoradi; tel. (31) 2026094.

Chief Imam: Sheikh USMAN NUHU SHARABUTU.

BAHÁ'Í FAITH

National Spiritual Assembly: POB AN 7098, Accra-North; tel. (30) 2222127; e-mail bahaighana@yahoo.com; Sec. KOBINA AMISSAH-FYNN.

The Press

DAILY NEWSPAPERS (PRINT AND ONLINE)

The Daily Dispatch: 1 Dade Walk, North Labone, PMB CCC 17, Cantonments, Accra; tel. (30) 2763339; e-mail thedailydispatchgh@gmail.com; internet thedailydispatchgh.com; Editor BEN EPHSON.

Daily Graphic: Graphic Communications Group Ltd, 3 Graphic Rd, POB 742, Accra; tel. (30) 2684001; e-mail info@graphic.com.gh; internet graphic.com.gh; f. 1950; state-owned; Editor VINCENT KOBINA ASHAM.

Daily Guide: POB 115, Accra; tel. (30) 2229576; e-mail dailyguidenews@yahoo.com; internet dailyguideghana.com; owned by Western Publications Ltd; Editor FORTUNE ALIMI.

The Daily Statesman: House No. 359/4, Faanofa Rd, Kokomlemle, Accra; tel. 244217504; e-mail editor@thestatesmanonline.com; internet www.thestatesmanonline.com; f. 1949; official publ. of the New Patriotic Party; Editor-in-Chief ASARE OTCHERE-DARKO; Editor KWABENA AMANKWAH.

Ghanaian Chronicle: 37 Lomoko St, Abeka, Accra-North; tel. (20) 8167110; internet thechronicle.com.gh; Editor EMMANUEL AKLI.

The Ghanaian Times: New Times Corpn, Ring Rd West, POB 2638, Accra; tel. (30) 2223285; e-mail info@ghanaiantimes.com.gh; internet www.ghanaiantimes.com.gh; f. 1958; state-owned; Editor DAVID AGBENU.

The Mail: POB CT 4910, Cantonments, Accra; e-mail mike@accra-mail.com; Editor Alhaji ABDUL RAHMAN HARUNA ATTAH.

Modern Ghana: POB DT 2235, Adentan, Accra; tel. 559000181; e-mail info@modernghana.com; internet www.modernghana.com; f. 2005; Online-only; Editor EMMANUEL AJARFOR.

PERIODICALS

Thrice-weekly

The Independent: 22 St John's Rd, Achimota, POB TN 99, Accra; tel. 570019020; e-mail independentghana@gmail.com; internet theindependentghana.com; f. 1989; Editor FIIFI MENSAH.

Network Herald: 34 Crescent Rd, Labone, Accra; tel. (30) 2701184; e-mail support@ghana.com; internet www.networkherald.gh; f. 2001; Editor ELVIS QUARSHIE.

Bi-weekly

The Ghanaian Lens: Accra; Editor KOBBY FIAGBE.

Weekly

Business and Financial Times: PMB CT 16, Cantonments, Accra; tel. (30) 2785869; e-mail info@thebftonline.com; internet www.thebftonline.com; f. 1989; 5 a week; Editor WILLIAM SELASSY ADJADOGO.

The Catholic Standard: Standard Newspapers & Magazines Ltd, POB KA 9712, Accra; tel. (30) 2424725; e-mail catholicstandard75@gmail.com; internet www.cathstandardgh.com; Roman Catholic; Editor ISAAC FRITZ ANDOH.

The Crusading Guide: Kofi Baako's Residence, North Labone Estates, POB 8523, Accra-North; tel. (30) 2770361; e-mail info@thenewcrusadingguideonline.com; internet thenewcrusadingguideonline.com; Editor KWEKU BAAKO, Jr.

Graphic Showbiz: Graphic Communications Group Ltd, 3 Graphic Rd, POB 742, Accra; tel. (30) 2684001; e-mail info@graphic.com.gh; internet www.graphic.com.gh; f. 2000; state-owned.

Graphic Sports: Graphic Communications Group Ltd, POB 742, Accra; tel. (30) 2228911; e-mail info@graphicghana.com; internet www.graphic.com.gh/graphicsports; state-owned; Editor FELIX ABAYATEYE.

The Mirror: Graphic Communications Group Ltd, POB 742, Accra; tel. (30) 2684001; e-mail mirror@graphic.com.gh; internet www.graphic.com.gh/mirror; f. 1953; state-owned; Sat.

The National Democrat: Democrat Publications, POB 13605, Accra; Editor ELLIOT FELIX OHENE.

Other

AGI Newsletter: c/o Asscn of Ghana Industries, POB 8624, Accra-North; tel. (30) 2779023; e-mail agi@agighana.org; internet www.agighana.org; f. 1974; monthly; Editor CARLO HEY.

Business World: Ghana House, 6th Floor, Accra; tel. 545553535; Editor-in-Chief EMMANUEL KWABLAH.

Ghana Review International (GRi): POB GP 14307, Accra; tel. (30) 2677437; e-mail accra@ghanareview.com; internet www.ghanareview.com; publishes in Accra, London (UK) and New York (USA); CEO NANA OTUO ACHEAMPONG.

The Watchman: Watchman Gospel Ministry, POB GP 4521, Accra; tel. (24) 3780716; e-mail watchmannewspaper@yahoo.com; f. 1986; Christian news; monthly; Pres. and CEO DIVINE P. KUMAH; Chair. Dr E. K. OPUNI.

REGULATORY AUTHORITY

National Media Commission (NMC): Gamel Abdul Nasser Ave, POB SD 114, Accra; tel. (30) 2662409; e-mail info@nmc.org.gh; internet fb.com/national.media.commission.ghana; Exec. Sec. GEORGE SARPONG.

NEWS AGENCIES

Ghana News Agency (GNA): POB 2118, Accra; tel. (30) 2662381; e-mail ghnews@ghana.com; internet www.gna.org.gh; f. 1957; Gen. Man. ALBERT KOFI OWUSU; 10 regional offices and 110 district offices.

PRESS ASSOCIATIONS

Ghana Journalists' Association: Press Centre, Abdul Nasser Ave, Ringway Estates, POB 4636, Accra; tel. (30) 2234694; e-mail info@gjaghana.org; internet gjaghana.org; Pres. ROLAND AFFAIL MONNEY; Gen. Sec. KOFI YEBOAH.

Publishers

Advent Press: Labadi Rd, POB 0102, Osu, Accra; tel. (30) 3930696; e-mail info@theadventpress.com; internet theadventpress.com; f. 1937; publishing arm of the Ghana Union Conference of Seventh-day Adventists; Gen. Man. KINGSLEY OSEI.

Adwinsa Publications (Ghana) Ltd: 17 Suncity Rd, Agbogba North Legon, POB 92, Legon, Accra; tel. (24) 2366537; e-mail adwinsa@yahoo.com; internet www.fb.com/pages/category/Media-News-Company/Adwinsa-Publications-Ghana-Limited-1665297323726050; f. 1977; general printing, educational materials, supplementary readers; Man. Dir KWAKU OPPONG AMPONSAH.

Afram Publications: C 184/22 Midway Lane, Abofu-Achimota, POB M 18, Accra; tel. (30) 4314103; e-mail info@aframpubghana.com; internet aframpubghana.com; f. 1973; textbooks and general; Chair. Prof. ESI SUTHERLAND ADDY; Man. Dir HARRIET TAGOE.

Asempa Publishers: Plot No. 8, 13th Street Close, Atomic Gate, Haatso, POB GP919, Accra; tel. 261602575; e-mail info@asempapublishers.com; internet asempapublishers.com; f. 1970; religion, social issues, African music, fiction, children's; Gen. Man. EMMANUEL AMOO.

Ghana Universities Press: POB GP 4219, Accra; tel. (30) 2513401; f. 1962; scholarly, academic and general and textbooks; CEO Dr JOHN K. BOSOMTWE (acting).

Sam-Woode Ltd: A979/15 1st Adoley Link, Sahara-Dansoma, POB 12719, Accra-North; tel. (30) 2305287; e-mail info@samwoode.com; internet samwoode.com; f. 1984; educational and children's; Chair. KWESI SAM-WOODE; Man. Dir KOJO E. SAM-WOODE.

Smartline (Publishing) Ltd: C3 Coastal Estates, DTD Batsonaa, Spintex Rd, Accra; tel. (30) 2810555; e-mail info@smartlinepublishers.com; internet smartlinepublishers.com; f. 1997; CEO ELLIOT AGYARE.

Sub-Saharan Publishers: POB 358, Legon, Accra; tel. (30) 2233371; e-mail info@subsaharanpublishers.com; internet www.subsaharanpublishers.com; Man. Dir AKOSS OFORI-MENSAH.

Waterville Publishing House: 101 Miamona Cl., South Industrial Area, POB 195, Accra; tel. (30) 2689973; f. 1963; general fiction and non-fiction, textbooks, paperbacks, Africana; Man. Dir EMMANUEL AMOH.

Woeli Publishing Services: 19 ECOWAS Rd, POB NT 601, Accra New Town; tel. (30) 289535570; e-mail woeli@woelipublishing.com; internet www.woelipublishing.com; f. 1984; children's, fiction, academic; Dir WOELI A. DEKUTSEY.

PUBLISHERS' ASSOCIATIONS

Ghana Book Development Council (GBDC): Ground Floor, NABPTEX Bldg, Tertiary Education Complex, Bawaleshie Traffic, Trinity College Rd, Okponglo, East Legon, POB M 430, Accra; tel. (30) 3936871; e-mail gbdc.moe@gmail.com; internet www.gbdc.gov.gh; f. 1975; govt-financed agency; promotes and co-ordinates writing, production and distribution of books; Exec. Dir ERNESTICIA LARTEY ASUINURA.

Ghana Publishers' Association (GPA): POB LT 471, Laterbiokorshie, Accra; tel. (30) 2912764; e-mail info@ghanabookpublishers.org; internet www.ghanabookpublishers.org; f. 1976; Pres. ASARE KONADU YAMOAH.

Broadcasting and Communications

REGULATORY AUTHORITY

National Communications Authority (NCA): 6 Airport City, KIA, POB 1568, Cantonments, Accra; tel. (30) 2776621; e-mail info@nca.org.gh; internet nca.org.gh; f. 1996; regulatory body; Chair. ISAAC EMMIL OSEI-BONSU; Dir-Gen. JOE ANOKYE.

TELECOMMUNICATIONS

AirtelTigo: Ghana Barnes Rd, Accra; e-mail info@airteltigo.com.gh; internet www.airteltigo.com.gh; f. 2008; provides both mobile and fixed-line telephone services; Man. Dir (vacant); 3,489 fixed-line and 7.9m. mobile subscribers (June 2021).

Glo Mobile Ghana: 19 Spintex Rd, opp. Furniture City, Accra; tel. 230010100; e-mail customercare@glomobileghana.com; internet www.gloworld.com/gh; Head of Business HARDEEP KHETERPAL; 814,475 subscribers (June 2021).

MTN Ghana: Plot OER 6, Independence Ave, Accra; tel. 244300000; e-mail customercare@mtn.com.gh; internet mtn.com.gh; f. 1994; Ghana's largest mobile telephone provider, through the network MTN (fmrly Areeba); 100% owned by MTN (South Africa); CEO SELORM ADADEVOH; 4,093 fixed-line and 23.5m. subscribers (June 2021).

Vodafone Ghana: Airport Bypass Rd, Accra; tel. 501000300; e-mail info.gh@vodafone.com; internet vodafone.com.gh; f. 1995; present name adopted in 2008, following acquisition of 70% shares in Ghana Telecommunications Company (GT) by Vodafone Group PLC (UK), 30% govt-owned; operates mobile, fixed-line networks and data services; CEO PATRICIA OBO-NAI; 307,585 fixed-line and 9.4m. mobile subscribers (June 2021).

BROADCASTING

There are internal radio broadcasts in English, Akan, Dagbani, Ewe, Ga, Hausa and Nzema, and an external service in English and French. There are three transmitting stations, with a number of relay stations. The Ghana Broadcasting Corporation operates two national networks, Radio 1 and Radio 2, which broadcast from Accra, and four regional FM stations. In December 2018 there were 136 authorized television stations and 398 FM radio stations operating in Ghana. The Government intended to switch off the analogue television signal and replace it with digital broadcasting throughout the country in 2020, but the transition was delayed as a result of the coronavirus pandemic.

Ghana Broadcasting Corpn (GBC): Broadcasting House, Ring Rd Central, Kanda, POB 1633, Accra; tel. (30) 2771245; e-mail info@gbcghana.com; internet www.gbcghana.com; f. 1935; 4 digital channels launched in 2014; Dir-Gen. Prof. AMIN ALHASSAN; Chair. EMMANUEL ADOW OBENG.

CitiFM: 11 Tettey Loop, Adabraka, Accra; tel. (30) 2226013; e-mail info@citifmonline.com; internet citifmonline.com; f. 2004; Man. Dir SAMUEL ATTA MENSAH.

Joy FM: 355 Faanofa St, Kokomlemle, Accra; tel. (30) 2233558; e-mail info@myjoyonline.com; internet www.myjoyonline.com; f. 1995; news, information and music broadcasts; Dir KWESI TWUM.

Live FM: opp. Premier Betting, Adabraka, Accra; tel. 595919919; e-mail livefmghanaofficial@gmail.com; internet fb.com/Livextragh; educational.

Metro TV: 59 Josiah Tongogara St, North Labone, POB C 1609, Cantonments, Accra; tel. (30) 2765701; e-mail admin@metroworld.tv; internet mymetrotv.tv; Chair. KWADWO DABO FRIMPONG; Man. Dir KAYODE AKINTEMI.

Radio Ada: POB KA9482, Accra; tel. (20) 1427760; e-mail radioada@kalssinn.net; internet fb.com/RadioAda; f. 1998; community broadcasts in Dangme; Dirs ALEX QUARMYNE, WILNA QUARMYNE.

Sky Broadcasting Co Ltd: 45 Water Rd, Kanda Overpass, North Ridge, POB CT 3850, Cantonments, Accra; tel. (30) 2225716; e-mail vayiku@yahoo.com; internet www.spirit.fm; f. 2000; Gen. Man. STEVE ESHUN.

TV3: 12th Rd, Kanda (opp. French embassy), Accra; tel. (30) 2763458; e-mail tv3netghana@gmail.com; internet 3news.com; f. 1997; private television station; programming in English and local languages; CEO BEATRICE AGYEMANG ABBEY.

Finance

BANKING

Central Bank

Bank of Ghana: 1 Thorpe Rd, POB 2674, Accra; tel. (30) 2666174; e-mail bogsecretary@bog.gov.gh; internet www.bog.gov.gh; f. 1957; bank of issue; Gov. Dr ERNEST KWAMINA YEDU ADDISON.

Banks

At April 2022 there were 23 banks operating in the country.

Absa Bank Ghana Ltd (UK): Absa House, John Evans Atta Mills High St, POB 2949, Accra; tel. (30) 2429150; e-mail service.excellence.GH@absa.africa; internet www.absa.com.gh; f. 1971; fmrly Barclays Bank of Ghana Ltd; name changed as above in 2020; owned by Absa Group Ltd; Man. Dir ABENA OSEI-POKU.

Access Bank Ghana PLC: Starlets' 91 Rd, POB GP353, Accra; tel. (30) 2661769; e-mail info@ghana.accessbankplc.com; internet www.ghana.accessbankplc.com; f. 2009; Chair. AMA SARPONG BAWUAH; Man. Dir ABENA OSEI-POKU.

Agricultural Development Bank (ADB): Accra Financial Centre, 3rd Ambassadorial Development Area, POB 4191, Accra; tel. (30) 2770403; e-mail customercare@agricbank.com; internet www.agricbank.com; f. 1965; 60.5% owned by Financial Investment Trust, 32.3% owned by the Government of Ghana and 7.2% owned by retail investors and ADB staff; credit facilities for farmers and commercial banking; Chair. ALEX BERNASKO, IV; Man. Dir Dr JOHN KOFI MENSAH.

Bank of Africa (Ghana) Ltd: The Octagon, Block A&B, 1st Floor, Independence Ave, Cantonments, POB C 1541, Accra; tel. (30) 2249690; e-mail enquiries@boaghana.com; internet www.boaghana.com; f. 1997; fmrly Amalgamated Bank Ltd, present name adopted 2011; Man. Dir KOBBY ANDAH.

CAL Bank Ltd: 23 Independence Ave, POB 14596, Accra; tel. (30) 2680062; e-mail info@calbank.net; internet calbank.net; f. 1990; Chair. PAAROCK VANPERCY; CEO and Man. Dir PHILIP OWIREDU.

Consolidated Bank Ghana Ltd: Manet Tower 3, South Liberation Link, Airport, POB CT363, Accra; tel. (30) 2216000; e-mail talktous@cbg.com.gh; internet www.cbg.com.gh; f. 2018; Chair. NANA ABRA-APPIAH; CEO DANIEL WILSON ADDO.

Ecobank Ghana Ltd (EBG): 2 Morocco Lane, off Independence Ave, POB 16746, Accra; tel. (30) 2681146; e-mail ecobankenquiries@ecobank.com; internet www.ecobank.com; f. 1989; 92.2% owned by Ecobank Transnational Inc (Togo, operating under the auspices of the Economic Community of West African States); merged with The Trust Bank Ltd June 2012; Chair. TERENCE RONALD DARKO; Man. Dir DANIEL KWEI-KUMAH SACKEY.

FBN Bank Ghana Ltd: Plot Nos 6, 7 and 9, Liberation Rd, PMB 16, Accra; tel. (30) 2236133; e-mail fbn@fbnbankghana.com; internet www.fbnbankghana.com; f. 1996; fmrly International Commercial Bank (Ghana) Ltd, name changed as above in 2014; Chair. JOSEPH YIELEH CHIREH; Man. Dir and CEO VICTOR YAW ASANTE.

Fidelity Bank: Ridge Towers, PMB 43, Cantonments, Accra; tel. (30) 2214490; e-mail wecare@myfidelitybank.net; internet www.fidelitybank.com.gh; f. 2006; Chair. EDWARD EFFAH; Man. Dir JULIAN OPUNI.

First Atlantic Bank Ltd: Atlantic Pl., 1 Seventh Ave, Ridge West, POB C 1620, Cantonments, Accra; tel. (30) 2682203; e-mail info@firstatlanticbank.com.gh; internet www.firstatlanticbank.com.gh; f. 1994; Chair. AMARQUAYE ARMAR; Man. Dir ODUN ODUNFA.

First National Bank Ghana Ltd: Accra Financial Centre, 6th Floor, cnr Independence and Liberia Aves, Ridge, POB TU23, Accra; tel. (30) 2435050; e-mail info@firstnationalbank.com.gh; internet www.firstnationalbank.com.gh; a subsidiary of FirstRand Group; CEO DOMINIC ADU.

GCB Bank Ltd: Thorpe Rd, POB 134, Accra; tel. (30) 2663964; e-mail customerservice@gcb.com.gh; internet www.gcbbank.com.gh; f. 1953; 21.4% state-owned; Chair. JUDE ARTHUR; Man. Dir ANSELM RAYMOND SOWAH.

Guaranty Trust Bank (Ghana) Ltd: 25A Castle Rd, Ambassadorial Area Ridge, PMB CT416, Accra; tel. (30) 2611560; e-mail gh.corporateaffairs@gtbank.com; internet www.gtbghana.com; f. 2004; 70% owned by Guaranty Trust Bank PLC, 15% owned by Netherlands Development Finance Co (FMO), 15% owned by Alhaji Yusif Ibrahim; Chair. KWASI MBOUMBA TAGBOR; Man. Dir THOMAS ATTAH JOHN.

National Investment Bank Ltd (NIB): 37 Kwame Nkrumah Ave, POB 3726, Accra; tel. (30) 2661701; e-mail info@nib-ghana.com; internet www.nib-ghana.com; f. 1963; 86.4% state-owned; Chair. (vacant); Man. Dir SAMUEL SARPONG.

OmniBSIC Bank Ghana: C9/14 Olusegun, Obasanjo Way, Dzorwulu, POB KN 5569, Kaneshie, Accra; tel. (30) 7086000; e-mail info@omnibank.com.gh; internet www.omnibank.com.gh; f. 2018; Man. Dir PHILIP OTI-MENSAH.

Prudential Bank Ltd: 8 John Harmond St, Ring Rd Central, PMB GPO, Accra; tel. (30) 2781201; e-mail headoffice@prudentialbank.com.gh; internet www.prudentialbank.com.gh; f. 1996; Chair. MURIEL SUSAN EDUSEI; Man. Dir JOHN KPAKPO ADDO.

Republic Bank: 35 Sixth Ave, North Ridge, POB CT4603, Cantonments, Accra; tel. (30) 2242090; e-mail email@republicghana.com; internet www.republicghana.com; f. 1990 as HFC Bank Ghana Ltd; present name adopted in 2018; a subsidiary of Republic Financial Holdings Ltd (Trinidad and Tobago); Chair. CHARLES WILLIAM ZWENNES; Man. Dir BENJAMIN DZOBOKU.

Société Générale Ghana Ltd: Ring Rd Central, POB 13119, Accra; tel. (30) 2202001; e-mail sgghana.info@socgen.com; internet www.societegenerale.com.gh; f. 1976 as Social Security Bank; 51.0% owned by Société Générale, France; Chair. KOFI AMPIM; Man. Dir HAKIM OUZZANI.

Stanbic Bank Ghana: Stanbic Heights, 25 Liberation Link, Airport City, POB CT 2344, Cantonments, Accra; tel. (30) 2687670; e-mail customercare@stanbic.com.gh; internet www.stanbicbank.com.gh; f. 1999; subsidiary of Standard Bank of South Africa Ltd; Man. Dir KWAMINA ASOMANING.

Standard Chartered Bank Ghana Ltd (UK): Head Office Bldg, Ground Floor, 87 Independence Ave, POB 768, Accra; tel. (30) 2664591; e-mail feedback.ghana@sc.com; internet www.sc.com/gh; f. 1896 as Bank of British West Africa; Country CEO MANSA NETTEY.

United Bank for Africa (Ghana) Ltd: Heritage Tower, Ambassadorial Enclave, off Liberia Rd, Ridge, PMB 29, Accra; tel. (30) 2634060; e-mail cfcghana@ubagroup.com; internet www.ubaghana.com; f. 2004; Chair. KWEKU ANDOH AWOTWI; Man. Dir and CEO OLALEKAN BALOGUN.

Universal Merchant Bank (Ghana) Ltd: Airport City, SSNIT Emporium, Liberation Rd, POB 401, Accra; tel. (30) 2666331; e-mail info@myumbbank.com; internet www.myumbbank.com; f. 1972; fmrly Merchant Bank (Ghana) Ltd; present name adopted 2014; Chair. RAS A. BOATENG; Man. Dir and CEO BENJAMIN AMENUMEY.

Zenith Bank Ghana Ltd (Nigeria): Zenith Heights, 31 Independence Ave, PMB CT 393, Accra; tel. (30) 2611500; e-mail info@zenithbank.com.gh; internet www.zenithbank.com.gh; Chair. FREDA YAHAN DUPLAN; Man. Dir and CEO HENRY CHINEDU ONWUZURIGBO.

Banking Association

Ghana Association of Bankers (GAB): Accra Financial Centre, 5th Floor, 3rd Ambassadorial Development Area, Liberia Rd, Ridge, POB 41, Accra; tel. (30) 2667138; e-mail info@gab.com.gh; internet gab.com.gh; f. 1980; Pres. MANSA NETTEY; CEO JOHN AWUAH.

STOCK EXCHANGE

Ghana Stock Exchange (GSE): Cedi House, 5th Floor, Liberia Rd, POB 1849, Accra; tel. (30) 2669908; e-mail info@gse.com.gh; internet www.gse.com.gh; f. 1990; 42 listed cos at Sept. 2018; Chair. Dr ALBERT ESSIEN; Man. Dir EKOW AFEDZIE.

INSURANCE

Donewell Life Co: 22 Josip Broz Tito Ave, Cantonments, POB GP 3958, Accra; tel. (30) 2772778; e-mail info@donewelllife.com.gh; internet donewelllife.com.gh; f. 2008; life insurance; owned by Pinnacle Equity Investments Ltd; Chair. SAMUEL KWAKU OWUSU-MANU; Man. Dir ERIC ATO BOTCHWAY.

Enterprise Insurance Co Ltd: Enterprise House, 11 John Evans Atta Mills High St, POB GP 50, Accra; tel. (30) 2634777; e-mail info@enterprisegroup.com.gh; internet enterprisegroup.net.gh; f. 1972; Chair. TREVOR TREFGARNE; Group CEO KELI GADZEKPO.

ESICH Life Assurance Co Ltd: C939/3, 2nd Ridge Link, North Ridge Residential Area, POB CT 8309, Cantonments, Accra; tel. (30) 2201980; e-mail info@esichlife.com; internet www.esichlife.com; f. 2013; life insurance; Chair. Dr KWADWO AYISI-AHWIRENG; CEO RICHARD ADU-MARFO.

Ghana Life Insurance Co: House No. 17, Aviation Rd, Airport Residential Area, POB 8168, Accra; tel. (30) 2771298; e-mail info@ghanalifeinsurance.com.gh; internet www.ghanalifeinsurance.com.gh; f. 1980; Chair. Eng. Chief CYRIL U. O. AJAGU; Man. Dir and CEO SHERIFF ABUDU.

Ghana Union Assurance Co Ltd: F828/1 Ring Rd East, POB 1322, Accra; tel. (30) 2780627; e-mail gua@ghanaunionassurance.com; internet ghanaunionassurance.com; f. 1973; insurance underwriting; Chair. NANA AGYEI DUKU; Man. Dir ARETHA DUKU.

Metropolitan Life Insurance Co Ltd: Metropolitan House, 81 Tabon Link, North Ridge Cres., PMB CT456, Cantonments, Accra; tel. (30) 2633933; e-mail met@metinsurance.com; internet www.metropolitan.com.gh; f. 1991; Chair. CHARLES AKUN EGAN; CEO TAWIAH BEN-AHMED.

Phoenix Life Assurance Co: House No. 244/3, 6th Ringway Estates, POB 17753, Kanda Highway, Accra; tel. (30) 2246319; e-mail info@phoenixinsurancegh.com; internet www.phoenixinsurancegh.com; Chair. D. K. D. LETSA; Man. Dir HENRY BUKARI.

Saham Life Insurance Ghana Ltd: Sethi Plaza, 4th Floor, Kwame Nkrumah Ave, POB AD 190, Accra; tel. (30) 2224299; e-mail sahamlife.gh@sahaminsurance.com; internet www.sahaminsurance.com.gh; CEO GIFTY AMA FIAGBE-ALABI.

SIC Insurance Co Ltd: 28/29 Ring Rd East, Osu, POB 2363, Accra; tel. (30) 2780600; e-mail sicinfo@sic-gh.com; internet www.sic-gh.com; f. 1962; 60% state-owned; all classes of insurance; Chair. Dr JIMMY HEYMANN; Man. Dir STEPHEN ODURO.

Social Security and National Insurance Trust (SSNIT): Pension House, POB MB 149, Accra; tel. (30) 2611622; e-mail contactcentre@ssnit.org.gh; internet www.ssnit.org.gh; f. 1972; Chair. ELIZABETH AKUA OHENE; Dir-Gen. Dr JOHN OFORI-TENKORANG.

Star Assurance Group Ltd: 1 Mankata Ave, Airport Residential Area, POB AN 5783, Accra; tel. (30) 2739605; e-mail info@starlife.com.gh; f. 2020; formed through merger of Star Assurance Co Ltd, StarLife Assurance Co Ltd (f. 2005) and Star Microinsurance Co Ltd; Chief Exec. KOFI DUFFUOR.

Vanguard Assurance Co Ltd: 25 Independence Ave, POB 1868, Accra; tel. (30) 2666485; e-mail vacmails@vanguardassurance.com; internet www.vanguardassurance.com; f. 1974; foreign travel, general accident, marine, motor and life insurance; Chair. DANIEL AWUAH-DARKO; CEO FREDERICK ADOTEY SAKA.

Regulatory Authority

National Insurance Commission: Insurance Pl., 67 Independence Ave, POB CT 3456, Cantonments, Accra; tel. (30) 2238300; e-mail info@nicgh.org; internet www.nicgh.org; f. 1989; Chair. EMMANUEL RAY ANKRAH; Commr of Insurance JUSTICE YAW OFORI.

Insurance Association

Ghana Insurers Association (GIA): 248/9 Kanda, Sunyani Ave, Accra; tel. (30) 2251091; e-mail info@ghanainsurers.org.gh; internet ghanainsurers.org.gh; f. 1988; Pres. SETH KOBLA AKLASI; CEO KINGSLEY KWESI KWABAHSON.

Trade and Industry

GOVERNMENT AGENCIES

Environmental Protection Agency (EPA): POB M 326, Accra; tel. (30) 2664697; e-mail info@epa.gov.gh; internet www.epa.gov.gh; f. 1974; Chair. KWESI ENYAN; Exec. Dir HENRY KOKOFU.

Forestry Commission of Ghana (FC): 4 Third Ave, Ridge, POB MB 434, Accra; tel. (30) 2401210; e-mail info@hq.fcghana.com; internet www.fcghana.org; CEO JOHN ALLOTEY.

Ghana Enterprises Agency (GEA): 4 Abdul Gamel Nasser Ave, Ridge, POB M85, Accra; tel. (36) 2196909; e-mail info@gea.gov.gh; internet gea.gov.gh; f. 1985 as the National Board for Small-scale Industries; name changed as above in 2020; part of Ministry of Trade and Industry; promotes and supports micro, small and medium-scale enterprises; Exec. Dir KOSI ANTWIWAA YANKEY-AYEH.

Ghana Export Promotion Authority (GEPA): Export Trade House, Liberia Rd, Accra; tel. (30) 2689889; e-mail gepa@gepaghana.org; internet www.gepaghana.org; f. 1974; CEO AFUA ASABEA ASARE.

Ghana Free Zones Authority (GFZA): 5th Link Rd, East Cantonments, POB M626, Accra; tel. (30) 2780535; e-mail info@gfzb.gov.gh; internet gfzb.gov.gh; f. 1995; approves establishment of cos in export processing zones; Chair. ALAN KYEREMATENG; CEO MICHAEL AARON NII OQUAYE YAW, Jr.

Ghana Infrastructure Investment Fund (GIIF): Accra World Trade Centre, 9th Floor, Ridge Ambassadorial Enclave No. 29, Independence Ave, Accra; tel. (24) 6482838; e-mail info@giif.gov.gh; internet giif.gov.gh; Chair. PHILIP ADDISON; CEO SOLOMON ASAMOAH.

Ghana Investment Promotion Centre (GIPC): Vivo Place, A1 Rangoon Lane, Cantonments, POB M193, Accra; tel. (30) 2665125; e-mail info@gipc.gov.gh; internet gipc.gov.gh; f. 1994; negotiates new investments, approves projects, registers foreign capital and decides extent of govt participation; Chair. ALEX APAU DADEY; CEO REGINALD YOFI GRANT.

Ghana Minerals Commission (MINCOM): 12 Switchback Rd Residential Area, POB M 248, Cantonments, Accra; tel. (30) 2771318; e-mail info@mincom.gov.gh; internet www.mincom.gov.gh; f. 1986 to regulate and promote Ghana's mineral industry; Chair. BARBARA OTENG GYASI; CEO MARTIN KWAKU AYISI.

Ghana National Petroleum Authority (NPA): 6 George Bush Highway, Dzorwulu, POB GA156, Accra; tel. (30) 2766196; e-mail info@npa.gov.gh; internet www.npa.gov.gh; f. 2005; oversees petroleum sector; Chair. JOE ADDO-YOBO; Chief Exec. Dr MUSTAPHA ABDUL-HAMID.

Ghana Standards Authority (GSA): POB MB245, Accra; tel. (30) 2500065; e-mail info@gsa.gov.gh; internet www.gsa.gov.gh; f. 1967; establishes and promulgates standards; promotes standardization, conformity assessment and metrology for industrial development and efficiency; operates certification mark scheme and conformity assessment; 402 mems; Chair. AKWASI ACHAMPONG; Exec. Dir Prof. ALEX DODOO.

Ghana Trade Fair Co Ltd: Trade Fair Centre, POB 111, Accra; tel. (20) 6774582; e-mail ghtradefair@gmail.com; internet www.tradefairgh.com; f. 1989; Chair. DANIEL MCKORLEY; CEO Dr AGNES ADU.

GNPA Ltd: Nii Tetteh Ankama St, POB 15331, Accra-North; tel. (30) 2228321; e-mail info@gnpa-ghana.com; internet www.gnpa-ghana.com; f. 1976 as Ghana National Procurement Agency; state-owned; part of Ministry of Trade and Industry; procures and markets a wide range of goods and services locally and abroad; CEO Dr EDWARD NANA YAW OFORI-KURAGU.

Public Procurement Authority (PPA): SSNIT Emporium, 6th Floor, Airport City, Accra; tel. (30) 2738140; e-mail info@ppaghana.org; internet ppa.gov.gh; Chair. Prof. DOUGLAS BOATENG; CEO FRANK MANTE (acting).

State Interests and Governance Authority (SIGA): 5–7 Liberia Rd, POB 393, Ministries, Accra; tel. (30) 2666799; e-mail info@siga.gov.gh; internet siga.gov.gh; f. 2019 to replace State Enterprises Commission; Dir-Gen. STEPHEN ASAMOAH BOATENG (acting).

DEVELOPMENT ORGANIZATIONS

Agence Française de Développement (AFD): 8th Rangoon Close, Ring Rd Central, POB 9592, Airport, Accra; tel. (30) 2778755; e-mail afdaccra@afd.fr; internet www.afd.fr; f. 1985; fmrly Caisse Française de Développement; Country Dir CHRISTOPHE COTTET.

Ghana Irrigation Development Authority (GIDA): opp. Customs Head Office, Accra; tel. (30) 2662050; e-mail ghanairrigation@gmail.com; develop and market efficiently irrigation, drainage, water management, stock water and aquaculture services and facilities; Chair. OSEI OWUSU AGYEMANG.

Private Enterprise Federation (PEF): 7 Prempeh II St, GIMPA, POB CT 1671, Cantonments, Accra; tel. (30) 2974983; e-mail info@pef.org.gh; internet pef.org.gh; f. 1994; promotes development of private sector; CEO NANA OSEI-BONSU.

Social Investment Fund: off El-Wak Stadium Rd, nr Agricultural Engineering Dept, POB 3919, Cantonments, Accra; tel. (30) 2778920; e-mail info@sifinghana.org; internet sifinghana.org; f. 1998; Chair. JOHN OWUSU AGYEMAN; Exec. Dir KOFI FRIMPONG.

Tema Development Co. Ltd (TDC): POB 46, Tema; tel. (30) 3202731; e-mail info@tdctema.org; internet www.tdctema.org; f. 1952; plan, lay out and develop the Tema Acquisition Area; Chair. ELIZABETH MANSA BANSON; Man. Dir ALICE A. OFORI-ATTA.

CHAMBER OF COMMERCE

Ghana Chamber of Commerce and Industry (GCCI): World Trade Centre, 1st Floor, POB 2325, Accra; tel. (30) 2662860; e-mail info@ghanachamber.org; internet www.ghanachamber.org; f. 1961; promotes and protects industry and commerce, organizes trade fairs; 3,500 individual mems and 10 mem. chambers; Pres. CLEMENT OSEI AMOAKO; CEO MARK BADU-ABOAGYE.

INDUSTRIAL AND TRADE ORGANIZATIONS

Federation of Associations of Ghanaian Exporters (FAGE): Ghana Highway Authority Bldg, 2nd Floor, POB M 124, Accra; tel. (24) 3457783; e-mail info@fageghana.com; internet www.fageghana.com; non-governmental, not-for-profit org. for exporters of non-traditional exports; Pres. ANTHONY SIKPA; over 2,500 mems.

Forestry Commission of Ghana, Timber Industry Development Division (TIDD): 4 Third Ave, Ridge, POB MB434, Accra; tel. (30) 2221315; e-mail info@hq.fcghana.com; internet www.ghanatimber.org; f. 1985; promotes the development of the timber industry and the sale and export of timber; Exec. Dir Dr BEN DONKOR.

Ghana Cocoa Board (COCOBOD): Cocoa House, 41 Kwame Nkrumah Ave, POB 933, Accra; tel. (30) 2661872; e-mail public_affairs@cocobod.gh; internet cocobod.gh; f. 1947; monopoly purchaser of cocoa until 1993; responsible for purchase, grading and export of cocoa, coffee and sheanuts; also encourages production and scientific research aimed at improving quality and yield of these crops; controls all exports of cocoa; subsidiaries include the Cocoa Marketing Co (Ghana) Ltd and the Cocoa Research Institute of Ghana; CEO JOSEPH BOAHEN AIDOO.

Grains and Legumes Development Board: POB 4000, Kumasi; tel. (32) 2024231; e-mail gldb@africaonline.com.gh; f. 1970; subsidiary of Ministry of Agriculture; produces, processes and stores seeds and seedlings, and manages national seed security stocks; Chair. Dr GODFRIED ADJEI DIXON; Exec. Dir Dr ROBERT AGYEIBI ASUBOAH.

EMPLOYERS' ORGANIZATIONS

Ghana Employers' Association (GEA): 14 Tafawa Balewa St, North Ridge, POB GP 2616, Accra; tel. (30) 2678455; e-mail gea@ghanaemployers.com; internet ghanaemployers.com.gh; f. 1959; Pres. DANIEL ACHEAMPONG; CEO ALEX FRIMPONG.

Affiliated Bodies

Association of Ghana Industries (AGI): Addison House, 2nd Floor, Trade Fair Centre, POB AN 8624, Accra-North; tel. (30)

2779023; e-mail agi@agighana.org; internet www.agighana.org; f. 1957; Pres. Dr HUMPHREY KWESI AYIM-DARKE; Exec. Dir SETH TWUM-AKWABOAH; c. 500 mems.

Ghana Chamber of Mines: Gulf St, South Legon, POB 991, Accra; tel. (30) 2760652; e-mail chamber@ghanachamberofmines.org; internet www.ghanachamberofmines.org; f. 1928; Pres. JOSHUA MORTOTI; CEO SULEMANU KONEY.

UTILITIES
Regulatory Bodies

Energy Commission (EC): Ghana Airways Ave, Airport Residential Area, Plot 40, Spintex Rd, PMB Ministries, Accra; tel. (30) 2813756; e-mail info@energycom.gov.gh; internet www.energycom.gov.gh; f. 2001; Chair. Prof. EBENEZER ODURO OWUSU; Exec. Sec. OSCAR OFOSU AMONOO-NEIZER.

Public Utilities Regulatory Commission (PURC): Olympic Committee Bldg, 2nd Floor, 53 Liberation Rd, African Liberation Circle, POB CT 3095, Cantonments, Accra; tel. (30) 2244181; e-mail info@purc.com.gh; internet www.purc.com.gh; f. 1997; Chair. EBO QUAGRAINIE; Exec. Sec. Dr ISHMAEL ACKAH.

Electricity

Bui Power Authority: 11 Dodi Link Airport Residential Area, Accra; tel. (30) 2522444; e-mail info@buipower.com; internet buipower.com; f. 2007; Chair. KWASI AMEYAW-CHEREMEH; CEO SAMUEL KOFI DZAMESI.

Electricity Co of Ghana (ECG): Electro-Volta House, POB 521, Accra; tel. (30) 2676727; e-mail ecgho@ecggh.com; internet www.ecgonline.info; Chair. KELI GADZEKPO; Man. Dir KWAME AGYEMAN-BUDU.

Ghana Grid Company Ltd (GRIDCo): off the Tema–Aflao Rd, POB CS 7979, Tema; tel. (30) 3318700; e-mail gridco@gridcogh.com; internet gridcogh.com; f. 2006; Chair. KABRAL BLAY-AMIHERE; CEO EBENEZER ESSIENYI.

Volta River Authority (VRA): Electro-Volta House, 28th February Rd, POB MB 77, Accra; tel. (30) 2664941; e-mail corpcomm@vra.com; internet www.vra.com; f. 1961; govt owned; controls the generation and distribution of electricity; Northern Electricity Department of VRA f. 1987 to distribute electricity in northern Ghana; Chair. KOFI TUTU AGYARE; CEO EMMANUEL ANTWI-DARKWA.

Water

The Volta Basin Authority (VBA) was created by Ghana, Benin, Burkina Faso, Côte d'Ivoire, Mali and Togo in 2006 to manage the resources of the Volta River basin.

Community Water and Sanitation Agency: off Legon-Tetteh Quarshie Rd, Accra; tel. (30) 2983104; e-mail info@cwsagh.org; internet www.cwsa.gov.gh; f. 1998; facilitates the provision of sustainable potable water and related sanitation services as well as hygiene promotion to rural communities and small towns; Chair. KWESI EDUAFO YANKEY; Chief Exec. WORLANYO KWADJO SIABI.

Ghana Water Co Ltd (GWCL): 28th February Rd, POB MB 194, Accra; tel. (30) 22218240; e-mail info@gwcl.com.gh; internet www.gwcl.com.gh; f. 1965 to provide, distribute and conserve water supplies for public, domestic and industrial use, and to establish, operate and control sewerage systems; jointly managed by Aqua Vitens (Netherlands) and Rand Water (South Africa); Chair. PATRICK YAW BOAMAH; Man. Dir CLIFFORD A. BRAIMAH.

MAJOR COMPANIES

The following are among the largest companies in terms of capital investment or of employment.

African Concrete Products Ltd (ACP): 5 Feo Eyeo St, North Industrial Area, POB AN 6357 Accra-North; tel. (30) 2221133; e-mail sales@africanconcrete.com; internet www.africanconcrete.com; f. 1956; mfrs of concrete products; Chair. CARL F. RICHARDS; Gen. Man. MICHAEL ADJEI-DJAN.

AngloGold Ashanti: Gold House, Patrice Lumumba Rd, Roman Ridge, POB 2665, Accra; tel. (30) 2722190; e-mail investors@anglogold.com; internet www.anglogoldashanti.com; f. 1897 as Ashanti Goldfields; merged 2004 with AngloGold; gold-mining at the Obuasi and Iduapriem mines; leases mining and timber concessions from the Govt, which holds a 17% interest; CEO ERIC ASUBONTENG.

Architectural and Engineering Services Ltd (AESLtd): Hall of Technology, Kinbu Rd, POB 3969, Accra; tel. (30) 2663871; e-mail info@aesl.com.gh; internet aesl.com.gh; Chair. Dr KWAME ASAMOAH; Man. Dir ARC ISAAC AGYEI MARFO.

Asap Vasa Gold Refinery: Plot No. 15, West Abossey Okai, opp. Matahek Pharmacy, POB ST 447, Accra; tel. (30) 2325466; e-mail info@asapvasa.com; internet www.asapvasa.com; f. 2006; Chair. and CEO HENRY VROOM PARKER.

Azar Chemical Industries Ltd: 88 Spintex Rd, POB 5205, Accra; tel. (30) 2811299; e-mail info@azargroup-gh.com; internet www.azarghana.com; mfrs of paints.

Bamson Company Ltd: Old Fadama Rd, POB AN1111, Accra; tel. (30) 2689421; e-mail info@bamson.org; internet www.bamson.org; f. 1983; mfrs of paints; Man. Dir KWAME OFOSU BAMFO.

Bulk Oil Storage and Transportation Co. Ltd (BOST): Plot No. 12, 1st Dzorwulu Cres., West Airport Residential Area, POB MB 499, Accra; tel. (30) 2775497; e-mail bost@bost.com.gh; internet www.bost.com.gh; f. 1993; storage and transmission of fuels; Chair. EKOW HACKMAN; Man. Dir EDWIN ALFRED PROVENCAL.

Chase Petroleum: CH Group Bldg, 5th Floor, 1 Rangoon Lane, Cantonments, POB CT 10481, Accra; tel. (30) 2215700; e-mail info@chaseghana.com; internet chaseghana.com; f. 1999; trading and distribution of petroleum products; Exec. Chair. KWAKU BEDIAKO; Man. Dir KINGSLEY SARPONG.

Cocoa Processing Co Ltd: PMB, Tema; tel. (30) 3212153; e-mail info@goldentreeghana.com; internet www.goldentreeghana.com; f. 1981; produces high-grade cocoa products for export and domestic consumption; wholly-owned subsidiary of COCOBOD; 2 factories divested to WAMCO Ltd in 1992 and 1993; Man. Dir NANA AGYENIM BOATENG (acting).

Equatorial Coca-Cola Bottling Co (ECCBC) (Coca-Cola Bottling Co of Ghana Ltd): Accra–Tema Motorway, Industrial Area, Spintex Rd, POB C 1607, Accra; tel. (30) 2812626; internet www.ghana.coca-cola.com; bottling plants in Accra and Kumasi.

GHACEM Ltd: Harbour Area, POB 646, Tema; e-mail info@ghacem.com; internet www.ghacem.com; f. 1967; cement; subsidiary of Heidelberg Cement Group; Chair. HAKAN GURDAL; Man. Dir STEFANO GALLINI.

Ghana Bauxite Co Ltd: 10 Sixth St, Airport Residential Area, PMB, Accra; tel. (30) 2765830; e-mail bauxite@ghana.com; f. 1940; 20% state-owned, 80% owned by Bosai Minerals Group (People's Republic of China); fmrly British Aluminium Co Ltd; mining of bauxite at Awaso with loading facilities at Takoradi.

Ghana Gas Company Ltd: 225 Osibisa Close, Airport West, POB CT 3686, Cantonments, Accra; tel. (30) 2744200; e-mail media@ghanagas.com.gh; internet ghanagas.com.gh; provides and operates infrastructure required for gathering, processing and delivering of natural gas resources; Chair. KENNEDY OHENE AGYAPONG; CEO Dr BEN ASANTE.

Ghana Manganese Co Ltd (GMC): POB 2, Nsuta-Wassaw, Western Region; tel. (31) 2320225; e-mail info@ghamang.com; internet ghamang.com.gh; transferred to private ownership in 1995; Man. Dir JURGEN EIJGENDAAL.

Ghana National Petroleum Corpn (GNPC): Harbour Rd, PMB, Tema, Accra; tel. (30) 3206020; e-mail info@gnpcghana.com; internet www.gnpcghana.com; f. 1983; exploration, development, production and disposal of petroleum; Chair. FREDDIE BLAY; CEO Dr KOFI KODUAH SARPONG.

Ghana Oil Company Limited: Kojo Thompson/Adjabeng Rd, POB GP 3183, Accra; tel. (30) 2688215; e-mail info@goil.com.gh; internet www.goil.com.gh; marketing and distribution of petroleum products; Chair. KWAMENA BARTELS; Man. Dir and Group CEO KWAME OSEI-PREMPEH.

Ghana Rubber Estates Ltd (GREL): POB TD 228, Takoradi; tel. (31) 2002600; e-mail info@grelgh.com; internet grelgh.com; f. 1957; rubber plantation; Chair. PIERRE BILLON; Man. Dir LIONEL BARRE.

GIHOC Distilleries: 2 Dadeban Rd, North Industrial Area, POB 7147, Accra; tel. (55) 2564456; e-mail info@gihocdistil.com; internet www.gihocdistil.com; 1958; state-owned; alcoholic and non-alcoholic beverages; Chair. EBENEZER EBO BARTELS; Man. Dir MAXWELL KOFI JUMAH.

Goldfields Ghana Ltd: 6 Akosombo St, Airport Residential Area, Airport Residential Area, POB KA 30742, Accra; tel. (30) 2770189; f. 1995; operates a gold mine, Tarkwa, and one at Damang, through its subsidiary Abosso Goldfields Ltd; 70% owned by Gold Fields Ltd, South Africa; Man. Dir ALFRED BAKU.

Guinness Ghana Breweries Ltd (GGBL): POB 3610, Achimota, Accra; tel. (30) 2428000; e-mail ggbl@diageo.com; internet www.diageo.com/en/our-business/where-we-operate/africa/guinness-ghana-breweries-plc; f. 1955; Chair. SIMON HARVEY; Man. Dir FRANCIS AGBONLAHOR.

Interplast Ltd: POB AD 330, Accra; tel. (30) 2819000; e-mail pipes@interplastghana.com; internet interplastghana.com; f. 1970; producer of high quality pipes and profiles; Chair. SAIDE FAKHRY; Man. Dir HAYSSAM FAKHRY.

John Bitar & Co. Ltd: Plot No. 1/20, Mempeasem St, POB 406, Essikadu, Sekondi; tel. (31) 2046321; e-mail info@johnbitar.com; f. 1955; wood products; Man. Dir GHASSAN JOHN BITAR.

Kama Group Ltd: Labone, Nyaniba Estate Junction, Ring Rd East, POB 5437, Accra; tel. (30) 2782705; e-mail info@aspenghana.com;

internet www.aspenghana.com; f. 1999; pharmaceutical products; acquired by Aspen Pharmacare Holdings Ltd in 2015; Chair. CHRIS MYNHARD BOTHA; CEO SANJAY MOHAN ADVANI.

Kasapreko Co. Ltd: DTD No 64, off Spintex Rd, Baatsonaa, Accra; tel. (30) 2810956; e-mail info@kasaprekogh.com; internet www .kasaprekogh.com; alcoholic and non-alcoholic beverage mfrs; Chair. P. A. KURANCHIE; Man. Dir RICHARD ADJEI.

Latex Foam: Dadeban Rd, North Industrial Area, Kaneshie, POB 533, Accra; tel. (30) 2231155; e-mail sales@latexfoamghana.com; internet www.latexfoamghana.com; manufacturers of foam and spring mattresses and related products.

Micheletti & Co. Ltd: PMB 281, Accra; tel. (30) 2511561; e-mail info@michelettighana.com; internet michelettighana.com; f. 1955; engineering, design and construction of civil works; Man. Dir ERNEST TARICONE.

Nestlé Ghana Ltd: Plot 33, South Legon Commercial Area, Motorway Extension, PMB KIA, Accra; tel. (30) 2517020; e-mail consumerservices@gh.nestle.com; f. 1957; Man. Dir FREDA DUPLAN.

Phyto-Riker (GIHOC) Pharmaceuticals Ltd: Mile 7, off Nsawam Rd, POB AN 5266, Dome, Accra-North; tel. (30) 2400482; e-mail info@phyto-riker.com; internet www.phyto-rikergh.com; fmrly Ghana Industrial Holding Corpn Pharmaceuticals Ltd (f. 1962); Chair. KWASI ATUAH; Exec. Dir THERESA YAMSON.

Precious Minerals Marketing Co Ltd (PMMC): Diamond House, Kinbu Rd, POB M 108, Accra; tel. (30) 2953279; e-mail enquiries@ pmmc.gov.gh; internet www.pmmc.gov.gh/pmmc; f. 1963; govt-owned; Chair. KISTON OHEMMENG KISSI; Man. Dir NANA AKWASI AWUAH.

PZ Cussons Ghana Ltd: Plot 27/3–27/7, Sanyo Rd, Heavy Industrial Area, POB 628, Tema; tel. (30) 3302701; internet www .pzcussons.com/ghana; f. 1958; mfrs of soaps, toiletries, cosmetics, pharmaceuticals, electrical goods and nutritional products; Chair. PAUL PEPRA; Man. Dir JAMES B. JUDSON.

Qualiplast Ltd: 37/38 Abotia St, North Industrial Area, POB 7136, Accra; tel. (30) 2227807; e-mail info@qualiplastgh.com; internet qualiplastghana.com; f. 1973; mfrs of industrial plastic packaging products and household plastic wares; Man. Dir FARES AKL.

Real Products Ltd: Apowa Industrial Area, Takoradi; tel. (31) 2096420; internet www.realproductsghana.com; f. 2010; cocoa powder, cocoa liquor and cocoa butter.

RLG Communications: Loko St, POB CT 6027, Cantonments, Accra; tel. (30) 2764263; f. 2001; manufacturer of mobile telephones; CEO ROLAND AGAMBIRE.

State Housing Co Ltd: Ring Rd West, POB 2753, Accra; tel. (30) 2232829; e-mail info@statehousing.gov.gh; internet statehousing .gov.gh; f. 1956 as Gold Coast Housing Corpn; Chair. BENJAMIN OWUSU MENSAH; Man. Dir KWABENA AMPOFO APPIAH.

Takoradi Gas Ltd: Plot No. E156, Efia Light Industrial Area, POB TD 1050, Takoradi; tel. (24) 4330594; e-mail tgl@tglgh.com; internet www.takoradigas.com; f. 1992; industrial and refrigerant gases, welding consumables and welding accessories; CEO ANURA KALUARACHI.

Tema Oil Refinery Ltd (TOR): POB 599, Tema; tel. (24) 4089146; e-mail info@torghana.com; internet www.tor.com.gh; f. 1963; sole oil refinery in Ghana; state-controlled since 1977; Chair. TONGRAAN KUGBILSONG NANLEBEGTANG; Man. Dir FRANCIS ADU TUTU BOATENG.

TotalEnergies Ghana Ltd: Total House, 25 Liberia Rd, POB 553, Accra; tel. (30) 2611530; e-mail totalgh.inquiry@totalmktgh.com; internet gh.totalenergies.com; f. 1960 as Total Ghana Ltd; name changed in 2006 to Total Petroleum Ghana Ltd; present name adopted 2021; distribution of petroleum products, incl. liquefied petroleum gas; Man. Dir ERIC FANCHINI.

Tullow Oil Ghana Ltd: George Walker Bush Highway, Plot No. 70, North Dzorwulu, Accra; tel. (30) 2742200; internet www.tullowoil .com/our-operations/africa/ghana; Man. Dir WISSAM AL-MONTHIRY.

Unilever Ghana Ltd: POB 721, Tema; tel. (30) 3218247; e-mail vicky.wireko@unilever.com; internet www.unileverghana.com; f. 1955 as United Africa Co of Ghana Ltd; comprises 6 divisions and assoc. cos; subsidiary of Unilever plc (UK); agricultural, industrial, specialized merchandising, distributive and service enterprises; Chair. EDWARD EFFAH; Man. Dir GEORGE OWUSU-ANSAH.

Volta Aluminium Co Ltd (VALCO): POB 625, Tema; tel. (30) 3200048; e-mail info@valcotema.com; internet www.valcotema.com; f. 1962; 100% govt-owned; operates an aluminium smelter at Tema (annual capacity 200,000 metric tons); Chair. Dr HENRY BENYAH; CEO DANIEL ACHEAMPONG.

CO-OPERATIVES

Ghana Co-operatives Council Ltd (GACOCO): POB 4034, Accra; tel. 242936551; e-mail gacopco@yahoo.com; f. 1951; co-ordinates activities of all co-operative socs and plays advocacy role

for co-operative movement; comprises 11 active nat. asscns and 2 central orgs; Sec.-Gen. EMMANUEL APUA KONAMOAH.

The national associations and central organizations include the Ghana Co-operative Marketing Asscn Ltd, the Ghana Co-operative Credit Unions' Asscn Ltd, the Ghana Co-operative Distillers' and Retailers' Asscn Ltd, and the Ghana Co-operative Poultry Farmers' Asscn Ltd.

TRADE UNIONS

Ghana Federation of Labour: POB Trade Fair 509, Accra; tel. (30) 2252105; e-mail info@gflghana.org; internet www.gflghana.org; f. 1999; Pres. CALEB NARTEY; Gen. Sec ABRAHAM KOOMSON.

Ghana National Association of Teachers (GNAT): POB 209, Accra; tel. (30) 2221576; e-mail info@ghanateachers.com; internet fb .com/GNAT.HQTRS; f. 1931; Pres. PHILIPPA LARSEN; Gen. Sec. THOMAS TANKO MUSAH.

Ghana Trades Union Congress (GTUC): Hall of Trade Unions, Liberia Rd, POB 701, Accra; tel. (30) 2662568; e-mail info@ghanatuc .org; internet www.ghanatuc.org; f. 1945; 17 affiliated unions; Chair. RICHARD KWASI YEBOAH; Sec.-Gen. ANTHONY YAW BAAH.

> **General Agricultural Workers' Union (GAWU):** Hall of Trade Unions, 5th Floor, Liberia Rd, POB 701, Accra; tel. (30) 2665514; e-mail gawughanatuc@yahoo.com; f. 1959; Gen. Sec. EDWARD T. KAREWEH.

> **Ghana Mineworkers' Union (GMWU):** Hall of Trade Unions Bldg, off Barnes and Liberia Rds, Tudu, POB 701, Accra; tel. (21) 665563; e-mail admin@gmwu.org; f. 1944; Chair. KWARKO MENSAH GYAKAR; Gen. Sec. ABDUL-MOOMIN GBANA.

> **Teachers' and Educational Workers' Union (TEWU):** Hall of Trade Unions, Liberia Rd, POB 701, Accra; tel. (30) 2663050; e-mail tewu@vodafone.com.gh; internet www.tewu-ghana.org; f. 1958; Gen. Sec.- MARK DANKYIRA KORANKYE.

Transport

RAILWAYS

Ghana's railway network connects Accra, Kumasi, Awaso and Takoradi.

Ghana Railway Co Ltd (GRC): POB 251, Takoradi; f. 1901; responsible for the operation and maintenance of all railways; Chair Dr CLEMENT HAMMAH.

Ghana Railway Development Authority (GRDA): PMB 54, Accra; tel. (30) 2732534; e-mail info@grda.gov.gh; internet grda .gov.gh; f. 2005; regulatory and devt authority; Chair. Dr MARTIN AMOGRE AYANORE; Man. Dir RICHARD DOMBO DIEDONG.

ROADS

Ghana Highway Authority: POB 1641, Accra; tel. (30) 2666591; e-mail eokonadu@highways.mrt.gov.gh; internet www.highways .gov.gh; f. 1974 to plan, develop, administer and maintain trunk roads and related facilities; Chair. Alhaji BASHIRU LOMO-TETTEH SAKIBU.

Intercity State Transport Company (STC) Coaches Ltd: POB 7384, 1 Adjuma Cres., Ring Rd West Industrial Area, Accra; tel. (30) 2221912; e-mail stc@ghana.com; internet stc.oyawego.com; f. 1965; fmrly State Transport Co; 80% owned by the Social Security and National Insurance Trust, 20% state-owned; above name adopted in 2003; regional and international coach services; Chair. E. K. ASANTE; Man. Dir SAMUEL NUAMAH DONKOR.

SHIPPING

The two main ports are Tema (near Accra) and Takoradi, both of which are linked with Kumasi by rail. There are also important inland ports on the Volta, Ankobra and Tano rivers.

Ghana Maritime Authority (GMA): 19 Mayor Rd, PMB 34, Accra; tel. (30) 2684392; e-mail info@ghanamaritime.org; internet www .ghanamaritime.org; f. 2002; policymaking body; part of Ministry of Transport; regulates maritime industry; Dir-Gen. THOMAS KOFI ALONSI.

Ghana Ports and Harbours Authority (GPHA): POB 150, Tema; tel. (30) 3202631; e-mail headquarters@ghanaports.net; internet www.ghanaports.gov.gh; f. 1986; holding co for the ports of Tema and Takoradi; Chair. ISAAC OSEI; Dir-Gen. MICHAEL ACHAGWE LUGUJE.

Liner Agencies and Trading (Ghana) Ltd: POB 214, Tema; tel. (30) 3202987; e-mail enquiries@liner-agencies.com; international freight services; shipping agents; Dir J. OSSEI-YAW.

Maersk Ghana Ltd: Obourwe Bldg, Torman Rd, Fishing Harbour Area, POB 8800, Community 7, Tema; tel. (30) 3218700; e-mail gnamkt@maersk.com; internet www.maerskline.com/ghana;

f. 2001; owned by Maersk Line (Denmark); offices in Tema, Takoradi and Kumasi; Man. Dir NAVED ZAFAR.

Shipping Association

Ghana Shippers' Authority: Ghana Shippers House, 7th Floor, Ridge, POB 1321, Accra; tel. (30) 2666915; e-mail info@shippers-gh .com; internet shippers.org.gh; f. 1974; fmrly Ghana Shippers' Council, present name adopted 2010; represents interests of 28,000 registered Ghanaian shippers; also provides cargo-handling and allied services; Chair. G. M. GRIFFITHS; CEO BENONITA BISMARCK.

CIVIL AVIATION

The main airport is at Kotoka (Accra); in 2021 Kotoka Airport was the only airport in Ghana that handled international flights. There are also airports at Kumasi, Takoradi, Sunyani, Tamale, Yendi, Navrongo and Wa. Following upgrade work, Tamale Airport and Kumasi Airport were granted international status in 2008 and 2015, respectively, but continued to operate solely domestic services.

Ghana Airports Co Ltd (GACL): Kotoka International Airport, PMB 36, Accra; tel. (30) 2550612; e-mail info@gacl.com.gh; internet www.gacl.com.gh; f. 2006; Chair. PAUL ADOM-OTCHERE; Man. Dir PAMELA DJAMSON-TETTEY.

Ghana Civil Aviation Authority (GCAA): PMB, Kotoka International Airport, Accra; tel. (30) 2776171; e-mail info@caa.com.gh; internet www.gcaa.com.gh; f. 1986; Chair. REXFORD G. M. ACQUAH; Dir-Gen. CHARLES KRAIKUE.

Africa World Airlines Ltd (AWA): SSNIT Emporium, Ground Floor, Airport City, Liberation Rd, PMB CT67, Cantonment, Accra; tel. (30) 7012024; e-mail awaoffice@flyafricaworld.com; internet www.flyafricaworld.com; f. 2011; CEO MICHAEL CHENG LUO.

Air Ghana: Block 12, KIA Cargo Village, POB 9892, Kotoka International Airport, Accra; tel. (30) 2774007; e-mail info@airghana.com; internet www.airghana.com; f. 1993; cargo and passenger services; Chair. MARWAN TRABOULSI; Man. Dir MICHAEL MAGUIRE.

Antrak Air: 50 Senchi St, Airport Residential Area, Accra; tel. (30) 2782814; e-mail info@antrakair.com; internet www.antrakair.com; f. 2003; passenger and cargo services for domestic and international routes; Chair. ASOMA BANDA.

Tourism

Ghana Tourism Authority: POB GP 3106, Accra-North; tel. (30) 2682601; e-mail gtb@africaonline.com.gh; internet www.ghana .travel; f. 1968; fmrly Ghana Tourist Board; name changed as above in 2011; Exec. Dir CHARLES OSEI BONSU.

Ghana Association of Tourist and Travel Agencies (GATTA): Swamp Grove, Asylum Down, POB 7140, Accra-North; tel. (30) 2222398; e-mail info@gattagh.com; internet www.gattagh.com; Pres. HILLARIUS MCCASH AKPAH; Exec. Sec. TINA OSEI.

Ghana Tourist Development Co Ltd: POB AN8710, Accra-North; tel. (30) 2770720; e-mail info@gtdc.com.gh; internet www.gtdc.com .gh; f. 1974; develops tourism infrastructure, incl. hotels, restaurants and casinos; operates duty-free shops; CEO KWADWO ODAME ANTWI.

Defence

As assessed at November 2021, Ghana's total armed forces numbered 15,500 (army 11,500, navy 2,000 and air force 2,000). In 2000 the Government restructured the armed forces; the army was subsequently organized into north and south commands, and the navy into western and eastern commands. In 2004 a peacekeeping training centre, which was primarily to be used by ECOWAS, was established in Accra. At November 2021 a total of 2,030 Ghanaian troops were stationed abroad.

Defence Budget: 2,100m. cedis in 2021.

Commander-in-Chief of the Armed Forces: Pres. NANA AKUFO-ADDO.

Chief of Defence Staff: Vice-Adm. SETH AMOAMA.

Chief of Air Staff: Air Vice-Marshal FRANK HANSON.

Chief of Army Staff: Maj.-Gen. THOMAS OPPONG-PEPRAH.

Chief of Naval Staff: Rear-Adm. ISSAH ADAMS YAKUBU.

Education

Education is officially compulsory and free of charge for eight years, between the ages of six and 14 years. Primary education begins at the age of six and lasts for six years, comprising two cycles of three years each. Secondary education begins at the age of 12 and lasts for a further seven years, comprising a first cycle of three years and a second of four years. Following three years of junior secondary education, pupils are examined to determine admission to senior secondary school courses, or to technical and vocational courses. In 2017/18, according to the United Nations Educational, Scientific and Cultural Organization (UNESCO), pre-primary enrolment included 73% of children in the relevant age-group (males 72%; females 75%). In 2018/19 primary enrolment included 99% of children in the relevant age-group (boys 99%; girls 100%), while the comparable ratio for secondary enrolment was equivalent to 75% (boys 75%; girls 75%). In the budget for 2021 the allocation for education (15,632m. Ghana cedis) was equivalent to 14.2% of total projected expenditure (110,050m. Ghana cedis).

Bibliography

Agbodeka, F. *An Economic History of Ghana from the Earliest Times*. Accra, Ghana Universities Press, 1992.

Ahlman, J. S. *Kwame Nkrumah: Visions of Liberation* Athens, OH, Ohio University Press, 2021.

Amenumey, D. E. K. *The Ewe Unification Movement: A Political History*. Accra, Ghana Universities Press, 1989.

Amoah, L. G. A. *Five Ghanaian Presidents and China*. Accra, University of Ghana Press, 2020.

Amoah, L. G. A. (Ed.) *Sixty Years of Ghana-China Relations: Friendship, Friction and the Future*. Accra, University of Ghana Press, 2020.

Amoah, M. *Reconstructing the Nation in Africa: The Politics of Nationalism in Ghana*. London, I. B. Tauris, 2007.

Aryeetey, E., Harrigan, J., and Nissanke, M. (Eds). *Economic Reforms in Ghana: The Miracle and the Mirage*. Oxford, James Currey, 1999.

Asamoah, O. Y. *The Political History of Ghana (1950-2013): The Experience of a Non-Conformist*. Bloomington, IN, AuthorHouse, 2014.

Ayensu, K. B., and Darkwa, S. N. *The Evolution of Parliament in Ghana*. Accra, Sub-Saharan Publishers, 2006.

Babatope, E. *The Ghana Revolution from Nkrumah to Jerry Rawlings*. Enugu, Fourth Dimension Publishers, 1984.

Baynham, S. *The Military and Politics in Nkrumah's Ghana*. Boulder, CO, Westview Press, 1988.

Danso-Boafo, A. J. J. *Rawlings and the Democratic Transition in Ghana*. Accra, Ghana Universities Press, 2014.

Frempong, A. K. D. *Electoral Politics in Ghana's Fourth Republic: In the Context of Post-Cold War Africa*. Accra, YAMENS Press, 2012.

Frimpong-Ansah, J. H. *The Vampire State in Africa. The Political Economy of Decline in Ghana*. London, James Currey. 1991.

Fuller, H. *Building the Ghanaian State: Kwame Nkrumah's Symbolic Nationalism*. Basingstoke, Palgrave Macmillan, 2014.

Gocking, R. S. *The History of Ghana*. Westport, CT, Greenwood Press, 2005.

Gyimah-Boardi, E. (Ed.). *Ghana under PNDC Rule*. Dakar, CODESRIA, 1993.

Hansen, E. *Ghana under Rawlings: Early Years*. Oxford, ABC and Malthouse Press, 1991.

Hasty, J. *The Press and Political Culture in Ghana*. Bloomington, IN, Indiana University Press, 2005.

Herbst, J. *The Politics of Reform in Ghana, 1982–1991*. Berkeley, CA, University of California Press, 1993.

Hutchful, E. *Ghana's Adjustment Experience: The Paradox of Reform*. Oxford, James Currey, 2002.

Jackson, K. A. *When Gun Rules: A Soldier's Testimony of the Events Leading to June 4 Uprising in Ghana and its Aftermath*. Accra, Woeli Publishing Services, 1999.

Kanbur, R., and Aryeetey, E. (Eds). *Economy of Ghana: Analytical Perspectives on Stability, Growth and Poverty.* Oxford, James Currey, 2008.

Killick, T. *Development Economics in Action. A Study of Economic Policies in Ghana.* 2nd edn. Abingdon, Routledge, 2010.

Luna, J. *Political Financing in Developing Countries: A Case from Ghana.* Abingdon, Routledge, 2019,

Mahama, J. D. *My First Coup d'Etat: Memories from the Lost Decades of Africa.* London, Bloomsbury, 2012.

Manuh, T. (Ed.). *At Home in the World? International Migration and Development in Contemporary Ghana and West Africa.* Accra, Sub-Saharan Publishers, 2006.

Milne, J. *Kwame Nkrumah—A Biography.* London, Panaf Books, 2000.

Nathan, N. *Electoral Politics and Africa's Urban Transition: Class and Ethnicity in Ghana.* Cambridge, cambridge University Press, 2018.

Ninsin, K. A. (Ed.). *Issues in Ghana's Electoral Politics.* Dakar, CODESRIA, 2016.

Ninsin, K. A., and Drah, F. K. (Eds). *The Search for Democracy in Ghana: A Case Study in Political Instability in Africa.* Accra, Asempa Publishers, 1987.

   Ghana's Transition to Constitutional Rule. Accra, Ghana University Press, and Oxford, ABC, 1991.

Nugent, P. *Big Men, Small Boys and Politics in Ghana: Power, Ideology and the Burden of History, 1982–1994.* London, Pinter, 1995.

Obeng, S. G., and Debrah, E. (Eds). *Ghanaian Politics and Political Communication.* London, Rowman & Littlefield International, 2019.

Okafor, G. M. *Christianity and Islam in West Africa; the Ghana Experience: A Study of the Forces and Influence of Christianity and Islam in Modern Ghana.* Würzburg, Oros, 1997.

Okeke, B. E. *4 June: A Revolution Betrayed.* Enugu, Ikenga Publishers, 1982.

Opoku, D. K. *The Politics of Government-Business Relations in Ghana, 1982–2008.* Basingstoke, Palgrave Macmillan, 2010.

Osei, A. P. *Ghana: Recurrence and Change in a Post-Independence African State.* New York, P. Lang, 1999.

Owusu-Ansah, D., and McFarland, M. D. *Historical Dictionary of Ghana.* 2nd edn. Lanham, MD, Scarecrow Press, 1995.

Paller, J. W. *Democracy in Ghana: Everyday Politics in Urban Africa.* Cambridge, Cambridge University Press, 2019.

Perbi, A. A. *A History of Indigenous Slavery in Ghana, From the 15th to the 19th Century.* Accra, Sub-Saharan Publishers, 2004.

Pierre, J. *The Predicament of Blackness: Postcolonial Ghana and the Politics of Race.* Chicago, IL, University of Chicago Press, 2013.

Rathbone, R. J. A. R. *Nkrumah and the Chiefs: The Politics of Chieftaincy in Ghana, 1951–60.* Oxford, James Currey, 2000.

Sackeyfio, N. *Energy Politics and Rural Development in Sub-Saharan Africa: The Case of Ghana.* London, Palgrave Macmillan, 2017.

Sapong, N. Y. B., and Pohl, J. O. *Replenishing History: New Directions to Historical Research in the 21st Century in Ghana.* Legon, University of Ghana, 2014.

Stockwell, S. E. *The Business of Decolonization: British Business Strategies in the Gold Coast.* Oxford, Clarendon Press, 2000.

Tsikata, D. *Living in the Shadow of the Large Dams: Long Term Responses of Downstream and Lakeside Communities of Ghana's Volta River Project.* Leiden, Brill Academic Publishers, 2006.

Yeebo, Z. *Ghana: The Struggle for Popular Power—Rawlings: Saviour or Demagogue?* Accra, New Beacon Books, 1992.

GUINEA

Physical and Social Geography

R. J. HARRISON CHURCH

The Republic of Guinea covers an area of 245,857 sq km (94,926 sq miles), containing exceptionally varied landscapes, peoples and economic conditions. The census of 2014 recorded a population of 10,523,261 (giving an average density of 42.8 inhabitants per sq km). According to official projections, the population had increased to 13,261,638 by mid-2022 (53.9 inhabitants per sq km). The population is concentrated in the plateau area of central Guinea. The capital, Conakry, had a population of 2,095,705 at mid-2022, according to official projections.

The official language is French, but Soussou, Manika and six other national languages are widely spoken. Some 87% of the population are Muslims, while around 7% are Christians and 2% follow traditional animist beliefs.

Guinea's coast is part of the extremely wet south-western sector of West Africa, which has a monsoonal climate. Thus Conakry has five to six months with almost no rain, while 4,300 mm fall in the remaining months. The coastline has shallow drowned rivers and estuaries with much mangrove growing on alluvium eroded from the nearby Fouta Djallon mountains. Much of the mangrove has been removed, and the land bunded for rice cultivation. Only at two places, Cape Verga and Conakry, do ancient hard rocks reach the sea. At the latter they have facilitated the development of the port, while the weathering of these rocks has produced exploitable deposits of bauxite on the offshore Los Islands.

Behind the swamps a gravelly coastal plain, some 65 km wide, is backed by the steep, often sheer, edges of the Fouta Djallon, which occupies the west-centre of Guinea. Much is over 900 m high, and consists of level Primary sandstones (possibly of Devonian age) which cover Pre-Cambrian rocks to a depth of 750 m. The level plateaux, with many bare lateritic surfaces, are the realm of Fulani (Peul) herders. Rivers are deeply incised in the sandstone. These more fertile valleys were earlier cultivated with food crops by slaves of the Fulani, and then with bananas, coffee, citrus fruits and pineapples on plantations under the French. Falls and gorges of the incised rivers have great hydroelectric potential. This is significant in view of huge deposits of high-grade bauxite located at Fria and Boké. The climate is still monsoonal but, although the total rainfall is lower—about 1,800 mm annually—it is more evenly distributed than on the coasts, as the rainy season is longer. In such a mountainous area there are sharp variations in climatic conditions over a short distance, and from year to year.

On the Liberian border the Guinea highlands rise to 1,752 m at Mt Nimba, where there are substantial deposits of haematite iron ore. These rounded mountains contrast greatly with the level plateaux and deep narrow valleys of the Fouta Djallon. Rainfall is heavier than in the latter, but is again more evenly distributed, so that only two or three months are without significant rain. Coffee, kola and other crops are grown in the forest of this remote area. Diamonds are mined north of Macenta and west of Beyla, and gold at Siguiri and Léro.

History

MARIE GIBERT

THE SÉKOU TOURÉ PERIOD

On 2 October 1958, having rejected membership of a proposed community of self-governing French overseas territories, French Guinea became the independent Republic of Guinea. Ahmed Sékou Touré, the Secretary-General of the Parti Démocratique de Guinée—Rassemblement Démocratique Africain (PDG—RDA), which had led the campaign for independence, became the Republic's first President, and the PDG—RDA the sole political party. The departing French authorities took punitive economic reprisals, and French aid and investment were suspended. Sékou Touré's Government initially obtained assistance from the Union of Soviet Socialist Republics and withdrew from the Franc Zone in 1960, but after 1961 the USA became a more significant source of aid. In 1978 it was decided to merge the PDG—RDA and the state, and in January 1979 the country was renamed the People's Revolutionary Republic of Guinea.

CONTÉ AND THE MILITARY COMMITTEE

Sékou Touré died suddenly in March 1984. Before a successor could be chosen, the army staged a coup in April and seized power. Col (later Gen.) Lansana Conté and Col Diarra Traoré, who became President and Prime Minister, respectively, had both held senior military positions for some years. A semi-civilian Government was appointed, and efforts were made to improve regional relations and links with potential sources of economic aid (most notably France). In May the country resumed the designation of Republic of Guinea. The PDG—RDA and organs of Sékou Touré's 'party state' were dismantled under this Second Republic. State surveillance and control were ended, and many political detainees were freed. Conté adopted an open style of government, inviting constructive advice and criticism from all sectors of society.

Undercurrents of Opposition

In December 1984 Conté abolished the office of Prime Minister, demoting Traoré to a lesser ministerial post. In July 1985, while Conté was attending a regional summit meeting in Togo, Traoré attempted a coup, supported mainly by members of the police force. Troops loyal to Conté swiftly regained control, and the President returned two days later. Traoré and many of his family were among more than 200 people arrested, and the armed forces conducted a purge of his suspected sympathizers. Traoré and a half-brother of Sékou Touré were executed in the immediate aftermath of the coup attempt, and about 60 other military officers were later sentenced to death.

The coup attempt strengthened Conté's position, allowing him to pursue the extensive economic reforms demanded by the World Bank and the International Monetary Fund. In December 1985 Conté reorganized the Council of Ministers, introducing a majority of civilians and creating resident 'regional' ministries.

In October 1988 Conté established a committee to draft a new constitution, which would be submitted for approval in a national referendum. In October 1989 Conté revealed plans whereby a Comité Transitoire de Redressement National (CTRN) would oversee a five-year transitional period, prior to the establishment of a two-party political system under an elected president and legislature.

Conté appealed in November 1990 for the return to Guinea of political exiles. However, three members of an illegal opposition movement, the Rassemblement Populaire Guinéen (RPG), were imprisoned later in the month. Rejecting widespread demands for an accelerated programme of political reform, the Government proceeded with its plan for a gradual transition to a two-party political system. The draft Constitution was submitted to a national referendum in December, and was declared to have been approved by 98.7% of those who voted (97.4% of the registered electorate). In February 1991 the 36-member CTRN was inaugurated, under the chairmanship of Conté. In October Conté announced that the registration of an unlimited number of political parties would come into effect on 3 April 1992, and that legislative elections would take place before the end of 1992 in the context of a full multi-party political system.

CONTÉ AND THE THIRD REPUBLIC

The Constitution of the Third Republic was promulgated on 23 December 1991. In January 1992 Conté ceded the presidency of the CTRN, in accordance with constitutional provision for the separation of the powers of the executive and legislature. In February most military officers and all *Guinéens de l'extérieur* (former dissidents who had returned from exile after the 1984 coup) were removed from the Government: it later became apparent that some of these long-serving ministers had left public office in order to establish a pro-Conté political party, the Parti de l'Unité et du Progrès (PUP). The RPG was among the first opposition parties to be legalized in April 1992. The most prominent other challengers to the PUP were the Parti pour le Renouveau et le Progrès (PRP), led by a well-known journalist, Siradiou Diallo, and the Union pour la Nouvelle République (UNR), led by Mamadou Boye Bâ. Clashes between pro- and anti-Conté activists (apparently fuelled by ethnic rivalries) occurred frequently from mid-1992, and in October the Government again banned all unauthorized public gatherings.

A presidential election was held on 19 December 1993. Despite reports of opposition appeals for a boycott of the election (and the absence of voters' lists in some polling stations), the official rate of participation was 78.5% of the registered electorate. Conté was elected in the first round of voting, having secured 51.7% of the votes cast. His nearest rival—the leader of the RPG, Alpha Condé—took 19.6% of the votes. Conté (who had, as required by the Constitution, resigned from the armed forces in order to contest the presidency) was inaugurated as President on 29 January 1994.

It was announced in March 1995 that elections to the new Assemblée Nationale (National Assembly) would take place on 11 June. Parties of the so-called 'radical' opposition (principally the RPG, the PRP and the UNR) frequently alleged harassment of their activists by the security forces. According to the official results, the PUP won 71 out of 114 seats; eight other parties won representation, among them the RPG, which took 19 seats, and the PRP and the UNR, which each won nine seats. A turnout of 63% of the electorate was reported. The results were confirmed by the Supreme Court in July, whereupon the new legislature formally superseded the CTRN. The three radical opposition parties joined forces with nine other organizations in July, creating a new opposition front—the Coordination de l'Opposition Démocratique—which indicated its willingness to enter into a dialogue with the authorities.

Military Unrest

In February 1996 Conté was reportedly seized as he attempted to flee the presidential palace during a mutiny by disaffected elements of the military. He was released after making several concessions, including a doubling of salaries and immunity from prosecution for those involved in the uprising. About 50 people were killed and 100 injured as rebels clashed with forces loyal to the Conté regime. By June 42 members of the armed forces had reportedly been charged in connection with the coup plot. (In September 1998 38 defendants received custodial sentences ranging from seven months to 15 years, on charges related to the attempted coup; a further 51 were acquitted.)

In July 1996 Conté announced the appointment of a Prime Minister (the first to be installed under the Third Republic)—non-partisan economist Sidya Touré—who also assumed responsibility for the economy. In February 1997 Touré relinquished control of the economy portfolio to two ministers-delegate, one of whom being Ibrahima Kassory Fofana, who became Minister of the Economy and Finance.

Trials and Tensions

In the presidential election on 14 December 1998, Conté was challenged by four candidates, including Boye Bâ, representing the Union pour le Progrès et le Renouveau (UPR—formed in September through a merger of the UNR and the PRP) and Condé (who had been resident abroad since early 1997, owing to fears for his personal safety) for the RPG. Renewed violence followed the arrest, two days after the poll, of Condé, who was accused of attempting to leave the country illegally (Guinea's borders had been sealed prior to the election) and of seeking to recruit troops to destabilize Guinea. By the end of December 1998 at least 12 people were reported to have been killed as a result of violence in Conakry (the capital), Kankan, Siguiri and Baro. Condé was formally charged in late December; some 100 other opposition activists remained in detention. The official results, subsequently confirmed by the Supreme Court, showed a decisive victory for Conté, with 56.1% of the valid votes cast. Boye Bâ took 24.6%, and Condé 16.6%. Turnout was recorded at 71.4% of the registered electorate.

In March 1999 Sidya Touré was dismissed as premier and replaced by Lamine Sidimé, hitherto the Chief Justice of the Supreme Court and an of no party political affiliation. Fofana, widely credited with Guinea's recent economic successes, was reappointed Minister of the Economy and Finance.

From 1999 opposition groups and human rights organizations urged the release from detention of Condé, as did the National Assembly in February 2000. Nevertheless, in April the trial began of Condé and his 47 co-defendants. In September Condé was sentenced to five years' imprisonment, and six other defendants also received prison terms.

Regional Upheavals

An armed rebellion in south-eastern Guinea in September 2000 reportedly resulted in at least 40 deaths. Instability subsequently intensified in regions near the borders with Sierra Leone and Liberia, with incidences of cross-border attacks on Guinean civilians and the military. The Government attributed the upsurge in violence to forces supported by the Governments of Liberia and Burkina Faso and to members of a Sierra Leonean rebel group, the Revolutionary United Front (RUF), who, the Government alleged, were acting in alliance with Guinean dissidents. Continued cross-border attacks later in that year were reportedly staged by forces associated with the RUF and former members of a faction of a dissolved Liberian dissident group—the United Liberation Movement of Liberia for Democracy (ULIMO). The President postponed Guinea's legislative elections, citing the state of insecurity in the country and in January 2001 assumed responsibility for the defence portfolio.

Conté Extends his Rule

In May 2001 Condé and two of his co-defendants were released from prison, following the granting of a presidential pardon. However, Condé was prohibited from participating in political activities for an unspecified period. In June President Conté announced his intention to hold a national referendum on a proposed constitutional amendment that would permit the President of the Republic to seek longer and limitless terms of office, justifying it by reference to the ongoing instability in border regions.

The referendum was held on 11 November 2001. According to the official results, 98.4% of voters endorsed the constitutional revisions, with a turnout of 87.2% of the registered electorate recorded, although opposition and media sources claimed that participation was lower than 20%. The presidential term of office was thus extended from five years to seven, with effect from the presidential election due in 2003, and the constitutional provision restricting the President to two terms of office was rescinded. Moreover, the President was to be permitted to appoint local government officials, who had hitherto been elected.

In April 2002 President Conté issued a decree scheduling the repeatedly postponed elections to the National Assembly for 30 June. In May four opposition parties that had expressed concerns about the transparency of the forthcoming polls and declared their intention to boycott them, including the RPG and the Union des Forces Républicaines (UFR) of Sidya Touré, announced the formation of a political alliance, the Front de l'Alternance Démocratique (FRAD). At the elections a voter turnout of 71.6% of the registered electorate was recorded; the PUP increased its majority in the legislature to 85 seats. The UPR became the second largest party in the Assembly, securing 20 seats, while four other parties shared the remaining nine seats. In October Boye Bâ was elected as President of a new party, the Union des Forces Démocratiques de Guinée (UFDG), which was composed largely of a faction of the UPR that had boycotted the elections to the National Assembly. The UFDG was affiliated to the FRAD, which announced its intention of nominating a common opposition candidate at the presidential election scheduled to be held in December 2003.

The FRAD opposition alliance boycotted the December 2003 presidential election, owing to a perceived lack of independence on the part of the electoral commission and the alliance's lack of access to the state-controlled media. The only rival to Conté was Boye Bâ, and Conté was declared the winner with 95.3% of the vote. The Government claimed that voter turnout was 82%. The European Union (EU) had declined to send observers, on the grounds that the conditions for the vote were neither free nor fair.

In February 2004 President Conté dismissed Sidimé as Prime Minister, replacing him with François Lonsény Fall, who had held the position of Minister at the Presidency, responsible for Foreign Affairs since June 2002. In April 2004 Fall resigned as Prime Minister and fled the country, claiming that he had been obstructed in trying to implement economic reforms. During 2004 public protests took place in Conakry against the rising cost of living. The post of Prime Minister remained vacant until December, when it was assigned to Cellou Diallo, hitherto Minister of Fishing and Aquaculture.

Following an alleged assassination attempt against the President in January 2005, when shots were fired at a presidential convoy, thousands of suspects were rounded up for questioning. In an atmosphere of increasing anarchy, the opposition parties in the FRAD alliance demanded Conté's resignation, and in July Condé returned from exile.

The political crisis deepened in March 2006 following the President's return from medical treatment in Switzerland. On 4 April it appeared that Prime Minister Diallo had won the President's support for increased powers and an extensive government reorganization. However, before the radio announcement of the presidential decree authorizing these changes was completed, troops invaded the radio and television headquarters to halt the broadcast. On the following day another presidential decree was issued, restoring the previous members of the Government to office and dismissing Diallo for having committed a 'grave error'. Those perceived to have been responsible for the Prime Minister's sudden removal were the Chief of Staff of the Armed Forces, Gen. Kerfalla Camara, and the erstwhile Minister, Secretary-General to the Presidency, Fodé Bangoura, who was promoted to the position of Minister of State for Presidential Affairs, in which capacity he held effective control of defence, security and economic and financial affairs.

Mounting Political Crisis

The sudden dismissal of Diallo, who had won widespread respect for his commitment to reform, was perceived largely to be linked to his efforts to expose corrupt dealings between the central bank and Conté's close business associate Mamadou Sylla, who was alleged to have withdrawn US $22m. in cash from the bank in recompense for arms that he had delivered to the Government in 2000–01. The country's trade unions planned protests demanding better economic management and lower prices of essential goods; strikes took place in June 2006, and the unions suspended their action only after prices were cut by up to 30%. Investigations were launched into the case against Sylla, who was eventually detained later in the year, together with a former Deputy Governor of the central bank, Fodé Soumah.

On 27 December 2006 Conté, whose declining health prevented him from managing government affairs effectively, again augmented the powers of Bangoura, without naming a premier. Shortly afterwards Conté ordered the release from detention of Sylla and Soumah, precipitating large protests led by the main trade unions, which called for a general strike in January 2007. Protesters demanded the return to jail of Sylla and Soumah, but the unions, with the support of the opposition parties, added more far-reaching demands such as the appointment of a new premier, lower fuel prices and the enforcement of heavier taxation on foreign mining companies.

In January 2007 some 60 people died in nationwide protests. Many foreign companies and organizations suspended operations and evacuated staff. On 19 January Conté raised expectations that he was considering appointing a Prime Minister when he removed Bangoura from the position of Minister of State. A negotiation process was initiated by the Speaker of the National Assembly, Aboubacar Somparé, resulting in an agreement on the prime ministerial role on 27 January, under which the Prime Minister would head and appoint the Council of Ministers and senior officials, and hold responsibility for public finance and economic policy. The trade unions subsequently ordered the suspension of the general strike. However, on 9 February, when Conté named his close associate and former minister Eugène Camara as his choice for Prime Minister, protests erupted again, and over the following days several demonstrators were shot dead. On 12 February Conté declared a state of emergency.

A new round of discussions under the aegis of the Economic Community of West African States (ECOWAS) led to the appointment, on 26 February 2007, of former ECOWAS Executive Secretary Lansana Kouyaté as Prime Minister. The new administration announced in March comprised mostly pro-Kouyaté technocrats with no previous experience in government. The new Prime Minister outlined a comprehensive reform agenda.

However, instability continued, and on 4 May 2007 soldiers staged violent street protests in Conakry, demanding the payment of salary arrears. After refusing to meet Kouyaté, on 15 May the mutinous soldiers held talks with Conté, agreeing to suspend their protests in return for the dismissal of five senior officers and the appointment of Gen. Bailo Diallo as defence minister and Gen. Diarra Camara as Chief of Staff of the Army. Conté also promised partial compensation for unpaid salary arrears. During 2007 the legislative elections were repeatedly postponed, owing to logistical obstacles, a lack of resources and the need to set up an independent electoral commission—the Commission Electorale Nationale Indépendante (CENI).

On 1 January 2008 Conté indicated his growing unease with the reforms being pursued by Kouyaté's Government. On 20 May the President dismissed Kouyaté, appointing former education minister and close ally Ahmed Tidiane Souaré as the new Prime Minister.

A further army mutiny in May 2008 rapidly spread across Conakry. Following the new Prime Minister's failure to appease the soldiers, Conté agreed to meet them, and the Government promised to disburse arrears amounting to US $1,100 per person. An attempt by the police to stage a similar mutiny in June was swiftly suppressed by the army.

In June 2008 Souaré announced the appointment of a broad-based Council of Ministers, with all principal portfolios being allocated to close allies of the President or politically neutral technocrats. Only two key ministers from the previous Government retained their positions, although both were dismissed over the next few months and replaced with officials professing greater loyalty to the President.

Guinea celebrated 50 years of independence on 2 October 2008, amid renewed fears about the poor health of Conté, who was unable to attend most of the public festivities. In the same month the CENI announced the further postponement of the legislative elections until March 2009 at the earliest, owing to continued logistical and financial difficulties. In late 2008 protests took place across the country against the lack of basic services, the high cost of many goods and poor pay.

CAMARA AND THE CONSEIL NATIONAL POUR LA DÉMOCRATIE ET LE DÉVELOPPEMENT

Conté died on 22 December 2008. Within a few hours a group of young mid-ranking army officers seized key positions in Conakry. On 23 December the national radio station proclaimed a military takeover. Protests by Prime Minister Soaré and Speaker Somparé were to no avail, and both men eventually recognized the military junta—the Conseil National pour la Démocratie et le Développement (CNDD).

On 24 December 2008 the national television station broadcast an address by the new, self-proclaimed head of state, Capt. Moussa Dadis Camara. He had played a decisive mediating role in the military mutinies that erupted in 2007–08. The newly formed CNDD encompassed various parts of the army, including the presidential guard and a large number of mid-ranking officers from the country's main ethnic groups, thus apparently constituting a consensual base for Camara's rule. Some initial clashes underlined the fragility of the junta, however, and Col Aboubacar Sidiki Camara was dismissed from the Government, after rejecting Moussa Dadis Camara's decision to prolong the detention of several army officers who were accused of plotting a counter-coup.

The junta swiftly began to dismantle Conté's patronage networks by dismissing or retiring 22 generals. In early January 2009 the CNDD appointed Kabiné Komara—a technocrat—as the new Prime Minister. Later that month the new Council of Ministers was announced, with 10 ministries, including the most important portfolios, being allocated to members of the military. Camara also announced that the new Government would review all contracts with mining companies, initiate a vast anti-corruption campaign and prosecute people involved in drug trafficking. This was followed by the arrest of four former mining ministers suspected of embezzlement and fraud and of the late President's son, Ousmane Conté, who was accused of involvement in the cocaine trade.

Despite widespread support for the coup among the population, opposition parties and trade unions, the CNDD maintained the suspension of all forms of political and trade union activity until late February 2009 to avoid unrest. In March it was announced that the legislative polls would take place on 11 October, followed by the first round of the presidential election on 13 December. Camara announced in May that he would not stand in the presidential election and that neither the Prime Minister nor any of the members of the CNDD would be permitted to present their candidacies either.

Camara, who had made public his displeasure with the initial electoral timetable, readily accepted alternative proposals by the Forces Vives (FV—a coalition of Guinea's main political forces and civil society organizations), under which the first round of the presidential election would take place on 31 January 2010, followed by legislative elections on 26 March. In August 2009, however, members of the FV stopped attending election preparation meetings with the CNDD, as they feared that Camara would soon announce his candidacy.

Tensions increased in September 2009 as protesters demanded that Camara keep his promise not to stand in the presidential election, and increasing harassment of opposition members and journalists was reported. On 28 September—the anniversary of Guinea's independence referendum—tens of thousands of Guineans marched to a stadium in Conakry and entered the site, despite the security forces' attempts to block the entrances. Before the opposition leaders could deliver their speeches, army units started to shoot directly into the crowd. Soldiers also publicly raped women and beat and arrested opposition leaders. Independent observers claimed that 150 demonstrators were killed and more than 1,000 injured. The CNDD claimed that there had been 58 deaths: four from gunshot injuries and the rest in the ensuing stampede.

The international community overwhelmingly condemned the events of 28 September 2009 and ceased all co-operation with Guinea. ECOWAS suspended Guinea from the group, imposed an international arms embargo and appointed the President of Burkina Faso, Blaise Compaoré, as mediator between the CNDD and opposition forces. Compaoré's mediation made little progress, however, as the opposition demanded Camara's immediate resignation and replacement by a transitional, civilian administration.

In early December 2009 Camara was shot by his aide-de-camp, Lt Aboubacar 'Toumba' Diakité. The incident was rumoured to have been linked to the events of 28 September; Diakité, who had been observed giving orders to troops and threatening demonstrators on that day, apparently feared that he would be made the scapegoat for Camara and the CNDD leadership. Camara survived the incident and was flown to Morocco, where he spent the following weeks recovering. The Minister at the Presidency, in charge of National Defence, Gen. Sékouba Konaté, assumed control of the junta and declared himself Interim President. In December a United Nations (UN) commission of inquiry formed after the 28 September massacre ruled that Camara, Diakité and Moussa Tiegboro Camara—a member of Camara's presidential cabinet—could be subjected to international criminal proceedings. The CNDD's own internal inquiry, published in February 2010, blamed Diakité alone.

TRANSITION UNDER KONATÉ

Camara's disappearance from the Guinean political scene eased the mediation process with the opposition. Konaté gave a national address on 6 January 2010, announcing the creation of a transitional ruling body led by a Prime Minister from the opposition and pledging that elections, in which the junta would not participate, would be organized promptly. On 15 January Konaté and Camara signed the Ouagadougou Accord in the capital of Burkina Faso, by which both leaders agreed that Guinea would return to civilian rule within six months. Although Camara's supporters staged violent demonstrations, Konaté maintained control over the armed forces.

The junta selected as the new Prime Minister Jean-Marie Doré, the leader of the Union pour le Progrès de la Guinée and the spokesman for the opposition, while Rabiatou Serah Diallo, head of one of the country's principal trade unions, the Confédération Nationale des Travailleurs de Guinée, was appointed to lead the Conseil National de la Transition (CNT), which was to have legislative responsibilities during the transition. Doré's new 34-member Government was announced in February 2010; the posts were evenly distributed among the FV, the CNDD and academics, civil servants and professionals, under the clear assumption that no minister would be allowed to contest the presidential election.

In May 2010 Konaté confirmed that the presidential election would take place on 27 June. On the following day he signed a decree adopting a new Constitution, which had been drafted by the CNT. The Supreme Court approved 24 candidates, including the longstanding opposition figure, Condé, and four former Prime Ministers under Conté—Cellou Diallo, Sidya Touré, Fall and Kouyaté. Konaté, meanwhile, disbanded personal militias and set up a 16,000-strong special military force to oversee the election, the Force Spéciale de la Sécurisation du Processus Electoral (Fossepel).

The presidential election proceeded calmly on 27 June 2010. On the following day the CENI acknowledged widespread technical failings, but ECOWAS observers confirmed that no deliberate systematic fraud had been carried out. On 2 July the CENI announced that Cellou Diallo and Condé would contest a second round. Protests against the results, in particular from Touré (who came third in the first round of the poll, with 13.0% of the vote) and his supporters, continued until 7 July, when Konaté threatened to resign but was persuaded to remain in his post after foreign diplomats intervened and politicians, including Touré, apologized.

After considering the complaints filed by 20 presidential candidates, the Supreme Court confirmed on 20 July 2010 that Diallo, who had received 43.7% of the votes, and Condé, with 18.3%, would contest the presidency in the second round. During the following weeks Condé was able to bring together 16 political parties into his Alliance Arc-en-Ciel (Rainbow Coalition).

After repeated postponements, the second round of the presidential election finally took place, peacefully, on 7 November 2010. International observers concluded that the result could be regarded as credible. The CENI announced on

15 November that Condé was the provisional winner, with 52.5% of the vote. After the announcement there was an outbreak of violence in the capital and across the country, essentially between members of Fossepel and pro-Diallo activists, and a state of emergency was declared. On 3 December the Supreme Court confirmed Condé's victory. Diallo immediately conceded defeat and urged his supporters to remain calm.

CONDÉ AND GUINEA'S FIRST DEMOCRATIC GOVERNMENT, 2010–15

Condé was sworn into office on 21 December 2010. The new President was obliged to consider the multiple loyalties within his Alliance Arc-en-Ciel and appointed a multi-party Council of Ministers of more than 40 members on 5 January 2011. Condé selected two technocrats—Mohamed Saïd Fofana and Kerfalla Yansané—as Prime Minister and Minister of the Economy and Finance, respectively, and assumed the position of Minister of National Defence himself, underlining the importance that he placed on army reform. Condé also appointed three members of the Peul community to government posts to counter further accusations of an anti-Peul stance.

Among the Government's first announcements in January 2011 were a suspension of rice exports, an immediate reduction in the price of rice and free maternal health care services. Although these and other economic stabilization measures proved popular, in February the national civil society platform—the Conseil National des Organisations de la Société Civile Guinéenne—accused Condé of violating the Constitution by failing to propose a schedule for the legislative and local elections.

From April 2012 the repeated postponement of the legislative elections led to public protests and riots against the ongoing political stalemate. Condé's Government and the opposition disagreed on three main issues: the updating of the voter register, which the opposition considered unnecessary; the composition of the CENI, which the opposition regarded as biased towards Condé's party; and the right for Guineans living abroad to vote, which could potentially benefit the opposition.

In May 2012 it was revealed that government officials had attempted to embezzle an estimated US $1.8m. of state funds. Condé confirmed that high-ranking officials had been arrested following the disclosure and that he intended to continue his drive against corruption. However, the assassination in November of the head of the Treasury, Aïssatou Boiro, who had been instrumental in ending the fraud operation, demonstrated the dangers of this tough anti-corruption stance.

An opposition march held in the capital in August 2012 was violently suppressed, and opposition leaders Kouyaté, Cellou Diallo and Sydia Touré were directly targeted. In response, several opposition parties announced their withdrawal from the transitional institutions. In September the CENI's President, Lounceny Camara, announced his resignation. He was replaced in November by former foreign minister and civil society activist Bakary Fofana.

Following the temporary withdrawal of the opposition from the electoral process in February 2013 and a series of riots in Conakry in March, in which at least 10 people were killed and some 240 injured, a compromise over the legislative elections was eventually reached in July, setting the date of the polling within the next 84 days. It was also agreed that the poorly managed CENI would be closely monitored by a commission in which all political movements in Guinea would be represented, that Guineans living abroad would be able to participate in the poll, and that an open tender procedure would be undertaken to revise the voter register for the presidential election of 2015.

The legislative elections took place peacefully on 28 September 2013. Over the following weeks, however, all parties issued accusations of mass fraud, and the opposition withdrew from the vote-counting process on 9 October, demanding that a new poll be organized. On 19 October the CENI announced that Condé's RPG had secured 53 of the 114 seats in the National Assembly, and that the UFDG and the UFR had won 37 and 10 seats, respectively; 12 smaller parties shared the remaining 14 seats. The Supreme Court confirmed the official results on 15 November.

On 15 January 2014 President Condé accepted the resignation of his Government. Prime Minister Mohamed Saïd Fofana, despite growing criticism directed at the limited results of his three years in office, was promptly reappointed, together with 18 other former ministers, and the new Cabinet included no member of the opposition.

In March 2014 the Government confirmed that 78 people had died in a recent outbreak of the Ebola Virus Disease (EVD) in the south-eastern Guinée Forestière region. Guinea received international assistance to address the crisis, and neighbouring Senegal and Côte d'Ivoire were placed on high alert. By mid-2014 the outbreak had spread to Liberia, Sierra Leone and Nigeria. By 29 December 2015, when Guinea was officially declared free of EVD, the final official death toll in the country was 2,544, out of a total of 3,814 persons who had been infected.

In March 2015 the CENI announced the electoral calendar for 2015–16, with the first round of the presidential elections to be held on 11 October 2015 and the local elections to be postponed until March 2016. Although the Government cited the Ebola crisis as the main reason for the new delay to the local elections, the opposition claimed that this was a strategy for President Condé to benefit from the backing of influential local leaders. On 17 March 2015 the opposition announced the suspension of its participation in parliamentary proceedings. In April–May violent clashes took place between protesters and the security forces in Conakry and Mamou, an opposition stronghold.

CONDÉ'S SECOND PRESIDENTIAL MANDATE, 2015–2020

In May 2015 former junta leader Moussa Dadis Camara announced that he was to stand as a candidate in the presidential election. In July, however, three Guinean judges indicted Camara for his alleged role in the violent repression of 28 September 2009, prompting accusations from the opposition that the indictment was politically motivated. A few days later Cellou Diallo announced that he would contest the presidential election as the UFDG candidate. In August 2015 an agreement was eventually reached between the Government and the opposition ahead of the presidential poll, providing for the monitoring of the compilation of a new voters' register, the appointment of two opposition members to the CENI and the partial reorganization of local authorities.

Despite violent clashes between supporters of the RPG and opposition activists in early October 2015 and opposition appeals to the Constitutional Court about alleged irregularities on the electoral register, the first round of the presidential election proceeded as planned on 11 October. The vote was conducted peacefully, and a turnout of 68.4% was recorded. Although Diallo and Sidya Touré issued allegations of malpractice, African Union (AU) and EU observer missions validated the conduct of the elections, while citing organizational difficulties. The CENI announced on 19 October that President Condé had secured a second five-year term, after winning 57.8% of the valid votes cast, ahead of Diallo with 31.5% and Touré of the UFR with 6.0%. The Constitutional Court confirmed the result at the end of the month.

Following the resignation of Fofana's Government, in December 2015 President Condé appointed Mamady Youla, hitherto director of the Guinea Alumina Corporation, as the new Prime Minister. Condé formed a new Government in January 2016. Like the new Prime Minister, most of the appointees, including the new Minister of the Economy and Finance, Malado Kaba, had a technocratic background. Condé appointed Sidya Touré as his High Representative, in a move designed to embrace the opposition and isolate Diallo.

In August 2016 the CENI announced that no date had been set for the next local elections (the most recent of which had been held in 2005), despite the fact that July 2016 had been set as the deadline in the agreement concluded in August 2015. Following renewed tensions between rival factions of the UFDG and the fatal shooting of a demonstrator by a police officer during a large opposition rally in Conakry in February 2016, Condé met Diallo in September. The President promised greater political dialogue with the opposition, a reduction in the rate of value added tax on staple goods and investment in national infrastructure.

Further talks in October 2016 led to the signing of a new agreement between the Government and the opposition, under the aegis of international organizations including the UN, the EU and ECOWAS. Both sides agreed that the local elections would take place in February 2017. (These were postponed indefinitely, however, in January.) Although it was also decided that the existing electoral register could be used for these elections, the authorities pledged to reform the CENI and revise the electoral code before the legislative elections, scheduled for 2018. The authorities also pledged to compensate victims of the pre-election violence in 2013. The National Assembly duly approved a new electoral code in July 2017, despite it being initially rejected by the opposition. In the following month Bakary Fofana was removed as President of the CENI after a vote to oust him by the CENI commissioners.

Meanwhile, in early February 2017 teachers' unions began strike action, demanding improvements in salaries and training. On 20 February at least five people were killed in Conakry when security forces violently suppressed an associated protest, which had been joined by students. Although the Government signed an agreement on pay increases with two of the main teachers' unions later on that day, it was reported that two other protesters had been killed. On 28 February President Condé removed the three ministers who were responsible, respectively, for pre-university education and literacy; civil service, state reform and modernization of administration; and the environment, water and forests.

The extradition of Diakité from Senegal in March 2017 opened the way for the long-awaited trial of those responsible for the stadium massacre of September 2009. Although the investigation was reported to have concluded in December 2017, no date was set for a trial.

In August 2017 the opposition organized a rally to protest against the high cost of living, government corruption and a lack of security. In an apparent attempt to assuage protesters, in September President Condé replaced five more ministers. September was nevertheless marked by a popular uprising against power and water shortages in the mining towns of Boké and Kamsar, which left two people dead and 60 injured and led to the dismissal of Boké's unpopular prefect. This was followed in November by another teachers' strike, which President Condé declared a 'rebellion', while forbidding radio stations from negotiating with the organizers. Two stations that ignored this order—BTA FM and Gangan FM—were subsequently shut down by Guinea's broadcasting regulatory body, the Haute Autorité de la Communication. Four more radio stations were shut down in December, prompting demonstrations by journalists.

In December 2017 a decree set the date of the local and municipal elections for 4 February 2018. Although these elections had long been awaited, participation rates did not rise above 50%. President Condé's RPG was the overall winner, securing 3,248 of the more than 6,000 local seats, followed by the UFDG (2,156 seats). However, the RPG performed poorly in Conakry, where the UFDG won 69 of the available 193 seats.

Violent clashes took place in February and March 2018 between protesters and the security forces, leaving at least seven people dead. From mid-February a strike by the teachers' union, the Syndicat Libre des Enseignants et Chercheurs de Guinée (SLECG), paralysed the education system for more than two months. A deal was eventually reached with the Government which included a 40% pay rise that had been promised in October 2017 and the reinstatement of the union's Secretary-General and main organizer of the strike, Aboubacar Soumah.

Once again, President Condé responded to popular dissatisfaction with a government reorganization. Following the mass resignation of the Government on 17 May 2018, Condé appointed Ibrahima Kassory Fofana—previously the investment and public-private partnerships minister—as the new Prime Minister. A new Council of Ministers was appointed on 27 May. However, fresh protests were organized in July in response to an increase in the price of petrol. In the same month the National Assembly passed legislation modifying the composition of the CENI to seven members from the ruling coalition, seven from the opposition, two from civil society and one from the Ministry of Territorial Administration and Decentralization.

In October 2018 President Condé removed the President of the Constitutional Court, Kéléfa Sall, and replaced him with the erstwhile Vice-President of the Court, Mohamed Lamine Bangoura. The opposition viewed this as an attempt to silence a powerful voice against any effort by Condé to seek a third presidential term. In the same month the SLECG appealed for an indefinite strike, claiming that the Government had failed to increase base salaries as agreed in March.

President Condé issued a decree in January 2019 authorizing the National Assembly to continue functioning beyond the end of its mandate in mid-January. The two main opposition groups—the UFDG and the UFR—had indeed failed to agree on their representatives for the new CENI, and therefore parliamentary elections could not be scheduled. The Government also reached a new agreement with the SLECG, including a new system that guaranteed the automatic payment of salaries and the creation of a joint commission to oversee the overhaul of the national teachers' payroll. Schools reopened in mid-January.

In April 2019 the main opposition parties, civil society organizations and trade unions created the Front National pour la Défense de la Constitution (FNDC), which aimed to prevent Condé from amending the Constitution to allow him to run for a third presidential term in 2020. On 20 May 2019 the Minister of Justice, Cheick Sako, resigned in protest at being excluded from the constitutional reform process—an apparent confirmation of rumours that a new constitution was in fact being prepared. Former Prime Minister Mohamed Lamine Fofana, currently serving as Minister, Adviser to the President, was allocated the justice portfolio. In late May Prime Minister Fofana stated that the Government was in favour of drafting a new constitution.

The CENI announced in September 2019 that legislative elections, which had initially been due to take place the previous year, would be held on 28 December. Later in September, during an official visit to the USA, President Condé prompted renewed speculation that he intended to amend the Constitution to allow him to contest a third term. The FNDC called for demonstrations against any constitutional amendment to this end, and protests commenced in October. In response, the security forces arrested several civil society leaders, including Abdourahmane Sanoh, the co-ordinator of the FNDC, confining the two main opposition leaders, Cellou Diallo and Sidya Touré, to their homes and a harsh crackdown on protesters, which left nine people dead and several more injured. In November the CENI postponed the legislative elections once again, to 20 February 2020, on the grounds that the necessary preparations could not be made for the polls to take place in December 2019.

In December 2019 President Condé proposed a new draft constitution, to be put to the public for approval by referendum at an undisclosed date in 2020. Although the proposed constitution did not increase the number of terms that a President could serve, it increased the duration of presidential terms from five to six years. In addition, the President of the Constitutional Court would no longer be elected by its members but instead nominated by the President of the Republic. This, together with the expectation that President Condé could use the new constitution to seek a third term by claiming that he had not served under the new constitutional rules, intensified protests across the country. In early February 2020 Condé announced that the referendum on the new constitution would be held on 1 March, concurrently with the legislative elections. Between October 2019 and March 2020 between 20 and 30 people were reported to have been killed during violent street protests against the constitutional reforms in Conakry and other towns.

The referendum and legislative elections took place on 22 March 2020—three weeks later than scheduled, owing to concerns about the validity of the electoral register; the opposition parties boycotted the vote. The new Constitution was approved by 89.8% of those who voted (based on a reported turnout of 58.2% of the registered electorate). The results of the legislative elections were confirmed, by the Constitutional

Court on 15 April: President Condé's RPG won 79 of the 114 seats, the Union Démocratique de Guinée, led by Sylla, was a distant second, with just four seats, and the remaining 31 seats were won by 20 small parties.

The newly elected legislature was expected to focus on tackling the COVID-19 pandemic and its impact on the country. The first confirmed case of COVID-19 in Guinea was reported on 12 March 2020, and the Government introduced measures, including a ban on large gatherings in Conakry, on the following day in order to contain the spread of the disease. Conakry's international airport was closed on 23 March, and a dusk-to-dawn curfew and a ban on movement in and out of the capital were imposed on 30 March. Some of these restrictions were partly relaxed from July, when the international airport was reopened.

In July 2020 the CENI announced that it intended to update the electoral register in preparation for the presidential election scheduled to take place on 18 October. In August the RPG nominated Condé to be its presidential candidate, and he submitted his nomination papers to the Constitutional Court in early September. Protests immediately erupted in Conakry and were violently suppressed. The FNDC declared Condé's candidacy to be 'illegal and illegitimate', announcing the organization of peaceful protests and calling for a boycott of the election. A few days later the UFDG's Cellou Diallo declared his intention to contest the poll.

In the run-up to the presidential election, the opposition accused the RPG of stoking ethnic violence at election rallies; notably, Cellou Diallo was forced to abandon a rally in Kankan for his own personal safety. Although 11 opposition candidates contested the election, Cellou Diallo was in effect the only serious challenger to Condé. Although the AU and ECOWAS declared the polling to have taken place freely and fairly, the EU, the USA and France raised concerns about the conduct of the election. An immediate outbreak of violence nationwide was severely repressed by the security forces. Hundreds of opposition and FNDC supporters were arrested and imprisoned, pending trial. The UFDG accused the CENI, which reported a voter turnout of 78.9%, of inflating the rate of participation. Although on 19 October Cellou Diallo claimed to have won the election, at the end of the month the CENI awarded victory to Condé, claiming that he had secured 59.5% of the total vote, ahead of Cellou Diallo with 33.5%. Despite a petition challenging the result, presented by Diallo and three other presidential candidates, the Constitutional Court confirmed the result in November.

CONDÉ'S THIRD PRESIDENTIAL MANDATE

Condé was sworn in as President on 15 December 2020 to serve a third term, the duration of which, according to the new Constitution, would be six years. The formation of a new Government, again headed by Fofana, was announced in January 2021. Many members of the previous administration were reappointed.

On 14 February 2021 the Government declared a fresh epidemic of EVD, after the disease killed three people and infected four others. A campaign of contact tracing, self-isolation and vaccination was immediately launched, while Guinea received international aid to support its response to the outbreak. By the time that the outbreak was officially declared to be over, in June, it had caused 12 deaths.

Meanwhile, the COVID-19 pandemic continued. In March 2021 Guinea received a shipment of 200,000 doses of the Sinovac COVID-19 vaccine from the People's Republic of China and launched a national vaccination campaign; in April the country received a further 300,000 (purchased) doses of Sinovac and 194,400 of the Oxford-AstraZeneca vaccine, donated through the World Health Organization's COVAX Facility scheme. Amid a rise in new infections, in August President Condé announced further restrictions in order to contain the virus. At mid-September 2022 a total of 37,652 confirmed cases of COVID-19, including 449 deaths, had been reported in Guinea since March 2020, and nearly 22% of the population had been fully vaccinated against the disease.

THE MILITARY COUP OF SEPTEMBER 2021

Following several weeks of growing unrest caused by the Government's attempts to boost its much-depleted finances by sharply increasing taxes and raising the price of fuel by 20%, on 5 September 2021 President Condé was detained by disaffected members of an elite military unit, who announced the formation of a Comité National pour le Rassemblement et le Développement (CNRD). The new ruling body, which cited poverty and endemic corruption as the main reasons for the staging of the coup, temporarily closed Guinea's land and air borders and announced the annulment of the Constitution and the dissolution of the Government. The junta strengthened its hold on power by appointing eight army officers to head the country's eight administrative entities (the city of Conakry and seven administrative regions), replacing the appointed Governors. While appearing to be widely supported by the local population and prompting no violent backlash or protest, the military takeover was immediately condemned by the international community, and the AU, the UN, the EU and ECOWAS all demanded Condé's immediate release. The leader of the CNRD, Col Mamady Doumbouya, stated that a 'government of national union' would be installed to lead the country through a transitional period culminating in the peaceful restoration of constitutional order. Cellou Diallo announced that the UFDG would be willing to participate in such an administration. On 15 September the junta instigated a four-day conference in Conakry, attended by political party leaders, including political prisoners who had been arrested and detained during President Condé's rule and released just after the coup, civil society organizations, diplomats, religious emissaries and even mining operators, to discuss the transition process. All stakeholders committed to policy continuity and sharing proposals with the CNRD with regard to Guinea's restoration of civilian rule.

At the end of September 2021 Col Doumbouya unveiled a transition charter intended to guide Guinea's transition back to civilian rule. The charter provided *inter alia* for an 81-member legislative body, the Conseil National de Transition (CNT), which would be responsible for drafting a new constitution. The charter also established that no individual member involved in any of the transitional government institutions would be allowed to participate in national or local elections. On 1 October Col Doumbouya was sworn in as interim President. On 7 October he appointed Mohamed Béavogui, a former civil servant, as Prime Minister. A new Government was formed during late October and early November, which included two retired generals (and allies of Col Doumbouya) as Minister of National Defence and Minister of Security and Civil Protection. Meanwhile, Col Doumbouya asserted control over the security forces by removing 42 army generals, including several close associates of Condé, appointing the junta's second-in-command, Col Sadiba Koulibaly, as Chief of General Staff of the Armed Forces and retiring several hundred soldiers and police officers. In late November Condé was released from prison and placed under house arrest, and in January 2022 he was allowed to travel out of the country for medical reasons. Meanwhile, on 2 December 2021 the CNRD created an anti-corruption court, the Cour de Répression des Infractions Economiques et Financières (CRIEF). At the end of that month former Presidents Konaté and Moussa Dadis Camara were allowed to return to Guinea from an exile of more than 10 years. In early January 2022 Minister of Justice Fatoumata Yarie Soumah was dismissed and replaced by Alphonse Charles Wright, after criticizing the CNRD's intrusion in the judiciary.

In January 2022, following extensive talks, Col Doumbouya announced the composition of the CNT, which, as previously announced, comprised representatives of political parties, civil society, the armed forces, employers' organizations, trade unions and specific interest groups and led by civil society leader Danso Kourouma. The CNT held its first session in February. In the following months tensions rose between the CNRD and the political parties, with the latter criticizing plans by the CNT to set an age limit for presidential candidates, while Wright referred an embezzlement case against Cellou Diallo to the CRIEF. In March a national dialogue conference was initiated to discuss a new institutional framework. However, the opposition parties boycotted the discussions, citing a lack of consultation on the agenda. In April several former government officials and members of the former ruling RPG were charged with corruption by the CRIEF and placed in detention; the RPG consequently suspended its participation in the national dialogue. On 30 April Col Doumbouta proposed a 39-month transition to civilian rule, which was immediately denounced by the opposition.

The CNT approved a 36-month transition period in May 2022, prompting immediate criticism from the leading political parties, including the RPG, and a call by the FNDC for widespread public protests. The CNRD responded by banning all political demonstrations. The FNDC called for a nationwide demonstration against the ban in mid-June, but later withdrew the appeal after Prime Minister Béavogui convened talks. In early July a second round of the national dialogue was launched and once again boycotted by the opposition parties. Three FNDC members were arrested at around the same time, precipitating public protests in the following days; the three were released on 8 July, after they were acquitted of the charges against them at a court hearing. On 10 July the CNRD instructed the CNT to suspend the process of drafting the new constitution until the publication of a final report by the national conference. Further anti-CNRD protests were held in late July, in which at least five protesters were killed and about 100 others arrested. Two FNDC leaders were arrested on 31 July, and the group called for another day of protests on 17 August, when a further two demonstrators were shot dead by security forces. Meanwhile, on 8 August the Government ordered the dissolution of the FNDC. Nevertheless, protests continued in the following month.

EXTERNAL AFFAIRS

Guinea's relations with its neighbours were generally cordial in the early post-independence period. In 1980 Guinea joined the Mano River Union (MRU)—originally founded by Liberia and Sierra Leone—which aimed to promote economic and political co-operation among its members. However, the outbreak of civil conflicts in Liberia and Sierra Leone in the early 1990s prevented the MRU from operating effectively, as its members supported rival rebel factions in each other's territories.

Guinea played a role in Sierra Leone's and Liberia's civil wars during the 1990s and early 2000s, with the repeated deployment of its troops to those countries' borders, its participation in regional peacekeeping missions in Sierra Leone and the support provided by Conté to the country's ousted leaders and to rebel movements, including ULIMO, which were fighting against Liberian President Charles Taylor's National Patriotic Front of Liberia. Guinean territory, particularly the Forestière region, was the object of numerous rebel attacks. Conté used these external threats to legitimize his rule and amass popular support within Guinea and international assistance for his regime and army.

Guinea sought to play a more positive role in the region, however, and became a member of the ECOWAS 'committee of four' (with Côte d'Ivoire, Ghana and Nigeria) charged with ensuring the implementation of decisions and recommendations pertaining to the situation in Sierra Leone in 1997. In the early 2000s relations between the Guinean authorities and their Sierra Leonean and Liberian counterparts improved. In May 2004 the MRU was reactivated by a summit of the leaders of Guinea, Sierra Leone and Liberia. Although the Guinean army continued to occupy the Sierra Leonean territory of Yenga, which is believed to contain significant diamond deposits, and was accused of forays into Liberia in 2010, Guinea's democratic transition in that year raised hopes that relations with its neighbours would soon be normalized. In March 2012 Guinea and Sierra Leone agreed to demarcate the boundaries of their continental shelves in order to prevent future disagreements, predominantly about fishing rights but also about proceeds from possible deep-sea oil deposits. The demilitarization of Yenga was confirmed in August.

The outbreak of EVD in early 2014 (see above) caused new tensions with Guinea's neighbours, as countries also affected, such as Sierra Leone, and others that were not, such as Senegal, unilaterally closed their borders. Tensions eased after the Ebola epidemic had receded by mid-2015.

The presence of gold deposits near the Malian border has also resulted in local tensions between Guinea and Mali, despite the historically good relations between the two countries (partly born from common ideological positions in the early years of their independence). In November 2017 clashes between artisanal gold miners from both sides of the border left 22 people dead, and in May 2018 violent confrontations between Malian youths and Guinean police resulted in the deaths of six people. The regional authorities of both countries promptly held joint meetings in order to prevent a further escalation of violence.

After the suspension of co-operation with France that immediately followed Guinea's declaration of independence, diplomatic relations were resumed in 1976, and in the following year the two countries reached an agreement on economic co-operation. In general, the Conté administration maintained good relations with the French Government, which continues to be Guinea's primary source of financial and technical assistance. France, like the rest of the international community, condemned the coup that followed Conté's death in December 2008 but maintained its co-operation with the army. After the attack on the opposition gathering on 28 September 2009, France announced that it was indefinitely suspending military and institutional co-operation and urged Camara to agree to a transition to civilian rule.

One of newly elected President Condé's first visits abroad was to France, in March 2011. Following this visit, the former colonial power promised its support for military reform and for Guinea's electricity and agricultural sectors. Official delegations of French business leaders visited Guinea on several occasions between 2010 and 2015, demonstrating an interest in increasing investments in the country.

Guinea's international relations after the coup that followed the death of President Conté were deeply affected by the internal political situation. The USA and the EU strongly criticized the CNDD's assumption of power, and the USA suspended all but humanitarian aid to Guinea. West African states in general agreed to frame their responses within ECOWAS, which issued a strong condemnation of the coup, suspended Guinea from all ECOWAS activities pending a restoration of constitutional order and demanded that elections take place before the end of 2009. An international contact group on Guinea, comprising representatives of the African and international communities, was formed in January 2009 to monitor and support the country's democratic transition.

Reactions to the violent suppression of the Guinean opposition in September 2009 were equally severe. The international community called for an international inquiry into the events, and the AU and the EU imposed targeted sanctions on members of the CNDD. Following the signing of the ECOWAS-mediated Ouagadougou Accord in January 2010, the international community provided funds in support of electoral preparation and organization, but all other forms of international assistance remained suspended.

The international community welcomed the election of Condé to the presidency in November 2010 and expressed its willingness to resume support to Guinea and assist in its political and economic reforms. Following the lifting of sanctions against Guinea in December, the President attended the 16th AU summit in Ethiopia in January 2011. The Chinese Minister of Foreign Affairs, Yang Jiechi, visited Guinea in February and announced that China would make available US $27m. in aid. In May the EU announced that the Guinean Government would now have access to suspended funds from the ninth European Development Fund (EDF). Although Guinea's main donors supported the new Government's ambitious economic reforms, notably by agreeing to waive two-thirds of the country's debt in September 2012, they expressed growing frustration during 2012 and 2013 about the indefinite postponement of the legislative elections and the lack of progress towards full democracy.

International pressure and mediation provided by the UN Office for West Africa were instrumental in pursuing the agreements over the legislative elections reached in July and September 2013. Following the confirmation of the election results, in December the EU announced the full resumption of aid. In December 2014 the normalization of Guinea's relations with the EU was confirmed by the signature of a €244m. co-operation agreement for 2014–20, under the 11th EDF.

In September 2016 Condé led a presidential mediation mission to Guinea-Bissau in response to a prolonged political crisis in that country between the Government and opposition, and in October, as the main ECOWAS mediator, hosted negotiations in Conakry, which resulted in the conclusion of a reconciliation agreement between the Guinea-Bissau representatives. Condé assumed the rotating chairmanship of the AU for a one-year term in January 2017.

The political unrest and violence arising from the repeated postponement of the legislative elections that were due to take place in September 2018 and that were eventually held in March 2020, as well as Condé's decision concurrently to hold a constitutional referendum, were met with criticism from the international community. In February ECOWAS had cancelled a goodwill mission to Guinea, and the Organisation Internationale de la Francophonie had withdrawn its electoral observation team, owing to inconsistencies in the electoral register.

The run-up to the 2020 presidential election, when Condé used provisions in the newly adopted Constitution to contest a controversial third term, was marked by further tensions between Guinea and the international community. In September the EU, ECOWAS and the UN expressed their concerns about increasing political polarization and electoral violence in Guinea. Guinea's relations with its neighbours also soured and compounded existing enmity between Condé and his Senegalese and Guinea-Bissau counterparts, when in late September Condé unilaterally closed Guinea's borders with Guinea-Bissau, Sierra Leone and Senegal, citing security reasons. The border with Sierra Leone was reopened in February 2021, following a visit to Conakry by Sierra Leone's President, Julius Maada Bio, and despite the further EVD outbreak. Guinea and Senegal concluded a technical and military co-operation agreement at the ECOWAS summit in Accra, Ghana, in June. Guinea's land borders were closed upon the military coup of 5 September, but shortly afterwards the CNRD announced the staged reopening of all borders (including with Guinea-Bissau and Senegal) from mid-September.

Chinese investments in Guinea's mining and infrastructure sectors under Condé's presidency confirmed China's growing economic involvement in the country (see *Economy*). President Condé made a state visit to China in October 2016, meeting his counterpart, Xi Jinping; 10 agreements covering various areas were signed, and it was announced that a comprehensive strategic bilateral partnership would be established. In September 2018 China and Guinea signed a bilateral co-operation agreement, with one of the first results being China's financing of the rehabilitation of Guinea's roads (see *Economy*). President Condé also sought closer diplomatic and commercial links with Iran, India and the Gulf countries, in an effort to diversify Guinea's international relations.

President Condé's ousting in the military coup of 5 September 2021 was widely condemned internationally and regionally. Guinea's membership of ECOWAS was suspended on 8 September and its membership of the AU two days later. ECOWAS also imposed sanctions on members of the Guinean junta, freezing their financial assets and imposing a travel ban from mid-September, while sending a delegation to the country to urge a transition back to civilian rule. ECOWAS sanctions were reinforced in November, in the absence of a detailed transition timetable, and the bloc called for the organization of elections by March 2022. In early July ECOWAS announced that it was maintaining its sanctions against the junta and threatened to impose economic sanctions on the country if the CNRD failed to publish a detailed transition timetable within a month. In late July ECOWAS reported that an agreement had been reached in principle with the Guinean Government to reduce the transitional period from 36 to 24 months, but a government spokesman subsequently denied that the duration of the transition had been shortened. The local representatives of the UN, the EU, ECOWAS, France and the USA criticized the violent repression of public protests at the end of July, calling on the CNRD to conduct a public inquiry into the killing of demonstrators.

Economy

MARIE GIBERT

INTRODUCTION

With successful management of its substantial mineral deposits and excellent agricultural potential, Guinea could eventually become one of the richest countries in West Africa. However, the country's economic record since independence has been significantly below expectations. The country's gross domestic product (GDP) expanded, in real terms, at an average annual rate of 3.0% in 1970–80, reflecting the rapid development of the bauxite sector, but declined by an average of 1.4% per year in 1980–85. The causes of Guinea's relatively poor performance during this 15-year period were largely political. First, there was the abrupt severance of the country's links with France in 1958, which was followed by the discontinuation of aid and the loss of the leading traditional market for Guinea's exports. Second, the newly independent Guinea immediately sought to set up a socialist economy, with direct state control of production and consumption in virtually every sector—an objective demanding a level of managerial input that Guinea lacked, which resulted in great inefficiency and waste. Under President Ahmed Sékou Touré (1958–84), the economy developed a large informal sector in response to the near monopoly of the state over formal economic activity.

During the 1990s, in an attempt to remove at least the domestic constraints on growth, the Lansana Conté regime (1984–2008) introduced policy reforms that had been agreed with the International Monetary Fund (IMF) and the World Bank. These included the transfer to private interests, or elimination, of parastatal organizations, the liberalization of foreign trade and the abolition of price controls, together with monetary and banking reforms and a reduction in the number of civil service personnel. The recovery programme initially received substantial international support, in the form of debt relief and new funds from bilateral and multilateral sources. However, the reform process collapsed in 2002 as the country began to build up budget deficits in an inflationary environment. Most international financial assistance was suspended until more rational economic management could be imposed. In 2004 the economic situation began seriously to deteriorate, without effective political management, even as mineral revenues increased, owing to higher global demand and prices. Rising inflation provoked widespread social unrest, and the differential between the official and unofficial exchange rates of the Guinean franc widened.

The lack of a clear economic direction after 2003 brought about not only high inflation but a deterioration in living standards, and the ratio of the population living below the poverty line rose to 53% in 2007–08. Annual average inflation surged to 34.7% in 2006, coinciding with the collapse of economic reform during protracted political upheaval, but by 2009 had fallen back to 4.7%, initially as a result of tighter monetary policy by the central bank and the depreciation of the Guinean franc and then as a result of a decline in commodity prices following the onset of the global financial crisis. Inflation rose again sharply in 2010 and 2011, to 15.5% and 21.4%, respectively, owing essentially to nominal exchange rate depreciation and increasing global commodity prices, before receding to 8.2% in 2015, as a result of the stabilization policies of the new

Government and the central bank. It averaged 10% in 2018–20 and reached 12.6% in 2021, owing mainly to higher food prices.

Following a deceleration in growth to 1.5% in 2007 owing to national strikes during the first two months of the year, it accelerated to 4.5% in 2008 as mining and construction sector activity increased. The death of President Conté in December 2008 precipitated the assumption of power by the Conseil National pour la Démocratie et le Développement. A period of great economic uncertainty followed as donors froze their development assistance, and the military junta reassessed and renegotiated major mining contracts. Amid the political crisis following the massacre of protesters in the capital, Conakry, in September 2009, several controversial contracts were signed with Chinese and other new investors attracted by the prospects of shares in substantial new production of minerals. Unsurprisingly, given the political uncertainty and the suspension of donor assistance, Guinea's real GDP contracted by 0.3% in 2009.

Following the election of Alpha Condé to the presidency in November 2010, the new Government appointed in January 2011 planned ambitious economic reforms, which included stabilizing the currency and encouraging investment in agriculture and mining. As a result of these policies and increased mining output, Guinea's real GDP expanded by 3.6% in 2011; it rose by 4.5% in 2012, despite a fall in alumina production, following industrial action, and in diamond production, owing to a government decree banning artisanal diamond mining in an effort to boost agriculture. GDP growth slowed to 2.3% in 2013, amid decreasing international market prices and investments in iron ore and bauxite and political turmoil prior to the legislative elections. In 2014 and 2015 the rate of GDP growth slowed to 0.4% and 0.1%, respectively, owing to an outbreak of Ebola Virus Disease (EVD), which resulted in more than 2,500 fatalities and had a heavy socioeconomic impact. The end of the outbreak in June 2016 allowed for a rebound in economic activity. GDP growth reached 5.2% in 2016 and 12.7% in 2017 as the mining sector experienced a boom, before falling to 6.2% in 2018 and 5.6% in 2019 as strikes and protests against proposed constitutional amendments disrupted economic activity.

By August 2020 Guinea had managed to curtail the spread of the COVID-19 pandemic, notably by closing its borders in March and isolating Conakry from the rest of the country. However, these measures and the sharp contraction in global trade triggered by the pandemic seriously affected Guinea's economy. In April the Government approved a package worth about US $318m. to mitigate the domestic impact of the pandemic. The poorest households were exempted from paying utility bills for three months from April, and several taxes for small and medium-sized enterprises were suspended. The economic impact of the pandemic and the ensuing global crisis accounted for a further deceleration in the rate of GDP growth to 4.6% in 2020 and 3.1% in 2021 (according to the World Bank).

POPULATION AND EMPLOYMENT

According to the United Nations (UN), the estimated total population stood at 13,261,638 as at mid-2022, and the urban population comprised 37% of the total in 2021.

According to the World Bank, the total labour force was estimated at 4.8m. in 2021. Although agriculture remains the principal sector of employment, since the 1980s an increasing proportion of the population has been engaged in industrial activities (6% in 2019, according to World Bank estimates) and service activities (34% in 2019). The reduction in job opportunities in the public sector, which was previously guaranteed to all university graduates, has caused a rise in urban unemployment and fuelled student unrest.

AGRICULTURE, FORESTRY AND FISHING

Despite the rapid development and potential of the mining sector, agriculture remains an important economic activity in terms of employment (engaging 61% of the labour force in 2019, according to World Bank estimates), even if the value of its output has progressively decreased (contributing an estimated 25.5% of GDP in 2021, according to the World Bank). Under the Sékou Touré regime, agricultural production was depressed by

the demands and inefficiencies of the collectivist regime. On taking office, the Conté Government abolished collectives, raised producer prices and ended the production tax. Improvements to infrastructure (notably the road network) and the easier availability of farm credits stimulated higher production by small-scale farmers.

Production of foods has recovered, and annual production in the late 1990s and early 2000s was about 20% more than the average annual output recorded in 1979–81. In 2020 output of paddy rice (cultivated mainly in the south-eastern Guinée Forestière region) was estimated by the Food and Agriculture Organization (FAO) of the UN at 2.9m. metric tons, while production of cassava was 2.5m. tons, maize 907,900 tons and sweet potatoes 322,100 tons. However, the rise in output has failed to keep pace with population growth, so that Guinea—a net exporter of food in the past—now imports large quantities, representing about double the value of its agricultural exports. The staple crops are supplemented by the substantial livestock herd (raised using traditional methods), which FAO estimated at 8.4m. cattle, 2.5m. sheep and 3.7m. goats in 2020.

The major commercial crops are bananas, coffee, pineapples, oil palm, groundnuts and citrus fruit. The banana plantations, which suffered in the late 1950s from disease and, following independence, from the withdrawal of European planters and the closing of the protected French market, have recovered well, and output reached 221,440 metric tons in 2020, according to FAO. Coffee production averaged 20,000 tons per year in the late 1990s and early 2000s and rose from the mid-2010s to reach an estimated 38,570 tons in 2020 (according to FAO). Annual pineapple production, which measured some 16,000 tons in the late 1970s, had increased to more than 70,000 tons by the late 1990s and was estimated at 132,100 tons by FAO in 2020. An export trade in fruit and vegetables for the European market has been developed as quality control and transportation links have improved, and there have been significant attempts to increase rubber and oil palm cultivation. Guinea's rubber production was estimated at 14,950 tons in 2020 (according to FAO). In 2016 the Government announced major investment in the cashew nut sector in order to increase the total area devoted to the crop from 200,000 ha to 1m. ha. Cashew nut production reached an estimated 20,860 tons in 2020, according to FAO.

There is considerable potential for timber production, with forests covering 25.2% of the total land area in 2020, according to the World Bank. Timber resources are used mainly for fuel, and production of wood fuel totalled an estimated 12.4m. cu m in 2020, according to FAO. In June 2021 the Government announced a ban on woodcutting in an attempt to combat illegal logging and its devastating effects on the country's forests.

The fishing sector remains relatively undeveloped. Only about one-third of the total catch from Guinean waters—363,000 metric tons in 2019, according to FAO estimates—is accounted for by indigenous fleets, the remainder being taken by factory ships and industrial trawlers. Since 1983 the Guinean Government has concluded a series of fishing accords with the European Community (EC, now European Union—EU). An agreement has since been reached to award foreign licences exclusively to EU fleets, in an effort to preserve the viability of fish stocks on the continental shelf. The EU and Guinea concluded a Fisheries Partnership Agreement in May 2009, but the European Commission suspended the payment of the financial compensation, initially because of the ongoing political instability and from 2014 in reaction to the Government's incapacity to combat illegal fishing in Guinean waters. In December 2016 the Government enacted the requisite legal measures and inspection systems to allow fish exports to the EU to resume and in January 2017 announced an action plan, developed in co-operation with the EU, to combat illegal fishing that was estimated to cost Guinea about US $100m. annually. Attempts to negotiate a new fisheries agreement with the EU broke down in 2017, and as at August 2022 negotiations had not resumed.

MINING

Mining has long been Guinea's most dynamic sector and the most important source of foreign exchange, providing more than 90% of recorded export revenues for much of the 1980s and about 80% in the 1990s. The share of GDP supplied by natural resource revenue reached 18.9% in 2017, but fell to 4.1% in 2020, according to the World Bank.

Minerals accounted for more than 94% of export earnings in 2021. In 1995 the Government revised the mining code to encourage foreign investment and announced the foundation of the Centre de Promotion et de Développement Miniers to act as the sector's advisory and regulatory body. Bauxite, diamonds and gold are exploited commercially, and deposits of nickel and titanium could also prove viable.

Following the military coup in December 2008 all mining contracts were to be reviewed in order to eradicate corruption, and the mining rights of some international companies were subsequently cancelled and awarded elsewhere, while others were able to negotiate new contracts. In October 2009 the Government signed contracts worth US $7,000m. with two institutions in the People's Republic of China with links to mining interests: the China International Fund (CIF—a Hong Kong-based investment company) and China Sonangol (a joint venture between the Angolan national oil company, Sonangol, and Dayuan International Development, the main shareholder of the CIF) pledged to build electric power-generating capacity, railways, roads and bridges and to launch a new airline.

President Condé announced in January 2011 that the existing mining contracts would not be amended, but that the Government would seek to increase its stake from 15% to at least 35%. In August the transitional parliament, the Conseil National de la Transition (CNT), adopted a law establishing a new state mining company, the Société Guinéenne du Patrimoine Minier (SOGUIPAMI), to manage funds for geological exploration and the state's interest in foreign mining operations. In September the CNT adopted a new mining code, which sought to increase transparency and improve the management of the country's mineral resources, notably through the creation of SOGUIPAMI and the Commission Nationale des Mines—the latter to manage licences. However, the new code was withdrawn after only two weeks, owing to the adverse reaction of investors. A revised code, adopted in April 2012, reduced mining profit tax, bauxite royalties and import duties on mining-related equipment. The minimum investment was cut by one-half to US $500m., while maximum concession areas were increased for bauxite and iron ore. Although the revised code maintained the state's automatic 15% stake in mining projects, it tapered it to encourage value-added activity. In July 2014 Guinea became the 28th country to agree to the Extractive Industries Transparency Initiative conditions of transparency and good governance and to achieve 'compliant' status under the initiative. Since the coup of September 2021, the military junta has sought to renegotiate contracts, notably in the bauxite and iron ore sectors, in an effort to defend national interests.

Bauxite and Alumina

The country possesses the world's largest bauxite reserves, estimated at some 7,400m. metric tons in 2020 by the US Geological Survey, with a very high-grade ore. In 2020 Guinea ranked second in terms of ore production (behind Australia) and is one of the world's largest exporters of bauxite. Annual output averaged some 12m.–17m. tons between the early 1980s and mid-2000s. Expansion and rehabilitation programmes at the country's mines were projected to increase annual output to 20m. tons, and the reduction in the state interest to 15% of equity was expected to enhance investment and efficiency. However, in 2006–09, despite advances in negotiations with foreign investors, the deteriorating political situation brought many mining operations to a halt. The stabilization of the political situation in 2010–13 encouraged bauxite investment and production, which increased from 17.6m. tons in 2011 to reach a record 87.7m. tons in 2020. In April 2022 the Government demanded that the bauxite mining companies operating in Guinea, in accordance with their

contracts, submit plans by the end of May for the development of refineries to process bauxite in the country.

The exploitation of bauxite reserves at Fria, north of Conakry, by the Compagnie Internationale pour la Production de l'Alumine Fria (an international consortium), commenced in the 1930s. Processing into alumina began in 1960 at what remains the country's only refinery, located near Kindia. Following independence, the Government took a 49% share in the company (renamed Friguia), increasing its share to 100% in 1998. In 1999 the Government formed a controlling company, the Alumina Company of Guinea Ltd (ACG). However, in 2002 Russian Aluminium (RUSAL) took a majority stake in ACG as part of a US $350m. plan to expand Friguia's annual production capacity to 1.4m. metric tons; in 2006 RUSAL increased its stake in ACG to 100%. The military junta that took power in December 2008 ordered an independent audit on the privatization of the Friguia refinery, and in September 2009 a local court declared it null and void, as it had been bought for one-tenth of its actual value. In the absence of a new agreement, the case was referred to an international arbitration court, which ruled in favour of RUSAL in July 2014. Meanwhile, from April 2012 the Russian company faced prolonged strike action at the Friguia complex as workers demanded a monthly minimum wage of $400 and medical expenses. Following an agreement between RUSAL and the Guinean Government in April 2016, the former announced that operations at Friguia would resume and that production would increase gradually to 550,000–600,000 tons per year. Renovation works began in early 2017, and the Friguia plant resumed full operations in June 2018. Meanwhile, in December 2012, despite the ongoing dispute over Friguia, the Government gave RUSAL exclusive access to the concession of Dian-Dian, which holds the world's largest bauxite deposit, with an estimated total capacity of 566m. tons. Production at Dian-Dian commenced in June 2018, with an annual projected capacity of 3m. tons. Following the Russian invasion of Ukraine in February 2022, RUSAL redirected its exports of bauxite for refining in Ireland.

The country's principal bauxite mine is at Sangarédi, in the north-west Boké region, which was commissioned in 1973 by the Compagnie des Bauxites de Guinée (CBG)—a joint venture between the Government and the Halco group (an international consortium). CBG exports some 16m. metric tons of bauxite ore annually. In June 2014 the Guinean legislature approved an agreement permitting a joint multinational venture led by the Global Alumina Corporation, a subsidiary of Emirates Global Aluminium (EGA) of the United Arab Emirates (UAE), to develop and operate a bauxite mine and alumina refinery at Sangarédi. The venture also involved plans to expand facilities at the port of Kamsar to facilitate exports from the refinery, and a new quay and container terminal were opened in October 2016. In its first year of operation (August 2019–August 2020), EGA exported 6.1m. tons of bauxite ore.

In August 2011 China Power Investment Corpn announced that it would invest US $6,000m. in the development of a bauxite mine and alumina refinery near the town of Boffa, in Boké region. Production at the facility, carried out by Chalco, a subsidiary of China's Aluminium Corporation of China (Chinalco), began in early 2020. In 2012 British-based Alufer Mining also announced plans to invest $400m. to develop a bauxite project near Boffa through its Guinean subsidiary, Bel Air Mining; an exploitation licence was granted in 2013. Following a $205m. agreement with the multilateral development finance institution Africa Finance Corporation, production commenced in August 2018. Alufer predicted that production would rise from an initial 5.5m. metric tons per year to 10m. tons over the following two years. The company was also building its own dedicated export facility, with a berth linked to the mainland by a 1.5-km causeway. However, high investment costs and the depressed international market following the COVID-19 pandemic led to Bel Air Mining operating at a loss in 2019–21, and Alufer consequently sought new investors to boost its operations.

In 2015 a vertically integrated joint venture, the Société Minière de Boké-Winning Africa Port (SMB-WAP), comprising Guinea's United Mining Supply, Singapore's Winning Africa Port (shipping) and Shandong Weiqiao Group (China's largest private sector aluminium producer) became Guinea's latest bauxite producer/exporter. SMB-WAP commenced operations in July at a new mine, in Katougouma, in Boké region. Output reached 12m. metric tons in 2016 and accounted for a significant increase in bauxite exports. In 2018 the Government signed an agreement with SMB-WAP worth US $3,000m. for the development of a new mine and related infrastructure. The agreement involved new mining licences for production of bauxite in the Santou 2 and Houda areas, the construction of an aluminium refinery in the Boké special economic zone and a 135-km railway line connecting Boké and Boffa. The new mines were scheduled to start operating in 2022, with annual bauxite production expected to reach 30m. tons in 2024.

Diamonds

Diamond mining was suspended in the late 1970s to prevent smuggling and theft. In 1980 the Government allowed the resumption of diamond mining by private companies, and AREDOR-Guinée was founded in 1981 with Australian, Swiss and British participation, as well as support from the International Finance Corporation (IFC), the private sector lending arm of the World Bank. The Government had a 50% holding and was to take 65% of net profits. AREDOR-Guinée began production in 1984, and output reached a peak of 204,000 carats in 1986. However, mining was suspended in 1994. AREDOR was subsequently restructured, with Canada's Trivalence Mining taking a majority stake with a view to developing new kimberlite resources. In 2006 South Africa's De Beers negotiated a resumption of activities and was awarded permits for exploration in the Macenta area. In July 2008 the Ministry of Mines and Energy recommended that the Government cancel the diamond mining licence granted for the AREDOR mine, owing to recent inactivity. The rights to the mine were eventually granted to the Guinean-owned Batax Bouna International Mining Corporation. In 2009 West African Diamonds (WAD) began producing small amounts of diamonds at its Bomboko and Mandala mines. WAD, which changed its name to Stellar Diamonds in February 2010, also continued its exploration activities on the Droujba and Bouro North properties. According to the African Diamond Producers Association, Guinea's diamond production totalled 128,600 carats in 2020 (down from 293,000 carats in 2018).

Gold

Gold is mined both industrially and by individuals (the latter smuggle much of their output abroad). Alluvial production in the Siguiri and Mandiana districts began in 1988; however, extraction ceased in 1992, owing to financial and technical difficulties and conflicts with artisanal miners. It resumed in early 1998, and production peaked at 283,000 troy oz in 2001 but fell to 100,000 oz in 2004, following a dispute with the Government, which placed an embargo on exports from the mine. After the lifting of the ban, production rose to a new high of 372,000 oz in 2009, before decreasing again in the first half of the 2010s, owing to the mining of lower-grade areas following the depletion of the high-grade Bidini and Santchoro pits. The elimination of export taxes on gold in February 2016 led to a strong revival in exports, which surged to a record 158 metric tons in 2020 (up from 18.5 tons in 2015), but fell to 65 tons in 2021, according to the International Trade Centre.

The Société Minière de Dinguiraye (a joint venture with Norwegian, Australian and French interests) began production at the Léro site in 1995; output in 2004 was estimated at 70,000 troy oz. The Norwegian-based Kenor developed an extension of the mine east of the Karta river, at Fayalala, which increased overall production to an estimated 400,000 oz in 2006. The current owner, OAO Severstal Resources of the Russian Federation, revised potential targets, and gold production at the mine totalled 214,000 oz in 2015. A Canadian company, Semafo, has developed a mine at Kiniero, which produced an estimated 20,000 oz in 2013. Semafo abandoned the mine in 2014, and the Government signed a new agreement with Cypriot-based Sycamore Mining in 2019 to exploit and expand the facility. Sycamore Mining merged with Canadian-based Robex Resources in early 2022, and the new entity planned to restart exploitation at Kiniero, with the development of a new solar power plant, by 2025. Russian mining company Nordgold has also developed a mine at Lefa. In 2013 Nordgold announced that it would conduct an infill drilling

programme in 2014 and invest US $4.6m. in exploration. Following the resolution of operational difficulties, gold production at the Lefa mine increased from 162,700 oz in 2013 to 208,800 oz in 2017. In 2019 the Government granted Nordgold a new licence to operate the Lefa mine for another 15 years. Several other foreign enterprises are also actively prospecting for gold. In June 2020 Hummingbird Resources, a British-based gold mining company, signed an agreement with Cassidy Gold, a Canadian mining firm, to acquire the Kouroussa gold project, located in the Siguiri Basin. The Government granted Hummingbird Resources a 15-year renewable licence in May 2021 against a 5% loyalty payable to the state, a 1% contribution to a local development fund and 30% tax on profits, and on the condition that construction would start within 12 months. The project was expected to produce more than 100,000 oz of gold annually. A licence was granted in 2016 to the Société des Mines de Mandiana, 85% owned by Morocco's Managem, with the remaining 15% owned by SOGUIPAMI, to exploit the mine of Tri-K, north-east of Kankan. Production began in June 2021, and the mine was expected to produce 130,000 oz of gold annually. Canadian-based Sanu Gold was granted a permit to exploit the Daina sites in the Siguiri Basin and announced in July 2022 that it had identified significantly elevated gold in rock chip samples of up to 12.5 g gold per metric ton.

Iron Ore

In May 2008 the multinational mining company Rio Tinto revealed that it was seeking a Chinese partner to develop the world's largest unexploited iron reserves, estimated at 2,250m. metric tons, at Simandou, at a cost of US $6,000m. However, in June the Government indicated that it would review Rio Tinto's contract to ensure that it complied with the proposed new mining code, and in December the Government withdrew Rio Tinto's rights to the northern half of the concession. It was confirmed in February 2009 that the northern sector had been awarded to BSG Resources (BSGR), an Israeli company owned by the Beny Steinmetz Group. In March 2010 Chinalco and Rio Tinto agreed to develop jointly Rio Tinto's Simandou concession, whereby Chinalco agreed to pay $1,350m. for about 45% of Rio Tinto's concession, while Rio Tinto retained just over 50%, and 5% remained with the IFC. In April Vale of Brazil, the world's largest iron ore producer, announced that it had acquired a majority 51% stake in BSGR's Guinean concession. In April 2011 the new Government formally approved the acquisition by Rio Tinto and Chinalco of two blocks of the Simandou concession. In July 2016 Rio Tinto announced that it was shelving the Simandou project, owing to low international prices for iron ore.

The Government announced in January 2012 that it would review BSGR's permit for the other two Simandou blocks, which could be subject to cancellation. In October Vale stated that it was abandoning its 51% stake in blocks 1 and 2 of the Simandou concession. In March 2013 Rio Tinto announced that it was to reduce sharply its local budget and its staff. Suspicions about the conditions under which the mining concession had initially been awarded to BSGR arose again in April, when the US Department of Justice arrested Frédéric Cilins, a French national and former BSGR representative, accusing him of having offered money to the wife of former President Conté to facilitate the transfer of the mining concession to BSGR. In April 2014 the Government withdrew BSGR's licence to exploit its northern share of the Simandou concession, on the grounds that the company had obtained it corruptly. In response, BSGR appealed to the International Centre for Settlement of Investment Disputes (ICSID) in May, in the hope that no third party would be allowed to develop any activity in the concession during the arbitration period. Meanwhile, Rio Tinto filed a suit in New York, USA, in April, accusing BSGR and Vale of fraudulently appropriating its rights to the Simandou north concession. In February 2015 the Government announced that it was planning to sell the two Simandou blocks, despite the pending case before the ICSID. In November 2016 BSGR declared its intention to file a lawsuit against Rio Tinto over its alleged theft of BSGR's mining rights in Simandou. In March 2018 BSGR, burdened with the cost of multiple arbitration and litigation cases, was placed in administration. In February 2019 BSGR and the Guinean Government agreed to withdraw the mutual corruption allegations and the arbitration case, and BSGR surrendered its rights to Simandou (while being allowed to maintain an interest in the smaller Zogota deposit). In January 2021 Israeli mining magnate Beny Steinmetz was sentenced by a Swiss court to five years in prison for corruption in the Simandou case.

In June 2020 the Guinean Government awarded a 25-year concession to the SMBWAP joint venture for the development of the Simandou north concession. The Government owns a 10% stake in SMB-WAP through SOGUIPAMI. SMB-WAP was expected to invest US $14,000m. towards developing Simandou north, including the construction of the 700-km Trans-Guinea Railway (TGR) to transport the ore to the coast and the development of a new deep-water port near Conakry. In May 2021 Liberia's parliament ratified a deal that would allow Guinea to transport iron ore from its south-eastern mining operations via the Liberian port of Buchanan, as a potential alternative to the TGR. In March 2022, however, the Guinean Government ordered a temporary halt on all activities at Simandou in an effort to encourage greater collaboration between the various owners of the facility in favour of Guinea's national interests, notably through infrastructural development, thus underlining Guinea's preference for the TGR option, and local employment. Two weeks later, a US $15m. tripartite agreement was signed between the Government, SMB-WAP and Rio Tinto that reaffirmed the three parties' intention to co-develop the deposit and to build the TGR and a deep-water port by 2024, with production to start in 2025. Operations were halted again in June 2022, when the Government proposed the establishment of a new company, the Compagnie du Trans-Guinéen, to be co-owned by the three parties. A new agreement was reached in July.

In May 2010 the Australian company Bellzone Mining acquired a 25-year concession to develop the Kalia iron ore mine, located near Faranah. In a joint venture with the CIF, the latter agreed to spend US $2,700m. on infrastructure to facilitate the production and export of iron ore. The Yomboyeli mine, on the Kalia site, (which was operated by Forécariah Guinea Mining—a subsidiary of Bellzone Mining) came on stream in June 2012—the mine had estimated reserves of 40m. metric tons of iron ore, and annual production was expected to rise eventually from an initial 4m. tons to 10m. tons. However, transport constraints and a sharp decline in international prices for iron ore resulted in the suspension of shipments, and drilling was halted in the first half of 2014. Following the liquidation of Forécariah Guinea Mining in October, the mine remained dormant. In June 2019 the Guinean Government and the Indian mining company Ashapura signed an agreement jointly to relaunch operations at the mine and rehabilitate the port of Konta. Iron exports from Yomboyeli resumed in late 2020.

In February 2019 the Guinean Government signed an agreement with Niron Metals, a British-based private mining venture, for the development of an iron ore mine in Zogota. This was followed in May by an agreement between Niron and the Liberian Government to use the railway line between Yekepa near the Guinean border and Buchanan. In September Canadian-based High Power Exploration acquired an 85% stake in the Nimba iron ore concession on the Guinean-Liberian border; the remaining 15% is held by the Guinean Government. The Nimba mine holds reserves of an estimated 1,000m. metric tons of high-grade iron ore and at full capacity is estimated to be capable of producing 30m. tons of iron ore annually. In October 2020 the Guinean and Liberian Governments agreed to allow several Guinean mines, including Nimba, to export through Liberian ports. The Nimba mine is expected to produce an initial 15m. tons of iron ore per year, with exports forecast to commence by 2025–26.

Uranium

In August 2007 the Government announced that a uranium deposit in Firawa and Bohoduo, in the Guinée Forestière region, had been discovered by an Australian company, Murchison International, which planned to develop the deposits. Murchison International, now Forte Energy NL, has conducted mineralogical and metallurgical studies at the 286-sq-km Firawa prospect, which indicate the presence of rare earth elements and uranium. Forte Energy commenced pre-feasibility activities at the site in January 2011. In 2019 Forte Energy was reported to have completed its exploration drilling programmes in Firawa and Bohoduo; it was estimated that the former site contained 11.6m. lb of uranium (5,262 metric tons).

Petroleum

From 2002 the US company Hyperdynamics acquired 80,000 sq km of Guinea's offshore territory to explore for potential oil reserves. However, the company faced difficulties in funding the exploration work, and in September 2009 it concluded an agreement with the Guinean Government to relinquish some of the offshore blocks in return for greater leniency over the ongoing delays. In October China Sonangol acquired 74% of the acreage relinquished by Hyperdynamics. In October 2011 Hyperdynamics drilled Guinea's first deepwater oil well, Sabu-1, situated 57 km from the Société Guinéenne des Pétroles 2B-1 well—the only offshore area where oil reserves had previously been identified, in 1977. Hyperdynamics confirmed in February 2012 that drilling had revealed oil deposits. In January 2013 London-listed Tullow Oil took a 40% stake in Hyperdynamics' Guinea operations. In September Hyperdynamics asked the Guinean Government to renew its exploration period to September 2017, with the appraisal of any discovery to be completed by September 2018. In March 2014, however, Tullow Oil declared *force majeure* on its offshore exploration block in Guinea, following a regulatory investigation into Hyperdynamics by the US authorities, and work was suspended. The declaration of *force majeure* was lifted in May. In August 2016 Tullow Oil and Dana Petroleum (which had purchased a 23% stake in 2010) relinquished their stakes in the offshore block, leaving Hyperdynamics with a 100% share. In September 2016 Hyperdynamics was granted an extension until September 2017 to drill a new offshore well, but no hydrocarbons had been located by that time. The Government then refused to grant Hyperdynamics a further extension, and the company filed for bankruptcy in December.

Energy

Installed electricity generation capacity was estimated at 1,100 MW in 2022. In 2020, despite significant recent reforms and investment, Guinea's national electrification rate was just 44.7% (19.3% in rural areas, 88.1% in urban areas), according to the World Bank. The country has a very large—but as yet little exploited—hydroelectric potential, estimated at over 6,000 MW. In 1999 a 75-MW plant was commissioned on the Konkouré river at Garafiri, and a further major scheme (with a capacity of 240 MW), at Kaléta, 100 km downstream, was inaugurated in 2015. Despite Guinea's electricity deficit amounting to 400 MW before the Kaléta hydroelectric dam came on stream, one-third of the power produced by the dam was to be exported to Senegal, Guinea-Bissau and The Gambia. China International Water and Electric (which constructed the Kaléta dam) began work in 2016 on another, 450-MW dam on the Konkouré river, at Souapiti, which commenced commercial operations in June 2021. In January 2018 Tebian Electric Apparatus (China) commenced construction of a hydroelectric dam at Amaria, also on the Konkouré river. The dam was expected to be completed in 2022 and to generate 300 MW–320 MW of energy annually. In April 2021 the European Investment Bank (EIB) granted Guinea and Mali a €330m. loan to build an interconnecting grid between their hydroelectric dams to improve regional electricity provision. In November Côte d'Ivoire agreed to export 11 MW of electricity to Guinea annually in 2022 and 2023.

In December 2014 the Government reached an agreement with the EIB, under which the latter would cover 38% of the costs for the rehabilitation of Guinea's hydroelectric dams—Grandes Chutes, Donkea, Baneah and Garafiri—together with Conakry's distribution network. Also in December the Government signed an agreement with a Mauritanian-based conglomerate, Groupe AON, for the rehabilitation of Conakry's old thermal power station and related distribution infrastructure linking Tombo to Guinea's coastal and interior regions. In 2014 the World Bank approved a US $1,500m. restructuring plan for Guinea's energy sector, financed by the World Bank, the African Development Bank (AfDB) and France, among others. In May 2015 the French energy company Veolia announced that it would oversee the restructuring project. Upon its completion, in October 2019, Electricité de Guinée reverted to being a state-owned utility. The company remained loss-making and performed below potential, as a higher capacity for power generation had not resulted in better distribution, and power outages remained frequent.

MANUFACTURING

The principal aim of Guinea's small manufacturing sector, which accounted for 10% of GDP in 2020, according to World Bank data, has been import-substitution, but the experience of the state-run projects that were established under Sékou Touré was disappointing. Lack of foreign exchange for raw materials, of skilled workers and of technical expertise, combined with poor management and low domestic purchasing power, meant that most of the plants operated well below capacity. The sector was rationalized under the Conté administration—the former state-run textile and fruit processing companies closed, and no new factories were established. Manufacturing is now largely limited to food, drinks and cigarettes, and basic inputs such as cement, metal manufactures and fuel products—all geared towards the domestic market. The Government's 2016–20 National Economic and Social Development Plan aimed to attract foreign direct investment (FDI) to bolster the manufacturing sector and transform the economy from a commodities producer to an exporter of agriculture products, energy and commodities with value added.

TRANSPORT AND INFRASTRUCTURE

The inadequacy of Guinea's transport infrastructure has been cited by the World Bank as the 'single most severe impediment to output recovery'. However, some improvements have been made since the mid-1980s. The road network is being almost entirely reconstructed, to restore links between Conakry and the country's interior, and road tracks have been built to open up rural areas. The network comprised over 43,000 km of roads (of which just 5% were paved) in 2021. In 2001 work commenced on an EU-financed road link from Kankan to the Malian capital, Bamako. The first section, between the Malian town of Naréna and Bamako, was inaugurated in 2008. In May 2011 a new bridge, built with EU funding, was inaugurated in Forécariah, on the road linking Conakry to Sierra Leone. In September 2018 the Government announced that it had signed two agreements, worth US $598m., with a consortium of Chinese banks to finance the reconstruction of the Coyah-Mamou-Dabola national road and the urban road network in Conakry. In August 2021 the Government launched an emergency road maintenance programme, including the paving of 1,500 km of roads, at a cost of $62.5m.

The rail network is better developed but geared entirely towards serving the bauxite sector: a 136-km heavy-gauge railway links the Boké bauxite deposits with the deep-water port at Kamsar, which handles about 9m. metric tons annually and is the country's major export outlet. Another, 135-km railway was inaugurated in June 2021 to link the bauxite mines of Santou, near Kindia, to the port of Boké-Dapilon. Attempts by successive governments to convince mining companies with concessions in Guinea to invest in its railway system have proved unsuccessful to date.

The port of Conakry, which has the capacity to handle some 6m. metric tons of international seaborne freight traffic annually, has been extended and modernized as part of a programme that envisages the construction of naval-repair and deep-water port facilities. In March 2011 the French conglomerate Bolloré became the new manager of the port of Conakry. However, in May 2018 the French judiciary arrested Vincent Bolloré, the director of the group, on suspicion of winning the contract to manage the port of Conakry in exchange for financing President Condé's election campaign in 2010 (and the election campaign of Togolese President Faure Gnassingbé in the same year). In October 2016 President Condé inaugurated the new port of Dapilon in Boké region, which was destined to facilitate the export to China of bauxite produced at the Katougouma mine. In the same month the Guinean Government signed a deal with China Harbour Engineering Company worth US $774m. for the upgrade of Conakry port, with funding to be provided by the Export-Import Bank of China.

The international airport at Conakry-Gbèssia handled some 573,600 passengers in 2019, before the impact of the COVID-19 pandemic on international travel; there are also 13 smaller airfields nationwide. In February 2020 the Government signed a 25-year concession agreement with the AfDB's infrastructure investment platform Africa50 and Groupe ADP of France to establish a new management body, the Société de Gestion de l'Aéroport de Gbèssia, and to co-develop and finance the upgrade and expansion of Conakry-Gbèssia International Airport, with the aim of increasing its annual handling capacity to 1m. passengers by 2031. Modernization and expansion works were contracted to Weihai International Economic & Technical Cooperative. Several international airlines have regular connections to Conakry, including Air France; Turkish Airlines and Ethiopian Airlines commenced services in 2017. After the closure of the national airline, Air Guinée, in 2002, Guinea Airlines was inaugurated in February 2017, following the establishment of a partnership between Guinea's Groupe Business Marketing and French-based Regourd Aviation.

The mobile telephone network has expanded dramatically in recent years, and by December 2020 the sector's three operators had an estimated combined total of 13.8m. subscribers. Guinea joined several other West African countries in 2016 to introduce tariff-free mobile roaming in the region. Access to the internet increased from just 0.4% of the population in 2010 to 26% in 2020.

FINANCE

State revenue remains heavily reliant on income from the mining sector, and the Government has struggled to improve fiscal management and reduce the budget deficit. Following reports of a budget deficit of 14.4% of GDP in 2010 (compared with 1.3% of GDP in 2008), the Government that took office in January 2011 confirmed that the military junta had printed an unprecedented quantity of money to finance expenditure. The new Government set about completing the audit of state finances that had been initiated by the preceding transitional administration. The new IMF staff-monitored programme also encouraged the Government to implement tighter controls on spending, which, together with windfall revenue received from the mining sector in May, led to a sharp decline in the budget deficit in 2011 to an estimated 2.5% of GDP. The deficit widened thereafter, notably in 2014 and 2015, to 6.5% of GDP and 7.6%, respectively, as a result of lower revenue and higher expenditure during the EVD outbreak. The end of the Ebola crisis, higher revenues and lower government spending helped steadily to reduce the budget deficit to 0.3% by 2018. The budget was balanced in 2019 but recorded a deficit of 2.9% of GDP in 2020, owing to a revenue shortfall and much higher expenditure as a result of the COVID-19 pandemic. The budget deficit narrowed to 2.3% in 2021 owing largely to higher tax revenue following the digitization of the financial system.

Relations with the IMF have been difficult, owing to the unwillingness or inability of successive governments to adhere to the Fund's reform agenda. In January 2008 the IMF approved a Poverty Reduction and Growth Facility (PRGF), running retroactively from July 2007 until June 2010. The PRGF was worth US $75m., in addition to budgetary support valued at €45m. from France and the EU. However, the PRGF was suspended following the military coup in December 2008. In June 2011, after the appointment of a new Government, the agreement of a staff-monitored programme for the remainder of the year marked a full restoration of relations between the Fund and Guinea. In February 2012 the IMF approved a three-year arrangement for Guinea under the Extended Credit Facility (ECF). Regular disbursements amounting to $231.9m. were made thereafter, confirming that the Government was on schedule with the agreed economic and fiscal reforms, despite a challenging political environment and the EVD outbreak. In response to the latter, the IMF provided emergency grants to Guinea, Sierra Leone and Liberia and modified the performance criteria under the ECF. Following an

IMF staff mission to Guinea in July–August 2017 and talks in the US capital, Washington, DC, in October, the IMF and the Government agreed a new three-year ECF worth $170m. Guinea was also granted $650m. in non-concessional loans from the IMF, and the Government announced that China had agreed to provide funding of $20,000m. over 20 years, in exchange for bauxite concessions. The first IMF staff review under the new ECF, in May 2018, commended surging mining exports and FDI in that sector, while noting the fiscal shortfall caused by large-scale public investments and lower tax revenues. The second, third and fourth reviews under the ECF, held in January 2019, June 2019 and April 2020, respectively, were equally positive, and total disbursements under the ECF reached $119.2m. by April 2020. In addition, in June the IMF approved the disbursement of $148m. to Guinea under the Rapid Credit Facility to address urgent balance-of-payments and fiscal financing needs stemming from the COVID-19 pandemic. The fifth and sixth reviews under the ECF were conducted jointly and virtually in October 2020, and Guinea's performance was declared satisfactory, despite the adverse effects of the pandemic; a disbursement of $49m. was consequently approved by the IMF. The Fund concluded an Article IV consultation in June 2021, noting the country's high growth rate, while highlighting the increasingly marked effects of the pandemic, in particular accelerating inflation as a result of rising food prices and freight rates associated with pandemic-related supply disruptions. After a staff visit in June 2022, the Fund reported that the Guinean economy remained resilient, owing to a buoyant mining sector, although the non-mining sector was affected by higher inflation, caused mainly by the global effects of the war in Ukraine and domestic uncertainties.

The Sékou Touré and Conté regimes reformed the banking sector, ending the state monopoly by allowing the establishment of private commercial banks and then closing the six state-controlled institutions. Government plans fully to privatize the Banque Internationale pour le Commerce et l'Industrie de la Guinée (BICIGUI) have not materialized; however, by 2016 BICIGUI had become a subsidiary of the French banking group BNP Paribas, and the Government had reduced its share in the bank from 51% to 15.1%. In mid-2022 a total of 17 banks, including BICIGUI, Ecobank and the Guinean subsidiary of the French banking group Société Générale, were operating in Guinea, and foreign-owned banks were responsible for some three-quarters of deposits and outstanding credit in the country. In 2018 the Government launched a national investment bank, the Banque Nationale d'Investissement de Guinée, to support local entrepreneurs by offering low-interest loans.

FOREIGN TRADE AND PAYMENTS

As bauxite resources were developed from the early 1970s, the country's external trade position improved greatly. The sharp rise in bauxite exports resulted in strong growth in export earnings after 1975, and sales of bauxite and alumina contributed more than 90% of recorded earnings in the early 1980s. Export earnings were subsequently increased by sales of diamonds and gold. The sustained growth in exports allowed a strong rise in spending on imports, largely reflecting capital investment in the mining sector. However, as earnings from bauxite and alumina declined from 1991, the trade account moved into deficit, but registered annual surpluses in 1996–98. The trade account fluctuated throughout the late 1990s and early 2000s. During 2004–15 the total value of Guinea's imports rose at a faster rate than its exports. Burgeoning exports of bauxite and gold, however, meant that Guinea recorded a trade surplus of US $2,100m. in 2017, which rose to a record $7,170m. in 2020, owing to a surge in gold production and exports. The trade surplus narrowed to $3,620m. in 2021, however, following a fall in gold production. India was Guinea's most important export market in 2021, accounting for 28.7% of total exports, consisting mostly of bauxite, alumina and gold, followed by the UAE (17.8%) and China (5.3%). The main source of imports in 2021 was China (18.4%), followed by India (12.7%) and Japan (7.9%). The current account is generally in deficit, owing to high outflows on services (including interest payments and profit remittances). According to the IMF, a current account deficit equivalent to 18.7% of GDP was registered in

2018, but the deficit narrowed to 10.8% in 2019. The deficit widened to 13.4% of GDP in 2020, reflecting an increase in imports of management, freight and telecommunications services, which offset strong export growth in the mining sector. The current account deficit then narrowed to around 4% in 2021, owing to a substantial reduction in the trade deficit. Foreign exchange reserves, which had remained uncomfortably low throughout the 2000s, increased from $134.5m. at the end of 2010 to an estimated $1,715m. at the end of 2021.

Inflows of FDI, primarily into the mining sector, have grown strongly in recent years. According to the United Nations Conference on Trade and Development, annual FDI inflows rose from an average of US $21m. during 1990–2000 to $382m. in 2008. From 2009 inflows fluctuated according to the political situation in the country, rising to a record $956m. in 2011 and falling to $134m. in 2013. The EVD outbreak largely accounted for the very low FDI inflows in 2014 and 2015, of $77m. and $48m., respectively. Inflows rebounded in 2016, to $1,618m., but declined thereafter, to a low of $44m. in 2019, partly recovering to $325m. in 2020.

In 1986, following final agreement between the IMF and the Conté administration about an economic stabilization programme (which included a 93% devaluation of the currency), the country's Western creditors agreed to a rescheduling of debt, covering arrears and debt service due up to 1987. The 'Paris Club' of official creditors rescheduled debt between 1990 and 1992, with the result that the debt-service ratio was kept at a manageable 11%–14% in 1992–94. New rounds of restructuring took place in 1995 and 1997. Further debt relief under the IMF's Heavily Indebted Poor Countries (HIPC) initiative was not granted, however, following the collapse of the IMF's PRGF programme in 2002.

Guinea reached HIPC 'decision point' in December 2000, but by 2007 it had failed to reach 'completion point', when it would become eligible for further bilateral debt relief under the Multilateral Debt Relief Initiative. A new PRGF programme was agreed in January 2008. In the same month the 'Paris Club' wrote off US $180m. of debt and agreed to restructure a further $120m. Total external debt was estimated at $3,092m. at the end of 2008 (equivalent to 59.5% of GDP). The military coup in December of that year, however, once again resulted in the suspension of co-operation between the IMF and the Guinean Government and halted progress towards HIPC completion. The new Government appointed following Condé's election announced in early 2011 that it would seek to reconnect with the HIPC initiative, and contacts were re-established with the IMF. Total external debt amounted to $3,139m. at the end of 2011, of which $2,849m. was public and publicly guaranteed debt. In April 2012 the 'Paris Club', to which Guinea owed $750m., announced that it would provide $344m. of debt relief to Guinea over eight years. Guinea reached HIPC completion point and received debt relief of $2,100m. in September. The amount represented 66% of the country's future external debt-servicing obligations over 40 years and reduced debt-servicing costs by 70%. In October the 'Paris Club' announced that it had agreed further debt relief, of $655.9m., leading to a total write-off of 99.2% of Guinea's outstanding 'Paris Club' obligations. The country's total external debt was $2,931m. at the end of 2019, of which $2,240m. was public and publicly guaranteed debt. In the context of the ongoing COVID-19 pandemic, from mid-2020 Guinea participated in the World Bank's Debt Service Suspension Initiative, which was aimed at alleviating debt-servicing pressures on low-income countries. The Initiative, which was initially planned to last until December 2020, was subsequently extended to December 2021 and expected to reduce Guinea's debt-service payments by the equivalent of about 1% of GDP.

Following the military coup of 5 September 2021, the international community froze financial support to the Guinean Government, demanding the restoration of civilian rule. The Economic Community of West African States (ECOWAS), in addition to targeted sanctions, suspended Guinea's membership shortly afterwards (see *Recent History*). The US Government suspended Guinea from the African Growth and Opportunity Act in January 2022. According to the IMF, however, exports from Guinea to the USA amounted to only US $11.4m. in 2020, thus limiting the effects of this measure.

Statistical Survey

Source (unless otherwise stated): Direction Nationale de la Statistique, BP 221, Conakry; tel. 300-21-33-12; e-mail dnstat@biasy.net; internet www.stat-guinee.org.

Area and Population

AREA, POPULATION AND DENSITY

Area (sq km)	245,857*
Population (census results)	
31 December 1996†	7,156,406
1 March–2 April 2014	
Males	5,084,307
Females	5,438,954
Total	10,523,261
Population (official projections at mid-year)	
2020	12,559,623
2021	12,907,395
2022	13,261,638
Density (per sq km) at mid-2022	53.9

* 94,926 sq miles.

† Including refugees from Liberia and Sierra Leone (estimated at 640,000).

POPULATION BY AGE AND SEX
('000, UN projections at mid-2022)

	Males	Females	Total
0–14 years	2,958.1	2,916.1	5,874.2
15–64 years	3,617.8	3,959.1	7,576.9
65 years and over	155.7	259.0	414.6
Total	6,731.6	7,134.1	13,865.7

Note: Totals may not be equal to the sum of components, owing to rounding.

Source: UN, *World Population Prospects: The 2019 Revision.*

ADMINISTRATIVE DIVISIONS
(official population projections at mid-2022)

Region	Area (sq km)	Population	Density (per sq km)
Boké	31,186	1,366,583	43.8
Conakry	450	2,095,705	4,657.1
Faranah	35,581	1,188,046	33.4
Kankan	72,156	2,476,006	34.3
Kindia	28,873	1,968,868	68.2
Labé	22,869	1,252,857	54.8
Mamou	17,074	922,150	54.0
N'Zérékoré	37,668	1,991,421	52.9
Total	245,857	13,261,638	53.9

Note: Totals may not be equal to the sum of components, owing to rounding.

PRINCIPAL LOCALITIES
(official population projections of prefectures at mid-2022)

Conakry (capital) .	2,095,705	Mandiana . . .	424,173
Siguiri . . .	855,494	Dubreka . . .	416,583
Kankan . . .	595,403	Beyla	411,727
Boké	567,873	Mamou . . .	402,530
Kindia . . .	554,224	Labé	401,215
N'Zérékoré . . .	500,513		

BIRTHS AND DEATHS
(official estimates)

	2018	2019	2020
Birth rate (per 1,000) . . .	37.6	37.1	36.6
Death rate (per 1,000) . . .	10.0	9.7	9.4

Life expectancy (years at birth, official estimates): 62.4 (males 59.5; females 61.0) in 2020.

ECONOMICALLY ACTIVE POPULATION
('000, FAO estimates at mid-year)

	2013	2014	2015
Agriculture, etc.	4,470	4,571	4,675
Total labour force (incl. others) .	5,697	5,862	6,032

Source: FAO.

Health and Welfare

KEY INDICATORS

Total fertility rate (children per woman, 2020)	4.6
Under-5 mortality rate (per 1,000 live births, 2020) . . .	95.6
HIV/AIDS (% of persons aged 15–49, 2020)	1.4
COVID-19: Cumulative confirmed deaths (per 100,000 persons at 31 August 2022)	3.3
COVID-19: Fully vaccinated population (% of total population at 28 August 2022)	19.3
Physicians (per 1,000 head, 2018)	0.2
Hospitals (per 100,000 head, 2013)	0.4
Domestic health expenditure (2019): US $ per head (PPP) .	26.9
Domestic health expenditure (2019): % of GDP . . .	0.9
Domestic health expenditure (2019): public (% of total current expenditure)	22.5
Access to improved water resources (% of persons, 2020) .	64
Access to improved sanitation facilities (% of persons, 2020) .	30
Total carbon dioxide emissions ('000 metric tons, 2018) . .	3,120
Carbon dioxide emissions per head (metric tons, 2018) . .	0.3
Human Development Index (2021): ranking	182
Human Development Index (2021): value	0.465

Note: For data on COVID-19 vaccinations, 'fully vaccinated' denotes receipt of all doses specified by approved vaccination regime (Sources: Johns Hopkins University and Our World in Data). Data on health expenditure refer to current general government expenditure in each case. For more information on sources and further definitions for all indicators, see Health and Welfare Statistics: Sources and Definitions section (europaworld.com/credits).

Agriculture

PRINCIPAL CROPS
('000 metric tons)

	2018	2019	2020
Bananas*	220.0	221.3	221.4
Cassava (Manioc)	1,895.4	2,145.5	2,503.6
Coconuts*	53.0	52.6	52.7
Coffee, green	50.0	56.7*	38.6*
Fonio (Millets)	477.4	530.2	566.0
Groundnuts, with shell . .	770.1	957.7	1,074.4
Mangoes, mangosteens and guavas*	180.5	181.9	183.2
Maize	818.5	871.4	907.9
Maize, green*	297.7	298.2	298.7
Millet	214.7	223.2	213.4
Oil palm fruit*	845.1	846.2	847.4
Pineapples*	132.2	132.5	132.1
Plantains and others* . . .	483.2	484.9	486.6
Potatoes	151.3	162.2	266.9
Rice, paddy	2,339.7	2,599.2	2,916.4

—continued					2018	2019	2020
Rubber, natural*	.	.	.	.	15.0	14.9	15.0
Seed cotton*					43.5	43.6	43.7
Sugar cane*	.				311.9	314.0	316.2
Sweet potatoes	.	.	.		265.3	281.7	322.1
Taro (Cocoyam)	.	.	.		107.7	110.0	117.5
Yams	.	.	.	.	187.9	195.8	268.9

* FAO estimate(s).

Aggregate production ('000 metric tons, may include official, semi-official or estimated data): Total cereals 3,911.0 in 2018, 4,286.4 in 2019, 4,666.9 in 2020; Total fruit (primary) 1,308.0 in 2018, 1,313.8 in 2019, 1,317.8 in 2020; Total oilcrops 1,713.7 in 2018, 1,902.3 in 2019, 2,020.6 in 2020; Total roots and tubers 2,607.6 in 2018, 2,895.3 in 2019, 3,478.9 in 2020; Total vegetables (primary) 562.1 in 2018, 559.8 in 2019, 561.2 in 2020.

Source: FAO.

LIVESTOCK

('000 head, year ending September)

					2018	2019	2020
Cattle	.	.	.	.	7,520	7,933	8,368
Chickens*	.	.	.	.	34,028	36,254	34,074
Goats	.	.	.	.	3,249	3,465	3,697
Pigs	.	.	.	.	140	147	160
Sheep	.	.	.	.	2,708	2,890	2,528

* FAO estimates.

Source: FAO.

LIVESTOCK PRODUCTS

('000 metric tons)

				2018	2019	2020*
Cattle hides, fresh*	.	.	.	15.8	16.7	17.6
Cattle meat	.	.	.	94.4	99.6	105.2
Cattle offals, edible*	.	.	.	17.6	18.5	19.6
Cows' milk	.	.	.	180.5	225.4	177.0
Chicken meat	.	.	.	10.6	11.2	12.4
Game meat*	.	.	.	6.2	6.3	6.3
Goat meat	.	.	.	15.4	16.5	17.5
Goats' milk*	.	.	.	36.8	38.4	40.0
Sheep meat	.	.	.	10.9	11.6	10.1
Hen eggs	.	.	.	28.8*	32.0	28.9

* FAO estimate(s).

Source: FAO.

Forestry

ROUNDWOOD REMOVALS

('000 cubic metres, excl. bark, FAO estimates)

				2018	2019	2020
Sawlogs, veneer logs and logs for sleepers	.	.	.	138	138	138
Other industrial wood	.	.	.	513	513	513
Fuel wood	.	.	.	12,340	12,380	12,420
Total	.	.	.	12,991	13,031	13,071

Source: FAO.

SAWNWOOD PRODUCTION

('000 cubic metres, incl. railway sleepers, FAO estimates)

			2018	2019	2020
Total (all broadleaved)	.	.	31	31	31

Source: FAO.

Fishing

('000 metric tons, all capture, live weight)

					2018	2019	2020*
Freshwater fishes	.	.	.	.	39.0*	51.7	40.0
Royal threadfin	.	.	.	.	36.9	37.9	35.0
Sea catfishes	.	.	.	.	25.9	70.5	38.0
Bobo croaker	.	.	.	.	7.3	8.5	8.7
West African croakers	.	.	.		—	n.a.	1,485
Sardinellas	.	.	.	.	38.8	36.6	33.0
Bonga shad	.	.	.	.	72.6	85.5	80.0
Total catch (incl. others)		.	.	293.7*	360.6	310.7

* FAO estimate(s).

Source: FAO.

Mining

('000 metric tons unless otherwise indicated)

				2016	2017	2018
Bauxite (dry basis)*	.	.	.	31,500	46,160	57,000†
Gold (kilograms)	.	.	.	15,561	18,388	18,000†
Diamonds ('000 carats)†‡	.	.		113	181	293

* Estimated to be 7% water.
† Estimate(s).
‡ Including artisanal production.

Salt (unrefined) ('000 metric tons): 15 in 2011 (estimate).

Source: US Geological Survey.

Industry

SELECTED PRODUCTS

('000 metric tons unless otherwise indicated)

				2017	2018	2019
Palm oil (unrefined)*†	.	.	.	50	50	50
Beer of barley*†	.	.	.	30.0	30.0	35.0
Alumina (calcined equivalent)	.		n.a.	169	345
Electrical energy (million kWh)‡	.	1,753	1,914	2,019

* Data from FAO.
† Unofficial figures.
‡ Data from UN Energy Statistics Database.

2020: Alumina (calcined equivalent) 453,000 metric tons.

Finance

CURRENCY AND EXCHANGE RATES

Monetary Units
100 centimes = 1 franc guinéen (FG or Guinean franc).

Sterling, Dollar and Euro Equivalents (31 May 2021)
£1 sterling = 13,770.4 Guinean francs;
US $1 = 9,749.0 Guinean francs;
€1 = 11,894.7 Guinean francs;
100,000 Guinean francs = £7.26 = $10.26 = €8.41.

Average Exchange Rate (Guinean francs per US $)
2018   9,011.1
2019   9,183.9
2020   9,565.1

BUDGET
('000 million Guinean francs)

Revenue*	2019	2020†	2021‡
Mining-sector revenue . . .	2,373	2,294	2,999
Other revenue	14,932	15,027	19,875
Tax revenue	13,495	14,293	18,403
Taxes on domestic production and trade	7,583	8,237	10,359
Taxes on international trade .	3,349	3,121	4,090
Non-tax revenue	1,437	733	1,353
Total	17,305	17,321	22,874

Expenditure§	2019	2020†	2021‡
Current expenditure	13,830	18,309	20,429
Wages and salaries	4,430	6,162	6,589
Other goods and services . .	4,253	5,037	5,891
Subsidies and transfers . .	4,570	6,097	6,344
Interest due on external debt .	186	226	317
Interest due on domestic debt .	391	788	1,168
Capital expenditure	4,545	4,703	8,963
Domestically financed . . .	2,766	1,159	2,774
Externally financed . . .	1,779	3,544	6,189
Total	18,375	23,012	29,392

* Excluding grants received ('000 million Guinean francs): 597 in 2019; 1,539 in 2020 (preliminary); 2,901 in 2021 (projection).
† Preliminary.
‡ Projections.
§ Excluding lending minus repayments ('000 million Guinean francs): 117 in 2019; 74 in 2020 (preliminary); 184 in 2021 (projection).

Source: IMF, *Article IV Consultation—Press Release; Staff Report; and Statement by the Executive Director for Guinea* (July 2021).

INTERNATIONAL RESERVES
(US $ million at 31 December)

	2018	2019	2020
Gold (national valuation) . . .	62.66	190.55	253.80
IMF special drawing rights . .	239.80	96.27	85.77
Reserve position in IMF . . .	37.34	37.13	38.67
Foreign exchange	902.06	1,055.19	1,120.88
Total	1,241.86	1,379.14	1,499.12

2021: IMF special drawing rights 370.7; Reserve position in IMF 37.6.

Source: IMF, *International Financial Statistics*.

MONEY SUPPLY
(million Guinean francs at 31 December)

	2019	2020	2021
Currency outside depository corporations	8,816,456	11,541,601	12,074,180
Transferable deposits . . .	18,053,372	21,109,391	23,145,745
Other deposits	2,404,881	3,297,951	3,844,542
Broad money	29,274,710	35,948,943	39,064,468

Source: IMF, *International Financial Statistics*.

COST OF LIVING
(Consumer Price Index; base: 2002 = 100)

	2019	2020	2021
Foodstuffs, beverages and tobacco.	1,931.1	2,166.7	2,494.0
Clothing and shoes	588.5	596.0	607.9
Housing, water, electricity and gas	704.7	735.3	754.9
All items	1,104.1	1,220.9	1,373.9

NATIONAL ACCOUNTS
('000 million Guinean francs at current prices, estimates)
Expenditure on the Gross Domestic Product

	2018	2019	2020
Government final consumption expenditure	16,541.7	19,015.3	22,213.4
Private final consumption expenditure	78,574.8	89,326.1	105,990.4
Gross fixed capital formation . .	20,800.0	21,526.6	24,093.0
Changes in inventories . . .	85.4	9,537.7	10,674.8
Total domestic expenditure .	116,001.8	139,405.7	162,971.6
Exports of goods and services . .	42,959.4	37,184.2	86,222.0
Less Imports of goods and services	52,115.9	52,480.8	108,068.5
Statistical discrepancy . .	—	—	6,062.8
GDP at market prices . . .	106,845.3	124,109.1	147,187.8
GDP at constant 2015 prices .	85,582.8	90,415.0	96,822.2

Gross Domestic Product by Economic Activity

	2018	2019	2020
Agriculture, livestock, forestry and fishing	23,854.2	30,020.3	35,498.7
Mining and utilities	18,852.5	20,301.6	29,757.9
Manufacturing	10,357.2	10,687.0	12,952.3
Construction	3,782.1	4,426.1	6,382.4
Trade, restaurants and hotels .	19,060.3	22,077.3	25,275.2
Transport, storage and communications	4,280.0	4,936.9	5,642.9
Other services	19,242.3	22,575.8	25,645.8
Sub-total	99,428.7	115,024.9	141,155.0
Net taxes on products* . . .	7,416.6	9,084.2	6,032.8
GDP at purchasers' values .	106,845.3	124,109.1	147,187.8

* Figures obtained as residuals.

Source: UN National Accounts Main Aggregates Database.

BALANCE OF PAYMENTS
(US $ million)

	2019	2020	2021
Exports of goods	3,945.4	8,931.2	10,238.9
Imports of goods	−3,470.0	−3,727.4	−4,187.4
Balance on goods	475.4	5,203.8	6,051.5
Exports of services	95.4	64.8	27.0
Imports of services	−850.1	−2,586.1	−1,165.8
Balance on goods and services	−279.4	2,682.5	4,912.8
Primary income received . .	86.8	32.5	9.1
Primary income paid	−200.9	−177.3	−672.8
Balance on goods, services and primary income	−393.5	2,537.7	4,249.1
Secondary income received . .	354.1	365.5	477.2
Secondary income paid . . .	−275.3	−218.5	−87.5
Current balance	−314.6	2,684.8	4,638.7
Capital account (net)	40.7	147.1	159.0
Direct investment assets . . .	−1.0	−2.4	3.1
Direct investment liabilities . .	44.4	176.4	197.6
Portfolio investment assets . .	—	—	−19.6
Portfolio investment liabilities .	5.6	−12.0	—
Other investment assets . . .	61.8	−3,116.2	−3,795.9
Other investment liabilities . .	408.6	170.2	−403.9
Net errors and omissions . . .	−128.1	−88.3	−446.3
Reserves and related items .	117.3	−40.4	332.7

Source: IMF, *International Financial Statistics*.

External Trade

PRINCIPAL COMMODITIES
(distribution by HS, '000 million Guinean francs)

Imports c.i.f.	2018	2019	2020
Vegetables and vegetable products	1,658.5	1,628.4	1,526.5
Prepared foodstuffs; beverages, spirits, vinegar; tobacco and articles thereof	1,603.6	1,955.6	1,958.7
Mineral products	7,711.2	9,602.4	8,157.3
Chemicals and related products	3,061.1	2,847.3	3,335.9
Plastics, rubbers, and articles thereof	935.8	1,269.4	1,425.0
Pulp of wood, paper and paperboard, and articles thereof	291.5	291.6	3,142.4
Iron and steel, other base metals and articles of base metal	2,388.3	2,162.8	2,526.0
Machinery and mechanical appliances; electrical equipment; parts thereof	5,807.4	6,868.6	6,339.0
Vehicles, aircraft, vessels and associated transport equipment	4,502.7	6,091.9	4,378.8
Total (incl. others)	30,524.3	35,766.0	35,653.0

Exports f.o.b.	2018	2019	2020
Mineral products	18,873.6	22,068.8	49,781.0
Plastics, rubber, and articles thereof	345.4	311.6	433.4
Pulp of wood, paper and paperboard, and articles thereof	44.4	195.7	27.4
Pearls, precious stones, metals, coins, etc.	9,248.3	11,167.4	30,867.2
Machinery and mechanical appliances; electrical equipment; parts thereof	5,649.2	393.6	214.4
Vehicles, aircraft, vessels and associated transport equipment	271.9	890.7	674.3
Total (incl. others)	35,867.0	36,276.5	83,718.4

PRINCIPAL TRADING PARTNERS
('000 million Guinean francs)

Imports c.i.f.	2015	2016	2017
Belgium	1,302.2	1,486.3	2,198.7
Brazil	276.6	172.6	303.4
China, People's Republic	2,766.8	2,900.9	3,839.1
France (incl. Monaco)	1,139.1	1,182.4	1,487.5
Germany	393.3	260.0	359.6
Ghana	427.6	110.3	210.2
India	1,799.4	1,684.3	1,960.3
Italy	233.0	148.0	328.5
Japan	116.3	31.8	53.3
Lebanon	376.2	440.3	72.1
Malaysia	215.2	90.2	168.8
Morocco	231.8	97.8	495.2
Netherlands	3,207.4	2,578.2	3,931.7
Pakistan	22.8	4.2	3.6
Portugal	184.1	76.9	210.5
Saudi Arabia	183.4	142.3	167.1
Senegal	286.3	213.6	111.9

Imports c.i.f.—*continued*	2015	2016	2017
Singapore	570.0	17,694.1	648.8
South Africa	165.1	3,169.4	356.5
Spain	262.8	254.3	2,409.7
Thailand	44.7	293.6	94.4
Türkiye	277.2	254.3	410.1
United Arab Emirates	1,074.1	3,067.5	771.0
United Kingdom	104.9	48.4	195.4
USA	430.2	474.3	1,579.2
Viet Nam	81.5	29.6	20.9
Total (incl. others)	18,221.4	39,231.9	31,608.2

Exports f.o.b.	2015	2016	2017
Angola	0.6	1.2	66.0
Belgium	115.7	295.0	2,849.9
Canada	367.0	363.8	438.2
China, People's Republic	285.2	4,014.3	29,139.9
Eswatini	170.1	—	568.5
France (incl. Monaco)	779.2	1,279.8	1,032.0
Germany	956.1	851.7	684.7
Ghana	2,900.6	0.6	260.8
India	2,144.9	1,958.6	205.6
Ireland	823.1	1,222.0	988.4
Mali	209.7	155.2	276.5
Spain	1,131.3	1,269.5	1,032.0
Switzerland	220.5	1,649.4	378.2
Ukraine	407.7	435.2	404.1
United Arab Emirates	1,299.1	5,801.2	1,032.0
USA	705.7	137.8	423.9
Total (incl. others)	13,277.9	20,724.0	41,678.5

2018: Total imports 30,524.3; Total exports 35,867.0.
2019: Total imports 35,766.0; Total exports 36,276,5.
2020: Total imports 35,653.0; Total exports 83,718.4.

Transport

ROAD TRAFFIC
('000, motor vehicles in use, estimates)

	2017	2018	2019
Passenger cars	186.6	205.7	226.8
Vans	8.8	9.1	9.4
Buses and coaches	28.2	28.8	29.4
Motorcycles and mopeds	80.5	92.5	106.7
Trucks	49.9	58.1	67.6
Total	354.0	394.2	440.0

SHIPPING
Flag Registered Fleet
(at 31 December)

	2019	2020	2021
Number of vessels	34	35	36
Total displacement ('000 grt)	23.7	24.0	25.0

Source: Lloyd's List Intelligence (www.bit.ly/LLintelligence).

International Seaborne Freight Traffic
(Port of Conakry, '000 metric tons)

	2018	2019	2020
Goods loaded	3,917	3,660	3,767
Goods unloaded	6,422	6,728	7,258

CIVIL AVIATION
(traffic at Conakry-Gbèssia airport)

	2018	2019	2020
Passengers carried ('000)	527.6	573.6	247.9
Freight handled ('000 metric tons)	4.6	5.3	5.1

Tourism

FOREIGN VISITOR ARRIVALS*

Country of origin	2014	2015	2016
Belgium	939	1,285	2,266
Canada	640	695	1,320
China, People's Republic . . .	2,908	2,551	5,002
Côte d'Ivoire	1,799	1,832	3,718
France	5,828	6,452	11,030
Germany	559	626	1,351
India	1,093	935	1,722
Mali	898	877	1,520
Morocco	1,093	716	1,147
Senegal	2,060	2,636	4,869
Sierra Leone	557	859	1,112
USA	1,950	2,251	4,367
Total (incl. others)†	32,772	35,320	60,226

* Arrivals of non-resident tourists at national borders, by nationality.
† Air arrivals at Conakry-Gbèssia airport.

Tourism receipts (US $ million, excl. passenger transport): 16 in 2017; 3 in 2018; 9 in 2019 (provisional) (Source: World Tourism Organization).

Communications Media

	2018	2019	2020
Mobile telephone subscriptions ('000) .	12,013	12,873	13,795
Broadband subscriptions, fixed . .	1,213	1,250	1,000
Broadband subscriptions, mobile ('000)	2,959	2,959	3,170
Internet users (% of population) . .	21.8	23.0	26.0

Telephones ('000 main lines in use): 18 in 2011.

Source: International Telecommunication Union.

Education

(2019/20 unless otherwise indicated)

	Institutions	Teachers	Students ('000)		
			Males	Females	Total
Pre-primary* .	2,983	6,169	116.9	112.8	229.7
Primary . .	10,685	43,914	1,147.4	960.2	2,107.7
Secondary . .	n.a.	22,490†	435.7‡	280.0‡	715.7‡
General . .	2,062	31,790	424.8	289.2	714.1
Tertiary* . .	49	6,487	60.6	27.2	87.7

* 2020/21.
† 2012/13.
‡ 2013/14.

Note: Totals may not be equal to the sum of components, owing to rounding.

Source: partly UNESCO Institute for Statistics.

Pupil-teacher ratio (primary education, UNESCO estimate): 75.5 in 2019/20 (Source: UNESCO Institute for Statistics).

Adult literacy rate (UNESCO estimates): 39.6% (males 54.4%; females 27.7%) in 2018 (Source: UNESCO Institute for Statistics).

Directory

The Constitution

On 6 April 2020 President Alpha Condé enacted a new Constitution (of the Fourth Republic) which had been approved by 89.8% of participants in a national referendum on 22 March. The main provisions of this are summarized below.

The Constitution defines the clear separation of the powers of the executive, the legislature and the judiciary. The President of the Republic, who is head of state, must be elected by an absolute majority of the votes cast, and a second round of voting is held should no candidate obtain such a majority at a first round. The duration of the presidential mandate is six years, renewable only once, and elections are by universal adult suffrage. A President may not serve more than two terms. Any candidate for the presidency must be more than 35 years old. The President appoints a Prime Minister, who is head of government, and proposes the structure and composition of the Government for approval by the President. Legislative power is vested in the National Assembly, members of which must be more than 18 years old. The legislature is elected, by universal suffrage, for a term of five years. No single gender should constitute more than two-thirds of each government body.

However, following a military coup on 5 September 2021, a new ruling body, the Comité National du Rassemblement et du Développement (CNRD), was created, the Constitution was suspended and government institutions were dissolved. On 27 September the CNRD released a transitional charter, which designated its leader as Transitional President, and provided for the establishment of a government, headed by a civilian Prime Minister, and an 81-member interim legislature, the Conseil National de la Transition.

The Government

HEAD OF STATE

Transitional President: Col MAMADY DOUMBOUYA (inaugurated 1 October 2021).

COUNCIL OF MINISTERS
(October 2022)

Prime Minister: Dr BERNARD GOUMOU.

Minister, Secretary-General of the Presidency: Col AMARA CAMARA.

Minister, Director of Cabinet of the Presidency: DJIBA DIAKITÉ.

Keeper of the Seals, Minister of Justice: ALPHONSE CHARLES WRIGHT.

Minister-delegate to the Presidency, in charge of National Defence: Gen. (retd) ABOUBACAR SIDIKI CAMARA.

Minister of Territorial Administration and Decentralization: MORY CONDÉ.

Minister of Security and Civil Protection: Col BACHIR DIALLO.

Minister of Foreign Affairs, International Co-operation, African Integration and Guineans Abroad: Dr MORISSANDA KOUYATÉ.

Minister of the Budget: Dr LANCINÈ CONDÉ.

Minister of the Economy, Finance and Planning: MOUSSA CISSÉ.

Minister of Labour and of the Civil Service: JULIEN YOUMBOUNO.

Minister of the Environment and Sustainable Development: LOPOU LAMAH.

Minister of Agriculture and Stockbreeding: MAMOUDOU NAGNALEN BARRY.

Minister of Energy, Water Resources and Hydrocarbons: ALY SEYDOUBA SOUMAH.

Minister of Mining and Geology: MOUSSA MAGASSOUBA.

Minister of Infrastructure and Transport: YAYA SOW.

Minister of Information and Communication: AMINATA KABA.

Minister of Postal Services, Telecommunications and the Digital Economy, Government Spokesperson: OUSMANE GAOUAL DIALLO.

Minister of Town Planning, Housing and Land Management: Col IBRAHIMA SORY BANGOURA.

Minister of Fisheries and the Maritime Economy: CHARLOTTE DAFFÉ.

Minister of Higher Education, Scientific Research and Innovation: Dr DIAKA SIDIBÉ.

Minister of Pre-University Education and Literacy: GUILLAUME HAWING.

Minister of Technical Education and Professional Training: ALPHA BACAR BARRY.

Minister of Health and Public Hygiene: MAMADOU PATHÉ DIALLO.

Minister of Trade, Industry and Small and Medium-sized Enterprises: ROSE POLA PRICEMOU.

Minister of Youth and Sport: LANSANA BÉA DIALLO.

Minister of Women's Promotion, Childhood and Vulnerable Persons: AÏCHA NÉNETTE CONTÉ.

Minister of Culture, Tourism and Handicrafts: ALPHA SOUMAH.

Minister, Secretary-General of the Government: ABDOURAHMANE SIKHÉ CAMARA.

Secretary-General for Religious Affairs: Elhadj KARAMO DIAWARA.

MINISTRIES

Office of the President: BP 1000, Boulbinet, Conakry; tel. 664-87-96-59; internet www.presidence.gov.gn.

Office of the Prime Minister: Palais des Colombes, BP 5141, Conakry; tel. 622-00-00-00; internet www.primature.gov.gn.

Ministry of Agriculture and Stockbreeding: BP 576, Conakry; tel. 664-24-72-63; internet www.agriculture.gov.gn.

Ministry of the Budget: blvd du Commerce, BP 519, Conakry; internet mbudget.gov.gn.

Ministry of Citizenship and National Unity: Conakry; tel. 622-53-03-28; e-mail info@citoyennetegn.org; internet www.citoyennetegn.org.

Ministry of Co-operation and African Integration: Conakry; tel. 657-21-21-87; internet fb.com/CooperationIntegrationAfricaineGN.

Ministry of Culture, Tourism and Handicrafts: BP 1304, Conakry; tel. 623-33-77-68; internet fb.com/MCSPHGN.

Ministry of the Economy, Finance and Planning: blvd du Commerce, BP 579, Conakry; tel. 300-45-17-95; internet www.mef.gov.gn.

Ministry of Energy, Water Resources and Hydrocarbons: route du Niger, Coléah, Conakry; tel. 620-74-80-10; internet fb.com/EnergieGN.

Ministry of the Environment and Sustainable Development: BP 761, Conakry; tel. 657-33-46-38; internet medd-guinee.org.

Ministry of Fisheries and the Maritime Economy: face à la Cité du Port, BP 307, Conakry; tel. 624-12-20-10; internet fb.com/pecheguinee.

Ministry of Foreign Affairs, International Co-operation, African Integration and Guineans Abroad: Quartier Almamya, face au Port Autonome de Conakry, Commune de Kaloum, BP 2519, Conakry; tel. 656-28-12-35; internet fb.com/MAEGEGN.

Ministry of Health and Public Hygiene: blvd du Commerce, BP 585, Conakry; tel. 611-71-71-71; e-mail info@sante.gov.gn; internet sante.gov.gn.

Ministry of Higher Education, Scientific Research and Innovation: Almamya, BP 2201, Conakry; tel. 625-48-72-79; internet www.mesrs.gov.gn.

Ministry of Information and Communication: Conakry; internet infocommunication.gov.gn.

Ministry of Infrastructure and Transport: BP 715, Conakry.

Ministry of Investment and Public-Private Partnerships: Corniche Nord, Société Navale, Conakry; tel. 656-31-11-30; e-mail info@invest.gov.gn; internet invest.gov.gn.

Ministry of Justice: face à l'Immeuble 'La Paternelle', Almamya, BP 564. Conakry; e-mail contact@justiceguinee.gov.gn; internet justiceguinee.gov.gn.

Ministry of Labour and of the Civil Service: Boulbinet, Conakry; tel. 622-54-13-38; internet fb.com/MFPREMAGN.

Ministry of Mining and Geology: blvd du Commerce, BP 295, Conakry; tel. 625-21-55-67; e-mail info@mines.gov.gn; internet mines.gov.gn.

Ministry of National Defence: Camp Samory-Touré, Conakry; tel. 620-39-43-18; internet fb.com/DefenseNationaleGN.

Ministry of Planning and Economic Development: BP 1210, Conakry; tel. 657-21-21-87; internet www.mplan.gov.gn.

Ministry of Postal Services, Telecommunications and the Digital Economy: BP 3000, Conakry; tel. 623-06-64-90; e-mail contact@mpten.gov.gn; internet fb.com/MptenGN.

Ministry of Pre-University Education and Literacy: Kaloum, Conakry; tel. 628-06-13-37; internet fb.com/MepuaGN.

Ministry of Security and Civil Protection: Coléah-Domino, Conakry; tel. 656-16-65-66; internet fb.com/MSPCGN.

Ministry of Social Action and Childhood: Corniche-Ouest, face au Terminal Conteneurs du Port de Conakry, BP 527, Conakry; tel. 628-21-89-94; internet fb.com/MaspfeGN.

Ministry of Technical Education and Professional Training: Conakry; tel. 611-25-99-99; e-mail infos@metfp.gov.gn; internet metfp.gov.gn.

Ministry of Territorial Administration and Decentralization: face aux Jardins du 2 Octobre, Tombo, BP 2201, Conakry; internet fb.com/AdministrationTDGN.

Ministry of Town Planning, Housing and Land Management: Kaloum Almamya, BP 846, Conakry; tel. 627-27-01-01; e-mail contact@urbanismehabitat.gov.gn; internet habitatguinee.org.

Ministry of Trade, Industry and Small and Medium-sized Enterprises: Kaloum Almamya, Côté Portuaire, BP 13, Conakry; tel. 623-46-00-35; internet commerce.gov.gn.

Ministry of Water Supply and Sanitation: BP 1200, Conakry; tel. 657330078; e-mail hydrauliqueassainissement224@gmail.com; internet fb.com/MHAGUINEE.

Ministry of Women's Promotion, Childhood and Vulnerable Persons: Conakry; tel. 628-21-89-94; internet fb.com/MaspfeGN.

Ministry of Youth and Sport: ave du Port Secrétariat, BP 262, Conakry; tel. 664-90-14-90; e-mail info@jeunesse.gov.gn; internet fb.com/MJSGUINEE.

President

Presidential Election, 18 October 2020

Candidate	Valid votes	% of valid votes
Alpha Condé (RPG)	2,438,815	59.50
Cellou Dalein Diallo (UFDG) . . .	1,372,920	33.49
Ibrahima Abé Sylla (NGR) . . .	63,676	1.55
Ousmane Kaba (PADES)	48,623	1.19
Ousmane Doré (MND)	46,235	1.13
Others*	128,652	3.14
Total	4,098,921†	100.00

* There were seven other candidates.
† Excluding 168,653 spoiled ballots. According to results released by the Constitutional Court, the total number of valid votes cast was 4,099,152, although the totals attributed by the same body to each candidate amounted to the figure given in the table.

Legislature

Following the assumption of power by the military-led Comité National du Rassemblement et du Développement in September 2021, the National Assembly (to which elections last took place in March 2020) was dissolved. On 22 January 2022 the 81-member Conseil National de la Transition (CNT), which was to act as the legislative body during the transitional period, was appointed by presidential decree; the members included 15 representatives of political parties, and nine of the defence and security forces, while the remainder represented the country's socio-professional organizations. A civil society activist, Dr Dansa Kourouma, was appointed as President of the CNT, which was officially installed on 5 February.

Election Commission

Commission Electorale Nationale Indépendante (CENI): Quartier Cameroun, Commune de Dixin, BP 1032, Conakry; tel. 622-79-04-71; e-mail ceniguineeconakry@gmail.com; f. 2005; comprises 10 representatives of the parliamentary majority, 10 representatives of the parliamentary opposition, 3 representatives of civil society and 2 representatives of the state administration; Pres. KABINET CISSÉ; Sec.-Gen. (vacant).

Advisory Council

Economic and Social Council: Immeuble Fote Yoy Camara, ave 6ème. BP 2947, Conakry; tel. 300-45-31-23; e-mail contact@cesguinee.com; internet cesecguinee.com; f. 1997; 45 mems; Pres. RABIATOU SÉRAH DIALLO.

Political Organizations

Alliance Nationale pour le Progrès (ANP): Conakry; Leader Dr SAGNO MOUSSA.

Changement, Progrès et Unité pour la Guinée (CPUG): Conakry; e-mail contact@cpu-guinee.com; internet www.cpu-guinee.com; Pres. Dr IBRAHIMA SACKO.

Génération pour la Réconciliation, l'Union et le Prospérité (GRUP): Conakry; Pres. PAPA KOLY KOUROUMA.

Guinée pour la Démocratie et l'Equilibre (GDE): Conakry; Pres. ABOUBACAR SOUMAH.

Guinée pour Tous (GPT): Conteyah, derrière UNC, Commune de Ratoma, BP 72, Conakry; tel. 628-84-85-93; e-mail mbmarouff@gmail.com; internet www.gptweb.org; Pres. IBRAHIMA KASSORY FOFANA.

Guinée Unie pour le Développement (GUD): Conakry; f. 2002; Pres. Dr SÉKOU BENNA CAMARA.

Mouvement Populaire Démocratique de Guinée (MPDG): Conakry; Pres. SIAKA BARRY.

Nouvelle Génération pour la République (NGR): Kissosso; tel. 664-29-05-72; Leader IBRAHIMA ABE SYLLA.

Parti Démocratique de Guinée—Rassemblement Démocratique Africain (PDG—RDA): Conakry; f. 1946; revived 1992; Sec.-Gen. MOHAMED TOURÉ.

Parti Dyama: Conakry; e-mail mansourkaba@yahoo.fr; internet www.guinea-dyama.com; moderate Islamist party; Pres. MOHAMED MANSOUR KABA.

Parti Ecologiste de Guinée (PEG—Les Verts): BP 3018, Quartier Boulbinet, 5e blvd, angle 2e ave, Commune de Kaloum, Conakry; tel. 300-44-37-01; Leader OUMAR SYLLA.

Parti de l'Espoir pour le Développement National (PEDN): Commune Ratoma, BP 1403, Conakry; tel. 655-55-00-00; Pres. LANSANA KOUYATÉ.

Parti Guinéen pour la Renaissance et le Progrès (PGRP): Conakry; Pres. ALPHA IBRAHIMA SILA BAH.

Parti National pour le Renouveau: Conakry; Pres. ALPHA SOULEYMANE BAH FISHER.

Parti du Peuple de Guinée (PPG): BP 1147, Conakry; socialist; Leader CHARLES-PASCAL TOLNO.

Parti du Travail et de la Solidarité (PTS): Pres. MAMADOU DIAWARA.

Parti de l'Unité et du Progrès (PUP): Camayenne, Conakry; Pres. El Hadj FODÉ BANGOURA; Sec.-Gen. El Hadj Dr SÉKOU KONATÉ.

Rassemblement pour la Défense de la République (RDR): Leader PAPA KOLY KOUROUMA.

Rassemblement pour le Développement Intégré de la Guinée (RDIG): Leader JEAN-MARC TELLIANO.

Rassemblement du Peuple de Guinée (RPG): Quartier Aéroport, Commune de Matoto, Conakry; tel. 669-90-51-06; e-mail info@rpg-arc-en-ciel.org.gn; f. 1980 as the Rassemblement des Patriotes Guinéens; socialist; Acting Pres. IBRAHIMA KASSORY FOFANA; Sec.-Gen. Dr SALOUM CISSÉ.

Union Démocratique de Guinée (UDG): Dixinn Centre, Conakry; tel. 601-52-40-26; f. 2009; Leader El Hadj MAMADOU SYLLA.

Union des Forces Démocratiques (UFD): BP 3050, Conakry; tel. 622-81-51-42; e-mail ufdconakry@yahoo.fr; Pres. MAMADOU BAADIKKO BAH.

Union des Forces Démocratiques de Guinée (UFDG): Carrefour Chinois, Belle-Vue, BP 3036, Conakry; e-mail baggelmalal@yahoo.fr; internet www.ufdgonline.org; f. 2002 by faction of UPR in protest at that party's participation in elections to National Assembly; Pres. CELLOU DALEIN DIALLO.

Union des Forces Républicaines (UFR): Immeuble 'Le Golfe', 4e étage, BP 6080, Conakry; tel. 664-30-47-50; e-mail contact@ufrguinee.com; internet www.ufrguinee.com; f. 1992; liberal-conservative; Pres. SIDYA TOURÉ; Exec. Sec. BAÏDY ARIBOT.

Union Guinéenne pour la Démocratie et le Développement (UGDD): BP 4600, Conakry; tel. 640-00-00-23; Sec.-Gen. KEAMOU BOGOLA HABA.

Union pour le Progrès de la Guinée (UPG): Conakry; Leader JEAN-MARIE DORÉ; Sec.-Gen. AHMED KOUROUMA.

Union pour le Progrès et le Renouveau (UPR): Quartier Minière, Commune de Dixinn, BP 690, Conakry; tel. 655-41-09-90; f. 1998 by merger of the Parti pour le Renouveau et le Progrès and the Union pour la Nouvelle République; Pres. OUSMANE BAH.

Union pour le Progrès National—Parti pour l'Unité et le Développement (UPN—PUD): Conakry; Leader MAMADOU BHOYE BARRY.

Diplomatic Representation

EMBASSIES IN GUINEA

Algeria: Cité des Nations, Quartiers Kaloum, BP 1004, Conakry; tel. 662-05-55-55; e-mail ambalg-cky@hotmail.fr; internet www.ambassadealgerieconakry.info; Ambassador ABDELFETAH DAGHMOUN.

Angola: Conakry; tel. 664-56-24-21; e-mail emaruas@live.com; Ambassador MARIA CUANDINA TCHILEPA DE CARVALHO.

Belgium: Immeuble Koubia, Appartement 402, Corniche Nord, Camayenne, Conakry; tel. 625256444; e-mail conakry@diplobel.fed.be; internet fb.com/ambassadebelgiqueguinee; Ambassador GUY HAMBROUK.

Brazil: Résidence 2000, Immeuble de la DHL, 5e étage, Conakry; tel. 664-20-21-11; e-mail brasemb.conacri@itamaraty.gov.br; internet www.gov.br/mre/pt-br/embaixada-conacri; Ambassador ANTÔNIO CARLOS DE SALLES MENEZES.

China, People's Republic: Quartier Donka, Cité Ministérielle, Commune de Dixinn, BP 714, Conakry; tel. 664-00-80-00; e-mail chinaemb_gn@mfa.gov.cn; internet gn.china-embassy.gov.cn; Ambassador HUANG WEI.

Congo, Democratic Republic: Quartier Almamya, ave de la Gare, Commune de Kaloum, BP 880, Conakry; tel. 300-45-15-01; e-mail missionrdcconakry@yahoo.fr; Ambassador (vacant).

Côte d'Ivoire: blvd de la République, Boulbinet, Commune de Kaloum, BP 5228, Conakry; tel. 656-34-34-34; e-mail info@guinee.diplomatie.gouv.ci; internet guinee.diplomatie.gouv.ci; Ambassador YOUSSOUF MIFOUGO DIARRASSOUBA.

Cuba: Cité des Nations, Villa 18, à côté du Tribunal Militaire, Commune de Kaloum, Conakry; tel. 628-86-08-00; e-mail embacuba@gn.embacuba.cu; internet misiones.minrex.gob.cu/es/guinea-conakry; Ambassador CARLOS MOYA RAMOS.

Egypt: Corniche Sud 2, BP 389, Conakry; tel. 300-46-85-08; e-mail ambconakry@hotmail.com; Ambassador TAMER MOHAMED KAMAL ELMILIGY.

Equatorial Guinea: Guinea Kipe, Centre Emetteur, Conakry; tel. 622-27-13-25; e-mail embarege.conakry@gmail.com; Ambassador ANTONIO EBALE AYINGONO.

France: ave du Commerce, BP 373, Conakry; tel. 621-00-00-10; e-mail ambafrance.conakry@diplomatie.gouv.fr; internet gn.ambafrance.org; Ambassador MARC FONBAUSTIER.

Germany: Quartier Almamya, Kaloum, BP 540, Conakry; tel. 621-22-17-06; e-mail amball@sotelgui.net.gn; internet conakry.diplo.de; Ambassador ULRICH MEIER-TESCH.

Ghana: Immeuble Ex-Urbaine et la Seine, BP 732, Conakry; tel. 664-26-01-91; e-mail ghanaem13@yahoo.co.uk; internet ghanaembconakry.com; Ambassador JANE GASU-AHETO.

Guinea-Bissau: Quartier Bellevue, Commune de Dixinn, BP 298, Conakry; tel. 628-97-13-05; e-mail ambaguineebi.conakry@yahoo.fr; Ambassador ERNESTO MUNTAGA DJALÓ.

Holy See: La Minière, DI 777, BP 2016, Conakry; tel. 664-58-49-59; e-mail nunziaturaguinea@gmail.com; Apostolic Nuncio (vacant).

India: Corniche Nord, Camayenne, Commune de Dixinn, Conakry; e-mail hcicky@gmail.com; tel. 626-26-26-31; e-mail hoc.conakry@mea.gov.in; internet eoiconakry.gov.in/index.php; Ambassador T. C. BARUPAL.

Iran: Donka, Cité Ministérielle, Commune de Dixinn, BP 310, Conakry; tel. 300-01-03-19; e-mail iranemb.cky@mfa.gov.ir; internet conakry.mfa.ir; Ambassador MOHAMMAD HOSSEIN MIRZA AGHAEI CHALKSARAEI.

Italy: 1141 rue 777, Commune de Ratoma, BP 5545, Conakry; tel. 662-85-07-97; e-mail conakry.ambitalia@esteri.it; internet ambconakry.esteri.it; Ambassador STEFANO PONTESILLI.

Japan: Quartier Landréah Port, Corniche Nord, Commune de Dixinn, BP 895, Conakry; tel. 628-68-38-38; internet www.gn.emb-japan.go.jp; Ambassador HIDEO MATSUBARA.

Korea, Democratic People's Republic: Quartier Bellevue/Quartier Minière, Commune de Dixinn, BP 723, Conakry; tel. 664-00-92-32; e-mail arpdcgn@yahoo.fr; Ambassador RI CHONG GYONG.

Lebanon: Immeuble PZ, Almamya, rue de Commerce, BP 5005, Conakry; tel. 664-74-44-44; e-mail lebembconakry@gmail.com;

internet www.conakry.mfa.gov.lb/guinea/arabic/home; Ambassador FADI ZAIN.

Liberia: Cité Ministérielle, Donka, Commune de Dixinn, BP 18, Conakry; tel. 666-41-46-51; e-mail conakry.leb@gmail.com; internet conakry.mfa.gov.lb/guinea; Ambassador VIVIAN WREH.

Libya: Commune de Kaloum, BP 1183, Conakry; tel. 300-41-41-72; e-mail ambalibye_conakry@yahoo.com; Ambassador B. AHMED.

Malaysia: Quartier Mafanco, Corniche Sud, BP 5460, Conakry; tel. 622-66-78-79; e-mail mwconakry@kln.gov.my; internet www.kln .gov.my/web/gin_conakry; Chargé d'affaires a.i. AHMAD IRSHAD RAZIB.

Mali: rue D1–15, Camayenne, Corniche Nord, BP 299, Conakry; tel. 300-46-14-18; e-mail ambamaliguinee@yahoo.fr; Ambassador MODIBO TRAORÉ.

Morocco: Cité des Nations, Villa 12, Commune du Kaloum, BP 193, Conakry; tel. 300-41-36-86; e-mail sifamgui@biasy.net; Ambassador ISSAM TAIB.

Nigeria: Corniche Sud, Quartier de Matam, BP 54, Conakry; tel. 666-37-59-19; e-mail nigeria.conakry@foreignaffairs.gov.ng; Ambassador MOHAMED SARKI ABUBAKAR.

Russian Federation: Matam-Port, km 9, BP 329, Conakry; tel. 625-25-26-90; e-mail ambrusgui@mid.ru; internet guinea.mid.ru; Ambassador VADIM VLADILENOVICH RAZUMOVSKIY.

Saudi Arabia: BP 611, Conakry; tel. 664-00-00-98; e-mail gnemb@ mofa.gov.sa; internet embassies.mofa.gov.sa/sites/Guinea; Ambassador Dr HUSSEIN BIN NASSER AL-DAKHILULLAH.

Senegal: Bâtiment 142, Coléah, Corniche Che Sud, BP 842, Conakry; tel. 300-44-61-32; e-mail ambassenconakry@aol.fr; Ambassador ANNA SÉMOU FAYE.

Sierra Leone: Quartier Bellevue, face aux cases présidentielles, Commune de Dixinn, BP 625, Conakry; tel. 631-35-82-03; e-mail slconakry@foreignaffairs.gov.sl; Ambassador ALMAMY HASSANE BANGOURA.

South Africa: Coléah, Mossoudougou, BP 4703, Conakry; tel. 664-90-47-71; e-mail conakry@dirco.gov.za; Ambassador Maj.-Gen. LEKOA SOLOMON MOLLO.

Spain: Plaza Almany Samory Touré, Immeuble R2000, BP 706, Conakry; tel. 631-35-87-30; e-mail emb.conakry@maec.es; internet www.exteriores.gob.es/embajadas/conakry; Ambassador CRISTIAN FONT CALDERON.

Türkiye (Turkey): Résidence Sandervalia, angle rues KA 019 et KA 022, Conakry; tel. 621-63-05-05; e-mail ambassade.conakry@mfa .gov.tr; internet konakri.be.mfa.gov.tr; Ambassador VOLKAN TÜRK VURAL.

United Arab Emirates: Taouya, Corniche Nord, Cité Guissé Villa No. 4. Commune de Ratoma, Conakry; tel. 624932323; e-mail conakryemb@mofaic.gov.ae; internet www.mofaic.gov.ae/ar-ae/ missions/conakry; Chargé d'affaires a.i. KHALED ALI RABIE ALI AL-HOSANI.

United Kingdom: Villa 1, Residence 2000, Corniche Sud, Conakry; tel. 626-26-40-40; e-mail BritishEmbassy.Conakry@fco.gov.uk; internet www.gov.uk/world/organisations/british-embassy -conakry; Ambassador DAVID MCILROY.

USA: Koloma, Ratoma, BP 603, Conakry; tel. 655-10-40-00; e-mail conconakry@state.gov; internet gn.usembassy.gov; Ambassador TROY DAMIAN FITRELL.

Judicial System

The judicial system comprises a Constitutional Court, a Supreme Court, two Courts of Appeal, 10 Tribunals of First Instance and 26 Tribunals of Justice of Peace. The Constitution of 6 April 2020 embodies the principle of the independence of the judiciary, and delineates the competencies of each component of the judicial system, including the Supreme Court and the Revenue Court.

Constitutional Court (Cour Constitutionnelle): Immeuble Hadja Foulé (Almamya), Kaloum, BP 3968, Conakry; tel. 628-51-68-26; e-mail contact@cour-constitutionnnelle.gov.gn; consists of nine mems; Pres. MOHAMED LAMINE BANGOURA.

Supreme Court (Cour Suprême): Corniche-Sud, Camayenne, Conakry; tel. 627-00-95-38; e-mail guineejuristes@gmail.com; internet www.coursupgn.org; Pres. FODÉ BANGOURA.

Court of Appeal (Cour d'Appel): Conakry: First Pres. ABDOULAYE CONTÉ; Kankan: First Pres. VICTORIEN HABA.

Revenue Court (Cour des Comptes): Conakry; consists of 11 judges; Pres. MOHAMED DIARÉ.

Religion

An estimated 87% of the population are Muslims and 7% Christians, while 2% follow animist beliefs.

ISLAM

National Islamic League: BP 386, Conakry; tel. 300-41-23-38; f. 1988; Sec.-Gen. Elhadj ABDOULAYE DIASSY.

CHRISTIANITY

The Roman Catholic Church

Guinea comprises one archdiocese and two dioceses.

Bishops' Conference: Conférence Episcopale de la Guinée, BP 1006 bis, Conakry; tel. 300-41-32-70; e-mail dhewara@eti.met.gn; Pres. Most Rev. RAPHAËL BALLA GUILAVOGUI (Bishop of N'Zérékoré).

Archbishop of Conakry: Most Rev. VINCENT COULIBALY, Archevêché, BP 2016, Conakry; tel. 662-90-28-72; e-mail conakriensis@ yahoo.fr.

The Anglican Communion

Anglicans in Guinea are adherents of the Church of the Province of West Africa (CPWA). The diocese of Guinea was established in 1985 as the first French-speaking diocese in the Province. In September 2012 the CPWA was subdivided into two internal provinces: the Internal Province of Ghana, comprising the 10 (now 11) dioceses in Ghana, and the Internal Province of West Africa, comprising the remaining five (now six) dioceses. The Archbishop of the CPWA is the Bishop of Liberia.

Bishop of Guinea: Rt Rev. JACQUES BOSTON, Cathédrale Toussaint, BP 1187, Conakry; tel. 631-20-46-60; e-mail agomezd@yahoo.fr.

BAHÁ'Í FAITH

Assemblée Spirituelle Nationale: BP 2010, Conakry 1; e-mail asngunee@yahoo.fr; Sec. MAMMA TRAORÉ.

The Press

REGULATORY AUTHORITY

Haute Autorité de la Communication (HAC): en face Primature, BP 2955, Conakry; internet hacgn.org; f. 2010; regulates the operations of the press, and of radio and television; regulates political access to the media; 13 mems; Pres. BOUBACAR YACINE DIALLO.

NEWSPAPERS AND PERIODICALS (PRINT AND ONLINE)

Bingo: Mifergui, ave du Port, face à la Douane, Almamya, Kaloum, Conakry; tel. 622-91-60-74; e-mail barryyoussoufben@gmail.com; internet www.journalsatiriquebingo.com; fortnightly; political and social satire; Dir of Publication BEN BARRY YOUSSOUF.

Le Démocrate: Quartier Ratoma Centre, Commune de Ratoma, BP 2427, Conakry; tel. 601-20-01-01; e-mail mamadoudianb@yahoo.fr; weekly; Dir of Publication and Editor-in-Chief MAMADOU DIAN BALDÉ.

Le Diplomate: BP 2427, Conakry; tel. 655-51-51-51; e-mail hawasanouci@yahoo.fr; internet www.lediplomateguinee.com; f. 2002; weekly; Dir SANOU KERFALLAH CISSÉ.

L'Enquêteur: Coléah Lanséboundji, Commune de Matam, BP 6474, Conakry; tel. 657-94-46-97; e-mail habib@boubah.com; f. 2001; weekly; Editor HABIB YAMBERING DIALLO.

Horoya (Liberty): Enceinte de RTG, Boulbinet, Kaloum, BP 341, Conakry; tel. 628-21-47-32; e-mail horoye2010@yahoo.fr; internet journalhoroya.net; govt daily.

L'Indépendant: Quartier Ratoma Centre, Commune de Ratoma, BP 2427, Conakry; tel. 601-20-01-01; e-mail lindependant@afribone .net.gn; weekly; also *L'Indépendant Plus*; Dir of Publication and Editor-in-Chief MAMADOU DIAN BALDÉ.

Le Jour: Koloma II, Ratoma, Conakry; tel. 656-12-94-13; e-mail lejourinfo@gmail.com; internet www.lejour.info; fortnightly; Dir of Publication MAMADOU BAILO DIALLO.

Journal Officiel de Guinée: BP 156, Conakry; fortnightly; organ of the Govt.

La Lance: Immeuble Baldé Zaïre, BP 4968, Conakry; tel. 300-41-23-85; weekly; general information; Dir SOULEYMANE E. DIALLO.

Le Lynx: Immeuble Baldé Zaïre, Sandervalia, BP 4968, Conakry; tel. 621-22-22-22; e-mail maryoudi@yahoo.fr; internet lelynx.net; f. 1992; weekly; satirical; Editor SOULEYMAN DIALLO.

Nouvelle Elite: Conakry; tel. 655-58-27-27; e-mail sekoubasavane@ yahoo.fr; weekly; Dir of Publication SÉKOUBA SAVANÉ.

La Nouvelle Tribune: blvd Diallo Tally, entre 5e et 6e ave, BP 35, Conakry; tel. 300-22-33-02; e-mail abdcond@yahoo.fr; internet www .lanouvelletribuneguinee.com; weekly, Tuesdays; independent; general information and analysis; Dir of Publ. and Editing ABDOULAYE CONDÉ.

L'Observateur: Immeuble Baldé, Conakry; tel. 300-40-05-24; e-mail ibrahimanouhou@yahoo.fr; weekly; independent; Dir NOU-HOU BALDÉ.

Le Populaire: Immeuble Baldé Zaïre, 5 ave Manquepas, Kaloum, Conakry; tel. 664-29-48-51; internet www.lepopulaireguinee.com; weekly; general; Dir of Publication ALPHA ABDOULAYE DIALLO.

Sanakou: Labé, Foutah Djallon, Moyenne-Guinée; tel. 622-82-94-74; e-mail sanakoulabe@gmail.com; f. 2000; monthly; general news; Publr IDRISSA SAMPIRING DIALLO; Editor-in-Chief MAMADOU CHÉRIF DIALLO.

Le Standard: 4e ave, Boulbinet, Kaloum, Conakry; tel. 622-98-34-97; e-mail contact@lestandardguinee.com; internet www .lestandardguinee.com; weekly; Dir of Publication ALPHA CAMARA; Editor-in-Chief IBRAHIMA SORY BAH.

3P Plus (Parole-Plume-Papier) Magazine: 7e ave Bis Almamyah, BP 5122, Conakry; tel. 631-35-04-90; e-mail 3p-plus@mirinet .net.gn; internet www.3p-plus.net; f. 1995; journal of arts and letters; supplements *Le Cahier de l'Economie* and *Mag-Plus: Le Magazine de la Culture*; monthly; Pres. MOHAMED SALIFOU KEÏTA; Editor-in-Chief SAMBA TOURÉ.

NEWS AGENCY

Agence Guinéenne de Presse: BP 1535, Conakry; tel. 300-41-14-34; e-mail info@agpguinee.net; internet www.agpguinee.com; f. 1960; Dir-Gen. ALPHA KABINET DOUMBOUYA.

PRESS ASSOCIATION

Association Guinéenne des Editeurs de la Presse Indépendante (AGEPI): Conakry; f. 1991; an asscn of independent newspaper publishers; Chair. HASSANE KABA.

Publishers

Editions du Ministère de l'Education Nationale: BP 561, Conakry; tel. 300-43-02-66; e-mail dnrst@mirinet.net.gn; f. 1959; general and educational; Deputy Dir Dr TAMBA TAGBINO.

L'Harmattan Guinée: Conakry; tel. 657-20-85-08; internet fb.com/ lharmattanguinee.

Société Africaine d'Edition et de Communication (SAEC): Belle-Vue, Commune de Dixinn, BP 6826, Conakry; tel. 300-29-71-41; e-mail dtniane@yahoo.fr; social sciences, reference, literary fiction; Editorial Assistant OUMAR TALL.

Broadcasting and Communications

TELECOMMUNICATIONS

In 2022 there were three providers of mobile telephone services and one provider of fixed-line telephone services in Guinea.

Cellcom Guinée: Immeuble WAQF-BID, Almamya, C/Kaloum, BP 6567, Conakry; tel. 655-10-01-00; e-mail info@gn.cellcomgsm.com; internet fb.com/cellcomgsm; f. 2008.

MTN Guinée: Quartier Almamya, Commune de Kaloum, BP 3237, Conakry; tel. 660-22-22-22; e-mail businesssales@mtn.com.gn; internet mtn.com.gn; f. 2005; mobile telephone provider; 75% owned by MTN (South Africa); Dir-Gen. PAPA SOW.

Orange Guinée: Conakry; tel. 624-93-00-00; e-mail serviceclientguinee@orange-sonatel.com; internet www .orange-guinee.com; f. 2007; 85% owned by Groupe Sonatel (Senegal); Dir-Gen. ABOUBACAR SADIKH DIOP.

Regulatory Authority

Autorité de Régulation des Postes et des Télécommunications (ARPT): Centre Directionnel de Koloma, Immeuble APRT, Conakry; tel. 669-22-10-10; e-mail contact@arpt .gov.gn; internet www.arpt.gov.gn; f. 2008; Dir-Gen. SÉKOU OUMAR BARRY.

BROADCASTING

Regulatory Authority

Haute Autorité de la Communication (HAC): see The Press.

Radio

Bolivar FM Guinée: Mamou; tel. 622-50-50-50; e-mail badicko@ bolivarfm.com; internet www.bolivarfm.com; Dir BADICKO DIALLO.

Espace FM: Quartier Matoto, Immeuble Mouna, BP 256, Conakry; tel. 664-20-20-92; e-mail services@espacefmguinee.info; internet espacefmguinee.info; Dir-Gen. LAMINE GUIRASSY.

Sweet FM: Quartier Matoto, Immeuble Mouna, BP 256, Conakry; tel. 664-20-20-92.

Love FM: Conakry; tel. 624-515-151; e-mail contact@lovefmguinee .info; internet www.lovefmguinee.info.

Milo FM: BP 215, Kankan; tel. 300-72-00-82; e-mail info@milo-fm .com; internet www.milo-fm.com; Dir-Gen. LANCINÉ KABA.

Nostalgie Guinée (98.2 FM): Conakry; internet nostalgieguinee .net.

Radio Bonheur FM: Conakry; tel. 622-99-51-73; e-mail radiobonheurfmguinee@gmail.com; internet bonheurfmguinee.com.

Radio Télévision Guinéenne (RTG): BP 391, Conakry; tel. 300-44-22-01; broadcasts in French, English, Créole-English, Portuguese, Arabic and local languages; Dir-Gen. YAMOUSSA SIDIBÉ; Dir of Radio ISSA CONDÉ.

Radio Rurale de Guinée: BP 391, Conakry; tel. 628-76-51-05; e-mail nouhankonate24@gmail.com; internet fb.com/R .ruralekerouane; network of rural radio stations; Dir-Gen. DOUSSOU MORY CONDÉ.

Renaissance FM: Marché Koloma, Conakry; tel. 622-70-05-51; e-mail contact@renaissancefmguinee.com; internet renaissancefmguinee.com.

Sabari FM: rue Nongo 501, Conakry; tel. 623-47-83-83; e-mail hawasanouci@gmail.com; internet sabarifm.com; f. 2008.

Soleil FM: ave du Port, Conakry; tel. 666-10-62-12; internet soleilfmguinee.net; f. 2006; Dir KEITA KABASSAN.

Television

Espace TV: Quartier Matoto, Immeuble Mouna, BP 256, Conakry; tel. 664-20-20-92; e-mail infos.solamedia@gmail.com; internet www .espacetvguinee.info; f. 2013; Pres. and Dir-Gen. LAMINE GUIRASSY.

Kalac TV: Quartier Matoto, Immeuble Mouna, BP 256, Conakry; tel. 664-20-20-92; e-mail infos.solamedia@gmail.com; internet www.espacetvguinee.info/kalac-tv; f. 2019; music and entertainment.

Radio Télévision Guinéenne (RTG): see Radio; transmissions in French and local languages; one channel; f. 1977.

Finance

BANKING

Central Bank

Banque Centrale de la République de Guinée (BCRG): 6 blvd du Commerce, BP 692, Kaloum, Conakry; tel. 664-67-77-77; e-mail secretariat.gouv@bcrg-guinee.org; internet www.bcrg-guinee.org; f. 1960; bank of issue; Gov. KARAMO KABA.

Commercial Banks

Afriland First Bank Guinée: Almamya, Commune de Kaloum, BP 343, Conakry; tel. 669-93-93-93; e-mail guinee@afrilandfirstbank .com; internet afrilandfirstbankgin.com; Dir-Gen. GUY LAURENT FONDJO.

Banque pour le Commerce et l'Industrie: 6e ave de la République, Sandervalia, Kaloum, BP 359, Conakry; tel. 628-68-75-19; e-mail infogn@bci-banque.com; internet www.bci-banque.com; f. 2012; Pres. ISSELMOU TAJIDINE; Dir-Gen. SIDY MOHAMED CHERIF.

Banque Internationale pour le Commerce et l'Industrie de la Guinée (BICIGUI): ave de la République, BP 1484, Conakry; tel. 624-93-11-11; e-mail dg.bicigui@africa.bnpparibas.com; internet www.bicigui.org; f. 1985; Pres. IBRAHIMA SOUMAH; Dir-Gen. DENIS RUBRICE.

Banque Nationale de Guinée: blvd Télly Diallo, Kouléwondy, Kaloum, BP 1787, Conakry; tel. 624-22-20-31; e-mail info@bng-gn .com; internet bng-gn.com; f. 2014; Pres. MOHAMED SALEM ZAMEL.

Banque Populaire Maroco-Guinéenne (BPMG): Immeuble BPMG, blvd du Commerce, Kaloum, BP 4400, Conakry 01; tel. 631-22-26-30; f. 1991; 55% owned by Crédit Populaire du Maroc; 42% state-owned; Dir-Gen. MOSTAFA DAFIR.

BSIC Guinée: 7e ave, angle route de Niger, Kaloum, BP 4614, Conakry; tel. 666-55-55-57; e-mail bsic.guinee@bsicbank.com; internet www.bsic-guinee.com; f. 2009; Dir-Gen. MOHAMED ATTAHER MAÏGA.

Coris Bank International Guinée: angle ave de la Gare, Quatier Almamyah, BP 3048, Conakry; tel. 610888888; e-mail corisbank-gn@coris-bank.com; internet guinee.coris.bank; f. 2021; Dir-Gen. MAMBO TETÉ BENISSAN.

Ecobank Guinée: Immeuble Al Iman, ave de la République, BP 5687, Conakry; tel. 666-70-14-34; e-mail ecobankgn@ecobank.com; internet www.ecobank.com; f. 1999; wholly owned by Ecobank Transnational Inc (Togo); Pres. BOUBACAR KEITA; Man. Dir MOUKARAM CHANOU ALAO.

FBN Bank Guinea: Koulewondy, blvd Diallo Telly, BP 3547, Conakry; tel. 624-93-20-20; internet www.fbnbankguinea.com; f. 1997; fmrly International Commercial Bank SA; Chair. IBUKUN A. AWOSIKA; Dir-Gen. Dr ADESOLA KAZEEM ADEDUNTAN.

NSIA Banque Guinée: ave de la République, Kaloum, BP 483, Conakry; tel. 628-91-58-88; e-mail nsiaguinee@groupensia.com; internet www.groupensia.com/fr/nsia-en-guinee; Dir-Gen. CHRISTELLE DIENG ZONGO.

Orabank Guinée: ave de la République, angle 5e blvd, BP 324, Conakry; tel. 622-35-00-70; e-mail info-gn@orabank.net; internet www.orabank.net/fr/filiale/guinee; f. 1988; fmrly the Union Internationale de Banques en Guinée, present name adopted in 2011; 54.0% owned by Oragroup SA (Togo), 14.3% owned by Orabank Tchad; Dir-Gen. MAMBO TETE-BENISSAN.

Skye Bank Guinée SA: Immeuble Immovie UGAR, 5e ave, Commune de Kaloum, BP 4606, Conakry; tel. 667-47-77-00; e-mail cservice@skyebankgn.com; internet www.skyebankgn.com; Pres. KABINÉ KOMARA; Man. Dir GABRIEL O. BANKOLE.

Société Générale Guinée: Immeuble Boffa, Cité du Chemin de Fer, BP 1514, Conakry; tel. 664-88-84-44; e-mail sgguinee.contact@socgen.com; internet guinee.societegenerale.com; f. 1985; 53% owned by Société Générale (France); Dir-Gen. JOSE C. GARCIA REBOLLAR.

United Bank for Africa Guinée: rue du Château d'Eau, Marché Niger, Kaloum, BP 1198, Conakry; tel. 664-10-02-00; e-mail cfcguineaconakry@ubagroup.com; internet www.ubaguinea.com; Dir-Gen. TONY ODEIGAH.

Vista Bank: Immeuble Lola, Cité des Chemins de Fer, BP 557, Conakry; tel. 662-46-46-46; e-mail info@vistabankgroup.com; internet vistabankgroup.com/gn/particuliers; fmrly FiBank Guinée SA; name changed as above in 2015; Pres. El Hadj MOUSTAPHA KABA; Dir-Gen. YASSIN BAYO.

Islamic Bank

Banque Islamique de Guinée: Immeuble Nafaya, 6e ave de la République, BP 1247, Conakry; tel. 622-84-53-99; e-mail contact@big-bank.com; internet www.ta-holding.com/fr/intl/guinee; f. 1983; 68.45% owned by Tamweel Africa Holding, 31.54% owned by Islamic Development Bank (Saudi Arabia); Dir-Gen. SIDY DIEYE.

INSURANCE

International Insurance Co (IIC): Immeuble Mirna, ave de la République, Kaloum, BP 4476, Conakry; tel. 656-14-31-80; e-mail infos@iicassuranceguinee.com; f. 2007; Dir-Gen. MORIBA FOFANA.

Mutragui: BP 1189, Conakry; tel. 657-05-00-00; e-mail info@mutragui.com.

NSIA Assurances: Immeuble NSIA, ave de la République, Kaloum, BP 5884, Conakry; tel. 629-00-00-20; e-mail nsiaguinee@groupensia.com; internet nsiassurancesguinee.com; acquired Sanlam Guinée in 2022; Dir-Gen. MAÏMOUNA BARRY BALDÉ.

Société Guinéenne d'Assurances et de Réassurance (SOGAM): Immeuble Chérif Abdoul Rahim, Carrefour Constantin, Matam BP 4340, Conakry; tel. 622-34-40-78; e-mail sogamsa2013@gmail.com; internet sogamguinee.com; f. 1989; Dir THIERNO MAMADOU BAÏLO DIALLO.

Société Nouvelle d'Assurances de Guinée (SONAG): Cité Chemin de Fer, Almamya, Commune de Kaloum, BP 805, Conakry; tel. 628-68-94-94; e-mail info@sonagassurances.com; internet sonag-assurances.com; f. 1989; Dir-Gen. CHARLES DÉLAMOU.

Sunu Assurances IARD Guinée: Immeuble MAKKA, rue KAO15, Almamya Niger, Kaloum, BP 1618, Conakry; tel. 666-10-10-27; e-mail guinee.sunu@sunu-group.com; internet www.sunu-group.com; Pres. THIERNO OURY BAH; Dir-Gen. MANDIAYE GUEYE.

Union Guinéenne d'Assurances et de Réassurances (UGAR): 14 pl. des Martyrs, BP 179, Conakry; tel. 656-96-00-00; e-mail contactgn@group-activa.com; internet www.group-activa.com/guinee; f. 1989; 40% owned by AXA (France), 35% state-owned; Pres. ISMAËL BANGOURA; Man. Dir IBRAHIMA CAMARA.

Activa-Vie: BP 179, Conakry; tel. 656-96-00-10; life insurance; Dir-Gen. MOUSSA DIAKITÉ.

Trade and Industry

GOVERNMENT AGENCIES

Agence Nationale d'Aménagement des Infrastructures Minières (ANAIM): Ex Immeuble Enipra, 6eme étage, BP 4596, Kaloum, Conakry; tel. 664-23-35-63; e-mail info@anaimgn.com; internet anaimgn.com; Dir-Gen. MOHAMED YAGO BANGOURA.

Agence Nationale d'Inclusion Economique et Sociale (ANIES): Conakry; tel. 629-00-57-00; e-mail contact@anies.gov.gn; internet anies.gov.gn; f. 2019; Co-ordinator-Gen. ANSOUMANE CAMARA; Dir-Gen. SAYON DAMBÉLÉ.

Agence de Promotion des Investissements Privés-Guichet Unique (APIP–GUINEE): 252 rue KA 022, BP 2024, Conakry; tel. 656-31-11-14; e-mail info@apip.gov.gn; internet www.apip.gov.gn; f. 1992; promotes private investment; Dir-Gen. NAMORY CAMARA.

Centre de Promotion et de Développement Miniers (CPDM): BP 295, Conakry; tel. 665-37-61-30; f. 1995; promotes investment and co-ordinates devt strategy in mining sector; Dir MOHAMED LAMINE SY SAVANÉ.

DEVELOPMENT ORGANIZATIONS

Agence Française de Développement (AFD): 5e ave, KA022, BP 283, Conakry; tel. 626-26-89-89; e-mail afdconakry@afd.fr; internet www.afd.fr; Country Dir OLIVIER PANNETIER.

France Volontaires: BP 570, Conakry; tel. 628-04-97-45; internet www.france-volontaires.org; f. 1987; name changed as above in 2009; devt and research projects; Nat. Rep. TELNGAR RASSEMBEYE.

Maison Guinéenne de l'Entrepreneur (MGE): Quartier Hermakonon, Matam, Conakry; tel. 622-60-74-15; e-mail kerfalla.camara@mge-guinee.org; internet www.mge-guinee.org; f. 1998; Exec. Dir KERFALLA CAMARA.

Service de Coopération et d'Action Culturelle: BP 373, Conakry; tel. 621-00-00-10; administers bilateral aid; Dir in Guinea FRÉDÉRIC BRIGNOT.

CHAMBERS OF COMMERCE

Chambre de Commerce, d'Industrie et de Artisanat de Guinée (CCIAG): Quartier Almamya, Commune de Kaloum, BP 545, Conakry; tel. 622-62-90-79; e-mail cciag06@gmail.com; f. 1985; Pres. MAMADOU BALDÉ; Sec.-Gen. FODÉ MOHAMED FOFANA.

Chambre des Mines de Guinée (CMG): Immeuble Labé, 4e étage, Cité Chemin de Fer, BP 2624, Conakry; tel. 622-35-10-36; e-mail mkeita@chambredesminesgn.com; internet www.chambredesminesgn.org; f. 1997; Pres. ISMAEL DIAKITÉ; 66 mems.

TRADE AND EMPLOYERS' ASSOCIATIONS

Association des Commerçants de Guinée: BP 2468, Conakry; tel. 664-21-92-42; e-mail thouca_acic@yahoo.fr; f. 1976; Sec.-Gen. THIERNO OUMAR CAMARA.

Association des Femmes Entrepreneurs de Guinée (AFEG): BP 104, Kaloum, Conakry; tel. 657-28-02-95; e-mail afeguine@yahoo.fr; f. 1987; Pres. HADJA RAMATOULAYE SOW.

Conseil National du Patronat Guinéen (CNPG): Boulbinet, Kaloum, BP 6403, Conakry; tel. 621-29-09-33; e-mail contact@cnpguinee.com; internet cnpguinee.com; f. 1992; Pres. ANSOUMANE KABA.

UTILITIES

Electricity

Electricité de Guinée (EDG): Immeuble EDG, Cité Chemin de Fer, Commune de Kaloum, BP 1463, Conakry; tel. 626-11-11-11; e-mail contact@edg.com.gn; internet edg.com.gn; f. 2001 to replace Société Guinéenne d'Electricité; majority state-owned; production, transport and distribution of electricity; Dir-Gen. BANGALY MATY.

Water

Service National des Points d'Eau de Guinée (SNAPE): Quartier Almamya, Commune de Kaloum, BP 2064, Conakry; tel. 622-87-46-75; e-mail infosdgsnape@gmail.com; internet www.snapeguinee.org; supplies water in rural areas; Dir-Gen. ALADJI FODÉ KABA.

Société des Eaux de Guinée (SEG): Quartier Almamya, BP 150, Conakry; tel. 601-29-01-50; e-mail contact@segguinee.com; internet www.segguinee.com; f. 2001 to replace SONEG; national water co; Dir-Gen. ABOUBACAR CAMARA.

MAJOR COMPANIES

The following are among the largest companies in terms either of capital investment or employment.

Alumina Company of Guinea (Friguia/ACG): BP 554, Conakry; f. 1999 to control Friguia (f. 1957); majority owned by Russian

Aluminium (RUSAL), 15% state-owned; mining of bauxite and production of alumina; technical and management agreement with Alcoa (USA); Dir-Gen. MALICK N'DIAYE.

AngloGold Ashanti Guinea (SAG): BP 1006, Conakry; tel. 300-41-58-09; f. 1985 as Société Aurifère de Guinée; name changed 1997; 85% owned by AngloGold Ashanti Goldfields (Ghana/South Africa); gold prospecting and exploitation at Siguiri; Man. Dir TERRY MULPETER.

BEGEC-TP: Quartier Sandervalia, ave de la République, BP 170, Conakry; tel. 628-21-30-96; e-mail btpbelco@yahoo.fr; internet begecgroup.com; construction; Dir-Gen. ABDOURAHAME BELLA KEÏTA.

Compagnie des Bauxites de Guinée: BP 523, Conakry; tel. 629-00-60-98; e-mail info@cbg-guinnee.com; internet cbg-guinee.com; f. 1964; 51% owned by Halco (Mining) Inc (a consortium of interests from USA, Canada, France, Germany and Australia), 49% state-owned; bauxite mining at Boké; Pres. MOUSSA MAGASSOUBA; Dir-Gen. SOULEYMANE TRAORÉ.

Compagnie des Bauxites de Kindia (CBK): BP 613, Conakry; tel. 623-23-01-43; f. 1969 as Office des Bauxites de Kindia, a jt venture with the USSR; production began 1974; name changed 1992; managed by Russian Aluminium (RUSAL) for 25-year (2001–26) contract; bauxite mining at Debélé; Man. Dir ANATOLII PANCHENKO.

Compagnie des Eaux Minérales de Guinée (CEG): BP 3023 Conakry; tel. 628-95-95-96; f. 1987; mineral water bottling plant.

Guinea Alumina Corpn Ltd: Quartier Taouyah, Commune de Ratoma, BP 5090, Conakry; tel. 623-23-80-65; e-mail gaccommunication@ega.ae; internet www.gacguinee.com; Pres. ABDULLA JASSEM KALBAN; CEO STEEVE TREMBLAY.

Guinée Industries: Kissosso, Commune de Matoto, BP 3835, Conakry; tel. 660-23-24-25; e-mail groupegi@guineeindustries .com; internet www.guineeindustries.com; started production of cement in 2013; Dir-Gen. ADEL FAKHREDDINE.

LafargeHolcim Guinée: Immeuble Macenta, Kaloum, Cité Chemins de Fer, BP 3621, Conakry; tel. 628-68-60-00; internet lafargeholcim-gn.com; fmrly Ciments de Guinée; present name adopted in 2016; one cement plant (Sinfonia); Dir-Gen. BRUNO SILETE HOUNKPATI.

Société des Bauxites de Dabola-Tougué (SBDT): BP 2859, Conakry; tel. 300-41-47-21; f. 1992; owned jtly by Govts of Guinea and Iran; bauxite mining at Dabola and Tougué; Dir-Gen. FODE DIABY.

Société des Brasseries de Guinée (Sobragui): Madina, Km 7 route du Niger, BP 345 Conakry; tel. 664-87-59-02; e-mail contact@ sobragui.com; internet www.sobragui.com; f. 1948; mfrs beer and soft drinks; brewery at Kissidougou; Dir-Gen. XAVIER DE BOISSET.

Société Guinéenne de Distribution: rue DI 266, Immeuble Hadja, 1er étage, Nagnouma Magassouba, Landréah, BP 4630, Dixinn; tel. 620-69-58-55; e-mail info@soguidi.com; internet soguidi.com; f. 2012.

Société Guinéenne de Lubrifiants et d'Emballages (SOGUI-LUBE): BP 709, Conakry; tel. 631-35-14-95; blends lubricants; 50% owned by Royal Dutch Shell (Netherlands/United Kingdom), 50% by Govt of Guinea.

Société Guinéenne des Pétroles (SGP): blvd Maritime, BP 656, Conakry; tel. 622-35-92-00; f. 1990; 47% owned by Total Guinée, 17% owned by Compagnie Shell de Guinée; Dir-Gen. IBRAHIMA KALIL MAGASSOUBA.

Société Minière de Boké: Immeuble WAZNI, Tombo, BP 2162, Conakry; internet www.smb-guinee.com; f. 2014; Dir-Gen. FRÉDÉRIC BOUZIGUES.

Société Minière de Dinguiraye (SMD): BP 2162, Conakry; tel. 300-46-36-81; 85% owned by Crew Gold Corpn (Canada), 15% state-owned; exploitation of gold deposits in the Lefa corridor and devt of other areas of Dinguiraye concession; Man. Dir Dr MARTIN WHITE.

Société Nationale des Pétroles (SONAP): Conakry; f. 2021 following merger of the Office National des Pétroles and the Société Nationale d'Importation des Pétroles; Dir-Gen. AMADOU DOUMBOUYA.

Total Guinée: route du Niger, Coleah Km 4, BP 306, Conakry; tel. 623-23-62-62; e-mail contact@totalgn.com; internet gn.totalenergies .com; f. 1988; storage of petroleum products; Dir-Gen. NICOLAS LISIECKI.

Vivo Energy Guinée: BP 312, Conakry; tel. 631-40-78-61; e-mail corporate@csgcky.simis.com; internet www.vivoenergy.com; a Shell licensee and a jt venture between Vitol (40%), Helios Investment Partners (40%) and Shell (20%); distribution of petroleum products; Dir-Gen. ABOU SOW.

TRADE UNIONS

Confédération Nationale des Travailleurs de Guinée (CNTG): Bourse du Travail, Corniche Sud 004, BP 237, Conakry; e-mail cntg60@yahoo.fr; internet www.gui-cntg.net; f. 1984; Sec.-Gen. AMADOU DIALLO.

Syndicat National des Mines, Industries Chimiques et Carrières (SYNAMIC/ONSLG): BP 4033, Conakry; tel. 655-85-95-65; e-mail dialloms57@gmail.com; f. 1991; Sec.-Gen. MAMADOU SALIOU DIALLO.

Union Syndicale des Travailleurs de Guinée (USTG): BP 1514, Conakry; tel. 300-41-25-65; e-mail fofi1952@yahoo.fr; independent; Sec.-Gen. ABDOULAYE SOW.

Transport

RAILWAYS

Office National des Chemins de Fer de Guinée (ONCFG): BP 589, Conakry; tel. 300-44-46-13; f. 1905; Man. Dir NABY BADRA YOULA.

Chemin de Fer de Boké: BP 523, Boké; operations commenced 1973.

Chemin de Fer Conakry–Fria: BP 334, Conakry; operations commenced 1960; Gen. Man. A. CAMARA.

Chemin de Fer de la Société des Bauxites de Kindia: BP 613, Conakry; tel. 300-41-38-28; operations commenced 1974; Gen. Man. K. KEITA.

ROADS

An 895-km cross-country road links Conakry to Bamako, in Mali, and the main highway connecting Dakar (Senegal) to Abidjan (Côte d'Ivoire) also crosses Guinea. The road linking Conakry to Freetown (Sierra Leone) forms part of the Trans West African Highway, extending from Morocco to Nigeria.

Fonds d'Entretien Routier (FER): Quartier Almamya, Commune de Kaloum, Immeuble C, 3e étage (ex-ENIPRA), BP 2691, Conakry; tel. 631-70-17-14; e-mail dgfer@hotmail.com; Dir-Gen. SOULEYMANE TRAORÉ.

SHIPPING

Conakry and Kamsar are the international seaports.

Alport Conakry: Conakry; tel. 621-74-56-52; e-mail operations@ conakryport.com; internet conakryport.com; subsidiary of Albayrak Group; stevedoring; Dir-Gen. MOUSTAPHA LEVENT ADALI.

Getma Guinée: Immeuble KASSA, Cité des Chemins de Fer, BP 1648, Conakry; tel. 300-41-26-66; e-mail info@getmaguinee.com; internet www.getma.com; f. 1979; fmrly Société Guinéenne d'Entreprises de Transports Maritimes et Aeriens; marine transportation; Chair. and CEO JEAN-JACQUES GRENIER.

Port Autonome de Conakry (PAC): BP 805, Conakry; tel. 655-80-00-80; e-mail info@portconakry.com; internet portconakry.com; Gen. Man. AISSATA ARIBOT.

Société Navale Guinéenne (SNG): Cité Chemin de Fer, Almamya, Kaloum, BP 522, Conakry; tel. 631-89-28-28; e-mail contact@ societenavaleguineenne.gov.gn; internet www .societenavaleguineenne.gov.gn; f. 1968; state-owned; shipping agents; Dir-Gen. FATOUMATA CISSÉ.

Transmar: Immeuble Zaidan, blvd du Commerce, Kaloum, BP 3115, Conakry; tel. 622-35-00-42; e-mail contact@transmarguinee.com; shipping, stevedoring, inland transport.

CIVIL AVIATION

There is an international airport at Conakry-Gbèssia, and some 13 smaller airfields elsewhere in the country. In February 2020 the Government signed a 25-year concession agreement with the infrastructure investment platform Africa50 and Groupe ADP of France to co-develop and finance the upgrade and expansion of Conakry-Gbèssia International Airport (which was renamed Ahmed-Sékou-Touré International Airport in late 2021), with the aim of increasing its annual handling capacity from some 500,000 passengers to 1m. passengers by 2031.

Autorité Guinéenne de l'Aviation Civile (AGAC): Rond Point Aéroport Gbessia, Route Bambeto, Commune de Matoto, Conakry; tel. 656-88-81-00; e-mail contact@agac-gn.com; internet agac-gn .com; f. 2013; Dir-Gen. MOHAMED KOBÉLÉ KEÏTA.

Guinea Airlines: Conakry; f. 2017; domestic and regional services; Gen. Man. ALAIN REGOURD.

Société de Gestion et d'Exploitation de l'Aéroport de Conakry (SOGEAC): BP 3126, Conakry; tel. 300-46-48-03; internet www .aeroport-conakry.com; f. 1987; manages Conakry-Gbèssia int. airport; 51% state-owned; Dir-Gen. OULABA KABASSAN KEÏTA.

Tourism

Office National du Tourisme: Immeuble al-Iman, 6e ave de la République, BP 1275, Conakry; tel. 622-09-34-36; f. 1997; Dir-Gen. LAYE MAMADY CONDÉ.

Defence

As assessed at November 2021, Guinea's active armed forces numbered 9,700, including an army of 8,500, a navy of an estimated 400 and an air force of 800. Paramilitary forces comprised a republican guard of 1,600 and a 1,000-strong gendarmerie, as well as a reserve 'people's militia' of 7,000.

Defence Expenditure: Estimated at 2,410,000m. Guinean francs in 2021.

Chief of General Staff of the Armed Forces: Col SADIBA KOULIBALY.

Chief of Staff of the Air Force: Col YACOUBA TOURÉ.

Chief of Staff of the Army: Col BALLA KOÏVOGUI.

Chief of Staff of the Navy: Capt. MAMADOU YAYA DIALLO.

Commander of the National Gendarmerie: Col BALLA SAMOURA.

Education

Education is provided free of charge at every level in state institutions. Primary education, which begins at seven years of age and lasts for six years, is officially compulsory. According to United Nations Educational, Scientific and Cultural Organization (UNESCO) estimates, in 2019/20 enrolment at pre-primary level was equivalent to 18% of children in the relevant age-group (males 18%; females 17%). In 2015/16 enrolment in primary education included 78% of children in the relevant age-group (males 85%; females 71%), while enrolment at secondary schools in 2013/14 was equivalent to 39% of children in the appropriate age-group (boys 47%; girls 31%). Secondary education, from the age of 13, lasts for seven years, comprising a first cycle (collège) of four years and a second (lycée) of three years. There are universities at Conakry and Kankan, and other tertiary institutions at Manéyah, Boké and Faranah. In 2021 government spending on education represented 11.9% of total government expenditure, according to the World Bank.

Bibliography

Bah, I. *Les Transitions Politiques en Guinée de son Indépendance à 2010*. Paris, L'Harmattan, 2013.

Bah, M. B. *Les Défis de la Démocratie en Guinée*. Paris, L'Harmattan, 2014.

Bangoura, D. (Ed.). *Quelle transition politique pour la Guinée?* Paris, L'Harmattan, 2006.

Bari, N. *L'accusé: Sékou Touré devant le TPI*. Paris, L'Harmattan, 2014.

Barry, A. O. *Les racines du mal guinéen*. Paris, Editions Karthala, 2004.

Binns, M. *Guinea*. Oxford, Clio Press, 1996.

Camara, D. K. *La diaspora Guinéenne*. Paris, L'Harmattan, 2003.

Camara, M. S. *Le pouvoir politique en Guinée sous Sékou Touré*. Paris, L'Harmattan, 2007.

  Political History of Guinea Since World War Two. New York, Peter Lang, 2014.

  Clés pour le Développement de la Guinée. Paris, L'Harmattan, 2015.

Camara, S. S. *La Guinée sans la France*. Paris, Presses de la Fondation Nationale des Sciences Politiques, 1976.

Condé, A. *La décentralisation en Guinée: une expérience réussie*. Paris, L'Harmattan, 2003.

Cournanel, A. *L'économie politique de la Guinée (1958–2010): des dictatures contre le développement*. Paris, L'Harmattan, 2013.

Diallo, B. Y. *La Guinée, un demi-siècle de politique (1945–2008): Trois hommes, trois destins*. Paris, L'Harmattan, 2011.

Diallo, El Hadj M. *Histoire du Fouta Djallon*. Paris, L'Harmattan, 2002.

Dicko, A. A. *Journal d'une défaite: autour du référendum du 28 septembre 1958 en Afrique noire*. Paris, L'Harmattan, 1992.

Faye, O. T. *Guinée: Chronique d'une démocratie annoncée*. Victoria, BC, Trafford Publishing, 2007.

Goudoussi, A. D. *Et Vint le Virus Ebola: Rumeurs, Stupeurs et Réalités en Guinée*. Paris, L'Harmattan, 2015.

Iffono, A. G. *La Guinée: de Ahmed Sékou Touré à Alpha Condé ou le Chemin de Croix de la Démocratie*. Paris, L'Harmattan, 2013.

Ii Mara, F. *Alpha Condé, l'opposant historique: Une école de la démocratie pour les Guinéens*. Paris, L'Harmattan, 2017.

Jeanjean, M. *Sékou Touré: un totalitarisme africain*. Paris, L'Harmattan, 2004.

Kaba, L. *Le "non" de la Guinée à de Gaulle*. Paris, Chaka, 1990.

Keita, S. K. *Des complots contre la Guinée de Sékou Touré 1958–84*. Boulbinet, Les Classiques Guinéens—SOGUIDIP, 2002.

Kobele-Keita, S. *L'Indépendance de la Guinée en 1958: Chronologie et Commentaires*. Paris, L'Harmattan, 2014.

Lewin, A. *Ahmed Sékou Touré (1922–1984), president de la Guinée*. (7 vols). Paris, L'Harmattan, 2009.

McGovern, M. *Unmasking the State: Making Guinea Modern*. Chicago, IL, University of Chicago Press, 2012.

O'Toole, T. E. *Historical Dictionary of Guinea*. Metuchen, NJ, Scarecrow Press, 1988.

Philipps, J. *Ambivalent Rage: Youth Gangs and Urban Protest in Conakry, Guinea*. Paris, L'Harmattan, 2013.

Rivière, C. *Guinea: The Mobilization of a People* (trans. by Thompson, V., and Adloff, R.). Ithaca, NY, Cornell University Press, 1977.

Said, M. B. *La Guinée en marche, mémoires inédits d'un changement*. Paris, L'Harmattan, 2008.

Sidibé, Y. *Capitaine Moussa Dadis Camara: Une parenthèse guinéenne*. Paris, L'Harmattan, 2017.

Soumah, I. *L'avenir de l'industrie minière en Guinée*. Paris, L'Harmattan, 2009.

Soumah, M. *Guinée: de Sékou Touré à Lansana Conté*. Paris, L'Harmattan, 2004.

  Guinée: la démocratie sans le peuple. Paris, L'Harmattan, 2006.

Tolno, C.-P. *Transition Militaire et Election Présidentielle 2010 en Guinée: L'indépendance Piégé*. Paris, L'Harmattan, 2015.

Touré, S. *L'expérience guinéenne et l'unité africaine*. Paris, Présence africaine, 1959.

Vieira, G. *L'Eglise catholique en Guinée à l'épreuve de Sékou Touré (1958–1984)*. Paris, Editions Karthala, 2005.

GUINEA-BISSAU

Physical and Social Geography

RENÉ PÉLISSIER

The Republic of Guinea-Bissau lies on the west coast of Africa and is bounded on the north by Senegal and on the east and south by the Republic of Guinea. Its territory includes a number of coastal islets, together with the offshore Bissagos or Bijagós archipelago, which comprises 18 main islands. The capital is Bissau.

The country covers an area of 36,125 sq km (13,948 sq miles), including some low-lying ground that is periodically submerged at high tide. Except for some higher terrain (rising to about 300 m above sea level), close to the border with Guinea, the relief consists of a coastal plain deeply indented by *rias*, which facilitate internal communications, and a transition plateau, forming the Planalto de Bafatá in the centre, and the Planalto de Gabú, which abuts on the Fouta Djallon.

The country's main physical features are its meandering rivers and wide estuaries, where it is difficult to distinguish mud, mangrove and water from solid land. The principal rivers are the Cacheu, also known as Farim on part of its course, the Mansôa, the Geba and Corubal complex, the Rio Grande and, close to the Guinean southern border, the Cacine. Ocean-going vessels of shallow draught can reach most of the main population centres, and there is access by flat-bottomed vessels to nearly all significant outposts except in the north-eastern sector.

The climate is tropical, hot and wet with two seasons. The rainy season lasts from mid-May to November and the dry season from December to April. April and May are the hottest months, with temperatures ranging from 20°C to 38°C, and December and January are the coldest, with temperatures ranging from 15°C to 33°C. Rainfall is abundant (1,000 mm–2,000 mm per year in the north), and excessive on the coast. The interior is savannah or light savannah woodland, while coastal reaches are covered with mangrove swamps, rainforest and tangled forest.

At the census of March 2009 the population was enumerated at 1,449,230, giving a population density of 40.1 persons per sq km. By mid-2022, according to official projections, the population had increased to 1,637,184 (45.3 persons per sq km). The main population centre is Bissau, which had an estimated 620,974 inhabitants at mid-2021, according to United Nations figures. Gabú, Bafatá, Bissorã, Bigene, Farim, Mansôa and Pitche are the other major towns. As recorded in 1996, the main indigenous groups were the Balante/Balanta (about 30% of the population), the Fulani or Fula (20%), the Mandyako or Mandjak (14%), the Malinké, Mandingo or Mandinka (12%) and the Papel (7%). The non-Africans were mainly Portuguese civil servants and traders, and Syrian and Lebanese traders. Although Portuguese is the official language, a Guinean *crioulo* is the lingua franca; there are, in addition, 19 local languages. According to the 2009 census, adherents of Islam represented 45.1% of the total population; Christians accounted for 22.1% and animists 14.9%.

History

MARIE GIBERT

The campaign for independence in Portuguese Guinea (now the Republic of Guinea-Bissau) commenced in the 1950s with the formation of the Partido Africano da Independência da Guiné e Cabo Verde (PAIGC), led by Amílcar Cabral, and armed conflict began in 1963. Cabral was assassinated by PAIGC dissidents in 1973, but by that time the pro-independence movement already controlled a large part of the territory. Guinea-Bissau unilaterally declared independence from Portugal on 24 September 1973, under the presidency of Luís Cabral (brother of Amílcar Cabral). Portugal withdrew its forces in August 1974 (in the wake of its own revolution), and on 10 September officially recognized independent Guinea-Bissau. The PAIGC, the sole party, laid the foundations for a socialist state. The party oversaw the administration of both Cabo Verde and Guinea-Bissau, with a view to eventual unification. In its foreign relations, the Government adopted a non-aligned stance, receiving military aid from the Eastern bloc, but also economic assistance from Western countries and Arab states. Amicable relations with Portugal were renewed.

Cabral was overthrown by the Prime Minister, João Bernardo Vieira, in 1980. A military-dominated revolutionary council took control, and numerous cadres of Caboverdian origin were dismissed from positions of power within the PAIGC and the administration.

VIEIRA AND THE PAIGC

A new Constitution was introduced in 1984, following elections to a new legislative assembly, which consolidated the position of President Vieira as head of state, Chief of Government, Commander-in-Chief of the Armed Forces and head of the PAIGC. Vieira reinforced his grip on power with the arrest, in 1985, and subsequent trial, on charges of plotting a coup, of about 40 military and government officials, most of whom were members of the Balante ethnic group. Six of these officials were executed. This would prove to have lasting consequences: resentment on the part of the Balante, who constitute a majority in Guinea-Bissau's military to the present day, is widely believed to have played an important role in the 1998 army rebellion and Vieira's assassination in 2009 (see below).

Vieira was confirmed as President for another five-year term in 1989, but domestic and external pressure for political liberalization, including from exiled political organizations, was inescapable.

Constitutional Transition

It was announced in 1990 that members of the legislature, the Assembleia Nacional Popular (ANP—National People's Assembly), would in future be elected by universal adult suffrage. Constitutional amendments were unanimously approved by the ANP in May 1991, terminating the PAIGC's role as the sole political force, severing the link between the party and the armed forces and guaranteeing the operation of a free-market economy. The post of Prime Minister, abolished in 1984, was revived in December 1991.

In November 1991 the Frente Democrática became the first party to be legalized by the Supreme Court. Several other opposition parties were subsequently registered, including the Resistência da Guiné-Bissau—Movimento Bafatá, the Partido para a Renovação Social (PRS), the Frente Democrática Social, the Partido Unido Social Democrático (PUSD) and the Partido da Convergência Democrática.

Multi-party presidential and legislative elections finally took place in July 1994. The PAIGC secured a clear majority in the ANP, winning 62 of the 100 seats. In the presidential election, Vieira won 46.3% of the valid votes cast, and his nearest rival, PRS leader Kumba Yalá, 21.9%. Both proceeded to a second round in August, at which Vieira was re-elected with 52.0% of the votes cast.

The Political-Military Conflict of 1998–99

In June 1998 a group of dissident troops, led by Brig. (later Gen.) Ansumane Mané, who had recently been dismissed as Chief of Staff of the Armed Forces, seized control of the international airport and the Bra military barracks in the capital, Bissau. Mané formed a 'military junta for the consolidation of democracy, peace and justice' and demanded the resignation of the Vieira administration and the holding of democratic elections. Forces loyal to the Government, assisted by troops from Senegal and Guinea, failed to regain control of rebel-held areas of Bissau. A truce was agreed in July, following mediation by a delegation from the Comunidade dos Países de Língua Portuguesa (CPLP), which became a ceasefire in August, after representatives of the Government and the rebels met under the auspices of the CPLP and the Economic Community of West African States (ECOWAS).

Further talks were held in October 1998, with tentative agreement being reached on the creation of a demilitarized zone separating the opposing forces in the capital. However, the ceasefire then collapsed as fighting erupted in the capital and several other towns. The Government imposed a nation-wide curfew, and Vieira subsequently declared a unilateral ceasefire, with most government troops having defected to the rebel side. Further negotiations, under the aegis of ECOWAS, in Abuja, Nigeria, resulted in the signing of a peace accord in November: the two sides reaffirmed the August ceasefire and resolved that the withdrawal of Senegalese and Guinean troops from Guinea-Bissau be conducted simultaneously with the deployment of an ECOMOG (ECOWAS Ceasefire Monitoring Group) interposition force. A government of national unity would be established, and presidential and legislative elections would be held by March 1999. Francisco José Fadul was appointed Prime Minister in December 1998. In January 1999 Fadul announced that presidential and legislative elections would not take place in March, but at the end of the year.

A new ceasefire was agreed in early February 1999. The composition of the new Government of National Unity was announced later that month. The disarmament of rebel and loyalist troops, as provided for under the Abuja accord, began in March, and the withdrawal of Senegalese and Guinean troops was completed in the same month.

TRANSITIONAL GOVERNMENT

Vieira was overthrown in May 1999 by the rebel junta, which claimed that its action had been in response to Vieira's refusal to allow his presidential guard to be disarmed. Vieira signed an unconditional surrender. The President of the ANP, Malam Bacai Sanhá, was appointed acting head of state, pending a presidential election, and the Government of National Unity remained in office. ECOWAS condemned the overthrow of Vieira and demanded that he be allowed to leave Guinea-Bissau; in June, he was granted asylum in Portugal. ECOMOG forces were withdrawn from Guinea-Bissau in the same month.

Constitutional amendments were introduced in July 1999, limiting the President to two terms and abolishing the death penalty. In September the PAIGC voted to expel Vieira from the party. The Minister of Defence and Freedom Fighters, Francisco Benante, was appointed as the party's new leader.

POST-CONFLICT POLITICAL DEVELOPMENTS, 2000–11

The Yalá Presidency

Presidential and legislative elections were conducted in November 1999. No candidate received the necessary 50% of the votes to win the presidential election outright. Thus, the two leading candidates, Yalá of the PRS and Sanhá of the PAIGC, proceeded to a second round, in January 2000, at which Yalá won a decisive 72% of the votes cast. The PRS, meanwhile, secured the most seats in the enlarged ANP (38 of the now 102 seats). Caetano N'Tchama of the PRS was appointed Prime Minister in February, heading a Council of Ministers that included members of several former opposition parties.

In August 2000 the ANP approved a measure formally making the head of state the Supreme Commander of the Armed Forces. Existing tensions between the civilian Government and members of the military loyal to the coup leader, Gen. Mané, worsened in November, after Mané rejected several promotions of high-ranking officers made by President Yalá and declared himself Commander-in-Chief. Forces loyal to the Government defeated a rebellion led by Mané, who was killed in late November.

Following the insurgency, the PAIGC split into various factions, the two most significant of which comprised, respectively, hardliners and young moderate reformers. Another outcome of the crisis was the increasing dominance of the Balante over state institutions. A thorough overhaul of the military leadership structure in December 2000 brought Balante into most positions of authority. As friction increased between Yalá and his own party, the President dismissed the increasingly unpopular N'Tchama in March 2001. His replacement, Faustino Fudut Imbali, was himself replaced as Prime Minister (following accusations by President Yalá of abuse of power) after just nine months, in December, by Almara Nhassé, hitherto Minister of Internal Administration. A new, PRS-dominated Council of Ministers was sworn in.

In January 2002 the PRS elected Prime Minister Nhassé as party President. In the same month the PAIGC selected Carlos Gomes Júnior as its new leader and took the controversial step of pardoning and reintegrating former members who had either abandoned or been expelled from the PAIGC, among them former President Vieira.

Political uncertainty intensified in November 2002, when President Yalá dissolved the ANP and dismissed Nhassé and the Council of Ministers, accusing them of creating a political stalemate and failing adequately to address the prevailing economic crisis. Yalá appointed Mário Pires of the PRS to lead a transitional Government. The announcement of elections for April 2003 (subsequently postponed until July, and then to October) precipitated a broad realignment of political forces, including the creation of several new political parties and the formation of two coalitions. Further government changes were effected in mid-2003. Notably, the Minister of Defence, Marcelino Cabral, and Minister of the Presidency of the Council of Ministers, José de Pina, were dismissed and subsequently detained for several weeks. The arrest of the former ministers caused serious friction between the Government and the military.

Military Intervention and Elections

In September 2003, following a further postponement of the scheduled elections, President Yalá was detained by soldiers on the orders of the Chief of Staff of the Armed Forces, Gen. Veríssimo Seabra, who declared himself interim President. The coup leaders belonged to the army faction of Mané that had ousted President Vieira in 1999. Seabra and a newly appointed Military Committee for the Restoration of Constitutional Order and Democracy held talks with civil society representatives and political organizations, with a view to forming a transitional, civilian-led government. The United Nations (UN), the African Union (AU) and several African countries condemned the coup, and ECOWAS dispatched a mission to Bissau to mediate between the military authorities and the deposed President. However, the mission withdrew its demand that Yalá be reinstated, once the scale of his unpopularity became clear. National support for the new regime was strong, including from all political parties (including Yalá's PRS). Yalá formally resigned in September 2003. Later that month Henrique Rosa, a businessman and former head of the national electoral commission, was appointed as President. Artur Sanhá, the Secretary-General of the PRS, was named as Prime Minister, despite protests by most parties that they had been promised a politically neutral premier.

A Comissão Nacional de Transição (CNT—National Transitional Commission) was formed in October 2003, comprising military officials, politicians and representatives of civil society, to oversee legislative elections scheduled for March 2004. President Rosa was to remain in office until a presidential election completed the democratization process in 2005. Seeking to distance itself from the ousted President, the PRS replaced Yalá with Alberto Nambeia as party leader.

Legislative elections proceeded as scheduled in March 2004, and were declared free and fair by international observers. According to the Comissão Nacional de Eleições (CNE—National Election Commission), some 75% of the registered electorate cast ballots. The PAIGC won 45 of the 100 seats in the ANP, while the PRS took 35 seats and the PUSD 17. The PAIGC subsequently formed a coalition administration with the PRS. Gomes Júnior, the PAIGC leader, was appointed Prime Minister and formed a Government in May, upon the completion of the six-month term of the CNT.

In October 2004 there was a mutiny by members of an army contingent that had recently returned from a UN peacekeeping mission in Liberia. The rebellion, seemingly to demand the payment of overdue salaries, resulted in the death of Gen. Seabra. The new Chief of Staff of the Armed Forces, Maj.-Gen. Baptista Tagmé Na Wai, pledged to unify the army and respect the authority of the future head of state, regardless of political affiliation.

In March 2005 the Government announced that a presidential election would take place in June. The PRS nominated ex-President Yalá as its candidate, and former President Vieira subsequently returned from exile in Portugal with the intention of contesting the presidency as an independent. The participation of both men in the election contravened the terms of the transitional agreement, which barred them from political activity for five years. In April the Supreme Court overturned legal obstacles to the candidacies of both Vieira and Yalá on grounds that were not made clear. Meanwhile, the PAIGC nominated Malam Bacai Sanhá as its presidential candidate.

At the presidential election in June 2005, Sanhá won 35.5% of the votes cast, Vieira 28.9% and Yalá 25.0%. The rate of voter participation was recorded at 87.6%. At a run-off ballot between the two leading candidates, held in July, Vieira (for whom Yalá had meanwhile announced his support) was elected with 52.4% of the votes cast. Turnout was 78.6%. Despite allegations by Sanhá of widespread electoral fraud, the Supreme Court upheld the result in August.

Vieira's Return to Power

Vieira was sworn in as President in October 2005. In his inaugural address to the ANP, he promised to respect the constitutional separation of powers and work with the Government of Prime Minister Gomes Júnior. Less than two weeks later, however, 14 of the PAIGC's 45 deputies defected to join the PRS and the PUSD in a new coalition—the Fórum de Convergência para o Desenvolvimento (FCD)—with the aim of removing the Prime Minister from power. Gomes Júnior and his Government were subsequently dismissed by Vieira, who in early November appointed his own ally, former PAIGC Vice-President Aristides Gomes, as the new Prime Minister in an FCD coalition Government.

Political tensions flared in January 2007, after the former Navy Chief of Staff, Mohamed Lamine Sanhá, was shot dead in Bissau. Sanhá was a member of the military junta formed following the 1998 rebellion and the third of its senior members to be killed (after Mané in 2000 and Seabra in 2004). His death sparked violent protests in Bissau, leaving one person dead and many injured. The Government denied involvement in the assassination, but Gomes Júnior publicly alleged that Vieira had masterminded the murder of former members of the junta that overthrew him. The Government subsequently issued an arrest warrant against Gomes Júnior, who took refuge in a building of the UN Peacebuilding Support Office in Guinea-Bissau (UNOGBIS). Two weeks later, under a UN-brokered agreement, the Government withdrew the arrest warrant.

A new political crisis erupted in March 2007 when the PRS and the PUSD withdrew from the FCD governing coalition and signed a political stability pact with the PAIGC, pledging to form a government of national unity. The Government subsequently lost a vote of no confidence in the ANP, and Aristides Gomes tendered his resignation as Prime Minister at the end of the month. In April Vieira appointed Martinho N'Dafa Cabi as Prime Minister, and a new Government was formed, heavily weighted in favour of the PAIGC and the PRS. Notably, however, Vieira's former security adviser Baciro Dabó was allocated the interior portfolio. The Government was soon judged to be competent, prompting donors, led by the World Bank and the International Monetary Fund, to re-engage fully in Guinea-Bissau and release large inflows of aid.

Concerns surfaced in mid-2007 regarding the use of Guinea-Bissau, with its extensive mangrove deltas and network of offshore islands, as a conduit for illegal drug shipments from South America to countries of the European Union (EU). Seizures of drugs spiralled, and the country's military and political leadership were suspected of involvement with the traffickers. In June Dabó established an inter-ministerial commission to investigate the involvement of politicians in drug trafficking. Several ministers and senior officials were questioned, but the Government refused to publish the commission's findings, thereby undermining the process.

In June 2008 the PAIGC congress re-elected Gomes Júnior as party President. Earlier that month Aristides Gomes had founded a new pro-Vieira party, the Partido Republicano para a Independência e o Desenvolvimento (PRID), prompting speculation that this might draw support away from the PAIGC at legislative elections scheduled for November.

The PAIGC withdrew from the Government in July 2008, following the unexpected dismissal by Cabi of four high-ranking ministers. In August Vieira issued a decree dissolving the ANP and formally ending the tenure of the coalition Government. Shortly thereafter, he appointed veteran politician Carlos Correia as Prime Minister. Correia subsequently announced the formation of a new, PAIGC-dominated Government. There was further upheaval in August, when it was reported that the Navy Chief of Staff, Rear-Adm. José Americo Bubo Na Tchuto, had been dismissed and placed under house arrest following his involvement in an alleged coup plot.

The 2008 Elections

At legislative elections held in November 2008 the PAIGC increased its representation in the ANP to 67 seats, thereby achieving a parliamentary majority for the first time since 1999, while the PRS suffered a decline in its representation to just 28 seats. The PRID won a mere three seats, ending its hopes of challenging the PAIGC's electoral base.

A week after the elections—and just two days after the CNE had announced the provisional results—the presidential residence was attacked by a group of soldiers. Following an armed confrontation between the assailants and members of the presidential guard, Vieira and his wife emerged unhurt. The army identified the suspected architect of the attack as Alexandre Tchama Yalá, a navy sergeant and nephew of former President Yalá. Sgt Yalá, who was later arrested in Senegal, was believed to have close links to Na Tchuto, who had been accused of organizing a coup attempt in August. However, despite Yalá's arrest and that of seven other members of the armed forces suspected of collusion, doubts remained over the identity of the instigators of the attack and what their motive had been. Vieira subsequently demanded the protection of the 400-strong Aguentas militia, which had protected him during the 1998–99 military rebellion.

The Supreme Court confirmed the election results in December 2008, despite complaints filed by the PRS and an opposition coalition, the Aliança de Forças Patrióticas. Vieira subsequently appointed Gomes Júnior as the new Prime Minister, and a new Government was formed, composed exclusively of members of the PAIGC.

Assassination of Vieira

In January 2009 members of the Aguentas militia opened fire on the vehicle of the Chief of Staff of the Armed Forces, Na Wai, in what the latter claimed was an assassination attempt. He declared the militia illegal, thus forcing Vieira to disband it. Na Wai was killed in a bomb explosion at the army headquarters on 1 March (the third Chief of Staff to be assassinated since the 1998–99 conflict). In the early hours of 2 March 2009 a group of soldiers entered the presidential residence and murdered Vieira. There was widespread speculation in the international media that Vieira had ordered Na Wai's murder, and that the President was killed in retaliation by soldiers and officers loyal to the Chief of Staff. Despite the arrest of five soldiers and the establishment of a civilian commission of inquiry into both assassinations, as well as a military commission of inquiry into the assassination of Na Wai, little substantiated information emerged.

The military swiftly denounced the killings as the work of isolated elements and confirmed its support for a constitutional transition. The President of the ANP, Raimundo Pereira, was appointed interim President on 3 March 2009, while the deputy navy chief, Commdr José Zamora Induta, was appointed interim Chief of Staff of the Armed Forces, and in April the Government announced that a presidential election would take place in June.

In early June 2009 one of the presidential candidates, former interior minister Baciro Dabó, was shot dead at his home. A former defence minister, Helder Proença (who, like Dabó, was closely associated with Vieira), was shot dead shortly thereafter, together with a bodyguard and a driver. Other senior members of the PAIGC were arrested. The Ministry of the Interior stated that Dabó and Proença had resisted arrest in the context of a thwarted coup plot. However, the full circumstances of the killings were unclear, and longstanding antagonism between the two victims and senior government and military figures prompted speculation that the killings had been planned.

The first round of the presidential election none the less proceeded without incident in late June 2009, and voting was deemed free and transparent by international election observers. According to official results, Malam Bacai Sanhá of the PAIGC received 39.6% of the votes, followed by Mohamed Yalá Embaló (as Kumba Yalá, who had converted to Islam in 2008, was now known) with 29.4% and independent candidate Henrique Rosa with 24.2%. At the second round, in July, Sanhá secured 63.3% of the votes.

The Sanhá Presidency

Malam Bacai Sanhá was sworn in as President in September 2009. He appointed a new Council of Ministers, again headed by Gomes Júnior, in October. In December it emerged that former Navy Chief of Staff Na Tchuto, who had been in exile in The Gambia since August 2008, had returned to the country. The Government promptly sought his arrest and prosecution. Claiming to fear for his life, Na Tchuto sought refuge in the UNOGBIS headquarters. In January 2010 UN officials, the Government and the Attorney-General reached an agreement whereby Na Tchuto would be handed over to the authorities in return for guarantees regarding his physical safety and his right to a fair trial. However, the agreement was not implemented, and Na Tchuto remained at what was now, following the completion of the UNOGBIS mission at the end of December 2009, the headquarters of its successor body, the UN Integrated Peacebuilding Office in Guinea-Bissau (UNIOGBIS).

In April 2010 the Deputy Chief of Staff of the Armed Forces, António Indjai, led an attempted coup. Soldiers loyal to Indjai went to the UNIOGBIS headquarters and requested that Na Tchuto be handed over to them. The latter left voluntarily, and his subsequent appearance alongside Indjai prompted speculation that he had been involved in the planning of the coup from within UNIOGBIS's facilities. Chief of Staff of the Armed Forces Induta was arrested, together with the head of military intelligence, Samba Djaló, and several other officers. Having assumed control of the armed forces, Indjai detained Gomes Júnior. Hundreds of civilians gathered outside the government building where the Prime Minister was being detained to protest against the coup. Gomes Júnior was transferred to the army headquarters, but was released a few hours later and returned to his office. Although the coup failed, its immediate consequences were the overthrow of Induta as Chief of Staff, his de facto replacement by Indjai and Na Tchuto's return to the political-military arena.

Throughout April 2010 there were rumours of fresh attempts to arrest the Prime Minister. Gomes Júnior, who was reported to have sought refuge in foreign embassies, subsequently left the country; he remained abroad for several weeks, officially for health reasons, but returned to Bissau in June. The lengthy impasse that arose over the formal nomination of the new Chief of Staff of the Armed Forces was eventually resolved in Indjai's favour by a presidential decree in late June, which legitimized his authority. Earlier that month Na Tchuto was formally acquitted of the charges pending against him since 2008; he was reinstated as Navy Chief of Staff in October 2010.

While on a trip to France in May 2010, President Sanhá stated before foreign media that senior government figures had been involved in the assassinations of Vieira and Na Wai, but gave no further details. Further strain between the offices of the President and Prime Minister emerged over the latter's dismissal, in October, of the Minister of the Interior, Hadja Satu Camará Pinto, who was considered to be close to the President. Former Chief of Staff Induta was released in December, after more than eight months in detention; also freed were the former head of military intelligence, Samba Djaló, and several figures suspected of involvement in the murders of Vieira and Na Wai.

The succession of events following the April 2010 rebellion marked a shift in the relative pre-eminence of Guinea-Bissau's Northern and Southern partners, as the former continued to demand that Indjai and Na Tchuto not be rewarded for taking control of the armed forces, while Southern partners such as Angola and ECOWAS exhibited more pragmatism and were able to adopt more central roles. ECOWAS, subsequently joined by the CPLP, began in August to design a new Security Sector Reform (SSR) initiative. Once this framework was adopted, in November, Angola took the lead at the bilateral level, signing a technical and military co-operation agreement with the Government in Guinea-Bissau, whereby the Angolan Armed Forces Security Mission in Guinea-Bissau (MISSANG) was established in January 2011. The Angolan contingent comprised about 200 personnel, who arrived in Bissau in March to assist in the reduction of the number of national servicemen, the renovation of the army barracks and the reform of Guinea-Bissau's military and police forces.

Tensions increased again in July–August 2011 as hundreds of people protested in Bissau, accusing Gomes Júnior of plotting Vieira's assassination in 2009 and demanding the Prime Minister's resignation. President Sanhá's health deteriorated in 2011, and he travelled to Europe for treatment on several occasions. In late December, during one of these absences, another military rebellion reportedly took place, although the actual circumstances were unclear. There was sporadic shooting around Bissau, checkpoints were set up, and several dozen people were arrested, most notably Na Tchuto for allegedly masterminding the plot. The rebellion also reportedly aimed to oust Prime Minister Gomes Júnior, but he was apparently rescued by Angolan soldiers and given refuge at the Angolan embassy. Gomes Júnior subsequently declared that the rebellion had constituted an attempt on his life, but 15 opposition parties issued a joint statement claiming that the alleged coup had been 'a parody', contrived by the Government and the armed forces high command in order to provide a pretext for a purge.

THE 2012 COUP AND TRANSITIONAL PROCESS

President Sanhá died in Paris, France, in January 2012, after several years of ill health. In accordance with the Constitution, Raimundo Pereira, President of the ANP and an associate of Prime Minister Gomes Júnior, became interim President, and preparations began to hold a presidential election within 60 days. The central committee of the PAIGC convened in February to appoint the party's presidential candidate; however, its members were presented with a *fait accompli*, Gomes Júnior having already been selected by the party's political bureau. Two of the most prominent members of the PAIGC opposition to Gomes Júnior—Manuel Serifo Nhamadjo and Baciro Djá—who sought to dispute the nomination, eventually decided to run as independent candidates, openly challenging the party leadership.

The presidential election took place on 18 March 2012. Turnout, at 55%, was the lowest ever recorded in Guinea-Bissau. Official results showed that Gomes Júnior, with 49.0% of the vote, had narrowly failed to win the election outright. Former President Kumba Yalá took 23.4% and Nhamadjo 15.8%. Meanwhile, on the night after the election Col. Samba Djaló, erstwhile head of military intelligence and a close associate of former Chief of Staff Induta, was murdered outside his home. Subsequently, claiming to fear for his own life, Induta (himself deemed a close associate of Gomes Júnior) was granted refuge at the EU delegation in Bissau. (He fled to The Gambia in May.) Yalá, who, as the second-placed candidate in the poll, would ordinarily have proceeded with Gomes Júnior to a run-off, announced that he was withdrawing his candidacy. In late March the CNE, which had been seized by defeated candidates over irregularity claims, ruled against their case, maintaining that the alleged irregularities had not altered the ranking of the candidates. The second round of the presidential election was scheduled for late April.

In early April 2012 Henrique Rosa, who had come fourth in the first round of the presidential election, accused the Angolan security presence, MISSANG, of functioning as Gomes Júnior's 'Praetorian Guard'. On the same day, after weeks of mounting tension between Guinea-Bissau's military leadership and MISSANG, Chief of Staff Indjai ordered the Angolan contingent to withdraw from the country, maintaining that the Angolan Government had been covertly sending heavy weapons to Guinea-Bissau without informing the Guinea-Bissau armed forces, thereby contravening the terms of MISSANG's presence. Gomes Júnior countered that MISSANG's presence was legitimized by an official agreement between the two states and that it was not in the Chief of Staff's power to order its withdrawal. The Angolan Minister of Foreign Affairs, George Rebelo Chicoty, promptly travelled to Bissau and announced that MISSANG would indeed be withdrawn in response to 'hostility on the part of some Bissau-Guineans'. It would, however, be replaced by a multinational force, to be co-ordinated by the CPLP, of which the Angolan contingent would form a part—the implication thus being that the Angolans would remain in Guinea-Bissau.

The gradual escalation in political tension culminated, on 12 April 2012, in a coup by a self-styled Military Command. Gomes Júnior's residence was attacked with grenades, and he and interim President Pereira were arrested. On the same day the Command justified the coup as an act of self-defence from Guinea-Bissau armed forces, in the face of 'imminent aggression'. Alleged evidence of this was produced a few days later, in the form of a letter purportedly written by Gomes Júnior to UN Secretary-General Ban Ki-Moon, in which the former requested that a UN peacekeeping force be dispatched to the country to control the Guinea-Bissau military. It soon became clear that Indjai was the mastermind of the coup and the leader of the Military Command. The situation deteriorated on the night of 12 April, when the homes of several ministers and other high-ranking political figures were pillaged by elements of the armed forces. Tens of thousands of people left the capital for the countryside in the days that followed. Meanwhile, the international community condemned the coup, demanding that constitutional order be re-established and calling for the immediate release of Gomes Júnior and Pereira.

The Military Command swiftly convened a meeting with members of the opposition to prepare a transfer of power. The aim of the coup had apparently been to oust Gomes Júnior before the second round of the presidential election—thus ensuring that he would be unable to control the PAIGC, the Government and the presidency combined—and not for the military to assume direct power. The transitional arrangement negotiated between the Military Command and the political opposition consequently involved the appointment as interim President of Nhamadjo, the PAIGC dissident who had come third in the first round of the presidential election. On 18 April 2012 Nigeria's stated willingness to accept the negotiated arrangement (such a solution apparently suited Nigeria's own aims, given its own continental rivalry with Angola) breached the international community's unanimous resolve to reject an unconstitutional solution. That breach was then exploited by ECOWAS, which brokered a settlement with Guinea-Bissau's military leaders that ended up legitimizing the coup and consolidating its outcome. Included in the agreement were the release of Gomes Júnior and Pereira (who subsequently fled to Côte d'Ivoire and thence to Portugal); a one-year transitional period, to be followed by presidential and parliamentary elections; the confirmation of Nhamadjo as interim President; and the replacement of MISSANG with an ECOWAS contingent.

In mid-May 2012 Nhamadjo appointed Rui Duarte de Barros, a former Minister of Finance, to head the transitional Government. His Council of Ministers, comprising elements of several parties (predominantly the PRS) and factions opposed to Gomes Júnior, took office later that month. MISSANG completed its withdrawal in early June, two weeks after the first contingent of what was to become the 600-strong, successor ECOWAS Mission in Guinea-Bissau (ECOMIB) had arrived in the country. In late June Na Tchuto was released from prison, after six months in custody for his alleged involvement in the December 2011 uprising.

An attack on the headquarters of an elite army unit in October 2012 left six people dead and led to the closing of the country's borders and a hunt for the alleged leader of the assailants, Capt. Pansau N'Tchama (a former aide of Induta and Indjai, who had admitted to having been present when Vieira was assassinated). It remained unclear whether an attempted counter-coup had taken place and been successfully repressed, or whether the incident had been contrived in order to discredit Gomes Júnior and provide cover for yet another purge within the armed forces. N'Tchama was captured a few days later and paraded in front of journalists wrapped in a Portuguese flag, in an attempt to suggest that the alleged counter-coup attempt had been masterminded by Gomes Júnior and Induta, in collaboration with the Portuguese authorities. In April 2013 N'Tchama and eight other individuals were sentenced to between three and five years in prison for their roles in the October 2012 incident.

In mid-November 2012 the ANP, in which the PAIGC still held a majority, resumed its activities after a seven-month suspension; the hiatus had resulted from the April coup and subsequent disagreements between the PAIGC and PRS over which party should rightfully appoint the new President of the ANP (following the designation of the PAIGC's Pereira as interim ANP President in January). As the pro-coup hardliners raised the possibility of dissolving the ANP and appointing an extra-constitutional legislative body as a means of breaking the deadlock, the PAIGC conceded, allowing the PRS to appoint Ibraima Sory Djaló as the new ANP President. In January 2013 the PAIGC announced its willingness to endorse the transition pact and participate in a new government of national unity.

In April 2013 it was reported, to widespread shock, that the US Drug Enforcement Administration (DEA) had conducted an operation off the coast of Guinea-Bissau, luring Na Tchuto to an offshore encounter with DEA agents posing as Colombian drug traffickers with links to the Fuerzas Armadas Revolucionarias de Colombia rebel militia. The arrest of the former Navy Chief of Staff was the culmination of a complex operation involving months of contacts between undercover DEA agents and senior members of Guinea-Bissau's military hierarchy. Na Tchuto was flown to the USA, where his trial began in July on charges including international drug trafficking and conspiracy to engage in narco-terrorism. Shortly after Na Tchuto's arrest, the US Department of Justice announced that it had gathered sufficient evidence to indict Indjai for the trafficking of drugs and weapons.

This unexpected high-profile international operation by US law enforcement agencies forced Indjai and the pro-coup hardliners onto the defensive, and the prospect of a swifter re-establishment of constitutional order suddenly improved. Throughout May 2013 interim President Nhamadjo oversaw discussions involving all Guinea-Bissau's key political figures, which eventually resulted in the signing, approval by the ANP and entry into force of a new political agreement among the various parties and a new transitional programme. In June a new, more broad-based Government was formally appointed. Duarte de Barros remained as transitional Prime Minister, the military retained control of the national defence and interior portfolios, and the PAIGC received five ministerial posts. Nhamadjo announced that presidential and legislative elections would take place in November, for which international partners including the EU and the USA pledged financial and logistical support. In October, however, the Government announced the indefinite postponement of the elections. In November Nhamadjo signed a decree scheduling the legislative and presidential elections for March 2014.

In February 2014 the PAIGC elected former CPLP Executive Secretary Domingos Simões Pereira as party President amid alleged irregularities in the selection of party delegates. Tensions were also heightened within the main opposition party, the PRS, in the pre-election period, with the selection of Abel Incada as the party's presidential candidate prompting the candidacy of two PRS Vice-Presidents in competition. (One of these was Sory Djaló.) Meanwhile, former President Yalá, who had previously declared his intention to stand, announced that he would instead support the independent candidate, Nuno Gomes Nabiam.

In late February 2014 interim President Nhamadjo announced a further postponement of the elections, to April, citing further logistical difficulties. ECOWAS declared that it would strengthen its ECOMIB military contingent in Guinea-Bissau in advance of the polls. In early March the PAIGC central committee elected José Mário Vaz, who had held the finance portfolio in the Government deposed in April 2012, as its presidential candidate. (Earlier in March 2014 Gomes Júnior had stated that he would accept his party's decision and not run for the presidency if it elected another candidate.) The sudden death of former President Yalá in early April raised concerns over potential further divisions within the PRS.

Despite security incidents during the election campaign and the army's open support for Nabiam, voting proceeded peacefully in the legislative elections held in April 2014. According to the official results, the PAIGC secured 57 of the 102 seats in the ANP, while the PRS, with 41 seats, consolidated its position as the main opposition party. In the presidential election, Vaz won 40.9% of the vote and Nabiam took 24.8%. During the run-off presidential campaign, seven parties, in addition to the PAIGC, endorsed Vaz, while Nabiam received the support of the PRS and 15 smaller parties. The campaign and voting, held in May, were largely peaceful. The CNE declared that Vaz had won the run-off, with 61.9% of votes cast. Turnout was 78.1%.

THE VAZ PRESIDENCY

In July 2014 the PAIGC leader, Domingos Simões Pereira, was sworn in as Prime Minister, together with a 31-member administration that included three ministers and two secretaries of state from the PRS and two ministers from smaller political parties. President Vaz and Prime Minister Simões Pereira focused their efforts on persuading donors to resume the provision of aid to the country and drafting reforms such as civil service cuts and changes to the military hierarchy.

In September 2014 Indjai was dismissed as Chief of Staff of the Armed Forces; he was replaced by Brig.-Gen. Biague Na Ntam, a veteran of the independence war. Ntam clarified that the military would defer to civilian authority and that security sector reforms would proceed. In November a list was issued of military members who would be removed through retirement. In January 2015 Ntam announced a series of measures, including the creation of a permanent military force to be deployed to discipline any misconduct by members of the armed forces. Another sign of the new regime's determination to accelerate security sector reforms was the appointment, in May, of José António Marques and Armando da Costa Marna as the new heads of the police and the National Guard, respectively, in both cases replacing close associates of Indjai.

The first half of 2015 was marked by increasing tensions within the ruling PAICG and between President Vaz and Prime Minister Simões Pereira, with senior PAIGC figures accusing Simões Pereira of neglecting the party. In June the Secretary of State for Communities, Idelfrides Fernandes, a member of the PAIGC and a close colleague of Simões Pereira, was detained on suspicion of trafficking diplomatic passports. He was later released on bail. Simões Pereira strengthened his

position in the party at an internal meeting in June, following which Baciro Djá, the Minister of State in charge of the Presidency of the Council of Ministers and Parliamentary Affairs, and one of the Prime Minister's sternest critics, resigned from the Government. Simões Pereira was confirmed in his position in early July, after receiving a unanimous vote of confidence in the ANP. However, a corruption investigation was opened against Minister of Foreign Affairs and International Co-operation Mário Lopes de Rosa, another close ally of Simões Pereira.

President Vaz dissolved the Government in August 2015, citing irreconcilable differences with Simões Pereira about how the country should be governed and widespread corruption and mismanagement of public funds within the administration. Vaz appointed Djá as the new Prime Minister, despite Simões Pereira's renomination as the PAIGC's candidate to the position and public demonstrations demanding his reinstatement. In early September President Vaz named a new PAIGC-PRS coalition Government, in which the PAIGC retained the most important portfolios, with lesser posts being allocated to the PRS. Amid criticism from PAIGC parliamentary deputies over his appointment, Djá began his premiership by dismissing the heads of the state-owned radio and television services, claiming that their coverage of recent events had been politically biased. On 9 September the Supreme Court declared Djá's appointment by presidential decree—without consultation with the PAIGC and other parliamentary parties—unconstitutional. Djá immediately announced his resignation. In mid-September, following consultations with the PAIGC leadership, Vaz nominated Carlos Correia, a senior member of the party, to the premiership. A new Government was installed in October.

A few months later, a fresh political crisis, over the adoption of the 2016 budget bill, threatened to bring the Government down. In late December 2015 15 dissident PAIGC members of the ANP abstained from the vote, leaving the Government short of the 52 votes required to carry the motion. The PAIGC subsequently expelled those members from the party, on the basis that they had abused their power as legislators, and replaced them with new deputies. The budget was approved in late January 2016.

In March 2016 the local media reported that several people had been arrested on suspicion of plotting a coup. Brig.-Gen. Ntam warned that any soldier involved in a coup would be executed. In May President Vaz dismissed the Government, citing poor internal party discipline and demanding that legislators prioritize national, rather than personal, interests. Correia declared the dismissals to be a 'constitutional coup'; his ministers refused to leave their posts, and sporadic protests broke out in the streets.

Vaz appointed Baciro Djá (who had served as premier for 20 days during the previous cabinet crisis) as the new Prime Minister in May 2016. A new Council of Ministers was named in June but was unable to govern in the face of PAIGC opposition. In July the Supreme Court, which had been seized by the PAIGC, ruled that Djá's appointment was constitutional. The PAIGC's deputies responded by boycotting parliamentary sessions. An ECOWAS delegation headed by Guinean President Alpha Condé arrived in the country in September to seek a solution to the crisis. Guinea-Bissau's political stakeholders agreed on a 'road map', which included plans to hold a round-table meeting, appoint an inclusive government and draft reforms of the Constitution, electoral legislation and the laws governing political parties (although no deadlines were set for the completion of these transitional steps). The six-point road map, known as the Conakry Accord, was formally signed in October; both parties agreed that Djá would remain Prime Minister until the holding of legislative elections scheduled for 2018.

On 14 November 2016 President Vaz once again dissolved the Government, following the PAIGC legislators' refusal to work with Prime Minister Djá. On 18 November Vaz appointed Umaro El Mokhtar Sissoco Embaló, a former presidential special adviser, as the new Prime Minister. PAIGC dissidents expressed their opposition to the appointment, claiming that there had not been sufficient consensus within the ANP over the selection of Embaló. In mid-December a new Council of

Ministers was sworn in, with most ministers from the previous cabinet retaining their positions.

The new Government was prevented from functioning, however, as PAIGC deputies refused to debate or approve its programme. In the context of further international mediation by the so-called P5 group (comprising ECOWAS, the UN, the EU, the AU and the CPLP), the President of the ANP, Cipriano Cassamá, proposed in March 2017 that the five parties represented in the legislature form a new government, to be led by the PAIGC. In the same month, protesters in Bissau demanded that President Vaz resign, in order to resolve the constitutional crisis.

In April 2017, amid growing impatience among ECOWAS leaders, the regional organization declared that Guinea-Bissau's leaders had 30 days to implement the Conakry Accord, failing which it would impose targeted sanctions. ECOWAS commenced the withdrawal of ECOMIB peacekeepers in May. In the same month the UN Security Council requested that President Vaz appoint a new Prime Minister. In response, Vaz threatened to dissolve the Government if the ANP voted against its programme. In light of the continuing impasse, at a summit meeting held in June ECOWAS extended ECOMIB's mandate for three months, until the end of September, despite the commencement of the mission's staged withdrawal. (ECOMIB's mandate was extended thereafter at regular intervals until the end of December 2020 when it was officially ended.) In August 2017 a dialogue was resumed between the different factions of the PAIGC, but failed again to agree on a programme to implement the Conakry Accord and break the political deadlock. In December ECOWAS gave the PAIGC 30 days to reach agreement on a nominee for Prime Minister.

In mid-January 2018 the Executive Secretary of the CNE, Pedro Sambú, announced that the Commission was ready to organize legislative elections in May, when the mandate of the current ANP was due to expire. President Vaz made no announcement on this development, but at the end of January, following the resignation of Embaló from the premiership two weeks earlier, Vaz unilaterally appointed Augusto Artur António Silva as the new Prime Minister, without consulting the ANP. In February ECOWAS announced sanctions, including travel and visa restrictions and the freezing of financial assets, against 19 Guinea-Bissau politicians and businessmen (including the President's son, Emerson Goudiaby Vaz, and members of his parliamentary faction) for obstructing the implementation of the Conakry Accord. ECOWAS's imposition of sanctions was denounced by Vaz's supporters, who staged mass demonstrations in protest.

Prime Minister Silva resigned in early April 2018 after failing to form a government. President Vaz subsequently appointed Aristides Gomes (who had served as premier in 2005–07) to the position, following discussions with the PRS and the PAIGC, and signed a decree postponing the legislative elections until November 2018. A new consensus Government was appointed in mid-April. Two days later the ANP was convened for the first time in about two years and voted to extend its mandate, which was due to expire in that month, until the holding of the elections in November. In early June the 15 dissident parliamentary deputies who had been expelled by the PAIGC in December 2015 created a new political group, the Movimento para a Alternância Democrática da Guiné-Bissau (MADEM-G15). In mid-June 2018 the ANP finally approved the budget, which had been suspended since 2016. In August 2018 ECOWAS and the West African Economic and Monetary Union pledged US $2m. to support the legislative elections, and ECOWAS announced the lifting of its sanctions.

The second half of 2018 was marked by several strikes over salaries (see *Economy*) and tensions over the upcoming legislative elections. Following delays in the voter registration process, the elections were postponed once again, to March 2019, amid serious concerns from the international community. Although a deal had been signed in January between the Government and the main teachers' union, the Sindicato Nacional dos Professores, the latter called for a new wave of strikes in February, claiming that the Government had not fulfilled its promises. This prompted demonstrations by students, who feared that they would miss classes for the entire academic year; 19 students were injured and 20 arrested during violent clashes with police.

The legislative elections finally took place on 10 March 2019, contested by 21 parties and attended by observers from the AU, ECOWAS and other multilateral bodies, as well as country representatives. According to the results, as announced by the CNE on 13 March, the PAIGC won 47 seats (down from 57 in the previous parliament) and the PRS 21 seats (down from 41). In second place was MADEM-G15, with 27 seats. The Assembleia do Povo Unido–Partido Democrática da Guiné Bissau (APU–PDGB) secured five seats, and the Partido para a Nova Democracia (PND) and the União para a Mudança (UM) each retained a single seat. President Vaz immediately announced that the PAIGC would form a coalition with the APU–PDGB, the PND and the UM, giving the alliance a narrow majority in the ANP.

In April 2019 a dispute over the election of the Second Vice-President of the ANP erupted between the ruling coalition and MADEM-G15, with President Vaz announcing that he would not appoint a premier until the dispute was resolved. In late May, as the dispute continued, thousands of PAIGC supporters demonstrated in Bissau and called on the President to nominate the party leader, Simões Pereira, as the Prime Minister. In late June, with the issue of the ANP second vice-presidency still unresolved and under international pressure, President Vaz reached a compromise with the PAIGC and appointed Aristides Gomes, now of MADEM-G15, as Prime Minister. Vaz also announced that the first round of the presidential election would be held on 24 November, with a run-off round (if required) on 29 December. On 30 June ECOWAS announced that, as President Vaz's mandate had expired one week earlier, the country's affairs should be managed by the new premier (Gomes) until the presidential polls took place. ECOWAS also stipulated that a new administration had to be formed by 3 July. A new Government was duly announced on that date, comprising 16 ministers, most of whom were from the PAIGC, with a few portfolios being allocated to the coalition's junior member parties.

In the following weeks, several leading politicians announced that they would contest the presidential election. Former Prime Minister Gomes Júnior was the first to declare his candidacy, as an independent, in mid-July 2019, followed by Embaló, the candidate of MADEM-G15. In late August the PAIGC announced that Simões Pereira would be the party's official candidate. This prompted President Vaz to announce a few days later that he would seek re-election as an independent candidate. In mid-October the Supreme Court confirmed these four candidacies, as well as a further eight, with the latter being either independents or the nominees of smaller parties.

On 28 October 2019 President Vaz dismissed the Gomes Government, accusing it of compromising the upcoming electoral process. Former premier Faustino Imbali was appointed Prime Minister the next day, with his new Government comprising members from the three main opposition parties—MADEM-G15, the PRS and the APU–PDGB, the last having changed sides. ECOWAS swiftly agreed to double the size of ECOMIB, in a move expressing its opposition to Imbali's appointment. Imbali tendered his Government's resignation on 8 November, and Gomes (de facto) remained in charge.

The first round of the presidential election took place peacefully on 24 November 2019. The PAIGC's Simões Pereira led, with 40.1% of the votes, followed by Embaló with 27.7%, Nuno Gomes Nabiam, with 13.2%, and Vaz with 12.4%. (Gomes Júnior received just 2.7% of the first-round votes.) Voter turnout was recorded at 74.4%. The second round was held on 29 December. According to the CNE, the winner, with 53.6% of the votes cast, was Embaló, who had been able to pool support from most of the unsuccessful first-round candidates. Simões Pereira, however, contested the results by making several appeals to the Supreme Court, citing malpractice, as did the PAIGC-led National Assembly. Despite the ongoing challenges at the Supreme Court against the election outcome, on 25 February 2020 the CNE again certified the victory of Embaló, who was inaugurated as President in a ceremony at a hotel in Bissau on 27 February. Meanwhile, the military, breaking with is proclaimed neutrality and in support of the President-elect, seized government offices and the state broadcasting services, prompting some observers to describe his investiture as a 'coup'. The PAIGC majority in the ANP rejected Embaló's inauguration as illegitimate (as it had not taken place within the parliamentary complex) and on 28 February voted to appoint its speaker, Cipriano Cassamá, as interim President, pending the Supreme Court's final ruling. However, on the following day Cassamá resigned from his designated new position, claiming that his life had been threatened, and Embaló, after issuing a decree dismissing the Gomes Government, appointed Nabiam of the APU-PDGB as the new Prime Minister. It was subsequently reported that troops had surrounded the Supreme Court and the residence of Gomes, who refused to recognize his removal from office. On 10 March Gomes, fearing for his personal safety, sought refuge at the headquarters of UNIOGBIS. (In February 2021 Gomes left Guinea-Bissau on a UN plane, reportedly for France, after having been granted permission by the Government to leave on medical grounds.)

THE EMBALÓ PRESIDENCY

The confirmation of two cases of COVID-19 in Guinea-Bissau on 25 March 2020, which signalled the beginnings of an outbreak in the country, heightened existing political tensions and led the self-proclaimed President Embaló to declare a national state of emergency on 28 March, some nine days after the Government had closed the country's land and sea borders and commercial air links as a preventative measure to curb the further spread of the disease, which had first appeared in the People's Republic of China in late 2019.

On 30 April 2020, following weeks of dispute, Attorney-General Ladislau Embassa resigned, officially for reasons of professional ethics. Meanwhile, on 23 April ECOWAS recognized Embaló as the winner of the presidential election, followed a few days later by the AU. President Embaló immediately called for fresh legislative elections, in order to seek a more reliable parliamentary majority, and confirmed the nominations of Nabiam and his Government. In May Embaló established a technical committee which was given the task of revising Guinea-Bissau's Constitution.

The opposition accused the Government of using the COVID-19-related state of emergency to exert pressure on the National Assembly, particularly to approve the adoption of its legislative programme. The latter was endorsed on 30 June 2020 in a parliamentary session boycotted by the PAIGC. Moreover, the opposition claimed that the emergency measures had led to the illegal detention of certain of its members, notably PAIGC central committee member Armando Correia Dias, who was arrested on 20 June on suspicion of the illegal possession of arms but released two days later, and former Minister of the Interior Juliano Fernandes of the APU–PDGB, who was detained on his return from Senegal in July and released the following day without charge.

From late May 2020 some of the restrictive measures introduced by the Government in response to the COVID-19 pandemic began to be eased; land borders were reopened, local travel was permitted and international commercial flight (albeit limited) resumed in August. In early September the state of emergency was downgraded to a state of calamity and in the following month schools were reopened. Although the COVID-19 situation in Guinea-Bissau was further downgraded to a public health alert in early December, the state of calamity designation was reintroduced in late January 2021 and regularly extended thereafter, until it was replaced with a state of alert in early February 2022. A mass COVID-19 vaccination campaign was launched in Guinea-Bissau in early April 2021. By 18 September 2022 around 20.7% of the population had been fully vaccinated, and 34.4% had received at least one dose. According to World Health Organization figures, 8,796 confirmed cases of COVID-19 had been reported in the country by 3 October, with 175 fatalities.

Meanwhile, in mid-December 2020 the ANP approved the 2021 budget, although most of the 47 PAIGC deputies boycotted the vote. President Embaló summoned political party representatives to discuss the proposed dissolution of the legislature but failed to win their support. At the end of December the Attorney-General issued an international arrest warrant (on charges of corruption) against Simões Pereira, who was living in exile in Portugal. In March Simões Pereira returned to Guinea-Bissau, with police forcibly dispersing a crowd of supporters who had gathered outside the PAIGC's headquarters to welcome him. A few days later a radio presenter who had reported on Simões Pereira's return, was attacked by unidentified armed men in an attempted kidnapping in Bissau.

In October 2021 President Embaló and his Senegalese counterpart, Macky Sall, signed an agreement with regard to the two countries' joint economic area. The agreement caused great controversy and heightened tensions between Embaló and the ANP, due to allegations that it provided for future revenue from the area to be unevenly split between the two countries, with Senegal receiving 70% of any oil receipts and Guinea-Bissau the remaining 30%. Although the two Presidents and the Agence de Gestion et Coopération, the organization in charge of jointly managing the area, denied the allegations and insisted that the deal sought to improve co-ordination and management of the common economic zone, the ANP, including members of Embaló's own MADEM-G15, adopted a resolution declaring the agreement null and void in late December.

On 1 February 2022 heavy gunfire broke out in Bissau, near the government offices where Embaló and Prime Minister Nabiam were chairing a cabinet meeting. Some 11 people were killed in the fighting and Embaló declared the situation to be under control a few hours later. He later linked the coup attempt to drug trafficking. On 10 February President Embaló announced that the attempted coup had been instigated by three figures previously detained by the US authorities on drug-trafficking charges, including former Navy Chief of Staff Na Tchuto, and that all three had been arrested. PAIGC leader Simões Pereira, however, noted in an interview that the President's narrative conveniently justified an intensification of the repression against opposition figures and internal critics. On 22 February the Attorney-General's office barred Simões Pereira from leaving the country, citing legal cases against him. In March the PAIGC was banned from holding its 10th congress following a complaint lodged by the leader of a rival party faction, Bolom Conté. The PAIGC members who tried to meet despite the ban were violently dispersed by police; seven were injured. In May Simões Pereira criticized ECOWAS for sending a stabilizing mission to the country (see *Foreign Affairs*) and accepting Embaló's account of the coup attempt.

On 16 May 2022 President Embaló, following consultations with ANP President Cassamá and party leaders, dissolved the ANP, citing persistent and irreconcilable differences between the Government and the legislature. He scheduled early legislative elections to take place on 18 December.

FOREIGN AFFAIRS

In its foreign relations, Guinea-Bissau is motivated primarily by the need to secure aid, and, in this context, it has actively promoted co-operation with both Northern and Southern donors. Until recently, Guinea-Bissau's main development partners comprised European bilateral donors, especially Portugal, and multilateral partners such as the EU, the UN and ECOWAS. In recent years, however, South-South co-operation, especially with Angola, China and Brazil, has assumed a greater role.

Angola has emerged as a key partner by virtue of its investments in mineral resource extraction and infrastructure, and its leadership of the ECOWAS-CPLP SSR process, which involved the deployment of the 270-strong MISSANG in 2011–12. In 1996 Guinea-Bissau was among the five lusophone African nations that, together with Brazil and Portugal, formally established the CPLP—a lusophone commonwealth promoting co-operation in technical, cultural and social affairs.

China has also become an important bilateral partner, particularly in the infrastructural domain, and from the mid-2000s the Chinese Government financed and undertook several large-scale construction projects in Guinea-Bissau. The two countries signed an economic and technical co-operation agreement worth US $7.4m. in April 2021, notably involving the financing of infrastructure projects.

Among Guinea-Bissau's Northern bilateral partners, the former colonial power, Portugal, has traditionally played the foremost role, and relations have generally been very cordial since the independence of Guinea-Bissau. Several Portuguese non-governmental organizations have been actively involved in development projects throughout Guinea-Bissau and played an important role in education, health care and rural development. Following the 2012 coup, Portugal remained steadfast in its support of Carlos Gomes Júnior and its refusal to accept the transitional arrangement negotiated between the Military Command, the opposition parties and ECOWAS. In addition to suspending a large part of its co-operation activities in Guinea-Bissau, Portugal announced that it would reduce its diplomatic representation in the country, pending the restoration of constitutional order. Following the political transition in May–July 2014, Portugal pledged its support for the new Government in mobilizing much-needed international financial assistance. However, the crisis arising from the dismissal of Prime Minister Simões Pereira by President Vaz in August 2015 cast a new shadow over Guinea-Bissau's relations with Portugal and other donors. Relations with donors resumed from mid-2018 as Guinea-Bissau achieved some political stability, but they remained fragile amid tensions relating to the 2019 legislative and presidential elections.

In a bid to diversify its Northern partners, but also to improve ties with its francophone neighbours, Guinea-Bissau has sought to establish closer relations with them and France. Guinea-Bissau thus joined the West African Economic and Monetary Union and its Franc Zone in 1997 (see *Economy*), and France has since been an important donor and international political player in the country. In July 2022 France's President, Emmanuel Macron, became the first French head of state to visit Guinea-Bissau. During the visit, Macron held discussions with President Embaló, then ECOWAS Chairman, on regional security issues, as well as Guinea-Bissau's own political context, condemning the alleged coup attempt of 1 February. He also promised to provide further development assistance and to establish a French school in Bissau in 2023.

Guinea-Bissau's foreign relations are also heavily influenced by a sense of vulnerability to the interests of its larger francophone neighbours, Senegal and Guinea. Relationships with Senegal, in particular, have been characterized by several acute crises over the demarcation of maritime borders, the common land border and the conflict between the Senegalese armed forces and separatists of the Mouvement des Forces Démocratiques de la Casamance (MFDC). The issue of Casamance constituted a triggering factor in the 1998–99 political-military conflict (see above), during which President Vieira obtained the support of military forces from both Senegal and Guinea. Military intervention by these neighbours, albeit in response to a request for assistance by Vieira, was regarded by most Guinea-Bissau citizens as an invasion, and represented a low point in relations with the countries in question. After the military junta's victory, incidents continued in the border area between Guinea-Bissau and Senegal for some time, despite diplomatic efforts to resolve the crisis.

In the years after the 1998–99 conflict, relations between Guinea-Bissau and Senegal improved, as the Government of Guinea-Bissau displayed willingness to collaborate with the Senegalese Government's efforts to bring stability to the Casamance region. In December 2004 a general peace accord was finally signed between the Senegalese Government and the MFDC. However, in June 2005 a dissident faction of the MFDC, which was opposed to the peace deal, launched attacks in Casamance, prompting fears that the ceasefire might collapse. Tensions at the border continued to be reported in the 2010s, with one of the most notable incidents involving Minister of Internal Administration Botche Candé, whose convoy was blocked by Casamance separatists in November 2014. Candé demanded that the rebels leave Guinea-Bissau and subsequently resigned over the incident. The conflict in Casamance remained largely dormant over the following years, until the Senegalese Government launched a large-scale offensive against the MFDC in January 2021. As ECOWAS Chairman, President Embaló facilitated and presided over the signature of a peace agreement between an emissary of Senegal's President Sall and MFDC leaders César Atoute Badiate and Lansana Fabouré in August 2022, under which the southern wing of the MFDC agreed to disarm and to support a return to peace in the region.

Relations between President Embaló and Guinean President Condé have been poor for several years, particularly since Embaló, while in his role as Prime Minister, criticized the mediation efforts conducted by Condé in Guinea-Bissau in 2017. As well as accusing Condé of supporting the PAIGC's candidate Simões Pereira during the presidential election campaign in Guinea-Bissau in 2019, Embaló also denounced Condé for seeking, and obtaining, a third term in office in the Guinean presidential election in October 2020 (see Guinea) and for unilaterally closing Guinea's borders with Guinea-Bissau, Senegal and Sierra Leone ahead of the polls. In late October Guinea's Minister of Security and Civil Protection, Albert Damantang Camara, accused Guinea-Bissau of sending weapons into Guinea; Guinea-Bissau's defence minister, Sandji Fati, immediately denied the charges. In December President of the Republic of the Congo Denis Sassou Nguesso offered to mediate between Embaló and Condé in order to defuse tensions between them. As ECOWAS Chairman, President Embaló actively engaged with the military junta that took power in Guinea in a coup in September 2021, notably pressing for a transition to restore civilian rule.

The UN has played a central role in international efforts to contribute to the political stabilization of Guinea-Bissau. In 1999 the UN Secretary-General established UNOGBIS, with a mandate to aid peacebuilding efforts, support democracy and the rule of law, encourage friendly relations with Guinea-Bissau's neighbours and assist in the election process. In 2007 Guinea-Bissau was added to the agenda of the new UN Peacebuilding Commission—a specific Guinea-Bissau configuration of the Commission, led by Brazil, was charged with co-ordinating the international community's conflict-prevention efforts in Guinea-Bissau and identifying key programmes to stop the country from sliding back into conflict. In 2008, in response to the numerous signals that Guinea-Bissau had become a hub for drug trafficking between Latin America and Europe, the UN Office on Drugs and Crime established a project office in Bissau to support the Government's counter-trafficking efforts and training a special judicial police task force. In January 2010 UNOGBIS was succeeded by UNIOGBIS, whose mandate was subsequently regularly extended until its departure at the end of 2020. The majority of agencies belonging to the UN system, including the Office of the UN High Commissioner for Refugees, the World Food Programme, the UN Development Programme, the UN Children's Fund and the World Health Organization, are present in Guinea-Bissau and actively implementing a variety of projects and programmes.

Several other international and regional organizations have played an important role in assisting Guinea-Bissau, including the EU, ECOWAS and the CPLP. The EU, a major donor in Guinea-Bissau, has provided support to state and rule of law reform programmes through the European Development Fund. In 2008 Guinea-Bissau joined the European Agency for the Management of Operational Co-operation at the External Borders (Frontex), extending European naval patrols into Guinea-Bissau's territorial waters. Also in 2008 the EU approved the deployment of the EU Security Sector Reform in Guinea-Bissau (EU SSR Guinea-Bissau). However, the pursuit of the mission's objectives was repeatedly hampered by resistance from elements of the armed forces, and in the wake of the events of April 2010 the EU announced that the mission would be suspended and that its mandate would not be extended beyond 30 September. In January 2011 the EU opened Article 96 consultations with the Guinea-Bissau Government, in view of the perceived risk of gross disrespect for the rule of law. These were concluded in March, with agreement between the two parties on a list of necessary reforms. Following the April 2012 coup, the EU extended the suspension of its aid and imposed a travel ban and asset freeze on six coup leaders, including António Indjai. However, the EU maintained its humanitarian operations and programmes that directly benefited the population. Following the peaceful elections in 2014, the EU sent a mission to define key priorities for budgetary support and swiftly announced that it would unblock an initial tranche of pre-pledged assistance and revive the ratification process for a fishing partnership. In November the normalization of relations with the EU was further confirmed with the signing of a new fisheries agreement, providing compensation and an important source of revenue to the Government in exchange for the right for up to 40 EU vessels to operate in Guinea-Bissau's territorial waters. A donor conference held in Brussels, Belgium, in March 2015 secured pledges of US $1,100m. to fund strategic projects during 2015–25.

ECOWAS played a prominent role in the resolution of the 1998–99 political-military conflict and has engaged actively in the country's subsequent political developments. In 2003, following the overthrow of President Yalá, ECOWAS once again dispatched a special mission to act as mediator. After the attempted coup in Bissau in April 2010, ECOWAS condemned the disruption to constitutional order and called for urgent military reform. In this context, ECOWAS began in the following months to draft a new SSR initiative, which was adopted in November and became the ECOWAS-CPLP SSR agreement, under which MISSANG was deployed to Guinea-Bissau in March 2011. In April 2012, following the coup, ECOWAS distanced itself significantly from the CPLP and assumed an entirely new role as it became the key international partner in negotiations regarding the transitional arrangement with the Military Command, thereby in effect legitimizing the de facto situation. In subsequent months ECOWAS invited Guinea-Bissau's post-coup authorities to attend its regional summits and pledged financial support for the transition. Included in this arrangement was the deployment of the 600-strong ECOMIB, which was to help to maintain peace and security during the transitional period; ECOMIB troops began to arrive in the country in May 2012, and the mission's mandate was regularly extended thereafter. ECOWAS once again played a prominent role in the cabinet crises that shook the country in 2015–18, sending prominent mediators (including Guinea's President Condé and Sierra Leone's Ernest Bai Koroma) to the country on several occasions to foster political dialogue. It was supported in this by the other multilateral members of the P5. In August 2016 the head of the ECOWAS Commission none the less announced that ECOMIB would withdraw from Guinea-Bissau within the coming year, citing the high costs of maintaining the force. A partial withdrawal process began in May 2017, in a move that ECOWAS justified in part as a response to the ongoing deadlock between President Vaz and the PAIGC members of the ANP over the appointment of a new Prime Minister. In February 2018 ECOWAS imposed targeted sanctions on 19 leading Guinea-Bissau politicians and businessmen for obstructing the implementation of the Conakry Accord. The sanctions were lifted in August, following the appointment of a consensus Prime Minister and a new Government. ECOWAS once again played a key role in resolving the potential power vacuum as President Vaz's mandate expired in June 2019, by securing the nomination of a new Government in July, following intense negotiations between President Vaz, the PAIGC and the opposition parties. Moreover, ECOWAS exercised pressure on President Vaz to maintain the Government in power until the presidential election, notably by doubling the size of ECOMIB, to 1,000 troops, and sending a high-level mission to Bissau in November (see *The Vaz Presidency*). Following the lengthy dispute over the results of the second round of the 2019 presidential election, ECOWAS, together with the AU, refrained from acknowledging the result until late April 2020, by which time President Embaló had effectively already established his authority (see *The Embaló Presidency*). In September ECOWAS officially announced its decision to undertake a phased withdrawal of ECOMIB from Guinea-Bissau and by the end of December all of the mission's troops had left the country. ECOWAS promptly condemned the alleged coup attempt of 1 February 2022 against its then Chairman, President Embaló, and announced two days later that it would deploy a stabilizing force to Guinea-Bissau. The regional organization also called for constitutional reform to resolve the competing power claims between the President and the ANP. The stabilizing force, which comprised 631 troops from Nigeria, Senegal, Côte d'Ivoire and Ghana, was deployed in the country from late April. In July Embaló, as ECOWAS Chairman, also proposed the creation of an ECOWAS special 'anti-coup' force.

Economy

MARIE GIBERT

INTRODUCTION

According to the International Monetary Fund (IMF), Guinea-Bissau's gross domestic product (GDP), measured at current prices, totalled an estimated US $1,640m. in 2021, equivalent to $813 per head. Poverty is widespread, and, not surprisingly, the country's social and human development indicators are among the lowest in the world: the United Nations (UN) Development Programme ranked Guinea-Bissau 177th out of 191 countries in its 2021 Human Development Index, reflecting the country's low levels of productivity and economic diversification, as well as the serious difficulties that it faces in the health and education domains.

Despite a steady decline, more than one-half of the country's population (55.0% in 2021, according to the World Bank) still lives in rural areas, for the most part subsisting on a combination of smallholder agriculture, fishing, forestry and cattle farming. Among those activities that take on a monetized form, the harvesting and sale of cashew nuts, typically undertaken on an independent smallholder basis, play a paramount role: this crop constitutes the single main source of income for most rural households and accounts for the overwhelming majority of the country's total exports (as much as 98% in some years). Extractive and manufacturing industries remain at a very early stage of development, although recent developments in the area of natural resource extraction (particularly bauxite, phosphates and petroleum) suggest the potential for a resource-driven boost to GDP. The contribution of the services sector to GDP (53.2% of GDP in 2020, according to UN estimates) is accounted for largely by public administration and commerce, with incipient foreign investment in telecommunications, banking, hotels and restaurants, and petrol distribution. Budget receipts have traditionally been dominated by foreign aid and the sale of fishing licences to international partners.

After the considerable economic upheaval caused by the 1998–99 conflict, including an estimated 28.1% contraction in GDP in 1998, growth briefly resumed around the turn of the millennium, but the economy suffered a decline in 2002, following a fall in prices and production of cashews, a reduction in foreign aid and renewed political instability. From 2004 onwards, however, economic growth recovered, averaging 2.9% per year in 2004–09, although if population growth over the same period is taken into account, growth in average annual GDP per capita was only 0.5%. After moderate GDP growth in 2010 (of 4.6%), a record cashew harvest in 2011 resulted in a GDP growth rate surge to 8.1% in 2011, but political instability in 2012 caused GDP to contract by 1.7%. GDP growth resumed, albeit modestly, from 2013, and averaged 4.5% in 2013–17, in the context of the ongoing political transition. Growth slowed to 1.3% in 2018, owing partly to a decline of some 25% in cashew nut exports, before increasing to 4.5% in 2019. Growth contracted by 2.4% in 2020, due to the effects of the global COVID-19 pandemic and a sharp fall in levels of international trade, before rebounding to 3.8% in 2021.

Inflationary pressures have been kept broadly in check since Guinea-Bissau joined the Franc Zone in 1997 (its currency being pegged to the euro at a fixed rate of €1 = 655.957 francs CFA), but have fluctuated in accordance with international prices for the country's main imports, particularly foodstuffs and oil. This was especially apparent in 2008, when the consumer price index increased by 10.5%. After a brief interlude in 2009 (when the index fell by 1.7%), consumer prices rose each year between 2010 and 2013, by an annual average of 2.7%, before registering a contraction of 1.5% in 2014 as a result of low domestic demand. Consumer price inflation averaged 0.9% per year in 2015–19. It rose again, to 1.5% in 2020 and 3.3% in 2021, as a result of the COVID-19 pandemic.

The roots of the country's economic difficulties originate far in the past. Portugal, the colonial power, was itself relatively undeveloped, and until a very late stage was never willing or able to develop its colony. Instead, it opted for the maintenance of traditional economic structures with a view to ensuring political control, alongside the extraction of mercantile profits from a small number of crops. Following independence in 1974, the Government of Guinea-Bissau established a centrally planned economy, and an ambitious investment programme—financed mainly by foreign borrowing—was initiated, with emphasis on the industrial sector. However, the economy, which had been adversely affected by the campaign for independence, continued to deteriorate, and by the early 1980s Guinea-Bissau had an underdeveloped agricultural sector, growing external debt, dwindling exports and escalating inflation. Furthermore, the production of many goods had been halted, as the depletion of the country's foreign exchange reserves made it difficult to import fuel or spare parts.

In response to the worsening economic situation, the Government initiated a process of economic liberalization in 1984. A Structural Adjustment Programme was adopted for 1987–90, which aimed to correct macroeconomic and foreign imbalances, increase producer prices and strengthen the private sector. In 1990 the Government began the reform of the country's public enterprises and launched the first phase of a privatization programme. The liberalization process was relatively successful in addressing macroeconomic and foreign imbalances, but it also brought about a deterioration in human development indicators. The privatization of public enterprises was often undertaken to the benefit of the ruling elite and its associates and eventually led to the dismantling of several of those companies.

Current economic prospects are mixed. While the country's dependence on the export of cashew nuts constitutes a major cause for concern in view of the recent significant fluctuations in this crop's international price, the exploration of the country's rich mineral wealth could boost future domestic income considerably. However, as has traditionally been the case in Guinea-Bissau, any progress will depend on developments in the political and security domains.

AGRICULTURE AND FISHING

Agriculture is the principal economic activity. The primary sector (including forestry, fishing and cattle farming) engaged an estimated 60% of the total labour force in 2019, according to the World Bank, and, with forestry and fishing, accounted for 32.6% of GDP in 2020 according to UN estimates. Political instability caused exports of cashew nuts (the main cash crop) to decline from a 2011 peak of 200,000 metric tons to 120,000 tons in 2012. Exports increased steadily thereafter, again reaching 200,000 tons in 2016. They gradually decreased over the next few years to an estimated 160,000 tons in 2020, owing in part to a fall in the volume of sales to India (the main customer for Guinean cashews), which in turn resulted from the Indian Government's decision to eliminate the subsidy that it granted to local cashew nut producers, causing a fall in the price. From 2019 Guinea-Bissau was able to diversify its export market slightly as Viet Nam was reported to have dramatically increased its purchases of West African cashew nuts. However, in 2020 and 2021 India remained the destination for most of Guinea-Bissau's cashew nut exports, owing to pandemic-related border closures preventing potential new buyers from entering the market. In

addition to cashew nuts, rice, roots and tubers, maize, beans, millet, sorghum, cassava, sweet potatoes, fruits, sugar cane, cotton, coconuts and groundnuts are produced in considerable quantities. Livestock and timber production are also significant. Artisanal fishing provides a key source of protein, especially for island, coastal and riverside communities, and the sale of industrial fishing licences to other countries constitutes a major source of government revenue.

Under the Constitution of Guinea-Bissau, the land is the common property of all the people. However, the Government does grant private concessions to work it and has maintained the rights of those tilling their fields. The post-independence regime confiscated some properties and introduced state control over foreign trade and domestic retail trade through 'People's Stores'; these were soon characterized by inefficiency and corrupt practices, contributing to the downfall of the regime of Luís Cabral in 1980. In 1983–84 the Government partly privatized the state-controlled trading companies and raised producer prices by about 70%, in an attempt to boost agricultural output. Despite these measures, Guinea-Bissau continued to operate a 'war economy', superimposed on a rudimentary peasant economy where most products were bought and sold by the state. From 1987, however, price controls were removed on most agricultural products, except essential goods, and internal marketing systems were liberalized. A new Land Law was drafted in 1998 but never implemented, and further efforts at reform stalled as civil war broke out. At present, a combination of customary tenure and government concessions is in practice, which has fuelled localized conflicts between commercial farmers and local communities.

Rice is the staple food crop. The southern region of Tombali has historically been the 'rice basket' of Guinea-Bissau, accounting for more than one-half of total national production. According to the Food and Agriculture Organization of the UN (FAO), production of paddy rice increased from a low point during the 1998–99 conflict (80,300 metric tons in 1999), to reach a record 209,700 tons in 2013. Production has remained stable over recent years and reached 198,000 tons in 2021. The overall increase in production, however, has not been enough to offset a significant increase in rice imports over the past two decades, which has been the result of population growth, rice field deterioration, lack of seeds and fertilizers, and a shift to the cultivation of cashew nuts and their barter for imported rice. Thus, according to FAO, the country has imported 20%–30% of its total rice consumption in recent years. In 2016 the Government launched the Rice Value Chain Development Project, which included an ambitious target of achieving self-sufficiency in rice by 2020, and received a US $5.7m. grant from the African Development Bank (AfDB).

Food insecurity is a major concern for Guinea-Bissau, especially because of low agricultural productivity, dependence on imported cereals, high global food prices and a long-term downward trend in the international price for cashew nuts. A Food Security and Vulnerability Analysis undertaken by the World Food Programme (WFP) in October 2017 found that 20% of the country's rural households could be considered food insecure at that time, with food insecurity reaching 27% in Quinara region. In order to address this problem, WFP has implemented several projects, including food-for-work, school feeding and nutritional assistance for mothers and children. Similar projects have been implemented by several development non-governmental organizations (NGOs).

Among Guinea-Bissau's traditional exports during the colonial period were groundnuts (grown in the interior as an extension of the Senegalese cultivation), cotton, oil-palm products on the islands and the coast, and coconuts. In 1977 groundnut exports, totalling 16,335 metric tons, accounted for 60% of total export earnings. However, according to the IMF, exports of groundnuts had ceased by 1993 and have not since resumed. According to FAO, production of groundnuts (in shell) totalled an estimated 42,625 tons in 2020.

Cashew nuts have become by far the country's principal cash crop over the past two or three decades. Although cashews were being harvested as far back as the colonial period, the crop only began to dominate from the late 1980s. As more of the country's land area was allocated to cashew groves, and as the trees gradually matured, production steadily increased, offsetting the long-term downward trend in the global price for cashew nuts. However, the country's trade in cashew nuts has been hampered on several occasions by disputes between producers, buyers and the Government over prices and export taxes. In 2006, for example, a buyers' dispute over government-fixed prices led to a sharp decline in annual production and export revenue. The pricing policy was subsequently amended, with the Government setting an 'indicative' price for the season. In May 2015, with the aim of increasing exports and curbing smuggling to neighbouring Senegal, the Government announced that it would raise the cashew price by 20%, to 300 francs CFA (US $0.51) per kg. The authorities also pledged to strengthen controls at ports and border points, impose higher penalties for those caught smuggling and introduce incentives for individuals reporting illicit activities, who would be entitled to 40% of the revenue from the sale of the seized merchandise. The Government raised the cashew nut price in both 2016 (following a strong harvest in 2015) and 2017, to 500 francs CFA ($0.90) per kg, to reflect higher international prices. This was not enough, however, to prevent the smuggling of cashew nuts to Senegal, where prices were reportedly between 80% and 120% higher. Attempts by the Government to regulate the sector, particularly the role played by intermediaries, created further incentives for smuggling. The following years were characterized by continued attempts by the Government to regulate the sector, offer a fair price and set an export tax that would encourage producers to sell their production in the country. In 2017–20 total production of cashew nuts averaged 160,630 metric tons annually. Guinea-Bissau exported an estimated 160,000 tons of cashew nuts in 2020, despite a late start to the campaign owing to the COVID-19 pandemic. In early April 2021 the Government announced that it had set the cashew reference price at 360 francs CFA ($0.66) per kg and introduced a farmers' tax of 15 francs CFA ($0.03) per kg; the campaign national marketing was launched on 7 April. However, confronted with a depressed market, notably because India was contending with a dramatic increase in COVID-19 cases, the Guinea-Bissau Government reduced the cashew reference price to 350 francs CFA ($0.65) per kg, down from 360 francs CFA ($0.66), removed the farmers' tax and lowered two other taxes (on intermediaries and exporters) in June. Cashew nut production reportedly reached 238,500 tons in 2021, of which 231,000 tons were exported. In April 2022 the Government announced a reference price of 375 francs CFA ($0.57) per kg for the forthcoming season.

The fishing industry has expanded rapidly since the late 1970s, and it has been estimated that the potential annual catch in Guinea-Bissau's waters totals some 300,000 metric tons. The local fishing sector is principally artisanal, while industrial fishing is conducted largely by foreign vessels operating under licence, depriving Guinea-Bissau of a potential revenue source in processing. The first of a subsequent series of fishing agreements between the Government and the European Union (EU) was signed in 1980. Protracted negotiations from 2017 culminated in the signing in November 2018 of a new Sustainable Fishing Partnership Agreement with the EU, under which the EU agreed to pay Guinea-Bissau €15.6m. (compared with €9.2m. under the previous agreement), of which €11.6m. would be channelled into the Guinea-Bissau Government's general budget, and €4m. would be used to support fisheries facilities, the supervision of territorial waters and research. Other agreements have been negotiated by the Government of Guinea-Bissau with the People's Republic of China, Senegal, Côte d'Ivoire and the West Africa Fisheries Sub-Regional Commission. The fisheries sector has contributed more than 40% of government budget receipts annually in recent years. However, the high level of illegal fishing—estimated in a study by the Environmental Justice Foundation at 23% of the total catch—continues to deprive Guinea-Bissau of an important source of revenue, while contributing to stock depletion. Several dozen foreign vessels have been impounded in recent years, having been caught fishing illegally in Guinea-Bissau's waters, but many go undetected.

Cattle farming is a very important activity among the Balante ethnic group, as well as the Muslim populations of the interior. Members of some hinterland communities practise transhumance, moving with their herds to riverside areas during the dry season. In 2020 there were 720,800 cattle, 473,800 pigs, 816,800 goats and 527,700 sheep, according to FAO estimates. Meat consumption is significant in parts of the country, and some hides and skins are exported.

Illegal logging became a major concern in the context of the political instability that followed the April 2012 coup, as reports emerged of conflicts between the local population and Chinese logging companies in some areas, as well as the illicit export of containers filled with timber. The issue was highlighted in 2012–14 by conservation NGOs and local organizations, and in media reports, some of which suggested the involvement of senior administration figures. In May 2015 the Government announced the imposition of a five-year moratorium on logging and suspended the export of cut logs, pending further clarification of the conditions under which they were cut. Some 104,000 logs awaiting export to China were consequently seized. Media reports have suggested that the increase in illegal logging was due to a crackdown on cocaine smuggling, with corrupt army and government officials moving from one sector to the other. There is, however, little concrete evidence about the scale of the activity. In 2020 Guinea-Bissau produced some 3.1m. cu m of wood (nearly all non-coniferous wood fuel), according to FAO estimates.

INDUSTRY, MINING, TRANSPORT AND TELECOMMUNICATIONS

There is little industrial activity other than food processing, brewing and wood processing. Industry (including mining, manufacturing, construction and energy) employed an estimated 9% of the working population in 2019, and the industrial sector contributed 14.2% of GDP in 2020, according to UN estimates.

Energy is derived principally from thermal and hydroelectric power. A total of 33.3% of the population (15.2% in rural areas) in Guinea-Bissau were estimated to have regular access to electricity in 2020: this was supplied mostly by private generators. The state-owned Empresa de Eletricidade e Aguas da Guiné-Bissau (EAGB) performs poorly, and attempts by the Government to restructure the company and attract private sector investment have proved unsuccessful. In 2006 the Chinese Government agreed to finance the construction of the 20-MW Saltinho Rapids dam on the Corubal river, 100 km south-east of Bissau, at an estimated cost of US $87m. Construction of the dam did not take place, however, and a Portuguese company was awarded a €1.5m. contract in early 2019 to develop feasibility and design studies for the run-of-river project, the investment costs of which were now estimated at up to €100m. Guinea-Bissau is part of the Gambia River Basin Development Organization (Organisation pour la Mise en Valeur du Fleuve Gambie—OMVG), which oversees development projects in the three river basins of The Gambia, Guinea-Bissau, Guinea and Senegal. The OMVG planned to build two new dams on the Gambia and Konkouré rivers, which would supply Guinea-Bissau with 42% of its power needs, and to construct 15 transformers across the country to facilitate the transport and distribution of electricity. In June 2011 a project to provide street lighting in Bissau using solar power was jointly announced by the UN Integrated Peacebuilding Office in Guinea-Bissau and the Bissau municipal authorities. However, public lighting was installed on only one-half of one of the avenues designated by the project. In February 2017, during the visit of a trade delegation from China, the Chinese embassy in Bissau announced plans to construct a 30-MW biomass power plant, costing $184m., in Mansôa, central Guinea-Bissau, which was to supply electricity to the capital; work commenced in March. A World Bank-sponsored three-year programme to improve the management of the EAGB commenced in late 2018. It involved a change in fuel supplies to Bissau's power station, from diesel to fuel oil, as the former tended to be stolen for private generators, leading to further power cuts. In October the Government signed a contract with Karpowership, a Turkish-based company, to supply electricity via a floating power station, which was expected to deliver 17.7 MW during 2019 and 30 MW annually during 2020–24. In March 2020 the Chinese company Sinohydro was awarded a contract to construct a 20-MW solar power plant at Gardete, near Bissau. The project was to be financed by a $42.9m. loan from the West African Development Bank.

The mining sector is at an incipient stage of development, but the phosphate reserves at Farim are promising. Canada's GB Minerals completed a feasibility study in December 2012, which indicated the viability of exporting 1m. metric tons of phosphate rock concentrate per year; production was initially scheduled to begin in 2017, but was subsequently delayed amid the ongoing political crisis related to the dissolution of the Government in May 2016 (see *History*). In February 2018 the Itafos Group, based in the Cayman Islands, acquired all the capital not yet owned by GB Minerals at Farim. Itafos announced that exploration would start at the end of 2020, but the site was still under construction as of mid-2022.

The exploitation of the country's bauxite reserves, located in the south-eastern region of Boé, near the border with Guinea, has also been the subject of negotiations in recent years. In 2007 Guinea-Bissau and Angola signed an agreement to explore jointly for bauxite in the region. A private Angolan company, Bauxite Angola, took a 70% share in the project (with the Governments of Angola and Guinea-Bissau, respectively, holding the remaining 20% and 10% shares), paying the Guinea-Bissau Government US $13m. for an exploration licence. In 2008 the Government announced that Bauxite Angola would invest some $300m. for the development of the bauxite reserves, including the construction of a mine that was expected to produce 2m. metric tons of bauxite per year over 56 years, a new deep-water port at Buba and a railway linking the two. Depending on the results of feasibility studies, the project was also expected to include an alumina plant, using bauxite from the mine and powered by a hydroelectric dam on the Geba river. Angola froze its investments in Guinea-Bissau in response to the April 2012 coup, pending the restoration of constitutional order, and a few months later the transitional authorities threatened to revoke the licence, on the grounds of allegedly irregular and unfavourable terms. Bauxite Angola announced in April 2018 that it would resume its activities in Guinea-Bissau later in that year; at mid-2022, however, operations had not recommenced.

Exploratory mining of other minerals has also been undertaken: West Africa Mining AG of Switzerland announced in April 2010 that prospecting for gold ore deposits in 46 areas of Guinea-Bissau had yielded positive results, and negotiations between the Government and two Russian and Chinese corporations have been conducted about the possibility of commercial exploitation of the ilmenite and zircon deposits in the north of Guinea-Bissau.

There have also been important developments in offshore petroleum exploration, as the increase in international oil prices in 2009–14 improved the commercial viability of Guinea-Bissau's reserves. In 1993 an agreement was signed with Senegal, providing for the joint management of the countries' maritime zones. The agreement, which was to operate for an initial 20-year period, provided for an 85%:15% division of petroleum resources between Senegal and Guinea-Bissau, subsequently altered to 80%:20% in 2000. Guinea-Bissau formally ratified the agreement in 1995, and the Agence de Gestion et Coopération was created to administer petroleum and fishing activity in the 100,000-sq-km joint area. A further agreement, signed in October 2021 by the two Governments, was declared null and void by Guinea-Bissau's parliament, the Assembleia Nacional Popular (ANP—National People's Assembly), amid controversy over an alleged uneven split of future oil revenues (see *History*). The southern section of the area, on the border with Guinea, which may contain significant deposits, was contested until 1985, when a joint commission was formed with Guinea to facilitate exploration in the two countries' maritime border area. Since 2004 a number of international petroleum companies have been granted licences to undertake offshore exploratory drilling and stakes in the country's offshore petroleum blocks. Guinea-Bissau's total offshore reserves are estimated to exceed 1,000m. barrels of heavy crude oil. Norwegian company PetroNor announced in November 2020 that it had acquired two licences from Svenska Petroleum of Sweden and planned to commence drilling in Guinea-Bissau waters in 2021 or 2022.

Although Guinea-Bissau is a small country, road access to many areas is problematic: there are only about 770 km of paved roads. Many areas, especially in the south, are cut off during the rainy season. Road rehabilitation projects in the 2000s were funded, *inter alia*, by the EU, the AfDB, the Economic Community of West African States, Portugal, France and China. In 2003 Guinea-Bissau's largest civil engineering project, the 750-m Ponte Amílcar Cabral over the Mansôa river at João Landim, was completed. The bridge, which links the north and south of the country, was financed by the EU. Another bridge, over the Cacheu river, at São Domingos, which is on the direct road link between Bissau and the border with Senegal, was completed in 2009, with funding from the EU and the Union Economique et Monétaire Ouest-Africaine (UEMOA). In November 2016 China announced that it would finance the construction of a 15-km motorway linking Bissau to Safim, to the north of the capital. Construction of the road began in January 2021 and was expected to be completed by 2023. Meanwhile, in August 2018 the World Bank announced that it was to finance the replacement and installation of road signs across the country in order to reduce the high rate of traffic accidents nationally.

The development of water transport holds considerable potential, as 85% of the population live within 20 km of a navigable waterway. The country's main commercial port is Bissau, which handles about 90% of the country's foreign trade. In 2007 the Angolan Government announced that a consortium of private Angolan companies would fund a US $500m. project to build a deepwater port at Buba, which could provide an outlet for future bauxite exports from the Boé deposits and serve as an alternative point of access to the continental hinterland. However, these plans were suspended following the April 2012 coup, although they were expected to resume after the 2014 elections and the normalization of relations with the country's international partners. In April 2016 it was announced that China Machinery Engineering Corporation (CMEC) had signed a memorandum of understanding (MoU) with the Government of Guinea-Bissau to build a number of new facilities, including the deep-water port at Buba and a new fishing port at Pikil in the north-east of the country. Meanwhile, a new, €10m. fishing harbour was inaugurated in Bissau in September 2011, with the capacity to hold four large vessels. In August 2018 the Government and the AfDB agreed to fund dredging work at the port of Bissau in a deal worth 15,000m. francs CFA (US $26.8m.).

There is one international airport—Osvaldo Vieira International Airport, OVIA—in Bissau, and there are smaller airstrips in other parts of the country, including on the island of Bubaque. In November 2010 the Spanish companies Petromiralles and Saicus Air were granted a 30-year licence to rehabilitate and operate OVIA. Guinea-Bissau's national airline, Transportes Aéreos da Guiné-Bissau, was liquidated in 1997 after an unsuccessful privatization. Following the illegal boarding of Syrian refugees on a Bissau–Lisbon flight in December 2013 and a three-year suspension of its service on that flight route, in December 2016 the Portuguese national airline, TAP, resumed its thrice-weekly direct flights between Bissau and Lisbon, the Portuguese capital. Royal Air Maroc also flies between Bissau and Casablanca, Morocco, five times a week. In April 2016, as part of an MoU signed with the Government (see above), CMEC agreed to build a new international airport in Guinea-Bissau. In July 2018 new facilities aimed at improving aviation safety and services were inaugurated at the OVIA, financed by the Senegalese-based air traffic control agency, Agence pour la Sécurité de la Navigation Aérienne en Afrique et à Madagascar. As part of its strategy aimed at curbing the further spread of COVID-19 in the country, the Government closed Guinea-Bissau's airports on 18 March 2020; regional flights resumed on 26 July, and international flights on 1 August.

Guinea-Bissau's telecommunications infrastructure has deteriorated sharply, as prolonged political instability has stifled investment. By 2014 the fixed-line telephone network had fallen to an estimated 5,000 functioning lines, according to the International Telecommunication Union (ITU), from 9,800 in 2004. Attempts by successive governments to revitalize the state-owned telecommunications operator, Guiné Telecom, through partial privatization have stalled repeatedly. However, this has been partly related to, and certainly offset by, the astonishingly rapid increase in the number of mobile telephone users. In 2003 the Government opened bids for licences to operate cellular services and established a national mobile telecommunications company, Guinetel, which began operations in Guinea-Bissau, with competition from just one other company, MTN of South Africa. In 2007 the Government awarded a third mobile telephone licence to Orange Sénégal, and a new service provider, Orange Bissau, started operations. The current level of network coverage across the entire country is high, with the exception of a few remote rural and island areas. According to the ITU, there were 1.9m. mobile telephone subscribers in Guinea-Bissau in 2020, compared with just 39,500 in 2004. The number of internet users in 2020 was estimated at 22.9 per 100 inhabitants.

EXTERNAL TRADE AND FINANCE

The total value of Guinea-Bissau's exports of goods and services, according to the International Trade Centre (ITC), increased steadily after the turn of the millennium, from US $67.4m. in 2001 to an estimated $249.8m. in 2019. Exports fell, however, to an estimated $166.2m. in 2020 and $181.6m. in 2021, as a result of the COVID-19 pandemic and a sharp contraction in the volume of international trade. ITC figures indicate that India, a major importer of cashew nuts, was the largest market for Guinea-Bissau's merchandise exports in 2021 (accounting for 79.2% of total exports), followed by Pakistan (12.2%) and Türkiye (2.7%).

Before the adoption of the franc CFA to replace the peso in 1997, demand for manufactured goods, machinery, fuel and food had ensured a high level of imports, the value of which on average exceeded 40% of annual GDP throughout the 1980s. However, foreign exchange controls and the closure of some state enterprises caused a large decline in imports of industrial raw materials in the subsequent decade, which was compounded by the upheaval caused by the 1998–99 conflict. According to ITC data, imports of goods and services experienced a significant expansion, from US $86.0m. in 2002 to an estimated $400.9m. in 2021, after contracting slightly in 2020 to an estimated $331.9m. The largest import categories (in terms of value) in 2020, according to the ITC, were mineral fuels, oils and distillates ($53.2m.), cereals and preparations of cereals ($35.3m.) and beverages ($33m.). In 2021 the principal sources of imports were Portugal (which provided 27.2% of total imports), China (22.2%) and Senegal (15.1%).

Every year since 2013 the approval of the annual budget has provoked considerable negotiations and tension between the Government and the ANP, and within the dominant Partido Africano da Independência da Guiné e Cabo Verde (PAIGC). The budget for 2013 was not endorsed by the legislature until July of that year, because of the extra-constitutional procedures and political instability that characterized the transitional period. In 2014 approval of the budget was delayed until the holding of elections (which eventually took place in April) and the appointment of a new Government able to prepare a new budget for the remainder of the year. Following the elections, the new administration successfully issued 15,000m. francs CFA in treasury bonds to clear wage arrears and submitted the 2014 and 2015 budgets, which were approved unanimously by the legislature. By July 2015 the Government had reduced wage arrears accumulated over the transitional period, from four months to two, and was expected to regularize these fully with the aid of a grant from the World Bank. In December 2015 a total of 15 PAIGC deputies abstained from a vote on the 2016 budget, accusing the Government of squandering public funds. Following the rapid dismissal and replacement of the dissident deputies, the budget was approved in January 2016 by the ANP, although the parliamentary opposition boycotted the session. Further tensions from May between President Vaz and the PAIGC over the appointment of a new Prime Minister (see *History*) meant that legislative proceedings ground to a near halt and further delayed the parliamentary vote on the 2017 budget. The budget was finally approved in June 2018, following the installation of a consensus Government in April. The adoption of the 2019

budget was similarly delayed by the holding of legislative elections in March and the appointment of a new Government in July (see *History*). The 2021 budget was approved in December 2020 by 54 of the 102 members of the ANP, although most of the 47 PAIGC deputies boycotted the vote. The budget for 2022, which included expenditures worth US $424m., was approved in December 2021 amid growing tensions between President Sissoco Embaló and the ANP.

An extensive reorganization of Guinea-Bissau's banking system took place after 1989, involving the replacement of the Banco Nacional da Guiné-Bissau by three institutions: a central bank, a commercial bank (Banco Internacional da Guiné-Bissau—BIG—which began operations in March 1990) and a national credit bank, established in September 1990, to channel investment. A fourth financial institution was responsible for managing aid receipts. The banking sector was severely weakened by the 1998–99 military conflict, which forced all banks to close temporarily. Major changes to the country's financial sector took place in the 2000s, with the closure of BIG and the Banco Totta e Açores and the emergence of several new private banks and many microfinance institutions. By 2015 five commercial banks together operated 22 branches across the country, and there were 18 licensed microfinance institutions. However, bank usage remained extremely low. While it was hoped that a decision by the regional bank, the Banque Centrale des Etats de l'Afrique de l'Ouest (BCEAO), to make most banking services free throughout the eight-country zone from October 2014 would encourage those currently excluded from the formal financial system to open a bank account, in 2020 only 155.8 out of every 1,000 adults held deposit accounts in commercial banks (up from 114 in 2017), according to the World Bank.

Guinea-Bissau applied to join the Franc Zone in November 1987, but withdrew its application in January 1990 following the formulation of an exchange rate agreement with Portugal linking the Guinea peso to the Portuguese escudo. However, Guinea-Bissau renewed its application in 1993 and joined UEMOA and the Franc Zone in 1997. The Guinea peso and the franc CFA co-existed for three months to allow for the gradual replacement, at foreign exchange offices, of the national currency at a rate of 1 franc CFA = 65 Guinea pesos. With the entry of Guinea-Bissau into the Franc Zone, the Banco Central da Guiné-Bissau ceased to operate as the country's central bank; its functions were assumed by the BCEAO, which has its headquarters in Senegal. Since the replacement of the French franc with the euro in 1999, the franc CFA has had a fixed peg to the euro of €1 = 655.957 francs CFA. Plans were under way in 2020 to replace the franc CFA with a new unit of currency—the eco—by the end of the year in at least eight countries (Benin, Burkina Faso, Guinea-Bissau, Côte d'Ivoire, Mali, Niger, Senegal and Togo). The eco would also be pegged to the euro, but France's financial support would be downgraded to an informal level. However, in light of dramatically higher levels of public spending by member states of the Franc Zone in 2020–21 as a result of the COVID-19 pandemic, the adoption of the eco was expected to be postponed by several years, as the convergence criteria for participation in the currency required limiting the budget deficit to below 3% of GDP, which few states appeared unlikely to achieve at that time.

DEVELOPMENT AND AID

Multilateral aid forms the major source of international assistance. According to the Organisation for Economic Co-operation and Development, in 2020 multilateral aid to Guinea-Bissau accounted for 77.1% of gross official development assistance (ODA) totalling US $156.4m. The largest donors in 2019–20, in terms of ODA, were the World Bank's International Development Association, which provided $34.8m. of gross ODA, the EU institutions, with $21.9m., and Portugal—traditionally the single most important bilateral donor—with $18.0m. The 2012 coup caused most donors to suspend their activities and disbursements, and aid inflows have fluctuated since then, reaching a peak of $153.6m. in 2014 but falling to $112.8m. in 2019, according to the IMF. Net aid inflows rose to an estimated $147.2m. in 2020.

Guinea-Bissau has been a signatory to the Lomé Conventions and their successor, the Cotonou Agreement—signed in Cotonou, Benin, in 2000 and ratified by Guinea-Bissau in 2003—and has been a regular recipient of European Development Fund assistance. Following the April 2010 attempted coup in Guinea-Bissau, the EU suspended part of its co-operation programmes; this suspension was extended in response to the April 2012 coup, pending a return to constitutional order. Immediately after the inauguration of the new Government in July 2014, the EU sent a mission to Guinea-Bissau to define key priorities for budgetary support and announced that it would release €60m. in pre-pledged assistance. The EU had ended all restrictions on the resumption of full co-operation with Guinea-Bissau by March 2015, and at a donor conference in the same month pledged US $172m. (out of $1,100m. in total pledges) to finance projects during 2015–25.

Guinea-Bissau's external debt rose dramatically throughout the post-independence period, from US $7.9m. in 1975 to $319m. in 1985 and to $936m. in 1996, according to the World Bank. Before the military conflict of 1998–99, faced with a stock of external debt of $921m. in 1997, equivalent to 362% of gross national income, the Government undertook efforts to renegotiate the country's external debt. In 1998 the IMF announced its approval of the Government's execution of its Structural Adjustment Programme for 1995–98, thus improving Guinea-Bissau's eligibility for debt relief under the initiative for heavily indebted poor countries (HIPC).

After preparing and submitting its first Poverty Reduction Strategy Paper in 2004, Guinea-Bissau was awarded two Staff-Monitored Programmes, two Emergency Post-Conflict Assistance programmes and one Extended Credit Facility (ECF) by the IMF between 2005 and 2010. In December 2010 the IMF and World Bank announced that the country had undertaken the requisite policy actions and, accordingly, had reached HIPC completion point. Debt relief amounting to about US $700m. of the estimated $1,200m. external debt was thus granted under the HIPC initiative, and Guinea-Bissau became eligible for additional assistance of $370m. under the Multilateral Debt Relief Initiative. This announcement was followed by several similar decisions by bilateral partners, including Brazil and Angola in May 2011. In June the 'Paris Club' of official creditors announced that a collective decision had been made to cancel $256m. of Guinea-Bissau's $285m. bilateral debt.

In July 2015 the IMF approved a new ECF for Guinea-Bissau, which was expected to enable the release of a total of US $23.9m. over the next three years. The first IMF staff visit to review the arrangement, in April 2016, cautiously noted that a good cashew harvest and favourable terms of trade, combined with an enhanced supply of electricity and water, had contributed to an economic recovery in 2015. The IMF delegation, however, emphasized that lack of progress in structural reforms, including in the banking sector, and a related weakening of development partner support, and spending pressure in the aftermath of recent political crises (see *History*), would hamper further growth. In June 2016 the IMF announced that it was suspending payments under the ECF (which were due to total $10.3m. in that year), following the Government's decision to bail out the country's two largest commercial banks, the Banco da União and Banco da Africa Ocidental, with some $16m. of public funds, against the IMF's previous advice. It was likely, however, that the IMF's decision was in part taken in reaction to the ongoing political uncertainty and absence of a unified new cabinet, following the dissolution of the Government in May and the appointment of a new Prime Minister by the President, against constitutional convention, and the wishes of the ruling PAIGC. As a result of the Government's decision later in 2016 to abandon the bank bailout and undertake further reforms, as well as owing to signs of greater political stability, relations with the IMF improved. The Executive Board of the Fund approved a disbursement of $6.9m. at the end of 2016 and another disbursement, of $4.1m., in July 2017, following a third review under the ECF. Satisfactory fourth and fifth reviews enabled two further disbursements, of $4.3m. each, in December 2017 and June 2018, respectively. At the end of 2017 the Government requested, and was granted, a one-year extension of the

ECF. Further IMF staff visits in late 2018 and early 2019 underlined the financing gap and growing budget deficit (estimated at 5.1% of GDP assessed on a commitment basis in May 2019), owing to higher expenditure and the uncertainty of the political situation (see *History*).

The Government expressed interest in a new ECF, and it was agreed that discussions about this would be held during the next IMF staff visit, which took place in September 2019. This visit enabled the IMF to conduct a diagnostic of weaknesses in governance and to outline the next steps towards reform, before developing a new programme in Guinea-Bissau. In April 2020, in response to the COVID-19 pandemic, the IMF approved debt relief for the country under its adapted Catastrophe Containment and Relief Trust. The relief was extended by six months in October and again in April 2021 as the negative economic effects of the health crisis continued. Meanwhile, in February the IMF approved a disbursement of US $20.5m. under its Rapid Credit Facility to help Guinea-Bissau to meet urgent balance-of-payments and fiscal needs stemming from the pandemic. In May the Fund approved a nine-month Staff Monitored Programme (SMP) to support the Government's reform package and to pave the way for a new ECF. Reviews of the SMP were completed in November 2021, and in February and April 2022, when an Article IV consultation procedure was also completed. Progress on the agreed fiscal consolidation and reform programme was considered satisfactory. Following this, the Government once again expressed interest in reaching agreement on a new ECF arrangement with the IMF.

INDUSTRIAL ACTION

Reflecting the characteristics of its largely rural and informal economy, Guinea-Bissau's formal employment spectrum is relatively small, and to a large extent accounted for by the public sector. For this reason, industrial negotiations and labour unrest in the country have typically been centred on various branches of public administration. A single, state-controlled trade union confederation was created after independence. Only much later, in the context of economic and political liberalization, were independent trade unions legalized and a new trade union confederation, the Confederação Geral dos Sindicatos Independentes da Guiné-Bissau, established.

A period of chronic labour unrest occurred in the early 2000s, as a result of the Government's financial problems and its difficulties in paying civil servants' wages on time. Strikes took place in 2002–03, and by August 2003 many civil servants had not been paid for nine months. The lack of resources and the huge accumulation of wage arrears led to further strikes in early 2004. In 2008 the World Bank granted an additional US $20m. in budgetary support to pay the salary arrears of primary school teachers. The Government that was appointed in January 2009 immediately began paying salary arrears, with financial support from various sources (particularly the IMF), which tended to reduce the frequency and intensity of strikes. However, industrial action was not motivated solely by unpaid salaries: for example, magistrates and court officials staged strike action on several occasions in 2010–13, in support of their demands for better pay and working conditions. Following the April 2012 coup, the entire public administration went on strike, to demand the restoration of constitutional order and protest against the non-payment of public sector salaries. This strike was ended in late May, after the new transitional Government settled part of the arrears. However, the 2012/13 and 2013/14 school years were severely affected by teachers' strikes prompted by salary arrears, with schools across the country closed for weeks at a time on several occasions, and the cancellation of the 2012/13 academic year was only narrowly averted. Guinea-Bissau has since experienced numerous further strikes by different public sector bodies, generally motivated by a combination of the non-payment of salaries and the ongoing political ferment.

From June 2018 the União Nacional dos Trabalhadores da Guiné (UNTG)—the country's largest civil servants' trade union, with about 8,000 members out of a total of some 13,000 civil servants—commenced an open-ended strike to call for higher salaries. Public radio and television workers joined the strike from early August. In October a strike was launched by the Federação Nacional de Transportadores Rodoviários in protest against extortion by the police. Regular waves of strikes marked the first half of 2019, as civil servants exercised pressure on the Government before and after the legislative elections that took place in March. In September 2020 the Sindicato de Enfermeiros e Técnicos de Saúde e Afins (the union representing nurses and health care workers) launched a seven-day strike demanding the disbursement of salary arrears and COVID-19-related subsidies; the provision of protective equipment to prevent the spread of the virus; and the provision of a structured career path for health care workers. The strike was called off after one day, following discussions with government representatives. The UNTG organized further strikes between December 2020 and September 2021 to protest against new taxes and tax increases, the unauthorized recruitment of employees in a number of government departments and poor working conditions, as well as to demand the payment of arrears to contract workers in the health care and education sectors.

Statistical Survey

Source (unless otherwise stated): Instituto Nacional de Estatística Guiné-Bissau, Av. Amílcar Cabral, CP 6, Bissau; tel. 443225457; e-mail inegbissau@gmail .com; internet www.stat-guinebissau.com.

Area and Population

AREA, POPULATION AND DENSITY

Area (sq km)	36,125*
Population (census results)	
1 December 1991	979,203
15–29 March 2009	
Males	702,826
Females	746,404
Total	1,449,230
Population (official projections at mid-year)	
2020	1,624,979
2021	1,619,869
2022	1,637,184
Density (per sq km) at mid-2022	45.3

* 13,948 sq miles.

POPULATION BY AGE AND SEX
(official projections at mid-2022)

	Males	Females	Total
0–14 years	368,069	351,755	719,824
15–64 years	444,417	473,789	918,206
65 years and over	12,661	17,218	29,879
Total	825,147	842,762	1,667,909

POPULATION BY REGION
(2009 census)

Bafatá . . .	200,884		Quinará . . .	60,777
Biombo . . .	93,039		Sector Autónomo	
Bolama/Bijagós . .	32,424		Bissau (SAB) .	365,097
Cacheu . . .	185,053		Tombali . . .	91,089
Gabú	205,608		**Total**	1,449,230
Oio	215,259			

PRINCIPAL TOWNS
(population at 2009 census)

Bissau (capital) .	365,097*		Bigene	51,412
Gabú†	81,495		Farim	48,264
Bafatá	68,956		Mansôa	46,046
Bissorã	56,585		Pitche	45,594

* Figure for Sector Autónomo Bissau (SAB) administrative division.
† Formerly Nova Lamego.

Mid-2021 (incl. suburbs, UN projection): Bissau (capital) 620,974 (Source: UN, *World Urbanization Prospects: The 2018 Revision*).

BIRTHS AND DEATHS

	2015	2016	2017
Birth rate (per 1,000)	40.5	39.8	39.2
Death rate (per 1,000)	12.2	11.8	11.4

2020: Birth rate 36.4 per 1,000 persons.

Life expectancy (years at birth, estimates): 58.6 (males 56.6; females 60.5) in 2020 (Source: World Bank, World Development Indicators database).

ECONOMICALLY ACTIVE POPULATION
('000, FAO estimates at mid-2015)

	Males	Females	Total
Agriculture, etc.	281	238	519
Total labour force (incl. others) .	415	254	669

Source: FAO.

Health and Welfare

KEY INDICATORS

Total fertility rate (children per woman, 2020)	4.3
Under-5 mortality rate (per 1,000 live births, 2020) . . .	76.8
HIV/AIDS (% of persons aged 15–49, 2019) . . .	3.4
COVID-19: Cumulative confirmed deaths (per 100,000 persons at 31 August 2022)	8.5
COVID-19: Fully vaccinated population (% of total population at 28 August 2022)	17.5
Physicians (per 1,000 head, 2020)	0.2
Hospitals (per 100,000 head, 2013)	56.4
Domestic health expenditure (2019): US $ per head (PPP) .	11.9
Domestic health expenditure (2019): % of GDP . . .	0.5
Domestic health expenditure (2019): public (% of total current expenditure)	6.4
Access to improved water resources (% of persons, 2020) .	59
Access to improved sanitation facilities (% of persons, 2020) .	18
Total carbon dioxide emissions ('000 metric tons, 2018) .	310
Carbon dioxide emissions per head (metric tons, 2018) . .	0.2
Human Development Index (2021): ranking	177
Human Development Index (2021): value	0.483

Note: For data on COVID-19 vaccinations, 'fully vaccinated' denotes receipt of all doses specified by approved vaccination regime (Sources: Johns Hopkins University and Our World in Data). Data on health expenditure refer to current general government expenditure in each case. For more information on sources and further definitions for all indicators, see Health and Welfare Statistics: Sources and Definitions section (europaworld.com/credits).

Agriculture

PRINCIPAL CROPS
('000 metric tons, FAO estimates unless otherwise indicated)

	2018	2019	2020
Cashew nuts	161.7	159.2	160.6
Cassava (Manioc)	47.6	45.0	46.5
Coconuts	40.7	40.9	40.9
Groundnuts, with shell . . .	42.8	42.5	42.6
Maize*	7.0	7.0	7.0
Millet*	18.0	20.0	24.0
Oil palm fruit	80.5	80.6	81.0
Oranges	6.9	6.8	6.9
Plantains and others . . .	54.0	54.1	53.9
Rice, paddy*	176.0	187.0	198.0
Sorghum*	21.0	22.0	21.0
Sugar cane	6.7	6.7	6.7

* Unofficial figure(s).

Aggregate production ('000 metric tons, may include official, semi-official or estimated data): Total cereals 224.6 in 2018, 238.6 in 2019, 252.6 in 2020; Total fruit (primary) 109.3 in 2018, 109.3 in 2019, 109.1 in 2020; Total oilcrops 169.2 in 2018, 169.2 in 2019, 169.8 in 2020; Total roots and tubers 128.1 in 2018, 126.0 in 2019, 127.9 in 2020; Total vegetables (primary) 39.5 in 2018, 39.6 in 2019, 39.4 in 2020.

Source: FAO.

LIVESTOCK
('000 head, year ending September, FAO estimates)

	2018	2019	2020
Cattle	697	709	721
Chickens	2,076	2,125	2,180
Goats	782	799	817
Pigs	476	483	474
Sheep	494	509	528

Source: FAO.

LIVESTOCK PRODUCTS
('000 metric tons, FAO estimates)

	2018	2019	2020
Cattle hides, fresh	1.6	1.6	1.7
Cattle meat	7.0	7.2	7.3
Cows' milk	18.0	19.0	19.2
Chicken meat	3.0	3.1	3.2
Goats' milk	14.6	14.8	15.1
Pig meat	13.8	14.0	14.1
Sheep's (Ewe's) milk	7.2	7.3	7.5

Source: FAO.

Forestry

ROUNDWOOD REMOVALS
('000 cubic metres, excluding bark, FAO estimates)

	2018	2019	2020
Sawlogs, veneer logs and logs for sleepers	1.9	1.9	1.9
Other industrial wood	130.0	130.0	130.0
Fuel wood	2,893.7	2,893.7	2,963.6
Total	3,025.6	3,025.6	3,095.5

Source: FAO.

SAWNWOOD PRODUCTION
('000 cubic metres, including railway sleepers, FAO estimates)

	2018	2019	2020
Total	16	16	16

Note: Annual production assumed to be unchanged from 1971.

Source: FAO.

Fishing

(metric tons, live weight)

	2018	2019*	2020
Capture	52,254	60,150	62,392
Atlantic chub mackerel . . .	3,049	2,110	1,114
Grunts and sweetlips . . .	280	1,270	2,233
Jacks and crevalles	4,970	4,380	3,672
Sardinellas	34,421	41,090	46,596
Other marine fishes	9,162	10,990	8,567
Aquaculture	25	5	0
Total catch*	52,279	60,155	62,392

* FAO estimates.

Source: FAO.

Industry

SELECTED PRODUCTS
('000 metric tons unless otherwise indicated)

	2001	2002	2003
Hulled rice	69.1	68.4	67.7
Groundnuts (processed) . . .	6.8	6.7	6.6
Bakery products	7.6	7.7	7.9
Frozen fish	1.7	1.7	1.7
Dry and smoked fish	3.6	3.7	3.8
Vegetable oils (million litres) . .	3.6	3.6	3.7
Beverages (million litres) . . .	3.5	0.0	0.0
Dairy products (million litres) .	1.1	0.9	0.9
Wood products	4.7	4.5	4.4
Soap	2.6	2.5	2.4
Electrical energy (million kWh) .	18.9	19.4	15.8

Source: IMF, *Guinea-Bissau: Selected Issues and Statistical Appendix* (March 2005).

Electrical energy (million kWh, estimates): 81 in 2018; 82 in 2019; 82 in 2020 (Source: UN Energy Statistics Database).

Finance

CURRENCY AND EXCHANGE RATES
Monetary Units
100 centimes = 1 franc de la Communauté Financière Africaine (CFA).

Sterling, Dollar and Euro Equivalents (31 May 2022)
£1 sterling = 770.825 francs CFA;
US $1 = 612.300 francs CFA;
€1 = 655.957 francs CFA;
10,000 francs CFA = £12.97 = $16.33 = €15.24.

Average Exchange Rate (francs CFA per US $)
2019   585.911
2020   575.586
2021   554.531

Note: An exchange rate of 1 French franc = 50 francs CFA, established in 1948, remained in force until January 1994, when the CFA franc was devalued by 50%, with the exchange rate adjusted to 1 French franc = 100 francs CFA. This relationship to French currency remained in effect with the introduction of the euro on 1 January 1999. From that date, accordingly, a fixed exchange rate of €1 = 655.957 francs CFA has been in operation.

BUDGET
('000 million francs CFA)

Revenue*	2019	2020	2021†
Tax revenue	79.1	67.8	93.5
Non-tax revenue	26.5	32.0	28.9
Total	105.6	99.8	122.4

Expenditure	2019	2020	2021†
Current expenditure	125.2	143.4	148.5
Wages and salaries	47.5	57.0	58.2
Goods and services	18.7	25.4	28.7
Transfers	27.1	27.3	25.9
Other current expenditures .	22.7	20.5	20.3
Scheduled interest payments .	9.2	13.2	15.4
Capital expenditure and net lending	38.5	75.7	87.8
Total	163.7	219.1	236.3

* Excluding budget grants received ('000 million francs CFA): 24.5 in 2019; 35.0 in 2020; 60.1 in 2021 (projection).
† Preliminary.

Source: IMF, *Guinea-Bissau: 2022 Article IV Consultation and Third Review under the Staff-Monitored Program; Press Release; and Statement by the Executive Director for Guinea-Bissau* (June 2022).

CENTRAL BANK RESERVES
(US $ million at 31 December)

	2019	2020	2021
IMF special drawing rights . .	25.09	26.16	83.41
Reserve position in IMF . . .	5.59	5.82	5.70
Foreign exchange	1.39	4.60	1.59
Total	32.07	36.58	90.70

Source: IMF, *International Financial Statistics.*

MONEY SUPPLY
('000 million francs CFA at 31 December)

	2019	2020	2021
Currency outside depository corporations	235.26	246.53	251.38
Transferable deposits	74.29	88.83	106.53
Other deposits	56.41	63.88	71.80
Broad money	365.97	399.24	429.71

Source: IMF, *International Financial Statistics.*

COST OF LIVING
(Consumer Price Index; base: 2003 = 100 unless otherwise indicated)

	2010	2011	2012
Food*	99.4	106.7	110.1
All items (incl. others) . . .	122.2	128.3	131.1

* Base: 2008=100.
Source: ILO.

All items (Consumer Price Index; base: 2010 = 100): 112.0 in 2017; 112.4 in 2018; 112.7 in 2019 (Source: IMF, *International Financial Statistics*).

NATIONAL ACCOUNTS
(million francs CFA at current prices)

Expenditure on the Gross Domestic Product

	2018	2019	2020
Government final consumption expenditure	112,253	123,831	117,076
Private final consumption expenditure	667,250	756,363	700,213
Gross fixed capital formation . .	52,248	39,229	57,498
Change in inventories	−13,679	−1,566	609
Total domestic expenditure .	818,073	917,857	875,396
Exports of goods and services . .	210,295	169,752	118,667
Less Imports of goods and services	239,914	278,470	249,396
Statistical discrepancy	−20,574	−34,406	12,228
GDP in purchasers' values	767,879	774,732	756,895
GDP at constant 2015 prices .	720,941	753,384	742,836

Gross Domestic Product by Economic Activity

	2018	2019	2020
Agriculture, hunting, forestry and fishing	256,771	256,395	254,344
Mining, quarrying and utilities .	11,380	7,580	8,449
Manufacturing	76,384	91,591	87,926
Construction	17,847	12,450	14,465
Trade, restaurants and hotels .	210,305	218,427	205,730
Transport and communications .	53,285	54,042	52,322
Public administration and other services	158,156	161,492	157,250
Sub-total	784,129	801,978	780,485
Indirect taxes (net)*	−16,250	−27,246	−23,590
GDP at purchasers' values .	767,879	774,732	756,895

* Figures obtained as residuals.
Source: UN, National Accounts Main Aggregates Database.

BALANCE OF PAYMENTS
('000 million francs CFA)

	2019	2020*	2021†
Exports of goods f.o.b.	145.7	114.8	154.4
Imports of goods f.o.b.	−196.4	−180.0	−189.9
Balance on goods	−50.6	−65.2	−35.5
Services and incomes (net) . .	−72.6	−69.5	−82.0
Balance on goods, services and primary income	−123.3	−134.7	−117.5
Unrequited current transfers (net)	48.9	66.3	78.6
Current balance	−74.4	−68.4	−38.9
Capital account (net)	16.1	22.6	23.6
Direct investment (net) . . .	41.8	7.0	10.1
Other investment (net) . . .	34.2	12.2	15.1
Net errors and omissions . . .	−4.3	6.3	—
Overall balance	13.2	−20.3	9.9

* Preliminary.
† Projections.

Source: IMF, *Guinea-Bissau: First Review Under the Staff Monitored Program* (November 2021).

External Trade

PRINCIPAL COMMODITIES
(US $ million)

Imports c.i.f.	2017	2018	2019
Cereals	49	36	36
Mineral fuels and oils	—	33	33
Beverages, spirits and vinegar	—	14	14
Electrical machinery and equipment	—	13	13
Vehicles other than railway or tramway	—	12	12
Total (incl. others)	66	190	190

Exports f.o.b.	2017	2018	2019
Edible fruit and nuts	198	172	172
Wood and articles of wood, charcoal	—	81	81
Total (incl. others)	196	253	253

Source: African Development Bank.

Trade aggregates ('000 million francs CFA, preliminary): Total imports c.i.f. 201.4 (Food products 59.3; Petroleum products 32.7) in 2021; Total exports f.o.b. 158.0 (Cashew nuts 152.8) in 2021 (Source: IMF, *Guinea-Bissau: 2022 Article IV Consultation and Third Review under the Staff-Monitored Program; Press Release; and Statement by the Executive Director for Guinea-Bissau*—June 2022).

PRINCIPAL TRADING PARTNERS
(US $ million)

Imports	2017	2018	2019
China, People's Republic . . .	0	11	11
Netherlands	0	12	12
Pakistan	—	15	15
Portugal	6	73	73
Senegal	5	19	19
Total (incl. others)	66	190	190

Exports	2017	2018	2019
China, People's Republic . . .	0	17	17
India	124	15	15
United Arab Emirates	4	—	—
Viet Nam	27	2	2
Total (incl. others)	196	253	253

Source: African Development Bank.

Transport

SHIPPING

Flag Registered Fleet
(at 31 December)

	2019	2020	2021
Number of vessels	26	26	28
Total displacement (grt) . . .	24,033	25,802	24,813

Source: Lloyd's List Intelligence (www.bit.ly/LLintelligence).

Tourism

TOURIST ARRIVALS BY NATIONALITY

	2005	2006	2007
Cabo Verde	159	401	1,498
China, People's Republic . . .	46	659	1,488
Cuba	29	329	309
France	599	834	2,984
Italy	213	343	1,871
Korea, Republic	36	523	1,289
Portugal	1,552	2,599	2,245
Senegal	235	921	2,798
Spain	324	231	1,458
USA	57	320	265
Total (incl. others)	4,978	11,617	30,092

Total tourist arrivals ('000): 55 in 2018; 52 in 2019 (provisional).

Tourism receipts (US $ million, excl. passenger transport): 12 in 2016; 16 in 2017; 20 in 2018.

Source: World Tourism Organization.

Communications Media

	2018	2019	2020
Mobile telephone subscriptions ('000)	1,481	1,590	1,914
Broadband subscriptions, fixed .	1,204	1,227	2,383
Broadband subscriptions, mobile ('000)	332	705	705
Internet users (% of population) .	22.0	28.0	n.a.

Telephones ('000 main lines in use): 5.0 in 2014.

Source: International Telecommunication Union.

Education

(2009/10 unless otherwise indicated, UNESCO estimates)

	Teachers	Students Males	Students Females	Students Total
Pre-primary . .	309	4,360	4,590	8,950
Primary	5,371	144,075	134,815	278,890
Secondary: general .		46,445	31,581	78,026
Secondary: technical and vocational . .	} 1,913* {	656†	239†	895†
Tertiary† . . .	32	399	74	473

* 1999.
† 2000/01.

Institutions (1999): Pre-primary 54; Primary 759.

Students (2005/06): Primary 269,287; Secondary 55,176; Tertiary 3,689.

Teachers (2005/06): Primary 4,327; Secondary 1,480; Tertiary 25.

Source: UNESCO Institute for Statistics.

Pupil-teacher ratio (primary education, UNESCO estimate): 51.9 in 2009/10 (Source: UNESCO Institute for Statistics).

Adult literacy rate (UNESCO estimates): 59.8% (males 71.7%; females 48.1%) in 2015.

Directory

The Constitution

A new Constitution for the Republic of Guinea-Bissau was approved by the National People's Assembly (Assembleia Nacional Popular—ANP) on 16 May 1984 and amended in May 1991, November 1996 and July 1999 (see below). The main provisions of the 1984 Constitution are:

Guinea-Bissau is an anti-colonialist and anti-imperialist Republic and a state of revolutionary national democracy, based on the people's participation in undertaking, controlling and directing public activities.

The economy of Guinea-Bissau shall be organized on the principles of state direction and planning. The state shall control the country's foreign trade.

The representative bodies in the country are the ANP and the regional councils. Other state bodies draw their powers from these. The members of the regional councils shall be directly elected. Members of the councils must be more than 18 years of age. The ANP shall have 150 members, who are to be elected by the regional councils from among their own members. All members of the ANP must be over 21 years of age.

The ANP shall elect a 15-member Council of State, to which its powers are delegated between sessions of the Assembly. The ANP also elects the President of the Council of State, who is also automatically Head of the Government and Commander-in-Chief of the Armed Forces. The Council of State shall subsequently elect two Vice-Presidents and a Secretary. The President and Vice-Presidents of the Council of State form part of the Government, as do Ministers, Secretaries of State and the Governor of the National Bank.

The Constitution can be revised at any time by the ANP on the initiative of the deputies themselves, or of the Council of State or the Government.

Note: Constitutional amendments providing for the operation of a multi-party political system were approved unanimously by the ANP in May 1991. The amendments stipulated that new parties seeking registration must obtain a minimum of 2,000 signatures, with at least 100 signatures from each of the nine provinces. (These provisions were adjusted in August to 1,000 and 50 signatures, respectively.) In addition, the amendments provided for the ANP (reduced from 150 to 100 members) to be elected by universal adult suffrage, and for the operation of a free-market economy. Multi-party elections took place in July 1994.

In November 1996 the legislature approved a constitutional amendment providing for Guinea-Bissau to seek membership of the Union Economique et Monétaire Ouest-Africaine and of the Franc Zone.

In July 1999 constitutional amendments were introduced limiting the tenure of presidential office to two terms and abolishing the death penalty. It was also stipulated that the country's principal offices of state could be held only by Guinea-Bissau nationals born of Guinea-Bissau parents. In the legislative elections held in November, the total number of seats in the ANP was increased to 102 through the creation of two new seats reserved for Guinea-Bissau citizens living abroad.

The Government

HEAD OF STATE

President: UMARO SISSOCO EMBALÓ (took office 27 February 2020).

COUNCIL OF MINISTERS
(October 2022)

Prime Minister: NUNO GOMES NABIAM.

Deputy Prime Minister, Minister of the Presidency of the Council of Ministers and of Parliamentary Affairs, Economic Co-ordinator: SOARES SAMBÚ.

Minister of State for Foreign Affairs, International Co-operation and Communities: SUZI CARLA BARBOSA.

Minister of State for the Interior and Public Order: BOTCHE CANDÉ.

Minister of State for Defence and Liberation War Veterans: MARCIANO SILVA BARBEIRO.

Minister of Natural Resources: DIONÍSIO CABI.

Minister of Agriculture and Rural Development: SANDJI FATI.

Minister of Fisheries: ORLANDO MENDES VIEGAS.

Minister of Territorial Administration and Local Government: FERNANDO GOMES.

Minister of Justice and Human Rights: TERESA ALEXANDRINA DA SILVA.

Minister of Energy and Industry: AUGUSTO POQUENA.

Minister of the Economy, Planning and Regional Integration: JOSÉ CARLOS VARELA CASIMIRO.

Minister of Finance: ILÍDIO VIEIRA TÉ.

Minister of Tourism and Handicrafts: FERNANDO VAZ.

Minister of Social Communication: FERNANDO MENDONÇA.

Minister of Transport and Communications: ARISTIDES OCANTE DA SILVA.

Minister of Trade: ABAS DJALÓ.

Minister of National Education: MARTINA MONIZ.

Minister of Higher Education and Scientific Research: TIMÓTEO SABA M'BUNDE.

Minister of Public Administration, Labour, Employment and Social Security: CIRILO MAMASALIU DJALÓ.

Minister of Public Health: Dr DIONÍSIO CUMBA.

Minister of Women, the Family and Social Solidarity: MARIA DA CONCEIÇÃO EVORA.

Minister of Public Works, Housing and Town Planning: FIDÉLIS FORBS.

Minister of the Environment and Biodiversity: VIRIATO SOARES CASSAMÁ.

Minister of Culture, Youth and Sport: AUGUSTO GOMES.

There were also 11 secretaries of state.

MINISTRIES

Office of the President: Bissau; e-mail gab.comunicacao.presidenciagb@gmail.com; internet fb.com/generaldepovo12.

Office of the Prime Minister: Av. dos Combatentes da Liberdade da Pátria, CP 137, Bissau; tel. 443211308; internet www.gov.gw.

Ministry of Agriculture and Rural Development: Av. dos Combatentes da Liberdade da Pátria, CP 102, Bissau; tel. 443221200.

Ministry of Culture, Youth and Sport: Bissau.

Ministry of Defence and Liberation War Veterans: Amura, Bissau; tel. 443223646.

Ministry of the Economy, Planning and Regional Integration: Av. dos Combatentes da Liberdade da Pátria, CP 67, Bissau; tel. 443203670.

Ministry of the Environment and Biodiversity: Bissau.

Ministry of Finance: Bissau.

Ministry of Fisheries: Av. Amilcar Cabral 102, Bissau.

Ministry of Foreign Affairs, International Co-operation and Communities: Av. dos Combatentes da Liberdade da Pátria, Bissau; tel. 443204301.

Ministry of the Interior and Public Order: Av. Unidade Africana, Bissau; tel. 443203781.

Ministry of Justice and Human Rights: Av. Amílcar Cabral, CP 17, Bissau; tel. 443202185.

Ministry of National Education: Rua Areolino Cruz, Bissau; tel. 443202244.

Ministry of Natural Resources and Energy: CP 311, Bissau; tel. 443215659.

Ministry of the Presidency of the Council of Ministers and Parliamentary Affairs: Bissau.

Ministry of Public Administration, Labour, Employment and Social Security: Bissau.

Ministry of Public Health: CP 50, Bissau; tel. 443204438.

Ministry of Public Works, Housing and Town Planning: Av. dos Combatentes da Liberdade da Pátria, CP 14, Bissau; tel. 443206575.

Ministry of Social Communication: Bissau.

Ministry of Territorial Administration and Local Government: Bissau.

Ministry of Tourism and Handicrafts: Bissau.

Ministry of Trade and Industry: Bissau.

Ministry of Transport and Communications: Bissau.

Ministry of Women, the Family and Social Solidarity: Bissau.

President

Presidential Election, First Round, 24 November 2019

Candidate	Valid votes	% of valid votes
Domingos Simões Pereira (PAIGC) . .	222,870	40.13
Umaro Sissoco Embaló (MADEM-G15) .	153,530	27.65
Nuno Gomes Nabiam (APU-PDGB) . .	73,063	13.16
José Mário Vaz 'Jomav' (Ind.) . . .	68,933	12.41
Carlos Gomes Júnior (Ind.)	14,766	2.66
Others*	22,186	3.99
Total	555,348†	100.00

* There were seven other candidates.
† In addition, there were 5,821 blank and 5,304 spoiled ballots.

Presidential Election, Second Round, 29 December 2019

Candidate	Valid votes	% of valid votes
Umaro Sissoco Embaló (MADEM-G15) .	293,359	53.55
Domingos Simões Pereira (PAIGC) . .	254,468	46.45
Total	547,827*	100.00

* In addition, there were 3,466 blank and 2,228 spoiled ballots.

Legislature

Assembleia Nacional Popular: Palácio Colinas de Boé, Av. Francisco Mendes, CP 219, Bissau; tel. 443201991; e-mail contato@anpguinebissau.org; internet www.parlamento.gw.
President: CIPRIANO CASSAMÁ.

General Election, 10 March 2019

Party	Valid votes	% of valid votes	Seats
Partido Africano da Independência da Guiné e Cabo Verde (PAIGC) . .	212,148	35.21	47
Movimento para a Alternância Democrática (MADEM-G15).	126,935	21.07	27
Partido para a Renovação Social (PRS)	127,104	21.10	21
Assembleia do Povo Unido-Partido Democrático da Guiné-Bissau (APU-PDGB) .	51,049	8.47	5
Partido para a Nova Democracia (PND) . . .	9,019	1.50	1
União para a Mudança (UM) .	8,535	1.42	1
Others	67,591	11.22	—
Total	602,381*	100.00	102

* Excluding 42,704 invalid votes.

Election Commission

Comissão Nacional de Eleições (CNE): Av. Unidade Africana, CP 44, Bissau; tel. 966900976; e-mail info@cne.gw; internet cne.gw; Pres. Dr N'PABI CABI (acting).

Political Organizations

Assembleia do Povo Unido-Partido Democrático da Guiné-Bissau (APU-PDGB): Av. da Unidade Africana, Bissau; tel. 955557111; e-mail apu.pdgb2014@gmail.com; internet www.apu-pdgb.com; f. 2014; Leader NUNO GOMES NABIAM.

Centro Democrático (CD): Bissau; f. 2006; Pres. EMPOSSA Ié; Sec.-Gen. VICTOR DJELOMBO.

Frente Patriótica de Salvação Nacional (FREPASNA): Bissau; f. 2018; Leader BACIRO DJÁ.

Movimento para a Alternância Democrática da Guiné-Bissau (MADEM-G15): Av. da Unidade Africana, Bissau; e-mail info.geral@mademg15.org; internet www.mademg15.org; f. 2018; Nat. Co-ordinator BRAIMA CAMARÁ.

Movimento Patriótico (MP): Bissau; internet www.mp-gb.com; Pres. JOSÉ PAULO SEMEDO.

Partido Africano da Independência da Guiné e Cabo Verde (PAIGC): Praça dos Heróis Nacionais, CP 329, Bissau; tel. 6877014; e-mail contato@partidopaigc.com; internet partidopaigc.com; f. 1956; fmrly the ruling party in both Guinea-Bissau and Cabo Verde; although Cabo Verde withdrew from the PAIGC following the coup in Guinea-Bissau in Nov. 1980, Guinea-Bissau has retained the party name and initials; Pres. DOMINGOS SIMÕES PEREIRA; Nat. Sec. ALY HIJAZI.

Partido da Convergência Democrática (PCD): Bissau; Pres. VICENTE FERNANDES.

Partido Democrático Socialista (PDS): Bissau; f. 2006; Pres. JOÃO SECO MAMADÚ MANÉ.

Partido para a Nova Democracia (PND): Bissau; f. 2007; Pres. IAIA DJALÓ.

Partido Popular Democrático (PPD): Bissau; f. 2006; Pres. MARIA LUIZA EMBALÓ.

Partido para a Renovação Social (PRS): c/o Assembleia Nacional Popular, Bissau; internet www.fb.com/prsgb1992; f. 1992; Pres. ALBERTO NAMBEIA EMBALÓ; Sec.-Gen. FLORENTINO MENDES PEREIRA.

Partido Republicano para a Independência e o Desenvolvimento (PRID): Bissau; f. 2008; Leader AFONSO TÉ.

Partido dos Trabalhadores (PT): Bissau; f. 2002; left-wing; Pres. ARREGADO MANTENQUE TÉ.

Partido da Unidade Nacional (PUN): Bissau; tel. 955334952; internet fb.com/Partido-da-Unidade-Nacional-PUN-112085990691954/; f. 2002; Leader IDRIÇA DJALÓ.

União para a Mudança (UM): Bissau; Pres. AGNELO REGALA.

União Nacional para Democracia e Progresso (UNDP): Bissau; f. 1998; Pres. ABUBACAR BALDÉ.

União Patriótica Guinéense (UPG): Bissau; f. 2004 by dissident members of the RGB; Pres. FRANCISCA VAZ TURPIN.

Diplomatic Representation

EMBASSIES IN GUINEA-BISSAU

Angola: Av. Combatentes de Liberdade da Pátria, Rua Abodoulaye Fadiga, Ex-Palace Hotel, CP 132, Bissau; tel. 969132525; e-mail embaixada.guinebissau@mirex.gov.ao; internet www.embaixadadeangola.gw/index.php; Ambassador DANIEL ANTÓNIO ROSA.

Brazil: Rua São Tomé, Esquina Rua Moçambique, CP 29, Bissau; tel. 443212549; e-mail brasemb.bissau@itamaraty.gov.br; internet www.gov.br/mre/pt-br/embaixada-bissau; Ambassador FÁBIO GUIMARÃES FRANCO.

Cabo Verde: Bissau; Ambassador CAMILO LEITÃO DA GRAÇA.

China, People's Republic: Bairro de Penha, CP 66, Bissau; tel. 955804048; e-mail gw@mofcom.gov.cn; internet gw.china-embassy.gov.cn; Ambassador GUO CE.

Cuba: Rua Joaquim N'Com 1, y Victorino Costa, CP 258, Bissau; tel. 443213579; e-mail embagbisau@eguitel.com; internet misiones.minrex.gob.cu/es/guinea-bissau; Ambassador C. RAÚL DE LA PEÑA SILVA.

France: Bairro de Penha, Av. dos Combatentes da Liberdade da Pátria, CP 195, 1011 Bissau; tel. 955393280; e-mail cad.bissao-amba@diplomatie.gouv.fr; internet gw.ambafrance.org; Ambassador TERENCE WILLS.

The Gambia: 47 Victorino Costa, Chao de Papel, CP 529, 1037 Bissau; tel. 443205085; e-mail gambiaembbissau@hotmail.com; Ambassador AMIE FABUREH.

Guinea: Rua 14, No. 9, CP 396, Bissau; tel. 443212681; e-mail ambaguibissau@mae.gov.gn; Ambassador Gen. ANSOUMANE CAMARA.

Libya: Rua 16, CP 362, Bissau; tel. 443212006; Representative DOKALI ALI MUSTAFA.

Nigeria: 6 Av. 14 de Novembro, CP 199, Bissau; tel. 443201018; e-mail nigeria.bissau@foreignaffairs.gov.ng; Ambassador JOHN JAMES USANGA.

Portugal: Av. Cidade de Lisboa, CP 76, 1021 Bissau; tel. 966990000; e-mail bissau@mne.pt; internet bissau.embaixadaportugal.mne.gov.pt; Ambassador JOSÉ RUI VELEZ CAROÇO.

Russian Federation: Av. dos Combatentes da Liberdade da Pátria, Bairro Penha, CP 308, Bissau; tel. 966268604; e-mail russiagb@eguitel.com; internet guinea-bissau.mid.ru; Ambassador ALEKSANDR R. EGOROV.

Senegal: Rua Omar Torrijos 43A, Bissau; tel. 443212944; Ambassador Gen. ABDOULAYE DIENG.

South Africa: Av. Amilcar Cabral (opp. UDIB Bldg), CP 1334, Bissau; tel. 966678910; e-mail bissau@dirco.gov.za; internet www .dirco.gov.za/guinea-bissau; Ambassador MPHAKAMA NYANGWENI.

Spain: Praza Dos Hèroes Naçionais, Bissau; tel. 966722246; e-mail emb.bissau@maec.es; internet www.exteriores.gob.es/embajadas/ bissau; Ambassador ANTÓNIO GONZÁLEZ ZAVALA PEÑA.

Türkiye (Turkey): Bissau; Ambassador ALI SAIT AKIN.

Judicial System

The judicial system comprises a Supreme Court, a Court of Appeal, nine Regional Courts (of which five are functional) and 42 Sectoral Courts (of which 21 are functional). The Supreme Court is the final court of appeal in criminal and civil cases and consists of nine judges. The Regional Courts are courts of first instance and deal with felony cases and major civil cases. They also hear appeals from the Sectoral Courts. The Sectoral Courts hear minor civil cases with maximum fines of 1m. francs CFA and criminal cases punishable by sentences of up to three years' imprisonment. There are plans to establish a second Court of Appeal, in Bafatá, and other Regional and Sectoral Courts envisaged by law.

Supreme Court (Supremo Tribunal de Justiça): Rua Guerra Mendes, CP 341, Bissau; tel. 443211003; Pres. JOSÉ PEDRO SAMBÚ.

Attorney-General of the Republic: BACARI BIAI BIAI.

Religion

According to the 2009 census, adherents of Islam represented 45.1% of the total population; Christians accounted for 22.1% and animists 14.9%. Some 0.2% of the population were without religious affiliation, while 15.7% did not indicate adherence to any religion.

ISLAM

Associação Islâmica Nacional: Bissau; Sec.-Gen. Alhaji ABDÚ BAIO.

Conselho Superior dos Assuntos Islâmicos da Guiné-Bissau (CSAI-GB): Bissau; Exec. Sec. MUSTAFA RACHID DJALÓ.

CHRISTIANITY

The Roman Catholic Church

Guinea-Bissau comprises two dioceses, directly responsible to the Holy See. The Bishops participate in the Episcopal Conference of Senegal, Mauritania, Cabo Verde and Guinea-Bissau, currently based in Senegal. Approximately 10% of the total population are adherents of the Roman Catholic Church.

Bishop of Bafatá: Rev. CARLOS PEDRO ZILLI, CP 17, Bafatá; tel. 6625409; e-mail domzilli@yahoo.com.br.

Bishop of Bissau: Rev. JOSÉ LAMPRA CÁ, Av. 14 de Novembro, CP 20, 1001 Bissau; tel. 6778231; e-mail diocesebissau@yahoo.it.

The Press

REGULATORY AUTHORITY

Conselho Nacional de Comunicação Social (CNCS): Bissau; f. 1994; dissolved in 2003, recreated in November 2004; Pres. (vacant).

NEWSPAPERS AND PERIODICALS (PRINT AND ONLINE)

Expresso de Bissau: Rua Vitorino Costa 30, Bissau; tel. 966666647.

Gazeta de Notícias: Av. Caetano Semeao, CP 1433, Bissau; tel. 966606642; e-mail monteirohumberto@hotmail.com; internet gnbissau.com; f. 1997; weekly; Dir HUMBERTO MONTEIRO.

Jornal Nô Pintcha: Av. do Brasil, CP 154, Bissau; tel. 443213713; internet jornalnopintcha.gw; Dir SIMÃO ABINA TOMOU.

Jornal O Democrata: Av. Combatentes da Liberdade de Pátria, Bairro Internacional, Bissau; tel. 5123860; internet www .odemocratagb.com.

Última Hora: Av. Combatentes da Liberdade da Pátria (Prédio Suna Ker), Bissau; tel. 955932236; e-mail damil@portugalmail.com; Dir ATHIZAR PEREIRA.

NEWS AGENCY

Agência de Notícias da Guiné-Bissau (ANG): Edificio da Inacep, Av. Domingos Ramos, CP 248, Bissau; tel. 955401515; internet www .ang.gw; f. 1975; Dir-Gen. SALVADOR GOMES.

Publishers

Ku Si Mon Editora: Bairro d'Ajuda, Rua José Carlos Schwarz, CP 268, Bissau; tel. 966280100; e-mail info@kusimon.com; internet www.kusimon.com; f. 1994; Portuguese language; Dir ABDULAI SILA.

Broadcasting and Communications

REGULATORY AUTHORITY

Autoridade Reguladora Nacional das Tecnologias de Informação (ARN): Bairro de Enterramento, Atras do Hospital Militar, CP 1372, Bissau; tel. 443204874; e-mail info@arn.gw; internet arn .gw; f. 2010 to replace Instituto das Comunicações da Guiné-Bissau; also manages radio spectrum; Pres. GIBRIL MANÉ.

TELECOMMUNICATIONS

Guiné Telecom (GT): Bissau; tel. 443202427; internet www .gtelecom.gw; f. 2003 to replace the Companhia de Telecomunicações da Guiné-Bissau (Guiné Telecom—f. 1989); state-owned; privatization pending.

MTN Guinea Bissau: 7 Av. Unidade Africana, CP 672, Bissau; tel. 966121200; e-mail mtnguinebissau@gmail.com; internet www .mtngbissau.com; f. 2007; mobile operator; CEO ELIANE HOUPHOUET-BOIGNY.

Orange Bissau: Praça dos Herois Nacionais, BP 1087, Bissau; tel. 955603030; e-mail abdul.dapiedadeTMP@orange-sonatel.com; internet orange-bissau.com; f. 2007; mobile operator.

RADIO AND TELEVISION

Radiodifusão Nacional da República da Guiné-Bissau (RDN): Av. Domingos Ramos, Praça dos Martires de Pindjiguiti, CP 191, Bissau; tel. 443212426; internet fb.com/rdngbissau; f. 1974; govt-owned; broadcasts in Portuguese on short-wave, MW and FM; Dir-Gen. ABDURAHAMANE TURÉ.

Rádio Jovem: Bairro de Ajuda, Bissau; tel. 955555555; e-mail contato@radiojovem.info; internet radiojovem.info; f. 2005.

Rádio Mavegro: Rua Eduardo Mondlane, CP 100, Bissau; tel. 443201216.

Televisão da Guiné-Bissau (TGB): Bairro de Luanda, CP 178, Bissau; tel. 956601862; internet fb.com/tgbecp24; f. 1997; Dir-Gen. Dr AMADÚ DJAMANCA.

Finance

BANKING

Central Bank

Banque Centrale des Etats de l'Afrique de l'Ouest (BCEAO): Av. dos Combatentes da Liberdade da Pátria, Brá, CP 38, Bissau; tel. 443256325; internet www.bceao.int; HQ in Dakar, Senegal; f. 1955; bank of issue for the mem. states of the Union Economique et Monétaire Ouest-Africaine (UEMOA, comprising Benin, Burkina Faso, Côte d'Ivoire, Guinea-Bissau, Mali, Niger, Senegal and Togo); Gov. JEAN-CLAUDE KASSI BROU; Dir in Guinea-Bissau HELENA MARIA JOSÉ NOSOLINI EMBALO.

Other Banks

Banco da Africa Ocidental, SARL: Rua Guerra Mendes 18, CP 1360, Bissau; tel. 956210808; e-mail bao@baogb.com; internet www .bao.gw; f. 2000; 15% owned by International Finance Corporation, 15% Grupo Montepio Geral (Portugal), 15% Carlos Gomes Júnior; Man. Dir RÓMULO CLAUDEMIR PIRES.

Banco da União (BDU): Av. Domingos Ramos 33, CP 874, Bissau; tel. 955152037; e-mail info@bdu-sa.com; internet www.bdu-sa.com; f. 2005; 70% owned by Banque de Développement du Mali; CEO HUGO DOS REIS BORGES.

Banque Atlantique Guinée-Bissau: Av. Pansau Na Isna n° 5, CP 228, Bissau; tel. 956000008; e-mail infobagb@banqueatlantique.net; internet www.banqueatlantique.net/gnb; Dir-Gen. SERGE KOFFI BABACAUH.

Coris Bank International Guinée-Bissau: Bissau; f. 2022; Dir-Gen. MYRIAM KONÉ.

Ecobank Guinea-Bissau: Av. Amílcar Cabral, BP 126, Bissau; tel. 443207360; e-mail ecobankgw@ecobank.com; internet www.ecobank .com; Chair. JOSUÉ GOMES DE ALMEIDA; Man. Dir TÉNÉ SONIA MARILYSE KAFANDO ABO.

Orabank Bissau: Av. Pansau Na Isna, CP 391, Bissau; tel. 966672907; e-mail info-gw@orabank.net; internet www.orabank

.net/en/filiale/guinea-bissau; fmrly Banco Regional de Solidariedade; present name adopted 2014; Dir-Gen. BILALY DIARRA.

Banking Association

Associação Profissional de Bancos e Cifrão Estabelecimentos Financeiros da Guiné-Bissau (APBCE-GB): Rua António N'bana 13, 1° andar, CP 340, Bissau; tel. 443207559; internet www.apbef-gb.com; Pres. RÓMULO PIRES.

STOCK EXCHANGE

In 1998 a regional stock exchange, the Bourse Régionale des Valeurs Mobilières (BRVM), was established in Abidjan, Côte d'Ivoire, to serve the member states of the Union Economique et Monétaire Ouest-Africaine (UEMOA). In April 2021 the BRVM had 65 listed companies, none of which, however, was from Guinea-Bissau.

INSURANCE

GUINEBIS—Guiné-Bissau Seguros SA: Rua Dr Severino Gomes de Pina 28, CP 280, Bissau; tel. 966871244; e-mail geral@guinebis .com; internet www.guinebis.com.

NSIA Assurances: Av. Pansau Na Isna 27, Bissau; tel. 955803131; e-mail amadou.thiam@groupensia.com; Dir-Gen. AMADOU THIAM.

Trade and Industry

DEVELOPMENT ORGANIZATION

Ajuda de Desenvolvimento de Povo para Povo ná Guiné Bissau (ADPP): Bairro Internacional, Av. Combatentes da Liberdade da Patria, CP 420, Bissau; tel. 966955000; e-mail adpp@adpp-gb .org; internet www.adpp-gb.org; f. 1992; Exec. Dir FERNANDO BINHAFA.

CHAMBERS OF COMMERCE

Câmara de Comércio da Guiné-Bissau (CDC-GB): Bissau; Chair. MAMADÚ SALIU LAMBA.

Câmara de Comércio, Indústria, Agricultura e Serviços da Guiné-Bissau (CCIAS): Av. Pansau N'Isna No. 1C, CP 361, Bissau; tel. 956601673; e-mail contato@ccias.gw; internet ccias.gw; f. 1987; Pres. MAMA SAMBA EMBALO (acting).

INDUSTRIAL AND TRADE ASSOCIATIONS

Associação Comercial, Industrial e Agricola (ACIA): CP 88, Bissau; tel. 443222276.

Direcção Geral de Promoção do Investimento Privado (DPIP): Av. Amilcar Cabral 37, Bissau Velho, CP 1276, Bissau; tel. 446613294; e-mail carimoly@hotmail.com; Dir-Gen. JOSÉ ABDUL CARIMO LY.

Fundaçao Guineense para o Desenvolvimento Empresarial Industrial (FUNDEI): Rua Gen. Omar Torrijos 49, Bissau; tel. 443202470; internet www.fundei.net; f. 1994; industrial devt org.; Pres. MACÁRIA BARAI.

NAFORE Procajú: Bissau; tel. 5201212; e-mail madjenstrading@ gmail.com; f. 2013; private sector association of cashew producers; Public and International Relations Dir MAMADJAM DJALÓ.

MAJOR COMPANIES

Grupo Carlos Gomes Júnior (GRUCAR): CP 329, Bissau; tel. 443213709; owned by Carlos Gomes Júnior.

Internegoce: CP 429, Bissau; tel. 3203701.

PetroGuin: Rua Eduardo Mondlane 20, CP 387, Bissau; tel. 443221155; e-mail dg.petroguin@yahoo.com.br; internet www .petroguin.com; state-owned; fmrly Empresa Nacional de Pesquisas e Exploração Petrolíferas e Mineiras (PETROMINAS); exploration for and production of petroleum and natural gas; Dir-Gen. LEONARDO CARDOSO.

Petromar—Sociedade de Abastecimentos Petrolíferos Lda: Rua 7, CP 838, Bissau; tel. 443214281; f. 1990; 65% owned by Petrogal GB and 35% by Grucar; import and distribution of petroleum, gas and lubricants; Administrator JORGE MANUEL ALMEIDA.

TRADE UNIONS

Confederação Geral dos Sindicatos Independentes da Guiné-Bissau (CGSI-GB): Rua No. 10, Bissau Apartado 693, Bissau; tel. 443204110; e-mail cgsi-gb@hotmail.com; Sec.-Gen. MALAM LY BALDÉ.

Sindicato Nacional dos Professores (SINAPROF): CP 765, Bissau; tel. 443204070; Pres. DOMINGOS CARVALHO.

União Nacional dos Trabalhadores da Guiné Bissau—Central Sindical (UNTGB—CS): 13 Av. Osvaldo Vieira, CP 98, Bissau; tel. 966727704; e-mail untgcs.gb@hotmail.com; f. 1965; Sec.-Gen. JÚLIO ANTÓNIO MENDONÇA.

Transport

SHIPPING

Plans have been announced to build a major deep-water port at Buba, the projected capacity of which would make it one of the largest in West Africa.

Empresa Nacional de Agências e Transportes Marítimos: Rua Guerva Mendes 4–4A, CP 244, Bissau; tel. 443212675; state shipping agency; Dir-Gen. M. LOPES.

Instituto Marítimo Portuário (IMP): Bissau; Pres. (vacant).

CIVIL AVIATION

There is an international airport at Bissau and 10 smaller airports serving the interior. In April 2016 China Machinery Engineering Corporation signed an agreement with the Government to build a new international airport in Guinea-Bissau and to expand the existing one. Senegal Airlines, Royal Air Maroc, EuroAtlantic Airways and Transportes Aéreos de Cabo Verde (TACV) fly to Bissau.

Tourism

Secretaria de Estado do Turismo: Palácio do Governo, Av. Combatentes da Liberdade da Pátria, Bissau; tel. 969256609.

Defence

As assessed at November 2021, the armed forces officially totalled an estimated 4,450 men (army 4,000, navy 350, air force 100). Military service was made compulsory from 2007, as part of a programme of reform of the armed forces. Following the seizure of power by the military in April 2012, the ECOWAS Mission in Guinea-Bissau (ECOMIB), comprising 629 security personnel, was deployed in May. ECOMIB's mandate was formalized in November and periodically renewed thereafter in light of continuing political unrest. In September 2020 ECOWAS announced its decision to end the ECOMIB mission and by the end of December all of the troops had been withdrawn from the country.

Defence Budget: 13,000m. francs CFA in 2014.

Chief of the General Staff of the Armed Forces: Gen. BIAGUE NA N'TAM.

Army Chief of Staff: Gen. ESTEVE LASSANA MASSALI.

Navy Chief of Staff: Rear Adm. HÉLDER NHANQUE.

Chief of Staff of the Air Force: Col JOAQUIM FILINTO SILVA FERREIRA.

Education

Education is officially compulsory only for the period of primary schooling, which begins at six years of age and lasts for seven years. Secondary education, beginning at the age of 13, lasts for up to five years (a first cycle of three years and a second of two years). According to estimates by the United Nations Educational, Scientific and Cultural Organization (UNESCO), in 2009/10 enrolment at pre-primary level included only 5% of children in the relevant age-group (boys 4%; girls 5%). In that year enrolment at primary schools included 71% of children in the relevant age-group (boys 73%; girls 69%). There are three tertiary level institutions in Guinea-Bissau: the Universidade Amílcar Cabral (public); the Universidade Colinas do Boé (private); and the Faculdade de Direito de Bissau (a law school funded and run within the ambit of Portuguese co-operation). In 2017 public expenditure on education was equivalent to 15% of total government spending.

Bibliography

Bigman, L. *History and Hunger in West Africa: Food Production and Entitlement in Guinea-Bissau and Cape Verde*. Westport, CT, Greenwood Press, 1993.

Bock, A. J. *Segurança Alimentar: Potencialidade dos Recursos na Guiné-Bissau e Política Alimentar*. Lisbon, Instituto Superior de Agronomia, 2009.

Boubacar-Sid, B., Creppy, E., and Gacitua-Mario, E. (Eds). *Conflict, Livelihoods, and Poverty in Guinea-Bissau*. Washington, DC, World Bank Publications, 2007.

Cabral, A. *Documentário*. Lisbon, Cotovia, 2008.

Cabral, L. *Crónica da Libertação*. Lisbon, O Jornal, 1984.

Cann, J. P. *Counter-insurgency in Africa: The Portuguese Way of War 1961–1974*. Westport, CT, Greenwood Press, 1997.

Chabal, P. *Amílcar Cabral: Revolutionary Leadership and People's War*. 2nd edn. London, C. Hurst & Co., 2001.

Chabal, P., and Green, T. *Guinea-Bissau: Micro-State to 'Narco-State'*. London, C. Hurst & Co., 2016.

Forrest, J. B. *Guinea-Bissau: Power, Conflict and Renewal in a West African Nation*. Boulder, San Francisco, CA, and Oxford, Westview Press, 1992.

Lineages of State Fragility: Rural Civil Society in Guinea-Bissau. Athens, OH, University of Ohio Press, 2003.

Kohl, C. *Translationsprobleme bei der Reform des Polizeisektors in Guinea-Bissau*. Frankfurt am Main, Hessische Stiftung Friedens- und Konfliktforschung, 2014.

Lopes, C. *Guinea-Bissau: From Liberation Struggle to Independent Statehood*. Boulder, CO, Westview Press, 1987.

Manji, F., and Fletcher, B. *Claim no Easy Victories: The Legacy of Amílcar Cabral*. Dakar, CODESRIA, 2013.

Mendy, P., and Karibe, M. *Historical Dictionary of the Republic of Guinea-Bissau*. 4th edn. Lanham, MD, The Scarecrow Press, 2013.

Morier-Genoud, E. *Sure Road? Nationalisms in Angola, Guinea-Bissau and Mozambique*. Leiden, Brill, 2012.

Nóbrega, A. *A luta pelo poder na Guiné Bissau*. Lisbon, Instituto Superior de Ciências Sociais e Políticas, 2003.

Pereira, L. T., and Moita, L. *Guiné-Bissau: Três Anos de Independência*. Lisbon, CIDAC, 1976.

Semedo, Odete Costa. *Guiné-Bissau: Histórias, Culturas, Sociedades e Literatura*. Belo Horizonte, Nandyala, 2011.

Silva, A. *A Independência da Guiné-Bissau e a Descolonização Portuguesa*. Porto, Afrontamento, 1997.

da Silva, F. H., and Santos, B. *Da Guiné Portuguesa à Guiné-Bissa: Um Roteiro*. Porto, Fronteira do Caos, 2014.

Sousa, J. S. *Amílcar Cabral (1924–1973) Vida e Morte de um Revolucionário Africano*. Lisboa, Nova Vega, 2011.

Tomás, A. *Amílcar Cabral The Life of a Reluctant Nationalist*. Oxford, Oxford University Press, 2020.

Venter, A. J. *Portugal's Guerrilla Wars in Africa. Lisbon's Three Wars in Angola, Mozambique and Portuguese Guinea 1961-74*. Solihull, Helion & Co., 2013.

Vigh, H. E. *Navigating Terrains of War: Youth and Soldiering in Guinea-Bissau*. Oxford, Berghahn Books, 2006.

World Bank. *Guinea-Bissau: A Prescription for Comprehensive Adjustment*. Washington, DC, 1988.

Guinea-Bissau Integrated Poverty and Social Assessment (IPSA) – Transitions from Post Conflict to Long-Term Development: Policy Considerations for Reducing Poverty. 2 Vols. Washington, DC, 2006.

Zeverino, G. *O Conflito Político-Militar na Guiné-Bissau (1998–1999)*. Lisbon, Instituto Português de Apoio ao Desenvolvimento, 2005.

KENYA

Physical and Social Geography

W. T. W. MORGAN

PHYSICAL FEATURES

The total area of the Republic of Kenya is 591,971 sq km (228,561 sq miles) or 580,609 sq km (224,174 sq miles) excluding inland waters (mostly Lake Turkana and part of Lake Victoria). Kenya is bisected by the Equator and extends from approximately 4°N to 4°S and 34°E to 41°E.

The physical basis of the country is composed of extensive erosional plains, cut across ancient crystalline rocks of Pre-Cambrian age. These are very gently warped—giving an imperceptible rise from sea level towards the highlands of the interior, which have their base at about 1,500 m above sea level. The highlands are dominated by isolated extinct volcanoes, including Mt Kenya (5,200 m) and Mt Elgon (4,321 m), while outpourings of Tertiary lavas have created plateaux at 2,500 m–3,000 m. The Great Rift Valley bisects the country from north to south and is at its most spectacular in the highlands, where it is some 65 km across and bounded by escarpments 600 m–900 m high. The trough is dotted with lakes and volcanoes which are inactive but generally associated with steam vents and hot springs. Westwards the plains incline beneath the waters of Lake Victoria, and eastwards they have been down-warped beneath a sediment-filled basin.

CLIMATE AND NATURAL RESOURCES

Although Kenya lies on the Equator, its range of altitude results in temperate conditions in the highlands above 1,500 m, with temperatures that become limiting to cultivation at about 2,750 m, while Mt Kenya supports small glaciers. Average temperatures may be roughly calculated by taking a sea-level mean of 26°C and deducting 1.7°C for each 300 m of altitude. For most of the country, however, rainfall is more critical than temperature. Only 15% of the area of Kenya can be expected to receive a reliable rainfall adequate for cultivation (750 mm in four years out of five). Rainfall is greatest at the coast and in the west of the country, near Lake Victoria and in the highlands, but the extensive plains below 1,200 m are arid or semi-arid. In the region of Lake Victoria and in the highlands west of the Rift Valley, rain falls in one long rainy season. East of the Rift Valley there are two distinct seasons: the long rains (March–May) and the short rains (September–October).

The high rainfall areas tend to be intensively cultivated on a small-scale, semi-subsistence basis with varying amounts of cash cropping. Food crops are in great variety, but most important and widespread are maize, sorghum, cassava and bananas. The principal cash crops, which provide the majority of exports, are tea, coffee (mainly *Coffea arabica*), pyrethrum and sisal. The first three are particularly suited to the highlands and their introduction was associated with the large-scale farming on the alienated lands of the former 'White Highlands'. Horticultural produce (in particular, cut flowers) is an increasingly significant export. The dairy industry is important both for domestic consumption and for export. The herds of cattle, goats, sheep and camels of the dry plains support a low density of mainly subsistence farmers. Fisheries are of local importance around Lake Victoria and are of great potential at Lake Turkana.

Soda ash is mined at Lake Magadi in the Rift Valley. Deposits of fluorspar, gemstones (including sapphires and rubies), lead, gold, salt, vermiculite, iron ore and limestone are also exploited. However, mineral resources make a negligible contribution to Kenya's economy.

POPULATION AND CULTURE

A total population of 47,564,296, excluding adjustment for underenumeration, was recorded at the census of August 2019. The resultant overall density of 81.9 inhabitants per sq km is extremely unevenly distributed, with a large proportion of the population contained in only 10% of the area; densities approach 400 per sq km on the small proportion of the land that is cultivable. None the less, by 2020 about 28% of the population resided in urban areas, principally in Nairobi (where, according to the 2019 census, the population was about 4.4m.) and Mombasa (1.2m.). The towns also contain the majority of the non-African minorities of Asians, Arabs and Europeans.

Kenya has been a point of convergence of major population movements in the past, and, on a linguistic and cultural basis, the people have been divided into Bantu, Nilotic, Nilo-Hamitic (Paranilotic) and Cushitic groups. Persian and Arab influence at the coast is reflected in the Islamic culture. Kiswahili (or Swahili) and English are the country's two official languages, although Kikuyu and Luo (or Dholuo) are widely understood. The majority of the population profess Christianity (some 85.5%, according to the 2019 census), while there is a sizeable Muslim minority (10.9%).

History

MICHAEL JENNINGS

COLONIAL RULE TO THE KENYATTA ERA

Kenya, formerly known as British East Africa, was declared a British protectorate in 1895. By the early 1920s African political activity had begun to be organized against colonial occupation; the Kenya African Union (KAU) was formed in 1944. Leadership of the movement, which drew its main support from the Kikuyu, passed in 1947 to Jomo Kenyatta, himself a Kikuyu. During 1952–56 a campaign of violence was conducted by the Mau Mau, a predominantly Kikuyu secret society. A state of emergency was declared by the British authorities, Kenyatta was detained, and a ban on all political activity remained in force until 1955. Following the removal of the state of emergency in January 1960, a transitional Constitution was introduced, legalizing political parties and according Africans a large majority in the legislative council. The KAU was reorganized as the Kenya African National Union (KANU), and Tom Mboya and Oginga Odinga (who later left to form an opposition party), both of the Luo people, were elected to the party's leadership. Following his release in August 1961, Kenyatta assumed the presidency of KANU, which won a decisive victory at the general election of May 1963. Kenyatta became Prime Minister in June, and independence followed on 12 December. The country was declared a republic (with Kenyatta as President) exactly one year later. During the early 1970s President Kenyatta became increasingly reclusive and autocratic. He was elected, unopposed, for a third five-year term in September 1974, but died in August 1978.

THE MOI PRESIDENCY

Daniel arap Moi succeeded to the presidency in October 1978. Despite initial signals of greater openness, Moi became increasingly intolerant of criticism, and in June 1982 Kenya's Constitution was amended to create a one-party state. Amid growing concern over his human rights record, Moi was returned unopposed for a third term in March 1988. Following his re-election, Moi moved to entrench further the power of the presidency.

In the early 1990s, responding to international and domestic pressures, Moi undertook a programme of reform and introduced a multi-party political system. By early 1992 several new parties were registered, but, with a divided opposition, Moi won a fourth term as President in December. During this period, the Government was accused of inciting ethnic tensions and violence to undermine the opposition. Clashes between 1992 and 1995 left at least 3,500 people dead, and more than 320,000 homeless. Government-sponsored clashes were particularly fierce in the Rift Valley, and between Kikuyu and Kalenjin. Tensions continued to grow throughout the next decade.

In May 1996 the opposition-dominated public accounts committee accused several senior members of the Government of withholding information vital to its investigation into the collapse of a number of Kenyan banks. This was linked to the loss of an estimated US $430m. in public funds from fraudulent claims for export tax rebates. (The affair was to become known as the Goldenberg scandal.)

In August 1998 a car bomb exploded at the US embassy in Nairobi (concurrently with a similar attack on the US mission to Dar es Salaam, Tanzania). A total of 254 people were killed in Nairobi, and more than 5,000 suffered injuries. The attacks were believed to have been co-ordinated by international Islamist fundamentalist militants led by the Saudi Arabian-born Osama bin Laden.

Meanwhile, presidential and legislative elections on 29 December 1997 returned Moi and KANU to Government, amid allegations of electoral fraud and political violence. Furthermore, international concern over corruption, and the Government's ineffectual response to it, began to shape Kenya's relationship with international donors.

Following an agreement with the National Development Party (NDP) in January 2001, in June Moi formed Kenya's first coalition Government, with the appointment of the NDP leader, Raila Odinga (the son of Oginga Odinga), as Minister of Energy. Internal struggles for power led to Odinga and deputies linked to his faction resigning and joining the opposition. In October an electoral alliance of 14 opposition parties, including Odinga's new party, the Liberal Democratic Party (LDP), was established under the leadership of Mwai Kibaki (a former Minister of Health who had founded the Democratic Party a decade earlier); the alliance became known as the National Rainbow Coalition (NARC).

THE KIBAKI ADMINISTRATION

Presidential and legislative elections took place on 27 December 2002. The opposition won an emphatic victory, with Kibaki taking 62.3% of the votes cast (as against Uhuru Kenyatta's 31.2%) in the presidential election, and NARC taking 125 of the 210 elected seats in the National Assembly. KANU won just 64 seats in the legislature. Raila Odinga became Minister of Roads, Public Works and Housing in Kibaki's first Cabinet, and soon began competing for power within the coalition Government. In response, Kibaki brought in KANU members to the cabinet to shift the balance of power away from the LDP. Meanwhile, Uhuru Kenyatta became acting Chairman of KANU in late 2003, and was elected substantively to the post in February 2005.

Political Fragmentation and Crisis

Following the opening of a constitutional review conference in April 2003, constitutional reform became a touchstone for rivalries within NARC. Odinga led the 'no' campaign in

opposition to the proposed draft, with Kibaki leading the 'yes' campaign. The draft was rejected by some 57% of voters at a referendum held in November 2005. The governing NARC coalition collapsed in mid-2006. After a succession of attempts to secure control over NARC, Kibaki established a new governing party, NARC—Kenya. Meanwhile, Odinga's LDP had left NARC to establish the Orange Democratic Movement (ODM).

The 2007 Elections and their Aftermath

High rates of voter turnout were recorded in the presidential and legislative elections of 27 December 2007, especially in western Kenya. On 30 December the Electoral Commission of Kenya (ECK) declared Kibaki to have won the presidential election, with 4,584,721 votes. Odinga, suggested by unofficial results to be in the lead, received 4,352,993 votes by the official count. The ODM claimed a parliamentary victory, although international observers questioned the results, with allegations of widespread electoral fraud. Odinga refused to accept the results, claiming victory in the presidential poll. None the less, Kibaki was sworn in as President shortly after the announcement of the official results.

The announcement of Kibaki's victory prompted an upsurge in violence, and by 31 December 2007 some 120 people had been killed in clashes between rival supporters and police. The Government, for its part, accused opposition politicians of fomenting violence against Kibaki's supporters, following attacks by Kalenjin militia on Kikuyu. Violence and killings escalated rapidly, particularly in the Rift Valley, where clashes between Kalenjin, Luo and Kikuyu ethnic groups sparked repeated revenge attacks.

The violence occurred in two main waves: the first took place between 30 December 2007 and 10 January 2008, focused on the Rift Valley and especially around Eldoret; the second occurred on 24–28 January in Nakuru and Naivasha, involving clashes between Luo, Kalenjin and Kikuyu communities. In the north, the violence centred on longstanding tensions between Kalenjin and Kikuyu, with Kalenjin armed gangs turning on Kikuyu soon after the results were announced. In mid-January the United Nations (UN) estimated that 500 people had been killed since the elections, with a further 250,000 displaced. Armed militia set up roadblocks, targeting rival ethnic groups and property. Widespread instances of rape, maiming and killing were reported, and in several attacks large numbers of people were killed. In one incident in early January, 35 people—mostly women and children who had sought refuge inside the Kiambaa Pentecostal church in Eldoret—were killed when the church was set on fire.

Negotiations to end the political impasse and violence proceeded slowly and fitfully. Former UN Secretary-General Kofi Annan succeeded in persuading Kibaki and Odinga to commence talks in late January 2008. On 28 February, with more than 1,000 people dead and at least 500,000 having fled their homes in the post-election violence, the two sides signed a power-sharing agreement. Under its terms, the post of executive Prime Minister would be established; two Deputy Prime Ministers would be appointed, one nominated by the ODM and one by the Party of National Unity (PNU); and ministerial posts would be divided between the two parties.

The Coalition Government

The settlement resulted in an end to the fighting, although serious tensions remained, and continued deadlock in the negotiations for the allocation of cabinet positions led to renewed violence in the ODM strongholds of Kibera and Kisumu. International pressure forced the renewal of negotiations, and on 12 April 2008 Kibaki and Odinga announced an agreement. The Cabinet would consist of 40 members, and 52 assistant ministers, with the PNU retaining the strategically important finance, foreign affairs, internal security, roads and energy portfolios. On 17 April Odinga was sworn in as Prime Minister, while Kenyatta was named Deputy Prime Minister and Minister of Trade.

Two official reports in 2008 implicated several senior politicians in the post-election violence. In August the Kenya National Commission on Human Rights issued a report naming Kenyatta and five members of the ODM, including Minister of Agriculture William Ruto and Henry Kosgey, Chairman of the ODM and Minister of Industrialization. Moreover, it suggested that violence had been planned before the elections, and that state security forces had adopted a shoot-to-kill policy. The Commission of Inquiry into the Post-Election Violence (CIPEV) issued its report in October. In addition, a sealed envelope containing the names of 10 individuals most directly linked to organizing the violence was handed to Annan. The ODM was accused of organizing violence in the North Rift, with Ruto, although not explicitly named in this report, rumoured to have been included on the secret list handed to Annan. The CIPEV report also suggested that meetings had taken place in State House (the official residence of the President in Nairobi) to organize the violence in Naivasha.

Tensions soon arose within the ODM between Odinga and Ruto, particularly over a proposed new constitution. The Constitution was approved by 67% of votes cast in a national referendum on 4 August 2010. Under its provisions, power was devolved to 47 new counties, which were to be represented by a new parliamentary chamber, the Senate.

In December 2010 the Chief Prosecutor for the International Criminal Court (ICC) in The Hague, Netherlands, Luis Moreno-Ocampo, named six Kenyans whom he accused of having been primarily responsible for organizing the post-election violence: Kenyatta, Ruto, Cabinet Secretary Francis Muthaura, former head of police Mohammed Hussein Ali, Kosgey, and radio executive Joshua arap Sang. Ruto, Sang and Kosgey were named in connection with acts of violence on the side of the ODM, while Kenyatta, Muthaura and Ali were widely viewed as allies of Kibaki. All six denied the accusations. After the ICC issued a formal summons, the six accused appeared voluntarily before it in April 2011. Despite appeals from the Kenyan Government for proceedings to be halted, in January 2012 the ICC announced that Kenyatta, Muthaura, Ruto and Sang would all stand trial. Kenyatta resigned as Minister of Finance (although he remained Deputy Prime Minister).

Political alliances shifted as campaigning began for the presidential and legislative elections scheduled for March 2013. In December 2012 Ruto and Kenyatta (on opposing sides during the 2007 elections, and in the violence that followed) formed an alliance known as the Jubilee Coalition (JC) between Kenyatta's The National Alliance (TNA) and Ruto's United Republican Party (URP); Kenyatta was to contest the presidency, with Ruto as his running mate. Meanwhile, Odinga brought his ODM into the Coalition for Reform and Democracy (CORD), with erstwhile political rival Kalonzo Musyoka and his Wiper Democratic Movement—Kenya (WDM—K). CORD also incorporated several smaller parties, including the Forum for the Restoration of Democracy—Kenya and the Federal Party of Kenya.

THE 2013 ELECTIONS AND THE KENYATTA ADMINISTRATION

The presidential and legislative elections took place on 4 March 2013. According to the official results, Uhuru Kenyatta received 50.5% of the votes cast in the presidential election, and Raila Odinga 43.7%. With a narrow overall majority, Kenyatta thus avoided a second round.

In the legislative elections the ODM won 78 of the 290 directly elected constituency seats in the expanded National Assembly, while the TNA received 72 seats, and the URP 62. Under the terms of the 2010 Constitution, elections were also held for a new Senate, at which the ODM and the TNA both obtained 11 of the 47 directly elected seats, and the URP nine. Overall, following the additional nomination of deputies, the JC secured 167 of the total 349 seats in the National Assembly, and 30 of the 67 seats in the Senate, while the ODM-led CORD took 141 seats in the lower and 28 in the upper chamber. Kenyatta was sworn in as President on 9 April, with Ruto as Deputy President.

Kenya's inquiry into the post-2007 election violence, the Truth, Justice and Reconciliation Commission, published its findings in May 2013. The report named Ruto and Kenyatta as complicit in organizing and financing the violence of 2007–08. It listed several suspects whose involvement should, it recommended, be further investigated: these included the incumbent

Secretary for Mining, Najib Balala, and the former Chairman of the Commission itself, Bethuel Kiplagat, who was allegedly implicated in a massacre by Kenyan security forces at Wagalla.

In October 2014 Kenyatta appeared before the ICC, the first serving head of state to do so. However, in December all charges against the President were dropped. In April 2016 the ICC process finally ended with the court abandoning its attempts to prosecute Ruto and Sang. The court alleged that interference and intimidation of witnesses (a key witness against Ruto was found murdered in January 2015) had undermined the prosecution.

From mid-2016 leaders of all the main parties began to mobilize their supporters ahead of the elections, although the Government was accused of undermining opposition efforts to campaign. Polling in late 2016 showed Odinga with about 22% support, compared with Kenyatta, who enjoyed a large lead, with about 50% of declared voting intentions. In response to the significant gap, Odinga began negotiations with other opposition parties over the creation of a single opposition coalition, similar to the 2002 coalition that had defeated KANU. Talks concluded in January 2017 with the creation of the National Super Alliance (NASA), a coalition of five opposition parties dominated by Odinga's ODM (although officially the alliance was described as a power-sharing structure). In April Odinga was selected as the alliance's official presidential candidate, with former Vice-President Musyoka selected as the vice-presidential candidate. Meanwhile, in January 2015 the ruling JC had been reconstituted as a political party, which in September 2016 merged with several smaller parties to form the Jubilee Party (JP).

The party primaries, held over the final two weeks of April 2017, resulted in chaos, with both NASA, led by Odinga, and Kenyatta's JP, having to cancel the initial voting and re-run the primary elections. Delays in the polls led to tensions within the parties, as rivals accused each other of seeking to rig the primaries; some clashes were reported, leaving at least two people dead and many injured. At least 62 people were arrested and charged with various electoral offences during the primary election process. Several incumbents lost their seats as dissatisfaction with their performance played out in the polls. In Baringo, the Governor and key ally of Ruto, Benjamin Cheboi, was deselected, alongside other key candidates. Three incumbent parliamentary deputies for the JP were also deselected, as were several of Odinga's allies.

In 2017 tensions between pastoralist communities and large-scale farmers erupted into violent confrontations during the severe drought caused by the El Niño weather phenomenon. In February Kenyatta declared the drought affecting large parts of the country to be a national disaster, committing to supplying food aid for affected areas. The drought led to increased tensions between pastoralist and large-scale private farmers in Laikipia county, where pastoralists herded their livestock onto private land in order to find food for their stock. Several clashes broke out, with allegations that the violence was being incited by politicians. In one clash in March a former British army officer was killed, and Italian-born Kuki Gallmann was shot and injured a month after a safari lodge on her Laikipia Nature Conservancy reserve was burned down by suspected pastoralists. The army was mobilized in the region, and pastoralists accused police of deliberately killing their cattle. At least 12 people were killed in the various clashes. In May a local politician being investigated for involvement in the raids, Thomas Minito, was found murdered.

THE 2017 ELECTIONS

The presidential and legislative elections, which took place as scheduled on 8 August 2017, were largely peaceful, but the technology used led to delays in voting and in counting the votes cast. When the final results were released by the Independent Electoral Boundaries Commission (IEBC—established in 2011 to replace the ECK) on 11 August 2017, Kenyatta had secured 54.2% of the valid votes cast in the presidential poll, while Odinga took 44.9%. None of the six other candidates won more than 0.3% of the votes cast. In the legislative elections the JP won the greatest number of seats (163 out of a total of 337), while the ODM took 73 and the

WDM—K garnered 22. A total of 18 other parties secured representation in the National Assembly. Odinga refused to accept the result, and he launched a legal challenge in mid-August after calling on his supporters to remain calm.

In a dramatic and unprecedented turn of events, on 1 September 2017 the Supreme Court annulled the results of the presidential election, citing irregularities and failings by the IEBC, and stipulated that a new poll should take place within 60 days. The ruling was the first time that a Supreme Court had overturned a presidential poll in Africa.

Odinga and NASA boycotted the re-run presidential election, which was held on 26 October 2017, together with the other main opposition leaders, claiming that the IEBC had not been sufficiently reformed to guarantee a fair election. Without a significant challenge, Kenyatta won the poll with 98.3% of the votes cast, but turnout, at 34%, was significantly lower than in August. Efforts by NASA to challenge the results of this election were rejected by the Supreme Court. Following the re-run vote, NASA continued to argue that Odinga was the true victor of the August election, and renamed itself the National Resistance Movement (NRM—although it did not register this name officially).

Meanwhile, in January 2018 the EU published its report into the August and October 2017 elections. The Government did not invite the EU mission to present the report in Nairobi, and shortly before its publication sought to have the findings toned down and its release delayed. Foreign diplomats were widely critical of all parties in the elections, as well as of the Government's repressive measures after the re-run poll in October.

In March 2018 Odinga and Kenyatta publicly shook hands as evidence of a rapprochement between the two. It emerged that Odinga had dropped his claims over the disputed elections, and both men agreed to work together to restore unity to the country. Odinga travelled to South Africa on behalf of Kenyatta in April and on several subsequent visits, representing the Kenyan Government.

Although relations between Odinga and Kenyatta improved, those between the President and his deputy worsened, as Ruto considered that Kenyatta was seeking to marginalize him and undermine his chances of victory in the presidential polls in 2022. In June 2018 Ruto and Kenyatta attended a crisis meeting aimed at ending disunity within the ruling JP. However, supporters of Ruto attacked Kenyatta's brother, Muhoho Kenyatta, for his alleged role in a corruption scandal, while Ruto himself sought to build alliances with several NASA deputies who felt betrayed by Odinga's reconciliation with Uhuru Kenyatta.

In May 2018 the Government proposed legislation covering computer misuse and cybercrimes, which would criminalize the dissemination of 'false information' through social media, with a penalty of a US $50,000 fine and up to two years in prison. The draft legislation was criticized by media organizations, notably the US non-governmental organization (NGO) the Committee to Protect Journalists, which argued that it would stifle press freedom and freedom of expression.

The JP's Vice-Chairman, David Murathe, resigned in January 2019 (although some speculated that he had been dismissed as part of the factional fighting), announcing that he would do all he could to prevent Ruto from becoming President. The alliance between the two politicians had always been viewed as one of convenience, concealing deep differences and tensions between them and their supporters. Murathe alleged that Ruto was complicit in several corruption scandals and that he was unsuited to high office. The failure of Kenyatta to censure his ally was regarded as further proof of the growing rift between Ruto and Kenyatta.

In April 2019 the parliamentary Public Accounts Committee delivered a highly critical report into the activities of the IEBC during the 2017 elections, accusing it of budget mismanagement and poor decisions regarding technology. The report particularly criticized the IEBC's former Chief Executive, Ezra Chiloba, and six other commissioners, and claimed that the elections had cost more than five times the global average for an election.

In May 2019 the High Court ruled against a challenge that Kenya's laws on homosexuality violated the Constitution, in a case that had been brought by gay activists in 2016. In the ruling, the presiding judge argued that repealing the law would encourage same-sex unions and defended the court's decision as upholding Kenyan traditions. With a worsening environment for gay people also being reported in other East African countries, donors expressed concerns about the treatment of gay individuals and respect for sexual rights.

In November 2019 the report of the Building Bridges Initiative (BBI) was published. The task force, which had been set up in 2018 following Kenyatta and Odinga's rapprochement, had been called upon to recommend reforms to Kenya's political system aimed at reducing tensions. Among its proposals, the BBI called for the creation of the post of non-executive Prime Minister, to be appointed by the President, with the head of state retaining power. The BBI also recommended that principal secretaries should be appointed directly by the President without the need for prior parliamentary approval and that the independent Ethics and Anti-Corruption Commission should be placed under the Office of the President. Almost immediately after its publication, the BBI report became a fresh source of tension between Kenyatta and Ruto and their respective allies. Although Ruto and his faction favoured implementing reforms through parliament, Kenyatta (supported by Odinga) advocated the holding of a popular referendum to approve any changes. The debates led to a shifting political alignment around support for the BBI, which deepened political divisions at the centre of government.

In late January 2020 the largest locust swarms to be recorded in East Africa in about 70 years reached Kenya and started to decimate crops. The World Bank provided US $13.7m. to the Kenyan Government to tackle the swarms as fears grew about the impact of the insect invasion on food security in Kenya and the wider affected region. However, as national efforts were diverted to curb the COVID-19 pandemic in early 2020, financial support to deal with the locust infestation was slow to arrive and insufficient to contain the swarms.

President Kenyatta continued to try to assert his control over the JP and isolate Ruto and his allies in the Cabinet. In May 2020 Kenyatta replaced the majority leader and the majority chief whip in the Senate with his own allies and signed a formal coalition agreement with KANU (led by Gideon Moi, the son of Daniel arap Moi)—a move that suggested that Kenyatta might favour Gideon Moi as a presidential challenger to Ruto in the 2022 elections. Other political parties, including Chama Cha Mashinani and the WDM—K, also explored possibilities for greater co-operation, citing the need to combine efforts to address the COVID-19 pandemic. In June 2020 the majority leader in the National Assembly, Aden Duale, who was a key ally of Ruto, was replaced, reinforcing Kenyatta's control of the JP.

In mid-2020 there were indications that political alliances were beginning to shift as attention began to be focused on the 2022 elections. President Kenyatta was reported to have begun talks with the opposition NASA with a view to his supporting its candidate in the presidential election, leading Ruto to claim that the President was seeking to undermine the JP. Talks were subsequently reported to have commenced between the JP and the opposition ODM over the formation of an electoral alliance. Meanwhile, Musyoka stated that he would not support Odinga in the 2022 elections and instead established the One Kenya Alliance (OKA) with other party leaders in NASA, including Gideon Moi. As tensions grew between Kenyatta and Ruto, clashes between supporters of the two rivals in October left two people dead.

Paul Gicheru, a Kenyan lawyer, surrendered himself to the ICC in November 2020, having been accused of bribing and intimidating witnesses in the failed ICC case against Ruto and Sang concerning the alleged orchestration of violent attacks following the disputed 2007 elections. In July 2021 the ICC confirmed the charges against Gicheru and committed him to face trial.

A NEW ROUND OF CONSTITUTIONAL REFORM

In late October 2020 the final report of the BBI was launched jointly by Odinga and Kenyatta, who claimed that it would stabilize and make Kenyan politics more democratic. The following month, the Government sought to implement the

BBI's recommendations through The Constitution of Kenya (Amendment) Bill 2020. The draft legislation contained provisions for: the creation of the posts of Prime Minister, Deputy Prime Ministers and leader of the official opposition; the appointment of cabinet ministers from among elected legislators (reviving the link between the Cabinet and the legislature that had existed prior to the 2010 reforms); the appointment of an independent judicial ombudsman to investigate complaints against court officials; the establishment of 70 new electoral constituencies; and the implementation of affirmative action processes to increase the number of women elected to parliament. The bill also contained provision for the creation of Ward Development Funds, similar to the Constituency Development Funds controlled by legislators, as part of an attempt to court the support of the county assemblies.

The BBI and consequent constitutional amendment bill were reportedly opposed by Ruto, whose supporters viewed them as a mechanism for a joint Odinga-Kenyatta alliance to undermine Ruto's bid for the presidency in 2022. However, Ruto did not oppose the bill outright, perhaps hoping that it would fail to be approved and that he could then reap the benefits from any subsequent dispute between Odinga and Kenyatta, thereby strengthening his position against his probable main rival in 2022, Odinga.

In May 2021 both houses of parliament (and most county assemblies) voted by a large majority to put the constitutional reform bill to a national referendum by the end of February 2022. Ruto announced that he would now openly support the bill, although his backing appeared lukewarm. Despite rapid progress through parliament, plans for the holding of a referendum in mid-2021 were thrown into disarray in late May, when the High Court ruled that constitutional reform under the BBI was unconstitutional. Potentially even more disruptive to the plans, the court also ruled that no referendum could take place until a new voter registration system had been put in place. This meant that even if the ruling on the legality of the process of the bill were overturned on appeal, the referendum might need to be delayed, possibly even until after the 2022 elections.

In May 2021 Lady Justice Martha Karambu Koome was appointed as the first female Chief Justice of Kenya. Her appointment came as relations between the Government and the judiciary further deteriorated following the High Court's ruling on the constitutional reform bill. In June President Kenyatta again refused to confirm the appointment of six judges who had been recommended by the Judicial Service Commission in 2019, despite two court orders requiring him to do so. Critics argued that although the President had the authority to reject some of the recommendations, he was not permitted to reject all of them.

THE COVID-19 PANDEMIC IN KENYA

Kenya recorded its first confirmed case of COVID-19 on 13 March 2020, on which date the Government banned public gatherings; over the following days it closed schools, sealed the country's borders to most foreigners and restricted flights. On 25 March, by which time 25 confirmed cases of infection had been officially recorded, the Government announced a series of further restrictions designed to contain the spread of the virus in the country: a dusk-to-dawn curfew was imposed nationwide, with partial lockdowns put in place in the four counties with the highest infection rates (Kilifi, Kwale, Mombasa and Nairobi) in the first week of April.

Despite the relatively rapid response to the onset of COVID-19 in the country, the Government faced criticism for failing to put in place a stricter lockdown (as had happened in neighbouring Uganda), for inconsistently applying the restrictions in place (senior politicians apparently faced no barriers to travel) and for failing to provide sufficient support to those whose livelihoods were disrupted. Kenyatta was criticized for using the crisis to undermine his political rival, Ruto. Government promises of support, including free face masks for all citizens, were not fulfilled, and financial support measures targeted the formal economy, leaving those in the informal sector (especially women) with almost no support.

These criticisms were compounded by a heavy-handed police response in enforcing the curfew and other restrictions. In April 2020 an official at the Ministry of Health announced that anybody who violated the restrictions could be placed in mandatory quarantine for 14 days. The Government was accused of treating the COVID-19 crisis as a law and order issue, rather than a public health emergency. By May the public health response to COVID-19 in Kenya was fast becoming overshadowed by the violence of certain police officers in enforcing lockdown restrictions and associated human rights abuses. In June an investigation was launched into the conduct of a number of police officers after a woman was tied up behind a police motorcycle and dragged along the street in Nakuru county in western Kenya. Meanwhile, many politicians were seen to be flouting the restrictions with apparent impunity.

In the first week of July 2020 the Government relaxed the lockdown restrictions that it had put in place in March, with a phased reopening of social and economic life. However, by November Kenya was facing a second wave of COVID-19 infections, with the number of new cases more than double those recorded in the previous two months combined. New lockdown measures were put in place, and large public gatherings were again banned. Police made almost 1,000 arrests in November alone of individuals accused of flouting the new restrictions. In December health care professionals, including nurses and doctors, went on strike in protest at low pay and the poor working conditions arising from the pandemic, and in January 2021 it was reported that several hundred doctors and nurses had been dismissed for participating in the industrial action.

At the beginning of March 2021 the first delivery of 1m. COVID-19 vaccines arrived in the country as part of an expected allocation of 3.5m. doses under the COVAX Facility of the World Health Organization (WHO). Kenya also received vaccines that were intended for delivery to South Sudan, but which could not be distributed in that country by health care professionals before their use-by date. Kenya's frontline health care workers were prioritized to be given the first vaccinations. The nationwide curfew was extended for another 60 days in March, and later that month further restrictions were implemented in five counties, including Nairobi, which had witnessed a particularly sharp rise in the rate of infection. Opposition leader Raila Odinga tested positive for the virus and was briefly hospitalized in March. Most hospitals faced shortages of beds and oxygen to treat patients infected with the virus.

Following the rapid spread of a new wave of infections in western Kenya in May 2021, the Government announced a new lockdown in that part of the country, restricting travel to and from 13 affected counties and implementing a curfew and a ban on public gatherings. By the end of June almost 1m. people had been given their first inoculation against COVID-19, around 300,000 were fully vaccinated, and further shipments of vaccines were arriving. In order to boost vaccination capacity, the Government announced that it would build a vaccine manufacturing plant which could undertake the final part of the process—filling vials and packaging doses for distribution—and planned to construct another general vaccine facility which would manufacture different types of doses, including those for COVID-19. By the end of 2021 less than 10% of the population (around 6.4m. people) had been vaccinated against COVID-19. After stepping up the pace of the campaign, by June 2022 some sources indicated that just over 30% of the adult population had been fully vaccinated, significantly higher than the 17.7% average for Africa's vaccination rate as a whole. The Government announced in that month that it would work with pharmaceutical companies and the largest African health-focused NGO, Amref Health Africa, to roll out mobile vaccination clinics across the country to expand coverage.

THE 2022 ELECTION CAMPAIGN

Election campaigning began in earnest in 2022, with both leading challengers for the presidency formally announcing their candidacies, and the final coalitions and informal alliances coming together to contest the August election.

Ruto announced that he would be standing as the presidential candidate for the Kenya Kwanza (Kenya First) coalition of the UDA and several other parties. His campaign—Ruto's first for the presidency—focused on economic pledges, with promises to grow the economy and reduce unemployment. Ruto pitched himself as a champion of those struggling to make ends meet, or the 'hustler nation', as his campaign has described them. At the start of 2022 opinion polls suggested that Ruto was enjoying a large lead over his rival, Odinga.

Meanwhile, Odinga was making his fifth attempt at the presidency. In February 2022 the OKA, bringing together the WDM—K, KANU, the United Democratic Party and NARC—Kenya, signed a deal under which each had an equal say on coalition decisions. Later that month the OKA, the JP and the ODM began talks to establish the Azimio la Umoja coalition. The agreement of Kalonzo Musyoka (leader of the WDM—K) to join was seen as a victory for Odinga. Previously, Musyoka had declared that he would not support an Odinga bid for the presidency. With Gideon Moi and President Uhuru Kenyatta also part of the coalition, Odinga had the weight of the political establishment behind him, and his campaign resembled that of a continuity candidate, who was promising to build on the Government's platform in addressing Kenya's economy and to address poverty and health inequalities. Kenyatta gave a speech in February in which he strongly criticized his deputy, Ruto, and praised Odinga, formalizing his support for the latter in the August elections. Odinga's endorsement by President Kenyatta since their 2018 agreement added to the feeling that he was indeed campaigning as the continuity candidate, building on the Government's platform. Azimo was a larger coalition of regional leaders than Kenya Kwanza, although whether this would translate into votes was unclear.

The third most prominent candidate, George Wajackoyah, managed to win some support among Kenyan youth in particular, not least with a platform that included legalizing marijuana and blaming 'migrants' for the country's economic problems. However, he trailed the two main candidates, with around 4% support in national opinion polls.

In March 2022 the Supreme Court ruled against the process of implementing reforms under the BBI. The ruling meant that efforts to introduce the post of Prime Minister could not go ahead. There had been speculation that Odinga had agreed to appoint Kenyatta to the role in return for his support in the campaign. However, the Supreme Court argued that constitutional reforms required approval from Kenya's citizens rather than the head of state. Ruto, who had always proclaimed the BBI as an initiative to undermine his authority, welcomed the ruling, which was widely regarded as strengthening his campaign. However, the ruling was based on process rather than content, raising the prospect of a further push for reforms depending on the outcome of the election.

In May 2022 Ruto announced that he had picked Rigathi Gachagua as his running mate for the elections, despite Gachagua facing charges of corruption and money laundering. Although Gachagua was widely regarded as an effective political mobilizer and had campaigned strongly on economic issues, the main reason for the selection was because he was a Kikuyu, and Ruto hoped to use this to gain support in the central region.

A few days later Odinga announced former Minister of Justice Martha Karua, inevitably also a Kikuyu, as his running mate, despite their past political rivalry and tensions. The appointments were a reminder that this would be Kenya's first election with no prominent candidate from this ethnic group, with both leading candidates seeking to do all they could to win this constituency. More widely known than Gachaugua, early indications suggested that Karua's appointment was gaining support for the Odinga campaign, especially in electorally critical central Kenya.

Campaigning was marked by bitter attacks on rivals, and misinformation published on social media by all sides. Opponents of the two leading candidates questioned whether Ruto and Odinga had legitimate educational qualifications, falsely suggesting that their degree certificates were faked. While misinformation and fake claims were not new to Kenyan politics (for example, during the 2007 elections a false memorandum of understanding between Odinga and Kenya's

Muslim community was circulated by his rivals), the larger scale of social media saw such platforms emerge as major conduits of false attacks, rumours and claims, emphasizing the importance of youth in the election.

The presidential and general elections were held concurrently on 9 August 2022. They were largely peaceful, although issues with the technology (including the biometric voter identification) led to some queues and delays in the process. Ruto won the presidential election with 50.5% of the vote (7,176,141 votes), while Odinga secured 48.9% (6,942,930 votes). Some 14.2m. people cast valid ballots, and the result was not announced until 15 August, when the electoral commission confirmed Ruto's victory. Odinga claimed irregularities, with a number of election officials also alleging electoral fraud. Observers noted, however, that many of those making such claims had been appointed by outgoing President Kenyatta, who had aligned himself with Odinga in the campaign. Odinga stated that he would accept the ruling of the Supreme Court, which on 5 September confirmed the election as free and fair, and Ruto's victory. Ruto was sworn in as President on 13 September.

In the National Assembly the elections resulted in the Odinga-led Azimio la Umoja securing 168 seats, while Ruto's Kenya Kwanza took 167, while 14 independent deputies were returned.

CORRUPTION

Corruption continued to dominate Kenyan politics and its relationship with donors throughout the presidencies of both Mwai Kibaki and Uhuru Kenyatta, despite both initially promising to take tough action. By 2005 the official who had been appointed to lead the Government's anti-corruption campaign, John Githongo, had fled to the United Kingdom in fear of his life, and the Kenyan courts had failed to prosecute several officials who had been named in reports into major scandals. Furthermore, in 2007 legislation was passed to prevent the investigation of historic corruption cases, effectively removing the threat of prosecution from several senior politicians and officials.

Corruption scandals continued to plague the new Kenyatta administration that took office in late 2017, with several scandals extending into 2018 providing reminders of the scale of graft in the country. As public concerns over the scale of corruption grew in mid-2018, on 14 June Kenyatta announced that all senior officials would undergo a lifestyle audit, beginning with himself and Ruto (who was reportedly given no warning about the announcement). The decision led to a serious rift between Kenyatta and the Deputy President.

The move did little to prevent new scandals from emerging. In one instance, former Secretary for Sports, Culture and the Arts Hassan Wario was charged with corruption in relation to the 2016 Olympic Games. In September 2021 he chose to pay a fine of Ks. 3.6m. to avoid a six-year prison sentence. Several ministers were questioned over suspected links to graft scandals, as were aides to Ruto. In July 2019 Henry Rotich became the first incumbent government minister to appear in court on charges of corruption, in relation to a scandal over the construction of a dam, which had killed 47 people when it collapsed in May 2018. Rotich appeared in court with the Deputy Secretary for Finance, Kamau Thugge. However, the trial collapsed in 2021.

The Governor of Nairobi, Mike Mbuvi Sonko was forced to hand over responsibility for four key sectors in the city—health, transport, public works and planning—to the central Government in February 2020, after being impeached and charged with criminal offences over corruption allegations.

In June 2020 John Waluke, a member of the National Assembly, was found guilty of corruption relating to a scandal at the National Cereals and Produce Board and received a conditional sentence of 67 years' imprisonment if he failed, together with a fellow official who had been convicted on the same charge, to pay a large fine.

The Jersey Government confirmed in March 2022 that it was to return around US $5m. to the Kenyan Government. The money had allegedly been hidden in Jersey's offshore banks by the former Managing Director of Kenya Power, Samuel

Gichuru, and former Secretary for Finance, Chris Okemo. The agreement was reached after a nine-year investigation into the affair, and the returning money was to be used to purchase medical equipment to respond to the COVID-19 crisis.

SECURITY CONCERNS

In November 2002 a simultaneous attack on a hotel just outside Mombasa and on an Israeli charter aircraft taking off from the city's airport killed 16 people and injured about 80 others. The attack was believed to have been carried out by a Somali militant Islamist group—al-Ittihad al-Islam—with support from the militant Islamist al-Qa'ida organization.

In response to the reported involvement of Kenyan forces in the conflict in Somalia in March 2011, the Somali militant Islamist group al-Shabaab launched attacks within Kenya from late 2011; such attacks were to continue for the next decade. Many of the attacks have taken place in northern Kenya near the border with Somalia, but al-Shabaab has also perpetrated a number of large-scale attacks further south in Kenya over the years, killing many people.

An attack on Nairobi's Westgate shopping centre in September 2013 by al-Shabaab gunmen and the siege that ensued left at least 67 people dead and many more injured. In October 2020 two Kenyan men were convicted for their role in the attack. Although these were the first convictions of individuals involved in the attack, none of those on trial were key actors, but were rather accused of providing material support to the perpetrators.

Further attacks took place in succeeding years: in mid-June 2014 more than 60 people were killed in an assault by armed men on hotels and a police station in the coastal town of Mpeketoni, in Lamu county, and in April 2015 al-Shabaab gunmen launched a major attack on Garissa University. During a 12-hour siege 148 people were killed—mostly students on the campus. In the immediate aftermath of the incident, the Kenyan Government was challenged over its failure to provide security for the university (despite warnings from European and North American intelligence agencies signalling an imminent attack) and over its slow response in ending the siege. The Government subsequently ordered air strikes against two suspected al-Shabaab camps in Somalia, claiming to have destroyed them. In January 2019 al-Shabaab gunmen entered a hotel in Nairobi, killing 21 people and injuring 30 others during the 19-hour siege that followed. Al-Shabaab spokesmen asserted that the attack on the hotel, which was popular with foreign nationals, was in response to US President Donald Trump's recent recognition of Jerusalem as the capital of Israel, although it also notably occurred on the third anniversary of an al-Shabaab assault against Kenyan forces in Somalia in which 140 Kenyan soldiers had died. In January 2020 suspected al-Shabaab militants launched attacks against various targets: several schools in Kenya near the Somali border, in which four teachers and one pupil were killed; a police post; and a military base on Manda Island, in which three US soldiers were killed and a US aircraft was reportedly destroyed.

The Kenyan security forces responded with increasing ferocity to the attacks by al-Shabaab fighters, and questions were raised about their conduct. The security forces were accused of arbitrary arrests, of orchestrating the disappearance of persons suspected of links to radical groups, and of operating a policy of pre-emptive killing of those suspected of being connected to al-Shabaab. In December 2016 a human rights group accused Kenyan police of deliberately targeting Muslim men in the coastal region in a number of cases of extrajudicial killings, including the fatal shooting in Mombasa in June 2014 of the chairman of the Council of Imams and Preachers of Kenya, Sheikh Mohammed Idris, and two other Muslim clerics.

The Kenyan Government was also accused of targeting Somali refugees and Kenyans with Somali heritage as part of its anti-terrorism operations. In March 2014, for example, the Government announced that all Somali refugees would be required to live in designated camps, and checks were stepped up on Somalis living in Kenya. In April police arrested around 4,000 Somalis; many were detained at a sports stadium, where they were questioned about possible links to al-Shabaab. Some were subsequently deported as illegal immigrants. The

Government was accused of raising tensions and of increasing hostility within the country towards all Somalis. In December the Kenyan parliament passed controversial new anti-terrorism legislation, which critics claimed undermined civil liberties and freedom of speech. The legislation increased the length of time that police could detain terrorist suspects from 90 days to almost 12 months; gave more powers to investigators secretly to monitor telephone conversations; and empowered the Government to prosecute and imprison journalists whose reports were considered to undermine security operations. Independent media outlets warned against a government attack on press freedom, and scuffles broke out between parliamentary deputies during the vote on the controversial legislation.

The Kenyan security forces continued to launch operations against suspected al-Shabaab fighters. In March 2020 three Islamist assailants were killed by the Kenyan armed forces in Garissa county during military operations, and another assailant was captured. Police officers reported in July that they had successfully repulsed three al-Shabaab attacks in Garissa, Mandera and Wajir counties, including the prevention of a kidnapping by a group of suspected al-Shabaab gunmen. Later that month an alleged al-Shabaab militant was killed when an explosive device that he was attempting to plant detonated.

In November 2021 three Islamist militants, including one convicted for his role in the 2015 attack on Garissa University, escaped from a maximum-security prison in Nairobi. Seven prison warders were arrested in response to the escape.

Towards the end of 2021 concerns over forced disappearances of Kenyans allegedly committed by Kenyan police and security forces came to a head. Evidence suggested that at least 43 families had reported family members being detained and subsequently remaining missing during the year. A report published in 2022 suggested that police had killed over 187 people in 2021. Many of those who had been killed or who disappeared were Muslim men, and areas with high proportions of Muslim residents appeared to have been particularly targeted. Critics suggested that the police were using such tactics as part of operations against suspected al-Shabaab members or sympathizers. In September the Somali scholar and director of the Institute for Horn of Africa Strategic Studies was abducted by unknown men. Following widespread protests, he was released after more than a week. Although he gave no details of his ordeal, he said that he had been warned not to comment in future on regional politics. In October a lawyer and Islamic scholar was abducted, also by unknown assailants, and refused to give details of his captivity after his release. Cases of abductions, violence and murders continued into 2022. Muslim and human rights organizations rejected police claims that these were the result of criminal gangs, and called for an inquiry into the forced disappearances and killings by police.

As the worst regional drought in 40 years continued to affect northern Kenya, ethnic tensions in the northern Marsabit county were exacerbated by the election campaigning. Dozens of people had been killed during the first months of 2022, with 10 people shot and killed by unknown gunmen in a 10-day period in early April alone. In response to the growing violence, a 30-day curfew was imposed, and police increased efforts to crack down on illegal ownership of firearms and ammunition, much of which has traditionally been smuggled across the border from Ethiopia.

EXTERNAL RELATIONS

In July 2000 the newly constituted East African Community (EAC) came into effect. In 2005 a customs union was established between the members of the EAC and in the following year Burundi and Rwanda joined the Community, expanding it to include some 90m. people.

After relations between Uganda and Rwanda deteriorated in 2019, Kenya sought to play a mediating role in resolving the dispute between the two. Kenya was keen that the tensions did not result in Rwanda attempting to develop import routes through Tanzania in order to avoid Uganda, which would have the additional effect of diverting those routes away from Kenya. Meanwhile, Uganda accused Kenya of seeking to ensure more favourable terms in the planned construction of an oil pipeline connecting Ugandan oilfields to Kenyan ports, and in 2016 announced plans to develop a pipeline through Tanzania instead.

In October 2012 the High Court in London, UK, ruled that Mau Mau veterans could proceed with their legal case against the British Government for atrocities committed by British forces under the colonial administration. In June 2013, responding to the release of a previously hidden cache of official records outlining some of the abuses perpetrated by the British during the Mau Mau emergency of the 1950s, the British Government reached an out-of-court settlement with the prosecution, to the value of almost £20m., whereby each of the 5,228 Kenyan plaintiffs would receive about £3,000. These pay-outs did not bring an end to the matter, however, and in October 2014 a second group litigation action was launched in London involving allegations of the physical abuse, mistreatment and torture of some 40,000 Kenyans by British colonial forces during the Mau Mau uprising. This second group action was dismissed by the High Court in November 2018.

In February 2019 the Kenyan Government accused Somalia of organizing a licensing round for hydrocarbon exploration blocks in waters over which Kenya claimed territorial rights. The dispute over the delimitation of the Kenyan–Somali maritime border was already under adjudication by the International Court of Justice (ICJ). Kenya recalled its ambassador to Somalia, but following mediation by Ethiopia, diplomatic relations were normalized in November.

In April 2020 the Council of Ministers of the EAC formulated a regional COVID-19 response plan. It included proposals for co-ordination between member states in medical training and procurement, protocols for national laboratories and agreed rules on cross-border movement, security and trade. However, efforts to create a meaningful regional response were undermined by tensions between the administrations of the various member states and the failure of Tanzania and Burundi to participate fully in the plan.

Relations between Kenya and Somalia deteriorated in November 2020, after the Somali Government accused Kenya of interfering in its domestic politics (with specific regard to the autonomous state of Jubaland) and of supporting Somali opposition parties in the run-up to Somalia's general election. In December the Somali Government expelled the Kenyan ambassador and severed diplomatic ties. In response, Kenya banned flights to and from Mogadishu, the Somali capital.

In March 2021 Kenya announced renewed plans—first suggested in 2013—to close down the refugee camps in Dadaab and Kakuma in eastern Kenya (inhabited mainly by Somalis), giving the UN High Commissioner for Refugees (UNHCR) two weeks to make arrangements for their disbandment. As on previous such occasions, although there was little likelihood of the Kenyan Government following through with its threat, the announcement immediately drew criticism from international organizations and human rights groups. At the end of April 2021 the Kenyan Government declared that it would postpone shutting down the camps and establish a joint task force with UNHCR to plan for their closure by mid-2022. This further heightened tensions between Kenya and Somalia, which were compounded by the opening in March 2021 of the maritime boundary case between the two countries at the ICJ. By mid-2021 bilateral relations between the two countries appeared to be warming, after Somalia restored diplomatic ties with Kenya in May and in the following month Kenya lifted its ban on flights to and from Mogadishu. In October the ICJ ruled on the Kenyan–Somali maritime border, upholding the principle of equidistance from each coastline as the boundary. Somalia claimed this as a victory, as the borderline looked closer to its original claims. Kenya welcomed the ruling, but added that it did not recognize the jurisdiction of the international court.

Economy

DUNCAN WOODSIDE

INTRODUCTION

In the third decade of the 21st century, it has become common to refer to Kenya as a 'regional economic powerhouse'. It possesses the largest economy in the East African Community (EAC) and hosts the regional headquarters of United Nations (UN) agencies and non-governmental organizations. It is also an information technology and transport hub, a status that is increasingly exploited not only by foreign organizations, but also by home-grown businesses and entrepreneurs. Kenya's banking sector has strong international links and serves much of the wider region, while its stock exchange hosts companies from neighbouring EAC nations. Meanwhile, the capital, Nairobi, has undergone an extraordinary construction boom.

However, a number of factors have exerted a drag on Kenya's economic performance, particularly in terms of poor governance. Election cycles have periodically been accompanied by significant violence, the most dramatic of recent times occurring at the end of 2007 and in early 2008, in a context where the distribution of wealth has long been heavily orientated towards ethnically structured patronage networks. The entrenched nature of these networks has resulted in high levels of corruption, as evidenced by Kenya's lowly position of joint 128th out of 180 countries in Transparency International's 2021 Corruption Perceptions Index (ahead of Uganda, under the increasingly authoritarian rule of President Yoweri Museveni, but far behind other fellow EAC members Rwanda and Tanzania).

The Government has also built up a significant external debt burden in recent years, through the repeated hefty insurance of Eurobonds. In January 2020 the International Monetary Fund (IMF) estimated that it would cost around US $10,000m. in additional funds to revive hundreds of poorly managed infrastructure projects, which were conceived as an attempt to accelerate the country's transition to middle-income status. Secretary for Finance—National Treasury and Planning Henry Rotich was arrested in July 2019 on suspicion of financial mismanagement of funds relating to two dam projects. He was suspended from his cabinet position, but denied the allegations, with his supporters arguing that the case was politically motivated, amid intensified rivalries within a precarious coalition headed by President Uhuru Kenyatta, a Kikuyu, who had served two full terms by 2022 (see *History*). Rotich's loyalties lay with Deputy President William Ruto, the most senior Kalenjin politician. Both Kenyatta and Ruto had been indicted by the International Criminal Court in relation to the 2007–08 post-election violence, when the two men had been on opposite sides of a deadly ethnic cleavage, before they formed an improbable alliance to contest jointly—and successfully—the 2013 polls, and went on to see the charges against them dropped amid prosecutors' repeated difficulties in maintaining the confidence and co-operation of witnesses. Despite consistent promises to address corruption (and detailed reports of wrongdoing in government departments by the Auditor-General), no major political figures have, to date, been convicted, although court proceedings were initiated against several former ministers.

Headline economic performance was strong in the decade before the onset of the coronavirus disease (COVID-19) pandemic, propelled in part by the high level of investment, even as funds went astray. Real gross domestic product (GDP) growth was 5.6% in 2019, thanks to a strong performance by the services sector, and average annual GDP growth during 2010–19 was 5.0%, according to the IMF, allowing a steady improvement in living standards.

Kenya also appeared to be improving aspects of its business environment, moving up 19 places to a ranking of 61st (out of 190 countries) in the World Bank's 2019 *Doing Business* report and rising further, to 56th place, in the 2020 report.

However, from early March 2020 the COVID-19 pandemic left the Kenyan economy exposed, especially in view of the hefty increase in external debt accumulated in recent years. In mid-May the IMF raised the country's risk of debt distress from 'moderate' to 'high', in a context where the Government's debt burden had increased from 50.2% of GDP at the end of 2015 to 61.7% in 2019. The economy contracted by 0.3% in real terms in 2020.

In April 2021 the IMF approved a 38-month Extended Fund Facility (EFF) and Extended Credit Facility (ECF) for Kenya, worth a total of US $2,340m. in funding, on the back of $739m. in emergency funding approved in May 2020. The IMF in April 2022 concluded its third review of the ECF/EFF, unlocking a $236m. tranche of funding upon formal completion of the review by the IMF board in July. Despite a slow roll-out of vaccinations against COVID-19 in Kenya and most of Africa, the country's economy recovered very strongly in 2021. The Secretary for National Treasury and Planning, Ukur Yatani, announced in May 2022 that real GDP growth totalled 7.5% in 2021, the fastest rate in 11 years. A recovery of the global economy, helped by accommodative fiscal and monetary policies worldwide, was a key factor in Kenya's recovery, alongside a release of pent-up domestic demand. Manufacturing, the retail sector, real estate and financial services all performed well in 2021, according to the Kenya National Bureau of Statistics (KNBS). Yatani noted that GDP growth would have accelerated further, were it not for fuel and food inflation, a weak agriculture sector and a weak shilling, which depreciated to Ks. 113 per US $ across the course of the year, from 109 per $ at the end of 2020 and 101 per $ at the end of 2019. The Secretary for National Treasury and Planning forecast slightly lower real GDP growth, of 6.7%, in 2022, noting that although agriculture should return to modest positive overall growth, the Russian Federation's invasion of Ukraine in February 2022 would continue to drive inflation and global interest rates higher. This would limit demand in Kenya's export markets and feed into tighter domestic monetary policy, especially given the weakness of the shilling, thus also constraining domestic economic activity. Yatani also noted that renewed COVID-19 lockdowns in the People's Republic of China, which was continuing to pursue a policy of COVID-19 elimination, rather than containment, would undermine Kenya's exports. Meanwhile, the IMF predicted that real GDP growth would total 5.7% in 2022, lower than the Government's forecast, even as it envisaged that the direct economic impact on Kenya of the conflict in Ukraine would be limited. It, too, cited a partial recovery in agriculture, alongside a continued recovery in the services sector as drivers of growth for 2022. The IMF also noted that Kenya's fiscal position had been bolstered by both the strong economic recovery and by tax reforms, both of which had boosted revenues significantly and reduced concerns about the country's debt vulnerabilities.

AGRICULTURE AND HORTICULTURE

Agriculture remains significant in Kenya, accounting (together with forestry and fishing) for a provisional 23.9% of GDP in 2021. The principal cash crops are tea, horticultural produce and coffee. In 2021 agriculture and forestry engaged 11.6% of the working population in paid employment in the formal sector, according to provisional figures. More than one-half of total agricultural output is subsistence production. For many Kenyans, the staple food is ugali, a porridge-like substance that is derived from maize. The agriculture sector (including forestry and fishing) contracted by 0.2% in real terms in 2021, according to the KNBS. Drought through much of the year affected production of maize, beans and vegetables, although there were steady production volumes in the crucial tea sector and improved coffee exports. Yatani noted in May 2022 that the agriculture sector should return to positive growth in 2022, helped by better rains and fertilizer subsidies. The moderately improved rains were also expected to help limit food price inflation, which was spurred higher worldwide by Russia's invasion of Ukraine, a major wheat producer.

With regard to externally orientated agriculture, the tea sector is a key driver of Kenya's export revenues. The sector is overseen by the Tea Board of Kenya (TBK), and produce is sold through auction at Mombasa. Output has fluctuated moderately in recent years, but not alarmingly, given the sensitivity of cash crops to poor weather and other forms of volatility. Tea production slumped in 2017 by some 20%, after the impact of drought on the country from late 2016. The TBK estimated production during January–April 2018 at 144,340 metric tons—a rise of 18% from the 121,550 tons recorded in the first four months of the previous year. According to preliminary statistics provided in Kenya's April 2021 IMF staff report, receipts from tea exports rose from US $1,115m. in 2019 to $1,248m. in 2020, although they remained below the $1,370m. achieved in 2018 and $1,424m. in 2017. In 2021 tea export earnings rose by 13% in local currency terms to Ks. 136,000m., according to TBK data. Based on the exchange rate at the end of 2021, this translated into a fall in tea earnings in dollar terms, to some $1,203m., despite increased export volumes, which rose from 518m. kg to 558m. kg. Receipts from coffee exports increased to $209m. in 2020, according to preliminary data, up slightly from $205m. in 2019, but down substantially from $232m. in 2018. Coffee exports totalled Ks. 26,100m. in 2021, according to the KNBS, marking a significant rise in dollar terms, to $231m., based on the exchange rate at the end of 2021. This marked improvement was driven by strong global coffee prices, as export volumes fell from 43,386 tons in 2020 to 37,477 tons in 2021.

Another key export-orientated agricultural sector in Kenya is the flower industry. Intensive farming of flowers, largely around Lake Naivasha, generates significant employment and moderate foreign exchange earnings. Kenya exported an estimated 136,601 metric tons of cut flowers in 2014, yielding revenue of Ks. 54,600m., according to the Kenya Flower Council (KFC). The principal export destinations are the Netherlands, the United Kingdom and Germany. The flower industry was one of the first sectors in Kenya to feel the adverse impact of the spread of COVID-19 through Europe in March 2020. Late that month Clement Tulezi, the CEO of the KFC, told the Agence France-Presse news agency that the country's 170 horticultural farms were losing a total of Ks. 250m. (US $2.3m.) per day. At that stage, the KFC estimated that the industry employed some 150,000 people and indirectly supported about 4m. people in Kenya. Losses within Kenya's horticulture industry subsequently reached $3.5m. per day, according to the British newspaper the *Financial Times*, before a partial return of demand from key European markets saw losses pared back to $1m. per day by late May/early June, in line with the easing of COVID-19 lockdowns in some of those markets. However, over the year as a whole, the horticulture sector performed remarkably well. IMF data indicated that export receipts from this crucial sector increased from $991m. in 2019 to $1,097m. in 2020. Horticulture revenues totalled Ks. 158,100m. ($1,398m.) in 2021, according to the KNBS. However, Tulezi warned in May 2022 that the sector was likely to be hit by new standards introduced by the European Union (EU) that required flower farmers to limit the use not only of pesticides, but also of water and fertilizer. He noted that the new measures would adversely affect crop yields and quality, at a time when profitability was also under pressure from high energy and air freight transport costs, owing to the effect of Russia's invasion of Ukraine on already elevated global energy prices.

The global COVID-19 crisis seriously affected the food production sector in Kenya, especially externally orientated firms. The Fresh Produce Exporters Association of Kenya estimated in early June 2020 that export volumes from the country's farms stood at 50% of normal levels. Some farms suspended shipments entirely. However, as with flower exports, figures for the full year were better than initially feared. In terms of volume, fruit exports rose from 81.9m. kg in 2019 to 103.8m. kg in 2020, although vegetable exports decreased from 72.7m. kg in 2019 to 60.3m. kg in 2020, according to the Fresh Produce Exporters' Association of Kenya (FPEAK). Overall, export revenue from fruit, vegetable and horticulture totalled

Ks. 151,159m. in 2020, according to FPEAK, with fruit accounting for 12%, vegetables 16% and flowers 72%.

A new threat emerged at the end of 2019, in the form of Kenya's worst desert locust invasion in decades. The Secretary for Agriculture, Livestock, Fisheries and Co-operatives, Mwangi Kiunjuri, declared that the swarms had first moved into the country from Somalia in late December, spreading through the counties of Mandera and Marsabit, alongside the east of Wajir, Garissa, central Isiolo and Samburu during the first 10 days of January 2020. Police shot at the swarms with guns and tear gas canisters, to little effect. By late January 70,000 ha of land in Kenya was infested or ruined, and one swarm had measured 60 km long by 40 km wide, according to the Associated Press. The Food and Agriculture Organization of the UN (FAO) reported in early April that the situation in East Africa remained 'extremely alarming', stating that hopper bands and an increasing number of new swarms were forming in Kenya, southern Ethiopia and Somalia. The same body had reported in late March that there were an 'increasing number of first-generation immature swarms in northern and central counties' of Kenya. It also noted that further concentrations of the pest were expected in Marsabit and Turkana counties.

Kenya had an estimated 21.7m. head of cattle in 2020, according to FAO. The country has traditionally exported butter, cheese and skimmed milk powder, and maintains strategic stocks of these products. In 2020 FAO reported that Kenya had an estimated 57.2m. chickens, 36.0m. goats, 25.3m. sheep, 4.7m. camels and 649,300 pigs.

Sugar is an additional significant sector for Kenya's agriculture. The market is overseen by the Kenya Sugar Board, which has estimated that the sector accounts for some 15% of agricultural GDP and supports the livelihoods of at least one-quarter of Kenya's population, with production centred largely in Nyanza, Rift Valley and Western Provinces. Mumias Sugar Co Ltd is the country's biggest miller of the commodity, but experienced difficulties in the 2010s, receiving a Ks. 1,000m. bailout from the Government in mid-2015. The company has struggled to maintain its competitiveness, particularly in a context of cheap imports.

BANKING SECTOR AND MONETARY POLICY

Kenya's financial sector has expanded significantly in recent years, stoked by rising middle-class incomes and an extended property boom. As of May 2020 the Central Bank of Kenya (CBK) stated that there was a total of 42 commercial banks licensed to operate in the country, down from 43 in 2014. Of those commercial banks, 24 were private locally owned institutions, 15 were private institutions majority-owned by foreign entities, and three were publicly owned institutions (the Consolidated Bank of Kenya, Development Bank of Kenya and National Bank of Kenya). Major operators in Kenya include Kenya Commercial Bank (KCB), Barclays Bank of Kenya and Standard Chartered Bank Kenya (SCB Kenya). The CBK issued two new banking licences in the first half of 2017. The first went to Dubai Islamic Bank, based in the United Arab Emirates (UAE), and is focused on *Shari'a*-compliant lending. Then in June the CBK confirmed that it had granted a licence to Mayfair Bank Ltd, which would initially maintain branches in Nairobi and Mombasa. These were the first licences to be granted since the CBK imposed a moratorium on permitting new banks to operate in October 2015. A survey by the CBK, released in April 2019, revealed that the proportion of Kenya's adult population with access to financial services had increased to an all-time high of 83%, from 75% in 2016. The rise was driven overwhelmingly by persistently strong uptake of mobile money services, predominantly Safaricom's M-Pesa service (see below), but also the services offered by Airtel Kenya and Telkom Kenya. According to the survey, at that time only 41% of the adult population had bank accounts.

Alongside strong growth in the assets of Kenya's conventional banking sector in recent years, there has been significant innovation in the development of so-called 'mobile money'. This entails the use of mobile telephones to transfer credit, which is used as a means of exchange. Initially, such transactions took place on an informal basis, typically involving individuals in relatively wealthy urban environments transferring credit to poorer relatives in rural areas. Safaricom, Kenya's principal mobile cellular telephone company, capitalized on this trade by imposing a small charge for the use of such services. In addition, Safaricom has developed the M-Pesa platform, which is increasingly being used to pay utility bills and settle invoices between private commercial enterprises. The system involves the payer sending credit via their mobile telephone to a receiver, who is then able to redeem the credit into cash at a Safaricom outlet.

Several major Kenyan banks—the KCB, Equity, Diamond Trust, Co-operative and SCB Kenya—were hit by fines totalling Ks. 385m. in March 2020 for failing to report suspicious transactions under lenders' obligations to counter money laundering. The punishment came on top of a similar sized fine two years earlier in connection to the same case, which had involved the embezzlement of nearly US $100m. from the National Youth Service. The scandal had resulted in businessmen and senior officials being charged with various offences. However, Director of Public Prosecutions (DPP) Noordin Haji deferred any prosecution of the banks, in order to allow them more time to enhance their internal controls.

The CBK cut interest rates aggressively in response to the COVID-19 pandemic. On 29 April 2020 it reduced its benchmark rate—the central bank rate (CBR)—by 0.25 percentage points to 7.0%, having already slashed it by one percentage point at a monetary policy meeting in March. In the same month the central bank had also lowered commercial banks' reserve requirements from 5.25% to 4.25%. It was clear by early May that the COVID-19 crisis—and in particular, the inability of companies and individuals that held bank loans to maintain interest repayments—was already having a significant impact on the health of commercial lenders' loan books, despite the easing of liquidity conditions by the CBK. Joshua Oigara, the CEO of the KCB Group, told *Business Daily* that his bank had restructured Ks. 80,000m. (about 15%) of its loan book. The SCK declared that it had restructured Ks. 8,000m., representing around 6% of its loan book. The CBK maintained the CBR at 7.0% at its monetary policy meeting in March 2021, and although the bank's Governor, Patrick Njoroge, announced that there was leeway to reduce rates in the future, it remained unchanged at 7.0% in March 2022, marking two years without any change to the benchmark cost of borrowing. However, the monetary policy committee in late May raised the CBR by 0.5 percentage points to 7.5%, citing significant changes in the global outlook, notably 'elevated global inflationary pressures, heightened geopolitical tensions, rising commodity prices' and 'measures taken around the world by authorities in response' notably rate rises engineered by the US Federal Reserve. It also took into account a rise in domestic annual inflation from 5.6% in March to 6.5% in April.

Major banks reported strong results in 2021, more than recovering from the COVID-induced downturn that had undermined profitability in 2020. The KCB generated a net profit of Ks. 34,200m. in 2021, an increase of 74% from 2020 (when net profit had registered Ks. 19,600m., a 22% fall from 2019). KCB's 2021 revenues were up by 13.5%, at Ks. 108,600m., thanks largely to a 15.0% rise in net interest income to Ks. 77,700m. However, KCB's non-performing loan (NPL) book climbed from 14.7% of total loans in 2020 to 16.5% in 2021, 'signalling', it said, 'the longer-term effects of the COVID-19 impact'. KCB's NPL ratio had stood at 10.9% in 2019, the last year before the pandemic. Meanwhile, Equity Group recorded a 99% rise in its annual net profit, which reached Ks. 40,100m. in 2021, compared to Ks. 20,100m. in 2020, on the back of total income rising from Ks. 92,900m. to Ks. 112,400m., an increase of 21% year on year. Encouragingly, Equity Group's NPL portfolio declined from 11% of its loan book in 2020 to 8.3% in 2021. Equity Group's provisioning for bad loans had risen more than fivefold in 2020, to Ks. 26,630m., from Ks. 5,300m. in 2019. In 2020 the EU and the European Investment Bank provided Equity Bank with a combined Ks. 15,800m. in funds to help small and medium-sized enterprises, including (but not limited to) those operating in the agriculture sector, to help them to cope with the financial fallout from the pandemic. The arrangement consisted of Ks. 13,200m. in the form of loans and Ks. 2,600m. in grants. Like KCB and Equity Group, SCB

Kenya reported dramatically improved profitability in 2021. Profit before tax surged to Ks. 12,600m., a rise of 70.2% from Ks. 7,400m. in 2020, and higher than the Ks. 12,200m recorded in 2019.

In a staff report in April 2021, the IMF noted that Kenya needed closely to monitor potential risks to financial stability, even as it described the CBK's monetary policy as being 'appropriately accommodative' in response to the challenges generated by the pandemic. While stating that Kenya's banking sector remained well capitalized and liquid, the Fund warned that the pandemic had 'exacerbated pre-existing asset quality issues'. NPLs stood at 14.1% of gross loans in the banking sector in December 2020, up significantly from 12.3% in February, at the onset of the health crisis.

SERVICES

Aside from the banking sector, the other main services sectors in Kenya's economy are tourism and the information and communications technology (ICT) market. The principal attractions are safaris, with the country's various national parks offering the opportunity to see wildlife, and the Indian Ocean coast, which boasts a tropical climate and long stretches of beach.

The tourism sector has been adversely affected by repeated periods of insecurity, most notably the unprecedented 2007–08 election violence and attacks by al-Shabaab insurgents in response to the Kenyan military's 2011 incursion into—and ongoing presence in—southern Somalia. In 2018 the country finally surpassed the 2011 peak for arrivals. The Ministry of Tourism and Wildlife reported a surge in arrivals in that year to just over 2.0m., from just below 1.5m. in 2017, while tourism receipts rose by 31.3%, from Ks. 119,900m. in 2017 to Ks. 157,386m. in 2018. The strong performance in 2018 came despite the issue of yet another revised travel advisory by the British Government regarding the likelihood of terrorist attacks. An attack perpetrated by al-Shabaab against the Dusit Hotel and office complex in Nairobi on 15 January 2019 killed 21 people, prompting fears of a renewed drop in tourist arrivals. None the less, arrivals in 2019 rose by 1% to 2.05m., while earnings in the sector increased by 3.9% to Ks. 163,560m. (US \$1,610m.), according to the Ministry of Tourism and Wildlife. The Secretary for Tourism and Wildlife, Najib Balala, stated that tourism growth during the year had been constrained by the Dusit Hotel attack, but had still shown a degree of resilience. Tourism in 2020, however, was seriously affected by the COVID-19 pandemic. Tourist arrivals through the two key air entry points—Jomo Kenyatta International Airport in Nairobi and Moi International Airport in Mombasa—fell to just below 440,000m. in that year, from 1.54m. in 2019, according to the KNBS.

Total foreign visitor arrivals registered just 579,600 in 2020 and close to 1.2m. tourism jobs were lost in Kenya during the pandemic, according to the Ministry of Tourism and Wildlife. The top five source markets for foreign tourist arrivals in 2020, according to provisional figures, were Germany (15.2%), the USA (10.1%), Italy (9.7%), the UK (6.7%) and France (4.7%). There was a marked improvement in 2021, as foreign visitor arrivals rose by 50.3% to reach 871,300. Tourism earnings rose from a paltry Ks. 88,560m. (US \$811m.) in 2020 to Ks. 146,510m (\$1,296m.) in 2021, according to the Ministry. Domestic tourism also partially recovered, with the number of visits to national parks and game reserves increasing to 1.5m. in 2021 from 1.0m. in 2020. The 2022/23 budget set aside Ks. 15,800m. for boosting tourism, and the Government targeted 1,030,000 visitor arrivals for that fiscal year.

The national airline, Kenya Airways, reported a full-year loss of Ks. 5,950m. in 2018/19 as the company grappled with accumulated financial difficulties provoked in large part by a downturn in tourism earlier in the decade and a sustained rise in competition from Middle Eastern carriers. Nearly a quarter of a century after the airline was privatized, the Kenyan parliament's transport committee proposed in June 2019 that Kenya Airways be renationalized, through the creation of a national holding company with four subsidiaries—the carrier itself, Jomo Kenyatta International Airport, the Kenya Airports Authority and a flying school. At that stage, the airline was already 48.9% owned by the Government, while 7.8% was held by Air France-KLM and 38.1% by a group of 11 banks that had converted their debt into equity in 2017. The Government would need to buy the remaining private creditors out of their shares if the proposal were to succeed. The Government quickly backed the committee's proposal and a full legislative vote was carried in favour of the move in July 2019. However, the outlook for the airline, Kenya's aviation sector and air companies around the globe darkened to an unprecedented extent in March 2020, with the far-reaching spread of COVID-19. A supplementary budget presented to parliament in February 2021 saw the carrier receive an additional Ks. 10,000m. in government support, in the form of Ks. 2,000m. from the Ministry of Transport, Infrastructure, Housing, Urban Development and Public Works and Ks. 8,000m. from the National Treasury. In March Kenya Airways announced a pre-tax loss of Ks. 36,570m. for 2020—its worst ever annual performance. In 2021 the airline's net loss totalled Ks. 15,800m., equating to US \$139.8m., based on the exchange rate at the end of that calendar year. Cost reductions, including renegotiated airplane leases, helped pare back the annual loss, alongside a partial recovery in airline traffic from the pandemic-provoked trough of 2020. However, the extent of the airline's drag on Kenya's overall fiscal performance was laid bare by the Government's 2021/22 and 2022/23 budgets, which set aside \$473m. in direct budgetary support for Kenya Airways, according to the IMF.

Kenya's ICT sector experienced very strong growth in the first two decades of the 21st century, owing to the proliferation of mobile telephones. The number of mobile subscriptions in Kenya increased from 24,000 in 1999 to 49.5m. in 2018—a year that saw a record surge in subscriptions, from 42.8m. in 2017. The following year, the number of mobile phone subscribers per 100 people exceeded 100 for the first time, reaching 104, from 96 in 2018, ahead of a further rise to 114 subscriptions per 100 people in 2020, according to World Bank data. The largest company in the Kenyan telecommunications market is Safaricom, which is 40% owned by the UK's Vodafone. Airtel Kenya and Telkom Kenya have repeatedly complained that Safaricom has unfairly dominated the market. However, in December 2019 the Communications Authority approved a merger between Airtel Kenya and Telkom Kenya, which represented a significant potential challenge to Safaricom's market dominance. Safaricom had lost market share to Airtel in 2018, and by the end of that year Safaricom accounted for 63.3% of the market, a decline from 71.9% at the end of September 2017, while the market share of Airtel rose from 14.9% to 23.4% over the same period, according to official data from Kenya's telecommunications regulator. Safaricom announced in March 2019 that it had secured an agreement that would enable its mobile payment service to be used on the platform of AliExpress.com, a subsidiary of Chinese online retail giant Alibaba Group. The deal permitted Kenyan consumers to purchase products in Kenyan shillings using M-Pesa, via Alibaba's own payment service affiliate, Ant Financial. Safaricom then won a licence in Kenya's neighbour Ethiopia in 2021, providing access to a market of 100m. people that had previously been off limits to foreign investors. It teamed up with CDC Group, a development finance company based in the UK, for the successful bid, which was reported by Reuters to have totalled US \$850m. Safaricom's net profit fell to Ks. 68,670m. in 2020/21, down from Ks. 73,650m. in 2019/20, as revenues were hit by the COVID-19 pandemic. This was the first time that Safaricom's annual profit had fallen since 2011/12. Net profit fell by a further 1.7%, to Ks. 67,496m., in 2021/22, despite total revenues rising by 12.9% to Ks. 298,078m. The company cited heightened regulatory risk, including unfavourable taxation changes, and inflationary pressures as headwinds affecting recent performance and the immediate outlook.

The retail sector has expanded significantly in Kenya since 2000, thanks in part to the emergence of a sizeable middle class, with supermarket and café chains establishing significant operations. Nakumatt Holdings was for a long time the most visible supermarket operator, with major stores across Kenya and other countries in the region, including Rwanda, Uganda and Tanzania, as well as convenience store outlets. Tuskys Supermarkets, established in 1990, maintained over

60 outlets in Kenya and Uganda at mid-2020. The Westgate shopping mall in Nairobi, where Nakumatt's flagship store was located, reopened in July 2015 after being largely destroyed during the siege of September 2013. In 2016 major international retail chains began to enter the market as France's Carrefour opened its first store, later expanding to five outlets. It was followed in March 2018 by South Africa's Shoprite (the continent's largest retailer in terms of sales), which announced the planned opening of two stores in Nairobi. The arrival of foreign enterprises came as the principal operators in the Kenyan retail sector struggled. Nakumatt suffered a dramatic collapse in 2017, leading to store closures and finally the decision to file for administration in October, with debts reported to be over US $300m. The deterioration was in part caused by a fatal fire in one store, the destruction of another and the Westgate attack. However, deeper issues included a failure to modernize management and address the endemic theft of cash and stock, in the context of poorly executed expansion plans. In January 2018 the High Court allowed Nakumatt to go into voluntary administration, granting it protection from its creditors. In January 2020 Nakumatt's creditors voted to liquidate the firm.

Twiga Foods, a company set up in Nairobi in 2014 as a fresh and processed foods distributor, reported in October 2019 that it had raised a total of US $30m. to fund ambitious expansion plans. Twiga disclosed that it was sourcing food from over 17,000 producers, while delivering three times per week to more than 8,000 retailers. In November 2021 Twiga announced that it had secured a further $50m. in funding to digitize food distribution not only in Kenya, but also to extend such operations to Uganda and Tanzania and potentially also other African markets.

FISCAL POLICY, CORRUPTION AND DEVELOPMENT AID

Kenya successfully launched US $2,000m. in Eurobonds on international capital markets in June 2014. Two separate bonds were offered; a $500m. five-year bond and a $1,500m. 10-year bond. In the event, the offer was oversubscribed by a factor of more than four, as $8,800m. of bids were received. The five-year bonds were floated with a coupon of 5.875% and the 10-year bonds at 6.875%, completing a remarkably successful initiative, given the backdrop of escalating terrorist attacks in Kenya and faltering economic growth. Proceeds from the sales of the bonds were earmarked for repaying a $600m. syndicated loan and an array of infrastructure projects. Further substantial foreign borrowing followed in subsequent years, including the flotation of a further $2,000m. of bonds at competitive rates in February 2018, on the back of bids amounting to $14,000m., despite an aborted investigation in 2015 and 2016 by the public prosecutor into the alleged misappropriation of up to $1,400m. of the $2,000m. in Eurobonds floated in 2014.

Also in February 2018 the IMF announced that it had blocked Kenya's access to the $1,500m. Stand-By Credit Facility for the past eight months, after it was unable to complete a review in June 2017 following disagreements with the Government on fiscal restraint. The revelation came shortly after rating agency Moody's caused alarm by downgrading Kenya's sovereign credit rating from B1 to B2 as the authorities were preparing their Eurobond issue. The Government subsequently implemented corrective fiscal measures as it sought to put relations with the IMF back onto a firmer footing and to maintain the confidence of international bond markets. As part of the 2018/19 budget, Rotich announced a new 'Robin Hood' tax on financial transactions, imposing a levy of 0.05% on transfers of Ks. 500,000 placed through banks or other financial institutions. On 21 September 2018 President Kenyatta signed into law the Finance Act for that year, which included the introduction of an 8% value-added tax on petroleum products.

Despite the Government's efforts to plug the fiscal gap, the IMF failed to renew the country's Stand-By Credit Facility when its US $990m. arrangement expired in September 2018, owing to concerns surrounding policy, particularly the ongoing interest rate cap. In May 2019 Kenya launched another $2,100m. of Eurobonds, with tenors (terms to maturity) of

seven and 12 years. Despite the continued absence of an IMF Stand-By Credit Facility, market demand for the new offering was again firm. The seven-year bonds were priced with a coupon of 7.0% and the 30-year bonds at 8.0%, according to a notice published by the National Treasury, which announced that the proceeds would be allocated to infrastructure spending, general budgetary expenditure and redeeming the five-year Eurobonds that had been issued in 2014.

Rotich was arrested in July 2019, on suspicion of financial misconduct in relation to the proposed construction of two dams by the Italian firm CMC di Ravenna. Earlier in his tenure, in December 2015 he had denied that any money was unaccounted for in connection with the investigation into the alleged misappropriation of the Eurobonds floated in 2014. Kenya's DPP, Haji, declared that Rotich and 27 co-accused—including Kamau Thugge (Rotich's Principal Secretary) and Paolo Porcelli, the CEO of CMC di Ravenna—faced charges ranging from financial misconduct to conspiring to defraud over the dams. Haji alleged that the National Treasury had borrowed Ks. 63,000m. to fund the two dams, yet the two projects were budgeted to cost only Ks. 46,000m. Although Rotich and CMC di Ravenna denied any wrongdoing, Rotich and Thugge were suspended from their government positions. The IMF subsequently cancelled a planned trip to Kenya and did not complete plans for a precautionary Stand-By Credit Facility in 2019.

Nevertheless, in May 2020, despite continued concerns about corruption and the high-level management of money, the IMF approved US $739m. in emergency lending under a Rapid Credit Facility, to help Kenya to manage the effects of the COVID-19 pandemic crisis. The World Bank, meanwhile, approved loans totalling $1,000m.: a $750m. facility repayable over 30 years at a rate of 1.35% and $250m. at a floating rate of about 2%.

Seeking to press the Government into limiting the fiscal shortfall, the Kenyan parliament's Budget and Appropriations Committee in March 2021 announced that it would reject the proposed 2021/22 budget if it failed to stipulate a maximum deficit of 7.5% of GDP. This announcement followed a statement by the National Treasury in February 2021 that it expected the deficit for the next fiscal year to be recorded at around this level. The parliamentary committee also recommended a rationalization of the most fiscally burdensome and loss-making state-owned enterprises, including through possible privatizations. In early April 2021 the IMF announced that it had approved Kenya's request for an extension to the EFF and also for an arrangement under the ECF. This would unlock a total of US $2,340m. in funds over a period of three years, with the money being targeted to help those citizens left most vulnerable by the pandemic and to ameliorate the country's state debt vulnerabilities. In mid-May the Fund announced that had reached an agreement with the Government on policies that enabled the conclusion of a first review of the EFF/ECF programme, which would unlock an initial $410m. in financing, pending approval by the IMF's executive board. In a further measure of direct budgetary support, in May the World Bank provided Kenya with funds of $750m. through its Development Policy Operations facility; the loan was to be repayable at an interest rate of 3.1%. The IMF commended a number of efforts to bolster Kenya's fiscal governance, notably the expected publication of information on all firms that win public procurement contracts, including the identification of beneficial owners, and the planned adoption of a common payroll system for both central government and county administrations.

In a staff report published in December 2021, the IMF projected that Kenya's overall fiscal deficit would reach 8.2% of GDP in 2021/22, unchanged as a percentage of GDP from 2020/21. These projections reflected a projected rise in revenues and grants in 2021/22, to Ks. 2,119,500m., up from an estimated Ks. 1,815,100m. in 2020/21. Meanwhile, after a pandemic-necessitated surge in spending in 2020/21 to a projected Ks. 2,749,500m., from a preliminary Ks. 2,545,000m. in 2019/20, a further significant rise in spending was factored in for 2021/22, to Ks. 3,153,200m. The IMF had already noted in its April 2021 report that although an interruption in planned fiscal consolidation in 2020/21—through temporary tax cuts and pandemic-related spending—was appropriate, given the exceptional circumstances, Kenya was at high risk of debt distress in the future. The Fund emphasized that the Government should rely as far as possible on concessional lending. In nominal terms, inclusive of small adjustments, the overall fiscal deficit was forecast to rise from Ks. 929,300m. in 2020/21 to Ks. 1,033,700m. in 2021/22. In an April 2022 press release following a third review of Kenya's EFF and ECF, the IMF expressed its confidence that 'Kenya is on track to meet its fiscal objectives and put debt as a percentage of GDP firmly on a downward path.'

EXTERNAL ACCOUNTS

Kenya has maintained a heavy imbalance on its current account in recent years, reaching a deficit of US $5,287m. in 2019, a substantial increase compared with $3,653m. in 2016 and $4,299m. in 2015. The widening current account deficit was overwhelmingly due to the rising trade deficit, which increased to $10,683m. in 2019, from $7,890m. in 2016, as a result of surging imports. Imports rose from $13,637m. in 2016 to $16,554m. in 2019. The services balance—positive to the amount of an estimated $1,746m. in 2019—did little to offset the negative effect of the trade balance on the overall current account.

According to IMF figures, Kenya's current account deficit fell to $4,797m. in 2020, owing largely to goods imports decreasing to $14,482m. as demand waned during the pandemic. The external picture was also supported by an improved export performance in 2020, as total exports rose from $5,871m. in 2019 to $6,052m. in 2020, aided by tea and horticulture shipments rising by double digits in percentage terms. Indeed, the horticulture sector had a good year, despite interruptions to global aviation traffic caused by the pandemic and shrinking disposable income in end-user markets. The trade balance therefore recorded a deficit of $8,078m. in 2020, compared with $8,937m. in 2019. However, the IMF predicted a significant deterioration in the external picture in 2021, including a current account deficit of $5,649m. and a trade deficit of $10,170m. Although the Fund expected goods exports to rise to $7,068m. in 2021, helped again by further substantial rises in revenue from tea and horticulture, it forecast that imports would surge to $17,239m. as pent-up demand in Kenya led to a rise in goods from abroad.

On a visit to Washington, DC, USA, in February 2020, President Kenyatta and US President Donald Trump announced that talks were to open between the two countries on a bilateral trade deal. US Trade Representative Robert Lighthizer declared that such a deal, if agreed, could serve as a template for use between the USA and other African countries. The US Chamber of Commerce pointed to Kenya's medical device industry, technology and textiles as key areas of interest. Negotiations on the proposed free trade agreement commenced in July.

Kenya maintains a diverse range of export partners. According to the International Trade Centre, Uganda was the leading destination of the country's exports in 2021, receiving a 12.3% share, followed by the Netherlands (8.3%), the USA (8.0%), Pakistan (7.2%) and the UK (6.7%). China was the largest provider of imports in 2021, accounting for 20.5% of the total, followed by India (10.8%), the UAE (8.3%) and Saudi Arabia (5.3%). The principal single export in 2021 was tea (accounting for 17.7% of the total), while the principal imports in that year were refined petroleum products (15.6%), machinery and electrical equipment (14.2%), and chemicals and related products (11.5%).

MINING AND INDUSTRY

Traditionally, Kenya has not been categorized as having major natural resources potential. However, recently it has become apparent that the country possesses significant hydrocarbon reserves. Anglo-Irish oil exploration company Tullow Oil announced in March 2012 that it had discovered a potentially significant source of petroleum in Kenya's Turkana district. The company revealed two months later that it had encountered a total net oil pay of over 100 m, having increased the depth of drilling at the deposit to 1,515 m at the Ngamia-1 well

on Block 10BB. Tullow added that it would extend its exploration further, partly through activity at nearby Block 10A, where it planned to locate another rig. It also intended to begin drilling at its Twiga-1 well, situated in Block 13T. In July 2013 Tullow announced a new discovery at the Etuko-1 well, which, taken together with the potential generated by Twiga-1 and Ngamia-1, indicated potential for 250m. barrels of oil. Danish corporation A. P. Moeller-Maersk bought equity in the blocks, but sold its stake in January 2018 to Total of France, which acquired a 25% share. Modest extraction had initially been tentatively scheduled to begin in June 2017 but Kenya delayed the start of oil production, owing to the lack of an official agreement over revenue sharing between the central Government, the Turkana county administration and the local community; draft legislation was pending at the Senate.

Kenya's subsequent protracted electoral crisis and the accompanying political uncertainty delayed the finalization of a revenue-sharing deal and progress of the legislation. Once the political turmoil had subsided, however, the Turkana regional administration and the central Government were in May 2018 finally able to agree on the division of revenues expected to be generated when production reached full capacity (scheduled for 2022). The agreement on revenue sharing removed a major obstacle and allowed the approval of a law governing petroleum production that enabled Tullow to begin shipping oil that it had been holding in storage. In early June 2018 Kenya initiated a landmark pilot scheme to begin its first exports of crude oil via Mombasa port. However, the programme transporting oil by road to the coast was severely disrupted within weeks of its launch, as angry local residents blocked the passage of trucks in a protest over insecurity caused by bandit attacks in the Turkana region. Tullow planned eventually to build a pipeline transporting crude oil to a port in the coastal town of Lamu, and hired the UK-based Wood Group as the designers for the project. Tullow estimated the cost of the pipeline at US $1,100m., and announced that it would need to spend an additional $2,900m. on upstream operations. Overall, Tullow estimated potential resources at the Amosing and Ngamia oilfields at about 560m. barrels, predicting that production could reach 100,000 barrels per day (b/d).

Kenya is the most industrially developed country in East Africa, with increasingly good infrastructure, extensive transport facilities and considerable private sector activity. However, productive capacity in the industrial sector remains low compared with other emerging markets, since the Kenyan economy is predominantly orientated towards agriculture and services.

In 2021, according to provisional figures, the manufacturing sector contributed 7.7% of GDP and accounted for 11.6% of workers engaged in paid employment in the formal sector. The country maintains a small vehicle manufacturing capacity, with Toyota and General Motors East Africa (GMEA) both possessing small production outlets. As of early 2013 GMEA had a production capacity of 10 trucks and buses per day, while Toyota had just begun production of such vehicles at a plant in Mombasa, with an initial production capacity of 40 vehicles per month, rising eventually to 200. Overall, however, Kenya remains highly dependent on vehicle imports. Overall, manufacturing growth remained sluggish in the five years to the beginning of 2018. In 2017 the gross value added of the sector increased by just 0.2%, compared with a rise of 2.7% in 2016. The sector was adversely affected by political uncertainty, but also by high production costs and competition from cheaper imported goods.

Kenya's brewing industry has long been a significant contributor to the manufacturing component of GDP, and in recent times has comprised close to 1.0% of the country's overall GDP. East African Breweries Ltd (EABL), owned by UK-based Diageo, reported a 9% year-on-year increase in pre-tax profits to Ks. 10,600m. in the six months to the end of December 2019, on the back of a 10% year-on-year increase in net sales, which reached Ks. 45,900m. Net profit was bolstered by strong sales of Senator Keg, a mass-produced beer, although the most recognizable brand, Tusker, saw a decline in sales. Output was boosted by the opening—and ramping up—of capacity at a new factory dedicated to the production of Senator Keg, in the city of Kisumu, which involved creating and sustaining approximately 100,000 direct and indirect jobs. The US \$149.2m. plant had opened after a successful production test was confirmed in July 2018. At full capacity, the new facility was able to produce 1.0m. hl of Senator Keg over five years, with a view potentially to producing other brands under the same roof. However, EABL registered a 39% reduction in net profit for 2019/20, as a result of the impact of the COVID-19 pandemic.

Despite having not yet capitalized on its oil production capacity, Kenya maintained refinery operations for many years. The country's first refinery, in Mombasa, entered production in 1963, followed by a second in 1974. However, the refineries were shut down in 2013. There had been plans for a US \$1,200m. upgrade, but these were abandoned after an evaluation concluded that it would not be viable. Hence, Kenya became dependent on imports of refined products via Mombasa.

An oil pipeline operated by Kenya Pipeline Co (KPC) conveys petroleum products from Mombasa to Nairobi ('Line I') and from Nairobi to Eldoret to Kisumu. Line I, completed in 1978, is 450 km long, has a diameter of 35.6 cm (14 in) and can transport 440 cu m per hour. At the time of its construction, provision was made to enable the capacity to be increased to 800 cu m per hour. Beyond Nairobi, Line II, with a diameter of 20.3 cm (8 in), and Line III, with a diameter of 15.2 cm (6 in), can transport 160 cu m per hour. In October 2009 KPC signed a contract with China Petroleum Pipeline Engineering Corpn for the construction of a 325-km Line IV pipeline from Nairobi to Eldoret. Construction of a new refined products pipeline between Mombasa and Nairobi began in July 2014, under the auspices of Lebanon's Zakhem International Construction Ltd; in July 2015 a US \$350m. loan agreement was signed between KPC and a consortium of six commercial lenders, including the Co-operative Bank of Kenya, to fund construction of the pipeline. In July 2018 local media reported that the first consignment of fuel had been dispatched from Mombasa to Nairobi via the new pipeline.

The Ministry of Petroleum and Mining announced in February 2019 that crude oil reserves thus far discovered in Kenya were not sufficient to make the construction of a new refinery viable. The ministry's Principal Secretary, Andrew Kamau, referred to a global consensus that refineries are only profitable once they start to process 400,000 b/d or more. At that time, Kenya's oil discoveries amounted to 560m. barrels in proven and probable reserves, which Tullow Oil calculated would amount to gross output of between 60,000 b/d and 100,000 b/d.

President Kenyatta signed into law a petroleum bill in March 2019, which was designed to regulate exploration, production and revenue sharing. The National Assembly had ratified an earlier draft in 2016, but Kenyatta had not signed that version into law. The final version of the bill stipulated that 75% of oil revenues would be received by the central Government, 20% by local government and 5% by the communities where the reserves were actually located. The earlier version of the bill had allocated 10% of oil earnings to the local communities. The enacted legislation stipulated that the revenue-sharing formula would be revised within a decade.

UTILITIES AND INFRASTRUCTURE

Kenya's extensive transport system includes road, rail, air, and coastal and inland waterways. In 2017 there were a total of 14,420 km of paved roads in the country, including 8,500 km of highways, 1,872 km of urban roads and 4,048 km of rural roads. Routes connecting major cities, together with bypasses around Nairobi, have been funded in recent years by the EU and China. The country has 16 airports with paved runways, and 3,819 km of railway tracks were in use in 2018.

The 1-m-gauge railway in Kenya was built between 1896 and 1901 and it runs from the coast at Mombasa, through Nairobi, to western Kenya, and on to destinations in Tanzania and Uganda. Construction work on a US \$3,200m. standard-gauge railway between Mombasa and Nairobi commenced in December 2014. The new railway opened to commercial services in mid-2017, owing to the continued support of President Kenyatta; the railway was a key pledge in his 2013 election manifesto.

The 472-km stretch connecting Nairobi to Mombasa was inaugurated on 31 May 2017, just ahead of the presidential election. This express line between Kenya's two principal cities reduced the journey time from 12 hours to just four hours. In October 2019 Kenyatta inaugurated a \$1,500m. stretch of railway between Nairobi and Naivasha, which complemented the route between the capital and Mombasa. Extending the line to Naivasha had been conceived in part on the basis of a new industrial park in the town, which would be served by electricity generated from the area's geothermal deposits. However, the industrial park was still awaiting construction at that stage. Plans to extend the railway from Naivasha to Malaba on Uganda's border for a further \$3,700m. were abandoned in April 2019, after China baulked over the funding amid concerns about Kenya's burgeoning fiscal deficit.

The chief port is Mombasa, which is now the largest port on the East African coast. It is operated by the Kenya Ports Authority (KPA). At times, the port of Mombasa also serves Sudan, South Sudan, landlocked Ethiopia, parts of Somalia and north-western Tanzania. Prospects for an extensive modernization of the port of Mombasa improved in January 2015, when the Government signed a US \$270m. deal with Japan. The funds were to be used to part-finance the ongoing construction of the container terminal at Kilindini Harbour, together with the building of a further new terminal and the acquisition of new cargo handling equipment. The first phase of the project was completed in February 2016, raising the port's capacity to 1.63m. Twenty-foot Equivalent Units (TEUs). The second phase got under way in mid-2018 and was reported to be complete in May 2022, adding a further 0.45m. TEUs and increasing overall capacity at the port to 2.08m. TEUs, according to Construction Kenya.

The construction of a new port in the historic town of Lamu formally began in March 2012. The port was to form the core of the Lamu Port South Sudan Ethiopia Transport Corridor (LAPSSET), which would also include rail links, highways, oil pipelines and a refinery. The project, if completed, would involve the construction of a 32-berth deep-water port at Lamu on Kenya's coast, a 120,000-b/d oil refinery, 1,260 km of oil pipelines between South Sudan and the port (together with 980 km between Ethiopia and Kenya), 1,710 km of standard-gauge railway, 880 km of highway and an international airport. However, the LAPSSET project was beset by significant delays. The outbreak of civil war in South Sudan in December 2013 represented a huge setback, given that the project was designed in large part to convey that country's oil output to Kenya's coast for export. Meanwhile, the project was also undermined by legal challenges in Kenya. In November 2014 the country's High Court ordered a halt to the project, in order to allow a compensation lawsuit initiated by affected landholders to proceed.

Despite the legal and geopolitical challenges, various deals centred on LAPSSET continued to be signed. In August 2014 the KPA concluded a Ks. 42,000m. agreement with the China Communications Construction Company to build three berths at the new port, while in November the Governments of Kenya and Uganda commissioned the Japanese company Toyota Tsusho Mechanical & Engineering to undertake a feasibility study for an oil pipeline between Hoima (in Uganda) and the Kenyan towns of Lokichar and Lamu. A further significant setback for LAPSSET emerged in April 2016, when Uganda opted to route a crude oil pipeline through Tanzania, rather than Kenya. Uganda and Kenya had tentatively agreed in October 2015 to link pipelines. However, a feasibility study conducted on behalf of the Ugandan Government estimated the cost of routing the pipeline to Lamu to be US \$5,000m., compared with the \$4,000m. proposed by Tanzania for a route to its own Tanga port. None the less, Kenya's Ministry of Energy and Petroleum announced in April 2016 that it would begin the search for a contractor to build its own pipeline. In 2018 the Lamu pipeline project advanced as the Kenyan authorities and Tullow Oil engaged the Wood Group to design the 800-km project. Tullow estimated that construction of the pipeline would cost \$1,100m. and be completed by 2021/22, when the oil project in the South Lokichar basin was scheduled to commence production (subsequently pushed back to 2024). Tullow furnished the Government with a final development plan for the project in December 2021. In March 2022 Bloomberg reported that Indian Oil had 'looked at potentially investing' in the project, citing sources familiar with the matter. Tullow had earlier in the month announced that 'constructive discussions with interested parties' were 'progressing'.

Kenya's total installed generating capacity stood at 2,545 MW at mid-2019. Kenya Electricity Generating Co Ltd (KenGen) accounted for some 75% of this capacity. KenGen's sources of power are hydro (45.3% in 2020), geothermal (39.2%), thermal (14.1%) and wind (1.4%).

In August 2011 Kenya began working with the International Development Association, a division of the World Bank, on the Lake Turkana Wind Power Project (LTWPP), a US $853m. venture designed to provide 310 MW of inexpensive power to Kenya's national grid. At that time, 310 MW was equivalent to 20% of the country's total installed generating capacity. Harnessing wind power would help to reduce Kenya's overdependence on hydroelectric generation, an energy source that is vulnerable to drought. Plans for LTWPP entailed building 365 turbines on some 16,000 ha of territory in Loiyangalani district, at altitudes ranging from 450 m to 2,300 m above sea level; on completion, the LTWPP would be Africa's largest wind farm. Despite the World Bank withdrawing its support for the project in October 2012, and continuing problems and delays arising from opposition from environmentalists and indigenous rights' groups, construction work finally commenced in mid-2015 and the power facility reached full commercial operation in March 2019.

Plans for a major biogas plant on Lake Victoria were under way in mid-2017. Equinox Energy Capital, a British firm,

claimed that it was close to completing fundraising for a US $250m. plant that would use invasive water hyacinth from the lake to power a gas plant, which would be capable of generating 35 MW. Hyacinth has spread rapidly in Lake Victoria, compromising fishing routes and access to ports. An initial phase, located at Homa Bay, would generate 8 MW, followed by a second phase to produce 27 MW. The hyacinth would be harvested and broken down with bacteria, with the resultant methane being harnessed as fuel. However, at mid-2017 Equinox had yet to reach an agreement with Kenya Power and Lighting Co, which would determine the value of payments and modalities of bringing electricity to the national grid.

The Office of the President announced in April 2019 that the country had secured Ks. 67,500m. (US $666m.) in loans from China to fund the construction of a technological city at Konza, near Nairobi, and a highway linking Jomo Kenyatta International Airport with the capital's key suburbs. The funding would come in the form of Ks. 17,500m. from telecommunications giant Huawei, which would finance the technological city, and a further Ks. 50,000m. for the highway. The latter would be built by China Road and Bridge Corporation, in an effort to ease severe congestion on the main existing route into and out of Nairobi, which also serves as the principal road to both the airport and Mombasa. In February 2021 China's Xinhua news agency reported Will Meng, the CEO of Huawei Kenya, as saying that his company was working with Kenya's Ministry of Information Communication Technology, Youth and Innovation to build the Konza Technopolis data centre, with the aim of further digitizing Kenya's government operations.

Statistical Survey

Source (unless otherwise stated): Kenya National Bureau of Statistics, POB 30266, Nairobi; tel. (20) 2911000; e-mail directorgeneral@knbs.or.ke; internet www.knbs.or.ke.

Area and Population

AREA, POPULATION AND DENSITY

Area (sq km)	
Land area	580,609
Inland water	11,362
Total	591,971*
Population (census results)†	
24 August 2009	38,610,097
24 August 2019	
Males	23,548,056
Females	24,014,716
Total‡	47,564,296
Density (per sq km) at 2019 census§	81.9

* 228,561 sq miles.
† Excluding adjustment for under-enumeration.
‡ Including 1,524 persons identifying as neither male nor female.
§ Land area only.

Mid-2022 (UN projection): 56,215,224 (Source: UN, *World Population Prospects: The 2019 Revision*). Note: UN estimate not adjusted to take account of 2019 census results.

POPULATION BY AGE AND SEX
('000, UN projections at mid-2022)

	Males	Females	Total
0–14 years	10,605.5	10,423.4	21,028.9
15–64 years	16,692.4	16,987.0	33,679.5
65 years and over	636.4	870.5	1,506.9
Total	27,934.3	28,280.9	56,215.2

Note: Totals may not be equal to the sum of components, owing to rounding; UN estimates not adjusted to take account of results of 2019 census.

Source: UN, *World Population Prospects: The 2019 Revision*.

PRINCIPAL ETHNIC GROUPS
(population at 2019 census)

African	47,362,842	European . . .	28,491
American . . .	14,377	Other	9,038
Arab	59,021	**Total** . . .	47,564,296
Asian	90,527		

Note: Classification of ethnicity reflects self-declaration and national census methodology.

COUNTIES
(population at 2019 census)

	Area (sq km)*	Population	Density (per sq km)
Baringo	10,717	666,763	62.2
Bomet	2,355	875,689	371.8
Bungoma	3,033	1,670,570	550.8
Busia	1,686	893,681	530.1
Elgeyo	3,018	454,480	150.6
Embu	2,828	608,599	215.2
Garissa	43,591	841,353	19.3
Homa Bay	2,696	1,131,950	419.9
Isiolo	25,382	268,002	10.6
Kajiado	21,783	1,117,840	51.3
Kakamega	3,023	1,867,579	617.8
Kericho	2,617	901,777	344.6
Kiambu	2,569	2,417,735	941.1
Kilifi	12,396	1,453,787	117.3
Kirinyaga	1,475	610,411	413.8
Kisii	1,321	1,266,860	959.0
Kisumu	2,110	1,155,574	547.7
Kitui	30,437	1,136,187	37.3
Kwale	8,165	866,820	106.2
Laikipia	9,544	518,560	54.3
Lamu	5,832	143,920	24.7
Machakos	6,016	1,421,932	236.4
Makueni	8,172	987,653	120.9
Mandera	25,986	867,457	33.4
Marsabit	71,905	459,785	6.4

—continued	Area (sq km)*	Population	Density (per sq km)
Meru	7,057	1,545,714	219.0
Migori	3,165	1,116,436	352.7
Mombasa	151	1,208,333	8,002.2
Murang'a	2,527	1,056,640	418.1
Nairobi	707	4,397,073	6,219.3
Nakuru	7,287	2,162,202	296.7
Nandi	2,847	885,711	311.1
Narok	17,943	1,157,873	64.5
Nyamira	901	605,576	672.1
Nyandarua . . .	3,267	638,289	195.4
Nyeri	3,336	759,164	227.6
Samburu	21,024	310,327	14.8
Siaya	2,453	993,183	404.9
Taita Taveta . . .	17,090	340,671	19.9
Tana River . . .	39,153	315,943	8.1
Tharaka Nithi . . .	2,514	393,177	156.4
Trans-Nzoia . . .	2,496	990,341	396.8
Turkana	68,307	926,976	13.6
Uasin Gishu . . .	3,407	1,163,186	341.4
Vihiga	563	590,013	1,048.0
Wajir	56,649	781,263	13.8
West Pokot	9,108	621,241	68.2
Total	580,609	47,564,296	81.9

* Land area only.

PRINCIPAL TOWNS
(at 2019 census)

Nairobi (capital) .	4,397,073	Garissa	163,399
Mombasa . . .	1,208,333	Kitale	162,174
Nakuru . . .	570,674	Juja	156,041
Ruiru	490,120	Kitengela . . .	154,436
Eldoret	475,716	Kiambu	147,870
Kisumu	397,957	Mlolongo . . .	136,351
Kikuyu	323,881	Malindi	119,859
Thika	251,407	Mandera . . .	114,718
Naivasha . . .	198,444	Kisii	112,417
Karuri	194,342	Kakamega . . .	107,227
Ongata Rongai . .	172,569	Ngong	102,323

Mid-2021 (incl. suburbs, UN projections): Nairobi (capital) 4,922,192; Mombasa 1,340,913; Eldoret 410,622; Ruiru 407,129; Nakuru 395,141; Kisumu 366,510 (Source: UN, *World Urbanization Prospects: The 2018 Revision*).

BIRTHS AND DEATHS
(annual averages, UN estimates)

	2005–10	2010–15	2015–20
Birth rate (per 1,000) . . .	37.1	32.9	28.9
Death rate (per 1,000) . . .	8.7	6.6	5.5

Source: UN, *World Population Prospects: The 2019 Revision*.

Registered births: 1,138,654 in 2018; 1,186,144 in 2019; 1,138,667 in 2020 (provisional).

Registered deaths: 192,019 in 2018; 191,495 in 2019; 184,185 in 2020 (provisional).

Life expectancy (years at birth, estimates): 67.0 (males 64.6; females 69.4) in 2020 (Source: World Bank, World Development Indicators database).

EMPLOYMENT
(labour force survey, selected urban and rural settlements, '000 persons in formal sector)*

	2019	2020	2021†
Agriculture and forestry . . .	338.6	322.3	337.2
Mining and quarrying	15.9	14.4	14.7
Manufacturing	353.3	316.9	336.8
Electricity and water . . .	39.2	37.1	37.2
Construction	221.5	221.5	226.5
Wholesale and retail trade; repair of motor vehicles, motorcycles and personal and household goods	269.2	251.9	258.5
Hotels and restaurants . . .	82.9	51.5	63.4
Transport, storage and communications	224.9	196.2	218.1
Financial intermediation . . .	78.0	77.6	77.8
Real estate, renting and business activities	81.5	72.2	79.8
Public administration and defence; compulsory social security . .	304.6	311.4	323.0
Education	597.8	563.0	609.2
Health and social work . . .	158.0	148.8	153.2
Community, social and personal services	45.5	39.6	44.9
Private households with employed persons	116.4	117.0	117.9
Extraterritorial organizations and bodies	1.4	1.4	1.4
Total	2,928.5	2,742.7	2,899.6

* Data are for salaried employees in the formal sector only, and therefore exclude self-employed and unpaid family workers and a vast number of workers in the informal sector (9.3 million in 2011, according to official estimates). According to ILO, the 1999 census recorded an employed population of 14,474,200.
† Provisional figures.

Note: Totals may not be equal to the sum of components, owing to rounding.

Health and Welfare

KEY INDICATORS

Total fertility rate (children per woman, 2020)	3.4
Under-5 mortality rate (per 1,000 live births, 2020) . . .	41.9
HIV/AIDS (% of persons aged 15–49, 2020)	4.2
COVID-19: Cumulative confirmed deaths (per 100,000 persons at 31 August 2022)	10.7
COVID-19: Fully vaccinated population (% of total population at 21 August 2022)	17.7
Physicians (per 1,000 head, 2018)	0.2
Hospitals (per 100,000 head, 2013)	1.5
Domestic health expenditure (2019): US $ per head (PPP) .	95.5
Domestic health expenditure (2019): % of GDP	2.1
Domestic health expenditure (2019): public (% of total current expenditure)	46.0
Access to improved water resources (% of persons, 2020) .	62
Access to improved sanitation facilities (% of persons, 2020) .	33
Total carbon dioxide emissions ('000 metric tons, 2018) . .	18,400
Carbon dioxide emissions per head (metric tons, 2018) . .	0.4
Human Development Index (2021): ranking	152
Human Development Index (2021): value	0.575

Note: For data on COVID-19 vaccinations, 'fully vaccinated' denotes receipt of all doses specified by approved vaccination regime (Sources: Johns Hopkins University and Our World in Data). Data on health expenditure refer to current general government expenditure in each case. For more information on sources and further definitions for all indicators, see Health and Welfare Statistics: Sources and Definitions section (europaworld.com/credits).

Agriculture

PRINCIPAL CROPS
('000 metric tons)

	2018	2019	2020
Avocados	233.9	264.0	322.6
Bananas	1,414.2	1,715.8	1,856.7
Barley	78.3	85.8	35.0
Beans, dry	837.0	747.0	774.4
Beans, green*	43.8	43.4	42.9
Cabbages and other brassicas	674.3	829.3	943.6
Carrots and turnips	239.5	329.0	363.2
Cashew nuts	13.9	12.8	12.7
Cassava (Manioc)	946.0	845.3	898.1
Coconuts	105.4	109.9	110.0
Coffee, green	41.4	44.5	36.9
Cow peas, dry	193.9	222.4	264.2
Groundnuts, with shell	21.3	15.5	15.6
Lemons and limes	20.6	25.9	98.9
Maize	4,013.8	3,582.0	3,789.0
Mangoes, mangosteens and guavas	676.4	806.1	819.3
Millet	72.0	135.0	153.0
Onions, dry	34.9	116.5	197.0
Oranges	71.6	73.5	145.4
Papayas	134.4	105.0	118.0
Peas, green	63.5	73.1	74.9
Pigeon peas	85.7	107.5	123.6
Pineapples	349.4	335.4	330.3
Plantains and others*	33.2	33.0	32.9
Potatoes	1,870.4	1,979.0	1,860
Rice paddy	112.6	160.6	180.9
Seed cotton	5.9	6.1	6.2
Sisal*	22.6	22.9	22.8
Sorghum	189.0	288.0	315.0
Spinach	169.4	180.3	243.3
Sugar cane	5,262.2	4,606.1	6,799.9
Sweet potatoes	871.0	976.7	685.7
Tea (made)	493.0	458.9	569.5
Tobacco, unmanufactured*	10.7	10.6	10.5
Tomatoes	599.5	567.9	1,046.2
Watermelons	188.8	333.6	381.5
Wheat	336.6	366.2	404.7

* FAO estimates.

Aggregate production ('000 metric tons, may include official, semi-official or estimated data): Total cereals 4,806.0 in 2018, 4,621.3 in 2019, 4,881.3 in 2020; Total fruit (primary) 3,391.4 in 2018, 3,960.4 in 2019, 4,373.8 in 2020; Total pulses 1,244.0 in 2018, 1,194.4 in 2019, 1,283.2 in 2020; Total roots and tubers 3,715.5 in 2018, 3,892.3 in 2019, 3,472.0 in 2020; Total vegetables (primary) 2,523.7 in 2018, 2,837.5 in 2019, 3,602.4 in 2020.

Source: FAO.

LIVESTOCK
('000 head, year ending September)

	2018	2019	2020
Camels	3,273.4	4,721.9	4,669.7
Cattle	19,635.1	20,898.8	21,653.6
Chickens	49,889	56,435	57,162
Goats	26,711	35,173	36,021
Pigs	567.8	596.4	649.3
Sheep	19,485.7	27,440.9	25,345.9

Source: FAO.

LIVESTOCK PRODUCTS
('000 metric tons)

	2018	2019	2020
Camel meat*	57.8	79.9	61.3
Camel offals, edible*	38.5	63.2	46.9
Camels' milk*	837.3	1,134.2	1,124.5
Cattle hides, fresh*	32.5	53.3	39.6
Cattle meat	200.8	329.2	244.2
Cows' milk	3,778.2	3,983.3	4,048.1
Chicken meat	131.7	88.7	69.2
Game meat*	29.6	29.2	29.4
Goat meat	37.1	55.9	80.7
Goats' milk*	260.0	271.7	276.2
Goats' skins, fresh*	11.9	17.8	25.8
Pig meat	18.5	14.4	25.8
Sheep meat	25.3	50.8	79.7
Sheep's (Ewes') milk*	66.2	67.7	66.8
Hen eggs*	91.1	98.5	110.4
Honey (natural)	25.6	13.9	17.8

* FAO estimates.

Source: FAO.

Forestry

ROUNDWOOD REMOVALS
('000 cubic metres, excluding bark, FAO estimates)

	2018	2019	2020
Sawlogs, veneer logs and logs for sleepers	514	514	486
Pulpwood	170	170	163
Other industrial wood	348	348	320
Fuel wood	26,400	26,400	24,948
Total	27,432	27,432	25,917

Source: FAO.

SAWNWOOD PRODUCTION
('000 cubic metres, including railway sleepers)

	2018*	2019	2020
Coniferous (softwood)	266	226	251
Broadleaved (hardwood)	30	30	28*
Total	296	256	279*

* FAO estimate(s).

Source: FAO.

Fishing

('000 metric tons, live weight)

	2018*	2019*	2020
Capture	126.1	126.1	122.8*
Silver cyprinid	61.2	61.2	54.0
Nile tilapia	8.1	8.1	19.5
Nile perch	17.5	17.5	18.9
Aquaculture	15.3	18.6	20.0
Nile tilapia	12.2	14.9	15.6
Total catch	141.4	144.7	142.8*

* FAO estimate(s).

Note: Figures exclude crocodiles, recorded by number rather than by weight. The number of Nile crocodiles caught was: 7,946 in 2018; 6,152 in 2019; 6,250 in 2020.

Source: FAO.

Mining

('000 metric tons)

	2016	2017	2018
Soda ash	301.7	303.6	339.0
Fluorspar	42.7	n.a.	n.a.
Salt	262.8	289.9	290.0*
Lime*	52.0	52.0	44.0

* Estimate(s).

Source: US Geological Survey.

Industry

SELECTED PRODUCTS
('000 metric tons unless otherwise indicated)

	2019	2020	2021
Wheat flour	1,356.6	n.a.	n.a.
Raw sugar	440.9	603.8	700.2
Soft drinks ('000 hectolitres) . .	6,309.4	5,505.9	5,775.9
Paint ('000 hectolitres)	786.6	n.a.	n.a.
Soap	254.2	n.a.	n.a.
Cement	5,967.2	7,406.9	9,247.7
Galvanized metal sheets . . .	274.4	247.5	250.1
Assembled vehicles	7,802	7,725	9,989
Electrical energy (million kWh) .	11,409	11,474	12,127

2016: Beer ('000 hectolitres) 5,287.7; Cigarettes (million) 22,757.9 (Source: UN Industrial Commodity Statistics Database).

Finance

CURRENCY, EXCHANGE RATES AND FISCAL YEAR

Monetary Units
100 cents = 1 Kenya shilling (Ks.).
Ks. 20 = 1 Kenya pound (K£).

Sterling, Dollar and Euro Equivalents (31 May 2022)
£1 sterling = Ks. 146.96;
US $1 = Ks. 116.74;
€1 = Ks. 125.06;
Ks. 1,000 = £6.80 sterling = $8.57 = €8.00.

Average Exchange Rate (Ks. per US $)
2019	101.991
2020	106.451
2021	109.638

Fiscal Year
The fiscal year ends on 30 June.

BUDGET
(Ks. '000 million, year ending 30 June)

Revenue*	2014/15	2015/16†	2016/17‡
Tax revenue	958.2	1,073.9	1,267.3
Taxes on income and profits .	508.6	566.0	659.8
Taxes on goods and services .	375.6	428.7	517.1
Value-added tax	259.7	289.2	338.7
Excise duties	115.9	139.5	178.4
Taxes on international trade .	74.0	79.2	90.4
Import duties	74.0	79.2	90.4
Non-tax revenue	148.2	163.9	251.2
Total	1,106.4	1,237.8	1,518.5

Expenditure§	2014/15	2015/16†	2016/17‡
Recurrent expenditure . . .	1,126.3	1,291.6	1,465.9
Current transfers to counties .	229.3	264.0	284.8
Wages and benefits	298.0	319.3	344.8
Defence	93.7	113.7	125.2
Interest payments	172.9	215.3	231.0
Internal	139.6	172.9	172.6
External	33.3	42.5	58.4
Other expenditure	332.4	379.3	480.1
Development expenditure . .	508.6	479.0	597.7
Domestically financed . . .	266.0	301.3	400.8
Foreign financed	240.4	175.5	194.7
Total (incl. others)	1,638.1	1,779.7	2,072.4

* Excluding grants received (Ks. '000 million): 27.4 in 2014/15; 29.6 in 2015/16 (preliminary); 40.1 in 2016/17 (projection).
† Preliminary.
‡ Projections.
§ Excluding net lending (Ks. '000 million): 2.2 in 2014/15; 2.2 in 2015/16 (preliminary); 2.2 in 2016/17 (projection).

Source: IMF, *Kenya: First Review Under the Twenty-Four Month Stand-By Arrangement and the Arrangement Under the Standby Credit Facility and Requests for Waivers of Applicability, Rephasing of Disbursements, and Modification of Performance Criterion—Press Release; Staff Report; and Statement by the Executive Director for Kenya* (February 2017).

2018/19 (Ks. '000 million, year ending 30 June, preliminary): *Revenue:* Tax revenue 1,400.6 (Taxes on income and profits 685.4, Taxes on goods and services 607.5, Taxes on international trade 107.7); Non-tax revenue 270.5; Total revenue 1,671.1 (excl. grants 19.7). *Expenditure:* Recurrent expenditure 1,857.0; Development expenditure 546.5; Total expenditure (incl. net lending 2.5) 2,405.9 (Source: IMF, *Republic of Kenya: Request for Disbursement under the Rapid Credit Facility—Press Release; Staff Report; and Statement by the Executive Director for the Republic of Kenya* (May 2020)).

2019/20 (Ks. '000 million, year ending 30 June, preliminary): *Revenue:* Tax revenue 1,383.9 (Taxes on income and profits 706.9, Taxes on goods and services 579.0, Taxes on international trade 98.0); Non-tax revenue 349.7; Total revenue 1,733.6 (excl. grants 19.8). *Expenditure:* Recurrent expenditure 1,961.1; Development expenditure 583.9; Total expenditure (incl. net lending 0.7) 2,545.0 (Source: *First Reviews of the Extended Arrangement under the Extended Fund Facility and an arrangement under the Extended Credit Facility and Requests for Modifications of Performance Criteria and Structural Conditionality—Press Release; Staff Report; and Statement by the Executive Director for Kenya* (June 2021)).

2020/21 (Ks. '000 million, year ending 30 June, preliminary): *Revenue:* Tax revenue 1,429.5 (Taxes on income and profits 694.1, Taxes on goods and services 627.1, Taxes on international trade 108.4); Non-tax revenue 354.2; Total revenue 1,783.7 (excl. grants 31.3). *Expenditure:* Recurrent expenditure 2,195.6; Development expenditure 553.9; Total expenditure (incl. net lending 0.0) 2,749.5 (Source: IMF, *Kenya: 2021 Article IV Consultation; Second Reviews Under the Extended Arrangement Under the Extended Fund Facility and Under the Arrangement Under the Extended Credit Facility, and requests for Modifications of Performance Criteria and Structural Conditionality—Press Release; and Staff Report* (December 2021)).

INTERNATIONAL RESERVES
(excl. gold, US $ million at 31 December)

	2019	2020	2021
IMF special drawing rights . .	59.0	26.3	686.1
Reserve position in IMF . . .	18.5	19.3	18.7
Foreign exchange	9,037.3	8,250.5	8,785.0
Total	9,114.9	8,296.1	9,489.8

Source: IMF, *International Financial Statistics*.

MONEY SUPPLY
(Ks. million at 31 December)

	2019	2020	2021
Currency depository corporations .	192,395	228,240	247,666
Transferable deposits	1,557,780	1,782,966	1,944,864
Other deposits	2,147,377	2,403,679	2,496,909
Broad money	3,897,552	4,414,885	4,689,439

Source: IMF, *International Financial Statistics*.

COST OF LIVING
(Consumer Price Index; base: February 2019 = 100)

	2019	2020	2021
Food and non-alcoholic beverages .	107.03	116.73	126.65
Clothing and footwear . . .	101.05	103.50	105.91
Housing and utilities . . .	101.00	103.33	108.26
All items (incl. others) . . .	103.16	108.69	115.33

NATIONAL ACCOUNTS
(Ks. million at current prices)

Expenditure on the Gross Domestic Product

	2019	2020	2021*
Final consumption expenditure .	9,172,334	9,441,477	10,602,069
Households	7,818,862	7,988,961	9,023,553
Non-profit institutions serving households	107,459	115,541	112,129
General government . . .	1,246,013	1,336,975	1,466,387
Gross capital formation . . .	1,980,164	2,109,248	2,455,882
Changes in inventories . .	38,930	35,358	84,748
Gross fixed capital formation .	1,941,234	2,073,890	2,371,134
Total domestic expenditure .	11,152,498	11,550,725	13,057,951
Exports of goods and services .	1,169,967	1,032,976	1,278,675
Less Imports of goods and services	2,081,481	1,885,418	2,431,743
Statistical discrepancy . . .	−3,258	17,751	193,317
GDP at market prices . .	10,237,727	10,716,034	12,098,200
GDP at constant 2016 prices .	8,756,946	8,735,040	9,391,684

Gross Domestic Product by Economic Activity

	2019	2020	2021*
Agriculture, forestry and fishing .	2,135,709	2,424,075	2,713,414
Mining and quarrying	72,769	76,327	91,849
Manufacturing	809,253	815,666	876,420
Electricity, gas and water . .	220,628	222,920	240,389
Construction	630,653	750,153	847,422
Wholesale and retail trade, restaurants and hotels . . .	957,499	944,315	1,077,704
Transport, storage and communications	1,460,249	1,426,544	1,677,934
Finance, insurance, real estate and business services	1,899,191	1,972,267	2,206,264
Public administration and defence	541,367	592,610	632,165
Education	431,876	413,026	515,129
Human health and social work .	197,969	213,215	232,623
Other services	240,867	216,226	241,198
Sub-total	9,598,030	10,067,344	11,352,511
Less Financial intermediation services indirectly measured .	226,631	218,991	241,849
Indirect taxes, less subsidies .	866,330	867,680	987,540
GDP in market prices . . .	10,237,727	10,716,034	12,098,200

* Provisional.

BALANCE OF PAYMENTS
(US $ million)

	2018	2019	2020
Exports of goods	6,086.6	5,870.7	6,051.7
Imports of goods	−16,286.2	−16,553.6	−14,481.6
Balance on goods . . .	−10,199.6	−10,682.9	−8,429.9
Exports of services . . .	5,477.5	5,600.5	3,724.4
Imports of services . . .	−3,881.1	−3,854.8	−3,372.6
Balance on goods and services	−8,603.3	−8,937.2	−8,078.1
Primary income received . .	169.6	188.6	117.9
Primary income paid	−1,604.1	−1,822.2	−1,788.5
Balance on goods, services and primary income . . .	−10,037.9	−10,570.7	−9,748.8
Secondary income received .	5,052.7	5,338.3	5,028.7
Secondary income paid . . .	−47.9	−54.7	−77.1
Current balance	−5,033.0	−5,287.1	−4,797.1

—continued	2018	2019	2020
Capital account	262.5	207.3	131.7
Direct investment assets . .	47.1	−8.5	77.6
Direct investment liabilities .	767.8	469.9	426.3
Portfolio investment assets . .	−1,151.3	−865.4	−1,054.3
Portfolio investment liabilities .	1,812.2	2,102.1	−271.1
Financial derivatives and employee stock options (net) . . .	−23.5	8.3	16.2
Other investment assets . .	−945.2	−577.0	−1,023.9
Other investment liabilities . .	5,695.1	4,477.9	4,443.0
Net errors and omissions . .	−295.0	546.4	522.2
Reserves and related items .	1,136.6	1,074.0	−1,529.4

Source: IMF, *International Financial Statistics.*

External Trade

PRINCIPAL COMMODITIES
(distribution by HS, US $ million)

Imports c.i.f.	2019	2020	2021
Vegetables and vegetable products	1,018.8	984.8	1,230.2
Cereals	858.0	797.3	1,035.1
Animal or vegetable fats and oils, and products thereof .	561.2	864.8	1,056.0
Palm oil and its fraction . . .	521.2	830.1	990.7
Prepared foodstuffs; beverages, spirits, vinegar; tobacco and articles thereof .	776.9	654.3	734.7
Mineral products	3,442.9	2,310.8	3,626.3
Mineral fuels, oils, distillation products, etc.	3,323.5	2,185.9	3,513.9
Refined petroleum products .	3,014.8	1,890.3	3,058.6
Chemicals and related products	1,720.4	1,942.8	2,243.7
Pharmaceutical products . .	557.2	690.5	776.8
Medicaments	468.4	536.7	615.8
Plastics, rubber, and articles thereof	956.5	927.7	1,231.7
Plastics and articles thereof . .	734.4	727.0	982.3
Textiles and textiles articles .	861.0	770.7	1,004.3
Iron and steel, other base metals and articles of base metal	1,512.3	1,513.0	2,075.8
Iron and steel	916.7	932.2	1,284.6
Machinery and mechanical appliances; electrical equipment; parts thereof .	2,908.9	2,633.2	2,788.7
Machinery and boilers, etc. . .	1,641.1	1,433.8	1,596.0
Electrical and electronic equipment	1,267.8	1,199.4	1,192.7
Vehicles, aircraft, vessels and associated transport equipment	1,784.0	1,374.8	1,897.1
Vehicles other than railway and tramway	1,209.4	1,120.8	1,373.5
Passenger cars (incl. station wagons)	553.5	442.5	482.9
Total (incl. others)	17,220.4	15,415.4	19,594.1

Exports f.o.b.	2019	2020	2021
Vegetables and vegetable products	2,489.3	2,699.4	2,958.8
Live trees, plants and cut flowers, etc.	644.0	635.4	805.2
Cut flowers and flower buds .	584.2	572.2	725.5
Edible vegetables, certain roots and tubers	224.6	295.4	302.4
Edible fruit and nuts; peel of citrus fruit or melons	204.4	216.3	282.3
Coffee, tea, mate and spices . .	1,338.5	1,469.7	1,471.6
Coffee	204.9	215.8	248.0
Tea	1,113.4	1,224.3	1,192.8
Prepared foodstuffs; beverages, spirits, vinegar; tobacco and articles thereof .	487.1	574.9	541.6
Mineral products	709.3	698.1	699.0
Ores, slag and ash	195.3	206.4	258.6
Mineral fuels, oils, distillation products, etc.	451.7	407.2	280.6
Refined petroleum products .	440.9	402.7	273.9
Chemicals and related products	456.1	481.1	574.3
Textiles and textile articles .	429.1	406.2	488.6
Articles of apparel and clothing accessories, not knitted or crocheted	231.1	198.6	231.4
Iron and steel, other base metals and articles of base metal	264.6	244.6	334.0
Machinery and mechanical appliances; electrical equipment; parts thereof .	201.9	141.6	220.5
Total (incl. others)	5,836.0	6,025.4	6,751.4

Source: Trade Map-Trade Competitiveness Map, International Trade Centre, marketanalysis.intracen.org.

PRINCIPAL TRADING PARTNERS
(US $ million)

Imports c.i.f.	2019	2020	2021
Argentina	147.1	154.4	136.5
Australia	52.3	66.0	236.2
Belgium	139.6	174.6	219.7
China, People's Republic . . .	3,590.4	3,396.2	4,025.7
Egypt	416.8	421.5	445.9
France (incl. Monaco) . . .	233.3	219.1	205.2
Germany	435.4	377.9	392.1
India	1,706.2	1,772.4	2,106.7
Indonesia	482.6	589.2	405.1
Italy	199.5	221.7	225.4
Japan	947.1	823.3	892.3
Korea, Republic	140.9	192.1	494.5
Malaysia	250.1	428.2	855.1
Netherlands	309.1	393.6	427.0
Oman	91.1	94.2	200.8
Pakistan	243.4	201.6	173.2
Russian Federation	313.4	357.1	343.5
Saudi Arabia	1,247.0	648.5	1,046.0
South Africa	688.1	430.2	402.0
Tanzania	269.8	258.3	489.8
Thailand	187.6	144.4	179.9
Türkiye	189.9	188.3	223.9
Uganda	336.1	229.3	305.2
United Arab Emirates	1,632.8	867.3	1,628.4
United Kingdom	327.5	274.3	302.3
USA	591.3	531.5	801.8
Total (incl. others)	17,220.4	15,415.4	19,594.1

Exports f.o.b.	2019	2020	2021
Belgium	72.1	64.4	72.3
Burundi	66.0	55.2	68.7
China, People's Republic . . .	148.6	139.0	199.6
Congo, Democratic Republic . .	132.0	134.4	223.1
Egypt	185.6	178.4	193.1
Ethiopia	63.8	74.0	106.1
France (incl. Monaco) . . .	78.7	87.0	90.9
Germany	110.8	136.6	130.1
India	53.0	72.2	94.9
Netherlands	470.1	458.0	562.5
Pakistan	443.4	513.7	485.0
Russian Federation	62.2	75.3	95.5
Rwanda	227.3	237.0	278.4
Saudi Arabia	87.3	76.6	70.2
Somalia	116.0	106.9	122.5
South Sudan	122.9	216.5	155.4
Sudan	57.1	77.7	66.0
Tanzania	329.5	295.0	409.8
Uganda	624.1	674.6	831.9
United Arab Emirates	379.3	323.6	315.2
United Kingdom	392.0	469.2	450.6
USA	508.5	464.1	543.3
Total (incl. others)	5,836.0	6,025.4	6,751.4

Source: Trade Map-Trade Competitiveness Map, International Trade Centre, marketanalysis.intracen.org.

Transport

RAILWAYS
(traffic)

	2019	2020	2021*
Passengers carried ('000)	4,025	1,899	4,498
Passenger-km (million) . . .	146	49	112
Freight carried ('000 metric tons) .	667	652	644
Freight ton-km (million) . . .	375	393	343

* Provisional.

ROAD TRAFFIC
(motor vehicles in use)

	2018	2019	2020*
Motor cars	1,047,855	1,130,338	1,196,054
Light vans	329,392	339,581	345,646
Lorries, trucks and heavy vans .	165,642	172,160	178,636
Buses and mini-buses . . .	106,676	112,327	114,311
Motorcycles and autocycles .	1,497,224	1,714,649	1,967,250
Other motor vehicles . . .	80,714	83,985	95,490

* Provisional.

SHIPPING

Flag Registered Fleet
(at 31 December)

	2019	2020	2021
Number of vessels	38	47	48
Total displacement (grt) . . .	21,036	25,434	26,632

Source: Lloyd's List Intelligence (www.bit.ly/LLintelligence).

International Seaborne Freight Traffic
('000 metric tons at Kenyan ports)

	2019	2020	2021*
Goods handled	34,440	34,116	34,551

* Provisional.

CIVIL AVIATION
(traffic on scheduled services)

	2013	2014	2015
Kilometres flown (million) . .	89	94	91
Passengers carried ('000) . . .	4,517	4,401	4,875
Passenger-km (million) . . .	9,793	10,000	10,197
Total ton-km (million)	258	269	286

Source: UN, *Statistical Yearbook*.

2020 (domestic and international): Departures 33,178; Passengers carried 1.9m.; Freight carried 113m. ton-km (Source: World Bank, World Development Indicators database).

Tourism

FOREIGN TOURIST ARRIVALS
('000 overnight stays at accommodation establishments)

	2018	2019	2020*
China, People's Republic . . .	230.5	297.2	26.4
France	193.3	166.7	56.5
Germany	934.2	1,132.6	182.7
India	167.2	202.2	28.9
Italy	103.1	184.6	117.4
South Africa	74.9	92.0	17.5
Switzerland	85.3	109.4	20.4
Tanzania	58.9	77.5	23.6
Uganda	81.1	105.8	32.7
United Kingdom	285.6	341.3	81.1
USA	346.0	426.9	122.3
Total (incl. others) . . .	4,013.4	4,911.9	1,205.9

* Provisional.

Tourism receipts (US $ million, excl. passenger transport): 824 in 2016; 919 in 2017; 1,072 in 2018 (Source: World Tourism Organization).

Communications Media

	2018	2019	2020
Telephones ('000 main lines in use)	65.6	70.4	66.6
Mobile telephone subscriptions ('000)	49,501	54,555	61,409
Broadband subscriptions, fixed ('000)	371.5	491.2	674.2
Broadband subscriptions, mobile ('000)	21,543.4	21,595.6	25,144.7
Internet users (% of population)* .	19.5	22.6	29.5

* Estimates.

Source: International Telecommunication Union.

Education

(2021/22 unless otherwise indicated, provisional)

	Institutions*	Teachers	Pupils
Primary	32,437	220,744	10,285,100
Secondary	10,413	} 120,279	{ 3,692,000
Teacher training colleges† .	122		16,429
Higher education institutions‡	2,365	3,456§	498,326

* 2020/21.

† Includes private and public institutions for pre-primary, primary and secondary (diploma) training.

‡ Includes universities, national polytechnics, institutes of technology and youth polytechnics.

§ 2016/17 figure.

Pupil-teacher ratio (primary education, UNESCO estimate): 30.7 in 2014/15 (Source: UNESCO Institute for Statistics).

Adult literacy rate (UNESCO estimates): 81.5% (males 85.0%; females 78.2%) in 2018 (Source: UNESCO Institute for Statistics).

Directory

The Constitution

A new Constitution replacing the charter introduced at independence on 12 December 1963 (and as subsequently amended) was approved at a national referendum on 4 August 2010 and entered into force on 27 August.

The territory of Kenya is divided into 47 counties. There shall be a County Government for each county, consisting of a County Assembly and a County Executive. The latter is headed by a County Governor elected directly by the people.

Legislative authority is vested in and exercised by Parliament, which consists of the National Assembly and the Senate. Members of Parliament serve concurrent five-year terms. The National Assembly consists of 290 members, each elected by the registered voters of single–member constituencies; 47 women members, each elected by the registered voters of the counties, each county constituting a single–member constituency; 12 members nominated by parliamentary political parties according to their proportion of members of the National Assembly to represent special interests, including the youth, persons with disabilities and workers; and the Speaker, who is an ex officio member. The Senate consists of 47 members, each elected by the registered voters of the counties, each county constituting a single–member constituency; 16 women members nominated by political parties according to their proportion of members of the Senate; two members, being one man and one woman, representing the youth; two members, being one man and one woman, representing persons with disabilities; and the Speaker, who is an ex officio member.

The President is the Head of State and Government and exercises the executive authority of the Republic, with the assistance of the Deputy President and Cabinet Secretaries. The President is also Commander-in-Chief of the Kenya Defence Forces and is the Chairperson of the National Security Council. An election of the President shall be held on the same day as a general election of Members of Parliament. A candidate shall be declared elected as President if the candidate receives more than one-half of all the votes cast in the election and at least 25% of the votes cast in each of more than one-half of the counties. If no candidate is elected, a fresh election shall be held within 30 days after the previous election and in that fresh election the only candidates shall be the candidate, or the candidates, who received the greatest number of votes and the candidate, or the candidates, who received the second greatest number of votes. When a vacancy occurs in the office of President the Deputy President shall assume office as President for the remainder of the term of the President. If the office of Deputy President is vacant, or the Deputy President is unable to assume the office of President, the Speaker of the National Assembly shall act as President and an election to the office of President shall be held within 60 days after the vacancy arose in the office of President.

The Deputy President shall be the principal assistant of the President and shall deputize for the President in the execution of the President's functions.

The Cabinet consists of the President, the Deputy President, the Attorney-General and not fewer than 14 or more than 22 Cabinet Secretaries. The President shall nominate and, with the approval of the National Assembly, appoint Cabinet Secretaries. A Cabinet Secretary shall not be a Member of Parliament.

The Constitution can be amended either by a simple majority of the citizens voting in a referendum, or by the adoption of a bill by not less than two-thirds of the members of both Houses of Parliament.

The Government

HEAD OF STATE

President: William Samoei Ruto (inaugurated 13 September 2022).

Deputy President: Rigathi Gachagua.

CABINET
(October 2022)

President: WILLIAM SAMOEI RUTO.

Deputy President: RIGATHI GACHAGUA.

Prime Cabinet Secretary: MUSALIA MUDAVADI.

Secretary for the Interior and National Administration: Prof. ABRAHAM KITHURE KINDIKI.

Secretary for National Treasury and Planning: Prof. NJUGUNA NDUNG'U.

Secretary for Public Service, Gender and Affirmative Action: AISHA JUMWA KARISA KATANA.

Secretary for Defence: ADEN BARE DUALE.

Secretary for Water, Sanitation and Irrigation: ALICE MUTHONI WAHOME.

Secretary for Foreign and Diaspora Affairs: ALFRED MUTUA.

Secretary for Trade, Investment and Industry: MOSES KURIA.

Secretary for East African Community, Arid and Semi-Arid Lands and Regional Development: REBECCA MIANO.

Secretary for Roads, Transport and Public Works: ONESIMUS KIPCHUMBA MURKOMEN.

Secretary for the Environment and Forestry: ROSELINDA SOIPAN TUYA.

Secretary for Lands, Housing and Urban Development: ZACHARIAH MWANGI NJERU.

Secretary for Tourism, Wildlife and Heritage: PENINA MALONZA.

Secretary for Agriculture and Livestock Development: FRANKLIN MITHIKA LINTURI.

Secretary for Health: SUSAN NAKHUMICHA WAFULA.

Secretary for Information, Communications and the Digital Economy: ELIUD OWALO.

Secretary for Education: EZEKIEL MACHOGU.

Secretary for Energy and Petroleum: DAVIS CHIRCHIR.

Secretary for Youth Affairs, Sports and the Arts: ABABU NAMWAMBA.

Secretary for Co-operatives and Micro, Small and Medium Enterprises Development: SIMON CHELUGUI.

Secretary for Mining, the Blue Economy and Maritime Affairs: SALIM MVURYA.

Secretary for Labour and Social Protection: FLORENCE BORE.

CABINET-LEVEL OFFICIALS

Advisor on Women's Rights Agency: HARRIET CHIGAI.

National Security Advisor: MONICA JUMA.

Attorney-General: JUSTIN BEDAN MUTURI NJOKA.

Secretary to the Cabinet: MERCY WANJAU.

MINISTRIES

Office of the President: State House, State House Rd, POB 40530, 00100 Nairobi; tel. (20) 2227436; internet www.president.go.ke.

Office of the Deputy President: POB 74434, 00200 Nairobi; tel. (20) 3247000; e-mail dp@deputypresident.go.ke; internet www.deputypresident.go.ke.

Ministry of Agriculture and Livestock Development: Kilimo House, off Cathedral Rd, POB 34188, 00100 Nairobi; tel. (20) 2718870; e-mail info@kilimo.go.ke; internet kilimo.go.ke.

Ministry of Co-operatives and Micro, Small and Medium Enterprises Development: Nairobi.

Ministry of Defence: Ulinzi House, Lenana Rd, POB 40668, 00100 Nairobi; tel. (20) 2712054; e-mail publicaffairs@mod.go.ke; internet mod.go.ke.

Ministry of East African Community, Arid and Semi-Arid Lands and Regional Development: State Department of EAC Integration, Co-op Bank House, 16th Floor, Haile Selassie Ave, POB 8846, 00200 Nairobi; tel. (20) 2245741; e-mail ps@meac.go.ke; internet meac.go.ke.

Ministry of Education: Jogoo House 'B', Harambee Ave, POB 30040, 00100 Nairobi; tel. (20) 318581; internet www.education.go.ke.

Ministry of Energy and Petroleum: Kawi Complex, Off Red Cross Rd, POB 30582, 00100 Nairobi; tel. (20) 4841000; e-mail info@energy.go.ke; internet energy.go.ke.

Ministry of the Environment and Forestry: NHIF Bldg, 12th Floor, Ragati Rd, POB 30126, 00100 Nairobi; tel. (20) 2730808; e-mail psoffice@environment.go.ke; internet www.environment.go.ke.

Ministry of Foreign and Diaspora Affairs: Old Treasury Bldg, Harambee Ave, POB 30551, 00100 Nairobi; tel. (20) 3318888; e-mail info@mfa.go.ke; internet mfa.go.ke.

Ministry of Health: Medical HQ, Afya House, Cathedral Rd, POB 30016, 00100 Nairobi; tel. (20) 2717077; e-mail ps@health.go.ke; internet www.health.go.ke.

Ministry of Information, Communications and the Digital Economy: Uchumi House, 5th Floor, Agha Khan Walk, POB 30025, 00100 Nairobi; tel. (20) 4920000; e-mail info@information.go.ke; internet www.information.go.ke.

Ministry of the Interior and National Administration: POB 350100, 00100 Nairobi; tel. (20) 2227411; e-mail ps.interior@kenya.go.ke; internet www.interior.go.ke.

Ministry of Labour and Social Protection: Social Security House, Bishop Rd, POB 40326, 00100 Nairobi; tel. (20) 2729801; e-mail info@labour.go.ke; internet labour.go.ke.

Ministry of Lands, Housing and Urban Development: Ardhi House, 12th Floor, 1st Ngong Ave, POB 30450, 00100 Nairobi; tel. (20) 2718050; internet www.lands.go.ke.

Ministry of Mining, the Blue Economy and Maritime Affairs: Nyayo House, Kenyatta Ave, POB 51614, 00100 Nairobi; tel. (20) 3310112; e-mail info@petroleumandmining.go.ke; internet www.petroleumandmining.go.ke.

Ministry of Public Service, Gender and Affirmative Action: Harambee House, Harambee Ave, POB 30050, 00100 Nairobi; tel. (20) 227411; e-mail info@psyg.go.ke; internet www.psyg.go.ke.

Ministry of Roads, Transport and Public Works: Transcom House, Ngong Rd, POB 52692, 00200 Nairobi; tel. (20) 2729200; e-mail ps@transport.go.ke; internet www.transport.go.ke.

Ministry of Tourism, Wildlife and Heritage: NSSF Bldg, Block A, 15th Floor, Eastern Wing, POB 30027, 00100 Nairobi; tel. (20) 3313010; e-mail ps@tourism.go.ke; internet www.tourism.go.ke.

Ministry of Trade, Investment and Industry: Social Security House, Block A, 17th and 23rd Floors, POB 30418, 00100 Nairobi; tel. (20) 2731531; e-mail ps@industrialization.go.ke; internet www.industrialization.go.ke.

Ministry of Water, Sanitation and Irrigation: Maji House, Upper Hill, off Ngong Rd, POB 49720, 00100 Nairobi; tel. (20) 2716103; e-mail ps@water.go.ke; internet www.water.go.ke.

Ministry of Youth Affairs, Sports and the Arts: Kencom House, 3rd Floor, Moi Ave, POB 49849, 00100 Nairobi; tel. (20) 2251164; e-mail csoffice@sportsheritage.go.ke; internet sportsheritage.go.ke.

National Treasury: Treasury Bldg, Harambee Ave, POB 30007, Nairobi; tel. (20) 2252299; e-mail ps@treasury.go.ke; internet www.treasury.go.ke.

President

Election, 9 August 2022

Candidate	Valid votes	% of valid votes
William Samoei Arap Ruto (UDA) . .	7,176,141	50.49
Raila Amollo Odinga (Azimio La Umoja)	6,942,930	48.85
George Luchiri Wajackoyah (RPK) .	61,969	0.44
David Mwaure Waihiga (AP) . . .	31,987	0.23
Total	14,213,027*	100.00

* In addition, there were 113,614 rejected votes.

Legislature

NATIONAL ASSEMBLY

National Assembly: Parliament Bldgs, POB 41842, 00100 Nairobi; tel. (20) 2221291; e-mail clerk@parliament.go.ke; internet www.parliament.go.ke.

Speaker: MOSES MASIKA WETANGULA.

General Election, 9 August 2022

Party*	Constituency seats	Women members	Total seats
UDA	119	21	140
ODM	73	10	83
JP	24	3	27
WDM—Kenya . .	21	4	25
ANC	6	1	7
UDM	6	1	7
FORD—Kenya . .	5	1	6
KANU	5	1	6
DAP—Kenya . .	5	—	5
PAA	3	—	3
KUP	2	1	3
MCCP	2	—	2
UPIA	2	—	2
TSP	1	1	2
CCM	1	—	1
DP	1	—	1
GDDP	1	—	1
MDG	1	—	1
NAPK	1	—	1
NOPEU	1	—	1
UPA	1	—	1
Ind.	9	3	12
Total	**290**	**47**	**337†**

* The ANC, the CCM, the DP, FORD—Kenya, the TSP and the UDA were members of the alliance Kenya Kwanza, while the JP, the DAP—Kenya, KANU, the MCCP, the MDG, the ODM, the PAA, the UDM, the UPA, the UPIA and the WDM—Kenya were members of the alliance Azimio La Umoja.

† In addition to the 290 directly elected constituency seats and 47 women members elected in each of the counties, 12 members are nominated by parliamentary political parties according to their respective proportion of members of the National Assembly to represent special interests, including the country's youth, persons with disabilities and workers. The Speaker is also, ex officio, a member of the National Assembly.

SENATE

Senate: KICC Bldg, 1st Floor, POB 41842, 00100 Nairobi; tel. (20) 3261304; e-mail csenate@parliament.go.ke; internet www.parliament.go.ke.

Speaker: AMASON KINGI JEFFAH.

General Election, 9 August 2022

Party	Seats
UDA	22
ODM	13
JP	4
WDM—Kenya	3
UDM	2
FORD—Kenya	1
DP	1
NRA	1
Total	**47***

* In addition, 16 women members are nominated by political parties according to their proportion of members of the Senate. A further two members represent the country's youth and two members represent persons with disabilities. The Speaker is also, ex officio, a member of the Senate.

Election Commission

Independent Electoral and Boundaries Commission (IEBC): Anniversary Towers, 6th Floor, University Way, POB 45371, 00100 Nairobi; tel. (20) 2877000; e-mail info@iebc.or.ke; internet www.iebc.or.ke; f. 2011 to replace Electoral Commission of Kenya; Chair. WAFULA W. CHEBUKATI; CEO MARJAN HUSSEIN MARJAN.

Political Organizations

Agano Party (AP): Nairobi; tel. 723909362; e-mail info@aganoparty.com; internet www.aganoparty.com; Leader DAVID MWAURE WAIHIGA.

Alliance for Real Change (ARK): Optimum House, Suite 1, General Waruinge St, POB 78943, 006200 Nairobi; tel. 791077058;

internet fb.com/Alliance-For-Real-Change-466435626727886; f. 2010; Leader MOHAMED ABDUBA DIDA; Sec.-Gen. AMINA GUYO.

Amani National Congress (ANC): Amani House, Loyangalani Dr., off James Gichuru Rd, Lavington, POB 11095, 00100 Nairobi; tel. 725179855; internet fb.com/amaninationalcongress; Leader MUSALIA MUDAVADI.

Azimio La Umoja: Lavington, Nairobi; tel. 709605400; e-mail info@azimio.ke; internet azimio.ke; f. 2022; multi-party coalition incl. NARC Kenya, the Jubilee Party, KANU, the Orange Democratic Movement, the Wiper Democratic Movement and the Upia Party; Leader RAILA AMOLLO ODINGA.

Chama Cha Uzalendo (CCU): Viewpark Towers, 1st Floor, West Wing, POB 51871, 00100 Nairobi; tel. 706697629; e-mail chamachauzalendokenya@gmail.com; Chair. WAVINYA NDETI.

Communist Party of Kenya: Swiss Cottages, off Ring Rd, Kileleshwa, POB 4403, 00100 Nairobi; tel. 721158008; internet fb.com/CommunistKenya; f. 1992 as the Social Democratic Party of Kenya; present name adopted in March 2019; Chair. MWANDAWIRO MGHANGA; Sec.-Gen. BENEDICT WACHIRA.

Democratic Party of Kenya (DP): Muhu Holdings House, 3rd Floor, Kenyatta Market, off Mbagathi Rd, POB 53695, 00200 Nairobi; tel. (20) 2625977; e-mail info@democraticpartyofkenya.co.ke; internet www.democraticpartyofkenya.co.ke; f. 1991; Leader JOSEPH MUNYAO; Sec.-Gen. JACOB HAJI.

Economic Freedom Party (EFP): Cool Waters Apts, M3 Flat, Woodlane, Hurlingham, POB 13521, 00400 Nairobi; tel. 722496898; internet fb.com/Economicfreedompartykenya; f. 2017; Chair. ISSACK HASSAN ABEY; Sec.-Gen. ABDULLAHI GESSEY.

Federal Party of Kenya (FPK): Annex House, Ground Floor, Limuru Rd, POB 34463, Nairobi; tel. 722302368; e-mail federalpartyofkenya07@gmail.com; internet federalpartyofkenya.yolasite.com; Chair. PHILIP OBONYO ABUBA; Sec.-Gen. KENNEDY OKELLO OLUOCH.

Forum for the Restoration of Democracy—Asili (FORD—Asili): Kwarara Rd, off Bogani Rd, Karen, POB 69564, 00400 Nairobi; e-mail fordasili@gmail.com; tel. 722779005; f. 1992; Chair. ISSAC ONEKA MUNANAIRI.

Forum for the Restoration of Democracy—Kenya (FORD—Kenya): Simba House, Gatundu Cres., Kileleshwa, off Gatundu Rd, POB 43591, 00100 Nairobi; tel. (20) 5286925; e-mail info@fordkenya.co.ke; internet www.fordkenya.co.ke; f. 1992; predominantly Luo support; Leader WAFULA WAMUNYINYI; Sec.-Gen. Dr DAVID ESELI SIMIYU.

Kenya African Democratic Union—Asili (KADU—Asili): Door 1, Dockworkers Union Bldg, Makuli Fagia, Kenyatta Ave, 2nd Floor, POB 83229, Mombasa; tel. 722829313; Sec.-Gen. PATIENCE M. CHOME.

Kenya African National Union (KANU): Yaya Center, Chania Rd, POB 72394, 00200 Nairobi; tel. 720237682; e-mail info@kanuparty.com; internet www.kanuparty.com; f. 1960; sole legal party 1982–91; absorbed the National Development Party (f. 1994) 2002; Sec.-Gen. NICK SALAT.

Kenya National Congress (KNC): Mbabane Rd, POB 1498, 00100 Nairobi; tel. (20) 2604013; f. 1992; Leader PETER KENNETH.

Jubilee Party (JP): Jubilee House, Pangani Interchange, Exit 3, Thika Rd, POB 38601-00623, Nairobi; tel. 709175000; e-mail info@jubileepamoja.co.ke; internet jubileepamoja.co.ke; f. 2016; Pres. UHURU KENYATTA; Sec.-Gen. RAPHAEL TUJU.

Maendeleo Chap Chap Party (MCCP): House No. 38, Convent Rd, Lavington, POB 10790, 00100 Nairobi; tel. 796622376; internet fb.com/MaendeleoChapChapParty; f. 2016; Chair. ALFRED MUTUA.

Maendeleo Democratic Party (MDP): Maendeleo House, 15 Kakamega Mumias Rd, POB 1980, 50100 Kakamega; f. 2007; Chair. OMUKANDA AMISI.

Mazingira Greens Party of Kenya (MPK): PAA Cres., Estate No 122/8, South C, POB 51855, Nairobi; tel. 705337848; f. 2007; campaigns for the equitable sharing of wealth, sustainable use of natural resources, women's rights and the defence of Kenyan cultural values; Leader WANGARI MAATHAI.

Muungano Party (MP): Nyahururu House, Kilome Rd, POB 19080, 00100 Nairobi; tel. (20) 8059439; e-mail muungano developmentparty@yahoo.com; internet muunganoparty.or.ke.

National Rainbow Coalition—Kenya (NARC—Kenya): Woodlands Rd, off Lenana Rd, Kilimani, POB 34200, 00100 Nairobi; tel. (20) 2726783; e-mail narckenya06@yahoo.com; internet www.narckenya.org; f. 2006 by former mems of NARC; Chair. MARTHA W. KARUA; Sec.-Gen. MWANYENGELA NGALI.

Orange Democratic Movement (ODM): Orange House, Menelik Rd, Kilimani, POB 42242, 00202 Nairobi; tel. (20) 2053481; e-mail info@odm.co.ke; internet www.odm.co.ke; f. 2005; Leader RAILA AMOLO ODINGA; Sec.-Gen. EDWIN SIFUNA.

Peoples Democratic Party (PDP): Cannon Annex, Parliament Lane, POB 10734, 00400 Nairobi; tel. 7212019203; Leader JAMES OMINGO MAGARA; Sec.-Gen. ERIC MBIU.

Restore and Build Kenya (RBK): Juma House, Makasembo St, POB 2670, 30100 Eldoret; tel. 720661812; Leader JAMES OLE KIYIAPI.

Roots Party of Kenya (RPK): Cara House, Karen Rd, POB 13678, Karen; internet rootspartyofkenya.org; Leader GEORGE LUCHIRI WAJACKOYAH; Sec.-Gen. ADAM MOHAMEDHANIF KADERNANI.

Safina ('Noah's Ark'): Amboseli Rd, off Gitanga Rd, Lavington, POB 14746-00100 Nairobi; tel. (20) 5202211; f. 1995; aims to combat corruption and human rights abuses and to introduce proportional representation; Chair. PAUL KIBUGI MUITE.

Thirdway Alliance Kenya (TAK): 57 Chalbi Dr., Lavington, Nairobi; tel. (20) 3860296; e-mail leader@thirdwayalliance.org; internet fb.com/Thirdwayalliancekenya; Leader EKURU AUKOT.

United Democratic Alliance (UDA): Hustler Center, Makindi Rd, off Ngong Rd, Nairobi; tel. (20) 2020405; e-mail info@uda.co.ke; internet www.uda.co.ke; f. 2012 as the Party of Action; subsequently the Party of Development and Reforms; present name adopted 2020; Leader WILLIAM SAMOEI RUTO; Chair. JOHNSON MUTHAMA; Sec.-Gen. VERONICA NDUATI MAINA.

United Democratic Movement (UDM): Matambato Rd, Upper-hill, POB 44820, Nairobi; tel. 722752156; e-mail uniteddemocraticmovement@yahoo.com; internet www.uniteddemocraticmovement.com; Chair. Rev. PAUL CHEBOI; Sec.-Gen. STANLEY K. ROTICH.

United Democratic Party (UDP): Matumbato Rd, Nairobi; tel. 722740760; f. 2017; Leader CYRUS SHAKHALAGA KHWA JIRONGO.

Wiper Democratic Movement—Kenya (WDM—Kenya): Wiper House, 408 Othaya Rd, POB 403-00100, Nairobi; tel. (20) 2663336; e-mail wiper@wipermovement.com; internet www.wiper.co.ke; f. 2007 following split in the ODM; Leader STEPHEN KALONZO MUSYOKA; Chair. CHIRAU ALI MWAKWERE; Sec.-Gen. JUDITH ACHIENG SIJENY (acting).

Diplomatic Representation

EMBASSIES AND HIGH COMMISSIONS IN KENYA

Algeria: 37 Muthaiga Rd, Mobil Plaza, POB 64140, 00620 Nairobi; tel. (20) 4055559; e-mail algeria@algerianembassy.co.ke; internet www.algerianembassy.co.ke; Ambassador SELMA MALIKA HADDADI.

Angola: 294 Runda Grove, Runda Estate, POB 44029, 00100 Nairobi; tel. (20) 7120313; e-mail embassyofangolain.kenya@gmail.com; internet embassyofangolainkenya.org/pt; Ambassador SYANGA KIVUILA SAMUEL ABÍLIO.

Argentina: Eaton Place Bldg, 4th Floor, United Nations Cres. Rd, Gigiri, POB 30283, 00100 Nairobi; tel. (20) 2324673; e-mail ekeny@cancilleria.gob.ar; internet ekeny.cancilleria.gob.ar; Ambassador GABRIELA MARTINIC.

Australia: ICIPE House, Riverside Dr., off Chiromo Rd, POB 39341, 00623 Nairobi; tel. (20) 4277100; e-mail australian.hc.kenya@dfat.gov.au; internet kenya.embassy.gov.au; High Commissioner LUKE WILLIAMS.

Austria: 536 Limuru Rd, Muthaiga, POB 30560, 00100 Nairobi; tel. (20) 4060022; e-mail nairobi-ob@bmeia.gv.at; internet www.bmeia.gv.at/oeb-nairobi; Ambassador Dr CHRISTIAN FELLNER.

Bangladesh: House No. 337, Runda Rd, Runda, POB 41645, Nairobi; tel. (20) 3870467; e-mail nairobi.mission@mofa.gov.bd; internet bdhcnairobi.com; High Commissioner TAREQUE MUHAMMAD.

Barbados: Nairobi; High Commissioner WILLIAM MCDONALD.

Belarus: Dik Dik Gardens, House No. 8, Nairobi; tel. 757075217; e-mail kenya@mfa.gov.by; internet kenya.mfa.gov.by; Ambassador PAVEL VZIATKIN.

Belgium: Muthaiga, Limuru Rd, POB 30461, 00100 Nairobi; tel. 730842000; e-mail nairobi@diplobel.fed.be; internet kenya.diplomatie.belgium.be; Ambassador PETER MADDENS.

Botswana: LR Block 91/238, Gigiri Dr., off United Nations Ave, Nairobi; tel. (20) 7123412; e-mail tsekao@gov.bw; internet fb.com/BostwanaHighMissionKenya; High Commissioner GOBOPANG DUKE LEFHOKO.

Brazil: 123 Gardenia Rd, Gigiri, POB 30754, 00100 Nairobi; tel. (20) 7125765; e-mail brasemb.nairobi@itamaraty.gov.br; internet www.gov.br/mre/pt-br/embaixada-nairobi; Ambassador SILVIO JOSE ALBUQUERQUE E SILVA.

Burkina Faso: Nairobi; Ambassador MADINA DIABY KASSAMBA GANOU.

Burundi: International Life House, 1st Floor, along Mama Ngina St, off Bunyala Rd, POB 61165, 00200 Nairobi; tel. (20) 3310826; e-mail info@burundiembassy-kenya.org; internet burundiembassy-kenya.org; Ambassador REMY BARAMPANA.

Canada: Limuru Rd, Gigiri, POB 1013, 00621 Nairobi; tel. (20) 3663000; e-mail nairobi@international.gc.ca; internet www.canadainternational.gc.ca/kenya; High Commissioner CHRISTOPHER THORNLEY.

Chile: 49 Gigiri Court, off UN Cres., POB 45554, 00100 Nairobi; tel. (20) 4452950; e-mail echile.kenya@minrel.gob.cl; internet chile.gob.cl/kenya; Ambassador MARÍA ALEJANDRA GUERRA.

China, People's Republic: Woodlands Rd, Kilimani, POB 30508, Nairobi; tel. (20) 2722559; e-mail chinaemb_ke@mfa.gov.cn; internet ke.china-embassy.gov.cn; Ambassador ZHOU PINGJIAN.

Colombia: Magnolia Close, off UN Ave, House No 57, Nairobi; tel. 714829792; e-mail ekenia@cancilleria.gov.co; internet kenia.embajada.gov.co; Ambassador MÓNICA DE GREIFF LINDO.

Congo, Democratic Republic: Electricity House, 12th Floor, Harambee Ave, POB 48106, 00100 Nairobi; tel. (20) 2229772; e-mail ambardckenyal@yahoo.com; Ambassador JOHN NYAKERU KALUNGA.

Congo, Republic: 162 Wispers Ave, Gigiri, POB 1722-00621, Nairobi; tel. 727037408; e-mail ambacoken@yahoo.com; Ambassador JEAN-PIERRE OSSEY.

Costa Rica: Eaton Place, 2nd Floor, UN Crescent, Gigiri, POB 63946, 00619 Nairobi; tel. (20) 5143583; e-mail embcr-ke@rree.go.cr; internet costaricanembassy.co.ke; Ambassador GIOVANNA VALVERDE STARK.

Cuba: Fame Tree Dr., 93-B, Runda, POB 198, 00606 Nairobi; tel. 774137859; e-mail consulado@ke.embacuba.cu; internet misiones.minrex.gob.cu/kenya; Ambassador JUAN MANUEL RODRIGUEZ VÁZQUEZ.

Czech Republic: 745 Tende Dr., Lavington, POB 25639, Nairobi; tel. 774420460; internet www.mzv.cz/nairobi; Ambassador MARTIN KLEPETKO.

Denmark: 13 Runda Dr., Runda, POB 40412, 00100 Nairobi; tel. (20) 4253000; e-mail nboamb@um.dk; internet kenya.um.dk; Ambassador OLE THONKE.

Djibouti: Nairobi International House, Mama Ngina St, POB 34446, 00100 Nairobi; tel. (20) 2122859; e-mail info@ken-djiboutiembassy.com; internet www.ken-djiboutiembassy.com; Ambassador YACIN ELMI BOUH.

Egypt: Othaya Rd, off Gitanga Rd, Kileleshwa, POB 30285, 00100 Nairobi; tel. (20) 3870360; e-mail eg.emb_nairobi@mfa.gov.eg; Ambassador (vacant).

Eritrea: New Rehema House, 2nd Floor, Westlands, POB 38651, Nairobi; tel. (20) 4443164; e-mail eritreanembassy@yahoo.com; Ambassador BEYENE RUSSOM.

Ethiopia: State House Ave, POB 45198, 00100 Nairobi; tel. (20) 2732052; internet fb.com/EthiopiainKE; Ambassador BACHA DEBELE.

Finland: Eden Sq., Blk 3, 6th Floor, Greenway Rd, off Westlands Rd, POB 30379, 00100 Nairobi; tel. (20) 3750721; e-mail sanomat.nai@formin.fi; internet finlandabroad.fi/web/ken; Ambassador PIRKKA TAPIOLA.

France: Peponi Gardens, off Peponi Rd, POB 41784, 00100 Nairobi; tel. (20) 7605555; e-mail ambafrance.nairobi@diplomatie.gouv.fr; internet ke.ambafrance.org; Ambassador ARNAUD SUQUET (designate).

Germany: Ludwig Krapf House, Riverside Dr. 113, POB 30180, Nairobi; tel. (20) 4262100; e-mail info@nairobi.diplo.de; internet nairobi.diplo.de; Ambassador ANNETT GÜNTHER.

Ghana: 328 Runda Grove, Runda, POB 42824, 00100 Nairobi; tel. (20) 2421801; e-mail ghanahighcomnairobi@gmail.com; internet nairobi.mfa.gov.gh; Ambassador DAMPTEY BEDIAKO ASARE.

Greece: Nation Centre, 7th Floor, Kimathi St, POB 30543, 00100 Nairobi; tel. (20) 340722; e-mail gremb.nai@mfa.gr; internet www.mfa.gr/nairobi; Ambassador (vacant).

Holy See: 151 Manyani Rd West, Waiyaki Way, POB 14326, 00800 Nairobi; tel. (20) 2148971; e-mail nunciokenya@nunciokenya.org; Apostolic Nuncio HUBERTUS MATHEUS MARIA VAN MEGEN (Titular Archbishop of Novaliciana).

Hungary: Kabarsiran Gardens, off James Gichuru Rd, Lavington, POB 61146, Nairobi; tel. 738905187; e-mail mission.nai@mfa.gov.hu; internet nairobi.mfa.gov.hu; Ambassador ZSOLT MÉSZÁROS.

India: Jeevan Bharati Bldg, 2nd Floor, Harambee Ave, POB 30074, Nairobi; tel. (20) 2225104; e-mail hoc.nairobi@mea.gov.in; internet www.hcinairobi.gov.in; High Commissioner VIRANDER KUMAR PAUL.

Indonesia: Menengai Rd, Upper Hill, POB 48868, Nairobi; tel. (20) 2714197; e-mail indonbi@indonesia.or.ke; internet www.kemlu.go.id/nairobi; Ambassador MOHAMAD HERY SARIPUDIN.

Iran: Villa Golestan, L. R. No. 29551, Lower Kabete Rd, POB 49170, Nairobi; tel. (20) 2002470; e-mail iranconkenya@gmail.com; internet kenya.mfa.gov.ir; Ambassador JAFAR BARMAKI.

Iraq: off UN Ave, Gigiri Dr., UN Crescent, House No. 176, Nairobi; tel. (20) 7122960; e-mail iraqembassynairobi@gmail.com; internet www.mofamission.gov.iq/en/KenyaNa; Ambassador BURHAN NAMIK AL-JAF.

Ireland: Delta Office Suites, 4th Floor, Waiyaki Way, Muthangari, Nairobi; tel. (20) 5135300; internet www.dfa.ie/irish-embassy/kenya; Ambassador FIONNUALA QUINLAN.

Israel: Bishop's Rd, POB 30354, 00100 Nairobi; tel. (20) 4927500; e-mail info@nairobi.mfa.gov.il; internet nairobi.mfa.gov.il; Ambassador MICHAEL LOTEM.

Italy: United Nations Cres., Gigiri, Muthaiga, POB 63389, 00100 Nairobi; tel. (20) 5137500; e-mail ambasciata.nairobi@esteri.it; internet ambnairobi.esteri.it/ambasciata_nairobi/it; Ambassador ROBERTO NATALI (designate).

Japan: Mara Rd, Upper Hill, POB 60202, 00200 Nairobi; tel. (20) 2898000; e-mail jinfocul@nb.mofa.go.jp; internet www.ke.emb-japan.go.jp; Ambassador KEN OKINAWA.

Jordan: 175 Ruaka Dr., Runda, POB 37554, 00100 Nairobi; tel. (20) 2400734; e-mail nairobi@fm.gov.jo; Ambassador FIRAS FARHAN SALEH KHOURI.

Korea, Republic: Misha Tower, 1st and 2nd Floors, Westlands Rd, POB 30455, 00100 Nairobi; tel. (20) 3615000; e-mail emb-ke@mofa.go.kr; internet overseas.mofa.go.kr/ke-ko/index.do; Ambassador YEO SUNG-JUN.

Kuwait: Muthaiga Rd, POB 42353, 00100 Nairobi; tel. (20) 3761614; e-mail kuwaitembassy@ymail.com; Ambassador QUSAI RASHED AL-FARHAN.

Libya: Jamahiriya House, Loita St, POB 47190, Nairobi; tel. (20) 250380; Chargé d'affaires a.i. MABRUK DAIA.

Malawi: Sports Rd, POB 30453, 00100 Nairobi; tel. (20) 4443805; e-mail info@malawihckenya.org; High Commissioner Dr CALLISTA MUTHARIKA.

Malaysia: Block 91/404, Gigiri Grove, Gigiri, POB 42286, 00200 Nairobi; tel. (20) 7123374; e-mail mwnairobi@kln.gov.my; internet www.kln.gov.my/web/ken_nairobi; Ambassador LOH SECK TIONG.

Mexico: Kibagare Way, off Loresho Ridge, POB 14145, 00800 Nairobi; tel. 728389813; e-mail inforken@sre.gob.mx; internet embamex.sre.gob.mx/kenia; Ambassador ERASMO ROBERTO MARTÍNEZ.

Morocco: UN Ave, Gigiri, POB 617, 00621 Nairobi; tel. (20) 7120765; e-mail sifmanbi@clubinternetk.com; Ambassador ABDERRAZZAK LAASSEL.

Mozambique: Bruce House, 3rd Floor, Standard St, POB 66923, Nairobi; tel. (20) 2221979; e-mail embamoc.quenia@minec.gov.mz; High Commissioner JERONIMO ROSA JOAO CHIVAVI.

Netherlands: Block B, Keystone Park, 95 Riverside Dr., POB 41537, 00100 Nairobi; tel. (20) 4288000; e-mail nai@minbuza.nl; internet www.netherlandsworldwide.nl/countries/kenya; Ambassador MAARTEN A. BROUWER.

Nigeria: Lenana Rd POB 30516, Nairobi; tel. (20) 2633941; e-mail info@nhc.org; internet www.nigeriankenya.or.ke; Ambassador YUSUF YUNUSA.

Norway: 58 Red Hill Rd, Gigiri, POB 2472-00621, 00100 Nairobi; tel. (20) 4251000; e-mail emb.nairobi@mfa.no; internet www.norway.no/kenya; Ambassador GUNNAR ANDREAS HOLM.

Oman: Gigiri Rd, off Limuru Rd, POB 76834, 00620 Nairobi; tel. (20) 4248348; e-mail trifoil@nbnet.co.ke; Ambassador SALEH BIN SULIMAN BIN AHMED AL HARTHY.

Pakistan: St Michel Rd, off Church Rd, off Waiyaki Way, Westlands, POB 30045, 00100 Nairobi; tel. (20) 4443911; e-mail pahicnairobi@gmail.com; internet www.pakhc.or.ke; High Commissioner SAQLAIN SAYEDA.

Philippines: Mzima Springs Rd, POB 47941, 00100 Nairobi; tel. 73445001; e-mail nairobipe@dfa.gov.ph; internet nairobipe.dfa.gov.ph; Ambassador MARIE CHARLOTTE G. TANG.

Poland: 58 Red Hill Rd, POB 30086, 00100 Nairobi; tel. (20) 7120019; e-mail nairobi.secretary@msz.gov.pl; internet www.gov.pl/web/kenya; Ambassador JACEK BAZAŃSKI.

Portugal: Eliud Mathu St 1090, Runda Estate, Nairobi; tel. 715883361; e-mail nairobi@mne.pt; internet nairobi.embaixadaportugal.mne.gov.pt; Chargé d'affaires e.p. ANA FILOMENA DA COSTA ROCHA.

Qatar: 178 Runda Dr., Runda, Nairobi; tel. (20) 7121300; e-mail nairobi@mofa.gov.qa; internet nairobi.embassy.qa; Ambassador JABIR ALI HUSSAIN AL-HAWASHELA AL-DOSARI.

Romania: Eliud Mathu St, Runda, POB 63240, 00619 Nairobi; tel. 721214073; e-mail nairobi@mae.ro; Ambassador DRAGOŞ VIOREL RADU ŢIGĂU.

Russian Federation: Lenana Rd, POB 30049, Nairobi; tel. (20) 2728700; e-mail russembkenya@mail.ru; internet russembkenya.mid.ru; Ambassador DMITRY I. MAKSIMYCHEV.

Rwanda: Limuru Rd, Gigiri, POB 30619, Nairobi; tel. 722207844; e-mail consular@kenya.embassy.gov.rw; internet www.rwandainkenya.gov.rw; High Commissioner Dr RICHARD MASOZERA.

Saudi Arabia: Muthaiga Rd, POB 58297, Nairobi; tel. (20) 762781; e-mail keemb@mofa.gov.sa; internet embassies.mofa.gov.sa/sites/kenya; Ambassador KHALID BIN ABDULLAH AL-SALMAN.

Senegal: House No. 192, Gigiri Close, off United Nations Ave, POB 2738, 00621 Nairobi; tel. (20) 2344077; e-mail ass@ambassenekenya.org; internet www.ambasenegal-ke.org; Ambassador NDONGO DIENG.

Serbia: Benin Dr. 1032, Runda, POB 30504, 00100 Nairobi; tel. 704588515; e-mail nairobi@embassyofserbia.or.ke; internet nairobi.mfa.gov.rs; Ambassador DRAGAN ŽUPANJEVAC.

Sierra Leone: 57 Gigiri Court, off United Nations Cres., POB 8242, 00100 Nairobi; tel. (20) 2189220; e-mail info@ke.slhc.gov.sl; internet slhckenya.org; High Commissioner ISATU AMINATA BUNDU.

Slovakia: Jakaya Kikwete Rd, POB 30204, Nairobi; tel. (20) 2721898; e-mail emb.nairobi@mzv.sk; internet www.mzv.sk/web/nairobi; Ambassador KATARÍNA ŽUFFA LELIGDONOVÁ.

Somalia: Denis Pritt Rd, POB 623, 00606 Nairobi; tel. (20) 2736618; e-mail admin@somaliembassy.co.ke; Ambassador MOHAMOUD AHMED NUR.

South Africa: Roshanmaer Place, Lenana Rd, POB 42441, 00100 Nairobi; tel. 709127000; e-mail sahc@africaonline.co.ke; High Commissioner MNINWA JOHANNES MAHLANGU.

South Sudan: Bishops Gate, 6th Floor, 5 Ngong Ave, cnr Bishop Rd, POB 73699, 00200 Nairobi; tel. (20) 2711382; e-mail goss@iconnect.co.ke; Ambassador CHOL MAWUT UNGUEC AJONGO.

Spain: CBA Bldg, Mara and Ragati Rds, Upper Hill, POB 45503, 00100 Nairobi; tel. (20) 2720222; e-mail emb.nairobi@maec.es; internet www.exteriores.gob.es/embajadas/nairobi; Ambassador CRISTINA DIAZ FERNADEZ-GIL.

Sri Lanka: Lenana Rd, POB 48145, Nairobi; tel. (20) 3872627; e-mail slhckeny@africaonline.co.ke; internet www.slhcnairobi.net; High Commissioner VELUPPILLAI KANANATHAN.

Sudan: Kabarnet Rd, off Ngong Rd, POB 48784, 00100 Nairobi; tel. 731280000; e-mail embassy@sudanembassyke.org; internet www.sudanembassyke.org; Ambassador GARIBALLA KHIDIR ELDAW.

Sweden: United Nations Cres., Gigiri, POB 30600, 00100 Nairobi; tel. 709964000; e-mail ambassaden.nairobi@gov.se; internet www.swedenabroad.com/nairobi; Ambassador CAROLINE VICINI.

Switzerland: Rosslyn Green Estate, Rosslyn Green Dr., off Red Hill Rd, POB 2600, 00100 Nairobi; tel. 730694000; e-mail nairobi@eda.admin.ch; internet www.eda.admin.ch/nairobi; Ambassador VALENTIN ZELLWEGER.

Tanzania: Re-Insurance Plaza, 9th Floor, Taifa Rd, POB 47790, 0100 Nairobi; tel. (20) 3311948; e-mail nairobi@nje.go.tz; internet ke.tzembassy.go.tz; High Commissioner Dr JOHN STEPHEN SIMBACHAWENE.

Thailand: Rose Ave, off Dennis Pritt Rd, POB 58349, 00200 Nairobi; tel. (20) 2919100; e-mail thaiembassy.nib@mfa.mail.go.th; internet www.thaiembassy.org/nairobi; Ambassador SASIRIT TANGULRAT.

Tunisia: Nairobi; Ambassador HATEM LANDOULSI.

Türkiye (Turkey): 30 Gigiri Rd, off Limuru Rd, POB 64748, 00620 Nairobi; tel. (20) 7126929; e-mail embassy.nairobi@mfa.gov.tr; internet nairobi.emb.mfa.gov.tr; Ambassador CEMIL MIROĞLU.

Uganda: Riverside Paddocks, off Riverside Dr., POB 60853, 00200 Nairobi; tel. (20) 4449096; e-mail info@ugahicom.co.ke; internet nairobi.mofa.go.ug; High Commissioner Dr HASSAN WASSWA GALIWANGO.

Ukraine: Limuru Rd 674, Muthaiga, POB 63566, 00619 Nairobi; tel. (20) 5224545; e-mail emb_ke@mfa.gov.ua; internet kenya.mfa.gov.ua/ua; Ambassador ANDRII PRAVENDNYK.

United Arab Emirates: Nyerere Rd, POB 42222, 00100 Nairobi; tel. 709991777; e-mail cons.nairobi@mofa.gov.ae; Ambassador KHALID KHALIFA ABDULLAH RASHID al-MUALLA.

United Kingdom: Upper Hill Rd, POB 30465, 00100 Nairobi; tel. (20) 2844000; e-mail nairobi.enquiries@fcdo.gov.uk; internet www.gov.uk/world/organisations/british-high-commission-nairobi; High Commissioner JANE MARRIOTT.

USA: UN Ave, Village Market, POB 606, 00621 Nairobi; tel. (20) 3636000; e-mail kenya_acs@state.gov; internet ke.usembassy.gov; Chargé d'affaires a.i. ERIC W. KNEEDLER.

Venezuela: UN Crescent, Gigiri, POB 2437, 00621 Nairobi; tel. (20) 7120648; e-mail embavene@swiftkenya.com; internet kenia.embajada.gob.ve; Ambassador JESÚS AGUSTÍN MANZANILLA PUPPO.

Yemen: cnr Ngong and Kabarnet Rds, POB 44642, Nairobi; tel. (20) 2145670; e-mail yemb-nairobi@mofa.gov.ye; Chargé d'affaires ABDUSSALAM AL-AWADHI.

Zambia: Nyerere Rd, POB 48741, Nairobi; tel. (20) 2593059; e-mail zambiacom@swiftkenya.com; internet fb.com/zamhighcomkenya; High Commissioner JOYCE KASOSA.

Zimbabwe: 111/192 Mumwe Ave, Runda, POB 693, 00621 Nairobi; tel. (20) 8164113; e-mail zimnairobi@gmail.com; Ambassador WINPEG MOYO.

Judicial System

The superior courts are the Supreme Court, the Court of Appeal and the High Court, the Employment and Labour Relations Court, and any court established to hear matters concerning the environment, and the use, occupation of and title to land.

Chief Justice: MARTHA KARAMBU KOOME.

Supreme Court: Supreme Court Bldg, City Hall Way, POB 30041, Nairobi; e-mail info@judiciary.go.ke; internet www.judiciary.go.ke; comprises the Chief Justice, who acts as the president of the court, the Deputy Chief Justice and 5 other judges; has jurisdiction to hear and determine disputes relating to the elections to the office of President and appellate jurisdiction to hear and determine appeals from the Court of Appeal and any other court or tribunal as prescribed by national legislation.

Court of Appeal: POB 30187, Nairobi; tel. 730181000; e-mail courtofappeal@judiciary.go.ke; comprises not fewer than 12 judges; the final court of appeal for Kenya in civil and criminal process; sits at Nairobi, Mombasa, Kisumu, Nakuru, Eldoret and Nyeri; Pres. WILLIAM OUKO.

High Court: between Taifa Rd and City Hall Way, POB 30041, Nairobi; tel. (20) 221221; e-mail hck-lib@nbnet.co.ke; has unlimited criminal and civil jurisdiction at first instance; jurisdiction to determine the question whether a right or fundamental freedom in the Bill of Rights has been denied, violated, infringed or threatened; jurisdiction to hear an appeal from a decision of a tribunal appointed under the Constitution to consider the removal of a person from office; and jurisdiction to hear any question respecting the interpretation of the Constitution; Principal Judge LYDIA AWINO ACHODE.

The subordinate courts are the Magistrates' courts, the Kadhis' courts, the Courts Martial and any other court or local tribunal as may be established by an Act of Parliament.

Resident Magistrates' Courts: have countrywide jurisdiction, with powers of punishment by imprisonment for up to five years or by fines of up to Ks. 500. If presided over by a chief magistrate or senior resident magistrate, the court is empowered to pass any sentence authorized by law. For certain offences, a resident magistrate may pass minimum sentences authorized by law.

District Magistrates' Courts: of first, second and third class; have jurisdiction within districts and powers of punishment by imprisonment for up to five years, or by fines of up to Ks. 500.

Kadhis' Courts: have jurisdiction within districts, to determine questions of Islamic law; comprise a Chief Kadhi and no fewer than three other Kadhis.

Religion

According to the 2019 census, some 85.5% of the population are Christian: Protestant 33.4%, Roman Catholic 20.6%, Evangelical 20.4%, African Instituted Churches 7.0% and other Christian denominations 4.1%. Approximately 10.9% of the population practises Islam, 0.1% practises Hinduism and the remainder follow various traditional indigenous religions. There are very few atheists. Muslim groups dispute government estimates; most often they claim to represent 15% to 20% of the population, sometimes higher. Members of most religious groups are active throughout the country, although certain religions dominate particular regions. Muslims dominate North-Eastern Province, where the population is chiefly Somali. Muslims also dominate Coast Province, except for the western areas of the Province, which are predominantly Christian. Eastern Province is approximately 50% Muslim (mostly in the north) and 50% Christian (mostly in the south). The rest of the country is largely Christian. Many foreign Christian missionary groups operate in the country.

CHRISTIANITY

National Council of Churches of Kenya: Jumuia Pl., 3rd Floor, Lenana Rd, POB 45009, 00100 Nairobi; tel. (20) 2721249; e-mail gsoffice@ncck.org; internet www.ncck.org; f. 1943 as Christian Council of Kenya; 29 mem. churches and 17 Christian orgs; Chair.

Archbishop Dr TIMOTHY NZYOKI NDAMBUKI; Sec.-Gen. Rev. CHRIS KINYANJUI KAMAU.

The Anglican Communion

Anglicans are adherents of the Church of the Province of Kenya, which was established in 1970. It comprises 36 dioceses, and has about 2.5m. members.

Primate and Archbishop of All Kenya: Most Rev. JACKSON NASOORE OLE SAPIT, Eastern Wing, ACK Garden House, 2nd Floor, 1st Ngong Ave, POB 40502, Nairobi; tel. (20) 2718001; e-mail info@ackenya.org.

The Roman Catholic Church

Kenya comprises four archdioceses, 20 dioceses, one Apostolic Vicariate and one military ordinariate.

Kenya Conference of Catholic Bishops: Kenya Catholic Secretariat, Waumini House, 4th Floor, Westlands, POB 13475, Nairobi; tel. (20) 443133; e-mail kccb@catholicchurch.or.ke; internet www.kccb.or.ke; f. 1976; Chair. Bishop PHILIP ARNOLD SUBIRA ANYOLO (Archbishop of Kisumu); Sec.-Gen. Rev. Fr DANIEL KIMUTAI RONO.

Archbishop of Kisumu: Most Rev. PHILIP ARNOLD SUBIRA ANYOLO, POB 1728, 40100 Kisumu; tel. 717507727; e-mail archdiocese-kisumu@africaonline.co.ke.

Archbishop of Mombasa: Most Rev. MARTIN KIVUVA MUSONDE, Catholic Secretariat, Nyerere Ave, POB 84425, Mombasa; tel. (41) 2311526; e-mail catholicsecretariat@msarchdiocese.org.

Archbishop of Nairobi: Most Rev. PHILIP ANYOLO, Archbishop's House, POB 14231, 00800 Nairobi; tel. (20) 2223906; internet archdioceseofnairobi.org.

Archbishop of Nyeri: Most Rev. ANTHONY MUHERIA, POB 288, 10100 Nyeri; tel. (61) 2030446; internet adnyeri.org.

Other Christian Churches

Africa Gospel Church: POB 418, Karen 00502; tel. 703940667; e-mail agc@agckenya.org; internet www.agckenya.org; Bishop Rev. Dr ROBERT LANG'AT.

Baptist Convention of Kenya: Jogoo Rd, POB 14907, 00800 Nairobi; tel. (20) 2494462; e-mail baptconvkenya@gmail.com; internet baptistconventionofkenya.com; f. 1972; Pres. STEPHEN ANYENDA; Gen. Sec. JOSHUA RUTERE MUCHEKE.

Church of God in East Africa: POB 160, 40105 Maseno; tel. 705671317; e-mail churchofgodeag@yahoo.com; internet www.churchofgodeak.org; Pres. Rev. Dr BYRUM MAKOKHA.

Evangelical Alliance of Kenya (EAK): Community Presbyterian Church, Makadara, Langata Rd, POB 26513, 00100 Nairobi; tel. 706444714; e-mail secretariat@eakenya.org; internet www.eakenya.org; f. 1975; Chair. Dr DAVID OGINDE; Gen. Sec. Dr NELSON MAKANDA.

Evangelical Lutheran Church in Kenya (ELCK): Luther Plaza, POB 44685, 00100 Nairobi; tel. 711187232; e-mail elckchurch@gmail.com; internet www.elck.org; f. 1948; Archbishop Most Rev. JOSEPH OCHOLA OMOLO; Gen. Sec. Rev. BENJAMIN LEMOSI.

Kenya African Church of the Holy Spirit: POB 183, Kakamega; internet kenyaafricanchurchoftheholyspirit.org; f. 1927.

Kenya Evangelical Lutheran Church: POB 54128, 00200 City Sq., Jogoo Rd, off Nile Rd, Nairobi; tel. (20) 2480545; e-mail info@kelckenya.org; internet kelckenya.org; Bishop ZACHARIAH W. KAHUTHU.

Methodist Church in Kenya: POB 47633, 00100 Nairobi; tel. (20) 2403437; e-mail mckconf@insightkenya.com; internet www.methodistchurchkenya.org; f. 1862; autonomous since 1967; Presiding Bishop Rev. Dr JOSEPH NTOMBURA MWAINE.

Presbyterian Church of East Africa (PCEA): Jitegemea House, Muhoho Ave, South C, POB 27573, 00506 Nairobi; tel. 722205051; e-mail info@pcea.or.ke; internet pcea.or.ke; f. 1891; Moderator Rt Rev. JULIUS GUANTAI MWAMBA; Sec.-Gen. Rev. ROBERT WAIHENYA NGUGI.

United Church of God: POB 75261, Nairobi; e-mail eastafrica@ucg.org; internet east-africa.ucg.org; Senior Pastor JOHN ELLIOTT.

BAHÁ'Í FAITH

National Spiritual Assembly: POB 47562, Nairobi; tel. (20) 2711364; e-mail nsa.kenya@gmail.com.

ISLAM

Supreme Council of Kenya Muslims (SUPKEM): Islamia House, 2nd and 3rd Floors, Njugu Lane, POB 415163, 00100 Nairobi; tel. (20) 2243109; e-mail info@supkem.org; internet www.supkem.org; Nat. Chair. Al-Hajj HASSAN OLE NAADO (acting); Sec.-Gen. (vacant).

Chief Kadhi: SHEIKH AHMED MUHDHAR.

The Press

DAILY NEWSPAPERS (PRINT AND ONLINE)

Business Daily: Nation Center, 2nd Floor, Kimathi St, POB 49010, 00100 Nairobi; tel. (20) 3288104; e-mail bdfeedback@ke.nationmedia.com; internet www.businessdailyafrica.com; Editorial Dir MUTUMA MATHIU; Man. Editor NG'ANG'A MBUGUA.

Daily Nation: Nation Centre, Kimathi St, POB 49010, 00100 Nairobi; tel. (20) 3288000; e-mail newsdesk@nation.co.ke; internet www.nation.co.ke; f. 1960; English; owned by Nation Media Group; Exec. Editor PAMELA MAKOTSI-SITTONI.

The People's Daily: DSM Place, 2nd Floor, Kijabe St, POB 103618, 00100 Nairobi; tel. (20) 4944100; e-mail editor.people@mediamax.co.ke; internet www.pd.co.ke; f. 1993; Group Editor-in-Chief ERIC OBINO.

The Standard: Mombasa Rd, POB 30080, 00100 Nairobi; tel. (20) 3222111; e-mail ads@standardmedia.co.ke; internet www.standardmedia.co.ke; f. 1902 as African Standard; renamed East African Standard before adopting present name in 2004; Group Editor-in-Chief OCHIENG RAPURO.

The Star: Lion Place, Waiyaki Way, POB 74497-0200, Nairobi; tel. (20) 4244000; e-mail webmaster@the-star.co.ke; internet www.the-star.co.ke; f. 2007; owned by Radio Africa Group; Convergence Dir WILLIAM PIKE.

Taifa Leo: POB 49010, Nairobi 00100; tel. (20) 3288419; e-mail taifa@ke.nationmedia.com; internet taifaleo.nation.co.ke; f. 1960; daily and weekly edns; Kiswahili; owned by Nation Media Group; Man. Editor NICHOLAS MUEMA.

Kenya also has a thriving vernacular press, but titles are often short-lived.

SELECTED PERIODICALS

Weeklies and Fortnightlies

Coastweek: Oriental Bldg, 2nd Floor, Nkrumah Rd, POB 87270, Mombasa; tel. (41) 2230125; e-mail coastwk@africaonline.co.ke; internet www.coastweek.com; f. 1978; English, with German section; Friday; Editor ADRIAN GRIMWOOD; Man. Dir SHIRAZ D. ALIBHAI.

Diplomat East Africa: Vision Plaza, Ground Floor, Suite 37, Mombasa Rd, POB 23399, Nairobi; tel. (20) 2525253; e-mail editor@diplomateastafrica.com.

The East African: POB 49010, 00506 Nairobi; tel. (20) 3288020; e-mail eastafrican@ke.nationmedia.com; internet www.theeastafrican.co.ke; f. 1994; weekly; English; owned by Nation Media Group; Editor-in-Chief TOM MSHINDI; Man. Editor OCHIENG RAPURO.

Kenya Gazette: POB 10443, 00100 Nairobi; tel. (20) 2712767; e-mail info@kenyalaw.org; internet www.kenyalaw.org; f. 1994; official notices; publ. by the National Council for Law Reporting; weekly.

Kenya Today: c/o Office of Public Communications, KICC Bldg, 3rd Floor, POB 45617, 00100 Nairobi; e-mail kenyatodaycorp@gmail.com; f. 2009; govt-owned; weekly; Dir JERRY OKUNGU.

Saturday Nation: POB 49010, Nairobi; English; owned by Nation Media Group; Man. Editor WAYUA MULI.

Taifa Jumapili: POB 49010, Nairobi; tel. (20) 3288419; e-mail taifa@ke.nationmedia.com; f. 1987; Kiswahili; owned by Nation Media Group; Man. Editor NICHOLAS MUEMA.

NEWS AGENCIES

Kenya News Agency (KNA): Uchumi House, Aga Khan Walk, Nairobi; tel. (20) 2211932; e-mail mawasiliano@information.go.ke; internet www.kenyanews.go.ke; f. 1963; Chief Editor WANGUI MUGO.

Publishers

AMECEA Gaba Publications: Amecea Pastoral Institute, POB 4002, 30100 Eldoret; tel. (53) 2061218; e-mail gabapubs@africaonline.co.ke; f. 1958; anthropology, religious; owned by AMECEA Bishops; Editor and Dir Sister JUSTINE C. NABUSHAWO.

Camerapix Publishers International: ABC Place, 3rd Floor, Waiyaki Way, POB 45048, 00100 Nairobi; tel. (20) 4448923; e-mail camerapixuk@btinternet.com; f. 1960; travel, topography, natural history; Man. Dir RUKHSANA HAQ.

East African Educational Publishers: Elgeyo Marakwet Close, off Elgeyo Marakwet Rd, Kilimani, POB 45314, 00100 Nairobi; tel. 722205661; e-mail info@eastafricanpublishers.com; internet www.eastafricanpublishers.com; f. 1965 as Heinemann Kenya Ltd; present name adopted 1992; academic, educational, creative writing;

some books in Kenyan languages; Chair. Dr HENRY CHAKAVA; CEO KIARIE KAMAU.

Evangel Publishing House: Lumumba Drive, off Kamiti Rd, Thika Rd, Private Bag 28963, 00200 Nairobi; tel. (20) 2320565; e-mail info@evangelpublishing.org; internet www.evangelpublishing.org; f. 1952; Christian literature; current back-list of over 300 titles; marriage and family, leadership, Theological Education by Extension (TEE); Gen. Man. MUSYOKI MULI.

Jomo Kenyatta Foundation: Industrial Area, Enterprise Rd, POB 30533, 00100 Nairobi; tel. (20) 6531965; e-mail info@jkf.co.ke; internet www.jkf.co.ke; f. 1966; primary, secondary, university textbooks; Man. Dir ROSEMARY K. A. BARASA.

Kenya Literature Bureau (KLB): Bellevue Area, Popo Rd, off Mombasa Rd, POB 30022, 00100 Nairobi; tel. 711318188; e-mail info@kenyaliteraturebureau.com; internet fb.com/klbkenya; f. 1947 as East African Literature Bureau; present name adopted in 1980; educational and general books; Chair. FRANCIS BAYAH; CEO EVE A. OBARA.

Longman Kenya Ltd: Kijabe St, next to Simlaw Seeds, POB 10679, 00100 Nairobi; tel. (20) 2119177; e-mail kkarani@longmankenya.com; internet www.longmanafrica.co.za/kenya.

Moran (EA) Publishers Ltd: Judda Complex, Prof. Wangari Maathai Rd, POB 30797, 00100 Nairobi; tel. (20) 2013580; e-mail info@moranpublishers.co.ke; internet www.moranpublishers.com; f. 1970 as Macmillan Kenya Publishers Ltd; present name adopted in 2010; publishes textbooks, atlases, maps, storybooks for all levels of education; CEO DAVID NUGUNA MUITA.

Oxford University Press (Eastern Africa): Elgon Rd, Upper Hill, The Oxford Place, POB 72532, Nairobi; tel. (20) 2732047; e-mail enq@oxford.co.ke; internet www.oxford.co.ke; f. 1954; children's, educational and general; Regional Dir JOHN MWAZEMBA.

Paulines Publications Africa: POB 49026, 00100 Nairobi; tel. (20) 447202; e-mail publications@paulinesafrica.org; internet www.paulinesafrica.org; f. 1985; African bible, theology, children's, educational, religious, psychology, audio CDs, tapes, videos; Pres. Sister MARIA KIMANI; Dir Sister TERESA MARCAZZAN.

Phoenix Publishers: Kijabe St, POB 18650, 00500 Nairobi; tel. (20) 2609087; e-mail info@phoenixpublish.com; internet www.phoenixpublishers.co.ke; Man. Dir JOHN MWAZEMBA.

Spotlight Publishers (E.A.) Ltd: Devan Plaza, 2nd Floor, Chiromo Rd, Westlands, POB 13433, 00800 Nairobi; tel. (20) 4441345; e-mail info@spotlightpublishers.co.ke; internet www.spotlightpublishers.co.ke; f. 2008; Man. Dir and CEO SIMON SOSSION.

Storymoja Publishers: Njamba House, Shanzu Rd, off Lower Kabete Rd, Westlands, POB 264, 00606 Nairobi; tel. (20) 2089595; e-mail info@storymojaafrica.co.ke; internet www.storymojaafrica.co.ke; f. 2008; CEO MUHIDDIN NGASHE.

University of Nairobi Press: Jomo Kenyatta Memorial Library Bldg, 3rd Floor, University of Nairobi, University Way, POB 30197, 00100 Nairobi; tel. (20) 4910000; e-mail nup@uonbi.ac.ke; internet uonpress.uonbi.ac.ke; Man. Editor PAMELLAH ASULE.

Vita Books: POB 62501-00200, Nairobi; e-mail info.vitabkske@gmail.com; internet vitabooks.co.uk; f. 1986.

WordAlive Publishers: 12 Riara Rd, Kilimani, POB 4547, 00100 Nairobi; tel. 728787675; e-mail info@wordalivepublishers.com; internet wordalivepublishers.com; Man. Dir DAVID WAWERU.

PUBLISHERS' ASSOCIATION

Kenya Publishers' Association: Occidental Plaza, 2nd Floor, Westlands, POB 42767, 00100 Nairobi; tel. (20) 2635498; e-mail info@kenyapublishers.org; internet www.kenyapublishers.org; f. 1971; organizes Nairobi International Book Fair each Sept; Chair. LAWRENCE NJAGI; 41 mems.

Broadcasting and Communications

TELECOMMUNICATIONS

In 2022 there were five providers of mobile telephone services in Kenya, one of which, Telkom Kenya Ltd, was also the sole provider of fixed-line services.

Airtel Kenya: Parkside Towers, Mombasa Rd, Nairobi; tel. (20) 6910000; e-mail customerservice@ke.airtel.com; internet www.airtelkenya.com; f. 2004; mobile telephone network provider; fmrly Celtel; present name adopted in 2010; Chair. LOUIS ONYANGO OTIENO; Man. Dir ASHISH MALHOTRA; 17.0m. subscribers (Sept. 2021).

Finserve Africa Ltd (Equitel): POB 104443, 00100 Nairobi; tel. 763063000; e-mail info@equitel.com; internet equitel.com; Chair. JAMES MWANGI; Man. Dir JACK NGARE; 1.4m. subscribers (Sept. 2021).

Jamii Telecommunications Ltd (JLT) (Faiba): POB 47419, 00100 Nairobi; tel. (20) 8405100; e-mail csc@jtl.co.ke; internet jtl .co.ke; CEO C. K. JOSHUA; 214,299 subscribers (Sept. 2021).

Safaricom Ltd: Safaricom House, Waiyaki Way, Westlands, POB 66827, 00800 Nairobi; tel. (20) 4273272; e-mail prcomms@safaricom .co.ke; internet www.safaricom.co.ke; f. 2000; owned by Telkom Kenya Ltd and Vodafone Airtouch (UK); operates a national mobile telephone network; Chair. MICHAEL JOSEPH; CEO PETER NDEGWA; 40.8m. subscribers (Sept. 2021).

Telkom Kenya Ltd: Telkom Plaza, Ralph Bunche Rd, POB 30301, Nairobi; tel. (20) 4952000; e-mail customercare@telkom.co.ke; internet www.telkom.co.ke; f. 1999; 51% owned by France Telecom; provides both fixed-line and mobile telephone services; Chair. EDDY NJOROGE; CEO MUGO KIBATI; 4.1m. mobile subscribers (Sept. 2021).

Regulatory Authority

Communications Authority of Kenya (CA): Waiyaki Way, POB 14448, Westlands, 00800 Nairobi; tel. (20) 4242000; e-mail info@ca .go.ke; internet ca.go.ke; f. 1999 as Communications Commission of Kenya; present name adopted in 2013; Chair. KEMBI GITURA; Dir-Gen. EZRA CHILOBA.

BROADCASTING

Radio

Kenya Broadcasting Corpn (KBC): Broadcasting House, Harry Thuku Rd, POB 30456, Nairobi; tel. 723892654; e-mail feedback@kbc .co.ke; internet www.kbc.co.ke; f. 1989; state corpn responsible for radio and television services; Chair. BENJAMIN K. MAINGI; Man. Dir SIMON MAINA.

Radio: National service (Kiswahili); General service (English); Vernacular services (Borana, Burji, Hindustani, Kalenjin, Kikamba, Kikuyu, Kimasai, Kimeru, Kisii, Kuria, Luhya, Luo, Rendile, Somali, Suba, Teso and Turkana).

Capital FM: Lonrho House, 19th Floor, City Sq., POB 74933, Nairobi; tel. (20) 2210020; e-mail info@capitalfm.co.ke; internet www.capitalfm.co.ke; f. 1999; commercial station broadcasting to Nairobi and environs.

Ghetto Radio (89.5 FM): Security Bldg, 4th Floor, Park Rd, Ngara, POB 387979, Nairobi; tel. (20) 2691900; internet ghettoradio.co.ke; f. 2007; Man. Dir MAJIMAJI JULIUS ONDIJO OWINO.

Hope FM: CITAM, Valley Rd, Nairobi; tel. 709861180; e-mail info@ hopefm.com; internet hopemediakenya.org; religious.

IQRA Broadcasting Network: Kilimani Rd, off Elgeyo Marakwet Rd, POB 21186, 00505 Nairobi; tel. 727444454; e-mail newsiqra@ yahoo.com; internet fb.com/Idhaalliotofauti; Islamic radio station broadcasting religious programmes in Nairobi; Man. Dir SHARIF HUSSEIN OMAR.

Kameme FM: Longonot Pl., Kijabe St, POB 49640, 00100 Nairobi; tel. (20) 2217963; e-mail info@kamemefm.co.ke; internet kameme.co .ke; f. 2000; commercial radio station broadcasting in Kikuyu in Nairobi and its environs; Man. Dir ROSE KIMOTHO.

Kitambo Communications Ltd: Bishop's Tower, 4th Floor, Bishop's Rd, POB 56155, Nairobi; tel. (20) 22247434; commercial radio and television station broadcasting Christian programmes in Mombasa and Nairobi; Man. Dir Dr R. AYAH.

Radio Africa Ltd (KISS FM): Lion Pl., Waiyaki Way, POB 74497, 00200 Nairobi; tel. 711046000; e-mail kiss100kenya@ radioafricagroup.co.ke; internet kiss100.co.ke; Man. Dir KIPRONO KITTONY.

Radio Citizen: Communication Centre, Maalim Juma Rd, off Dennis Pritt Rd, POB 7468, Nairobi; tel. (20) 2721415; e-mail citizen@royalmedia.co.ke; internet radiocitizen.co.ke; commercial radio station broadcasting in Nairobi and its environs; owned by Royal Media Services Ltd; Chair. SAMUEL KAMAU MACHARIA.

Sauti ya Rehema RTV Network: off Kaptagat Rd, opp. AIC Mission College, Eldoret; tel. 712178748; e-mail info@sayare.co.ke; internet www.sayare.co.ke; f. 1998; Christian, broadcasts in Eldoret and its environs; Man. Dir Rev.Dr ELI ROP.

Television

Kenya Broadcasting Corpn (KBC): see Radio

Television: KBC–TV; services in Kiswahili and English; operates 3 channels—KBC1, KBC2 and Metro TV.

Citizen TV: Communication Centre, Maalim Juma Rd, off Dennis Pritt Rd, POB 7468, Nairobi; tel. 719060000; e-mail info@royalmedia .co.ke; internet www.citizentv.co.ke; f. 1990, relaunched 2006; commercial station broadcasting in Nairobi and its environs; owned by Royal Media Services; Chair. SAMUEL KAMAU MACHARIA.

Family Media: Dik Dik Gardens, off Gatundu Rd, Kileleshwa, POB 2330, 00202 Nairobi; tel. 700316316; e-mail promotions@

familymedia.tv; internet familymedia.tv; f. 1999; CEO LEO SLINGERLAND.

Inooro TV: Maalim Juma Rd, off Dennis Pritt Rd, POB 7468, Nairobi; tel. 719060000; e-mail digitalsales@royalmedia.co.ke; internet inoorotv.co.ke; f. 2015; broadcasts in Kikuyu; owned by Royal Media Services.

K24 TV: Kijabe St, POB 103618, 00100 Nairobi; tel. 709824000; e-mail info@mediamax.co.ke; internet www.mediamaxnetwork.co .ke; f. 2009.

Kenya Television Network (KTN–TV): Nyayo House, 22nd Floor, POB 56985, Nairobi; tel. (20) 3222111; e-mail news@ktnkenya.com; internet www.ktnkenya.tv; f. 1990; commercial station operating in Nairobi and Mombasa; Man. Dir D. J. DAVIES.

NTV: Nation Centre, Kimathi St, POB 49010, Nairobi; tel. (20) 3288430; e-mail newsdesk@ke.nationmedia.com; internet ntv .nation.co.ke; f. 1999 as Nation TV; commercial station; owned by Nation Media Group; Man. Dir LINUS KAIKAI.

Regulatory Authority

Media Council of Kenya: Britam Centre, Ground Floor, cnr Mara and Ragati Rds, Upper Hill, POB 43132, 00100 Nairobi; tel. (20) 2716265; e-mail info@mediacouncil.or.ke; internet mediacouncil.or .ke; f. 2013; Chair. MAINA MUIRURI; CEO DAVID OMWOYO.

Finance

BANKING

Regulatory Body

Capital Markets Authority (CMA): Embankment Plaza, 3rd Floor, Longonot Rd, off Kilimanjaro Ave, Upperhill, POB 74800-00200, Nairobi; tel. (20) 2264400; e-mail corporate@cma.or.ke; internet www.cma.or.ke; f. 1989; independent government regulating agency; Chair. NICHOLAS NESBIT; CEO WYCKLIFFE SHAMIAH.

Central Bank

Central Bank of Kenya (Banki Kuu Ya Kenya): City Sq., Haile Selassie Ave, POB 60000, 00200 Nairobi; tel. (20) 2861000; e-mail comms@centralbank.go.ke; internet www.centralbank.go.ke; f. 1966; bank of issue; Chair. MOHAMMED NYAOGA; Gov. Dr PATRICK NGUGI NJOROGE.

Commercial Banks

Absa Bank Kenya PLC: West End Bldg, Level 6, off Waiyaki Way, POB 30120, 00100 Nairobi; tel. (20) 4254000; e-mail absa.kenya@ absa.africa; internet www.absabank.co.ke/personal; f. 1916; fmrly Barclays Bank Kenya Ltd; name changed as above in 2020; Chair. CHARLES MUCHENE; Man. Dir JEREMY AWORI.

Access Bank Kenya: Transnational Plaza, 2nd Floor, City Hall Way, POB 34353, 00100 Nairobi; tel. (20) 2224235; e-mail customerservice@tnbl.co.ke; internet www.tnbl.co.ke; f. 1985 as Transnational Bank Ltd; present name adopted 2020; Chair. Dr HENRY KIPLANGAT; CEO SAMMY LANGAT.

African Banking Corpn Ltd: ABC-Bank House, Mezzanine Floor, Koinange St, POB 46452, Nairobi; tel. (20) 4263000; e-mail talk2us@ abcthebank.com; internet www.abcthebank.com; f. 1984 as Consolidated Finance Co; converted to commercial bank and adopted present name 1995; Chair. RICHARD OMWELA; Group Man. Dir SHAMAZ SAVANI.

Bank of Africa—Kenya: BOA House, Karuna Close, off Waiyaki Way, Westlands, POB 69562, 00400 Nairobi; tel. (20) 3275000; e-mail yoursay@boakenya.com; internet www.boakenya.com; f. 2004; Chair. DENNIS AWORI; Man. Dir RONALD MARAMBII.

Consolidated Bank of Kenya Ltd: Consolidated Bank House, 6th Floor, 23 Koinange St, POB 51133, 00200 Nairobi; tel. 703016000; e-mail tellus@consolidated-bank.com; internet www .consolidated-bank.com; f. 1989; Chair. PETER NTOYIAN MUSEI; CEO THOMAS KIPKEMEI KIYAI.

Diamond Trust Bank Kenya Ltd (DTB): DTB Centre, Mombasa Rd, POB 61711, 00200 Nairobi; tel. 719031888; e-mail contactcentre@dtbafrica.com; internet dtbk.dtbafrica.com; f. 1945; established as a non-bank financial institution; commenced full commercial banking services in 1997, when it assumed present name; Chair. LINUS GITAHI; Man. Dir NASIM MOHAMED DEVJI.

Ecobank Kenya Ltd: Ushuru Pension Plaza, Muthangari Dr., off Waiyaki Way, Westlands, POB 49584, 00100 Nairobi; tel. (20) 22883000; e-mail kenya@ecobank.com; internet www.ecobank .com; f. 1972 as Akiba Bank Ltd, present name adopted 2008; Chair. MARTIN MBOGO; Man. Dir CHEIKH TRAVALLY.

Equity Bank: Equity Centre, 9th Floor, Hospital Rd, Upper Hill, POB 75104, 00200 Nairobi; tel. 763063000; e-mail info@equitybank

.co.ke; internet equitygroupholdings.com/ke; f. 1984; Chair. ERASTUS J. O. MWENCHA; Man. Dir GERALD WARUI.

Family Bank: Family Bank Tower, Muindi Mbingu St, POB 74145, 00200 Nairobi; tel. 703095000; e-mail info@familybank.co.ke; internet www.familybank.co.ke; f. 1984; Chair. WILFRED DAVID KIBORO; Man. Dir and CEO REBECCA MBITHI.

First Community Bank: FCB Mihrab Bldg, Mez 1, Ring Rd, Killimani, POB 26219, 00100 Nairobi; e-mail contactcenter@fcb.co.ke; internet www.firstcommunitybank.co.ke; f. 2007; Islamic banking; Chair. Sheikh MOHAMED MBAYE.

Guaranty Trust Bank Ltd: Plot 1870, Woodvale Close, Westlands, POB 20613, 00200 Nairobi; tel. (20) 3084000; e-mail customercareke@gtbank.com; internet www.gtbank.co.ke; f. 1986 as The Finance Institute of Africa Ltd; subsequently became a commercial bank in 1996 (Fina Bank Ltd); name changed as above in 2014; Chair. DHANJI HANSRAJ CHANDARIA; Man. Dir OLABAYO VERACRUZ.

Gulf African Bank (GAB): Geminia Insurance Plaza, Kilimanjaro Ave, Upper Hill, POB 43683, 00100 Nairobi; tel. (20) 2740000; e-mail info@gulfafricanbank.com; internet www.gulfafricanbank.com; f. 2007; 20% owned by Bank Muscat International (BMI), 10% owned by International Finance Corpn (IFC); Chair. RAFIK NAYED; Man. Dir ABDALLA ABDULKHALIK.

I&M Bank Kenya Ltd: I&M Bank House, 2nd Ngong Ave, POB 30238, 00100 Nairobi; tel. (20) 3221000; e-mail customercare@imbank.co.ke; internet www.imbank.com; f. 2013; acquired Giro Commercial Bank Ltd in 2017; Chair. S. B. R. SHAH; Man. Dir KIHARA MAINA.

Kenya Commercial Bank Ltd: Kencom House, Moi Ave, POB 48400, 00100 Nairobi; tel. (20) 3270000; e-mail contactcentre@kcb.co.ke; internet ke.kcbgroup.com; f. 1970; 23.1% state-owned; Group CEO PAUL RUSHDIE RUSSO.

M Oriental Bank Ltd: Finance House, 7 Koinange St, POB 44080, 00100 Nairobi; tel. (20) 2228461; e-mail info@moriental.co.ke; internet www.moriental.co.ke; f. 1991; fmrly Oriental Commercial Bank Ltd; name changed as above in 2016; Chair. SHANTI V. SHAH; CEO ALAKH KOHLI.

Middle East Bank Kenya Ltd: Mebank Tower, Milimani Rd, POB 47387, 00100 Nairobi; tel. (20) 2723120; internet www.mebkenya.com; f. 1981; 17.84% owned by Primecorp Holdings, 11.57% owned by Baumann Management Services, 11.57% owned by Meb Holdings, 11.57% owned by Good Fortune, 10.47% owned by Mustang; Chair. A. A. K. ESMAIL; Man. Dir ISAAC MWIGE.

National Bank of Kenya Ltd (Banki ya Taifa La Kenya Ltd): National Bank Bldg, Harambee Ave, POB 72866, 00200 Nairobi; tel. (20) 2828000; e-mail corporateaffairs@nationalbank.co.ke; internet nationalbank.co.ke; f. 1968; 42% owned by National Social Security Fund, 22.5% state-owned; Chair. JOHN NYERERE; Man. Dir PAUL RUSSO.

NCBA Bank Kenya PLC: Mara Rd, Upper Hill, POB 44599, POB 30437, 00100 Nairobi; tel. (20) 2884444; internet ke.ncbagroup.com; f. 2019 following the merger of Commercial Bank of Africa Ltd and National Industrial Credit Bank Ltd; Chair. ISAAC O. AWUONDO; Group Man. Dir JOHN GACHORA.

Paramount Universal Bank Ltd: Sound Plaza, 4th Floor, Woodvale Grove, Westlands, POB 14001, 00800 Nairobi; tel. (20) 4449266; e-mail info@paramountbank.co.ke; internet www.paramountbank.co.ke; f. 1993 as Combined Finance Ltd; name changed as above in 2000; 18.75% owned by Anwarali Noorali Merali Padany, 25% owned by Tormount Holdings Ltd, 25% owned by Tasneem Ashifali Padamshi, 25% owned by Noorez Karim Hassanali Padamshi, 6.25% owned by Kentrac Agencies Ltd; Chair. ANWARALI NOORALI MERALI PADANY; Man. Dir AYAZ MERALI.

SBM Bank Kenya Ltd: POB 34886, 00100 Nairobi; tel. 730175000; e-mail atyourservice@sbmbank.co.ke; internet www.sbmbank.co.ke; f. 1993 as Fidelity Finance; name changed to Fidelity Commercial Bank Ltd in 1996; present name adopted in 2017; CEO MOEZZ MIR.

Spire Bank: Mwalimu Towers, Hill Lane, Upper Hill, POB 52467, 00200 Nairobi; tel. (20) 4981777; e-mail letstalk@spirebank.co.ke; internet www.spirebank.co.ke; f. 1983; fmrly Equatorial Commercial Bank Ltd; present name adopted in 2016; Chair. DAVID NDEGWA WACHIRA; Man. Dir BRIAN KILONZO (acting).

Stanbic Bank Kenya Ltd: CFC Centre, Chiromo Rd, Westlands, POB 30550, 00100 Nairobi; tel. (20) 3268000; e-mail customercare@stanbic.com; internet www.stanbicbank.co.ke; formed by merger of CFC Bank Ltd and Stanbic Bank Kenya Ltd in June 2008; 100% owned by CFC Stanbic Holdings Ltd; Chief Exec. CHARLES MUDIWA.

Standard Chartered Bank Kenya Ltd: Stanbank House, Level 2, 48 Westlands Rd, POB 30003, 00100 Nairobi; tel. (20) 3293900; e-mail straight2bank.ke@sc.com; internet www.sc.co.ke; f. 1911; 74.5% owned by Standard Chartered Holdings (Africa) BV (Netherlands); Chair. PATRICK OBATH; CEO KARIUKI NGARI.

Co-operative Banks

Co-operative Bank of Kenya Ltd: Co-operative House, Haile Selassie Ave, POB 48231, 00100 Nairobi; tel. (20) 3276000; e-mail customerservice@co-opbank.co.ke; internet www.co-opbank.co.ke; f. 1965; Chair. JOHN MURUGU; Man. Dir and CEO GIDEON MURIUKI.

Development Banks

Development Bank of Kenya Ltd: Finance House, 16th Floor, Loita St, POB 30483, 00100 Nairobi; tel. (20) 3340401; e-mail dbk@devbank.com; internet www.devbank.com; f. 1963 as Development Finance Co of Kenya; current name adopted 1996; owned by Industrial and Commercial Devt Corpn (89.3%), Commonwealth Development Corpn (10.7%); Chair. WILLIAM HAGGAI; CEO VICTOR J. O. KIDIWA.

East African Development Bank: The Oval Bldg, 7th Floor, Ring Rd, Westlands, POB 47685, Nairobi; tel. (20) 2992000; e-mail cok@eadb.org; internet eadb.org; f. 1967; Country Man. LOISE MUIGAI.

IDB Capital Ltd: National Bank Bldg, 18th Floor, Harambee Ave, POB 44036, Nairobi; tel. (20) 2247142; e-mail bizcare@idbkenya.com; internet www.idbkenya.com; f. 1973 as Industrial Development Bank Ltd; adopted present name in 2005; 49% state-owned; Chair. Prof. MICHAEL KIPYEGO BOWEN; Man. Dir KAREN KANDIE.

STOCK EXCHANGE

Nairobi Securities Exchange (NSE): 55 Westlands Rd, POB 43633, 00100 Nairobi; tel. (20) 2831000; e-mail info@nse.co.ke; internet www.nse.co.ke; f. 1954; Chair. KIPRONO KITTONY; CEO GEOFFREY OTIENO ODUNDO.

INSURANCE

Insurance Regulatory Authority: Zep-Re Place, Longonot Rd, Upper Hill, POB 43505, 00100 Nairobi; tel. (20) 4996000; e-mail commins@ira.go.ke; internet www.ira.go.ke; f. 2006; Chair. ABDIRAHIN HAITHAR ABDI; CEO GODFREY K. KIPTUM.

Africa Merchant Assurance Co Ltd (AMACO): Nextgen Mall, 4th Floor, Mombasa Rd, POB 61599, 00200 Nairobi; tel. (20) 2204000; e-mail info@amaco.co.ke; internet www.amaco.co.ke; f. 2000; Chair. SILAS SIMATWO; CEO ELIZABETH KOSKEI.

AIG Kenya Co Ltd: Eden Sq. Complex, Chiromo Rd, POB 49460, 00100 Nairobi; tel. (20) 3676000; e-mail aigkenya@aig.com; internet www.aig.co.ke; Man. Dir CATHERINE IGATHE.

APA Insurance Ltd: 7 Ring Rd, Parklands, Westlands, POB 30065, 00100 Nairobi; tel. (20) 2862000; e-mail info@apainsurance.org; internet www.apainsurance.org; f. 2003; Chair. DANIEL NDONYE; CEO VINOD BHARATAN.

APA Life: Apollo Centre, Ring Rd, Parklands, Westlands, POB 30389, 00100 Nairobi; tel. (20) 3641000; e-mail info@apainsurance.org; internet www.apainsurance.org/apa-life; f. 1977; fmrly Apollo Life Assurance Ltd, name changed as above in 2013; life; CEO CATHERINE KARIMI.

British-American Insurance Co (BRITAM): Britam Centre, Mara and Ragati Rds Junction, Upper Hill, POB 30375, 00100 Nairobi; tel. 705100100; e-mail info@britam.co.ke; internet www.britam.com; f. 1965; operates under the trade name of Britam; Chair. KURIA MUCHIRU; Group Man. Dir TOM GITOGO.

CIC Insurance Group Ltd: CIC Plaza, Mara Rd, Upper Hill, POB 59485, 00200 Nairobi; tel. (20) 2823000; internet cic.co.ke; f. 1968; fmrly The Co-operative Insurance Co of Kenya Ltd, name changed as above in 2010; later demerged into CIC Life Assurance, CIC General Insurance Ltd and CIC Asset Management Ltd; Chair. JAPHETH ANAVILA MAGOMERE; Group CEO PATRICK NYAGA.

East Africa Reinsurance Co Ltd: EARe House, 98 Riverside Dr., POB 20196, 00200 Nairobi; tel. (20) 4443588; e-mail info@eastafricare.com; internet eastafricare.com; f. 1993; Chair. J. P. M. NDEGWA; CEO PETER K. MAINA.

Fidelity Shield Insurance Ltd: Equatorial Fidelity Centre, 5th Floor, Waridi Lane, off Waiyaki Way, Westlands, POB 47435, 00100 Nairobi; tel. (20) 4225000; e-mail info@fidelityshield.com; internet fidelityshield.com; Chair. RICHARD KEMOLI; Man. Dir MATHEW KOECH.

First Assurance Co Ltd: Gitanga Rd, Lavington, POB 30064, 00100 Nairobi; tel. (20) 2900000; internet firstassurance.co.ke; f. 1979 as Prudential Assurance Co. of Kenya Ltd; present name adopted 1991; 63.3% owned by Barclays Africa; life and general; Chair. MARY NGIGE; Man. Dir FREDRICK RUORO.

GA Insurance Ltd: GA Insurance House, 4th Floor, Ralph Bunche Rd, POB 42166, 00100 Nairobi; tel. (20) 626000; e-mail insure@gakenya.com; internet www.gakenya.com; general, medical, life; Chair. SURESH B. R. SHAH; CEO VIJAY SRIVASTAVA.

Heritage Insurance Co Ltd: Liberty House, Mamlaka Rd, POB 30390, 00100 Nairobi; tel. (20) 2783000; e-mail info@heritage.co.ke;

internet www.heritageinsurance.co.ke; f. 1976; general; Chair. PETER N. GETHI; Man. Dir GODFREY KIOI.

Jubilee Insurance Co Ltd: Jubilee Insurance House, Wabera St, POB 30376, 00100 Nairobi; tel. (20) 3281000; e-mail info@ jubileekenya.com; internet jubileeinsurance.com/ke; f. 1937; 66% owned by Allianz (Germany); long-term (life and pensions) and short-term (general and medical) insurance; Chair. NIZAR N. JUMA; CEO Dr JULIUS KIPNG'ETICH.

Kenindia Assurance Co Ltd: Kenindia House, Loita St, POB 40512, Nairobi; tel. (20) 3316099; e-mail kenindia@kenindia.com; internet www.kenindia.com; f. 1978; life and general; Chair. M. N. MEHTA; Man. Dir B. S. SHARMA.

Kenya Reinsurance Corpn Ltd (KenyaRe): Reinsurance Plaza, Taifa Rd, POB 30271, Nairobi; tel. (20) 2202000; e-mail kenyare@ kenyare.co.ke; internet www.kenyare.co.ke; f. 1970; Chair. CHIBOLI INDULI SHAKABA; Man. Dir JADIAH MWARANIA.

Liberty Life Assurance Kenya Ltd: Liberty House, Processional Way, POB 30364, 00100 Nairobi; tel. (20) 2866000; e-mail csc@ libertylife.co.ke; internet www.liberty.co.ke; f. 1964; fmrly CfC Life Assurance Co Ltd; present name adopted 2014; life and general; Chair. PETER NDERITU GETHI; Man. Dir ABEL MUNDA.

Madison Insurance Co Kenya Ltd: Madison House, Upper Hill Close, POB 47382, 00100 Nairobi; tel. 709922000; e-mail madison@ madison.co.ke; internet www.madison.co.ke; f. 1988 following merger of Crusader PLC and Kenya Commercial Insurance Corpn; life and general; Chair. SAMUEL G. NGARUIYA; Man. Dir JOSHUA NJIRU.

Metropolitan Cannon: Gateway Business Park, Mombasa Rd, Block D, POB 46783, 00100 Nairobi; tel. (20) 3966000; e-mail info@metcannon.co.ke; internet www.metcannon.co.ke; f. 2015 following merger of Metropolitan Life Kenya and Cannon Assurance; life and general; Chair. AIDA KIMEMIA.

Monarch Insurance Co Ltd: Monarch House 664, Olenguruone Ave, off James Gichuru Rd, Lavington, POB 44003, Nairobi; tel. (20) 4292000; e-mail info@monarchinsurance.co.ke; internet www .monarchinsurance.co.ke; f. 1975; life and general; Man. Dir STEPHEN OKUNDI.

Phoenix of East Africa Assurance Co Ltd: The Mirage, Tower 1, 7th Floor, Chiromo Rd, POB 30129, 00100 Nairobi; tel. 732178000; e-mail infoke@mua.co.ke; internet www.phoenix-assurance.com; general; Chair. BERTRAND CASTERES; Man. Dir ASHRAF MUSBALLY.

Prudential Life Assurance Kenya: Prudential House, 1st Floor, Wing A, Wabera St, Nairobi; tel. (20) 2712591; internet www .prudentiallife.co.ke; f. 2014 following acquisition of Shield Assurance Co Ltd; life; Chair. TITUS NAIKUNI; CEO Dr MATT LILLEY.

PTA Reinsurance Co (ZEP-RE): Zep-Re Pl.,8th Floor, Longonot Rd, Upper Hill, POB 42769, 00100 Nairobi; tel. (20) 4973000; e-mail mail@zep-re.com; internet www.zep-re.com; f. 1992; Chair. WILLIAM ERIO; Man. Dir HOPE MURERA.

Saham Assurance Co Kenya Ltd: Ecobank Towers, 16th Floor, Muindi Mbingu St, POB 20680, Nairobi; tel. (20) 2219486; e-mail mercantile@mercantile.co.ke; internet www.sahamassurance.co.ke; fmrly Mercantile Insurance Co Ltd; name changed as above in 2014; Chair. N. P. G. WARREN; Man. Dir SUPRIYO SEN.

Sanlam Kenya: Sanlam Tower, Waiyaki Way, Westlands, POB 10493, 00100 Nairobi; tel. (20) 5138200; e-mail info@sanlam.co.ke; internet www.sanlam.com/kenya; f. 1946; fmrly Pan Africa Life Assurance Ltd; present name adopted in 2016; life and general; Chair. Dr JOHN SIMBA; CEO PATRICK TUMBO.

UAP Insurance Co Ltd: UAP Old Mutual Tower, Upper Hill Rd, POB 43013, 00100 Nairobi; tel. (20) 2850000; e-mail uapinsurance@ uap-group.com; internet www.uapoldmutual.com; f. 1980; general and health insurance; UAP Life Assurance Ltd is also part of the UAP group; Chair. JOSEPH BARRAGE WANJUI; Group CEO ARTHUR OGINGA.

Insurance Association

Association of Kenya Insurers (AKI): AKI Centre, Mimosa Rd, Muchai Dr., off Ngong Rd, POB 45338, 00100 Nairobi; tel. 722204149; e-mail info@akinsure.com; internet www.akinsure.or .ke; f. 1987; Chair. MATHEW KOECH; Exec. Dir and Sec. TOM GICHUHI.

Trade and Industry

GOVERNMENT AGENCIES

Export Processing Zones Authority (EPZA): Administration Bldg, Viwanda Rd, Athi River Export Processing Zone, off Nairobi–Namanga Highway, Athi River, POB 50563, Nairobi; tel. (45) 6621000; e-mail info@epzakenya.com; internet epzakenya.com; f. 1990; est. by the Govt to promote investment in export processing zones; Chair. BEN OLUOCH OLUNYA.

Kenya Accreditation Service (KENAS): Embankment Plaza, 2nd Floor, Longonot Rd, Upper Hill, POB 47400, 00100 Nairobi; tel. 725227640; e-mail info@kenyaaccreditation.org; internet www .kenas.go.ke; f. 2009; provision of accreditation services that promote fair trade, health and safety as well as protection of the environment; Chair. Dr CATHERINE NYAKI ADEYA; CEO MARTIN CHESIRE.

Kenya Export Promotion and Branding Agency (KEPROBA): Anniversary Towers, 1st and 16th Floors, University Way, POB 40247, Nairobi; tel. (20) 2228534; e-mail chiefexe@brand.ke; internet brand.ke; f. 2019 to replace Export Promotion Council; Chair. JASWINDER SINGH BEDI; CEO WILFRED NYAKWANYA MARUBE.

Kenya Investment Authority: UAP Old Mutual Tower, 15th Floor, Upper Hill Rd, POB 55704, 00200 Nairobi; tel. 730104200; e-mail inquire@invest.go.ke; internet www.invest.go.ke; f. 1986; promotes and facilitates local and foreign investment; Chair. DENNIS WAWERU; Man. Dir OLIVIA RACHIER (acting).

Kenya National Trading Corpn Ltd: Yarrow Rd, off Nanyuki Rd, POB 30587, Nairobi; tel. (20) 2430861; e-mail kntc@kntc.co.ke; internet kntc.co.ke; f. 1965; promotes wholesale and retail trade; Chair. PETER KABERIA NKUBITU; Man. Dir PAMELA MUTUA.

Kenya Revenue Authority: Times Tower, Haile Selassie Ave, POB 48240, 00100 Nairobi; tel. (20) 2810000; e-mail callcentre@kra.go.ke; internet kra.go.ke/en; f. 1995; Chair. Dr FRANCIS MUTHAURA; Commr-Gen. GITHII MBURU.

Kenya Trade Network Agency (KENTRADE): Embankment Plaza, 1st Floor, Longonot Rd, Upper Hill, POB 36943, 00200 Nairobi; tel. (20) 4965000; e-mail contactcentre@kentrade.go.ke; internet www.kentrade.go.ke; f. 2011; mandated to facilitate cross-border trade and to establish, manage and implement the National Electronic Single Window System as a Vision 2030 flagship project; Chair. MUGAMBI IMANYARA; CEO AMOS WANGORA.

Privatization Commission: Social Security House, 10th Floor, Annex (Parking Silo), POB 34542, 00100 Nairobi; tel. (20) 2212346; e-mail info@pc.go.ke; internet www.pc.go.ke; f. 2005; Chair. PAUL N. OTUOMA; Exec. Dir and CEO JOSEPH KOSKEY.

State Corporations Advisory Committee: Kenyatta International Conference Centre, 9th Floor, Harambee Ave, POB 42145, 00100 Nairobi; tel. (20) 3343511; e-mail info@scac.go.ke; internet www.scac.go.ke; Chair. JEREMIAH MATAGARO; Sec. WANJIKU WAKOGI.

DEVELOPMENT ORGANIZATIONS

Agricultural Development Corpn: Development House, 10th Floor, Moi Ave, POB 47101, Nairobi; tel. (20) 2250695; e-mail info@adc.or.ke; internet adc.or.ke; f. 1965 to promote agricultural devt and reconstruction; Chair. NICHOLAS SALAT; CEO MOHAMMED M. BULLE.

Agricultural Finance Corpn: Development House, Moi Ave, POB 30367, Nairobi; tel. (20) 317199; e-mail info@agrifinance.org; internet agrifinance.org; a statutory organization providing agricultural loans; Chair. FRANKLIN KIPNGETICH BETT; Man. Dir LUCAS MESO.

Agriculture and Food Authority (AFA): Tea House, Naivasha Rd, off Ngong Rd, POB 37962, 00200 Nairobi; tel. 722200556; e-mail info@afa.go.ke; internet agricultureauthority.go.ke; f. 2014; following merger of 8 agricultural institutions: Coffee Board of Kenya, Sugar Board of Kenya, Tea Board of Kenya, Coconut Development Authority, Cotton Development Authority, Sisal Board of Kenya, Pyrethrum Board of Kenya and Horticultural Crops Development Authority; regulation and promotion of agriculture; Dir-Gen. HARSAMA P. KELLO.

Coast Development Authority (CDA): Mama Ngina Dr., POB 1322, 80100 Mombasa; tel. (20) 8009196; e-mail cda@cda.go.ke; internet www.cda.go.ke; Chair. PHILIP KITSAO CHARO; Man. Dir MOHAMED KEINAN HASSAN.

HF Group of Kenya Ltd: Rehani House, cnr Kenyatta Ave and Koinange St, POB 30088, 00100 Nairobi; tel. 709438000; e-mail customer.service@hfgroup.co.ke; internet www.hfgroup.co.ke; f. 1965; Group Chair. Prof. OLIVE M. MUGENDA; Group CEO ROBERT KIBAARA.

Kenya Development Corpn Ltd (KDC): Uchumi House, 17th Floor, Aga Khan Walk, POB 45519, Nairobi; tel. 727534572; e-mail info@kdc.go.ke; internet kdc.go.ke; f. 2020; following merger of Industrial and Commercial Development Corpn, Tourism Finance Corporation and IDB Capital Ltd; devt finance; Chair. MICHAEL NYACHAE; Dir-Gen. CHRISTOPHER G. HUKA.

Kenya Fishing Industries Corpn (KIFC): Liwatoni Fisheries Complex, Ganjoni, Mombasa; tel. 742407768; e-mail info@kfic.go.ke; internet kfic.go.ke; f. 2018; Chair. JOHN G. MSAFARI; Dir-Gen. Dr MIKAH O. NYABERI (acting).

Kenya Industrial Estates Ltd: Nairobi Industrial Estate, Likoni Rd, POB 78029, Nairobi; tel. (20) 6651348; e-mail admin@kie.co.ke; internet kie.co.ke; f. 1967 to finance and develop small-scale industries; Chair. MUTHONI KIMANI; Man. Dir Dr PARMAIN OLE NARIKAE.

Kenya Industrial Research and Development Institute (KIRDI): South C Campus, Popo Rd, off Mombasa Rd, POB 30650, Nairobi; tel. (20) 2388216; e-mail dir@kirdi.go.ke; internet www.kirdi.go.ke; f. 1942; reorg. 1979; restructured 1995; research and devt in industrial and allied technologies, including engineering, agro-industrial, mining and environmental technologies; Chair. Dr DINAH MWINZI; CEO Dr-Ing. CALVIN ONYANGO.

Kenya Medical Supplies Authority (KEMSA): Commercial St, Industrial Area, POB 47715, 00100 Nairobi; tel. (20) 3922000; e-mail info@kemsa.co.ke; internet www.kemsa.co.ke; f. 2013; procures, warehouses and distributes drugs and medical supplies for prescribed public health programmes; CEO TERRY KIUNGE RAMADHANI.

Kenya Tea Development Agency (KTDA): Moi Ave, POB 30213, Nairobi; tel. (20) 3227000; e-mail info@ktdateas.com; internet www.ktdateas.com; f. 1964 as Kenya Tea Development Authority to develop tea growing, manufacturing and marketing among African smallholders; operates 65 tea factories and 6 subsidiaries; privatized in 2000; Chair. DAVID MUNI ICHOHO; CEO WILSON MUTHAURA.

Micro and Small Enterprise Authority (MSEA): Utalii House, 10th Floor, Utalii Lane, 00100 Nairobi; tel. 770666000; e-mail info@msea.go.ke; internet msea.go.ke; f. 2012; promotion, development and regulation of micro and small enterprises; Chair. JAMES MUREU; CEO HENRY M. RITHAA.

National Irrigation Authority: Unyunyizi House, Lenana Rd, POB 30372, 00100 Nairobi; tel. 711061000; e-mail communication@irrigation.go.ke; internet www.irrigation.go.ke; f. 2019 to develop and improve irrigation infrastructure; Chair. Eng. JOSHUA N. TORO; CEO GITONGA MUGAMBI.

CHAMBER OF COMMERCE

Kenya National Chamber of Commerce and Industry (KNCCI): Heritan House, Ground Floor, Woodlands Rd, off Argwings Kodhek Rd, Hurlingham, POB 47024, Nairobi; tel. 782392700; e-mail info@kenyachamber.or.ke; internet www.kenyachamber.or.ke; f. 1965; Pres. RICHARD NGATIA; CEO SAMUEL MATONDA; 47 brs.

INDUSTRIAL AND TRADE ASSOCIATIONS

East African Tea Trade Association (EATTA): Tea Trade Centre, 1st Floor, Nyerere Ave, POB 85174, 80100 Mombasa; tel. (41) 2220093; e-mail info@eatta.co.ke; internet eatta.com; f. 1957; organizes Mombasa weekly tea auctions; Chair. A. D. SEWE; Man. Dir EDWARD K. MUDIBO; 178 mems in 9 countries.

Fresh Produce Exporters' Association of Kenya (FPEAK): New Rehema House, 4th Floor, Rhapta Rd, Westlands, POB 40312, 00100 Nairobi; tel. (20) 5160333; e-mail info@fpeak.org; internet fpeak.org; Chair. APOLLO OWUOR; CEO HOSEA MACHUKI.

Kenya Association of Manufacturers (KAM): 15 Mwanzi Rd, opposite Westgate Mall, Westlands, POB 30225, Nairobi; tel. (20) 2324817; e-mail info@kam.co.ke; internet kam.co.ke; f. 1959; Chair. RAJAN SHAH; CEO ANTHONY MWANGI; 950 mems.

Kenya Dairy Board: NSSF Bldg, 10th Floor, Bishops Rd, POB 30406, Nairobi; tel. 722573432; e-mail info@kdb.co.ke; internet www.kdb.go.ke; f. 1958; Chair. Dr IGANTIUS KAHIU; Man. Dir MARGARET KIBOGY.

Kenya Fish Processors' and Exporters' Association: 5th Floor, New Rehema House, Rhapta Rd, Westlands, POB 345, 00606 Nairobi; tel. (20) 4440858; e-mail info@afipek.org; internet www.afipek.org; f. 2000; Chair. JOHN G. MSAFARI; CEO BETH WAGUDE.

Kenya Flower Council: Green House Bldg, 4th Floor, Suite 12, Adams Arcade, Ngong Rd, POB 56325, 00200 Nairobi; tel. 733639523; e-mail info@kenyaflowercouncil.org; internet www.kenyaflowercouncil.org; f. 1996; association of independent growers and exporters of flowers and ornamentals; Chair. RICHARD FERNANDES; CEO CLEMENT TULEZI.

Kenya Meat Commission: off Mombasa Rd, POB 2, 00204 Athi River; tel. (45) 6626041; e-mail info@kenyameat.co.ke; internet www.kenyameat.co.ke; state-owned; f. 1953; purchasing, processing and marketing of beef livestock; Chair. Lt-Gen. JOSEPH K. KASAON; Man. Commr Brig. JAMES GITHANGA.

National Cereals and Produce Board (NCPB): Machakos Rd, Industrial Area, POB 30586, Nairobi; tel. (20) 6536028; e-mail info@ncpb.co.ke; internet www.ncpb.co.ke; f. 1985; grain marketing and handling, provides drying, weighing, storage and fumigation services to farmers and traders, stores and manages strategic national food reserves, distributes famine relief; Chair. MUTEA IRINGO; Man. Dir JOSEPH MUNA KIMOTE.

Nyayo Tea Zones Development Corpn (NTZDC): Nyayo House, 11th Floor, Kenyatta Ave, POB 48552, 00100 Nairobi; tel. (20) 3315650; e-mail info@teazones.co.ke; internet teazones.co.ke;

f. 1986; Chair. Prof. ELIZABETH PANTOREN; Man. Dir and CEO PETER KORIR.

Pyrethrum Processing Company of Kenya (PPCK): POB 420, Nakuru; tel. (51) 2211567; f. 1935; Man. Dir JOSEPH WAWERU.

EMPLOYERS' ORGANIZATIONS

Federation of Kenya Employers (FKE): Waajiri House, Argwings Kodhek Rd, POB 48311, Nairobi; tel. (20) 2721929; e-mail fkehq@fke-kenya.org; internet fke-kenya.org; Nat. Pres. HABIL OLAKA; Exec. Dir JACQUELINE MUGO.

Kenya Association of Hotelkeepers and Caterers: Applewood Adams, 12th Floor, Office Suite 1201, Ngong Rd, POB 9977, 00100 Nairobi; tel. 707402504; e-mail info@kahc.co.ke; internet www.kahc.co.ke; f. 1944; Chair. CHRISTOPHER MUSAU; CEO MIKE MACHARIA.

Kenya Bankers' Association: International Life House, 13th Floor, Mama Ngina St, POB 73100, 00200 Nairobi; tel. (20) 2221704; e-mail info@kba.co.ke; internet www.kba.co.ke; f. 1962; Chair. JOHN GACHORA; CEO HABIL O. OLAKA; 47 mem. orgs.

Kenya Coffee Producers' Association (KCPA): Wakulima House, 4th Floor, Room 408, Haile Selassie Ave, Ronald Ngala, POB 8100, 00300 Nairobi; tel. 748141214; e-mail info@kcpa.or.ke; internet kcpa.co.ke; f. 2009; Chair. PETER GIKONYO.

Kenya Vehicle Manufacturers' Association: Garissa Rd, POB 1436, Thika; tel. (20) 350309; e-mail kvm@kvm.co.ke; f. 1974; name changed as above in 1989; Chair. KENNETH KEBAARA.

UTILITIES

Electricity

Energy and Petroleum Regulatory Authority (EPRA): Eagle Africa Centre, Longonot Rd, Upperhill, POB 42681, 00100 Nairobi; tel. 709336000; e-mail info@epra.go.ke; internet www.epra.go.ke; f. 1997 as Energy Regulatory Board; subsequently the Energy Regulatory Commission; present name adopted in 2019; Chair. JACKTON B. OJWANG; Dir-Gen. DANIEL KIPTOO.

Kenya Electricity Generating Co Ltd (KenGen): KenGen Pension Plaza, POB 47936, Nairobi; tel. (20) 3666000; e-mail pr@kengen.co.ke; internet www.kengen.co.ke; f. 1997 as Kenya Power Co; present name adopted 1998; generates 82% of Kenya's electricity requirements; partially privatized in 2006; Chair. SAMSON MWATHETHE; Man. Dir and CEO REBECCA MIANO.

Kenya Electricity Transmission Co Ltd (KETRACO): KAWI Complex, Popo Lane, off Red Cross Rd, South C, POB 34942, 00100 Nairobi; tel. (20) 4956000; e-mail info@ketraco.co.ke; internet www.ketraco.co.ke; f. 2008; designs, constructs, operates and maintains new high-voltage electricity transmission infrastructure; state-owned; Chair. Capt. JOE MUSYIMI MUTAMBU; Man. Dir and CEO Eng. FERNANDES BARASA.

Kenya Power and Lighting Co (KPLC): Electricity House, Harambee Ave, POB 301779, Nairobi; tel. 703070707; e-mail custcare@kplc.co.ke; internet www.kplc.co.ke; partially privatized in 2006; 4% owned by Transcentury Group; co-ordinates electricity transmission and distribution; Chair. VIVIENNE YEDA; Acting Man. Dir and CEO GEOFFREY MULI.

Rural Electrification and Renewable Energy Corpn: Kawi House, off Red Cross Rd, Bellevue South C, POB 34585, 0010 Nairobi; tel. 709193000; e-mail info@rea.co.ke; internet www.rea.co.ke; f. 2019 to replace Rural Electrification Authority; Chair. SIMON GICHARU; CEO PETER MBUGUA.

WATER

Nairobi City Water and Sewerage Co (NWSC): Kampala Rd, off Enterprise Rd, POB 30656, 00100 Nairobi; tel. (20) 3988000; internet www.nairobiwater.co.ke; f. 2002; Chair. BERYL OKUMU; Man. Dir NAHASHON MUGUNA.

MAJOR COMPANIES

The following are among the largest companies in terms either of capital investment or employment.

ARM Cement Ltd (ARM): Rhino House, Chiromo Rd, Westlands, POB 41908, 00100 Nairobi; tel. 733636456; e-mail info@armcement.com; internet www.armcement.com; f. 1974; present name adopted in 2012; mines and processes industrial minerals and chemicals; ISO-certified manufacturer of cement and lime; manufactures cement, quick and hydrated lime, sodium silicate, industrial minerals, special cements and building products and fertilizers; Man. Dir PRADEEP H. PAUNRANA.

Bamburi Cement Ltd: Kenya-Re Towers, 6th and 9th Floors, Upper Hill, off Ragati Rd, Upper Hill, POB 10921, 00100 Nairobi; tel. (20) 2710487; e-mail corp.info@bamburi.lafarge.com; internet www.lafarge.co.ke; f. 1951; 29.3% owned by Fincem Holdings Ltd, 29.3% owned by Kencem Holdings Ltd; produces Portland cement;

Chair. Dr JOHN P. N. SIMBA; Group Man. Dir SEDDIQ HASSANI; 932 employees (2014).

BAT (Kenya) Ltd: 8 Likoni Rd, Industrial Area, POB 30000, Nairobi; tel. 711062000; e-mail info_ke@bat.com; internet www .batkenya.com; f. 1956; subsidiary of British American Tobacco Co Ltd, UK; mfrs of tobacco products; Chair. RITA KAVASHE; Dir-Gen. CRISPIN ACHOLA.

Bata Shoe Co (Kenya) Ltd: POB 23, Limuru 00217; tel. (20) 2010620; e-mail bata.kenya@bata.com; internet www.batakenya .com; f. 1943; mfrs of footwear; Country Man. JEDDIDAH THOTHO.

Bedi Investments Ltd: Lower Factory Rd, Industrial Area, POB 230, Nakuru; tel. (51) 2212320; e-mail info@bedi.com; internet www .bedi.com; f. 1972; manufactures finished fabrics, yarns and garments; Chair. JARNAIL BEDI; CEO JASWINDER S. BEDI.

Bidco Africa Ltd: General Kago Rd, POB 239, 01000 Thika; tel. (67) 2821000; e-mail happy@bidcoafrica.com; internet www.bidcoafrica .com; agribusiness, manufacturer and marketer of consumer products; CEO TARUN SHAH.

BOC Kenya Ltd: Kitui Rd, Industrial Area, POB 18010, 00500 Nairobi; tel. (20) 6944000; e-mail bocinfo@boc.co.ke; internet www .boc.co.ke; f. 1940; a member of The Linde PLC; supplier of industrial and medical gasses and accessories; Man. Dir (vacant).

Brollo Kenya Ltd: Miritini, POB 90651, 80100 Mombasa; tel. (41) 2312123; e-mail info@brollokenya.com; internet brollokenya.com; manufactures value-added steel and tubular products; Chair. L. P. DOSHI.

Brookside Dairy Ltd: POB 236, 00232 Ruiru; tel. (20) 2506210; e-mail maziwa@brookside.co.ke; internet www.brookside.co.ke; manufacture of dairy products; in July 2014 the French food products co Groupe Danone announced that it was purchasing a 40% stake in Brookside Dairy; Gen. Man. JOHN GETHI.

Chemelil Sugar Co Ltd: POB 177, Muhoroni 40107; tel. (20) 2031883; e-mail csc@chemsugar.co.ke; internet chemelil.adevinci .co.ke; f. 1965; production and processing of sugar; Man. Dir GABRIEL NYANGWESO (acting); 1,244 employees.

CMC Motors Group Ltd: Lusaka Rd, POB 30135, 00100 Nairobi; tel. 722509868; e-mail ceo@cmcmotors.com; internet www .cmcmotors.com; f. 1948; acquired by Al-Futtaim Group (UAE) in 2014; Man. Dir MARK JAMES KASS.

East African Breweries PLC: Thika Rd, Ruaraka, POB 30161, Nairobi; tel. (20) 8644000; e-mail eabl.info@eabl.com; internet www .eabl.com; f. 1922; brews Tusker, Pilsner, Whitecap, Allsopps, Bell Lager and Kibo Gold; Group Man. Dir JANE KARUKU.

East African Cables Ltd: Addis Ababa Rd, Industrial Area, POB 18243, 00500 Nairobi; tel. (20) 6607000; e-mail info@eacables.com; internet www.eacables.com; manufacture and sale of electrical cables and conductors; Chair. MICHAEL G. WAWERU; CEO PAUL MUIGAI.

East African Packing Industries Ltd (EAPI): Kitui Rd, off Kampala Rd, POB 30146, Nairobi; tel. (20) 3955000; e-mail sales@ eapi.co.ke; internet www.eapi.co.ke; f. 1959; produces multiwall paper bags, corrugated cardboard containers and toilet tissue; Chair. A. P. HAMILTON; Man. Dir RON FASOL.

East African Portland Cement Co Ltd: Namanga Rd, off Mombasa Rd, Athi River, POB 20, Nairobi; tel. 709855000; e-mail customercare@eapcc.co.ke; internet www.eastafricanportland.com; f. 1932; cement mfrs; Chair. EDWIN MURIITHI KINYUA; Man. Dir DANIEL KIPRONO (acting).

Eveready East Africa Ltd: MCFL Logistics Centre, 1st Floor, Mombasa Rd, POB 44765, 00100 Nairobi; tel. (20) 2980000; e-mail info@eveready.co.ke; internet www.eveready.co.ke; manufactures batteries, lights and personal care products; Chair. LUCY WAGUTHI WAITHAKA; Man. Dir THOMAS MONG'ARE MASAKI (acting).

Geothermal Development Co: Kawi House, South C Bellevue, off Mombasa Rd, POB 100746, 00101 Nairobi; tel. 719036000; e-mail ewamanji@gdc.co.ke; internet www.gdc.co.ke; f. 2006; development of geothermal resources; state-owned; Chair. JOHN NJIRAINI; Man. Dir Eng. JARED O. OTHIENO.

Insteel Ltd: Ol Kalou Rd, Industrial Area, POB 78161, 00507 Nairobi; tel. 734333163; e-mail info.insteel@safalgroup.com; internet www.insteellimited.com; f. 1983; manufactures steel water pipes and hollow sections; COO and Dir H. P. MODI.

Kakuzi Ltd: Punda Milia Rd, Makuyu, POB 24, Thika; tel. (20) 2184111; e-mail mail@kakuzi.co.ke; internet www.kakuzi.co.ke; f. 1927; 26.1% owned by Bordure Ltd, 24.6% by Lintak Investments Ltd, 5.0% by Kenya Reinsurance Corpn; tea and coffee growing, livestock farming, horticulture, forestry development; Chair. GRAHAM MCLEAN; Man. Dir CHRISTOPHER FLOWERS.

Kaluworks Ltd: Mariakani, off Mombasa Rd, POB 89128, Mombasa; tel. (41) 2220342; e-mail enquiries@kaluworks.com; internet www.kaluworks.com; f. 1929; mfr of aluminium kitchenware and

catering equipment for export, mfrs of aluminium sheets, coils and circles; COO VENU NAIR; Exec. Dir RAKESH CHANDRA SHARMA.

Kapa Oil Refineries Ltd (KAPA): Main Mombasa Rd, POB 18492, 00500 Nairobi; tel. (20) 6420000; e-mail info@kapa-oil.com; internet www.kapa-oil.com; f. 1975; mfrs of cooking fats and edible oils, margarines, baking powder, detergents, laundry soaps and glycerine; CEO NITIN SHAH; 2,000 employees.

KenolKobil Ltd: Ave 5 Bldg, 5th Floor, Rose Ave, off Lenana Rd, POB 44202, Nairobi; tel. 703022000; e-mail info@ke.kenolkobil.com; internet www.kenolkobil.com; f. 1959; fmrly Kenya Oil Co Ltd; present name adopted in 2008; acquired by Rubis Energie in 2019; import of crude petroleum; marketing of fuel and lubricants; Chair. JAMES MATHENGE; Group Man. Dir JEAN-CHRISTIAN BERGERON.

Kenya Heavy Vehicle Manufactures Ltd (KVM): Garissa Rd, POB 1436, Thika; tel. (20) 3540309; e-mail kvm@kvm.co.ke; internet www.kvm.co.ke; 35% state-owned, 32.5% owned by CMC Holdings Ltd and 32.5% owned by D. T. Dobie & Co (K) Ltd; Man. Dir MARTYN BROADFIELD.

Kenya Petroleum Refineries Ltd (KPRL): Refinery Rd, Changamwe, POB 90401, 80100 Mombasa; tel. (41) 3433511; e-mail refinery@kprl.co.ke; internet www.kprl.co.ke; f. 1960 as East African Oil Refineries Ltd; state-owned; CEO JOSEPH NDOTI (acting).

Kenya Pipeline Co Ltd (KPC): Kenpipe Plaza, Sekondi Rd, off Nanyuki Rd, Industrial Area, POB 73442, 00200 Nairobi; tel. (20) 2606500; e-mail info@kpc.co.ke; internet www.kpc.co.ke; f. 1973; state-owned; Chair. JOHN NGUMI; Man. Dir JOE SANG.

Kenya Seed Co Ltd: Teachers Plaza, 2nd Floor, POB 553, Kitale; tel. 739480663; e-mail info@kenyaseed.co.ke; internet www .kenyaseed.com; f. 1956; seed growers and merchants; Chair. FRANCIS OKWARA; Man. Dir FRED OLOIBE (acting).

Simlaw Seeds: Kijabe St, POB 40042, Nairobi; tel. 722200545; e-mail info@simlaw.co.ke; internet www.simlaw.co.ke; Chair. LAWRENCE MARK NJIRU; Gen. Man. DAVID KIPLAGAT.

Kenya Tea Packers Ltd (KETEPA): POB 413, 20200 Kericho; tel. 726555550; e-mail info@ketepa.com; internet ketepa.com; f. 1977; 70% owned by Kenya Tea Development Agency Ltd; production of packed tea; Chair. PAUL MURITHI RINGERA; Man. Dir ALBERT OTOCHI.

Kwale International Sugar Co. Ltd (KISCOL): Unifresh Exotics Bldg, Baba Dogo Rd, POB 46279, Ruaraka; tel. 722456546; e-mail info@kwale-group.com; internet www.kwale-group.com; f. 2007; Gen. Man. PAMELA OGADA.

Libya Oil Kenya Ltd: Oilibya Plaza, Muthaiga Rd, POB 64900, 0620 Nairobi; tel. 719020300; e-mail info@oilibya.co.ke; internet fb .com/OLAEnergyKenya; f. 2006; operates under the trade name of Ola Energy; Gen. Man. MILLICENT ONYONYI.

Mabati Rolling Mills Ltd: Athi River, POB 271, 00204 Nairobi; tel. (20) 6247000; e-mail sales@mabati.com; internet www.mabati.com; owned by Safal Group; CEO ANDREW HEYCOTT.

Mumias Sugar Co Ltd: Kakamega-Bungoma Rd, Private Bag, Mumias; tel. 711094000; e-mail msc@mumias-sugar.com; internet www.mumias-sugar.com; f. 1971; privatized in 2001; sugar production; Chair. KENNEDY NGUMBAU MULWA; Man. Dir ISAAC SHEUNDA.

National Oil Corporation of Kenya Ltd (NOCK): KAWI House, South C, Popo Lane, off Red Cross Rd, POB 58567, Nairobi; tel. (20) 6952000; e-mail feedback@nockenya.co.ke; internet www.nockenya .co.ke; f. 1981; 100% owned by Govt of Kenya; Chair. PATRICK OBATH; CEO LEPARAN GIDEON MORINTAT.

New KCC Ltd: Creamery House, Dakar Rd, POB 30131, Nairobi; tel. (20) 3980000; e-mail info@newkcc.co.ke; internet www.newkcc .co.ke; f. 1925 as Kenya Co-operative Creameries Ltd; name changed as above in 2009; processes and markets the bulk of dairy produce; Chair. Dr GATHIGI KAHIU; Man. Dir Dr NIXON KIPKEMOI SIGEY.

Njoro Canning Factory (Kenya) Ltd: POB 7076, Nakuru; tel. 724253050; e-mail info@njorocanning.com; internet www .njorocanning.co.ke; f. 1978; produces canned, dried and frozen vegetables; Chair. T. K. PATEL; Man. Dir G. KARAN.

Numerical Machining Complex Ltd (NMC): Workshops Rd, POB 70660, 00400 Nairobi; tel. (20) 2241701; e-mail enquiries@ nmc.co.ke; internet nmc.co.ke; f. 1994; manufacturer of machinery and components; Man. Dir Eng. GEORGE S. ONYANGO.

Nzoia Sugar Co: POB 285, 50200 Bungoma; tel. (55) 30500; e-mail md@nzoiasugar.com; internet www.nzoiasugar.co.ke; f. 1975; Chair. JOASH WAMANG'OLI; Man. Dir MICHEAL WANJALA.

Orbit Chemical Industries Ltd (OCIL): POB 48870, Nairobi; tel. (20) 2338200; e-mail orbit@orbitchem.com; internet www.orbitchem .com; f. 1972; manufacture of chemicals, soaps and detergents; Chair. V. D. CHANDARIA.

Sameer Africa Ltd: cnr Mombasa and Enterprise Rds, POB 30429, 00100 Nairobi; tel. (20) 3962000; e-mail customercare@sameerafrica .com; internet www.sameerafrica.com; f. 1969; formerly Firestone East Africa (1969) Ltd; corporate identity changed to Sameer Africa

Ltd in 2005; tyre and tube mfrs; Chair. ERASTUS K. MWONGERA; Man. Dir PETER M. GITONGA.

Sasini Ltd: Sasini House, Loita St, POB 30151, 00100 Nairobi; tel. (20) 342166; e-mail info@sasini.co.ke; internet www.sasini.co.ke; f. 1952; public co with majority shares owned by Sameer Investments Ltd; tea and coffee farming and production; Chair. Dr JAMES BOYD MCFIE; Group Man. Dir STEPHEN MAINA GITHIGA.

South Nyanza Sugar Co Ltd (SonySugar): Kisii-Migori Highway, POB 107, 40405 Sare, Awendo; tel. (20) 8029201; e-mail administration@sonysugar.co.ke; internet www.sonysugar.co.ke; f. 1976; Chair. CHARLES OWINO; Man. Dir JANE PAMELA ODHIAMBO.

Tata Chemicals Magadi: POB 1, 00205 Magadi; tel. (20) 6999000; e-mail info@magadisoda.co.ke; internet www.tatachemicals.com/operations/magadi; f. 1911; fmrly Magadi Soda Co., name changed as above in 2005; mfr of soda ash sodium carbonate and salt; Man. Dir JACKSON MUCHIRA MBUI.

Total Kenya Ltd: Regal Plaza, 6 Ave Parklands, Limuru Rd, POB 30736, Nairobi; tel. (20) 2897333; e-mail customercare@total.co.ke; internet www.total.co.ke; f. 1963; name changed as above in 1991; distribution of petroleum products; Man. Dir OLAGOKE ALUKO.

Trans-Century Ltd: Westend Towers, 8th Floor, Waiyaki Way, POB 42334-00100 GPO, Nairobi; tel. 709916000; e-mail info@transcentury.co.ke; internet www.transcentury.co.ke; f. 1997; Chair. SHAKA KARIUKI; CEO and Man. Dir NGANGA NJIIINU.

> **Civicon Ltd:** West End Towers, 8th Floor, Muthangari Dr., POB 99491-80107, Mombasa; tel. 733615433; e-mail info@civicongroup .com; internet www.civicongroup.com; f. 1975; engineering and construction; Chair. NGUGI KIUNA; Group CEO JASON HORSEY.

Unga Group Ltd: Ngano House, Commercial St, POB 30386, Nairobi; tel. (20) 3933000; e-mail information@unga.com; internet ungagroup.com; f. 1928; 51% owned by Victus Ltd; mfrs of flour, maize meal, porridges, animal feed and animal minerals; Chair. ISABELLA OCHOLA-WILSON; Man. Dir NICHOLAS HUTCHINSON.

Unilever Tea Kenya Ltd (UTKL): POB 42011, Nairobi; tel. (20) 532520; e-mail richard.fairburn@unilever.com; internet www .unilever-esa.com; f. 1825 as Brooke Bond Kenya Ltd; present name adopted in 2004; growth, production and sale of tea; Man. Dir RICHARD FAIRBURN.

Vivo Energy Kenya: Vienna Court, East Wing, State House Cres. Rd, off State House Ave, POB 43561, 00100 Nairobi; tel. 703025000; e-mail csc.helpdesk@vivoenergy.com; internet www.vivoenergy .com; a Shell licensee; jt venture between Vitol (40%), Helios Investment Partners (40%) and Shell (20%); Man. Dir PETER MURUNGI.

Williamson Tea Kenya Ltd: Karen Office Park, Langata Rd, POB 42281, Nairobi; tel. (20) 3882522; e-mail info@williamson.co.ke; internet www.williamsontea.com; f. 1952; fmrly George Williamson Kenya Ltd; 50.41% owned by Williamson Tea Holdings PLC (UK); tea cultivation and production; Man. Dir ALAN CARMICHAEL.

TRADE UNIONS

Central Organization of Trade Unions (Kenya) (COTU): Solidarity Bldg, Digo Rd, POB 13000, Nairobi; tel. (20) 2383367; e-mail info@cotu-kenya.org; internet www.cotu-kenya.org; f. 1965 as the sole trade union fed.; Chair. RAJABU W. MWONDI; Sec.-Gen. FRANCIS ATWOLI.

> **Amalgamated Union of Kenya Metalworkers:** Avon House, Mfangano St, POB 73651, Nairobi; tel. (20) 2211060; e-mail aukmw@clubinternetk.com; internet fb.com/aukmwworkers; Gen. Sec. ROSE OMAMO.

> **Bakery, Confectionery Manufacturing and Allied Workers' Union (Kenya):** Lengo House, 3rd Floor, Room 20, Tom Mboya St, opposite Gill House, POB 57751, 00200 Nairobi; tel. (20) 330275; e-mail bakers@form-net.com; Gen. Sec. DANCHEL MWANGURE.

> **Communication Workers' Union of Kenya:** Hermes House, Tom Mboya St, POB 48155, Nairobi; tel. (20) 219345; e-mail cowuk@clubinternet.com; Gen. Sec. BENSON OKWARO.

> **Dockworkers' Union (DWU):** Dockers House, Kenyatta Ave, POB 98207, Mombasa; tel. (41) 2491974; f. 1954; Gen. Sec. SIMON SANG.

> **Kenya Airline Pilots' Association:** RUBANI House, off Airport North Rd, POB 57509, 00200 Nairobi; tel. 722778844; e-mail kalpa .kenya@gmail.com; internet www.kalpa.org; Gen. Sec. and CEO PAUL GICHINGA.

> **Kenya Building, Construction, Timber, Furniture and Allied Industries Employees' Union:** Munshiram Bldg, POB 49628, 00100 Nairobi; tel. (20) 2223434; e-mail kbtfaie@yahoo .com; Gen. Sec. FRANCIS KARIMI MURAGE.

> **Kenya Chemical and Allied Workers' Union:** Hermes House, Tom Mboya St, POB 73820, Nairobi; tel. (20) 249101; Gen. Sec. WERE DIBI OGUTO.

> **Kenya County Government Workers' Union:** Dundee House, Country Rd, POB 55827, Nairobi; tel. (20) 2217213; e-mail klgwuhq@yahoo.com; Gen. Sec. ROBA DUBA.

> **Kenya Electrical Trades Allied Workers' Union:** Rainbow Plaza, 1st Floor, Suite 13, cnr Ngara and Munea Rds, POB 47060, Nairobi; tel. (20) 3752087; e-mail admin@ketawu.or.ke; Nat. Gen. Sec. ERNEST NADOME.

> **Kenya Engineering Workers' Union:** Simla House, Tom Mboya St, POB 73987, Nairobi; tel. (20) 311168; Gen. Sec. CHARLES NATILI.

> **Kenya Game Hunting and Safari Workers' Union:** Comfood Bldg, Kilome Rd, POB 47509, Nairobi; tel. 733861930; e-mail huntingunion2014@gmail.com; Gen. Sec. JOSEPHAT M. NDOLO.

> **Kenya Jockey and Betting Workers' Union:** Kirim and Sons Bldg, 3rd Floor, POB 55094, Nairobi; tel. 722792286; Gen. Sec. WILSON MAKUMI.

> **Kenya Petroleum Oil Workers' Union (KPOWU):** KCB Bldg, 4th Floor, Jogoo Rd, POB 10376, Nairobi; tel. (20) 2302640; e-mail kpow.union@yahoo.com; Gen. Sec. GILBERT AMOLO.

> **Kenya Plantation and Agricultural Workers' Union:** Co-operative House, Kenyatta St, POB 1161, 20100 Nakuru; tel. (51) 2212310; e-mail kpawu@africaonline.co.ke; Gen. Sec. FRANCIS ATWOLI.

> **Kenya Quarry and Mine Workers' Union:** Coffee Plaza, Exchange Line Off Hailesellasie Ave, POB 48125, Nairobi; tel. (20) 229774; e-mail wmusamia@yahoo.com; f. 1961; Gen. Sec. WAFULA WA MUSAMIA.

> **Kenya Railway Workers' Union (KRWU):** RAHU House, Mfangano St, POB 72029, Nairobi; tel. (20) 340302; f. 1952; Nat. Chair. FRANCIS O'LORE; Sec.-Gen. JOHN T. CHUMO.

> **Kenya Scientific Research, International Technical and Allied Institutions Workers' Union:** Ngumba House, Tom Mboya St, POB 55094, Nairobi; tel. 724727129; Sec.-Gen. MARTIN ODUOR.

> **Kenya Shipping, Clearing and Warehouse Workers' Union:** Yusuf Ali Bldg, 3rd Floor, POB 84067, Mombasa; tel. 725914968; e-mail kscwwu@yahoo.com; Gen. Sec. JAMES O. TONGI.

> **Kenya Shoe and Leather Workers' Union:** NACICO Plaza, 3rd Floor, POB 49629, Nairobi; tel. (20) 2228992; e-mail kshlwuheadoffice@yahoo.com; Gen. Sec. JULIUS MAINA.

> **Kenya Union of Commercial, Food and Allied Workers:** Comfood Bldg, Kilome Rd, POB 2628, 00100 Nairobi; tel. (20) 2245054; e-mail info@kucfaw.co.ke; Sec.-Gen. BONIFACE KAVUVI.

> **Kenya Union of Domestic, Hotel, Educational Institutions, Hospitals and Allied Workers (KUDHEIHA):** Sonalux House, 4th Floor, POB 41763, 00100 Nairobi; tel. (20) 2241509; e-mail info@kudheiha.org; internet www.kudheiha.org; f. 1952; Sec.-Gen. ALBERT NJERU.

> **Kenyan Union of Entertainment and Music Industry Employees:** Coffee Plaza, 4th Floor, POB 8305, Nairobi; tel. (20) 2243249; Gen. Sec. JOB MUCUHA.

> **Kenya Union of Journalists:** International House, 1st Floor, 19 Mama Ngina St, POB 47035, 00100 Nairobi; tel. 721230016; e-mail info@kenyaunionofjournalists.org; internet www .kenyaunionofjournalists.org; f. 1962; Chair. OSCAR KWENA OBO-NYO; Gen. Sec. ERIC ODUOR.

> **Kenya Union of Printing, Publishing, Paper Manufacturers, Pulp & Industries Industries Workers:** Nacico Plaza, 5th Floor, POB 72358, Nairobi; tel. (20) 2215981; e-mail kupripupa04@yahoo.com; Gen. Sec. RAJABU W. MWONDI.

> **Kenya Union of Sugar Plantation Workers:** POB 19019, Kisumu; tel. (57) 2021595; Gen. Sec. FRANCIS BUSHURU WANGARA.

Trade Union Congress of Kenya (TUC-Ke): UNIAFRIC House, 3rd Floor, Koinange St, POB 51809, 00100 Nairobi; tel. 725712538; e-mail info@tuckenya.org; an umbrella body for unions representing teachers, civil servants, lecturers and other workers; Nat. Chair. TOM MBOYA ODEGE; Gen. Sec. CHARLES MUKHWAYA (acting).

> **Kenya National Union of Teachers (KNUT):** POB 30407, 00100 Nairobi; tel. (20) 2220387; internet www.knut.or.ke; f. 1957; Nat. Chair. PATRICK KARIGA; Sec.-Gen. COLLINS OYUU.

Transport

RAILWAYS

In 2011 plans were announced to construct a railway line linking the proposed port of Lamu with oilfields in South Sudan and eventually with Ethiopia. Construction work on the project began in 2012. Construction work on a US $3,800m., 487-km standard-gauge railway between Mombasa and Nairobi commenced in December 2014, and was completed in mid-2017. Passenger services were inaugurated in May 2017 and commercial operations in January 2018. A second phase of the project (Phase 2A), linking Nairobi to Naivasha, was completed in October 2019.

Kenya Railways Corpn: Workshops Rd, off Haille Selassie Ave, opposite Technical University of Kenya, POB 30121, Nairobi; tel. 709907000; e-mail info@krc.co.ke; internet www.krc.co.ke; f. 1977; management of operations assumed by Rift Valley Railways consortium in Nov. 2006; Chair. Maj.-Gen. (retd) PASTOR AWITTA; Man. Dir PHILIP J. MAINGA.

ROADS

An all-weather road links Nairobi to Addis Ababa, in Ethiopia, and there is a 590-km road link between Kitale (Kenya) and Juba (South Sudan).

Kenya Bus Service Management Ltd: Utali Lane, View Park Towers, 10th Floor, Rm 1010, POB 41001, 00100 Nairobi; tel. (20) 2019685; e-mail info@kenyabus.net; internet www.kenyabus.net; promotes and develops transport enterprises; Man. Dir EDWINS MASSIMBA MUKABANAH.

Kenya National Highways Authority (KeNHA): Barabara Plaza, off Airport South Rd, along Mazao Rd, opp. KCAA HQs, POB 49712, 00100 Nairobi; tel. 700423606; e-mail dg@kenha.co.ke; internet www.kenha.co.ke; Chair. Eng. WANGAI NDIRANGU; Dir-Gen. PETER M. MUNDINIA.

Kenya Roads Board: Kenya Re Towers, 3rd Floor, Ragati Rd, Upper Hill, POB 73718, Nairobi; tel. (20) 4980000; e-mail info@krb.go.ke; internet www.krb.go.ke; f. 2000 to co-ordinate maintenance, rehabilitation and devt of the road network; Exec. Dir JACOB RUWA.

Kenya Rural Roads Authority (KeRRA): Barabara Plaza, Block B, Airport South Rd, opp. KCAA, POB 48151, 00100 Nairobi; tel. (20) 7807600; e-mail kerra@kerra.go.ke; internet www.kerra.go.ke; f. 2007; Chair. (vacant); Dir-Gen. Eng. PHILEMON K. KANDIE (acting).

Kenya Urban Roads Authority (KURA): Barabara Plaza JKIA, off Airport South Rd, along Mazao Rd, opp. Aviation House, POB 41727, 00100 Nairobi; tel. 717105233; e-mail info@kura.go.ke; internet kura.go.ke; Dir-Gen. Eng. SILAS KINOTI.

National Transport and Safety Authority (NTSA): 316 Upper-hill Chambers, 2nd Ngong Ave, POB 3602, 00506 Nairobi; tel. (20) 6632000; e-mail info@ntsa.go.ke; internet ntsa.go.ke; f. 2012; co-ordinates the operations of the key road transport departments; Chair. AGNES ODHIAMBO; Dir-Gen. GEORGE NJAO.

SHIPPING

The major international seaport of Mombasa has 16 deep-water berths, with a total length of 3,044 m, and facilities for the off-loading of bulk carriers, tankers and container vessels. In 2012 the construction of a second international port, at Lamu, commenced; the port, which was to have 32 deep-water berths, was officially commissioned in June 2021.

Kenya Ferry Services Ltd: POB 96242, 80110 Mombasa; tel. (20) 2118344; e-mail info@kenyaferry.co.ke; internet www.kenyaferry.co.ke; Man. Dir BAKARI GOWA.

Kenya Maritime Authority (KMA): White House, Moi Ave, POB 95076, 80104 Mombasa; tel. (20) 2381204; e-mail info@kma.go.ke; internet www.kma.go.ke; f. 2004; regulates, co-ordinates and over-sees maritime affairs; Chair. GEOFREY NGOMBO MWANGO; Dir-Gen. GEORGE N. OKONGO.

Kenya Ports Authority: POB 95009, Mombasa; tel. (41) 2112999; e-mail customerfeedback@kpa.co.ke; internet www.kpa.co.ke; f. 1978; sole operator of coastal port facilities; also operates two inland container depots at Nairobi and Kisumu; Chair. Gen. (retd) JOSEPH KIBWANA; Man. Dir JOHN MWANGEMI (acting).

Inchcape Shipping Services Kenya Ltd: Inchcape House, Archbishop Makarios Cl., off Moi Ave, POB 90194, 80100 Mombasa; tel. (41) 2221885; e-mail isskenyaenquiries@iss-shipping.com; internet www.iss-shipping.com; covers all ports in Kenya, Tanzania, Uganda, South Africa, Namibia, Nigeria, Ghana and Mauritius; Sr Gen. Man. SANJEEV SUKUMARAN.

Kenya National Shipping Line Ltd (KNSL): Canon Towers II, 1st Floor, Mbaraki Wing, Moi Ave, POB 88206–80100, Mombasa; tel. (11) 2300015; e-mail md@knsl.co.ke; internet knsl.go.ke; f. 1987; Chair. Lt-Gen. LEVI FRANKLIN MGHALU; Man. Dir JOSEPH JUMA (acting).

Mitchell Cotts Kenya Ltd: Voi St, Shimanzi, POB 42485, 80100 Mombasa; tel. 730111000; e-mail sales@mitchellcotts.co.ke; internet mitchellcotts.co.ke; f. 1926; transport and shipping agents; freight handling and distribution; warehousing; Man. Dir DANIEL TANUI.

Motaku Shipping Agencies Ltd: Motaku House, Tangana Rd, POB 80419, 80100 Mombasa; tel. (41) 2229065; e-mail motaku@motakushipping.com; internet motakushipping.googlepages.com/home; f. 1977; ship managers; Man. Dir KARIM KUDRATI.

PIL (Kenya) Ltd: Inchcape House, 2nd Floor, Mikanjuni Rd, POB 43050, Mombasa; tel. (41) 2225361; e-mail gencomm@mba.pilship.com; internet www.pilship.com.

Shipmarc Ltd: POB 94081, Mombasa; tel. 742957626; e-mail info@shipmarcltd.com; internet www.shipmarcltd.com.

CIVIL AVIATION

Kenya has four major international airports: Jomo Kenyatta International Airport, in south-eastern Nairobi, Moi International Airport, at Mombasa, Eldoret International Airport and Kisumu International Airport. Wilson Airport, in south-western Nairobi, and the airport at Malindi handle internal flights. Kenya also has about 250 smaller airfields.

Kenya Airports Authority: Jomo Kenyatta International Airport, POB 19001, Nairobi; tel. (20) 6611000; e-mail talk2us@kaa.go.ke; internet www.kaa.go.ke; f. 1991; state-owned; responsible for the provision, management and operation of all airports and private airstrips; Chair. ISAAC AWUONDO; Man. Dir ALEX GITARI.

Kenya Civil Aviation Authority: Jomo Kenyatta International Airport, POB 30163, 00100 Nairobi; tel. (20) 6827470; e-mail info@kcaa.or.ke; internet www.kcaa.or.ke; f. 2002; regulatory and advisory services for air navigation; Chair. JOSEPH N. NKADAYO; Dir-Gen. Capt. GILBERT MACHARIA M. KIBE.

African Express Airways: Airport North Rd, Jomo Kenyatta International Airport, POB 19202, 00501 Nairobi; tel. (20) 2014746; e-mail afex@africanexpress.co.ke; internet africanexpress.net; f. 1986.

Airkenya Express Ltd: Wilson Airport, POB 30357, 00100 Nairobi; tel. (20) 3916000; e-mail info@airkenya.com; internet www.airkenya.com; f. 1985; operates internal scheduled and charter passenger services; Gen. Man. DINO BISLETI.

Astral Aviation: Jomo Kenyatta International Airport, POB 594, 00606 Nairobi; tel. (20) 6827222; e-mail info@astral-aviation.com; internet www.astral-aviation.com; f. 2001; cargo services; CEO SANJEEV S. GADHIA.

Blue Bird Aviation Ltd (BBA): Wilson Airport, Langata Rd, POB 52382, 00200 Nairobi; tel. 732189000; e-mail enquiries@bluebirdaviation.com; internet bluebirdaviation.com; f. 1992; chartered regional services; CEO Col (retd) H. A. FARAH; Gen. Man. Capt. HUSSEIN MOHAMED.

Five Forty Aviation Ltd (fly540.com): Watermark Business Park, Karen, POB 10293, Nairobi; tel. 722540540; e-mail bookings@fly540.com; internet www.fly540.com; f. 2006; low-cost airline operating domestic and regional flights; CEO DONALD SMITH.

Jambojet: Jambojet House, KQ Base North Airport Rd, Nairobi; tel. (20) 3274545; e-mail info@jambojet.com; internet www.jambojet.com; f. 2014; wholly-owned subsidiary of Kenya Airlines Ltd; low-cost, domestic flights; Chair. VINCENT RAGUE; Man. Dir KARANJA NDEGWA.

Kenya Airways Ltd (KQ): Airport North Road, Jomo Kenyatta International Airport, POB 19142, Nairobi; tel. (20) 6422000; e-mail contact@kenya-airways.com; internet www.kenya-airways.com; f. 1977; in private sector ownership since 1996; passenger services to Africa, Asia, Europe and Middle East; freight services to Europe; internal services from Nairobi to Kisumu, Mombasa and Malindi; also operates a freight subsidiary; Chair. MICHAEL JOSEPH; Man. Dir and CEO ALLAN KILAVUKA.

Safarilink Aviation: Phoenix House, Wilson Airport, POB 5616, 00506 Nairobi; tel. (20) 206690000; e-mail res@flysafarilink.com; internet www.flysafarilink.com; f. 2004; safari airline with a network of connecting domestic scheduled services to all the major safari destinations within Kenya and across the border into northern Tanzania; Chair. MBUVI NGUNZE; Man. Dir ALEX AVEDI.

Tourism

Kenya Tourism Board: Kenya-Re Towers, Ragati Rd, POB 30630, 00100 Nairobi; tel. (20) 2711262; e-mail info@ktb.go.ke; internet www.magicalkenya.com; f. 1997; promotes Kenya as a tourist destination, monitors the standard of tourist facilities; Chair. JOANNE MWANGI-YELBERT; Man. Dir Dr BETTY RADIER.

Kenya Tourism Federation: KWS Complex, Langata, POB 15013, 00509 Nairobi; tel. 7220745645; internet www.ktf.co.ke; represents the private sector in tourism industry; Chair. FRED ODEK.

Kenya Wildlife Service: POB 40241, 00100 Nairobi; tel. (20) 2379407; e-mail customerservice@kws.go.ke; internet www.kws.go.ke; f. 1990; conserves and manages national parks, wildlife conservation areas, and sanctuaries under its jurisdiction; Chair. (vacant); Dir-Gen. KITILI MBATHI.

Tourism Finance Corpn: Utalii House, 11th Floor, Uhuru Highway, POB 42013, Nairobi; tel. (20) 2229751; e-mail md@

tourismfinance.go.ke; internet www.tourismfinance.go.ke; f. 1965; fmrly Kenya Tourist Development Corpn; present name adopted in 2013; CEO and Man. Dir JONAH T. ORUMOI.

Tourism Fund: Tourism Fund Bldg, 5th Floor, Nairobi; tel. (20) 2714900; e-mail info@tourismfund.co.ke; internet tourismfund.co.ke; f. 2011 to replace Catering and Tourism Development Levy Trustees; CEO JOSEPH CHERUTOI.

Tourism Regulatory Authority: Utalii House, 5th Floor, Utalii Lane, off Uhuru Highway, POB 30027, 00100 Nairobi; tel. 701444777; e-mail info@tourismauthority.go.ke; internet www.tourismauthority.go.ke; f. 2014; Dir-Gen. LAGAT KIPKORIR.

Defence

As assessed at November 2021, Kenya's armed forces numbered 24,100, comprising an army of 20,000, an air force of 2,500 and a navy of 1,600. Military service is voluntary. The paramilitary police general service unit was 5,000 strong. At November 2021 a total of 4,311 troops were stationed abroad.

Defence Budget: Ks. 120,000m. in 2021.

Commander-in-Chief of the Defence Forces: Pres. WILLIAM SAMOEI RUTO.

Chief of Defence Forces: Gen. ROBERT KARIUKI KIBOCHI.

Army Commander: Lt-Gen. PETER MBOGO NJIRU.

Air Force Commander: Maj.-Gen. JOHN M. OMENDA.

Navy Commander: Maj.-Gen. JIMSON LONGIRO MUTAI.

Education

The Government provides, or assists in the provision of, schools. In 2007/08 enrolment at the pre-primary level was 26% (26% of boys; 26% of girls). Primary education, which is compulsory, is provided free of charge. The education system involves eight years of primary education (beginning at six years of age), four years at secondary school and four years of university education. According to estimates by the United Nations Educational, Scientific and Cultural Organization (UNESCO), in 2018/19 pre-primary enrolment was equivalent to 65% of children in the relevant age-group (males 66%; females 64%). In 2011/12 enrolment at primary schools included 80% of pupils in the relevant age-group (males 78%; females 82%), while in 2008/09 enrolment at secondary schools included 48% of children in the relevant age-group (males 50%; females 47%). There are seven public universities and 18 private universities (of which 11 are chartered and seven have received letters of interim authority). In the budget for the financial year 2021/22, education was allocated Ks. 202,800m., equivalent to some 5.5% of total projected expenditure.

Bibliography

Aiyar, S. *Indians in Kenya: The Politics of Diaspora*. Cambridge, MA, Harvard University Press, 2015.

Angelo, A. *Power and the Presidency in Kenya: The Jomo Kenyatta Years*. Cambridge, Cambridge University Press, 2019.

arap Moi, D. T. *Kenya African Nationalism: Nyayo Philosophy and Principles*. London, Macmillan, 1986.

Azam, J.-P., and Daubrée, C. *Bypassing the State: Economic Growth in Kenya, 1964–1990*. Paris, OECD, 1997.

Bailey, J. *Kenya: The National Epic*. Nairobi, East African Education Publishers, 1993.

Bates, R. H. *Beyond the Miracle of the Market: The Political Economy of Agrarian Development in Kenya*. (2nd edn). Cambridge, Cambridge University Press, 2005.

Branch, D. *Kenya: Between Hope and Despair, 1963–2011*. New Haven, CT, Yale University Press, 2011.

Cheeseman, N., Kanyinga, K., and Lynch, G. (Eds). *The Oxford Handbook of Kenyan Politics*. Oxford, Oxford University Press, 2020.

Collins, R. L. *Kenya: The Evolution of Independence*. Ilfracombe, Arthur H. Stockwell, 2014.

Coombes, A. E. *Managing Heritage, Making Peace: History, Identity and Memory in Contemporary Kenya*. London, I. B. Tauris, 2014.

Cullen, P. *Kenya and Britain after Independence: Beyond Neo-Colonialism*. London, Palgrave Macmillan, 2017.

Faulkner, C. *A Two Year Wonder: The Kenya Police 1953–1955*. Elgin, Librario Publishing Ltd, 2005.

Durrani, S. *Mau Mau the Revolutionary, Anti-Imperialist Force from Kenya: 1948–1963*. Nairobi, Vita Books, 2018.

Fazan, S. H. *Colonial Kenya Observed: British Rule, Mau Mau and the Wind of Change*. London, I. B. Tauris, 2015.

Gibbon, P. (Ed.). *Markets, Civil Society and Democracy in Kenya*. Uppsala, Nordic Africa Institute, 1995.

Hassan, M. *Regime Threats and State Solutions: Bureaucratic Loyalty and Embeddedness in Kenya*. Cambridge, Cambridge University Press, 2020.

Haugerud, A. *The Culture of Politics in Modern Kenya*. Cambridge, Cambridge University Press, 1995.

Hope, Sr, K. *The Political Economy of Development in Kenya*. New York, Continuum Publishing, 2012.

Hornsby, C. *Kenya: A History Since Independence*. London, I. B. Tauris, 2011.

Horowitz, J. *Multiethnic Democracy: The Logic of Elections and Policymaking in Kenya*. Oxford, Oxford University Press, 2022.

Hughes, L. *Moving the Maasai: A Colonial Misadventure*. Basingstoke, Palgrave Macmillan, 2006.

Kenyatta, J. *Facing Mount Kenya*. London, Heinemann, 1979.

Kimenyi, M. S. (Ed.), et al. *Restarting and Sustaining Economic Growth and Development in Africa: The Case of Kenya* (Contemporary Perspectives on Developing Societies). Brookfield, VT, Ashgate Publishing, 2003.

Kithinji, M., Koster, M., and Rotich, J. (Eds) *Kenya After 50: Reconfiguring Historical, Political, and Policy Milestones*. Basingstoke, Palgrave Macmillan, 2016.

Klaus, K. *Political Violence in Kenya: Land, Elections, and Claim-Making*. Cambridge, Cambridge University Press, 2020.

Knighton, B. *Religion and Politics in Kenya*. Basingstoke, Palgrave Macmillan, 2009.

Koster, M. M. *The Power of the Oath. Mau Mau Nationalism in Kenya, 1952–1960*. Rochester, NY, University of Rochester Press, 2016.

Kusimba, S. *Reimagining Money: Kenya in the Digital Finance Revolution*. Palo Alto, CA, Stanford University Press, 2021.

Kyle, K. *The Politics of the Independence of Kenya*. London and Basingstoke, Palgrave, 1999.

Leakey, L. *Defeating Mau Mau*. London, Routledge, 2004.

Lewis, J. *Empire State-Building: War and Welfare in Kenya, 1925–52*. Athens, OH, Ohio University Press, 2001.

Lynch, G. *I Say to You: Ethnic Politics and the Kalenjin in Kenya*. Chicago, IL, University of Chicago Press, 2011.

   Performances of Injustice: The Politics of Truth, Justice and Reconciliation in Kenya Cambridge, Cambridge University Press, 2018.

Maloba, W. O. *Kenyatta and Britain: An Account of Political Transformation, 1929–1963*. London, Palgrave Macmillan, 2017.

Mbaya, B. *Kenya's Foreign Policy and Diplomacy: Evolution, Challenges and Opportunities*. Nairobi, East African Educational Publishers, 2019.

Manji, A. *The Struggle for Land and Justice in Kenya*. Woodbridge, James Currey, 2020.

Morton, A. *Moi: The Making of an African Statesman*. London, Michael O'Mara Books, 1998.

Murunga, G. R., and Nasong'o, S. W. (Eds). *Kenya: The Struggle for Democracy*. London, Zed Books, 2007.

Mwangi, S., Opongo, E., and Wahome, E. *The State and Nation-Building Processes in Kenya Since Independence: Remembering the Marginalised and Forgotten Issues and Actors*. Bamenda, Langaa RPCIG, 2019.

Odhiambo, E. S. *Mau Mau and Nationhood*. Athens, OH, Ohio University Press, 2003.

Ogot, B. A., and Ochieng, W. R. (Eds). *Decolonization and Independence in Kenya, 1940–1993*. London, James Currey, 1995.

Okanja, O. *Kenya at Forty-five: 1963–2008 (Economic Performance, Problems and Prospects)*. Twickenham, Athena Press, 2010.

Otiende, J. E., Wamahiu, S. P., and Karugu, A. M. *Education and Development in Kenya: An Historical Perspective.* Nairobi, Oxford University Press, 1992.

Owino, J. *Kenya into the 21st Century.* London, Minerva Press, 2001.

Oyaya, C., and Poku, N. *The Making of the Constitution of Kenya: A Century of Struggle and the Future of Constitutionalism.*Abingdon, Routledge, 2016.

Paarlberg, R. L. *The Politics of Precaution.* Baltimore, MD, Johns Hopkins University Press, 2001.

Rotberg, R. I. (Ed.). *Kenya (Africa: Continent in the Balance Series).* Broomall, PA, Mason Crest Publishers, 2005.

Sabar, G. *Church, State and Society in Kenya.* London, Frank Cass Publishers, 2001.

Shilaho, W. K. *Political Power and Tribalism in Kenya.* London, Palgrave Macmillan, 2017.

Shitemi, N. L., and Kamaara, E. *Wanjiku: A Kenyan Sociopolitical Discourse.* Nairobi, Goethe-Institut Kenya, Native Intelligence, 2014.

Sunman, H. *A Very Different Land: Agriculture, Development and the Foundation of Modern Kenya.* London, I. B. Tauris, 2014.

Wakhungu-Githuku, S. *50 Years since Independence: Where is Kenya?* Nairobi, Footprints Press, 2013.

wa Wamwere, K. *The People's Representative and the Tyrants: or, Kenya, Independence without Freedom.* Nairobi, New Concept Type-setters, 1993.

I Refuse to Die. New York, Seven Stories Press, 2004.

Weitzberg, K. *We Do Not Have Borders: Greater Somalia and the Predicaments of Belonging in Kenya.* Athens, OH, Ohio University Press, 2017.

Whittaker, H. *Insurgency and Counterinsurgency in Kenya: A Social History of the Shifta Conflict, c. 1963–1968.* Leiden, Brill, 2015.

Widner, J. A. *The Rise of a Party State in Kenya: From 'Harambee' to 'Nyayo'.* Berkeley, CA, University of California Press, 1992.

LESOTHO

Physical and Social Geography

A. MacGREGOR HUTCHESON

PHYSICAL FEATURES

The Kingdom of Lesotho, a small, landlocked country of 30,355 sq km (11,720 sq miles), is enclosed on all sides by South Africa. It is situated at the highest part of the Drakensberg escarpment on the eastern rim of the South African plateau. About two-thirds of Lesotho is very mountainous. Elevations in the eastern half of the country are generally more than 2,440 m above sea level, and in the north-east and along the eastern border they exceed 3,350 m. This is a region of very rugged relief, bleak climate and heavy annual rainfall (averaging 1,905 mm), where the headstreams of the Orange river have incised deep valleys. Westwards the land descends through a foothill zone of rolling country, at an altitude of 1,830 m–2,135 m, to Lesotho's main lowland area. This strip of land along the western border, part of the Highveld, averages 40 km in width and lies at an altitude of about 1,525 m. Annual rainfall averages in this region are 650 mm–750 mm, and climatic conditions are generally more pleasant. However, frost may occur throughout the country in winter, and hail is a summer hazard in all regions. The light, sandy soils that have developed on the Karoo sedimentaries of the western lowland compare unfavourably with the fertile black soils of the Stormberg basalt in the uplands. The temperate grasslands of the west also tend to be less fertile than the montane grasslands of the east.

POPULATION AND NATURAL RESOURCES

At the census of April 2016 the *de jure* population was 2,007,201, giving an average density of 66.1 inhabitants per sq km. According to United Nations estimates, the population totalled 2,175,695 at mid-2022 (71.7 inhabitants per sq km). The noticeable physical contrasts between east and west Lesotho are reflected in the distribution and density of the population. While large parts of the mountainous east (except for valleys) are sparsely populated, most of the fertile western strip, which carries some 70% of the population, has densities in excess of 200 inhabitants per sq km. Such population pressure, further aggravated by steady population growth, has resulted in: (i) the permanent settlement being pushed to

higher levels (in places to 2,440 m) formerly used for summer grazing, and on to steep slopes, thus adding to the already serious national problem of soil erosion; (ii) an acute shortage of cultivable land and increased soil exhaustion, particularly in the west; (iii) land holdings that are too small to maintain the rural population; and (iv) the country's inability, in its current stage of development, to support all of its population, thus necessitating the migration of large numbers of workers to seek paid employment in South Africa. A migratory labour system on this scale has grave social, economic and political implications for the country involved, and Lesotho's economy depends heavily on the remitted earnings. However, the number of Basotho employed in South Africa declined substantially in the late 1990s and 2000s, and by the late 2000s the level of remittances had fallen considerably.

Lesotho's long-term development prospects largely rely upon the achievement of optimum use of its soil and water resources. According to the World Food Programme, less than 10% of the land is arable, and, since virtually all of this is already cultivated, only more productive use of the land can make Lesotho self-sufficient in food (the majority of domestic needs are currently imported from South Africa). The high relief produces natural grasslands, well suited for a viable livestock industry, but this has been hindered through inadequate pasture management, excessive numbers of low-quality animals and disease. Lesotho and South Africa are jointly implementing the Lesotho Highlands Water Project (see *Economy*), which has provided employment for thousands of Basotho and has greatly improved Lesotho's energy infrastructure through its advancement of the hydroelectricity sector. Large-scale exploitation of diamond reserves in the mountainous north-east of the country ceased in 1982, although small surface workings continued to operate at Lemphane, Liqhobong and Kao. However, the Lets'eng-la-Terae diamond mine reopened in the late 1990s and industrial mining at Liqhobong and Kao commenced in the 2000s. Uranium deposits have been located near Teyateyaneng in the north-west, but their exploitation awaits a sustained improvement in world prices. The search for other minerals continues.

History

CHRISTOPHER SAUNDERS

Lesotho, formerly known as Basutoland, became a British protectorate in 1868, and from 1884 was administered as one of the High Commission territories in Southern Africa. Unlike the other territories—Bechuanaland (now Botswana) and the protectorate of Swaziland—Basutoland was entirely surrounded by South African territory.

Modern party politics began in 1952, when Ntsu Mokhehle founded the Basutoland Congress Party (BCP). Basutoland's first general election, held on the basis of universal adult suffrage, took place in April 1965. The majority of seats in the new Legislative Assembly were won by the Basutoland National Party (BNP, renamed the Basotho National Party at independence), a conservative group backed by South Africa. The BNP's leader, Chief Leabua Jonathan, became Prime Minister, and Moshoeshoe II, the paramount chief, was recognized as King. Basutoland gained its independence, as the Kingdom of Lesotho, on 4 October 1966.

When, in the general election held in January 1970, the BCP appeared to have won a majority of seats in the National Assembly (the lower house of the bicameral legislature introduced under the 1966 Constitution), Jonathan declared a state of emergency, suspended the Constitution and arrested Mokhehle and other BCP leaders. The election was annulled, and Lesotho in effect came under the Prime Minister's control. King Moshoeshoe went briefly into exile but returned in December after agreeing to take no part in politics. The BCP split into an 'internal' faction, whose members were acquiescent in the political status quo, and an 'external' faction, whose members were prepared to take up arms to overthrow Jonathan. The latter group was led by Mokhehle after he fled the country in 1974, following a coup attempt.

The Jonathan regime was initially supported by South Africa, but as Jonathan's support among the Basotho, most of whom disliked his pro-South African policies, declined, he became increasingly critical of the South African Government, winning international credit for opposing its policy of apartheid. In November 1974 he revived Lesotho's claim to 'conquered territory' in South Africa's Orange Free State (now the Free State Province). The vigorous anti-South African stance that Lesotho adopted at the United Nations (UN) and the Organization of African Unity (OAU, now the African Union—AU) in 1975 increased tensions. Although Jonathan met the South African Prime Minister, P. W. Botha, in 1980 and accepted a preliminary agreement on the Lesotho Highlands Water Project (LHWP), whereby Lesotho would supply water to South Africa, he openly criticized apartheid and supported the prohibited African National Congress of South Africa (ANC). In April 1983 Jonathan announced that a state of war in effect existed between Lesotho and South Africa.

On 1 January 1986 South Africa blockaded its border with Lesotho, impeding access to vital supplies of food and fuel. Two weeks later troops of the Lesotho paramilitary force, led by Maj.-Gen. Justin Lekhanya, surrounded government buildings. On 20 January, having returned from 'security consultations' in South Africa, Lekhanya, together with the chief of police, deposed the Jonathan Government.

The new regime established a Military Council, led by Lekhanya and including senior officers of the paramilitary force (which subsequently became the Royal Lesotho Defence Force—RLDF). The legislature was dissolved, and all executive and legislative powers were vested in the King, who acted on the advice of the Military Council. One week after the coup some 60 members of the ANC were deported from Lesotho, and the South African blockade was lifted. The main opposition groups initially welcomed the military takeover. However, all formal political activity was suspended in March 1986. In October the Military Council signed a treaty with South Africa to initiate the LHWP, which involved building the Mohale and Katse dams to supply water to what was then South Africa's Transvaal province.

In April 1988 the five main opposition parties appealed to the OAU, the Commonwealth and South Africa to restore civilian rule. In May, after 14 years of exile, Mokhehle and other members of the BCP were allowed to return to Lesotho for peace talks. It was widely believed that the South African Government had played a part in this reconciliation. In 1989 the BCP's armed wing was reportedly disbanded, and by 1990 the two factions had reunited under Mokhehle's leadership.

In early 1990 conflict developed between Lekhanya and King Moshoeshoe. Following the King's refusal to approve changes made by Lekhanya to the Military Council, Lekhanya suspended his executive and legislative powers. Lekhanya promised that a return to civilian government would take place in 1992, and, to reassure business interests, announced a programme for privatizing state enterprises. In March 1990 the Military Council assumed the executive and legislative powers that had been vested in the King, and Moshoeshoe (who remained head of state) went into exile in the United Kingdom. When Lekhanya invited him to return in October, the King stated that he would do so only if military rule was ended and an interim government was formed by representatives of all political parties, pending the restoration of the 1966 Constitution and the holding of an internationally supervised general election. On 6 November 1990 Lekhanya promulgated an order deposing the King with immediate effect, and Lesotho's 22 principal chiefs elected Moshoeshoe's eldest son, Prince Bereng Seeisa, as his successor. He succeeded to the throne as King Letsie III, having undertaken not to involve himself in political life. In April 1991 Lekhanya was removed as Chairman of the Military Council in a coup led by Col (later Maj.-Gen.) Elias Phitsoane Ramaema, a member of the Council. Shortly thereafter Ramaema repealed the 1986 law banning party political activity, and by July 1991 a new Constitution had been drafted. Following talks in the UK with Ramaema, hosted by the Commonwealth Secretary-General, former King Moshoeshoe returned to Lesotho in July 1992. A general election, returning Lesotho to democracy, finally took place in March 1993.

FROM THE MOKHEHLE GOVERNMENT TO THE 1998 CRISIS

The BCP swept to power in the election of March 1993, winning all 65 seats in the new National Assembly. In April Mokhehle was inaugurated as Prime Minister, and King Letsie swore allegiance to the new Constitution. Although independent local and international observers called the election broadly free and fair, the BNP, supported by members of the former military regime, alleged widespread irregularities and rejected the results.

In July 1994 Mokhehle appointed a commission of inquiry into the circumstances surrounding the dethronement of former King Moshoeshoe in 1990. After petitioning the High Court to abolish the commission on the grounds of members' bias, King Letsie dissolved Parliament, dismissed the Mokhehle Government and suspended sections of the Constitution, citing 'popular dissatisfaction' with the BCP administration. A provisional government was to be established, pending a general election, which was to be organized by an independent commission. A prominent human rights lawyer, Hae Phoofolo, was appointed Chairman of the transitional Council of Ministers, declaring his intention to amend the Constitution and thereby restore Moshoeshoe as monarch. Meanwhile, Letsie acted as executive head of state.

The suspension of constitutional government was widely condemned outside Lesotho. Several countries threatened economic sanctions, and the USA withdrew financial assistance. In September 1994 Letsie and Mokhehle signed an agreement, guaranteed by Botswana, South Africa and Zimbabwe, providing for the restoration of Moshoeshoe as reigning monarch and for the immediate restitution of the elected organs of government; the commission of inquiry into Moshoeshoe's dethronement was to be abandoned; persons involved in the 'royal coup' were to be immune from prosecution; the political neutrality of the armed forces and public service was to be guaranteed; and consultations were to be undertaken with the expressed aim of broadening the democratic process.

On 25 January 1995 Moshoeshoe was restored to the throne, following the voluntary abdication of Letsie, who took the title of Crown Prince. When Moshoeshoe was killed in a car crash in January 1996, the Crown Prince was formally elected by the College of Chiefs to succeed his father and was returned to the throne, resuming the title King Letsie III, in February. Letsie undertook not to involve the monarchy in any aspect of political life.

Following a protracted struggle between rival factions for control of the party, in June 1997 Mokhehle resigned from the BCP and, with the support of a majority of BCP members of the National Assembly, formed a new political party, the Lesotho Congress for Democracy (LCD), to which he transferred executive power. In early 1998 Mokhehle resigned as leader of the LCD and was replaced by his deputy, Bethuel Pakalitha Mosisili. At a general election held in May the LCD secured 78 of the 80 seats, and the BNP won only one seat.

Despite the pronouncement of regional and international observers that the election had been fair, demonstrators in Maseru, the capital, protested against the results and accused the LCD and the Independent Electoral Commission (IEC) of irregularities. Although Mosisili was elected Prime Minister by the National Assembly, and a new Cabinet was appointed in June 1998, more than 200 defeated opposition candidates filed petitions in the High Court demanding the annulment of the election results and a re-examination of the ballot papers. In July, after evidence of irregularities began to emerge, anti-Government protests broke out in Maseru.

As protests escalated the Southern African Development Community (SADC), under South African leadership, intervened. A commission was appointed under Pius Langa, the Deputy President of South Africa's Constitutional Court, to investigate the allegations of electoral fraud. His report (released in September 1998) stated that, while voting irregularities had occurred, they were insufficient to invalidate the election results. Meanwhile, influential elements within the Lesotho Defence Force (LDF, as the RLDF had been redesignated) openly declared their support for the opposition. Prime Minister Mosisili, fearing a collapse of law and order and an imminent military coup, sought assistance from SADC. South African troops arrived in late September, followed by a contingent from Botswana. Operation Boleas, as the military intervention was named, was poorly conducted and met considerable resistance from the LDF. There were at least 68 deaths, and extensive looting spread to other towns, causing serious damage to the economy. Thousands of people fled into the countryside and to South Africa.

FROM THE 1998 CRISIS TO THE 2015 ELECTIONS

With South African mediation, a multi-party Interim Political Authority (IPA) was formed to prepare for a new general election, which was to be held within 18 months. The remaining SADC troops were withdrawn in May 1999. The IPA rapidly became embroiled in controversy over arrangements for the proposed elections. The Government wanted the existing voting system to remain, while the BNP demanded full proportional representation. In October a tribunal proposed a system combining both simple majority voting (for 80 seats) and proportional representation. The IPA and the Government accepted this proposal in December. However, when the relevant draft legislation was introduced to Parliament in February 2000, the LCD-dominated National Assembly rejected it, prompting the IPA to accuse the Government of reneging on its undertaking to abide by the tribunal's decision and the agreement reached in December 1999.

Following international mediation, the opposition parties agreed to the LCD remaining in office, in return for assurances that the electoral system would be changed as soon as possible. The LCD wanted 40 seats to be elected by proportional representation and 80 by constituencies; this arrangement for the new 120-seat National Assembly was finally agreed by all parties and approved by Parliament in January 2002. Meanwhile, in September 2001 internal divisions prompted a group of LCD deputies, led by Kelebone Maope, hitherto Deputy Prime Minister, to split from the party and establish the Lesotho People's Congress (LPC), which subsequently became the main opposition party.

A general election was held on 25 May 2002. The voting process was generally accepted as being free and fair by observers. The ruling LCD won 77 of the 78 contested constituency seats (voting was postponed in two constituencies). The LPC gained the remaining contested seat and four of the 40 seats allocated by proportional representation. The BNP secured 21 of the seats allocated by proportional representation. The BNP leader, Lekhanya, demanded a forensic audit of the results, claiming that they had been manipulated. He refused to attend the ceremony at which Mosisili was sworn in as Prime Minister for another five-year term and threatened to boycott the new National Assembly. However, there was no widespread support for Lekhanya's legal challenge, and he was persuaded that the BNP should participate in Parliament.

Mosisili identified three main challenges confronting his new Government when it took office in June 2002. First, almost one-third of the adult population of Lesotho was estimated to be living with HIV/AIDS. Second, over 50% of the population was unemployed. Finally, there was a major food crisis, precipitated partly by the failure to keep sufficient grain reserves. In response to a poor harvest and the high cost of importing maize, the Government declared a state of famine in April, hoping to attract foreign aid. By June the World Food Programme and the Food and Agriculture Organization of the UN estimated that some 500,000 people (almost one-quarter of the population) needed emergency food aid. All three crises intensified in subsequent years.

In March 2004 Mosisili and the Roman Catholic Archbishop of Lesotho took public HIV tests to try to increase awareness of the disease and encourage others to be tested. However, the adult prevalence rate remained at about 23% of the population over the following years—the second highest in the world—and only a fraction of those who needed antiretrovirals actually received them. Nurses and doctors were scarce, and efforts to import medical staff were largely unsuccessful. By 2006 the country had about 100,000 AIDS orphans and a rising number of urban street children.

Meanwhile, in March 2004 President Thabo Mbeki of South Africa and King Letsie held a ceremony to mark the completion of the first phase of the LHWP, which had become the world's largest water transfer operation, with the royalties that Lesotho received from South Africa for it constituting the largest source of the country's foreign exchange. Lesotho had gained international credit for its handling of corruption that had taken place, and Masupha Sole, the former chief executive of the LHWP, was found guilty in May 2002 of accepting bribes totalling some US $2m. over a 10-year period. He was sentenced to a 15-year prison term. In September a Canadian construction company was found guilty of paying bribes to Sole in return for a contract to work on the LHWP, and Germany's largest engineering consultancy, Lahmeyer International, was fined $1.9m. in the following year. In August 2011 Lesotho and South Africa formally agreed to implement Phase 2 of the LHWP. This included the construction of a new dam on the Senqu river, which would be connected by tunnel to the Katse dam. Lesotho would build a hydroelectric plant and relocate some 2,500 people.

Mosisili reorganized his Cabinet in November 2004, demoting Motsoahae Thomas Thabane, who had been Minister of Home Affairs and was regarded as a potential challenger to Mosisili, to the position of Minister of Communications, Science and Technology. In October 2006 Thabane resigned from the Cabinet and the LCD, accusing the party of rampant corruption. Along with 17 other dissident LCD deputies, he formed a new party, the All Basotho Convention (ABC), which began to attract large crowds at urban rallies. In response to this challenge, the Government announced that the parliamentary elections would be brought forward by three months, giving the electoral authorities little time to register new voters and preventing the ABC from organizing effectively. (Fewer than 1m. people were registered in time for the elections.) Wary of its now fragile legislative majority, and in response to the ABC allying itself with the Lesotho Workers' Party, the LCD proposed an electoral alliance with the smaller National Independent Party (NIP). The NIP leader, Anthony Manyeli, strongly opposed the idea, but the LCD made an agreement with his deputy, Tsibiso Motikoe, and Manyeli was removed from the party. The alliances subverted the spirit of the mixed electoral system, which was supposed to ensure that votes cast for the ruling party via proportional representation would be discounted to ensure overall proportionality. Constituency members were allowed to cross the floor, but not those elected by proportional representation.

In the legislative elections, which took place on 17 February 2007, fewer than one-half of the registered voters cast their ballots. The LCD was re-elected for a third term, winning 61 of the 80 contested constituency seats, while the ABC won 17 constituency seats. Of the 40 seats allocated by proportional representation, the NIP was awarded 21, giving the LCD-NIP alliance control of 82 seats in the 120-member National Assembly. Amid growing discontent about the allocation of proportional representation seats, a coalition of opposition parties, including the ABC, called a national strike in March, which paralysed much of the country. The Government emphasized that SADC and other observers had described the elections as free and fair. Tensions persisted, however, and in April 2009 armed men attacked Mosisili's residence in a failed assassination attempt. Government officials blamed the ABC for the attack but did not produce any firm evidence to support their allegations. In May 2011 seven people were extradited from South Africa and charged with plotting to assassinate Mosisili.

Challenged by opponents within the LCD, in February 2012 Mosisili, along with 43 other deputies, formed a new party, the Democratic Congress (DC). With the support of 44 members of the National Assembly, including the Speaker, Mosisili survived a no-confidence vote and remained as Prime Minister. The rump of the LCD became the main opposition party, led by former Minister of Communications, Science and Technology Mothetjoa Metsing.

In March 2012 King Letsie dissolved Parliament, in preparation for the forthcoming legislative elections. The most significant challenge to Mosisili came from the ABC, but that party had been weakened by internal disputes. During the campaign the country's sole television channel, controlled by the Government, was accused of demonstrating bias towards the DC. In the event, the elections, held on 26 May, were the closest in Lesotho's history: the DC won the most seats (48 out of 120) but not an overall majority. Thabane's ABC (which secured 30 seats), the LCD (26 seats) and the BNP (five seats) formed a coalition to oust Mosisili. Thabane was sworn in as Prime Minister in June, and later that month King Letsie approved the new Cabinet. Metsing was appointed Deputy Prime Minister and Minister of Local Government and Chieftainship Affairs, and the LCD secured nine other ministerial portfolios.

By early 2013 a challenge to the leadership of the LCD threatened to split that party: 12 branches, complaining about a lack of democracy in the party, adopted a motion of no confidence in the LCD's executive and demanded new leadership. Furthermore, while the coalition had promised to adopt a firm stance against corruption, two cabinet ministers were accused of graft. The Minister of Energy, Meteorology and Water Affairs (a member of the LCD) was dismissed in November, following accusations that he had diverted funds from a programme to assist small-scale farmers, and the Minister of Health, of the ABC, was sued for allegedly interfering in her ministry's tender process. After a dispute about seniority between the country's two highest-ranking judges—the Chief Justice, Mahapela Lehohla, and the President of the Court of Appeal, Mathealira Ramodibedi—had led to the cancellation of the Court session, the Prime Minister demanded the resignation of both judges. Lehohla agreed to relinquish his post, but Ramodibedi refused to stand down and accused Thabane of violating the Constitution by interfering with judicial independence. In September Ramodibedi was suspended, and in June 2015 he was dismissed.

In June 2014 the LCD withdrew from the coalition Government, claiming that it could no longer work with the ABC. Thabane, apparently fearing that a vote of no confidence in his Government would be carried, persuaded the King to suspend Parliament for nine months. The ABC, the DC and the LCD engaged in crisis talks mediated by the Christian Council of Lesotho and met South African President Jacob Zuma but were unable to resolve their differences. When rumours surfaced of a possible military coup, the South African Government warned that it would not accept any unconstitutional change of government in Lesotho. Thabane ordered the dismissal of the Commander of the LDF, Lt-Gen. Tlali Kamoli, who was loyal to Metsing, but Kamoli refused to step down. There were clashes between the military and the police, and Thabane fled to South Africa in August, claiming that his life was in danger.

President Zuma, as chairman of the SADC Organ on Politics, Defence and Security, met Thabane and Metsing in early September 2014 and persuaded the Prime Minister to return to Lesotho. An SADC meeting later that month appointed a facilitation mission, led by South Africa's Deputy President, Cyril Ramaphosa, who in early October persuaded the parties to agree that Parliament would be reconvened, but only to discuss the budget and the holding of a general election. Later in October, to help to stabilize the security situation, a second accord was signed in Maseru, under which Kamoli and two other senior officers were to take a leave of absence. The presence of an SADC police force, comprising mostly South Africans, helped to maintain calm in the months leading up to the general election held on 28 February 2015.

FROM THE 2015 ELECTIONS TO THE 2017 ELECTIONS

Although the 2015 general election was declared credible, free and fair by SADC and other observers, it failed to bring stability. Although the ABC won more constituencies than the DC, after seats were allocated on a proportional basis the DC was able to form a coalition Government with six smaller parties. Mosisili was sworn in as Prime Minister again, on 17 March. The LCD leader, Metsing, became his deputy. At the end of March the SADC mission was terminated, but the situation soon deteriorated after Mosisili dismissed the commander of the LDF appointed by Thabane, Brig. Maaparankoe Mahao, and reappointed Kamoli to lead the army.

In May 2015 Thabane fled again to South Africa, in fear of his life. Thabane appealed to Zuma for SADC assistance to deal with the continuing political and security instability, and the crisis worsened in June, when Mahao was killed outside Maseru by LDF members who had been sent to arrest him for allegedly plotting a mutiny. Some observers held Kamoli responsible, and Zuma again dispatched Ramaphosa to Lesotho to try to calm the situation. SADC appointed an independent commission to investigate the killing, but the Mosisili administration only reluctantly engaged with the commission and launched a legal challenge to block the release of its report. In February 2016, however, after SADC had threatened to suspend Lesotho from the regional organization, Mosisili released the report and implemented its recommendations. These included Kamoli's dismissal as army commander, the suspension of any soldier implicated in Mahao's murder and the initiation of criminal investigations into the killing. The report also stated that security sector reform should be undertaken to ensure civilian control of the military, and that other constitutional reforms, including granting greater power to the king, were needed to bring stability to the country. However, Kamoli was not dismissed, and the Government consequently claimed that it needed more time to consider the other recommendations. When the residence of the Pro-Vice Chancellor of the National University, a critic of the ruling coalition, was attacked in May, the AU expressed its concern about the deteriorating situation in Lesotho and urged implementation of the recommendations of the SADC report. In November Kamoli finally resigned from his post, owing partly to pressure from the USA.

The USA tied Lesotho's continued eligibility to benefit from the African Growth and Opportunity Act (AGOA) of 2000 to the country's implementation of SADC recommendations. Exemption from duties on exports to the USA was critical for Lesotho's textile and garment industry, which in 2008 employed some 40,000 people in 20 clothing factories, many established to take advantage of the AGOA preferences. That South Africa in effect removed benefits to clothing imports from Lesotho in December 2008 was a setback, and although the USA renewed Lesotho's eligibility for trade preferences under AGOA in 2015, there was concern that the kingdom's failure to meet AGOA criteria could result in its future suspension. At the end of 2016 US President Barack Obama agreed that Lesotho's eligibility should continue, despite its failure to carry out the reforms demanded by SADC.

In November 2016 factionalism in the DC, the dominant party in the ruling seven-party coalition, came to a head. Prime Minister Mosisili dismissed several ministers for allegedly colluding with the opposition and removed responsibility for policing from deputy party leader, Monyane Moleleki. The latter left the Government with several of his colleagues and initiated talks with Thabane, who remained in self-imposed exile in South Africa. This eventually led to an agreement between Moleleki, who in January 2017 launched a new party, the Alliance of Democrats (AD), and the ABC. Although Thabane and the other opposition leaders returned from exile, the Speaker suspended sessions of the National Assembly to prevent a no-confidence motion from being introduced. In March, however, the opposition joined forces in Parliament to pass a motion of no confidence in Mosisili's Government. King Letsie was asked to appoint Moleleki as the new Prime Minister; by agreement, Moleleki would be succeeded by Thabane after 18 months. However, Mosisili did not resign and instead asked Letsie to dissolve Parliament and set a date for a new general election, which was duly scheduled for 3 June.

As Moleleki and Thabane had co-operated on the no-confidence vote, they were expected to form an electoral pact. However, Thabane rejected this option and committed his party to fielding candidates in all 80 constituencies, stating that he would only consider a coalition after the election. The election took place peacefully on 3 June 2017, albeit with a considerable military presence. Thabane's ABC won 48 seats, and the DC 30. Thabane declared that he would join a coalition with the AD, the BNP and the Reformed Congress of Lesotho to achieve a legislative majority. Thabane was sworn in as the new Prime Minister in mid-June at the head of a new Cabinet.

All but one of the new ministers were members of the four-party governing coalition, which held a total of 63 seats in the National Assembly.

POLITICAL INSTABILITY CONTINUES

In March 2014 President Zuma of South Africa had joined King Letsie and Prime Minister Thabane at Polihali to launch Phase 2 of the LHWP.; however, the start of work on the project was delayed over disputes about the contracts. Although it began in 2019, the date for completion was postponed to 2025. The projected cost of the new dam and the Polihali–Katse tunnel was US $1,300m. Some feared that an increase in the occurrence of dry spells would reduce the yield of Lesotho's dams, leading to lower volumes of water being exported to South Africa and less royalty income for Lesotho. With disruption caused both by the COVID-19 pandemic and by protests in early 2021 by villagers who had to relocate, a new completion date was set for 2027. In May 2021 King Letsie travelled visited the site of the new dam to launch an Integrated Catchment Management System, co-financed by the European Union (EU).

In September 2017 Lt-Gen. Khoantle Motšomotšo, the Commander of the LDF since late 2016, was shot dead in his office by two military officers, who were subsequently killed by his bodyguards. It was subsequently claimed that Motšomotšo had refused to protect the two officers from prosecution for involvement in Mahao's murder. While Thabane appealed for calm SADC intervened again, agreeing to send a 'preventive' mission, comprising military, police and civilian personnel, to oversee the process of security and constitutional reform. Meanwhile, Kamoli had been arrested in October. He was tried, convicted of involvement in Mahao's murder and imprisoned.

The 258-member the SADC Preventive Mission in Lesotho (SAPMIL) was officially launched in Maseru in December 2017. It was initially scheduled to remain in Lesotho for six months, but in April 2018 a SADC summit extended its mandate for another six months. SADC then ignored a request by Thabane that SAPMIL remain for a further three months, and the mission withdrew in November. In May 2018 Ramaphosa, Zuma's successor as South African President, had delegated his role as head of the SADC facilitation mission to former Deputy Chief Justice of South Africa Dikgang Moseneke, who established a team that held talks with stakeholders in Lesotho. In late 2018 Lesotho's opposition parties demanded that the Government overturn the suspension, in September, of the country's Chief Justice, Nthomeng Majara, whom Prime Minister Thabane had accused of threatening national stability; Majara was reinstated in October but agreed to retire, with a generous retirement package, in February 2019. The exile in South Africa of opposition leader Metsing, whom the Government wished to extradite to stand trial in Lesotho on corruption charges, threatened to create even more unrest, until Moseneke persuaded the Government to drop its request. The opposition parties consequently agreed to participate in a Multi-Stakeholder National Dialogue, held in Maseru in November 2018, to discuss the constitutional, security and governance reforms required to end political and military instability. In December Metsing and two other leading opposition figures returned from exile, and meetings were held in districts throughout Lesotho to canvass local reactions to the constitutional reform process. By May 2019, however, when Moseneke's mandate as facilitator was set to expire, the task of drafting a new constitution that guaranteed the independence of the judiciary, police and army from state interference had barely begun.

In 2019 factionalism within the ABC—the main party in the ruling coalition—increased. Thabane and his influential young wife sought to prevent Prof. Nqosa Mahao, the former Vice-Chancellor of the National University of Lesotho, from being elected as the ABC's deputy leader, at the party's elective conference in February. The dispute over those elected at the conference lasted for several months, and Thabane dismissing from the Cabinet those he now saw as political opponents. To forestall a possible vote of no confidence in the National Assembly, Thabane arranged for Parliament to be suspended and rejected calls for a snap general election. Demands for his resignation mounted, and some in the ABC accused him of granting his wife too much power. When Ramaphosa visited Lesotho in July, he persuaded Thabane to reconvene Parliament to establish a National Reform Authority (NRA) to oversee a second national dialogue, which took place in September. Out of this process emerged a set of reforms designed to end the chronic political and security instability. These included depoliticizing the army and police and amending the Constitution to clarify that the army should not perform police functions, to prevent floor crossings and to limit the number of parties in Parliament. The number of parliamentary seats would be reduced to 80. However, further political instability prevented these reforms from being enacted.

In December 2019 it was reported that the police were investigating Thabane's role in the murder of his estranged former wife in 2017, immediately before his inauguration as Prime Minister. Phone records from the murder scene included his mobile number. Charges were first brought against Thabane's wife, Maesaiah, and in January 2020, after police had issued a warrant for her arrest, the now 80-year-old Thabane stated that he would step down at the end of July. His lawyer claimed that a Prime Minister had immunity from prosecution. Pressure mounted on Thabane, not least from within the ruling ABC and its coalition partners, to resign immediately. In March, after the National Assembly adopted legislation barring Thabane from calling fresh elections if he lost a no-confidence vote, he again prorogued the legislature for three months. However, the High Court (acting as the Constitutional Court) swiftly set this aside. In April, fearing that he would be ousted by a vote of no confidence, Thabane ordered troops onto the streets of Maseru to 'restore order'. He accused unnamed law enforcement agencies of undermining democracy and called on the army to enforce the lockdown that he had initiated in March to contain the spread of COVID-19, which meant that the borders with South Africa were largely closed. Thabane subsequently lifted some of the restrictions, and by mid-May Lesotho had recorded only one case of the virus.

South African pressure helped to force Thabane from office. President Ramaphosa, acting on behalf of SADC, sent a former South African government minister, Jeff Radebe, to Lesotho, and he persuaded all parties to agree that Thabane should be allowed to step down in a dignified way. On 19 May 2020 he reluctantly resigned. On the following day Moeketsi Majoro, a technocrat who had worked for the International Monetary Fund and been Minister of Finance, was sworn in as the new Prime Minister. Majoro reduced the Cabinet from 26 to 17 ministers and began tackling urgent issues. An estimated 40% of the country's population was food-insecure. Remittances from South Africa, where perhaps one-quarter of Lesotho's population resided, had fallen sharply. Majoro was aware of Lesotho's vulnerability to drought and its dependence on declining tariff income from the Southern African Customs Union. Owing largely to the AGOA, Lesotho had become a garment manufacturing hub—the textile sector employed some 45,000 people and contributed 10% of the country's gross domestic product (GDP), but as COVID-19 spread that sector increasingly struggled.

When Majoro made his first official visit to South Africa, in June 2020, he and Ramaphosa agreed to work towards the freer movement of people between the two countries. In November they agreed to revive a Joint Bilateral Commission of Co-operation and discussed creating one-stop border crossings at Maseru and Ficksburg. However, the COVID-19 pandemic led to new restrictions on cross-border movement. In July Lesotho went into another lockdown, in which non-essential travel was banned. These restrictions were progressively lifted, but in January 2021 there was another spike in infections, following seasonal migration between Lesotho and South Africa. After South Africa closed its border posts, including the main one outside Maseru, Lesotho introduced another lockdown. In March the country launched its vaccination campaign after receiving vaccines through the COVID-19 Vaccines Global Access (COVAX) Facility, but the supply soon ran out. By May 2022 most of the lockdown restrictions had been removed, and the economic continued to recover, after a recession in 2020. However, an internal audit effected in

2021 had reported that much state funding had been wasted on accommodating and feeding those involved in tackling COVID-19, and payments had been made for fumigation of public spaces that had never been carried out. As at 1 August 2022, over 34,000 cases had been recorded, including 702 deaths (although this was probably a significant underestimate), and only 38.3% of the population had been vaccinated.

Meanwhile, Prime Minister Majoro led a very fragile coalition. In April 2021 tensions between him and Nqosa Mahao, a cabinet minister, who was Deputy President of the ruling ABC and had ambitions to take over as its leader, came to a head. Majoro dismissed Mahao, who announced that he was forming a new party, the Basotho Action Party. He claimed to have sufficient support to threaten Majoro's majority support in the legislature. Worried that Majoro would be ousted and instability return, further delaying the implementation of the reforms that SADC had called for in 2016, Radebe, Ramaphosa's special envoy, led a new mission to Lesotho in May 2021. It was reassured by the Prime Minister and his deputy, Mathibeli Mokhothu, the DC leader, that the coalition would continue and be able to survive a no-confidence motion in Parliament. Thabane's attempts to force Majoro from office failed; however, in November the Director of Public Prosecutions finally brought charges against Thabane for the murder of his former wife. In January 2022 he was replaced as ABC leader by Nkaku Kabi, who unsuccessfully attempted to withdraw the ABC from the ruling coalition. Majoro remained as Prime Minister, surviving a vote of no confidence in April, but the Government became increasingly unstable. Notably, in March deputies had prevented the finance minister from presenting the budget.

The disarray in Government further delayed reforms. Metsing had returned to Lesotho under a SADC-brokered agreement that he would not be prosecuted for any crimes until the country had implemented the multi-sector reforms recommended by SADC, and Moseneke, the special envoy for the SADC mediator Ramaphosa, urged the Government to suspend proceedings against Metsing until the reform process was concluded, but the Government insisted that the judiciary was independent and that the cases could not be linked to the reforms. Meanwhile, the NRA prepared a reform package that ended floor-crossing in Parliament, provided that a prime minister could be impeached only by a two-thirds majority vote and required the head of government to appoint senior officials on merit. Two bills embodying these reforms, which reduced the Prime Minister's powers and made King Letsie the army's Commander-in-Chief, were introduced in Parliament in May 2022. However, because it necessitated an amendment to the Constitution, it required two-thirds of the members to support it and it was not approved before Parliament was dissolved in July prior to the general election called for early October. Nevertheless, SADC insisted that the electoral reforms be enacted before the election, so when Masisi was at an SADC conference held in the Democratic Republic of the Congo in August he declared a state of emergency, under the terms of which the King then recalled Parliament for six days in order to pass the two pieces of legislation. The legality of the state of emergency and the reconvening of Parlament was challenged in the courts by a media activist and the Law Society of Lesotho. In September the Constitutional Court ruled that both were null and void, which meant that the reform legislation had been passed by a Parliament without due authority. The Government announced that it would appeal the ruling, but the general election went ahead.

Several court cases had delayed the replacement of members of the IEC for over two years. When new commissions were appointed, they promised to organize overdue by-elections in five constituencies in July and August 2022. However, Parliament's five-year term ended in July, and a general election was called for early October. In March the EU had sent a delegation to Lesotho to report on whether it should send observers before the general election. As electoral campaigning got under way there was a rise in thuggery linked to the rivalry between the 60 political parties that were preparing for the polls. In July the murder charges against Thabane and his wife were dropped. The new Revolution for Prosperity (RP) party, led by Sam Matekane, reportedly the country's richest man, was seen by some as a breath of fresh air in a stale political environment and he attracted large crowds at rallies. Matekane, who had made his fortune in transport, construction and mining, had donated funds for educational and other philanthropic ventures and led a private-sector initiative to increase the supply of COVID-19 vaccines. Although the new party suffered when there was much dissension and contestation over the selection of candidates for the 7 October general election, according to the official results of the polls, the RP won 56 seats and became the largest party in the legislature.

Lesotho had been awarded a grant from the US-based Millennium Challenge Corporation (MCC) in 2007 to fund projects to reduce poverty and boost economic growth, but the MCC consequently refused to grant new funds owing to alleged human rights abuses in Lesotho and delays in addressing the SADC-recommended reform process. However, after the Majoro-led Government had addressed concerns about human trafficking, in May 2022 the MCC awarded Lesotho a US $300m. grant for projects in horticulture, business assistance and health care. By that time the fall in remittances and rising prices for food and agricultural inputs, caused in part by the Russian invasion of Ukraine, had resulted in greater food insecurity. The textile industry, which had been hit hard during the pandemic, had only partially recovered and Lesotho continued to rely heavily on the LHWP for revenue. Whether a new government and legislature would pick up the reform agenda after the October election remained to be seen.

Economy

MALEFA ROSE MALEFANE

INTRODUCTION

Lesotho is unique in its geographic location, and, as a result of it being entirely landlocked by one country, South Africa, the economic relations between the two countries influence Lesotho's possibilities to a large extent. It is, therefore, not surprising that the South African currency is a legal tender in Lesotho, owing to both countries being members of the Common Monetary Area (CMA). Apart from the CMA membership, both Lesotho and South Africa serve in other regional agreements such as the South African Customs Area, the Southern African Customs Union, and the recently established African Continental Free Trade Area. Although Lesotho is an independent state, its economic performance is hugely influenced by the changes in the South African economy, especially considering the significant number of Lesotho's labour force who are migrant workers in South Africa. According to the Lesotho Ministry of Labour and Employment, the present poor economic performance in South Africa was likely to result in dire effects on both job creation and the prospects for inclusive growth in Lesotho.

KEY INDICATORS

The economy of Lesotho is mainly dependent on the manufacturing and services sectors, which have contributed the largest share to gross domestic product (GDP) in recent years. Manufacturing activities comprise mainly clothing and textiles production for export under the Africa Growth and Opportunity Act (AGOA) concession. The AGOA is a time-bound trade privilege aimed at granting duty-free access to selected products entering the USA. However, the AGOA concession for

Lesotho is set to expire in 2025. Over the past decade Lesotho has recorded an exceptional performance in the manufacturing sector as witnessed by the increase in the sector's contribution to GDP during the period between 2010 and 2022. As previously alluded to by the World Bank (in 2001), Lesotho's ability and success in attracting several ventures leading in manufacturing exports was primarily due to the country's comparative advantage concerning productive labour and favourable trade arrangements such as the AGOA.

Looking at the trends in various economic indicators for the period between 2010 and 2020, on average, Lesotho recorded positive economic growth rates prior to 2020; however, during that year the COVID-19 pandemic crippled the socioeconomic potential of many economies worldwide. According to 2021 data from the World Bank's World Development Indicators (WDI), Lesotho's GDP increased from US $2,234m. in 2010 to $2,330m. in 2020. This increase can be mainly attributed to various factors that drove up output in the primary sector, particularly during the first half of the decade. One of the factors, as documented by the Central Bank of Lesotho (CBL), was the recovery in the mining and quarrying sub-sectors, with strong global demand for diamonds resulting from the economic recovery in major developed economies. Between 2018 and 2020 mining and quarrying output more than doubled in volume. The second factor explaining the increase in Lesotho's output relates to the expansion in livestock and crop production, both of which also contributed to output growth in the primary sector. For example, between 2018 and 2020, the value of overall agricultural output increased from 1,438m. maloti to 1,757m. maloti.

Apart from the impetus from the primary sector, output growth in Lesotho around the beginning of the 2010s was also accelerated by expansion in the secondary and tertiary sectors. For instance, the secondary sector, which mainly comprises manufacturing and construction, grew by 5.8% in 2012, while the tertiary sector grew by 4.6%, according to the CBL. In recent years, however, Lesotho's GDP has been deteriorating and it declined by 1.2% in 2018 and by 11.1% in 2020, according to the World Bank. The poor outlook in GDP growth was due to the decline in the overall performance of the primary, secondary and tertiary sectors. For instance, in 2020, the primary sector declined by 9.2% as a result of a slowdown in agriculture, forestry and fishing coupled with a sharp decline in the mining and quarrying sub-sector.

The 2020 decline in Lesotho's output growth coincided with the temporary nationwide lockdown, which was enforced as part of the COVID-19 prevention measures. During the lockdown only essential services could continue with their normal operations, whereas the rest of the other economic sectors had to cease operation until the lockdown measures were lifted. Furthermore, according to the CBL, the recent decline in the demand for Lesotho's exports from the USA and South Africa has led to a contraction in the manufacturing sub-sector and ultimately the slowing down of the overall performance of the secondary sector.

Looking at the trends in Lesotho's real GDP per capita during the reviewed period, it fell from US $1,119.8 in 2010 to $1,088.0 in 2020. This decline reflects the increase in Lesotho's population size, which, during 2011–20 increased at an average annual rate of 0.7%. Apart from the increase in population size, the decline in Lesotho's real GDP per capita in recent years could also be attributed to the contraction in the country's output growth as explained above.

Compared to the rest of sub-Saharan Africa, Lesotho's real GDP growth has recently been far below the regional average. The 2021 *World Economic Outlook* revealed that in 2020 sub-Saharan African GDP averaged a decline of 1.9%, whereas Lesotho recorded a decline of 11.1%. In terms of the inflation rate, however, the expansion in Lesotho's consumer price index is about one-half of that of the sub-Saharan region. The sub-Saharan African average for 2020 was 10.8%, according to the *World Economic Outlook*, whereas Lesotho recorded a rate of 5.0%, according to the WDI. One of the factors affecting the inflation rate in Lesotho relates to the fact that its currency, the loti, is pegged at par with the South African rand. Thus, the pegging of the loti to the rand helps maintain the price stability in Lesotho.

THE DEPENDENT ECONOMY

Owing to the country's geographic location, Lesotho's economy has historically been dependent on South Africa mainly for trade and labour employment. At the time Lesotho introduced its second National Development Plan (NDP) covering the period 1975/76–1979/80, the Government identified the reduction of Lesotho's dependence on South Africa as one of the target areas for development. Around the time of the implementation of the first NDP (which ran from 1970/71–1974/75), about 45% of the male labour force of Lesotho were employed as migrant labourers in South Africa. Unfortunately, the absenteeism of the male labour force in Lesotho has proven to have contributed to the stagnation of rural development, particularly considering that most of the rural population relies on subsistence agriculture. In many cases, in the absence of the male labour force, women and children in rural Lesotho have been forced to take over the management of animal husbandry and crop farming activities, which they often conduct with limited resources.

In recent years, the trends in labour migration from Lesotho to South Africa indicate that a high proportion of labour migrants are from rural areas. According to the Lesotho Bureau of Statistics (LBS) 2019 Labour Force Survey, about 70.3% of Lesotho's labour migrants were from rural areas (52.0% were male and 20.3% were female). In comparison, 14.4% of male and 7.1% of female migrants were reported to originate from urban areas, whereas 3.3% of male and 2.9% of female migrants were from peri-urban areas of Lesotho. This finding indicates the severity of economic deprivation in rural areas of Lesotho relative to urban and peri-urban areas.

While South Africa has been providing a 'safety-net' for the unskilled labourers from Lesotho, it has emerged that the prospects of Lesotho's income benefits from migrant labour are not favourable because of the low wages paid to Basotho workers. As Lesotho continues to be integrated into South Africa and the global economy, it would be ideal for the policymakers in the country to address the socioeconomic problems associated with labour migration, which are continuing to cripple rural development.

TRADE PATTERNS AND EXPORT COMPETITIVENESS

Since the beginning of the 2000s the Lesotho trade sector has experienced surges in trade flows. For instance, according to the United Nations (UN) COMTRADE, between 2000 and 2004 the value of Lesotho's imports increased substantially from US $487.0m. to $1,399.0m. On the exports side, while the value of Lesotho's exports dropped slightly between 2000 and 2004, a recovery occurred from 2002 with exports reaching a peak of $968.4m. in 2004. Lesotho's leading five export products are garments, diamonds, electricity, wool and mohair, with South Africa being the top export destination in 2020 followed by Belgium and the USA.

One of the factors that historically resulted in improvements in the volume and value of Lesotho's exports was the increased demand from the USA for Lesotho's exports of textiles and clothing. However, since 2004 the competitiveness of Lesotho's exports has been threatened by various factors that have resulted in a decline in the country's exports. One of the threats to Lesotho's export competitiveness was the lifting of quotas under the World Trade Organization's Agreement on Textiles and Clothing, which was adopted in 2004. With the lifting of the quotas on textiles and clothing, Lesotho's exports of those goods faced stiff competition from countries like India and the People's Republic of China, which are far more productive and relatively cheaper than Lesotho. Despite these challenges, Lesotho's manufacturing exports have consistently accounted for more than two-thirds of total exports, with the exceptions of 2013 and 2014, when the share dropped to 41.6% and 53.1%, respectively.

A closer look at the structure of Lesotho's exports indicates that although about 80% of the population is engaged in agricultural activities, the share of agricultural exports in total merchandise exports remains significantly low compared to the share of exports from the manufacturing sector. For instance, the share of agricultural raw materials in total merchandise exports stood at just 0.1% in 2000 and only 5.3% in 2010. (By 2016 the share had improved slightly to 6.4%.) While agricultural activities dominate other sectoral activities in Lesotho's economy, subsistence agriculture (as opposed to commercial agriculture) is the one being practised in most parts of the country. For this reason, it is not surprising that the share of agricultural exports in total merchandise exports has traditionally remained relatively low. Furthermore, agricultural raw materials exports mainly comprise crude materials and fertilizers, which are sparsely produced in Lesotho.

THE AGOA MIRACLE

The economy of Lesotho has been one of the main beneficiaries of the trade concessions offered under the AGOA. Incepted in 2000 the AGOA is a non-reciprocal and unilateral programme offered by the US Administration to the qualifying economies in Africa. In the case of Lesotho, through the AGOA, selected textiles and apparel products from the country are granted duty-free access to the US market. Following the inception of the AGOA in Lesotho, there has been evidence of increased manufacturing output and the creation of several jobs for low-skilled workers in the country, while about 40 factories have been established, employing over 40,000 persons. In turn, the establishment of these factories has directly created an informal trading market in their proximity, where local hawkers sell food items, fresh produce and other merchandise for household use.

While exports from Lesotho to the USA increased tremendously during the period following the inception of the AGOA in 2000, there was a sharp decline in AGOA exports from Lesotho after 2008. The fiscal year 2008/09 corresponds with the emergence of the global financial crisis during which major economies, including the USA, were negatively affected by recession, and subsequently reduced their consumption and thus domestic demand for exports declined. Between 2008 and 2009 the value of AGOA exports from Lesotho to the USA declined from US $374.1m. to $304.2m. The value reached $305.3m. in 2020 and $333.7m. in 2021, but it has never recovered to reach pre-2008 levels.

Although the AGOA has provided much economic relief to Lesotho, for instance, through contributing to job creation and income, the programme will expire in September 2025 and thus the Lesotho economy faces a potential loss in jobs and income, which could exacerbate the level of poverty and unemployment in the country unless mitigating strategies are put in place.

AGRICULTURE

The agriculture sector is one of the most significant contributors to Lesotho's economy in terms of it being the main source of livelihood for the majority of the population. Although the agriculture sector accounts for the smallest share of Lesotho's GDP (around 6%), it continues to be a mainstay in the country and is a solace to some of the retrenched mineworkers who previously worked in South Africa. The 2019 Labour Force Survey indicated that about 10% of the economically active population was employed in agriculture, forestry and fishing. Moreover, according to the International Labour Organization (ILO), about two-fifths of the economically active population is involved in subsistence agriculture. Thus, the sector provides the sought-after relief to the labour force that otherwise cannot be absorbed in other formal sectors of employment.

Agricultural activities in Lesotho are small-scale in nature and mainly comprise crop production where maize, sorghum and pulses (beans, peas and lentils) are cultivated. Apart from crop farming, livestock production and poultry farming are also practised. Currently, livestock production is the main contributor to Lesotho's leading agricultural export commodities, namely, wool and mohair. The World Bank has been providing financial aid for the Smallholder Agricultural Development Project which aims to assist Basotho farmers in adopting 'climate smart' agricultural technologies. Furthermore, the project supports the Government's efforts to empower women and young people as it aims to reach at least 50% of women and youth in its total beneficiaries.

Although some of the subsistence farmers in Lesotho rely on primitive methods of farming, others have adopted resource-saving farming practices such as conservation farming. Through the initiative of the UN Food and Agriculture Organization (FAO) and collaboration with local non-governmental organizations, a planting basins system, which is one of the conservation farming methods, was introduced in the early 2000s in some of the rural areas in the highland districts. This conservation method has succeeded in improving agricultural productivity as a result of improved soil structure and efficiency in the use of resources such as seeds and fertilizers.

INDUSTRY

The manufacturing sector is one of the significant drivers of the economy in Lesotho although the sector depends on a narrow industrial base. In 2020 manufacturing contributed 16% of GDP, which was 1% lower than the 2018 figure. The recent decline in the manufacturing sector is due to the COVID-19 pandemic, which affected clothing and textile production during the lockdown in 2020. In the pre-COVID-19 era Lesotho's manufacturing sector witnessed buoyant growth of 34% in 2014–19.

Despite the significance of the manufacturing sector in the economy of Lesotho, traditionally industry in Lesotho has been mostly based on a few product categories, typically in the clothing and footwear, food processing and construction subsectors. This concentration of industrial activities can partly be linked to the privileges that were granted to the manufacturing sector through various trade arrangements. For instance, the Cotonou Agreement, which is part of the Everything But Arms (EBA) initiative, granted non-reciprocal access to all products from Lesotho except arms to the European Union, while the AGOA (see above) grants duty-free access of selected Lesotho products to the US market.

Historically, the activities of the clothing and textiles subsector, have been based in the urban centres including the capital city, Maseru, and the Maputsoe urban area in the north-western part of the country. The industrial factories are mainly managed and owned by Chinese and Taiwanese investors, although the workers are mostly local women and men. The clothing, textiles and footwear industry is the largest private sector employer in Lesotho employing approximately 46,500 workers, 86% of whom are women.

After manufacturing, the construction sub-sector is the second largest contributor to industry in Lesotho. The Lesotho Highlands Water Project (LHWP), currently in its second phase, is one of the key operations in the construction subsector. The project is an extension of the construction involving a water dam and reservoir for delivery of water to South Africa and establishing a hydropower station to improve the capacity of the generation of electricity in Lesotho. According to the African Union's Programme for Infrastructure Development in Africa, the amount of water received by South Africa from Lesotho is 24.6 m^3 per second, which is expected to increase further to a cumulative total of 45.5 m^3 after the completion of the LHWP Phase II. In 2020, however, the LHWP halted its operations temporarily due to the COVID-19 pandemic, which resulted in a sharp contraction in the construction sub-sector. As documented by the CBL in 2020, the construction sub-sector contracted by 24.9% in that year, which was far higher than the 3.7% decline recorded in 2019. The LHWP has now resumed its operations and in the ministerial meeting held between Lesotho and South Africa in late October 2021, the two parties committed to fast-tracking the completion of the project by 2027.

Compared to manufacturing and construction, food processing contributes a very small proportion of Lesotho's GDP. The sub-sector comprises two milling companies, a brewing company, a dairy farm, and retail outlets such as butcheries and bakeries. Overall, the food processing industry in Lesotho is not well-developed nor of sufficient size to cater for the demand in the domestic economy. Consequently, the country depends on food and consumer imports, some of which come from South Africa. In 2017, for example, according to the World Bank, Lesotho purchased 59.5% of consumer imports and 10.5% of food imports from South Africa, and that country remains the largest source of Lesotho's total imports, with 90% of all imports originating from there.

SERVICES

Compared to agriculture and manufacturing, the services sector dominates in GDP and currently accounts for some 52% thereof. The key sub-sectors in the services sector, as indicated in the Lesotho Services Policy Review of 2018, are financial services, tourism and professional medical services. The financial services sector encompasses the banking systems, non-bank financial institutions, microfinance institutions and savings schemes. The financial services industry is, however, facing the problem of limited access to financial services, especially by communities based in remote rural areas. This problem undermines service delivery and the achievement of the financial inclusion objective.

The other main sub-sector in the services sector, tourism, is very much unexplored in Lesotho, although it has the potential to bring economic emancipation through job creation and income generation. Lesotho is renowned for its beautiful mountainous scenery and is one of the few countries on the African continent that receives snowfall in winter. There is currently one ski resort in the Butha-Buthe district, the Afriski Mountain Resort, which extends up to an altitude of 3,222 m above sea level. Considering that all 10 districts of Lesotho receive snowfall every winter, it could benefit the economy to have more ski resorts and seasonal ice-skating facilities in other parts of the country. Not only would the tourism industry attract tourists into the country, but most importantly, it could create jobs for the local people and help promote the handicrafts made by community members.

KEY ECONOMIC CHALLENGES

Lesotho's economy faces various challenges including unemployment, poverty and inequality. Lesotho continues to be ranked as a least developed country (LDC) even though some of its trading partners such as Botswana and Eswatini have moved out of LDC status. Poverty levels in Lesotho remain much higher than the sub-Saharan African average. In 2017, for example, the poverty headcount ratio based on the World Bank data for Lesotho was 49.7%, indicating that about one-half of the population lives below the poverty line. In comparison, the 2017 poverty headcount ratio for sub-Saharan Africa was 40%, which is lower than that of Lesotho by 9.7%. In 2019 the poverty headcount ratio for sub-Saharan Africa slightly decreased to 38.3%.

According to the World Bank, poverty is more prevalent in the rural areas of Lesotho where deprived members of society typically have limited access to basic services such as infrastructure, education and health care. The problem of food security also characterizes the rural areas, and the World Food Programme projected that about 312,000 people from rural areas (in contrast to 158,000 people from the urban areas) of Lesotho, will suffer from food insecurity between October 2021 and March 2022. The main factors contributing to poverty and food insecurity in Lesotho can be linked to the high unemployment levels in the country and recent job losses resulting from the retrenchment of mine workers in South Africa and the COVID-19 related lockdown. According to ILO, in 2012, there were about 41,000 mineworkers from Lesotho working in South Africa, which was a steep decline in the number of migrant mineworkers considering that in 2005 these numbered about 145,000. The number has edged back up in recent years, and there were believed to be about 46,000 Lesotho migrant mineworkers currently in South Africa.

The COVID-19 outbreak is another factor that has in recent years significantly affected the Lesotho economy due to the nationwide lockdown that was enforced by the Government in March 2020. During the initial nationwide lockdown, all non-essential services were put on hold until the restrictions were officially relaxed. According to a UN Survey on the impact of the COVID-19 pandemic in Lesotho, the pandemic affected the youth more than other age categories as 26% of those surveyed pointed to the negative impact of the pandemic on their education and skills development. This is because when the lockdown was introduced in Lesotho, schools were closed from March to October and later in other months depending on the state of the infections in the country.

While Lesotho is battling the problem of general poverty that is savaging the economy, child poverty and child labour have recently emerged as other aspects of poverty in the country. According a 2018 study by the United Nations Children's Fund (UNICEF), 64.5% of children under the age of 17 are classified as poor, and deprivation rates are more pronounced among children living in rural areas compared to those living in urban areas. There are different dimensions of child poverty in Lesotho varying in the deprivation in nutrition, education and housing. In addition to these dimensions of child poverty, HIV/AIDS prevalence is very high among children and young adults below the age of 23 compared with the prevalence rate among mature adults. (The HIV/AIDS prevalence rate for persons aged under 23 is 74% and it is 63% for those aged 24–59.) Looking at another aspect, which is child labour, statistics for Lesotho indicate that 62.8% of children aged 10–17 who are engaged in work activities originate from rural areas as opposed to 6.8% from the peri-urban settlements. Most child labourers (79.1%) are male, while the remaining 20.9% are female.

Unemployment is one of the main economic challenges in Lesotho; however, the country's unemployment rate, based on the broad definition of unemployment, has actually decreased over the past two decades. Between 2000 and 2020 the unemployment rate decreased from 35.3% to 24.7%. Nevertheless, the expanded definition of unemployment, which includes discouraged job seekers, remains relatively high at 38.5%. Unemployment in Lesotho results from various factors including labour market deficiencies, an undiversified economy and inadequate skill development. According to ILO, the deficiencies in the labour market are due to the lack of responsive (government driven) labour market policies and supportive labour market information systems in Lesotho.

Overall, the unemployment rate among females is higher in the rural and urban areas in comparison to the peri-urban areas of Lesotho. However, the proportion of unemployed males in the peri-urban areas remains higher than in the urban and rural areas. In 2019, for example, the unemployment rate among females was 17.4%, 28.0% and 24.1% for the urban, rural and peri-urban areas, respectively. For males the respective unemployment rates for the urban, rural and peri-urban settlements were 15.5%, 27.8% and 25.8%. These findings suggest that the labour market presents more favourable conditions for men than is the case for women. For instance, the trends in the labour force participation rate by industry and gender show that a total of 53.6% of males are employed in a secondary job in the agriculture, manufacturing or services sector as opposed to 46.4% for females.

Because of the small size of the economy of Lesotho, the formal labour market in the country is unable to absorb the labour force at a rate that could maintain the unemployment rate at a single digit level. As indicated by FAO, the Lesotho economy generates around 6,000 jobs per year yet approximately 22,000 to 25,000 persons enter the labour force each year. Consequently, the economy finds itself having two-fifths of its labour force working in the informal sector. According to the 2019 Labour Force Survey, more males than females are employed in the informal sector with a distribution of 66.9% and 33.1% respectively.

Like other economies in sub-Saharan Africa, the economy of Lesotho is undiversified, and GDP is driven by a somewhat narrow export base. The undiversified nature of Lesotho's economy has been evidenced in production and industrial ventures being concentrated in the textiles and clothing subsector, which as the data shows, is the largest contributor to the manufacturing sector. About 80% of the clothing and textiles exports are destined for the US market, which again is an indication of overdependence on one customer. As previously mentioned, the expiration of the AGOA concessions, which are currently granting duty-free access to Lesotho's textiles and clothing exports to the US market, will have severe effects on jobs and income.

ECONOMIC REFORMS

Over the past two decades, the Government of Lesotho has been making efforts to enhance the development of the domestic economy through the implementation of various economic reforms. The reforms that took place in Lesotho between 2000 and 2020 can be broadly categorized according to their target objectives as follows: first, there are reforms with a macroeconomic focus, including the Fiscal Consolidation Strategy. Second, there are reforms targeting industrialization, food security and employment. The third category of reforms comprises those that focus on the empowerment of youth and women, but also address the demographic dynamics arising from the rural-urban migration.

The origins of these economic reforms point to the desire of the country's authorities to undertake additional supportive measures commensurate with the short-to-medium-term targets as stipulated in the National Development Plans. Again, the existence of impediments to private sector growth and job creation prompted the direction and focus of some of the economic reforms implemented in Lesotho. For instance, while the 1990s marked a decade of buoyant economic growth rates in Lesotho, the economy was still characterized by some impediments that throttled the business environment and consequently affected the prospects for economic growth and job creation. Some of the impediments at that time related to the slow growth in the private sector coupled with the high cost of doing business in Lesotho. According to the CBL, some of the costs of doing business in Lesotho stem from the lengthy and cumbersome processes that accompany company registration and business licensing. As an example, it takes about 183 days to obtain a construction permit in Lesotho and this has led to Lesotho ranking 171st out of 193 countries on the indicator for dealing with business permits, in the World Bank's Ease of Doing Business Index. To harness a conducive business environment and support economic diversification, the Government of Lesotho, with external assistance from the World Bank, embarked on the Private Sector Competitiveness and Economic Diversification Project (PSCEDP). The first phase of this project was launched in 2007 while the second phase began in 2013. The PSCEDP project focuses on diversifying Lesotho's economy away from the textile and clothing sub-sector, recommending that the focus of economic activities must be directed towards other sub-sectors such as tourism and horticulture. Accordingly, the project is envisaged to bring about a 5% increase in Lesotho's annual GDP growth.

Considering the transformative reforms targeting industrialization, agriculture and employment, the proposed strategies underscored the need to intensify infrastructure development and bring innovations in agroindustry, while also ensuring that the women and youths are afforded opportunities to engage in productive activities. These proposed strategies were put together with further emphasis on the need to provide education and training interventions to improve skills development in the country. However, the success of these strategies depends on a host of factors such as good governance, institutional reforms and political stability.

Rural–urban migration is predominant in Lesotho and can, to some extent, be regarded as having resulted in the underdevelopment of the rural areas. In most cases, the allocation of resources tends to be biased towards the urban and peri-urban areas as budgets are formulated and disbursed at a centralized government level, usually leaving little room, if any, for local government involvement. With the implementation of the Decentralization Policy, effective linkages between the local and central governments could be fostered. Furthermore, decentralization would ensure that economic plans and budgets are formulated at a local government level, which could empower the local authorities and possibly bring economic benefits to the previously disadvantaged communities. Currently, the Decentralization Policy cannot be said to have been successful in Lesotho, although it was conceptualized in 1993 under the auspices of the National Constitution and officially inaugurated in 2014.

CONCLUSION

Lesotho is one of the least developed economies in sub-Saharan Africa but is integrated into several regional economic associations and is a beneficiary of other trade arrangements outside the African continent. The downside of Lesotho's economy is its heavy reliance on manufactured exports, most of which are dependent on time-bound privileges. Without a well-diversified and growing economy, it would be impossible for Lesotho to overcome some of the challenges that are currently negatively impacting on the economy. Unemployment, poverty and rural–urban migration continue to make the country's development prospects grim, and require immediate alternative strategies to be implemented in the country. It appears, however, that the slow implementation of some of the economic reforms that have been drafted to aid the Lesotho economy, is the major obstacle to the achievement of national objectives.

Statistical Survey

Sources (unless otherwise stated): Bureau of Statistics, POB 455, Maseru 100; tel. 22323852; internet www.bos.gov.ls; Central Bank of Lesotho, POB 1184, Maseru 100; tel. 22314281; e-mail cbl@centralbank.org.ls; internet www.centralbank.org.ls.

Area and Population

AREA, POPULATION AND DENSITY

Area (sq km)	30,355*
Population (*de jure* census results)	
9 April 2006	1,876,633
10 April 2016	
Males	982,133
Females	1,025,068
Total	2,007,201
Population (UN estimates at mid-year)†	
2020	2,142,252
2021‡	2,159,067
2022‡	2,175,695
Density (per sq km) at mid-2022‡	71.7

* 11,720 sq miles.
† Source: UN, *World Population Prospects: The 2019 Revision*.
‡ Projection.

POPULATION BY AGE AND SEX
('000, UN projections at mid-2022)

	Males	Females	Total
0–14 years	349.1	347.4	696.4
15–64 years	686.4	682.0	1,368.4
65 years and over	39.6	71.2	110.8
Total	1,075.1	1,100.6	2,175.7

Note: Totals may not be equal to the sum of components, owing to rounding.

Source: UN, *World Population Prospects: The 2019 Revision*.

DISTRICTS
(population at 2016 census)

District	Area (sq km)	Population	Density (per sq km)
Berea	2,222	262,616	118.2
Butha-Buthe	1,767	118,242	66.9
Leribe	2,828	337,521	119.3
Mafeteng	2,119	178,222	84.1
Maseru	4,279	519,186	121.3
Mohale's Hoek	3,530	165,590	46.9
Mokhotlong	4,075	100,442	24.6
Qacha's Nek	2,349	74,566	31.7
Quthing	2,916	115,469	39.6
Thaba-Tseka	4,270	135,347	31.7
Total	30,355	2,007,201	66.1

Principal Town (including suburbs, population at mid-2018, UN estimate): Maseru (the capital) 201,851 (Source: UN, *World Urbanization Prospects: The 2018 Revision*).

BIRTHS AND DEATHS
(annual averages, UN estimates)

	2005–10	2010–15	2015–20
Birth rate (per 1,000)	29.7	28.4	27.0
Death rate (per 1,000)	20.4	17.5	14.3

Source: UN, *World Population Prospects: The 2019 Revision*.

2020 (official figures, registered data): Births 9,047; Marriages 1,738; Deaths 13,268.

Life expectancy (years at birth, estimates): 54.8 (males 51.7; females 58.1) in 2020 (Source: World Bank, World Development Indicators database).

ECONOMICALLY ACTIVE POPULATION
(labour force survey, persons aged 15 years and over, 2019)

	Males	Females	Total
Agriculture, forestry and fishing .	47,887	18,719	66,606
Mining and quarrying	22,853	1,374	24,227
Manufacturing	20,516	44,988	65,504
Electricity, gas and water supply .	4,256	1,486	5,742
Construction	44,103	2,225	46,328
Wholesale and retail trade; repair of motor vehicles, motorcycles and household goods . .	33,007	38,514	71,521
Hotels and restaurants . . .	3,671	14,786	18,457
Transport, storage and communications . . .	18,411	1,597	20,008
Financial intermediation . . .	1,930	2,586	4,516
Real estate, renting and business activities	12,914	4,449	17,363
Public administration and defence; compulsory social security . .	19,208	12,107	31,315
Education	8,904	22,136	31,040
Health and social work . . .	4,601	9,889	14,490
Other community, social and personal service activities . .	4,791	6,569	11,360
Households with employed persons	25,596	61,445	87,041
Extraterritorial organizations and bodies	1,547	2,396	3,943
Sub-total	274,195	245,216	519,411
Not classified by economic activity	927	1,107	2,034
Total employed	275,122	246,323	521,445
Unemployed	80,320	70,946	151,266
Total labour force	355,442	317,369	672,711

Note: Figures for employment in the primary sector exclude subsistence farmers (estimated at some 250,000 in 2008).

Health and Welfare

KEY INDICATORS

Total fertility rate (children per woman, 2020)	3.1
Under-5 mortality rate (per 1,000 live births, 2020) . . .	89.5
HIV/AIDS (% of persons aged 15–49, 2020)	21.1
COVID-19: Cumulative confirmed deaths (per 100,000 persons at 31 August 2022)	30.9
COVID-19: Fully vaccinated population (% of total population at 17 July 2022)	38.3
Physicians (per 1,000 head, 2018)	0.5
Hospital beds (per 1,000 head, 2006)	1.30
Domestic health expenditure (2019): US $ per head (PPP) .	136.5
Domestic health expenditure (2019): % of GDP . . .	4.9
Domestic health expenditure (2019): public (% of total current expenditure)	43.5
Access to improved water resources (% of persons, 2020) .	72
Access to improved sanitation facilities (% of persons, 2020) .	50
Total carbon dioxide emissions ('000 metric tons, 2018) .	2,570
Carbon dioxide emissions per head (metric tons, 2018) . .	1.2
Human Development Index (2021): ranking	168
Human Development Index (2021): value	0.514

Note: For data on COVID-19 vaccinations, 'fully vaccinated' denotes receipt of all doses specified by approved vaccination regime (Sources: Johns Hopkins University and Our World in Data). Data on health expenditure refer to current general government expenditure in each case. For more information on sources and further definitions for all indicators, see Health and Welfare Statistics: Sources and Definitions section (europaworld.com/credits).

Agriculture

PRINCIPAL CROPS
('000 metric tons)

	2018	2019	2020
Beans, dry	6.8	0.9	2.4*
Maize	109.9	24.6	70.0†
Peas, dry	0.5	0.1	0.1*
Potatoes*	126.9	128.2	128.8
Sorghum	40.3	8.4	20.0†
Wheat	7.0	1.4	8.0†

* FAO estimate(s).
† Unofficial figure.

Aggregate production ('000 metric tons, may include official, semi-official or estimated data): Total cereals 158.0 in 2018, 35.3 in 2019, 98.8 in 2020; Total fruit (primary) 15.4 in 2018, 15.4 in 2019, 15.4 in 2020; Total pulses 7.3 in 2018, 1.0 in 2019, 2.5 in 2020; Total roots and tubers 126.9 in 2018, 128.2 in 2019, 128.8 in 2020; Total vegetables (primary) 31.9 in 2018, 31.9 in 2019, 31.9 in 2020.

Source: FAO.

LIVESTOCK
('000 head, year ending September)

	2018	2019	2020*
Asses	117	102	107
Cattle	453	361	425
Chickens	419	286	380
Goats	910	749	877
Horses	11	50	49
Pigs	49	54	47
Sheep	1,613	1,540	1,732

* FAO estimates.

Source: FAO.

LIVESTOCK PRODUCTS
('000 metric tons, FAO estimates)

	2018	2019	2020
Cattle meat	1.7	1.4	1.7
Cows' milk	170.0	180.0	173.3
Chicken meat	2.3	1.5	1.9
Game meat	5.3	5.3	5.3
Pig meat	0.6	0.7	0.7
Sheep meat	0.6	0.5	0.5
Hen eggs	1.4	1.4	1.4
Wool, greasy	3.7	3.7	3.7

Source: FAO.

Forestry

ROUNDWOOD REMOVALS
('000 cubic metres, excluding bark, FAO estimates)

	2018	2019	2020
Total (all fuel wood)	2,153.9	2,156.6	2,159.4

Source: FAO.

Fishing

(metric tons, live weight, FAO estimates)

	2018	2019	2020
Capture	52	52	57
Common carp	14	14	17
North African catfish	10	10	10
Other freshwater fishes	28	28	30
Aquaculture	2,500	2,550	2,600
Rainbow trout	2,500	2,549	2,599
Total catch	2,552	2,602	2,657

Source: FAO.

Mining

(cubic metres unless otherwise indicated)

	2016	2017	2018
Fire clay*	26,000	n.a.	n.a.
Diamond (carats)	342,014	1,126,409	1,294,283

* Estimated production, including clay and shale.

Gravel and crushed rock (estimate): 300,000 in 2010.

Source: US Geological Survey.

Finance

CURRENCY, EXCHANGE RATES AND FISCAL YEAR

Monetary Units
100 lisente (singular: sente) = 1 loti (plural: maloti).

Sterling, Dollar and Euro Equivalents (31 May 2022)
£1 sterling = 19.686 maloti;
US $1 = 15.638 maloti;
€1 = 16.753 maloti;
100 maloti = £5.08= $6.39 = €5.97.

Average Exchange Rate (maloti per US $)
2019   14.4484
2020   16.4732
2021   14.7834

Note: The loti is fixed at par with the South African rand.

Fiscal Year
The fiscal year ends on 31 March.

BUDGET
(million maloti, fiscal year)

Revenue*	2018/19	2019/20†	2020/21‡
Tax revenue	7,438	7,505	5,959
Taxes on net income and profits	4,100	4,052	3,275
Taxes on goods and services	3,300	3,453	2,683
Taxes on international trade	38	—	—
Non-tax revenue	1,764	1,650	1,815
Property income	682	532	477
Sales of goods and services	1,081	1,116	1,333
Other non-tax revenue	0	1	5
SACU	5,542	6,226	8,981
Total	14,744	15,381	16,755

Expenditure and net lending	2018/19	2019/20†	2020/21‡
Compensation of employees	5,995	5,891	7,180
Wages and salaries	5,469	5,425	6,644
Social contributions	526	465	537
Goods and services	3,112	3,161	3,391
Subsidies	340	346	1,068
Interest payments	449	480	505
Grants	1,022	1,133	1,119
Social benefits	1,734	1,687	2,201
Other expenditures	630	837	952
Total	13,282	13,535	16,416

* Excluding grants received (million maloti): 1,373 in 2018/19; 1,256 in 2019/20 (estimate); 1,108 in 2020/21 (budget figure).
† Estimates.
‡ Budget figures.

Source: IMF, *Kingdom of Lesotho: Requests for Disbursement Under the Rapid Credit Facility and Purchase Under the Rapid Financing Instrument—Press Release; Staff Report; and Statement by the Executive Director for the Kingdom of Lesotho* (July 2020).

INTERNATIONAL RESERVES
(excl. gold, US $ million at 31 December)

	2017	2018	2019
IMF special drawing rights	43.03	30.39	16.19
Reserve position in IMF	17.96	17.59	17.52
Foreign exchange	596.68	680.55	740.38
Total	657.67	728.53	774.10

2020: IMF special drawing rights 3.12; Reserve position in IMF 18.35.

2021: IMF special drawing rights 95.26; Reserve position in IMF 17.83.

Source: IMF, *International Financial Statistics*.

MONEY SUPPLY
(million maloti at 31 December)

	2017	2018	2019
Currency outside depository corporations	1,111.09	1,044.72	1,148.90
Transferable deposits	5,049.68	5,118.14	4,185.00
Other deposits	5,945.20	7,213.12	6,861.32
Broad money	12,105.97	13,375.98	12,195.22

Source: IMF, *International Financial Statistics.*

COST OF LIVING
(Consumer Price Index; base: December 2016 = 100)

	2019	2020	2021
Food and non-alcoholic beverages .	116.4	128.5	140.9
Clothing and footwear	106.7	110.6	114.6
Rent and utilities	124.2	121.8	130.2
All items (incl. others) . . .	113.5	119.2	126.4

NATIONAL ACCOUNTS
(million maloti at current prices)

Expenditure on the Gross Domestic Product

	2018	2019	2020
Final consumption expenditure .	40,096	42,289	43,733
General government	12,885	13,073	12,693
Households	26,648	28,587	30,400
Non-profit institutions serving households	562	628	640
Changes in inventories . . .	−1,405	329	3,037
Gross fixed capital formation . .	9,053	8,984	8,233
Total domestic expenditure .	47,743	51,601	55,003
Exports of goods and services .	16,951	16,249	15,001
Less Imports of goods and services	31,422	32,390	32,552
GDP in purchasers' values .	33,272	35,460	37,452
GDP at constant 2012 prices .	21,531	22,087	20,649

GDP in purchasers' values (million maloti at current prices): 35,417 in 2019 (revised figure); 37,045 in 2020 (revised figure); 37,220 in 2021.

GDP at constant 2012 prices (million maloti): 22,048 in 2019 (revised figure); 20,382 in 2020 (revised figure); 20,589 in 2021.

Gross Domestic Product by Economic Activity

	2019*	2020*	2021
Agriculture	1,538	1,757	1,825
Mining and quarrying	1,830	5,316	4,848
Manufacturing	5,952	5,471	5,731
Electricity, gas and water . . .	1,691	1,684	1,828
Construction	1,067	667	663
Wholesale and retail trade, restaurants and hotels . . .	3,434	2,568	2,674
Transport and communication .	1,667	1,369	1,335
Finance, insurance, real estate and business services . . .	6,200	6,374	6,243
Public administration and defence	6,853	6,935	7,015
Education, health and social work activities	653	693	645
Other services	262	258	243
Sub-total	31,147	33,091	33,049
Indirect taxes, less subsidies . .	4,270	3,954	4,171
GDP in purchasers' prices .	35,417	37,045	37,220

* Revised figures.

BALANCE OF PAYMENTS
(US $ million)

	2019	2020	2021
Exports of goods	1,063.5	888.8	1,064.4
Imports of goods	−1,782.6	−1,602.3	−1,814.0
Balance on goods	−719.1	−713.5	−749.6
Exports of services	29.2	11.9	8.0
Imports of services	−458.6	−390.0	−459.2
Balance on goods and services	−1,148.5	−1,091.6	−1,200.8
Primary income received . . .	603.6	517.3	604.8
Primary income paid	−127.6	−108.1	−119.9
Balance on goods, services and primary income	−672.4	−682.4	−715.9
Secondary income received . .	609.5	674.4	639.6
Secondary income paid . . .	−20.9	−33.3	−24.0
Current balance	−83.8	−41.3	−100.2
Capital account (net)	86.0	93.4	130.0
Direct investment from liabilities .	35.7	29.6	26.6
Portfolio investment liabilities .	0.2	0.2	0.2
Other investment assets . . .	−34.9	−157.0	−122.0
Other investment liabilities . .	117.9	3.1	155.1
Net errors and omissions . . .	−49.6	150.0	−7.2
Reserves and related items .	71.6	78.0	82.5

Source: IMF, *International Financial Statistics.*

External Trade

PRINCIPAL COMMODITIES
(distribution by HS, US $ million)

Imports	2018	2019	2020
Live animals and animal products	41.0	49.1	62.0
Vegetables and vegetable products	70.8	123.1	137.7
Products of the milling industry; malt; starches; inulin; wheat gluten	21.1	47.0	55.7
Prepared foodstuffs; beverages, spirits, vinegar; tobacco and articles thereof .	91.8	157.2	206.7
Preparations of meat, of fish or of crustaceans, molluscs or other aquatic invertebrates . . .	11.1	16.1	71.5
Prepared or preserved fish; caviar and caviar substitutes prepared from fish eggs . .	3.1	4.1	57.8
Beverages, spirits and vinegar .	26.5	45.7	36.3
Mineral products	113.0	200.3	148.9
Mineral fuels, oils, distillation products	102.4	188.6	131.0
Petroleum oils, etc. (excl. crude)	89.0	168.9	110.5
Chemicals and related products	76.2	91.7	125.6
Pharmaceutical products . . .	24.3	37.3	52.4
Medicaments consisting of mixed or unmixed products for therapeutic or prophylactic uses	21.4	33.6	47.0
Plastics, rubber, and articles thereof	39.1	35.0	39.7
Textiles and textile articles .	254.9	253.9	267.7
Cotton	70.9	63.1	55.7
Man-made filaments; strip and the like of man-made textile materials	37.6	38.1	39.5
Knitted or crocheted fabric . .	76.0	83.8	96.7
Iron and steel, other base metals and articles of base metal	47.7	48.6	60.0

Imports—*continued*	2018	2019	2020
Machinery and mechanical appliances; electrical equipment; parts thereof .	145.7	182.6	167.7
Machinery and boilers, etc. . .	59.4	100.2	85.0
Electrical, electronic equipment .	86.3	82.3	82.6
Vehicles, aircraft, vessels and associated transport equipment	111.2	94.1	79.7
Road vehicles	109.5	93.8	79.3
Motor cars and other motor vehicles	55.6	40.6	38.3
Optical, medical apparatus, etc.; clocks and watches; musical instruments; parts thereof	10.1	10.4	52.2
Optical, photographic, cinematographic, measuring, checking, precision, medical or surgical	9.6	10.2	51.9
Instruments and appliances used in medical, surgical, dental or veterinary sciences . . .	2.2	3.2	44.5
Total (incl. others)	1,128.8	1,369.3	1,480.8

Exports	2018	2019	2020
Textiles and textile articles .	448.1	434.4	445.8
Wool and fabrics thereof . .	14.0	23.2	42.0
Wool, not carded or combed .	4.0	21.7	37.2
Cotton	22.5	20.0	21.4
Articles of apparel, accessories, knitted or crocheted . . .	240.9	242.0	214.2
Men's suits, ensembles, jackets, blazers, trousers etc. . . .	27.0	27.5	24.3
Women's suits, and dresses, knitted or crocheted . . .	106.6	81.5	92.3
Men's shirts, knitted or crocheted	27.9	28.7	24.4
T-shirts, singlets and other vests, knitted or crocheted . . .	35.9	52.0	27.7
Jerseys, pullovers, cardigans, waistcoats, etc.	33.4	42.5	33.6
Men's suits, jackets, trousers .	84.2	77.4	99.2
Women's suits, jackets, and dresses	46.4	34.1	31.0
Articles of apparel, accessories, not knitted or crocheted	151.3	128.8	149.5
Pearls, precious or semi-precious stones, precious metals, and articles thereof .	139.2	111.3	267.9
Diamonds, whether or not worked, but not mounted or set . . .	139.1	111.3	267.9
Machinery and mechanical appliances; electrical equipment; parts thereof .	90.5	51.2	45.6
Machinery, mechanical appliances, boilers; parts thereof . . .	42.8	18.0	12.2
Electrical, electronic equipment .	47.7	33.2	33.4
Electrical apparatus	22.2	17.4	22.2
Total (incl. others)	733.1	645.8	818.5

Source: Trade Map-Trade Competitiveness Map, International Trade Centre, marketanalysis.intracen.org.

PRINCIPAL TRADING PARTNERS
(US $ million)

Imports c.i.f.	2018	2019	2020
China, People's Republic . . .	77.1	84.5	125.9
Hong Kong	8.7	15.6	21.4
India	26.2	35.8	48.3
Japan	33.9	25.2	26.4
South Africa	828.6	1,052.9	1,052.2
Taiwan	85.6	83.9	81.8
Zambia	16.1	8.9	11.2
Total (incl. others)	1,128.8	1,369.3	1,480.8

Exports f.o.b.	2018	2019	2020
Belgium	139.1	111.3	267.9
China, People's Republic . . .	2.3	17.7	1.0
Eswatini	6.3	7.0	7.3
Germany	3.8	4.9	8.3
Lebanon	47.1	0.0	0.0
South Africa	256.1	241.7	273.1
USA	265.3	245.8	241.4
Total (incl. others)	733.1	645.8	818.5

Source: Trade Map-Trade Competitiveness Map, International Trade Centre, marketanalysis.intracen.org.

Transport

CIVIL AVIATION
(traffic on scheduled services)

	1997	1998	1999
Kilometres flown (million) . .	0	1	0
Passengers carried ('000) . . .	10	28	1
Passenger-km (million) . . .	3	9	0
Total ton-km (million)	0	1	0

Source: UN, *Statistical Yearbook*.

2008 (domestic and international traffic): Flights 2,769; Arriving passengers 22,206; Departing passengers 19,453.

Tourism

FOREIGN TOURIST ARRIVALS BY COUNTRY OF RESIDENCE

	2017	2018	2019
Botswana	7,513	6,916	8,791
China, People's Republic . . .	7,830	6,099	7,971
Eswatini	3,930	4,897	5,439
Germany	8,913	9,477	8,957
India	4,745	3,614	4,950
Netherlands	9,275	8,840	8,177
South Africa	1,009,856	1,056,433	1,009,982
United Kingdom	5,554	4,880	5,724
USA	8,589	8,732	9,239
Zimbabwe	20,991	20,407	23,228
Total (incl. others)	1,137,166	1,172,648	1,142,381

Source: Lesotho Tourism Development Corporation, Maseru.

Tourism receipts (US $ million, excl. passenger transport): 23 in 2017; 24 in 2018; 22 in 2019 (provisional) (Source: World Tourism Organization).

Communications Media

	2018	2019	2020
Telephones ('000 main lines in use)	8.3	12.9	11.6
Mobile telephone subscriptions ('000)	1,582.1	1,681.6	1,562.6
Broadband subscriptions, fixed ('000)	5.8	4.6	5.1
Broadband subscriptions, mobile ('000)	1,210.9	1,314.7	1,385.5
Internet users (% of population) .	40.8	42.3	n.a.

Source: International Telecommunication Union.

Education

(2018/19 unless otherwise indicated)

			Students		
	Institutions	Teachers	Males	Females	Total
Pre-primary .	2,094	2,711	23,538	23,909	47,447
Primary . . .	1,486	10,193	168,486	161,284	329,770
Secondary:					
general . .	348	5,322	58,423	76,661	135,084
technical and vocational .	25*	198†	1,938†	2,646†	4,584†
Tertiary . . .	15†	1,097‡	8,820†	13,982†	22,802†

* 2013/14.
† 20107/18.
‡ 2015/16.

Source: Ministry of Education, Maseru.

Pupil-teacher ratio (qualified teaching staff, primary education, UNESCO estimate): 32.9 in 2017/18 (Source: UNESCO Institute for Statistics).

Adult literacy rate (UNESCO estimates): 79.4% (males 70.1%; females 88.3%) in 2015 (Source: UNESCO Institute for Statistics).

Directory

The Constitution

The Constitution of the Kingdom of Lesotho, which took effect at independence in October 1966, was suspended in January 1970. A new Constitution was promulgated following the March 1993 general election. Its main provisions, with subsequent amendments, are summarized below:

Lesotho is an hereditary monarchy. The King, who is head of state, has no executive or legislative powers. Executive authority is vested in the Cabinet, which is headed by the Prime Minister, while legislative power is exercised by the 120-member National Assembly, which comprises 80 members elected on a single-member constituency basis and 40 selected by a system of proportional representation. The National Assembly is elected, at intervals of no more than five years, by universal adult suffrage in the context of a multi-party political system. There is also a Senate, comprising 22 traditional chiefs and 11 nominated members. The Prime Minister is the official head of the armed forces.

The Government

HEAD OF STATE

King: HM King LETSIE III (acceded to the throne 7 February 1996).

CABINET
(October 2022)

The Cabinet is a coalition formed by the All Basotho Convention (ABC), the Basotho National Party (BNP), the Democratic Congress (DC), the Movement for Economic Change (MEC) and the Popular Front for Democracy (PFD).

Prime Minister: Dr MOEKETSI MAJORO (ABC).

Deputy Prime Minister, responsible for Parliamentary Affairs: MATHIBELI MOKHOTHU (DC).

Minister of Communications, Science and Technology: TŠOIUNYANE RAPAPA (ABC).

Minister of Home Affairs: MOTLALENTOA LETSOSA (DC).

Minister of Forestry and Land Reclamation: MOTLOHI MALIEHE (ABC).

Minister of Defence and National Security: HALEBONOE SETŠABI (ABC).

Minister of Public Service: LEHLOHONOLO MORAMOTSE (ABC).

Minister of Mining: SERIALONG QOO (DC).

Minister of Agriculture and Food Security: KEKETSO SELLO (ABC).

Minister of Social Development: 'MATEBATSO DOTI (ABC).

Minister of Transport: TŠOEU MOKERETLA (DC).

Minister of Finance: THABO SOPHONIA (ABC).

Minister of Tourism, Environment and Culture: NTLHOI MOTSAMAI (DC).

Minister of Health: SEMANO SEKATLE (ABC).

Minister of Gender, and Youth, Sports and Recreation: LIKELELI TAMPANE (DC).

Minister of Small Business Development, Co-operatives and Marketing: MACHESETSA MOFOMOBE (BNP).

Minister in the Prime Minister's Office: LIKOPO MAHASE (ABC).

Minister of Development and Planning: SELIBE MOCHOBOROANE (MEC).

Minister of Labour and Employment: SELEMO MANGOBE (ABC).

Minister of Foreign Affairs and International Relations: 'MATS'EPO RAMAKOAE (ABC).

Minister of Law and Justice: LEKHETHO RAKUOANE (PFD).

Minister of Education and Training: 'MAMOOKHO PHIRI (DC).

Minister of Public Works: LEBOHANG MONAHENG (BNP).

Minister of Local Government and Chieftainship Affairs: MOSHE LEOMA (ABC).

Minister of Water: KEMISO MOSENENE (ABC).

Minister of Police and Public Safety: LEPOTA SEKOLA (ABC).

Minister of Energy and Meteorology: MOHAPI MOHAPINYANE (ABC).

Minister of Trade and Industry: Dr THABISO MOLAPO (DC).

In addition, there were seven deputy ministers.

MINISTRIES

Office of the Prime Minister: Government Office Complex, Phase 1, Qhobosheaneng, POB 527, Maseru 100; tel. 22320415; internet gov.ls/prime-ministers-office.

Ministry of Agriculture and Food Security: 80 Constitution Rd, POB 24, Maseru 100; tel. 22324651.

Ministry of Communications, Science and Technology: Moposo House, Kingsway Rd, POB 36, Maseru 100; tel. 22310264; e-mail info@communication.gov.ls; internet www.communications.gov.ls.

Ministry of Defence and National Security: Kingsway, opp. National Library, Private Bag A166, Maseru 100; tel. 22326651.

Ministry of Development and Planning: POB 24, Maseru 100; tel. 22311100; e-mail info.planning@gov.ls; internet www.planning.gov.ls.

Ministry of Education and Training: Constitution Rd, POB 47, Maseru 100; tel. 22313045; e-mail info@education.org.ls; internet education.org.ls.

Ministry of Energy and Meteorology: POB 772, Maseru 100; tel. 22311742.

Ministry of Finance: Finance House, Kingsway Rd, POB 395, Maseru 100; tel. 22219900; internet www.finance.gov.ls.

Ministry of Foreign Affairs and International Relations: Qhobosheaneng Govt Complex, Griffith Hill Rd, POB 1387, Maseru 100; tel. 22311150; internet www.foreign.gov.ls/home.

Ministry of Forestry and Land Reclamation: Industrial Site, opp. Lesotho Standard Bank, cnr Raboshabane and Senate Rds, POB 92, Maseru 100; tel. 22323600; e-mail mfrsc.mail@gov.ls; internet www.forestry.gov.ls.

Ministry of Gender, and Youth, Sports and Recreation: POB 729, Maseru 100; tel. 22311006; internet gender.gov.ls.

Ministry of Health: Constitution Rd, POB 1095, Maseru 100; tel. 22312836; e-mail info.health@gov.ls; internet health.gov.ls.

Ministry of Home Affairs: cnr Moshoeshoe and Lerotholi Rds, POB 174, Maseru 100; tel. 22215900; e-mail info.homeaffairs@gov.ls; internet www.homeaffairs.gov.ls.

Ministry of Labour and Employment: LNDC, Development House, 7th and 8th Floors, Blk D, Constitutional Rd, Private Bag A116, Maseru 100; tel. 22323565; e-mail info.ministryoflabourandemployment@yahoo.com; internet www.labour.gov.ls.

Ministry of Law and Justice: POB 33, Maseru 100; tel. 22315983.

Ministry of Local Government and Chieftainship Affairs: POB 686, Maseru 100; tel. 22325331.

Ministry of Mining: cnr Constitution and Parliament Rds, POB 750, Maseru 100; tel. 22311447; internet www.mining.gov.ls.

Ministry of Police and Public Safety: Private Bag A166, Maseru 100; tel. 22312222.

Ministry of Public Service: POB 228, Maseru 100; tel. 22311130; e-mail publicservice@gov.ls; internet www.mps.gov.ls.

Ministry of Public Works and Transport: Moshoeshoe Rd, Industrial Area, POB 20, Maseru 100; tel. 22310695; e-mail cio@mopwt.gov.ls; internet www.mopwt.gov.ls.

Ministry of Small Business Development, Co-operatives and Marketing: POB 747, Maseru 100; tel. 22325272.

Ministry of Social Development: Private Bag A222, Maseru 100; tel. 22226004.

Ministry of Tourism, Environment and Culture: Post Office Bldg, 6th and 7th Floors, Kingsway St, POB 52, Maseru 100; tel. 22313034; e-mail info@tourism.gov.ls; internet www.tourism.gov.ls.

Ministry of Trade and Industry: POB 747, Maseru 100; tel. 22325272.

Ministry of Water: POB 2222, Maseru 100; tel. 22320127; e-mail info@water.gov.ls; internet www.water.org.ls.

Legislature

NATIONAL ASSEMBLY

National Assembly: POB 190, Maseru; tel. 22323035; internet nationalassembly.parliament.ls.

Speaker: SEPHIRI MOTANYANE.

General Election, 7 October 2022

Party	Constitu-ency seats	Compen-satory seats*	Total seats
Revolution for Prosperity . .	56	—	56
Democratic Congress . . .	18	11	29
All Basotho Convention . .	—	8	8
Basotho Action Party . .	—	6	6
Alliance of Democrats . .	2	3	5
Movement for Economic Change	1	3	4
Lesotho Congress for Democracy	—	3	3
Socialist Revolutionaries . .	1	1	2
Basotho Covenant Movement .	—	1	1
Basotho National Party . .	—	1	1
HOPE	—	1	1
Mpulule Political Summit . .	—	1	1
National Independent Party .	1	—	1
Popular Front for Democracy .	—	1	1
Total	**79†**	**40**	**119**

* Allocated by proportional representation.
† The results in one constituency were not immediately declared.

SENATE

Senate: POB 553, Maseru 100; tel. 22315338; internet senate.parliament.ls.

President: MAMONAHENG MOKITIMI.

The Senate is an advisory chamber, comprising 22 traditional chiefs and 11 members appointed by the monarch.

Election Commission

Independent Electoral Commission (IEC): MGC Park, 2nd and 3rd Floors, cnr Pope John Paul II Rd and Mpilo Blvd, Kingsway, POB 12698, Maseru 100; tel. 22314991; internet www.iec.org.ls; f. 1997 as successor to the Constituency Delimitation Commission; Chair. MPHASA MOKHOCHANE.

Political Organizations

In 2022 a total of 65 parties were registered by the Independent Electoral Commission.

All Basotho Convention (ABC): Rm 147, Met Cash Bldg, Kingsway, POB 11967, Maseru 100; tel. 22310706; e-mail abc4lesotho@gmail.com; internet www.abc.org.ls; f. 2006 by fmr mems of the Lesotho Congress for Democracy; Leader NKAKU KABI; Sec.-Gen. LEBOHANG HLAELE.

Alliance of Democrats: Maseru; internet www.ad.org.ls; f. 2016; Leader MONYANE MOLELEKI; Sec.-Gen. (vacant).

Basotho Action Party (BAP): Qoatsaneng, Maseru 100; tel. 63872752; e-mail info@bap.org.ls; internet bap.org.ls; f. 2021 as a breakaway faction of the All Basotho Convention; Leader NQOSA MAHAO; Sec.-Gen. LEBOHANG THOTANYANA.

Basotho National Party (BNP): BNP Centre, POB 124, Maseru 100; f. 1958; Leader MACHESETSA MOFOMOBE; Sec.-Gen. (vacant).

Basotho Patriotic Party (BPP): Maseru; f. 2021; Leader TEFO MAPESELA.

Democratic Congress: POB 12002, Maseru 100; tel. 22322944; e-mail ralehlathebonang@yahoo.com; internet fb.com/democraticcongress; f. 2012; Leader MATHIBELI MOKHOTHU; Sec.-Gen. TŠITSO CHEBA.

HOPE: Maseru; f. 2020; Leader ʻMACHABANA LEMPHANE-LETSIE; Sec.-Gen. RETŠELISITSOE LESANE.

Lesotho Congress for Democracy (LCD): 9863–9867, Maseru 100; tel. 22327912; f. 1997; Leader MOTHETJOA METSING; Sec.-Gen. TEBOHO SEKATA.

Lesotho People's Congress (LPC): f. 2001 following split in the LCD; Leader MABUSETSA MAKHARILELE; Sec.-Gen. BOKANG RAMATŠELLA.

Maremakou Freedom Party (MFP): POB 0443, Maseru 105; tel. 22315804; f. 1962 following merger between the Marema Tlou Party and Basutoland Freedom Party; Leader TLHORISO LEKATSA.

Movement for Economic Change (MEC): Rm 301, Carlton Center, 3rd Floor, Maseru; tel. 22325109; internet fb.com/MovementforEconomicChange; f. 2017; Leader SELIBE MOCHOBOROANE.

National Independent Party (NIP): Maseru; f. 1984; Pres. KIMETSO MATHABA.

Popular Front for Democracy (PFD): Maseru; f. 1991; left-wing; Leader LEKHETHO RAKUOANE.

Progressive Democrats: Maseru; f. 2014; Leader MOPHATO MONYAKE.

Reformed Congress of Lesotho (RCL): Maseru; Leader KEKTSO RANTŠO; Sec.-Gen. (vacant).

Revolution for Prosperity (RFP): cnr Kingsway and Maluti Rds, Maseru W, Maseru 100; tel. 56896378; e-mail info@rfp.org.ls; internet rfp.org.ls; f. 2022; Leader SAM MATEKANE.

Socialist Revolutionaries (SR) (Kanana Ea Basotho): Maseru; tel. 22320890; e-mail wesvant@gmail.com; internet www.srlesotho.co.za; f. 2017; Leader TEBOHO MOJAPELA.

United for Change (UFC): Maseru; f. 2020; registered in 2021; Chair. ʻMALINEO LETŠENG; Leader ʻMALICHABA LEKHOABA; Sec.-Gen. LISEBO MOSITSI.

Diplomatic Representation

EMBASSIES AND HIGH COMMISSIONS IN LESOTHO

China, People's Republic: United Nations Rd, POB 380, Maseru 100; tel. 22316521; e-mail chinaemb_ls@mfa.gov.cn; internet ls.china-embassy.gov.cn; Ambassador LEI KEZHONG.

Libya: 173 Tona-Kholo Rd, Maseru West, POB 432, Maseru 100; tel. 22320148; Chargé d'affaires a.i. ABDEL-HAFIZ MUHAMMAD MESBAH JABER.

South Africa: cnr Kingsway and Old School Rd, Private Bag A266, Maseru 100; tel. 22225800; e-mail madibam@dirco.gov.za; High Commissioner CONSTANCE SEOPOSENGWE.

United Kingdom: Maseru; internet gov.uk/world/organisations/british-high-commission-maseru; High Commissioner HARRY MAC-DONALD (designate).

USA: 254 Kingsway Ave, POB 333, Maseru 100; tel. 22312666; e-mail infomaseru@state.gov; internet ls.usembassy.gov; Ambassador MARIA BREWER.

Judicial System

The Constitution provides for an independent judicial system, consisting of a Court of Appeal, a High Court, Magistrates' Courts, and traditional courts that exist predominantly in rural areas. Apart from the Magistrates' Courts, there are also Judicial Commissioners' Courts and Central and Local Courts that are subordinate to the Court of Appeal and the High Court. Their jurisdiction is limited to civil and criminal appeals.

Court of Appeal: POB 90, Maseru; tel. 22312188; Pres. Dr KANANELO MOSITO.

High Court: POB 90, Maseru; tel. 22312188; the High Court is a superior court of record, and in addition to any other jurisdiction conferred by statute it is vested with unlimited original jurisdiction to determine any civil or criminal matter; it also has appellate jurisdiction to hear appeals and reviews from the subordinate courts; appeals may be made to the Court of Appeal; Chief Justice SAKOANE PETER SAKOANE.

Magistrates' Courts: each of the 10 districts possesses subordinate courts, presided over by magistrates; Chief Magistrates 'MATANKISO NTHUNYA (Central region), 'MAKHOTSO KABI (Northern region; acting), MANYATHELA KOLOBE (Southern region).

Attorney-General: POB 402, Maseru 100; tel. 22322683RAPELANG MOTSIELOA.

Religion

CHRISTIANITY

African Federal Church Council (AFCC): POB 70, Peka 340; f. 1927; co-ordinating org. for 48 African independent churches.

Christian Council of Lesotho (CCL): POB 547, Maseru 100; tel. 22313639; e-mail generalsecretary@ccl.org.ls; internet www.ccl.org.ls; f. 1965; ecumenical fellowship of 6 churches/denominations; Chair. Archbishop TLALI LEROTHOL.

The Anglican Communion

Anglicans in Lesotho are adherents of the Anglican Church of Southern Africa (formerly the Church of the Province of Southern Africa). The Primate is the Archbishop of Cape Town, South Africa. Lesotho forms a single diocese.

Bishop of Lesotho: Rev. VICENTIA KGABE, 70 Lancers Rd, Maseru W, POB 87, Maseru 100; tel. 22311974; e-mail dioceselesotho@ecoweb.co.ls; internet lesotho.tacosa.org.

The Roman Catholic Church

Lesotho comprises one archdiocese and three dioceses.

Lesotho Catholic Bishops' Conference: LCBC Bldg, Catedral Area, Opp. Captain Dorego Main North 1, POB 200, Maseru 100; tel. 22310294; internet www.lcbc.org.ls; f. 1972; Pres. Most Rev. GERARD TLALI LEROTHOLI (Archbishop of Maseru).

Archbishop of Maseru: Most Rev. GERARD TLALI LEROTHOLI, Archbishop's House, 19 Orpen Rd, POB 267, Maseru 100; tel. 22312565.

Other Christian Churches

African Methodist Episcopal Church: POB 223, Maseru 100; tel. 22311801; internet www.ame-church.com; f. 1903; Presiding Prelate Rt Rev. STAFFORD J. N. WICKER.

Lesotho Evangelical Church: Casalis House, Cathedral Area, Phamola Rd, POB 260, Maseru 100; tel. 22313942; e-mail lecmaseru@ilesotho.com; internet www.lecsakereke.wordpress.com; f. 1833; independent since 1964; Moderator Rev. MOJAKI BERNARD KOMETSI; Exec. Sec. Rev. NELSON POSHOLI.

BAHÁ'Í FAITH

National Spiritual Assembly of the Bahá'ís of Lesotho: POB 508, Maseru 100; tel. 22312346; e-mail bahai.lesotho@gmail.com; f. 1953.

The Press (Print and Online)

Lesotho does not have a daily newspaper.

Informative: Suite 03, Metcash Complex, Kingsway Rd, Maseru; tel. 22327228; e-mail editor@informativenews.co.ls; internet informativenews.co.ls; weekly; owned by BAM Media; Editor LINTLE TSITA.

Lesotho Times: 220A Lower Thetsane, POB 9098, Maseru; tel. 22315335; e-mail editor@lestimes.co.ls; internet lestimes.com; owned by Africa Media Holdings; Publr BASILDON PETA; Editor HERBERT MOYO.

Moeletsi oa Basotho: Mazenod, POB 18, Maseru, 160; tel. 28350466; e-mail moeletsioabasotho@gmail.com; internet fb.com/mooabasotho; f. 1933; weekly; Sesotho; publ. by the Roman Catholic Church; Editor MOKOAILANE MOKOAILANE.

Mosotho: Florida Industrial Park, Florida Industrial Park, Maseru; tel. 22325494; e-mail editor@mosotho.co.ls; internet mosotho.co.ls; weekly; Sesotho and other local languages.

The Post: cnr Lepoqo and Caledon Sts, Maseru; tel. 63258013; e-mail editor@thepost.co.ls; internet www.thepost.co.ls; f. 2014; CEO ABEL CHAPATARONGO; Editor-in-Chief SHAKEMAN MUGARI.

Public Eye: House 14A3, cnr Princess Margaret and Mabile Rds, Old Europa, POB 14129, Maseru 100; tel. 22321414; e-mail editor@publiceyenews.com; internet www.publiceyenews.com; f. 1997; weekly; English and Sesotho; publ. by Voice Multimedia.

The Reporter: House 7 STC Race Course, Maseru; tel. (266) 22326006; e-mail adverts@thereporter.co.ls; internet www.thereporter.co.ls; f. 2019; weekly (print); daily (online); English.

Sunday Express: 5C Happy Villa, Maseru; tel. 22315356; e-mail webmaster.lestimes@gmail.com; internet sundayexpress.co.ls; f. 2006; weekly; English.

PERIODICALS

Achiever: Metcash Complex, Kingsway Rd, POB 1803, Maseru 100; tel. 22327228; e-mail editor@achievermagazine.co.ls; internet fb.com/AchieverMagazineLesotho; f. 2012; quarterly; education and entertainment; owned by BAM Media; Gen. Man. LEBOHANG THAANYANE.

Finite: Suite No. 3, Metcash Complex, Kingsway Rd, Maseru; tel. 22327228; internet finitemagazine.co.ls; f. 2009; monthly; owned by BAM Media.

NEWS AGENCY

Lesotho News Agency (LENA): Lerotholi St, POB 36, Maseru 100; tel. 22325317; e-mail lesothonewsagency@gmail.com; internet www.lena.org.ls; f. 1985; Editor and Acting Dir MOROA MOPELI; Editor MOROA MOPELI, LITEBOHO MAHULA.

Publishers

Macmillan Boleswa Publishers Lesotho (Pty) Ltd: 30 Oblate House, Kingsway St, Maseru 100; tel. 22317340; internet www.macmillanenglish.com/ls; Man. Dir PAUL MOROLONG.

Pearson Lesotho: Christie House, 1st Floor, Orpen Rd, Old Europa, POB 1174, Maseru 100; tel. 22314254; e-mail teboho.khalieli@pearson.com; internet www.pearson.com/africa; Man. TEBOHO KHALIELI.

GOVERNMENT PUBLISHING HOUSE

Government Printer: POB 268, Maseru; tel. 22313023; e-mail gpsec@printer.gov.ls; Govt Printer MOKHACHANE ALOYSIUS POSHOLI (acting).

Broadcasting and Communications

TELECOMMUNICATIONS

In 2022 there were two providers of mobile telephone services and one provider of fixed-line telephone services.

Lesotho Communications Authority (LCA): 30 Princess Margaret Rd, Old Europa, Maseru 100; tel. 22224300; e-mail info@lca.org.ls; internet www.lca.org.ls; f. 2000; fmrly Lesotho Telecommunications Authority (LTA); regulates telecommunications, broadcasting and postal services; Chair. (vacant); CEO NIZAM GOOLAM (acting).

Econet Telecom Lesotho (ETL): Kingsway Rd, POB 1037, Maseru 100; tel. 22211000; e-mail escalations@etl.co.ls; internet www.etl.co.ls; 70% holding acquired by the Econet Wireless Group in 2008; 30% state-owned; fixed-line and mobile services; Chair. STRIVE MASIYIWA; CEO DENNIS PLAATJIES.

Vodacom Lesotho (Pty) Ltd: 585 Mabile Rd, POB 7387, Maseru 100; tel. 52212201; e-mail customercare@vodacom.co.ls; internet www.vodacom.co.ls; f. 1996; 80% owned by Vodacom Group (South Africa), 20% owned by Sekha-Metsi Enterprises (Lesotho); mobile telecommunications provider; Man. Dir MOHALE RALEBITSO.

BROADCASTING

Radio

Harvest FM: Rm 312, Carlton Centre Bldg, 3rd Floor, POB 442, Maseru 100; tel. 22313858; e-mail mlekhoaba@harvestfm.co.ls; internet www.harvestfm.co.ls; f. 2003; operated by HCJB World Radio (USA); current affairs and Christian programmes; Man. Dir 'MALICHABA MOSHOESHOE-LEKHOABA.

MoAfrika FM: Carlton Centre, Kingsway St, Maseru 100; tel. 22321956; internet moafrikafmradio.co.ls; f. 1999; Sesotho, Xhosa and Mandarin; news and entertainment; Man. and Editor-in-Chief Prof. SEBONONOLA R. K. RAMAINOANE.

People's Choice Radio (PC FM): Avani Lesotho Hotel & Casino, Hilton Rd, POB 8800, Maseru 100; tel. 22322122; e-mail mkhauta@pcfm.co.ls; internet www.pcfm.co.ls; f. 1996; news and entertainment; Station Man. KHAUTA MPEQA.

Radio Lesotho: Lerotholi St, opp. Royal Palace, POB 552, Maseru 100; tel. 22316429; e-mail radiolesotho@gmail.com; internet www.lnbs.org.ls; f. 1964; state-owned; part of Lesotho Nat. Broadcasting Services; Sesotho and English.

Ts'enolo FM: Patlalla Lower Thamae, opp. Thamae Shopping Center, Maseru 100; tel. 22335344; e-mail retsmaloi@gmail.com; internet www.tsenolofm.co.ls; f. 2012; owned by Tse'enolo Media Services; Station Man. MSHENGU TSHABALALA.

Television

Lesotho Television (LTV): Lesotho News Agency Complex, Lerotholi St, opp. Royal Palace, POB 552, Maseru 100; tel. 22323808; e-mail mfalatsa@yahoo.com; internet www.lnbs.org.ls; f. 1988 in association with M-Net, South Africa; state-owned; part of Lesotho Nat. Broadcasting Services; Sesotho and English.

Finance

BANKING

Central Bank

Central Bank of Lesotho: cnr Airport and Moshoeshoe Rds, POB 1184, Maseru 100; tel. 22314281; e-mail info@centralbank.org.ls; internet www.centralbank.org.ls; f. 1978 as the Lesotho Monetary Authority; present name adopted in 1982; bank of issue; Gov. and Chair. Dr MALUKE LETETE.

Commercial Banks

In 2022 there were four commercial banks in Lesotho.

First National Bank Lesotho: cnr Kingsway St and Parliament Rd, POB 11902, Maseru 100; tel. 22241000; internet www.fnb.co.ls; f. 2004; subsidiary of FNB, division of FirstRand Bank Limited; Chair. IAN LEYENAAR; CEO DELAKAZI MOKEBE.

Lesotho PostBank (LPB): Oblate House, Kingsway St, Private Bag A121, Maseru 100; tel. 22317842; e-mail csc_dept@lpb.co.ls; internet www.lpb.co.ls; f. 2004; state-owned; Chair. LEFA MOKOTJO; Man. Dir MOLEFI LEQHAOE.

Nedbank Lesotho Ltd: 115–117 Griffith Hill, Kingsway St, POB 1001, Maseru 100; tel. 22282100; internet www.nedbank.co.ls; f. 1997; fmrly Standard Chartered Bank Lesotho Ltd; 100% owned by Nedbank Ltd (South Africa); Acting Group Chair. MPHO MAKWANA; Man. Dir NKAU MATETE.

Standard Lesotho Bank: LHDA, Tower Bldg, Kingsway St, Kingsway Town Centre, POB 1053, Maseru 100; tel. 22212000; e-mail lesothoccc@stanbic.com; internet www.standardlesothobank.co.ls; f. 2006 following merger between Lesotho Bank (1999) Ltd (f. 1972) and Standard Bank Lesotho Ltd (fmrly Stanbic Bank Lesotho Ltd); owned by Standard Bank Group (South Africa); CEO ANTON NICOLAISEN.

STOCK EXCHANGE

Maseru Securities Market: Central Bank of Lesotho Bldg, cnr Airport and Moshoeshoe Rds, Maseru; tel. 22232101; internet www.msm.org.ls; f. 2014.

INSURANCE

Alliance Insurance Co Ltd: Alliance House, 4 Bowker Rd, POB 01118, Maseru West 105; tel. 22215600; e-mail info@alliance.co.ls; internet www.alliance.co.ls; f. 1993; life and short-term insurance; CEO ANGUS YEATS.

Lesotho National General Insurance Co Ltd (LNIG): LNIC Hse Constitution Rd, Kingsway, Private Bag A65, Maseru 100; tel. 22313031; e-mail info@lngic.com; internet lnig.co.ls; f. 1976; 60% owned by Regent Insurance Co Ltd (South Africa), 20% state-owned, 20% owned by Molepe Investment Holdings (Pty) Ltd; part-privatized in 1995; incorporating subsidiaries specializing in life and short-term insurance; Chair. Dr TIMOTHY THAHANE; Man. Dir R. J. LETSOELA.

Liberty Life Lesotho: Maseru Mall, Unit 39, Maseru; tel. 22212719; e-mail info@libertyhealthblue.com; internet www.liberty.co.ls; f. 2015; life insurance Co; subsidiary of Liberty Holdings Ltd (Standard Bank Group, South Africa); Chair. Dr KELELLO LEROTHOLI; Man. Dir MAKHAKHE MALIEHE.

Metropolitan Lesotho Ltd: Metropolitan Bldg, Kingsway St, POB 645, Maseru; tel. 22222300; e-mail info@metropolitan.co.ls; internet www.metropolitan.co.ls; f. 2003; subsidiary of Metropolitan Holdings Ltd, South Africa; Man. Dir MAMELLO PHOMANE.

Trade and Industry

GOVERNMENT AGENCY

Lesotho Revenue Authority (LRA): Govt Office Complex, Finance House Bldg, Ground Floor, Kingsway St, POB 1085, Maseru; tel. 22313796; e-mail info@lra.org.ls; internet www.lra.org.ls; f. 2003; Chair. ROBERT LIKHANG; Commr-Gen. THABO KHASIPE.

DEVELOPMENT ORGANIZATIONS

Basotho Enterprises Development Corpn (BEDCO): BEDCO Sebaboleng Estate, POB 1216, Maseru; tel. 22216100; e-mail business@bedco.org.ls; internet www.bedco.org.ls; f. 1980; promotes and assists in the establishment and devt of Basotho-owned enterprises; CEO (vacant).

Lesotho Council of Non-Governmental Organizations (LCN): House 544, Hoohlo Ext., Private Bag A445, Maseru 100; tel. 22317205; e-mail admin@lcn.org.ls; internet www.lcn.org.ls; f. 1990; promotes sustainable management of natural resources, socioeconomic devt and social justice; Exec. Dir SEABATA MOTSAMAI.

Lesotho Highlands Development Authority (LHDA): LHDA Tower Bldg, 3rd Floor, Kingsway St, POB 7332, Maseru 100; tel. 22311280; e-mail lhwp@lhda.org.ls; internet www.lhda.org.ls; f. 1986 to implement the Lesotho Highlands Water Project (LHWP), being undertaken jtly with South Africa; Chief Exec. TENTE TENTE.

Lesotho National Dairy Board (LNDB): 89 Constitution Rd, Maseru; e-mail info@lndb.org.ls; f. 1991; prescribes standards of production, storage, packaging, processing and distribution of dairy products; CEO ABIEL MASHALE.

Lesotho National Development Corpn (LNDC): Development House, Blk A, Kingsway St, Private Bag A96, Maseru 100; tel. 22312012; e-mail info@lndc.org.ls; internet www.lndc.org.ls; f. 1967; state-owned; interests in manufacturing, mining, food processing and leisure; Interim CEO MOLISE RAMAILI.

National Reforms Authority (NRA): LNDC, Blk B, Level 7, Maseru; tel. 57836954; e-mail info@nra.org.ls; internet www.nra.org.ls; f. 2019 to oversee the implementation of reforms backed by the Southern African Development Community (SADC); Chair. Chief PELELE LETSOELA; CEO MAFIROANE MOTANYANE.

Rural Self-Help Development Association (RSDA): POB 0523, Maseru West 105; tel. 22311279; e-mail rsda@rsda.org.ls; internet www.rsdalesotho.com; f. 1991; Man. Dir 'MAMPHO THULO.

CHAMBERS OF COMMERCE

Lesotho Chamber of Commerce and Industry: cnr Orpen and Princess Margaret Rds, POB 79, Maseru 100; tel. 22311066; e-mail lcci@leo.co.ls; internet www.lcci.org.ls; f. 1976; Pres. NTAOTE SEBOKA.

EMPLOYERS' ORGANIZATIONS

Association of Lesotho Employers and Business: 18 Bowker Rd, POB 1509, Maseru 100; tel. 22315736; e-mail alemp@leo.co.ls; internet www.aleb.org.ls; f. 1961; represents mems in industrial relations and on govt bodies, and advises the Govt on employers' concerns; CEO LINDIWE SEPHOMOLO.

UTILITIES

Lesotho Electricity and Water Authority (LEWA): Moposo House, 7th Floor, Kingsway, Private Bag A315, Maseru; tel. 22312479; e-mail secretary@lewa.org.ls; internet www.lewa.org.ls; f. 2004 as Lesotho Electricity Authority; present name adopted in 2013; Chair. C. RELEBOHILE MOSITO; Chief Exec. Prof. MOTLATSI RAMAFOLE.

Lesotho Electricity Co (LEC): 53 Moshoeshoe Rd, Industrial Area, POB 423, Maseru 100; tel. 22312236; e-mail info@lec.co.ls; internet www.lec.co.ls; f. 1969; state-owned; Chair. LEJONE MPOT-JOANE; Man. Dir MOHATO SELEKE.

Water and Sewerage Co (WASCO): POB 426, Maseru 100; tel. 22262000; e-mail info@wasco.co.ls; internet www.wasco.co.ls; f. 2010 to replace Lesotho Water and Sewerage Authority; Chair. CHABELI RAMOLISE; Chief Exec. THELEJANE THELEJANE (acting).

MAJOR COMPANIES

Engen Lesotho: Maseru; Man. Dir TEBOGO MOSEHLA.

Lesotho Flour Mills: 44 Lioli Rd Industrial Area, Maseru; tel. 22313498; e-mail inquiries@lfm.co.ls; internet fb.com/lesothoflour .mill; f. 1979; mfrs of maize and wheat products and animal feed; incorporates Lesotho Maize Mills, Lesotho Farm Feed Mills, and Lesotho Sugar Packers; privatized in 1998; Gen. Man. CHARLES WILLIAMS.

Lesotho Milling Co (Pty) Ltd: Seretse Khama Rd, POB 39, Maputsoe 350; tel. 22430622; e-mail info@lesco.co.za; internet lesco.co.za; f. 1971; milling and export of maize; Man. Dir GRAHAM GATCKE.

Lesotho Stone Enterprises (Pty) Ltd: BNP Centre, Suite 10, POB 15518, Maseru; tel. 22327485; e-mail lesothosandstone@gmail.com; internet www.lesothostone.co.za; produces natural sandstone products.

Lets'eng Diamonds: Lets'eng Diamonds House, cnr Kingsway and Old School Rds, Maseru 100; tel. 22221800; e-mail communications@ letseng.co.ls; internet www.letsengdiamonds.co.ls; f. 1995; 70% owned by Gem Diamonds Ltd; 30% owned by Lesotho Govt; CEO KELEBONE LEISANYANE.

Mofaya Lesotho: K-Ash Bldg, Thetsane Industrial Area, Maseru; tel. 62304471; internet fb.com/Mofaya-Lesotho-938135779579959; food and beverages co.

TRADE UNIONS

Lesotho National Farmers Union (LENAFU): Moshoeshoe II, cnr Airport and Majara Rds, nr Department of Livestock, POB 11911, Maseru 100; tel. 22327009; e-mail info@lenafu.co.ls; internet lenafu .org.ls; f. 2008; Pres. MOHLALEFI MOTEANE; CEO MOTSAU KHUELE.

Lesotho Teachers' Trade Union (LTTU): POB 0509, Maseru West 105; tel. 22322774; e-mail lttu@leo.co.ls; Gen. Sec. VUYANI TYHALI.

Transport

RAILWAYS

Lesotho is linked with the South African railway system by a short line (2.6 km in length) from Maseru to Marseilles, on the Bloemfontein–Bethlehem main line.

ROADS

Roads Directorate: cnr Senate and Lepoqo Rds, Industrial Area, POB 194, Maseru 100; tel. 22229000; e-mail info@rd.org.ls; internet www.rd.org.ls; responsible for construction, upgrading, rehabilitation and maintenance of roads and bridges in Lesotho; Chair. MOTHABATHE HLALELE; Dir-Gen. SEBOKA THAMAE.

Road Fund: cnr Moshoeshoe and Senate Rds, Industrial Area, POB 14644, Maseru 100; tel. 22216000; e-mail info@roadfund.org.ls; internet www.roadfund.org.ls; f. 1995; CEO NKEKELETSE MAKARA.

CIVIL AVIATION

King Moshoeshoe I International Airport is at Thota-Moli, some 20 km from Maseru. International services between Maseru and Johannesburg, South Africa, are operated by South African Airways, while MGC Aviation provides internal services.

Department of Civil Aviation: POB 629, Maseru 100; tel. 22312499; internet www.civilair.org.ls; Dir KETSO Z. MOEKETSI.

MGC Aviation: MGC Park, cnr Mpilo Blvd, Pope John Paul II Rd, Maseru; tel. 52216200; e-mail info@mgc.co.ls; internet www.mgc.co .ls; f. 2009; provides business and commercial aviation services.

Tourism

Lesotho Council of Tourism (LCT): Maseru; f. 2009; re-launched in 2022; Chair. MAKHETHA MOTŠOARI.

Lesotho Tourism Development Corpn (LTDC): cnr Linare and Parliament Rds, POB 1378, Maseru 100; tel. 22312238; e-mail touristinfo@ltdc.org.ls; internet visitlesotho.travel; f. 2000; successor to the Lesotho Tourist Board; CEO MPAIPHELE D. MAQUTU.

Defence

Military service is voluntary. As assessed at November 2021, the Lesotho Defence Force (LDF) comprised an estimated 2,000 men, including an air wing of 110 men. In 2021 a total of 71 troops were stationed abroad.

Defence Budget: M519m. in 2021.

Commander of the Lesotho Defence Force: Lt-Gen. MOJALEFA EXAVERY LETSOELA.

Education

All primary education is available free of charge, and is provided mainly by the three main Christian missions (Lesotho Evangelical, Roman Catholic and Anglican), under the direction of the Ministry of Education and Training. Education at primary schools is officially compulsory for seven years between six and 13 years of age. Secondary education, beginning at the age of 13, lasts for up to five years, comprising a first cycle of three years and a second of two years. According to estimates by the United Nations Educational, Scientific and Cultural Organization (UNESCO), in 2015/16 enrolment at pre-primary institutions included 27% of children (27% of boys; 28% of girls) in the appropriate age-group, while total enrolment at primary schools in 2016/17 included 98% of children (97% of boys; 98% of girls). In 2015/16 enrolment at secondary schools included 41% of children (33% of boys; 50% of girls) in the relevant age-group. In 2021/22 the Ministry of Education and Training was allocated M2,484.3m., representing 19.8% of total projected government recurrent expenditure.

Bibliography

Aerni-Flessner, J. *Dreams for Lesotho: Independence, Foreign Assistance, and Development*. Notre Dame, IN, University of Notre Dame Press, 2018.

Ashton, H. *The Basuto: A Social Study of Traditional and Modern Lesotho, Vol. 3*. Abingdon, Routledge, 2018

Chigara, B. *Southern African Development Community Land Issues Volume I: Towards a New Sustainable Land Relations Policy*. Abingdon, Routledge, 2011.

Crush, J. *Migration, Remittances and 'Development' in Lesotho*. Cape Town, Southern African Migration Programme, 2010.

Eldredge, E. A. *Power in Colonial Africa: Conflict and Discourse in Lesotho*. Madison, WI, University of Wisconsin Press, 2007.

Ferguson, J. (Ed.). *The Anti-Politics Machine: Development, Depoliticization and Bureaucratic State Power in Lesotho*. Cambridge, Cambridge University Press; Cape Town, David Philip, 1990.

Gill, S. J. *A Short History of Lesotho, From the Late Stone Age Until the 1993 Elections*. Morija, Morija Museum and Archives, 1993.

Kabemba, C. (Ed.), *et al. From Military Rule to Multiparty Democracy: Political Reforms and Challenges in Lesotho*. Johannesburg, Electoral Institute of Southern Africa (EISA), 2003.

Kenworthy, N. *Mistreated: The Political Consequences of the Fight Against AIDS in Lesotho*. Nashville, TN, Vanderbilt University Press, 2017.

Kimyaro, S. S. (Ed.), et al. *Turning a Crisis into an Opportunity: Strategies for Scaling up the National Response to the HIV/AIDS Pandemic in Lesotho*. New York, New Rochelle, 2004.

Lundahl, M., McCarthy, C., and Petersson, L. *In the Shadow of South Africa: Lesotho's Economic Future*. Aldershot, Ashgate, 2003.

Machobane, L. B. B. J. *Government and Change in Lesotho, 1800–1966: A Study of Political Institutions*. Maseru, Macmillan Lesotho, 1990.

The King's Knights: Military Governance in the Kingdom of Lesotho, 1986–1993. Roma, Institute of Southern African Studies, National University of Lesotho, 2001.

Makoa, F. K. *Elections, Election Outcomes and Electoral Politics in Lesotho*. Pretoria, Africa Institute of South Africa, 2002.

Beyond the Electoral Triumphalism: Reflections on Lesotho's Coalition Government and Challenges. Maseru, Transformation Resource Centre, 2012.

Maloka, E. T. *Basotho and the Mines: A Social History of Labour Migrancy in Lesotho and South Africa, c. 1890–1940*. Dakar, Council for the Development of Social Science Research in Africa, 2004.

Maqutu, W. C. M. *Democracy and Constitutionalism in Lesotho in 2012*. Maseru, Transformation Resource Centre, 2012.

Mphanya, N. *A Brief History of the Basutoland Congress Party: Lekhotla la Mahatammoho, 1952–2002*. Morija, 2004.

Murray, C. *Families Divided: The Impact of Migrant Labour in Lesotho*. Cambridge, Cambridge University Press, 2009.

Olaleye, W. *Democratic Consolidation and Political Parties in Lesotho*. Johannesburg, Electoral Institute of Southern Africa (EISA), 2004.

Pule, N. W., and Thabane, M. (Eds). *Essays on Aspects of the Political Economy of Lesotho, 1500–2000*. Roma, Department of History, National University of Lesotho, 2002.

Rosenberg, S., Weisfelder, R. F., and Frisbie-Fulton, M. *Historical Dictionary of Lesotho*. 2nd edn. Lanham, MD, Scarecrow Press, 2013.

Rwelamira, M. *Refugees in a Chess Game: Reflections on Botswana, Lesotho and Swaziland Refugee Policies*. Trenton, NJ, Red Sea Press, 1990.

Sanders, P. *'Throwing Down White Man': Cape Rule and Misrule in Colonial Lesotho, 1871-1884*. Pontypool, Merlin Press, 2011.

Southall, R., and Petlane, T. (Eds). *Democratisation and Demilitarisation in Lesotho: The General Election of 1993 and its Aftermath*. Pretoria, Africa Institution of South Africa, 1996.

LIBERIA

Physical and Social Geography

CHRISTOPHER CLAPHAM

The Republic of Liberia was founded in 1847 by freed black slaves from the USA who were resettled from 1821 onwards along the western Guinea coast between Cape Mount and Cape Palmas. Liberia occupies an area of 97,754 sq km (37,743 sq miles) between Sierra Leone to the west, the Republic of Guinea to the north and Côte d'Ivoire to the east.

PHYSICAL FEATURES AND POPULATION

An even coastline of 570 km, characterized by powerful surf, rocky cliffs and lagoons, makes access from the Atlantic Ocean difficult, except at the modern ports. The flat coastal plain, which is 15 km–55 km wide, consists of forest and savannah. The interior hills and mountain ranges, with altitudes of 180 m–360 m, form part of an extended peneplain, covered by evergreen (in the south) or semi-deciduous (in the north) rainforests. The northern highlands contain Liberia's greatest elevations, which include the Nimba mountains, reaching 1,752 m above sea level, and the Wologisi range, reaching 1,381 m. The descent from the higher to the lower belts of the highlands is characterized by rapids and waterfalls.

Liberia has two rainy seasons near Harper, in the south, and one rainy season (from May to October) in the rest of the country. From Monrovia, on the coast in north-west Liberia, with an average of 4,650 mm per year, rainfall decreases towards the south-east and the hinterland, reaching 2,240 mm per year at Ganta. Average temperatures are more extreme in the interior than at the coast. Monrovia has an annual average of 26°C, with absolute limits at 33°C and 14°C, respectively. At Tappita temperatures may rise to 44°C in March and fall to 9°C during cool harmattan nights in December or January. Mean water temperature on the coast is 27°C.

The drainage system consists of 15 principal river basins, of which those of the Cavalla river, with an area of 30,225 sq km (including 13,730 sq km in Liberia), and of the St Paul river, with an area of 21,910 sq km (11,325 sq km in Liberia), are the largest. The water flow varies considerably and may reach over 100,000 cubic feet per second (cfs) at the Mt Coffee gauge of the St Paul river in August or decrease to 2,000 cfs during the dry season in March.

The fourth Liberian census, conducted on 21 March 2008, enumerated a population of 3,476,608, an increase of 66% compared with the total population at the 1984 census. The population was projected by the United Nations (UN) to have increased to 5,305,119 by mid-2022.

The demographic pattern of Liberia is characterized by a number of features typical of developing countries: a high birth rate (estimated at 33.2 per 1,000 in 2015–20); a high proportion of children under 15 years of age (estimated at 39.7% of the total population at mid-2022; and a low expectation of life at birth (estimated at 64.4 years in 2020). The average population density is low (54.3 inhabitants per sq km at mid-2022), but urbanization has been rapid. The population of Monrovia increased from 80,992 in 1962 to 421,058 in 1984; influxes of people displaced by the fighting may have taken the population above 1.3m. during the 1989–96 war. At mid-2021, according to the UN, the population of Monrovia (including the suburbs) was estimated at 1,569,013.

The war of 1989–96 caused massive displacements of population: at many times during the conflict one-third of the population fled to neighbouring countries, and a further one-third were internally displaced. The mass repatriation of Liberian refugees commenced in 1997. Following further rebel activity in Liberia from early 2001, some 119,293 Liberian refugees were in Guinea and about 43,000 in Côte d'Ivoire at 1 January 2003, according to the office of the UN High Commissioner for Refugees (UNHCR). The advance of hostilities to Monrovia in mid-2003 precipitated a further humanitarian crisis. Following the signing of a comprehensive peace agreement in August, the security situation improved significantly, with the deployment of UN peacekeeping troops and the initiation of a disarmament programme for former combatants. During 2004 more than 50,000 refugees returned to Liberia, while UNHCR completed the voluntary repatriation programme for some 13,000 Sierra Leonean refugees. The increase in the rate of return of Liberian refugees from Côte d'Ivoire in the early 2010s was as a result of the conflict that broke out in that country after the disputed presidential election of November 2010. At the end of 2011 some 128,067 refugees from Côte d'Ivoire were in Liberia; although this figure had decreased to 8,152 by December 2019, renewed violence following the presidential election in Côte d'Ivoire in October 2020 led to an increase in the number of refugees to 36,145 by the end of August 2021.

History

FRED VAN DER KRAAIJ

INTRODUCTION

Liberia was created on 26 July 1847, some 25 years after the successful landing of the first group of African-American colonists on the Malagueta or Grain Coast, a sparsely populated, densely forested coastal region of West Africa. The colonists—freed slaves and free-born black and coloured people—created Liberia with the permission of the white-dominated, private American Colonization Society (ACS), which, aided by the US Government, organized and financed the colonization. After the creation of Liberia, they referred to themselves as 'Americo-Liberians'. The ACS supporters were motivated by abolitionist principles and humanitarian and religious objectives. Moreover, many of them wanted to remove a fast-growing black and coloured population which was considered a threat to white dominance.

THE CREATION OF THE REPUBLIC

The new Republic consisted of a few dozen colonial settlements scattered in a coastal strip about 240 km long and stretching some 65 km inland. The 1847 Constitution excluded the indigenous population from citizenship and had two other noteworthy clauses. One stipulated that 'none but persons of color shall be admitted to citizenship', and the other stated that 'only citizens can own land and hold real estate'.

The population of Liberia also included slaves from intercepted slave ships who were brought to the then colony by US marine boats patrolling the Upper and Lower Guinea Coast to enforce the prohibition of the slave trade. Since many freed slaves originated from the Lower Guinea region they were called 'Congo-people'. A number of them, mainly adult males, acquired land through the ACS and became colonists. Children were often placed as a ward in settler families and used as cheap labour.

A CENTURY OF SURVIVAL, 1847–1944

Between 1820 and 1944 more than 90 deadly clashes between colonists and local indigenous peoples were recorded, while a further threat to the existence of the country was the 'scramble for Africa'. The settler community was also divided, with a sharp distinction existing along a 'colour-line' separating light-skinned and dark-skinned colonists. Finally, the climate was harsh and the death toll among newly arrived colonists was high.

By 1862 nearly 13,000 African-Americans and some 6,000 recaptives had entered Liberia. However, the emigration of African-Americans from the USA to Liberia slowed dramatically after the American Civil War (1862–65). By 1900 the indigenous population, divided into about 16 different tribes—mostly living in the hinterland, and considered 'uncivilized' by the 10,000–12,000 Americo-Liberians who lived on the coast—was believed to number 100,000–200,000. However, the ward system and formation of amorous relations between individuals made the distinction between the two main groups less rigid than indicated by their traditional mutual hostility.

Eleven Liberian heads of state were born in the USA. Under the administration of Arthur Barclay (1904–12, born in Barbados and Liberia's last President born outside Africa) the 1847 Constitution was amended in 1907, granting citizenship to the indigenous population and replacing the word 'colored' with 'Negro' in the clause that defined eligibility for citizenship (the 'Negro clause').

THE PRE-CONFLICT PERIOD, 1944–80

William V. S. Tubman became Liberia's 19th President in 1944. The two cornerstones of his administration were an economic 'open door' policy and a political 'national unification' policy. Tubman introduced universal adult suffrage, granting voting rights to Americo-Liberian women and the indigenous population, although with a property clause, and introduced Hinterland representation in the House of Representatives (in 1946) and the Senate (in 1964), abolishing the Hinterland administration. Overall, Tubman's unification policy was one of appeasement. He significantly improved the position of the indigenous population, but the historical divide between it and the descendants of the founders of the Republic remained. His foreign policy was based on an anti-communist doctrine, although in African affairs he held a moderate view. Tubman was both admired and feared, and an unprecedented personality cult developed around his administration, with Liberia becoming a de facto one-party state under his rule.

Tubman died in 1971 and was succeeded by the Vice-President, William R. Tolbert, who was re-elected as President in 1975. One of Tolbert's first measures was to relax the stringent security measures of the Tubman era, as well as the anti-communist focus. In 1977 Liberia and the People's Republic of China established diplomatic relations. Tolbert began renegotiating rubber and iron ore concession agreements with foreign investors. His progressive policies collided with conservative forces within the ruling True Whig Party (TWP). The most controversial domestic policy issue was the inclusion of the indigenous population in the polity. Tolbert's flight into nepotism, favouring members of his extended clan, opened the door to unrestrained corruption and abuse of power, and created much resentment.

Civil society organizations began to demand greater reforms, multi-party democracy and an end to corruption and nepotism. The tense domestic situation culminated in a violent climax on 14 April 1979 (the so-called 'Rice Riot'). Earlier that year Tolbert had lost the support of several elite settler families when he refused to pardon two of their prominent sons, who had been found guilty in one of Liberia's most notorious ritual murder cases (known as the 'Hanging of the Harper Seven'). A change of leadership appeared imminent; a 'palace coup' by TWP hardliners was among the possibilities. In the same year Tolbert refused to allow the bunkering of the US Rapid Deployment Force at Robertsfield International Airport. His growing alienation from the USA ensured that the US

Central Intelligence Agency and the US Department of Defense were also prospecting for leadership change in Liberia.

THE CONFLICT PERIOD, 1980–2003

The 1980 Coup

On 12 April 1980 a military coup in which Tolbert was assassinated ended the Americo-Liberian rule over Liberia. The leader of the coup was a 28-year-old Master Sgt (later Gen.) of the Armed Forces of Liberia (AFL), Samuel Doe, who became head of the newly created People's Redemption Council (PRC). All putschists were indigenous Liberians, and the coup was followed by widespread arrests of Americo-Liberians, lootings, murders, rape and summary executions. However, the military takeover was generally met with popular support. Thirteen former members of Tolbert's Government and high-ranking TWP officials were publicly executed after they had been found guilty of treason by a kangaroo court.

The PRC consisted of 17 non-commissioned members of the AFL. As Doe was the highest ranked of the 17 conspirators—mainly ethnic Gio, Mano, Krahn and Kru—he was appointed as its Chairman and, consequently, Liberia's 21st head of state, and the first Liberian of indigenous descent to hold that office. Doe was a tribal Krahn, while the second highest ranking of the putschists was Sgt Thomas Quiwonkpa, a tribal Gio. After the coup Quiwonkpa became Commander-in-Chief of the AFL, while Thomas Weh-Syen, a tribal Kru, became Vice-Chairman of the PRC.

Doe, who lacked political experience, appointed George Boley, a highly educated fellow Krahn, to be his most senior adviser, and later in 1980, Quiwonkpa introduced an Americo-Liberian economist (and his relative by marriage), Charles Taylor, into the ruling military regime. Tribal hostility became a defining feature of Liberian politics for the first time under the rule of the PRC. The coup surprised the outside world, notably the USA, which, fearing a leftist takeover, quickly established cordial relations with the new rulers.

During the early 1980s Doe gradually lost popular support for the military takeover, alienated progressive civil society organizations, whose leaders had initially joined the Government, and eliminated most of his fellow putschists. Doe transformed the PRC along tribal lines, appointing fellow Krahns to prominent positions and sidelining and persecuting Gio, Mano and Kru. Weh-Seyen was executed in 1981, while Quiwonkpa fled to the USA in 1983 (as did Taylor, who was accused of embezzlement). However, Doe maintained the support of the US Government despite evidence of human rights violations, economic and financial mismanagement, corruption and the theft of state resources.

Return to Civilian Rule

In July 1984 the four-year ban on political activities was lifted. Samuel Doe created the National Democratic Party of Liberia (NDPL), while opposition to his regime was led by the Liberian Action Party (LAP), headed by the unrelated Jackson Doe (a Gio who had been raised in an elite Americo-Liberian family), and which included among its founding members Harry Greaves and Ellen Johnson Sirleaf.

Samuel Doe won the presidential election held in October 1985 with 50.9% of the vote—just sufficient to avoid a run-off. The LAP claimed that the election had been fraudulent and that Jackson Doe had won with 62.8% of the votes cast, which was reportedly confirmed by independent observers. However, the USA supported the outcome of the election.

In November 1985 Quiwonkpa and a small group of heavily armed men invaded Liberia in an attempt to depose Samuel Doe and install Jackson Doe in the presidency. The involvement of LAP politicians in the invasion has never been proven, although several sources alleged that Greaves and Johnson Sirleaf played some role. Quiwonkpa and his National Patriotic Forces were defeated by Doe's troops. Quiwonkpa was killed, his body mutilated and cannibalized, then publicly displayed. In the aftermath of the coup attempt thousands of people were detained, while in the capital, Monrovia, and in Quiwonkpa's home county of Nimba a campaign of terror and reprisals against the Mano and Gio tribes was launched. Liberia's military also paid a heavy toll: several hundred troops were killed, and many were castrated, disembowelled and beheaded.

The Second Republic

In January 1986 Samuel Doe was inaugurated as the first President of the Second Republic. However, support for his presidency continued to be largely drawn from his Krahn tribesmen in an alliance with the Mandingo tribe, and a de facto one-party state re-emerged. By the late 1980s the ending of the Cold War had led to a waning of US interest in Liberia, although Liberian dissidents in the USA, including Amos Sawyer and Johnson Sirleaf, created the Association for Constitutional Democracy in Liberia (ACDL), a non-violent advocacy group. Members of the Liberian diaspora there also created a military organization, the National Patriotic Front of Liberia (NPFL), led by Taylor, which aimed to overthrow the Doe regime. Notably Tom Woewiyu, the ACDL Chairman, advocated supporting the NPFL. However, his plea to support Charles Taylor caused a split within the ACDL, with Sawyer reportedly opposed to any ACDL support of the NPFL, while a pro-NPFL faction led by Johnson Sirleaf pursued the opposite path.

The 1989–97 Civil War

In December 1989 the NPFL invaded Liberia from Côte d'Ivoire. A group of about 200 armed Liberians, mostly ethnic Mano and Gio, supported by soldiers from Burkina Faso, had been trained in Libya and was financed by powerful individuals in that country, in Côte d'Ivoire, in Burkina Faso and by Liberian dissidents in the USA.

In 1990 the situation in Liberia deteriorated rapidly. Doe's brutal reprisals against ethnic Gio and Mano people in Nimba County led to both increased local support for the NPFL and the displacement of hundreds of thousands of refugees to Côte d'Ivoire and Guinea. In Monrovia, Doe reacted by arresting his real and perceived opponents. By mid-1990 Taylor claimed to control the countryside and was targeting the capital (in the 'First Battle of Monrovia'). Meanwhile, Prince Yormie Johnson, a rebel fighter from Nimba County, had defected from the NPFL and created his own splinter group, the Independent National Patriotic Front of Liberia (INPFL), which soon entered into conflict with NPFL forces and with Doe's AFL. All three forces were accused of war crimes and human rights violations.

The Economic Community of West African States (ECOWAS) dispatched a regional military force (the ECOWAS Cease-Fire Monitoring Group—ECOMOG) to Liberia in August 1990. The USA refused to intervene, but evacuated its own citizens and embassy personnel. In early September Doe headed to the temporary ECOMOG headquarters at the Free Port of Monrovia, but was captured by Prince Johnson and was tortured and killed. The bicameral legislature ceased to function.

Meanwhile, in June 1990 Taylor formed the National Patriotic Reconstruction Assembly Government (NPRAG), seated in Gbarnga, Bong County. Two months later an ECOWAS conference led to the creation of an Interim Government of National Unity (IGNU), which was headed by Sawyer as Interim President and which excluded the warring factions. The IGNU was officially installed in Monrovia in late November. Liberia now had two competing administrations: the IGNU was internationally recognized and was supported by ECOMOG, but only controlled Monrovia, while the NPRAG occupied large areas of rural Liberia, giving Taylor access to precious natural resources which enabled him to finance the war. In October 1992 the Firestone rubber plantation at Harbel was the launch pad for the NPFL's Operation Octopus. In this 'Second Battle of Monrovia', which lasted for four months, thousands of civilians from different tribes were killed, tortured and raped.

The following years were marked by a proliferation of fighting factions, peace conferences and broken peace agreements. (During 1990–97 as many as 15 peace agreements were signed and subsequently broken.) Moreover, much of the West African region was affected by the crisis: hundreds of thousands of Liberian refugees entered neighbouring countries, notably Sierra Leone, Guinea, Côte d'Ivoire and Ghana, threatening their stability. Furthermore, relations between several of the

protagonists and regional leaders were extremely complex and threatened to involve more countries in the conflict. President Félix Houphouët-Boigny of Côte d'Ivoire, who had been a close ally of Tolbert, lent his support to Taylor and not to Samuel Doe, who had been ultimately responsible for Tolbert's killing and the disappearance of Tolbert's son (Houphouët-Boigny's son-in-law). Relations between Taylor and Burkina Faso's President Blaise Compaoré were more complex. Following Taylor's mysterious escape from a US prison in 1985, he had resurfaced in Ghana and Burkina Faso. His NPFL rebels had used the Burkinabè capital, Ouagadougou, as a stopover between Liberia and Libya, where NPFL leaders developed close relations with the Libyan leader, Col Muammar al-Qaddafi. NPFL rebels, then led by Prince Johnson, were also believed to have assisted in the 1987 assassination of Compaoré's predecessor, Thomas Sankara. It was presumed that, in exchange for this assistance, Compaoré supported the NPFL in order to remove Doe.

In May 1991 a former minister in Doe's administration, and an ethnic Mandingo, Alhaji Kromah, and another member of Doe's Government, and a fellow Krahn, Albert Karpeh, created the United Liberation Movement of Liberia for Democracy (ULIMO). ULIMO also included former AFL soldiers. Subsequent disagreement between ULIMO leaders led to an ethnic split, with the formation of a Mandingo faction, led by Kromah (ULIMO—K), and a Krahn faction, led by Gen. Roosevelt Johnson (ULIMO—J). Doe's trusted adviser Boley led the Liberia Peace Council (LPC), also consisting of former AFL soldiers. Furthermore, three NPFL leaders—Woewiyu, Sam Dokie and Lavell Supuwood—created their own faction, the Central Revolutionary Council (CRC). Finally, there existed a number of smaller splinter groups.

Each of these warring factions was responsible for horrific atrocities, including summary executions, murder, mutilation, torture, rape, looting and arson. The savage internecine war was predominantly a tribal conflict, but one with an important traditional-religious component. One of the worst atrocities committed, notably by members of the AFL, the LPC, the NPFL, and the ULIMO—J and ULIMO—K factions, was the eating of human flesh. Economic motives for the fighting mainly concerned access to natural resources which were sold to European companies, the proceeds of which financed the purchase of weapons, also primarily from Europe. The fighting and atrocities led to hundreds of thousands of internally displaced persons (IDPs) and refugees. An estimated one-third of Liberia's population of almost 3m. people had fled or were internally displaced, while one-third resided in Monrovia under ECOMOG protection, and the remaining one-third attempted to survive in the rural areas.

In March 1994 the IGNU, led by Sawyer, was replaced by the Liberia National Transitional Government (LNTG), headed by Prof. David Kpormakpor. In August 1995, however, the LNTG was replaced by LNTG-II, chaired by Prof. Wilton Sankawulo, with Paramount Chief Tamba Taylor as his deputy and in which the warlords Charles Taylor (of the NPFL), Kromah (of ULIMO—K), Roosevelt Johnson (of ULIMO—J) and Boley (of the LPC), as well as Oscar Quiah (of the Liberian National Conference, representing various civil society organizations) all secured representation.

In April 1996 heavy fighting (the 'Third Battle of Monrovia') erupted between the warlord members of LNTG-II, devastating large parts of Monrovia, killing at least 2,000 people and leading to the collapse of LNTG-II. In September LNTG-III was created, headed by Ruth Perry, a former senator and peace activist. Perry, a Vai from Grand Cape Mount County, thus became Liberia's first female head of state (although she was appointed, not elected).

Presidential and legislative elections were held in July 1997, prior to which Charles Taylor's supporters threatened to restart the war were he not victorious. In the event, Taylor secured an outright victory in the presidential poll, with 75% of the votes cast. Johnson Sirleaf (representing the Unity Party—UP) took 10%, while Kromah (of the All Liberia Coalition Party—ALCOP) secured 4%. Numerous election observers, including those from the European Union (EU), ECOWAS and the Carter Center, called the elections free and fair despite an atmosphere of intimidation. Taylor's political party, the

National Patriotic Party (NPP), won an overwhelming majority of the seats in the legislature (49 of the 64 seats in the House of Representatives and 21 of the 29 seats in the Senate). On 2 August Taylor was inaugurated as the 22nd President of Liberia, with Enoch Dogolea, an ethnic Gio from Nimba County, as his Vice-President.

Charles Taylor's Presidency, 1997–2003

Taylor moved swiftly to silence and eliminate his enemies. During 1998 the political climate deteriorated with the harassment of civil society activists, extra-judicial killings, and the repression of freedom of the press and of speech. Taylor refused to demobilize approximately 35,000 ex-combatants in violation of the Abuja Agreement that had ended the civil war. Instead, he manipulated the transformation of the defunct NPFL into the national army. In April 1999 a new rebel group backed by the Guinean Government, Liberians United for Reconciliation and Democracy (LURD), consisting of former ULIMO members and other opponents of Taylor, led by Sekou Conneh, invaded Voinjama, Lofa County, from Guinea, triggering the second civil war.

This conflict was also characterized by widespread atrocities committed by the fighting forces, including murder, looting, rape, arson, the use of child soldiers, and once again reports of decapitation, disembowelment, ritualistic killings and cannibalism. Heavy fighting again forced many Liberians to flee, giving rise to tens of thousands of IDPs and refugees. Taylor supported numerous rebel movements in West Africa and for this reason the United Nations (UN) imposed sanctions, including the freezing of bank accounts and the imposition of travel restrictions on Taylor and his closest associates. Furthermore, in May 2001 the UN placed an embargo on the export of all rough diamonds from Liberia (only lifted in April 2007), and in July 2003 also imposed a ban (periodically extended until mid-2006) on imports of round logs and timber products from the country.

Most notably, it was discovered that Taylor was supplying arms and training facilities to rebels of the Revolutionary United Front (RUF) and other armed groups in Sierra Leone in exchange for diamonds. In 2000 Taylor's troops invaded Guinea in a concerted action with RUF fighters and Guinean rebels who invaded Guinea from Sierra Leone. From that point onwards the Government of Sierra Leone supported LURD's attempts to oust Taylor.

In 2003 LURD, which was involved in fighting in western and central Liberia, was joined by another rebel group, the Movement for Democracy in Liberia (MODEL), comprising mainly Krahn combatants and led by Thomas Nimely, who invaded eastern Liberia from Côte d'Ivoire, rapidly assuming control of a large area after a series of confrontations with Taylor's forces that were accompanied, again, by gruesome atrocities. The support given by Côte d'Ivoire's President, Laurent Gbagbo, to the incursion was motivated by Taylor's backing of Ivorian rebels who supported Gbagbo's rival, Alassane Ouattara.

By mid-2003 LURD controlled one-third of Liberia (in the west), MODEL ruled one-third (in the east) and Taylor held power over the remainder of the country. In the ensuing battle for Monrovia thousands of people perished, tens of thousands fled, and the city was further destroyed. In June a ceasefire agreement was signed by the Government of Liberia, LURD and MODEL in Accra, Ghana (see below). On 11 August Taylor resigned, as his position had become untenable, rebel forces were already in Monrovia and the international pressure was overwhelming. His Vice-President, from Nimba County, Moses Zeh Blah, who had replaced Dogolea after his sudden, mysterious death in 2000, was inaugurated as Liberia's 23rd President.

Despite being indicted by the Sierra Leone Special Court (SLSC), Taylor was granted asylum in Nigeria under certain conditions. However, in March 2006 Johnson Sirleaf (who had been elected as President of Liberia in late 2005—see below) formally requested that Nigeria extradite Taylor as he had violated the terms of his asylum. He was captured, transferred to the Sierra Leonean capital, Freetown, and delivered to the SLSC. For security reasons and out of the fear of increasing political instability in the region, Taylor was tried in The

Hague, Netherlands, where a Trial Chamber of the SLSC had been created, within the facilities of the International Criminal Court (ICC). (In June 2006 the United Kingdom had agreed that Taylor could serve any custodial term in a British prison, and Taylor was transferred to the custody of the ICC with the assent of the UN Security Council.)

In April 2012 the SLSC found Taylor guilty of 11 counts of war crimes, crimes against humanity, and serious violations of international humanitarian law committed between November 1996 and January 2002 during Sierra Leone's civil war. He was sentenced to 50 years' imprisonment, and in October 2013 was transferred to a prison in the UK.

THE POST-CONFLICT PERIOD, 2003–

The Comprehensive Peace Agreement and UNMIL

In mid-August 2003 a Comprehensive Peace Agreement (CPA) was initialled in Accra, Ghana. The ensuing election for the head of the transitional administration was won by Johnson Sirleaf; however, the warring factions opposed her assuming this position and imposed their choice, who had been placed third in the contest, Gyude Bryant, a founder of the LAP. In October Bryant was installed as Chairman of the National Transitional Government of Liberia (NTGL). Meanwhile, in September, the UN Security Council approved the creation of a 15,000-strong peacekeeping force, the UN Mission in Liberia (UNMIL). It was tasked with disarming the warring parties, co-ordinating humanitarian aid and maintaining peace. The reconstruction task facing the country was immense. The two back-to-back civil wars (1989–97 and 1999–2003) may have claimed the lives of 250,000 people and resulted in the displacement of 750,000 Liberians. The two wars had undoubtedly left countless people traumatized and wounded, and had destroyed the country's infrastructure and economy.

The National Transitional Government of Liberia, 2003–06

The CPA provided for the creation of a National Transitional Legislative Assembly, consisting of 76 members, split between various groups, including Taylor's forces, LURD and MODEL, while the NTGL's institutions (the ministries, state agencies and state-owned enterprises) were also divided among the former warring factions. The NTGL inherited an empty treasury; the Liberian state was virtually bankrupt. In the 2004/05 financial year, the Government operated on the basis of a US $80m. national budget. Although in February 2004 international donors pledged more than US $500m. in reconstruction aid, much of this was squandered, mismanaged or stolen. In 2005 the NTGL and the international community agreed on a controversial Governance and Economic Management Assistance Programme (GEMAP, see *Economy*) under which Liberia's financial transactions were subjected to international supervision.

A national dialogue for the creation of a Truth and Reconciliation Commission (TRC) was initiated in January 2004, and in June 2005 legislation establishing the TRC was signed into law by Bryant. In February 2006 the Johnson Sirleaf administration authorized the TRC to start its investigations. The TRC Act mandated the TRC to act in conformity with international law.

The NTGL was also tasked with organizing presidential and legislative elections. The 64 seats available in the House of Representatives were contested by 513 candidates, while the 30 seats in the Senate were contested by 205 candidates and 22 presidential candidates were registered. The pre-election period was marred by extreme violence.

At the first round of the presidential election in October 2005, George Manneh Weah (a former professional footballer representing the Congress for Democratic Change, CDC) won 28.3% of the votes cast, followed by Johnson Sirleaf of the UP with 19.8%, and Charles Brumskine (Liberty Party—LP) with 13.9%. The second round on 8 November was won by Johnson Sirleaf, who obtained 59.4% of the votes. Weah contested the results, alleging 'massive and systematic' fraud; however, after the overwhelming majority of regional and international observers qualified the poll as free, fair and transparent, he withdrew his protests. Voter turnout was 75% in the first round, and 61% in the second. Due to the large number of political parties contesting the legislative elections, no party obtained a parliamentary majority.

The Johnson Sirleaf Presidency, 2006–18

On 16 January 2006 Johnson Sirleaf was inaugurated as Liberia's 24th President, thus becoming the first democratically elected female head of state in Africa. Joseph Boakai, an ethnic Kissi from Lofa County, was installed as Vice-President. Controversially, the new Government included some of the President's relatives and friends. Johnson Sirleaf quickly gave precedence to the reconstruction of the national economy and invested significantly in two pre-conditions: internal political stability and the cancellation of Liberia's excessive international debt. Within three months she had requested Nigeria's extradition of Taylor (see above), ordered the arrest and prosecution of former NTGL Chairman Bryant on corruption charges, revoked the concession agreements signed by the Taylor and Bryant Governments, and commenced debt cancellation negotiations. She also appeased former warlords and political opponents, notably through the payment of high salaries and allowances to legislators and senior government officials.

The achievements of President Johnson Sirleaf in the areas of human rights and the protection of vulnerable people were noteworthy. In 2005 a National Commission on Disabilities was created and in 2008 Liberia ratified the UN Convention on the Rights of Persons with Disabilities. In 2007 she made primary school education compulsory and free, and in 2010 she signed into law a Freedom of Information Act, which granted both individuals and media organizations the right to demand information from government institutions and private entities that performed public functions. Furthermore, in 2012 Liberia ratified the Protocol to the African Charter on Human and Peoples' Rights on the Rights of Women in Africa (the Maputo Protocol) and in January 2018 Johnson Sirleaf outlawed female genital mutilation (FGM) practices in Liberia.

President Johnson Sirleaf's foreign policy focused on regional and continental African organizations: the Mano River Union (MRU), ECOWAS and the African Union (AU); strengthening relations with the USA; and bolstering diplomatic relations with the People's Republic of China, in exchange for Chinese funds and assistance, notably for infrastructural projects. In 2007 Hu Jintao was the first Chinese President officially to visit Liberia, reciprocating President Sirleaf's state visit to China in 2006.

However, a major impediment to the smooth functioning of Johnson Sirleaf's presidency during her first term was the final report of the TRC, which was published in mid-2009. It focused on the war crimes, human rights violations and transgressions of Liberian laws committed between January 1979 and October 2003, and listed 10 recommendations, five of which merit specific mention. The foremost among these concerned the establishment of an Extraordinary Criminal Tribunal for Liberia, which was to try all persons specified by the TRC. Second, the TRC recommended the prosecution of individual warlords, including Charles Taylor (NPFL), Prince Johnson (INPFL), Roosevelt Johnson (deceased, ULIMO—J), Kromah (ULIMO—K), Boley (LPC), Thomas Nimely (MODEL) and Sekou Conneh (LURD). Third, 52 individuals, including political leaders, financiers and commanders of the various former warring factions, were recommended for public sanctions, notably to be barred from public office for 30 years. The most surprising name on this list was Johnson Sirleaf herself. She had admitted to the TRC having supported the NPFL in the early phases of the first civil war, but denied any military role or further involvement beyond an initial contribution of US \$10,000. Fourth, the TRC named 21 individuals responsible for committing economic crimes, including international arms traffickers Viktor Bout, Guus Kouwenhoven and Leonid Minin, as well as high-profile Liberians Emmanuel Shaw, Edwin Snowe and Benoni Urey (see below). Finally, the TRC also recommended that no prosecution be brought against 36 individuals, despite their involvement in heinous acts and crimes.

The formal response to the TRC's recommendations lay in the hands of President Johnson Sirleaf and the legislature, in which former members of the warring factions held powerful positions. Not surprisingly the TRC report was largely ignored. After a complaint lodged by one of the 52 individuals recommended for sanctioning, the Supreme Court ruled in January 2011 that the recommendation that public sanctions be applied to the 52 named individuals was unconstitutional, and stipulated that all the names included in this section of the report be removed.

Johnson Sirleaf confirmed her intention to stand as a candidate in the 2011 presidential election, despite her 2005 pledge to resign from the presidency after one six-year term. Shortly before the election, Johnson Sirleaf was awarded the 2011 Nobel Peace Prize jointly with Liberian peace activist Leymah Gbowee. Her opponents protested in vain against what they perceived as an unwarranted influencing of Liberian politics.

The presidential election was held on 11 October 2011 and contested by 16 candidates, while at the concurrent legislative elections 15 seats in the Senate and 73 seats in the House of Representatives were contested (after the creation of nine additional seats). Johnson Sirleaf was placed first in the presidential poll, with 43.9% of the votes cast, while Winston A. Tubman of the CDC, a nephew of the former President, came second with 32.7%. Former rebel leader Prince Yormie Johnson was placed third with 11.6% of the votes and was thus cast into the role of kingmaker. Turnout in the first round was 72%. Tubman claimed that the election had been fraudulent and four days before the run-off poll called for an opposition boycott. Clashes between police and CDC protesters on the eve of the election resulted in two deaths. However, the run-off took place as scheduled in early November, prior to which Prince Johnson had declared his support for Johnson Sirleaf. Turnout was just 39%, mainly due to the CDC boycott, and Sirleaf Johnson won convincingly with 90.7% of the vote. She was inaugurated for her second term as President in January 2012.

The political landscape in the legislature remained fragmented. The UP remained the largest party in the enlarged House of Representatives with 24 deputies, while the CDC was the second largest (11). No other party had more than 10 deputies. In the Senate, the UP also remained, with 10 senatorial seats, the largest party, while the NPP, now led by Jewel Howard-Taylor, former wife of Charles Taylor, had six senators and the CDC three.

Johnson Sirleaf's new Cabinet included five women. There were other noteworthy, and controversial, appointments. Three of President Johnson Sirleaf's four children were given senior positions: her eldest son, Robert Sirleaf, was appointed Chairman of the state-owned National Oil Company of Liberia (NOCAL), while another, Charles Sirleaf, was reconfirmed as Deputy Governor of the Central Bank of Liberia (CBL), and a third, Fumba Sirleaf, was appointed Director of the National Security Agency.

Johnson Sirleaf's second term was overshadowed by the Ebola Virus Disease (EVD) epidemic. Lack of funds, a weak public health system, unfavourable socio-cultural traditions and beliefs, an underestimation of the disease and consequently an inadequate response to the outbreak in March 2014 resulted in a catastrophic outcome. According to official figures, by June 2016, when the epidemic was declared over, the number of deaths resulting from the virus in the country totalled 4,809 (including a reported 500 health workers), while 10,675 people had been infected. Before the outbreak Liberia had just 44 doctors for a total population of well over 4m. people.

The EVD epidemic was more than a health crisis. It was also a sanitary and management crisis and it destroyed the country's nascent economic recovery. Moreover, the outbreak demonstrated the alienation between the governing elite and the wider population; at the peak of the epidemic, demands were made for President Johnson Sirleaf's resignation. According to the UN Office for the Coordination of Humanitarian Affairs, international aid to Liberia during the EVD crisis amounted to US \$1,000m., with an additional US \$150m. coming from the private sector. However, there were several reports of fraud, embezzlement and mismanagement of funds designated to combat Ebola.

Upon taking office in 2006, Johnson Sirleaf had announced a zero-tolerance policy towards corruption. In 2008 she established the Liberia Anti-Corruption Commission (LACC), yet during most of her presidency the organization was under-staffed, underfunded and lacked authority. In January 2012 Johnson Sirleaf made it mandatory for officials of the executive branch of government to make financial disclosures and declare their assets to the LACC. Despite various measures, corruption in Liberia, in its various forms, remains endemic and rampant, particularly within (and throughout) the justice system. The executive branch is also significantly affected by corruption, while in schools and hospitals bribery is widely reported.

The governance indicators for Liberia during the Johnson Sirleaf administration also revealed that corruption was deteriorating. In Transparency International's 2017 Corruption Perception Index, Liberia ranked 122nd out of 180 countries, while in 2019 it ranked 137th out of 198 countries—compared with an average ranking of 88th out of 179 countries in 2009–16. One of the most notable corruption cases during Johnson Sirleaf's presidency involved the Speaker of the House of Representatives, Edwin Snowe (the former son-in-law of Charles Taylor), who resigned in February 2007 following bribery allegations, while in 2016 Snowe's successor, Alex Tyler, resigned after facing multiple charges of bribery, aggravated assault, criminal solicitation and human rights violations. The Sable Mining bribery scandal also emerged in 2016, implicating legislators, ministers and high-ranking politicians and civil servants. Leymah Gbowee resigned as head of the Peace and Reconciliation Commission in 2012, in protest against the President's failing anti-corruption policy and increasing nepotism. Liberia had also reintroduced the death penalty in 2008, in violation of the Second Optional Protocol to the International Covenant on Civil and Political Rights, to which Liberia acceded in 2005.

The 2017 presidential and legislative elections were the first to be organized by the National Elections Commission (NEC). (At the 2005 and 2011 elections responsibility for security had rested with UNMIL, but in July 2016 Liberia had reassumed full responsibility for its own security, although UNMIL's mandate remained effective until 30 March 2018, when its remaining troops and police personnel left Liberia). The two main presidential candidates were Vice-President Joseph Boakai, for the UP, and George Weah. In November 2016 Weah's CDC had joined with the NPP and the much smaller Liberia People Democratic Party, led by Alex Tyler, in the Coalition for Democratic Change. The NPP Chairperson, Jewel Howard Taylor, was selected as Weah's running mate and proved important in winning the votes in her native Bong County.

A reported 75.2% of the electorate voted in the elections held on 10 October 2017. None of the presidential candidates was able to secure a majority, with Weah receiving 38.4% of the votes cast, followed by Boakai (28.8%) and Charles Brumskine of the LP (9.6%). Weah won in 11 of Liberia's 15 counties; Boakai won Lofa and Gbarpolu Counties, Brumskine in Grand Bassa County and Prince Johnson in Nimba County. The run-off, originally scheduled for 7 November, was postponed following protests led by Brumskine and Boakai, who alleged large-scale fraud and irregularities. After the complaint was rejected by the Supreme Court, the second round was held on 26 December, at which Weah secured a convincing victory, taking 61.5% of the vote on a turnout of just 55.8%.

The Presidency of George Weah, 2018–

The inauguration of George Weah as Liberia's 25th President on 22 January 2018 was an historic event for several reasons, most notably as Weah, an ethnic Kru, was the first opposition candidate to defeat the ruling party's candidate since 1870. He was also the first wholly indigenous Liberian to be democratically elected in the country's 170-year history. In his inaugural address, President Weah pledged to: respect human rights; fight corruption; promote the private sector and invite foreign investment; change the structure of the economy; and conduct pro-poor governance. Later that month he outlined the major issues confronting the country: the economy risked collapse, the Government being virtually bankrupt with foreign reserves at an all-time low and unemployment at an unprecedented high level. Weah sought urgently to: remove the constitutional limitation of citizenship to black people; remove the constitutional restriction of land ownership to Liberian citizens; and end the legal restriction on Liberians holding dual citizenship. He announced that he was reducing his salary and benefits by 25%. Budgetary provisions in subsequent years, however, have not reflected his avowed intention. Much criticism followed after Weah refused to publish a declaration of his assets and reports emerged concerning his numerous property acquisitions and construction activities.

Following his inauguration, Weah appointed CDC stalwarts and allied politicians to key positions. CDC Chairman Nathaniel McGill became Minister of State for Presidential Affairs, while the finance and development planning portfolio was entrusted to Samuel D. Tweah, Jr. McGill and Tweah are among Weah's closest confidants, together with Jefferson Koijee, who became Mayor of Monrovia in January 2018. (In August 2022 Weah suspended McGill following the latter's designation for sanctions under the US Magnitsky Act—see *Human Rights Abuses, Corruption Scandals and Democratic Decline* and he was replaced in October in an acting capacity by George Wesseh Blamoh after McGill had tendered his resignation.) Maj.-Gen. Daniel Dee Ziankahn, hitherto Chief of Staff of the AFL, was appointed Minister of Defence, and Varney Sirleaf, the nephew of the former President and one of her cabinet members, Minister of Internal Affairs. The prestigious role of Minister of Foreign Affairs was allocated to Gbehzohngar Findley, a former UP senator who had defected to the CDC in 2017. (Findley resigned in July 2020 to contest a senatorial seat in the December elections, thereby contravening the National Code of Conduct, which mandates resignation from ministerial posts at least two years prior to an election. He was succeeded by Dee-Maxwell Saah Kemayah, Liberia's Permanent Representative to the UN.) Finally, in January 2018 Maryland County legislator Dr Bhofal Chambers, of the CDC, was elected Speaker of the House of Representatives.

The political scene during the Weah presidency remained as fragmentated as it had been under the preceding administration. By mid-2022 each of the two major political blocs, the ruling CDC and the Collaborating Political Parties (CPP—see below), showed tensions and even splits. Meanwhile, the various political parties, civil society organizations, Liberian diaspora organizations and other diverse groups—including the Council of Patriots (COP)—found that their initial importance as an opposition force had virtually vanished.

Within months of Weah becoming President, cracks began to appear within the ruling three-party alliance. There were indications of strained relations between Weah and Howard-Taylor, despite official denials. In March 2022 Howard-Taylor distanced herself from Weah's CDC by declaring that she was an NPP member. However, her position as NPP Standard Bearer was seriously compromised after she and NPP Acting Chairman James Biney clashed. Meanwhile, several high-profile NPP politicians defected to the CDC, partly explained by the turmoil within the party and its division in early 2022, which was caused by a disagreement over the selection of senior party officials. In mid-2022 a number of other opposition lawmakers also crossed over to the ruling coalition. Other politicians from the CDC and NPP indicated that they would stand as independents or defected to the opposition in an effort to defeat Weah in 2023. The return to Liberia of Agnes Reeves Taylor (another former wife of Charles Taylor) threatened further to destabilize the NPP and ruling coalition. Reeves Taylor had been arrested in the UK in 2017 on charges relating to war crimes allegedly committed during the early stages of the first civil war. Following the dismissal of these charges, she was freed from custody in December 2019. Upon her arrival in Monrovia in July 2020, Reeves Taylor was welcomed by NPP stalwarts as its 'founding mother'.

From February 2019 parliamentary opposition was organized into a new alliance, the CPP, comprising the LP, the UP, the All Liberian Party (ALP) and the Alternative National Congress (ANC). The four parties combined had won more than 47% of the votes cast in the 2017 presidential election and joined forces 'to make George Weah a one-term President'.

However, by the end of 2019 the alliance had suffered serious clashes between businessman-turned-politician, ANC Chairman and then CPP leader Alexander Cummings, and a wealthy businessman and former associate of Charles Taylor, Benoni Urey of the ALP, who was the CPP founder and its first leader. These divisions were compounded by a lack of strong leadership in the UP, headed by Joseph Boakai, and a crisis within the LP after the unexpected death of its leader, Charles Brumskine, in November 2019. Brumskine was succeeded by Senator Nyonblee Karnga-Lawrence. However, in late 2021 the LP elected a new party leader, Harrison Karnwea, and suspended Senators Nyonblee Karnga-Lawrence and Abe Darius Dillon, who both supported Boakai as the CPP's presidential candidate. The existing division in the CPP was deepened as ALP leader Urey had also declared his support for Boakai six months earlier. Furthermore, a number of prominent UP politicians left the party to join the ruling CDC.

In early 2022 Urey accused Cummings of fraud and of forging the CPP framework document—an accusation supported by the UP and the Karnga-Lawrence faction of the LP. Subsequently, criminal charges were levelled against the ANC and Cummings. However, in June, after a five-month trial, the Solicitor-General (on behalf of the Government) unexpectedly dropped all charges against Cummings. This did not prevent the CPP's collapse. In February 2022 the LP's Karnga-Lawrence faction had also withdrawn from the CPP, followed by the UP. In July the leadership of the People's Liberation Party (PLP—established in late 2020) accepted Cummings' invitation to join the CPP, although the position of PLP Standard Bearer, Dr Daniel Cassell, who is embroiled in criminal charges in the USA (having been arrested in March on fraud charges), remained unclear. Cassell is a vocal critic of President Weah for his perceived failure to fight corruption. Also in late July Boakai was elected unopposed as UP Standard Bearer. In late August 2022 LP faction leader Musa Hassan Bility and ANC leader Cummings signed a new framework agreement reviving the now two-party opposition CPP, with Bility named as Chairman and Cummings as Standard Bearer.

The COP, a broad-based civil society movement comprising a number of opposition groups, had revealed its strength as an opposition voice against the Weah Government in June 2019 when it organized a large peaceful demonstration in Monrovia under the banner 'Save the State'. The demonstrators protested against the administration's economic policies and the deteriorating economic conditions. Towards the end of 2019 the COP launched a campaign urging Weah to step down from the presidency, which culminated in a further large protest in January 2020. Marching under the same slogan, over 3,000 protesters denounced: the rampant corruption and poor governance that they claimed characterized Weah's Government; the delays in payment of salaries to civil servants; the shortage of Liberian dollar banknotes; the ongoing economic crisis, including soaring inflation; and deteriorating living conditions, including a petrol shortage. The peaceful march descended into violent clashes between demonstrators and police. The COP was considerable weakened in April 2020 when two high-profile members left: Montserrado County Representative Yekeh Kolubah, a former child soldier and a vocal critic of President Weah, and Telia Urey (daughter of Benoni Urey and former Montserado County Representative). In May 2021 the COP Secretary-General, Mulbah Yorgbor, announced that he was joining the ANC and supporting Cummings as the CPP's presidential candidate. Yorgbor left the COP in January 2022, by which time it had lost much of its importance.

Meanwhile, in December 2019 an 'All Liberian Diaspora Conference' was held in Maryland, USA, jointly sponsored by the principal Liberian diaspora organizations. (Many of these are united under the umbrella of the All-Liberian Conference on Dual Citizenship, which is reported to represent some 500,000 diaspora Liberians.) The conference followed the parliamentary approval in October of a constitutional amendment that would permit dual citizenship. On 8 December 2020 a national referendum was held, jointly with the mid-term senatorial elections (see below), on the proposed change and several others, including the reduction of the presidential and vice-presidential terms of office (from six years to five) and the tenure of members of the House of Representatives

(also from six years to five) and of the Senate (from a maximum of nine years to seven). The NEC did not announce the results of the referendum until April 2021 following allegations of fraud and other irregularities. Each of the proposed amendments failed to secure the constitutionally required two-thirds' majority of the (valid) votes. (In the mid-term senatorial the results were contested in at least seven of the 15 counties after complaints of irregularities and intimidation of local government officials. Nineteen political parties and several independent candidates competed for the 15 available seats, with the CPP taking six. The ruling CDC won just three seats.)

None the less, on 22 July 2022 President Weah signed an amended Alien and Nationality Law, which had been passed by the House of Representatives and the Senate on 19 July. It officially became law in August. The amended law legalized dual citizenship for Liberians and people of 'Negro' descent, while maintaining the clause based on the 1847 Constitution (restricting citizenship to people of African descent). An important aspect of the amended law prohibits people with dual citizenship from holding elected positions in the legislature and certain positions in the executive, including those of president, CBL governor, and ministers of defence and of finance and development planning. Dual citizens wishing to run for certain elected positions must reject the citizenship of the other country at least one year prior to the election date. Interestingly, President Weah's wife is Jamaican, one of his sons is a well-known football player in the USA, whereas Weah himself holds a French passport. It is a public secret that many in the elite hold two passports. Dual citizenship allows people to acquire land and to operate businesses under the 'Liberianization' policy, and gives access to certain government jobs. The amended law could thus act as a catalyst for increased investment, but concerns have also been voiced that dual citizenship could lead to land grabbing and unfair competition, notably in view of Liberia's considerable Lebanese community and the dominant position of Lebanese businessmen, who occupy a quasi-monopoly on the wholesale of imported consumer goods (see *Economy*).

After the four opposition parties in the CPP had separated in 2022, having failed to agree on a candidate to oppose President Weah in the 2023 presidential election, two main contenders remained: Joseph Boakai (UP) and Alexander Cummings (ANC). An important test for the forthcoming election was the outcome of the senatorial by-election held in Lofa County on 28 June 2022. Independent candidate Joseph Jallah, who was heavily backed by the CDC, narrowly defeated the UP candidate, Galakpai Kortimai, in a UP stronghold. There were allegations of fraud and of massive vote-buying. However, the UP failed to produce evidence, and Jallah was inducted into the Senate in July.

Upon the retirement of the Chief Justice of the Supreme Court, Francis Korkpor, in September 2022, Associate Justice Sie-A-Nyene Gyapay Yuoh (the wife of Edwin Snowe) became Chief Justice of Liberia. Justice Yuoh is the third woman ever to occupy this position. Her appointment meant that all three branches of government would be headed by Liberians hailing from the south-east and was therefore politically sensitive.

Mysterious Deaths, Unexplained Murders and Ritualistic Killings

The weak security situation meant that violent crimes, including armed robbery, gender-related violence, murders and unexplained deaths, which existed during the Sirleaf administration further deteriorated during the Weah presidency. After the final report of the TRC was published in 2009, many TRC commissioners received death threats. Another major factor triggering violence was corruption. On 1 November 2009, a few months after NTGL Chairman Gyude Bryant and Liberia Petroleum Refining Co (LPRC) Managing Director Edwin Snowe had been acquitted in a major corruption trial, the head of the Public Procurement and Concessions Commission (PPCC), Keith Jubah, was shot dead, his body hacked and burned, at his farm in Kakata, Margibi County. The PPCC had cancelled most of the concession agreements and procurement contracts awarded by the NTGL and the preceding Taylor Government.

At the end of President Sirleaf's first term, the Ministry of Justice was investigating more than 100 corruption-related cases, most of them involving public officials, but there were few arrests and most accused officials retained their position after the initial turmoil fizzled out. In February 2015 a whistleblower, consultant to NOCAL, Michael Allison was found dead on a Monrovia beach under suspicious circumstances. Notably, a number of former managers and executive staff members of NOCAL, then headed by President Sirleaf's eldest son, Robert, had been indicted, accused of economic sabotage, bribery and criminal conspiracy (see *Economy*). Allison had drawn attention to irregularities at NOCAL and revealed illegal payments to members of the legislature involving House Speaker Alex Tyler. Allison's death was never explained. In January 2016 the body of prominent LAP politician Harry Greaves was found off a beach on Capitol Hill, in Monrovia. Greaves was a Managing Director of the LPRC during President Sirleaf's first term. Allegedly, he and Sirleaf played a role in the 1985 coup attempt led by Quiwonkpa (see above). Later, the relationship between Greaves and Sirleaf soured. Neither the circumstances nor exact cause of his sudden, mysterious death were ever elucidated.

Liberia has a long history of ritualistic murders, notably during election campaigns. The TRC final report stated that hundreds of Liberians were killed for ritual purposes during the country's back-to-back civil wars (1989–2003). During the Johnson Sirleaf administration ritualistic killings continued, with President Sirleaf publicly condemning these criminal practices. In 2015 she promised to crack down on ritual murderers after another rise in such crimes, amid speculation that presidential candidates wishing to replace her were involved. However, during her two terms, arrests of perpetrators were few, and condemnation of those accused even rarer. The culture of impunity for perpetrators of ritual murders continued after President Weah took office. The public reacted to the growing insecurity and inaction of the authorities with mob justice and riots. In May 2019, following a wave of ritual killings, two men suspected of ritual murder were mobbed to death in Nimba County. A few months later the discovery of the mutilated dead bodies of two missing children led to riots in Montserrado County. At least one person was shot dead by the police.

In March 2021 violent unrest erupted in Maryland County over a series of suspected ritualistic murders. The property of the Speaker of the House of Representatives, Bhofal Chambers, was set alight and the Government was forced to impose a curfew to quell the unrest. In April a civil society organization, 'Citizens United Against Secret Killings', petitioned the US Government, through its embassy in Monrovia, drawing attention to an alarming increase in the number of mysterious, unexplained deaths, ritualistic murders and secret killings under Weah's leadership. In October another such organization linked to the opposition CPP protested against the alleged wave of ritual murders across the country, with some church leaders also speaking out. The bishop of the Lutheran Church in Liberia, Rev. Daniel Jensen Seyenkulo, publicly accused ambitious politicians of being responsible. Amid all this turmoil, ritual killings were reported in Montserrado, Bomi, Bong, Nimba, and Maryland Counties. This coincided with by-elections scheduled for November 2021 in Bomi, Bong, Grand Gedeh and Nimba Counties. Opposition leaders Cummings (ANC), Karnga-Lawrence (LP) and Cassell (PLP) urged President Weah to take action to end the mysterious and often gruesome killings of Liberians. The brutal murder of John Hilary Tubman, a son of former President Tubman, in his Monrovia residence in September 2021, as well as the sudden, unexplained death of Liberia's peace ambassador, Rev. William Tolbert III, youngest son of slain President Tolbert, in October shocked many Liberians. The ruling CDC was increasingly being mentioned in connection with reported violence, unexplained deaths and murders, while law enforcement agencies were accused of involvement in extraordinary violence and/or disappearances.

In March 2019, shortly after the 'missing-millions-scandal' had emerged (see *Economy*), Matthew Innis, a senior staff member at the CBL, died in an unexplained hit-and-run accident. Shortly afterwards, another CBL employee who may also have had information on the 'missing' L \$16,000m., truck driver Kollie Ballah, also died in an accident. In early 2020 Zenu Miller, a radio journalist, died after reportedly being beaten by presidential security personnel. Furthermore, in October the deaths of three senior employees of the Liberian Revenue Authority and the Director-General of the Internal Audit Agency were all unexplained.

In May 2021 Dr Howard White, the former Chief Investigator of the Special Court for Sierra Leone, revealed in a radio interview that he had narrowly escaped an assassination attempt in Monrovia in 2004. The would-be assassins accidentally killed another American, John Auffrey. Liberian police investigators and authorities then claimed that the killing was a robbery which had gone wrong. However, White accused them of a cover-up, presumably because of the alleged involvement of close associates of exiled President Charles Taylor. He revealed that new intelligence linked unnamed officials of the Weah administration to the assassination attempt and the killing of John Auffrey.

In December 2021 Morris Tidball-Binze, the independent UN Special Rapporteur on extrajudicial, summary and arbitrary executions urged the Liberian authorities to investigate fully the suspected ritual murders for occult purposes. The Government, however, continued to deny the existence of a problem and in 2022 the unexplained disappearances and deaths, ritualistic killings, violent murders, political and police violence continued. Suspected ritual murders were reported in Grand Bassa, Grand Kru, Nimba and Montserrado Counties.

On 26 July 2022, Liberia's 175th independence anniversary, a peaceful demonstration of University of Liberia students before the US embassy in Monrovia, protesting against the poor performance of the Weah administration, was attacked by a pro-Weah group allegedly led by officials of the CDC-COP, including CDC loyalist Ben Topkah, who later claimed to be acting upon orders of Jefferson Koijee (which the latter denied). Several protesters were severely injured in the violence, with one student protester stripped naked, mobbed and tortured. The CDC denied any responsibility for the brutal attack, video footage of which circulated widely on social media. After the violence was condemned by President Weah, many national politicians and community and religious leaders, and representatives of the international community residing in Liberia, seven CDC-COP members were arrested in early August and indicted for attempted murder and aggravated assault.

War Crimes and Economic Crimes Court

After the December 2020 senatorial elections, which weakened the position of the ruling CDC, demands for the establishment of a war crimes and economic crimes court intensified. The establishment of such a court, as requested in the TRC's final report in 2009, has been a long simmering issue in Liberian politics. While in opposition under the Johnson Sirleaf presidency, the CDC had consistently declared itself in favour of implementing all the TRC's recommendations, with Weah having pleaded for the establishment of a war crimes court. However, shortly after Weah's inauguration as President (his candidacy having been supported by popular former rebel leader Prince Johnson), CDC Chairman Mulbah Morlu announced that the creation of such a court was no longer a priority for his party. In September 2019 a resolution of the House of Representatives calling for the establishment of a war crimes and economic crimes court was endorsed by the required two-thirds' majority but blocked by the Speaker, Chambers. While opposition leaders such as Alexander Cummings and Musa Bility have spoken out in favour of a war crimes court, during 2021 CDC support also increased for an end to impunity for suspected war criminals. The National Civil Society Council of Liberia (NCSCL) and the Liberian Council of Churches also advocated the establishment of a war crimes and economic crimes court. In June the newly established National Consortium to Eliminate Impunity in Liberia, comprising 20 professional, religious and civil society organizations including the Liberian National Bar Association and the NCSCL, held a peaceful rally to promote this campaign. However, later that month, in a move which supporters of the court interpreted as a delaying tactic, the Senate proposed establishing a Transitional Justice Commission to analyse the TRC's recommendations and determine why they had not been implemented. In July 2022 Solicitor-General Syrenius Cephas qualified the establishment of an economic and war crimes tribunal as a violation of the Constitution and any presidential act to create such a court as treason. His position likely reflected the thinking of the Government and notably President Weah, who was delaying the creation of such a court despite his numerous pledges at international forums, including the UN General Assembly.

Therefore, 19 years after the end of the second civil war, no Liberian court has yet prosecuted a former warlord or fighter for war crimes or human rights violations. Former President Charles Taylor was convicted and sentenced by the Special Court for Sierra Leone (SCSL) in 2012 for aiding and abetting Sierra Leonean rebels. The arrest of a substantial number of other Liberians abroad, suspected of war crimes in their home country, is a significant indication of the spread of former fighters across the world and their escape routes from justice. To date, 10 Liberians have been arrested in the USA. Charles Taylor's son, 'Chuckie' Taylor, was found guilty of torture in 2009 by a US judge, but he was tried as a US citizen. In 2018 Charles Taylor's right-hand man, Tom Woewiyu, was found guilty by a US court of immigration fraud and lying about his past as a rebel leader, but he died from COVID-19 in 2020 before being sentenced. Another former NPFL commander, Alexander Zinnah, was arrested in the USA in 2017 and was deported to Liberia in April 2020, echoing the deportation in 2012 of former LPC warlord George Boley and of Charles Cooper, a former member of the NPFL and bodyguard of Taylor, in 2018. Furthermore, in April 2018 former ULIMO-K commander Mohammed Jabbateh was sentenced by a US court to 30 years' imprisonment, having been found guilty of immigration fraud and of lying about his past as a rebel leader. Moses Thomas, a former senior commander of President Doe's Special Anti-Terrorist Unit was arrested in the USA in 2018, charged with responsibility for the massacre in 1990 of some 600 people who were seeking refuge in a church in Monrovia; however, while awaiting trial, Thomas managed to flee to Liberia in 2020. In August 2022 a US court ordered him to pay US \$84m. to four victims of the massacre.

Other Liberians arrested on suspicion of war crimes, indicted and awaiting trial include Martina Johnson in Belgium, Kunti Kamara in France, Jankuba Fofana in the UK, and an unnamed person in the UK who was arrested in September 2022. A former NPFL commander, Bill Horace, who had allegedly been involved in war crimes, was shot dead by unidentified assailants in June 2020 in Canada, where he had taken refuge. In June 2021 a Swiss court found former ULIMO-K commander Alieu Kosiah guilty of murder, rape, looting and the use of a child soldier, and sentenced him to 20 years in prison. Meanwhile, in early 2021 the trial of Gibril Massaquoi commenced in Finland where he had obtained permanent residence status. Massaquoi, a Sierra Leonean national and former RUF rebel commander, played a key role in the SCSL trial of Charles Taylor and had, for that reason, been granted protected witness status. He was charged with war crimes and human rights violations during Liberia's second civil war. Objections were consequently raised to his trial, on the alleged grounds that such an action violated his protected witness status. Two months after he was released from prison, in April 2022 the Finnish court acquitted Massaquoi, citing 'resasonable doubt'; the Finnish prosecutors appealed the acquittal. The trial of Massaquoi represents a historic milestone: the Finnish court travelled twice to Liberia and once to Sierra Leone to hear witnesses—the first time that a war crime hearing was held in Liberia.

Two Nationwide Crises

The year 2020 was dominated by two nationwide crises. A shortage of petrol in the first three months led to widespread dissatisfaction with the Government's failure to address corruption and mismanagement in the public sector. In June 2022 it became known that 1.5m. gallons of petrol products worth about US \$6m. was missing from the storage facilities of the LPRC. Its Managing Director confirmed that the country's stockpile of gasoline would only last for three weeks. Hence a

massive shortage loomed large, reminiscent of the petroleum crisis of 2020, which—in combination with the rising fuel prices occasioned by the Russian Federation's invasion of Ukraine in February 2022—could contribute to serious social and political unrest (see *Economy*).

From March 2020 Liberia was impacted by the global outbreak of COVID-19. The first confirmed case of COVID-19 was reported in Monrovia on 16 March. The Ministry of Health immediately declared a national health emergency in the country's most populated county, Montserrado, as well as in Margibi, issuing a series of health protocols and other measures, including the suspension of all commercial flights, and the closure of educational institutions. On 8 April President Weah declared a national state of emergency. Officially, Liberia registered 7,548 confirmed cases of COVID-19 with 294 deaths in the 16 March 2020–5 August 2022 period. However, official data need to be treated with some caution owing to fraud, limited testing and inaccuracies in the attribution of cause of death to COVID-19.

In March 2021 Liberia received 96,000 doses of vaccines under the international COVAX programme and another 27,000 donated by the AU. However, by early July only 85,000 doses had been administered, covering just 1.7% of the population and the vaccination programme only really started in early October.

The pandemic reached a peak in mid-2021, with the Government barring entry into Liberia for persons travelling from India, Pakistan and Bangladesh within the last 14 days, banning gatherings of more than 20 people, and reinforcing the existing (but little respected) health protocols, such as social distancing and mandatory mask wearing in public spaces. The Government's handling of the COVID-19 crisis was widely criticized, with the former Head of the National Public Health Institute of Liberia (NPHIL), Tolbert Nyenswah, accusing officials of complacency and inaction in their response.

In early July 2022 Liberia was officially declared COVID-free, although the virus had not disappeared completely. As of mid-2022 2.3m. Liberians, or 46% of the population, had been fully vaccinated. The NPHIL has acknowledged the existence of extortion cases and fraud, including the swapping of results in COVID-19 testing processes at Liberia's international airport and the lack of basic health precautions. Weah's Government inherited a service which had suffered from years of underfunding, understaffing and poor management, resulting in poorly administered health care facilities, shortages of vital medical equipment and of drugs, and undermotivated personnel.

Human Rights Abuses, Corruption Scandals and Democratic Decline

In December 2019 US Congressman Chris Smith issued a scathing public criticism of the Weah administration and the deteriorating political conditions in Liberia. Smith cited allegations made by the International Justice Group (IJG), a US-based non-governmental organization, which implicated Koijee, the Mayor of Monrovia, in human and civil rights violations—including unlawful arrest, detention, torture, rape and attempted murder—allegedly committed by the Liberian National Security Agency in collusion with the Government. The US Department of State's *Liberia Human Rights Report* has in recent years invariably echoed the accusations of significant human rights violations on the part of the authorities, including arbitrary detention by government officials and killings by police officers; life-threatening prison conditions; violations of the independence of the judiciary; government inaction in cases of violence against women, including rape, domestic violence and FGM; human trafficking; the use of forced or compulsory child labour; the existence or use of laws criminalizing consensual same-sex sexual conduct between adults; and the imposition of substantial restrictions on freedom of expression and on the press. Numerous incidents have been reported including harassment, assaults or detention of journalists by security forces, and the seizure and destruction of their equipment. A local broadcast journalist, Zenu Koboi Miller, died in January 2020 after being assaulted by President Weah's bodyguards. In March a reporter was flogged by executive protection agents while covering a demonstration for the establishment of a war crimes court in Monrovia. In early 2022 Isaac Vah Tukpah, the co-author of an unauthorized biography on Weah, received several death threats for humiliating the President and his wife. In June the police in Lofa County threatened to shoot two journalists who were covering the senatorial elections.

In January 2020 Jerome Verdier, IJG Executive Director and former TRC Chairman, sent a letter to the ICC requesting it to investigate crimes against humanity in Liberia. Verdier accused Koijee of inciting, ordering and overseeing violent actions by vigilante groups loyal to the CDC and the Weah administration. (Koijee later denied any wrongdoing.) Earlier in January two Liberian human rights organizations had published a report on the 'Save the State' demonstration in which they denounced the excessive use of force by state security organizations against peaceful and unarmed protesters.

In September 2020 the US Treasury designated a senior Liberian government official, the former Director of Passports and Visas Andrew Wonplo, for 'significant corruption and passport fraud', after discovering the selling of Liberian travel documents, including diplomatic passports. (Wonplo implicated then Minister of Foreign Affairs Gbehzohngar Findley and President Weah in the passport fraud.) The US action was triggered by the discovery of a Liberian diplomatic passport during a search in the US residence of a Liberian national, Sheik Basirou Kante, following his arrest on charges of money laundering. Kante, who is not entitled to a diplomatic passport, identified himself as the Managing Director of a gold trading company in Liberia (see *Economy*). The search also implicated Vice-President Howard-Taylor. Meanwhile, a controversial Ivorian businessman Ousmane Bamba was also granted a diplomatic passport, allegedly on the President's orders. Since the late 2010s corruption scandals have been reported in the Ministries of Agriculture, Health, Finance and Development Planning, Lands and Mines, and Posts and Telecommunications, as well as in the AFL, police, judiciary and legislature.

In December 2020 the US Treasury imposed economic sanctions on Cape Mount County Senator Varney Sherman, who was accused of significant involvement in the Sable Mining corruption scandal (see *Economy*). The US Department of State's *Human Rights Report on Liberia* for 2020 and 2021 noted no substantial improvements compared with its findings from 2019. The reports mentioned several cases of government agents committing arbitrary and unlawful killings, arbitrary arrests and detention, and abuse, harassment, and intimidation of persons in custody as well as those seeking protection. It was reported that impunity in the security forces was a serious problem as was the continued impunity enjoyed by former warlords and rebel fighters suspected of war crimes.

The election in May 2021 of Prince Johnson as Chairman of the Liberian Senate Committee on Defense and Intelligence was denounced by the US Government under the Global Magnitsky Human Rights Accountability Act (2012), which authorizes the USA to sanction those who are 'responsible for extrajudicial killings, torture, or other gross violations of internationally recognized human rights'. Prince Johnson resigned from the post in July. Relations between the Liberian and US Governments appeared to have hit an all-time low under Weah's leadership. In February 2022 the US House of Representatives adopted a resolution reaffirming its commitment to support progress towards transparency, accountable institutions and other tenets of good governance in Liberia, as it approached the bicentennial of the arrival of the first free Black Americans to Providence Island.

On 15 August 2022 the US Department of the Treasury designated and sanctioned the Minister of State for Presidential Affairs, Nathaniel McGill, the Solicitor-General, Syrenius Cephas, and the Managing Director of the National Port Authority, Bill Twehway, for their alleged involvement in ongoing public corruption including bribery, misappropriation of governments assets, stealing of public funds, rigging contracts, conniving with money launderers, intimidation of prosecutors, obstruction of the rule of law, and organizing warlords to threaten political rivals. The three senior officials were designated and sanctioned under the Global Magnitsky Act.

On 16 August Weah suspended the officials with immediate effect to enable them to face an investigation and they resigned in the following month.

Foreign Affairs

President Weah's foreign policy has, to date, not contrasted greatly from that of his predecessor's, although there are interesting differences. The focus remains on regional and continental African organizations, notably the MRU, ECOWAS and the AU; however, Weah's first official trip outside Africa was to France in February 2018. The many years spent by Weah in France, where he gained cult status as an internationally acclaimed football star, his French citizenship and his proficiency in French have all contributed to a more French-orientated foreign policy than that of his predecessors. Therefore, Liberia's traditionally strong bilateral relations with the UK and Germany have in recent years shifted towards a closer affiliation with France. In June 2021 the French Minister for Europe and Foreign Affairs, Jean-Yves Le Drian, visited Monrovia for talks on regional security matters. He was the first French foreign affairs minister to visit Liberia for more than 40 years. In July President Weah travelled to France at the head of a large delegation. A meeting between Weah and his French counterpart, Emmanuel Macron, resulted in increased French commitments for projects in Liberia, the provision of COVID-19-related equipment, and a pledge by France to strengthen collaboration between the French military and the AFL with regard to the ongoing UN peacekeeping mission in Mali.

As Liberia shares borders with Sierra Leone, Guinea and Côte d'Ivoire, members of some ethnic groups live on both sides of these borders. The four countries together form the MRU, which was originally a regional economic grouping but gradually expanded to address security-related issues in the wake of the civil conflicts in Liberia, Sierra Leone and Côte d'Ivoire. The security component of the organization has recently grown in importance due to the worsening instability in the Sahel region, fuelling fears that rebel attacks and terrorism may spread into West African coastal countries. There is a significant economic aspect to relations between Liberia and Guinea on account of the latter's plans to mine the rich iron ore deposits of Simandou and to transport the ore via Liberia (see *Economy*). President Weah's continued use of a private jet lent to him by a rich business colleague from Burkina Faso for his trips abroad has been much criticized by the opposition, who have also expressed disapproval at the huge costs incurred by Weah's large travelling delegations. The Presidents of Burkina Faso, Côte d'Ivoire, Guinea, Nigeria, Senegal and Sierra Leone all attended Liberia's independence celebrations in Monrovia in July 2019. However, the COVID-19 pandemic led to a decrease in diplomatic travel from early 2020.

In May 2021 Weah attended an extraordinary ECOWAS summit meeting in Ghana on the military coup in Mali. In September 2020 the AU relegated Liberia from full membership to observer status owing to the country's non-payment of its financial obligations to the bloc since 2017 and its failure to submit regular reports on agreed issues. Having settled its debts, in February 2021 Liberia regained its full membership of the AU.

On two occasions in 2022 Liberia was host to a number of foreign dignitaries. In February Liberia celebrated the 200th anniversary of the first successful landing of African American colonists on the shores of what was to become Liberia. The ceremonies and festivities were attended by the heads of state of The Gambia, Niger, Sierra Leone and Togo, the Vice-President of Nigeria, the ECOWAS Chairman, the UN Secretary-General and official delegations, civil society organizations and individuals from Gabon, Ghana, South Africa and the USA. On 26 July Liberia celebrated the 175th anniversary of the founding of the republic, which was attended by the Presidents of The Gambia, Niger and Guinea-Bissau, the latter in his capacity as the new ECOWAS Chairman.

Outside Africa, Liberia's relations with China and Israel merit special attention. Over the years China has become a major development partner and has provided substantial assistance in the areas of infrastructure, agriculture, education and health. As part of efforts undertaken by President

Weah to secure further funding for planned infrastructure projects, he and other government officials attended the 2018 Forum on China-Africa Cooperation in the Chinese capital, Beijing, in September. In June 2021 the Minister of Foreign Affairs, Dee-Maxwell Saah Kemayah, reaffirmed Liberia's continuing commitment to the 'One China Policy', a major cornerstone of China's foreign policy. Weah visited Israel in 2019. In June 2022 a high-level Liberian delegation, headed by McGill and including the Ministers of Agriculture and of Commerce and Industry, visited Israel and met with President Isaac Herzog; the visit may lead to a reopening of Liberia's embassy in Israel. Traditionally the two countries share strong ties, dating back to 1947 when Liberia voted in favour of the establishment of the State of Israel at the UN.

Relations between Liberia and the EU were traditionally based on the Cotonou Agreement, a partnership agreement between the EU and members of the Organisation of African, Caribbean and Pacific States (OACPS). The basic components of the Agreement were continued political dialogue, smaller sectoral and thematical meetings, and a multi-year plan which formed the framework for the expenditure of a determined amount of funds for project financing and budget support. On 15 April 2021 the EU and the OACPS initialled a new 'post-Cotonou' agreement.

Liberia's poor record on human rights, rampant corruption and lack of good governance have led the US Government to keep bilateral relations at a low level. An accusation of sexual harassment levelled against Dee-Maxwell Saah Kemayah by a female staffer of Liberia's mission in New York in early 2021 further complicated the smooth communication between the two countries. Kemayah has since avoided travelling to the USA, where police in New York want to question him. In Liberia the Minister of Foreign Affairs is also involved in a dubious passport affair. The US Government has reportedly turned down several requests by Liberia for an official visit to the White House in Washington, DC, despite Weah's hiring of several well-known US lobbying firms to improve Liberia's image and to enhance US-Liberia relations. However, in mid-2022 Weah received an invitation from the US Government to participate in a US-Africa Leaders Summit in Washington, DC, in December, which, although not a state visit, would finally bring him to the White House. Liberia's vote at the UN General Assembly in March supporting the USA and 139 other countries in condemning Russia's invasion of Ukraine may have contributed to the softening of the US position *vis-à-vis* the Government.

Economy

FRED VAN DER KRAAIJ

INTRODUCTION

Although Liberia possesses abundant natural resources, most of its economic potential remains unexploited. The country's climate and soil are very well suited to the production of rubber and palm oil products, and the cultivation of pineapples, bananas, cocoa beans, coffee, mangoes and other tropical crops. Its numerous rivers and a coastline of some 590 km offer rich fishery resources. Much of the country is covered with tropical hardwood rainforests. Liberia's mineral wealth includes iron ore, gold and diamonds, base metals, and industrial minerals. There are also indications of offshore natural gas and petroleum in commercial quantities. None the less, Liberia ranks among the world's 10 poorest countries. Some 2m. of its 5.3m. population are unable to meet their basic food requirements, with around two-thirds of them living in rural areas. There is widespread and often extreme poverty.

Liberia's economy is characterized by a duality. A modern economy in which foreign investors dominate exists alongside a traditional economy from which the rural population of 2.5m. derives a livelihood. The main economic activities of the rural population are in agriculture, fishing, trading and artisanal mining. Production methods and productivity levels have not changed substantially since the arrival of African-American settlers in the early 19th century. The informal sector of the economy is estimated to contribute between one-third and one-half of gross domestic product (GDP).

The modern economy effectively came into being in the 1920s with the arrival of the US rubber company Firestone, which in 1926 concluded a 99-year Planting Agreement with the Liberian Government. Nevertheless, in the 1930s and 1940s barter trade was still common in the Hinterland, where Liberian money, the British pound and later the US dollar (predominantly used in the 'Americo-Liberian' settlements and the Firestone enclave) were rare.

Liberia's failure to experience even the beginnings of economic growth prior to 1947 can be attributed to the country's need to survive politically. Under its 'Open Door' policy, Liberia hoped to preserve its national territory and sovereignty by attracting foreign investors. Both in earlier years and in recent times, internal factors, such as deficient human resources in the modern economy and low productivity in the traditional economy, in combination with bad governance practices,

formed significant impediments to sustained economic expansion.

THE ECONOMY IN THE PRE-CONFLICT PERIOD, 1944–80

Aided by foreign loans and grants, President William V. S. Tubman (1944–71) developed the infrastructure needed to exploit and export Liberia's rubber, iron ore and timber, which were in high demand during the post-Second World War economic boom. In order to attract foreign capital and expertise, Liberia offered foreign investors generous privileges and incentives, including: extensive tax holidays; freedom from import and export duties; exclusive rights in large concession areas; long concession periods; low wages; and the absence of an active or combative labour movement.

Annual government revenue, which prior to 1940 had been less than US \$1m., rose sharply after Tubman acceded to power. In the last full calendar year of his rule (1970) domestic revenue totalled US \$67m., of which US \$23m. originated from foreign companies. Notwithstanding the large inflow of funds into the Treasury, the Tubman administration borrowed heavily.

Within 25 years the total value of foreign investments exceeded US \$1,000m., mainly in agricultural, mining and forestry operations. Liberia's annual exports increased dramatically from US \$9m. in 1943 to US \$537m. in 1979, the last full year in office of Tubman's successor, William R. Tolbert.

Liberia held some impressive records. It hosted the world's largest rubber plantation, had the largest mercantile fleet, and was Africa's primary (and the world's third largest) exporter of iron ore. At the height of the economic boom during the Tubman administration, Liberia recorded double-digit economic growth figures, while per head GDP was among the highest in sub-Saharan Africa. However, all commodities left the country unprocessed, and Liberia thus squandered opportunities to create value-added locally, develop processing industries and diversify the economy.

President Tolbert acknowledged that the benefits of economic growth were very unevenly shared and instigated several renegotiations of the concession agreements. A complicating factor was the chaotic administration of the concession sector. The Concession Secretariat in the Ministry of Finance, created in 1974, was underfunded and understaffed, while foreign investors' reporting obligations were mostly non-existent and investors frequently refused to provide information to government officials. Consequently, the Government lacked a complete overview of the concession sector, and thus granted exclusive rights in the same area to different investors, for different purposes and under different concession agreements. In the late 1970s the total concession area granted for logging operations actually exceeded Liberia's total forested area.

During the Tolbert administration, domestic revenue almost tripled, reaching US $200m. in the 1978/79 financial year. However, the global recession of the mid-1970s impacted negatively on Liberia's economy and public finances. With domestic revenue declining and expenditure rising, budgetary deficits began to increase. Tolbert's Government reacted with irresponsible borrowing. By mid-1979 public external debt had risen to US $600m.–$700m., twice the size of the national budget.

THE ECONOMY IN THE CONFLICT PERIOD, 1980–2003

After the military takeover of April 1980, the number of dubious business transactions which had characterized the Tolbert administration increased under the regime of Samuel Doe (1980–90). Greedy soldiers, joined by unscrupulous politicians, connived with dishonest foreign investors, and such behaviour increased during the civil wars.

Virtually all foreign investors left the country when the first civil war started in 1989. Warring factions looted abandoned rubber plantations, stole leftover iron ore from mining sites, conspired with illegal logging firms to fell precious trees, and mined diamonds illegally. A handful of foreign investors and traders also took advantage of the anarchy that prevailed during the civil wars, most notably Guus Kouwenhoven (see *Forestry*), a Dutch business partner of the warlord Charles Taylor (who became President in 1997). During 1999–2003 Kouwenhoven was Liberia's most important foreign timber trader. The only major foreign investor to remain during the first civil war was Firestone (purchased in 1988 by Bridgestone of Japan). In 1992 Firestone signed an agreement with Taylor, paying millions of US dollars (which were used to fund the conflict) to the National Patriotic Front of Liberia (NPFL) in order to resume operations at its Harbel plantation.

Upon seizing power in April 1980, Doe tripled the salaries of soldiers and doubled those of civil servants. Employment in the civil service grew by 300% in 1980–83. Consequently, the Government's recurrent expenditure rose sharply, and large budgetary deficits ensued. Mismanagement, including unlimited looting of public finances, large-scale embezzlement and rampant corruption led to the 'vanishing' of at least US $60m. per year out of an annual budget of around US $200m. However, the US Administration came to Doe's rescue: eager to keep Liberia within its sphere of influence, it provided massive financial support. In 1980–85 US aid to Liberia amounted to US $500m., the highest amount per capita in sub-Saharan Africa.

By the end of the 1980s Liberia's economy had foundered. The International Monetary Fund (IMF) and World Bank had ceased lending to the country, which had accumulated debt service arrears of some US $400m. As Liberia was also defaulting on US loans, the USA suspended (temporarily) its aid to the Doe regime.

THE ECONOMY IN THE POST-CONFLICT PERIOD, 2003–22

The National Transitional Government of Liberia (NTGL), which was installed in 2003 after 24 years of conflict, inherited an empty Treasury, while the net reserves of the Central Bank of Liberia (CBL) were close to zero. Government institutions had ceased to function, and the economy was in total ruins. Capacity had disappeared as a result of the fleeing of competent persons and related brain drain, conflict-related deaths and destroyed infrastructure. In 2004 GDP was below US $500m., less than one-half of its value in 1998. Agriculture, the most important economic activity, had completely

disintegrated. Official mining activities had ceased, and that sector's share of GDP had dwindled from 12% in 1988 to less than 0.1% in 2004. Meanwhile, the contribution of the tertiary sector had declined from 50% of GDP to 17%. Unemployment was estimated at 85% of the total labour force in the formal sector, and overall, around 1m. people were unemployed, most of them living in urban areas, and notably in the capital, Monrovia. Poor living conditions were endemic: three-quarters of Liberians lived on less than US $1 per day and around one-half on less than US $0.50. There was no electricity, unless produced by privately owned generators. Basic facilities (such as clean drinking water), if available, could only be enjoyed by a privileged few. Traditionally, the main trading activities were controlled by a substantial Lebanese community—except for the numerous street vendors and local markets—but the purchasing power of the urban population was extremely low.

The NTGL adopted a US $80m. national budget for the 2004/05 financial year. This represented per capita spending of less than US $25 per Liberian (on an annual basis), which was one of the lowest levels in the world.

In February 2004 international donors pledged more than US $500m. in reconstruction aid for Liberia. However, when the leading aid-providing agencies—the Economic Community of West African States (ECOWAS), the African Union (AU), the IMF, the World Bank and the European Union (EU)—discovered that systematic fraud, embezzlement, mismanagement and outright theft within the NTGL were so pervasive that they were obstructing economic reconstruction and a durable peace, a Governance and Economic Management Assistance Programme (GEMAP) was drawn up. Following pressure from the International Contact Group on Liberia (ICGL, representing the major international donors), including a threat to cut off all international aid if the proposed programme were not accepted, the GEMAP document was signed by NTGL Chairman Gyude Bryant and the ICGL in September 2005.

Under GEMAP (2006–10), foreign financial and management experts were placed in senior positions in key ministries, state corporations and state-owned enterprises. Most notably, they were appointed to roles in and given co-signatory authority over the financial affairs of the CBL, the ministries of finance and of lands, mines and energy, and in five revenue-generating state organizations where former combatants were also in positions of responsibility: the National Port Authority; Robertsfield International Airport; the Forestry Development Authority; the Liberian Petroleum Refining Company; and the Bureau of Maritime Affairs. The expert delegated to work alongside the Executive Director of the CBL was also given co-signatory powers in all operational matters, and all foreign specialists were given such powers over the procurement of goods and services. The revenues generated by the five agencies were placed into a separate account. The programme was overseen by an Economic Governance Steering Committee, co-chaired by the President of Liberia and the US ambassador to Liberia.

The Administration of President Johnson Sirleaf, 2006–18

After Ellen Johnson Sirleaf became President in January 2006, she faced a number of major economic problems, including a huge external debt, a devastated infrastructure, and lack of investment funds. Aided by her extensive network resulting from many years of working in international organizations, Johnson Sirleaf successfully sought financial assistance from abroad. The international community wanted a stable economy to maintain the fragile peace in the country and was prepared to assist in the reconstruction of Liberia, not only with a costly peacekeeping operation, the United Nations Mission in Liberia (UNMIL—established in 2003 and which operated until 2018), but also with aid funds.

One of the main issues to be tackled was the elimination of the external debt. An interim Poverty Reduction Strategy Paper (PRSP), covering 2006–08, preceded a fully fledged second PRSP (2008–11), which was required to qualify for access to the Heavily Indebted Poor Countries (HIPC) initiative of the World Bank and the IMF. The PRSP policy goals were linked to the UN Millennium Development Goals

(MDGs), although Johnson Sirleaf cautioned that due to Liberia's post-conflict status it was highly unlikely that it would meet any of the MDGs by 2015.

In 2006 Liberia had the highest debt-to-GDP ratio in the world, with external debt amounting to US \$4,700m. In December 2007 Liberia's arrears with the World Bank and the African Development Bank (AfDB) were reduced by US \$400m. and US \$240m., respectively, using bridging loans, which restored Liberia's voting rights with these multilateral agencies. In March 2008 an agreement with the IMF ended Liberia's suspension from the Fund. Meanwhile, the second PRSP had been approved by the IMF and World Bank, thereby enabling Liberia to meet the decision point qualifications under the enhanced HIPC initiative, begin the debt relief process and embark on a three-year, IMF-supported programme. In June 2010 Liberia reached the HIPC completion point, and external debt to the value of US \$4,600m. (some 90% of the total outstanding) was cancelled.

Liberia's inadequate power infrastructure constituted one of the greatest challenges for the Johnson Sirleaf Government. In 2007 only 3% of the Liberian population had access to electricity. The reconstruction of the country's largest hydropower plant, Mount Coffee in Montserrado County, which had been looted and destroyed by Taylor's forces in 1990, was crucial to the rehabilitation of the electricity network and the rebuilding of the modern economy. The first phase of reconstruction of the Mount Coffee plant, the cost of which (estimated at US \$360m.) was funded by the international donor community, took 10 years to complete. In July 2017 the plant's four hydropower turbines became operational, with a total installed capacity of 88 MW, which doubled Liberia's existing power generation capacity.

Another major task was increasing government revenues. In 2005/06 domestic revenue amounted to just US \$90m., but by 2007/08 it had increased to US \$200m. Interestingly, this was equivalent to the value of domestic revenue (in nominal terms) almost 30 years earlier, when Johnson Sirleaf served briefly as Minister of Finance. Domestic revenue reached US \$509m. in 2012/13, although this amount was largely surpassed by the aid funds from the international donor community. Thus, in the post-HIPC period (2011–13) some US \$1,000m. per year was available to finance the priority areas agreed upon between the Government, the international donor community and the population. However, a large proportion of government expenditure in the early 2010s (on average 60%–80%) was recurrent expenditure, which reduced the amount of funds available for investment purposes.

With scarce domestic funds to stimulate the local economy, modernize the agricultural sector and exploit Liberia's abundant resources, President Johnson Sirleaf turned to foreign investors, as her predecessors Tolbert and Tubman had done.

The Private Sector—The Concession Sector

In Liberia all investments over US \$10m. require a concession agreement to become operational. Investments in priority areas may benefit from special incentives granted by an inter-ministerial concession committee, which is chaired by the National Investment Commission (NIC). Key roles in the relations between the Government and concessionaries have also been allocated to the National Concessions Bureau (NCB), the Public Procurement and Concessions Commission (PPCC) and the Extractive Industries Transparency Initiative (EITI).

The mandate of the NCB, created in 2011, includes the monitoring and evaluation of concession agreements and the provision of technical assistance in the bid award process. The Bureau is also mandated to provide technical assistance to the various government entities responsible for granting and regulating the various concessions. The PPCC, another autonomous public institution, was created in 2006 to guarantee that public procurement and concessions processes take place in a transparent and non-discriminatory way and to ensure the efficient use of public funds. The Liberia EITI was created as an autonomous agency in 2009 to promote revenue transparency and accountability in the extractive sectors and operates on a partnership basis between the Government, investors and civil society. Liberia is the only EITI-compliant

country to have added agriculture and forestry to the traditional EITI scope of hydrocarbons and mining.

Johnson Sirleaf was very successful in attracting foreign investors, notably following the HIPC debt cancellation, and had initially claimed that foreign investments into Liberia could surpass US \$20,000m. However, by the end of her second term it became clear that this was unrealistic, partly due to a fall in commodity prices, the protracted effects of the Ebola Virus Disease (EVD) epidemic of 2014, and an over-optimism about the reliability of foreign investors. Furthermore, some of the mistakes made by her predecessors continued into many of the concession agreements granted after 2006. The size of the areas granted, the duration of the concessions, and the interests of the indigenous population in these areas were among the concerns raised. Additionally, the trustworthiness and financial strength of potential investors was a persistent issue. Moreover, indications of bribery, corruption, covert agreements, and a lack of transparency were far from absent. The start of George Weah's presidency in 2018 brought no substantial alterations.

Agriculture

Liberia is not self-sufficient in food. Rice constitutes the main imported food item, with annual rice imports showing a rising trend. Population growth, urbanization, displacement of people during civil conflict, changing consumer preferences and large-scale commercial export-orientated farming diverting land and labour away from food production for local consumption are among the main factors behind the increase in annual rice imports since the early 1970s. In 2020 Liberia imported 380,000 metric tons of rice, equating to an average of 74–75kg per person.

Liberia's two main commercial agricultural products are rubber and oil palm fruit, and both are exported unprocessed. Production of both commodities are long-term activities. It takes about four years before an oil palm tree becomes productive, and seven years before a rubber tree starts producing rubber. Both species have a productive life of around 25 years. Liberia, once a significant player on the international rubber market, no longer ranks among the world's most important rubber producers, while its aim to become a major exporter of palm oil products has not been achieved. Rubber production decreased from 68,285 metric tons in 2019 to 63,734 tons in 2020, reportedly owing to lower levels of output among smallholders due to lockdown measures introduced following the onset of COVID-19 pandemic in March 2020. Rubber production in 2021 showed a substantial increase to 87,777 tons, mainly resulting from increased production by smallholders. (In 2022 some 1,500 smallholders, concentrated in Margibi, Bong and Nimba Counties, were registered for tax purposes). Rubber exports rose from US \$82.6m. in 2020 to US \$109.9m. in 2021, partly resulting from higher world market prices, which also had a positive impact on the value of crude palm oil exports. Crude palm oil production increased to 25,041 tons in 2021, compared to 22,465 tons in 2019 and 22,286 tons in 2020, with pandemic-related limitations on labour mobility explaining the stagnation in 2020.

In 2021 the Government concluded a US \$20m. Investment Incentive Agreement with local Indian businessman Upjit Singh Sachdeva for a rubber processing factory, which could end a nearly century-old practice of exporting unprocessed natural rubber. The Jeety Rubber Factory will process some 25,000 metric tons of rubber yearly, create about 300 jobs and produce tyres and other rubber products, targeting the ECOWAS market. The (renewable) agreement has a life span of 15 years. Construction of the factory, in Margibi County, began in June 2022; its first output is expected in 2026. In 2021 six companies (five of which were foreign-owned) were operating nine rubber and oil palm plantations of various sizes. Following the initial establishment of plantations by US and European companies under President Tubman's 'Open Door' policy, there has been a recent shift to Asian-owned companies. An unknown number of Liberian-owned rubber and oil palm plantations also exist, varying in size, age, productivity, employment and profitability. The largest active Liberian-owned plantation is operated by the Morris American Rubber Company in Todee District, Montserrado County, covering around 10,000 ha. The Sinoe Rubber Corporation, also Liberian-owned, is the former African Fruit Company (founded in 1952) and covers more than 240,000 ha; however, the plantation is currently in a state of neglect. Most of Liberia's rubber output is produced on three foreign-owned plantations.

The oldest and largest foreign-owned rubber plantation is operated by the Japanese Bridgestone Group (Firestone Liberia), currently the parent company of the Firestone Plantations Company, which itself was a wholly owned subsidiary of the Firestone Tire and Rubber Company (USA) from 1926 until 1988, when it was sold for US $2,650m. Firestone Liberia operates the world's largest single natural rubber plantation, at Harbel, Margibi County, which covers about 48,000 ha. The original 1926 Planting Agreement had a lifespan of 99 years. A revised concession agreement approved by the NTGL in 2005, which extended the lease term generously to 2091, was cancelled and renegotiated by President Johnson Sirleaf in 2008, and the new agreement is due to expire in 2041. Accumulated investments since 2003 exceed US $2,000m. The Liberian Government has an ambivalent relationship with Firestone, which recently has become the second largest private employer in the country, employing more than 4,000 workers who, besides their salary, benefit from free housing, medical care and education for themselves and their dependants. Firestone finances and operates the largest concession-run school system in Liberia, incorporating 24 schools with over 7,000 students. The company operates a 300-bed medical centre in Duside, Margibi County, which is highly regarded. However, in 1930 Firestone was accused of using forced labour on its plantations, and during the civil war it reportedly paid millions of US dollars to Charles Taylor in exchange for being permitted to continue to operate. Moreover, in its nearly 100 years of operations in Liberia the company has continuously failed to add value to its produce by processing rubber locally into a final product. In December 2021 a new bridge built by Firestone and connecting major parts of the concession area was officially opened, replacing the old bridge which collapsed in 2017. Some 60% of the costs of the rebuilt bridge—amounting to US $1.8m., including access roads—will be returned to Firestone as tax relief in the future.

In 2007 the Government and the Societé Financière des Caoutchoucs (SocFin), a Luxembourg-registered (and Belgian-based) rubber company, signed an agreement for the rehabilitation of two plantations, one in Bong County (operated by the Salala Rubber Corporation—SRC, on the basis of a 1959 agreement granting a concession area of 40,000 ha for 70 years) and the other in Grand Bassa County (operated by the Liberian Agricultural Company—LAC, initially on a 70-year concession for 240,000 ha, also granted in 1959).

The LAC plantation is Liberia's second largest rubber plantation in terms of size (covering 12,800 ha planted; actual concession size: 121,407 ha) and production. Output is around 25,000 metric tons of rubber per year (28,363 tons in 2020) and the company is the largest private employer in Liberia with some 4,300 workers, while more than 30,000 people depend on LAC's economic activities and social infrastructure. As a public electricity network was absent in the region and to reduce fuel consumption, the LAC constructed a biomass facility (operational from 2014) and a hydropower dam in 2016. It also operates a rubber processing plant. SocFin has adopted a similar approach at the SRC plantation. The company rehabilitated the old plantation, invested in the social infrastructure, and works with local smallholders. At present the plantation covers 4,400 ha and employs 700 people, directly and indirectly. SRC's production, with 327 tons in 2020, is still low, but LAC and SRC's combined production accounts for about 18% of SocFin's total rubber production. However, in 2019 four non-governmental organizations (NGOs) representing 22 communities in Margibi and Bong Counties accused SocFin of: 'grabbing' ancestral territory; forced eviction; lack of consultation; economic displacement and loss of livelihood; violations of employment conditions and labour rights; water pollution; gender-based violence; and threats of reprisals and intimidation. An official complaint was submitted to the World Bank's International Finance Corporation (IFC), which had provided SocFin with a US $10m. loan to develop the SRC plantation. In early 2020 SocFin declined to participate in a dispute resolution process under the auspices of the IFC, accusing the latter of being biased. After the IFC ruled later in the year that the communities' complaint was valid, the SRC resorted to delaying tactics. By early 2022 the situation remained unresolved.

In 2022 the Government launched a five-year National Oil Palm Strategy and Action Plan (2021–26) for the promotion and guidance of sustainable oil palm production. In recent years, oil palm cultivation has been increasing in importance, with more than 1m. ha now planted with oil palm trees. An estimated 220,000 people work in the oil palm sector, approximately 10% of agricultural employment, with one out of every five households producing palm oil. Palm oil producers are Liberian medium and smallholders, as well as foreign concessionaires.

Among the major palm oil concessions is a 169,000 ha area in Grand Bassa and Sinoe Counties, with an expansion area of 80,000 ha in Rivercess County, operated by the UK-based (majority Malaysian-owned) Equatorial Palm Oil (EPO). The concession area includes forested lands owned and occupied by local communities which were not consulted or involved in the negotiations preceding the concession agreement. Following the signing of the agreement in 2008, EPO commenced the rehabilitation and replanting of two plantations that had been abandoned during the civil war. However, EPO's relations with local communities and its workers have been far from harmonious. Since September 2018 EPO has operated a palm oil mill at its Palm Bay plantation in Grand Bassa County, with the capacity to process up to 30 (and ultimately 60) metric tons per hour; the first shipments from the mill were made in early 2019 via the ports of Monrovia and Buchanan. It was reported in 2021 that EPO had been renamed Capital Metals, and it subsequently shut down its operations in Liberia, due to persistent land acquisition conflicts. Little is known about the settlement of the company's obligations under its concession agreement and the follow-up of the concession.

In 2009 the Malaysian-owned Sime Darby Group concluded a 63-year concession agreement with the Government for the development of oil palm and rubber plantations. Sime Darby was granted a concession area of more than 300,000 ha in Bomi, Grand Cape Mount, Bong and Gbarpolu Counties, of which 220,000 ha were designated for oil palm plantations. Like other concessionaires, the company (with a 4,000-strong workforce) also clashed with local communities over customary rights of ownership and use of land. Its planting activities were impeded by the EVD epidemic, such that by mid-2019 only 10,400 ha had been planted with oil palm trees and just 107 ha with rubber trees. In December Sime Darby sold its loss-making Liberian subsidiary for a token US $1 (plus an earn-out payment) to Mano Palm Oil Industries (MPO), a Liberian company and subsidiary of the Lebanese-owned Mano Manufacturing Company (MANCO), the largest manufacturer of household health and cleaning products in Liberia. MPOI was granted a 15-year tax break and in 2022 its oil palm plantations covered 10,401 ha, mainly in Grand Cape Mount, Bomi and Lofa Counties. (MPOI also runs a 120-ha rubber plantation in Bomi County.). MPOI is in the process of applying for Roundtable on Sustainable Palm Oil (RSPO) certification.

In 2010 Golden Veroleum Liberia (GVL, backed by Golden Agri-Resources of Singapore, the world's second largest palm oil producer) concluded a 65-year concession agreement with the Liberian Government for the development of more than 220,000 ha of oil palm plantations in the south-east of the country (incorporating parts of Sinoe, Grand Kru, Rivercess, River Gee and Maryland Counties). By late 2020, however, GVL had developed only about 19,000 ha of land, mainly owing to the actions of local communities, who accused the company of 'land grabbing', destroying precious wetlands and the habitat of endangered species through vast deforestation, and human rights violations, notably the desecration of sacred and burial sites. GVL is an RSPO member and in July 2018 announced a Sustainability Action Plan. Due to low world market prices for crude palm oil and the economic effects of the COVID-19 pandemic, GVL laid off more than 10% of its workforce in May 2020. This fuelled bitterness within the local communities which had given up their lands in exchange for jobs created by the company. In August 2021 the Sustainable

Development Institute, a Liberian NGO, and Milieudefensie, its Dutch partner organization, accused GVL of violating an agreement signed in 2014 with local communities resulting in human rights abuses and environmental damage, including deforestation. In contrast, the Association of Liberian Journalists in Peace Building honoured GVL in August 2022 as 'Liberia's Most Outstanding Corporate Concessionaire for the Year 2021/2022' because of the more than 3,000 jobs created, housing facilities provided, free health care for its employees and their dependents, construction and rehabilitation of schools, and the company's annual contributions to Community Development Funds.

In 2011 the industrial group SIFCA of Côte d'Ivoire and the Government concluded a 25-year concession agreement for the development of rubber and oil palm plantations in Liberia. SIFCA Rubber and Oil Palm Plantations operates the Maryland Oil Palm Plantation (MOPP—formerly owned by Firestone) and the Cavalla Rubber Plantation (CRP), both of which are in Maryland and River Gee Counties. SIFCA agreed to increase the extent of the CRP from 8,100 ha to 35,000 ha, although this project too was beset by controversy. In 2019 the Government concluded an Oil Palm Investment Incentive Agreement with Golden SIFCA, a Liberian-registered corporation and a 50:50 joint venture between GVL and MOPP for the development of oil palm plantations in south-eastern Liberia (Maryland, Sinoe and Grand Kru Counties). The 28-year agreement also aims to develop and operate a US $34m. oil palm processing plant in Pleebo, Maryland County, with an initial capacity of 40 metric tons per hour, to be doubled over the term of the agreement. The construction of the Golden SIFCA Palm Mill commenced in 2021. However, in December the local population protested against the lack of progress, complained of broken promises and demanded a copy of the Golden SIFCA concession agreement to know their rights and the company's obligations.

In July 2020 Liberia's legislature approved another Investment Incentive Agreement, for the construction and operation of a crude oil palm refinery by the Liberian-registered Fouani Brothers Corporation, at an estimated cost of US $30m. The output of the refinery would be for the local market and for export to neighbouring Mano River Union member states (Côte d'Ivoire, Guinea and Sierra Leone). By mid-2022 no progress had been reported with respect to the project.

Forestry

The Forestry Development Authority (FDA), a semi-public autonomous corporation created in 1976, is mandated sustainably to manage and conserve the forests and related resources of Liberia, including by protecting the National Parks and supervising the community forest system. In economic terms, the forestry sector contributes approximately 10% to the national economy. The Liberia Timber Association comprises some 30 investment and trading companies, both Liberian and foreign-owned.

A National Forest Inventory Report published by the FDA and the UN's Food and Agriculture Organization (FAO) in March 2021 revealed that Liberia's tropical forests, long thought to cover just one-third of the country, actually comprise some 6.6m. ha, or about 68% of the total land area. Liberia incorporates the largest part of the remaining forested area of the Upper Guinean rainforest. The forests have a high biodiversity, with around 250 different tree species, of which about 60 are of commercial interest. The Sapo National Park in Sinoe County, covering an area of 1,804 sq km, ranks among the top 10 rainforests in the world and reportedly has the highest mammal species diversity of any region worldwide. However, it has suffered from illegal farming and hunting, while the Government has also granted concessions and licences for logging and mining activities in violation of the FDA's mandate. The forest cover and biodiversity of another national park, the East Nimba Nature Reserve, are also under threat due to logging activities, mining operations and population growth.

By 2003 annual timber exports were valued at US $100m., representing 20% of GDP. The 'conflict timber' issue, as it was termed by the international NGO Global Witness, led to the imposition of bans on timber exports from Liberia by the UN

Security Council and the EU in 2003, which remained in force until 2006.

Shortly after Johnson Sirleaf took office as President in January 2006, she cancelled all of the 70 or so timber concession agreements concluded by her predecessors. This decision followed the revelation by the Forest Concession Review Committee that nearly two-and-a-half times the entire forested area of Liberia had been granted to logging companies. The review documented widespread illegal logging, irregular financial transactions of logging companies, and their active involvement in the civil war. Aided by the lifting of the ban on timber exports, President Johnson Sirleaf started to reform the forestry sector. In 2006 the National Forestry Reform Law was adopted. From 2009 commercial logging operations gradually resumed. However, fraud, corruption and mismanagement persisted. In 2012 President Johnson Sirleaf ordered the suspension of all logging operations, including the so-called Private Use Permits (PUPs—which authorized private owners to exploit their own forest resources), dissolved the FDA Board and deferred any further reform of the forestry sector. Several FDA officials were put on trial for their involvement in the illegal issuing of 61 PUPs (out of the 66 granted) and were found guilty in September 2015.

The Land Rights Policy, adopted in 2013, and the Land Rights Act, signed into law in September 2018, play an important role in the management and exploitation of Liberia's forest resources. The new legal framework recognizes the rights of communities to their customary lands, as well as their rights to participate in the management of the local forests and to receive a share of forestry revenue. Customary land is now recognized as a formal category of land holding. However, abuses still exist both in the forestry and productive agriculture sectors. Under the Community Rights Law, Community Forest Management Agreements (CFMAs) are concluded between local communities and commercial parties with the FDA's consent. There were at least 23 active CFMAs as of mid-2021. The FDA is paid the commercial party's rental fees but often fails to transfer these funds to local communities. In 2021 the Government—through the FDA—reportedly owed forest communities some US $3m. in land rental fees accrued through commercial logging activities over the previous four years.

In mid-2022 it was reported that the Universal Forestry Corporation (UFC), a mining and logging company co-owned by Minister of Posts and Telecommunications Cooper Kruah, was involved in the unauthorized harvesting of logs in Nimba County. Moreover, the UFC subcontracted a company ineligible for any logging operations because it is owned by a former Superintendent of Grand Cape Mount County, who in 2015 had been dismissed for 'misuse of public funds'. In late 2021 a group of civil society organizations reported that two companies—the Liberian-owned Renaissance Group Inc and Freedom Group Liberia, owned by Liberian and US shareholders, while being subcontracted by the Liberian owned Tarpeh Timber Company—had illegally felled logs outside a concession area in Grand Bassa County and exported the logs with a value of US $2.5m. During 2018–21 Sing Africa Plantation Liberia Ltd, a Singaporean company owned by the Gupta family, illegally cut high-value trees ('ekko wood', one of the most expensive tree species on the world market, with an estimated value of US $2.2m.) outside its concession area in Lofa County. Despite violating the National Forestry Reform Law, the FDA had authorized the harvesting.

Mining

The Ministry of Mines and Energy is responsible for the administration and supervision of the mining sector, including the granting of mining rights and licences, in collaboration with the NIC and NCB. The Minerals and Mining Law of 2000 forms the sector's legal framework, while the Liberia Revenue Code provides its fiscal regime. Mining companies in principle pay tax on taxable income, royalties and surface rent, but practices may vary in accordance with the Mineral Development Agreement (MDA) concerned.

The Ministry of Mines and Energy reported that by September 2022 there were 920 registered active licences out of a total of 7,148 agreed licences for trading purposes, industrial operations and artisanal mining activities. Artisanal or small-scale mining activities accounted for 66.4% of active licences, trading licences for 10.3%, and industrial licences for large scale-mining operations for 23.3%, including several MDAs with foreign companies.

The mining sector is characterized by land disputes with local communities, overlapping mining claims between concession holders and an unequal relationship between the host country and foreign investors. The Liberian Government is dealing with powerful large-scale international mining corporations which are better equipped and have more financial resources and experience than the understaffed and ill-equipped Ministry of Mines and Energy.

In economic terms the mining sector is dominated by foreign investors, who engage in large-scale operations on the basis of long-term concession agreements, mining the country's iron ore, gold and diamond deposits. The gold and diamond mining sectors also have important small-scale, artisanal (and largely non-registered, illegal) components which operate mostly outside government control. In 2021, according to official preliminary figures, iron ore, gold and diamonds accounted for a combined 80.0% of total exports (although due to inaccurate reporting and illegal exports, actual values may vary).

Liberia was a leading world exporter of iron ore during the 1960s and 1970s from just four pioneering mines. After the civil war, there was a considerable revival of investor interest in Liberia's rich iron ore deposits. Seven concession agreements (now known as MDAs) were concluded with foreign investors, from India (ArcelorMittal, Sesa Sterlite), People's Republic of China/Hong Kong (China-Union Investment), Russia (Putu Iron Ore Mining), Australia (Tawana Resources), South Africa (Cavalla Resources) and the UK (Iron Bird Resources, a subsidiary of Hummingbird Resources). From the early days of Liberia's dealings with foreign investors, the negotiating trajectories of the concession agreements were frequently beset by allegations of corruption and complicated financial constructions. In 2016 it was revealed that a British company, Sable Mining, had allegedly bribed senior government officials and legislators to 'facilitate' the conclusion of an MDA that would have given the company access to the rich iron ore deposits of the Wologisi Range, in Lofa County. By 2021 only ArcelorMittal remained active in Liberia's iron ore mining sector. In June 2022 Western Cluster Liberia (WCL) began mining operations in Bomi Hills, Bomi County, on the site of Liberia's first successful iron ore mine (1951–77). The Indian-owned WCL operates on the basis of a 25-year MDA originally concluded in 2011 with the Elenilto Group. The WCL concession area contains three important iron ore deposits: Bomi Hills, the Mano River reserves in Gbarpolu County and the Bea Mountain reserves in Grand Cape Mount County.

In 2019 the Government granted Solway Mining, a subsidiary of a Swiss-based Estonian-Russian investment company, the Solway Investment Group, a three-year exploration licence. However, three communities in Nimba County accused the company of illegal encroaching on community-owned forestland. A complicating issue is that the Community Rights Law, which grants communities all legal rights over their communal lands, conflicts with the Minerals and Mining Law, which stipulates that minerals on the surface of the ground or in the soil, rivers, streams and territorial waters are state property.

In 2021, according to official figures, exports of iron ore (all produced by ArcelorMittal) accounted for a preliminary 39.5% of Liberia's total exports, compared with 47.6% in 2020.

In 2005 ArcelorMittal, the world's leading steel producer, and the NTGL concluded a 25-year MDA for the development of iron ore mines in northern Liberia. President Johnson Sirleaf renegotiated the agreement in 2006. Under the amended MDA, ArcelorMittal agreed to: reopen the mines formerly operated by the Liberian American-Swedish Minerals Company Joint Venture (created in 1953) at Yekepa, in Nimba County; surface the 72 km of road between Yekepa and Ganta; reconstruct the 265-km Yekepa–Buchanan railway; and rehabilitate part of the port of Buchanan. In 2011 the (symbolic) shipment of iron ore took place. In September 2021 a third amendment to the MDA was signed between the Government and ArcelorMittal to allow for the company's

expansion project, known as Phase II, with investments of US $800m.–$1,000m. bringing its total investments in Liberia to over US $2,500m. Upon the completion of Phase II, ArcelorMittal's annual output in Liberia would rise from its current level of 5m. metric tons of direct shipment ore to 15m. tons of high-value concentrate product, and even expand to 30m. tons. At least 2,000 new jobs would be created and ArcelorMittal's tax and other payments to Liberia would increase from an annual US $30m.–$40m. to more than US $75m. Production of concentrate under the project was originally expected to commence in 2023. However, due to objections raised by the legislature, ratification of the amendment was still pending as of September 2022. A major issue was the use of the Yekepa–Buchanan railway and Buchanan port (see below).

Over the years a number of developments have damaged relations between ArcelorMittal and the Liberian Government. In 2019 the Government concluded a 25-year concession agreement with the Bulgarian-based Prista Oil Holding, allowing it to manage the port of Buchanan. ArcelorMittal objected, claiming that the concession area overlapped its own infrastructure in Buchanan and interfered with its Phase II expansion project. ArcelorMittal also protested vehemently when Solway Mining was granted exploration rights in the eastern Nimba mountain range—over which ArcelorMittal claimed exclusive concession rights. In July 2022 President Weah publicly supported Solway Mining, whose main financier is a Russian-Estonian businessman with strong ties to the Russian leadership. ArcelorMittal has also invested US $500m. in the rehabilitation of the Yekepa–Buchanan railway and infrastructure of Buchanan port (both state-owned), and planned to invest an additional US $200m. as part of Phase II. However, in early 2022 the Liberian Government allowed High Power Exploration Inc (HPX), a US-based mining company, to use the Nimba–Buchanan railway and Buchanan port to export iron ore from its planned Nimba Iron Ore Project in Guinea—a major investment of hundreds of millions of US dollars.

Gold reserves exist in most of Liberia's counties, and small-scale mining is very important to local economies. Artisanal gold miners use simple tools and methods and operate in often dangerous circumstances, resulting in frequent accidents. In February 2019 more than 60 illegal miners died at the Gboanipea gold mine in Nimba County, after being trapped underground following a landslide, while in May 2020 about 50 miners died in a mine collapse in Grand Cape Mount County. Data on the informal gold mining sector are scarce and unreliable. Several thousand artisanal miners are known to operate (many without a licence) in the Sapo National Park in Sinoe County. The Minister of Mines and Energy, Gesler Murray, stated in February 2022 that illegal mining was increasing, referring specifically to Gbarpolu County. Liberia's porous borders with Guinea, Sierra Leone and Côte d'Ivoire, the proliferation of illicit buyers from Senegal, Mali, Guinea and Côte d'Ivoire, and the connivance of government officials with illegal miners and traders are part of the problem.

Around 100,000 people are believed to be involved—as miners, buyers and intermediaries—in Liberia's informal gold sector, providing support for about 500,000 dependants (10% of the population). Official gold exports show a remarkable increase in the past few years, from US $165.8m. in 2017 to some US $340.3m. in 2021, partly owing to higher world prices for gold. It is estimated that up to 10 times the amount of gold mined by artisanal miners that is officially reported is smuggled out of the country. International gold prices rose to a record high due to greater investment in gold during the COVID-19 crisis. The resulting 'gold rush' led to increased interest among international mining companies and a rise in the number of unlicensed and illegal miners.

There are known to be significant deposits of diamonds in Grand Cape Mount, Gbarpolu, Lofa, Montserrado, Nimba, Grand Bassa and Sinoe Counties. Traditionally, diamond mining is illegal and shrouded in secrecy. 'Conflict diamonds' contributed to financing the civil war, and led to the UN and EU banning imports of diamonds from Liberia from 2001 until April 2007. The following month Liberia was admitted to the Kimberley Process Certification Scheme. Small-scale artisanal alluvial diamond mining provides a livelihood for tens of thousands of artisanal miners. In 2013 the Government estimated that over 75% of the diamonds produced in western Liberia were smuggled to Sierra Leone. Given that the value of official diamond exports decreased from US $31.8m. in 2018 to US $12.1m. in 2020 (although it rose slightly to a preliminary US $15.2m. in 2021), this situation does not appear to have improved in recent years.

Under the 2000 Minerals and Mining Law it is mandatory to obtain a licence before engaging in mining activities. However, in practice, only a small fraction of artisanal miners possess a Class C Licence, which is only available to Liberian citizens. The remote location of gold and diamond deposits render government monitoring of mining activities difficult. In general, the informal gold and diamond sectors are unregulated and linked to corruption, money laundering and other illegal financial transfers. In recent years, an increase in the illegal presence of foreign national miners has met with xenophobic accusations and attacks, and increased insecurity. Consequently, the Government loses tens of millions of US dollars each year in tax revenues from the informal gold and diamond mining sectors.

In the large-scale gold and diamond mining sectors, frequent changes of ownership occur, which, in combination with the remote location of the mines, hinders government efforts to acquire current information about company activities. By mid-2022 six foreign-owned gold mining companies had acquired licences for exploratory activities or had signed an MDA for actual mining operations. In Grand Cape Mount County, Avesoro Resources has taken over the 25-year concession awarded to the UK's Mano River Resources in 2001 for the Mano River area (and a subsequent mining licence, agreed in 2009, for the Bea Mountain area). The MDA was revised in 2013 at the request of the Government. Avesoro Resources thus has the following concession rights: the New Liberty gold project (the largest in Liberia), the Weaju project area and the Ndablama and Leopard Rock gold sites, with a mining licence area of 457 sq km and five contiguous exploration licences covering 581.2 sq km. It is one of Liberia's most important foreign investors, with over 2,000 employees and significant levels of gold production through its subsidiaries Bea Mountain Mining Corporation and MNG Gold (Liberia). The latter company operates a mining site in Kokoyah, Bong County, under an agreement concluded with the Government in 2020 which allows it to carry out underground mining for gold. In December 2019 Avesoro Resources was bought by a major shareholder, Turkish businessman Murathan Nazif Günal.

The New Liberty project commenced operations in 2014, and commercial production of gold started officially in 2016. However, production at New Liberty was halted twice during 2019 owing to flooding and the collapse of a pit wall. Nevertheless, the steep rise in gold prices from mid-2020 indicated favourable prospects, at least in the short term.

Following the granting in 2010 to the UK's Hummingbird Resources of exploration rights in a concession area in southeastern Liberia known as the Dugbe Shear Zone, the company claimed to have discovered the largest gold site in the country. In 2019 Hummingbird resources and the Government signed a 25-year MDA for this promising gold mining project, which covers an area of 2,355 sq km. In 2020 Hummingbird sold a 49% stake in the Dugbe project to ARX Resources of Canada. Field work in the Bukon Jedeh area was carried out in 2021; its report became available in August 2022 and production at the Dugbe site is scheduled to begin in 2025.

The high price for gold on the world market from mid-2020 resulted in the emergence of new potential investors in Liberia's gold mining sector, including Zodiac Gold of Canada, which was granted a gold exploration licence covering 417 sq km along the Todi Shear zone in western Liberia. In 2022 Hamak Gold, a Liberian-owned company, registered in the British Virgin Islands, started exploration activities after it had acquired two gold mineral exploration licences covering 1,752 sq km in Nimba and River Cess Counties. Notably, some of the gold deposits included in these recent concession agreements were already known deposits which had been sold (without having been developed) by previous concession holders.

In 2000 a Petroleum Law was enacted, establishing the National Oil Company of Liberia (NOCAL) with a mandate to implement government policy on the exploration and exploitation of oil and gas reserves, both onshore and offshore. A reform of the oil sector, initiated in 2011, resulted in the enactment of a new Petroleum Law in 2013. During 2004–15 NOCAL awarded 10 offshore Production Sharing Contracts (PSCs) to foreign companies. Virtually all exploration activities were concentrated on possible offshore deposits in the Liberia Basin. In February 2012 President Johnson Sirleaf appointed Robert Sirleaf (a naturalized US citizen and her eldest son), as Director of the NOCAL Board, who thus became the de facto head of the company until September 2013, reportedly remaining influential in its affairs thereafter. Malpractices reminiscent of the Tubman era took place during 2004–15, including the granting of PSCs to companies with little or no experience in the oil sector, the signing of contracts without international bidding, and the selling on of PSCs for substantial amounts by concession holders who lacked expertise, investment funds and serious plans. As in the gold sector, governmental monitoring of activities was challenged by frequent changes of ownership and complex financing constructions. NOCAL suffered from gross mismanagement, including overstaffed offices and declining revenues. In 2016 it became insolvent and entered a three-year period of dormancy.

Among the five foreign companies to obtain concession rights in the Liberia Basin during 2004–15 were the US oil giants Chevron, ExxonMobil and Anadarko. Other concession owners were the Australian-based African Petroleum Corporation, Spanish-owned Repsol YPF, the Liberty Petroleum Corporation and Canadian-owned Simba Energy.

The exploration activities of the concession holders experienced a setback during the EVD outbreak of 2014. When the epidemic was over, either the fall in international oil prices discouraged the resumption of activities or the expiry of their PSCs caused companies to leave, with the exception of the African Petroleum Corporation, Chevron and ExxonMobil (the latter two in partnership with Nigeria's Oranto Petroleum and Canadian Overseas Petroleum, respectively). By the end of 2018, however, these three remaining oil companies had also shut down their Liberian operations.

Global Witness reported on Liberia's oil and gas sector in September 2011 and March 2018. The latter report referred to ExxonMobil's controversial acquisition in 2013 (through a Canadian intermediary, thereby avoiding the risk of exposure to US anti-corruption laws) of an exploration block that had been awarded to Peppercoast Petroleum, a small company with a weak financial status and no experience in the oil sector which was allegedly owned by former government officials. The publication of the 2018 report prompted President Weah immediately to order an investigation in a number of former senior officials, including Robert Sirleaf and former Ministers of Lands, Mines and Energy, of Finance and of Justice. Robert Sirleaf acknowledged the payment of bonuses worth US $500,000 to a group of high-ranking government officials, but stated that this was common practice within all state-owned enterprises. Moreover, he stated that, as a result of the transaction, ExxonMobil had paid a US $50m. signature bonus to the Government (in 2013), and emphasized that this amount was larger than the total of all signature bonuses received by the Government from all the previous exploration contracts combined. In May 2018 the investigating committee recommended that former government officials who had received bonus payments must refund them or be indicted for misuse of public money.

Liberia amended its 2016 Petroleum Laws in 2019, redrawing the licence block map to comprise 33 blocks in total, 24 in the Liberia Basin and nine in the offshore Harper Basin. The offshore blocks of the Liberia Basin are situated between the Mano River, in the west, and Greenville, Sinoe County in the east. The Harper Basin lies south of the Liberia Basin, along the remaining coastline. The Liberia Petroleum Regulatory Authority (LPRA) was established in 2016. Its mandate was to include the technical evaluation of areas available for exploration; the management of tenders; the conclusion of concession agreements and the monitoring of associated activities; the administration of concession rights; the supervision of data storage; and the provision of assistance to the Liberia Revenue Authority in collecting fees, taxes and all types of revenues accruing to the state under the concession agreements concluded. Meanwhile, in 2019 NOCAL assumed responsibility for the management of well data collected since the 1970s by companies undertaking exploration activities in Liberia. In April 2020 the LPRA launched the first licensing round for the Harper Basin offshore blocks, with bidding to be conducted online in view of the COVID-19 pandemic. In mid-2021, however, the LPRA suspended the 2020 licensing round. In collaboration with NOCAL, it now offered the 33 offshore blocks to interested parties for direct negotiations. The process was expected to run until 31 May 2022. By September limited information was available, but it was reported that potential investors including ExxonMobil had bought the original data of Blocks 8 and 9.

The Administration of President Weah, January 2018–

President George Weah faced a multitude of economic and financial problems when he succeeded Johnson Sirleaf as head of state—falling international prices for Liberia's main commodities, a deterioration of the exchange rate, high inflation, rising unemployment, corruption, and, once again, an empty Treasury—but these problems were overshadowed from mid-2018 by the mismanagement of state funds, and notably by irregularities within the CBL. The latter had serious political repercussions, leading in early 2019 to the arrest of high-ranking officials and a mass protest. At the centre of the turmoil were four (partly overlapping) issues: (i) the apparent disappearance of newly printed Liberian dollar bills worth L $15,500m. (equivalent to approximately US $104m.) from the Free Port of Monrovia; (ii) the manner in which a US $25m. injection into the weak Liberian economy was managed (the so-called 'mop-up' exercise); (iii) the unauthorized printing of Liberian dollar banknotes; and (iv) a suspicious US $14m. damaged banknote exchange.

The reporting of the 'missing billions' in mid-2018 caused much confusion with cabinet ministers and CBL Executive Governor Nathaniel Patray contradicting one another. Almost simultaneously with the disclosure, the CBL announced a US $25m. 'mop-up' exercise, with the double objective of replacing older Liberian dollar notes with US dollar bills and reducing the amount of Liberian dollars in circulation to bring to a halt a deterioration of the exchange rate, which was contributing to high inflation. The exercise took place between July and October: while US $17m. of the funding allocation was used, the remainder appeared not to have been accounted for.

The confusion and unrest which ensued from the allegations of mismanagement and corruption led President Weah to order two investigations—one by a Presidential Investigative Team (PIT), another by Kroll, an external organization. The PIT and Kroll found that there was no evidence to confirm that funding money was missing, but noted serious shortcomings in the implementation of government policies—both in the 'mop-up' exercise and in the case of the 'missing billions'—and discovered inexplicable differences in the ordering and printing of the amount agreed upon between the Government and Crane Currency, the Swedish currency printing company. In March 2019 former CBL Executive Governor Milton Weeks, his Deputy Governor for Operations, Charles Sirleaf (son of former President Johnson Sirleaf) and three other CBL officials were arrested and indicted for economic sabotage, the illegal disbursement and expenditure of public money, and criminal conspiracy. Weah also reformed the CBL in May, announcing the retirement of Governor Patray (who was succeeded by Jolue Aloysius Tarlue in November). In May 2020 all charges against Charles Sirleaf and his three co-defendants were dropped and Sirleaf was released. The others were to face lesser charges, with only Weeks remaining accused of the original charges.

The court cases conducted against the former CBL officials accused of the unauthorized (hence illegal) printing of Liberian banknotes failed to provide answers to many questions regarding the missing monies. In August 2020 Weeks and the other defendants were acquitted after the Criminal Court ruled that the unauthorized printing by the CBL was not a specific crime under Liberian criminal law and found the defendants not guilty.

The 2020/2021 Liberian Dollar Liquidity Crisis

Liberia's monetary policy is entrusted to the CBL, but the National Assembly decides when and how much money is printed and grants permission to the CBL to print new banknotes. Behind the scenes there is often conflict between the National Assembly, the CBL and the presidency over the authority to print new banknotes, fuelling rumours that bribery takes place in the legislature to influence the outcome of debates on increasing the money supply. In late 2020 a Liberian dollar liquidity crisis emerged which paralyzed the national economy. The liquidity crisis affected all sectors of Liberia's cash-based economy and had a negative impact on the transfer of remittances from abroad, which represent a lifeline for many families. In an effort to resolve the crisis, the National Assembly in May 2021 granted a request of the CBL Executive Governor Tarlue to print a new batch of banknotes worth L $48,734m. (US $300.8m.) to replace the notes that were currently in use over the following three years. The new batch would include L $1,000 banknotes for the first time. In addition, L $5 and L $10 coins would be introduced. The new coins and banknotes were expected to enter circulation in October 2022.

The Petroleum Situation

The first three months of 2020 were dominated by a national shortage of petroleum and related products. A Special Presidential Petroleum Task Force concluded in February that the planning, inventory and internal control systems of the Liberia Petroleum Refining Company (LPRC) had failed. (The LPRC is not, strictly speaking, a refinery. Its main role is to store petroleum imported by private companies and supervise its distribution.) In early March the company's Deputy Managing Director for Operations was dismissed for gross negligence and fraudulent activities; the Government also suspended all petroleum import licences, announcing that they would only be reactivated on a case-by-case basis. The shortage affected businesses severely and resulted in higher consumer prices for petrol and other petroleum products. Increased transportation costs led to a rise in the price of food and other commodities, thereby providing a further impetus to an already high rate of inflation. On 7 March 2022, following the Russian invasion of Ukraine in late February and the resulting rise in international oil and gas prices, prices for petroleum products in Liberia were considerably increased: gasoline by 26% and diesel by 32%.

In June 2022 importers of petroleum products and the Ministry of Commerce and Industry clashed over further price increases, and the accompanying uncertainty for consumers led to hoarding, unofficial price increases and shortages on the market, as well as political unrest. Further complications arose when 1.5m. gallons of petroleum products with a value of US $6m. was found missing from LPRC's storage facilities in July. It is unclear if this was the result of a stock accounting problem at LPRC or a criminal act.

Macroeconomic Trends: External Trade and Evolution of GDP

Traditionally, Liberia has a trade deficit, which amounted to US $390m. in 2020 and an estimated US $459m. in 2021. The largest single import category consisted of food imports—notably rice, mainly to feed the country's growing urban population.

All exports consist of unprocessed raw materials: agricultural products (mainly natural rubber, palm oil products, cocoa and coffee), mining products (iron ore, gold and diamonds) and wood products (logs and timber). The reported values of exported rubber fluctuated between US $56m. and US $110m. during 2016–20. In the same period the export of palm oil products oscillated between US $4m. and US $10m., with an estimated value of US $33m. in 2021. The bulk of exports consist of mining products. Iron ore exports rose from US $48m. in 2016 to US $289m. in 2020 and to some US $347m. in 2021. Estimated gold exports during 2016–21 also showed strong growth, from US $116m. in 2016 to an estimated US $340m. in 2021, almost matching iron ore exports, with each representing nearly 40% of total exports. Diamond exports, reportedly at US $29m. in 2016, rose to US $34m. in 2017, but have been in the range of US $12–$16m. in recent years. However, diamond and gold statistics are notoriously unreliable; reported values may be considered minimum amounts. To a lesser extent, this also applies to timber exports, which officially oscillate between US $30m. and US 45m. per year.

In 2021 82% of Liberia's exports went to Europe (notably iron ore and gold), 8% to the USA (mainly rubber, Liberia's main producer being Firestone) and 6% to Asia (with iron ore and palm oil products going to China and India). Switzerland, which before 2018 hardly figured in Liberia's trade statistics, became a leading export destination during the Weah administration: according to preliminary figures, it accounted for 38% of exports in 2021.

Evolution of GDP

In 2006, the first year of the Johnson Sirleaf administration, GDP was reportedly US $1,120m., representing 50% growth compared to 2003. In 2012, the first year of her second term, President Johnson Sirleaf could boast that GDP had reached more than double that of 2006: US $2,790m. However, from 2013 GDP growth first slowed down, then stagnated, partly as a result of the EVD epidemic of 2014–16, with GDP fluctuating at around US $3,200m. –$3,400m. during that period. This, in combination with a growing population, resulted in an actual decrease in per capita income. After 2018 the economy even contracted in absolute terms (in current US dollar prices), with GDP declining to US $3,040m. in 2020. GDP (in current prices) reportedly then grew to US $3,490m. in 2021.

Developments in the National Budget

Liberia's Public Finance Management Act (enacted in 2009 and amended in 2019) stipulates that the budget and accompanying documentation must be submitted by the President to the National Assembly no later than two months before the start of the fiscal year. In October 2020 the Government officially changed Liberia's fiscal year from 1 July to 30 June, to 1 January to 31 December, thereby aligning it with other ECOWAS member states.

The national budget (excluding official development assistance—ODA) decreased yearly during 2014–19, from US $660.2m. in 2014/15 to US $518.9m. in 2019/20, before increasing to US $570.1m. in 2020/21—to which a supplementary budget of US $347.9m. for July–December 2021 should be added, thus totalling US $918.0m. for the 1 July 2020–31 December 2021 period.

In July 2022 the legislature approved (without much scrutiny) a recast national budget for 2022 of US $811.6m., which received presidential approval on 22 July. The recast budget, the highest in Liberia's history, was US $25m. or 3.2% higher than the original approved budget of US $786.6m.

On average, 80%–90% of total expenditure is recurrent expenditure. In recent years, deficit financing has grown in importance. Since the Weah administration took office, yearly public expenditure has amounted to US $100–110 per capita, one of the lowest levels in sub-Saharan Africa, although this figure hides important discrepancies in budgetary allocations. The impact of the insufficiency of the various sectoral budgets is worsened by dysfunctional governmental services. Actual availability of public funds is sometimes lower than the amounts allocated. Mismanagement, corruption and outright theft further reduce the efficiency and effectiveness of what spending actually takes place. A survey conducted by Transparency International in 2018/19 indicated that 53% of public service users in Liberia had paid a bribe, presumably to 'buy' access to public services. In 2021 Liberia ranked 136th out of 180 countries on Transparency International's Corruption Perceptions Index. The level of public corruption under the Weah administration justified the US Treasury in August 2022 to impose sanctions on three senior government officials under the Global Magnitsky Act (see *History*).

The originally approved budget for 2019/20 of US $525.9m. was revised to US $518.0m. due to the onset of the COVID-19 crisis, representing a decrease of 9% compared to the 2018/19 budget of US $570.1m. The actual fiscal out-turn for 2019/20 showed that total available resources amounted to

US $543.3m., including revenues (US $435.1m.), grants (US $14.3m.) and loans (US $93.9m.). Expenditure (on a commitment basis) amounted to US $518.5m., of which 91.8% was recurrent expenditure and only 8.2% (US $42.8m.) for investment purposes under the Public Sector Investment Programs (PSIPs). The Government relies heavily on external sources (in the form of foreign aid) to finance the PSIPs, but in 2019/20 only 31% of projected aid for investment purposes (US $128.1m.) was actually disbursed.

Budgetary provisions for 2020/21 did not differ much from the actual fiscal out-turn in 2019/20. Recurrent expenditure was forecast to account for 89.9% of total envisaged expenditure, leaving just over 10% for investment-related expenditure. Other budgetary provisions also differed little from those in 2019/20 and in some cases were even lower. Notably, despite the ongoing COVID-19 pandemic, the budgetary allocation for health amounted to only US $70.6m., compared with actual spending on health of US $90.0m. in 2019/20.

The Weah administration has resorted increasingly to public borrowing to finance the fiscal deficit. At the end of June 2019 Liberia's total public debt amounted to US $1,170.5m. By 30 June 2020 it had risen to US $1,519.6m., mainly due to an 89% increase in domestic debt owed to the CBL and commercial banks from US $319.6m. to US $603.5m. Over the same period the external debt increased by only 7.7%, from US $850.9m. to US $916.1m., while debt service increased by 119%, from US $13.7m. to US $30.0m. Further analysis of available data shows that the CBL was instrumental in a high level of deficit financing, expanding the value of Liberian dollars in circulation on various occasions, which, in turn, was a key factor in a steep increase in inflation, accompanied by a rapid depreciation in the exchange rate against the US dollar. The CBL's actions contrast sharply with its main stated objective of achieving and maintaining domestic price stability. The resulting macro- and micro-economic impacts of these economic developments include a growing reluctance on the part of foreign investors to engage in economic activities in Liberia and a constant and deepening loss of purchasing power for ordinary Liberians, with the unemployed and poor bearing the brunt of the Government's fiscal policy and performance. By 31 March 2022 total public debt stood at US $1,806.8m., compared to a public debt stock of US $1,639.6m. in 2021, an overall increase of 10.2%, which equalled the growth rate of the domestic debt (to US $744.9m., or 41% of total public debt) and of the external debt (to US $1,061.9m., or 59%). The bulk of domestic debt (89.8%) was owed to the CBL (US $525.5m., or 70.5%) and commercial banks (US $143.4m., or 19.3%). With respect to the total external debt of US $ 1,061.9m. on 31 March 2022, bilateral debt constituted 10.7% (US $113.2m.) whereas the debt to multilateral institutions amounted to US $948.7m. (89.3%).

The 2022 national budget is the ninth since the launch of the Medium Term Expenditure Framework (MTEF) in 2012/13, an annual, rolling three-year expenditure planning system which was developed and agreed with the Bretton Woods institutions. The focus of the MTEF was based on the Government's medium-term Pro-Poor Agenda for Prosperity and Development (2018–23). The official objectives of this ambitious development agenda were to raise the incomes of 1m. Liberians and to reduce absolute poverty by 23.0% through sustained and inclusive economic growth based on investments in agriculture, infrastructure, human resource development and social protection. However, the national budget lacks a clear development focus, as illustrated by the sectoral breakdown of planned expenditure. In 2022 the four sectors which are essential for 'running the state'—public administration, security and rule of law, municipal government, and transparency and accountability—together were allocated 59.7% of envisaged total expenditure, leaving about 40% for expenditure in the domain of economic and social development, corresponding with actual spending in previous years. Allocations for the agricultural sector, within which most of the population earns its living, are only 0.9% of total expenditure, US $7.3m., all of which is for civil servants' salaries and functioning. Liberia is a signatory to the AU's 2003 Maputo Declaration on Agriculture and Food Security in Africa as well as the Comprehensive Africa Agriculture Development Program Malabo Framework

(2013), which include a commitment to allocate at least 10% of national budgetary resources to agriculture and rural development policy implementation. In the 2021 Global Hunger Index, Liberia was ranked 110th out of 116 qualifying countries, which is an extremely poor performance for a country so well endowed with natural resources. Planned expenditure on education accounts for US $92.3m., or 11.7% of total expenditure, well below the UN recommendation of 26%. Allocated funds for health services amount to US $78.4m., or 10.0% of total expenditure, also less than spent in previous years. Given the prevalence of COVID-19 and other serious diseases, this level of spending is obviously insufficient to cover the needs of the 5.3m. Liberians.

Development Assistance and Relations with External Donors

Since the signing of the Comprehensive Peace Agreement in 2003, the international community has spent huge sums of aid money in Liberia. Continued support from the international donor community is important for the Government as budgetary spending from its own revenue sources does not allow for much investment-related expenditure. However, owing to the mismanagement and corruption that prevail in the country, several important donors have been reluctant to provide aid in recent years. Projections of ODA disbursements in 2019/20 were high (US $412.7m.) but were not realized. The international donor community only disbursed US $128.1m., of which US $56.7m. was in the form of bilateral aid and US $71.4m. (including both grants and loans) was from multilateral sources. However, in 2020/2021 disbursements were high and beyond expectations.

Development assistance in 2020/21 exceeded slightly the national budget for the same period and amounted to US $574.3m. Available data for the first quarter of 2022, with actual foreign aid disbursements amounting to US $88.8m., indicate a possibly much lower disbursement level for 2022.

In 2020/21 the bulk of external assistance was in the form of project aid (91%). External funding of off-budget projects implemented through government institutions and NGOs amounted to US $522.6m. Only 6.3% (US $35.9m.) was provided as budget support; 2.7% (US $15.7m.) went to the Liberia Reconstruction Trust Fund. Most aid was provided as a grant: US $366.1m., or 63.8%, whereas US $208.2m., or 36.2%, was added to the public debt.

Multilateral aid accounted for 67.3% of ODA (US $386.3m.), while 32.7% came from bilateral sources (US $188.0m.). Liberia benefits from a fairly large number of multilateral funds. In 2020/21 the bulk of multilateral funds originated from five sources: the International Development Association (IDA), the UN, the EU, the AfDB and the IMF, which together accounted for 74% of all multilateral financing (US $363.3m.). The USA continues to be Liberia's main bilateral donor, providing US $73.5m. (equalling all UN assistance). Sweden and Germany occupy the second and third places on the list of bilateral donors, with US $32.5m. and US $29.9m., respectively.

In April 2019 the UN Resident Coordinator in Liberia warned the Minister of Finance and Development Planning, Samuel D. Tweah, Jr that continued lack of accountability over government expenditure could lead to the discontinuation of UN-funded programmes and projects. The ECOWAS Representative in Liberia echoed these concerns, warning the Government against the squandering of funds from the international community. In May 2020 Germany, a major bilateral donor, announced that it was to remove Liberia from its list of aid-receiving countries owing to the lack of reform, notably in the areas of good governance, human rights and combating corruption. However, in 2020/2021 Germany was still one of Liberia's most important bilateral donors. Against this background, President Weah's efforts to strengthen bilateral ties with Türkiye (Turkey) are noteworthy. In May 2022 a 16-member senior Liberian delegation visited the capital, Ankara, following Weah's talks with President Recep Tayyip Erdoğan in March. Recently, bilateral aid (as well as bilateral trade and Turkish investments in Liberia, notably in gold mining) has been increasing.

In March 2020 the World Bank agreed to provide budgetary support of US $40m. for 2019/20, comprising an IDA credit of US $20m. and a matching grant of US $20m. In June 2021 the World Bank/IDA approved a US $55m. Rural Development Transformation Project and the Second Inclusive Growth Development Policy Operation, amounting to US $40m. The World Bank also pledged US $15m. to aid Liberia in combating the spread of COVID-19, followed in June 2022 by additional financing of US $9m. to tackle the pandemic with an IDA grant of US $6.2m. and an IDA loan of US $2.8m. Overall, the World Bank's lending to Liberia has registered a remarkable increase since 2018.

In 2021 the AfDB provided a loan of US $10m. to support the Liberian Government's efforts to control the spread of COVID-19, while in 2020 the EU granted US $17.6m. in budgetary support and supplied US $2.4m. worth of personal protective equipment. The EU aid was in addition to its regular support to Liberia under the Cotonou Agreement. Under the 11th European Development Fund (covering 2014–20), Liberia was allocated €279m. Indicative allocations for the 2021–24 period under the Multiannual Indicative programme for 2020–27 amount to €191m. for specified priority areas, including natural resources preservation, employment promotion and the improvement of financial and democratic governance; the indicative allocations for 2025–27 are subject to a decision by the EU after an evaluation of the 2020–24 performance. The EU aid is predominantly channelled through the European Development Fund. Liberia also benefits from regional funds earmarked for West Africa and from several thematic funds. The European Investment Bank mainly supports infrastructural projects.

In December 2019 the IMF approved a four-year Extended Credit Facility (ECF) arrangement totalling US $214.3m. to help restore macroeconomic stability, with an immediate disbursement of US $48.9m., of which US $38m. was to cover the fiscal financing gap arising from the impact of COVID-19. In April 2020 the IMF Board approved immediate debt service relief for 25 low-income countries, which included a US $50m. disbursement for Liberia to address the pandemic. In mid-2021 the IMF announced a new allocation of Special Drawing Rights from which Liberia could benefit from about US $350m. to support economic growth through investments in infrastructure, to finance expenses related to the COVID-19 pandemic (particularly a vaccination programme) and to cancel part of the country's outstanding debt. In November the IMF disbursed about US $23.6m. under the ECF and in mid-2022 another US $22.1m.; total disbursements under the ECF approved in 2019 thus amounted to some US $110.7m.

OUTLOOK

Liberia's economic outlook and political perspectives for 2023 are closely related. The political campaign preceding the presidential and legislative elections of October 2023 (see *History*) is likely to be intense and, based on recent experience, violence cannot be excluded. The stakes are high, since in Liberia politics are about access to resources rather than ideologies.

Economically, three separated though inter-related economies exist: a modern economy dominated by foreign investors, a traditional economy of mainly rural people, and an informal economy concentrated in urban centres. Foreign investments finance the exploitation of the country's rich natural resources, thereby providing public revenues and infrastructure and creating jobs. Liberia's traditionally favourable attitude towards foreign investment is expected to continue, with a Government which is responsible for an attractive investment climate. However, although Liberia's labour force is characterized by low cost, it is one of the least skilled in sub-Saharan Africa, most of its infrastructure is in a deplorable state, indispensable facilities such as electricity and internet are expensive, unreliable or absent, and the weak rule of law and omnipresent corruption increase investment costs or may deter serious investors.

The prospects for substantial changes in the traditional economy from which 47.4% of the population (or 2.5m. people) depend, are limited. Farmers' savings are insufficient or lacking for the much-needed modernization of traditional farming methods, whereas budgetary allocations for the agricultural sector are extremely low. Also, external aid funds are insufficient, with donors prioritizing other economic sectors. As for the informal economy, 52.6% of the population (2.75m. people) live in urban centres. The urban population is concentrated in Monrovia, which has a population of around 1.5m. people. Urban unemployment is estimated at 85%–95%, so the jobless and their families depend on the informal economy to make ends meet. The chances for substantial improvements in the short term, however, are nil. Consequently, the prevailing unemployment in urban centres contributes to a politically fragile situation which may impact the overall national economy negatively if unexpected events, including election-related incidents, were to get out of control.

The COVID-19 pandemic brought much hardship and uncertainty. The pandemic disrupted many sectors of the economy, which contracted in 2019 and 2020. However, the World Bank and IMF expect per capita GDP to return to pre-COVID-19 levels by 2023; the economy as a whole is projected to grow from an estimated 4.0% in 2021 to 4.4% in 2022, assuming continued recovery from the pandemic and domestic political stability. In view of an estimated population growth rate of 2.5% per year, the development of the inflation rate and of the exchange rate, this means a slight improvement in per capita GDP. It should be noted, however, that economic projections are based on demographic data emanating from the latest available population census of 2008. Liberia's Fifth National Housing and Population Census, initially scheduled for 2018, is now scheduled for October–November 2022.

Economic growth will be driven mainly by the mining sector. Growth projections are largely dependent on ArcelorMittal's speedy implementation of Phase II, which will increase the annual capacity of its iron ore mines from 5m. metric tons a year to 15m. and eventually 30m. Furthermore, it is expected that the gold mining sector will contribute substantially to future economic growth, given the current high prices for gold on the world market.

Inflation fell from 17.4% in 2020 to 7.9% in 2021 and may stay in single digits, provided that prudent monetary and fiscal policies are continued. However, inflation figures could show an upward trend resulting from the increasing food and energy prices caused by Russia's invasion of Ukraine in early 2022. The conflict in Ukraine creates uncertainties and increased risks of unplanned or uncontrolled public spending. The 2023 elections may also constitute a risk and lead to extra public expenses and an increasing fiscal deficit, which, when financed by increased borrowing, could result in a higher public debt and trigger inflation.

Popular discontent with his economic policies and performance, together with the approach of the 2023 presidential election, may induce President Weah to yield to increasing domestic and international pressure to establish a war crimes and economic crimes court. This would certainly meet with stiff opposition from former warlords and their associates occupying powerful positions in the legislature, political parties and civil society. Political agitation and unrest in the country would spread, with the additional risk of creating an attractive breeding ground for foreign terrorists who have already taken advantage of weak states in the Sahel region.

Liberia is highly dependent on external funds for its functioning. Investor confidence remains crucial for attracting much-needed investment to increase the country's productive capacity and to provide both domestic revenue and a source of job creation. Liberia's weak public sector performance, the impunity of corruption, and apparent lack of political will to introduce substantial changes also threaten its relations with bilateral and multilateral donors. Despite dissatisfaction with the Government's handling of aid funds, the major sources of such finance, the multilaterals (the Bretton Woods institutions, the AU, EU and UN) and the bilateral donors (notably the USA), are none the less expected to continue their substantial support—albeit at a lower level than in 2020/21, when ODA disbursements exceeded the national budget.

Statistical Survey

Sources (unless otherwise stated): Liberia Institute of Statistics and Geo-Information Services, POB 629, Tubman Blvd, Sinkor, Monrovia; internet www.lisgis.net; Central Bank of Liberia, POB 2048, cnr of Warren and Carey Sts, Monrovia; tel. 776225685; internet www.cbl.org.lr.

Area and Population

AREA, POPULATION AND DENSITY

Area (sq km)	97,754*
Population (census results)	
1 February 1984	2,101,628
21 March 2008	
Males	1,739,945
Females	1,736,663
Total	3,476,608
Population (UN estimates at mid-year)†	
2020	5,057,677
2021‡	5,180,208
2022‡	5,305,119
Density (per sq km) at mid-2022‡	54.3

* 37,743 sq miles.
† Source: UN, *World Population Prospects: The 2019 Revision.*
‡ Projection.

POPULATION BY AGE AND SEX
(’000, UN projections at mid-2022)

	Males	Females	Total
0–14 years	1,073.9	1,031.4	2,105.4
15–64 years	1,514.5	1,504.9	3,019.4
65 years and over	80.4	100.0	180.3
Total	**2,668.8**	**2,636.3**	**5,305.1**

Note: Totals may not be equal to the sum of components, owing to rounding.

Source: UN, *World Population Prospects: The 2019 Revision.*

COUNTIES
(population at 2008 census)

Bomi	84,119	Margibi . . .	209,923
Bong	333,481	Maryland . . .	135,938
Gbarpolu	83,388	Montserrado .	1,118,241
Grand Bassa . . .	221,693	Nimba	462,026
Grand Cape Mount .	127,076	Rivercess . . .	71,509
Grand Gedeh . . .	125,258	River Gee . . .	66,789
Grand Kru . . .	57,913	Sinoe	102,391
Lofa	276,863	**Total**	3,476,608

PRINCIPAL TOWNS
(population at 2008 census, provisional)

Monrovia (capital) .	1,010,970	Zwedru	23,903
Ganta	41,106	Harbel	23,402
Buchanan . . .	34,270	Pleebo	22,963
Gbarnga . . .	34,046	Foya	19,522
Kakata	33,945	Harper	17,837
Voinjama . . .	26,594	Greenville	16,434

Mid-2021 (incl. suburbs, UN projection): Monrovia 1,569,013 (Source: UN, *World Urbanization Prospects: The 2018 Revision*).

BIRTHS AND DEATHS
(annual averages, UN estimates)

	2005–10	2010–15	2015–20
Birth rate (per 1,000)	38.6	35.6	33.2
Death rate (per 1,000)	10.6	9.0	7.6

Source: UN, *World Population Prospects: The 2019 Revision*.

Life expectancy (years at birth, estimates): 64.4 (males 63.0; females 65.8) in 2020 (Source: World Bank, World Development Indicators database).

EMPLOYMENT
(formal sector only)

	2008	2009	2010*
Agriculture and forestry . . .	22,616	34,882	38,615
Mining	1,421	1,907	1,691
Manufacturing	2,215	2,075	1,367
Construction	390	1,659	3,856
Wholesale and retail trade . .	10,028	10,998	7,536
Transport and communications .	4,984	5,563	9,423
Banking and insurance . .	2,189	4,044	6,426
Business services	6,231	9,467	10,179
Social and community services .	9,213	20,160	28,020
Government	47,681	34,000	37,532
Total	106,968	124,755	144,647

* Estimates.

Total employed in informal sector: 487,000 in 2008; 569,790 in 2009; 672,352 (estimate) in 2010.

Mid-2015 ('000 persons, estimates): Agriculture, etc. 985; Total labour force 1,668 (Source: FAO).

Health and Welfare

KEY INDICATORS

Total fertility rate (children per woman, 2020)	4.2
Under-5 mortality rate (per 1,000 live births, 2020) . . .	78.3
HIV/AIDS (% of persons aged 15–49, 2020)	1.1
COVID-19: Cumulative confirmed deaths (per 100,000 persons at 31 August 2022)	5.7
COVID-19: Fully vaccinated population (% of total population at 3 July 2022)	44.8
Physicians (per 1,000 head, 2018)	0.05
Hospitals (per 100,000 head, 2013)	0.4
Domestic health expenditure (2019): US $ per head (PPP) .	20.3
Domestic health expenditure (2019): % of GDP . . .	1.4
Access to improved water resources (% of persons, 2020) .	75
Access to improved sanitation facilities (% of persons, 2020) .	18
Total carbon dioxide emissions ('000 metric tons, 2018) .	1,320
Carbon dioxide emissions per head (metric tons, 2018) . .	0.3
Human Development Index (2021): ranking	178
Human Development Index (2021): value	0.481

Note: For data on COVID-19 vaccinations, 'fully vaccinated' denotes receipt of all doses specified by approved vaccination regime (Sources: Johns Hopkins University and Our World in Data). Data on health expenditure refer to current general government expenditure in each case. For more information on sources and further definitions for all indicators, see Health and Welfare Statistics: Sources and Definitions section (europaworld.com/credits).

Agriculture

PRINCIPAL CROPS
('000 metric tons)

	2018	2019	2020
Bananas*	136.0	136.2	135.8
Cassava (Manioc)	578.8	581.2*	632.6*
Cocoa beans†	11.0	12.0	14.0
Maize, green*	23.9	23.7	23.8
Oil palm fruit*	176.0	176.1	177.9
Oranges*	8.0	7.9	7.9
Pineapples*	8.9	8.9	9.0
Plantains and others* . . .	49.5	49.6	49.7
Rice, paddy	258.0	269.0†	270.0†
Rubber, natural*	55.0	42.2	64.9
Sugar cane*	271.9	272.7	273.4
Sweet potatoes*	24.3	24.0	24.1
Taro (Cocoyam)*	27.9	27.9	28.0
Yams*	21.0	21.0	21.0

* FAO estimate(s).
† Unofficial figure(s).

Aggregate production ('000 metric tons, may include official, semi-official or estimated data): Total cereals 258.0 in 2018, 269.0 in 2019, 270.0 in 2020; Total fruit (primary) 205.6 in 2018, 205.9 in 2019, 205.6 in 2020; Total roots and tubers 652.0 in 2018, 654.1 in 2019, 705.7 in 2020; Total vegetables (primary) 121.1 in 2018, 120.2 in 2019, 120.8 in 2020.

Source: FAO.

LIVESTOCK
('000 head, year ending September, FAO estimates)

	2018	2019	2020
Cattle	45.2	45.0	45.5
Chickens	8,083	8,380	8,713
Ducks	334	344	354
Goats	361.2	372.6	385.9
Pigs	318.2	338.5	362.8
Sheep	287.4	294.9	303.6

Source: FAO.

LIVESTOCK PRODUCTS
(metric tons, FAO estimates)

	2018	2019	2020
Cows' milk	9,378	9,358	9,435
Chicken meat	14,373	14,840	15,308
Game meat	7,842	7,796	7,809
Pig meat	12,716	13,318	13,921
Hen eggs	6,109	6,238	6,379

Source: FAO.

Forestry

ROUNDWOOD REMOVALS
('000 cubic metres, FAO estimates, excluding bark)

	2018	2019	2020
Sawlogs, veneer logs and logs for sleepers	422	422	422
Other industrial wood . . .	42	42	42
Fuel wood	9,166	9,465	9,773
Total	9,630	9,928	10,237

Source: FAO.

SAWNWOOD PRODUCTION
('000 cubic metres, including railway sleepers, FAO estimates)

	2015	2016	2017
Total (all broadleaved) . . .	132	132	133

2018–20: Production assumed to be unchanged from 2017.

Source: FAO.

Fishing

(metric tons, live weight)

	2018	2019	2020
Capture	14,122	16,134	31,629*
Freshwater fishes . . .	305	517	500*
African red snapper . .	n.a.	1,271	966
Barracudas	5,287	828	1,984
Bobo croaker	847	138	124
Cassava croaker . . .	204	250	1,010
Longneck croaker . . .	n.a.	211	1,350
Lesser African threadfin . .	1,035	585	1,370
Bonga shad	—	1,110	105
Skipjack tuna	29	21	6,770
Yellowfin tuna	1	—	1,730
Atlantic bumper	213	503	789
Sardinellas	330	593	2,207
Aquaculture*	240	250	255
Total catch*	14,362	16,384	31,884

* FAO estimate(s).

Source: FAO.

Mining

	2019	2020	2021
Diamonds ('000 carats) . . .	56	55	63
Iron ore ('000 metric tons) . . .	4,429	4,874	5,000
Gold (kilograms)	4,619	4,007	7,164

Industry

SELECTED PRODUCTS
(litres unless otherwise indicated)

	2019	2020	2021
Beverages	16,890,776	14,169,521	17,239,963
Cement (metric tons) . . .	343,219	416,444	534,993
Paint	212,943	213,166	206,223
Candles (kilograms) . . .	94,416	71,274	48,416
Bleach	1,195,428	1,246,431	829,241
Rubbing alcohol	308,650	493,786	306,268
Mattresses (number) . . .	100,040	103,353	129,454
Treated (finished) water (million gallons)	1,334	1,160	1,134

Electrical energy (million kWh): 444 in 2017; 456 in 2019; 502 in 2020 (Source: UN Energy Statistics Database).

Finance

CURRENCY AND EXCHANGE RATES

Monetary Units
100 cents = 1 Liberian dollar (L $).

Sterling, Dollar and Euro Equivalents (31 August 2021)
£1 sterling = L $236.548;
US $1 = L $171.797;
€1 = L $203.305;
L $1,000 = £4.23 = US $5.82 = €4.92.

Average Exchange Rate (L $ per US $)
2018   144.0556
2019   186.4297
2020   191.5180

Note: The aforementioned data are based on market-determined rates of exchange. Prior to January 1998 the exchange rate was a fixed parity with the US dollar (L $1 = US $1).

BUDGET
(US $ million)

Revenue	2020/21	2021/22*	2022/23†
Tax revenue	430.5	492.2	516.6
Taxes on income and profits .	176.1	199.8	209.6
Taxes on property	5.7	5.9	6.2
Taxes on goods and services .	50.2	56.0	59.0
Taxes on international trade and transactions	195.0	227.1	238.2
Other taxes	3.6	3.4	3.4
Non-tax revenue	99.2	149.4	155.6
Property income	83.5	129.6	135.9
Interest income and dividends	54.7	94.8	49.1
Royalties and rent . . .	28.8	34.8	86.8
Administrative fees . . .	15.2	19.2	19.1
Fines, penalties and forfeits .	0.4	0.6	0.6
Miscellaneous and unidentified.	0.2	0.0	0.0
Grants	138.1	145.0	—
Cash carry-forward . . .	17.7	—	—
Total	685.5	786.6	677.2

Expense by economic type	2020/21	2021/22*	2022/23†
Compensation of employees . .	316.6	292.6	292.6
Use of goods and services . . .	115.5	138.5	73.2
Social benefits	1.3	14.0	12.6
Other expenses	106.9	341.5	293.8
Total	540.2	786.6	672.2

Outlays by function of government	2020/21	2021/22*	2022/23†
Agriculture	5.5	7.3	6.3
Education	74.1	92.3	78.8
Energy and environment . . .	13.4	35.6	26.3
Health	64.8	78.4	71.6
Industry and commerce . . .	6.8	9.2	8.1
Infrastructure and basic services .	32.8	70.5	57.8
Municipal government . . .	17.3	27.2	24.1
Public administration . . .	200.5	297.4	257.4
Security and rule of law . . .	89.7	102.0	86.0
Social development services . .	10.9	24.5	20.4
Transparency and accountability .	24.2	42.1	35.4
Other	0.2	—	—
Total	540.2	786.6	672.2

* Estimates.
† Budget figures.

Source: Ministry of Finance and Development Planning, Monrovia.

INTERNATIONAL RESERVES
(US $ million at 31 December)

	2018	2019	2020
IMF special drawing rights . .	211.79	196.85	197.16
Reserve position in IMF . .	44.97	44.71	46.57
Foreign exchange	306.50	306.46	294.81
Total	563.26	548.02	538.53

2021: IMF special drawing rights 538.25, Reserve position in IMF 45.25.

Source: IMF, *International Financial Statistics*.

MONEY SUPPLY
(L $ million at 31 December)

	2019	2020	2021
Currency outside depository corporations*	20,535.4	22,591.3	22,227.3
Transferable deposits	58,155.6	63,804.6	62,934.0
Other deposits	42,315.4	40,900.9	40,249.4
Broad money	121,006.3	127,296.9	125,410.7

* Figures refer only to amounts of Liberian coin in circulation. US notes and coin also circulate, but the amount of these in private holdings is unknown. The amount of Liberian coin in circulation is small in comparison to US currency.

COST OF LIVING
(Consumer Price Index; base: January 2017 = 100)

	2017	2018
Food and non-alcoholic beverages	99.7	120.7
Housing, water, electricity, gas and other fuels .	103.3	123.1
Clothing and footwear	115.7	148.3
All items (incl. others)	104.7	129.4

NATIONAL ACCOUNTS
(US $ million at current prices)

Expenditure on the Gross Domestic Product

	2018	2019	2020
Government final consumption expenditure	673	750	693
Private final consumption expenditure	1,741	1,383	1,326
Gross capital formation . . .	599	994	836
Total domestic expenditure .	3,013	3,127	2,854
Exports of goods and services . .	860	893	855
Less Imports of goods and services	1,403	1,382	1,271
Statistical discrepancy	275	−56	43
GDP in purchaser's values .	2,745	2,582	2,481
GDP at constant 2015 prices .	2,755	2,693	2,615

Gross Domestic Product by Economic Activity

	2018	2019	2020
Agriculture	1,770	1,747	1,828
Mining and utilities	70	63	56
Manufacturing	107	97	95
Construction	51	46	41
Trade, restaurants and hotels .	124	114	111
Transport, storage and communications	137	125	122
Other service activities . . .	184	168	164
Sub-total	2,442	2,360	2,418
Indirect taxes (net)*	303	222	63
GDP in market prices . . .	2,745	2,582	2,481

* Figures obtained as a residual.

Source: UN Statistics Division, National Accounts Main Aggregates Database.

BALANCE OF PAYMENTS
(US $ million)

	2019	2020	2021*
Exports of goods	542.9	607.7	878.5
Imports of goods	−933.8	−998.0	−1,337.7
Balance on goods	−390.9	−390.3	−459.3
Exports of services	11.1	11.7	4.9
Imports of services	−310.0	−314.7	−290.6
Balance on goods and services	−689.8	−693.4	−745.0
Primary income received . . .	23.8	21.0	21.8
Primary income paid	−136.2	−120.4	−127.3
Balance on goods, services and primary income	−802.2	−792.8	−850.5
Secondary income received . .	339.1	367.4	348.1
Secondary income paid . . .	−217.7	−119.6	−104.7
Current balance	−680.8	−545.1	−607.1
Capital account (net)	229.6	390.5	215.6
Direct investment liabilities . .	86.8	66.1	95.0
Other investment assets . . .	−4.4	−39.1	−103.8
Other investment liabilities . .	135.8	180.8	438.9
Net errors and omissions . .	202.1	29.3	362.2
Reserves and related items .	−30.9	82.5	400.8

* Preliminary.

External Trade

PRINCIPAL COMMODITIES
(US $ million)

Imports c.i.f.	2019	2020	2021*
Food and live animals (including animal and vegetable oils) . .	264.3	254.7	356.0
Rice	133.3	122.1	185.7
Mineral fuels and lubricants . .	145.2	189.2	222.0
Petroleum	115.6	161.6	137.2
Basic manufactures	125.6	106.4	—
Machinery and transport equipment	210.2	231.3	355.7
Total (incl. others)	933.8	998.0	1,337.7

Exports f.o.b.	2019	2020	2021*
Rubber	85.6	82.2	110.0
Palm oil	11.3	3.9	32.5
Diamonds	16.1	12.1	15.2
Gold	164.3	194.4	340.3
Iron ore	234.6	289.0	346.9
Total (incl. others)	542.9	607.7	878.5

* Preliminary.

SELECTED TRADING PARTNERS
(US $ million)

Imports c.i.f.	2019	2020	2021*
China, People's Republic . . .	190.3	177.7	193.2
Côte d'Ivoire	118.7	164.7	174.9
India	183.4	175.7	278.0
USA	58.8	67.4	64.4
Total (incl. others)	933.8	998.0	1,337.7

Exports f.o.b.	2019	2020	2021*
China, People's Republic . . .	31.9	33.4	3.2
Switzerland	151.1	179.5	334.3
United Arab Emirates	24.6	17.3	10.2
USA	51.5	42.9	70.5
Total (incl. others)	542.9	607.7	878.5

* Preliminary.

Transport

SHIPPING

Flag Registered Fleet
(at 31 December)

	2019	2020	2021
Number of vessels	4,451	4,668	5,018
Displacement ('000 grt) . . .	176,013.4	189,578.6	211,437.3

Source: Lloyd's List Intelligence (www.bit.ly/LLintelligence).

Communications Media

	2015	2016	2017
Telephones ('000 main lines in use)	9.0	8.0	n.a.
Mobile telephone subscriptions ('000)	3,652.0	3,117.0	2,660.0
Broadband subscriptions, fixed ('000)	7.0	8.0	9.0
Broadband subscriptions, mobile ('000)	236.0	463.4	550.0
Internet users (% of population)* .	10.0	15.7	16.3

* Estimates.

2020: Internet users (% of population): 25.6.

Source: International Telecommunication Union.

Education

(2015 unless otherwise indicated)

	Institutions	Teachers	Students Males	Students Females	Total
Pre-primary . .	5,080	14,311	273,608	266,052	539,660
Primary . . .	5,178	30,438	334,730	320,319	655,049
Secondary . .	2,472	19,532	143,917	128,915	272,832
Technical and vocational . .	n.a.	1,168	6,324	5,547	11,871
Higher* . . .	33	1,517	27,585	16,258	43,843

* 2012 figures.

Source: Ministry of Education, Monrovia.

Pupil-teacher ratio (qualified teaching staff, primary education, UNESCO estimate): 31.8 in 2016/17 (Source: UNESCO Institute for Statistics).

Adult literacy rate (UNESCO estimates): 48.3% (males 62.7%; females 34.1%) in 2017 (Source: UNESCO Institute for Statistics).

Directory

The Constitution

The Constitution of the Republic of Liberia entered into effect on 6 January 1986, following its approval by national referendum in July 1984. Its main provisions (including subsequent amendments) are summarized below:

PREAMBLE

The Republic of Liberia is a unitary sovereign state, which is divided into counties for administrative purposes. There are three separate branches of government: the legislative, the executive and the judiciary. No person is permitted to hold office or executive power in more than one branch of government. The fundamental human rights of the individual are guaranteed.

LEGISLATURE

Legislative power is vested in the bicameral National Assembly, comprising a Senate and a House of Representatives. Deputies of both chambers are elected by universal adult suffrage. Each county elects two members of the Senate (for a term of nine years), while members of the House of Representatives are elected by legislative constituency for a term of six years. Legislation requires the approval of two-thirds of the members of both chambers, and is subsequently submitted to the President for endorsement. The Constitution may be amended by two-thirds of the members of both chambers.

EXECUTIVE

Executive power is vested in the President, who is Head of State and Commander-in-Chief of the armed forces. The President is elected by universal adult suffrage for a term of six years, and is restricted to a maximum of two terms in office. A Vice-President is elected at the same time as the President. The President appoints a Cabinet, and members of the judiciary and armed forces, with the approval of the Senate. The President is empowered to declare a state of emergency.

JUDICIARY

Judicial power is vested in the Supreme Court and any subordinate courts, which apply both statutory and customary laws in accordance with standards enacted by the legislature. The judgments of the Supreme Court are final and not subject to appeal or review by any other branch of government. The Supreme Court comprises one Chief Justice and five Associate Justices. Justices are appointed by the President, with the approval of the Senate.

POLITICAL PARTIES AND ELECTIONS

Political associations are obliged to comply with the minimum registration requirements imposed by the Elections Commission. Organizations that endanger free democratic society, or that organize, train or equip groups of supporters, are to be denied registration. Prior to elections, each political party and independent candidate is required to submit statements of assets and liabilities to the Elections Commission. All elections of public officials are determined by an absolute majority of the votes cast. If no candidate obtains an absolute majority in the first ballot, a second ballot is conducted between the two candidates with the highest number of votes. Complaints by parties or candidates must be submitted to the Elections Commission within seven days of the announcement of election results. The Supreme Court has final jurisdiction over challenges to election results.

The Government

HEAD OF STATE

President: GEORGE MANNEH WEAH (inaugurated 22 January 2018).
Vice-President: JEWEL HOWARD-TAYLOR.

THE CABINET
(October 2022)

Acting Minister of State for Presidential Affairs: GEORGE WESSEH BLAMOH.

Minister of Foreign Affairs: DEE-MAXWELL SAAH KEMAYAH, Sr.

Minister of Finance and Development Planning: SAMUEL D. TWEAH, Jr.

Minister of Justice: MUSA F. DEAN.

Minister of Defence: Maj.-Gen. DANIEL DEE ZIANKAHN.

Minister of Gender, Children and Social Protection: WILLIAMETTA PISO SAYDEE-TARR.

Minister of Labour: CHARLES GIBSON.

Minister of Commerce and Industry: MAWINE G. DIGGS.

Minister of Information: LEDGERHOOD JULIUS RENNIE.

Minister of Mines and Energy: GESLER E. MURRAY.

Minister of Youth and Sports: D. ZOGAR WILSON.

Minister of Education: Prof. ANSU D. SONII.

Minister of Internal Affairs: VARNEY SIRLEAF.

Minister of State without Portfolio: TROKON A. KPUI.

Minister of Health: Dr WILHELMINA JALLAH.

Minister of Public Works: RUTH COKER-COLLINS.

Minister of Transport: SAMUEL A. WLUE.

Minister of Agriculture: JEANINE COOPER.

MINISTRIES

Office of the President: Executive Mansion, POB 10-9001, Capitol Hill, 1000 Monrovia 10; e-mail info@emansion.gov.lr; internet www.emansion.gov.lr.

Ministry of Agriculture: Tubman Blvd, POB 10-9010, 1000 Monrovia 10; tel. 880745449; internet www.moa.gov.lr.

Ministry of Commerce and Industry: Ashmun St, POB 10-9014, 1000 Monrovia 10; tel. 777604576; e-mail info@moci.gov.lr; internet www.moci.gov.lr.

Ministry of Defence: UN Dr., POB 10-9007, 1000 Monrovia 10; tel. 778718584; e-mail info@mod.gov.lr; internet mod.gov.lr.

Ministry of Education: 3rd Ave and Tubman Ave, POB 10-9012, 1000 Monrovia 10; tel. 777403676; internet www.moe.gov.lr.

Ministry of Finance and Development Planning: Broad St, POB 10-9013, 1000 Monrovia 10; e-mail info@mfdp.gov.lr; internet www.mfdp.gov.lr.

Ministry of Foreign Affairs: Mamba Point, POB 10-9002, 1000 Monrovia 10; internet www.mofa.gov.lr.

Ministry of Gender, Children and Social Protection: UN Dr. and Gurley St, Monrovia; e-mail info@mogcsp.gov.lr; internet mogcsp.gov.lr.

Ministry of Health: Congo Town, Tubman Blvd, POB 10-9009, 1000 Monrovia 10; tel. 886401228; internet moh.gov.lr.

Ministry of Information, Culture and Tourism: Capitol Hill, POB 10-9021, 1000 Monrovia 10; internet fb.com/micatliberia1.

Ministry of Internal Affairs: cnr Warren and Benson Sts, POB 10-9008, 1000 Monrovia 10; tel. 226346; internet www.mia.gov.lr.

Ministry of Justice: cnr Gardiner Ave and 9th St, Sinkor, POB 10-9006, 1000 Monrovia 10; tel. 770133197; internet www.moj.gov.lr.

Ministry of Labour: Mechlin St, POB 10-9040, 1000 Monrovia 10; internet www.mol.gov.lr.

Ministry of Mines and Energy: Capitol Hill, POB 10-9024, 1000 Monrovia 10; tel. 770132540; internet mme.gov.lr.

Ministry of Posts and Telecommunications: cnr Carey and McDonald Sts, 1000 Monrovia 10; tel. 881709675; e-mail info@mopt.gov.lr; internet mopt.gov.lr.

Ministry of Public Works: Lynch St, POB 10-9011, 1000 Monrovia 10; internet www.mpw.gov.lr.

Ministry of Transport: Parker Bldg, Broad St, 1000 Monrovia 10; tel. 888960960; internet mot.gov.lr.

Ministry of Youth and Sports: Monrovia; e-mail info@moys.gov.lr; internet www.moys.gov.lr.

President

Presidential Election, First Round, 10 October 2017

Candidate	Valid votes	% of valid votes
George Manneh Weah (Coalition for Democratic Change)	596,037	38.37
Joseph Nyuma Boakai (Unity Party)	446,716	28.76
Charles Walker Brumskine (Liberty Party)	149,495	9.62
Prince Y. Johnson (Movement for Democracy and Reconstruction)	127,666	8.22
Alexander B. Cummings (Alternative National Congress)	112,067	7.22
Others*	121,367	7.81
Total	1,553,348†	100.00

* There were 15 other candidates.

† Excluding 88,574 invalid votes.

Presidential Election, Second Round, 26 December 2017

Candidate	Valid votes	% of valid votes
George Manneh Weah (Coalition for Democratic Change)	732,185	61.54
Joseph Nyuma Boakai (Unity Party)	457,579	38.46
Total	1,189,764†	100.00

† Excluding 28,360 invalid votes.

Legislature

HOUSE OF REPRESENTATIVES

House of Representatives: Capitol Bldg, Monrovia; internet fb.com/Liberia-House-of-Representatives-346078425435582.

Speaker: Dr BHOFAL CHAMBERS.

General Election, 10 October 2017

Party	Seats
Coalition for Democratic Change	21
Unity Party	19
Independents	12
People's Unification Party	5
All Liberian Party	3
Liberty Party	3
Movement for Democracy and Reconstruction	2
Liberia National Union	1
Liberian People's Party	1
Liberia Transformation Party	1
Movement for Economic Empowerment	1
Victory for Change Party	1
United People's Party	1
Total	73

SENATE

Senate: Capitol Bldg, Monrovia; tel. 775947558; e-mail liberiansenate1847@gmail.com; internet fb.com/The-Liberian-Senate-1484662195117109.

President Pro Tempore: Prof. ALBERT T. CHIE.

There are 30 senators who are elected for nine-year terms. One-half of the seats were elected on 20 December 2014 and 15 seats were contested at elections held on 8 December 2020.

Distribution of Seats, May 2021

Party	Seats
Independents	7
Collaborating Political Parties	6
Congress for Democratic Change	5
Unity Party	4
Liberty Party	2
People's Unification Party	2
Alternative National Congress	1
Movement for Democracy and Reconstruction	1
National Democratic Coalition	1
National Patriotic Party	1
Total	30

Election Commission

National Elections Commission: Tubman Blvd Sinkor, Monrovia; tel. 777558685; e-mail info@necliberia.org; internet www.necliberia.org; independent; Chair. DAVIDETTA BROWNE LANSANAH.

Political Organizations

A total of 23 political parties were registered by the National Elections Commission in 2022. The most significant of these parties are listed below:

All Liberian Party (ALP): Old Rd, Monrovia; tel. 88098305; internet fb.com/allliberianparty; f. 2015; Leader BENONI W. UREY.

Coalition for Democratic Change (CDC): Bernard's Compound, Congo Town, Monrovia; tel. 886524899; e-mail info@cdcliberia.org; f. 2004; Chair. MULBAH MORLU, Jr; Leader GEORGE MANNEH WEAH.

Grassroots Democratic Party of Liberia (GDPL): Monrovia; Chair. GLADYS BEYAN.

Liberia National Union (LINU): 16th St, Sinkor, Monrovia; tel. 777059282; Chair. AARON S. M. WESSEH.

Liberia Transformation Party (LTP): Monrovia; internet fb.com/liberiatransformationparty; f. 1984; Leader KENNEDY GBLEYAH SANDY; Chair. JULIUS SUKU.

Liberty Party (LP): Old Rd, Sinkor, Opposite Haywood Mission, POB 1340, Monrovia; tel. 886547921; internet libertypartyliberia.com; f. 2005; Chair. MUSA HASSAN BILITY.

Movement for Progressive Change (MPC): Fiama, 21st St, Sinkor, Monrovia; Leader SIMEON FREEMAN.

National Patriotic Party (NPP): Sinkor, Tubman Bldg, Monrovia; f. 1997 from the fmr armed faction the National Patriotic Front of Liberia; Leader JEWEL HOWARD-TAYLOR.

People's Unification Party (PUP): Monrovia; Chair. SAMUEL G. KOGAR.

Unity Party (UP): 86 Broad St, Monrovia; f. 1984; Chair. Rev. J. LUTHER TARPEH; Nat. Sec. Rev. AMOS TWEH.

Diplomatic Representation

EMBASSIES IN LIBERIA

Cameroon: 18th St and Payne Ave, Sinkor, POB 414, Monrovia; tel. 880324366; e-mail cameroon_mission@yahoo.com; Ambassador BEN-G'YELA AUGUSTINE GANG.

China, People's Republic: POB 5970, Monrovia; tel. 886555556; e-mail chinaemb_lr@mfa.gov.cn; internet lr.china-embassy.gov.cn; Ambassador REN YISHENG.

Congo, Democratic Republic: Spriggs Payne Airport, Sinkor, POB 1038, Monrovia; Ambassador (vacant).

Côte d'Ivoire: 17–18 Warner Ave, Sinkor, Monrovia; tel. 880556361; e-mail ambaci.monrovia@diplomatie.gouv.ci; internet liberia.diplomatie.gouv.ci; Ambassador FENI KOUAKOU.

Egypt: Coconut Plantation, Randall St, Mamba Point, POB 462, Monrovia; tel. 886583486; Ambassador AHMED EL-SAYED HELAL.

France: 98A UN Dr., Mamba Point, Monrovia; tel. 770599373; e-mail ambafrance.liberia@yahoo.fr; internet lr.ambafrance.org; Ambassador MICHAËL ROUX.

Germany: Tubman Blvd C-86, Congo Town, Monrovia; tel. 886438365; e-mail info@monrovia.diplo.de; internet monrovia.diplo.de; Ambassador Dr JAKOB HASELHUBER.

Ghana: 15th St, Sinkor, POB 6421, Monrovia; tel. 777000813; e-mail monrovia@mfa.gov.gh; internet monrovia.mfa.gov.gh; Ambassador KWABENA OKUBI APPIAH.

Guinea: 23rd St, Tubman Blvd, POB 461, Monrovia; tel. 886564615; e-mail dore10032@yahoo.com; Ambassador (vacant).

Holy See: Gordan St, Mamba Point, Monrovia; tel. 777324473; e-mail nuntiusliberia@gmail.com; Apostolic Nuncio WALTER ERBÌ.

India: No. 16, Coconut Plantation, Mamba Point, Monrovia; internet www.indianembassymonrovia.gov.in; Ambassador PRADIP KUMAR YADAV.

Ireland: 12th St, Sinkor, Monrovia; tel. 880060832; internet www.dfa.ie/irish-embassy/liberia; Ambassador CLAIRE BUCKLEY.

Lebanon: 12th St, cnr Warner Ave, Sinkor, Monrovia; tel. 886477444; e-mail emb.lebanon.mon@gmail.com; Ambassador HENRI KASTOUN.

Libya: 14th St, Sinkor, Monrovia; Ambassador MUHAMMAD UMARAT-TABI.

Nigeria: Tubman Blvd, Congo Town, POB 366, Monrovia; tel. 777024195; e-mail nigeria.monrovia@foreignaffairs.gov.ng; internet nigeriaembassymonrovia.org; Ambassador GODFREY A. E. ODUDIGBO.

Qatar: 16th St, Sinkor, Monrovia; tel. 555765555; e-mail monrovia@mofa.gov.qa; internet monrovia.embassy.qa/en; Chargé d'affaires a.i. SHAMSAN ABDULLAH AL-SADA.

Sierra Leone: Tubman Blvd, POB 575, Monrovia; tel. 886888825; e-mail slembmnvia@yahoo.com; Ambassador EDDIE SIDIKIE MASSALLY.

South Africa: Sophie Rd, House No 5, Congo Town, Monrovia; tel. 880885544; e-mail molefej@dirco.gov.za; Ambassador M. IGBAL JHAZBHAY.

Sweden: LCL Compound, 12th St, Sinkor, Monrovia; tel. 770173801; e-mail ambassaden.monrovia@gov.se; internet www.swedenabroad.com/monrovia; Ambassador URBAN SJÖSTRÖM.

United Kingdom: Leone Compound, 12th St, Beach-side, Sinkor, Monrovia; tel. 777530320; e-mail monrovia.generalenquiries@fco.gov.uk; internet www.gov.uk/government/world/liberia; Ambassador NEIL BRADLEY.

USA: 502 Benson St, POB 98, Monrovia; tel. 776777000; e-mail ConsularMonrovia@state.gov; internet lr.usembassy.gov; Ambassador MICHAEL A. MCCARTHY.

Judicial System

The five-member Supreme Court was established in January 1992 to adjudicate in electoral disputes.

Supreme Court: Temple of Justice, Capitol Hill, Monrovia; tel. 886458993; e-mail info@judiciary.gov.lr; internet judiciary.gov.lr; consists of a Chief Justice and 4 Associate Justices; Chief Justice SIE-A-NYENE GYAPAY YUOH.

Religion

Christianity and Islam are the two main religions. According to the 2008 census, about 86% of the population are Christians, predominantly Anglicans, while around 12% are Muslims. A very small number of Liberians hold traditional beliefs.

CHRISTIANITY

Liberian Council of Churches: 15th St, Sinkor, POB 10-2191, 1000 Monrovia; tel. 886234674; e-mail lccsecretariat2018@gmail.com; internet fb.com/Liberia-Council-of-Churches-151416415568912; f. 1982; 13 mems, 11 assoc. mems, 4 fraternal mems; Pres. Rev. Dr SAMUEL B. REEVES; Gen. Sec. CHRISTOPHER WLEH TOE, I.

The Anglican Communion

The diocese of Liberia forms part of the Church of the Province of West Africa (CPWA), incorporating the local Episcopal Church. In September 2012 the CPWA was subdivided into two internal provinces: the Internal Province of Ghana, comprising the 10 (now 11) dioceses in Ghana, and the Internal Province of West Africa, comprising the remaining five (now six) dioceses, including the diocese of Liberia. The Archbishop of the CPWA is the Bishop of Liberia.

Archbishop of the Church of the Province of West Africa and Bishop of Liberia: Rt Rev. Dr JONATHAN BAU-BAU BONAPARTE HART, POB 10-0277, 1000 Monrovia 10; tel. 886516343; e-mail bishop@liberia.net.

The Roman Catholic Church

Liberia comprises the archdiocese of Monrovia and the dioceses of Cape Palmas and Gbarnga.

Catholic Bishops' Conference of Liberia (CABICOL): Gaye Town, Old Rd, POB 10-2078, 1000 Monrovia 10; tel. 888910825; e-mail frdnimene@gmail.com; internet cabicol.org; f. 1998; Pres. ANTHONY FALLAH BORWAH (Bishop of Gbarnga).

Archbishop of Monrovia: (vacant), Archbishop's Office, 46 Ashmun St, POB 2078, 1000 Monrovia 10; tel. 886554578; e-mail apostolic_adm@yahoo.com.

Other Christian Churches

Assemblies of God in Liberia: POB 1297, Monrovia; tel. 886539480; internet fb.com/agliberia; f. 1908; Gen. Supt EDWIN A. GBELLY; c. 75,000 adherents, 400 churches.

Lutheran Church in Liberia (LCL): 13th St, Payne Ave, Sinkor, POB 10-1046, 1000 Monrovia 10; tel. 886213894; e-mail lutheranchurchinliberia@yahoo.com; internet fb.com/LCL1860; f. 1947 as Evangelical Lutheran Church, reorg. in 1965 under indigenous leadership as LCL; Bishop Rt Rev. G. VICTOR PADMORE; Gen. Sec. VICTOR KAYDOR.

Providence Baptist Church: cnr Broad and Center Sts, Monrovia; tel. 77534172; e-mail admin@providencebc.net; internet www.providencebc.net; f. 1821; 2,500 adherents, 300 congregations, 6 ministers, 8 schools; Senior Pastor Rev. Dr SAMUEL BROOMFIELD REEVES, Jr.

Liberia Baptist Missionary and Educational Convention, Inc: Baptist House, 98 Tubman Blvd, Sinkor, POB 390, Monrovia; tel. 880224305; f. 1880; Pres. Dr SAMUEL B. REEVES; Exec. Sec. Rev. JUSTUS R. REEVES.

United Methodist Church in Liberia: cnr 13th St and Tubman Blvd, POB 10-1010, 1000 Monrovia 10; tel. 880421686; e-mail liberiaumc@yahoo.com; internet liberiaunitedmethodistchurch.org; f. 1833; Resident Bishop Rev. Dr SAMUEL QUIRE.

Other active denominations include the National Baptist Mission, the Pentecostal Church, the Presbyterian Church in Liberia, the Prayer Band and the Church of the Lord Aladura.

ISLAM

National Muslim Council of Liberia: POB 417, Monrovia; e-mail nmclib2013@gmail.com; internet fb.com/nationalmuslimcouncilofliberia; Chair. SHEIKH OMARU A. KAMARA; Sec.-Gen. SHEIKH AKBU SHERIFF.

The Press

NEWSPAPERS (PRINT AND ONLINE)

Concord Times: 120 Ashmun St, Monrovia; tel. 886572523; e-mail lyndonponnie@yahoo.com; daily; Man. Editor J. LYNDON PONNIE.

Daily Observer: ELWA Junction, Paynesville; tel. 777274772; e-mail liberianobserver@gmail.com; internet www.liberianobserver.com; f. 1981; independent; daily; Man. Dir BAI SAMA G. BEST.

Focus: Gurley St, Monrovia; tel. 776583266; e-mail info@focus.com.lr; internet focus.com.lr; f. 2011; daily; Man. JOHN C. HARRIS.

FrontPage Africa: Oldest Congo Town, Monrovia; tel. 886738666; e-mail editor@frontpageafricaonline.com; internet www.frontpageafricaonline.com; f. 2005; daily; Man. Editor RODNEY D. SIEH.

Heritage: cnr Broad and Nelson Sts, Monrovia; tel. 777548878; e-mail info@heritagenewslib.com; internet www.heritagenewslib.com; f. 1977; Man. Editor MOHAMMED M. KANNEH.

Informer: Caesar Bldg, cnr Carey and Johnson Sts, Monrovia; tel. 886519515; e-mail informerkevin@yahoo.com; f. 2003; Man. Editor DARKOLLIE SUMO.

In Profile Daily: Capitol By-Pass, Monrovia; tel. 886452864; e-mail inprofilecontact@gmail.com; internet www.inprofiledaily.com; f. 2008; Man. Editor CARLTON BOAH.

The Inquirer: Gurley St, POB 3600, Monrovia; tel. 886516533; e-mail theinquirer.era@gmail.com; internet www.theinquirer.com.lr; f. 1991; daily; Man. Editor (vacant).

Insight: 33 Gurley St, Monrovia; tel. 777636364; e-mail insightadvertisment@gmail.com; internet insight.com.lr; f. 2010; daily; Man. Editor JOE K. ROBERTS.

National Chronicle: Carey St, POB 20-1598, Monrovia; tel. 886543189; e-mail nationalchronicle2011@gmail.com; f. 1996; Editor WEDEO R. JOHNSON.

New Dawn: UN Dr., POB 1266, Monrovia; tel. 886484201; e-mail info@thenewdawnliberia.com; internet www.thenewdawnliberia.com; f. 2010; CEO OTHELLO B. GARBLAH.

New Republic: Maxim Bldg, 153 Benson St, Monrovia; tel. 886400050; e-mail tnrliberia@outlook.com; internet newrepublicliberia.com; Publr ALPHONSO TOWEH; Editor-in-Chief ELLIS TOGBA.

PERIODICALS

Business Liberia: Monrovia; f. 2009; publ. by Baker Pearson Communications, Inc; Editor-in-Chief SEANAN DENIZOT.

Liberia Travel & Life: Monrovia; internet fb.com/ATLmagazine; 4 a year; publ. by Baker Pearson Communications, Inc; Editor-in-Chief HESTA BAKER PEARSON.

PRESS ORGANIZATIONS

Liberia Media Center: LMC Box 1153, 1st St, Sinkor, Jallah Town, Monrovia; tel. 866523144; f. 2005; Chair. (vacant).

Press Union of Liberia: 44 Clay St, Monrovia; tel. 886522334; e-mail info@pul.org.lr; internet www.pul.org.lr; f. 1985; Pres. CHARLES B. COFFEY, Jr.

NEWS AGENCIES

Liberian News Agency (LINA): Ministry of Information Bldg, POB 9021, Capitol Hill, Monrovia; tel. 881102511; e-mail directorgeneral@linagov.org; internet liberianewsagency.com; f. 1978; Dir-Gen. KWAME O. WEEKS.

Broadcasting and Communications

TELECOMMUNICATIONS

Libtelco: 18th St and Tubman Blvd, Sinkor, Monrovia; tel. 778228592; e-mail info@libtelco.com.lr; internet libtelco.com.lr;

f. 1973 as the Liberia Telecommunications Corpn; Chair. ALEXANDRA ZOE; Man. Dir RICHMOND N. TOBII.

Lonestar Cell MTN: LBDI Bldg, Congo Town, Monrovia; tel. 880501822; e-mail product@lonestarcell.com; internet lonestarcell.com; f. 2001; mobile telephone provider; subsidiary of Mobile Telephone Networks (Pty) Ltd, South Africa; CEO RAHUL DE.

Orange Liberia: Haile Selassie Ave, Capital By-Pass, POB 1611, Monrovia; tel. 777000100; internet www.orange.com.lr; mobile telephone provider; fmrly Cellcom; present name adopted in 2017; owned by Orange (France); CEO JEAN MARIUS YAO.

Regulatory Authority

Liberia Telecommunications Authority: Menetamba Rd, Cooper's Beach Community, Paynesville; tel. 888929349; e-mail info@lta.gov.lr; internet www.lta.gov.lr; f. 2007; Chair. EDWINA CRUMP ZACKPAH (acting).

BROADCASTING
Radio

Buffalo VoA 94.1 FM: cnr Broad and Buchanan Sts, Monrovia; tel. 886514414; e-mail jimnardy@yahoo.com; owned by Buffalo Investment Liberia Inc; CEO OJIMBA IFEANYI DAVIES.

Farbric 101.1 FM: 14th and 15th Sts, Sinkor, Tubman Blvd, Monrovia; tel. 886933684; internet www.farbric.net; f. 2010; Station Man. AUGUSTA V. FREEMAN; Operations Man. PRESTON GAYFLOR.

Hott FM 107.9: Prall Bldg, 1st Floor, 12 Broad St, Snapper Hill, Monrovia; tel. 886807372; e-mail hotttvch12@gmail.com; internet fb.com/hottfmliberia.

Power FM: Carey St, Snapper Hill, Monrovia; tel. 886518418; f. 2003.

Radio Veritas: POB 3569, Monrovia; tel. 994712834; e-mail radioveritas@hotmail.com; f. 1981; Catholic; independent; nationwide shortwave broadcasts; Dirs Fr ANTHONY BOWAH, LEDGERHOOD RENNIE.

SKY FM 107: King Burger Bldg, 42 Broad St, POB 2941, Monrovia; tel. 777521162; e-mail skyliberiainc@gmail.com; internet fb.com/SkyFMandTV; f. 2005; Man. MARTIN BROWN.

Star Radio: 12 Broad St, Snapper Hill, Monrovia; tel. 777104411; e-mail star@liberia.net; internet www.starradio.org.lr; independent news and information station; f. July 1997 by Fondation Hirondelle, Switzerland, with funds from the US Agency for International Development; broadcasts in English, French and 14 African languages; Man. JAMES K. MORLU.

Teach FM 92.7: St. Joseph Campus, Capitol Hill, 00231 Monrovia; tel. 777333316; f. 2010.

Television

Liberia Broadcasting System: POB 594, Paynesville City, Monrovia; tel. 777137435; e-mail ledgeehood@elbcradio.com; internet elbcradio.com; f. 1960; govt-owned; Chair. EUGENE L. NAGBE; Dir-Gen. ESTELLA LIBERTY-KEMOH.

Real TV: Duport Rd, Monrovia; tel. 770142319; e-mail lkbility@yahoo.com; internet fb.com/RealTV3; f. 2005; Gen. Man. LYEE BILITY.

Sky TV (Channel 6): King Burger Bldg, Broad St, POB 2941, Monrovia; tel. 777747747; e-mail skyliberiainc@gmail.com; internet fb.com/SkyFMandTV; f. 2005; CEO MARTIN BROWN.

Finance

BANKING
Central Bank

Central Bank of Liberia: cnr Warren and Carey Sts, POB 2048, 1000 Monrovia; internet www.cbl.org.lr; f. 1974 as National Bank of Liberia; present name adopted in March 1999; bank of issue; Exec. Gov. JOLUE ALOYSIUS TARLUE, Jr.

Other Banks

AccessBank Liberia Ltd: 20th St, Sinkor, POB 1230, Monrovia; tel. 881983429; e-mail info@accessbank.com.lr; internet www.accessbank.com.lr; f. 2008; Chair. BERND ZATTLER; CEO JONAS NYAYE.

Afriland First Bank Liberia: Crown Hill, Broad St, POB 1935, Monrovia; tel. 880232400; e-mail afbankliberia@afrilandfirstbank.com; internet afrilandfirstbanklb.com; f. 2011; Man. Dir ROBERT NKOUS.

Ecobank Liberia Ltd: Ashmun and Randall Sts, POB 4825, Monrovia; tel. 886974494; e-mail ecobanklr@ecobank.com;

internet www.ecobank.com; commenced operations Aug. 1999; Chair. T. NEGBALEE WARNER; Man. Dir GEORGE MENSAH-ASANTE.

Global Bank Liberia Ltd (GBLL): 6th St, Sinkor, POB 2053, 1000 Monrovia; tel. 886522460; f. 2005; Italian-owned; Man. Dir ROTIMI SANGODEYI.

Groupe Nduom Bank Liberia Ltd (GNBLL): Luke Bldg, Broad St, Monrovia; tel. 555014065; e-mail info@gnbankliberia.com; internet gnbankliberia.com; f. 2016; fmrly First International Bank (Liberia) Ltd; CEO JOSEPH K. ANIM.

Guaranty Trust Bank (Liberia) Ltd (GTBLL): 13th St, Tubman Blvd, POB 0382, Monrovia; tel. 776498652; internet www.gtbanklr .com; f. 2007; Chair. OPRAL MASON BENSON; CEO IKENNA ANEKWE.

International Bank (Liberia) Ltd: Tubman Blvd, between 11th and 12th Sts, POB 10292, 1000 Monrovia; tel. 886511823; e-mail customercare@ibliberia.com; internet www.ibliberia.com; f. 1948 as International Trust Co of Liberia; present name adopted in April 2000; 75.5% owned by Liberian Financial Holdings; 19.1% Trust Bank Ltd (The Gambia); Chair. ESTRADA BERNARD; CEO HENRY SAAMOI.

Liberian Bank for Development and Investment (LBDI): 9th St, Sinkor, POB 547, Monrovia; e-mail lbdi@lbdi.net; internet www .lbdi.net; f. 1961; 18.7% govt-owned; Chair. AMARA M. KONNEH; Pres. and CEO JOHN B. S. DAVIES, III.

United Bank for Africa Liberia Ltd: cnr Broad and Nelson Sts, POB 4523, Monrovia; tel. 880560509; e-mail cfcliberia@ubagroup .com; internet www.ubaliberia.com; f. 2006; Man. Dir and CEO NKECHI JOYCE ARIZOR.

Financial Institutions

Liberian Enterprise Development Finance Co.: Tubman Blvd, Congo Town, Monrovia; tel. 888514424; e-mail info@ledfcliberia .com; internet ledfcliberia.com; f. 2007; Gen. Man. AMBROSE HOUPHOUET.

Banking Associations

Liberia Bankers' Association: POB 292, Monrovia; mems include commercial and devt banks; Pres. JOHN B. S. DAVIES, Jr.

INSURANCE

American National Underwriters, Inc: Carter Bldg, 39 Broad St, POB 180, Monrovia; general; Gen. Man. S. B. MENSAH.

Insurance Co of Africa: 2nd Floor, International Bank Building, 64 Broad St, Monrovia; internet www.ica-liberia.com; f. 1969; life and general; Pres. SAMUEL OWAREE MINTAH.

Omega Insurance Co.: cnr Tubman Blvd and 5th St, Sinkor, POB 260, Monrovia; tel. 881795639; e-mail info@omegalr.com; internet www.omegalr.com; f. 2007; Chair. CHARLES N. ANANABA; Pres. and CEO GAJAY L. ANANABA.

Trade and Industry

GOVERNMENT AGENCIES

General Services Agency (GSA): Old USTC Compound, UN Dr., POB 10-9027, Monrovia; tel. 886901333; e-mail info@gsa.gov.lr; internet www.gsa.gov.lr; Dir-Gen. MARY T. BROH.

National Bureau of Concessions: Monrovia; tel. 775950341; internet fb.com/nbcliberia; f. 2011; Exec. Dir EDWIN N. DENNIS.

DEVELOPMENT ORGANIZATIONS

Forestry Development Authority: POB 10-3010, Kappa House, Eli Saleby Compound, Monrovia; tel. 886798425; e-mail info@fda.gov .lr; internet www.fda.gov.lr; f. 1976; responsible for forest management and conservation; Chair. HARRISON KARNWEA; Man. Dir C. MIKE DONYEN.

Liberia National Investment Commission (LNIC): Sekou Toure Ave, Monrovia; tel. 777405511; e-mail info@investliberia.gov.lr; internet www.investliberia.gov.lr; f. 1979; autonomous body negotiating investment incentives agreements on behalf of Govt; promotes agro-based and industrial devt; Chair. MOLEWULEH B. GRAY; Exec. Dir MORRIS SACKOR.

CHAMBER OF COMMERCE

Liberia Chamber of Commerce: Queen's Ave, Capitol Hill, POB 92, Monrovia; tel. 777857805; e-mail info@liberiachamber.org; internet www.liberiachamber.org; f. 1951; Pres. N. OSWALD TWEH; Sec.-Gen. SALAMARTU STEPHANIE DUNCAN.

INDUSTRIAL AND TRADE ASSOCIATIONS

Liberia Agriculture Commodity Regulatory Authority: Bushrod Island, Monrovia; tel. 880825097; tel. info@lacra.gov.lr; f. 2015 to replace Liberian Produce Marketing Corpn; govt-owned; exports Liberian produce, provides industrial facilities for processing of agricultural products and participates in agricultural devt programmes; Man. Dir NYAH MARTEIN.

UTILITIES

Liberia Electricity Corpn (LEC): Waterside, UN Dr., POB 10-165, Monrovia; tel. 777444156; e-mail info@lecliberia.com; internet lecliberia.com; f. 1973; Chair. MONIE R. CAPTAN; Man. Dir ERNEST R. HUGHES.

National Oil Co of Liberia (NOCAL): Episcopal Church Plaza, 3rd and 4th Floors, Ashmun and Randall Sts, 1000 Monrovia; tel. 777019768; e-mail info@nocal.com.lr; f. 2000; Chair. RICHARD B. DEVINE; Pres. and CEO SAIFUAH MAI GRAY.

Water

Liberia Water and Sewer Corpn: King Sao Bosso St, POB 1079, Monrovia; tel. 207313501; internet www.lwsc.gov.lr; f. 1973; Chair. GEORGE HARRIS; Man. Dir DUANNAH A. KAMARA.

Regulatory Authority

Liberia Electricity Regulatory Commission: Tubman Blvd, Monrovia; tel. 776004350; e-mail info@lerc.gov.lr; internet www .lerc.gov.lr; f. 2017; Chair. LAWRENCE D. SEKAJIPO; Man. Dir AUGUSTUS V. GOANUE.

MAJOR COMPANIES

The following are among the largest companies in terms either of capital investment or employment.

Firestone Liberia Inc: POB 140, Harbel; internet www .firestonenaturalrubber.com; f. 1926 by Firestone Rubber Co (USA); acquired by Japanese co, Bridgestone, in 1988, although Firestone retained control of local management; Gen. Man. DON DARDEN.

Liberia Cement Corpn (CEMENCO): Bushroda Island, Somalia Dr., POB 150, Monrovia; e-mail robert.marshall@hcafrica.com; internet www.cemenco.com/en; mfrs of Portland cement; Man. Dir WILLIAM PHILLIPPE GAIGNARD.

Liberia Petroleum Refining Co (LPRC): POB 90, Monrovia; sole producer of domestically produced fuels, with designed capacity of 15,000 b/d; products include diesel fuel, fuel oils, liquid petroleum gas; supplies domestic market and has limited export facilities for surplus products; Chair. JOSEPH T. PAH; Man. Dir MARIE UREY COLEMAN.

TRADE UNIONS

Liberian Labor Congress: J. B. McGill Labor Center, Gardnersville Freeway, POB 415, Monrovia; internet fb.com/LLCLiberia; f. 2008 following merger of Liberian Federation of Labor Unions and Congress of National Trade Unions; Pres. ELITHA T. MANNING, Jr; Sec.-Gen. DAVID D. SACKOR.

Transport

RAILWAYS

Bong Mine Railway: POB 538, Monrovia; f. 1958; Gen. Man. HANS-GEORG SCHNEIDER.

ROADS

The main trunk road is the Monrovia–Sanniquellie motor road, extending north-east from the capital to the border with Guinea, near Ganta, and eastward through the hinterland to the border with Côte d'Ivoire. Trunk roads run through Tapita, in Nimba County, to Grand Gedeh County and from Monrovia to Buchanan. A bridge over the Mano river connects with the Sierra Leone road network, while a main road links Monrovia and Freetown (Sierra Leone).

National Transit Authority (NTA): Monrovia; internet nta.com .lr; f. 2008; govt-owned bus operator in 7 counties; Man. Dir TECONBLA MCCAULEY.

SHIPPING

Liberia Maritime Authority (LiMA): Tubman Blvd, Sinkor, Monrovia; tel. 777206108; internet www.lima.gov.lr; Chair. THERESA LEIGH-SHERMAN; Commissioner EUGENE LENN NAGBE.

National Port Authority: Freeport of Monrovia, Bushrod Island, POB 1849, Monrovia; tel. 777718937; e-mail info@npaliberia.com; internet www.npaliberia.com; f. 1967; administers Monrovia

Freeport and the ports of Buchanan, Greenville and Harper; Chair. RICHARD DIVINE; Man. Dir (vacant).

CIVIL AVIATION
Liberia's principal airports are Robertsfield International Airport, at Harbel, 56 km east of Monrovia, and James Spriggs Payne Airport, at Monrovia.

Liberia Airport Authority (LAA): POB 1, Robertsfield; tel. 777010192; e-mail info@robairport.com; internet fb.com/LiberiaLAA; Chair. MUSA SHANNON (acting); Man. Dir (vacant).

Liberia Civil Aviation Authority: Monrovia; internet lcaa.gov.lr; Dir-Gen. MOSES Y. KOLLIE.

Tourism

Liberia National Tourism Association (LINTA): 10th St, Sinkor, Monrovia; tel. 888879879; e-mail info@linta.org.lr; internet linta.wildapricot.org; Pres. MAI UREY.

Defence

As assessed at November 2021, the total strength of the Liberian armed forces was 2,010 (an army of 1,950 and a coast guard of 60).

Defence Budget: L $19.6m. in 2021.

Chief of Staff of the Armed Forces of Liberia: Maj. Gen. PRINCE CHARLES JOHNSON, III.

Education

Education is provided by a mixture of government, private, church and mosque schools. Education in Liberia is officially compulsory for 10 years, between six and 16 years of age. Primary education begins theoretically at six years of age and lasts for six years (grades 1–6). Secondary education, beginning theoretically at 12 years of age, lasts for a further six years, and is divided into two three-year cycles, known in Liberia as 'junior high school' (grades 7–9) and 'senior high school' (grades 10–12). Pre-primary education is undertaken from the age of five or younger and is important for those students whose mother language is not English, since English is the language of instruction throughout the school system. School attendance is not enforced. According to estimates by the United Nations Educational, Scientific and Cultural Organization (UNESCO), in 2016/17 enrolment at pre-primary level included 59% of pupils in the relevant age-group (58% boys; 59% girls). In that year enrolment at primary schools included 79% of pupils in the relevant age-group (78% boys; 79% girls), while in 2014/15 enrolment at secondary schools was equivalent to 38% of pupils in the relevant age-group (43% boys; 33% girls). Although the Constitution includes the aspiration to provide universal free education, and fees in public primary schools have been officially abolished, school attendance is discouraged by the poor quality of education offered, by the remaining school fees, by charges and by the cost of uniforms and travel. The higher education sector consists of the University of Liberia in Monrovia, Cuttington University College in Bong County, the Booker Washington Institute in Kakata, Margibi County, and the William V. S. Tubman College in Maryland County. According to the 2020/21 budget figures, government spending on education represented 13.9% of total proposed budgetary expenditure.

Bibliography

Aboagye, F. B., and Bah, Alhaji M. S. *A Tortuous Road to Peace: The Dynamics of Regional, UN and International Humanitarian Interventions in Liberia.* Pretoria, Institute for Security Studies, 2005.

Abramowitz, S. A. *Searching for Normal in the Wake of the Liberian War.* Philadelphia, PA, University of Pennsylvania Press, 2014.

Adebajo, A. *Liberia's Civil War: Nigeria, Ecomog and Regional Security in West Africa.* Boulder, CO, Lynne Rienner Publishers, 2002.

Afolabi, B. T. *The Politics of Peacemaking in Africa. Non-State Actors' Role in the Liberian Civil War.* Woodbridge, Boydell and Brewer, 2017.

Alao, A. *The Burden of Collective Goodwill: The International Involvement in the Liberian Civil War.* Aldershot, Ashgate, 1998.

Alao, A., Mackinlay, J., and Olonisakin, F. *Peacekeepers, Politicians and Warlords: The Liberian Peace Process (Foundations of Peace Series).* Tokyo, United Nations University Press, 2000.

Banton, C. A. *More Auspicious Shores: Barbadian Migration to Liberia, Blackness, and the Making of an African Republic.* Cambridge, Cambridge University Press (2019).

Beevers, M. *Peacebuilding and Natural Resource Governance After Armed Conflict: Sierra Leone and Liberia.* London, Palgrave Macmillan, 2018.

Bjarnesen, M. *Repurposed Rebels Postwar Rebel Networks in Liberia.* Athens, GA, University of Georgia Press, 2020.

Clegg, C. A. *The Price of Liberty: African Americans and the Making of Liberia.* Chapel Hill, NC, University of North Carolina Press, 2004.

Cooper, H. *Madame President: The Extraordinary Journey of Ellen Johnson Sirleaf.* New York, Simon & Schuster, 2017.

Deme, M. *Law, Morality, and International Armed Intervention: The United Nations and Ecowas (African Studies: History, Politics, Economics and Culture).* Abingdon, Routledge, 2005.

Dolo, E. *Democracy versus Dictatorship: The Quest for Freedom and Justice in Africa's Oldest Republic, Liberia.* Lanham, MD, University Press of America, 1996.

Dunn, D. E., Bevan, A. J., and Burrowes, C. P. *Historical Dictionary of Liberia.* 2nd edn. Metuchen, NJ, Scarecrow Press, 2001.

Dunn, D. E., and Tarr, S. B. *Liberia: A National Polity in Transition.* Metuchen, NJ, Scarecrow Press, 1988.

Dwyer, J. *American Warlord: A True Story.* New York, Alfred A. Knopf, 2015.

Ellis, S. *The Mask of Anarchy: The Destruction of Liberia and the Religious Dimension of an African Civil War.* New York, New York University Press, 2006.

Everill, B. *Abolition and Empire in Sierra Leone and Liberia.* Basingstoke, Palgrave Macmillan, 2013.

Gerdes, F. *Civil War and State Formation: The Political Economy of War and Peace in Liberia.* Frankfurt, Campus Verlag, 2013.

Gershoni, Y. *Black Colonialism: The Americo-Liberian Scramble for the Hinterland.* Boulder, CO, Westview Press, 1985.

Gifford, P. *Christianity and Politics in Doe's Liberia.* Cambridge, Cambridge University Press, 2003.

Gobewole, S. H. *Liberia's Political Economy: An Examination of Public Institutional Quality.* Indianapolis, IN, Dog Ear Publishing, 2016

Graef, J. *Practicing Post-Liberal Peacebuilding: Legal Empowerment and Emergent Hybridity in Liberia.* Basingstoke, Palgrave Macmillan, 2015.

Hardgrove, A. *Life after Guns: Reciprocity and Respect among Young Men in Liberia.* New Brunswick, NJ, Rutgers University Press 2017.

Harris, D. *Civil War and Democracy in West Africa: Conflict Resolution, Elections and Justice in Sierra Leone and Liberia.* London, I.B. Tauris, 2012.

Harris, J. *Mother Liberia.* New York, Vantage Press, 2004.

Hoffman, D. *The War Machines: Young Men and Violence in Sierra Leone and Liberia.* Durham, NC, Duke University Press, 2011.

Huffman, A. *Mississippi in Africa: The Saga of the Slaves of Prospect Hill Plantation and their Legacy in Liberia Today.* New York, Gotham Books, 2004.

Hyman, L. S. *United States Policy Towards Liberia, 1822 to 2003: Unintended Consequences.* New Jersey, Africana Homestead Legacy Publications, 2003.

Jaye, T. *Issues of Sovereignty, Strategy and Security in the Economic Community of West African States (Ecowas) Intervention in the Liberian Civil War.* Lewiston, NY, Edwin Mellen Press, 2003.

Johnson Sirleaf, E. *This Child Will Be Great: Memoir of a Remarkable Life by Africa's First Woman President.* New York, HarperCollins, 2010.

Kastfelt, N. *Religion and African Civil Wars.* London, Palgrave Macmillan, 2005.

Keih, G. K., Jr. *Dependency and the Foreign Policy of a Small Power.* Lewiston, NY, Edwin Mellen Press, 1992.

The First Liberian Civil War. New York, Peter Lang, 2008.

Levitt, J. *The Evolution of Deadly Conflict in Liberia: From 'Paternaltarianism' to State Collapse.* Durham, NC, Carolina Academic Press, 2005.

Illegal Peace in Africa: An Inquiry into the Legality of Power Sharing with Warlords, Rebels, and Junta. Cambridge, Cambridge University Press, 2012.

Lindsey, S. E. *Liberty Brought Us Here. The True Story of American Slaves Who Migrated to Liberia*. Lexington, KY, University Press of Kentucky, 2020.

Lyons, T. *Voting for Peace: Postconflict Elections in Liberia* (Studies in Foreign Policy). Washington, DC, Brookings Institution Press, 1999.

McDaniel, A. *Swing Low, Sweet Chariot: The Mortality Cost of Colonizing Liberia in the Nineteenth Century* (Population and Development). Chicago, IL, University of Chicago Press, 1995.

Mgbeoji, I. *Collective Insecurity: The Liberian Crisis, Unilateralism and Global Order*. Vancouver, BC, University of British Columbia Press, 2003.

Moran, M. H. *Liberia: The Violence of Democracy (Ethnography of Political Violence)*. Philadelphia, PA, University of Pennsylvania Press, 2005.

Morse, K., and Sawyer, A. *Beyond Plunder: Toward Democratic Governance in Liberia*. Boulder, CO, Lynne Rienner Publishers, 2005.

Moses, W. J. (Ed.), *Liberian Dreams: Back-to-Africa Narratives from the 1850s*. Philadelphia, PA, University of Pennsylvania Press, 1998.

Mulbah, S. *State-building Interventions in Post-Conflict Liberia: Building a State without Citizens*. Abingdon, Routledge, 2017.

Nass, I. A. *A Study in Internal Conflicts: The Liberian Crisis and the West African Peace Initiative*. Enugu, Fourth Dimension Publishing, 2001.

Olukoju, A. *Culture and Customs of Liberia*. Westport, CT, Greenwood Press, 2006.

Perry, J., and Debey Sayndee, T. *Social Mobilization and the Ebola Virus Disease in Liberia*. Lanham, MD, Hamilton Books, 2016.

Pailey, R. *Development, (Dual) Citizenship and its Discontents in Africa: The Political Economy of Belonging to Liberia*. Cambridge, Cambridge University Press, 2021.

Pal Chaudhuri, J. *Whitehall and the Black Republic: A Study of Colonial Britain's Attitude Towards Liberia, 1914–1939*. Cham, Palgrave Macmillan (2018).

Pham, J.-P. *Liberia: Portrait of a Failed State*. New York, Reed Press, 2004.

Saha, S. C. *Culture in Liberia: An Afrocentric View of the Cultural Interaction between the Indigenous Liberians and the Americo-Liberians*. Lewiston, NY, Edwin Mellen Press, 1998.

Sawyer, A. *The Emergence of Autocracy in Liberia: Tragedy and Challenge*. San Francisco, CA, ICS Press, 1992.

Shellum, B. G. *African American Officers in Liberia: A Pestiferous Rotation, 1910–1942*. Lincoln, NE, Potomac Books, 2018.

Sirleaf, A. M. *The Role of the Economic Community of the West African States: Ecowas—Conflict Management in Liberia*. New York, 1stBooks Library, 2003.

Söderström, J. *Peacebuilding and Ex-Combatants: Political Reintegration in Liberia*. Abingdon, Routledge, 2015.

Stryker, R. L. *Forged from Chaos: Stories and Reflections from Liberia at War*. New York, 1stBooks Library, 2003.

Sundiata, I. *Brothers and Strangers: Black Zionism, Black Slavery, 1914–1940*. Durham, NC, Duke University Press, 2004.

Tellewoyan, J. *The Years the Locusts have Eaten: Liberia 1816–2004*. Philadelphia, PA, Xlibris Corporation, 2005.

Tyler-McGraw, M. *An African Republic: Black and White Virginians in the Making of Liberia*. Chapel Hill, NC, University of North Carolina Press, 2007.

Vogt, M. A. (Ed.). *Liberian Crisis and ECOMOG: A Bold Attempt at Regional Peace-keeping*. Lagos, Gabumo Publishing Co, 1992.

Waugh, C. M. *Charles Taylor and Liberia: Ambition and Atrocity in Africa's Lone Star State*. London, Zed Books, 2011.

Wilén, N. *Justifying interventions in Africa: (de)stabilizing sovereignty in Liberia, Burundi and the Congo*. Basingstoke, Palgrave Macmillan, 2012.

Wodon, Q. *Poverty and the policy response to the economic crisis in Liberia*. Washington, DC, World Bank, 2011.

Yoder, J. C. *Popular Political Culture, Civil Society, and State Crisis in Liberia*. Lewiston, NY, Edwin Mellen Press, 2003.

MADAGASCAR

Physical and Social Geography

VIRGINIA THOMPSON

PHYSICAL FEATURES

The Republic of Madagascar comprises the island of Madagascar, the fourth largest island in the world, and several much smaller offshore islands, in the western Indian Ocean. Madagascar lies 390 km from the east African mainland across the Mozambique Channel. It extends 1,600 km from north to south and is up to 570 km wide. The whole territory covers an area of 587,295 sq km (226,756 sq miles). Geologically, the main island is basically composed of crystalline rock, which forms the central highlands that rise abruptly from the narrow eastern coastal strip and descend gradually to the wide plains of the west coast.

Topographically, Madagascar can be divided into six fairly distinct regions. Antsiranana province, in the north, is virtually isolated by the island's highest peak, Mt Tsaratanana, rising to 2,800 m above sea level. Tropical crops can be grown in its fertile valleys, and the natural harbour of Antsiranana is an important naval base. Another rich agricultural region lies in the north-west, where a series of valleys converge on the port of Mahajanga. To the south-west along the coastal plains lies a well-watered region where there are large animal herds and crops of rice, cotton, tobacco and manioc. The southernmost province, Toliary (Tuléar), contains most of Madagascar's known mineral deposits, as well as extensive cattle herds, despite the almost total lack of rainfall. In contrast, the hot and humid climate of the east coast favours the cultivation of the island's most valuable tropical crops—coffee, vanilla, cloves and sugar cane. Although this coast lacks sheltered anchorages, it is the site of Madagascar's most important commercial port, Toamasina. Behind its coral beaches a continuous chain of lagoons, some of which are connected by the Pangalanes Canal, provides a partially navigable internal waterway. The island's mountainous hinterland is a densely populated region of extensive rice culture and livestock farming. Despite its relative inaccessibility, this region is Madagascar's administrative and cultural centre, the focal point being the capital city of Antananarivo.

Climatic conditions vary from tropical conditions on the east and north-west coasts to the hotness and dryness of the west coast, the extreme aridity of the south and the temperate zone in the central highlands. Forests have survived only in some areas of abundant rainfall, and elsewhere the land has been eroded by over-grazing and slash-and-burn farming methods. Most of the island is savannah-steppe, and much of the interior is covered with laterite. Except in the drought-ridden south, rivers are numerous and flow generally westward, but many are interspersed by rapids and waterfalls, and few are navigable except for short distances.

POPULATION AND CULTURE

Geography and history account for the diversity and distribution of the population, which was enumerated at 25,674,196 at the census of May–June 2018, giving an average density of 43.7 inhabitants per sq km. At mid-2022 the population stood at 29,178,075, according to estimates by the United Nations (UN). The island's 18 principal ethnic groups are the descendants of successive waves of immigrants from such diverse areas as South-East Asia, continental Africa and Arab countries. Two of the dominant ethnic groups, the Merina (Hova) and the Betsileo, who inhabit the most densely populated central provinces of Antananarivo and Fianarantsoa, are of Asian-Pacific origin. In the peripheral areas live the tribes collectively known as côtiers, of whom the most numerous are the Betsimisaraka on the east coast, the Tsimihety in the north, and the Antandroy in the south. Although continuous migrations, improved means of communication and a marked cultural unity have, to some extent, broken down geographical and tribal barriers, traditional ethnic antagonisms—notably between the Merina and the côtiers—remain close to the surface.

With the population increasing at an average annual rate of 2.7% during 2011–20, the Malagasy are fast exceeding the island's capacity to feed and employ them. The UN estimated that 39.6% of the population were under 15 years of age at mid-2022, and that the urban component was steadily growing, thus aggravating urban socioeconomic problems. Antananarivo, the capital, is by far the largest city (with a population of over 3.5m.—including the suburbs—at mid-2021, according to UN estimates) and continues to expand, as do all the six provincial capitals.

History

JULIAN COOKE

INDEPENDENCE

After Madagascar's increasing engagement with Europe in the latter part of the 19th century and its annexation by France in 1896, there were moves to full independence as the Malagasy Republic on 26 June 1960. Even the imposition of colonial rule did not resolve the long-established ethnic conflict between the dominant Merina tribe from the central plateau and the coastal peoples (côtiers), represented by two opposing parties: the Mouvement Démocratique pour la Rénovation Malgache, a predominantly Merina group, and the Parti des Déshérités de Madagascar, a côtier party. There had been violent ethnic and partisan confrontations during 1947, in which some 80,000 people were killed. In October 1958 Madagascar became a self-governing republic within the French Community. Philibert Tsiranana of the moderately socialist Parti Social Démocrate (PSD) was elected President in 1959.

A serious agrarian uprising in 1971 followed a period of economic decline in the late 1960s. In January 1972, as the sole candidate, Tsiranana was re-elected as President, but a resurgence of violent protest led him in May to relinquish power to Gen. Gabriel Ramanantsoa, the Merina Chief of Staff of Madagascar's armed forces.

MILITARY GOVERNMENT

Ramanantsoa moved swiftly to restore public order, and in a referendum in October 1972 96% of those who voted endorsed a transitional period of five years under a new constitutional structure, with Malagasy as the official language. Madagascar withdrew from the Franc Zone and renegotiated its co-operation agreements with France, which closed its air and naval bases, while establishing diplomatic relations with the

People's Republic of China, the Soviet bloc countries and Arab nations.

Ramanantsoa's authority was weakened by the country's worsening financial position, and a radical faction led by Col Richard Ratsimandrava demanded administrative and political reform, based on a revival of the traditional communities, known as *fokonolona*. In February 1975 Ramanantsoa transferred power to Ratsimandrava, who was assassinated six days later. Gen. Gilles Andriamahazo immediately assumed power, imposing martial law and suspending political parties. In June Andriamahazo was succeeded as head of state by Lt-Commdr (later Adm.) Didier Ratsiraka, a *côtier* and former Minister of Foreign Affairs. Ratsiraka established a Conseil Supreme de la Révolution (CSR—Supreme Revolutionary Council), and the country was renamed the Democratic Republic of Madagascar. At a referendum held in December, 94.7% of participants approved a new Constitution, based on the *fokonolona*. Ratsiraka assumed the presidency in January 1976 for a seven-year term.

THE SECOND REPUBLIC

Unable to establish a single-party state, Ratsiraka formed the Avant-garde de la Révolution Malgache (AREMA) as the nucleus of the Front National pour la Défense de la Révolution Socialiste Malgache (FNDR), the only permitted political organization and a coalition of parties that included the extreme left-wing Mouvement pour le Pouvoir Prolétarien (MFM), led by Manandafy Rakotonirina, the left-wing Parti du Congrès de l'Indépendance de Madagascar (Antoko'ny Kongresi'ny Fahaleovantenan'i Madagasikara—AKFM), led by Richard Andriamanjato, and the PSD-derived Elan Populaire pour l'Unité Nationale (known as Vonjy). In November 1982 Ratsiraka was re-elected as President with 80% of the vote.

Ratsiraka's regime declined in popularity, owing in part to continued economic hardship. The press, now free from censorship, and the Christian Council of Churches in Madagascar (Fiombonan'ny Fiangonana Kristiana eto Madagasikara—FFKM) demanded reforms including an end to the FNDR's political monopoly. At the presidential election held in March 1989 Ratsiraka received 62% of the vote, although in the legislative elections in May AREMA further increased its parliamentary majority to 120 of the 137 seats (albeit with a high abstention rate). In August the President reorganized both the CSR and the Government, appointing several members of the opposition.

In September 1989 AREMA made large gains in local elections, and in December a constitutional amendment abolished the requirement to adhere to the FNDR. Consequently, in March 1990 a number of new parties were established, including the centre-right Mouvement des Démocrates Chrétiens Malgaches, a reformed PSD and the Union Nationale pour le Développement et la Démocratie (UNDD), led by a medical professor, Albert Zafy.

Confrontation and General Strike

In December 1990 16 opposition factions established an informal alliance, the Forces Vives (FV), together with trade unions and other groups, to co-ordinate proposals for constitutional reform. In June 1991 the FV demanded a constitutional conference and, when the Government failed to respond, organized a general strike, which was widely supported.

In July 1991 negotiations between the FV and AREMA failed, because Ratsiraka refused to resign as the FV demanded. The FV appointed its own 'Provisional Government', with a retired army general, Jean Rakotoharison, as President and with Albert Zafy of the UNDD as Prime Minister. Ratsiraka dissolved his Government and pledged to organize a referendum on a new constitution by the end of the year. In early August Ratsiraka nominated a new Prime Minister, Guy Razanamasy, the Mayor of Antananarivo (the capital city), who invited the FV to join the Government. The FV rejected the offer and organized a large but peaceful protest march on the President's residence to demand his resignation. The deaths of 120 people as a result of the authorities' violent suppression of this march and one in Mahajanga led the French Government to suspend military aid and to advise Ratsiraka to resign. Ratsiraka used his support in the five provinces other than the capital to be declared President of a federal Madagascar. In late August Razanamasy formed a new Government, which included some from the FV.

Interim Settlement

The stalemate continued until an interim agreement was reached on 31 October 1991 to create a transitional government for a maximum period of 18 months, pending the adoption of a new constitution and the holding of elections. Under the agreement, Ratsiraka relinquished all executive powers but remained as a ceremonial President and titular Head of the Armed Forces. Zafy became President of a 31-member Haute Autorité de l'Etat (High State Authority), while Andriamanjato and Rakotonirina were appointed joint Presidents of a 131-member advisory body, the Conseil de Redressement Economique et Social (Council of Economic and Social Recovery).

The draft Constitution for a Third Republic, drawn up in March 1992 by a National Forum, provided for a largely ceremonial President, with executive power vested in a Prime Minister elected by a National Assembly, the lower house of a bicameral legislature, with a Senate as the upper house. At a referendum in August the new Constitution was approved by 72% of votes cast, with a turnout of some two-thirds of the electorate.

The presidential election took place peacefully in November 1992 with eight candidates. Zafy received 45% of votes cast, while Ratsiraka took 29% and Rakotonirina 10%. In a second round for the two leading candidates in February 1993, Zafy obtained 67% of the votes and was formally invested as President in late March, amid violent clashes between security forces and federalists in the north of the country.

In June 1993 elections to the new National Assembly took place under a system of proportional representation. Hery Velona Rasalama (HVR or Forces Vives Rasalama), proved the most successful group, securing 46 of the 138 seats; Rakotonirina's MFM obtained 15 seats, while a new coalition of pro-Ratsiraka parties won 11. In the election held in August, Francisque Ravony, son-in-law of former President Tsiranana, obtained a majority of votes for Prime Minister.

THE THIRD REPUBLIC

In August 1993 Ravony formed a new Council of Ministers. Effective action on the economy proved difficult, in part given the fragmented nature of the National Assembly, with some 25 parties in two largely informal coalitions of equal size, the HVR group and the G6. A number of deputies opposed measures that the World Bank and International Monetary Fund (IMF) required as a precondition to the approval of financial credit. Ravony's position was also undermined by public opposition from President Zafy and Andriamanjato (now the President of the National Assembly), who rejected the demands as an affront to national sovereignty. Nevertheless, in January 1995 Ravony did dismiss the Governor of the central bank as demanded and assumed the post of Minister of Finance; the Government pledged to undertake further austerity measures. In mid-1995 Ravony strengthened his parliamentary position by recruiting additional deputies to his party, the Committee for the Support of Democracy and Development in Madagascar (CSDDM). The CSDDM then joined the G6, which became the G7 and had a clear majority in the National Assembly.

President Zafy announced that he could not co-operate with Ravony and called a referendum for 17 September 1995 to endorse a constitutional amendment empowering the President, rather than the National Assembly, to select the Prime Minister. Ravony declined to campaign against the referendum and announced that he would resign in October on the formal announcement of the result, which showed an approval rate of 64%. Zafy appointed Emmanuel Rakotovahiny, the leader of the UNDD, as Prime Minister.

Zafy failed to recommence negotiations with the IMF over the budget, and the G7 with the newly formed Rassemblement pour la Troisième République (Rally for the Third Republic) joined forces in May 1996 in a successful motion of censure against the Government. Rakotovahiny resigned as Prime Minister and Zafy appointed the non-political Norbert Ratsirahonana, President of the Haute Cour Constitutionnelle

(HCC—High Constitutional Court), although he vetoed the proposed new Government.

On 26 July 1996 the National Assembly voted by 99 votes to 32 to impeach President Zafy for various violations of the Constitution, which the HCC endorsed on 5 September when Zafy announced his resignation. The HCC appointed Ratsirahonana as interim President and he formed a new Government, excluding five UNDD ministers whom Zafy had forced him to accept.

The Return of Ratsiraka

In the first round of the presidential election, in November 1996, Ratsiraka won 37% of the votes, with Zafy on 23%. In the second round, in December, Ratsiraka secured a narrow victory with 51% of the votes, but some 52% of the electorate abstained or spoiled their votes. In February 1997 Ratsiraka appointed as Prime Minister Pascal Rakotomavo, who formed a Government consisting largely of technocrats. Ratsirahonana had successfully completed negotiations with the IMF, which led to the resumption of international aid and debt relief arrangements.

The new Government proposed extensive revisions to the Constitution, greatly increasing the President's powers, weakening the independence of the judiciary and providing for a decentralization of government to the provinces. In a referendum held on 15 March 1998, the amendments were only narrowly adopted, by 51% of the votes cast (on a turnout of 66% of the electorate) even though most opposition parties had not campaigned actively against them. The amended Constitution allowed the President to complete his term of office and to be re-elected twice.

Elections to an enlarged 150-member National Assembly took place in May 1998, under a new electoral law that favoured the larger parties. Ratsiraka's AREMA secured only 25% of the votes but 63 of the 150 seats, while its coalition partners, Libéralisme Economique et Action Démocratique pour la Reconstruction Nationale/Fanilo (LEADER/Fanilo) and AKFM/Fanavaozana, a breakaway faction of the AKFM, together won 19 seats, thus forming a majority in the Assembly. In July Ratsiraka appointed as Prime Minister Tantely Andrianarivo, who installed a coalition Government dominated by AREMA.

Although the Government secured the backing of the Rassemblement pour le Socialisme et la Démocratie (RPSD—Rally for Socialism and Democracy) and 24 independent deputies, it lost support over its economic performance. The opposition divided into two groups: radicals, including Zafy's new party Asa, Fahamarinana, Fampandrosoana, Arinda (Action, Truth, Development and Harmony) and Rakotonirina's MFM, which demanded the overthrow of the Government; and moderates, led by Ratsirahonana's Ny Asa Vita No Ifampitsara (AVI—People Are Judged By The Work They Do). Elections for provincial councillors in the six newly introduced 'autonomous provinces' took place in December 2000. AREMA received the most votes in all six provinces, with an absolute majority in all except Antananarivo, and all the governors were members of AREMA. In March 2001 the provincial councillors joined with the mayors of the communes to elect two-thirds of the 90-member Senate, with the remaining one-third to be nominated by the President. AREMA was again victorious, winning 49 of the 60 seats, thus completing the presidential party's dominance at all levels of both government and legislature.

Disputed Presidential Election

The country was plunged into crisis after the presidential election of December 2001. The official results for the first round, confirmed by a newly appointed HCC, gave Marc Ravalomanana, Mayor of Antananarivo, 46% of the votes cast and Ratsiraka 41%, necessitating a second round of voting. However, Ravalomanana, supported by a consortium of observers, claimed that he had won 52% of the votes. He declared himself President and appointed a Government, headed by Jacques Sylla, which subsequently took over government offices. Ratsiraka withdrew his Government to the port of Toamasina, while his supporters erected roadblocks and destroyed bridges on all roads leading to the capital.

At a meeting in Dakar, Senegal, called by the Organization of African Unity (OAU—subsequently the African Union, AU),

the two contenders agreed in mid-April 2002 to a recount (followed by a second round if necessary). The Supreme Court in Madagascar reinstated the former HCC, the members of which carried out the recount and declared Ravalomanana the winner, with 51.5% of the votes cast against Ratsiraka's 35.9%. Ravalomanana was duly inaugurated as President on 6 May. However, Ratsiraka refused to accept the recount and demanded a second round of voting; the blockade and the violence in coastal towns continued.

There were further OAU attempts at mediation, which became more urgent when Ravalomanana's troops occupied the area around Sambava in the north-east. In June 2002 Ravalomanana agreed to bring forward the legislative elections and reorganized his cabinet to include two former supporters of Ratsiraka, although the OAU suspended Madagascar's membership until new elections were held. However, in late June the USA officially recognized Ravalomanana as President, while recognition by France and the European Union (EU) in July, following the inclusion of two more AREMA members in the Government, effectively ended Ratsiraka's resistance; he subsequently sought exile in France.

Peace and Reconciliation

Although President Ravalomanana proclaimed a policy of national reconciliation, more than 200 supporters of Ratsiraka, were imprisoned for varying periods of time. In legislative elections held in December 2002, under amended electoral rules which abolished the remaining limited element of proportional representation, the President's party, Tiako i Madagasikara (TIM—I Love Madagascar), won 104 of the 160 seats in the enlarged National Assembly. Allies from AVI and the RPSD joined in a Front Patriotique, which secured 22 seats. AREMA came second in many constituencies, but the new 'first-past-the-post' system limited it to three seats, while 23 independent candidates also won.

TIM dominated the new Government formed by Prime Minister Sylla in January 2003. In August former President Ratsiraka was sentenced *in absentia* to 10 years' hard labour for embezzling public funds.

While the President retained much of his popularity, support for his party declined. In January 2004 Ravalomanana restructured the Council of Ministers, appointing several former supporters of Ratsiraka to diversify its ethnic composition. Public protests took place against large increases in the cost of consumer goods and there was an alleged attempt on the President's life. In May 2006, prompted by the United Nations (UN), the Government organized a national dialogue, but it was boycotted by most of the opposition groups when the Government refused to accept their proposals (notably a revision of the electoral law).

Ravalomanana Re-elected

The Government brought forward the date of the presidential election to December 2006 with the approval of the HCC. The official results gave Ravalomanana 54.8% of the vote, well ahead of his closest rival candidate, Jean Lahiniriko, with 11.7%. Voter turnout was 62% and international observers commented favourably on the conduct of the election. In January 2007 the President appointed Gen. Rabemananjara as the new Prime Minister.

Although turnout was low, at 44%, in a referendum held in April 2007, 75% of participants approved amendments to the Constitution that granted extended powers to the President, including the right to rule by decree in times of emergency. Further changes included the abolition of the autonomous powers of the six provinces, a reduction in the size of the National Assembly to 127 seats, and the introduction of English as a third official language alongside French and Malagasy.

Political rivalries intensified following the President's decision in July 2007 to dissolve the National Assembly and to schedule legislative elections for September. The campaign was subdued, and the eventual turnout only 46%; TIM won 105 of the 127 seats. Two other small parties won seats, with the remainder going to independent candidates, a number of whom subsequently allied themselves to the Government.

Rabemananjara retained his position as Prime Minister in the new Government, which saw several cabinet changes, including the appointment of Cécile Manorohanta as Minister of National Defence. This was the first time a woman or a civilian had held that post.

The Rise of Andry Rajoelina

In elections to the Senate (reduced in size from 90 to 33 members) in April 2008, TIM won all of the 22 directly elected seats and the President used his right to nominate one-third of the house to appoint new senators from outside his party.

There was unrest in the capital and other cities during August and September 2008, with an intensification in the discord between the Government and the Mayor of Antananarivo, Andry Rajoelina, the leader of the Tanora malaGasy Vonona (TGV—Determined Malagasy Youth). Tensions arising from economic hardship and an increasing sense of the autocratic nature of the President's regime were exacerbated by the Government's decision in December to close the Rajoelina-owned broadcasting station Télévision Viva, which had broadcast an interview with former President Ratsiraka. Rajoelina orchestrated protest marches that led to clashes with security forces, in which at least 44 people died in January and early February 2009 when the Government replaced him as Mayor with a special delegation. Rajoelina in turn appointed his own successor and named Monja Roindefo, the son of the late Monja Jaona, as prime minister of a rival government, the Haute Autorité de Transition (HAT—High Transitional Authority).

In protest against the increasingly violent actions of the security forces, Manorohanta resigned as Minister of National Defence. After discussions in February 2009, Ravalomanana and Rajoelina agreed an end to the street protests and political arrests but failed to reach agreement on how to end the unrest conclusively. However, in mid-March Ravalomanana dissolved the Government and resigned as President. Before heading into exile, he transferred power to a three-man military executive committee; the latter in turn transferred executive powers to Rajoelina. Rajoelina was inaugurated as President of the HAT on 21 March. As the Constitution stipulated that the minimum age for the President of Madagascar was 40 years, the 34-year-old Rajoelina announced that a new charter would be drawn up. The HCC approved Rajoelina's appointment but it drew strong criticism from overseas; most aid was halted, and Madagascar was suspended from both the AU and the Southern African Development Community (SADC).

The National Assembly was dissolved in mid-March 2009, and in late March Rajoelina appointed a 22-member Government, retaining those ministers he had named in February. The HAT announced a draft timetable for the transition of power, which attracted criticism for the proposed length of time before the staging of a presidential election. The HAT also faced criticism for its intolerance of opposition in the media and for its, at times, arbitrary treatment of opponents. In April soldiers arrested Pety Rakotonirina, the 'prime minister' recently appointed by Ravalomanana, who himself was sentenced in June *in absentia* to four years in prison and fined US $70m. for the misuse of public funds relating to the purchase of a new presidential jet.

Negotiations to resolve the crisis continued intermittently from April 2009 under the aegis of various bodies, but with limited progress. The four parties involved were Rajoelina's HAT, Ravalomanana's TIM, the Comité pour la Réconciliation Nationale, a group formed in 2002 by former President Zafy, and representatives of former President Ratsiraka's AREMA party. A key issue was the return from exile and the eligibility to stand in a presidential election of Ravalomanana and Ratsiraka. Following a summit held in Maputo, Mozambique, in August, with mediation by the Groupe International de Contact (GIC—comprising representatives from the UN, the AU, SADC and the Organisation Internationale de la Francophonie), the four parties agreed upon a Transitional Charter, which was to remain in place for a maximum of 15 months, after which presidential and legislative elections would be held. The Charter provided for a bicameral transitional legislature and a National Union Government of Transition, with a Prime Minister selected by consensus and officially appointed by Rajoelina, who would exercise the functions of head of state.

A new constitution was to be drafted for a Fourth Republic, and an amnesty was to cover events from 2002 up to the date of signing.

In early September 2009 Rajoelina appointed as Prime Minister Monja Roindefo, who announced a new Government. The three former Presidents rejected the moves as unilateral and not in accordance with the Maputo agreement, a view endorsed by the AU and SADC. The opposition held a series of protest meetings that were dispersed by the authorities; several Ravalomanana supporters were arrested and in late September Rakotonirina received a two-year suspended sentence.

In early October 2009 the GIC reached an agreement with the opposition parties whereby Rajoelina would remain President of the Transition, with Rakotovahiny as Vice-President and Eugène Mangalaza, an academic, as Prime Minister. However, Roindefo refused to stand down, and Cécile Manorohanta was appointed as interim Prime Minister while the HCC reviewed the issue. After a further round of talks in the Ethiopian capital, Addis Ababa, in November, under the threat of economic sanctions from the EU, there was an agreement whereby Rajoelina would remain as President, would share power with two Vice-Presidents—Rakotovahiny representing Zafy, and Fetison Andrianirina representing Ravalomanana—and Mangalaza, an ally of Ratsiraka, would continue as Prime Minister. Following pressure from the army, the three opposition leaders met again in Maputo, without Rajoelina, and announced in early December a timetable for the installation of the new institutions and the division of ministerial posts. Rajoelina denounced the declaration as treason, and refused permission for the aircraft carrying the three men with their delegations to land in Madagascar.

Rajoelina pursued his unilateral approach, announcing that legislative elections would be held in March 2010. In December 2009 he appointed a new Prime Minister, Col (later Gen.) Albert Camille Vital, and declared a new constitutional law that returned the country largely to the position when he had assumed power in March. The GIC held a further meeting in Addis Ababa, in January 2010, at which it rejected Rajoelina's actions. Amid continuing tension, Jean Ping, the AU representative, visited Madagascar and recommended the deferral of elections, to which Rajoelina agreed in late January. Rajoelina proposed the creation of a new election commission, the Commission Electorale Nationale Indépendante (CENI), which was established in March without the participation of the opposition parties. Meanwhile, pressure on Rajoelina mounted in mid-February when the AU imposed a deadline of one month for implementation of the Maputo and Addis Ababa agreements. In response to Rajoelina's continued intransigence, in mid-March the AU imposed sanctions on him and 108 other members of the HAT.

Three days of negotiations in April 2010 in Pretoria, South Africa, chaired by that country's President, Jacob Zuma, proved unsuccessful, and Rajoelina declined to attend a second round of talks. On 27 July a national dialogue was launched, which involved a debate on the transition, the constitution and the electoral code. On 11 August the Government signed an agreement (known as the Ivato agreement) rescheduling the constitutional referendum from August to November, with legislative and presidential elections to follow in March and May 2011, respectively; Rajoelina would for now continue to hold office as head of the HAT, which was to be reconstituted as a transitional parliament. On 24 August 2010 the trial commenced of 19 people implicated in the killings of 28 protesters by security forces in early February 2009; Ravalomanana, who rejected what he called a 'mock trial', was sentenced *in absentia* to life imprisonment.

On 7 October 2010 the HCC approved a decree by Rajoelina establishing a Parlement de la Transition (Transitional Parliament) with a 256-member lower parliamentary chamber—the Congrès de la Transition (Transitional Congress). The Espace de Concertation des Partis Politiques (ESCOPOL), received 62 seats, TIM 52, the TGV 52 and an alliance of parties supporting Rajoelina, the Union des Démocrates et Républicains—Fanovana (UDR—Fanovana) 29. In the 90-member upper chamber—the Conseil Supérieur de la Transition (Transitional Superior Council)— there were 25 deputies for UDR—Fanovana, 21 TIM, 18 ESCOPOL and 10 TGV. The official campaign for the constitutional referendum was boycotted by the opposition. The draft Constitution included provisions reducing the minimum age for the President from 40 to 35 years, thus enabling Rajoelina legitimately to assume the presidency, and removing English as an official language. The referendum, which was held as scheduled on 17 November, was overshadowed by a mutiny by troops at a base near the capital. The new Constitution of the Fourth Republic was approved by 74.2% of those who voted, according to the HCC, on a turnout of 53%. The CENI highlighted a number of irregularities with the vote, but while the result was not accepted by the international community, it strengthened the position of Rajoelina, who later received some de facto recognition at the UN. He officially inaugurated the Fourth Republic on 12 December.

THE FOURTH REPUBLIC

In January 2011 the elections planned for March and May were postponed indefinitely. There were further attempts at conciliation: negotiations took place between members of TIM and the TGV, but foundered on the issues of the choice of Prime Minister and on Ravalomanana's return from exile. In February the SADC envoy, Leonardo Simão, presented new proposals for a 'road map' towards a solution to the crisis. The details were largely based on the Ivato agreement of 2010 and were favourable to the HAT: Rajoelina would be confirmed as President and head of state and would have the right to designate a Prime Minister from a list proposed by the different parties, with a broad amnesty covering 2002–09 and Ravalomanana to stay in exile until a stable situation after the holding of elections, in which Rajoelina and other members of the HAT could stand.

The HAT blocked attempts by both Ravalomanana and Ratsiraka to return to Madagascar and declared that elections would be held in September 2011. On 9 March the new transitional programme proposed by the SADC mediators was approved by eight of the country's 11 principal political groups, but rejected by the parties of Ravalomanana, Ratsiraka and Zafy. As agreed, Vital resigned as Prime Minister but was promptly reappointed. A new Government, supposedly of national unity, was announced on 26 March.

Following continued SADC mediation, on 17 September 2011 10 political groups (including those representing Ravalomanana and Zafy) signed a further agreement regarding a timetable for the restoration of democratic rule; this was widely welcomed by the international community, including the UN. Rajoelina attended that month's session of the UN General Assembly in New York, USA.

A further SADC visit facilitated the reaching of an agreement on 14 October 2011 over the timetable of the transitional programme, including the appointment by mid-November of a new Prime Minister and government of national unity. Vital duly submitted the resignation of his Government on 17 October, and Rajoelina announced the appointment of Jean Omer Beriziky of LEADER/Fanilo as the new Prime Minister on 28 October. Beriziky's appointment was supported by the Zafy movement, but rejected by Ravalomanana's supporters on the grounds that Beriziky was too close to Rajoelina. The Zafy and Ravalomanana movements formed a new front with Monja Roindefo's MONIMA (the Mouvement National pour l'Indépendance de Madagascar, founded by his father in the 1970s), and claimed one-half of the new ministerial seats. Following intense negotiations over its composition, the new Government was finally announced on 21 November.

Ratsiraka returned from nine years in exile in France on 24 November 2011, but refused to join a Government that he saw as non-consensual. Thus, the new Transitional Parliament formed on 1 December had fewer members than stipulated. Rajoelina's meeting in France with its President, Nicolas Sarkozy, on 7 December provided further recognition of the HAT. The AU, however, said that it would not lift its suspension of Madagascar until further progress had been made on the return of exiles and the holding of elections.

Ravalomanana attempted to return to Madagascar from exile in South Africa on 21 January 2012, in accordance with the transitional agreement, but the flight was turned back; there were violent clashes between his supporters and the security forces. The opposition boycotted the opening of the new parliamentary session on 23 January and the HAT missed SADC's deadline of the end of February to agree an amnesty law. A new independent electoral commission, the Commission Electorale Nationale Indépendante pour la Transition (CENIT), started in mid-March. The amnesty law was finally approved in April, but controversially excluded those who had been found guilty of human rights abuses, including those sentenced for murder, notably Ravalomanana over the incidents in February 2009.

The continuing political impasse was compounded by the decision of the Ravalomanana movement to suspend its participation in the transitional institutions. However, following a visit by a UN mission in June 2012, the first round of the presidential election was scheduled for May 2013, with the legislative elections due in July.

Legislation adopted in July 2012 banned convicted criminals from standing in elections, although Ravalomanana's conviction in absentia in August 2010 had been challenged. His wife, Lalao, who had been prevented from returning from exile earlier, returned briefly to Madagascar, but was promptly deported to Thailand. Rajoelina and Ravalomanana attended a summit in South Africa in August 2012, which again proved inconclusive.

In October 2012 the new Cour Electorale Spéciale (CES—Special Electoral Court) was constituted, as was the Conseil de Réconciliation Malagasy (Madagascar Reconciliation Council), although the latter's composition was met with such criticism that new members were proposed in November. In late October 2012 Ravalomanana formally announced his candidature for the presidential election, although SADC had yet to adjudicate on his potential return from exile. At a meeting in early December, SADC proposed that neither Ravalomanana nor Rajoelina should contest the election. Ravalomanana accepted this proposal at talks in Tanzania in December; Rajoelina proved more reluctant but announced in January 2013 that he too would not stand, although he revealed that he might seek the premiership instead. Rajoelina's relations with Prime Minister Beriziky became increasingly strained.

In February 2013 the CENIT announced that, owing to logistical issues, the presidential election was to be rescheduled for July, and legislative elections for September. The TGV selected Edgard Razafindravahy, the head of the municipal administration in Antananarivo, as its presidential candidate. Lalao Ravalomanana, who had returned to Madagascar in March, was chosen as the candidate of the Ravalomanana movement, although she was unable to meet the six-month residency requirement, as was former President Ratsiraka, who in April also resumed residency and confirmed that he would stand.

By the deadline of 29 April 2013 49 presidential candidates had registered. Rajoelina subsequently announced that he would also stand in the election, notwithstanding the expiry of the registration deadline and his declaration in January that he would not contest the poll. The CES controversially approved Rajoelina's candidature, as well as those of Lalao Ravalomanana and Ratsiraka, prompting criticism and threats of sanctions from the GIC. When the three candidates refused to withdraw, various donors suspended their financing of the poll, which was once again delayed, until 23 August.

On 17 August 2013, in a move that was widely welcomed and prompted the restoration of donor financing, a reconstituted CES barred Rajoelina, Lalao Ravalomanana, Ratsiraka and five other candidates. The CENIT subsequently set a new date, of 25 October, for the presidential election, with, if necessary, a second round on 20 December, when the delayed legislative polls were also scheduled to be held. Rajoelina was allowed to continue as transitional President, and in early September the AU ended the sanctions imposed in 2010 against 109 officials, including Rajoelina, in recognition of progress in the electoral process. Ravalomanana announced his support for former Minister of Health Jean Louis Robinson, while Rajoelina favoured former Minister of Finance and Budget Hery Rajaonarimampianina.

Although there were concerns over irregularities in the electoral list and campaign finances, international observers declared the first round of the presidential election, held on 25 October 2013, to have been free and credible. The final results gave Robinson 21.2% of the vote and Rajaonarimampianina 15.9%, ahead of former Deputy Prime Minister Hajo Andrianainarivelo with 10.5%, Roland Ratsiraka with 9.0% and Albert Camille Vital with 6.9%.

Prior to the run-off between the two leading candidates, Rajoelina gave more explicit backing to Rajaonarimampianina, who stated that he would in turn appoint Rajoelina as Prime Minister if elected, while Robinson was supported by Marc Ravalomanana and promised the premiership to the former President's wife, Lalao. Each candidate claimed victory following the poll on 20 December 2013, but provisional results released in early January 2014 gave Rajaonarimampianina 53.5% of the votes, which was confirmed two weeks later. Turnout was 50.7%, the lowest level in a presidential election since 1965. Robinson and Ravalomanana initially rejected the outcome but subsequently accepted the official results, as did the international community. Rajaonarimampianina, who was inaugurated on 25 January, claimed to represent a move away from past regimes. Both the AU and SADC subsequently announced the restoration of Madagascar's membership.

The Rajaonarimampianina Presidency

Prime Minister Beriziky had resigned after the legislative elections, also on 20 December 2013, but was asked to remain in office until a new Government had been formed. The CES finally announced the results in early February 2014: on a turnout of 50.8%, the coalition that supported Rajoelina, Miaraka amin'ny Prezidà Andry Rajoelina (MAPAR), took 49 of the 151 seats in the enlarged National Assembly, the Mouvance Ravalomanana 19, Vondrona politika miara-dia Malagasy Miara-Miainga, led by Andrianainarivelo, 14 and Vital's Parti Hiaraka Isika and LEADER/Fanilo five each; there were 25 nominally independent candidates and smaller parties took the remaining seats. The convening of the new National Assembly on 18 February marked the official end of the transitional period. MAPAR claimed the right as the largest party to nominate the new Prime Minister; however, the HCC decided that in the circumstances the President should agree. On 11 April President Rajaonarimampianina named Roger Kolo, a physician, in the role and he announced a new Government comprising technocrats and politicians from all of the country's six regions; Prime Minister Kolo himself took charge of the Ministry of Public Health. Although two new ministers were MAPAR representatives, it was reported that most members of the party, which disputed Kolo's appointment, had refused to join the Government.

In mid-August 2014 the National Assembly approved the legislation required to establish new decentralized local authorities. In October Ravalomanana unexpectedly returned from exile; he was placed under house arrest on the naval base at Antsiranana. In December the FFKM convened discussions between Rajaonarimampianina and the four former heads of state (Ravalomanana under military escort), in an attempt to promote national reconciliation.

On 12 January 2015 Prime Minister Kolo and his Government resigned, following persistent electricity outages and the violent suppression of protests by police; two days later Gen. Jean Ravelonarivo, a former air force commander, was appointed as Prime Minister. A further inconclusive reconciliation meeting took place on 14 January between Rajaonarimampianina, Zafy, Ratsiraka and Ravalomanana. Ravelonarivo announced a new Government on 26 January, with nine new ministers, including Béatrice Atallah as Minister of Foreign Affairs. The seventh summit of past and current Presidents organized by the FFKM met in February, albeit with representatives for Rajoelina and Ratsiraka, who were both overseas. In May the Council of Ministers repealed the decree that had confined Ravalomanana under house arrest; his wife, Lalao, confirmed that she would stand as TIM's candidate in Antananarivo in the long-delayed municipal elections scheduled for July 2015.

On 26 May 2015 the National Assembly voted to impeach President Rajaonarimampianina for alleged repeated violations of the Constitution and for high treason; the motion was reported to have been approved by 121 of the 125 deputies who participated, thereby securing the requisite two-thirds' majority. On 12 June, however, the HCC dismissed the attempted impeachment, asserting that the allegations were unfounded. On 3 July the Government survived a parliamentary motion of no confidence, although fewer than two-thirds of the deputies voted in its favour.

In the municipal elections of 31 July 2015, President Rajaonarimampianina's party, Hery Vaovao ho an'i Madagasikara (HVM—New Forces for Madagascar, founded in 2013), secured 42% of the seats, winning the majority of mayoral contests in rural areas and taking control of Antsiranana, Mahajanga, Toliary and Toamasina. However, HVM's candidate obtained only 4% of the vote in the mayoral election in Antananarivo, which was won by Lalao Ravalomanana with 56%. Turnout was recorded at only 30% nationally, reflecting both a degree of disillusionment and issues relating to voter registration.

In October 2015 the HCC approved the establishment of a new nine-member CENI (to replace the now defunct CENIT), which was to have greater powers to investigate electoral anomalies. Yves Herinirina Rakotomanana, a lawyer who had been involved in the constitutional referendum in 2010, was appointed to head the new body.

In elections to the Senate held in Madagascar's 22 regions on 29 December 2015, the President's HVM party gained 65% of the votes in the electoral college (comprising National Assembly deputies, regional councillors and mayors) who selected 42 of the 63 senators. On 21 January 2016 the HCC confirmed that HVM had won 34 of the 42 seats, while TIM had won three and MAPAR two. On 1 February the President appointed a further 21 senators, in accordance with the Constitution: these included former Prime Minister Kolo and Honoré Rakotomanana, who resumed his role as President of the Senate first held under President Ratsiraka.

After a short period of considerable confusion, Olivier Mahafaly, the Minister of the Interior and Decentralization, was appointed as the new Prime Minister on 11 April 2016. On 15 April Mahafaly appointed a new Government, in which he retained his existing portfolio.

Tensions continued in the country, with a reported planned coup attempt and public protests in the capital. On 26 June 2016 three people died and more than 80 were injured in a grenade attack staged during Independence Day celebrations at a stadium in the capital attended by President Rajaonarimampianina and his family. The unrest persisted into July when security forces surrounded the house of former Prime Minister Roindefo, who had been vocal in demanding that the perpetrators of the stadium attack be brought to justice.

In February 2017 the Government, the CENI and the international community agreed a new electoral programme, for regional and provincial polls to be held later that year, followed by legislative and presidential elections in 2018. However, there was a deterioration in the security situation, with violent disturbances in the northern town of Antsakabary. In mid-April 2017 the regional and provincial elections were postponed.

On 25 August 2017 a new body was established, the Conseil du Fampihavanana Malagasy (CFM—Council for National Reconciliation), which included former ministers, generals and journalists, as well as representatives of the various former Presidents. President Rajaonarimampianina announced a cabinet reorganization; six new ministers were appointed, including Henry Rabary-Njaka, who replaced Béatrice Atallah as Minister of Foreign Affairs.

On 31 October 2017 Honoré Rakotomanana resigned as President of the Senate, ceding the position to HVM President Rivo Rakotovao, who had been nominated as a senator shortly before; Rakotovao's appointment was approved by 52 of the 55 votes, reflecting the dominance of the ruling party.

In early February 2018 Prime Minister Mahafaly announced plans to rationalize the large number of political parties in the country, which totalled some 195. In late February an extraordinary session of the National Assembly was convened to consider a proposed new electoral law. Voting was postponed until 3 April, when 79 of the 151 deputies approved the draft legislation, while opposition deputies staged a walkout, then organized a series of protests against the proposed new electoral law. One such demonstration on 21 April escalated into a violent confrontation with the security forces, in which two protesters were killed. The President claimed that the events had the semblance of a planned coup and the international community pressed for dialogue: SADC organized a visit to Madagascar by former Mozambican President Joaquim Chissano, although the reaction to his attempted mediation was mixed and the 73 opposition deputies declined to meet him.

On 3 May 2018 the HCC rejected many of the provisions of the new electoral law, ruling that private media could not be subject to the same rules as state outlets (which would have benefited Rajoelina) and that election candidates would not need to declare criminal charges (which allowed the candidacy of Ravalomanana). The opposition continued its calls for the resignation of the Government. On 22 May the CENI gave the country's political parties a deadline of 13 June to find a solution in order to avoid a postponement of the elections. On 25 May 2018 the HCC ruled that President Rajaonarimampianina should not be obliged to resign, but should appoint within seven days a new consensus Prime Minister from a proposed list of three candidates from the largest elected party.

Prime Minister Mahafaly duly offered his resignation; however, the opposition deputies continued to demand that the President resign and refused to join a consensus government. A dispute arose as to whether MAPAR, which had the highest number of deputies elected in 2013, or HVM, which had the largest current representation, should present the list. On 1 June 2018 the new Haute Cour de Justice (High Court of Justice) was inaugurated. After a first list of candidates for the new Prime Minister was rejected, on 4 June the President selected Christian Ntsay from a second. Ntsay, who had served as Minister of Tourism in 2002–03, took office on 6 June 2018. On 11 June a new Government of National Unity was announced, with seven members of MAPAR and four from TIM becoming ministers, leaving the majority of posts still with HVM. Seven ministers retained their portfolios, including those at finance and defence. Although opposition deputies and their supporters expressed continued discontent, the number of participants at protest rallies in the capital decreased, with a split emerging between MAPAR and TIM.

Rajoelina Returns to the Presidency

At the end of June 2018 the Government agreed to a proposal by the CENI that the first round of voting in the presidential poll would take place on 7 November, after a campaign period of one month, and the second round on 19 December. A total of 46 candidates subsequently registered, including the former Presidents Rajaonarimampianina, Ravalomanana, Rajoelina and Ratsiraka, and former Prime Ministers Jean Beriziky, Olivier Mahafaly and Gen. Jean Ravelonarivo. The HCC disqualified 10 candidates.

On 7 September 2018 Rajaonarimampianina resigned as President to be eligible to stand and was replaced temporarily by Rakotovao (President of the Senate). After a campaign marked by some violence and a dispute over the electoral list, voting took place as scheduled on 7 November. The provisional results published by the CENI on 18 November indicated that Rajoelina had won the first round; the HCC confirmed this on 27 November when it announced the official results, which gave Rajoelina 39.2% of the votes cast, Ravalomanana 35.4% and Rajaonarimampianina just 8.8%, on a turnout of 54%. The second round, on 19 December, resulted in victory for Rajoelina, according to the provisional results released by the CENI on the following day, on a lower turnout of 48%. While Ravalomanana and his supporters lodged a number of complaints at the HCC, alleging irregularities, observers from the EU and SADC said that the vote had been conducted in a regular and peaceful manner. The HCC rejected most of the complaints made by Ravalomanana's supporters and released the official results on 8 January 2019, confirming that Rajoelina had won with 55.7% of the votes cast in the second round.

On 19 January 2019 Rajoelina was inaugurated as President; he confirmed that Ntsay would remain in his role as Prime Minister. Ntsay's new Government was smaller than its predecessor, comprising 22 ministers. Notable appointments included Richard Randriamandrato, a technocrat, as Minister of the Economy and Finance, Naina Andriantsitoahina as Minister of Foreign Affairs, and Alexandre Georget, leader of the Antoko Maitso Hasin'i Madagasikara (Madagascar Green Party), as Minister of the Environment and Sustainable Development.

At the end of January 2019 the CENI proposed that the next legislative elections be held on 27 May. The National Assembly subsequently allowed Rajoelina to rule the country by presidential decree until the new legislature was convened in July. On 19 April 2019 Rajoelina issued a decree providing for the holding of a referendum on constitutional reform concurrent with the forthcoming elections, under which the Senate would be abolished and regional governors appointed. Following a ruling by the HCC against the proposal to abolish the Senate, Rajoelina declared that he would postpone plans to appoint regional governors. On 23 May he announced revised proposals, involving a reduction in the number of senators from the current 63 to 18, of whom 12 would be elected (two from each of the six provinces) and six appointed by the President; the HCC subsequently ruled that these proposals were constitutional.

Rajoelina's electoral coalition (Isika Rehetra Miaraka amin'i Andry Rajoelina—IRMAR—We Are All With Andry Rajoelina), comprising around 10 parties that supported him during the 2018 presidential poll, won an absolute majority of 84 of the 151 seats in the National Assembly in the legislative elections of 27 May 2019, with the CENI announcing the final results on 14 June. TIM took 16 seats, while five smaller parties obtained one seat each and independents the remaining 46; turnout was low, at just 31%. The voting was conducted peacefully according to a SADC observer mission, although there were several allegations of fraud.

A special parliamentary session in July 2019 ended the interim period in which the President had governed by decree. Christine Razanamahasoa, a member of IRMAR and a former Minister of Justice in the HAT, was elected unanimously as President of the National Assembly. Ntsay's Government offered its resignation, and he was asked to select a new cabinet. On 25 July Ntsay announced a 22-member Council of Ministers, unchanged other than the appointment of a new Minister of Higher Education and Scientific Research. In August a new opposition alliance, the Rodoben'ny Mpanohitra ho an'ny Demokrasia eto Madagasikara (RMDM—Group of Opposition Parties for Democracy), was formed under the leadership of Ravalomanana.

There were municipal elections on 27 November 2019. While the RMDM selected its Secretary-General, Tahiry Randriamasinoro, as its candidate for Mayor of Antananarivo, it was the Minister of Foreign Affairs, Naina Andriantsitohaina, who won by a narrow margin for Rajoelina's IRMAR—the first time since independence that the capital had voted in a candidate representing the incumbent Government, albeit on a turnout of only 23.2%. IRMAR secured five of the six provincial capitals, with the mayoralty in Antsiranana being won by an independent.

In a government reorganization on 29 January 2020 six ministers were dismissed, ostensibly for their failure to meet targets, and two new posts created, for a Minister of Water, Sanitation and Hygiene, and a Deputy Minister of New Cities and Housing, who would be responsible for overseeing the controversial project for a new city on the outskirts of the capital. Djacoba Tehindrazanarivelo was appointed to the vacant post of Minister of Foreign Affairs.

From 21 March 2020, when President Rajoelina announced the first three cases of COVID-19 in Madagascar, the ensuing crisis dominated events in the country. The Government shortly declared a 14-day state of health emergency, which was extended repeatedly under the provisions of legislation introduced in 1991 that had conferred far-reaching powers on the President. Rajoelina personally espoused the use of a controversial untested plant-based remedy for the disease, COVID-Organics. As part of a ministerial reorganization on 20 August 2020, Prof. Hanitrala Rakotovao replaced as Minister of Public Health Prof. Ahmad Ahmad, whose request for international aid had been criticized by President Rajoelina.

On 5 September Rajoelina announced that the virus was apparently under control and that restrictions would be eased, while later that month Prime Minister Ntsay noted that 93% of victims had recovered and that the mortality rate was 1.1%. On 18 October Rajoelina announced an end to the emergency measures first imposed in March; by that time the country had reported a total of 238 deaths resulting from 16,810 cases of COVID-19.

The opposition boycotted elections for 12 seats in the smaller Senate on 11 December 2020, when IRMAR secured 10 seats, while the reconstituted Malagasy Miara-Miainga (MMM) party led by Andrianainarivelo, an ally of Rajoelina, took two. On 19 January 2021 Rajoelina appointed the additional six members of the Senate.

Political tensions rose in February 2021 over opposition plans to demonstrate in Antananarivo and the CFM appealed for calm. On 22 February various opposition groups formed a new alliance, Tolon'ny Vahoaka Malagasy (Struggle of the Malagasy People), as a movement against abuse of power; its members included the TIM, the RMDM and the wide-ranging Groupe Panorama. Ravalomanana demanded the release of demonstrators arrested in the capital and protested at an increased police presence at his residence. On 27 May the Senate unanimously approved a new statute which required the official leader of the opposition to be a deputy in the National Assembly, thereby excluding Ravalomanana.

On 20 March 2021 Rajoelina acknowledged that the country was facing a second wave of COVID-19 infections, after a sharp rise in cases and related deaths from late February. On 25 March the Government approved the use of vaccination against the disease, despite Rajoelina's opposition, and the country joined the World Health Organization's COVAX programme (which aimed to provide global access to vaccines). On 19 April the Government announced that Madagascar would acquire the Chinese-manufactured vaccine Sinopharm and on 8 May it received 250,000 doses of AstraZeneca's Covishield vaccine; by that time the country had registered 38,874 cases and 716 deaths. The Ministry of Public Health announced on 17 May that the second wave of infections had peaked in mid-April and further adjustments were made to the restrictions in place. At the end of May Rajoelina maintained the state of health emergency but lifted lockdown measures. In mid-August Prof. Arivelo Zely Randriamanantany replaced Rakotovao at the Ministry of Public Health.

Former President Ratsiraka died on 28 March 2021, following a brief period in hospital; Rajeolina declared a day of national mourning. Political tensions continued and in July the Government arrested a number of prominent military personnel and foreign nationals on suspicion of organizing a coup attempt; 20 went on trial. On 16 December a Franco-Malagasy citizen, Paul Rafanoharana, received the heaviest penalty of 20 years in prison with hard labour, while Philippe François (a former French military officer and adviser to Rajoelina under the HAT) and Aina Razafindrakoto received 10 years, with Rafanoharana's wife, artist Yvon Randriazanakolona (known as Sareraka and an adviser to Madagascar Oil) and Gen. Victor Ramahatra (a former Prime Minister under Ratsiraka) each being sentenced to five years in gaol.

On 15 August 2021 Rajoelina appointed a new Government still under Ntsay as Prime Minister, with a former special adviser Patrick Rajoelina (not a relation) as Minister of Foreign Affairs and Rindra Hasimbole Rabarinirinarison, a senior figure in the ministry, as Minister of the Economy and Finance. Prof. Arivelo Zely became the fourth Minister of Public Health since 2019 and Sophie Ratsiraka, the former President's daughter, became Minister of Handicrafts and Trades.

On 3 September 2021 Rajoelina announced an end to the state of health emergency introduced to deal with the COVID-19 epidemic; data from the Ministry of Public Health indicated that the total number of reported cases amounted to 42,878, with 956 deaths recorded since March 2020. The number of vaccinations had stood at 1,297,653 at the end of March 2022, equivalent to some 4% of the population.

Following a further ministerial reshuffle on 16 March 2022, the cabinet comprised 30 ministers, of whom nine were women. There were seven new appointments, with Richard Randriamandrato and Fidiniavo Ravokatra returning to government as Minister of Foreign Affairs and Minister of Water, Sanitation and Hygiene, respectively.

Madagascar has seen preparations for the next presidential election, which is due at the end of 2023. A poll in April 2022 indicated that 53% wanted to see President Rajoelina re-elected, while 34% did not and 13% were undecided. There were reported divisions in April within the presidential platform IRD, from which the MMM party had already seceded. Ravalomanana looked to relaunch his party, which had suffered from its own divisions when its deputies Hanitra Razafimanantsoa and Fidèle Razara Pierre left to form a new coalition. In May the Government confirmed that there would be a full revision to the electoral list—the first such change since 2010, at an estimated cost of 50,000m. ariary.

FOREIGN AFFAIRS

President Ratsiraka had adopted a foreign policy that was nominally non-aligned, if close to the Union of Soviet Socialist Republics (USSR). In the early 1990s Ravony's Government reversed this approach and established relations with Israel, South Africa, the Republic of Korea (South Korea) and the Republic of China (Taiwan). Ratsiraka did not alter these arrangements on his return as President in 1997, although by 2000, under pressure from the People's Republic of China, the Taiwan office had been closed. France remained the principal trading partner and supplier of bilateral aid, especially after the 1998 settlement of a longstanding dispute over compensation for nationalized French assets. Disagreement remained over the sovereignty of the Iles Eparses (Scattered Islands—a small group of coral islands in the Mozambique Channel over which France claims sovereignty), which, it was agreed in 2000, would be co-administered by France, Madagascar and Mauritius, without prejudice to the question of sovereignty. In 2002 relations with African countries were adversely affected by the support of the OAU (now the AU) for the outgoing President, Ratsiraka, and Madagascar's exclusion from that organization, to which Madagascar was only formally readmitted in July 2003. In 2004 Madagascar joined SADC.

In November 2005 a visit by a Chinese delegation, headed by the Deputy Prime Minister, highlighted the extent of Chinese involvement and investment in many areas of the Malagasy economy. Ravalomanana visited the Chinese capital of Beijing in April 2007 to attend the Forum on China-Africa Cooperation.

The political crisis that began in late 2008 and Rajoelina's subsequent assumption of power isolated Madagascar from the international community. The country was promptly suspended from SADC and the AU, losing the right to host the AU summit in July 2009; the USA excluded Madagascar from the benefits due under its African Growth and Opportunity Act (AGOA), and did not replace its retiring ambassador. The HAT announced in December 2010 that it would recall various ambassadors appointed by Ravalomanana, including those in France and the USA, to replace them with chargés d'affaires, as there was no international recognition of the regime; the Malagasy embassy in the United Kingdom was also closed. However, the UK reopened its embassy in Madagascar in October 2012 (and Madagascar reopened its embassy in the UK in September 2017).

While the HAT received some support from France and the Organisation Internationale de la Francophonie (La Francophonie), the USA remained critical of the regime, particularly over human rights. After the first round of the presidential election in October 2013, sanctions were lifted; in January 2014 Madagascar was readmitted to the AU and its suspension from SADC ended. In June the USA announced that Madagascar could again participate in AGOA.

Ban Ki-Moon, the Secretary-General of the UN, visited Madagascar in May 2016. Madagascar hosted the summit of the Common Market for Eastern and Southern Africa (COMESA) in October and the summit of La Francophonie in the following month. In November King Mohammed VI of Morocco visited Madagascar and promoted commercial links between the two countries.

In June 2017 President Rajaonarimampianina, in his capacity as head of state of the country currently chairing La Francophonie, met his new French counterpart, Emmanuel Macron, in Paris, France. He met Chinese President Xi Jinping in September 2018 at the Forum on China-Africa Co-operation in Beijing, when he expressed support for China's Belt and Road Initiative. In February 2019 the recently inaugurated President Rajoelina attended the 32nd summit of the AU in Addis Ababa.

Pope Francis visited Madagascar in September 2019 as part of a wider tour that also included Mauritius and Mozambique; he celebrated Mass at the Soamandrakizay stadium in Androhibe, which was attended by an estimated 1m. people.

During a visit to France in May 2019 Rajoelina met President Macron, at which the two leaders agreed to set up a joint commission to seek a resolution over the Iles Eparses by June 2020, the 60th anniversary of Madagascar's independence. A controversial visit by Macron to Ile Glorieuse, the largest of the islets in the group, in October 2019 prompted renewed negotiations in Antananarivo between the two countries. During a visit to Madagascar in February 2020, the French Minister for Europe and Foreign Affairs, Jean-Yves Le Drian, indicated further talks on the sovereignty of the Iles Eparses. At the UN General Assembly in October, the Malagasy Minister of Foreign Affairs, Djacoba Tehindrazanarivelo, called on the Non-Aligned Movement to support the country's claim to the islets. In November the French Government returned to Madagascar (apparently as a loan) a crown which had surmounted the throne of Queen Ranavalona III, and declared its support for Madagascar's bid to have the royal palace complex (Rova) inscribed on the UN Educational, Scientific and Cultural Organization (UNESCO) list for World Heritage.

Rajoelina met President Macron again in Paris in August 2020. Macron pledged to provide further French support in dealing with the drought in the south of Madagascar and the impact of the COVID-19 pandemic, as well as a constructive discussion on the Iles Eparses. Rajoelina announced that the Malagasy diaspora in France would be entitled to vote in the presidential election due in 2023, and in September 2021 he raised the matter of the Iles Eparses at the UN General Assembly, stating that he expected a positive outcome.

On 2 March 2022 Madagascar was one of 35 countries that abstained when the UN General Assembly voted by 141 to five to condemn the Russian Federation's invasion of Ukraine. The new Minister of Foreign Affairs, Richard Randriamandrato, had to defend a secret pact on military co-operation signed with Russia in January, which extended one from October 2018. In April 2022 the Russian ambassador stated that his country supported Madagascar's legitimate right to restore sovereignty over the Iles Eparses. In June a date for a second round of negotiations over the disputed territory was set for September.

Economy

JULIAN COOKE

INTRODUCTION

Madagascar is a country that is rich in resources while still ranking among the poorest countries in the world. Political issues and pressure from a growing population have impeded economic advancement, as have the impact of climate issues and the COVID-19 pandemic, notably in the tourism sector.

The economy is largely agricultural, with subsistence farming based on rice cultivation, and with substantial production of crops such as vanilla and cloves. The country has experienced considerable deforestation and increased exploitation of marine resources. There is limited industrial production, although the country has benefited from a favourable environment to develop textile exports. Mining was predominantly artisanal until the development of substantial projects in nickel, cobalt and graphite. The country has suffered from cyclone damage and struggled with poor infrastructure, although sizeable amounts of international aid have made an important contribution to the Government's budgets.

ECONOMIC AND SOCIAL DEVELOPMENTS

In 2021 Madagascar's gross national income (GNI), at current prices, was US $515 per head for an estimated population of 28.4m. (compared with $500 for a population of 8.7m. in 1980), according to the World Bank. On an international purchasing-power parity basis, GNI amounted to $1,635 per head in 2021. The country's gross domestic product (GDP) in 2021 was $14,637m.

The rate of economic expansion accelerated from 2006, reaching 6.7% in 2008 before a contraction of 4.0% in 2009, with the global economic crisis and Madagascar's own political unrest (see *History*). There was a revival in growth to 4.4% in 2019, a level that was expected broadly to continue before the crisis precipitated by the pandemic in 2020 led to an economic contraction in that year of 4.2%. However, a subsequent economic recovery led to growth of 4.4% in 2021.

A high rate of population growth, which the World Bank estimated at an average annual level of 2.7% in 2011–19, offset the economic growth, so that Madagascar's GDP per head decreased, in real terms, by an average of 0.2% per year during that period, although it increased by 1.3% in 2019. The official population census carried out in 2018 indicated a total population of 25.7m., compared with 12.2m. in 1993; the Ministry of the Economy and Finance reported growth to 28.5m. by mid-2021 and forecasts suggest further increases to 60m. by 2050. In 2021 the rural population was 61% of the total, according to the World Bank, while the urban population had grown to 39% from only 11% in 1960.

Average incomes in the country are among the lowest in the world and Madagascar was ranked 162nd out of 189 countries in the 2021 United Nations (UN) Human Development Index (based on 2020 data). The level of poverty deteriorated from 68.0% of the population in 2008 to 77.7% in 2014, before improving to reach an estimated 74.1% in 2019, according to the World Bank; however, there has been a more recent deterioration. The political crisis of the late 2000s reduced the number of jobs in the formal sector and prompted greater economic migration; the Government has estimated the number of Malagasy currently living abroad at over 200,000, with their remittances representing 3% of GDP in 2019.

Madagascar has seen some progress in meeting the UN's Millennium Development Goals, including a sizeable reduction in the number of deaths in childbirth from 97 per 1,000 births in 1997 to an estimated 33.5 in 2017. The country has been vulnerable to disease, such as pneumonic plague, of which 2,348 cases were reported in 2017 (claiming 202 lives), and measles, from which 1,249 people died in an outbreak in 2018–19. Lack of funding has affected social conditions. Madagascar saw a higher incidence of malaria in 2020 than in previous years, with cases estimated at over 1m. In the education sector, school attendance averages 6.1 years, according to the UN; the number of pupils taking the baccalaureate examination declined from 174,822 in 2019 to 164,396 in 2020. The World Bank estimated in 2022 that the level of education in Madagascar was 10% behind the sub-Saharan average and 7% behind that of low-income countries.

The World Food Programme (WFP) has ranked Madagascar as among the 10 countries most vulnerable to disasters, estimating that 83% of those in rural areas faced food insecurity, and in 2018 it estimated that 47% of children under five years of age suffered from malnutrition. The south of the country in particular has faced a prolonged drought. Despite extensive military operations, cattle rustling and banditry have continued into 2022, resulting in heavy loss of life—estimated at 1,781 fatalities during 2016–21, including 43 gendarmes (and some criticism over the impunity of the perpetrators). The impact of the pandemic has contributed to an increase in crime in the capital, Antananarivo. Moreover, Madagascar's Gini coefficient (a standard measure of inequality) was high, at 42.6, as measured in 2021.

The informal sector is significant and accounted for an estimated 36% of GDP in 2021. As a result of the growth in microfinance, an estimated 29% of the adult population had access to financial services in 2016, and the country has benefited from improved internet access following its connection to a fibre-optic cable system (see *Transport and Communications*).

In 2021 the Economist Intelligence Unit (EIU) placed Madagascar 83rd in the world, if among the top 10 African countries, in its survey on democracy. Madagascar was ranked 147th out of 180 countries in Transparency International's global Corruption Perceptions Index 2021; while there was a slight improvement in its score to 26/100, this remained far short of the Government's target score of 40/100 by 2030.

AGRICULTURE, FORESTRY AND FISHING

Madagascar has traditionally been dependent on agriculture and a subsistence economy, in which 80% of the country's population worked, as estimated by the African Development Bank (AfDB) in 2017, with the wider agricultural sector accounting for 26.7% of GDP in 2020. Madagascar's agricultural area was 40.9m. ha out of a total land area of 58.2m. ha, as measured in 2016, and the average farm size is small. Agricultural products represented 39.2% of merchandise exports totalling US $ 1,987m. in 2020, and 17.9% of imports totalling $3,224m., according to World Trade Organization (WTO) data. Increases in mining and manufacturing production have reduced the relative proportion of food exports, as have poor harvests and variable prices for vanilla.

The agricultural sector has struggled due to adverse climatic conditions, a lack of insecticides or fertilizers, poor road conditions, and the impact of the traditional *tavy* culture of slash-and-burn. Persistent pressures meant that, according to UN figures, agricultural GDP increased at an average annual rate of only 0.3% in 2009–18, if by 3.7% in 2018 and 5.9% in 2019. While the political crisis of 2009–10 heavily curtailed development aid and government reforms, the agricultural sector has proved relatively resilient, although its GDP grew by just 0.6% in 2020.

Cyclones can have a substantial impact on Madagascar, albeit varying in intensity and frequency each year. In 2018 Cyclone Ava caused 51 deaths and displaced some 20,000 people and in 2020 heavy storms caused over 30 deaths, while in 2022 a succession of six tropical storms or cyclones from January to April, notably Cyclone Batsirai in February, caused at least 214 deaths and affected 571,100 people overall.

Locusts have threatened agricultural production, particularly in 2013–15 when the Food and Agricultural Organization of the UN (FAO) undertook a programme of extensive and effective insecticide spraying, although there have been recurrent occurrences, such as in 2022. Since 2015 a persistently severe drought has affected the south of Madagascar, where UN agencies in June 2022 estimated that 1.68m. people still faced food insecurity, even after the provision of substantial aid and various irrigation projects.

Paddy rice is a staple food and the main crop, a legacy of the origin of settlers from south-east Asia. Average annual consumption per head of some 135 kg is one of the highest rates in the world, and rice occupies about 1.2m. ha, or between one-third and one-half of the total area under cultivation. The use of faster-yielding seeds, improved land registration and reduced cyclone damage have offset challenges from a shortage of quality seeds, equipment and fertilizer. Annual rice production has varied and output increased to 4.7m. metric tons in 2020, although the finished product of 2.4m. did not meet end demand, of 2.8m. tons; the International Trade Centre (ITC) estimated the value of rice imports at US $179.8m. The World Bank has estimated that the rice harvest would be 4m. tons in

2021/22, 6% lower than in the previous season. The price of rice is politically sensitive and the Government subsidizes the cost while planning for self-sufficiency, as in 2022 when President Andry Rajoelina called for improved rice production; the Indian Exim Bank financed a state project worth $38m.

Madagascar is the world's largest producer of natural vanilla, produced from approximately 25,000 ha of plants grown in the north-east of the country. The USA, France and Germany are the main purchasers. The Government and producer confederations follow a policy of limited exports to manage prices, but output has fluctuated widely in recent years, at between 600 metric tons and 4,400 tons per year; tropical storms can cause the loss of up to 30% of the annual crop. After the price peaked at US $400 per kg in 2003, competition from cheap synthetic substitutes contributed to a collapse in prices, to $20 per kg, by 2006; for 2022 the price was in the range of $395–455 per kg. Production increased to an estimated 1,800 tons in 2020 with improved quality and maturity, given a lower incidence of early picking and theft. The ITC estimated that revenue from vanilla exports increased steadily to a peak of $855.4m. in 2018 (equivalent to 28.5% of total export revenue), before falling to $509.6m. in 2020 (26.3% of the total).

Another important cash crop is cloves. Annual production fell sharply to around 10,000 metric tons in 2005–10, partly given cyclone damage and the felling of trees to extract essential oils, before recovering to 23,325 tons in 2018, according to FAO; it totalled some 15,000 tons in 2022. The ITC reported export revenue increasing substantially in 2017 to US $228.2m. before a decline to just $63.0m. by 2020. Much of Madagascar's clove production goes to Singapore for re-export.

Coffee was an important agricultural export, although the International Coffee Organization estimated that production fell from 584,000 bags in 2013/14 to 370,000 bags in 2020, while the exported volume was just 19,490 bags in 2021/22. Madagascar has also exported sisal, ylang ylang and litchis (or lychees), being the principal supplier of litchis to Europe. Sugar production has suffered from underinvestment and the country imports 100,000 metric tons annually, although in 2020 the processing plant in Brickaville reopened. Madagascar resumed exports of tobacco in 2019, after a hiatus of 30 years. Groundnuts, bananas, pineapples, coconuts, butter beans and tobacco are also grown on a small scale, while Madagascar has yet to realize its initial potential in biofuels, including the cultivation of jatropha, an oil-producing plant.

There is little in the way of a forestry sector, although FAO estimated in 2018 that forested and wooded land totalled 12.5m. ha, or one-fifth of the total land area. The majority of forest products are the wood and charcoal that generate over 80% of domestic fuel consumption, and contribute heavily to deforestation; the Government reported in November 2019 that 14m. ha of forest had been lost to bush fires in the 60 years since Madagascar's independence. The development of the country's national parks was closely associated with potential for the eco-tourism sector and helped by external funding, although illegal logging, especially of rosewood, is a serious problem that political conditions have exacerbated. There have been extensive efforts at reforestation: in 2021 the World Bank agreed funding for Madagascar of US $50m. under its Forest Carbon Partnership Facility in part to promote sustainable forest management in some 7m. ha of land in the east of Madagascar. The Government announced plans in 2021 for the reforestation of 150,000 ha of land in 2021–22, and in 2022 Madagascar signed a resolution based on the pledges made at the UN Climate Change Conference (COP26)—held in Glasgow, UK, in October–November 2021—to stop the degradation of forests and to restore 4m. ha of degraded land by 2030.

Madagascar has sizeable potential in its coastal resources, with FAO indicating that the output of the country's fishing industry rose from less than 20,000 metric tons in 1950 to 159,100 tons in 2007. As with other products and according to FAO estimates, the total catch has varied in recent years and was 115,800 tons in 2020. Shrimp fishing expanded considerably in the 1990s to become an important source of export revenue, albeit with concerns about overfishing; the shrimp and prawn catch declined to 12,100 tons in 2020. Fish farming has developed in recent years, with around 50,000 ha of suitable territory in swamps along the western coast. Aquaculture production rose rapidly from the 1990s to reach a peak in 2006 of over 16,000 tons, before falling sharply to only 5,500 tons in 2020. Illegal fishing in Malagasy waters is increasingly problematic and Madagascar lacks sufficient resources to police the area, although FAO agreed a three-year project worth US \$4.4m. in 2019. In 2017 the World Bank provided funds totalling \$83.2m. to Madagascar and other member countries of the Indian Ocean Commission to improve the management of their fishing industries. Meanwhile, agreements with the European Union (EU) concerning fishing around the island expired at the end of 2018 and have yet to be renewed; Madagascar had earned €6.1m. from the industry in 2015–18.

Madagascar had an estimated 8.9m. head of cattle in 2020, according to FAO, down from some 20m. in 1980. Cattle are generally regarded as an indication of wealth rather than as a source of income; some beef is exported, but volumes have declined in recent years to about 800 metric tons annually. In 2019 the International Finance Corporation helped to fund a new meat-processing plant near Taolagnaro (Fort Dauphin), in the south-east of the island. There remains a pressing need to revive veterinary services and rehabilitate abattoirs, partly to meet EU import standards. There has also been an increase in cattle theft related to rural banditry. There are growing numbers of dairy cattle, with production of cow's milk being estimated by FAO at 491,300 tons in 2020. FAO also estimated that there were 1.5m. goats, 0.9m. sheep and 1.8m. pigs in 2020, when meat production included around 34,900 tons of cattle meat, 26,900 tons of pig meat and 51,400 tons of chicken meat.

INDUSTRY

Industry accounted for an estimated 20.7% of Madagascar's GDP in 2020. Growth in extractive industries and the export processing zones (EPZs) contributed to average annual growth in I industrial GDP of 6.6% in 2010–19, according to the UN. The island's major industrial centres, other than mines, are located in the High Plateaux or near the port of Toamasina. Food processing accounts for a significant portion of all industrial value added, while brewing, paper and soap are also important sectors. Textile production benefited from the success of the EPZs under the preferential terms of the USA's African Growth and Opportunity Act (AGOA). However, Madagascar's exclusion from the Act in 2010, owing to US disapproval of the regime change in 2009, saw exports to the USA decline sharply in 2019–10 from US \$279m. in 2008, one-half of Madagascar's total export revenue, before the country's readmission in 2014. According to the ITC, total textile exports declined from \$580.1m. in 2017 to \$422.2m. in 2020 (accounting for 21.8% of total export revenue). Madagascar's reported clothing exports were worth \$838m. in the year to March 2022, with the USA, France, South Africa, Germany and the United Kingdom accounting for 75% of the total.

Demand for cement has varied depending on mining and construction projects, although the estimated overall level of 1m. metric tons in 2020 was similar to the 0.94m. tons in 2010. There are cement plants at Mahajanga and Toamasina, where Raysut Cement, an Omani company, planned a new plant with an annual capacity of 750,000 tons; this is due to become operational in 2022. Overall production fell significantly to 240,000 tons in 2015 and further, to some 150,000 tons, in 2022. A fertilizer plant at Toamasina produces some 90,000 tons per year of urea- and ammonia-based fertilizers. Other industries include the manufacture of wood products and furniture, agricultural machinery, and the processing of agricultural products, especially tobacco. The food industry overall remains underdeveloped and, according to the AfDB, represented just 1.7% of GDP in 2019.

The EPZs, which were established in the 1980s, attracted foreign investors, particularly from South-East Asia, Mauritius and France; by 2004 1,276 companies employed an estimated 115,000 people in the zones. Poor infrastructure and high transportation costs have constrained development of manufacturing, as did the political crisis in 2009–10 which led to the closure of a number of businesses. However, call centre operations have grown and are estimated to employ around 50,000 people; in 2021 the French company Teleperformance had 1,200 employees on two sites in Antananarivo.

There have been political efforts to attract investment. President Rajoelina has encouraged domestic industry, and in June 2020 he presented prototypes of a new brand of locally manufactured cars as well as motorcycles, due to be launched by 2023, and initially involving the assembly of parts from German and Chinese manufacturers that are shareholders in the project; the GasyCar is the second locally manufactured brand of vehicle, after the Karenjy model, which the Government launched in 1984. However, the economic crisis arising from the COVID-19 pandemic in 2020 led nine out of 10 firms in the Special Economic Zones to lay off some employees, with an estimated 150,000 redundancies in total. The Government launched an economic stimulus package, worth approximately US \$75m. to support more than 980,000 small businesses. Madagascar had ranked 161st out of 190 countries in the World Bank's *Doing Business 2020* report.

MINING

Madagascar has sizeable deposits of a wide range of minerals, although it has yet to ensure adequate official commercialization of them due to political crises and the challenges of operating in remote locations. Successive governments have encouraged investment, if with limited success, while the major projects that do exist have given rise to considerable social and environmental issues, as well as economic development.

One major project is the exploitation of nickel and cobalt deposits at Ambatovy in the Moramanga area, in which a consortium led by Korea Resources Corpn and Sherritt International of Canada invested some US \$8,000m. from 2006. Sherritt has operated the mine, which has an annual capacity of 60,000 metric tons of nickel and 5,600 tons of cobalt, as well as 210,000 tons of ammonium sulphate fertilizer, a by-product. In 2015, the first full year, production amounted to 47,271 tons of nickel and 3,464 tons of cobalt. However, nickel production declined to 33,185 tons in 2018 and cobalt production to 2,852 tons. Sherritt reduced its interest in the project from 40% to 12% in 2017 and to zero in 2020, when its partners Sumitomo Corpn of Japan and Korea Resources Corpn held 54% and 46%, respectively. Production at the mine halted during the pandemic, when many foreign personnel left the country; it resumed, for nickel initially, in March 2021, after a stoppage that had lasted a year.

Another major project is an ilmenite (titanium ore) mine which Rio Tinto operates through its subsidiary QIT Madagascar Minerals Ltd near Taolagnaro, where the 60% titanium dioxide content makes it one of the higher-grade resources in the world. There was a first shipment in 2009, via a new deep-sea port at Ehoala, and ore is shipped to Canada for processing. Lower demand from the People's Republic of China contributed to lower exports of 600,000 metric tons in 2014–15; Rio Tinto adjusted production to reduce stocks and deferred further investment given limited profitability, and in 2020 it raised further capital, with the Malagasy Government providing US \$16m. in line with its 20% stake. A Chinese state company, Mainland Mining Ltd, started production of ilmenite in 2007 at a site near Toamasina, with capacity of 100,000 tons. The Australian company Base Resources, which has a stock market listing in the UK, is still developing the Toliara Sands ilmenite project that it assumed from World Titane in 2018, with a prospective 34.8m. tons of ilmenite, zircon and rutile giving a mine life of 38 years; however, local opposition led to a suspension of operations in 2019.

Madagascar has seen substantial activity in graphite mining, as demand for the mineral for renewable energy uses has increased. Bass Metals Ltd of Australia operates the Graphmada mine, which underwent a US \$3.1m. upgrade in 2018 intended to increase annual output to 6,000 metric tons. Canadian-based NextSource Materials (formally known as Energizer Resources) manages a graphite resource at Molo (near the coal fields at Sakoa), which has estimated reserves of 141m. tons, although it delayed starting operations to the third quarter of 2022; the company raised a further \$6.5m. in 2021 and signed a supply agreement with German conglomerate ThyssenKrupp. Another Canadian company, DNI Metals Inc, began the construction in 2020 of a graphite pilot plant with a potential annual capacity of 20,000 tons at Vohitsara, south of Toamasina, with an estimated inferred resource of 4m. tons. BlackEarth Minerals of the Netherlands has a graphite project at Ianapera in southern Madagascar, with an exploration target of 20m.–35m. tons; the company signed a supply agreement for 25,000 tons per year from its Maniry mine with the German firm Luxacarbon. London-listed Tirupati Graphite produces 3,000 tons at the Sahamamy project and in September 2021 commissioned one at Vatomina near Toamasina, with an initial annual capacity of 9,000 tons; the company planned to expand to 81,000 tons by 2024.

Other mineral projects have not been developed in full. Thankys Exports of India holds the Manantenina bauxite project in the south-east of the country, which had estimated reserves of 10m. metric tons but has seen limited development to date. Bushveld Minerals of South Africa has since 2013 owned the Lemur Resources coal project at Imaloto in south-west Madagascar, with deposits of 136m. tons, as well as a 60-MW coal power station due to be completed in 2022. Another coal project in the Sakoa basin is operated by the Thai company PTT, which in 2012 invested US $50.2m. to buy the remaining two-thirds' stake in the project from Red Island Minerals, with initial plans to double production to 22m. tons by 2020. Jubilee Platinum and Impala Platinum carried out exploratory drilling at the Londokomanana prospect at Ambodilafa, south-east of the capital, in 2008.

Official production of gold in Madagascar has been limited, although, unofficially, an estimated 3–4 metric tons were produced annually from 1995 to 2008, when legal exports were just 39–50 kg per year. However, reforms to regulate artisanal production and to curb illegal trade, including an agreement by the central bank of Madagascar with 16 operators in 2020, have contributed to a substantially larger level of gold exports, at 2,833 kg in 2017 and then 3,051 kg in 2018, when they had a value of US $97m., although exports decreased in 2019 to 2,423 kg. There are deposits of iron ore at Soalala, near Mahajanga in the west, where a Chinese joint venture led by Wuhan Iron & Steel paid $100m. in 2010 for the right to mine reserves estimated at up to 800m. tons, and at Bekisopa in the south, first developed by Cline Mining Corpn. The Australian company Akora Resources assumed control from Cline of its stake in the Bekisopa project, for which it raised funds in 2020.

Madagascar has significant potential deposits of heavy minerals, with test results on the Ambohimirahavavy volcano in the north of the country indicating a clay composition that is identical to those in southern China, the world's main source of rare earth minerals. Reenova Holdings (formerly ISR Capital) of Singapore held a majority and Tantalus Rare Earths of Germany a minority share in a project at Ampasindava in the north-west of the island, with an estimated 348,000 metric tons of oxides including tantalum, niobium, zirconium and gallium potentially worth over US $8,000m., although any planned production has stalled. NextSource Materials of Canada also has a joint venture with Malagasy Minerals in rare earths, while UMC Energy of the USA has a uranium project at Morondava.

Madagascar has exported small quantities of chromite, graphite and mica. The main deposits of chromium ore, at Andriamena, produced over 100,000 metric tons in 2005, while the reopened Bemanevika pit, with reserves of 2.2m. tons, boosted production in subsequent years. According to estimates by the US Geological Survey (USGS), output of chromite increased from 88,000 tons in 2013 to 197,750 tons in 2015, before declining to 79,345 tons in 2016. The state-owned company Kraomita Malagasy reported annual exports of chromium ore of 100,000–140,000 tons in the latter half of the 2000s. In March 2019 Kraomita Malagasy became part of a joint venture with the Russian company Ferrum Mining, with the latter taking a 70% stake in a new holding company, Kraoma Mining, which suspended mining during the pandemic in 2020.

There was a first discovery of sapphires north of Taolagnaro in the early 1990s and another in 1997 in the north of the island, where the arrival of thousands of unofficial miners caused serious damage to the Ankarana nature reserve. A further discovery in 1998, at Ilakaka in the south-west, prompted another influx and aroused the interest of foreign investors. Sapphires worth some US $100m. were reported to have been mined by early 1999, and although the country received little in the way of tax income, unauthorized mining has seen Madagascar become a significant global producer. The country's anti-corruption agency estimated in 2018 that annual exports amounted to around 20 metric tons, of which only 2 tons were traded officially. Rubies are mined at Vatomandry on the east coast, and emeralds at Mananjary. The Canadian company Diamond Fields Resources has a zircon project at Beravina, with inferred resources of 1.5m. tons.

In 2000 a new mining code set out the legal and environmental framework for the sector; this code was revised in 2005. Most mining companies signed up to the international Extractive Industries Transparency Initiative (EITI) in 2012. While investment in the mining sector has been substantial and has previously strengthened the country's economy and currency, royalties and fees remain low. In 2015 the Government proposed a revision to the 2005 mining law, with an increase in the royalty rate from 2% to 5%; the Ambatovy mine pays a discounted rate of only 1% However, in 2017 President Hery Rajaonarimampianina said that there would be no changes to the code, to reassure investors, and even with a revised proposal of a 4% rate in 2019 there has been no revision to date. The initial report under the EITI indicated that Madagascar had received 115,000m. ariary (US $52m.) in revenues from extractive activities in 2012, this figure rising to 231,000m. ariary in 2018. In February 2019 Madagascar was suspended from the EITI for missing a reporting deadline; by 2022 it had made meaningful progress in meeting the EITI targets.

ENERGY

Madagascar has considerable potential in terms of hydroelectric and solar power, which would help to reduce its dependence on fuel imports (which accounted for 15.7% of total imports in 2021, according to the ITC), while development of its own hydrocarbon resources has been limited.

Fuel wood and charcoal still provide an estimated 84% of Madagascar's total energy requirements, with petroleum products accounting for 11% and electricity 5%. The country's hydroelectric stations supplied an estimated 54% of electricity production in 2018, while most of the remainder came from thermal installations. The Government estimated the national access rate in 2017 at only 15%, with 84% in urban areas and 6% in rural areas. Installed capacity comprised 446 MW of thermal power (with only 3 MW in rural areas) and 162 MW of hydroelectric power, with minimal amounts of solar, wind and biomass power. The Government's target was to have an access rate of 70% by 2030 and to generate 7,900 MW, of which 85% would come from renewable sources, mainly hydroelectric power.

The Andekaleka hydroelectric scheme, which began operations in 1982, supplies the regions of Antananarivo and Antsirabe, as well as the Andriamena chromite mine; it suffered a fire in January 2022 that reduced output. In 2016 contracts were awarded for five new hydroelectric projects, including to the New Onive Hydroelectric Energy (NEHO) consortium, comprising the French company Eiffage, the Moroccan company Themis and the Franco-African Eranove, which won a bid to build a new 205-MW capacity hydroelectric scheme at Sahofika, at a cost of €797m.; commissioning was expected in 2024. In 2019 the Italian firm Tozzi Green was awarded a US $90m. contract to build a 40-MW hydroelectric plant at Tsinjoarivo, while the Malagasy industrial company Jovena signed a shareholders' agreement with the pan-African infrastructure investment platform Africa50, Norway's SN Power and civil engineering company Colas to co-develop a 120-MW run-of-river hydropower plant on the Ivondro River, which was due to commence operations by 2023.

The country has seen increased investment in solar power, while there has been limited development of wind power in spite of a planned US $80m. project in 2021. In 2017 the US Trade and Development Agency provided a grant to the

Malagasy energy company Henri Fraise to develop mini-grids with capacity of 10 MW, and in 2018 a new 20 MW solar park opened at Ambohiphaonana, operated by GreenYellow in a joint venture with Axian Group, which in June 2020 announced plans to double the size of the park in a €17m project by the end of 2021. In 2019 the Malagasy company Filatex announced a $50m., 50-MW solar energy project in partnership with Canada's DERA Energy.

Madagascar has yet to exploit fully its sizeable onshore and offshore petroleum reserves. From the 1980s foreign companies signed concession agreements to prospect for oil in a number of areas, particularly in the Morandava basin in western Madagascar, while work continued on deposits of heavy petroleum at Tsimiroro, where in 2014 Madagascar Oil started to develop. Madagascar Oil was privatized in 2016 as part of the Government's plans to raise US $20m. towards the funding of the project, which came into production in 2016, if with limited output or commercial sales. In 2008 a Chinese consortium announced plans to develop a US $300m. onshore block, while Niko Resources of Canada took a 75% stake in EnerMad's offshore block by funding a $125m. seismic programme. By 2016 only 10% of available exploration blocks had been licensed and the Malagasy state agency, Office des Mines Nationales et des Industries Stratégiques (OMNIS), announced a new licensing round in 2018 (the first since 2006) to cover 44 offshore blocks in the Morondava basin. However, it subsequently cancelled the auction, which has been deferred indefinitely. In October 2020 BP renounced its rights to four offshore oil blocks where initial work had been carried out, citing its decision to focus on renewable energy.

The average electricity usage in Madagascar is only 75 KWh, well below the 500 KWh average for the sub-Saharan region The national electricity and water utility Jiro sy Rano Malagasy (JIRAMA) has experienced serious financial problems, exacerbated by economic conditions and poor contracts. The company has struggled to ensure adequate production, with the country facing persistent power outages compounded by a fire at the Andekaleka hydroelectric power station in 2022, as well as revenue for its services, and it has made substantial losses since 2008, necessitating extensive assistance from the Government; by June 2022 the accumulated deficit was 200,000m. ariary (US $35m.) There have been offers of external finance, while other operators, such as the US company Symbion Power, have looked to develop new power plants. In 2020 the EU funded the majority of the $83m. cost of a project to improve the drinking water supply system in Antananarivo.

TRANSPORT AND COMMUNICATIONS

Madagascar's poor infrastructure was one factor in its ranking of 132nd out of 141 nations in the 2019 Global Competitiveness Index produced by the World Economic Forum. The country's mountainous topography has hindered the development of adequate communications, and the limited existing infrastructure is prone to cyclone damage, making even major routes impassable in bad weather. In 2000 the Government launched a road development programme funded by the World Bank and the EU, and from 2003 Japan assisted in the building of a bypass road in Antananarivo, which opened in 2007. However, the suspension of international aid that resulted from the regime change in 2009 had a material impact. In 2012 there were an estimated 31,640 km of classified roads and only about 16.3% of the road network was paved. In 2018 Kuwait agreed to provide US $10m. towards the total estimated cost of $64m. of a project to construct a new bridge over the Mangoky river, which was to be the longest in the country, with Saudi Arabia contributing a further $20m. Also in 2018 China announced that it was to provide $155m. in finance for the rehabilitation of the RN5A highway linking the northern cities of Ambilobe and Vohémar. In November the World Bank granted $140m. towards a scheme aiming to enhance rural transport connectivity in the priority regions of Alaotra Mangoro, Anosy and Atsimo-Atsinanana. In December 2020 the Ministry of Public Works noted that nearly 90% of the country's roads were in poor condition, a proportion that the Government hoped to reduce to 70% by 2023. In May 2022 the World Bank noted that only 12% of the rural population had access to roads, the lowest

level in the world. The Government announced that an Egyptian company would undertake the rebuilding of the RN2 highway between the capital and Toamasina. Meanwhile, the European Investment Bank agreed to finance the rehabilitation of the RN13 between Tolagnaro and Ambovombe, a key project for President Rajoelina, as well as the RN6 between Antsiranana and Ambanja.

Madagascar has a limited railway network of some 836 km. Three lines totalling 673 km in the north of the country run from Antananarivo to the port of Toamasina and to Antsirabe as well as from Moramanga to the rice-growing region of Lake Alaotra, while a fourth, 163-km line in the south runs between Fianarantsoa and the east coast port of Manakara. The Government of Madagascar signed memorandums of understanding with Chinese companies in 2018 for a new railway between Antananarivo and Fianarantsoa and a tramway system in the capital. In 2021 President Rajoelina committed to development of the new tramway, as well as to a cable car system in the capital at a cost of €151m., with funding from France.

Domestic air services are important to Madagascar given its size, terrain and limited road and rail networks. The main international airport, Ivato, is at Antananarivo. The national airline Madagascar Airlines was formed in 2021 from the merger of the former operator Air Madagascar, which had struggled with debts of some US $72m. and an operating deficit of $80m., and its domestic subsidiary, Tsaradia, launched in 2019. On international routes, there was effectively a duopoly with Air France, although other operators have introduced routes. Serious safety shortcomings led the EU to ban two Air Madagascar Boeing 767-300 aircraft from its airspace in 2021; the airline subsequently leased replacement aircraft and appointed a new Chief Executive, and it was finally removed from the EU's blacklist in 2016. In October 2017 the Government chose the French airline Air Austral, based in Réunion, as a strategic partner which was due to provide $40m. of capital for a minority stake of 49%; in April 2018 the Government wrote off nearly one-half of the outstanding debt of Air Madagascar. The airline faced significant competition and there was friction with Air Austral, which by mid-2020 had only committed some $10m. of the pledged investment. Air Madagascar's fleet was grounded from mid-March 2020 as a consequence of the suspension of international flights during the COVID-19 pandemic. In July 2021 Air Madagascar formally ended its agreement with Air Austral, and the latter's 40% stake was returned to the Government, while pressure remained on a start-up airline Madagasikara Airways, after its flights were suspended over a minor irregularity in 2020. In April 2020 Madagascar Airlines was still in need of $69m. in funding and was reported to be looking again for a partner, possibly Air France.

In 2016 a consortium comprising Aéroports de Paris (ADP), Bouygues Bâtiment International, Colas Madagascar and Meridian Africa was appointed to operate the airports at Ivato and Nosy Be under a 28-year contract; the consortium invested in improving the airports. A new US $200m. terminal at Ivato came into operation ahead of schedule in October 2019, and in December 2021 a further new terminal opened, which was intended to increase capacity to 1.5m. passengers a year after a project that cost some $225m. The Government also confirmed a new contract for this airport and that at Nosy Be with Ravinala Airports (a consortium of ADP, Bouygues and Meridian).

The principal port in Madagascar is Toamasina, which handles some two-thirds of the country's foreign trade; the port's volume of traffic is estimated at 1.7m. metric tons per year, of which 70% is in containers. However, the port is vulnerable to cyclones, which destroyed it in 1986 and caused further serious damage in 1994, 2003 and 2007 (the last of these cyclones also damaging the port at Mahajanga). The Philippine company International Container Terminal Services, Inc (ICTSI) manages the port of Toamasina and in 2007 completed the first phase of a modernization programme, at a cost of US $30m. In 2016, as part of a planned $500m. financial package to redevelop the port, the Japanese International Cooperation Agency allocated $3m. towards a survey regarding the improvement of the RN2 highway between Toamasina and the capital, while China provided a 30-year preferential loan in

2018 to fund the construction of a link road from the port to the RN2. ICTSI reached an agreement to extend its concession for the Madagascar International Container Terminal at Toamasina by 15 years from 2025 to 2040; the port is currently undertaking a planned $639m. expansion project. Japan stated that it would proceed with the second phase of improvements to the port at Toamasina, at an estimated cost of $411m. The Malagasy Ports Authority operates the country's other general ports, and in 2006 upgraded those at Mahajanga, Toliary and Antsiranana/Nosy Be. As part of the development of the Ilikaka ilmenite mine, a new deep-sea port began operations in 2008 at Ehoala, near Taolagnaro, while a $200m. project to rehabilitate the port of Manakara in the south-east of Madagascar was under way in 2022, with funding from the Chinese Government. Coastal shipping is conducted mainly by private companies.

Madagascar has benefited from its initial connection in 2010 to the fibre-optic Eastern Africa Submarine Cable System and from subsequent upgrades to the system, which have enabled lower communication costs and the development of service outsourcing activities. According to the World Bank, mobile telephone subscriptions stood at 34.1 per 100 of the population in 2017, when Madagascar ranked 169th out of 176 countries in a survey by the International Telecommunication Union on access to and use of telecommunications. In July 2019 TELMA signed a US $100m. agreement with the Swedish company Ericsson to upgrade its network in 2019–23, including the launching of commercial 5G services in June 2020. Meanwhile, in December 2019 Madagascar signed a technical assistance agreement worth $47m. with the Chinese Government which was to fund the installation of 130 km of fibre-optic connections and the establishment of data management centres. The Government raised the excise duty on telecommunications from 8% to 10% in 2020, before reversing the move in 2021.

TOURISM

With its unique biodiversity and strikingly varied scenery, Madagascar has considerable potential for the development of eco-tourism. The political crisis of the late 2000s had a substantial impact on tourist arrivals, which declined by 57% year on year, to reach 162,687 in 2009 before a steady recovery to 255,942 in 2012. However, following a deterioration in the security situation, the number of visitors fell to 196,375 in 2013, before rallying to reach 244,321 in 2015. The number of visitors increased further to 293,185 in 2016, with some 10,000 having attended the summit meetings of the Common Market for Eastern and Southern Africa (COMESA) and the Organisation Internationale de la Francophonie, and some 38,800 tourists arriving on cruise ships. However, in 2017 the number of arrivals fell to 255,460, due to the impact of an outbreak of plague in the second half of the year. In spite of insecurity and political tensions, the number of arrivals increased to 291,299 in 2018 and further rose to 383,717 in 2019. The COVID-19 crisis from March 2020 had a severe impact on the tourism industry. In August the Government announced the reopening of the resort of Nosy Be to tourists from the beginning of October, with an initial 1,000 visitors a week subject to strict control. Tourist numbers in 2020 overall declined to 68,330 and, according to the Institut National de la Statistique de Madagascar, totalled only 31,689 in 2021. In response to a second wave of COVID-19 cases in the country beginning in March 2021, national restrictions were reinstated, including the suspension of international flights. The Government reopened the country to visitors in October, although after further issues it was only in March 2022 that the country reopened to air travel, albeit with a ban on flights to and from South Africa for three months due to a dispute over gold smuggling. Madagascar reopened the country to maritime travel in April.

Revenue from tourism decreased from US $668m. in 2017 to $489m. in 2018, and amounted to $534m. in 2019. In March 2021 the Confédération du Tourisme de Madagascar estimated that the sector had lost some $500m. in revenue in 2020 due to the COVID-19 pandemic, with other estimates at $750m. Prior to the crisis, the tourism sector had accounted for some 44,000 direct jobs and a substantial number indirectly.

ECONOMIC POLICY, TRADE AND AID

Madagascar's balance of payments became increasingly unfavourable in the 1980s, such that the Government yielded to pressure from the International Monetary Fund (IMF) and the World Bank to liberalize trade and to adjust the Malagasy franc exchange rate. The reforms succeeded in reducing the external current account deficit, as export earnings improved, although it continued to fluctuate, being equivalent—according to the IMF—to some 21% of GDP in 2009 and 0.3% in 2014.

In 2000 Madagascar participated in the formation of a free trade area between nine (subsequently increased to 11) of the 20 countries of COMESA, which eliminated all tariff barriers. The International Development Association (IDA) and the IMF agreed to a comprehensive debt reduction package under the Heavily Indebted Poor Countries (HIPC) initiative, amounting to US $1,500m., or 40% of Madagascar's total debt.

Following the disputed presidential election in December 2001 (see *History*), international financial organizations froze Madagascar's assets and the central bank was closed, rendering the country unable to service its debts. During the following six months of economic blockades, destruction of infrastructure and general strikes, the economy largely ceased to function.

In July 2002 donors pledged some US $2,300m. in aid over four years, while the new Government emphasized its commitment to good governance and to private sector development. The international aid allowed the country to repay accumulated arrears from the crisis, and from August the foreign exchange markets reopened, with the currency settling to a relatively stable level. The IMF provided credit as well as loans towards reforming public sector management and developing the private sector, and, following elections in December, disbursed $15m. under the Poverty Reduction and Growth Facility (PRGF, agreed in March 2001).

In 2003 a lengthy drought and some cyclone damage weakened Madagascar's economy; France, Germany and the UK cancelled further significant amounts of debt, and in June the IMF granted an additional US $15.9m. under the PRGF. From July the country began to reintroduce its former currency, the ariary, and on 1 January 2005 it replaced the franc as the official currency.

In response to further severe cyclones in March 2004, the IMF released US $35m. in funds and extended the PRGF until March 2005. In July 2004 the World Bank granted a Poverty Reduction Support Credit of $88m. and a credit of $37m. In August 2004 Madagascar joined the Southern African Development Community (SADC); the country's membership was suspended in 2009 but reinstated in 2014. Following the successful fulfilment of the criteria of the HIPC initiative in October 2004, the 'Paris Club' of creditors once more restructured the country's debt. Subsequently, Madagascar also successfully completed the PRGF.

In April 2005 Madagascar was the first country to negotiate an agreement with the USA under its Millennium Challenge Corporation programme, whereby some US $110m. was to be disbursed over five years. In July Madagascar qualified as a primary candidate for debt cancellation, owing to its success in the HIPC schedule, and received a second Poverty Reduction Support Credit, of $80m., from the World Bank.

In mid-2006 the World Bank approved a new PRGF arrangement of US $81m. over three years Meanwhile, the EU's approval of the Government's policies prompted an increased allocation of funds under the ninth European Development Fund (EDF) (2000–07) and a commitment of €462m. under the 10th EDF (2008–13).

In 2007 the World Bank and the IMF confirmed their support for the country and its prudent macroeconomic policies, agreeing a further US $140m. per year for 2007–11 under the Strategic Country Assistance programme and $69m. of finance for investment in various sectors. The EU increased its allocation under the 10th EDF to €588m., of which 40% was scheduled for improving the road network. Continued problems with the power supply affected industry and prompted civil unrest. In addition, the severe cyclone seasons during 2006–08 caused extensive damage to infrastructure and crops.

In early 2008 an IMF review allowed the country to draw down a further US $25m. of low-interest loans, while in June the World Bank approved a $50m. Poverty Reduction Support Credit. However, the regime change in March 2009 prompted widespread suspension of bilateral and multilateral aid (with the exception of humanitarian aid). The EU ended any new projects, affecting $180m. worth of road rehabilitation works; the World Bank suspended payments to its projects; and the Millennium Challenge Corporation terminated its 2002 agreement one year early (having already disbursed $85m. of the proposed $110m.

The Government sought finance and investment from new sources, such as Saudi Arabia, while the US $100m. Chinese purchase of rights to the Soalala iron ore prospect in May 2010 provided a crucial injection of money. A state-funded construction programme and a recovery in the tourism sector still left limited GDP growth in 2011, while the completion of the Ambatovy mining project boosted the economy in 2012. In 2014 the IMF noted that the Malagasy authorities had maintained macroeconomic and financial stability during a difficult period, but that weak tax revenue and declining donor support had led to reduced spending and accumulated arrears; the UN estimated that sanctions during the political crisis had cost the country US $600m. Humanitarian aid continued, such as $35m. from the US Agency for International Development (USAID) for health care projects and the UN's $151m. for a range of programmes. The USA excluded Madagascar from the benefits of its AGOA until June 2014.

The IMF formally re-established relations with Madagascar in March 2014, and approved US $47m. of funding under its Rapid Credit Facility. In May the EU announced that it would resume aid under the 11th EDF (2014–20).

An increase in development aid and tourism revenue after the presidential election helped to underpin higher levels of economic growth in 2013–14. However, the IMF remained concerned at the burden of continuing support for the state utility JIRAMA, as well as the low level of tax receipts.

In 2015 the Government set out the basis for a National Development Plan, with ambitious expectations of GDP growth of over 10% in 2018 and outside funding to cover one-half of the US $14,000m. needed in 2015–19. In 2016 the IMF expressed its satisfaction at the reduced inflation rate, and agreed an Extended Credit Facility (ECF) amounting to $320m.

During an official visit to China in March 2017, President Rajaonarimampianina signed several investment agreements, including one concerning the building of a new link road between the port of Toamasina and the RN2 highway. In June the IMF agreed to provide a second tranche of credit equivalent to US $85m., an amount higher than first proposed owing to the damage costs of Cyclone Enawo. In August the Fund offered a further loan of $50m. to clear the debts of Air Madagascar and to help offset the impact of the cyclone, while the World Bank provided $250m. towards social projects in the south of Madagascar and committed to provide $1,300m. for the period 2017–21 to support economic resilience and growth.

In August 2017 the Minister of Economy and Planning set out the basis for the National Development Plan, with its focus on good governance, macroeconomic stability, inclusive growth, human capital and natural capital with resilience to disasters. GDP growth in 2017 was marginally lower than in the previous year, in part due to the impact of Cyclone Enawo.

In late 2017 the AfDB proposed an allocation of US $2,000m. to Madagascar over five years, with a focus on infrastructure, energy, transport and agriculture, the German Government committed €65m. in support of the environment and renewable energy, and the World Bank a further $45m. to promote financial stability. The EU agreed to a loan of €120m. and aid of €120m. to improve roads, while the IMF approved a further $45m. under the credit arrangement agreed in 2016. Further aid followed in 2017.

In January 2018 President Rajaonarimampianina announced a plan called *Fisandratana 2030* (Regeneration 2030), which was intended to increase the rate of annual GDP growth to over 10%, create 5m. new jobs and raise Madagascar to a ranking of 70th on the UN's Human Development Index by 2030. The IMF approved the release of a further US $44.3m. of credit, and although it called for further action to reduce corruption, it gave broadly positive reports; further

disbursements brought the total amount under the ECF to some $304m. by July. President Rajoelina launched a new 13-pronged action plan in 2019, Initiative Emergence Madagascar, covering the period 2019–23. The World Bank approved financing for a wide range of projects, including $150m. towards the Government's target of doubling electricity access across the country from 15%. In January 2020 the EU provided funding of €65m. to help to provide better sanitation and water supplies in Antananarivo.

The substantial impact of the COVID-19 pandemic led to reduced growth expectations and to an eventual contraction in the economy of 4.2% in 2020, with particular weakness in the mining and tourism sectors.

Madagascar received significant overseas aid to help to manage the impact of the pandemic, calculated at some US $672m. by July 2020, including loans at favourable rates and of which $381m. had been disbursed by November. There was apparent progress in debt relief following an earlier accord with the IMF, under which Madagascar would be spared $16m. in monthly payments as interest or capital on debts to Group of 20—G20) countries. In September the World Bank agreed to provide a further $75m. to alleviate the impact of the crisis, while the EU committed a further €36m. with a focus on infrastructure spending and job creation. By November the Ministry of the Economy and Finance stated that the country had received $673.4m. in aid, of which $381m. had been disbursed. A report in January 2021 noted that only 9% (of now an estimated $836m. in emergency expenditure) had been spent on health, compared with one-third on infrastructure projects (notably sports stadia), and there were concerns that funds had been misappropriated.

As part of longer-term aid, the World Bank committed US $143m. in October 2020 to help Madagascar to computerize its system for identification requirements, as one-quarter of the population was estimated not to have an official identity. In July 2021 the World Bank announced funding for Madagascar of US $470m., including $200m. for the rehabilitation of 1,200 km of the road network and $140m. for the purchase of vaccines against COVID-19. In August the Bank provided a loan of $40m. to improve irrigation and to promote sustainable agriculture. In December the World Bank allocated $100m. for the upgrading of water points and anti-locust surveillance over a period of up to four years.

The budget for 2021, published in November 2020, forecast GDP growth of 4.5% in 2021 and allocated further funds to a number of presidential projects. The Government estimated that the budget deficit would narrow from 6.3% of GDP in 2020 to 5.5% in 2021, based on a 39% increase in net revenue to 6,400,000m. ariary, with budgeted expenditure (still dependent on external grants) amounting to 11,400,000m. ariary. The IMF forecast a more modest rate of growth in 2021 of 3%, while in January of that year the World Bank warned that Madagascar's economic recovery would be limited by a second wave of the virus, as well as potentially by the impact of natural disasters and social unrest. The World Bank noted that the country's medium-term prospects depended on an increase in productivity in agriculture and in formal employment in other sectors.

In February 2021 USAID agreed a new strategic plan for Madagascar, involving the provision of US $490m. in development assistance over the next five years. In March the IMF approved a new, $312m. ECF arrangement for Madagascar, which was to support efforts to mitigate the effects of the COVID-19 pandemic and of climate-related shocks, with an immediate disbursement of $69m. In July the World Bank provided $490m. of project funding. Madagascar also received aid to counter the worsening drought and food insecurity in the south of the country. WFP estimated in November 2020 that $35m. was needed, while in January 2021 the UN appealed for $76m. in aid. The USA promised up to $40m. in additional support to provide emergency food aid and to treat malnutrition, as well as for rebuilding wells to ensure access to clean water, while the UN released $8m. from its Central Emergency Response Fund.

Public finances improved during the late 2010s, with tax collection rates increasing from 10.5% in 2015 to 12.2% in 2019, according to the AfDB. However, the budget deficit widened, from 1.5% of GDP in 2018 to 2.4% in 2019, and was forecast to reach 4.1% in 2020, even before the onset of the COVID-19 crisis. Moreover, the current account of the balance of payments moved from a small positive balance of 0.8% of GDP in 2018 to a deficit of 0.2% in 2019. Inflation rose to 8.6% in 2018, before declining to 5.7% in 2019 and 4.2% in 2020; it then increased to 5.8% in 2021.

In 2021, according to the ITC, Madagascar's total imports amounted to US $4,400m., up by 35% on 2020 as a result of the recovery in the economy and a further small weakening in the ariary. China and other Asian countries accounted for 63.9% of imports and Europe 17.9%. The main imports in 2021 were mineral products, cereals and machinery. Exports also recovered strongly in 2021, when France accounted for 19.8% of the total, followed by the USA (18.9%), China and Japan. The main products exported in that year were agricultural products (principally vanilla), textiles, nickel and fish.

In January 2022 the World Bank provided further financing of US $40m to fund the country's vaccination programme, which was intended to cover 27% of the population in 2022 and a little over 50% by June 2023. The IMF agreed to release a further $67.5m. under its ECF arrangement, while calling for a detailed report into the use of funds during the pandemic. The World Bank provided $135m. to help with Madagascar's preparedness for a future pandemic and with basic health. In February the Ministry of Justice released a first audit report from the Court of Audit in relation to the initial funding of COVID-19 measures worth 1,800m., for which it identified a range of irregularities, such as insufficient paperwork and the use of cash payments; the Government had delayed its publication from December 2021. In March the Court of Audit released two further reports relating to social measures during the pandemic, which as with the first (and as with many countries) pointed to a range of irregularities. In June the World Bank confirmed funds of $220m. to improve water supply and sanitation for 3.4m. people in urban centres, of which one-half was in the form of a non-repayable donation. The World Bank also signed an accord for $158m. of funds to improve food security in the south of the country, as part of financing that totalled $2,300m. for 11 African countries under the Food Systems Resilience Programme.

Madagascar has in 2022 seen the impact of a further rise in the price of food and fuel arising from the Russian Federation's invasion of Ukraine in February, while there may be some benefit from the higher prices for commodities such as nickel. The country has previously imported 120,000 metric tons of cooking oil mostly from the Russian Federation and Ukraine, which accounted for 85% of total demand; it also took 50% of its wheat imports from Ukraine and 25% from Russia. The IMF revised its forecast for the rate of inflation in 2022 from 6.3% to 8.8%. The Government froze the price of a number of essential products in April, and in May President Rajoelina announced that minimum salaries in the private sector would rise from 200,000 ariary to 250,000 ariary, with the state covering the cost of the balance from the 10% rise offered by employers. Rajoelina led a delegation to Washington, DC, USA in April to hold meetings with the World Bank and the IMF. The institutions agreed funding of US $535m. to assist with two projects to provide resilience to the population against future shocks, as well as $415m. to support a plan for post-cyclone recovery; USAID also committed to a further $25m. of support.

In a 2022 report, the World Bank requested that Madagascar make further reforms to counter the impact of the pandemic, recent cyclones and the Russian invasion of Ukraine, which it estimated would lead to limited economic growth of 2.6% in 2022 as against 4.4% in 2021, with poverty levels set to remain at 81% of the population. The reforms included: a clear policy to accelerate the level of vaccination against COVID-19 of vulnerable people in urban and tourist areas; the rebuilding of infrastructure and restoration of public services after the cyclone damage; measures to boost the agricultural sector; changes to tariffs for fuel and electricity; a further push on access to the internet; and greater accountability in the public sector.

In April 2022 the Standard & Poor's agency gave Madagascar a rating of B–/B along with a positive outlook, which it said was in line with the average for sub-Saharan countries and reflected the benefit of recent reforms.

Statistical Survey

Sources (unless otherwise stated): Institut National de la Statistique de Madagascar, BP 485, Anosy Tana, 101 Antananarivo; tel. (20) 2221652; e-mail spdg@instat.mg; internet www.instat.mg; Ministry of the Economy and Planning, Bâtiment Commerce, Ambohidahy, 101 Antananarivo; internet www.economie.gov.mg.

Area and Population

AREA, POPULATION AND DENSITY

Area (sq km)	587,295*
Population (census results)	
1–19 August 1993	12,238,914
18 May–25 June 2018	
Males	12,658,945
Females	13,015,251
Total	25,674,196
Population (UN estimates at mid-year)	
2020	27,691,019
2021†	28,427,333
2022†	29,178,075
Density (per sq km) at mid-2022†	49.7

* 226,756 sq miles.
† Projection.

POPULATION BY AGE AND SEX
('000, UN projections at mid-2022)

	Males	Females	Total
0–14 years	5,828.3	5,713.3	11,541.6
15–64 years	8,300.6	8,395.0	16,695.7
65 years and over	430.9	510.0	940.9
Total	**14,559.8**	**14,618.3**	**29,178.1**

Note: Totals may not be equal to the sum of components, owing to rounding.

Source: UN, *World Population Prospects: The 2019 Revision.*

REGIONS
(at 2018 census)

	Area (sq km)	Population	Density (per sq km)
Alaotra Mangoro . . .	31,948	1,249,931	39.1
Amoron'i Mania . . .	16,141	837,116	51.9
Analamanga . . .	16,911	3,623,925	214.3
Analanjirofo . . .	21,930	1,150,089	52.4
Androy	19,317	900,235	46.6
Anosy	25,731	809,051	31.4
Atsimo Andrefana . .	66,236	1,797,894	27.1
Atsimo Antsinanana . .	18,863	1,030,404	54.6
Atsinanana	21,934	1,478,472	67.4
Betsiboka	30,025	393,278	13.1

—continued	Area (sq km)	Population	Density (per sq km)
Boeny	31,046	929,312	29.9
Bongolava	16,688	670,993	40.2
Diana	19,266	889,962	46.2
Haute Matsiatra . . .	21,080	1,444,587	68.5
Ihorombe	26,391	417,312	15.8
Itasy	6,993	898,549	128.5
Melaky	38,852	308,944	8.0
Menabe	46,121	692,463	15.0
Sava	25,518	1,123,772	44.0
Sofia	50,100	1,507,591	30.1
Vakinankaratra . . .	16,599	2,079,659	125.3
Vatovavy Fitovinany . .	19,605	1,440,657	73.5
Total	587,295	25,674,196	43.7

PRINCIPAL TOWNS
(population at 2018 census)

Antananarivo (capital) . . .	1,274,225	Mahajanga (Majunga) . . .	246,022
Toamasina (Tamatave) . .	325,857	Fianarantsoa . .	191,776
Antsirabé . . .	246,354	Toliary (Tuléar) . .	168,756
		Antsiranana (Diégo-Suarez) . . .	129,320

Mid-2021 (incl. suburbs, UN projections): Antananarivo 3,531,887; Toamasina 457,595; Antsirabé 372,920 (Source: UN, *World Urbanization prospects: The 2018 Revision*).

BIRTHS AND DEATHS

	2017	2018	2019
Birth rate (per 1,000) . . .	39.2	38.9	38.6
Death rate (per 1,000) . . .	7.4	7.2	7.1

Source: African Development Bank.

Life expectancy (years at birth, estimates): 67.4 (males 65.7; females 69.1) in 2020 (Source: World Bank, World Development Indicators database).

ECONOMICALLY ACTIVE POPULATION
(labour force survey, '000 persons aged 10 years and over, October–December 2012)

	Males	Females	Total
Agriculture, hunting, forestry and fishing	4,175.7	3,683.8	7,859.4
Mining and quarrying . . .	77.8	54.6	132.4
Electricity, gas and water . .			
Manufacturing	199.0	348.6	547.6
Construction	137.9	4.2	142.2
Wholesale and retail trade, transportation, accommodation and food; business and administrative services	517.8	586.4	1,104.3

—continued	Males	Females	Total
Public administration, community, social and other services and activities . .	304.0	352.0	656.0
Total employed . . .	5,412.3	5,029.6	10,441.9
Unemployed	55.4	78.1	133.5
Total labour force . . .	5,467.7	5,107.7	10,575.4

Source: ILO.

2015 (labour force survey, '000 persons aged 10 years and over): Agriculture, hunting, forestry and fishing 8,234; Mining and quarrying 105; Electricity, gas and water 13; Manufacturing 727; Construction 162; Wholesale and retail trade, repair of motor vehicles, motorcycles 800; Hotels and restaurants 51; Transport, storage and communications 160; Real estate, renting and business activities 64; Public administration and defence, compulsory social security 129; Education 197; Health and social work 40; Other community, social and personal service activities 169; Private households with employed persons 202; *Total employed* 11,052 (Source: ILO).

Health and Welfare

KEY INDICATORS

Total fertility rate (children per woman, 2020)	4.0
Under-5 mortality rate (per 1,000 live births, 2020) . . .	50.2
HIV/AIDS (% of persons aged 15–49, 2020)	0.3
COVID-19: Cumulative confirmed deaths (per 100,000 persons at 31 August 2022)	4.9
COVID-19: Fully vaccinated population (% of total population at 28 August 2022)	5.0
Physicians (per 1,000 head, 2018)	0.20
Hospitals (per 100,000 head, 2013)	0.5
Domestic health expenditure (2019): US $ per head (PPP) .	21.0
Domestic health expenditure (2019): % of GDP	1.2
Domestic health expenditure (2019): public (% of total current expenditure)	32.2
Access to improved water resources (% of persons, 2020) .	53
Access to improved sanitation facilities (% of persons, 2020) .	12
Total carbon dioxide emissions ('000 metric tons, 2018) . .	3,370
Carbon dioxide emissions per head (metric tons, 2018) . . .	0.1
Human Development Index (2021): ranking	173
Human Development Index (2021): value	0.501

Note: For data on COVID-19 vaccinations, 'fully vaccinated' denotes receipt of all doses specified by approved vaccination regime (Sources: Johns Hopkins University and Our World in Data). Data on health expenditure refer to current general government expenditure in each case. For more information on sources and further definitions for all indicators, see Health and Welfare Statistics: Sources and Definitions section (europaworld.com/credits).

Agriculture

PRINCIPAL CROPS
('000 metric tons)

	2018	2019	2020
Avocados*	27	27	27
Bananas*	375	376	374
Beans, dry	86	63	69
Cashew apples*	76	77	77
Cassava (Manioc)*	2,500	2,914	2,600
Cinnamon (Canella)* . . .	3	4	4
Cloves	24	23	24
Coconuts	58†	58*	56*
Coffee, green	56*	66	42
Groundnuts, in shell . . .	58	59	59*
Maize	215	219	
Mangoes, mangosteens and guavas*	304	309	304
Oil palm fruit*	21	21	21
Oranges*	84	84	84
Peas, dry*	20	20	20

—continued	2018	2019	2020
Pineapples*	86	85	85
Potatoes	257	250	247*
Rice, paddy	4,030	4,231	4,232
Sisal*	18	18	18
Sugar cane*	3,021	3,026	3,017
Sweet potatoes	1,089	1,113	1,131*
Taro (Cocoyam)*	229	228	227
Tobacco, unmanufactured* . .	1	1	1
Tomatoes*	40	40	40
Vanilla*	3	3	3

* FAO estimate(s).
† Unofficial figure.

Aggregate production ('000 metric tons, may include official, semi-official or estimated data): Total cereals 4,251 in 2018, 4,457 in 2019, 4,459 in 2020; Total fruit (primary) 1,262 in 2018, 1,265 in 2019, 1,259 in 2020; Total roots and tubers 4,075 in 2018, 4,505 in 2019, 4,205 in 2020; Total vegetables (primary) 458 in 2018, 454 in 2019, 456 in 2020.

Source: FAO.

LIVESTOCK
('000 head, year ending September)

	2019	2020*
Cattle	8,606	8,700	8,949
Chickens	39,488	40,276	41,318
Ducks	4,459*	4,486*	4,452
Geese and guinea fowls . . .	3,026*	3,027*	3,028
Goats	1,541	1,468	1,479
Pigs	1,731	1,763	1,769
Sheep	841	856	868
Turkeys	2,353*	2,333*	2,354

* FAO estimate(s).

Source: FAO.

LIVESTOCK PRODUCTS
('000 metric tons)

	2018	2019	2020*
Cattle hides, fresh	5.3*	5.3*	5.0
Cattle meat	37.0	37.4	34.9
Cattle offals, edible . . .	7.4*	7.5*	7.0
Cows' milk	476.7*	480.9*	491.3
Chicken meat	49.8*	50.5*	51.4
Duck meat	12.4*	12.4*	12.5
Goat meat	3.4	3.4	3.3
Goose meat	12.8	12.8	12.8
Pig meat	26.2	26.7	26.9
Turkey meat	9.9*	9.9*	10.0
Hen eggs	17.7*	17.6*	17.7
Other eggs	4.8*	4.8*	4.8
Honey (natural)	4.0*	4.0*	4.0

* FAO estimate(s).

Source: FAO.

Forestry

ROUNDWOOD REMOVALS
('000 cubic metres, excl. bark, FAO estimates)

	2018	2019	2020
Sawlogs, veneer logs and logs for sleepers	155	155	155
Pulpwood	10	10	10
Other industrial wood	8	8	8
Fuel wood	14,682	14,946	15,210
Total	14,855	15,120	15,384

Source: FAO.

SAWNWOOD PRODUCTION
('000 cubic metres, incl. railway sleepers)

	2016	2017	2018
Coniferous (softwood)	23	64	25
Broadleaved (hardwood) . . .	45	23	51
Total	68	87	76

2019–20: Production assumed to be unchanged from 2018 (FAO estimates).

Source: FAO.

Fishing
('000 metric tons, live weight)

	2018	2019	2020
Capture*	128.8	113.0	110.4
Cichlids	2.4	1.1	3.1
Other freshwater fishes . . .	12.9	10.9	13.1
Narrow-barred Spanish mackerel	3.8	3.8	3.8
Other marine fishes	64.4	48.2	57.6
Shrimps and prawns . . .	18.8	16.7	12.1
Aquaculture*	7.4	5.2	5.5
Giant tiger prawn	4.9	4.3	5.3
Total catch*	136.2	118.2	115.8

* FAO estimates.

Note: Figures exclude aquatic plants ('000 metric tons, capture only): 0.8 in 2018–20. Also excluded are crocodiles, recorded by number rather than weight, and shells.

Source: FAO.

Mining
(metric tons)

	2016	2017	2018
Chromite*†	107,735	208,100	109,200
Salt (marine)	107,295	110,000‡	110,000‡
Graphite (natural)*	9,200	13,300	47,900
Mica*	22,311	34,817	48,763

* Exports.
† Figures refer to gross weight. The estimated chromium content is 27%.
‡ Estimate.

Source: US Geological Survey.

Industry

SELECTED PRODUCTS
(metric tons unless otherwise indicated)

	2016	2017	2018
Raw sugar	87,000	—	—
Cement*	150,000	180,000	210,000
Electrical energy (million kWh)† .	1,886	1,994	2,095

* Estimated figures.
† Production by the state-owned utility only, excluding electricity generated by industries for their own use.

Raw sugar (million kWh): 57,210 in 2014; 86,950 in 2015 (Source: UN Industrial Commodity Statistics Database).

Electrical energy (million kWh): 2,162 in 2019; 2,119 in 2020 (Source: UN Energy Statistics Database).

Sources: US Geological Survey; UN Industrial Commodity Statistics Database; UN Energy Statistics Database.

Finance

CURRENCY AND EXCHANGE RATES

Monetary Units
5 iraimbilanja = 1 ariary.

Sterling, Dollar and Euro Equivalents (31 May 2022)
£1 sterling = 5,011.68 ariary;
US $1 = 3,981.00 ariary;
€1 = 4,264.85 ariary;
10,000 ariary = £2.00 = $2.51= €2.34.

Average Exchange Rate (ariary per US $)
2019   3,618.3
2020   3,787.8
2021   3,830.0

BUDGET
('000 million ariary, central government operations)

Revenue and grants	2018	2019	2020*
Tax revenue	5,003	5,618	4,845
Domestic tax revenue . . .	2,575	2,870	2,658
Taxes on international trade and transactions	2,428	2,748	2,187
Non-tax revenue	133	141	163
Grants	1,231	1,586	919
Total	6,367	7,346	5,926

Expenditure	2018	2019	2020*
Current expenditure	4,619	5,089	5,263
Wages and salaries . . .	2,331	2,497	2,780
Goods and services . . .	1,412	1,909	2,246
Interest payments	353	356	355
Domestic	248	249	246
Foreign	105	107	109
Other	524	328	−118
Capital expenditure	2,449	2,936	2,986
Total	7,068	8,025	8,248

* Provisional.

Source: Central Bank of Madagascar, Antananarivo.

INTERNATIONAL RESERVES
(excl. gold, US $ million at 31 December)

	2019	2020	2021
IMF special drawing rights . .	2.9	11.4	339.9
Reserve position in IMF . .	42.4	44.1	42.9
Foreign exchange	1,647.9	1,925.3	1,951.8
Total	1,693.2	1,980.8	2,334.6

Source: IMF, *International Financial Statistics*.

MONEY SUPPLY
('000 million ariary at 31 December)

	2019	2020	2021
Currency outside depository corporations	3,294.09	3,553.76	4,096.24
Transferable deposits . . .	5,435.87	6,128.57	6,534.24
Other deposits	3,744.28	4,175.56	4,784.41
Securities other than shares . .	88.61	92.92	66.19
Broad money	12,562.85	13,950.81	15,481.08

Source: IMF, *International Financial Statistics*.

COST OF LIVING
(Consumer Price Index for Malagasy in Antananarivo; base: 2016 = 100)

	2019	2020	2021
Food	127.0	131.8	141.6
Clothing	115.2	120.3	127.7
Housing, water, electricity, gas and other fuels	128.4	134.4	137.7
All items (incl. others) . . .	124.6	129.8	137.3

NATIONAL ACCOUNTS
('000 million ariary at current prices)

Expenditure on the Gross Domestic Product

	2018	2019	2020
Government final consumption expenditure	6,242	7,709	9,061
Private final consumption expenditure	33,047	36,182	37,990
Increase in stocks	−151	733	−678
Gross fixed capital formation . .	9,651	10,844	9,699
Statistical discrepancy . . .	−714	−1,497	−2,305
Total domestic expenditure .	48,075	53,971	53,767
Exports of goods and services . .	14,471	14,506	9,957
Less Imports of goods and services	16,659	17,442	14,271
GDP in purchasers' values .	45,886	51,035	49,453
GDP at constant 2007 prices .	20,956	21,881	20,319

Gross Domestic Product by Economic Activity

	2018	2019	2020
Agriculture, hunting, forestry and fishing	11,000	11,716	12,423
Mining and quarrying	2,118	2,116	980
Manufacturing	4,299	5,149	4,808
Electricity, gas and water . . .	359	397	404
Construction	3,081	3,793	3,432
Wholesale and retail trade, restaurants and hotels . . .	6,054	6,876	5,948
Transport and communications .	3,524	3,901	4,253
Finance, insurance, real estate and business services	5,285	5,804	5,115
Public administration and defence	4,617	5,775	6,091
Education	1,345	1,535	1,543
Health and social work . . .	1,540	1,526	1,594
Sub-total	43,222	48,588	46,590
Less Financial intermediation services indirectly measured (FISIM)	775	950	1,053
GDP at basic prices . . .	42,447	47,638	45,537
Indirect taxes, less subsidies . .	3,439	3,397	3,916
GDP in purchasers' values .	45,886	51,035	49,453

BALANCE OF PAYMENTS
(US $ million)

	2018	2019	2020
Exports of goods f.o.b.	3,035.7	2,612.1	1,948.3
Imports of goods f.o.b.	−3,493.3	−3,456.5	−2,848.6
Balance on goods	−457.5	−844.4	−900.2
Exports of services	1,371.8	1,484.3	648.6
Imports of services	−1,327.8	−1,240.8	−904.4
Balance on goods and services	−413.5	−600.9	−1,156.0
Primary income received . . .	52.7	60.7	45.6
Primary income paid	−513.2	−579.1	−496.7
Balance on goods, services and primary income	−874.0	−1,119.3	−1,607.1
Secondary income received . .	1,055.3	873.8	965.1

—continued			2018	2019	2020
Secondary income paid	.	. .	−83.3	−80.8	−75.8
Current balance	.	. .	98.0	−326.3	−717.7
Capital account (net)	.	. .	239.8	335.3	214.7
Direct investment assets	.	. .	−117.9	−101.6	−119.1
Direct investment liabilities	.	.	612.0	474.3	358.5
Portfolio investment assets	.	.	−0.4	−0.1	2.3
Other investment assets	.	. .	−343.0	1.3	−103.1
Other investment liabilities	.	.	−156.0	−440.9	103.3
Net errors and omissions	.	. .	−198.8	−61.1	116.1
Reserves and related items		.	133.8	−119.1	−145.0

Source: IMF, *International Financial Statistics*.

External Trade

PRINCIPAL COMMODITIES
(distribution by HS, US $ million)

Imports c.i.f.	2019	2020	2021
Vegetables and vegetable products	270.0	281.1	436.1
Cereals and cereal preparations .	164.3	205.5	351.6
Rice	144.7	180.3	272.9
Animal or vegetable fats and oils, and products thereof .	115.7	153.8	200.7
Prepared foodstuffs; beverages, spirits, vinegars; tobacco and articles thereof .	211.2	186.9	257.2
Mineral products	826.6	481.4	876.3
Salt, sulphur, earth, stone, plaster, lime and cement	141.0	76.4	187.9
Mineral fuels, oils, distillation products, etc.	685.3	404.8	688.2
Petroleum oils, not crude . .	621.9	369.1	604.0
Chemicals and related products	338.9	315.9	389.2
Medicinal and pharmaceutical products	146.4	140.8	161.1
Medicaments consisting of mixed or unmixed products . . .	118.5	104.0	109.0
Plastics, rubber, and articles thereof	175.4	148.0	194.6
Plastics and articles thereof . .	132.6	110.8	147.4
Pulp of wood, paper and paperboard, and articles thereof	109.7	105.7	94.8
Textiles and textile articles .	569.8	501.5	663.2
Iron and steel; other base metals and articles of base metal	214.2	185.9	195.3
Machinery and mechanical appliances; electrical equipment; parts thereof .	470.8	419.0	565.0
Machinery, boilers, etc. . . .	289.9	258.2	345.4
Electrical, electronic equipment .	180.9	160.8	219.6
Vehicles, aircraft, vessels and associated transport equipment	315.6	217.2	219.2
Vehicles other than railway, tramway	281.5	188.3	201.0
Motor vehicles for the transport of goods, incl. chassis with engine and cab	130.5	61.4	76.0
Total (incl. others)	3,896.9	3,227.3	4,380.3

Exports f.o.b.	2019	2020	2021
Live animals and animal products	115.8	114.6	112.3
Fish, crustaceans and molluscs and preparations thereof	114.7	113.8	111.1
Crustaceans	98.3	97.1	95.9
Vegetables and vegetable products	769.3	698.1	871.2
Coffee, tea, cocoa, spices . . .	663.4	595.9	753.9
Vanilla	573.2	511.5	620.4
Cloves	74.9	63.6	115.4
Prepared foodstuffs; beverages, spirits, vinegar; tobacco and articles thereof .	109.9	108.2	94.4
Mineral products	213.7	180.2	251.6
Ores, slag and ash	130.1	129.4	187.3
Titanium ores and concentrates.	81.8	96.5	143.5
Chemicals and related products	78.2	81.8	110.8
Essential oils and resinoids; perfumery, cosmetic	60.5	70.5	77.3
Essential oils concretes and absolutes	60.1	69.8	77.0
Textiles and textile articles	513.4	424.0	524.7
Articles of apparel and clothing accessories	485.6	391.6	489.6
Jerseys, pullovers, cardigans (knitted or crocheted) . . .	116.6	101.1	91.9
Men's or boys' suits, ensembles, jackets, blazers, trousers . .	82.5	79.4	110.1
Pearls, precious or semi-precious stones, precious metals, and articles thereof .	117.3	96.6	43.4
Gold, incl. gold plated with platinum, unwrought . . .	84.6	68.9	0.0
Iron and steel; other base metals and articles of base metal	559.6	181.6	623.8
Nickel and articles thereof . .	451.1	146.8	514.3
Unwrought nickel	451.1	143.2	507.6
Other base metals, cermets, and articles thereof	102.9	33.7	106.2
Cobalt mattes and other intermediate products of cobalt metallurgy	102.9	33.1	106.1
Total (incl. others)	2,564.4	1,956.9	2,718.7

Source: Trade Map-Trade Competitiveness Map, International Trade Centre, /marketanalysis.intracen.org.

PRINCIPAL TRADING PARTNERS
(US $ million)

Imports	2019	2020	2021
Argentina	32.3	21.4	64.5
Belgium	43.5	40.5	40.2
Brazil	28.7	43.4	70.7
China, People's Republic . . .	874.6	818.1	999.8
Egypt	107.3	114.3	118.3
France	261.7	232.1	247.5
Germany	98.8	78.5	94.4
India	314.9	276.1	391.8
Indonesia	57.8	48.5	58.1
Italy	66.3	59.5	68.8
Japan	104.1	39.1	108.8
Korea, Republic	37.9	47.5	47.7
Malaysia	87.0	108.8	149.0
Mauritius	100.8	98.2	125.8
Myanmar	41.4	32.9	0.0
Netherlands	51.1	20.7	24.6
Oman	9.1	50.5	389.0
Pakistan	109.4	65.5	124.3

Imports—*continued*	2019	2020	2021
Qatar	76.3	8.4	48.8
Saudi Arabia	46.0	77.0	60.4
South Africa	175.0	134.3	194.0
Spain	50.9	40.3	46.9
Taiwan	39.5	31.8	31.8
Thailand	42.2	28.9	25.6
Türkiye	84.6	79.5	71.8
United Arab Emirates . . .	381.7	212.7	227.1
USA	84.4	76.4	105.3
Total (incl. others)	3,896.9	3,227.3	4,380.3

Exports	2019	2020	2021
Belgium	25.6	17.3	24.0
Canada	73.0	63.0	148.2
China, People's Republic . . .	167.2	117.5	368.5
France	525.7	452.6	536.8
Germany	142.9	162.1	126.6
India	73.9	77.1	105.3
Indonesia	23.4	22.3	41.2
Japan	166.0	61.7	239.8
Korea, Republic	123.5	35.9	12.3
Mauritius	41.2	20.1	29.2
Netherlands	115.3	85.4	143.8
Singapore	11.4	14.9	32.8
South Africa	86.2	58.8	90.2
Spain	43.8	31.8	18.6
Sweden	37.3	15.9	11.3
Switzerland	15.7	17.3	32.1
Taiwan	47.1	14.0	46.0
United Arab Emirates . . .	95.7	76.3	22.9
United Kingdom	45.6	27.3	27.2
USA	513.5	440.5	506.9
Total (incl. others)	2,564.4	1,956.9	2,718.7

Source: Trade Map-Trade Competitiveness Map, International Trade Centre, marketanalysis.intracen.org.

Transport

ROAD TRAFFIC
(new vehicle registrations in Antananarivo)

	2018	2019	2020
Passenger cars	3,048	5,539	6,146
Other private vehicles	4,306	4,327	3,546
Commercial vehicles . . .	5,376	3,460	n.a.
Motorcycles	2,325	1,353	1,353

SHIPPING

Flag Registered Fleet
(at 31 December)

	2019	2020	2021
Number of vessels	43	43	42
Displacement ('000 grt) . . .	24.8	24.8	24.2

Source: Lloyd's List Intelligence (www.bit.ly/LLintelligence).

CIVIL AVIATION
(traffic on scheduled services)

	2013	2014	2015
Kilometres flown (million) . .	10	11	10
Passengers carried ('000) . . .	539	520	547
Passenger-km (million) . . .	1,372	1,309	1,302
Total ton-km (million)	35	31	31

Source: UN, *Statistical Yearbook*.

2020 (domestic and international): Departures 4,225; Passengers carried 186,314; Freight carried 5.4m. ton-km (Source: World Bank, World Development Indicators database).

Tourism

TOURIST ARRIVALS BY NATIONALITY

	2018	2019	2020
China, People's Republic . . .	6,285	9,085	2,514
Comoros	6,084	6,221	2,465
France	70,886	115,115	15,365
Germany	5,449	8,415	2,138
Italy	43,984	98,525	4,548
Mauritius	5,448	7,667	2,411
South Africa	2,513	3,864	1,007
Spain	3,653	4,638	1,318
United Kingdom	3,561	5,212	3,864
USA	6,383	7,909	3,678
Total (incl. others)	291,299	383,717	68,330

Source: World Tourism Organization.

Total tourist arrivals: 383,717 in 2019; 68,330 in 2020; 31,689 in 2021 (provisional).

Tourism receipts (US $ million): 668 in 2017; 489 in 2018; 534 in 2019.

Communications Media

	2018	2019	2020
Telephones (main lines in use) .	69,046	69,000	69,000
Mobile telephone subscriptions ('000)	10,654.7	13,003.0	15,869.0
Broadband subscriptions, fixed .	27,211	30,000	32,000
Broadband subscriptions, mobile ('000)	4,097.4	5,061.0	6,176.0
Internet users (% of population) .	15.0	n.a.	n.a.

Source: International Telecommunication Union.

Education

(public and private schools, 2018/19 unless otherwise indicated)

		Pupils		
	Teachers	Males	Females	Total
Pre-primary (all programmes)	40,521	433,518	468,442	901,960
Primary (all programmes) .	126,649	2,324,032	2,324,568	4,648,600
Secondary: General . .	82,444	735,733	758,787	1,494,520
Secondary: Vocational* .	4,318	23,755	12,338	36,093
Tertiary†	5,748	77,411	75,018	152,429

* 2017/18 figures.
† 2019/20.

Source: UNESCO Institute for Statistics.

2005/06: 6 universities; 14 private institutes of higher education.

Pupil-teacher ratio (qualified teaching staff, primary education, UNESCO estimate): 36.8 in 2018/19 (Source: UNESCO Institute for Statistics).

Adult literacy rate (UNESCO estimates): 76.7% (males 78.4%; females 75.1%) in 2018 (Source: UNESCO Institute for Statistics).

Directory

The Constitution

On 17 November 2010 the Constitution of the Fourth Republic of Madagascar was approved at a national referendum by some 74% of the participating electorate. The Constitution entered into effect on 11 December. The President of the Republic is the head of state and is elected by direct universal suffrage for a five-year mandate, renewable only once. Candidates for the presidency must be at least 35 years of age and have resided in Madagascar for a minimum of six months prior to the date of the submission of their candidacy. The President nominates a Prime Minister from the party or group of parties that secures the largest number of seats in the Assemblée Nationale (National Assembly). The President also nominates members of the Government, upon the advice of the Prime Minister. Members of the National Assembly are elected by direct universal suffrage for a term of five years. The Constitution also provides for the election of members to the Sénat (Senate); each senator serves a five-year mandate.

The Government

HEAD OF STATE

President: ANDRY NIRINA RAJOELINA (inaugurated 19 January 2019).

COUNCIL OF MINISTERS
(October 2022)

Prime Minister: CHRISTIAN NTSAY.

Minister of National Defence and Acting Minister of Foreign Affairs: Gen. LÉON JEAN RICHARD RAKOTONIRINA.

Keeper of the Seals, Minister of Justice: FRANÇOIS RAKOTOZAFY.

Minister of Territorial Management and Land Affairs: PIERRE HOLDER RAMAHOLIMASY.

Minister of the Economy and Finance: RINDRA HASIMBELO RABARINIRINARISON.

Minister of the Interior and Decentralization: JUSTIN TOKELY.

Minister of Public Security: FANOMEZANTSOA RODELLYS RANDRIANARISON.

Minister of Industrialization, Trade and Consumer Affairs: EDGARD RAZAFINDRAVAHY.

Minister of Labour, Employment, the Civil Service and Social Law: GISÈLE RANAMPY.

Minister of Tourism: JOËL RANDRIAMANDRANTO.

Minister of Youth and Sport: TINOKA ROBERTO RAHAROARILALA.

Minister of Communication and Culture: LALATIANA ANDRIATONGARIVO RAKOTONDRAZAFY.

Minister of Higher Education and Scientific Research: ELIA BÉATRICE ASSOUMACOU.

Minister of National Education: MARIE MICHELLE SAHONDRARIMALALA.

Minister of Public Health: Prof. ARIVELO ZELY RANDRIAMANANTANY.

Minister of Transport and Meteorology: ROLLAND RANJATOELINA.

Minister of Public Works: JERRY HATREFINDRAZANA.

Minister of Agriculture and Stockbreeding: HARIFIDY RAMILISON.

Minister of Fishing and the Blue Economy: PAUBERT MAHATANTE.

Minister of Energy and Hydrocarbons: LANTONIAINA RASOLOELISON.

Minister of Water, Sanitation and Hygiene: FINDINIAVO RAVOKATRA.

Minister of Handicrafts and Trades: SOPHIE RATSIRAKA.

Minister of Technical Education and Professional Training: RAHANTANIRINA GABRIELLA VAVITSARA.

Minister of Digital Development, Digital Transformation, Postal Services and Telecommunications: TAHIANA RAZAFINDRAMALO.

Minister of Population, Social Protection and the Promotion of Women: PRINCIA SOAFILIRA.

Minister of Mining and Strategic Resources: HERINDRAINY OLIVIER RAKOTOMALALA.

Minister of the Environment and Sustainable Development: MARIE-ORLÉA VINA.

Secretary of State at the Ministry of National Defence, responsible for the National Gendarmerie: Gen. SERGE GELLE.

Secretary of State at the Presidency of the Republic, responsible for New Cities and Housing: GÉRARD ANDRIAMANOHISOA.

Deputy Minister at the Ministry of Agriculture and Stockbreeding, responsible for Stockbreeding: Dr RAYMOND.

MINISTRIES

Office of the President: BP 955, 101 Antananarivo; tel. (20) 2254703; internet www.presidence.gov.mg.

Office of the Prime Minister: Palais d'Etat Mahazoarivo, BP 248, 101 Antananarivo; tel. (20) 2265010; e-mail cellcom@primature.gov.mg; internet www.primature.gov.mg.

Ministry of Agriculture and Stockbreeding: rue Pierre Stibbe, BP 301, Anosy, 101 Antananarivo; tel. (20) 2261002; internet www.minae.gov.mg.

Ministry of Communication and Culture: BP 305, Anosy, 101 Antananarivo; internet www.mcc-gov.mg.

Ministry of Digital Development, Digital Transformation, Postal Services and Telecommunications: pl. Philibert Tsiranana, Antaninarenina, 101 Antananarivo; tel. 341610259; e-mail contact.dcp@mndpt.gov.mg; internet www.mptdn.gov.mg.

Ministry of the Economy and Finance: Immeuble Antaninarenina, Porte 305, Antananarivo; tel. (20) 2264683; internet www.mefb.gov.mg.

Ministry of Energy and Hydrocarbons: BP 896, rue Farafaty Ampandrianomby, 101 Antananarivo; tel. (20) 2259556; e-mail memcab@yahoo.fr; internet www.mineau.gov.mg.

Ministry of the Environment and Sustainable Development: rue Fernand Kasanga, Tsimbazaza, BP 610, 101 Antananarivo; tel. 340562073; e-mail meddcom5@gmail.com; internet www.environnement.mg.

Ministry of Fishing and the Blue Economy: Antananarivo; e-mail mpeb.contact@gmail.com; internet fb.com/MPEBMADAGASCAR.

Ministry of Foreign Affairs: rue Andriamifidy, Anosy, BP 836, 101 Antananarivo; tel. (20) 2221196; internet www.diplomatie.gov.mg.

Ministry of Handicrafts and Trades: 101 Antananarivo.

Ministry of Higher Education and Scientific Research: 101 Antananarivo; internet www.mesupres.gov.mg.

Ministry of Industrialization, Trade and Consumer Affairs: BP 527, Antananarivo; tel. 343080069; internet www.industrie.gov.mg.

Ministry of the Interior and Decentralization: BP 833, Anosy, 101 Antananarivo; tel. (20) 2223084; internet www.mid.gov.mg.

Ministry of Justice: rue Joel Rakotomalala, BP 231, Faravohitra, 101 Antananarivo; tel. (20) 2237684; internet www.justice.mg.

Ministry of Labour, Employment, the Civil Service and Social Law: pl. Philibert Tsiranana, Antaninarenina, BP 207, 101 Antananarivo; tel. 341610259; e-mail contact.dcp@mndpt.gov.mg; internet www.mndpt.gov.mg.

Ministry of Mining and Strategic Resources: rue Farafaty Ampandrianomby, BP 280, 101 Antananarivo; tel. 320311099; internet mmrs.gov.mg.

Ministry of National Defence: BP 08, Ampahibe, 101 Antananarivo; tel. (20) 2222211; e-mail mdndico@gmail.com; internet www.defense.gov.mg.

Ministry of National Education: BP 247, Anosy, 101 Antananarivo; tel. (20) 2224308; e-mail mlraharimalala@yahoo.fr; internet www.education.gov.mg.

Ministry of Population, Social Protection and the Promotion of Women: 41 rue Razanakombana, Ambohijatovo, 101 Antananarivo; tel. 330968906; internet www.population.gov.mg.

Ministry of Public Health: BP 88, Ambohidahy, 101 Antananarivo; tel. (20) 2223697; e-mail communication.msanp2@gmail.com; internet www.sante.gov.mg.

Ministry of Public Security: rue Pierre Stubbe, Anosy, BP 23 bis, 101 Antananarivo; tel. (20) 2221029; internet www.pn.gov.mg.

Ministry of Public Works: rue Jules Ranaivo, 101 Antananarivo; tel. (20) 2228715; internet www.mahtp.gov.mg.

Ministry of Technical Education and Professional Training: Complexe Scolaire Ampefiloha, Bâtiment H, BP 793, 101 Antananarivo; e-mail contact.metfp@gmail.com; internet www.metfp.gov.mg.

Ministry of Territorial Management and Land Affairs: Antananarivo.

Ministry of Tourism: rue Jules Ranaivo Anosy, BP 4139, Antananarivo; tel. (20) 2224604; e-mail mtmmadagascar@gmail.com; internet fb.com/MTTMMadagascar.

Ministry of Transport and Meteorology: 101 Antananarivo; tel. (20) 2262816; internet fb.com/MTTMMadagascar.

Ministry of Water, Sanitation and Hygiene: Antananarivo; e-mail scomeah@gmail.com; internet fb.com/meahmadagascar.

Ministry of Youth and Sport: pl. Goulette Ambohijatovo, BP 681, 101 Antananarivo; internet www.mjs.gov.mg.

President

Presidential Election, First Round, 7 November 2018

Candidate	Votes	% of votes
Andry Nirina Rajoelina	1,954,023	39.23
Marc Ravalomanana	1,760,837	35.36
Hery Martial Rajaonarimampianina Rakotoarimanana	439,070	8.82
André Christian Dieudonné Mailhol	63,391	1.27
Joseph Martin Randriamampionona	57,903	1.16
Ny Rado Rafalimanana	57,476	1.15
Others	647,904*	13.01
Total	4,980,604†	100.00

* There were 30 other candidates.

† Excluding 386,946 blank or invalid votes.

Presidential Election, Second Round, 19 December 2018

Candidate	Votes	% of votes
Andry Nirina Rajoelina	2,586,938	55.66
Marc Ravalomanana	2,060,847	44.34
Total	4,647,785*	100.00

* Excluding 119,557 blank or invalid votes.

Legislature

NATIONAL ASSEMBLY

National Assembly: Antananarivo; e-mail poste@assemblee-nationale.mg; internet assemblee-nationale.mg.

President: CHRISTINE RAZANAMAHASOA.

General Election, 27 May 2019

Party	Seats
Isika Rehetra Miaraka amin'i Andry Rajoelina (IRD)	84
Tiako i Madagasikara (TIM)	16
Groupement des Jeunes Malagasy Patriotiques (GJMP)	1
Malagasy Tia Tanindrazana (MATITA)	1
Malagasy Tonga Saina (MTS)	1
Mouvement pour la Démocratie à Madagascar (MDM)	1
Rassemblement pour le Socialisme et la Démocratie—Nouveau (RPSD—Nouveau)	1
Independents	46
Total	151

SENATE

Senate: Antananarivo; e-mail commsenatmada@gmail.com; internet fb.com/SenatdeMadagascar.

President: HERIMANANA RAZAFIMAHEFA.

Senatorial Election, 11 December 2020

Party	Seats
Isika Rehetra Miaraka amin'i Andry Rajoelina (IRMAR)	10
Malagasy Miara-Miainga (MMM)	2
Total	12*

* Two senators are elected from each of the six provinces by an electoral college of regional councillors and mayors in each province. An additional six senators are appointed by the President.

Election Commission

Commission Electorale Nationale Indépendante (CENI): Immeuble Microréalisation, 4e étage, 67 ha, 101 Antananarivo; tel. (20) 2225179; internet www.ceni-madagascar.mg; f. 2010; temporarily replaced by the Commission Electorale Nationale Indépendante pour la Transition (CENIT) during 2012–14; 9 mems; Pres. YVES HERINIRINA RAKOTOMANANA.

Political Organizations

Antoko Maitso Hasin'i Madagasikara (AMHM) (Madagascar Green Party): Lot VK 99, Fenomanana, Morarano, BP 682, 101 Antananarivo; tel. 340220664; e-mail madahasin@gmail.com; internet hasinimadagasikara.mg; f. 2009; Pres. ALEXANDRE MARIE GEORGET.

Antoko Malagasy Miara-Miainga (MMM): Lot II H 41, M Ankadindramamy Ankerana, Antananarivo; tel. (34) 9683394; e-mail malagasymiaramiainga2014@gmail.com; internet malagasy-miara-miainga.org; Pres. HAJO ANDRIANAINARIVELO.

Antoko ny Vahoaka Aloha no Andrianina (AVANA): mem. of the Alliance pour la Restauration de la Démocratie (ARD); Leader JEAN LOUIS ROBINSON.

Comité pour la Réconciliation Nationale (CRN): Villa la Franchise, Lot II-I 160 A, Alarobia, Antananarivo; tel. (20) 2242022; f. 2002; radical opposition; Leader ALBERT ZAFY.

Hasin'i Madagasikara: Lot VK 99, Fenomanana, Morarano, BP 682, 101 Antananarivo; tel. 340220664; e-mail madahasin@gmail.com; internet hasinimadagasikara.mg; f. 2009; green party; Pres. GEORGET ALEXANDRE.

Hery Vaovao ho an'i Madagasikara (HVM): Antananarivo; Leader HERY MARTIAL RAJAONARIMAMPIANINA RAKOTOARIMANANA.

Libéralisme Economique et Action Démocratique pour la Reconstruction Nationale (LEADER/Fanilo) (Torch): f. 1993 by Herizo Razafimahaleo; Sec.-Gen. MANASSÉ ESOAVELOMANDROSO.

Malagasy Tonga Saina (MTS): Antananarivo; Pres. IAROVANA ROLAND RATSIRAKA.

Miaraka amin'ny Prezidà Andry Rajoelina (MAPAR): Antananarivo; Leader ANDRY RAJOELINA.

Mouvement pour la Démocratie à Madagascar (MDM): Villa Khannet, Maibahoaka, Ambohidratrimo; tel. (34) 3118672; internet www.mdm-iarivo.mg; Pres. PIERROT RAJAONARIVELO.

Mouvement pour le Progrès de Madagascar (Mpitolona ho Amin'ny Fandrosoan'ny Madagasikara) (MFM): 42 & 44 Cité Ampefiloha Bldg, 101 Antananarivo; tel. (20) 2437560; f. 1972 as Mouvement pour le Pouvoir Prolétarien (MFM); adopted present name in 1990; advocates liberal and market-orientated policies; Leader MANANDAFY RAKOTONIRINA; Sec.-Gen. OLIVIER RAKOTOVAZAHA.

Parti Hiaraka Isika (PHI): Leader Brig.-Gen. ALBERT CAMILLE VITAL.

Parti Socialiste et Démocratique pour l'Union de Madagascar (PSDUM): f. 2006; Pres. JEAN LAHINIRIKO.

Rassemblement pour le Socialisme et la Démocratie (RPSD): f. 1993; Leader EVARISTE MARSON.

TAMBATRA: Antananarivo; internet tambatra.free.fr; Pres. PETY RAKOTONIAINA.

Tiako i Madagasikara (TIM) (I Love Madagascar): f. 2002; supports former Pres. Ravalomanana; Pres. YVAN RANDRIASANDRATRINIONY.

Diplomatic Representation

EMBASSIES IN MADAGASCAR

Algeria: rue Reverend Pere Callet, Antananarivo; tel. (20) 2222864; e-mail ambalg.tnr@moov.mg; Ambassador MALEK DJAOUD.

China, People's Republic: Nanisana Ambatobe, BP 1658, 101 Antananarivo; tel. (20) 2240129; e-mail ambchinemada@yahoo.com; internet mg.china-embassy.gov.cn; Ambassador GUO XIAOMEI.

Comoros: Lot IB 50, rue du Dr Théodore Villette, Isoraka, 101 Antananarivo; tel. (20) 2224982; e-mail amba.comores_tana@yahoo.fr; internet fb.com/ambacomorestana; Ambassador CAABI EL-YACHROUTU.

Egypt: Lot MD 378 Ambalatokana Mandrosoa Ivato, BP 4082, 101 Antananarivo; tel. (20) 2245497; e-mail embassy.antananarivo@mfa.gov.eg; internet www.mfa.gov.eg/french/embassies/egyptian_embassy_antananarivo; Ambassador USAMA SAEED MAHMOUD KHALIL.

France: 3 rue Jean Jaurès, BP 204, 101 Antananarivo; tel. (20) 2239898; e-mail ambatana@moov.mg; internet mg.ambafrance.org; Ambassador ARNAUD GUILLOIS (designate).

Germany: 101 rue du Pasteur Rabeony Hans, BP 516, Ambodirotra, 101 Antananarivo; tel. (20) 2223802; e-mail info@antananarivo.diplo .de; internet antananarivo.diplo.de; Ambassador MICHAEL GERHARD KARL HÄUSLER.

Holy See: Amboniloha Ivandry, BP 650, 101 Antananarivo; tel. (20) 2242376; Apostolic Nuncio TOMASZ GRYSA (Titular Archbishop of Rubicon).

India: 4 Làlana Emile Rajaonson, Tsaralalana, BP 1787, 101 Antananarivo; tel. (20) 2223334; e-mail amb.aanarivo@mea.gov.in; internet www.eoiantananarivo.gov.in; Ambassador BANDARU WILSONBABU (designate).

Indonesia: Lot II, J Ter A, Ivandry, 26–28 rue Patrice Lumumba, BP 3969, 101 Antananarivo; tel. (20) 2224915; e-mail antananarivo .kbri@kemlu.go.id; internet www.kemlu.go.id/antananarivo; Chargé d'affaires BENNY YAN PIETER SIAHAAN.

Iran: route Circulaire, Lot II L43 ter, Ankadivato, 101 Antananarivo; tel. (20) 2228527; e-mail iranemb.tnr@mfa.gov.ir; internet madagascar.mfa.gov.ir; Chargé d'affaires a.i. HASSAN ALI BAKHSHI.

Japan: Villa Chrysanthème III, Ambohijatovo-Analamahitsy, BP 3863, 101 Antananarivo; tel. (20) 2249357; internet www.mg .emb-japan.go.jp; Ambassador YOSHIHIRO HIGUCHI.

Korea, Republic: Immeuble Fitaratra, 9ème étage nord, rue Ravoninahitriniarivo, Ankorondrano, 101 Antananarivo; tel. (20) 2222933; e-mail ambcoreemg@mofa.go.kr; internet overseas.mofa .go.kr/mg-fr/index.do; Ambassador SON YONG-HO.

Libya: Lot IIB, 37A route Circulaire Ampandrana-Ouest, 101 Antananarivo; tel. (20) 2221892; e-mail libyanembassy_tana@ yahoo.com; Chargé d'affaires a.i. Dr MOHAMED ALI SHARFEDIN AL-FITURI.

Mauritius: Office No 1105, Lot II J 172B, rue Ranaivo Paul, Ivandry, 101 Antananarivo; tel. (20) 2221864; e-mail tanaemb@govmu.org; internet mauritius-antananarivo.govmu.org/Pages/index.aspx; Ambassador MARIE NOËLLE FRANÇOISE LABELLE.

Morocco: Bâtiment D1, Rez-de-Chaussée, Ankorondrano, BP 12, 104 Antananarivo; tel. (20) 2221347; e-mail ambmaroctana@gmail .com; internet fb.com/ambassadedumarocmadagascar; Ambassador MOHAMED BENJILANI.

Russian Federation: Ivandry-Ambohijatovo, BP 4006, 101 Antananarivo; tel. (20) 2242827; e-mail madagascar@mid.ru; internet madagascar.mid.ru; Ambassador ANDREI V. ANDREEV.

South Africa: Lot IVO 68 bis, rue Ravoninahitriniarivo, Ankorondrano, BP 12101-05, 101 Antananarivo; tel. (20) 2243350; e-mail antananarivo.consular@dirco.gov.za; internet www.dirco.gov.za/ madagascar; Ambassador SISA NGOMBANE.

Switzerland: Immeuble ARO, Solombavambahoaka, Frantsay 77, BP 118, 101 Antananarivo; tel. (20) 2262997; e-mail ant.vertretung@ eda.admin.ch; internet www.eda.admin.ch/antananarivo; Ambassador ROLF STALDER.

Türkiye (Turkey): Hotel Carlton, Chambre No. 1410, rue Pierre Stibbe, BP 959, 101 Antananarivo; tel. (20) 2226060; internet antananarivo.be.mfa.gov.tr; Ambassador ISHAK EBRAR ÇUBUKÇU.

United Kingdom: Tour Zital Ankorondrano, 9th Floor, Ravoninahitriniarivo St, 101 Antananarivo; tel. (20) 2233053; e-mail british .embassyantananarivo@fcdo.gov.uk; internet www.gov.uk/world/ organisations/british-embassy-antananarivo; Ambassador DAVID ASHLEY.

USA: Lot 207A, Point Liberty, Andranoro-Antehiroka, BP 5253, 105 Antananarivo; tel. (20) 2348000; e-mail paoantananarivo@state.gov; internet mg.usembassy.gov; Ambassador CLAIRE A. PIERANGELO.

Judicial System

According to the Constitution of the Fourth Republic of Madagascar, endorsed by national referendum on 17 November 2010, justice is administered by the Supreme Court, the High Constitutional Court, the High Court of Justice and any courts of appeal that may be established.

Supreme Court (Cour Suprême): Palais de Justice, Anosy, 101 Antananarivo; internet www.cour-supreme.gov.mg; 9 mems; First Pres. ROBERTSON RANARY RAKOTONAVALONA; Attorney-General JOHNNY RICHARD ANDRIAMAHEFARIVO.

High Constitutional Court (Haute Cour Constitutionnelle): BP 835, Ambohidahy, 101 Antananarivo; tel. (20) 2266061; internet www.hcc.gov.mg; interprets the Constitution and rules on constitutional issues; 9 mems; Pres. FLORENT RAKOTOARISOA.

High Court of Justice (Haute Cour de Justice): Lot III, M33 BL Ouest, Ambohijanahary; tel. (34) 6671138; internet

hautecourdejustice-mada.mg; 9 mems; Pres. ANDRIAMANANKIANDRIANANA RAJAONA.

Tribunaux de Première Instance: at Antananarivo, Toamasina, Antsiranana, Mahajanga, Fianarantsoa, Toliary, Antsirabé, Ambatondrazaka, Antalaha, Farafangana and Maintirano; for civil, commercial and social matters, and for registration.

Cours Criminelles Ordinaires: tries crimes of common law; attached to the Cour d'Appel in Antananarivo but may sit in any other large town. There are also 31 Cours Criminelles Spéciales dealing with cases concerning cattle.

Tribunaux Spéciaux Economiques: at Antananarivo, Toamasina, Mahajanga, Fianarantsoa, Antsiranana and Toliary; tries crimes specifically relating to economic matters.

Tribunaux Criminels Spéciaux: judges cases of banditry and looting; 31 courts.

Religion

It is estimated that more than 50% of the population follow traditional animist beliefs, some 41% are Christians (about two-thirds of whom are Roman Catholics) and some 7% are Muslims.

CHRISTIANITY

Fiombonan'ny Fiangonana Kristiana eto Madagasikara (FFKM)/Conseil Chrétien des Eglises de Madagascar (Christian Council of Churches in Madagascar): Vohipiraisana, Ambohijatovo-Atsimo, BP 798, 101 Antananarivo; tel. (20) 2623433; e-mail ffkmfoibe@gmail.com; f. 1980; 4 mems and 2 assoc. mems; Pres. Pastor ODON MARIE ARSÈNE RAZANAKOLONA.

Fiombonan'ny Fiangonana Protestanta eto Madagasikara (FFPM)/Fédération des Eglises Protestantes à Madagascar (Federation of the Protestant Churches in Madagascar): VK 3 Vohipiraisana, Ambohijatovo-Atsimo, BP 4226, 101 Antananarivo; tel. (20) 2415888; e-mail zakazafyetienne@gmail.com; f. 1958; 2 mem. churches; Gen. Sec. Rev. ETIENNE ZAKAZAFY.

The Anglican Communion

Anglicans are adherents of the Church of the Province of the Indian Ocean, comprising eight dioceses (six in Madagascar, one in Mauritius and one in Seychelles). The Archbishop of the Province is the Bishop of Seychelles.

Bishop of Antananarivo: Rt Rev. SAMOELA JAONA RANARIVELO, Evêché anglican, Lot VK 57 ter, Ambohimanoro, 101 Antananarivo; tel. (20) 2220827; e-mail eemdanta@yahoo.com.

Bishop of Antsiranana: Rt Rev. THEOPHILE BOTOMAZAVA, Evêché anglican, 4 rue Grandidier, BP 278, 201 Antsiranana; tel. (20) 8222776; e-mail rinaldoulrick@yahoo.fr.

Bishop of Fianarantsoa: Rt Rev. GILBERT RATELOSON RAKOTONDRAVELO, Evêché anglican, BP 1418, 531 Fianarantsoa; tel. 340522681; e-mail eemdiofianara@yahoo.fr.

Bishop of Mahajanga: Rt Rev. SAMUEL HALL SPEERS, Evêché anglican, BP 365, 401 Mahajanga; e-mail hallspeers@gmail.com.

Bishop of Toamasina: Rt Rev. JEAN PAUL SOLO, Evêché anglican, rue James Seth, BP 531, 501 Toamasina; tel. 341921195; e-mail solojeanpaulmgr@gmail.com.

Bishop of Toliary: Rt Rev. TODD MCGREGOR, BP 408601, Toliara; tel. 333742745; e-mail bishopmctodd@yahoo.com.

The Roman Catholic Church

Madagascar comprises five archdioceses and 17 dioceses.

Bishops' Conference: Conférence Episcopale de Madagascar, 102 bis, rue Cardinal Jerôme Rakotomalala, BP 667, 101 Antananarivo; tel. (20) 2220478; f. 1969; Pres. Most Rev. DÉSIRÉ TSARAHAZANA (Archbishop of Toamasina).

Archbishop of Antananarivo: ODON MARIE ARSÈNE RAZANAKOLONA, Archevêché, Andohalo, BP 3030, 101 Antananarivo; tel. (20) 2220726; e-mail didih@simicro.mg.

Archbishop of Antsiranana: Most Rev. BENJAMIN MARC BALTHASON RAMAROSON, Archevêché, 5 blvd le Myre de Villers, BP 415, 201 Antsiranana; tel. (32) 4072782; internet www .dioceseantsiranana-oloraiky.com.

Archbishop of Fianarantsoa: Most Rev. FULGENCE RABEMAHAFALY, Archevêché, pl. Mgr Givelet, BP 1440, Ecar Ambozontany, 301 Fianarantsoa; tel. (20) 7550027.

Archbishop of Toamasina: Cardinal DÉSIRÉ TSARAHAZANA, 11 rue du Commerce, BP 98, 501 Toamasina; tel. (20) 5332128.

Archbishop of Toliary: Most Rev. FULGENCE RABEONY, Archevêché, Maison Saint Jean, BP 30, 601 Toliary; tel. (20) 9442416; e-mail rajeanchrys@yahoo.it.

Other Christian Churches

Fiangonan'i Jesoa Kristy eto Madagasikara/Eglise de Jésus-Christ à Madagascar (FJKM): Lot 11 B18, Tohatohabato Ranavalona 1, Trano 'Ifanomezantsoa', BP 623, 101 Antananarivo; tel. (20) 2228237; e-mail fjkm@fjkm.mg; internet www.fjkm.mg; f. 1968; Pres. ANDRIAMAHAZOSOA AMMI IRAKO.

Fiangonana Loterana Malagasy (Malagasy Lutheran Church): BP 1741, 19 rue Jules Pochard, 101 Antananarivo; tel. (20) 2422703; e-mail drmodeste@yahoo.fr; internet loterana-malagasy.org; f. 1867; Pres. Rev. Dr DAVID RAKOTONIRINA.

The Press

DAILY NEWSPAPERS (PRINT AND ONLINE)

Ao Raha: Antananarivo; Malagasy; Editor RIANA RASOAVA.

L'Express de Madagascar: Z.I. Nord, route des Hydrocarbures, Ankorondrano, BP 3893, 101 Antananarivo; tel. (20) 2221934; e-mail lexpress@lexpressmada.com; internet lexpress.mg; f. 1995; French and Malagasy; Editor-in-Chief SYLVAIN RANJALAHY.

Gazetiko: rue Ravoninahitriniarivo, BP 1414 Ankorondrano, 101 Antananarivo; tel. (20) 2269779; e-mail gazetiko@midi-madagasikara.mg; internet fb.com/gazetiko; Malagasy; Dir of Publication HERIVONJY RAJAONAH.

La Gazette de la Grande Ile: Lot II, W 23 L Ankorahotra, route de l'Université, BP 8678, Antananarivo; tel. 340561396; e-mail administration@lagazette-dgi.com; internet www.lagazette-dgi.com; French; 24 pages; Editor-in-Chief CHRISTIAN ANDRIANARISOA.

Jejoo: Antananarivo; tel. (33) 1530089; internet www.jejooweb.net.

La Ligne de Mire: Village des Jeux, Ankorondrano, Antananarivo.

Madagascar Matin: Antananarivo; tel. (33) 3741020; internet www.matin.mg; Editor-in-Chef DOMINIQUE VALOHERY.

Madagascar Tribune: Immeuble SME, rue Ravoninahitriniarivo, BP 659, Ankorondrano, 101 Antananarivo; tel. (20) 2222635; e-mail contact@madagascar-tribune.com; internet www.madagascar-tribune.com; f. 1988; independent; French and Malagasy; Editor ANSELME RANDRIAKOTO.

Midi Madagasikara: Làlana Ravoninahitriniarivo, BP 1414, Ankorondrano, 101 Antananarivo; tel. (20) 2269779; e-mail contact@midi-madagasikara.mg; internet www.midi-madagasikara.mg; f. 1983; French and Malagasy; Dir/CEO JEREMY RABESAHALA.

Les Nouvelles: 8/10, rue Rainizanabololona, BP 194, 101 Antananarivo; tel. (20) 2235433; e-mail administration@les-nouvelles.com; French and Taratra; f. 2003; Dir-Gen. NAINA ANDRIANTSITOHAINA.

Tia Tanindrazana: Antananarivo; tel. (33) 0337739; e-mail titanindrazana@gmail.com; internet www.tiatanindrazana.mg; Malagasy.

La Vérité: Immeuble SODIAT, Mandrosoa Ivato, BP 5068, 105 Antananarivo; tel. (20) 2629521; e-mail tatauto@yahoo.fr; internet www.laverite.mg.

PERIODICALS (PRINT AND ONLINE)

Diva: Alarobia Amboniloha 9, Cité des Travaux Publics, Antananarivo; tel. (20) 2642027; Dir of Publication LUCIANA G. LINDA; Editor-in-Chief JEAN RO.

Essentielle Madagascar: Antananarivo; tel. (20) 2221934; e-mail redaction.essentielle@lexpressmada.com; monthly.

Expansion: Immeuble Premium, 3e étage, ex-Village des Jeux, Antananarivo; tel. (20) 2224007; internet www.expansion-madagascar.mg; bimonthly; publ. by the Syndicat des Industries de Madagascar; Dir of Publication FREDY RAJAONERA; Editor-in-Chief TOKY RAJAONA.

Gazetinao: Lot IPA 37, BP 1758, Anosimasina, 101 Antananarivo; tel. (20) 1198161; e-mail mitantanasymitarika@yahoo.fr; f. 1976; French and Malagasy; monthly; religion and culture; Editor-in-Chief DAVID ALDEN EINSTEN RAKOTOMAHANINA.

L'Hebdo de Madagascar: Z.I. Nord Route des Hydrocarbures, Ankorondrano, BP 3893, 101 Antananarivo; tel. (20) 2222287; e-mail contact@lhebdomada.com; internet www.lhebdomada.com; f. 2005; French and Malagasy; weekly; Editor-in-Chief NASOLO VALIAVO ANDRIAMIHAJA.

Journal Officiel de la République de Madagascar/Gazetim-Panjakan' Ny Repoblika Malagasy: BP 248, 101 Antananarivo; tel. (20) 2265010; f. 1883; official announcements; Malagasy and French; weekly; Dir HONORÉE ELIANNE RALALAHARISON.

Jureco: BP 6318, Lot IVᴅ 48 bis, rue Razanamaniraka, Behoririka, 101 Antananarivo; tel. (20) 2255271; e-mail jureco@malagasy.com; law and economics; monthly; French; Dir MBOARA ANDRIANARIMANANA.

Lakroan'i Madagasikara/La Croix de Madagascar: BP 7524, CNPC Antanimena, 101 Antananarivo; tel. (20) 2266128; e-mail lakroa@moov.mg; internet www.lakroa.mg; f. 1927; Roman Catholic; French and Malagasy; weekly; Dir Fr JACQUES MANANTO REHAMA.

Ny Mpamangy-FLM: 9 rue Général Gabriel Ramanantsoa Isoraka, 101 Antananarivo; tel. (20) 2228943; f. 1882; monthly; Dir LUCIE NOROSOANOMENJANAHARY.

Ny Sakaizan'ny Tanora: BP 538, Antsahaminitra, 101 Antananarivo; tel. (20) 2228943; internet fb.com/gazety.nysakaizannytanora; f. 1878; monthly; Editor-in-Chief ELISABETH RAHELINORO.

Ny Valosoa Vaovao: Antananarivo; tel. 347907600; e-mail gvalosoa@yahoo.com; internet www.gvalosoa.net; f. 2010; 3 a week; Dir of Publication ARPHINE RAHELISOA.

Prime Magazine: Antananarivo; e-mail direction.commercial@primemedia.international; internet www.primemedia.international; monthly.

Revue de l'Océan Indien: Immeuble Madprint, Antsakaviro, BP 46, 101 Antananarivo; tel. 3432904; e-mail roi@moov.mg; f. 1980; monthly; French; Dir of Publication NORO RAZAFIMANDIMBY.

Triatra: Ankorondrano, Antananarivo; tel. (34) 1190502; Malagasy; weekly.

NEWS AGENCY

Dépêche Informative Taratra: 7 rue Jean Ralaimongo, Ambohiday, 101 Antananarivo; tel. 321291299; e-mail redactiondepechetaratra@gmail.com; internet depeche-taratra.mg; f. 1977; fmrly Agence Nationale d'Information 'TARATRA'; name changed as above in 2021; Dir RAZAFIMANANTSOA ANITRA RAKOTOARISOA.

Publishers

CITE: rue Samuel Rahamefy Ambatonakanga, BP 74, 101 Antananarivo; tel. (20) 2225386; internet www.cite.mg; Dir-Gen. HAINGONIRINA RANDRIANARIVONY.

Editions Mixte: BP 3204, 101 Antananarivo; tel. (20) 2225130; e-mail librairiemixte@moov.mg; Dir AINA JEAN RAZAKASOA.

Presse Edition et Diffusion: 51 rue Tsiombikibo Ambatovinaky, 101 Antananarivo; tel. (20) 2256658; e-mail prediff@prediff.mg; internet www.prediff.mg; f. 1995; owns the imprint Editions Jeunes Malgaches; Dir of Publication MARIE MICHÈLE RAZAFINTSALAMA.

Société Malgache d'Edition (SME): BP 659, Ankorondrano, 101 Antananarivo; tel. (20) 2222635; f. 1943; general fiction, university and secondary textbooks; Man. Dir RAHAGA RAMAHOLIMIHASO.

Société Nouvelle de l'Imprimerie Centrale (SNIC): Route des Hydrocarbures, BP 1414, 101 Antananarivo; tel. (20) 2221118; internet www.snic.mg; f. 1961; books, newspapers and magazines; CEO JEREMY RABESAHALA.

Trano Printy Fiangonana Loterana Malagasy (TPFLM): 9 rue Général Gabriel Ramanantsoa, BP 538, 101 Antananarivo; tel. (20) 2223340; e-mail impluth@yahoo.fr; f. 1877; religious, educational and fiction; owned by the Malagasy Lutheran Church; Dir JOSEPH RANDRIANARIVELO.

GOVERNMENT PUBLISHING HOUSE

Imprimerie Nationale: BP 38, 101 Antananarivo; tel. (20) 2223675; internet www.mefb.gov.mg/imprimerie-nationale; all official publs; Dir JEAN ANGELSON RANDRIAMBOAVONJY.

ASSOCIATION

Association des Editeurs de Madagascar: rue Samuel Rahamefy, 101 Antananarivo; tel. (20) 2225386; e-mail contact@aedim.mg; internet www.aedim.mg; f. 2010; Pres. JEAN DONNÉ LAHIVELO.

Broadcasting and Communications

REGULATORY AUTHORITY

Autorité de Régulation des Technologies de Communication de Madagascar (ARTEC): Immeuble ARTEC, Andohatapenaka, 101 Antananarivo; tel. (20) 2242119; e-mail artec@artec.mg; internet www.artec.mg; f. 1997 as Office Malagasy d'Etudes et de Régulation des Télécommunications; present name adopted in 2015; Pres. LAURENT RICHARD RAKOTOMALALA.

TELECOMMUNICATIONS

Airtel Madagascar: Explorer Business Park, Ankorondrano, 101 Antananarivo; tel. (33) 3300121; e-mail corporate.support@mg.airtel

.com; internet www.airtel.mg; f. 1997 as Madacom; fmrly Celtel and subsequently Zain Madagascar; present name adopted in 2010; Man. Dir EDDY KAPUKU.

blueline: Immeuble Fitaratra, 4e étage, Ankorondrano, 101 Antananarivo; tel. (20) 2332028; e-mail contact@blueline-business.mg; internet www.blueline.mg; f. 1998; internet and digital television service provider; owned by Gulfsat Madagascar; Dir-Gen. DAMIEN DE LAMBERTERIE.

Orange Madagascar: La Tour, rue Ravoninahitriniarivo, BP 7754, 101 Antananarivo; tel. (32) 3456789; e-mail contact.oma@orange .com; internet www.orange.mg; f. 1998; fmrly Antaris, la Société Malgache de Mobiles; present name adopted in 2003; mobile telecommunication GSM network provider; CEO FRÉDÉRIC DEBORD.

Télécom Malagasy SA (TELMA): BP 763, 101 Antananarivo; tel. (20) 2532705; e-mail telmacorporate@telma.mg; internet www.telma .mg; majority share owned by Groupe Axian; owns DTS Wanadoo internet service provider; Dir-Gen. PATRICK PISAL-HAMIDA.

BROADCASTING

Radio

Le Messager Radio Evangélique: BP 1374, 101 Antananarivo; tel. (20) 2234495; internet mreradio.com; broadcasts in French, English and Malagasy; Dir JOCELYN RANJARISON.

Radio Antsiva: Ankorondrano enceinte SITRAM, 101 Antananarivo; tel. 2254849; e-mail radioantsiva@gmail.com; internet www .antsiva.mg; f. 1994; broadcasts in French and Malagasy; Editor-in-chief MICHEL RALIBERA.

Radio Don Bosco: Maison Don Bosco, Ivato Aéroport, BP 60, 101 Antananarivo; tel. (20) 2244387; e-mail rdbradiodonbosco2@gmail .com; internet www.rdb.mg; f. 1996; Catholic, educational and cultural; Dir Fr ERIC FRANCK RANDRIAMIANDRINIRINARIVO.

Radio Lazan'iarivo (RLI): Lot V A49, Andafiavaratra, 101 Antananarivo; tel. (20) 2229016; broadcasts in French, English and Malagasy; privately owned; specializes in jazz music; Dir IHOBY RABARIJOHN.

Radio MBS (Malagasy Broadcasting System): BP 11137, Anosipatrana, Antananarivo; tel. (20) 2266702; internet malagasynews.com/radio; broadcasts by satellite; Man. SARAH RAVALOMANANA.

Radio Nationale Malagasy: BP 442, Anosy, 101 Antananarivo; tel. (20) 2221745; e-mail r.radiomadagaskara@yahoo.fr; internet fb.com/radio.madagasikara; state-controlled; part of the Office de Radiodiffusion et de Télévision de Madagascar (ORTM); broadcasts in French and Malagasy; Dir RATOVONDRAHONA HARISON.

Radio Viva: Immeuble INJET, Parcelle No. 34, Zone Water Front, Ambodivona, 101 Antananarivo; tel. (20) 2256788; e-mail viva .madagascar@gmail.com; internet www.viva-madagascar.com; f. 2017; Owner ANDRY RAJOELINA.

Television

MA TV: BP 1414 Ankorondrano, 101 Antananarivo; tel. (20) 2236469; e-mail matv@matv.mg; internet matv.mg; f. 1995; Pres. FREDY ANDRIAMBELO; Dir-Gen. WILLY FREDY ANDRIAMBELO.

MBS Television (Malagasy Broadcasting System): BP 11137, Anosipatranaa, Antananarivo; tel. (20) 346037607; e-mail mbsonline@yahoo.com; internet malagasynews.com; broadcasts in French and Malagasy.

Radio Télévision Analamanga (RTA): Immeuble Fiaro, 101 Antananarivo; tel. (20) 2224503; internet www.rta.mg; incl. 4 provincial radio stations; Dir-Gen. SELVEN NAIDU.

Télévision Nationale Malagasy (Televiziona Malagasy—TVM): BP 1202, Anosy, 101 Antananarivo; tel. (20) 2222381; f. 1967; state-controlled; part of the Office de Radiodiffusion et de Télévision de Madagascar (ORTM); broadcasts in French and Malagasy; Dir-Gen. (vacant).

Finance

BANKING

Central Bank

Banque Centrale de Madagascar (Banky Foiben'i Madagasikara—BFM): rue de la Révolution Socialiste Malgache, BP 550, 101 Antananarivo; tel. (20) 2221751; e-mail banky-foibe@bfm.mg; internet www.banky-foibe.mg; f. 1973; bank of issue; Gov. HENRI RABARIJOHN.

Other Banks

AccèsBanque Madagascar: Immeuble Bir Hackeim, Lot IBG, 21 Ter Antsahavola, 101 Antananarivo; tel. (20) 2232234; e-mail info@

accesbanque.mg; internet www.accesbanque.mg; f. 2006; Dir-Gen. MIKHAIL VELICHKO.

Bank of Africa (BOA)—Madagascar: 2 pl. de l'Indépendance, BP 183, 101 Antananarivo; tel. (20) 2239100; e-mail boa@boa.mg; internet www.boa.mg; f. 1976 as Bankin'ny Tantsaha Mpamokatra; name changed as above 1999; 61.11% owned by BOA Group, 9.37% state-owned; commercial bank, specializes in microfinance; Pres. ALPHONSE RALISON; Man. Dir OTHMANE ALAOUI.

Banque Malgache de l'Océan Indien (BMOI) (Indian Ocean Malagasy Bank): pl. de l'Indépendance, BP 25 bis, Antaninarenina, 101 Antananarivo; tel. (20) 2234609; e-mail bmoi@bmoi.mg; internet www.bmoinet.net; f. 1989; 71% owned by BCP (Morocco); Pres. ANDRIANTSITOHAINA NAINA; Dir ALAIN MERLOT.

Banque SBM Madagascar: rue Andrianary Ratianarivo Antsahavola 1, 101 Antananarivo; tel. (20) 2266607; e-mail hotlinemada@sbmgroup.mu; internet www.sbmgroup.mu; f. 1998; owned by SBM Holding Ltd; Gen. Man. GILBERT LAGAILLARDE.

Baobab Banque Madagascar: Immeuble Ariane, 5A Zone Galaxy, Andraharo, BP 7119, Antananarivo 101; tel. 342000650; e-mail contactmadagascar@baobab.bz; internet www.microcred.com/mg; f. 2006 as Microcred Banque Madagascar; name changed as above in 2018; Dir-Gen. CHRISTOPHE LASSUS-LALANNE.

BGFIBANK Madagascar SA: Explorer 19A, ex Village des Jeux, Ankorondrano, BP 770, Antananarivo; tel. (33) 1558304; e-mail a .moussirou@bgfi.com; internet madagascar.groupebgfibank.com; Dir-Gen. FRANÇOIS BARNABÉ.

BM Madagascar: 22 ave de l'Indépendance, Analakely, 101 Antananarivo; tel. (32) 2300600; f. 2011; Dir-Gen. RACHID MOUHTAJY.

BNI Madagascar: 74 rue du 26 Juin 1960, BP 174, 101 Antananarivo; tel. (20) 2222800; e-mail info@bni.mg; internet www.bni.mg; f. 1976 as Bankin 'ny Indostria; 53% owned by Indian Ocean Financial Holding, 32.58% state-owned; Pres. HERINTSALAMA RAJAONARIVELO; Man. Dir ALEXANDRE MEY.

Mauritius Commercial Bank (Madagascar) SA (MCB): 77 rue Solombavambahoaka Frantsay, Antsahavola, BP 197, 101 Antananarivo; tel. (20) 2227262; internet www.mcbmadagascar.com; f. 1992 as Union Commercial Bank; name changed as above in 2007; 70% owned by Mauritius Commercial Bank Ltd; Chair. JEAN FRANÇOIS DESVAUX DE MARIGNY; Gen. Man. JEAN-PHILIPPE LEBON.

Société Générale Madagasikara: 14 rue Général Rabehevitra, BP 196, Antananarivo 101; tel. (20) 2220691; e-mail relation.client@socgen.com; internet societegenerale.mg; f. 1977 as Banky Fampandrosoana ny Varotra; subsequently BFV—Société Générale; name changed as above in 2019; wholly owned by Société Générale (France); Pres. JOSÉPHINE SOANORONDRIAKA ANDRIAMAMONJIARISON; Dir-Gen. ZDENEK METELAK.

Société d'Investissement pour la Promotion des Entreprises à Madagascar (SIPEM): A216H, Andavamamba, Antananarivo 101; tel. (20) 2269103; e-mail assdg@sipem.mg; internet www.sipem .mg; Dir-Gen. BRILLIANT RAKOTOARISON.

Banking Association

Association Professionnelle des Banques: c/o MICROCRED Banque Madagascar, Bâtiment Ariane 5A, Zone Galaxy, Andraharo, Antananarivo 101; Pres. RACHID MOUTHAJY.

INSURANCE

ARO (Assurances Réassurances Omnibranches): Lalana Solombavambahoaka Frantsay 77, Antsahavola, BP 42, 101 Antananarivo; tel. (20) 2220154; e-mail aro1@moov.mg; internet www.aro .mg; state-owned; Pres. RINDRA HASIMBELO RABARINIRINARISON; CEO LANTONIRINA ANDRIANARY.

ASCOMA Madagascar: 13 rue Patrice Lumumba, BP 673, 101 Antananarivo; tel. (20) 2223162; e-mail madagascar@ascoma.com; internet www.ascoma.com; f. 1952; Dir-Gen. EDOUARD BERSON.

Compagnie Malgache d'Assurances et de Réassurances 'Ny Havana': Immeuble 'Ny Havana', Zone des 67 Ha, BP 3881, 101 Antananarivo; tel. (20) 2226760; e-mail info@nyhavana.mg; internet www.nyhavana.mg; f. 1968; 47% state-owned; Pres. MIHAMINA RATOVOHARINONY; Dir-Gen. OLIVIER RANDRIANTIANA.

Mutuelle d'Assurances Malagasy (MAMA): Lot IF, 12 bis Ambalavao-Isotry, BP 185, 101 Antananarivo; tel. (20) 2261882; f. 1968; Dir SETH AIMÉ RANDRIANARIJAONA.

Saham Assurance Madagascar: BP 1118, Antananarivo; tel. (20) 2222882; e-mail madagascar@sahamassurance.com; internet www .sahamassurance.mg.

Insurance Association

Comité des Entreprises d'Assurances à Madagascar: Immeuble de la Résidence des Assureurs, Ampefiloha, Rez-de-Chaussée de l'Escalier, BP 112, Antananarivo 101; tel. (20) 2223337; Pres. PATRICK ANDRIAMBAHINY.

Trade and Industry

GOVERNMENT AGENCIES

Autorité de Régulation des Marchés Publics (ARMP): Antananarivo; internet armp.mg; f. 2005; Dir-Gen. HARISON VONJY RAZAFY.

Fonds d'Intervention pour le Développement: Lot III M39, Ouest Ambohijanahary, 101 Antananarivo; tel. (20) 2236150; e-mail dirgen@fid.mg; internet www.fid.mg; f. 1993; Dir-Gen. PIERRETTE RASOARIVELO.

Madagascar Development Learning Center (MDLC): Làlana Andriamifidy, Anosy, Antananarivo; tel. (20) 2269725; e-mail contact@madagascar-dlc.com; internet www.madagascar-dlc.com.

DEVELOPMENT ORGANIZATIONS

Agence Française de Développement: 23 rue Razanakombana Ambohijatovo, BP 557, Antananarivo; tel. (20) 2220046; e-mail afdantananarivo@afd.fr; internet www.afd.fr; Dir YVES GUICQUÉRO.

Agence Nationale d'Appui au Logement et à l'Habitat (ANA-LOGH): Lot III i Soanierana Ankadimbahoaka, blvd Gal Richard, Ratsimandrava, 101 Antananarivo; tel. 341191130; e-mail contact@analogh.mg; internet www.analogh.mg; f. 2011; Dir-Gen. HASINA LANDRY RAZAFINDRAKOTO.

Centre d'Information Technique et Economique de Madagascar (CITE): rue Samuel Ramahefy Ambatonakanga, BP 74, 101 Antananarivo; tel. (20) 2225386; internet www.cite.mg; f. 1967; supports and promotes Malagasy businesses; Pres. GÉDÉON RAJAONSON; Dir-Gen. HAINGONIRINA RANDRIANARIVONY.

Economic Development Board of Madagascar (EDBM): Immeuble EDBM, ave Gal Gabriel, Antaninarenina, 101 Antananarivo; tel. (20) 2268121; e-mail edbm@edbm.mg; internet edbm.mg; f. 2006; service for the facilitation and promotion of investment in Madagascar; advisory service for starting a business, obtaining visas and land acquisition; Pres. DERA NIAINA ZAFINDRAVAKA; CEO ANDRY TIANA RAVALOMANDA.

Office des Mines Nationales et des Industries Stratégiques (OMNIS): 21 Làlana Razanakombana, BP 1 bis, 101 Antananarivo; tel. (20) 2224283; e-mail secdg@omnis.mg; internet omnis.mg; f. 1976; promotes the exploration and exploitation of mining resources, in particular oil resources; Pres. STÉPHANIE DELMOTTE; Dir-Gen. NANTENAINA RASOLONIRINA.

CHAMBERS OF COMMERCE

Fédération des Chambres de Commerce et d'Industrie de Madagascar (FCCIM): Lot IVR 42, Espace Conquête Antanimena, BP 166, 101 Antananarivo; tel. (20) 2221322; e-mail federationcci@gmail.com; internet www.fccim.mg/sitefccim; 20 mem. chambers; Pres. VIVIANE DEWA; Dir-Gen. BERNARDIN RAMIANDRISOA.

Chambre de Commerce et d'Industrie d'Antananarivo (CCIA): 20 rue Henri Razanatseheno, Antaninarenina, BP 166, 101 Antananarivo; tel. (20) 2220211; internet www.cci.mg; f. 1993; Pres. RIVO RAKOTONDRASANJY.

Chambre des Mines de Madagascar (CMM): QMM-Rio Tinto, Villa 3H, Lot II, J169 Ivandry, BP 4003, 101 Antananarivo; tel. (32) 1126185; e-mail cmm@mineschamber.mg; internet www.mineschamber.mg/CMM/web; f. 2005; Pres. JEAN LUC MARQUETOUX; 27 mems.

EMPLOYERS' ORGANIZATIONS

Global Entrepreneurship Network Madagascar (GEN Madagascar): Immeuble Jacaranda, Lalana Ranavalona III, Antananarivo; tel. (34) 5495751; e-mail sg@gen-madagascar.org; internet www.gen-madagascar.org; Dir-Gen. PROSPÉRIN TSIALONINA (acting).

Groupement des Entreprises de Madagascar (GEM): Kianja MDRM sy Tia Tanindrazana, Ambohijatovo, BP 1338, 101 Antananarivo; tel. (20) 2223841; e-mail gem@iris.mg; internet www.gem-madagascar.com; f. 1975; 20 nat. syndicates and 7 regional syndicates comprising 1,900 cos and 95 directly affiliated cos; Pres. THIERRY-MARIE RAJAONA; Sec.-Gen. ZINAH RASAMUEL RAVALOSON.

Malagasy Entrepreneurs' Association (FIV.MPA.MA): Immeuble BNI, Escallier A, rue Pasteur Rabary Ankadivato, 101 Antananarivo; tel. (34) 2000261; e-mail contact@fivmpama.mg; internet fivmpama.mg; comprises 10 trade assocs, representing 400 mems, and 200 direct business mems; Chair. RIVO RAKOTONDRASANJY.

Syndicat des Industries de Madagascar (SIM): Immeuble Prémium Ankorondrano, Ex-Village des Jeux, Antananarivo 101; BP 1695, 101 Antananarivo; tel. (20) 2224007; e-mail syndusmad@sim.mg; internet www.sim.mg; f. 1958; Pres. AMIRALY HASSIM; Exec. Dir EVELYNE RAKOTOMANANA; 102 mems (2021).

Syndicat Professionel des Producteurs d'Extraits Aromatiques, Alimentaires et Medicinaux de Madagascar (SYPEAM): 7 rue Rakotoson Toto Radona, Antsahavola, BP 5038, Antananarivo 101; tel. (20) 2235363; e-mail itd.madagascar@moov.mg; f. 1994; Pres. CHARLES RANDRIAMBOLOLONA.

UTILITIES

Electricity and Water

Agence de Développement de l'Électrification Rurale: Logement 12, Cité des Travaux Publics, Alarobia, Antananarivo 101; tel. 332353794; e-mail ader@ader.mg; internet ader.mg.

Office de Regulation de l'Electricité (ORE): rue Tsimanindry, Ambatoroka, Antananarivo; tel. (20) 2264813; e-mail ore@ore.mg; internet www.ore.mg; f. 2004; Exec. Sec. RIVOHARILALA RASOLOJAONA.

Jiro sy Rano Malagasy (JIRAMA): 149 rue Rainandriamampandry, Faravohitra, BP 200, 101 Antananarivo; tel. (20) 2220031; internet www.jirama.mg; f. 1975; controls production and distribution of electricity and water; managed by local manager; Chair. SOLO ANDRIAMANAMPISOA; Gen. Man. VONJY ANDRIAIMANGA.

MAJOR COMPANIES

The following are some of the largest in terms either of capital investment or employment.

Ambatovy: Immeuble Tranofitaratra, 6ème étage, rue Ravoninahitriniaivo, Ankorodrano, Antananarivo 101; tel. (32) 3366565; e-mail media@ambatovy.mg; internet www.ambatovy.com; f. 2003; nickel and cobalt mining at Ambatovy; Pres. GUSTAVO GOMES.

Brasseries STAR Madagascar: rue Dr Raseta, Andranomahery, BP 3806, 101 Antananarivo; tel. (20) 2327711; e-mail bsm@star.mg; internet www.star.mg; f. 1953; mfrs of beer and carbonated drinks; Pres. and Dir-Gen. MARC POZMENTIER.

    La Nouvelle Brasserie de Madagascar (NBM): Antananarivo; acquired by Groupe Star in 2014.

    Société d'Exploitation des Sources d'Eaux Minérales Naturelles d'Andranovelona SA (Sema Eau Vive): BP 22, 101 Antananarivo; tel. (20) 2227711; produces mineral water.

Compagnie Salinière de Madagascar: Propriété Salines Plion, Antsahampano, BP 29, 201 Antsiranana; tel. (34) 0569002; internet www.csm.mg; f. 1895; exploitation of salt marshes (60,000 metric tons a year); Pres. PANAYOTIS TALOUMIS; Dir-Gen. DIMITRI CHARALAMBAKIS.

COTONA: route d'Ambositra, BP 45, Antsirabé; tel. (20) 4449422; e-mail sag@cotona.com; internet www.groupesocota.com; f. 1952; owned by Socota Textile Mills Ltd; spinning, weaving, printing and dyeing of textiles; Chair. SALIM ISMAIL; Dir-Gen. HAKIM FAKIRA.

Etablissements Gallois: 15 rue Béniowsky, BP 159, 101 Antananarivo; tel. (20) 2222951; internet www.ets-gallois.com; leading producer of graphite and sisal; Pres. ROBERT FÉLIX; Man. Dir JEAN-CLAUDE FÉLIX-GALLOIS.

Galana Distribution Petrolière SA: Immeuble Pradon Trade Centre, rue Rainizanabololona, Antanimena, BP 60, 118 Antananarivo; tel. (20) 2246803; internet www.galana.mg; subsidiary of Galana, Kenya; owns the national petroleum refinery at Toamasina: Galana Raffinerie Terminale SA; Dir-Gen. PHILIPPE GULDEMONT.

Groupe Basan: 24 rue Radama, 1er Tsaralalàna, BP 207, 101 Antananarivo; tel. (20) 2222373; internet www.basan.mg; agrobased.

Groupe Sipromad: Antananarivo; tel. 321148004; e-mail contact@sipromad.com; internet www.sipromad.com; f. 1972; Pres. YLIAS AKBARALY.

Groupe SODIAT: Immeuble Pradon Trade Center, 9e étage Antanimena, BP 5068, 101 Antananarivo; tel. (20) 2221237; internet sodiatgroupe.mg; f. 1990; Pres. and Dir-Gen. MAMINIAINA RAVATOMANGA.

Jovena: Complexe Kube, Bâtiment A, Zone Galaxy Andraharo, BP 12087, Antananarivo; tel. (20) 2369470; internet www.jovena.mg; 80% owned by Jovena International Holding Madagascar, 20% owned by Govt of Madagascar; one of three petroleum distributors to purchase the assets of the state company Solitany Malagasy; Man. Dir BENJAMIN MEMMI.

Kraomita Malagasy SA (KRAOMA): rue Andrianaivoravelona Zanany, BP 930, Ampefihola, 101 Antananarivo; tel. (20) 2224304; e-mail kraoma@moov.mg; internet www.kraoma.mg; f. 1966 as Cie Minière d'Andriamena (COMINA); 100% state-owned; mining and concentration of chrome; Man. Dir NIRINA RAKOTOMANANTSOA.

Cementis Madagascar: 1 bis, rue Patrice Lumumba, BP 332, 101 Antananarivo; tel. (20) 2232908; e-mail contact@cementis.io; fmrly Matériaux de Constructions Malgaches—MACOMA, subsequently Lafarge-Holcim Madagascar; present name adopted 2021; annual production capacity is 0.4m. metric tons; operates a cement plant in Antsirabé and three concrete plants; Dir-Gen. FRANÇOIS DE LESQUEN.

LMM Farine SA: Enceinte Gare Soarano, BP 361, 101 Antananarivo; tel. (20) 2266533; internet www.lesmoulinsdemadagascar.com;

f. 2007; reopened 2011; annual production capacity of 4,500 metric tons of flour; Man. GREG STOUGH.

Madagascar Oil: Immeuble Trano Fitaratra, 8e étage, Antananarivo; e-mail info@madagascaroil.com; internet www.madagascaroil.com; f. 2004; Chair. ANDREW JAMES MORRIS; COO and Gen. Man. STEWART AHMED.

QIT Madagascar Minerals (QMM): BP 4003, Villa 3H, Lot II J-169 Ivandry, 101 Antananarivo; tel. (20) 2242559; e-mail media.enquiries@riotinto.com; internet www.riotintomadagascar.com; f. 2001; 80% owned by Rio Tinto plc (UK/Australia), 20% state-owned; construction of an ilmenite mine and deep-sea port in the Fort Dauphin region; CEO NY FANJA RAKOTOMALALA.

Société d'Etudes de Constructions et Réparations Navales SA (SECREN): 1 rue Lavigerie, BP 135, Antsiranana; tel. (20) 8229321; e-mail secren@moov.mg; internet secren.mg; 37.5% state-owned; f. 1975; transfer to the private sector pending; shipbuilding and repairs; Gen. Man. ABEL NTSAY.

Société Malgache de Pêcherie (SOMAPECHE): Quai Barriquand, BP 324, Mahanga; tel. (20) 6222093; e-mail secr.somapeche@moov.mg; f. 1963; 33% state-owned; sea fishing; Pres. CLAUDE BRUNOT; Dir-Gen. XUEWEN ZHANG.

Société des Produits Chimiques de Madagascar SA (PROCHIMAD): Mandrosoa Ivato, BP 3145, 101 Antananarivo; tel. (20) 2244140; e-mail prochimad@blueline.mg; manufactures chemicals and fertilizers; Pres. and Dir-Gen. CHARLES ANDRIANTSITOHAINA.

TotalEnergies Madagascar: Immeuble Titaratra, Ankolondrano, 101 Antananarivo; tel. (20) 2239040; e-mail total.madagasikara@total.com.mg; internet www.total.mg; fmrly Total Madagascar; present name adopted 2021; subsidiary of TotalEnergies, France; Man. Dir BIOVA AGBOKOU.

Vivo Energy Madagascar: Bâtiment B4, Golden Business Center, Morarano Alarobia, BP 12029, 101 Antananarivo; tel. (20) 2242708; internet www.vivoenergy.com; Dir-Gen. MONDHER BOUCHOUCHE.

TRADE UNIONS

Confédération des Travailleurs Malagasy Révolutionnaires (FISEMARE): Lot IVN 76-A, Ankadifotsy, BP 1128, Befelatanana-Antananarivo 101; tel. (20) 2221989; f. 1985; Pres. PAUL RABEMANANJARA.

Confédération des Travailleurs Malgaches (Fivomdronamben'ny Mpiasa Malagasy—FMM): Lot IVM 133 A Antetezanafovoany I, BP 846, 101 Antananarivo; tel. 331121526; e-mail rjeannot2002@yahoo.fr; f. 1949; Sec.-Gen. JEANNOT RAMANARIVO; 8,000 mems.

Fédération des Syndicats des Travailleurs de Madagascar (Firaisan'ny Sendika eran'i Madagaskara—FISEMA): Lot III, rue Pasteur Isotry, BP 172, 101 Antananarivo; tel. (33) 1187414; e-mail fisema@gmail.com; internet fisema.mg; f. 1956; Sec.-Gen. JOSÉ RANDRIANASOLO; 8 affiliated unions representing 60,000 mems.

Sendika Kristianina Malagasy (SEKRIMA) (Christian Confederation of Malagasy Trade Unions): Soarano, route de Mahajanga, BP 1035, 101 Antananarivo; tel. (32) 6772998; internet www.sekrima.org; f. 1937; Pres. WILLIS CLARITY RAJAONAH; Gen. Sec. Dr VOLOLONA RAKOTOMALALA; 158 affiliated unions representing 40,000 mems.

Union des Syndicats Autonomes de Madagascar (USAM): Lot IIIM 33 BC, Andrefan'Ambohijanahary, BP 1038, 101 Antananarivo; tel. (20) 2227485; e-mail usam@moov.mg; f. 1954; Pres. THÉOPHILE JOËL RUFIN RAZAKARIASY; Sec.-Gen. MBOLA NOMENA; 49 affiliated unions representing 30,000 mems.

Transport

RAILWAYS

The northern system links the east coast with Antsirabé, in the interior, via Moramanga and Antananarivo, with a branch line from Moramanga to Lake Alaotra. The southern system links Manakara, on the east coast, with Fianarantsoa.

Fianarantsoa-Côte Est (FCE): FCE Gare, 301 Fianarantsoa; tel. (34) 5549917; e-mail fce@blueline.mg; internet www.fce-madagascar.net; f. 1936; southern network, 163 km; Man. JEAN PHILIPPE DAUPHIN RAMONJARSOLO.

Madarail: Gare de Soarano, 1 ave de l'Indépendance, BP 1175, 101 Antananarivo; tel. (20) 2234599; internet www.madarail.mg; f. 2001; operated by VECTURIS (Belgium); 75% owned by Madarail Holding, 25% state-owned; operates the northern network of the Malagasy railway (673 km); Pres. PATRICK CLAES.

INLAND WATERWAYS

The Pangalanes canal runs for 600 km near the east coast from Toamasina to Farafangana.

SHIPPING

There are 18 ports, the largest being at Toamasina, which handles about 70% of total traffic, and Mahajanga; several of the smaller ports are prone to silting problems. A new deep-sea port was constructed at Ehoala, near Taolagnaro (Fort Dauphin), in order to accommodate the activity of an ilmenite mining development; the first vessel docked at the port in December 2008.

Agence Portuaire Maritime et Fluviale (APMF): route des Hydrocarbures, Alarobia, BP 581, Antananarivo; tel. (20) 202253995; e-mail apmf@apmf.mg; internet www.apmf.mg; f. 2003; Dir-Gen. JEAN EDMOND RANDRIANANTENAINA.

CMA—CGM Madagascar: Immeuble Fitaratra Ankorondrano, 3e étage, 101 Antananarivo; tel. (20) 2249901; e-mail tnr.mrajaonarison@cma-cgm.com; internet www.cma-cgm.com; maritime transport; Chair. and CEO PAUL BOULARD.

SCAC-SDV Shipping Madagascar: rue Rabearivelo Antsahavola, BP 514, 102 Antananarivo; tel. (20) 2220631; operates the harbour in Antananarivo Port.

Société du Port à Gestion Autonome de Toamasina: blvd Ratsimilaho, Ampasimazava Est, BP 492, Toamasina; tel. (20) 5332155; e-mail spat@port-toamasina.com; internet www.port-toamasina.com; Dir-Gen. CHRISTIAN EDDY AVELLIN.

CIVIL AVIATION

The Ivato international airport is at Antananarivo, while the airports at Mahajanga, Toamasina and Nosy Be can also accommodate large jet aircraft.

Aeromarine: 3è étage, Immeuble ARO, Antsahavola, BP 3844, 101 Antananarivo; tel. 321144444; e-mail aeromarine@gmail.com; internet www.aeromarine.mg; f. 1991; Dir-Gen. RIAZ BARDAY.

Air Madagascar: Immeuble La City 3000, Ivandry Rez-de-Chaussée, BP 029, 101 Antananarivo; tel. (20) 202251000; e-mail groupe@airmadagascar.com; internet www.airmadagascar.com; f. 1962; 51% owned by Govt; internal services to principal towns; external services to the People's Republic of China, the Comoros, Kenya, Mauritius, Mayotte, Réunion, South Africa and Thailand; Chair. (vacant); Dir-Gen. HANITRA RASETARINERA (acting).

Tsaradia: Immeuble La City 3000, Ivandry Rez-de-Chaussée, BP 029 Antananarivo 101; tel. (20) 2344444; internet tsaradia.com; a subsidiary of Air Madagascar; Dir-Gen. JEAN-FRANÇOIS DEVAUX.

Aviation Civile de Madagascar (ACM): 13 rue Fernand Kasanga, BP 4414, 101 Tsimbazaza-Antananarivo; tel. (20) 2222438; e-mail acm@acm.mg; internet www.acm.mg; f. 2000; Chair. CHRISTIAN RAZAFINDRAKOTO; Dir-Gen. BAKO ALAIN RAMANANJANAHARY.

Madagasikara Airways: La City Ivandry, Anatananarivo; tel. (20) 2249369; e-mail ankoay@madagasikaraairways.com; internet www.madagasikaraairways.com; f. 2015; operates domestic services.

Tourism

Office National du Tourisme de Madagascar (ONTM): Lot IBG 29C, Antsahavola, BP 1780, 101 Antananarivo; tel. (20) 2266115; e-mail ontm@moov.mg; internet madagascar-tourisme.com; f. 2003; Pres. BODA NARIJAO.

Association des Tours Opérateurs Professionnels Réceptifs de Madagascar (TOP): Immeuble Aro, Escalier A, 2ème étage, Ex-Village des Jeux, Ankorondrano, 101 Antananarivo; tel. (34) 2049627; e-mail topmad@moov.mg; internet www.top-madagascar.com; Pres. JONAH RAMAMPIONONA.

Fédération des Hôteliers et Restaurateurs de Madagascar (FHORM): Antaninarenina, pl. de l'Indépendance, Enceinte Hôtel Colbert Antaninarenina, BP 4040, 101 Antananarivo; tel. (20) 2224690; e-mail de.fhorm@moov.mg; internet www.hotels-madagascar-island.com/la-fhorm; Pres. RITA RAVELOJAONA.

Madagascar National Parks: BP 1424, Ambatobe, 103 Antananarivo; tel. (32) 40010; e-mail contact@mnparks.mg; internet www.parcs-madagascar.com; maintains and manages the national network of parks and reserves; Dir-Gen. MAMY RAKOTOARIJAONA.

National Tourism Development: Lot IIA, 42 Ter, Antaninandro, 101 Antananarivo; internet www.national-tourism-development.com; Dir-Gen. LOVA MIRELLA RAKOTOMALALA.

Defence

As assessed at November 2021, Madagascar's total armed forces numbered 13,500 men: army 12,500, navy 500 and air force 500. There was also a paramilitary gendarmerie of 8,100.

Defence Budget: 390,000m. ariary in 2021.
Chief of Staff of the Armed Forces: Gen. LALA MONJA DELPHIN SAHIVELO.

Education

Education is officially compulsory between six and 13 years of age. Madagascar has both public and private schools, although legislation enacted in 1978 envisaged the progressive elimination of private education. Primary education generally begins at the age of six and lasts for five years. Secondary education, beginning at 11 years of age, lasts for a further seven years, comprising a first cycle of four years and a second of three years. According to estimates by the United Nations Educational, Scientific and Cultural Organization (UNESCO), in 2018/19 pre-primary enrolment was equivalent to 40% of children in the relevant age-group (males 38%; females 42%), while primary enrolment included 98% of children in the relevant age-group (males 95%; females 100%). In that year enrolment at secondary schools was equivalent to 35% of children in the relevant age-group (males 34%; females 35%). In 2021 education was allocated 15.7% of total government expenditure.

Bibliography

Allen, P. *Madagascar: Conflicts of Authority in the Great Island.* Boulder, CO, Westview Press, 1995.

Allen, P., and Covell M. *Historical Dictionary of Madagascar.* Lanham, MD, Scarecrow, 2005.

Bat, J. P., and Courtin, N. *Maintenir l'Ordre Colonial: Afrique et Madagascar (XIXe-XXe Siècles).* Rennes, Presses Universitaires de Rennes, 2012.

Bloch, M. *From Blessing to Violence.* Cambridge, Cambridge University Press, 1996.

Bradt, H., and Brown, M. *Madagascar.* Oxford, Clio Press, 1993.

Covell, M. *Madagascar. Politics, Economics and Society.* London, Frances Pinter, 1987.

Deschamps, H. *Histoire de Madagascar.* 4th edn. Paris, Berger-Levrault, 1972.

Feeley-Harnick, G. *A Green Estate: Restoring Independence in Madagascar.* Washington, DC, Smithsonian Institution Press, 1991.

Fernandes, G., and Ranaivo Rabetokotany, N. *ESS-ISTS: cinquante ans pour le développment social à Madagascar, 1960–2010.* Antananarivo, CAPDAM, 2010.

Goodman, S., and Benstead, J. *The Natural History of Madagascar.* Chicago, IL, Chicago University Press, 2004.

Grehan, J. *The Forgotten Invasion: Madagascar 1942.* Pulborough, Historic Military Press, 2007.

Imbiki, A. *La réconciliation nationale à Madagascar: une perspective complexe et difficile.* Paris, L'Harmattan, 2014.

Jackson, J. *Political Oratory and Cartooning: An Ethnography of Democratic Processes in Madagascar.* Chichester, Wiley-Blackwell, 2013.

Jolly, A. *Thank You Madagascar: Conservation Diaries of Alison Jolly.* London, Zed Books, 2015.

Litalien, R. *Madagascar 1956–1960. Étape vers la décolonisation.* Paris, Ecole Pratique des Hautes Etudes, 1975.

Massiot, M. *L'organisation politique, administrative, financière et judiciaire de la République malgache.* Antananarivo, Librairie de Madagascar, 1970.

Pascal, R. *La République malgache: Pacifique indépendance.* Paris, Berger-Levrault, 1965.

Pryor, F. L. *Malawi and Madagascar: The Political Economy of Poverty, Equity and Growth.* New York, Oxford University Press, 1991.

Radrianja, S., and Ellis, S. *Madagascar: A Short History.* Chicago, IL, Chicago University Press, 2009.

Raison-Jourde, F. *Les souverains de Madagascar.* Paris, Editions Karthala, 1983.

Rajoelina, P. *Quarante années de la vie politique de Madagascar, 1947–1987.* Paris, L'Harmattan, 1988.

Rajoelina, P., and Ramelet, A. *Madagascar, la grande île.* Paris, L'Harmattan, 1989.

Ralaimihoatra, E. *Histoire de Madagascar.* 2 vols. Antananarivo, Société Malgache d'Editions, 1966–67.

Ramahatra, O. *Madagascar: une économie en phase d'ajustement.* Paris, L'Harmattan, 1989.

Ratsiraka, D. *Didier Ratsiraka. Transition démocratique et pauvreté à Madagascar.* Paris, Editions Karthala, 2015.

Réseau des observatoires ruraux (Madagascar). *Madagascar dans la tourmente: analyses socioéconomiques de la crise en zones rurales.* Paris, L'Harmattan, 2011.

Roubaud, F. *Identités et transition démocratique: l'exception malgache.* Paris, L'Harmattan, 2001.

Schuurman, D., and Ravelojoana, N. *Madagascar.* London, New Holland, 1997.

SeFaFi. *L'Observatoire de la Vie Publique à Madagascar 2001–13.* Paris, L'Harmattan, 2014.

Sodikoff, G. M. *Forest and Labor in Madagascar: From Colonial Concession to Global Biosphere.* Bloomington, IN, Indiana University Press, 2012.

Spacensky, A. *Madagascar: cinquante ans de vie politique (de Ralaimongo à Tsiranana).* Paris, Nouvelles Editions Latines, 1970.

Tronchon, J. *L'insurrection malgache de 1947.* Paris, Editions Karthala, 1986.

Tyson, P. *The Eighth Continent: Life, Death and Discovery in the Lost World of Madagascar.* New York, William Morrow & Co, 2000.

Vivier, J.-L. *Madagascar, une île à la dérive: les années 2007–2010: de Ravalomanana à Rajoelina.* Paris, L'Harmattan, 2010.

MALAWI

Physical and Social Geography

A. MacGREGOR HUTCHESON

The landlocked Republic of Malawi extends some 840 km from north to south, varying in width from 80 to 160 km. It has a total area of 118,760 sq km (45,853 sq miles), including 24,208 sq km (9,347 sq miles) of inland water, and is aligned along the southern continuation of the east African Rift Valley system. There are land borders with Tanzania to the north, with Zambia to the west, and with Mozambique to the south and east. Frontiers with Mozambique and Tanzania continue to the east, along the shores of Lake Malawi.

Malawi occupies a plateau of varying height, bordering the deep Rift Valley trench, which averages 80 km in width. The northern two-thirds of the Rift Valley floor are almost entirely occupied by Lake Malawi, which is 568 km in length and varies in width from 16 km to 80 km. The lake covers an area of 23,310 sq km, and has a mean surface of 472 m above sea level. The southern third of the Rift Valley is traversed by the Shire river, draining Lake Malawi, via the shallow Lake Malombe, to the Zambezi river. The plateau surfaces on either side of the Rift Valley lie mainly at 760 m–1,370 m, but elevations up to 3,000 m are attained; above the highlands west of Lake Malawi are the Nyika and Viphya plateaux (at 2,606 m and 1,954 m, respectively) and the Dedza mountains and Kirk Range, which rise to between 1,524 m and 2,440 m in places. South of Lake Malawi are the Shire highlands and the Zomba and Mulanje mountain ranges; the Zomba plateau rises to 2,087 m, and Mt Mulanje, the highest mountain in central Africa, to 3,050 m above sea level.

The great variations in altitude and latitudinal extent are responsible for a wide range of climatic, soil and vegetational conditions within Malawi. There are three climatic seasons. During the cool season, from May to August, there is very little cloud, and mean temperatures in the plateau areas are 15.5°C–18°C, and in the Rift Valley 20°C–24.5°C. The coldest month is July, when the maximum temperature is 22.2°C and the minimum 11.7°C. In September and October, before the rains, a short hot season occurs when humidity increases: mean temperatures range from 27°C–30°C in the Rift Valley, and from 22°C–24.5°C on the plateaux at this time. During October–November temperatures exceeding 37°C may be registered in the low-lying areas. The rainy season lasts from November to April, and over 90% of the total annual rainfall occurs during this period. Most of Malawi receives an annual rainfall of 760 mm–1,015 mm, but some areas in the higher plateaux experience over 1,525 mm.

Malawi possesses some of the most fertile soils in south-central Africa. Of particular importance are those in the lake-shore plains, the Lake Chilwa-Palombe plain and the upper and lower Shire valley. Good plateau soils occur in the Lilongwe-Kasungu high plains and in the tea-producing areas of Thyolo, Mulanje and Nkhata Bay districts. In 2016 some 61.4% of the total land area was agricultural land. The lakes and rivers have been exploited for their considerable hydro-electric and irrigation potential.

Malawi is one of the more densely populated countries of Africa, with 17,563,749 inhabitants (giving an average density of 185.8 per sq km) according to the September 2018 census. By mid-2022 the population had, according to official projections, increased to 19,351,892, with a density of 204.7 inhabitants per sq km. Population patterns are affected by the high rate of incidence of HIV/AIDS, which is particularly prevalent in urban areas. Labour has been a Malawian resource for many years, and thousands of migratory workers seek employment in neighbouring countries, particularly in South Africa.

As a result of physical, historical and economic factors, Malawi's population is unevenly distributed. According to the September 2018 census, the Southern Region, the most developed of the three regions, contained 44.1% of the population, while the Central Region had 42.9% and the Northern Region only 13.0%.

History

CHRISTOPHER SAUNDERS

INTRODUCTION

On 6 July 1964 the British colony of Nyasaland became the independent state of Malawi. For almost three decades thereafter the country was dominated by Dr Hastings Kamuzu Banda, who had led the struggle against British rule. He ruled dictatorially from 1971 as President-for-life. His Malawi Congress Party (MCP) was the only legal political organization, and no opposition was tolerated. Banda established diplomatic relations with apartheid South Africa in 1967. Malawi's relations with its independent neighbours were strained, and during the 1980s Mozambique alleged that members of the Resistência Nacional Moçambicana were operating from Malawi. It was not until the mid-1990s that most Mozambican refugees were repatriated from Malawi.

In the early 1990s the Banda regime came under increasing pressure to reform. In March 1992 the bishops of the influential Roman Catholic Church publicly condemned the state's abuses of human rights. Political exiles from Malawi began to organize in Lusaka, Zambia, and in May anti-Government riots in the southern Malawian city of Blantyre spread to the capital, Lilongwe. Shortly afterwards international donors suspended non-humanitarian aid pending reform, and in September the Alliance for Democracy (AFORD), a pressure group for political reform, and the United Democratic Front (UDF), a political party to challenge Banda, were formed. In October Banda reluctantly agreed to a national referendum by secret ballot on the introduction of multi-party democracy.

Despite efforts by the Government to disrupt the opposition, 63.2% of voters in the referendum of June 1993 supported the reintroduction of a multi-party system. Banda established a National Executive Council to oversee this transition and a National Consultative Council to draft a new constitution. He also announced an amnesty for political exiles and promised to hold a multi-party general election within a year. The Constitution was duly amended to allow the registration of political parties other than the MCP; these subsequently included AFORD and the UDF.

Banda became seriously ill in October 1993 and underwent surgery in South Africa. A three-member Presidential Council assumed executive power in his absence. In November the National Assembly adopted constitutional amendments that, *inter alia*, repealed the institution of life presidency and the requirement that election candidates belong to the MCP. After making an unexpected recovery, Banda resumed full presidential powers in December. Banda stood as the MCP's presidential candidate in the May 1994 election, but Bakili Muluzi, the UDF leader, was placed first with 47.3% of the votes. Banda took 33.6%, and Chakufwa Chihana, the AFORD leader, 18.6%. The UDF won 84 of the 177 seats in the National Assembly, the MCP 55, and AFORD 36.

THE MULUZI PRESIDENCY, 1994–2004

Although President Muluzi included smaller parties in his Cabinet, AFORD and the MCP agreed to work together in opposition, thereby depriving the Government of a parliamentary majority. In June 1994 Muluzi established an independent commission of inquiry to investigate the deaths in 1983 of Dick Matenje, then MCP Secretary-General, and three other senior politicians in an alleged road accident. In January 1995 Banda, now a chief suspect, was placed under house arrest, and John Tembo, who had been Governor of the Reserve Bank of Malawi (RBM—the central bank) and a rival of Matenje, and two former police officers were arrested and charged with murder and conspiracy to murder. In December, however, all the defendants were acquitted. In November 1997 Banda died in South Africa.

Presidential and legislative elections were held on 15 June 1999. Muluzi was re-elected to the presidency, securing 51.4% of the votes, while Gwandaguluwe Chakuamba, the MCP President, obtained 43.3%. In the elections to the expanded, 193-member National Assembly, the ruling UDF won 93 seats, the MCP 66, and AFORD 29. Although international observers considered the elections largely free and fair, the MCP-AFORD alliance challenged Muluzi's victory and several results. Nevertheless, Muluzi was inaugurated for a second term in late June, and a new Cabinet was appointed. In August the UDF regained a parliamentary majority, when four independent deputies resumed their support for the party.

In December 1999 a Southern African Development Community (SADC) report criticized the Malawi Electoral Commission (MEC) and recommended that its membership should be entirely without political affiliation. After a recount of votes cast in the presidential election, lawyers representing the MCP-AFORD alliance claimed to have discovered evidence of electoral fraud in favour of the UDF. However, in May 2000 the High Court dismissed the opposition's case and declared Muluzi's election to the presidency lawful. Meanwhile, the MCP was weakened by a power struggle between Chakuamba and its Vice-President, Tembo.

From early 2001 senior UDF officials campaigned for the Constitution to be amended to enable President Muluzi to seek a third five-year term. After this was rejected by opposition parties and church leaders, Muluzi banned assemblies or demonstrations that either supported or condemned the proposal, on security grounds. Militant young UDF activists attacked opposition supporters.

Amid a food crisis and drought, in February 2002 the President declared a state of famine, in the hope of securing large amounts of aid. However, donor countries held the Government partly responsible for failing to manage the crisis properly, and initially aid was not forthcoming. It was revealed that sizeable emergency stores of maize had been sold during the previous two years, primarily to Kenya. In August the Minister of Poverty Alleviation, Leonard Mangulama, was dismissed and charged with abuse of office for selling off the grain stores while Minister of Agriculture. By mid-2002 an estimated 3m. people required food aid, which began to arrive from the USA, the European Union and the United Kingdom. The severity of the situation was compounded by an outbreak of cholera and the HIV/AIDS crisis. By the end of 2003 about 14% of the adult population (aged 15–49 years) were living with HIV/AIDS, and, despite government measures, the rate of infection continued to increase. From December 2002 the food situation began to improve as rain and mostly British supplies of seed and fertilizer packs enabled new crops to be planted.

As criticism continued to build, the UDF abandoned its efforts to secure a third term for Muluzi. In April 2003 Muluzi dissolved the Cabinet and named Bingu wa Mutharika, the new Minister of Economic Planning and Development, as the party's candidate in the presidential election scheduled for 20 May 2004. The MEC initially claimed to have registered

some 6.6m. voters, but following opposition complaints, almost 1m. people were removed from a revised voters' roll. While the election body blamed incorrect information given to its officials by those registering, opposition parties accused the MEC of mismanagement. The Supreme Court nevertheless ordered the election to proceed.

Polling proceeded peacefully, although opposition parties subsequently alleged electoral malpractice and threatened legal challenges. Mutharika was declared the winner of the presidential election, with 35.9% of the vote. Tembo received 27.1%, and Chakuamba, who now led the newly formed Republican Party (RP), 25.7%. In the concurrent legislative elections, the UDF won only 49 seats in the 193-member National Assembly. The MCP won the most seats, taking 56, the RP secured 15, the National Democratic Alliance eight, and AFORD six. Election observers generally described the polling as free but not fair, owing to the flawed registration process and pro-UDF media. There were widespread demands for the MEC to be disbanded owing to its chaotic handling of the polls.

THE MUTHARIKA PRESIDENCY, 2004–12

Mutharika was sworn in as Malawi's new President on 24 May 2004. The UDF swiftly secured a working majority in the National Assembly, as Muluzi, who remained National Chairman of the party, attracted opposition support for the new Government. However, as Mutharika began investigations into associates of Muluzi on suspicion of corruption, relations between the two men deteriorated. In February 2005 Mutharika resigned from the UDF leadership, dismissed three Muluzi loyalists from the Government, announced his intention to form a new political party and began to create a parliamentary support base from small parties, independents and disaffected UDF members. Mutharika formally launched his Democratic Progressive Party (DPP) in May, and 18 UDF deputies had joined the new party by July. He pledged that it would promote good governance and transparency and develop the economy. One of Mutharika's first acts as President was to introduce a programme providing subsidized fertilizer and seed to farmers. In 2005 1.7m. of Malawi's 11m. people required food aid after the recurrence of drought; however, within a few years the distribution of subsidized seed and fertilizer had transformed the agricultural sector, and the country had become a net maize exporter.

During 2005 the political infighting intensified. In May the Minister of Education and Human Resources, Yusuf Mwawa, was arrested on charges of corruption, fraud and misuse of public funds. When the opposition accused Mutharika of acting dictatorially, he accused the UDF of seeking to curb his clampdown on corruption and undermine his moves to modernize the economy. After the UDF and Tembo agreed to co-operate, the National Assembly voted in October to begin proceedings to impeach the President. Mutharika was summoned to face an indictment; however, the impeachment process was halted by the High Court on constitutional grounds, and the motion was withdrawn in January 2006. Other UDF members subsequently joined the DPP. Following a judgment of the Constitutional Court in November that placed restrictions on deputies who switched party allegiance, Mutharika's political opponents requested a court ruling on whether the Speaker of the National Assembly should declare a seat vacant when a deputy crossed the floor. This would have a potentially serious impact on the DPP: most of the 80 deputies liable to be affected were from the President's new party.

Mutharika's dismissal in February 2006 of Cassim Chilumpha, his Vice-President and a close ally of Muluzi, for neglecting his duties, resulted in the High Court ordering his reinstatement. However, in April Chilumpha was arrested and charged with treason and conspiring with South African mercenaries to assassinate the President. Lawyers for Chilumpha argued that he was immune from prosecution while in office, but he remained in custody, before being placed under house arrest and then released. In March 2007 Muluzi announced that he would stand as the UDF candidate in the 2009 presidential election. In April, however, constitutional revisions were approved that limited a President to two terms and established the minimum requirement of a first university degree for candidates. Muluzi, who did not have a degree, claimed that the two-term rule applied only to consecutive terms.

Opposition parties welcomed the High Court ruling in June 2007 that the Speaker could declare a seat vacant in the event of a deputy crossing the floor, subsequently refusing to approve the 2007/08 budget in an attempt to force the issue. In September the UDF finally agreed to adopt the budget. Mutharika then prorogued the National Assembly, stating that it was wasting taxpayers' money by debating issues that had no bearing on the lives of ordinary Malawians. The legislature was not convened until April 2008, as the President wished to prevent the Speaker, an MCP member, from invoking the section of the Constitution that prohibited deputies from switching party allegiance. The opposition initially boycotted the parliamentary sessions and again threatened to block the budget, unless the Speaker removed those deputies who had crossed the floor. However, in August 2008 an agreement was reached between the Government and the opposition parties, which had a parliamentary majority, whereby the latter would approve the 2008/09 budget in return for a government assurance that a special session would be held to resolve the floor crossing issue.

Meanwhile, Mutharika warned his predecessor Muluzi that he could face charges of treason for plotting to overthrow the Government, and in February 2009 Mulizi was arrested and charged with redirecting donor funds into his private bank account while President. This, together with confirmation by the Constitutional Court that he was ineligible to contest the election, having already served two terms, ended Muluzi's bid for the presidency and left Tembo as Mutharika's main opponent.

After a bitter campaign, Malawi's fourth multi-party elections took place on 19 May 2009. Mutharika was returned for a second term as President with 64.4% of the votes. The DPP and its allies secured control of the National Assembly in the legislative elections, with the party winning 112 of the 192 contested seats (voting in one constituency was postponed owing to the death of a candidate); the MCP took only 27 seats, and the UDF 18 seats. Tembo, who secured 29.9% of the votes in the presidential election, claimed that the vote had been rigged, and the Commonwealth observer mission reported state media bias. However, Muluzi quickly accepted the result.

The scale of Mutharika's victory was largely a consequence of his record in economic affairs, having transformed Malawi into a food exporter and achieved three years of strong growth. However, the international financial crisis was beginning to affect Malawi. The country obtained 40% of its state revenues from the sale of tobacco, earnings from which declined in 2010. In 2008 Malawi severed ties with the Republic of China (Taiwan) and subsequently established diplomatic relations with the People's Republic of China, which became a new market for Malawi's tobacco exports and agreed to fund the construction of a new parliamentary building. However, hopes for economic recovery rested primarily on large uranium deposits located in the north of the country; it was hoped that Malawi could become one of Africa's largest uranium producers.

In December 2010 Joyce Banda, the country's first female Vice-President, was expelled from the DPP for refusing to endorse Mutharika's brother, the Minister of Education, Science and Technology, Prof. Arthur Peter Mutharika, as the ruling party's presidential candidate for the 2014 election. Members of the DPP sought to undermine the Vice-President, suspecting that she planned to run for the presidency herself. (Banda formed a new political party, the People's Party—PP, in March 2011.) Meanwhile, in February 2011 a lecturer at Chancellor College (the largest constituent college of the University of Malawi) spoke to his students about the popular uprisings in North Africa and the Middle East. Spies in his class informed the police, who subsequently interrogated him. Other lecturers then abandoned classes in protest at their colleague's detention. The President accused the lecturers of promoting 'academic anarchy' and ordered that both Chancellor College and another constituent college, the Polytechnic, be shut down.

Following the online release by WikiLeaks, an organization publishing leaked private and classified content, of a diplomatic cable in which the British High Commissioner had referred to Mutharika as 'ever more autocratic and intolerant of criticism', the High Commissioner was expelled from Lilongwe in April 2011. The UK responded by expelling Malawi's acting High Commissioner from London. The donor community had by this time become increasingly uneasy about the apparent trend towards authoritarianism in Malawi and the leadership's lack of accountability. The USA's Millennium Challenge Corporation (MCC) had delayed approving a US $350m. grant for Malawi's collapsing electricity network in response to the Government's threats to media freedom and its opposition to homosexual marriages, but the grant was finally approved in April. However, the UK—Malawi's single largest bilateral donor—announced in May that it had frozen new aid to Malawi, pending a review of bilateral ties.

Peaceful protests took place across Malawi on 20–21 July 2011, organized by various civil society groups. The protests, influenced by similar activity in the Arab world, were met with live police fire, and at least 19 demonstrators were killed. In response, the USA suspended the recent MCC agreement. Further protests against the President were postponed, after he agreed to mediation with civil society groups, including trade unions and religious organizations, under the auspices of the United Nations (UN). The talks began in August but produced no satisfactory outcome.

In September 2011 Mutharika appointed a new Cabinet, which included his wife as National Co-ordinator of Maternal, Infant and Child Health and HIV/Nutrition/Malaria and Tuberculosis. In his final months in office, President Mutharika continued to ignore appeals by civil society groups and Malawi's donors to engage with his critics and introduce reforms. As the economy deteriorated, poverty increased. Urban protests took place over fuel and electricity shortages, the lack of political freedom and extensive government corruption. On 5 April 2012 President Mutharika died suddenly of a heart attack. Initially, his death was not announced, and his body was sent to South Africa, giving time for his brother Peter, a former law professor who was now Minister of Foreign Affairs, to engineer his own succession. Following the official announcement of the President's death, the plotters of what in effect would have been a coup were pre-empted, when the head of the army confirmed that he would support Joyce Banda as the rightful successor, in accordance with the Constitution. On 7 April Banda was sworn in as southern Africa's first female President. The change in leadership precipitated mass defections from the DPP and the UDF to the PP, giving Banda's party a majority in the National Assembly.

THE BANDA PRESIDENCY, 2012–14

Once in office, Banda moved quickly to break with the policies of her autocratic predecessor. She removed from her Cabinet the late President's brother and widow and replaced the chief of police, who had been blamed for the July 2011 shootings, with a human rights advocate. She made key changes at the central bank, the Treasury, the Ministry of Information and Civic Education and elsewhere. Banda pledged to restore good relations with Malawi's donors and pressurized the US Secretary of State, Hillary Clinton, to release US $350m. from the MCC, informing her that Malawi was 'committed to restoring the rule of law, respect for human rights and freedoms, and demonstrating good economic governance'. To boost the economy and mend relations with donors, Banda agreed to abandon the peg between the kwacha and the US dollar.

In May 2012 the central bank removed the peg, allowing the kwacha to devalue by one-third. The International Monetary Fund (IMF), which had appealed for this reform, responded by providing a three-year loan package worth US $157m. In June the $350m. MCC grant was restored, with the immediate aim of improving Malawi's electricity supply. Meanwhile, Banda reduced her presidential salary, sold the presidential jet and ordered her ministers to relinquish their luxury cars. The price of fuel was raised, and state expenditure was reduced by cutting subsidies to farmers. The UK responded by dispatching a new High Commissioner to Lilongwe and pledged funds to stabilize the Malawian economy and support the health care system.

The African Union had planned to hold its mid-year summit in Lilongwe in 2012, but Banda warned that if the President of Sudan, Lt-Gen. Omar Hassan Ahmad al-Bashir, attended he would be arrested, owing to his indictment by the International Criminal Court. The meeting was therefore moved to Ethiopia. In her first state of the nation address, in May, Banda announced that she would urge the National Assembly to legalize homosexuality. In November Malawi's laws against same-sex relationships, which provided for a maximum prison sentence of 14 years, were suspended.

Shortly after becoming President, Banda disclosed that she had uncovered evidence that former President Mutharika had tried to arrange her assassination. After a commission of inquiry published its findings on his death, in March 2013, several DPP leaders, including his brother Peter, were arrested. They were subsequently charged with treason for their alleged involvement in a reported plot to prevent Banda's accession. Notwithstanding the charges against him, Peter Mutharika was elected as DPP President in April. Although the resumption of aid allowed the Government to increase public sector salaries and restore fertilizer subsidies, the rising cost of living provoked anti-Government protests in early 2013. From February Banda's PP was confronted with growing opposition in the National Assembly and thus required the support of smaller parties to adopt legislation. Banda herself was accused of pandering to international donors and criticized for her extensive foreign travel.

Meanwhile, a longstanding border dispute with Tanzania became acrimonious in 2012, when Malawi granted the British firm Surestream Petroleum the right to explore for oil in the north-eastern area of Lake Malawi. Tanzania argued that the boundary between the two countries lay in the middle of the lake, while Malawi, citing an Anglo-German treaty of 1890, claimed that it owned the entire lake. Following unsuccessful bilateral talks, the issue went to SADC mediation. A proposed compromise, whereby Malawi and Tanzania would agree to share Lake Malawi and later tackle border delimitation, was not accepted, and the dispute flared up again in January 2016, after Tanzania issued a map showing the border running down the middle of the lake. When the respective leaders met in January 2017, they agreed to revive the mediation process, but in March President Peter Mutharika stated that drilling for oil and gas in Lake Malawi would proceed, despite environmental concerns and opposition from Tanzania. Malawi's Government announced in May that it would take the matter to the International Court of Justice in The Hague, Netherlands. The dispute remained unresolved at mid-2022.

In September 2013 a major scandal broke, when the Anti-Corruption Bureau (ACB) disclosed that large sums of government money (as much as US $250m.) had been transferred into private bank accounts. In that month an assassination attempt was apparently made on the budget director in the Ministry of Finance, Paul Mphwiyo, who had been tasked with combating high-level corruption. It was revealed that civil servants had been exploiting loopholes in the state's payment system to private companies to divert substantial funds to themselves. In response to the revelations in what the media dubbed 'Cashgate', Banda dismissed her Cabinet on 10 October and five days later appointed a new Government, which excluded those implicated in the scandal. A parliamentary investigation was instigated, various arrests were made, and a ministerial portfolio for good governance was created. In November the former Minister of Justice and Constitutional Affairs, Ralph Kasambara, was detained by the police and charged with the attempted murder of Mphwiyo. (He received a 13-year prison sentence but in March 2018 was released on bail by a Supreme Court of Appeal judge, pending an appeal.) Legal proceedings against those accused of involvement in the Cashgate scandal (predominantly lower-ranking public servants) began in January 2014.

In response to the financial scandal, the UK joined other states in freezing aid to Malawi, pending an IMF review. As donor aid accounted for up to 40% of Malawi's development budget, the freeze threatened to halt the country's economic revival. In December 2013 the head of Malawi's Catholic Commission for Justice and Peace claimed that Banda was herself involved in the scandal, and that the PP had used state funds for its campaign ahead of the general election scheduled for 20 May 2014. Banda denied the allegations, reiterating her determination to eradicate corruption, and during the election campaign she publicly claimed credit for uncovering the fraud scandal. However, Peter Mutharika continued to claim that some of the money siphoned off in the Cashgate scandal had been used to fund Banda's campaign.

Eleven candidates contested the presidency in the May 2014 election, which was chaotic, with many polling stations opening late, and some recording more votes than there were registered voters. When the preliminary results suggested that she had lost the presidency, Banda claimed that the polls had been marred by serious irregularities and were therefore null and void. She demanded that fresh elections be held within 90 days. However, the MEC stated that it would conduct a recount. When the High Court ruled against this, the MEC announced that Peter Mutharika of the DPP had won 36.4% of the votes cast in the presidential poll, Lazarus Chakwera of the MCP 27.8%, and Banda only 20.2%. The MCP, which had supported a recount, announced its intention to challenge the results in court. In the concurrent legislative elections, the DPP took 50 of the 192 contested seats, while the MCP secured 48, the PP 26, the scandal-ridden UDF only 14, and AFORD just one. When civil society organizations described the elections as neither fair nor credible, there were demands for Malawi's electoral processes to be reformed and the MEC's independence and technical capacity expanded.

THE MUTHARIKA PRESIDENCY, 2014–20

Peter Mutharika was sworn in as President on 31 May 2014. He assumed the defence portfolio and appointed Atupele Muluzi of the UDF, son of the former President, who had come fourth in the presidential election, Minister of Natural Resources, Energy and Mining. (Muluzi was transferred to head the Ministry of Home Affairs and Internal Security in April 2015.) Mutharika and his Vice-President, Saulos Chilima, a former telecommunications executive, deferred large increases in their salaries, but members of parliament declined to follow suit, despite Malawi's poverty.

Shortly after Mutharika's installation as President, which afforded him immunity from prosecution, the Director of Public Prosecutions dismissed the treason charges against him. In December 2014 a warrant of arrest was issued against Banda for her alleged involvement in the Cashgate scandal. She had left Malawi and claimed that there was a plot to assassinate her, if she returned. The Government, accusing her of being the main beneficiary of Cashgate and of evading the law, refused to pay her retirement salary. Meanwhile, several PP members defected to the ruling DPP.

In May 2015 a former Commander of the Malawi Defence Force (MDF), Gen. Henry Odillo, who had been dismissed by Peter Mutharika in June 2014, and another senior officer were arrested for allegedly authorizing fraudulent payments to a firm that had not actually supplied any services to the military. Meanwhile, several trials of people implicated in the Cashgate affair were held. In October 2015 the first of those charged were convicted and imprisoned. A forensic audit into the scandal conducted by British-based auditors PricewaterhouseCoopers had found that corrupt practices had been taking place for several years, and that the PP, the DPP and the MCP had all used stolen money for campaign purposes. The report, released in May 2015, found that K577,000m. (US $1,400m.) was unaccounted for.

When a senior ACB official, Issa Njauju, was murdered in Lilongwe in July 2015, it was widely assumed that his killing was linked to the Cashgate scandal. Although this subsequently appeared not to be the case, several ACB officials left the organization following the murder, and the rate of prosecutions related to the scandal slowed. Nevertheless, many of those who were put on trial claimed that Banda was the mastermind behind the siphoning off of government funds. The ACB continued to pursue a case against Bakili Muluzi, who was accused of diverting K1,700m. of public funds into his personal account. Muluzi argued that the charges amounted to political persecution and that Bingu Wa Mutharika had interfered with ACB operations by ordering his arrest on corruption charges. While the opposition criticized President Peter Mutharika for weak leadership, deteriorating public services and his failure to tackle poverty, he blamed the country's difficulties on the Cashgate scandal. In May 2017 the Director of Public Prosecutions announced that the state had seized property, including houses and vehicles belonging to those responsible for theft of public resources, valued at K600m., as well as K175m. in cash.

After severe floods in southern Malawi caused serious destruction and displaced over 200,000 people in January 2015, the UN provided US $9.2m. of emergency relief. However, major Western donors continued to suspend budgetary aid, and the IMF refused to release a K20,000m. tranche of its Extended Credit Facility until the Government balanced its books. In March the Global Fund to Fight AIDS, Tuberculosis and Malaria cancelled $574m. in grants to Malawi and asked for the return of funds already disbursed, owing to concerns about financial mismanagement, following claims that some of the money had been diverted to Mutharika's relatives. In October, however, Malawi received $332m. from the Global Fund to procure more anti-retroviral drugs and combat malaria and tuberculosis. Nevertheless, Malawi continued to have one of the highest HIV prevalence rates in the world (9% of the adult population in 2021). It also remained one of the poorest countries in the world, with about one-third of the population living on less than US $1 per day. Malawi was the first country to repatriate its citizens from South Africa after an upsurge in xenophobic violence there in April 2015.

In 2015/16 Malawi was severely affected by drought conditions associated with the climatic phenomenon known as El Niño. In April 2016 the President declared a state of disaster over the resultant food crisis. By this time, with maize production having dropped significantly, almost 3m. people faced food insecurity, and Mutharika appealed for international humanitarian aid. In May the World Food Programme, the main provider of aid, confirmed that Malawi's food crisis was the worst in decades. After good rains, in 2017 Malawi removed its ban on the export of maize. However, the food crisis had given rise to the so-called 'Maizegate' scandal: it was alleged that there had been large-scale corruption, involving government officials, in procuring maize from Zambia, which had waived its own maize export ban to help its neighbour. The Office of the Director of Public Procurement and the ACB opened investigations, while the President appointed a commission of inquiry. After the publication of the commission's report, together with the findings of a joint parliamentary committee, the ACB raided the home of the Minister of Agriculture, George Chaponda, where large quantities of cash were discovered. Chaponda was dismissed in February 2017. He was later arrested and charged, but later freed on bail.

The Malawi Law Commission recommended in April 2017 that the existing 'first-past-the-post' system of electing the President should be replaced by one requiring the winning candidate to secure more than 50% of the national vote, failing which a run-off would take place between the two leading candidates. The DPP benefited from the existing system, which favoured presidential candidates from more populated regions, such as the Southern region. Opposition parties and faith-based and civil society groups urged that the proposed new system be adopted. However, when the Government reluctantly brought draft electoral reform legislation before the National Assembly in November 2017, it was rejected by the DPP and some PP deputies. Meanwhile, factionalism within opposition parties increased, and both the PP and the UDF were divided over the issue of co-operation with the DPP. The MCP President, Chakwera, rejected a demand by his party's Secretary-General, Gustav Kaliwo, that an emergency convention be held to choose a new leader before the 2019 elections. Kaliwo and other officials were suspended from their party posts, and, following lengthy legal disputes, an MCP convention was held in May 2018, at which Chakwera was re-elected party President. Meanwhile, in April the first large anti-Government demonstrations since 2011 took place, with thousands chanting 'Peter Must Resign'.

After a four-year absence, former President Banda returned to Malawi in April 2018. A warrant for her arrest in connection with the Cashgate scandal was not served, sparking speculation that she had reached an agreement with President Mutharika. While the police claimed to have evidence that she had committed offences relating to abuse of office and money laundering, she insisted that she had merely, on learning of the corruption, requested a forensic audit to reveal its extent. Meanwhile, a high-profile Cashgate case in which the former budget director and others were charged with fraud, negligence, money laundering and theft, stalled, when the defence lawyer withdrew. Critics accused the ACB of being ineffectual, and some commentators considered entrenched corruption to be a major reason for Malawi's continued impoverishment.

Political tensions increased prior to the 2019 national and local elections. One faction in the ruling DPP sought to advance Chilima as the DPP's presidential candidate instead of Mutharika. When this was rejected, Chilima and others left the party, and in July 2018 Chilima announced that he would contest the presidency as leader of the new United Transformation Movement (UTM). Chakwera, leader of the parliamentary opposition, called on Chilima to resign as Vice-President, as did members of the DPP, but he refused to do so. Chakwera accused Mutharika of involvement in a scandal concerning a US $4m. contract to provide rations to Malawi's police force. Mutharika, denying the allegations, insisted that a political donation from the contractor had been returned, as soon as the DPP discovered possible links to corruption. Chakwera received a major boost in March 2019, when Banda withdrew from the presidential race and pledged to support his candidacy. The funding of political parties was to be regulated for the first time.

With Transparency International's 2017 Corruption Perceptions Index ranking Malawi 122nd out of 180 countries, the country's donors remained sceptical that the Government was serious about tackling corruption. In May 2018 the Minister of Finance, Economic Planning and Development, Goodall Gondwe, announced the provision of major budgetary support from the World Bank but added that there would be no donor support for the 2019 elections. The economy remained fragile, relying heavily on agriculture—particularly tobacco exports—for foreign exchange. Unemployment was high, and only 10% of Malawians had access to electricity. In March 2019 Cyclone Idai caused major flooding, and many refugees left Mozambique for Malawi. Intermittent power outages continued.

THE 2019 AND 2020 ELECTIONS

Presidential and legislative elections were held on 21 May 2019. Observer missions praised the MEC for its organization of the polls, which included the use of a new biometric system of voting, but there was not a level playing field. The 78-year-old President Mutharika had the advantage of incumbency. A month before the elections the Government awarded 20,000 teachers and 7,000 police officers pay increases, despite the recommendation of the IMF and the World Bank that the Government control its wage bill. The Government also provided agricultural subsidies to farmers. Civil servants subsequently demanded better working conditions and threatened to strike. When early results suggested that Chakwera had not won the presidential election, the MCP obtained a court injunction to delay the release of the final results, owing to alleged irregularities, and demanded a recount in some districts. The final results, as announced by the MEC, gave Mutharika 38.6% of the votes and Chakwera 35.4%. Mutharika was sworn in for a second five-year term as President on 28 May. Chilima, who came third in the presidential poll, with 20.2% of the votes cast, rejected the result and called for fresh elections. Meanwhile, in the legislative elections the DPP won 62 seats, the MCP 55, and 55 independents were elected. Although several independents immediately joined the DPP in the National Assembly, the DPP did not control a majority, and the MCP elected one of its members to be Malawi's first female Speaker.

Following the elections, opposition parties and the Human Rights Defenders Coalition organized a series of nationwide protests, which steadily gained momentum. Some became violent and led to clashes with the police. The Government attempted to ban further protests, but in August 2019 the High Court upheld the right to protest. Meanwhile, the Constitutional Court started to hear a challenge to the results of the presidential election which had been brought by Chakwera and Chilima. The protests continued in early 2020. On 3 February the Constitutional Court annulled the results, ruling that the election had been flawed and that a fresh poll should be held within 150 days. The Court cited widespread irregularities, including duplicate forms and the use of correction fluid, as well as missing signatures on some result sheets, and determined that 'majority' in Section 80 of the Constitution should be interpreted as a 50% +1 majority electoral system. It directed the National Assembly's Public Appointments Committee (PAC) to assess the competence of the MEC's commissioners. For showing independence from the executive, the judges were given a prestigious award in October by the Royal Institute of International Affairs in London. In April 2021 the judiciary received further praise, when the Supreme Court of Appeal declared the death penalty unconstitutional and ordered the re-sentencing of all convicts facing execution. Although no executions had taken place since 1994, capital punishment had been mandatory for prisoners convicted of murder or treason and optional for rape and violent robbery.

The National Assembly adopted electoral reform legislation to meet the Constitutional Court's requirements, while 23 June 2020 was set as the date for the new presidential election. The PAC recommended that the MEC commissioners be replaced. Mutharika and the MEC rejected the Court's ruling and filed an appeal with the Supreme Court, arguing that there was no evidence that the election result had been affected by any irregularities. Mutharika refused to ratify the National Assembly's electoral reform bills or to replace the MEC commissioners. Instead, he appointed a new Cabinet, reflecting an alliance between the ruling DPP and the UDF, and dismissed the head of the MDF. Meanwhile, the President declared a 'state of disaster', without reference to parliament, over the COVID-19 pandemic. He closed schools and banned large gatherings, but his announcement of a three-week lockdown led to protests in Malawi's major cities. The High Court granted a temporary interdict against the implementation of the lockdown, on the grounds that the Government had not introduced measures to cushion the impact of the crisis. Mutharika then announced an emergency cash transfer programme targeting 172,000 households, each of which would receive a monthly grant of US $50 for six months, beginning in May. In that month the Supreme Court rejected his appeal and confirmed that the presidential election should proceed.

As COVID-19 spread, in late May 2020 over 400 people recently repatriated from South Africa and elsewhere, many of whom had tested positive for the virus, fled from a quarantine centre in Blantyre. Meanwhile, Chakwera and Chilima forged the broad-based Tonse (meaning 'All of Us' in Chewa) Alliance between the MCP, the UTM and seven small parties. It was agreed that if the alliance won the presidential election, Chakwera would become President and Chilima Vice-President. Despite the ongoing pandemic, election campaigning proceeded, and all the main parties held large rallies. Former President Muluzi endorsed the candidacy of Mutharika, whose running mate was Muluzi's son, Atupele, the leader of the UDF.

In early June 2020 President Mutharika cast doubt on whether any credible election could be held after the annulment of the 2019 poll. However, civil society had been energized, and most Malawians were desperate for change. Although the MEC, under new and impressive leadership, had little time to organize the election (which took place amid growing numbers of COVID-19 cases), it nevertheless went ahead on 23 June 2020, with only local observers. Within days it was clear that Chakwera had decisively won the election, securing 59.3% of the vote, according to official figures. Mutharika obtained 39.9%. Although the DPP claimed election irregularities, Chakwera was sworn in as President on 28 June, with Chilima as his Vice-President. This was the first time in Africa that an incumbent leader had won an election, but then been defeated in a subsequent poll after the

previous result was overturned. In view of this, *The Economist* magazine in December named Malawi its 'country of the year'.

THE CHAKWERA PRESIDENCY 2020–

Once in office, President Chakwera announced plans to tackle Malawi's entrenched poverty—over 70% of the population lived on less than US $1.90 per day. He pledged to attract foreign investment, prevent the illegal export of minerals and encourage agribusiness in a country that was highly dependent on subsistence farming. He also promised to reduce the powers of the presidency and to initiate greater transparency accountability in governance and closer scrutiny of the executive. However, his ambitious agenda was impeded by the ongoing pandemic and other challenges.

In November 2020 Chakwera's first official foreign visit, to South Africa, ended with the departure of his plane being delayed, after the South African police suspected wrongly that a self-styled Malawian prophet, Shepherd Bushiri, and his wife, who were sought on charges of fraud, theft and money laundering, might be on board. Although Bushiri and his wife were later arrested in Malawi, a court in Lilongwe rejected the South African authorities' request for their extradition, straining relations between the two countries.

After several DPP officials were arrested for corruption in early 2021, Mutharika accused the Government of persecuting him and his party. In April the DPP called for Chakwera's election as President to be nullified, after he dismissed two electoral commissioners, on the grounds that they had been declared incompetent in June 2020 by the Constitutional Court for their handling of the polls in May 2019 that had led to Chakwera's election. However, Chakwera invited the DPP to submit new names and the issue was resolved.

Owing to the fact that some two-thirds of Malawi's population is under the age of 24, the rate of severe infection from COVID-19 remained low, and in October 2020 the country's borders and airports were partly reopened, but from December the number of cases increased dramatically. In January 2021 two cabinet ministers died from illness related to COVID-19. Uptake of the vaccine was slow, owing partly to availability and partly to vaccine hesitancy among the population, and Malawi became the first country in Africa to admit to destroying vaccine doses, after they expired unused. Further waves of COVID-19 infections were recorded in July and December. At 12 September 2022, according to the World Health Organization, 87,842 cases of COVID-19 had been reported in Malawi, with 2,675 deaths, although this was widely considered to be an underestimate.

In 2021 Malawian soldiers were deployed to the province of Nord-Kivu in the Democratic Republic of the Congo, as part of Malawi's contribution to the UN Organization Stabilization Mission in the Democratic Republic of the Congo, and by mid-2022 order had largely been restored in the area they were stationed in. But in Malawi itself corruption remained rampant. Malawi dropped to 129th out of 180 countries in Transparency International's 2020 Corruption Perceptions Index. When a parliamentary committee rejected the appointment of Martha Chizuma-Mwangonde, who was widely recognized as a person of integrity, to lead the ACB, there was a public outcry, and anti-Government demonstrations were planned, before she was confirmed in the post. Once in office, she investigated scandals involving the misuse of funds to tackle COVID-19 and the appointment of individuals to public office without the appropriate qualifications. In March 2021 it was reported that the Malawian authorities had seized assets worth over US $2m. from the bodyguard of former President Peter Mutharika. Chakwera in April dismissed his Minister of Labour for misappropriating COVID-19 funds, and among those arrested on corruption-related charges were two of his senior aides and the energy minister. In late July the Secretary to the President and the Cabinet was accused of appropriating some of the funds for independence day celebrations earlier in that month. In August Chakwera's special assistant on religious affairs was arrested for abuse of office and dismissed. In December a former finance minister, a RBM governor and a local government minister were arrested on charges of abuse of office and fraud over the sale of a state-owned bank. Chakwera was criticized for appointing relatives to office and for favouritism towards individuals from his home city of Lilongwe.

Structural reforms that aimed to tackle the country's deep-rooted socioeconomic problems were not initiated, and an application for loan funding from the IMF was put on hold. With little of Chakwera's ambitious agenda achieved, owing partly to the pandemic but also because of poor governance, popular anger increased. The coalition Government was accused of incompetence, corruption and nepotism. In August 2021 the Catholic Commission for Justice and Peace accused the administration of having 'lost direction' and claimed that wrangling among the coalition partners was preventing it from achieving progress, and the Human Rights Defenders' Coalition called for public protests if economic issues were not addressed urgently, notably rising unemployment and the cost of living.

By May 2021 the government coalition was under severe strain, amid disagreements about appointments to public positions and accusations of bribe-taking and illegal payments from private contractors. After the UTM announced that it would leave the coalition Government unless its grievances were addressed, a meeting of the leaders of the MCP, the UTM and AFORD in June calmed tensions, but following President Chakwera's dismissal of Attorney-General Chikosa Silungwe,

a UTM member, in the following month, there were again calls for Chilima to leave the coalition, which remained extremely fragile. In January 2022 Chakwera dismissed his Cabinet and appointed a significantly changed administration, but public criticism of his rule continued to grow. He was accused of excessive international travel, and there was public anger about revelations in a British court concerning a British-based Malawian businessman, Zuneth Sattar, who was under investigation both by Malawi's ACB and by the UK's National Crime Agency on suspicion of paying bribes to Malawian officials over the course of a decade. Chakwera was unable to dismiss Chilima as Vice-President, owing to his role as leader of the UDM in the ruling coalition, but he nevertheless removed Chilima's delegated powers. Together with other senior officials, Chilima was alleged to have received illicit payments from Sattar in exchange for government contracts. Chilima considered the allegation as a means by Chakwera to renege upon the coalition agreement signed in March 2020, which, he claimed, provided for a rotational presidency, although the MCP denied this. Meanwhile the economy deteriorated further, and most Malawians sank deeper into poverty. As the cost of living escalated, in part because of the Russian invasion of Ukraine, demands for Chakwera and Chilima to resign grew stronger.

Economy

DONALD L. SPARKS

Revised for this edition by the editorial staff

INTRODUCTION

Malawi is a small, poor, landlocked country (with a population of 20.4m. at mid-2022, according to United Nations—UN—estimates), which suffers from many of the similar development constraints as its neighbours and ranks among the world's least developed countries. According to the World Bank, in 2021 it had a gross domestic product (GDP) per head of only around US $1,658 (based on purchasing-power parity), and in 2020 about 76% of its population lived below the international poverty line of $1.90 per day. The same source noted in May 2021 that progress in tackling poverty in Malawi had actually stagnated during the past 15 years, in contrast with other regional countries. The UN Development Programme (UNDP) ranked it 174th out of 189 countries on its 2019 Human Development Index, putting it in the 'low human development' category. Furthermore, Malawi was not ranked highly on most other aggregate indicators: it was 128th (out of 141 countries) in the World Economic Forum's 2019 Global Competitiveness Index, and was placed in the middle of countries in the World Bank's 2019 Ease of Doing Business Index (at 109th out of 190 countries).

Malawi does not have a particularly diversified economy. Services accounted for 53.1% of GDP in 2020, with agriculture contributing 26.7% and industry 20.2%. About 80% of the population live in rural areas, and agriculture, which has benefited from fertilizer subsidies since 2006, provides around 90% of export revenue (although most farmers are engaged in subsistence agriculture). The performance of the tobacco sector is key to short-term growth as tobacco accounts for a large percentage of exports. The economy depends on significant amounts of foreign economic assistance from the International Monetary Fund (IMF), the World Bank and individual donor nations, which together provide, on average, 35% of annual government revenue.

RECENT ECONOMIC DEVELOPMENTS

Although Malawi's GDP grew at an average annual rate of 7.1% in 2006–10, it experienced serious economic setbacks in 2011, including a general shortage of foreign exchange, which damaged its ability to pay for imports, and fuel shortages, which hindered transportation and overall productivity. In

that year donors suspended general budget support for Malawi due to a negative IMF review and governance problems. Real GDP growth slowed to 4.3% in 2011. Due to an improved food harvest and higher tobacco production, according to African Development Bank (AfDB) figures, overall GDP grew by 6.1% in 2013 and by an estimated 5.7% in 2014. Growth slowed to some 3.0% in 2015, owing to the late arrival of rains and the severe floods experienced in January, which damaged crops and infrastructure (see below). Following a drought in early 2016, growth in that year declined further, to 2.5%, and the country faced its worst food shortage in over a decade. However, as better weather conditions enabled a bumper harvest, GDP was officially reported to have grown by 5.2% in 2017.

Growth slowed to 3.9% in 2018, mainly because of sluggish expansion in agriculture. Maize output declined during 2018/19, as a result of drought and an infestation of armyworm, and an estimated one-sixth of Malawi's population were at risk of food insecurity. In March 2019 Cyclone Idai—a Category 2 storm, and the most powerful storm ever to strike the southern hemisphere—made landfall in Mozambique and travelled west, causing severe flooding in its wake. This was followed by another storm, Cyclone Kenneth, in April. Nevertheless, despite the impact of these storms (at least 60 people were killed in Malawi and more than 125,000 displaced), the agricultural sector generally performed well, with maize production increasing significantly. According to official figures, GDP grew by 5.6% in 2019.

In mid-April 2020 the Malawian Government instituted a partial lockdown of the country, in an effort to contain the spread of a new coronavirus disease (COVID-19), which had first appeared in the People's Republic of China in December 2019 and which in March 2020 was categorized by the World Health Organization (WHO) as a global pandemic. Schools were closed, public gatherings were restricted, all international flights to Malawi were suspended, and a 14-day quarantine period for people arriving from high-risk countries was introduced. President Arthur Peter Mutharika stated that the country needed around US $200m. to implement a national plan in response to the outbreak; he ordered the lowering of fuel prices to assist those struggling financially during the pandemic, as well as a 10% reduction in the salaries of government ministers (including his own) for three months. The

World Bank pledged US $37m. to support the Government's response to the COVID-19 crisis, while in early May the IMF agreed to disburse $91m. In May 2021 official sources estimated GDP growth of just 0.9% for 2020. Amid a sharp rise in the number of infections from late December 2020, on 12 January 2021 the Government declared a state of disaster. However, the situation started to improve in March, and growth of 3.0% was recorded for 2021, aided by a better harvest than in the previous year. Although a fourth wave of COVID-19 infections occurred in December 2021, this had a smaller economic impact. According to WHO figures, 87,842 confirmed cases of COVID-19 had been reported in Malawi by 5 September 2022, with 2,675 fatalities, a rate of 13.4 per 100,000 of the population; by that time just 10.7% of the population had been fully vaccinated.

During her term of office (April 2012–May 2014) former President Joyce Banda (who inherited an economy with a gloomy outlook) introduced bold economic policy reforms that appeared to reverse the downward trend of the previous few years. These reforms included devaluing the kwacha by 49% to encourage a more flexible foreign exchange regime and removing fuel subsidies. Her Government re-engaged with the IMF by signing a new three-year agreement worth US $157m., and direct budgetary support by donors was resumed. The administration of President Mutharika, which came to power in May 2014, indicated that it would continue to pursue these market-based policies.

Following a re-run of the May 2019 elections, which took place in June 2020 and brought to power President Lazarus Chakwera (see *History*), a new Government took office in the following month. This change of administration complicated Malawi's response to the COVID-19 pandemic, with Chakwera deciding to reduce drastically the number of people and businesses eligible to receive pandemic-related benefits. There have also been claims that the disbursement of aid has been poorly managed by the authorities and unnecessarily slow.

The widespread misappropriation of public funds that was uncovered in late 2013 (and referred to by the media as the 'Cashgate' scandal—see *History*) prompted several donors to suspend their aid disbursements to the Malawian Government (amounting to about US $150m.). Malawi, like many of its neighbours, has a mixed record in governance: the 2020 Ibrahim Index of African Governance ranked it 23rd out of 54 African countries. It ranked 78th (of 167 countries) in the Economist Intelligence Unit's 2021 Democracy Index (and is one of 14 countries in sub-Saharan Africa considered to have a 'hybrid regime'). The Heritage Foundation placed Malawi at 134th (of 184 countries) in its 2022 Index of Economic Freedom, putting Malawi in the 'mostly unfree' category. Finally, the country ranked 110th (of 180) in Transparency International's 2021 Corruption Perceptions Index, although this was an improvement compared with its 2020 ranking (129th). (In early 2017 financial crimes legislation was adopted which would bring the country in line with global best practices, and in February of that year the Minister of Agriculture was dismissed over allegations in the 'Maizegate' scandal—see *History*. In April 2021, after President Chakwera declared that he would not tolerate any corruption or abuse of office during his tenure, the Minister of Labour was also removed over the misuse of COVID-19 funds.)

From mid-November 2021 numerous anti-Government protests were held, as Malawians vented their frustration at deteriorating living standards, high unemployment, rising food prices and government corruption. Further corruption allegations involving several cabinet ministers led Chakwera to appoint a new Government in late January 2022 (see *History*), including new Ministers of Finance and Economic Affairs, of Labour and of Energy.

AGRICULTURE

Agriculture continues to play the key role in Malawi's economy, contributing almost 27% of GDP in 2020 and employing about 72% of the workforce, according to the 2018 census. Most of these employees work in smallholdings at the subsistence level, and their main crop is maize. The Government recognizes the importance of the sector and has introduced a number

of support policies. For example, the Farm Input Subsidy Programme (FISP), introduced in 2005, was aimed at increasing smallholder access to vital inputs such as fertilizers and seeds. Over 1.5m. farmers have received support from the FISP, which was replaced in 2020 by the Affordable Inputs Programme (AIP). The 2021/22 budget allocated K142,000m. to the AIP, with the Government planning to assist 3.5m. farmers.

Malawi used to produce enough maize for its own population and exported a surplus to its neighbours. While maize production has been helped by the FISP since 2005, much of the sector's success depends on the weather. Delayed rains in 2012 resulted in food shortages in the south, where nearly 2m. people required food relief. Such shortages highlight the need to diversify the production base from maize, while at the same time increasing support for irrigation and extension services. In 2015 there was an increase in the price of maize and the Consumer Association of Malawi asked the Government to regulate the price and force farmers to sell their stocks which would, in turn, lower consumer prices. None the less, the severe El Niño-induced drought of 2016 resulted in a smaller crop output and widespread food shortages in 2017. The agricultural sector, in particular maize production (which rose by 11%) helped to prevent Malawi from experiencing a recession in 2020, despite the widespread economic impact of the COVID-19 pandemic.

Tobacco traditionally has been the major source of foreign exchange for Malawi, but due to decreased worldwide demand it is not likely to remain a critical component of future export earnings. In 2020 tobacco constituted some 53% of export earnings. Tobacco is grown on about 150,000 ha in most years in both large estates and smallholdings, employing over 1m. Malawians. Malawi is the only significant African producer of burley, which is the most important of the six types of tobacco cultivated in the country; it accounts for approximately 25% of global exports of burley tobacco. Burley tobacco production totalled 193m. kg in 2013, and burley was likely to remain the dominant variety for some time into the future. In 2020 Malawi earned US $413.1m. from tobacco export revenue, according to the International Trade Centre. Tobacco production was estimated at 93,600 metric tons in that year, compared with 100,300 tons in 2019. In recent years overproduction has been one of the factors responsible for low prices, while an attempt to increase prices through the Integrated Production System has been unsuccessful. Furthermore, due to weak global demand and soil degradation, the industry is likely to remain in structural decline. In an effort to combat tobacco's negative long-term prospects, in February 2020 the National Assembly passed a medical cannabis and industrial hemp bill to legalize the farming of cannabis. Malawi thereby joined other regional countries (South Africa, Lesotho and Zimbabwe) in decriminalizing marijuana.

Malawi has one of Africa's largest lakes, and fish provides about 70% of animal protein consumption. The fisheries sector employs some 250,000 people. The annual catch recorded a low of 54,194 metric tons in 2003, but reached a new high of 123,600 tons in 2012, according to figures from the UN Food and Agriculture Organization (FAO). Total fish output decreased in 2014, but then rose steadily to reach a new record of 230,900 tons in 2018. Output declined sharply to 163,200 tons in 2019, before rising to 180,500 tons in 2020. Much of the commercial fishing activity centres on Nkhotakota, on the western shore of Lake Malawi. The lake has more than 500 species of fish, including several species of tilapia. The country's total tilapia catch amounted to 7,700 tons in 2018, according to FAO data, but declined to 6,200 tons in 2019 and further, to 5,000 tons in 2020. Fish stocks in some of Malawi's lakes have been almost obliterated by a combination of overfishing, declining water levels and pollution.

Malawi is Africa's second largest producer and exporter of tea (after Kenya). Tea is Malawi's second largest single export commodity after tobacco; according to FAO estimates, production totalled 48,100m. metric tons in 2019 and 47,900m. tons in 2020. However, according to the International Trade Centre, exports of tea decreased from US $80.1m. in 2019 to $74.6m. in 2020. The main destinations for Malawi's tea exports are the

United Kingdom, South Africa, the USA, Canada and Pakistan.

Large estates control more than four-fifths of the land under tea cultivation, and around 5,200 smallholders work the remainder. Tea production is dominated by commercial farmers who cultivate 18,000 ha in the southern Malawi highland districts. For the long term, Malawi must diversify its agricultural sector. One alternative crop is sorghum, which was grown in the country for centuries before the British planted maize. The Government is also trying to encourage the cultivation of cassava (manioc), which is more drought-resistant than maize. Cassava production rose steadily from 2005 onwards, reaching almost 5.9m. tons in 2020, according to FAO. However, cassava is not as nutritious as maize, and supplies are erratic. Growth in agriculture will continue to be hampered by logistic bottlenecks, the lack of credit and technology, and low productivity.

INFRASTRUCTURE, COMMUNICATIONS AND ENERGY

Malawi has a total road network of some 15,500 km, of which around 4,000 km are paved. Road transport is the most widely used mode of transport for both passengers and goods, and for conducting external trade. The road network is relatively wide and well maintained, at least by regional standards. Paved, two-lane highways connect Malawi's major cities of Blantyre, Lilongwe, Mzuzu and Zomba. Paved roads extend from Blantyre to the borders of Mozambique, from Lilongwe to the Zambian border, and from Karonga to the Tanzanian border. Road cargo haulage is important for the delivery and collection of goods from seaports in Tanzania, Mozambique and South Africa.

Although road infrastructure deteriorated significantly during the period between 1990 and the mid-2000s, the Government has since made noticeable improvements following the establishment in 2006 of the Roads Authority and the Road Fund Administration. None the less, inadequate drainage often contributes to the premature break-up of road surfaces, which are subject to washouts during the rainy season (November–April); many dirt roads are unusable in that period.

Malawi has seven airports with paved runways (and 25 unpaved ones), and airports on the outskirts of Lilongwe and Blantyre handle international air traffic. In March 2014 Chileka International Airport (located 16 km from Malawi's business capital of Blantyre) was closed after the appearance of several large potholes on its main runway. The airport had not undergone any significant rehabilitation since 1966. The resultant disruption seriously affected business and tourist travel, and highlighted the poor state of the country's infrastructure. Following repair work costing more than K4,000m., Chileka International Airport was eventually reopened for large aircraft in January 2020, although later that year international air travel was significantly impacted by the COVID-19 pandemic. There are daily scheduled flights to Addis Ababa (Ethiopia), Nairobi (Kenya) and Johannesburg (South Africa). The Government identified Air Malawi (a state-owned enterprise) as a candidate for privatization, and in 2013 it was announced that Ethiopian Airlines had acquired a 49% stake in the company, which had then been renamed Malawian Airlines (now known as Malawi Airlines).

There are 797 km of railways, and in 2000 the Central East African Railways Company (CEAR) took over the operations of the former Malawi Railways Limited. CEAR operates limited passenger service in the southern part of the country, and freight service between Lilongwe, Blantyre and the Mozambican port of Nacala. Freight service also extends south to the town of Makhanga, near the Mozambique border. In 2010 a 27-km track extension was completed connecting Malawi's network (from Mchinji) to the Zambian network (at Chipata); however, a scheduled service to Zambia did not commence until 2014. There is also a proposal eventually to connect Malawi's rail network to the Tanzania–Zambia Railway Authority (TAZARA) line. Mozambique and Malawi have co-operated on the commencement of a high-volume rail link built across Malawi to connect to the new coal mines in Mozambique's Tete province with Nacala, a port on the Indian Ocean.

In 2020 Malawi had only around 12,500 landline subscribers, and there were 10.0m. mobile telephone subscribers. The telecommunications sector is fast growing but underdeveloped, and telephone penetration rates in Malawi are the lowest in the Southern African Development Community (SADC) region. The mobile subscriber rate is about 52 per 100 persons. Mobile network coverage—while growing—is limited and based around urban areas, where only about 15% of the population lives. Furthermore, mobile telephone services are expensive and unreliable, with frequent dropped calls and daily congestion. Only 15.5% of the population were internet users in 2019, but access to the internet (including wireless) is improving.

The majority of Malawi's household energy requirements are supplied by fuel wood, which accounts for more than 90% of energy needs (compared with 3% for hydropower, 4% for petroleum products and 1% for coal). Dependence on wood for fuel is a leading cause of deforestation (see below). Only 11% of the total population has reliable electricity supplies, most of whom live in urban areas, although the Government's goal is for 30% of the population to have access to electricity by 2030 and 60% by 2040. This is vital as shortage of reliable electricity supply is often cited as a factor hindering growth in the manufacturing and mining sectors. Blackouts are a continual occurrence, with load shedding scheduled almost daily. The state-owned Electricity Supply Corporation of Malawi (ESCOM) operates both thermal and hydroelectric power stations in its grid; the latter supply 98% of the central grid generating capacity. ESCOM estimates that Malawi will need five consecutive years of above average rainfall to return to normal operating capacity. According to the company, electricity generation has already been reduced by more than 40%—with average production of 200 MW, compared with its maximum capacity of 351 MW—and the situation is expected to deteriorate further. In the mean time, the Government has purchased diesel-powered generators capable of generating 55 MW (which are more expensive than hydropower), after power shortages reached a crisis situation in 2017.

In 2000 a hydroelectric power plant, with a generation capacity of 64 MW, was opened at Kapichira. The completion of the Kapichira Hydroelectric Power Phase II Project in January 2014 doubled the capacity of the plant and increased the total generation capacity of Malawi's hydroelectric power plants to 352 MW (against a forecast peak national demand of 350 MW). A tropical storm damaged the plant in January 2022, leading to power outages, although in August the World Bank agreed to fund Kapichira's restoration. Meanwhile, in April 2013 an agreement was signed to connect Malawi's electricity system to Mozambique's Cahora Bassa hydroelectric power plant (later scheduled for 2023), which would increase Malawi's power supply by some 200 MW. Although the central grid in Malawi is currently operating at below capacity, ESCOM has invested in new capacity in an attempt to satisfy projected future demand, as well as to reinforce the existing grid. In 2015 the Government signed a memorandum of understanding with the China Gezhouba Group Company (a Chinese consortium), financed by the Export and Import Bank of China (China Exim Bank), to build a 300-MW coal-fired power plant with generating capacity of up to 1,000 MW in the Neno district of Malawi. A feasibility study for the Kamwamba power plant project (involving capacity of 300 MW) was completed in February 2022, with the plant likely to open in 2025. In 2017 US $8m. worth of large generators were imported to complete a substation at Phombeya, which was to connect with the Matambo substation in Mozambique; the power line between the two substations was scheduled to come online by 2023. In 2018 Malawi commenced construction of a 60-MW solar project in Salima district, one of the world's first commercial-scale solar photovoltaic plants. The plant, which began to supply electricity in November 2021, was to operate under a 20-year power purchase agreement with ESCOM. With electricity demand totalling just over 450 MW in late 2020, in May 2021 President Chakwera announced plans to increase Malawi's national grid by 1,000 MW in four years. In addition to Salima Solar, Chakwera named 14 other power projects that would come to fruition during 2021–25.

INDUSTRY AND TOURISM

Industry plays an important role in Malawi's economy, contributing 20.2% of GDP in 2020. Manufacturing alone accounted for 12.8% of GDP in that year.

Tourism has been held back by the poor road infrastructure, which has made much of the country inaccessible to tourists, who number approximately 800,000 annually. None the less, the travel and tourism sector plays an increasingly important role in the economy; it contributed 7.3% of GDP in 2019 (providing 7.7% of all jobs), according to the World Travel and Tourism Council (WTTC). This share declined to 5.7% of GDP (and 6.5% of employment) in 2020, due to the severe impact of the COVID-19 pandemic on the tourism industry; it stood at 5.8% of GDP (and 6.4% of all jobs) in 2021. Domestic travel spending generated 89% of direct travel and tourism revenues in 2019, compared with 11% for foreign visitors; the proportion of domestic spending increased to 97% in 2021. In 2017 foreign tourist arrivals totalled 837,233, and receipts from tourism amounted to US $31m. Tourist arrivals increased to 870,722 in 2018, and receipts rose to $38m. However, although this trend continued in 2019 (with receipts rising to some $42m.), the WTTC estimated that the amount spent by foreign visitors to Malawi declined by about 47% in 2020 and 57% in 2021. The majority of foreign tourists are from nearby African countries, mainly Mozambique, Zambia, Zimbabwe and South Africa, although there are also many visitors from the UK, Ireland and North America.

Malawi promotes its five national parks, including Nyika National Park, with its high escarpment providing views of the north shore of Lake Malawi; Kasungu National Park, with its rolling woodlands, grassy river channels and elephant herds; and Liwonde National Park, with its reed swamps, floodplains and tropical birds. A tourism development plan has identified potential areas for eco-tourism at Likhubula Falls, Manchewe Falls, Likoma Island, the three Maleri Islands and the Nkhotakota Wildlife Reserve.

NATURAL RESOURCES AND MINING

Malawi has diverse natural resources, many of which are underexploited. For example, only 0.5% of the irrigable land is under irrigation despite the large potential from Lake Malawi. The country's natural resource base is subject to increasing pressure given the high population growth rate of around 2.8%. In addition, Malawi's ecology is fragile and is suffering from deforestation as urban areas expand. Indeed, large areas of Malawi's 9.4m. ha of land under forest cover are disappearing, at the rate of 2.6 ha per year. Another environmental concern is land degradation, as a result of the loss of soil fertility, soil erosion, water depletion, pollution and a loss of biodiversity. A 2010 report by the UNDP-UN Environment Programme Poverty Environment Initiative estimated that 5.3% of GDP is lost annually because of unsustainable natural resources management. The Government's recently announced plan to develop oil and gas on Lake Malawi has raised concerns from environmentalists who fear that such activities will damage the area's ecology.

Malawi recognizes the importance of its vulnerability to climate change and launched a National Programme of Action in 2008. The Government has also instigated a number of initiatives, such as cash transfers to farmers to help tree planting and conservation efforts.

Unlike most of its neighbours, Malawi has little history of mining, although that is changing rapidly: output from mining expanded by 9.1% in 2014 (although the rate of increase had slowed to 2.3% in 2020). Mineral exploration began in earnest only in 2009 with the opening of the US $200m. Kayelekera uranium mine (85% owned by a local subsidiary of Australia's Paladin Energy and 15% owned by the Malawian Government) in the north of the country. Although uranium may well play an important role in future foreign exchange revenues, production at the Kayelekera mine was suspended in early 2014 due to depressed world uranium prices. Paladin Energy sold its majority share in the mine to the Australian-based Lotus Resources Ltd in March 2020. In mid-2022 Lotus was pursuing the possibility of reopening the Kayelekera mine if uranium prices had risen sufficiently. In 2012 a Canadian-based firm,

Mkano Resources, announced discoveries of a variety of rare earth minerals at Songwe Hill, and in 2021 plans were advancing to explore for uranium in the Thambani area. The returns from mining can be very high; however, Malawi's mining sector is very isolated and remote, and there is no secure regulatory framework to ensure that the country can escape the 'resources curse' (although in October 2015 Malawi was accepted as a candidate country to the Extractive Industry Transparency Initiative).

The country's only operating coal mine is Mchenga, in the Livingstonia coalfield, which was privatized in 1999. Mchenga is estimated to contain some 2.3m. metric tons of bituminous coal, and the Livingstonia coalfield contains a further 5m. tons of probable reserves. At full capacity, Mchenga is capable of producing 8,000 tons per month, supplying a regional demand of about 12,500 tons per month. Further coal deposits, as yet unexploited, have been identified at coalfields at Ngana (15m. tons proven, plus another 5m. tons probable), Nthalire (15m. tons possible, according to the Government), Lengwe (10m. tons probable), Mwabvi (5m. tons proven, 50m. tons possible), Lufira (600,000 tons proven, 50m. tons probable) and North Rukuru (500,000 tons proven, 5m. tons probable and as much as 165m. tons possible). Coal production has fallen substantially from 2014, owing to low international prices.

FOREIGN TRADE, INVESTMENT, AID AND DEBT

As a landlocked country, Malawi faces high transport costs and border delays. It has begun to establish one-stop border posts (which should streamline commercial transit), with funds being provided by the World Bank and the AfDB. Malawi is also negotiating an Economic Partnership Agreement under the African Caribbean Pacific-European Union (EU) Everything But Arms initiative and is a member of both Common Market for East and Southern Africa (COMESA) and SADC (regional trade blocs). None the less, infrastructure bottlenecks are important factors in limiting the country's export potential.

According to the IMF, in 2020 the total value of Malawi's exports was US $912m., while imports totalled $2,696m., resulting in a merchandise trade deficit of $1,785m. The major exports in 2020 were virtually all primary agricultural commodities, including tobacco (representing 52.8% of the total, in terms of value), vegetables and vegetable products, tea, sugar and coffee. In 2020 Malawi's major export partners were Belgium (accounting for 20.8% of the total), South Africa, the UK and Kenya. In that year its principal sources of imports were South Africa (providing 20.6% of the total), China, the United Arab Emirates and India. Major imports in that year were chemicals, machinery and electrical equipment, mineral products, wood pulp and products, and vehicles and transport equipment.

Malawi has traditionally depended on foreign economic assistance to meet its budgetary obligations. It received an estimated US $1,170m. in official development assistance (ODA) in 2019 and $1,450m. in 2020, according to the World Bank. Foreign direct investment (FDI) averaged $174.2m. annually during 1994–2017). According to the IMF, FDI inflows totalled some $104.8m. in 2019 and $91.8m. in 2020.

Malawi and the EU signed a three-year US $126m. budget support agreement in late 2012. The EU has been one of Malawi's major donors, but it suspended its support in 2011 as a result of its opposition to the policies of President Bingu wa Mutharika. The renewal of EU support, along with that of the IMF, was expected to trigger further economic assistance from other donors, many of whom had remained on the sidelines in order to gauge the seriousness of the commitment of Mutharika's successor, President Joyce Banda, to economic reform. However, in late 2013 a group of development partners in Malawi's Common Approach to Budget Support mechanism again put financial support on hold after an audit found that the Malawian authorities had lost $32m. over a six-month period due to fraud and theft. None the less, a number of donor countries, including the UK, were to continue to provide assistance for specific programmes such as drugs and medical supplies. In addition, closer relations with non-traditional donors, including China, had the potential to produce much-needed financial support.

The IMF authorized a US $112m. Extended Credit Facility (ECF) for Malawi in mid-2012 (which had been signed by the previous administration). The programme, which was to cover the period 2012–17, included government commitments to strengthen public financial management and structural reform; closer adherence to such pledges was expected to boost donor and investor confidence. However, the Government faced criticism for its poor performance in making the required economic policy reforms in a timely manner, and the IMF began to withhold funds in late 2015. As a result of the Government's implementation of budgetary reforms (see below), in early 2016 the IMF released $30m. In March 2017 IMF staff completed a review mission to Malawi and reached a preliminary ECF agreement with the Government for a further three years. Fiscal reforms and debt management remained important conditions of the new programme, as domestic debt at that time amounted to 25% of GDP (above the self-imposed government maximum of 20%).

In 2006 Malawi was approved for debt relief under the World Bank's initiative for heavily indebted poor countries (HIPC). By early 2022 39 countries—34 of them in Africa, including Malawi—had received the full amount of debt relief for which they were eligible under HIPC. Nevertheless, Malawi's debt stock increased to an estimated US $2,940m. in 2020, from $488m. in 2006.

PUBLIC FINANCE, INFLATION AND THE FINANCIAL SECTOR

Following the IMF's decision to withhold funding (see above), the Government revised the 2015/16 budget in mid-2015. It planned to cut spending by reducing civil servants' salaries, ministerial budgets and farm subsidies, and by implementing tax reforms. None the less, given Malawi's economic slowdown and the Government's inability to raise domestic revenue, the budget deficit was expected to increase to 5.8% in 2015/16, before declining to 3.0% of GDP in 2016/17. Although the budget for 2017/18 provided for increased government revenues, including tax rises for the highest earners, the budget deficit was forecast to widen to 4.4% of GDP in that year and to 6.4% in 2018/19, according to the World Bank. The increase in the latter year was primarily owing to higher levels of public expenditure on maize imports and preparations for the May 2019 elections. Following an anticipated rise in development spending for 2019/20, the impact of the COVID-19 outbreak on state finances resulted in projected budget deficits of 8.8% of GDP in 2020/21 and 8.0% in 2021/22.

The Reserve Bank of Malawi, the central bank, has remained independent of the Government and it continues to push for price stability. According to the National Statistical Office, food price inflation (which accounts for 58% of the consumer price index) is the main driver of the overall high inflation rate. In an effort to encourage price stability, in late 2015 the central bank raised its benchmark interest rate from 25% to 27%. By 2017 the RBM had reduced the benchmark rate to 16%, and in January it lowered it yet again, to 14.5%. Further reductions were implemented, to 13.5% in May 2019 and 12.0% in November 2020, before the benchmark rate was increased to 14% in April 2022 in an effort to counter strong inflationary pressures (see below). The depreciated kwacha and food price increases resulting from widespread flooding in early 2015 contributed to an inflation rate of 22% in 2016. In 2017 the inflation rate declined to some 13%, which was based on a more stable currency outlook and improved crop production. Inflation of 4.7% was recorded in 2018, due to increased food output combined with lower government spending. However, inflation doubled to 9.4% in 2019, following a significant rise in the price

of maize. The inflation rate fell to 8.6% in 2020, largely as a result of lower fuel prices, but rose again to 9.2% in 2021. Amid ongoing supply issues resulting from the global response to the COVID-19 pandemic, Russia's invasion of Ukraine in February 2022 led to even higher international food and energy prices. In July Malawi's annual inflation rate reached 24.6% (the highest rate since 2015), with maize prices having increased sharply.

In 2012 the foreign currency exchange rate was liberalized and allowed to be determined by the market (a floating exchange rate system). The flotation caused the kwacha to depreciate overnight from US $1 = K167 to $1 = K250. The kwacha continued to lose value, and had depreciated to a rate of $1 = K384 by mid-2014. The rate had deteriorated even further, to $1 = K822, by September 2021. In May 2022 the kwacha was devalued by 25%, as the central bank acted to ease the shortage of foreign currency, which had in turn led to serious food and fuel shortages. There has been speculation that the Government might link the kwacha to the US dollar in an attempt to lower inflation, but Malawi probably lacks adequate foreign reserves to maintain a pegged currency system.

The private financial sector in Malawi is underdeveloped and small in comparison to other African countries, consisting mainly of nine deposit banks, with two banks accounting for nearly one-third of the banking industry's assets in 2011. The Malawi Stock Exchange, which was established in 1996, is small (with only 16 listed companies and market capitalization of around K2,930,000m. in August 2022) and hampered by an outdated operational framework.

PROSPECTS

Official sources recorded an increase in real GDP growth to 5.6% in 2019 (from 3.9% in 2018), based primarily on improved agricultural output. This growth was achieved despite the effects of Cyclones Idai and Kenneth, as discussed above. However, in 2020 the COVID-19 pandemic had a dramatic impact on economic growth in Malawi, with GDP estimated by the Ministry of Finance to have expanded by just 0.9%. Nevertheless, the same source recorded growth of 3.0% in 2021, as the country began to emerge from the crisis, and predicted higher growth of 4.1% in 2022. The private sector will be Malawi's growth engine for the long term; however, this sector has deteriorated in recent years and the regulatory environment continues to hinder the establishment and operation of local firms. As noted above, Malawi ranks very low in ease of doing business. The major constraints are the country's weak infrastructure and high transport costs, limited access to finance, poor education and a low skills base, corruption, and burdensome regulations in starting and maintaining a business.

Malawi faces many other challenges over which it has no control. Adverse weather conditions exacerbated by climate change could again play havoc with agriculture, since that sector is so dependent on rain. Lower agricultural production would have a significant impact on overall output. Furthermore, should the Government slow its implementation of recent policy reforms, international confidence would slip. In addition, aside from COVID-19, there are a number of other significant health challenges (principally the need to combat HIV/AIDS).

Over the long term, growth could gain momentum as aid flows gradually recover and investor confidence improves. None the less, the Government must try to find ways to increase the country's defences against external shocks by diversifying the economy, investing in education and infrastructure, and generally strengthening the enabling environment for business (for example, by reducing bureaucracy and creating a more attractive destination for FDI).

Statistical Survey

Sources (unless otherwise indicated): National Statistical Office of Malawi, POB 333, Zomba; tel. 1524377; e-mail enquiries@statistics.gov.mw; internet www.nsomalawi.mw; Reserve Bank of Malawi, POB 30063, Capital City, Lilongwe 3; tel. 1770600; e-mail reserve-bank@rbm.mw; internet www.rbm.mw.

Area and Population

AREA, POPULATION AND DENSITY

Area (sq km)	
Land	94,552
Inland water	24,208
Total	118,760*
Population (census results)	
8–28 June 2008	13,029,498
3–23 September 2018	
Males	8,521,460
Females	9,042,289
Total	17,563,749
Population (official projections at mid-year)	
2020	18,449,828
2021	18,898,441
2022	19,351,892
Density (per sq km) at mid-2022	204.7†

* 45,853 sq miles; figure for total area is provisional, as no data on inland water were published at 2018 census.
† Land area only.

POPULATION BY AGE AND SEX
(official projections at mid-2022)

	Males	Females	Total
0–14 years	4,021,027	4,002,872	8,023,899
15–64 years	5,065,665	5,582,905	10,648,570
65 years and over	293,137	386,286	679,423
Total	9,379,829	9,972,063	19,351,892

REGIONS
(population at census of September 2018)

Region	Area (sq km)*	Population ('000)	Density (per sq km)	Regional capital
Central . . .	35,641	7,523.3	211.1	Lilongwe
Northern . . .	27,131	2,289.8	84.4	Mzuzu
Southern . . .	31,780	7,750.6	243.9	Blantyre
Total . . .	94,552	17,563.7	185.8	

* Excluding inland waters, totalling 24,208 sq km.

PRINCIPAL TOWNS
(population at census of September 2018)

Lilongwe (capital) .	989,318	Karonga	61,609
Blantyre . . .	800,264	Kasungu . . .	58,653
Mzuzu	221,272	Mangochi . . .	53,498
Zomba	105,013	Salima	36,789

BIRTHS AND DEATHS
(annual averages, UN estimates)

	2005–10	2010–15	2015–20
Birth rate (per 1,000)	42.3	37.9	34.3
Death rate (per 1,000)	13.3	8.6	6.8

Source: UN, *World Population Prospects: The 2019 Revision.*

2008 (official estimates): Live births 609,487 (birth rate 46.5 per 1,000); deaths 195,014 (death rate 14.9 per 1,000).

Life expectancy (years at birth, estimates): 64.7 (males 61.5; females 67.9) in 2020 (Source: World Bank, World Development Indicators database).

EMPLOYED
(persons aged 15–64 years, employees and self-employed only, 2018 census)

	Males	Females	Total
Agriculture, forestry and fishing .	1,301,744	1,761,418	3,063,162
Mining and quarrying	6,900	2,451	9,351
Manufacturing	49,348	21,409	70,757
Electricity, gas and water . . .	14,167	2,558	16,725
Construction	109,363	8,521	117,884
Wholesale and retail trade; repair of motor vehicles and motorcycles	51,279	30,563	81,842
Transport, storage and communications	71,844	9,668	81,512
Hotels and restaurants . . .	32,212	39,560	71,772
Financial intermediation . . .	9,394	5,458	14,852
Real estate, renting and business activities	35,811	12,833	48,644
Public administration and defence; compulsory social security . .	27,090	5,068	32,158
Education	47,127	37,644	84,771
Human health and social work activities	23,727	21,077	44,804
Other community, social and personal service activities . .	283,982	169,567	453,549
Private households with employed persons	30,609	27,101	57,710
Activities of extraterritorial organizations and bodies . .	8,206	3,644	11,850
Total employed	2,102,803	2,158,540	4,261,343

Note: Figures exclude unpaid family workers, numbering 858,979 (Agriculture, forestry and fishing 777,092) at the time of the census.

Total unemployed: 1,224,602 (males 539,774, females 684,828).

Health and Welfare

KEY INDICATORS

Total fertility rate (children per woman, 2020)	4.1
Under-5 mortality rate (per 1,000 live births, 2020) . . .	38.6
HIV/AIDS (% of persons aged 15–49, 2020)	8.1
COVID-19: Cumulative confirmed deaths (per 100,000 persons at 31 August 2022)	13.5
COVID-19: Fully vaccinated population (% of total population at 21 August 2022)	10.3
Physicians (per 1,000 head, 2020)	0.05
Hospitals (per 100,000 head, 2013)	0.4
Domestic health expenditure (2019): US $ per head (PPP) .	26.6
Domestic health expenditure (2019): % of GDP	2.4
Domestic health expenditure (2019): public (% of total current expenditure)	32.6
Access to improved water resources (% of persons, 2020) . .	70
Access to improved sanitation facilities (% of persons, 2020) .	27
Total carbon dioxide emissions ('000 metric tons, 2018) . .	1,570
Carbon dioxide emissions per head (metric tons, 2018) . .	0.1
Human Development Index (2021): ranking	169
Human Development Index (2021): value	0.512

Note: For data on COVID-19 vaccinations, 'fully vaccinated' denotes receipt of all doses specified by approved vaccination regime (Sources: Johns Hopkins University and Our World in Data). Data on health expenditure refer to current general government expenditure in each case. For more information on sources and further definitions for all indicators, see Health and Welfare Statistics: Sources and Definitions section (europaworld.com/credits).

Agriculture

PRINCIPAL CROPS
('000 metric tons)

	2018	2019	2020
Avocados	92.2	93.3*	93.6*
Bananas*	408.9	404.9	406.3
Beans, dry	188.2	215.5	233.7
Cabbages and other brassicas .	187.9	173.0*	212.6*
Cassava (Manioc)	5,410.5	5,708.0	5,858.7
Coffee, green	11.1	11.0†	10.0†
Cow peas, dry	42.5	49.5	56.5†
Groundnuts, with shell . . .	344.6	350.0†	350.0†
Maize	2,698.0	3,391.9	3,691.9
Mangoes, mangosteens and guavas	1,694.4	1,492.7*	1,938.1*
Millet	31.3	44.7	48.9
Onions, dry	171.8	170.5*	188.5*
Oranges	58.5	66.8*	69.1*
Papayas	62.9	64.5*	66.8*
Pigeon peas	434.8	403.5	424.0
Pineapples	319.9	300.0*	309.2*
Plantains and others* . . .	384.0	385.2	385.1
Potatoes	1,125.9	1,113.1	1,318.2
Pumpkins, squash and gourds .	480.2	368.2*	429.3*
Rice, paddy	112.3	132.7	145.4
Sorghum	82.9	133.2	141.3
Soybeans (Soya beans) . . .	175.5	170.0†	180.0†
Sugar cane*	2,903.0	2,881.0	3,058.5
Sweet potatoes	5,668.5	6,369.5	6,918.4
Tangerines, mandarins, etc. . .	144.6	140.7*	146.4*
Tea*	48.1	48.1	47.9
Tobacco, unmanufactured . .	95.4	100.3*	93.6*
Tomatoes	583.2	627.3*	684.2*
Tung nuts*	4.5	4.4	4.5

* FAO estimate(s).
† Unofficial figure.

Aggregate production ('000 metric tons, may include official, semi-official or estimated data): Total cereals 2,925.2 in 2018, 3,703.1 in 2019, 4,028.2 in 2020; Total fruit (primary) 3,460.3 in 2018, 3,245.8 in 2019, 3,713.9 in 2020; Total oilcrops 571.8 in 2018, 569.0 in 2019, 580.2 in 2020; Total roots and tubers 12,204.9 in 2018, 13,190.7 in 2019, 14,095.4 in 2020; Total vegetables (primary) 1,750.3 in 2018, 1,664.9 in 2019, 1,824.6 in 2020.

Source: FAO.

LIVESTOCK
('000 head, year ending September)

	2018	2019	2020
Cattle	1,656	1,867	1,946
Chickens*	18,810	18,559	18,813
Goats	8,374	10,029	10,727
Pigs	6,388	8,383	7,795
Sheep	318	351	366

* FAO estimates.

Source: FAO.

LIVESTOCK PRODUCTS
('000 metric tons)

	2018	2019*	2020*
Cattle hides, fresh*	5.0	5.5	5.6
Cattle meat	50.0	55.2	55.6
Cows' milk*	58.6	63.6	65.5
Chicken meat	190.6	105.2	109.2
Goat meat	51.7	49.2	57.9
Goat offals, edible*	9.6	9.1	10.7
Goats' milk*	117.4	132.4	138.5
Goats' skins, fresh*	9.1	8.7	10.2
Pig fat*	16.3	16.4	13.8
Pig meat	268.1	270.0	226.4
Pig offals, edible*	10.9	11.0	9.2
Hen eggs*	23.1	22.9	23.1

* FAO estimates.

Source: FAO.

Forestry

ROUNDWOOD REMOVALS
('000 cu m, excluding bark, FAO estimates)

	2018	2019	2020
Sawlogs, veneer logs and logs for sleepers	230	230	230
Other industrial wood	1,200	1,200	1,200
Fuel wood	5,912	5,978	6,045
Total	7,342	7,408	7,475

Source: FAO.

SAWNWOOD PRODUCTION
('000 cu m, including railway sleepers, FAO estimates)

	2013	2014	2015
Coniferous (softwood)	30	30	38
Broadleaved (hardwood) . . .	65	65	65
Total	95	95	103

2016–20: Production assumed to be unchanged from 2015.

Source: FAO.

Fishing

('000 metric tons, live weight)

	2018	2019	2020
Capture	221.8	154.9	171.1
Lake Malawi sardine . . .	156.7	98.5	105.2
Lake Malawi utaka	19.1	13.5	16.4
Tilapias	7.7	6.2	5.0
Cichlids	25.1	21.1	22.5
Torpedo-shaped catfishes . .	4.8	5.4	5.8
Aquaculture	9.0	8.3	9.4
Total catch	230.9	163.2	180.5

Note: Figures exclude aquatic mammals, recorded by number rather than weight. The number of Nile crocodiles caught was: 1,757 in 2018; 8,267 in 2019, 5,100 in 2020 (FAO estimate).

Source: FAO.

Mining

('000 metric tons unless otherwise indicated)

	2016	2017	2018
Bituminous coal	43.3	45.2	49.8
Lime	38.3	43.7	48.5
Gemstones (kg)	110.1*	135.2	1,197.0
Stone (crushed for aggregate) .	1,990.0	2,500.0	2,679.3
Limestone	128.7	43.7	48.0

* Estimate.

Source: US Geological Survey.

Industry

SELECTED PRODUCTS
('000 metric tons unless otherwise indicated)

	2017	2018	2019
Raw sugar	264.0	198.0	144.7
Cement	163.1	173.7	150.1
Electrical energy (million kWh) .	1,457.8	1,384.1	1,633.0

2020: Cement 150.1.

Finance

CURRENCY AND EXCHANGE RATES

Monetary Units
100 tambala = 1 Malawi kwacha (K).

Sterling, Dollar and Euro Equivalents (30 September 2021)
£1 sterling = 1,104.579 kwacha;
US $1 = 822.165 kwacha;
€1 = 951.985 kwacha;
10,000 Malawi kwacha = £9.05 = $12.16 = €10.50.

Average Exchange Rate (kwacha per US $)
2018   732.333
2019   745.541
2020   749.527

CENTRAL GOVERNMENT BUDGET
(K '000 million)

Revenue*	2019	2020	2021
Tax revenue	1,033	1,087	1,257
Income tax	290	291	281
Corporate tax	150	190	247
Import duty	85	119	127
Value added tax	293	305	374
Excise duty	169	170	191
Non-tax revenue	44	61	83
Total	1,078	1,148	1,340

Expenditure	2019	2020	2021
Recurrent expenditure	1,270	1,622	1,972
Wages and salaries	423	491	606
Interest payments	251	281	402
Other expenditure	596	849	964
Development expenditures . .	289	387	306
Domestically financed . . .	91	139	125
Foreign financed	198	216	247
Total	1,559	2,008	2,278

* Excluding grants received (K '000 million): 153 in 2019; 177 in 2020; 183 in 2021.

INTERNATIONAL RESERVES
(US $ million at 31 December)

	2018	2019	2020
IMF special drawing rights . .	6.15	1.28	6.34
Reserve position in IMF . . .	3.39	3.38	3.52
Foreign exchange	750.07	819.95	565.13
Total	759.61	824.61	574.99

2021: IMF special drawing rights 6.09; Reserve position in IMF 3.42.

Source: IMF, *International Financial Statistics*.

MONEY SUPPLY
(K '000 million at 31 December)

	2019	2020	2021
Currency outside banks . . .	202	237	300
Demand deposits at commercial banks	406	476	592
Total money	608	713	892

Source: Reserve Bank of Malawi, Lilongwe.

COST OF LIVING
(Consumer Price Index; base: December 2017 = 100)

	2019	2020	2021
Food (incl. non-alcoholic beverages)	119.0	134.6	149.9
Clothing (incl. footwear) . . .	113.4	120.6	128.3
Housing and utilities	110.2	112.8	122.0
All items (incl. others) . . .	114.5	124.4	136.0

NATIONAL ACCOUNTS
(K million at current prices)

Expenditure on the Gross Domestic Product

	2018	2019	2020
Government final consumption expenditure	685,318	770,625	1,012,694
Private final consumption expenditure	6,221,615	6,996,070	9,193,676
Increase in stocks	735,994	827,609	17,295
Gross fixed capital formation . .	935,897	1,052,395	646,211
Total domestic expenditure .	8,578,823	9,646,698	10,869,876
Exports of goods and services . .	1,350,718	1,373,916	1,247,000
Less Imports of goods and services	2,696,241	2,795,704	3,300,643
GDP in purchasers' values	7,233,301	8,224,910	8,816,233
GDP at constant 2015 prices .	5,104,120	5,387,697	5,436,379

Source: UN National Accounts Main Aggregates Database.

Gross Domestic Product by Economic Activity

	2018	2019	2020
Agriculture, hunting, forestry and fishing	1,565,093	1,890,768	2,222,603
Mining and quarrying	53,465	60,238	62,575
Manufacturing	824,618	948,775	1,066,082
Electricity, gas and water . . .	218,221	251,641	276,284
Construction	232,666	263,092	276,941
Wholesale and retail trade, restaurants and hotels . . .	1,042,146	1,155,520	1,137,282
Transport, storage and communications	732,781	844,083	874,709
Financial intermediation . . .	446,297	491,857	522,726
Real estate, renting and business activities	571,323	616,429	642,112
Public administration and defence, compulsory social security . .	231,201	255,916	269,825
Education	296,645	326,562	327,627
Health and social work . . .	422,922	467,750	484,531
Other service activities . . .	128,026	154,478	156,807
Sub-total	6,765,403	7,727,161	8,320,106
Taxes, less subsidies, on products .	467,897	497,750	496,127
GDP in purchasers' values .	7,233,301	8,224,910	8,816,233

BALANCE OF PAYMENTS
(US $ million)

	2018	2019	2020
Exports of goods f.o.b.	945.4	1,084.9	911.7
Imports of goods f.o.b.	−2,603.7	−2,815.0	−2,696.3
Balance on goods	**−1,658.4**	**−1,730.2**	**−1,784.6**
Exports of services	207.5	223.4	206.7
Imports of services	−389.1	−432.6	−353.2
Balance on goods and services	**−1,840.0**	**−1,939.4**	**−1,931.2**
Primary income received	17.6	11.1	6.9
Primary income paid	−338.5	−290.2	−314.3
Balance on goods, services and primary income	**−2,160.9**	**−2,218.5**	**−2,238.6**
Secondary income received	465.3	576.0	858.9
Secondary income paid	−9.2	−25.6	−32.8
Current balance	**−1,704.8**	**−1,668.0**	**−1,412.4**
Capital account (net)	859.1	930.6	817.8
Direct investment assets	102.2	23.5	18.7
Direct investment liabilities	77.0	55.3	45.2
Portfolio investment liabilities	190.8	453.9	383.5
Financial derivatives and employee stock options liabilities	7.2	3.7	4.0
Other investment assets	135.8	5.2	−101.0
Other investment liabilities	204.8	270.9	260.6
Net errors and omissions	121.5	−29.1	−440.6
Overall balance	**−6.3**	**46.0**	**−424.3**

Source: IMF, *International Financial Statistics*.

External Trade

PRINCIPAL COMMODITIES
(distribution by HS, US $ million)

Imports c.i.f.	2018	2019	2020
Animal or vegetable fats and oils, and products thereof	43.6	67.5	87.6
Prepared foodstuffs; beverages, spirits, vinegar; tobacco and articles thereof	122.0	138.2	207.1
Mineral products	362.5	292.8	278.7
Mineral fuels, oils, distillation products, etc.	304.1	232.0	217.1
Petroleum oils, not crude	281.1	213.1	196.8
Chemicals and related products	514.2	575.6	602.9
Pharmaceutical products	132.2	176.3	163.4
Medicaments consisting of mixed or unmixed products for therapeutic or prophylactic uses	87.5	131.7	115.8
Fertilizers	192.1	214.9	235.6
Mineral or chemical fertilizers, nitrogenous	110.4	90.8	109.6
Plastics, rubber, and articles thereof	152.7	148.9	148.6
Plastics and articles thereof	120.0	115.7	115.5
Pulp of wood, paper and paperboard, and articles thereof	288.3	333.4	301.9
Printed books, newspapers, pictures, etc.	237.5	282.3	255.1
Unused stamps, cheque forms, banknotes, and bond certificates	219.5	266.8	248.1

Imports c.i.f.—*continued*	2018	2019	2020
Textiles and textile articles	141.5	119.5	135.8
Other made textile articles, sets, worn clothing, etc.	89.2	71.9	93.2
Iron and steel; other base metals and articles of base metals	160.3	235.7	162.6
Articles of iron or steel	57.0	130.5	49.9
Machinery and mechanical appliances; electrical equipment; parts thereof	434.7	531.1	349.0
Machinery and boilers, etc.	246.3	293.8	211.6
Electrical, electronic equipment	188.5	237.3	137.4
Vehicles, aircraft, vessels and associated transport equipment	233.3	242.8	204.9
Vehicles other than railway, tramway	212.0	214.8	191.8
Total (incl. others)	2,707.1	2,941.1	2,730.3

Exports f.o.b.	2018	2019	2020
Vegetables and vegetable products	205.9	221.9	201.4
Edible vegetables and certain roots and tubers	38.4	39.9	40.8
Dried leguminous vegetables	36.8	39.6	40.0
Edible fruit and nuts; peel of citrus fruit or melons	27.2	32.0	22.9
Coffee, tea, cocoa and spices	90.9	83.7	77.2
Tea	87.7	80.1	74.6
Oil seed, oleagic fruits, grain, seed, fruit, etc.	40.6	61.2	57.2
Prepared foodstuffs; beverages, spirits, vinegar; tobacco and articles thereof	598.0	618.2	523.0
Sugars and sugar confectionery	38.0	85.5	76.1
Cane or beet sugar and chemically pure sucrose	38.0	85.4	76.0
Miscellaneous edible preparations	27.2	1.5	1.9
Residues, wastes of food industry, animal fodder	37.2	26.2	27.2
Oilcake and other solid residues	30.3	21.8	24.2
Tobacco and tobacco products	493.7	501.4	413.1
Tobacco (unmanufactured) and tobacco refuse	492.3	498.5	410.9
Total (incl. others)	879.8	913.0	782.0

Source: Trade Map-Trade Competitiveness Map, International Trade Centre, marketanalysis.intracen.org.

PRINCIPAL TRADING PARTNERS
(US $ million)

Imports	2018	2019	2020
China, People's Republic	386.8	541.2	441.9
Germany	29.7	33.6	40.0
Hong Kong	23.5	61.3	30.0
India	249.0	256.7	211.1
Indonesia	40.7	39.5	58.5
Japan	107.5	101.2	90.7
Kenya	33.2	35.6	39.8
Kuwait	119.9	86.5	69.9
Malaysia	33.6	44.3	65.2
Mozambique	38.8	37.8	102.5
Netherlands	50.4	36.8	23.2
Norway	0.4	83.8	4.9
Russian Federation	27.2	11.9	19.6
Saudi Arabia	42.3	28.7	44.8
South Africa	500.8	490.9	561.2
Tanzania	57.3	62.8	40.8
United Arab Emirates	235.7	279.1	274.5
United Kingdom	226.5	224.2	125.1
USA	39.3	39.1	29.8
Zambia	87.5	105.3	120.0
Zimbabwe	26.8	27.6	31.2
Total (incl. others)	2,707.1	2,941.1	2,730.3

Exports	2018	2019	2020
Armenia	4.6	9.8	1.7
Belgium	133.7	151.1	162.9
China, People's Republic . . .	31.2	35.3	34.1
Egypt	46.6	65.7	31.8
Germany	40.3	25.2	19.9
India	14.9	15.0	4.7
Italy	30.5	5.6	2.1
Jordan	4.9	4.3	11.0
Kenya	43.7	67.9	39.8
Korea, Republic	11.1	15.5	7.9
Mozambique	15.1	16.6	14.7
Netherlands	43.9	36.2	28.9
Poland	19.3	9.9	12.8
Russian Federation	21.6	32.9	14.1
Rwanda	2.0	10.1	11.6
Singapore	10.5	11.4	9.8
South Africa	86.4	61.3	48.7
Spain	3.7	5.6	23.7
Sweden	1.6	10.1	0.5
Switzerland	5.7	28.7	26.4
Tanzania	16.1	31.9	33.5
Ukraine	27.4	23.5	7.2
United Arab Emirates	15.6	25.4	15.2
United Kingdom	33.1	28.0	46.7
USA	48.1	49.9	36.0
Zambia	49.3	31.1	26.9
Zimbabwe	37.5	23.0	35.3
Total (incl. others)	**879.8**	**913.0**	**782.0**

Source: Trade Map-Trade Competitiveness Map, International Trade Centre, marketanalysis.intracen.org.

Transport

RAILWAYS
(traffic)

	2019	2020	2021
Passengers carried ('000) . . .	304	253	241
Passenger-km ('000)	255,388	246,780	248,579
Net freight ton-km ('000) . . .	89,147	39,899	n.a.

ROAD TRAFFIC
(new registrations)

	2012	2013	2014
Passenger cars	11,978	16,467	15,779
Commercial goods vehicles . .	6,200	8,204	6,756
Buses	1,389	1,669	1,518
Motorcycles	2,235	2,460	2,837

SHIPPING

Inland Waterways
(lake transport)

	2017	2018	2019
Passengers carried ('000) . . .	52	29	53
Passenger-km ('000)	4,458	2,367	51,296
Net freight-ton km ('000) . . .	n.a.	1,801	3,504

CIVIL AVIATION
(traffic on scheduled services)

	2007	2008	2009
Kilometres flown (million) . .	3	5	5
Passengers carried ('000) . . .	116	160	157
Passenger-km (million) . . .	83	209	200
Total ton-km (million)	8	24	23

Source: UN, *Statistical Yearbook*.

2020 (domestic and international): Departures 367; Passengers carried 179 (Source: World Bank, World Development Indicators database).

Tourism

FOREIGN TOURIST ARRIVALS BY COUNTRY OF RESIDENCE

	2016	2017	2018
Mozambique	279,200	253,025	263,146
North America	49,876	35,385	36,800
Southern Africa*	64,400	90,819	94,452
United Kingdom and Ireland .	56,057	40,056	41,658
Zambia	66,739	139,000	144,560
Zimbabwe	100,007	110,740	110,740
Total (incl. others)	**849,156**	**837,233**	**870,722**

* Comprising Botswana, Eswatini, Lesotho and South Africa.

Tourism receipts (US $ million, excl. passenger transport): 31 in 2017; 38 in 2018; 42 in 2019 (provisional).

Source: World Tourism Organization.

Communications Media

	2018	2019	2020
Telephones ('000 main lines in use)	15.0	13.1	12.5
Mobile telephones ('000 subscriptions)	7,076.9	8,901.0	10,004.7
Broadband subscriptions, fixed ('000)	11.4	11.4	12.3
Broadband subscriptions, mobile ('000)	4,936.4	5,932.5	6,822.6
Internet users (% of population) .	13.9	15.5	n.a.

Source: International Telecommunication Union.

Education

(2020 unless otherwise indicated)

	Institutions	Teachers	Students
Primary	6,468	83,031	5,419,637
Secondary	1,494	14,497*	415,013
Tertiary	6†	747‡	8,702‡

* 2015 figure.
† 2003 figure.
‡ 2013 figure.

Pupil-teacher ratio (primary education): 65.0 in 2019/20.

Adult literacy rate (UNESCO estimates): 62.1% (males 69.8%; females 55.2%) in 2015 (Source: UNESCO Institute for Statistics).

Directory

The Constitution

A new Constitution, replacing the (amended) 1966 Constitution, was approved by the National Assembly on 16 May 1994, and took provisional effect for one year from 18 May. During this time the Constitution was to be subject to review, and the final document was promulgated on 18 May 1995. The main provisions (with subsequent amendments) are summarized below:

THE PRESIDENT

The President is both head of state and head of government. The President is elected for five years, by universal adult suffrage, in the context of a multi-party political system. The Constitution provides for up to two Vice-Presidents.

PARLIAMENT

Parliament comprises the President, the Vice-President(s) and the National Assembly. The National Assembly has 193 elective seats, elections being by universal adult suffrage, in the context of a multi-party system. Cabinet ministers who are not elected members of parliament also sit in the National Assembly. The Speaker is appointed from among the ordinary members of the Assembly. The parliamentary term is normally five years. The President has power to prorogue or dissolve Parliament.

EXECUTIVE POWER

Executive power is exercised by the President, who appoints members of the Cabinet.

The Government

HEAD OF STATE

President: Dr Lazarus McCarthy Chakwera (inaugurated 28 June 2020).
Vice-President: Dr Saulos Klaus Chilima.

CABINET
(October 2022)

The Government comprises members of the Malawi Congress Party (MCP), the United Transformation Movement (UTM), the Citizens for Transformation Movement (CFT), the People's Party (PP), the People's Progressive Movement (PPM) and independents (Ind.).

President, Commander-in-Chief of the Malawi Defence Force, and Minister of Defence: Dr Lazarus McCarthy Chakwera (MCP).

Vice-President and Minister responsible for Public Sector Reforms: Dr Saulos Klaus Chilima (UTM).

Minister of Agriculture: Lobin Clarke Lowe (MCP).

Minister of Tourism, Culture and Wildlife: Dr Michael Bizwick Usi (UTM).

Minister of Finance and Economic Affairs: Sosten Alfred Gwengwe (MCP).

Minister of Foreign Affairs: Nancy Tembo (MCP).

Minister of Natural Resources and Climate Change: Eisenhower Nduwa Mkaka (MCP).

Minister of Gender, Community Development and Social Welfare: Patricia Annie Kaliati (UTM).

Minister of Youth and Sports: Richard Chimwendo Banda (MCP).

Minister of Justice: Titus Songiso Mvalo (MCP).

Minister of Education: Agnes Makonda Nyalonje (UTM).

Minister of Health: Khumbize Kandodo Chiponda (MCP).

Minister of National Unity: Timothy Pagonachi Mtambo (CFT).

Minister of Information and Digitalization: Gospel Kazako (Ind.).

Minister of Homeland Security: Jean Muonaowauza Sendeza (MCP).

Minister of Labour: Vera Kamtukule (UTM).

Minister of Water and Sanitation: Abida Sidik Mia (MCP).

Minister of Transport and Public Works: Jacob Hara (MCP).

Minister of Local Government: Prof. Blessings Darlo Chinsinga (Ind.).

Minister of Mining: Dr Albert Mbawala (MCP).

Minister of Energy: Ibrahim Matola (PP).

Minister of Trade and Industry: Mark Katsonga Phiri (PPM).

Minister of Lands: Samuel Dalitso Kawale (MCP).

There were also nine deputy ministers.

MINISTRIES

Office of the President and Cabinet: Capital Hill Circle, Capital City, Private Bag 301, Lilongwe 3; tel. 1789411; e-mail opc@malawi.gov.mw; internet www.opc.gov.mw.

Office of the Vice-President: Capital Hill, POB 30399, Lilongwe; tel. 1788444; e-mail vicepres@malawi.gov.mw; internet fb.com/gov.mw.

Ministry of Agriculture: Capital Hill, POB 30134, Lilongwe 3; tel. 1788738; e-mail agriculture@agriculture.gov.mw; internet www.agriculture.gov.mw.

Ministry of Education: Capital Hill Circle, Area 24, off Chilembwe Dr., Capital City, Private Bag 328, Lilongwe 3; tel. 1789422; e-mail info-edu@education.gov.mw; internet www.education.gov.mw.

Ministry of Energy: Capital House, City Center, 2nd Floor, Private Bag 309, Lilongwe 3; tel. 1770688; e-mail info@energy.gov.mw; internet www.energy.gov.mw.

Ministry of Finance and Economic Affairs: Capital Hill, POB 30049, Lilongwe 3; tel. 1789355; e-mail finance@finance.gov.mw; internet www.finance.gov.mw.

Ministry of Foreign Affairs: Capital City, POB 30315, Lilongwe 3; tel. 1789088; e-mail foreign.affairs@foreignaffairs.gov.mw; internet www.foreignaffairs.gov.mw.

Ministry of Natural Resources and Climate Change: City Centre, off Kenyatta Dr., Private Bag 350, Lilongwe 3; tel. 1770344; internet fb.com/NaturalResourcesMalawi.

Ministry of National Unity: Capital Hill, Lilongwe 3; internet fb.com/CivicEducationAndNationalUnity.

Ministry of Gender, Community Development and Social Welfare: Gemini House, City Centre, Capital City, Private Bag 330, Lilongwe 3; tel. 1770411; e-mail PS.gender@gender.gov.mw; internet www.gender.gov.mw.

Ministry of Health: Capital City, POB 30377, Lilongwe 3; tel. 1789400; internet www.health.gov.mw.

Ministry of Homeland Security: Capital City, Private Bag 331, Lilongwe 3; tel. 1789177.

Ministry of Information and Digitalization: Capital City, Private Bag 310, Lilongwe; tel. 1772702; e-mail principal.secretary@information.gov.mw; internet ict.gov.mw.

Ministry of Justice: Capital Hill, Capital City, Private Bag 333, Lilongwe 3; tel. 1788433; e-mail enquiries@justice.gov.mw; internet www.justice.gov.mw; also comprises the Attorney-General's Chambers and the Directorate of Public Prosecutions.

Ministry of Labour: Capital Hill, Private Bag 344, Lilongwe 3; tel. 1773277; internet www.malawi.gov.mw/labour.

Ministry of Lands: Zowe House, Lilongwe; tel. 1776098; internet www.lands.gov.mw.

Ministry of Local Government: Capital City, POB 30312, Lilongwe 3; tel. 1789388; e-mail inquiriesmlgrd@gmail.com; internet www.localgovt.gov.mw.

Ministry of Mining: Matamando House, City Center, POB 251, Lilongwe; tel. 1755303; internet www.mining.gov.mw.

Ministry of Trade and Industry: Gemini House, POB 30366, Lilongwe 3; tel. 1770244; e-mail trademin@trade.gov.mw; internet fb.com/MoITTMW.

Ministry of Transport and Public Works: Capital City, Private Bag 322, Lilongwe 3; tel. 1789377; internet www.motpwh.gov.mw.

Ministry of Tourism, Culture and Wildlife: POB 394, Lilongwe 3; internet 1775499.

Ministry of Water and Sanitation: Lilongwe.

Ministry of Youth and Sports: Capital City, Private Bag 384, Lilongwe 3; tel. 1788755; e-mail youthandsports@youth.gov.mw; internet www.youth.gov.mw.

President

Presidential Election, 23 June 2020

Candidate	Valid votes	% of valid votes
Dr Lazarus Chakwera (MCP) . . .	2,604,043	59.34
Prof. Arthur Peter Mutharika (DPP) .	1,751,877	39.92
Peter D. S. D. Kuwani (MMD) . . .	32,456	0.74
Total	4,388,376*	100.00

* In addition, there were 57,323 spoiled ballots.

Legislature

National Assembly: Presidential Dr., Private Bag B362, Lilongwe 3; tel. 1770090; e-mail parliament@parliament.gov.mw; internet www.parliament.gov.mw.

Speaker: CATHERINE GOTANI HARA.

General Election, 21 May 2019

Party	Seats
Democratic Progressive Party	62
Malawi Congress Party	55
United Democratic Front	10
People's Party	5
United Transformation Movement	4
Alliance for Democracy	1
Independents	55
Total	**192***

* Voting in one constituency did not take place due to the death of a candidate.

Election Commission

Malawi Electoral Commission (MEC): Chisankho House, opp. Mwaiwathu Hospital, Private Bag 113, Blantyre; tel. 1822033; e-mail ceo@mec.org.mw; internet mec.org.mw; f. 1998; Chair. Dr CHIFUNDO KACHALE; Chief Elections Officer ANDREW MPESI.

Political Organizations

Alliance for Democracy (AFORD): Private Bag 28, Lilongwe; f. 1992; Pres. ENOCK CHIHANA; Sec.-Gen. CHRISTOPHER RITCHIE.

Assembly for Democracy and Development (ADD): Lilongwe; f. 2015; Pres. CASSIM CHILUMPHA.

Democratic Progressive Party (DPP): Lilongwe 3; tel. 1750034; e-mail officeddp@yahoo.com; internet fb.com/Democratic ProgressivePartyMalawi; f. 2005 following Bingu wa Mutharika's resignation from the UDF; Pres. Prof. ARTHUR PETER MUTHARIKA; Sec.-Gen. GELZEDER JEFFREY.

Leadership with Compassion (LCP): Lilongwe; f. 2017; Pres. SALLY KUMWENDA.

Malawi Congress Party (MCP): Private Bag 388, Lilongwe 3; tel. 999223228; e-mail editor@malawicongress.party; internet www .malawicongress.party; f. 1959; sole legal party 1966–93; Pres. Dr LAZARUS CHAKWERA; Gen. Sec. EISENHOWER MKAKA.

Malawi Forum for Unity and Development (MAFUNDE): f. 2002; aims to combat corruption and food shortages; Pres. GEORGE NNESA.

Mbakuwaku Movement for Development Party (MMD): Lilongwe; Pres. PETER D. S. D. KUWANI.

New Republican Party (NRP): f. 2009; Pres. (vacant).

People's Party (PP): Lilongwe; f. 2011 by Joyce Banda following her expulsion from the DPP; Pres. JOYCE BANDA; Sec.-Gen. IBRAHIM MATOLA.

People's Progressive Movement (PPM): f. 2003 by fmr mems of the UDF; Pres. MARK KATSONGA; Sec.-Gen. (vacant).

People's Transformation Party (PETRA): POB 31964, Chichiri, Blantyre 3; tel. 1871577; f. 2002; Pres. KAMUZU CHIBAMBO.

Umodzi Party (UP): Lilongwe; e-mail umodziparty@yahoo.com; f. 2013; Pres. Prof. JOHN EUGENES CHISI.

United Democratic Front (UDF): POB 5446, Limbe; internet fb .com/udf92party; f. 1992; Acting Pres. LILIAN PATEL; Sec.-Gen. KANDI PADAMBO.

United Independence Party: Blantyre; f. 2014; Leader CHIMBUNA BELEKIAH.

United Transformation Movement (UTM): Lilongwe; internet fb .com/UTMSKCMalawi; f. 2018; Pres. SAULOS KLAUS CHILIMA; Sec.-Gen. PATRICIA KALIATI.

Diplomatic Representation

EMBASSIES AND HIGH COMMISSIONS IN MALAWI

Brazil: Plot 399, Area 12, POB 30521, Lilongwe; tel. 1772559; e-mail brasemb.lilongue@itamaraty.gov.br; internet fb.com/ brasemblilongue; Ambassador ARTUR JOSE SARAIVA DE OLIVEIRA.

China, People's Republic: City 188, Area 13, POB 31799, Lilongwe; tel. 1794750; e-mail chinaemb_mw@mfa.gov.cn; internet mw.china-embassy.gov.cn; Ambassador LONG ZHOU.

Egypt: 1Area 43/2/354A, Lilongwe; tel. 1794657; e-mail embassy .malawi@mfa.gov.eg; internet fb.com/EgyptMalawi; Ambassador MOHAMED EL-SHARIF.

Germany: Convention Dr., Lilongwe 3; tel. 994437057; e-mail info@ lilongwe.diplo.de; internet www.lilongwe.diplo.de; Ambassador RALPH TIMMERMANN.

Holy See: c/o Catholic Secretariat of ECM, Chimutu Rd, Area 11, POB 31671, Lilongwe 3; tel. 1772259; e-mail na.malawi@diplomat .va; Apostolic Nuncio GIANFRANCO GALLONE (Titular Archbishop of Motula).

Iceland: 13/13 Samala House, Lilongwe; tel. 1771141; e-mail lilongwe@mfa.is; internet government.is/diplomatic-missions/ embassy-of-iceland-in-lilongwe; Chargé d'affaires a.i. INGA DÓRA PÉTURSDÓTTIR.

India: Plot 55, Area 9, POB 1482, Lilongwe; tel. 1759337; e-mail com .malawi@mea.gov.in; internet hcililongwe.gov.in; High Commissioner SUBBIA GOPALAKRISHNAN.

Ireland: Arwa House, 3rd Floor, 13/14 City Centre, Lilongwe; tel. 1776408; e-mail lilongweemdiplomats@dfa.ie; internet dfa.ie/ irish-embassy/malawi; Ambassador SÉAMUS O'GRADY.

Japan: Plot 14/191, Petroda Glass House, POB 30780, Lilongwe 3; tel. 888985352; e-mail embmalawi@lw.mofa.go.jp; internet www.mw .emb-japan.go.jp; Ambassador SATOSHI IWAKIRI.

Morocco: Lilongwe; Chargé d'affaires ABDELKADER NAJI.

Mozambique: Area 40/14A, POB 30579, Lilongwe 3; tel. 1774100; e-mail embamoc.malawi@minec.gov.mz; High Commissioner ELIAS JAIME ZIMBA.

Nigeria: Plot 12/529, New Area 12, nr Mlambe Lodge, POB 31259, Lilongwe; tel. 14567890; e-mail nigeria.lilongwe@yahoo.com; internet www.nigeriahcl.com; High Commissioner ZAHRA MUAZU OMAR.

Norway: Arwa House, City Centre, Private Bag B323, Lilongwe 3; tel. 1779400; e-mail emb.lilongwe@mfa.no; internet norway.no/ malawi; Ambassador INGRID MARIE MIKELSEN.

South Africa: Plot 19, Convention Dr., Area 40, POB 30043, Lilongwe 3; tel. 1773722; e-mail lilongwe.dha@dirco.gov.za; High Commissioner AHLANGENE SIGCAU.

Tanzania: Plaza House, Capital City, POB 922, Lilongwe 3; tel. 1770150; e-mail lilongwe@nje.go.tz; internet mw.tzembassy.go.tz; High Commissioner HUMPHREY POLEPOLE (designate).

United Kingdom: off Convention Dr., POB 30042, Lilongwe 3; tel. 1772123; e-mail bhclilongwe@fcdo.gov.uk; internet www.gov.uk/ world/malawi; High Commissioner FIONA RICHIE.

USA: 16 Jomo Kenyatta Rd, Lilongwe 3; tel. 1773166; e-mail consularlilong@state.gov; internet mw.usembassy.gov; Ambassador DAVID YOUNG.

Zambia: Area 40/2, City Centre, POB 30138, Lilongwe 3; tel. 1772100; e-mail zambiahighcom@sdnp.org.mw; High Commissioner Lt-Col. (retd) PANJI KAUNDA.

Zimbabwe: Gemini House, 7th Floor, POB 30187, Lilongwe 3; tel. 1784988; e-mail zimlilongwe@zimfa.gov.zw; Ambassador Dr NANCY SAUNGWEME.

Judicial System

The courts administering justice are the Supreme Court of Appeal, High Court and Subordinate Courts.

The High Court, which has unlimited jurisdiction in civil and criminal matters, and reviews any law and any action and decision of the Government for conformity with the Constitution, is headed by the Chief Justice. Appeals from the High Court are heard by the Supreme Court of Appeal, in Blantyre.

Supreme Court of Appeal: POB 30244, Chichiri, Blantyre 3; tel. 1870225; e-mail malawijudiciary@judicary.mw; internet www .judiciary.mw/supreme; consists of the Chief Justice and not fewer than 3 other judges; Judge Pres. (vacant).

High Court of Malawi: POB 30244, Chichiri, Blantyre 3; tel. 1670255; e-mail malawijudiciary@judicary.mw; internet www .judiciary.mw/highcourt; Judge Pres. HEALEY POTANI.

Chief Justice: REZINE ROBERT MZIKAMANDA.

Attorney-General: THABO CHAKAKA NYIRENDA.

Religion

According to the 2018 census, 77.3% of the population professed Christianity, while Islam was practised by about 13.8% of the population.

CHRISTIANITY

Malawi Council of Churches (MCC): POB 30068, Capital City, Lilongwe 3; tel. 1783499; f. 1942; Chair. Rt Rev. FANUEL EMMANUEL MANGANI; Gen. Sec. Bishop GILFORD MATONGA; 24 mem. churches.

The Anglican Communion

Anglicans are adherents of the Church of the Province of Central Africa, covering Botswana, Malawi, Zambia and Zimbabwe. The Church comprises 15 dioceses, including four in Malawi. The current Archbishop of the Province is the Bishop of Northern Zambia.

Bishop of Lake Malawi: Rt Rev. FRANCIS KAULANDA, POB 30349, Capital City, Lilongwe 3; tel. 1796463; e-mail info@anglicandioceseoflakemalawi.org; internet www.anglicandioceseoflakemalawi.org.

Bishop of Northern Malawi: Rt Rev. FANUEL EMMANUEL CHIOKO MAGANGANI, POB 120, Mzuzu; tel. 1331486; e-mail fanuelmagangani@yahoo.com; internet www.nmalawianglican.org.

Bishop of Southern Malawi: Rt Rev. ALINAFE KALEMBA, POB 30220, Chichiri, Blantyre 3; tel. 1641218; e-mail info@angdiosoma.org; internet www.angdiosoma.org.

Bishop of Upper Shire: Rt Rev. BRIGHTON VITTA MALASA, Private Bag 1, Chilema, Zomba; tel. 1539203; e-mail angus@globemw.net.

Protestant Churches

Baptist Convention of Malawi (BACOMA): POB 249, Lilongwe; tel. 993721410; e-mail generalsecretary@bacoma.org; Pres. Rev. RUSTIN KALENGA.

Church of Central Africa Presbyterian (CCAP): POB 413, Blantyre; tel. 1836744; internet www.ccapblantyresynod.org; comprises 3 synods in Malawi (Blantyre, Livingstonia and Nkhoma); Moderator Rev. EDNA NAVAYA.

Evangelical Association of Malawi: POB 30296, Lilongwe 3; tel. 999831258; e-mail eam@eamalawi.org; internet www.eamalawi.org; f. 1962; Chair. Rev. Dr MARK KAMBALAZAZA; Gen. Sec. Rev. FRANCIS MKANDAWIRE.

Evangelical Lutheran Church in Malawi: Plot 22/22, Chidzanja Rd, POB 650, Lilongwe; tel. 999063044; e-mail mphatsothole@yahoo.com; internet elcm.weebly.com; f. 1982; Bishop Dr JOSEPH P. BVUMBWE.

Malawi Assemblies of God (MAOG): off Paul Kagame Rd, POB 1220, Lilongwe; tel. 888779952; e-mail info@malawiassembliesofgod.org; internet www.malawiassembliesofgod.org; Pres. Rev. Dr ANDREW DUBE; Sec.-Gen. Rev. MATILDA MATABWA.

Seventh-day Adventist Church: Robins Rd, Kabula Hill, POB 951, Blantyre; tel. 1820264; Pres. Pastor FRACKSON KUYAMA; Exec. Sec. Pastor INNOCENT CHIKOMO.

The African Methodist Episcopal Church, the Churches of Christ, the Free Methodist Church, the New Apostolic Church and the United Evangelical Church in Malawi are also active.

The Roman Catholic Church

Malawi comprises two archdioceses and six dioceses.

Episcopal Conference of Malawi: Catholic Secretariat, Area 11, Chimutu Rd, POB 30384, Capital City, Lilongwe 3; tel. 1772204; e-mail ecm@ecmmw.org; internet www.ecmmw.org; f. 1961; Chair. Most Rev. THOMAS LUKE MSUSA (Archbishop of Blantyre); Sec.-Gen. Rev. Fr HENRY SAINDI.

Archbishop of Blantyre: Most Rev. THOMAS LUKE MSUSA, Archbishop's House, POB 385, Blantyre; tel. 1637905; e-mail archdblantyre@africa-online.net.

Archbishop of Lilongwe: Most Rev. GEORGE DESMOND TAMBALA, Archbishop's House, POB 33, Lilongwe; tel. 1754667; e-mail archbziyaye@africa-online.net.

ISLAM

Muslim Association of Malawi (MAM): POB 497, Blantyre; tel. 1622060; e-mail mam@malawi.net; f. 1946 as the Nyasaland Muslim Asscn; umbrella body for Muslim orgs; provides secular and Islamic education; Chair. SHEIKH IDRISA MUHAMMAD; Sec.-Gen. Alhaji TWAIBU LAWE.

BAHÁ'Í FAITH

National Spiritual Assembly: POB 30922, Capital City, Lilongwe 3; tel. 884201121; e-mail admin@bahaimalawi.com; f. 1970; mems resident in over 1,200 localities; Desk Information Officer GANIE NEESHU CAMRUDINE.

The Press

The Daily Times: Scott Rd, Private Bag 39, Blantyre; tel. 1871663; e-mail dailytimes@bnltimes.com; internet times.mw; f. 1895; fmrly the *Nyasaland Times*; Mon.–Fri., Sun.; English; publ. by Blantyre Newspapers Ltd (Chayamba Trust); affiliated to the MCP; Editor-in-Chief (vacant); Editor REX CHIKOKO.

The Eye Magazine: Ginnery cnr, POB E756, Post Dot Net, Blantyre; tel. 888709223; e-mail theeyemalawi@gmail.com; internet www.theeyemw.com; quarterly.

The Lamp Magazine: Montfort Media, POB 280, Balaka; tel. 1522267; e-mail montfortmedia@gmail.com; f. 1995; monthly; Roman Catholic and ecumenical; part of Montfort Media SLD; Editor Fr GAMBA PIERGIORGIO.

Malawi 24: 7 AGMA House, Maselema, Chichiri, Blantyre; tel. 889904184; e-mail editor@malawi24.com; internet malawi24.com; affiliated with the Media Institute of Southern Africa (MISA); daily; Man. Editor MACMILLAN MHONE.

Malawi Government Gazette: Government Printer, POB 37, Zomba; tel. 1523155; f. 1894; weekly.

Malawi News: Scott Rd, Private Bag 39, Blantyre; tel. 1871679; internet timesmediamw.com; f. 1959; weekly; English and Chichewa; publ. by Blantyre Newspapers Ltd (Chayamba Trust); Editor (vacant).

The Nation: POB 30408, Chichiri, Blantyre 3; tel. 1874419; e-mail emunthali@mwnation.com; internet mwnation.com; f. 1993; daily; publ. by Nation Publs Ltd, also the Publr of *The Weekend Nation* and *Nation on Sunday*; English and Nyanja; Man. Editor EPHRAIM MUNTHALI.

Nyasa Times: Lilongwe; e-mail editor.nyasatimes@gmail.com; internet www.nyasatimes.com; f. 2006; English; Man. Dir EDGAR CHIBAKA.

PERIODICALS

Fairlane Magazine: POB 1745, Blantyre; tel. 1880205; f. 2006; 6 a year; lifestyle magazine; English and Chichewa; Man. Dir MARIE FRANCE CHIKUNI.

Pride: POB 51668, Limbe; tel. 1840569; e-mail pridemagazine@yahoo.com; f. 1999; quarterly; Publr JOHN SAINI.

Together: Montfort Media, POB 280, Balaka, Zomba; tel. 1552267; e-mail together@sdnp.org.mw; f. 1995; quarterly; Roman Catholic and ecumenical, youth; Editor BARTHOLOWMEW BOAZ.

Other publications include *Dzukani*, *Inspiration* and *Msilikali*.

PRESS ASSOCIATIONS

Media Council of Malawi: Mtolankhani House, Acacia Lilaga, off Kasiya Rd, Lilongwe; tel. 999558052; e-mail info@mediacouncil-mw.org; internet fb.com/mediaCouncilmw; f. 2007; Exec. Dir MOSES KAUFA.

Media Institute of Southern Africa—Malawi (MISA—Malawi): Mtolankhani House, Acacia, Lilaga Community, off Lilongwe-Kasiya Rd, POB 30463, Lilongwe; tel. 1758091; internet malawi.misa.org; Chair. TERESA TEMWEKA NDANGA; Nat. Dir AUBREY CHIKUNGWA.

NEWS AGENCIES

Malawi News Agency (MANA): Gemini House, Ground Floor, City Centre, Capital City, Lilongwe; tel. 1774171; e-mail manaheadquarters@gmail.com; internet www.manaonline.gov.mw; f. 1966; Man. Editor WALLACE CHIPETA.

Publishers

Likuni Press and Publishing House: Likuni Parish, POB 133, Lilongwe; tel. 997766122; e-mail likunipressph@gmail.com; internet fb.com/likunipress; f. 1949; English and Chichewa; general and religious; Gen. Man. FRANCIS LEKALEKA.

Montfort Press and Popular Publications: POB 5592, Limbe; tel. 1651833; f. 1961; general and religious; owned by Archdiocese of Blantyre (Roman Catholic Church); Chief Editor SISTER LUISA.

GOVERNMENT PUBLISHING HOUSE

Government Press: Government Printer, POB 37, Zomba; tel. 1525515.

Broadcasting and Communications

REGULATORY AUTHORITY

Malawi Communications Regulatory Authority (MACRA): 9 Salmin Amour Rd, PMB 261, Blantyre; tel. 1810497; e-mail dg-macra@macra.mw; internet www.macra.org.mw; f. 1998; Chair. Dr STANLEY KHAILA; Dir-Gen. DAUD SULEMAN.

TELECOMMUNICATIONS

In 2011 dual licences were awarded to all telecommunications operators, permitting them to provide both fixed-line and mobile services. In 2022 there were two mobile telephone operators, one fixed-line telephone operator and one fixed wireless operator in Malawi.

Access Communications Ltd: Accord Bldg, Masauko Chipembere Hwy, Limbe, POB 343, Blantyre; tel. 212200200; e-mail switch@ access.mw; internet www.access.mw; f. 2010; fixed wireless; CEO FAIZAL OKHAI; Gen. Man. MAC MTILA.

Airtel Malawi: Airtel Complex, Chilembwe Rd, POB 57, Lilongwe; tel. 1774800; e-mail customercare@mw.airtel.com; internet www .airtel.mw; f. 1999; fmrly Zain Malawi, present name adopted in 2010; Man. Dir CHARLES KAMOTO.

Malawi Telecommunications Ltd (MTL): Lunjika House, Moi Rd, POB 537, Blantyre; tel. 1846977; e-mail info@mtl.mw; internet www.mtl.mw; f. 2000 following division of Malawi Posts and Telecommunications Corpn into two separate entities; partially privatized in 2006; 52.7% owned by Press Corpn, 16.1% owned by Old Mutual, 9% owned by Nico Holdings, 2.2% owned by Investment Alliance, 20% state-owned; fixed-line operator; Chair. ELIZABETH MAFENI; CEO HARRY GOMBACHIKA.

Telekom Networks Malawi (TNM): Livingstone Towers, 5th Floor, Glyn Jones Rd, POB 3039, Blantyre; tel. 888800800; e-mail customercare@tnm.co.mw; internet www.tnm.co.mw; f. 1995; 41.31% owned by Press Corpn Ltd, 24.07% owned by Old Mutual Life Assurance Co Ltd (Malawi); operates mobile telephone network; launched the Internet of Good Things (IoGT) with UNICEF Malawi to provide free information on education and health in 2018; Chair. Prof. GEORGE PATRIDGE; CEO Arnold KWEYANI MBWANA.

BROADCASTING

Radio

Malawi Broadcasting Corpn (MBC): POB 30133, Chichiri, Blantyre 3; tel. 1871257; e-mail dgmbc@malawi.net; internet www.mbc .mw; f. 1964; merged with Television Malawi in July 2010; state-run; 2 channels: Radio 1 and Radio 2; programmes in English, Chichewa, Chitonga, Chitumbuka, Kyangonde, Lomwe, Sena and Yao; Chair. Rev. VASCO KACHIPAPA; Dir-Gen. GEORGE KASAKULA.

Private commercial and religious radio stations include:

African Bible College Radio (Radio ABC): Plot 530, Area 47, POB 1028, Lilongwe; tel. 1761910; internet africanbiblecolleges.com/ abcmalawi; f. 1995; regional Christian religious programming.

Calvary Family Radio: POB 30239, Blantyre 3; tel. 1671627; operated by the Calvary Family Church; religious community radio station; Founder and Pres. Apostle MADILITSO MBEWE.

Capital Radio Malawi: Pamdozi Park, 1st Floor, Ali Hassen Mwinyi Rd, Blantyre; PMB 437, Chichiri, Blantyre 3; tel. 1875400; e-mail info@capitalradiomalawi.com; internet capitalradiomalawi .com; f. 1999; commercial radio station; music, news and entertainment; Man. Dir and Editor-in-Chief ALAUDIN OSMAN.

MIJ FM: POB 30165, Chichiri, Blantyre 3; tel. 1875154; e-mail mijonline2019@gmail.com; internet fb.com/mijmw; f. 2000; operated by students of the Malawi Institute of Journalism; community radio station; Exec. Dir ANTHONY PHANGA.

Nkhotakota Community Radio: Stambuli Dr., 265 Nkhotakota, PMB 48, Nkhotakota; tel. 1292388; e-mail nkkcommradio@yahoo .com; internet fb.com/RadioNkhotakota; f. 2003; focus on social and devt issues; Chair. BLESSINGS MKOLOLA; Station Man. EDWARD KWACHA.

Power 101 FM: Raynor Ave, Limbe, POB 761, Blantyre; tel. 1841101; e-mail fm101power@gmail.com; f. 1998; commercial radio station; music and entertainment; Dir and Station Man. OSCAR THOMSON.

Radio Alinafe: Maula Parish, POB 631, Lilongwe; tel. 998733593; e-mail alinafecomm1@gmail.com; internet radioalinafe.com; f. 2002; Chichewa and English; operated by the Archdiocese of Lilongwe; regional Roman Catholic religious programming; Dir Fr LOUIS CHIKANYA.

Radio Islam: Agason Bldg, POB 5400, Blantyre; tel. 1841408; e-mail info@radioislam.org.mw; internet radioislam.org.mw; f. 2001; operated by the Islamic Zakaat Fund; religious programming;

programmes in English, Yao, Urdu, Tumbuka, and Chichewa; Pres. YUSUF JAMES; Station Man. ALI BLESSINGS IDI.

Radio Maria Malawi: Area 43, Ali Maunde, Lilongwe; tel. 1599626; e-mail info.mlw@radiomaria.org; internet www.radiomaria.mw; f. 1999; operated by Asscn of Radio Maria Malawi as part of the World Family of Radio Maria, Italy; Roman Catholic religious programming; Chichewa, Chiyao, Chitumbuka and English; Pres. LEVI PHERANI; Dir of Programmes Fr JOSEPH KIMU.

Timveni Radio: Area 47, Sector 5, POB 712, Blantyre; tel. 992677092; e-mail info@timveni.org; internet timveni.com; f. 2006; fmrly Star Radio; present name adopted in 2016; commercial radio station; owned by Timveni Child and Media Organizations; also operates Timveni Television; Owner MIKE CHILEWE, Jr; Exec. Dir HERBERT CHIDAYA.

Zodiak Broadcasting Station (ZBS): Artbridge House, Area 47, Sector 5, Lilongwe; tel. 1762557; e-mail editor@zodiakmalawi.com; internet www.zodiakmalawi.com; f. 2005; operated by Zodiak Broadcasting Services; programmes in Chichewa and English; Man. Dir GOSPEL KAZAKO.

Television

Calvary Family Television: Blantyre; Christian; Founder and Pres. Apostle Dr MADILITSO MBEWE.

Hope Channel Malawi: Kabula Hill, Robins Rd, POB 951, Blantyre; tel. 886757957; internet malawi.hopechannel.de; f. 2015; operated by the Seventh Day Adventist Church, Malawi; religious programmes; Dir CHARLES THANGALIMODZI.

Luntha Television: Andiamo Loop, POB 137, Balaka; tel. 1553009; e-mail lunthatvdirector@gmail.com; internet www.lunthatv.com; f. 2007; religious broadcaster; also operates from Lilongwe; Dir Fr DAVID NIWAGABA.

MBC: see Radio.

Finance

BANKING

Central Bank

Reserve Bank of Malawi: Convention Dr., City Centre, POB 30063, Capital City, Lilongwe 3; tel. 1770600; e-mail reserve-bank@rbm.mw; internet www.rbm.mw; f. 1965; bank of issue; Gov. Dr WILSON TONGANI BANDA.

Commercial Banks

Ecobank Malawi Ltd: cnr Victoria Ave and Henderson St, Private Bag 389, Chichiri, Blantyre; tel. 1822099; e-mail ecobankenquiries@ ecobank.com; internet www.ecobank.com; fmrly Loita Bank Ltd; present name adopted in 2008; Chair. MASAUKO MSUNGAMA; Man. Dir RAYMOND FORDWUO.

FDH Bank: Umoyo House, 1st Floor, 8 Victoria Ave North, POB 512, Blantyre; tel. 1820219; e-mail callcentre@fdh.co.mw; internet www .fdh.co.mw; f. 1994; fmrly Malawi Savings Bank; Chair. CHARITY JOY MSEKA; Man. Dir NOEL MKULICHI.

National Bank of Malawi: 7 Henderson St, POB 945, Blantyre; tel. 1820622; e-mail chiefexec@natbankmw.com; internet www.natbank .co.mw; f. 1971 following merger of Barclays Bank DCO and Standard Bank; acquired with Indebank Ltd 2016; Chair. GEORGE B. PARTRIDGE; CEO MACFUSSY KAWAWA.

NBS Bank Ltd: Ginnery Cnr, cnrs Chipembere Highway and Johnstone Rd, POB 32251, Chichiri, Blantyre 3; tel. 1876222; e-mail nbs@nbs.mw; internet www.nbs.mw; f. 2003; 50.1% owned by NICO Holdings Ltd, 23.9% owned by general public; fmrly New Building Society; Chair. VIZENGE M. KUMWENDA; CEO KWANELE NGWENYA.

Nedbank (Malawi) Ltd: Plantation House, Victoria Ave, POB 750, Blantyre; tel. 1820477; e-mail info@nedbank.co.mw; internet www .nedbank.co.mw; f. 1999; fmrly Fincom Bank of Malawi Ltd; 98.8% owned by Ned Group Investments Africa, 1.1% owned by Nedbank Group Ltd; Chair. MAZIKO SAUTI PHIRI; Man. Dir PAUL GUTA.

Standard Bank Ltd: Standard Bank Centre, Victoria Ave, City Centre, POB 30380, Capital City, Lilongwe 3; tel. 9999015001; e-mail callcentre@standardbank.co.mw; internet www.standardbank.co .mw; f. 1969 as Commercial Bank of Malawi; present name adopted June 2003; 60.18% owned by Stanbic Africa Holdings Ltd, 20.00% owned by NICO Holdings Ltd; Chair. NYEGI KANYONGOLO; CEO PHILLIP MADINGA.

Discount Houses

CDH Investment Bank: CDH House, 5 Independence Dr., POB 1444, Blantyre; tel. 1821300; e-mail info@cdh-malawi.com; internet www.cdh-malawi.com; f. 1998; 80% owned by Trans-Africa Holdings,

13% owned by Press Trust; Chair. FRANKLIN KENNEDY; Man. Dir and CEO MISHECK ESAU.

First Discount House Ltd: Umoyo House, 1st Floor, 8 Victoria Ave North, POB 512, Blantyre; tel. 1820397; e-mail callcentre@fdh.co .mw; internet www.fdh.co.mw; f. 2001; subsidiary of FDH Financial Holding Ltd; Group CEO Dr THOMSON MPINGANJIRA; Man. Dir MIKE CHIWALO.

Merchant Banks

First Capital Bank Ltd: Livingstone Towers, Glyn Jones Rd, Private Bag 122, Blantyre; tel. 1821955; e-mail info@ firstcapitalbank.co.mw; internet firstcapitalbank.co.mw; f. 1984; fmrly First Merchant Bank Ltd; present name adopted in 2018; acquired Barclays Bank of Zimbabwe, Opportunity International Bank of Malawi (q.v.) and Leasing and Finance Co of Malawi Ltd in 2017; Chair. HITESH ANADKAT; Interim Group Man. Dir MAHENDRA GURUSAHANI.

STOCK EXCHANGE

Malawi Stock Exchange: Old Reserve Bank Bldg, 14 Victoria Ave, Private Bag 270, Blantyre; tel. 1824233; e-mail info@mse-mw.com; internet mse.co.mw; f. 1996; owned by the Reserve Bank of Malawi; 15 cos listed in 2020; Chair. Dr WINFORD HENDERSON MASANJALA; CEO JOHN ROBSON KAMANGA.

INSURANCE

General Alliance Insurance Ltd: Alliance House, cnr Sharp Rd, POB 1811, Blantyre; tel. 1822100; e-mail info@generalalliancemw .com; internet www.generalalliancemw.com; f. 1996; two subsidiaries: General Alliance Insurance (Zambia) Ltd, Star General Insurance (Tanzania) Ltd; Chair. RAMESH H. SAVJANI; CEO PRAKASH PATIL.

NICO Holdings Ltd: Chibisa House, 19 Glyn Jones Rd, POB 501, Blantyre; tel. 1831902; e-mail csnico@nicomw.com; internet www .nicomw.com; f. 1970; fmrly National Insurance Co Ltd; transferred to private sector in 1996; incorporates NICO Gen. Insurance Co Ltd, NICO Life Insurance Co Ltd, NICO Technologies Ltd and Nico Asset Managers; offices at Blantyre, Lilongwe, Mzuzu and Zomba; agencies countrywide; Chair. GAFFAR HASSAM (acting); Group Man. Dir VIZENGE M. KUMWENDA.

Old Mutual Malawi: 30 Glyn Jones Rd, Old Mutual Building, POB 393, Blantyre; tel. 1820677; e-mail info@oldmutual.co.mw; internet www.oldmutual.co.mw; f. 1954 as a mutual life insurance co; demutualized in 1997; subsidiary of Old Mutual PLC, UK; Chair. Dr RONALD MANGANI; Group CEO EDITH JIYA.

United General Insurance Co Ltd (UGI): Michiru House, Victoria Ave, POB 383, Blantyre; tel. 1821770; e-mail ugi@ugi.mw; internet www.ugi.mw; f. 1986 as Pearl Assurance Co Ltd; latterly Property and Gen. Insurance Co Ltd; present name adopted following merger with Fide Insurance Co Ltd in July 1998; 47% owned by National Bank of Malawi; CEO BYWELL CHIWONI.

Vanguard Life Assurance Co Ltd: Zeka Office Park, 1st Floor, Robins Rd, POB 1625, Blantyre; tel. 1832216; e-mail vanguard@ vanguardlifemw.com; internet www.vanguardlifemw.com; f. 1999; 90% owned by Fidelity Life Assurance Ltd, Zimbabwe; Chair. G. KAMBALE; Man. Dir NOAH MUPFURUTSA.

Trade and Industry

GOVERNMENT AGENCIES

Agricultural Development and Marketing Corpn Ltd (ADMARC): Tsiranana Rd, Limbe, POB 5052, Blantyre; tel. 1840044; e-mail admce@admarc.co.mw; internet www.admarc.co .mw; f. 1971; involved in cultivation, processing, marketing and export of grain and other crops; Chair. ALEXANDER KUSAMBA DZONZI; CEO DHLELISILE MATANDA PHIRI (acting).

Malawi Housing Corpn: opp. Njamba Park, Soche, POB 414, Blantyre; tel. 1686401; e-mail ceo@mhcmw.org; internet www .mhcmw.org; f. 1964; 4 regional offices; Chair. JUSTIN DZONZI; CEO JORDAN CHIPATALA (acting).

Malawi Investment and Trade Centre (MITC): Aquarius House, 1st Floor, PMB 302, Lilongwe 3; tel. 1770800; e-mail info@mitc.mw; internet mitc.mw; f. 2010 following merger of the Malawi Investment Promotion Agency (MIPA) and Malawi Export Promotion Council (MEPC); promotes and facilitates export and investment, and provides technical assistance and training to exporters; Chair. KARL CHOKHOTHO; CEO PAUL KWENGWERE.

Malawi Revenue Authority: Msonkho House, PMB 247, Blantyre; tel. 1822588; e-mail mrahq@mra.mw; internet www.mra.mw; f. 2000; responsible for assessment, collection and accounting for tax revenues; Chair. VIZENGE M. KUMWENDA; Commr-Gen. JOHN S. BIZIWICK.

National Food Reserve Agency: Kanengo Silos Complex, PMB B450, Lilongwe 3; tel. 887082356; internet www.nframw.com; f. 1999; Chair. DENNIS KALEKENI; CEO (vacant).

Public Private Partnership Commission: Livingstone Towers, 2nd Floor, Glyn Jones Rd, POB 937, Blantyre; tel. 1823655; e-mail info@pppc.mw; internet www.pppc.mw; f. 1996 as Privatisation Commission of Malawi; present name adopted in 2011; has sole authority to oversee divestiture of govt interests in public enterprises; Chair. LEKANI KATANDULA; CEO PATRICK KABAMBE.

Tobacco Commission: Plot 29/190, M1 Rd, Kanengo, POB 40045, Lilongwe 4; tel. 1712777; e-mail tclib@tc.mw; internet www.tccmw .com; f. 1938; fmrly Tobacco Control Commission; regulates tobacco production and marketing; advises Govt on sale and export of tobacco; divisional offices in Kasungu, Mzuzu and Limbe; CEO JOSEPH CHIDANTI MALUNGA.

DEVELOPMENT ORGANIZATIONS

Council for Non-Governmental Organizations in Malawi (CONGOMA): Amina House, Ground Floor, Units 11 and 12, off Paul Kagame Rd, POB 2264, Lilongwe; tel. 1759881; e-mail congoma@gmail.com; internet www.congoma.net; f. 1992; promotes social and economic devt; Chair. KOSSAM MUNTHALI; Exec. Dir RONALD MTONGA.

National Oil Co of Malawi Ltd (NOCMA): Kang'ombe Bldg, 4th Floor, City Centre, PMB 370, Lilongwe 3; tel. 1770875; e-mail info@ nocma.mw; internet www.nocma.mw; f. 2010; state-owned; Acting CEO HELLEN BULUMA.

Small and Medium Enterprise Development Malawi (SMEDI): Amina House, Area 4, West Wing, off Paul Kagame Rd, PMB 393, Lilongwe 3; tel. 1772714; e-mail smediheadquarters@ gmail.com; internet www.smedi.org.mw; f. 2013 following merger of Medium Enterprise Development Institute, Small Enterprise Development Organization of Malawi and Development of Malawi Enterprises Trust; promotes the devt and growth of micro, small and medium enterprises in Malawi; Chair. TEMWA SIMWAKA; CEO RODRICK CHATTAIKA.

CHAMBER OF COMMERCE

Malawi Chamber of Mines and Energy: Press Properties Bldg, off Kamuzu Procession Rd, POB 687, Lilongwe 2; tel. 991019196; e-mail malawichamberofmines@yahoo.com; f. 2016 to promote, advance and protect the mining industry of Malawi; Pres. BURTON KACHINJIKA.

Malawi Confederation of Chambers of Commerce and Industry (MCCCI): 61 Masauko Chipembere Hwy, Chichiri Trade Fair Grounds, POB 258, Blantyre; tel. 1871988; e-mail mccci@mccci.org; internet www.mccci.org; f. 1892; promotes trade and encourages competition in the economy; also a mem of Asscn of SADC Chambers of Commerce and Industry; Pres. L. KATANDULA; CEO CHANCELLOR L. KAFERAPANJIRA; 400 mems.

INDUSTRIAL AND TRADE ASSOCIATIONS

Coffee Association of Malawi (CAMAL): Kidney Cres., POB 930, Blantyre; tel. 1983737; e-mail admin@coffeemalawi.org; internet www.coffeemalawi.org; f. 1981; Chair. ROBIN SAUNDERS.

Leather Industries Association of Malawi (LIAMA): Lilongwe; f. 2016; Pres. EDWARD MALUNGA.

TAMA Farmers Trust: Tama House, Independence Ave, POB 31360, Lilongwe 3; tel. 1773099; e-mail tama@tamalawi.com; internet tamalawi.com; f. 1929 as Nyasaland Tobacco Asscn; registered as trust in 1983; fmrly Tobacco Association of Malawi (TAMA); Pres. ABEL MASACHE KALIMA-BANDA; CEO NIXON LITA; brs in Mzuzu, Limbe and Chinkhoma.

Tea Association of Malawi Ltd (TAML): Kidney Cres., POB 930, Blantyre; tel. 888890152; e-mail secretariat@teamalawi.com; internet www.teamalawi.org; f. 1934; Chair. SANGWANI HARA; CEO TONDA CHINANGWA.

EMPLOYERS' ORGANIZATIONS

Employers' Consultative Association of Malawi (ECAM): Plot CH/M/114, The Ridge, off Chilomoni Ring Rd, POB 2134, Blantyre; tel. 995189391; e-mail ecam@ecammw.com; internet www.ecammw .com; f. 1963; Pres. ANNE CHAVULA; Exec. Dir GEORGE KHAKI; 250 mem. orgs, incl. 6 affiliates representing over 277,000 mems.

UTILITIES

Electricity

Electricity Generation Co Ltd (EGENCO): Chayamba Bldg, 7 Victoria Ave, POB 1567, Blantyre; tel. 1836000; e-mail egenco@ egenco.mw; internet www.egenco.mw; f. 2017 to take over generation assets from ESCOM; state-owned; Chair. ZANGAZANGA CHIKHOSI; CEO WILLIAM LIABUNYA.

Electricity Supply Corpn of Malawi (ESCOM): ESCOM House, 9 Haile Selassie Rd, POB 2047, Blantyre; tel. 1822000; e-mail info@escom.mw; internet www.escom.mw; f. 1986; controls electricity distribution; Chair. CHOKANI MHANGO; CEO KAMKWAMBA WAYERA KUMWENDA.

Malawi Energy Regulatory Authority (MERA): Development House, 2nd Floor, City Centre, PMB B496, Lilongwe 3; tel. 1775810; e-mail mera@mera.mw; internet mera.mw; f. 2004; Chair. RECKFORD KAMPANJE; CEO HENRY KACHAJE.

Water

Blantyre Water Board: POB 30369, Chichiri, Blantyre 3; tel. 1895000; e-mail bwb@bwb.mw; internet www.bwb.mw; f. 1995; supplies potable water to Blantyre City and its environs; Chair. GEORGE NNESA; Chief Exec. Dr ROBERT T. HANJAHANJA.

Lilongwe Water Board: POB 96, Lilongwe; tel. 1750366; e-mail madzi@lwb.mw; internet www.lwb.mw; f. 1947; Chair. GEORGE KAJANGA; CEO SILLI MBEWE.

There are also three regional water boards—Central Region Water Board, Northern Region Water Board, Southern Region Water Board—serving the population in small towns and rural areas.

MAJOR COMPANIES

The following are among the largest companies in terms of capital investment or employment.

AHL Group: Plot 29/78, POB 40035, Kanengo, Lilongwe 4; tel. 1710377; f. 1962 following the amalgamation of Tobacco Auctions Ltd and Producers Warehouse Ltd; fmrly Auction Holdings Ltd; present name adopted in 2015; privatized 1997; tobacco and tobacco products; auction floor operators; 42.6% owned by ADMARC, 5% owned by the Nat. Investment Trust Ltd; Chair. FOSTER MULUMBE; Chief Exec. ALFRED NKHONO (acting).

Alliance One Tobacco (Malawi) Ltd: Plot 29/86, Kanengo Industrial Site, POB 30522, Lilongwe 3; tel. 1710044; f. 2005 through merger of Standard Commercial Tobacco (Malawi) Ltd and Dimon (Malawi) Ltd; growing and processing tobacco for tobacco manufacturers; Man. Dir HUGH SAUNDERS.

Bakhresa Malawi Ltd: Charterland Rd, POB 5847, Limbe; tel. 1841198; e-mail malawi@bakhresa.com; internet bakhresa.com; f. 2003 as Bakhresa Grain Milling (Malawi) Ltd; fmrly Grain and Milling Co Ltd (GRAMIL); present name adopted in 2013; 100% owned by Bakhresa Family; Chair. SAID SALIM AWADH BAKHRESA; Man. Dir ABUBAKAR SAID SALIM BAKHRESA.

Bio Energy Resources Ltd (BERL): Mchinji Rd, Njewa Farm, opp. ARET, POB 1075, Lilongwe; tel. 1737136; e-mail hello@bioenergyresources.ltd; internet www.bioenergyresources.ltd; f. 2006; CEO LAURIE WEBB.

BNC Packaging Ltd: POB 30575, Chichiri, Blantyre 3; tel. 1874255; CEO DEVANG SHAH.

British American Tobacco Malawi Ltd: Chipembere Highway, POB 428, Blantyre; tel. 1870033; internet www.bat.com; f. 1942; mfrs and distributors of cigarettes; Regional Dir LUCIANO COMIN.

Capital Foods Ltd: Plot 29/93 Salima Rd, Kanengo Industrial Site, POB 1009, Lilongwe; tel. 1711055; e-mail info@capitalfoodsmw.com; internet www.capitalfoodsmw.com; f. 1976; producer and supplier of flour; Chair. NAZMA BANU VALIMAHOMED; Man. Dir AYOB MAHOMED SALIM.

Capital Oil Refining Industries Ltd (CORI): Chirimba Industrial Estate, POB 2826, Blantyre; tel. 999915990; e-mail info@corilimited.com; internet www.corilimited.com; f. 1988; Man. Dir SHIRAZ KARIM.

Chombe Foods Ltd: MBL Compound, Viphya Ave, POB 500, Blantyre; tel. 1870559; e-mail chombefoods2021@gmail.com; internet chombefoods.com; f. 1969; Gen. Man. MAQSOOD RAHMAN BORA.

Glens (Malawi) Ltd: Makata Industrial Area, Blantyre; tel. 1871888; e-mail glens_blz@glensmw.com; internet glensmw.com; f. 1954; freight and logistics services; Man. Dir S. J. MUKUNDAM.

Illovo Sugar (Malawi) Ltd: Churchhill Rd, PMB 580, Limbe; tel. 1843988; e-mail infomalawi@illovo.co.za; internet www.illovosugar.co.za; f. 1965; fmrly Sugar Corpn of Malawi Ltd (SUCOMA); present name adopted 2004; 76% owned by Illovo Sugar Group, South Africa, 10% owned by Old Mutual Life Assurance Co; sugar mills at Dwangwa and Nchalo; sugar production and processing; Man. Dir LEKANI KATANDULA.

Kentam Products Ltd: Luwinga Industrial Site, POB 898, Mzuzu; tel. 1320643; e-mail kentam@africa-online.net; internet fb.com/KentamProducts; pharmaceutical, and chemical manufacturing co; Man. Dir Dr K. J. M. THINDWA.

LafargeHolcim Malawi Ltd: Plot NY318, Makata Heavy Industrial Area, POB 523, Blantyre; tel. 1871933; e-mail lafarge.mwcem@lafarge.com; internet www.lafarge.mw; f. 1974 as Portland Cement Co; subsidiary of LafargeHolcim Group; CEO (vacant).

Malawi Cotton Co Ltd: Blantyre; internet www.ca-cotton.com; subsidiary of China-Africa Cotton Development Ltd; Chinese-owned; Chair. JU WENBIN; CEO SHI JINGRAN.

Mapeto (DWSM) Ltd: cnr Macleod and Makata Rds, Makata Industrial Site, Blantyre; tel. 1870027; e-mail mm@mapetodwsm.com; textiles; Man. Dir MOHAMED GAFFAR; Gen. Man. MARTIN C. MPATA.

Nampak Malawi: POB 30533, Chichiri, Blantyre 3; tel. 1884533; e-mail hrm@mw.nampak.com; internet www.nampak.com; f. 1969 as Packaging Industries (Malawi) Ltd; present name adopted in 2013; mfrs of cardboard boxes, paper sacks and liquid packaging containers; Man. Dir SHAUN DU PLESSIS.

Petroleum Importers Ltd (PIL): Unit House, 5th Floor, Victoria Ave, PMB 200, Blantyre; tel. 1822886; e-mail pil@pilmalawi.mw; internet pilmw.com; f. 2000 following liberalization of the petroleum industry; industry consortium incl. national and international oil cos; owned by Puma Malawi Ltd, Total Malawi Ltd, Petroda Malawi Ltd and Engen Malawi; imports 80% of the country's fuel requirements; Chair. HILDA SOKO; Gen. Man. MARTIN MSIMUKO.

Pharmanova Malawi Ltd: Plot 264/267, Scott Rd, Ginnery Corner, Chichiri, POB 30075, Blantyre 3; tel. 1870747; e-mail admin@pharmanovamw.com; internet www.pharmanovamalawi.com; mfrs of pharmaceutical products; Man. Dir YUSUF PATEL.

Press Corpn Ltd: NBM Top Mandala House, Kaohsiung Rd, POB 1227, Blantyre; tel. 1833569; e-mail companysec@presscorp.com; internet www.presscorp.com; f. 1983 as Press Group Ltd; diversified co with eight subsidiaries, four assoc. and one jt venture co in distribution, banking, insurance, manufacturing and processing; Chair. RANDSON MWADIWA; Group CEO Dr LYTON CHITHAMBO (acting).

Subsidiaries incl. Castel Malawi Ltd, Presscane Ltd and also:

Ethanol Co Ltd (ETHCO): POB 50, Dwangwa; tel. 1295200; e-mail ethco@ethanolmw.com; internet www.ethanolmw.com; f. 1982; producer and distributor of ethanol fuel; 66% owned by Press Corpn Ltd, 26% by INDETrust and 8% by Illovo Sugar (Malawi) Ltd; distillery at Dwangwa; Chair. JOHN BIZIWICK; CEO LUSUBILO CHAKANIZA.

Limbe Leaf Tobacco Co Ltd: Plot 29/125–126, Area 29, POB 40044, Kanengo, Lilongwe 4; tel. 1710355; e-mail lmuhara@lltcmw.com; internet www.universalcorp.com; 58% owned by Universal Leaf Tobacco Co and 42% owned by Press Corpn Ltd; Chair., Pres. and CEO Dr GEORGE C. FREEMAN, III.

Macsteel (Malawi) Ltd: Raynor Ave, POB 5651, Limbe, Blantyre; tel. 881934369; e-mail steel@macsteelmw.com; internet fb.com/macsteelmdubs; fmrly Press Steel and Wire Ltd; present name adopted in 2003; steel processors; jt venture Co between Press Corpn Ltd and Macsteel South Africa.

Maldeco Fisheries: POB 45, Mangochi; tel. 1580300; e-mail customercare.maldeco@maldeco.mw; internet www.maldeco.mw; f. 2003; 100% subsidiary of Press Corpn Ltd; Gen. Man. ANDREW SANTHE.

Press Properties Ltd (PPL): PCL House, 2nd and 3rd Floors, Top Mandala, Kaohsiung Rd, POB 925, Blantyre; tel. 1824444; e-mail info@pressproperties.com; internet www.pressproperties.com; f. 1969; Chair. JOHN BIZIWICK; Gen. Man. MARTIN CHIMANGENI.

Puma Energy Malawi: Standard Bank Bldg, 3rd Floor, Glyn Jones Rd, POB 469, Blantyre; tel. 1895900; e-mail malawi@pumaenergy.com; internet pumaenergy.com; f. 1963; fmrly BP Malawi Ltd, present name adopted in 2011; fuel and oil distributor; owned by Press Corpn Ltd and Puma Energy; Man. Dir DAVIS LANJESI.

Raiply Malawi Ltd: Chikangawa, PMB 1, Mzimba; tel. 1340212; e-mail raiplymw@raiplymalawi.com; internet raiplymalawi.com; f. 1999; fmrly Viphya Plywoods and Allied Industries (Viply); acquired by T. S. Rai Ltd, Kenya in 1999; mfrs of plywood, blockboard, timber, treated poles and furniture; CEO KRISHNA DAS.

Salima Sugar Co Ltd: Plot 588, Area 3, POB 200, Lilongwe,; tel. 991999889; e-mail info@salimasugars.com; internet www.salimasugars.com; 40% state-owned; Chair. SHIRIEESH BETGIRI.

Toyota Malawi Ltd: Queens cnr, Masauko Chipembere Highway, POB 430, Blantyre; tel. 1841933; e-mail info@toyotamalawi.com; internet www.toyotamalawi.com; f. 1964; import and distribution of motor vehicles and parts; Man. Dir KENNEDY KABAGHE.

Unilever Malawi Ltd: cnr Tsiranana Rd and Citron Ave, POB 5151, Limbe; tel. 1841100; e-mail charles.cofie@unilever.com; internet www.unilever.com; f. 1963; present name adopted in 2003; subsidiary of Unilever PLC, UK; mfrs of soaps, detergents, cooking oils, foods, beverages and chemicals; Man. Dir TARISAI VAMBE MAEREKA.

Van Rees Ltd: Plot NK 132, Maone Industrial Area, POB 451, Blantyre; tel. 1684817; e-mail trading-MW@vanrees.com; internet vanrees.com; tea sourcing and blending; Gen. Man. JAN BAS VAN VEELEN.

TRADE UNIONS

Malawi Congress of Trade Unions (MCTU): POB 1271, Lilongwe; tel. 1752162; e-mail mctusecretariat@gmail.com; internet www.mctusolidarity.org; f. 1995 as successor to the Trade Union Congress of Malawi (f. 1964); Pres. LUTHER MAMBALA; Sec.-Gen. DENIS KALEKENI.

Affiliated unions include:

Building Construction, Civil Engineering and Allied Workers' Union (BCCEAWU): c/o MCTU, POB 5094, Limbe; tel. 1620381; e-mail johnmwafulirwa@yahoo.com; f. 1995; also affiliated to global Building and Wood Worker's International; Pres. WEZZIE GRACE MKANDAWIRE; Gen. Sec. JOHN O. MWAFULIRWA.

Commercial Industrial and Allied Workers' Union (CIAWU): Amarsi Odhavji Bldg, POB 5099, Limbe; tel. 1820716; e-mail mareydzinyemba@yahoo.com; f. 1998; also affiliated to International Union of Food; Pres. VIWEMI MZUMARA; Gen. Sec. MARY DZINYEMBA.

Communications Workers' Union of Malawi (COWUMA): PMB 186, Blantyre; tel. 1830830; e-mail cowuma@yahoo.co.uk; f. 2002; also affiliated to Union Network International; Pres. SWEENY CHIMKANGO; Gen. Sec. HAMILTON DELEZA.

ESCOM Staff Union: POB 2047, Blantyre; tel. 1773447; Pres. CHARITY HARAWA; Gen. Sec. WILLIAM MNYAMULA.

Malawi Housing Co-operation Workers' Union: POB 414, Mzuzu; tel. 1332655; e-mail rachealpilirani@yahoo.co.uk; Pres. KONDWANI CHITIMBE; Gen. Sec. RACHEL LIMBE.

Plantation and Agriculture Workers' Union (PAWU): POB 237, Mzuzu, Kawalazi; e-mail banda.denis@gmail.com; f. 1995; Pres. GRACIAN KHEMBO; Gen. Sec. DENNIS BANDA.

Private Schools Employees' Union of Malawi (PSEUM): PMB A 210, Lilongwe; tel. 1755614; e-mail lemanifalison@gmail .com; f. 2001; also affiliated to Education International; Pres. JOYCE MBEBA; Gen. Sec. FALLISON LEMANI.

Teachers' Union of Malawi: Aphunzitsi Centre, off Malangalanga Rd, PMB 11, Lilongwe; tel. 1727302; e-mail kumchengacharles@gmail.com; Pres. WILLIE MALIMBA; Gen. Sec. CHARLES KUMCHENGA.

Textile, Garment, Leather and Security Services Workers' Union: POB 5094, Limbe; tel. 888389801; e-mail textilegarmentunion@yahoo.com; f. 1995; Gen. Sec. CHARLES MIKUNDI.

Tobacco and Allied Workers' Union of Malawi (TOAWUM): POB 477, Nkhotakota; tel. 1292288; e-mail raphaelsandramu@ gmail.com; f. 1992; also affiliated to International Union of Food; Gen. Sec. RAPHAEL SANDRAM-NKHOTAKOTA.

Transport and General Workers' Union (TGWU): POB 2778, Blantyre; tel. 888877795; e-mail raphaelsandramu@gmail.com; f. 1995; also affiliated to International Transport Federation; Gen. Sec. RAPHAEL SANDRAM.

Water Employees' Trade Union of Malawi (WETUM): c/o Lilongwe Water Board, POB 96, Lilongwe; tel. 1750344; f. 2000; also affiliated to Public Services International; Pres. GERALD NGULUWE; Gen. Sec. GANIZANI THYANGATHYANGA.

Transport

RAILWAYS

The Central East African Railways Co (fmrly Malawi Railways) operates between Nsanje (near the southern border with Mozambique) and Mchinji (near the border with Zambia) via Blantyre, Salima and Lilongwe, and between Nkaya and Nayuchi on the eastern border with Mozambique. The Central East African Railways Co and Caminhos de Ferro de Mozambique connect Malawi with the Mozambican ports of Beira and Nacala. There is a rail/lake interchange station at Chipoka on Lake Malawi, from where vessels operate services to other lake ports in Malawi.

Central East African Railways Co Ltd (CEAR): Station Rd, POB 5144, Limbe; tel. 1840841; e-mail cear@cearcdn.mw; internet www .cear.mw; f. 1994 as Malawi Railways Ltd; operates jointly with Corredor de Desenvolvimento Do Norte (Mozambique); owned by a consortium of Brazilian, Japanese and Mozambican companies; freight and passenger service; CEO ROBERT E. MORTENSEN.

ROADS

In Malawi all main roads, and most secondary roads, are all-weather roads. Major routes link Lilongwe and Blantyre with Harare (Zimbabwe), Lusaka (Zambia) and Mbeya and Dar es Salaam (Tanzania). A 480-km highway along the western shore of Lake Malawi links the remote Northern Region with the Central and Southern Regions.

Department of Road Traffic: c/o Ministry of Transport and Public Infrastructure, PMB 257, Capital City, Lilongwe 3; tel. 1756138; comprises the Roads Authority and the Road Fund Administration.

Roads Authority: Functional Bldg, off Paul Kagame Rd, PMB B346, Lilongwe 3; tel. 1759154; e-mail rahq@ra.org.mw; internet www.ra.org.mw; f. 2006 following the division of the National Roads Authority into two separate bodies—the other being the Roads Fund Administration; Chair. (vacant); Acting CEO Eng. FRANCIS DIMU.

Roads Fund Administration: Ngerengere House, Ground Floor, Off Queens Dr., Lilongwe 3; tel. 1762733; e-mail info@ rfamw.com; internet rfamw.com; f. 2006 following the division of the National Roads Authority into two separate bodies—the other being Roads Authority; Chair. CHANCY GONDWE; CEO STEWART MALATA.

SHIPPING

There are 23 ports and landing points on Lake Malawi. The four main ports are at Chilumba, Nkhata Bay, Chipoka and Monkey Bay. Ferry services carry around 60,000 passengers annually; the principal cargoes transported are sugar, fertilizer, dried fish and maize. Smaller vessels are registered for other activities, including fishing and tourism.

Malawi Shipping Co (MSC): Nasra Bldg, City Centre, Lilongwe; tel. 1773723; f. 1994; fmrly Malawi Lake Services Ltd; privatized 2010; conceded to Mota-Engil (Portugal) for 35 years; operates passenger and freight services to Mozambique, and freight services to Tanzania; Gen. Man. CAROS MATOS; 9 vessels, incl. 3 passenger and 4 cargo vessels.

CIVIL AVIATION

Kamuzu (formerly Lilongwe) International Airport was opened in 1982. There is also an international airport at Chileka (Blantyre) and domestic airports at Mzuzu and Karonga in the Northern Region and at the Club Makokola resort near Mangochi.

Malawi Airlines: Golden Peacock Shopping Complex, City Centre, Capital City, POB 2095, Lilongwe; tel. 1774518; e-mail info@ malawian-airlines.com; internet www.malawian-airlines.com; f. 2013 as Malawian Airlines to replace Air Malawi Ltd; present name adopted in 2016; 49% owned by Ethiopian Airlines, 51% state-owned; scheduled domestic and international services; CEO HAILE-MELEKOT MAMO.

Tourism

Department of Tourism: off Convention Dr., Private Bag 326, Lilongwe 3; tel. 1775499; e-mail info@visitmalawi.mw; internet www .visitmalawi.mw; f. 1969; responsible for tourism policy; inspects and licenses tourist facilities, sponsors training of hotel staff and publishes tourist literature; Dir of Tourism ISAAC DALTON KATOPOLA.

Defence

As assessed at November 2021, Malawi's defence forces comprised a land army of 10,500, a marine force of 220 and an air force of 200: all form part of the army. There was also a paramilitary police force of 4,200. In 2021 a total of 732 Malawian troops were stationed abroad.

Defence Budget: K65,800m. in 2021.

Commander-in-Chief of the Malawi Defence Force: Dr LAZARUS MCCARTHY CHAKWERA.

Commander of the Malawi Defence Force: Gen. VINCENT NUNDWE.

Commander of the Air Force: Maj.-Gen. IAN MACLEOD CHIRWA.

Commander of the Land Forces: Maj.-Gen. ELIAS MPAPSO.

Commander of the Navy: Maj.-Gen. FRANCIS BLESSINGS KAKHUTA BANDA.

Education

Primary education, which is provided free of charge but is not compulsory, begins at six years of age and lasts for eight years. Secondary education, which begins at 14 years of age, lasts for four years, comprising two cycles of two years. According to estimates by the United Nations Educational, Scientific and Cultural Organization (UNESCO), in 2014/15 pre-primary enrolment was equivalent to 84% of children in the relevant age-group (males 83%; females 84%), while primary enrolment in 2018/19 included 98% of children in the relevant age-group (males 96%; females 100%). Secondary enrolment in 2018/2019 was equivalent to 37% of children in the relevant age-group (males 41%; females 34%). Education was allocated some K462.240m. in the budget for 2022/23, equivalent to around 16.3% of total projected expenditure.

Bibliography

Aberman, N., Meerman, J., and Benson, T. (Eds). *Agriculture, Food Security, and Nutrition in Malawi: Leveraging The Links*. Washington, DC, International Food Policy Research Institute, 2018.

Banik, D., and Chinsinga, B. (Eds). *Political Transition and Inclusive Development in Malawi: The Democratic Dividend*. Abingdon, Routledge, 2016.

Burton, P., Pelser, E., and Gondwe, L. *Understanding Offending: Prisoners and Rehabilitation in Malawi*. Pretoria, Institute for Security Studies, 2005.

Conroy, A. C. (Ed.), et al. *Poverty, AIDS and Hunger: Breaking the Poverty Trap in Malawi*. Basingstoke, Palgrave Macmillan, 2006.

Englund, H. (Ed.). *A Democracy of Chameleons: Politics and Culture in the New Malawi*. Uppsala, Nordic African Institute; London, Global, 2002.

Gilman, L. *The Dance of Politics: Gender, Performance and Democratization in Malawi*. Philadelphia, PA, Temple University Press, 2009.

Hartmann, C. *Malawi before the 2014 Tripartite Elections: Actors, Issues, Prospects & Pitfalls: An Analytical Stocktaking*. Gaborone, Friedrich Ebert Stiftung, 2014.

Henk, D. *The Botswana Defense Force in the Struggle for an African Environment (Initiatives in Strategic Studies: Issues and Policies)*. Basingstoke, Palgrave Macmillan, 2011.

Immink, B., Lembani, S., Ott, M., and Peters Berries, C. (Eds). *From Democracy to Empowerment: Ten Years of Democratisation in Malawi*. Maputo, Konrad-Adenauer-Stiftung, 2003.

Kalinga, O. J. *Historical Dictionary of Malawi*. 4th edn. Lanham, MD, Scarecrow Press, 2012.

Langwe, K. J. *Impact of Structural Adjustment and Stabilisation Programmes in Malawi*. Manchester, University of Manchester, 2005.

Levy, S. *Starter Packs: A Strategy to Fight Hunger in Developing Countries?: Lessons from the Malawi Experience 1998–2003*. Cambridge, MA, CABI Publishing, 2005.

Lwanda, J. L. C. *Kamuzu Banda of Malawi: A Study in Promise, Power and Paralysis: Malawi under Dr Banda, 1961 to 1993*. Glasgow, Dudu Nsomba Publrs, 1993.

   Promises, Power Politics and Poverty: Democratic Transition in Malawi, 1961–1996. Glasgow, Dudu Nsomba Publrs, 1996.

   Politics, Culture and Medicine in Malawi. Zomba, Kachere Series, 2005.

McCracken, J. (Ed.). *Twentieth Century Malawi: Perspectives on History and Culture*. Stirling, University of Stirling, 2001.

   A History of Malawi, 1855-1966. Woodbridge, James Currey, 2012.

Maliyamkono, T. L., and Kanyongolo F. E. *When Political Parties Clash*. Dar es Salaam, TEMA Publrs, 2003.

Manda, M. A. Z. *State and Labour in Malawi*. Glasgow, Dudu Nsomba Publications, 2000.

Mandala, E. C. *The End of Chidyerano: A History of Food and Everyday Life in Malawi, 1860–2004*. Portsmouth, NH, Heinemann, 2005.

Mawdsley, E., and McCann, G. (Eds). *India in Africa: Changing Geographies of Power*. Oxford, Pambazuka Press, 2011.

Mchenga, R. G. *Macroeconomic Stabilisation and Structural Adjustment Programmes: Policy Objectives and Outcomes. A Case Study of Malawi*. Manchester, University of Manchester, 2005.

Meinhardt, H., and Patel, N. *Malawi's Process of Democratic Transition: An Analysis of Political Developments between 1990 and 2003*. Maputo, Konrad-Adenauer-Stiftung, 2003.

Mulwafu, W. O. *Conservation Song: A History of Peasant-State Relations and the Environment in Malawi, 1860-2000*. Cambridge, White Horse Press, 2013.

Muula, A., and Cahnika, E. T. *Malawi's Lost Decade: 1994–2004*. Limbe, Montfort Press, 2005.

Ndalama, J. S. *Impact of Economic Reform Programmes on Economic Growth of Malawi*. Manchester, University of Manchester, 2005.

Nzunda, M. S., and Ross, K. R. (Eds). *Church, Law and Political Transition in Malawi 1992–1994*. Gweru, Mambo, 1995.

Patel, N., and Svasand, L. (Eds). *Government and Politics in Malawi*. Zomba, Kachere Series, 2007.

Phiri, D. D. *History of the Tumbuka*. Blantyre, Dzuka Publishing Co Ltd, 2000.

   History of Malawi: From Earliest Times to the Year 1915. Blantyre, Christian Literature Asscn of Malawi (CLAIM), 2004.

Phiri, K. M., McCracken, J., and Mulwafu, W. O. *Malawi in Crisis: The 1959/60 Nyasaland State of Emergency and its Legacy*. Zomba, Kachere Series, 2012.

Power, J. *Political Culture and Nationalism in Malawi*. Rochester, NY, University of Rochester Press, 2010.

Sindima, H. J. *Malawi's First Republic: An Economic and Political Analysis*. Lanham, MD, University Press of America, 2002.

Tengatenga, J. *Church, State and Society in Malawi*. Zomba, Kachere Series, 2006.

Thompson, T. J. (Ed.). *Colonialism to Cabinet Crisis. A Political History of Malawi*. Zomba, Kachere Series, 2009.

MALI

Physical and Social Geography

R. J. HARRISON CHURCH

With an area of 1,240,192 sq km (478,841 sq miles), the Republic of Mali is only slightly smaller than Niger, West Africa's largest state. Like Niger and Burkina Faso, Mali is landlocked. Bordering seven countries, it extends about 1,600 km from north to south, and roughly the same distance from east to west, with a narrowing at the centre. The population was 14,528,662 according to the census of April 2009, and was projected by the United Nations (UN) to have risen to 21,473,776 by mid-2022 (giving an average density of 17.3 inhabitants per sq km). The capital city, Bamako, had a population of 2,816,943 at mid-2022, according to UN estimates. The official language is French, but a number of other languages, including Bambara, Maasina Fulfulde, Sonrai, Tamashek, Soninke and Dogon, are widely spoken. According to census figures, in 2009 a total of 94.8% of the population were Muslims, while 2.4% were Christians and 2.0% followed traditional animist beliefs.

The ancient Basement Complex rocks of Africa have been uplifted in the mountainous Adrar des Iforas of the north-east, whose dry valleys bear witness to formerly wetter conditions. Otherwise the Pre-Cambrian rocks are often covered by Primary sandstones, which have bold erosion escarpments at, for example, Bamako and east of Bandiagara. At the base of the latter live the Dogon people. Where the River Niger crosses a sandstone outcrop below Bamako, rapids obstruct river navigation, giving an upper navigable reach above Bamako, and another one below it from Koulikoro to Ansongo, near the border with Niger.

Loose sands cover most of the rest of the country and, as in Senegal and Niger, are a relic of drier climatic conditions. They are very extensive on the long border with Mauritania and Algeria.

Across the heart of the country flows the River Niger, a vital waterway and source of fish. As the seasonal floods retreat, they leave pasture for thousands of livestock desperate for food and water after a dry season of at least eight months. The retreating floods also leave damp areas for man, equally desperate for cultivable land in an arid environment. Flood water is sometimes retained for swamp rice cultivation, and has been made available for irrigation, particularly in the 'dead' south-western section of the inland Niger delta.

The delta is the remnant of an inland lake, in which the upper River Niger once terminated. In a more rainy era this overflowed to join the then mighty Tilemsi river, once the drainage focus of the now arid Adrar des Iforas. The middle and lower courses of the Tilemsi now comprise the Niger below Bourem, at the eastern end of the consequential elbow turn of the Niger. The eastern part of the delta, which was formed in the earlier lake, is intersected by 'live' flood-water branches of the river, while the relic channels of the very slightly higher western part of the delta are never occupied naturally by flood water and so are 'dead'. However, these are used in part for irrigation water retained by the Sansanding barrage, which has raised the level of the Niger by an average of 4.3 m.

Mali is mainly dry throughout, with a rainy season of four to five months and a total rainfall of 1,120 mm at Bamako, and of only seven weeks and an average fall of 236 mm at Gao. North of this there is no rain-fed cultivation, but only semi-desert or true desert, which occupies nearly one-half of Mali. The exploitation of gold reserves, most of which are located near the borders with Senegal and Guinea, has become an increasingly important activity since the latter half of the 1990s. Modest quantities of diamonds are mined near the border with Senegal.

The distance to the nearest foreign port from most places in Mali is at least 1,300 km, and, not surprisingly, there is much seasonal and permanent emigration.

History

STEPHEN HARMON

Revised for this edition by the editorial staff

LATE COLONIAL AND DECOLONIZATION PERIOD

The former French colony of Soudan merged with the neighbouring colony of Senegal in April 1959 to form the Mali Federation, which became independent on 20 June 1960. Senegal seceded two months later, and the French Soudan proclaimed itself the Republic of Mali on 22 September. Prior to decolonization, France increasingly allowed the formation of political parties and local and regional elections within its African colonies, including Soudan. Modibo Keïta, who became independent Mali's first President, was an important anti-colonialist and leader of the Rassemblement Démocratique Africain (RDA), the largest political party in the French African colonies. Keïta served as the Secretary-General of the RDA for Soudan and became head of the party's Soudanese affiliate Union Soudanaise–RDA (US—RDA). He also served as mayor of Bamako (the Malian capital) and as a member of the French legislature. Like other RDA leaders, Keïta had been influenced by French socialists and communists who were prominent in the decolonization movement.

Significantly for Mali's later history, Soudan included an arid northern region, historically dominated by nomadic and transhumant peoples, including desert-dwelling Tuareg and Arabs and cattle raising and town dwelling Fulbe (Fulani), as well as the agricultural and commercial Songhai along the Niger river which skirts the southern edge of the Sahara. Soudan also included a rich farming region to the south of the river, dominated by Mande-speaking peoples, notably Bambara and Mandinka, as well as Soninke. Keïta, like most of his US—RDA colleagues, the future leaders of independent Mali, was of the Bambara ethnic group, which came to dominate the country numerically and linguistically. Historic tensions between the relatively fair-skinned, pastoral Tuareg and Arab peoples of the north and the black farming peoples of the south, including the Bambara, dated from pre-colonial times. The nomadic peoples of the desert lived in economic symbiosis with the riverine farming peoples, but also raided them for slaves. Such tensions were accentuated and exacerbated during the colonial period by French officials who, though committed to ending slavery, had, none the less, brought their own ideas about race and ethnicity. These historic tensions have had a significant impact on independent Mali.

THE KEÏTA PERIOD

President Modibo Keïta declared the country a one-party state under the leadership of his US—RDA, and the anti-colonial, socialist regime severed links with France and sought relations with the Soviet bloc countries. Keïta moved quickly to assert Mali's national sovereignty in three key areas: diplomacy, defence, and monetary policy. During the first two months of his administration Keïta opened diplomatic relations with the rebel government of Algeria, which was fighting for independence from France, and also requested the complete removal of French troops from Malian territory. In 1962 he also took Mali out of the Franco-African monetary community (Communauté Financière Africaine, CFA) and created the Malian franc. While Keïta's strong anti-colonial stance secured him popularity among many sectors of Malian society, his socialist economic policies did little to spur development. In addition, the Malian army's brutal reactions against both rebels and civilians in what became known as the *Alfellaga*, the first of several post-independence rebellions by northern Tuareg and Arabs, reinforced historic tensions and caused lasting resentment against the Malian Government. This and other missteps contributed to the overthrow of Keïta's regime in a coup in November 1968 staged by junior army officers led by Lt (later Gen.) Moussa Traoré.

THE REGIME AND DEPOSITON OF TRAORÉ

Traoré and his Comité Militaire pour la Libération Nationale seized power and banished US—RDA militants to newly established desert prison camps. Traoré's regime was less doctrinaire than its predecessor, and attempted some economic diversification while maintaining a non-aligned stance in international affairs. In 1976 Traoré formed a new political party, the Union Démocratique du Peuple Malien (UDPM), which continued the single-party style rule of the US—RDA but pledged a return to 'normal constitutional life'. The army-sponsored UDPM won all 82 seats in the Assemblée Nationale (National Assembly) in the 1979 elections and again in 1985. Traoré ran unopposed for the presidency in both years.

The Traoré regime's general ineptness gave way to endemic corruption in the 1980s, and eventually to outright predation towards its own people. In July 1990 the Traoré Government declared a state of emergency in the northern regions of Gao and Tombouctou, claiming that Tuareg and Arab rebels were attempting to form a secessionist state. This state of emergency marked the beginning of a five-year rebellion (known as the *Aljebha*), the most serious northern uprising thus far. Meanwhile, Demba Diallo, a human rights activist, seized the opportunity to form an association, knowing that it would be difficult for Traoré to deny its establishment, given his chairmanship of the Organization of African Unity (OAU—later the African Union—AU) whose charter endorsed the Universal Declaration of Human Rights. Emboldened by Diallo's bid, Mali's first credible opposition movements emerged in 1990. These included the Comité National d'Initiative Démocratique (CNID) and the Alliance pour la Démocratie au Mali (ADEMA). By the end of 1990 the CNID and ADEMA were organizing mass pro-democracy demonstrations. Seeking a free hand to deal with the political opposition in the capital, in January 1991 the Traoré Government accepted a hastily negotiated agreement (the Tamanrasset Accords) with the main Tuareg and Arab rebel groups, including the Mouvement Populaire de l'Azawad (MPA) and the Front Islamique-Arabe de l'Azawad. (Since the 1990s the name for Mali's northern territories in the Tuareg language—Tamasheq—has been Azawad.)

However, the demonstrations continued in early 1991, growing ever larger and more tumultuous. Following the harsh repression of rallies by security forces in March, resulting in more than 200 deaths, Traoré was deposed on 26 March. The next day Diallo formally announced to a jubilant crowd that President Traoré had been arrested by Lt-Col Amadou Toumani Touré, commander of the elite paratroopers. Touré declared his intention to transfer power to civilian rule. To this end he formed the Conseil de Réconciliation Nationale (CRN), after abrogating the 1978 Constitution and dissolving the UDPM. Touré's intentions became even clearer when the CRN was replaced by the 25-member Comité de Transition

pour le Salut du Peuple (CTSP), chaired by himself but including a majority of civilians to oversee transition to a democratic, non-military political system. In May ADEMA was reconstituted as a political party, the Alliance pour la Démocratie au Mali—Parti Pan-Africain pour la Liberté, la Solidarité et la Justice (ADEMA-PASJ). A national conference was convened in July 1991 consisting of some 1,800 delegates representing political parties, trade unions, women's and student associations, religious leaders and senior civil society figures. Among their tasks was the drafting of a constitution for Mali's Third Republic. The new Constitution was approved by 99.8% of voters (about 43% of the electorate) in a referendum in January 1992. Legislative elections were held in February and March. ADEMA-PASJ candidates won 76 of the 129 seats in the new National Assembly. ADEMA-PASJ's leader, Alpha Oumar Konaré, became Mali's first democratically elected President in April, winning 69% of the vote in a second round run-off poll.

The National Pact of 1992

The *Aljebha* rebels included many Tuareg who had been part of the Teshumara exile community. Dissatisfaction on the part of the *ishumar* ('exile') leadership with the Tamanrasset Accords, negotiated in the waning months of the Traoré regime, led to calls for the opening of talks with Mali's transitional government. The CTSP negotiated with an umbrella group of rebel factions (the Mouvements et Fronts Unifiés de l'Azawad—MFUA) and, following talks in Algiers, Algeria, the National Pact was signed in April 1992. The Pact included special administrative structures for the north, including the new region of Kidal which had been established in May 1991. It also provided for: the incorporation of Tuareg fighters into the Malian army; the demilitarization of the north; efforts to integrate Tuareg, including *ishumar*, into the economy and politics of Mali; the establishment of joint military patrols; and new development funds for the north. Significantly, the MFUA did not seek independence. However, substantial problems emerged with the agreement. Mali could not pay its share of the cost, outside support was late and below promised levels, and much of the development funding for the north was hijacked by Tuareg elites who did not wish to share scarce development resources with other northern groups whom they considered their clients or their former slaves. The sedentary communities near the Niger river believed that the Pact favoured Tuareg and Arab communities. Furthermore, Algeria, which was supposed to oversee compliance, could not focus effectively on Mali because it was confronted with its own national crisis in 1992, namely the onset of what proved to be a brutal civil war.

THE KONARÉ PRESIDENCY

Alpha Konaré took office in June 1992; however, the dysfunction of 23 years of dictatorship and the tradition of single-party rule, as well as the entrenched habits of corruption, were not easily overcome. By 1994 Konaré found his administration in crisis. While the political situation was stabilized somewhat by the appointment of Ibrahim Boubacar Keïta as Prime Minister, a position he would retain until February 2000, the economic crisis was significant. A notorious currency devaluation in 1994 resulted in the halving in value of the CFA franc, while salaries remained unchanged—Mali had rejoined the CFA franc zone in the late 1980s. The devaluation, imposed by France, affected many West African nations across the CFA franc zone, but was particularly damaging for Mali, which had no significant export sector, leading to rampant inflation and severe economic hardship.

The new Government of Prime Minister Keïta, who was also chosen as President of the ruling ADEMA-PASJ, helped to stabilize the political and economic situation, as well as to abate the northern rebellion. By 1995, with new commitments of development aid for the north, the integration of former rebels into the Malian army and administration, and promises of decentralization in local government and aid distribution, the fighting had slowly subsided. Refugees and internally displaced persons (IDPs), numbering some 160,000, began to return to their northern homes. The long peace process culminated in a 'Flame of Peace' ceremony in March 1996, featuring a bonfire of surrendered weapons.

However, new problems surfaced during the 1997 election process. The first round of elections for the expanded 147-seat National Assembly was held in April, but the results were annulled by the Constitutional Court owing to 'serious irregularities'. Despite this setback, the presidential election went ahead in May. Opposition parties, angered over the alleged irregularities in the legislative elections and fearful that ADEMA-PASJ was reverting to the old single-party methods of the UDPM, boycotted the presidential election. However, this merely resulted in a massive win for Konaré, despite a low turnout. Fresh legislative elections were then held, in July and August. These were also boycotted, by the umbrella group Collectif des Partis Politiques de l'Opposition (COPPO), which included most of the opposition parties. ADEMA-PASJ won 130 of the 147 assembly seats and COPPO's claims that the vote was illegitimate because of low voter turnout went unheeded. Keïta was reappointed Prime Minister and formed a new Government.

Following the flawed 1997 elections, COPPO led a campaign of civil disobedience to oppose the Konaré administration, which it considered illegitimate. By 2000 the political situation had calmed somewhat, but rifts were opening within the ruling ADEMA-PASJ. Keïta resigned as Prime Minister in February and as President of ADEMA-PASJ in October. ADEMA-PASJ split, with Dioncounda Traoré becoming the party's President, and Keïta, who defected from ADEMA-PASJ partly because of widespread popular dissatisfaction with the party and partly to contest the presidential election in 2002, formed a new party, the Rassemblement pour le Mali (RPM).

THE TOURÉ ADMINISTRATION

Prior to the 2002 elections, Amadou Toumani Touré, hero of the pro-democracy coup of 1991, announced his intention to stand in the presidential election as an independent. Touré had served on peacemaking commissions in other African countries on behalf of international organizations, including the United Nations (UN), but returned to Mali in 2001 and resigned his commission in the army to present his candidature. A total of 23 parties jointly supported Touré's candidacy. ADEMA-PASJ's candidate was Soumaïla Cissé, while Keïta stood as the RPM candidate with the support of Espoir 2002, a consortium of 15 parties, including the CNID and the US—RDA. Touré won the largest share of votes in the first round, but not a majority and therefore faced a run-off against Cissé. With the support of 40 parties, including Espoir 2002, Touré secured 65% of the vote in the second round, although again turnout was only 25%. Touré appointed Ahmed Mohammed Ag Hamani as Prime Minister, the first Tuareg to hold the premiership. Donor countries welcomed Touré's accession to the presidency.

However, the criminal networks that had taken root in the north continued to thrive under Touré's presidency, abetted by corrupt officials in government, the police and the military. Furthermore, from 2003 the Algerian-based Islamist terrorist Groupe Salafist pour la Prédication et le Combat (GSPC), later known as al-Qa'ida in the Islamic Maghreb (AQIM), began to expand its violent and illegal activities south into the Sahara. The GSPC became involved in smuggling and the trafficking of migrant workers, offering protection for the Tuareg and Arab drivers and taking a share of the profits. It also added a new dimension to the broader issue of human trafficking, with the kidnapping for ransom of European tourists, aid workers and oil workers. By his second term in office, all of these problems—endemic corruption, smuggling, human trafficking, kidnapping and the presence of armed and ideologically committed foreign fighters in the barren north—had significantly worsened.

Touré won 71% of the votes at the presidential election held on 29 April 2007; turnout was 36%. The legislative elections, held in July, were also marred by low voter turnout: around 33% of the electorate voted in the first round and only 10%–12% in the second round. Parties supporting Touré took a majority of seats in the legislature. Dioncounda Traoré was elected President of the National Assembly.

Meanwhile, a third northern rebellion began in February 2006. Fighting broke out among splinter groups of Ifoghas Tuareg, based in the Adagh Mountains, who had instigated the earlier rebellions. By 2006 this area had become heavily infiltrated by AQIM fighters and also served as a key transit area for the smuggling of commodities and illegal drugs, especially cocaine. The fighting was as much about control of smuggling routes as it was about Tuareg separatism. Touré was reluctant to see the rebellion escalate into full-blown war, and thus was prepared to negotiate. Dissension among Ifoghas Tuareg led to an abatement in the rebellion, and Algeria was asked, yet again, to help negotiate a settlement. An agreement signed in Algiers in May brought the fighting to a temporary end. It seemed to many Malians that the Tuareg rebels were being bought off with more sinecures in the administration, more development funds and more discretion for regional assemblies. However, the violence resumed in 2007 when the terms of the Accord were not fully implemented. Indeed, low-level violence, related to the drug trade as well as to secessionist sentiment on the part of the Tuareg, continued until 2011.

THE COUP OF MARCH 2012

The first round of Mali's fifth presidential election was scheduled to take place in late April 2012. President Touré was not standing for election, having served his two constitutionally allowed terms. Dioncounda Traoré was the ADEMA-PASJ candidate, while Ibrahim Boubacar Keïta was to contest the election for the RPM, and Soumaïla Cissé and Modibo Sidibé were also to stand. However, prior to the election date, Mali would receive two shocks that would preclude any chance of the vote taking place. First, was the start of the fourth northern rebellion since independence. Second, a coup was staged, ousting Touré and forcing him to flee into exile. However, the most significant incident was to come some weeks after the scheduled election date, as hitherto little-known Islamist militias seized control of Mali's three northern regional capitals, Gao, Tombouctou and Kidal, from the secular, separatist Tuareg and Arab rebels who had earlier seized them from the hapless Malian army.

The fourth northern rebellion started as a secular-nationalist separatist movement. From late 2011 large numbers of Teshumara refugees returned to Mali from Libya following the death of that country's deposed leader, Col Muammar al-Qaddafi. They possessed heavy weapons and military experience since many of them had fought in Qadaffi's various wars. Touré allowed them to settle in Kidal without surrendering their arms. Insurrection against the central authority began officially in January 2012 when the key town of Ménaka, east of Gao, was seized by the rebels under the banner of their new separatist organization, the Mouvement National de Libération de l'Azawad (MNLA). Later that month more than 80 Malian army troops who had earlier surrendered in the town of Aguelhok were killed. This massacre deeply angered Malians across the country, who held the MNLA responsible, although later reports indicated that the Islamist militia Ansar Dine (Defenders of Faith—founded in late 2011 by the Ifoghas Tuareg leader and political figure Iyad Ag Agaly) was present in Aguelhok at the time. The Malian army fled, abandoning important positions in the north, including Kidal and Gao, and MNLA fighters secured all three northern regional capitals. Islamist militiamen of both Ansar Dine and from a splinter group of AQIM, the Mouvement Unité pour le Jihad en Afrique de l'Ouest—MUJAO, fought alongside MNLA fighters in these attacks.

Termed an 'accidental coup' by critics, the removal of Touré appeared to begin as a mutiny by soldiers from the Kati Barracks, near Bamako, who were angered by the precipitous collapse of the army in the north. On 21 March 2012, scarcely a month before the scheduled national elections, disaffected troops led by Capt. Amadou Sanogo appeared at the presidential palace at Koulouba. Touré and other senior military and civilian leaders fled, abandoning the palace to Sanogo's followers. Sanogo declared himself the head of a Comité National pour le Redressement de la Démocratie et la Restauration de l'Etat (CNRDRE), and some 14 members of Touré's Government, including Prime Minister Modibo Sidibé, were detained at the barracks.

Many regional and international organizations, including the Economic Community of West African States (ECOWAS), the AU, the European Union (EU) and the UN, condemned Sanogo's coup. Faced with ECOWAS sanctions that effectively shut down Mali's borders, the CNRDRE agreed to reinstate a constitutional article that allowed for the President of the National Assembly to act as interim head of state in the absence of the President of the Republic. Thus, Dioncounda Traoré became interim President on 12 April 2012. This compromise gave ECOWAS cover to remove the crippling sanctions and also allowed for a transitional Government to be formed by Cheikh Modibo Diarra, serving as interim Prime Minister. This arrangement set up three poles of power in Mali: Sanogo in virtual charge of the armed forces, Traoré as President, and Diarra as Prime Minister.

The political tensions in Bamako came to the surface, however, during late April and early May 2012, when military supporters of Touré clashed with supporters of the CNRDRE and Sanogo, leaving 27 soldiers dead. On 21 May a group of pro-coup demonstrators attacked Traoré in his offices at Koulouba, leaving him unconscious. He was subsequently flown to France for several months of medical care. These incidents revealed not only a significant rift in the army, but also lingering resentment among many Malians over the corruption of ADEMA-PASJ officials. By mid-August, when the AU reinstated Mali after a four-month suspension following the coup, the political situation had somewhat calmed in the capital, and the organization had approved a road map for the restoration of constitutional rule providing for new elections within 12 months. Nevertheless, Malians were still outraged over the 'betrayal' by the MNLA for starting the new rebellion and especially for the Aguelhok massacre. However, most alarming to observers was the hijacking of the ongoing northern rebellion by Ansar Dine and MUJAO. The Islamists turned on their former allies in late June, forcing MNLA fighters out of the three northern capitals, leaving Gao in the hands of MUJAO and Tombouctou, as well as Kidal, under the control of AQIM with support from Ansar Dine fighters. The Islamist occupation of the north had begun.

THE ISLAMIST OCCUPATION, JUNE 2012–JANUARY 2013

MUJAO at Gao

MUJAO combatants arrived in Gao with MNLA rebels in early 2012 and initially participated in the occupation and looting of the city with MNLA fighters; however, by June they began to distance themselves from their secular partners, criticizing them for looting shops and molesting women. They posed as defenders of the people of Gao, protecting them from the excesses of the MNLA. They subsequently clashed with their erstwhile allies and finally expelled them from the city. MUJAO managed to establish some goodwill among Gao residents, but began imposing harsh, supposedly Koranic, penalties for minor infractions, such as petty theft, alcohol and tobacco use, and improper relations with women. These penalties, including amputations and stoning, shocked the Gaois, sending thousands of them into exile. Displaced Gao residents claimed that neighbouring Burkina Faso provided fuel and medical supplies to the MNLA. Reportedly, such aid, including food and money, was later brought in by trucks paid for by wealthy donors from Qatar after MUJAO had taken over the city. This aid allowed MUJAO to provide minimal services, such as electric power, running water, food and medicines, for Gao residents. MUJAO launched an aggressive recruitment effort, targeting adolescent boys in the Koranic secondary schools in Gao and towns to the east of the city. MUJAO leaders were allowed into the schools to recruit openly, especially in those between Ansongo and Ménaka where radical teachers were already promoting an Islamist agenda. Many students left their classes to join MUJAO.

Ansar Dine at Tombouctou

Ansar Dine fighters occupied the fabled city of Tombouctou from June 2012. They too expelled the MNLA rebels who they had helped to seize the city some weeks earlier. The militia ordered the closure of all government offices, including schools, and burned furniture and documents, forcing many, if not all, government employees into exile or displacement in southern Mali. They also forced bars, theatres, clubs and some restaurants to shut. They imposed harsh penalties, including amputations, on residents and issued petty edicts aimed at controlling social behaviour. What drew the most international attention and outrage, however, was Ansar Dine's destruction of historical sites, tombs of saints and certain mosques which they deemed inappropriate for their restrictive Salafist agenda. Also destroyed were some of Tombouctou's precious documents that had been preserved for centuries in small private libraries in the region. Many of these documents, some dating from medieval times, had recently been brought together at the Ahmed Baba Institute. The apparent issue with both the tombs and the documents was their links to Sufism, seen as an unlawful innovation (*bidat*) and therefore considered heretical to extreme Salafists.

AQIM in the Far North of Mali

AQIM continued to operate from its bases in the Adagh. Indeed, AQIM appeared to act in a supervisory role with respect to both MUJAO and Ansar Dine, and some of the leaders of these groups appeared to have originally been AQIM recruits. These included Oumar Ould Hamaha, from the far north of Mali, who had been a member of AQIM and had participated in kidnappings before the occupation. He served as MUJAO amir (commander) at Gao and later arrived in Tombouctou. He was killed by a French air strike in May 2014. Other AQIM commanders were also involved with the occupation. Algerian-born Abdelhamid Abou Zeid, formerly AQIM's 'southern amir', in charge of kidnapping operations in the Sahara, was also based in the far north of Mali, where he had trading and smuggling links with the Bidan clan. He too was killed by French troops in the Adagh, in March 2013, during the follow-up to Operation Serval (see below). The exact nature of the relationship between the Islamist militias that occupied Gao and Tombouctou and AQIM remains unclear, although the AQIM leadership was clearly in charge of the occupation. AQIM continued to facilitate and draw revenue from the smuggling and trafficking operations in the region. With Malian troops expelled from the north, the Islamist militants had a free hand to manage the traffic in commodities, drugs and migrants. They also continued to hold hostages, most of whom had been seized earlier.

By late 2012, as it became increasingly clear that some sort of international intervention force would soon be dispatched to the Malian north, the Islamist militias began competing for advantageous positions. Ansar Dine indicated that a rapprochement with the Malian Government might be possible, pointing out that they, unlike MUJAO, which was composed of radicalized fighters mostly from Mauritania, Algeria and Niger, were actually Malians. By December MUJAO and Ansar Dine had begun to fight among themselves. Having expelled Ansar Dine from Tombouctou, MUJAO was left in control of Gao and Tombouctou, while Ansar Dine and AQIM occupied Kidal. Meanwhile, Algeria, which had taken limited interest in the Malian conflict throughout most of 2012, began urging the MNLA and Ansar Dine to work with the Malian Government to isolate MUJAO. The political situation in Bamako, however, remained murky. Despite the supposed return to constitutionality with the installation of the interim Government, coup leader Sanogo still held considerable power through his control of much of the army. On 12 December Prime Minister Diarra suddenly resigned amid rumours that he had been briefly detained, and possibly threatened, by Sanogo.

OPERATION SERVAL

The awaited international intervention was finally precipitated on 10 January 2013 by attacks by MUJAO and Ansar Dine on two central Malian towns when Islamist fighters seized control of the strategic town of Konna, near Mopti, and, two days later, of Diabaly, north-east of Bamako. These attacks were the last co-ordinated offensive operations of the Islamist forces. The Malian interim Government appealed for assistance, and on 11 January French military forces launched a series of air strikes on the rebel-held towns. These were followed by strikes on rebel targets at Tombouctou and Gao; by the end of January French ground troops had regained control of the two cities.

Malian army troops participated in the recapture of Konna and Diabaly and were also present in the early stages of the fighting at Gao. However, after complaints by French officers that Malian troops had engaged in reprisals and revenge killings in Gao, the French were reluctant to allow Malian army personnel to proceed to the far north, instead relying on Chadian troops who had been deployed as part of the international force that made up Operation Serval. Malians were outraged when the French chose not to fight the MNLA, allowing the Tuareg separatist movement to retake Kidal from the Islamists. Many Malians still blamed the MNLA for starting the fighting in January 2012 and especially for the Aguelhok massacre. This difference of opinion regarding the MNLA would cause a rift between Mali and France that cost the latter much of the goodwill that it had earned by intervening against the Islamist occupation.

By the time the rollback of the Islamist occupation by Operation Serval reached the Kidal region, the willingness of the French to ally themselves with the MNLA had caused lingering resentment. While the Bamako elites were pleased when the French and their Chadian allies liberated Kidal City and Tessalit, with its strategic airstrips, they were most displeased when the French appeared to allow the MNLA to take control of Kidal. As for the Islamist militias, sweeping them from the cities was accomplished with relative ease. However, confronting them in the vast, arid countryside posed much more of a challenge. Even in the cities, sporadic attacks continued. Gao witnessed a spate of suicide bombings in the weeks after French intervention forces took control of the city. The situation in the Adagh was even more problematic. Intense combat persisted in the area during early 2013, with Chadian forces sustaining many casualties.

Before and during Operation Serval troops from several West African countries, including Togo, Nigeria and Niger, had been deployed to Mali, where they were to form part of an international intervention force that had been planned prior to the French intervention. This force, the African-led International Support Mission to Mali (AFISMA), authorized in December 2012, was reconstituted as the UN Multidimensional Integrated Stabilization Mission in Mali (MINUSMA) by a UN Security Council resolution in April 2013. MINUSMA was mandated to support the 'legitimate political processes in Mali and carry out security-related tasks'. Eventually, MINUSMA would take over peacekeeping duties, with an authorized strength of 11,200 troops.

By mid-2013, as promised elections neared, most of the fighting was being handled by the remaining French troops with the support of MNLA combatants, as they tried to root the Islamists out of the towns near Kidal. Meanwhile, the Islamist militias were also undergoing changes and reorganization. Flushed out of the major towns, the fighters either went underground, or relocated to neighbouring countries, including southern Libya. In some cases, the groups splintered. In August remnants of MUJAO merged with the al-Mulathameen Brigade, newly formed by Algerian commander Mokhtar Belmokhtar, to create a new movement called al-Mourabitoun.

THE ELECTIONS OF JULY 2013

Several factors militated for the holding of elections even as the fighting continued in parts of northern Mali and large numbers of refugees and IDPs still feared returning to their homes in the conflict zones. One factor was that the term of the interim Government, formed in mid-2012, was stipulated as one year, after which elections were supposed to be held. In addition, the USA and other donor nations were legally prohibited from sending aid money to countries where democratically elected governments had been overthrown. In December 2012 Mali's National Assembly agreed on a road map for the transition which provided for elections to be held before the end of July 2013. The road map sought serious discussions with the 'legitimate representatives of the populations of the north' and with 'non-terrorist armed groups which recognize Mali's territorial integrity'. These conditions would exclude the

Islamist militias but include the MNLA, assuming it was willing to renounce separatism. The terms were in accordance with UN Security Council Resolution 2018 of December 2012, and the first round of the presidential election was subsequently fixed for 28 July 2013. Traoré agreed not to stand as a candidate, and in May 2013 an international conference in Brussels, Belgium, pledged €3,250m. towards the Malian Government's Sustainable Recovery Plan for 2013–14.

The presidential election duly took place on 28 July 2013, contested by 27 candidates. Despite acknowledging some flaws, most notably concerns that electoral authorities were not completely free to carry out their business in the northern city of Kidal due to it largely being controlled by the rebel MNLA, observers praised the peaceful and orderly conduct of the ballot. Former Prime Minister Ibrahim Boubacar Keïta, representing the RPM, secured 40% of the votes cast, while his closest rival, Soumaïla Cissé of the Union pour la République et la Démocratie (URD), won 20%. Dramane Dembélé, the ADEMA-PASJ candidate, obtained 10% of the vote, with no other candidate attracting more than 5%. At a second round of voting, held on 11 August, Keïta defeated Cissé with 78% of the ballot.

THE PEACE PROCESS

Little was done to advance serious peace negotiations during the second half of 2013. This failure to work towards a settlement was due to a variety of factors, one of which was that the new Government needed to resolve certain political tensions that still simmered in Bamako, in particular regarding the fate of Sanogo following the restoration of constitutional government. In November Sanogo was arrested and charged with complicity in the disappearance of 'Red Beret' soldiers who had participated in an attempted counter-coup in April 2012. Shortly after his arrest, mass graves were discovered at the Kati Barracks; these were believed to contain the bodies of some of the disappeared soldiers. Sanogo remained in detention pending his trial on charges of murder and conspiracy to commit murder.

By January 2014 the Malian Government had requested that Algeria again take the diplomatic initiative to instigate talks. However, what finally precipitated peace talks was the 'Kidal Debacle' of May. In mid-May the Malian Prime Minister, Moussa Mara, who had been appointed in April, reignited tensions between the Government and the MNLA with an 'ill-advised' visit to Kidal, which remained under MNLA control. Fighting broke out between the security force that accompanied him and the rebel troops that controlled the city, and Mara was forced to retreat to safety. On 21 May the Malian army attempted to retake Kidal, resulting in the deaths of over 40 people. With AU mediation, the separatists and government representatives concluded a ceasefire agreement on 23 May. However, following what was perceived as its humiliating defeat, the Malian army abandoned all of its positions in the Kidal region, as well as those in the areas to the north and east of Gao, leaving only MINUSMA forces and a relatively small number of French troops in the territory. Mali was effectively cut in two again, as it had been before Operation Serval.

Meanwhile, France abandoned its plans for a major troop withdrawal from Africa and instead announced a new deployment across the Sahara-Sahel zone. Operation Serval was replaced by a more expansive security mission, Operation Barkhane (see below), focused on stabilizing the broader Sahara-Sahel region. The number of French troops in Mali was to be reduced to 1,000, with the bulk of French forces henceforth to be stationed in Chad. The MNLA, for its part, was emboldened by the defeat of the Malian government force, and in the wake of the 'Kidal Debacle' neither MINUSMA nor Barkhane were able to contain the political armed groups of the north of Mali.

Negotiations Begin

Following Algerian mediation, representatives of the major factions met in Algiers in early June 2014. The eventual outcome of this meeting was the signing later in that month by several factions of a declaration in support of the peace process itself, termed the Algiers Declaration. According to the Declaration, the plan was to address the 'legitimate claims' of local northern populations within a framework of respect for the territorial integrity of Mali. Among the signatories of the Declaration were the Malian Government, along with major rebel factions, including the MNLA and all or part of two rebel umbrella groups, the Haut Conseil pour l'Unité de l'Azawad (HCUA) and the secular faction of the Mouvement Arabe de l'Azawad (MAA). A timetable was announced on 16 June, and the AU and MINUSMA agreed to a peace process that was now out of their control. The first round of the peace talks was held in Algiers on 14–27 July. All parties formally recognized Algeria as the chief mediator in the talks, and agreed upon a road map addressing four key sets of issues.

The negotiating teams returned to Algiers in early September 2014 to discuss issues outlined in the road map. A draft agreement was eventually reached on 28 November, which included provisions similar to those drawn up in earlier peace negotiations (a degree of autonomy for the north, as well as the decentralization of political control and of the distribution of aid funds). However, the agreement fell short of establishing a true federal system, as demanded by the rebel factions, and it did not recognize Azawad as a distinct northern polity or jurisdiction. At least three significant problems with the draft agreement were identified by observers. First, the agreement reduced the conflict to a problem of 'centre versus periphery'. This interpretation disregarded communal disagreements within the north itself, minimizing the grievances of the Songhai, the Fulbe and the Bellah (black Tamasheq-speaking former slaves of the Tuareg), as well as those of the Imghad Tuareg. A second problem was that the draft agreement excluded the views of ordinary Malians. When negotiations began in mid-2013, civil society representatives were promised a voice. However, that process stalled, and became two-party talks between the Malian Government and the rebels, with civil society representatives barred from attending. The third problem was that, with various parties appearing eager to conclude the peace negotiations, the agreement did not allow sufficient time for the consolidation of the peace process. The final round of the peace talks ended without a conclusive agreement, and new talks were planned for early 2015.

Continued Fighting

Meanwhile, on 16 July 2014 France and Mali signed a new defence pact, replacing an earlier treaty from 1985. The new treaty, renewable after five years, allowed for the transition from Operation Serval to Operation Barkhane. Mali's vulnerability to outside terrorist groups convinced the Government of the advisability of such a mutual defence pact with the former colonial power. However, despite the signing of the treaty, in August 2014 violence in the north began to recur. On 3 October the worst single attack on MINUSMA peacekeepers took place when nine Nigerien troops were killed by MUJAO remnants east of Gao. The upsurge in casualties and attacks in the north intensified after MINUSMA took over security duties from Operation Serval as the al-Qa'ida-linked groups, including the newly formed al-Mourabitoun battalion, were once again becoming active.

Three particular areas of the north witnessed concentrations of violence from late 2014: the Ménaka-Ansongo region; Tabankort in the Tilemsi Valley between Gao and Kidal; and the area between Tombouctou and Léré near the south-east corner of Mauritania. After France moved its main force to Chad as part of Operation Barkhane, the UN strengthened its peacekeeping contingent, notably bringing in 450 troops from the Netherlands, deployed at Gao, and 200 troops from Sweden, deployed near Tombouctou. An attack on 5 January 2015 against a Malian army garrison at Nampala, south-west of Léré, resulted in the deaths of 11 Malian troops, along with some UN peacekeepers.

In a particularly severe incident on 20 January 2015 at Tabankort, MNLA forces attacked UN peacekeepers with heavy weapons and Dutch reinforcements were called in. Dutch helicopters fired on an MNLA column, killing five rebels. In response to the clash at Tabankort, pro-MNLA demonstrators attacked UN peacekeepers at the airport at Kidal the following day. After the fighting at Tabankort, MNLA leaders claimed that MINUSMA was openly siding with the Malian Government and announced that co-operation with the UN

mission would be suspended. The MNLA also threatened to boycott the planned resumption of the peace talks scheduled for early February 2015. In late January, in a bid to save the faltering peace talks, Algerian mediators summoned representatives from the Government and the armed groups to a new round of meetings in Algiers.

The Signing of the 2015 Algiers Accord

The fifth round of talks began in mid-February 2015. By early March a preliminary peace proposal, the Algiers Accord, had emerged as a blueprint for a more enduring agreement to be signed later. The Malian Government signed the preliminary Algiers Accord on 1 March, and the UN urged the MNLA to follow suit. The proposals outlined in the new Algiers document included: more developed powers for the north (including a degree of autonomy); a regional security force that incorporated Tuareg troops; a special northern development plan; and a decision on the final political status of the north (i.e. autonomy, federal status or independence) to be left in the hands of a future national conference. The Ifoghas Tuareg were displeased with the proposed Accord and demonstrations against the document were mounted in Kidal. The MNLA sought stronger political recognition of Azawad, a more defined local security force, and the creation of a regional assembly. The position of the Government, however, had strengthened by March. Several influential individuals switched sides and abandoned the MNLA, including the military chief of the MAA.

The emergence of rival ethnic- and clan-based militias as important participants in the conflict also helped shift the balance in the Government's favour. In the absence of properly trained desert fighters in the Malian army, the use of northern militias with desert fighting experience as a proxy force enabled President Keïta to claim that he was supporting the peace process. A new armed group, the pro-Government Groupe Autodéfense Touareg Imghad et Alliés (GATIA), emerged and played a role in the fighting in the Tilemsi Valley, including the clashes at Tabankort. Pro-Government militias, including GATIA, assumed a leading role in fighting the separatist rebels, especially the MNLA. GATIA undermined the MNLA's claim to represent and speak on behalf of the Tuareg. As a result, the separatist groups (the HCUA, the MNLA and the anti-Government faction of the MAA) appeared determined to prevent GATIA from securing representation at any future peace talks. In late April 2015 fighting between GATIA and the MNLA threatened once again to derail the talks. GATIA militia and their allies managed to capture the key town of Ménaka, east of Gao, on 27 April.

Following eight months of negotiations, the final round of the Algiers talks culminated in a signing ceremony on 15 May 2015 in Bamako. On 14 May the two main factions had initialled the agreement, indicating their willingness formally to sign the document pending the finalization of certain details. These two factions comprised the Malian Government supported by the Plateforme coalition, which included a number of rebel groups such as the pro-Government faction of the MAA, and the Coordination des Mouvements de l'Azawad (CMA)—a recently formed separatist umbrella group composed of the main rebel factions, including the MNLA, the HCUA and the pro-separatist MAA faction. The details outlined by the CMA included its objection to the tactics of the ethnic-based militias that were allied with the Government, especially GATIA, and the refusal of the Government to consider stronger degrees of autonomy. A key reason for the Government declaring itself unwilling to relinquish further ground on the autonomy issue was Malians' widespread mistrust of both France and MINUSMA, both of which they regarded as pro-MNLA. Despite these issues remaining unresolved, the international mediators, led by Algeria, insisted that the signing ceremony should proceed as scheduled. President Keïta signed the Algiers Accord on behalf of the Government and the Plateforme coalition, but the CMA refused to sign the document, despite having earlier initialled it. Thousands of demonstrators took to the streets of Bamako on 26 May, denouncing France and MINUSMA and demanding that the CMA sign the Accord; it finally did so on 20 June.

However, the Islamist armed groups operating in northern Mali, including Ansar Dine, MUJAO, AQIM and al-

Mourabitoun, were not addressed by the peace process. Meanwhile, following an ideological divide within al-Mourabitoun, a new militant group in the region, the Islamic State in the Greater Sahara (ISGS), was formed in early 2015.

THE KEÏTA ADMINISTRATION, 2013–17

Meanwhile, Ibrahim Boubacar Keïta was sworn in as President of Mali in early September 2013. His election was welcomed by major donor nations, including the USA, because it represented Mali's return to democratic elections, and thus clearance for the renewal of military and development aid. Keïta's leading priority was the re-establishment of government control over the formerly rebel-held northern regions, especially Kidal. There, only a limited government presence was tolerated by MNLA leaders whom the French had allowed to occupy Kidal city after the expulsion of the Islamist militias by the troops of Operation Serval. Another stated priority of Keïta was a campaign against Mali's endemic corruption and nepotism. Yet few results with regard to either of these priorities were forthcoming. In January 2014 Keïta controversially secured the election of Issaka Sidibé, a close ally, as the new President of the National Assembly; Sidibé's daughter was married to the President's son, Karim Keïta. In addition, Karim Keïta's recent rise to prominence prompted speculation that his father might be preparing him as his successor. Furthermore, the new President suffered a number of damaging political reverses. Keïta's first Prime Minister, technocrat Oumar Tatam Ly, resigned, along with his entire Government, on 5 April. This was believed to be as a consequence of the mishandling of negotiations with the MNLA leadership by the Minister of Reconciliation, Cheikh Oumar Diarrah, which led to the rebels abandoning the ceasefire agreement that had enabled the elections of 2013. Ly was replaced as Prime Minister by Moussa Mara, a former minister and a rival of Keïta in the 2013 presidential contest. Mara's administration was soon marred by his 'ill-advised' May 2014 visit to Kidal (see *The Peace Process*). Mara's resignation in January 2015 led to the appointment of Modibo Keïta, who had been President Keïta's chief representative in the peace negotiations in Algiers, as the new premier.

In September 2016 four RPM deputies resigned from the ruling party owing to their dissatisfaction with Keïta's leadership. In the same month, following an upturn in militant violence in central Mali, Tiéman Hubert Coulibaly was dismissed as Minister of Defence and War Veterans and replaced by Abdoulaye Idrissa Maïga. Opposition parties organized a large anti-Government demonstration in Bamako in October to protest against alleged high-level corruption, the Keïta regime's domination of the media, and the National Assembly's recent approval of a steep increase in the registration fee for presidential candidates.

In December 2016 the Keïta administration survived a no-confidence motion introduced in the National Assembly by opposition deputies in response to the electoral fraud allegations and the Government's failure to improve the security climate. Also in that month, the Assembly voted in favour of initiating legal action against former premier Mara in connection with the deadly violence that his 2014 visit to Kidal had provoked. The Government presented a constitutional reform bill to the legislature in March 2017. Proposed amendments included the creation of a Senate to act as an upper legislative chamber, with two-thirds of the senators being elected and the remaining third appointed by the President; the empowerment of the President to dismiss the Prime Minister and appoint the head of the Constitutional Court; and the extension of official recognition to the Tuareg's ethnic homeland of Azawad. The proposals met with strong opposition, on the grounds that they gave excessive powers to the executive and that, according to the Constitution, no reform of the charter could be pursued when the territorial integrity of the country was being undermined (as was the case, so opponents claimed, in various parts of Mali that were still under rebel control). None the less, in early June the bill was approved by 111 votes to 35 in the National Assembly and a referendum on the proposed constitutional amendments was scheduled to be held on 9 July. However, with public opposition to the proposals growing, and

following a large protest march held in Bamako, on 21 June the Government announced the referendum's indefinite postponement. Under continuing pressure from various political and civil society organizations, on 18 August President Keïta decided officially to suspend the referendum.

Meanwhile, in April 2017 Keïta effected a major government reorganization, appointing erstwhile defence minister and close ally of the President Abdoulaye Idrissa Maïga as the new Prime Minister; the vacated defence portfolio was allocated to Tiéna Coulibaly. Tiéman Hubert Coulibaly, another former defence minister and Keïta loyalist, was given responsibility for the crucial post of Minister of Territorial Administration, charged with organizing the presidential and legislative elections in late 2018.

Maïga unexpectedly announced the resignation of his Government on 29 December 2017. On the following day President Keïta appointed as his successor Soumeylou Boubèye Maïga, a close associate of the President who had previously served as Minister of Defence until his resignation in 2014 following military defeats in the north. The formation of Maïga's Government was announced shortly afterwards; notably, Tiéman Hubert Coulibaly became Minister of Foreign Affairs and International Co-operation (and was succeeded as Minister of Territorial Administration and Decentralization by Mohamed Ag Erlaf).

CONTINUED ATTACKS AND PEACE AGREEMENT IMPLEMENTATION

Despite the signing of the Algiers Accord in mid-2015, militant attacks across Mali continued. With deaths mounting, the effectiveness of MINUSMA became eroded as it focused increasingly on force protection. MINUSMA personnel, together with French and Malian government troops and security personnel, were targets of frequent gun and land mine attacks. On 9 August five UN workers and eight others were killed in a militant attack against the Hotel Byblos in Sévaré, the site of a strategic military airbase. The surge in Islamist attacks was seen as an attempt to disrupt the implementation of the peace deal by Islamist militias, excluded from the negotiations. The most notorious of the attacks took place in mid-November, when at least 19 people were killed in an attack on the Radisson Blu Hotel in central Bamako. As many as 170 people were temporarily held hostage inside the hotel before Malian security agents, supported by French and US special operations personnel, ended the siege, killing two of the militants. Among the victims of the attack, for which al-Mourabitoun claimed responsibility, were Russian and Chinese nationals, along with one US aid worker. Only eight days later unidentified attackers fired rockets at a UN base in Kidal, killing three peacekeepers. Keïta on 20 November declared a national state of emergency (which was subsequently extended at intervals by the National Assembly, in response to continued violence).

Following continued fatalities among MINUSMA peacekeepers due to Ansar Dine ambushes and landmine attacks, by mid-2016 even some of those responsible for MINUSMA and the implementation of the peace terms had issued critical assessments of the mission. UN Secretary-General Ban Ki-Moon, in his report to the UN Security Council on 9 June, requested that it approve an additional 2,500 troops and retain the mission until June 2017. Accordingly, the Security Council extended MINUSMA's mandate for another year and raised its authorized force levels to 13,289 military personnel and 1,920 police officers. (In July 2017 the UN Security Council extended MINUSMA's mandate by another year and maintained its strength at the levels set in 2016.)

In addition, a new regional counter-terrorism force was established by the so-called G5 Sahel countries (Niger, Burkina Faso, Chad, Mali and Mauritania): the creation of the Force Conjointe du G5 Sahel (FC-G5S) was authorized by the AU Peace and Security Council in April 2017 and endorsed by a UN Security Council resolution in June. The FC-G5S subsequently comprised some 5,000 troops from the G5 Sahel countries, which were concentrated in the border areas of Mali to support Operation Barkhane in its campaign to suppress jihadist activity. Financial backing for the FC-G5S was provided by powers including the EU, the USA and Saudi Arabia.

Al-Mourabitoun staged a suicide attack in January 2017 at an encampment for government soldiers and militia members in Gao, killing 77 people. Ansar Dine, al-Mourabitoun and two smaller jihadist groups merged in March to form Jama'at Nusrat al-Islam wal-Muslimeen (JNIM), which immediately pledged allegiance to AQIM. However, in early 2017 significant progress was reported in implementing some interim provisions of the 2015 peace agreement. Notably, the first joint patrol, comprising government forces and those of MINUSMA, the CMA and GATIA, was conducted in Gao on 23 February, while interim regional authorities were installed in Kidal later that month. Interim authorities were also established in Ménaka and Gao in early March and, following delays caused by the resistance of armed Tuareg factions, in Tombouctou and Taoudénit on 13 April (representing the restoration of state authority in the north). A peace conference convened on 27 March was partially attended by the CMA and opposition representatives, which had initially announced a boycott, and ended on 2 April with the adoption of a resolution calling for negotiations with jihadist leaders.

AQIM claimed responsibility for an attack by gunmen on 18 June 2017 at the tourist resort of Le Campement Kangaba in Dougourakoro, east of Bamako, in which at least five people were killed and hostages taken. On 14 August eight people were killed by armed militants in two separate attacks on MINUSMA targets—seven in an attack on the mission's headquarters in Tombouctou and one at a MINUSMA camp in Douentza. Following negotiations mediated by MINUSMA, on 20 September CMA and GATIA leaders signed a further agreement in Kidal providing for a renewed ceasefire and the exchange of prisoners. However, activities by jihadist groups in central Mali, as well as in the north, intensified, and the CMA and Platforme alliances reportedly lost territorial control. Four UN peacekeepers and a Malian soldier were killed in attacks in the north-eastern Menaka region and in central Douentza in November, and in the following month (when an International Investment Forum was held in Bamako) four Malians and a Togolese working for a Chinese telecommunications firm were kidnapped and murdered while laying fibre-optic cables near the town of Niafunke, in central Mali.

In response to the continued violations of the 2015 peace agreement, the UN Security Council in September 2017 established a sanctions regime for Mali, providing for the introduction of travel ban and assets freeze on individuals and entities engaged in actions that threatened peace, security or stability in the country; a Panel of Experts was also to be created. In January 2018 26 civilians died in a landmine explosion in central Boni, and shortly afterwards at least 18 soldiers were killed in an attack on an army camp in Tombouctou. JNIM declared responsibility for the attacks. Operations by French troops in northern Mali, near the border with Algeria, on 13–14 February resulted in the deaths of six JNIM leaders and the arrest of several others (prompting large-scale reprisal attacks by JNIM against the army headquarters and French embassy in Burkina Faso on 2 March). JNIM forces were also believed to have killed more than 40 Tuareg civilians in two retaliatory attacks in the Menaka region. UN Secretary-General António Guterres visited Mali at the end of May, meeting representatives of the parties to the peace agreement, and issued a statement urging an inclusive political dialogue to enable the organization of a credible election. The Security Council maintained the existing maximum strength of MINUSMA when extending its mandate in June.

KEÏTA'S RE-ELECTION

The organization of planned local and regional elections (originally scheduled for December 2017) was further postponed in March 2018 to the end of the year, owing to the continued insecurity. However, in April the Government confirmed that the next presidential election would take place on 29 July, as scheduled. In May Keïta confirmed that he would seek re-election for a second term. Former interim President Traoré announced shortly afterwards that he would not contest the

election on behalf of ADEMA-PASJ, indicating his support for Keïta's candidacy. On 2 June protests organized by opposition leaders, including Soumaïla Cissé, to demand transparent elections and equal access to state media were violently suppressed by police; at least 25 demonstrators were injured. Another candidate, Aliou Boubacar Diallo of the Alliance Démocratique pour la Paix (ADP-MALIBA), claimed that the bodyguard of Prime Minister Maïga had fired into a crowd of his supporters (although this was officially strongly denied). Following criticism from the EU, and mediation by the UN and the AU, the authorities permitted an opposition rally to proceed peacefully on 8 June. Meanwhile, JNIM issued a video recording warning the public not to vote and obstructed electoral preparations in the north with targeted attacks. In addition, recurrent ethnic violence between nomadic Fulani people and farmers from the Dogon community again erupted in the central Mopti region in mid-2018. On 4 July the Constitutional Court endorsed the registration of 24 presidential candidates, rejecting six; the successful applicants included Cissé of the URD (Keïta's previous opponent in the 2013 presidential election), the Mayor of Sikasso, Kalifa Sanogo, as the candidate of ADEMA-PASJ, former Prime Minister and leader of the Forces Alternatives pour le Renouveau et l'Emergence (FARE) Modibo Sidibé, and several former ministers.

Keïta's electoral campaign focused on the achievement of his administration in signing the 2015 Algiers Accord, while opposition candidates emphasized its failure to improve the security situation. On 25 July 2018 the arrest of Arab youths in Tombouctou, in response to a robbery, precipitated violent protests there against worsening insecurity and alleged ill-treatment by security forces, followed by ethnic clashes. At the presidential poll on 29 July, Keïta was the leading candidate with 41.6% of the votes cast, followed by Cissé, who received 17.7%, Diallo (8.0%) and Cheick Mohamed Abdoulaye Souad 'Modibo' Diarra of the Rassemblement pour le Développement du Mali (7.4%). Voter turnout of only 43.7% was reported, after attacks and other violent incidents prevented voting in more than 600 polling stations and disrupted proceedings in many others, particularly in Mopti. Observers from large EU and ECOWAS monitoring missions reported irregularities in some areas, including the theft of ballot boxes, but in general endorsed the conduct of the poll. Since Keïta had failed to secure an outright majority, a run-off between him and Cissé was scheduled for 12 August. Both Cissé and Diarra submitted allegations of violations to the Constitutional Court. On 12 August Keïta defeated Cissé by a decisive 67.2% of votes cast (but representing a fall of around 10% compared with his victory of 2013). The voter turnout was even lower than in the first round, at only 34.5%, with further reported violence in central and northern areas. Despite Keïta's decline in popularity, following his perceived failure to curb corruption and Islamist militancy, the fractured nature of the opposition and lack of strong alternative figures (since Cissé was also identified with the political establishment) was believed to have favoured his victory. Cissé again rejected the results and organized a protest by his supporters in Bamako. However, the Constitutional Court ratified Keïta's re-election for a second term on 20 August, rejecting Cissé's malpractice allegations. The UN Security Council welcomed 'the generally peaceful conduct of the polls', while emphasizing the need to accelerate the implementation of the 2015 peace agreement. Keïta was sworn in for a second term on 4 September 2018 and appointed a new Government, in which Maïga was retained as Prime Minister, on 9 September.

INCREASING VIOLENCE AND INTERNATIONAL STABILIZATION EFFORTS

Despite the success of Operation Serval when French troops and their Chadian allies quickly pushed the Islamist militias back into the extreme north of Mali, and the continued deployment of French and international troops, the Islamist groups succeeded in retaining their foothold in the north and in extending the range of their attacks deep into central Mali and across the Sahel into neighbouring countries, including Burkina Faso and Niger. In addition, new ethnic dimensions to the violence emerged. By mid-2019 most of the violence was occurring in the central regions of Mali, although attacks also continued to be carried out in the northern region of Kidal. In mid-March JNIM militants (including many Fulani) attacked an army camp at Dioura in the Mopti region, killing 23 soldiers. A few days after the incident at Dioura, Dogon militiamen attacked Fulani herders in the town of Ogossagou, also in the Mopti region, killing 160 people. On 18 April, following popular protests in Bamako expressing growing frustration over the Government's inability to disarm the Islamist militias or to stem the surge of ethnic-based violence (often precipitated by disputes over access to land and water), Prime Minister Maïga resigned, together with his entire cabinet. On 22 April President Keïta appointed former finance minister Dr Boubou Cissé as the new Prime Minister; a new Council of Ministers was installed in early May.

In response to the increase in jihadist attacks in Mali during the first half of 2019, the donor community increased its support for international troop deployments. In June the Dogon town of Sobane-Kou in central Mali was attacked by some 50 suspected Fulani on motorcycles, who killed nearly 100 civilians. At that time, the international and regional forces based in Mali and neighbouring countries to contain the jihadist threat comprised France's Operation Barkhane (which was deployed across several Sahel states), MINUSMA, the EU-led training mission intended to rebuild the Malian armed forces, and the regional FC-G5S. Several hundred US special operations personnel were also deployed in Mali to assist the anti-terrorism efforts and stabilize the Malian Government, as well as to train Malian troops. Meanwhile, by December the UN Security Council had imposed targeted sanctions against eight prominent members of militant armed groups, under the sanctions regime introduced in 2017.

Plans were announced for the creation of an additional military task force. The establishment of Task Force Takuba, as part of a more unified international 'Coalition pour le Sahel', followed a summit of G5 Sahel leaders, convened at the initiative of French President Emmanuel Macron, in January 2020. Under the command of France's Operation Barkhane, Takuba, which means 'sabre' in the Tuareg language, was to comprise some 600 European special operations troops to support the Malian army in fighting terrorism, with focus on the sensitive tri-border area between Mali, Niger and Burkina Faso. The French Minister for the Armed Forces, Florence Parly, subsequently announced the reinforcement of Operation Barkhane by an additional 600 troops, to number around 5,100. Task Force Takuba was deployed at three military bases in northern Mali from mid-2020, and was to become fully operational in 2021 with an initial mandate of three years. Parly announced on social media on 8 June 2020 that Abdelmalek Droukdal, the Algerian head of AQIM and of its Malian affiliates, including JNIM, had been killed, along with 'several of his collaborators'.

FRESH POLITICAL CRISIS

Several factors fuelled political discontent on the streets of Bamako in 2020. These included President Keïta's insistence on holding the delayed legislative elections on 29 March according to a new timetable, despite the introduction of restrictions in response to the COVID-19 pandemic, and the abduction shortly beforehand, in Niafunke, of prominent opposition figure Soumaïla Cissé and six members of his electoral campaign delegation by JNIM. Concerns over the already controversial legislative elections were exacerbated, when the Constitutional Court, following a second round on 19 April, annulled the outcomes in 31 of the 147 seats at the end of that month. The revised results added 10 seats to the total held by the ruling RPM (51 seats), making Keïta's supporters the largest bloc in the National Assembly. Angered by these events, religious and civil society organizations began to demand the President's resignation. These calls intensified as dissidents cited his poor record of governance and the persistent state corruption that had called into question the legitimacy of Malian Governments since the pro-democracy coup of March 1991.

In addition to these factors, the army's continuing failure to restore security contributed to a rising crescendo of anti-

Government protest. Traditional religious figures, who were not associated with militant Islamist movements, emerged as de facto political leaders. Notable among them was Imam Dicko, a Salafist imam and former political supporter of President Keïta, who had launched a civil organization (Coordination des Mouvements, Associations et Sympathisants) in September 2019, subsequently establishing himself as the unofficial leader of the opposition. Dicko convened two huge opposition rallies in Bamako in June 2020, when participants demanded that the President step down, protested against the clearly political decision of the Constitutional Court, and demanded the release of Soumaïla Cissé. Following the deaths of at least 14 people in violence during further protest rallies on 10–12 July, Dicko called for calm, but repeated his demand that Keïta resign. President Keïta's subsequent dissolution of the Constitutional Court on 12 July, along with other political concessions, did little to quell popular appeals for his resignation. A new wide-ranging opposition coalition, known as the Mouvement du 5 Juin-Rassemblement des Forces Patriotiques (M5-RFP), reiterated demands for the President to step down. The leaders of five ECOWAS countries—Ghana, Côte d'Ivoire, Niger, Nigeria and Senegal—arrived in Bamako, in late July, in an unsuccessful effort to resolve Mali's the volatile political crisis.

MILITARY TAKEOVER

On 18 August 2020 disaffected army officers at the Soundiata Keïta military base at Kati, some 15 km outside the capital, staged a mutiny, then marched into Bamako, arresting the President, Prime Minister Boubou Cissé and other officials. The military coup promptly received the support of the M5-RFP coalition, whose supporters rejoiced in the streets. Before resigning, in a statement read on the state broadcaster on 19 August, Keïta also dissolved the National Assembly with immediate effect. M5-RFP spokesperson Nouhoun Togo signalled support for the takeover, calling it 'not a military coup, but a popular insurrection'. Protesters complained that those in power had not addressed the systemic corruption and violence across the country, and accused Keïta of attempting to manipulate the outcome of the parliamentary elections in March with the connivance of the Constitutional Court.

The military junta behind the coup declared itself as the Comité National pour le Salut du Peuple (CNSP). The participating soldiers and officers were under the command of Col Malick Diaw, and led by Deputy Chief of Staff of the Air Force Col-Maj. Ismaël Wagué. Wagué later announced that the coup leaders would put a 'civil-political transition' administration in charge that would conduct new elections. On 19 August 2020 the CNSP declared Col Assimi Goïta as its President, and therefore as head of state. Condemnations of the coup and demands for the reinstatement of President Keïta promptly ensued, including from ECOWAS, European leaders and the USA, as well from the UN. The UN Security Council on 19 August adopted a resolution condemning the coup and demanding the release of the detained officials, while the AU and ECOWAS suspended Mali's membership and ECOWAS additionally imposed sanctions suspending commercial and financial transactions with the country. Keïta was released from detention on 27 August, and he subsequently left the country for medical treatment in the United Arab Emirates.

Following negotiations with political and civil society representatives, amid international pressure, on 12 September 2020 the CNSP adopted a Transitional Charter providing for an 18-month transitional period prior to elections; the M5-RFP, in particular, criticized the failure of the charter to stipulate that the interim President be a civilian. In accordance with its provisions, on 21 September a former Minister of Defence, Col-Maj. (retd) Bah N'Daw, was nominated as Transitional President by a 17-member committee established by the CNSP, with Goïta as Transitional Vice-President. N'Daw was inaugurated on 25 September, appointing a civilian, former Minister of Foreign Affairs Moctar Ouane, as Prime Minister shortly afterwards. The Transitional Charter, which granted amnesty to CNSP, members, was promulgated on 1 October. A 25-member transitional Government was formed by N'Daw on 5 October; senior CNSP members Col Sadio Camara, Col Modibo Koné and Wagué received principal posts as, respectively, Minister of Defence and War Veterans, Minister of Security and Civil Protection, and Minister of National Reconciliation. Civilian representatives, and members of the M5-RFP and former rebel groups signatory to the 2015 peace agreement also received ministerial portfolios. On the following day ECOWAS announced the removal of all punitive measures imposed on Mali, and the AU ended its suspension of Mali's membership shortly afterwards. In accordance with ECOWAS demands, on 8 October the new transitional authorities released the remaining officials detained since 18 August. On the same day they announced the release by JNIM of opposition leader Soumaïla Cissé, who had been seized in March, together with a French aid worker held hostage since December 2016 and two Italian nationals, following a controversial negotiated prisoner exchange believed to involve some 200 militants.

On 3 December 2020 Transitional President N'Daw issued a decree appointing a 121-member interim legislative body, the Conseil National de Transition (CNT); 22 seats were allocated to representatives of the defence and security forces, 11 to political parties and groups, nine to civil society organizations, and eight to the M5-RFP. At the inaugural session of the CNT in Bamako two days later, Diaw, the second-ranking CNSP leader, was elected unopposed as its President. Civil society groups and political parties criticized the selection process for the new body and the level of representation granted to the military. Later that month a radio presenter and four prominent officials were placed in detention and charged with conspiring to overthrow the Government; former premier Boubou Cissé, who remained at large, was also accused by the authorities of involvement in the alleged coup plot. Following continued international pressure, on 28 January 2021 N'Daw decreed the official dissolution of the CNSP.

Meanwhile, in mid-March 2021 a court in Bamako ended the long-delayed trial of former coup leader Amadou Sanogo, who had remained in detention until early 2020, accused of responsibility for the killing of 21 'Red Beret' soldiers during violence following the 2012 coup. The court dismissed proceedings against Sanogo and 15 other defendants, citing a 2019 reconciliation law that offered amnesty for crimes committed during the 2012 crisis. In early April 2021 a French journalist, Olivier Dubois, was kidnapped by JNIM forces in Gao, where he had travelled to interview a jihadist commander.

In mid-April 2021 the Government announced that, in accordance with pledges for an 18-month transitional period, a constitutional referendum would be held on 31 October, followed by local and regional elections on 26 December, and the first round of presidential and legislative elections on 27 February 2022.

EXTENSION OF THE TRANSITIONAL PERIOD

However, the slow pace of the transitional process and the continued dominance of former members of the CNSP in the transitional Government drew increasing criticism, with the M5-RFP, in particular, demanding its dissolution. On 14 May 2021 the Office of the Presidency announced plans to form a more 'broad-based' administration, and on the same day Prime Minister Ouane resigned, but was immediately returned to office. In the ensuing reorganized Government announced on 24 May, the military retained control of strategic portfolios but former CNSP members Camara and Koné were replaced. Later that day, however, Transitional President N'Daw and Ouane were detained and transferred to the Kati military base at the orders of Transitional Vice-President Goïta, who complained that he had been not been consulted over the reorganization, describing it as a breach of the Transitional Charter. In a statement read on public television, Goïta announced that N'Daw and Ouane had been removed for seeking to 'sabotage' the transition, and reaffirmed his commitment to the electoral timetable. Despite renewed international condemnation and rapid ECOWAS mediation, two days later the resignation of N'Daw and Ouane was announced, prior to their release. On 29 May the Constitutional Court named Goïta as Transitional President, in view of the 'vacancy in the presidency', and he was

sworn into office on 7 June. The AU and ECOWAS again suspended Mali's membership at the beginning of June. In addition, the French Government announced the suspension of military co-operation with the Malian armed forces, including joint operations and training; President Macron declared in an interview with French newspaper *Le Journal du Dimanche* that he had informed G5 Sahel leaders that France would not support 'a country where there is no longer any democratic legitimacy or transition'. However, the military coup was reported to have received some popular support, particularly after Goïta confirmed his intention to appoint a member of the M5-RFP as the new Prime Minister, in early June naming the leader of the opposition Mouvement Patriotique pour le Renouveau and former minister, Choguel Kokalla Maïga, to the post. On 11 June Maïga became premier of a new, 28-member transitional Government, which included several other M5-RFP representatives; however, four army officers held principal portfolios, among them Camara, who was reinstated as Minister of Defence and War Veterans, and a former deputy Chief of Staff of the Armed Forces, Col-Maj. Daouda Aly Mohammedine, as Minister of Security and Civil Protection.

Meanwhile, on 10 June 2021 President Macron announced plans for the extensive revision of France's military operations in the Sahel as the jihadist threat began to shift south, involving the phased withdrawal of the 5,100-member Operation Barkhane and closure of French bases, although it was envisaged that around 2,500 French special forces would continue to participate in international anti-terrorism missions in the region, notably Task Force Takuba. Shortly afterwards, French Minister for the Armed Forces Parly announced that French forces had killed four terrorists in an operation in northern Mali on 5 June, including Bayes Ag Bakabo, who was believed to be responsible for the murder of two French journalists by AQIM in 2013. In addition, a senior ISGS commander, Dadi Ould Chouaib (also known as Abou Dardar), who had been released by the Malian authorities as part of the criticized hostage exchange the previous October, was rearrested by French forces in the tri-border region between Niger, Mali and Burkina Faso. The UN Security Council on 29 June extended the mandate of MINUSMA for a further year, tasking it with supporting the country's political transition towards the planned presidential and legislative elections. In early July France announced that its troops would resume joint operations with the Malian armed forces. However, following a virtual G5 Sahel meeting on 9 July, Macron confirmed that three military bases in northern Mali would be closed by the end of the year. In a further of a series of attacks in the Sahel region, at least 51 people were killed in early August when jihadists simultaneously attacked three villages in central Mali near the border with Niger. In mid-September Macron announced as 'another major success' the killing of ISGS leader Adnan Abu Walid al-Sahrawi, who had died in a French air strike in the tri-border region the previous month. Parly visited Mali later in September, in a reported attempt to dissuade the transitional authorities from finalizing a contract with a Russian private security company, the Wagner Group, under which up to 1,000 Russian paramilitary forces would be deployed to Mali to train its army and protect high-level figures. ·

On 4 September 2021 armed members of the country's elite Special Anti-Terrorist Force marched on a prison in central Bamako and forced the release of their commander, Oumar Samaké, who had been detained in connection with the deaths of at least 14 anti-Government protesters in July 2020. Following widespread criticism, however, it was reported that Samaké had surrendered to police and again been taken into detention. Meanwhile, an ECOWAS mission, led by former Nigerian President Goodluck Jonathan, which made a three-day visit to Mali to assess progress in September 2021, expressed concerns about the lack of 'concrete actions in the effective preparation of the electoral process'. However, in late October the Government declared the ECOWAS special representative in Mali, Hamidou Boly, *persona non grata*.

Following a summit meeting on 7 November 2021, when heads of state were informed by Goïta that the presidential and legislative elections would not be held according to the original timetable, ECOWAS announced the imposition of targeted sanctions (comprising a travel ban and asset freeze) on members of the transitional authorities and their relatives. After ECOWAS threatened further measures unless a new plan to organize elections was presented by the end of the year, on 28 December the Government launched a delayed National Conference on Reform in Bamako to decide on a timetable for returning the country to civilian rule. However, at the end of December the 1,600 participating delegates issued recommendations that the transitional period be extended by up to five years, due to security concerns and to allow the implementation of reforms. At a summit on 9 January 2022, having rejected a Malian proposal for a five-year extension to the transition, ECOWAS imposed economic and financial sanctions, including the closure of land and air borders between member states and Mali, the freezing of Malian assets, and the suspension of non-essential commercial transactions and of financial assistance; it was also decided to recall the ambassadors of member states from Bamako. The transitional Government condemned the measures as illegitimate and announced the retaliatory withdrawal of its ambassadors from member states; public protests against the sanctions were staged in Bamako and other cities on 14 January. On 21 February the CNT unanimously adopted a proposal by the Government to amend the Transitional Charter, providing for extension of the transition and thereby allowing the incumbent authorities to remain in office for a further five years; in addition, the post of Vice-President was abolished and the CNT was to be expanded from 121 to 147 members. The main opposition parties strongly criticized the revision and demanded the establishment of new transitional institutions. During a further visit by ECOWAS envoy Jonathan to the country in March, the transitional authorities proposed a two-year timetable as a compromise; however, ECOWAS again rejected the extension.

WITHDRAWAL OF OPERATION BARKHANE

Meanwhile, the relations of the military junta with France also deteriorated sharply. In early October 2021 the Government summoned the French ambassador to Bamako over critical remarks made by President Macron that were considered to question the legitimacy of the transitional authorities. However, in December France and a further 14 European states, together with Canada, issued a joint statement condemning the deployment of the Russian mercenaries in Mali (which was denied by the transitional authorities), and claiming that the Wagner Group was sponsored by the Government of the Russian Federation. In January 2022 the transitional authorities demanded the withdrawal from Mali of some 90 Danish special forces, which had been newly deployed under Task Force Takuba, stating that they had arrived without official permission. In response to remarks by French Minister for Europe and Foreign Affairs Jean-Yves Le Drian denouncing the decision of the transitional authorities, the Malian Government expelled the French ambassador to Bamako at the end of January. A co-ordinated withdrawal from Mali of the French, other European and Canadian forces operating in both Operation Barkhane and Task Force Takuba was then announced in a joint statement issued on 17 February. (France pledged to continue anti-jihadist operations in the Sahel region, particularly under increased military co-operation with Niger.) In support of the ECOWAS measures, on 4 February the EU adopted sanctions, including a travel ban and an assets freeze, against five senior members of the transitional Government.

Intensified fighting between the ISGS, JNIM and other armed groups was reported in the northern regions of Menaka and Gao from March 2022. The Malian media regulator ordered the suspension of broadcasts by France 24 television and RFI radio in the country in that month, after the Government accused the French state-funded outlets of reporting 'false allegations' of abuse by the Malian army. In early April Human Rights Watch reported that some 300 civilians had been summarily executed in the village of Moura, in the central Mopti region, in late March, during a security operation by the Malian armed forces together with Russian paramilitary personnel. In early April Russia vetoed a proposal submitted by France at the UN Security Council for an independent investigation into the alleged massacre, and later that month the UN expressed extreme concerns at the continued refusal of the Malian authorities to allow its investigators access to the site. The EU on 11 April announced the end of its military training missions in Mali, on the grounds that the junta was unable to guarantee non-interference from the Russian military contractors. On 2 May the Malian Government unilaterally revoked the Status of Forces Agreement reached in 2013 that had provided the framework for French military intervention, and also a bilateral defence co-operation treaty signed in 2014 with France, which it accused of 'violations of Mali's national sovereignty'. Shortly afterwards, in mid-May, the Government announced its decision to withdraw from the G5 Sahel group and its FC-G5S (with effect from the end of June), after it was blocked by some member states from assuming the body's rotating presidency. Two days later the Government announced that an attempted coup, led by dissident army officers and 'supported by a Western state', had been suppressed on 11–12 May. Meanwhile, a court in Bamako issued a summons for Le Drian to attend an investigation over a contract for the manufacture of Malian biometric passports in 2015.

On 6 June 2022 Transitional President Goïta issued a decree under which the transitional period would end in March 2024 (with a duration of two years from 26 March 2022), presenting it as a demonstration of willingness to engage in dialogue with ECOWAS. Later that month Goïta declared three days of national mourning following the massacre by jihadists of at least 132 civilians in the central town of Diallassagou and surrounding areas. At the end of June the UN Security Council extended the mandate of MINUSMA for a further year, maintaining its previous strength of 13,289 military personnel and 1,920 international police; for the first time, Russia and the People's Republic of China abstained from the vote in the Security Council. At an ECOWAS summit in the Ghanaian capital, Accra, on 3 July the heads of state accepted Mali's new transitional timetable (reportedly following mediation by Togolese President Faure Gnassingbé), and announced a decision to lift the economic and financial sanctions imposed against the country, while maintaining its suspension from the bloc.

However, a further dispute erupted soon afterwards, when the Malian authorities on 10 July 2022 detained 49 soldiers from Côte d'Ivoire at Bamako airport, announcing that they had arrived in the country without official permission and would be charged as mercenaries. The Government of Côte d'Ivoire maintained that the personnel had been deployed under a security support contract signed with MINUSMA and demanded their immediate release. Four days later the Malian Government suspended its approval of the rotation of MINUSMA personnel for 'national security' reasons. In addition, on 20 July it announced the expulsion of the MINUSMA spokesman, Olivier Salgado, who had supported the statements of the Ivorian Government in posts on social media network Twitter. In early August Mali received a further delivery of armaments from Russia, comprising five military jets and a combat helicopter. Although the rotation of MINUSMA troops resumed in mid-August under a new mechanism, following discussions between the Government and UN officials on revised procedures for deployments of mission personnel, the Ivorian soldiers remained in custody and were formally charged by a Mali court with attempting to destabilize state security.

In the most severe attack against the military recorded since 2019, ISGS forces killed 42 Malian soldiers and injured 22 in Tessit, in Gao, on 7 August 2022; the Malian authorities reported that 37 ISGS militants were also killed in the fighting. On 15 August the French military announced that the final troops deployed under Operation Barkhane had been withdrawn from Mali (after the mission of Task Force Takuba in Mali had officially been terminated at the end of June); around 2,500 French personnel remained in the Sahel region, with many stationed in Niger. On the same day Mali's Minister of Foreign Affairs and International Co-operation, Abdoulaye Diop, dispatched a letter to the UN Security Council requesting an emergency meeting on the situation in the country, while accusing France of repeatedly violating Malian airspace and of providing intelligence and military support to jihadist forces.

The French Government condemned the allegations. Meanwhile, Prime Minister Choguel Kokalla Maïga was reported to have been hospitalized on 13 August. Lt-Col Abdoulaye Maïga, the Minister of Territorial Administration and Decentralization, and the Government Spokesperson since the previous December, was appointed by Transitional President Goïta as his interim replacement on 21 August. Three women among the imprisoned group of Ivorian soldiers were released on 3 September, following Togolese mediation; however, Goïta demanded the extradition of Malian former politicians in exile in Côte d'Ivoire in exchange for the release of the other Ivorian army personnel. Addressing the UN General Assembly in New York on 24 September, Interim Prime Minister Abdoulaye Maïga denounced the French military withdrawal from Mali as a 'unilateral decision', also criticizing the leaders of Côte d'Ivoire and Niger. A high-level ECOWAS mission, comprising Gnassingbé, Ghanaian President Nana Akufo-Addo and Gambian President Adama Barrow, visited Bamako on 29 September, in continued mediation efforts to secure the release of the remaining 46 Ivorian soldiers.

In an indication of some progress in the transition, a commission established by Goïta in June 2022 presented the draft of a new constitution on 11 October; among its provisions, the previous National Assembly was to be replaced by a bicameral parliament, with the creation of an upper Haut Conseil de la Nation. The draft constitution was to be submitted to the transitional Government and the CNT, prior to a referendum envisaged for March 2023.

Economy

PAUL MELLY

INTRODUCTION

Mali presently remains trapped in a profound crisis of violent insecurity that has spread across vast areas of the north and the centre of the country, its destabilizing impacts compounded by years of political tension and a marked deterioration in the country's relations with its neighbours and much of the international community. This complex and multi-layered crisis has wide economic and social impacts, largely the operation of the state and public services in some regions where the spread of terrorism and inter-communal tensions has hugely disrupted everyday rural life and the support services and commerce that underpin it—and effectively shut down a tourism sector that used to be a valuable source of livelihoods and income for a number of communities in the north and the centre, and for the capital, Bamako. Even regions that have escaped the worst insecurity are rendered more fragile by the wider national crisis and its erosion of the functionality of the state machine and networks of economic life.

The troubled state of Mali's relations with neighbours such as Côte d'Ivoire, and key Western partners such as France, the European Union (EU) and the USA weakens its access to aid funding, at a time when the unstable and insecure condition of many regions is already a serious impediment to any prospect of sustained development progress. Should Mali successfully complete its planned transition back to constitutional democracy in March 2024, as agreed with the Economic Community of West African States (ECOWAS), that would do much to revive both its trade and co-operation partnerships with its neighbours and the confidence of key external partners, with which relationships have become seriously degraded since the military coups of August 2020 and May 2021. Such an improved diplomatic context would not itself resolve the country's huge security challenges, but it would create easier conditions for Mali to develop a coherent strategy for maintaining public services and development initiatives in those regions of the country where security conditions were less difficult. For since the second coup, and the subsequent breakdown in key ECOWAS and Western relationships, the transitional regime has had little capacity to focus on much beyond urgent crisis management, and managing economic and development policy on a caretaker basis.

For now, Mali remains in a highly fragile situation. Yet, if the country can recover a measure of stability and strategic focus, it has deep social, geographical and economic roots on which to rebuild. Dialogue and the resolution of differences through discussion and negotiation are very much part of social culture in a country that has a distinct sense of its historical identity—and that is an identity also profoundly connected to landscape and the patterns of rural production and village life.

The roots of today's modern state can be traced back to the Mali empire of the medieval era—a history that is itself an important consequence of geography and climate. The fertility brought by the river Niger and its tributaries such as the Bani, but also by the upper reaches of the Senegal river in the far west, sustains a substantial agricultural and pastoral economy, still the principal sources of livelihood. These rivers endow Mali with a much greater rural productive potential than that of some fellow Sahelian countries, which are more heavily dependent on the region's brief annual rainy season. If today's violent instability can be overcome, Mali could become a major supplier of cereals for West Africa as a whole; and it also has large potential as a livestock producer. Important areas of cotton production extend south and east from the river and from Bamako, the capital, while in the much less populated desert north nomadic pastoralism and trans-Saharan trading remain longstanding economic foundations. However, competition for the crucial resources of reasonably well-watered grazing and farmland is also one of the drivers behind the tensions and violence that have scarred central Mali in recent years.

Gold mining has also for many centuries played an important economic role. Today both industrial mines and smaller scale commercial and artisanal diggings are key providers of employment, income and government fiscal revenue. Commerce, government and service activities are the fundamentals of the urban economy of Bamako and major towns. During the first decade of this century tourism was also an important generator of livelihoods in historic centres such as Timbuktu, Mopti and Djenné and also for the Dogon villages of the Bandiagara escarpment; however, the sector has been almost completely shut down by the security crisis of the past decade.

In Mali, as in most West African countries, the COVID-19 pandemic had a less impact on health than on economic activity. By October 2022 only 742 deaths had been recorded, although many cases were probably unrecorded and the true death toll was probably higher. The economic impact was more severe, as real gross domestic product (GDP) contracted by 1.2% in 2020, compared with expansion of 4.8% in the previous year.

Moreover, Mali's route back to stability and hopes of a renewed focus on development and economic diversification have been further undermined by insecurity and political upheavals. After seizing power in the August 2020 military coup, Col Assimi Goïta negotiated a transitional timetable for the restoration of civilian rule with ECOWAS (to which Mali belongs). However, Goïta's second coup, in May 2021, derailed this framework and in January 2022 ECOWAS imposed economic and financial sanctions against Mali. In theory, these were designed to hinder trade and investment while protecting the flow of essential imports; but the sanctions proved to be an imperfect instrument, particularly in a context of political tension and at a time when global prices for key imported commodities such as cereals and fuel were rising anyway, as a result of the Russian Federation's invasion of Ukraine in February. Hence, the regime could conveniently blame the effects of soaring consumer price inflation on ECOWAS rather than Russia. Eventually, in mid-2022, Goïta reached a new agreement with ECOWAS on extension of the transition to March 2024 and the bloc agreed to lift sanctions.

Even before the military takeover of 2020, the effectiveness of government services and development strategy had been undermined by the weak governance standards and feeble policy leadership during the presidency of Ibrahim Boubacar Keïta (2013–20). Thus the potential for enhancing agricultural output and diversifying the commercial and service base had gone largely unfulfilled for a decade or so. Indeed, even under President Amadou Toumani Touré (2002–12), repeated corruption scandals were eroding donors' confidence. Concerns regarding Mali's ongoing security crisis have kept the international community engaged; but a combination of poor government leadership, fragile state capacity and the violent insecurity that affects much of the north and centre have hampered economic and social development for Mali's 21.5m. people for more than a decade.

FUNDAMENTALS OF THE ECONOMY

Beyond the Bamako conurbation, Mali remains fundamentally a rural society, with most families dependent on agriculture, livestock husbandry and informal trading and craft activity. Rural activities account for almost one-half of annual GDP. However, located in the Sahel and already exposed to periodic droughts, Mali now faces the risk of climate change impacts that could further increase the pressure on resources of land, water and vegetation. There is therefore a need to diversify economic activity, to offer more varied and resilient livelihood opportunities for young people.

Gold mining is the principal export earner: the metal is produced at a number of industrial mines and numerous informal digging sites, which are a major source of employment but do also have serious environmental impacts. The manufacturing sector is small, its development partly hampered by the additional transport costs imposed by Mali's landlocked location; however, there is also substantial artisanal production of textiles and clothing. Commerce and other service activities are important in Bamako but the tourism sector, formerly a major activity in Bamako and in the north and centre of the country, has been almost completely shut down by the decade-long security crisis. With options for diversification thus blocked or constrained, Mali has been forced back into reliance on its economic fundamentals—agriculture, pastoralism, gold mining and formal and informal artisanal activity and services.

The country has thus lost a decade of development progress and potential for the broadening of value-added activities that could have diversified employment and state revenues and helped reduce poverty amongst its fast growing population.

Even in Bamako and the south, transport imposes serious cost and time burdens on both import purchases and the competitiveness of exports such as cotton; for the more distant central and northern regions it is an even greater constraint, compounded in many areas by security risks. These also hamper the provision of basic public administration and services, and development activities, with large parts of the north almost 'no go' areas for many public servants and international personnel. Mali previously benefited from extensive European non-governmental organization engagement in grassroots development, but insecurity has severely curtailed activity in some areas. Since early 2020 the COVID-19 pandemic has brought further complications, albeit rather less than those resulting from a decade of continuous security crisis.

Mali has also suffered from serious flaws in governance and large-scale corruption. Scandals in vaccination and HIV treatment programmes were followed by those regarding military uniforms procurement and the supply of agricultural fertilizer.

Yet elements of the state machine, notably the analysis of agriculture and food security indicators, and local delivery of emergency support, have proved resilient and capable, in large part thanks to the efforts of the many skilled and committed specialist personnel in technical public services. Moreover, Malian society also has considerable strengths that have enabled most people and communities to sustain an economic and family life, despite the ongoing security crisis and the political upheavals of 2020 and 2021. The culture of consensus and negotiation is deeply embedded.

The stability of Mali's economy is underpinned by its membership of the eight-country Union Economique et Monétaire de l'Afrique de l'Ouest (UEMOA) single currency bloc and, more broadly, ECOWAS. Moreover, the country also belongs to the Sahel's food security early warning and resilience system, through its membership of the Comité Permanent Inter-Etats de Lutte Contre la Sécheresse dans le Sahel (CILSS), a crucial support to rural sectors and the overall supply of food to communities nationwide. Furthermore, it is a member of the Organisation pour la Mise en Valeur du Fleuve Sénégal (OMVS), which manages water and power in the Senegal river basin.

In the Sahelian climate rainfall is concentrated mainly in a wet season running from late June to early September. It is during this period that the main cereal crops and cotton (the main cash export crop) must be planted; this is also the period of vegetation growth, replenishing grazing areas. In the inland delta of the Niger much of the land is flooded by the seasonal rains and irrigation networks extend the areas of farmland with longer-lasting water supply. Even so, overall rural production is mainly reliant on the distinct seasonal cycle, with the well-watered months of planting and growth, followed by harvest, and long months of almost no rainfall before the next annual farming period comes around. From April onwards Mali enters the lean season (*la soudure*), when temperatures are at their highest—routinely 50°C or more—and villagers must eke out their remaining grain stocks; supplies are at their lowest during the final rainy months, when the new crops are still growing and not yet ready for harvest.

However, rains often fail locally or across wide areas, or at the wrong time, causing flood damage without assisting agricultural production. This means that Mali, like other Sahelian states, lives permanently with the risk of food crisis. In response to the catastrophic drought of 1973, Sahelian countries created CILSS, based in Ouagadougou (Burkina Faso), which oversees national systems for collecting data on weather conditions, grazing and agricultural conditions and results, market prices for crops and animals and levels of reserve grain stocks. Collated at provincial and central government level, and by CILSS, this data enables governments, CILSS and international donors to monitor the risks of food crises, whether local or more widely spread, and thus to provide emergency support ahead of time, averting crisis and famine. The system has become steadily more subtle and detailed, with data based on harmonized standards. CILSS and its technical analyst team based in Niamey (Niger) oversee the performance of individual national systems.

The 15-member ECOWAS bloc now plays a major role in managing political and security issues on a consensual regional basis. However, the last 10 years have also seen a reinvigoration of efforts to develop West Africa as a more integrated regional market and trading bloc and, potentially, future single monetary zone. From 2015 member states began to implement a Common External Tariff (CET) regime for all imports from outside the bloc while, within the ECOWAS space, trade in food is supposedly subject to no tariff or customs dues other than a minimum technical charge—which should facilitate Malian exports of grain to regional neighbours. The bloc has also established a standardized market regime for the cross-border sale of electricity. Mauritania, Mali's neighbour to the north-west, is not a member of ECOWAS but is part of the bloc's economic space in most respects (although not free movement of people).

ECOWAS members are committed to the creation of a common currency, to be called the eco, and for some years they have been measuring their performance under agreed economic and fiscal convergence criteria. However, the practical and institutional arrangements for the currency are yet to be agreed, while the COVID-19 pandemic had disrupted compliance with the convergence targets. Consequently, in June 2021 member states decided to postpone the launch of the eco until 2027, after a fresh period of convergence, also leaving time for other unresolved issues to be settled.

The UEMOA bloc (Benin, Burkina Faso, Côte d'Ivoire, Guinea-Bissau, Mali, Niger, Senegal and Togo) already has a common currency, the CFA franc, and a single politically independent central bank, the Banque Centrale des Etats de l'Afrique Centrale (BCEAO), based in Dakar, Senegal, with a national office in each member state. UEMOA also has a central commission, in Ouagadougou, and operates a common regime of bank regulation and a regional capital market; an electronic regional stock exchange, the Bourse Régionale des Valeurs Mobilières (BRVM), is based in Abidjan, Côte d'Ivoire. The system was originally set up under French colonial rule and the value of the CFA franc was pegged against the French franc and, subsequently, the euro, at a rate guaranteed by the French Treasury. (There has been just one devaluation of the CFA franc, by 50% in 1994.) The euro peg means that BCEAO aligns its monetary policy with the tight stance maintained by the European Central Bank. There is also a six-member block of central African countries using the CFA franc, but the two blocs operate separately, with separate bank notes and institutions.

In practical economic terms, the system has provided monetary stability and low inflation, and facilitated co-operation between member states and a degree of regional economic integration. In recent years, however, there has been pressure for reforms to a system that many regarded as a colonial legacy and in 2017 France's President, Emmanuel Macron stated that his country would accept reform if UEMOA member states decided on it. They chose Côte d'Ivoire's President, Alassane Ouattara, a former deputy managing director of the International Monetary Fund (IMF), to develop a reform plan, which was agreed with France and announced in late 2019. This comprised the abolition of the requirement for member countries to deposit one-half of their foreign exchange reserves in a special Operations Account at the French Treasury to underpin the exchange rate guarantee and France's withdrawal from the governing boards of the UEMOA core institutions. However, the French-guaranteed peg to the euro would be retained.

Ouattara also proposed replacing the CFA franc name and banknotes with new notes and coins, under the eco name. However, Nigeria and several other West African states outside UEMOA felt this would appropriate the eco name already chosen for the future all-ECOWAS single currency. The onset of the COVID-19 pandemic derailed the prospect of negotiations over the name, and in late 2022 that particular issue remained unresolved. However, France proceeded with the domestic legislation required to allow the implementation of the other elements of Ouattara's reform package, which in technical monetary and central banking terms were more important, particularly in strengthening UEMOA's international credibility as a single currency bloc.

Like many other francophone African countries, Mali belongs to the Organisation pour l'Harmonisation en Afrique du Droit des Affaires (OHADA), a harmonized framework of business law with a supranational disputes tribunal.

The G5 Sahel bloc, to which Mali has belonged since its foundation in 2014, is mainly concerned with regional security and the fight against jihadist militants; but these military efforts are supported with a programme of 40 priority development projects for marginal areas. In mid-2022 the Goïta regime withdrew Mali from the G5 Sahel, but it remained unclear whether this was a permanent move or a temporary political gesture.

SOCIETY

Mali is amongst the world's least developed countries and some key development indicators are weaker than those for neighbouring countries that, in terms of economic output, are actually poorer. The country has substantial agricultural and mining capacity, but national economic output is not fully translated into effective core public services and development programmes—probably because the protracted security crisis has consumed the energy and focus of government. Real GDP per capita, according to the World Bank, at US $917.9 in 2021, was much higher than in Niger ($594.9) and around the same level as the figure for Burkina Faso ($918.2). Yet average life expectancy, at just 60.5 years for women and 58.9 years for men in 2020, was lower than in Niger (64.0 years for women and

61.6 for men) and Burkina Faso (62.7 and 61.1, respectively). Over the past decade political leaders gave little attention to a coherent long-term development strategy and this focus has weakened even further since the military coup of August 2020, since when the Government has been preoccupied with security issues and short-term crisis management. In the 2021 Human Development Index, produced by the United Nations Development Programme (UNDP), Mali was ranked 186th out of 189 countries, ahead of Niger (189th), but below Burkina Faso (184th).

There have been areas of significant progress in community level health service provision: some 67% of births are now attended by trained personnel and over the past 25 years the rate of maternal mortality has fallen from 940 deaths per every 100,000 live births to 562 deaths by 2017. Meanwhile, 70% of children aged 12–23 months are immunized against measles and 77% against diphtheria, whooping cough and tetanus. However, there is only one doctor for every 10,000 people, while the provision of hospital beds, also at one for 10,000 people, is just one-quarter of the level in Burkina Faso and Mauritania.

Serious health fragilities persist. For example, 79% of children under five suffer from anaemia and 22% are stunted. The causes include not just shortcomings in health provision but also economic factors—constraints on families' ability to grow enough food or earn sufficient income—and even dietary traditions. Rates of malnutrition are highest around Sikasso in the south, one of Mali's most productive and well watered regions. Violent insecurity also disrupts the community economic and social life that provides the means for healthy wellbeing, particularly in central Mali.

Social factors and family structure also play a significant role in these problems. Child marriage remains widespread, with 54% of Malians marrying by the age of 18 and Mali's adolescent birth rate is amongst the highest in the world. Young teenage pregnancy often has serious consequences for young women's physical health and ability to continue education or secure employment. Only 18% of women aged 15–49 use modern contraception, although a further 21% would like access to it. The consequence of widespread early marriage and low contraceptive use is a fertility rate of 5.7 children per woman in 2020, and a projected rate of population growth averaging 2.9% per year for 2020–25, leaving Mali with an estimated population of 21.5m. at mid-2022.

Some 47% of girls and 52% of boys complete primary education and 30% of children complete at least lower secondary education, but specialists believe such figures should be treated with caution amid doubts over true levels of continuing attendance at school, and the disruptive impact of insecurity. There is also widespread concern over the quality of free state school education and even many poor families therefore scrape together the money to pay for private schooling.

Mali's higher education system has some notable strengths, such as the specialist engineering and architecture college and the Ecole Nationale d'Administration (ENA) for training senior public servants; however, it suffers from intense geographical centralization. Most university provision is concentrated in Bamako, which is also home to two of the three teaching hospitals, with the third in Kati, a neighbouring military garrison town. A university has now been established in Ségou, but the development of higher education facilities in Mali's major provincial centres lags far behind that in Senegal, Burkina Faso or Niger.

ECONOMIC POLICY AND PERFORMANCE

Malian economic policy has been based on consistent fundamentals: a conservative monetary stance, piloted by the BCEAO regional central bank; relatively tight management of public finances, depending largely on external donors for the funding of major capital projects; a growing role for international investors, notably in gold mining and in cotton, and a high priority for agriculture and rural development. Policies have been closely co-ordinated with the IMF and major donors.

In reality, however, the execution of this strategy has been inconsistent, disrupted by the recent military coups and interludes of unconstitutional government and undermined by serious failures of public finance governance and corruption scandals that have shaken public confidence and damaged relations with the IMF and other international partners. The past 20 years have seen scandals over the embezzlement of funds for vaccination and HIV/AIDS treatments, the deliberate over-stating of cereal harvest data and questions about the procurement of military uniforms; but under the Goïta regime, the investigation of past alleged corruption has in part become a politically motivated campaign.

Reformist ministers and Prime Ministers have sometimes tried to tighten up financial management and tackle technical priorities such as the modernization of the mining code, and some technical arms of the state machine have functioned well. Moreover, despite the huge political and security challenges to stability, the Government has sustained a consistent economic strategy and relatively stable public finances. Mali has not toppled into debt crisis.

However, opportunities have been missed over the past 10 years. Although the state and public service machine has not collapsed, it has often failed to perform well. The political leadership has proved unable to provide clear and creative long-term strategic leadership on economic policy and development—in contrast, for example, to the Emerging Senegal Plan or Niger's '3N' programme for food security and rural community resilience. Moreover, the security crisis has inhibited the implementation of many programmes in northern and central regions.

The IMF approved an Extended Credit Facility (ECF) programme in August 2019, which provided for (US $191.9m.) in highly concessional support, phased over three years. At this stage the economy was doing relatively well, despite the security crisis: real GDP growth in 2019 was 4.8%, comfortably outstripping demographic growth and thus providing a basis for increasing average per-capita income; moreover, inflation was actually negative, with consumer prices declining by 3% in real terms, thus strengthening household purchasing power, at least in urban areas. (The impact in rural areas, where most families earn their income from the sale of basic agricultural products, may have been less clearly positive.)

In 2020, however, the adverse effects of the COVID-19 pandemic began, slowing global trade and international investor confidence. While Mali was only marginally affected in health terms, the economy soon suffered from the impact both of the global slowdown and domestic lockdown measures. Real GDP contracted by 1.2% that year, while consumer price inflation resurged, albeit at a mere 0.5%. Moreover, the Government had to bolster some areas of expenditure, to preserve economic stability and protect the progress that had been made in development and so the public deficit surged to 6.1% of GDP in 2020, compared with a mere 2.6% the previous year. The Fund estimated the cost of extra medical care and testing, and income support for the poorest households and weakest businesses at 0.8% of GDP and therefore provided US $200m. in emergency support from its Rapid Credit Facility. It also agreed debt relief on the repayments that it had been due to receive from Mali and relaxed performance targets under the ECF programme.

Yet while the economy slowed down, Mali's current account position actually strengthened in 2020, because the country benefited from a surge in the price of gold, its main export. As so often happens in times of crisis, gold was favoured by international investors as a store of safe value. As an energy importing country Mali also benefited from the pandemic-induced slump in oil prices. Consequently, the deficit on Mali's current account, excluding official transfers, actually contracted to 3.7% of GDP—less than one-half of the 7.5% recorded in 2019. Transfers from Malians abroad remained stable, despite the difficult economic conditions in countries with large Malian diaspora populations such as France. However, foreign direct investment slumped, albeit probably because of the episodic nature of major project investment rather than due to the pandemic.

In 2021 the economy rebounded quite strongly, with real GDP growth of 3.1%. However, the recovery slowed in 2022, with growth for that year projected at 2.5%—a reflection both of the steadily worsening security situation, with violent attacks occasionally reaching the outskirts of Bamako, and the global consequences of the Russian invasion of Ukraine.

The war in Ukraine resulted in a sharp increase in global prices of fuel, which Mali has to import, and of imported cereals; the net impact of the rise in cereal prices is hard to gauge, since Mali imports some items such as wheat flour but is also a major cereals producer. In its February 2021 review of performance under the ECF programme, the IMF relaxed some targets, due to the impact of COVID during the preceding year. The Fund advised the Government to focus on expenditure essentials and basic fiscal revenue reform. However three months later, in May, there was a second military coup, rapidly followed by a sharp deterioration in Mali's relations with France and other Western European governments. Security and politics increasingly dominated the government agenda. The regime's failure to implement the previous transitional agreement with ECO-WAS led the West African bloc to impose wide-ranging sanctions against Mali in January 2022, with some disruptive economic effect, until agreement on a new timetable was negotiated in July. In this context, the final out-turn for growth in 2022 was likely to be lower than projected, while inflation was higher than expected.

Before the pandemic, government revenues rose from 16.7% of GDP in 2016 to 18.4% in 2017; although they fell back to just 14.3% in 2018, they rebounded to 19.6% in both 2019 and 2020. In cash terms, this resulted in a rise in budget receipts from 1,389,700m. francs CFA in 2016 to 1,645,600m. francs CFA in 2017, before a decline in 2018 to 1,358,800m. francs CFA, and then a new surge to 1,982,000m. francs CFA in 2019, slipping back to 1,958,800m. francs CFA in 2020. Within this overall figure, the main contribution came from fiscal revenues, climbing from 1,239,300m. francs CFA in 2016 to 1,353,700m. francs CFA in 2017, then a drop in 2018 to just 1,125,800m. francs CFA, before recovery to 1,495,800m. francs CFA in 2019, slipping to 1,442,400m. francs CFA in 2020. Grant aid increased from 132,500m. francs CFA in 2016 to 144,200m. francs CFA in 2017, but then fell to 117,100m. francs CFA in 2018—perhaps reflecting donor caution during a presidential election year—before rising to 191,300m. francs CFA in 2019. In 2020, however, with the ousting of the elected civilian Government in August, donor disbursements of grant aid fell back sharply, to just 113,400m. francs CFA.

Total expenditure rose from 1,858,000m. francs CFA in 2016 to 2,055,100m. francs CFA in 2017; with voters going to the polls, the Government managed to sustain spending at 1,932,400m. francs CFA in 2018, despite constrained public revenues, and with revenues surging the following year, spending jumped sharply, to 2,349,700m. francs CFA and then 2,632,300m. francs CFA in 2020. Current expenditure was predominant within the overall outlays, rising steadily from 1,013,000m. francs CFA in 2016 to 1,105,100m. francs CFA in 2017, then 1,140,500m. francs CFA the next year and 1,280,600m. francs CFA in 2019, and finally 1,567,700m. francs CFA in 2020—of which public sector salaries and benefits accounted for 620,000m. francs CFA. Capital spending rose from 740,000m. francs CFA in 2016 to 784,500m. francs CFA in 2017, but then dropped to 614,700m. francs CFA in 2018, followed by a limited resurgence to 658,000m. francs CFA the following year and then a fall back to just 613,800m. francs CFA in 2020. That decline may reflect both the disruptive impact of insecurity on some development projects and the disruption to normal government decision making and the administrative approval of projects and programmes after the August 2020 coup.

AGRICULTURE

Smallholder agriculture, animal husbandry and related rural activities remain the foundation of the domestic economy and the main source of livelihood for the large majority of the population, and the Niger river and its tributaries and inland delta are a vital artery of fertility, stretching from south-west to north-east. However, the rural economy is heavily influenced by Mali's Sahelian weather cycle. The whole country—except for the Sahara itself—is subject to the broad seasonal contrast between a rainy season from late June to early September and nine months with almost no rainfall. December and January are cool, before temperatures quickly rebound; from March to early June they are routinely around or well above 40°C in daytime. Furthermore, a total failure of the main annual rains is not uncommon.

Although gold dominates Mali's export accounts, cotton and livestock are also significant contributors, while farmers grow large volumes of cereals, fruit and vegetables for sale to in domestic urban consumer markets. Bamako is the only large city and there is a deep economic interdependence between towns large and small and the surrounding rural areas: markets, cereal stores and a range of government and commercial services cater for villagers' supply needs and provide a key sales outlet for their produce. There are regional variations, but rural communities across the country have many features in common: most farmers are smallholders, cultivating small plots mainly by hand or with animal drawn ploughs; women typically cultivate market gardens, watered from wells and thus able to continue producing vegetables and sometimes even small quantities of cereals, during much of the nine-month dry season.

Certain ethnic groups have a deeply rooted culture of pastoralism, and in central Mali competition between Peul livestock herders and Dogon or Bambara farmers over access to land and water has fuelled violent tensions. Climate change and drought can of course intensify these pressures, as rainfall becomes less reliable and predictable, accentuating the pressure on limited resources of grazing, arable land and water. However, farming and pastoralism can also be complementary to each other: pastoralists buy supplies that farmers have grown and sell livestock in return, farmers often allow herds to graze the crop stalks and roots remaining on their land after harvest, and thus fertilize the soil with their droppings. Moreover, farming and livestock husbandry are not mutually exclusive: many pastoralist households will also cultivate some land, while most farming households have poultry and often sheep and goats too.

There are significant geographical variations in the pattern of rural economic activity: north of Ségou is a large area of seasonally irrigated land managed under the aegis of the Office du Niger (ON) and producing rice, while large parts of the south produce cotton. In central Mali the west of the Mopti region and the south of the Tombouctou region are dominated by the vast inland delta of the River Niger, subject to seasonal flooding and a major producer of forage for animals; however, eastern Mopti region is upland, including the Bandiagara escarpment, home to many Dogon farming villages. Where the Niger flows through the fringes of the Sahara desert irrigation allows the farming of extensive areas, notably around the outskirts of Tombouctou, but the north and most of the north-east is desert or the more arid band of Sahel grazing land and scrub.

Agriculture has frequently suffered from serious governance failings, notably corruption in the procurement and distribution of fertilizer, with malpractice sometimes depriving farmers of the promised supply subsidies. Even so, the Compagnie Malienne pour le Développement du Textile (CMDT) in cotton growing regions in the south and west, and the ON, in the rice producing areas around Ségou, are crucial sources of support for smallholders.

Of the major cereal crops, millet and sorghum are particularly suitable for conditions in the more arid regions, while paddy rice is grown in large tracts of the Niger river basin and inland; maize is also important. Sorghum and millet production slipped from 3.2m. metric tons in 2016/17 to 2.9m. tons in the following crop year, but recovered to 3.3m. tons in 2018/19, almost 3.4m. tons in 2019/20 and then exceeded 3.7m. tons in 2020/21. Maize output soared from 2.8m. tons in 2016/17 to 3.6m. tons in 2017/18 and 2018/19 and reached 3.8m. tons in 2019/20, but fell back to 3.5m. tons in 2020/21. Mali's paddy rice harvest fell back from 2.8m. tons in 2016/17 to 2.7m. in 2017/18, but then rebounded to almost 3.2m. tons in 2018/19 and 2019/20, but also slipped back, to 3m. tons, in the following year. Groundnuts make a significant contribution to rural incomes, with harvests on a steady upward trend, rising from 453,100 tons in 2016/17 to 472,600 tons in 2017/18, then to 497,200 tons in 2018/19 and an impressive 511,400 tons in 2019/20, but this crop also suffered a modest decline in output, to 485,800 tons, in 2020/21.

With 716 permanent staff and a turnover of 7,500m. francs CFA in 2019, the ON maintains one of the largest irrigated zones in West Africa (of some 100,000 ha), extending north from the Markala dam, near Ségou. Farmers in its zone of operation grew 808,102 metric tons of paddy rice in 2019/20, together with 325,390 tons of horticultural produce and 51,605 tons of other crops aimed at diversifying the production base. The ON is hoping for a substantial increase in output in 2020/21. The ON zone also grows sugar cane, to supply the sugar manufacturer Sukalasa; fish farming is being developed. Yet, despite ambitious talk of boosting crop production and food security in its zone of operation, and success in reducing the local incidence of household poverty to around 60% (compared with a national average of about 80%) the ON model for agricultural development has suffered numerous shortcomings and some of the policies associated with the project have proved highly contentious, particularly the allocation of land to foreign concessionaires for the production of food crops for their home markets at a time when the security of Mali's own food supply is inconsistent. Moreover, many smallholders have insecure land tenure.

Mali is among West Africa's main producers of cotton, which plays a crucial role in the economics of many smallholder households is a key source of their cash income. Hungry for fertilizer, it can be grown in rotation with cereals and legumes, which then benefit from the fertilizer residues in fields where cotton had been planted the previous year. These are all annual crops, and therefore farmers can adjust the division of their land between cotton and food crops year by year, in response demand and prices. However, Mali and fellow West African producers struggle to compete with low cost Asian cotton output and heavily subsidized US production. So they have begun to target niche opportunities, such as the growing Western consumer market for organic cotton hand-picked by small farmers. In 2019 the French retail group Carrefour agreed to buy 3,000 metric tons of Malian organic cotton over three years to stimulate this sub-sector. Output climbed from 645,000 tons in 2016/17 to 728,700 tons in 2017/18, before slipping back to 700,000 tons in 2018/19. It recovered to reach 773,500 tons in 2019/20, but in 2020/21 production slumped to a mere 192,600 tons as the COVID-19 pandemic severely restricted export demand and farmers went on strike in protest at the low producer price set by the Government. After three years at 250 francs CFA per kg, and a rise to 275 francs CFA per kg for 2019/20, the producer price was slashed to just 200 francs CFA per kg in 2020/21, seriously discouraging growers. After the resulting collapse in output, the Government announced that the price would be raised to 280 francs CFA per kg for 2021/22 as it set an ambitious recovery target of producing 810,000 tons. Production fell short of that goal but nevertheless staged a dramatic recovery, reaching a record 760,000 tons. The imposition of sanctions against Mali by ECOWAS prevented the export of this harvest by the usual routes to ports such as Abidjan and Dakar, so the Government organized road transport to take the crop over Mali's north-west border into Mauritania—not an ECOWAS state and thus not participating in the sanctions regime—where it could be loaded onto ships in the port of Nouakchott.

The Compagnie Malienne pour le Développement des Textiles (CMDT), established in 1974, has four subsidiaries in which farmers organizations hold 20% stakes and plays a huge strategic role in southern and western Mali. It provides inputs, credit and training for cotton production, buys the crop and gins it (the first stage of processing which transforms raw cotton into cotton fibre), and it also provides the framework for the production of maize, millet, sorghum and legumes in cotton-farming regions. These crops are produced by 212,670 mostly small farmer households, on average each farming a mere 10 ha, one-third of which is planted with cotton, and two-thirds with food crops, which ensures local self-sufficiency in basic foods, with a surplus for sale to other regions. The CMDT's area of operation (all of Sikasso region, and parts of the regions of Kayes, Koulikoro and Ségou) has more than 4.1m. people, spread among 3,346 villages, with farmers organized into 7,259 producer co-operatives. The company operates 18 ginning plants and by mid-2020 had three more planned; it is also responsible for 5,000 km of rural roads.

Although Mali is landlocked, fishing is an important economic activity and part of the local diet in many areas, thanks to the Niger and Bani rivers and their numerous tributaries, the inland delta of the Niger, and lakes behind dams at Sélingué and Manantali. Much of the fish is dried or smoked, to conserve it for transport and sale through local markets. The national wild catch was 117,700 metric tons in 2020, according to estimates by the UN Food and Agriculture Organization, with a further 7,700 tons from aquaculture. Mali even exports small amounts of fish. However, researchers have discovered that catches contain levels of lead and mercury that in some cases are clearly above European norms; this may be the consequence of the widespread use of mercury in the extraction of gold from the ore mined by artisanal diggers, who are active across much of southern Mali.

EXTRACTIVES AND ENERGY

Gold mining dates back many centuries in Mali. Over recent decades the sector has developed on a modern industrial-scale, but artisanal digging and small-scale commercial mining has also hugely expanded. Concentrated is mostly in the south and the far west of the country, the regions least affected by Mali's ongoing security crisis and in 2019 Mali was ranked as the third largest producer in Africa, behind Ghana and Sudan, and the sixth largest in the world. In January 2020 the Government adopted a fresh strategy for the mining and petroleum sector to run through to 2023.

Output of gold rose from 50.9 metric tons in 2016 to 60.9 tons in 2018, when production began at the Syama pit, operated by Australia's Resolute Mining. Output then reached 71.2 tons in 2019 and remained at that level in 2020, with industrial mines contributing 65.2 metric tons and artisanal digging an estimated 6.0 tons. However, in 2021 output fell slightly, to 69.4 tons, of which 63.4 tons were produced by industrial mines.

By early 2021 there were 13 industrial mine sites in operation, employing 11,000 people, and construction work at the country's 14th pit, Bagama, was completed by February. In December 2020 longstanding mine investor, Canada's Iamgold, sold its 41% stake in the Sadiola mine to Dubai-registered Allied Gold Corp. Largely as a result of the recent discovery or confirmation of resources at the Syama, Morila, Yanfolila and Nampala mines, the mines ministry estimated Mali's confirmed remaining gold deposits at around 703 metric tons, sufficient to sustain a further 10 years of output at current levels. Furthermore, there have been encouraging results from exploration work at Diba and Dandoko. Barrick, B2Gold, both Canadian, and Resolute Mining from Australia, account for about two-thirds of production, with the balance produced mainly by AngloGold Ashanti (UK-South African), Hummingbird (British) and Robex Gold (Canadian).

Tensions sometimes develop between industrial mine companies and the artisanal diggers. However, the Government has tried to develop a more organized structure for the sector, improving relations between these two groups and setting aside areas for the small local operators, many of whom are developing into increasingly mechanized small-scale industrial ventures.

Mali also has deposits of rock salt—mined in the Sahara—and semi-precious stones; phosphates are produced in the Tilemsi valley west of Goundam. However, enduring hopes of extensive oil exploration in the Malian Sahara have been largely stymied by the severe security problems affecting the region.

The national power utility Energie du Mali (EdM), which is owned 66% by the state and 34% by Industrial Promotion Services, a subsidiary of the Aga Khan Development Network, has overall responsibility for generation, transmission and distribution. The largest power station is the 200-MW Manantali dam on the Bafing river, a tributary of the River Senegal; this is part of the network operated by the OMVS, a multinational structure set up by Mali, Guinea, Senegal and Mauritania to manage the water and power generation resources of the Senegal river basin. Manantali and the much smaller OMVS power dam at Félou are operated by its offshoot Société de Gestion de l'Energie de Manantali. The other main power stations in the Malian generation system are the 46-MW Sélingué hydro plant on the Sankarani river, a tributary of the Niger, the Sotuba hydro plant and the Darsalam and Balingué thermal plants, together with at least 19 local stations not connected to the national grid but servicing surrounding local communities such as Gao, Tombouctou, Niafunké, Mopti, Djenné and Bandiagara. EdM is also responsible for water supply.

However, power supply is highly unreliable, constantly disrupted by outages—a reflection not just of indaequate generating capacity but also the run-down condition of EdM's infrastructure. Furthermore, the company is desperately short of the funds required to maintain and upgrade its network, because it operates at a chronic loss. In 2018 losses were equal to almost €100m. on a turnover of €277m. and by June 2019 EdM had accumulated debts of 319,000m. francs CFA (equal to €486m.). This is both because it sells electricity at a price below the cost of production and because almost one-quarter of the power that it supplies is leaked or stolen out of the network and never even billed to paying customers. EdM is also burdened by serious inefficiencies and high operating costs, with average connection costs around US $200, twice the sub-Saharan average. Struggling to sustain supplies, EdM regularly resorts to the services of short-term emergency suppliers, usually deploying thermal generation systems, and imports of around 60 MW–80 MW from Côte d'Ivoire. There are also plans for an interconnector link to Guinea. Mali has great solar power potential, but this has been little exploited on a large scale, although the African Development Bank (AfDB) group is funding a 33-MW solar plant at Ségou and a 50-MW solar plant is also being developed at Fana. The Agence Française de Développement (AFD) is funding the doubling of the capacity of the supply link between the Manantali dam and Bamako at a cost of €80m. EdM hopes that an additional 20-MW plant near Bamako and the modernization of the medium tension supply link around the city will ease local supply problems.

Despite these initiatives, about one-half of all Malians have no access to electricity. Many communities are still not connected to the network, although a growing number of villages and households get some power from local solar panels and windmills.

MANUFACTURING AND SERVICES

The manufacturing sector is small, producing some import substitution goods and foodstuffs. The textiles market is flooded with cheap imports and only 2% of Mali's cotton production is transformed into textile products locally, by traditional craftsmen or by the Chinese-owned Compagnie Malienne des Textiles factor near Ségou.

Mali has a vibrant trading culture, and a wide range of service businesses, but the hospitality sector has long suffered from the security crisis, which deterred most tourists even before the advent of the COVID-19 pandemic.

The banking sector saw its balance sheet grow by 6.6% in 2018, while the proportion of loans categorized as nonperforming fell to 10.4% (from 12.9% the year before). However, the sector's combined net profit shrank by 16.2% as assets were depreciated by write-offs and risk provisions. Microfinance is relatively well developed, notably through the Union des Caisses Mutuelles d'Epargne et de Crédit (Kafo Jiginew), which was originally set up largely to support cotton farmers but has since broadened its activities and also moved into urban areas.

TRANSPORT AND COMMUNICATIONS

Being landlocked the competitiveness of the Malian economy is burdened by the time and cost required to move goods to or from the gateway ports of the West African coast—principally the major container terminals Dakar and Abidjan. Most goods are moved from and to these gateways mainly by all-weather tarmac roads in a good state of repair; the rail line from Bamako to Dakar is in a very poor condition, although preparations for restoration of the main Senegalese section are well advanced. Freight is also carried by rail from Abidjan to Ouangolodougou in northern Côte d'Ivoire, then transferred to trucks for onward carriage to Bamako. While Dakar and Abidjan have generally been the main trade gateways, when

ECOWAS imposed sanctions during the first half of 2022 significant volumes of trade were diverted through Nouakchott, the capital of Mauritania, and also through Conakry, the capital of Guinea, an ECOWAS member whose Government decided not to join the sanctions regime. Conakry is also the port that is geographically closest to Bamako.

Internally, the main highways to towns in the centre or south such as Kita, Bougouni or Mopti, and even some medium-sized towns are tarmac surfaced. However, the northern road network, notably to Gao, is in a much poorer state and there is no all-weather direct route from central Mali to Tombouctou, even though it is a regional capital.

Commercial air transport has developed slowly. A national carrier, Compagnie Aérienne du Mali, later renamed Air Mali, only operated from 2005 until the 2012 security crisis, but the Al-Sayegh group, based in the United Arab Emirates (UAE), has launched Sky Mali, which was granted an operator's certificate in July 2020. This newcomer operates scheduled flights from Bamako to Kayes, Mopti, Tombouctou and Gao, and to regional destinations including Dakar, Cotonou (Benin) and Libreville (Gabon). Malian Aéro Company operates air taxi and charter flights, often for mining companies, while the UN Humanitarian Air Service flies to towns in the centre and the north, in support of UN operations and development. Mali's sole international air gateway is the now expanded Senou airport at Bamako, served by African carriers and international companies, including Air France and Turkish Airlines. Political difficulties and sanctions led to the periodic suspension of some foreign airline services to Bamako for limited periods in the first half of 2022.

As across Africa, mobile telecommunications and the expansion of internet access have transformed consumers' ability to communicate locally and internationally, notably through products such as WhatsApp. Orange, Telecel and Malitel (the mobile subsidiary of the national telecommunications company Société des Télécommunications du Mali—Sotelma) provide services and in May 2021 the Government indicated that it would consider offering a fourth licence, to increase competition and reduce prices. Fixed-line services are provided by Sotelma, which is a subsidiary of Maroc Telecom, part of the Abu Dhabi-based Etisalat group.

FOREIGN TRADE AND PAYMENTS

Recent years have seen a gradual erosion of the structural deficit in Mali's current account balance of payments, contracting from 704,300m. francs CFA in 2017 to just 459,900m. francs CFA the following year, before a dramatic rebound to 755,100m. francs CFA in 2019, but a further contraction to just 375,200m. francs CFA in 2020. The scale of the deficit is heavily influenced by fluctuations in the cost of the fuel that Mali has to import and in the value of the gold that it exports, reflecting shifts in world commodity prices. The values of other imports and exports also tend to fluctuate, but to a smaller degree. Remittances from the Malian diaspora had been growing and remained stable, at 530,700m. francs CFA, in 2020, despite the pandemic-induced economic slowdown in countries with large expatriate communities, such as France and Côte d'Ivoire.

Within the overall current account, merchandise trade has recorded deficits of 342,100m. francs CFA in 2016 and 409,600m. francs CFA in 2017, but just 212,600m. francs CFA in 2018 and 373,600m. francs CFA the next year—and a mere 99,700m. francs CFA in 2020. Total imports were expanding steadily before the pandemic, from 2,402,300m. francs CFA in 2016 to 2,494,600m. francs CFA in 2017 and 2,623,900m. francs CFA in 2018, and then to 3,008,300m. francs CFA in 2019, but shrank slightly, to 2,807,100m. francs CFA in 2020. The cost of petroleum product imports surged from 445,700m. francs CFA in 2015 to 751,300m. francs CFA in 2019, but contracted to 609,600m. francs CFA as activity slowed in the 2020 pandemic year, whereas the cost of capital equipment—including goods for the investment-heavy mining

sector has slowly but steadily risen, from 543,200m. francs CFA in 2017 to 600,600m. francs CFA in 2020. The value of food imports, which of course partly reflects fluctuations in the volume of domestic harvests, was 412,600m. francs CFA in 2020.

Exports—dominated by gold—have been steadily rising, from 1,675,900m. francs CFA in 2016 to 1,685,900m. francs CFA in 2017 and 1,991,400m. francs CFA the year after, then 2,153,400m. francs CFA in 2019 and 2,258,300m. francs CFA in 2020. Gold has been the key driver of this trend, with exports rising from 1,120,400m. francs CFA in 2016 to 1,175,700m. francs CFA in 2017 and 1,388,400m. francs CFA in 2018, and then to 1,566,100m. francs CFA in 2019 and 1,833,300m. francs CFA in 2020. Sales of cotton climbed from 183,100m. francs CFA in 2015 to 270,700m. francs CFA in 2018, but fell back to 256,800m. francs CFA the following year and then slumped to just 149,900m. francs CFA in 2020, after farmers had reduced planting because of the low producer price. Livestock, often exported to coastal West African cities, is also an important earner, with sales worth 115,100m. francs CFA in 2019. The geographical pattern of Mali's good exports reflects the importance of the gold mining sector, with the UAE a key market, accounting for an annual average of 47.9% of all exports in 2015–19. Other key markets were Switzerland (21.9%), South Africa (11.3%) and the Asia-Pacific region (10.7%).

The services balance also records regular deficits, although these declined from 1,061,000m. francs CFA in 2016 to 868,000m. francs CFA in 2017 and to 839,900m. francs CFA in 2019, before rebounding to 998,100m. francs CFA in 2020. Within that overall total, freight and insurance costs accounted for 449,200. francs CFA in 2020. On the positive side of the balance, remittances from Malians expatriates rose from 460,200m. francs CFA in 2015 to 530,700m. francs CFA in 2020.

Mali is hugely reliant on support from external donors, amid European and US concerns about the country's protracted crisis and its impact on western Africa as a whole. The country receives large volumes of both humanitarian aid, budget support and long-term development assistance. Budget aid inflows totalled 45,500m. francs CFA in 2016 and 48,600m. francs CFA in 2018, but surged to 104,200m. francs CFA in 2019 and 250,100m. francs CFA in 2020. However, donors' confidence and readiness to sustain support has been sorely tested by repeated corruption scandals and weak governance, the military coups of 2012, 2020 and 2021 and the confrontational stance that the transitional regime has adopted towards European countries since mid-2021. When final figures for the levels of aid disbursed in 2021 and 2022 become available they may well show a decline in donor support. Moreover, insecurity hampers the implementation of projects and programmes in the northern and central regions.

Major partners include both multilateral and bilateral actors. The World Bank in December 2019 approved a US $250m. package of assistance for poverty reduction and stabilization and it has since approved projects to support COVID-19 emergency response and recovery, education, entrepreneurship and local services. The AfDB has a portfolio of 25 projects, of which the largest elements concern roads, agriculture, governance, energy, business, water and sanitation and measures to tackle the impacts of climate change; its new strategy for operations in Mali over 2021–25 includes a particular focus on supporting the agricultural sector value chain, to reduce economic fragilities. Other key partners include the EU, which provided a €665m. programme for 2014–20, as well as humanitarian aid, the UNDP and other UN agencies. Islamic and Arab donors, and key Western bilateral agencies such as the AFD, which focuses particularly on sanitation and water management, and the US Agency for International Development (USAID), which is heavily engaged in supporting agriculture education and health, are also active in Mali.

Statistical Survey

Source (unless otherwise stated): Institut National de la Statistique, BP 12, Avenue du Mali Hamdallaye ACI 2000, Bamako; tel. 2022-2455; e-mail direction@instat.gouv.ml; internet www.instat-mali.org.

Area and Population

AREA, POPULATION AND DENSITY

Area (sq km)	1,240,192*
Population (census results)	
17 April 1998†	9,790,492
1 April 2009	
Males	7,204,990
Females	7,323,672
Total	14,528,662
Population (UN estimates at mid-year)‡	
2020	20,250,834
2021§	20,855,724
2022§	21,473,776
Density (per sq km) at mid-2022§	17.3

* 478,841 sq miles.
† Figures are provisional and refer to the *de jure* population.
‡ Source: UN, *World Population Prospects: The 2019 Revision.*
§ Projection.

POPULATION BY AGE AND SEX
(UN projections at mid-2022)

	Males	Females	Total
0–14 years	5,065.9	4,898.6	9,964.5
15–64 years	5,466.5	5,514.7	10,981.2
65 years and over	232.6	295.5	528.1
Total	10,765.0	10,708.8	21,473.8

Source: UN, *World Population Prospects: The 2019 Revision.*

ADMINISTRATIVE DIVISIONS
(population at 2009 census)

District			Koulikoro	. . .	2,422,108
Bamako	. . .	1,810,366	Mopti	. . .	2,036,209
Regions			Ségou	. . .	2,338,349
Gao	. . .	542,304	Sikasso	. . .	2,643,179
Kayes	. . .	1,993,615	Tombouctou	. .	674,793
Kidal	. . .	67,739	**Total**	. . .	14,528,662

Note: In January 2016 two new regions—Taoudéni and Ménaka—were created in the north of the country in accordance with the peace agreement concluded between the Government and insurgents in mid-2015.

PRINCIPAL TOWNS*
(population at 2009 census)

Bamako (capital)	.	1,810,366	Ségou	. . .	133,501
Sikasso	. . .	226,618	Mopti	. . .	120,786
Kayes	. . .	149,129	Gao	. . .	86,353
Koutiala	. . .	141,444	Kati	. . .	84,500

* With the exception of Bamako, figures refer to the population of communes (municipalities).

Mid-2022 (incl. suburbs, UN projections): Bamako 2,816,943; Sikasso 424,574 (Source: UN, *World Urbanization Prospects: The 2018 Revision*).

BIRTHS AND DEATHS
(annual averages, UN estimates)

	2005–10	2010–15	2015–20
Birth rate (per 1,000) . . .	47.7	44.8	41.8
Death rate (per 1,000) . . .	13.6	11.6	9.8

Source: UN, *World Population Prospects: The 2019 Revision.*

Life expectancy (years at birth, estimates): 59.7 (males 58.9; females 60.5) in 2020 (Source: World Bank, World Development Indicators database).

EMPLOYMENT
('000 persons, 2009 census)

	Males	Females	Total
Agriculture, hunting and forestry .	2,264.2	1,239.0	3,503.2
Fishing	60.4	25.1	85.5
Mining	29.9	8.9	38.7
Manufacturing	133.5	55.5	189.0
Electricity, gas and water . . .	11.4	0.5	12.0
Construction	86.7	2.6	89.3
Wholesale and retail trade; repair of motor vehicles, motorcycles and personal household goods .	310.7	176.4	487.1
Hotels and restaurants . . .	4.3	4.2	8.5
Transport, storage and communications	137.5	21.2	158.7
Financial intermediation . . .	3.8	2.8	6.6
Real estate	41.7	7.9	49.6
Public administration	52.3	16.6	68.8
Education	169.8	87.6	257.3
Health and social work . . .	14.1	13.4	27.6
Other social services	59.3	114.3	173.6
Sub-total	3,379.6	1,776.0	5,155.5
Activities not adequately defined .	174.8	139.9	314.7
Total employed	3,554.1	1,915.9	5,470.1

Mid-2015 (estimates in '000): Agriculture, etc. 3,144; Total labour force 4,395 (Source: FAO).

Health and Welfare

KEY INDICATORS

Total fertility rate (children per woman, 2020)	5.7
Under-5 mortality rate (per 1,000 live births, 2020) . . .	91.0
HIV/AIDS (% of persons aged 15–49, 2020) . . .	0.9
COVID-19: Cumulative confirmed deaths (per 100,000 persons at 31 August 2022)	3.4
COVID-19: Fully vaccinated population (% of total population at 28 August 2022)	7.4
Physicians (per 1,000 head, 2018)	0.13
Hospitals (per 100,000 head, 2013)	0.46
Domestic health expenditure (2019): US $ per head (PPP) . .	31.8
Domestic health expenditure (2019): % of GDP	1.3
Domestic health expenditure (2019): public (% of total current expenditure)	33.6
Access to improved water resources (% of persons, 2020) . .	83
Access to improved sanitation facilities (% of persons, 2020) .	45
Total carbon dioxide emissions ('000 metric tons, 2018) . .	5,620
Carbon dioxide emissions per head (metric tons, 2018) . .	0.3
Human Development Index (2021): ranking	186
Human Development Index (2021): value	0.428

Note: For data on COVID-19 vaccinations, 'fully vaccinated' denotes receipt of all doses specified by approved vaccination regime (Sources: Johns Hopkins University and Our World in Data). Data on health expenditure refer to current general government expenditure in each case. For more information on sources and further definitions for all indicators, see Health and Welfare Statistics: Sources and Definitions section (europaworld.com/credits).

Agriculture

PRINCIPAL CROPS
('000 metric tons)

	2018	2019	2020
Bananas	196.4	196.4	200.5
Beans, dry*	150.0	161.2	163.2
Cashew nuts, with shell . .	167.6	167.6	173.2
Cassava (Manioc)	138.0	70.3	164.8
Cottonseed	656.6	710.7	147.2
Fonio (Millets)	27.9	40.5	44.0
Groundnuts, with shell . .	491.5	368.7	260.0
Karité nuts (Sheanuts) . . .	144.9	226.1	168.0
Maize	3,625.0	3,816.5	3,516.9
Mangoes, mangosteens and guavas	813.5	814.9	793.2
Millet	1,840.3	1,878.5	1,921.2
Onions, dry*	83.8	81.0	81.9
Rice, paddy	3,167.5	3,196.3	3,010.0
Sorghum	1,469.7	1,511.1	1,822.7
Sugar cane*	356.5	353.9	355.2
Sweet potatoes	504.6	312.5	573.2
Tomatoes	204.7	160.0	233.7
Watermelons	396.6	551.2	594.3
Yams	91.0	63.9	109.8

* FAO estimates.

Aggregate production ('000 metric tons, may include official, semi-official or estimated data): Total cereals 10,159.7 in 2018, 10,451.4 in 2019, 10,352.1 in 2020; Total fruit (primary) 1,865.0 in 2018, 2,023.9 in 2019, 2,350.3 in 2020; Total oilcrops 1,388.1 in 2018, 1,407.5 in 2019, 669.9 in 2020; Total pulses 435.7 in 2018, 403.1 in 2019, 390.4 in 2020; Total roots and tubers 1,044.5 in 2018, 750.0 in 2019, 1,073.7 in 2020; Total vegetables (primary) 2,022.4 in 2018, 2,092.7 in 2019, 2,535.3 in 2020.

Source: FAO.

LIVESTOCK
('000 head, year ending September)

	2018	2019	2020
Asses	1,122	1,144	1,167
Camels	1,217	1,241	1,266
Cattle	11,758	12,111	12,474
Chickens	47,255	49,618	52,098
Goats	25,225	26,486	27,811
Horses	573	584	596
Pigs	85	86	87
Sheep	18,270	19,184	20,143

Source: FAO.

LIVESTOCK PRODUCTS
('000 metric tons)

	2018	2019	2020
Camels' milk	265.7	271.0	271.0
Cattle hides, fresh*	7.9	7.9	11.0
Cattle meat	51.5*	54.6	71.3
Cattle offals, edible*	8.8	9.3	12.1
Cows' milk	268.6	276.6	284.9
Chicken meat*	52.9	55.3	57.8
Game meat*	24.8	24.6	24.6
Goat meat	8.2*	9.5	13.1
Goat offals, edible*	1.5	1.8	2.4
Goats' milk	231.5	243.1	255.2
Goats' skins, fresh*	1.2	1.4	1.9
Sheep meat	5.4*	6.6	7.8
Sheep offals, edible*	1.1	1.4	1.6
Sheep's (Ewe's) milk . . .	167.7	176.1	184.9
Sheepskins, fresh*	1.2	1.4	1.7
Hen eggs*	14.9	22.4	18.7

* FAO estimate(s).

Source: FAO.

Forestry

ROUNDWOOD REMOVALS
('000 cubic metres, excl. bark, FAO estimates)

	2018	2019	2020
Sawlogs, veneer logs and logs for sleepers	388	388	388
Other industrial wood	429	429	429
Fuel wood	5,783	5,835	5,889
Total	6,600	6,652	6,706

Source: FAO.

SAWNWOOD PRODUCTION
('000 cubic metres, incl. railway sleepers,)

	2018	2019	2020
Total (all broadleaved) . . .	130*	273	141*

* FAO estimate.

Source: FAO.

Fishing

('000 metric tons, live weight)

	2018	2019	2020
Capture	90.4	109.4	117.7
Nile tilapia	29.0	32.8	35.6
Elephantsnout fishes . . .	2.4	7.7	7.6
Characins	—	5.5	5.5
Black catfishes	1.2	4.4	4.3
North African catfish . . .	25.0	27.3	31.4
Nile perch	3.5	6.6	6.0
Other freshwater fishes . . .	29.3	25.2	27.3
Aquaculture	5.3*	7.0*	7.7
Total catch	95.7*	116.3*	125.4

* FAO estimate.

Source: FAO.

Mining

	2017	2018	2019*
Gold (kg)	46,483	55,029	61,000

* Estimate.

Source: US Geological Survey.

Industry

SELECTED PRODUCTS
('000 metric tons unless otherwise indicated)

	2016	2017	2018
Raw sugar	95	—	—
Electrical energy (million kWh) .	2,613	3,068	3,261*

* Estimate.

2007: Fish (dried, salted or in brine), smoked fish and edible fish meal 8.8.

Electrical energy (million kWh, estimate): 3,298 in 2019.

Sources: UN Industrial Commodity Statistics Database; UN Energy Statistics Database.

Finance

CURRENCY AND EXCHANGE RATES

Monetary Units
100 centimes = 1 franc de la Communauté Financière Africaine (CFA).

Sterling, Dollar and Euro Equivalents (31 May 2022)
£1 sterling = 770.824 francs CFA;
US $1 = 612.300 francs CFA;
€1 = 655.957 francs CFA;
10,000 francs CFA = £12.97 = $16.33 = €15.24.

Average Exchange Rate (francs CFA per US $)
2019   585.91
2020   575.59
2021   554.53

Note: An exchange rate of 1 French franc = 50 francs CFA, established in 1948, remained in force until January 1994, when the CFA franc was devalued by 50%, with the exchange rate adjusted to 1 French franc = 100 francs CFA. This relationship to French currency remained in effect with the introduction of the euro on 1 January 1999. From that date, accordingly, a fixed exchange rate of €1 = 655.957 francs CFA has been in operation.

BUDGET
('000 million francs CFA)*

Revenue†	2019‡	2020§	2021§
Budgetary revenue	1,571	1,488	1,692
Tax revenue	1,496	1,427	1,559
Non-tax revenue	75	60	134
Special funds and annexed budgets	411	397	420
Total	1,982	1,884	2,112

Expenditure‖	2019‡	2020§	2021§
Budgetary expenditure . . .	1,939	2,192	2,483
Current expenditure . . .	1,281	1,573	1,680
Wages and salaries . .	517	615	758
Interest payments (scheduled)	104	121	141
Other current expenditure .	659	838	781
Capital expenditure	658	618	803
Externally financed . .	192	187	348
Special funds and annexed budgets	411	397	420
Total	2,350	2,588	2,903

* Figures represent a consolidation of the central government budget, special funds and annexed budgets.
† Excluding grants received ('000 million francs CFA): 191 in 2019 (estimate); 140 in 2020 (projection); 202 in 2021 (projection).
‡ Estimates.
§ Projections.
‖ Excluding net lending ('000 million francs CFA): –6 in 2019 (estimate); –6 in 2020 (projection); n.a. in 2021 (projection).

Source: IMF, *Mali: Second and Third Reviews Under the Extended Credit Facility Arrangement. Requests for Waivers for Nonobservance of Performance Criteria and Modification of Performance Criterion—Press Release; Staff Report; and Statement by the Executive Director for Mali* (March 2021).

INTERNATIONAL RESERVES
(excl. gold, US $ million at 31 December)

	2019	2020	2021
IMF special drawing rights . .	229.4	476.1	769.8
Reserve position in IMF . . .	46.1	48.0	46.6
Foreign exchange	3.6	3.6	6.0
Total	279.1	527.7	822.4

Source: IMF, *International Financial Statistics.*

MONEY SUPPLY
('000 million francs CFA at 31 December)

	2019	2020	2021
Currency outside depository corporations	641.01	964.41	1,042.60
Transferable deposits . . .	1,478.72	1,660.38	2,030.06
Other deposits	879.97	1,040.23	1,216.80
Broad money	2,999.70	3,665.02	4,289.47

Source: IMF, *International Financial Statistics.*

COST OF LIVING
(Consumer Price Index: base: 2014 = 100)

	2019	2020	2021
Food and non-alcoholic beverages .	98.7	101.2	106.4
Clothing and footwear	103.8	106.0	107.0
Housing, water, electricity, gas and other fuels	106.8	107.6	106.5
All items (incl. others) . . .	100.8	101.3	105.2

NATIONAL ACCOUNTS
('000 million francs CFA at current prices)

Expenditure on the Gross Domestic Product

	2018	2019	2020
Government final consumption expenditure	1,505	1,594	1,618
Private final consumption expenditure	7,089	7,490	7,637
Changes in inventories . . .	167	136	–566
Gross fixed capital formation . .	1,773	2,029	1,992
Total domestic expenditure .	10,534	11,249	10,681
Exports of goods and services . .	2,325	2,530	2,640
Less Imports of goods and services	3,378	3,653	3,345
GDP in purchasers' values .	9,482	10,126	9,976
GDP at constant 2015 prices .	9,615	10,220	10,209

Gross Domestic Product by Economic Activity

	2018	2019	2020
Agriculture, hunting, forestry and fishing	3,517	3,727	3,519
Mining and utilities	82	90	92
Manufacturing	1,479	1,646	1,678
Construction	405	435	416
Wholesale and retail trade, restaurants and hotels . . .	1,012	1,055	1,017
Transport, storage and communications	459	483	503
Other services	1,846	1,959	2,009
Gross value added	8,801	9,394	9,234
Indirect taxes (net)*	681	732	742
GDP in purchasers' values .	9,482	10,126	9,976

* Figures obtained as a residual.

Source: UN National Accounts Main Aggregates Database.

BALANCE OF PAYMENTS
(US $ million)

	2018	2019	2020
Exports of goods f.o.b.	3,585.3	3,675.3	4,794.0
Imports of goods f.o.b.	–3,968.0	–4,312.9	–4,290.0
Trade balance	–382.8	–637.6	504.0
Exports of services	600.9	766.7	401.5
Imports of services	–2,113.0	–2,245.7	–2,049.1
Balance on goods and services	–1,894.8	–2,116.6	–1,143.6
Other income received . . .	176.2	142.0	154.4
Other income paid	–686.4	–837.5	–893.2
Balance on goods, services and income	–2,405.0	–2,812.1	–1,882.4
Current transfers received . .	1,717.2	1,706.9	1,669.8
Current transfers paid	–182.6	–216.0	–200.1

—continued	2018	2019	2020
Current balance	−870.5	−1,321.2	−412.7
Capital account (net) . . .	239.4	194.5	219.7
Direct investment assets . . .	−0.3	−1.0	−1.2
Direct investment liabilities . .	467.3	859.1	536.9
Portfolio investment assets . .	−49.0	−177.6	−322.1
Portfolio investment liabilities .	212.7	259.6	368.9
Other investment assets . .	−127.4	−42.1	−131.3
Other investment liabilities . .	235.0	401.6	−170.9
Net errors and omissions . . .	48.2	62.6	69.6
Reserves and related items .	155.4	235.5	156.9

Source: IMF, *International Financial Statistics*.

External Trade

PRINCIPAL COMMODITIES
(distribution by HS, US $ million)

Imports c.i.f.	2017	2018	2019
Vegetables and vegetable products	296.0	254.7	269.5
Cereals and cereal preparations .	170.6	142.5	161.4
Prepared foodstuffs; beverages, spirits, vinegar; tobacco and articles thereof .	281.0	304.1	309.7
Mineral products	1,275.8	1,553.8	1,702.4
Mineral fuels, lubricants, etc. .	1,037.4	1,307.6	1,475.5
Petroleum oil	998.3	1,263.9	1,361.3
Salt, sulphur, earth, stone, plaster, lime and cement	238.3	244.1	226.8
Cement	212.5	215.8	201.4
Chemicals and related products	581.8	553.2	630.6
Medicinal and pharmaceutical products	243.1	207.6	204.2
Medicaments	232.5	175.8	193.0
Fertilizers	163.2	148.3	208.9
Plastics, rubber, and articles thereof	152.2	175.4	176.3
Iron and steel, other base metals and articles of base metal	269.3	277.4	287.0
Articles of iron or steel . . .	143.5	119.9	121.0
Machinery and mechanical appliances; electrical equipment; parts thereof .	648.4	689.3	750.7
Machinery, boilers, etc. . . .	362.9	361.7	349.0
Electrical, electronic equipment .	285.5	327.6	401.8
Vehicles, aircraft, vessels and associated transport equipment	358.8	303.8	357.3
Road vehicles	300.6	278.4	338.7
Total (incl. others)	4,336.6	4,605.5	5,049.2

Exports f.o.b.	2017	2018	2019
Live animals and animal products	195.1	200.1	215.2
Live animals	190.7	195.2	210.9
Chemicals and related products	105.2	82.2	70.9
Fertilizers	90.5	61.4	52.7
Textiles and textile articles .	139.0	476.3	425.9
Cotton	134.6	474.0	425.2
Pearls, precious or semi-precious stones, precious metals, and articles thereof .	1,254.1	2,644.0	2,656.4
Total (incl. others)	1,902.7	3,624.3	3,642.3

Source: Trade Map-Trade Competitiveness Map, International Trade Centre, marketanalysis.intracen.org.

PRINCIPAL TRADING PARTNERS
('000 million francs CFA)

Imports c.i.f.	2017	2018	2019
Belgium	53.3	49.9	51.3
Benin	79.8	155.7	104.7
Brazil	67.9	52.1	87.2
China, People's Republic . . .	660.1	650.4	796.0
Côte d'Ivoire	419.3	457.6	536.2
Finland	52.3	36.5	40.0
France (incl. Monaco) . . .	341.7	398.4	401.5
Germany	156.0	158.3	149.9
Ghana	58.5	65.9	79.1
India	107.4	127.4	156.1
Italy	71.0	51.7	125.8
Japan	86.6	79.7	98.3
Morocco	80.0	80.0	78.5
Netherlands	152.0	40.9	44.5
Niger	101.5	73.5	109.9
Russian Federation	57.8	54.4	72.1
Senegal	889.8	1,062.4	1,136.0
South Africa	153.3	139.3	117.6
Spain	52.2	47.4	47.4
Türkiye	45.5	94.5	71.6
United Arab Emirates	37.1	35.1	51.4
United Kingdom	21.6	47.8	31.5
USA	144.6	143.0	142.3
Total (incl. others)	4,336.6	4,605.5	5,049.2

Exports f.o.b.	2017	2018	2019
Bangladesh	111.2	283.1	258.5
Burkina Faso	116.7	87.9	100.7
Côte d'Ivoire	93.9	100.5	154.4
India	52.2	22.3	55.2
Malaysia	6.2	78.5	36.5
Senegal	88.5	126.0	97.4
South Africa	780.2	1,364.0	1,328.1
Switzerland-Liechtenstein . .	407.8	1,239.8	1,297.6
Türkiye	23.4	19.4	5.5
United Arab Emirates . . .	29.5	40.8	19.5
Total (incl. others)	1,902.7	3,624.3	3,642.3

Source: Trade Map-Trade Competitiveness Map, International Trade Centre, marketanalysis.intracen.org.

Transport

RAILWAYS
(traffic)

	2014	2015	2016
Passenger carried ('000) . . .	81.9	29.1	8.8
Passenger-km (million) . . .	40.3	14.7	4.3
Freight carried ('000 metric tons) .	253	211	76

CIVIL AVIATION
(traffic on scheduled services at Bamako-Sénou Airport)

	2018	2019	2020
Aircraft movements	13,402	16,502	11,966
Passengers carried ('000) . . .	841.1	919.2	428.9
Freight carried ('000 metric tons) .	10.2	11.2	12.2

Tourism

FOREIGN TOURIST ARRIVALS BY NATIONALITY*

	2018	2019	2020
Algeria	1,610	1,290	388
Belgium	2,060	1,391	203
Burkina Faso	5,664	5,214	2,347
Cameroon	2,146	1,749	386
China, People's Republic	4,671	4,947	469
Congo, Republic	3,206	1,169	885
Côte d'Ivoire	10,901	10,491	5,558
France	30,269	34,577	35,792
Gabon	872	631	947
Germany	2,663	1,758	215
Guinea	6,037	4,821	1,126
Morocco	3,034	2,598	2,404
Senegal	11,071	10,029	5,206
South Africa	2,313	2,148	349
Spain	1,962	1,656	1,070
USA	6,744	6,518	1,340
Total (incl. others)	202,741	217,050	75,155

* International tourists passing through Bamako-Sénou Airport.

Tourism receipts (US $ million, excl. passenger transport): 200 in 2016; 206 in 2017; 227 in 2018.

Source: World Tourism Organization.

Communications Media

	2018	2019	2020
Telephones ('000 main lines in use)	228.1	242.2	281.6
Mobile telephone subscriptions ('000)	21,955.6	22,925.5	25,315.6
Broadband subscriptions, fixed ('000)	120.9	142.5	243.8
Broadband subscriptions, mobile ('000)	5,776.7	6,894.5	9,372.1
Internet users (% of population)*	21.4	24.2	27.4

* Estimates.

Source: International Telecommunication Union.

Education

(2017/18 unless otherwise indicated)

	Institutions*	Teachers	Students ('000)		
			Males	Females	Total
Pre-primary	212	6,677	65.6	65.5	131.1
Primary	2,871	65,485	1,323.1	1,154.0	2,477.1
Secondary	n.a.	58,364†	580.9	465.6	1,046.5
Tertiary†	n.a.	2,356	51.4	21.2	72.6

* 1998/99 figures.
† 2016/17 figures.

Note: Totals may not be equal to the sum of components, owing to rounding.

2005/06: *Pre-primary*: 412 institutions; 1,510 teachers; 51,071 students; *Primary and Secondary (lower)*: 8,079 institutions; 39,109 teachers; 1,990,765 students (1,137,787 males, 852,978 females); *Secondary (higher)*: 121 institutions; 1,904 teachers; 47,279 students (31,724 males, 15,555 females—estimates); *Secondary (technical and vocational)*: 119 institutions; 41,137 students; *Secondary (teacher-training)*: 10,467 students (Source: Office of the Secretary-General of the Government, Bamako).

Source: mainly UNESCO Institute for Statistics.

Pupil-teacher ratio (primary education, UNESCO estimate): 37.8 in 2017/18 (Source: UNESCO Institute for Statistics).

Adult literacy rate (UNESCO estimates): 35.5% (males 46.2%; females 25.7%) in 2018 (Source: UNESCO Institute for Statistics).

Directory

The Constitution

The Constitution of the Third Republic of Mali was approved in a national referendum on 12 January 1992. The document upholds the principles of national sovereignty and the rule of law in a secular, multi-party state, and provides for the separation of powers of the executive, legislative and judicial organs of state.

Executive power is vested in the President of the Republic, who is head of state and is elected for five years by universal adult suffrage. The President appoints the Prime Minister, who, in turn, appoints other members of the Council of Ministers.

Legislative authority is exercised by the unicameral 147-member National Assembly, which is elected for five years by universal adult suffrage.

The Constitution guarantees the independence of the judiciary. Final jurisdiction in constitutional matters is vested in a Constitutional Court.

The rights, freedoms and obligations of Malian citizens are enshrined in the Constitution. Freedom of the press and of association are guaranteed.

Following the assumption of power by the Comiteé National pour le Salut du Peuple on 18 August 2020, the National Assembly was dissolved; under a Transitional Charter, a Transitional President was inaugurated with a mandate to oversee an 18-month transitional period. A 121-member interim legislative body, the Conseil National de Transition (CNT), was appointed by the Transitional President on 3 December. On 21 February 2022 the CNT voted to amend the Transitional Charter, providing for extension of the transitional period for a further five years; an increase in the size of the CNT to 147 members was also approved.

The Government

HEAD OF STATE

Transitional President: Col ASSIMI GOÏTA (assumed power 27 May 2021; inaugurated 7 June 2021).

COUNCIL OF MINISTERS
(October 2022)

Interim Prime Minister, Minister of Territorial Administration and Decentralization, Government Spokesperson: Lt-Col ABDOULAYE MAÏGA.

Minister of Defence and War Veterans: Col SADIO CAMARA.

Minister of Justice and Human Rights, Keeper of the Seals: MAHAMADOU KASSOGUÉ.

Minister of State Reconstruction, in charge of Relations with the Institutions: IBRAHIM IKASSA MAÏGA.

Minister of Security and Civil Protection: Col-Maj. DAOUDA ALY MOHAMMEDINE.

Minister of Reconciliation, Peace and National Cohesion, in charge of the Peace Accord and National Reconciliation: Col-Maj. ISMAËL WAGUÉ.

Minister of Transport and Infrastructure: MADINA DEMBÉLE SISSOKO.

Minister of Foreign Affairs and International Co-operation: ABDOULAYE DIOP.

Minister of the Economy and Finance: ALOUSSÉNI SANOU.

Minister of National Education: DEDEOU SIDIBÉ OUSMANE.

Minister of Higher Education and Scientific Research: AMADOU KEÏTA.

Minister of Mining, Energy and Water: LAMINE SEYDOU TRAORÉ.

Minister of Health and Social Development: DIÉMINATOU SANGARÉ.

Minister of Labour, the Civil Service and Social Dialogue: AOUA PAUL DIALLO DIAWARA.

Minister of Youth and Sport, in charge of Civic Education and Citizen-Building: MOUSSA AG ATTAHER.

Minister of Malians Abroad and African Integration: ALHAMDOU AG ILYENE.

Minister of Rural Development: MODIBO KEÏTA.

Minister of National Entrepreneurship, Employment and Professional Training: BAKARY DOUMBIA.

Minister of the Promotion of Women, Children and the Family: FOUNÈ COULIBALY WADIDIÉ.

Minister of Industry and Trade: MAHMOUD OULD MOHAMED.

Minister of Town Planning, Housing, Properties, Land Management and Population: BRÉHIMA KAMENA.

Minister of the Environment, Sanitation and Sustainable Development: MODIBO KONÉ.

Minister of Communication, the Digital Economy and Administrative Modernization: HAROUNA MAMADOU TOUREH.

Minister of Handicrafts, Culture, the Hotel Industry and Tourism: ANDOGOLY GUINDO.

Minister of Religious Affairs, Cults and Customs: MAMADOU KONÉ.

Minister-delegate to the Prime Minister, in charge of Political and Institutional Reform: FATOUMATA SÉKOU DICKO.

Minister-delegate to the Minister of Health and Social Development, in charge of Humanitarian Action, Solidarity, Refugees and Displaced Persons: OUMAROU DIARRA.

Minister-delegate to the Minister of Rural Development, in charge of Stockbreeding and Fisheries: YOUBA BA.

MINISTRIES

Office of the President: BP 10, Koulouba, Bamako; tel. 2070-2000; internet www.koulouba.ml.

Office of the Prime Minister: Quartier du Fleuve, BP 790, Bamako; tel. 2022-4310; internet www.primature.gov.ml.

Ministry of Communication, the Digital Economy and Administrative Modernization: Bamako; e-mail segal@communication.gouv.ml; internet communication.gouv.ml.

Ministry of Defence and War Veterans: route de Koulouba, BP 2083, Bamako; tel. 2022-5021.

Ministry of the Economy and Finance: BP 234, Bamako; tel. 2222-5858; internet finances.ml.

Ministry of the Environment, Sanitation and Sustainable Development: Bamako; internet www.environnement.gouv.ml.

Ministry of Foreign Affairs and International Co-operation: BP 11, Koulouba, Bamako; tel. 2023-0733; internet diplomatie.gouv.ml.

Ministry of Handicrafts, Culture, the Hotel Industry and Tourism: Cité Administrative, Bâtiment No. 05, BP E4075, Bamako; tel. 2001-5000; e-mail malibiennale@yahoo.fr; internet www.culture.gouv.ml.

Ministry of Health and Social Development: BP 232, Koulouba, Bamako; tel. 2023-4266; internet www.sante.gov.ml.

Ministry of Higher Education and Scientific Research: BP E5466, Bamako; tel. 2001-5900; e-mail contact.mesrs@gmail.com; internet fb.com/mesrs.

Ministry of Industry and Trade: Cité Administrative, Batiment No. 6 RDC, 1er Étage, BP 234, Koulouba, Bamako; tel. 2001-6000; e-mail info@investmali.gouv.ml; internet www.investir.gouv.ml.

Ministry of Justice and Human Rights: Cité Administrative, Bâtiment No 12, 3e Étage, BP 97, Bamako; tel. 2001-5914; internet www.justice.gouv.ml.

Ministry of Labour, the Civil Service and Social Dialogue: Bamako; tel. 76338261.

Ministry of Malians Abroad and African Integration: Cité Administrative, Bâtiment 6, Hamdallaye ACI 2000, Bamako; tel.

2001-6000; e-mail maliensdelexterieur@yahoo.fr; internet www.maliens-exterieur.gouv.ml.

Ministry of Mining, Energy and Water: BP 238, Bamako; tel. 2001-3500; e-mail info@mines.gouv.ml; internet www.mines.gouv.ml.

Ministry of National Education: Bamako; e-mail education2010@gmail.com; internet www.education.gouv.ml.

Ministry of National Entrepreneurship, Employment and Professional Training: Bamako.

Ministry of the Promotion of Women, Children and the Family: porte G9, rue 109, Badalabougou, BP 2688, Bamako; tel. 2022-6659; e-mail contact@mpfef.gouv.ml; internet mpfef.gouv.ml.

Ministry of Reconciliation, Peace and National Cohesion: Cité Administrative, Hamdallaye, Bâtiment No. 2, Bamako; tel. 2020-9600; e-mail mrpcr32@gmail.com; internet reconciliation.gouv.ml.

Ministry of Religious Affairs, Cults and Customs: Bamako; internet fb.com/MARCCMALI.

Ministry of Rural Development: Bamako.

Ministry of Security and Civil Protection: BP E 4771, Bamako; tel. 2022-0082; internet securite.gouv.ml.

Ministry of State Reconstruction: Bamako.

Ministry of Territorial Administration and Decentralization: Bamako; tel. 2022-4212; e-mail info@matcl.gouv.ml; internet www.matcl.gov.ml.

Ministry of Town Planning, Housing, Properties, Land Management and Population: Bamako.

Ministry of Transport and Infrastructure: Bamako; tel. 6512-1221; internet fb.com/mieccom.

Ministry of Youth and Sport: Bamako; tel. 6678-3123; internet fb.com/MJSREPMALI.

President

Presidential Election, First Round, 29 July 2018

Candidate	Valid votes	% of valid votes
Ibrahim Boubacar Keïta (RPM)	1,331,132	41.57
Soumaïla Cissé (URD)	567,679	17.73
Aliou Boubacar Diallo (ADP-Maliba)	256,404	8.00
Cheick Mohamed Abdoulaye Souad 'Modibo' Diarra (RpDM)	236,025	7.37
Housseini Amion Guindo (CODEM)	124,506	3.89
Others*	686,403	21.44
Total	3,202,149†	100.00

* There were 19 other candidates.
† The figure declared by the Constitutional Court for the total number of valid votes was 3,192,149. In addition, there were 224,069 invalid or cancelled votes.

Presidential Election, Second Round, 12 August 2018

Candidate	Valid votes	% of valid votes
Ibrahim Boubacar Keïta (RPM)	1,791,926	67.16
Soumaïla Cissé (URD)	876,124	32.84
Total	2,668,050*	100.00

* In addition, there were 85,648 invalid votes.

Legislature

Following the resignation of President Ibrahim Boubacar Keïta on 18 August 2020 and the subsequent assumption of power by the Comité National pour le Salut du Peuple, the National Assembly was dissolved. On 5 December the appointment of 121 members to an interim legislative body—the Conseil National de Transition, CNT—was announced. On the following day Col Malick Diaw was elected to the presidency of that body. On 21 February 2022 the CNT voted to amend the Transitional Charter, providing for extension of the transitional period for a further five years; an increase in the size of the CNT to 147 members was also approved.

Election Commission

Commission Electorale Nationale Indépendante (CENI): Bamako; Pres. AMADOU BAH.

Advisory Councils

Economic, Social and Cultural Council: BP E 15, Koulouba, Bamako; tel. 2022-4368; internet cesc-mali.ml; f. 1987; Pres. Dr YACOUBA KATILÉ.

High Council of Communities: Bamako; compulsorily advises the Govt on issues relating to local and regional devt; comprises national councillors, elected indirectly for a term of five years; Pres. MAMADOU SATIGUI DIAKITÉ.

Political Organizations

Alliance pour la Démocratie au Mali-Parti Pan-Africain pour la Liberté, la Solidarité et la Justice (ADEMA-PASJ): rue Fankélé, porte 145, BP 1791, Bamako-Coura; tel. 2023-0368; internet www.adema-pasj.org; f. 1990 as Alliance pour la Démocratie au Mali; Pres. TIEMOKO SANGARÉ; Sec.-Gen. ASSARID AG IMBARCAOUANE.

Alliance Démocratique pour la Paix (ADP-MALIBA): Bamako; internet fb.com/adpmaliba; Leader ALIOU BOUBACAR DIALLO.

Alliance pour la Solidarité au Mali-Convergence des Forces Patriotiques (ASMA-CFP): rue 662, porte 537, Tomikorobougou, Bamako; Pres. SOUMEYLOU BOUBÈYE MAÏGA.

Ansar Dine: f. 2012; Islamist; seeks to impose *Shari'a* law in Mali; Pres. IYAD AG AGALY.

Bloc des Alternances pour le Renouveau, l'Intégration et la Coopération Africaine (BARICA): Faladié Sema, ave de l'OUA, Bamako; Pres. MAMADOU SINAYOKO.

Congrès National d'Initiative Démocratique—Faso Yiriwa Ton (CNID—FYT): 192 rue du Commissariat Garantiguibougou, 300 Logements, BP 2572, Bamako; tel. 77117777; e-mail mc_tall@ hotmail.com; f. 1991; Chair. MOUNTAGA TALL; Sec.-Gen. Dr AMADOU SY.

Convention Démocratique et Sociale (CDS): Quinzambougou, rue 535, porte 112, Bamako; tel. 2029-2625; f. 1996; Chair. MAMADOU BAKARY SANGARÉ.

Convention Parti du Peuple (COPP): Hippodrome, rue 234, angle rue 287, porte 1345, BP 9012, Bamako; e-mail lawyergakou@datatech.toolnet.org; f. 1996; Pres. MAMADOU GACKOU.

Convergence pour le Développement du Mali (CODEM): rue 296, porte 162, Bamako; Pres. HOUSSEINOU AMION GUINDO.

Forces Alternatives pour le Renouveau et l'Emergence (FARE): Ex Imacy, ave Cheick Zayed, Dravela, Bamako; tel. 76374461; Leader MODIBO SIDIBÉ.

Mouvement pour l'Indépendance, la Renaissance et l'Intégration Africaine (MIRIA): Dravéla, Bolibana, rue 417, porte 66, Bamako; tel. 2029-2981; e-mail miria12002@yahoo.fr; f. 1994 following split in ADEMA; Pres. MAMADOU KASSA TRAORÉ.

Mouvement Islamique de l'Azawad (MIA): f. 2013 following breakaway from Ansar Dine; Tuareg; Sec.-Gen. ALGABAS AG INTALLA.

Mouvement National de Libération de l'Azawad (MNLA): internet www.mnlamov.net; f. 2011; Tuareg movement seeking independence for the Azawad region; Gen. Sec. BILAL AG ACHERIF.

Mouvement Patriotique pour le Renouveau (MPR): Quinzambougou, BP E 1108, Bamako; tel. 2021-5546; f. 1995; Pres. Dr CHOGUEL KOKALLA MAÏGA.

Mouvement Unité pour le Jihad en Afrique de l'Ouest (MUJAO): f. 2011; seeks to launch a *jihad* across West Africa; Leader SULTAN OULD BADI.

Parti Citoyen pour le Renouveau (PCR): Niaréla II, rue 428, porte 592, Bamako; tel. 66720988; internet pcrmali.net; f. 2005; Pres. OUSMANE BEN FANA TRAORÉ.

Parti pour le Développement Economique et la Solidarité (PDES): Hamdallaye, ACI 2000, rue 320, porte 200, Bamako; f. 2010; Pres. HAMED DIANE SÉMÉGA.

Parti pour l'Indépendance, la Démocratie et la Solidarité (PIDS): Hippodrome, rue 300, porte 426, BP E 1515, Bamako; tel. 2077-4575; f. 2001; Pres. DABA DIAWARA.

Parti pour la Renaissance Nationale (PARENA): rue Soundiata, porte 1397, BP E 2235, Ouolofobougou, Bamako; tel. 2023-4954; internet fb.com/parenamali; f. 1995 following split in CNID; Pres. TIÉBILÉ DRAMÉ; Sec.-Gen. DJIGUIBA KEÏTA.

Parti pour la Restauration des Valeurs du Mali—Fasoko (PRVM—Fasoko): Cité UNICEF, rue 58, porte 334, Niamakoro, Bamako; Pres. MAMADOU OUMAR SIDIBÉ.

Parti de la Solidarité Africaine pour la Démocratie et l'Indépendance (SADI): Djélibougou, rue 246, porte 559, BP 3140, Bamako; tel. 2024-1004; internet www.partisadi.net; f. 2002; Pres. Dr OUMAR MARIKO.

Parti pour la Solidarité et le Progrès (PSP): rue 552, porte 255, Quinzambougou, Bamako; tel. 2022-9960; internet psp-mali.jimdo .com; f. 1945; Pres. OUMAR HAMMADOUN DICKO.

Rassemblement pour la Démocratie et le Progrès (RDP): Niarela, rue 485, porte 11, BP 2110, Bamako; tel. 2021-3092; f. 1991; Pres. BISSI SANGARÉ.

Rassemblement pour le Développement du Mali (RpDM): rue 300, porte 320, Bamako; tel. 70217773; e-mail rpdmcom@gmail.com; internet rpdm.ml; Pres. CHEICK M. A. S. (MODIBO) DIARRA.

Rassemblement pour le Mali (RPM): Hippodrome, rue 232, porte 130, BP 9057, Bamako; tel. 2021-1433; e-mail siegerpmbko@yahoo .fr; internet rpm.ml; f. 2001; Pres. Dr BOCARY TRETA; Sec.-Gen. BABER GANO.

Union pour la Démocratie et le Développement (UDD): ave OUA, porte 3626, Sogoniko, BP 2969, Bamako; tel. 2020-4694; f. 1991; Leader HASSANE BARRY.

Union des Forces Démocratiques pour le Progrès—Sama-ton (UFDP): Quartier Lafiabougou, BP E 37, Bamako; tel. 2023-7273; f. 1991; Pres. (vacant).

Union Malienne du Rassemblement Démocratique Africain Faso Jigi (UM-RDA FASO JIGI): Commune II, Hippodrome, rue RDA, porte 41, face Champ Hippique, BP E 1413, Bamako; tel. 2021-4522; f. 2010; Pres. (vacant).

Union pour la République et la Démocratie (URD): Badalabougou, rue 105, porte 483, Bamako; tel. 2022-8642; e-mail segal@ urd-mali.org; internet urd-mali.org; f. 2003; Pres. (vacant); Sec.-Gen. MADANI TRAORÉ.

Yelema: Hamdallaye, BP E 2546, Bamako; tel. 75444534; e-mail yelema@yelema.net; internet www.yelema.net; Pres. (vacant); Sec.-Gen. ASSETOU SANGARE ROBICHAUD.

Diplomatic Representation

EMBASSIES IN MALI

Algeria: ave de l'OUA, Daoudabougou, BP 02, Bamako; tel. 2020-1883; e-mail bamakoalger@gmail.com; internet dzembassy-mali .com; Ambassador EL HAOUÉS RIACHE.

Belgium: rue 247, porte 209, Quartier Hippodrome, BP E1633, Bamako; tel. 2021-9622; e-mail bamako@diplobel.fed.be; internet mali.diplomatie.belgium.be; Ambassador JURGEN VAN MEIRVENNE.

Brazil: rue 113, porte 62, Badalabougou-ouest, Bamako; tel. 2022-9817; e-mail brasemb.bamako@itamaraty.gov.br; internet www.gov .br/mre/pt-br/embaixada-bamako; Ambassador CARLOS EDUARDO DE RIBAS GUEDES.

Burkina Faso: Quartier Hamdallaye ACI 2000, rue 204, porte 394, BP 9022, Bamako; tel. 2023-3171; e-mail info@ambfasomali.org; internet ambassadeburkina-ml.org; Ambassador KODIO LOUGUÉ.

Canada: route de Koulikoro, Immeuble Séméga, Commune II, BP 198, Bamako; tel. 4498-0450; e-mail bmakog@international.gc.ca; internet www.canadainternational.gc.ca/mali; Ambassador MICHAEL ELLIOT.

China, People's Republic: 2259 route de Koulikoro, Hippodrome, BP 112, Bamako; tel. 2021-3597; e-mail chinaemb_ml@mfa.gov.cn; internet ml.china-embassy.gov.cn; Ambassador CHEN ZHIHONG.

Côte d'Ivoire: square Patrice Lumumba, Immeuble CNAR, 3e étage, BP E 3644, Bamako; tel. 2022-0389; internet www.mali .diplomatie.gouv.ci; Ambassador CHEICK IBRAHIM BAKAYOKO.

Cuba: rue 23, porte 2394, Faso Kanu, Comunne V, BP 4105, Bamako; tel. 2020-0288; e-mail emcuba.mali@orangemali.net; internet misiones.minrex.gob.cu/es/mali; Ambassador LILIANA GARCÍA SOCCARAS.

Denmark: Lots 94–95, Cité du Niger II, BP E 1733, Bamako; tel. 2070-5300; e-mail bkoamb@um.dk; internet mali.um.dk; Ambassador ROLF PEREIRA HOLMBOE.

Egypt: Badalabougou-est, BP 44, Bamako; tel. 2022-3565; e-mail embassy.bamako@mfa.gov.eg; Ambassador KARIM MUHAMMAD SADAT ABDEL KARIM.

France: square Patrice Lumumba, BP 17, Bamako; tel. 4497-5757; e-mail cad.bamako-amba@diplomatie.gouv.fr; internet ml .ambafrance.org; Chargé d'affaires a.i. MARC DIDIO.

Germany: ave de l'OUA, rue 14, porte 330, Badalabougou-est, BP 100, Bamako; tel. 2070-0770; e-mail info@bamako.diplo.de; internet bamako.diplo.de; Ambassador DIETRICH POHL.

Ghana: ACI 2000 Hamdallaye, rue 408, porte 130, BP 3161, Bamako; tel. 2029-6083; e-mail bamako@mfa.gov.gh; internet bamako.mfa.gov.gh; Ambassador NAPOLEON ABDULAI.

Guinea: Immeuble Saybou Maïga, Quartier du Fleuve, BP 118, Bamako; tel. 2022-3007; e-mail ambaguibamako@mae.gov.gn; Ambassador Gen. FODÉ KEITA.

India: 101 ave de l'OUA, Badalabougou-est, BP 8008, Bamako; tel. 2023-5420; e-mail admn.bamako@mea.gov.in; internet www .embassyofindiabamako.gov.in; Ambassador ANJANI KUMAR.

Iran: ave al-Quds, Hippodrome, BP 2136, Bamako; tel. 2021-7638; e-mail akt_ambiranbko@yahoo.fr; internet mali.mfa.gov.ir; Ambassador HOSSEIN TALESHI SALEHANI.

Italy: Bamako; Ambassador STEFANO ANTONIO DEJAK.

Japan: ave du Mali, ACI 2000 Hamdallaye, Bamako; tel. 4497-9220; internet www.ml.emb-japan.go.jp; Ambassador DAISUKE KUROKI.

Korea, Democratic People's Republic: Bamako; Ambassador KIM JUN GAP.

Libya: Badalabougou-ouest, face Palais de la Culture, BP 1670, Bamako; tel. 2022-3496; Ambassador Dr ALI MUHAMMAD AL-MAGOURI.

Mauritania: route de Koulikoro, Hippodrome, BP 135, Bamako; tel. 2021-4815; e-mail ambarimbko@yahoo.fr; Ambassador AHMEDOU OULD AHMEDOU.

Morocco: Faso-Kanou, ave de l'OUA, BP 2013, Bamako; tel. 2022-2123; e-mail marocambamako@gmail.com; internet fb.com/ AmbassadeduRoyaumeduMarocauMali; Ambassador DRISS ISBAYENE.

Netherlands: Hamdallaye ACI 2000, rue 250, porte 31, BP 2220, Hippodrome, Bamako; tel. 4497-8200; e-mail bam@minbuza.nl; internet www.paysbasetvous.nl/votre-pays-et-les-pays-bas/mali; Ambassador MARCHEL GERRMANN.

Niger: rue 47, Cité du Niger II, Villa 2L 100, BP 856, Bamako; tel. 2021-4364; e-mail ambnigerml15@yahoo.com; internet ambniger-mali.org; Ambassador MAMOUDOU MOUMOUNI.

Nigeria: Badalabougou-est, BP 57, Bamako; tel. 2021-5328; e-mail nigeria.bamako@foreignaffairs.gov.ng; Ambassador CHIKEZIE OGBONNA NWACHUKWU.

Norway: Cité du Niger, Bamako; tel. 75430325; e-mail emb .bamako@mfa.no; internet www.norway.no/mali; Ambassador RIGMOR ELIANNE KOTI.

Qatar: Bamako; Ambassador AHMED BIN ABDULRAHMAN AL SUNAIDI.

Russian Federation: BP 300, Niarela, Bamako; tel. 2021-5592; e-mail ambassade.russe@mail.ru; internet rusembmali.mid.ru; Ambassador IGOR A. GROMYKO.

Saudi Arabia: Hamdallaye ACI 2000, BP 81, Bamako; tel. 2021-2528; internet embassies.mofa.gov.sa/sites/mali; Ambassador KHALID BIN MABROUK AL-KHALID.

Senegal: rue 50, porte 636, Badalabougou-ouest, BP 42, Bamako; tel. 2021-8273; e-mail ambassenemali@yahoo.fr; internet ambasenegal-mali.org; Ambassador ASSANE N'DOYE.

South Africa: Bâtiment Diarra, Hamdallaye ACI 2000, BP 2015, Bamako; tel. 2029-2925; e-mail bamako@dirco.gov.za; Ambassador (vacant).

Spain: Batîment Fondation de l'Enfance, 2ème étage, rue 260, Hamdallaye ACI 2000, BP 3230, Bamako; tel. 2070-7350; e-mail emb.bamako@maec.es; internet www.exteriores.gob.es/embajadas/ bamako; Ambassador JOSÉ HORNERO GÓMEZ.

Sweden: Immeuble UATT, 2ème étage, Quartier du Fleuve, BP E2093, Bamako; tel. 2070-7000; e-mail ambassaden.bamako@gov.se; internet www.swedenabroad.com/bamako; Ambassador KRISTINA KÜHNEL.

Tunisia: Hamdallaye ACI 2000, rue 329, porte 53, Bamako; tel. 2023-1754; e-mail at.bamako@diplomatie.gov.tn; Ambassador KHEMAIS MESTIRI.

Türkiye (Turkey): Cité du Niger, M-105/112, Niarela, Bamako; tel. 2021-0281; e-mail ambassade.bamako@mfa.gov.tr; internet bamako .be.mfa.gov.tr; Ambassador MURAT MUSTAFA ONART.

United Kingdom: Cité du Niger II, Bamako; tel. 4497-6913; e-mail bebamako@fco.gov.uk; internet www.gov.uk/world/organisations/ british-embassy-bamako; Ambassador BARRY LOWEN.

USA: ACI 2000, rue 243, porte 297, Bamako; tel. 2070-2300; e-mail webmaster@usa.org.ml; internet ml.usembassy.gov; Ambassador DENNIS B. HANKINS.

Venezuela: Badalabougou-ouest, rue 50, prés du Palais de la Culture, BP E34690, Bamako; tel. 2023-2531; e-mail ambavenemali@ orangemali.net; Ambassador OSCAR ERNESTO ROMERO VALLENILLA.

Judicial System

The 1992 Constitution guarantees the independence of the judiciary.

High Court of Justice: ACI 2000, pl. Can, Bamako; tel. 4497-8357; e-mail hautecourdejustice2017@gmail.com; internet hautecourdejustice.ml; competent to try the President of the Republic and government ministers for high treason and for crimes committed in the course of their duties, and their accomplices in any case where state security is threatened; mems designated by the mems of the Assemblée Nationale, and renewed annually; Pres. ISSIAKA SIDIBÉ.

Supreme Court: BP 7, Bamako; tel. 2022-2406; e-mail csupreme@ afribone.net.ml; f. 1969; comprises judicial, administrative and auditing sections; judicial section comprises five chambers, administrative section comprises two chambers, auditing section comprises three chambers; Pres. Dr FATOMA THÉRA; Sec.-Gen. ABOUBACAR GUISSÉ.

Constitutional Court: Hamdallaye ACI 2000, Commune IV, BP E 213, Bamako; tel. 2023-4239; internet www.courconstitutionnelle .ml; f. 1994; Pres. AMADOU OUSMANE TOURÉ.

There are three Courts of Appeal, seven Magistrates' Courts and also courts for labour disputes.

Religion

According to the 2009 census, 94.8% of the population were Muslims, while 2.4% were Christians and 2.0% followed traditional animist beliefs.

ISLAM

Association Malienne pour l'Unité et le Progrès de l'Islam (AMUPI): Annexe Grande Mosquée, Bamako; internet fb.com/ Association-Malienne-pour-lUnité-et-le-Pro- grès-de-lIslam-AMUPI-920039734799414; state-endorsed Islamic governing body; Pres. El Hadj ISSIAKA TRAORÉ.

Haut Conseil Islamique du Mali (HCIM): Bamako; tel. 2029-6078; internet fb.com/hciml; f. 2002; responsible for management of relations between the Muslim communities and the state; Pres. CHÉRIF OUSMANE MADANI HAÏDARA.

CHRISTIANITY

The Roman Catholic Church

Mali comprises one archdiocese and five dioceses.

Bishops' Conference: Conférence Episcopale du Mali, Archevêché, BP 298, Bamako; tel. 2022-5842; e-mail emission.catholique@gmail .com; internet eglisemali.org; f. 1973; Pres. Most Rev. JONAS DEMBÉLÉ (Bishop of Kayes).

Archbishop of Bamako: Cardinal JEAN ZERBO (Cardinal-Priest of San Silvestro in Capite), Archevêché, BP 298, Bamako; tel. 2222-5842.

BAHÁ'Í FAITH

National Spiritual Assembly: BP 1657, Bamako; e-mail bahaimali@hotmail.com.

The Press

DAILY NEWSPAPERS (PRINT AND ONLINE)

Les Echos: Hamdallaye, ave Cheick Zayed, porte 2694, BP 2043, Bamako; tel. 2029-6289; e-mail lesechos@jamana.org; internet lesechos.ml; f. 1989; daily; publ. by Jamana cultural co-operative; Editor-in-Chief ABOUBACAR SALIPH DIARRA.

L'Essor: sq. Patrice Lumumba, BP 141, Bamako; tel. 2022-3683; internet lessor.ml; f. 1949; daily; pro-Govt newspaper; Dir-Gen. BREHIMA TOURÉ.

L'Indépendant: rue 360, porte 276, ACI 2000, Djikoroni Para, BP E 1040, Bamako; tel. 2029-0602; e-mail contact@lindependant-mali .net; internet lindependant-mali.net; Dir El Hadj SAOUTI LABASS HAÏDARA.

Info Matin: 56 rue 350, Bamako Coura, BP E 4020, Bamako; tel. 7541-4141; internet info-matin.ml; independent.

Le Pays: Bamako; internet lepays.ml; Dir of Publication BOUBACAR YALCOUÉ.

Le Républicain: 116 rue 400, Dravéla-Bolibana, BP 1484, Bamako; tel. 2029-0900; f. 1992; independent; Dir BOUKARY DAOU.

PERIODICALS

L'Aurore: Niarela 298, rue 438, BP 3150, Bamako; tel. 2021-6922; e-mail aurore@timbagga.com.ml; f. 1990; 2 a week; independent; Dir KARAMOKO N'DIAYE.

Le Canard Déchaîné: Immeuble Koumara, bloc 104, Centre Commercial, Bamako; tel. 76212686; weekly; satirical; Dir OUMAR BABI.

Le Challenger: Bamako; f. 2002; independent.

Le Combat: Sotuba, Bamako; tel. 74494916; internet lecombat.fr; weekly.

L'Inspecteur: Immeuble Nimagala, bloc 262, BP E 4534, Bamako; tel. 66724711; e-mail inspecteurmali@yahoo.fr; f. 1992; weekly; Dir ALY DIARRA.

Jamana—Revue Culturelle Malienne: ave Cheick Zayed, porte 2694, Hamdalaye, BP 2043, Bamako; e-mail infos@jamana.org; f. 1983; quarterly; organ of Jamana cultural co-operative; Dir HAMIDOU KONATÉ.

Journal Officiel de la République du Mali: Koulouba, BP 14, Bamako; tel. 2022-5986; official gazette.

Liberté: Immeuble Sanago, Hamdallaye Marché, BP E 24, Bamako; tel. 2028-1898; f. 1999; weekly; Dir ABDOULAYE LADJI GUINDO.

Le Magazine du Mali (MagMa): Bamako; tel. 73150047; internet www.lemagazinedumali.com; monthly.

Match: 97 rue 498, Lafiabougou, BP E 3776, Bamako; tel. 2029-1882; e-mail bcissouma@yahoo.fr; f. 1997; 2 a month; sports; Dir BABA CISSOUMA.

Nyéléni Magazine: Kalaban Coro, Koulouba, rue 105, porte 406, BP E 1415, Bamako; tel. 77058781; e-mail nyelenimagazine@gmail.com; internet nyelenimagazine.org; f. 1991; weekly and monthly; Dir MAÏMOUNA TRAORÉ.

Le Scorpion: 230 ave Cheick Zayed, Lafiabougou Marché, BP 1258, Bamako; tel. 2029-1862; f. 1991; weekly; Dir MAHAMANE HAMÈYE CISSÉ.

22 Septembre: Bamako; Dir CHAHANA TAKIOU.

Le Sphinx: Immeuble Nioro du Sahel, 1er et 2ème étages, BP 14, Bamako; tel. 4439-1786; e-mail adrame4@gmail.com; internet lesphinxmali.com; weekly; Dir of Publication ADAMA DRAMÉ.

Le Tjikan: Ouolofobougou-Bolibana, ave Cheick Zayed, Bamako; tel. 2022-3774; e-mail journaletjikan@gmail.com; biweekly; Editor AMADOU DIALLO.

NEWS AGENCY

Agence Malienne de Presse et de Publicité (AMAP): sq. Patrice Lumumba, BP 141, Bamako; tel. 2022-2346; internet www.amap.ml; f. 1977; Dir BRÉHIMA TOURÉ.

PRESS ASSOCIATIONS

Association des Editeurs de la Presse Privée (ASSEP): BP E 1002, Bamako; tel. 66713133; e-mail belcotamboura@hotmail.com; Pres. OUSMANE DAO.

Association des Professionnelles Africaines de la Communication (APAC MALI): rue 428, BP E 731, Bamako; tel. 2021-2912; Pres. MARIÉTOU KONATÉ.

Groupement Patronal de la Presse Ecrite: Bamako; Pres. CHAHANA TAKIOU.

Union Nationale des Journalistes Maliens (UNAJOM): BP 1300, Bamako; tel. 2022-1915; e-mail ibrafam@yahoo.fr; Pres. FAKARA FAINKÉ.

Publishers

Cauris Livres: BP 1484, Bamako; tel. 2022-4079; e-mail contact@caurislivres.com; internet www.caurislivres.com; 2013; Man. BESNARD NADINE.

EDIM SA: ave Kassé Keïta, BP 21, Bamako; tel. 2022-4041; f. 1972 as Editions Imprimeries du Mali; general fiction and non-fiction, textbooks; Chair. and Man. Dir ALOU TOMOTA.

Editions Donniya: Cité du Niger, BP 1273, Bamako; tel. 2021-4646; internet www.editionsdonniya.com; f. 1996; general fiction, history, reference and children's books in French and Bambara.

Editions Jamana: ave Cheick Zayed, BP 2043, Bamako; tel. 2029-6289; e-mail infos@jamana.org; f. 1988; literary fiction, poetry, reference; Dir-Gen. HAMIDOU KONATÉ.

Editions des Trois Fleuves: ACI 2000, pl. CAN, 2ème Immeuble après COVEC, BP 1590, Bamako; tel. 2029-1290; internet groupesaga.com.

Nouvelles Editions Maliennes: Bamako; publishing division of the Institut Secondaire et Supérieur de Sciences Appliquées.

La Sahélienne: rue 593, porte 164, Bako Djikoroni ACI, Bamako; tel. 6679-2440; e-mail sahelienneedition@yahoo.fr; internet editionslasahelienne.net; books in French and national languages; Dir-Gen. ISMAÏLA SAMBA TRAORÉ.

Broadcasting and Communications

TELECOMMUNICATIONS

Orange Mali SA: Immeuble Orange Mali, Hamdallaye, ACI-2000, BP E 3991, Bamako; tel. 4499-9903; e-mail orange@orangemali.com; internet www.orangemali.com; f. 2003 as Ikatel; present name adopted in 2007; fixed-line and mobile telecommunications; jtly owned by France Télécom and Société Nationale des Télécommunications du Sénégal; Dir-Gen. BRELOTTE BA.

Moov Africa Mali: Hamdallaye ACI 2000, près du Palais des Sports, BP 740, Bamako; tel. 2021-5280; e-mail segal@sotelma.ml; internet www.moovafrica.ml; f. 1990; 51% owned by Itissalat al-Maghrib—Maroc Télécom (Morocco), 20% state-owned; operates fixed-line telephone services and also mobile telecommunications under the brand name Malitel; Dir-Gen. ABDEL AZIZ BEDDINI.

Regulatory Authority

Autorité Malienne de Régulation des Télécommunications/TIC et des Postes (AMRTP): Hamdallaye ACI 2000, BP 2206, Bamako; tel. 2023-1490; e-mail amrtp@amrtp.ml; internet amrtp.ml; f. 1999; Pres. CHEICK SIDI MOHAMED NIMAGA.

BROADCASTING

Regulatory Authority

Haute Autorité de la Communication (HAC): ACI 2000, BP 5551, Bamako; tel. 2023-0060; e-mail contact@hac.ml; internet hac.ml; f. 2015 to replace Conseil Supérieur de la Communication; Pres. FODIÉ TOURÉ.

Radio

Office de Radio et Télévision du Mali (ORTM): rue de la Marne, BP 171, Bamako; tel. 2021-5937; e-mail info@ortm.live; internet www.ortm.ml; Dir-Gen. HASSANE DIOMBELÉ; Dir of Radio MAHAMADOU KONÉ.

> **Radio Mali–Chaîne Nationale:** rue de la Marne, BP 171, Bamako; tel. 2021-5937; e-mail info@ortm.live; f. 1957; state-owned; radio programmes in French, Bambara, Peul, Sarakolé, Tamashek, Sonrai, Moorish, Wolof, English.

> **Chaîne 2:** rue de la Marne, Bozola, BP 171, Bamako; e-mail info@ortm.live; internet www.ortm.ml/radiochaine2; f. 1993; radio broadcasts to Bamako.

Joliba FM 105.0: Hamadallaye, ACI 2000 Bamako; tel. 7171-5916; e-mail jolibafm@gmail.com; internet www.jolibafm.com.

Radio Jamana: BP 2043, Bamako; tel. 2029-6289; e-mail infos@jamana.org; internet jamana.org.

Radio Kayira: Djélibougou Doumanzana, BP 3140, Bamako; tel. 2024-8782; f. 1992; community station; Dir OUMAR MARIKO.

Radio Klédu: Cité du Niger, BP 2322, Bamako; tel. 2021-0018; e-mail kledu@orangemali.com; internet www.info-mali.com; f. 1992; commercial; Dir-Gen. JACQUES DEZ.

Radio La Bonne Nouvelle (96.6 FM): BP 298, Bamako; tel. 2073-5049; e-mail radiolabonnenouvelle@yahoo.fr; internet radiolabonnenouvelle.com; f. 2013; Roman Catholic; Dir JANINE TRAORÉ.

Radio Patriote: Korofina-Sud, BP E 1406, Bamako; tel. 2024-2292; f. 1995; commercial station; Dir MOUSSA KEÏTA.

Radio Rurale de Kayes: Plateau, BP 94, Kayes; tel. 2158-0081; internet fb.com/radioruraledekayes; f. 1988; community stations established by the Agence de Coopération Culturelle et Technique (ACTT); transmitters in Niono, Kadiolo, Bandiagara and Kidal; Dir DARRAR BEN AZOUR MAGUIRAGA.

Radio Wassoulou: BP 24, Yanfolila; tel. 2165-1097; internet wassoulou.radio.org.ml; commercial.

Television

Office de Radio et Télévision du Mali (ORTM): see Radio; a second channel, Télévision Malienne 2, was launched on 31 December 2011; Dir of Television YOUSSOUF DEMBÉLÉ.

Cherifla TV: Koulikoro; tel. 2074-0917; e-mail info@cherifla.tv; internet fb.com/cheriflatelevision; f. 2015.

Hondou TV: BP 253, Bamako; e-mail hondoutv01@gmail.com; internet fb.com/tvhondou; lifestyle.

M7 TV: Titibougou, route de Koulikoro 00223, Bamako; tel. 97972727; e-mail info@m7tv.ml; internet m7tv.ml.

Multicanal SA: Quinzambougou, BP E 1506, Bamako; tel. 2020-2929; private subscription broadcaster; relays international broadcasts; Pres. ISMAÏLA SIDIBÉ; Dir-Gen. MOHAMED KEITA.

Renouveau TV: BP 2250, Bamako; tel. 7219-1979; e-mail renouveautv21@gmail.com; internet renouveau.tv.

Finance

BANKING

Central Bank

Banque Centrale des Etats de l'Afrique de l'Ouest (BCEAO): 94 ave Moussa Travele, BP 206, Bamako; tel. 2022-3756; internet www.bceao.int; f. 1962; HQ in Dakar, Senegal; bank of issue for the mem. states of Union Economique et Monétaire Ouest-Africaine (UEMOA, comprising Benin, Burkina Faso, Côte d'Ivoire, Guinea-Bissau, Mali, Niger, Senegal and Togo); Gov. JEAN-CLAUDE KASSI BROU; Dir in Mali KONZO TRAORÉ.

Commercial Banks

Bank of Africa—Mali (BOA—MALI): 418 ave de la Marne, Bozola, BP 2249, Bamako; tel. 2070-0500; e-mail information@boamali.com; internet www.boamali.com; f. 1983; 61.39% owned by BOA West Africa; Pres. PAUL DERREUMAUX; Dir-Gen. GEORGES NABI.

Banque Atlantique du Mali: ave Cheick Zayed, Hamdallaye, BP 1617, Bamako; tel. 2070-2828; Dir-Gen. MOUSSA TOURÉ.

Banque pour le Commerce et l'Industrie (BCI-Mali): Immeuble Baldé, ave Cheick Zayed, BP E 4373, Bamako; tel. 2029-5957; internet www.bci-banque.com/banque/mali; Chair ISSELMOU TAJIDINE; Dir-Gen. HAÏDARA ZEYNABOU KOUREICHY.

Banque Commerciale du Sahel (BCS–SA): ave Bozola 127, BP 2372, Bamako; tel. 2021-0535; e-mail dg@bcs-sa.com; f. 1977; fmrly Banque Arabe Libyo-Malienne pour le Commerce Extérieur et le Développement; 96.64% owned by Libyan-Arab Foreign Bank; Pres. MARIMANTIA DIARRA; Dir-Gen. JAMAL RAMADAN ELBENGHAZI.

Banque Internationale pour le Commerce et l'Industrie au Mali (BICIM): blvd du 22 octobre 1946, Quartier du Fleuve, BP 72, Bamako; tel. 2070-0700; e-mail bicim-dg@africa.bnpparibas.com; internet www.bicim.ml; f. 1998; 85% owned by BNP Paribas BDDI Participations (France); Dir-Gen. SAMIR MEZINE.

Banque Internationale pour le Mali (BIM): blvd de l'Indépendance, BP 15, Bamako; tel. 2022-5066; e-mail bim@bim.com.ml; internet www.bim.com.ml; f. 1980; present name adopted 1995; 51% owned by Attijariwafa Bank Group (Morocco), 10.5% state-owned; Pres. BOUBKER JAI; Dir-Gen. BRAHIM AHABBANE.

Coris Bank International—Mali (CBI—Mali): Quartier du Fleuve, blvd 22 Octobre, 03 BP 75, Bamako; tel. 2070-5900; internet mali.coris.bank; f. 2014; Pres. YACOUBA SARE; Dir-Gen. AISSATA KONÉ SIDIBÉ.

Ecobank Mali: Immeuble Amadou Sow, pl. de la Nation, Quartier du Fleuve, BP E 1272, Bamako; tel. 2070-0600; e-mail ecobankml@ecobank.com; internet www.ecobank.com; f. 1998; 49.5% owned by Ecobank Transnational Inc, 17.8% by Ecobank Bénin, 14.9% by Ecobank Togo, 9.9% by Ecobank Burkina; Pres. DAOUDA KANÉ; Dir-Gen. COUMBA SIDIBÉ TOURÉ.

Orabank Mali: Immeuble Soutra, Hamdallaye, ACI 2000, BP 1625, Bamako; tel. 2070-6100; internet www.orabank.net/fr/filiale/mali; f. 2005; fmrly Banque Régionale de Solidarité Mali (BRS-Mali); present name adopted in 2014; 52.6% owned by Oragroup SA (Togo); Pres. M'BAYE THIAM; Dir-Gen. TIGUIDA GUINDO DIARRA.

United Bank for Africa—Mali (UBA—Mali): Hamdallaye, ACI 2000, rue 360, Bamako; tel. 2029-2109; e-mail cfc@ubagroup.com; internet www.ubamali.com; f. 2018; Dir-Gen. HACKO ROKIA KONÉ.

Development Banks

Banque de Développement du Mali (BDM-SA): 525 ave Modibo Keita, Quartier du Fleuve, BP 94, Bamako; tel. 2070-0400; e-mail info@bdm-sa.com; internet www.bdm-sa.com; f. 1968; absorbed Banque Malienne de Crédit et de Dépôts in 2001; 32.3% owned by Banque Marocaine du Commerce Extérieur (Morocco), 19.6% state-owned, 16.0% by Banque Ouest-Africaine de Développement and 17.9% owned by Chambre de Commerce et d'Industrie du Mali; Dir-Gen. IBRAHIMA NDIAYE.

Banque Malienne de Solidarité (BMS): Immeuble BMS, ACI 2000, BP E 1280, Bamako; tel. 2070-3000; e-mail bms@bms-sa.ml; internet www.bms-sa.ml; f. 2002; Dir-Gen. ALIOUNE COULIBALY.

Banque Nationale de Développement Agricole—Mali (BNDA—Mali): Immeuble BNDA, blvd du Mali, ACI 2000, BP 2424, Bamako; tel. 2029-6464; e-mail bnda@bndamali.com; internet www.bnda-mali.com; f. 1981; 36.5% state-owned, 22.7% owned by Agence Française de Développement (France), 21.4%

owned by Deutsche Entwicklungsgesellschaft (Germany), 9.7% owned by BPCE—IOM, 9.7% owned by Crédit Coopératif; Pres. MOUSSA ALASSANE DIALLO; Dir-Gen. SOULEYMANE WAIGALO.

Financial Institutions

Alios Finance Mali: rue 286, porte 176, Hamdallaye, ACI 2000, BP E 3643, Bamako; tel. 2022-1849; e-mail mali@alios-finance.com; internet www.alios-finance.com; f. 1997 as Société Malienne de Financement (SOMAFI); Dir-Gen. IBRAHIM TOURÉ.

Fonds de Garantie Hypothécaire du Mali (FGHM): rue 382, porte 128, Hamdallaye, ACI 2000, BP E 5205, Bamako; tel. 2229-2380; e-mail fghm@fghm-sa.com; internet www.fghm-sa.com; f. 2000; home finance; Dir-Gen. SIDI MODIBO TRAORÉ.

Fonds de Garantie pour le Secteur Privé du Mali (FGSP-SA): Immeuble Me Kanda Keita, Hamdallaye, ACI 2000, BP 2890, Bamako; tel. 2029-0855; e-mail courrier@fgsp.ml; internet fgsp.ml; Dir-Gen. MOUSTAPHA ADRIEN SARR.

Banking Association

Association Professionnelle des Banques et Etablissements Financiers (APBEF): Siege Sébénikoro, route Nationale 5, Villa No G 18, Bamako; tel. 2029-2214; e-mail apbefmali@yahoo.fr; internet www.apbefmali.org; Pres. BRÉHIMA AMADOU HAÏDARA.

STOCK EXCHANGE

Bourse Régionale des Valeurs Mobilières (BRVM): Immeuble Sonavie, Hamdallaye, ACI 2000, BP E 1398, Bamako; tel. 4490-1810; e-mail abocoum@brvm.org; internet www.brvm.org; f. 1998; nat. br. of BRVM (regional stock exchange based in Abidjan, Côte d'Ivoire, serving the mem. states of UEMOA); Dir AMADOU DJÉRI BOCOUM.

INSURANCE

Les Assurances Bleues CNAR SA: Immeuble Siprovet, ACI 2000, BP 568, Bamako; tel. 2021-3117; internet lesassurancesbleues.com; f. 1969; fmrly Caisse Nouvelle d'Assurance et de Réassurance; present name adopted in 2012; state-owned; Dir-Gen. LÉOPOLD KEITA.

Assurances Lafia: Immeuble Assurances Lafia SA, Hamdallaye, ACI 2000, ave du Mali, BP 1542, Bamako; tel. 2029-0940; e-mail assurlafia@assurancelafia.com; internet www.assurancelafia.com; f. 1983; Dir-Gen. AMINATA DEMBÉLÉ CISSÉ.

Compagnie d'Assurance et de Réassurance Sabu Nyuman: Immeuble SONAVIE, Hamdalaye ACI 2000, BP 1822, Bamako; tel. 2022-6029; e-mail akouyate@sbnassurances.com; f. 1984; Dir-Gen. ABDRAHAMANE KOUYATÉ.

Nouvelle Alliance d'Assurance (NALLIAS): BP E4666, Bamako; tel. 2022-2244; e-mail contact@nalliasmali.com; internet nalliasmali.net; f. 2007; Dir-Gen. OUMAR N'DOYE.

Sanlam Mali SA: Immeuble SANLAM, Quartier du Fleuve, blvd du 22 Octobre, angle rue 303, Bamako; tel. 2022-5775; e-mail contact@ml.sanlam.com; internet ml.sanlam.com; f. 1990; fmrly Colina Mali SA, subsequently Saham Mali SA; present name adopted in 2021; life and general; acquired NSIA Mali in 2022; Dir-Gen. BIKIRY MAKANGUITÉ.

Société Nouvelle d'Assurance—Vie (SONA—VIE): Immeuble Sonavie, ACI 2000, BP E 2217, Bamako; tel. 2029-5400; e-mail sonavie@sonavie.com; internet sonavie.ml; f. 1996; Dir-Gen. MAMADOU TOURÉ.

SUNU Assurances IARD Mali: Immeuble SUNU, 560 ave de la Nation, BP E 4447, Bamako; tel. 2022-0802; e-mail mali.iard@sunu-group.com; internet sunu-group.com; f. 1998; Pres. DJIBRIL NGOM; Dir-Gen. LASSINA OUATTARA.

Insurance Association

Comité des Compagnies d'Assurances du Mali (CCAM): ACI 2000, Bamako; tel. 2016-4040; internet ccam.ml; f. 1959; Pres. OUMAR N'DOYE.

Trade and Industry

GOVERNMENT AGENCIES

Agence Nationale pour l'Emploi (ANPE): BP 211, Bamako; tel. 2022-3187; internet www.anpe-mali.org; f. 2001; Dir-Gen. IBRAHIM AG NOCK.

Agence pour la Promotion des Investissements au Mali (API-Mali): Quartier du Fleuve, BP 1980, Bamako; tel. 2022-9525; e-mail contact@apimali.gov.ml; internet apimali.gov.ml; f. 2005; CEO SIMBALLA SYLLA.

Autorité pour la Promotion de la Recherche Petrolière (AUREP): Médina Coura, rue 28, porte 189, BP E 4306, Bamako; tel. 2021-2948; f. 2003; Dir-Gen. AHMED AG MOHAMED.

Initiative pour la Transparence dans les Industries Extractives (ITIE): Immeuble Cinquantenaire, ave du Mali, Hamdallaye ACI 2000, Bamako; tel. 2079-1765; e-mail info_itiemali@itie.ml; internet itie.ml; Perm. Sec. DJANGO MADY COULIBALY.

Office National des Produits Pétroliers (ONAP): Quartier du Fleuve, rue 315, porte 141, BP 2070, Bamako; tel. 2022-2827; e-mail onapmali@afribone.net.ml; Dir-Gen. MODIBO GOURO DIALL.

Office du Niger (ON): BP 106, Ségou; tel. 2132-0292; e-mail info@on-mali.org; internet www.on-mali.org; f. 1932; taken over from the French authorities in 1958; restructured in mid-1990s; principally involved in cultivation of food crops, particularly rice; the Office du Niger zone is the western region of the Central Niger Delta; Pres. and Dir-Gen. ABDEL KADER KONATÉ.

Office des Produits Agricoles du Mali (OPAM): BP 132, Bamako; tel. 2021-4085; e-mail opam.bamako@gmail.com; internet opam.ml; f. 1965; state-owned; manages National (Cereals) Security Stock, administers food aid, responsible for sales of cereals and distribution to deficit areas; Pres. and Dir-Gen. Col OUSMANE DEMBÉLÉ.

DEVELOPMENT ORGANIZATIONS

Agence pour le Développement du Nord-Mali (ADN): Gao; f. 2005 to replace l'Autorité pour le Développement Intégré du Nord-Mali; govt agency with financial autonomy; promotes devt of regions of Tombouctou, Gao and Kidal; br. in Bamako; Dir MOHAMED AG MAHMOUD.

Agence Française de Développement (AFD): Quinzambougou, route de Sotuba, BP 32, Bamako; tel. 2021-2842; e-mail afdbamako@afd.fr; internet www.afd.fr; Country Dir (vacant).

Service de Coopération et d'Action Culturelle: sq. Patrice Lumumba, BP 84, Bamako; tel. 2021-8338; e-mail scac.bamako-amba@diplomatie.gouv.fr; administers bilateral aid from France; Dir NADÈGE CHOUAT.

CHAMBERS OF COMMERCE

Chambre de Commerce et d'Industrie du Mali (CCIM): pl. de la Liberté, BP 46, Bamako; tel. 2022-5036; e-mail info@cci.ml; internet www.cci.ml; f. 1906; Pres. YOUSSOUF BATHILY; Sec.-Gen. IDDRISA MOUSSA DIALLO.

Chambre des Mines du Mali (CMM): BP 1707, Bamako; e-mail tambourabelco@gmail.com; f. 2004; Pres. ABDOULAYE PONA; Sec. ABOUBACAR AMADOU TOURÉ.

EMPLOYERS' ASSOCIATIONS

Association Malienne des Exportateurs de Légumes et Fruits (AMELEF): BP 1291, Bamako; tel. 76317655; e-mail csp_mdbdn_amelef@yahoo.fr; f. 1984; Pres. BAKARY YAFFA.

Conseil National du Patronat du Mali (CNPM): Immeuble du Patronat, Hamdallaye, ACI 2000, derrière le Gouvernorat du District, route de Sotuba, BP 2445, Bamako; tel. 2021-6311; e-mail cnpm@cnpmali.org; internet www.cnpmali.org; f. 1980 as Fédération Nationale des Employeurs du Mali; Pres. MAMADOU SINSY COULIBALY; 39 professional groups and 7 regional employers' asscns.

Coordination Nationale des Organisations Paysannes du Mali (CNOP): Kalaban Coura, rue 325, porte 69, BP E 2169, Bamako; tel. 2028-6800; e-mail cnopmali@yahoo.fr; internet www.cnop-mali.org; Pres. IBRAHIMA COULIBALY.

Association des Organisations Professionnelles Paysannes: Kalaban Coura, rue 200, porte 533, BP 3066, Bamako; tel. 2028-6781; e-mail aopp@afribonemali.net; Pres. TIASSÉ BOUARÉ.

Fédération Nationale de la Filière Bétail et Viande: Ombevi, ave de la Liberté, Bamako; e-mail barbieren2001@yahoo.fr; Pres. RENÉ ALPHONSE BARBIÉ.

UTILITIES

Commission de Régulation de l'Electricité et l'Eau: rue 22, porte 21, Bamako; tel. 2023-4955; e-mail cree@creemali.org; internet www.creemali.ml; f. 2000; Pres. ISMAÏLA KONATÉ.

Electricity

Agence Malienne pour le Développement de l'Energie Domestique et l'Electrification Rurale (AMADER): colline de Badalabougou, BP E 715, Bamako; tel. 2023-8567; e-mail amader@amadermali.net; internet fb.com/AmaderMali; f. 2003; Pres. and Dir-Gen. AMADOU SIDIBÉ.

Energie du Mali (EdM): sq. Patrice Lumumba, BP 69, Bamako; tel. 2022-3020; e-mail edm@edm-sa.com.ml; internet www.edm-sa.com

.ml; f. 1960; 66% state-owned, 34% owned by Industrial Promotion Services (West-Africa); planning, construction and operation of power sector facilities; Pres. ABDRAMANE DEMBÉLÉ; Dir-Gen. KOURÉISSI KONARÉ.

Société de Gestion de l'Energie de Manantali (SOGEM): Parcelle 2501, ACI 2000, BP E 4015, Bamako; tel. 2023-3286; e-mail info@sogem-omvs.org; internet www.sogem-omvs.org; generates and distributes electricity from the Manantali hydroelectric project, under the auspices of the Organisation pour la Mise en Valeur du Fleuve Sénégal; Dir-Gen. CHEIKH OULD ABDELLAHI BEDDA.

Gas

SODIGAZ: Banankabougou, Bamako; tel. 2020-3381; internet www.sodigazmali.com; gas distribution.

Other gas distributors are: Fasogaz, Sigaz and Total.

Water

Société Malienne de Gestion de l'Eau Potable (SOMAGEP): rue 41, Djicoroni, Troukabougou, BP E 708, Bamako; tel. 2070-4100; e-mail somagep@somagep.ml; internet www.somagep.ml; f. 2010; responsible for the operation of public drinking water supplies; Dir-Gen. DRAMANE COULIBALY.

Société Malienne de Patrimoine de l'Eau Potable (SOMAPEP): Quartier Magnambougou Faso Kanu, BP 1528, Bamako; tel. 2022-0026; e-mail info@somapep.ml; internet www.somapep.ml; f. 2010; responsible for the management and development of infrastructure for supplying drinking water; Dir-Gen. BAKARY COULIBALY.

MAJOR COMPANIES

The following are among the major private and state-owned companies in terms of capital investment or employment.

Abattoir Frigorifique de Bamako (AFB): Zone Industrielle, BP 356, Bamako; tel. 2022-2467; f. 1965; transferred to 80% private ownership in 2002; Man. Dir ABDOUL WAHAB MOLÉKAFO.

Air Liquide Maligaz: route de Sotuba, BP 5, Bamako; tel. 2021-2394; internet www.airliquide.com/mali; f. 1966; mfrs of industrial gases; Chair. and CEO BENOÎT POTIER.

B2Gold Mali: Bamako; operates a gold mine at Fekola; Country Man. WILLIAM LYTLE.

Bakary Textile Commerce et Industrie (BATEX-CI): Zone Industrielle, BP 299, Bamako; tel. 2022-4647; e-mail batexci2006@yahoo.fr; f. 2005 following purchase of liquidated textile co Industrie Textile du Mali (ITEMA); Pres. and Dir-Gen. BAKARY CISSÉ.

Compagnie Malienne pour le Développement des Textiles (CMDT): 100 ave de la Marne Bozola, BP 487, Bamako; tel. 2070-7321; e-mail cmdt@cmdt.ml; internet www.cmdt-mali.net; f. 1974; restructured in 2001–03; 99.49% state-owned, 0.51% owned by GEOCOTON (France); cotton cultivation, ginning and marketing; Pres and Dir-Gen. Dr NANGO DEMBÉLÉ.

Compagnie Malienne des Textiles (COMATEX): route de Markala, BP 52, Ségou; tel. 2132-0183; f. 1994; owned by Covec (People's Republic of China); production of unbleached fibre and textiles; Dir-Gen. SAMBALA SISSOKO.

Fils et Tissus Naturels d'Afrique (Fitina): BP E 4024, Bamako; f. 2004; cotton products; Pres. AIMÉ ZINCK.

Groupe TOGUNA: route de Sénou, BP E1218, Bamako; tel. 4497-9400; e-mail toguna@gmail.com; internet www.groupetoguna.com; f. 1994; agro-based, mining; Pres. and Dir-Gen. SEYDOU NANTOUMÉ.

Groupe Tomota: Immeuble Tomota, ave Cheick Zayed, Hamdallaye, BP 2412, Bamako; tel. 2029-3000; e-mail atomota@groupe-tomota.com; internet www.groupe-tomota.net; Pres. and Dir-Gen. ALIOU TOMOTA.

Graphique Industrie: Immeuble Tomota, ave Cheick Zayed, Hamdallaye, BP 2412, Bamako; tel. 2029-3000; internet www.graphique-industrie.net; f. 1989; Dir-Gen. ALIOU TOMOTA.

Groupement AMI (GIE AMI): rue 839, BP 324, Bamako; tel. 2021-3664; e-mail ami@gieami.ml; internet gieami.net; f. 1950; agro-based; group comprises GAM Transit, Grande Confiserie du Mali, Grands Moulins du Mali, Société des Eaux Minérales du Mali; Dir CYRIL ACHCAR.

Huilerie Cotonnière du Mali (HUICOMA): Immeuble Graphique Industrie, ave Cheick Zayed, BP 2474, Bamako; tel. 2023-4261; f. 1979; processing of oilseeds; Pres. and Dir-Gen. ALIOU TOMOTA.

Initiative Malienne de Tannerie (IMAT): Zone Industrielle, Commune II, Bamako; tel. 2021-4470; f. 1994; fmrly Tannerie de l'Afrique de l'Ouest; jt venture by private Malian interests and Curtidos Corderroura (Spain); processing of skins and hides.

N-Sukala SA: M'bewani; f. 2009; 60% Chinese-owned, 40% state-owned; sugar production; Man. Dir WAN FU CHANG.

Petroma SA: rue 111, porte 63, Badalabougou, BP 8012, Bamako; tel. 2022-5425; f. 2007; Pres. ALIOU DIALLO.

Pharmacie Populaire du Mali (PPM): ave Moussa Travele, porte 724, BP 277, Bamako; tel. 2022-5059; e-mail spdg@ppm-mali.com; f. 1960; majority state-owned; import and marketing of medicines and pharmaceutical products; Pres. and Dir-Gen. MAMADY SISSOKO.

Société des Brasseries du Mali (BRAMALI/BGI): Sénou, Route de Bougouni, BP 442, Bamako; tel. 2079-4842; e-mail contacts@bramali.com; internet bramali.com; f. 1985; owned by Groupe Castel (France); mfrs of beer and soft drinks; Dir-Gen. BENJAMIN BRONNE.

Société d'Equipement du Mali (SEMA): Centre Commercial, rue Thira Diarra, BP 163, Bamako; tel. 4490-1340; e-mail direction.commerciale@sema-sa.com; internet sema-sa.com; f. 1961; construction and public works; Dir MAMADOU DIAKITE.

Société d'Exploitation des Mines d'Or de Sadiola (SEMOS): Sadiola; f. 1994; owned by AngloGold Ashanti (South Africa); devt of gold deposits at Sadiola Hill; Dir-Gen. Dr DAVID RENNER.

Société des Mines d'Or de Loulo (SOMILO): Faladié, 6448 ave de l'OUA, BP E1160, Bamako; tel. 2151-3000; f. 1987; 80% owned by Randgold Resources (South Africa), 20% state-owned; exploration and devt of gold deposits at Loulo; Man. Dir TAHIROU BALLO.

Société des Mines de Morila: 6448 Unity Chambers, ave de l'OUA, BP E1160, Bamako; Morila, près de Sanso; tel. 2020-3858; e-mail morila-sa@morila.com; f. 2000; 40% owned by Randgold Resources (South Africa), 40% by AngloGold Ashanti (South Africa), 20% owned by Govt of Mali; exploration and devt of gold deposits at Morila; Dir-Gen. ADAMA KONÉ.

Société Nationale des Tabacs et Allumettes du Mali (SONATAM): route de Sotuba, Zone Industrielle, BP 59, Bamako; tel. 2021-4965; f. 1968; production of cigarettes; Chair. SIDIBÉ MARIAM KAIDAMA CISSÉ; Gen. Man. YOUSSOUF TRAORÉ.

Star Oil Mali: Quartier TSF, Zone Industrielle, Niarela, BP 145, Bamako; tel. 2021-2597; internet staroilgroup.com; f. 2004 by purchase of Mobil Oil Mali; distribution of petroleum products; Dir-Gen. MOHAMED LEMINE ELY SENAD.

TotalEnergiesMali: ave Kasse Keita, BP 13, Bamako; tel. 2022-2976; e-mail info@totalmali.com; internet totalenergies.ml; f. 1999; fmrly Elf Oil Mali, subsequently TotalFinaElf Mali and Total Mali; present name adopted in 2021; subsidiary of TotalEnergies (France); distribution of petroleum; Dir-Gen. DAMIEN ROQUES.

Usine Malienne de Produits Pharmaceutiques (UMPP): Zone Industrielle, BP 2286, Bamako; tel. 2022-5161; f. 1983; Gen. Man. OUSMANE DOUMBIA.

TRADE UNION FEDERATIONS

Union Nationale des Travailleurs du Mali (UNTM): Bourse du Travail, blvd de l'Indépendance, BP 169, Bamako; tel. 2022-3699; f. 1963; 13 nat. and 8 regional unions, and 52 local orgs; Sec.-Gen. YACOUBA KATILÉ.

There are, in addition, several non-affiliated trade unions.

Transport

RAILWAYS

Mali's only railway runs from Koulikoro, via Bamako, to the Senegal border, and continues to that country's port of Dakar. In 1995 the Governments of Mali and Senegal agreed to establish a joint company to operate the Bamako–Dakar line, and the line passed fully into private ownership in 2003. In January 2020 the Government signed an agreement with the China Railway Construction Corporation for the renovation of the Bamako–Dakar line.

Société de Patrimoine Ferroviaire du Mali (SOPAFER-Mali): Immeuble la Roseraie, 310 ave de la Liberté, BP 4150, Bamako; tel. 2022-5967; f. 2017; fmrly Régie du Chemin de Fer du Mali, management of which was transferred to privately owned Transrail SA; Dir-Gen. IBRAHIM MAÏGA.

ROADS

A bituminized road between Bamako and Abidjan (Côte d'Ivoire) provides Mali's main economic link to the coast; construction of a road linking Bamako and Dakar (Senegal) was to be financed by the European Development Fund. The 344-km Kankan–Kouremale–Bamako road between Mali and Guinea, which was funded by the African Development Bank, was completed in December 2013. There are also plans to connect Mali to the Trans-Sahara Highway through the construction of a 700-km road link between Gao, in Mali, and the Algerian border town of Timiaouine.

Agence Nationale de la Sécurité Routière: ACI 2000, rue 425, porte 294, BP 231, Bamako; tel. 2029-3238; internet anasermali.net; f. 2009; road safety; Dir-Gen. MAMADOU SIDIKI KONATÉ.

Autorité Routière du Mali: rue 320, porte 153, Hamdallaye, ACI 2000, 03 BP 12, Bamako; tel. 2029-1125; internet www.arfer-mali.net; f. 2001; Dir-Gen. BABA MOULAYE HAIDARA.

INLAND WATERWAYS

The River Niger is navigable in parts of its course through Mali (1,693 km) during the rainy season from July to late December. The River Senegal was, until the early 1990s, navigable from Kayes to Saint-Louis (Senegal) only between August and November, but its navigability improved following the inauguration, in 1992, of the Manantali dam, and the completion of works to deepen the riverbed.

Compagnie Malienne de Navigation (COMANAV): BP 10, Koulikoro; tel. 2126-2094; e-mail samakedra@gmail.com; internet fb.com/CMNKOULIKORO; f. 1968; 100% state-owned; river transport; Pres. and Dir-Gen. ELWANGARY MAIMOUNA HAÏDARA.

Conseil Malien des Chargeurs (CMC): Dar-salam, BP E 4031, Bamako; tel. 2023-0486; internet www.cmchargeur.com; f. 1999; Pres. OUSMANE BABALAYE DAOU.

CIVIL AVIATION

The principal airport is at Bamako-Senou. The other major airports are at Bourem, Gao, Goundam, Kayes, Kita, Mopti, Nioro, Ségou, Tessalit and Tombouctou. There are about 40 small airfields. Mali's airports are being modernized with external financial assistance.

Aéroports du Mali: BP 230, Bamako; tel. 2020-4626; internet www.aeroports-mali.ml; f. 1970; responsible for commercial exploitation, maintenance and development of airports; Pres. and Dir-Gen. Col LASSINA TOGOLA.

Agence Nationale de l'Aviation Civile (ANAC): route de l'Aéroport de Bamako, Sénou, BP 227, Bamako; tel. 2020-5524; e-mail anacmali@hotmail.com; f. 2005 to replace Direction Nationale de l'Aéronautique Civile (f. 1990); Dir-Gen. Col DRISSA KONÉ.

Air Mali: Immeuble Tomota, ave Cheick Zayed, BP E 2286, Bamako; tel. 2022-2424; f. 2005; 1% owned by Fonds Aga Khan pour le Développement Economique (AKAFED), 20% state-owned; domestic and international flights; Dir-Gen. ABDERRAHMANE BERTHÉ.

Sky Mali: Immeuble TOMOTA, Hamdallaye, ave Cheick Zayed, près du Rond-Point de l'Eléphant, BP 7126, Bamako; tel. 4434-7282; e-mail agencebamako@flyskymali.com; internet www.flyskymali.com; f. 2020; Dir-Gen. TAHIR NDIAYE.

Tourism

Agence de Promotion Touristique du Mali (APTM): Hamdallaye ACI 2000, BP 191, Bamako; tel. 2022-5673; e-mail info@officetourismemali.com; internet officetourismemali.com; Dir-Gen. SIDY KEITA.

Defence

As assessed at November 2021, Mali's armed forces numbered an estimated 21,000, including an air force of some 2,000. Gendarmerie and paramilitary forces numbered 20,000. Military service is by selective conscription and lasts for two years. Following the escalation of an Islamist insurgency during 2012, in January 2013 some 4,000 French ground troops, together with military fighter jets, undertook an intervention mission in northern Mali. The UN Security Council had in December 2012 authorized the deployment of an African-led International Support Mission to Mali (AFISMA) to assist the Malian armed forces in combating the insurgency. In April 2013 the Security Council approved a resolution providing for the reconstitution of AFISMA (then numbering about 6,300 forces under the command of the Economic Community of West African States—ECOWAS) into the United Nations Multidimensional Integrated Stabilization Mission in Mali (MINUSMA), to comprise up to 11,200 military personnel and 1,440 police officers, with a 12-month mandate effective from 1 July. Having been extended by a year in 2014, 2015, 2016, 2017, 2018, 2019, 2020 and 2021, in June 2022 MINUSMA's mandate was once again extended, until 30 June 2023, and its authorized strength maintained at 13,289 military personnel and 1,920 police officers (to which level it had been raised in June 2016).

Defence Budget: 474,000m. francs CFA in 2021.

Chief of Staff of the Armed Forces: Brig.-Gen. OUMAR DIARRA.

Chief of Staff of the Air Force: Col ALOU BOI DIARRA.

Chief of Staff of the Land Army: Col-Maj. FÉLIX DIALLO.

Chief of Staff of the National Guard: Col ELISÉE JEAN DAO.

Education

Education is provided free of charge and is officially compulsory for nine years between seven and 16 years of age. Basic education, which includes six years of primary education, begins at the age of seven and lasts for nine years. Secondary education, from 16 years of age, lasts for a further three years. The rate of school enrolment in Mali is among the lowest in the world. According to the United Nations Educational, Scientific and Cultural Organization (UNESCO), in 2017/18 enrolment at pre-primary level was equivalent to 7% of children in the relevant age-group (males 7%; females 7%). In that year primary enrolment included 59% of children in the appropriate age-group (males 62%; females 56%), while secondary enrolment was equivalent to 41% of those in the appropriate age-group (males 45%; females 37%). Tertiary education facilities include the national university, developed in the mid-1990s. Hitherto many students have received higher education abroad, mainly in France and Senegal. In 2017 spending on education represented 16.5% of total government expenditure, according to the World Bank.

Bibliography

Bah, T. *Mali: le procès permanent*. Paris, L'Harmattan, 2010.

Bastian, D. E., Myers, R. A., and Stamm, A. L. *Mali*. Oxford, ABC-Clio, 1994.

Bingen, R. J., Staatz, J. M., and Robinson, D. (Eds). *Democracy and Development in Mali*. East Lancing, MI, The Michigan State University Press, 2000.

Bocquier, P., and Diarra, T. *Population et société au Mali*. Paris, L'Harmattan, 1999.

Boilley, P. *Les Touaregs Kel Adagh: dépendances et révoltes: du Soudan français au Mali contemporain*. Paris, Editions Karthala, 1999.

Bonneval, P., Kuper, M., Tonneau, J.-P. et al. *L'Office du Niger, grenier à riz du Mali: succès économiques, transitions culturelles et politiques de développement*. Paris, Editions Karthala, 2002.

Brenner, L. *Controlling Knowledge: Religion, Power, and Schooling in a West African Muslim Society*. Bloomington, IN, Indiana University Press, 2001.

Camara, B. *Migration et tensions sociales dans le sud du Mali*. Dakar, CODESRIA, 2011.

Camara, M. M. *Questions brûlantes pour démocratie naissante*. Dakar, Nouvelles éditions africaines du Sénégal, 1998.

Cathala, R. *Où va le Mali? Entre vulnrabilités et résilience*. Paris, Editions du Cygne, 2013.

Chivvis, C. S. *The French War on Al Qa'ida in Africa*. Cambridge, Cambridge University Press, 2015.

Cissé, A. *Mali: Une Démocratie à Refonder*. Paris, L'Harmattan, 2006.

Cissé, Y. T., and Kamissoko, W. *La grande geste du Mali, des origines à la fondation de l'empire*. Paris, Editions Karthala, 1988.

Couloubaly, P. B. *Le Mali d'Alpha Oumar Konaré: ombres et lumières d'une démocratie en gestation*. Paris, L'Harmattan, 2004.

Daniel, S. *Les mafias du Mali: Trafics et terrorisme au Sahel*. Paris, Descartes & Cie, 2014.

Davies, S. *Adaptable Livelihoods: Coping with Food Insecurity in the Malian Sahel*. New York, St Martin's Press, 1995.

Dayak, M. *Touareg, la tragédie*. Paris, J.-C. Lattès, 1992.

Diakite, Y. *La Fédération du Mali: sa création et les causes de son éclatement*. Bamako, Ecole Normale Supérieure de Bamako, 1985.

Diarrah, C. O. *Mali: Bilan d'une gestion désastreuse*. Paris, L'Harmattan, 2000.

Grevoz, D. *Les canonnières de Tombouctou: les français à la conquête de la cité mythique 1870–1894*. Paris, L'Harmattan, 1992.

Harmon, S. A. *Terror and Insurgency in the Sahara-Sahel Region: Corruption, Contraband, Jihad and the Mali War of 2012–2013*. Farnham, Ashgate, 2014.

Imperato, P. J. *Historical Dictionary of Mali*. 3rd edn. Lanham, MD, Scarecrow Press, 1996.

Jus, C. *Soudan français-Mauritanie: Une géopolitique coloniale (1880–1963)*. Paris, L'Harmattan, 2003.

Klein, M. A. *Slavery and Colonial Rule in French West Africa*. Cambridge, Cambridge University Press, 1998.

Konaré B. A. *Ces mots que je partage: discours d'une Première Dame d'Afrique, avec une introduction sur la parole*. Bamako, Editions Jamana, 1998.

Maïga, A. B. C. *La politique africaine du Mali de 1960 à 1980*. Bamako, Ecole Normale Supérieure de Bamako, 1983.

Maïga, M. T.-F. *Le Mali: De la secheresse à la rebellion nomade: Chronique et analyse d'un double phénomène du contre-développement en Afrique Sahélienne*. Paris, L'Harmattan, 1997.

Mariko, K. *Les Touaregs Ouelleminden*. Paris, Editions Karthala, 1984.

Notin, J.-C. *La guerre de la France au Mali*. Paris, Tallandier, 2014.

Tag, S. *Paysans, état et démocratisation au Mali: enquête en milieu rural*. Hamburg, Institut für Afrika-Kunde, 1994.

MAURITANIA

Physical and Social Geography

DAVID HILLING

Covering an area of 1,030,700 sq km (397,950 sq miles), the Islamic Republic of Mauritania forms a geographical link between the Arab Maghreb and black West Africa. Moors, heterogeneous groups of Arab/Berber stock, form about two-thirds of the population, which totalled 3,537,368 at the March–April 2013 census. At mid-2022 the population totalled 4,372,037, according to official projections, giving an average population density of 4.2 persons per sq km.

The Moors are divided on social and descent criteria, rather than skin colour, into a dominant group, the Bidan or 'white' Moors, and a group, probably of servile origin, known as the Harratin or 'black' Moors. All were traditionally nomadic pastoralists. The country's black African inhabitants traditionally form about one-third of the total population, the principal groups being the Wolof, the Toucouleur and the Fulani (Peul). They are mainly sedentary cultivators and are concentrated in a relatively narrow zone in the south of the country.

During the drought of the 1970s and early 1980s, there was mass migration to the towns, and the urban population increased from 18% of the total in 1972 to as much as 35% in 1984. The population of Nouakchott was 393,300 at the time of the 1988 census, but had risen to 958,399 by the census of 2013. The populations of towns such as Nouadhibou (59,200 in 1988) and Rosso (27,783 in 1988) had increased to 118,167 and 51,026, respectively, by 2013. By mid-2021, according to UN estimates, the population of Nouakchott had risen to 1,372,244. There has been a general exodus from rural areas and an associated growth of informal peri-urban encampments. In 1963 about 83% of the population was nomadic, and 17% sedentary, but by 1988 only 12% remained nomadic, while 88% were settled, mainly in the larger towns. By 2013 the nomadic population numbered only 71,122, equivalent to some 2% of the population.

Two-thirds of the country may be classed as 'Saharan', with rainfall absent or negligible in most years and always less than 100 mm. In parts vegetation is inadequate to graze even the camel, which is the main support of the nomadic peoples of the northern and central area. Traditionally this harsh area has produced some salt, and dates and millet are cultivated at oases such as Atar. Southwards, in the 'Sahelian' zone, the rainfall increases to about 600 mm per year; in good years

vegetation will support sheep, goats and cattle, and adequate crops of millet and sorghum can be grown. There is evidence that the 250 mm precipitation line has moved at least 200 km further south since the early 1960s, as Saharan conditions encroach on Sahelian areas. In 1983 rainfall over the whole country reached an average of only 27% of that for the period 1941–70, and was only 13% in the pasturelands of the Hodh Ech Chargui (Hodh Oriental) region. Average annual rainfall in the capital in the 1990s was 131 mm. In the early 1990s the Senegal river was at record low levels, and riverine cultivation in the seasonally inundated *chemama* lands was greatly reduced, although larger areas of more systematic irrigation could be made possible by dams that have been constructed for the control of the river.

Geologically, Mauritania is a part of the vast western Saharan 'shield' of crystalline rocks, but these are overlain in parts with sedimentary rocks, and some 40% of the country has a superficial cover of unconsolidated sand. Relief has a general north-east–south-west trend, and a series of westward-facing scarps separate monotonous plateaux, which only in western Adrar rise above 500 m. Locally these plateaux have been eroded, so that only isolated peaks remain, the larger of these being known as kedias and the smaller as guelbs. These are often minerally enriched; however, reserves of high-grade iron ore in the *djbel le-hadid* ('iron mountains') of the Kédia d'Idjil were nearing exhaustion in the late 1980s, and production ceased in 1992. Mining at a neighbouring guelb, El Rhein (some 40 km to the north), commenced in 1984, while the exploitation of the important M'Haoudat deposit (55 km to the north of Zouïrât) began in 1994. Gypsum, rock salt, gold and copper are also mined on a small scale. Other exploitable mineral resources include diamonds, phosphates, sulphur, peat, manganese and uranium. Many international companies were involved in offshore petroleum exploration in Mauritania in the early 2000s, with reserves at the offshore Shafr el Khanjar and Chinguetti fields estimated at 450m.–1,000m. barrels; production commenced at Chinguetti in 2006.

In 1991 Modern Standard Arabic was declared to be the official language. The principal vernacular languages, Pulaar, Wolof and Soninké, were, with Arabic, recognized as 'national languages'. French is still widely used, particularly in the commercial sector.

History

GIUSEPPE MAIMONE

INDEPENDENCE AND OULD DADDAH

Mauritania achieved independence from France on 28 November 1960. Its first head of state was Mokhtar Ould Daddah, a French-educated lawyer, leader of the Union Progressiste Mauritanienne (UPM). During Ould Daddah's first years of government, national policies took account of the dual nature of Mauritania both as a sub-Saharan and as a Maghreb country. A new Constitution was adopted in 1961. The President (elected by universal suffrage for a five-year term, with unlimited renewals) was also the head of government. Legislative power was vested in a National Assembly, initially comprising 40 members. Islam was the official religion, and the President was required to profess the Muslim faith.

At the presidential election in 1961, Ould Daddah received the support of Nahda (an Arab party) and from the black Union

Nationale Mauritanienne (UNM). In 1964 he consolidated his power by merging the UPM, Nahda, the UNM and the socialist Entente Mauritanienne into the Parti du Peuple Mauritanien (PPM), which declared itself to be non-aligned. Shortly afterwards, Ould Daddah declared Mauritania a one-party state and instigated a process of Arabicization. In 1966 Arabic was introduced as Mauritania's official language, eliciting strong reactions from the black communities, who feared Arab domination and their own exclusion from the public administration.

At the PPM congress in January 1968 Arabic was proposed as the national language. Protests by black Mauritanians were accompanied by strikes and demonstrations by miners in the northern town of Zouerate. These inspired many students to support the first Marxist opposition movements, namely the Mouvement National Démocratique and the Parti des

Kadihines Mauritaniens. In the 1970s Ould Daddah attempted to halt the Moroccan claims on Mauritania by forming alliances with Tunisia and Algeria and then with Egyptian President Gamal Abd al-Nasir (Nasser) and the Iraqi President Saddam Hussain.

Morocco withdrew its claims on Mauritanian territory in 1969. In 1973 Mauritania joined the League of Arab States (the Arab League) and abandoned the CFA franc, the currency of the former French West African colonies, replacing it with the ouguiya. In the following year Spain announced its intention to withdraw from Western Sahara. Mauritania and Morocco signed an agreement envisaging the division of this territory between the two countries, with two-thirds passing to Morocco and one-third to Mauritania. In 1976 Spain withdrew its troops, and the Frente Popular para la Liberación de Saguia el-Hamra y Río de Oro (Polisario Front) proclaimed the independence of the Sahrawi Arab Democratic Republic, with Algerian support. Mauritania refused Polisario's proposal of a federalist union, and conflict began. The war demonstrated the limitations of the Mauritanian military forces, which fought with Moroccan support.

FROM THE CMSN TO OULD TAYA

Ould Daddah was overthrown in July 1978 by the Comité Militaire de Redressement National (CMRN—Military Committee for National Recovery), which signed a ceasefire agreement with Polisario in December and withdrew Mauritanian troops from Western Sahara in August 1979. Meanwhile, the President of the CMRN, Lt-Col Moustapha Ould Saleck, suspended the Constitution and dissolved Ould Daddah's one-party system, but he was deposed in April 1979 by the Comité Militaire de Salut National (CMSN—Military Committee for National Salvation). The CMSN leader, Muhammad Khouna Ould Haidalla, ruled the country during 1979–84, first as Prime Minister and then as President.

Slavery was abolished in 1981, thus formally freeing the Haratins, former slaves of the Moorish society who were of black origin and who had in 1978 established the anti-slavery movement El-Hor (Free Man). The Haratins were estimated to be Mauritania's largest demographic group (some 40%–45% of the population), while the rest of the population was divided almost equally between Arab Berbers and black Mauritanians.

Maaouiya Ould Sid'Ahmed Taya, who had become Prime Minister in 1981, ousted Haidalla in a coup in December 1984. Taya soon assumed complete political control. He announced democratic elections but repressed opposition parties and movements—above all the black Mauritanian Forces de Libération Africaines de Mauritanie (FLAM). Many FLAM leaders were arrested, and others were forced into exile.

Persecution of the black Mauritanian population intensified during the late 1980s, and in 1989 clashes between black Mauritanian herders and Senegalese farmers degenerated into violence, and hundreds of deaths were reported in both countries. Senegal expelled some 230,000 Mauritanians; Mauritania, in turn, expelled large numbers of Senegalese citizens, along with about 80,000 undocumented black Mauritanians from the lands of the Senegal river valley, which were now needed for the resettlement of impoverished Arabs and Haratins, affected by the advancing desertification in the north. Opposition movements accused Taya of having planned the ethnic cleansing. He reinforced his alliance with Iraqi President Hussain and was strongly influenced by Baathism. Islamic movements and political speeches in mosques were banned.

REFORMS AND CONTINUITY

Iraq's defeat in the Gulf conflict of 1991 prompted Mauritanian isolation from traditional Arab allies such as Saudi Arabia and Kuwait, which had provided 97% of foreign economic assistance in 1990. Consequently, Taya was obliged to request assistance from the USA, the World Bank and the International Monetary Fund (IMF), in return for which a number of democratic measures were conceded. In July 1991 97.9% of voters in a national referendum (some 85% of the registered electorate) approved a new Constitution. Provision was made for a bicameral legislature, comprising the al-Jamiya al-

Wataniyah (National Assembly), to be elected by universal suffrage every five years, and the Majlis al-Shuyukh (Senate), to be indirectly elected by municipal leaders. The President of the Republic was to be elected, by universal suffrage, for a six-year term, with unlimited renewals of office. Mauritania was redefined as an Islamic Republic, and the President was again required to be a Muslim.

Multi-party elections were held in 1992, although parties based on clear ethnic, social or regional lines were proscribed. Among the first parties to receive official status were the pro-Government Parti Républicain Démocratique et Social (PRDS) and the Action pour le Changement (AC), founded by El-Hor leader Messaoud Ould Boulkheir. At the presidential election in January, Taya obtained 63% of the votes cast; his nearest rival, Ahmed Ould Daddah (the brother of the country's first President, and leader of the Union des Forces Démocratiques—UFD), received 33%. At legislative elections in March, the PRDS won a majority in both chambers. Taya formed a civilian Government, appointing Sidi Muhammad Ould Boubacar as Prime Minister, thus marking the definitive marginalization of the CMSN.

The PRDS again dominated at legislative elections in October 1996. In early 1997 the opposition parties joined forces in the Front Uni des Partis d'Opposition (FUPO). After Taya won 91% of the votes at the presidential election held in December, the FUPO alleged that the unusually high turnout (73.8%) indicated electoral fraud. The Union des Forces Démocratiques—Ere Nouvelle (UFD—EN, as the UFD had become) subsequently split into two rival factions.

Some critics of Taya formed the pro-Iraqi Baathist party Taliaa, which was banned for attempted subversion and violation of public order, after it criticized the Government's decision to establish full diplomatic relations with Israel. Following the renewed uprising in the Palestinian territories from September 2000, Mauritania's diplomatic ties with Israel also provoked protest by the UFD—EN; the party was subsequently dissolved by the Government, and several of its leaders were arrested. The party faction that was opposed to Ould Daddah subsequently formed the Union des Forces du Progrès (UFP), and in 2001 Ould Daddah established the Rassemblement des Forces Démocratiques (RFD).

Elections were held to an enlarged National Assembly in October 2001, under a new electoral system that prohibited independent candidates and introduced a form of proportional representation. The PRDS won 64 of the 81 seats in the new Assembly.

During 2001 Parliament debated legislation banning human trafficking—an issue that continued to afflict the Haratins. The Law Against Trafficking in Persons came into effect in 2003. Meanwhile, the Government dissolved the AC in early 2002, accusing the party of racism and extremism.

In March 2003 the invasion of Iraq by US-led coalition forces caused renewed tension in Mauritania between the Government and the Baathist opposition. Many members of Salafist or Muslim Brotherhood associations were arrested, as was Mohamed Ould Eya, leader of the Baathist opposition party, the Parti de la Renaissance Nationale (PRN). Police closed the PRN headquarters, accusing the party of attempting to re-establish the banned Taliaa.

Several coup attempts against Taya were foiled in 2003–04. In July 2003 Taya appointed Sghaïr Ould M'Barek, a Haratin and former member of the CMSN, as Prime Minister. At the November 2003 presidential election Taya was re-elected with 67% of votes cast. His principal rival, Haidalla, was arrested shortly after the election and charged with having organized a coup. In July 2004 a new, pro-Haidalla opposition party, Sawab (Reward), was established.

In August 2004 the President revealed a further coup plot by Arab officers. Opposition to Taya was increasing both in the army and in the Arab Berber community, particularly following his establishment in 1999 of diplomatic relations with Israel and to support the US-led campaign against the al-Qa'ida Organization in the Land of the Islamic Maghreb (AQIM) after the suicide attacks on the USA of September 2001. In November 2004 the trial commenced of 195 soldiers and civilians accused of participating in the coup attempts. The four main organizers of the plots were sentenced to life imprisonment; 111 were acquitted, and the others received lesser custodial sentences.

In June 2005 about 150 members of Algeria's Groupe Salafiste pour la Prédication et le Combat (GSPC) crossed into north-eastern Mauritania and killed 15 soldiers at Lemgheity, in apparent revenge for the persecution of Islamist movements in the country. A new anti-terrorism law was subsequently introduced to prevent threats against the state.

THE 'DEMOCRATIC TRANSITION'

In an effort to forestall further coup attempts and ensure his personal protection, Taya created three new corps within the armed forces. Nevertheless, on 3 August 2005 a group of 17 colonels, led by Ely Ould Mohamed Vall and Mohamed Ould Abdel Aziz, ousted Taya in a bloodless coup. The incoming Conseil Militaire pour la Justice et la Démocratie (CMJD—Military Council for Justice and Democracy) declared its intention to oversee a two-year transition period to prepare Mauritania for democratic elections. Parliament was dissolved, and the CMJD, under Vall's presidency, assumed legislative power and appointed Boubacar as Prime Minister. The CMJD freed some Islamists and activists from detention, not including detainees connected with the GSPC, thus reassuring Western allies of its commitment to fight terrorism. The CMJD notably appointed Ould Sidi Ahmed, who had been instrumental in Mauritania's establishment of diplomatic relations with Israel, as Minister of Foreign Affairs. Taya took up political exile in Qatar. The PRDS immediately distanced itself from Taya and in October changed its name to the Parti Républicain pour la Démocratie et le Renouveau (PRDR).

Constitutional reforms drafted under the transitional administration included a five-year term of office for the President, renewable only once; a maximum age of 75 for presidential candidates; a prohibition on the President holding any other post while in office; and a mixed electoral system for the National Assembly, with single-member constituencies for two-thirds of the seats and the remainder to be elected on a proportional basis. Senate members were to be appointed by mayors and city councils. Independent candidatures were to be allowed. The amendments were approved overwhelmingly at a national referendum held in June 2006.

Elections to the National Assembly took place in November–December 2006 and were overseen by international observers and by the country's Commission Electorale Nationale Indépendante (CENI—National Independent Electoral Commission). Both the National Assembly and the Senate (elected in February 2007) witnessed a sizeable victory for Al-Mithaq (The Pact), an alliance of 18 Islamist movements including some close to the former PRDS.

Nineteen candidates contested the first round of the presidential election, held in March 2007. Sidi Ould Cheikh Abdallahi and Ahmed Ould Daddah proceeded to the second round. Abdallahi, standing as an independent, was elected with 53% of the votes cast, having received the support of Ould Boulkheir, the veteran Haratin leader, who was subsequently appointed President of the new National Assembly.

In April 2007 President Abdallahi appointed the former head of the central bank, Zeine Ould Zeidane, as Prime Minister. A pro-presidential party, the Pacte National pour la Démocratie et le Développement (PNDD), was established, comprising largely former members of Taya's PRDS. For the first time, Islamist parties were officially authorized, among them al-Fadhila and Tawassoul (also known as the Rassemblement National pour la Réforme et le Développement). Furthermore, in November Mauritania, Senegal and the office of the United Nations High Commissioner for Refugees (UNHCR) reached a tripartite agreement for the return of 20,000 black Mauritanians, expelled in 1989–90, who remained in refugee camps in Senegal; however, most of the refugees' land had been assigned to others in Mauritania, thus provoking tensions.

Debates about Haratin slavery were a central focus of the presidential election campaign. The new administration established a human rights commission, the Commission Nationale des Droits de l'Homme, and criminal legislation requiring custodial sentences for the practice of slavery was introduced.

However, in August 2008 a bloodless coup, led by Abdel Aziz, brought an end to the 'democratic transition'.

ABDEL AZIZ AND THE FIGHT AGAINST TERRORISM

The coup followed Zeidane's resignation as Prime Minister in mid-2008. His successor, Yahya Ould Ahmed El Waghef, initially had the support of the PNDD and some opposition parties, including Tawassoul. Soon, however, the PNDD tabled a motion of no confidence in the Government. El Waghef formed a new Council of Ministers, but 25 PNDD deputies withdrew their support.

The protracted institutional crisis weakened President Abdallahi, and on 6 August 2008 he was deposed by the 11-member Haut Conseil d'Etat (HCE—High Council of State). Abdallahi and El Waghef were arrested, and Abdel Aziz designated himself President of the Republic. The HCE stated its intention to preserve democracy and announced that a new presidential election would take place. Moulaya Ould Mohamed Laghdaf, a diplomat, was appointed Prime Minister.

Abdel Aziz was opposed by the parliamentary opposition grouped in the Front National pour la Défense de la Démocratie, led by Ould Boulkheir. Nevertheless, the majority of the legislature declared their support for the coup. Among the opposition parties, Tawassoul, the RFD and the black Alliance pour la Justice et la Démocratie/Mouvement pour la Rénovation backed Abdel Aziz. Poor Mauritanians also legitimized Abdel Aziz, in response to his declared intention to be the 'President of the Poor'.

Abdel Aziz resigned from the army in April 2009 in order to contest the presidential election and established the Union pour la République (UPR), which 83 of the 151 members of the two parliamentary chambers joined. The President of the Senate, Ba Mamadou Mbaré, became interim President of the Republic.

The presidential election was held in July 2009. Abdel Aziz won the first round, with 53% of the votes cast. His closest rival was Ould Boulkheir (with 16%), followed by Ahmed Ould Daddah (with 14%). The defeated candidates denounced the process as fraudulent, and the President of the CENI resigned. Unexpectedly, Abdel Aziz received the support of Western governments, which apparently preferred the prospect of stability for Mauritania as a frontline state against terrorism in the Sahara region. After Ould Daddah and the RFD recognized the legitimacy of Abdel Aziz's presidency in September, followed by the PNDD, the rump of the opposition formed a new coalition, the Coordination de l'Opposition Démocratique (COD).

In July 2010 the National Assembly adopted anti-terrorism legislation that granted increased powers to the police. However, the opposition accused President Abdel Aziz of using the new measure to restrict freedoms.

A MAURITANIAN ARAB SPRING

The events of the 'Arab spring' in the Middle East and North Africa swiftly spread to Mauritania. The self-immolation of a man in front of the presidential palace in Nouakchott, the capital, in January 2011 prompted students to take to the streets in a series of large demonstrations. The students' Mouvement du 25 Février became a leading opposition group, demanding reforms in education, the economy, health care, women's rights and the fight against slavery and poverty.

More popular among black Mauritanians became the Touche Pas à Ma Nationalité movement, which demonstrated against the national registration programme implemented from June 2011. This programme was deeply unpopular among former refugee families, especially the approximately 17,000 who had returned to Mauritania in 2008–09. Planned elections for one-third of the Senate seats were postponed, as were legislative and municipal elections due in September–October 2011.

In April 2012 Biram Ould Dah Ould Abeid, the leader of the anti-slavery Initiative pour la Résurgence du Mouvement Abolitionniste en Mauritanie (IRA Mauritanie), was arrested, together with nine other IRA activists, after burning six Islamic law texts containing sentences that were claimed to condone slavery. All were freed in September, following international protests and a legal campaign.

A new electoral commission was inaugurated in June 2012, but the COD refused to recognize its legitimacy, and there were renewed street protests demanding Abdel Aziz's resignation. In October the President was shot and injured near the Tweila checkpoint, 40 km north of Nouakchott: it was officially reported that the shooting was accidental. Abdel Aziz was flown to France for surgery but returned to Mauritania in November.

The delayed legislative and municipal elections took place in November–December 2013. Several opposition parties boycotted the elections, and many smaller parties participated only in Nouakchott. At the first round of voting, the UPR won the largest share of the votes cast, with 21%, followed by Tawassoul (14%) and the APP (8%). The UPR thus won 56 of the 121 seats assigned, and Tawassoul 12. Defeated candidates denounced the process as fraudulent and criticized the CENI. Following the second round, in December, the UPR held 75 of the 146 declared seats in the National Assembly, Tawassoul 16 seats, El Wiam (the Party of the Democratic and Social Agreement) 10, and the APP seven. In the municipal elections, the UPR won control of about 70% of communes. Observers from the African Union (AU) reported electoral irregularities, confirming allegations by the APP, El Wiam and Tawassoul. A new 25-member Government led by Laghdaf, announced later in that month, included six female ministers.

At the beginning of 2014 a young Mauritanian, Cheikh Ould Muhammad Ould Mkheitir, was arrested for blasphemy after publishing an article online criticizing what the author identified as the marginalization of the *Mu'allmin* ('artisan') social class in the name of Islam. Mass protests were held to demand that he be put to death. In December the Penal Court in Nouadhibou found Ould Mkheitir guilty of blasphemy and imposed the death penalty. In November 2017 the Court of Appeals commuted Ould Mkheitir's sentence to two years' imprisonment (in an undisclosed location, to ensure his safety) and a fine. The court's decision led to further protests, and one week later, in an effort to restore calm, the Government adopted a law increasing penalties for blasphemy and apostasy, including the restoration of the death penalty. Ould Mkheitir was freed in July 2019 after a secret transfer to Dakar, Senegal.

The presidential election was scheduled for June 2014. The opposition parties again boycotted the vote. Abdel Aziz was challenged for the presidency by four other candidates, but won easily, with 82% of the votes cast, ahead of Abeid—who had received the UN Human Rights Prize in 2013—with 9%.

ABDEL AZIZ'S SECOND TERM: CONSTITUTIONAL REFORMS AND PARLIAMENTARY ELECTIONS

Abdel Aziz was sworn in for a second term as President in August 2014. Later in that month Laghdaf resigned as Prime Minister; former Minister of Transport Yahya Ould Hademine was appointed as his replacement. A largely unchanged 27-member Council of Ministers was announced.

A march from Boghé to Nouakchott was organized by IRA Mauritanie and other non-governmental organizations (NGOs) in November 2014 to raise awareness about the authorities' increasing land grabs. Some 10 IRA members, including Abeid, were arrested, accused of membership of an unauthorized organization, rebellion, incitation to violence and an outrage to public order. In January 2015 Abeid and his deputy were sentenced to two years' imprisonment, but both were freed following an appeal in May 2016.

In August 2015 the National Assembly approved new anti-slavery legislation, which defined slavery as a crime against humanity and doubled prison terms for offenders. Nevertheless, the Global Slavery Index published by the Australian NGO Walk Free in 2018 ranked Mauritania sixth out of 167 countries, with 2% of the population estimated to be living in modern slavery. Following a visit to Mauritania in May 2017, the UN Special Rapporteur for extreme poverty and human rights published a report highlighting the continued exclusion of Haratins and Afro-Mauritanians from positions of economic and social power.

President Abdel Aziz announced plans in May 2016 to dissolve the Senate, citing high running costs and delays to the legislative process. Instead he advocated the creation of regional assemblies, which would channel legislative proposals to the Government. These amendments were to be put to a public referendum (see below), but the proposals were strongly opposed by senators, who halted all legislative activity in protest. In September the Government launched a four-week National Inclusive Dialogue (NID), which was, however, boycotted by the largest opposition groups, the Forum National pour la Démocratie et l'Unité (FNDU) and the RFD, and was attended only by the Convention pour l'Unité et l'Alternance Pacifique et Démocratique, comprising three minor parties. Focusing on constitutional reform, the meeting notably proposed dissolving the Senate and creating regional assemblies; imposing a maximum age for presidential candidates; reforming the High Court of Justice; introducing the post of Vice-President; and choosing a new national flag. The UPR demanded an amendment to extend the presidential mandate to three terms.

The NID culminated in an agreement that a constitutional referendum on the future of the Senate and the design of the flag would take place by the end of 2016. The age limits for candidates and the two-term presidential mandate were upheld. In October thousands of protesters, supported by the FNDU, the RFD and IRA Mauritanie, demonstrated against the constitutional reforms. Even Tawassoul announced that it would boycott the referendum, which was subsequently postponed until 2017.

In March 2017 the National Assembly approved the constitutional reform bill. However, the bill was unexpectedly rejected by the Senate a week later. The date of the referendum was set for July, although it was later postponed until August. Meanwhile, in early July most opposition parties announced that they would boycott the referendum. The UPR and other smaller parties campaigned for a 'yes' vote.

The referendum duly took place on 5 August 2017. Two questions were submitted to the public: whether or not to modify the national flag and the national anthem; and whether or not to dissolve the Senate, create regional councils and consolidate the High Council of Islam and the Arbitrator of the Republic under the High Council of Fatwas and Appeals for Reprieve. According to the CENI, 85.6% voted in favour of amending the national flag and the anthem. On the question of institutional reform, the measure passed with 85.7% of the vote. Turnout was 54%. Despite allegations of electoral malpractice from the opposition parties, the constitutional changes were promulgated in mid-August.

On 28 November 2017 Abdel Aziz marked the 57th anniversary of Mauritania's independence by unveiling a new national flag and playing a new national anthem. An adjusted ouguiya, equivalent to 10 of the previous version of the currency, was introduced from 1 January 2018. Also in early January the National Assembly adopted legislation replacing the Senate with six regional councils; later in that month the first of two enlargements of the National Assembly was approved, with a second, bringing the membership to 157, implemented in March.

In April 2018 Abdel Aziz nominated the 11 members of the CENI ahead of municipal, regional and parliamentary elections, which were due to be held in September. Opposition groups complained that they had been excluded from the process and were unrepresented in the Commission. Legislation that was passed in June mandated the dissolution of political parties that did not obtain at least 1% of the votes cast in two elections or that did not compete in the two following municipal elections.

The first round of voting to the enlarged, 157-member National Assembly was held on 1 September 2018, with 73.4% of the electorate participating. The UPR won 67 seats, followed by Tawassoul, with 14. Other opposition parties took 17 seats, although significant fragmentation was apparent: the UDP was placed third; a further six parties won less than 3.5% of the votes cast; and more than 70 parties failed to secure 1%. Some of the latter would later merge with the UPR. Opposition parties protested about the high number of ballots that were invalidated (324,659 for the legislative elections and more than

200,000 in regional and municipal elections). At the second round of voting, on 15 September, the UPR secured all 22 remaining seats.

At the concurrent municipal elections, the UPR, which was the only party to present candidates in all municipalities, won two-thirds of those municipalities and six of the nine *moughataa* (departments led by mayors) in Nouakchott. The party also won all 13 regional assemblies. Meanwhile, three deputies from the IRA-Sawab coalition—including Abeid—were elected to the National Assembly.

Mohamed Salem Ould Béchir, hitherto Minister of Petroleum, Energy and Mines, was appointed Prime Minister in late September 2018, following Hademine's resignation. A new, largely unchanged Government was announced on the following day, comprising 21 ministers, including seven women.

Also in September 2018, a training centre for imams in Nouakchott was closed, after it was accused of extremism. This was followed by the closure of the Ibn Yassine University; both institutions were directed by Ould Deddew, a local Muslim Brotherhood leader.

THE 2019 PRESIDENTIAL ELECTION

In January 2019 Abdel Aziz announced his support for the candidacy of Ghazouani in the presidential election scheduled for June. Ghazouani received the official backing of the UPR in March and resigned as Minister of National Defence (he was replaced by Hademine). Abeid also confirmed his candidacy for the presidency. The opposition parties failed to find a common candidate and requested unsuccessfully a change in the board of the CENI, from which they were excluded. In March, in accordance with the 2018 legislation, the Ministry of the Interior and Decentralization dissolved more than 70 parties that had received less than 1% of the votes cast in the municipal elections of 2013 and 2018. In April several black Mauritanian parties and organizations established the Coalition Vivre Ensemble/Vérité et Réconciliation (CVE/VR); its leader, Hamidou Baba Kane, registered as a presidential candidate, as did Mohamed Sidi Mouldoud of the UFP, former Prime Minister Ould Boubacar (standing as an independent with support from Tawassoul and the Parti Mauritanien de l'Union et du Changement—Hatem, among others) and one pro-Government independent, Mohamed Lemine El Mourtaji El Wafi. The four opposition candidates declared themselves to be allied against Ghazouani and confirmed that they would support each other in the event of a second round of voting.

The first round of the presidential election was held on 22 June 2019. The Mauritanian authorities refused to permit the participation of European Union (EU) observers, allowing only those from the AU. The CENI declared the vote to be free and fair, although opposition candidates reported irregularities and the presence of the security forces in Nouakchott and around the CENI's offices. Turnout was 62.7%. Within hours of the polls closing, Ghazouani unilaterally proclaimed himself as the winner, provoking strong protests from the other candidates. On the following day, however, the CENI confirmed Ghazouani's victory with 52.0% of the votes, followed by Abeid (18.6%), Ould Boubacar (17.9%) and Baba Kane (8.7%). Opposition candidates protested against the result, and demonstrators took to the streets demanding a recount and a second round of voting. During a crackdown by the security forces, particular cruelty was reportedly shown against black Mauritanians, and some journalists were arrested. Ghazouani's victory was confirmed on 1 July, when the Constitutional Court rejected a challenge brought by Abeid and the other candidates against the outcome. In the following days Ghazouani visited France and Saudi Arabia—two of the countries that had supported his election as President.

THE GHAZOUANI PRESIDENCY

Two days after his inauguration, held on 1 August 2019, President Ghazouani appointed Ismail Ould Bedde Ould Cheikh Sidiya as Prime Minister. Of the 25 ministers appointed to the new Government a week later, six had served in the previous Government, and others were close to Abdel Aziz. No ministerial portfolio was given to the opposition.

In January 2020 the implementation in the National Assembly of a ruling that meant members' speeches were no longer to be translated into French gave rise to debate, with many (including black Mauritanians as well as francophone deputies) perceiving the measure as supporting the Arabicization of public affairs.

Meanwhile, former President Abdel Aziz's return to Mauritania in November 2019, following a period of absence, fuelled a power conflict within the UPR. At a party congress in late December, the 2,250 delegates backed Ghazouani and elected a new governing council. Meanwhile, in mid-December a group of 24 deputies requested the establishment of a parliamentary commission of inquiry to investigate allegations of corruption and mismanagement against former President Abdel Aziz. It was to examine seven financial dossiers, containing, *inter alia*, details of sales of state-owned property in Nouakchott, as well as information relating to the management of the state-owned mining company Société Nationale Industrielle et Minière (SNIM), the liquidation of the majority state-owned Société Nationale d'Importation et d'Exportation (SONIMEX), and the management of oil revenues.

Mauritania recorded its first confirmed case of COVID-19 in mid-March 2020. In response, all tourist flights to the country were cancelled, schools, universities, bars and restaurants were closed, a night-time curfew was declared, and all national borders were closed. In June the Government launched a programme of aid distribution to alleviate the economic impact of the COVID-19 crisis on some 200,000 families, with a budget of MRU 420m. (about US $11.2m.). The spread of the COVID-19 pandemic in Mauritania surged in December, when schools were closed for several weeks and other measures such as a night curfew were imposed. A vaccination programme in Mauritania began in April 2021. As at 12 October 2022 a total of 62,869 cases of COVID-19 infection had been recorded in the country, including 995 fatalities, and only 30.6% of the population had been fully vaccinated by that time.

Meanwhile, the work of the parliamentary commission of inquiry investigating the affairs of former President Abdel Aziz was interrupted in April 2020 as the global COVID-19 pandemic spread. When the commission resumed its work in June, the investigation was extended to cover the alleged gift to the former Amir of Qatar, Sheikh Hamad bin Khalifa Al Thani, of Mauritania's largest island, Tidra, situated in the Atlantic Ocean within the Banc d'Arguin National Park. Abdel Aziz refused to appear in front of the commission. Meanwhile, the opposition pushed for the re-establishment of the High Court of Justice, dissolved in 2017, which would have authority over former presidents in cases of high treason. The National Assembly approved a draft law to this effect in late July 2020 and approved the investigating commission's 800-page report detailing the extent of the mismanagement and fraud allegedly committed by Abdel Aziz during his term in office. The report was sent to the Ministry of Justice, which opened an inquiry. By early August six former ministers and several members of Abdel Aziz's family had been summoned to appear before the official investigation. On 6 August Prime Minister Ould Cheikh Sidiya tendered his Government's resignation, having been named along with three other ministers in the report; President Ghazouani appointed Mohamed Ould Bilal, a veteran administrator, as Sidiya's replacement. The smaller Government of 22 ministers that was appointed on 10 August notably included new appointees to the key portfolios of justice, the economy, and petroleum, mines and energy.

A World Bank report stated in November 2020 that some 10% of the Mauritanian population (including returned refugees) still had not been registered as civilians. The interior minister confirmed in May 2021 that 3,892,000 Mauritanians were officially registered, while the population at that time was estimated to be 4,271,197.

In May 2021 President Ghazouani effected a minor cabinet reorganization, notably replacing the Minister of Health. In July the Government reinforced measures at airports and borders in an effort to prevent a new spread of the pandemic. In August six opposition parties organized a joint press conference and criticized the lack of a dialogue with the Government' and its apparent inability to fight corruption and criminality.

In early 2021 renewed investigations were carried out against former President Abdel Aziz, and in June he was placed in preventive detention on corruption charges. In late August the High Court confirmed the imprisonment of Abdel Aziz in a special section of the Police National School in Nouakchott. In September he went on trial on a charge of misappropriating some US $90m. of state funds over a period of 10 years. His lawyers repeatedly asked for him to be released during the trial; this was eventually permitted in December, when his failing health required medical intervention.

Meanwhile, anti-Government protests in the city of R'Kiz in September 2021 led to the arrest of some 60 demonstrators. In early November new protests were held in front of the National Assembly building against the proposed 'Protections of Symbols' law (protecting, *inter alia*, the role of Islam in national life, as well as the prestige of the state and its symbols, especially when mentioned on social media), which opponents claimed would limit freedom of expression and human rights. The law, nevertheless, received parliamentary approval in November. A reform of education was also proposed at that time, whereby Arabic would replace French as the language of instruction for scientific subjects, but this was fiercely opposed by black Mauritanians. However, the law was approved in July 2022.

After public criticism of him by President Ghazouani, Prime Minister Ould Bilal resigned on 29 March 2022. However, the following day he was reappointed to form a new and much-changed Government. Notably, Dr Mohamed Salem Ould Merzoug, hitherto Minister of the Interior and Decentralization, was appointed as the new Minister of Foreign Affairs and Co-operation. He was succeeded in his previous post by Mohamed Ahmed Ould Mohamed Lemine.

The opposition brought an unsuccessful vote of no confidence in the new Government in April 2022, and in the following month a deputy left the main opposition party Tawassoul after accusing it of anti-black racism and having no real engagement in defending human rights in the country. After several months of discussion, the Government's proposal for a 'Conference of Co-operation for an Inclusive Dialogue' between parties failed.

In July 2022 the UPR changed its name to Al Insaf (Equity). It was to be led by Mohamed Melainine Ould Eyih, the Minister of National Education. In the same month the Government launched the first phase of the national registration programme of the population. A general election was expected to take place in 2023.

EXTERNAL RELATIONS

Mokhtar Ould Daddah chose to take Mauritania to independence in 1960 rather than opt to join with Senegal and the former French Soudan in the Federation of Mali and rejected Moroccan territorial claims over Mauritania. Ould Daddah sought French economic and diplomatic assistance, and consequently Mauritania joined the 'Brazzaville Group', formed by 12 former French colonies that opted for a pro-French political stance during a meeting in Brazzaville, the Republic of the Congo, in December 1960. The group subsequently became the Union Africaine et Malgache and then, in 1964, the Union Africaine et Malgache de Coopération Economique (UAMCE), with Ould Daddah as its first President.

Having consolidated his leadership, Ould Daddah sought to strengthen an independent role for Mauritania within the Arab League. The country's first Arab allies were Tunisia and Algeria, both of which had been supported by Mauritania in their struggle for independence. Economic agreements were concluded with Egypt in 1963. Mauritania left the Organisation Commune Africaine et Malgache (as the UAMCE had become) in 1965 and ended diplomatic relations with the United Kingdom. Algeria and Egypt helped Mauritania to secure recognition by Morocco in 1969 and to be admitted to the Arab League in 1973.

In 1972 Mauritania, together with Mali, Senegal and Guinea, established the Organisation pour la Mise en Valeur du Fleuve Sénégal, to promote the economic development of the Senegal river valley. An agreement with France in 1973 allowed for greater economic and military independence,

and Mauritania subsequently left the regional Union Economique et Monétaire Ouest-Africaine.

During the early 1970s Mauritania supported self-determination for the Sahrawi people, hoping that an independent Western Sahara would opt to merge with Mauritania. Moroccan claims over Western Sahara induced the two countries to subscribe to a secret pact to share the disputed territory, with the agreement of Spain. The Western Sahara conflict caused a rift in diplomatic relations with Algeria, which assisted the Polisario Front against Mauritania. From 1979 President Haidalla was accused of protecting Sahrawi fighters against Morocco; he shifted towards more radical Arab countries such as Libya and Iraq, and Baathism began to rise in Mauritania.

Mauritania and Senegal sponsored a resolution at the Organization of African Unity (OAU, now the AU) in 1983 to establish negotiations between Morocco and Polisario. This improved relations with Algeria. President Taya renewed diplomatic ties with Morocco and pursued a neutral stance in external affairs in order to secure economic support from the international community. In 1989 Mauritania, Morocco, Algeria, Tunisia and Libya established the Union du Maghreb Arabe, intended to promote economic co-operation.

Severe tensions with Senegal in 1988–89 prompted intervention by the President of Côte d'Ivoire, who organized a bilateral summit meeting, but further clashes brought the threat of war. Cross-border expulsions and the flow of refugees caused severe problems for Senegal, Mauritania and Mali, but Taya resisted the return of refugees to Mauritania. The USA, which supported Senegal in the dispute, suspended economic assistance to Mauritania, and Morocco also withdrew its support. Mauritania and Senegal eventually signed a peace treaty in July 1991. The only country to support Mauritania in its dispute with Senegal was Iraq.

Mauritania did not condemn Iraq's invasion of Kuwait in August 1990 and did not support the ensuing, Egyptian-sponsored Resolution 195 at the Arab League summit in Cairo, which denounced the deployment of Iraqi troops on the border with Saudi Arabia. The close relationship with the Iraqi regime caused Arab and Western donors to suspend economic support for Mauritania. In order to secure the restoration of ties with the Gulf states and to receive World Bank and IMF assistance, Taya was obliged to oust all Baathists from the country's leadership. As the Baathists represented the strongest anti-black faction in Mauritania, the purge also allowed Taya to normalize diplomatic relations with Senegal and France.

Mauritania formally recognized Israel in 1995, having established lower-level relations from 1991, and Israel opened an embassy in Nouakchott in 1999. Mauritania was the first Arab country in the Maghreb to forge such close relations with Israel; Libya closed its embassy in Mauritania in protest. In May 2001 a visit by the Mauritanian Minister of Foreign Affairs and Co-operation to Israel was strongly criticized by the Arab League but had a more positive impact on Mauritania's relations with the West. Mauritania joined the Pan-Sahel Initiative in 2002, with Chad, Mali and Niger, intended to promote border security against terrorism.

There was considerable international concern following the ousting of Taya and the seizure of power by the CMJD in August 2005. The USA suspended co-operation, demanding an immediate restoration of constitutional order, and the AU declared that the removal of Taya was unconstitutional. However, Mauritania slowly regained international support following the implementation of constitutional reforms and the holding of democratic elections. In April 2007 the Peace and Security Council of the AU readmitted Mauritania.

The coup led by Abdel Aziz in August 2008 prompted further regional and international concern. The EU condemned the action and blocked €156m. in planned funding for 2008–13, and the USA suspended all non-humanitarian assistance to Mauritania, including finance for training in peacekeeping operations and military co-operation. Abdel Aziz resisted the AU's demand that the elected President, Sidi Ould Cheikh Abdallahi, be reinstated. Mauritania's new Minister of Foreign Affairs and Co-operation visited Morocco to discuss the political situation with King Mohammed VI, and Morocco accorded recognition to the new military junta. Abdel Aziz gradually secured a degree of external support for Mauritania's new political course.

After declaring solidarity with the Palestinian territories, in January 2009 Abdel Aziz recalled the Mauritanian ambassador from Israel and suspended diplomatic relations with that country, thereby receiving support from Libya and Iran. Israel closed its embassy in Nouakchott in March at the request of the Mauritanian Government, and bilateral relations ended. The Libyan leader, Muammar al-Qaddafi, pledged funds to Mauritania of some US $500m. to compensate for losses from Western countries. Following the death of Qaddafi, in November 2011 the Mauritanian Government officially recognized the National Transitional Council as the legitimate Government of Libya.

The AU and President Abdoulaye Wade of Senegal sponsored the formation of an International Contact Group on Mauritania (ICGM), including the EU and the Arab League. Under ICGM auspices, the Dakar Agreement was signed by the Mauritanian Government and opposition parties in June 2009, and Mauritania was readmitted to the AU later in that month. Abdel Aziz's victory at the presidential election in July, together with the need to ensure stability in the country after further attacks by AQIM, motivated the EU to normalize relations with Mauritania in January 2010 and resume full development co-operation.

An agreement whereby Mauritania granted a Chinese company 25 years' fishing rights in its waters, in return for investments of some US $100m. in Nouadhibou, was approved by the Mauritanian legislature in June 2011, despite protracted protests by Mauritanian shipowners, opposition deputies and civil society organizations. The Chinese partner withdrew from the agreement in January 2013, provoking renewed criticism of Abdel Aziz. In December Mauritania and China signed an agreement on economic and technical co-operation, whereby Mauritania was to receive some MRU 17,000m. for infrastructure, sanitation and agricultural development projects in Nouadhibou. In August 2014 China granted a loan of $294m. to Mauritania to extend the port of Nouakchott, making China its most important commercial partner. In June 2015 Parliament approved an agreement with China that assigned Mauritania about $28m. on a part-donation/part-loan basis for a water purification system in Nouakchott.

In late 2012, following a shooting incident (see above), Abdel Aziz received prolonged medical treatment in France, allowing for improved relations with his host country. In April 2013 the French Minister of Foreign Affairs, Laurent Fabius, visited Mauritania, where he and Abdel Aziz discussed establishing a UN peacekeeping mission for Mali. At the conclusion of the AU-led International Support Mission to Mali operation in Mali in mid-2013, Mauritania contributed 1,800 troops to the successor UN Multidimensional Integrated Stabilization Mission in Mali (MINUSMA).

Relations between Mauritania and Mali deteriorated in 2013 following the refusal of the transitional administration in Mali to allow Mauritanian forces on to Malian territory as part of the MINUSMA peacekeeping operation. The transitional Malian authorities declared that this would violate Malian sovereignty and prove Mauritanian support for Tuareg and Arab rebel forces in northern Mali. The two countries' ministers responsible for foreign affairs met in Nouakchott in October, and a visit to Mauritania in January 2014 by the Malian President, Ibrahima Boubacar Keïta, marked the normalization of bilateral relations.

In January 2014 Abdel Aziz participated in the creation of the G5 Sahel—comprising Mauritania, Mali, Niger, Burkina Faso and Chad—to collaborate against terrorism in the region. This provoked criticism from Senegal and Algeria, which had been excluded from the alliance. Nouakchott was chosen as its headquarters. In March 2016 the G5 Sahel announced plans for a joint counter-terrorism rapid reaction force, following which Algeria suspended military co-operation with Mauritania.

In August 2014, as part of the G5 Sahel anti-terrorist initiative, France announced the launch of Operation Barkhane and its intention to create eight military bases in the five member countries, including in Atar in Mauritania. In December Mauritania announced that it had agreed to deploy 890 troops as part of the UN Multidimensional Integrated Stabilization Mission in the Central African Republic (MINUSCA). In December 2015 the first group of soldiers joined MINUSCA. (As at June 2022 Mauritania contributed a total of 787 personnel to MINUSCA.)

In June 2016 UNHCR, Mauritania and Mali signed an agreement to repatriate about 40,000 Malian refugees living in the Mbera camp in south-eastern Mauritania. However, in the second half of that year an additional 6,000 people were estimated to have crossed the border seeking refuge. A commission on the repatriation of refugees was formed by Mauritania, Mali and UNHCR, and its inaugural meeting was convened in Nouakchott in early 2017.

Meanwhile, in September 2016 the Executive President of the Palestinian National Authority, Mahmud Abbas, visited Nouakchott for meetings with Abdel Aziz. Abbas announced the inauguration of a Palestinian embassy in Mauritania, which was later opened in Nouakchott.

Tensions with Morocco increased in December 2016 when Hamid Chabat, Secretary-General of the Moroccan Istiqlal party, laid claim to La Güera (also known as Lagouira), a 'ghost town' in Western Sahara adjoining Nouadhibou, where the Mauritanian army had maintained a small garrison since the end of the 1975–78 war. In an attempt to alleviate the situation, President Abdel Aziz received an official call from King Muhammad VI to discuss bilateral relations. The Moroccan Prime Minister, Abdelilah Benkirane, subsequently visited Abdel Aziz in Nouakchott. On the same day, in Rabat, leaders of Morocco's largest party, the Parti de la Justice et du Développement, received representatives of pro-Government Mauritanian parties.

In July 2017 a G5 Sahel allied force was officially launched, to consist of about 5,000 troops from the five member countries and to be supported by France in the fight against terrorism in the region. In September Abdel Aziz attended the 72nd UN General Assembly in New York, USA, where he met his counterparts from countries supporting the G5 Sahel concerning the need for funds. In November Abdel Aziz met Jean-Marc Chataigner, Special Envoy of the French President for the Sahel, who declared French support for the G5 Sahel and announced an increase in French funding for Mauritania, from €600m. to €800m. Meanwhile, a series of reciprocal visits by French and Mauritanian officials in April showed a willingness to strengthen ties between the two countries.

Senegalese President Macky Sall visited Abdel Aziz in Nouakchott in February 2018 to discuss the exploitation of oil and natural gas resources along their borders. The meeting also marked the beginning of negotiations regarding a fishing treaty between the two countries, which had been suspended in 2015. In July 2018 Abdel Aziz and Sall finally signed the fishing treaty, marking the normalization of relations between Mauritania and Senegal. In December, following a brief visit to Senegal by Abdel Aziz, Senegalese President Sall visited Nouakchott to sign the agreement concerning exploitation of the gas deposits located across the maritime border between the two countries.

Meanwhile, in September 2018 Mauritania became the 15th West African country to sign the regional Economic Partnership Agreement, which seeks to promote trade between the EU and 16 West African countries. In October the EU announced funds worth €16.8m. in support of a project to improve the health care system in Mauritania, which was followed in November by a €13m. grant to finance land development in Mauritania.

In November 2018 US President Donald Trump announced that Mauritania would be removed from the African Growth and Opportunity Act, which offers incentives to African countries to open up their economies, from January 2019, owing to the continuation of forced labour and the legacy of slavery in the country.

Meanwhile, France's Minister for Europe and Foreign Affairs, Jean-Yves Le Drian, visited Mauritania in December 2018 for a G5 Sahel meeting, and assigned funds of €11.2m. to the country. In August 2019 a total of 11 West African heads of state, as well as representatives from European countries, the USA and the Russian Federation, attended the inauguration of

Ghazouani as Mauritania's new President. Ghazouani's first international event as President was a G5 Sahel meeting in Ouagadougou in September.

In November 2019 the Kuwait Fund for Arab Economic Development granted a loan of US $32.9m. for the construction of a new 150-km paved road linking the south-eastern town of Néma to the border with Mali. In January 2020 the National Assembly approved a bill authorizing the ratification of an $87m. loan agreement between the Government and the Export-Import Bank of China for the construction of a new fishing port at Nouakchott. President Ghazouani made an official visit to the United Arab Emirates (UAE) in late January, after which the UAE Government announced the allocation of funds totalling $2,000m. to aid investment and development projects in Mauritania.

A summit of the G5 Sahel heads of state was held in the French town of Pau in January 2020, following which a new military co-operation framework was announced, including an expansion of Operation Barkhane. During the summit the EU agreed to grant €24m. to improve the Mauritanian health care system, while France granted €9.8m. towards the amelioration of the national electricity network.

Also in January 2020, Ghazouani attended the UK-Africa Investment Summit in London, UK, reportedly meeting on its sidelines the chief executive of BP. In February Mauritania and Senegal signed a sale and purchase agreement with BP and Kosmos Energy, covering an annual total of 2.5m. metric tons of liquefied natural gas from the offshore Greater Tortue Ahmeyim project, located in waters on the two countries' maritime border.

The World Bank approved grants totalling US $52m. in March 2020 to support Mauritania in implementing an effective social 'safety net' system, including social transfers to poor and vulnerable households. In April the Bank's board approved a grant of $5.2m. in support of the country's public health response to the spread of COVID-19; a further grant of $70m. was approved by the World Bank's International Development Association in July. Meanwhile, in April, as the economic and social impact of the pandemic intensified, the IMF approved the disbursement of $130m. from its Rapid Credit Facility partly to address Mauritania's urgent balance of payments needs. The Fund increased Extended Credit Facility funding (agreed in December 2017) from $164m. to $193m. in September 2020.

Following the reopening of Mauritania's borders in early June 2020, the Algerian Minister of Foreign Affairs, Sabri Boukadoum, made an official visit to the country. Discussions focused on reviving bilateral co-operation and combating the further spread of COVID-19. French President Emmanuel Macron and Spanish Prime Minister Pedro Sánchez joined leaders of the G5 Sahel nations at a summit meeting in Nouakchott on 30 June, which also included the participation (by video link) of German Chancellor Angela Merkel and Italian Prime Minister Giuseppe Conte.

On 7 September 2020 the US Special Envoy for the Sahel visited President Ghazouani in Nouakchott to discuss security and human rights. Shortly afterwards, President Ghazouani received the Spanish interior minister in Nouakchott, together with an EU delegation, which announced a €48m. loan towards the Mauritanian development programme and €12m. for the health care sector.

On 25 September 2020 the USA announced a US $152m. loan to four Sahelian countries, including Mauritania, to improve development in the region. A meeting between G5 Sahel, MINUSMA, EU representatives and President Ghazouani was held in Nouakchott at the end of the month to discuss technical support for the G5 Sahel force. The meeting was followed in October by the eighth session of the G5 Sahel Council of Ministers in Nouakchott.

After Polisario troops blockaded a key road leading to the border crossing with Mauritania at Guerguerat, obstructing the import of goods, in October 2020 the Mauritanian Chief of General Staff of the Armed Forces, Maj.-Gen. Mohamed Ould Bamba Ould Meguett, met Polisario leaders in Tindouf, Algeria, to attempt a mediation. Nevertheless, the blockade of the passage continued, causing a huge increase in prices of imported goods from Morocco. In the following month the

Moroccan army intervened against Polisario in Guerguerat and reopened the passage. Meanwhile, in October the Saudi Minister of State for African Affairs visited Nouakchott to reinforce relations between Saudi Arabia and the G5 Sahel countries.

In February 2021 a Mauritanian delegation participated in the 2021 General Assembly of the Sahel Alliance in N'Djamena, Chad. On 17–18 May President Ghazouani visited the French capital, Paris, to attend first a G5 Sahel meeting and then a Summit on Financing African Economies with French President Macron, other African heads of state and several European leaders. On 28 May the Mauritanian Government signed an agreement with renewable energy company CWP Global for the development of a 30-GW 'Power-to-X' project, under which the largest solar and wind project in the world was to be created in the north of the country for the production of 'green' hydrogen. In June the French Government's announcement of the staged withdrawal of its Barkhane operation was strongly criticized in Mauritania. Meanwhile, pandemic-related restrictions were increased at airports and borders for visitors to the country.

Along with several other African countries, in early August 2021 Mauritania criticized the admission of Israel as an observer member of the AU. In late August the IMF launched a US $650,000m. plan to support the global economy, including a $175m. loan to Mauritania. On the same day, the Government concluded an agreement with Kuwait to cancel 95% of the interest payments due on the loans received from that country. The remaining 5% of payments would be reinvested by Kuwait in Mauritania.

On 31 August 2021 G5 Sahel Ministers of Defence met in Niamey, Niger, to devise a strategy against the increasing jihadist threat across their countries. In September the Mauritanian Chief of the Army met his counterpart in Saudi Arabia to discuss joint military co-operation.

President Ghazouani met his Togolese counterpart Faure Gnassingbé in Nouakchott in October 2021 to discuss co-operation between the two countries. Later in that month Mauritania participated in a meeting of EU and AU member states in Kigali, Rwanda. In November Mauritania's fishing licence with the EU was renewed for five years at the cost of €75m. per year. In the same month the UN Development Programme granted Mauritania US $17m. to tackle poverty in the country.

President Ghazouani visited Abu Dhabi, UAE, in mid-November 2021 to attend a summit on industrialization, where he met several senior Emirati officials with whom he agreed to establish a joint council dedicated to UAE investment in Mauritania's private sector.

In late November 2021 three radar posts were installed along Mauritania's border with Algeria in order to deter illicit trafficking of goods. On 30 November construction began of the bridge in Rosso connecting Mauritania and Senegal, the costs of which would be covered from a gift of EU (€20m.) and loans from the African Bank for Development (€41m.) and the European Investment Bank (€22m.). According to President Ghazouani, the Rosso bridge would strengthen African integration and co-operation. In early December President Ghazouani received a World Bank delegation in Nouakchott and the representatives of several other Sahelian countries. The World Bank consequently announced funding to Mauritania worth US $810m. Later in that month Ghazouani visited İstanbul, Turkey (now Türkiye), to attend an Africa-Turkey summit, and then Algiers, Algeria, in an attempt to bring about reconciliation between Algeria and Morocco.

In January 2022 an incident took place in the Malian border town of Nara that led to the deaths of seven Mauritanian livestock farmers, reportedly by Malian armed forces. After pressure from Mauritania, the Malian Government announced an inquiry. In early March further clashes took place around Nara, which reportedly had been the scene of activity by jihadist groups, and several Mauritanian livestock farmers went missing, prompting fresh protests from the Mauritanian Government, which accused Malian forces of being responsible. In mid-March Mali closed its border with Mauritania to civilians.

On 28 March 2022 the Agence Française de Développement (AFD) announced €9.75m. in funding to improve enterprises run by women in Mauritania. In the same month the World Health Organization announced US $9m. to fund country's welfare system. The AFD granted a further €6.5m. in June to improve the Mauritanian judicial system.

The eighth session of the Moroccan-Mauritanian High Commission closed on 11 March 2022 in Rabat with the signing of 13 co-operation treaties in various economic sectors. In mid-March President Ghazouani made an official visit to Madrid, Spain, to promote bilateral co-operation, and later in the month he visited Dakar to attend the ninth Water World Forum.

In April 2022 Saudi Arabia announced that it would convert a deposit of US $300m. that it had made with Mauritania's central bank in 2015 to a 'soft' loan, in order to support the local currency and Mauritania's balance of payments position. In May the EU made a grant of $40m. to Mauritania to improve education. In the same month the Chiefs of Staff of the armed forces of Mauritania, Algeria, Niger and Mali met in Nouakchott to discuss co-operation in the fight against terrorism and illegal immigration.

During the North Atlantic Treaty Organization (NATO) summit held in Madrid, Spain, in June 2022, the General Secretary of the alliance stated that Mauritania played an essential role in the stability of the Sahel. As a result of a prolonged drought affecting Mauritania (and the wider Sahel region), especially in the south of the country, where some 680,000 people were suffering from food insecurity, in July the US Government announced US $11m. in emergency funding to Mauritania.

Economy

PAUL MELLY

INTRODUCTION

Extending from the Atlantic coast eastwards across vast tracts of the Sahara and the Sahel, the Islamic Republic of Mauritania is not only a geographical bridge between the Maghreb and West Africa, but a social, economic and political bridge between these two regions. Thinly populated across its northern and central desert regions, the country is dotted with many more settlements across the southern pastoral and agricultural belt. However, no part of the country is densely inhabited, beyond Nouakchott, the capital.

Largely nomadic and rural for centuries, Mauritania has experienced a huge shift in the geographical balance of human settlement and economic activity since independence in 1960. Much of the population is now concentrated in urban areas, particularly Nouakchott, founded just 60 years ago, and now home to perhaps one-third of Mauritania's 4.9m. people. In desert regions the population is concentrated in Nouadhibou (the main fishing and export port), Zouerate (centre of the iron mining industry) and a few isolated towns, including several historic oasis settlements. Across the south many people live in farming villages. The local economies of Nouadhibou and Zouerate are built around iron ore production and fisheries—key export earnings—but the Nouakchott urban economy is more diverse, with government and the public sector complemented by trading and service businesses, artisanal fishing and port operations. Across the rural south, agriculture and livestock husbandry are the main providers of livelihoods.

Mauritania's dual regional attachments are reflected in its membership of the Union du Maghreb Arabe (UMA), its 2017 association agreement with the Economic Community of West African States (ECOWAS) and its membership of the G5 grouping of Sahelian countries. Each of these plays a distinct role, but each faces serious challenges. The UMA remains largely paralysed by the ongoing 'Cold Peace' between Morocco and Algeria, while ECOWAS faces serious difficulty in maintaining the bloc's commitment to democratic constitutional politics after military coups in Mali, Burkina Faso and Guinea, and the G5 Sahel was weakened by the withdrawal of Mali in mid-2022. Mauritania's then President Gen. Mohamed Ould Abdel Aziz played a key role in the creation of the G5 Sahel in 2014, with Mali, Burkina Faso, Niger and Chad. Initially set up to promote regional economic development, in order to defuse the pressures that fuel recruitment by jihadist and criminal groups, the G5 soon prioritized the military struggle against armed groups, although in 2018 it reinvigorated the development side of its agenda, drafting a list of priority projects, mostly in deprived outlying areas, which secured pledges of donor support.

However, ECOWAS is making steady progress in deepening economic integration, with a common external tariff, and the attractions of this regional trading space induced Mauritania to opt for the 2017 association accord, particularly as it was already aligned with the West African bloc for trade and development negotiations with the European Union (EU). Nevertheless, the country held back from fully rejoining ECOWAS—which it had left in 2000—partly because it wanted to stay outside the bloc's space for free movement of people. There are significant communities of expatriate Mauritanian traders in several West African countries, but the Government in Nouakchott prefers to retain the power to control migration. (It does have a bilateral migration agreement with Senegal and there is a large Senegalese population in Nouakchott.) Meanwhile, Mauritania belongs to both the League of Arab States (the Arab League) and the African Union (AU).

The Grand Tortue Ahmeyim (GTA) offshore gas project should become a major contributor to exports from 2023–24. It will generate extra Government revenue and hugely bolster a hydrocarbons sector that hitherto had struggled to achieve significant scale or commercial viability.

The impacts of the COVID-19 pandemic slowed the buoyant pace of economic activity. However, the International Monetary Fund (IMF) stepped in to provide additional emergency funding and steady growth resumed in 2021.

ECONOMIC FUNDAMENTALS

Heavily reliant on exports of iron ore, gold and fish, and with domestic agriculture and pastoralism dependent on the arid Sahelian climate, the Mauritanian economy is exposed to powerful influences beyond the Government's control: fluctuations in the prices of its extractive exports and the level of Atlantic fish stocks and the always fragile weather cycle. In the Sahel precipitation is concentrated in a single wet season, from late June to early September; and the total or partial failure of these rains—as happened in 2017—is not unusual. Moreover, occasional flash floods can also cause damage, as happened in September 2020. In the lowlands along the Senegal and Gorgol rivers, irrigation does partially mitigate this meteorological risk.

Despite these challenges, Mauritania has experienced an increase in rates of growth in real gross domestic product (GDP) from an annual average of 2.7% in 1980–1999. Since the turn of the century the overall long term trend has been steadily positive, with real GDP growth averaging 3.7% per annum over 2000–18, despite difficult years in 2014—when output from the small Chinguetti oil field, and world prices for iron ore, gold and oil, were disappointing—and 2018, marred by drought. There was a rebound to 5.8% in 2019 before COVID-19 pushed Mauritania into recession, with real GDP contracting by 1.8% in 2020. However, 2021 brought recovery, with real GDP rising by 3.0%. Initial projections suggested growth could reach 5.0% in 2022, but the knock-on effects of the Russian Federation's invasion of Ukraine, pushing up world cereal prices, may prove to have curbed the final out-turn.

Inflation averaged 5% per annum over 2000–18; in 2019 and 2020 it was 2.3%, rising to 3.8% in 2021.

There are marked contrasts between the performance of different parts of the economy, with the extractives sector experiencing sharp fluctuations.

Extractives real GDP rose by 4.2% in 2014 but shrank by 5.6% the following year, grew by just 0.7% in 2016 and then slumped by 6.2% in 2017 and a further 9.5% in 2018, only to recover by a dramatic 27.2% in 2019; in 2020, amid global trading conditions cooled by COVID-19, it rose by just 0.9%, before growing much more strongly, by around 5.0%, in 2021.

Non-extractives real GDP, influenced by different factors, has been on a much more consistent growth track: it rose by 5.8% in 2014 and 1.4% the year after, then by 2.0% in 2016, by 4.7% in 2017, by 3.5% in 2018 and by 3.2% in 2019. Amid the impacts of COVID-19, unsurprisingly, it contracted by 2.9% in 2020 but then recovered, with growth of about 2.5%, in 2021.

Development of the GTA gas project, and the manner in which government oversight has been smoothly co-ordinated with Senegal, which shares the field, has done much to enhance Mauritania's credibility as a location for international investment. That credibility has been further reinforced by the fact that BP, one of the largest global 'oil majors', is the main developer of the scheme. And the scale of the GTA deposit has stirred fresh interest in Mauritania among other hydrocarbons companies that had hitherto regarded the country as of only marginal interest for exploration. The Government has upgraded key infrastructure—notably, with a new airport for Nouakchott—and simplified tax rules and bureaucracy, while overhauling technical and engineering education to produce an expanded pool of specialist skilled potential employees. The results of this initiative were demonstrated by Mauritania's rise up the World Bank's *Doing Business* rankings, from 165th place out of 190 in 2016 to a much more creditable 152nd place in 2019. The parliamentary commission of inquiry into alleged poor governance during the Abdel Aziz presidency and the subsequent arrest and detention of the former head of state could temporarily damage Mauritania's image yet also strengthen the country's standing by demonstrating that there is a process of accountability—a message reinforced when an IMF team visited Nouakchott at the request of the Government, to advise on how good governance could be reinforced to curb the risks of corruption.

SOCIETY

Despite substantial social progress, the pattern of advances has been uneven and sections of the population, such as the Harratins (descendants of slaves), suffer serious disadvantage. President Mohamed Ould Cheikh Mohamed Ahmed Ould Ghazouani pledged to address these problems, announcing a programme of social measures in early 2020, halfway into his first year in office. The advent of COVID-19 initially hampered his ability to prioritize this agenda, but as the pandemic faded the Government regained more room to tackle societal inequality and meet basic development needs.

After setbacks during the 2008–09 global financial crisis—which reduced demand for Mauritania's commodity exports—and the 2014–16 commodity price slump, average per capita GDP has been on a fitful but broadly upward track, rising from US $1,136 in 2016 to $1,678 by 2019; it slipped back to $1,673, in the pandemic year, 2020, before recovering to $1,723 in 2021. This places Mauritania far behind the much more prosperous Morocco ($3,497) but slightly ahead of Senegal ($1,607). Mauritania ranked 157th out of 189 countries in the 2020 Human Development Index produced by the United Nations (UN) Development Programme (while Morocco was in 121st place and Senegal 168th). The IMF describes Mauritania's development needs as 'massive'.

In mid-2022 Mauritania had a population of around 4.9m., which was projected to increase by 2.6% per annum in 2020–25, according to the UN Population Fund. Although this rate is gradually slowing, 39% of Mauritanians were aged under 15 at mid-2022, presenting the state with a huge challenge to provide sufficient school places and stimulate job creation—tasks that were further complicated by the pandemic. Average life expectancy in 2021 was 64 years for men and 67 years for women. However, although 70% of births were attended by skilled health personnel, the maternal mortality ratio, at 766 deaths per 100,000 live births in 2017 (according to the UN Children's Fund, UNICEF), compares unfavourably with Senegal (315) and the much poorer Mali (562) and Niger (509). Only around 13% of women aged 15–49 use modern contraception, yet a further 18% of women in this age group would like to do so but do not have access. Only 68% of children aged 12–23 months are immunized against diphtheria, pertussis and tetanus—below the figures for Mali and Niger—and nutrition also remains a problem for many families, although indicators are improving: in 2021 some 17% of children under the age of five suffered from stunting.

COVID-19 posed severe challenges in 2020 and 2021. However, as in other Sahelian countries, the confirmed numbers of cases—at 63,041 by mid-October 2022—and deaths (995) were relatively low, even though the limited extent of testing means that these figures are probably an underestimate. Vaccinations began quite early, in February 2021, with doses donated by the United Arab Emirates (UAE), followed by the People's Republic of China and later France, the latter as part of the COVAX programme.

There has been notable progress in extending access to schooling and improving its quality: some 66% of boys and 80% of girls reach the final year of primary education and 46% complete at least lower secondary school education. Some 97% of primary school teachers are trained.

ECONOMIC POLICY AND PUBLIC FINANCE

The impact of COVID-19 significantly slowed the pace of growth but did not push Mauritania into deep recession or to a fundamental shift in economic strategy; with IMF support, the country was able to contain both the scale and the duration of the pandemic-induced downturn, with a clear rebound in 2021. Moreover, the Government can look ahead to the start of gas production at the GTA project in 2023–24, boosting exports and fiscal revenues and holding out the prospect of a broader energy generation base. However, as noted above, the advent of COVID-19 did slow the launch momentum of President Ghazouani's new drive to tackle deep-seated societal inequalities in household living standards and access to core public services, curbing its immediate political impact, even if progress towards the longer term socioeconomic goals has only been delayed rather than obstructed.

The political focus on the corruption probe into the financial stewardship of the former head of state, Abdel Aziz, and resulting prosecutions, has helped to divert public attention away from the performance of the Ghazouani administration. However, eventually the current head of state will come under some pressure to show that his more consensual political style and his proclaimed focus on tackling social inequality can deliver meaningful results—higher living standards, better services and greater opportunity for the most disadvantaged. This is not just a question of money; real progress may also depend on the Government sometimes making awkward choices about priorities, sensitive issues such as land rights or taking actions that erode the preferential position enjoyed by certain vested interests or powerful socioeconomic entities or sections of society.

Mauritania operates a liberal mixed economic model, with a continued production sector role for some state-owned entities beyond utility and public service provision—and, in particular, the national iron ore mining company Société Nationale Industrielle et Minière (SNIM). This parastatal has long acted both as a conventional mining operator and as the spine of economic activity and development in the far north. During the Abdel Aziz presidency it was also often used as a cash cow for state projects outside its own sector and it remained effectively integrated into the political and public service personnel structure, with a frequent crossover of senior personnel between SNIM and the higher reaches of government. It seems possible that the recent investigation into the Abdel Aziz administration's conduct of public affairs, and the Government's decision in 2022 to seek detailed IMF advice on governance and transparency, might lead to a tightening of the constraints on SNIM's freedom to invest in, or finance, activities and projects beyond its core mineral sector remit.

The Government is keen to encourage the diversification of urban business and services, to stimulate the creation of jobs and open up entrepreneurial opportunities for technically educated young people, and to encourage more business growth beyond Nouakchott, for example, through development of a free zone in Nouadhibou. The state does try to assist the less well off through the Emel network of subsidized shops, but this approach is less effective than the food security mechanisms developed by some other Sahelian states.

Regional development also contributes to the strategy for countering the risk of jihadist terrorism: the Government has established local service hubs and even new communities in remote areas, to reinforce social and economic opportunity and counter the possibility of disenchantment among young people; around the Mbera camp for Malian refugees in the far southeast, programmes have been developed for the local host population as well as the Malians. Mauritania differs from other Sahelian states in being more urbanized; agriculture and pastoralism are proportionally less significant as sources of livelihood, although many Mauritanians have deep cultural and family connections to nomadic pastoralist culture.

The commodity price slump that began in 2014 exerted increasing economic and social pressure and eventually the Government sought the assistance of the IMF, which in December 2017 approved a three-year recovery programme, supported by Extended Credit Facility (ECF) concessional funding of US $163.9m. This sought to stabilize the fiscal and macroeconomic position, strengthen action to tackle deprivation and the social safety net, and encourage a diversification of activity and employment. Monetary policy was overhauled to reinforce the autonomy of the central bank and allow greater flexibility in the foreign exchange market, to enhance private sector access to hard currency. In September 2020 the IMF bolstered the programme's funding and extended its timeframe to December that year, to help the Government cope with the impacts of COVID-19; it had already, in April 2020, approved an extra SDR 95.68m. in extra support, to assist with pandemic costs.

At its final review of performance under the ECF programme, in March 2021, the Fund gave a strongly positive verdict on Mauritania's performance. It advised the Government to continue to prioritize health, education and support for the most vulnerable, while maintaining a careful monetary stance; it also argued for close monitoring of the banking sector and endorsed the Government's commitment to transparency and proper auditing of pandemic-related contracts. The Fund also warned that Mauritania still had 'massive' development needs and remained at 'high risk' of debt distress.

The Abdel Aziz Government had drawn up a Strategy for Accelerated Growth and Shared Prosperity (SCAPP) for 2016–30, with the goal of halving poverty over the long term and also responding to the threat of climate change. After the earlier prioritizing of infrastructure projects and the extractives sector, the plan laid new stress on agriculture, pastoralism and fishing, vocational training, health and education; it also promised transparency reforms, reinforcement of the statistics service and the judicial system, and the promotion of gender equality. Although the SCAPP was drafted under Abdel Aziz, its underlying priorities are broadly compatible with Ghazouani's approach.

The Government's capacity to tackle these goals is of course contingent on the strength of public finances, albeit seconded by support from international donors. The Government's primary fiscal balance (excluding the net impact of grant aid) had moved from a deficit equivalent to 4.5% of GDP in 2015 to a comfortable surplus of 3.5% in 2018, slipping back to a surplus of 1.7% in 2019. Unsurprisingly, the pandemic year 2020 saw further weakening, although there was still a surplus, of 1.3%; however, in 2021 that finances slid back into the red, with a deficit equal to 3.0% of GDP.

Until the pandemic, the Mauritanian state managed to maintain a broadly stable level of current expenditure, and which actually declined from 20.6% of GDP in 2015 to a mere 13.7% in 2019. Understandably, 2020 brought a rebound, to 15.8%, before a surge to an estimated 18.2% in 2021. Capital expenditure had been cut sharply from 15.8% of GDP in 2015 to just 8.3% by 2019; amid pandemic disruption the following year capital spending rose only slightly, to 8.7% of GDP, before climbing further, to an estimated 10.0%, in 2021. It seems likely that expenditure at these slightly higher levels will at least be maintained over the years ahead: Ghazouani's Presidential Priority Programme of spending set out sectoral spending targets equal to 3.1% of GDP for 2021 alone and a total of 6.8% of GDP for 2020–22. The main priorities are infrastructure, health, education, income support, agriculture and fisheries, subsidies for both existing and start up businesses, water and sanitation and additional 'greening' support for agriculture.

Yet to pay for these enhanced outlays, the Government needs to sustain domestic revenue collection, while retaining the confidence of international donors and development lenders. Positively, government income has been on a fluctuating but broadly upward track, with total revenues and grant aid income rising from 22.8% of GDP in 2017 to 25.0% the next year, slipping to 24.4% in 2019, but then rebounding to 27.2% in 2020, before settling back at an estimated 24.5% in 2021. Within this overall total, extractive sector revenue rose from 1.7% of GDP in 2016 to 3.5% in 2018, then fell back to 1.9% in 2019 before rebounding to 2.8% in 2020 and to 3.2% in 2021, whereas non-extractive revenue fell from 26.8% in 2015 to 21.0% in 2018 and 20.5% the following year. It recovered slightly, to 21.6% in 2020, but fell back to a projected 20.7% in 2021. Inflows of grant aid have fluctuated between 0.5% of GDP and 1.9%, except in the pandemic year 2020, when they surged to 2.7%.

AGRICULTURE

The Sahara desert covers most of northern and central Mauritania, giving way to more Sahelian landscapes that can support livestock pastoralism towards the south. Outside oases, agriculture is mainly confined to southern regions, particularly the Senegal and Gorgol river valleys, where irrigation is feasible on much lower lying land. About 45% of the population still lives in rural areas. The UN's Food and Agricultural Organization (FAO) categorizes only 0.5% of Mauritanian territory as useful agricultural land. Much more extensive areas can support pastoralism, and nomadic traditions remain deeply rooted, a powerful social influence on attitudes among many communities.

Livestock husbandry can generate up to 12% of GDP in some years. The size of the national herd fluctuates in response to the seasonal availability of grazing, but sheep and goats, were estimated to number 23.6m. in 2019, while the number of cattle amounted to 2.2m. and the camel herd just over 1.5m. With climate change, the weather has been getting drier and hotter, pushing many pastoralist communities further south in search of grazing, edging into the narrow southern narrow band of less arid territory that supports widespread farming.

The rural development ministry estimates total potential arable land at 502,000 ha. However, in reality competition with pastoralist needs and the constraints of access to water limit how much land is actually cultivated: in drought years, rain-fed production can be severely depressed, leaving the country more reliant on those areas that can be irrigated with river water. In broad terms, Mauritania can grow about one-third of the grain required to feed its population and in most years it usually needs to import some 500,000–600,000 metric tons.

Farming on the 220,000 ha of rain-fed arable land, producing about 60% of the grain harvest, is reliant on the extent of the late June to early September rainy season, when the main cereal crop is planted, with the harvest following in September–November. By April of the following year household grain stocks start to come under pressure and villagers have to eke out their remaining reserves through the six months or so of the lean season (*la soudure*) until the new harvest. There are extensive tracts of irrigated low-lying land along the Senegal and Gorgol rivers, and small tracts of irrigated agriculture in oases in the Sahara. The irrigated riverside plains, producing paddy rice and other crops, provide a shield against the worst drought impacts and extend the growing season; however, local geographical reality within a village can produce stark inequalities, with households that have irrigated riverside land in a much more secure food supply and income position; those who have only rain-fed fields, on higher ground, are more vulnerable to drought and, if their own crops fail, they sometimes have no choice but to work as paid labourers for their more fortunate neighbours. Traditional manual or animal-drawn techniques are supplemented with tractors in many areas, particularly in the flatlands of the lower Senegal river valley, much of which has been taken over by extensive commercial scale mechanized agriculture.

Good farmland is mainly concentrated along the valley of the Senegal river, which forms the frontier with Mauritania's southern neighbour and its tributary the Gorgol. The water resources of the Senegal basin are managed by the Organisation pour la Mise en Valeur du Fleuve Sénégal (OMVS), with irrigation, power generation and navigation managed through a series of dams, including Diama, on the Mauritania–Senegal border. Around Rosso in the lower Senegal valley, traditional smallholder farming has largely given way to big estates, mainly owned by outside investors from Nouakchott or abroad. This is a politically charged issue for local Afro-Mauritanian families, some of whom were expelled into neighbouring Senegal in 1989, before being allowed to return later, having been deprived of many of their civil and land rights.

More generally across the south, as across the rest of the Sahel, farmers and pastoralists compete for resources of land, water and vegetation, yet they also complement each other: animals graze the stalks of crops left after the harvest that have been harvested and their droppings fertilize the soil for the next season. Peul pastoralists engage in transhumance, moving between southern Mauritania and Senegal in search of grazing. However, climate change intensifies competition for access to land, water and vegetation, putting the interaction between farmers and pastoralists under pressure.

Millet, sorghum and maize are largely grown as rain-fed crops and FAO has also encouraged the cultivation of wheat. However, harvests of these crops are far outstripped by the production of paddy rice on irrigated land. Vegetables are produced in small market gardens watered from wells; and on some plots local solar power units fuels water pumps. Gum arabic, tapped from acacia trees, is also a significant earner for some villages. Harvest volumes fluctuate in response to the weather, but the previous Government set the goal of almost doubling national production of the main cereal crops between 2014 and 2025, and almost tripling horticultural output. Progress has varied, reflecting the complex impacts of weather and irrigation. In 2017 the failure of rainfall left many farmers unable to produce a significant harvest, while in the 2020–21 season planting started late in many areas, flooding caused some disruption, and agricultural activity and food trade was significantly disrupted by the COVID-19 pandemic—yet these setbacks were more than outweighed by the overall benefit of sustained good rains. The sorghum and millet harvest was 82,000 metric tons in the 2016/17 agricultural year, but the widespread failure of the mid-2017 rainy season sent the output plunging, to just 59,800 tons in 2017/18; then came a recovery to 90,200 tons in 2018/19, followed by a fresh decline, to 69,500 tons, in 2019/20 and then a resurgence to 79,300 tons in 2020/21. Harvests of maize, wheat and barley have fluctuated to a smaller extent, sinking from 17,100 tons in 2016/17 to just 12,400 tons in 2017/18, before recovering to 14,600 tons in 20218/19 and 16,100 tons the year after, and improved further, to 16,800 tons, in 2020/21. Paddy rice is irrigated with water channelled through the OMVS system, and thus partially shielded against drought: output surged from 207,300 tons in 2016/17 to 312,600 tons in 2017/18 but declined slightly, to 305,300 tons, in 2018/19, before a more significant decrease, to 255,400 tons, was recorded in 2019/20. In 2020/21 it rebounded to 309,000 tons. All this means that the total national cereal crop was 306,400 tons in 2016/17, rising to 384,700 tons in 2017/18 and 410,200 tons in 2018/19, but a slump to 341,100 tons followed in 2019/20 before a recovery to 405,100 tons in 2020/21. With national production rising, cereal imports in both 2018/19 and 2019/20 were estimated at around 550,000 tons, compared with a five-year annual average of almost 600,000 tons.

Mauritania participates in the food crisis early warning system overseen by the Ouagadougou-based Comité Permanent Inter-Etats de Lutte contre la Sécheresse dans le Sahel (CILSS), which maintains a harmonized set of data standards and co-ordinates with international donors through the Réseau de Prévention des Crises Alimentaires (RPCA). Data is collected at local level and analysed nationally to spot communities at risk of food crisis, reserve stocks are maintained and essential supplies provided to households in need through the Emel network of subsidized shops; however, subventions are limited and customers can face lengthy queues—so many take paid work instead, and then buy food at market prices. Each March–April the RPCA issues projections of the numbers of people at risk during the forthcoming lean season, so that national agencies, non-governmental organizations and international partners can organize the distribution of the necessary assistance. In March–April 2022 the RPCA warned that according to projections by the CILSS-supervised framework, during the most severe phase of the 2022 lean season, from June to August, some 678,543 people in Mauritania would be in food crisis or emergency or famine. In mid-October 2022, according to the UN High Commissioner for Refugees, Mauritania was still hosting 71,000 refugees, mainly from Mali, in Hodh Chargui, in the south-east; most were at the Mbera camp and supported by humanitarian aid. An estimated additional 11,000 refugees and asylum seekers are living in the cities of Noukchott and Nouadhibou.

FISHING

Off Mauritania's long Atlantic coast lie rich fishing grounds and the sector employs 180,000 people and in some years generates up to one-half of all export income, according to FAO, which stated that in 2018 there were 3,800 locally-based boats operating. In addition to the maritime fish catch, some 15,000 metric tons per year are caught in the Senegal river and its tributaries, and much of this is consumed locally. The total national catch in 2021 amounted to 627,100 tons, according to central bank figures. The Imraguen community fish the Banc d'Arguin area of shallows, sandbanks and islands by traditional methods, while many Senegalese migrants based in Nouakchott, Nouadhibou and the southern town of Ndiago operate sea-going canoes. Mauritanian society is culturally oriented towards the desert, but the Government has tried to encourage more locals to engage in inshore fishing using modern boats.

Meanwhile, industrial deep-sea fishing is a major economic activity, with Mauritanian waters attracting fleets from Europe and Asia, usually operating under long-term agreements with the Government. In 2021 fish exports amounted to 330,859 metric tons. Nouadhibou is the main base for the commercial deep-water fishing sector: international vessels, largely crewed by Mauritanians, land much of the catch at the port for processing and the sub-sector employs 40,000 people and indirectly generates additional livelihoods. Europe—and Spain in particular—is a key market.

Fisheries agreements with the EU are renegotiated on a rolling basis, seeking maintain catches and, government revenue and jobs while protecting fish stocks on a sustainable basis, with an annual two-month rest period (September–October) during the peak reproductive season. The first accord was signed in 1987 and since 2006 they have taken the form of renewable six-year Fisheries Partnership Agreements (FPAs) for 2006–2011 and then 2012–18, within which four-year protocols are renegotiated on a rolling basis. With the normal schedule of talks disrupted by the COVID-19 pandemic, in July 2020 the agreement was extended for a further year, and on 15 November 2021 the EU and Mauritania signed a new five-year deal, under which the EU will pay €57.5m. per annum for the right to catch up to 287,050 tons a year of shrimp, demersal fish, tuna and small pelagic fish, plus a further €16.5m. for development in Mauritanian coastal communities. The provisions are subject to regular reviews and catch limits can be adjusted in light of stocks, to ensure that fishing is carried out on a sustainable basis.

The Mauritanian Government uses the accords with the EU as a benchmark for the agreements that it strikes with other partners such as Russia and China. Licences with some Chinese companies were at one stage revoked because of concern over compliance with the conservation rules. Poaching is also a concern and the Government has been expanding the offshore patrol capacities of the small Mauritanian navy, with the delivery of a new Chinese-built vessel in 2019.

EXTRACTIVES AND ENERGY

Mauritania is a major producer of iron ore production and development of the rich deposits of the Kédia d'Idjil mountain and surrounding hills in the north, near the border with Western Sahara, is the cornerstone of the industrial mining sector that has diversified the economy away from reliance on rural sectors. Industrial mines also exploit the Tasiast gold deposit, 300 km north of Nouakchott, and the Guelb Moghrein copper and gold deposit, near Akjoujt. More broadly, the extractives sector has diversified with the growth of offshore hydrocarbons exploration and development, a process that is expected to advance significantly with the completion of the GTA gas project.

Iron ore mining is overwhelmingly the preserve of SNIM and the town of Zouerate has grown up as the urban hub for these operations, with a 704-km rail line to an export terminal loading the ore on to ships at Nouadhibou. Nationalized in 1974 and now 78.4% state-owned, SNIM is a pillar of Mauritania's production economy, directly employing about 6,000 people and generating up to 15% of GDP. The company is also a key provider of technocratic appointees to some of the highest posts in political life. Total reserves of iron ore are estimated at more than 1,000m. metric tons. Commercial production began in 1963 and by 2014 the country was the world's 12th largest exporter, with iron ore typically accounting for about one-half of all exports in 2000–13. The Kédia d'Idjil and M'Haoudatt mines were the main sources of production, but in 2013 SNIM announced the discovery of an 830m.-ton deposit 40 km north of Zouerate, and it invested US $750m. in a second magnetite enrichment plant—the Guelb II project—which began operations in 2016.

Output averaged about 11m. metric tons annually over 2006–09, rising to 13.6m. tons in 2015. By 2018 it had fallen back to 11m. tons but reached the 12m–13m. tons range in 2019–20; in 2021 it amounted to 12.8m. tons. SNIM's finances are under pressure but the company hopes to boost output to 18m. tons a year by 2026 and it has pursued a series of joint projects with international partners, although these have not all come to fruition. An agreement with steel giant Arcelor-Mittal to develop a mine at El Agareb was abandoned in 2013. Proposals were drawn up for a mine at Guelb el Aouj, in partnership with Australia's Sphere Minerals, later absorbed into Glencore, but the latter withdrew from Mauritania in 2015 because of low world ore prices. Another project, Tazadit 1, envisaged annual deliveries of 1.5m. metric tons of ore to China's Minmetals Corp.

Canada-based Kinross took over the Tasiast gold mine in 2010. Past difficulties in relations with the Government and the workforce have been gradually smoothed out and in 2019 Kinross confirmed that a US $300m. second phase expansion to extend the mine's life until 2033 would proceed with funding support from the World Bank's International Finance Corporation, Canada's Export Development Corporation (EDC) and commercial banks. In 2021 gold output from Tasiast was 170,502 oz.; some gold is also produced from artisanal diggings and from First Quantum's Guelb Moghrein mine and so total national output in 2021 reached 202,500 oz.

The Guelb Moghrein copper and gold deposit, near Akjoujt, was first developed in the 1970s but soon closed. In 2004 Canada's First Quantum acquired an 80% stake and began mining two years later; in 2010 it took its holding to 100%. The project is operated by the group's subsidiary Mauritanian Copper Mines (MCM), employing some 1,150 people. With estimated proven and probable reserves of 29m. metric tons, some 15,000 tons of copper-gold concentrate are extracted each month from the Guelb Moghrein site. In 2020 the mine produced 28,491 tons of copper, 47,637 oz of gold and 543,719 tons of magnetite and in 2021 output was 18,845 tons of copper, 38,431 oz of gold and 375,268 tons of magnetite.

Further diversification in the mining sector is in prospect. SNIM has been prospecting for tungsten (wolfram), iron, petroleum, phosphates and uranium, while Australian companies have reported encouraging exploration results for uranium. The SNIM subsidiary Société Arabe des Industries Métallurgiques produces about 60,000 metric tons of gypsum per year and has been granted a licence to mine phosphates near Bofal, where reserves are estimated at 135m. tons. There are deposits of high value blue granite in the north.

Mauritania was a late entrant into the hydrocarbons sector, after disappointing results from early exploration efforts after independence. Eventually promising finds were made offshore, with the Chinguetti field estimated to hold 120m. barrels of oil equivalent (BOE), while gas deposits of 265m. BOE were discovered in the Banda field. Production from Chinguetti began in 2006 and rose to 75,000 barrels per day (b/d), but soon sank back to a mere 5,512 b/d by 2014. With the estimate of reserves revised downwards to just 34m. BOE and export receipts sinking to just UM 20.4m in 2016 the project operator, Malaysia's Petronas, prepared to decommission the field. Banda's gas deposit was declared commercially viable in 2012, but the Islamic Development Bank (IDB) opted not to fund a proposed scheme to pipe the gas to an onshore power plant.

However, discovery of the Grand Tortue Ahmeyim (GTA) gas deposit—a major find by international standards—has transformed the sector's prospects and attracted BP to become the operator of the project. The gas deposit, located astride the maritime boundary with Senegal, was discovered by US-based Kosmos Energy in 2015 and as the serious commercial potential became clear, with reserves estimated at 15,000,000m. cu ft, BP came in to lead development and production. In December 2018 Mauritania and Senegal signed a framework bilateral inter-governmental accord, enabling BP to take its own final investment decision and a sale and purchase agreement for BP Gas Marketing to take 2.5m. metric tons of LNG per annum for 20 years, for export to international markets, was signed in early 2020, After an interruption at the height of the COVID-19 pandemic, development of the project resumed in 2021 and commercial production is expected to begin in 2023 or 2024. Besides LNG, plans also provide for two possible pipelines to carry natural gas onshore to both Mauritania and Senegal, for local power generation.

GTA has catalysed a renewal of investor interest in the Mauritanian offshore. In December 2018 Total took on two further exploration blocks, in addition to the three it already held, and announced plans for drilling. Tullow (United Kingdom), Sonatrach (Algeria) and Qatar Petroleum have also been active and there has been a fair degree of interest from other companies.

Mauritania has 486 MW of installed power-generating capacity and in 2019 some 1178.6 GWh were generated, overwhelmingly under arrangements operated or contracted by the parastatal Société Mauritanienne d'Electricité (SOMELEC), which produced 1151.30 GWh and also operates a 5,450-km transmission network. However, the country has difficulty ensuring a reliable supply of electricity and outages are not uncommon. SOMELEC's own generation plants—the largest of which is Nouakchott Nord (180 MW)—accounted for 62% of power output. Some 17% was acquired from the Mananatali and Félou dams operated by the OMVS in Mali, in the Senegal river basin; the OMVS operates a 933-km distribution network that extends to Nouakchott and nine towns across the south. SOMELEC's main windfarm (30 MW) produces 10% of national power output, while a further 10% is produced by solar plants, notably a 50-MW facility in Nouakchott, and 1% is generated by SNIM in Nouadhibou.

Wind and solar power are technologies well suited to servicing isolated locations and thus ideal for Mauritania's many remote settlements. These renewable sources were underexploited until recently, but the UAE is now funding the installation of a series of solar plants; a 15-MW unit in Nouakchott can supply 10,000 homes. A 100-MW windfarm is already under construction between Nouakchott and Nouadhibou. The Australian group CWP Global has now signed an agreement to develop a 30-GW wind and solar power hub in the

Sahara, which would both supply energy to the local market and produce green hydrogen for export.

The vast distances between towns of often moderate size make it difficult to operate a long-distance distribution network on a viable basis, but two major connections are being built, from Nouakchott to Nouadhibou and also from the capital to Akjoujt, Atar and Zouerate. Two other major lines from Nouakchott are planned, one linking it to Keur Macène, on the Senegal border, and the other running to Néma in the far south-east.

MANUFACTURING, INFRASTRUCTURE AND SERVICES

With such a small home market, Mauritania has little manufacturing activity. It is not a cost-competitive location for most activities not directly related to its natural resource base and the main industry is fish processing, concentrated principally in Nouadhibou. Yet there is still scope for economic diversification in technical business and service sectors that require skilled personnel, which explains the Government's drive to enhance higher level technical and engineering education.

Roads are the main form of domestic transport, although the railway from Zouerate to Nouadhibou does carry passengers. Major roads link Nouakchott to Nouadhibou, to Akjoujt and Atar in the centre, to Rosso on the Senegal border and the Route de l'Espoir to Aleg, Kiffa and the far south-east, which also provides a route to Mali and Burkina. The Government is developing a freeport in Nouadhibou. An €87.6m. bridge is under construction to replace the current ferry over the Senegal river at the Rosso border crossing with Senegal, funded mainly by the African Development Bank (AfDB), the European Investment Bank and the EU. The river itself is navigable for 210 km throughout the year, with major river ports, at Rosso, Kaédi and Gouraye.

The main air transport hub is Nouakchott's Oumtounsy airport, the base of national carrier Mauritania Airlines International. Created in 2010, the company flies to Nouadhibou and Zouerate, to Spain's Canary Islands and to numerous North and West African capitals.

Mauritel, owned by Maroc Telecom (now part of the Etisalat group) operates the terrestrial telecommunications network. There are 106 mobile telephone subscriptions for every 100 people, although a significant minority of the population live in communities without network coverage. Mauritel, Mattel and Chinguitel provide mobile services and were awarded licences in 2020.

FOREIGN TRADE AND PAYMENTS

Amid the commodity market slump exports totalled just US $1,388m. in 2015—of which iron ore contributed only $340m—but they edged back up to $1,401m. in 2016 and then $1,767m. in 2017 and $1,895m. in 2018, before surging to $2,319m. in 2019 and an estimated $2,398m. in 2020, despite the impact of the pandemic on global demand. Within this total, exports of iron ore increased in value from $418m. in 2016 to an estimated $879m. in 2020, while exports of gold rose from $289m. to $772m. over the same period. However, exports of copper—which amounted to $138m. in 2016 and $131m. in 2020—have been stable. Exports of fish are of course constrained by the need to manage stocks and their capacity for renewal: these expanded from $421m. in 2016 to $750m. in 2018, before slipping back to an estimated $571m. in 2020. Hydrocarbon exports—$87m. in 2016—finally ceased in 2018, when a mere $11m. was brought in; however, this sector is set for revival in the medium term.

Mauritania has a chronic structural deficit in visible trade and the overall current account of the balance of payments, with the value of imports consistently outweighing export earnings. The 2014–15 economic downturn depressed imports to just $1,948m. in 2015 and $1,900m. in 2016. However, imports then rebounded to $2,094m. in 2017 and $2,601m. in 2018 before increasing further, to $2,889m. in 2019, and to estimated $2,948m. in 2020. The upward trend is evident across the main sectors, with food imports growing in value from $334m. in 2016 to an estimated $693m. in 2020, petroleum products growing from $355m. in 2016 to $624m. two years later, before sinking back to $425m. in 2020 as COVID-19 slowed economic activity and thus demands for fuel. Imports of capital goods fluctuate, reflecting the episodic procurement needs of large mining and development projects and the GTA offshore project: these rose from $538m. in 2016 to $928m. in 2020. Mauritania imports significant quantities of fresh fruit and vegetables from Morocco, and is also heavily reliant on a range of imports from Senegal and international suppliers in Europe and Asia. Iran is a supplier of quality household items such as carpets. Overall, China is the country's largest trade partner.

The deficit in merchandise trade contracted from US $559m. in 2015 to just $327m. in 2017, before expanding to $706m. in 2018. It then contracted again, to $570m. in 2019 and an estimated $550m. in 2020. The current account deficit shrank from $956m. in 2015 to just $681m. by 2017, but rebounded sharply to $976m. in 2018, before falling back to $831m. in 2019, and then expanding again in 2020 to an estimated $945m.

The overall balance includes large and fluctuating inward flows of foreign direct investment, largely a reflection of specific business transactions or projects, and the flows fluctuate sharply, plunging from a net US $502m. in 2015 to $271m. in 2016, before rebounding to $588m. in 2017. They increased further, to $772m., in 2018 and to $884m. in 2019, but slipped to an estimated $783m. in 2020. The current account balance also includes loan and debt service flows by SNIM—a net outflow of $63m. in 2017 but a net inflow of $40m. in 2020; however, these must be seen against the importance of SNIM's contribution to the export account and overall economic activity. The company's net positive contribution to the balance of payments in 2020 was $617m. Loan disbursement inflows for the GTA gas project were $117m. in that year.

Government borrowing is also a factor. The authorities have been careful to keep external public debt below 70% of GDP over recent years, although debt service payments have risen from US $161m. in 2016 to $276m. in 2019 before declining to an estimated $186m. in 2020. Foreign exchange reserves have been stable at between four and six months' worth of imports.

International multilateral and bilateral partners are important sources of development assistance and, in some cases, non-developmental financial support. Their support also remains valuable in terms of expertise and specialist technical assistance. Official grant support to help Mauritania cope with the impacts of COVID-19 was US $134m. in 2020, of which the EU provided $12m., the AfDB $10m. and the World Bank $70m. Disbursements of largely highly concessional support from the IMF were $46m. in 2019 and probably much greater in 2020, after the Fund's approval of large sums in emergency support.

Flows from individual partners vary from year to year. By far the largest net donor is the Arab Fund for Economic and Social Development, contributing US $110m. in 2018 and $164m. the following year. Contributions from the IDB have declined from $83m. in 2015 to just $7m. in 2019. Other key partners are the World Bank ($34m. in 2019), the EU ($13m. in 2019), the AfDB (albeit just $3m. in 2019), China ($11.4m. in 2018), India ($39m. in 2019) and Saudi Arabia ($49m. in 2018 and $35m. in 2019). Moreover, in 2015 Saudi Arabia deposited $300m. in the central bank as a support to overall state finances.

Statistical Survey

Sources (unless otherwise stated): Agence Nationale de la Statistique et de l'Analyse Démographique et Economique, BP 240, Nouakchott; tel. 45-25-30-70; e-mail oumarba70@hotmail.mr; internet www.ansade.mr; Banque Centrale de Mauritanie, Avenue de l'Indépendance, BP 623, Nouakchott; tel. 45-25-00-44; e-mail info@bcm.mr; internet www.bcm.mr.

Area and Population

AREA, POPULATION AND DENSITY

Area (sq km)	1,030,700*
Population (census results)†	
1–15 November 2000	2,508,159
25 March–8 April 2013	
Males	1,743,074
Females	1,794,294
Total	3,537,368
Population (official projections at mid-year)	
2020	4,173,077
2021	4,271,197
2022	4,372,037
Density (per sq km) at mid-2022	4.2

* 397,950 sq miles.
† Figures include nomads, totalling 128,163 in 2000 and 71,122 (males 38,006, females 33,116) in 2013.

POPULATION BY AGE AND SEX
('000, official projections at mid-2022)

	Males	Females	Total
0–14 years	898.8	860.5	1,759.3
15–64 years	1,183.5	1,268.8	2,452.3
65 years and over	79.2	81.2	160.4
Total	2,161.5	2,210.5	4,372.0

REGIONS
(official projections at mid-2021)

Region	Area ('000 sq km)	Population	Density (per sq km)	Chief town
Adrar . . .	215	60,913	0.3	Atâr
Assaba . . .	37	395,928	10.7	Kiffa
Brakna . . .	33	331,838	10.1	Aleg
Dakhlet-Nouadhibou .	22	153,757	7.0	Nouadhibou
Gorgol . . .	14	382,172	27.3	Kaédi
Guidimagha .	10	323,087	32.3	Sélibabi
Hodh Echargui .	183	527,973	2.9	Néma
Hodh el Gharbi .	53	335,019	6.3	Aïoun el Atrous
Inchiri . . .	47	26,129	0.6	Akjoujt
Nouakchott (district) .	1	1,280,183	1,280.2	Nouakchott
Tagant . . .	95	85,294	0.9	Tidjikja
Tiris Zemour .	253	57,643	0.2	Zouerate
Trarza . . .	68	311,261	4.6	Rosso
Total . . .	1,030	4,271,197	4.1	

PRINCIPAL TOWNS
(population at 2013 census*)

Nouakchott (capital)	958,399	Bougadoum . . .	40,341
Nouadhibou . .	118,167	Ghabou	34,924
Vassale	65,927	Mal	33,301
Kiffa	60,005	Sélibabi	29,786
Rosso	51,026	Boutilimit . . .	26,926
Kaédi	49,152	Atâr	26,144
Adel Bagrou . .	47,829	Gouraye	26,142
Zouerate . . .	44,649	Hamed	25,916
Boghé	42,759	Guerou	25,368

* With the exception of Nouakchott, figures refer to the population of communes (municipalities), and include nomads.

Mid-2021 (incl. suburbs, UN estimate): Nouakchott (capital) 1,372,244 (Source: UN, *World Urbanization Prospects: The 2018 Revision*).

BIRTHS AND DEATHS
(annual averages, UN estimates)

	2005–10	2010–15	2015–20
Birth rate (per 1,000) . . .	36.9	35.9	33.9
Death rate (per 1,000) . . .	8.6	8.0	7.3

Source: UN, *World Population Prospects: The 2019 Revision*.

Life expectancy (years at birth, estimates): 65.1 (males 63.5; females 66.7) in 2020 (Source: World Bank, World Development Indicators database).

EMPLOYMENT
(national survey of employment and the informal sector, '000 persons aged 14–64 years, 2017)

	Males	Females	Total
Agriculture, forestry and fishing .	157.2	66.2	223.4
Mining	8.9	0.5	9.3
Manufacturing	37.0	46.7	83.7
Electricity, gas and water . . .	6.0	0.4	6.4
Construction	33.0	0.7	33.7
Wholesale and retail trade; repair of motor vehicles, motorcycles and personal household goods .	72.4	84.8	157.3
Hotels and restaurants . .	2.9	8.0	10.9
Transport, storage and communications . .	37.3	2.6	39.9
Financial intermediation . . .	2.1	1.0	3.0
Real estate, renting and business activities	19.7	4.0	23.8
Public administration . . .	19.1	3.1	22.2
Education	20.6	16.2	36.8
Health and social work . . .	4.9	3.8	8.7
Other social services	29.0	40.4	69.4
Sub-total	449.9	278.5	728.4
Activities not adequately defined .	1.9	4.0	5.8
Total employed	452.0	282.4	734.3

Health and Welfare

KEY INDICATORS

Total fertility rate (children per woman, 2020) . . .	4.4
Under-5 mortality rate (per 1,000 live births, 2020) .	70.7
HIV/AIDS (% of persons aged 15–49, 2020) . .	0.3
COVID-19: Cumulative confirmed deaths (per 100,000 persons at 31 August 2022)	21.5
COVID-19: Fully vaccinated population (% of total population at 21 August 2022)	30.9
Physicians (per 1,000 head, 2018)	0.2
Hospitals (per 100,000 head, 2013)	1.03
Domestic health expenditure (2019): US $ per head (PPP) .	70.1
Domestic health expenditure (2019): % of GDP . . .	1.2
Domestic health expenditure (2019): public (% of total current expenditure)	37.5
Access to improved water resources (% of persons, 2020) .	72
Access to improved sanitation facilities (% of persons, 2020) .	50
Total carbon dioxide emissions ('000 metric tons, 2018) . .	4,000
Carbon dioxide emissions per head (metric tons, 2018) . .	0.9
Human Development Index (2021): ranking	158
Human Development Index (2021): value	0.890

Note: For data on COVID-19 vaccinations, 'fully vaccinated' denotes receipt of all doses specified by approved vaccination regime (Sources: Johns Hopkins University and Our World in Data). Data on health expenditure refer to current general government expenditure in each case. For more information on sources and further definitions for all indicators, see Health and Welfare Statistics: Sources and Definitions section (europaworld.com/credits).

Agriculture

PRINCIPAL CROPS
('000 metric tons, FAO estimates unless otherwise indicated)

	2018	2019	2020
Beans, dry	13.8	14.0	14.3
Cow peas, dry	7.9	7.9	7.9
Dates	22.2	21.9	22.0
Maize*	12.0	16.0	15.0
Millet	2.7	2.7	2.6
Peas, dry	8.7	8.5	8.3
Rice, paddy	323.0	383.0	365.0
Sorghum*	87.0	68.0	93.0
Sweet potatoes	4.9	5.2	5.3
Wheat	8.3	8.6	8.9

* Unofficial figures.

Aggregate production ('000 metric tons, may include official, semi-official or estimated data): Total cereals 434.5 in 2018, 479.8 in 2019, 486.1 in 2020; Total fruit (primary) 29.5 in 2018, 28.7 in 2019, 29.1 in 2020; Total pulses 51.9 in 2018, 52.0 in 2019, 52.4 in 2020; Total roots and tubers 10.1 in 2018, 10.4 in 2019, 10.5 in 2020; Total vegetables (primary) 4.7 in 2018, 4.8 in 2019, 4.8 in 2020.

Source: FAO.

LIVESTOCK
('000 head, year ending September, FAO estimates)

	2018	2019	2020
Asses	325	326	328
Camels	1,493	1,500	1,510
Cattle	1,915	1,933	1,954
Chickens	4,675	4,704	4,733
Goats	7,420	7,519	7,571
Sheep	10,665	11,066	11,102

Source: FAO.

LIVESTOCK PRODUCTS
('000 metric tons, FAO estimates)

	2018	2019	2020
Camel meat	25.5	25.8	26.2
Camels' milk	26.1	26.2	26.3
Cows' milk	155.0	147.8	149.0
Chicken meat	4.6	4.6	4.6
Goat meat	18.7	18.9	19.2
Goats' milk	108.7	109.7	110.3
Sheep meat	35.9	36.7	37.4
Sheep's (Ewe's) milk . . .	76.6	78.5	78.7
Hen eggs	5.5	5.5	5.6

Source: FAO.

Forestry

ROUNDWOOD REMOVALS
('000 cubic metres, excl. bark, FAO estimates)

	2018	2019	2020
Sawlogs, veneer logs and logs for sleepers	30	30	30
Other industrial wood	2	2	2
Fuel wood	2,169	2,209	2,251
Total	2,201	2,241	2,283

Source: FAO.

SAWNWOOD PRODUCTION
('000 cubic metres, incl. railway sleepers, FAO estimates)

	2018	2019	2020
Broadleaved (hardwood)	14	14	14
Total	14	14	14

Note: Production assumed to be unchanged from 2007 (FAO estimates).

Source: FAO.

Fishing

('000 metric tons, live weight of capture)

	2018	2019*	2020*
Freshwater fishes*	15.0	15.0	15.0
Leaping African mullet . . .	35.9	22.9	21.5
Sardinellas	340.2	245.6	230.9
Bonga shad	30.2	21.8	20.5
European pilchard (sardine) . .	325.0	234.6	220.6
Atlantic Chub mackerel . . .	19.0	13.7	12.9
Octopuses	29.2	41.5	39.0
Total catch (incl. others)* . .	967.7	720.9	678.4

* FAO estimates.

Source: FAO.

Mining

('000 metric tons)

	2016	2017	2018
Gypsum	70.0*	200.0	200.0*
Iron ore: gross weight . . .	13,268	11,714	10,711
Iron ore: metal content . . .	8,290	7,320	6,694
Copper concentrates†	32,818	28,791	28,137
Gold (kg)	7,127	9,096	9,235

* Estimate.

† Figures refer to the metal content of concentrates.

Source: US Geological Survey.

Industry

SELECTED PRODUCTS
('000 metric tons unless otherwise indicated)

	2016	2017	2018
Cement	630	640	670
Crude steel	5	n.a.	n.a.
Salt*	1,000	1,000	1,000
Electrical energy (million kWh) .	1,042	1,183	1,271

* Estimates.

2019: Electrical energy (million kWh) 1,347.

Sources: US Geological Survey; UN Energy Statistics Database.

Finance

CURRENCY AND EXCHANGE RATES

Monetary Units
5 khoums = 1 adjusted ouguiya (MRU).

Sterling, Dollar and Euro Equivalents (31 May 2022)
£1 sterling = 45.748 ouguiyas;
US $1 = 36.340 ouguiyas;
€1 = 38.931 ouguiyas;
1,000 ouguiyas = £21.86 = $27.52 = €25.69.

Average Exchange Rate (ouguiyas per US $)
2019   36.691
2020   37.189
2021   36.063

Note: An adjusted ouguiya, equivalent to 10 of the previous version of the currency, was introduced from 1 January 2018.

BUDGET
('000 million adjusted ouguiyas)

Revenue*	2019	2020	2021†
Tax revenue	37.9	36.9	42.5
Taxes on income and profits	11.9	13.1	13.5
Taxes on goods and services .	18.1	17.8	21.0
Value-added tax	13.2	11.5	11.9
Tax on petroleum products .	1.7	1.6	3.1
Other excises	1.8	1.9	1.7
Taxes on international trade .	6.4	5.7	7.1
Non-tax revenue	12.6	20.1	25.0
Fishing royalties and penalties .	8.9	7.5	8.4
Revenue from public enterprises	1.3	1.4	1.9
Capital revenue	0.3	0.1	2.0
Special accounts	0.7	6.0	5.6
Petroleum revenue	3.0	0.6	—
Total	**53.6**	**57.6**	**67.5**

Expenditure‡	2019	2020	2021†
Current expenditure	33.1	36.8	52.0
Wages and salaries	15.6	16.8	19.2
Goods and services	6.9	7.4	11.8
Special accounts	0.2	0.9	4.9
Interest on public debt . . .	3.1	2.9	3.0
Capital expenditure	22.7	20.3	28.5
Total	**55.7**	**57.1**	**80.5**

* Excluding grants received ('000 million adjusted ouguiyas): 2.9 in 2019; 6.2 in 2020; 2.5 in 2021 (estimate).
† Estimates.
‡ Excluding restructuring expenditure and net lending ('000 million adjusted ouguiyas): 0.8 in 2019; 0.2 in 2020; 0.0 in 2021 (estimate).

Source: Trésor Public, Nouakchott.

INTERNATIONAL RESERVES
(excluding gold, US $ million at 31 December)

	2019	2020	2021
IMF special drawing rights . .	1.6	6.8	11.5
Reserve position in the IMF . .	22.5	23.4	22.8
Foreign exchange	1,004.6	1,463.0	2,004.3
Total	**1,028.7**	**1,493.2**	**2,038.6**

Source: IMF, *International Financial Statistics*.

MONEY SUPPLY
(million adjusted ouguiyas at 31 December)

	2017	2018	2019
Currency outside depository corporations	14,981	15,651	17,549
Transferable deposits . . .	44,514	49,547	54,245
Other deposits	7,999	9,660	10,513
Broad money	**67,494**	**74,859**	**82,306**

Source: IMF, *International Financial Statistics*.

COST OF LIVING
(Consumer Price Index; base: 2014 = 100)

	2019	2020	2021
Food (incl. beverages) . . .	114.7	117.0	124.0
Clothing (incl. footwear) . . .	105.3	106.2	107.0
Rent and utilities	102.5	103.1	105.6
All items (incl. others) . . .	110.4	113.0	117.1

NATIONAL ACCOUNTS
(million adjusted ouguiyas at current prices, provisional)

Expenditure on the Gross Domestic Product

	2019	2020	2021
Government final consumption expenditure	36,023	40,241	52,760
Private final consumption expenditure	159,546	167,605	179,138
Gross fixed capital formation . .	109,764	114,754	175,569
Increase in stocks	29,167	31,669	30,495
Total domestic expenditure	**334,500**	**354,269**	**437,962**
Exports of goods and services . .	123,057	127,106	142,225
Less Imports of goods and services	161,604	168,782	219,689
GDP in purchasers' values .	**295,953**	**312,593**	**360,498**

Gross Domestic Product by Economic Activity

	2019	2020	2021
Agriculture, hunting, forestry and fishing	64,080	61,324	66,976
Mining and quarrying	45,231	63,310	78,539
Manufacturing and utilities . .	23,814	25,424	26,052
Construction	13,348	12,591	14,003
Wholesale and retail trade, restaurants and hotels . . .	34,609	34,901	40,324
Transport, storage and communications	20,113	18,801	20,778
Public administration	18,039	19,261	23,454
Other activities	51,930	54,197	61,046
Sub-total	**271,165**	**289,809**	**331,171**
Indirect taxes, less subsidies . .	24,787	22,784	29,327
GDP in purchasers' values .	**295,953**	**312,593**	**360,498**

BALANCE OF PAYMENTS
(US $ million)

	2019	2020	2021
Exports of goods f.o.b.	2,319.2	2,590.8	2,913.8
Imports of goods f.o.b.	−2,889.5	−2,878.9	−3,519.5
Trade balance	**−570.3**	**−288.1**	**−605.7**
Services (net)	−480.8	−524.2	−472.3
Balance on goods and services	**−1,051.1**	**−812.3**	**−1,078.0**
Other income (net)	−96.2	−105.7	−146.2
Balance on goods, services and income	**−1,147.3**	**−918.3**	**−1,224.2**
Current transfers (net) . . .	316.2	341.7	415.7
Private unrequited transfers (net)	101.7	152.6	143.4
Official transfers	214.5	189.1	272.3
Current balance	**−831.1**	**−576.3**	**−808.4**
Capital account (net)	22.3	72.6	987.1
Direct investment (net) . . .	883.6	927.9	1,061.5
Official medium- and long-term loans	63.4	34.2	−151.4
Other capital	−69.1	−414.6	80.5
Net errors and omissions . . .	18.6	82.8	112.1
Overall balance	**87.6**	**126.6**	**1,281.5**

External Trade

PRINCIPAL COMMODITIES
('000 million adjusted ouguiyas)

Imports	2018	2019	2020
Food products	19.8	22.1	29.5
Cosmetic chemical products . .	2.5	2.9	3.7
Petroleum products	37.1	37.4	29.6
Construction materials . . .	9.2	10.2	8.3
Road vehicles and parts . . .	4.9	6.7	5.2
Capital goods	25.5	31.6	15.7
Total (incl. others)	113.2	125.7	102.1

Exports	2018	2019	2020
Iron ore	19.1	32.0	37.1
Gold	11.8	22.3	27.5
Copper	7.0	7.0	8.0
Fish	39.1	40.7	30.6
Total (incl. others)	77.7	103.2	105.6

PRINCIPAL TRADING PARTNERS
('000 million adjusted ouguiyas)

Imports c.i.f.	2018	2019	2020
Belgium	12.4	10.1	7.2
Brazil	1.0	0.8	3.5
China, People's Republic . . .	8.6	13.5	9.0
France	6.8	9.8	8.3
Germany	1.5	1.4	1.8
Italy	1.2	2.4	n.a.
Japan	4.9	3.2	2.2
Morocco	5.6	3.4	3.5
Netherlands	6.6	5.2	4.1
Russian Federation	4.1	5.1	6.2
Senegal	0.9	1.5	0.4
Singapore	1.4	2.2	2.0
Spain	12.4	14.3	14.6
Türkiye	3.0	3.1	3.1
United Arab Emirates	16.3	14.3	14.5
United Kingdom	7.0	2.0	n.a.
USA	2.5	4.3	2.6
Total (incl. others)	113.2	125.7	102.1

Exports c.i.f.	2018	2019	2020
Australia	n.a.	n.a.	2.7
China, People's Republic . . .	23.3	31.3	35.6
Côte d'Ivoire	3.3	3.1	2.7
France	0.9	2.1	1.6
Germany	2.5	2.6	3.4
Greece	0.8	0.7	n.a.
Italy	2.4	3.8	4.8
Japan	6.7	6.8	4.6
Nigeria	1.2	1.6	1.4
Russian Federation	4.9	5.8	3.6
Spain	11.0	12.3	6.9
Switzerland	n.a.	n.a.	17.9
Total (incl. others)	77.7	103.2	105.6

Transport

ROAD TRAFFIC
(motor vehicles registered)

	2004	2005	2006
Passenger cars	6,033	6,040	6,182
Government vehicles	251	317	369
Specialist vehicles	413	542	504

SHIPPING
Flag Registered Fleet
(at 31 December)

	2019	2020	2021
Number of vessels	77	81	86
Total displacement ('000 grt) . .	29.5	30.6	32.1

Source: Lloyd's List Intelligence (www.bit.ly/LLintelligence).

International Seaborne Freight Traffic
(Port of Nouakchott, '000 metric tons)

	2018	2019	2020
Goods loaded	867	1,044	1,081
Goods unloaded	4,141	3,923	4,016

CIVIL AVIATION
(traffic on scheduled services)

	2013	2014	2015
Kilometres flown (million) . .	4	4	4
Passengers carried ('000) . . .	262	271	248
Passenger-km (million) . . .	360	375	338

Total ton-km (million): 6 in 2009.

Source: UN, *Statistical Yearbook*.

2020 (domestic and international): Departures 2,205; Passengers carried 100,904 (Source: World Bank, World Development Indicators database).

Communications Media

	2018	2019	2020
Telephones ('000 main lines in use)	60.0	61.9	62.1
Mobile telephone subscriptions ('000)	4,566.5	4,710.8	4,932.6
Broadband subscriptions, fixed .	13,222	10,815	19,246
Broadband subscriptions, mobile ('000)	2,331.3	2,513.1	2,894.3

Internet users (% of population, estimate): 20.8 in 2017.

Source: International Telecommunication Union.

Education

(2018/19 unless otherwise indicated)

	Institutions	Teachers	Students Males	Females	Total
Pre-primary* .	n.a.	1,587	4,921	6,215	11,136
Primary . .	4,430†	17,518	333,222	344,294	677,516
Secondary . .	569‡	9,029	127,675	130,916	258,591
Tertiary . . .	4§	712†	13,602†	6,678†	20,280†

* 2013/14.
† 2014/15.
‡ 2015/16.
§ 1995/96.

Pupil-teacher ratio (primary education, UNESCO estimate): 34.3 in 2017/18 (Source: UNESCO Institute for Statistics).

Adult literacy rate (UNESCO estimates): 53.5% (males 63.7%; females 43.4%) in 2017 (Source: UNESCO Institute for Statistics).

Directory

While no longer an official language, French is still widely used in Mauritania, especially in the commercial sector. Many organizations are therefore listed under their French names, by which they are generally known.

The Constitution

The Constitution of the Islamic Republic of Mauritania was approved in a national referendum on 12 July 1991; amendments were adopted following a referendum conducted on 25 June 2006, following approval by the National Assembly on 6 March 2012, and after a further referendum held on 5 August 2017.

The Constitution vests executive power in the President, who is elected, by universal adult suffrage, for a term of five years, renewable only once. Legislative power is vested in the National Assembly, which is elected by universal suffrage for a period of five years. All elections are conducted in the context of a multi-party political system. The President of the Republic appoints the Prime Minister and, on the recommendation of the latter, the members of the Council of Ministers.

The Constitution states that the official language is Arabic, and that the national languages are Arabic, Pulaar, Wolof and Soninké.

The Government

HEAD OF STATE

President: Mohamed Ould Cheikh Mohamed Ahmed Ould Ghazouani (inaugurated 1 August 2019).

COUNCIL OF MINISTERS
(October 2022)

Prime Minister: Mohamed Ould Bilal.

Minister, Secretary-General of the Presidency: Moulaye Ould Mohamed Laghdaf.

Minister of Justice: Mohamed Mahmoud Ould Cheikh Abdoullah Ould Boyé.

Minister of Foreign Affairs, Co-operation and Mauritanians Abroad: Dr Mohamed Salem Ould Merzoug.

Minister of National Defence: Hanena Ould Sidi.

Minister of the Interior and Decentralization: Mohamed Ahmed Ould Mohamed Lemine.

Minister of Islamic Affairs and Original Education: Dah Ould Sidi Ould Amar Taleb.

Minister of the Economy and the Promotion of Productive Sectors: Ousmane Mamoudou Kane.

Minister of Finance: Isselmou Ould Mohamed M'Bady.

Minister of National Education and the Reform of the Education System: Brahim Vall Ould Mohamed Lemine.

Minister of Health: Moktar Ould Dahi.

Minister of the Civil Service and Labour: Zeinabou Mint Hmednah.

Minister of Digital Transformation, Innovation and the Modernization of the Administration: Moctar Ahmed Yedaly.

Minister of Petroleum, Mines and Energy: Abdessalem Ould Mohamed Saleh.

Minister of Fisheries and the Maritime Economy: Mohamed Ould Abdine Ould Maayif.

Minister of Agriculture: Yahya Ould Ahmed el-Waghef.

Minister of Stockbreeding: Mohamed Ould Abdallahi Ould Ethmane.

Minister of Trade, Industry, Handicrafts and Tourism: Lemrabott Ould Bennahi.

Minister of Employment and Professional Training: Niang Mamoudou.

Minister of Housing, Urban Development and Territorial Management: Sid'Ahmed Ould Mohamed.

Minister of Equipment and Transport, Government Spokesperson: Nany Ould Chrougha.

Minister of Water Resources and Sanitation: Sidi Mohamed Ould Taleb Amar.

Minister of Higher Education and Scientific Research: Mohamed Lemine Ould Aboyé Ould Cheikkh El Hadrami.

Minister of Culture, Youth and Sports, and Relations with Parliament: Mohamed Ould Soueidatt.

Minister of Social Action, Childhood and Families: Savia Mint N'Tahah.

Minister of the Environment and Sustainable Development: Lalya Ali Camara.

Minister, Secretary-General of the Government: Lam Moctar Alhousseyni.

MINISTRIES

Office of the President: BP 184, Nouakchott; tel. 45-25-26-36; internet www.presidence.mr.

Office of the Prime Minister: BP 237, Nouakchott; tel. 45-25-33-37; internet www.primature.gov.mr.

Office of the Secretary-General of the Government: 562 ave du Roi Faissal, BP 184, Nouakchott; tel. 45-29-63-60; e-mail infomsgg@msgg.gov.mr; internet www.msgg.gov.mr/fr.

Ministry of Agriculture: Nouakchott; internet www.agriculture.gov.mr.

Ministry of the Civil Service and Labour: BP 193, Nouakchott; tel. 45-25-67-63; e-mail asabdalla@gmail.com; internet www.fonctionpublique.gov.mr.

Ministry of Culture, Youth and Sports, and Relations with Parliament: BP 223, Nouakchott; tel. 45-25-11-30; internet www.culture.gov.mr.

Ministry of Digital Transformation, Innovation and the Modernization of the Administration: Nouakchott; internet mtnima.gov.mr.

Ministry of the Economy and the Promotion of Productive Sectors: 303 Ilôt C, BP 5150, Nouakchott; tel. 44-48-04-59; e-mail ouldmodou@gmail.com; internet www.economie.gov.mr.

Ministry of Employment and Professional Training: Ancienne Primature, Nouakchott; tel. 45-00-00-00; e-mail contact@mefp.gov.mr; internet mefp.mr.

Ministry of the Environment and Sustainable Development: BP 1666, Nouakchott; internet www.environnement.gov.mr.

Ministry of Equipment and Transport: BP 237, Nouakchott; tel. 45-25-19-61; e-mail metsec@yahoo.fr; internet www.transports.gov.mr.

Ministry of Finance: Nouakchott.

Ministry of Fisheries and the Maritime Economy: BP 137, Nouakchott; tel. 45-25-99-70; internet www.peches.gov.mr.

Ministry of Foreign Affairs, Co-operation and Mauritanians Abroad: ave Moustapha Ould Mohamed Saleck, BP 230, Nouakchott; tel. 45-29-63-01; e-mail rimmaec@diplomatie.gov.mr; internet www.diplomatie.gov.mr.

Ministry of Health: ave Gamel Abdel, BP BP 115, Nouakchott; tel. 45-25-20-52; e-mail med.khatry@sante.gov.mr; internet www.sante.gov.mr.

Ministry of Higher Education and Scientific Research: BP 5758, Nouakchott; tel. 45-25-04-48; e-mail info@mesrstic.gov.mr; internet www.mesrs.gov.mr.

Ministry of Housing, Urban Development and Territorial Management: BP 115, Nouakchott; tel. 45-25-22-37; e-mail contact@habitat.gov.mr; internet habitat.gov.mr.

Ministry of the Interior and Decentralization: BP 195, Nouakchott; tel. 45-25-36-61; e-mail communication@mid.mr; internet www.interieur.gov.mr.

Ministry of Islamic Affairs and Original Education: Immeuble Soukouk, 3e étage, Nouakchott; tel. 45-24-33-61; internet www.affairesislamiques.gov.mr.

Ministry of Justice: BP 350, Nouakchott; tel. 45-25-10-83; internet www.justice.gov.mr.

Ministry of National Defence: Nouakchott.

Ministry of National Education and the Reform of the Education System: BP 227, Nouakchott; tel. 45-29-60-74; internet education.gov.mr.

Ministry of Petroleum, Mines and Energy: Route de la Plage Carrefour, Hôpital Sabah, BP 4921, Nouakchott; tel. 45-25-95-15; e-mail contact.mpemi@gmail.com; internet www.petrole.gov.mr.

Ministry of Social Action, Childhood and Families: Nouakchott; tel. 45-25-80-18; e-mail sitemasef@masef.gov.mr; internet www.masef.gov.mr.

Ministry of Stockbreeding: Nouakchott.

Ministry of Trade, Industry, Handicrafts and Tourism: BP 182, Nouakchott; tel. 45-25-81-82; e-mail mail@commerce.gov.mr; internet www.commerce.gov.mr.

Ministry of Water Resources and Sanitation: BP 4913, Nouakchott; tel. 45-25-71-44; e-mail saadouebih@yahoo.fr; internet www.hydraulique.gov.mr.

President

Presidential Election, 22 June 2019

Candidate	Valid votes	% of valid votes
Mohamed Ould Cheikh Mohamed Ahmed Ould Ghazouani	483,007	52.00
Biram Ould Dah Ould Abeid	172,649	18.59
Sidi Mohamed Ould Boubacar Boussalef .	165,995	17.87
Hamidou Baba Kane	80,777	8.70
Mohamed Sidi Mouldoud	22,656	2.44
Mohamed Lemine El Mourtaji El Wafi .	3,688	0.40
Total	928,772*	100.00

* In addition, there were 28,796 invalid and 9,504 blank votes.

Legislature

NATIONAL ASSEMBLY
(Al-Jamiya al-Wataniyah)

National Assembly: ave de l'Indépendance, BP 545, Nouakchott; tel. 45-24-38-44; e-mail contact@assembleenationale.mr; internet www.assembleenationale.mr.

President: CHEIKH AHMED OULD BAYE.

A general election to the newly enlarged legislature (157 seats compared with 146 in the outgoing Assembly) was held over two rounds on 1 and 15 September 2018. Full results were not immediately made available; however, at the first round the Union pour la République (UPR) was reported to have won 67 seats, while the Rassemblement National pour la Réforme et le Développement (Tawassoul) took 14, with a further 17 secured by other parties. All 22 seats contested in the second round were reportedly won by the UPR. Of the 157 deputies, 117 were selected on a constituency basis (with 18 of these being in the capital, Nouakchott), while 20 were chosen under a national list system, and a further 20 were chosen from a national list of women.

Election Commission

National Independent Electoral Commission (Commission Electorale Nationale Indépendante—CENI): 230 ave Moktar Ould Daddah, BP 4550, Nouakchott; tel. 45-24-15-40; e-mail ceni@ceni.mr; internet www.ceni.mr; 15 mems; Pres. MOHAMED VALL OULD BELLAL.

Advisory Council

Economic, Social and Environmental Council: E-Nord 386, Nouakchott; tel. 45-24-18-38; e-mail conseil.e.s@hotmail.fr; internet www.cese.mr; 6 mems; Pres. MESSAOUD OULD BOULKHEIR.

Political Organizations

Alliance pour la Justice et la Démocratie/Mouvement pour la Rénovation (AJD/MR): Nouakchott; tel. 36-30-42-92; internet www.ajd-mr.org; Leader IBRAHIMA MOCTAR SARR.

Alliance Populaire Progressiste (APP): Nouakchott; f. 1991; Pres. MESSAOUD OULD BOULKHEIR.

Alternative (Al-Badil): Nouakchott; f. 2006; mem. of Coordination de l'Opposition Démocratique coalition, formed in 2010; Leader MOHAMED YEHDHIH OULD MOKTAR EL HASSEN.

Coalition Vivre Ensemble/Vérité et Réconciliation (CVR/VR): Nouakchott; f. 2019; Pres. Dr DIA ALASSANE.

Forum National pour la Démocratie et l'Unité (FNDU): Nouakchott; f. 2014; Pres. MOHAMED OULD MAOULOUD.

Pacte National pour la Démocratie et le Développement (PNDD/ADIL): Nouakchott; Leader YAHYA OULD AHMED EL WAGHEF.

Parti El Karama: Nouakchott; Pres. Dr CHEIKHNA OULD HAJBOU.

Parti El Wiam Démocratique et Social: Leader BOYDIEL OULD HOUMEID.

Parti pour la Liberté, l'Egalité et la Justice (PLEJ): Nouakchott; Pres. MAMADOU ALASSANE BÂ.

Parti Mauritanien de l'Union et du Changement—Hatem: Nouakchott; f. 2005 by leadership of the fmr prohibited Knights of Change militia and reformist elements of the fmr ruling Parti Républicain Démocratique et Social; Pres. SALEH OULD HNANA; Sec.-Gen. ABDERAHMANE OULD MINI.

Parti Radical pour une Action Globale (RAG): Nouakchott; f. 2013, fmrly known as Initiative pour la Résurgence du Mouvement Abolitionniste en Mauritanie (IRA Mauritanie).

Parti du Rassemblement du Peuple Mauritanien: Nouakchott; f. 2009 by parliamentary deputies in support of ruling military junta; Leader Dr LOULEID OULD WEDAD.

Parti Ravah: Nouakchott; tel. 46-31-77-31; internet fb.com/erravahrim; f. 2008.

Parti Républicain pour la Démocratie et le Renouveau (PRDR): ZRB, Tevragh Zeina, Nouakchott; tel. 45-29-18-36; e-mail info@prdr.mr; f. 2006 to replace Parti Républicain Démocratique et Social, the fmr ruling party, prior to coup of Aug. 2005; Leader SIDI MOHAMED OULD MED VALL DIT GHRINY.

Rassemblement des Forces Démocratiques (RFD): Ext. NOT No 31, BP 5381, Nouakchott; tel. 45-24-01-02; internet www.rfd-mauritanie.org; f. 2001; Pres. AHMED OULD DADDAH.

Rassemblement National pour la Réforme et le Développement (RNRD) (Tawassoul): internet www.tewassoul.mr/fr; f. 2007; Islamist; mem. of Coordination de l'Opposition Démocratique coalition, formed in 2010; Leader MOHAMED MAHMOUD OULD SIDI.

Reward (Sawab): Nouakchott; f. 2004; social democratic; Chair. of Central Council MOHAMED MAHMOUD OULD GHOULMA; Pres. ABDESSELAM OULD HORMA.

Sursaut de la Jeunesse pour la Nation: Nouakchott; Leader GUISSET DIALLEL ABOU.

Union du Centre Démocratique (UCD): Nouakchott; f. 2005 by fmr mems of the Parti Républicain Démocratique et Social, the fmr ruling party; Pres. CHEIKH SID'AHMED OULD BABA.

Union pour la Démocratie et le Progrès (UDP): Ilot V, 70 Tevragh Zeina, BP 816, Nouakchott; tel. 45-25-52-89; f. 1993; Pres. NAHA HAMDI MINT.

Union des Forces de la Majorité Présidentielle: Nouakchott; coalition comprising 8 political parties supporting Pres. Mohamed Ould Abdel Aziz.

Union des Forces du Progrès (UFP) (Ittihad Quwa al-Taqaddum): Nouakchott; tel. 45-29-32-66; e-mail infos@ufpweb.org; f. 2000; Pres. MOHAMED OULD MAOULOUD.

Union de la Jeunesse Démocratique (UJD): f. 2008; promotes patriotism and moderate Islamic values, opposes extremism; Pres. JEDDOU OULD AHMAD.

Union pour la République (UPR): Nouakchott; internet upr.mr/fr; f. 2009; Chair. MOHAMED MELAININE OULD EYIH; Sec.-Gen. FALL N'GUISSALY.

The clandestine **Forces de Libération Africaines de Mauritanie (FLAM)** was founded in 1983 in Senegal to represent Afro-Mauritanians (BP 5811, Dakar-Fann, Senegal; tel. +221 822-80-77; e-mail flammauritanie@gmail.com; internet flam-mauritanie.org; Pres. MAMADOU SIDI BÀ); a faction broke away from this organization and returned to Mauritania in early 2006, forming the Forces de Libération Africaines de Mauritanie—Rénovation. A further group based in exile is the **Front Arabo-Africain de Salut contre l'Esclavage, le Racisme et le Tribalisme—FAAS** (e-mail faas@caramail.com; internet membres.lycos.fr/faas).

Diplomatic Representation

EMBASSIES IN MAURITANIA

Algeria: Ilôt A, Tevragh Zeina, BP 625, Nouakchott; tel. 45-25-35-69; Ambassador MOHAMED BEN ATTOU.

Brazil: rue 502, Tevragh Zeina, BP 5458, Nouakchott; tel. 45-29-49-82; e-mail brasemb.nouakchott@itamaraty.gov.br; internet www.gov.br/mre/pt-br/embaixada-nouakchott; Ambassador LEONARDO CARVALHO MONTEIRO.

China, People's Republic: rue 42–133, Tevragh Zeina, BP 257, Nouakchott; tel. 45-25-20-70; e-mail chinaemb_mr@mfa.gov.cn; internet mr.china-embassy.gov.cn; Ambassador LI BAIJUN.

Congo, Democratic Republic: Tevragh Zeina, BP 5714, Nouakchott; tel. 45-25-46-12; Chargé d'affaires a.i. ERNEST BONGA DINZO.

Egypt: Villa 468, Tevragh Zeina, BP 176, Nouakchott; tel. 45-25-21-92; Ambassador KHALED FATHI YOUSSEF.

France: rue Ahmed Ould Hamed, Tevragh Zeina, BP 231, Nouakchott; tel. 45-29-96-99; e-mail ambafrance.nouakchott-amba@diplomatie.gouv.fr; internet mr.ambafrance.org; Ambassador ALEXANDRE GARCIA.

The Gambia: BP 1202, Nouakchott; tel. 45-29-80-32; e-mail gambia.embassy-nktt@hotmail.com; Ambassador SHEIKH OMAR FAYE.

Germany: rue Mamadou Konaté, Tevragh Zeina, BP 372, Nouakchott; tel. 45-29-40-75; e-mail info@nouakchott.diplo.de; internet nouakchott.diplo.de; Ambassador ISABEL HÉNIN.

Iran: Nouakchott; tel. 20-20-62-44; e-mail emrani110@gmail.com; Ambassador AMIRALI EMAM JOM'E SHAHIDI.

Iraq: Tevragh Zeina, Nord Villa 399, Nouakchott; tel. 45-24-32-77; e-mail nokemb@mofa.gov.iq; internet mofamission.gov.iq/en/Mauritan; Ambassador AHMED NAEEF RASHID AL-DULAIMI.

Japan: Tevragh Zeina, BP 7810, Nouakchott; tel. 45-25-09-77; internet www.mr.emb-japan.go.jp; Ambassador NORIO EHARA.

Kuwait: Tevragh Zeina, BP 345, Nouakchott; tel. 45-25-33-05; e-mail nouakchott@mofa.gov.kw; Ambassador BEDAH MAGHAAD DOUSRY.

Libya: BP 673, Nouakchott; tel. 45-25-52-02; Ambassador MOUSSA ABDEL NABI TRABELSI.

Mali: Tevragh Zeina, BP 5371, Nouakchott; tel. 45-25-40-81; e-mail ambmali@hotmail.com; Ambassador MOHAMED DIBASSY.

Morocco: 569 ave Charles de Gaulle, Tevragh Zeina, BP 621, Nouakchott; tel. 45-25-14-11; e-mail sifmanktt@mauritel.mr; Ambassador HAMID CHABAR.

Oman: Nouakchott; Ambassador SAIF BIN HILAL BIN ALI AL-MAAMARI.

Qatar: ZRB blvd 449, rue Zaina, Nouakchott; tel. 45-25-23-99; internet nouakchott.embassy.qa; Ambassador MOHAMMED ABDERRAHMANE AL-KEBISSI.

Russian Federation: rue Abu Bakr, BP 221, Nouakchott; tel. 45-25-19-73; e-mail ambrussmaur@mid.ru; internet mauritanie.mid.ru; Ambassador BORIS A. ZHILKO.

Saudi Arabia: Las Palmas, Zinat, BP 498, Nouakchott; tel. 45-25-26-33; e-mail mremb@mofa.gov.sa; internet embassies.mofa.gov.sa/sites/mauritania; Ambassador MOHAMED AL-BULAWI.

Senegal: Villa 500, Tevragh Zeina, BP 2511, Nouakchott; tel. 45-25-72-90; Ambassador MAMADOU MOUSTAPHA N'DOUR.

South Africa: NOT 135/137, Tevragh Zeina, BP 2006, Nouakchott; tel. 45-24-55-90; e-mail molalad@dirco.gov.za; Ambassador PETER GOOSEN.

Spain: rue Mamadou Konate S/N, BP 232, Nouakchott; tel. 45-25-20-80; e-mail emb.nouakchott@mae.es; internet www.exteriores.gob.es/embajadas/nouakchott; Ambassador MIRIAM ÁLVAREZ DE LA ROSA RODRÍGUEZ.

Sudan: Tevragh Zeina 12, Nouakchott; tel. 45-09-99-08; e-mail sudannouakchott@yahoo.com; internet www.sudanembassy-rim.info; Ambassador BILAL GASMALLA AL-SIDDIQ.

Syrian Arab Republic: Tevragh Zeina, BP 288, Nouakchott; tel. 45-25-27-54; Ambassador SAID EL-BENI.

Tunisia: rue des Ambassades, TVZ, BP 631, Nouakchott; tel. 45-25-28-71; e-mail at.nouakchott@diplomatie.gov.tn; internet www.diplomatie.gov.tn/nc/mission/etranger/ambassade-de-tunisie-a-nouakchott-mauritanie; Ambassador SABER CHAÂBANI.

Türkiye (Turkey): cnr Stade Olympique, Tevragh Zeina, BP 5155, Nouakchott; tel. 45-25-78-00; Ambassador AKIF MENEVŞE.

United Arab Emirates: ZRA 742 bis, Tevragh Zeina Quarter, Nouakchott; tel. 45-24-22-00; e-mail nouakchott@mofa.gov.ae; internet www.mofaic.gov.ae/en/Missions/Nouakchott; Ambassador HAMAD GHANIM AL-MUHAIRI.

United Kingdom: Rue 42–163, BP 213, Nouakchott; tel. 45-25-69-86; internet www.gov.uk/world/organisations/british-embassy-nouakchott; Ambassador COLIN WELLS.

USA: rue Abdallaye, BP 222, Nouakchott; tel. 45-25-26-60; e-mail PASNouakchott@state.gov; internet mr.usembassy.gov; Ambassador CYNTHIA KIERSCHT.

Yemen: Tevragh Zeina, BP 4689, Nouakchott; tel. 45-25-55-91; Ambassador Dr SALEM SALEH AL-ERADA.

Judicial System

The Code of Law was promulgated in 1961 and subsequently modified to incorporate Islamic institutions and practices. The President of the Republic guarantees the independence of judicial power and is assisted in this task by the Higher Council of the Magistracy. The main courts comprise a Supreme Court, three Courts of Appeal, 15 Regional Tribunals, 13 Labour Tribunals and 44 Departmental Civil Courts. An Audit Court has jurisdiction in financial matters. The members of the High Court of Justice are elected by the National Assembly.

Shari'a (Islamic) law was introduced in February 1980. A special Islamic court was established in March of that year, presided over by a magistrate of Islamic law, assisted by two counsellors and two *ulemas* (Muslim jurists and interpreters of the Koran). A High Council of Fatwas and Appeals for Reprieve, comprising nine members, renewable every two years, was established in 2012.

Audit Court: ave Jemal Abd'Enassir, BP 592, Nouakchott; tel. 45-25-34-04; e-mail ccomptes@cc.gov.mr; internet www.cdcmr.mr; audits all govt institutions; Pres. HAMID OULD AHMED TALEB.

Constitutional Council: Ilôt C, Lot 281, Tevrag Zeina, BP 3205, Nouakchott; internet ccfr.rimpresse.com; f. 1992; 9 mems; Pres. DIALLO MAMADOU BATHA; Sec.-Gen. SY ADAMA.

Courts of Appeal: at Aleg, Kiffa, Nouadhibou and Nouakchott.

High Council of Fatwas and Appeals for Reprieve (Haut Conseil de la Fatwa et des Recours Gracieux): Nouakchott; f. 2012; comprises 9 members, renewable every 2 years; issues fatwas with respect to interpretations of Islamic law; also has the authority to resolve disputes that are not under any court of law; Pres. ISSELMOU OULD SID'EL-MOUSTAPH.

High Court of Justice: Nouakchott; f. 1961; comprises nine mems; comprises appointees elected by the National Assembly from its membership, following each partial or general renewal of the legislature; competent to try the President of the Republic in case of high treason, and the Prime Minister and members of the Government in case of conspiracy against the state; Pres. JEMAL MOHAMED EL-YEDALI.

Supreme Court: Palais de Justice, BP 201, Nouakchott; tel. 45-25-67-40; internet www.coursupreme.mr; f. 1961; comprises an administrative chamber, two civil and social chambers, a commercial chamber and a criminal chamber; Pres. EL HOUCEIN OULD NAGI.

Religion

ISLAM

Islam is the official religion, and the population are almost entirely Muslims of the Malekite rite. The major religious groups are the Tijaniya and the Qadiriya. Chinguetti, in the region of Adrar, is the seventh Holy Place in Islam.

CHRISTIANITY

Roman Catholic Church

Mauritania comprises the single diocese of Nouakchott, directly responsible to the Holy See. The Bishop participates in the Bishops' Conference of Senegal, Mauritania, Cabo Verde and Guinea-Bissau, based in Dakar, Senegal.

Bishop of Nouakchott: Most Rev. MARTIN ALBERT HAPPE, Evêché, BP 5377, Nouakchott; tel. 45-25-04-27; e-mail mgrmartinhappe@yahoo.fr.

The Press

Al-Akhbar: ave Charles de Gaulle, BP 5346, Nouakchott; tel. 22-00-03-90; e-mail fr.redaction@alakhbar.info; internet www.fr.alakhbar.info; f. 2003; weekly; Arabic and French; Exec. Dir EL HAÏBA OULD CHEIKH SIDATI; Editor-in-Chief MOHAMED DIOP.

Biladi: Immeuble BMCI, 5e étage, Apt 508, BP 1122, Nouakchott; tel. 45-24-02-75; e-mail oneina1@gmail.com; internet www.rmibiladi.com; weekly; French; Dir of Publication MOUSSA OULD HAMED; Editor-in-Chief ABDELVETAH OULD MOHAMED.

Le Calame/Al-Qalam: rue 42–62, Tevragh Zeina, 348 Kennedy ave Ouest, BP 1059, Nouakchott; tel. 45-24-08-29; e-mail lecalame@yahoo.fr; internet www.lecalame.info; f. 1993; weekly; Arabic and French; independent; Editors-in-Chief RIYAD OULD AHMED EL-HADI (Arabic edn), AHMED OULD CHEIKH (French edn).

Châab: BP 371, Nouakchott; tel. 45-25-29-40; internet www.ami.mr; f. 1975; daily; Arabic; also publ. in French *Horizons*; publ. by Agence Mauritanienne de l'Information; Dir of Publication YARBA OULD SGHAÏR.

Ech-tary: BP 1059, Nouakchott; tel. 45-25-50-65; fortnightly; Arabic; satirical.

Essirage Hebdo: Nouakchott; tel. 45-29-18-51; e-mail info@essirage.net; internet www.essirage.net; weekly.

L'Essor: BP 5310, Nouakchott; tel. 22-30-21-68; e-mail sidiel2000@ yahoo.fr; monthly; the environment and the economy; Dir SIDI EL-MOCTAR CHEÏGUER.

L'Eveil-Hebdo: BP 587, Nouakchott; tel. 46-41-28-76; e-mail symoudou@yahoo.fr; internet www.eveilhebdo.info; f. 1991; weekly; independent; Dir of Publication MAMADOU SY.

Financial Afrik: Immeuble Abou Khaled Socogim, Nouakchott; tel. 45-24-10-94; e-mail ibrahima.dia@financialafrik.com; internet www .financialafrik.com; f. 2012; monthly; Gen. Man. El Hadj DIA IBRAHIMA.

Mauritanies1: ave Charles de Gaulle, Immeuble Tewvigh, Nouakchott; tel. 45-24-10-94; e-mail contact@lesmauritanies.com; monthly; Dir-Gen. DIA EL HADJI IBRAHIMA; Dir of Publication ADAMA WADE.

Nouakchott-Info: Immeuble Abbas, Tevragh Zeina, BP 1905, Nouakchott; tel. 45-25-02-71; e-mail nouakchottinfo@yahoo.fr; internet ani.mr; f. 1995; daily; independent; Arabic and French.

Points Chauds Online: Ilôt O63, Tevrag Zeina, face de Bana Bleu, Nouakchott; tel. 45-25-06-04; e-mail infopointschauds@gmail.com; internet www.pointschauds.info; f. 2002; Dir of Publication MOULAYE NAJIM MOULAYE ZEINE.

Le Quotidien de Nouakchott: BP 1153, Nouakchott; tel. 45-24-53-74; internet www.lequotidien.mr; French; Editor-in-Chief KHALILOU DIAGANA.

Tahalil Hebdo: BP 5205, Nouakchott; tel. 46-31-92-07; e-mail contact@journaltahalil.com; internet www.journaltahalil.com; weekly; French; Editor SALIHI ISSELMOU.

NEWS AGENCIES

Agence Mauritanienne de l'Information (AMI): Ksar 1540, rue 22-006 Habib Bourguiba, BP 371, Nouakchott; tel. 45-25-29-40; e-mail amiakhbar@gmail.com; internet www.ami.mr; fmrly Agence Mauritanienne de Presse; state-controlled; news and information services in Arabic and French; Man. Dir MOHAMED FALL OUMEIR BEYE.

Publishers

Imprimerie Commerciale et Administrative de Mauritanie: BP 164, Nouakchott; textbooks, educational.

Imprimerie Nationale: BP 618, Nouakchott; tel. 45-25-44-38; f. 1978; state-owned; Pres. RACHID OULD SALEH; Man. Dir ISSIMOU MAHJOUB.

GOVERNMENT PUBLISHING HOUSE

Société Nationale d'Impression: BP 618, Nouakchott; Pres. MOUSTAPHA SALECK OULD AHMED BRIHIM.

Broadcasting and Communications

TELECOMMUNICATIONS

Chinguitel: Carrefour Cité SMAR, Nouakchott; tel. 22-00-02-91; internet www.chinguitel.mr; f. 2007; provides mobile, fixed-line and internet services; Dir-Gen. HANI ARABI KARRAR.

Moov Mauritel: 563 ave du Roi Fayçal, BP 7000, Nouakchott; tel. 45-25-76-00; e-mail webmaster@mauritel.mr; internet www .mauritel.mr; f. 1999; fmrly Société Mauritanienne des Télécommunications; provides fixed-line and mobile telephone services; 46% state-owned, 51% owned by the Compagnie Mauritanienne de Communication (created by Maroc Télécom), 3% owned by Mauritel employees; Dir-Gen. (vacant).

Société Mauritano-Tunisienne de Télécommunications (Mattel): ave Moctar Ould Daddah, Tevragh Zeina, BP 3668, Nouakchott; tel. 36-17-12-12; e-mail contact@mattel.mr; internet www.mattel .mr; f. 2000; operates mobile communications network; Pres. and Dir-Gen. ELYÉS BEN SASSI.

Regulatory Authority

Autorité de Régulation: 428 rue 23023 Ksar, BP 4908, Nouakchott; tel. 45-29-12-70; internet www.are.mr; f. 1999; Pres. CHEIKH AHMED OULD SID'AHMED.

BROADCASTING
Regulatory Authority

Haute Autorité de la Presse et de l'Audiovisuel (HAPA): ave du Roi Fayçal, en face de l'UTM, BP 3192, Nouakchott; tel. 45-24-10-88; internet www.hapa.mr; f. 2006; Pres. Dr EL HUSSEIN OULD MEDDOU.

Radio

Radio Mauritanie (RM): ave Gamal Abdel Nasser, BP 200, Nouakchott; tel. 45-25-93-94; e-mail radiomauritaniesa@gmail .com; internet www.radiomauritanie.mr; f. 1958; state-controlled; broadcasts 2 channels; 5 transmitters; radio broadcasts in Arabic, French, Sarakolé, Toucouleur and Wolof; Dir MOHAMED CHEIKH OULD SIDI MOHAMED.

Radio Mauritanie also operates 10 local radio stations. Broadcasts from RFI (FM), Africa N°1 and Radio Monte Carlo Doualiya are also received in the country.

Television

Télévision de Mauritanie (TVM): BP 5522, Nouakchott; tel. 45-25-32-66; e-mail mauritaniantv@gmail.com; internet www.tvm.mr; f. 1982; Dir MOHAMED MAHMOUD ABDOU MAALI.

El Mourabitoune TV: Nouakchott; tel. 41-99-48-93; e-mail elmourabitounetv@gmail.com; internet elmourabiton.tv; f. 2011.

Sahel TV: Nouakchott; tel. 45-25-28-22; e-mail saheltv3@gmail .com; internet fb.com/tvsahel; Dir (vacant).

Finance
BANKING
Central Bank

Banque Centrale de Mauritanie (BCM): ave de l'Indépendance, BP 623, Nouakchott; tel. 45-20-00-44; e-mail info@bcm.mr; internet www.bcm.mr; f. 1973; bank of issue; Gov. MOHAMED LEMINE OULD DHEHBI.

Commercial Banks

Attijari Bank Mauritanie: 91/92 rue Mamadou Konaté, BP 415, Nouakchott; tel. 45-29-63-74; internet www.attijaribank.mr; Dir-Gen. MOHAMED BOUBRIK.

Banque El Amana (BEA): rue Mamadou Konaté, BP 5559, Nouakchott; tel. 45-25-59-53; internet www.bea.mr; f. 1996; 72% privately owned, 27% owned by Société Nationale Industrielle et Minière; Pres. AHMED SALEM BOUNA MOCTAR; Gen. Man. AHMED SALEM ELY EL KORY.

Banque pour le Commerce et l'Industrie (BCI): 57 ave Gamal Abdel Nasser, BP 5050, Nouakchott; tel. 45-29-28-76; e-mail info@ bci-banque.com; internet www.bci-banque.com; f. 1999; Pres. and Dir-Gen. ISSELMOU OULD DIDI OULD TAJEDINE.

Banque Mauritanienne pour le Commerce International (BMCI): ave de l'Unité Nationale, BP 622, Nouakchott; tel. 45-25-28-26; e-mail info@bmci.mr; internet www.bmci.mr; f. 1974; 96.31% owned by Group Abbas; Pres. and Dir-Gen. MARHOUM SIDI MOHAMED ABASS.

Banque Nationale de Mauritanie (BNM): ave du Roi Fayçal Nouackott 291, BP 614, Nouakchott; tel. 45-25-26-02; e-mail bnm10@ bnm.mr; internet www.bnm.mr; f. 1989; privately owned; Pres. and Dir-Gen. MOHAMED OULD NOUEIGUED.

Chinguitty Bank: 57 ave Gamal Abdel Nasser, BP 626, Nouakchott; tel. 45-25-21-73; e-mail chinguittybank@mauritel.mr; internet www.chbank.mr; f. 1972; 71.42% owned by Libyan Arab Foreign Bank, 28.58% state-owned; Pres. SHEIKH SIDI MUKHTAR OULD SHEIKH ABDULLAH; Gen. Man. OSAMA RAMI AL-SARRAJ.

Générale de Banque de Mauritanie pour l'Investissement et le Commerce SA (GBM): 6 ave de l'Indépendance, BP 5558, Nouakchott; tel. 45-25-36-36; e-mail dco@gbm-mr.com; internet www.gbm-banque.com; f. 1995; 70% privately owned; Dir-Gen. Dr LEILA BOUAMATOU.

Orabank Mauritanie: 54 ave du Général Charles de Gaulle, rue 42-060, Tevragh Zeina, RC 1673, BP 1268, Nouakchott; tel. 45-29-19-00; e-mail info-mr@orabank.net; internet www.orabank.net; f. 2002 as Bacim-Bank; present name adopted 2012; 62.36% owned by Mauritania Gulf SAS, 34.39% owned by Oragroup SA; Dir-Gen. PIERRE MARAZZATO.

Société Générale Mauritanie (SGM): ave Charles de Gaulle, BP 5085, Nouakchott; tel. 45-29-70-00; e-mail espace.client@socgen .com; internet societegenerale.mr; f. 2005; present name adopted 2007; Dir-Gen. (vacant).

Islamic Banks

Banque al-Wava Mauritanienne Islamique (BAMIS): 758 rue 22–018, ave du Roi Fayçal, BP 650, Nouakchott; tel. 45-25-14-24; e-mail bamis@bamis.mr; internet www.bamis.mr; f. 1985; fmrly Banque al-Baraka Mauritanienne Islamique; 38.9% owned by Société Nationale d'Assurance et de Réassurance (NASR); Pres. and Dir-Gen. MOHAMED ABDELLAHI OULD ABDELLAHI.

Mouamalat Assahiha Bank: BMS Bldg, Ilôt P 21, Tevragh Zeina, POB 5243, Nouakchott; tel. 45-29-62-15; internet www.bms.mr; f. 2013; Pres. AHMED HAMDY MOUKNASS; Dir-Gen. MOUHIDINE AHMED SALECK.

Nouvelle Banque de Mauritanie (NBM): Immeuble al-Baraka, rue de l'Ambassade du Sénégal, Nouakchott; tel. 45-25-16-79; e-mail nbm@nbm.mr; f. 2014; Pres. JAMES CLAYTON; Dir-Gen. DIENG ADAMA.

Banking Association

Association Professionnelle des Banques de Mauritanie (APBM): Immeuble BMCI, 2e étage, N° 204, BP 749, Nouakchott; tel. 45-25-24-18; Pres. ISSELMOU OULD DIDI OULD TAJEDINE.

INSURANCE

Assurances Générales de Mauritanie: ave Charles de Gaulle, TZA Ilot A 667, BP 2141, Nouakchott; tel. 45-29-29-00; e-mail info@agm.mr; internet agm.mr; Man. MOULAYE ELY BOUAMATOU.

CNA Assurances: 21 ZGE, route de l'Aéroport, Nouakchott; tel. 45-24-04-91.

DAMANE Assurances SA: BP 5080, Nouakchott; tel. 45-25-25-08; e-mail dg@damane.mr; internet damaneassurances.com; Dir-Gen. MOHAMED AHMEDOU JEIREB.

Mauritanienne d'Assurances et de Réassurances (MAR): Nouakchott; tel. 45-24-12-18; e-mail mar@mar-assur.mr; internet www.mar-assur.mr; f. 2002.

TAAMIN: BP 5164, Nouakchott; tel. 45-29-40-00; e-mail info@assurancestaamin.com; internet www.assurancestaamin.com; Pres. and Dir-Gen. MOULAYE EL HASSEN OULD MOCTAR EL HASSEN.

Trade and Industry

GOVERNMENT AGENCIES

Agence de Promotion des Investissements en Mauritanie (APIM): ave Mokhtar Ould Daddah, Tevragh Zeina, Nouakchott; tel. 38-81-90-51; e-mail info-apim@apim.gov.mr; internet apim.gov.mr/fr; f. 2020; Dir-Gen. AÏSSATA LAM.

Autorité de Régulation des Marchés Publics (ARMP): 306 E Nord, Tevragh Zeina, BP 4424, Nouakchott; tel. 45-24-13-03; e-mail contact@armp.mr; internet armp.mr; Pres. AHMED SALEM OULD TABAKH; Dir-Gen. ELY OULD DADE.

Commission des Marchés des Secteurs de l'Economie et des Finances: BP 5193, Nouakchott; tel. 45-29-41-88; internet www.cmsef.mr.

Commission Nationale de Contrôle des Marchés Publics (CNCMP): BP 184, Nouakchott; tel. 45-25-25-94; internet www.cncmp.mr; Pres. MOHAMED ABBA SIDI JEILANY.

Commission de Passation des Marchés Publics du Secteur Rural: Immeuble Mouna, No ZRB 180, 2e étage, ave Moctar Ould Daddah, Carrefour cité SMAR, Nouakchott; tel. 45-24-21-74; Pres. YACOUB OULD HAÏBELTY.

Commission de Passation des Marchés Publics des Secteurs des Infrastructures: BP 5357, Nouakchott; tel. 45-25-32-24; internet www.cpmpsi.mr; Pres. SIDI MOHAMED OULD NEMINE.

DEVELOPMENT ORGANIZATIONS

Agence Française de Développement (AFD): rue Mamadou Kouaté prolongée, BP 5211, Nouakchott; tel. 45-25-25-25; e-mail afdnouakchott@afd.fr; internet www.afd.fr; Country Dir BÉNÉDICTE BRUSSET.

Office National de la Recherche et du Développement de l'Elevage (ONRDE): Nouakchott; Dir MOHAMED LEMINE OULD HAKKI.

Service de Coopération et d'Action Culturelle: BP 203, Nouakchott; tel. 45-29-95-59; administers bilateral aid from France; Dir BERNARD RUBI.

Société Nationale pour le Développement Rural (SONADER): BP 321, Nouakchott; tel. 45-21-18-00; internet www.sonader.mr; f. 1975; Dir-Gen. MOMMA BEIBATTA.

CHAMBERS OF COMMERCE

Chambre de Commerce, d'Industrie et d'Agriculture de Mauritanie (CCIAM): 303 ave de l'Indépanda, BP 215, Nouakchott; tel. 45-25-22-14; e-mail info@cciam.mr; internet cciam.mr; f. 1954; Pres. AHMED BABA OULD ELEYA; Sec.-Gen. ABDEL AZIZ WANE.

EMPLOYERS' ORGANIZATIONS

Union Nationale du Patronat Mauritanien (UNPM): 824 ave du Roi Fayçal, Ksar, BP 383, Nouakchott; tel. 45-25-33-01; internet www.unpm.mr; f. 1960; professional asscn for all employers active in Mauritania; Pres. ZEINE EL ABIDINE OULD CHEIKH AHMED; Sec.-Gen. MOHAMED LEMINE OULD SIDI.

UTILITIES

Electricity

Agence de Développement de l'Electrification Rurale: Ilôt C, Tevragh Zeina, BP 2920, Nouakchott; tel. 45-29-38-36; e-mail ader@mauritel.mr; internet www.ader.mr; Dir-Gen. EL-KORY OULD H'MEITY.

Société Mauritanienne d'Electricité (SOMELEC): 47 ave de l'Indépendance, BP 355, Nouakchott; tel. 45-29-66-04; e-mail somelec@somelec.mr; internet www.somelec.mr; f. 2001; state-owned; transfer to majority private sector ownership proposed; production and distribution of electricity; Pres. MOHAMED LEMINE SALEM DAH; Dir-Gen. CHEIKH OULD ABDALLAHI OULD BODDÉ.

Gas

BSA GAZ SA: Ilôt E, Zone Industrielle, Tevragh Zeina, BP 5528, Nouakchott; tel. 45-25-87-90; e-mail kabich@bsagaz-mr.com; f. 2009; Dir-Gen. MOHAMED KABICH.

Rim Gaz: ZRB 515, Tevragh Zeina, BP 7708, Nouakchott; tel. 45-29-10-40; e-mail rimgaz@gmail.com; internet rimgaz.business.site; f. 2010.

Société Mauritanienne de Gaz (SOMAGAZ): Ilôt K No. 207, POB 5089, Nouakchott; tel. 45-24-28-58; e-mail somagazinfo@somagaz.com; internet somagaz.com; f. 1987; production and distribution of butane gas; Dir-Gen. KHADIJETOU MINT BOUKA.

Water

Office National des Services de l'Eau en Milieu Rural: Nouakchott; Dir-Gen. EL MOUDIR OULD BOUNA.

Société Nationale d'Eau (SNDE): 106 ave 42-096, Tevragh Zeina, BP 796, Nouakchott; tel. 45-25-22-70; e-mail dg.snde@gmail.com; internet www.snde.mr; f. 2001; Dir-Gen. MOHAMED MAHMOUD OULD JAFAAR.

MAJOR COMPANIES

The following are some of the largest companies in terms of either capital investment or employment:

Ciment de Mauritanie SA: 10 rue Mamadou Konaté, Immeuble Al-Khaima City Center, 7e étage, BP 40029, Nouakchott; tel. 45-25-71-01; e-mail info@ciment.mr; internet www.ciment.mr/index.php; f. 1979; Pres. and Dir-Gen. AHMED SALECK MOHAMED LAMINE.

Compagnie Mauritanienne de Sucre et Dérivés: Ex-Siège MAEC, Ilôt C, Tevragh Zeina, Nouakchott; tel. 25-21-06-06; e-mail contact@comasud.mr; internet www.comasud.mr; Dir-Gen. MOHAMED TAGHIOLLAH OULD CHEIKH BOUYA.

Entreprise de Bâtiment, Travaux et Routes (EBTR): Zone Industrielle de la Foire, BP 5501, Nouakchott; tel. 45-25-82-34; f. 1992; construction; Pres. and Dir-Gen. MOHAMED LAFDAL BETTAH.

Mauritano-Française des Ciments (MAFCI): Zone du Port, Lot no 1, BP 5291, Nouakchott; tel. 45-25-82-55; e-mail info@mafci.mr; internet mafci.mr; f. 1995; Pres. and Dir-Gen. MOHAMMAD LAMINE OULD ZAIN.

Pact-Industrie: Nouakchott; tel. 45-74-60-56; e-mail pactndb@yahoo.fr; Pres. and Dir-Gen. MAURICE BENZA.

Société Arabe du Fer et de l'Acier en Mauritanie (SAFA): BP 114, Nouadhibou; tel. 45-74-61-28; e-mail safa@snim.com; internet www.safa-mr.com; f. 1985; 100% owned by SNIM; steel-rolling mill; Chair. MOHAMED ALI OULD SIDI MOHAMED; Man. Dir MOHAMED YARBANA OULD MOHAMED EL MAMY.

Société Arabe des Industries Métallurgiques (SAMIA): Zone Industrielle el-Mina, route de Rosso, BP 6247-1248, Nouakchott; tel. 45-25-44-55; e-mail samia@samia.mr; internet www.samia.mr; f. 1974; 50% owned by SNIM, 50% owned by Kuwait Real Estate Investment Consortium; extraction of gypsum and production of plaster of Paris; Man. Dir MOHAMED EL MOUSTAPHA OULD ELEYA.

Société de Construction et de Gestion Immobilière de la Mauritanie (SOCOGIM): BP 28, Nouakchott; tel. 45-25-47-75; e-mail socogim@mauritel.mr; f. 1974; 89% state-owned; Chair. DIALLO MAMADOU BATHIA; Dir-Gen. MOHAMED LEMINE OULD KHATTRI.

Société Mauritanienne de Commercialisation de Poissons, SA (SMCP): blvd Median, BP 250, Nouadhibou; tel. 45-74-52-81; e-mail info@smcpsa.com; internet smcp.mr; f. 1984; 70% state-owned; until 1992 monopoly exporter of demersal fish and crustaceans; Dir-Gen. MOCTAR BOUCEIF.

Société Mauritanienne des Hydrocarbures et du Patrimoine Minier (SMHPM): Ilôt K, rue 42-133, N° 349, Nouakchott; tel. 45-25-59-93; e-mail info@smhpm.mr; internet www.smhpm.mr; f. 2014; established to replace the Société Mauritanienne des Hydrocarbures; 100% state-owned.

Société des Mines du Cuivre de Mauritanie (MCM): BP 5576, Nouakchott; tel. 45-25-64-23; f. 2005 to acquire operations of Guelb Moghrein Mines d'Akjoujt (GEMAK); exploitation of copper and other ores at Akjoujt; 80% owned by First Quantum Minerals (Canada); Dir-Gen. MERLIN THOMAS.

Société Nationale des Aménagements Agricoles et Travaux (SNAAT): BP 12, Rosso; tel. 45-56-90-90; e-mail info@snaat.mr; internet snaat.mr; f. 2009; Dir-Gen. KHATTRY OULD EL-ATIGH MOHAMED MAHMOUD.

Société Nationale d'Importation et d'Exportation (SONIMEX): ave Bourguiba, BP 290, Nouakchott; tel. 45-25-22-24; internet www.sonimex.mr; f. 1966; 74% state-owned; import of foodstuffs and textiles, distribution of essential consumer goods, export of gum arabic; Pres. HAMOUD OULD AHMEDOU; Dir-Gen. CHEIKH OULD ZEIDANE.

Société Nationale Industrielle et Minière (SNIM): BP 42, Nouadhibou; tel. 45-74-51-74; e-mail snim@snim.com; internet www.snim.com; f. 1972; 78.4% state-owned; balance held by Islamic Development Bank (Saudi Arabia) and private Kuwaiti and Jordanian interests; operates mining centre at Zouerate, three open-pit cast iron mines, port facilities, and 700-km railway line; Man. Dir MOHAMED VALL OULD TELMIDI.

Société de Gestion des Installations Pétrolières (GIP): BP 73, Nouadhibou; tel. 45-74-52-40; f. 1981 as Société Mauritanienne des Industries de Raffinage (SOMIR); 67.85% owned by SNIM.

Tasiast Mauritanie Ltd SA (TMLSA): ZRA 741, BP 5051, Nouakchott; tel. 45-20-00-08; e-mail tmlsa_local_business@kinross.com; internet www.kinrosstasiast.mr; gold mining; Pres. BRAHIM OULD M'BARECK.

TIVISKI SA: BP 2069, Nouakchott; tel. 45-25-17-56; e-mail contact@tiviski.com; internet www.tiviski.com; f. 1989; dairy products; Dir-Gen. NAGI ICHOUDOU.

Total Mauritanie: E Nord, Lot no 110, BP 4973, Nouakchott; tel. 45-29-00-19; internet totalenergies.com/fr/en-mauritanie; f. 1999; distribution of petroleum; Man. Dir ABDELLATIF BOUMEDIANE.

TRADE UNIONS

Confédération Générale des Travailleurs de Mauritanie (CGTM): BP 6164, Nouakchott; tel. 45-25-60-24; internet cgtm.org; f. 1992; obtained official recognition in 1994; Sec.-Gen. KHADIJETTOU MAMADOU DIALLO.

Confédération Libre des Travailleurs de Mauritanie (CLTM): BP 6902, Nouakchott; f. 1995; Sec.-Gen. SAMORY OULD BÈYE.

Confédération Nationale des Travailleurs de Mauritanie (CNTM): Nouakchott; tel. 45-00-17-01; internet www.cntm.mr/index.php/fr; Sec.-Gen. MOHAMED AHMED OULD SALECK.

Union Générale des Travailleurs de Mauritanie (UTM): Bourse du Travail, BP 630, Nouakchott; internet rim-utm.org; f. 1961; Sec.-Gen. EL-KORY OULD ABDEL MOLA.

Transport

RAILWAYS

A railway connects the iron ore deposits at Zouerate with Nouadhibou; an extension services the reserves at El Rhein, and another those at M'Haoudat. The Société Nationale Industrielle et Minière (SNIM) operates one of the longest (2.4 km) and heaviest (22,000 metric tons) trains in the world.

SNIM—Direction du Chemin de Fer et du Port: BP 42, Nouadhibou; tel. 45-74-51-74; internet www.snim.com; f. 1963; Gen. Man. MOCTAR OULD DIAY.

ROADS

The 1,100-km Trans-Mauritania highway, completed in 1985, links Nouakchott with Néma in the east of the country. The construction of a 470-km highway between Nouakchott and Nouadhibou was completed in 2004. Plans exist for the construction of a 7,400-km highway, l'Autoroute Transmaghrébine, linking Nouakchott with the Libyan port of Tubruq (Tobruk).

Autorité de Régulation des Transports: Nouakchott; Pres. CHEIKH SID'AHMED OULD BABA.

Entreprise Nationale de l'Entretien Routier: Nouakchott; Dir-Gen. AHMEDOU TDJANE THIAM.

INLAND WATERWAYS

The Senegal river is navigable in the wet season by small coastal vessels as far as Kayes (Mali) and by river vessels as far as Kaédi; in the dry season it is navigable as far as Rosso and Boghé, respectively. The major river ports are at Rosso, Kaédi and Gouraye.

SHIPPING

The principal port, at Point-Central, 10 km south of Nouadhibou, is almost wholly occupied with mineral exports. There is also a commercial and fishing port at Nouadhibou. The deep-water Port de l'Amitié at Nouakchott, built and maintained with assistance from the People's Republic of China, was inaugurated in 1986, and has a total annual capacity of about 1.5m. metric tons.

Mauritanienne de Transport Maritime: Nouakchott; tel. 45-25-44-79; e-mail mtm@mtm.mr; internet www.mtm.mr; f. 1996; Pres. and Dir-Gen. A. KADER KAMIL.

Port Autonome de Nouadhibou: BP 236, Nouadhibou; tel. 45-74-51-36; e-mail contact@pan.mr; internet www.pan.mr; f. 1973; state-owned; Dir-Gen. TALEB OULD SID'AHMED.

Port Autonome de Nouakchott (Port de l'Amitié): El Mina, BP 5103, Nouakchott; tel. 45-25-38-59; e-mail contact@port-nouakchott.com; internet www.port-nouakchott.com; f. 1986; deep-water port; Dir-Gen. SIDI AHMED OULD RAIS.

Société des Services Maritimes de Nouakchott (SSMN): Nouakchott; f. 2021; subsidiary of BOLUDA France; Dir-Gen. MATHIEU MOAL.

Shipping Companies

Société d'Acconage et de Manutention en Mauritanie (SAMMA): BP 258, Nouadhibou; tel. 45-74-52-63; e-mail ekhyarhoum.medlemine@snim.com; internet www.samma.mr; f. 1960; 52.5% owned by SNIM; freight and handling, shipping agent, forwarding agent, stevedoring; Man. Dir EKHYARHOUM OULD MOHAMED LEMINE.

Société Générale de Consignation et d'Entreprises Maritimes (SOGECO): 1765 rue 22-002, Commune du Ksar, BP 351, Nouakchott; tel. 45-25-22-02; e-mail sogeco@sogeco-sa.mr; internet www.sogecosa.com; f. 1973; 50% owned by Bolloré Logistics Mauritania; shipping agent, forwarding, stevedoring; Man. Dir SID'AHMED OULD ABEIDNA.

CIVIL AVIATION

There are international airports at Nouakchott, Nouadhibou and Néma, and 23 smaller airstrips.

Agence Nationale de l'Aviation Civile (ANAC): BP 91, Nouakchott; tel. 45-24-40-05; e-mail anac@anac.mr; internet w3.anac.mr; f. 2004; Gen. Man. NGAIDÉ ABDOULAYE ABBAS.

Class Aviation: BP 776, Nouakchott; tel. 27030303; e-mail seyniducros@classaviation.aero; internet www.classaviation.aero; f. 2008; air taxi service; CEO SEYNI DUCROS.

Mauritania Airlines International: Aéroport International de Nouakchott, Ancienne Aérogare, BP 7991, Nouakchott; tel. 45-24-12-53; e-mail mai@mauritaniaairlines.mr; internet www.mauritaniaairlines.mr; f. 2010; Dir-Gen. AMAL MINT MAOULOUD.

Tourism

Office National du Tourisme (ONT): BP 2884, Nouakchott; tel. 45-29-03-44; internet fb.com/ONT.Mauritanie; f. 2002; Dir MAHFOUDH OULD JIYID.

SOMASERT: BP 42, Nouadhibou; tel. 45-74-29-91; e-mail somasert@snim.com; internet www.somasertsa.com; f. 1987; subsidiary of SNIM; responsible for promoting tourism, managing hotels and organizing tours; Dir-Gen. SAAD CHEIK SAAD BOUH.

Defence

As assessed at November 2021, the armed forces numbered an estimated 15,850 men: army 15,000, navy about 600, air force 250. Full-time membership of paramilitary forces totalled about 5,000. Military service is by authorized conscription, and lasts for two years. In 2021 a total of 472 troops were stationed abroad.

Defence Budget: UM 7,770m. in 2021.

Chief of General Staff of the Armed Forces: Maj.-Gen. MOCTAR OULD BELLAA OULD CHAABANE.

Chief of Staff of the Army: Brig.-Gen. MOHAMED EL MOCTAR OULD CHEIKH OULD MENNY.

Chief of Staff of the Navy: Rear-Adm. MOHAMED OULD CHEIKHNA OULD TALEB MOUSTAPH.

Chief of Staff of the Air Force: Gen. HAMADI OULD ELY MAHMOUD.

Chief of Staff of the National Gendarmerie: Brig.-Gen. ABDALLAHI OULD AHMED AICHA.

Education

Primary education, which is officially compulsory, begins at six years of age and lasts for six years. Secondary education begins at 12 years of age and lasts for seven years, comprising a first cycle of four years and a second of three years. According to estimates by the United Nations Educational, Scientific and Cultural Organization (UNESCO), in 2014/15 enrolment at pre-primary level was equivalent to 10% of children in the relevant age-group (9% of boys; 12% of girls). In 2018/19 total enrolment at primary schools included 77% of children in the relevant age-group (75% of boys; 79% of girls), while the comparable ratio for secondary education was equivalent to 39% of children in the appropriate age-group (38% of boys; 40% of girls). In 2020 spending on education represented 9.7% of total government expenditure, according to the World Bank.

Bibliography

Abdoul, M., et al. *Regards sur la Mauritanie. L'ouest saharien: cahiers d'études pluridisciplinaires*; Vol. 4. Paris, L'Harmattan, 2004.

Bonte, P. *La montagne de fer: la SNIM, Mauritanie: une entreprise minière saharienne à l'heure de la mondialisation*. Paris, Editions Karthala, 2001.

Boye, A. H., and Thiam, S. *J'étais à Oualata: le racisme d'Etat en Mauritanie*. Paris, L'Harmattan, 1999.

Calderini, S., Cortese, D., and Webb, J. L. A. *Mauritania*. Oxford, ABC Clio, 1992.

Clausen, U. *Demokratisierung in Mauritanien: Einfuehrung und Dokumente*. Hamburg, Deutsches Orient-Institut, 1993.

Désiré-Vuillemin, G. *Histoire de la Mauritanie: des origines à l'indépendance*. Paris, Editions Karthala, 1997.

Devey, M. *La Mauritanie*. Paris, Editions Karthala, 2005.

Dia, A. O. *Peuls et paysans: Les Halaye de Mauritanie*. Paris, L'Harmattan, 2013.

Diaw, M. *La politique étrangère de la Mauritanie*. Paris, L'Harmattan, 1999.

Foster, N. *Mauritania: The Struggle for Democracy*. Boulder, CO, First Forum Press, 2011.

Garnier, C., and Ermont, P. *Désert fertile: un nouvel état, la Mauritanie*. Paris, Hachette, 1960.

El Haycen, M. L. O. *La Mauritanie et ses présidents de 1958 à 2008*. Dakar, Editions Silex, 2010.

Jus, C. *Soudan français–Mauritanie, une géopolitique coloniale (1880–1963): tracer une ligne dans le désert*. Paris, L'Harmattan, 2003.

McBrewster, J., Miller F. P., and Vandome, A. (Eds). *History of Mauritania*. Mauritius, Alphascript Publishing, 2009.

N'Diaye, B. *Mauritania's Colonels: Political Leadership, Civil-Military Relations and Democratization*. Abingdon, Routledge, 2018.

Ould Ahmed Salem, M. *L'économie mauritanienne: le bilan de la planification économique depuis l'indépendance* (trans. from Arabic by Ould Moulaye Ahmed, A.). Nouakchott, Imprimerie Atlas, 1994.

Ould Cheikh, A. W. *Etat et société en Mauritanie: Cinquante ans après l'indépendance*. Paris, Karthala, 2014.

Ould Ciré, M. Y. *La Mauritanie: Entre l'esclavage et le racisme*. Paris, L'Harmattan, 2014.

Ould Daddah, M. *La Mauritanie contre vents et marées*. Paris, Editions Karthala, 2003.

Ould Meymoun, M. *La Mauritanie entre le pouvoir civil et le pouvoir militaire*. Paris, L'Harmattan, 2011.

Ould Saleck, El-A. *Les Haratins: La paysage politique mauritanien*. Paris, L'Harmattan, 2003.

Pazzanika, A. G. *Historical Dictionary of Mauritania*. Lanham, MD, Scarecrow Press, 1996.

Robinson, D. *Sociétés musulmanes et pouvoir colonial français au Sénégal et en Mauritanie 1880–1920*. Paris, Editions Karthala, 2004.

Sy, A. A. *L'Enfer d'Inal: Mauritanie—l'horreur des camps*. Paris, L'Harmattan, 2000.

MAURITIUS

Physical and Social Geography

The Republic of Mauritius, comprising the islands of Mauritius and Rodrigues, together with the Agalega Islands and the Cargados Carajos Shoals, lies in the Indian Ocean 800 km east of Madagascar. The island of Mauritius covers 1,868 sq km (721 sq miles) in area. It is a volcanic island, consisting of a plain rising from the north-east to the highest point on the island, Piton de la Rivière Noire (827 m above sea level) in the south-west, interspersed by abrupt volcanic peaks and gorges, and is almost completely surrounded by a coral reef. Including Rodrigues and its other islands, the republic occupies a land area of 2,007 sq km (775 sq miles).

The climate is sub-tropical maritime, but with two distinct seasons; additionally, the warm dry coastal areas contrast with the cool rainy interior. Mauritius and Rodrigues are vulnerable to cyclones, particularly between September and May.

Rodrigues, a volcanic island of 110 sq km (42 sq miles) surrounded by a coral reef, lies 585 km east of the island of Mauritius. Its population was officially estimated at 44,216 in 2021. Mauritius has two dependencies (together covering 29 sq km, with 274 inhabitants at mid-2021): Agalega, two islands 935 km north of Mauritius; and the Cargados Carajos Shoals (or St Brandon Islands), 22 islets without permanent inhabitants but used as a fishing station, 370 km north-north-east of Mauritius.

Mauritius claims sovereignty over Tromelin, a small island without permanent inhabitants, 556 km to the north-west. This claim is disputed by Madagascar and France. Mauritius also seeks the return of the Chagos Archipelago (notably the coral atoll of Diego Garcia), about 2,000 km to the north-east. The archipelago was formerly administered by Mauritius but in 1965 became part (and in 1976 all) of the British Indian Ocean Territory.

The population of the Republic of Mauritius was enumerated at 1,237,091 at the July 2011 census, giving a density of 606.4 inhabitants per sq km. In mid-2021 the total population was officially estimated at 1,266,334. Almost 42% of the population reside in the urban area extending from Port Louis (the capital and business centre) on the north-west coast, to Curepipe in the island's centre. The population is of mixed origin, including people of European, African, Indian and Chinese descent. English is the official language, and Creole (Kreol), derived from French, the lingua franca. The most widely spoken languages at the 2011 census were Creole (40.5%) and Bhojpuri (19.3%), a Hindi dialect.

History

MANORAMA AKUNG

INTRODUCTION

The Republic of Mauritius, situated in the middle of the Indian Ocean, with its multi-ethnic population of approximately 1.2m., has been qualified as an exemplary democracy, despite pessimistic initial conditions upon its accession to independence in 1968. According to the Economist Intelligence Unit's Democracy Index (of 2020), it is ranked first in Africa, and, globally, it is placed 20th out of 167 countries, ahead of countries such as France, the USA and South Africa.

HISTORICAL BACKGROUND

Mauritius inherited modern political institutions, which were mainly inspired by Europe. The island was successively colonized by the Dutch (1638–1710), the French (1715–1810), and the British (1810–1968). Without an indigenous population before its colonization, the country has been a 'welcoming land' for successive waves of immigrants, including European settlers, slaves (mainly from Africa, Madagascar and smaller numbers from India), indentured workers (largely Indians and a few Malagasy, Comorians and Africans), free immigrants (Europeans, Indians, Chinese and the 'Coloured People' who were of mixed origins) and numerous others.

The formation of the state and the organization of general elections in Mauritius dates back to the 18th century during the French colonial period. Democratic institutions were installed, with a first Constitution with an elective principle and the separation of powers between the judiciary and the executive in 1791. Henceforth, the free people of the colony—the Whites and the 'Coloured People'—could vote for elected representatives to the Colonial Assembly.

However, ministerial despotism returned with the rule of Napoleon Bonaparte from 1803 and continued during the early British rule. The elective principal was regained in 1885 but the suffrage was a restrictive one—only those who possessed the minimum property qualifications could vote. After much procrastination and debate the suffrage was enlarged in 1948 to grant voting rights to any citizen aged 21 and older who could read and write a simple sentence in any nine recognized languages of the colony. In 1958 universal suffrage was granted and voting rights were extended to all citizens of 21 years an above. The main political parties, on the eve of independence, were the Parti Travailliste (PTr, Mauritius Labour Party), founded in 1936, the Parti Mauricien Social Démocrate (PMSD), the Independent Forward Bloc (IFB) and the Comité d'Action Musulman (CAM), founded in the 1950s.

POST-INDEPENDENCE INSTITUTIONAL FRAMEWORK

Mauritius attained independence on 12 March 1968 and, as a member of the Commonwealth, Queen Elizabeth II, represented by a Governor-General, remained the head of the state. Mauritius became a republic in 1992 with a President (holding very few executive powers) as the head of the state. Mauritius has a Westminster system adapted to the multi-ethnic setting of the country. During the 1960s, throughout the process of democratization and constitutional development, the main concern of the authorities was to find the right balance between majority rule and minority right. Hindus are referred to as the majority (although this group is sub-divided in terms of castes, linguistic differences and geographical origins) and the minorities include the remaining ethnic groups, namely Muslims, Sino-Mauritians, Creoles (of African and mixed origins) and Whites (mainly Franco-Mauritian). Mechanisms such as the 'best loser' system and other entrenched clauses (requiring a parliamentary three-quarter majority for any amendment) were incorporated into the independence Constitution as safeguards for the minorities and to ensure power-sharing.

The National Assembly includes members of the elected opposition, government deputies, and the Cabinet system where the Prime Minister (the head of government) and his ministers sit. There are a maximum of 70 members in this unicameral legislature, 62 of which are elected through the first-past-the-post system and a maximum of eight can be nominated via the best loser system. The best losers are seats allocated to ensure a fair and adequate representation of each community and party in the Assembly. For the specific nomination of best losers, the Constitution divides the population in four ethnic groups—Hindus and Muslims (classified according to religion), Chinese and General Population, categorized in terms of race and mode of life, respectively. The General Population is composed of citizens who do not fall into the first three mentioned ethnic groups and includes mainly those of Christian faith—the Creoles and the Whites and those of mixed origins. Of the eight best losers' seats, the top four go to the best loser candidates representing the under-represented ethnic groups, regardless of party affiliation, and the remaining four seats go to the best losers of the victorious party.

Legislative elections are scheduled to be held at regular intervals (every five years) and have always been qualified as relatively fair and transparent. The main parties are the PTr, the PMSD, the Mouvement Militant Mauricien (MMM) founded in 1969 and the Mouvement Socialiste Mauricien (MSM) founded in 1983. The PTr and the MSM, traditionally, have had a mostly Hindu-majority rural-based electorate and the PMSD and the MMM have had the support of urban Creole-minority groups. Throughout the years, many small parties emerged but most of them have been short-lived.

The consociational nature of the Mauritian political system and the institutional constraints of the electoral system promoted pre-electoral coalition making as a power-sharing device. The gerrymandering in the delimitation of the electoral boundaries along communal lines has created an urban-rural dichotomy, where 40% of the constituencies (mostly rural) are predominantly composed of the Hindu majority, 40% (mostly urban) are largely inhabited by the minorities and 20% are marginal districts. This induces mainstream parties to nominate candidates from both the majority and minority groups. As aforementioned, despite having a cross-ethnic membership, the four main parties are perceived as representing one main ethnic group, respectively, and mainly draw support from specific segments of the population. Hence, no party on its own can win a majority. Coalition governments have been instrumental in alleviating polarization and promoting national unity by ensuring that all the ethnic groups have their share of the national cake. Through further informal institutional practices—with regards to nomination to key posts within the Cabinet, to parastatal bodies, ambassadorships, etc.—successive governments have ensured that the different ethnic and religious groups feel integrated and empowered in the governance of the multi-ethnic society.

THE SIR SEEWOOSAGUR RAMGOOLAM ERA

At the general election of 1967 a PTr-CAM-IFB coalition (the Independence Party) was formed to compete against the PMSD which advocated for integration into and/or association with the United Kingdom. In 1968 the status of independence, acclaimed on one hand (by 55% of votes for the PTr-CAM-IFB alliance) and decried on the other (by 44% of votes for the PMSD), created a considerable political divide between pro- and anti-independence Mauritians. This political bipolarity was accompanied by a difficult economic situation, the inter-ethnic conflict (mainly linked to a gang warfare rather than of political origins) of January 1968 and the fear of a Hindu hegemony among the minority groups.

At the beginning of 1969 speculation about a PTr-PMSD alliance caused upheavals within the Government and the opposition, and in October the PTr-PMSD-CAM coalition was officially sealed. According to Sir Seewoosagur Ramgoolam (Prime Minister, leader of the PTr and commonly known as the Father of the Nation) and Sir Gaëtan Duval (leader of the PMSD and former Leader of the Opposition), this coalition would be a symbol of national unity, essential to promote political and economic stability and the appeasement of inter-ethnic tensions.

For many observers, the PTr-PMSD-CAM coalition created a political vacuum with only a few members of the IFB and the Union Démocratique Mauricienne forming the parliamentary opposition. It was claimed by some observers that the PTr, previously a proletarian party close to the trade unions, had abandoned the workers' struggle, while the PTr-PMSD coalition was viewed as the symbol of state-private (between the state bourgeoisie of Indo-Mauritian origin and the historical bourgeoisie of Franco-Mauritian origin) power-sharing. Several documents show the influence of Western foreign powers in the conclusion of this alliance—as an attempt to thwart the rise of communism in the midst of the ongoing Cold War.

The years between 1969 and 1980 were marked by a challenge to the traditional parties after the formation of the MMM, a 'New Left' party, which was launched in September 1969 by Paul Bérenger (who became the party leader), Dev Virahsawmy and Jooneed Jeerooburkhan, among others. It owed its origin to a number of graduate students who set up the Club des Etudiants Militants in 1968. Conditions were ripe to favour the rapid rise of the MMM. As well as the tensions linked to the inter-ethnic riots, Mauritius, akin to other African and Latin American countries, was facing an acute economic crisis, with increasing unemployment, especially among the youth. The country's economy was still mainly dependent on the sugar industry and the few steps towards diversification—with the cultivation of other commercial plants, the development of tourism, the creation of a development bank to help entrepreneurs—were insufficient to meet the demands of the situation.

The programme of the MMM included, for instance, the nationalization of, *inter alia*, the sugar industry, the docks and the transport sector, as well as the emancipation of women, and resistance against neo-colonialism and communalism. The party's ideology attracted the support of people from several ethnic groups, whether Hindu, Muslim or Creole. However, its success was a consequence of its internal organization. Unlike the traditional parties, which at that point had no proper structure or party discipline, the MMM was organized around an ideology and not around individuals. The party was well structured with regional cells which disseminated its programme throughout the island.

By 1970 the MMM had created numerous trade unions to rally workers to the party, and which were grouped under the General Workers' Federation (GWF). Initially the MMM advocated direct democracy instead of parliamentary democracy and the party limited its activities to organizing street protests to criticize the Government. However, in 1970 the party decided to participate in a by-election, following the death of the IFB deputy. The MMM candidate, Virahsawmy was victorious with 71.5% of the votes, against the candidate proposed by the Government.

The MMM used its influence on the unions and organized a series of strikes, the first of which took place in September 1971. This strike disconcerted the authorities and also surprised Bérenger, who realized that the control of the situation was slipping out of his hands. The party was accused of receiving foreign aid and causing shortages of foodstuffs such as eggs, milk and meat, among other provisions. Thereafter Bérenger changed tactics, and the party broadened its membership criteria and also recruited members of the new middle class including Sir Aneerood Jugnauth, Vishnu Lutchmeenaraidoo, Jean-Claude de l'Estrac.

During the strikes in November 1971 the first post-independence political murder took place. A partisan of the MMM, Azor Adelaide, was killed and riots broke out. A state of emergency was declared in December 1971 and the by-elections, municipal elections and the general election of 1972 were cancelled through constitutional amendments. All political gatherings were banned and some leaders of the MMM—including Bérenger and Virahsawmy—were arrested and detained for a year. The GWF was shut down and the press was censored. The Prime Minister appointed an independent mediator to settle the disputes that had led to the strikes; however, this was in vain and the strikes continued. In 1972 the leaders of the MMM were released but the state of emergency remained still in force. Pro-MMM unions slowly started to function again. However, the party faced internal divisions leading to the resignation of several party members, among them Virahsawmy, who accused the party of becoming communal and bourgeois.

In late 1973 the PTr-PMSD coalition collapsed and the PMSD joined the opposition. The main tensions were due to the contradictory policies pursued by the two party leaders: for instance, Duval, then Minister of Foreign Affairs, in contradiction with the Government's policies, worked for the strengthening of links with South Africa and was opposed to diplomatic ties between the People's Republic of China and Mauritius, Ramgoolam was determined to maintain a policy of non-alignment and to receive aid from China. Duval had also personally made an offer to the French Government that it could establish a naval base in Mauritius in contradiction with the Government's policies. Electoral strategies accentuated these conflicts, as in 1973 negotiations took place between the MMM and the PTr regarding the formation of a coalition. However, these failed and the MMM continued its attack on the PTr-CAM Government.

Meanwhile, the economy began to recover after a decade of financial difficulties. In 1973, benefiting from the European Economic Community's Sugar Protocol, the sugar boom contributed to the growth of the economy. The Export Processing Zone, created in 1970, benefited from the Yaoundé II and Lomé Conventions, and increased exports while attracting foreign investors, without harming local enterprises. The Government established, *inter alia*, policies to develop tourism and boost the export of sugar. However, in 1975 thousands of students took to the streets to express their dissatisfaction with the failings of the education system. In 1976 secondary school education became free and the voting age was reduced from 21 years to 18.

It was in this context that the general election of 1976 took place. Negotiations towards the formation of alliances began again with renewed vigour. The MMM first unsuccessfully negotiated with the PMSD, and there were proposals from the MMM for a coalition with the IFB; however the leader of the latter refused this option. The MMM also negotiated with the PTr for an equal sharing of seats in the event of victory but this endeavour also failed. Eventually, all parties contested the polls individually. The MMM obtained 38.7% of votes (34 seats), the PTr-CAM 38.1% of votes (28 seats) and the PMSD, 16.5% of votes (eight seats).

Despite its victory, it was not the MMM that formed the Government. To do so, according to the electoral system, a party must have an absolute majority but this was not the case for the MMM, and the party refused offers from both the PMSD and the PTr to form a coalition. Eventually, it was an alliance of the PTr and the PMSD, with Ramgoolam as Prime Minister, that took power. Jugnauth, who was presented as the next Prime Minister by the MMM during the election campaign, became the Leader of the Opposition.

The MMM continued to use its influence on the trade unions and campaigned for the abolition of the Industrial Relations Act which controlled the development of these bodies. The Government's refusal to amend this law, or to allocate salary compensations, gave rise to a general strike in August 1979. With the lingering world economic crisis (aggravated by four devastating cyclones between December 1979 and March 1980), the Government became increasingly unpopular. Yet, the post-1979 strike marked the end of revolutionary socialism within the MMM. Thereafter, the party faced incessant internal squabbles regarding its deviating leftist ideology. Some party members resigned from the MMM accusing it of becoming bourgeois, centre-left and giving in to ethnic politics.

On the eve of the 1982 general election, the Government was already weakened by internal dissensions. Young deputies, including Harish Boodhoo, had formed a Protest Group to restore the credibility of the PTr, but it was expelled from the party in 1979. This group created the Parti Socialiste Mauricien (PSM) and joined the opposition. Holding a narrow majority in the Parliament, the PTr also faced a leadership succession crisis between Satcam Boolell and Veerasamy Ringadoo as Ramgoolam reached the age of 80 and retirement. In 1981 the PMSD left the governing coalition. In the same year the MMM contracted an alliance with the PSM. The MMM-PSM coalition also made an agreement with the Organisation du Peuple Rodriguais (OPR) from Rodrigues Island. The MMM once again presented Jugnauth as the next Prime Minister. Given the realities of the Mauritian society, this choice was seen as a strategy to reassure the Hindu community. The PTr tried to conclude an alliance with the PMSD and

the Rassemblement pour le Progrès et la Liberté, but Duval refused. The CAM, meanwhile, did not stand for election.

THE ANEROOD JUGNAUTH ERA 1982–94

In the legislative elections held in June 1982 the MMM-PSM-OPR alliance won 64.1% of votes and secured all 62 of the directly elected seats, resulting in the appointment to the premiership of Jugnauth. The PTr received 25.7% of the votes (taking two best loser seats) and the PMSD 7.7% of votes (and also garnered two best loser seats). After the proclamation of the results, the Electoral Commission deemed it unnecessary to appoint best losers since the victorious alliance fairly represented all the communities. However, the Supreme Court's advice was sought and it recommended the appointment of best losers as stipulated by law.

The Government of the MMM-PSM-OPR alliance lasted only nine months. Conflicts between Bérenger and Boodhoo broke out at the start of the mandate. There were clashes over the Mauritius Broadcasting Corporation and the policies set out to resolve the country's economic crises. Bérenger, then Minister of Finance, decided that the Government had to continue the Structural Adjustment Programmes started by the previous Government to benefit from the loans offered by the International Monetary Fund (IMF) and the World Bank. These reforms meant reducing subsidies on foodstuffs and wages, and setting a ceiling on government spending. For the PSM these conditions were too draconian. Despite protests, Bérenger, with the support of the Prime Minister, decided to comply with the conditions of the IMF and the World Bank. The situation degenerated and MMM leaders appealed to the party members to dismiss the ministers of the PSM. However, Jugnauth, asserting his prerogative as Prime Minister, rejected this demand. Consequently, Bérenger and 12 other ministers resigned from the Government and joined the opposition in the legislature.

Expelled from the MMM, Jugnauth formed a new party, the MSM, dissolved the National Assembly and called a general election for August 1983. As soon as the elections were announced, bargaining for alliances began. Eventually, a PTr-MSM-PMSD coalition was struck. The MMM, presenting Bérenger as its candidate for Prime Minister, contested the elections alone. According to the Mauritian scholar Jocelyn Chan Low, these elections marked the consecration of the ethnic politics illustrated by divisions opposing 'minority and majority', and an urban-rural dichotomy. The PTr-MSM-PMSD alliance was victorious with 52.2% of votes (41 seats) against 46.6% of votes (19 seats) for the MMM. The OPR, re-elected with 2 seats, later joined the PTr-MSM-PMSD governmental coalition. Jugnauth became the Prime Minister and Ramgoolam, the Governor-General. Bérenger secured a best loser seat and was appointed as Leader of Opposition.

However, after only six months, the Government began to face internal discord. In early 1984 Sir Satcam Boolell, the new leader of the PTr, was dismissed and he joined the opposition benches with some members of the PTr. The PTr split into two factions: some PTr deputies decided to stay in the Government and they formed a new party, the Rassemblement des Travaillistes Mauriciens (RTM). In the same year, the controversial Newspaper and Periodical Bill and the amendment of the Criminal Code in 1985 led to uproar among the press and civil society. In 1985 four members of the Government were arrested in Amsterdam, Netherlands, (one of whom was found guilty of possession of 20 kg of heroin). Boodhoo and several other deputies resigned after the Government refused to set up a commission of inquiry on the issue. Faced with numerous dissidences, Jugnauth once again appealed to Boolell and the latter agreed to return to the Government. This period was also marked by the emergence of sustained economic prosperity that lasted until the early 1990s. The signing of the Double Taxation Avoidance Treaty with India in 1983 allowed the start of the offshore financial sector and made Mauritius the then largest source of foreign direct investment in India.

For the general election of 1987, the MMM first negotiated with the PTr, but was unsuccessful. The MMM offered Dr Navin Ramgoolam, the son of Seewoosagar Ramgoolam (who died in 1985), the opportunity to run as Prime Minister but he refused. The MMM then announced Prem Nababsing as its candidate for the premiership and entered into an alliance with the Mouvement des Travaillistes Démocrates (MTD), dissident of the PTr, and the Front des Travailleurs Socialistes (FTS). The MSM, once again, made a coalition with the PTr and the PMSD.

The PTr-MSM-PMSD alliance won the 1987 elections with 39 seats against the MMM-MTD-FTS which obtained 21 seats. Bérenger was not elected and Nababsing became the Leader of the Opposition. Tensions again emerged between Duval and Jugnauth and in August 1988 the PMSD left the Government. In 1989 Duval was arrested following the testimony of a former supporter of the PMSD, who had been convicted of the murder of Azor Adelaide. However, the case was later dismissed.

In 1990, to the surprise of most analysts, the MMM and the MSM announced that they would contest the 1991 election in coalition, and this was successful in securing 56.3% of the votes (57 seats) against 40% of the votes (seven seats) for the PTr-PMSD alliance. Jugnauth became Prime Minister for the fourth time, while Navin Ramgoolam, the new leader of the PTr, became the Leader of the Opposition. In 1992 the Government transformed Mauritius into a republic (mostly based on the Indian model). Sir Veerasamy Ringadoo became the first President of the Republic of Mauritius.

In 1993 Jugnauth learnt that Bérenger was secretly negotiating an alliance with Navin Ramgoolam. Bérenger was dismissed and joined the opposition; however, 15 deputies of the MMM under the leadership of Nababsing decided to remain in the Government. The MMM split into two factions: one group under the leadership of Bérenger, and the other under that of Nababsing. Each group claimed to be the real MMM. A legal dispute ensued and a ruling was made in favour of Bérenger's group. Nababsing created another party, the Renouveau Militant Mauricien (RMM).

Following the resignation of Bérenger and de l'Estrac in January 1995, a by-election was organized in constituency number 19. Bérenger and James Burty David of the PTr were elected against the candidates of the MSM-RMM and the PMSD, respectively. Following these elections, the PMSD joined the Government and Charles Gaëtan Xavier-Luc Duval, the son of Sir Gaëtan Duval, was appointed Minister of Industry and Industrial Technology and Minister of Tourism. However, in November, Xavier-Luc Duval resigned, protesting against legislation aimed at allowing the counting of marks obtained in Oriental languages for the final examinations at the primary level. This bill was considered to be detrimental to students (mostly Creole children) who had not opted to study these languages. The opposition voted against the bill, some government deputies abstained and the Supreme Court, whose advice was sought, ruled the amendment as unconstitutional. This incident led to a decline in Jugnauth's popularity and was used by the opposition in the subsequent electoral campaigns.

THE 1995 GENERAL ELECTION

For the November 1995 legislative elections, the MSM joined the RMM while the PTr entered into coalition with the MMM. The PTr-MMM obtained 63.7% of votes against 19.3% of votes for the MSM/RMM. Navin Ramgoolam was appointed Prime Minister. The results of these elections were similar to those of 1982. Not only did the victorious PTr-MMM alliance secure all 60 seats, but it also ousted Jugnauth, who had served as Prime Minister for 13 years, as had been the case in 1982 when Seewoosagur Ramgoolam who was Prime Minister for 15 years was removed. In 1996 Sir Gaëtan Duval died and Hervé, his brother, succeeded him as the leader of the PMSD. Quickly, the endemic dynamics of Mauritian politics came to the forefront, and the PTr-MMM coalition crumbled. In 1997 all the ministers of the MMM (with the exception of Dr Rachid Beebeejaun) resigned from the Government and joined the opposition.

In 1999 Xavier-Luc Duval (who in protest against the nomination of his uncle to the post of leader, left the PMSD and created his own party, the Parti Mauricien Xavier Duval—PMXD), with the support of the PTr, was successful in a by-election and the PMXD joined the Government. However, the declining socioeconomic situation, the inter-ethnic tensions and riots between February and May 1999 and a number of politico-financial scandals, weakened the Government. This period also saw the rise of identity politics through the virulent communal discourse of some socio-cultural groups and the discourse of Malaise Creole.

SHARING OF THE PREMIERSHIP

On the eve of the general election of 2000, as had become usual, negotiations to contract alliances began. The MSM and the MMM formed a coalition including other small parties: the FTS (Les Verts Fraternels) of Sylvio Michel, the Mouvement Republicain (MR) of Rama Valayden and the PMSD. The PTr allied itself with the PMXD, the Rassemblement Populaire pour le Renouveau (RPR) of Sheila Bappoo and the Mouvement Militant Socialiste Mauricien (MMSM) of Madun Dulloo. One of the conditions that helped to consolidate the MMM-MSM alliance despite their initial differences, was the sharing of the post of Prime Minister where Jugnauth would assume the post for the first three years and Bérenger, the last two years during which Jugnauth would become the President of the Republic. Furthermore, the agreement provided for an equal sharing of seats between the two parties.

The MMM-MSM-FTS-MR-PMSD won the elections with 52.3% of votes (58 seats) against 36.5% of votes (eight seats) for the PTr-PMXD-RPR-MMSM. However, once again, internal conflicts reappeared almost immediately. The MR and the FTS left the government alliance and joined the opposition. In 2002 Rodrigues Island was granted its autonomy with the creation of the Rodrigues Regional Assembly. In the same year, the President of the Republic, Cassam Uteem, resigned in disagreement with the proposed Prevention of Terrorism Bill. Despite efforts to diversify the economy with new sectors such as the seafood hub and the cyber-city, the Government faced a deteriorating economy in the wake of the dismantling of the Multi-Fibre Agreement (see *Economy*). Discontent was growing among the population because of the loss of purchasing power and the proposed reform of the old age pension. In 2003 Jugnauth, as agreed, resigned as Prime Minister to become President of Mauritius, with Bérenger succeeding him. Subsequently, a by-election was organized in constituency number 7. The victory of the PTr candidate, Rajesh Jeetah, over that of the MMM-MSM indicated the Government's loss of popularity. More notably, however, for the first time, in the country's history, a non-Hindu had become Prime Minister, creating a rupture in the tradition of appointing someone who belonged to the majority caste within the Hindu community.

THE DECADE OF THE PTR-PMSD, 2005-14

In anticipation of the general election of 2005, negotiations for the formation of alliances began. The MMM and the MSM again entered into an alliance, called the 'Remake 2000', on the same basis as in 2000, except that on this occasion, Pravind Jugnauth, the son of Anerood Jugnauth, was presented as the candidate for the premiership. Meanwhile, the PTr focused its campaign on the democratization of the economy and entered into alliance with the PMXD, the MMSM, the MR, the FTS and the Mouvement Socialiste Démocrate, which won with 48% of the votes (42 seats) against the MMM-MSM-PMSD alliance with 42% (24 seats). This election witnessed an unprecedented rise in the number of elected women in the National Assmebly from four to 12. Navin Ramgoolam became the Prime Minister and Paul Bérenger the Leader of Opposition. Following the election, the PMSD withdrew from the opposition alliance and in April 2006 joined the Government.

The early years of this mandate (until the renewal of the President's tenure in 2008) was marked by a conflictual cohabitation between Prime Minister Ramgoolam and the President, Anerood Jugnauth. In 2009, following the decision of the Judicial Committee of the Privy Council confirming the invalidation of the election of Ashock Jugnauth (brother of Anerood Jugnauth), who had been accused of electoral fraud, a by-election was organized. Pravind Jugnauth, leader of the MSM, and who had lost his seat in the 2005 general election, secured the seat with the support of the PTr against Ashock Jugnauth, supported by the MMM.

The PTr and the PMSD contested the 2010 general election in alliance with the MSM, and secured 49% of the votes (45 seats) against 42% of votes (20 seats) for the MMM-UN-MMSD alliance. Navin Ramgoolam remained the Prime Minister. Yet, from the beginning of the mandate the Government faced internal clashes. In 2011 the MSM left the Government and joined the opposition. In 2012 Anerood Jugnauth resigned as President to return to active politics and a MMM-MSM alliance, again with a sharing of the post of Prime Minister, was initially concluded. However, in September 2014, the MMM announced that it would contest the next general election coalition with the PTr. Furthermore, the PMSD, which has been in alliance with the PTr since 2005, had left the Government in June 2014. The PMSD and the Muvman Liberater (ML), formed by dissident members of the MMM, also joined the opposition.

THE PERENNITY OF THE POLITICAL SYSTEM, 2014–19

In October 2014 the National Assembly was dissolved and the country was called to the polls. The central themes discussed during the electoral campaign were the constitutional reform (Second Republic) project proposed by the PTr-MMM alliance and the assessment of the Ramgoolam regime. Akin to previous elections, the alliances contracted in 2014 were tied up at the last minute with the main objective of obtaining the maximum number of votes. These elections were contested by 73 parties (including independent candidates) but with the bipolarization of the Mauritian politics, the main choice laid either in a 'continuity' of Ramgoolam's regime (under the PTr-MMM alliance), following 10 years of his reign or in a 'rupture' with the MSM-PMSD-ML alliance under the aegis of Anerood Jugnauth. At the same time, the electorate had to choose between a continuity of the constitutional system proposed by the MSM-PMSD-ML alliance or a transition to a Second Republic proposed by the PTr-MMM.

The MSM-PMSD-ML alliance won the elections with 49.8% of votes (51 seats) against 38.5% of votes (16 seats) for the PTr-MMM alliance. Anerood Jugnauth became the new Prime Minister and Bérenger, the Leader of Opposition. Ramgoolam was not elected. In terms of the organization of the electoral campaign, particularly regarding communication, YouTube, Facebook and other social media/interactive platforms became an important battleground, whether at the level of mainstream parties or small parties/independent candidates. In addition to the folkloric aspects (organizing rallies, distributing leaflets and posters) of the electoral campaign, there was extensive use of private radios, meme videos and social networks. It should be noted that the media, especially newspapers, have always played a decisive role in Mauritian politics, even before independence. With the partial liberalization of the airwaves and with about 60% of the population having access to internet, these elections demonstrated the advent of the transformation of political communication in Mauritius.

Shortly after the elections the country witnessed some major political upheavals. Former Prime Minister Navin Ramgoolam was arrested in February 2015 and charged with conspiracy and money laundering. He was released on bail and all the charges against him were dismissed in November 2019. Meanwhile, in July 2015 Pravind Jugnauth was convicted of a conflict of interest in the 'MedPoint' affair (the Government had, allegedly, purchased a medical clinic owned by the private company MedPoint, in which Jugnauth was a shareholder, for an inflated sum), but after appeal, he was exonerated by Supreme Court in May 2016.

In December 2016, the PMSD resigned from the Government in disagreement over a constitutional amendment to reduce the power of the Director of Public Prosecutions. Xavier-Luc Duval became the Leader of Opposition. In January 2017 Anerood Jugnauth resigned as Prime Minister and the post was transferred to his son, Pravind. While for some observers, this transfer of power was unethical, for others, it was carried out within the constitutional parameters.

Similar to previous governmental mandates, this administration was also rocked by internal dissidence and politico-financial scandals. However, prior to the 2019 general elections, some major successful events (for example the victory of Mauritius in the Chagos Archipelago case at the United Nations and the International Court of Justice, the inauguration of the Metro Express light rail transit system, and the introduction of social measures including the minimum wage and the Negative Income Tax system) brought back a positive limelight on the Government.

Meanwhile, the MMM witnessed many instabilities and setbacks from 2014, and a number of senior members left the party to join the governmental alliance. The PTr, on the other hand, was reinvigorated with the acquittal of Navin Ramgoolam, and it entered into coalition with the PMSD in October 2019, prior to the general election the following month. These were a triangular contest between the MSM-ML, led by Pravind Jugnauth, the PTr-PMSD alliance led by Navin Ramgoolam and the MMM led by Bérenger. The MSM-ML came out victorious with 36.9% of votes (42 seats) against the PTr-PMSD with 33.5% of votes (17 seats) and the MMM which obtained 22% (nine seats).

THE MAURITIAN DEMOCRATIC PARADOX

The first decade of the 21st century witnessed an acute paradox. On the one hand, democracy, as an ideal and a set of political institutions and practices, triumphed in most countries. On the other hand, in recent years, citizens—whether from 'old democracies' or 'emerging democracies'—have suffered from great disenchantment with the practices and workings of democracy. Mauritius has not been spared from this paradox. Mauritius is recognized as a successful multi-party democracy and boasts an impressive array of achievements, such as an enduring socio-political stability, a sustained and resilient level of economic growth, with a consequent reduction in inequality, and a high level of human development. Yet, the country is increasingly witnessing democratic failings.

Several indexes measuring the quality of democracy showed a downward tendency in Mauritius' ranking. For instance, in 2002 the country was ranked in 36th position in the World Press Freedom Index published by Reporters Without Borders, but had declined to 62nd by 2022. V-Dem Institute's latest report (2022) on the state of democracy in the world in the wake of the COVID-19 pandemic also commented on the declining trends of the Mauritian democracy.

Strong institutions and consensual politics have fostered a democratic political culture that goes beyond ethnic and partisan lines, particularly with regards to core issues such as the respect of religious and ethnic diversity and fundamental rights and freedoms, the rule of law and an independent judiciary, inclusiveness with a strong civil society, the economic development strategies, a strong welfare state and the restoration of territorial sovereignty (with regards to the Chagos Archipelago and Tromelin Island). Yet, in recent years Mauritian society has also witnessed growing popular protests against democratic loopholes. Again, while the power-sharing and interdependence between the political (public sector) and economic (private sector) elites have promoted the country's economic success, the country is also facing perceptions of growing socioeconomic inequalities, with 1% of the population owning over 65% of productive assets and more than one-half of the land.

As a result of the recurring game of alliances, since the 1980s the country has also been facing a bipolarization of politics between two major blocs composed mainly of parties organized around political entrepreneurs and dynasties, with the Ramgoolam, Duval, Mohamed, Bérenger, Jugnauth and Uteem families to the fore. Despite the chronic instabilities within successive governmental coalitions and the accompanying dissidences, power struggles and factionalism, the existence of these two blocs are legitimized by the majority of the Mauritian citizens during each general elections which have been so far held in a free and fair manner. However, according to Chan Low, in the midst of the existing endemic political volatility and against a backdrop of politico-financial scandals, there has been the rise of a new phenomenon—the 'lawfare'—where court cases are being instrumentalized to delegitimize the opponent.

For many observers, institutional failure lies at the heart of the democratic weaknesses in Mauritius. The concern to find the 'ideal' norms/institutions for the multi-ethnic Mauritian society has existed since the British period. Since the 1980s civil society, political actors and observers have pressed for constitutional reforms to abolish obsolete institutions and improve the state of governance. Some of the major issues which have been recurrently in the limelight are the reform of the electoral system (namely, the abolition of the best loser system, the correction of the discrepancies between the number of votes obtained and the number of seats won and the elimination of ethnic politics and the block vote/dualistic system to provide more opportunities for new and small parties) and for the political nomination practices to consider competence along with communal representativeness.

There have also been proposals for a Second Republic, a Freedom of Information Act, and mechanisms to strengthen human rights and gender equality in politics, and to reduce the concentration of power in the hands of the executive (particularly that of the Prime Minister's Office). The lack of a regulatory framework on the conduct and funding of political parties and electoral campaigns and the ineffective mechanisms to control public expenditures, resulting in malpractices and wastage of public funds, are other decried issues, which are constantly on the reform agenda along with finding solutions to impede money politics and improve accountability, transparency and good governance.

Since independence, the Constitution has undergone more than 20 amendments, but without upsetting the system itself. The analysis of the majority of amendments shows that it was generally circumstantial factors that led politicians to initiate these changes, and not the desire to improve obsolete or deficient mechanisms. Whenever there were in depth proposals to reassess the Constitution, the debates became stuck in an impasse and the prospects for reforms are still not encouraging. As long as these institutions are favourable to the politicians in power, they will have every interest in maintaining them. Yet, in the event of reform, it is hoped that this would be more democratic—with the advent of referendums or the increased participation of the civil society, because, to date, almost all reform processes have been decided by the political elite—and that any reform would allow the continuity of the socioeconomic and political stability.

Economy

VERENA TANDRAYEN-RAGOOBUR, SHEEREEN FAUZEL and BOOPEN SEETANAH

INTRODUCTION

Since its independence in 1968 Mauritius has engaged in a strong growth-oriented developmental path, undergoing a striking economic transformation from a low-income country (with a per head gross national income of just US $260 in 1968), mainly based on agriculture (particularly sugar), to a relatively diversified economy. Overall, the country's economy is driven by the services sector (which accounts for around two-thirds of gross domestic product—GDP), with tourism (catering, accommodation, leisure, etc.) and financial services being the most vital sectors. In recent decades the island has also consolidated its industrial and information and communications technology (ICT) sectors, and promoted new growth sectors such as the ocean (or 'blue') economy, renewable energy, outsourcing and medicine, creating new employment opportunities. It is noteworthy that the island's development has also been founded on a combination of political stability, a strong institutional framework, a good state-business relationship and a favourable regulatory environment. The open trade and investment policies have also both been particularly instrumental in sustaining growth.

Before the COVID-19 pandemic, GDP per capita stood at US $11,360 and over $25,000 (on an international purchasing-power parity—PPP—basis) in 2019, with a growth rate averaging 3.8% per year during 2015–19, and Mauritius was one of the most dynamic and vibrant economies in sub-Saharan Africa. However, the pandemic had a severe impact on the economy and GDP plummeted by an estimated 15.8% in 2020, mostly due to restrictions in international travel and strict sanitary protocols.

In 2021, with a remarkable vaccination campaign (the country eventually attained a vaccination rate of 75% in February 2022 and covered over 90% of the eligible population in May) and following the relaxation of sanitary protocols and the reopening of international borders, the economy gradually started to recover from the pandemic. Real GDP grew by an estimated 3.9% in 2021. According to the International Monetary Fund (IMF), GDP per capita in PPP terms reached almost US $22,030 in 2021, although subsequent COVID-19 waves dampened growth and output remains below pre-pandemic levels (a 4.8% year-on-year growth as registered in the first quarter of 2022). The 2022/23 budget estimated economic growth for 2022 at 8.5%, conditional on the expectation that all sectors of the economy would exceed pre-pandemic economic output, particularly the tourism sector.

However, an increase in food and transport costs prompted a rise in inflation, which rose from 2.5% in 2020 to 6.8% at the end of December 2021 and further, to 10.7%, at the end of March 2022. Unemployment, heavily affected by the negative economic impact of the COVID-19 pandemic, was estimated at 9.2% in 2020 (mostly due to many redundancies in the tourism sector) but fell to around 8.0% in 2021.

The island had been progressively reducing its debt-to-GDP ratio in recent years before the pandemic, but this rose after 2020 mainly due to the costs of tackling the pandemic. It was contained at 87.1% in June 2021 and was projected to fall to around 77.3% in June 2022. Meanwhile, higher revenue collection contributed to a reduction in the 2021 budget deficit to 5% (from 11% in 2019/20), and this was expected to follow a downward trend in 2022 to around 4%, according to the recent 2022/23 budget speech. It is noteworthy that the budget deficit will remain under pressure over the coming financial year should global prices result in higher domestic prices.

Mauritius has made substantial progress in its campaign for social equality and poverty reduction, and represents an exemplary model of development. The island is classified as an upper-middle-income country by the World Bank, with a high level of human development, and is seeking to become a high-income country within the next decade. Poverty was contained because the Government decided to increase the level of existing social protection schemes, with priority given to the most vulnerable segments of the population.

On the external front, imports grew faster than exports in 2021, resulting in the trade deficit widening by 39.4%. However, the country recorded a fall in the current account deficit from 12.5% to 11.1% of GDP, supported by net income inflows. Tourist arrivals plummeted by over 41% in 2021 compared to 2020, even after the full reopening of borders from 1 October 2021. However, this sector is expected to pick up rapidly in 2022. Foreign direct investment (FDI) for 2021 has been lower than 2020 (Rs 15,400m. compared to Rs 16,900m.) and was projected to exceed Rs 20,000m. in 2022. The Mauritian rupee took another severe blow in 2021, with a depreciation of around 9% against the US dollar. The rupee also lost around 8% of its value against the major trading partner currencies during that year.

After a subsequent cut in the interest rate in response to the COVID-19 pandemic (in March 2020 by 50 basis points and April by 100 basis points), to reach a historic low rate of 1.85%), the Key Repo Rate was maintained at 1.85% per annum during the last meeting of the Monetary Policy Committee in February

2021. However, the rate was raised by 15 basis points to 2% on 9 March 2022 and by a further 25 basis points to reach 2.25% on 3 June 2022, in response of rising inflation.

In June 2022 the Minister of Finance, Economic Planning and Development presented his 2022/23 budget called 'With the People, for the People', focusing on rebooting and reshaping the Mauritius economy through investing in its people. The Government firmly believes that the various sectors (particularly tourism) will recover to a significant extent and that the economy will exceed pre-pandemic levels in 2022/23.

RECENT ECONOMIC FUNDAMENTALS

Despite registering a low yet steady growth rate over the last decade or so, GDP per capita continued to trend upward. On 1 July 2020 Mauritius was officially propelled to the rank of high-income country by the World Bank, and this marked a milestone in this small island nation's development trajectory from a poor, remote mono-crop producer at independence into one of Africa's most successful development stories. (It is important to note that this classification was made using 2019 data, and thus does not yet reflect the economic impact of the COVID-19 pandemic.)

However, it also remains a cruel irony that the country achieved such a status during one of the worst years in its history due to COVID-19. It should be highlighted that Mauritius successfully responded to the pandemic through drastic, fast and strict lockdown and quarantine measures, and has effectively contained the disease, being 'COVID-free' from April 2020 to March 2021, when a second outbreak occurred. With a total of 261,976 cases and 1,026 deaths by 27 September 2022, Mauritius has so far been able to avoid the large-scale health crisis observed in many other countries. Nevertheless, the drastic sanitary measures that probably allowed it to avoid the worst of the pandemic brought severe disruptions, and entailed a very high cost for the economy. (An oil spill in August 2020 and Mauritius' inclusion by the European Union—EU— on its list of High-Risk Third Countries for Money Laundering in October added further pressure.)

GDP plummeted by an estimated 15.8% in 2020, mostly due to restrictions in international travel which engendered a collapse in tourist arrivals. This dramatic decline of the tourism sector, which represents one-fifth of the island's GDP and over 20% of employment, resulted in significant spillover effects on the whole economy. At the same time, exports of textiles and apparel, seafood and sugar were hurt by global demand disruptions. Only the ICT and financial services sectors grew, the former supported by heavy use of technological and teleworking services during the lockdown. Investment fell by around 20%, while household consumption registered a 12% decrease.

Unemployment was estimated at 9.2% in 2020 (up from 6.7% one year earlier, itself a 10-year high), mostly due to large-scale redundancies in the tourism sector. It should be highlighted that unemployment numbers would have been considerably worse in the absence of non-cyclical government interventions, namely in the form of wage support (the Wage Assistance Scheme—WAS—and the Self-Employed Assistance Scheme— SAS).

As far as public finance is concerned, an increase in public expenditure targeted at social and economic safety nets, coupled with a contraction in revenues due to the severe economic downturn, led to a fiscal deficit of 5.6% for the fiscal year 2020/21 (it remained in a stable range of 3.0%–3.5% until 2019, but increased to 13.6% in 2019/20 due to COVID-19 assistance programmes). As most of the measures were extended into 2021 and will continue to weigh on public finances, the budget deficit-to-GDP ratio was projected to reach 5.0% in 2021/22. The public sector debt-to-GDP ratio was expected to rise from 78.8% in 2020/21 to 82.8% 2021/22. Poverty was contained because the Government decided to increase the level of existing social protection schemes, with priority given to the most vulnerable segments of the population.

On the external front, the current account deficit widened to around 12.0% in 2020 from 5.5% in 2019 (after over a decade of being contained to single digits) due to the decline in export and tourist receipts, while the rupee depreciated in 2020, in real effective terms, by 8.1% compared to its 2019 level. FDI inflows also felt the effect of the pandemic, falling from Rs 14,893m. to Rs 9,080m. (for the first three-quarters of 2020 compared to the corresponding period of 2019).

Turning to monetary policy, since the mid-2010s the Bank of Mauritius (BoM) has pursued an expansionary path in an effort to stimulate the economy through several reductions (between 2015 and 2019) in the KRR. In response to the COVID-19 pandemic, the BoM further lowered the interest rate in early 2020 (see *Introduction*) to reach a historic low of 1.85%, before it was raised to reach 2.25% in June 2022.

HUMAN DEVELOPMENT, POVERTY AND DEMOCRACY

According to the 2021 Human Development Index (HDI), compiled by the United Nations (UN) Development Programme, the island is in the high human development category (with a rank of 63 and a value of 0.802). In the 2020 HDI it had progressed slightly from 0.8 to 0.804, and between 1990 and 2019 Mauritius' HDI value increased by almost 30%. It is noteworthy that the sub-Saharan African average stood at 0.547, while the very high human development group average stood at 0.898). However, when inequality is factored in, the discounted HDI drops to 0.694 (which is still well above the regional average of 0.38). The Gender Development Index, which measures gender inequalities in the achievement of human development, stood at 0.976, placing Mauritius into the Group 1 ranking.

The country has over the last decade made progress in its campaign for social equality and poverty reduction, although the proportion of households living below the relative poverty line was estimated at 9.4% in 2017, unchanged from 2012. Based on an international poverty line of US $1.90 per capita per day, it was reported that 0.5% of the population lived below this threshold, while the figure stood at 1.5% based on an international poverty line of $3.20. Only about 10% of Mauritians were living below the upper middle-income class poverty line before the pandemic. Poverty, however, reportedly increased in 2020 from 10.7% to 12%, and was expected to decline more slowly than expected to reach 9.5% by 2022, due principally to the economic impact of COVID-19.

Although the latest available figures indicate a slight improvement in the income distribution in the country (with a decreased Gini coefficient from 0.413 in 2012 to 0.400 in 2017), the income of the bottom 40% of the population has been growing at an average annual rate of 1.8%, compared to 3.1% for the rest of the population. This confirms that prosperity may have not been shared as hoped, with high-skilled service sectors benefiting more relative to the most vulnerable and least educated.

Mauritius is known for its welfare state philosophy, particularly with respect to maintaining free health, social protection and education (the latter even extended to the tertiary level in 2019). Recent government budgets (including the 2022/23 budget) allocated over 50% of projected expenditure to these three essential elements. In addition to its continued support for social housing and its pursuance of policies to safeguard people's economic livelihood, ensure the stability of the financial system and to procure COVID-19 vaccines for the whole population, the 2022/23 budget outlined a range of measures to support the population in the face of rising food and energy prices, which are a direct consequence of disruptions in supply chains and the Russian Federation's invasion of Ukraine in February 2022. These include a direct monthly financial grant of Rs 1000 for those earning less than Rs 50,000 (including pensioners) as well as a reduction of income tax up to 10%. Such measures are expected to increase the post-tax income of an estimated 100,000 income earners, thus partly alleviating the burden of higher living costs on the lower income households while also improving income redistribution between the rich and poor. Municipal tax in urban areas has also been abolished and there have been various increases in allowances under the social aid and Social Register of Mauritius schemes.

Mauritius has established itself as a viable democracy and market economy since independence. The island enjoys stable and mature institutions, and also a stable multi-party parliamentary democracy overall. The Economist Intelligence Unit, in its Democracy Index 2021, classified Mauritius as a 'full democracy', ranking it 19th out of 167 jurisdictions and the only African country in this category. Moreover, the Heritage Foundation's 2022 Index of Economic Freedom reports a score of 70.9 for the country, making it the 30th freest globally (and in the category of 'mostly free') and the first among 47 countries in the sub-Saharan Africa region. While property rights and judicial effectiveness are strong components, those of government integrity and fiscal health components require improvement.

As far as corporate governance is concerned, according to the Chandler Good Government Index 2022 (which measures the capabilities and effectiveness of 104 Governments globally), the island leads the African continent and ranks among the top 40 countries worldwide. The 2020 Ibrahim Index on African Governance consolidates Mauritius' first place, with an average score of 77.2 compared with the African average of 48.8.

Mauritius is ranked 13th among 190 economies in the 2020 Ease of Doing Business Index, according to the latest World Bank ratings (up from 20th in 2019), remaining the leader of the continent (before Rwanda, Kenya and South Africa) and among the most business-friendly countries in the world. The country has consistently transformed its business environment and has climbed the index over recent years (it was placed 49th in 2016). Mauritius has improved significantly in the area of construction permits and registration of properties, with streamlined procedures resulting from the automation of licensing permits and the implementation of the National Electronic Licensing System. However, more effort on the dimensions of trading across borders, as well as obtaining credit, are required and the Economic Development Board is well aware of this.

INDUSTRY

A competitive and sustainable industrial sector contributes positively to economic growth through innovation, technology upgrading, higher productivity, as well as high skilled employment. Mauritius relies on its industrial sector, which accounted for 20.7% of GDP in 2021. The sector declined by 17% in 2020 compared with growth of 1.2% in 2019, and has faced difficult challenges with the COVID-19 pandemic and health containment measures imposed by the authorities.

In terms of the sub-sectors, which consist of mining and quarrying, manufacturing, electricity, gas and water supply, sewerage and waste management, the performance declined in 2020, in the midst of the pandemic, but recovered in 2021. From a 16.6% decline in the real growth rate of gross value added in 2020 (compared to growth of 3.3% in 2019), the mining and quarrying sub-sector grew by 8.4% in 2021. A similar picture is observed for manufacturing, which recovered to achieve growth of 11.3% in 2021 after having contracted by 17.8% in 2020. Water, supply, sewerage and waste management has also experienced an improvement with expansion of 8.0% recorded in 2021, after a decline of 3.8% in 2020.

The number of large establishments in the industrial sector was 559 in 2020, compared to 575 in 2019 and 598 in 2018. Employment in these large establishments stood at 68,623 in 2020 compared to 71,319 in 2019, showing a decline of 3.8%. Real investment in the industrial sector was around Rs 6,046 m. compared with Rs 7,942m. in 2019, representing a fall of 23.9%. The decline in investment, employment and the number of large establishments in operation can all be attributed to the COVID-19 pandemic, which had important economic repercussions.

Manufacturing

The manufacturing sector has by and large made a very significant contribution to economic growth, being the most dominant sector in the country with a contribution to GDP of around 13.2% in 2021. Its performance in 2021 can be ascribed to the different industrialization measures put forward to mitigate the impact of the pandemic on the sector. The real growth rate in gross value added for the manufacturing sector stood at 11.3% in 2021, compared to a decline of 17.8% in 2020 and growth of just 0.5% in 2019. This recovery has been possible as Mauritius has reinforced its reputation as a reliable and high-quality player on both the domestic and foreign markets. This has been achieved via a diversification of its manufacturing base. In essence, during the 1970s manufacturing was largely concentrated in the production of consumer goods, essentially food, beverages, tobacco, footwear, clothing, paints and board for furniture, and refining sugar. The sector has in recent years diversified into chemicals and chemical products, including basic pharmaceutical products and pharmaceutical preparations to furniture, fabricated metal products, rubber and plastic products, as well as leather products. The key component of the manufacturing sector remains, however, clothing and food products. Manufacturing remains the largest employer and generator of employment within the industrial sector. The number of workers employed in large manufacturing establishments (i.e. enterprises with more than 10 employees) was 62,772 in 2021, compared to 65,792 in 2020 and 70,152 in 2019.

The core of Mauritius' industrial development policy in the 1970s was the establishment of export-processing zones (EPZs) to encourage FDI in labour-intensive textile manufacturing for exports, thus prompting the diversification of the textile sector. The creation of the EPZ with duty free access for imported inputs, raw materials and capital goods, tax incentives, free repatriation of capital, profits and dividends, as well as a segmented labour market with abundant cheap labour which could easily be trained, represented a major comparative advantage and attracted foreign investors from Hong Kong, France and South Africa, among others. Beyond FDI and cheap labour, a key element in the expansion of the manufacturing sector was the preferential treatment for Mauritian exports in the European and US markets. The Multi-Fibre Agreement (MFA), signed in 1973, provided protected access of Mauritian textile products to the EU. Being labour intensive, the EPZ sector became a major source of employment and contributed significantly to export earnings and economic growth. Export-oriented enterprises (EOEs) were also effective in raising export diversification and promoting inward FDI.

While the EPZ provided a sound and solid base for growth and development, over the years there have been various measures implemented to expand the EOE sector. In the late 1980s and 1990s the EOEs remained the main source of employment creation, representing one-third of total employment, and, with continuous devaluations of the local currency and the adoption, in 1983, of a flexible exchange rate, the textiles industry grew faster than the sugar sector. However, with India and the People's Republic of China becoming members of the World Trade Organization, Mauritius lost its advantages within the textile industry. In addition, Mauritius was not categorized as a 'least developed country' and was thus not eligible for the third-country fibre benefit, which allows the sourcing of fabrics from any country. Mauritius was compelled to source its fabrics regionally or from the USA. Hence, nations like Lesotho, Madagascar and Eswatini (Swaziland), began to erode Mauritian textile exports. The dismantling of the MFA in 2003 had major implications for the textile industry. Several textile factories made huge losses and had to close, and the performance of the EOE sector started to decline. The number of enterprises in the sector was 558 in December 1992, 411 in 2009 and 239 in 2019; as at December 2021, there were only 233 enterprises. The largest decline has been in the wearing apparel sub-sector, with 307 enterprises in December 1992, falling to 83 in December 2021. Over the same period, the number of enterprises specializing in the production and export of flowers fell from 51 to two.

In terms of employment, the number of employed was 86,937 in 1992, rising to 90,682 in 2000 but falling to 53,601 in 2015 and dropping further to 36,736 in 2020 and 35,024 in 2021. In the first quarter of 2022 total employment in the EOEs stood at 34,904, representing a decline of around 0.34% over a three-month period. The largest decline in employment has been in the wearing apparel sector, while the food sector has been employing more workers over the years. The employment trend across EOEs can also be analysed in terms of the number of local and foreign workers. In 2016 there were around 29,608 Mauritians and 22,994 expatriates working in the EOE sector, and by 2021 the number had declined to 19,908 Mauritians and

15,116 expatriates, representing a fall of 32.8% and 34.3%, respectively. In the first quarter of 2022 the figures stood at 20,202 local workers and 14,702 expatriates. The gender-disaggregated data shows that there are more female Mauritian workers in the EOE sector, while foreign workers tend to be mainly male. The ratio of female to male local workers was 1.5:1 while that of expatriates stood at 0.4:1 as at March 2022.

Total exports of the EOEs increased to Rs 42,657m. in 2021 from Rs 37,289 in 2020. The performance was better than the level of exports of Rs 42,319m. in 2019, prior to the COVID-19 pandemic. During the first quarter of 2022 EOE exports were Rs 10,932m., 16.5% higher compared with the same quarter in 2021. This performance has been mainly attributed to a relative upturn in export orders from the main markets, namely the UK, France and South Africa. The positive impact of support schemes like the Freight Rebate Scheme and the Support for Trade Promotion and Marketing Scheme have enhanced export competitiveness. Total imports from the EOE sector was Rs 7,483m. in the first quarter of 2022., compared with Rs 7,767m. in the last quarter of 2021. Annual imports from EOEs in 2021 rose to Rs 25,673m., compared with Rs 19,629m. in 2020 and Rs 24,645m. in 2019.

Despite the many challenges encountered over the years, the manufacturing industry remains an important engine of growth and has been playing an instrumental part in employment creation, trade performance and investment trends. The Eurocentric focus of the sector, born out of preferential agreements, has become a risk factor in the sustainable development of the economy. However, the preferential market access of Mauritius to the Common Market for Eastern and Southern Africa (COMESA), the Southern African Development Community (SADC) and the Indian Ocean Commission (IOC), as well as through the interim Economic Partnership Agreement (EPA) with the EU, the USA's African Growth and Opportunity Act (AGOA) and recently the African Continental Free Trade Area (AfCFTA) Agreement, is helping the country to achieve a competitive edge in sectors like textile and apparel, seafood processing, sugar and agro-processing and harness new segments such as medical devices, pharmaceutical products, high-end jewellery and optical products.

While the world economy is still struggling to recover from the contractions induced by COVID-19, Russia's invasion of Ukraine is another growing concern to the global economy. Furthermore, the effects of the Russian invasion are likely to operate through various channels in terms of a rise in commodity prices, disruption of trade, rising interest rates and widening fiscal pressures, having both direct and indirect effects on the Mauritian economy. Although Russia and Ukraine do not have significant trade linkages with Mauritius, a knock-on effect can be experienced through the re-export of goods to Mauritius and a disruption in the global value chain.

With the assistance of the UN Conference on Trade and Development, Mauritius devised an Industrial Policy and Strategic Plan 2020–2025, which contains a wide range of recommendations to support the continued growth and development of Mauritius' industrial capacity and capabilities. These recommendations aimed to support the 2030 National Vision, which intended to shift the country towards a highly productive manufacturing sector contributing one-quarter of GDP. A Trade Development and Intelligence Cell has been set up to undertake research into market dynamics, distribution channels and buyers, as well as detailing the necessary standards, requirements and non-tariff barriers available for selected products where Mauritius has preferential access. An Export Development Programme is also in place, targeting specifically exporting enterprises or those which have the export readiness, under the Comprehensive Economic Co-operation and Partnership Agreement (CECPA) with India, the Mauritius-China Free Trade Agreement (M-CFTA), the AfCFTA and other trade agreements. Various measures have also been set out in the budget for 2022/23, where specific policies target the promotion of both locally manufactured products and exports. In terms of exports promotion, the Freight Rebate Scheme and the Trade Promotion and Marketing Scheme have been extended to June 2023. Small and medium-sized enterprises (SMEs) will benefit from the Freight Rebate Scheme for South Africa. A 50% reduction in port charges on exports will further benefit export-oriented enterprises. Two regional feeder vessels will connect Mauritius to markets regionally and to Asia, further supporting the business community amid rising global freight costs.

AGRICULTURE AND FISHERIES

At independence, Mauritius was mainly an agrarian economy, relying almost entirely on the sugar-growing sector. However, in the absence of economies of scale and with comparative disadvantage in most food production, Mauritius imports many of its essential food requirements. It is a net food importer and has an overall self-sufficiency ratio of less than 30%. In 2021 agriculture's contribution to GDP was just 3.7%, and a total of 29,300 people (equivalent to about 5.7% of the employed labour force) were employed in the sector.

Agricultural imports accounted for US $1,100m. in 2020, which represented 26.1% of total Mauritian imports. France was the leading source of agricultural imports, followed by South Africa, India, Spain and Australia. The main products imported are rice, meat and fish, certain fruits (oranges, mandarins and grapes), pulses, milk and dairy products, fresh and frozen vegetables, coffee, tea and spices, cereals, oil, beverages, wheat, and food preparations. The Government has launched the National Agri-Food Development Programme, which was announced in its 2021/22 budget speech and aims to reduce dependence on imports.

The sugar sub-sector accounts for roughly one-half of agricultural output. Sugar cane is cultivated on 72,000 ha (around 85% of the arable land in Mauritius) and some 600,000 metric tons of sugar is produced each year, with about 530,000 tons exported to the EU. Around 40,000 tons is consumed locally. The sugar sector was successful mainly because of the preferential agreements which the country gained initially from the UK and then from the EU. The sugar protocol under the first Lomé Convention transformed Mauritius into the principal exporter of sugar to the EU, and Mauritius benefited from a guaranteed price which was three times higher than the actual price on the world market, resulting in stable revenues from the export of the commodity. However, with the diversification mentioned above, the importance of sugar declined. Furthermore, the EU abolished the African, Caribbean and Pacific sugar quota regime in 2017 due to accusations of unfair competition from Australia, Brazil and Thailand. By 2021 sugar production contributed only 0.4% of GDP and the number of sugar refineries had dropped from 11 to four (Mauritius now exports only high-value refined sugar).

Nevertheless, the sugar sub-sector is still important as it represents about 19% of foreign exchange earnings, although in 2020 sugar cane production declined by 23.0%, to 2.6m. metric tons, compared with 3.4m in 2019. The average yield decreased from 75.6 tons per ha in 2019 to 60.0 in 2020, while the area harvested decreased from 45,054 ha in 2019 to 43,711 ha in 2020, and production of sugar declined to 270,875 tons in 2020 from 331,105 tons in 2019. However, the average extraction rate was 10.3% in 2020, compared with 9.7% in 2019. There remain many small sugar planters who are grouped into co-operatives and supply cane to the factories. Mauritius has the third biggest sugar bulk terminal in the world, with an annual capacity of 350,000 tons.

Mauritius is also classified as the 21st largest exporter of sugar in the world, as it exported US $197m. of raw sugar in 2020. It is also the second most exported product in Mauritius. Sugar is mainly exported to the following main destinations: Kenya ($42.1m.), Spain ($35.8m.), the UK ($20.3m.), Greece ($18.0m.) and Italy ($17.2m.). However, Mauritius also imported sugar, and this amounted to $22.7m. in raw sugar, making Mauritius the 122nd largest importer of raw sugar in the world. Raw sugar is imported mainly from: Brazil ($11.7m.), Egypt ($3.56m.), Mozambique ($2.96m.), Thailand ($2.21m.) and India ($2.0m.).

Mauritius is also engaged in the production of tea. The area under tea plantation was 685 ha in 2021, the same as in 2020. However, the production of green tea leaves declined from 5,105 metric tons in 2020 to 5,034 tons in 2021. The production of manufactured tea increased from 1,083 tons to 1,097 tons over that period.

Food crop production is becoming increasingly important. A total area of 7,922 ha under food crops was harvested in 2021, representing an increase of 7.8% over the figure of 7,352 ha in 2020. Production increased by 6.8%, from 95,029 metric tons to 101,537 tons in 2021.

In terms of livestock production, a significant number of people are involved in subsistence farming. However, only a small amount is produced locally. In 2021 beef production from live cattle was 1,823 metric tons, 0.2% lower than the production of 1,826 tons in 2020. Production of beef from the slaughter of imported cattle increased by 0.2% and that of local beef fell by 38.9%. Production of goat meat and mutton decreased by 2.4%, from 42 tons in 2020 to 41 tons in 2021, while the production of pork decreased by 4.0%. Poultry production increased by 3.4%, from 47,500 tons in 2020 to 49,100 tons in 2021. Finally, fish production increased by 8.6%, from 26,415 tons in 2020 to 28,696 tons in 2021. The Government supports this industry and technical assistance is provided.

TOURISM

Tourism, with a pre-pandemic estimated contribution of over 20% of the country's GDP and employment, remains one of the important pillars of the economy. The sector has suffered the most from COVID-19, resulting in sizeable effects on the economy, employment and foreign currency inflows. The sector has registered constant growth in the number of tourism arrivals over the last decade (from 964,700 in 2011 to 1.38m. in 2019) and tourism receipts (Rs 41,000m. in 2011 to Rs 63,100m. in 2019). However, following the outbreak of COVID-19, accentuated by air travel restrictions and national lockdowns, it plunged and in 2020 only 308,980 tourists visited the island, while an even smaller number, of 179,780 (a decline of 41.8%), was recorded for 2021. Tourism receipts were estimated at Rs 17,664m. in 2020 and just Rs 15,253m. in 2021. Mauritius reopened its international borders fully on 1 October 2021. (The borders were reopened to tourists in October 2020 under certain sanitary conditions, but were closed again in March 2021, amid the second wave of the pandemic). It was reassuring to welcome over 100,000 tourists in the following 50 days and this gave the tourism industry the kickstart it needed. As at June 2022, 376,556 people had visited the island in that year, compared to 3,225 in the same period of 2021—but still far from the pre-pandemic figure of 650,082 in that period of 2019.

Conscious of the critical importance of the tourism sector in achieving pre-pandemic growth, the Government has consolidated the various measures taken to support the sector since 2020. In addition to the extension of the WAS and SAS schemes to tourism-related companies up to September 2021, and the full opening of the international borders in October 2021, as well as various measures outlined in the 2021/22 budget (including an increased tourism marketing budget, the deferral of lease payments on state lands, introduction of a Tourism Business Continuity loan for SMEs at an annual rate of 0.5%, temporary waiving of the rental fee of counters by hotels and operators at the airport, and more incentivized investment hotel and integrated resort schemes), the Government announced further support measures for the sector in the 2022/23 budget. The marketing budget of the Mauritius Tourism Promotion Agency has been increased from Rs 360m. to Rs 400m., with the aim of both consolidating existing markets and exploring new opportunities. To support hotels in their refurbishment, the 50% lease rent waiver is being extended up to June 2023. Finally, a 10-year strategy blueprint has been announced for the tourism industry. The Government is quite optimistic in achieving 1.0m. tourists by the end of 2022 and a pre-pandemic level of 1.4m. tourists by 2023.

INFRASTRUCTURE AND ICT

Transport is also an important component of the economy. Given that the island is very small, the main form of land transport is by road and the country's total road network is 2,428 km. However, as a consequence of the increased demand for private transport, the public bus transport fleet decreased from 2,034 in 2017 to 1,962 in June 2020. As a result, there was a considerable increase in road traffic congestion and gridlocks,

road accidents, and pollution and greenhouse gas emissions. In order to deal with these challenges, the Government started a development programme in the transport sector. Hence, in October 2019 a light rail transit system (Metro Express) was introduced. An initial 13-km stretch of line was opened in that month, with a further 13 km scheduled to be completed by the end of 2022. The project design includes the creation of a multi-modal urban transit solution, connecting 12 stations and stops to give commuters access to bus services.

The sea port located at Port Louis is one of the deepest container ports in the sub-Saharan African region. It has the capacity to accommodate fifth-generation container vessels with draughts of up to 13 m. To be in line with the latest technology, the cargo handling corporation has made a massive investment of Rs 1,775m. in recent years, mostly in port handling equipment, in order to provide quality and efficient services.

Mauritius has emerged as an international ICT destination and is becoming a regional ICT hub. The ICT sector comprises manufacturing activities, telecommunications services, wholesale and retail trade, and other activities such as call centres, software and website development, and IT consulting. The value added at current prices by the sector was at Rs 21,576m. in 2021, and it contributed 5.1% of GDP in that year. In 2020 Mauritius had some 1.6m. internet broadband subscribers. There are around 600 ICT companies operating in the country presently in various activities, including major international ICT firms such as Oracle, Microsoft, IBM, HP, Cisco, France Télécom, Orange Business Services, Accenture, Infosys and Hinduja Group. The percentage of the population covered by mobile telephony was 99% as at 2020, while the number of mobile cellular subscriptions per 100 inhabitants was 151.1 and there were 130.2 internet subscriptions per 100 inhabitants.

THE EXTERNAL SECTOR

Mauritius follows a liberal economic and trade policy, with the objective of becoming globally competitive and at the same time integrating fully in the world trade system. The country is relatively open, with few trade barriers and low custom duties. The main exports in 2021 were manufactured products in terms of articles of apparel and clothing accessories, followed by food and live animals (of which fish and fish preparations and cane sugar comprised the largest share). Manufactured goods also form part of total exports, where textile yarns, fabrics and made-up articles along with pearls, precious and semi-precious stones top up the list. In 2021 the main export markets were the EU, with 41% of total exports; the UK and France took the largest shares of total exports to the EU, with 22% and 21%, respectively, followed by Spain and Italy, with 13% and 12%. Africa has been increasingly considered as a vital export destination for Mauritian products, with 33% of total exports targeted to the continent. The African export destinations tend to be mainly focused on South Africa, with a share of 42% of total merchandise exports to the region, followed by Madagascar with 24%. Mauritius also exports to Asia, which represents the third major destination with a share of 17% of total merchandise exports. The main imports from Mauritius are machinery and transport equipment (19.6% of total merchandise imports), of which electrical machinery, apparatus and appliances and electrical parts of household type form a major component. The second import component is food and live animals (18.5% of total merchandise imports). Mauritius also imports manufactured goods (17.5% of total merchandise imports) in terms of iron and steel and manufactured metals, and the third main imported goods are mineral fuels, lubricants and other related products, which comprise 17.2% of total imports. Most of the country's imports come from Asian countries (55.7% of total imports), with the biggest share coming from China (31.8% of total imports from Asia) and India (28.0%). Around 24% of total merchandise imports come from European countries, mainly from France, Germany, Turkey, Italy and Spain.

Mauritius imports more than it exports, generating a consistent trade deficit over the years. The external current account deficit is estimated at about Rs 14,900m. for the first quarter of 2022, with the goods account deficit widening as exports of goods rose by 26.2% but imports of goods increased by 40.3% (due to higher imports of mineral fuels, lubricants and related products, machinery and transport equipment, food and live animals, and manufactured goods). The services account recorded a surplus of Rs 4,100m. in the first quarter of 2022 against a deficit of Rs 3,100m. in the same period of 2021, reflecting the significant rise in tourism earnings to Rs 12,500m., which was, however, partly offset by a 68% rise in freight costs.

Much effort has been made to improve the trade and economic partnership with other countries. As noted above, Mauritius is a member of several regional trading blocs in the African and Indian Ocean regions, notably COMESA and SADC, whereby Mauritius participates in the Tripartite Free Trade Area, which is an agreement between COMESA, SADC and the East African Community. Within COMESA, Mauritius benefits from, *inter alia*, a wider and competitive market, greater industrial productivity and competitiveness, higher agricultural production and food security, along with a better use of natural resources. In addition, being a member of SADC also offers Mauritian exporters duty free access (or partial tariff reductions) to most member states. Hence, Mauritius benefits from a margin of preference for its exporters as compared to imports from other third countries such as China and India. The other trade bloc is the IOC, which is an intergovernmental organization that links the islands of the region (namely Comoros, Madagascar, Mauritius, Réunion, Mayotte and Seychelles) together to encourage co-operation. The IOC principally aims to promote diplomatic co-operation and consolidate and strengthen economic and commercial ties among the islands. It is noteworthy that so far only Madagascar and Mauritius have granted trade preferences under this trade regime. In fact, there are no customs duties for products meeting the IOC rules of origin between the two countries.

In October 2019 Mauritius ratified the AfCFTA Agreement, the single continental market for goods and services in order to expand intra-Africa trade and introduce free movement of investment and people. With 54 countries, covering a market of 1,300m. people with a combined GDP of US $3,400,000m., the AfCFTA is a significant milestone towards the realization of the African Union's Agenda 2063 for the socioeconomic transformation of the continent. Mauritius is likely to benefit as its total exports and imports are expected to increase by 2.5% and 1.8%, respectively, compared to a situation without the AfCFTA. It is forecast that Mauritian exports to the rest of Africa would rise most in services (by 41%) and then in industry (19%), agri-food (18%), and energy and mining (16%) by 2045.

Mauritius also signed the C-MFTA in October 2019, and the agreement entered into force on 1 January 2021. Mauritius will benefit from immediate duty free access to the Chinese market on some 7,504 tariff lines. Mauritius and China have also agreed to remove restrictions in more than 100 sectors, including financial services, telecommunications, ICT, professional services, construction and health services. In addition, Mauritius and India have embarked on new avenues of bilateral co-operation with the signing of the CECPA. This represents an important milestone in their trade and economic relationship as it provides access to a market of more than 1,300m. inhabitants to Mauritius. Under the CECPA, Mauritius is granted preferential access by India on various products, including medical services, food preparation and jewellery, and the application of specific tariff by Mauritius on over 600 products such as special sugar, garments, spirits and rum. The non-tariff barriers that hinder mutual trade between the two countries, as well as import and export restrictions, will be eliminated. In terms of trade in services, both countries will be granted full access to some 31 subsectors, including insurance and insurance related services, banking and other financial services, telecommunication, professional services tourism and related services.

To fully take advantage of the opportunities of these trade agreements and promote a business-friendly environment, various trade facilitation measures as well as ease of doing business strategies were announced in the 2022/23 budget. Together with the promotion of international trade, FDI plays a crucial role in the Mauritian investment landscape.

Mauritius recorded an estimated FDI of Rs 15,417 m. in 2021, compared to Rs 16,944 m. in 2020. The real estate activities sector was the main recipient, with 54% of total inflows, amounting to Rs 8,373m. The financial and insurance services sector recorded significant inflows of Rs 1,815m., followed by the accommodation and food services activities sector, which registered Rs 958m. in 2021. The primary sources of FDI flows into Mauritius are France and South Africa. FDI flows from the United Arab Emirates experienced the highest rise in 2021, surging to Rs 2,000m. from Rs 286m. in 2020. The share of FDI to GDP stood at 3.3% in 2021 and was expected to rise to 4% in 2022.

THE FINANCIAL SERVICES SECTOR

Financial intermediation continues to play a key role in the development of the island's economy. To further benefit from this sector, the Government regularly adopts policies to ensure that there is development of the financial hub in Mauritius, and continues to take new measures to attract capital from all over the world. Indeed, financial development witnessed an upward trend between 1993 and 2019. Development in banking and the stock market, as captured by the domestic credit to private sector and market capitalization ratio, has been on the rise despite the numerous challenges faced along the way.

According to Statistics Mauritius, the contribution of financial and insurance activities to GDP was 13.9% in 2021. In accordance with the Government's objectives of enhancing business processes and boosting investment, the Government has relaxed regulations for global business corporations. While it was obligatory to apply for a global business licence, the Financial Services Commission issued new rules in January 2019 whereby certain categories of residents do not have to apply for such a licence.

Due to the outbreak of COVID-19 in March 2020, several sectors in Mauritius contracted. However, the ICT sector grew, supported by the heavy use of technological and teleworking services during the lockdown. The financial services sector also registered a positive growth of 1.1%.

As far as the financial market is concerned, the all-share index of the Stock Exchange of Mauritius (SEM) has performed relatively well since the mid-2000s, rising steadily since 2003 to reach a value of 1,967 in 2010 and 2,218 in 2018, before registering a slight drop, to 2,177, in 2019. It fell as low as 1,463 in November 2020, but by July 2021 had recovered to 1,979.

During 2020/21 several transformational changes were proposed by the SEM in order to further strengthen the competitive position of the SEM as a multi-asset class internationalized stock exchange and create the enabling environment for the listing and trading of niche international products. The SEM also successfully innovated through the use of its new multi-asset Automated Trading System, which comprises a rich and robust desktop trading front-end for brokers and a modern web and mobile mySEM App for investors at large. This new system enable SEM to have an attractive multi-currency capital-raising and listing platform, also allowing further growth and development of the market.

In terms of transactions by types of investors, purchases by local institutions amounted to Rs 5,700m., whereas sales stood at Rs 3,800m., resulting in a net inflow of Rs 1,900m. Purchases and sales effected by local individuals amounted to Rs 2,700m. and Rs 3,100m., respectively. Foreign investors acquired shares worth Rs 4,600m., while sales amounted to Rs 6,100m.

ECONOMIC PROSPECTS

Mauritius is gradually recovering from COVID-19, as appropriate health, social and economic support measures have been implemented to mitigate the socioeconomic effects of the pandemic. Real GDP growth was estimated to have reached 3.9% in 2021 and was expected to be 6.1% in 2022, as most sectors were gradually rebounding to pre-COVID-19 levels of economic activity. However, the performance of the tourism sector in 2022 was still foreseen to be sub-optimal relative to pre-pandemic trends. Although Mauritius was recovering in 2021/22, the economy is highly vulnerable to new challenges facing the global economy, especially as a result of the Russian invasion of Ukraine, which is threatening economic recovery from the pandemic, leading to rising inflation—which reduces real disposable income and increases costs of living. Other downside risks are high fuel and food prices resulting in high food insecurity, rising freight costs, and supply-chain pressures and disruptions.

The country's macroeconomic indicators have been improving. Unemployment was expected to decline to 7.8% in 2022, compared to 9.5% in 2021 and 9.2% in 2020. As the economy recovers and returns to a more stable trend in the medium term, employment levels will improve, given that employment creation features high on the Government's agenda. One important measure in the 2022/23 budget targeting job creation among the most affected segments of the population is the 'Prime à L'Emploi' scheme, which provides a benefit of Rs 15,000 to all youth and women currently searching for a job, on top of the current unemployment benefit. Another macroeconomic fundamental is the annual inflation rate. Inflation rate rose substantially, from 2.7% at the end of 2020 to 6.8% in 2021 and further, to 11%, in April 2022. It is expected to increase further during 2022 due to surging fuel and food prices, rising freight costs, global supply bottlenecks, high commodity prices, past depreciation of the rupee and recovering domestic demand.

The different budget support measures provided to cushion the effects of the pandemic on the economy and vulnerable segments of the Mauritian population have created pressures on both fiscal and monetary policies. The fiscal and debt position of the country deteriorated significantly in 2020/21 although debt as a percentage of GDP stood at 86.4% in July 2022, marking a gradual decline since June 2021. Public debt is expected to fall below 80% of GDP, fuelled by cautiously planned government expenditure and a higher GDP growth rate, as well as the possibility of recalibrating the medium-term debt anchor to 80% of GDP. The budget deficit of 4% in 2021/22 further reflects the prudent approach of the Government to attempt all means to ensure a strong recovery.

With respect to the country's monetary policy position, the BoM has maintained an accommodative monetary policy stance since 2021, with the interest rate increased to 2% in March 2022 from 1.85% in April 2020. Despite the fact that excess rupee liquidity declined from its peak in 2020, a low short-term interest rate was maintained. Exchange rate adjustments were also made, as the BoM made substantial foreign exchange sales interventions and borrowed foreign currency to maintain official reserves. The rupee depreciated by about 10% in nominal terms and 9% in real effective terms in 2021. Normalization of the monetary policy will help in minimizing the potential effects from supply side shocks and also act as a means of controlling inflation in the medium term. Within an increasingly complicated global environment, engineering tighter monetary policy is vital for the economy.

CHALLENGES AND OPPORTUNITIES

New challenges have emerged in the midst of the COVID-19 pandemic, namely the Russian invasion of Ukraine and China's zero-COVID strategy, which among others, are disrupting supply chains and having enormous repercussions for small economies highly dependent on international trade and investment. The widespread increase in prices of important commodities such as oil and gas as well as food items is exercising tremendous pressure on the Mauritian economy and fuelling growing discontent among its population. The intensification of inflationary pressures will hurt national economic prospects by increasing production costs and exerting downward pressures on household purchasing power. The main economic challenge for the Government is to find the right balance between supporting recovery and controlling inflation while consolidating the fiscal stance.

Mauritius' economic recovery is expected to continue, albeit at a slower pace than projected due to the uncertainties prevailing in the global economy. The worsening terms of trade, rising trade deficit, less optimistic prospects for tourist flows (owing to lower growth rates in major source countries), high fuel and food prices, and fast depreciation of the rupee all represent major challenges for Mauritius as it seeks to accelerate its growth rate and create sustainable and inclusive development in order to move from an upper-middle income to a high income economy.

As an open small island economy, highly dependent on international trade, tourism and food imports, the conflict in Ukraine has confirmed the urgency for Mauritius to become resilient and reduce its dependence on imports. The global food shortages arising from supply chain disruptions and shipping issues have stressed the importance of food security; this is another challenge for the Mauritian population. With the pressing need to reduce dependence on food imports, the budget for 2022/23 provides subsidies on fertilizers and loans to support innovation and mechanization to address the rising production costs and the possibility of expanding production capacity. As an island destination far from its main markets, air flights represent a significant portion of tourists' spending on Mauritius. A clearer air access policy to support the sector is expected to be covered in the strategy blueprint due to be developed by the Government and the private sector.

Mauritius remains one of the most dynamic economies of the continent. However, like most countries globally, the island was severely affected by COVID-19, which pushed the economy into recession in 2020/21, although it recovered in 2021/22 and growth of 8.5% was forecast for 2022/23. This recovery is expected to be led by all sectors of the economy, and in particular the tourism industry.

Mauritius is also expected to leverage on its various Free Trade Agreement (FTA) markets, to diversify its export market as well as sourcing partners, and to boost exports while also promoting foreign investment. Such FTAs are poised to allow Mauritius to fully integrate into global and regional markets.

The country has good potential to embrace structural transformation in order to continue along the path to sustainable and resilient long-term growth. Its priorities should be on enhancing diversification and competitiveness, including greater digitalization of the economy and adaptation and mitigation policies to tackle climate change vulnerabilities.

Mauritius' good ranking on the Ease of Doing Business Index, sound legislation, business environment and appropriate infrastructure provide an excellent opportunity to position itself as an important hub for Africa, particularly for African technology entrepreneurs who can choose the country to incubate their ideas, raise funding and operate their companies from Mauritius to deliver technology products and services to Africa. The growing market for education in Africa means that Mauritius is also positioning itself as an education hub for the region.

Although the island is relatively tiny in terms of land mass, it is surrounded by a vast maritime zone (2.3m. sq. km and an additional sea area of approximately 396,000 sq. km, which is co-managed with Seychelles). The blue sector, represented by coastal tourism, fishing, seafood processing and seaport activities, surely offers good potential for the economy in the medium term, and the development of emerging sectors such as aquaculture, maritime services, marine biotechnology, and oil and gas exploration are serious candidates to be explored. Following the country's exit from the Financial Action Task Force list of jurisdictions under increased monitoring during the year, Mauritius can continue to work towards being a viable and trusted environment, and can thus expect to boost this sector in the short and medium term.

Statistical Survey

Source (unless otherwise stated): Statistics Mauritius, LIC Bldg, President John F. Kennedy St, Port Louis; tel. 208-1800; e-mail statsmauritius@govmu.org; internet statsmauritius.govmu.org.

Area and Population

AREA, POPULATION AND DENSITY

Area (sq km)	2,007*
Population (census results)	
2 July 2000	1,179,137
3–4 July 2011	
Males	611,022
Females	626,069
Total	1,237,091
Population (official estimates at mid-year)	
2019	1,265,711
2020	1,265,740
2021	1,266,334
Density (per sq km) at mid-2021	631.0

* 775 sq miles.

POPULATION BY AGE AND SEX

(Mauritius and Rodrigues islands only, official estimates at mid-2021)

	Males	Females	Total
0–14 years	107,000	103,563	210,563
15–64 years	450,148	445,844	895,992
65 years and over	68,855	90,650	159,505
Total	626,003	640,057	1,266,060

ISLANDS

(official population estimates at mid-2021)

	Area (sq km)	Population	Density (per sq km)
Mauritius . .	1,868	1,221,844	654.1
Rodrigues . .	110	44,216	402.0
Other islands . .	29	274	9.4
Total	2,007	1,266,334	631.0

DISTRICTS

(Mauritius and Rodrigues islands only, '000 official population estimates at 31 December 2020)

Black River . . .	84.8	Port Louis . . .	117.7
Flacq	138.7	Riv du Rempart .	108.1
Grand Port . . .	112.7	Rodrigues . . .	44.0
Moka	83.7	Savanne . . .	68.2
Pamplemousses .	142.1	**Total**	1,265.8
Plaine Wilhems .	365.8		

PRINCIPAL TOWNS

(official population estimates at 31 December 2020)

Port Louis (capital) .	145,406	Curepipe . . .	78,114
Vacoas/Phoenix .	105,614	Quatre Bornes . .	77,005
Beau Bassin/Rose Hill	103,304		

BIRTHS, MARRIAGES AND DEATHS*

	Registered live births		Registered marriages		Registered deaths	
	Number	Rate (per 1,000)	Number	Rate (per 1,000)	Number	Rate (per 1,000)
2017	13,479	10.7	9,757	15.4	10,140	8.0
2018	12,965	10.2	10,034	15.9	10,787	8.5
2019	12,862	10.2	9,709	15.3	11,174	8.8
2020	13,465	10.6	6,929	10.9	11,060	8.7
2021	12,982	10.3	8,186	12.9	13,274	10.5

* Figures refer to the islands of Mauritius and Rodrigues only. The data are tabulated by year of registration, rather than by year of occurrence.

Life expectancy (years at birth, estimates): 74.2 (males 70.9; females 77.7) in 2020 (Source: World Bank, World Development Indicators database).

ECONOMICALLY ACTIVE POPULATION

('000 persons aged 16 years and over, incl. foreign workers)

	2019	2020	2021*
Agriculture, forestry and fishing .	40.3	35.4	29.3
Sugar cane	9.0	6.2	5.4
Mining and quarrying	2.3	2.0	1.5
Manufacturing	96.3	90.4	85.0
Electricity, gas and water . .	5.4	5.4	5.4
Construction	44.0	41.4	41.9
Wholesale and retail trade, repair of motor vehicles and household goods	96.2	89.0	89.1
Hotels and restaurants . .	44.0	40.1	36.0
Transport, storage and communications	57.8	55.5	55.6
Financial intermediation . . .	13.9	14.4	14.0
Real estate, renting and business activities	40.0	37.0	34.9
Public administration and defence; compulsory social security . .	44.3	44.7	42.5
Education	31.8	31.2	29.5
Health and social work . . .	20.2	20.0	18.9
Other community, social and personal service activities . .	45.5	43.2	30.8
Total employed	582.0	549.7	514.4
Unemployed	39.7	52.2	48.4
Total labour force	621.7	601.9	562.8
Males	379.2	361.5	342.8
Females	242.5	240.4	220.0

* Provisional.

Health and Welfare

KEY INDICATORS

Total fertility rate (children per woman, 2020)	1.4
Under-5 mortality rate (per 1,000 live births, 2020) . . .	16.5
HIV/AIDS (% of persons aged 15–49, 2020)	1.7
COVID-19: Cumulative confirmed deaths (per 100,000 persons at 31 August 2022)	78.8
COVID-19: Fully vaccinated population (% of total population at 28 August 2022)	75.3
Physicians (per 1,000 head, 2020)	2.7
Hospitals (per 100,000 head, 2013)	1.0
Domestic health expenditure (2019): US $ per head (PPP) .	694.3
Domestic health expenditure (2019): % of GDP	2.9
Domestic health expenditure (2019): public (% of total current expenditure)	47.0
Access to improved sanitation facilities (% of persons, 2017) .	96
Total carbon dioxide emissions ('000 metric tons, 2018) . .	4,130
Carbon dioxide emissions per head (metric tons, 2018) . .	3.3
Human Development Index (2021): ranking	63
Human Development Index (2021): value	0.802

Note: For data on COVID-19 vaccinations, 'fully vaccinated' denotes receipt of all doses specified by approved vaccination regime (Sources: Johns Hopkins University and Our World in Data). Data on health expenditure refer to current general government expenditure in each case. For more information on sources and further definitions for all indicators, see Health and Welfare Statistics: Sources and Definitions section (europaworld.com/credits).

Agriculture

PRINCIPAL CROPS
('000 metric tons)

	2018	2019	2020
Aubergines (Eggplants) . . .	2.5	3.4	3.5
Bananas	7.3	7.3	8.5
Beans, green	1.4	1.5	1.5
Cabbages and other brassicas .	3.6	3.5	4.0
Carrots and turnips . . .	4.9	5.3	3.3
Cauliflowers and broccoli . . .	1.5	0.8	0.9
Chillies and peppers, green . .	1.4	2.0	2.6
Coconuts	0.8*	0.8†	0.8†
Cucumbers and gherkins . .	7.8	6.1	5.3
Lettuce and chicory	1.1	1.3	0.8
Okra	1.0	1.3	1.2
Onions, dry	4.5	4.6	3.1
Pineapples	10.0	8.5	9.6
Potatoes	17.0	14.8	15.8
Pumpkins, squash and gourds .	17.4	22.8	18.6
Sugar cane	3,154.5	3,405.3	2,620.9
Tea	1.5	1.6	1.1
Tobacco, unmanufactured† . .	0.3	0.2	0.2
Tomatoes	9.2	8.7	8.3

* Unofficial figure.
† FAO estimate(s).

Aggregate production ('000 metric tons, may include official, semi-official or estimated data): Total cereals 0.4 in 2018, 0.5 in 2019, 0.8 in 2020; Total fruit (primary) 23.7 in 2018, 22.1 in 2019, 24.4 in 2020; Total roots and tubers 18.9 in 2018, 16.8 in 2019, 18.3 in 2020; Total vegetables (primary) 59.9 in 2018, 64.8 in 2019, 56.6 in 2020.

Source: FAO.

LIVESTOCK
('000 head, year ending September)

	2018	2019	2020*
Cattle	4.0	3.5	3.8
Chickens	15,954*	16,218*	16,481
Goats	26.0	25.8	25.8
Pigs	19.7	20.9	22.0
Sheep	3.8	4.6	3.8

* FAO estimate(s).

Source: FAO.

LIVESTOCK PRODUCTS
('000 metric tons)

	2018	2019	2020
Cattle meat*	1.8	1.8	1.4
Cows' milk	2.5	2.5	1.8
Chicken meat	49.0	51.0	47.5
Hen eggs*	12.8	13.5	12.4

* FAO estimates.

Source: FAO.

Forestry

ROUNDWOOD REMOVALS
('000 cubic metres, excl. bark, FAO estimates)

	2018	2019	2020
Sawlogs, veneer logs and logs for sleepers	1.2	1.2	1.2
Other industrial wood	0.2	0.2	0.2
Fuel wood	5.2	5.2	3.7
Total	6.5	6.6	5.0

Source: FAO.

SAWNWOOD PRODUCTION
('000 cubic metres, incl. railway sleepers)

	2015	2016	2017
Coniferous (softwood)	0.4	0.9	0.9
Broadleaved (hardwood) . . .	0.2	0.1	0.1
Total	0.6	1.0	1.0

2018–20: Production assumed to be unchanged from 2017 (FAO estimates).

Source: FAO.

Fishing

(metric tons, live weight)

	2018	2019	2020
Capture	28,314	34,143	25,989
Groupers and seabasses . .	204	213	79
Snappers and jobfishes . .	344	480	378
Emperors (Scavengers) . . .	1,379	1,460	1,449
Skipjack tuna	9,295	12,756	9,220
Yellowfin tuna	11,655	12,681	9,779
Bigeye tuna	1,871	2,008	1,515
Octopuses	723	665	622
Aquaculture	2,070	3,251	3,298
Red drum	1,948	3,132	3,224
Total catch	31,409	37,493	29,287

Note: Figures exclude aquatic animals, recorded by number rather than weight. The number of Nile crocodiles captured was: 0.0 in 2018; 160 in 2019; 0.0 in 2020.

Source: FAO.

Industry

SELECTED PRODUCTS
('000 metric tons unless otherwise indicated)

	2018	2019	2020*
Fish	74.1	76.9	64.7
Frozen	23.3	28.2	21.0
Canned	50.3	48.1	43.1
Raw sugar	323.4	331.1	270.9
Molasses	106.9	119.5	86.9
Beer and stout ('000 hectolitres) .	435.5	464.1	439.0
Electrical energy (million kWh) .	3,131.6	3,236.6	2,882.4

* Provisional.

2016 ('000 metric tons): Iron bars and steel tubes 20.2; Fertilizers 15.5.

2017 ('000 metric tons): Iron bars and steel tubes 26.2.

2021 ('000 metric tons, provisional): Fish 28.7; Raw sugar 255.8; Molasses 90.4; Electrical energy (million kWh) 2,992.2.

Finance

CURRENCY, EXCHANGE RATES AND FISCAL YEAR

Monetary Units
100 cents = 1 Mauritian rupee.

Sterling, Dollar and Euro Equivalents (31 May 2022)
£1 sterling = 54.72 rupees;
US $1 = 43.47 rupees;
€1 = 46.57 rupees;
1,000 Mauritian rupees = £18.27 = $23.01 = €21.47.

Average Exchange Rate (Mauritian rupees per US $)
2019   35.474
2020   39.347
2021   41.692

Fiscal Year
The fiscal year ends on 30 June.

BUDGET
(fiscal year, million rupees, estimates)

Revenue

	2020/21	2021/22	2022/23
Tax revenue	82,905	107,680	129,535
Taxes on income, profits and capital gains	23,535	31,925	38,525
Taxes on property . . .	28	51	105
Domestic taxes on goods and services	55,664	71,210	86,165
Taxes on international trade .	1,140	1,595	1,830
Other tax revenue	2,538	2,899	2,910
Non-tax revenue	72,495	28,805	20,465
Social contributions . . .	6,300	10,120	11,756
Grants	2,480	4,245	2,280
Other non-tax revenue . . .	63,715	14,440	6,429
Total	155,500	136,485	150,000

Expense/Outlays

Expense by economic type	2020/21	2021/22	2022/23
Expenditure	136,400	138,299	154,500
Wages and salaries . . .	32,283	36,810	36,644
Other purchases of goods and services	11,300	12,194	12,621
Interest payments . . .	12,570	12,800	13,100
Subsidies and other current transfers	30,083	26,193	27,902
Social benefits	45,710	47,234	55,535
Other expense	4,454	3,068	8,709
Net acquisition of non-financial assets	43,700	23,320	18,391
Total	180,099	161,618	172,891

Outlays by function of government	2020/21	2021/22	2022/23
General public services . . .	73,383	46,644	45,171
Public order and safety . . .	11,944	14,194	15,195
Community and social services .	83,099	90,244	99,310
Education	15,866	18,165	19,037
Health	13,692	16,388	15,330
Social security and welfare . .	48,729	50,878	59,401
Housing and community amenities	2,631	2,565	2,831
Recreational, cultural and religious services	1,069	1,031	1,306
Environmental protection . .	1,112	1,217	1,405
Economic services	11,667	10,536	12,216
Agriculture, forestry, fishing and hunting	3,010	2,580	2,769
Fuel and energy	92	108	99
Mining, manufacturing and construction	681	717	891
Transportation and communications	5,099	4,656	5,660
Tourism	700	296	356
General economic, commercial and labour affairs . . .	1,080	1,166	1,271
Other economic affairs . . .	1,008	445	465
Infrastructure projects in preparation	5	—	200
Contingencies	—	—	800
Total expenditure	180,099	161,618	172,891

Source: Ministry of Finance and Economic Development, Port Louis.

INTERNATIONAL RESERVES
(US $ million at 31 December)

	2019	2020	2021
Gold (market prices)	609.9	756.9	726.8
IMF special drawing rights . .	124.6	129.9	317.0
Reserve position in IMF . . .	34.5	50.0	48.9
Foreign exchange	6,594.3	6,355.2	7,469.2
Total	7,363.3	7,292.0	8,561.9

Source: IMF, *International Financial Statistics*.

MONEY SUPPLY
(million rupees at 31 December)

	2019	2020	2021
Currency outside depository corporations	35,365.4	39,610.5	43,542.0
Transferable deposits	393,473.0	493,926.8	566,394.0
Other deposits	146,312.0	150,023.9	140,857.1
Securities other than shares . .	26,822.9	20,031.6	15,054.3
Broad money	601,973.2	703,592.7	765,847.4

Source: IMF, *International Financial Statistics*.

COST OF LIVING
(Consumer Price Index; base: 2017 = 100)

	2019	2020	2021
Food and non-alcoholic beverages .	106.6	113.2	118.1
Clothing and footwear	104.8	106.6	109.1
Housing, water, electricity and fuels	97.8	94.9	92.1
All items (incl. others) . . .	103.7	106.3	110.6

NATIONAL ACCOUNTS
(million rupees in current prices)

National Income and Product

	2019	2020	2021
Compensation of employees .	181,051	169,097	183,516
Operating surplus			
Consumption of fixed capital .	264,552	224,773	241,371
Gross domestic product (GDP) at factor cost . .	445,603	393,870	424,887
Taxes on production and imports	68,258	57,011	58,278
Less Subsidies	1,870	2,386	2,654
GDP in purchasers' values .	511,991	448,495	480,511
Primary incomes received from abroad			
Less Primary incomes paid abroad	11,920	8,662	7,132
Gross national income . .	523,911	457,157	487,644
Current transfers from abroad .			
Less Current transfers paid abroad	411	−26	−2,704
Gross national disposable income	524,322	457,131	484,940

Expenditure on the Gross Domestic Product

	2019	2020	2021
Private final consumption expenditure	375,746	326,044	350,019
Government final consumption expenditure	75,416	78,314	80,958
Gross fixed capital formation . .	97,745	76,916	93,820
Increase in stocks	1,788	4,846	−320
Total domestic expenditure .	550,695	486,120	524,477
Exports of goods and services . .	225,695	176,631	211,683
Less Imports of goods and services	267,408	208,640	258,356
Statistical discrepancy	3,010	−5,615	2,707
GDP in purchasers' values .	511,991	448,495	480,511

Gross Domestic Product by Economic Activity

	2019	2020	2021
Agriculture, hunting, forestry and fishing	13,864	14,103	15,694
Sugar cane	1,296	1,202	1,519
Mining and quarrying	1,615	1,472	1,822
Manufacturing	53,874	48,552	56,013
Electricity, gas and water . . .	8,296	7,642	7,817
Construction	22,817	17,033	22,419
Wholesale and retail trade, repair of motor vehicles and personal goods	54,673	48,932	50,751
Hotels and restaurants . . .	31,714	11,633	10,574
Transport, storage and communications	48,109	42,272	44,751
Financial intermediation . . .	55,178	55,561	59,064
Real estate, renting and business activities	64,283	58,394	61,927
Public administration and defence; compulsory social security . .	27,399	28,656	30,965
Education	20,821	20,713	21,616
Health and social work . . .	20,288	20,579	22,583
Other services	22,671	18,328	18,892
Gross value added in basic prices	445,603	393,869	424,888
Taxes, less subsidies, on products	66,388	54,626	55,624
GDP in market prices . . .	511,991	448,495	480,511

BALANCE OF PAYMENTS
(US $ million)

	2019	2020	2021
Exports of goods	2,223	1,789	1,964
Imports of goods	−5,294	−3,915	−4,652
Balance on goods	−3,071	−2,126	−2,688
Exports of services	3,035	1,300	1,233
Imports of services	−2,071	−1,307	−1,430
Balance on goods and services	−2,106	−2,134	−2,884
Primary income received . . .	10,184	8,543	6,444
Primary income paid	−8,387	−6,676	−4,707
Balance on goods, services and primary income	−309	−267	−1,147
Secondary income received . .	411	364	337
Secondary income paid . . .	−820	−1,099	−716
Current balance	−718	−1,003	−1,527
Direct investment assets . . .	5,190	−2,649	−5,561
Direct investment liabilities . .	−1,645	−10,084	9,159
Portfolio investment assets . .	3,307	2,595	−4,139
Portfolio investment liabilities .	269	4,155	1,659
Financial derivatives and employee stock options (net)	−788	77	−85
Other investment assets . . .	−7,132	3,029	−950
Other investment liabilities . .	2,518	3,329	2,816
Net errors and omissions . .	−61	15	−77
Reserves and related items .	939	−537	1,294

Source: IMF, *International Financial Statistics*.

External Trade

PRINCIPAL COMMODITIES
(million rupees)

Imports c.i.f.	2019	2020	2021
Food and live animals . . .	35,828	35,805	39,878
Fish and fish preparations . .	9,989	9,197	9,453
Crude materials, inedible, except fuel	4,998	3,619	5,034
Mineral fuels, lubricants, etc. . .	36,373	24,571	37,030
Refined petroleum products . .	30,645	20,542	30,293
Chemicals and related products	17,325	16,647	24,810
Basic manufactures	31,906	26,850	37,717
Machinery and transport equipment	47,156	36,611	42,089
General industrial machinery, equipment and parts . . .	6,580	5,830	6,387
Telecommunications and sound equipment	8,047	5,801	7,003
Other electrical machinery, apparatus, etc.	7,049	5,455	6,636
Road motor vehicles . . .	14,130	10,882	13,141
Miscellaneous manufactured articles	19,118	15,748	21,255
Total (incl. others)	198,639	165,722	215,186

Exports f.o.b.*	2019	2020	2021
Food and live animals . . .	23,449	23,175	23,607
Chemicals and related products	3,068	3,118	3,495
Basic manufactures	9,567	8,603	10,970
Machinery and transport equipment	2,534	2,446	3,021
Miscellaneous manufactured articles	25,330	20,589	25,534
Total (incl. others)	66,351	60,427	69,993

*Excluding stores and bunkers for ships and aircraft (million rupees): 12,448 in 2019; 9,796 in 2020; 12,112 in 2021.

PRINCIPAL TRADING PARTNERS
(million rupees)*

Imports c.i.f.	2019	2020	2021
Argentina	1,902	2,100	2,834
Australia	2,728	2,692	2,595
Belgium	4,051	2,834	4,374
China, People's Republic	33,234	27,564	38,128
France	13,818	11,914	14,282
Germany	5,960	5,377	5,828
India	27,579	15,859	33,565
Indonesia	3,961	3,594	4,028
Italy	4,662	4,017	4,847
Japan	6,143	4,899	5,203
Korea, Republic	3,909	2,246	1,900
Madagascar	1,501	913	1,159
Malaysia	4,072	4,314	3,757
New Zealand	1,804	1,943	2,580
Saudi Arabia	1,283	248	283
Seychelles	2,244	1,966	2,742
South Africa	16,008	12,741	17,173
Spain	6,208	5,798	4,569
Switzerland	1,503	1,081	1,521
Thailand	3,910	2,870	3,486
Türkiye	3,160	3,103	5,150
United Arab Emirates	14,161	20,041	18,938
United Kingdom	6,016	3,264	3,355
USA	4,009	2,724	4,944
Total (incl. others)	198,639	165,722	215,186

Exports f.o.b.	2019	2020	2021
Belgium	997	1,207	1,350
China, People's Republic	1,137	934	1,072
France	6,271	4,848	5,955
Germany	1,380	1,148	1,208
India	848	1,269	1,852
Italy	3,644	3,960	3,314
Japan	1,203	795	596
Kenya	1,961	1,914	2,115
Madagascar	4,684	4,148	5,387
Netherlands	2,601	2,685	2,880
Portugal	606	306	427
Réunion	1,715	1,680	3,036
Seychelles	982	928	1,000
Singapore	1,206	866	549
South Africa	6,948	7,187	9,684
Spain	2,937	3,415	3,454
Switzerland	878	832	1,052
United Kingdom	7,328	6,085	6,434
USA	7,106	5,827	5,871
Total (incl. others)	66,351	60,427	69,993

* Imports by country of origin; exports by country of destination (including re-exports, excluding ships' stores and bunkers).

Transport

ROAD TRAFFIC
(motor vehicles registered at 31 December)

	2019	2020	2021
Private vehicles:			
Cars	307,081	320,064	334,104
Motorcycles and mopeds	216,863	221,988	229,563
Commercial vehicles:			
Buses	3,088	3,101	3,151
Lorries and trucks	16,086	16,512	17,040

SHIPPING
Flag Registered Fleet
(at 31 December)

	2019	2020	2021
Number of vessels	127	125	126
Total displacement ('000 grt)	207.2	207.7	204.9

Source: Lloyd's List Intelligence (www.bit.ly/LLintelligence).

Seaborne Freight Traffic
('000 metric tons)

	2018	2019	2020
Goods unloaded	6,787	7,102	6,120
Goods loaded	1,278	1,414	1,292

CIVIL AVIATION
(traffic)

	2018	2019	2020
Aircraft landings	11,652	12,118	4,174
Freight unloaded ('000 metric tons)	32.9	33.3	12.8
Freight loaded ('000 metric tons)	32.7	30.4	12.9

Tourism

FOREIGN TOURIST ARRIVALS

Country of residence	2019	2020	2021*
China, People's Republic	42,740	5,189	499
France	302,038	79,510	51,525
Germany	129,100	36,047	18,605
India	75,673	12,781	2,845
Italy	41,991	7,567	3,954
Réunion	137,570	30,581	5,288
South Africa	118,556	19,370	8,061
Switzerland	42,045	7,328	7,011
United Kingdom	141,520	22,687	34,194
Total (incl. others)	1,383,488	308,980	179,780

* Provisional.

Tourism receipts (gross earnings, million rupees): 63,107 in 2019; 17,664 in 2020; 15,253 in 2021 (provisional).

Communications Media

	2018	2019	2020
Telephones ('000 main lines in use)	434.3	458.7	478.7
Mobile telephone subscriptions ('000)	1,918.0	1,866.6	1,912.9
Fixed internet subscriptions ('000)	275.0	307.2	323.2
Broadband subscriptions, fixed ('000)*	274.2	307.2	322.1
Broadband subscriptions, mobile ('000)*	1,001.3	1,109.5	1,245.6
Television sets licensed ('000) .	383.3	350.7	349.9
Daily newspapers	8	7	n.a.
Non-daily newspapers	59	63	n.a.

* Source: International Telecommunication Union.

Education

(2021 unless otherwise indicated)

	Institutions	Teachers	Students*
Pre-primary	789	3,087	23,603
Primary	319	8,819	84,129
Secondary	178	9,379	102,722
Technical and vocational† .	15	n.a.	7,603
Tertiary‡	45	n.a.	49,205

* By enrolment.
† 2017.
‡ 2019.

Pupil-teacher ratio (qualified teaching staff, primary education, UNESCO estimate): 14.0 in 2020/21 (Source: UNESCO Institute for Statistics).

Adult literacy rate (UNESCO estimates): 91.3% (males 93.4%; females 89.4%) in 2018 (Source: UNESCO Institute for Statistics).

Directory

The Constitution

The Mauritius Independence Order, which established a self-governing state, came into force on 12 March 1968, and was subsequently amended. Constitutional amendments providing for the adoption of republican status were approved by the Legislative Assembly (henceforth known as the National Assembly) on 10 December 1991, and came into effect on 12 March 1992. The main provisions of the revised Constitution, including subsequent amendments, are listed below:

HEAD OF STATE

The head of state is the President of the Republic, who is elected by a simple majority of the National Assembly for a five-year term of office. The President appoints the Prime Minister (in whom executive power is vested) and, on the latter's recommendation, other ministers.

COUNCIL OF MINISTERS

The Council of Ministers, which is headed by the Prime Minister, is appointed by the President and is responsible to the National Assembly.

THE NATIONAL ASSEMBLY

The National Assembly, which has a term of five years, comprises the Speaker, 62 members elected by universal adult suffrage, a maximum of eight additional members and the Attorney-General (if not an elected member). The island of Mauritius is divided into 20 three-member constituencies for legislative elections. Rodrigues returns two members to the National Assembly. The official language of the National Assembly is English, but any member may address the Speaker in French.

The Government

HEAD OF STATE

President: PRITHVIRAJSING ROOPUN (took office 2 December 2019).

Vice-President: (MARIE CYRIL) EDDY BOISSEZON.

COUNCIL OF MINISTERS

(October 2022)

Prime Minister, Minister of Defence, Home Affairs and External Communications, Minister for Rodrigues and Outer Islands and Territorial Integrity: PRAVIND KUMAR JUGNAUTH.

Deputy Prime Minister, Minister of Housing and Land Use Planning, Minister of Tourism: LOUIS STEVEN OBEEGADOO.

Vice-Prime Minister, Minister of Education, Tertiary Education, Science and Technology: LEELA DEVI DOOKUN-LUCHOOMUN.

Vice-Prime Minister, Minister of Local Government and Disaster Risk Management: Dr MOHAMMAD ANWAR HUSNOO.

Minister of Land Transport and Light Rail, and Foreign Affairs, Regional Integration and International Trade: ALAN GANOO.

Minister of Finance, Economic Planning and Development: Dr RENGANADEN PADAYACHY.

Minister of Energy and Public Utilities: GEORGES PIERRE LESJONGARD.

Minister of Social Integration, Social Security and National Solidarity: FAZILA JEEWA-DAUREEAWOO.

Minister of Industrial Development, Small and Medium-sized Enterprises and Co-operatives: SOOMILDUTH BHOLAH.

Minister of Environment, Solid Waste Management and Climate Change: KAVYDASS RAMANO.

Minister of Financial Services and Good Governance: MAHEN KUMAR SEERUTTUN.

Attorney-General, Minister of Agro-industry and Food Security: MANEESH GOBIN.

Minister of Youth Empowerment, Sports and Recreation: JEAN CHRISTOPHE STEPHAN TOUSSAINT.

Minister of National Infrastructure and Community Development: MAHENDRANAUTH SHARMA HURREERAM.

Minister of Information Technology, Communication and Innovation: DARSANAND BALGOBIN.

Minister of Labour, Human Resource Development and Training, and Commerce and Consumer Protection: SOODESH SATKAM CALLICHURN.

Minister of Health and Wellness: Dr KAILESH KUMAR SINGH JAGUTPAL.

Minister of the Blue Economy, Marine Resources, Fisheries and Shipping: SUDHEER MAUDHOO.

Minister of Gender Equality and Family Welfare: KALPANA DEVI KOONJOO-SHAH.

Minister of Arts and Cultural Heritage: AVINASH TEELUCK.

Minister of Public Service and Administrative and Institutional Reforms: TEERUTHRAJ HURDOYAL.

MINISTRIES

Office of the President: State House, Le Réduit, Port Louis; tel. 454-3021; e-mail president@govmu.org; internet president.govmu.org.

Office of the Vice-President: 30 Farquhar Ave, Quatre Bornes, Port Louis; tel. 427-0737; e-mail ovp@govmu.org; internet vice-president.govmu.org.

Office of the Prime Minister: New Government Centre, 4th Floor, Port Louis; tel. 201-2409; e-mail pmo@govmu.org; internet pmo.govmu.org.

Ministry of Agro-industry and Food Security: Renganaden Seeneevassen Bldg, 8th and 9th Floor, cnr Jules Koenig and Maillard Sts, Port Louis; tel. 212-0854; e-mail moaheadoffice@govmu.org; internet agriculture.govmu.org.

Ministry of Arts and Cultural Heritage: Renganaden Seeneevassen Bldg, 7th Floor, cnr Pope Hennessy and Maillard Sts, Port Louis; tel. 212-2112; e-mail moac@govmu.org; internet culture.govmu.org.

Ministry of the Blue Economy, Marine Resources, Fisheries and Shipping: LIC Centre, 4th Floor, John F. Kennedy St, Port Louis; tel. 211-2470; e-mail blueconomy@govmu.org; internet blueconomy.govmu.org.

Ministry of Commerce and Consumer Protection: SICOM Tower, Level 2, Wall St, Cyber City, Ebene; tel. 460-2500; e-mail mcom@govmu.org; internet commerce.govmu.org.

Ministry of Defence, Home Affairs and External Communications, and Ministry for Rodrigues and Outer Islands and Territorial Integrity: New Government Centre, 6th Floor, Port Louis; tel. 201-3593; internet mroiti.govmu.org.

Ministry of Education, Tertiary Education, Science and Technology: MITD House, Pont Fer, Phoenix; tel. 601-5200; e-mail moeps@govmu.org; internet education.govmu.org.

Ministry of Energy and Public Utilities: Air Mauritus Centre, 6th Floor, John Kennedy St, Port Louis; tel. 210-3774; e-mail mpu@govmu.org; internet publicutilities.govmu.org.

Ministry of the Environment, Solid Waste Management and Climate Change: Ken Lee Tower, cnr Barracks and St Georges Sts, Port Louis; tel. 203-6200; e-mail menv@govmu.org; internet environment.govmu.org.

Ministry of External Communications: Newton Tower, 1st Floor, Sir William Newton St, Port Louis; tel. 201-2410; e-mail mexc@govmu.org; internet externalcom.govmu.org.

Ministry of Finance, Economic Planning and Development: Government House, Ground Floor, Port Louis; tel. 260-1300; e-mail mofed-registry@govmu.org; internet mof.govmu.org.

Ministry of Financial Services and Good Governance: SICOM Tower, Levels 9 and 14, Wall St, Ebene; tel. 404-2400; e-mail financialservices@govmu.org; internet financialservices.govmu.org.

Ministry of Foreign Affairs, Regional Integration and International Trade: Newton Tower, 8th–11th and 14th Floors, Sir William Newton St, Port Louis; tel. 405-2500; e-mail mfa@govmu.org; internet foreign.govmu.org.

Ministry of Gender Equality and Family Welfare: Newton Tower, 7th Floor, Sir William Newton St, Port Louis; tel. 405-3300; e-mail mwfwcd@govmu.org; internet gender.govmu.org.

Ministry of Health and Wellness: Emmanuel Anquetil Bldg, 5th Floor, Sir Seewoosagur Ramgoolam St, Port Louis; tel. 201-2175; e-mail moh@govmu.org; internet health.govmu.org.

Ministry of Housing and Land Use Planning: Plot 52, Ebene Tower, Ebene; tel. 401-6808; e-mail mhou@govmu.org; internet housing.govmu.org.

Ministry of Industrial Development, Small and Medium-sized Enterprises and Co-operatives: Newton Tower, 16th Floor, Sir William Newton St, Port Louis; tel. 405-3100; e-mail mbe@govmu.org; internet enterbusiness.govmu.org.

Ministry of Information Technology, Communication and Innovation: SICOM Tower, Level 7, Wall St, Ebene Cyber City, Ebene; tel. 401-3500; e-mail mtci@govmu.org; internet mtci.govmu.org.

Ministry of Labour, Human Resource Development and Training: Victoria House, 1st–9th Floor, cnr St Louis and Barracks Sts, Port Louis; tel. 207-2600; e-mail mol@govmu.org; internet labour.govmu.org.

Ministry of Land Transport and Light Rail: Air Mauritius Bldg, 12th Floor, Port Louis; tel. 210-2761; e-mail nta@govmu.org; internet landtransport.govmu.org.

Ministry of Local Government and Disaster Risk Management: Emmanuel Anquetil Bldg, 3rd Floor, cnr Sir Seewoosagur Ramgoolam and Jules Koenig Sts, Port Louis; tel. 201-2155; e-mail mlg@govmu.org; internet localgovernment.govmu.org.

Ministry of National Infrastructure and Community Development: National Development Unit, Citadelle Mall, Level 11, cnr Louis Pasteur, Dr Eugene Laurent and Sir Virgil Naz Sts, Port Louis; tel. 405-0700; e-mail ndu@govmu.org; internet ndu.govmu.org.

Ministry of Public Service and Administrative and Institutional Reforms: SICOM Bldg 2, cnr Chevreau and Rev. Jean Lebrun Sts, Port Louis; tel. 405-4100; e-mail civser@govmu.org; internet civilservice.govmu.org.

Ministry of Social Integration, Social Security and National Solidarity: Renganaden Seeneevassen Bldg, Jules Koenig St, Port Louis; tel. 207-0625; e-mail mss@govmu.org; internet socialsecurity.govmu.org.

Ministry of Tourism: Air Mauritius Centre, 5th Floor, John F. Kennedy St, Port Louis; tel. 211-7930; e-mail mtou@govmu.org; internet tourism.govmu.org.

Ministry of Youth Empowerment, Sports and Recreation: Citadelle Mall, Level 7/8, cnr Louis Pasteur and Sir Virgil Naz Sts, Port Louis; tel. 206-1555; e-mail mysopenreg@govmu.org; internet mys.govmu.org.

Legislature

National Assembly: Parliament House, Place d'Armes, Port Louis; tel. 201-1414; e-mail clerk@govmu.org; internet mauritiusassembly.govmu.org.

Speaker: Sooroojdev Phokeer.

General Election, 7 November 2019

Party	Seats		
	Directly elected	Additional*	Total
Alliance Morisien†	38	4	42
L'Alliance Nationale‡ . . .	14	3	17
Mouvement Militant Mauricien .	8	1	9
Organisation du Peuple Rodriguais .	2	—	2
Total	62	8	70

* Awarded to those among the unsuccessful candidates who attracted the largest number of votes, in order to ensure that a balance of ethnic groups is represented in the Assembly.
† Alliance comprising the Mouvement Socialiste Militant and the Muvman Liberater.
‡ Alliance comprising the Parti Travailliste and the Parti Mauricien Social Démocrate.

Election Commission

Office of the Electoral Commissioner (OEC): Max City Bldg, 4th Floor, cnr Louis Pasteur and Remy Ollier Sts, Port Louis; tel. 241-7000; e-mail electcom@govmu.org; internet electoral.govmu.org; under the aegis of the Prime Minister's Office; Commissioner appointed by the Judicial and Legal Service Commission; Electoral Commissioner Mohammad Irfan Abdool Rahman.

Political Organizations

Forum des Citoyens Libres (FCL): Mahébourg; Leader Georges Ah-Yan.

Front Solidarité Mauricienne (FSM): internet fb.com/officialfsm; f. 1990; Leader Cehl Meeah.

LALIT: 153 Main Rd, Grand River North West; tel. 208-2132; e-mail lalitmail@intnet.mu; internet www.lalitmauritius.org; f. 1976.

Les Verts Fraternels/The Greens: Port Louis; f. 2002; Leader Sylvio Michel.

Mouvement Mauricien Social Démocrate (MMSD): Morcellement Piat, Forest-Side, POB 1, Port Louis; tel. 670-4000; internet fb.com/mmsdmru; f. 2009; Leader Eric Guimbeau.

Mouvement Militant Mauricien (MMM): 21 Poudrière St, Port Louis; tel. 212-6553; e-mail ajaygunness@intnet.mu; internet mmm.mu; f. 1969; socialist; Leader Paul Bérenger; Sec.-Gen. Ajay Gunness.

Mouvement Patriotique (MP): Mirah Bldg, route St Jean, Quatre Bornes; internet fb.com/MPLaNouvelleForceOfficialPage; f. 2015; formed by breakaway group from the Mouvement Militant Mauricien (q.v.); Pres. Jean-Claude Barbier; Sec.-Gen. (vacant).

Mouvement Rodriguais (MR): Port Mathurin, Rodrigues; tel. 52556984; e-mail nvmally@intnet.mu; internet fb.com/mouvementrodriguais; f. 1992; represents the interests of Rodrigues; Leader Louis Joseph (Nicholas) Von-Mally.

Mouvement Socialiste Militant (MSM): Sun Trust Bldg, 1st Floor, 31 Edith Cavell St, Port Louis; tel. 212-8787; internet fb.com/msmparty; f. 1983 by fmr mems of the MMM; Leader Dr Pravind Kumar Jugnauth; Pres. Joe Lesjongard; Sec.-Gen. Maneesh Gobin.

Muvman Liberater: Port Louis; f. 2014; Leader Ivan Collendavelloo.

Organisation du Peuple Rodriguais (OPR): Mont Lubin, Rodrigues; represents the interests of Rodrigues; f. 1976; Leader Louis Serge Clair.

Parti Mauricien Social Démocrate (PMSD): Astor Court, 1st Floor, Port Louis; tel. 212-6945; e-mail rosemay@lepmsd.mu; internet lepmsd.mu; centre-right; Leader Charles Gaëtan Xavier-Luc Duval.

Parti Réformiste: Port Louis; f. 2017; Leader Roshi Badain.

Parti Travailliste (PTr) (Mauritius Labour Party): 7 Guy Rozemont Sq., Port Louis; tel. 212-6691; e-mail info@labourparty.mu;

internet www.labourparty.mu; f. 1936; Leader Dr NAVINCHANDRA RAMGOOLAM; Pres. PATRICK ASSIRVADEN; Sec.-Gen. RITESH RAMFUL.

Party Malin: Royal Rd, Curepipe; tel. 696-1224; internet fb.com/partimalin1; Leader DANRAJSINGH AUBEELUCK.

Diplomatic Representation

EMBASSIES AND HIGH COMMISSIONS IN MAURITIUS

Australia: Rogers House, 2nd Floor, 5 John F. Kennedy St, POB 541, Port Louis; tel. 202-0160; e-mail ahc.portlouis@dfat.gov.au; internet mauritius.embassy.gov.au; Chargé d'affaires KEARA SHAW.

Bangladesh: Hennessy Court, 8th Floor, Pope Hennessy St (cnr Suffren Rd), Port Louis; tel. 212-9527; e-mail mission.portlouis@yahoo.com; internet portlouis.mofa.gov.bd; High Commissioner REZINA AHMED.

China, People's Republic: Royal Rd, Belle Rose, Rose Hill; tel. 467-4600; e-mail chinaemb_mu@mfa.gov.cn; internet mu.china-embassy.gov.cn; Ambassador ZHU LIYING.

Egypt: Sun Trust Bldg, 2nd Floor, Edith Cavell St, Port Louis; tel. 213-1765; e-mail egypt.embassy.mru@gmail.com; internet fb.com/EmbassyofEgyptinMauritius; Ambassador Dr ALYA'A SAMIR BORHAN.

France: 14 St George St, Port Louis; tel. 202-0100; e-mail consulat.port-louis-amba@diplomatie.gouv.fr; internet mu.ambafrance.org; Ambassador FLORENCE CAUSSÉ-TISSIER.

India: Plot 65C, Cyber City, Ebene; tel. 460-6600; e-mail admn.portlouis@mea.gov.in; internet hcimauritius.gov.in; High Commissioner K. NANDINI SINGLA.

Japan: Tower C, Level 6, Cyber City, Ebene; tel. 460-2200; e-mail japanembassy@mx.mofa.go.jp; internet www.mu.emb-japan.go.jp; Ambassador SHUICHIRO KAWAGUCHI.

Libya: John F. Kennedy St (ex-Residence of Dr Malleck), Port Louis; tel. 686-1801; e-mail libyambass@intnet.mu; Chargé d'affaires a.i. RABEA M. K. TAILAMUN.

Madagascar: Theveneau Ave, Floreal, Port Louis; tel. 686-5015; e-mail consulat@ambamadmaurice.org; internet ambamadmaurice.org; Ambassador ALBERT CAMILLE VITAL.

Pakistan: 9A Queen Mary Ave, Floreal, Port Louis; tel. 698-8501; e-mail pareportlouis@hotmail.com; internet mofa.gov.pk/port-louis-mauritius; High Commissioner MUHAMMAD ARSHAD JAN PATHAN.

Russian Federation: Queen Mary Ave, Floreal, POB 10, Port Louis; tel. 696-1545; e-mail rusemb.mu@yandex.ru; internet mauritius.mid.ru; Ambassador KONSTANTIN KLIMOVSKY.

South Africa: British American Insurance Bldg, 4th Floor, 25 Pope Hennessy St, POB 908, Port Louis; tel. 212-6925; e-mail sahc@intnet.mu; High Commissioner Dr HLAMALANI NELLY MANZINI.

United Kingdom: Sir Hesketh Bell St, Floreal, POB 2, Plaines Wilhems; tel. 660-4900; e-mail bhc@intnet.mu; internet www.gov.uk/world/mauritius; High Commissioner CHARLOTTE PIERRE.

USA: Rogers House, 4th Floor, John F. Kennedy St, POB 544, Port Louis; tel. 202-4400; e-mail usembass@intnet.mu; internet mu.usembassy.gov; Chargé d'affaires a.i. SATRAJIT (JITU) SARDAR.

Judicial System

The laws of Mauritius are derived both from the French Code Napoléon and from English Law. The Judicial Department is divided into two tiers: the Supreme Court and subordinate courts. The Supreme Court is presided over by the Chief Justice and exercises unlimited jurisdiction. The Supreme Court also comprises a Senior Puisne Judge and a number of Puisne Judges recommended by the Parliament. Subordinate courts include the Intermediate Court, the Industrial Court, the District Courts, the Bail and Remand Court and the Court of Rodrigues.

Supreme Court: Pope Henessy St, Port Louis; tel. 212-0275; e-mail croffice@govmu.org; internet supremecourt.govmu.org.

Chief Justice: REHANA MUNGLY-GULBUL.

Senior Puisne Judge: NIRMALA DEVAT.

Religion

The principal religious group are Hindus, who comprised 48.5% of the population, according to the 2011 census. At that time, about 32.7% were Christians (the majority of whom being Roman Catholics) and 17.3% were Muslims.

CHRISTIANITY

The Anglican Communion

Anglicans in Mauritius are within the Church of the Province of the Indian Ocean, comprising eight dioceses (six in Madagascar, one in Mauritius and one in Seychelles). The Archbishop of the Province is the Bishop of Seychelles.

Bishop of Mauritius: Rt Rev. JOSEPH STÉNIO ANDRÉ, Diocesan Church House, 37 St Paul Rd, Vacoas; tel. 686-5158; e-mail dioang@intnet.mu; internet www.anglican.mu.

The Presbyterian Church of Mauritius

Chairman: Pasteur MAURICE DAVANTIN, cnr Farquhar and Royal Rds, Coignet, Rose Hill; tel. 464-5265; e-mail presby@intnet.mu; internet www.presbyterian.mu.

The Roman Catholic Church

Mauritius comprises a single diocese, directly responsible to the Holy See, and the Apostolic Vicariate of Rodrigues.

Bishop of Port Louis: Cardinal MAURICE E. PIAT, Evêché, 13 Mgr Gonin St, Port Louis; tel. 208-3068; e-mail eveche@intnet.mu; internet www.dioceseportlouis.org.

BAHÁ'Í FAITH

National Spiritual Assembly: 40 Volcy Pougnet St, Port Louis; tel. 212-2179; e-mail mauritiusnsa@gmail.com; internet bahaimauritius.org; mems resident in 190 localities.

ISLAM

World Islamic Mission (Mauritius): 30 Old Moka Rd, Bell Village, Port Louis; tel. 57705270; e-mail wim.mauritius@gmail.com; internet www.wimmauritius.org; f. 1975; Chair. Sheikh MOHAMMAD NASSER JAULIM NOORANI; Gen. Sec. HAMADE AUBDOOLLAH.

The Press

DAILY NEWSPAPERS (PRINT AND ONLINE)

China Times: 34 Emmanuel Anquetil St, POB 325, Port Louis; tel. 240-3067; f. 1953; Chinese; Editor-in-Chief LONG SIONG AH KENG; Dir LI KOOK TSEUNG.

Chinese Daily News: 32 Remy Ollier St, POB 316, Port Louis; tel. 240-0472; f. 1932; Chinese.

Le Défi Quotidien: 4B rue Labourdonnais, Port Louis; tel. 207-0666; e-mail redaction@defimedia.info; internet defimedia.info; French; Chief Editor MANOOURAJ GUNGEA.

L'Express: 3 rue des Oursins, Riche-Terre, Baie du Tombeau, POB 247, Port Louis; tel. 206-8200; e-mail digital@lasentinelle.mu; internet www.lexpress.mu; f. 1963; daily; owned by La Sentinelle Ltd; weekend edns: L'Express Samedi and L'Express Dimanche; French; Editor-in-Chief JÉRÔME BOULLE.

Le Mauricien: 8 rue St George St, POB 7, Port Louis; tel. 207-8200; e-mail lemauricien.redaction@gmail.com; internet www.lemauricien.com; f. 1907; English and French; Dir-Gen. (vacant).

WEEKLY NEWSPAPERS (PRINT AND ONLINE) AND FORTNIGHTLY PERIODICALS

5-Plus Dimanche: 3 rue des Oursins, Baie du Tombeau; tel. 206-8200; e-mail prod@5plus.mu; internet www.5plus.mu; f. 1994; French; Editor-in-Chief MICHAËLLA SEBLIN.

Business Magazine: 3 Brown-Sequard St, 3rd Floor, Port Louis; tel. 206-8200; e-mail contact@business-magazine.mu; internet www.businessmag.mu; f. 1992; part of La Sentinelle Group; French; Editor-in-Chief (vacant).

La Vie Catholique: 28 Nicolay Rd, Port Louis; tel. 242-0975; e-mail viecatho@intnet.mu; internet laviecatholique.org; f. 1930; weekly; French and Creole; publ. by Catholic diocese; Editor-in-Chief DANIÈLE BABOORAM.

Le Défi-Plus: 4B rue Labourdonnais, Port Louis; tel. 212-4820; e-mail marketing@defimedia.info; internet defimedia.info; weekly; Dir ESHAN KHODABUX.

L'Hebdo: cnr Antonio and Labourdonnais St, Port Louis; tel. 203-4800; e-mail marketing@defimedia.info; internet defimedia.info; weekly.

Lalit de Klas: 153 Main Rd, Grand River North West, Port Louis; tel. 208-2132; e-mail lalitmail@intnet.mu; internet www.lalitmauritius.org; English, French and Creole; Editor RADA KISTNASAMY.

Mauritius Times: Rm 406, Pearl House, Sir Virgil Naz St, Port Louis; tel. 212-1313; e-mail mtimes@intnet.mu; internet www

.mauritiustimes.com; f. 1954; weekly; English and French; Editor-in-Chief MADHUKAR RAMLALLAH.

News on Sunday: cnr Antonio and Labourdonnais St, Port Louis; tel. 203-4800; e-mail marketing@defimedia.info; internet defimedia .info; f. 1996; weekly; owned by Le Défi Group; English; Editor NAGUIB LALLMAHOMED.

Scope: 8 rue St George St, POB 7, Port Louis; tel. 207-8200; e-mail wes@lemauricien.com; internet www.lemauricien.com/scope; f. 1989; English and French; owned by Le Mauricien Ltd; Editor-in-Chief JACQUES ACHILLE.

Star: Sir Virgil Naz St, Port Louis; tel. 212-2736; e-mail star_press@live.com; internet starpress.info; English and French; Editor-in-Chief REZA ISSACK.

Week-End: 8 rue St George St, POB 7, Port Louis; tel. 207-8200; e-mail lemauricien.redaction@gmail.com; internet www.lemauricien.com; f. 1966; French and English; owned by Le Mauricien Ltd; Chief Editor GAËTAN SÉNÈQUE.

OTHER SELECTED PERIODICALS

CCI–INFO: Anglo-Mauritius House, 2nd Floor, 6 Adolphe de Plevitz St, Port Louis; tel. 203-4830; e-mail mcci@intnet.mu; internet www .mcci.org; f. 1995; quarterly; English and French; publ. of the Mauritius Chamber of Commerce and Industry; Man. FAEEZA IBRAHIMSAH.

Le Message de L'Ahmadiyyat: Darus Salaam Sq., Dr Maurice Cure St, Rose Hill; tel. 464-0374; e-mail jamaatmu@gmail.com; internet ahmadiyya.mu; annual; French; Editor-in-Chief MOUSSA TAUJOO.

Publishers

Business Publications Ltd: 3 rue des Oursins, Baie du Tombeau; tel. 206-8200; e-mail businessmag@intnet.mu; internet www .business-magazine.mu; f. 1992; part of La Sentinelle Group; English and French; Editor-in-Chief RICHARD LE BON.

Editions de l'Océan Indien: 22B Marcel Cabon St, Stanley, Rose Hill; tel. 464-6761; e-mail eoi-info@intnet.mu; internet eoibooks .gov-mu.org; f. 1977; general, textbooks, dictionaries, literature; English, French and Asian languages; privately owned; Dir YASHVIN HASSAMAL.

Editions Vizavi: 3 Nahaboo Solim St, Port Louis; tel. 211-2435; e-mail info@vizavi.mu; internet www.vizavi.mu; f. 1993; Man. Dir PASCALE SIEW.

Broadcasting and Communications

TELECOMMUNICATIONS

Cellplus Mobile Communications Ltd: Telecom Tower, 17th Floor, Edith Cavell St, Port Louis 11302; tel. 203-7000; e-mail ceo@telecom.mu; internet www.telecom.mu; f. 1996; introduced the first GSM network in Mauritius and recently in Rodrigues (Cell-Oh); a fully-owned subsidiary of Mauritius Telecom.

Emtel: 10 Ebene Cyber City, Ebene 72201; tel. 57295400; e-mail emtel@emtelnet.com; internet www.emtel.com; f. 1989; collaboration of Currimjee Jeewanjee Group and Bharti Enterprises, India; CEO KRESH GOOMANY.

Mahanagar Telephone Mauritius Ltd (MTML): MTML Sq., 63 Cyber City, Ebene; tel. 52943333; e-mail mtmlinfo@mtmltd.net; internet chili.mu; f. 2004; launched GSM service 'Chile' in Nov. 2011; subsidiary of Mahanagar Telephone Nigam Ltd (India); CDMA and GSM technology based telecom and internet service provider; CEO SANJAY GARG.

Mauritius Telecom Ltd: Telecom Tower, Edith Cavell St, Port Louis 11302; tel. 203-7000; e-mail ceo@telecom.mu; internet www .telecom.mu; f. 1988 as Mauritius Telecommunication Services; present name adopted 1992 following merger with Overseas Telecommunications Services; 40% owned by Rimcom Ltd and 33.49% owned by Govt of Mauritius; Chair. MAXIME SAUZIER; CEO KAPIL REESAUL.

Outremer Télécom Maurice: Cyber Tower 2, 5th Floor, Ebene; tel. 800-1400; e-mail info@outremer-telecom.mu; internet www .outremer-telecom.mu; f. 2004.

Regulatory Authority

Information and Communication Technologies Authority (ICTA): The Célicourt, 12th Floor, 6 Sir Célicourt Antelme St, Port Louis 11302; tel. 211-5333; e-mail info@icta.mu; internet www.icta.mu; f. 2002; regulatory authority; Chair. DICK CHRISTOPHE NG SUI WA.

BROADCASTING

Independent Broadcasting Authority: The Célicourt, 6 Sir Célicourt Antelme St, Port Louis; tel. 213-3890; e-mail iba@intnet .mu; internet www.iba.mu; Chair. BHOONESWAR RAJKUMARSINGH.

Radio

Mauritius Broadcasting Corpn: 1 Royal Rd, Moka; tel. 402-8000; e-mail dirgen@mbc.intnet.mu; internet www.mbcradio.tv; f. 1964; parastatal organization operating 6 national radio services, 3 analogue television channels and 17 digital television channels; radio channels incl. Radio Maurice, Radio Mauritius, Taal FM, Kool FM, Best FM and MBC Rodrigues; Chair. PREMODE NEERUNJUN; Dir-Gen. MOONENDRA NUDHI SHARMA (ANOOJ) RAMSURRUN (acting).

Radio One: United Docks Business Park, Caudan Waterfront, Port Louis; tel. 211-4555; e-mail reception@r1.mu; internet www.r1.mu; f. 2002; owned by Sentinelle media group; news and entertainment; Editor-in-Chief GÉRALDINE GEOFFROY.

Radio Plus: 4B Labourdonnais St, Port Louis; tel. 208-6002; e-mail redaction@radioplus.mu; internet live.radioplus.mu; f. 2008; owned by Le Défi Media Group; Head VENEN COOLEN.

Top FM: The Peninsula, Caudan Bldg, 7th Floor, 2A Falcon St, Caudan, Port Louis; tel. 213-6666; e-mail topfm@intnet.mu; internet www.topfmradio.com; f. 2002; Man. Dir and Editor-in-Chief BALKRISHNA KAUNHYE.

Radio France International and France Inter are also broadcast to Mauritius.

Television

Independent television stations commenced broadcasting from 2002. In June 2015 all analogue terrestrial television signals in Mauritius were switched off, marking the transition to digital only services.

Mauritius Broadcasting Corpn: see Radio.

Finance

BANKING

Central Bank

Bank of Mauritius: Sir William Newton St, POB 29, Port Louis; tel. 202-3800; e-mail communications@bom.mu; internet www.bom.mu; f. 1967; bank of issue; Gov. HARVESH KUMAR SEEGOLAM.

Principal Commercial Banks

ABC Banking Corpn Ltd: WEAL House, Duke of Edinburgh Ave, Place d'Armes, Port Louis 11328; tel. 206-8000; e-mail info@abcbanking.mu; internet www.abcbanking.mu; f. 1997; fmrly a leasing co under name of ABC Finance & Leasing Ltd, started banking operations in 2010; 70.47% owned by ABC Group Cos and other corpns and 29.53% owned by individuals; Chair. Y. K. J. YEUNG SIK YUEN; Man. Dir Prof. DONALD AH-CHUEN.

Absa Bank Mauritius Ltd: Barclays House, 2nd Floor, 68–68A Cyber City, POB 284, Ebene; tel. 402-1000; e-mail customer.contact@absa.africa; internet www.mu.barclaysafrica.com; f. 1919; fmrly Barclays Bank Mauritius Ltd; present name adopted in 2020; part of Absa Group Ltd; Chair. IQBAL RAJAHBALEE; Man. Dir RAVIN DAJEE.

AfrAsia Bank Ltd: Bowen Sq., 10 Dr Ferriere St, Port Louis; tel. 208-5500; e-mail afrasia@afrasiabank.com; internet www .afrasiabank.com; f. 2007; majority shares held by IBL Ltd, National Bank of Canada and Intrasia Capital Pvt Ltd; Interim Chair. JEAN-RAYMOND REY; Interim CEO THIERRY VALLET.

Bank of Baroda: 32 Sir William Newton St, POB 553, Port Louis; tel. 208-1504; e-mail bobgen@intnet.mu; internet www .bankofbaroda-mu.com; f. 1962; Vice-Pres. (Mauritius Operations) RITESH KUMAR; Chief Man. S. K. PANDE.

Bank One Ltd: 16 Sir William Newton St, POB 485, Port Louis; tel. 202-9200; e-mail info@bankone.mu; internet bankone.mu; f. 1991 as the Delphis Bank Ltd; merged with Union International Bank in 1997; present name adopted in 2008; 50% owned by Investments & Mortgages Bank Ltd (Kenya), 50% by Ciel Investments Ltd; Chair. ROSELYNE RENEL; Exec. Dir and CEO MARK WATKINSON.

BanyanTree Bank Ltd: Nexteracom Tower I, 13th Floor, Cyber City, Ebene; tel. 468-1101; e-mail info@banyantreebank.com; internet www.banyantreebank.com; f. 2012; Chair. JAGDISH CAPOOR; CEO ROBERT GREEN.

Deutsche Bank (Mauritius) Ltd: Barkly Wharf East, 4th Floor, Le Caudan Waterfront, POB 615, Port Louis; tel. 202-7878; e-mail dbml .enquiries@list.de.com; internet www.db.com/mauritius; f. 1995; Chief Country Officer FRIEDRICH PHILIPPS.

Habib Bank Ltd: 30 Louis Pasteur St, Port Louis; tel. 217-7600; e-mail hbl@hbl.intnet.mu; internet www.hbl.com/mauritius; f. 1964; part of Habib Bank (Pakistan); Country Man. IMRAN AHMER SIDDIQUI.

Hongkong and Shanghai Banking Corpn Ltd (HSBC): HSBC Centre, 18 Cyber City, Ebene; tel. 403-8333; e-mail hsbcmauritius@hsbc.co.mu; internet www.hsbc.co.mu; f. 1916; CEO BONNIE QIU; Man. Dir DEAN LAM.

Investec Bank (Mauritius) Ltd: Dias Pier Bldg, 6th Floor, Le Caudan Waterfront, Port Louis; tel. 207-4000; e-mail infomru@investec.co.mu; internet www.investec.com/en_mu/welcome-to-investec.html; f. 1997; subsidiary of Investec Group, South Africa; Chair. DAVID M. LAWRENCE; CEO CRAIG C. MCKENZIE.

MauBank Ltd: 25 Bank St, Cyber City, Ebene 72201; tel. 405-9400; e-mail info@maubank.mu; internet www.maubank.mu; f. 2016 by merger of National Commercial Bank and Mauritius Post and Cooperative Bank; Chair. SOOKUN GOOROODEO; CEO PREMCHAND MUNGAR.

Mauritius Commercial Bank Ltd: MCB Centre, 9–15 Sir William Newton St, POB 52, Port Louis; tel. 202-5000; e-mail contact@mcb.mu; internet www.mcb.mu; f. 1838; Chair. JEAN-FRANÇOIS DESVAUX DE MARIGNY; CEO ALAIN LAW MIN.

SBI Mauritius Ltd (SBIML): SBI Tower Mindspace, 7th Floor, 45 Cyber City, Ebene; tel. 404-4900; e-mail info@sbimauritius.com; internet www.sbimauritius.com; f. 1978 as Indian Ocean International Bank Ltd; merged with SBI International and present name adopted in 2008; 96.6% owned by State Bank of India, 1.17% owned by Indian Ocean General Assurance Co Ltd and 2.23% owned by others; Chair. VENKAT NAGESWAR CHALASANI; Man. Dir and CEO SHASHI PRABHA.

SBM Bank (Mauritius) Ltd: SBM Tower, 1 Queen Elizabeth II Ave, POB 152, Port Louis; tel. 202-1111; e-mail sbm@sbmgroup.mu; internet www.sbmgroup.mu; f. 1973; fmrly State Bank of Mauritius Ltd, present name adopted 2014; mem of SBM Holdings Ltd; Chair. (vacant); CEO ANOOP KUMAR NILAMBER.

Standard Bank (Mauritius) Ltd: Tower A, Level 9, 1 Cyber City Ebene, 72201; tel. 402-5200; e-mail clientservices@standardbank.mu; internet www.standardbank.mu; fully owned subsidiary of Standard Bank Group Limited (South Africa); Chair. DUNCAN WESTCOTT; CEO FRANÇOIS GAMET.

Standard Chartered Bank (Mauritius) Ltd: Raffles Tower, 6th Floor, 19 Cyber City, Ebene; tel. 403-6500; e-mail CIB.mu@sc.com; internet www.sc.com/mu; f. 2002; wholly owned subsidiary of Standard Chartered Bank PLC; offshore banking unit; CEO MATHIEU MANDENG.

Development Banks

Development Bank of Mauritius Ltd: rue La Chaussée, POB 157, Port Louis; tel. 203-3600; e-mail dbm@intnet.mu; internet www.dbm.mu; f. 1964; present name adopted in 1991; 96.3% govt-owned; Chair. JAIRAJSING LUCHOO; Man. Dir JAYWANT PANDOO.

Principal Offshore Banks

BCP Bank (Mauritius) Ltd: Maeva Tower, 9th Floor, cnr Silicon Ave and Bank St, Cyber City, Ebene; tel. 207-1000; e-mail serviceclient@bcpbank.mu; internet www.bcpbank.mu; f. 2004; fmrly Banque des Mascareignes Ltée; present name adopted 2019; part of BCP Group; CEO ABDELWAFI ATIF.

AfrAsia Bank Ltd, Bank of Baroda, Barclays Bank PLC, HSBC Bank PLC, Investec Bank (Mauritius) and Standard Chartered Bank (Mauritius) also operate offshore banking units.

Islamic Banks

Century Banking Corpn Ltd: 15 Sir Seewoosagur Ramgoolam St, Port Louis; tel. 213-3400; e-mail info@cbc.com.mu; internet cbc.com.mu; f. 2010; CEO MUNIRUDDEEN LALLMAHOMOODC.

Banking Organizations

Mauritius Bankers Association Ltd (MBA): Newton Tower, Level 15, Sir William Newton St, Port Louis; tel. 213-2390; e-mail mba@mba.mu; internet www.mba.mu; f. 1967; Chair. BONNIE QIU; CEO DANIEL ESSOO; 18 mems (2).

STOCK EXCHANGE

Stock Exchange of Mauritius Ltd: 1 Cathedral Sq., 4th Floor, 16 Jules Koenig St, Port Louis; tel. 212-9541; e-mail stockex@sem.intnet.mu; internet www.stockexchangeofmauritius.com; f. 1989; 9 mems; Chair. JAIYANSING SHAILEN SOOBAH; Chief Exec. SUNIL DUTT BENIMADHU.

REGULATORY AUTHORITIES

Financial Services Commission: FSC House, 54 Cyber City, Ebene 72201; tel. 403-7000; e-mail fscmauritius@intnet.mu; internet www.fscmauritius.org; f. 2001; integrated regulator for the non-bank financial services sector and global business; Chair. MARDAYAH KONA YERUKUNONDU; Chief Exec. DHANESSWURNATH THAKOOR.

INSURANCE

Eagle Insurance Co Ltd: Eagle House, 15 A5 Wall St, Cyber City, Ebene; tel. 460-9200; e-mail info@eagle.mu; internet www.eagle.mu; f. 1973; fmrly Mauritian Eagle Insurance Co Ltd; present name adopted in 2019; Chair. JEAN-CLAUDE BÉGA; CEO DEREK WONG WAN PO.

Indian Ocean General Assurance Ltd (IOGA): 12 Volcy Pougnet St, Port Louis; tel. 208-9000; e-mail info@iogaltd.com; internet www.ioga.mu; f. 1970; Chair Dr SOOPRAMANIEN M. CUNDEN; CEO NATARAJAN M. CUNDEN.

Jubilee Insurance (Mauritius) Ltd: Mezzanine Floor, 1 Cathedral Sq., Pope Hennessy St, Port Louis; tel. 202-2200; e-mail info@jubileemauritius.com; internet jubileeportal.com; f. 1997; Chair. NIZAR N. JUMA; CEO MARIE ANNICK PAMELA BUSSIER.

Lamco International Insurance Ltd: 12 Barracks St, Port Louis; tel. 212-4494; e-mail info@lamcoinsurance.com; internet www.lamcoinsurance.com; f. 1978; CEO SHAIK MAHOMED LATIFF.

Life Insurance Corpn of India: LIC Centre, John F. Kennedy St, POB 310, Port Louis; tel. 211-5702; e-mail liccmm@intnet.mu; internet www.licindia.in; f. 1956; Chief Man. BISWAJEET GANGULY.

Mauritius Union Assurance Co Ltd (MUA): 4 Léoville l'Homme St, POB 233, Port Louis; tel. 207-5500; e-mail info@mua.mu; internet www.mua.mu; f. 1948; Chair. DOMINIQUE GALEA; CEO JÖRG WEBER.

National Insurance Co Ltd: NIC Centre, 217 Royal Rd, Curepipe; tel. 602-3000; e-mail customerservice@nicl.mu; internet www.nicl.mu; f. 2015; Chair. VIKASH PEERUN; COO RISHI SOOKDAWOOR.

New India Assurance Co Ltd: Bank of Baroda Bldg, 3rd Floor, 15 Sir William Newton St, POB 398, Port Louis; tel. 208-1442; e-mail niasurance@intnet.mu; f. 1935; general insurance; part of New India Assurance (owned by Govt of India); COO DEEPAK PAWLAS PATHARE.

Phoenix Insurance (Mauritius) Ltd: 36 Sir William Newton St, POB 852, Port Louis; tel. 405-5080; e-mail phoenixins@intnet.mu; internet phoenixins.mu; f. 2002; Chair. AJITH ROHAN GUNAWARDENA; CEO TILAK FERNANDO.

State Insurance Co of Mauritius Ltd (SICOM): SICOM Bldg, Sir Célicourt Antelme St, Port Louis; tel. 203-8400; e-mail email@sicom.intnet.mu; internet www.sicom.mu; f. 1975; Chair. MUHAMMAD YOOSUF SALEMOHAMED; Group CEO NANDITA RAMDEWAR.

Swan General Ltd: Swan Group Centre, 10 Intendance St, POB 364, Port Louis; tel. 207-3500; e-mail info@swanforlife.com; internet www.swanforlife.com; f. 1855; fmrly Swan Insurance Co Ltd; present name adopted in 2015; Chair. NICOLAS MAIGROT; Group CEO LOUIS RIVALLAND.

Swan Life Ltd: Swan Centre, 10 Intendance St, POB 8370, Port Louis; tel. 207-3500; e-mail info@swanforlife.com; internet www.swanforlife.com; f. 1951; fmrly Anglo-Mauritius Assurance Society Ltd; present name adopted in 2015; Chair. NICOLAS MAIGROT; Group CEO LOUIS RIVALLAND.

Trade and Industry

GOVERNMENT AGENCIES

Agricultural Marketing Board (AMB): Dr Georges Leclézio Ave, Moka; tel. 433-4025; e-mail amb@ambmauritius.mu; internet ambmauritius.mu; f. 1964; operates under the aegis of the Ministry of Agro-industry and Food Security; markets certain locally produced and imported food products (such as potatoes, onions, garlic, spices and seeds); provides storage facilities to importers and exporters; Chair. Dr KESSAWA PAYANDI PILLAY; Gen. Man. GOWKARAN OREE.

Economic Development Board: 1 Cathedral Sq. Bldg, 10th Floor, 16 Jules Koenig St, Port Louis; tel. 203-3800; e-mail contact@edbmauritius; internet www.edbmauritius.org; f. 2018 following the merger between the Board of Investment, Enterprise Mauritius and the Financial Services Promotion Agency; Chair. HEMRAJ RAMNIAL; CEO KEN POONOOSAMY.

Mauritius Cane Industry Authority (MCIA): Moka Rd, Réduit 80835; tel. 454-1061; e-mail cs@mcia.mu; internet mcia.mu; f. 201; regulatory body for the sugar industry; also supervises Mauritius Sugar Industry Research Institute (MSIRA); CEO SATISH PURMESSUR.

Mauritius Meat Authority: Abattoir Rd, Roche Bois, POB 612, Port Louis; tel. 242-5884; e-mail mauritiusmeat@intnet.mu; f. 1974; controls and regulates sale of meat and meat products; also purchases and imports livestock and markets meat products; Chair. ZAID ZOUBERE HEERA.

DEVELOPMENT ORGANIZATIONS

Agence Française de Développement (AFD): Bâtiment Dias Pier, Le Caudan Waterfront, Port Louis; tel. 213-6400; e-mail afdportlouis@afd.fr; internet www.afd.fr; provides financial and technical support for the devt and promotion of green infrastructure projects in Mauritius; Group CEO RÉMY RIOUX.

National Housing Development Co Ltd (NDHC Ltd): Royal Complex, 4th and 5th Floors, rue St Ignace, Rose-Hill 71319; tel. 403-7333; e-mail nhdcom@intnet.mu; internet nhdcmauritius.com; f. 1991; 99.5% state-owned; Chair. ABDOOL RAHMAN MOHAMMAD EHSAN AHMAD; Group CEO SONOO JAIRAJ.

National Productivity and Competitiveness Council (NPCC): The Catalyst, 3rd Floor, Silicon Ave, Cyber City, Ebene 72201; tel. 467-7700; e-mail npccmauritius@intnet.mu; internet www .npccmauritius.org; f. 2000; Chair. SANJIV MULLOO; Exec. Dir ASHIT KUMAR GUNGAH.

SME Mauritius: Pope Hennessy Bldg, 25 Pope Hennessy St, Port Louis; tel. 202-0040; e-mail info@smemu.org; internet www.smemu .org; f. 2017 to replace the Small and Medium Enterprises Development Authority; Chair. VIRENDRA KUMAR BISSOONAUTH; CEO RAMPERSAD RAMPERSAD.

State Investment Corpn Ltd (SIC): Air Mauritius Centre, 15th Floor, John F. Kennedy St, Port Louis; tel. 202-8900; e-mail contactsic@stateinvestment.com; internet stateinvestment.com; f. 1984; provides support for new investment and transfer of technology in agriculture, industry and tourism; Chair. JAIRAJ SONOO; Man. Dir. GOOLABCHUND GOBURDHUN.

CHAMBERS OF COMMERCE

Chinese Chamber of Commerce: Jade Court, Fifth Floor, Jummah Mosque St, Port Louis; tel. 242-0156; e-mail ccoc1908@intnet .mu; internet fb.com/ChineseChamberofCommerce; f. 1908; Pres. PASCAL FOK KOW.

Mauritius Chamber of Commerce and Industry: Anglo-Mauritius House, 2nd Floor, 6 Adolphe de Plevitz St, Port Louis; tel. 203-4830; e-mail mcci@mcci.org; internet www.mcci.org; f. 1850; Pres. NAMITA JAGARNATH HARDOWAR; Sec.-Gen. Dr YOUSOUF ISMAËL.

INDUSTRIAL ASSOCIATIONS

Association des Hôteliers et Restaurateurs de l'île Maurice (AHRIM): Suite 83, Level 2, Médine Mews, rue La Chaussée, Port Louis; tel. 208-8181; e-mail secretariat@ahrim.mu; internet www .ahrim.mu; f. 1973; non-profit organization to represent and promote the interests of hotels and restaurants in Mauritius; Pres. JEAN MICHEL PITOT; over 90 hotel mems.

Association of Mauritian Manufacturers (AMM): Les Kocottes, Old Post Office Rd, Citroën Lane, St Pierre; tel. 433-6762; e-mail info@mauritianmanufacturers.mu; internet www.mauritian manufacturers.mu; f. 1995; Pres. YANNIS FAYD'HERBE.

EMPLOYERS' ORGANIZATIONS

Business Mauritius: BM-MCCI Bldg, rue du Savoir, Cyber City, Ebene; tel. 466-3600; e-mail info@businessmauritius.org; internet www.businessmauritius.org; f. 2015 by merger of the Mauritius Employers Federation and the Joint Economic Council; Pres. JEAN-PIERRE DALAIS; CEO KEVIN RAMKALOAN.

UTILITIES

Utility Regulatory Authority (URA): 1 Cyber City Bldg, 8th Floor, Ebene; tel. 454-8079; e-mail info@uramauritius.mu; internet uramauritius.mu; f. 2016; Chair. PHILIP AH-CHUEN; CEO EUNICE HARRIS POTANI.

Electricity

Central Electricity Board: rue du Savoir, Cyber City, POB 134, Ebene; tel. 404-2000; e-mail ceb@intnet.mu; internet ceb.mu; f. 1952; state-operated; Chair. RADHAKRISHNA CHELLAPERMAL.

Water

Central Water Authority: Royal Rd, St Paul, Phoenix; tel. 601-5000; e-mail cwa@intnet.mu; internet cwa.govmu.org; parastatal body; f. 1973; Chair. ASHISH NEELUMBUR; Gen. Man. PRAKASH MAUNTHROOA.

Wastewater Management Authority (WMA): Jerningham St, Curepipe; tel. 206-3000; e-mail wma@intnet.mu; internet

wmamauritius.mu; f. 2001; Chair. NANDA VEERAPA; Officer-in-Charge NAVINDRANATH JOWAHEER.

MAJOR COMPANIES

Cementis Maurice: Maeva Tower, Level 10, cnr Silicon Ave and Bank St, Cyber City, Ebene; tel. 452-2210; e-mail lafarge.mtius@ lafargeholcim.com; internet cementis.io/mu; f. 1959 as Lafarge Mauritius Cement Ltd; fmrly part of LafargeHolcim (Switzerland); present name adopted following acquisition by Cementis Océan Indien in 2021; Man. Dir HEBA CAPDEVILA-JANGEERKHAN.

CMT International Ltd: La Tour Koenig, Pointe aux Sables; tel. 234-2898; e-mail info@cmt-intl.com; internet www.cmt-intl.com; f. 1995; textiles and pharmaceuticals; subsidiaries in Hong Kong, China, Madagascar and Zimbabwe; Man. Dir KRIS POONOOSAMY.

Consolidated Investments and Enterprises Group (CIEL): Ebene Skies, 5th Floor, rue de l'Institut, Ebene; tel. 404-2200; e-mail info@cielgroup.com; internet www.cielgroup.com; f. 1977; diversified investment group; comprises CIEL Agro-Industry (Deep River—Beau Champ sugar estate), CIEL Investment Ltd and CIEL Textile Ltd; Chair. P. ARNAUD DALAIS; Group CEO JEAN-PIERRE DALAIS.

Currimjee Jeewanjee and Co Ltd: 38 Royal St, Port Louis 11602; tel. 650-6200; e-mail contact@currimjee.com; internet www .currimjee.com; f. 1890; media and communications, financial services, building materials, real estate, hospitality, travel, distribution, food and beverages, personal care and household products; Group Chair. BASHIR A. CURRIMJEE; Man. Dir ANIL C. CURRIMJEE.

ENL Ltd: ENL House, Vivea Business Park, Moka; tel. 404-9500; e-mail info@enl.mu; internet www.enl.mu; f. 1944; fmrly Espitalier Noël Ltd; present name adopted in 2009; holding co; agriculture, manufacturing and services; comprises more than 100 cos; notable subsidiaries include Ascencia, Axess, ENL Investment Ltd, ENL Agri-business and ENL Commercial Ltd (fmrly General Investment & Development Co Ltd); Chair. and Group CEO HECTOR ESPITALIER-NOËL.

Gamma-Civic Ltd: HSBC Centre, 4th Floor, 18 Bank St, Cyber City, Ebene; tel. 403-8000; e-mail headoffice@gamma.mu; internet gamma.mu; f. 1987; supply of building materials, civil engineering, construction and lottery gaming; Chair. TOMMY AH TECK.

General Construction Co Ltd: Industrial Zone, Plaine Lauzun, Port Louis; tel. 202-2000; e-mail gcc@gcc.mu; internet www.gcc.mu; f. 1958; civil engineering and construction; Man. Dir DIDIER ADAM.

Harel Mallac & Co Ltd: 18 Edith Cavell St, Port Louis; tel. 207-3000; e-mail communication@harelmallac.com; internet www .harelmallac.com; f. 1830; multiple activities, incl. 6 divisions: technologies; office equipment; travel, tourism and retail; reprographics; engineering and outsourcing; Chair ANTOINE L. HAREL; CEO CHARLES P. L. HAREL.

IBL Together: IBL House, Le Caudan Waterfront, Port Louis; tel. 203-2000; e-mail corporate@gmlmail.com; internet www.iblgroup .com; f. 1830 as Ireland Fraser and Blyth Brothers; fmrly Ireland Blyth Ltd; present name adopted in 2016 following merger with GML Investissement Ltée; sugar, tourism, industry, commerce, manufacturing, biotechnologies, etc.; 285 subsidiaries and affiliates; notable subsidiaries: IBL Energy and Cervonic; Chair. JAN BOULLÉ; Group CEO ARNAUD LAGESSE.

 Alteo Ltd: Vivéa Business Park, St Pierre; tel. 402-9050; e-mail info@alteogroup.com; internet www.alteogroup.com; f. 2012 as a merged entity of Deep River-Beau Champ (DRBC) and Flacq United Estates Ltd (FUEL); sugar cane growing and milling, also supplies electricity derived from coal/bagasse to the national grid; notable subsidiaries: Alteo Milling Ltd, Alteo Refinery Ltd, Alteo Energy Ltd, Alteo Properties Ltd and TPC Ltd; jt venture of CIEL Ltd and IBL Ltd; Chair. JÉRÔME DE CHASTEAUNEUF; CEO FABIEN DE MARASSÉ ENOUF.

IndianOil (Mauritius) Ltd (IOML): Terminal, Mer Rouge, Port Louis; tel. 217-2710; e-mail indianoil@ioml.mu; internet www.ioml .mu; f. 2001; wholly owned by IndianOil Corpn (India); Chair. RANJAN K. MOHAPATRA; Man. Dir K. NAVIN CHARAN.

Innodis Ltd: Innodis Bldg, Caudan; tel. 206-0800; e-mail info@ innodisgroup.com; internet www.innodisgroup.com; f. 1973 as Mauritius Farms Ltd; present name adopted in 2006; owned by Altima Group; distributes and markets dry, chilled and frozen consumer goods; also has chicken farming and processing units; operates five outlets under Supercash, a cash and carry concept, in Mauritius and Rodrigues; Chair. VICTOR SEEYAVE; CEO JEAN-PIERRE LIM KONG.

International Distillers (Mauritius) Ltd: POB 661, Plaine Lauzun; tel. 212-6896; e-mail idm@idm.intnet.mu; internet greenislandrummauritius.com; f. 1972; fmrly known as Gilbeys (Mauritius) Ltd; mfrs, importers and distributors of wines and spirits; Chief Exec. JACQUES T. LI WAN PO; Man. Dir W. L. SHEPHERD.

Landscope (Mauritius) Ltd: Shri Atal Bihari Vajpayee Tower, Level 7, Wing A, Ebene; tel. 467-6900; e-mail info@landscopemauritius.com; internet landscopemauritius.com; f. 2016 following merger of State Land Development Co Ltd, the State Property Development Co Ltd, Business Parks Mauritius Ltd, Belle Mare Tourist Village Ltd, Le Val Development Ltd and Les Pailles Conference Centre Ltd; govt-owned; develops, constructs and manages high technology business parks, including Ebene Cyber City; Chair. PREETAM BOODHUN.

Ingenia: chaussée Tromelin, Fort George, POB 344, Port Louis; tel. 261-3965; e-mail customerservice@mcfi.mu; internet www.mcfi.mu; f. 1975 as Mauritius Chemical and Fertilizers Industry Ltd; present name adopted in 2022; mfrs of agricultural chemicals and fertilizers; Chair. ANTOINE L. HAREL; Man. Dir YANNIS FAYD'HERBE.

Omnicane Ltd: Omnicane House, Mon Trésor Business Gateway, New Airport Access Rd, Plaine Mangnien; tel. 660-0600; e-mail info@omnicane.com; internet www.omnicane.com; f. 2009 following the rebranding of Mon Tresor & Mon Desert Ltd; sugar, energy and bioethanol; Chair. HAROLD MAYER; CEO JACQUES M. D'UNIENVILLE.

Phoenix Beverages Ltd: Phoenix House, Pont-Fer, Phoenix; tel. 601-2000; e-mail contact@phoenixbev.mu; internet phoenixbev.mu; f. 1960; fmrly Mauritius Breweries Ltd, now part of the Phoenix Beverages Group; present name adopted in 2004; brews, bottles and distributes alcoholic and soft drinks; Chair. ARNAUD LAGESSE; CEO and Exec. Dir BERNARD THEYS.

Rogers Group: Rogers House, 5 John F. Kennedy St, POB 60, Port Louis 11302; tel. 202-6666; e-mail communication@rogers.mu; internet www.rogers.mu; f. 1899; aviation, chemicals and pharmaceuticals, construction materials, engineering, food, financial services, property development, shipping, tourism and hospitality; Chair. JEAN PIERRE MONTOCCHIO; CEO PHILIPPE ESPITALIER-NOËL.

State Trading Corpn (STC): 55 Business Zone, Cyber City, Ebene; tel. 401-0800; e-mail stc@stcmu.com; internet www.stcmu.com; f. 1982; responsible for the importation of essential commodities, such as petroleum products, cement, rice and wheat flour and liquefied petroleum gas; state-owned; operates under Ministry of Industry, Commerce and Consumer Protection; Chair. Dr RAMCHANDRA BHEENICK; Gen. Man. RAJIV SERVANSINGH.

Sugar Investment Trust (SIT): NG Tower, Ground Floor, Cyber City, Ebene; tel. 406-4747; e-mail info@sit.mu; internet www.sit.mu; f. 1994; part of SIT group; subsidiaries incl. SIT Leisure Ltd and SIT Property Development Ltd; Chair. PREETAM BOODHUN; CEO DINESHRAO BABAJEE.

Sugar Storage and Handling Unit (SSHU): Les Salines, Port Louis; tel. 211-1327; e-mail sugar.tech@intnet.mu; f. 1980; fmrly Mauritius Sugar Terminal Corpn (MSTC); part of Mauritius Cane Industry Authority (MCIA); provides facilities for storage, sampling, bagging, packing, loading and unloading of sugar; Dir LUCKRAJ JHURRY.

Sun Ltd: Ebene Skies, rue de l'Institut, Ebene; tel. 402-0000; e-mail info@sunresorts.mu; internet www.sunresortshotels.com; f. 1983; holding co, with interests in the hotel and leisure business; Chair. JEAN-PIERRE DALAIS; CEO FRANÇOIS EYNAUD.

Tamak Textile Ltd (Tamaktex): 2 Royal Rd, Coromandel, Port Louis 71625; tel. 233-0020; e-mail tamak@tamak.com; internet tamakgroup.com; f. 1983; mfr of quality casual garments for men, ladies and children; sells under Citadel brand; CEO EMMANUEL TSANG MANG KIN.

Terra Mauricia Ltd: Beau Plan Business Park, Pamplemousses 21001; tel. 204-0808; e-mail terra@terra.co.mu; internet terra.co.mu; f. 1838 as Harel Frères; present name adopted 2012; investment group; Chair. ALAIN REY; Man. Dir NICOLAS MAIGROT.

United Basalt Products Ltd (UBP): Trianon, Quatre Bornes; tel. 454-1964; e-mail customercare@ubpgroup.com; internet www.ubp.mu; f. 1953; mfrs of building materials; Chair. MARC FREISMUTH; Group CEO STÉPHANE ULCOQ.

Vivo Energy Mauritius Ltd: Shell House, Cemetery Rd, Roche Bois, POB 85, Port Louis; tel. 206-1234; internet www.vivoenergy.com; f. 2011; marketing and distribution of Shell-branded petroleum products; part of Vivo Energy (owned by Vitol, Helios Investment Partners and Shell); Chair. ERIC GOSSE; Man. Dir MATTHIAS DE LARMINAT.

TRADE UNIONS

Federations

Federation of Civil Service and Other Unions (FCSOU): Jade Court, 3rd Floor, 28 Jummah Mosque St, Port Louis; tel. 216-1977; e-mail fcsou@intnet.mu; internet www.fcsou.org; f. 1957 as Federation of Civil Service Unions; Pres. NARENDRANATH GOPEE; Gen. Sec. HAROLD APPASAMY.

Mauritius Labour Congress (MLC): 8 Louis Victor de la Faye St, Port Louis; tel. 212-4343; e-mail mlcongress@intnet.mu; f. 1963; Pres. HANIFF PEERUN; Gen. Sec. BHOLANATH JEEWUTH.

Mauritius Trade Union Congress (MTUC): Emmanuel Anquetil Labour Centre, James Smith St, Port Louis; tel. 210-8567; e-mail mtuc_mu@hotmail.com; f. 1946; Pres. Dr MOHUN PRASADSING ODIT; Gen. Sec. DEWAN QUEDOU.

Principal Unions

Government Services' Employees Association: Unity House, 107A Royal Rd, Beau Bassin; tel. 464-4242; e-mail gsa@intnet.mu; internet www.gseamauritius.org; f. 1945; fmrly Government Servants Association; Pres. RADHAKRISNA SADIEN; Sec.-Gen. POONIT RAMJUG.

Mauritius Nursing Association: 159 Royal Rd, Beau Bassin; tel. 464-5850; e-mail nur.ass@intnet.mu; f. 1955; Pres. RAM NOWZADICK.

Port Louis Harbour and Docks Workers' Union (PLHDWU): Port Louis; tel. 208-2276; Pres. JOSE FRANÇOIS.

Transport

RAILWAYS

The first phase of the Metro Express light rail project was officially inaugurated by Prime Minister Pravind Kumar Jugnauth at a ceremony on 3 October 2019. The 13-km north–south route serves nine stops between Immigration Square in Port Louis and Rose Hill. The second phase will add another 13 km from Rose Hill to Curepipe with 10 stops.

ROADS

National Transport Corpn: Bonne Terre, Vacoas; tel. 427-5000; e-mail cnt.bus@intnet.mu; internet www.ntcmauritius.com; Chair. ASHVIN JAIN GOKOOL; Gen. Man. HOOLASS LOCHEE.

United Bus Service Ltd: Royal Rd, Les Cassis, Port Louis; tel. 212-2026; e-mail ubsltd@intnet.mu; internet ubsgroup.mu; f. 1954; Man. Dir SWALEH RAMJANE.

SHIPPING

Mauritius is served by numerous foreign shipping lines. In 1990 Port Louis was established as a free port to expedite the development of Mauritius as an entrepôt centre.

Mauritius Ports Authority (MPA): H. Ramnarain Bldg, Mer Rouge, Port Louis; tel. 206-5400; e-mail info@mauport.com; internet www.mauport.com; f. 1976; fmrly Mauritius Marine Authority; Chair. ASHIT KUMAR GUNGAH; Dir-Gen. SHEKUR SUNTAH.

Cargo Handling Corpn Ltd (CHCL): Chaussée Tromelin, Mer Rouge, Port Louis; tel. 206-1700; internet www.chcl.mu; f. 1983; Pres. MENON MUNIEN.

Ireland Blyth Ltd: IBL House, 5th Floor, Le Caudan Waterfront, Port Louis; tel. 203-2000; e-mail iblinfo@iblgroup.com; internet www.iblgroup.com; f. 1972; part of IBL Group; Chair. ARNAUD LAGESSE; Exec. Dir DIPAK CHUMMUN.

Mauritius Freeport Development Co Ltd: Freeport Zone 5, Mer Rouge, Port Louis; tel. 206-2000; e-mail info@mfd.mu; internet www.mfd.mu; f. 1997; manages and operates Freeport Zone 5, more than 40,000 sq m of storage facility; facilities include dry warehouses, cold warehouses, processing and transformation units, open storage container parks and a container freight station; Chair. RENÉ LECLÉZIO; CEO DOMINIQUE DE FROBERVILLE.

Mauritius Shipping Corpn Ltd: Nova Bldg, 1 Military Rd, Port Louis 11601; tel. 217-2284; internet www.mauritiusshipping.net; f. 1985; state-owned; operates two passenger-cargo vessels between Mauritius, Rodrigues, Réunion and Madagascar; Man. Dir RISHI RONOOWAH.

CIVIL AVIATION

Sir Seewoosagur Ramgoolam International Airport is at Plaisance, 4 km from Mahébourg.

Civil Aviation Department: Sir Seewoosagur Ramgoolam International Airport, Plaine Magnien; tel. 603-2000; e-mail civil-aviation@govmu.org; internet civil-aviation.govmu.org; under the aegis of Prime Ministers Office; Dir POKHUN ISWARDUTH.

Air Mauritius: Air Mauritius Centre, John F. Kennedy St, POB 441, Port Louis; tel. 207-7070; e-mail contact@airmauritius.com; internet www.airmauritius.com; f. 1967; 94.04% owned by Airport Holdings Ltd; services to 20 destinations in Europe, Asia, Australia and Africa; Chair. MARDAY VENKATASAMY; CEO (vacant).

Tourism

Mauritius Tourism Promotion Authority (MTPA): Victoria House, 4th and 5th Floors, St Louis St, Port Louis; tel. 203-1900; e-mail mtpa@intnet.mu; internet www.mymauritius.travel; f. 1996; Chair. (vacant); Dir ARVIND BUNDHUN.

Tourism Authority (TA): Victoria House, 1st Floor, St Louis St, Port Louis; tel. 203-1000; e-mail tourism.authority@intnet.mu; internet www.tourismauthority.mu; f. 2003; parastatal; responsible for licensing, regulating and supervising the activities of tourist enterprises; Dir LINDSAY MORVAN.

Defence

The country has no standing defence forces, although as assessed at November 2021 paramilitary forces were estimated to number 2,550, comprising a special 1,750-strong mobile police unit, to ensure internal security, and a coastguard of 800.

Defence Budget: Rs 10,400m. in 2022.

Education

Education is officially compulsory and free of charge for 11 years between the ages of five and 16. Primary education begins at five years of age and lasts for six years. Secondary education, beginning at the age of 11, lasts for up to seven years, comprising a first cycle of five years and a second of two years. According to estimates by the United Nations Educational, Scientific and Cultural Organization (UNESCO), in 2018/19 enrolment at pre-primary institutions was equivalent to 98% of pupils in the relevant age-group (males 98%; females 98%), while enrolment at primary schools included 99% of pupils in the relevant age-group (males 97%; females 100%). Secondary school enrolment in that year was equivalent to 97% of pupils in the relevant age-group (males 96%; females 98%). The education system provides for instruction in seven Asian languages. The Government exercises indirect control of the large private sector in secondary education (in 2005 only 70 of 188 schools were state administered). In 2021/22 spending on education represented 11% of total projected government expenditure.

Other Islands

RODRIGUES

The island of Rodrigues covers an area of 104 sq km. Its population was enumerated at 40,434 at the 2011 census. Formerly also known as Diego Ruys, Rodrigues is located 585 km east of the island of Mauritius, and is administered by a resident commissioner. Rodrigues is currently represented in the National Assembly by two members. In 2001 a constitutional amendment provided for the establishment of the Rodrigues Regional Assembly (RRA). The most recent elections to the RRA were held on 27 February 2022 at which the Organisation du Peuple Rodriguais secured eight of the Assembly's 17 seats, while the Alliance (FPR-PMSD) Rodriguais took five seats and the Lalians UPR-MIR-MMR the remaining four. Fishing and farming are the principal activities, while the main exports are cattle, salt fish, sheep, goats, pigs and onions.

Rodrigues Regional Assembly: Passenger Terminal Bldg, Fisherman Lane; tel. 831-0683; e-mail regionalassembly@intnet.mu; internet rra.govmu.org; Chair. JOSEPH CHRISTIAN LÉOPOLD; Chief Commissioner JOHNSON ROUSSETY.

THE LESSER DEPENDENCIES

The Lesser Dependencies (area 71 sq km, population enumerated at 274 at the 2011 census) are the Agalega Islands, two islands about 935 km north of Mauritius, and the Cargados Carajos Shoals (St Brandon Islands), 22 islets without permanent inhabitants, lying 370 km north-north-east. Mauritius also claims sovereignty over Tromelin Island, 556 km to the north-west. This claim is disputed by Madagascar, and also by France, which maintains an airstrip and weather station on the island.

Bibliography

Addison, J., and Hazareesingh, K. *A New History of Mauritius*. Oxford, ABC; Rose Hill, Editions de l'Océan Indien, 1991.

Bissoonoyal, B. *A Concise History of Mauritius*. Bombay, Bharatiya Vidya, 1963.

Bowman, L. W. *Mauritius: Democracy and Development in the Indian Ocean*. Boulder, CO, Westview Press, 1991.

Cuttaree, J. *Behind the Purple Curtain: A Political Autobiography*. Mauritius, ELP Publications, 2012.

Dukhira, C. D. *Mauritius and Local Government Management*. Oxford, ABC; Port Louis, Editions de l'Océan Indien; Bombay, LSG Press, 1992.

Favoreu, L. *L'Île Maurice*. Paris, Berger-Levrault, 1970.

Frankel, J. A. *Mauritius: African Success Story*. National Bureau of Economic Research Working Paper No. 16569, December 2010.

Grégoire, E., Hookoomsing, V. Y., and Lemoine G. *Maurice: de l'Île Sucrière à l'Île des Savoirs*. Mauritius, ELP Publications, 2011.

Mahadeo, T. *Mauritian Cultural Heritage*. Port Louis, Editions de l'Océan Indien, 1995.

Ng, P. C. *Alice in Dodoland: Looking to the Mauritian Economy*. Port Louis, PluriConseil, 2012.

Ramgoolam, Sir S. *Our Struggle: 20th Century Mauritius*. New Delhi, Vision Books, 1982.

Ramtohul, R., Eriksen, T. (Eds). *The Mauritian Paradox: Fifty Years of Development, Diversity and Democracy*. Réduit, University of Mauritius Press, 2018.

Selvon, S. *Historical Dictionary of Mauritius*. 2nd edn. Metuchen, NJ, Scarecrow Press, 1991.

Seetanah, B., Sannassee, R., and Nunkoo, R. (Eds). *Mauritius: A Successful Small Island Developing State*. Abingdon, Routledge, 2019.

Tang, V., Shaw, T., and Holden, M. (Eds). *Development and Sustainable Growth of Mauritius*. Cham, Palgrave Macmillan, 2019.

MAYOTTE

Physical and Social Geography

Mayotte forms part of the Comoros archipelago, which lies between the island of Madagascar and the east coast of the African mainland. The territory comprises a main island, Mayotte (Mahoré), and a number of smaller islands. The climate is tropical, and temperatures average between 24°C and 28°C (75°F to 82°F) throughout the year.

The population of Mayotte was 256,518 at the census of 2017, and this had risen, according to official estimates, to 299,348 by January 2022, giving a population density of 800.4 inhabitants per sq km. At that time 43.8% of Mayotte's opulation was under 14 years of age, while 53.6% of the population was aged between 15 and 64 years. The capital is Mamoudzou, with 71,437 inhabitants at the 2017 census. Other major towns include Koungou with 32,156 inhabitants and Dzaoudzi with 17,831.

History

Since the Comoros unilaterally declared independence in July 1975, Mayotte (Mahoré) has been administered separately by France. The independent Comoran state claims Mayotte as part of its territory and officially represents it in international organizations, including the United Nations (UN). In December 1976, following the holding of a referendum in Mayotte in April (in which the population voted to renounce the status of an overseas territory), France introduced the special status of Collectivité Territoriale (Territorial Collectivity) for the island.

Following a coup in the Comoros in May 1978, Mayotte rejected a proposal by the new Comoran Government that it should rejoin the other islands under a federal system, and reaffirmed its intention of remaining linked to France. In December 1979 the Assemblée Nationale (National Assembly) in Paris, France, approved legislation that extended Mayotte's special status for another five years, during which the islanders were to be consulted. In October 1984, however, the National Assembly further extended Mayotte's status, and the referendum on the island's future was postponed indefinitely. The UN General Assembly adopted several resolutions reaffirming the sovereignty of the Comoros over the island, and urging France to reach an agreement with the Comoran Government as soon as possible. The Organization of African Unity (now the African Union—AU) endorsed this view.

At the elections to the National Assembly in March 1986, Henry Jean-Baptiste, representing an alliance of the Centre des Démocrates Sociaux (CDS) and the Union pour la Démocratie Française (UDF), was elected as deputy for Mayotte (one representative from Mayotte was also elected to the Sénat/Senate in Paris—the number of senators from Mayotte was increased to two in 2003).

In November 1989 the island's directly elected legislature, the Conseil Général (General Council), demanded that the French Government introduce measures to curb immigration to Mayotte from neighbouring islands, particularly from the Comoros, as the growing number of immigrants was heightening racial tension. In June 1992 increasing concern about the number of Comorans seeking employment on the island resulted in further attacks against the immigrants. In early September representatives of the main political party on Mayotte, the Mouvement Populaire Mahorais (MPM), met the French Prime Minister, Pierre Bérégovoy, to request the reintroduction of entry visas to restrict immigration from the Comoros. Later that month the MPM organized a boycott of Mayotte's participation in the French referendum on the Treaty on European Union, in support of the provision of entry visas.

At elections to the National Assembly in March 1993, Jean-Baptiste was returned with 53.4% of the votes cast, while Mansour Kamardine, the Secretary-General of the local branch of the right-wing French mainland party, the Rassemblement pour la République (RPR), obtained 44.3% of the vote. Elections to the General Council (which was enlarged from 17 to 19 members) took place in March 1994; the MPM retained 12 seats, while the local branch of the RPR secured four seats and independent candidates three. During an official visit to Mayotte in November, the French Prime Minister, Edouard Balladur, announced the reintroduction of entry visas as a requirement for Comoran nationals, and the adoption of a number of security measures, in an effort to reduce illegal immigration to the island. None the less, illegal immigration from the Comoros continued to be a major concern for the authorities on Mayotte. The relative prosperity of Mayotte was thought to have prompted separatist movements on the Comoran islands of Nzwani and Mwali to demand the restoration of French rule, and subsequently to declare their independence from the Comoros in August 1997.

In elections to the French Senate in September 1995, the incumbent MPM representative, Marcel Henry, was returned with a large majority. Partial elections to fill nine seats in the General Council were held in March 1997; the MPM secured three seats (losing two that it had previously held), the RPR won three seats, the local Parti Socialiste (PS) one, and independent right-wing candidates two. In elections to the National Assembly, Jean-Baptiste, representing an alliance of the UDF and the Force Démocrate, defeated Kamardine, securing 51.7% of the votes cast in the second round of voting, which took place in June.

Meanwhile, uncertainty remained over the future status of Mayotte. In April 1998 a commission charged with examining the issue submitted its report, which concluded that the existing status of Territorial Collectivity was no longer appropriate, but did not advocate an alternative. In May the MPM declared its support for an adapted form of departmental administration, and urged the French authorities to schedule a referendum. In May 1999 draft legislation was introduced to the National Assembly, which proposed the holding of a referendum regarding the island's future before the end of the year. In August, following negotiations with the French Secretary of State for Overseas Departments and Territories, Jean-Jack Queyranne, Mayotte members of the RPR and the PS, as well as the leader of the MPM, Younoussa Bamana, signed a draft document providing for the transformation of Mayotte into a Collectivité Départementale (Departmental Collectivity), subject to approval at a referendum. However, both Henry and Jean-Baptiste rejected the document. The two politicians subsequently left the MPM and formed a new political party, the Mouvement Départementaliste Mahorais (MDM), while reiterating their demands that Mayotte be granted the status of a full Département d'Outre-mer (Overseas Department). Following the approval of Mayotte's proposed new designation as a Departmental Collectivity by the General Council (by 14 votes to five) and the municipal councils, an accord to this effect was signed by Queyranne and political representatives of Mayotte on 27 January 2000. On 2 July a referendum was held, in which the population of Mayotte voted overwhelmingly in favour of the January accord, granting Mayotte the status of Departmental

Collectivity for a period of 10 years. The French Parlement (Parliament) approved Mayotte's new status on 11 July 2001.

At elections to the General Council held in March 2001, no party achieved a majority. The MPM experienced significant losses, with only four of its candidates being elected, while the RPR won five seats, the Mouvement des Citoyens (MDC) two, the MDM one, the PS one and various right-wing independent candidates six. Bamana was re-elected as President of the General Council (head of government).

At the first round of the French presidential election in April 2002, Jacques Chirac, the candidate of the RPR, received the highest number of votes on Mayotte (and overall), winning 43% of votes cast on the island; the second round, held in May, was also won by Chirac, who secured 88.3% of votes cast on the island, defeating the candidate of the extreme right-wing Front National (FN), Jean-Marie Le Pen. At elections to the National Assembly, held in June, Kamardine, representing the recently formed Union pour la Majorité Présidentielle (UMP, which incorporated the RPR, the Démocratie Libérale and significant elements of the UDF), defeated the MDM-UDF candidate, Siadi Vita. In November the UMP was renamed the Union pour un Mouvement Populaire (retaining the same acronym).

At elections to the General Council in March 2004, the UMP won eight seats in alliance with the MPM, which secured one seat, while the MDM and the MDC, also in alliance, obtained five and two seats, respectively; independent candidates were elected to the remaining three seats. With the election of Saïd Omar Oili, an independent, as President of the General Council on 2 April, executive power was transferred from the Prefect—the appointed representative of the French Government—to the Council. (Although the position of Prefect was scheduled to be abolished by 2007, it still remained in existence—and with an incumbent—as of September 2022.)

In May 2005 a national referendum on ratification of the European Union (EU) constitutional treaty was held. More than 80% of those who took part in the poll on Mayotte voted in favour of adopting the treaty; however, it was ultimately rejected by a majority of French voters.

Nicolas Sarkozy of the UMP secured 30.5% of the votes cast on Mayotte in the first round of the 2007 French presidential election, held in April. Although Ségolène Royal of the PS won 60.0% of the votes cast on the island in the second round, held in May, Sarkozy was elected to the presidency. At elections to the National Assembly conducted in June, the incumbent deputy, Kamardine, was defeated by Abdoulatifou Aly, who was affiliated to the centrist Mouvement Démocrate (MoDem), which had been formed following the presidential election by François Bayrou, the erstwhile leader of the UDF, to oppose Sarkozy's UMP.

Meanwhile, in February 2007 new legislation approved by the National Assembly introduced statutory and institutional measures granting Mayotte many of the powers afforded to territories with full overseas departmental status, with the exception of certain fiscal, financial and social welfare powers. This followed a constitutional amendment in 2003 whereby Mayotte acquired the status of Collectivité d'Outre-mer (Overseas Collectivity) and expedited the process towards the territory becoming an Overseas Department. The 2007 legislation provided a framework for measures to facilitate the transfer of full fiscal control to Mayotte by January 2014.

Elections for 10 of the 19 seats in the General Council took place over two rounds in March 2008. The UMP, the MDM and the Nouvel Elan pour Mayotte (founded in 2007 by Omar Oili) each secured two seats, the PS won one and three seats were taken by independent candidates. Later in March 2008 Ahamed Attoumani Douchina was elected to replace Oili as President of the General Council.

In April 2008 the General Council adopted a resolution providing for the transition of Mayotte's status from that of Overseas Collectivity to Overseas Department. The resolution required that a public consultation on the matter be held within 12 months. At the subsequent referendum, which was held on 29 March 2009, 95.2% of participants approved of Mayotte attaining the status of an Overseas Department within the French Republic (in contradiction to the recognition of the island by the AU and the Comoran Government as an inseparable part of the Comoran state). Some 61% of the electorate took part in the ballot. In October 2010 the French Senate endorsed the departmentalization of Mayotte and the following month the National Assembly approved the requisite legislation.

On 31 March 2011 Mayotte officially became the 101st Department of France and the fifth Overseas Department. On 3 April Daniel Zaïdani was elected President of the General Council. In October the authorities of Mayotte made an official request to the EU to recognize Mayotte as a Région Ultrapériphérique (RUP—Outermost Region) of France. Recognition as an RUP would allow Mayotte to draw upon EU funds to aid its economic development. In July 2012 the European Council published its decision that, effective from 1 January 2014, Mayotte would cease to be classified as an overseas country or territory and would acquire the status of RUP.

Meanwhile, persistent unrest on the island caused by the continuing high cost of living led to a 44-day general strike in October and early November 2011, followed by a further two days' shutdown in December. Following talks between the trade unions, employers and the Government (mediated by former Prefect Denis Robin), in late December an agreement was signed, imposing until March 2012 a reduction in the price of 11 staple goods; in addition, families with modest incomes were to receive food tokens.

In the first round of the 2012 French presidential election, held in April, President Sarkozy received 48.7% of the votes cast on Mayotte, while François Hollande of the PS secured 36.6%; both proceeded to a second ballot, held in early May. Sarkozy narrowly defeated Hollande in the second Mayotte vote, receiving 51.0% of the votes cast, compared with 49.1% for Hollande. However, Hollande triumphed nationally and was sworn in as President in mid-May. In the French legislative elections held in June, Mayotte's representation in the National Assembly was increased to two seats; these were won by Ibrahim Aboubacar, representing the PS, and Boinali Saïd, an independent left-wing candidate.

The French Minister of Overseas Territories, Victorin Lurel, visited Mayotte in July 2012 to hold discussions with the local authorities regarding the high cost of living on the island. A bill to address the problem of inflated prices (and related social unrest) in the French Overseas Territories was promulgated in November. Most notably, the legislation provided for the imposition of price controls on a range of staple goods.

In October 2013, in response to further public sector strikes, Lurel, during a visit to Mayotte, signed a decree approving price indexation for public employees of up to 5%, with retroactive effect from 1 January; nevertheless, industrial unrest continued. In November Lurel announced a further decree, which was to enter into force on 1 January 2014, to regulate fuel prices in the Overseas Departments. The French Minister of the Interior, Bernard Cazeneuve, visited Mayotte in June 2014 for discussions with island officials on new measures to combat illegal immigration. According to Cazeneuve, annual deportations from Mayotte averaged around 16,000.

Departmental elections were held in March 2015, at which, in accordance with national legislation adopted in May 2013, the General Council was renamed the Conseil Départemental (Departmental Council) and was expanded to comprise 26 members. Of these, 10 were representatives of the UMP, eight represented a grouping of right-wing parties, four were from the Union Démocrates et Indépendants, and four represented a grouping of left-wing parties. In early April 2015 Soibahadine Ibrahim Ramadani of the UMP replaced Zaïdani as head of government, assuming the new title of President of the Departmental Council.

During a visit to Mayotte in June 2015 French Prime Minister Manuel Valls signed a 10-year institutional and economic reform agreement ('Mayotte 2025') and a €378.5m. infrastructural development plan for the territory. The Prime Minister also announced the deployment of additional police officers to the island to help tackle crime and illegal immigration.

During March–April 2016 trade unions organized a number of protests in Mayotte (including another general strike) to demand that the island's working conditions, living standards and social benefits be aligned with those of mainland France. Amid rising social tension, riots erupted in Mamoudzou in mid-April, prompting the Hollande administration to deploy police reinforcements to the island. Later that month, following talks with the French Government, the unions agreed to suspend their protest action. After a meeting with Mayotte officials in late April, Prime Minister Valls announced that the island would be granted financial assistance totalling over €50m. In the following month Cazeneuve stated that, as part of a campaign to counter rising levels of violent crime on Mayotte, the local police presence would be 'significantly increased', and in June the Hollande administration presented a new 25-point security plan for the territory. A wave of anti-immigrant violence during the first half of 2016, which resulted in the expulsion of hundreds of Comoran migrants from their homes and the destruction of their settlements, compounded the island's unstable security climate. The French Government condemned the xenophobic attacks and announced that the perpetrators of the violence would be prosecuted.

In January 2017 the Senate adopted further legislation aimed at reducing economic inequality between mainland France and its Overseas Territories. The Loi Egalité Réelle Outre-mer (Real Overseas Equality Act), which was promulgated in February, was intended to address the high cost of living and the lack of socioeconomic development in the territories.

In the first round of the 2017 French presidential election, held on 23 April, François Fillon, the candidate of Les Républicains (as the UMP had been rebranded in May 2015), took the largest number of votes in Mayotte (32.6%), while Marine Le Pen of the FN received 27.2%. Le Pen was placed second nationally and contested the run-off election on 7 May against Emmanuel Macron of the En Marche! movement (subsequently restyled as La République En Marche—REM). Macron secured a decisive victory in the poll, winning 66.1% of the valid votes cast nationally (and 57.2% of those cast in Mayotte). In the elections to the National Assembly on 11 and 18 June, Mayotte's two seats were won by Ramlati Ali, representing the PS—although she subsequently joined REM—and the first female deputy from Mayotte, and Kamardine, representing Les Républicains. Ali's victory was annulled by the Constitutional Council in January 2018, owing to polling irregularities, but she was re-elected in a re-run of the vote, held on 18 and 25 March.

Meanwhile, in mid-September 2017 the French and Comoran foreign ministers signed a 'road map' agreement to encourage greater bilateral co-operation. However, the agreement provoked anti-immigration demonstrations in Mayotte as it included a clause suggesting that visa controls on Comoran nationals entering the territory would be eliminated. In response to the unrest, and to pressure from the territory's elected officials, at the end of September the Macron administration suspended implementation of the 'road map'. In March 2018 the Comoran authorities announced that undocumented Comoran migrants who had been deported from Mayotte would no longer be permitted to return to the Comoros. The French authorities consequently suspended the issuance of visas to Comoran nationals seeking to enter French territory (including Mayotte). These measures were rescinded in November following bilateral negotiations.

The Assises des Outre-Mer, a series of public and institutional consultations on the socioeconomic development needs of the overseas territories, commenced in October 2017. In the subsequent report, which President Macron presented in June 2018, it was stated that the French Government's priorities in Mayotte included security, immigration and health care. The policies that emerged from the Assises des Outre-Mer were expected to replace those devised as part of the 'Mayotte 2025' plan.

A series of at times violent anti-immigration protests took place during February–April 2018, with the demonstrators accusing migrants of overstretching local public services and contributing to rising levels of crime. Xenophobic attacks against Comoran migrants were also reported. In response, the French Government announced a range of new security measures to combat crime and illegal immigration, and police reinforcements were deployed to the island. Additional development funding was also promised. None the less,

demonstrations continued to be organized—albeit sporadically—throughout 2018.

President Macron, Minister of the Interior Christophe Castaner and Minister of Overseas Territories Annick Girardin all visited Mayotte during 2019. Discussions with local officials focused on the island's ongoing immigration, security and socioeconomic issues, and the Macron administration pledged to dispatch additional police and patrol boats to the territory, to establish a new police station in Mamoudzou, and to expand aerial surveillance operations. In addition, in July Mayotte concluded a 'convergence and transformation contract' with the French Government, which provided for €1,600m. of development financing for the island during 2019–22. Later that month France and the Comoros signed a bilateral framework agreement; in exchange for €150m. of French aid, the Comoran authorities agreed to introduce measures to restrict unlawful migratory flows between the Comoros and Mayotte.

In mid-March 2020 Mayotte reported its first case of COVID-19, which had first been detected in the People's Republic of China in late 2019 and subsequently became a global pandemic. The French Government declared a national state of health emergency on 23 March 2020. The territory's airport was closed to commercial flights at the end of March, and various other social and economic measures were implemented in that month in an effort to curb the spread of the virus. Amid growing concerns over the capacity of Mayotte's health system to cope with the increasing number of cases of COVID-19, in May Girardin made a surprise visit to the island bringing medical supplies and personnel. Following the detection of a case of a variant of the virus in Mayotte, in mid-January 2021 all international air and sea links to the territory were suspended. Later that month a COVID-19 vaccination programme was initiated on Mayotte. Strict lockdown measures were again imposed in early February, while the French Government sent reinforcements of medical personnel to the territory and patients in intensive care were evacuated to the neighbouring island of Réunion. Although some of the lockdown restrictions were eased in mid-2021, the authorities reintroduced them in December to halt the highly contagious Omicron variant. The state of health emergency was finally lifted on 2 March 2022. According to World Health Organization figures, 40,204 confirmed cases of COVID-19 had been reported in Mayotte by 19 September, with 187 fatalities, a rate of 65.3 per 100,000 of the population. By 12 September 2022 46.8% of the population had received two doses of the vaccine.

Meanwhile, levels of crime and unrest in Mayotte remained high. Three nights of violence on the island of Pamandzi in January 2021 left three people dead, including two minors, prompting the French Government to dispatch additional police reinforcements to the territory. In February 2022 France again sent extra security to Mayotte to tackle the rise in violent crime being committed by youth gangs. However, further gang violence occurred in June, with several police officers wounded as they attempted to restore order.

At elections to the Departmental Council held on 20 and 27 June 2021, a grouping of centrist parties secured 12 of the 26 seats; of the remainder, six were won by a grouping of right-wing parties, four by Les Républicains, two by a grouping of left-wing parties and two by the Union au Centre et à Gauche. On 1 July Ben Issa Ousseni of Les Républicains defeated Maymounati Moussa Ahamadi (the first woman to run for the post of head of government), by 14 votes to 12, to be elected as the new President of the Departmental Council, replacing Ramadani.

In the first round of the 2022 French presidential election, held on 10 April, Le Pen of the Rassemblement National (as the FN had been restyled in 2018) secured 42.7% of the votes cast in Mayotte, while Jean-Luc Mélenchon, representing La France Insoumise, won 24.0%. Le Pen was placed second nationally and contested the run-off poll on 24 April against Macron (REM). Le Pen attracted 59.1% of the vote in Mayotte, but was defeated nationally. In the elections to the National Assembly on 12 and 19 June, incumbent deputy Kamardine retained his seat for Les Républicains, while Estelle Youssouffa—a former journalist representing Divers Droite—won Mayotte's second seat.

Economy

Mayotte's gross domestic product (GDP) per head was €9,706 in 2021, according to official figures. Total GDP in 2021 amounted to an estimated €2,700m. Between the censuses of 2012 and 2017 the population of Mayotte increased at an average annual rate of 3.8%. The official population of Mayotte was 256,518 at the census of 5 September 2017. At mid-2022 the population totalled 286,254, according to United Nations (UN) estimates. In 2019, according to the French national statistics institute, 48% of Mayotte's inhabitants were foreigners (the vast majority being Comoran), around one-half of whom were illegal immigrants.

The economy of Mayotte is based mainly on agriculture. In 2017 some 1.5% of the employed labour force were actively engaged in this sector. Vanilla and ylang ylang (an ingredient of perfume) are the main export crops, but exports are limited by production costs and the local market is small. Mayotte imports large quantities of foodstuffs, which comprised 22.1% of the value of total imports in 2019. Cassava, maize and pigeon peas are cultivated for domestic consumption; although rice is widely eaten, there is little domestic production. More than 90% of farms grow bananas, often together with coconuts (grown for their milk and oil, both of which are used in cooking); combined, banana and coconut plantations occupy around 45% of agricultural land (approximately 20,000 ha in total, some 55% of the surface area of Mayotte). Mangoes are also widespread, and around one-third of mango trees grow wild. Livestock farming (of cattle, goats—for meat—and chickens) and fishing are also important activities. Aquaculture was first introduced in 1998, and by 2005 there were five producers catering mainly to the export market. Mayotte's total fishing catch amounted to an estimated 1,237 metric tons in 2020, according to the Food and Agriculture Organization of the UN. Industry (which is dominated by the construction sector) engaged 14.1% of the employed population in 2017. Total electricity production was 374.6m. kWh in 2020, while consumption of electricity in that year amounted to 344.3m. kWh. There are no mineral resources on the island. Services engaged 84.3% of the employed population in 2017. Tourist arrivals (excluding cruise ship passengers) totalled 65,500 in 2019; receipts from tourism in 2006 amounted to €16.3m.

In 2020 Mayotte's total budgetary revenue was €394.8m., while total expenditure was €349.8m., giving a surplus of €45.0m. The annual rate of inflation averaged 0.8% in 2010–19; consumer prices contracted by 0.2% in 2019, before increasing by 1.2% in 2020 and 1.8% in 2021. As Mayotte's labour force has continued to grow, owing to elevated birth and immigration levels, the persistently high unemployment rate (30.1% in April–June 2021) is a cause of concern and is particularly prevalent among the island's youth. The territory suffers from a chronic high trade deficit, owing to its reliance on imports, and is largely dependent on French aid. The principal source of imports in 2020 was France (56.9%); another major supplier was the United Arab Emirates (5.5%). France was also the single principal market for exports in 2020 (taking some 25% of exports); other significant purchasers were the following five countries of the Indian Ocean region—the Comoros, Réunion, Madagascar, Mauritius and South Africa—which together accounted for 35.9% of total exports. The principal imports in 2021 were capital goods (providing 29.8% of the total), non-

durable consumer goods (29.4%), intermediate goods (23.1%) and energy products (10.2%). The principal exports in that year were capital goods (41.4%), non-durable consumer goods (27.1%) and intermediate goods (10.0%). In 2021 Mayotte recorded an increased trade deficit of €867.1m. (imports €874.1m., exports €7.0m.)

The island's drinking water supply system and waste water sanitation network are coming under increasing pressure, owing to the growing population and rising urbanization. In December 2015 the Schéma Directeur d'Aménagement et de Gestion des Eaux (SDAGE) was approved for the period 2016–21. The plan, aimed at improving the management of water resources on Mayotte, allocated €622m. in funds to provide, *inter alia*, equipment for the treatment of waste water and rainwater. The SDAGE for 2022–27 was approved in April 2022, highlighting the need to prevent waste and tackle pollution; it will cost over €233m. (the figure cited after 70% of the plan had been costed).

Mayotte's economic prospects are hampered by the small size of its private sector, high levels of public debt, an uncompetitive agricultural sector and undeveloped tourism infrastructure. From late 2011 public sector strikes disrupted trade and deterred visitors; despite measures undertaken by the French Government to address social discontent by reducing inequalities with mainland France, industrial unrest has persisted. After the European Union (EU) granted Mayotte the status of Région Ultrapériphérique (Outermost Region) of France on 1 January 2014, the island was expected to benefit from increased development funding. The economy expanded by 6.8% in 2015 and by 7.2% in 2016, with growth driven primarily by high levels of domestic demand—a consequence of the territory's rising population. However, trade, construction, tourism and agricultural indicators for 2015–16 were largely mixed or negative. Although the construction and agricultural sectors were subdued in 2017, GDP rose by an estimated 7.5% in that year, supported by an increase in exports, investment, household and government consumption, and visitor arrivals. Social unrest during early 2018 caused widespread economic disruption, although an upturn in household consumption helped to generate economic growth of around 3.2% in that year. The economy grew by 6.6% in 2019. The COVID-19 pandemic, which emerged in early 2020, had a significant impact on Mayotte's economy and the standard of living of its poorest inhabitants. The important tourism sector was effectively shut down as a result of COVID-related travel restrictions and an economic recession was widely predicted. In March the French Government established a solidarity fund to support companies severely affected by the crisis and in April Minister of Overseas Territories Annick Girardin announced the creation of a support system for families in the form of financial aid or direct food aid for the duration of the health emergency. In November the Departmental Council voted in favour of investing €80m. towards a €250m. project to extend the runway at Mayotte's airport, which would make the territory more accessible to the lucrative long-haul flight market. The Departmental Council's budget for 2021, approved in April, showed a gradual reduction in the support measures introduced since the start of the pandemic.

Statistical Survey

Source (unless otherwise stated): Institut National de la Statistique et des Etudes Economiques (INSEE) de Mayotte; Z.I. Kawéni, BP 1362, 97600 Mamoudzou; tel. 269-61-36-35; e-mail antenne-mayotte@insee.fr; internet www.insee.fr.

AREA AND POPULATION

Area: 374 sq km (144 sq miles).

Population: 212,645 at census of 21 August 2012; 256,518 at census of 2017. *2022* (official estimate at 1 January): 299,348.

Density (at 1 January 2022): 800.4 per sq km.

Population by Age and Sex ('000, official estimates at 1 January 2022): *0–14 years:* 131.0 (males 65.1, females 65.9); *15–64 years:* 160.3 (males 73.5, females 86.8); *65 years and over:* 8.0 (males 4.0, females 4.0); *Total* 299.3 (males 142.6, females 156.7).

Population by Place of Origin (2002, before adjustment for double counting): Mayotte 103,705; France 6,323; Comoros 45,057; Madagascar-Mauritius-Seychelles 4,601; Total (incl. others) 160,301.

Principal Towns (population of communes at 2017 census): Mamoudzou (capital) 71,437; Koungou 32,156; Dzaoudzi 17,831; Dembeni 15,848; Bandraboua 13,989; Tsingoni 13,934; Pamandzi 11,442; Sada 11,156; Bandrele 10,282; Ouangani 10,203.

Births and Deaths (2021): Registered live births 10,329 (birth rate 34.0 per 1,000); Registered deaths 1,103 (death rate 3.4 per 1,000).

Life expectancy (years at birth, 2021): Males 72.5; females 73.9.

Employment (persons aged 15 years and over, 2017 census): Agriculture and fishing 613; Construction 3,527; Other industry 2,144; Wholesale and retail trade 4,350; Hotels and restaurants 888; Transport, storage and telecommunications 2,342; Financial activities and real estate 496; Public administration 10,125; Education, health and social care 12,121; Other services 3,534; *Total employed* 40,140. *2021* (labour force survey, persons aged 15 years and over, April–June): Total employed 51,000; Unemployed 22,000; Total labour force 73,000.

HEALTH AND WELFARE

Total Fertility Rate (children per woman, 2021): 4.4.

Physicians (per 1,000 head, 1997): 0.4.

Hospital Beds (per 1,000 head, 2007): 1.5.

Note: For sources and definitions, see Health and Welfare Statistics: Sources and Definitions section (europaworld.com/credits).

AGRICULTURE, ETC.

Livestock (2003): Cattle 17,235; Chickens 80,565; Goats 22,811.

Fishing (metric tons, live weight, all capture, 2020, FAO estimates): Skipjack tuna 123; Yellowfin tuna 156; Swordfish 41; Other marine fishes 918; *Total catch* 1,237. Source: FAO.

INDUSTRY

Electrical Energy (million kWh): 367 in 2019 (Source: Électricité de Mayotte, Mamoudzou).

FINANCE

Currency and Exchange Rates: 100 cent = 1 euro. *Sterling and Dollar Equivalents* (31 May 2022): £1 sterling = €1.175; US $1 = 0.933; €10 = £8.51 = US $10.71. *Average Exchange Rate* (euros per US dollar): 0.8933 in 2019; 0.8755 in 2020, 0.8455 in 2021. The French franc was used until the end of February 2002. Euro notes and coins were introduced on 1 January 2002, and the euro became the sole legal tender from 18 February.

Budget of the Collectivity (€ million, 2020): Total revenue 394.8 (Current revenue 316.8, Capital revenue 78.0); Total expenditure 349.8 (Current expenditure 260.6, Capital expenditure 89.2) (Source: Institut d'Emission des Départements d'Outre-mer, *Rapport Annuel 2021*).

French State Expenditure (€ million, 2021): Direct expenditure 1,163.1; Indirect expenditure 346.1; *Total expenditure* 1,509.2 (Source: Institut d'Emission des Départements d'Outre-mer, *Rapport Annuel 2021*).

Cost of Living (Consumer Price Index; base: December 2006 = 100): 118.8 in 2017; 119.2 in 2018; 119.0 in 2019.

Expenditure on the Gross Domestic Product (€ million, 2019, INSEE estimates): Government final consumption expenditure 1,655; Private final consumption expenditure 1,148; Gross fixed capital formation 561; *Total domestic expenditure* 3,364; Net exports of goods and services –704; *GDP in purchasers' values* 2,660.

EXTERNAL TRADE

Principal Commodities (€ million, 2021): *Imports:* Capital goods 260.1; Durable consumer goods 46.7; Non-durable consumer goods 257.4; Intermediate goods 201.9; Energy products 89.0; Total (incl. others) 874.1. *Exports:* Capital goods 2.9; Durable consumer goods 0.4; Non-durable consumer goods 1.9; Intermediate goods 0.7; Total (incl. others) 7.0.

Principal Trading Partners (€ million, 2019): *Imports:* Belgium 10.9; Bahrain 62.1; China, People's Republic 29.6; France (Metropolitan) 404.0; Germany 7.9; Italy 9.6; Netherlands 8.6; Poland 10.5; Spain 10.9; Türkiye 10.1; United Arab Emirates 14.2; Thailand 13.6; Viet Nam 13.5; Total (incl. others) 697.5. *Exports* (incl. re-exports): Total 11.6. Note: The principal markets for exports are France (Metropolitan—some 44% of exports in 2019), Comoros and Réunion. *2021:* Total imports 874.1 (Belgium 18.3; Bahrain 20.6; France—Metropolitan 485.0; Germany 21.6; Italy 19.3; Netherlands 12.1; Poland 15.4; Spain 10.8; Türkiye 16.4; United Arab Emirates 62.1); Total exports 7.0.

Source: Institut d'Emission des Départements d'Outre-mer, *Rapport Annuel 2021*.

TRANSPORT

Road Traffic (new vehicle registrations, 2021): Private vehicles 2,059; Commercial vehicles 463; Other motor vehicles and public transport 139.

Shipping (2014 unless otherwise indicated): *Maritime Traffic:* Vessel movements 530 (2005); Goods unloaded 381,043 metric tons; Goods loaded 45,816 metric tons; Passengers 36,872 (arrivals 9,607, departures 27,265) (Source: Institut d'Emission des Départements d'Outre-mer, *Rapport Annuel 2015*).

Civil Aviation (2021): Passengers carried 255,289; Freight carried 2,988 metric tons; Post carried 1,011 metric tons (Source: Institut d'Emission des Départements d'Outre-mer, *Rapport Annuel 2021*).

TOURISM

Foreign Tourist Arrivals (excl. cruise ship passengers): 61,800 in 2017; 56,300 in 2018; 65,500 in 2019.

Foreign Tourist Arrivals by Country of Residence (2019): France (metropolitan) 38,700; Réunion 24,400; Total (incl. others) 65,500.

Tourism Receipts (€ million): 13.7 in 2004; 14.5 in 2005; 16.3 in 2006.

COMMUNICATIONS MEDIA

Telephones ('000 main lines in use, 2015): 10.0.

Mobile Telephone Subscriptions ('000, 2008): 48.1.

Internet Users (% of population, 2000): 1.2.

Source: International Telecommunication Union.

EDUCATION

Pre-primary (2020/21 unless otherwise indicated): 71 schools; 17,680 pupils (2018/19).

Primary (2020/21 unless otherwise indicated): 140 schools; 37,102 pupils (2018/19).

General Secondary (2020/21): 36 schools; 47,644 pupils.

Vocational and Technical (2015/16 unless otherwise indicated): 10 institutions; 11,656 students (2013/14).

Students Studying in France or Réunion (2009): Secondary 1,452; Higher 2,253; *Total* 3,705.

Teaching Staff (2020/21 unless otherwise indicated): Primary 3,024; Secondary 3,180; Higher 16 (2013).

Directory

The Government
(October 2022)

HEAD OF STATE

President: EMMANUEL MACRON (took office 14 May 2017; re-elected 24 April 2022).

Prefect: THIERRY SUQUET.

DEPARTMENTAL ADMINISTRATION

President of the Departmental Council: BEN ISSA OUSSENI, 8 blvd Halidi Sélémani, BP 101, 97645 Mamoudzou; tel. 269-66-10-00; internet www.cg976.fr.

Election, Departmental Council, 20 and 27 June 2021

Party	Seats
Divers Centre	12
Divers Droite	6
Les Républicains	4
Divers Gauche	2
Union au Centre et à Gauche	2
Total	26

REPRESENTATIVES TO THE FRENCH PARLIAMENT

Deputies to the French National Assembly: ESTELLE YOUSSOUFFA (Divers), MANSOUR KAMARDINE (Les Républicains).

Representatives to the French Senate: THANI MOHAMED SOILIHI (La République En Marche), ABDALLAH HASSANI (La République En Marche).

GOVERNMENT DEPARTMENTS

Office of the Prefect: BP 676, Kawéni, 97600 Mamoudzou; tel. 269-63-50-00; e-mail communication@mayotte.pref.gouv.fr; internet www.mayotte.gouv.fr.

Department of the Economy, Employment, Labour and Solidarity: 3 rue Mahabou, BP 174, 97600 Mamoudzou; tel. 269-61-16-57; e-mail 976.direction@dieccte.gouv.fr; internet www.mayotte.dieccte.gouv.fr.

Department of the Environment, Planning and Housing: BP 109, 97600 Mamoudzou; tel. 269-61-12-54; internet www.mayotte.developpement-durable.gouv.fr.

Department of Food, Agriculture and Forestry: 15 rue Mariaze, BP 103, 97600 Mamoudzou; tel. 269-61-12-13; e-mail daaf976@agriculture.gouv.fr; internet daaf.mayotte.agriculture.gouv.fr.

Department of Youth, Sports and Social Cohesion: 13 rue Mariazé, BP 104, 97600 Mamoudzou; tel. 269-61-60-50; internet mayotte.drjscs.gouv.fr.

Political Organizations

Fédération du Rassemblement National (RN): 97640 Sada; tel. 639-05-17-57; e-mail contact@rassemblement-national976.fr; internet rassemblementnational.fr/federation/976-mayotte; Regional Sec. ALI-MANSOIB SOIHIBOU.

Fédération du Mouvement National Républicain (MNR) de Mayotte: 15 rue des Réfugiers, 97615 Pamandzi; tel. 269-60-33-21; Departmental Sec. ABDOU MIHIDJAY.

Mouvement pour la Developpement de Mayotte (MDM): 97610 Dzaoudzi; tel. 639-69-58-33; e-mail mdm.mayotte@yahoo.fr; internet fb.com/Mouvement-pour-le-Développement-de-Mayotte-MDM-102069717822757; Pres. MOIZARI AHAMADA.

Parti Socialiste (PS): pl. Boinatavi, 97680 Combani; e-mail abdou-alimlanao@orange.fr; internet fb.com/partisocialiste.mayotte; local branch of the metropolitan party; Fed. Sec. MOULA ISSOUF MADI.

Les Républicains de Mayotte: rue Massakini, 97600 Mamoudzou; tel. 269-61-64-64; e-mail mansour@mkamardine.fr; internet fb.com/lesrepublicains.976; known as the Union pour un Mouvement Populaire until May 2015; centre-right; local branch of the metropolitan party; Departmental Pres. MANSOUR KAMARDINE.

Renaissance: Mamoudzou; e-mail aminat.hariti@en-marche.fr; internet dpt.en-marche.fr/mayotte.

Judicial System

Palais de Justice: Immeuble Espace, BP 106 (Kawéni), 97600 Mamoudzou; tel. 269-61-11-15.

Tribunal Judiciaire: 16 rue de l'hôpital, BP 106, 97600 Mamoudzou; tel. 269-61-11-15; e-mail accueil.tj-mamoudzou@justice.fr; Pres. CATHERINE VANNIER.

Procureur de la République: YANN LE BRIS.

Religion

Muslims comprise about 98% of the population. Most of the remainder are Christians, mainly Roman Catholics.

CHRISTIANITY

The Roman Catholic Church

Mayotte is within the jurisdiction of the Apostolic Administrator of the Comoros.

Office of the Apostolic Administrator: 7 rue de l'Hôpital, BP 1012, 97600 Mamoudzou; tel. 269-61-11-53.

ISLAM

Conseil Représentatif des Musulmans à Mayotte (CREMM): e-mail info@cremm-mayotte.fr; internet www.cremm-mayotte.fr; Pres. BAKAR HAMADA.

The Press

Flash Infos Mayotte: Société Mahoraise de Presse, 7 rue Salamani Cavani/M'Tsapéré, BP 60, 97600 Mamoudzou; tel. 269-61-20-04; e-mail flash-infos@somapresse.com; internet www.mayottehebdo.com; f. 1999; owned by Somapresse; daily e-mail bulletin; Dir LAURENT CANAVATE.

Horizon Austral: Société Mahoraise de Presse, 7 rue Salamani Cavani/M'Tsapéré, BP 60, 97600 Mamoudzou; tel. 269-61-20-04; e-mail contact@mayottehebdo.com; internet www.mayottehebdo.com; f. 2007; owned by Somapresse; Dir of Publication LAURENT CANAVATE.

Mayotte Hebdo: Société Mahoraise de Presse, 7 rue Salamani Cavani/M'Tsapéré, BP 60, 97600 Mamoudzou; tel. 269-61-20-04; e-mail redaction@somapresse.com; internet www.mayottehebdo.com; f. 2000; weekly; French; incl. the economic supplement *Mayotte Eco* and cultural supplement *Tounda* (weekly); owned by Somapresse; Dir LAURENT CANAVATE.

Broadcasting and Communications

TELECOMMUNICATIONS

BJT Partners: Mamoudzou; internet www.bjtpartners.com; mobile telephone operator.

Only—Mayotte: 97600 Mamoudzou; tel. 639260221; e-mail infotelco@trm.yt; internet only.yt; mobile telephone operator.

Orange Mayotte: rue de la Grande Traversée, Kawéni, 97600 Mamoudzou; tel. 69393900; internet mayotte.orange.fr; Dir JEAN-MARC ESCALETTES.

SFR Mayotte: BP 418, Kawéni, 97600 Mamoudzou; tel. 639692000; e-mail scclient@srr.fr; internet www.sfr.yt; Dir CHRISTOPHE HULIN.

RADIO AND TELEVISION

Mayotte 1ère: piste de la Carrière, Les Hauts-Vallons, 97600 Mamoudzou; tel. 269-60-10-17; e-mail mayotte1erecvous@gmail.com; internet la1ere.francetvinfo.fr/mayotte; f. 1977; acquired by Groupe France Télévisions in 2004; fmrly Réseau France Outre-mer, name changed as above in 2010; radio broadcasts in French and more than 70% in Mahorian; television transmissions began in 1986; a satellite service was launched in 2000; Regional Dir (vacant).

Finance

BANKS

Issuing Authority

Institut d'Emission des Départements d'Outre-mer: rue de la Préfecture, BP 500, 97600 Mamoudzou; tel. 269-61-05-05; internet agence@iedom-mayotte.fr; internet www.iedom.fr; Dir VICTOR-ROBERT NUGENT.

Commercial Banks

Banque Française Commerciale Océan Indien: route de l'Agriculture, BP 222, 97600 Mamoudzou; tel. 269-61-10-91; e-mail pleclerc@bfcoi.com; internet www.bfcoi.com; f. 1976; jtly owned by Société Générale and Mauritius Commercial Bank Ltd; Dir JEAN-PHILIPPE LEBON.

Banque de la Réunion: Immeuble de la Palme d'Or, 30 pl. Mariage, 97600 Mamoudzou; tel. 269-60-82-82; internet www.banquedelareunion.fr; owned by Groupe Banque Populaire et Caisse d'Epargne (France); Dir PATRICK TACOUN.

BRED Banque Populaire: Résidence Espace, RN1, Kawéni, 97600 Mamoudzou; tel. 269-60-51-51; internet www.bred.fr; owned by Groupe Banque Populaire et Caisse d'Epargne (France); Dir YVES FARINAS.

INSURANCE

Groupama: Immeuble Mahafa 2, Z.I. Nel, Lot 7, ave de l'Archipel, BP 665, 97600 Mamoudzou; tel. 269-62-59-92; Dir-Gen. ALAIN BAUDRY.

Prudence Créole: Centre Commercial et Médical de l'Ylang, BP 480, 97600 Mamoudzou; tel. 269-61-11-10; e-mail prudencecreolemayotte@wanadoo.fr; 87% owned by Groupe Générali.

Trade and Industry

DEVELOPMENT ORGANIZATION

Agence Française de Développement (AFD): Résidence Sarah, pl. du Marché, BP 610, Kawéni, 97600 Mamoudzou; tel. 269-64-35-00; e-mail afdmamoudzou@afd.fr; internet www.afd.fr; Dir IVAN POSTEL-VINAY.

EMPLOYERS' ORGANIZATIONS

Mouvement des Entreprises de France Mayotte (MEDEF): Immeuble Archipel, Kawéni, BP 570, 97600 Mamoudzou; tel. 269-61-44-22; e-mail contact@medef-mayotte.com; internet www.medef-mayotte.com; Pres. CARLA BALTUS; Sec.-Gen. ANDJIB ABDOURRAQUIB.

UTILITIES

Electricity

Electricité de Mayotte (EDM): BP 333, Z.I. Kawéni, 97600 Kawéni; tel. 269-62-96-80; internet www.electricitedemayotte.com; f. 1997; 50.01% owned by Conseil Général de Mayotte, 24.99% owned by EDEV 24.99% owned by SAUR; Dir-Gen. FADY HAJJAR.

Water

Mahoraise des Eaux: Z.I Kawéni 97600, BP 22, Mamoudzou; tel. 269-61-11-42; e-mail contact@mahoraisedeseaux.com; internet www.mahoraisedeseaux.com.

Syndicat Intercommunal de l'Eau et de l'Assainissement de Mayotte (SIEAM): Z.I. Kaweni, route Nationale, BP 289, 97600 Mamoudzou; tel. 269-62-11-11; e-mail sieam@sieam.fr; internet www.sieam.fr; Pres. MOUSSA MOUHAMADI.

MAJOR COMPANIES

Cementis Mayotte: BP 818 Kaweni, 97600 Mamoudzou; tel. 269624497; e-mail contact@cementis.io; internet cementis.io/yt; fmrly Lafarge Mayotte; name changed as above in 2021; Dir-Gen. LOUIS MALIKITÉ.

Entreprise de Travaux Publics et de Concassage (ETPC): BP 256, 97600 Mamoudzou; tel. 269-62-04-82; e-mail etpc@etpc-mayotte.fr; internet www.etpc-mayotte.fr.

Groupe Cananga: Z.I. Kawéni, BP 10, 97600 Mamoudzou; tel. 269-61-12-11; e-mail cananga@cananga.net; internet www.cananga.net; subsidiary cos: Batimax, Distrimax and Mr Bricolage; Pres. GAMIL KAKAL.

SAS SODIFRAM: Z.I. Kawéni, BP 70, 97600 Mamoudzou; tel. 269-61-10-76; internet groupe-sodifram.com.

Somaco: Z.I. Kawéni, BP 15, 97600 Mamoudzou; tel. 269-63-63-03; e-mail somaco@maharajah.fr; internet www.somaco.fr.

Somiva SAS: Z.I. Kawéni, BP 87, 97600 Mamoudzou; tel. 269-61-06-44; internet www.groupe-marill.com/fr/societe/somiva-sas; f. 1991; a subsidiary of Groupe Marill; importer and distributor of Renault vehicles.

TRADE UNIONS

Fédération Départementale des Syndicats d'Exploitants Agricoles de Mayotte (FDSEAM): 150 rue Mbalamanga-Mtsapéré, 97600 Mamoudzou; tel. 269-61-34-83; f. 1982; Pres. LAÏNA MOGNÉ-MALI; Dir AHMED CHAMSIDINE.

SNES Mayotte (SNES-FSU): 12 Résidence Bellecombe, 110 Lotissement Les Trois Vallées, Majicavo, 97600 Mamoudzou; tel. 269-62-50-58; e-mail mayotte@snes.edu; internet www.mayotte.snes.edu; represents teaching staff in secondary education; Sec. FRÉDÉRIC LOUVIER.

Union Départementale Force Ouvrière de Mayotte (FO): Z. I. de Kaweni, Rond Point El-Farouk, BP 1109, 97600 Mamoudzou; tel. 269-61-18-39; Sec.-Gen. HAMIDOU MADI M'COLO.

Union Interprofessionnelle CFDT de Mayotte (UI-CFDT): 1 rue Mahabou, Cavani, M'tsapéré, BP 1038, 97600 Mamoudzou; tel. 269-61-00-81; e-mail cisma3@wanadoo.fr; f. 1993; fmrly Confédération Inter-Syndicale de Mayotte; name changed as above in 2015; Sec.-Gen. OUSSENI BALAHACHI.

Affiliated unions incl.:

ScDEN-CGT: BP 793, Kawéni, 97600 Mamoudzou; tel. 269-62-53-35; e-mail scdencgt.mayotte@free.fr; represents teaching staff; Sec.-Gen. KHÉMAÏS SAIDANI.

SGEN-CFDT: 32 rue Marindrini, BP 1038, 97600 Mamoudzou; tel. 0639665132; e-mail mayotte@sgen.cfdt.fr; internet mayotte.sgen-cfdt.fr; represents teaching staff; Sec.-Gen. TANGUY SEMBIC.

Transport

SHIPPING

Coastal shipping is provided by locally owned small craft. There is a deep-water port at Longoni.

Mayotte Channel Gateway: BP 553, Kawéni, 97600 Mamoudzou; tel. 269-62-15-45; e-mail contact@channel-gateway.yt; internet www.mcg-mayotte.com; Pres. IDA NEL.

Service des Transports Maritimes (STM): BP 186, 97600 Dzaoudzi; tel. 269-64-39-72; e-mail denys.cormy@cg976.fr; internet www.stm-mayotte.com; Dir DENYS CORMY; 8 vessels.

Société de Gestion et de Transport Maritime (SGTM): BP 288, 97610 Dzaoudzi; tel. 269-61-20-69; e-mail info@sgtm.com; internet www.sgtm.com; f. 2004; Dir-Gen. MICHEL LABOURDERE.

CIVIL AVIATION

There is an airport at Dzaoudzi, serving commercial flights to the Comoros, Réunion, Madagascar, Paris (France), Kenya and Mozambique. A new terminal at the airport, with the capacity to allow the passage of 600,000 passengers annually, became operational in 2014.

Air Austral: pl. Mariage, BP 1429, 97600 Mamoudzou; tel. 269-60-90-90; e-mail mayotte@air-austral.com; internet www.air-austral.com; Pres. MARIE JOSEPH MALÉ.

Tourism

Comité Départemental du Tourisme de Mayotte (CDTM): BP 1169, 97600 Mamoudzou; tel. 269-61-09-09; e-mail mayottetourisme.lareunion@orange.fr; internet www.mayotte-tourisme.com; Dir MICHEL AHAMED.

MOZAMBIQUE

Physical and Social Geography

RENÉ PÉLISSIER

The Republic of Mozambique covers a total area of 799,380 sq km (308,641 sq miles). This includes 13,000 sq km of inland water, mainly comprising Lake Niassa, the Mozambican section of Lake Malawi. Mozambique is bounded to the north by Tanzania, to the west by Malawi, Zambia and Zimbabwe, and to the south by South Africa and Eswatini (formerly known as Swaziland).

With some exceptions towards the Zambia, Malawi and Zimbabwe borders, Mozambique is generally a low-lying plateau of moderate height, descending through a sub-plateau zone to the Indian Ocean. The main reliefs are Monte Binga (2,436 m above sea level), the highest point of Mozambique, on the Zimbabwe border in Manica province, Monte Namúli (2,419 m) in Zambézia province, the Serra Zuira (2,227 m) in Manica province and several massifs that are a continuation into northern Mozambique of the Shire highlands of Malawi. The coastal lowland is narrower in the north but widens considerably towards the south, so that terrain less than 1,000 m high comprises about 45% of the total Mozambican area. The shoreline is 2,470 km long and generally sandy and bordered by lagoons, shoals and strings of coastal islets in the north.

Mozambique is divided by at least 25 main rivers, all of which flow to the Indian Ocean. The largest and most historically significant is the Zambezi, whose 820-km Mozambican section is navigable for 460 km. Flowing from eastern Angola, the Zambezi provides access to the interior of Africa from the eastern coast.

Two main seasons, wet and dry, divide the climatic year. The wet season has monthly averages of 26.7°C–29.4°C, with cooler temperatures in the interior uplands. The dry season has June and July temperatures of 18.3°C–20.0°C in Maputo. Mozambique is vulnerable to drought and attendant famine, which severely affected much of the country during the 1980s, particularly during 1982–84 and again during 1986–87. In 2000 serious flooding struck the centre and south of Mozambique, displacing an estimated 500,000 people and causing serious damage to the country's infrastructure.

The population totalled 27,909,798, according to the census of 1 August 2017, giving a density of 34.9 inhabitants per sq km. According to official projections, the population amounted to 31,616,078 at mid-2022 (39.6 inhabitants per sq km).

North of the Zambezi, the main ethnic groupings among the African population, which belongs to the cultural division of Central Bantu, are the Makua-Lomwe groups, who form the principal ethno-linguistic subdivision of Mozambique and are believed to comprise about 40% of the population. South of the Zambezi, the main group is the Thonga, who feature prominently as Mozambican mine labourers in South Africa. North of the Thonga area lies the Shona group, numbering more than 1m. Southern ethnic groups have tended to enjoy greater educational opportunities than those of other regions. The Government has sought to balance the ethnic composition of its leadership, but the executive is still largely of southern and central origin.

Portuguese is the official language (spoken by 47.3% of the population at the time of the 2017 census), while there are some 39 indigenous languages, the most widely spoken being Makhuwa, Tsonga, Sena and Lomwe. Many of the inhabitants follow traditional beliefs. According to the 2017 census, 59.8% of the population were Christian and 18.9% were Muslim.

Mozambique is divided into 11 administrative provinces, one of which comprises the capital, Maputo, a modern seaport with a population of 1.1m. at mid-2022, according to official projections. The country's second seaport is Beira. Other towns of importance include Matola and Nampula, on the railway line to Niassa province and Malawi.

History

MARISÉ CASTRO

The Republic of Mozambique gained independence from Portugal on 25 June 1975, the culmination of a long guerrilla war launched in 1964 by the Frente de Libertação de Moçambique (Frelimo). On the day of independence, Frelimo's leader, Samora Machel, took office as the first President of the nascent People's Republic of Mozambique. The new Frelimo-led Government faced enormous economic and social problems, exacerbated by the vacuum left by the departing Portuguese administration. In addition, Frelimo's radical policy of *socialização do campo* (socialization of the countryside) antagonized much of Mozambique's peasantry (then around 80% of the population) as collectivized agriculture was promoted, traditional beliefs and ceremonies were prohibited, and *regulos* (tribal kings) were stripped of their powers. Nevertheless, major advances were made in public health, social welfare and education. Within a few years, however, a brutal civil war began, fomented and supported from abroad. Thousands of people were killed and an estimated 1.7m. Mozambicans fled to neighbouring countries, while the number of internally displaced people (IDPs) exceeded 4m.

Mozambique as an independent nation was born into an inherently hostile neighbourhood, flanked by the last two white minority regimes in Africa: (Southern) Rhodesia (to become Zimbabwe upon independence in 1980) and apartheid South Africa. The political orientation of the new Frelimo Government was the polar opposite: it pledged to support liberation movements within the region and other Front-Line States (FLS—a loose grouping of southern African countries set up to combat apartheid and South African expansionism), making confrontation inevitable. The Government was soon forced to deal with a crippling civil war, driven initially by Rhodesia through its creation in 1976 of the Movimento Nacional de Resistência de Moçambique (MNR), and later by South Africa. With the economy devastated, the Government drew economic and military support from the socialist Eastern bloc countries and from other FLS members, while also establishing good relations with a number of Western countries.

The new Government swiftly implemented a centrally planned economy and one-party state. In 1977 Frelimo declared itself to be a 'Marxist-Leninist vanguard party', committed to establishing socialism in Mozambique. Its foreign policy was based on solidarity and international activism, expressed through its membership of the FLS. Accordingly, the Government imposed sanctions against the white regime in Rhodesia by cutting off its main transport route to the sea via the Mozambican port of Beira, and allowed Rhodesia's opposition forces to establish bases on Mozambican territory and mount cross-border raids. The Rhodesian authorities retaliated by supporting and arming the MNR in a guerrilla war against the Frelimo Government. The latter also allowed South Africa's African National Congress (ANC) to launch attacks on South Africa from Mozambique, and granted sanctuary to South African exiles. After Zimbabwe attained independence in 1980, South Africa became the main sponsor of the MNR (subsequently renamed Resistência Nacional Moçambicana—Renamo), which grew rapidly into a force of some 8,000 guerrilla fighters.

Viewed against the backdrop of the civil war, the Government's achievements during this period were impressive. Health centres and schools were built nationwide, resulting in greatly improved health care and a huge reduction in adult illiteracy. Along with other social and infrastructure projects, these symbols of Frelimo's achievements became the main targets of Renamo's attacks.

CIVIL WAR AND CONFLICT WITH SOUTH AFRICA

With South Africa's support, Renamo was able to inflict widespread disruption on all aspects of life in Mozambique. Despite several major offensives by government forces against the guerrillas, by mid-1984 Renamo forces were active in all of Mozambique's provinces, with the capital, Maputo, increasingly under threat. The high economic and human cost of the conflict drove the Government to seek talks with the South African authorities in late 1983, leading to the signing of the Nkomati Accord in March 1984. Both sides agreed to cease providing material aid to opposition movements operating in each other's territory, and to establish a joint security commission. However, the South African Government effectively ignored the Accord, and the conflict continued to escalate. In August the Mozambican Government informed South Africa that the Accord was at risk unless Renamo activity was halted. South Africa responded by convening a series of separate but parallel talks with Renamo and the Mozambican Government, which in October culminated in the 'Pretoria Declaration'. A ceasefire was agreed in principle between the Government and Renamo, and a tripartite commission, comprising Frelimo, Renamo and South African representatives, was established to implement the truce. In November, however, Renamo withdrew from the peace negotiations, and in April 1985 it severed rail links between Mozambique and South Africa.

As the security situation worsened, in June 1985 President Machel met Zimbabwean Prime Minister Robert Mugabe and Tanzanian President Julius Nyerere in Harare, Zimbabwe, where both countries pledged their support, with Zimbabwe committing to increase its military presence in Mozambique. This arrangement led to the capture two months later of major Renamo bases in Sofala province. As well as weapons, documents were seized revealing the extent of South African support for Renamo since the signing of the Nkomati Accord. In October Mozambique unilaterally suspended the joint security commission.

In October 1986 President Machel and 33 others were killed when the aircraft flying them back from an FLS meeting in Zambia crashed in South Africa. Although South African involvement in the crash has long been suspected, in January 1987 a joint report compiled by Mozambican, Soviet and South African experts, concluded that pilot error—and not sabotage—had caused the accident. However, doubts remained about the thoroughness of the investigation. In October 2008 a former member of South Africa's special services alleged that he had taken part in a covert operation to divert the aircraft off course and cause it to crash. The investigation was eventually wound down, but the controversy surrounding possible South African involvement in the crash persists to the present day.

The recapture of five northern towns by Zimbabwean and Mozambican troops in February 1987 marked a major shift in the balance of power, with Renamo encroaching further south, while government troops registered important successes in the north and along the coast. Under the new President, Joaquim Chissano, Mozambique pressurized its northern neighbour Malawi to cease accommodating Renamo. In December Mozambique and Malawi signed a joint security agreement which provided for the deployment of Malawian troops in Mozambique to protect the railway line from the Malawian

border to the northern Mozambican port of Nacala. Meanwhile, an open raid in May by South African security forces on alleged ANC bases in metropolitan Maputo signalled the effective demise of the Nkomati Accord.

PEACE AGREEMENT AND END OF CIVIL WAR

Following the death of President Machel, Frelimo revised its policies, largely prompted by the urgent need to achieve a negotiated solution to the civil war. In July 1989 Frelimo renounced Marxist-Leninism, adopting in its place a multiparty political system, and began to liberalize the economy. A new Constitution was approved by the legislature in November 1990. This provided for direct election by universal suffrage of the President and the legislature (voting rights were extended to Renamo members who renounced violence and recognized the legitimacy of the Frelimo Government); the separation of the Frelimo party and the Mozambique state; and the independence of the judiciary. The country was renamed the Republic of Mozambique, and the Assembleia Popular (People's Assembly) became the Assembleia da República (Assembly of the Republic). The new Constitution, which also enshrined fundamental human rights including freedom of expression and an end to censorship, was welcomed by Western aid donors but rejected by Renamo as the product of an unrepresentative unelected body. In December the Assembly of the Republic passed legislation enabling the establishment of political parties.

Meanwhile, the collapse of the Nkomati Accord prompted new peace proposals. In June 1989 the Government launched a peace initiative, which demanded the cessation of acts of terrorism and guaranteed all those renouncing violence the right to political participation. In addition, it recognized the principle that no group should forcibly impose its will on another, and demanded that all parties respect the legitimacy of the state and the Constitution. Although Renamo rejected the initiative, the two sides signed a partial ceasefire agreement in December 1990 following talks in Rome, Italy. Nevertheless, the peace negotiations stalled repeatedly. In early 1991 Renamo resumed its attacks, which were intermittently sustained right up to the signing of the Acordo Geral de Paz (AGP—General Peace Accord) on 4 October 1992. In October 1991 the two sides signed a protocol whereby Renamo recognized the Government's legitimacy. In the following month Renamo agreed to reconstitute itself as a political party upon the cessation of hostilities. Another protocol, signed in March 1992, provided for a system of proportional representation for the legislature, and for legislative and presidential elections to take place simultaneously within one year of the signing of a ceasefire agreement.

The AGP provided for a general ceasefire to come into force immediately after its ratification by the Assembly of the Republic. Renamo and government forces were to withdraw to assembly points within seven days of ratification of the peace accord. A new 30,000-strong national defence force, the Forças Armadas de Defesa de Moçambique (FADM), would be created, incorporating equal numbers from each side, with the remaining troops surrendering their weapons to a United Nations (UN) peacekeeping force within six months. A Ceasefire Commission would be established to supervise the implementation of the truce, while overall political control of the peace process would rest with the Comissão de Supervisão e Controlo (CSC—Supervision and Control Commission). The Ceasefire Commission and the CSC were to incorporate representatives of the Government, Renamo and the UN. Presidential and legislative elections, under UN supervision, were to be held one year after the signing of the AGP, provided that it had been fully implemented and the demobilization process completed.

In October 1992 the UN Security Council appointed a special representative for Mozambique, and in December it approved the establishment of the UN Operation in Mozambique (ONUMOZ) and the deployment of some 7,500 troops, police and civilian observers to oversee the implementation of all aspects of the AGP and to supervise the forthcoming elections. However, in March 1993 Renamo refused to demobilize its troops until the UN force was in place, and withdrew from the CSC and the Ceasefire Commission. The first UN troops became operational in the Beira Corridor on 1 April, prompting the withdrawal of the Zimbabwean troops guarding the Beira and Limpopo corridors. Renamo, however, continued to violate the peace accord and to delay demobilization, demanding US $100m. to transform itself into a political party. In June the CSC agreed to postpone the elections by one year until October 1994, while appealing for immediate action on the establishment of assembly points and unified national armed forces. Although aid donors expressed growing impatience with the repeated delays and with Renamo's escalating financial demands, they nevertheless pledged additional funds, bringing their total to $520m., to support the peace process, the repatriation of refugees from neighbouring countries, the resettlement of IDPs and the reintegration of around 80,000 former combatants into civilian life, as well as emergency relief and reconstruction. The UN also agreed to establish a trust fund of $10m. to finance Renamo's transformation into a political party.

In November 1993 an agreement was signed which provided for the confinement of troops from the end of that month. To expedite the process, in March 1994 the Government unilaterally began demobilizing its troops, prompting Renamo to do likewise, and in April the high command of the FADM was inaugurated. Demobilization progress was slow, however, and the deadline for troop confinement was repeatedly extended. In August the Forças Armadas de Moçambique were formally dissolved and their functions transferred to the FADM.

In December 1994 the Ceasefire Commission's final report revealed that ONUMOZ had registered a total of 91,691 government and Renamo troops during the confinement process, of whom 11,579 had enlisted in the FADM, compared with the 30,000 envisaged in the AGP. Demobilization had continued until 15 September, with some cases still being processed on the day before the elections were held in late October. By that time, the UN High Commissioner for Refugees had resettled an estimated 3m. IDPs. By May 1995 some 1.7m. refugees had returned to Mozambique from neighbouring countries.

MULTI-PARTY ELECTIONS

Mozambique's first multi-party elections were held on 27–28 October 1994, marking the completion of the peace process. All subsequent elections have been won by Frelimo and its presidential candidates, with increased majorities in each successive poll. Although elections have usually passed off peacefully and been declared free and fair by international observers, irregularities have been consistently noted, but never deemed significant enough to affect the result. Since 2000, however, each election has been followed by political violence, with Renamo regularly contesting the results and accusing Frelimo of electoral fraud and harassment, while threatening violence if its demands for a greater share of power were not fully met.

Just hours before polling began on 27 October 1994, Renamo withdrew, claiming that conditions were not conducive to free and fair elections. Fearing a repeat of what had happened in Angola in late 1992 (when disputed elections had led to a resumption of civil war), the international community applied intense pressure on Renamo, which abandoned its electoral boycott on the following day, in exchange for further funds. Voting was then extended by one day. In the presidential election, Chissano won an outright majority with 53.3% of the vote, while Renamo's leader, Afonso Dhlakama, received 33.7%, with a reported turnout of 80%. In the legislative elections, Frelimo also secured an overall majority, winning 129 of the 250 seats in the Assembly of the Republic, while Renamo obtained 112 seats and the União Democrática—a coalition of three opposition parties—the remaining nine. The UN declared the elections to have been free and fair, while acknowledging minor irregularities.

Subsequent elections followed similar patterns. In December 1999 Chissano secured 52.3% of the vote, while Frelimo increased its majority in the legislative elections, winning 133 seats. Renamo and 10 other opposition parties, which had formed a coalition, Renamo—União Eleitoral, with a single list of legislative candidates and Dhlakama as its presidential candidate, took the remaining seats in the Assembly of the

Republic. Renamo, however, contested the results and threatened to regroup its demobilized soldiers and seize control of the country.

The December 2004 elections were widely disputed, and Frelimo was accused of extensive electoral fraud. Voter turnout reached a record low of 36% in that year, reflecting public apathy and disillusionment with the political system. (Voter participation improved in subsequent elections, but remained below 55%.) Frelimo won a decisive victory, increasing its majority in both parliamentary and presidential polls. Armando Guebuza, Frelimo's presidential candidate, won 63.7% of the vote and the party took 62.0% in the parliamentary elections, while Renamo (the only other party to secure representation) obtained just 29.7% in the parliamentary elections, with Dhlakama securing 31.7% of the presidential vote. In February 2005 Guebuza was sworn in as President, in a ceremony boycotted by Renamo.

The October 2009 elections included, for the first time, contests for provincial governors and assemblies. Frelimo won an overwhelming victory in the legislative poll, increasing its strength to 191 seats in the Assembly of the Republic, while Renamo suffered a humiliating defeat, with its parliamentary representation reduced to just 51 seats. The Movimento Democrático de Moçambique (MDM), a party launched in March by Renamo dissidents, came third, winning eight seats—the first serious challenge to exclusive political domination by the two main parties. In the concurrent presidential election Guebuza won decisively with 75.0% of the vote, while Dhlakama secured just 16.4%. The MDM's leader, Daviz Simango, garnered 8.6%. Frelimo had stood unopposed in several constituencies where 11 political parties, including the MDM, and 17 presidential candidates, had been excluded, allegedly owing to procedural errors. From the outset the campaign was beset by sporadic violence between Frelimo and Renamo supporters, and attempts by both parties to undermine the MDM threat to their political dominance. Both the MDM and Renamo complained of obstruction and intimidation tactics by Frelimo and the Government during campaigning. Election observers criticized Frelimo's misuse of state resources and monopoly of the media, and noted numerous irregularities, albeit not considered significant enough to affect results. The electoral shortcomings were serious enough to provoke a temporary suspension of funding by Mozambique's international donors, who demanded immediate action on reform of the electoral law, corruption and conflicts of interest, with particular emphasis on the blurred distinction between Frelimo and the state. Funding was resumed in March 2010, after the Government had made a number of concessions on governance.

Only a few parties and three presidential candidates participated in the October 2014 elections. Although polling day itself passed off peacefully, the campaign period witnessed widespread violence by supporters of the three main parties, resulting in dozens of injuries and numerous arrests. The police and courts, however, exhibited notable leniency towards Frelimo adherents, while strongly penalizing opponents from the two other parties. Frelimo won the parliamentary elections, securing 144 seats; Renamo's representation in the legislature rose to 89 seats, while the MDM's share increased to 17 seats. Frelimo's candidate, Filipe Nyusi, won the presidential poll with 57.0% of the vote; Dhlakama received 36.6% and Simango 6.4%. Dhlakama repeated his earlier demands for a government of national unity, claiming that Renamo had secured a majority in five provinces, and threatened to establish a parallel government unless Frelimo agreed to his demands. He also called for a boycott of the inauguration of the Assembly of the Republic and the provincial assemblies, scheduled for January 2015.

The elections held on 15 October 2019 took place amid heightened political tensions, particularly in northern and central provinces, which seriously called into question people's freedom to vote. The pattern of political violence during the election campaign was repeated, involving political killings (including those of Renamo leaders in Tete province and civil society election monitors), disappearances and other human rights violations. Widespread electoral irregularities were reported. Incumbent President Nyusi won the presidential election, securing an overwhelming 73.5% of the vote (against the 21.5% garnered by Renamo's Ossufo Momade), while Frelimo took 184 seats in the Assembly of the Republic, Renamo 60 seats and the MDM just six. Frelimo also won all the provincial governorships and gained control of all the provincial assemblies. Renamo disputed the results and demanded a re-run of the elections. The Election Observation Mission (EOM) of the European Union (EU) strongly criticized the conduct of the elections and denounced the results as highly implausible, citing numerous irregularities and malpractices before and during polling. The EU EOM also criticized the Comissão Nacional de Eleições (CNE—National Election Commission) for its alleged lack of transparency and claimed that electoral legislation had been violated. Nevertheless, the Constitutional Council validated the results in December, and in January 2020 the new Assembly of the Republic was inaugurated and President Nyusi sworn in. A new Government was appointed shortly thereafter, differing little from its predecessor, with the most notable change being the appointment of two civilians to head the Ministries of National Defence and of the Interior (although both were unexpectedly dismissed in November 2021).

Municipal elections were held in November 2008, two years after legislation had been passed on the electoral system governing provincial and municipal assemblies, which provided for directly elected provincial assemblies. The elections, with an estimated 48% turnout, resulted in an overwhelming victory for Frelimo, which won control of 41 of the 43 municipalities, including 10 new municipalities and three previously under Renamo control. In February 2009 a run-off mayoral election held in Nacala was won by Frelimo's candidate, unseating the Renamo incumbent. Frelimo thereby secured control of 42 of the 43 municipal councils, and in March Renamo lost control of its sole remaining municipality—Beira—when Simango, the city's mayor, left Renamo to launch his own party, the MDM (see above).

Despite the violent unrest in parts of the country, and a campaign marred by politically motivated attacks, municipal elections took place peacefully in November 2013. Frelimo gained control of 49 of the now 53 municipalities, and the MDM won the remaining four, including the major cities of Beira, Nampula and Quelimane; Renamo boycotted the polls. With support from the MDM, in March 2018 Renamo's candidate won the mayoral by-election in Nampula, which had been called following the assassination of the MDM mayor in January. Nationwide municipal elections were held in November. The campaign was marked by unprecedented levels of political violence, particularly in the north and in Maputo province. Frelimo was victorious in 44 municipalities, Renamo in eight, including Nampula, Quelimane and Nacala, while the MDM retained power in Beira. Renamo claimed that serious electoral fraud had taken place in five municipalities. There was, indeed, evidence of serious irregularities in four municipalities, where Frelimo and Renamo demanded a recount in constituencies where they had been defeated.

POLITICS IN THE POST-WAR PERIOD

Frelimo continues to dominate political life in Mozambique. Each new election has served to increase its majority and consolidate its control over government, the judiciary and the security forces. Renamo has routinely challenged Frelimo's dominance, contesting the legitimacy of every new administration, demanding a share of power, economic resources, and even control of parts of the country, and often resorting to violent protest. The ever-present friction between the two parties worsened during President Chissano's second term. In January 2000 Dhlakama rejected the legitimacy of the new Government and threatened to regroup Renamo's demobilized soldiers to seize power. The threats were not entirely idle: in May former Renamo soldiers attacked a police station in Nampula province, killing five people. This was followed by riots in northern Mozambique in November. Conciliatory talks between Chissano and Dhlakama collapsed in January 2001, when Chissano rejected Dhlakama's demands for an early election and the appointment of Renamo governors in provinces where the opposition party had won a majority of votes.

Following his victory in the presidential election of December 2004, on assuming office in February 2005 Guebuza appointed a new cabinet in which Luísa Dias Diogo retained her post as Mozambique's first female Prime Minister. Guebuza announced that the twin priorities of his presidency were to overhaul the justice system and combat police corruption. In December he inaugurated a new statutory consultative body, the Conselho de Estado (Council of State). Meanwhile, in an effort to restore faith in the electoral process following the controversy surrounding the mayoral election in Moçimboa da Praia in May and the subsequent unrest there in September, Frelimo amended the system for appointing members to the CNE, whereby the allocation of seats reserved for political parties would be reduced to one-third, with the remainder split between appointees from the Government, the judiciary and civil society. Given Frelimo's control over the Government and judiciary, however, the changes made little impact.

In November 2006 the Assembly of the Republic passed legislation creating 10 directly elected provincial assemblies—a key Renamo demand since negotiations on constitutional changes began in early 2004. The following month the legislature approved three amendments to the electoral law, covering voter registration, electoral procedures and the composition of the CNE, which was to be reduced from 18 members to 13. Five CNE members were henceforth to be legislators, while the remainder were to be drawn from civil society, subject to parliamentary approval. Another key change was the removal of the 5% threshold required for parties to win seats in the Assembly of the Republic, thereby enabling smaller political parties to gain representation.

Frelimo emerged strengthened from the elections in October 2009, having increased its presence in the hitherto Renamo-dominated northern and central regions. As expected, Dhlakama rejected the outcome, demanding the creation of a transitional government to organize new elections, and ordered his party to boycott the parliamentary swearing-in ceremony (although 16 Renamo members, including the party's Secretary-General, defied Dhlakama to attend). In contrast with 2004, Guebuza retained most of the cabinet following the elections, with the notable exception of Prime Minister Diogo, who was replaced by Aires Ali, a Guebuza loyalist. Despite opposition from Renamo, in April 2010 the Constitutional Council modified the legislation governing *bancada* or 'bench' status in the Assembly of the Republic, and reduced from 11 to eight the number of parliamentary seats needed by a party to raise questions in the Assembly or to propose legislation and participate in parliamentary commissions. This measure officially confirmed the MDM as the third *bancada* in the legislature. Simango's unexpected death in February 2021, however, cast a shadow over the MDM's future. His brother, Lutero, was elected as the new MDM leader in December.

Following a constitutional review (initiated in late 2011), a draft revised Constitution was presented to the Assembly of the Republic for consideration in 2013, before public consultation began in February of that year. A Frelimo-dominated parliamentary commission set up to draft the amendments approved them all unchallenged, including a proposal for the establishment of a Constitutional Court with a broader mandate than the existing Constitutional Council. Renamo boycotted the entire process.

Growing discontent over Guebuza's authoritarian leadership style took root among Frelimo ranks during his second term in office, and open challenges soon emerged. In September 2012 the Frelimo congress foiled Guebuza's planned alternative to a third term, whereby Prime Minister Aires Ali would take over as puppet party President for an intermediate term. In the event, Ali failed even to secure election to Frelimo's Political Commission. In October Guebuza countered with a cabinet reshuffle, appointing Alberto António Vaquina as Prime Minister and replacing several other ministers.

In March 2014 Nyusi was designated Frelimo's candidate for the presidential election due in October. For the first time, Frelimo's presidential candidate was not the party's President, since Guebuza had already served two consecutive terms in the national presidency, as allowed by the Constitution. Following Frelimo's victory in the poll, in January 2015 a new legislature was inaugurated (in a ceremony again boycotted by the

Renamo deputies), and Nyusi was sworn in as President, raising high hopes of a fresh start.

Tensions within Frelimo festered following the 2014 elections. In March 2015 Guebuza stood down as Frelimo's President and was replaced by Nyusi, who was elected almost unanimously, thus strengthening his authority within the party. However, Nyusi inherited the legacy of heightened tensions with Renamo, chronic corruption and political killings, as well as lingering disenchantment with the ruling party, both internally and among the general public. On the positive side, Nyusi's promise to improve governance and transparency was welcomed after Guebuza's authoritarian rule. Upon taking office, he appointed a new Government, headed by a new Prime Minister, Carlos Agostinho do Rosário but several ministers from the previous administration were retained. President Nyusi invested much of his early political capital in peace negotiations with Renamo and attempts to accommodate its demands, the most persistent of which being the decentralization of power. None the less, in 2015 the Assembly of the Republic twice rejected a proposal for a partial revision of the Constitution aimed at meeting Renamo's demand for the right to appoint governors in provinces where it emerged victorious in the provincial polls.

In February 2018 President Nyusi announced a decentralization package that he had agreed with Dhlakama in December 2017, which would effectively increase the power of provincial and municipal assemblies. Starting from the municipal elections scheduled for October 2018, voters would no longer elect mayors directly, only municipal assemblies. The winning party would then nominate the mayor from among the newly elected assembly members. Similarly, from the general election scheduled for October 2019, each provincial governor would be appointed by the party that secured the most votes in the provincial assembly. Their appointment would then be approved by the President. Governors would thus become accountable to the provincial assemblies. The proposals suited both Frelimo and Renamo, which preferred not to risk the emergence of popular and independent-minded provincial governors and mayors with their own power bases challenging the country's two main parties; the proposals also served to increase the power of each party's leader. The package additionally provided for the creation of a Secretary of State in each province, who would be appointed by the President and would assume responsibility for state functions that were not decentralized to provincial level.

The decentralization package, which called for immediate constitutional amendments, met with opposition from many quarters opposed to the transfer of control from the electorate to the parties. The MDM President, Simango, denounced the package as an undemocratic measure aimed at ensconcing party loyalists in key posts. Deputies in the Assembly of the Republic rejected a request to table the amendments within 15 days, on the grounds that proposed constitutional changes must be submitted to the legislature 90 days prior to parliamentary debate. Moreover, at an extraordinary meeting of Frelimo's political commission held in March 2018, the decentralization package was rejected as being unconstitutional. None the less, in late May (some three weeks after Dhlakama's sudden death) the legislature unanimously approved all of the proposed constitutional amendments and changes to the electoral law. In February 2019 the Assembly officially passed the decentralization legislation, which was duly promulgated in May.

Midway through his second term in March 2022, President Nyusi dismissed Prime Minister do Rosário and appointed a reorganized Government, headed by Adriano Maleiane, hitherto Minister of the Economy and Finance. Among the changes, Ernesto Max Elias Tonela was transferred from the mineral resources and energy portfolio to succeed Maleiane as Minister of the Economy and Finance, while Carlos Joaquim Zacarias, previously Chairman of the Instituto Nacional de Petróleo (National Petroleum Institute), became the new Minister of Mineral Resources and Energy.

Meanwhile, Renamo's difficulties in evolving into a credible political party were obvious, exemplified by its persistent reversion to threats and actual use of violence in support of its demands. In contravention of the AGP, Renamo refused to disband its sizeable armed force, which it claimed was Dhlakama's personal bodyguard. Despite growing dissent within the party at his leadership style, in late 2001 Dhlakama was re-elected as Renamo's President, and Joaquim Vaz, Renamo's representative in Portugal, was elected as its Secretary-General. In July 2002, however, the latter was dismissed by Dhlakama, who then proceeded to dissolve the party's national political commission, assuming the role of Secretary-General himself. Dhlakama's announcement in 2005 that he would seek re-election as Renamo's leader at the party congress in November provoked further resentment among reformist elements within the party.

In March 2009 Simango left Renamo to establish his own party, the MDM, taking several senior Renamo figures with him. In June Simango was the target of an assassination attempt at an MDM rally in Nacala, when his motorcade came under fire from Dhlakama's bodyguards. Renamo denied any involvement in the incident, but a police investigation discovered the weapon allegedly used in the attack at Dhlakama's residence in Nacala, and 10 Renamo members were later accused of involvement in the incident.

Following Dhlakama's death in May 2018, Momade was appointed as Renamo's interim leader; he was formally elected as party leader in January 2019. However, he failed to resolve internal dissension within Renamo. Dissatisfaction with Momade grew and his leadership was contested. In August a group of guerrilla dissidents established a self-styled military junta (Junta Militar da Renamo—JMR), led by Mariano Nhongo, who declared himself to be the 'real' Renamo President, thereby exacerbating party divisions. In addition, hundreds of Renamo members including some senior local leaders in Sofala province, left the party, with many defecting to Frelimo. The party has since remained deeply divided.

CONFLICT WITH RENAMO

Up to the death of Dhlakama, the pattern of Renamo's post-election violence, as summarized above, persisted largely unabated. In November 2000 riots instigated by Renamo broke out in northern parts of the country, resulting in the deaths of 41 people, including police officers. Hundreds of rioters were arrested, 83 of whom subsequently died owing to extreme overcrowding inside a police cell in Montepuez, in Cabo Delgado province. Controversy over a mayoral election in Moçímboa da Praia in May 2005 led to clashes between the police and Renamo, in which at least eight Renamo supporters were killed.

Tensions escalated sharply during 2013. In April a raid by security forces on a Renamo compound in the central town of Muxúnguè and a counter-attack by Renamo resulted in the deaths of four police officers. One month later, government and Renamo forces exchanged fire near Dhlakama's base in Gorongosa. Talks between the two parties, which had been suspended since December 2012, resumed in May 2013. In June, however, Renamo threatened to restrict road and rail traffic in central Mozambique. Shortly afterwards, armed groups conducted a series of attacks on the country's main north–south transport corridor, although Renamo did not claim responsibility. These incidents, in which a number of civilians were killed, adversely affected shipping and temporarily delayed coal deliveries by the Sena railway service to the port of Beira. The security environment in central and northern Mozambique deteriorated further in October, when at least 11 people were killed in a series of clashes, and Dhlakama's encampment at Gorongosa was seized by the FADM. Although it was generally accepted that Renamo lacked the offensive capacity to initiate large-scale conflict, the group's announcement in late October that it was withdrawing from the AGP triggered widespread alarm. Approximately 25 people died in renewed skirmishes and alleged Renamo ambushes between November 2013 and January 2014, while internal displacement of the population was again becoming a serious problem.

Talks between the Government and Renamo resumed in January 2014. In the following month Renamo secured a major concession when the Assembly of the Republic approved legislation increasing party representation in an enlarged CNE, which was expanded from 13 to 17 members; Renamo was granted two additional seats on the commission, bringing its total to four. Reports of low-level clashes between armed Renamo members and government forces continued throughout 2014. In an attempt to end the ongoing hostilities prior to the elections in October, in August the Assembly approved an amnesty law that would allow Dhlakama and his supporters to contest the polls after a peace accord had been signed by both sides. A general peace agreement was subsequently reached which included provisions to integrate the remaining Renamo troops (believed to number some 1,000 men) into the FADM and to release Renamo prisoners, including those captured in recent fighting and others who had instigated or been involved in acts of violence. The two sides signed a memorandum of understanding (MoU) to end the two-year conflict. A ceasefire, which was formally signed by President Guebuza and Dhlakama in early September, came into immediate effect. The demilitarization and integration of 300 Renamo residual forces commenced in late October, with 200 joining the police force and 100 the FADM. However, demilitarization of the remaining Renamo forces was left pending. According to Dhlakama, the process was complex and required more time. As skirmishes between government troops and Renamo became increasingly frequent, the security situation continued to worsen, and demilitarization of Renamo forces effectively ground to a halt. Partly in an attempt to appease Dhlakama, in December the Assembly of the Republic approved the Special Statute of the Leader of the Opposition, as promised by President Guebuza when the ceasefire had been signed.

Two days after the new Government under Nyusi was installed in January 2015, Dhlakama threatened to set up a centre-north republic if his demands for a government of national unity were not met. In an effort to defuse tension and encourage Renamo parliamentarians to take up their seats in the Assembly of the Republic, talks between the Government and Renamo resumed in early February. It was the first such meeting since the elections, as well as the first between President Nyusi and Dhlakama. The latter had abandoned his request for a national unity government in favour of the creation of autonomous regions. Nyusi agreed to consider the proposals, which were duly presented to the legislature in March, only to be rejected as unconstitutional. Political friction increased, with sporadic clashes between armed Renamo members and the security forces, particularly in Sofala province. On 2 May Dhlakama issued another ultimatum to the Government, giving it 60 days to reconsider its position on regional autonomy 'or face serious consequences'. One month later, he declared that he would forcibly establish autonomous provinces. After more than 100 rounds, negotiations between the Government and Renamo had reached deadlock by the end of June. During that month there were further clashes between Renamo residual forces and the police in Inhambane, Gaza and Tete provinces, resulting in several casualties in the latter province. Several people were killed in an attack by men in civilian clothing on Dhlakama's motorcade in September in Gondola (Manica province). The security forces denied accusations by Renamo of involvement in the attack. Subsequently, armed clashes between the two sides became more frequent and spread to all the central provinces, forcing people to flee their homes. Between December 2015 and April 2016 some 11,000 Mozambicans fled into neighbouring Malawi, while thousands more became IDPs.

There was no contact between the Government and Renamo after August 2015. In early March 2016 Dhlakama expressed willingness to meet with the Government to seek an end to the political and military crisis, while at the same time reiterating his threat to take over local government by the end of the month in the six central and northern provinces where Renamo had won a majority in the elections: Sofala, Manica, Zambézia, Tete, Nampula and Niassa. A new Government-Renamo joint commission was established by the Government to draw up the agenda and terms of reference for a future meeting between President Nyusi and Dhlakama. However, in late March security forces raided several Renamo properties, including Dhlakama's residence in Maputo, and seized dozens of guns. On 1 April—the day after Renamo's takeover deadline—state security forces launched an attack on Renamo's base at Gorongosa.

Armed clashes continued unabated throughout 2016, resulting in several hundred deaths as the political and military crisis worsened. In May there were several attacks along the EN1 Highway, in which a number of civilians were killed and many more injured, for which the Government blamed Renamo. There were also reports in the same month of activity by 'death squads' in Sofala, Manica and Zambézia provinces, which were believed to be responsible for a wave of kidnappings and killing since March. At least 12 Renamo members, including several senior figures, were killed in the first quarter of the year. In addition, a number of government critics, as well as the Maputo provincial prosecutor, were killed after being kidnapped by unknown assailants. During May and June there were numerous reports of the discovery of mass graves around Gorongosa and in Manica province. Following its own investigation, the Parliamentary Commission in charge of Constitutional Affairs, Human Rights and Legality concluded that no mass graves existed. These findings were disputed by the opposition and the media, including some international media, who carried out their own investigation and found at least 25 bodies at the alleged grave sites.

Attacks on villages in the central provinces and the destruction of infrastructure by Renamo intensified in July and August 2016, when, according to the international non-governmental organization Human Rights Watch, armed Renamo members raided several hospitals and health centres, mainly in Zambézia province. Dhlakama admitted that he had ordered some of these attacks as part of a military strategy aimed at dispersing government forces surrounding Renamo positions in Gorongosa. Meanwhile, talks between the Government and Renamo initiated in July under international mediation broke down the following month. Renamo rejected the mediators' proposal for a truce unless the government forces withdrew from Gorongosa; similarly, a proposal for a demilitarized corridor in Sofala province to enable the mediators to access Dhlakama was rejected by Renamo. Talks resumed in September, and a sub-commission was established to prepare a legislative package to facilitate political and administrative decentralization. As well as the Constitution itself, the package sought to reform laws and regulations pertaining to local elections, provincial assemblies and provincial governing bodies. By December, however, no agreement had been reached on any of these issues, and the negotiations collapsed again, triggering the resignation of the international mediators. Renamo then intensified attacks and ambushes on civilian and military vehicles in central Mozambique, causing several civilian deaths. In January 2017 Dhlakama declared a 60-day truce, which was subsequently extended, although not without several violations.

Despite his declaration two months earlier that international mediation would no longer be sought unless considered imperative, when peace negotiations resumed in late February 2017, President Nyusi invited several foreign ambassadors resident in Maputo and the head of the EU mission to Mozambique to join the Contact Group to support the peace dialogue. In June Dhlakama announced that he expected the dialogue to last until the end of the year, blaming delays on intransigent elements within the armed forces. An agreement on decentralization was finally reached in December, which required modifications to electoral legislation, as well as to the Constitution itself. These amendments were approved by the Assembly of the Republic in May 2018, although no agreement was achieved on disarming Renamo forces. Dhlakama's interim successor, Momade, pledged to honour the peace agreements that had been reached by Dhlakama and the Government, and in August he and Nyusi signed an MoU to establish a framework for the demilitarization, disarming and integration of Renamo fighters into the security forces. However, progress proved slow.

In an attempt to accelerate the peace process, President Nyusi and Momade met in March 2019 and again in June, when they committed themselves to signing a permanent peace accord in August. Prior to the conclusion of the peace accord, in late July the Assembly of the Republic approved a broad amnesty law which exempted from prosecution members of both Renamo and government forces for human rights abuses committed during 2014–16. The two leaders duly signed a cessation of hostilities agreement at a ceremony held in Gorongosa National Park, near the Renamo headquarters, on 1 August 2019. Five days later, they signed the National Peace and Reconciliation Accord in Maputo, and pledged to ensure that the elections scheduled for 15 October would be conducted peacefully. The disarming of Renamo fighters commenced in June, and was to be followed by their demobilization and reintegration into civilian life from July. The Maputo peace accord envisaged the completion of this process by 21 August.

The dissident JMR, however, rejected the peace accord, claiming that Renamo's military wing had not been consulted on its terms, and demanded the resignation of Momade and the election of a new Renamo leader. The JMR further demanded that the Government renegotiate the peace agreement with them, and threatened to resort to violence if their demands were not met. Political tension and insecurity persisted in the central provinces, where, since August 2019, there had been several attacks attributed to the JMR, some of which had resulted in fatalities. Despite the JMR's announcement in December 2020 of a unilateral ceasefire and its readiness to start negotiations with the Government, attacks in Sofala continued.

With the JMR refusing to surrender its weapons, little progress was made. By the end of 2020 only three Renamo bases were known to have been dismantled; about 1,000 fighters had been disarmed. In early 2021 it was hoped that the process would be completed by October, involving the demobilization of over 5,000 combatants, but actual advances were minimal. However, the death in October of the JMR leader, Mariano Nhongo, marked the end of two fruitless years during which he contested Renamo's leadership and demanded the renegotiation of the August 2019 peace agreement. Moreover, it effectively ended the armed conflict between Renamo and the Government, as well as removing the driving force behind much of the internecine feuding within Renamo itself. With the JMR lacking resources to sustain further attacks, the prospect of a durable peace finally appeared attainable. None the less, by the end of 2021 five bases were yet to be closed, and some 2,000 fighters to be demobilized. The process continued throughout 2022, with its completion now expected by the end of the year.

ISLAMIST INSURGENCY

In 2017 attacks by suspected Islamist extremists in Cabo Delgado province precipitated a major security crisis, jeopardizing the country's prosperity and plunging the province into war. Five years later, the conflict continues unabated, and hopes for an early peaceful resolution have faded. The attacks began in October, in the northern port town of Moçímboa da Praia, where official buildings and security personnel were targeted. They soon spread to the nearby Palma and Macomia districts and similar incidents have since occurred on a regular basis. The attacks, which initially focused on security or state facilities, subsequently shifted to 'easier' civilian targets, in a manner reminiscent of Renamo atrocities committed during the civil war. Insurgent raids intensified in the aftermath of Cyclone Kenneth, which struck Mozambique in April 2019, resulting in at least 30 deaths. By April 2021 the number of IDPs had risen to about 700,000, and those killed by the insurgents to over 2,000.

Initially, Renamo involvement in the atrocities was suspected, but this hypothesis was soon discarded. Although several sources attributed the raids to an Islamist organization linked to the Somali militant Islamist group al-Shabaab ('The Youth'), the Government denied such links and characterized the attackers as bandits, rather than terrorists. None the less, the authorities responded to the attacks with a crackdown on Muslim communities, shutting down a number of mosques in Cabo Delgado and arresting about 470 people, including over 300 Mozambicans, as well as foreign nationals from Tanzania, Uganda and Somalia, and about 100 unidentified individuals. More than 180 of the detainees, including 50 Tanzanian nationals, were charged with illegal arms possession, murder, mercenary activities and terrorism, and were tried in October 2018. In April 2019 a number of the defendants were acquitted,

owing to lack of evidence, partly attributable to the courts' lack of experience in dealing with terrorism cases. Some reportedly rejoined the insurgent groups and were believed to have carried out the attacks in May. Following further trials, by September 2020 some 120 defendants had been convicted and 130 acquitted. Meanwhile, in January 2018 Mozambique and Tanzania signed an MoU to co-operate in preventing such attacks, and in June the Mozambican Government confirmed that forces of the Democratic Republic of the Congo had been dispatched to Mozambique to support the security forces.

The attacks have caused considerable disquiet among multinational oil and gas companies operating in the area, notably Anadarko Petroleum Corporation of the USA and Eni of Italy, and now constitute a serious threat to potentially lucrative investments in Mozambique. Although these companies were not initially targeted by the attackers, they nevertheless reported that security problems in the Moçimboa da Praia and Palma districts were preventing safe onshore access for their employees. However, in February 2019 an Anadarko convoy on the road linking the two districts suffered an attack in which a company employee was beheaded and six others were injured. Anadarko temporarily suspended operations in Mozambique. Several days after operations were resumed in May, another company employee was killed in a further attack. In January 2021 the French oil company Total (rebranded as TotalEnergies in May), which was developing a liquefied natural gas project in the Afungi peninsula in Palma, temporarily suspended activities, citing insurgent attacks and the failure of the Mozambican Government to secure the area. In late March—three days after announcing the resumption of operations—Total suspended its activities indefinitely, withdrawing all its personnel after an attack on the town of Palma, in which several dozen people, including company employees, were killed. The Mozambican security forces only regained control of the town after four days of heavy fighting. The Islamic State militant group claimed responsibility for the attack, though this was widely dismissed. Earlier in March, the US State Department had designated the insurgents a foreign terrorist organization. It is estimated that since October 2017, excluding the impact of the attack on Palma in March 2021, the insurgency has caused losses of US $209m., including lost agricultural production, and has precipitated the closure of some 1,110 companies.

The attacks escalated after January 2020, occurring on an almost daily basis and with ever-increasing levels of brutality. Massacres have spread well beyond the districts of Moçímboa da Praia and Palma. In March and April insurgents briefly seized the towns of Quissanga and Moçímboa da Praia, killing an undetermined number of people. Also in April, for the first time, the Catholic Church was targeted by the insurgents, with the Catholic mission in Nangololo coming under attack. A week earlier, militants had killed 52 youths in the Muidumbe district who had refused to join their ranks. After intense fighting in August, insurgents seized Moçímboa da Praia, which remained under their control until 9 August 2021 when it was recaptured by Rwandan troops deployed to assist the Mozambican Government in its counter-insurgency operations (see below).

The attacks increased at the end of 2021, when violence also spread to Niassa and Zambézia provinces, becoming particularly intense in the first quarter of 2022. The districts of Macomia, Meluco and Mueda became the prime targets, and some villages (such as Nova Zambézia in Macomia district) were attacked repeatedly; Meluco district suffered 10 attacks in January alone, displacing tens of thousands of people. The frequency of these attacks appeared to diminish from March. Although Islamic State has increasingly issued claims of responsibility for the attacks, they continue to lack credibility, and an official connection between the insurgents and the wider Islamic State grouping has yet to be demonstrated.

The failure of the security forces to crush the insurgency led the Mozambican Government to seek foreign military assistance. In October 2019 some 200 Russian troops were dispatched to Mozambique to provide training and intelligence to Mozambican security forces in Cabo Delgado. In the same month, in an ambush in the Namala region, 20 security forces personnel—including five Russians—were shot dead and then beheaded. In April 2020 President Nyusi also hired the services of personnel from the Dyck Advisory Group, a South African private military contractor, allegedly after the South African Government failed to respond to his request for military assistance. In the aftermath of the attack on Palma in March 2021, the Mozambican Government accepted offers of training in counter-insurgency for the Mozambican security forces by US marines and the Portuguese military. In June Nyusi agreed to the deployment of standby forces from the member states of the Southern African Development Community (SADC) in Mozambique to assist in operations against the Islamist insurgency. The SADC Mission in Mozambique (SAMIM) became operational in July, the largest contingent being provided by South Africa. The mission has been extended at three-month intervals. After some initial successes in restoring sufficient security to enable the return of some IDPs, SAMIM lost momentum, and has since proved unable to contain insurgent advances in areas under the mission's control. Rwanda, which is not a member of SADC, also dispatched a 1,000-strong contingent of troops to Mozambique in late July to support operations against the insurgents. Rwandan troops have achieved greater success, and were instrumental in recapturing some areas; reportedly, there have been no further insurgent attacks in areas under their control. Nevertheless, overall the deployment of foreign forces has so far only had a limited impact on efforts to contain the insurgency and stabilize security.

CORRUPTION

The liberalization of the economy in the late 1980s opened the door to corruption on an unprecedented scale, and it is now endemic in Mozambique, particularly in the police, judiciary and civil service. High-ranking Frelimo party and government members have been implicated, but few corruption cases have ever been prosecuted—particularly those involving senior officials. In 2021 Mozambique remained among the bottom 35 countries of the 180 ranked in Transparency International's Corruption Perceptions Index.

Two major banking corruption scandals broke out during President Chissano's second presidency. In the first case, investigative journalist Carlos Cardoso was shot dead in Maputo in November 2000 while investigating fraudulent activities connected to the privatization of Mozambique's largest bank, the Banco Comercial de Moçambique. After much international pressure, Cardoso's murderer was captured, tried and convicted in 2003. During his trial the defendant implicated Chissano's son Nyimpine in both the banking fraud and the killing of Cardoso. However, Nyimpine Chissano died before an investigation into these allegations was concluded. In the second case, which remains unresolved, in August 2001 economist António Siba-Siba Macuácua was murdered while investigating corruption at Austral Bank.

Upon taking office in 2005, President Guebuza pledged to eradicate corruption within the police and judiciary. However, corruption continued unabated and with apparent impunity, particularly in many of the cases involving senior officials. Nevertheless, during Guebuza's presidency thousands of police officers were dismissed for corrupt practices, along with members of the judiciary, civil servants, and education and health personnel; some subsequently faced criminal charges and were imprisoned. Many observers noted, however, that only political enemies or those who had fallen foul of the Frelimo leadership were ever brought to justice.

In September 2008 former Minister of the Interior Almerino Manhenje was charged with 49 counts of embezzlement of public funds worth an estimated US $8.8m. during his 10 years in office (1995–2005); a further eight officials at the ministry were also arrested. Manhenje was sentenced to two years' imprisonment in May 2011, although the number of charges against him was reduced on appeal. In 2009 the chairman of the state-owned airport management body Aeroportos de Moçambique (ADM), Diodino Cambaza, was arrested and charged with embezzling public funds; the former Minister of Transport and Communications António Munguambe was subsequently charged with involvement in the fraud. In February 2010 Cambaza was sentenced to 22 years' imprisonment,

while Munguambe and former ADM finance director, Antenor Pereira, each received 20-year prison terms. Munguambe's sentence was reduced on appeal to four years and five months in May 2011. The sentencing in the ADM case coincided with anti-corruption negotiations between the Government and Mozambique's aid donors, and the revelation that Frelimo had benefited directly from the embezzlement undermined the ruling party's anti-corruption agenda.

In late 2015 former President Guebuza himself, by then one of Mozambique's wealthiest businessmen, was implicated in corruption. Documents published by WikiLeaks revealed his involvement in business dealings related to major projects worth millions of US dollars. These included his involvement in the purchase of the Cahora Bassa hydroelectric plant from the Portuguese state in April 2012 for US $950m, for which he reportedly received a commission of between $35m. and $50m.

In April 2016 a further scandal erupted when it was reported that former President Guebuza and other senior members of his Government had been involved in 2013–14 in the fraudulent creation and funding of three state-owned enterprises— the tuna fishing company Empresa Moçambicana de Atum, the maritime security firm ProIndicus and Mozambique Asset Management—under the pretext of instigating a number of projects, including the construction of a new port and improving the country's maritime security. Guebuza had contracted almost US $2,000m. in covert loans with Credit Suisse and VTB Bank of the Russian Federation. The funds channelled through the three companies were secretly and illegally guaranteed by the Mozambican state, bypassing the Assembly of the Republic. The companies never became operational but accumulated huge debts, now known as the 'hidden debt', owed by the state to international creditors. In response to the revelations, in May 2016 the International Monetary Fund suspended financial support to Mozambique, while international donors suspended aid. In July Guebuza and 17 others, including two of his sons and several advisers, were placed under investigation by the Public Prosecutor's Office, after evidence emerged of violation of budgetary laws and abuse of power and public position. An independent international audit confirmed the alleged wrongdoing in early 2017. Consequently, in April the Public Prosecutor's Office requested the suspension of the right of Guebuza and his associates to financial privacy, in order to ascertain whether the secret loans had been deposited in their bank accounts. Five of those under investigation, including two former heads of the Mozambique's intelligence services and Guebuza's former private secretary, were arrested in February 2019. Their trial and those of 14 others began in August 2021 and continued until March 2022, with a verdict expected in August. However, in July the verdict was postponed until 30 November, apparently so that it would occur after the conclusion of Frelimo's congress.

Meanwhile, in December 2018 former Minister of Finance Manuel Chang was arrested in South Africa at the request of the US authorities, who sought his extradition to the USA to face charges of fraud and money laundering. The US authorities accused Chang of taking advantage of the US financial system to defraud US investors in connection with the 'hidden debts' case. In April 2019 the court hearing Chang's extradition case ruled that he could be extradited to either the USA or Mozambique, which had also requested his extradition to face charges of abuse of power, violations of fiscal law, passive corruption, money laundering and embezzlement. In May the South African judiciary ruled that Chang should be extradited to Mozambique. The USA appealed against this decision. In November the High Court in Gauteng, South Africa, ruled that SADC protocol on extradition prohibited Chang's extradition to Mozambique, and ordered the South African justice minister to decide on the issue. The Mozambican Attorney-General, Beatriz Buchili, contested the ruling and sought permission to appeal to the South African Supreme Court of Appeal. However, in February 2020 Buchili dropped the appeal case after a suspect implicated in the 'hidden debts' case (who was also sought by the Mozambican judiciary) was acquitted by a court in New York, USA. Buchili hoped that this acquittal would persuade the South African Government to extradite Chang to Mozambique, and insisted that only Mozambique had the jurisdiction to try Chang. For its part, the US authorities accused Mozambique of pursuing Chang's extradition to protect Guebuza and other high-ranking Frelimo officials. In December 2021 South Africa's High Court ordered Chang's extradition to the USA. Mozambique again appealed against the ruling, but its challenge was dismissed by South Africa's Constitutional Court in June 2022. Mozambique has one further recourse to appeal against this decision, and has declared its intention to pursue the case.

The case brought by the Mozambican state against Credit Suisse and those involved in the 'hidden debts' affair opened in the Commercial Division of the High Court in London, United Kingdom, in February 2021. In the following month the Court dismissed the case against Credit Suisse and Privinvest (a United Arab Emirates-based shipbuilding company that had also been implicated in the scandal), and in May it authorized the latter to instigate its own legal proceedings against President Nyusi. In October the UK Financial Conduct Authority found Credit Suisse guilty of 'serious financial crime due diligence failings' and fined it over US $200m. The bank also agreed to waive another $200m. of debt owed by Mozambique. Then, in July 2022 the bank agreed to pay over $23m. in restitution to US investors defrauded by the bank in connection with the 'hidden debts'.

Further cases of high-level corruption in Mozambique have attracted attention and condemnation. In December 2016 a company owned by former agriculture minister Tomas Mandlate was fined the equivalent of US $270,000 for attempting illegally to export 33,000 cu m of logs to the People's Republic of China, which would have defrauded the Mozambican state of at least $830,000 in lost revenue. In January 2018 former transport minister Paulo Zucula, alongside the former chairman of the Mozambican airline Linhas Aéreas de Moçambique, José Viegas, and a former senior manager at the hydrocarbons company Sasol Petroleum Temane, Mateus Zimba, were arrested (and subsequently released on bail, pending trial) on charges of corruption and money laundering. During 2008–09, the three men, in collaboration with the Brazilian aircraft manufacturer Embraer, devised a scheme that inflated the price of two aircraft to facilitate the illicit payment to them of commissions by Embraer. A company was created in São Tomé e Príncipe to enable the transfer of the commission money. The Embraer case trial commenced in Maputo in March 2020. In September 2021 the court sentenced both Zucula and Zimba to 10 years' imprisonment, but acquitted Viegas.

In June 2019 Zucula was arrested again, on suspicion of receiving bribes amounting to US $315,000 from the Brazilian company Odebrecht in exchange for the contract to build Nacala International Airport, one of the largest airports in Mozambique, despite low passenger numbers. Former finance minister Chang was also alleged to have received bribes, of $250,000, from Odebrecht in relation to the airport contract.

In another high-profile case, in July 2022 a former Minister of Labour, Maria Helena Taipo, was convicted of crimes of embezzlement and illicit business transactions during her term in office (2005–14) and was sentenced to 16 years' imprisonment.

FOREIGN RELATIONS

Relations with the former colonial power, Portugal, were initially strained but were eventually normalized and became closer following the creation of the Comunidade dos Países de Língua Portuguesa (Community of Portuguese-speaking Countries) in 1996.

Mozambique has maintained the good relations established during the war of independence with several countries of the former Union of Soviet Socialist Republics and the socialist eastern European bloc, which provided economic and military support to Frelimo. Russia remains a major supplier of arms and other military equipment. In April 2018 Mozambique and Russia signed an agreement facilitating the Russian navy's access to Mozambican ports, as well as a memorandum on military and naval co-operation. In October 2019 Russian troops were dispatched to Mozambique to train and provide intelligence to Mozambican security forces in Cabo Delgado, where an Islamist insurgency was ongoing (see *Islamist Insurgency*). Mozambique in March 2022 abstained from voting on a UN General Assembly resolution that condemned Russia's invasion of Ukraine in February.

Upon independence from Portugal in 1975, the new Government established relations with Western countries, which were strengthened at the end of the civil war. In 1995 Mozambique became a full member of the Commonwealth. The USA and Western European countries, either unilaterally or as member states of the EU, became major aid providers and budget support donors, as well as becoming important commercial partners. Other significant budget support donors include Switzerland and Japan, which, together with the EU and other countries, suspended aid to Mozambique, including budget support, in the wake of the 'hidden debt' revelations in 2017. In 2011 budget support donors had temporarily suspended aid owing to high levels of government corruption. Despite the country's lack of progress in terms of good governance, in November 2020 the EU approved €100m. in funding to support Mozambique's budget.

Regionally, Mozambique has been a member of SADC since its creation in 1992, and enjoys good relations with other member states, particularly the former Front-Line States. Relations with South Africa were tense for many years after independence, but improved greatly following the end of apartheid in that country and the establishment of SADC. However, there has been sporadic tension between the two countries as Mozambican migrant workers are often victims of xenophobic attacks in South Africa. Troops from SADC countries were deployed in Mozambique from July 2021 against the insurgents in Cabo Delgado (see *Islamist Insurgency*).

Relations with Malawi have frequently been strained, owing to Malawi's perceived support for Renamo and border-related disputes. Diplomatic relations came under pressure in October 2010, when Malawi inaugurated a shipping route from its fluvial port, Nsanje, down the Shire and Zambezi rivers to the Mozambican port of Chine. Although plans for the route had been ongoing since 2005, the Mozambican authorities seized the first Malawian ship to cross the border in October 2010, and arrested the Malawian military attaché on board. In May 2012, at the insistence of the Mozambican Government, President Guebuza and his Malawian counterpart, Joyce Banda, signed an agreement to conduct environmental impact assessments on the shipping route. Several observers voiced their suspicions that the Mozambican Government's actions were motivated mainly by concerns that the new trade route might prove financially detrimental to Mozambique's coastal ports.

Political and military co-operation and friendship ties with Zimbabwe are longstanding and remain close. In January 2018 the new Zimbabwean President, Emmerson Mnangagwa, made an official visit to Mozambique in a bid further to strengthen relations and revitalize commercial co-operation.

China has been a significant aid donor to Mozambique in recent years. Since the 2000s, commercial relations between the two countries have intensified and reciprocal visits by dignitaries have increased in frequency. By 2019 China had become a major funder and overseer of Mozambican infrastructure projects, as well as Mozambique's main source of investment. President Nyusi has been instrumental in ensuring China's financial support to help to deal with the economic crisis afflicting Mozambique and the impact of reduced financial support from other international partners. His first official visit to China, in May 2016, was believed to have been motivated by the need to seek help regarding Mozambique's external debt. During the visit, a co-operation framework agreement was signed between Mozambique's oil and gas company, Empresa Nacional de Hidrocarbonetos de Moçambique, and the China National Petroleum Corporation for the exploration, production and marketing of hydrocarbons. In May 2018 a delegation of Chinese government officials and businessmen visited Mozambique, where they concluded several trade agreements.

Mozambique maintains good relations with other Asian countries, including India; a significant proportion of the Mozambican population, particularly in the northern provinces, is of Indian sub-continent origin. The Democratic People's Republic of Korea (North Korea) provided much-needed aid to Mozambique, particularly for health and sanitation, during the 1980s. In February 2018 the US television news channel Cable News Network (CNN) accused Mozambique of violating UN economic sanctions on North Korea by allowing it to use Mozambican fishing vessels and businesses in order to avoid the restrictions, an accusation denied by the Mozambican Government.

Mozambique was elected as a non-permanent member of the UN Security Council in June 2022 and was to take up the position in January 2023.

Economy

ROBERT E. LOONEY

INTRODUCTION

Following its independence from Portugal in 1975, Mozambique's economy suffered prolonged periods of instability brought on by internal conflicts, natural disasters, poor policy-making, and volatile international economic conditions. Mozambique was one of the world's lowest-income countries at its independence. Conditions deteriorated even further under socialist mismanagement and in the course of a civil war lasting from 1977 to 1992. During much of this period, the economy stagnated, with an inefficient socialist development model producing little or no growth or improvements in living conditions. Poverty was pervasive, with only negligible increases in productive investment.

There were significant regional variations in rates of improvement in economic well-being. The south of the country remained considerably more prosperous than the north. Maputo, the capital, attracted the bulk of new foreign direct investment (FDI) in the south, while the northern provinces received paltry amounts.

PATTERNS OF GROWTH

Gradually, the country transitioned to relative peace, leading to its first democratic elections in 1994. The Frente de Libertação de Moçambique (Frelimo) emerged as Mozambique's dominant political party. With peace and increased political stability, the economy recovered and sustained one of the emerging world's highest rates of economic expansion before being hit by a debt crisis in 2016. International Monetary Fund (IMF) data show that the rate of growth of gross domestic product (GDP), after stagnating at an average annual rate of 0.7% in 1980–92, accelerated to 9.1% per year in 1993–99 and 7.5% per year in 2000–09. However, during 2010–21 growth declined to an average annual rate of 4.7%. Growth remained at about 7.0% until 2015, when it decreased to 6.7%. A steep decline followed the 2016 debt crisis, with growth rates of 3.8% in 2016, 3.7% in 2017, 3.4% in 2018 and 2.3% in 2019. In 2020, with the COVID-19 pandemic spreading to southern Africa, Mozambique's GDP contracted by 1.2%, before recovering to 2.2% in 2021. The country's per capita income (in international dollars, at purchasing power parity) increased from US $475 in 1993 to $1,027 in 2010 and $1,221 in 2021.

Since the return of relatively peaceful conditions in the 1990s, Mozambique's economic policies have primarily adapted to meet the challenges at hand. During the first phase (1993–2002), the emphasis was on reconstruction. The Government also focused on developing the institutions needed to shift the economy from state control to one driven mainly by market forces. In the second phase (2003 onwards), the Government, consolidating and building on the framework developed earlier, turned its attention to sustaining high economic expansion rates. Specifically, while privatization and market liberalization dominated the first phase, the second phase primarily involved investments in major projects (so-called 'megaprojects'—large, capital-intensive, usually foreign-owned and export-orientated activities based on the extraction and transformation of natural resources). Donor support was influential throughout the second period, with aid inflows covering a significant portion of the Government's fiscal deficits.

The two phases witnessed shifts in the relative importance of the major sources of growth, labour, capital, technological progress, and efficiency. Over both periods, as in most developing economies, Mozambique's economic growth has relied heavily on capital accumulation (investment). However, the importance of this factor has decreased, from accounting for approximately 66% of growth in the first period (1993–2002) to 44% in the second (since 2003). In contrast, labour's contribution to growth was similar in both periods, at around 21%–22%. There has been a noticeable increase in technological progress and efficiency. This factor contributed 13% to the country's growth in the first period, but it rose to 36% during the second period.

These shifts in the relative importance of Mozambique's sources of growth probably stem from the fact that the second period was more stable, relatively free from conflict, experiencing sound macroeconomic management, and characterized by institutional development and the increasing replacement of socialist controls with market forces. In this environment, firms take a long-term view of sounder investment decisions and focus on efficiency measures to increase output and profits. The technological progress and efficiency improvement in recent years also suggest that the country is transitioning to the point where high growth rates are sustainable, even in adverse external conditions.

However, in the near term, Mozambique faces a mounting financial crisis stemming from an unsustainable level of government debt. The country is also recovering from two devastating cyclones, the first in 2019 and the second in 2020, and the effects of the COVID-19 pandemic and global recession in 2020. Relations with the IMF deteriorated, and many donors froze aid in response to revelations in early 2016 of massive undisclosed public borrowing and endemic corruption. The Government is attempting to rectify the situation, and relations with the IMF have improved to the extent that in May 2022 the Fund agreed to provide the country with a US $456m. Extended Credit Facility arrangement. None the less, it may take years before Mozambique's economy returns to its high-growth path

SOCIOECONOMIC DEVELOPMENT

Despite the country's impressive growth record, most of the population remains impoverished and predominantly rural, with GDP per head in 2021 of just US $501, down from $674 in 2014. Approximately 62.4% of Mozambique's 32.2m. citizens lived in rural areas in 2021. Progress in poverty alleviation occurred mainly in the more affluent south and urban areas, especially in Maputo. The proportion of the population living in extreme poverty (defined as living on less than $1.90 a day) declined from 69% in 1996/97 to 54% in 2003, owing mainly to growing agricultural income and improved educational levels. However, much of the progress in this area disappeared with the onset of the COVID-19 pandemic. By 2021 World Bank data indicated a poverty rate of 63.7%, with 82.4% living on less than $3.20 a day.

None the less, significant socioeconomic advances have occurred in many areas. There has been a dramatic reduction in the infant mortality rate, from 165.1 per 1,000 live births in 1990 to 54.8 in 2019, and life expectancy has increased from 49.0 years at birth in 2001 to 60.9 years in 2019, before falling during the pandemic, to 59.3 in 2021. However, overall, the country ranks poorly in terms of human development. The 2022 United Nations (UN) Development Programme's *Human Development Report* (HDR), with figures for 2021, ranked Mozambique 185th out of 191 countries in the Human

Development Index (HDI), down from 181st in the previous year. Furthermore, improvement in the country's HDI score has slowed over time, increasing at an average annual rate of 3.1% during the 1990s before decelerating to 2.7% in the 2000s and just 0.9% in 2010–21.

As with poverty, Mozambique's income distribution is relatively unequal, with the poorest 40% accounting for only 11.8% of total income between 2010 and 2018. The upper 10% received 45.5% of income during this period, with the wealthiest 1% taking 30.9%. In the 2020 *HDR*, Mozambique recorded a relatively high average Gini coefficient (the summary measure of wealth inequality) during 2010–18 of 54.0 (where 0 represents absolute equality and 100 absolute inequality), giving the country one of the most unequal income distributions in Africa.

Poverty and income inequality will persist if the current levels of education among the population remain unchanged. The proportion of primary-school-age children completing that level of education is only 15% (30% in urban areas, compared with just 7% in rural areas), with an overall literacy rate of 47% for those aged 15 years or older (and only 33% for females). Educational completion rates have not improved for many years. Owing to inadequate infrastructure, flawed teaching methodology, limited instruction and time in school, combined with high absenteeism among students, teachers and school administrators, less than 2% of students reach an adequate reading fluency level. Gender inequality is also high. In 2018 males had nearly twice the mean schooling as females (4.6 years, compared with 2.5 years).

The Legatum Institute's Index of Prosperity (incorporating 12 dimensions for gauging well-being) ranked Mozambique 146th out of 167 countries in 2021. The country ranked particularly poorly in economic quality (163rd), education (159th), living conditions (157th) and health (150th)

Thus, after several decades of independence, Mozambique struggles with a dualistic economy—pockets of prosperity surrounded by vast stretches of rural impoverishment. Reversing the deceleration of poverty reduction while maintaining high rates of inclusive economic growth are the fundamental challenges facing the country. However, before much progress can occur, the Government will have to address the recent deterioration in governance in critical areas. Between 1996 and 2020 World Bank data show the country declining from the 50th percentile in government effectiveness to the 24th, from the 23rd percentile in the rule of law to the 15th, and from the 41st percentile in control of corruption to the 26th. Overall governance (the average of the World Bank's six governance dimensions) fell from the 42nd percentile in 2010 to the 22nd by 2019. In mid-2019 the Government faced a protracted financial crisis involving US $2,000m. in secret loans and unpaid debts—an unfortunate direct consequence of the erosion in good governance.

AGRICULTURE

Mozambique's agricultural sector is still critical to the economy. The sector employed 70.2% of the working population in 2019. Mozambique's agricultural sector has several strengths. The Government's market liberalization policies have opened up agriculture to private foreign capital, and international agri-businesses have made considerable investments. However, the sector also faces many obstacles, including poor infrastructure, limited access to bank credit, periodic droughts, and regular flooding. Irrigation facilities are inadequate in many parts of the country.

In 2021 crop production dominated the sector, representing 83.9% of agricultural GDP, while the shares of livestock, forestry, and fisheries were 6.4%, 4.6% and 5.0%, respectively. In 2003 their respective shares were 79.2%, 8.1%, 7.4% and 5.4%. The leading agricultural products are cassava, sugar cane, maize, sweet potatoes, sorghum, coconuts, pulses, vegetables, rice, and fresh fruits. Livestock farming consists mostly of chickens for household consumption. However, pigs, sheep, and goats are also important sources of income. A census carried out in 1974 (before the civil war) showed some 1.4m. cattle in the country. By 1992, however, the destruction wrought by the civil conflict had reduced this number to 215,000. Since then, the Government, with the support of

aid agencies, has succeeded in rebuilding the stock, with the number of cattle reaching 2.6m. by 2020. Beef production increased from 24,750 metric tons in 1961 to 36,750 tons in 1985. Production then declined dramatically to 14,250 tons in 1990. After falling further to just 3,531 tons in 2002, production gradually increased thereafter, reaching 16,184 tons by 2020.

The contribution of agriculture to GDP fell from 35.0% in 1991 to 23.0% in 2000 but increased to 29.8% in 2010 after substantial investment in commercial firms. By 2021, however, the sector's contribution had fallen to 29.2%. These patterns are partly because of the gradual deceleration in the agriculture sector's growth rate from an average of 9.7% per year during 1993–99 to 5.8% in the 2000s and 3.3% in 2010–21. The declining growth rate stems mainly from the crop subsector, which expanded by an average of 7.8% per year in the 2000s, before decelerating to 3.1% in 2010–21. Between the same periods, average annual growth in the livestock subsector increased from 3.3% to 4.6%, while growth in the forestry sub-sector decreased from 3.4% to 2.8%, and expansion in the fisheries sub-sector fell from 7.1% to 6.5%.

As noted above, a key factor affecting agricultural growth is the weather. On the one hand, the sector is vulnerable to flooding, which occurs regularly. Droughts are an increasingly disruptive factor. Floods in January 2015 and again in early 2017 caused significant damage to infrastructure. In May 2019 the Government reported that at least 126,000 ha of land planted with various crops were affected by drought in three southern provinces during the 2018/19 agricultural season. Over 60,000 households were directly affected. The three provinces—Maputo, Gaza, and Inhambane—suffered crop losses of up to 60%. As many as 1.5m. people required emergency food aid.

Furthermore, during March and April 2019 the agriculture sector was severely affected by tropical Cyclones, Idai and Kenneth, which brought destructive winds and massive flooding. Cyclone Idai, which flooded and partly destroyed towns and villages across Mozambique, will have a lasting effect inland, particularly on maize farmers, seed suppliers, and infrastructure. Fortunately, the two cyclones that struck Mozambique in late 2019 and early 2021 caused less damage to agriculture.

Approximately 30% of Mozambique's agricultural products never reach market because of poor logistics, warehousing, and processing methods. In certain provinces such as Tete and Sofala, in the central part of the country, up to 50% of the harvest is lost because of poor handling and storage capabilities. The UN's World Food Programme (WFP) notes that subsistence farming is the primary source of food production, and severe shortages exist in agricultural knowledge and techniques. The WFP's Zero Post-Harvest Loss project in Tete assists with improved logistics, farm-to-fork techniques, and optimal storage methods, including hermetic bags. Similarly, the Government of the Republic of Korea (South Korea) donated US $5.7m. to the WFP's ongoing effort in Sofala to reduce harvest losses.

The progress in transforming the agriculture sector will be critical in shaping Mozambique's growth pattern, trade, and income distribution. Food security is problematic nationwide. In planning future strategies and policies for the sector, the Government has considered two contrasting agricultural development models. The first focuses on using giant agribusiness. The idea is for such firms to control vast stretches of farmland using state-of-the-art production methods and business practices. Inherent in this strategy is the creation of value chains in which smallholder units link up and provide input to the agri-businesses.

The second model, proposed by the Africa Progress Panel (APP, a Swiss-based non-profit organization), focuses directly on improving the situation of smallholders. This approach assumes that much agricultural technology for producing crops in Mozambique and elsewhere in Africa is mainly scale-invariant and that there is consequently no inherent benefit from large-scale farms.

The Government's current agricultural development strategy favours the agri-business/small shareholder value chain approach. However, the plan is not without considerable controversy. Many groups in Mozambique view the endeavour as a form of 'land grab', which will displace the peasant farmers who work and live in the Nacala Logistics Corridor (which runs west to east through Mozambique, connecting the coal mines of western Mozambique—via Malawi—by rail with the port of Nacala on the Indian Ocean). Peasant groups contend that there has been little transparency in the Government's handling of the project and that farmers in the region had no input on the venture. Many affected farmers believe that the project will remove their independence and transform them into rural labourers working for the giant agri-businesses.

Peasant groups and their advocates favour adopting the APP approach of developing small shareholder farming and thus supporting the peasant economy. They view peasant farming as providing rural stability and increased employment, thereby enabling rural towns to thrive. In contrast to the agri-business approach, the APP strategy would upgrade millions of peasant farms to up to 5 ha each, using most of the available land. Initial support would involve subsidizing inputs, including mechanical ploughing, together with guaranteed markets for produce. Only time will tell which of the two approaches will lead to a more significant reduction in poverty and better use of Mozambique's land.

In 2022 Mozambique faced a food crisis resulting from the Islamist insurgency in Cabo Delgado province (see *History*) and inclement weather. By February the displacement of 784,560 people (compared with around 172,190 displaced people at April 2020) intensified food insecurity in the province as farmers fled their land. This disaster prompted the WFP to distribute food, cash transfers, and vouchers to displaced people in the region. The rain and cyclone seasons (from October 2021 to May 2022) have been more severe than usual. Tropical Storms Ana and Dumako and Tropical Cyclone Gombe between January and March damaged over 200,000 ha of agricultural land across seven provinces, reducing food supply and placing upward pressures on food prices.

MINING

Mozambique's mining sector is driven, in large part, by coal. The country possesses vast deposits of untapped high-grade coal reserves. Furthermore, the industry is geographically well-positioned to export coal to Asia. However, the sector has some severe disadvantages. Currently, mining infrastructure is inadequate. Until there is substantial investment in power, ports and railways, production levels will continue to suffer. However, the Government's dire fiscal situation (see *Fiscal Policy*) suggests that it is likely to make only minimal investments in the short term.

After growing at an average annual rate of 8.9% during 1993–99, the mining sector averaged growth of 25.3% per year in the 2000s, before decelerating to 12.9% in 2010–21. The surge in sectoral growth stemmed mainly from a sharp increase in coal production and exports. However, growth has declined in recent years, falling from 32.1% in 2017 to 11.3% in 2018, and the sector registered contractions of 2.6% in 2019 and 15.4% in 2020, before recovering to grow by 2.5% in 2021. Mining's contribution to total GDP increased from 0.2% in 2000 to 1.4% in 2010 and 13.6% in 2018, before decreasing to 11.2% in 2021.

With reserves estimated at more than 20,000m. metric tons, coal mining currently dominates the sector. The increase in coal production is a recent development, with production amounting to only around 35,400 tons in 2010. Production increased rapidly to reach 6.2m. metric tons in 2016 and 15.2m. tons in 2018, before falling by 10.4% in 2019. In recent years the sector has experienced severe infrastructure constraints on the supply side and wide price fluctuations on the demand side. These factors together exacted a significant ton on profitability. The average international price for a ton of coal fell from US $107 in 2018 to $77.9 in 2019 and $60.8 in 2020. Prices then rose swiftly in 2021, reaching $138.1 per ton.

Owing to the fall in the price of coal in the early 2010s, Rio Tinto, a leading international mining group, was forced to sell its Mozambican operations to India's International Coal Ventures Private Ltd in 2014. Rio Tinto had acquired its coal holdings in Mozambique for US $3,700m. in 2011, but sold them for just $50m. In February 2016 another major

international mining company, Vale of Brazil, reported that its coal operations in Mozambique were making annual losses of $500m. With substantial commitments already made in the coal industry, the foreign mining companies in Mozambique have been waiting for prices and demand to increase before making any significant investments in the sector.

In early 2017 a more favourable export environment for coal began to develop. With increased import demand from the People's Republic of China, international prices recovered. The security situation in Mozambique improved, with a marked decrease in attacks by the insurgent group Resistência Nacional Moçambicana (Renamo) on coal-carrying infrastructure. By mid-2017 coal was Mozambique's biggest export, and it remained so. In 2020 India was the largest destination for Mozambique's coal exports, receiving 4.0m metric tons, followed by South Korea (860,500 tons), Viet Nam (769,999 tons) and the United Arab Emirates (755,800 tons). Mozambique's coal exports were valued at US $719.2m. 2016, increasing to $1,680.2m. in 2017 and $1,752.8m. in 2018, before falling to $1,225.8m. in 2019 and $648,700m. in 2020.

However, as prices began steadily to fall again, in April 2020 Vale announced the Moatize coal mine would remain closed for an indefinite period as the economic impact of the COVID-19 pandemic widened. In late 2019 Vale had announced that, following sizeable operational losses in that year, the mine would shut down for three months for maintenance in 2020. In January 2021 Vale agreed to acquire Mitsui's 15% stake in the Moatize coal mine and the Nacala Logistics Corridor project. Vale planned to divest the assets as a first step towards its sale of the entire coal-mining operation (in line with the company's goal to become carbon-neutral by 2050).

In April 2022 Vale sold its interests in Moatize and the associated Nacala transportation corridor to a subsidiary of the Indian Jindal Group, which expected demand for coking coal and thermal coal to continue to rise over the medium term. In the longer term, planned expansion projects at Mozambique's principal ports of Maputo, Beira and Nacala aim to facilitate coal exports. Nacala's port expansion will increase its handling capacity to meet larger shipments from Malawi once a 44-km cross-border expansion from Mutarara to a dry port in Marka in Malawi is completed. A planned new coal terminal at Beira, sponsored by India-based Essar Ports, targets coal freight volumes from the Moatize coal basin. Beira port is much closer to the Moatize coal mines, which may considerably reduce overall transport costs.

Although Mozambique possesses significant gold deposits, mining of the precious metal is likely to remain a small share of the sector's value, as informal or artisanal mining, which goes unreported, accounts for most of the country's output. Political instability and underdeveloped infrastructure will continue to deter foreign investment in gold mining. However, the Government is attempting to encourage formal production. There are also proposals to designate specific areas for artisanal mining and to promote safer techniques to protect the environment from mercury pollution.

While there are grounds for optimism, Mozambique's mining sector is unlikely to sustain the growth rates experienced in the past. In 2014 the Government announced plans to increase taxes on the mining sector for redistributive purposes. Flooding remains a critical risk to the sector's development, as unpredictable rains can halt mining operations and export routes.

PETROLEUM AND NATURAL GAS

Mozambique has few proven oil reserves. However, there is the potential for significant discoveries of hydrocarbons, as the country lies at the southern end of the East African Rift, northern sections of which, in Uganda, Kenya and Somalia, have been found to contain deposits of hydrocarbons. Before the discovery of vast offshore reserves in the early 2010s, Mozambique's proven natural gas reserves comprised three onshore gas fields in the Mozambique basin: Pande, Buzi and Temane. However, following the discovery of sizeable offshore gas fields (notably the large deepwater reservoirs in the Rovuma Basin), Mozambique's official proven gas reserves increased from 130,000m. cu m in 2013 to an estimated

2,900,000m. cu m at the end of 2019. Mozambique's national energy company, Empresa Nacional de Hidrocarbonetos, estimates that natural gas reserves could total around 7,000,000m. cu m.

Anticipating a surge in offshore natural gas production, Anadarko Petroleum of the USA (acquired by Occidental Petroleum in August 2019) and Eni of Italy planned jointly to develop four liquefied natural gas (LNG) plants in Mozambique in order to export the commodity globally. However, given the uncertainties and complexities of developing the Rovuma gas fields, it will be some years before the LNG complex generates significant revenue. Mozambique currently produces only a small volume of natural gas, mainly from two of its onshore gas fields, most of which goes to South Africa via the 865-km ROMPCO (Republic of Mozambique Pipeline Company) pipeline.

The Government's Natural Gas Master Plan, adopted in June 2014, envisaged the construction of six LNG plants at Palma in the northern province of Cabo Delgado (two in 2018, 2020, and 2022, respectively) and power generation plants in Palma and Ressano Garcia, together with gas processing and exports to Secunda in South Africa via the ROMPCO pipeline. Under this scenario, total government revenue from natural gas could reach US $6,260m. per year—a figure exceeding the Government's current total annual budget. However, much uncertainty underlay these projections, and by 2015 most experts were already scaling down estimates of both production and revenue.

In September 2019 the French multinational energy company Total (rebranded as TotalEnergies in May 2021) announced its acquisition of Anadarko's interest in the Mozambique LNG project. This deal was concluded after Total reached a binding agreement with Occidental in May to acquire Anadarko's assets in Africa (Mozambique, Algeria, Ghana and South Africa) and signed the subsequent Purchase and Sale Agreement in August. The Mozambique LNG project ownership now comprises TotalEnergies (with a 26.5% participating interest), alongside ENH Rovuma Area Um (15%), Mitsui E&P Mozambique Area1 (20%), ONGC Videsh (10%), Beas Rovuma Energy Mozambique (10%), BPRL Ventures Mozambique (10%) and PTTEP Mozambique Area 1 (8.5%).

Further scaling down took place following the collapse of oil prices in early 2020 and the steep decline in demand arising from the ongoing COVID-19 pandemic. Most observers expected these factors to slow further exploration efforts in Mozambique to a minimum for the foreseeable future. By June 2020 companies were facing a bleak oil price environment, with delays and cancellations for many 'non-essential' or high-risk/high-cost projects increasingly likely. However, a recovery in oil prices from late 2020 gave some cause for optimism.

The volatility in oil prices could also affect final investment decisions for the ExxonMobil/Eni LNG Rovuma project (initially planned for 2020), as most of the 15m. metric tons of LNG sold each year is typically oil-indexed. Depressed oil prices could increase financing costs and reduce the project's returns. Indeed, ExxonMobil announced in March 2020 that it would probably reduce its near-term capital expenditure and operating costs.

In April 2021 Total declared *force majeure* on its Mozambique LNG project after withdrawing all of its staff from its construction site on the Afungi peninsula near Palma, following a deterioration in the security situation over the preceding month. Total stated that it hoped 'that the actions carried out by the government ... and its regional and international partners will enable the restoration of security and stability in Cabo Delgado ... in a sustained manner'. A spokesperson for the company stated that *force majeure* was 'the only way to best protect the project interest, until work can resume'. Total had reportedly already cancelled or suspended contracts relating to the project. The severe damage to Palma and its surrounding infrastructure resulting from the fighting between insurgents and government forces in March–April is likely to cause plans for further development of complex infrastructure in the area to be abandoned for the foreseeable future.

POWER

Mozambique's power sector benefits from the country's abundant energy resources, including natural gas, coal, oil, and renewable sources such as hydropower, solar and wind power. Furthermore, the Government has understood the need to increase foreign investment in the energy sector. However, Mozambique's advantage of having lower electricity tariffs than most southern African neighbours is undermined by the fact that it has one of the lowest electrification rates in the region, at just 30.6% of the population in 2020. This figure masks a significant divide—75.0% of those living in urban areas had access to electricity, but only 4.5% of those in rural areas. In 2021 55% of the population reported having no electricity access or connection. Of the remainder, 8% had a connection with supply working about one-half of the time, while 37% reported supply working most or all the time.

Limited power transmission and distribution infrastructure leave most parts of the country without access to the grid, which tends to restrict businesses to urban areas. As most of Mozambique's population has limited income, with almost one-half living in poverty, the ability of Electricidade de Moçambique to raise electricity prices to cost-effective levels for investors is restricted. Finally, the national grid's deficiencies oblige Mozambique to import electricity at a high cost from South Africa, despite Mozambique being an exporter of electricity to South Africa, mainly from the Cahora Bassa hydroelectric plant in the west of the country.

The power sector has experienced slowing growth in recent years. Annual growth averaged 59.9% during 1993–99, before decelerating to 12.0% in the 2000s and to just 1.9% in 2010–21 (with contractions of 4.0% in 2017, 3.2% in 2018, 1.4% in 2019 and 1.8% in 2021). The power sector's contribution to GDP increased from 0.3% in 1991 to 1.6% in 2000 and 3.4% in 2010. However, in 2021 its contribution declined to 3.1%. In 2021 the country generated 18,300m. kWh of electricity, of which it consumed 12,800m. kWh. Around 80% of the country's electricity is from hydropower, with thermal power accounting for 18%.

Most of Mozambique's electricity generation occurs at the Cahora Bassa hydroelectric plant on the Zambezi river. The plant has a capacity of about 2,000 MW, thus providing a considerable surplus (over Mozambique's immediate needs) for export, with sufficient amounts remaining for energy-intensive projects such as the Mozal aluminium smelter in Maputo. Mozal was Mozambique's first 'megaproject'. Given the country's high population growth rate, energy demand has increased by 7%–8% per year and is rapidly catching up with available supply. In mid-2021 the Government announced the construction of a hydroelectric dam some 70 km downstream of Cahora Bassa—the Mphanda Nkuwa plant—was to be delayed until 2024. The plant would have an initial generating capacity of 1,500 MW (to be expanded to 2,500 MW in a second phase), with some electricity exported to South Africa.

However, while the Mphanda Nkuwa hydropower project is the current priority for capacity expansion, the planned Cahora Bassa Norte project (involving a 1.2-GW expansion of the existing Cahora Bassa dam) is currently on hold. One risk factor in the construction of additional hydropower plants is that the Mozambican power market is thereby further exposed to the risk of droughts.

As noted above, a boom in natural gas production is anticipated in Mozambique, with ample amounts available for the domestic power sector. Some forecasts expect gas-fuelled electricity generation to increase by an annual average of 5.6% between 2021 and 2031, to reach nearly 5,500m. kWh annually and account for 25% of the electricity generation mix. If this occurs, it will represent a significant increase from its share of just under 18% in 2021. While Mozambique has substantial renewable energy potential, the installed capacity base remains limited, primarily as a consequence of the underdeveloped regulatory environment.

MANUFACTURING

Mozambique's industries primarily involve the processing of primary materials, and the country remains dependent on imports for many of its manufactured products. About one-half of Mozambican manufacturers are located in or around Maputo, although the Government is encouraging decentralization towards Beira and northern Mozambique. Food processing forms the traditional basis of the sector, with sugar refining and the processing of cashews and wheat predominating. Other industries include cement, fertilizers, agricultural implements, textiles, glass, ceramics, paper, tyres, and railway carriages. The Mozal aluminium smelting plant is the most significant manufacturing operation, with aluminium contributing 30.6% of the country's export earnings in 2020. However, manufacturing employment is not significant, accounting for only about 3% of the country's workforce.

The average annual growth rate in manufacturing was 10.8% in 1993–99, decreasing to 10.1% in the 2000s and 2.5% in 2010–21. More recently, growth has been weak, with rates of 1.8% in 2018, 1.4% in 2019, and a contraction of 1.5% in 2020 as the effects of the COVID-19 pandemic curbed activity and suppressed demand. The sector recovered to grow by 1.5% in 2021.

The contribution of manufacturing to GDP increased from 14.8% in 1991 to 15.4% in 2000, but fell to 11.1% in 2010. The sector's importance had declined further by 2021, when it contributed just 8.7% of GDP. Much of the sector's growth between 1993 and 2003 reflected the ongoing conflict and civil war recovery. By 2002 the restoration and catch-up phase was over, and, in the absence of solid linkages to the country's 'megaprojects', the manufacturing sector faced several constraints that limited continued expansion.

The Survey of Manufacturing Industries 2012 found that many companies were operating at a low level of productivity, yet still surviving at much higher rates than elsewhere in southern Africa. However, few firms appeared to be expanding and transforming themselves into more efficient production units. Recent research by the World Bank uncovered a similar pattern and found that manufacturing industries employed only 7.5% of the formal workforce and that new job creation had been insufficient in recent years and was confined mainly to a few large companies. The predominance of larger firms in employment generation again reflects the lack of expansion in small and medium-sized enterprises.

Both findings are consistent with the latest figures released in the Global Competitiveness Index 2019 of the World Economic Forum (WEF), where Mozambique ranked 137th out of 141 countries. The country scored consistently poorly in many critical areas: institutions (133rd), infrastructure (133rd), health (140th), skills (139th), labour market (138th), financial system (119th) and innovation capacity (125th). More specific deficiencies included: incidence of corruption (132nd), organized crime (129th), reliability of police services (133rd), quality of vocational training (137th), skill set of graduates (138th) and prevalence of non-tariff barriers to trade (132nd). When asked to specify the most problematic factors for doing business in Mozambique, firms listed: access to financing, corruption, inefficient government bureaucracy, an inadequately educated workforce and political instability.

In 2015 the Government introduced a new industrial policy with an emphasis on creating new special economic zones. The Government intended to implement the plan by providing various tax incentives, subsidies, and institutional support. The new strategy was to adopt both the free market and interventionist strategies. However, it was unclear whether the subsidies and special incentives outlined in the plan would be sufficient to overcome the infrastructural and bureaucratic impediments to new corporate development.

TRANSPORT AND COMMUNICATIONS

Traditionally, Mozambique's transport system has centred on 'transport corridors', which include rail, road and energy infrastructure, linking the interior and neighbouring countries with Mozambique ports. There are four main corridors: the Beira Corridor from the Zimbabwean border to the port of Beira; the Limpopo Corridor from north-east South Africa to the Xai-Xai district north of Maputo; the Maputo Corridor linking Johannesburg, South Africa, to Maputo; and the Nacala Corridor from the northern port of Nacala to the coalfields of western Mozambique, via Malawi. Since 2010,

there has been a renewed focus on the corridor zones to integrate road, rail, and sea infrastructure to support Mozambique's expanding coal industry.

In general, however, Mozambique's transport network is underdeveloped and unable to respond to national and subregional demand, particularly in the port and rail sectors. Although the road network handles much internal freighting and offers connection to regional peers, it remains limited. Much of it is unpaved, constituting a significant barrier to intraregional trade flows. The extent of the railway network is also limited, and its quality is poor. It is unable to meet the enormous demand for heavy freight, mainly in the form of agricultural produce and coal exports. While Mozambique boasts a long coastline along the Indian Ocean, many years of underinvestment, coupled with robust traffic growth, have left seaport infrastructure overburdened. Meanwhile, the air transport sector remains relatively underdeveloped in terms of its ability to meet domestic demand and plays an insignificant role in facilitating international and regional freighting.

These limitations are readily apparent in the WEF's 2019 Global Competitiveness Index, where the overall quality of Mozambique's infrastructure ranked 133rd out of 141 countries. The condition of the roads and the efficiency of air transport services are significant problems, with Mozambique ranked 134th for each. However, the country ranked more highly in terms of efficiency of train services (80th) and was placed 101st for seaport services efficiency. Deficiencies in the transport sector have made it difficult for the sector to keep pace with overall economic activity and have accordingly imposed growing constraints on the country's economic expansion.

The transportation and warehousing sector expanded at an average annual rate of 9.5% in 1993–99, 6.8% in the 2000s and 3.9% in 2010–21. Growth has decelerated sharply in recent years, falling to just 3.9% in 2018 and 3.7% in 2019 and contracting by 3.4% in 2020. The sector expanded by only 0.8% in 2021. The transport sector's contribution to GDP rose from 11.0% in 1991 to 13.7% by 2000. Since then, however, the sector's share has progressively declined: from 9.5% in 2010 to 6.1% in 2021.

International air transport continues to be operated by the state-owned Linhas Aéreas de Moçambique (LAM), and domestic and regional routes by the Sociedade de Transporte e Trabalho Aéreo (TTA). There are 18 airports in Mozambique, of which eight handle international flights—Beira, Maputo, Nampula, Pemba, Ponto Douro, Quelimane, Tete, and Vilankulo. Following pressure from the World Bank, the Government privatized TTA in 1997. In 2007 the Government adopted a new civil aviation policy, which authorized foreign or domestic carriers to operate routes not serviced by LAM. The new policy led to the establishment of direct flights from Johannesburg to Inhambane, Pemba and Vilankulo.

TELECOMMUNICATIONS

After expanding at an average annual rate of 7.7% during 1993–99, Mozambique's information and communications sector grew per year by 9.1% in the 2000s and 5.8% in 2010–20. However, the sector's contribution to total GDP remains relatively small, increasing only slightly from 2.6% in 1991 to 2.7% in 2000 and then to 3.7% in 2010, before decreasing to 3.5% in 2021. Mozambique's sector is very underdeveloped compared with South Africa and other more economically advanced countries. The WEF's 2019 Global Competitiveness Index ranked Mozambique's mobile cellular telephone subscriptions per 100 population at 135th out of 141 countries.

Mozambique, like many African states, has lagged in investment in fixed-line telecommunications. As recently as 2007, owing to many years of underinvestment and neglect, Telecomunicações de Moçambique (TDM) maintained a network of only 78,000 fixed lines, giving Mozambique one of the smallest fixed-line markets in the region. Underinvestment has also affected the country's internet sector, which increasingly depends on wireless.

TOURISM

One of Mozambique's most promising industries is tourism. The country has long, unspoiled coastlines, which are ideal for the development of beachside holiday resorts. Furthermore, its wildlife reserves are on a par with those that have drawn visitors in large numbers to other parts of Africa for many years. The sector expanded rapidly from the turn of the century, with international arrivals increasing from 323,000 in 2001 to 578,000 in 2005, 1.7m. in 2010 and 2.1m. in 2012. However, the trend thereafter was generally downwards, with arrivals declining to 1.8m. in 2014, 1.6m. in 2015 and 1.5m. in 2017. While a significant increase in visitor numbers, to 2.9m., was recorded in 2018, a drop of 29.2% followed in 2019, bringing the total that year down to 2.0m. The spread of violence to several areas near the country's main tourist areas was partly responsible for the earlier decline. The recent economic slump experienced by South Africa has also exerted a toll on the industry.

Owing to the pandemic-related suspension of international travel, tourism's contribution to GDP declined from 6.2% in 2019 to 4.2% in 2020. The number of jobs in the tourism sector fell from 671,100 (or 5.3% of employment) to 530,100 (4.1%) in the same period. The sector's contribution to exports, meanwhile, fell from US $352.1m. (20.6%) in 2019 to $132.4m. (10.1%) in 2020.

The tourism industry experienced a mild recovery in 2021, and operators hoped that the December season, traditionally the busiest, would be a turning point. However, after major Asian and Western countries imposed travel restrictions on southern Africa in response to the emergence of the Omicron variant of COVID-19 there in November, most tour operators reported booking cancellations. The sector's contribution to GDP dropped to 4.1% in 2021 (although the dollar value increased from US $691.1m. in 2020 to $696.8m. in 2021. Similarly, tourism employment declined to 4.0% of the total in 2021, but the number of jobs in tourism increased to 532,400. However, the sector's contribution to exports continued to fall, amounting to 6.0% of exports in 2021. Visitors spent $132.4m. in 2020, but only $100.6m. in 2021. In the absence of state support (which would be difficult owing to the tight fiscal situation in Mozambique), further bankruptcies and job losses are likely in 2022.

In 2019 Mozambique attracted a growing international clientele, with South Africa accounting for 51% of tourist arrivals, followed by Zimbabwe (10%), the United Kingdom (4%), Portugal (4%) and the USA (3%). Mozambique's primary travel market remains South Africa. Although cross-border travel has not yet been affected directly by the international restrictions, the sector has shrunk significantly owing to economic disruptions in South Africa itself and other barriers, including the requirement to present a negative coronavirus test as a requirement for entry to Mozambique (which is prohibitively expensive for many crossing the border). In 2021 tourism in Mozambique was primarily regional, with South Africa's share of arrivals increasing to 72%, followed by Zimbabwe (12%), Malawi (11%), Eswatini (2%) and Tanzania (1%).

BANKING AND FINANCE

The banking sector in Mozambique is dominated by foreign-owned institutions, with only a few domestic players. The largest banks are the Banco Comercial e de Investimentos and Millennium bim (formerly known as the Banco Internacional de Moçambique), both of which have Mozambique and Portuguese shareholders; Absa Bank Moçambique (formerly Barclays Bank Mozambique); South Africa's Standard Bank; and the domestic Moza Banco (formerly Banco Terra Moçambique), which failed in September 2016 when its solvency dropped to zero but was rescued by an injection of liquidity from the pension fund of the central bank, the Banco de Moçambique, which is now the majority owner. The entrenched position of these banks makes it difficult for smaller companies to gain a foothold. These banks control approximately 95% of the system's financial assets, raising concerns about competition in the sector and the public's access to financial services.

Mozambique's banking system has a low level of financial depth, and supervision is weak. Furthermore, by 2016 approximately 80% of Mozambicans still did not have access to formal financial institutions, and only about 3% of the population had access to credit. However, in recent years growth in the GDP of the financial sector has been impressive. After contracting at an average annual rate of 0.3% during 1993–99, the GDP of the financial sector expanded at average annual rates of 21.7% in the 2000s and 13.0% in 2010–20. The industry's rate of growth was faster than that of the economy as a whole. As a result, the financial sector's contribution to overall GDP grew from 1.7% in 1991 to 2.6% in 2000 and 5.4% by 2021.

However, from 2016 Mozambique's banking sector started to come under stress, owing to high inflation, sharp devaluations in the national currency and slowing overall economic growth. Banco Terra Moçambique, the country's fourth-largest bank, failed in September of that year, and the portfolios of many other banks continued to be at risk, as a result of their extensive holdings of bad government debt. Although the three largest banks (as well as the revived Banco Terra Moçambique in the form of Moza Banco) will probably survive, many smaller banks remain in danger of closing.

The relatively poor quality of assets and the dominance of public lending remain the critical characteristics of Mozambique's banking sector. Non-performing loans (NPLs) as a percentage of total loans increased from 9.1% in January 2021 to 10.6% in December 2021 and remained higher than the pre-pandemic six-year average of 7.9%. This probably reflects the increased cost of borrowing in 2021 (the Bank of Mozambique raised its key policy rate by a cumulative 300 base points to 13.25% in that year—the first rise since 2016), limiting the ability of consumers to repay their outstanding debt. Banks are likely to remain cautious about lending to consumers in 2022 and 2023.

TRADE

Mozambique has sought to liberalize its trade regime in recent decades. Currently, the country's average tariff rate is only 4.8%. Mozambique also scores highly in the Heritage Foundation's Index of Economic Freedom. However, customs delays often act as de facto tariffs by adding costs to imports. Mozambique is a member of the Southern African Development Community's free trade area; it also has preferential access to European Union (EU) markets under an Economic Partnership Agreement signed in 2009 and has concluded bilateral agreements with Malawi and Zimbabwe. In 2014, Mozambique became eligible to participate in the USA's African Growth and Opportunity Act. In March 2018 Mozambique, together with 43 other African nations, became a member of the newly established African Continental Free Trade Area (AfCFTA), which came into force in May 2019. One of AfCFTA's central goals is to boost African economies by harmonizing trade liberalization across subregions and at the continental level.

Data from the IMF show that imports and exports of goods and services have undergone notable changes over time. During 1980–92 Mozambique's exports of goods and services decreased at an average annual rate of 0.6%. However, since then, there has been substantial growth in exports of goods and services, averaging 9.3% annually in 1993–99 and 14.2% in 2000–09, before decelerating to 5.5% during 2010–20.

The pattern for imports of goods and services is considerably different, with average annual growth of 2.7% during 1980–92, 9.0% in 1993–99, 6.1% in 2000–09 and 7.7% in 2010–21. These trade patterns have produced high, chronic deficits in the country's current account balance, averaging 13.3% of GDP in 1980–92, 16.3% in 1993–99 and 10.3% in 2000–09, and soaring to 28.8% in 2010–21. The current account deficit reached a record high of 41.5% of GDP in 2012, before gradually declining to 19.6% by 2017. However, the deficit increased again in 2018, to 30.3% of GDP, before falling to 19.1% in 2019 and then widening sharply in 2020, to 27.6%, as a result of extraordinary government borrowing to support the economy during the COVID-19 pandemic. In 2021 the current account deficit declined to a still extremely high 22.4% of GDP.

The increase in trade and current account deficits in recent years reflects Mozambique's low saving rates and rising investment levels. Investment, which averaged 25.9% of GDP per year in 2000–09, rose to an average of 48.9% in 2010–21, reflecting the high level of imports required by 'megaprojects' and infrastructure construction associated with the country's newly discovered offshore natural gas deposits. At the same time, Mozambique's gross national savings as a percentage of GDP increased slightly from 16.1% of GDP in 2000–09 to 17.0% in 2010–21. Net inflows of FDI have covered much of the current account deficits. FDI as a percentage of GDP averaged 4.8% per year during 2000–09 but increased to 23.4% in 2010–21. However, FDI inflows gradually declined, falling from 39.5% in 2013 to 14.3% in 2019. Remittances played only a minor role, averaging 1.3% of GDP during 2010–20.

FISCAL POLICY

IMF data show that both the revenue and expenditure of the Mozambican Government have increased over time, with the rate of growth of spending tending to outpace that of revenue. The result has been widening budget deficits since the 1990s and higher government debt. Specifically, in 1993–99 government revenue averaged 16.6% of GDP annually, increasing to 17.6% in 2000–09 and 26.8% in 2010–21. However, expenditure averaged 18.7% of GDP annually in 1993–99, increasing to 20.6% in 2000–09 and 31.1% in 2010–21. The resulting annual fiscal deficit averaged 2.1% of GDP in 1993–99, increasing to 3.0% in 2000–09 and 4.3% in 2010–21.

Total public debt in Mozambique has been rising rapidly since the country received debt relief from the Heavily Indebted Poor Countries initiative in 2001 and the Multilateral Debt Relief Initiative in 2005–06. The debt was at a manageable level of 32.3% of GDP in 2007, but it rose steadily to reach 64.3% in 2014. The debt level subsequently rocketed to reach 119.9% of GDP in 2016. Although debt fell to 96.1% of GDP in 2019, it increased to 119.0% in the pandemic year of 2020, before falling to 102.3% in 2021. An indication of how dire Mozambique's debt situation has become is that these levels are about one-quarter higher than the average for sub-Saharan Africa.

Complicating the country's fiscal problems, the IMF discovered in early 2016 that the Mozambique state had borrowed more than US $2,000m., which had previously remained undisclosed, casting doubt on its ability to meet its mounting debt obligations. The Government issued an $850m. Eurobond in 2013, supposedly to finance a tuna fishing fleet. Further examination revealed that some $500m. from the bond sale was spent on defence equipment without being disclosed publicly. These revelations prompted many donor countries to suspend or considerably reduce their aid efforts in Mozambique. As a result, the Government had to reduce expenditure significantly, causing a sharp drop in economic growth.

On a positive note, however, in September 2019 the Government announced that creditors holding 99.5% of the total volume of Eurobonds (well above the minimum requirement of 75%) had agreed to a debt restructuring proposal that would involve the face value of the principal and outstanding interest being reduced by 8% to $900m., while the interest rate would be cut from 10.5% to 5.0% until 2023, and would subsequently remain at 9.0% until maturity in 2033.

In April 2020 the IMF approved debt service relief to Mozambique totalling SDR 39.3m. under its Catastrophe Containment and Relief Trust. This injection of funding increased the Government's fiscal resources, but total debt servicing costs remained high. In the same month, the IMF also approved a disbursement of SDR 227.2m. through its Rapid Credit Facility to help the country meet its urgent balance-of-payments needs.

In May 2022 the IMF approved a three-year US $456.0m. Extended Credit Facility arrangement for Mozambique. According to the IMF, the arrangement aimed to support Mozambique's post-pandemic economic recovery and public debt reduction, 'creating space for priority investment in human capital, climate adaptation, and infrastructure'.

ECONOMIC PROSPECTS

Mozambique has the potential to sustain high rates of economic expansion for many years through increased coal production, development of the natural gas sector (including LNG plants), further 'megaprojects' and continued public investment in infrastructure. However, the country needs to address the current financial crisis effectively and make significant progress in governance and institution building before it can join the ranks of emerging economies.

In the short term, government policy will focus on improving the security situation in Cabo Delgado, addressing the cost-of-living crisis caused by the global rise in food and energy prices ensuing from Russia's invasion of Ukraine in February 2022, and recovering from the COVID-19 pandemic. Despite a slow start, the Government's COVID-19 vaccine programme has made marked progress in recent months, with about 93% of adults having received two doses by the end of June. Total COVID-19 cases increased sharply during the global Omicron wave in late 2021 and January 2022, but stabilized thereafter. With the vaccination campaign supporting economic recovery and a natural gas project expected to come online in the next few years, the IMF forecast that growth would increase from 2.2% in 2021 to 3.8% in 2022, 5.0% in 2013 and 8.3% in 2024.

Finally, with the imposition of international sanctions against Russia following its invasion of Ukraine, the need for European governments and the EU to seek alternative sources of natural gas has increased interest in Mozambique's gas reserves. It is likely that this interest will stimulate greater investment and accelerate the development of the country's vast gas fields.

Statistical Survey

Source (unless otherwise stated): Instituto Nacional de Estatística, Comissão Nacional do Plano, Av. Ahmed Sekou Touré 21, CP 493, Maputo; tel. 21491054; e-mail webmaster@ine.gov.mz; internet www.ine.gov.mz.

Area and Population

AREA, POPULATION AND DENSITY

Area (sq km)	799,380*
Land	786,380
Inland waters	13,000
Population (census results)	
1 August 2007	20,226,296
1 August 2017	
Males	13,348,446
Females	14,561,352
Total	27,909,798
Population (official projections at mid-year) . . .	
2020	30,066,648
2021	30,832,244
2022	31,616,078
Density (per sq km) at mid-2022	39.6

* 308,641 sq miles.

POPULATION BY AGE AND SEX
(official projections at mid-2022)

	Males	Females	Total
0–14 years	7,104,598	7,107,134	14,211,732
15–64 years	7,704,562	8,629,633	16,334,195
65 years and over	470,509	599,642	1,070,151
Total	15,279,669	16,336,409	31,616,078

PROVINCES
(official projections at mid-2022)

Province	Area (sq km)	Population	Density (per sq km)
Cabo Delgado	82,625	2,670,078	32.3
Gaza	75,709	1,465,802	19.4
Inhambane	68,615	1,564,289	22.8
Manica	61,661	2,235,836	36.3
Maputo (City)	300	1,130,319	3,767.7
Maputo Province . . .	26,058	2,390,673	91.7
Nampula	81,606	6,490,271	79.5
Niassa	129,056	2,132,767	16.5
Sofala	68,018	2,600,754	38.2
Tete	100,724	3,080,446	30.6
Zambézia	105,008	5,854,843	55.8
Total	799,380	31,616,078	39.6

PRINCIPAL TOWNS
(at 2017 census)

Maputo (capital) .	1,080,277	Tete	307,338
Matola . . .	1,032,197	Quelimane . . .	246,915
Nampula . .	663,212	Lichinga . . .	242,204
Beira . . .	592,090	Pemba . . .	200,529
Chimoio . . .	363,336	Xai-Xai . . .	132,884

BIRTHS AND DEATHS

	2019	2020	2021
Crude birth rate (per 1,000) . .	37.9	37.6	37.2
Crude death rate (per 1,000) . .	12.4	12.3	12.1

Life expectancy (years at birth, official estimates): 55.3 (males 52.5; females 58.2) in 2021.

ECONOMICALLY ACTIVE POPULATION
('000, FAO estimates at mid-year)

	2013	2014	2015
Agriculture, etc.	9,544	9,788	10,046
Total labour force (incl. others) .	11,968	12,341	12,681

Source: FAO.

Health and Welfare

KEY INDICATORS

Total fertility rate (children per woman, 2020)	4.7
Under-5 mortality rate (per 1,000 live births, 2020) . . .	70.6
HIV/AIDS (% of persons aged 15–49, 2020)	11.5
COVID-19: Cumulative confirmed deaths (per 100,000 persons at 31 August 2022)	6.9
COVID-19: Fully vaccinated population (% of total population at 28 August 2022)	40.0
Physicians (per 1,000 head, 2020)	0.08
Hospital beds (per 1,000 head, 2011)	0.7
Domestic health expenditure (2019): US $ per head (PPP) .	22.3
Domestic health expenditure (2019): % of GDP . . .	1.7
Domestic health expenditure (2019): public (% of total current expenditure)	21.3
Access to improved water resources (% of persons, 2020) .	63
Access to improved sanitation facilities (% of persons, 2020) .	37
Total carbon dioxide emissions ('000 metric tons, 2018) . .	6,640
Carbon dioxide emissions per head (metric tons, 2018) . .	0.2
Human Development Index (2021): ranking	185
Human Development Index (2021): value	0.446

Note: For data on COVID-19 vaccinations, 'fully vaccinated' denotes receipt of all doses specified by approved vaccination regime (Sources: Johns Hopkins University and Our World in Data). Data on health expenditure refer to current general government expenditure in each case. For more information on sources and further definitions for all indicators, see Health and Welfare Statistics: Sources and Definitions section (europaworld.com/credits).

Agriculture

PRINCIPAL CROPS
('000 metric tons)

	2018	2019	2020
Bananas*	669	733	775
Beans, dry	361	400	393*
Cashew nuts, with shell . . .	130	140	128*
Cassava (Manioc)	6,346	6,019	5,404*
Castor oil seed*	73	72	72
Coconuts*	252	252	251
Cow peas, dry*	90	91	92
Groundnuts, with shell . . .	123	151	103†
Maize	1,407	1,452	1,632
Onions, dry*	227	231	202
Oranges†	66	67	68
Papayas*	43	43	43
Pineapples*	56	55	56
Potatoes	323	298	313
Rice, paddy	170	180	137
Seed cotton	97	101	89*
Sesame seed	74	80	132†

—continued		2018	2019	2020
Sorghum	. . . . .	148	158	142
Sugar cane	. . . . .	3,139	3,913	2,738
Sweet potatoes	. . . .	487	505	525*
Tea	. . . .	31	32	34*
Tobacco, unmanufactured	. .	115	142	159*
Tomatoes	. . . . .	700	685	571*

* FAO estimate(s).
† Unofficial figure(s).

Aggregate production ('000 metric tons, may include official, semi-official or estimated data): Total cereals 1,776 in 2018, 1,848 in 2019, 1,949 in 2020; Total fruit (primary) 1,030 in 2018, 1,095 in 2019, 1,138 in 2020; Total oilcrops 723 in 2018, 757 in 2019, 769 in 2020; Total roots and tubers 7,165 in 2018, 6,831 in 2019, 6,251 in 2020; Total vegetables (primary) 1,136 in 2018, 1,124 in 2019, 981 in 2020.

Source: FAO.

LIVESTOCK
('000 head, year ending September)

		2018	2019	2020*
Asses	. . . .	49*	49*	49
Cattle	. . . . . .	2,382	2,483	2,604
Chickens	. . . . .	15,885	48,351	27,746
Goats	. . . . . .	3,407	3,211	3,425
Pigs	. . . . . .	1,676*	1,734*	1,695
Sheep	. . . . . .	228*	236*	226

* FAO estimate(s).

Source: FAO.

LIVESTOCK PRODUCTS
('000 metric tons)

		2018	2019	2020
Cattle meat	. . . . .	14	15	16*
Cows' milk*	. . . . .	540	540	539
Chicken meat	. . . .	98	108	115*
Goats' milk*	. . . .	19	18	19
Pig meat*	. . . . .	138	92	92
Hen eggs*	. . . . .	46	46	48

* FAO estimate(s).

Source: FAO.

Forestry

ROUNDWOOD REMOVALS
('000 cubic metres, excl. bark, FAO estimates)

		2012	2013	2014
Sawlogs, veneer logs and logs for sleepers	. . . .	336	336	480
Other industrial wood	. . . .	1,191	1,191	1,504
Fuel wood	. . . . .	16,724	16,724	16,724
Total	. . . . . .	18,251	18,251	18,708

2015–20: Production assumed to be unchanged from 2014.

Source: FAO.

SAWNWOOD PRODUCTION
('000 cubic metres, incl. railway sleepers, FAO estimates)

		2018	2019	2020
Coniferous (softwood)	. . . .	12	12	12
Broadleaved (hardwood)	. . .	649	649	550
Total	. . . .	661	661	562

Source: FAO.

Fishing
(metric tons, live weight)

		2018	2019	2020
Capture	. . . . . .	349,426*	401,122	399,954*
Dagaas	. . . . .	6,970*	15,163	7,215
Other freshwater fishes	. .	95,000*	102,267	90,000*
Marine fishes	. . . .	221,716*	253,451	274,597
Marine crabs	. . . .	3,585*	8,233	9,483
Shrimps	. . . . .	16,040*	14,263	14,631
Aquaculture (all tilapias)	. . .	2,654	2,458	3,162
Total catch	. . . . . .	352,080*	403,580	403,116*

* FAO estimate.

Note: Figures exclude crocodiles, recorded by number rather than by weight. The number of Nile crocodiles caught was: 38,868 in 2018; 59,966 in 2019; 1,950 in 2020.

Source: FAO.

Mining
('000 metric tons unless otherwise indicated)

		2018	2019	2020
Bauxite	. . . . . .	9.9	8.0	6.5
Coal (coking)	. . . . .	8,355.3	5,356.4	4,670.6
Coal (thermal)	. . . . .	6,891.2	4,983.1	3,370.6
Gold (metric tons)	. . . .	507	430	488
Quartz (kg)	. . . . .	361,390	123,572	163,355
Natural gas (million cu m)	. .	5,038.2	4,548.9	4,801.5

Industry

SELECTED PRODUCTS
('000 metric tons unless otherwise indicated)

		2013	2014	2015
Wheat flour	. . . . .	216	218	336
Raw sugar	. . . . . .	557	369	308
Groundnut oil ('000 metric tons)	.	8.0	12.4	0.0
Beer ('000 hl)	. . . . .	2,081	2,168	2,535
Soft drinks ('000 hl)	. . . .	894	1,013	1,239
Cigarettes (metric tons)	. . .	2,326	2,557	2,255
Footwear (excl. rubber, '000 pairs)		41	82	83
Cement	. . . .	1,299	1,512	1,585
Electrical energy (million kWh)	.	15,123	17,739	19,641

2016: Electrical energy (million kWh) 18,697; Raw sugar 350; Cement 2,446.

2017: Electrical energy (million kWh) 17,641; Cement 2,350.

2018: Electrical energy (million kWh) 17,140; Cement 2,400.

2019: Electrical energy (million kWh) 18,981.

Sources: UN Industrial Commodity Statistics Database; US Geological Survey; UN Energy Statistics Database.

Finance

CURRENCY AND EXCHANGE RATES

Monetary Units
  100 centavos = 1 metical (plural: meticais).

Sterling, Dollar and Euro Equivalents (29 April 2022)
  £1 sterling = 80.231 meticais;
  US $1 = 63.830 meticais;
  €1 = 67.277 meticais;
  1,000 meticais = £12.46 = $15.67 = €14.86.

Average Exchange Rate (meticais per US $)
  2019   62.55
  2020   69.47
  2021   65.47

Note: A devaluation of the metical, with 1 new currency unit becoming equivalent to 1,000 of the former currency, was implemented on 1 July 2006.

BUDGET
('000 million meticais)

Revenue*	2017†	2018‡	2019‡
Taxation	168.0	177.0	239.7
Taxes on income and profits .	94.8	90.4	144.3
Domestic taxes on goods and services	53.8	63.7	71.5
Taxes on international trade .	12.0	14.9	17.1
Other taxes	7.3	8.0	6.8
Non-tax revenue	43.1	36.1	36.8
Total	211.1	213.0	276.4

Expenditure§	2017†	2018‡	2019‡
Current expenditure	162.6	194.6	212.0
Compensation of employees .	89.3	101.7	117.3
Goods and services	26.1	33.6	41.2
Interest on public debt . . .	25.0	39.6	31.2
Transfer payments	22.3	19.7	22.3
Capital expenditure	56.7	72.2	68.8
Statistical discrepancy . . .	7.7	−1.0	—
Total	227.0	265.8	280.8

* Excluding grants received ('000 million meticais): 16.3 in 2017 (preliminary figure); 117.7 in 2018 (estimate); 9.3 in 2019 (estimate).
† Preliminary figures.
‡ Estimates.
§ Excluding net lending ('000 million meticais): 24.9 in 2017 (preliminary figure); 13.9 in 2018 (estimate); 6.4 in 2019 (estimate).

Source: IMF, *Request for Disbursement Under the Rapid Credit Facility—Press Release; Staff Report; and Statement by the Executive Director for the Republic of Mozambique* (April 2020).

INTERNATIONAL RESERVES
(US $ million at 31 December)

	2019	2020	2021
IMF special drawing rights . .	6.03	5.92	310.46
Reserve position in IMF . . .	39.47	41.11	39.95
Foreign exchange	3,649.77	3,805.14	3,200.10
Total	3,695.28	3,852.18	3,550.51

Source: IMF, *International Financial Statistics.*

MONEY SUPPLY
('000 million meticais at 31 December)

	2019	2020	2021
Currency outside depository corporations	41,965.5	50,871.5	55,629.8
Transferable deposits	265,219.2	333,689.7	328,969.2
Other deposits	160,992.4	194,284.4	210,392.9
Broad money	468,177.1	578,845.5	594,991.8

Source: IMF, *International Financial Statistics.*

COST OF LIVING
(Consumer Price Index; base: 2016 = 100)

	2019	2020	2021
Food and non-alcoholic beverages .	120.2	129.4	143.5
Clothing (incl. footwear) . . .	130.7	134.6	139.8
Housing, utilities and fuels . .	124.9	124.4	131.1
All items (incl. others) . . .	122.9	126.8	134.0

NATIONAL ACCOUNTS
(million meticais at current prices)

Expenditure on the Gross Domestic Product

	2019	2020	2021
Government final consumption expenditure	219,047	200,637	196,450
Private final consumption expenditure	622,321	641,217	708,566
Gross capital formation . . .	578,134	499,680	514,593
Total domestic expenditure .	1,419,502	1,341,533	1,419,609
Exports of goods and services . .	310,622	288,354	324,143
Less Imports of goods and services	767,503	646,481	710,926
GDP in purchasers' values .	962,621	983,407	1,032,826
GDP at constant 2014 prices .	675,763	667,663	683,203

Gross Domestic Product by Economic Activity

	2019	2020	2021
Agriculture, livestock and forestry	220,232	242,086	269,752
Fishing	12,833	13,548	14,228
Mining	103,459	93,507	103,418
Manufacturing	85,020	77,182	80,630
Electricity and water . . .	26,902	28,463	28,770
Construction	12,295	11,564	13,415
Wholesale and retail trade; repairs	95,249	105,663	96,448
Restaurants and hotels . . .	15,308	12,244	11,923
Transport and communications .	87,196	85,986	88,843
Financial services	40,549	43,128	49,534
Real estate and business services	35,936	33,434	28,359
Public administration and defence	64,691	66,074	69,991
Education	35,094	39,030	43,278
Health	14,047	16,049	18,537
Other services	6,470	6,702	7,060
Gross value added in basic prices	855,281	874,659	924,183
Taxes on products . . . . *Less* Subsidies on products . .	107,340	108,747	108,642
GDP in market prices . .	962,621	983,407	1,032,826

BALANCE OF PAYMENTS
(US $ million)

	2019	2020	2021
Exports of goods	4,668.9	3,588.5	5,579.0
Imports of goods	−6,752.6	−5,882.7	−7,837.3
Balance on goods	−2,083.6	−2,294.2	−2,258.3
Exports of services	931.0	781.4	821.9
Imports of services	−2,750.0	−2,747.4	−2,564.9
Balance on goods and services	−3,902.6	−4,260.2	−4,001.3
Primary income received . . .	260.5	216.0	219.4
Primary income paid	−536.9	−502.7	−559.2
Balance on goods, services and primary income	−4,179.0	−4,547.0	−4,341.1
Secondary income received . .	1,350.6	814.6	853.4
Secondary income paid . . .	−105.9	−137.0	−127.1
Current balance	−2,934.3	−3,869.4	−3,614.9

—*continued*	2019	2020	2021
Capital account (net)	105.9	135.1	64.9
Direct investment assets . .	30.9	−153.4	−193.7
Direct investment liabilities . .	3,379.3	3,187.9	5,295.4
Portfolio investment assets . .	3.4	14.2	−13.4
Portfolio investment liabilities .	10.0	3.1	0.0
Financial derivatives and employee stock options (net)	—	−9.0	−16.0
Other investment assets . . .	−495.4	−91.2	−1,079.4
Other investment liabilities . .	408.4	736.4	−1,219.7
Errors and omissions (net) . .	−112.3	−312.1	−9.5
Reserves and related items .	395.9	−358.4	−786.2

Source: IMF, *International Financial Statistics.*

External Trade

PRINCIPAL COMMODITIES
(distribution by HS, US $ million)

Imports c.i.f.	2019	2020	2021
Vegetables and vegetable products	601.7	644.1	859.7
Cereals	486.9	521.3	676.2
Wheat and meslin	198.4	213.6	252.2
Rice	240.4	250.6	377.3
Animal or vegetable fats and oils, and products thereof .	224.3	231.6	426.2
Palm oil	154.9	163.8	295.7
Prepared foodstuffs; beverages, spirits, vinegar; tobacco and articles thereof .	242.6	232.9	294.8
Mineral products	1,687.1	1,103.4	1,578.9
Mineral fuels, oils, distillation products, etc.	1,569.7	977.4	1,458.5
Petroleum oils, not crude . .	1,161.8	704.2	1,050.3
Electrical energy	171.6	180.5	
Chemicals and related products	912.0	940.2	1,169.9
Inorganic chemicals; organic or inorganic compounds of precious metals	332.8	291.9	376.6
Fluorides; fluorosilicates and other fluoroaluminates and other complex fluorine salts . .	296.0	273.7	306.2
Pharmaceutical products . . .	211.0	286.4	306.6
Medicaments consisting of mixed or unmixed products for therapeutic or prophylactic uses, put etc.	162.0	250.6	213.3
Plastics, rubber, and articles thereof	300.0	254.3	312.4
Textiles and textile articles .	207.6	201.5	236.4
Iron and steel, other base metals and articles of base metal	577.7	481.1	829.0
Articles of iron or steel . . .	223.4	210.0	293.1
Machinery and mechanical appliances; electrical equipment; parts thereof .	1,440.4	1,125.5	1,340.0
Machinery, boilers, etc. . . .	981.7	755.9	818.4
Electrical, electronic equipment .	458.7	369.6	521.7
Vehicles, aircraft, vessels and associated transport equipment	671.7	540.8	749.1
Vehicles other than railway, tramway	592.4	442.4	610.3
Trucks and motor vehicles for transport of goods	229.2	142.7	222.7
Total (incl. others)	7,638.7	6,437.6	8,622.7

Exports f.o.b.	2019	2020	2021
Vegetables and vegetable products	340.0	286.4	408.8
Edible vegetables, roots and tubers	87.5	59.1	155.1
Edible fruit and nuts; peel of citrus fruit or melons	138.7	126.0	118.6
Prepared foodstuffs; beverages, spirits, vinegar; tobacco and articles thereof .	347.9	234.8	274.5
Tobacco and manufactured tobacco substitutes	230.5	162.3	144.8
Tobacco, unmanufactured . .	230.5	162.1	144.8
Mineral products	2,357.4	1,543.6	2,724.0
Ores, slag and ash	272.7	238.0	433.4
Titanium ores and concentrates.	199.3	180.5	335.8
Mineral fuels, lubricants, etc. .	2,001.4	1,258.7	2,201.0
Coal; briquettes and similar solid fuels manufactured from coal .	1,016.7	590.8	1,079.3
Coke and semi coke of coal, lignite and peat	212.1	34.6	334.4
Petroleum gases	271.4	230.5	292.8
Electrical energy	435.2	371.2	454.4
Pearls, precious or semi-precious stones, precious metals, and articles thereof .	185.6	11.4	108.3
Precious stones and semi-precious stones, whether or not worked or graded, but not strung	179.7	1.6	101.9
Iron and steel, other base metals and articles of base metal	1,094.5	1,103.2	1,192.1
Aluminium and articles thereof .	1,061.8	1,060.0	1,128.3
Unwrought aluminium . . .	940.3	970.1	686.9
Aluminium bars, rods and profiles	0.1	0.0	294.3
Aluminium wire	105.2	72.9	136.5
Total (incl. others)	4,722.3	3,460.0	5,111.7

Source: Trade Map-Trade Competitiveness Map, International Trade Centre, marketanalysis.intracen.org.

PRINCIPAL TRADING PARTNERS
(US $ million)

Imports c.i.f.	2019	2020	2021
Argentina	49.3	55.0	92.0
Australia	36.4	9.3	94.5
China, People's Republic . . .	861.5	694.6	946.4
France	42.8	41.0	205.9
Germany	127.7	82.0	67.3
Hong Kong	83.6	44.6	82.3
India	464.1	619.8	739.8
Indonesia	94.2	71.6	70.8
Italy	123.4	109.9	68.7
Japan	238.1	160.9	230.3
Malaysia	96.0	136.7	250.2
Netherlands	149.0	54.0	54.7
Oman	24.7	100.1	75.3
Pakistan	108.8	103.5	105.7
Portugal	269.4	230.3	302.9
Russian Federation	72.6	59.7	52.5
Saudi Arabia	49.5	44.2	99.1
Singapore	513.1	362.9	532.4
South Africa	2,131.2	1,884.5	2,252.5
Thailand	123.9	76.0	105.6
United Arab Emirates . . .	733.8	429.7	716.8
United Kingdom	96.5	176.5	147.3
USA	208.5	154.1	240.8
Viet Nam	72.8	72.0	71.4
Total (incl. others)	7,638.7	6,437.6	8,622.7

Exports f.o.b.	2019	2020	2021
Belgium	196.0	121.4	80.1
China, People's Republic . . .	323.8	255.2	489.4
Hong Kong	160.5	5.6	74.9
India	803.9	423.1	803.2
Italy	302.4	237.8	134.9
Japan	101.8	33.3	91.7
Korea, Republic	138.2	80.2	193.3
Netherlands	246.6	233.5	561.6
Poland	127.1	64.7	100.2
Singapore	168.1	120.9	150.5
South Africa	890.8	731.1	855.2
Spain	170.9	106.3	105.6
United Arab Emirates	74.2	61.8	73.2
United Kingdom	220.2	373.4	372.3
USA	83.0	60.4	102.3
Viet Nam	52.8	68.6	45.6
Zambia	31.0	30.6	53.8
Zimbabwe	69.2	109.8	211.1
Total (incl. others)	**4,722.3**	**3,460.0**	**5,111.7**

Source: Trade Map-Trade Competitiveness Map, International Trade Centre, marketanalysis.intracen.org.

Transport

RAILWAYS
(traffic)

	2018	2019	2020
Passenger carried ('000) . . .	8,383	7,433	3,543
Passenger-km (million) . . .	875	793	185
Freight transported ('000 tons) .	23,719	20,576	16,791
Freight ton-km (million) . . .	13,456	10,520	7,895

ROAD TRAFFIC
(motor vehicles in use)

	2018	2019	2020
Light vehicles	523,580	562,022	597,514
Heavy vehicles	153,660	161,349	169,838
Trailers	21,269	23,051	24,995
Tractors	7,814	8,271	8,531
Motorbikes	76,434	80,914	83,581
Total	**782,757**	**835,607**	**884,514**

SHIPPING

Flag Registered Fleet
(at 31 December)

	2019	2020	2021
Number of vessels	81	87	91
Total displacement ('000 grt) . .	41.4	46.0	47.3

Source: Lloyd's List Intelligence (www.bit.ly/LLintelligence).

Freight Handled
('000 metric tons)

	2018	2019	2020
Goods loaded and unloaded . .	45,999	44,621	44,995

CIVIL AVIATION
(traffic on scheduled services)

	2013	2014	2015
Kilometres flown (million) . .	17	18	18
Passengers carried ('000) . . .	701	752	687
Passenger-km (million) . . .	766	837	787
Total ton-km (million)	6	6	5

Source: UN, *Statistical Yearbook*.

2020 (domestic and international): Departures 6,779; Passengers carried 327,742; Freight carried 2m.ton-km (Source: World Bank, World Development Indicators database).

Tourism

TOURIST ARRIVALS BY COUNTRY OF RESIDENCE

Country	2018	2019	2020
Eswatini	34,645	25,463	7,483
Malawi	6,614	43,527	29,169
Portugal	57,007	78,784	48,986
South Africa	1,871,147	1,043,339	478,492
United Kingdom	60,156	79,437	39,882
USA	65,826	68,555	37,506
Zimbabwe	178,264	208,058	62,893
Total (incl. others)	**2,869,870**	**2,032,923**	**958,588**

Tourism receipts (US $ million, excl. passenger transport): 151 in 2017; 242 in 2018; 252 in 2019 (provisional).

Source: World Tourism Organization.

Communications Media

	2018	2019	2020
Telephones ('000 main lines in use)	63.0	80.8	89.0
Mobile telephone subscriptions ('000)	14,074.2	14,773.4	15,463.2
Broadband subscriptions, fixed ('000)	70.1	70.0	70.0
Broadband subscriptions, mobile ('000)	4,444.0	5,365.6	5,233.9
Internet users (% of population) .	10.9	15.1	16.5

Source: International Telecommunication Union.

Education

(2020 unless otherwise indicated)

	Institutions	Teachers	Students
Pre-primary*†	5,689	28,705	1,745,049
Primary‡			
First level	12,929	88,892	5,977,463
Second level	8,623	29,870	1,073,069
Secondary§			
First level	618	17,090	767,314
Second level	340	7,656	216,175
Technical	252	7,716	93,463
Teacher training‖	18	n.a.	9,314

* Public education only.
† 1997 figures.
‡ Primary education is divided into two cycles of five years followed by two years.
§ Secondary education is divided into two cycles of three years followed by two years.
‖ 2002 figures.

Source: mainly Ministry of Education.

Pupil-teacher ratio (qualified teaching staff, primary education, UNESCO estimate): 58.8 in 2019/20 (Source: UNESCO Institute for Statistics).

Adult literacy rate (UNESCO estimates): 60.7% (males 72.6%; females 50.3%) in 2017 (Source: UNESCO Institute for Statistics).

Directory

The Constitution

The Constitution came into force on 30 November 1990, replacing the previous version, introduced at independence on 25 June 1975. Its main provisions, as amended in 1996 and 2004, are summarized below.

GENERAL PRINCIPLES

The Republic of Mozambique is an independent, sovereign, unitary and democratic state of social justice. Sovereignty resides in the people, who exercise it according to the forms laid down in the Constitution. The fundamental objectives of the Republic include:

the defence of independence and sovereignty;

the defence and promotion of human rights and of the equality of citizens before the law; and

the strengthening of democracy, of freedom and of social and individual stability.

POLITICAL PARTICIPATION

The people exercise power through universal, direct, equal, secret, personal and periodic suffrage to elect their representatives, by referendums and through permanent democratic participation. Political parties are prohibited from advocating or resorting to violence.

FUNDAMENTAL RIGHTS AND DUTIES OF CITIZENS

All citizens enjoy the same rights and are subject to the same duties, irrespective of colour, race, sex, ethnic origin, place of birth, religion, level of education, social position or occupation. In realizing the objectives of the Constitution, all citizens enjoy freedom of opinion, assembly and association. All citizens over 18 years of age are entitled to vote and be elected. Active participation in the defence of the country is the duty of every citizen. Individual freedoms are guaranteed by the state, including freedom of expression, of the press, of assembly, of association and of religion. The state guarantees accused persons the right to a legal defence. No court or tribunal has the power to impose a sentence of death upon any person.

STATE ORGANS

Public elective officers are chosen by elections through universal, direct, secret, personal and periodic vote. Legally recognized political parties may participate in elections.

THE PRESIDENT

The President is the head of state and of the Government, and Commander-in-Chief of the armed forces. The President is elected by direct, equal, secret and personal universal suffrage on a majority vote, and must be proposed by at least 10,000 voters, of whom at least 200 must reside in each province. The term of office is five years. A candidate may be re-elected on only two consecutive occasions, or again after an interval of five years between terms. The President is advised by a Council of State, but is not obliged to follow its advice.

COUNCIL OF STATE

The Council of State is an advisory body presided over by the President of the Republic. It comprises the President of the Assembly of the Republic, the Prime Minister, the President of the Constitutional Council, the President of the Supreme Court, those former Presidents of the Republic not deposed, the former Presidents of the Assembly and the second placed candidate in the most recent presidential election. In addition, seven representatives are nominated by the President of the Assembly for the term of the legislature and four representatives are nominated by the President of the Republic for the duration of the presidential mandate. The Council of State rules on the dissolution of the Assembly and the declaration of war and oversees general elections and public referenda.

THE ASSEMBLY OF THE REPUBLIC

Legislative power is vested in the Assembly of the Republic. The Assembly is elected by universal direct adult suffrage on a secret ballot, and is composed of 250 Deputies. The Assembly is elected for a maximum term of five years, but may be dissolved by the President before the expiry of its term. The Assembly holds two ordinary sessions each year. The Assembly, with a two-thirds' majority, may impeach the President.

THE COUNCIL OF MINISTERS

The Council of Ministers is the Government of the Republic. The Prime Minister assists and advises the President in the leadership of the Government and presents the Government's programme, budget and policies to the Assembly of the Republic, assisted by other ministers.

THE JUDICIARY

Judicial functions shall be exercised through the Supreme Court and other courts provided for in the law on the judiciary, which also subordinates them to the Assembly of the Republic. Courts must safeguard the principles of the Constitution and defend the rights and legitimate interests of citizens. Judges are independent, subject only to the law.

LOCAL STATE ORGANS

The Republic is administered in provinces, municipalities and administrative posts. The highest state organ in a province is the provincial government, presided over by a governor, who is answerable to the central Government. There shall be assemblies at each administrative level.

CONSTITUTIONAL COUNCIL

The Constitutional Council rules, *inter alia*, on the constitutionality of legislation, the eligibility of presidential candidates and the legitimacy of electoral results. The Constitutional Council also formally declares the death or deposition of the head of state and rules on the incapacity of the President of the Republic to remain in office. It comprises seven judges: one nominated by the President of the Republic, five elected by the Assembly of the Republic according to proportional representation and one nominated by the Supreme Court, each to serve a term of five years, which is renewable. Councillors must be aged 35 years or over.

The Government

HEAD OF STATE

President of the Republic and Commander-in-Chief of the Armed Forces: FILIPE JACINTO NYUSI (took office 15 January 2015; re-elected 15 October 2019).

COUNCIL OF MINISTERS
(October 2022)

Prime Minister: ADRIANO MALEIANE.

Minister of Foreign Affairs and Co-operation: VERÓNICA NATANIEL MACAMO DLHOVO.

Minister of the Economy and Finance: ERNESTO MAX ELIAS TONELA.

Minister of National Defence: Maj.-Gen. CRISTÓVÃO ARTUR CHUME.

Minister of the Interior: ARSÉNIA FELICIDADE FÉLIX MASSINGUE.

Minister of Agriculture and Rural Development: CELSO ISMAEL CORREIA.

Minister of State Administration and Public Service: ANA COMOANA.

Minister of Labour, Employment and Social Security: MARGARIDA ADAMUGY TALAPA.

Minister in the Presidency: CONSTANTINO ALBERTO BACELA.

Minister of the Sea, Inland Waters and Fisheries: LÍDIA DE FÁTIMA DA GRAÇA CARDOSO.

Minister of Mineral Resources and Energy: CARLOS JOAQUIM ZACARIAS.

Minister of Justice and Constitutional and Religious Affairs: HELENA MATEUS KIDA.

Minister of Health: ARMINDO DANIEL TIAGO.

Minister of Gender, Children and Social Welfare: NYELETI BROOKE MONDLANE.

Minister of Education and Human Development: CARMELITA RITA NAMASHALUA.

Minister of Industry and Commerce: SILVINO AUGUSTO JOSÉ MORENO.

Minister of Transport and Communications: MATEUS MAGALA.

Minister of Land and Environment: IVETE MAIBASE.

Minister of Science, Technology and Higher Education: Prof. DANIEL DANIEL NIVAGARA.

Minister of Public Works, Housing and Water Resources: CARLOS ALBERTO FORTES MESQUITA.

Minister of Culture and Tourism: EDELVINA MATERULA.

Minister of Veterans' Affairs: JOSEFINA BEATO MATEUS MPELO.
There were also 14 secretaries of state.

MINISTRIES

Office of the President: Av. Julius Nyerere 1780, Maputo; tel. 21491121; internet www.presidencia.gov.mz.

Office of the Prime Minister: Praça da Marinha Popular, Maputo; tel. 21426861; internet www.portaldogoverno.gov.mz.

Ministry of Agriculture and Rural Development: Praça dos.Heróis, CP 1406, Maputo; tel. 21468200; e-mail geral@ agricultura.gov.mz; internet www.agricultura.gov.mz.

Ministry of Culture and Tourism: Av. 24 de Julho, CP 443, Maputo; tel. 21492582; e-mail micultur@micultur.gov.mz; internet www.micultur.gov.mz.

Ministry of the Economy and Finance: Av. 10 de Novembro, Praça da Marinha 929, CP 272, Maputo; tel. 21315015; e-mail info@ mef.gov.mz; internet www.mef.gov.mz.

Ministry of Education and Human Development: Av. 24 de Julho 167, CP 34, Maputo; tel. 21480700; e-mail l_suporte@mined .gov.mz; internet www.mined.gov.mz.

Ministry of Foreign Affairs and Co-operation: Av. 10 de Novembro 640, Maputo; tel. 21327000; e-mail minec@minec.gov .mz; internet www.minec.gov.mz.

Ministry of Gender, Children and Social Welfare: Av. Ahmed Sekou Touré 908, Maputo; tel. 21350300; internet www.mgcas.gov .mz.

Ministry of Health: Av. Eduardo Mondlane 1008, CP 264, Maputo; tel. 21427131; internet www.misau.gov.mz.

Ministry of Industry and Commerce: Av. Praça 25 de Junho 300, CP 1831, Maputo; tel. 21343500; e-mail infomic@mic.gov.mz; internet www.mic.gov.mz.

Ministry of the Interior: Av. Olof Palme 46/48, CP 290, Maputo; tel. 21303510; internet www.mint.gov.mz.

Ministry of Justice and Constitutional and Religious Affairs: Av. Julius Nyerere 33, Maputo; tel. 21491613; internet www.minjust .gov.mz.

Ministry of Labour, Employment and Social Security: Av. 24 de Julho 2351, CP 281, Maputo; tel. 21428301; e-mail admin@mitrab .com; internet www.mitess.gov.mz.

Ministry of Land and Environment: Rua de Resistência 1746/7, Maputo; tel. 823063020; internet www.mta.gov.mz.

Ministry of Mineral Resources and Energy: Av. Fernão Magalhães 34, 1º andar, Maputo; tel. 21314843; internet mireme.gov.mz.

Ministry of National Defence: Av. Mártires de Mueda 280 e 373, CP 3216, Maputo; tel. 21492081; e-mail mdn@mdn.gov.mz; internet www.mdn.gov.mz.

Ministry of Public Works, Housing and Water Resources: Av. Karl Marx 606, CP 268, Maputo; tel. 21430028; internet www.moph .gov.mz.

Ministry of Science, Technology and Higher Education: Av. Patrice Lumumba 770, Maputo; tel. 21352800; e-mail mctes@mctes .gov.mz; internet www.mctes.gov.mz.

Ministry of Sea, Inland Water and Fisheries: Rua Marquês de Pombal 285, Maputo; tel. 21357100; internet www.mozpesca.gov.mz.

Ministry of State Administration and Public Service: Rua da Rádio Moçambique 112, CP 4116, Maputo; tel. 21304037; e-mail maefp@maefp.gov.mz; internet www.maefp.gov.mz.

Ministry of Transport and Communications: Av. Mártires de Inhaminga 336, CP 276, Maputo; tel. 21389819; internet www.mtc .gov.mz.

Ministry of Veterans' Affairs: Rua General Pereira d'Eça 35, CP 3697, Maputo; tel. 21494912; internet www.mico.gov.mz.

PROVINCIAL GOVERNORS
(October 2022)

Cabo Delgado: VALIGE TAUABO.

Gaza: MARGARIDA MAPANZENE.

Inhambane: DANIEL FRANCISCO CHAPO.

Manica: FRANCISCA TOMÁS.

Maputo: JULIO PARRUQUE.

Nampula: MANUEL RODRIGUES.

Niassa: ELINE JUDITE MASSANGELE.

Sofala: LOURENÇO BULHA.

Tete: DOMINGOS VIOLA.

Zambézia: PIO AUGUSTO MATOS.

President

Presidential Election, 15 October 2019

Candidate	Valid votes	% of valid votes
Filipe Jacinto Nyusi (Frelimo)	4,639,172	73.46
Ossufo Momade (Renamo)	1,356,786	21.48
Daviz Mbempo Simango (MDM) . .	273,599	4.33
Mário Albino (Partido AMUSI) . . .	46,048	0.73
Total*	**6,315,605**	**100.00**

* Excluding 221,342 invalid votes and 283,429 blank votes.

Legislature

Assembly of the Republic: Av. 24 de Julho 3773, CP 1516, Maputo; tel. 21255100; e-mail administrator@parlamento.mz; internet www .parlamento.mz.

President: ESPERANÇA BIAS.

General Election, 15 October 2019

Party	Valid votes	% of valid votes	Seats
Frelimo	4,195,072	70.78	184
Renamo	1,346,009	22.71	60
MDM	251,347	4.24	6
Others	134,390	2.27	—
Total*	**5,926,818**	**100.00**	**250**

* Excluding 275,055 invalid votes and 420,980 blank votes.

Election Commission

Comissão Nacional de Eleições (CNE): Rua Almeida Ribeiro, Maputo; tel. 21415669; e-mail dci@cne.org.mz; internet www.cne.org .mz; f. 1997; 17 mems; Chair. Rev. CARLOS MATSINHE.

Political Organizations

Aliança Independente de Moçambique (ALIMO): f. 1998; Leader KHALID HUSSEIN SIDAT.

Frente de Libertação de Moçambique (Frelimo): Rua da Frelimo, Maputo; tel. 21490181; e-mail info@frelimo.org.mz; internet www.frelimo.org.mz; f. 1962 by merger of 3 nationalist parties; reorg. 1977 as a 'Marxist-Leninist vanguard movement'; in 1989 abandoned its exclusive Marxist-Leninist orientation; Pres. FILIPE JACINTO NYUSI; Sec.-Gen. FERNANDO FAUSTINO.

Movimento Democrático de Moçambique (MDM): Av. 25 de Setembro, 1123, Prédio Cardoso, Maputo; tel. 21312041; e-mail info@ mdm.org.mz; internet fb.com/MDM.Movimento.Democratico .Mocambique; f. 2009; Pres. LUTERO SIMANGO; Sec.-Gen. LEONOR ELISA LOPES DE SOUSA.

Movimento Patriótico para Democracia (MPD): f. 2009; Leader MATIAS DIANHANE BANZE.

Partido Amusi: Acção Do Movimento Unido Para Salvação Integral-Nampula: tel. 841229765; f. 2010 following split from the MDM (q.v.); Leader MÁRIO ALBINO.

Partido Ecologista—Movimento da Terra (PEC—MT): tel. 863063370; e-mail ecologista.movterra@gmail.com; f. 1999; Leader JOÃO PEDRO MASSANGO.

Partido Humanitário de Moçambique (Pahumo): Nampula; f. 2010 by fnr mems of the Frente de Libertação de Moçambique (Frelimo), Resistência Nacional Moçambicana (Renamo) and Partido para a Paz, Democracia e Desenvolvimento (PDD); Pres. CORNÉLIO QUIVELA; Sec.-Gen. FILOMENA MUTOROPA.

Partido para a Paz, Democracia e Desenvolvimento (PDD): Av. Amílcar Cabral 570, Maputo; tel. 21486759; f. 2003; liberal; Leader RAÚL MANUEL DOMINGOS.

Partido para a Reconciliação Nacional (PARENA): Maputo; f. 2004; Leader ANDRÉ BALATE.

Partido Independente de Moçambique (PIMO): Maputo; Leader YAQUB SIBINDY.

Partido Trabalhista (PT): f. 1993; Pres. MIGUEL MABOTE; Sec.-Gen. LUÍS MUCHANGA.

Resistência Nacional Moçambicana (Renamo): Av. Ahmed Sekou Touré 657, Maputo; tel. 843981313; e-mail secgeral@renamo.org.mz; internet www.renamo.org.mz; f. 1976; fmr guerrilla group, in conflict with the Govt between 1976 and Oct. 1992; obtained legal status in 1994; Leader OSSUFO MOMADE; Sec.-Gen. (vacant).

Diplomatic Representation

EMBASSIES AND HIGH COMMISSIONS IN MOZAMBIQUE

Algeria: Rua de Mukumbura 121–125, CP 1709, Maputo; tel. 21492070; e-mail ambalgmaputo@tvcabo.co.mz; internet www.ambalgmaputo.org.mz; Ambassador MOHAMED MEZIANE.

Angola: Av. Kenneth Kaunda 783, CP 2954, Maputo; tel. 21493641; e-mail geral@embaixadadeangola.co.mz; Ambassador JOSÉ JOÃO MANUEL.

Argentina: Edifício JAT V-1, Rua dos Desportistas 833, 9º Piso, CP 1100, Maputo; tel. 21421242; e-mail emoza@mrecic.gov.ar; internet emoza.cancilleria.gob.ar; Chargé d'affaires a.i. ANDRÉS VENTAFRIDDA.

Botswana: Av. Julius Nyerere 3812, Sommershield, Maputo; tel. 21494918; e-mail infobotmoz@gov.bw; internet fb.com/botswanahighcommissionmozambique; High Commissioner GOBE PITSO.

Brazil: Av. Kenneth Kaunda 296, CP 1167, Sommerschield, Maputo; tel. 21484800; e-mail embaixada.maputo@itamaraty.gov.br; internet maputo.itamaraty.gov.br; Ambassador ADEMAR SEABRA DA CRUZ JUNIOR.

Canada: Av. Kenneth Kaunda 1138, Maputo; tel. 21244200; e-mail consul.mputo@international.gc.ca; internet www.canada international.gc.ca/mozambique; High Commissioner SARA NICHOLLS (designate).

China, People's Republic: Av. Julius Nyerere 3142, CP 4668, Maputo; tel. 21491560; e-mail chinaemb_mz@mfa.gov.cn; internet mz.china-embassy.gov.cn; Ambassador WANG HEJUN.

Congo, Democratic Republic: Av. Kenneth Kaunda 127, CP 2407, Maputo; tel. 21497154; Ambassador ANTOINE KOLA MASALA NE BEBY.

Congo, Republic: Av. Kenneth Kaunda 783, CP 4743, Maputo; tel. 21490142; Ambassador CONSTANT-SERGE BONDO.

Cuba: Av. Kenneth Kaunda 492, CP 387, Maputo; tel. 21492444; e-mail consulcuba.mozambique@tvcabo.co.mz; internet misiones .minrex.gob.cu/es/mozambique; Ambassador JORGE LUÍS LÓPEZ TORMO.

Egypt: Av. Mao Tse Tung 851, CP 4662, Maputo; tel. 21491118; e-mail egypt@tvcabo.co.mz; internet www.mfa.gov.eg/maputo_emb; Ambassador WALID ADEL ABDELAZIZ ELMELIGY.

Equatorial Guinea: Maputo; Ambassador BIENVENIDO ESONO ENGONGA OKOMO.

Eswatini: Av. Kwame Nkrumah, CP 4711, Maputo; tel. 21491601; High Commissioner MLONDI SOLOMON DLAMINI.

Finland: Av. Julius Nyerere 1128, CP 1663, Maputo; tel. 21482400; e-mail sanomat.map@formin.fi; internet finlandabroad.fi/mozambique; Ambassador ANNA-KAISA HEIKKNEN.

France: Av. Julius Nyerere 2361, CP 4781, Maputo; tel. 21484600; internet mz.ambafrance.org; Ambassador YANN PRADEAU (designate).

Germany: Rua Damião de Góis 506, CP 1595, Maputo; tel. 21482700; e-mail info@maputo.diplo.de; internet maputo.diplo.de; Ambassador LOTHAR FREISCHLADER.

Holy See: Av. Kwame Nkrumah 224, CP 2738, Maputo; tel. 21491144; e-mail namoz.secret@tvcabo.co.mz; Apostolic Nuncio Most Rev. PIERGIORGIO BERTOLDI (Titular Archbishop of Hispellum).

India: Av. Kenneth Kaunda 167, CP 4751, Maputo; tel. 21492437; e-mail cons.maputo@mea.gov.in; internet www.hcimaputo.gov.in; High Commissioner ANKAN BANERJEE.

Indonesia: Rua de Dar Es Salaam 141, Sommerschield 1102, Maputo; tel. 21494227; e-mail maputo.kbri@kemlu.go.id; internet kemlu.go.id/maputo/id; Ambassador HERRY SUDRAJAT.

Ireland: Av. Julius Nyerere 3630, Sommerschield, Maputo; tel. 21491440; e-mail maputoembassy@dfa.ie; internet www.dfa.ie/irish-embassy/mozambique; Ambassador PATRICK EMPEY (designate).

Italy: Av. Kenneth Kaunda 387, CP 976, Maputo; tel. 21492229; e-mail ambasciata.maputo@esteri.it; internet ambmaputo.esteri.it; Ambassador GIANNI BARDINI.

Japan: Av. Julius Nyerere 2832, CP 2494, Maputo; tel. 21499819; e-mail embjpmoz@mp.mofa.go.jp; internet www.mz.emb-japan.go .jp; Ambassador HAJIME KIMURA.

Kenya: Maputo; High Commissioner NDUNG'U PAUL KAMWERU.

Korea, Republic: Torres Rani, 7º andar, Av. Marginal 141, Maputo; tel. 21495625; e-mail embassy-mz@mofa.go.kr; internet overseas .mofa.go.kr/mz-ko/index.do; Ambassador CHOI WON SOK.

Libya: Rua Pereira Marinho 274, CP 4434, Maputo; tel. 21490662; Ambassador SALEH MUHAMMAD MUHAMMAD AL-BOAYSHI.

Malawi: Av. Kenneth Kaunda 75, CP 4148, Maputo; tel. 21492676; e-mail malawmoz@tdm.co.mz; High Commissioner WEZI MOYO.

Mauritius: Rua da Nwamatibyane 42, Sommershield, Maputo; tel. 21494624; e-mail maputo@govmu.org; internet mauritius-maputo .govmu.org/Pages/index.aspx; High Commissioner JEAN FRANÇOIS CHAUMIERE.

Morocco: Av. Julius Nyerere 4337, Maputo; tel. 21483330; Ambassador ABDELALI RAHALI.

Netherlands: Av. Kwame Nkrumah 324, CP 1163, Maputo; tel. 21484200; e-mail map@minbuza.nl; internet www .nederlandwereldwijd.nl/landen/mozambique; Ambassador (vacant).

Nigeria: Av. Kenneth Kaunda 821, CP 4621, Maputo; tel. 21492457; e-mail admin@nigerianhcmaputo.gov.ng; internet nigerianhc maputo.gov.ng; High Commissioner YAMAH MOHAMMED MUSA.

Norway: Av. Julius Nyerere 1162, CP 828, Maputo; tel. 21480100; e-mail emb.maputo@mfa.no; internet www.norway.no/mozambique; Ambassador HAAKON GRAM-JOHANNESSEN.

Portugal: Av. Julius Nyerere 720/730, CP 4696, Maputo; tel. 21490316; e-mail maputo@mne.pt; internet maputo .embaixadaportugal.mne.pt; Ambassador ANTÓNIO MANUEL COELHO DA COSTA.

Russian Federation: Av. Vladimir I. Lénine 2445, CP 4666, Maputo; tel. 21417372; e-mail embmozambic@mid.ru; internet mozambik.mid.ru; Ambassador ALEXANDER SURIKOV.

Rwanda: Av. de Barnabe Thawe 720–3, Bairro da Polana, Maputo; tel. 21488982; e-mail ambamaputo@minaffet.gov.rw; internet fb .com/RwandainMozambique; High Commissioner CLAUDE NIKOBISANZWE.

Saudi Arabia: Av. Julius Nyerere 3268, Maputo; tel. 21498832; e-mail saudiembassyinmaputo@gmail.com; internet fb.com/KSAembassyMOZ; Ambassador FAHAD ABDULLAH FAHAD AL-ISSA.

South Africa: Av. Eduardo Mondlane 41, CP 1120, Maputo; tel. 21490059; e-mail sahcmaputoenquiries@dirco.gov.za; internet www .dirco.gov.za/maputo; High Commissioner Gen. (Retd) SIPHIWE NYANDA.

Spain: Rua Damião de Góis 347, CP 1331, Maputo; tel. 21492025; e-mail emb.maputo@maec.es; internet www.exteriores.gob.es/embajadas/maputo; Ambassador ALBERTO CEREZO SOBRINO.

Sudan: Av. Kenneth Kaunda 842, Maputo; tel. 21485590; e-mail sudanembassy2014maputo@gmail.com; Ambassador (vacant).

Sweden: Av. Julius Nyerere 1128, CP 338, Maputo; tel. 21480300; e-mail ambassaden.maputo@gov.se; internet www.swedenabroad .se/maputo; Ambassador METTE SUNNERGREN.

Switzerland: Av. Ahmed Sekou Touré 637, CP 135, Maputo; tel. 21321337; e-mail maputo@eda.admin.ch; internet www.eda.admin .ch/maputo; Ambassador OLIVIER BÜRKI.

Tanzania: Martires da Machava 852, Maputo; tel. 21490110; e-mail tanzrep-maputo@tvcabo.co.mz; internet www.mz.tzembassy.go.tz; High Commissioner PHAUSTINE MARTIN KASIKE.

Thailand: Av. Julius Nyerere 4317, Maputo; tel. 843924698; e-mail thaiembassy.mpm@mfa.mail.go.th; internet maputo.thaiembassy .org; Ambassador SORADJAK PURANASAMRIDDHI.

Timor-Leste: Av. do Zimbábwe 1532, Maputo; tel. 823349468; Ambassador FRANCISCO MIRANDA BRANCO.

Türkiye (Turkey): Av. Marginal, CP 3901, Maputo; tel. 21494122; e-mail embassy.maputo@mfa.gov.tr; internet maputo.be.mfa.gov.tr; Ambassador HUSEYIN AVNI AKSOY.

United Arab Emirates: Av. Marginal 141, CP 1100, Maputo; tel. 21246200; e-mail maputoemb@mofaic.gov.ae; internet fb.com/UAEinMaputo; Chargé d'affaires a.i. SALIM ALJABERI.

United Kingdom: Av. Vladimir I. Lénine 310, CP 55, Maputo; tel. 21356000; e-mail maputo.consularenquiries@fco.gov.uk; internet www.gov.uk/world/mozambique; High Commissioner HELEN LEWIS (designate).

USA: Av. Marginal 5467, Maputo; tel. 840958000; e-mail maputoirc@state.gov; internet mz.usembassy.gov; Ambassador PETER HENDRICK VROOMAN.

Venezuela: Rua dos Bougainvilea Flora 3350, Nº 57, Sommerchield II, Maputo; tel. 21494960; e-mail embve.mzmpt@mppre.gob.ve; internet mozambique.embajada.gob.ve; Ambassador JUAN CARLOS FERNANDES JUÁREZ.

Viet Nam: Av. Francisco Orlando Magumbwe 1026/1048, CP 4501, Maputo; tel. 21497912; e-mail sqvnmoz@yahoo.com; internet vnembassy-maputo.mofa.gov.vn; Ambassador PHAM HOANG KIM.

Zambia: Av. Kenneth Kaunda 1286, CP 4655, Maputo; tel. 21492452; e-mail zhcmmap@tvcabo.co.mz; High Commissioner PAUL LUMBI.

Zimbabwe: Av. Mártires da Machava 1657, CP 743, Maputo; tel. 21490404; e-mail zimmaputo@tdm.co.mz; Ambassador Dr VICTOR MATEMADANDA.

Judicial System

The Constitution of November 1990 provides for a Supreme Court and other judicial courts, a Constitutional Council, an Administrative Court, courts-martial, customs courts, maritime courts and labour courts. The Supreme Court consists of professional judges, appointed by the President of the Republic, and judges elected by the Assembly of the Republic. It acts in sections, as a trial court of primary and appellate jurisdiction, and, in plenary session, as a court of final appeal. The Administrative Court controls the legality of administrative acts and supervises public expenditure.

Supreme Court: Av. Vladimir I. Lénine 103, CP 278, Maputo; tel. 21323306; internet www.ts.gov.mz; Pres. Dr ADELINO MANUEL MUCHANGA.

Constitutional Council: Rua Mateus Sansão Muthemba 493, CP 2372, Maputo; tel. 21487431; e-mail correiocc@cconstitucional.org.mz; internet www.cconstitucional.org.mz; f. 1990; Pres. LÚCIA RIBEIRO.

Administrative Court: Praça da Independência 1117, Maputo; tel. 21345002; e-mail ta@ta.gov.mz; internet www.ta.gov.mz; Pres. LUCIA DO AMARAL.

Attorney-General: BEATRIZ BUCHILI.

Religion

According to the 2017 census, 59.8% of the population were Christian and 18.9% were Muslim. There are, in addition, small Hindu, Jewish and Bahá'í communities.

CHRISTIANITY

There are many Christian organizations registered in Mozambique.

Conselho Cristão de Moçambique (CCM) (Christian Council of Mozambique): Av. Ahmed Sekou Touré 1037, Maputo; tel. 21322043; f. 1948; Pres. Rt Rev. FELICIDADE CHIRINDA; Gen. Sec. Rev. JOÃO DAMIÃO MUHALE.

The Roman Catholic Church

Mozambique comprises three archdioceses and nine dioceses. According to the 2017 census, the number of adherents represented some 27.2% of the total population.

Bishops' Conference: Conferência Episcopal de Moçambique (CEM), Secretariado Geral da CEM, Av. Paulo Samuel Kankhomba 188/RC, CP 286, Maputo; tel. 21490766; f. 1982; Pres. Rt Rev. LUCIO ANDRICE MUANDULA (Bishop of Xai-Xai).

Archbishop of Beira: Most Rev. CLAUDIO DALLA ZUANNA, Cúria Arquiepiscopal, Rua Correia de Brito 613, CP 544, Beira; tel. 23322313; e-mail arquidbeira@teledata.mz.

Archbishop of Maputo: Most Rev. FRANCISCO CHIMOIO, Paço Arquiepiscopal, Av. Eduardo Mondlane 1448, CP 258, Maputo; tel. 826425603; e-mail arcemaputosecretaria@gmail.com; internet www.arquidiocesedemaputo.org.

Archbishop of Nampula: Most. Rev. INÁCIO SAÚRE, Paço Arquiepiscopal, CP 84, 70100 Nampula; tel. 26213024; e-mail info@arquidiocesenampula.org; internet www.arquidiocesenampula.org.

The Anglican Communion

A new Anglican province for Mozambique and Angola—the Igreja Anglicana de Moçambique e Angola—was formed in September 2021; eight of the 12 dioceses were to be in Mozambique.

Igreja Anglicana de Moçambique e Angola (IAMA): Maputo; f. 2021; Acting Presiding Bishop CARLOS MATSINHE.

Other Churches

Baptist Convention of Mozambique: Rua da Coimbra 15, Maputo; tel. 2126852; e-mail info@cbmnet.org; internet www.cbmnet.org; Pres. Pastor LOURENÇO ANTEIRO.

Evangelical Lutheran Church in Mozambique: Av. Kim Il Song 520, CP 1488, Sommerschield, Maputo; tel. 212489200; e-mail bispo.ielm@tvcabo.co.mz; Bishop EDUARDO SINALO.

Igreja Congregacional Unida de Moçambique: Rua 4 Bairro 25 de Junho, CP 930, Maputo; tel. 21475820; Pres. Sec. of the Synod A. A. LITSURE.

Igreja Maná: Rua Francisco Orlando Magumbwe 528, Maputo; tel. 21491760; e-mail adm_mocambique@igrejamana.com; Bishop DOMINGOS COSTA.

Igreja Reformada em Moçambique (IRM) (Reformed Church in Mozambique): CP 3, Vila Ulongue, Anogonia-Tete; f. 1908; Gen. Sec. Rev. SAMUEL M. BESSITALA.

Presbyterian Church of Mozambique: Av. Ahmed Sekou Touré 1822, CP 21, Maputo; tel. 21421790; e-mail ipmoc@zebra.uem.mz; f. 1887; Pres. of Synodal Council Rev. OBEDE BALIO.

Seventh-Day Adventist Church: Av. Maguiguana 300, CP 1468, Maputo; tel. 21427200; e-mail mozambiqueunion@gmail.com; internet mzm.adventist.org; Pres. ALFREDO JOTAMO CHILUNDO.

Other denominations active in Mozambique include the Church of Christ, the Church of the Nazarene, the Greek Orthodox Church, the United Methodist Church of Mozambique, the Wesleyan Methodist Church, the Zion Christian Church, and Jehovah's Witnesses.

ISLAM

Comunidade Mahometana: Av. Albert Luthuli 291, Maputo; tel. 21425181; e-mail cmahometana@gmail.com; internet fb.com/Comunidademahometanamaputo; Pres. SALEEM AHMED ABDUL KARIM.

Conselho Islâmico de Moçambique (CISLAMO) (Islamic Council of Mozambique): CP 4510, Maputo; tel. 21405271; e-mail cislamo@fdm.co.mzgmail.com; internet cislamo.org; f. 1983; Pres. AMINUDIN MUHAMMAD; Sec.-Gen. (vacant).

The Press

DAILY NEWSPAPERS (PRINT AND ONLINE)

Club of Mozambique: Av. Marginal 8874, Maputo; tel. 21451739; e-mail info@clubofmozambique.com; internet clubofmozambique.com; f. 2007; English; Founder ADRIAN FREY.

Correio da Manha: Rua das Dálias 49, 2° andar, CP 1756, Maputo; tel. 21305322; e-mail correiodamanha@tvcabo.co.mz; internet www.correiodamanhamoz.com; f. 1997; published by Sojornal, Lda; also publishes weekly *Correio Semanal*; Dir REFINALDO CHILENGUE.

Folha de Maputo: Av. Julius Nyerere 360, 21° andar, Prédio Mont'Alto Arganil, Maputo; tel. 21494065; e-mail editor@folhademaputo.co.mz; internet www.folhademaputo.co.mz; Editorial Co-ordinator M. CHIDIMA.

mediaFax: Av. Amílcar Cabral 1049, CP 73, Maputo; tel. 21301737; e-mail mediafax@mediacoop.co.mz; f. 1992 by co-operative of independent journalists Mediacoop; news-sheet by subscription only, distribution by fax and internet; Editor FERNANDO MBANZE.

Notícias: Rua Joe Slovo 55, CP 327, Maputo; tel. 21420119; internet jornalnoticias.co.mz; f. 1926; publ. by Sociedade do Notícias, SA; Dir LÁZARO MANHIÇA.

WEEKLIES

Desafio: Rua Joe Slovo, 55, CP 327 Maputo; tel. 21320119; e-mail info@snoticias.co.mz; internet jornaldesafio.co.mz; Dir ALMIRO SANTOS; Chief Editors REGINALDO CUMBANA, GIL CARVALHO.

Domingo: Rua Joe Slovo 55, CP 327, Maputo; tel. 21431026; e-mail jornaldomingo@snoticias.co.mz; internet www.jornaldomingo.co.mz; f. 1981; Sun.; Dir ANDRÉ MATOLA; Editor-in-Chief ANTÓNIO MONDLHANE.

Fim de Semana: Prédio Cardoso, Flat D-E-F, 1° andar, Av. Setembro 25 1123, Maputo; tel. 21321946; e-mail fimdomes@tvcabo.co.mz; internet fimdesemana.co.mz; f. 1997; independent; Editor MARCELO MACHAVA.

Savana: Av. Amílcar Cabral 1049, CP 73, Maputo; tel. 21301737; e-mail savana@mediacoop.co.mz; internet savana.co.mz; f. 1994; owned by mediacoop, SA; CEO NÍDIA CHIZIANE; Editor FERNANDO GONÇALVES.

@Verdade: Av. 25 de Setembro 57A, Maputo; tel. 843998624; e-mail averdademz@gmail.com; internet www.verdade.co.mz; f. 2008; Founder ERIK CHARAS; Editor-in-Chief SAMBO EMILDO.

Zambeze: Rua José Sidumo, Maputo; tel. 21302019; Dir JOÃO CHAMUSSE.

PERIODICALS

Boletim da República: Rua da Imprensa 283, CP 275, Maputo; tel. 21427022; e-mail imprensanac@minjust.gov.mz; internet www.portaldogoverno.gov.mz; govt and official notices; publ. by Imprensa Nacional da Moçambique.

Mozambique Inview: c/o Mediacoop, Av. Amílcar Cabral 1049, CP 73, Maputo; tel. 21430722; e-mail inview@savana.co.mz; f. 1994; bimonthly; economic bulletin in English.

NEWS AGENCY

Agência de Informação de Moçambique (AIM): Rua da Rádio Moçambique 112, 5º andar, CP 896, Maputo; tel. 21313225; e-mail aim@aim.org.mz; internet www.aim.org.mz; f. 1975; daily reports in Portuguese and English; Dir BERNARDO MAVANGA.

Publishers

Arquivo Histórico de Moçambique (AHM): Travessa do Varietá 58, CP 2033, Maputo; tel. 21323428; e-mail ahm@uem.mz; internet www.ahm.uem.mz; f. 1934; unit of Eduardo Mondlane University, Maputo; Dir JOEL DAS NEVES TEMBE.

Centro de Estudos Africanos: Universidade Eduardo Mondlane, Av. Julius Nyerere, CP 1993, Maputo; tel. 21430239; e-mail cea@uem.ac.mz; internet www.cea.uem.mz; f. 1976; social and political science, regional history, economics, humanities; Dir Dr CARLOS ARNALDO.

Fundo Bibliográfico de Língua Portuguesa: Av. 25 de Setembro 1230, 7º andar, Maputo; tel. 21429531; e-mail palop@zebra.uem.mz; internet fb.com/fundoblp.gov; f. 1990; state owned; Pres. NATANIEL NGOMANE.

Imprensa Universitária: Universidade Eduardo Mondlane, Av. Julius Nyerere, Maputo; tel. 21410100; e-mail feedback@uem.mz; internet www.uem.mz; university press; Pres. Prof. Dr ORLANDO ANTÓNIO QUILAMBO.

Minerva-Continental: Av. 25 de Setembro 1521/1531, ângulo com a Av. Samora Machel, Maputo; tel. 843018782; e-mail comercial@minerva.co.mz; internet fb.com/MinervaMZ; f. 1908; fmrly Minerva Central; stationers and printers, educational, technical and medical textbooks; Man. Dir J. F. CARVALHO.

Moçambique Editora: Rua Armando Tivane 1430, Bairro de Polana, Maputo; tel. 21495017; e-mail info@me.co.mz; internet www.me.co.mz; f. 1996; educational textbooks, dictionaries.

Plural Editores: Av. Patrice Lumumba 765, Maputo; tel. 21360900; e-mail plural@pluraleditores.co.mz; internet www.pluraleditores.co.mz; f. 2003; educational textbooks; part of the Porto Editora Group.

GOVERNMENT PUBLISHING HOUSE

Imprensa Nacional de Moçambique: Rua da Imprensa, CP 275, Maputo; tel. 21427021; e-mail e-br.reclamacoes@inm.gov.mz; internet www.inm.gov.mz; f. 1854; Chair. JAIME BESSA NETO.

Broadcasting and Communications

TELECOMMUNICATIONS

Movitel: Av. Guerra Popular 1086, Maputo; internet movitel.co.mz; f. 2012; mobile telecom operator; joint venture of Viettel, Vietnam and SPI, Mozambique; Chair. SAFURA DA CONCEIÇÃO.

Moçambique Telecom, SA (TMCEL): Rua Belmiro Obadias Muianga 384, CP 1483, Maputo; tel. 21351100; e-mail contactcenter@tmcel.mz; internet fb.com/tmcel.mz; f. 1981 as Telecomunicações de Moçambique; merged with Moçambique Celular (mCel, f. 1997) in 2019; Chair. MOHAMED RAFIQUE JUSOB; Man. Dir MAMUDO IBRAIMO.

Vodacom Moçambique (VM): Rua dos Desportistas 649, Maputo; tel. 840900000; e-mail social.media@vm.co.mz; internet www.vm.co.mz; f. 2003; mobile telephone provider; owned by Vodacom Group (South Africa) and local shareholders; CEO SIMON KARIKARI.

Regulatory Authority

Instituto Nacional das Comunicações de Moçambique (INCM): Praça 16 de Junho 340, Bairro da Malanga, CP 848, Maputo; tel. 21227100; e-mail info@incm.gov.mz; internet www.incm.gov.mz; f. 1992; regulates post and telecommunications systems; Chair. TUAHA CHABANE MOTE.

BROADCASTING

Radio

Rádio Encontro: Av. Francisco Manyanga 359, CP 366, Nampula; tel. 842857346; e-mail info@radioencontro.co.mz; internet radioencontro.co.mz; f. 1995; owned by the diocese of Nampula.

Rádio Maria: House 31, Praça da OMM, Rua de França, Rua 1398; tel. 823004785; e-mail info.moz@radiomaria.org; internet www.radiomaria.org.mz; f. 1995; part of Associazione Radio Maria (Italy); evangelical radio broadcasts; Dir MIGUEL GONÇALVES.

Rádio Miramar: Rede de Comunicação, Av. Julius Nyerere 1555, Maputo; tel. 843108693; e-mail comercial@miramar.co.mz; internet fb.com/radiomiramar.mz; owned by Rede de Comunicação Miramar; CEO JOSÉ GUERRA.

Rádio Moçambique: Rua da Rádio 2, CP 2000, Maputo; tel. 21429908; e-mail dinfoweb@rm.co.mz; internet www.rm.co.mz; f. 1975; state-owned; programmes in Portuguese, English and vernacular languages; Chair. FARUCO SADIQUE.

Rádio Trans Mundial Moçambique: Av. Eduardo Mondlane 2998, CP 1526, Maputo; tel. 21440003; internet fb.com/radiocapital907; f. 2001.

Television

RTP África: Rua Pero de Anaia 248, Maputo; tel. 21497344; e-mail rtp.a.moc@teledata.mz; f. 1998; part of Portuguese international channel RTP África.

Televisão Miramar: Av. Julius Nyerere 1555, Polana Cimento, Maputo; tel. 21498440; e-mail comercial@miramar.co.mz; internet miramar.co.mz; f. 1998; owned by RecordTV (Brazilian International Media Group); Gen. Man. LEANDRO MAQUINEZ.

Televisão de Moçambique, EP (TVM): Av. 25 de Setembro 154, CP 2675, Maputo; tel. 21308117; e-mail tvm@tvm.co.mz; internet www.tvm.co.mz; f. 1981; Pres. of Administrative Council FARUCO IBRAIMO; Dir of Programmes HOLDEN GUEDES.

tvcabo Moçambique: Av. dos Presidentes 68, CP 4268, Maputo; tel. 21480550; e-mail tvcabo@tvcabo.co.mz; internet www.tvcabo.co.mz; f. 1996; cable television and internet services in Maputo; jointly owned by Telecomunicações de Moçambique and Grupo Visabeira, Portugal; Dir-Gen. FRANCISCO FERREIRA.

Finance

BANKING

Central Bank

Banco de Moçambique: Av. 25 de Setembro 1695, CP 423, Maputo; tel. 21354600; e-mail gci_mail@bancomoc.mz; internet www.bancomoc.mz; f. 1975; bank of issue; Gov. ROGÉRIO LUCAS ZANDAMELA.

Other Banks

Absa Bank Moçambique: Av. 25 de Setembro 1184, CP 757, Maputo; tel. 21344400; e-mail linhacliente@absa.africa; internet www.absa.co.mz; f. 1995 as Banco Popular de Desenvolvimento (BPD); name changed to Banco Austral SARL in 1998 and to Barclays Bank Mozambique in 2007; present name adopted in 2019; part of ABSA Group LTD; Chair. LUÍSA DIAS DIOGO; CEO PEDRO CARVALHO.

BancABC Moçambique: Edifício JAT 6-3, Rua dos Desportistas, No. 733, Maputo; tel. 21482100; e-mail allmozJATVI@bancabc.com; internet www.bancabc.co.mz; f. 1999 as BNP Nedbank (Moçambique); present name adopted in 2009; 100% owned by African Banking Corpn Holdings Ltd (Botswana); Interim Chair. LUISA CAPELÃO; Man. Dir TAWANDA MUNAIWA.

Banco Mais—Banco Moçambicano de Apoio aos Investimentos SA: Av. Julius Nyerere 3504, Bloco A2, Maputo; tel. 823058130; e-mail info@bancomais.co.mz; internet www.bancomais.co.mz; Chair. NARCISO MATOS; Man. Dir Eng. LUIS ALMEIDA.

Banco Nacional de Investimentos (BNI): Av. Julius Nyerere 3504, Bloco A2, 4668, Maputo; tel. 21498581; e-mail info@bni.co.mz; internet www.bni.co.mz; f. 2010; state-owned; managed by govt agency IGEPE (Instituto de Gestão das Participações do Estado); Chair. TOMÁS MATOLA.

Banco Société Générale Moçambique: Av. Julius Nyerere 140, 4º andar, CP 1568, Maputo; tel. 21481900; e-mail sgmoz-apoio.cliente@socgen.com; f. 1999; fmrly Mauritius Commercial Bank (Moçambique); present name adopted in 2015; Chair. SIONLÉ SEYDOU YEO; CEO LAURENT THONG VANH.

BCI (Banco Comercial e de Investimentos, SARL): Av. 25 de Setembro 1465, CP 4745, Maputo; tel. 21353700; e-mail bci@bci.co.mz; internet www.bci.co.mz; f. 1996; present name adopted in 2003 following merger between Banco Comercial e de Investimentos and Banco de Fomento.

Ecobank Moçambique SA: Av. Vladimir Lénine 210, CP 1106, Maputo; tel. 21341300; e-mail ecobankenquiries@ecobank.com; internet www.ecobank.com; f. 2000 as NovoBanco, subsequently Banco ProCredit; present name adopted in 2014; Chair. SILVINO AUGUSTO JOSÉ MORENO; Exec. Dir and Man. Dir JOSÉ MANUEL CORREIA MENDES.

First Capital Bank SA Moçambique: Edifício Maryah, 7º andar, Av. 25 de Setembro, Aterro do Maxaquene, Maputo; tel. 21320760; e-mail suporte.ao.cliente@firstcapitalbank.co.mz; internet firstcapitalbank.co.mz; f. 2013 as Capital Bank SA; present name adopted in 2019; owned by FMB Capital Holdings PLC; Chair. HITESH ANADKAT; CEO TIAGO CONTENTE.

FNB Moçambique: Av. 25 de Setembro 420, 1° andar, sala 8, Maputo; tel. 21355999; e-mail call.center@fnb.co.mz; internet www.fnb.co.mz; f. 2000; fmrly Banco de Desenvolvimento e de Comércio de Moçambique; present name adopted in 2007; subsidiary of FirstRand Group (South Africa); CEO GRAÇA PEREIRA.

Millennium bim: Rua dos Desportistas 873–879, 1800, 11° andar, CP 865, Maputo; tel. 21350035; e-mail cac@millenniumbim.co.mz; internet ind.millenniumbim.co.mz; f. 1995; fmrly Banco Internacional de Moçambique; present name adopted in 2006; 66.7% owned by Banco Comercial Português; Chair. RUI CIRNE PLÁCIDO DE CARVALHO FONSECA; Vice-Chair. and CEO JOSÉ DA COSTA.

Moza Banco (BTM): Edifício JAT, Rua dos Desportista 715, Maputo; tel. 21342000; e-mail dcq@mozabanco.co.mz; internet www.mozabanco.co.mz; f. 2008; fmrly Banco Terra Moçambique; present name adopted in 2019 following merger; provides access to a full range of financial services to the rural and peri-urban population in Mozambique; Chair. JOÃO FIGUEIREDO.

MyBucks Banking Corpn: Av. 25 de Setembro 1821, 3rd Floor, Maputo; tel. 21422247; e-mail info@mbc.finance; internet www.mbc.finance; f. 2005; fmrly Opportunity Bank; present name adopted in 2018; acquired by MyBucks (Luxembourg); Group Chair. DAVE VAN NIEKERK.

Nedbank Moçambique: Av. Julius Nyere 585, Maputo; tel. 21488400; internet www.nedbank.co.mz; f. 2011; fmrly Banco Unico; present name adopted in 2021 following acquisition by Nedbank Group (South Africa); Chair. ABDUL MAGID OSMAN; CEO JOEL RODRIGUES.

Socremo—Banco de Microfinanças SA: Av. 24 de Julho 426, Maputo; tel. 21499543; e-mail secretariado@socremo.com; internet www.socremo.com; f. 1998 as Mozambique Credit Society; present name adopted in 2003; 39% owned by ACCION, 36% by Arise BV, 13% by Sociedade de Investimentos SA and 12% by Nordic Microcap; Chair. TITOS MACIE; CEO WELLINGTON CHINANZVAVANA.

Standard Bank, SARL (Moçambique): Av. 10 de Novembro 420, CP 2086, Maputo; tel. 21329777; e-mail linhadocliente@standardbank.co.mz; internet www.standardbank.co.mz; f. 1966 as Banco Standard Totta de Moçambique; 98.1% owned by Stanbic Africa Holdings, UK; Chair. TOMAZ AUGUSTO SALOMÃO; CEO BERNARDO APARÍCIO.

United Bank for Africa Moçambique SA: Edifício do INCM, Praça 16 de Junho 312, 2° andar, Maputo; tel. 43008601; e-mail cfcmozambique@ubagroup.com; internet www.ubamozambique.com; Group Chair. TONY O. ELUMELU.

STOCK EXCHANGE

Bolsa de Valores de Moçambique: Av. 25 de Setembro 1230, Prédio 33, 5° andar, Maputo; tel. 21308826; e-mail info@bvm.co.mz; internet www.bvm.co.mz; f. 1999; 10 listed cos; CEO SALIM CRIPTON VALA.

INSURANCE

Empresa Moçambicana de Seguros, EE (EMOSE): Av. 25 de Setembro 1383, CP 1165, Maputo; tel. 21356300; e-mail comercial@emose.co.mz; internet www.emose.co.mz; f. 1977 as state insurance monopoly; 80% govt-owned, 20% private; Chair. Eng. JOAQUIM MAQUETO LANGA; CEO ANTONIO CARRASCO.

Global Alliance Seguros (Moçambique): Av. Marginal, Parcela 141C, Maputo; tel. 21493110; e-mail info@ga.co.mz; internet www.ga.co.mz; f. 2001; Man. Dir BUSANI NGWENYA.

Moçambique Companhia de Seguros SA: Av. Kenneth Kaunda 518, Maputo; tel. 21485020; e-mail mcs@mcs.co.mz; internet www.mcs.co.mz; life and non-life.

Sanlam Moçambique: Av. Kenneth Kaunda 1202, Maputo; tel. 21494821; e-mail info@sanlam.co.mz; internet www.sanlam.com/mozambique; f. 2012; 51% owned by Sanlam Emerging Markets; CEO SIMBA MANUNURE.

Trade and Industry

GOVERNMENT AGENCIES

Agência para a Promoção de Investimento e Exportações (APIEX): Av. Ahmed Sekou Touré 2539, Maputo; tel. 823056432; e-mail info.apiex@apiex.gov.mz; internet www.apiex.gov.mz; f. 2016 following merger of Centro de Promoção de Investimentos (CPI), Gabinete das Zonas Económicas de Desenvolvimento Acelerado (GAZEDA) and Instituto para a Promoção de Exportações (IPEX); promotes and facilitates investment and exports; evaluates and negotiates investment proposals; Dir-Gen. GIL BIRES.

Autoridade Reguladora da Concorrência (ARC) (Competition Regulatory Authority): Av. 25 de Setembro 1502, Maputo; internet fb.com/arcmoz; f. 2021; Chair. IACUMBA ALI AIUBA.

Instituto de Amêndoas de Moçambique: Rua Gavea N33, Cruzamento entre 25 de Setembro e Karl Marx, Maputo; tel. 873069660; e-mail iam@iam.gov.mz; internet iam.gov.mz; fmrly Instituto do Fomento do Cajú; present name adopted in 2020; responsible for the promotion and devt of the dry fruit industry; Dir-Gen. ILÍDIO BANDE.

Instituto do Algodão e Oleaginosas de Moçambique (IAOM): Av. Eduardo Mondlane 2221, Maputo; tel. 21431016; e-mail info@iaom.gov.mz; internet iaom.mechanical.co.mz; f. 1991 as the Instituto do Algodão e Moçambique (IAM); present name adopted in 2020; responsible for promotion and devt of the cotton and oilseed industries; Dir-Gen. YOLANDA MILENA GONÇALVES.

Instituto Nacional de Petróleo (INP): Rua dos Desportistas, Parcela 259 E, CP 4724, Maputo; tel. 21248300; e-mail comunicacao@inp.gov.mz; internet www.inp.gov.mz; f. 2005; regulates energy sector; Chair. NAZÁRIO BANGALANE.

CHAMBERS OF COMMERCE

American Chamber of Commerce, Mozambique (AMCHAM): Rua Matheus Sansão Muthemba 476, Maputo; tel. 21492904; e-mail info@ccmusa.org.mz; internet ccmusa.org.mz; f. 1993; Sec. ROBERTO BUQUE.

Câmara de Comércio de Moçambique (CCM): Rua Mateus Sansão Muthemba 452, CP 1836, Maputo; tel. 21491970; e-mail info@ccmoz.org.mz; internet ccmoz.org.mz; f. 1980; Pres. ÁLVARO MASSINGUE.

INDUSTRIAL AND TRADE ASSOCIATIONS

Associação Algodoeira de Moçambique (AMM) (Cotton Association of Mozambique): Av. de Angola 2850, Maputo; tel. 21467600; e-mail geral@aam.org.mz; internet aam.org.mz; f. 1998; Pres. FRANCISCO DOS SANTOS.

Câmara de Energia de Moçambique: Maputo; f. 2020 as Câmara de Petróleo e Gás de Moçambique; present name adopted in 2022; Exec. Chair. FLORIVAL MUCAVE.

Confederação das Associações Económicas de Moçambique (CTA): Av. Patrice Lumumba 927, CP 2975, Maputo; tel. 21321002; e-mail cta@cta.org.mz; internet cta.org.mz; f. 1996; Pres. AGOSTINHO VUMA; 140 mem. cos.

STATE INDUSTRIAL ENTERPRISES

Empresa Nacional de Hidrocarbonetos de Moçambique (ENH): Rua dos Desportistas 918, Prédio JAT V-III, Maputo; tel. 21427634; e-mail info@enh.co.mz; internet www.enh.co.mz; f. 1981; controls concessions for petroleum exploration and production; Chair. ESTÊVÃO PALE.

Petróleos de Moçambique (PETROMOC): Praça dos Trabalhadores 9, CP 417, Maputo; tel. 21356600; e-mail cac@petromoc.co.mz; internet www.petromoc.co.mz; f. 1977 to take over the Sonarep oil refinery and its associated distribution co; fmrly Empresa Nacional de Petróleos de Moçambique; state directorate for liquid fuels within Mozambique, incl. petroleum products passing through Mozambique to inland countries; Exec. Chair. HÉLDER CHAMBISSE.

UTILITIES

Electricity

Electricidade de Moçambique (EDM): Av. Agostinho Neto 70, CP 2447, Maputo; tel. 21490636; internet www.edm.co.mz; f. 1977; 100% state-owned; production and distribution of electric energy; Chair. MARCELINO GILDO ALBERTO.

Companhia de Transmissão de Moçambique, SARL (MOTRACO) (Mozambique Transmission Co): Av. 25 de Setembro 420, Prédio JAT, Maputo; tel. 21313427; e-mail info@motraco.co.mz; f. 1998; jt venture between power utilities of Mozambique, South Africa and Eswatini (Swaziland); electricity distribution; Gen. Man. HIGINO FABIÃO.

Water

Direcção Nacional de Águas (DNA): Rua da Imprensa 162, CP 1611, Maputo; tel. 21302811; e-mail watco@zebra.uem.mz; internet www.dnaguas.gov.mz.

MAJOR COMPANIES

Afrisal do Mar, SARL: Av. Marginal 2555, Matola; tel. 21721740; subsidiary of Grupo Epsilon Investimentos; producer of salt.

British American Tobacco Mozambique (BAT) (Sociedade Agricola de Tabacos Lda): Av. de Angola 2289, CP 713, Maputo; tel. 21466538; internet www.bat.com; production of cigarettes; Group Chair. LUC JOBIN; Regional Dir LUCIANO COMIN.

Cervejas de Moçambique, SARL (CDM): Rua do Jardim 1329, CP 3555, Maputo; tel. 21352300; e-mail souCDM@mz.ab-inbev.com; internet www.ab-inbev.com; f. 1995; production and sale of beer; fmrly part of SABMiller PLC, UK; absorbed by AB InBev in 2016; Dir.-Gen. SANDRO FERNANDO DE ASSIS.

CETA Engenharia e Construção: Av. 25 de Setembro 420, 4° andar, CP 2783, Maputo; tel. 21355600; e-mail info@ceta.co.mz; internet www.ceta.co.mz; f. 1999; construction and civil engineering; Chair. NELSON MUIANGA; Dir-Gen. EUGÉNIO ABU-BACAR.

Cimentos de Moçambique, SA (CM): Av. 24 de Julho 7, 9° e 10° andar, Maputo; tel. 21482500; e-mail atendimento.cm@intercement .com; internet www.cimentosdemocambique.co.mz; f. 1924; cement; owned by Cimentos de Portugal (mem. of InterCement, Brazil); Dir-Gen. EDNEY VIEIRA.

Coca Cola Sabco (Mozambique), SARL: Av. OUA 270, Maputo; tel. 21400189; internet www.ccbagroup.com; f. 1994; bottling co; Man. Dir BASIL GADZIOS.

Companhia Industrial da Matola (CIM): Via Impasse 76, Matola, Maputo; tel. 21726700; e-mail customercare@cim.co.mz; internet www.cim.co.mz; f. 1948; food processing; Man. Dir ALFREDO LOPES.

Forjadora, SARL (Fábrica de Equipamentos Industriais): Av. de Angola 2850, CP 3078, Maputo; tel. 21466583; internet www.jfs.co .mz; f. 1969; motor vehicle and truck bodies; Group Chair. JOÃO FERREIRA DOS SANTOS.

Grupo de Empresa Issufo Nurmamade (GEIN): Av. Francisco Manyanga 15, 1° andar, CP 536, Nampula; tel. 26214959; e-mail inquiry@gein.co.mz; internet geingroup.com; f. 1986; comprises Sanam Cotton, Sanam Oil Industries and Sanam Soap Industries; production of cotton, palm oil and soap; Chair. ISSUFO NURMAMADE; Man. Dir DILAVAR HUSSEIN ISSUFFO.

Grupo Maëva: Rua Gago Coutinho 401, Unidade 7, Maputo; tel. 21477797; e-mail groupomaeva@gmail.com; internet fb.com/ MaevaGroup; f. 1998; manufacturer of soap, vegetable oil and other agro-based products; consists of Sabimo Lda (Maputo), Southern Refineries Lda (Matola), Maëva Plast Lda (Matola), Maxi Oils Lda (Maxixe), Maëva Oils Lda (Inhacoongo) and Azania Lda (Maputo); Dir DANIEL MONDLANE.

Hidroeléctrica de Cahora Bassa, SARL (HCB): Cahora Bassa Dam, Songo Village, Tete; tel. 25282200; e-mail cas.songo@hcb.co .mz; internet www.hcb.co.mz; f. 1975; 92.5% state-owned; production and transmission of electricity; operates Cahora Bassa Dam; Chair. BOAVIDA JOSÉ LOPES MUHAMBE.

Higest: Av. Josina Machel, km 15, Machava, Maputo; tel. 21750046; e-mail expedicao@higest.co.mz; internet www.higest.co.mz; f. 1993; produces poultry feed, chickens and eggs.

Maragra Açúcar SARL: KM75 EN1, Maciana, Distrito de Man-hica, CP 2789, Maputo; tel. 21810023; e-mail webmz@illovo.co.za; internet www.illovosugar.co.za; f. 1968; a subsidiary of Illovo Sugar Ltd (South Africa); Man. Dir FILIPÉ RAPOSO.

Medimoc SA: Av. Julius Nyerere 500, 1° andar, CP 600, Maputo; tel. 21491211; e-mail medimoc@medimoc.co.mz; internet www.medimoc .co.mz; f. 1977 as Empresa Estatal de Importação e Exportação de Medicamentos (MEDIMOC); pharmaceuticals, medical equipment and supplies (import and export); CEO SHIZAN RAHIM.

Mota-Engil Africa Moçambique, Lda: Av. Vladimir Lenine 179, Edif. Millennium Park, 14° e 15° andar, Maputo; tel. 21305484; e-mail geral@mota-engil.co.mz; internet www.mota-engil.com; f. 1991; civil engineering and construction; Chair. MANUEL ANTÓNIO DA MOTA.

Mozal Aluminium: Beluluane Industrial Park, Boane, CP 1235, Maputo; tel. 21735000; internet www.south32.net; f. 1998; aluminium smelting and production; 63.7% owned by South32 (Australia); Dir GIL CUMAIO.

Mozfoods SA: Rua Joseph Ki-Zerbo 255, CP 2112, Maputo; tel. 21483760; e-mail apoiocliente@mozfoods.com; internet www .mozfoods.com; f. 2004; group comprising Companhia de Vanduzi SA (Manica), Moçfer Industrias Alimentares SA (Chokwe) and Moz-seeds (Chokwe); food and agricultural products.

Olam Mozambique: Av. União Africana 7752, CP 1128, Maputo; tel. 20972572; e-mail mozambique@olamnet.com; internet olamgroup.com; f. 1999; produces cotton, edible oils and rice; Head SRIDHAR KRISHNAN.

Sociedade de Águas de Moçambique (SAM): Av. das Industrias 749, Machava, Matola; tel. 21754513; e-mail geral@sam.co.mz; internet www.sam.co.mz; f. 1972; produces mineral water the brand name of 'Água da Namaacha'; Dir MIGUEL PADRÃO.

Topack Moçambique, SARL: Av. do Trabalho 826, Maputo; tel. 21400281; e-mail topack@topack.net; internet www.topack.net; f. 1995; plastic products; CEO MANUEL VARA.

TRADE UNIONS

Freedom to form trade unions, and the right to strike, are guaranteed under the 1990 Constitution.

Confederação de Sindicatos Livres e Independentes de Moçambique (CONSILMO): Av. de Julho 1106, Maputo; tel. 823654021; e-mail info@consilmo.com; internet consilmo.com; f. 1998; Sec.-Gen. JEREMIAS TIMANE.

Organização dos Trabalhadores de Moçambique—Central Sindical (OTM—CS) (Mozambique Workers' Organization—Trade Union Headquarters): Rua Manuel António de Sousa 36, Maputo; tel. 21327574; e-mail otmdiz@hotmail.com; internet www.otm.org.mz; f. 1983; 15 affiliated unions with over 94,000 mems; Pres. SAMUEL MATSINHE; Sec.-Gen. ALEXANDRE MUNGUAMBE.

Sindicato Nacional dos Empregadores Bancários (SNEB): Av. Fernão de Magalhães 785, 1° andar, CP 1230, Maputo; tel. 21428627; e-mail info@snebmoz.co.mz; internet www.snebmoz.co .mz; f. 1992; Sec.-Gen. RAMIRO SIMBE.

Sindicato Nacional dos Empregados do Comércio, Seguros e Serviços (SINECOSSE): Av. Ho Chi Minh 365, 1° andar, CP 2142, Maputo; tel. 21428561; e-mail sincosse@teledata.mz; Sec.-Gen. AMÓS MATSINHE.

Sindicato Nacional da Função Pública (SINAFP): Av. Ho Chi Min 365, Maputo; tel. 21310019; e-mail mausseliazario@yahoo.co .br; Sec.-Gen. ELIAZÁRIO MAÚSSE.

Sindicato Nacional dos Profissionais da Estiva e Ofícios Correlativos (SINPEOC): Av. Paulo Samuel Kakhomba 1568, Maputo; tel. 21309535; Sec.-Gen. DAMIÃO SIMANGO.

Sindicato Nacional dos Trabalhadores da Indústria Meta-lúrgica, Metalomecânica e Energia (SINTIME): Av. Samora Machel 30, 6° andar, CP 1868, Maputo; e-mail sintimeorg@gmail .com; Sec.-Gen. MATEUS MUIANGA.

Sindicato Nacional dos Trabalhadores da Indústria Química e Afins (SINTIQUIAF): Av. Olof Palme 255, CP 4439, Maputo; tel. 21320288; e-mail sintiquigra@tvcabo.co.mz; f. 2008 by merger of SINTEVEC and SINTIQUIGRA; clothing, leather and footwear workers' union; Sec.-Gen. JÉSSICA GUNE.

Sindicato Nacional de Jornalistas (SNJ): Av. 24 de Julho 231, Maputo; tel. 21492031; e-mail snj@snjmocambique.co.mz; internet snj.org.mz; f. 1978; Sec.-Gen. EDUARDO CONSTANTINO.

Transport

Improvements to the transport infrastructure since the signing of the General Peace Agreement in 1992 have focused on the development of 'transport corridors', which include both rail and road links and promote industrial development in their environs. The Beira Corridor, with rail and road links and a petroleum pipeline, runs from Manica, on the Zimbabwean border, to the Mozambican port of Beira, while the Limpopo Corridor joins southern Zimbabwe and Maputo. Both corridors form a vital outlet for the landlocked southern African countries, particularly Zimbabwe. The Maputo Corridor links Ressano Garcia in South Africa to the port at Maputo, and the Nacala Corridor runs from Malawi to the port of Nacala. Two further corridors were planned: the Mtwara Corridor was to link Mozambique, Malawi, Tanzania and Zambia, while the Zambezi Corridor was to link Zambézia province with Malawi.

Instituto Ferro-Portuario de Moçambique (IFEPOM): Maputo; f. 2021 to supervise, regulate and monitor the activities of the combined railway and port system.

RAILWAYS

There are both internal routes and rail links between Mozambican ports and South Africa, Eswatini, Zimbabwe and Malawi. During the hostilities many lines and services were disrupted. In the early 2000s work commenced on upgrading the railway system and private companies were granted non-permanent concessions to rehabilitate and operate the railways. Rehabilitation work on the 670-km Sena railway line linking Beira with Moatize was completed in 2013. The construction of a line connecting Moatize in western Mozambique with the Malawian railway south of Blantyre was completed in 2017.

Portos e Caminhos de Ferro de Moçambique (CFM): Praça dos Trabalhadores, CP 2158, Maputo; tel. 21431705; e-mail gci@cfm.co .mz; internet www.cfm.co.mz; fmrly Empresa Nacional dos Portos e Caminhos de Ferro de Moçambique; privatized and restructured in 2002; Chair. MIGUEL JOSÉ MATABEL; comprises 4 separate systems linking Mozambican ports with the country's hinterland, and with other southern African countries, including South Africa, Eswatini, Zimbabwe and Malawi:

CFM—Centro (CFM—C): Largo dos CFM, CP 236, Beira; tel. 23325200; lines totalling 994 km linking Beira with Zimbabwe and Malawi, as well as a link to Moatize (undergoing rehabilitation); Exec. Dir AUGUSTO ABUDO.

CFM—Norte: Av. Paulo Samuel Kamkomba 4, Nampula; tel. 26212927; lines totalling 872 km, including link between port of Nacala with Malawi; management concession awarded to Nacala Corridor Development Co (a consortium 67% owned by South African, Portuguese and US cos) in January 2000; Exec. Dir JEREMIAS DO REGO.

CFM—Sul: Praça dos Trabalhadores, CP 2158, Maputo; tel. 21429357; lines totalling 1,070 km linking Maputo with South Africa, Eswatini and Zimbabwe, as well as Inhambane–Inharrime and Xai-Xai systems; Exec. Dir CÂNDIDO JONE.

ROADS

Administraçao Nacional de Estradas (ANE): Av. de Moçambique 1225, CP 403, Maputo; tel. 21476163; internet ane.gov.mz; f. 1999 to replace the Direcção Nacional de Estradas e Pontes; implements government road policy through the Direcção de Estradas Nacionais (DEN) and the Direcção de Estradas Regionais (DER); Pres. Eng. LUCIANO DE CASTRO; Dir-Gen. MARCO ALEXANDRE DOS ANJOS.

SHIPPING

Mozambique has three main sea ports, at Nacala, Beira and Maputo, while inland shipping on Lake Niassa and the river system remain underdeveloped.

Portos e Caminhos de Ferro de Moçambique (CFM-EP): Praça dos Trabalhadores, CP 2159, Maputo; tel. 823078124; e-mail cfm@cfm.co.mz; internet www.cfm.co.mz; fmrly Empresa Nacional dos Portos e Caminhos de Ferro de Moçambique; privatized and restructured in 2002; Chair. MIGUEL MATABEL; Port Dir CFM-Sul CÂNDIDO JONE; Port Dir CFM-Norte JEREMIAS DO REGO; Port Dir CFM-Centro Dr AUGUSTO ABUDO.

Manica Freight Services, SARL: Praça dos Trabalhadores 51, CP 557, Maputo; tel. 21356500; e-mail operations.maputo@manica.co.mz; internet www.manica.co.mz; international shipping agents; Man. Dir AHMAD Y. CHOTHIA.

Maputo Port Development Co, SARL (MPDC): Port Director's Building, Porto de Maputo, CP 2841, Maputo; tel. 21340500; e-mail info@portmaputo.com; internet www.portmaputo.com; f. 2003; private sector international consortium with concession (awarded 2003) to develop and run port of Maputo until 2033; Chair. ALAN OLIVIER; CEO OSÓRIO LUCAS.

CIVIL AVIATION

In 2020 there were three international airports in Mozambique.

Aeroportos de Moçambique: Av. Acordos de Lusaka 3267, CP 2631, Maputo; tel. 21465375; internet www.aeroportos.co.mz; under Ministry of Transport and Communications; Chair. and CEO AMÉRICO MUCHANGA.

Instituto de Aviação Civil de Moçambique (IACM): Alameda do Aeroporto, CP 227, Maputo; tel. 823021250; e-mail geral@iacm.gov.mz; internet www.iacm.gov.mz; f. 2009; civil aviation institute; Pres. JOÃO MARTINS DE ABREU.

Linhas Aéreas de Moçambique, SARL (LAM): Aeroporto Internacional de Maputo, CP 2060, Maputo; tel. 21465137; e-mail jrviegas@lam.co.mz; internet www.lam.co.mz; f. 1980; 80% state-owned; operates domestic services and international services to South Africa, Tanzania, Mayotte, Zimbabwe and Portugal; Dir-Gen. JOÃO CARLOS PÓ JORGE.

Sociedade de Transportes Aéreos/Sociedade de Transporte e Trabalho Aéreo, SARL (STA/TTA): Rua da Tchamba 405, CP 665, Maputo; tel. 21491765; e-mail sta.tta@sta.co.mz; f. 1991; domestic airline and aircraft charter transport services; acquired Empresa Nacional de Transporte e Trabalho Aéreo in 1997; Chair. JOSÉ CARVALHEIRA; Dir of Operations FERNANDO CARREIRA.

Other airlines operating in Mozambique include Serviço Aéreo Regional, South African Airlines, Moçambique Expresso, SA—Airlink International, Transairways (owned by LAM) and TAP Air Portugal.

Tourism

Instituto Nacional Do Turismo (INATUR): Av. 25 de Setembro 1018, CP 4758, Maputo; tel. 21307320; e-mail tourismmozambique@gmail.com; internet www.visitmozambique.gov.mz; f. 2008 to replace Fundo Nacional do Turismo; promotion and development of tourism sector; Dir-Gen. GEREMIAS MANUSSE.

Defence

As assessed at November 2021, total active armed forces were estimated at 11,200 (army 10,000, navy 200, air force 1,000).

Defence Budget: 9,350m. meticais in 2021.

Commander-in-Chief of the Armed Forces: Pres. FILIPE JACINTO NYUSI.

Chief of General Staff of the Armed Forces: Adm. JOAQUIM RIVAS MANGRASSE.

Commander of the Army: Brig. TIAGO ALBERTO NAMPELE.

Commander of the Navy: Rear-Adm. EUGÉNIO DIAS DA SILVA MUATUCA.

Commander of the Air Force: Brig. CANDIDO JOSE TIRANO.

Education

Primary education is officially compulsory for seven years from the age of six. It is divided into two cycles, of five and two years. Secondary schooling, from 13 years of age, lasts for five years and comprises a first cycle of three years and a second of two years. According to estimates by the United Nations Educational, Scientific and Cultural Organization (UNESCO), in 2018/19 98% of children in the relevant age-group were enrolled at primary schools (males 99%; females 96%), while secondary enrolment in 2016/17 was equivalent to 35% of children in the relevant age-group (males 37%; females 33%). Two privately owned higher education institutions, the Catholic University and the Higher Polytechnic Institute, were inaugurated in 1996. In 2003 it was announced that education would no longer be conducted solely in Portuguese, but also in some Mozambican dialects. In the budget for 2021 the education sector was allocated 63,973.7m. meticais, equivalent to 17.4% of total projected budgetary spending in that year.

Bibliography

Abrahamsson, H., and Nilsson, A. *Mozambique: The Troubled Transition from Socialist Construction to Free Market Capitalism*. London, Zed Books, 1995.

Alden, C. *Mozambique and the Construction of the New African State: From Negotiations to Nation Building*. Basingstoke, Palgrave Publishers, 2001.

Allina, E. *Slavery by any Other Name: African Life Under Company Rule in Colonial Mozambique*. Charlottesville, VA, University of Virginia Press, 2012.

Armon, J., et al. (Eds). *Accord: The Mozambique Peace Process in Perspective*. London, Conciliation Resources, 1998.

Tragedy and Triumph: Mozambique Refugees in Southern Africa, 1977–2001. Westport, CT, Greenwood Publishing Group, 2002.

Bekoe, D. *Implementing Peace Agreements: Lessons from Mozambique, Angola, and Liberia*. Basingstoke, Palgrave Macmillan, 2008.

Cabrita, J. *Mozambique (The Tortuous Road to Democracy)*. Basingstoke, Palgrave Publishers, 2001.

Christie, F., and Hanlon, J. *Mozambique and the Great Flood of 2000*. Bloomington, IN, Indiana University Press, 2001.

Englund, H. *From War to Peace on the Mozambique–Malawi Borderlands*. New York, Columbia University Press, 2002.

Fox, L. *Beating the Odds: Sustaining Inclusion in Mozambique's Growing Economy*. Washington, DC, World Bank Publications, 2009.

Funada-Classen, S. *The Origins of War in Mozambique: A History of Unity and Division*. Cape Town, African Minds, 2012.

Hanlon, J., and Smart, T. *Do Bicycles Equal Development in Mozambique?* London, James Currey, 2010.

Isaacman, A., and Isaacman, B. *Mozambique from Colonialism to Revolution, 1900–82*. Boulder, CO, Westview Press, 1983.

Jentzsch, C. *Violent Resistance: Militia Formation and Civil War in Mozambique*. Cambridge, Cambridge University Press, 2022.

Manning, C. *The Politics of Peace in Mozambique*. Westport, CT, Praeger Publishers, 2002.

Marcum, J. A. *Conceiving Mozambique*. London, Palgrave MacMillan, 2018.

Mazula, B. *Mozambique: Elections, Democracy and Development*. Maputo, Manila, 1996.

Minter, W. *Apartheid's Contras: An Inquiry into the Roots of War in Angola and Mozambique*. London, Zed Press, 1994.

Morier-Genoud, E. *Sure Road? Nationalisms in Angola, Guinea-Bissau and Mozambique*. Leiden, Brill, 2012.

Morier-Genoud, E., Cahen, M., and do Rosário, D. (Eds). *The War Within: New Perspectives on the Civil War in Mozambique, 1976–1992*. Woodbridge, James Currey, 2018.

Müller, T. R. *Legacies of Socialist Solidarity: East Germany in Mozambique*. Lanham, Lexington Books, 2014.

Newitt, M. *A Short History of Mozambique*. London, C. Hurst & Co, 2017.

Penvenne, J. *Women, Migration & the Cashew Economy in Southern Mozambique, 1945–1975*. Woodbridge, James Currey, 2015.

Pitcher, A. *Transforming Mozambique: The Politics of Privatization, 1975–2000*. Cambridge, Cambridge University Press, 2002.

Rafael, S. D. *Dicionário Toponímico, Histórico, Geográfico e Etnográfico de Moçambique*. Maputo, Arquivo Histórico de Moçambique, 2002.

Schafer, J. *Soldiers at Peace: The Post-war Politics of Demobilized Soldiers in Mozambique*. Basingstoke, Palgrave MacMillan, 2007.

Soderbaum, F. *Regionalism and Uneven Development in Southern Africa: The Case of the Maputo Development Corridor*. Aldershot, Ashgate, 2003.

Trindade, J. C., and Meneses, M. P. *Law and Justice in a Multicultural Society: The Case of Mozambique*. Dakar, CODESRIA, 2006.

Young, T., and Hall, M. *Confronting Leviathan: Mozambique Since Independence*. London, Hurst, 1997.

NAMIBIA

Physical and Social Geography

A. MacGREGOR HUTCHESON

The Republic of Namibia, lying across the Tropic of Capricorn, covers an area of 825,615 sq km (318,772 sq miles). It is bordered by South Africa on the south and south-east, by Botswana on the east, and by Angola on the north, while the narrow Zambezi Region (formerly known as the Caprivi Strip), between the two latter countries, extends Namibia's boundaries to the Zambezi river and a short border with Zambia.

The Namib Desert, a narrow plain 65 km–160 km wide and extending 1,600 km along the entire Atlantic seaboard, has a mean annual rainfall of less than 100 mm; long lines of huge sand dunes are common and it is almost devoid of vegetation. Behind the coastal plain the Great Escarpment rises to the plateau, which forms the rest of the country. Part of the Southern African plateau, it has an average elevation of 1,100 m above sea level, but towards the centre of the country it rises to altitudes of 1,525 m–2,440 m. A number of mountain masses rise above the general surface throughout the plateau. Eastwards the surface slopes to the Kalahari Basin and northwards to the Etosha Pan. Much of Namibia's drainage is interior to the Kalahari. There are no perennial rivers apart from the Okavango and the Cuando, which cross the Zambezi Region, and the Orange, Kunene and Zambezi, which form parts of the southern and northern borders.

Temperatures in the coastal areas are modified by the cool Benguela Current, while altitude modifies plateau temperatures (Walvis Bay, sea level: January 19°C, July 14.5°C; and Windhoek, 1,707 m: January 24°C, July 14°C). Average annual rainfall varies from some 50 mm on the coast to 550 mm in the north. Most rain falls during the summer (September–March), but is unreliable and there are years of drought. Grasslands cover most of the plateau; they are richer in the wetter north, but merge into poor scrub in the south and east.

Most of the population (which totalled 2,596,037 at mid-2022, according to official projections) reside on the plateau. Figures for the density of population (3.1 inhabitants per sq km at mid-2022) are misleading, as the better-watered northern one-third of the plateau contains more than one-half of the total population and about two-thirds of the African population, including the Ovambo (the largest single ethnic group), Kavango, East Caprivians and Kaokovelders. Almost the entire White population (80,000 in 1988, including the European population of Walvis Bay, an exclave of South Africa that was ceded to Namibia in March 1994) are concentrated in the southern two-thirds of the plateau, chiefly in the central highlands around Windhoek, the capital, together with the other main ethnic groups, the Damara, Herero, Nama, Rehoboth (Baster) and Coloured. Excluding ports and mining centres in the Namib, and apart from small numbers of Bushmen (San) in the Kalahari, the desert regions are largely uninhabited.

Namibia possesses scattered deposits of valuable minerals, and its economy is dominated by the mining sector. Of particular importance are the rich deposits of alluvial diamonds, which are exploited by surface mining, notably in the area between Oranjemund and !Nami#nus (formerly Lüderitz). Furthermore, the development of new diamond fields off shore has also proved very successful. Uranium ore (although of a low grade) is mined open cast at Rössing, 39 km north-east of Swakopmund, which, on a global scale, is one of the largest open-pit uranium oxide complexes and the sixth largest producer of uranium oxide. A joint Sino-Namibian venture began construction of a major new uranium mine—the Husab mine, located in the western Erongo region—in 2013; the mine began producing uranium in 2016. Tin, copper, rock salt, lead and zinc are also mined, and Namibia is believed to have significant reserves of coal, iron ore and platinum, although these have yet to be fully assessed. Other minerals currently produced or awaiting exploitation include vanadium, manganese, gold, silver, tungsten (wolfram), cadmium and limestone. There are also considerable reserves of offshore natural gas. In May 2013 the Government announced that deposits of petroleum (although not in commercially viable quantities) had been discovered in the Walvis Basin off the coast of central Namibia.

Despite the limitations imposed by frequent drought, agriculture is a significant economic activity. With the help of water from boreholes, large areas are given over to extensive ranching. Rivers, notably the Orange, Kunene and Okavango, are potential water resources for irrigation and hydroelectric power, while swamps, such as those situated in the Zambezi Region, could be drained to enhance arable output.

Namibia possesses potentially the richest inshore and deep-water fishing zones in tropical Africa, as a consequence of the rich feeding provided by the Benguela Current. Measures are being taken to counter the effects of decades of overfishing by both domestic and foreign fleets.

History

CHRISTOPHER SAUNDERS

HISTORICAL BACKGROUND

The origins of modern Namibia lay in the protectorate established by Germany in 1884. The present boundaries, which in the north cut through the Ovambo-speaking peoples, were demarcated in the late 19th and early 20th centuries. The port of Walvis Bay, initially ruled by the United Kingdom, was from 1884 part of the Cape Colony and therefore of the Union of South Africa from 1910. Following the outbreak of the First World War, South African forces occupied the German colony of South West Africa (SWA). After the war, the League of Nations awarded South Africa a mandate to administer the territory. No trusteeship agreement was concluded with the United Nations (UN) after the Second World War, and the UN's refusal in 1946 to allow South Africa to annex SWA led to a protracted legal dispute. In 1950 the International Court of Justice (ICJ) ruled that South Africa did not have to place SWA under UN trusteeship but could not alter its legal status unilaterally. In 1966, after the ICJ had failed to make a substantive judgment on the legality of South Africa's rule, the UN General Assembly terminated South Africa's mandate and assumed responsibility for SWA. A Council for South West Africa was appointed in 1967, and in 1968 the UN renamed the territory Namibia (although it remained under South African occupation). Meanwhile, in August 1966 the South West Africa People's Organisation (SWAPO)—founded in 1960 under the leadership of Sam Nujoma—began an armed insurgency in the north of the territory.

In 1971 the ICJ issued an advisory opinion that South Africa's presence in Namibia was illegal and that it should withdraw. In December 1973 the UN General Assembly recognized SWAPO as the 'authentic representative of the people of Namibia' and appointed the first UN Commissioner for Namibia to undertake 'executive and administrative tasks'. South Africa's unsuccessful military intervention in Angola in 1975 prompted an escalation of the Namibian armed struggle. With support from the new Angolan Government, SWAPO's military wing, the People's Liberation Army of Namibia (PLAN), established bases close to Namibia's borders. South Africa responded by expanding counter-insurgency forces in the territory. In September 1975 a constitutional conference was convened to discuss Namibia's future. The Turnhalle Conference (named after a historic building in the capital, Windhoek) designated 31 December 1978 as the target date for Namibian independence, and in March 1977 it produced a draft constitution for a pre-independence interim government. This constitution, providing for 11 ethnic administrations, was denounced by the UN and SWAPO, which proposed a parliamentary system with universal adult suffrage.

A 'contact group' comprising the five Western members of the UN Security Council was established in 1977 to persuade South Africa to adopt a plan that the UN could accept. In September South Africa appointed an Administrator-General for Namibia, and the territory's representation in the South African Parliament was terminated. Proposals presented by the 'contact group' providing for UN-supervised elections, a reduced number of South African troops in Namibia and the release of political prisoners were accepted by South Africa in April 1978 and by SWAPO in July; they were incorporated into UN Security Council Resolution 435 in September. South Africa held its own election for a Namibian Constituent Assembly in the territory in December; with SWAPO boycotting the election, 41 of the 50 seats were won by the Democratic Turnhalle Alliance (DTA), a conservative coalition of the ethnic groups involved in the conference. The DTA leader, Dirk Mudge, became Chairman of a Ministerial Council, which had limited executive powers.

In January 1981 the UN convened a conference in Geneva, Switzerland, which was attended by SWAPO, South Africa, the DTA and other internal parties. The 'contact group' and the 'front-line' states (Angola, Botswana, Mozambique, Tanzania, Zambia and Zimbabwe) acted as observers. However, South Africa and the internal parties failed to agree on a ceasefire date and the implementation of the UN plan.

A major obstacle was South Africa's insistence that the Cuban troops who had supported the Angolan Government from 1975 withdraw from that country before it would agree to implement Resolution 435. The idea of linking South Africa's withdrawal from Namibia with the withdrawal of Cuban military forces from Angola was introduced by the USA to persuade the South African Government to withdraw. For SWAPO and its allies, however, it gave South Africa an excuse not to implement Resolution 435, for as long as South African forces were active in southern Angola there seemed no likelihood that the Angolan Government and the Cubans would agree to withdraw Cuban forces.

In February 1984 a ceasefire agreement was concluded in Lusaka, Zambia, following talks between South African and US government officials. A joint commission was established to monitor the withdrawal of South African troops from Angola, and Angola undertook to permit neither SWAPO nor Cuban forces to move into the area. SWAPO promised to abide by the agreement but pledged to continue PLAN operations until a ceasefire was established in Namibia as the first stage of implementing UN Resolution 435. In November, in response to US proposals, Angola suggested a timetable for the withdrawal of Cuban troops from the south of the country; however, a settlement involving the implementation of Resolution 435 seemed unlikely.

South Africa took advantage of the delay in Namibia's transition to independence to build an anti-SWAPO front. The DTA was weakened in 1982 by losing support among the Ovambo, Namibia's largest ethnic group. After disputes with the South African Government over the DTA's future role, Mudge resigned as Chairman of the Ministerial Council in January 1983, and the Council was dissolved. The Administrator-General, in turn, dissolved the National Assembly and

assumed direct rule of Namibia on behalf of the South African Government. He promoted the establishment of a multi-party conference (MPC), made up of the DTA and smaller internal parties. In June 1985 South Africa installed a 'Transitional Government of National Unity' in Windhoek, consisting of a Cabinet and a National Assembly; members were appointed from among the MPC's constituent parties. A 'bill of rights', drawn up by the MPC, prohibited racial discrimination, and a Constitutional Council was established, under a South African judge, to prepare a constitution for an independent Namibia. South Africa retained responsibility for foreign affairs, defence and internal security.

As the Cold War came to an end and the Union of Soviet Socialist Republics sought to settle its regional conflicts, Angola and Cuba accepted, in principle, US demands for a complete withdrawal of Cuban troops from Angola in January 1988. In March South Africa rejected proposals for the withdrawal, but its troops were unable to gain advantage over the Angolan and Cuban forces at Cuito Cuanavale, in southern Angola, and the Cuban forces began moving towards the Namibian border. As the threat of a major confrontation between the Cuban and South African armies loomed, in May South Africa joined US-mediated negotiations with Angola and Cuba. South Africa agreed to implement Resolution 435, providing that a timetable for the withdrawal of Cuban troops could be drawn up. Having agreed in July a document containing 14 'essential principles' for a peaceful settlement, in early August the negotiating parties agreed to implement Resolution 435 from 1 November. South African troops withdrew from southern Angola by the end of August. The November deadline expired, however, owing to disagreement about an exact schedule for the evacuation of Cuban troops. These arrangements were formally ratified in December.

On 22 December 1988 South Africa, Angola and Cuba signed an agreement designating 1 April 1989 as the implementation date for Resolution 435. Another treaty, signed by Angola and Cuba, required Cuban troops to leave Angola by July 1991. A joint commission was established to monitor the implementation of the trilateral treaty. Under the terms of Resolution 435, South African forces in Namibia were to be confined to their bases, and their numbers reduced to 1,500 by 1 July 1989; all South African troops were to have left Namibia one week after the election. A multinational UN observer force, the UN Transition Assistance Group (UNTAG), was to monitor this withdrawal and supervise the election, and the UN Secretary-General's Special Representative, Martti Ahtisaari of Finland, would consider whether the election was free and fair.

By 1 April 1989 few of the UNTAG forces (which were eventually to comprise 4,650 troops, with a further 500 police and about 1,000 civilian observers) had arrived. Meanwhile, PLAN forces began to reveal themselves in Ovamboland. They probably hoped to be settled in UN-supervised bases, but the South African Government obtained Ahtisaari's agreement to release its forces from their base, and more than 300 PLAN troops were killed in the subsequent fighting. On 9 April the joint commission produced conditions for an evacuation of the PLAN forces, after Nujoma, President of SWAPO, had ordered their withdrawal to Angola. At a meeting of the joint commission in May, the ceasefire was certified to be in force. In June most racially discriminatory legislation was repealed, and an amnesty was granted to Namibian refugees and exiles. By September nearly 42,000 of those who had gone into exile, including Nujoma, had returned to Namibia.

The pre-independence election was conducted peacefully in November 1989, and voter turnout exceeded 95%. SWAPO received 57.3% of all votes cast and won 41 of the 72 seats in the Constituent Assembly, while the DTA, with 28.6% of the votes, secured 21 seats. Ahtisaari pronounced the election to have been free and fair, after which the remaining South African troops left Namibia, and SWAPO's bases in Angola were disbanded.

In February 1990 the Constituent Assembly unanimously adopted a draft Constitution, providing for a multi-party system based on universal adult suffrage, with an independent judiciary and a 'bill of rights'. Executive power was to be vested in a President, who could serve a maximum of two five-year terms, while a 72-member National Assembly was to have legislative power. The Constituent Assembly subsequently elected Nujoma as Namibia's first President. On 21 March 1990 Namibia became independent: the Constituent Assembly became the National Assembly, and the President and his Cabinet (led by Prime Minister Hage Geingob, hitherto Chairman of the Constituent Assembly) took office.

SWAPO IN GOVERNMENT

Namibia became a full member of the Southern African Customs Union; the South African Development Co-ordination Conference (SADCC), which sought to reduce the dependence of southern African states on South Africa; the UN; the Organization of African Unity (from 2002 the African Union); and the Commonwealth. Full diplomatic relations were established with many states, and partial diplomatic relations with South Africa, with which negotiations began over the future of Walvis Bay. These led to a joint administration of the port and then its incorporation into Namibia in early 1994. In August 1992 Namibia joined the other SADCC members in recreating the organization as the Southern African Development Community (SADC), to which South Africa was admitted in August 1994.

In November 1991 the DTA reorganized itself as a single party, but its support continued to dwindle. In November–December 1992 the first elections were held for Namibia's 13 regional councils and 48 local authorities. SWAPO won nine regional councils, while the DTA won three. SWAPO thus secured control of the newly established second house of parliament, the National Council, which comprised two members from each regional council.

Namibia's first post-independence presidential and legislative elections took place on 7–8 December 1994, resulting in overwhelming victories for SWAPO. Nujoma was elected for a second term as President, securing 76.3% of the vote; his only challenger was the DTA President, Mishake Muyongo. SWAPO secured 53 of the elective seats in the National Assembly. Although SWAPO thus had a two-thirds' majority in the Assembly, Nujoma gave assurances that the Constitution would not be amended without prior approval by national referendum. He was sworn in again on 21 March 1995.

In May 1997, at SWAPO's second party congress since independence, a resolution endorsing the proposal that Nujoma should seek re-election for a third term as President was justified on the grounds that he had initially been chosen by the Constituent Assembly and had only once been elected President on a popular mandate. Hifikepunye Pohamba, one of Nujoma's closest associates during the exile, replaced Moses Garoëb as SWAPO Secretary-General. In October 1998 an exceptional amendment to the Constitution, allowing Nujoma to seek a third presidential term, was approved by the requisite two-thirds' majority in the National Assembly; it was endorsed by the National Council in November.

REGIONAL CONCERNS

With the resumption of civil war in Angola in late 1992, the Namibian Government's concerns about security along its northern border increased. In March 1993 the Angolan insurgent movement União Nacional para a Independência Total de Angola (UNITA) claimed that members of the Namibian Defence Force had crossed into southern Angola to assist Angolan government forces in offensives against it. The Namibian authorities denied any involvement in the Angolan civil conflict, but in 1996 a special field force of the Namibian police was deployed along the Okavango river on the Angolan border to deter possible UNITA attacks.

In 1996 Namibia and Botswana referred their dispute over the demarcation of their joint border on the Chobe river (specifically, the issue of the sovereignty of the sparsely inhabited island of Kasikili-Sedudu) for adjudication by the ICJ. In December 1997 a new dispute began concerning two further islands, Situngu and Luyondo, when Botswanan soldiers allegedly harvested crops planted on the islands by Namibian villagers.

In August 1998 President Nujoma sent Namibian troops to support President Laurent-Désiré Kabila of the Democratic

Republic of the Congo (DRC) against rebel forces backed by Uganda and Rwanda. Within weeks almost 2,000 Namibian troops were fighting in the DRC alongside troops from Angola and Zimbabwe, helping to secure the Matadi corridor from Kinshasa, DRC, to the sea. Although Nujoma claimed that Namibia was acting in solidarity and support for the territorial integrity of the DRC in the face of external aggression, many observers considered that he was seeking to increase Namibia's chances of benefiting from future mineral exploitation there. Nujoma played a prominent role in efforts towards a negotiated settlement between Kabila and the rebels. While denying again that Namibian troops were supporting the Angolan Government against UNITA, he stated that, if requested, Namibia would assist its neighbour under SADC auspices. In April Namibia signed a regional defence pact with Angola, the DRC and Zimbabwe, providing for mutual assistance in the event of aggression against any of the signatories.

Efforts to resolve the DRC conflict were accelerated in early 2001, following the assassination of Laurent-Désiré Kabila and the succession to the presidency of his son, Maj.-Gen. Joseph Kabila. Proposals for the withdrawal of foreign (including Namibian) troops were subsequently approved by the participating countries, under the aegis of the UN Security Council, and Namibian forces completed their withdrawal in September.

Relations with Botswana were further complicated from October 1998, when refugees began entering that country from the Caprivi Strip, a thin section of Namibian territory extending its north-eastern corner and bordering Angola, Zambia and Botswana. The refugees cited police harassment, after a man was reportedly killed at a secret military training base that the Namibian Government alleged was being used by the secessionist Caprivi Liberation Movement (CLM). The Caprivi people had long sought closer links with their neighbours to the east, believing that the Government in Windhoek was ignoring the region's development, as they did not support SWAPO. It emerged that the leading refugee figure was Muyongo, and in August 1998 the DTA's executive suspended him as President and dissociated the party from his overt support for the Caprivi secession. With 14 other members of the CLM, he was granted asylum by the Botswana Government in February 1999. In March Botswana and Namibia agreed that the secessionist leaders could be accorded refugee status, on condition that they be resettled in a third country; the approximately 2,500 remaining refugees would be able to return without fear of punishment or persecution. Muyongo and another CLM leader were granted political asylum in Denmark.

In early August 1999, however, an attack by members of the Caprivi Liberation Army on the regional capital, Katima Mulilo, resulted in 12 deaths. The Namibian Government imposed a state of emergency in Caprivi, while Zimbabwe and Zambia offered support against the separatists. Although the state of emergency was revoked in late August, human rights groups in Namibia produced evidence that Namibian troops had committed acts of brutality against those believed to support the rebels. More than 120 of those arrested first appeared in court in 2001, charged with high treason, murder and sedition. In July 2007 10 of the alleged secessionists were convicted of high treason and sentenced to prison terms of 30–32 years; the others remained on trial (see below).

Tensions along the Namibian–Angolan border escalated from late 1999, after the two countries began joint patrols targeting UNITA, and the Namibian Government authorized Angolan forces to launch attacks against UNITA from Namibia. UNITA responded by launching sporadic attacks in the Caprivi Strip. By June 2000 more than 50 Namibians had been killed in cross-border raids by the Angolan rebels. However, following the death of Jonas Savimbi, the UNITA leader, and the signing of a ceasefire between the Angolan Government and UNITA in April 2002, the situation in north-eastern Namibia improved. As Angola became more peaceful, its trade with Namibia increased, and in August Namibian refugees in Botswana began to be repatriated. Meanwhile, the return of Angolan refugees in Namibia to their country began; about 20,000 returned home in the second half of 2003, under the auspices of the UN High Commissioner for Refugees.

In March 1999 Namibia and Botswana confirmed that they would both respect the judgment of the ICJ regarding sovereignty of Kasikili-Sedudu. In December the Court ruled in Botswana's favour. The two countries then established a joint commission to settle the remaining disputes in the Chobe river area. In March 2003 both Governments accepted the commission's demarcation of their joint border along the Kwando, Linyanti and Chobe rivers. The issue of Namibia's border with South Africa remained unresolved: Namibia claimed that its southern border extended to the middle of the Orange river, while South Africa claimed its territory stretched to the northern bank. How the boundary ran out to sea (and thus to diamond deposits) was also disputed.

In 2004 the Shesheke bridge across the Zambezi river was opened. This linked the Trans-Caprivi Highway in Namibia to the Zambian Copperbelt and enabled exports from Zambia and the southern DRC to be sent to the Namibian port of Walvis Bay. In addition, SADC promoted the 'Western Power Corridor' from South Africa through Namibia to Angola; the boldest proposal was to route the delivery of power from the Inga hydroelectric dam in the DRC through Angola to Namibia.

NUJOMA'S THIRD TERM

A potential challenge to SWAPO's dominance emerged with the establishment in March 1999 of a new political party, the Congress of Democrats (CoD), under a former trade union leader and senior SWAPO official, Ben Ulenga. Ulenga had resigned as Namibia's High Commissioner to the UK in August 1998, in protest against SWAPO's decision to alter the Constitution to allow Nujoma to seek a third term. Ulenga also opposed Namibia's involvement in the DRC conflict and criticized the Government's failure adequately to address the issue of unemployed former combatants. Concerned about the CoD's prospects in the presidential and legislative elections due in late 1999, Nujoma appointed two key figures from the labour movement as deputy ministers, and the Government set aside N \$255m. in the 1999/2000 budget for the social integration of about 9,000 former combatants, who were to be offered employment in the public service (including the police force).

The elections, held on 30 November and 1 December 1999, resulted in an overwhelming victory for Nujoma and SWAPO. In the presidential election Nujoma won 76.8% of the votes cast, while Ulenga took 10.5%. SWAPO won 55 of the elective seats in the National Assembly, with 76.1% of the votes; the CoD and the DTA each won seven seats (taking, respectively, 9.9% and 9.5% of the votes), but the DTA kept its status as the official opposition by forming an alliance with the ethnic Damara United Democratic Front, which secured two seats. Geingob was reappointed Prime Minister in a cabinet reorganization announced in March 2000. Pohamba was elevated to SWAPO Vice-President at the party's congress in 2002. In January 2001 he had been appointed Minister of Lands, Resettlement and Rehabilitation. In August 2002 Nujoma dismissed Geingob, a potential successor, as Prime Minister and replaced him with the long-serving Minister of Foreign Affairs, Theo Ben-Gurirab.

As Namibia entered the new millennium, one of its major problems was HIV/AIDS. By 2003 21.3% of Namibia's adult population (aged 15–49) were living with HIV, and the Government responded tardily to the pandemic. The effect of AIDS in reducing the agricultural labour force and production was cited as one of the reasons for the serious food crisis that had developed by mid-2002, when about 70,000 people in the northeastern Caprivi region needed urgent food aid. The Government's decision to allocate more than N \$80m. in the 2003/04 budget to purchase antiretroviral drugs for people infected with HIV was widely welcomed, as was the announcement in May 2003 that it would support the manufacture of generic medication for the treatment of HIV/AIDS.

In April 2004 Nujoma confirmed that he would not seek a fourth presidential term. Hidipo Hamutenya was widely viewed as his likely successor, but Nujoma dismissed him from the Cabinet, and Pohamba was chosen as SWAPO's presidential candidate. Hamutenya later broke away from SWAPO (see below).

After Zimbabwe's President Robert Mugabe allowed the forcible seizure of land from white farmers and its redistribution to the black population, the issue of land reform gained more prominence in Namibia. The Government remained firm that it would not permit land invasions, and by 2000 only 35,000 black farmers had been settled on land obtained from white farmers. However, during a visit to Germany in mid-2002, Nujoma sought financial aid for the purchase of land from white commercial farmers for landless blacks. In August Nujoma warned white farmers to co-operate with the Government's scheme for land redistribution. Representatives of the Herero people, meanwhile, proceeded with cases against the German Government, Deutsche Bank and a shipping firm, demanding compensation of some US \$4,000m. for their involvement in the atrocities committed against them under German colonial rule. The Namibian Government refused to support this claim, declaring that Namibia should continue to work with the German Government and industry.

In 2003 the Namibian Government compiled a list of 192 farms owned by foreigners—mostly South Africans and Germans—for expropriation. In February 2004 the Government, citing the slow pace of land reform under the 'willing buyer, willing seller' programme, announced that it would consider using compulsory expropriation to accelerate the process of redistributing land to the estimated 240,000 landless people. By 2004 some 700 farms had been sold to the Government for land reform purposes over a decade, and some 4,000 white commercial farmers owned about 30m. ha of land, although much of that was arid and unsuitable for peasant agriculture. In March Pohamba wrote to 15 landowners informing them that they were required to sell their property to the state and had 14 days to respond. The Namibia Agricultural Union stated that it would accept expropriation, providing that compensation was paid at market value and that those targeted were allowed to contest expropriation under the law. Expropriation with compensation meant that budgetary constraints would determine the rate of redistribution, and some Namibians spoke out against paying for land that had been seized in the process of colonial settlement. Given Nujoma's continued support for Mugabe, many white farmers feared that their land would also be forcibly seized. In May Nujoma confirmed that his Government would not only target underused land, but expropriate land as a punitive step against whites who maltreated their labourers.

THE POHAMBA PRESIDENCY

In the legislative elections held on 15–16 November 2004, SWAPO won 76.1% of the vote and retained its 55 seats in the 72-seat National Assembly. Pohamba overwhelmingly defeated his opponents in the presidential election, taking 76.4% of the votes cast. Following the elections, the CoD, which became the official opposition, with five seats (one more than the DTA), and the Republican Party, which won a seat for the first time, alleged widespread voting irregularities and instigated proceedings at the High Court. In March 2005 the Court ordered a recount of the results, although the allocation of seats remained unchanged.

At regional elections held in November 2004, SWAPO won an overwhelming victory, and the party's majority in the upper house grew. Parliament was increasingly marginalized and unable to provide any effective check on executive power.

On 21 March 2005 Pohamba was inaugurated as Namibia's second President and swiftly appointed an Anti-Corruption Commission, which began its work in 2006. However, the Commission was given limited resources and unable to prevent large-scale self-enrichment or bring to account all those responsible for corruption at several state agencies, including the Social Security Commission, the Ministry of Defence and the railway company TransNamib. Namibia nevertheless ranked near the top of tables on African governance.

Implementation of the Government's land reform programme remained slow. By mid-2006 only 10,000 people had been resettled on some 150 commercial farms. The new owners were often unable to operate the farms commercially, and valuable equipment was stolen or lay idle. The Government made available about US \$7.7m. annually to buy commercial farms, and all farms for sale had to be offered to the state in the first instance. Although an Affirmative Action Loan Scheme (see *Economy*) allowed individual black Namibians to buy commercial farms on preferential terms, often those who bought under this scheme could not keep up their loan repayments.

Namibia remained among the most unequal societies in the world. While the country had moved up to 125th place out of the 177 countries in the 2005 UN Human Development Index, with over 90% of primary-age children attending school, and water and electricity reaching over 80% of the population, 35% of the population still lived on less than US \$1 per day. HIV prevalence was 19.6% among adults. Although the number of Namibians receiving antiretroviral medication for HIV increased substantially, HIV remained the leading cause of the continued decline in life expectancy, which the World Health Organization estimated at 57 years in 2009. By 2021 the adult HIV prevalence rate had declined to 11.8%, owing largely to an education campaign and the greater availability of antiretroviral drugs, and life expectancy was 64 years.

In October 2007 Nujoma announced that the party's fourth congress should choose his successor as SWAPO President, to which position Pohamba was elected in November. In his first government reorganization, in April 2008, Pohamba appointed former Prime Minister Geingob as Minister of Trade and Industry.

Before the 2007 SWAPO congress, Hamutenya had established a breakaway party, the Rally for Democracy and Progress (RDP). When the RDP was heavily defeated in a local government election, it blamed widespread intimidation and claimed that the election had been neither free nor fair. As the 2009 general election approached, there was intimidation and violence, especially between supporters of SWAPO and the RDP.

At the presidential and legislative elections held on 27–28 November 2009, SWAPO won 75.3% of the vote for the National Assembly and 54 of the 72 seats. President Pohamba received 76.4% of the vote in the presidential election. The RDP won 11.3% of the vote and eight seats in the Assembly and thus became the official opposition. Hamutenya obtained 11.1% of the vote in the presidential election. The opposition parties, led by the RDP, challenged the result in the High Court, alleging electoral fraud. After this Court dismissed the challenge on a technicality, the parties appealed to the Supreme Court. In February 2011 the Judge President, while acknowledging voting irregularities, dismissed the case.

Meanwhile, in March 2010 President Pohamba formed a new Government, again led by Prime Minister Nahas Angula. Utoni Nujoma, son of the founding President, became Minister of Foreign Affairs. In April SWAPO marked 50 years since its foundation. Although much was made of Namibia's undoubted achievements since independence, some of those arrested at the time of the Caprivi secession in 1999 remained in prison without having been put on trial. The authorities ignored appeals for an amnesty, although some claims against the Government for human rights abuses in the Caprivi Strip at the time of the secession attempt were settled out of court. In February 2011 the presiding judge refused to admit any new evidence in the main trial, but the case continued. More than 20 of those detained had by then died in gaol, while Muyongo remained in exile in Denmark. The main trial ended in September 2015, with 30 being found guilty and 79 not guilty. In December those convicted of high treason were imprisoned for up to 18 years.

In 2013 Namibia suffered severe drought; with some 14% of the population experiencing food insecurity, in May President Pohamba declared a national emergency. In November President Jacob Zuma of South Africa pledged N \$100m. in drought relief; however, this took two years to arrive. In 2015 intensifying drought reduced Namibia's maize crop, leading to a shortage of food, especially in the north.

Geingob was reappointed SWAPO Vice-President at the party congress in December 2012. This meant that he would be SWAPO's presidential candidate in the election scheduled for November 2014. Immediately after the congress, Pohamba reorganized his Cabinet, appointing Geingob as Prime Minister and promoting his supporters, thereby strengthening the

position of SWAPO moderates. Geingob was seen by some as too close to business interests, although SWAPO itself had increasingly accepted a larger role for the state in the economy.

Despite a resurgence in ethnic sentiment, which in the former Caprivi Strip—renamed the Zambezi Region in 2013—was tied to a feeling of socioeconomic deprivation, Namibia's opposition parties remained fragmented in the run-up to the general election in 2014. The largest of these, the RDP, re-elected Hamutenya as its President in November 2013 but suffered internal ructions, while the DTA President made fruitless appeals for opposition parties to present a united challenge against SWAPO.

Although in 2014 Namibia could boast that it held the highest position among African nations in the Reporters Without Borders' rankings for press freedom, it remained one of the most unequal countries on the continent, and about one-half of the population lacked proper sanitation. Although Namibia faced no military threat, annual military spending doubled during 2004–14, and it became the third largest arms importer in sub-Saharan Africa.

THE 2014 ELECTIONS AND THE GEINGOB PRESIDENCY

SWAPO gained a record 80.0% of the votes in the parliamentary election on 28 November 2014 and won 77 seats in the expanded, 96-seat legislature. The DTA became the official opposition in the Assembly, although it took only five seats. The RDP obtained three seats, while the radical Workers' Revolutionary Party, with two seats, gained representation for the first time. Turnout was 72%. With the ruling party having established gender parity in its parliamentary representation—one-half of its elected members were female—Namibia was ranked third out of 52 African countries in the African Development Bank's Gender Equality Index. SWAPO's presidential candidate, Geingob, obtained 86.7% of the votes cast in the concurrent presidential election. At his inauguration on 21 March 2015 he pledged a 'war on poverty'. Former Minister of Finance Saara Kuugongelwa-Amadhila was named as Prime Minister. The new Government was confronted with the challenges of combating corruption, nepotism and self-enrichment. In April 2016 Geingob launched his Harambee (from a Swahili word meaning 'pull together') programme, which aimed at greater transparency, improved service delivery and a significant reduction in poverty. In December he cancelled a N \$6,000m. tender awarded to a Chinese construction company for the upgrading and expansion of Windhoek's airport.

Meanwhile, in November 2014 young SWAPO activists cleared a piece of land in an upmarket Windhoek suburb with a view to occupying it illegally, to protest against high property prices and the Government's failure to address the land issue. In April 2015 their Affirmative Repositioning (AR) Movement persuaded over 50,000 people to apply for land at local authorities, and the AR threatened that land would be occupied, if it were not given. The issue was diffused in a meeting with President Geingob that secured a promise of 200,000 serviced sites. The AR continued to mobilize around issues such as anti-corruption and the burgeoning cost of the proposed new parliament building in Windhoek.

In the regional and local elections held in November 2015, SWAPO won 54 of the 57 local councils and 40 of the 42 seats in the National Council. In May 2016 SWAPO opened a party school in Windhoek, something proposed since 2002 and based on a Cuban model. Those who called themselves 'children of the liberation struggle' engaged in several protests and marches, and in early 2017 Geingob set aside considerable funding for their training.

In January 2017 Namibia acceded to the African Peer Review Mechanism, thereby agreeing to undergo a transparent review process of all aspects of governance. Meanwhile, Herero and Nama representatives filed a class-action lawsuit in New York, USA, under the Alien Tort Act, seeking compensation for 'incalculable damages' for what they termed the 'genocide' of 1904–08. The Namibian Government had begun negotiations with its German counterpart in 2015. The latter would not accept the term 'genocide' or pay direct reparations, on the grounds that its development aid to Namibia, more per head than to any other country, was for all Namibians. The Namibian Government nevertheless announced that it would launch a US $30,000m. lawsuit against Germany for the genocide. Some of the 16,000 ethnic Germans in Namibia feared that their properties might be confiscated. In April 2017, on a state visit to Zimbabwe, President Geingob praised Mugabe's land policy and promised to hold a second land conference in Namibia. Geingob was overwhelmingly elected party President at SWAPO's November congress and thus confirmed as the party's presidential candidate in the elections scheduled for 2019. Geingob's Minister of Sport, Youth and National Service, Jerry Ekandjo, ran against him on a ticket with the Minister of Home Affairs and Immigration, Pendukeni Iivula-Ithana. Both had served in government since Namibian independence. In February 2018 Geingob reorganized his Cabinet, removing both Iivula-Ithana and Ekandjo. Nangolo Mbumba, a party veteran, became Vice-President. The promotion of three ministers in the new Cabinet was, according to Geingob, part of 'leadership succession planning'. Meanwhile, in November 2017 the DTA was renamed the Popular Democratic Movement (PDM), in an attempt to reinvent the party as one untainted by its past association with South Africa.

By 2018 Namibia's poverty rate had fallen to 23% from 53% at independence, but with little economic growth there was no new source of large-scale employment on the horizon. A draft National Equitable Economic Empowerment Framework bill, which aimed to force white-owned companies to sell 25% of their stake to the previously disadvantaged, concerned foreign investors and Namibia fell below Botswana in a ranking of the most attractive jurisdictions in which mining companies could invest. In April Geingob announced that the 25% equity stake requirement would be dropped to create a more conducive business environment.

In 2014 some human skulls had been returned to Namibia from a German museum, and in February 2019 a bible and whip that the Germans had looted from the Namibian resistance hero Hendrik Witbooi in 1893 were returned from another German museum to Gideon, Witbooi's home. There were pleas for other looted artefacts to be returned, as well as human remains. In March 2019 a New York federal court dismissed the lawsuit brought by the Herero and Nama for compensation for the genocide; they subsequently appealed the judgment.

With a downturn in mineral prices and a crippling drought, Namibia entered recession in 2017 (see *Economy*). On a high-profile visit to the People's Republic of China in March–April 2018, President Geingob sought further Chinese investment. In April 2020 it was announced that China had offered to lend funds to upgrade Namibia's main airport, outside Windhoek. Meanwhile, Rio Tinto announced that it would close its Rössing uranium mine in 2020, unless it could arrange to sell it to the China National Uranium Corporation; this sale was completed in July 2019.

The second national land conference, held in October 2018, passed resolutions appealing for the 'willing buyer, willing seller' principle to be abolished, for foreign-owned land to be expropriated with compensation, and for a principle of 'one Namibian, one farm' to be upheld, although how these would be implemented was unclear.

After several years of below-average rainfall, another drought-related state of emergency was declared in May 2019; the end of the rainy season left much of Namibia's north and east parched, and the drought was reported to be the worst in a century. The Government launched an urgent appeal for international aid while increasing its own assistance, including distributing maize to almost half a million people. In October the state of emergency was extended, and the drought continued in much of the country until February 2020. In June 2019 a former Minister of Education, Arts and Culture, Katrina Hanse-Himarwa, was found guilty of corruption in the allocation of housing, and in November evidence appeared of high-level corruption in the Government's awarding of fishing concessions.

Meanwhile, in 2017, after Bernadus Swartbooi, the Deputy Minister of Lands, Resettlement and Rehabilitation, was dismissed by President Geingob for insubordination in December

2016, he founded the Landless People's Movement (LPM) to campaign in support of repossessing and redistributing ancestral land, especially in the south of the country.

THE 2019 ELECTIONS AND AFTER

Parliamentary and presidential elections were held on 27 November 2019, after the most competitive campaign in Namibia's democratic history. Panduleni Itula, who remained a member of SWAPO, campaigned for the presidency as an independent. However, the 77-year-old Geingob was re-elected with 56.2% of the vote. Itula received 29.4%. In the elections to the National Assembly, SWAPO lost 14 seats, winning 63 of the 96 elected seats and thus losing its two-thirds' majority. The PDM increased its seats from five to 16, while the relatively new LPM took four seats. The remainder were split between eight smaller parties. Itula challenged the results, partly on the grounds that electronic voting without a verifiable paper record was unconstitutional; he demanded a re-run of the presidential election. In February 2020 the Supreme Court unanimously declined to order a re-run, clearing the way for Geingob to be sworn in again for his second and final term as President on 21 March. On the previous day SWAPO had expelled Itula from the party. He went on to found the Independent Patriots for Change (IPC) party in August.

In the regional and local elections held in November 2020, in which the turnout was under 35%, SWAPO's share of the vote declined to 56.8% and it lost several constituencies in the main urban areas. The LPM won 12 constituencies, the IPC 17.5% of the vote and the PDM just under 7%. Job Amupanda, a young former activist in the AR Movement, emerged as the new mayor of Windhoek.

Meanwhile, in the so-called 'Fishrot' scandal, an investigation by the Qatari-based satellite television station Al Jazeera revealed that bribes had been accepted by Namibian cabinet ministers for licences given to Iceland's largest fishing company, and money laundered to the ruling party. The Minister of Justice, Sacky Shanghala, and the Minister of Fisheries and Marine Resources, Bernhardt Esau, resigned in November 2019. They were then arrested, charged with fraud, corruption and money laundering and refused bail. The case against them was postponed, owing to the outbreak of coronavirus disease (COVID-19) but was transferred to the High Court in December 2020. It was further delayed when the Government tried to obtain an order for three Icelanders to be extradited. In early 2021 allegations surfaced that President Geingob had instructed associates to use money from the national fishing company to ensure his re-election. In mid-2022 those charged in the case remained in prison, and their trial had not yet begun. Meanwhile, the Minister of Defence and Veterans Affairs, Peter Vilho, resigned in April 2021, after it was reported that he had a bank account in Hong Kong allegedly linked to illicit proceeds.

In response to the COVID-19 pandemic, Geingob announced a state of emergency on 17 March 2020. The Government imposed a partial lockdown on 24 March, and on 1 April offered a stimulus and relief package of N $8,100m. to support businesses and households, while labour regulations were relaxed to protect jobs. The lockdown began to be eased from May, as the number of confirmed infections relatively low. A sharp rise in COVID-19 cases in August led the Government to reintroduce some restrictions. Further spikes were recorded in January, June and December 2021 as the virus mutated. Namibia was slow to acquire vaccines, and the rollout of these, after it began in April, was slow. As the rate of new infections fell in early 2022, in March President Geingob removed the requirement to wear protective masks in public. By 1 August some 166,000 cases had been recorded, including 4,072 deaths, and only about 18% of the population had been fully vaccinated.

Before the pandemic, Namibia was already one of the most unequal countries in the world, and poverty and unemployment increased as a result of the COVID-19 crisis. Over one-half of all eligible young people were not in formal employment, and tourism activity dried up. One of the many casualties was the national airline, Air Namibia, which in February 2021 ceased operations and entered voluntary liquidation. In August the liquidators announced that the airline's liabilities stood at some N $3,500m., including around N $693m. in outstanding taxes. Recognizing the damage that the pandemic had inflicted, President Geingob convened a task force to propose legislation that would assist distressed enterprises and encourage entrepreneurship.

With the economy in recession, the Government granted a licence to a Canadian company, Reconnaissance Energy Africa (ReconAfrica), to drill an exploratory well in the Kavango basin, from which it hoped to extract 120,000m. barrels of oil. Protests took place, in Windhoek and elsewhere, by those predicting an environmental disaster in an ecologically fragile area, but in April the Government welcomed the first petroleum discovery, and a second find, at another well, followed in June. In early 2022 Shell (UK) and TotalEnergies (France) announced significant oil discoveries off the Namibian coast, and there was much discussion of green hydrogen projects, funded from outside Namibia. A Namibian government delegation that toured Europe to market the country as a potential powerhouse of clean energy claimed that Namibia could soon be self-sufficient in electricity due to solar power and that, by the end of the decade, it could become an exporter of green hydrogen.

In May 2021 the Namibian and German Governments announced that they had reached an agreement, after nine rounds of negotiations, under which Germany would pay Namibia €1,100m. (N $18,400m.) for development projects over a 30-year period, and would formally apologize for what it now accepted had been genocide against the Herero and Nama people during 1904–08. The agreement did not mention reparations, due to the German Government's concerns that the term might set a legal precedent for other colonies or victims of human rights abuses during the Nazi era (1933–45). Some €600m. was earmarked to buy commercial farms from whites on a 'willing buyer, willing seller' basis; white farmers continued to own 70% of commercial farmland in Namibia. However, most Herero leaders rejected the agreement, as the descendants of those who had died had not been party to the negotiations, and because what Germany offered was deemed to be grossly inadequate. The Namibian Government accepted the German offer, stating that a special fund would be created separate from the national budget, but when the proposal was presented to Parliament in September, it was not approved. Many in the Herero and Nama communities stated that they doubted that the funds would ever reach them and that they distrusted SWAPO, as it was a largely Ovambo party.

In June 2022 the Namibian Government became embroiled in the so-called 'Farmgate' scandal in South Africa, after the main suspect in theft from President Ramaphosa's game farm in February 2020 had fled to Namibia, where he had been arrested and jailed. President Geingob found it necessary to issue a statement denying that he had been involved in any cover-up of the crime, and a meeting of the Namibia-South Africa Bi-National Commission was postponed. Relations with South Africa deteriorated in August 2022 when, along with Botswana, Namibia stopped agricultural imports from South Africa to protect its local agricultural industry. In September Geingob travelled to Gaborone for the inaugural meeting of a Namibia-Botswana Bi-National Commission, which was expected to meet on a regular basis.

SWAPO held a policy conference in July, although it did not discuss the controversial rule in the SWAPO constitution that candidates for senior positions had to have served as a member of the party's central committee for 10 years. This left SWAPO Vice-President Netumbo Nandi-Ndaitwah and Prime Minister Saara Kuugongelwa-Amadhila as favourites to succeed Geingob. SWAPO was to hold an elective congress in late November to confirm the succession.

Economy

TERESIA KAULIHOWA, JACOB M. NYAMBE and VALDEMAR J. UNDJI

INTRODUCTION AND RECENT ECONOMIC DEVELOPMENTS

The World Bank ranks Namibia as a upper middle-income country with an estimated annual gross national income (GNI) per capita, of US $5,160 in 2019 and of US $4,500 in 2020. In sub-Saharan Africa, it is grouped together with Botswana, Mauritius and South Africa, which also fall under middle-income status. However, Namibia is characterized by extreme inequalities in income distribution and standards of living. It ranks as one of the most unequal economies in the world, with a Gini coefficient of 57.6 in 2015/16. Based on the national poverty line of N $520.8 per month in 2015/16 prices (equivalent to approximately US $40.8 using the average exchange rate in 2015), 17.4% of Namibians were poor in 2015/16, although this was a significant reduction from 37.5% in 2003/04. Despite this progress, however, World Bank estimates indicated that 13.4% of the population lived on less than US $1.9 per person per day in 2015/16—relatively high for an upper middle-income country.

Namibia's comparative wealth reflects a large primary sector dominated by mining and quarrying, producing diamonds, uranium and base metals for export. Although the country is prone to frequent drought, this mainly affects dry-land crop production, whereas its commercial livestock sector provides significant exports of beef and karakul sheepskin. The economy is highly dependent on the extractive industry and is not optimally integrated. According to the Namibia Statistics Agency (NSA), some 37.8%, 36.6% and 38.1% of the goods that Namibia produced were exported in 2019, 2020 and 2021, respectively. Pearls and precious stones (diamonds) dominated the export basket in 2021, accounting for 19.4% of the total, followed by uranium (15.2%), fish (14.8%), non-monetary gold (9.5%) and copper blisters (7.9%). The import penetration index reveals that over a period of five years (2017–21), imports on average have accounted for about 44.1% of aggregate demand in Namibia. Petroleum oils headed the list of products that Namibia imported from the rest of the world in 2021, accounting for 12.7% of total imports, followed by copper ore and concentrates (5.4%), motor vehicles for transport of goods (3.1%), pearls and precious stones (2.8% and vessels (2.4%). The measure of trade dependence for Namibia increased from 41.7% in 2020 to 45.9% in 2021, while it stood at 43.9% in 2019—an indication that Namibia's economy has been, and continues to be, strongly dependent on international trade. The coronavirus disease (COVID-19) pandemic hit Namibia's economy hard—its gross domestic product (GDP) contracted by 7.9% in 2020 because of declines in tourism, retail, trade and investments, health and education.

The United Nations Development Programme (UNDP) 2020 *Human Development Report* indicated that Namibia's Human Development Index (HDI) value for 2019 was 0.646, which placed the country in the medium human development category, and it ranked 130th out of 189 countries and territories worldwide. In sub-Saharan Africa, Namibia is broadly comparable with Botswana and South Africa, which had HDI rankings of 100 and 114, respectively. Between 1990 and 2019 Namibia's HDI value increased by 11.2% from 0.581 to 0.646. In terms of the disaggregated components, over that period Namibia's life expectancy at birth increased by 2.1 years, mean years of schooling rose by 1.4 years and expected years of schooling by 1.5 years, while GNI per capita increased by 57.0%. Although Namibia's HDI for 2019 was 0.646, it fell to 0.418 when discounted for inequality. This constitutes a loss of 35.3% due to inequality in the distribution of the HDI dimension indices. In comparison, South Africa shows a loss due to inequality of 34.0%, whereas the average loss due to inequality for medium category HDI countries is 26.3% and for sub-

Saharan Africa 30.5%. Other disparities such as access to land or housing pose a major challenge, while women remain at a disadvantage in income, health and protection. Moreover, education disparities in Namibia are defined by urban/rural divides, regional variations, and income/wealth differences.

In 2020 about 84% and 35% of Namibia's population had access to improved water resources and sanitation facilities, respectively. The World Health Organization (WHO) Global Health Expenditure database reported that the Government spent on average US \$427 in 2019 per capita compared to US \$464 in 2018. Namibia's health expenditure in 2019 ranked below its neighbours Botswana (US \$482) and South Africa (US \$547). Namibia's health spending growth is proportionately linked to its economic performance. Current health expenditure rose from 8.3% of GDP in 2018 to 8.5% in 2019. However, HIV/AIDS has had a negative implication on Namibia's health indicators: in 2020 HIV prevalence in Namibia was 11.6%, although this represented a decline from 13.6% in 2000. HIV/AIDS prevalence in Namibia is much lower compared with Botswana and South Africa, where prevalence rates of 19.9% and 19.1%, respectively, were reported in 2020. Although Namibia appears to have been successful in reducing the HIV/AIDS prevalence rate, it still ranks above the global average of 1.8% for 2020. According to Namibia's first ever population-based HIV survey, the country exceeded many of the 90-90-90 targets set by the Joint UN Programme on HIV/AIDS in 2014. (The targets required countries to ensure that 90% of people living with HIV were diagnosed, that 90% of those diagnosed were accessing treatment, and that 90% of people on treatment had suppressed viral loads by 2020.) According to the Namibia National Human Development Report (2019), the rate of new HIV/AIDS infection has reduced by more than three-fold from over 15,000 in 2002 to only 4,500 in 2018. Similarly, HIV/AIDS-related deaths have roughly halved during the same period, from approximately 10,000 in 2002.

The Namibian economy experienced robust economic expansion in 1991–2015, when it recorded average annual growth of 4.4%. However, economic growth has stagnated since 2016, and recessions were reported in 2017, 2019 and 2020, although a recovery was estimated for the year 2021. The NSA projected that real GDP would grow by 2.4% in 2021, compared with the deep contraction of 7.9% in 2020. The 2021 estimate ranked Namibia below the average GDP growth for the sub-Saharan African region, which, according to International Monetary Fund (IMF) projections, would reach 4.5% in 2021. The recovery in that year was mainly driven by improved performances in primary and tertiary industries, and, in particular, by expansion in the production of diamonds and uranium, as well as value addition in the wholesale and retail trade, hotels and restaurants, information and communication, and public administration and defence sectors.

At independence in 1990, the country inherited an economy characterized by a narrow industrial base and heavy dependence on the production and export of primary commodities such as beef, fish and minerals. Although mining remains the pillar of Namibia's economy, being among the largest contributors to GDP and foreign exchange earnings, the economy has made progress towards diversification in recent years. According to the NSA, primary industry recorded a growth rate of 18.8% in 2018, but declined by 6.9% in 2019 and by a further 5.9% in 2020. Secondary industry declined by 0.7% in 2018, but expanded by 2.2% in 2019 before contracting by 13.0% in 2020, while tertiary industry declined by 1.0% in 2018, grew by 1.1% in 2019 and fell by 5.7% in 2020. The central bank, the Bank of Namibia (BoN), reported that value addition in the mining and quarrying sector increased by 13.6% in 2021, compared to a contraction of 15.0% registered in the preceding year. During the same year primary industry expanded by 8.0%, and tertiary industry by 1.9% but secondary industry declined by 6.6%, due to a decline in construction, as well as in the electricity and water sector.

In line with global trends, the COVID-19 pandemic has had a drastic impact on Namibia's economy and has exacerbated pre-existing structural challenges such as high unemployment rate and poverty levels. On 17 March 2020 the Namibian Government declared the COVID-19 pandemic a state of emergency, outlined lockdown measures to combat the spread of the virus, and implemented various policy interventions. At the macro level the Government, through the Ministry of Finance, enacted a stimulus and relief package of N \$8,100m. (about 4.3% of GDP) to serve as a safety net for affected businesses and individuals. At the end of July the Government requested an emergency loan worth N \$4,500m. (US \$273m.) from the IMF. According to WHO figures, 160,074 confirmed cases of COVID-19 had been reported in Namibia by 16 May 2022, with 4,028 fatalities. Nevertheless, despite the significant detrimental effects of the pandemic, with the GDP contraction of 7.9% in 2020, the Namibian economy proved somewhat resilient and was able to bounce back in 2021 when the BoN expected GDP growth of 2.4%.

PRIMARY INDUSTRY

Minerals and Mining

With exception of the years 2019 and 2020, the mining sector has had a consistently higher contribution to economic growth in Namibia than any of the other sub-sectors in the primary industry sector (agriculture, forestry and fisheries). Each year it has contributed 10% to GDP on average, and in 2021 the contribution of mining and quarrying to overall GDP was 9.8% (with diamonds alone accounting for 2.9% of the total). With regards to job creation, a total of 12,087 persons were employed in the sector, of which 9,943 were male and 2,144 were female, according to the NSA in 2019. Moreover, the sector indirectly contributes to 100,000 citizens' livelihoods. Namibia produces diamonds, uranium, copper, magnesium, zinc, silver, gold, lead, semi-precious stones and industrial minerals.

The reserves of the country's offshore diamonds are estimated to be more than 80m. carats, making it the largest global offshore miner. Precious stones (mainly diamonds) are among the top five export products and are mostly destined for Botswana, the United Arab Emirates (UAE) and Belgium. Diamond output has seen a major increase in recent years, from 1.7m. carats in 2016 to 2.0m. carats in 2019. This figure would have been much higher if it were not for the onshore mines producing less in 2019. Nevertheless, the diamond industry was expected to grow by 17.2% in 2022, according to the BoN. This is because of increasing diamond output through the new diamond mining vessel which began production in the second quarter of 2022.

In addition to diamond production, the country has one of the largest uranium mines in the world. In 2018 the Husab open-pit uranium mine produced 3,028 metric tons of uranium, making it the third largest uranium mine in the world. Moreover, in 2019 Namibia was ranked in fourth place in the world's largest producers of uranium. However, decreased nuclear power demand due to past nuclear disasters around the globe has depressed world uranium prices.

Namibia is also a leading producer of zinc, which is becoming one of the country's largest export revenue sources. In 2000 Skorpion Zinc mine became active and produced over 47,000 metric tons for export in the following year. By 2009 the mine was producing 150,000 tons, thus becoming the largest integrated zinc producer in Africa, and was ranked the 10th largest zinc mine in the world. However, refined zinc production had declined to 66,000 tons by 2019, although among the reasons for the fall in output were a shutdown of production during the first quarter of 2019 and an illegal strike from 22 February to 6 March of that year. It is thus not surprising that, after Namdeb Diamond Corporation and Rössing (which operates the Husab mine), sales from Skorpion are considered the main source of export earnings in Namibia.

In recent years minerals such as copper have also seen a considerable increase in production. The output of copper from Chelopech mines and later smelted at Tsumeb increased from an estimated 185,000 metric tons in 2013 to about 220,000 tons in 2017. Overall, the contribution of the mining sector to the Namibian economy includes export involvement, government tax revenue and a foreign currency earner for the country.

Namibia, like any other developing country, has used a growth strategy of actively participating in developing sectors that are already industrialized in other countries. For this reason, developing countries have rarely been leaders but rather followers of technology. This is evident in the diamond cutting, diamond polishing and garment manufacturing industries in Namibia. Despite this historic trend, Namibia is set to be a new global industry leader through the development of its own green hydrogen and ammonia industry. This has been viewed as another growth opportunity by the Government, since the country is one of a few global regions with favourable conditions for green hydrogen production and export.

At the 26th UN Climate Change Conference of the Parties (COP26) held in Glasgow, United Kingdom, in late 2021, a US $9,400m. vertically integrated green hydrogen project was announced by the Namibian Government. The preferred bidder for this development, to be undertaken in Tsau //Khaeb National Park, was the German consortium Hyphen Hydrogen Energy. The project will be undertaken in stages that will target the production of 300,000 metric tons of green hydrogen in the form of pure hydrogen or green ammonia (hydrogen in derivative form). The annual quantity produced will be sold in both regional and global markets. Moreover, the German consortium will be granted the right to construct and operate the project for a period of 40 years.

The first stage, which is scheduled to enter into production in 2026, will produce 2 GW of renewable electricity generation capacity. This will be used to produce green hydrogen, which will be converted to green ammonia at an approximate cost of US $4,400m. Expansion stages scheduled to commence in the late 2020s will increase joint renewable generation capacity to 5 GW, raising the joint total investment to the US $9,400m. mentioned above.

The Namibian Government hopes to have an operational stake of between 10% and 24% in the project. This is not surprising because the project will contribute to a significant increase in foreign direct investment (FDI) and employment once fully developed. The investment amount is roughly equivalent to the total value of the Namibian economy. In the four-year construction of both stages, 15,000 jobs will be directly created, while an extra 3,000 jobs will be permanently created during the operational stage. It is believed that more than 90% of these roles will be occupied by local citizens. Most importantly, the Namibian Government will receive royalties, concession fees and a sovereign wealth fund contribution, as well as an environment levy.

In addition to the green hydrogen project announcement, large petroleum and gas discoveries have recently been made by Total Energies and Shell off Namibia's coast. It was believed that these deposits hold roughly 3,000m. barrels of oil overall, offering the Namibian Government a potential income of approximately US $3,500m. per year in taxes and royalties. The country aims to expedite the development of its first oilfield to begin production by 2026.

Agriculture and Fisheries

The agriculture sector, which comprises both commercial and subsistence farming, is one of the highest contributors to employment creation in Namibia. The principal crops with the highest aggregate production in the three years to 2020 were millet, grapes, maize, dry onions and potatoes. In 2020 aggregate production ranged from 14,300 metric tons (for potatoes) to an estimated 95,000 tons (for millet), which represented an improvement from the previous year's figures. In 2021 the agricultural, forestry and fishing sector provided 10.1% of GDP.

While the NSA's 2019 Labour Force Survey reported a rise in the overall employment rate (to 46.1% of the total labour force) the agricultural sector was not a significant driver of this. Over the past 30 years the agricultural sector, through commercial farming, has experienced a transition from labour intensive to capital intensive. The agriculture sub-sector mainly comprises livestock farming (which expands when farmers are increasing their herds), crop farming, and forestry. It has been stated that to support growth in farming and major marketable areas, necessary resources should be assigned to farmers. There was a slight increase by the Ministry of Finance in the budget allocation for appropriation for investment to the Ministry of Agriculture, Water and Land Reform, from N $1,700m. in 2021/22 to N $1,900m. in 2022/23. This budget allocation was still just 3%, however, which was well below the 10% suggested

by the Comprehensive African Agricultural Development Program (CAADP) of the African Union.

The fishing sector is considered important for the Namibian economy, due to it having one of the highest levels of employment creation in the country. It boasts approximately 24,000 employees, who are either seasonal personnel or engage in onshore processing. Despite having a much lower contribution to GDP (3.0% on average), overall, this has been stable and not open to wide fluctuations. (In 2021 the sector contributed 2.7% of the country's GDP.) However, the value addition in the sector has not yet been used as a source of economic development. Hence it is not surprising that the fifth National Development Plan (NDP) claims that on an annual basis 5,000 metric tons of quality fish could be produced by the country's freshwater fisheries through sustainable fishery management. Namibia's fish species captured include Cape hake (stokvis), Southern Africa pilchard and Cape horse mackerel (Maasbanker). In 2017 the total number of fish captured was 501,400 tons, but the amount declined to 490,200 tons in 2018, to 467,100 tons in 2019 and to 429,600 tons in 2020.

THE SECONDARY SECTOR

Manufacturing and Construction

The manufacturing sub-sector contributed an average of 11% per year to GDP in 1990–2019, and accounted for 11.8% in 2021. As the sub-sector is dependent on inputs coming from the primary sector, the goods produced in this sector have largely remained the same since independence. In 1990 food and beverages, wood products and metal, and non-metal products dominated the sector. During this same period textiles, clothing, and leather industries were still undeveloped. However, over the past 30 years the manufacturing sector has gradually established cosmetics, chemicals and non-chemical products.

Although the sector had not reached its set target contribution to GDP, as stipulated in the fifth NDP, of 52% in 2019 and of 60% in 2021, the country is still focused on increasing manufacturing output, and the Namibian Industrial Policy of 2015 aims to increase manufacturing's contribution to GDP significantly by 2030.

Construction is also an important component of the Namibian economy. However, this sector is very sensitive to interest rates and is also affected by cement prices and availability. In 2019, according to the NSA, the construction sector contracted by 4.4%, while in the following year a 9.8% decrease in real value added was recorded. According to the BoN, the construction sector was still expected to remain in contraction in 2022 but was projected to recover in 2023. Many of the reasons for the significant 2020 contraction, including low construction activity in the private and public sectors, were still prevailing. Despite the recent contraction trend, the sector's predicted recovery might lead to the rates of positive growth that were seen in the past, especially in 2002–06.

Energy (Electricity)

The energy and water sector plays an important role in terms of providing electricity to households and to the production sector. Regarding electricity, the Government has strongly emphasized that providing greater access to it is a major tool in poverty reduction. The company responsible for generating, transmitting and distributing electricity in Namibia is the Namibia Power Corporation, commonly known as NamPower. The corporation's main sources of power are the thermal, coal-fired Van Eck power station outside the capital, Windhoek, the hydroelectric plant at the Ruacana falls in the Kunene region, and the standby diesel-driven Paratus power station at Walvis Bay. One of the NamPower's major aims is to deliver the sustainable security of electricity supply, as well as a least-cost reflective tariff path to support economic growth.

Of equal importance are the additional supplies of power from neighbouring Southern African Development Community (SADC) countries, which have helped to ensure that sufficient electricity is available for local consumer demand in the country. Namibia reduced the volume of electricity imported from the SADC region from 71.0% of the country's total requirement in 2018/19 to 59.2% in 2019/20. One of the major reasons for the reduction of the county's electricity imports was the plentiful rainfall that was received. This then led to an increase in the electricity generated by NamPower's Raucana hydro power plant, which recorded a rise in its provision from 22.7% in 2018/19 to 33.4% in 2019/20.

THE TERTIARY SECTOR

Tourism

According to the fourth and fifth NDPs, improving the tourism sector's contribution to GDP (by attracting tourists in greater numbers) will be key in reaching developmental goals for the country. The tourism sector comprises private commercial operators and major state operators, and in the immediate pre-pandemic era Namibia received around 1.7m. tourists per year, attracted by the nation's peace and political stability, abundant wildlife resources, spectacular landscape, good infrastructure and low population density. Countries that provided the highest number of foreign tourist arrivals were Angola, South Africa, Zambia and Germany, and the number of Angolan tourists increased from 447,295 in 2017 to 606,818 in 2019, while the figures from South Africa were 345,376 and 284,431, respectively.

The COVID-19 pandemic had a huge negative impact on the tourism sector, with figures for total tourist arrivals reduced to just 169,565 in 2020 and only a small recovery, to 233,692, recorded in 2021. Even so, through its strong multiplier effect, the sector has traditionally made major contributions to the economy. These include investments, employment, generation of foreign exchange and rural development. Due to Namibia being part of the SADC grouping on tourism known as the Regional Tourism Organization of Southern Africa, the country has benefited from the implementation of strategies that improve natural resources management and the establishment of lodges and hotels. This has helped the country to receive a high number of international tourists. Tourists also obtain satisfaction from visiting areas that are rich in landscapes, natural vegetation cover and wildlife.

Transport

The transport sector in Namibia covers road, rail, air and maritime transportation modes. Due to the country's vastness and the sparsity of its population, road, rail and air transport infrastructures are of great economic importance. Namibia's transport infrastructure includes well developed and well maintained road networks which are ranked among the best in the world. The country received a score of 5.2 out of 7.0 in the 2019 World Economic Forum (WEF) *Global Competitiveness Report* placing it first in Africa in terms of having the best road infrastructure network (a position it has held for the last five years). Furthermore, the country was ranked 23rd in the world, ahead of countries such as the People's Republic of China, India and Italy. The ports of Walvis Bay and !Nami#nus (formerly Lüderitz) receive some 1,800 and 2,500 vessels each year, respectively. The latter handled 6,320 containers in 2017/18, 5,355 in 2018/19 and 5,685 in 2019/20, while Walvis Bay handled 176,335 containers in 2017/18, 144,109 in 2018/19 and 142,957 in 2019/20. In 2019 a new container terminal at Walvis Bay was inaugurated and entered into operation. This terminal was estimated to have increased capacity to 750,000 20-ft equivalent units per annum. However, due to the COVID-19 pandemic, port operations were slowed down until conditions normalized again.

Communications

The communications sector is crucial to the Namibian economy and plays an important role in the success of all trade activities and in the 4th industrial revolution drive. The country has been striving for better infrastructure development, including the bolstering of information and communication technology as a catalyst for economic growth and development. Internet services have improved in terms of bandwidth and accessibility during the last 10 years. In 2018 the number of fixed broadband subscriptions totalled 62,000, and this increased slightly, to 63,300 in 2019, and then to 71,100 in 2020. A total of 1.67m. mobile broadband subscriptions was recorded in 2018, but this figure decreased slightly in 2019 to 1.65m. before rising again to 1.78m. in 2020. Overall, the number of internet users as a percentage of population (aged 18 years and over) has increased slightly from 40.0% in 2018 to 40.5% in 2019.

Finance

Prior to Namibia's independence in 1990, South Africa was an important source of public finance; however, upon attainment of independence, South Africa made its final financial contribution (of R 83m.) and ceased acting as guarantor of Namibian loans. Since then the revenue from the Southern African Customs Union (SACU) pool has been an important source of Government income, contributing an average of about one-third of annual revenue over the past five years. The Customs Union was renegotiated in 2002, and a new SACU secretariat was established in Windhoek. The new agreement, effective from July 2004, guaranteed a duty rate of 17%, reducing the yearly fluctuations of the past. In addition, each member state now receives customs revenues based on its average relative share of SACU GDP, towards which Namibia contributes 2.4%. However, this source of revenue has been volatile, and many observers (including the IMF) want the Government to use such windfalls to pay off debt. Indeed, over the long term the level of revenue is expected to decline because of planned amendments to the revenue sharing formula.

Transfers of SACU revenue to Namibia decreased by 5.5% year-on-year, to an estimated N \$17,100m., in 2015/16 (equivalent to 29.3% of total government revenue) from an estimated N \$18,100m. in 2014/15. In 2020/21 Namibia received a total of N \$22,600m. from the SACU revenue pool. However, this increase was followed by a drastic decline of N \$7,900m. in 2021/22 (to N \$14,700m.) brought about by external factors exacerbated by the impacts of the COVID-19 pandemic. South Africa has been advocating a further revision of the revenue sharing formula, and this could additionally affect the amount of revenue that Namibia receives from the SACU revenue pool. None the less, such re-evaluation has been delayed until a consensus among the member states can be reached. In the meantime, the economic contraction which started in 2016, as well as the uncertain growth prospects for 2023, continue to undermine the Government's efforts towards domestic revenue mobilization (i.e., in the form of income and company tax revenue), which is crucial to implement the Medium Term Expenditure Framework objectives.

The Namibian Stock Exchange (NSX) is currently home to about 40 companies with a market capitalization of US \$136,000m., making it the second biggest exchange in Africa after the Johannesburg Stock Exchange in South Africa. The reason for its size is the large number of dual or secondary listings. The NSX actively pursues dual listings and focuses on ease of listings to diversify its market as well as deepen it with more local content. The stability of the Namibian stock market has been reflected in the investment grade credit rating the country has enjoyed over the years as well the country's macroeconomic solidity. However, in December 2017 the European Union placed Namibia on its draft list of non-co-operative tax jurisdictions (because the Government failed to give clear details about preferential tax treatment in the Export Processing Zones).

The Namibian dollar, linked at parity to the South African rand, was valued at US \$1 = N \$9.72 in May 2013, but had depreciated to a rate of US \$1 = N \$15.903 by December 2021. This depreciation was the result of several factors, including weak global mineral prices. Namibia's foreign exchange reserves totalled US \$2,169m. in 2020, up from US \$1,209m. in 2014. The flow of FDI over the past five years has dwindled, and has done so particularly since the COVID-19 global outbreak, thereby affecting the deteriorating Namibian economy. First Capital Namibia argues that there is a strong link between GDP and FDI in Namibia. For instance, in 2014 FDI stood at 22% (the highest in years), and in that same year Namibia's economy grew by 6.8%. In 2016 Namibia registered a contraction in FDI of 27%, and in that year GDP declined by 0.3%. Lack of recovery in FDI flows has kept the economy in a poor state, as it registered a decline of 1.1% in 2019 and of 7.9% in 2020. Namibia is one of many mineral-rich African countries that are dependent on FDI, and it is not an exception in regard to low inflows of FDI leading to negative consequences for the broader economy, but it is certainly among the most severely affected countries in the world.

Inflation and Monetary Policy

Since 1980 Namibia has not traditionally experienced very high levels of inflation. In 1980–89 the average annual rate was 13.0%, and since attaining independence inflation has been well within a reasonable single digit range with the exception of the 1992 drought year when it registered 17.7%. In 2021 Namibia recorded an annual inflation rate of 3.6%, which was the lowest among the SACU member states. Furthermore, its moderate inflation environment is among the lowest in sub-Saharan Africa. Despite the annual rate of inflation being slightly more volatile in recent years, it has been well under control. Higher electricity prices resulted in inflation of around 4.9% in 2014, but inflationary pressures subsequently eased due to the continued decline in global oil prices. Consumer prices increased by 3.6% in 2015 and rose sharply by 7.3% in 2016, due to a weakened currency and higher food prices, before the rate of growth steadily declined with an inflation rate of 3.8% recorded in 2019 and, as noted above, of 3.6% in 2021.

The currency peg agreement entered between the countries in the Common Monetary Area (CMA), of which Namibia is a member, continues to ensure credible monetary policy management by the monetary authority in Namibia. Its principal aim is to ensure price stability for sustainable economic development. Namibia's monetary policy framework is also underpinned by a fixed currency peg to the South African rand. In addition, Namibia's inflation rate is highly influenced by South African price levels, not least because over 62% of goods (mainly food) imported in 2021 came from South Africa.

Following the emergence of COVID-19, the BoN introduced successive monetary policy measures to mitigate the adverse effects of the pandemic and to stimulate economic activities, most notably by lowering the repo rate from 6.75% in July 2019 to 3.75% in August 2020 (the lowest repo rate ever recorded in Namibia) and it remained unchanged throughout 2021. However, the repo rate was increased to 4.25% in April 2022, with the BoN's Governor stressing the need to safeguard the one-to-one link between the Namibian dollar and South African rand. The repo rate was expected to rise further during 2022 due to global inflationary pressures, which had led many central banks, including the South African Reserve Bank (SARB), the central bank of South Africa), to raise rates. In June the BoN matched the SARB and increased its repo rate by 50 basis point to 4.75%. Current projections indicated that the SARB was likely to hike the repo rate again during the third quarter of 2022 as South Africa struggled to maintain its inflation target of between 3% and 6%. Namibia was expected to follow suit, with more repo rate increases predicted in 2022 and early 2023.

Unemployment

Namibia's economic growth trends have varied since the 1980s, reaching their high point in 2001–15 when the average annual rate of increase was 5.5%. Yet the growth that Namibia has experienced so far falls short of the required yearly growth rate of 7% needed to diminish the high rate of unemployment in the country, and has had little impact in creating employment opportunities capable of absorbing the majority of the unemployed youth population. The NSA estimated that the broad unemployment rate had increased from 27.4% in 2012 to 37.7% in 2018. As of 2019 youth unemployment was estimated to be 72.8%, and this figure is believed to have increased significantly due to the impact of the COVID-19 pandemic. Given the high unemployment rate among the country's youth, it is imperative for the Government to scale-up the numbers of profitable projects to better the future of unemployed youths in the country. The areas to focus on should include entrepreneurial coaching, and increasing the availability of start-up capital and skills training. Moreover, the issue of skills mismatch needs to be addressed through the transformation of curriculums of existing academic institutions of higher learning.

Foreign Trade and Balance of Payments

Foreign trade is an integral part of Namibia's economic development due to the role it facilitates in linking countries that have certain comparative and/or absolute advantages in the global economy. As such, Namibia is highly integrated into the global economy through trade, free flow of capital and tourism. Like so many countries around the world, Namibia is an open economy, endowed with an abundance of natural resources, but heavily dependent on other countries in terms of international trade. Namibia's major trading partner for both imports and exports has, since independence in 1990, been South Africa. More specifically, the top five import markets in 2021 were: South Africa (62.3%), followed by China (6.8%), India (5.5%), the eurozone (5.3%) and Oman (2.3%). These imports were largely dominated by food products, petroleum products and fuel, machinery and equipment, and chemicals. In the same year the top five export destination markets were: South Africa (23.7%), followed by China (21.2%), the eurozone (17.2%), Botswana (13.0%), and the UAE (4.1%). These exports, which are also responsible for providing a significant portion of foreign currency earnings in Namibia, are largely dominated by minerals, fish and meat products.

Based on official statistics, it is evident that Namibia's economic growth is highly susceptible to external shocks that emanate primarily from South Africa and then the rest of the global economy. Certainly, the inconsistent GDP growth has posed challenges to policy makers, since the source of the volatility in growth in Namibia is largely exogenous through the trade transmission mechanism of global commodity prices, as well as endogenous through domestic factors such as the prolonged drought period. This implies that a decline in the demand for Namibia's export commodities is rapidly transmitted to other sectors thereby negatively affecting the overall growth of the economy.

Namibia's trade balance has been widening for a number of years and during the COVID-19 era it has worsened. For instance, the trade balance deteriorated by N $12,700m. to N $28,400m. in 2021. The deterioration was significantly driven the by rise in the value of merchandise imports, which increased by 19.9% to N $80,900m. in that year, reflecting improved domestic demand following weak economic activity exacerbated by the COVID-19 pandemic lockdowns and restrictions during 2020. Against this background, Namibia's trade balance was expected to remain in large deficit until there was a drastic recovery from the adverse effects of COVID-19 and from the geopolitical instability in Europe caused by the war in Ukraine (following the Russian invasion in February 2022).

Given that Namibia continues to export primary products, mostly in their raw format, especially from the agriculture, forestry, fishing and mining sectors, it becomes almost impossible to improve the country's balance of trade. Unless there are concerted efforts to narrow the gap between high import value and low export value through value addition to its raw materials, it is inconceivable that an improvement can be made. Value addition is indispensable for Namibia's economic development given its abundant natural resource base, which has the potential to boost the value of its export earnings while causing the value of its imports to be cheaper and lower, thereby improving the terms of trade. In addition, the recent formation of the African Continental Free Trade Area (AfCFTA), of which Namibia is a member, accords it an unprecedented trade opportunity through which its exports have access to a much wider African market. Nevertheless, the establishment of the AfCFTA will only be beneficial if aspects of value addition, which will lead to a wider variety of export goods, are adopted.

Although Namibia experienced a persistent deficit on the current account of the balance of payments in 2009–16, in 2020 the country recorded a current account surplus of 2.8% of GDP. This was short-lived, as by the end of 2021 Namibia reverted back to recording a current account deficit, which reached 9.1% of GDP. The deficit had widened further to 15.0% of GDP by the first quarter of 2022. The deterioration can be explained by a range of factors, including that the country is a net borrower, that there has been a deterioration of merchandise trade deficit, that the country import bill has risen due to high food and oil prices, and that there has been a sharp decline in secondary income inflows, such as those from the SACU revenue pool. Policymakers should pay close attention to the persistence of the current account deficit as it is indicative of impending instabilities.

Aid

Aid to Namibia has been provided in the form of systematic aid (bilateral and multilateral), humanitarian aid and charity-based aid. The major contributors of bilateral aid to Namibia since independence have been Germany, the Nordic countries, the UK and the USA. In 2019 according to the World Bank total net bilateral aid flows from the Development Assistance Committee (DAC) donors reached US $115.8m. Germany is the country's largest development partner and has rendered aid through the Deutsche Gesellschaft für Internationale Zusammenarbeit and Kreditanstalt für Wiederaufbau. Between 2017 and 2019 Germany's aid payments (net bilateral aid flows from DAC donors) increased from US $36.5m. to US $70.2m.

The USA, EU institutions and China are also among the largest development partners to Namibia. The USA through the Millennium Challenge Corporation focuses on education, tourism, health and livestock. According to the World Bank, net aid flows from the USA to Namibia in 2019 totalled US $33.3m. However, this figure was lower than the aid flow in the previous year (US $66.3m.). In 2019 net bilateral aid flows from EU institutions stood at US $14.6m., which was an increase from the figure of the previous year (US $11.4m.).

China's rise to becoming one of the largest providers of bilateral development aid has stemmed from the fact that Namibia has found it challenging to access concessionary loans from international bodies. The reason is because Namibia is placed in the middle-income category. China has delivered aid in the mining, construction and retail sectors. Some projects that have benefited from Chinese loans are the Engela–Outapi road (roughly 90 km in length), the Omakange–Ruacana road (roughly 60 km), and the installation of security scanners at all the country's borders.

Namibia has nevertheless received multilateral aid payments from institutions such as the World Bank and the IMF. In March 2021 the IMF executive board approved a US $270.8m. payment to Namibia to address the COVID-19 pandemic. This was disbursed under the Rapid Financing Instrument (RFI) to meet urgent balance of payment and financing needs resulting from negative consequences of the pandemic. Most importantly, the payment was intended to fund the purchase of vaccines and a vaccination campaign.

Humanitarian aid to Namibia has provided necessary help to deal with disasters such as floods, droughts, epidemics and tropical cyclones, with international organizations assisting with the management and control of the country's HIV and tuberculosis outbreaks. Programmes such as Project HOPE, the Office of US Foreign Disaster Assistance (OFDA, a former unit within the US Agency for International Development) and the UN Children's Fund (UNICEF) have had a positive impact on the country. For instance, the OFDA has assisted Namibia at times of natural disasters by improving food security in vulnerable households with relief funds that have focused on enhancing agriculture and harvesting needs. Likewise, agencies such as the UN Population Fund have assisted in the prevention of gender-based violence and sexual exploitation of women and adolescent girls. Apart from systematic and humanitarian aid, Namibia has also received charity-based aid disbursed by charitable organizations to institutions or people on the ground.

ECONOMIC PROSPECTS

The Namibian economy was on a recovery trajectory in 2021—a positive prospect that comes after five years of recession. Although the COVID-19 pandemic triggered Namibia's highest ever GDP contraction of 7.9% (as revised) in 2020, the economy is now making a steady recovery, as evidenced by its quick rebound in 2021, when the NSA estimated GDP growth of 2.4%. However, economic growth remains weak due to increased headwinds from low credit growth, surging international food prices, soaring energy prices and supply shocks caused by the conflict in Ukraine, as well as renewed pandemic

lockdowns in China. In addition, in May 2022 Namibia was declared to have entered its fifth wave of COVID-19 cases, while a high vaccine hesitancy rate posed a potential obstacle in fighting the pandemic. According to WHO, just 16% of the Namibian population were fully vaccinated at May. This was much lower compared to its neighbours such as South Africa and Botswana, where the figures were 31% and 57%, respectively. Notwithstanding these issues, the BoN predicted that the Namibian economy would grow by a further by 3.3% in 2022. Namibia has recently set up a sovereign wealth fund that is aimed to serve as a buffer against future economic shocks. Royalties from the sale of natural, renewable and non-renewable mineral resources, taxes, divestiture from public investment holdings and contributions from certain state-owned enterprises will finance the fund, which is expected to build investor confidence.

Namibia's economic growth is mainly driven by the expansion prospects of the mining industry and most of the tertiary industries, whereas the contribution of the secondary sector (which predominantly comes from manufacturing) is expected to remain low. This indicates that the country is not fully industrialized and has an underdeveloped manufacturing sector. The mining sector was ultimately set for another year of growth in 2022, as marine diamond production was expected to increase with the operation of a new recovery vessel by leading mining company Debmarine Namibia (a 50-50 joint venture between De Beers and the Namibian Government) in March, ahead of schedule. The custom-built vessel, the AMV3. was predicted to increase Debmarine Namibia's annual production by 45%, adding some 500,000 carats of high-value diamonds. This new development will support Namibia's long-term sustainable future for the diamond sector, as the country is the source of some of the most prized diamonds in the world.

The production of other commodities, such as uranium and copper, was also expected to increase. The Husab uranium mine was expected to gear up to capacity in 2022 while simultaneously taking advantage of the rise in uranium prices. Kombat copper mine has been brought back into production by Trigon Metals and was also expected to ramp up to full production in 2022—after resuming output in 2021. Meanwhile, several exploration projects in mine development are currently in progress. A pre-feasibility study (PFS) for the Twin Hills gold exploration project was completed in 2021, while the uranium exploration company Reptile Mineral Resources and Exploration is at an advanced stage of a definitive feasibility study (DFS) for its Tumas project. In addition, another uranium exploration company, Bannerman Resources, has completed a PFS while its DFS was projected to near completion by mid-2022. The investment on these projects, if realized, was expected to enhance job creation and support economic development.

Furthermore, Namibia's new green hydrogen project offers good growth prospects. As noted above, Hyphen Hydrogen Energy was selected by the Government of Namibia as the preferred bidder for the green hydrogen project in the Tsau // Khaeb National Park, and Namibia is set to receive approximately US $6.3m. in concessional fees from Hyphen. These revenues will enable the country to fast track its green hydrogen development while ensuring that economic growth is not only maintained but accelerated. In early 2022 the Namibian President, Dr Hage Geingob, announced that the country would secure an initial N $100m. in concession fees from the preferred bidder, bringing immediate fiscal relief and translating the vision of a synthetic fuel industry into immediate FDI flows. Cleanergy, a joint venture between Namibia's Ohlthaver & List Group and CMB.Tech of Belgium, launched the first green hydrogen plant (at Walvis Bay) in February 2022, with an initial investment of N $270m. It was expected to be operational in 2023—an indication of the potential of Namibia's green hydrogen strategy and the possibility of unlocking even greater investments and of establishing Namibia as a regional and global decarbonization champion.

According to the World Bank, Namibia was ranked 104th out of 190 economies in the Ease of Doing Business Index in 2020. Its Global Innovation Index ranking improved in 2021 to 100th position (from 104th in 2020), although the country performed better in innovation input than in innovation output in 2021

(88th compared with 110th, respectively). In terms of sub-Saharan Africa performance, Namibia was ranked sixth among the 27 economies assessed in the region. The 2021 Corruption Perception Index (CPI) compiled by Transparency International ranked Namibia 58th out of 180 countries, down from 57th place in 2020. Despite a slight fall, it is important to note that Namibia's CPI ranking is higher than most other economies in the region. In terms of global competitiveness, the WEF's 2019 *Global Competitiveness Report* ranked Namibia as the 94th most competitive economy out of 140 countries in the world. As mentioned above, Namibia heads the African region in the quality of its road infrastructure.

Namibia's recent participation in the Dubai World Expo and the WEF are two of the key highlights from major investment promotion events. This follows the establishment of the Namibia Investment Promotion and Development Board (NIPDB) in March 2020. By March 2022 the NIPDB indicated that it had secured investment to the value of N $94,000m. with the potential to create 122,000 jobs. This excludes Total Energies

and Shell's significant discovery of light oil off the country's southern coast. The country is aiming to fast track this development into production by 2026.

Since independence in 1990 Namibia has experienced comparatively little social or economic upheaval, has had relatively sound macroeconomic policies, and has possessed a physical infrastructure that should serve as catalyst to long-term development and growth. The country boasts political stability and good fiscal management. Namibia's biggest challenges will be to transform the economy towards a green and blue economy to ensure sustainable future growth in a manner that creates more jobs and lowers the current high unemployment rate. However, the conflict in Ukraine and current inflationary pressures constitute watershed moments in history that are reshaping geopolitical developments and straining financial institutions around the globe, including in Namibia—an indication that countries are facing serious headwinds and downside risks through various channels.

Statistical Survey

Source (unless otherwise indicated): Namibia Statistics Agency, POB 2133, Windhoek; tel. (61) 4313200; e-mail info@nsa.org.na; internet www.nsa.org.na.

Area and Population

AREA, POPULATION AND DENSITY

Area (sq km)	825,615*
Population (census results)	
28 October 2001	1,830,330
28 August 2011	
Males	1,021,912
Females	1,091,165
Total	2,113,077
Population (official projections at mid-year)	
2020	2,504,498
2021	2,550,226
2022	2,596,037
Density (per sq km) at mid-2022	3.1

* 318,772 sq miles.

POPULATION BY AGE AND SEX
(official projections at mid-2021)

	Males	Females	Total
0–14 years	471,405	462,821	934,226
15–64 years	727,009	783,217	1,510,226
65 years and over	41,881	63,893	105,774
Total	1,240,295	1,309,931	2,550,226

POPULATION BY ETHNIC GROUP
(population, 1988 estimates)

Ovambo . . .	623,000	Caprivian . . .	47,000
Kavango . . .	117,000	Bushmen . . .	36,000
Damara . . .	94,000	Baster	31,000
Herero . . .	94,000	Tswana	7,000
White . . .	80,000	Others	12,000
Nama . . .	60,000	**Total**	1,252,000
Coloured . . .	51,000		

Note: Classification of ethnicity reflects national methodology.

REGIONS
(official population projections at mid-2022)

	Area (sq km)	Population	Density (per sq km)
Caprivi*	14,785	109,160	7.4
Erongo	63,539	222,380	3.5
Hardap	109,781	96,626	0.9
Karas*	161,514	96,015	0.6
Kavango*	48,742	255,978	5.3
Khomas	36,964	513,044	13.9
Kunene	115,260	112,130	1.0
Ohangwena	10,706	270,452	25.3
Omaheke	84,981	77,652	0.9
Omusati	26,551	259,554	9.8
Oshana	8,647	205,336	23.7
Oshikoto	38,685	212,160	5.4
Otjozondjupa	105,460	165,550	1.6
Total	825,615	2,596,037	3.1

* In August 2013 it was announced that henceforth Kavango region would be divided into two new regions to be known as Kavango East and Kavango West. Furthermore, the regions of Caprivi and Karas were to be renamed Zambezi and !Karas (or ‖Karas), respectively. Area and population data for the new regions were not available at mid-2022.

PRINCIPAL TOWNS
(population at 2011 census)

Windhoek . .	325,858	Rehoboth . . .	28,843
Rundu . . .	63,431	Katima Mulilo . .	28,362
Walvis Bay . .	62,096	Otjiwarongo . .	28,249
Swakopmund . .	44,725	Ondangwa . . .	22,822
Oshakati . .	36,541	Okahandja . . .	22,639

Mid-2022 (incl. suburbs, UN projection): Windhoek (capital) 461,123 (Source: UN, *World Urbanization Prospects: The 2018 Revision*).

BIRTHS AND DEATHS
(annual averages, UN estimates)

	2005–10	2010–15	2015–20
Birth rate (per 1,000)	30.0	30.5	28.8
Death rate (per 1,000)	13.1	9.5	8.2

Source: UN, *World Population Prospects: The 2019 Revision*.

Life expectancy (years at birth, estimates): 64.0 (males 61.0; females 66.9) in 2020 (Source: World Bank, World Development Indicators database).

ECONOMICALLY ACTIVE POPULATION
(labour force survey, 2018, '000 persons)

	Males	Females	Total
Agriculture, hunting, forestry and fishing	90.1	77.2	167.2
Mining and quarrying	9.9	2.1	12.1
Manufacturing	28.2	16.8	45.1
Electricity, gas and water	5.4	2.0	7.4
Construction	41.8	3.3	45.1
Wholesale and retail trade, repair of motor vehicles, motorcycles and personal and household goods	41.9	39.0	80.9
Restaurants and hotels	19.2	63.9	83.1
Transport, storage and communications	27.6	4.3	31.9
Financial intermediation	4.7	9.2	13.9
Real estate, renting, administrative and business activities	21.6	18.1	39.6
Public administration and defence; compulsory social security	21.2	13.0	34.2
Education	14.3	32.6	46.9
Health and social work	5.5	14.0	19.5
Other community, social, cultural and personal services	9.1	16.6	25.8
Private households with employed persons	20.4	51.7	72.2
Extraterritorial organizations and bodies	0.6	0.4	1.0
Total employed	361.5	364.2	725.7
Unemployed	173.9	190.5	364.4
Total labour force	535.4	554.7	1,090.2

Note: Totals may not be equal to the sum of components, owing to rounding.

Health and Welfare

KEY INDICATORS

Total fertility rate (children per woman, 2020)	3.3
Under-5 mortality rate (per 1,000 live births, 2020)	40.2
HIV/AIDS (% of persons aged 15–49, 2020)	11.6
COVID-19: Cumulative confirmed deaths (per 100,000 persons at 31 August 2022)	161.1
COVID-19: Fully vaccinated population (% of total population at 21 August 2022)	19.8
Physicians (per 1,000 head, 2018)	0.6
Hospitals (per 100,000 head, 2013)	1.9
Domestic health expenditure (2019): US $ per head (PPP)	406.8
Domestic health expenditure (2019): % of GDP	4.0
Domestic health expenditure (2019): public (% of total current expenditure)	46.9
Access to improved water resources (% of persons, 2020)	84
Access to improved sanitation facilities (% of persons, 2020)	35
Total carbon dioxide emissions ('000 metric tons, 2018)	4,250
Carbon dioxide emissions per head (metric tons, 2018)	1.7
Human Development Index (2021): ranking	139
Human Development Index (2021): value	0.615

Note: For data on COVID-19 vaccinations, 'fully vaccinated' denotes receipt of all doses specified by approved vaccination regime (Sources: Johns Hopkins University and Our World in Data). Data on health expenditure refer to current general government expenditure in each case. For more information on sources and further definitions for all indicators, see Health and Welfare Statistics: Sources and Definitions section (europaworld.com/credits).

Agriculture

PRINCIPAL CROPS
('000 metric tons)

	2018	2019	2020
Cabbages and other brassicas*	6.3	6.2	6.3
Carrots and turnips*	2.7	2.7	2.7
Grapes*	28.5	30.1	32.7
Maize	59.3	45.0	64.0†
Millet	83.5	18.7	95.0†
Onions, dry*	26.3	25.8	26.0
Potatoes*	14.5	14.2	14.3
Sorghum	4.0	1.0	3.3*
Tomatoes*	8.8	8.7	8.7
Watermelons*	3.6	3.6	3.6
Wheat	6.1	6.1	12.0†

* FAO estimate(s).
† Unofficial figure.

Aggregate production ('000 metric tons, may include official, semi-official or estimated data): Total cereals 152.9 in 2018, 70.8 in 2019, 174.3 in 2020; Total fruit (primary) 57.8 in 2018, 59.2 in 2019, 61.9 in 2020; Total roots and tubers 385.5 in 2018, 381.7 in 2019, 383.4 in 2020; Total vegetables (primary) 65.8 in 2018, 65.1 in 2019, 65.4 in 2020.

Source: FAO.

LIVESTOCK
('000 head, year ending September, FAO estimates)

	2018	2019	2020
Asses	148	148	149
Cattle	2,896	3,005	2,948
Chickens	4,401	4,391	4,381
Goats	1,892	1,862	1,854
Horses	44	44	43
Pigs	97	101	105
Sheep	1,646	1,475	1,349

Source: FAO.

LIVESTOCK PRODUCTS
('000 metric tons, FAO estimates)

	2018	2019	2020
Cattle hides, fresh	3.6	3.5	3.6
Cattle meat	31.7	31.3	32.0
Cows' milk	110.5	113.4	112.0
Chicken meat	11.0	11.0	11.1
Game meat	7.0	6.9	6.9
Sheep meat	8.7	7.9	7.3
Hen eggs	3.7	3.7	3.7

Source: FAO.

Fishing

('000 metric tons, live weight)*

	2018	2019	2020
Capture†	490.2	467.1	429.6
Cape hakes (Stokvisse)	158.2	152.0	122.4
Cape horse mackerel (Maasbanker)	306.4	296.3	182.3
Aquaculture†	0.3	0.4	0.3
Total catch†	490.5	467.4	429.9

* Figures include quantities caught by licensed foreign vessels in Namibian waters and processed in !Nami#nus (formerly Lüderitz) and Walvis Bay. The data exclude aquatic mammals (whales, seals, etc.). The number of South African fur seals caught was: 20,419 in 2018; 13,527 in 2019; 4,465 in 2020. The number of Nile crocodiles caught was: 250 in 2018; 271 in 2019; nil in 2020.
† FAO estimates.

Source: FAO.

Mining

(metric tons unless otherwise indicated)

	2017	2018	2019
Copper ore*	15,466	15,177	14,940
Lead concentrates*	7,100	8,200	7,000
Zinc concentrates*	132,584	118,435	117,002
Silver ore (kilograms)* . . .	7,014	4,666	6,220
Uranium oxide	4,224	5,525	5,476
Gold ore (kilograms)* . . .	7,272	6,171	6,526
Salt (unrefined)	886,586	1,221,803	1,041,407
Diamonds ('000 metric carats) .	1,948	2,397	2,018

* Figures refer to the metal content of ores and concentrates.

Source: US Geological Survey.

Industry

SELECTED PRODUCTS
(metric tons)

	2014	2015	2016
Unrefined (blister) copper (unwrought)	49,600*	49,027	41,100
Electrical energy (million kWh) .	1,530	1,576	1,479

* Estimate.

Electrical energy (million kWh): 1,307 in 2018; 1,052 in 2019; 1,917 in 2020.

Sources: US Geological Survey; UN Energy Statistics Database.

Finance

CURRENCY, EXCHANGE RATES AND FISCAL YEAR

Monetary Units
100 cents = 1 Namibian dollar (N $).

Sterling, US Dollar and Euro Equivalents (31 May 2022)
£1 sterling = N $19.593;
US $1 = N $15.564;
€1 = N $16.673;
N $100 = £5.10 = US $6.43 = €5.99.

Average Exchange Rate (N $ per US $)
2019   14.4487
2020   16.4633
2021   14.7787

Note: The Namibian dollar was introduced in September 1993, replacing (at par) the South African rand. The rand remained legal tender in Namibia.

Fiscal Year
The fiscal year ends on 31 March.

CENTRAL GOVERNMENT BUDGET
(N $ million, fiscal year)

Revenue	2020/21	2021/22*	2022/23*
Taxation	52,427	48,512	48,706
Taxes on income and profits .	20,906	21,960	23,053
Taxes on property . . .	141	155	167
Domestic taxes on goods and services	9,037	11,536	13,038
Taxes on international trade and transactions	22,252	14,750	12,328
Other taxes	91	111	120
Non-tax revenue	2,764	3,479	3,704
Grants	266	73	73
Total	**55,457**	**52,065**	**52,483**

Expenditure	2020/21	2021/22*	2022/23*
Current expenditure	65,350	61,921	61,182
Personnel expenditure . . .	28,681	28,459	28,598
Expenditure on goods and other services	9,413	7,771	7,956
Interest payments	7,738	8,500	9,219
Subsidies and other current transfers	19,518	17,191	15,410
Capital expenditure	6,756	6,029	7,156
Capital investment	5,336	4,706	5,234
Capital transfers	1,420	1,323	1,922
Total	**72,106**	**67,950**	**68,338**

* Estimates.

Source: Ministry of Finance, Windhoek.

INTERNATIONAL RESERVES
(excluding gold, US $ million at 31 December)

	2019	2020	2021
IMF special drawing rights . .	2.43	1.95	255.74
Reserve position in IMF . . .	0.21	0.22	0.21
Foreign exchange	2,046.60	2,168.99	2,508.07
Total	**2,049.24**	**2,171.15**	**2,764.02**

Source: IMF, *International Financial Statistics*.

MONEY SUPPLY
(N $ million at 31 December)

	2019	2020	2021
Currency outside depository corporations	2,873.46	2,914.25	3,131.86
Transferable deposits . . .	54,092.65	58,371.26	64,714.60
Other deposits	58,370.32	63,366.71	62,101.79
Broad money	**115,336.43**	**124,652.21**	**129,948.26**

Source: IMF, *International Financial Statistics*.

COST OF LIVING
(Consumer Price Index: December 2012 = 100)

	2019	2020	2021
Food and non-alcoholic beverages .	148.0	155.7	164.7
Clothing and footwear	103.4	99.8	96.4
Housing, fuel and power . . .	134.6	133.3	135.0
All items (incl. others) . . .	**137.6**	**140.6**	**145.7**

NATIONAL ACCOUNTS
(N $ million at current prices)

National Income and Product

	2019	2020	2021
Compensation of employees . .	81,249	80,366	80,294
Operating surplus	65,881	62,294	65,586
Domestic factor incomes . .	**147,130**	**142,660**	**145,880**
Consumption of fixed capital . .	20,227	20,900	22,574
Gross domestic product (GDP) at factor cost	**167,357**	**163,561**	**168,454**
Taxes, less subsidies, on production and imports	13,872	10,335	12,381
GDP in purchasers' values .	**181,229**	**173,896**	**180,836**
Primary income received from abroad	4,457	3,999	5,297
Less Primary income paid abroad .	8,904	4,709	8,137
Gross national income . . .	**176,783**	**173,186**	**177,995**
Less Consumption of fixed capital .	20,227	20,900	22,574

—continued	2019	2020	2021
National income in market prices	156,556	152,286	155,422
Other current transfers from abroad	21,640	24,984	19,909
Less Other current transfers paid abroad	2,755	2,697	2,581
National disposable income .	175,441	174,573	172,750

Expenditure on the Gross Domestic Product

	2019	2020	2021
Government final consumption expenditure	46,307	47,070	46,957
Private final consumption expenditure	127,663	119,933	136,522
Change in stocks	−1,323	−427	2,751
Gross fixed capital formation . .	28,542	23,367	26,042
Total domestic expenditure .	201,190	189,942	212,272
Exports of goods and services . .	65,898	58,215	57,761
Less Imports of goods and services	85,859	74,262	89,199
GDP in purchasers' values .	181,229	173,896	180,836
GDP in constant 2015 prices .	144,752	133,366	136,608

Gross Domestic Product by Economic Activity

	2019	2020	2021
Agriculture and forestry . . .	8,155	11,403	12,401
Fishing	4,682	4,571	4,592
Mining and quarrying	16,388	16,131	16,476
Diamond mining	5,970	4,733	4,828
Manufacturing	22,692	19,220	19,872
Electricity and water	6,191	6,361	5,656
Construction	3,765	3,237	3,279
Wholesale and retail trade, repairs, etc.	18,190	17,038	18,121
Hotels and restaurants . . .	3,692	2,527	2,782
Transport, storage and communications	8,285	7,576	8,107
Financial intermediation . . .	12,632	12,193	13,934
Real estate and business services .	13,148	13,144	13,414
Public administration and defence	20,829	20,236	18,958
Education	18,590	18,754	19,298
Health	6,017	6,410	6,724
Community, social and personal services	3,299	3,303	3,449
Private households with employed persons	1,202	1,135	1,235
GDP at basic prices	167,756	163,238	168,297
Taxes, less subsidies, on products .	13,473	10,658	12,538
GDP in purchasers' values .	181,229	173,896	180,836

BALANCE OF PAYMENTS
(US $ million)

	2019	2020	2021
Exports of goods	3,879.1	3,153.3	3,540.1
Imports of goods	−5,181.4	−4,138.5	−5,466.0
Balance on goods	−1,302.3	−985.2	−1,926.0
Exports of services	697.7	411.9	413.1
Imports of services	−615.8	−475.1	−589.1
Balance on goods and services	−1,220.5	−1,048.4	−2,102.1
Primary income received . . .	309.1	241.3	345.2
Primary income paid	−615.9	−279.8	−539.7
Balance on goods, services and primary income	−1,527.2	−1,086.9	−2,296.6
Secondary income received . .	1,497.1	1,524.1	1,352.2
Secondary income paid . . .	−189.8	−166.1	−175.7
Current balance	−219.9	271.1	−1,120.1

—continued	2019	2020	2021
Capital account (net)	105.5	101.6	98.4
Direct investment assets . . .	−9.0	−51.4	−17.0
Direct investment liabilities . .	−176.5	−159.3	408.5
Portfolio investment assets . .	−113.4	140.0	938.5
Portfolio investment liabilities .	−7.5	−92.3	−504.0
Financial derivatives and employee stock options (net)	−9.6	−5.0	23.8
Other investment assets . . .	246.1	−186.6	54.2
Other investment liabilities . .	−133.1	123.7	448.4
Net errors and omissions . . .	101.8	−112.1	98.0
Reserves and related items .	−215.9	29.7	428.8

Source: IMF, *International Financial Statistics*.

External Trade

PRINCIPAL COMMODITIES
(distribution by HS, US $ million)

Imports c.i.f.	2018	2019	2020
Prepared foodstuffs, beverages, spirits and vinegars, tobacco and articles thereof	544.5	557.5	461.9
Mineral products	1,252.4	1,497.2	1,220.1
Mineral fuels, oils, distillation products, etc.	859.6	944.8	586.8
Petroleum oils, not crude . .	828.0	898.2	550.9
Ores, slag and ash	365.7	538.2	608.7
Copper ores and concentrates .	339.3	514.6	582.5
Chemicals and related products	657.8	580.1	590.5
Plastics, rubbers, and articles thereof	300.4	315.8	269.8
Textile and textile articles .	205.5	188.6	155.8
Pearls, precious or semi-precious stones, precious metals, and articles thereof .	331.0	267.1	79.5
Diamonds, not mounted or set .	325.5	262.0	75.0
Iron and steel, base metals and articles of base metals . .	1,557.9	1,670.0	1,883.1
Copper and articles thereof . .	1,146.0	1,273.4	1,583.0
Unrefined copper and copper anodes for electrolytic refining	1,007.6	1,043.0	1,209.1
Articles of iron or steel . . .	227.0	209.2	143.4
Machinery and mechanical appliances; electrical equipment; parts thereof .	984.5	849.8	678.0
Machinery, boilers, etc. . . .	603.0	540.0	428.0
Electrical, electronic equipment .	381.5	309.8	250.0
Vehicles, aircraft, vessels and associated transport equipment	1,456.5	800.0	461.2
Vehicles other than railway, tramway	588.3	553.1	359.7
Motor vehicles for the transport of goods	216.3	193.8	116.3
Ships, boats and other floating structures	816.1	224.0	85.4
Total (incl. others)	8,288.9	7,715.2	6,612.7

Exports f.o.b.	2018	2019	2020
Live animals and animal products	1,018.8	941.6	737.3
Fish, crustaceans, molluscs, aquatic invertebrates . . .	731.1	695.2	596.8
Fish, frozen, whole	331.7	307.7	253.0
Fish fillets and pieces, fresh, chilled or frozen	345.0	323.4	294.3
Mineral products	932.5	1,049.7	895.2
Ores, slag and ash	825.4	893.7	757.9
Copper ores and concentrates .	0.1	12.0	17.3
Uranium or thorium ores and concentrates	658.0	754.7	638.8
Pearls, precious or semi-precious stones, precious metals, and articles thereof .	1,958.6	1,459.1	1,160.5
Diamonds, not mounted or set .	1,670.3	1,133.4	758.3
Gold	287.4	324.5	401.1
Iron and steel, base metals and articles of base metals . .	1,850.8	1,937.5	1,886.4
Copper and articles thereof . .	1,557.7	1,637.4	1,756.5
Refined copper and copper alloys, unwrought	243.3	224.9	337.8
Unrefined copper and copper anodes for electrolytic refining	1,277.8	1,338.9	1,349.9
Zinc and articles thereof . . .	201.1	186.9	61.0
Unwrought zinc	199.3	186.8	60.8
Vehicles, aircraft, vessels and associated transport equipment	1,017.7	348.4	140.2
Ships, boats and other floating structures	884.7	217.6	61.3
Vessels, incl. warships and lifeboats	408.2	193.6	51.5
Total (incl. others)	7,488.3	6,439.3	5,424.1

Source: Trade Map-Trade Competitiveness Map, International Trade Centre, marketanalysis.intracen.org.

2021 (N $ million): Total imports 95,222; Total exports 128,609.

PRINCIPAL TRADING PARTNERS
(US $ million)

Imports c.i.f.	2018	2019	2020
Bahamas	429.9	0.0	0.0
Botswana	338.0	192.4	59.7
Bulgaria	205.4	247.8	262.2
China, People's Republic . .	468.8	309.8	313.0
Congo, Democratic Republic . .	10.5	125.1	382.0
Germany	78.4	88.5	68.2
India	142.4	226.9	177.2
Italy	35.5	88.0	29.6
Peru	118.7	134.1	133.7
South Africa	3,683.7	3,475.8	2,515.0
Spain	104.3	67.6	57.2
Türkiye	35.7	54.2	64.3
United Arab Emirates . . .	122.5	100.4	49.8
United Kingdom	198.7	71.6	58.7
USA	165.6	170.7	169.0
Zambia	1,169.3	1,198.3	1,328.8
Total (incl. others)	8,288.9	7,715.2	6,612.7

Exports f.o.b.	2018	2019	2020
Belgium	707.4	476.6	299.3
Botswana	703.0	644.9	458.7
Canada	23.5	102.2	78.6
China, People's Republic . .	1,248.0	1,646.0	1,954.6
Congo, Democratic Republic . .	153.4	190.4	150.6
France	272.6	140.6	43.4
Germany	58.8	90.3	134.4
Hong Kong	56.6	93.0	134.4
Italy	230.9	151.3	85.2
Marshal Islands	356.9	10.8	0.8

Exports f.o.b.—*continued*	2018	2019	2020
Netherlands	108.2	147.9	101.2
Norway	3.0	3.0	56.2
Singapore	131.1	14.1	52.9
South Africa	1,132.0	1,093.9	832.3
Spain	292.0	311.4	264.3
United Arab Emirates . . .	183.0	221.5	115.8
United Kingdom	469.5	49.8	38.1
USA	112.7	136.5	72.8
Zambia	264.6	247.1	242.5
Total (incl. others)	7,488.3	6,439.3	5,424.1

Source: Trade Map-Trade Competitiveness Map, International Trade Centre, marketanalysis.intracen.org.

2021 (N $ million): Total imports 95,222; Total exports 128,609.

Transport

SHIPPING

Flag Registered Fleet
(at 31 December)

	2019	2020	2021
Number of vessels	159	165	167
Displacement (gross registered tons)	182,644	194,692	196,084

Source: Lloyd's List Intelligence (www.bit.ly/LLintelligence).

Seaborne Freight Traffic
('000 freight tons*, fiscal year)

	2018/19	2019/20	2020/21
Port of !Nami#nus (Lüderitz):			
Goods loaded	236.2	98.3	813.6
Goods unloaded	155.6	40.0	54.6
Containers handled (total TEUs)	5,355	5,685	1,773
Port of Walvis Bay:			
Goods loaded	1,747.5	1,757.3	1,718.7
Goods unloaded	3,458.3	3,090.9	3,264.1
Goods transshipped	168.9	112.1	344.8
Containers handled (total TEUs)	144,109	142,957	154,207

* One freight ton = 40 cu ft (1.133 cu m) of cargo capacity.

Source: Namibian Ports Authority.

CIVIL AVIATION
(traffic on scheduled services)

	2013	2014	2015
Kilometres flown (million) . .	13	13	15
Passengers carried ('000) . . .	510	522	553
Passenger-km (million) . . .	1,445	1,485	1,402
Total ton-km (million)	1	34	30

Source: UN, *Statistical Yearbook*.

2020 (domestic and international): Departures 593; Passengers carried 0.1m.; Freight carried 2m. ton–km (Source: World Bank, World Development Indicators database).

Tourism

FOREIGN TOURIST ARRIVALS

Country of origin	2017	2018	2019
Angola	447,295	554,496	606,818
Botswana	57,950	57,109	68,410
France	32,388	31,142	28,431
Germany	124,971	126,139	98,464
South Africa	345,376	307,285	284,431
United Kingdom	34,252	31,269	28,119
USA	31,674	28,749	26,423
Zambia	213,184	246,457	258,215
Zimbabwe	96,028	65,600	83,141
Total (incl. others)	1,608,018	1,659,762	1,681,336

Total tourist arrivals: 169,565 in 2020; 233,692 in 2021.

Source: Ministry of Environment, Forestry and Tourism, Windhoek.

Tourism receipts (US $ million, excl. passenger transport): 188 in 2017; 383 in 2018; 350 in 2019 (provisional) (Source: World Tourism Organization).

Communications Media

	2018	2019	2020
Telephones ('000 main lines in use)	154.8	142.2	141.3
Mobile telephone subscriptions ('000)	2,530.9	2,575.6	2,594.4
Broadband subscriptions, fixed ('000)	62.0	63.3	71.1
Broadband subscriptions, mobile ('000)	1,669.6	1,651.8	1,765.0
Internet users (% of population)* .	40.0	40.5	n.a.

* Population aged 18 years and over.

Source: International Telecommunication Union.

Education

(2017/18 unless otherwise indicated)

		Students		
	Teachers	Males	Females	Total
Pre-primary	1,920	21,326	22,112	43,448
Primary	19,557	249,209	241,510	490,719
Secondary	11,343*	86,085†	96,860†	182,945†
Tertiary	3,689	19,587	39,621	59,208

* 2016/17.
† 2011/12.

Source: UNESCO, Institute for Statistics.

Pupil-teacher ratio (qualified teaching staff, primary education, UNESCO estimate): 32.6 in 2018/19 (Source: UNESCO Institute for Statistics).

Adult literacy rate (UNESCO estimates): 91.5% (males 91.6%; females 91.4%) in 2018 (Source: UNESCO Institute for Statistics).

Directory

The Constitution

The Constitution of the Republic of Namibia took effect at independence on 21 March 1990. Its principal provisions, including subsequent amendments, are summarized below:

THE REPUBLIC

The Republic of Namibia is a sovereign, secular, democratic and unitary state, and the Constitution is the supreme law.

FUNDAMENTAL HUMAN RIGHTS AND FREEDOMS

The fundamental rights and freedoms of the individual are guaranteed regardless of sex, race, colour, ethnic origin, religion, creed, or social or economic status. All citizens shall have the right to form and join political parties. The practice of racial discrimination shall be prohibited.

THE PRESIDENT

Executive power shall be vested in the President and the Cabinet. The President shall be the Head of State and of the Government and the Commander-in-Chief of the Defence Force. The President shall be directly elected by universal and equal adult suffrage, and must receive more than 50% of the votes cast. The term of office shall be five years; one person may not hold the office of President for more than two terms. The President shall appoint a Vice-President from the members of the National Assembly.

THE CABINET

The Cabinet shall consist of the President, the Vice-President, the Prime Minister and such other ministers as the President may appoint from members of the National Assembly. The President may also appoint a Deputy Prime Minister. The functions of the members of the Cabinet shall include directing the activities of ministries and government departments, initiating bills for submission to the National Assembly, formulating, explaining and assessing for the National Assembly the budget of the state and its economic development plans, formulating, explaining and analysing for the National Assembly Namibia's foreign policy, and foreign trade policy and advising the President on the state of national defence.

THE NATIONAL ASSEMBLY

Legislative power shall be vested in the National Assembly, which shall be composed of 96 members elected by general, direct and secret ballots and not more than eight members appointed by the President by virtue of their special expertise, status, skill or experience. These eight presidential appointees have qualified voting rights. Every National Assembly shall continue for a maximum period of five years, but it may be dissolved by the President before the expiry of its term.

THE NATIONAL COUNCIL

The National Council shall consist of three members from each region (elected by regional councils from among their members) and shall have a life of six years. The functions of the National Council shall include considering all bills approved by the National Assembly, investigating any subordinate legislation referred to it by the National Assembly for advice, and recommending legislation to the National Assembly on matters of regional concern.

OTHER PROVISIONS

Other provisions relate to the administration of justice (see under Judicial System), regional and local government, the public service commission, the security commission, the police, defence forces and prison service, finance, and the central bank and national planning commission. The repeal of, or amendments to, the Constitution require the approval of two-thirds of the members of the National Assembly and two-thirds of the members of the National Council; if the proposed repeal or amendment secures a majority of two-thirds of the members of the National Assembly, but not a majority of two-thirds of the members of the National Council, the President may make the proposals the subject of a national referendum, in which a two-thirds' majority is needed for approval of the legislation.

The Government

HEAD OF STATE

President and Commander-in-Chief of the Defence Force: Dr HAGE GEINGOB (inaugurated 21 March 2015; re-elected 27 November 2019).

Vice-President: NANGOLO MBUMBA.

THE CABINET
(October 2022)

President: Dr HAGE GEINGOB.

Vice-President: NANGOLO MBUMBA.

Prime Minister: SAARA KUUGONGELWA-AMADHILA.

Deputy Prime Minister and Minister of International Relations and Co-operation: NETUMBO NANDI-NDAITWAH.

Minister of Presidential Affairs: CHRISTINA //HOEBES.

Minister of Gender Equality, Poverty Eradication and Social Welfare: DOREEN SIOKA.

Minister of Agriculture, Water and Land Reform: CALLE SCHLETTWEIN.

Minister of Defence and Veterans Affairs: FRANS KAPOFI.

Minister of Education, Arts and Culture: ANNA NGHIPONDOKA.

Minister of Environment, Forestry and Tourism: POHAMBA SHIFETA.

Minister of Finance and Acting Minister of Public Enterprises: IIPUMBU SHIIMI.

Minister of Fisheries and Marine Resources: DEREK KLAZEN.

Minister of Health and Social Services: Dr KALUMBI SHANGULA.

Minister of Home Affairs, Immigration, Safety and Security: ALBERT KAWANA.

Minister of Higher Education, Technology and Innovation: Dr ITAH KANDJII-MURANGI.

Minister of Industrialization and Trade: LUCIA IIPUMBU.

Minister of Information and Communications Technology: Dr PEYA MUSHELENGA.

Minister of Justice: YVONNE DAUSAB.

Minister of Labour, Industrial Relations and Employment Creation: UTONI NUJOMA.

Minister of Mines and Energy: TOM ALWEENDO.

Minister of Sport, Youth and National Service: AGNES TJONGARERO.

Minister of Urban and Rural Development: ERASTUS UUTONI.

Minister of Works and Transport: JOHN MUTORWA.

Attorney-General: FESTUS MBANDEKA.

In addition, there were 16 deputy ministers. The Secretary to the Cabinet and the Director-General of the National Planning and of the Intelligence Service were also *ex officio* members of the Cabinet.

MINISTRIES

Office of the President: 1 Engelberg St, Auasblick, PMB 13339, Windhoek; tel. (61) 2707111; e-mail info.op@op.gov.na; internet op.gov.na.

Office of the Prime Minister: Robert Mugabe Ave, PMB 13338, Windhoek; tel. (61) 2872002; e-mail info@opm.gov.na; internet opm.gov.na.

Ministry of Agriculture, Water and Land Reform: Government Office Park, Luther St, PMB 13184, Windhoek; tel. (61) 2087111; e-mail kalom@mawrd.gov.na; internet mawf.gov.na.

Ministry of Defence and Veterans Affairs: c/o Sam Nujoma and Tall St, PMB 13307, Windhoek; tel. (61) 2049111; e-mail ps@namdefence.org; internet modva.gov.na.

Ministry of Education, Arts and Culture: Government Office Park, Luther St, PMB 13186, Windhoek; tel. (61) 2933111; e-mail info@moe.gov.na; internet www.moe.gov.na.

Ministry of Environment, Forestry and Tourism: Phillip Troskie Bldg, PMB 13306, Windhoek; tel. (61) 2842111; internet www.meft.gov.na.

Ministry of Finance: Fiscus Bldg, John Meinert St, PMB 13295, Windhoek; tel. (61) 2099111; internet mof.gov.na.

Ministry of Fisheries and Marine Resources: Brendan Simbwaye Sq., Blk C, cnr Dr Kenneth David Kaunda and Goethe Sts, PMB 13355, Windhoek; tel. (61) 2053911; e-mail MFMRenquiries@mfmr.gov.na; internet mfmr.gov.na.

Ministry of Gender Equality, Poverty Eradication and Social Welfare: Juvenis Bldg, Independence Ave, PMG 13359, Windhoek; tel. (61) 2833111; e-mail genderequality@mgecw.gov.na; internet mgecw.gov.na.

Ministry of Health and Social Services: Ministerial Bldg, Harvey St, PMB 13198, Windhoek; tel. (61) 2039111; e-mail public.relations@mhss.gov.na; internet mhss.gov.na.

Ministry of Higher Education, Technology and Innovation: Luther St, PMB 13391, Windhoek; tel. (61) 2933111; internet www.mheti.gov.na.

Ministry of Home Affairs, Immigration, and Safety and Security: cnr Hosea Kutako Dr. and Harvey St, Erf 6971, opp. Electoral Commission of Namibia, PMB 13200, Windhoek; tel. (61) 2922111; internet mha.gov.na.

Ministry of Industrialization and Trade: Brendan Simbwaye Sq., Blk B, cnr Kenneth Kaunda and Goethe Sts, PMB 13340, Windhoek; tel. (61) 2837334; e-mail nic@mti.gov.na; internet www.mti.gov.na.

Ministry of Information and Communications Technology: Parliament Office Bldg, Robert Mugabe Ave, Windhoek; tel. (61) 2839111; e-mail info@mict.gov.na; internet mict.gov.na.

Ministry of International Relations and Co-operation: Govt Bldgs, Robert Mugabe Ave, PMB 13347, Windhoek; tel. (61) 2829111; e-mail headquarters@mirco.gov.na; internet mirco.gov.na.

Ministry of Justice: Justitia Bldg, Independence Ave, PMB 13302, Windhoek; tel. (61) 2805111; e-mail info@moj.gov.na; internet moj.na.

Ministry of Labour, Industrial Relations and Employment Creation: 32 Mercedes St, Khomasdal, PMB 19005, Windhoek; tel. (61) 2066111; internet mol.gov.na.

Ministry of Mines and Energy: 6 Aviation Rd, PMB 13297, Windhoek; tel. (61) 2848111; e-mail info@mme.gov.na; internet www.mme.gov.na.

Ministry of Public Enterprises: Sanlam Center, 3rd and 9th Floors, Independence Ave, Windhoek; tel. (61) 2023600; e-mail info@mpe.gov.na; internet mpe.gov.na.

Ministry of Sport, Youth and National Service: NIDA Bldg, 4th Floor, Goethe St, PMB 13391, Windhoek; tel. (61) 2706528; e-mail ed.secretary@msyns.gov.na; internet www.msyns.gov.na.

Ministry of Urban and Rural Development: Govt Office Park, Luther St, PMB 13289, Windhoek; tel. (61) 2975111; e-mail murd.enquiries@murd.gov.na; internet www.murd.gov.na.

Ministry of Works and Transport: 6719 Bell St, Snyman Circle, PMB 13341, Windhoek; tel. (61) 2088111; internet mwt.gov.na.

President

Presidential Election, 27 November 2019

Candidate	Votes	% of votes
Dr Hage G. Geingob (SWAPO) . .	464,703	56.24
Dr Panduleni Fillemon Bango Itula		
(Ind.)	242,657	29.37
McHenry Venaani (PDM) . . .	43,959	5.32
Bernadus Clinton Swartbooi (LPM) .	22,542	2.73
Apius Auchab (UDF)	22,115	2.68
Others*	30,222	3.66
Total	826,198	100.00

* There were six other candidates.

Legislature

NATIONAL ASSEMBLY

National Assembly: Parliament Bldg, 14A Love St, Private Bag 13323, Windhoek; tel. (61) 2889111; e-mail national.assembly@parliament.na; internet www.parliament.na.

Speaker: PETER KATJAVIVI.

General Election, 27 November 2019

Party	Votes	% of votes	Seats
SWAPO	536,861	65.45	63
PDM	136,576	16.65	16
LPM	38,956	4.75	4
NUDO	16,066	1.96	2
APP	14,644	1.79	2
UDF	14,644	1.79	2
RP	14,546	1.77	2
NEFF	13,580	1.66	2
RDP	8,953	1.09	1
CDV	5,841	0.71	1
SWANU	5,330	0.65	1
Others	14,210	1.73	—
Total	820,207	100.00	96*

* In addition to the 96 directly elected members, the President of the Republic is empowered to nominate as many as eight members (who enjoy qualified voting rights).

NATIONAL COUNCIL

National Council: Parliament Bldg, 14A Love St, Private Bag 13371, Windhoek; tel. (61) 2028000; e-mail national.council@parliament.na; internet www.parliament.na.

Chairperson: LUKAS SINIMBO MUHA.

The second chamber of parliament is the advisory National Council, comprising three representatives from each of the country's 14 Regional Councils, elected for a period of six years.

Election Commission

Electoral Commission of Namibia (ECN): 67–71 Van Rijn St, POB 13352, Windhoek; tel. (61) 376200; e-mail info@ecn.na; internet www.ecn.na; f. 1992; independent; Chair. ELSIE NGHIKEMBWA; Chief Electoral and Referenda Officer THEO MUJORO.

Political Organizations

In 2022 there were 20 registered political parties in Namibia.

All People's Party (APP): POB 80207, Olympia, Windhoek; tel. (61) 2882595; e-mail nakatanal@yahoo.com; internet app.org.na; f. 2008 in Kavango region; splinter group of the CoD, which split in late 2007; Pres. (vacant); Sec.-Gen. VINCENT KANYETU.

Christian Democratic Voice Party (CDV): POB 136, Usakos; e-mail christiandemocraticvoice@gmail.com; f. 2013; Pres. IGNATIUS VRIES; Sec.-Gen. VIOLA GEIRISES.

Congress of Democrats (CoD): 8 Storch St, POB 40905, Windhoek; tel. (61) 256954; f. 1999 after split from SWAPO; Pres. ELAGO AMUTHENU (acting).

Democratic Party of Namibia (DPN): Maltahöhe, POB 206, Windhoek; tel. (63) 293567; e-mail aisaak12@gmail.com; f. 2008; Pres. ADAM ISAAK.

Independent Patriots for Change: SWAMED Bldg, 1st Floor, John Meinert St, POB 7094, Katutura, Windhoek; tel. 814114448; e-mail information@ipc.com.na; internet www.ipc.com.na; f. 2020; Pres. Dr PANDULENI ITULA; Gen. Sec. CHRISTINE AOCHAMUS.

Landless People's Movement (LPM): 11 Sauer St, Windhoek; tel. (61) 400693; internet www.lpmparty.org; f. 2016; Leader BERNADUS CLINTON SWARTBOOI.

Monitor Action Group (MAG): 55 Van Coller St, POB 90396, Olympia, Windhoek; tel. (61) 229931; e-mail mag@iway.na; f. 1991 by mems of the National Party of South West Africa alliance; Chair. GERNOT SCHAAF.

Namibia Economic Freedom Fighters (NEFF): cnr Grimm St and Independence Ave, Bldg 392, POB 142, Windhoek; tel. 811299393; e-mail namibiaeconomicfreedomfighters@gmail.com; f. 2014; Pres. EPAFRAS JAN MUKWIILONGO.

National Democratic Party of Namibia (NDP): Daily Park, Ngweze, POB 2438, Katima Mulilo; e-mail martinlukato@yahoo.com; f. 2004; Pres. MARTIN LUKATO.

National Empowerment Fighting Corruption (NEFC): Erf 4124, Moon St, Kuisebmond POB 1215, Walvis Bay; tel. 814948572; f. 2020; Pres. KENNETH IILONGA.

National Patriotic Front (NPF): POB 7624, Katutura; e-mail uapirukapapama@gmail.com; Sec.-Gen. SIMEON PAPAMA (acting).

National Unity Democratic Organization (NUDO): Clemence Kapuuo St, POB 62691, Soweto, Katutura; tel. (61) 211550; e-mail nudoparty@iway.na; internet fb.com/nudoofnamibiaparty; f. 1964 by the Herero Chiefs' Council; joined the DTA in 1977; broke away from the DTA in 2003; Pres. ESTHER UTJIUA MUINJANGUE; Sec.-Gen. JOSEPH KAUANDENGE.

Popular Democratic Movement (PDM): POB 173, Windhoek; tel. (61) 2882563; e-mail mvenaani@yahoo.com; internet fb.com/OfficialOppositionNamibia; f. 1977 as a coalition of 11 ethnically based political groupings; reorg. in 1991 to allow dual membership of coalition groupings and the main party; fmrly known as Democratic Turnhalle Alliance of Namibia and later as DTA of Namibia; present name adopted in Nov. 2017; Pres. MCHENRY VENAANI; Sec.-Gen. MANUEL NGARINGOMBE.

Rally for Democracy and Progress (RDP): 18 Schönlein St, POB 81500, Olympia, Windhoek; tel. (61) 255973; e-mail hq@rdp.org.na; internet www.rdp.org.na; f. 2007 by fmr mems of ruling SWAPO party; Pres. MIKE RATOVENI KAVEKOTORA; Sec.-Gen. BRUNHILDE CORNELIUS.

Republican Party of Namibia (RP): Parliament Bldg, POB 3062, Windhoek; tel. (61) 244040; e-mail hfmudge@gmail.com; f. 1977; Pres. HENRY (HENK) FERDINAND MUDGE.

Swanu of Namibia (SWANU): Katutura, POB 2976, Windhoek; tel. (61) 2882325; e-mail tciijambo@gmail.com; f. 1959 by mems of the Herero Chiefs' Council; formed alliance with the Workers' Revolutionary Party in 1999; Pres. Dr TANGENI IIJAMBO; Sec.-Gen. EVILASTUS KAARONDA.

SWAPO Party of Namibia (SWAPO): Plot 2464, Hans-Dietrich Genscher St, Katutura, POB 1071, Windhoek; tel. (61) 238364; internet www.swapoparty.org; f. 1957 as the Ovamboland People's Congress; renamed South West Africa People's Organization in 1960; Pres. HAGE GEINGOB; Sec.-Gen. SOPHIA SHANINGWA.

United Democratic Front of Namibia (UDF): POB 20037, Windhoek; tel. (61) 230683; f. 1989 as a centrist coalition of 8 parties; reorg. as a single party in 1999; Pres. APIUS !AUXAB; Sec.-Gen. ELIJAH HAGE / GAWASEB.

United People's Movement (UPM): POB 4621, Rehoboth; tel. 811404573; e-mail nam.unitedpeople@yahoo.com; f. 2010; Nat. Chair. EMMA FARMER; Pres. PETRUS JUNIUS; Sec.-Gen. CELESTE BECKER.

Workers' Revolutionary Party (WRP): POB 3349, Windhoek; tel. (61) 260647; f. 1989; Nat. Chair. AUGUST MALETZKY; Leader SALMON FLEERMUYS.

Diplomatic Representation

EMBASSIES AND HIGH COMMISSIONS IN NAMIBIA

Algeria: 96 Joseph Mukwayu Ithana St, Ludwigsdorf, POB 3079, Windhoek; tel. (61) 221507; e-mail ambalg.w@mweb.com.na; Ambassador SEDDIK SAOUDI.

Angola: Angola House, 3 Dr Agostinho Neto St, Ausspannplatz, POB 1220, Windhoek; tel. (61) 227535; e-mail embaixada.namibia@mirex.gov.ao; Ambassador JOVELINA ALFREDO ANTÓNIO IMPERIAL DA COSTA.

Botswana: 101 Nelson Mandela Ave, POB 20359, Windhoek; tel. (61) 221941; e-mail botnam@gov.bw; internet fb.com/BotswanaHighCommissionNamibia; High Commissioner Dr BATLANG COMMA SEREMA.

Brazil: 52 Simeon Lineekele Shixungileni St, POB 24166, Windhoek 9000; tel. (61) 237368; e-mail brasemb.windhoek@itamaraty.gov.br; internet www.gov.br/mre/pt-br/embaixada-windhoek; Ambassador VIVIAN LOSS SANMARTIN.

China, People's Republic: 28 Hebenstreit St, Ludwigsdorf, POB 22777, Windhoek 9000; tel. (61) 402598; e-mail chinaemb_na@mfa.gov.cn; internet na.china-embassy.gov.cn; Chargé d'affaires YANG JUN.

Congo, Democratic Republic: 56 Bismarck St, POB 9064, Windhoek; tel. (61) 256287; Ambassador ANASTAS KABOBA KASONGO WA-KIMBA.

Congo, Republic: 9 Marien Ngouabi St, POB 22970, Windhoek; tel. (61) 257517; e-mail embcongo@iway.na; Ambassador LAURIA NGAYINO.

Cuba: 37 Quenta St, Ludwigsdorf, POB 23866, Windhoek; tel. (61) 227072; e-mail embajada@cubanembassy.net; internet misiones.minrex.gob.cu/es/namibia; Ambassador SIDENIO ACOSTA ADAY.

Egypt: 10 Berg St, POB 11853, Windhoek; tel. (61) 221501; e-mail embassy.windhoek@mfa.gov.eg; Ambassador WAEL M. LOFTY.

Finland: 2 Crohn St, POB 3649, Windhoek 9000; tel. (61) 221355; e-mail sanomat.win@formin.fi; internet finlandabroad.fi/web/nam/frontpage; Ambassador LEENA VILJANEN.

France: 24 Willemien St, POB 20484, Windhoek; tel. (61) 276700; e-mail cad.windhoek-amba@diplomatie.gouv.fr; internet na .ambafrance.org; Ambassador SÉBASTIEN MINOT.

Germany: Sanlam Centre, 6th Floor, 145 Independence Ave, POB 231, Windhoek; tel. (61) 273100; e-mail info@windhuk.diplo.de; internet windhuk.diplo.de; Ambassador HERBERT BECK.

Ghana: 5 Nelson Mandela Ave, POB 24165, Windhoek; tel. (61) 221341; internet ghanahighcommission-namibia.com; High Commissioner YAKUBU ALHASSAN.

India: 97 Nelson Mandela Ave, POB 1209, Windhoek; tel. (61) 226037; e-mail hoc.windhoek@mea.gov.in; internet hciwindhoek .gov.in; High Commissioner PRASHANT AGRAWAL.

Indonesia: 103 Nelson Mandela Ave, POB 20691, Windhoek; tel. (61) 2851000; e-mail windhoek.kbri@kemlu.go.id; internet kemlu.go .id/windhoek; Ambassador WISNU EDI PRATIGNYO.

Iran: 4 Breiting St, POB 23022, Windhoek; tel. (61) 249700; e-mail iranembassywhk@yahoo.com; internet namibia.mfa.gov.ir; Ambassador SEYED ALI SHARIFI SADATI.

Japan: 78 Sam Nujoma Dr., POB 23025, Windhoek; tel. (61) 426700; e-mail info@wh.mofa.go.jp; internet www.na.emb-japan.go.jp; Ambassador NISHIMAKI HISAO.

Kenya: Kenya House, 5th Floor, 134 Robert Mugabe Ave, POB 2889, Windhoek; tel. (61) 226836; e-mail windhoek@mfa.go.ke; internet fb .com/KenyaHighCommissionNamibia; High Commissioner MICHAEL SIALAI.

Libya: 8 Conrad Rust St, Ludwigsdorf, POB 124, Windhoek; tel. (61) 234454; e-mail libya.emb.na@gmail.com; Chargé d'affaires a.i. OTMAN E. N. SALEM.

Malaysia: 98 Nelson Mandela Ave, Windhoek 9000; tel. (61) 259342; e-mail mwwindhoek@kln.gov.my; internet kln.gov.my/web/ nam_windhoek; High Commissioner HISHAMUDDIN IBRAHIM.

Nigeria: 4 Gen. Murtala Muhammed Ave, Eros Park, POB 23547, Windhoek; tel. (61) 232105; e-mail nigeria.windhoek@foreignaffairs .gov.ng; internet nigeriahighcommissionwindhoek.org; High Commissioner Dr TARZOOR TERHEMEN.

Portugal: 4 Karin St, Ludwigsdorf, POB 443, Windhoek; tel. (61) 259791; e-mail windhoek@mne.pt; internet windhoek .embaixadaportugal.mne.pt; Ambassador LUIS AUGUSTO FERNANDES GASPAR DA SILVA.

Russian Federation: 4 Christian St, POB 3826, Windhoek; tel. (61) 228671; e-mail rusembnamib@mid.ru; internet rusemwhk.mid.ru; Ambassador VALERY UTKIN.

South Africa: RSA House, cnr Jan Jonker St and Nelson Mandela Ave, POB 23100, Windhoek; tel. (61) 2057111; e-mail dibem@foreign .gov.za; internet dirco.gov.za/windhoek; High Commissioner THEN-JIWE ETHEL MTINSTO.

Spain: 58 Simeon Shixungileni St, POB 21811, Windhoek; tel. (61) 223066; e-mail emb.windhoek@maec.es; internet exteriores.gob.es/ embajadas/windhoek/es/Paginas/inicio.aspx; Ambassador ALBERTO PABLO DE CALLE GARCIA.

Türkiye (Turkey): 54 Toermalyn St, Eros, POB 090998, Windhoek; tel. (61) 246158; e-mail embassy.windhoek@mfa.gov.tr; internet windhoek.be.mfa.gov.tr; Ambassador FERAL ÇEKEREK ORUÇKAPTAN (designate).

United Kingdom: 116 Robert Mugabe Ave, POB 22202, Windhoek; tel. (61) 274800; e-mail general.windhoek@fco.gov.uk; internet www .gov.uk/world/namibia; High Commissioner CHARLES MOORE.

USA: 14 Lossen St, Windhoek; tel. (61) 2958500; e-mail embassywindhoek@state.gov; internet na.usembassy.gov; Chargé d'affaires JESSICA LONG.

Venezuela: 12 Nelson Mandela Ave, Private Bag 13353, Windhoek; tel. (61) 227905; e-mail embavenenam@gmail.com; Ambassador OMAR ERNESTO BERROTERAN PAREDES.

Zambia: 22 Mandume Ndemufayo St, PMB 22882, Windhoek; tel. (61) 237610; e-mail zahico@iway.na; internet www.zahico.iway.na; High Commissioner STEPHEN KATUKA.

Zimbabwe: 398 cnr Independence Ave and Grimm St, POB 23056, Windhoek; tel. (61) 227738; e-mail zimwindhoek@zimfa.gov.zw; internet www.zimwhk.com; Ambassador ROFINA NDAKAZIVA CHIKAVA.

Judicial System

Judicial power is exercised by the Supreme Court, the High Court, and a number of Magistrate and Lower Courts. The Constitution provides for the appointment of an Ombudsman.

Supreme Court: Private Bag 13398, Windhoek; tel. (61) 279900; e-mail chiefjustice@jud.gov.na; internet ejustice.jud.na; f. 1990; Chief Justice PETER SAM SHIVUTE.

High Court: Private Bag 13179, Windhoek; tel. (61) 4353000; e-mail registrar@jud.gov.na; internet ejustice.jud.na; Judge Pres. PETRUS DAMASEB.

Religion

CHRISTIANITY

Council of Churches in Namibia: 8521 Abraham Mashego St, POB 41, Windhoek; tel. (61) 217621; f. 1978; 8 mem. churches; Gen. Sec. Rev. LUDWIG BEUKE (acting).

The Anglican Communion

Namibia comprises a single diocese in the Anglican Church of Southern Africa (formerly the Church of the Province of Southern Africa). The Metropolitan of the Province is the Archbishop of Cape Town, South Africa.

Bishop of Namibia: Rev. PATRICK DJUULUME, POB 57, Windhoek; tel. (61) 238920; e-mail bishop@anglicanchurchnamibia.com.

Dutch Reformed Church

Dutch Reformed Church in Namibia (Nederduitse Gereformeerde Kerk in Namibië): 46A Schanzen Rd, POB 389, Windhoek; tel. (61) 374350; e-mail ngkn@ngkn.com.na; internet www.ngkn.com .na; f. 1898; Gen. Sec. THIJS VAN DER MERWE.

Evangelical Lutheran

Evangelical Lutheran Church in Namibia (ELCIN): POB 2018, Ondangwa; tel. (65) 240049; e-mail east.finance@elcin.org.na; internet www.elcin.org.na; f. 1870; became autonomous in 1954; Presiding Bishops Rev. HILYA NGHAANGULWA (Eastern Diocese); acting), Rev. GIDEON NIITENGE (Western Diocese); Sec.-Gen. Rev. ALPO ENKONO.

Evangelical Lutheran Church in the Republic of Namibia (ELCRN) (Rhenish Mission Church): POB 5069, 6 Church St, Ausspanplatz, 9000 Windhoek; tel. (61) 224531; e-mail egamxamub@yahoo.com; f. 1842 as a missionary church; became autonomous in 1957; Bishop Pastor SAGEUS /KEIB.

Evangelisch-Lutherische Kirche in Namibia (ELKIN—GELC): POB 233, 12 Fidel Castro St, Windhoek; tel. (61) 236002; e-mail windhoek@elcin-gelc.org; internet www.elcin-gelc.org; f. 1896 as the German Evangelical Congregation; present name adopted 1992; Pres. Bishop BURGERT BRAND.

Methodist

African Methodist Episcopal Church: POB 798, Keetmanshoop; tel. (63) 223457; e-mail webmaster@amechurchnamibia.com; internet www.amechurchnamibia.com; bishop resident in Cape Town, South Africa; Presiding Elder Rev. ANDREAS BIWA.

Methodist Church of Southern Africa: POB 143, Windhoek; tel. (61) 228921; e-mail central@iway.na; internet www.methodist.org .za; Rep. Rev. CHRISTOPHER BAUMANN GAYA.

The Roman Catholic Church

Namibia comprises one archdiocese, one diocese and one apostolic vicariate.

Bishops' Conference: Namibian Catholic Bishops' Conference, 17 Jan Jonker Rd, POB 11525, Windhoek 9000; tel. (61) 224798; e-mail gs@ncbc.com.na; internet www.rcchurch.na; f. 1996; Pres. LIBORIUS NDUMBUKUTI NASHENDA (Archbishop of Windhoek).

Archbishop of Windhoek: LIBORIUS NDUMBUKUTI NASHENDA, 91 Werner List St, POB 272, Windhoek 9000; tel. (61) 228376.

Other Christian Churches

Among other denominations active in Namibia are the Evangelical Reformed Church in Africa, the Presbyterian Church of Southern Africa, Seventh Day Adventists and the United Congregational Church of Southern Africa.

JUDAISM

Windhoek Hebrew Congregation: POB 563, Windhoek; tel. (61) 221990; Chair. LAURENCE PIETERS.

BAHÁ'Í FAITH

National Spiritual Assembly: POB 20372, Windhoek; tel. (61) 302663; e-mail bahainamibia@iway.na; Sec. ROSI STEVENSON.

The Press

AgriForum: Agri House, cnr Robert Mugabe Ave and John Meinert St, Windhoek; tel. (61) 256023; e-mail info@agrinamibia.com.na; internet www.agriforum.com.na; f. 1978; monthly; Afrikaans and English; publ. by AgriPublishers; Editor MARIETJIE VAN STADEN.

Allgemeine Zeitung: 11 Gen. Murtala Muhammed Ave, POB 3436, Eros, Windhoek; tel. (61) 2972300; e-mail azinfo@az.com.na; internet www.az.com.na; f. 1916; Mon.–Fri.; publ. by Newsprint Namibia; German; Editor-in-Chief FRANK STEFFEN.

The Caprivi Vision Newspaper: NDC Bldg, POB 2011, Ngweze Katima Mulilo; tel. (66) 253162; e-mail caprivinews@yahoo.com; internet www.caprivivision.com; f. 2002; owned by Close Corpn; weekly; English and siLozi; Editor RISCO MASHETE LUMAMEZI.

Confidénte: 127 John Meinert St, POB 5033, Ausspannplatz, Windhoek; tel. (61) 246136; e-mail editor@confidentenamibia.com; internet confidentenamibia.com; weekly; owned by Max Media; Owner and Editor MAX HAMATA.

Informanté: Dr Kenneth David Kaunda St, Windhoek; tel. (61) 2754178; e-mail editor@tgh.na; internet informante.web.na; owned by Trustco Group International; Editor NGHIDIPO NANGOLO.

Insight Namibia: IMLT Bldg, 70–72 Dr Frans Indongo St, POB 86058, Windhoek; tel. (61) 301437; e-mail advertising@insight.com .na; internet fb.com/insightnamibia; f. 2004; monthly; business and current affairs; Editor FREDERICO LINKS.

Namib Times: 8 Sam Nujoma Ave, POB 706, Walvis Bay; tel. (64) 205854; e-mail newsdesk@namibtimes.net; internet namibtimes .net; f. 1958; weekly; Afrikaans, English and German; Editor FLORIS STEENKAMP.

Namibia Economist: 7 Schuster St, POB 49, Windhoek 9000; tel. (61) 221925; e-mail info@economist.com.na; internet economist.com .na; f. 1991; weekly; English; business, finance and economics; Editor DANIEL STEINMANN.

Namibiamagazin: Deutsch-Namibische Gesellschaft eV, Sudetenland Str. 18, 37085 Goettingen, Germany; tel. (551) 7076870; e-mail mail@k-hess-verlag.de; internet www.dngev.de; f. 1990; quarterly; publ. by Klaus Hess Verlag; German; politics, tourism, culture, economics, and German-Namibian relations; Rep. KLAUS A. HESS.

The Namibian: 42 John Meinert St, POB 20783, Windhoek; tel. (61) 279600; e-mail info@namibian.com.na; internet www.namibian.com .na; f. 1985; daily; English; Editor TANGENI AMUPADHI.

Namibian Sun: 11B Gen. Murtala Muhammad Ave, Eros, POB 86829, Windhoek; tel. (61) 383400; e-mail sun@namibiansun.com; internet www.namibiansun.com; f. 2008; owned by Namibia Media Holdings; Mon.–Fri.; English; Editor TOIVO NDJEBELA.

NCCI Namibia Business Journal: National Youth Service House, 1st Floor, Haddy St, POB 9355, Windhoek; tel. (61) 228809; e-mail info@ncci.org.na; internet ncci.org.na; 6 a year; publ. by the Namibia Chamber of Commerce and Industry; English; CEO CHARITY MWIYA; Editor LEONARD KAMWI.

New Era: Daniel Tjongarero House, cnr Kerby and W. Kulz Sts, PMB 13364, Windhoek; tel. (61) 2080800; e-mail info@nepc.com.na; internet neweralive.na; f. 1991; daily; publ. by the Ministry of Information and Communication Technology; English; Chair. JOHN SIFANI; Man. Editor FESTUS NAKATANA.

Republikein: 11 Gen. Murtala Muhammed Ave, POB 3436, Eros, Windhoek; tel. (61) 2972000; e-mail republikein@republikein.com .na; internet www.republikein.com.na; f. 1977; Mon.–Fri.; owned by Namibia Media Holdings; Afrikaans and English; Editor DANI BOOYSEN.

The Southern Times: cnr Schonlein and Jenner Sts, Windhoek West, POB 32235, Windhoek; tel. 814292554; e-mail editor@ southerntimesafrica.com; internet southerntimesafrica.com; f. 2004; owned by New Era and Zimpapers, Zimbabwe; weekly (Sun.); printed in Namibia and Zimbabwe; regional; Gen. Man. GWEN SNYDERS; Editor INNOCENT GORE.

Windhoek Observer: cnr John Meinert and Rossini Sts, Windhoek; tel. (61) 411800; e-mail marketing@observer.com.na; internet www .observer.com.na; f. 1978; weekly; owned by Paragon Investment Holdings; English; Editor KUVEE KANGUEEHI.

NEWS AGENCIES

Namibia Press Agency (NAMPA): cnr Keller and Eugene Marais Sts, POB 26185, Windhoek 9000; tel. (61) 374000; e-mail news@ nampa.org; internet www.nampa.org; f. 1991; national news agency; Chair. NDEUHALA LEWIS; CEO LINUS CHATA.

Publishers

ELOC Printing Press: PMB 2013, Oniipa, Ondangwa; tel. (65) 240211; e-mail elocbook@iway.na; internet www.elocbook.iway.na; f. 1901; Exec. Dir JULIUS KAALE.

Namibia Publishing House (Macmillan Education Namibia): 19 Faraday St, POB 22830, Windhoek; tel. (61) 232165; e-mail info@nph .com.na; internet www.nph.com.na; imprints incl. New Namibia Books and Out of Africa; Gen. Man. DEON DE WAAL.

National Archives of Namibia: 1–9 Eugène Marais St, PMB 13250, Windhoek; tel. (61) 2935211; e-mail national.archives@nlas .gov.na; internet nan.gov.na; f. 1939; Chief Archivist BEAUTY MATONGO.

Pearson Namibia: Southern Industrial Area, 19 Joule St, POB 6025, Eros, Windhoek; tel. (61) 231214; e-mail catherine.sissing@ pearson.com; internet www.pearson.com/africa; Man. CATHERINE SISSING.

Broadcasting and Communications

REGULATORY AUTHORITY

Communications Regulatory Authority of Namibia (CRAN): Communication House, 56 Robert Mugabe Ave, PMB 13309, Windhoek; tel. (61) 222666; e-mail communications@cran.na; internet www.cran.na; f. 2011; issues broadcasting licences, supervises broadcasting activities and programme content; Chair. HEINRICH MIHE GAOMAB, II; CEO EMILIA NGHIKEMBUA.

TELECOMMUNICATIONS

Mobile Telecommunications Ltd (MTC): cnr Mosé Tjitendero and Hamutenya Wanahepo Ndadi Sts, Olympia, POB 23051, Windhoek; tel. (61) 2802000; e-mail feedback@mtc.com.na; internet www .mtc.com.na; f. 1995 as jt venture between Namibia Post and Telecommunications Holdings (NPTH), Telia and Swedfund; 100% owned by NPTH; Chair. THEOFELUS MBERIRUA; CEO Dr LICKY ERASTUS.

Telecom Namibia Ltd (Telecom): cnr Lüderitz and Daniel Munamava Sts, POB 297, Windhoek; tel. (61) 2019211; e-mail commpr@ telecom.na; internet www.telecom.na; f. 1992; operates fixed-line, fixed wireless and GSM network; state-owned; Chair. MELKIZEDEK UUPINDI; CEO Dr STANLEY SHANAPINDA.

TN Mobile: POB 40799, Windhoek; tel. 855550000; e-mail info@ leo.na; internet www.telecom.na; f. 2007; fmrly Cell One and Leo, present name adopted in 2012; owned by Telecom Namibia Ltd; Chair. CATHERINE M. BEUKES-AMISS; CEO ROBERTA DA COSTA.

BROADCASTING

Radio

Namibian Broadcasting Corpn (NBC): Pettenkofer St, Windhoek (W), POB 321, Windhoek; tel. (61) 2919111; e-mail tvlicence@ nbc.na; internet www.nbc.na; f. 1991; runs 10 radio stations, broadcasting daily to 98% of the population in English (24 hours), Afrikaans, German and 8 indigenous languages (10 hours); Chair. LAZARUS JACOBS; Dir-Gen. STANLEY SIMILO.

Base FM: Hahnemannstrasse, Windhoek; tel. (61) 256464; e-mail assit.basefmradio@gmail.com; internet fb.com/BaseFM; f. 1995 as Katutura Community Radio by non-governmental orgs; present name adopted in 2008; Chair. PENDAPALA NAKATHINGO; Station Man. JEHOIACKIM KATEVE (acting).

Channel 7/Kanaal 7: Hoek van Hendrik Witbooi Dr., and Ara St, Dorado Park, POB 20500, Windhoek; tel. (61) 420850; e-mail kanaal7@k7.com.na; internet www.k7.com.na; f. 1993; Christian community radio station; English, Afrikaans and Oshiwambo; Man. Dir NEAL VAN DEN BERG.

Ninety Nine FM (Pty) Ltd (99 FM): 44 Hyper Motor City Centre, Maxwell St, Windhoek; tel. (61) 383450; e-mail contact@99fm.com .na; internet 99fm.com.na; f. 1994; Gen. Man. CHRISTINE HUGO.

Omulunga Radio: Old Power Station, 3rd Floor, Armstrong St, Old Power Station, Windhoek; tel. 840009800; e-mail info@omulunga .com.na; internet www.omulunga.com.na; f. 2002; Ovambo interest station affiliated to Kudu FM; Oshiwambo and English; Man. Dir QUINTIN KOTZE.

Radiowave 96.7 FM: Old Power Station, Armstrong St, 3rd Floor, Windhoek; tel. 840009825; e-mail info@radiowave.com.na; internet www.radiowave.com.na.

Other radio stations include: Kosmos Radio and Radio France Internationale (via relay).

Television

Namibian Broadcasting Corpn (NBC): Cullinan St, Northern Industrial, POB 321, Windhoek; tel. (61) 2913111; e-mail tvlicence@nbc.na; internet www.nbc.na; f. 1990; broadcasts television programmes in English to 45% of the population, 18 hours daily; Chair. LAZARUS JACOBS; Dir-Gen. STANLEY SIMILO.

One Africa TV: Maxwell St, 44 Hyper Motor City, Windhoek; tel. (61) 383450; e-mail contact@oneafrica.com; internet www.oneafrica.tv; f. 2003; CEO STEFAN HUGO; Man. Dir MADRYN COSBURN.

Trinity Broadcasting Namibia: POB 74, Swakopmund; tel. (64) 401100; e-mail comments@tbnnamibia.tv; internet www.tbnnamibia.tv; f. 2002; religious broadcasts; CEO BE BOTHA.

Finance

BANKING

Central Bank

Bank of Namibia: 71 Robert Mugabe Ave, POB 2882, Windhoek; tel. (61) 2835111; e-mail info@bon.com.na; internet www.bon.com.na; f. 1990; Gov. JOHANNES !GAWAXAB.

Commercial Banks

Bank Windhoek Ltd: 119 Independence Ave, POB 15, Windhoek; tel. (61) 2991200; e-mail info@bankwindhoek.com.na; internet www.bankwindhoek.com.na; f. 1982; wholly owned subsidiary of Capricorn Investment Group; Chair. JOHAN SWANEPOEL; Man. Dir BARONICE HANS.

First National Bank of Namibia Ltd: Parkside, 130 Independence Ave, c/o Fidel Castro, POB 285, Windhoek; tel. (61) 2992222; e-mail info@fnbnamibia.com.na; internet www.fnbnamibia.com.na; f. 1987 as First Nat. Bank of Southern Africa Ltd; present name adopted in 1988; Chair. INGE ZAAMWANI-KAMWI; CEO CONRAD DEMPSEY.

Letshego Namibia: Schwerinsburg Rd, Windhoek; tel. (61) 2023500; e-mail namibia@letshego.com; internet www.letshego.com/namibia; f. 2002 as Edu Loan Namibia; present name adopted following acquisition by Letshego Holdings Ltd; Chair. MARYVONNE PALANDUZ; CEO ESTER KALI.

Nedbank Namibia Ltd: 12–20 Dr Frans Indongo St, POB 1, Windhoek; tel. (61) 2952052; e-mail serviceplus@nedbank.com; internet www.nedbank.com.na; f. 1973; fmrly Commercial Bank of Namibia Ltd; subsidiary of Nedbank Ltd, South Africa; Chair. PETER C. W. HIBBIT; Man. Dir MARTHA MURORUA.

Standard Bank Namibia Ltd: Erf 1378, 1 Chasie St, Kleine Kuppe, Windhoek; tel. (61) 2942126; e-mail CCCQueries@standardbank.com.na; internet www.standardbank.com.na; f. 1915; controlled by Standard Bank Africa; Chair. HERBERT MAIER; CEO MERCIA GEISES.

Trustco Bank Namibia: 1 Lossen St, Windhoek; tel. (61) 4348111; e-mail info@tbn.na; internet www.tbn.na; f. 2002 as Namibian-German Microfinance Ltd; subsequently FIDES Bank Namibia; present name adopted in 2014; microfinance institution; 100% owned by Trustco Group Holdings Ltd; Chair. TOM NEWTON; Group Man. Dir Dr QUINTON VAN ROOYEN.

Agricultural Banks

Agricultural Bank of Namibia (AgriBank): 10 Post St Mall, POB 13402, Windhoek; tel. (61) 2074111; e-mail info@agribank.com.na; internet agribank.com.na; f. 1922; state-owned; Chair. MICHAEL IYAMBO; CEO Dr RAPHAEL KARUAIHE.

Development Banks

Development Bank of Namibia (DBN): 12 Daniel Munamava St, POB 235, Windhoek; tel. (61) 2908000; e-mail info@dbn.com.na; internet www.dbn.com.na; f. 2004; state-owned; Chair. TANIA HANGULA; CEO SAREL VAN ZYL.

BANKING ASSOCIATION

Bankers Association of Namibia: First National Bank, POB 195, Windhoek; tel. (61) 2992116; internet www.ban.na; f. 1997; Chair. MARTHA MURORUA.

REGULATORY AUTHORITY

Namibia Financial Institutions Supervisory Authority (NAMFISA): 51-55 Werner List St, Gutenberg Plaza, Windhoek; tel. (61) 2905000; e-mail info@namfisa.com.na; internet www.namfisa.com.na; f. 2001; regulates non-banking financial institutions; Chair. GERSOM KATJIMUNE; CEO KENNETH S. MATOMOLA.

STOCK EXCHANGE

Namibia Stock Exchange (NSX): Robert Mugabe Ave 4, POB 2401, Windhoek; tel. (61) 227647; e-mail info@nsx.com.na; internet nsx.com.na; f. 1992; Chair. DAVID NUYOMA; CEO TIAAN BAZUIN.

INSURANCE

Corporate Guarantee and Insurance Co of Namibia Ltd (CGI): 1st Floor, 140 Mandume Ndemufayo Ave, POB 416, Windhoek; tel. (83) 3313000; e-mail clientcare@corporateguarantee.com; internet www.corporateguarantee.com; f. 1996; wholly owned subsidiary of Nictus Group Ltd since 2001; Chair. F. R. VAN STADEN; Man. Dir and Principal Officer W. O. FOURIE.

Momentum Metropolitan Namibia Ltd: MMI House, cnr Dr Frans Indongo and Werner List Sts, POB 3785, Windhoek; tel. (61) 2973000; e-mail ci.clientservice@momentum.com.na; internet www.momentummetropolitan.com.na; f. 1996 as Metropolitan Life Namibia Ltd; subsidiary of Metropolitan Group, South Africa; fmrly MMI Holdings Namibia; present name adopted in 2019; Chair. SAKARIA NGHIKEMBUA; Group CEO GRANT MARAIS.

Namibia National Reinsurance Corpn Ltd (NamibRe): NamibRe Bldg, 39 cnr Feld and Lazarett Sts, POB 716, Windhoek; tel. (61) 422800; e-mail info@namibre.com; internet namibre.com; f. 2001; 100% state-owned; Chair. LIBERTHA DEWINA KAPERE; Man. Dir PATTY KARUAIHE-MARTIN.

Old Mutual Life Assurance Co (Namibia) Ltd: Mutual Tower, 223 Independence Ave, POB 25548, Windhoek; tel. (61) 2993999; e-mail nam-csenquiries@oldmutual.com; internet www.oldmutual.com.na; Chair. PETER DE BEYER; Group CEO TASSIUS CHIGARIRO.

OUTsurance Insurance Co of Namibia Ltd: Maerua Mall, 2nd Floor, c/o Jan Jonker St and Robert Mugabe Ave, POB 79, Windhoek; tel. (61) 2306081; internet www.outsurance.com.na; f. 1990; fmrly Swabou Insurance Co Ltd; jointly owned by OUTsurance Holdings (South Africa) and FNB Namibia Holdings Ltd; short-term insurance; Chair. L. DIPPENAAR; CEO D. H. MATTHEE.

Sanlam Namibia: 145 Independence Ave, POB 317, Windhoek 9000; tel. (61) 2947440; e-mail marketing@sanlam.com.na; internet www.sanlam.com/namibia; f. 1928; subsidiary of Sanlam Ltd, South Africa; merged with Regent Life Namibia, Capricorn Investments and Nam-Mic Financial Services in Dec. 2004; CEO TERTIUS STEARS.

Santam Namibia Ltd: Tenbergen Village, cnr Robert Mugabe and Julius Nyerere Sts, Windhoek; tel. (61) 2928000; e-mail information@santam.com.na; internet www.santam.na; f. 1990; 60% owned by Santam, South Africa; 30% owned by Bank Windhoek Holdings Ltd and 10% owned by Nam-mic Financial Services; subsidiary of Capricorn Investments; Chair. VUSUMUZI PHILLIP KHANYILE.

Trustco Insurance Ltd: Trustco House, 2 Keller St, POB 11363, Windhoek; tel. (61) 2754000; e-mail info@tgh.na; internet www.tgh.na; f. 1992; legal, funeral and medical insurance; Chair. WINTON JOHN GEYSER; Group Man. Dir QUINTON VAN ROOYEN.

Trade and Industry

GOVERNMENT AGENCIES

Agro-Marketing and Trade Agency: Windhoek; tel. (61) 2023300; e-mail info@amta.na; internet www.amta.na; manages marketing and trading of agricultural produce in Namibia; Man. Dir LUCAS LUNGAMENI.

Meat Board of Namibia: 30 David Hosea Meroro Rd, POB 38, Windhoek; tel. (61) 275830; e-mail info@nammic.com.na; internet www.nammic.com.na; f. 1935; facilitates export of livestock, meat and processed meat products; Chair. PATRICIA GURUBES; Gen. Man. PAUL STRYDOM.

Meat Corpn of Namibia Ltd (Meatco): Northern Industrial Area St, POB 3881, Windhoek; tel. (61) 3216400; internet www.meatco.com.na; f. 1986; processors of meat and meat products at 4 abattoirs and 1 tannery; Interim Chair. ADOLF MUREMI; CEO MWILIMA MUSHOKABANJI.

Namibian Agronomic Board: 30 David Merero St, Ausspannplatz, POB 5096, Windhoek; tel. (61) 379500; e-mail nab.queries@nab.com.na; internet www.nab.com.na; f. 1985; Chair. MICHAEL IYAMBO; CEO Dr FIDELIS MWAZI.

National Fishing Corporation of Namibia (Fishcor): !Nami#nus; tel. (63) 208100; e-mail info@seaflower.com.na; internet www.seaflowergroup.com.na; f. 1991; subsidiaries include: Seaflower Lobster Corpn Ltd, Seaflower Whitefish Corpn Ltd and Seacope Freezer Fishing (Pty) Ltd (SEACOPE); Interim Chair. HEINRICH MIHE GAOMAB (II); CEO ALEX CLIVE GAWANAB.

National Petroleum Corpn of Namibia (NAMCOR): Petroleum House, 1 Aviation Rd, PMB 13196, Windhoek; tel. (61) 2045000; e-mail info@namcor.com.na; internet www.namcor.com.na; f. 1965 as Southern Oil Exploration Corpn (South-West Africa) (Pty) Ltd—SWAKOR; present name adopted 1990; state petroleum co; Chair. JENNIFER COMALIE; Man. Dir IMMANUEL MULUNGA.

National Planning Commission: Office of the President, Govt Office Park, Blk D2, Windhoek Luther St, PMB 13356, Windhoek; tel. (61) 2834225; e-mail info@npc.gov.na; internet www.npc.gov.na; Dir-Gen. OBETH KANDJOZE.

Swakara Board of Namibia: Pelt Centre, 8 Bessemer St, Southern Industrial, PMB 12011, Windhoek; tel. (61) 2909301; e-mail swakara@agra.com.na; internet www.swakara.net; f. 1982; promotes development of karakul wool and the pelt industry; Chair. JULENE MEYER.

DEVELOPMENT ORGANIZATIONS

Namibia Industrial Development Agency (NIDA): 11 Goethe St, PMB 13252, Windhoek; tel. (61) 2062111; e-mail info@nida.com.na; internet nida.com.na; f. 2018 following the merger of the Namibia Development Corpn and Offshore Development Corpn; Chair. LIONEL MATTHEWS; CEO MIHE GAOMAB (II).

National Housing Enterprise (NHE): 7 Gen. Murtala Muhammed Ave, Eros, POB 20192, Windhoek; tel. (61) 2927111; e-mail info@nhe.com.na; internet www.nhe.com.na; f. 1993; replaced Nat. Building and Investment Corpn; provides low-cost housing; manages Housing Trust Fund; 100% state-owned; Chair. SAM SHIVUTE; CEO GISBERTUS MUKULU.

Namibia Investment Promotion and Development Board (NIPDB): BRB Bldg, cnr Garten St and Dr A. B. May St, PMB 13340, Windhoek,; tel. 833338600; e-mail info@nipdb.com; internet nipdb.com; f. 1990; promotes foreign and domestic investment; CEO NANGULA UAANDJA.

Namibia Trade Forum: 15 Eugene Marais St, POB 5342, Windhoek; tel. (61) 235327; e-mail ntfadmin@ntf.org.na; internet www.ntf.org.na; facilitates public-private dialogue to influence trade policies and economic devt; Chair. GIDEON M. L. SHILONGO; CEO STACEY PINTO.

CHAMBERS OF COMMERCE

Chamber of Mines of Namibia (CoM): 3 Schutzen St, POB 2895, Windhoek; tel. (61) 237925; e-mail info@chamberofmines.org.na; internet chamberofmines.org.na; f. 1969; Pres. HILIFA MBAKO; CEO VESTON MALANGO.

Namibia Chamber of Commerce and Industry (NCCI): 6436 Church St, Windhoek; tel. (61) 228809; e-mail info@ncci.org.na; internet www.ncci.org.na; f. 1990; Pres. BISEY /UIRAB; CEO CHARITY MWIYA.

EMPLOYERS' ORGANIZATIONS

Construction Industries Federation of Namibia: cnr Stein and Schwabe Sts, POB 1479, Klein Windhoek; POB 1479, Windhoek; tel. (61) 417302; e-mail gm@cifnamibia.com; internet www.cifnamibia.com; f. 1952 as Master Builders Association; registered as above in 1993; Pres. NICO BADENHORST; Consulting Gen. Man. BÄRBEL KIRCHNER.

Namibia Agricultural Union (NAU): Robert Mugabe Ave, PMB 13255, Windhoek; tel. (61) 237838; e-mail elsabe@agrinamibia.com.na; internet www.agrinamibia.com.na; f. 1947; represents commercial farmers; Pres. P. S. GOUWS; Exec. Man. ROELIE VENTER.

Namibian Employers' Federation (NEF): Cargo City, South Bldg, 1st Floor, 5 Von Braun St, Southern Industrial Area, Windhoek; tel. (61) 244089; e-mail enquiries@nef.com.na; internet www.nef.com.na; Chair. TERENCE MAKARI; Pres. ELIA SHIKONGO.

Namibia National Farmers' Union (NNFU): Erf 4, Axalie Doeseb St, POB 3117, Windhoek; tel. (61) 271117; e-mail info@nnfu.org.na; internet www.nnfu.org.na; f. 1992; represents communal farmers; Pres. KUNIBERTH SHAMATHE; Sec. ELINA KALUNDU.

Namibia Professional Hunting Association (NAPHA): 318 Sam Nujoma Dr., Klein Windhoek; POB 11291, Windhoek; tel. (61) 234455; e-mail office@napha.com.na; internet www.napha-namibia.com; f. 1974; represents hunting guides and professional hunters; Pres. DANENE VAN DER WESTHUYZEN; CEO TANJA DAHL.

UTILITIES

Electricity

Electricity Control Board: 35 Theo-Ben Gurirab St, POB 2923, Windhoek; tel. (61) 374300; e-mail info@ecb.org.na; internet www.ecb.org.na; f. 2000; Chair. GOTTLIEB HINDA; CEO RACHEL BOOIS (acting).

Namibia Power Corpn (Pty) Ltd (NamPower): NamPower Centre, 15 Luther St, POB 2864, Windhoek; tel. (61) 2054111; e-mail webinfo@nampower.com.na; internet www.nampower.com.na; f. 1964 as South West Africa Water and Electricity Corpn; present name adopted in 1996; state-owned; Chair. DANIEL MOTINGA; Man. Dir SIMSON HAULOFU.

Water

Namibia Water Corpn Ltd (NamWater): 176 Iscor St, Northern Industrial Area, POB 13389, Windhoek; tel. (61) 710000; e-mail info@namwater.co.na; internet www.namwater.com.na; f. 1997; state-owned; Chair. THADDIUS MASWAHU; CEO ABRAHAM NEHEMIA.

MAJOR COMPANIES

Bidvest Namibia: 1 Ballot St, Ausspannplatz, POB 6964, Ausspannplatz, Windhoek; tel. (61) 417450; e-mail info@bidvest.com.na; internet www.bidvestnamibia.com.na; f. 1989 as Crown Mills Namibia (Pty) Ltd; present name adopted in 1993; automotive, freight and logistics services, food and distribution, commercial and industrial services and products; Chair. LINDSAY PETER RALPHS; Man. Dir SEBULON INOTILA KANKONDI.

Commercial Investment Corpn Namibia (CIC Namibia): United House, cnr Solingen and Iscor Sts, Northern Industrial Area, POB 98, Windhoek; tel. (61) 2855800; e-mail pro@cic.com.na; internet www.cic.com.na; f. 1946 as J. J. van Zyl (Pty) Ltd; present name adopted in 1984; part of CIC Holdings Ltd, South Africa; provides logistical and administrative services to consumer goods industry; Man. Dir DIVAN OPPERMAN.

Namdeb Diamond Corpn Ltd: Namdeb Centre, 10th Floor, 10 Dr Frans Indongo St, POB 1906, Windhoek; tel. (63) 2043333; internet www.namdeb.com; f. 1994; 50% state-owned, 50% owned by De Beers Centenary AG, Switzerland; operates alluvial diamond mine at Oranjemund; also recovers marine diamonds; Chair. CHRIS NGHAAMWA; CEO RIAAN BURGER.

Namib Desert Diamonds (Pty) Ltd (NAMDIA): c/o Sam Nujoma and Dr Kwame Nkrumah, Windhoek; tel. 833311111; e-mail info@namdia.com; internet www.namdia.com; f. 2016; Chair. BRIAN EISEB; CEO ALISA AMUPOLO.

Namib Mills (Pty) Ltd: POB 20276, Windhoek; tel. (61) 2901000; e-mail info@namibmills.com; internet www.namibmills.com; f. 1982; grain processing co; CEO IAN COLLARD.

Namibia Breweries Ltd (Nambrew): Iscor St, Northern Industrial Area, POB 206, Windhoek; tel. (61) 3204999; e-mail nambrew@ol.na; internet www.nambrew.com; f. 1920 as South West Breweries Ltd; present name adopted in 1990; owned by Ohlthaver & List Group; producers and distributors of beer, spirits and soft drinks; Chair. SVEN THIEME; Man. Dir MARCO WENK.

Namibia Diamond Trading Co (NTDC): Namdeb Bldg, 9th Floor, 10 Dr Frans Indongo St, POB 23316, Windhoek; tel. (61) 2043222; e-mail info@ndtc.com.na; internet ndtc.com.na; f. 2007; 50% state-owned, 50% owned by De Beers Namibia Holdings; CEO BRENT EISEB.

Nictus Furnishers: 140 Mandume Ndemufayo Ave, Windheok; tel. 833313333; e-mail nictsum@nictus.com.na; internet www.nictus.com.na; furniture, carpet and motor retail, and financial services; Man. Dir FRANCOIS WAHL.

Ohorongo Cement (Pty) Ltd: 11 Van Der Bijl St, Northern Industrial Area, Windhoek; POB 86842, Eros; tel. (61) 389300; internet www.ohorongo-cement.com; f. 2006; Chair. THOMAS SPANNAGL; Man. Dir HANS-WILHELM SCHÜTTE.

Rosh Pinah Zinc Corpn (RPZC): Rosh Pinah Mine, Rosh Pinah; tel. (63) 274201; f. 1999 to succeed Imcor Zinc (Pty) Ltd; lead and zinc producers; 90% owned by Trevali Mining Corpn, Canada; Pres. and CEO RICUS GRIMBEEK; Mine Man. CHRISTO ASPELING.

Rössing Uranium Ltd: Corporate Communications Dept, 1st Floor, The Dome, 5371 Welwitschia St, PMB 5005, Swakopmund; tel. (64) 5209111; e-mail rul.communications@rossing.com.na; internet www.rossing.com; f. 1970; began production in 1976; operates world's largest open-pit uranium mine in the Namib Desert; Chair. STEVE GALLOWAY; Man. Dir JOHAN COETZEE.

Skorpion Zinc: 26 km North of Rosh Pinah, Namzinc (Pty) Ltd, PMB 2003, Rosh Pinah; tel. (63) 2712100; e-mail info@vedantaresources.co.na; internet vedanta-zincinternational.com; f. 2000; entered commercial production 2004; owned and operated by Vedanta Zinc International, South Africa; producers of zinc; Gen. Man. IRVINNE SIMATAA.

Weatherly Mining Namibia: Ausspann Plaza, Unit 4, Ground Floor, Dr Agostinho Neto Rd, Ausspannplatz, Windhoek; tel. (61) 2931010; internet www.weatherlyplc.com; f. 2006 after acquisition of Ongopolo Mining and Processing Ltd assets by Weatherly International, UK; copper producers; Chair. JOHN BRYANT; Man. Dir JOHN SISAY.

TRADE UNIONS

Trade Union Federations

Namibia National Labour Organisation (NANLO): Windhoek; e-mail nanlooffice@gmail.com; f. 2014; 3 affiliated unions: the Metal, Mining, Maritime and Construction Union, the Namibia Parastatals and Civil Service Workers' Union and the Solidarity Union; Pres. EVILASTUS KAARONDA.

National Union of Namibian Workers (NUNW): 8506 Mungunda St, Katutura; POB 50034, Windhoek; tel. (61) 215037; f. 1972; affiliated to the SWAPO party; Sec.-Gen. JOB MUNIARO.

The NUNW has 10 affiliates, which include:

Metal and Allied Namibian Workers' Union (MANWU): NUNW Centre, 8506 Mingunda St, Windhoek; tel. (61) 263100; e-mail secretary1@iway.na; internet fb.com/manwu.org; f. 1987; Pres. ANGULA ANGULA; Gen. Sec. JUSTINA JONAS-EMVULA.

Mineworkers' Union of Namibia (MUN): 7353 Mungunda St, POB 1566, Windhoek; tel. (61) 261723; e-mail mun@mun-na.com; internet www.mun-na.com; f. 1986; Pres. MAYEMELO KALUMBU; Sec.-Gen. EBBEN ZARONDO.

Namibia Farm Workers' Union (NAFWU): NUNW Centre, Mungunda St, Katutura; POB 21007, Windhoek; tel. (61) 218653; f. 1994; Pres. CORNELIUS NTELAMO; Sec.-Gen. ROCCO NGUVAUVA.

Namibia Financial Institutions Union (NAFINU): POB 61791, Windhoek; tel. (61) 239917; f. 2000; Pres. and Gen. Sec. ASNATH ZAMUEE.

Namibia Food and Allied Workers' Union (NAFAU): Mungunda St, Katutura; POB 1553, Windhoek; tel. (61) 218213; f. 1986; Pres. MIKE KARUPU; Sec.-Gen. JACOB PENDA.

Namibia National Teachers' Union (NANTU): Mungunda St, Katutura, POB 61009, Windhoek; tel. (61) 262247; e-mail nantu@nantu.org.na; internet nantuweb.org; f. 1989; Pres. (vacant); Sec.–Gen. LOIDE SHAANIKA.

Namibia Public Workers' Union (NAPWU): 11 John Meinert St, Bachbrecht, POB 50035, Windheok; tel. (61) 261961; e-mail gs@napwu.org.na; internet www.napwu.org.na; f. 1987; Pres. EVANS MASWAHU; Sec.-Gen. PETRUS NEVONGA.

Namibia Transport and Allied Workers' Union (NATAU): 85 Mungunda St, Katutura, POB 7516, Windhoek; tel. (61) 218514; f. 1988; Gen. Sec. NARINA POLLMANN.

Trade Union Congress of Namibia (TUCNA): POB 2111, Windhoek; tel. (61) 246143; f. 2002 following the merger of the Namibia People's Social Movement (f. 1992 as the Namibia Christian Social Trade Unions) and the Namibia Fed. of Trade Unions (f. 1998); Pres. PAULUS HANGO; Sec.-Gen. MAHONGORA KAVIHUHA.

TUCNA has 14 affiliates, including:

Namibia Seamen and Allied Workers' Union (NASAWU): Nataniel Maxuilli St, Kuisebmund; POB 1341, Walvis Bay; tel. (64) 204237; f. 1996; Pres. PAULUS HANGO; Sec.-Gen. ERRKIE SHITANA.

Namibia Wholesale and Retail Workers' Union (NWRWU): 3930 Verbena St, Khomasdal; POB 22769, Windhoek; tel. (61) 212378; f. 1993; Sec.-Gen. VICTOR HAMUNYELA.

Public Service Union of Namibia (PSUN): 45/51 Kroon Rd, Khomasdal, POB 21662, Windhoek; tel. (61) 213083; e-mail info@psun.com.na; internet www.psun.com.na; f. 1981 as Govt Service Staff Asscn; present name adopted 1990; Pres. TITUS SITENTU; Sec.-Gen. NDJIZUVEE HAAKURIA.

Teachers' Union of Namibia (TUN): PSUN Bldg, 4551 Dollar St, Khomasdal, POB 30800, Windhoek; tel. (61) 229115; f. 1990; Pres. TOINI NAUYOMA; Sec.-Gen. MAHONGORA KAVIHUHA.

Transport

RAILWAYS

The main line runs from Nakop, at the border with South Africa, via Keetmanshoop to Windhoek, Kranzberg, Tsumeb, Swakopmund and Walvis Bay. There are three branch lines, from Windhoek to Gobabis, Otavi to Grootfontein and Keetmanshoop to !Nami#nus (formerly Lüderitz). Under phase one of the Northern Railway Line Extension Project, the Kranzberg–Tsumeb line was extended by 248 km to Ondangwa in 2006. Phase two of the project, a further 60-km extension of this line to Oshikango, was officially opened in July 2012, and phase three was to involve the eventual construction of a 58-km international link with Oshakati, Angola. In the late 2000s plans were under discussion regarding the proposed construction of a 1,500-km Trans-Kalahari Railway linking Walvis Bay with the Mmamabula coal deposits in Botswana. There were also plans to extend the rehabilitated Mulobezi railway line in Zambia to connect with the Namibian railway system.

TransNamib Holdings Ltd: cnr Independence Ave and Bahnhof Sts, PMB 13204, Windhoek; tel. (61) 2981111; e-mail pubrelation@transnamib.com.na; internet www.transnamib.com.na; f. 1998; state-owned; Chair. (vacant); CEO JOHNNY SMITH.

ROADS

Roads Authority: Snyman Circle, Ausspannplatz, Windhoek; tel. (61) 2847000; e-mail pr@ra.org.na; internet www.ra.org.na; Chair. LILY BRANDT; CEO CONRAD MUTONGA LUTOMBI.

SHIPPING

The ports of Walvis Bay and !Nami#nus (formerly Lüderitz) are linked to the main overseas shipping routes and handle almost one-half of Namibia's external trade. Walvis Bay has a container terminal, built in 1999, and eight berths; it is a hub port for the region, serving landlocked countries such as Botswana, Zambia and Zimbabwe. As part of a N $3,000m. expansion project, a new container terminal at Walvis Bay port was opened in August 2019. Traditionally a fishing port, a new quay was completed at !Nami#nus in 2000, with two berths, in response to growing demand from the offshore diamond industry.

Namibian Ports Authority (NAMPORT): 17 Rikumbi Kandanga Rd, POB 361, Walvis Bay; tel. (64) 2082111; e-mail customercare@namport.com.na; internet www.namport.com; f. 1994; Chair. GERSON S. HINDA; CEO ANDREW KANIME.

CIVIL AVIATION

There are international airports at Windhoek (Hosea Kutako) and Walvis Bay (Rooikop), as well more than 20 other, smaller airports and numerous landing strips throughout Namibia.

Namibia Civil Aviation Authority (NCAA): 12 Rudolf Hertzog St, Windhoek; tel. (61) 702201; e-mail avsec@dca.com.na; internet www.ncaa.com.na; f. 2016 to replace the Directorate of Civil Aviation; Exec. Dir TOSKA SEM.

Namibia Airports Company (NAC) Ltd: 5th Floor, Sanlam Centre, 154 Independence Ave, POB 23061, Windhoek; tel. (61) 2955000; e-mail pr@airports.com.na; internet www.airports.com.na; f. 1998; Chair. Dr LEAKE HANGALA; CEO BISEY /UIRAB.

Tourism

Federation of Namibian Tourism Associations (FENATA): 36 Bismarck St, POB 86495, Windhoek; tel. (61) 230337; e-mail welcome@fenata.org; internet www.fenata.org; f. 1991; umbrella body for tourism associations in the private sector; Chair. NETUMBO NASHANDI.

Namibia Tourism Board: c/o Haddy and Sam Nujoma Dr., Private Bag 13244, Windhoek; tel. (61) 2906000; e-mail info@namibiatourism.com.na; internet www.namibiatourism.com.na; Chair. BERND SCHNEIDER; CEO DIGU //NAOBEB.

Defence

As assessed at November 2021, the Namibian Defence Force numbered an estimated 9,000 men; there was also a 900-strong navy, operating as part of the Ministry of Fisheries and Marine Resources, and a paramilitary force of 6,000.

Defence Budget: N $5,430m. in 2021.

Commander-in-Chief of the Defence Force: Pres. HAGE GEINGOB.

Chief of Staff of the Defence Force: Air Marshal MARTIN PINEHAS.

Commander of the Army: Maj.-Gen. MATHEUS ALUEENDO.

Education

Education is officially compulsory and free of charge for 10 years between the ages of six and 16 years, or until primary education has been completed (whichever is the sooner). Under the Education Act of 2001, free basic education was extended to grade 12, although it is not compulsory beyond the limits set in the Constitution. Primary education begins at six years of age and lasts for seven years. Secondary education, beginning at the age of 13, lasts for up to five years, comprising a first cycle of three years and a second of two. According to estimates by the United Nations Educational, Scientific and Cultural Organization (UNESCO), in 2017/18 enrolment at pre-primary schools included 33% of children (males 32%; females 34%) in the relevant age-group, while enrolment at primary schools included 98% of children (males 97%; females 100%) in the relevant age-group. The comparable ratio for secondary enrolment in 2012/13 was 54% (males 48%; females 60%). Higher education is provided by the University of Namibia, the Technicon of Namibia, a vocational college and four teacher training colleges. Various schemes for informal adult education are also in operation in an effort to combat illiteracy. In 2021/22 education was allocated N $16,900m., equivalent to 28.5% of total projected government expenditure.

Bibliography

Akawa, M. *The Gender Politics of the Namibian Liberation Struggle.* Basel, Basler Afrika Bibliographien, 2014.

Bley, H. *Namibia under German Rule.* Uppsala, Nordiska Afrikainstitutet, 1997.

Bösl, A., Du Pisani, A., and Zaire, D. U. *Namibia's Foreign Relations: Historic Contexts, Current Dimensions, and Perspectives for the 21st Century.* Windhoek, Macmillan Education Namibia, 2014.

Cliffe, L., et al. *The Transition to Independence in Namibia.* Boulder, CO, Lynne Rienner Publishers, 1994.

Du Pisani, A., Kössler, R., and Lindeke, W. (Eds). *The Long Aftermath of War: Reconciliation and Transition in Namibia.* Freiburg, Arnold-Bergstraesser-Institut, 2010.

Gewald, J. *Herero Heroes: A Socio-Political History of the Herero of Namibia, 1890–1923.* London, James Currey Publishers, 1999.

Grotpeter, J. J. *Historical Dictionary of Namibia.* Metuchen, NJ, Scarecrow Press, 1994.

Hayes, P., Silvester, J., Wallace, M., and Hartmann, W. *Namibia under South African Rule.* London, James Currey Publishers, 1998.

Heribert, W., and Matthew, B. (Eds). *The Namibian Peace Process: Implications and Lessons for the Future.* Freiburg, Arnold-Bergstraesser-Institut, 1994.

Hofnie, K., Friedman, S., and Iipinge, S. *The Relationship Between Gender Roles and HIV Infection in Namibia.* Windhoek, University of Namibia, 2004.

Katjavivi, P. H. *A History of Resistance in Namibia.* London, James Currey Publishers, 2004.

Kern, T. *West Germany and Namibia's Path to Independence, 1969-1990: Foreign Policy and Rivalry with East Germany.* Walvis Bay, Brookridge Publishing, 2019.

Kössler, R. *Namibia and Germany: Negotiating the Past.* Windhoek, University of Namibia, 2015.

Kreike, E. *Environmental Infrastructure in African History: Examining the Myth of Natural Resource Management in Namibia.* Cambridge, Cambridge University Press, 2013.

Leys, C., and Saul, J. S. *Namibia's Liberation Struggle: The Two-Edged Sword.* London, James Currey Publishers, 1995.

Lush, D. *Last Steps to Uhuru: An Eye-Witness Account of Namibia's Transition to Independence (1988–1992).* Ibadan, Spectrum Books, 1993.

Mbuende, K. *Namibia: The Broken Shield: Anatomy of Imperialism and Revolution.* Uppsala, Scandinavian Institute for African Studies, 1986.

Melber, H. *Cross-examining Transition in Namibia: Socio-economic and Ideological Transformation since Independence.* Uppsala, Nordiska Afrikainstitutet, 2006.

Understanding Namibia: The Trials of Independence. London, C. Hurst & Co, 2014.

A Decade of Namibia: Politics, Economy and Society: The Era Pohamba, 2004–2015. Leiden, Brill, 2016.

Namibia: Gesellschaftspolitische Erkundungen seit der Unabhängigkeit. Frankfurt am Main, Brandes & Apsel, 2017.

Melber, H. (Ed.). *Transitions in Namibia: Which Changes for Whom?* Uppsala, Nordiska Afrikainstitutet, 2007.

Otaala, B. (Ed.). *Government Leaders in Namibia Responding to the HIV/AIDS Epidemic.* Windhoek, University of Namibia, 2003.

Soggot, D. *Namibia: The Violent Heritage.* London, Collings, 1986.

Southall, R. *Liberation Movements in Power: Party & State in Southern Africa.* Woodbridge, James Currey, 2013.

Thornberry, C. *A Nation is Born: The Inside Story of Namibia's Independence.* Windhoek, Gamsberg Macmillan, 2004.

Torreguitar, E. *National Liberation Movements in Office: Forging Democracy with African Adjectives in Namibia.* New York, Peter Lang, 2009.

Tötemeyer, G. *Obstacles to Reconciliation and Stability in the Namibian State and Society.* Windhoek, Namibia Institute for Democracy, 2013.

Tsokodayi, C. J. *Namibia's Independence Struggle.* Bloomington, IN, Xlibris, 2011.

Vergau, H.-J. *Negotiating the Freedom of Namibia: The Diplomatic Achievement of the Western Contact Group.* Basel, Basler Afrika Bibliographien, 2011.

Wallace, M. *A History of Namibia: From the Beginning to 1990.* London, C. Hurst & Co, 2011.

Winterfeldt, V., Fox, T., and Mufune, P. (Eds). *Namibia: Society, Sociology.* Windhoek, University of Namibia, 2002.

Zimmerer, J., and Zeller, J. (Eds). *Genocide in German South West Africa: the Colonial War (1904–1908) in Namibia and its Aftermath.* Monmouth, Merlin Press, 2008.

NIGER

Physical and Social Geography

R. J. HARRISON CHURCH

The landlocked Republic of Niger is the largest state in western Africa, with Algeria and Libya to the north of it, Nigeria and Benin to the south, Mali and Burkina Faso to the west, and Chad to the east. With an area of 1,267,000 sq km (489,191 sq miles), it is larger than Nigeria, its immensely richer southern neighbour, which is Africa's most populous country. The relatively small size of Niger's population, 17,138,707, according to the census of 10 December 2012, is largely explained by the country's aridity and remoteness. According to official projections, population density at mid-2022 averaged 19.3 persons per sq km (based on an estimated population of 24,463,374). Two-thirds of Niger consists of desert, and most of the north-eastern region is uninhabitable. The only large city is the capital, Niamey, which had a population of 978,029 at the 2012 census. Hausa tribespeople are the most numerous (representing some 55.4% of Nigerien nationals in 2001), followed by the Djerma and Sonraï (together amounting for a total of 21.0%), Tuareg (9.3%) and Peulh (8.5%).

In the north-centre is the partly volcanic Aïr massif, with many dry watercourses remaining from earlier wetter conditions. Agadez, in Aïr, receives an average annual rainfall of no more than about 180 mm. None the less, the Tuaregs keep considerable numbers of livestock by moving them seasonally to areas further south, where underground well-water is usually available. Further south, along the Niger–Nigeria border, are sandy areas where annual rainfall is just sufficient for the cultivation of groundnuts and millet by Hausa farmers. Cotton is also grown in small, seasonally flooded valleys and depressions.

In the south-west is the far larger, seasonally flooded Niger valley, the pastures of which nourish livestock that have to contend with nine months of drought for the rest of the year. Rice and other crops are grown by the Djerma and Sonraï peoples as the Niger flood recedes.

History

LUCA RAINERI

Based on an earlier article by ABDOURAHMANE IDRISSA

POLITICS IN POST-INDEPENDENCE NIGER

The First Republic, 1958–87

Formerly a part of French West Africa, Niger became a self-governing republic within the French Community in December 1958, and proceeded to full independence on 3 August 1960. Control of government passed to the Parti Progressiste Nigérien (PPN), the leader of which, Hamani Diori, favoured the retention of close economic links with France. This brought him in line with 'moderate' independentist leaders, such as Gabon's Albert-Bernard (later Omar) Bongo and Côte d'Ivoire's Dr Félix Houphouët-Boigny. Together, they ratified a treaty of mutual co-operation with France, according to which France ensured military support for the newly independent countries, which still lacked standing armies, in exchange for a priority right (also called 'relative exclusiveness') over the export of their natural resources. In the case of Niger, this concerned most notably uranium, the commercial exploitation of which started in 1968 through a joint venture controlled by the French public company Areva. The importance of Niger's uranium in French energy and military policies strengthened the relationships between the two countries.

Until the late 1960s favourable rains and commodity trade terms sustained the cautious hopes of the Government for economic development. However, the oil crisis in the early 1970s prompted a rapidly deteriorating trade situation, which, compounded by a prolonged drought, contributed to the undermining of Diori's rule. His regime became more authoritarian, and the French Government grew increasingly dissatisfied as Diori attempted to renegotiate uranium price exports, not least by establishing closer relationships with Libyan leader, Col Muammar al-Qaddafi.

Amid urban civil disorders, Diori was eventually ousted by a military coup in April 1974, led by the Chief of Staff of the Armed Forces Lt-Col (later Maj.-Gen.) Seyni Kountché. While early accounts tended to link Kountché's rise to French interference, recent historiography is more cautious. Indeed, Kountché swiftly renegotiated the military support agreement with France, which led to the departure of French troops from Niger in 1975. Kountché established the Conseil Militaire Suprême (CMS) and replaced the legislature with a consultative Conseil National de Développement (CND). Although political parties were outlawed, exiled opposition activists were permitted to return to the country under the condition of refraining from any involvement in politics. Plots to remove Kountché were thwarted in 1975, 1976 and 1983. An increase in world uranium prices led to a period of relative economic growth in Niger, which, however, deteriorated as soon as commodity prices started to decline. At the same time, the oil boom and the introduction of heavy subsidies on consumption goods in North Africa contributed to the development of a thriving smuggling economy across the Sahara. This was favoured by the presence of a significant Nigerien diaspora in Algeria and Libya who had fled the famines that struck Sahelian countries, including Niger, in the 1970s and 1980s. By the early 1980s the military regime had embarked on a 'normalization' process, as well as the gradual implementation of economic and political liberalization measures leading to the adoption, via a referendum, of a constitutional charter. When Kountché died in November 1987, this process was well under way. However, political freedom had released energies among the educated classes and their agitation soon grew into a full-blown democratization movement in the late 1980s, as the state was weakened by a fiscal crisis and wide-ranging austerity measures.

The Second Republic, 1987–92

Kountché was succeeded by the Chief of Staff of the Armed Forces, Col (later Brig.) Ali Saïbou, who was appointed as Chairman of the CMS and head of state on 14 November 1987. In an era popularly known as *décrispation* ('relaxation'), Saïbou introduced a number of reforms. In May 1989, however, Saïbou engineered the return of the country to a system of single-party rule with the foundation of the Mouvement National pour la Société de Développement (MNSD), later known as the MNSD Parti-Etat ('party state'). He appointed a consultative team of legal and administrative technocrats to draft a constitutional text which enshrined single-party rule and conferred extensive powers on the President of the Republic. This authoritarian Constitution was ratified by 99.3% of voters, although the democratic movement secured a victory in that the new legal framework fully endorsed freedom of expression. One offshoot of this development was the appearance of independent media and the emergence of public opinion as a political force.

The authoritarian credentials of the new regime were confirmed at the only elections it organized, which took place in December 1989. Saïbou was the sole candidate in the presidential poll, when he was confirmed as head of state, for a seven-year term, by 99.6% of voters. At the same time a single list of 93 MNSD-approved deputies to a new Assemblée Nationale (National Assembly), to replace the CND, was endorsed by a similar margin.

Nevertheless, a number of developments, both internal and external, brought about the swift collapse of the Saïbou regime, and precipitated a decade of great turbulence in Niger. On the one hand, the end of the Cold War led international donors to distance themselves from authoritarian regimes in Africa and to introduce good governance conditionalities for the disbursement of aid to developing countries. On the other hand, the highly unpopular austerity policies promoted by the International Monetary Fund (IMF) and the World Bank during the 1980s stirred major protests across the country. Facing mounting dissatisfactions throughout 1990–91, Saïbou sponsored the transformation of the MNSD into a political party under the name MNSD—Nassara, as well as a profound review of the Constitution. The new text that emerged from the process on 24 April 1991 established the first fully-fledged democratic framework in Niger since 1958. However, it was ill-fated, as the democratic movement sought a fresh start under conditions that involved the termination of the Second Republic through a National Conference. As a result of persisting protests, Saïbou resigned in July 1991 as Chairman of MNSD—Nassara. He was succeeded as party leader by Col (retd) Mamadou Tandja.

The eruption of an insurgency in the north of the country also contributed to the ending of the Second Republic. While Kountché, fearing Libyan interference, had adopted a repressive stance against the Tuaregs living in the north of the country, Saïbou, in pursuit of normalization, recalled the exiled and refugees, and most notably the Tuareg among them, promising the fostering of economic opportunities. During their exile, however, Tuareg youth had grown heavily politicized, and the slow implementation of the announced development programmes sparked protests. The Tuaregs were also frustrated by what they perceived as an unfair redistribution of the rents and externalities of the mining activities taking place in their native lands. In May 1990 clashes between Tuareg militants and Nigerien law enforcement officials in the north-western town of Tchintabaraden triggered harsh repressions by the authorities, with numerous reported civilian victims. With similar dynamics taking place in neighbouring Mali, the escalation led, in October 1991, to the establishment of the Front de Libération de l'Aïr et l'Azaouad (FLAA), under the leadership of Rhissa Ag Boula (military wing) and Mano Dayak (civilian wing).

The National Conference was convened on 29 July 1991 and lasted until November. Declaring the Conference sovereign, its 1,200 delegates voted to suspend the Constitution and to dissolve all organs of state. Pending the installation of elected democratic institutions, the Conference appointed Cheiffou Amadou (an officer of the International Civil Aviation Organization) to head a transitional Government, while André Salifou (a dean of the University of Niamey), was designated Chairman of a 15-member Haut Conseil de la République, which was to function as an interim legislature.

A new Constitution was approved by 89.8% of those who voted (56.6% of the electorate) at a referendum on 26 December 1992. At elections to the new 83-member National Assembly, which were held on 14 February 1993 and contested by 12 political parties, the MNSD—Nassara won the greatest number of seats (29), but was prevented from resuming power by the rapid formation of an opposition coalition, the Alliance des Forces de Changement (AFC), which grouped six parties

together with a total of 50 seats. Principal members of the AFC were the Convention Démocratique et Sociale—Rahama (CDS), the Parti Nigérien pour la Démocratie et le Socialisme—Tarayya (PNDS—Tarayya) and the Alliance Nigérienne pour la Démocratie et le Progrès Social—Zaman Lahiya (ANDP).

The MNSD—Nassara was similarly frustrated in the presidential election. In the first round, on 27 February 1993, Tandja won the largest share of the votes cast (34.2%), followed by Mahamane Ousmane, the leader of the CDS (26.6%). Ousmane was elected President at a second round, on 27 March, by 55.4% of those who voted (just over 35% of the electorate), aided by the support of four of the six other candidates from the first round, who were members of the AFC.

The Third Republic, 1993–96

Ousmane became President of the Third Republic on 16 April 1993, the first to be democratically elected since independence, and appointed another presidential candidate, Mahamadou Issoufou of the PNDS—Tarayya, to the post of Prime Minister.

The Ousmane administration identified the resolution of the Tuareg dispute as a major priority, and the rise of a civilian leadership made the prospect of peaceful negotiations more realistic. After some two years of low-intensity hostilities, in June 1993 Mano Dayak signed a formal, three-month truce agreement, providing for the demilitarization of the north and envisaging negotiations on the Tuaregs' political demands. The deal, however, was not unanimous: Ag Boula maintained that the FLAA could not support any agreement that contained no specific commitment to discussion of federalism, which prompted Mano Dayak (alongside with Mohamed Akotey) to form a splinter group, the Front de Libération de Tamoust (FLT), while another group of Tuareg hardliners created the Armée Révolutionnaire de Libération du Nord-Niger (ARLN) to denounce the accord. In October 1993, however, the FLAA and the ARLN joined the FLT in the Coordination de la Résistance Armée (CRA), with the aim of presenting a cohesive programme in future negotiations.

After the CRA managed to present the Nigerien Government a 'comprehensive and final' plan for the restoration of peace, a new accord was signed in October 1994 in Ouagadougou, Burkina Faso, under which the Government was to establish elected assemblies for decentralized communities, as well as take measures to ensure the security, rehabilitation and return of refugees in the areas affected by the conflict. A renewable three-month truce, to be monitored by French and Burkinabé military units, was to take immediate effect. Subsequent negotiations also led to the agreement that demobilized rebels were to be integrated into the Nigerien military and civilian sectors, that special military units were to be assigned responsibility for the security of the northern regions; and that the development of the north would receive particular attention. Furthermore, there was to be a general amnesty for all parties involved in the Tuareg rebellion and its suppression. The peace agreement, which was to be implemented within six months, was formally signed in Niamey on 24 April 1995, and its provisions were gradually enacted.

In the meantime, however, political developments contributed to the weakening of Ousmane's presidential mandate. In September 1994 the PNDS—Tarayya withdrew from the AFC, and Issoufou resigned as Prime Minister, in protest against the perceived transfer of some of the premier's powers to the President. A period of political instability followed. Unable to form a new coalition, Ousmane dissolved the National Assembly, and parliamentary elections were held on 12 January 1995. Ousmane's CDS increased its representation to 24 seats, while the AFC, having lost the support of the PNDS—Tarayya and also that of the PPN, still held 40 seats. However, it became clear that the MNSD—Nassara, combining its 29 seats with those of its allies, would be able to form a 43-strong majority group in the legislature. Ousmane was then obliged to accept the new majority's nominee, Hama Amadou (the Secretary-General of the MNSD—Nassara) as Prime Minister. The difficulties inherent in the 'cohabitation' situation precipitated an institutional crisis from July 1995, with a dispute over the appointment of new senior executives to state-owned organizations, which subsequently led to an impasse over the delineation of responsibilities between the President and Prime Minister.

On 27 January 1996 the state's democratic institutions were overthrown by the military, under the command of Col (later Brig.-Gen.) Ibrahim Baré Maïnassara, Chief of Staff of the Armed Forces. Declaring a state of emergency to overcome the institutional impasse, the coup leaders forced both the President and the Prime Minister to resign, dissolved the National Assembly, and formed a 12-member Conseil de Salut National (CSN), chaired by Maïnassara. In April the CSN proposed constitutional revisions that aimed to guarantee greater institutional stability, essentially by conferring executive power solely on the President of the Republic and requiring the Prime Minister to implement a programme stipulated by the head of state. The revised Constitution was approved by 92.3% of voters on 12 May; however, reportedly only 35% of the electorate participated. A presidential election was immediately planned under the new Constitution. The suspension of political parties was lifted and Maïnassara confirmed his intention to seek election to the presidency, forming the Union Nationale des Indépendants pour le Renouveau Démocratique (UNIRD), despite earlier assurances that he fostered no personal political ambitions.

Voting in the presidential election took place on 7 and 8 July 1996. Controversy arose when, shortly before the end of voting, the authorities announced the dissolution of the electoral supervisory body, the Commission Electorale Nationale Indépendante (CENI), in response to what they termed its 'obvious and deliberate' obstruction of the electoral process. (Early results had placed Maïnassara last among the candidates.) After a new commission was appointed to collate the election results, Maïnassara was declared the victor, with 52.2% of the votes cast; Ousmane secured 19.8% of the vote and Tandja 15.7%. The losing parties claimed that the vote was rigged by the Maïnassara-appointed CENI.

The Fourth Republic, 1996–99

Maïnassara became President on 7 August 1996, inaugurating the Fourth Republic. The new Government was headed by Boukary Adji, a former finance minister and Deputy Governor of the Banque Centrale des Etats de l'Afrique de l'Ouest. Legislative elections were held on 23 November 1996 and, according to official results, the successor party to the UNIRD, Mainassara's Rassemblement pour la Démocratie et le Progrès (RDP—Djamaa), took 52 of the 83 seats in the National Assembly. All other seats were filled by parties and individuals allied to the RDP, making the National Assembly in effect a single-party organ. Claiming that the electoral process was beset by irregularities, opposition parties, including the CDS, the MNSD—Nassara and the PNDS—Tarayya and five other groupings, boycotted the vote and united in the coalition Front pour la Restauration et la Défense de la Démocratie (FRDD).

The new Government quickly expressed its commitment to the peace process in the north of the country, and Maïnassara pursued negotiations to oversee the process of encampment, disarmament and reintegration of former combatants. Throughout the first half of 1997 several armed groups converged to support the Ouagadougou Agreement, including Ag Boula's Organisation de la Résistance Armée, the Union des Forces de la Résistance Armée (UFRA) led by Mohamed Anacko, and the Tebu-Arab Forces Armées Révolutionnaires du Sahara (FARS). The conclusion of the disarmament process was officially celebrated in Tchintabaraden in October 1997, and in the following month a peace accord was signed in Algeria between the Nigerien Government, the UFRA and the FARS. As part of this process, former rebel leaders were appointed to political and administrative roles: in late 1997 Ag Boula became Minister of Tourism, a position which granted him substantial control over all the informal cross-border trades taking place in the north of the country, while Anacko was appointed High Commissioner of Peace Restoration, a new body tasked with the redistribution of peace dividends. As a result of these developments, in September 2000 more than 1,200 guns, surrendered by the disarmed factions, were ceremoniously burned in Agadez, when Anacko announced the dissolution of several of the rebel groups and militias.

In Niamey, however, the stalemate between the Government and the political opposition contributed to the undermining of the stability of the Fourth Republic. The FRDD organized several protests demanding Maïnassara's resignation, and the trade unions initiated repeated demonstrations, ostensibly in protest against Maïnassara's endorsement of austerity proposals from the IMF. In subsequent years repeated political changes at the head of the Government, as well as international mediation attempts led by France, failed to achieve social peace. The crisis escalated when, following the regional elections of February 1999, which the opposition coalitions had won in most districts, the Supreme Court announced the annulment of results in nearly one-half of the districts, citing the impairment of vote counting by disturbances. In response, on 8 April, opposition parties appealed to the people to rise against Maïnassara. However, the following day Prime Minister Ibrahim Hassane Maiyaki made a broadcast to the nation, announcing the sudden death of Maïnassara in an 'unfortunate accident' at a military airbase in Niamey.

It soon became apparent that Maïnassara had in fact been assassinated by members of his presidential guard, whose head, Maj. Daouda Mallam Wanké, became the leader of a newly instituted military Conseil de Réconciliation Nationale (CRN). Although Niger's donors strongly denounced the apparent coup, as did the Economic Community of West African States (ECOWAS), the CRN assumed the responsibility of exercising executive and legislative authority during a nine-month transitional period in order to draft a new constitution and prepare the transfer of power to civilians. The newly drafted Constitution was approved by 89.6% of those who voted (about one-third of the registered electorate) at a referendum on 18 July 1999. Unlike the 1992 Constitution of the Third Republic, the new Constitution did not permit the President to dissolve the National Assembly for 12 months after an initial dissolution; in addition, an autonomous Constitutional Council was created.

The first round of the presidential election, contested by seven candidates, took place on 17 October 1999. Tandja (MNSD—Nassara) won 32.3% of the votes cast, followed by Issoufou (PNDS—Tarayya), with 22.8%, and former President Ousmane (CDS), with 22.5%. The rate of participation by voters was 43.7%. Having secured the support of Ousmane, Tandja was elected President at a second round of voting, held on 24 November, defeating Issoufou with 59.9% of the votes cast. The MNSD—Nassara was similarly successful in concurrent elections to the National Assembly, winning 38 of the 83 seats; the CDS took 17, the PNDS—Tarayya 16, the RDP eight and the ANDP four.

The Fifth Republic, 1999–2009

Tandja officially assumed the presidency on 22 December 1999, inaugurating the Fifth Republic. Hama Amadou was subsequently appointed Prime Minister, and a new Council of Ministers was announced in January 2000. Departing from the prevailing trend of the 1990s, the Fifth Republic managed to restore a degree of stability and democratic governance to the country over the next few years, and Tandja was successful at the presidential election held on 16 November 2004, winning 40.7% of the votes cast, followed by Issoufou, with 24.6%, and Ousmane, with 17.4%. Tandja succeeded in securing the support of all four eliminated candidates before the second round, which took place on 4 December. As in 1999 elections, Tandja comfortably defeated Issoufou, with 65.5% of the votes cast. The ruling MNSD—Nassara also performed well at concurrent elections to the enlarged 113-member National Assembly, winning 47 seats, while five other parties loyal to Tandja secured a further 41 seats, including 22 taken by the CDS. The opposition PNDS—Tarayya and its allies won a total of 25 seats. Amadou was reappointed to the premiership in late December 2004, and the formation of a new Council of Ministers, composed of members of the MNSD—Nassara and its allies, was announced.

Tandja's presidency was considerably influenced by changing international dynamics, brought about by the 11 September 2001 terrorist attack on the USA and the ensuing 'Global War on Terror' proclaimed by US President George W. Bush.

Niger was one of the key partners in the US counter-terrorism capacity-building programmes, and benefited from US military support. On the other hand, greater international instability generated a dramatic rise of the price of primary commodities, which had a considerable impact on Nigerien politics and on the economy. In mid-March 2005 the Coalition Contre la Vie Chère, comprising trade unions, human rights organizations and consumer movements, organized mass strikes and protests in Niamey, Maradi, Zinder and Tahoua against rising prices. The Government responded with arrests and charges of unauthorized association and plotting against state security.

Tandja's second term was dominated by the resumption of armed hostilities in the north of the country. The resurrection of Tuareg armed militancy in the north of Mali from mid-2006 contributed to the reigniting of the rebellion that was brewing just across the border among the Nigerien Tuareg. In February 2007 the Mouvement Nigérien pour la Justice (MNJ) attacked an army base near Iférouane, some 1,000 km north of Niamey, in which three soldiers were killed. The new rebel movement, led by the Tuareg Aghali Alambo, claimed to fight for the rights of Saharan dwellers, and sought a fairer redistribution of the revenues of uranium mined in northern Niger, and the full implementation of the 1995 Ouagadougou peace agreement terms. Insecurity in northern Niger intensified in mid-2007, leading President Tandja to declare a state of emergency in the region from August.

While endemic violence and sporadic escalations persisted for a couple of years, the rebel front fractured in May 2008, with the creation of a breakaway group, the Front des Forces de Redressement (FFR), led by Mohamed Aoutchiki Kriska (a leading member of the FLT in the 1990s); Rhissa Ag Boula, living in exile in France, was named as the FFR's Commissioner of War, although shortly thereafter, he was convicted *in absentia* in Niamey of allegedly ordering the murder of an MNSD—Nassara activist in January 2004 and sentenced to death. In March 2009 a further split within the MNJ led to the creation of the Front Patriotique du Niger (FPN). Raising hopes for a negotiated end of the rebellion, the FPN requested Libyan mediation to initiate peace negotiations with the Government, which in turn led to Tandja holding talks for the first time with representatives of the three Tuareg groups in May in Agadez. Although no formal peace agreement was ever signed, in the following months the second Tuareg insurrection rapidly subsided, as Qaddafi brokered an end to hostilities This led to an amnesty for the rebels who agreed to disarm, in exchange for generous reintegration packages.

Meanwhile, political developments towards the end of Tandja's second (and constitutionally final) mandate fuelled speculation about the President's intentions. Tandja's relations with Prime Minister Amadou began to deteriorate during the Tuareg rebellion, when the two took divergent positions, with the President adopting a hardline stance against the insurgents (describing them as 'armed bandits' and maintaining that the irredentists were receiving support from France and Libya) and the Prime Minister urging dialogue. The rift was confirmed by the division of the MNSD—Nassara into 'Tandjiste' and 'Hamiste' factions. In May, when the opposition proposed a vote of no confidence against the Prime Minister for his refusal to testify about his role in a scandal regarding education funding, the 'Tandjiste' faction supported the motion, leading to the fall of the Government. Three days later Tandja appointed a new Prime Minister, Seini Oumarou, hitherto Minister of State and Minister of Infrastructure. Amadou retained the chairmanship of the MNSD—Nassara, a position he intended to use to prepare for a presidential candidacy in 2009 (although his immunity from prosecution was lifted in June 2008). Yet it soon appeared that the incumbent President was seeking to circumvent the constitutional provisions on presidential terms limits. In December Prime Minister Oumarou and leading members of the Government were among thousands of participants at a rally in Niamey aimed at securing a three-year extension for Tandja. In February 2009, an extraordinary congress of the MNSD—Nassara designated Oumarou as President of the party, replacing Amadou, whose supporters declared the change of leadership

to be 'illegal' on the grounds that it contravened party regulations.

In the following months Tandja acknowledged that he would be willing to remain in power after the end of his second term, and announced his intention to organize a referendum on the extension of his mandate. Significantly, Tandja's bid for a third term was made official in March during a visit by the French President, Nicolas Sarkozy, theoretically held to celebrate the signature of a new deal granting a notable rise in the price of Niger's uranium sold to Areva. Sarkozy's seeming assent to Tandja's plan stirred controversies and speculation that France had been ready to trade democracy for stability in pursuit of its own strategic interests.

A political crisis swiftly developed over Tandja's referendum plan. The President dissolved the National Assembly, and created a committee to draft a new constitution (of what was to be designated the Sixth Republic) that would enable him to remain in office for a transitional period of three years, if endorsed at a national referendum, scheduled for 4 August. However, the Constitutional Court immediately annulled the decree on the organization of the referendum. Large-scale demonstrations took place in Niamey against Tandja's plan for a referendum, while allies of Amadou announced the formation of a new political party, the Mouvement Démocratique Nigérien pour une Fédération Africaine Moden (Moden/Fa Lumana Africa, FLA), and the CDS withdrew its eight ministers from the Government, stating that it could not be associated with a project deemed illegal by the Constitutional Court. In late June 2009 Tandja assumed emergency powers to rule by decree (claiming that Niger's independence was under threat), suspended the Constitution, dissolved the Constitutional Court, appointed members to a new Constitutional Court and again announced a constitutional referendum. This was eventually held, as scheduled, on 4 August. According to the CENI, 92.5% of those who participated in the vote (68.3% of the electorate, although the figure was widely disputed) were in favour of the new Constitution, which, in addition to prolonging Tandja's mandate by three years, provided for the removal of the limit on presidential terms, the significant expansion of the powers of the President and the creation of a Senate.

From the Sixth Republic to the Transition, 2009–11

The Constitution of the Sixth Republic entered into force on 18 August 2009. Legislative elections took place on 20 October, in spite of a boycott by the main opposition parties and an ECOWAS demand for their indefinite postponement. The MNSD—Nassara secured 76 of the 113 seats, while the Rassemblement Social-Démocratique—Gaskiya (which had been formed following a split in the CDS) won 15 seats, independent candidates 11 and the RDP seven. A turnout of 51.3% was recorded. On the day after the elections ECOWAS suspended Niger's membership pending a restoration of constitutional order, and in November the European Union (EU) suspended development aid to the country. Tens of thousands of protesters attended a demonstration in mid-December in support of demands that Tandja should step down from office by 22 December, when his presidential mandate would have ended under the previous Constitution.

On 18 February 2010 members of the armed forces seized power, capturing President Tandja and his government ministers during an attack on the presidential palace in which some 10 people were killed. Citing the need to resolve Niger's 'tense political situation', the coup leaders formed a Conseil Suprême pour la Restauration de la Démocratie (CSRD), headed by Squadron Commdr Salou Djibo, and announced the suspension of the Constitution and the dissolution of all state institutions. In March Djibo announced the formation of an interim Council of Ministers, largely comprising civilian technocrats, as well as five military officers, and installed a 131-member advisory council for the transitional period—the Conseil Consultatif National (CCN)—chaired by civil society activist Marou Amadou. In April 2010 Djibo appointed a 16-member committee to draft a new constitution, and in May, in an announcement that was welcomed by ECOWAS, the CSRD formally pledged to return power to civilians by 18 February 2011, one year after the power takeover, following a constitutional referendum and local, legislative and presidential elections.

At a referendum held on 31 October 2010 the Constitution of the Seventh Republic, which provided for a five-year presidential term (renewable only once) and an amnesty for the perpetrators of February's coup, was approved by 90.2% of those who participated in the vote (52.7% of the electorate). In the following month Tandja's immunity from prosecution was withdrawn, and in January 2011 the former President was moved from house arrest to prison, after being formally charged with corruption. Municipal and regional elections took place on 11 January. The democratic election of local authorities, a longstanding demand of the northern insurgents, was unprecedented in Niger. On 31 January 2011 legislative and presidential elections took place simultaneously, in the presence of AU, EU and ECOWAS observers, who praised the overall conduct of the elections. Turnout of 51.6% was recorded. Of the National Assembly's 113 seats, the PNDS—Tarayya secured 39, while the MNSD—Nassara won 26 and Moden/FLA 24; six other parties also gained representation. At the presidential election, four of the 10 presidential candidates attracted more than 5% of the votes cast: PNDS—Tarayya leader Issoufou, with 36.2%, former Prime Minister Oumarou, who ran for the MNSD—Nassara, with 23.2%, Hama Amadou of Moden/FLA, with 19.8%, and former President Ousmane, with 8.3%. At the second round, held on 12 March, Issoufou defeated Oumarou, securing 58.0% of the votes cast. Amadou and four other unsuccessful candidates from the first round had declared their support for Issoufou, although Ousmane had notably backed Oumarou. A participation rate of 49.0% was recorded. In March both the AU and ECOWAS lifted Niger's suspension from membership of those organizations.

The Seventh Republic, 2011–

Issoufou was sworn in as President on 7 April 2011, marking a return to civilian rule and the beginning of the Seventh Republic. He immediately appointed as Prime Minister Brigi Rafini, a Tuareg and a member of the RDP, who had served as a government minister under Maïnassara, perhaps in an attempt to assuage tensions still brewing in the north of the country. The 24-member Council of Ministers, formed later in April, was largely composed of members of the PNDS—Tarayya and other parties that had supported Issoufou in the second round of the election, which together held a comfortable legislative majority. Meanwhile, Hama Amadou was elected as President of the National Assembly. Measures aimed at diluting political tensions were among the first acts of the newly installed authorities: in accordance with the new Constitution, in May the National Assembly approved legislation according an amnesty to those responsible for ousting Tandja from office in February 2010, while the Court of Appeal ordered the release of Tandja from prison. The intervention of the judiciary in sensitive political issues became increasingly evident, as the immunity from prosecution of political figures such as Tandja, his entourage and members of the CSRD transitional authorities was revoked in subsequent months and years.

A changing international environment contributed to tempering the development and modernization ambitions of the new Government. On the one hand, the accident that occurred at the nuclear power plant of Fukushima, Japan, in March 2011 significantly constrained the global appetite for nuclear energy investment programmes. The decline in world uranium prices that ensued heavily impacted on Niger's sources of income—as illustrated by the closure of the large Imouraren uranium mine in 2014—and prompted Niamey's increasing reliance on local businessmen and traders. On the other hand, Nigerien authorities were soon forced to adjust their initiatives to a regional security environment which was experiencing a dramatic deterioration. The collapse of the Qaddafi regime in Libya in August 2011 and the eruption, from April 2012, of a Tuareg-led rebellion in Mali exposed Niger to flows of militants and smuggled weapons with the huge potential to fuel local insurgencies. On 23 May 2013 violence spilled over into Niger with the suicide terrorist attacks perpetrated against a military base in Agadez (killing 24 members of the Niger armed forces), and simultaneously against Areva's security personnel

in Arlit (see below). Furthermore, with growing volatility in the Lake Chad basin and in Burkina Faso, providing support to Niger's weak security sector became a major priority of foreign aid and internal budget allocations. The inherent opacity of military procurement, however, prompted allegations of corruption and embezzlement against the Minister of National Defence, Karidjo Mahamadou, one of the founding members of the PNDS—Tarayya, and his intermediaries.

In August 2013 Issoufou announced the formation of a new, more broadly-based Government, which included several opposition members, among them the Secretary-General of the MNSD—Nassara, Abouba Albadé. Rafini was retained as Prime Minister, as were most of the ministers responsible for key portfolios. However, Moden/FLA officially withdrew from the Government later that month in protest against its allocation of portfolios. A new opposition grouping, the Alliance pour la République, la Démocratie et la Réconciliation (ARDR), was formed in October 2013 by some 20 political parties, including the MNSD—Nassara and Moden/FLA, despite the continued participation in the Government of some of their members. However, opposition weakness was made apparent in November when the support of 12 nominally opposition deputies allowed the Government comfortably to defeat a motion of no confidence by 70 votes to 43. The ARDR organized a demonstration in Niamey in December, at which thousands of people protested against corruption, media censorship, living standards and allegedly poor governance.

In early 2014 political tensions mounted as a result of the consolidation of an opposition front, of which Hama Amadou was considered a potential leader. While the ruling coalition sought Amadou's removal from the post of President of the National Assembly, in May 2014 some 40 associates of Amadou were arrested and accused of planning a 'campaign of terror' with the aim of provoking a military coup, only to be released soon afterwards. The arrests followed gunfire at the home of a pro-Government deputy and an attack on the headquarters of the PNDS—Tarayya. In June 17 people, including Amadou's wife, Hadiza Amadou, were arrested as part of an investigation into allegations of child trafficking from Nigeria. Amadou fled to Paris, France, claiming that the investigation was politically motivated, but he was arrested upon his return to Niger in November that year. On 15 December several high-ranking military officers were arrested on suspicion of preparing a coup, allegedly masterminded by Gen. Souleymane Salou, Chief of Staff of the Armed Forces.

On 9 January 2016 the Constitutional Court approved 15 candidates to contest the presidency, including Issoufou, Oumarou and Amadou, although Amadou remained in detention. The Court of Appeal rejected a request from Amadou for conditional release in order to campaign, prompting the national bar association to call a strike against what it denounced as arbitrary detentions and denial of fair process in politically sensitive affairs.

The first round of the presidential election took place on 21 February 2016. With his main adversary in prison, Issoufou promised 'peaceful elections' and expected victory at the first round; however, he was attributed just 48.4% of the vote, with Amadou taking 17.7% and Oumarou 12.1%. Electoral observers from the AU and the Organisation Internationale de la Francophonie (OIF) noted logistical problems during the election. An opposition coalition, the Coalition pour l'Alternance en 2016 (COPA 2016), was formed to support Amadou's candidacy at the run-off election. However, after another failure to secure Amadou's release from detention, and claiming procedural irregularities, COPA 2016 decided to boycott the poll. While Amadou strategically maintained his candidacy, to safeguard the right to lodge appeals against the final results in the post-election period, some of the first-round candidates backed Issoufou.

At the second round, held on 20 March 2016, Issoufou won 92.5% of the vote, with the official turnout reported at some 60% of the electorate. Turnout was, however, much lower according to international observers, who also noticed minor irregularities—and as low as 11% according to COPA 2016. On 22 March COPA 2016 rejected the results as fraudulent, and appealed for a 'résistance citoyenne' (citizen's resistance).

In the legislative elections, held concurrently with the first round of the presidential election, the PNDS—Tarayya and its allies won a majority of 118 seats out of a total of 171. As President-elect with a strong parliamentary majority, Issoufou proposed an inclusive national union government, an offer that was ignored by COPA 2016. On 29 March, with the presidential and legislative electoral process completed, the Court of Appeal finally ruled in favour of the conditional release of Amadou, who upon being freed immediately departed for France. In April a new Council of Ministers, again headed by Rafini as Prime Minister, was announced. With 40 ministers, and a significant number of special advisers, some with ministerial rank, the Government was one of the largest in Niger's history.

The presidential majority was further strengthened when in August 2016 the MNSD, the third largest political party after the PNDS—Tarayya and Moden/FLA, agreed to join the Government. The creation of what President Issoufou termed a 'national unity Government', which comprised 42 ministers, prompted Moden/FLA and 10 other opposition parties, including former President Ousmane's CDS, to establish a new opposition coalition, the Front pour la Restauration de la Démocratie et la Défense de la République (FRDDR).

Local and municipal elections were originally scheduled to take place on 9 May 2016, but were repeatedly rescheduled. In addition to the continued militant activity, the delay was attributed to budgetary constraints, then to the alleged need to establish a biometric registry and to harmonize electoral legislation. The terms of local and municipal elected officials were extended by law and managing administrators were appointed.

As had been the case during his first term, Issoufou's second term was marked by judicial interventions in political affairs, and vice-versa. Shortly after its appointment, the Government indicted three close associates of Amadou for alleged crimes committed in 2004–05 under his premiership, while disregarding more recent allegations of financial misappropriation and corruption scandals that had erupted during Issoufou's first term. In June 2016 Karidjo Mahamadou was appointed as President of the High Court of Justice, the only body constitutionally entrusted with the power to prosecute the President of the Republic, while Hassoumi Massaoudou took his place at the Ministry of Defence. At the same time, three journalists were arrested for publishing documents revealing the perpetration of fraud during the civil service entry examinations, allegedly involving a number of prominent figures, including President Issoufou's second wife, the President of the Constitutional Court, the Chief of Army Staff and the Minister of Petroleum. In early 2017 the Court of Appeal sentenced Amadou to one year in prison, in connection with the 2014 child trafficking affair; Amadou's wife, and former minister Abdou Labo and his wife were also all imprisoned.

A financial scandal erupted in February 2017, when the journal *Le Courrier* published an account of a uranium transaction conducted in November 2011 by the Nigerien branch of Areva, in collaboration with President Issoufou's administration. According to transparency advocates, the operation involved the opaque provision of large commissions amounting to US $100m. to doubtful 'ghost' companies in Lebanon and the Russian Federation, as well as to the President's Office (then headed by Massaoudou). Pressure from civil society groups and the political opposition over what was dubbed 'Uraniumgate' led to the creation of an investigative parliamentary committee in March 2017. Just one month after its installation, however, the committee reported that there had been no breach of legality, with the opposition claiming a 'botched investigation'.

Amid continuing financial difficulties, growing insecurity and alleged corruption scandals, President Issoufou grew increasingly sensitive to criticism, and frequently resorted to repression against his opponents. The Government in April 2017 also ordered the violent repression of protests against scholarship cuts, which had been organized by the Union des Scolaires Nigériens (USN), the national student union, resulting in the death of one student. However, video footage of brutality on the part of the security forces released on social media prompted widespread condemnation, obliging the Government to introduce concessions to appease public indignation.

From October 2017 parliamentary discussion of the 2018 budget law raised the concerns of the political opposition, civil society organizations and Nigerien consumer rights group over a government proposal to increase taxes and the price of consumption goods. A rally on 29 October ended in clashes with the police, damage to public property and the incarceration of some protest leaders. On 26 November 2017, however, the National Assembly approved the budget for 2018, including the proposed tax increases, a substantial rise in the price of electricity and the introduction of new taxes, in accordance with the recommendations of the IMF. Protests against the budget continued into early 2018, with numerous demonstrations taking place in Niamey, Zinder and Dosso. Interior minister Mohamed Bazoum suggested that the anti-budget protests were being orchestrated by Moden/FLA, and alleged that the opposition party planned to seize power through insurrection. Citing security concerns, the police prohibited a rally called by the opposition for 25 March. Nevertheless, the demonstration took place, and 26 leading civil society activists were arrested. Most of them were released later in the year, but these repressive measures overall managed to quell activism against the budget.

In April 2018 Amadou lost his appeal against the one-year prison sentence that he had received in March 2017 for child trafficking. In May 2018 a tentative media campaign inviting Issoufou to run for a third term, in spite of the constitutional provisions outlawing this, was met with harsh repressive countermeasures by Minister of Interior Bazoum (considered the probable candidate to succeed Issoufou). Shortly thereafter Issoufou reiterated that he had no intention of standing for a third presidential mandate. In October 2018 the CENI launched a review of the electoral code, which included a proposed provision barring individuals convicted of one year in prison from contesting the presidency. The opposition believed that the measure explicitly targeted Amadou and boycotted the vote. In February 2019 the PNDS—Tarayya confirmed that Bazoum would be the party's candidate for the next presidential election. Immediately afterwards, Bazoum's main contender within the PNDS—Tarayya, Minister of Finance, Massoudou Hassoumi, resigned in a government reshuffle. In the meantime, Amadou continued to campaign as the opposition leader, obtaining the support of the global Inter-Parliamentary Union forum in March 2019. He returned to Niger in late 2019, but was immediately imprisoned.

The AU summit held in Niamey on 6–8 July 2019 represented the recognition of Niger's renewed diplomatic influence, largely as a result of Issoufou's contribution to the international efforts to combat terrorism and irregular migration. On the one hand, the summit marked the historic entry into force of the African Continental Free Trade Area Agreement (AfCFTA), while on the other hand the public investments linked to the organization of the summit (including the renovation of the airport and the building of new hotels) permanently changed the face of Niamey.

In September 2019 a further governmental reorganization propelled President Issoufou's longstanding supporter, Issoufou Katambé, to the Ministry of National Defence, where he was instructed to carry out a detailed audit of his predecessors' management. The audit identified major shortcomings in the procedures for awarding contracts and monitoring their implementation, revealing many cases of unfulfilled contracts, overcharging and embezzlements between 2014 and 2019, with an overall public loss estimated at 76,000m. francs CFA. (The actual figure may be higher, as inspectors were unable to examine international donors and external operations funds because they were not subject to public procurement procedures.) When rumours about the report spread in early 2020, the case became incendiary, as it prompted allegations of corruption and embezzlement against former Ministers of National Defence and key PNDS—Tarayya figures Karidjo Mahamadou and Kalla Moutari, who were in office, respectively, during most of Issoufou's first and second term. In mid-March civil society groups organized a rally demanding that the case be brought to court. Clashes between protesters and the police resulted in the incarceration of eight civil society leaders and the killing of three demonstrators, but in April the Government eventually agreed to launch a judicial procedure.

In the meantime, the global COVID-19 pandemic reached Niger in late March 2020. The number of confirmed COVID-19 cases peaked in December, then slowing down during the first half of 2021. The preventive measures adopted by the Government focused on the prohibition of mass gatherings, including political rallies and collective prayers, with the suppression of violations, prompting accusations of authoritarianism and anti-Islamic conduct. At the same time, as prisons were regarded as potential incubators of the virus, decongestion measures that were adopted led to the release of opposition leaders, including Amadou. Later, Niger also participated in the global vaccination campaign against COVID-19. By mid-2021 the country had reportedly received 780,000 vaccine doses, approximately one-half of which were provided through Chinese bilateral co-operation, and one-half through the COVAX Facility mechanism of the World Health Organization. Although the programme suffered from equipment shortages and lack of awareness, resulting in delays and inconsistencies, it arguably helped slow down the progress of the virus within Niger. In June 2021 the Government reopened Niger's borders, and a dramatic rise in COVID-19 cases in December caused fewer fatalities than in the previous year. At 13 October 2022 a total of 9,416 COVID-19 cases had been recorded in Niger, with 314 reported deaths, while approximately 12% of the population had been fully vaccinated.

The 2020–21 Elections

As the end of Issoufou's second mandate neared, a presidential election was scheduled to take place before the end of 2020. In November the Constitutional Court rejected 11 of the 41 presidential candidacies received, including that of Amadou, owing to his previous prison sentence. Controversy over alleged political interference proved shortlived, and eventually Amadou urged his supporters to rally behind the Renouveau Démocratique et Républicain—Tchanji (RDR—Tchanji) party newly formed by Ousmane.

The first round of the presidential election, together with legislative elections, took place on 27 December 2020, following the long-delayed local and municipal elections on 13 December. A voter turnout of 69.7% was recorded in the presidential poll. Bazoum, representing the PNDS—Tarayya, was placed first with 39.3% of the votes cast, followed by Ousmane of the RDR—Tchanji (with 17.0%), Oumarou of the MNSD—Nassara (with 9.0%), Albadé Abouba of the Mouvement Patriotique pour la République (MPR—Jamhuriya, with 7.1%) and Ibrahim Yacouba of the Mouvement Patriotique Nigérien (MPN—Kiishin Kassa, with 5.4%). The results were only validated by the Constitutional Court on 30 January 2021. Eventually, both Oumarou and Abouba, respectively the third- and fourth-placed candidates, decided to support Bazoum, although the late endorsement indicated long unofficial negotiations. In the concurrent legislative elections, the PNDS—Tarayya secured 79 of the 166 contested seats in the National Assembly (voting for the five seats allocated to the Nigerien diaspora did not take place), while Amadou's Moden/FLA obtained 19 seats, the MPR—Jamhuriya 14 and the MNSD—Nassara 13.

The second round of the presidential election between Bazoum and Ousmane took place on 21 February 2021. The official turnout was 62.9%. Violent incidents occurred in remote parts of the country where jihadist insurgencies continued, including the killing of seven electoral officials by a landmine in the region of Tillabéri. Apart from these incidents, however, the electoral observer missions that were deployed by the AU and the Community of Sahel–Saharan States considered the conditions of the polls to be 'satisfying', although it was later acknowledged that the international observers were only stationed in the main towns, and failed to monitor remote and rural areas effectively. In the regions of Tahoua and Agadez, in fact, significant irregularities reportedly occurred.

On 23 February 2021 the CENI proclaimed Bazoum to be the winner of the election, with 55.7% of the votes cast. Denouncing irregularities, Ousmane's campaign director urged the population to mobilize against what he described as 'electoral robbery'. The call precipitated rioting in the capital in which at least two people were killed, with protesters burning tyres, damaging shops, assaulting foreign journalists and attacking the headquarters of pro-Bazoum parties. During subsequent days the riots escalated across Niamey, and to other southern towns, including Zinder and Dosso. Ousmane himself did not explicitly condone the eruption of violence, while he challenged the results issued by the CENI at the Constitutional Court and maintained that he was the actual winner, with 50.3% of the votes in his favour.

The Government's response to the violent unrest led to hundreds of arrests, including that of Amadou, who was transferred to the high-security prison of Filingué, and former army Chief of Staff Moumouni Boureima, who was suspected of plotting a military coup. By 28 February 2021 the protests had been largely quelled across the whole country, although opposition parties and civil society organizations continued to dispute the outcome of the elections.

On 21 March 2021 the Constitutional Court confirmed the election results and declared Bazoum President-elect. On 22 March Ousmane appealed to the opposition not to participate in the National Assembly, and to the army to disregard orders coming from an 'illegal and illegitimate' authority. On the night of 30–31 March heavy gunfire targeted the presidential palace in Niamey, in what Bazoum later declared to have been an attempted coup. The attack prompted the arrest of some dissident officers of the armed forces, led by Capt. Sani Saley Gourouza.

Bazoum's Presidency

On 2 April 2021 Bazoum was sworn in as the new President of the Republic. The ceremony took place at a newly constructed conference building in Niamey, in the presence of international heads of state and government. The attendance of the Turkish Vice-President, Fuat Oktay, was particularly notable, demonstrating the development of Niger's new partnerships and alliances.

On 3 April 2021 Bazoum appointed Ouhoumoudou Mahamadou, a prominent member of the PNDS—Tarayya and President Issoufou's former Director of the Cabinet, as Prime Minister. On 7 April Mahamadou announced the composition of his new Government, which comprised 33 ministers, including five women (well below the legally required minimum 30% representation). The MNSD—Nassara was allocated four ministries, in addition to the appointment of its leader, Oumarou, as President of the National Assembly, and the MPR—Jamhuriya five ministries. The PNDS—Tarayya maintained control of key ministries, through the appointment of the party's most prominent leaders: Alkassoum Indattou became Minister of National Defence, Hassoumi Massaoudou Minister of State, Minister of Foreign Affairs and Co-operation, and Alkache Alhada Minister of Interior and Decentralization. The appointment of Issoufou's son, Mahamane Sani Mahamadou, to the crucial Ministry of Petroleum, Energy and Renewable Energy Sources reflected the legacy and influence of the former President on the early tenure of Bazoum.

President Bazoum's first year in office was characterized by an attempt to signal good intentions in promoting good governance. Expectations by influential international partners, including the issuance in April 2021 of a new EU Sahel Strategy based on good governance, arguably contributed to shaping this approach. Yet domestic political constraints led to ambiguities and hesitations in its implementation, particularly in the fight against corruption and impunity, which was among Bazoum's proclaimed priorities. On the one hand, the new President authorized the arrest and trial of long-unpunished prominent figures, including a Nigerien drug trafficking leader in March, and senior public officers allegedly involved in large-scale embezzlement in July. Further high-profile arrests followed in early 2022, including of the mayor of Dirkou for alleged involvement in drug trafficking, and of the Minister of Communication for corruption. On the other hand, some of the most politically sensitive trials inherited from Issoufou's tenure stalled, such as those against the alleged perpetrators of abuses against civilians in the army, and of large-scale embezzlement at the Ministry of Defence. A similar ambivalence characterized Bazoum's relationship with the political and social opposition. While the President exhibited a commitment to dialogue by promoting participatory forums and by expanding the legal guarantees to freedom of expression, legislative and executive measures were taken to ensure a stricter control on civil society organizations and independent media. Overall, expectations of radical changes during Issoufou's tenure were frustrated, as the former President's power networks retained considerable influence.

On the international front, the new President and his Government manifested their resolve to co-operate with international partners in curbing jihadist terrorism in the Sahel. As the only head of state of the G5 Sahel to join the July 2021 summit in Paris, Bazoum strongly criticized the rising nationalism of the Malian military junta (see *The Rise of Violent Extremism*). Yet in November the resupply of French forces in Mali through Niger triggered violent demonstrations in Tera, resulting in three civilian casualties, and demonstrating the unpopularity of a French military presence among the Nigerien people. The issue proved to be highly consequential a few months later, when acute diplomatic tensions precipitated the withdrawal of the French army from Mali from February 2022, and French President Emmanuel Macron announced that Niger would become the new focus for the French forces in the Sahel. Bazoum struggled to persuade his party and the Nigerien public in general of the benefits of a deployment of additional French and European forces in the country. The harsh polarization that ensued led to a vote of confidence on the Government's general policy in late April, which the PNDS and its allies won by a large majority. In the process, the MPN—Kiishin Kassa joined the parliamentary majority and the Government, with the appointment of four ministers from the party. MPN—Kiishin Kassa leader Ibrahim Yacouba became Minister of State, Minister of Energy and Renewable Energy Sources, thereby leaving Mahamane Sani Mahamadou with only the petroleum portfolio. Meanwhile, the ECOWAS Court of Justice in May rejected a case against Niger brought by the unsuccessful presidential candidate Ousmane, thereby further marginalizing the political opposition.

Building on the consolidation of its domestic authority, the Government continued the development of international partnerships to further its own security policy. In the first half of 2022 Niger received significant military equipment from Turkey, including six drone aircraft, while in July the EU allocated €25m. through the newly established European Peace Facility to increase the capacities of the Nigerien armed forces. At the same time, with a view to encouraging jihadists to negotiate, the Government implemented confidence-building measures and reintegration schemes.

NIGER IN THE 21ST CENTURY: SECURITY CHALLENGES

The Rise of Violent Extremism

Since the beginning of the 21st century, the rise of violent extremism (i.e. of armed groups boasting Islamist credentials and determined militarily to overthrow incumbent governments in the name of militant Salafism) has represented one of the major security challenges across the entire Sahelian region. Salafist armed groups of Algerian origin began targeting Saharan and Sahelian states when they were expelled from Algeria, and the rise of violent extremism in Niger was part of this dynamic. In early 2004, for instance, the Islamist militants belonging to the Algerian-based Groupe Salafiste pour la Prédication et le Combat (GSPC) attacked a group of tourists in northern Niger. Subsequent attacks took place mostly in Mali and Mauritania, and only resurfaced in Niger in the context of the second Tuareg rebellion, which had undermined governmental control over the northern regions. The abduction, in December 2008, of the UN Secretary-General's special envoy to Niger, Robert Fowler, his assistant and their driver about 40 km north-west of Niamey, near the border with Mali, was followed in January 2009 by that of four European tourists, also in the border area. In February al-Qa'ida in the Islamic Maghreb (AQIM, as the GSPC had been restyled) claimed to be holding those kidnapped; the driver was released in March and the diplomats and two of the tourists in April, all in Mali, where they had been held, raising strong suspicions that a ransom had been paid. The same group was subsequently believed to have killed the British hostage, but released the Swiss national in July. In late 2009 a Salafist

militant attacked and killed four Saudi Arabian tourists in northern Niger.

Amid increasing concern regarding the activities of AQIM, in April 2010 Algeria, Mali, Mauritania and Niger agreed on a plan for co-operation in combating terrorism and cross-border crime, and established a joint military command headquartered in the southern Algerian town of Tamanrasset to co-ordinate intelligence gathering and patrols in border areas. In the same month, however, a French national and his Algerian driver were abducted in northern Niger, near the Algerian border, with AQIM subsequently claiming responsibility; the driver was released later that month, but the French citizen was killed in Mauritania in July. In mid-September seven foreigners who were employees of Areva and one of its contractors (five French nationals, one Togolese and one Malagasy) were kidnapped near the northern Nigerien town of Arlit, before being transferred by their captors to Mali; AQIM claimed responsibility for the abductions. The French Government deployed 80 military personnel to Niamey to assist in the search for the hostages. Three of them (the two Africans and a French woman) were released in February 2011. The four remaining French nationals were eventually released in October 2013, following mediation by Nigerien officials including the former Tuareg rebel leader Mohamed Akotey; the French Government denied having paid a ransom for the hostages' release, although reports suggested that their captors had received €20m. In the mean time, in January 2011 an AQIM commando kidnapped two French nationals in Niamey, who were killed in the pursuit and liberation attempt by French special forces.

Since early 2012 the capture of northern Mali by a coalition of Tuareg insurgents and jihadist groups, including AQIM, has raised widespread fears of contagion in Niger. In aiming to prevent a spill-over from Mali, President Issoufou was, from mid-2012, a vocal supporter of a proposed regional military intervention in Mali. When this was launched in December, Niger contributed troops to the African-led International Support Mission in Mali (AFISMA). In January 2013 the French military commenced its own intervention, Operation Serval, against the Islamist militants, who now held sole control of much of northern Mali, having expelled the Tuareg separatists. This marked the official return of the French military to Niger, with Niamey becoming a logistical base for Operation Serval and its air force. The USA also contributed to Operation Serval with intelligence and drone capabilities, thereby gaining the opportunity to progressively increase its military presence in Niger, which shortly thereafter included not only a base in Niamey, but also one in Agadez and another in Dirkou, operated by the Central Intelligence Agency. President Issoufou confirmed in early February that French special forces were also protecting the Areva uranium mine near Arlit. The Malian, French and African forces had ousted the Islamists from the main towns of northern Mali by March, and AFISMA was reconstituted as a UN peacekeeping mission, the UN Multidimensional Integrated Stabilization Mission in Mali (MINUSMA), in July.

In May 2013 Niger suffered simultaneous suicide bombings at a military barracks in Agadez and at the uranium mining company Société des Mines de l'Aïr (SOMAÏR), a subsidiary of Areva partly owned by the Nigerien state, in Arlit. The veteran AQIM leader, Mokhtar Belmokhtar, claimed responsibility for the attacks on the behalf of his new splinter group the Mouvement pour l'Unicité et le Jihad en Afrique de l'Ouest (MUJAO), stating that the bombings were in retaliation for Nigerien and French military action against MUJAO and other Islamist insurgents in Mali. Following the eviction of Islamist groups from the main town in northern Mali, France replaced Operation Serval with the 3,000-strong, multi-country Operation Barkhane (later expanded to 5,100 military personnel) in order to enlarge its counter-terrorism operation to the entire Sahel region. Operation Barkhane, which was headquartered in Chad, commenced its missions in August 2014, and secured a mandate to operate across Mali, Niger and Chad, with most of the French troops stationed in northern Mali, and Niger retaining the role of logistical hub. A few days after the announcement of the new deployment the French President, François Hollande, made a state visit to Niger, during which six bilateral co-operation agreements were signed.

Meanwhile, the Nigerien authorities were confronted with the rise of a new front of violent Islamist militantism, with the expansion of Boko Haram activities across the Lake Chad region from Nigeria into Niger's south-eastern Diffa region. The need for co-operative efforts to curb cross-border insecurity thus became increasingly evident. In November 2013 the Governments of Niger and Nigeria agreed to establish a Joint Border Patrol Command. In May 2014 Issoufou and the Presidents of Benin, Cameroon, Chad, France and Nigeria pledged to share intelligence and co-ordinate action against Boko Haram, and in July the member states of the Lake Chad Basin Commission gathered in Niamey where they pledged to accelerate the planned creation of a 2,800-strong multinational force to restore order in the region, to which each country would contribute 700 troops.

The humanitarian and security situation in the impoverished region of Diffa further deteriorated, as a result of the sharp increase in refugee flows from Nigeria after August 2014. The Nigerien Government eventually accepted the establishment of three refugee camps by the Office of the UN High Commissioner for Refugees (UNHCR), following reluctance owing to concerns that such camps might become either targets for Boko Haram attacks or be used as bases by the militants. In early January 2015 Boko Haram attacked and overran the Nigerian troops affiliated to the multinational joint task force headquartered in Baga (Borno State), Nigeria. The offensive lasted four days, causing mass killings, the destruction of the surrounding villages and the forcible displacement of an estimated 20,000 locals. The event prompted the mobilization of Chadian troops, who arrived in the Nigerien town of Bosso on 4 February with the intention to recapture Baga. In response, Boko Haram launched land attacks and shelled Diffa and Bosso, and carried out a number of suicide attacks in Diffa on 7 February, prompting the population to evacuate the town. On 9 February Niger's National Assembly unanimously approved legislation authorizing the President to dispatch 750 combat troops to Diffa and to Nigeria. A 15-day state of emergency was also declared in the region. Nevertheless, in late April Boko Haram staged a massive attack on the Karamga island on the Nigerien side of Lake Chad. After at least 46 soldiers and 28 civilians were killed by Boko Haram rebels, the Government ordered the forcible evacuation of the 25,000-strong population of the island, which further aggravated the humanitarian crisis in the region. The response by Niger authorities, which included mass arrests of those who refused to co-operate, attracted the criticism of human rights and humanitarian organizations, to which the Government responded aggressively by threatening to withdraw their permission to operate.

Overall, between 2015 and mid-2017 Boko Haram attacks killed 319 civilians in Niger, primarily by retaliating against individuals that Boko Haram believed to have collaborated with the authorities or the families of members who had fled the movement. On 3 June 2016 Boko Haram militancy in Niger culminated with a large-scale assault on Bosso. The attack forced Nigerien troops to retreat, leaving at least 34 soldiers dead, while the complete destruction of the town forced the displacement of tens of thousands of civilians. While other attacks, smaller in scale, occurred in the following weeks, an overall decline of Boko Haram activities in Niger was recorded from the second half of 2016 onwards. Several possible factors could account for this outcome: the strengthening of the military support provided by French, US and Chadian forces to Nigerien authorities in the Diffa region; the greater effectiveness of the strategy against Boko Haram by the newly installed Nigerian authorities; or the split inside Boko Haram with recognition by the transnational Islamic State group of the splinter faction led by Abu Musab al-Barnawi, which styled itself as the Islamic State West Africa Province (ISWAP). In subsequent years ISWAP focused mainly on Nigeria, and became known as Islamic State's strongest external affiliate.

In 2017 and 2018 attacks—while limited in number—mostly targeted internally displaced persons and refugee camps, most notably in the area of Kablewa, raising concerns among the host population. In late 2017 the Government launched an ambitious program of 'deradicalization'. Representatives of local authorities and of the central government, including interior minister Bazoum, convened a solemn ceremony in Diffa and appealed for the social reintegration of the Nigerien youth who had joined Boko Haram, offering an amnesty in exchange for the cessation of the hostilities. However, in early June 2018 suicide bomb attacks occurred in Diffa at three different locations in the regional capital. The attack, which was carried out in the Islamic holy month of Ramadan, targeted religious sites—a mosque and a Koranic school—during evening prayers, and killed 10 people. From 2019 onwards, operations by Boko Haram and ISWAP in Niger remained relatively contained. Together with a series of low-intensity clashes along border areas, attacks focused mainly on Niger's security forces positions, including an attack on a Nigerien military checkpoint in Bilabrin in May 2020, which reportedly killed 12 soldiers and injured several more.

In May 2021 clashes between Boko Haram and ISWAP in Nigeria led to the death of Boko Haram's longstanding leader, Imam Muhammad Abubakar Shekau, and further eroded the capacity of the group to carry out armed incursions across the border. In subsequent months repeated clashes took place in the Lake Chad region between ISWAP and the remnants of Shekau's loyalists who were grouped under the Ba Koura faction. This conflict weakened both groups, and resulted in the deaths of commanders such as Bako Gorgore, Muhammad Mustapha, Mallam Baba, and most notably ISWAP's main leader, Abu Musab al-Barnawi. The dismantling of the jihadist insurrection's leadership in the Lake Chad region has contributed to securing Niger's border, paving the way for the recapture of territory by local state forces. Joint military efforts in early 2022 reportedly led to the killing of several hundred alleged jihadists who had been in hiding around the Lake Chad, mostly in Nigeria. The modicum of stability thus achieved increased the determination of the Nigerien authorities to implement the return of internally displaced families in Diffa. A much-publicized return of approximately 25,000 internally displaced residents to Diffa's villages had begun in June 2021, with the resettlement of 1,800 families in Baroua. Capitalizing on these dynamics, Bazoum has claimed a 'victory against Boko Haram' as a landmark achievement of his presidency, although independent observers questioned the Government's figures on resettlements and returns in Diffa.

Meanwhile, in late October 2014 the simultaneous attacks on the region of Tillabéry, some 50 km north-west of Niamey, opened up a new jihadist front in Niger. While initially unclaimed, the attacks were subsequently attributed to a new splinter jihadist faction led by Abu Walid al-Saharawi, a former leader of MUJAO and longtime right-hand man of Belmokhtar. In subsequent months al-Saharawi's group gained a clear jihadist status, culminating in October 2016 when the official press agency of Islamic State accepted the allegiance of the new group, which was then renamed Islamic State of the Greater Sahara (ISGS). In the same month ISGS staged a successful attack against the security garrison of a Malian refugee camp at Tazalit, in the region of Tahoua, killing 22 gendarmes and soldiers.

The continued attacks and soaring levels of violence across the region prompted a review of the counter-terrorism tactics used to confront ISGS, and from mid-2017 Nigerien authorities increasingly relied on both the support of French and US air forces, as well as pro-governmental, non-state Malian armed groups as ground forces. These included most notably the Tuareg-based armed groups the Mouvement pour le Salut de l'Azawad (MSA) and the Group Autodéfense Touareg Imghad et Alliés (GATIA). However, this actually provoked an escalation of violence. The rhetoric of jihadism and of counter-terrorism led to a dramatic rise in communal conflicts between the Tuareg and the Fulani, and abuses against civilians began to increase with the commencement of joint MSA-GATIA-French military operations. In October ISGS gained international prominence when four US special troopers as well as four Nigerien soldiers deployed in the region of Tillabéry were ambushed and killed by al-Saharawi's men.

These developments prompted an increasing hesitation by France and the USA to commit their own troops or to rely on the support of local non-state armed groups for ground operations. In addition to the weakness of Sahelian state armies, in Niger, as well as in neighbouring countries, the situation gave ISGS an opportunity progressively to gain territory in the borderlands straddling Niger, Mali and Burkina Faso. The Government's contested hold on its western provinces also precipitated a resumption of terrorist kidnappings, including of a German aid worker in April 2018 and an Italian priest in September. The latter was eventually released in Mali in October 2020, as part of a larger exchange of prisoners negotiated by Jama'at Nusrat al-Islam wal-Muslimeen (JNIM—Group for Support of Islam and Muslims), a jihadist group affiliated to AQIM. (The former was only released from Mali in August 2022.)

In March 2019 Islamic State officially proclaimed the incorporation of ISGS within ISWAP. However, subsequent months were marked by an unprecedented escalation of violence in the tri-border area of Liptako-Gourma. ISGS claimed responsibility for attacks that killed 28 Nigerien soldiers in May, 24 Burkinabé soldiers in August and 49 Malian soldiers in November, culminating with an onslaught against the Nigerien military camp of Chinégodar in January 2020, in which 89 soldiers were killed—the largest number of fatalities ever suffered by the Nigerien army.

Worried by the increasing incidence and violence of terrorist attacks in the region, Macron and his Sahelian counterparts convened in Pau, France, in January 2020, and agreed to reinvigorate counter-terrorism operations, targeting primarily ISGS operations in the tri-border area. Renewed international efforts, combining with infighting against JNIM, forced ISGS to reduce the level of its activities throughout 2020. Avoiding major attacks on military targets, ISGS exploited local populations, professing religious credentials to legitimize extortionary practices. However, as soon as the military pressure subsided, owing to the refocusing of Operation Barkhane towards JNIM in Mali, ISGS began reprisal attacks against Nigerien communities. In early 2021 ISGS thus claimed responsibility for unprecedented massacres targeting local populations, including villages in Tondikiwindi in January, and Banibangou and Tilia in March, with a total of more than 260 civilian victims overall. The Nigerien forces' inability to protect civilians prompted local populations in the Agadez, Tahoua and Tillabéry regions to set up community-based self-protection militias. The move proved contentious, forcing the Nigerien authorities to balance the competing needs of preventing an escalation in communal violence on the one hand, and maintaining a fragile ethnic equilibrium in the security apparatus on the other.

In subsequent months, however, a series of successful counter-terrorism operations by French, US and Nigerien forces—which also benefited from continued infighting between ISGS and JNIM—effectively netutralized the ISGS leadership, and considerably curtailed the capability of the group. Over the course of mid-2021 some of the most prominent senior commanders of the group were captured or killed, including its overall leader, Abu Walid al-Saharawi himself, who was killed in a French bombing in August. JNIM promptly took advantage of ISGS's difficulties in reconstituting a new leadership, and made inroads in Tillabéry. Following JNIM's first attack in Torodi in July, clashes between Nigerien forces and JNIM escalated in the south-west of the Tillabéry region in the first half of 2022. Meanwhile, ISGS appeared to have refocused its efforts in the Malian regions bordering Niger, where heavy clashes with Malian forces and aligned armed groups took place during the first half of 2022. The official propaganda of Islamic State has attributed these actions to a newly branded 'Islamic State Sahel Province', suggesting greater autonomy of local militants from ISWAP.

The recognition that violent extremism thrives in the remote borderland of fragile Sahelian states has led governments in the region, and Niger in particular, to place an increasing emphasis on enhanced border controls. To this end, in February 2014 President Issoufou and his counterparts from Burkina Faso, Chad, Mali and Mauritania announced plans to create the Group of Five Sahel Countries (later to be known as the G5 Sahel), a framework to promote cross-border co-operation on regional security matters in view of the ongoing

threat from Islamist militants. The project attracted some initial scepticism at the AU level given the exclusion of Algeria, which shares a long desert border with G5 Sahel countries, yet it gained traction due to the commitment of France, which in turn managed to mobilize the EU. In June 2017 the Security Council unanimously adopted a resolution welcoming the establishment of a G5 Sahel force for anti-terrorism purposes. The resolution, however, fell short of a formal endorsement of a specific mandate as well as funding commitments, owing to the scepticism of the USA and the newly installed Administration of Donald Trump. Drawing on the financial support of bilateral donors (including most notably the EU, France, the USA, Saudi Arabia and the United Arab Emirates), the first operational battalion was nevertheless deployed in November 2017 in the tri-border areas of Mali, Niger and Burkina Faso. Further joint operations in the same area were carried out in subsequent months, with the aim of tackling the rise of violent extremist groups in the central Sahel. In June 2018, however, the joint G5 Sahel military command based in Sévaré, Mali, suffered a suicide terrorist attack, in which three people were killed, and which led to a significant downscaling of its activities during the second half of 2018. While the G5 Sahel countries agreed to relocate the joint force command to the Malian capital, Bamako, several shortcomings continued to undermine the functioning of the G5 Sahel joint force, including a structural lack of funding and major bureaucratic complexities. The poor military performance and human rights abuses demonstrated by some local troops on the ground raised further doubts. While Malian and Burkinabé forces were initially implicated, subsequent investigations led by the UN and human rights organizations alleged that Nigerien forces were also responsible for cases of torture and extrajudicial killings since at least 2019.

Acknowledging the limits of a purely security-oriented approach to anti-terrorism, Niger, having assumed the rotating presidency of the G5 Sahel, placed a greater emphasis on development, and fostered the drafting of a G5 Sahel development strategy (which, in turn, was largely inspired by the EU Strategy for Security and Development in the Sahel). In December 2018 the international partners of the G5 Sahel pledged €2,400m. for the implementation of stabilization projects as part of the G5 Sahel development strategy 2019–21. The election of Joe Biden to the US presidency in 2020 led to greater US and NATO involvement from 2021 in providing assistance to the G5 Sahel joint military efforts. Yet at the same time the seizure of power by a military junta in Mali precipitated diplomatic tensions and undermined security co-operation. The proliferation of undemocratic power transitions in the region prompted President Bazoum to claim in a May 2022 interview that 'the G5 Sahel is dead'.

Acknowledging the limits of existing security co-operation schemes, European leaders sought to reconsider their strategic assistance to Sahelian countries. In early 2020 the creation of Task Force Takuba was announced, a grouping that was to consist of a few hundred European special forces under French command, and focus on the Liptako-Gourma area. The full deployment of Takuba was deferred to 2021, owing to the COVID-19 pandemic. In June Macron eventually announced the 'remodulation' of French military efforts in the Sahel, and the progressive scale-down of Operation Barkhane, with around one-half of its forces to remain in the region. From early 2022 the stance of the Malian junta and its increasing reliance on Russian military contractors fuelled an increasing deterioration in its relations with France and the wider international community, which precipitated the withdrawal of European military forces from Mali. In April Niger agreed to host the headquarters of the restructured Operation Barkhane, which fully withdrew from Mali in mid-August, while the discontinuation of Takuba was announced in June.

The Rise of Extralegal Economies

Niger's effective sovereignty over its northernmost territories has always been problematic. Throughout the past decade, however, the degradation of local and regional security—including initially during the second Tuareg rebellion of 2007–09, and then as a result of the destabilization of Libya since 2011—has contributed to the further erosion of Niamey's grip over its outer provinces, and the region of Agadez in particular. The limited capacity of control by Nigerien authorities has made Niger's borderlands a fertile ground for the consolidation of extralegal economies grafted onto cross-border flows of goods and people. These, however, have become progressively entrenched in Niger's social and political fabric as a result of patronage politics.

In the 1980s and 1990s northern Niger developed a thriving smuggling economy with subsidized goods entering Niger from northern African countries while trafficked cigarettes departed in the opposite direction. This was largely tolerated by local communities and central authorities as a valuable and relatively harmless source of jobs, cheap commodities and societal resilience. During the 2000s the Sahara Desert, and Niger in particular, progressively became a hub of the global drug trafficking supply chain, including hashish from Morocco and cocaine from Latin America. These flows were upscaled during the second Tuareg rebellion, benefiting from the insecurity prevailing in the northern regions of both Mali and Niger and from the connections between Malian and Nigerien traffickers. The large amounts of money thus accumulated were partly reinvested by local drug barons in real estate and transport companies (and investigations triggered by the so-called Panama Papers leak have raised suspicions about the sudden wealth of some among Niger's most successful businesses). At the same time, illicit profits were also used to pay for protection and political connivance at the highest levels. Major hashish seizures in Niger, including 10 metric tons from Morocco in April 2018 and 17 tons from Lebanon in March 2021, suggest that the country continues to harbour major drug flows. However, investigations and prosecutions have also been undertaken against the networks enabling these activities, and may be indicative of the Nigerien authorities' efforts to regain control over the country's porous borders.

Meanwhile, the downfall of the Qaddafi regime and the eruption of conflicts in neighbouring countries made Niger a fertile ground for the development of another type of illicit trafficking, namely of weapons. During mid-2011 large-scale flows of weapons transited Niger (mainly coming from Libya and heading for Mali). The massive military convoys were headed by Malian and Nigerien leaders of the former Tuareg rebellions, who were subsequently recruited into Qaddafi's security apparatus. The Nigerien Government was reluctant to acknowledge the ongoing regime change in Libya, and only in August formally recognized the National Transitional Council, which had been established in Libya by the anti-Qaddafi forces in February as the official authority representing the Libyan people. In September 2011 the Nigerien Government confirmed that more than 30 Qaddafi loyalists, including one of his sons, Saadi Gaddafi, had been permitted to enter Niger from Libya on humanitarian grounds. In October, as Nigerien Tuareg leaders were reported to have joined the meeting in the Adrar mountains which resulted in the creation of the MNLA (Mouvement de Libération de l'Azawad) and the ignition of the uprising in north Mali, Issoufou expressed concern that the renewed Tuareg insurgency in that country would spread to Niger. In an effort to avert such an eventuality, the Government, in partnership with the EU, immediately announced a five-year development and security strategy for the Sahel-Saharan regions of northern Niger, as well as a reintegration project providing income-generating skills and job opportunities to reabsorb (at least part of) the Nigerien diaspora returning from Libya. However, it was widely held that it was the defeat of the MNLA by jihadist forces in June 2012 that ultimately brought an end to the restiveness of some former Nigerien Tuareg rebel leaders. At the request of the Nigerien authorities, in July the EU authorized the deployment of EUCAP (EU Capacity Building Mission) Sahel Niger, a civilian mission mandated to support the implementation of Niger's security and development strategy by supporting the Nigerien security forces in their efforts to combat terrorism and organized crime, with a particular emphasis on rule of law, criminal investigation, forensic techniques and intelligence. Throughout 2013 and 2014 arms trafficking through Niger declined considerably, largely as a result of the interdiction and surveillance activities carried out by Operation Serval and Operation Barkhane.

In addition to the trafficking of drugs and weapons, the smuggling of migrants has become particularly prominent in Niger. Since the beginning of Libya's second civil war in 2014, the combination of border porosity in Niger, forbearance by local authorities, poor law enforcement in Libya and an economic downturn in many African countries, concurred to make Niger the main hub of the northbound smuggling of migrants en route from West Africa to Europe, via Libya and Italy. The northern Nigerien town of Agadez, in particular, became a crossing point of primary importance, through which it was estimated that more than one-half of the total number of refugees and migrants who reached Italian shores had passed. The growing demand of international mobility greatly stimulated the (informal) job market in Agadez. However, facing international pressure to ensure a more rigorous governance of migration and to curb irregular flows, in May 2015 the National Assembly of Niger adopted a law (Loi 036-2015) against illicit migrant smuggling. Drafted with the assistance of EUCAP Sahel Niger and the International Organization for Migration (IOM), the legislation introduced severe penalties for a variety of offences connected to migrant smuggling. Owing to widespread local perceptions of migration as socially acceptable and economically profitable, however, the Government was unwilling to implement the widely unpopular legislation prior to the 2016 elections. It was only in late 2016, after the PNDS—Tarayya had secured the control of key institutions and the EU had introduced aid conditionalities through the Migration Partnership Framework, that Loi 036-2015 began to be implemented, albeit reluctantly.

In July 2016 the Government adopted a national strategy to fight irregular migration, while EUCAP Sahel Niger was extended (and its budget considerably increased) and given the additional mandate of assisting Niger in addressing irregular migration and associated criminal activities, while the establishment of a permanent field office in Agadez was also authorized. By the end of 2016 many Agadez-based prominent smugglers had fled or had been convicted (although many managed to obtain short sentences or early release). In 2017 overall the migrant flows observed in Agadez fell sharply to 70,000. In 2019, however, migrant numbers rose again, to 187,000, although remaining well below the volume observed in 2016. Explanations for this fluctuation vary, ranging from an improvement in economic conditions in Libya, to the strengthening of migration data collection, to a relaxation of widely unpopular restrictions prior to the 2020 presidential and legislative elections. These developments concurred with emerging reports that alternative migration routes were being used, transporting migrants in smaller numbers and away from the main roads in order to escape detection.

Niger has become one of the primary beneficiaries of the EU Emergency Trust Fund for Africa (EUTF), which was introduced in conjunction with the 2015 EU Agenda on Migration with a view to addressing the root causes of migration in Africa. Starting in early 2017 EUTF-funded projects in Niger (of which 15 were in operation by mid-2022, with a total budget of €279m.) were conceived to target both long-term development and short-term recovery needs. Notwithstanding these initiatives, the EU-sponsored reconversion plans fell short of the expectations of former smugglers, whose revenues were estimated to contribute to the livelihoods of one-half of the population of Agadez. From October 2017 demobilized smugglers, as well as local authorities from Agadez, organized protests against what they considered to be the Government's submissiveness to the EU's priorities. Several former migrant smugglers reportedly turned to the smuggling of other goods, including drugs and gold, which in turn prompted a marked rise in organized crime, protection rackets, armed banditry and ethnic tensions in the Agadez region.

Meanwhile, Niger is becoming a hub of southbound flows linked to migration and forcible displacement. Between 2016 and 2019, an estimated 43,000 migrants have been deported from Algeria to Niger via the border post of Assamaka, including about 26,000 Nigeriens and 17,000 nationals of other sub-Saharan African countries. In December 2017 Niger agreed to a EU proposal regarding the launch of an Emergency Transit Mechanism (ETM) for the evacuation to Niger of asylum seekers detained in Libya. By the end of 2019 approximately

3,000 refugees and asylum seekers had benefited from this opportunity, with the majority of them being subsequently relocated to EU countries. The activation of the ETM humanitarian corridor prompted hundreds of asylum seekers—mostly of Sudanese origin—to arrive in Agadez with their families during the first half of 2018, before the Nigerien authorities and the UN clarified in June that asylum seekers reaching Niger outside of the ETM programme did not qualify for relocation. In late 2021 and early 2022 an intensification of anti-smuggling operations by armed groups in southern Libya led to the unprecedented expulsion of hundreds of migrants into Niger. Overall, these dynamics placed considerable strain on Niger's limited capacity to provide adequate protection, and risked exacerbating tensions with the host communities.

A further development of Niger's extralegal economies relates to a boom in artisanal gold mining. Since 2014, large gold deposits have been discovered in the region of Agadez. The most important gold mining sites in the Nigerien Sahara, including Djado, Tchibarakaten and Tabelot, reportedly attracted tens of thousands of miners from across the region, fuelling animosities with local residents and stimulating the demand for armed protection. While the remoteness of the finds weakened the prospects of industrial exploitation, the Government undertook to shut down informal gold mining initiatives fearing that its revenues would finance terrorism, organized crime and rebel groups. The Djado site was thus formally closed since late 2016. The ensuing protests prompted the Government to increase the militarization of the region and remove the most rebellious leaders. Nevertheless, the rising threat of illegal exploitation by armed groups and of violent escalations between these and local dwellers led local authorities to condone informal mining in Djado from 2021. At the same time, the Government acquiesced to the exploitation of the Tchibarakaten and Tabelot sites, in exchange for a slight formalization and minimum oversight by state security forces. This differential treatment can be attributed to the job absorption opportunities that artisanal gold mining in Tchibarakaten and Tabelot offered to former Tuareg rebels and migrant smugglers. Artisanal gold mining has thus served to dilute the social tensions that were rising in the region of Agadez as a result of repeated economic reverses: the crisis in the tourism sector, the partial closure of uranium mining sites and the measures against irregular migration.

Economy

PAUL MELLY

INTRODUCTION

Extending over a vast tract of the central Sahara and the arid Sahelian belt, Niger is one of the world's poorest nations, confronted by the dual challenges of climate change and violent insecurity which are exerting huge pressure on its always fragile socioeconomic development model. The country's landlocked location is a constraint on trade competitiveness, while rapid demographic growth drives the continual rise in demand for health and education services and new livelihood opportunities. For most of the past decade Niger has been ranked in the bottom two or three places of the United Nations (UN) Development Programme's Human Development Index (HDI). National territory covers 1.27m. sq km, and the distances between most major urban centres are vast.

However, the country does have significant strengths. Public administration and the armed forces have proved more resilient than those of some other Sahelian nations and the Government operates probably the most effective food security system of any nation in the region, while there has been significant development progress: for example, since 1980 life expectancy at birth has increased by some 20 years to reach 61.6 years for men and 64.0 for women in 2020. Niger's main southern neighbour, Nigeria, Africa's most populous country, is a major market for exports, particularly livestock—a crucial sector for the Nigerien economy—and a major supplier of grain and other essential imports. For decades Niger has been a major producer of uranium, mainly supplying the French nuclear power industry, while recent years have seen the rapid growth of informal gold mining in the Saharan north. Moreover, oil production from the Agadem area, hitherto sufficient only for local needs and sales to near neighbours, is anticipated to expand rapidly after the opening of an export pipeline to the coast of Benin (see *Mining and Power*), expected at the end of 2023.

Nevertheless, Niger is likely to remain a low-income country for the foreseeable future. Real gross domestic product (GDP) per capita in 2021 was just US $594.9, one of the lowest in Africa, while the population of 24.5m. (at mid-2022) is still increasing by a projected annual average of 3.7% over 2020–25, according to the UN Population Fund. With only 17% of Nigeriens living in urban areas, the prospects for a sustained improvement in living standards will be heavily dependent on the progress of efforts to diversify rural livelihoods and strengthen the basic viability of agriculture and community resilience and services—factors that are also closely linked to the drive to broaden secondary school attendance, particularly among girls, and steadily reduce the incidence of young teenage marriage. The Government has well developed strategies for addressing these issues, but implementation is complicated by the widespread extent of violent insecurity, particularly in the Tillabéri region, in the west, the Diffa region in the far east adjoining Lake Chad and, increasingly, also the Tahoua and Maradi regions in the centre-south.

FUNDAMENTALS OF THE ECONOMY

West Africa has a strong sense of regional identity and culture of co-operation between countries in addressing political, security and economic issues and Niger shares this outlook. Like its neighbours, the country belongs to a number of regional structures that provide a stable and highly integrated framework for monetary and trade co-operation—the 15-member Economic Community of West African States (ECOWAS), the eight-country Union Économique et Monétaire de l'Afrique de l'Ouest (UEMOA) single currency bloc, the Sahel's food security early warning and resilience system—co-ordinated by the Comité Permanent Inter-Etats de Lutte Contre la Sécheresse dans le Sahel (CILSS)—and the G5 Sahel grouping focused on regional security and supportive development measures.

ECOWAS now plays a major role in managing political and security issues on a consensual regional basis. During the last 10 years, however, there has also been a reinvigoration of the bloc's longstanding regional economic integration agenda. From 2015 member states began to implement a Common External Tariff (CET) regime for all imports from outside the bloc, while within the ECOWAS space, trade in food is supposedly subject to no tariff or customs dues other than a minimum technical charge. The bloc has also established a standardized market regime for the cross-border sale of electricity. The members of ECOWAS have decided to create a common currency, to be called the eco, although the project has been repeatedly delayed. Their performance has been measured under agreed economic and fiscal convergence criteria and in June 2021 a fresh convergence timetable was agreed, aiming towards a launch of the eco in 2027. However, there has been little progress in deciding the large practical and institutional arrangements for the currency, and the project still faces some international scepticism.

The members of UEMOA (Benin, Burkina Faso, Côte d'Ivoire, Guinea-Bissau, Mali, Niger, Senegal and Togo) already operate a long-established common currency, the CFA franc, inherited from the pre-independence era. Their politically independent common central bank, the Banque Centrale des Etats de l'Afrique Centrale (BCEAO), is based in Dakar, Senegal, with a national office in each member state. UEMOA also has a central commission in Ouagadougou, Burkina Faso, and it operates a common regime of bank regulation and a regional capital market; an electronic regional stock exchange, the Bourse Régionale des Valeurs Mobilières (BRVM), is based in Abidjan, Côte d'Ivoire. The CFA franc was originally pegged against the French franc, at a rate guaranteed by the French Treasury, and this peg was subsequently transferred to the euro when Europe's single currency was created, with France—rather than the European Union (EU) institutions—continuing to guarantee the fixed exchange rate. (The CFA franc was devalued just once, by 50%, in 1994.) The euro peg means that BCEAO aligns its monetary policy with the tight stance maintained by the European Central Bank. A six-member bloc of central African countries also uses the CFA franc, but the two blocs operate separately, with their own bank notes and institutions.

In practical economic terms, the system has provided monetary stability and low inflation, and facilitated co-operation between member states and a degree of regional economic integration. However, the arrangement has been increasingly criticized as a colonial legacy. Hence, in 2017 the French President, Emmanuel Macron, stated that his country would accept reform if it was proposed by UEMOA member states—who then chose Côte d'Ivoire's President, Alassane Ouattara, to design a reform plan. Ouattara, a former deputy managing director of the International Monetary Fund (IMF), drafted a three-pronged strategy, announced in late 2019: the abolition of a rule requiring UEMOA member countries to deposit one-half of their foreign exchange reserves in a special Operations Account at the French Treasury to underpin the exchange rate guarantee; the withdrawal of French representatives from the governing boards of the UEMOA core institutions; and the replacement of the CFA franc name and banknotes with new notes and coins, under the eco name. However, the French-guaranteed peg to the euro would be retained.

Ouattara regarded UEMOA as an advance guard in the creation of the all-ECOWAS eco currency and therefore envisaged that the euro peg could be dropped if other states such as Ghana wished to join the bloc. However, Nigeria and some of the non-member states interpreted this as appropriating the eco name. The onset of the COVID-19 pandemic prevented resolution of this dispute. Nevertheless, progress has been made towards the implementation of the other reforms proposed by Ouattara—which are in reality more important in demonstrating UEMOA's capacity to maintain a strong CFA franc, pegged to the euro, without the need to back this up with the deposit of one-half of its members' foreign exchange reserves in France.

Meanwhile, for Niger's still overwhelmingly rural population, the regional food security structures embodied in the CILSS system are also of critical importance. The populated regions of the country lie mainly in areas with a Sahelian climate—with a single annual rainy season and a high risk of drought. The challenge of ensuring a secure supply of food and sustaining a viable rural economy has been compounded over recent years by the spread of jihadist, criminal and intercommunal violence in the Sahel. This has only reinforced the importance of the early warning food supply monitoring and stocks co-ordination structures developed within individual Sahel countries and overseen by CILSS, which was established in response to the catastrophic drought of 1973 and is based in Ouagadougou. In Niger and other member states in the network, communities and government officials continually collect and report data on the weather, the state of crops and grazing vegetation, infant health, water supply and numerous other indicators; increasingly, smartphones and other informational technology are used to report this in real time. The central Government collates and analyses all of this information, to identify communities and regions at risk of food crisis, so that emergency support can be delivered on time. Reserve stocks are maintained at both local, national and West African regional level. CILSS, through its technical analyst team based

in the capital, Niamey, maintains a harmonized set of data standards adopted by all member countries and oversees the performance of individual national systems. It also co-ordinates with international donors through the Réseau de Prévention des Crises Alimentaires (RPCA).

Like many other francophone African countries, Mali belongs to the Organisation pour l'Harmonisation en Afrique du Droit des Affaires (OHADA), a harmonized framework of business law with a supranational disputes tribunal.

The G5 Sahel bloc, to which Niger has belonged since its foundation in 2014, is mainly concerned with regional security and the fight against jihadist militants; but these military efforts are supported with a programme of 40 priority development projects for marginal areas. In mid-2022 Mali's transitional military regime withdrew from the G5 Sahel. However, Niger has been at the forefront of efforts to maintain security co-operation between remaining members of the bloc and it co-operates closely with both Chad and Burkina Faso.

SOCIETY

With its population of 24.5m. at mid-2022 (according to official projections), Niger is an overwhelmingly youthful country: some 49% of Nigeriens are aged under 15. This creates huge demand for maternal and child health services and the continual expansion of the school system—and for the generation of new employment opportunities. Some 54% of boys and 49% of girls completed primary education in 2020, and about one-quarter attended secondary school. President Mohamed Bazoum has launched a drive to bolster girls' attendance at secondary school by building school boarding accommodation for girls in provincial towns, so that rural families are more willing to allow their daughters to leave their villages and lodge in the towns where the secondary schools are located. Bazoum believes that if girls remain at school until they are 18, they will not only be equipped to take on a wider range of jobs and economic opportunities but will also tend to marry later and thus have smaller families. At present, only 16% of Nigerien women use modern contraception, although a further 15% would like access to this.

Bazoum has openly talked about the need for Niger to slow the rate of population growth in order to support development progress. In many regions resources of farmland are already under huge pressure and with the inheritance subdivided at each generation, the size and viability of farms are becoming steadily smaller, increasing the risks of food insecurity and a decline in household incomes.

Health indicators remain fragile. The rate of maternal mortality, at 509 per 100,000 live births in 2017, is much lower than in Nigeria or Mali, but only 44% of births are attended by trained personnel, while 72% of children under five suffer from anaemia and 44% are stunted. However, 82% of infants are now vaccinated against diphtheria, whooping cough and tetanus.

ECONOMIC POLICY AND PERFORMANCE

Niger operates a mixed economy model. The strategic uranium mining sector is a state partnership with foreign investors, principally France, but in many other areas of activity the private sector is predominant. Most Nigeriens live in rural communities, and the agricultural and pastoral economy remains substantially informal, albeit supported by state services such as veterinary care and inspection. The country has a long history of close policy co-ordination with the IMF and the international donor community, which remain a crucial source of support both for longer-term development and the response to humanitarian emergencies resulting from drought, floods or violent insecurity. In December 2021 the IMF approved its latest three-year programme for Niger, a US $275.8m. Extended Credit Facility (ECF) arrangement. In June 2022, reporting on its first review of performance under the ECF, the Fund announced that most targets had been met, but while the economic outlook was favourable, particularly in view of the anticipated opening of the new oil export pipeline, the country faced a serious food crisis, due both to the weather and the disruptive impact of insecurity; moreover, the war in Ukraine from February resulted in additional global food and fertilizer price pressures.

For decades, rates of economic growth have often fluctuated, often as a result of weather conditions. The partial or total failure of the annual rainy season can have a drastic impact on agricultural output and the availability of grazing for animals. For example, real GDP grew by 8.6% in 2010 but by just 2.4% the next year, only to rebound by 10.5% in 2012. The position subsequently stabilized somewhat, with growth fluctuating between 4.4% and 7.2% between 2013 and 2019—more than keeping pace with the rise in population and thus at least laying the foundations for a potential rise in living standards. Even in the first year of the COVID-19 pandemic, real GDP growth was still 3.6%; it fell to 1.3% in 2021, but is projected to rebound by an impressive 6.7% in 2022. While the performance of the rural economy has generally been the biggest driver of growth rates, these have also been affected by the performance of the extractives sector and, in particular, the price of uranium, as well as the construction of new infrastructure in Niamey, prior to the hosting of an African Union (AU) summit there in July 2019.

The health impact of the COVID-19 pandemic was relatively limited: even by mid-October 2022 only 9,416 cases and 314 deaths had been confirmed, although the limited extent of testing means that the actual number of cases was certainly higher. However, the strict travel curbs and lockdown restrictions rapidly imposed by the Government at the start of the pandemic undoubtedly curtailed urban economic activity.

The Government's fiscal position has been consistently in deficit but relatively stable. Revenues sank from 12.1% of GDP in 2018 to 11.2% the following year and to an estimated 10.8% in 2020, the pandemic year. Total expenditure and net lending far outweighed these revenues, at 21.1% of GDP in 2018, 21.6% in 2019 and 22.9% in 2020, but included a heavy capital spending component. In cash terms, fiscal receipts rose from 619,900m. francs CFA in 2017 to 862,300m. francs CFA in 2018, before slipping back to 848,500m. francs CFA in 2019 and 852,400m. francs CFA in 2020. Total spending increased from 1,263,500m. francs CFA in 2017 to 1,505,400m. francs CFA in 2018, and then to 1,631,800m. francs CFA in 2019 and 1,769,400m. francs CFA in 2020.

AGRICULTURE

Niger is divided into four climatic zones in which average rates of rainfall determine the type of rural activities that are possible (together with the presence of aquifers and surface water bodies that may be used for irrigation). In a very small portion of the far south-western corner of the country, representing 1% of total surface area, a Sudanic-Sahelian climate dominates, with average rainfall of 600 mm–800 mm per year. North of this zone, 10% of the territory belongs in the Sahel, which receives on average 350 mm–600 mm of rainfall each year. The Sahel-Saharan zone, further north, covers 12% of total surface area and barely registers 150 mm–350 mm of rainfall each year. Beyond, the remaining 77% of Niger's territory is a desert receiving on average less than 150 mm of rainfall per annum. Most of the country's population reside in the two southern zones, where the majority of them live in villages (Niger's rate of urbanization is the lowest in West Africa, at just 17% in 2020, according to the World Bank) and practise settled farming. Rainfall is concentrated mainly in a wet season running from late June to early September, when the main cereal crops and cotton are planted; this is also the period of vegetation growth, replenishing grazing areas. The harvest follows, from September to November, and then long months of almost no rainfall, with temperatures often in the range of 45°C–50°C between March and May, before the next annual wet season arrives again in June or July. From April onwards, Niger enters the lean season (*la soudure*), when villagers must eke out their remaining grain stocks; the risk of food crisis is at its most intense after the rains have begun, with the new crops still growing and not yet ready for harvest. However, rains often fail locally or across wide areas—or they may fall at the wrong moment, causing flood damage without assisting agricultural production. So Niger, like other Sahelian states, always lives with the risk of food crisis.

The Sahel-Saharan zone was customarily devoted to livestock farming, although in recent years population growth in the south has led to a gradual agricultural colonization by farmers of the traditional haunts of nomadic herders—a situation not without conflicts. In the desert north, oases and aquifers sustain the production of citrus fruits, onions and potatoes, sold primarily in southern towns.

Agriculture, livestock husbandry and other rural pursuits accounted for an average 39.3% of GDP during 2016–20. In response to repeated droughts and food shortages in recent years, in 2012 the Government of President Mahamadou Issoufou launched the '3N' Initiative—'Les Nigériens Nourrissent les Nigériens'—which aimed to end famine and reduce poverty by enhancing sustainable agricultural development and the resilience of rural communities to food shortages. Government actions in support of this strategy, across the various ministerial portfolios, are co-ordinated by the High Commission of the 3N, whose head has senior ministerial rank. The cost of the initial 2013–15 phase of the initiative was estimated at some US $2,000m. A series of action plans were developed under the Government's 3N programme, with reported good results in terms of improved water resources management and increased productivity. In November 2018 the Government adopted its first ever 'national multisectoral nutrition security policy', which aimed to make nutrition programmes part of the development and resilience work in the country, rather than emergency-focused. Since Bazoum succeeded his close ally Issoufou in April 2021 he has maintained the focus on rural development and food security and the role of the 3N.

The main food crops are millet and sorghum—particularly well suited to coping with severe heat—and paddy rice, produced in irrigated low-lying land, groundnuts and beans and cowpeas (niébé). The millet and sorgum harvest in the 2018/19 agricultural year—planted and harvested in 2018 and then supplied to the market in late 2018 and early 2019—was just under 6m. metric tons; the next season saw the harvest sink to 5.2m. tons, but 2020/21 saw a recovery to 5.5m. tons. Production of beans and cowpeas was around 2.4m. tons in 2018/19. The groundnut harvest rose gently from 557,400 tons in 2018/19 to 575,800 tons the next year and 600,000 tons in 2020/21. Production of paddy rice has also edged steadily upwards, from 115,600 tons in 2018/19 to 119,500 tons the following year and then 124,400 tons in 2020/21.

The combination of several years without any major destructive droughts, together with investment in irrigation programmes to help promote better harvests, has enabled the Government to accumulate a national stock of cereals. However, agriculture remains vulnerable to climate change, drought and the exhaustion of soils where population growth has forced families to cultivate every scrap of land year after year, without ever leaving it fallow to recover fertility; this is particularly the case in the southern Maradi region, which has more rainfall than most areas but is also densely populated and thus has high levels of malnutrition. A growing number of men from farming households in the Maradi and Zinder regions now make their way north to work in the Tchibarakaten goldfields in the Sahara for at least past of the year—a trend that both reflects their need to earn cash income and the constraints that limit how much food and income they can generate from their farm plots back in their home villages.

In terms of cash crops, cowpeas and onions are the most important, with the country producing some 2.6m. metric tons of cow peas and an estimated 1.3m. tons of onions in 2020, according to the UN Food and Agriculture Organization (FAO). The dry desert conditions around Agadez, on the edge of the Sahara, with cool winters, are particularly good for producing onions and potatoes of much higher quality than could be grown further south or in the tropical zones of coastal West Africa. Hence, about 95% of the onion crop on average is exported, and Niger is West Africa's largest exporter of onions and the second largest producer of this crop (after Nigeria). Onions are exported mainly to Nigeria, Benin, Togo, Ghana and Côte d'Ivoire. The main competition comes from another Sahelian country, Burkina Faso.

Cow peas are Niger's second major agricultural export commodity. Production has risen in recent years and, typically,

80% is exported, mainly to Nigeria. Tiger nuts, sesame seed and chufa are also produced, as are red peppers, a speciality of the Komadougou river valley, which forms the boundary between south-east Niger and Nigeria. In the 1970s Niger also produced around 100,000 tons of cotton each year, but the crop was later neglected, with output sinking below 10,000 tons. In 2014 the Government struck a deal with the French company Géocoton to pursue a cotton revival strategy.

The most important traditional activity in Niger after crop farming is livestock farming, with the country estimated to possess some 16.1m. cattle, 13.7m. sheep and 18.8m. goats in 2020, according to FAO. Cattle and livestock products have historically been the second most significant export, in terms of foreign exchange earnings, after uranium, contributing an average 10% of export earnings per year during 2005–10. Most of this comprised a significant, if largely unrecorded, trade across the border with Nigeria. Pastoralists' terms of trade have been adversely affected in recent years by the sustained high cost of cattle feed and by falling livestock prices. The Government has been unable to promote either intensive commercial livestock operations or dairy farming, in part owing to Niger's ecological conditions, but also because of policy choices. However, efforts have intermittently been made to improve conditions in livestock farming, including a vaccination campaign in 2011, targeting an estimated 1m. head of cattle in the northern Agadez region. In 2013 the Government adopted the Strategy for the Sustainable Development of Livestock Farming for 2013–35, which aimed to intensify production by increasing the trading income of livestock farmers. The programme was intended to integrate the existing model of family-based farming better with domestic and regional markets. Nomadic pastoralists follow patterns of circular migration, moving south as local grazing on the Saharan fringe is exhausted, and crossing into Nigeria, Cameroon and even the Central African Republic to reach areas where grazing remains available for longer periods. Meanwhile, large numbers of animals are exported to the populous markets of the coastal West African states. To maintain animal health, in this context of transhumance and export, the Nigerien Government maintains a number of veterinary inspection posts and a system of livestock passport documents.

With about 90% of cultivable land believed to have been lost to drought in the 20th century, and losses recently averaging 200,000 ha per year, the anti-desertification campaign is a priority for the Nigerien Government, and a programme of afforestation and environmental protection has been under way for a number of years with positive results. In 2010 Niger gained access to funds from the Climate Investment Funds' Pilot Program for Climate Resilience to reduce desertification and food insecurity. A portion of the funds was to be used to fight desert encroachment and drought, to allow Niger to achieve its development goals in a sustainable manner. A new forestry code was adopted in June 2004 and better conservation through behavioural changes led to the successful recovery of hundreds of thousands of hectares of woodlands, especially in the densely populated region of Maradi. However, such efforts are not sufficient completely to protect Niger's farmers from the vagaries of the weather and the effects of climate change, such as the devastating floods experienced on several occasions in recent years, even in Agadez, on the edge of the desert.

As in most other West African countries, manufacturing primarily takes the form of the processing of agricultural commodities. The manufacturing sector contributed 7.7% of GDP in 2020, according to UN estimates, up from an annual average of less than 2.0% in 1990–2004. Ventures are concentrated in Niamey and include a brewery, dairy product plants, and tanneries. Most manufacturing units are parastatals privatized in the 1990s, with the tanneries of Niamey—which have a maximum output of 3.5m. hides and skins annually—being the property of the Burkina Faso group Tan Alize. A textile plant, the Entreprise Nigérienne de Textile (ENITEX), and a cement works, the Société Nigérienne de Cimenterie, were both transferred from state to majority private ownership in the late 1990s. Around 52,000 metric tons of cement were produced in 2018, increasing to 260,000 tons in 2019. The new

Malbaza cement plant in the western Tahoua region, with an annual production capacity of 650,000 tons, was officially completed in March 2019, following a construction project undertaken by Nigeria's Dangote Cement, financed by a consortium of local banks, the West African Development Bank and private investors. In October 2018 Dangote Cement began work on another plant in Keita, in the Tahoua region, which was expected to have an annual capacity of 2.5m. tons and reduce the country's import requirements for cement; the US $275m. project included the construction of a 100-MW coal-fired power station. In August 2020 the Government approved a project by local company Kao Cement to construct a further plant in the Tahoua region, at a cost of $287m.

MINING AND POWER

Mining and quarrying constitute a crucial part of Niger's economy, contributing 9.0% of GDP (along with utilities) in 2020, according to UN estimates, and consistently accounting for more than 40% of the country's exports. Niger has reserves of various minerals, including gypsum, limestone, salt, silver and tin. However, by far the most important commodities in terms of both production and earnings are uranium, gold and petroleum, all of which have attracted renewed foreign interest in recent years. Uranium production originally began in the early 1970s, commercial gold mining in 2004, and the extraction of oil commenced at the Agadem block north of Lake Chad in 2012. In March 2011 the Council of the Extractive Industries Transparency Initiative declared Niger to be a compliant country.

Niger is among the world's foremost producers of uranium (the fourth largest, after Kazakhstan, Canada and Australia, in 2017), but the sector's economic contribution has declined, owing to a fall in the price of uranium on the world market. Production began in 1971 at Arlit, north-west of the Aïr mountains. The French state-controlled Compagnie Générale des Matières Nucléaires (COGEMA—later Areva) held a majority share in the mining company, Société des Mines de l'Aïr (SOMAÏR), with the Nigerien Government's Office National des Ressources Minières du Niger (ONAREM) holding the remaining 36.4% share. Production at the country's second uranium mine, at Akouta, began in 1978, and was managed by the consortium Compagnie Minière d'Akouta (COMINAK), which included COGEMA, the Nigerien Government, the Japanese Overseas Uranium Resources Development Co and the Spanish Empresa Nacional del Uranio. The People's Republic of China later launched the Société des Mines d'Azelik (SOMINA), a joint venture between China Nuclear International Uranium Corporation (37.2%), the Nigerien Government (33%), ZXJOY Invest of China (24.8%) and Trendfield Holdings Ltd of Hong Kong (5%), which began to develop the Azelik uranium deposits in the Agadez region, with production at the Teguidda mine commencing in 2010. Then, in January 2009 the renamed Areva signed an agreement with the Government to invest €1,200m. over five years in developing a new mine at Imouraren near Agadez. Areva and the Korea Electric Power Corporation (Kepco) were to own 66.7% of the project, with the Government, through ONAREM and the Société du Patrimoine des Mines du Niger (SOPAMIN), holding the remainder in a joint venture. The Fukushima Daiichi nuclear power station disaster in Japan in March 2011 destabilized the uranium market, but Areva nevertheless agreed to a Government demand that royalties be increased from 5% to 12%–15%. However, eventually the weakening of world uranium prices led the French group, by now renamed Orano, to postpone the development of Imouraren indefinitely. The Azelik mine project also stalled. In July 2019 Orano confirmed the suspension of the operations of COMINAK, which had recorded significant losses in previous years, due to depletion at the Akouta mine and the continued low price of uranium; the mine was officially closed at the end of March 2021, jeopardizing more than 600 jobs—although a significant number of personnel would still be required for the carefully phased close-down and clean-up of the site.

During the brief revival in uranium extraction, both production and the sector's contribution to foreign earnings rose considerably. In 2013 Niger produced 4,528 metric tons, according to the World Nuclear Association, although output fell to 4,116 tons in 2015 and to 3,477 tons in 2016.

However, at a time of concern about global warming, many countries regard nuclear power as a valuable non-carbon complement to renewable sources such as the less consistently reliable solar and wind generation. This is sustaining international interest in uranium exploration and exploitation. Moreover, Western countries' interest in Niger as a source of uranium is likely to have been reinforced by their mistrust of the Russian Federation, after its February 2022 invasion of Ukraine and manipulation of gas supplies to Europe. Niger, by contrast, has a long history of reliable uranium production partnership with the French and other investors.

In February 2016 the Government issued a mining permit to United Kingdom-based GoviEx Uranium for a deposit of over 45,000 metric tons of uranium ore at Madaouela, 15 km from the old Arlit and Akouta mines, although the mines could be developed only if uranium market prices increased to US $70 per lb. Global Atomic Fuels Corporation of Canada has begun to develop four uranium deposits with a main interest in Dasa, which has estimated resources of over 40,000 tons, and in July 2017 the company signed an ore sales agreement with Orano to sell its ore for processing by SOMAÏR. At the end of 2018 Niger's uranium resources were estimated at 237,000 tons, principally located at Imouraren. According to government figures, uranium production dropped sharply to only 688 tons in 2018 (amid further production cuts by Areva), but partly recovered to 2,863 tons in 2019 and 2,992 tons in 2020. In that year uranium exports earned $285.1m., equivalent to 22.9% of total export revenue (a significant fall compared with more than 50% in 2015). The international price of uranium rose to above $30 per lb in April 2020, for the first time since February 2016, after which it was announced that GoviEx Uranium planned to undertake an updated feasibility study for its uranium project at Madaouela. In May 2021 GoviEx commenced a five-month drilling programme as part of the feasibility study for the Madaouela uranium project. The price of uranium remained steady at around $32 per lb at mid-2021; production in that year overall was 2,282 tons.

Niger has long been known to hold commercially viable gold reserves mainly in the Liptako region, near the border with Burkina Faso, and these have been exploited on a small scale since the early 1980s. Gold is produced both from artisanal diggings and through industrial mining. The Samira Hill gold mine began operations in 2004. Meanwhile, in April 2014 gold deposits were found in the Djado plateau, in the central Sahara south of the Libyan border; and soon afterwards gold was also discovered at Tchibarakaten, along the border with Algeria in the north-west. These discoveries precipitated a gold rush that attracted more than 20,000 prospectors from Niger itself and neighbouring countries, notably Chad and Sudan. In 2017 the Government closed down the north-eastern sites, on the grounds of security concerns related to terrorism and armed robbery, but it opted to allow informal and small-scale commercial mining to continue in the Tchibarakaten area—where the state does not get closely involved in regulation but does maintain a security force presence. Gold production had risen to 6,207 kg by 2019, but fell to 2,361 kg in 2020. However, following a dramatic rise in the international price of gold amid the global pandemic, in 2020 Niger earned a record US $630.9m. from gold exports (representing 50.6% of total exports), compared with $189.5m. (22.2% of the total) in the previous year, according to the International Trade Centre.

Exploration for oil in Niger dates back to the 1960s. However, early discoveries in the south-west were not deemed commercially exploitable. Interest in conducting oil exploration in Niger was renewed in 2005, when a consortium led by ExxonMobil (of the USA) and Petronas (of Malaysia) announced its first discovery of oil in the country, less than one year after it drilled three exploratory wells in the Agadem region. In 2008 the China National Petroleum Corporation (CNPC) signed a production-sharing agreement with the Government to develop the Agadem field, in the far eastern desert, north of Lake Chad, which held estimated reserves of 350m. barrels. The development strategy also comprised a 460-km pipeline to a new refinery to be built at Zinder, near the Nigerian border, with a capacity of 20,000 barrels per day

(b/d). Production began in 2011, with output rising to 19,000 b/d by the end of 2013. All the oil produced is refined in the Zinder refinery. Although output has been a modest 20,000 b/d this has usefully supplied the domestic market and export customers within the region—for example, in northern Nigeria. Petroleum exports earned Niger US $244.5m. in 2021—38.6% of total exports. In accordance with mining and petroleum legislation, the Government has a 15% ownership stake in the Agadem field. The capital cost of the oilfields and pipeline are financed by CNPC, with the Nigerien Government repaying the financing cost of its share through future cash flows of the project. The refinery in Zinder is managed as a corporation, with CNPC holding 60% and the Government contributing 40% of the capital costs. The national oil company, Société Nigérienne Distribution des Produits Pétroliers (SONIDEP), markets domestic production. Meanwhile, the UK-based independent oil and gas company Savannah Petroleum plans to develop the Amdigh field, in the Agadem basin.

However, a massive expansion of oil production is anticipated. Under a September 2019 agreement with the Governments of Niger and Benin, CNPC has begun the construction of a 1,980-km oil pipeline to connect Agadem and Zinder to an export terminal at Sèmè-Kpodji on the coast of Benin. This is expected to open up international markets, thus allowing Nigerien oil output to rise to around 110,000 b/d and perhaps eventually even 200,000 b/d, which would provide a substantial boost both to the country's exports and to government revenues. In October 2022 construction of the pipeline was reported to be 30% complete and its commissioning was expected at the end of 2023.

Domestic thermal sources, such as coal and diesel, provide a little less than one-half of Niger's electrical energy requirements, with much of the remainder being imported from Nigeria. According to the World Bank, in 2019 18.8% of the population had access to electricity. In 2020 425m. kWh of electrical energy were produced (representing a fall in output from 668m. kWh in 2018). A large proportion of the population use kerosene as their main source of lighting. Owing to the unreliability of the Nigerian supply, the development of a 130-MW hydroelectric dam at Kandadji, on the Niger river, began in 2009. In 2013 the Russian operator of the project was dismissed, with the Nigerien Government alleging that the company had failed to meet its commitments. In 2014 the Government secured €151m. from the World Bank, the Islamic Development Bank and the Agence Française de Développement, to revive the project. Following delays in securing a new operator and in funding (after the project cost increased from an initial US $785m. to around $1,290m.), in 2018 China Gezhouaba Group Company (CGGC) was selected to resume work on the dam, and in March 2019 the construction phase of the project was officially launched. The World Bank in June 2020 approved a $100m. loan and a $50m. grant to help fund a second phase of resettlement and livelihood support in the area. The first stage of the dam construction was expected to end in 2025 or 2026, followed by a second construction stage, to a height of 228 m, to be completed by the end of 2031. On completion, the dam and associated reservoir would regulate the water flow for the benefit of downstream areas, raising the irrigation potential in the Niger delta by up to 45,000 ha, increasing agricultural production and improving food security. Furthermore, in 2015 financing for a coal mine and power plant was completed by the US-based firm Source California Energy Services, to tap into a reserve of 92m. metric tons of coal in Salkadamna, in the region of Tahoua. At full capacity, the plant would produce 600 MW—a significant boost, given that current domestic generating capacities are less than 150 MW. In contrast to this longer-term project, a 100-MW diesel-fired power plant project was launched in 2013 in Gorou Banda, near Niamey, under a contract with the China-based Sinohydro Corporation. The 75,400m. francs CFA of funding was provided by the Nigerien Government, the West African Development Bank and the Islamic Development Bank. The project was inaugurated in April 2017, with the first phase due to generate a total of 80 MW. However, the investment has been criticized locally as a costly and inefficient means of overhauling Niamey's failing electricity network.

TRANSPORT, SERVICES AND TELECOMMUNICATIONS

Niger's transport system is still poorly developed and road rehabilitation depends heavily on funding from donors. In 2012 there were 19,675 km of classified roads, and in 2008 only 21% of roads were paved. Niger uses the Benin–Togo railway to carry goods from seaports to the Niger border and vice versa. In 2012 a multinational railway system was proposed to connect Benin, Niger, Burkina Faso and Côte d'Ivoire; as part of this project, Niger's first train station was inaugurated in Niamey in April 2014. The 630-km section connecting Parakou, in Benin, to Niamey was to be built by Bénirail, a concession railway company headed by the French firm Bolloré Transport and Logistics, which owned 40% of the shares. Bolloré commenced work on the Niger side in early 2014, 15 months before it signed the necessary agreements with the two Governments, leading to a lawsuit from Beninese company Petrolin and the suspension of work in November 2015. In March 2018, by which time some 140 km of the Niger section of the railway had been completed by Bolloré, negotiations between the Beninese and Nigerien authorities resulted in agreement that the contract would be ceded to the China Railway Construction Corporation. The extensive rehabilitation of Niger's Diori Hamani International Airport, 8 km south-east of Niamey, including the construction of new passenger and cargo terminals, was officially completed in June 2019; the Turkish construction company SUMMA, which had invested €154m. in the airport's new facilities and infrastructure, became the sole operator of the airport. In February 2021 Mota-Engil SGPS SA, a Portuguese construction company, commenced work on a 283-km railway line which was to link Nigeria's northern state and trading centre of Kano to the Nigerien border town of Maradi, at a cost of US $1,800m. The route was expected to have a capacity to transport more than 3m. passengers and 1m. tons of freight each year when operational.

For several years the Government of Niger has been promoting the country as a tourist destination; tourist arrivals increased from 39,190 in 1997 to 157,152 in 2018, when tourism receipts were US $98m. Tourist arrivals rose to 192,240 in 2019, but dropped to 85,472 in 2020, as a result of the COVID-19 pandemic. For a time, Agadez, the gateway to the Sahara and the Air massif, received direct tourist charter flights from Europe. However, as in the rest of the Sahel, tourism has been drastically curtailed by the security crisis of recent years.

Telecommunications in Niger have expanded with the arrival of three mobile cellular telephone and two internet service providers. With only 59 mobile subscriptions per 100 people, access to cellular communications is lower than in many West African countries, but this may in part be a reflection of both low income levels and of geographical reality: a significant proportion of the population live in locations where mobile network coverage is weak or non-existent.

Niger's banks were not severely affected by the COVID-19 pandemic in 2020 and they are well capitalized. However, the sector is quite concentrated and the country faces a challenge in extending wider access to credit to the rural and small town population to support growth and greater economic diversification.

FOREIGN TRADE AND PAYMENTS

Niger's trade balance has generally been characterized by deficits, with 1987 being the last year in which a surplus was recorded. In local currency terms, exports have been in decline, sinking from 701,800m. francs CFA in 2017 to 668,200m. francs CFA the following year, then to 659,700m.

francs CFA in 2019 and just 574,300m. francs CFA in 2020. They were far outweighed by imports, which have been rising steadily—from 1,431,600m. francs CFA in 2017 to 1,597,600m. francs CFA in 2018, then to 1,717,600m. francs CFA in 2019 and 1,726,100m. francs CFA in 2020. The overall current account balance has also recorded deficits: of 740,000m. francs CFA in 2017 and 902,600m. francs CFA the following year, increasing further to 921,300m. francs CFA in 2019 and 1,098,000m. francs CFA in 2020. In terms of ratio to GDP, the current account deficit was 11.4% in 2017, rising to 12.6% in 2018, contracting slightly to 12.1% in 2019 but resurging to 13.8% in 2020.

Niger's main exports in 2020 were uranium (134,400m. francs CFA), onions (90,200m. francs CFA), petroleum oils (79,500m. francs CFA) and livestock (61,800m. francs CFA). The main imports were capital equipment (456,100m. francs CFA), food products (397,600m. francs CFA) and petroleum products (73,900m. francs CFA). Remittances from the Nigerien diaspora amounted to 126,300m. francs CFA.

In October 2019 the Nigerian Government closed its borders with Niger and Benin to the movement of goods (after a partial closure from 20 August), with the aim of curbing the smuggling of large quantities of rice and other commodities, and arms. This hugely disrupted trade. Even after Nigeria officially reopened the border with Niger in January 2021, the entry of some commodities, including rice, remained banned.

During 2015–19 France took the largest share of Nigerien exports—averaging 21% of the total in that period, a reflection of the importance of uranium exports. Nigeria ranked second (17%), reflecting shipments of onions and other crops, and the movement of livestock. The third largest market was the United Arab Emirates (16%), ahead of other African countries (13%—again reflecting agricultural and livestock trade).

At the AU summit held in Niamey on 6–8 July 2019, the African Continental Free Trade Area Agreement (AfCFTA), providing for the creation of a continent-wide common market and currency union, officially entered its operational phase; 54 of the AU's 55 member states (the exception being Eritirea) had signed the AfCFTA, with future phases remaining under negotiation. Trading under the AfCFTA Agreement began on 1 January 2021. By October 2022 44 of the signatory countries had ratified the Agreement.

In terms of debt, Niger has traditionally relied on foreign aid and borrowing, although domestic borrowing has increased in recent years. Niger was a beneficiary of the Heavily Indebted Poor Countries (HIPC) initiative launched in 1996, under which its external debt was reduced by US $1,200m. in nominal terms, with $680.2m. provided by multilateral creditors. Furthermore, in June 2005 Niger was among 18 countries to be granted 100% debt relief on multilateral debt agreed by the Group of Eight (G8) leading industrialized nations. As a result of these initiatives, the debt-to-GDP ratio declined substantially, from 52.0% in 2005 to an estimated 11.8% in 2010, according to the IMF.

However, a fall in exports and a rise in external borrowing resulting from the COVID-19 pandemic left Niger with public debt equivalent to 41.8% of GDP in 2020, and forecast to reach 42.9% in 2021. Official development assistance (ODA) increased over the first half of the 2010s. After contracting to US $469m. during the period of political uncertainty in 2009, ODA almost doubled to $745m. during the military transition in 2010, reflecting in part donor contributions to the financing of the cycle of elections in that year. Net ODA rose annually thereafter to reach $952m. in 2016 and $1,225m. in 2017, according to the World Bank, increasing further to $1,308m. in 2018, $1,439m. in 2019 and $1,928m. in 2020.

Statistical Survey

Source (unless otherwise stated): Institut National de la Statistique, Immeuble sis à la Rue Sirba, derrière la Présidence de la République, BP 720, Niamey; tel. 20-72-35-60; e-mail ins@ins.ne; internet www.stat-niger.org.

Area and Population

AREA, POPULATION AND DENSITY

Area (sq km)	1,266,491*
Population (census results)	
20 May 2001	11,060,291
10 December 2012	
Males	8,518,818
Females	8,619,889
Total	17,138,707
Population (official projections at mid-year)	
2020	22,752,385
2021	23,591,983
2022	24,463,374
Density (per sq km) at mid-2022	19.3

* 488,995 sq miles.

POPULATION BY AGE AND SEX
('000, official projections at mid-2022)

	Males	Females	Total
0–14 years	6,073.2	6,007.0	12,080.2
15–64 years	5,778.0	5,972.5	11,750.5
65 years and over	307.2	325.5	632.7
Total	12,158.4	12,305.0	24,463.4

POPULATION BY ETHNIC GROUP
(2001 census, Nigerien citizens only)

	Population	%
Hausa	6,069,731	55.36
Djerma-Sonraï	2,300,874	20.99
Tuareg	1,016,883	9.27
Peulh	935,517	8.53
Kanouri-Manga	513,116	4.68
Toubou	42,172	0.38
Arab	40,085	0.37
Gourmantché	39,797	0.36
Others	5,951	0.05
Total	10,964,126	100.00

Note: Classification of ethnicity reflects national census methodology.

ADMINISTRATIVE DIVISIONS
(official population projections at mid-2022)

Agadez	669,004		Tahoua	4,776,698
Diffa	815,324		Tillabéri	3,903,596
Dosso	2,944,264		Zinder	5,075,308
Maradi	4,871,545		**Total**	24,463,374
Niamey (city) . .	1,407,635			

PRINCIPAL TOWNS
(population at 2012 census)

Niamey (capital) .	978,029		Tahoua	149,498
Maradi	267,249		Agadez	110,497
Zinder	235,605		Arlit	78,651

BIRTHS AND DEATHS
(annual averages, UN estimates)

	2005–10	2010–15	2015–20
Birth rate (per 1,000)	50.8	48.7	46.3
Death rate (per 1,000)	12.8	10.1	8.4

Source: UN, *World Population Prospects: The 2019 Revision.*

2017: Birth rate 45.5 per 1,000; Death rate 7.2 per 1,000 (Source: African Development Bank).

Life expectancy (years at birth, estimates): 62.8 (males 61.6; females 64.0) in 2020 (Source: World Bank, World Development Indicators database).

EMPLOYMENT
('000 persons at 31 December)

	2010	2011	2012
Agriculture, hunting, forestry and fishing	158	252	254
Mining and quarrying	31	33	33
Manufacturing	1,012	1,395	1,397
Electricity, gas and water . . .	181	262	280
Construction	603	888	903
Trade, restaurants and hotels .	1,419	1,543	1,563
Transport, storage and communications	635	706	717
Financing, insurance, real estate and business services . . .	224	347	349
Community, social and personal services	1,315	1,222	1,286
Total	5,578	6,648	6,782

2001 census (persons aged 10 years and over): Total employed 4,015,951 (males 2,706,910, females 1,309,041), Unemployed 64,987 (males 49,437, females 15,550), Total labour force 4,080,938 (males 2,756,347, females 1,324,591).

Mid-2015 (estimates in '000): Agriculture, etc. 5,212; Total labour force 6,409 (Source: FAO).

Health and Welfare

KEY INDICATORS

Total fertility rate (children per woman, 2020)	6.7
Under-5 mortality rate (per 1,000 live births, 2020) . . .	77.5
HIV/AIDS (% of persons aged 15–49, 2020)	0.2
COVID-19: Cumulative confirmed deaths (per 100,000 persons at 31 August 2022)	1.2
COVID-19: Fully vaccinated population (% of total population at 28 August 2022)	11.8
Physicians (per 1,000 head, 2016)	0.04
Hospital beds (per 100,000 head, 2017)	0.4
Domestic health expenditure (2019): US $ per head (PPP) .	25.9
Domestic health expenditure (2019): % of GDP	2.0
Domestic health expenditure (2019): public (% of total current expenditure)	35.7
Access to improved water resources (% of persons, 2020) .	47
Access to improved sanitation facilities (% of persons, 2020) .	15
Total carbon dioxide emissions ('000 metric tons, 2018) . .	2,290
Carbon dioxide emissions per head (metric tons per, 2018) .	0.1
Human Development Index (2021): ranking	189
Human Development Index (2021): value	0.400

Note: For data on COVID-19 vaccinations, 'fully vaccinated' denotes receipt of all doses specified by approved vaccination regime (Sources: Johns Hopkins University and Our World in Data). Data on health expenditure refer to current general government expenditure in each case. For more information on sources and further definitions for all indicators, see Health and Welfare Statistics: Sources and Definitions section (europaworld.com/ credits).

Agriculture

PRINCIPAL CROPS
('000 metric tons)

	2018	2019	2020
Bambara beans	46.9	44.8	55.6
Beans, green*	32.0	31.8	31.9
Cabbages and other brassicas .	346.7	410.2	514.1
Carrots and turnips . . .	42.1	53.8	58.8
Cassava (Manioc)	372.4	513.7	658.2
Chillies and peppers, green .	211.4	260.9	239.6
Cow peas, dry	2,376.7	2,386.7	2,637.5
Dates*	16.8	16.5	16.6
Groundnuts, with shell . . .	594.2	544.0	594.1
Lettuce and chicory	170.0	216.6	282.9
Millet	3,856.3	3,270.5	3,508.9
Okra	150.5	103.9	140.1
Onions, dry	1,180.3	1,313.2	1,310.4
Potatoes	168.6	198.4	235.6
Pumpkins, squash and gourds .	138.9	192.6	250.0
Rice, paddy	101.6	121.8	179.4
Sesame seed	90.2	97.7	88.2
Sorghum	2,100.2	1,896.6	2,132.3
Sugar cane	258.1	320.7	440.8
Sweet potatoes	130.0	173.2	209.9
Tobacco, unmanufactured . . .	1.7*	2.1	3.8
Tomatoes	289.8	310.9	344.3
Watermelons	49.7	79.0	115.3

* FAO estimate(s).

Aggregate production ('000 metric tons, may include official, semi-official or estimated data): Total cereals 6,100.2 in 2018, 5,339.0 in 2019, 5,878.5 in 2020; Total fruit (primary) 560.9 in 2018, 588.8 in 2019, 636.9 in 2020; Total oilcrops 744.4 in 2018, 699.2 in 2019, 737.9 in 2020; Total pulses 2,457.9 in 2018, 2,465.4 in 2019, 2,727.1 in 2020; Total roots and tubers 670.9 in 2018, 885.2 in 2019, 1,103.7 in 2020; Total vegetables (primary) 2,706.6 in 2018, 3,046.4 in 2019, 3,333.8 in 2020.

Source: FAO.

LIVESTOCK
('000 head, year ending September)

	2018	2019	2020
Asses	1,874	1,912	1,950
Camels	1,811	1,835	1,859
Cattle	14,364	15,225	16,139
Chickens	19,893	20,291	20,696
Goats	17,412	18,108	18,832
Horses	253	256	258
Pigs*	43	43	43
Sheep	12,747	13,193	13,655

* FAO estimates.

Source: FAO.

LIVESTOCK PRODUCTS
('000 metric tons)

	2018	2019	2020
Ass meat*	10.7	11.1	11.6
Camel meat	11.6	10.7	11.4*
Camels' milk, fresh . . .	109.1	110.6	112.0
Cattle hides, fresh*	10.7	10.1	12.1
Cattle meat	61.0	57.5	68.8*
Cattle offals, edible* . . .	11.9	11.2	13.4
Cows' milk, fresh	732.3	776.3	822.8
Chicken meat*	19.3	19.7	20.1
Game meat*	29.5	29.3	29.4
Goat meat	28.2	30.8	31.3*
Goats' milk, fresh	376.6	391.7	407.3
Sheep meat	19.2	18.6	21.3*
Sheep's (Ewe's) milk, fresh . .	157.6	163.1	168.8
Hen eggs*	10.1	10.0	10.1

* FAO estimate(s).

Source: FAO.

Forestry

ROUNDWOOD REMOVALS
('000 cubic metres, excl. bark, FAO estimates)

	2018	2019	2020
Industrial wood	701	701	701
Fuel wood	11,651	11,875	12,103
Total	12,352	12,576	12,804

Source: FAO.

SAWNWOOD PRODUCTION
('000 cubic metres, incl. railway sleepers, FAO estimates)

	2018	2019	2020
Total (all broadleaved) . . .	4	4	4

Note: Figures assumed to be unchanged from 1993.

Source: FAO.

Fishing

(metric tons, live weight)

	2018	2019	2020
Capture (freshwater fishes) . .	31,042	40,058	46,000
Aquaculture	350*	352	649
Total catch	31,392*	40,410	46,649

* FAO estimate.

Source: FAO.

Mining

	2019	2020	2021
Hard coal ('000 metric tons) . .	225.9	246.9	231.8
Petroleum ('000 barrels)* . . .	6,623	6,272	6,401
Uranium (metric tons)	2,863	2,992	2,282
Gold (kg)	6,207	2,361	4,010

* Barrels sold to refinery.

Industry

SELECTED PRODUCTS

	2018	2019	2020
Cement ('000 metric tons) . . .	52.0*	260.0	n.a.
Electrical energy (million kWh) .	667.9	555.0	425.0

* Estimate.

Sources: partly US Geological Survey.

Finance

CURRENCY AND EXCHANGE RATES

Monetary Units
100 centimes = 1 franc de la Communauté Financière Africaine (CFA).

Sterling, Dollar and Euro Equivalents (31 May 2022)
£1 sterling = 770.824 francs CFA;
US $1 = 612.300 francs CFA;
€1 = 655.957 francs CFA;
10,000 francs CFA = £12.97 = $16.33 = €15.24.

Average Exchange Rate (francs CFA per US $)
2019   585.911
2020   575.586
2021   554.531

Note: An exchange rate of 1 French franc = 50 francs CFA, established in 1948, remained in force until January 1994, when the CFA franc was devalued by 50%, with the exchange rate adjusted to 1 French franc = 100 francs CFA. This relationship to French currency remained in effect with the introduction of the euro on 1 January 1999. From that date, accordingly, a fixed exchange rate of €1 = 655.957 francs CFA has been in operation.

BUDGET
('000 million francs CFA)

Revenue	2020	2021*	2022†
Tax revenue	760	831	1,001
Income and profits	192	209	237
Goods and services	270	318	391
International trade	215	222	272
Other taxes	83	82	100
Non-tax revenue	74	51	58
Special accounts revenue	18	15	16
Total	**852**	**897**	**1,075**

Expenditure	2020	2021*	2022†
Current expenditure	813	887	964
Wages and salaries	298	318	344
Goods and services	131	135	147
Transfers and subsidies	269	323	340
Interest	83	94	106
Adjustments to fiscal expenditure	1	—	—
Special accounts expenditure	32	19	27
Capital expenditure	997	1,119	1,242
Total	**1,810**	**2,007**	**2,206**

* Estimates.
† Projections.

Source: IMF, *Niger: First Review Under the Extended Credit Facility Arrangement and Request for Modification of Performance Criteria–Press Release; Staff Report; and Statement by the Executive Director for Niger* (July 2022).

INTERNATIONAL RESERVES
(US $ million at 31 December, excl. gold)

	2019	2020	2021
IMF special drawing rights	136.0	296.2	519.7
Reserve position in IMF	34.7	36.1	35.1
Foreign exchange	3.7	5.8	7.5
Total	**174.4**	**338.1**	**562.3**

Source: IMF, *International Financial Statistics*.

MONEY SUPPLY
('000 million francs CFA at 31 December)

	2019	2020	2021
Currency outside depository corporations	527.23	579.07	545.09
Transferable deposits	500.73	605.76	723.09
Other deposits	268.53	332.14	381.93
Broad money	**1,296.49**	**1,516.96**	**1,650.11**

Source: IMF, *International Financial Statistics*.

COST OF LIVING
(Harmonized Consumer Price Index for Niamey; base: 2014 = 100)

	2019	2020	2021
Food and non-alcoholic beverages	97.5	102.5	110.2
Clothing and footwear	106.4	106.8	108.2
Housing, water, gas, electricity and other fuels	116.9	116.7	117.5
Health	103.2	103.0	102.6
Transport	103.7	104.3	102.0
All items (incl. others)	101.5	104.4	108.5

NATIONAL ACCOUNTS
('000 million francs CFA at current prices)

Expenditure on the Gross Domestic Product

	2018	2019	2020
Government final consumption expenditure	1,082.0	1,182.3	1,246.3
Private final consumption expenditure	4,980.0	5,174.5	5,661.1
Gross fixed capital formation	2,013.6	2,328.1	2,223.0
Changes in inventories	35.1	22.2	12.9
Total domestic expenditure	**8,110.7**	**8,707.1**	**9,143.3**
Exports of goods and services	874.8	849.9	813.7
Less Imports of goods and services	1,871.0	1,989.2	2,047.6
GDP at purchasers' values	**7,114.5**	**7,567.9**	**7,909.3**
GDP at constant 2015 prices	**6,815.0**	**7,219.9**	**7,478.4**

Gross Domestic Product by Economic Activity

	2018	2019	2020
Agriculture, hunting, forestry and fishing	2,679.4	2,793.7	3,036.0
Mining and quarrying (including utilities)	606.3	669.3	673.7
Manufacturing	526.4	554.8	578.9
Construction	271.8	330.6	341.2
Wholesale and retail trade; restaurants and hotels	965.8	1,017.4	1,055.1
Transport and communications	335.0	358.8	369.5
Other services	1,304.6	1,399.2	1,436.6
Gross value added in basic prices	**6,689.4**	**7,123.7**	**7,490.9**
Indirect taxes (net)*	425.1	444.2	418.4
GDP at purchasers' values	**7,114.5**	**7,567.9**	**7,909.3**

* Figures obtained as a residual.

Source: UN National Accounts Main Aggregates Database.

BALANCE OF PAYMENTS
(US $ million)

	2018	2019	2020
Exports of goods	1,203.0	1,126.0	1,115.5
Imports of goods	−2,282.3	−2,326.1	−2,466.4
Balance on goods . . .	−1,079.3	−1,200.1	−1,350.9
Exports of services	247.0	260.7	222.5
Imports of services	−1,086.2	−1,068.9	−1,075.9
Balance on goods and services	−1,918.5	−2,008.4	−2,204.3
Primary income received . . .	135.2	136.1	144.3
Primary income paid . . .	−327.9	−328.9	−352.3
Balance on goods, services and primary income . . .	−2,111.3	−2,201.2	−2,412.3
Secondary income received . .	608.9	747.9	936.1
Secondary income paid . . .	−122.6	−119.1	−339.5
Current balance	−1,625.0	−1,572.4	−1,815.7
Capital account (net) . . .	624.0	631.1	705.3
Direct investment assets . .	−38.6	−32.0	−15.0
Direct investment from liabilities .	466.0	717.1	360.7
Portfolio investment assets . .	−9.0	−35.0	−4.3
Portfolio investment liabilities .	171.7	300.8	21.5
Other investment assets . .	−76.5	−273.2	78.3
Other investment liabilities . .	289.6	747.4	555.6
Net errors and omissions . . .	−14.2	−4.8	−10.2
Overall balance	−212.1	479.1	−123.9

Source: IMF, *International Financial Statistics.*

External Trade

PRINCIPAL COMMODITIES
(distribution by HS, US $ million)

Imports c.i.f.	2019	2020	2021
Vegetables and vegetable products	381.4	459.7	545.3
Cereals	322.8	396.4	474.1
Rice	315.7	393.2	469.9
Animal or vegetable fats and oils, and products thereof	126.6	104.9	103.0
Palm oil and its fractions . .	121.1	103.2	100.2
Miscellaneous edible preparations	55.7	96.7	91.5
Prepared foodstuffs; beverages, spirits, vinegar; tobacco and articles thereof .	224.9	297.5	330.4
Mineral products	232.2	207.4	244.5
Salt, sulphur, earth, stone, plaster, lime and cement	102.8	86.8	99.9
Cement, incl. cement clinkers, whether or not coloured . .	77.6	55.0	79.6
Mineral fuels, oils, distillation products, etc.	129.2	120.0	143.9
Chemicals and related products	212.0	352.0	231.6
Pharmaceutical products . .	108.3	259.2	130.8
Human, animal blood prepared for therapeutic, uses . . .	32.5	173.0	52.2
Plastics, rubber, and articles thereof	57.0	46.6	50.2
Textiles and textile articles .	103.7	81.1	69.8
Iron and steel, other base metals and articles of base metals	174.6	188.3	172.7
Articles of iron and steel . . .	84.7	119.5	115.3
Machinery and mechanical appliances, electrical equipment	489.2	377.0	345.8
Machinery and boilers, etc. . .	268.0	253.0	225.8
Moving, grading, levelling, etc. .	17.2	11.3	11.5

Imports c.i.f.—*continued*	2019	2020	2021
Parts suitable for use solely or principally with the machinery	83.7	69.0	47.8
Electrical and electronic equipment	221.3	124.0	120.1
Vehicles, aircraft, vessels and associated transport equipment	480.4	508.2	464.6
Vehicles other than railway, tramway	204.0	212.8	229.2
Aircraft, spacecraft, and parts thereof	272.6	292.2	220.2
Aircraft parts	188.2	245.6	157.6
Arms, ammunition and parts thereof	98.2	238.8	80.0
Parts and accessories for weapons.	70.9	89.0	64.0
Bombs, grenades, missiles, etc. .	25.9	148.9	129.2
Total (incl. others)	2,772.5	3,026.1	2,784.7

Exports f.o.b.	2019	2020	2021
Live animals and animal products	26.5	13.5	20.4
Live animals	23.5	11.9	19.3
Live bovine animals . .	16.8	7.7	15.2
Vegetables and vegetable products	75.1	25.9	42.6
Edible vegetables and certain roots and tubers	58.6	17.5	35.9
Onions, shallots, garlic, and other alliaceous vegetables .	52.0	14.2	31.9
Animal or vegetable fats and oils, and products thereof	57.2	15.3	11.2
Palm oil and its fractions . .	55.3	15.2	11.2
Mineral products	446.7	470.0	426.8
Ores, slag and ash	226.4	285.1	181.0
Uranium or thorium ores and concentrates	226.4	285.1	181.0
Mineral fuels, oils, distillation products, etc.	219.1	183.4	244.6
Petroleum oils, not crude . .	219.0	183.1	244.5
Pearls, precious or semi-precious stones, precious metals and articles thereof .	189.5	631.2	76.0
Gold unwrought or in semi-manufactured forms	189.5	630.9	76.0
Total (incl. others)	854.3	1,247.2	633.0

Source: Trade Map-Trade Competitiveness Map, International Trade Centre, marketanalysis.intracen.org.

PRINCIPAL TRADING PARTNERS
(US $ million)

Imports c.i.f.	2019	2020	2021
Algeria	46.8	25.5	34.7
Belgium	49.6	191.4	39.2
Benin	42.0	38.9	45.0
Brazil	28.0	53.2	45.4
China, People's Republic . . .	565.3	558.2	519.9
Côte d'Ivoire	91.2	108.8	94.1
France (incl. Monaco) . . .	547.9	674.9	393.8
Germany	45.7	56.1	84.0
Ghana	59.9	68.1	77.5
India	97.8	124.4	237.6
Indonesia	55.4	25.0	29.9
Italy	28.6	13.6	20.1
Japan	81.1	86.6	116.8
Malaysia	50.1	36.2	29.8
Nigeria	149.0	139.5	209.3
Pakistan	11.8	54.6	33.3
Thailand	221.8	178.7	165.8
Togo	27.1	38.1	52.8
Türkiye	147.5	47.3	50.0
United Arab Emirates	30.0	24.0	27.4
USA	159.0	199.4	179.4
Total (incl. others)	2,772.5	3,026.1	2,784.7

Exports f.o.b.	2019	2020	2021
Algeria	3.1	19.9	0.6
Belgium	1.4	0.1	7.0
Benin	3.2	10.7	8.6
Burkina Faso	35.8	78.2	91.4
Canada	1.5	54.8	42.7
Chad	16.0	18.0	9.8
France (incl. Monaco) . . .	228.6	212.7	146.6
Ghana	53.9	15.8	33.1
Mali	100.3	108.2	137.9
Nigeria	199.5	40.5	63.4
South Africa	0.0	8.1	19.5
Spain	0.9	12.8	0.7
United Arab Emirates . . .	189.9	623.0	57.3
USA	3.9	21.9	0.2
Total (incl. others)	854.3	1,247.2	633.0

Source: Trade Map-Trade Competitiveness Map, International Trade Centre, marketanalysis.intracen.org.

Transport

ROAD TRAFFIC
(motor vehicles in use at 31 December, estimates)

	2015	2016	2017
Passenger cars	183,074	198,631	214,134
Buses and coaches	10,108	10,676	11,373
Tractors and semi-trailers . .	24,451	25,496	27,110

CIVIL AVIATION
(traffic on scheduled services at Niamey International Airport)

	2019	2020	2021
Aircraft movements	11,476	7,713	13,401
Passengers carried ('000) . . .	377	161	266
Freight carried (metric tons) . .	7,694	8,354	9,022

Tourism

FOREIGN TOURIST ARRIVALS BY NATIONALITY*

	2018	2019	2020
Africa	88,607	108,391	48,192
America	14,139	17,296	7,691
East Asia and the Pacific . . .	12,542	15,342	6,822
Europe	41,864	51,211	22,767
France	29,977	36,670	16,304
Total	157,152	192,240	85,472

*Figures refer to arrivals at national borders.

Source: World Tourism Organization.

Tourism receipts (US $ million, excl. passenger transport): 77 in 2016; 83 in 2017; 98 in 2018 (Source: World Tourism Organization).

Communications Media

	2015	2016	2017
Telephones ('000 main lines in use)	110.0	160.8	114.3
Mobile telephone subscriptions ('000)	8,959.0	7,471.8	8,778.9
Broadband subscriptions, fixed ('000)	27.2	7.7	8.7
Broadband subscriptions, mobile ('000)	354.0	409.5	849.6
Internet users (% of population) .	2.5	4.3	10.2

2018: Internet users (% of population) 5.3.

Source: International Telecommunication Union.

Education

(2018/19 unless otherwise indicated)

	Institutions	Teachers	Students
Pre-primary	1,936*	5,643	177,822
Primary	17,749*	67,285	2,666,748
Secondary	1,401†	26,456*	786,582*
Tertiary	7‡	5,512	80,415
University	5§	505§	30,066†

* 2016/17 figure.
† 2015/16 figure.
‡ 2012/13 figure.
§ 2013/14 figure.

Source: partly UNESCO Institute for Statistics.

Pupil-teacher ratio (primary education, UNESCO estimate): 40.2 in 2018/19 (Source: UNESCO Institute for Statistics).

Adult literacy rate (UNESCO estimates): 35.1% (males 43.6%; females 26.7%) in 2018 (Source: UNESCO Institute for Statistics).

Directory

The Constitution

On 31 October 2010 90.2% of those who voted in a national referendum approved the text of the Constitution of the Seventh Republic, which was promulgated on 25 November. The main provisions are summarized below:

The President of the Republic is the head of state and is elected by direct, universal suffrage for a term of five years, renewable only once. Candidates for the presidency must be at least 35 years of age. The President appoints a Prime Minister, upon whose recommendation he/she appoints the other members of the Council of Ministers. The Prime Minister is the head of government.

Legislative power is exercised by the National Assembly, members of which are elected by direct, universal suffrage for terms of five years.

The judiciary is independent and consists of a Constitutional Court, a Court of Cassation, a Council of State, a Court of Auditors, and other courts and tribunals instituted by law.

The Constitution also makes provision for an Economic, Social and Cultural Council and a Higher Council of Communications.

The initiative for the revision of the Constitution belongs jointly to the President of the Republic and members of the National Assembly, four-fifths of whom must approve the proposed amendment (and three-quarters of the members must vote).

French is the official language.

The Government

HEAD OF STATE

President: MOHAMED BAZOUM (inaugurated 2 April 2021).

COUNCIL OF MINISTERS
(October 2022)

Prime Minister: OUHOUMOUDOU MAHAMADOU.

Minister of State, Minister of Foreign Affairs and Co-operation: HASSOUMI MASSAOUDOU.

Minister of State at the Presidency of the Republic: RHISSA AG BOULA.

Minister of State, Minister of Energy and Renewable Energy Sources: IBRAHIM YACOUBA.

Minister of National Defence: ALKASSOUM INDATTOU.

Minister of the Interior and Decentralization: HAMADOU ADAMOU SOULEY.

Minister of Professional Training: KASSOUM MAMAN MOCTAR.

Minister of Higher Education and Research: MAMOUDOU DJIBO.

Minister of Public Health, Population and Social Affairs: Dr ILLIASSOU IDI MAÏNASSARA.

Minister of Mining: OUSSEINI HADIZATOU YACOUBA.

Minister of Postal Services and New Information Technologies: HASSANE BARAZÉ MOUSSA.

Minister of Transport: OUMAROU MALAM ALMA.

Minister of Humanitarian Action and Disaster Management: LAOUAN MAGAGI.

Minister of Stockbreeding, Government Spokesperson: TIDJANI IDRISSA ABDOULKADRI.

Minister of Equipment: GADO SABO MOCTAR.

Minister of Justice, Keeper of the Seals: IKTA ABDOULAYE MOHAMED.

Minister of Communication, in charge of Relations with the Institutions: MAHAMADOU LAOULI DAN DANO.

Minister of Finance: AHMAT JIDOUD.

Minister of Trade: ALKACHE ALHADA.

Minister of Agriculture: Dr ALAMBEDJI ABBA ISSA.

Minister of Town Planning, Housing and Sanitation: MAÏZOUMBOU LAOUAL AMADOU.

Minister of Planning: ABDOU RABIOU.

Minister of Petroleum: MAHAMANE SANI MAHAMADOU.

Minister of Culture, Tourism and Handicrafts: MOHAMED HAMID.

Minister of Land Management and Community Development: MAMAN IBRAHIM MAHAMAN.

Minister of the Promotion of Women and the Protection of Children: ALLAHOURY AMINATA ZOURKALEINI.

Minister of National Education: Prof. IBRAHIM NATATOU.

Minister of Water Resources: ADAMOU MAHAMAN.

Minister of the Civil Service and Labour: HADIZA DOURA KAFOUGOU.

Minister of the Environment and the Fight against Desertification: GARAMA SARATOU RABIOU INOUSSA.

Minister of Employment and Social Protection: Dr IBRAHIM BOUKARY.

Minister of Youth and Sport: SEKOU DORO ADAMOU.

Minister of Industry and Youth Entrepreneurship: GOUROUZA MAGAGI SALAMATOU.

Minister-delegate to the Minister of the Interior and Decentralization, in charge of Decentralization: DARDAOU ZANEIDOU.

Minister-delegate to the Minister of State, Minister of Foreign Affairs and Co-operation, in charge of African Integration: YOUSSOUF MOHAMED ELMOUCTAR.

Minister-delegate to the Minister of Finance, in charge of the Budget: TCHOUSSO RAHAMATOU OUMAROU.

MINISTRIES

Office of the President: BP 550, Niamey; tel. 20-72-23-80; internet www.presidence.ne.

Office of the Prime Minister: blvd de la République, BP 893, Niamey; tel. 20-45-73-77; internet www.primature.ne.

Ministry of Agriculture: BP 12091, Niamey; tel. 20-73-35-41; internet www.agricultureelevage.gouv.ne.

Ministry of the Civil Service and Labour: BP 11087, Niamey; tel. 20-73-22-42.

Ministry of Communication: Immeuble Stade Général Seyni Kountché, ave du Zarmaganda, BP 368, Niamey; tel. 20-72-28-74.

Ministry of Culture, Tourism and Handicrafts: Niamey; internet www.culture.gouv.ne.

Ministry of Employment and Social Protection: Niamey.

Ministry of Energy and Renewable Energy Sources: Niamey.

Ministry of the Environment and the Fight against Desertification: Niamey; internet www.environnement.gouv.ne.

Ministry of Equipment: Niamey; tel. www.equipement.gouv.ne.

Ministry of Finance: ave des Ministères, BP 389, Niamey; tel. 20-72-48-88; e-mail contact@finances.gouv.ne; internet www.finances.gouv.ne.

Ministry of Foreign Affairs and Co-operation: blvd de la République, BP 396, Niamey; tel. 20-72-21-49; internet www.diplomatie.gouv.ne.

Ministry of Higher Education and Research: BP 628, Niamey; tel. 20-72-26-20.

Ministry of Humanitarian Action and Disaster Management: Niamey; tel. 20-72-48-87; e-mail contact@mahgc.ne.

Ministry of Industry and Youth Entrepreneurship: Niamey.

Ministry of the Interior and Decentralization: BP 622, Niamey; tel. 20-72-32-62; internet www.interieur.gouv.ne.

Ministry of Justice: BP 466, Niamey; tel. 20-75-27-20; internet www.justice.gouv.ne.

Ministry of Land Management and Community Development: Niamey.

Ministry of Mining: BP 11700, Niamey; tel. 20-73-45-82; internet www.mines.gouv.ne.

Ministry of National Defence: BP 626, Niamey; tel. 20-20-30-95; internet www.defense.gouv.ne.

Ministry of National Education: BP 557, Niamey; tel. 20-20-38-60; e-mail dpi.education.niger@gmail.com; internet www.education.gouv.ne.

Ministry of Petroleum: BP 603, Niamey; tel. 20-37-22-50; e-mail minisenergie2018@gmail.com; internet www.energie.gouv.ne.

Ministry of Planning: blvd de la République, BP 403, Niamey; tel. 20-72-36-17; e-mail contact@plan.ne; internet www.plan.gouv.ne.

Ministry of Postal Services and New Information Technologies: ave des Ministères, BP 458, Niamey; tel. 20-72-69-68; e-mail infompten@gmail.com; internet www.telecoms.gouv.ne.

Ministry of Professional Training: BP 2501, Niamey; tel. 20-72-52-13; e-mail formationpro@gouv.ne; internet www.mept.gouv.ne.

Ministry of the Promotion of Women and the Protection of Children: Niamey; tel. 20-73-98-37; e-mail mpfpe.niger@gmail.com; internet www.promotionfemme.gouv.ne.

Ministry of Public Health, Population and Social Affairs: BP 623, Niamey; tel. 20-72-69-60; e-mail daidrp@msp.ne; internet www.sante.gouvne.org.

Ministry of Stockbreeding: Niamey.

Ministry of Town Planning, Housing and Sanitation: Niamey.

Ministry of Trade: BP 480, Niamey; tel. 20-73-29-74.

Ministry of Transport: BP 12130, Niamey; tel. 20-72-28-21.

Ministry of Water Resources: BP 257, Niamey; tel. 20-73-20-25; internet www.hydraulique.gouv.ne.

Ministry of Youth and Sport: BP 215, Niamey; tel. 20-72-32-35; e-mail info@mjs-niger.org.com; internet www.mjs-ne.org.

President

Presidential Election, First Round, 27 December 2020

Candidate	Valid votes	% of valid votes
Mohamed Bazoum (PNDS—Tarayya) .	1,879,629	39.30
Mahamane Ousmane (RDR—Tchanji) .	812,412	16.99
Seini Oumarou (MNSD—Nassara) .	428,083	8.95
Albadé Abouba (MPR—Jamhuriya) .	338,511	7.08
Ibrahim Yacouba (MPN—Kishin Kassa)	257,302	5.38
Salou Djibo (PJP—Generation Doubara)	142,747	2.99
Oumarou Malam Alma (RPP—Farrilla)	118,259	2.47
Hassane Baraze Moussa (ANDP—Zaman Lahiya)	114,965	2.40
Others*	690,472	14.44
Total	4,782,380†	100.00

* There were 22 other candidates.

† Excluding 406,752 blank or invalid votes.

Presidential Election, Second Round, 21 February 2021

Candidate	Valid votes	% of valid votes
Mohamed Bazoum (PNDS—Tarayya) .	2,490,049	55.66
Mahamane Ousmane (RDR—Tchandji)	1,983,072	44.33
Total	4,473,121*	100.00

* Excluding 211,650 blank or invalid votes.

Legislature

National Assembly: pl. de la Concertation, BP 12234, Niamey; tel. 20-72-27-38; e-mail an@assemblee.ne; internet www.assemblee.ne.

President: SEINI OUMAROU.

General Election, 27 December 2020

Party	Seats
PNDS—Tarayya	79
Moden/Fa Lumana Africa	19
MPR—Jamhuriya	14
MNSD—Nassara	13
CPR—Inganci	8
RDR—Tchandji	7
MPN—Kishin Kassa	6
ANDP—Zaman Lahiya	3
PJP—Generation Doubara	2
RDP—Djamaa	2
RPP—Farrilla	2
ARD—Adaltchi-Mutuntchi	2
Amen Amin	2
MDEN Falala	2
RSD—Gaskiya	1
ADEN—Karkara	1
PSD—Bassira	1
ADR—Mahita	1
RNDP—Anneima Banizoubou	1
Others	—
Total	166*

* Owing to administrative problems, elections to the five seats allocated to Nigeriens in the diaspora did not take place.

Election Commission

Commission Electorale Nationale Indépendante (CENI): Rue des Bâtisseurs, Quartier Gamkale, BP 13782, Niamey; tel. 20-33-03-86; e-mail ceniniger@ceniniger.org; internet www.ceniniger.org; Pres. ISSAKA SOUNA.

Political Organizations

In 2022 there were 163 parties registered with the Commission Electorale Nationale Indépendante.

Alliance pour la Démocratie et le Progrès (ADP—Zumunci): Niamey; tel. 20-73-67-57; f. 1992; Chair. (vacant).

Alliance Démocratique pour le Niger (ADN—Fusaha): Niamey; f. 2014; Founder HABI MAHAMADOU SALISSOU.

Alliance des Mouvements pour l'Emergence du Niger (AMEN—AMIN): Niamey; f. 2015; Founder OUMAROU HAMIDOU LADAN TCHIANA.

Alliance Nigérienne pour la Démocratie et le Progrès Social (ANDP—Zaman Lahiya): Quartier Abidjan, Niamey; tel. 20-74-07-50; internet fb.com/andpzamanlahiya; Pres. MOUSSA HASSANE BARAZÉ.

Alliance pour le Renouveau Démocratique (ARD—Adaltchi-Mutuntchi): Niamey; f. 2010; Sec.-Gen. MAMANE TOUANI OUSSEINI.

Congrès pour la République (CPR—Inganci): Niamey; internet fb.com/cpr.inganci; f. 2014; Founder KASSOUM M. MOCTAR.

Convention Démocratique et Sociale (CDS—Rahama): BP 11973, Niamey; tel. 20-74-19-85; f. 1991; mem. of Alliance des Forces Démocratiques (AFD); Pres. MAHAMANE OUSMANE.

Mouvement Démocratique Nigérien pour une Fédération Africaine (Moden/Fa Lumana Africa): Niamey; e-mail mdnloumana@gmail.com; f. 2009; Pres. HAMA AMADOU; Sec.-Gen. OMAR HAMIDOU TCHIANA.

Mouvement National pour la Société de Développement (MNSD—Nassara): rue Issa Beri 30, cnr blvd de Zarmaganda, porte 72, BP 881, Niamey; tel. 20-73-39-07; f. 1988; sole party 1988–90; est. as MNSD; restyled as MNSD—Nassara in 1991; Pres. SEINI OUMAROU.

Mouvement Nigérien pour le Renouveau Démocratique (MNRD—Hankuri): Niamey; tel. 96-58-05-05; internet fb.com/MNRD-Hankuri-581170395291411; f. 2009; Pres. SIDI MOULAYE HAROUNA HAMBALI.

Mouvement des Nigériens pour la Justice (MNJ): e-mail mnj.contact@gmail.com; internet m-n-j.blogspot.com; f. 2007; First Vice-Pres. Capt. ASHARIF MOHAMED-ALMOCTAR.

Mouvement Patriotique Nigérien (MPN—Kiishin Kassa): Niamey; internet fb.com/MPN-Kiishin-KASSA-1493301117637658/; f. 2015; est. by former government minister Ibrahim Yacouba following his expulsion from PNDS—Tarayya (q.v.); Pres. IBRAHIM YACOUBA.

Mouvement Patriotique pour la République (MPR—Jamhuriya): Niamey; tel. 98-33-33-83; internet fb.com/jamhuriyampr; f. 2015; est. by dissident mems of MNSD—Nassara (q.v.); Interim Pres. ALBADÉ ABOUBA; Sec.-Gen. SANI MAIGOCHI.

Parti des Masses pour le Travail (PMT—al Barka): Niamey; tel. 20-74-02-15; Pres. MAMALO ABDOULKARIM.

Parti Nigérien pour la Démocratie et le Socialisme (PNDS—Tarayya): pl. Toumo, Niamey; tel. 20-74-48-78; internet pnds-tarayya.net; f. 1990; Pres. MOHAMED BAZOUM; Sec.-Gen. HASSOUMI MASSAOUDOU.

Parti Social Démocrate (PSD—Bassira): Niamey; internet fb.com/psdbassiraofficiel; f. 2015; Founder MOHAMED BEN OMAR.

Parti Social-Démocrate Nigérien (PSDN—Alheri): tel. 20-72-28-52; f. 1992; Pres. LABO ISSAKA.

Rassemblement pour la Démocratie et le Progrès (RDP—Djamaa): pl. Toumo, Niamey; tel. 20-74-23-82; party of late Pres. Maïnassara; Chair. HAMID ALGABID; Sec.-Gen. MAHAMANE SOULEY LABI.

Rassemblement des Patriotes Nigériens (RPN—al Kalami): Niamey; f. 2009; Pres. OUSMANE ISSOUFOU OUBANDAWAKI.

Rassemblement pour un Sahel Vert (RSV—Ni'ima): BP 12515, Niamey; tel. 20-38-16-06; e-mail agarba_99@yahoo.com; f. 1991; Pres. ADAMOU GARBA.

Rassemblement Social-Démocratique (RSD—Gaskiya): Quartier Poudrière, Niamey; tel. 20-74-00-90; internet fb.com/RSD-Gaskiya-567845756687660; f. 2004 following split in the CDS; Pres. CHEIFFOU AMADOU.

Union pour la Démocratie et le Progrès Social (UDPS—Amana): Agadez; internet www.udps-amana.com; represents interests of Tuaregs; Chair. RHISSA AG BOULA.

Union pour la Démocratie et la République (UDR—Tabbat): Quartier Plateau, Niamey; f. 2002; Pres. AMADOU BOUABACAR CISSÉ.

Union des Nigériens Indépendants (UNI): Quartier Zabarkan, Niamey; tel. 20-74-23-81; Leader AMADOU DJIBO.

Union des Socialistes Nigériens (USN—Talaka): f. 2001; Leader ISSOUFOU ASSOUMANE.

Diplomatic Representation

EMBASSIES IN NIGER

Algeria: route des Ambassades-Goudel, BP 142, Niamey; tel. 20-72-35-83; e-mail ambalgniamey@gmail.com; Ambassador BEKHEDDA MEHDI.

Belgium: ave de Niamey, YN 39, Quartier Yantala Nouveau, BP 10192, Niamey; tel. 20-73-94-18; e-mail niamey@diplobel.fed.be; internet niger.diplomatie.belgium.be; Ambassador MYRIAM BACQUELAINE.

Chad: ave du Présidence, POB 12820, Niamey; tel. 20-75-34-64; e-mail minaffec@intnet.te; Ambassador OUSMAN SOUGUI KOKO.

China, People's Republic: 4 blvd des Ambassades, Quartier Goudel, BP 873, Niamey; tel. 20-72-32-83; e-mail chinaemb_ne@mfa.gov.cn; internet ne.china-embassy.gov.cn; Ambassador JIANG FENG.

Cuba: blvd Askia Mohamed, Kouara Kano, Niamey; tel. 20-37-05-94; e-mail embacuba@niger.cubaminrex.cu; internet misiones.minrex.gob.cu/niger; Ambassador JORGE JOSÉ HADAD CAPOTE.

Egypt: Terminus Rond-Point Grand Hôtel, BP 254, Niamey; tel. 20-73-33-55; e-mail ambegypteniger@yahoo.fr; Ambassador SAYED MOHAMED AHMED EL-SALAHI.

France: route des Ambassades, BP 10660, Niamey; tel. 20-72-24-32; internet ne.ambafrance.org; Ambassador SYLVAIN ITTÉ.

Germany: 71 ave du Général de Gaulle, BP 629, Niamey; tel. 20-72-35-10; internet niamey.diplo.de/ne-de; Ambassador HERMANN NICOLAI.

Ghana: rue KK 75, Kouara Kano, BP 927, Niamey; tel. 20-37-04-06; e-mail niamey@mfa.gov.gh; internet niamey.mfa.gov.gh; Ambassador JONATHAN REXFORD MAGNUSEN.

India: 14 rue des Ambassades, Kouara Kano, BP 201, Niamey; tel. 20-37-00-29; e-mail hoc.niamey@mea.gov.in; internet www.indembniamey.gov.in; Ambassador PREM KUMAR NAIR.

Iran: 138 ave des Lacs, Plateau 45, BP 10543, Niamey; tel. 20-72-21-98; e-mail iranemb.nim@mfa.gov.ir; internet niger.mfa.gov.ir; Chargé d'affaires Dr MEHDI KARDOUST.

Italy: ave Issa Beri, BP 940, Niamey; tel. 20-72-79-88; e-mail niamey.ambasciata@esteri.it; internet ambniamey.esteri.it; Ambassador EMILIA GATTO.

Libya: route de Goudel, BP 683, Niamey; tel. 20-72-40-19; e-mail boukhari@intnet.ne; Chargé d'affaires a.i. Dr ABDULLAH BESHIR.

Luxembourg: rue YN-129, Immeuble Lux-Development, BP 13254, Niamey; tel. 20-35-12-73; e-mail eric.dietz@mae.etat.lu; Chargé d'affaires ERIC DIETZ.

Mali: Niamey; Ambassador YOUNOUSSA BARAZI MAÏGA (designate).

Mauritania: Koura Kano, rue 29, BP 12519, Niamey; tel. 20-75-38-43; e-mail ambarimniger@yahoo.fr; internet ambarimniamey.com; Ambassador SIDATTY CHEIKH AHMED AICHA.

Morocco: ave du Président Lubke, face Clinique Kaba, BP 12403, Niamey; tel. 20-73-40-84; e-mail ambmang@intnet.ne; Ambassador ALLAL EL ACHAB.

Netherlands: Ave de Niamey, Quartier Yantala, Niamey; tel. 20-73-94-18; e-mail nia@minbuza.nl; internet www.netherlandsandyou.nl/your-country-and-the-netherlands/niger; Ambassador PAUL THOLEN.

Nigeria: ave du Gen. Ibrahim B. Babangida Goudel, BP 11130, Niamey; tel. 20-73-24-10; e-mail embnig@intnet.ne; internet nigerianniamey.com.ng; Ambassador MUHAMMAD SANI USMAN.

Pakistan: blvd Bero 50m, Yantala Nord, Ilot 1368, Parcelle I, Plateau I, BP 10426, Niamey; tel. 20-75-32-57; e-mail parepniamey@hotmail.com; internet mofa.gov.pk/niamey-niger-our-team; Ambassador AHMED ALI SIROHEY.

Saudi Arabia: ave Charles de Gaulle, BP 339, Niamey; tel. 20-72-53-72; internet embassies.mofa.gov.sa/sites/niger; Ambassador ZAID BIN MAKHLID AL-HARBI.

South Africa: ave de la Radio Nord-Quest, Cité ORTN, BP 13417, Niamey; tel. 20-72-60-83; e-mail niamey@dirco.gov.za; Chargé d'affaires a.i. P. MOTSILILI.

Spain: 151 rue de la Radio, Yantala Commune 1, BP 11888, Niamey; tel. 20-75-59-61; e-mail emb.niamey@maec.es; internet www.exteriores.gob.es/embajadas/niamey; Ambassador NURIA REIGOSA GONZÁLEZ.

Türkiye (Turkey): 54 rue AM 5, Zone des Ambassades, Kouara Kano, Niamey; tel. 20-72-51-20; internet niamey.be.mfa.gov.tr; Ambassador ÖZGÜR ÇINAR.

USA: rue des Ambassades, BP 11201, Niamey; tel. 20-72-26-61; e-mail NiameyPASN@state.gov; internet ne.usembassy.gov; Chargé d'affaires a.i. SUSAN N'GARNIM.

Judicial System

According to the Constitution of the Seventh Republic, promulgated on 25 November 2010, the judiciary is independent and consists of a Constitutional Court, a Court of Cassation, a Council of State, an Audit Court, and any other courts and tribunals instituted by law.

Constitutional Court (Cour Constitutionnelle): BP 10779, Niamey; tel. 20-72-35-29; internet cour-constitutionnelle-niger.org; f. 2013; 7 mems; Pres. BOUBA MAHAMANE.

High Court of Justice (Haute Cour de Justice): Niamey; mems elected by deputies of the National Assembly from among themselves; competent to indict the members of the Government; Pres. ALI MARIAMA ELHAJ IBRAHIM.

Council of State (Conseil d'Etat): Niamey; f. 2013; Pres. ALKACHE ALHADA.

Court of Cassation (Cour de Cassation): Zone Industrielle, BP 613, Niamey; tel. 20-74-26-36; e-mail ibseyha@gmail.com; internet www.courdecassation.ne; f. 2013; First Pres. ABDOU ZAKARI.

Courts of Appeal: at Niamey, Zinder and Tahoua; Niamey: Pres. GAYAKOYE SABI ABDOURAHAMANE; Zinder: Pres. IBBO LASSEINI; Tahoua: Pres. KALLA GARBA.

Audit Court: rue 239, pl. Nelson Mandela, BP 14034, Niamey; tel. 20-72-68-00; e-mail courdescomptes@courdescomptes.ne; internet www.courdescomptes.ne; Pres. NARAYE OUMAROU.

There are also nine Tribunaux de Grande Instance (at Agadez, Arlit, Birni N'Konni, Diffa, Dosso, Maradi, Tahoua, Tillabéri and Zinder), one Tribunal de Grande Instance hors classe (Niamey), one military court and 63 Tribunaux d'Instance (one in each department).

Religion

According to the 2012 census, more than 99% of the population were Muslims. The remainder of the population comprised a small Christian minority, adherents of traditional beliefs and those professing no religious belief.

ISLAM

The most influential Islamic groups in Niger are the Tijaniyya, the Senoussi and the Hamallists.

Association Islamique du Niger: BP 2220, Niamey; tel. 20-74-08-90; Dir CHEIKH DJIBRIL SOUMAILA KARANTA.

CHRISTIANITY

The Roman Catholic Church

Niger comprises one archdiocese and one diocese. The Archbishop and Bishop participate in the Bishops' Conference of Burkina Faso and Niger (based in Ouagadougou, Burkina Faso).

Archbishop of Niamey: Rt Rev. DJALWANA LAURENT LOMPO, Evêché, BP 10270, Niamey; tel. 20-73-32-59; e-mail cartateguymi@voila.fr; internet eglisecatholiqueauniger.org.

Bishop of Maradi: Rt Rev. AMBROISE OUÉDRAOGO, Evêché, BP 447, Maradi; tel. 20-41-03-30; e-mail evechemi@intnet.ne.

The Press

The following were among those newspapers and periodicals (print and online) believed to be appearing regularly in the early 2020s:

ActuNiger: Niamey; tel. 92555412; e-mail contact@actuniger.com; internet www.actuniger.com.

L'Actualité: Quartier Terminus, BP 383, Niamey; tel. 20-73-30-91; e-mail actualite98@yahoo.fr; f. 2010; weekly; Dir of Publication MAHAROU HABOU OUMAROU.

L'Alternative: BP 10948, Niamey; tel. 20-74-24-39; e-mail alter@intnet.ne; f. 1994; weekly; in French and Hausa; Dir MOUSSA TCHANGARI; Editor-in-Chief ABDRAMANE OUSMANE.

Le Canard Déchainé: BP 383, Niamey; tel. 96275535; e-mail redaction@lecanarddechaineniger.com; internet lecanarddechaineniger.com; satirical; weekly; Dir of Publication ABDOULAYE TIÉMOGO; Editor-in-Chief IBRAHIM MANZO.

Le Courrier: Niamey; weekly; independent; Founder and Dir of Publication ALI SOUMANA.

Le Démocrate: 21 rue 067, NB Terminus, BP 11064, Niamey; tel. 20-73-24-25; weekly; independent; f. 1992; Dir of Publication ALBERT CHAÏBOU; Editor-in-Chief OUSSEINI ISSA.

Les Echos du Sahel: Villa 4012, 105 Logements, BP 12750, Niamey; tel. 20-74-32-17; e-mail ecosahel@intnet.ne; f. 1999; rural issues and devt; quarterly; Dir IBBO DADDY ABDOULAYE.

L'Enquêteur: BP 172, Niamey; tel. 93901874; e-mail lenqueteur@yahoo.fr; internet www.lenqueteur-niger.com; fortnightly; Dir of Publication SOUMANA IDRISSA MAÏGA.

L'Evénement: Zabarkan, ave de L'Entente, Porte 654, BP 12679, Niamey; tel. 20-74-15-75; internet levenementniger.com; 2 a week; Dir of Publication MOUSSA AKSAR.

La Griffe: Quartier Nouveau Marché, BP 195, Niamey; tel. 96980540; e-mail lagriffeniger@yahoo.fr; weekly; social and political satire; Dir of Publication MOUSSA DOUKA.

Le Hérisson: Niamey; tel. 96969024; e-mail ibouplanet@yahoo.fr; weekly; social and political satire; Dir of Publication IBRAHIM AMADOU.

Journal Officiel de la République du Niger: BP 116, Niamey; tel. 20-72-39-30; f. 1960; fortnightly; govt bulletin; Man. Editor BONKOULA AMINATOU MAYAKI.

Journal du Niger.com: Niamey; tel. 22-44-56-47; e-mail contact@cynomedia.com; internet www.journalduniger.com; Dir of Publication CYRILLE T. NONO.

Libération: BP 10483, Niamey; tel. 96979622; e-mail liberation_niger@yahoo.fr; internet liberation-niger.com; f. 1995; weekly; Dir BOUBACAR DIALLO.

Le Monde d'Aujourd'hui: Siège Terminus, Niamey; tel. 93401407; e-mail lemonde_niger1@yahoo.fr; weekly; independent.

Le Républicain: Nouvelle Imprimerie du Niger, pl. du Petit Marché, BP 12015, Niamey; tel. 20-73-47-98; f. 1991; weekly; independent; Dir of Publication MAMANE ABOU.

Le Sahel Quotidien: pl. du Petit Marché, BP 13182, ONEP, Niamey; tel. 20-73-34-87; e-mail onep@intnet.ne; internet www.lesahel.org; f. 1960; publ. by Office National d'Edition et de Presse; daily; Dir MAHAMADOU ADAMOU; Editor-in-Chief ASSANE SOUMANA; also Sahel-Dimanche, Sundays.

La Source: Academie des Arts, BP 5320, Niamey; tel. 96539577; e-mail amanimb9@yahoo.fr; weekly; Dir of Publication AMANI MOUNKAÏLA.

Le Témoin: BP 10483, Niamey; tel. 96965851; e-mail istemoin@yahoo.fr; 2 a month; Dir of Publication IBRAHIM SOUMANA GAOH; Editors AMADOU TIÉMOGO, MOUSSA DAN TCHOUKOU, I. S. GAOH.

Le Visionnaire: quartier Plateau, Niamey; tel. 98156240; weekly; Dir of Publication SALIFOU SOUMAÏLA ABDOULKARIM.

NEWS AGENCIES

Agence Nigérienne de Presse (ANP): BP 11158, Niamey; tel. 20-74-08-09; e-mail anpniger@intnet.ne; internet www.anp.ne; f. 1987; state-owned; Dir-Gen. MALAM MAMANE DALATOU.

Sahel—Office National d'Edition et de Presse (ONEP): BP 13182, Niamey; tel. 20-73-34-87; e-mail onep@intnet.ne; internet www.lesahel.org; f. 1989; Dir-Gen. RABIBA ABOUBACAR BOUZOU.

PRESS ASSOCIATION

Association Nigérienne des Editeurs de la Presse Indépendante (ANEPI): Niamey; Pres. IBRAHIM SOUMANA GAOH; Sec.-Gen. IBRAHIM MANZO DIALLO.

Publishers

La Nouvelle Imprimerie du Niger (NIN): pl. du Petit Marché, BP 61, Niamey; tel. 90340500; e-mail ninmarketing@gmail.com; internet www.nouvelle-imprimerie-du-niger.com; f. 1962 as Imprimerie Nationale du Niger; govt publishing house; brs in Agadez and Maradi; Dir MAMAN ABOU.

Broadcasting and Communications

TELECOMMUNICATIONS

AFR-IX Telecom Niger: Yantala Haut, YN 03, Niamey; tel. 97327373; e-mail contact.niger@afr-ix.com; internet afr-ix.com/afr-ix-telecom-niger; internet service provider; CEO MOULAYE ALI.

Airtel Niger: route de l'Aéroport, BP 11922, Niamey; tel. 96799999; e-mail assistance.client@ne.airtel.com; internet www.airtel.ne; f. 2001 as Zain Niger; present name adopted in 2010; Dir-Gen. ABDELLATIF BOUZIANI; 6.0m. subscribers (Sept. 2021).

Bacorex: Cité Poudrière, rue CI-85, Porte 4212, Niamey; tel. 20-34-01-01; e-mail bacorexsarl@gmail.com; internet www.bacorex.com; f. 2009; internet service provider; Dir-Gen. AHAMED BABATI IBRAHIM.

Moov Africa Niger: route de l'Aéroport, 720 blvd du 15 Avril, BP 13379, Niamey; tel. 20-74-44-44; internet www.moov-africa.ne; f. 2001; 68% owned by Orascom Telecom (Egypt); Dir-Gen. MUSTAPHA DADI; 3.0m. subscribers (Sept. 2021).

Niger Telecom: blvd Mali, Béro Échangeur, BP 208, Niamey; tel. 20-72-20-00; e-mail clientnt@nigertelecoms.ne; internet www.nigertelecoms.ne; f. 2016 following merger of Société Nigérienne des Télécommunications and Société Sahélienne des Communications; Dir-Gen. ISSAKA JAHAROU; 334,870 subscribers (Sep. 2021).

Zamani Telecom: 1282 blvd Mali Bero, BP 2874, Niamey; tel. 90222222; e-mail service.client@zamanitelecom.com; internet www.zamanitelecom.com; fmrly Orange Niger; present name adopted 2020; provides mobile, fixed-line and internet services; Dir-Gen. SOULEYMANE DIALLO; 4.2m. subscribers (Sept. 2021).

Regulatory Authorities

Autorité de Régulation des Communications Electroniques et de la Poste (ARCEP): 64 rue des Bâtisseurs, BP 13179, Niamey; tel. 20-73-90-08; e-mail arcep@arcep.ne; internet www.arcep.ne; f. 2018 to replace Autorité de Régulation des Télécommunications et de la Poste (f.1999); Pres. BÉTY AÏCHATOU HABIBOU OUMANI; Dir-Gen. HACHIMOU HASSANE.

Haut Commissariat à l'Informatique et aux Nouvelles Technologies de l'Information et de la Communication: BP 259, Niamey; tel. 20-72-24-64; e-mail contact@hcntic.ne; internet www.hcntic.ne; High Commissioner IBRAHIMA GUIMBA SAÏDOU.

BROADCASTING

Regulatory Authority

Conseil Supérieur de la Communication du Niger (CSC): 636 ave de la République, BP 11284, Niamey; tel. 20-72-23-56; e-mail cscniger@gmail.com; internet www.csc-niger.ne; 15 mems; Pres. Dr SANI KABIR.

Radio

Anfani FM: blvd Nali-Béro, BP 2096, Wadata, Niamey; tel. 20-74-08-80; e-mail kgb_anfani@yahoo.fr; private radio station, broadcasting to Niamey, Zinder, Maradi and Diffa; Dir-Gen. GREMAH BOUKAR KOURA.

Office de Radiodiffusion-Télévision du Niger (ORTN): BP 309, Niamey; tel. 20-72-31-63; e-mail ortny@ortn-niger.com; internet www.ortn.ne; f. 1967; state broadcasting authority; Pres. OUMAROU HIMA ISSOUFI; Dir-Gen. SEYDOU OUSMANE.

> **La Voix du Sahel:** BP 361, Niamey; tel. 20-72-22-02; e-mail ortny@intnet.ne; internet www.ortn.ne; f. 1958; govt-controlled radio service; programmes in French, Hausa, Djerma, Kanuri, Fulfuldé, Tamajak, Toubou, Gourmantché, Boudouma and Arabic; Dir IBRO NA-ALLAH AMADOU.

RURANET: Niamey; f. 2000; network of rural radio stations, broadcasting 80% in national languages, with 80% of programmes concerned with devt issues.

Ténéré FM: BP 13600, Niamey; tel. 20-73-65-76; f. 1998; Dir ZÉNABOU HIMA SOULÈYE; Editor-in-Chief SOULEYMANE ISSA MAÏGA.

Television

Office de Radiodiffusion-Télévision du Niger (ORTN): see Radio.

Radio Télévision Bonferey: rue du Collège Mariama, BP 2260, Niamey; tel. 20-74-17-17; e-mail bonfereytv@yahoo.fr; internet fb.com/Bonferey; f. 2007; Dir-Gen. MOUSTAPHA ZONGOMA.

Télévision Ténéré (TTV): BP 13600, Niamey; tel. 20-73-65-76; f. 2000; independent broadcaster in Niamey; Dir ZÉNABOU HIMA SOULÈYE.

Other television channels include Dounia, Canal 3 and Bonferey. The independent operator, Télé Star, broadcasts several international or foreign channels in Niamey and its environs, including TV5 Monde, Canal Horizon, CFI, RTL9, CNN and Euro News. Canal+Media Overseas, another independent operator, broadcasts over 50 television channels, both international and African, as well as a number of radio channels.

Radio and Television Associations

Association des Promoteurs des Radios Privées du Niger (APRPN): Niamey; tel. 96963371; e-mail jamila_souley@yahoo.com; Dir JAMILA SOULEY.

Association des Promoteurs de Radio-Télévisions Privées du Niger (APRTPN): Niamey; tel. 93930446.

Co-ordination Nationale de Radios Communautaires: Niamey; tel. 95260305; Co-ordinator MOUSSA HASSANE.

Finance

BANKING

Central Bank

Banque Centrale des Etats de l'Afrique de l'Ouest (BCEAO): rue de l'Uranium, BP 487, Niamey; tel. 20-72-24–91; internet www.bceao.int; HQ in Dakar, Senegal; f. 1962; bank of issue for the mem. states of the Union Economique et Monétaire Ouest-Africaine (UEMOA, comprising Benin, Burkina Faso, Côte d'Ivoire, Guinea-Bissau, Mali, Niger, Senegal and Togo); Gov. JEAN-CLAUDE KASSI BROU; Dir in Niger MAMAN LAOUANE KARIM.

Commercial Banks

Bank of Africa—Niger (BOA—Niger): Immeuble BOA, rue du Gawèye, BP 10973, Niamey; tel. 20-73-36-20; e-mail information@boaniger.com; internet www.boaniger.com; f. 1994 to acquire assets of Nigeria International Bank Niamey; 59.6% owned by BOA West Africa; Pres. BOUREIMA WANKOYE; Dir-Gen. SÉBASTIEN TONI.

Banque Atlantique Niger: Rond Point Liberté, BP 375, Niamey; tel. 20-73-98-88; e-mail info@banqueatlantique.net; f. 2005; subsidiary of Groupe Banque Centrale Populaire (Morocco); Dir-Gen. N'GAN GBOHO COULIBALI.

Banque Commerciale du Niger (BCN): rue du Combattant, BP 11363, Niamey; tel. 20-73-39-14; e-mail dga@bcn.ne; f. 1975; 92.05%

owned by Libyan Arab Foreign Bank, 7.95% state-owned; Administrator ESSAM ABURGIA.

Banque Internationale pour l'Afrique au Niger (BIA—Niger): ave de la Mairie, BP 10350, Niamey; tel. 20-73-31-01; e-mail bia@bia-niger.com; internet www.bia-niger.com; f. 1980; a subsidiary of Groupe Banque Centrale Populaire (Morocco); Dir-Gen. NANA AÏSSA ANGO.

Banque Islamique du Niger (BIN): Immeuble BIN, rue de Gawèye, BP 12754, Niamey; tel. 20-73-27-30; e-mail bin@bin-bank.ne; internet www.ta-holding.com/fr/intl/niger; f. 1983; fmrly Banque Masraf Faisal Islami; 56.96% owned by Tamweel Africa Holding, 35% by Islamic Development Bank (Saudi Arabia); Dir-Gen. ALIOUNE TRAORE.

Ecobank Niger: blvd de la Liberté, angle rue des Bâtisseurs, BP 13804, Niamey; tel. 22-40-02-00; e-mail dcorrea@ecobank.com; internet www.ecobank.com; f. 1999; 99.85% owned by Ecobank Transnational Inc (Togo); Dir-Gen. DIDIER ALEXANDRE CORREA.

Société Nigérienne de Banque (SONIBANK): 21 ave de la Mairie, BP 891, Niamey; tel. 20-73-47-40; internet www.sonibank.com; f. 1990; 25% owned by Société Tunisienne de Banque; Pres. OUMAROU ALMA; Dir-Gen. SOULEY OUMAROU.

Financial Institutions

Groupe Al Izza: rue de l'Islam Kalley Est, BP 2002, Niamey; tel. 20-33-13-68; e-mail alizzatour@gmail.com; internet www.alizza-transfert.com; f. 2017; Pres. BADAGÉ BAWA; Dir-Gen. MOUSSA WAZIRI.

SAHFI SA: blvd Mali Bero 62, rue IB 063, BP 10346, Niamey; tel. 20-75-45-58; owned by Association TANYO, Sonibank, BIA—Niger and BOA—Niger; Dir-Gen. AMADOU TIDJANI ABDOU.

Savings Bank

FINAPOSTE: BP 11778, Niamey; tel. 20-73-24-98; fmrly Caisse Nationale d'Epargne; Chair. Mme PALFI; Man. Dir HASSOUME MATA.

STOCK EXCHANGE

Bourse Régionale des Valeurs Mobilières (BRVM): rue du Grand Hôtel, Quartier Terminus, BP 13299, Niamey; tel. 20-73-66-92; e-mail akndiaye@brvm.org; internet www.brvm.org; f. 1998; national branch of BRVM (regional stock exchange based in Abidjan, Côte d'Ivoire, serving the member states of UEMOA); Man. ABDELKADER NDIAYE.

INSURANCE

Compagnie d'Assurances et de Réassurances du Niger (CAREN): ave Général de Gaulle (PL32), angle ave Jules Brévié, BP 733, Niamey; tel. 20-73-34-70; e-mail info@caren-niger.com; internet caren-niger.com; insurance and reinsurance; Pres. and Dir-Gen. IBRAHIM IDI ANGO.

Leyma—Société Nigérienne d'Assurances et de Réassurances (SNAR—Leyma): BP 426, Niamey; tel. 20-73-57-72; f. 1973; restructured 2001; Pres. AMADOU HIMA SOULEY; Dir-Gen. GARBA ABDOURAHAMANE.

Mutual Benefits Assurances Niger SA: Quartier Bobiel, blvd Tanimoune, BP 11924, Niamey; tel. 88888111; e-mail info@mbaniger.com; internet www.mbaniger.com; f. 2013; general; Dir-Gen. ABDOULAYE MAMADOU TRAORÉ.

La Nigérienne d'Assurance et de Réassurance: BP 13300, Niamey; tel. 20-73-63-36; e-mail niaassurance@yahoo.fr; Dir-Gen. OUMAROU ALMA.

SAHAM Assurance Niger: BP 13567, Niamey; tel. 20-74-13-61; e-mail mamadou.talata.doulla@sahamassurance.com; internet www.sahamassurance.ne; Dir-Gen. MAMADOU TALATA DOULA.

Sunu Assurances Niger: 216 rue de Kalley, BP 11935, Niamey; tel. 20-73-54-06; e-mail niger.iard@sunu-group.com; internet www.sunu-group.com; f. 1985; fmrly Union Générale des Assurances du Niger (UGAN); name changed as above in 2015; Pres. PATHÉ DIONE; Dir-Gen. (non-life) PASCAL PLAZIAT; Dir-Gen. (life) BINTA TINI.

Trade and Industry

GOVERNMENT AGENCIES

Agence Nigérienne de Promotion de l'Electrification en Milieu Rural (ANPER): 82 ave de la Radio, Niamey; tel. 20-35-01-73; e-mail info@anperniger.org; internet anperniger.org; f. 2013; govt agency for the promotion and implementation of renewable energy projects; Dir-Gen. SALOUHOU HAMIDINE.

Agence de Promotion des Entreprises et Industries Culturelles du Niger (APEIC): BP 227, Niamey; tel. 20-37-00-89; e-mail apeic.niger@gmail.com; 2009; Dir OUMAROU MOUSSA.

Agence de Régulation des Marchés Publics: BP 725, Niamey; tel. 20-72-35-00; e-mail armp@intnet.ne; internet www.armp-niger.org; Exec. Sec. ADAMOU ISSOUFOU.

Centre National d'Energie Solaire (CNES): BP 621, Niamey; tel. 20-72-39-23; e-mail cnes@intnet.ne; f. 1965; fmrly Office National de l'Energie Solaire (ONERSOL), present name adopted 1998; govt agency for research and devt, commercial production and exploitation of solar devices; Dir MARIAMA SIDO.

Conseil Economique Social et Culturel (CESOC): blvd Mali Béro, Boukoki, BP 2805 Niamey; tel. 20-72-20-17; e-mail contact@cesocniger.org; internet cesocniger.org; Pres. MALAM LIGARI MAÏROU.

Initiative pour la Transparence des Industries Extractives (ITIE): BP 10692, Niamey; tel. 20-75-59-50; Exec. Sec. AKSAR ABDELKARIM.

Office des Produits Vivriers du Niger (OPVN): blvd Zarmaganda, BP 474, Niamey; tel. 20-73-44-43; e-mail opvn@opvn.info; internet www.opvn.info; govt agency for developing agricultural and food production; Dir-Gen. ALHOUSSEINI IKTAM.

Riz du Niger (RINI): BP 476, Niamey; tel. 20-71-13-29; f. 1967; 30% state-owned; transfer to 100% private ownership proposed; production and marketing of rice; Pres. YOUSSOUF MOHAMED ELMOCTAR; Dir-Gen. SEYDOU ASMAN.

DEVELOPMENT ORGANIZATIONS

Agence Française de Développement (AFD): 203 ave du Gountou-Yéna, BP 212, Niamey; tel. 20-72-22-00; e-mail afdniamey@afd.fr; internet www.afd.fr; Country Dir JEAN-CHRISTOPHE MAURIN.

Institut National de la Recherche Agronomique du Niger (INRAN): route Corniche Yantala, BP 429, Niamey; tel. 20-72-53-89; e-mail dginran@yahoo.com; f. 1975; Dir-Gen. ILLIASSOU MOSSI MAÏGA.

Laboratoire Central de l'Elevage (LABOCEL): BP 485, Niamey; Dir-Gen. ZANGUI IBRAHIMA MAHAMAN SANI.

Stichting Nederlandse Vrijwilligers Niger (SNV): ave des Zarmakoye, BP 10110, Niamey; tel. 20-75-36-33; e-mail niger@snv.org; internet snv.org/country/niger; present in Niger since 1978; projects concerning food security, agriculture, the environment, savings and credit, marketing, water and communications; operations in Tillabéri, Zinder and Tahoua regions; Country Dir MAMADOU DIALLO.

CHAMBERS OF COMMERCE

Chambre de Commerce et d'Industrie du Niger (CCIN): 168 pl. de la Concertation, BP 209, Niamey; tel. 20-73-22-10; e-mail ccaianiger@yahoo.fr; internet cciniger.org; f. 1954; fmrly entitled Chambre de Commerce, d'Industrie et d'Artisanat du Niger (CCIAN); comprises 80 full mems and 40 dep. mems; Pres. MOUSSA SIDI MOHAMED; Sec.-Gen. MAMAN OUSMANE.

Réseau National des Chambres d'Agriculture (RECA): rue de la Grande Chancellerie, PL21, Porte 97, BP 686, Niamey; tel. 21-76-72-94; e-mail recaniger@yahoo.fr; internet reca-niger.org; consists of 8 regional chambers of agriculture; Exec. Sec. YOUSSOUF ELMOCTAR.

UTILITIES

Electricity

Autorité de Régulation du Secteur de l'Energie (ARSE): Arrondissement 1, Plateau, blvd Mohamed 6, ave de l'Irhazer, Niamey; tel. 20-72-50-31; e-mail contact@arse.ne; internet www.arse.ne; f. 2015; regulatory authority for electricity; Dir-Gen. IBRAHIM NOMAO.

Société Nigérienne d'Electricité (NIGELEC): 46 ave du Gen. de Gaulle, BP 11202, Niamey; tel. 20-72-26-92; e-mail nigelec@intnet.ne; internet fb.com/nigelecofficiel; f. 1968; 95% state-owned; 51% transfer to private ownership proposed; production and distribution of electricity; Dir-Gen. HALID ALHASSANE; Sec.-Gen. ARZIKA MAHAMADOU.

Water

Autorité de Régulation du Secteur de l'Eau (ARSEAU): Niamey; f. 2019; regulatory authority for water; Dir-Gen. ATTAHIROU KARBO.

Société d'Exploitation des Eaux du Niger (SEEN): blvd Zarmaganda, BP 12209, Niamey; tel. 20-72-25-00; e-mail contact@seen-niger.com; internet www.seen-niger.com; fmrly Société Nationale des Eaux; 51% owned by Veolia Environnement (France); production and distribution of drinking water; Dir-Gen. DENIS REBOUL.

Société de Patrimoine des Eaux du Niger (SPEN): Immeuble Sonara II, 6ème étage, BP 10738, Niamey; tel. 20-73-43-40; e-mail contact@spen.ne; internet www.spen.ne; f. 2000; Dir-Gen. AMADOU MAMADOU SÉKOU.

MAJOR COMPANIES

The following are among the largest companies in terms of either capital investment or employment.

Entreprise Nigérienne de Textile (ENITEX): route de Kolo, BP 10735, Niamey; tel. 20-73-25-11; f. 1997; textile complex at Niamey; fmrly Société Nouvelle Nigérienne des Textiles (SONITEXTIL); 80% owned by China Worldbest Group (People's Rep. of China), 20% by Nigerien interests.

Malbaza Cement Co: BP 03, Malbaza; tel. 20-74-26-02; e-mail ventes@malbazacement.com; internet www.malbazacement.com; f. 1963; privatized 1998; fmrly Société Nigérienne de Cimenterie; present name adopted 2018; privately owned; production and marketing of cement at Malbaza; Pres. and Dir-Gen. IBRAHIM IDI ANGO.

Nigerlait SA: Zone Industrielle, route de Kalmaharo, BP 13324, Niamey; tel. 20-74-29-56; e-mail nigerlai@intnet.ne; internet www.niger-lait.com; f. 1994; Pres. and Dir-Gen. ISSOUFOU BOUBACAR KADO MAIDAH ZEINABOU.

Office National des Produits Pharmaceutiques et Chimiques (ONPPC): BP 11585, Niamey; tel. 20-74-27-92; e-mail onppc@intnet.ne; internet www.onppc-niger.com; f. 1962; state-owned; Dir Dr ABDOUL KARIM KATAMBÉ.

Société des Mines de l'Aïr (SOMAÏR): BP 10545, Niamey; tel. 20-72-29-70; f. 1971; 56.9% owned by AREVA NC (France), 36.6% by ONAREM (Niger Govt); uranium mining at Arlit; Chair. FRÉDÉRIC TONA; Dir-Gen. ABDOULAYE ISSA.

Société des Mines du Liptako (SML): blvd Mali Béro, angle 169IB 73 St, BP 12470, Niamey; tel. 20-75-30-32; internet www.nigersml.com; f. 2004; 75% owned by A Group International, 20% by Nigerien Govt; operates gold mine at Samira Hill; Dir-Gen. ABDELKADER CISSÉ.

Société Nigérienne du Charbon (SONICHAR): BP 51, Agadez; tel. 20-44-02-48; e-mail sonichar@intnet.ne; internet www.sonichar.com; f. 1975; 69.3% state-owned, 10.1% owned by the Islamic Development Bank (Saudi Arabia), 15.8% by COMINAK and SOMAÏR; exploitation of coal reserves at Anou Araren and generation of electricity; Dir-Gen. ALKASSOUM MOUSSANA.

Société Nigérienne de Distribution des Produits Pétroliers (SONIDEP): 361 rue NB1, angle ave Abdoulaye Fadiga, BP 11702, Niamey; tel. 20-73-33-34; e-mail info@sonidep-niger.com; internet www.sonidep-niger.com; f. 1977; distribution of petroleum products; Pres. BARMOU SALIFOU; Dir-Gen. ALIO TOUNE.

Société Nigérienne de l'Urbanisme et de Construction Immobilière (SONUCI): route Francophonie, BP 532, Niamey; tel. 20-72-28-12; e-mail sonuci@intnet.ne; Pres. DJIKA RÉKIATOU BAKO; Dir-Gen. TANKARI MAHAMADOU.

Société du Patrimoine des Mines du Niger (SOPAMIN): Quartier Kouara Kano, ave des Ambassades, BP 11500, Niamey; tel. 20-73-51-54; internet www.sopamin.com.

TotalEnergies Niger: route de l'Aéroport, BP 10349, Niamey; tel. 20-38-28-81; internet totalenergies.com/fr/au-niger; fmrly Total Niger; present name adopted 2021; distribution of petroleum; Dir-Gen. DAGNON AIMÉ SOUROU.

TRADE UNION FEDERATIONS

Confédération Démocratique des Travailleurs du Niger (CDTN): 1046 ave de l'Islam, BP 10766, Niamey; tel. 96870318; e-mail c_cdtn@yahoo.fr; f. 2000; Sec.-Gen. IDRISSA DJIBRILLA.

Confédération Générale des Syndicats Libres du Niger (CGSL): Niamey; Sec.-Gen. SOUMAILA BAGNA.

Transport

Autorité de Régulation du Secteur des Transports (ARST): Niamey; f. 2020; regulatory authority for roads, railways, inland waterways and civil aviation.

ROADS

Niger is crossed by highways running from east to west and from north to south, giving access to neighbouring countries. A road is under construction to Lomé, Togo, via Burkina Faso, and the 428-km Zinder–Agadez road, scheduled to form part of the Trans-Sahara Highway, has been upgraded.

Société Nigérienne de Transit (NITRA): Niamey; tel. 20-74-25-46; internet nitra-sa.com; f. 1974; Dir-Gen. ABDOULKADRI HAMA ASSAH.

Société des Transports Urbains de Niamey (SOTRUNI): BP 135, Niamey; tel. 20-72-24-55; e-mail stratech@intnet.ne; f. 1963; fmrly Société Nationale des Transports Nigériens; operates passenger and freight road-transport services; 49% state-owned; Dir-Gen. DANIEL MAÏNASSARA TCHIWAKÉ.

RAILWAYS

In 2012 a multinational railway system was proposed to connect Benin, Niger, Burkina Faso, Togo and Côte d'Ivoire; as part of this project, Niger's first train station was inaugurated, in the capital, Niamey, in April 2014. In 2016 a 143-km section of track (between Niamey and Dosso) that would eventually form part of a 1,050-km link between Niamey and Cotonou (Benin) was inaugurated.

Organisation Commune Bénin-Niger des Chemins de Fer et des Transports (OCBN): BP 38, Niamey; tel. 20-73-27-90; f. 1959; 50% owned by Govt of Niger, 50% by Govt of Benin; manages the Benin-Niger railway project (begun in 1978); also operates more than 500 km within Benin; extension to Niger proposed; transfer to private ownership proposed; Dir-Gen. CORNEILLE AHOSSI.

INLAND WATERWAYS

The River Niger is navigable for 300 km within the country. Access to the sea is available by a river route from Gaya, in south-western Niger, to the coast at Port Harcourt, Nigeria, between September and March. Port facilities at Lomé, Togo, are used as a commercial outlet for landlocked Niger.

CIVIL AVIATION

There are international airports at Niamey (Hamani Diori), Agadez (Mano Dayak) and Zinder, and major domestic airports at Diffa, Maradi and Tahoua.

Agence Nationale de l'Aviation Civile (ANAC-NIGER): BP 727, Niamey; tel. 20-72-32-67; e-mail anacniger@hotmail.com; internet anacniger.org; f. 2010; Pres. ADAMOU MAHAMADOU; Dir-Gen. AYAHA AHMED.

Niger Airlines: rue KK 37, Porte 529, Koira Kano, BP 12281, Niamey; tel. 20-37-09-91; e-mail airlinesniger@gmail.com; internet nigerairlines.net; f. 2012; Dir-Gen. ABDOUL AZIZ LARABOU.

Tourism

Centre Nigerien de Promotion Touristique (CNPT): ave de Président H. Luebke, BP 612, Niamey; tel. 20-73-24-47; e-mail CNPT2@yahoo.fr; Dir-Gen. BOULOU AKANO.

Defence

As assessed at November 2021, Niger's armed forces totalled 5,300 men (army 5,200, air force 100). Paramilitary forces numbered 5,400 men, comprising the gendarmerie (1,400 men), the republican guard (2,500) and the national police force (1,500). Conscription is selective and lasts for two years. At November 2021 a total of 881 Nigerien troops were stationed abroad.

Defence Expenditure: Estimated at 112,000m. francs CFA in 2021.

Chief of General Staff of the Armed Forces: Gen. SALIFOU MODI.

Chief of Staff of the Land Army: Brig.-Gen. ABO TAGUÉ MAHAMADOU.

Chief of Staff of the Air Force: Col SALIFOU MAÏNASSARA.

Education

Education is available free of charge, and is officially compulsory for eight years between the ages of seven and 15 years. Primary education begins at the age of six or seven and lasts for six years. Secondary education begins at the age of 13 years, and comprises a four-year cycle followed by a three-year cycle. According to estimates by the United Nations Educational, Scientific and Cultural Organization (UNESCO), in 2019/20 pre-primary enrolment was equivalent to 7% of children in the relevant age-group (males 7%; females 8%). In 2018/19 primary enrolment included 59% of children in the appropriate age-group (boys 63%; girls 55%), while secondary enrolment in 2016/17 was equivalent to only 24% of the relevant age-group (boys 28%; girls 21%). The Abdou Moumouni University was inaugurated (as the University of Niamey) in 1973, and the Islamic University of Niger, at Say (to the south of the capital), was opened in 1987. In December 2001 the National Assembly approved legislation providing for the introduction of teaching in all local languages, with the aim of improving the country's literacy rate—one of the lowest in the world. According to the World Bank, government expenditure on education in 2021 represented 11.9% of total public spending in that year.

Bibliography

Abba, S. *Niger: La junte militaire et ses dix affaires secrètes (2010–2011)*. Paris, L'Harmattan, 2013.

Abdourhame, B. *Crise institutionnelle et démocratisation au Niger*. Talance, Université de Bordeaux IV, 1997.

Asiwaju, A. I., and Barkindo, B. M. (Eds). *The Nigerian-Niger Transborder Co-operation*. Lagos, Malthouse Press, 1993.

Carlier, M. *Meharistes au Niger*. Paris, L'Harmattan, 2001.

Charlick, R. B. *Niger: Personal Rule and Survival in the Sahel*. Boulder, CO, Westview Press, 1991.

Decalo, S. *Historical Dictionary of Niger*. 3rd edn. Metuchen, NJ, Scarecrow Press, 1996.

Deschamps, A. *Niger 1995: Révolte touaregue: Du cessez-le-feu provisoire à la 'paix définitive'*. Paris, L'Harmattan, 2000.

Frère, M.-S. *Presse et démocratie en Afrique francophone: Les mots et les maux de la transition au Bénin et au Niger*. Paris, Editions Karthala, 2000.

Gilliard, P. *L'extrême pauvreté au Niger: Mendier ou mourir?* Paris, Editions Karthala, 2005.

Grégoire, E. *Touaregs du Niger: Le Destin d'un mythe*. Paris, Editions Karthala, 2000.

Hamani, A. *Les femmes et la politique au Niger*. Paris, L'Harmattan, 2001.

Hamani, D. *Quatorze siecles d'histoire du Soudan Central: Niger du VIIè au XXè siecle*. Niger, Editions Alpha, 2012.

Idrissa, K. (Ed.). *Le Niger: Etat et démocratie*. Paris, L'Harmattan, 2001.

   Armée et politique au Niger. Dakar, CODESRIA, 2008.

Koré, L. *La rébellion touareg au Niger*. Paris, L'Harmattan, 2010.

Lund, C. *Law, Power and Politics in Niger: Land Struggles and the Rural Code*. Uppsala, Nordiska Africainstitutet, 1998.

Luxereau, A., and Roussel, B. *Changements économiques et sociaux au Niger*. Paris, L'Harmattan, 1998.

Maignan, J.-C., et al. *La difficile démocratisation du Niger*. Paris, Centre des hautes études sur l'Afrique et l'Asie modernes (CHEAM), 2000.

Mamadou, A. *A la conquête de la souveraineté populaire: Les élections au Niger 1992–1999*. Niamey, Nouvelle Imprimerie de Niger, 2000.

Moussa, S. *La responsabilité des commissions électorales au Niger*. Paris, L'Harmattan, 2017.

Rossi, B. *From Slavery to Aid: Politics, Labour, and Ecology in the Nigerien Sahel, 1800–2000*. Cambridge, Cambridge University Press, 2015.

Salifou, A. *Le Niger*. Paris, L'Harmattan, 2002.

Séré de Rivières, E. *Histoire du Niger*. Paris, Berger-Levrault, 1966.

Sherif, E. *Elections et participation politique au Niger: Le cas de Maradi : contribution à l'analyse électorale en Afrique*. Paris, L'Harmattan, 2014.

van Walraven, K. *The Yearning for Relief: a History of the Sawaba Movement in Niger*. Leiden, Brill, 2013.

   A Decade of Niger: Politics, Economy and Society, 2008–2017. Leiden, Brill, 2019.

Zakari, M. *L'islam dans l'espace nigérien. De 1960 aux années 2000*. (2 vols) Paris, L'Harmattan, 2010.

NIGERIA

Physical and Social Geography

AKIN L. MABOGUNJE

The Federal Republic of Nigeria covers an area of 909,890 sq km (351,310 sq miles) on the shores of the Gulf of Guinea, with Benin to the west, Niger to the north, Chad to the north-east, and Cameroon to the east and south-east. The population was enumerated at 140,431,790, according to the census of March 2006, giving an average density of 154.3 persons per sq km. According to a projection by the United Nations (UN), the population had risen to an estimated 216,746,933 by mid-2022 (238.2 persons per sq km).

Nigeria became independent on 1 October 1960, and in 1968 adopted a new federal structure comprising 12 states. A federal capital territory was created in 1979. The number of states was increased to 19 in 1976, to 21 in 1987, to 30 in 1991 and to 36 in 1996.

PHYSICAL FEATURES

The physical features of Nigeria are of moderate dimensions. The highest lands are along the eastern border of the country and rise to a maximum of 2,040 m above sea level at Vogel Peak, south of the Benue river. The Jos plateau, which is located close to the centre of the country, rises to 1,780 m at Shere Hill and 1,698 m at Wadi Hill. The plateau is also a watershed, from which streams flow to Lake Chad and to the rivers Niger and Benue. The land declines steadily northwards from the plateau; this area, known as the High Plains of Hausaland, is characterized by a broad expanse of level sandy plains, interspersed by rocky dome outcrops. To the south-west, across the Niger river, similar relief is represented in the Yoruba highlands, where the rocky outcrops are surrounded by forests or tall grass and form the major watershed for rivers flowing northwards to the Niger and southwards to the sea. Elsewhere in the country, lowlands of less than 300 m stretch inland from the coast for over 250 km and continue in the trough-like basins of the Niger and Benue rivers. Lowland areas also exist in the Rima and Chad basins at the extreme north-west and north-east of the country, respectively. These lowlands are dissected by innumerable streams and rivers flowing in broad sandy valleys.

The main river of Nigeria is the Niger, the third longest river of Africa. Originating in the Fouta Djallon mountains of north-east Sierra Leone, it enters Nigeria for the final one-third of its 4,200 km course. It flows first south-easterly, then due south and again south-easterly to Lokoja, where it converges with its principal tributary, the Benue. From here the river flows due south until Aboh, where it merges with the numerous interlacing distributaries of its delta. The Benue rises in Cameroon, flows in a south-westerly direction into the Niger, and receives on its course the waters of the Katsina Ala and Gongola rivers. The other main tributaries of the Niger within Nigeria are the Sokoto, Kaduna and Anambra rivers. Other important rivers in the country include the Ogun, the Oshun, the Imo and the Cross, many of which flow into the sea through a system of lagoons. The Nigerian coastline is relatively straight, with few natural indentations.

CLIMATE

Nigeria has a climate that is characterized by relatively high temperatures throughout the year. The annual average maximum varies from 35°C in the north to 31°C in the south; the annual average minimum from 23°C in the south to 18°C in the north. On the Jos plateau and the eastern highlands altitude moderates the temperatures, with the maximum no more than 28°C and the minimum sometimes as low as 14°C.

The average annual rainfall total decreases from over 3,800 mm at Forcados on the coast to under 650 mm at Maiduguri in the north-east of the country. The length of the rainy season ranges from almost 12 months in the south to under five months in the north. Rain starts in January in the south and moves gradually across country. June, July, August and September are the rainiest months countrywide. In many parts of the south, however, there is a slight break in the rains for some two to three weeks in late July and early August. No such break occurs in the northern part of the country, and the rainy season continues uninterrupted for three to six months.

SOILS AND VEGETATION

The broad pattern of soil distribution in the country reflects both the climatic conditions and the geological structure; heavily leached, reddish-brown, sandy soils are found in the south, and light or moderately leached, yellowish-brown, sandy soils in the north. The difference in colour relates to the extent of leaching the soil has undergone.

The nutrient content of the soil is linked to the geological structure. Over a large part of the northern and south-western areas of the country the geological structure is that of old crystalline Basement complex rocks. These are highly mineralized and give rise to soils of high nutrient status, although variable from place to place. On the sedimentary rocks found in the south-east, north-east and north-west of the country the soils are sandy and less variable but are deficient in plant nutrients. They are highly susceptible to erosion.

The vegetation displays clear east-west zonation. In general, mangrove and rainforests are found in the south, occupying about 20% of the area of the country, while grassland of various types occupies the rest. Four belts of grassland can be identified. Close to the forest zone is a derived savannah belt, which is evidently the result of frequent fires in previously forested areas. This belt is succeeded by the Guinea, the Sudan and the Sahel savannah northwards in that order. The height of grass and density of wood vegetation decrease with each succeeding savannah belt.

RESOURCES

Although nearly 180,000 sq km of Nigeria is in the forest belt, only 23,000 sq km account for most of its timber resources. These forests are mainly in Ondo, Delta, Edo and Cross River States. Nigeria exports a wide variety of tropical hardwoods, and internal consumption has been growing rapidly.

Cattle, goats and, to a lesser extent, sheep constitute important animal resources. Most of the cattle are found in the Sudan grassland belt in the far north. Poultry and pigs are increasing in importance.

Coastal waters are becoming important fishing grounds. Traditionally, however, major sources of fish have been Lake Chad in the extreme north-east, the lagoons along the coast, the creeks and distributaries of the Niger Delta and the various rivers in the country.

Mineral resources are varied, although considerable exploration remains to be carried out. Tin and columbite are found in alluvial deposits on the Jos plateau. Extensive reserves of medium-grade iron ore exist, and iron and steel production is being developed. There are also plans to exploit several recently discovered significant deposits of uranium.

Fuel resources include deposits of lignite and sub-bituminous coal, exploited at Enugu since 1915; however, total reserves are small. More significant are the petroleum reserves, estimates of which alter with each new discovery in the offshore area. The oil produced, being of low sulphur content and high quality, is much in demand on the European and US markets. Since Libya restricted production in 1973, Nigeria has been Africa's leading producer of petroleum.

Natural gas is also found in abundance, and has been undergoing development since the mid-1980s.

POPULATION

The Nigerian population is extremely diverse. English is the country's official language; Nigerian English (a dialect of English) and Nigerian Pidgin are also widely spoken. There are more than 500 native languages, and well over 250 ethnic groups, some numbering fewer than 10,000 people. Ten groups, including the Hausa, Yoruba, Igbo, Kanuri, Tiv, Edo, Nupe, Ibibio and Ijaw, account for nearly 80% of the total population. Much of the population is concentrated in the southern part of the country, as well as in the area of dense settlement around Kano in the north. Between these two areas is the sparsely populated Middle Belt. According to the 2013 Nigeria Demographic and Health Survey, Muslims comprised 51.5% of the total population and Christians 47.0%.

Urban life has a long history in Nigeria, with centres of population such as Kano, Benin and Zaria dating from the Middle Ages. Recent economic development, however, has stimulated considerable rural–urban migration and led to the phenomenal growth of cities such as Lagos, Ibadan, Kaduna and Port Harcourt. In December 1991 the federal capital was formally transferred to Abuja (which then had an estimated population of 107,069); however, a number of government departments and non-government institutions have remained in the former capital, Lagos. According to UN projections, at mid-2022 Lagos had an estimated 15.4m. inhabitants, Kano 4.2m., Ibadan 3.8m., Abuja 3.7m. and Port Harcourt 3.3m.

History

MAX SIOLLUN

Revised for this edition by the editorial staff

INTRODUCTION

Nigeria is Africa's richest and most populous country. Its gross domestic product (GDP) is greater than the combined GDP of the 14 other members of the Economic Community of West African States. The United Nations (UN) estimates that by 2050 Nigeria will be the third most populous nation in the world (behind the People's Republic of China and India), with a population of 400m.

Nigeria is also one of the most ethnically and linguistically diverse countries in the world. It has over 300 ethnic groups and over 500 different languages. Its history and politics have been deeply influenced by multiple fault lines regarding ethnicity, geography and religion. The three most populous ethnic groups are the Hausa, who are mainly Muslim and live in the north of the country, the Igbo, who are mainly Christians and live in the south-east, and the Yoruba, who live in south-western Nigeria and are split roughly equally between Muslims and Christians.

Nigeria's wealth lies in the oilfields of the Niger Delta areas near its southern coastline. The so-called 'middle belt' of Nigeria, between the north and south, contains hundreds of different ethnic groups practising Christianity, Islam and animist religions. The fact that Muslims live predominantly in the north and Christians predominantly in the south has historically attached a geographic polarization to religious controversies.

Yet, contemporary Nigeria cannot be understood without reference to its past. The colonization of Nigeria began in 1861 when the United Kingdom annexed the coastal city of Lagos in the south-west. From there, British forces moved northwards and eastwards to conquer the land presently constituting Nigeria. The British conquest of Nigeria was completed in 1914 when it amalgamated the country's northern and southern regions. The British authorities ruled the north of the country via a system of 'indirect rule', using pre-existing local chiefs known as Emirs as their proxies. The same system of indirect rule could not be easily replicated in the south-east, as many areas there did not have pre-existing chiefs or emirates under the control of a single political authority. In 1939 the UK subdivided Nigeria into three regions (north, east and west), corresponding to the three largest ethnic groups (Hausa in the north, Igbo in the south-east and Yoruba in the south-west). Although the country has since been further subdivided into 36 states, the tripodal structure bequeathed by the British still maintains a psychological influence on Nigeria's contemporary affairs.

INDEPENDENCE AND CRISES, 1960–66

Nigeria became independent on 1 October 1960. Its Government was modelled on the British parliamentary system, with some modifications to take cognizance of Nigeria's diversity. Ironically, political leadership was inherited by those who opposed independence (northerners), rather than those who campaigned for it (southerners). The exceptionally eloquent Alhaji Abubakar (later Sir Abubakar) Tafawa Balewa (a Muslim Hausa from the north) of the Northern People's Congress (NPC) was elected as the country's first (and to date only) Prime Minister. Queen Elizabeth II of the UK remained Nigeria's ceremonial head of state until 1963 when Nigeria became a republic. Dr Nnamdi Azikiwe (an Igbo from the south-east), who had been a leader and symbol of the independence movement, became the non-executive President.

However, the cultural, geographic, numerical and developmental differences between the north and south fuelled each region's fear of domination by the other. The south was better educated and more economically advanced, and Igbos especially benefited from the massive educational disparity between the south and the north, migrating north to fill the administrative and technical jobs vacated by departing British colonial officers. Igbo migration into the north stoked fear among the northerners that they would be economically and educationally dominated by the southerners (particularly the Igbos). Southerners in turn were apprehensive that the numerical majority held by the northerners in the Federal Parliament would lead to permanent northern political domination of the country.

The 1963 census pushed the north and south into overt confrontation. The census had political ramifications, as its results determined each region's share of seats in the Federal Parliament. The initial census results revealed massive (and suspicious) population growth in the south, and that it had overtaken the north's population. Prime Minister Balewa ordered a verification exercise, after which an additional 8m. people were 'found' in the north, thus restoring its numerical advantage over the south. The census controversy damaged relations between the north and south, with each region accusing the other of inflating its population.

Two elections, in 1964 and 1965, pushed the country to the edge of the abyss. In the 1964 federal elections the Premier of the Western Region Samuel Akintola's party, the Nigerian National Democratic Party, formed an electoral coalition with the ruling NPC, known as the Nigerian National Alliance (NNA). The Igbo-led National Council of Nigerian Citizens joined forces with Obafemi Awolowo's Action Group to campaign as the United Progressive Grand Alliance (UPGA). The UPGA alleged that the NNA planned to rig the elections and decided to boycott them. The NNA ignored the UPGA's boycott and proceeded with the elections. As a result the NNA won unopposed in many districts and increased its parliamentary majority.

President Azikiwe was appalled by the electoral irregularities and refused to ask Balewa to form a new government, as was the custom, triggering a constitutional crisis. After weeks of tense negotiations, shuttle diplomacy and rumours of a military coup, Azikiwe called on Balewa and the NPC once again to form a government.

Another controversial election occurred in 1965 in the Western Region, where Akintola's opponents alleged that he had rigged the polls to ensure that he was returned to power. The region descended into near anarchy, with mass protests, riots, arson and political thuggery. The Government dispatched the army's fourth battalion (commanded by a northerner) to restore order. The three consecutive years of crisis (1963, 1964 and 1965) culminated in the events of January 1966.

THE MILITARY IN POLITICS (1966–79)

The first four decades of Nigeria's post-independence history were dominated by eight different increasingly authoritarian and repressive military governments. The military first seized power in January 1966 and stayed in power for nearly 29 years.

On 15 January 1966 a group of young, British-trained army majors overthrew the Government in a violent military coup. Most of the coup leaders were Igbo, while the majority of their victims were non-Igbo. They assassinated several northern leaders, including the four highest-ranking northern army officers, as well as Prime Minister Balewa and the Premier of the Northern Region, Ahmadu Bello. They also killed Akintola and the Minister of Finance, Festus Okotie-Eboh. Crucially, the coup leaders killed no Igbo politicians. The army's commander, Maj.-Gen. Johnson Aguiyi-Ironsi (also an Igbo), suppressed the coup, but the surviving cabinet ministers ceded power to the army under Aguiyi-Ironsi's leadership. The fact that Aguiyi-Ironsi was also Igbo reinforced northerners' interpretation of the coup as an Igbo-led conspiracy to displace the northern-led Government and impose 'Igbo domination' on Nigeria. The coup and Aguiyi-Ironsi's subsequent policies reignited and intensified northern hostility to Igbos.

On 29 July 1966 northern soldiers led by Lt-Col Murtala Muhammed staged a retaliatory coup, murdering Aguiyi-Ironsi and over 200 other Igbo soldiers. The initial intention of the mutineers was not to seize control of the Government, but for the Northern Region to secede from Nigeria. They were dissuaded from doing so after northern civil servants in Lagos convinced them that secession would be disastrous for the north and leave it landlocked and impoverished, without access to a sea outlet in the south.

The northern soldiers selected Lt-Col Yakubu 'Jack' Gowon as the new head of state. At the age of 32, Gowon became the youngest head of state in Africa. Although Gowon was northern, he was a Christian from a minority ethnic group (the Ngas) outside the core Hausa and Fulani areas of the north. However, the Eastern Region's Military Governor, Lt-Col Chukwuemeka Odumegwu-Ojukwu, refused to recognize Gowon as head of state, as Gowon was not the most senior officer. Gowon's leadership did not dissipate anti-Igbo sentiment in the north, and northern mobs killed over 30,000 Igbos in the Northern Region between May and October 1966. More than 1m. Igbos fled the Northern Region and returned to their homeland in the Eastern Region in a mass and rapid population transfer that stretched the Eastern Region to breaking point. Between October 1966 and May 1967 the Eastern Region and the Federal Government remained in a state of undeclared separation. On 27 May 1967 Gowon announced Nigeria's division into 12 states: six in the south and six in the north. The Igbo-dominated Eastern Region was split into three new states in a division that separated Igbos from minority groups and granted the minorities states of their own. Three days later Odumegwu-Ojukwu announced the secession of the Eastern Region from Nigeria and designated it a new, independent country, called the 'Republic of Biafra'.

The Civil War, 1967–70

Gowon ordered federal troops to reclaim the Eastern Region, in what he termed a brief 'police action'. Indeed, both sides believed that matters would be resolved through skirmishes lasting just a few days. Instead, 920 brutal days of civil war ensued. Igbo resistance and motivation to fight were reinforced by Biafran propaganda, which indoctrinated Igbos to believe that they would be exterminated by federal soldiers if they lost the war. The conflict evolved into a war of attrition, with the more numerous and far better equipped federal troops pushing Biafran forces back, while failing decisively to break their resistance. Biafran troops retreated into an ever shrinking enclave. Although they resisted tenaciously, they had no real chance of prevailing. The Federal Government imposed a land and sea blockade to try to break the Igbos' determined resistance. Between 1m. and 2m. people died in less than three years of fighting, mostly from malnutrition; 90% of the victims were civilians.

The secession formally ended when Biafra surrendered in January 1970. Nigeria's civil war was distinguished by the remarkably rapid peace and reconciliation that followed, without the involvement of international bodies such as the UN. Gowon proclaimed a general amnesty for wartime combatants on both sides. He also declared that there would be 'no victor, no vanquished', and insisted that Igbos should be treated as returning prodigal sons, rather than a defeated enemy. He refused to conduct war crimes trials or demand reparations, and allowed some Igbo students, civil servants and soldiers to resume their old jobs and positions, at the same level of seniority as before the war.

The Post-war Years, 1970–79

Gowon dedicated the post-war years to reconciliation, rehabilitation and reconstruction. His charisma, magnanimity in victory, and identity as a northerner and a Christian gave him appeal in both the north and the south. Reconstruction was accelerated by an 'oil boom' that brought unprecedented riches to Nigeria. National earnings from crude oil exports increased by over 500% between 1970 and 1974. Although the new-found oil wealth created a small coterie of overnight millionaires, it failed to stimulate mass economic mobility. Nigeria became a wealthy country with poor people. Gowon observed that Nigeria's problem was not lack of money, but how effectively to spend its sudden riches. As many scrambled to access that wealth, corruption increased, and a small elite became accustomed to growing rich rapidly without sacrifice. Although Gowon was a great wartime leader, he was accused of indecision and procrastination in peacetime. His critics also accused him of failing to punish corrupt governors in his administration, and his popularity dipped in 1974 when he indefinitely postponed the return to democracy that had been scheduled to take place in 1976. On 29 July 1975 a group of colonels, including Shehu Musa Yar'Adua, Muhammadu Buhari and Ibrahim Babangida, overthrew Gowon in a bloodless military coup and replaced him with Murtala Muhammed (a Hausa Muslim), who had led the coup that brought Gowon to power in 1966.

THE MUHAMMED-OBASANJO GOVERNMENT AND THE RETURN TO DEMOCRACY, 1975–83

Muhammed was a decisive (almost impulsive) leader. He dismissed over 10,000 civil servants in a massive campaign against corruption and inefficiency, announced that Nigeria's capital would relocate from Lagos to Abuja (in the geographic centre of the country) and pledged to restore Nigeria to democracy in 1979. These measures made Muhammed the most popular Nigerian leader to date; however, his popularity may have made him complacent about his security. He routinely travelled to work in an unescorted car without a long motorcade or heavy security. On 13 February 1976 soldiers from northern minority ethnic groups in the Middle Belt ambushed Muhammed on his way to work and assassinated him during a failed coup attempt. The majority of the army remained loyal, rallied behind the Chief of Army Staff, Lt-Gen. Theophilus Danjuma, and suppressed the coup. A special military tribunal sentenced to death 39 people (most of whom were Christians from the Middle Belt) for involvement in the coup, and they were executed by firing squad.

Muhammed was succeeded by his deputy, Lt-Gen. Olusegan Obasanjo. To assuage the feelings of the Muslim north, Lt-Col Yar'Adua (a Fulani Muslim from the far north-west) was double promoted to the rank of brigadier over several senior officers in order to make him Obasanjo's deputy. Obasanjo continued Muhammed's policies and the transition to democracy. He led Nigeria until 1 October 1979, when he and other senior military officers retired, promulgated a new Constitution and ceded power to a democratically elected government following the holding of multi-party legislative and presidential elections, which were won by Alhaji Shehu Shagari of the National Party of Nigeria. The new Constitution replaced the parliamentary system with a federal presidential system modelled on that of the USA. It also introduced new power-sharing provisions aimed at reducing ethnic, regional and religious rivalry in politics. It banned political parties from adopting names, emblems or mottoes with ethnic or religious connotations. Each party's headquarters had to be located in the national capital city. To be elected President, a candidate not only had to win the most votes, but also had to secure at least 25% of the votes in at least two-thirds of Nigeria's states. The President was also obliged to appoint at least one minister from each state. These measures were intended to oblige all parties to become multi-ethnic and multi-regional organizations.

THE RETURN OF MILITARY RULE, 1983–99

The return to democracy was short-lived. On 31 December 1983 the army overthrew the administration of President Shagari and returned to power under a new military government led by Maj.-Gen. Muhammadu Buhari.

The First Buhari Government, 1983–85

Buhari's Government launched the most severe anti-corruption campaign in Nigeria's history. It closed Nigeria's borders (trapping politicians inside), arrested nearly 500 politicians and businessmen, tried them by military tribunals with no juries or right of appeal to higher courts, and sentenced many of them to long prison terms for corruption (some were given jail sentences of over 100 years). In March 1984 Buhari's regime inaugurated a nationwide campaign termed 'War Against Indiscipline' (WAI) aimed at promoting patriotism, environmental sanitation, a strong work ethic, punctuality and civic virtues. The zenith of Buhari's anti-corruption campaign was the extraordinary kidnap of the former Minister of Transport, Umaru Dikko (who had fled to the UK to evade arrest) in 1984. The Nigerian security forces (acting with the assistance of Israeli agents) kidnapped Dikko in the British capital, London, in a spectacular attempt to return him to Nigeria to face trial for corruption. Although Dikko's forced repatriation was foiled by British police, the alleged involvement of Nigerian officials led to a two-year suspension of diplomatic relations between Britain and Nigeria.

The harshness of Buhari's policies dissipated his initial popularity. Buhari's Government enacted decrees that empowered it to arrest and detain anyone deemed a danger to state security without charge or trial, and approved the public execution of convicted drug dealers by firing squad. On 27 August 1985 Buhari was overthrown in a military coup and replaced by Maj.-Gen. (later Gen.) Ibrahim Babangida. Nigerians welcomed Buhari's overthrow, as Babangida was presumed to be more benevolent and progressive than the stern and uncompromising Buhari.

The Babangida Government, 1985–93

Babangida's Government was embroiled in controversy throughout its existence. Only four months after coming to office, the Government announced that it had uncovered a plot to overthrow Babangida, allegedly led by a close friend of the latter, Maj.-Gen. Mamman Vatsa. In March 1986 a special military tribunal sentenced Vatsa and nine other accomplices to death for treason, and they were executed by firing squad. Babangida had, in January, announced plans to return Nigeria to civilian-led democracy in 1990. However, the Government blocked the formation of independent political parties, and instead created two parties itself, with one party 'a little to the left' (the Social Democratic Party, SDP), and the other party 'a little to the right' (the National Republican Convention). It then asked politicians to join one of the two parties.

Babangida postponed the return to democracy three times before scheduling a presidential election for 12 June 1993. With preliminary results indicating that Moshood Abiola (a wealthy Yoruba Muslim from the south-west) of the SDP was likely to secure a convincing victory, the military abruptly annulled the election results and refused to cede power to Abiola. Yorubas were outraged, and the annulment engulfed the country in its most serious political crisis since the civil war. The ferment caused by the annulment convinced Babangida to resign on 27 August, but he refused to recognize Abiola's election victory, and instead ceded power to an Interim National Government (ING) led by Ernest Shonekan (who, like Abiola, was a Yoruba civilian from the south-west). However, Shonekan resigned on 17 November, and was replaced by the Minister of Defence, Gen. Sani Abacha, who dissolved the ING, dismissed all elected state governors and legislators, and inaugurated a new military Government.

The Abacha Government, 1993–98

Abacha was intolerant of dissent and opposition, and his security officers conducted the most ruthless suppression of opposition by any Nigerian military regime to date. In June 1994 Abacha ordered Abiola's arrest after the latter declared himself President on the first anniversary of the annulled June 1993 election. Abiola's supporters were either arrested, forced into exile and/or assassinated. Retired military officers who criticized the Government's excesses were not spared. Obasanjo and his former deputy, Yar'Adua, were arrested in March 1995 for their alleged involvement in a plot to overthrow Abacha. A sceptical Nigerian public dubbed the alleged planned coup a 'phantom coup' concocted by the Government to eliminate the opposition. Several journalists and pro-democracy campaigners who reported on the coup plot or criticized the Government were also arrested, and tried by a special military tribunal for being 'accessories after the fact'. The tribunal convicted and passed prison sentences on 43 people (including Obasanjo and Yar'Adua).

In November 1995 Nigeria became a pariah nation and was expelled from the Commonwealth after renowned author and screenwriter Ken Saro-Wiwa and eight other activists from the Movement for the Survival of the Ogoni People (MOSOP) were executed. Saro-Wiwa and MOSOP had been campaigning for compensation to be paid to the Ogoni people of the Niger Delta for the environmental damage caused to their lands by the drilling and spillages of major petroleum companies. A special tribunal convened by the Government convicted Saro-Wiwa and his co-defendants on charges of inciting the murder of four pro-Government Ogoni chiefs.

In February 1998 six Yoruba officers (including Abacha's deputy, Lt-Gen. Oladipo Diya) were convicted of plotting to overthrow Abacha, and sentenced to death. Abacha announced that he would hand over power to a democratically elected civilian President on 1 October and appeared on the verge of transforming from a military ruler into a civilian head of state after all five political parties unanimously adopted him as their presidential candidate. However, on 8 June Abacha died suddenly of a reported heart attack and was buried without an autopsy having been carried out (some Nigerians described his death as 'a coup from heaven').

The Abubakar Government, 1998–99

Abacha was succeeded as head of state by the hitherto Chief of Defence Staff, Maj.-Gen. Abdulsalami Abubakar. Abubakar released Obasanjo and many other political prisoners who had been detained by Abacha's security agents. In addition, he agreed to release Abiola from detention. However, on the brink of his release, Abiola died of a heart attack on 7 July 1998. The deaths of Abacha and Abiola removed from the political scene the two principal protagonists whose struggle for power had paralysed Nigerian politics since 1993.

Abubakar subsequently announced that Nigeria would return to democracy in May 1999. However, the deaths of Abacha and Abiola did not dissipate southern grievances with the north. Southerners complained bitterly of northern domination of the military and politics and of northerners having ruled Nigeria for 35 of its 38 post-independence years. Yorubas believed that the northern-led military assassinated Abiola and demanded an immediate end to military rule, with a political 'power shift' to the south. Influential retired northern generals coaxed Obasanjo into entering the presidential race. Obasanjo was duly selected as the presidential candidate of the People's Democratic Party (PDP), a new party formed by a coalition of wealthy retired military officers and veteran politicians. The opposition Alliance for Democracy and All People's Party also jointly fielded a Yoruba presidential candidate (Olu Falae). Nevertheless, on 27 February Obasanjo won the presidential election, with 62.8% of votes cast, and on 29 May was sworn in as Nigeria's first democratically elected President in over 15 years.

RETURN TO CIVILIAN RULE

Obasanjo became Nigeria's head of state almost 20 years after he last led the country as a military ruler. He inherited a politicized military, an embittered society and a debt-laden economy, with foreign debt of over US $30,000m. Furthermore, following its ostracization by the international community, Nigeria's reputation on the world stage had reached a nadir. However, Obasanjo possessed the political dexterity to bargain with foreign heads of state and international lending institutions, and he was equally successful in dealing with Nigeria's domestic political oligarchs. His first priority was to depoliticize the military. Within a month, Obasanjo had summarily retired 93 military officers who had been members of former military governments. He retired hundreds more officers over the next four years, replacing them with apolitical officers who had not served in previous military administrations. As a retired general, he was able to carry out military reforms more aggressively than a civilian head of state would have dared with a coup-prone army.

Obasanjo also embarked upon economic reforms and privatized state-owned enterprises. His reforms were enabled by a team of capable technocrats, including Ngozi Okonjo-Iweala (a renowned World Bank executive who returned from the USA to become Minister of Finance), Nasir El-Rufai (Minister of the Federal Capital Territory), Oby Ezekwesili (Minister of Education), and the Governor of the Central Bank of Nigeria (CBN) and renowned economist, Prof. Chukwuma Charles Soludo). Okonjo-Iweala's contacts and expertise with international financial institutions were instrumental in the rescheduling and repayment of Nigeria's 'Paris Club' debt in 2006. Nigeria thus became the first African country to pay off its debt to the group of creditor nations, while the economy was boosted by a large increase in global oil prices.

Obasanjo was re-elected for a second term in 2003 after defeating Buhari. Also in 2003 the Federal Government created a new anti-corruption agency, the Economic and Financial Crimes Commission (EFCC), headed by a young northern police officer, Nuhu Ribadu. The EFCC achieved notable success in its campaign against corruption, including arresting and securing corruption convictions against state governors and ministers.

In 2007, shortly before the expiry of Obasanjo's second elected term of office, his supporters made an unsuccessful bid to amend the Constitution in order to allow him to govern for an unprecedented third term. Obasanjo and his Vice-President, Atiku Abubakar, became estranged after Abubakar opposed the constitutional amendment, and instead sought the presidency for himself. Obasanjo retaliated by opposing Abubakar's presidential ambitions and commencing corruption investigations against him. Obasanjo instead persuaded the PDP to accept the Governor of Katsina State, Umaru Musa Yar'Adua (a Fulani Muslim from the north), as its presidential candidate for the 2007 election. Yar'Adua was favoured for three reasons. First, he was the younger brother of Obasanjo's deceased close friend and former deputy, Maj-Gen. Shehu Musa Yar'Adua. Second, Ribadu had revealed that he was preparing corruption charges against 31 of Nigeria's 36 state governors and Yar'Adua was not among those under investigation for corruption. Third, Obasanjo needed a northern candidate to reciprocate the north's 'power shift' to the south in 1999, by returning power to the north after the south had enjoyed its 'turn' in power.

THE YAR'ADUA PRESIDENCY, 2007–10

Yar'Adua secured a landslide victory in the presidential election (held in April 2007), winning 70% of votes cast. Buhari received 18.6% and Abubakar 7.2%. Although the defeated candidates rejected the outcome and claimed that the PDP had massively inflated its vote, Yar'Adua was sworn in as President on 29 May. In contrast to previous heads of state, he projected a quiet and reliable persona, having pledged extensive reforms to combat corruption. However, the new President inherited severe social and political problems, including an armed insurgency that threatened Nigeria's economy.

The Niger Delta Insurgency

Nigeria's Constitution vests ownership of mineral resources (including oil) in the Federal Government, which collects oil revenues and then divides it among the states under a revenue-sharing formula known as 'derivation'. Oil-producing states in the Niger Delta (principally Akwa Ibom, Bayelsa, Delta and Rivers states) became aggrieved that oil drilled from their land caused environmental devastation, polluted farms, crops and rivers, and was used to enrich other parts of Nigeria. Despite providing the vast majority of Nigeria's wealth, the oil-producing states remained among the poorest and least-developed regions in the country. Years of pent-up grievances, coupled with massive youth unemployment in the Niger Delta, erupted when youths formed militant groups and waged an insurgency from 2004 to protest against economic exploitation and environmental pollution in their states, demanding greater regional autonomy and control of oil extracted from their states. Militants groups included the Niger Delta People's Volunteer Force and the Movement for the Emancipation of the Niger Delta, and they sabotaged oil pipelines, attacked oil installations and kidnapped oil workers. Oil companies closed some of their facilities and evacuated their staff. The militancy was worsened by the activities of criminal syndicates, which engaged in piracy and the theft of oil from pipelines. The insecurity severely disrupted Nigeria's oil production and economy and caused an increase in global oil prices.

The armed forces launched a large-scale crackdown on the militants in 2008 and 2009, raiding camps, seizing weapons and using boats to patrol the creeks of the Niger Delta. The offensive demonstrated to both sides that neither could achieve their aim by military means alone. The inhospitable topography of the Delta proved a challenge for the military as its narrow creeks, waterways and marshes were dangerous for soldiers and provided hiding places for the militants and their weapons. Conversely, the militants could not win a war against the better-funded government troops. In June 2009 the Federal Government announced an amnesty, and more than 25,000 militants agreed to lay down their weapons in exchange for monthly cash stipends and training from the Government. Although the amnesty programme achieved its objective in ending the violence and allowing the resumption of oil extraction, it did not address underlying structural issues concerning the Nigerian federation. It also set a 'cash for guns' precedent by effectively adding the militants to the Government's payroll and paying them per weapon surrendered. Former militant leaders became wealthy from government patronage and contracts; some were even awarded security contracts to guard the oil installations that they had previously attacked.

Constitutional Crisis

In November 2009 Yar'Adua travelled to Saudi Arabia for medical treatment. Two months later he had yet to return to Nigeria and had been neither seen nor heard from, and speculation mounted about his health. The Constitution stipulated that power would be delegated to the Vice-President upon the President informing the Senate President and the Speaker of the House of Representatives of his absence from the country or incapacitation. Yar'Adua had failed to inform those office-holders and, unsurprisingly, the Constitution did not envisage a situation where the President would leave the country without informing the Vice-President or key political actors, and remain incommunicado thereafter. Yar'Adua's failure to make a formal handover contingency prior to his absence triggered a constitutional crisis. During his absence, Nigeria was leaderless.

Ethno-regional politics influenced Yar'Adua's reticence temporarily to delegate power to Vice-President Goodluck Jonathan. Yar'Adua's illness threatened not just him, but the political fortunes of an entire region. The ruling PDP had a policy of 'zoning' its candidate for the presidency, and for other key offices, to candidates from different parts of the country. Former President Obasanjo (a Yoruba Christian from the south) stood as the PDP's candidate for two terms of office, and when Obasanjo's term of office expired in 2007, the PDP 'zoned' the presidency to the north via Yar'Adua. The expectation was that Yar'Adua would serve two terms of office (i.e. until 2015) before the PDP 'zoned' the presidency back to the south. However, Yar'Adua's illness threatened to disrupt the regional reciprocity of Nigerian politics. Yar'Adua's supporters feared that allowing Vice-President Jonathan to deputize for Yar'Adua would truncate the north's 'turn' in the presidency.

In January 2010 Yar'Adua (or someone purporting to be him) broke his silence in a British Broadcasting Corporation audio interview, supposedly from his hospital bed; however, a Nigerian newspaper reported that Yar'Adua was comatose and 'brain dead'. After nearly three months of controversy and tension, the National Assembly appointed Jonathan as Acting President on 9 February by invoking a contrived doctrine of 'necessity' as the only way to end the constitutional impasse caused by Yar'Adua's absence. On 23 February Yar'Adua suddenly returned to Nigeria and was escorted directly to the presidential villa by troops from an elite military formation. Two Presidents were thus in residence at the presidential villa until Yar'Adua died on 5 May. Jonathan was sworn in as Nigeria's substantive President on the following day.

THE JONATHAN GOVERNMENT, 2010–15

Goodluck Jonathan lived up to his first name. Within 11 years he progressed from being the Deputy Governor of oil-rich Bayelsa State in the south to the President of Nigeria, without ever having contested, let alone won, an election. He acceded to the governorship of Bayelsa State when the incumbent, Diepreye Alamieyeseigha, was impeached on corruption charges in December 2005. The raging insurgency in the Niger Delta had incentivized PDP leaders to seek a Vice-President from the area during the 2007 presidential election campaign, in order to mollify the region. The unheralded Jonathan was their choice, after having served as a state governor for less than two years. Only two years after being sworn in as Vice-President, Jonathan found himself Acting President after President Yar'Adua fell ill, and he became President upon Yar'Adua's death. As an Ijaw, Jonathan became the first President from the Niger Delta in Nigeria's history, and he played a vital role in maintaining the fragile ceasefire agreement in that region.

Jonathan's presidency started with great goodwill. The cabal-like style of Yar'Adua's Government dissipated when Jonathan convinced political exiles such as Ribadu and El-Rufai to return to Nigeria. Jonathan was re-elected to the presidency in April 2011 (taking 58.6% of the votes, while Buhari received 32.0% and Ribadu 5.4%). However, opposition from within and outside the PDP intensified after the election. In February 2013 the four main opposition parties merged to form a new coalition party, the All Progressives Congress (APC). The manner in which Jonathan became President disturbed Nigeria's delicate ethno-regional balance. His presidency constituted a tacit suspension of the PDP's rotational arrangement, much to the chagrin of some northerners who felt that the north had been denied its full 'turn' in power. In August seven state governors (six of whom were northerners) and former Vice-President Atiku Abubakar resigned from the PDP. The pattern of the defections exposed regional antagonism against Jonathan. In September 57 PDP House of Representatives members and 22 of the 50 PDP Senate members also defected to join the rebel PDP faction. The PDP was weakened further when these and other PDP defectors joined the APC in 2013 and 2014.

Jonathan's opponents accused him of engaging in cronyism similar to that witnessed under former President Yar'Adua. For example, many powerful members in, or allied to, Jonathan's Government were from the Niger Delta, including the Minister of Petroleum Resources, Diezani Allison-Madueke (a former executive of the Shell Petroleum Development Co of Nigeria), and the Chief of Army Staff, Lt-Gen. Kenneth Minimah. Jonathan's wife, Patience, was appointed as a civil servant in her home state of Bayelsa, while in 2013 Jonathan pardoned Alamieyeseigha, who had pleaded guilty to corruption in 2007.

In February 2014 the Governor of the CBN, the respected Lamido Sanusi, alleged that $20,000m. worth of Nigerian oil revenue was unaccounted for by the state-owned Nigerian National Petroleum Corporation. Rather than investigating the claims, Jonathan dismissed Sanusi. Jonathan's apparent inability to respond decisively to mounting opposition and to his Government's lack of direction can perhaps best be explained by the fact that he was an accidental President, brought to power by the crises and misfortune of others around him. Furthermore, in addition to having to deal with feuding in his party and the most powerful opposition ever to challenge a Nigerian President, Jonathan also inherited the most serious religious insurgency in Nigeria's history.

THE BOKO HARAM INSURGENCY

After Nigeria had weathered the Niger Delta uprising, another insurgency emerged at the opposite end of the country and caught the Government and the security forces completely off guard. The Boko Haram insurgency that turned north-eastern Nigeria into a war zone was the result of the transformation of a local sect into a transnational organization that has presented deep security challenges to four West African countries simultaneously.

Boko Haram's strength and sway were enabled by multiple factors: the charismatic oratory and leadership of its founder, Mohammed Yusuf; financial support from politically connected individuals; its infectious doctrine; the ruthless brutality of the security forces; and a splintering of ideology from other Islamic groups. Boko Haram is not the first violent religious insurrection in Nigeria. In the early 1980s an Islamic sect led by the Cameroonian preacher Mohammed Marwa came to prominence in northern Nigeria. Marwa rejected Western materialism and influence, and was nicknamed 'Maitatsine' (a Hausa phrase meaning 'the one who curses'), owing to his habit of declaring curses upon those who disagreed with his religious views. The Maitatsine sect's belligerence, hostility to secular authority and clashes with police led to several weeks of rioting in late 1980 in the northern city of Kano. Over 5,000 people (including Maitatsine) were killed during the subsequent brutal military crackdown on the sect.

Boko Haram's rise can be contextualized within the modern emergence of reformist religious groups in Nigeria. Many Nigerians turned to religion as an antidote to the decadence, corruption, crime, and economic and political hardships of 1980s and 1990s. Although these issues existed all over Nigeria, the north lagged behind the south in socioeconomic and educational indicators. Extremist religious sects sprang up across the north. One of these was a proselytizing sect founded in Maiduguri (the Borno State capital) under the leadership of Mohammed Yusuf. He advocated a severe and puritanical brand of Islam, free of the influences of Western culture and education, which, in his view, contaminated and contradicted Islamic edicts. Although the sect refers to itself as the Jama'atu Ahlis Sunnah Lidda'awati Wal Jihad (Group for Proselytizing and Jihad), commentators dubbed it 'Boko Haram' (meaning 'Western culture is forbidden'), in a pejorative reference to its members' preoccupation with criticizing Western culture.

The sect was initially regarded as an eccentric curiosity rather than a national security threat. Yusuf's hostility to Western education arose from a combination of legacy issues of local Nigerian history and the influence of the Middle Eastern Islamic discourse that he read. Some Muslim areas of northern Nigeria harboured a longstanding scepticism towards Western education, owing to its association with the Christian missionaries who had introduced it to Nigeria. It was unsurprising that some Muslims did not wholeheartedly embrace concepts that had been used to colonize them and religiously convert their neighbours.

When Nigeria returned to democracy in 1999, Nigeria had a Christian President (Obasanjo) for the first time in 20 years. Religion once again became a national political issue. In 2000 the Governor of Zamfara State in the north-west, Ahmed Yerima, extended the application of Islamic *Shari'a* law to criminal matters in his state and eight other states followed suit. *Shari'a* had previously applied only to civil law matters such as divorce and inheritance. Its extension to criminal law prescribed punishments such as death by stoning for adultery, amputation for theft and flogging for drinking alcohol. *Shari'a* states forbade bars from serving alcohol and segregated public transport by gender. The extension of *Shari'a* law was initially popular, as some Muslims hoped that it would lead to a social and moral revival. However, many Christians opposed its extension to cover criminal law, arguing that it violated Nigeria's Constitution, which forbids states from adopting any religion, and feared that it would lead to the marginalization of Christians. President Obasanjo avoided a confrontation with the Muslim north over the *Shari'a* issue and casually dismissed it as 'political *Shari'a*', a political device concocted by his opponents that would eventually fizzle out. However, the extended application of *Shari'a* law substantially increased animosity between Christians and Muslims. Over 4,000 people were killed in the north during clashes between Christians and Muslims in 2000–03. Boko Haram initially supported the extension of *Shari'a* in Borno State in the north-east, but became disaffected after 2003 when the Borno State Government did not implement *Shari'a* with the stringency that the sect expected.

The Slide to Extremism

Extraordinarily, an argument about motorcycle helmets was the spark that turned Boko Haram into a full-fledged insurgent organization. In June 2009 police intercepted Boko Haram members who were en route to a funeral and challenged some, riding motorcycles, for not wearing safety helmets in accordance with new regulations. The police shot several Boko Haram members during the angry confrontation that ensued. In July several hundred Boko Haram members retaliated by attacking and burning down police stations and other government installations in northern cities and killing several police officers. President Yar'Adua dispatched the army to suppress Boko Haram and a brutal military crackdown followed. Security forces demolished Boko Haram's mosque and arrested and/or summarily executed hundreds of the sect's members, including Yusuf and Buji Foi (a wealthy local politician whom security forces suspected of being Boko Haram's financier). Photos and videos circulating on social media showed security forces executing Boko Haram members by the roadside using machine guns. More than 700 people died during four days of violence. The extrajudicial killing of Boko Haram's leaders and members turned Yusuf into a martyr and gave the sect legitimate grievances and leeway to portray itself as the victim of police brutality. Furthermore, the killings were a huge tactical mistake as they denied the security forces vital sources of intelligence on the sect's aims and methods.

However, the sect did not die with its leader during the 2009 onslaught. Security forces also inadvertently made Boko Haram more dangerous by eliminating the least violent faction within the sect and paving the way for its takeover by its most implacable and violent faction, led by Yusuf's deputy, Abubakar Shekau. Although Shekau had been shot (and was presumed dead) during the 2009 crackdown, he survived. Boko Haram's surviving members fled Nigeria for neighbouring countries such as Cameroon, Chad and Niger. While in exile, they re-armed, established ties with foreign *jihadi* groups, and prepared for a 'rematch' with the Nigerian security forces. Boko Haram returned to Nigeria in 2010 amid a sudden and suspicious amplification of its organization, violence and weaponry. The group advanced from attacking with knives and guns, to using explosives, armoured personnel carriers, vehicle columns with mounted machine guns, rocket-propelled grenades, improvised explosive devices and suicide bombings. In September 2010 Boko Haram staged a spectacular prison break in Bauchi State and released over 700 inmates, including more than 100 of its members who were detained there. They hunted down and killed civilians who had allegedly reported

their activities to the security forces, as well as Muslim clerics who had criticized them. This created a climate of fear and terrified the public into silence. In June 2011 a Boko Haram suicide attack at Nigeria's police headquarters in Abuja was the first suicide bombing in the country's history. In August, in another Boko Haram suicide attack, a car laden with explosives drove through two security barriers and crashed into the UN building in Abuja, before detonating a bomb that killed 23 people and injured 116 others. Thereafter Boko Haram unleashed a wave of drive-by shootings, bombings, arson and mass casualty attacks on markets, schools, churches, mosques, police stations and army barracks. Boko Haram made large areas of northern Nigeria inaccessible for civilians and security officers.

The timing of Boko Haram's reappearance coincided with other ethno-regional tensions in Nigerian politics. Jonathan's victory in the 2011 presidential election was bitterly disputed by many northerners, and supporters of the main opposition candidate, Buhari, who maintained that the election had been rigged. Over 800 people were killed in the course of protests and violence instigated by northerners aggrieved by the election result. Some in the President's circle interpreted the Boko Haram insurgency as an attempt by Muslim northerners to destabilize Jonathan's administration, owing to northern discontent about a southern Christian interrupting the north's 'turn' in leadership. The National Security Adviser, Gen. Owoye Andrew Azazi, publicly lent credence to this narrative in April 2012 by stating that the interruption of the PDP's zoning arrangement 'created the climate' for Boko Haram. In contrast, many northerners believed that the Government itself had created Boko Haram as part of a smear campaign against Muslims. Allegations of political collusion between the Government and Boko Haram had been given credence in November 2011 when the State Security Service arrested Senator Mohammed Ali Ndume of Borno State, claiming that he had telephoned a Boko Haram member more than 70 times in one month. In January 2012 the police re-arrested a Boko Haram member, Kabiru Sokoto, in the Abuja lodge of the Governor of Borno State, Kashim Shettima, a few days after Sokoto had escaped from police custody.

By the time the country realized that it was not dealing with a conspiratorial political plot, but with an unprecedented new insurgency, Boko Haram had become confident, well-funded and well-equipped. In May 2013 President Jonathan declared a state of emergency in the three north-eastern states worst affected by the insurgency (Adamawa, Borno and Yobe). Troops flooded into the north-east in the army's largest deployment since the civil war. Civilians formed vigilante patrol teams of youth volunteers dubbed the 'Civilian Joint Task Force' (CJTF). Although armed only with rudimentary weapons such as sticks, knives and aged rifles, the local knowledge of the members of the CJTF enabled them to identify Boko Haram members to the army. The CJTF's co-operation with regular security forces helped to push Boko Haram out of Maiduguri and into rural areas. However, Boko Haram's dispersal from Maiduguri made rural areas more vulnerable as the military's presence was less significant outside the cities.

In late February 2014 Boko Haram killed 59 boys at a boarding school in Buni Yadi in Yobe State, and set fire to all 24 buildings on the school's premises. Owing to such attacks, most schools in the north-east had been closed, including the Government Girls Secondary School in the town of Chibok in Borno State. However, the school was temporarily reopened to allow schoolgirls from neighbouring institutions to sit examinations, and on the night of 14 April several hundred teenage girls were in the school. Boko Haram members dressed in military camouflage gained entry to the building by masquerading as soldiers sent to take the girls to safety. They seized 276 girls, herded them onto a convoy of trucks and set fire to the school. Although 57 girls managed to escape while being transported to Boko Haram's camp, the rest remained in captivity. The abductions were widely reported by local and international media, and demonstrations were staged in Abuja, as well as abroad, demanding that the Government rescue the girls. Social media users deployed the Twitter hashtag 'BringBackOurGirls' to galvanize global opinion.

The abduction of the Chibok schoolgirls was not a new phenomenon. Boko Haram had been kidnapping young women and girls as 'brides' for some time and forcibly converting them to Islam. The few girls who managed to escape returned with horrendous accounts of being beaten, raped, impregnated and forced to kill during Boko Haram's raids. The kidnap of the Chibok schoolgirls attracted international media attention not because it was a new tactic, but because it was the most large-scale kidnap of its type. Perhaps more than any other event, the Government's mishandling of its response to the mass kidnap was the worst of the public relations disasters of President Jonathan's administration. Some of the President's supporters even suggested that the kidnap was an elaborate hoax concocted by Jonathan's political opponents to discredit him. Jonathan's failure publicly to speak about the kidnap for several weeks made him appear indifferent to the suffering of his people, a perception compounded when he was photographed celebrating his niece's lavish wedding a few days after Boko Haram had killed 2,000 people in the town of Baga in January 2015. Meanwhile, Boko Haram became more ambitious after the Chibok kidnap and instead of limiting itself to the hit-and-run tactics that it had used for years to torment the Nigerian military, it began to seize and hold territory, and declared an Islamic 'caliphate' in the areas that it captured.

THE 2015 PRESIDENTIAL ELECTION

The February 2015 presidential election was set to be the most closely contested in Nigeria's history, with opinion polls indicating equal levels of support for the PDP and APC. Prior to this election, every change of government since independence had been effected by the military. The APC's choice of former military ruler Buhari as its presidential candidate was astute. Boko Haram's insurgency and the numerous corruption scandals in the Government led the public to seek a leader who could simultaneously fight corruption and terrorism.

In July 2014 Buhari's car was targeted by a massive bomb blast attributed to Boko Haram that killed over 50 people. Buhari survived the attack owing to his car's armour plating. His calm demeanour immediately after the failed assassination attempt reinforced his 'iron man' image. Multiple factors coalesced to reinvigorate Buhari's popularity. When confronted by war or insecurity, electorates often gravitate towards strong leaders with military credentials. Despite being out of power for 30 years, Buhari's anti-corruption credentials remained unblemished. Nigeria's demographics also helped him: some 70% of Nigerians had not been born when Buhari last governed Nigeria, and did not necessarily share the older generation's apprehension about his past as a military dictator. Buhari campaigned on a theme of change. In an address at the Royal Institute of International Affairs (Chatham House) in London in February 2015, he deflected criticism about his past, stating: 'I stand before you a former military ruler, now a converted democrat'.

In February 2015 the Chairman of the Independent National Electoral Commission (INEC), Prof. Attahiru Jega, announced that INEC would postpone the election by six weeks on the advice of the military. The military chiefs claimed that their energies would be focused on fighting Boko Haram around the time the election was scheduled (thereby reducing the military's capacity to provide security at the polls). However, critics claimed that the Government had engineered the postponement in order to curb the APC's electoral momentum and buy time to improve its chances of winning.

Boko Haram's infiltration of Nigeria's neighbouring countries was the catalyst for the formation of a Multinational Joint Task Force coalition between Nigeria, Cameroon, Chad and Niger. Instead of one army, Boko Haram was suddenly confronted by four. Between January and April 2015 the Nigerian army finally expelled Boko Haram from the major towns and cities that it had captured, and released over 1,000 kidnapped women and children.

In the event, the postponement of the presidential election boosted the chances of a free and fair poll by enabling the military to improve the security environment in the north-east, and allowing more people to collect their Permanent Voter Cards (PVCs) and participate in the vote. By the time the election took place, 81% of PVCs had been collected.

The presidential election, which eventually took place on 28 March 2015, proceeded peacefully, without the mass vote rigging that had marred previous polls. Jega, a former university lecturer, oversaw a number of reforms intended to prevent customary rigging methods, including an elaborate system of voter registration, the training of thousands of electoral staff and the introduction of biometric readers. When initial results revealed that Buhari had gained a large lead, Jonathan avoided a political crisis by conceding defeat and congratulating his rival. Furthermore, Jonathan resisted the exhortations of his PDP allies to challenge the election result in court and made a nationwide television broadcast to affirm that 'nobody's ambition is worth the blood of any Nigerian'. Jonathan thus became the first incumbent President in Nigeria's history to lose an election. Buhari won 54.0% of the 28.6m. valid votes cast, compared with Jonathan's 45.0%. Buhari was sworn in as Nigeria's new President on 29 May.

THE RETURN OF BUHARI, 2015–

In accordance with his election campaign pledges, on returning to power Buhari gave priority to combating both corruption and the insurgency. He issued a deadline of the end of 2015 for the army to quash the insurgency, and in December he claimed that Boko Haram had been 'technically' defeated. Although this was not actually the case, Nigeria's security forces had weakened the insurgents' ability to launch mass casualty attacks.

Security

In April 2016 the State Security Service arrested senior Boko Haram commander Khalid al-Barnawi, who had been described as 'the most sophisticated extremist in Nigeria'. Al-Barnawi was affiliated with international Islamic insurgent groups, and an official hailed his arrest as 'our biggest breakthrough against terrorism in Nigeria ever'. Boko Haram was also beset by an internal power struggle. In August the Islamic State militant organization announced that Abu Musab al-Barnawi (the son of the former Boko Haram leader Mohammed Yusuf, and no relation of Khalid al-Barnawi) had been appointed as Boko Haram's new leader. ('Al-Barnawi' is a *nom de guerre* denoting that someone is from Borno State—where Boko Haram was founded). However, Shekau rejected Abu Musab al-Barnawi's appointment and insisted that he remained in charge. Abu Musab al-Barnawi and Shekau consequently became leaders of different Boko Haram factions, with al-Barnawi representing the Islamic State in West Africa Province (ISWAP). Internal conflict and factionalism among the insurgents increased from 2018. In August senior Boko Haram commander Mamman Nur was killed by his own men in what may have been an internal coup. The State Security Service had accused Nur of masterminding a bomb blast at the UN building in Abuja in 2011. In March 2019 Islamic State announced that it had deposed Abu Musab al-Barnawi as ISWAP leader and replaced him with Abu Abdullah ibn Umar al-Barnawi. Although these leadership changes indicated serious internal rifts within Boko Haram, they also made a comprehensive negotiated settlement to the crisis more difficult to achieve. With the emergence of multiple factions, it became difficult to know which faction to attribute attacks to or to negotiate with regarding hostage releases or an eventual armistice agreement.

By mid-2017 103 of the kidnapped Chibok schoolgirls had been released, after negotiations between Nigerian security forces and Boko Haram resulted in an exchange of the girls for five Boko Haram commanders who had been in Nigerian military custody. However, in February 2018 Boko Haram carried out another mass kidnap, abducting 110 schoolgirls in the north-eastern village of Dapchi. The militants released 104 of the girls (five had died, and one had refused to convert to Islam) and a boy from Dapchi. The circumstances of their release were unclear, but the Government denied having paid a ransom. In a surprising revelation, the Minister of Defence, Mansur Dan-Ali, stated that Boko Haram had released the girls because their kidnap violated the terms of ongoing truce talks between Boko Haram and the Government.

The focus on the Boko Haram insurgency has deflected attention from another source of insecurity. Conflict between nomadic cattle herders and farmers killed more people in 2016 than Boko Haram, and posed a growing security threat. The main catalyst of the conflict was ecology. The Sahara desert's southward expansion, at a rate of nearly 50 km a year, has dried up grazing areas, forcing nomadic cattle herders to head further south and west in search of new grazing and water sources for their cattle. Desertification has also shrunk farmers' crop yields, thereby making green land more scarce and valuable to both farmers and herders. Farmers accuse herders of allowing their cattle to eat crops and destroy farmland. Militant herders stage marauding attacks against farming communities, involving murder and rape. Herders, in turn, complain that farmers plant crops on established grazing routes, and steal or kill their cattle. The fact that the herders are predominantly Muslims of Fulani or Tuareg ethnicity, and that farmers in the areas to which they migrate are mainly Christians of other ethnic groups, introduces a lethal sectarian dynamic to the conflict. Although the Fulani and Tuareg are geographically dispersed across several West African countries, including Cameroon, Niger, Nigeria and Senegal, strong kinship networks between them result in deadly revenge attacks. The herders' nomadic lifestyle and the Boko Haram insurgency have dispersed the conflict across West Africa. Boko Haram attacks on civilians and cattle markets in northeastern Nigeria caused herders to adopt new cattle-grazing routes to avoid the worst-affected areas of the insurgency. This brought the herders into contact with communities that were not accustomed to their presence. In response to the conflict, some states in the south and Middle Belt have enacted laws against open cattle grazing.

Corruption and the Economy

In April 2017 the EFCC discovered more than US $43m. in cash in a flat in Lagos. When the National Intelligence Agency (NIA) claimed that it kept the cash there covert operations, Buhari suspended the NIA's Director-General, Ayodele Oke, from his post. Buhari also suspended the Secretary to the Government of the Federation, Babachir David Lawal, for alleged contract fraud related to the provision of humanitarian relief in the north-east. Furthermore, the Government froze assets in the UK and USA that were allegedly acquired in illicit deals by former Minister of Petroleum Resources Diezani Allison-Madueke and her allies. The Government's other anti-corruption tactic has been publicly to shame suspected offenders by leaking corruption allegations against them to the media.

Despite these high-profile actions against corruption, criticism of Buhari's policies has become more persistent and severe (especially in the south). His opponents accuse him of the same sectionalism and cronyism that was attributed to his predecessor, Jonathan. Recruitment statistics for the State Security Service in 2017 showed that Katsina State (Buhari's home state) had more recruits than any other state. At mid-2019 the President, the Minister of Defence, the National Security Adviser, the Minister of Petroleum Resources, the Minister of the Interior, the Inspector-General of Police, the Chief of Army Staff and the Director-Generals of all three intelligence agencies (the State Security Service, the Defence Intelligence Agency and the National Intelligence Agency) were all Muslims from the north. In a country as sensitive to allegations of nepotism and ethnic, religious or geographic favouritism as Nigeria, regionally unbalanced appointments inevitably increase tensions.

Nigeria's economic problems threatened to overshadow gains made against corruption. In 2016 the inflation rate reached a 10-year high, and Nigeria's economy entered recession for the first time in 25 years. Buhari's antiquated responses to Nigeria's economic problems aroused public discontent. One of Buhari's previously staunchest supporters, El-Rufai (the Governor of Kaduna State and a powerful member of the ruling party), sent a memorandum to the President in September 2016 stating that the Government 'has not only failed to manage expectations of a populace that expected overnight "change" but has failed to deliver even mundane matters of governance'.

Buhari's Second Term

For the second time in seven years, Nigeria's political stability became dependent on the fragile health of its President. In 2016–17 Buhari travelled to the UK three times in 11 months for treatment of an illness that he refused to disclose. He was on medical leave in the UK for nearly two months between January and March 2017, and was absent abroad and incommunicado between May and August. Although he subsequently claimed that he was in good health, his frequent sick leave and relatively advanced age called into question his continued capability to act as President.

In January 2018 former President Obasanjo (who remained an important figure, despite leaving power in 2007) addressed a public letter to the 75-year-old Buhari urging him to 'dismount from the horse' and retire from public office. However, in April Buhari announced that he would seek re-election in the presidential election scheduled for February 2019. Growing discontent within the ruling APC was demonstrated in July 2018 when 14 senators and 37 members of the House of Representatives defected from the APC to the PDP, in a reversal of the defections that had helped propel Buhari to power in 2015.

Buhari's main rival candidate in the 2019 election was former Vice-President Abubakar, who had defected from the PDP to the APC, but rejoined the PDP in 2017. This was Abubakar's fifth bid for the presidency. As both he and Buhari were ethnic Fulani Muslims from northern Nigeria, neither could appeal to ethno-regional or religious sentiment to divert votes from the other, making the election result unpredictable. In contrast to Buhari's conservative image, Abubakar presented himself as a gregarious, multi-billionaire businessman who could bring about economic liberalization. To the dismay of many voters who had made cross-country trips home to vote at their local polling stations, INEC announced only five hours before the polls were due to open on 16 February 2019 that the election would be postponed by a week, owing to logistical problems. Buhari won the delayed election, which was held on 23 February (although voting in some regions was further delayed until 9 March as a result of ongoing unrest), after securing 55.6% of the votes cast, ahead of Abubakar, who received 41.2%. Buhari was inaugurated for a second term as President on 29 May, but his new Cabinet was not sworn in until August. To the consternation of many observers, the appointment to cabinet posts of a large number of relatively elderly APC stalwarts (rather than technocrats with greater expertise) did not appear to presage the introduction of meaningful reform to bolster the fragile economic recovery or tackle deep-seated corruption.

The Government reacted rapidly to the COVID-19 pandemic, which spread across the world in early 2020, by closing its borders, halting inter-state travel within the country, setting up isolation centres for infected patients, and imposing lockdown restrictions. The Government provided loans and food assistance to poor households impacted by COVID-19. In early April 2022 the Government lifted a nationwide night-time curfew and ban on large social gatherings which had been imposed in response to the COVID-19 pandemic. (The level of COVID-19 infections in the country remained stable; at the end of August a total of 263,407 cases and 3,148 related deaths had been confirmed.)

Meanwhile, in addition to the Boko Haram insurgency, Nigeria has been rocked by increasing outbreaks of banditry, kidnapping and violence. Approximately 600 students were kidnapped between December 2020 and March 2021 alone. The second half of May 2021 was particularly tumultuous for the Nigerian security sector. Boko Haram leader Shekau was reportedly killed on 19 May in unclear circumstances during an intra-insurgency conflict between Boko Haram and ISWAP factions. Two days later, Nigeria's Chief of Army Staff, Lt-Gen Ibrahim Attahiru, and 10 senior military officers died in an aeroplane crash. A militant group known as the Indigenous People of Biafra (IPOB) has continued demands for the restoration of an independent state of Biafra in the south-east. The widespread insecurity often involves unidentified armed groups, and at times assumes ethno-regional overtones, with communities in different regions accusing each other of fomenting the violence. This has been a source of embarrassment for President Buhari, who has been unable to fulfil the pledge to suppress insecurity that played a large role in his 2015 election victory.

Nevertheless, counter-insurgency operations had significantly reduced Boko Haram's activities by 2021, with only 64 recorded attacks, resulting in 178 deaths, attributed to the group in that year (compared with 2,131 deaths in 2015). Largely as a result, terrorism-related deaths in Nigeria fell by 47% to a recorded total of 448 in 2021, the lowest level since 2011, with ISWAP becoming the most active group. In October 2021 the Nigerian military confirmed the death of ISWAP leader al-Barnawi (following media reports that he had died in factional clashes in August). Later in October al-Barnawi's successor, Malam Bako, was also killed in strikes by Nigerian troops. ISWAP, which had expanded its operations in the Lake Chad basin following the loss of Shekau, killed Nigerian troops, including senior officers, in attacks against military posts in November and December. Sani Shuwaram, who replaced Bako as leader of ISWAP in early November, was killed in government air strikes in February 2022; Bako Gorgore, who next assumed the leadership of ISWAP was also killed, in air strikes in May.

Meanwhile, in late March 2022, after bombing rail tracks, an armed group attacked a train travelling between Abuja and the northern city of Kaduna and abducted passengers. The federal authorities reported that local bandits had carried out the attack in collaboration with insurgent forces; 10 people were killed, while around 65 passengers were confirmed as missing. (By early August about one-half of the passengers were reported to have been freed in prisoner exchanges that resulted in the release of 30 militants from custody.) On 5 June at least 44 people were killed and 87 injured in a gun attack at a Catholic church in the south-western city of Owo, which was attributed by the Government to ISWAP (increasing concerns that the militant group's area of operations was expanding). ISWAP claimed responsibility for an attack against a prison in Kuje, around 40 km from Abuja, on 5 July, during which about 900 inmates escaped. In response to rising insecurity near the capital, later that month the Ministry of Education announced the closure of all federal government colleges in the Federal Capital Territory to ensure the safety of students.

The 2023 Presidential Candidates

Buhari was ineligible to seek a further term in office, and during early 2022 numerous political and business figures announced that they intended to seek nomination as party candidates for the presidential election scheduled for 25 February 2023. The political focus on the forthcoming election intensified with the party primary polls. On 28 May 2022 a PDP convention selected as its candidate former Vice-President and previous presidential candidate Atiku Abubakar. The APC nominated 70-year-old Bola Tinubu, a southern Muslim who was a former party Chairman and Governor of Lagos, as its candidate on 8 June. Tinubu, who had been dubbed the 'Godfather of Lagos', pledged to suppress violence and restore order, citing his record in curbing crime in Lagos during his 1999–2007 tenure as Governor. Following the conclusion of the party primaries, later in June INEC released a list of 18 nominated presidential candidates. Among them, the candidate of the social-democratic Labour Party, Peter Obi, a former Governor of Anambra State, was predicted by some observers to garner significant support. In early July Tinubu's final choice of Kashim Shettima, a former Governor of Borno State who was also a Muslim, as the APC vice-presidential nominee prompted immediate controversy (including within the APC), since it violated the informal convention for candidates to have vice-presidential running mates from both a different region and a different religion. Since Abubakar was a Muslim northerner, the PDP had also abandoned its 'zoning' arrangement (allowing power to alternate between the predominantly Muslim north and the mainly Christian south).

CONCLUSION

Nigeria is yet again at a crossroads. The country's political contests have gradually become more competitive and unpredictable. The spirit of optimism that followed Buhari's election in 2015 has dissipated, especially during his second and final term of office. The President has failed to deliver on his promises simultaneously to combat corruption, stimulate the economy and suppress insecurity, as Boko Haram and ISWAP continue to carry out gun attacks, bombings and kidnappings. The next President, who is due to succeed Buhari at the election of February 2023, is also likely to inherit enduring economic difficulties: in 2020 Nigeria suffered its second recession in five years, owing to the COVID-19 pandemic, with only a modest recovery recorded in the following year. Amid a worsening global economic environment, conditions had deteriorated further by mid-2022, with rising poverty, elevated levels of inflation and unemployment, and strike action in many sectors. However, the outcome of the presidential election is unlikely to bring new solutions to Nigeria's long-term problems, particularly in view of the nomination of veteran political figures to represent the two main parties, considered by some critics to reflect ongoing political polarization and cronyism.

Economy

ROBERT E. LOONEY

INTRODUCTION

Since 2000, and until the sudden decline in oil prices in 2014, Nigeria appeared to be Africa's new economic powerhouse. After average annual growth in gross domestic product (GDP) of only 1.7% in the 1970s, followed by an average annual contraction of 0.1% in the 1980s and an average rise of 1.7% per year in the 1990s, GDP expanded at average annual rates of 8.3% during 2000–09 and 6.4% during 2010–14. However, the sharp drop in the price of petroleum from mid-2014 and the emergence of the global coronavirus disease (COVID-19) pandemic in 2020 resulted in the annual growth rate in 2015–21 averaging only 1.1%. In 2016 the economy entered a recession, with GDP contracting by 1.6%, before recovering gradually to register growth of 0.8% in 2017, 1.9% in 2018 and 2.2% in 2019. Following the onset of the COVID-19 pandemic, the economy contracted by 1.8% in 2020, but recovered to record growth of 3.6% in 2021.

Earlier optimism had been encouraged not only by the country's high rates of growth but also by the fact that Nigeria had become Africa's largest economy based on a revision of the country's GDP in April 2014 (and indeed remained so). Growth seemed assured, with oil prices stabilizing at over US $100 per barrel and, with a young population of some 187m. (the largest in Africa and the fourth largest in the world), the country was on the verge of a significant demographic dividend. Confidence had risen in 2011 with the publication of the Government's 2011 transformation agenda—a bold strategy that had aimed to make Nigeria one of the world's leading 20 economies by 2020. In 2013 the British-based multinational professional services network PricewaterhouseCoopers (PwC) predicted that Nigeria would become one of the fastest-growing emerging economies.

Moreover, Nigeria's revised GDP figures suggested that the economy was much more diversified than previously thought. While the country remained a significant petroleum exporter, that sector progressively declined from 18.1% of GDP in 2000 to 15.4% by 2010. By 2021 the sector's share of GDP had fallen to just 5.6%. Oil rents as a share of GDP declined from 38.6% of GDP in 1979 to 20.7% by 2000, and then further, to 12.9% in 2010 and 4.4% in 2020. Overall, in 2021 services accounted for 44.4% of GDP, industry for 31.9%, and agriculture 23.7%. In 2000 services had contributed 44.3% of GDP, industry 34.2% and agriculture 21.6%.

In 2019 35.0% of the employed workforce remained in agriculture, with 53.0% in services and only 12.0% in industry (manufacturing, mining and construction), in comparison with the 1991 shares of 50.6% (agriculture), 36.0% services and 13.4% (industry). The changing employment patterns suggest that Nigeria is moving from an agrarian/resource-based economy to a service economy without first going through an industrial phase like that experienced at a similar stage of development by the now advanced countries.

SOCIOECONOMIC DEVELOPMENT

Dampening earlier optimism over the economy's progress, the United Nations (UN) Development Programme *Human Development Report* for 2020 (with data for 2019) ranked Nigeria 161st out of 189 countries (down from 152nd in 2016) on its Human Development Index (HDI). Nigeria's HDI ranking was 19 places below its ranking in terms of gross national income (GNI) per head, suggesting a significant underachievement in human development. Poverty is also a recurring problem, with the World Bank estimating that in 2021 40.7% of the population existed on less than US $1.90 per day, while 72.3% lived on less than $3.20 and 92.0% lived on less than $5.50.

Although Nigeria's income distribution is about average for the region (with a Gini coefficient of 0.351 in 2018), in 2010–18 the income share of the lowest 40% of the population averaged 15.1%, whereas the top 10% of the population received 32.7% of total income and the top 1% received 15.3%. There is also a widening gap in incomes and opportunities between the country's impoverished north and more affluent southern parts.

Unemployment varies considerably by state. In 2020 Benue had the highest unemployment rate, at 43.5%, followed by Zamfara (41.7%) and Jigawa (41.3%). During that year 10 states had unemployment rates higher than 30%. The lowest levels of unemployment were in Lagos (4.5%), Ogun (9.9%) and the Federal Capital Territory (13.1%). Twelve states had unemployment rates lower than 20%.

DEVELOPMENT CHALLENGES

Many of Nigeria's current range of problems will take time to address. The country's weak governance structures significantly limit the achievement of rapid, effective solutions. Nigeria ranked in the 13th percentile (with 100 being the highest) in the World Bank's 2020 Worldwide Governance Indicators for control of corruption (down from the 15th percentile in 2010) as well as for government effectiveness (up from the 10th percentile in 2010), and in the 21st percentile for rule of law (compared with 12th in 2010).

In addition to governance constraints, education and skill levels present further severe limitations to future growth. Significant quality and access constraints exist in Nigeria's education system, underpinned by limited state funding for the sector. There are wide disparities in educational attainment levels across different geographical and income groups, with rural communities less likely to acquire basic literacy, information and communications technology, and numeracy skills. Furthermore, Nigeria has the highest number of out-of-school children in the world, mainly due to institutional weakness, the prevalence of corruption, the impact of poverty, which exposes many children to neglect, child labour and child marriages, as well as the high levels of conflict risk in areas such as northern Nigeria and the Niger Delta, which have led to the displacement of millions of people. Although there are many graduates, few have on-the-job training, and many skilled workers are either based in urban areas or emigrate in search of better economic opportunities abroad.

AGRICULTURE

In 1960 agriculture accounted for about one-half of Nigeria's GDP and around 75% of its foreign exchange. However, with the development of the petroleum sector, attention and investment shifted from agriculture. From the mid-1980s the country went from being self-sufficient in basic foodstuffs to becoming heavily reliant on imports. Economist Impact's Global Food Security Index for 2021 ranked Nigeria 97th out of 113 countries, a decline from 88th place in 2012. In 2021 the country ranked 104th for affordability, 96th for availability and 94th for quality and safety.

The agricultural sector grew at an average annual rate of 10.9% in 2000–09, before slowing considerably, to 3.6%, in 2010–21. Agriculture's sub-components all declined over this period, with average annual growth for crops decelerating from 12.0% in 2000–09 to 3.6% in 2010–21, livestock from 5.5% to 2.6%, forestry from 4.2% to 3.5% and fishing from 6.3% to 4.2%. The expansion of agricultural GDP stems from increasing the area of land under cultivation and improving productivity. Value-added per worker in agriculture was stagnant from 1991 to 2001, increasing (at constant 2015 US $ prices) from $1,412 in 1991 to $1,610 by 2001. Subsequently, productivity increased each year to reach a high of $5,591 in 2019, down from $5,661 in 2017.

The composition of agriculture has gradually shifted over time, with crops increasingly dominating the sector. In 1981 crops accounted for 75.2% of agricultural output, increasing to 84.2% in 2000 and 88.4% in 2021. Livestock's share declined from 14.8% of agricultural production in 1981 to 11.4% in 2000 and 5.5% by 2021. In 2021 forestry accounted for only 0.7% of agricultural output (down from 6.8% in 1981) while fishing accounted for 5.4% (up from 3.2% in 1981). In 2018 agricultural land comprised 78.0% of Nigeria's total land area, while forest accounted for 9.5%.

Of the major crops, rice production reached 3.3m. metric tons in 1989, before falling to 2.8m. tons by 2001. Subsequently, production expanded rapidly, reaching 5.4m. tons in 2012 and 8.2m. tons by 2020. After reaching 6.5m. tons in 1995, maize production was only 4.0m. in 2000. Subsequently, however, production increased steadily, reaching 12.0m. tons in 2020. Vegetable production also increased rapidly from around 1983. In that year production was 4.0m. tons, rising to 11.7m. tons in 2006 and 16.7m. tons in 2019.

As part of its attempt to make the country more self-sufficient in food, the administration of President Muhammadu Buhari introduced the Agriculture Promotion Policy (APP) in 2016. The APP's main priorities included import substitution, economic diversification, food security and job creation. After Buhari's re-election to a second four-year term in February 2019, protectionism intensified, first with the partial closure of Nigeria's western border with Benin in August and then with the suspension of all land trade across its borders in October. However, all of Nigeria's land crossings had been reopened by the end of 2020.

At mid-2022 soaring food price inflation, fuelled by import restrictions and rising local prices, was contributing to widespread popular discontent. Using the five-point scale devised by the US Agency for International Development's Famine Early Warning Systems Network, in June most Nigerian states were at level 2 ('stressed'), while broad swathes of the north-west and north-east were at level 3 ('crisis') and part of the far north-east was at level 4 ('emergency'). The most food-stressed areas were also the most physically insecure, with jihadist violence in the north-east and banditry in the north-west disrupting livelihoods, markets and transportation. However, high food prices were also affecting the safer parts of the country.

In June 2022 the UN Office for the Coordination of Humanitarian Affairs (OCHA) issued an emergency warning for the north-eastern states of Borno, Adamawa and Yobe, which form part of the Lake Chad region. OCHA warned that over 8m. people in the three states needed help, with around 600,000 people encountering emergency levels of food insecurity owing to the jihadist insurgency.

OIL

The first commercial discoveries of petroleum in Nigeria occurred in 1956 in the Niger River Delta region. Exports began in 1958, and production advanced rapidly. By the early 1970s the petroleum industry was the country's most dynamic and significant contributor to overall economic growth. The sector now accounts for by far the largest share of exports (an estimated 88.3% in 2021) and government tax revenues (35.6% in 2020).

In 2020 Nigeria's proven petroleum reserves were the second largest in Africa, after Libya, and the country was the 11th largest oil producer in the world. However, exploration has declined considerably in recent years, owing to rising security concerns in the Niger Delta and regulatory uncertainty. The country's proven reserves expanded from 21,000m. barrels in 1993 to 37,050m. in 2021, or 2.4% of the total proven world reserves in that year. Reserves occur in the Niger River Delta and offshore, with current exploration confined mainly to offshore fields. Production costs for Nigerian petroleum are up to seven times higher than those in the Middle East; however, the Nigerian product's low sulphur content places it at the upper end of the price scale of the Organization of the Petroleum Exporting Countries (OPEC).

Nigeria produced over 2m. barrels per day (b/d) for the first time in 1973 and, although output recorded a decline in 2005–09, it reached a high of 2.5m. b/d by 2010. However, by early 2016 a series of attacks by a new militant group, the Niger Delta Avengers, and pipeline breakdowns were causing losses of up to 500,000 b/d. The group claimed that its objective was to shut down Nigeria's oil industry. The country's production decreased to 1.9m. b/d in that year, and remained at around 2.0m.–2.1m. b/d in 2017–19, before falling to 1.8m. b/d in 2020 and 1.6m. b/d in 2021.

Slow progress in securing legislative support for the Petroleum Industry Bill (PIB) of 2021 damaged the industry and economy through lost opportunities to build up external reserves, increased spending on infrastructure, and an estimated loss of US $80,000m. in foreign direct investment (FDI). After nine years of trying to pass the PIB into law, the Nigerian Minister of State for Petroleum Resources, Emmanuel Ibe Kachikwu, broke the Bill down into five separate pieces of legislation to make the process more manageable. The strategy proved successful. Nigeria's National Assembly approved the PIB in July 2021, and President Buhari signed it into law in August. Although the PIB introduces much-needed oil and gas sector reforms, by mid-2022 it had failed to spur a substantial increase in foreign investment in the petroleum industry. Production costs are likely to remain too high compared with other global producers, and corruption, insecurity and weak infrastructure are expected to persist.

Even with the approval of the PIB, the Dutch multinational oil and gas company Shell indicated that it intended to divest all its onshore operations in Nigeria, citing the ongoing insecurity surrounding infrastructure and incompatibility with its long-term strategy. The Department of Petroleum Resources was considering three potential scenarios: a takeover of operations by the Nigerian Petroleum Development Company; a takeover by a combination of national companies; and acquisition by other international oil companies. If Shell were to divest its onshore assets, it would represent a severe setback to future investment and threaten the long-term output of Nigeria's ageing oilfields.

Despite the loosening of OPEC+ production curbs in April 2022, Nigerian output continued to decline on a month-by-month basis, with industry experts forecasting a 9.2% decline for 2022 as a whole, representing only a modest improvement from an estimated 10% decline in 2021. According to monthly production figures from OPEC, in March 2022 Nigeria fell short of its production target by some 364,000 b/d.

Natural Gas

Nigeria has estimated proven natural gas reserves of 5,100,000m. cu m, according to the US Energy Information Administration, making the country one of the largest holders of gas reserves worldwide. Most of Nigeria's natural gas reserves are associated with oil and are not adequately captured. As a result, around 40% of natural gas produced in Nigeria is non-commercial. Nevertheless, international oil companies operating in Nigeria have increasingly turned their focus to gas developments. This shift stems from improved infrastructure and stricter regulations against gas flaring, and rising domestic demand and export opportunities.

Natural gas production totalled 420m. cu ft per day in 1999, increasing to 3,250m. cu ft per day in 2007. By 2021 production reached some 4,442m. cu ft per day. While production is forecast to maintain high rates of expansion, as with oil, pipeline sabotage and supply disruptions are common. At mid-2021 about three-quarters of Nigerian gas was being exported in the form of liquefied natural gas (LNG), of which Nigeria was the world's fourth largest exporter. The remainder of the country's gas output was being used for domestic consumption or was being exported through the West African Gas Pipeline to Cotonou in Benin, Lomé in Togo and three Ghanaian ports—Tema (serving the capital, Accra), Takoradi and Effasu.

In the future, the Nigerian Government intends to place more emphasis on domestic gas needs. However, increased gas availability will require considerable investment in an environment with security and regulatory problems akin to those faced by the country's oil industry. Furthermore, the lack of infrastructure in the gas industry is a far more significant constraint on production than is the case with oil.

Following the Russian invasion of Ukraine, which began in February 2022, and the subsequent imposition of economic sanctions against the Russian Federation by members of the international community, by mid-2022 many European countries were seeking alternative sources of natural gas. Although Nigeria—which, according to OPEC, had proven natural gas reserves of 5,848,000m. cu m at the end of 2021—is sufficiently close to Europe, it was unlikely to become a significant supplier, especially as Algeria and Egypt are better placed geographically. Proposed gas pipelines linking Nigeria to Europe are fraught with potential difficulties, including security risks and fractious relations between the relevant parties, with Algeria and Morocco in longstanding dispute over the political status of Western Sahara. The planned 4,128-km Trans-Saharan pipeline would traverse increasingly lawless parts of northern Nigeria before entering Niger, itself beset by terrorism-related insecurity.

MANUFACTURING

After recording an average annual contraction of 4.8% in the 1980s and 1.3% in the 1990s, manufacturing resumed growth in the 2000s, averaging 1.8% per year, before rising to 5.6% in 2010–21. More recent growth, however, has been quite erratic, with the sector expanding by 21.8% in 2013 and by 14.7% in 2014 before being adversely affected by the slowdown in overall economic activity stemming from low oil prices. The sector contracted by 1.5% in 2015, 4.3% in 2016 and 0.2% in 2017. Growth of 2.1% was recorded in 2018, slowing to 0.8% in 2019. As expected, manufacturing was severely affected by the COVID-19 pandemic, with the sector contracting by 2.8% in 2020. However, the sector recovered in 2021, recording growth of 3.4%. Manufacturing's share of GDP was 14.8% in 2021, compared with 20.3% in 1981 and 13.9% in 2000.

Food, beverages and tobacco dominate manufacturing, together accounting for 33.5% of the sector's total output in 2021 (compared with 67.1% in 2000). Cement was the next largest sub-sector in 2021, providing 22.0% of manufacturing output, followed by textiles, apparel and footwear (21.0%), non-metallic products (6.4%) and motor vehicles and assembly (4.0%).

During 2015–21 the manufacturing sub-components with the highest rates of average annual growth were cement (which expanded by an average of 4.7% per year), chemical and pharmaceutical products (4.5%), plastics and rubber products (3.5%) and electrical goods and electronics (3.5%). Over the same period food, beverages and tobacco (the largest manufacturing sub-sector) grew by an average annual rate of just 0.4%, while textiles, apparel and footwear (the third largest sub-sector) contracted by an average of 1.2% per year. Cement should maintain its healthy growth because, with rapid urbanization, there has been increasing demand. The

Government estimates that an additional 15m. residential units will be required, as new construction has failed to keep up with demand.

Historically, manufacturing in Nigeria has been heavily reliant on imported raw materials and components, and efforts to lessen that reliance have proven largely unsuccessful. The combination of import restrictions, overpricing and industrial disputes favours cheaper foreign goods and encourages smuggling and black-market activities. In recent years manufacturers have contended that inadequate development funds and the Government's stringent fiscal policy have also constrained the sector.

The Government has attempted to correct these impediments and has shown renewed interest in manufacturing. A globally competitive manufacturing sector was integral to the Government's Vision 2020, a long-term economic transformation plan launched in 2009. In 2012 the Ministry of Industry, Trade and Investment (the agency responsible for developing policies and programmes to promote growth) instigated the Nigeria Industrial Revolution Plan. A 12-member committee was created to propose tariffs to raise capacity in sectors prioritized by the Government, such as agri-business, solid minerals, and petrochemicals. The Government's foreign exchange policies have also benefited manufacturing (see Finance and Monetary Policy, below).

However, for manufacturing to thrive, more broad-based reforms are necessary. Nigeria was ranked 116th out of 141 countries in the World Economic Forum's Competitiveness Index for 2019, with significant deficiencies in infrastructure (ranking 128th), macroeconomic stability (130th), skills (129th) and the financial system (131st). Nigeria was placed 131st out of 190 countries in the World Bank's Ease of Doing Business 2020 Index, making it one of the world's most challenging places in which to establish and conduct business.

As with agriculture, President Buhari's approach towards manufacturing has emphasized his desire for the country to achieve self-sufficiency and includes many specific proposals. These involve significantly expanding government support for infrastructure, improving fiscal incentives for small and medium-sized enterprises, providing easier access to credit and more lending to the manufacturing sector by the banks, and expanding government procurement from local producers. Owing to a steep decrease in employment in Nigeria's textile industry, from around 320,000 workers to just 30,000, the President has also announced that he aims to revive the sector by providing incentives for investment in ailing factories.

POWER

In 2021 the electricity, gas and water sector accounted for only around 1.0% of GDP. Only 55.4% of the population had access to electricity in 2020; access followed urban–rural lines, with 83.9% of urban residents having access, but only 24.6% of those living in rural areas. Almost all industrial electricity users and those residential customers who can afford it have a backup diesel generator system. The widely varying rates of expansion (and contraction) in recent years reflect the difficulties experienced by the power sector. Electricity, gas, steam and air conditioning expanded by 14.6% in 2013, but contracted by 8.7% in 2014, 9.3% in 2015 and 15.0% in 2016. Growth resumed over the following two years, with the sector expanding by 16.4% in 2017 and 7.3% in 2018. Contractions of 4.9% in 2019 and 2.9% in 2020 were followed by an expansion of 27.6% in 2021.

In 2020 around 19% of Nigeria's electricity was generated by hydroelectric power, while natural gas accounted for the remaining 81%. In December the Government announced plans to install 5m. home solar systems to increase electrification rates. The estimated cost of the project was US $367m., of which the World Bank was to finance 20%. The project was also intended to stimulate job creation, with the Central Bank of Nigeria (CBN) providing funding to the solar energy companies involved in the project.

Gas is the preferred input for power plants, owing to its low costs and relatively low emissions compared with oil or coal. However, ensuring a reliable gas supply to power producers has been challenging, given the limited infrastructure. The capital costs of potentially expanding supply in the future are staggering, with investment of up to US $70,000m. required merely to reach the equivalent level of supply as in South Africa.

Reform of the power sector was one of the Government's primary objectives under President Goodluck Jonathan's Transformation Agenda (2011–15). The Government viewed the privatization of generation and distribution assets and enforcement of domestic supply obligations as the most appropriate method of expanding Nigeria's power supply. The Power Holding Company of Nigeria ceased operations in early 2012, and the Government initiated the privatization of the power sector. The new private owners of the country's power sector are a mixture of foreign and local investors.

In addition to privatizing power generation and distribution activities, the Government hopes to improve the sourcing of inputs and achieve greater supply diversification. Nigeria already possesses several hydroelectric facilities and is seeking to develop its capacity for renewable energy. However, the country's wealth in natural gas is the only feasible short-term option for achieving large-scale electricity production.

President Buhari's proposals for the power sector include completion of the privatization process but with more extensive supervision by the Nigerian Electricity Regulatory Commission, the acceleration of the connection of gas pipelines to power stations, and the provision of greater security to protect gas facilities. Despite Buhari's efforts, inadequate power supply and structural problems across the electricity and gas supply chains are likely to remain significant inhibitors of faster economic growth in Nigeria for at least the next five years.

In early 2022 two pieces of legislation seeking to overhaul the legal framework governing Nigeria's electricity sector were introduced in the National Assembly. In March the legislature approved a constitutional amendment allowing Nigeria's 36 states to generate, transmit and distribute electricity; at mid-2022 the amendment was awaiting ratification by the state assemblies. The National Assembly was also examining a bill that, if approved, would repeal and replace the Electric Power Sector Reform Act of 2005 and would enable generating companies to transact directly with electricity distributors.

TRANSPORT

Transport services accounted for only 2.0% of GDP in 2021. After expanding at an average annual rate of 11.3% in the 2000s, the growth rate of Nigeria's transport sector moderated to an average of 3.8% per year during 2010–21. Following a contraction of 22.3% in 2020, sectoral GDP increased by 16.25% in 2021. In 2021 some 90.1% of the sector's GDP was provided by road transport, while 6.1% was provided by air transport. However, during 2010–21 road transport grew at an average annual rate of only 3.5%, while air transport expanded by an average of 8.3% per year and rail transport expanded by 5.9%. The transport sector's overall relatively low growth during 2010–21 was the result of underinvestment, which led to a shortage of capacity and several bottlenecks that curbed the country's economic growth.

Nigeria's transport system involves a broad national network of highways and bridges. Road conditions vary significantly across the country. Many roads are in excellent condition, while others are barely adequate. A few areas are still unconnected to the main national routes. The Government estimated in 2011 that, between that year and 2020, it would need to spend US $340,200m. on the transport sector to bring it up to the requisite level. Of that total, about $285,000m. would be required to repair existing infrastructure and extend the network. The Government is relying increasingly on public-private partnerships (PPPs), especially in Lagos, to provide bus, rail and other modes of transport. The size and scope of Nigeria's PPP programme are in contrast to the situation in many other African countries, where such projects remain limited. In Nigeria, operations, concessions and management contracts are an integral part of transport policy and, in many cases, are bundled in with construction contracts, typically within build-operate-transfer structures.

Since undertaking a comprehensive reform of the port sector in 2000, there has been a considerable improvement in port operations. Nigeria's two most important ports are Apapa and Tin Can Island Port, which together form the Lagos Port Complex. Apapa, which handles 70% of Nigeria's container traffic, is West Africa's busiest container terminal. However, limited space at the port prompted plans to create additional capacity. In October 2019 the Lagos state Government signed a US $629m. financing facility with the China Development Bank for the Lekki Deep Seaport project. The seaport was to have two container berths, each with a length of 680 m and a depth of 16.5 m. Eleven port projects are under way, and, alongside Lekki, the Onne Port Complex expansion in Port Harcourt and the Olokola Deep Seaport in Ondo State are under construction.

Nigeria's rail network extends over 3,500 km. However, a lack of new investment and maintenance has led to a decline in rail traffic. The Government is attempting to restore the network, and in December 2019 it announced plans to construct a railway line connecting Ibadan and Kano, at an estimated cost of US $5,300m. China Civil Engineering Construction Company was to execute the project as part of the Lagos–Kano standard gauge railway line. The Ibadan–Kano line was due to be completed by 2023.

In October 2019 the Nigerian Government signed a US $3,900m. contract with China Railway Construction Corporation (CRCC) to build a railway line connecting Abuja with Itakpe and Warri. Under the agreement, CRCC was to complete the rail line from Warri Central Station to the new Warri Seaport and build a branch line to Lokoja in Kogi State. CRCC was to operate the project for 30 years before transferring it to the Nigerian Government.

Nigeria's aviation sector has burgeoned in recent years as domestic services have expanded. The country has 22 airports, four of which are international airports. However, maintenance has proved to be a problem.

Although Nigeria is making progress in improving services and facilities in the primary modes of transport, it will be several years before the country's transport system is up to international standards. In the mean time, added transport costs will have to be absorbed by firms and individuals, thus reducing overall economic growth.

FINANCE AND MONETARY POLICY

The CBN is responsible for the promotion and maintenance of a sound financial system that effectively serves the country's credit needs. To strengthen the competitive and operational capabilities of Nigeria's banks, the CBN launched a banking reform programme in January 2005. The consolidation exercise saw most of the country's banks merging to meet the recapitalization requirement of the CBN. This process reduced the number of banks from 89 to 20, with each of these 20 institutions having much higher capitalization. The remaining banks were in a much-improved position to expand their lending activities and develop new business areas, such as financing oil investments and infrastructure.

Since Nigerian banks had not significantly increased their holdings of sophisticated financial assets when the 2008–09 global financial crisis struck, their losses were minimal compared with other parts of the world. However, the instability in commodity markets and exchange rates that followed put considerable stress on their operations. The CBN found that 10 banks were either severely undercapitalized or insolvent, and 10 banks held nearly one-third of the total assets of the country's banking system. The CBN responded quickly and decisively by injecting liquidity into the system and reorganized the management of eight of the problem banks. With depositors reassured and a new financial body, the Asset Management Corporation of Nigeria, created to preserve bank equity by purchasing all non-performing loans, the crisis ended.

In 2022 the leading three banks in Nigeria held about 54% of the country's total banking assets. There were 22 licensed commercial banks. Foreign banks in Nigeria account for only 10% of total banking assets. However, Nigeria's banks actively seek opportunities to expand into other African markets. The finance sector has seen average annual growth rates decline from 10.1% in the 1980s to 9.1% in the 1990s, 5.2% in the 2000s and 4.2% in 2010–21. In 2021 the sector accounted for 2.7% of GDP.

According to 2022 edition of *The Global Payments Report* published by Worldpay, cash accounted for 63% of point-of-sale spending in Nigeria in 2021. Around one-half of Nigerian adults do not have a bank account, and Nigeria had one of the largest proportions of unbanked people in the world. As financial technology and mobile network operators have attempted to tap this market, the CBN has introduced new types of licences. For example, payment service banks can accept consumer and small business deposits, process payments, issue debit and credit cards, and offer financial advisory services. Still, they must have 25% of their 'touchpoints' in rural areas. Financial technology is making substantial progress, with Nigeria home to five out of seven 'unicorns' (privately owned start-ups with a valuation in excess of US $1,000m.).

The non-performing loan ratio for the banking sector overall has fallen significantly since 2018, but remains relatively high; however, there is wide variation across the sector. Nigerian banks have a low loan-to-deposit ratio, which is likely to result from a combination of risk aversion and a lack of high-quality lending opportunities. In addition to the promotion and maintenance of a sound domestic financial system, the CBN is also responsible for the country's monetary policy and maintaining price stability and foreign reserves to ensure the value of the national currency, the naira.

The annual rate of inflation in Nigeria averaged 13.6% in the 1990s, 12.3% in the 2000s and 12.4% in 2010–21, above that recorded in other large, emerging economies. Inflation increased from 11.4% in 2019 to 13.2% in 2020, and increased further to 16.9% in 2021, far above the CBN's 6.0%–9.0% target range. Periods of hyperinflation have often been sparked by currency devaluations, as in 2016 and 2020. While constitutionally independent, the CBN has often opted to allow inflation to remain far above target in order to focus on providing stimulus to the economy. In April 2022 the International Monetary Fund (IMF) forecast a modest deceleration in the rate of inflation in Nigeria, to 16.1%, in 2022. However, by June the annualized rate of inflation had increased to 18.6%, fuelled by soaring food and fuel prices within the context of the Russian invasion of Ukraine. In an attempt to control inflationary pressures, the CBN had increased its monetary policy rate by 150 basis points in May, to 13.0%, and a further increase, to 14.0%, was implemented in July.

In terms of exchange-rate management, sudden capital outflows and sharply declining US dollar revenues from oil have placed enormous pressure on the naira. The CBN's response has been controversial. For example, it maintained an artificially strong exchange rate for 16 months after a steep decline in petroleum prices in 2014. The CBN implemented its stable exchange rate policy in conjunction with a ban on access to foreign exchange markets for importers of some 50 agricultural and manufactured goods. However, by impeding imports of critical inputs, this policy reinforced the economic downturn. To avoid a repeat of this situation, on 20 March 2020 the CBN devalued its official exchange rate by 17.6%, to 360 naira per US $1, from 306 naira per $1 previously. The devaluation came as the Brent crude oil price fell to around $29 per barrel, one-half of the Government's (original) 2020 budget oil price of $57. The move signalled a fundamental policy shift away from an emphasis on preserving the value of the naira towards the preservation of dwindling foreign currency reserves.

Currently, Nigeria does not have a unified exchange rate. The CBN sets an official US dollar rate at which it sells foreign exchange to commercial banks, which differs considerably from black market rates. In May 2021 a further devaluation of the official rate was implemented, from 380 naira per $1 to 410 naira per $1, thereby reducing the disparity between the official rate and the black market rate, which at that time stood at around 480 naira per $1.

In January 2020 the CBN announced the introduction of a new foreign exchange bidding regime, which gave priority to selected local manufacturers, who would subsequently have easier access to foreign exchange at official rates. This formed part of a broader programme supporting chosen sectors to promote import substitution, increase local production and non-oil exports, and reduce pressure on foreign exchange holdings. As of mid-2022 the CBN had yet to provide a timeline for implementation of the new foreign exchange regime, which builds upon efforts dating back to 2015 to defend the official exchange rate in the face of downward pressure on foreign exchange reserves.

Critics have claimed that the new scheme will increase the scarcity of foreign exchange in other sectors, potentially widening the gap between official and parallel exchange rates. This policy may exert additional pressure on the naira, thereby complicating the CBN's efforts to defend the currency. Given constraints linked to limited infrastructure, irregular energy supplies, corruption and security risks, it remained unclear whether many local manufacturers would upgrade their production processes in competitive ways.

TRADE AND EXTERNAL ACCOUNTS

Even with oil exports, Nigeria's economy is relatively closed, with trade (the sum of total imports and exports of goods and services) accounting for only 25.4% of GDP in 2020, compared with 76.0% of GDP in Botswana, 71.1% in Ghana and 56.0% in South Africa. As is typical for an oil-exporting nation, Nigeria's exports comprise a narrow range of products. In 2021 mineral products (comprising primarily petroleum and petroleum products) accounted for 89.4% of total exports. Mineral products also accounted for the largest share of imports (31.5% of the total) in 2021, followed by machinery, mechanical appliances and electrical equipment (20.1%) and chemicals and related products (8.6%). Nigeria's leading export markets in 2021 were India (16.4%), Spain (11.8%), France (including Monaco—6.3%) and the Netherlands (6.0%), while its principal sources of imports were the People's Republic of China (24.7%), the Netherlands (10.3%), India (8.8%) and the USA (6.1%).

From 1990 imports and exports experienced contrasting patterns. Imports grew by average annual rates of 10.4% during the 1990s, 9.2% in the 2000s and 3.3% during 2010–21, while exports grew by average annual rates of only 2.5% in the 1990s and 2.9% in the 2000s, before contracting by an average of 1.8% per year during 2010–21. During these periods the current account of the balance of payments remained in surplus, increasing from an average of 1.0% of GDP in the 1990s to 9.4% in the 2000s, before falling to 0.7% during 2010–21.

Traditionally, Nigeria's balance of payments has had a large capital inflow component, with much of the FDI inflows helping to expand productive sectors such as manufacturing, oil and gas, banking and telecommunications. However, in recent years these flows have declined, owing to, *inter alia*, political uncertainty, internal instability and violence. As a result, net FDI inflows as a percentage of GDP remain low. The level of FDI declined progressively from 2.2% of GDP in 2011 to 1.6% in 2012, 1.1% in 2013, 0.9% in 2014 and 0.6% in 2015, and remained below 1.0% in each year during 2016–21; inflows declined to 0.2% of GDP in 2018, the lowest rate recorded since 1980, before increasingly slightly, to 0.5% in 2019 and to 0.6% in 2020.

PUBLIC FINANCE

As with most oil-dominated economies, Nigeria has suffered from periods of fiscal indiscipline and uncontrolled debt accumulation. The federal budget doubled each year between 1976 and 1978, fuelled by sharply rising oil receipts. Politicians and bureaucrats had little incentive to reduce spending as it provided them with privileged and non-transparent access to significant revenue streams. Uncontrolled spending has consistently also allowed otherwise weak political coalitions to 'buy' public support. Although these tendencies still exist, Nigeria has managed to keep them in check by establishing more formal budgetary procedures for the country's complex federal system of government. A formal system of revenue sharing now prevails among the different governmental jurisdictions. More than one-half of the distributable revenue goes to state and local governments. The revenue-sharing formulas

set by the National Assembly can be updated every five years by that body.

Data from the IMF show that both government revenue and expenditure as a share of GDP have decreased over time. Government revenue as a share of GDP declined from an average of 21.3% per year during 2000–09 to an average of 9.7% per year in 2010–21. In the latter period the decline was sharp, with the share of GDP provided by government revenue decreasing from 17.3% in 2011 to 13.4% in 2014, and finally to 7.2% by 2021. However, while also declining as a share of GDP, government expenditure has done so at a somewhat slower pace. Specifically, government expenditure averaged 19.5% of GDP between 2000 and 2009, falling to an average of 13.3% per year in 2010–21. The decline during this latter period was from 17.3% of GDP in 2011 to 13.3% by 2021. These revenue and expenditure patterns produced an average annual surplus of 1.8% of GDP in the 2000s. However, the fiscal position turned into an average annual deficit of 3.6% of GDP in 2010–21, with the deficit increasing from 2.4% of GDP in 2014 to 3.8% in 2015, 4.6% in 2016 and 5.4% in 2017, rising to 5.7% in 2020 and 6.0% in 2021, and the IMF projected a further increase, to 6.4%, in 2022.

In 2005 the 'Paris Club' of public sector creditors signed debt reduction agreements with Nigeria, whereby the country's debt would be reduced by US $18,000m. in exchange for an agreement to pay back the remaining $12,000m. by March 2006. Nigeria made the final repayment as agreed, following which the debt reduction commitments entered into force in April, eliminating the country's debt to the Paris Club. Although Nigeria initially kept its debt within a relatively safe range, in recent years the level of external debt has risen rapidly, with IMF statistics showing net debt increasing from 6.4% of GDP in 2010 to 13.8% in 2014 and 36.6% in 2021; the Fund projected that net debt would increase to 41.2% of GDP by 2025.

The Government's current fiscal difficulties stem primarily from the national fuel subsidy programme, which had been scheduled to end by February 2022. However, the Government decided to extend it until June 2022 and subsequently until June 2023, primarily on political grounds, amid fears within the Buhari administration that ending subsidies at that time would spark major protests and strikes, with potential ramifications for the presidential and general elections due to be held in 2023. Many Nigerians view the fuel subsidy, which keep the country's petrol prices at well below global market rates, as one of the few concrete benefits delivered by the Government, and previous efforts to remove it have met with significant opposition.

However, the decision to extend the fuel subsidy programme has considerably increased government financing needs. Amid increased oil prices and declining domestic oil production, the additional subsidy requirements have increased the budget deficit to around 4% of GDP, 0.5 percentage points more than projected. This increased Nigeria's overall debt profile by 2,000,000m. naira in the first quarter of 2022 alone, to some 41,000,000m. naira. In June the Minister of Finance, Budget and National Planning, Zainab Shamsuna Ahmed, announced the cancellation of a planned US $950m. Eurobond issue owing to adverse market conditions, reflecting broader investor concerns over the risk profile of Nigeria's debt.

The next presidential administration will face severe fiscal constraints. Global price conditions and falling domestic oil production will necessitate higher levels of borrowing to finance ongoing fuel subsidy payments at least until the end of President Buhari's tenure in February 2023. With increasing pressure on the naira and an increase in international interest rates, there is a risk that debt service costs could rise to unsustainable levels.

ECONOMIC PROSPECTS

At mid-2022 the Nigerian economy was facing various deteriorating trends, with economic prospects clouded by high inflation, stretched public finances and rising external debt. The Government and the CBN will struggle to control inflation, and food insecurity was expected to grow. Fuel subsidies could reach US $9,600m. in 2022, 10 times higher than the initially projected figure, which may effectively outweigh the rising profits from high oil prices. However, cutting fuel subsidies would threaten the economic survival of many precariously balanced households. The CBN projects that overall GDP growth for 2022 will remain above 3.2%, a more conservative estimate than the Government's projection of 4.2%.

In the longer term, the business environment is in dire need of reform, with a cumbersome bureaucracy and high levels of corruption acting as critical obstacles to private sector development. In early 2017 the IMF warned of potential economic collapse if Nigeria failed to progress with reforms. In April 2019 the Fund revisited previous themes by noting the country's massive infrastructure gap and that low revenue mobilization continued to constrain growth. The Fund also warned that Nigeria's health care and education spending were among the lowest globally, and recommended tax reform and increasing non-oil revenues to raise more funds to pay for public services.

In mid-2019, before the global oil price collapse and the COVID-19 pandemic, the IMF predicted that per capita income (on an international purchasing-power-parity basis) in Nigeria would continue to fall until at least 2023. In its April 2021 forecasts, the IMF extended the projected decline to at least 2026. To many observers, it is not a question of whether Nigeria will change but rather of how it will change. Will the process be one of ongoing and planned reform, or something more radical?

So far, the Government's approach has drawn extensive criticism. In December 2021 President Buhari formally announced Nigeria's Medium-Term Development Plan for 2021–25, which aimed to achieve an average annual growth rate of 5% during the plan period, as well as to create 21m. jobs and bring 35m. people out of poverty. The projected cost of the plan was estimated at some 350,000,000m. naira (US $850,000m.), of which 86% was to come from private sector investments, with the remainder to be funded by public spending. However, the national budget for 2022 did not incorporate the development plan's objectives into its line items, raising questions about how the plan was to be implemented. A significant increase in oil output would be required to provide the necessary funding, and as of mid-2022 this had failed to materialize.

To its critics, none of the plan's targets were achievable within the expected timeframe, as they would require a significant increase in the annual growth rate projected by the IMF (of around 3% in 2022–23). With political attention firmly focused on the 2023 presidential and general elections, implementation of the regulatory changes necessary to attract more private investment, such as exchange rate and tax reforms, seemed highly unlikely in the short term.

Statistical Survey

Sources (unless otherwise stated): National Bureau of Statistics, Plot 762, Independence Avenue, Central Business District, PMB 127, Garki, Abuja; tel. (9) 2731085; e-mail feedback@nigerianstat.gov.ng; internet www.nigerianstat.gov.ng; Central Bank of Nigeria, Plot 33, Abubakar Tafawa Balewa Way, Central Business District, PMB 187, Garki, Abuja; tel. (9) 46239701; e-mail contactcbn@cbn.gov.ng; internet www.cbn.gov.ng.

Area and Population

AREA, POPULATION AND DENSITY

Area (sq km)	909,890*
Population (census results)	
28–30 November 1991†	88,992,220
21–27 March 2006	
Males	71,345,488
Females	69,086,302
Total	140,431,790
Population (UN estimates at mid-year)‡	
2020	206,139,587
2021§	211,400,704
2022§	216,746,933
Density (per sq km) at mid-2022§	238.2

* 351,310 sq miles.
† Revised 15 September 2001.
‡ Source: UN, *World Population Prospects: The 2019 Revision*.
§ Projection.

POPULATION BY AGE AND SEX
('000, UN projections at mid-2022)

	Males	Females	Total
0–14 years	47,775.0	45,664.6	93,439.6
15–64 years	59,259.0	58,040.8	117,299.8
65 years and over	2,838.9	3,168.7	6,007.6
Total	109,872.9	106,874.1	216,746.9

Note: Totals may not be equal to the sum of components, owing to rounding.
Source: UN, *World Population Prospects: The 2019 Revision*.

STATES
(official population projections, 2015)

	Area (sq km)	Population	Density (per sq km)	Capital
Abia	4,900	3,622,862	739.4	Umuahia
Adamawa . . .	38,700	4,120,196	106.5	Yola
Akwa Ibom . . .	6,900	5,286,948	766.2	Uyo
Anambra . . .	4,865	5,366,909	1103.2	Awka
Bauchi . . .	49,119	6,304,513	128.4	Bauchi
Bayelsa . . .	9,059	2,209,200	243.9	Yenogoa
Benue . . .	30,800	5,562,423	180.6	Makurdi
Borno . . .	72,609	5,651,497	77.8	Maiduguri
Cross River . . .	21,787	3,749,566	172.1	Calabar
Delta . . .	17,108	5,474,015	320.0	Asaba
Ebonyi . . .	6,400	2,796,543	437.0	Abakaliki
Edo . . .	19,187	4,116,862	214.6	Benin City
Ekiti . . .	5,435	3,164,993	582.3	Ado-Ekiti
Enugu . . .	7,534	4,273,202	567.2	Enugu
Gombe . . .	17,100	3,148,070	184.1	Gombe
Imo . . .	5,288	5,227,922	988.6	Owerri
Jigawa . . .	23,287	5,652,239	242.7	Dutse
Kaduna . . .	42,481	7,994,351	188.2	Kaduna
Kano . . .	20,280	12,625,460	622.6	Kano
Katsina . . .	23,561	7,586,469	322.0	Katsina
Kebbi . . .	36,985	4,296,421	116.2	Birnin Kebbi
Kogi . . .	27,747	4,333,624	156.2	Lokoja
Kwara . . .	35,705	3,093,065	86.6	Ilorin
Lagos . . .	3,671	12,130,987	3,304.5	Ikeja
Nassarawa . . .	28,735	2,444,499	85.1	Lafia
Niger . . .	68,925	5,358,381	77.7	Minna
Ogun . . .	16,400	5,037,594	307.2	Abeokuta
Ondo . . .	15,820	4,525,632	286.1	Akure

—continued	Area (sq km)	Population	Density (per sq km)	Capital
Osun	9,026	4,548,265	503.9	Oshogbo
Oyo	26,500	7,561,640	285.3	Ibadan
Plateau . . .	27,147	4,082,696	150.4	Jos
Rivers	10,575	7,043,821	666.1	Port Harcourt
Sokoto	27,825	4,841,822	174.0	Sokoto
Taraba	56,282	2,974,262	52.8	Jalingo
Yobe	46,609	3,173,229	68.1	Damaturu
Zamfara . . .	37,931	4,364,460	115.1	Gusau
Federal Capital Territory (Abuja) .	7,607	3,195,116	420.0	Abuja
Total	909,890	186,939,754	205.5	—

PRINCIPAL TOWNS
('000, urban agglomerations, UN projections at mid-2022)

Lagos	15,387.6	Zaria	749.3
Kano	4,219.2	Akure	716.8
Ibadan	3,756.4	Sokoto	684.6
Abuja (federal capital) . .	3,652.0	Bauchi	645.0
Port Harcourt . .	3,324.7	Abakaliki . . .	631.8
Benin City . . .	1,841.1	Calabar	630.6
Onitsha	1,552.6	Ogbomosho . . .	602.3
Uyo	1,264.6	Abeokuta . . .	556.6
Nnewi	1,176.6	Gombe	550.8
Kaduna	1,158.0	Ado-Ekiti . . .	516.2
Aba	1,150.1	Katsina	504.9
Ikorodu	1,041.2	Okene	493.5
Ilorin	1,000.5	Okpogho	483.6
Owerri	945.0	Potiskum	483.3
Warri	942.7	Igbidu	478.8
Jos	942.2	Minna	478.6
Umuahia . . .	860.6	Gwagwalada . . .	475.1
Maiduguri . . .	822.3	Gboko	471.6
Enugu	819.8	Ondo	459.8
Lokoja	790.7	Oyo	455.5
Oshogbo	749.8	Makurdi	437.9

Source: UN, *World Urbanization Prospects: The 2018 Revision*.

BIRTHS AND DEATHS
(annual averages, UN estimates)

	2005–10	2010–15	2015–20
Birth rate (per 1,000) . . .	41.9	40.5	38.1
Death rate (per 1,000) . . .	15.1	13.5	12.0

Source: UN, *World Population Prospects: The 2019 Revision*.

Life expectancy (years at birth, estimates): 55.0 (males 54.1; females 56.0) in 2020 (Source: World Bank, World Development Indicators database).

ECONOMICALLY ACTIVE POPULATION
('000 persons aged 15–64 years, labour force survey at July–September 2017)

	Males	Females	Total
Agriculture, hunting, forestry and fishing	24,109.4	8,248.8	32,358.2
Mining and quarrying . . .	103.0	8.7	111.7
Manufacturing	3,008.0	1,913.9	4,921.9
Electricity, gas and water . .	74.1	16.7	90.7
Construction	1,581.3	32.6	1,613.9
Wholesale and retail trade; repairs of motor vehicles and motorcycles and personal and household articles .	3,591.0	6,423.8	10,014.8
Hotels and restaurants . .	114.5	820.1	934.6
Transport, storage and communications . .	2,671.8	106.7	2,778.5
Financial intermediation . .	568.5	315.6	884.1
Real estate, renting and business activities . .	63.6	2.6	66.2
Public administration, defence and compulsory social security .	3,147.6	1,634.4	4,782.0
Education	1,243.9	1,278.8	2,522.8

—continued	Males	Females	Total
Health and social welfare . .	755.2	1,218.8	1,973.9
Other community, social and personal service activities . .	3,543.3	2,493.3	6,036.6
Total employed	44,575.3	24,514.7	69,090.0
Unemployed	7,092.1	8,905.9	15,998.0
Total labour force	51,667.4	33,420.6	85,088.1

Note: Figures for unemployed include persons undertaking 1–19 hours of work per week (8,461,422 in July–September 2017).

2020 (labour force survey at January–March): Total employed 46,488.1; Unemployed 23,187.4; Total labour force 69,675.5.

Note: Totals may not be equal to the sum of components, owing to rounding.

Health and Welfare

KEY INDICATORS

Total fertility rate (children per woman, 2020)	5.2
Under-5 mortality rate (per 1,000 live births, 2020) . . .	113.8
HIV/AIDS (% of persons aged 15–49, 2020)	1.3
COVID-19: Cumulative confirmed deaths (per 100,000 persons at 31 August 2022)	1.5
COVID-19: Fully vaccinated population (% of total population at 21 August 2022)	13.6
Physicians (per 1,000 head, 2018)	0.4
Hospital beds (per 1,000 head, 2004)	0.5
Domestic health expenditure (2019): US $ per head (PPP) .	25.9
Domestic health expenditure (2019): % of GDP	0.5
Domestic health expenditure (2019): public (% of total current expenditure)	15.9
Access to improved water resources (% of persons, 2020) .	78
Access to improved sanitation facilities (% of persons, 2020) .	43
Total carbon dioxide emissions ('000 metric tons, 2018) . .	130,670
Carbon dioxide emissions per head (metric tons, 2018) . .	0.7
Human Development Index (2021): ranking	163
Human Development Index (2021): value	0.535

Note: For data on COVID-19 vaccinations, 'fully vaccinated' denotes receipt of all doses specified by approved vaccination regime (Sources: Johns Hopkins University and Our World in Data). Data on health expenditure refer to current general government expenditure in each case. For more information on sources and further definitions for all indicators, see Health and Welfare Statistics: Sources and Definitions section (europaworld.com/credits).

Agriculture

PRINCIPAL CROPS
('000 metric tons)

	2018	2019	2020
Carrots and turnips*	236	236	237
Cashew nuts*	100	100	99
Cassava (Manioc)*	55,868	59,412	60,002
Chillies and peppers, dry* . .	63	62	63
Chillies and peppers, green* . .	758	760	762
Cocoa beans*	340	348	340
Coconuts	228†	229*	226*
Cow peas, dry*	3,500	3,547	3,647
Ginger*	700	647	734
Groundnuts, with shell* . . .	4,600	4,461	4,493
Karité nuts (sheanuts)* . . .	343	347	346
Kolanuts*	168	165	167
Maize†	11,000	12,700	12,000
Maize, green*	757	760	761
Mangoes, mangosteens and guavas*	895	897	894
Melonseed*	558	554	556
Millet†	2,119	2,000	2,000
Oil palm fruit*	9,600	10,062	9,457
Okra*	1,732	1,835	1,838
Onions and shallots, green* . .	244	247	245
Onions, dry*	1,400	1,374	1,382
Papayas*	877	882	877
Pineapples*	1,510	1,514	1,508
Plantains and others*	3,081	3,086	3,077

—continued	2018	2019	2020
Potatoes*	1,206	1,194	1,199
Rice, paddy	8,403	8,435	8,172†
Rubber, natural*	148	148	148
Sesame seed†	480	510	490
Sorghum†	6,800	6,665	6,362
Soybeans (Soya beans)† . . .	660	700	600
Sugar cane*	1,481	1,499	1,517
Sweet potatoes*	3,877	3,884	3,868
Taro (Coco yam)*	3,228	3,212	3,205
Tomatoes*	3,500	3,799	3,694
Wheat†	60	60	55
Yams	50,000*	50,000	50,053

* FAO estimate(s).
† Unofficial figure(s).

Aggregate production ('000 metric tons, may include official, semi-official or estimated data): Total cereals 28,465 in 2018, 29,943 in 2019, 28,672 in 2020; Total fruit (primary) 11,553 in 2018, 11,568 in 2019, 11,530 in 2020; Total oilcrops 16,750 in 2018, 17,145 in 2019, 16,449 in 2020; Total roots and tubers 114,180 in 2018, 117,703 in 2019, 118,327 in 2020; Total vegetables (primary) 15,435 in 2018, 15,779 in 2019, 15,706 in 2020.

Source: FAO.

LIVESTOCK
('000 head, year ending September, FAO estimate)

	2018	2019	2020
Asses	1,301	1,308	1,313
Camels	280	289	291
Cattle	20,201	20,527	20,745
Chickens	184,347	167,385	166,125
Goats	80,245	82,634	83,715
Horses	102	102	103
Pigs	7,987	7,989	7,990
Sheep	45,713	46,842	47,744

Source: FAO.

LIVESTOCK PRODUCTS
('000 metric tons, FAO estimate)

	2018	2019	2020
Cattle hides, fresh	38	39	39
Cattle meat	317	328	326
Cattle offals, edible	48	50	49
Cows' milk	514	520	525
Chicken meat	264	240	238
Game meat	171	170	171
Goat meat	268	268	261
Goat offals, edible	43	43	42
Goats' skins, fresh	43	43	42
Pig meat	298	300	303
Sheep meat	156	154	151
Sheepskins, fresh	28	28	27
Hen eggs	640	640	647

Source: FAO.

Forestry

ROUNDWOOD REMOVALS
('000 cubic metres, excluding bark, FAO estimates)

	2018	2019	2020
Sawlogs, veneer logs and logs for sleepers	7,600	7,600	7,600
Pulpwood	22	22	22
Other industrial wood	2,400	2,400	2,400
Fuel wood	66,210	66,541	66,883
Total	76,232	76,563	76,905

Source: FAO.

SAWNWOOD PRODUCTION
('000 cubic metres, including railway sleepers)

	2003	2004	2005*
Coniferous (softwood) . . .	0†	0†	2
Broadleaved (hardwood) . . .	2,000*	2,000*	2,000
Total	2,000	2,000	2,002

* Unofficial figure(s).
† FAO estimate.

2006–20: Production assumed to be unchanged from 2005 (FAO estimates).

Source: FAO.

Fishing
('000 metric tons, live weight)

	2018	2019	2020
Capture	878.2	825.0	783.1
Tilapias	69.6	65.7	62.4
Bagrid catfish	31.2	33.6	31.9
Elephant snout fishes . . .	32.0	29.5	28.0
Torpedo-shaped catfishes . .	27.3	25.7	24.4
Giant African threadfin . . .	35.2	33.8	32.0
Sardinellas	55.2	50.6	48.1
Bonga shad	44.8	41.7	39.6
Other shrimps and prawns . .	28.6	27.2	25.9
Aquaculture	291.3	289.5	261.7
North African catfish . . .	160.1	156.7	141.6
Total catch	1,169.5	1,114.6	1,044.8

Source: FAO.

Mining
(metric tons unless otherwise indicated)

	2016	2017	2018
Coal, bituminous	104,425	638,062	352,679
Kaolin	26,710	46,935	11,707
Gypsum	25,000*	16,619	39,052
Crude petroleum ('000 barrels) .	670,049	689,743	701,432
Tin concentrates	3,443	12,324	11,721

* Estimated production.

Source: US Geological Survey.

Crude petroleum ('000 metric tons, estimates): 101,108 in 2019; 88,421 in 2020; 77,929 in 2021 (Source: BP, *Statistical Review of World Energy*).

Natural gas (million cu m, excl. gas flared or recycled, estimates): 49,279 in 2019; 49,431 in 2020; 45,913 in 2021 (Source: BP, *Statistical Review of World Energy*).

Industry

SELECTED PRODUCTS
('000 metric tons unless otherwise indicated)

	2016	2017	2018
Raw sugar*	20.0	n.a.	n.a.
Palm oil†‡	960	1,040	1,130
Beer of barley†‡	2,600	1,750	1,800
Plywood ('000 cubic metres)†‡ .	56	56	56
Wood pulp†§	23	23	23
Paper and paperboard†§ . . .	19	19	19
Liquefied petroleum gas ('000 barrels)	1,112	887	605
Motor spirit—petrol ('000 barrels)	7,942	5,757	3,142
Kerosene ('000 barrels) . . .	7,197	5,217	2,847
Gas-diesel (distillate fuel) oil ('000 barrels)	4,993	6,453	2,528
Residual fuel oils ('000 barrels) .	2,330	4,624	2,551
Cement§	22,000	19,000	21,000
Electrical energy (million kWh)‖ .	36,512	32,221	32,446

* Source: UN Industrial Commodity Statistics Database.
† Source: FAO.
‡ Unofficial figures.
§ Estimates.
‖ Source: UN Energy Statistics Database.

Electrical energy (million kWh): 31,422 in 2019 (Source: UN Energy Statistics Database).

2019 ('000 metric tons unless otherwise indicated, FAO estimates): Palm oil 1,220 (unofficial figure); Beer of barley 1,800 (unofficial figure); Plywood ('000 cubic metres) 56; Wood pulp 23; Paper and paperboard 19 (Source: FAO).

2020 ('000 metric tons unless otherwise indicated, FAO estimates): Plywood ('000 cubic metres) 56; Wood pulp 23; Paper and paperboard 19 (Source: FAO).

Source (unless otherwise indicated): US Geological Survey.

Finance

CURRENCY AND EXCHANGE RATES

Monetary Units
100 kobo = 1 naira (₦).

Sterling, Dollar and Euro Equivalents (29 October 2021)
£1 sterling = 566.867 naira;
US $1 = 411.250 naira;
€1 = 478.901 naira;
1,000 naira = £1.76 = $2.43 = 2.09.

Average Exchange Rate (naira per US $)
2018 306.084
2019 306.921
2020 358.811

FEDERAL BUDGET
(₦ '000 million)

Revenue	2018	2019	2020
Petroleum revenue	2,076	2,209	1,307
Non-petroleum revenue . . .	1,520	2,240	2,272
Import and excise duties . .	318	748	396
Companies' income tax . . .	660	695	674
Value-added tax	147	160	198
Federal government independent revenue . . .	395	637	1,003
Grants	0	0	93
Total	3,596	4,449	3,672

Expenditure	2018	2019	2020
Recurrent expenditure	7,364	8,896	9,891
Personnel and pensions . . .	2,417	2,596	3,187
Overhead costs	517	1,131	1,269
Interest payments	2,186	2,442	3,261
Transfers	1,912	2,147	1,735
Arrears clearance	331	580	439
Capital expenditure	1,682	2,084	1,602
Total	9,046	10,981	11,492

Source: IMF, *Nigeria: 2021 Article IV Consultation—Press Release; Staff Report; Staff Statement, and Statement by the Executive Director for Nigeria* (February 2022).

INTERNATIONAL RESERVES
(excl. gold, US $ million at 31 December)

	2018	2019	2020
IMF special drawing rights . .	2,085	2,073	2,122
Reserve position in IMF . .	244	243	253
Foreign exchange	40,510	36,021	34,355
Total	42,839	38,337	36,730

2021: IMF special drawing rights 5,318; Reserve position in IMF 246.

Source: IMF, *International Financial Statistics.*

MONEY SUPPLY
(₦ '000 million at 31 December)

	2019	2020	2021
Currency outside depository corporations	2,022.6	2,495.6	2,938.4
Transferable deposits	8,625.8	13,342.8	15,230.9
Other deposits	18,229.5	21,990.5	25,648.3
Securities other than shares . .	5,972.9	1,076.0	0.9
Broad money	34,850.9	38,904.9	43,818.5

Source: IMF, *International Financial Statistics.*

COST OF LIVING
(Consumer Price Index; base: November 2009 = 100)

	2019	2020	2021
Food (excl. beverages)	318.3	369.8	445.3
Clothing (incl. footwear) . . .	277.6	307.4	349.9
Housing and utilities	284.5	307.6	339.1
All items (incl. others) . . .	291.4	330.0	385.9

NATIONAL ACCOUNTS
(₦ '000 million at current basic prices)

Expenditure on the Gross Domestic Product

	2019	2020	2021
Government final consumption expenditure	8,115.0	13,431.8	9,004.0
Private final consumption expenditure	108,638.3	98,583.8	109,433.1
Increase in stocks	1,151.5	1,161.4	1,280.7
Gross fixed capital formation . .	35,864.0	41,253.5	58,293.9
Total domestic expenditure	153,768.8	154,430.5	178,011.7
Exports of goods and non-factor services	20,711.2	12,522.7	18,907.8
Less Imports of goods and non-petroleum services	28,840.8	12,700.9	20,844.0
GDP in basic prices . . .	145,639.1	154,252.3	176,075.5
GDP in constant basic 2010 prices	72,094.1	70,800.5	73,382.8

Gross Domestic Product by Economic Activity

	2019	2020	2021
Agriculture, hunting, forestry and fishing	31,904.1	37,241.6	41,126.1
Mining and quarrying	12,769.4	10,851.8	10,737.6
Crude petroleum	12,400.4	10,195.6	9,636.0
Manufacturing	16,781.1	19,539.6	25,725.9
Electricity, gas and water	1,332.3	1,500.0	2,250.7
Construction	8,996.9	11,639.5	16,586.8
Wholesale and retail trade	22,509.3	21,106.4	23,288.4
Hotels and restaurants	1,398.7	1,340.9	1,490.1
Transport and communications	18,455.4	19,448.4	21,152.5
Finance, insurance	4,230.9	4,737.8	5,300.7
Real estate and business services	14,044.1	13,440.9	14,092.7
Education	2,969.3	2,707.4	2,805.0
Health and social work	896.2	951.3	1,042.9
Government services	2,896.8	2,971.6	3,008.0
Other community, social and personal services	5,026.1	4,846.9	4,920.2
GDP at factor cost	144,210.5	152,324.1	173,527.7
Indirect taxes (net)	1,428.6	1,928.2	2,547.8
GDP in basic prices	145,639.1	154,252.3	176,075.5

BALANCE OF PAYMENTS

(US $ million)

	2018	2019	2020
Exports of goods	61,221	64,978	35,944
Imports of goods	−40,754	−62,110	−52,346
Balance on goods	20,467	2,868	−16,402
Exports of services	4,818	4,949	3,993
Imports of services	−30,884	−38,710	−19,833
Balance on goods and services	−5,599	−30,893	−32,241
Primary income received	2,050	2,319	1,559
Primary income paid	−14,325	−12,422	−7,316
Balance on goods, services and primary income	−17,874	−40,996	−37,998
Secondary income received	24,526	27,080	21,627
Secondary income paid	−392	−711	−605
Current balance	6,261	−14,627	−16,976
Direct investment assets	−566	−285	338
Direct investment liabilities	775	2,305	2,385
Portfolio investment assets	−401	−88	−17
Portfolio investment liabilities	395	3,178	−3,585
Other investment assets	−4,132	7,396	1,381
Other investment liabilities	7,116	4,439	2,907
Net errors and omissions	−6,162	−6,809	8,519
Reserves and related items	3,286	−4,490	−5,047

Source: IMF, *International Financial Statistics*.

External Trade

PRINCIPAL COMMODITIES

(distribution by HS, ₦ '000 million)

Imports c.i.f.	2019	2020	2021
Live animals and animal products	422.9	454.5	551.2
Vegetables and vegetable products	585.9	749.4	1,351.4
Prepared foodstuffs; beverages, spirits, vinegars; tobacco and articles thereof	676.4	594.1	903.5
Mineral products	2,718.8	2,965.2	6,563.0
Chemicals and related products	1,388.0	1,456.6	1,799.4
Plastics, rubber, and articles thereof	695.2	609.2	1,161.3
Iron and steel; other base metals and articles thereof	785.0	672.5	1,060.2
Machinery and mechanical appliances; electrical equipment; articles thereof	4,541.2	3,029.2	4,195.2
Vehicles, aircraft, vessels and associated transport equipment	2,352.0	1,149.4	1,555.9
Total (incl. others)	16,959.9	12,700.9	20,844.0

Exports f.o.b.	2019	2020	2021
Vegetables and vegetable products	155.2	189.9	259.3
Prepared foodstuffs; beverages, spirits, vinegars; tobacco and articles thereof	174.3	169.3	345.3
Mineral products	16,729.1	11,121.0	16,910.1
Chemicals and related products	67.8	79.0	405.9
Plastics, rubber, and articles thereof	31.5	10.6	44.6
Iron and steel; other base metals and articles thereof	805.3	35.6	152.2
Raw hides and skins, leather, furskins, etc., and articles thereof	26.9	23.5	37.2
Vehicles, aircraft and parts thereof; vessels, etc.	1,163.7	842.0	654.2
Total (incl. others)	19,192.2	12,522.7	18,907.8

PRINCIPAL TRADING PARTNERS

(₦ '000 million)*

Imports c.i.f.	2019	2020	2021
Brazil	252.5	283.3	462.9
China, People's Republic	4,317.9	3,227.0	5,155.7
France (incl. Monaco)	340.8	269.9	469.7
Germany	521.5	395.3	509.8
India	2,041.8	1,104.6	1,841.1
Italy	312.4	272.1	422.9
Japan	258.1	140.6	119.6
Netherlands	1,250.5	1,163.1	2,142.1
Spain	198.1	194.1	275.7
United Kingdom	481.4	282.1	326.0
USA	1,674.2	1,026.1	1,271.6
Total (incl. others)	16,959.9	12,700.9	20,844.0

Exports f.o.b.	2019	2020	2021
Brazil	304.8	53.9	496.8
Canada	481.0	287.0	857.9
China, People's Republic . . .	596.0	633.5	739.0
France (incl. Monaco)	1,270.7	565.6	1,190.5
Germany	415.1	116.9	330.7
India	2,957.8	1,880.5	3,095.9
Italy	761.7	440.2	759.2
Japan	102.6	100.5	153.9
Netherlands	1,742.6	1,072.3	1,135.1
Spain	1,903.8	1,362.0	2,232.1
United Kingdom	416.4	310.2	448.6
USA	1,008.3	382.2	800.3
Total (incl. others)	19,192.2	12,522.7	18,907.8

* Imports by country of consignment; exports by country of destination.

Transport

RAILWAYS
(traffic)

	2006	2007	2008
Passenger journeys ('000) . . .	708.8	1,478.7	1,996.3
Passenger-km (million) . . .	256.6	535.3	722.7
Freight ('000 metric tons) . .	41,219	31,405	47,409
Net freight ton-km (million) . .	34.3	26.0	41.1

Passenger journeys ('000): 3,019.7 in 2018; 2,890.1 in 2019; 1,020.4 in 2020.

ROAD TRAFFIC
(new registrations)

	2013	2014	2015
Motorcycles and mopeds . . .	254,667	418,417	269,795
Other motor vehicles . . .	1,004,469	560,987	303,274

SHIPPING

Flag Registered Fleet
(at 31 December)

	2019	2020	2021
Number of vessels	994	1,043	1,085
Total displacement ('000 grt) . .	3,276.3	3,316.8	3,487.0

Source: Lloyd's List Intelligence (www.bit.ly/LLintelligence).

CIVIL AVIATION
(traffic on scheduled services)

	2013	2014	2015
Kilometres flown (million) . .	39	40	36
Passengers carried ('000) . .	4,210	3,857	3,223
Passenger-km (million) . .	3,281	3,127	2,464
Total ton-km (million) . . .	12	12	22

Source: UN, *Statistical Yearbook*.

2020 (domestic and international): Departures 47,035; Passengers carried 3.4m.; Freight carried 1m. ton-km (Source: World Bank, World Development Indicators database).

Tourism

ARRIVALS BY NATIONALITY*

Country	2014	2015	2016
Benin	88,847	157,847	164,828
Cameroon	161,819	196,628	211,609
Chad	31,141	38,762	49,705
China, People's Republic . . .	117,424	200,436	207,927
Germany	50,742	55,197	34,816
Ghana	104,344	144,289	149,974
India	101,296	163,391	166,810
Niger	304,554	383,674	393,670
United Kingdom	152,296	303,754	213,384
USA	203,523	302,625	246,562
Total (incl. others)	4,803,213	6,017,338	5,265,453

* Figures refer to arrival at frontiers of visitors from abroad, including same-day visitors (excursionists). Nigerian nationals resident abroad accounted for 2,582,002 in 2014, 2,887,188 in 2015 and 2,346,481 in 2016.

Tourism receipts (US $ million, excl. passenger transport): 2,549 in 2017; 1,962 in 2018; 1,449 in 2019 (provisional).

Source: World Tourism Organization.

Communications Media

	2018	2019	2020
Telephones ('000 main lines in use)	140.5	107.2	107.0
Mobile telephone subscriptions ('000)	172,730.6	184,592.3	204,228.7
Broadband subscriptions, fixed ('000)	74.0	83.4	65.3
Broadband subscriptions, mobile ('000)	60,087.2	72,153.8	85,941.2
Internet users (% of population) .	31.9	33.6	35.5

Source: International Telecommunication Union.

Education

(2016 unless otherwise specified)

	Institutions	Teachers	Students ('000) Males	Females	Total
Primary . . .	85,286*	595,753*	13,435.9	12,155.2	25,591.2
Secondary . . .	19,549*	690,355	5,510.7	4,803.6	10,314.3
Poly/Monotechnic† .	178	16,499	n.a.	n.a.	237.7
University . . .	104‡	23,535†	475.6‡	214.4‡	690.0‡

* 2010 figure.
† 2005 figure.
‡ 2006 figure.

2017/18 (UNESCO estimates): *Pupils:* Pre-primary 1,391,030 (Source: UNESCO Institute for Statistics).

Pupil-teacher ratio (qualified teaching staff, primary education, UNESCO estimate): 49.1 in 2017/18 (Source: UNESCO Institute for Statistics).

Adult literacy rate (UNESCO estimates): 62.0% (males 71.3%; females 52.7%) in 2018 (Source: UNESCO Institute for Statistics).

Directory

The Constitution

The Constitution of the Federal Republic of Nigeria was promulgated on 5 May 1999, and entered into force on 31 May. The main provisions are summarized below:

PROVISIONS

Nigeria is one indivisible sovereign state, to be known as the Federal Republic of Nigeria. Nigeria is a Federation, comprising 36 States and a Federal Capital Territory. The Constitution includes provisions for the creation of new States and for boundary adjustments of existing States. The Government of the Federation or of a State is prohibited from adopting any religion as a state religion.

LEGISLATURE

The legislative powers of the Federation are vested in the National Assembly, comprising a Senate and a House of Representatives. The 109-member Senate consists of three Senators from each State and one from the Federal Capital Territory, who are elected for a term of four years. The House of Representatives comprises 360 members, representing constituencies of nearly equal population as far as possible, who are elected for a four-year term. The Senate and House of Representatives each have a Speaker and Deputy Speaker, who are elected by the members of the House from among themselves. Legislation may originate in either the Senate or the House of Representatives, and, having been approved by the House in which it originated by a two-thirds' majority, will be submitted to the other House for approval, and subsequently presented to the President for assent. Should the President withhold his or her assent, and the bill be returned to the National Assembly and again approved by each House by a two-thirds' majority, the bill will become law. The legislative powers of a State of the Federation will be vested in the House of Assembly of the State. The House of Assembly of a State will consist of three or four times the number of seats that the State holds in the House of Representatives (comprising not less than 24 and not more than 40 members).

EXECUTIVE

The executive powers of the Federation are vested in the President, who is the head of state, the Chief Executive of the Federation and the Commander-in-Chief of the Armed Forces of the Federation. The President is elected for a term of four years and must receive not less than one-quarter of the votes cast at the election in at least two-thirds of the States in the Federation and the Federal Capital Territory. The President nominates a candidate as his or her associate from the same political party to occupy the office of Vice-President. The Ministers of the Government of the Federation are nominated by the President, subject to confirmation by the Senate. Federal executive bodies include the Council of State, which advises the President in the exercise of his or her powers. The executive powers of a State are vested in the Governor of that State, who is elected for a four-year term and must receive not less than one-quarter of votes cast in at least two-thirds of all local government areas in the State.

JUDICIARY

The judicial powers of the Federation are vested in the courts established for the Federation, and the judicial powers of a State in the courts established for the State. The Federation has a Supreme Court, a Court of Appeal and a Federal High Court. Each State has a High Court, a *Shari'a* Court of Appeal and a Customary Court of Appeal. Chief Judges are nominated on the recommendation of a National Judicial Council.

LOCAL GOVERNMENT

The States are divided into 774 local government areas. The system of local government by democratically elected local government councils is guaranteed, and the Government of each State will ensure their existence. Each local government council within the State will participate in the economic planning and development of the area over which it exercises authority.

Federal Government

HEAD OF STATE

President and Commander-in-Chief of the Armed Forces: Maj.-Gen. (retd) MUHAMMADU BUHARI (inaugurated 29 May 2015; re-elected 23 February 2019, sworn in 29 May).

Vice-President and Chairman of the National Planning Commission: Prof. OLUYEMI OLULEKE OSINBAJO.

CABINET
(October 2022)

President and Minister of Petroleum Resources: Maj.-Gen. (retd) MUHAMMADU BUHARI.

Minister of Defence: Maj.-Gen. (retd) BASHIR SALIHI MAGASHI.

Minister of Finance, Budget and National Planning: ZAINAB SHAMSUNA AHMED.

Minister of the Interior: RAUF AREGBESOLA.

Minister for the Federal Capital Territory: MUHAMMADU MUSA BELLO.

Minister of Power: ABUBAKAR ALIYU.

Minister of Niger Delta Affairs: UMANA UMANA.

Minister of Education: ADAMU ADAMU.

Minister of Labour and Employment: Dr CHRIS NGIGE.

Attorney-General and Minister of Justice: ABUBAKAR MALAMI.

Minister of Youth and Sports: SUNDAY DARE.

Minister of Industry, Trade and Investment: OTUNBA ADENIYI ADEBAYO.

Minister of Information and Culture: Alhaji LAI MOHAMMED.

Minister of Foreign Affairs: GEOFFREY ONYEAMA.

Minister of Health: Dr OSAGIE EHANIRE.

Minister of Women's Affairs and Social Development: PAULINE TALLEN.

Minister of Works and Housing: BABATUNDE RAJI FASHOLA.

Minister of Science and Technology: ADELEKE MAMORA.

Minister of Transportation: MU'AZU JAJI SAMBO.

Minister of Mines and Steel Development: Dr OLAMILEKAN ADEGBITE.

Minister of Agriculture and Rural Development: Dr MUHAMMAD MAHMOUD ABUBAKAR.

Minister of Communications: Dr ALI ISA PANTAMI.

Minister of Water Resources: SULEIMAN ADAMU.

Minister of Police Affairs: MUHAMMADU MAIGARI DINGYADI.

Minister of Special Duties and Intergovernmental Affairs: GEORGE AKUME.

Minister of Humanitarian Affairs, Disaster Management and Social Development: SA'ADIYA UMAR FAROUK.

Minister of Aviation: HADI SIRIKA.

Minister of State for the Budget and National Planning: CLEMENT IKANADE AGBA.

Minister of State of the Federal Capital Territory: RAMATU TIJANI.

Minister of State for Science and Technology: IKECHUKWU IKOH.

Minister of State for Foreign Affairs: ZUBAIRU DADA.

Minister of State for Health: NKAMA EKUMANKAMA.

Minister of State for Niger Delta Affairs: SHARON IKEAZOR.

Minister of State for Power: GODWIN JEDY-AGBA.

Minister of State for the Environment: UDI ODUM.

Minister of State for Education: GOODLUCK OPIAH.

Minister of State for Agriculture and Rural Development: MUSTAPHA BABA SHEHURI.

Minister of State for Labour and Employment: FESTUS KEYAMO.

Minister of State for Industry, Trade and Investment: MARIAM YALWAJI KATAGUM.

Minister of State for Mines and Steel Development: GBEMISOLA SARAKI.

Minister of State for Petroleum Resources: TIMIPRE SYLVA.

Minister of State for Transportation: ADEMOLA ADEGOROYE.

Minister of State for Works and Housing: IBRAHIM EL-YAKUB.

MINISTRIES

Office of the Head of State: New Federal Secretariat Complex, Shehu Shagari Way, Central Area District, Abuja; tel. (9) 5233536; internet statehouse.gov.ng.

Ministry of Agriculture and Rural Development: Area 11, Secretariat Complex, 1 Capital Dr., Garki, PMB 135, Abuja; tel. (9) 3141931; e-mail adm@fmard.gov.ng; internet fmard.gov.ng.

Ministry of Aviation: New Federal Secretariat Complex, Shehu Shagari Way, Central Area District, PMB 146, Abuja; tel. (9) 5237487; e-mail info@aviation.gov.ng; internet www.aviation.gov.ng.

Ministry of Communications and Digital Economy: Federal Secretariat Complex, Phase 1, Annex 3, Shehu Shagari Way, Abuja; e-mail info@commtech.gov.ng; internet www.commtech.gov.ng.

Ministry of Defence: Ship House, Area 10, Garki, Abuja; tel. (9) 2340534; internet fb.com/DefenceInfoNG.

Ministry of Education: New Federal Secretariat Complex, Shehu Shagari Way, Central Area District, PMB 146, Abuja; tel. 9030009912; e-mail info@education.gov.ng; internet www .education.gov.ng.

Ministry of the Environment: Block C, Mabuchi, PMB 468, Abuja; tel. (9) 5233611; e-mail info@environment.gov.ng; internet environment.gov.ng.

Ministry of the Federal Capital Territory: 2 Kapital St, off Obafemi Awolowo St, Garki Area 11, PMB 24, Garki, Abuja; tel. (9) 4603600; e-mail info@fct.gov.ng; internet www.fct.gov.ng.

Ministry of Finance, Budget and National Planning: Ahmadu Bello Way, Central Area, PMB 14, Garki, Abuja; tel. (9) 2346290; internet finance.gov.ng.

Ministry of Foreign Affairs: Sir Tafawa Balewa House, Federal Secretariat, PMB 130, Abuja; tel. 84666876; e-mail info@ foreignaffairs.gov.ng; internet foreignaffairs.gov.ng.

Ministry of Health: Federal Secretariat Complex, Phase 3, Ahmadu Bello Way, Central Business District, Abuja; tel. (9) 5238362; e-mail info@health.gov.ng; internet health.gov.ng.

Ministry of Humanitarian Affairs, Disaster Management and Social Development: Federal Secretariat Complex, Phase 1, 6th Floor, Shehu Shagari Way, Central Area District, Abuja; tel. 8024175445; e-mail info@fmhds.gov.ng; internet www.fmhds.gov .ng.

Ministry of Industry, Trade and Investment: Old Secretariat, Area 1, Garki, PMB 88, Abuja; tel. (9) 2341662; e-mail info@fmiti.gov .ng; internet fmiti.gov.ng.

Ministry of Information and Culture: Phase II, Block A, 1st Floor, PMB 473, Sheh Shagari Way, Abuja; tel. (9) 5237183; internet fmic.gov.ng.

Ministry of the Interior: Block F, Old Federal Secretariat, Area 1, PMB 7007, Garki, Abuja; tel. 7000099999; internet interior.gov.ng.

Ministry of Justice: 71B Shehu Shagari Way, Maitama, PMB 192, Garki, Abuja; tel. 8050888806; e-mail info@justice.gov.ng; internet www.justice.gov.ng.

Ministry of Labour and Employment: New Federal Secretariat Complex, Phase I, Annex II, Shehu Shagari Way, Central Area, PMB 04, Garki, Abuja; tel. (9) 5235980; e-mail info@labour.gov.ng; internet labour.gov.ng.

Ministry of Mines and Steel Development: 2 Luanda Cres., off Adetokunbo Ademola Cres., Wuse II, Abuja; tel. (9) 5239064; internet www.minesandsteel.gov.ng.

Ministry of Niger Delta Affairs: Federal Secretariat, 11th Floor, Phase 1, Abuja; tel. 8055884477; e-mail dprs@nigerdelta.gov.ng; internet nigerdelta.gov.ng.

Ministry of Petroleum Resources: Block D, NNPC Towers, Herbert Macaulay Way, Central Business District, Abuja; tel. (9) 46084820; e-mail info@petroleumresources.gov.ng; internet petroleumresources.gov.ng.

Ministry of Police Affairs: Federal Secretariat Complex, Phase 3, Shehu Shagari Way, Abuja; e-mail info@policeaffairs.gov.ng; internet policeaffairs.gov.ng.

Ministry of Power: Power House, Plot No. 14, Zambezi Cres., Maitama, Abuja; e-mail info@power.gov.ng; internet www.power .gov.ng.

Ministry of Science and Technology: New Federal Secretariat Complex, Block D, Shehu Shagari Way, Central Area, PMB 331, Garki, Abuja; tel. 8059685843; e-mail info@scienceandtech.gov.ng; internet scienceandtech.gov.ng.

Ministry of Transportation: Dipcharima House, Central Business District, off 3rd Ave, PMB 0336, Garki, Abuja; tel. (9) 2347451; e-mail info@transportation.gov.ng; internet www.transportation .gov.ng.

Ministry of Water Resources: Federal Secretariat Complex, Area 1, PMB 135, Garki, Abuja; tel. 7061450955; e-mail info@ waterresources.gov.ng; internet www.waterresources.gov.ng.

Ministry of Women's Affairs and Social Development: Ahmadu Bello Way, Central Business District, PMB 229, Garki, Abuja; tel. (9) 5237112; e-mail enquiries@womenaffairs.gov.ng; internet www .womenaffairs.gov.ng.

Ministry of Works and Housing: Mabushi, Abuja; e-mail info@ worksandhousing.gov.ng; internet worksandhousing.gov.ng.

Ministry of Youth and Sports: 2nd Floor (257–237), Block 4A, New Federal Secretariat Complex, Shehu Shagari Way, Central Area, Abuja; tel. (9) 5231694; internet www.youthdevelopment.gov.ng.

President

Presidential Election, 23 February 2019

Candidate	Votes	% of votes
Maj.-Gen. (retd) Muhammadu Buhari (All Progressives Congress)	15,191,847	55.60
Atiku Abubakar (People's Democratic Party)	11,262,978	41.22
Obadiah Mailafia (African Democratic Congress)	97,874	0.36
Yabagi Sani Yusuf (Action Democratic Party)	54,930	0.20
Donald Duke (Social Democratic Party)	34,746	0.13
Omoyele Sowore (African Action Congress)	33,953	0.12
Others*	648,255	2.37
Total	27,324,583†	100.00

* There were 67 other candidates.
† In addition, there were 1,289,607 invalid votes.

Legislature

HOUSE OF REPRESENTATIVES

House of Representatives: The National Assembly Complex, 3 Arms Zones, PMB 141, Abujae-mail info@nass.gov.ng; internet nass .gov.ng.

Speaker of the House of Representatives: FEMI GBAJABIAMILA.

Election, 23 February 2019

Party	Seats
All Progressives Congress	218
Peoples Democratic Party	115
All Progressives Grand Alliance	9
Action Democratic Congress	2
Action Alliance	2
Peoples Redemption Party	2
African Democratic Party	1
Allied Peoples Movement	1
Labour Party	1
Social Democratic Party	1
Vacant	8
Total	360

SENATE

Senate: The National Assembly Complex, 3 Arms Zones, PMB 141, Abuja.

President of the Senate: AHMED IBRAHIM LAWAN.

Election, 23 February 2019

Party	Seats
All Progressives Congress	65
Peoples Democratic Party	39
Young Progressive Party	1
Total*	105

* The Independent National Electoral Commission did not announce results for four senatorial districts, including one in which the returning officer had allegedly declared a candidate the winner under duress.

Election Commission

Independent National Electoral Commission (INEC): Plot 436 Zambezi Cres., Maitama District Abuja; tel. 70022554632; e-mail iccc@inec.gov.ng; internet www.inecnigeria.org; f. 1998; Chair. MAHMOOD YAKUBU.

Political Organizations

Accord: Plot 488, 7 Yauri St, Area 3, Garki, Abuja; tel. 8062523829; Nat. Chair. MOHAMMAD LAWAL NALADO; Nat. Sec. Dr BUKOLA AJAJA.

Action Alliance (AA): 1977 Orlu St, Area 3, Garki, Abuja; tel. 7067277005; internet www.actionallianceng.org; Nat. Chair. KENNETH UDEZE; Nat. Sec. JAMES A. VERNIMBE.

Action Democratic Party (ADP): Plot 3379A, Mungo Park Close, off Jesse Jackson Asokoro New Extension, Abuja; tel. 9060000536; e-mail contact@adp.ng; internet www.adp.ng; f. 2016; Nat. Chair. YABAYI V. SANI; Nat. Sec. JAMES OKOROMA.

African Democratic Congress (ADC): 1 Capital Plaza, Nyanyan-Kuru Rd, Abuja; tel. 8059969415; Nat. Chair. Chief RALPH OKEY NWOSU; Nat. Sec. Alhaji SAID BABA ABDULLAHI.

African Peoples Alliance (APA): 7 Yauri St, Area 11, Garki, Abuja; tel. 8033493571; Nat. Chair. EMMANUEL URHUARHOVIE (acting); Nat. Sec. SAMAILA UMAR SIFAWA.

All Progressives Congress (APC): 40 Blantyre St, off Adetokunbo Ademola St, Wuse II, Abuja; tel. 8033345691; e-mail info@apc.com.ng; internet apc.com.ng; f. 2013 by a merger of the Action Congress of Nigeria, the Congress for Progressive Change, the All Nigeria People's Party (ANPP) and a faction of the All Progressives Grand Alliance; Chair. ABDULLAHI ADAMU; Nat. Sec. OTUNBA IYIOLA OMISORE.

All Progressives Grand Alliance (APGA): 41B Libreville Crescent, opp. Tulip Press, Wuse 11, Abuja; tel. 8035897127; internet fb.com/AllProgressivesGrandAlliance; regd June 2002; Chair. Dr VICTOR IKECHUKWU OYE; Nat. Sec. LABARAN MAKU.

Alliance for Democracy (AD): 4 Aba Close, Area 8, Garki, Abuja; tel. 8164495673; Nat. Chair. Chief JOSEPH AVAZI; Nat. Sec. FASOGBON P. AKINBOYE.

Allied Congress Party of Nigeria (ACPN): Suite D402, Global Plaza, 366 Obafemi Awolowo Way, Jabi Upstairs, Abuja; tel. 8038313424; internet fb.com/ACPNHOPE; Nat. Chair. Alhaji GANIYU O. GALADIMA; Nat. Secretary PAUL ISAMADE.

Democratic People's Party (DPP): 11 Nouakchott St, Zone 1, Wuse, Abuja; tel. 8033381764; Chair. GARSHON BENSON; Nat. Sec. AMINU SADIQ (acting).

Fresh Democratic Party: 4 Park Close, Aguyi Ironsi St, Maitma, Abuja; tel. 8033651678; Chair. Rev. CHRIS OKOTIE; Nat. Sec. FELA BINUTU.

KOWA Party (PSP): House No. 22, 23rd Ave, Phase 1, Federal Housing Authority, Abuja; tel. 8033354443; Nat. Chair. SAIDU BOBBOI; Nat. Sec. MARK ADEBAYO.

Labour Party: 29 Oke Agbe St, off Ladoke Akintola Blvd, Garki II, Abuja; tel. 8033005810; Nat. Chair. MARIA LEBEKE (acting); Nat. Sec. JULIUS ABURE.

National Conscience Party (NCP): 1 Younde St, Wuse Zone 6, Abuja; tel. 8033144131; Chair. Dr YUNUSA TANKO; Nat. Sec. (vacant).

People for Democratic Change (PDC): 2 Bitou St, off Parakou St, Wuse 2, Abuja; tel. 8023645376; Nat. Chair. IGWE EMEKA BENJAMIN; Nat. Sec. AMOS ELEGBE.

Peoples Democratic Party (PDP): Plot No. 1970, Wadata Plaza, Michael Okpara Way, Wuse, Abuja; tel. (9) 5232589; e-mail info@peoplesdemocraticparty.com.ng; internet www.peoplesdemocraticparty.com.ng; f. 1998; Chair. Dr IYORCHA AYU; Nat. Sec. UMARU IBRAHIM TSAURI.

People's Party of Nigeria (PPN): House 43, 6th Ave, Gwarimpa Estate, Abuja; tel. 7037674661; Chair. RAZAK EYIOWUAWI; Nat. Sec. Alhaji GARBA IBRAHIM YAKASAI.

Progressive People's Alliance (PPA): Warri St, off Emeka Anyoku St, Area 11, Garki, Abuja; tel. 8023137834; Nat. Chair. PETER OJONUGWA AMEH; Nat. Sec. KEHINDE EDUN.

Social Democratic Party: Plot 2105, Herbert Macaulay Way, opp. Sky Memorial Plaza, Block B3, Wuse Zone 6, Abuja; tel. 8036203435; Nat. Chair. TUNDE ADENIRON; Nat. Sec. Alhaji SHEHU MUSA GABAM.

Diplomatic Representation

EMBASSIES AND HIGH COMMISSIONS IN NIGERIA

Algeria: Plot No. 1398, Honourable Justice Mamman Nasir St, Cadastral Zone A4, Asokoro, POB 19739, Garki, Abuja; tel. (9) 4132840; e-mail ambalgabuja@yahoo.com; Ambassador HOCINE LATLI.

Angola: 321 Diplomatic Dr., 25 Pope John Paul II St, Maitama District, Abuja; tel. (9) 4614731; e-mail angola.embassy@yahoo.com; Ambassador EUSTÁQUIO JANUÁRIO QUIBATO.

Argentina: 30 Nelson Mandela St, Asokoro District, Abuja; tel. 8093664820; e-mail enige@mrecic.gov.ar; internet enige.cancilleria.gob.ar; Ambassador MARÍA DEL CARMEN SQUEFF.

Australia: 38 N'Djamena Cres., Wuse II, Abuja; PMB 5152, Abuja; tel. (9) 4606960; e-mail ahc.abuja@dfat.gov.au; internet www.nigeria.embassy.gov.au; High Commissioner JOHN DONNELLY.

Austria: Plot 9, Usuma St, Maitama, Abuja; tel. (9) 2915465; e-mail abuja-ob@bmeia.gv.at; internet www.bmeia.gv.at/en/austrian-embassy-abuja; Ambassador THOMAS SCHLESINGER.

Bangladesh: Plot 2609, Hassan Musa Kastina St, Asokoro, Abuja; tel. 9073859213; e-mail mission.abuja@mofa.gov.bd; internet abuja.mofa.gov.bd; High Commissioner MASUDUR RAHMAN.

Belarus: 1866 Deng Xioping St, Plot No. 2148, Asokoro, Abuja; tel. (9) 6233210; e-mail nigeria@mfa.gov.by; internet nigeria.mfa.gov.by; Ambassador VYACHESLAV BRIL.

Belgium: 9 Usuma St, Maitama, Abuja; tel. 8033016822; e-mail abuja@diplobel.fed.be; internet diplomatie.belgium.be/nigeria; Ambassador DANIEL BERTRAND.

Benin: Plot 328, Constitution Ave (Embassy Zone), Central Business District, POB 50457, Abuja; tel. 9061983632; e-mail ambassade.abuja@gouv.bj; Ambassador MARCELLINE PAULETTE ADJOVI.

Botswana: 1241 Oguta Lake St, Maitama Ext., Abuja; tel. (9) 7822818; e-mail botnig@yahoo.com; High Commissioner PULE BATIMANKI MPHOTHWE.

Brazil: 324 Diplomatic Dr., Central Business District, Garki, Abuja; tel. 8036590806; e-mail brasemb.abuja@itamaraty.gov.br; internet www.gov.br/mre/pt-br/embaixada-abuja; Ambassador RICARDO GUERRA DE ARAÚJO.

Bulgaria: 10 Euphrates St, off Aminu Kano Cres., Maitama, Abuja; tel. 8033078578; e-mail embassy.abuja@mfa.bg; internet www.mfa.bg/embassies/nigeria; Ambassador YANKO V. YORDANOV.

Burkina Faso: Plot 341, Diplomatic Dr., Garki, PMB 5104, Abuja; tel. 8129166772; e-mail ambassade@ambaburkina-ng.org; internet ambaburkina-ng.org; Ambassador (vacant).

Burundi: 59 T. Y. Danjuma St, Asokoro, Abuja; tel. 8085286039; e-mail ambabuja1@yahoo.com; Ambassador MARIE JEANNE NTAKIRUTIMANA.

Cabo Verde: Abuja; Ambassador BELARMINO MONTEIRO SILVA.

Cameroon: 469 Lobito Cres., Wuse II, Abuja; tel. (9) 2914485; e-mail haucocamabuja@yahoo.fr; internet www.cameroonhighcomabuja.com; High Commissioner ABBAS IBRAHIMA SALAHEDDINE.

Canada: 13010G, Palm Close, Diplomatic Dr., Central Business District, POB 5144, Abuja; tel. (9) 4612900; e-mail abuja@international.gc.ca; internet www.canadainternational.gc.ca/nigeria; High Commissioner JAMES CHRISTOFF.

Chad: 35 Mississippi St, Maitama District, PMB 488, Abuja; tel. 7040448557; e-mail ambatchad.nigeria@gmail.com; Ambassador ABAKAR SALEH CHAHAIMI.

China, People's Republic: Plot 302–303, Central Area, Abuja; tel. (9) 4618661; e-mail chinaemb_ng@mfa.gov.cn; internet ng.china-embassy.gov.cn; Ambassador CUI JIANCHUN.

Congo, Democratic Republic: 5 Malabo St, off Aminu Kano Cres., Wuse 2, Abuja; tel. 8110170630; e-mail congokinshasamission@yahoo.com; Ambassador PASCALINE GERENGBO YAKIVU.

Congo, Republic: 32 Lobito Cres., PMB 540, Garki, Abuja; tel. 8028192567; e-mail diplobrazzabuja@gmail.com; Ambassador JACQUES OBINDZA.

Côte d'Ivoire: 301 Diplomatic Dr., Central Area, Abuja; tel. (9) 2912123; e-mail ambaci.abuja@yahoo.fr; internet nigeria.diplomatie.gouv.ci; Ambassador TRAORÉ KALILOU.

Cuba: Plot 339, Diplomatic Zone, Area 10, Garki, Abuja; tel. (9) 4614821; e-mail embajada@ng.embacuba.cu; internet misiones.minrex.gob.cu/es/nigeria; Ambassador CLARA MARGARITA PULIDO ESCANDELL.

Czech Republic: 5 Gnassingbé Eyadéma St, Asokoro District, POB 4628, Abuja; tel. 7037571096; internet www.mzv.cz/abuja; Ambassador ZDENĚK KREJČÍ.

Denmark: 157 Adetokunbu Ademola Cres., Wuse II, Abuja; tel. (9) 9036635; e-mail abvamb@um.dk; internet nigeria.um.dk; Ambassador SUNE KROGSTRUP.

Ecuador: 10 Marakesh St, off Kumasi Cres., off Aminu Kano Cres., Wuse II, Abuja; tel. 9054545425; e-mail embecunigeria@gmail.com; internet nigeria.embajada.gob.ec; Ambassador LEOPOLDO ROVAYO VERDESOTO.

Egypt: 8 Buzi Close, off Amazon St, Maitama, Abuja; PMB 5069, Wuse, Abuja; tel. (9) 4136091; internet www.mfa.gov.eg/abuja_emb; Ambassador ASSEM HANAFI ELSEIFY.

Equatorial Guinea: F61003, Adekunle Fajuyi St, Abuja; tel. 7034977106; e-mail embaregeabuja@hotmail.com; internet www.egembassyabuja.org; Ambassador FRANCISCO EDÚ NGUA MANGUÉ.

Eritrea: Plot 1510, Yedseram St, off IBB Way, Maitama, Abuja; tel. 8139856889; e-mail eriemba_nigeria@yahoo.com; Ambassador MOHAMMED ALI OMARO.

Ethiopia: 322 Cadastral Zone, AO Mission Rd, Central Area, Garki, POB 2488, Abuja; tel. (9) 4618648; e-mail etemba2@yahoo.com;

internet fb.com/ethiopianembassyabuja; Ambassador AZANAW TADESSE.

Finland: 9 Iro Dan Musa St, Asokoro, Abuja; tel. 8037851150; e-mail sanomat.aba@formin.fi; internet www.finlandnigeria.org; Ambassador LEENA PYLVÄNÄINEN.

France: 37 Udi Hills St, off Aso Dr., Abuja; tel. 8059499786; e-mail cad.abuja-amba@diplomatie.gouv.fr; internet ng.ambafrance.org; Ambassador EMMANUELLE BLATMANN.

Gabon: 3680 Erie Cres., off Nile St, Abuja; tel. (9) 8734965; e-mail ambagabngr@yahoo.fr; High Commissioner CORENTIN BERNADIN MBOUROU HERVO-AKENDENGUE.

The Gambia: 7 Misratah St, off Parakou Cres., Wuse II, PMB 5058, Abuja; tel. 8057012927; e-mail info@thegambiahc.org.ng; internet www.thegambiahc.org.ng; Ambassador MOHAMADOU MUSA NJIE.

Germany: 9 Lake Maracaibo Close, off Amazon St, Maitama, POB 5177, Abuja; tel. (9) 2208010; e-mail info@abuja.diplo.de; internet nigeria.diplo.de; Ambassador BIRGITT ORY.

Ghana: Plot 301, Olusegun Obasanjo Way, Area 10, Garki, POB 2025, Abuja; tel. (9) 4615400; e-mail ghcom_abj@hotmail.com; internet ghanahighcommission-nigeria.com; High Commissioner Alhaji RASHID BAWA.

Greece: 24 Agadez St, Wuse II, POB 11525, Abuja; tel. 8099264095; e-mail gremb.abj@mfa.gr; internet www.mfa.gr/abuja; Ambassador LOANNIS PLOTAS.

Guinea: No. 349, Central Business District, opp. United Nations Premises, POB 591, Abuja; tel. (9) 2913607; e-mail ambaguineeab1@yahoo.fr; Ambassador SIAKA CISSOKO.

Guinea-Bissau: 2 Samura Michele St, Asokoro, Abuja; tel. 94618612; e-mail gbembassynigeria@gmail.com; Ambassador JOÃO RIBEIRO BUTIAM CÓ.

Holy See: Pope John Paul II Cres., Maitama, PMB 541, Garki, Abuja; tel. (9) 8725005; e-mail nuntiusabj@hotmail.com; Apostolic Nuncio ANTONIO GUIDO FILIPAZZI (Titular Archbishop of Sutrium).

Hungary: 11 River Niger St, Maitama, POB 5299, Abuja; tel. 8074949771; internet abuja.mfa.gov.hu; Ambassador Dr SÁNDOR GYÖRGY BEER.

India: Plot 364, Cadastral Zone, off Constitution Ave, Central Business District, Abuja; tel. 7080622800; e-mail info.abuja@mea.gov.in; internet www.hciabuja.gov.in/index.php; High Commissioner G. BALASUBRAMANIAN (designate).

Indonesia: 10 Katsina Ala Cres., Maitama District, Abuja; tel. 8166026466; e-mail kbri.abuja@gmail.com; internet www.kemlu.go.id/abuja; Ambassador Dr USRA HENDRA HARAHAP.

Iran: 1 Udi Hills St, off Aso Dr., Maitama, POB 701/2, Abuja; tel. 7037740223; e-mail iranabuja@yahoo.com; internet nigeria.mfa.gov.ir; Ambassador MOHAMMAD ALI BAK.

Iraq: Plot 338, Diplomatic Dr., Cadastral Zone A00, Central Area, Abuja; tel. 8026286023; internet www.mofa.gov.iq/abuja/ar; Chargé d'affaires a.i. NIHAD T. K. ALMAROOF.

Ireland: 11 Negro Cres., Maitama District, Abuja; tel. (9) 4621080; e-mail abujaembassy@dfa.ie; internet www.dfa.ie/irish-embassy/nigeria; Ambassador SÍLE MAGUIRE.

Israel: Plot 12, Mary Slessor St, Asokoro, POB 10924, Abuja; tel. (9) 4605500; e-mail info@abuja.mfa.gov.il; internet abuja.mfa.gov.il; Ambassador SHIMON BEN-SHOSHAN.

Italy: Europe House Complex, 21st Cres., off Constitution Ave, Central Business District, Abuja; tel. (9) 4602970; e-mail ambasciata.abuja@esteri.it; internet ambabuja.esteri.it/ambasciata_abuja/it; Ambassador (vacant).

Jamaica: Plot 247, Muhammadu Buhari Way, Central Area District, Abuja; tel. (9) 2345107; e-mail jamaicanembassy@yahoo.com; internet jis.gov.jm/government/agencies/jamaican-high-commission-abuja-nigeria; High Commissioner ESMOND ST CLAIR REID.

Japan: 9 Bobo St, off Gana St, Maitama, PMB 5070, Abuja; tel. (9) 4612713; internet www.ng.emb-japan.go.jp; Ambassador MATSUNAGA KAZUYOSHI.

Kenya: Plot 357, Diplomatic Dr., Central Business District, PMB 5160, Wuse Head Office, Abuja; tel. 9095446757; e-mail abuja@mfa.go.ke; internet kenyahighcom.org.ng; High Commissioner Maj.-Gen. (retd) ANDREW IKENYE (designate).

Korea, Democratic People's Republic: Plot 350, Central Area, Cadastral Zone AO, POB 407, Garki, Abuja; tel. (9) 2347200; e-mail dprk_abuja@yahoo.com; Ambassador JON YONG CHOL.

Korea, Republic: 9 Ovia Cres., off Pope John Paul II St, Maitama, POB 6870, Abuja; tel. 8103890991; e-mail emb-ng@mofa.go.kr; internet overseas.mofa.go.kr/ng-en/index.do; Ambassador KIM YOUNG-CHAE.

Kuwait: 3501 Ganges St, off Alvan Ikoku Way, Maitama District, Abuja; tel. (9) 4135247; Ambassador ABDULAZIZ AL-BISHER.

Lebanon: Plot 4 Cape Town St, Zone 4, Wuse, Abuja; tel. 8055001500; e-mail abuja.leb@gmail.com; internet www.abuja.mfa.gov.lb; Ambassador HOUSSAM DIAB.

Liberia: Plot 352 Cadastral Zone A0, Independence Ave, near United Nations House, Central Business District, Abuja; tel. 8168704549; e-mail liberiaembassyabuja@ymail.com; internet liberiaembassyabuja.org; Ambassador Prof. AL-HASSAN CONTEH.

Libya: Roseline Ukeje Close, Kyari Muhammed Cres., off Justice Sowemimo St, Asokoro, POB 435, Garki, Abuja; tel. 8169462714; e-mail info@libyaembassynigeria.com; Ambassador AYAD MESBAH AL-TAYARI.

Malaysia: 4A, Plot 2232B, Rio Negro Close, off Yedseram St, Maitama, Abuja; tel. (9) 2908488; e-mail mwabuja@kln.gov.my; internet www.kln.gov.my/web/nga_abuja/home; High Commissioner GLORIA CORINA ANAK PETER TIWET.

Mali: 3257 Ibrahim Babaguida Way, Maitama, Wuse, PMB 5082, Abuja; tel. 8031722702; e-mail ambassademaliabuja@yahoo.fr; internet ambamali-ng.ml; Ambassador MOUSTAPHA TRAORE.

Mauritania: 7 Danube Close, off Danube St, Maitama-Abuja; tel. 8073412886; e-mail ambarimnigeria@yahoo.com; Ambassador AMEDI CAMARA.

Mexico: 39 Usuma St, off Ghana St, Maitama District, PMB 718, Garki, Abuja; tel. 9070251902; internet embamex.sre.gob.mx/nigeria; Ambassador JUAN ALFREDO MIRANDA ORTIZ.

Morocco: 5 Mary Slessor St, off Udo Udoma Cres., Asokoro, Abuja; tel. (9) 8746697; e-mail mcherkaoui45@yahoo.fr; Ambassador MOHA OUALI TAGMA.

Namibia: Plot 16, T. Y. Danjuma St, Asokoro P.M.B 5097, Wuse, Abuja; tel. 9053862451; e-mail abuja@mirco.gov.na; internet www.namibiahc.com.ng; High Commissioner HUMPHREY DESMOND GEISEB.

Netherlands: EU Common Embassy Complex, European Union Cres., off Constitution Ave, Central Business District, Abuja; tel. (9) 4611200; e-mail abj@minbuza.nl; internet www.netherlandsworldwide.nl/countries/nigeria; Ambassador HARRY VAN DIJK.

Niger: 7 Sangha St, off Mississippi St, Maitama, Abuja; tel. (9) 5236275; e-mail ambniger@yahoo.fr; Ambassador MANDOUR MAMAN HADJ DADDA.

Norway: 54 T.Y. Danjuma St, Asokoro, Abuja; tel. (9) 8746989; e-mail emb.abuja@mfa.no; internet www.norway.no/nigeria; Ambassador KNUT EILIV LEIN.

Pakistan: Plot No. 358, Zone AO, Central Area, Abuja; tel. (9) 4610744; e-mail pahicabuja@mofa.gov.pk; internet www.pakistanhighcommissionabuja.com; High Commissioner MUHAMMAD TAYYAB AZAM.

Philippines: 453B, 14 St, off 2nd Ave, Gwarinpa, Abuja; tel. 8102541252; e-mail abuja.pe@dfa.gov.ph; internet abujape.dfa.gov.ph; Ambassador SHIRLEY HO-VICARIO.

Poland: 10 River Niger St., off Danube St. Maitama, Abuja; tel. 8076631021; internet www.gov.pl/web/nigeria; Ambassador JOANNA MAGDALENA TARNAWSKA.

Portugal: Plot 3655, Orinoco Cres., off River Kubani St, Maitama, Abuja; tel. 9037808670; e-mail abuja@mne.pt; Ambassador LUÍS FILIPE RIBEIRO DA SILVA BARROS.

Qatar: Transcorp Hilton, 1 Aguiyi Ironsi, Maitama, Abuja; tel. 9094264010; e-mail qatarabj412@gmail.com; Ambassador ALI BIN GHANIM AL-HAJRI.

Romania: Nelson Mandela St, No. 76, Plot 498, Asokoro, Abuja; tel. 9038411860; e-mail abuja@mae.ro; internet abuja.mae.ro; Ambassador FLORIN TALAPAN.

Russian Federation: Plot 1119, Constitution Ave, Central Business District, Abuja; tel. 8059080007; e-mail nigeria@mid.ru; internet nigeria.mid.ru; Ambassador ALEXEI L. SHEBARSHIN.

Rwanda: 1 Justice Mohammed Bello St, off Jose Marti Cres., Asokoro, Abuja; tel. 9077561181; e-mail ambaabuja@minaffet.gov.rw; internet www.rwandainnigeria.gov.rw; High Commissioner STANISLAS KAMANZI.

São Tomé and Príncipe: 10 Queen Elizabeth St, Asokoro, Abuja; tel. 97807820; e-mail drstpembassynigeria@gmail.com.

Saudi Arabia: 6 Orange Close, off Thames St, off Alvan lkoku Way, Ministers' Hill, Abuja; tel. (9) 8221442; e-mail ngemb@mofa.gov.sa; internet embassies.mofa.gov.sa/sites/nigeria; Ambassador FAISAL BIN IBRAHIM AL-GHAMDI.

Senegal: 12 Jose Marti St, off General Yakuba Gowon, Asokoro, Abuja; tel. (9) 2914519; e-mail ambassadesenegalabuja@yahoo.com; Ambassador NICOLAS AUGUSTE NIOUKY (designate).

Serbia: 11, Rio Negro Close, off Yedseram St, Cadastral Zone A6, Maitama District, Abuja; tel. 8059738141; e-mail serbconsabuja@gmail.com; internet www.abuja.mfa.gov.rs; Ambassador DJURA LIKAR.

Sierra Leone: Plot 308 Mission Rd, opp. Ministry of Defence (Ship House), Diplomatic Zone, Central Business District, Abuja; tel. (9) 8725413; e-mail info@slhcnigeria.org; internet www.slhcnigeria.org; High Commissioner RUPERT SYDNEY DOWU DAVIES.

Slovakia: European Union Delegation Complex, 21st Crescent, off Constitution Ave, Central Business District, Abuja; tel. 9092243995; e-mail emb.abuja@mzv.sk; internet www.mzv.sk/web/abuja; Ambassador TOMÁŠ FELIX.

South Africa: Plot No. 371, Diplomatic Zone, Central Business District, Abuja; tel. (9) 4624200; e-mail abuja.dha@dirco.gov.za; internet www.dirco.gov.za/abuja; High Commissioner THAMI MSELEKU.

South Sudan: 16 Lake Chad Cres., off IBB Way, Maitama, Abuja; tel. 8148465873; e-mail mails@embrssng.org; internet embrssng .org/web1; Ambassador DAVID BUOM CHOAT.

Spain: 8 Bobo Close, off Ghana St, Maitama, PMB 5120, Wuse, Abuja; tel. (9) 4603490; e-mail emb.abuja@maec.es; internet www .maec.es/embajadas/abuja; Ambassador (vacant).

Sri Lanka: Plot No. 1346, Cadastral Zone A05, Maitama, Abuja; tel. (9) 2916442; e-mail slemb.abuja@mfa.gov.lk; internet www.mfa.gov .lk/missions/sri-lanka-missions-overseas/africa/nigeria/; High Commissioner JANAKA BANDARA.

Sudan: Plot 337, Zone A0, Diplomatic Dr., Central Business District, Abuja; tel. (9) 6700668; e-mail sudaniabj124@hotmail.com; Ambassador (vacant).

Sweden: 41 T. Y. Danjuma St, Asokoro District, PMB 569 Garki, Abuja; tel. (9) 9047302; e-mail ambassaden.abuja@gov.se; internet www.swedenabroad.com/abuja; Ambassador CARL MICHAEL GRÄNS.

Switzerland: 157 Adetokunbo Ademola Cres., Wuse II, Abuja; tel. (9) 2200400; e-mail abu.vertretung@eda.admin.ch; internet www .eda.admin.ch/abuja; Ambassador GEORG STEINER.

Syrian Arab Republic: 318 Amazon St, Ministers Hill, Maitama, POB 393, Garki, Abuja; tel. (9) 2901323; e-mail syrembassy.abuja@ hotmail.com; Ambassador Dr SHAFIK DAIYOB.

Tanzania: 21B Yedseram St, Maitama, PMB 5125, Wuse, Abuja; tel. (9) 2910825; e-mail abuja@nje.go.tz; internet www.ng.tzembassy.go .tz; High Commissioner Dr BENSON ALFRED BANA.

Thailand: 34 Rhine St, Maitama, Abuja; tel. 7063080501; e-mail thaiembassy.abj@mfa.go.th; internet www.thaiembassynigeria .com; Chargé d'affaires a.i. KRIWAT PHAMORABUTRA.

Togo: 96 Kwame N'krumah Cres., Thomas Sankara St, Asokoro, Abuja; tel. 7031581407; e-mail ambatogoabuja@yahoo.com; internet ambatogoabuja.com; High Commissioner LÉNÉ DIMBAN.

Trinidad and Tobago: 7 Casablanca St, off Nairobi St, off Amino Kano Cres., Wuse II, Abuja; tel. (9) 6411118; e-mail trinitobagoabj@ yahoo.co.uk; High Commissioner WENDELL DE LANDRO.

Tunisia: 11 Kainji Cres., off Lake Cres., Maitama, Abuja; tel. 8172490723; e-mail at.abuja@diplomatie.gov.tn; Ambassador (vacant).

Türkiye (Turkey): Plot No. 333, Diplomatic Dr., Central Business District, Abuja; tel. 8036488981; internet abuja.emb.mfa.gov.tr/ Mission; Ambassador HIDAYET BAYRAKTAR.

Uganda: Plot No. 3, Mandara Cl., off Mambila St, Aso Dr., PMB 223, Abuja; tel. 8132666559; e-mail highcomabuja@yahoo.co.uk; internet abuja.mofa.go.ug; High Commissioner NELSON OCHEGER.

Ukraine: Plot 894, Olu Awotesu St, Jabi District, Abuja; tel. 8091155338; e-mail emb_ng@mfa.gov.ua; internet nigeria.mfa.gov .ua; Ambassador VALERII KIRDODA.

United Arab Emirates: 17 Kainji St, off Lake chad Cres., off IBB way, Miatama, Abuja; tel. 8099009003; e-mail abujaemb@mofaic.gov .ae; Ambassador FAHD OBAID MUHAMMAD AL-TAFAQ.

United Kingdom: Plot No. 1137, Diplomatic Dr., Central Business District, Abuja; tel. (9) 4623100; e-mail PPAInformation.abuja@fcdo .gov.uk; internet www.gov.uk/world/organisations/british-high -commission-abuja; High Commissioner CATRIONA LAING.

USA: Plot 1075, Diplomatic Dr., Central District Area, Abuja; tel. (9) 4614000; e-mail consularabuja@state.gov; internet ng.usembassy .gov; Ambassador MARY BETH LEONARD.

Venezuela: 1 Taraba Close, off Limpopo St, Maitama, Abuja; tel. 8093004444; e-mail evenigeria@yahoo.com; Ambassador DAVID NIEVES VALASQUEZ-CARABALLO.

Viet Nam: 1 Kyari Mohammed Cres., off Sowemimo St, Asokoro, Abuja; tel. (9) 079173669; e-mail dsqvnnigeria@yahoo.com; internet vnembassy-abuja.mofa.gov.vn; Ambassador LUONG QUOC THINH.

Zambia: 351 Mission Rd, Central Area District, Garki, Abuja; tel. (9) 4618605; internet zambiahcabuja.org.ng; High Commissioner SOLO-MON JERE.

Zimbabwe: 60 Parakou Cres., PMB 5138, Wuse 2, Abuja; tel. 9062834589; e-mail zimabuja@yahoo.co.uk; Ambassador MAXWELL RANGA.

Judicial System

The Constitution provides for both federal and state courts, in addition to election tribunals. The Supreme Court is the highest court of Nigeria. There are also Magistrate, Area and Customary Courts with limited jurisdiction, which are established by the National Assembly in respect of the Federal Capital Territory, Abuja, and the State House of Assembly in respect of a state.

Supreme Court: Three Arms Complex, Central District, PMB 308, Abuja; tel. 8152576253; internet supremecourt.gov.ng; consists of a Chief Justice and up to 15 Justices, appointed by the President, on the recommendation of the National Judicial Council (subject to the approval of the Senate); has original jurisdiction in any dispute between the Federation and a state, or between states, and hears appeals from the Federal Court of Appeal; Chief Justice OLUKAYODE ARIWOOLA.

Court of Appeal: First Ave, off Shehu Shagari Way, Central District, Abuja; tel. (9) 4138995; internet www.courtofappeal.gov .ng; consists of a President and at least 35 Justices, of whom 3 must be experts in Islamic (*Shari'a*) law and 3 experts in Customary law; has 12 divisions in various states; Pres. MONICA BOLNA'AN DONGBAN-MENSEM.

Federal High Court: 24 Shehu Shagari Way, Central District, Abuja; tel. (1) 2691439; e-mail info@fhc.gov.ng; internet www.fhc-ng .com; Chief Judge J. T. TSOHO.

Each state has a **High Court**, consisting of a Chief Judge and a number of judges, appointed by the Governor of the state on the recommendation of the National Judicial Council (subject to the approval of the House of Assembly of the state). If required, a state may have a **Shari'a Court of Appeal** (dealing with Islamic civil law) and a **Customary Court of Appeal. Special Military Tribunals** have been established to try offenders accused of crimes such as corruption, drug trafficking and armed robbery; appeals against rulings of the Special Military Tribunals are referred to a **Special Appeals Tribunal**, which comprises retired judges.

Religion

ISLAM

According to the 2013 Nigeria Demographic and Health Survey, Muslims comprised 51.5% of the total population.

Nigerian Supreme Council for Islamic Affairs (NSCIA): National Mosque Office Complex, Central Business District, Abuja; tel. 8139310727; e-mail info@nscia.com.ng; internet www.nscia.com .ng; aims to preserve, protect, promote and advance the interests of Islam and Muslims throughout Nigeria; Pres.-Gen. Alhaji MUHAM-MADU SA'AD ABUBAKAR (Sultan of Sokoto); Sec.-Gen. Prof. IS-HAQ OLANREWAJU OLOYEDE.

Spiritual Head: Alhaji MUHAMMADU SA'AD ABUBAKAR (Sultan of Sokoto).

CHRISTIANITY

According to the 2013 Nigeria Demographic and Health Survey, 47.0% of the population were Christians.

Christian Association of Nigeria (CAN): CAN Headquarters, National Christian Centre, Central Area, PMB 260, Garki, Abuja; tel. 8060816172; e-mail info@canng.org; internet canng.org; f. 1976; Pres. Rev. Dr SAMSON OLASUPO A. AYOKUNLE; Gen. Sec. JOSEPH BADE DARAMOLA.

Christian Council of Nigeria: 139 Ogunlana Dr., Surulere, POB 2838, Lagos; tel. 8034393548; f. 1929; 15 full mems and six assoc. mems; Pres. Most Rev. EMMANUEL UDOFIA; Gen. Sec. Rev. Dr IBRAHIM YUSUF WUSHISHI.

The Anglican Communion

Anglicans are adherents of the Church of Nigeria, which is divided into 14 provinces and comprises 159 dioceses.

Metropolitan, Primate of All Nigeria, Bishop of Abuja: Most Rev. HENRY NDUKUBA, 24 Douala St, Wuse Zone 5, POB 212, Abuja; tel. (9) 5236950; e-mail communicator1@anglican-nig.org; internet www.anglican-nig.org.

Archbishop of the Province of Aba and Bishop of Isiala-Ngwa South: Most Rev. Dr ISAAC NWAOBIA, St Stephen's Cathedral Church Compound, POB 96, Umuahia.

Archbishop of the Province of Bendel and Bishop of Ughelli: Most Rev. CYRIL O. ODUTEMU, Bishopscourt, POB 760, Ughelli, Delta; tel. 8035307114; e-mail ughellidiocese@anglican-nig.org.

Archbishop of the Province of Enugu and Bishop of Enugu: Most Rev. Dr EMMANUEL O. CHUKWUMA, 40 Nawfia St, POB 418, Enugu; tel. 8063443333; e-mail enugudodiocese@anglican-nig.org.

Archbishop of the Province of Ibadan and Bishop of Ibadan North: Most Rev. Dr SEGUN OKUBADEJO, POB 28961, Agodi; e-mail ibadannorthdiocese@anglican-nig.org.

Archbishop of the Province of Jos and Bishop of Yola: Most Rev. MARKUS IBRAHIM, 10 Hong Rd, Karewa GRA, POB 601, Jimeta-Yola, Adamawa; tel. 8030457576; e-mail yoladiocese@anglican-nig.org.

Archbishop of the Province of Kaduna and Bishop of Wusasa: Most Rev. ALI BUBA LAMIDO, POB 28, Wusasa, Zaria, Kaduna; tel. 8037272504; e-mail wusasadiocese@anglican-nig.org.

Archbishop of the Province of Kwara and Bishop of New Bussa: Most Rev. ISRAEL AFOLABI AMOO, Bishopscourt, Mokwa Rd, opp. NIFFR, POB 208, New Bussa, Niger; tel. 8036773839; e-mail newbusadiocese@anglican-nig.org.

Archbishop of the Province of Lagos and Bishop of Remo: Most Rev. MICHAEL OLUSINA FAPE, Bishopscourt, Ewusi St, POB 522, Sagama, Ogun; tel. 8037267949; e-mail remodiocese@anglican-nig.org.

Archbishop of the Province of Lokoja and Bishop of Minna: Most Rev. DANIEL ABU YISA, Bishopscourt, Zarumain Quarters, POB 2469, Minna, Niger; tel. 8030782525; e-mail minnadiocese@anglican-nig.org.

Archbishop of the Province of the Niger and Bishop of Awka: Most Rev. Dr ALEXANDER CHIBUZO IBEZIM, Bishopscourt, Emmaus House Complex, Arthur Eze Ave, POB 130, Awka, Anambra; tel. 8038652776; e-mail awkadiocese@anglican-nig.org.

Archbishop of the Niger Delta and Bishop of Calabar: Most Rev. TUNDE ADELEYE, Bishopscourt, 81 Calabar Rd, POB 74, Calabar; tel. 87232812; e-mail calabardiocese@anglican-nig.org.

Archbishop of the Province of Ondo and Bishop of Ekiti: Most Rev. CHRISTOHER TAYO OMOTUNDE, Bishopscourt, POB 12, Okesa St, Ado-Ekiti, Ekiti; tel. 8029191866; e-mail ekitidiocese@anglican-nig.org.

Archbishop of the Province of Owerri and Bishop of Ideato: Most Rev. CALEB MADUOMA, Bishopscourt, POB 2, Arondizuogu, Imo; tel. 8037454503; e-mail ideatodiocese@anglican-nii.org.

The Roman Catholic Church

Nigeria comprises nine archdioceses, 47 dioceses and one Eparchy for adherents of the Maronite rite.

Catholic Bishops' Conference of Nigeria (CBCN): Plot 459, Cadastral Zone B2, Southern Park, Durumi 1, Garki, POB 6523, Abuja; tel. (9) 5239413; e-mail csnabuja@cbcn.org; internet cbcn-ng.org; f. 1976; Pres. Most Rev. LUCIUS IWEJURU UGORJI (Archbishop of Owerri); Sec. Rt Rev. CAMILLUS RAYMOND UMOH (Bishop of Ikot Ekpene).

Archbishop of Abuja: Most Rev. IGNATIUS AYUA KAIGAMA, Archdiocesan Secretariat, 9 New Bussa Close, Area 3, Section 2, POB 286, Garki, Abuja; tel. 8034511635; e-mail info@abujacatholicarchdiocese.org; internet abujacatholicarchdiocese.org.

Archbishop of Benin City: Most Rev. AUGUSTINE OBIORA AKUBEZE, Archdiocesan Secretariat, 30 Airport Rd, POB 35, Benin City, Edo; tel. 8136443724; e-mail office@catholicarchdioceseofbenin.org; internet www.catholicarchdioceseofbenin.com.

Archbishop of Calabar: Most Rev. JOSEPH EFFIONG EKUWEM, Catholic Secretariat, 1 Bishop Moynagh Ave, PMB 1124, Calabar, Cross River; tel. 8063515177.

Archbishop of Ibadan: Most Rev. GABRIEL ‛LEKE ABEGUNRIN, Archbishop's House, 8 Bale Latosa Rd, Onireke, PMB 5057, Dugbe, Ibadan, Oyo; tel. 8099333340; e-mail ibcathad@yahoo.com; internet ibadanarchdiocese.org.

Archbishop of Jos: Most Rev. MATTHEW ISHAYA AUDU, Archdiocesan Secretariat, 20 Joseph Gomwalk Rd, POB 494, Jos, Plateau; tel. 8031152765; internet www.cadjos.org.

Archbishop of Kaduna: Most Rev. MATTHEW MAN-OSO NDAGOSO, Archbishop's House, 71 Tafawa Balewa Way, POB 248, Kaduna; tel. 8034657789; internet archkd.org.

Archbishop of Lagos: Most Rev. ALFRED ADEWALE MARTINS, Archdiocesan Secretariat, 19 Catholic Mission St, POB 8, Lagos; tel. 8033222081; e-mail info@lagosarchdiocese.org; internet lagosarchdiocese.org.

Archbishop of Onitsha: Most Rev. VALERIAN MADUKA OKEKE, Archdiocesan Secretariat, 1 Mission Rd, POB 411, Onitsha, Anambra; tel. 8021818008; e-mail secretariat@onitsha-archdiocese.org; internet www.onitsha-archdiocese.org.

Archbishop of Owerri: Most Rev. LUCIUS IWEJURU UGORJI, Villa Assumpta, POB 85, Owerri, Imo; tel. 8033389449; e-mail owcatsec@owerriarchdiocese.org.

Other Christian Churches

Church of the Brethren in Nigeria: c/o Kulp Bible School, POB 1, Mubi, Adamawa; f. 1923; Pres. Rev. JOEL STEPHEN BILLI; Gen. Sec. DANIEL Y. C. MBAYA.

Church of the Lord (Prayer Fellowship) Worldwide (Aladura): 10/12 Primate Oshitelu St, Ogere-Remo, POB 71, Shagamu, Ogun; tel. 8037263902; e-mail cla_primate@gmail.com; internet www.tclaw.org; f. 1925; Primate Most Rev. Dr RUFUS OKIKIOLA OSITELU; 3.8m. mems.

Lutheran Church of Christ in Nigeria (LCCN): Hospital Rd, Numan, POB 21, Adamawa; tel. 8039100978; e-mail nemuelbabba@hotmail.com; Pres. Archbishop PANTI FILIBUS MUSA; 2.2m. mems.

Lutheran Church of Nigeria (LCN): Obot Idim Ibesikpo, POB 49, Uyo, Akwa Ibom; tel. 8062556675; e-mail chrisekonglcn@yahoo.com; internet www.lutheranchurchnigeria.org; f. 1936; Pres. Most Rev. CHRISTIAN EKONG.

Methodist Church Nigeria: Wesley House, 21–22 Marina, POB 2011, Lagos; tel. 8058287979; internet methodistnigeria.org; Prelate SAMUEL CHUKWUEMEKA KANU UCHE.

Nigerian Baptist Convention: Baptist Bldg, PMB 5113, Ibadan; tel. 8159990096; e-mail ict@nigerianbaptist.org; internet nigerianbaptist.org; Rev. Dr MICHAEL ADEOYE ABODUNRIN; Pres. Dr SAMSON OLASUPO AYOKUNLE.

The Presbyterian Church of Nigeria: 26–29 Ehere Rd, Ogbor Hill, POB 2635, Aba, Imo; tel. 8144537676; e-mail emekalu54@yahoo.com; f. 1846; Prelate and Moderator Rev. NZIE NSI EKE; Principal Clerk Dr MIRACLE AJAH.

The Redeemed Church of Christ, the Church of the Foursquare Gospel, the Qua Iboe Church and the Salvation Army are prominent among numerous other Christian churches active in Nigeria.

AFRICAN RELIGIONS

The beliefs, rites and practices of the people of Nigeria are very diverse, varying between ethnic groups and between families in the same group.

The Press

NEWSPAPERS (PRINT AND ONLINE)

Al-Mizan: POB 686, Babban Dodo, Zariya, Kaduna; tel. 69335148; internet www.almizan.ng; Hausa; Editor IBRAHIM MUSA.

Aminiya: 20 POW Mafemi Cres., off Solomon Lar Way, Utako, Abuja; tel. 7001777577; e-mail info@dailytrust.com; internet aminiya.dailytrust.com; Hausa; Editor-in-Chief MANNIR DAN ALI.

Authority: 10 Oguda Close, off Lake Chad Cres., Maitama, Abuja; e-mail info@authoritynigr.com; internet authorityngr.com; f. 2015; Owner IFEANYI UBAH.

BusinessDay: 72 Festac Link Rd, Amuwo Odofin, Lagos; tel. 8034694482; internet businessday.ng; f. 2001; Editor PATRICK ATUANYA.

Daily Champion: Isolo Industrial Estate, Oshodi-Apapa, Lagos; tel. 8186166160; e-mail editor.championnews@gmail.com; internet www.championnews.com.ng; Man. Editor UGO ONUOHA.

Daily Independent: Independent Newspapers Ltd, Plot 8, Wempco Rd, Ogba, PMB 21777, Ikeja, Lagos; tel. (1) 4535267; e-mail info@independentnig.com; internet independent.ng; f. 2001; Editor DONATUS OKERE.

Daily Triumph: Triumph Publishing Co Ltd, Gidan Sa'adu Zungur, PMB 3155, Kano; tel. 8036133541; e-mail lawalsabot@gmail.com; internet triumphnews.org; Editor-in-Chief LAWAL SABO IBRAHIM.

Daily Trust: 20 POW Mafemi Cres., off Solomon Lar Way, Utako, Abuja; tel. (9) 6726241; e-mail dailytrust@yahoo.co.uk; internet www.dailytrust.com; f. 2001; Editor HAMZA IDRIS.

The Guardian: Guardian Newspapers Ltd, Rutam House, Isolo Expressway, Isolo, PMB 1217, Oshodi, Lagos; tel. (1) 4524111; internet guardian.ng; f. 1983; independent; Editor-in-Chief EMEKA IZEZE.

The Herald: Ilorin; tel. 9064873822; e-mail editor@herald.ng; internet www.herald.ng; f. 2012; online-only.

Leadership: 27 Ibrahim Tahir Lane, Utako, Abuja; tel. 7033592020; e-mail editor@leadership.ng; internet leadership.ng; Editor PEMBI DAVID-STEPHEN.

The Nation: Vintage Press Ltd, 27B Fatai Atere Way, Matori, Mushin, Lagos; tel. (1) 8168361; e-mail info@thenationonlineng.com; internet www.thenationonlineng.net; f. 2006; Editor ADENIYI ADESINA.

National Daily: 29B Emina Cres., off Toyin St, Ikeja, Lagos; e-mail publisher@nationaldailyng.com; internet nationaldailyng.com; f. 2006; Exec. Editor SYLVESTER EBHODAGHE.

New Nigerian: New Nigerian Newspapers Ltd, 4/5 Ahmadu Bello Way, POB 254, Kaduna; tel. 8028332521; e-mail news@ newnigeriannewspapers.com; internet www .newnigeriannewspaper.com; f. 1965; govt-owned; Editor-in-Chief NDANUSA ALAO.

Nigerian Compass: 10 Western Industrial Ave, Compass Media Village, Isheri, Ogun; tel. (1) 7400001; Editor GABRIEL AKINADEWO.

Nigerian Observer: Bendel Newspaper Co Ltd, 24 Airport Rd, PMB 1334, Benin City; tel. (52) 240050; e-mail observernigerian@yahoo .com; internet nigerianobservernews.com; f. 1968; Editor TONY IKEAKANAM.

Nigerian Tribune: African Newspapers of Nigeria Ltd, Imalefalafi St, Oke-Ado, POB 78, Ibadan; tel. (2) 2312844; e-mail editornigeriantribune@yahoo.com; internet tribuneonlineng.com; f. 1949; Editor EDWARD DICKSON.

Peoples Daily: 35 Ajose Adeogun St, Peace Park Plaza, 1st Floor, Utako, Abuja; tel. (9) 9702136; e-mail pmlnewsdesk@gmail.com; Editor AHMED SHEKARAU.

The Port Harcourt Telegraph: 33 Opobo Cres., GRA Phase I, Port Harcourt; tel. 8036002239; e-mail phctelegraph@gmail.com; internet phctelegraph.info; f. 1999; 3 a week; Editor-in-Chief OGBONNA NWUKE.

The Punch: 1 Olu Aboderin St, Onipetesi, PMB 21204, Ikeja, Lagos; tel. (1) 7748081; e-mail editor@punchontheweb.com; internet punchng.com; f. 1976; Editor-in-Chief DAYO OKETOLA.

The Sun: The Sun Publishing Ltd, 2 Coscharis St, Kirikiri Industrial Layout, Apapa, PMB 21776 Ikeja, Lagos; tel. (1) 5875560; e-mail sunonlineteam@gmail.com; internet www.sunnewsonline.com; f. 2003; Man. Dir ONUOHA UKEH; Editor IHEANACHO NWOSU.

This Day: 35 Creek Rd, Apapa, Lagos; tel. 8022924485; e-mail hello@thisdaylive.com; internet www.thisdaylive.com; f. 1995; Editor SHAKA MOMODU.

The Tide: Rivers State Newspaper Corpn, 1 Ikwerre Rd, POB 5072, Port Harcourt; tel. 8034780061; e-mail webmaster@ thetidenewsonline.com; internet www.thetidenewsonline.com; f. 1971; Editor (vacant).

Vanguard: 2 Vanguard Ave, Kirikiri Canal, PMB 1007, Apapa, Lagos; tel. 8023145566; e-mail citizenreport@vanguardngr.com; internet www.vanguardngr.com; f. 1984; Editor EZE ANABA.

SUNDAY NEWSPAPERS

New Nigerian on Sunday: 4/5 Ahmadu Bello Way, POB 254, Kaduna; tel. 8033118023; e-mail newnigeriannews@gmail.com; internet www.newnigeriannewspaper.com; f. 1981; weekly.

Sunday Compass: 10 Western Industrial Ave, Compass Media Village, Isheri, Ogun; tel. (1) 7400001; internet compassnews.net; Editor DOTUN OLADIPO.

Sunday Observer: Bendel Newspapers Co Ltd, 24 Airport Rd, PMB 1334, Benin City; e-mail observernigerian@yahoo.com; internet www.nigerianobservernews.com; f. 1968; Editor T. O. BORHA.

Sunday Sun: The Sun Publishing Ltd, 2 Coscharis St, Kirikiri Industrial Layout, Apapa, PMB 21776 Ikeja, Lagos; tel. (1) 5875560; e-mail sunonlineteam@gmail.com; internet www.sunnewsonline .com; Editor ABDULFATAH OLADEINDE.

Sunday Tribune: Tribune House, Imalefalafia St, Oke-Ado, POB 78, Dugbe, Ibadan; tel. 8116954632; e-mail onlineeditor55@gmail .com; internet tribuneonlineng.com; Editor SINA OLADEINDE.

WEEKLIES

Business Hallmark: 109B Adeniyi Jones Ave, Ikeja, Lagos; tel. (1) 8034026226; internet hallmarknews.com; Editor-in-Chief OKEY ONYENWEAKU.

Desert Herald: 24 Manona Rd, U/Sarki, Kaduna; tel. 8099138343; e-mail heraldnews@yahoo.com; internet desertherald.com; Publr TUKUR MAMU.

The News: 27 Acme Rd, Agidingbi, PMB 21531, Ikeja, Lagos; tel. (1) 7939286; e-mail info@thenewsng.com; internet thenewsng.com; independent; Editor-in-Chief JENKINS ALUMONA.

Newswatch: 3 Billingsway Rd, Oregun, Ikeja, Lagos; tel. (1) 7619660; internet www.newswatchngr.com; f. 1985; English; CEO RAY EKPU; Editor-in-Chief DAN AGBESE.

Nigerian Newsworld: A1 AMAC Plaza, Zone 3, Wuse, Abuja; tel. (9) 7816987; internet nigeriannewsworld.com; f. 2010; Editor-in-Chief DENNIS O. SAMI.

Technology Times: 26 Omodara St, off Ajanaku St, Awuse Estate, Ikeja, Lagos; tel. 8074016074; e-mail info@technologytimes.ng; internet technologytimes.ng; f. 2004.

Tell Magazine: Kilometre 22, Lagos Ibadan Expressway, Lagos; tel. 8033079498; internet tell.ng; f. 1991; Editor AYO AKINKUOTU.

ENGLISH-LANGUAGE PERIODICALS

The Catholic Ambassador: PMB 2011, Iperu-Remo, Ogun; tel. 8025048894; e-mail ambassadorpub1980@gmail.com; internet www .mspfathers.org; f. 1980; 2 a year; Roman Catholic; Editor Fr MARTIN YINA.

Economic Confidential: Abuja; e-mail editor@ economicconfidential.com; internet economicconfidential.com; f. 2007; monthly; Editor SANYA ADEJOKUN.

Financial Standard: 2 IPM Ave, CBD, Alausa-Ikeja, Lagos; tel. (1) 4934894; e-mail info@financialstandardnews.com; internet www .financialstandardnews.com; f. 1999; Mon.–Fri.; Editor-in-Chief SUNDAY SAMUEL ADEBOLA ONANUGA.

The Leader: 19A Assumpta Press Ave, Industrial Layout, PMB 1017, Owerri, Imo; tel. 8064918509; e-mail leaderpress@yahoo.com; internet theleader.ng; f. 1956; weekly; Roman Catholic; Editor-in-Chief Rev. RAYMOND NZEREOGU.

Nigerian Journal of Science: Science Asscn of Nigeria, c/o Dept of Computer Science, University of Ibadan, POB 4039, Ibadan, Oyo; tel. 8023382550; e-mail editor@sciencenigeria.org; internet journal .thescienceassociationofnigeria.org; publ. of the Science Asscn of Nigeria; f. 1966; 2 a year; Editor Prof. I. FAWOLE.

Nigerian Medical Journal: Department of Internal Medicine, University of Port Harcourt Teaching Hospital, PMB 6173, Port Harcourt; tel. 8033129421; e-mail nigerianmedjournal@gmail.com; internet nigerianmedjournal.org; f. 1959; publ. by the Nigerian Medical Association; bimonthly; Editor-in-Chief Dr DATONYE ALASIA.

Time Nigeria: A. A. Rano Filling Station Office Complex, 1st Floor, nr AYA Bridge, Asokoro, Abuja; tel. 8077726552; e-mail editor@ timenigeria.com; internet timenigeria.com.

VERNACULAR PERIODICALS

Gaskiya ta fi Kwabo: New Nigerian Newspapers Ltd, 4/5 Ahmadu Bello Way, POB 254, Kaduna; tel. (62) 245220; internet gaskiyatafikwabo.com; f. 1939; 3 a week; Hausa; Editor ALHAJI NASIRU GARBA TOFA (acting).

NEWS AGENCIES

News Agency of Nigeria (NAN): Independence Avenue, Central Business District, PMB 7006, Garki, Abuja; tel. (9) 6732189; e-mail nanhq@nanngr.com; internet www.nannews.ng; f. 1976; state-owned; Man. Dir BUKI PONLE.

Publishers

Africana First Publishers Ltd: Book House Trust, 1 Africana-First Dr., PMB 1639, Onitsha; tel. 8034770740; internet www .afpublishers-plc.com; f. 1973; study guides, general science, textbooks; Chair. JOHN C. ODIKE; Man. Dir AUSTIN CHIDUWEM ONWUBIKO.

Ahmadu Bello University Press: Ahmed Talib Bldg, Ring Rd, Ahmadu Bello University, Main Campus, PMB 1094, Zaria; tel. 8034405123; e-mail abupresslimited2005@yahoo.co.uk; internet abupress.org; f. 1972; history, Africana, social sciences, education, literature and arts; Chair. Prof. KABIR BALA; Man. Dir AHMAD IBRAHIM JAE.

Cassava Republic: 62B Arts and Crafts Village, opp Sheraton, Abuja; e-mail info@cassavarepublic.biz; internet www .cassavarepublic.biz; f. 2006; Publishers BIBI BAKARE-YUSUF, JEREMY WEATE.

Evans Brothers (Nigeria Publishers) Ltd: Jericho Rd, PMB 5164, Ibadan; tel. (2) 2918714; e-mail evans@evanspublishers.com; internet www.evanspublishers.com; f. 1966; general and educational; Man. Dir and CEO LUKMAN DAUDA.

HEBN Publishers PLC: 1 Ighodaro Rd, Jericho, PMB 5205, Ibadan; tel. (2) 2412268; e-mail info@hebnpublishers.com; internet www.hebnpublishers.com; f. 1962; educational, law, medical and general; Chair. AYO OJENIYI; Man. Dir OLAWEPO AFUERI SOGO.

Kachifo Ltd: 253 Herbert Macaulay Way, Yaba, Lagos; tel. 8077364217; e-mail info@kachifo.com; internet kachifo.com; f. 2004; publr of Farafina Books, Farafina Tuuti, Farafina Breeze, Kamsi and Prestige Books; Founder MUHTAR BAKARE.

Literamed Publications Ltd (Lantern Books): Plot 1, Morrison Cres., off Kudirat Abiola Way, Ikeja, PMB 21068, Lagos; tel. 8063367604; e-mail information@lantern-books.com; internet www .lantern-books.com; f. 1969; children's, medical and scientific; Chair. O. M. LAWAL-SOLARIN.

Spectrum Books Ltd: Spectrum House, Ring Rd, PMB 5612, Ibadan; tel. 8064477954; e-mail info@spectrumbookslimited.com; internet www.spectrumbookslimited.com; f. 1978; educational and fiction; Chair. DAYO OGUNNIYI; Man. Dir SINA OKEOWO.

University of Lagos Press and Bookshop: University of Lagos, Main Campus, Lagos; tel. (1) 4539983; e-mail info@unilagpress.com; internet www.unilagpress.com; university textbooks, monographs, lectures and journals; Chair. WAHAB BABATUNDE DABIRI.

University Press PLC: Three Crowns Bldg, Jericho, PMB 595, Ibadan; tel. 8008775264; internet universitypressplc.com; Chair. Dr LALEKAN ARE; Man. Dir SAMUEL KOLAWOLE.

West African Book Publishers Ltd: Ilupeju Industrial Estate, 28–32 Industrial Ave, Lagos; tel. (1) 7754518; e-mail info@wabp.com.ng; internet wabp.com.ng; f. 1963; textbooks, children's, periodicals and general; Chair. B. A. IDRIS-ANIMASHAUN; Man. Dir FOLASHADE B. OMO-EBOH.

PUBLISHERS' ASSOCIATION

Nigerian Publishers' Association: Premium House, 1st Floor, Jericho, POB 2541, Ibadan; tel. 8162489037; e-mail nigerianpublishers@ymail.com; internet nigerianpublishers.com; f. 1965; Pres. ADEDAPO GBADEGA.

Broadcasting and Communications

TELECOMMUNICATIONS

Airtel Nigeria: Plot L2, Banana Island, Foreshore Estate, Ikoyi, Lagos; tel. 8021500111; e-mail customercare.ng@airtel.com; internet www.airtel.com.ng; f. 2000; fmrly Celtel Nigeria, subsequently Zain Nigeria, present name adopted in 2010; Chair. Justice SALIHU ALFA BELGORE; Man. Dir C. SURENDRAN; 50.3m. subscribers (July 2021).

Bitflux Communications Ltd: Union Marble House 1, Alfred Rewane Rd, Falomo, Ikoyi, Lagos; tel. (1) 2714711; e-mail office@creatika.com; internet www.bitfluxng.com; f. 2014; internet service provider; Chair. ROTIMI OYEKANMI; Group CEO ABIODUN OMONIYI.

EMTS Ltd (Etisalat): Plot 19, Zone L, Banana Island, Ikoyi, Lagos; tel. 8090000200; e-mail care@9mobile.com.ng; internet 9mobile.com.ng; f. 2007; Chair. Alhaji NASIRU ADO BAYERO; CEO JUERGEN PESCHEL; 12.9m. subscribers (July 2021).

Galaxy Backbone: 61 Adetokunbo Ademola Cres., Wuse 2, Abuja; tel. 8073990518; e-mail servicedesk@galaxybackbone.com.ng; internet galaxybackbone.com.ng; f. 2006; state-owned; provides internet and technology services to public sector agencies and institutions; Man. Dir and CEO MUHAMMAD BELLO ABUBAKAR.

Globacom Nigeria Ltd: Mike Adenuga Towers, 1 Mike Adenuga Close., off Adeola Odeku, Victoria Island, Lagos; tel. 8050020121; e-mail customercare@gloworld.com; internet www.gloworld.com/ng; f. 2003; Chair. Dr MIKE ADENUGA, Jr; 51.1m. subscribers (July 2021).

Legend: 15 Bangui St, Wuse 2, Abuja; tel. 70069534363; e-mail experience@legend.ng; internet www.legend.ng; f. 2016; internet service provider.

MTN Nigeria Communications Ltd: Golden Plaza Bldg, Awolowo Rd, Falomo, Ikoyi, PMB 80147, Lagos; tel. 8032005638; e-mail customercareng@mtn.com; internet www.mtnonline.com; f. 2001; Chair. Dr ERNEST CHUKWUKA NDUKWE; CEO KARL TORIOLA; 73.1m. subscribers (July 2021).

ntel: NECOM House, 17th Floor, 15 Marina, Lagos; tel. 70068355483; e-mail care@ntel.com.ng; internet www.ntel.com.ng; trade name of NatCom Development and Investment Ltd; Man. Dir/CEO BABATUNDE OMOTOBA.

Smile Nigeria: 230 Awolowo Rd, Ikoyi, Victoria Island, Lagos; tel. 702044444; e-mail info@smile.com.ng; internet smile.com.ng; internet service provider; Group CEO AHMAD FARROUKH.

Spectranet: Plot 36B, Mobolaji Johnson Ave, Oregun Industrial Estate, Alausa, Ikeja, Lagos; tel. 7002345678; internet spectranet.com.ng; internet service provider; Chair. OBA RILWANU BABATUNDE OSUOLALE AREMU AKIOLU; CEO AJAY AWASTHI.

Telnet (Nigeria) Ltd: Plot 242, Kofo Abayomi St, Victoria Island, POB 53656, Falomi Ikoyi, Lagos; tel. (1) 4611747; e-mail contact@telnetng.com; internet www.telnetng.com; f. 1985; telecommunications engineering and consultancy services; Group Exec. Dir FOLORUNSO ALIU.

21st Century Technologies: 5 Jeremiah Ugwu St, off Babatunde Anjous, Lekki Phase 1, Lagos; tel. (1) 2707777; e-mail commercial@21ctl.com; internet www.21ctl.com; fixed-line services; Chair. TUNDE AJISOMO; CEO WALE AJISEBUTU.

Regulatory Authority

Nigerian Communications Commission (NCC): Plot 423, Aguiyi Ironsi St, Maitama, Abuja; tel. (9) 4617000; e-mail ncc@ncc.gov.ng; internet www.ncc.gov.ng; f. 1932; Chair. Prof. ADEOLU AKANDE; Exec. Vice-Chair. and CEO Prof. UMAR GARBA DANBATTA.

BROADCASTING

Regulatory Authority

National Broadcasting Commission: Plot 20, Ibrahim Taiwo St, Asokoro District, POB 5747, Garki, Abuja; tel. (9) 2913808; e-mail info@nbc.gov.ng; internet www.nbc.gov.ng; Dir-Gen. MALLAM ISHAQ MODIBO KAWU.

Radio

Federal Radio Corpn of Nigeria (FRCN): Radio House, Herbert Macaulay Way, Area 10, PMB 452, Garki, Abuja; tel. (9) 8734228; e-mail info@radionigeria.gov.ng; internet www.radionigeria.gov.ng; f. 1976; controlled by the Fed. Govt and divided into 6 zones: Lagos (English); Enugu (English, Igbo, Izon, Efik and Tiv); Ibadan (English, Yoruba, Edo, Urhobo and Igala); Kaduna (English, Hausa, Kanuri, Fulfulde and Nupe); Abuja (English, Hausa, Igbo and Yoruba); Chair. ALIYU HAYATU; Dir-Gen. MANSUR LIMAN.

The Beat 99.9 FM: 26 Keffi St, off Awolowo Rd, Ikoyi, Lagos; tel. (1) 2701020; e-mail enquiries@thebeat99.com; internet www.thebeat99.com; f. 2009; Man. Dir and CEO CHRIS UBOSI.

Brilla FM: 4 Oluwatunmike Disu, opp. Jakande First Gate, Lekki-Ajah Expressway, Lagos; tel. 8034439502; e-mail hello@brila.net; internet www.brila.net; f. 2002; sports; Chair. and CEO Dr LARRY IZAMOJE.

Freedom Radio: Phase 1, Sharada Industrial Estate, Kano; internet freedomradionig.com; Chair. Alhaji ADO MOHAMMED; Man. Dir ABBAS M. DALHATU.

Imo Broadcasting Corpn: Egbu Rd, PMB 1129, Owerri, Imo; tel. (42) 250327; operates one radio station in Imo State.

Inspiration 92.3 FM: Amazing Grace Plaza, Plot 2E–4E Ligali Ayorinde St, Victoria Island, Lagos; tel. (1) 2770923; e-mail info@ifm923.com; internet ifm923.com; CEO AZUBIKE OSUMILI.

Max 102.3 FM: 1 Continental Way, off CMD Rd, Magodo, Lagos; tel. 7080668003; e-mail pr@tvcontinental.tv; internet www.max1023.fm; f. 2017; owned by TVC Communications; CEO ANDREW HANLON.

Ray Power Radio 100.5 FM: Abeokuta Express Way, Ilapo, Alagbado, Lagos; tel. (1) 2644814; 100% owned by DAAR Communications Ltd; commenced broadcasting in Sept. 1994; Chair. Chief ALEOGHO RAYMOND DOKPESI.

Smooth 98.1 FM: 4 Amichi Close, off Eletu Ogabi St, Victoria Island, Lagos; tel. (1) 4489960; e-mail info@smooth981.fm; internet smooth981.fm; f. 2009; owned by Fenchurch Media and Broadcasting Network Ltd.

Splash 105.5 FM: Oba Abimbola Oluwo Rd, Felele, Ibadan, Lagos; tel. 8056998717; e-mail info@splashfm1055.com; internet splashfm1055.com; f. 2007; Chair. Chief ADEBAYO MURITALA AKANDE.

Voice of Nigeria (VON): Plot 1386, Oda Cres., off Aminu Kano Cres., Wuse II, Abuja; tel. (9) 2344017; e-mail info@von.gov.ng; internet von.gov.ng; f. 1990; controlled by the Fed. Govt; external services in English, French, Arabic, Ki-Swahili, Hausa and Fulfulde; Dir-Gen. OSITA OKECHUKWU.

Television

Nigerian Television Authority (NTA): Television House, Area 11, Garki, PMB 13, Abuja; tel. (9) 2345907; e-mail ntacorporateaffairs@gmail.com; internet www.nta.ng; f. 1976; controlled by the Fed. Govt; operates a network of 31 terrestrial broadcasters, which share national programming but also broadcast local programmes; also operates c. 70 regional channels; Chair. DURO ONABULE; Dir-Gen. YAKUBU IBN MOHAMMED.

Africa Independent Television (AIT): DAAR Communications Complex, Kpaduma Hills, Ladi Lawal Dr., off Gen. T. Y. Danjuma St, Asokoro, Abuja; e-mail info@aitonline.tv; internet ait.live; f. 1994; 100% owned by DAAR Communications Ltd; Man. Dir Dr OLUWATOSIN FOLAKE ABIMBOLA DOKPESI.

Channels Television: 44/48 Channels TV Ave, Isheri-North, Lagos; tel. (1) 4406464; e-mail info@channelstv.com; internet www.channelstv.com; Chair. and CEO JOHN MOMOH.

Galaxy Television: 25 Community Rd, off Allen Ave, Lagos; tel. 8130753244; e-mail info@galaxytvonline.com; internet www.galaxytvonline.com.

Murhi International Television (MITV): MITV Radiovision Plaza, Obafemi Awolowo Way, POB 4260, POB 4260, Ikeja, Lagos; tel. (1) 2954586; e-mail info@mitvonline.tv; internet mitvonline.ng; Chair. MURI GBADEYANKA BUSARI.

People's Television (PTV): 1282 Aderemi Adesoji St, Apo Legislative Quarters, Abuja; tel. 9080000054; e-mail info@ptvng.com.com; internet ptvng.com.

Silverbird Television: 133 Ahamadu Bello Way, Victoria Island, Lagos; tel. (1) 7936938; e-mail info@silverbirdtv.com; internet silverbirdtv.com; f. 2003.

Swift Networks Ltd: 31 Saka Tinubu St, Victoria Island, Lagos; tel. 8167002398; e-mail customercare@swiftng.net; internet www .swiftng.com; f. 2002; Chair. RICHARD KRAMER; Man. Dir and CEO CHARLES ANUDU.

Television Continental (TVC): 1 Continental Way, Ikosi Ketu, Lagos; tel. 7080668003; e-mail pr@tvcontinental.tv; internet www .tvcnews.tv; CEO ANDREW HANLON.

Finance

BANKING

In 2022 there were 22 commercial banks, six development finance institutions, five merchant banks and five discount houses in Nigeria. There were also 45 finance companies and 975 microfinance banks in the country. Stanbic IBTC Bank PLC provided Islamic banking services.

Central Bank

Central Bank of Nigeria: Plot 33, Abubakar Tafawa Balewa Way, Central Business District, Cadastral Zone, PMB 0187, Garki, Abuja; tel. (9) 46239701; e-mail contactcbn@cbn.gov.ng; internet www.cbn .gov.ng; f. 1958; bank of issue; Gov. GODWIN EMEFIELE.

Commercial Banks

Access Bank: 14/15 Prince Alaba Abiodun Oniru Rd, Victoria Island, Lagos; tel. (1) 2712005; e-mail contactcenter@ accessbankplc.com; internet www.accessbankplc.com; f. 1989; Chair. AJORITSEDERE AWOSIKA; Group Man. Dir HERBERT WIGWE.

Citibank Nigeria Ltd: Charles S. Sankey House, 27 Kofo Abayomi St, POB 6391, Lagos; tel. (1) 2798400; internet www.citigroup.com/ citi/about/countries-and-jurisdictions/nigeria.html; f. 1984; Chair. OLAYEMI CARDOSO; CEO IRETI SAMUEL-OGBU.

Ecobank Nigeria Ltd: Plot 21, Ahmadu Bello Way, Victoria Island, POB 72688, Lagos; tel. (1) 2710391; e-mail engcontactcentre@ ecobank.com; internet www.ecobank.com; f. 1989; Chair. BOLA ADESOLA; Man. Dir JUBRIL MOBOLAJI LAWAL.

Fidelity Bank PLC: 2 Kofo Abayomi St, Victoria Island, Lagos; tel. (1) 4485252; e-mail info@fidelitybankplc.com; internet www .fidelitybank.ng; f. 1988; Chair. MUSTAFA CHIKE-OBI; CEO NNEKA ONYEALI-IKPE.

First Bank Nigeria Ltd: Samuel Asabia House, 35 Marina, POB 5216, Lagos; tel. (1) 9052326; e-mail firstcontact@firstbanknigeria .com; internet www.firstbanknigeria.com; f. 1894 as Bank of British West Africa; Chair. TUNDE HASSAN-ODUKALE; CEO ADESOLA KAZEEM ADEDUNTAN.

First City Monument Bank Ltd: Primrose Tower, 17A Tinubu St, POB 9117, Lagos; tel. (1) 12793030; e-mail customerservice@fcmb .com; internet fcmb.com; f. 1983; Chair. OTUNBA OLUTOLA O. SENBORE; Man. Dir YEMISI EDUN.

Globus Bank: 6 Adeyemo Alakija St, Victoria Island, Lagos; tel. (1) 2259000; e-mail contactcenter@globusbank.com; internet globusbank.com; f. 2019; Chair. CHARLES OSEZUA; Man. Dir and CEO ELIAS IGBINAKENZUA.

Guaranty Trust Bank PLC: Plot 635, Akin Adesola St, PMB 75455, Victoria Island, Lagos; tel. (1) 2715227; e-mail complaints@ gtbank.com; internet www.gtbank.com; f. 1990; Chair. OSARETIN AFUSAT DEMUREN; Man. Dir MIRIAM OLUSANYA.

Heritage Bank PLC: Plot 292, Ajose Adeogun St, Victoria Island, Lagos; tel. (1) 2369000; e-mail info@hbng.com; internet www.hbng .com; Chair. JANI IBRAHIM (acting); Man. Dir IFIE SEKIBO.

Keystone Bank Ltd: 1 Keystone Bank Cres., off Adeyemo Alakija St, Victoria Island, Lagos; tel. (1) 4485742; e-mail contactcentre@ keystonebankng.com; internet www.keystonebankng.com; fmrly Bank PHB, name changed following nationalization in August 2011; Chair. Alhaji UMARU H. MODIBBO; Man. Dir and CEO OLANIRAN OLAYINKA.

Polaris Bank Ltd: 3 Akin Adesola St, Victoria Island, Lagos; tel. (1) 2705850; e-mail yescenter@polarisbanklimited.com; internet www .polarisbanklimited.com; 2018 to replace Skye Bank PLC; Chair. MUHAMMAD K. AHMED; Man. Dir and CEO INNOCENT C. IKE (acting).

Stanbic IBTC Bank PLC: IBTC Place, Walter Carrington Cres., POB 71707, Victoria Island, Lagos; tel. (1) 4222222; e-mail customercarenigeria@stanbic.com; internet www.stanbicibtcbank .com; f. 1989 as Investment Banking & Trust Co Ltd; name changed as above 2008 following merger with Stanbic Bank (Nigeria) Ltd; CEO WOLE ADENIYI.

Standard Chartered Bank Nigeria Ltd: 142 Ahmadu Bello Way, Victoria Island, Lagos; tel. (1) 2704611; e-mail clientcare.ng@sc.com; internet www.sc.com/ng; Chair. SOLA ADEPETUN; Man. Dir and CEO LAMIN MANJANG.

Sterling Bank: Sterling Towers, 20 Marina, POB 12735, Lagos; tel. (1) 4484481; e-mail customercare@sterlingbankng.com; internet sterling.ng; f. 2005 following merger of Indo-Nigerian Bank Ltd, Magnum Trust Bank, NAL Bank PLC, NBM Bank and Trust Bank of Africa Ltd; Chair. ASUE IGHODALO; Man. Dir and CEO ABUBAKAR SULEIMAN.

SunTrust Bank: 1 Oladele Olashore St, off Sansui Fafunwa St, Victoria Island, Lagos; tel. 9087331440; e-mail helpdesk@ suntrustng.com; internet suntrustng.com; Chair. OLANREWAJU SHITTU; CEO HALIMA BUBA.

Titan Trust Bank Ltd: 1680 Sanusi Fafunwa St, Victoria Island, Lagos; tel. 700200200; e-mail contactcentre@titantrustbank.com; internet www.titantrustbank.com; f. 2019; Man. Dir and CEO MUDASSIR AMRAY.

Union Bank of Nigeria Ltd: 36 Marina, PMB 2027, Lagos; tel. (1) 2716816; e-mail customerservice@unionbankng.com; internet www .unionbankng.com; f. 1917 as Colonial Bank, Barclays Bank acquired Colonial Bank in 1925; acquired by Titan Trust Bank Ltd (2022); Chair. FAROUK MOHAMMED; CEO MUDASSIR AMRAY.

United Bank for Africa (Nigeria) Ltd: 57 Marina, POB 2406, Lagos; tel. 7002255822; e-mail cfc@ubagroup.com; internet www .ubagroup.com; f. 1961; Group Chair. TONY O. ELUMELU; Group Man. Dir OLIVIER ALAWUBA.

Unity Bank PLC: Plot 42, Ahmed Onibudo St, Victoria Island, Lagos; tel. 7080666000; e-mail customercare@unitybankng.com; internet www.unitybankng.com; f. 2005; Chair. AMINU BABANGIDA; Man. Dir and CEO OLUWATOMI SOMEFUN.

Wema Bank Ltd: Wema Towers, 54 Marina, PMB 12862, Lagos; tel. (1) 2777700; e-mail info@wemabank.com; internet www.wemabank .com; f. 1945; Chair. Chief BABATUNDE KASALI; Man. Dir and CEO ADEMOLA ADEBISE.

Zenith Bank PLC: Plot 84, Ajose Adeogun St, Victoria Island, POB 75315, Lagos; tel. (1) 2787000; e-mail zenithdirect@zenithbank.com; internet www.zenithbank.com; f. 1990; name changed as above in 2004; Chair. JIM OVIA; Group Man. Dir EBENEZER N. ONYEAGWU.

Merchant Banks

Coronation Merchant Bank: 10 Amodu Ojikutu St, off Saka Tinubu St, PMB 12511, Marina, Lagos; tel. (1) 2797640; e-mail crc@coronationmb.com; internet www.coronationmb.com; f. 2015; Chair. BABATUNDE FOLAWIYO; Man. Dir and CEO BANJO ADEGBOHUNGBE.

FBNQuest Merchant Bank: 2 Broad St, Lagos; tel. (1) 2702290; e-mail info@fbnquest.com; internet fbnquest.com; fmrly FBN Merchant Bank; present name adopted in 2017; Chair. BELLO MACCIDO; Man. Dir and CEO KAYODE AKINKUGBE.

FSDH Merchant Bank Ltd: UAC House, 5th–8th Floors, Odunlami St, PMB 12913, Lagos; tel. (1) 2702880; e-mail info@fsdhgroup .com; internet www.fsdhgroup.com; fmrly First Securities Discount House Ltd; Chair. FEMI AGBAJE; Man. Dir BUKOLA SMITH.

NOVA Merchant Bank: 23 Kofo Abayomi St, Victoria Island, Lagos; tel. (1) 2804000; e-mail info@novambl.com; internet www .novambl.com; f. 2018; Chair. PHILLIPS ODUOZA; Man. Dir and CEO NATH UDE.

Rand Merchant Bank: Wings, East Towers, 3rd Floor, 17A Ozumba Mbadiwe St, Victoria, Lagos; tel. (1) 4637900; e-mail customercare@ rmb.com.ng; internet www.rmb.com.ng; CEO MICHAEL LARBIE.

Development Finance Institutions

Bank of Agriculture Ltd (BOA): 1 Yakubu Gowoh Way, PMB 2155, Kaduna; tel. 7040202222; e-mail info@boanig.com; internet www.boanig.com; f. 1973 for funds to farmers and co-operatives to improve production techniques; established as Nigerian Agricultural Bank, renamed Nigerian Agricultural and Co-operative Bank in 1978, and Nigerian Agricultural, Co-operative and Rural Development Bank Ltd in 2000; name changed as above in 2010; 40% owned by the Central Bank of Nigeria and 60% owned by the Federal Ministry of Finance Incorp; Man. Dir ALWAN HASSAN.

Bank of Industry (BOI) Ltd: 23 Marina, POB 2357, Lagos; tel. 7002255264; e-mail customercare@boinigeria.com; internet www .boi.ng; f. 1964 as the Nigerian Industrial Development Bank Ltd to provide medium- and long-term finance to industry, manufacturing, non-petroleum mining and tourism; name changed as above Oct. 2001; Man. Dir OLUKAYODE A. PITAN.

The Federal Mortgage Bank of Nigeria (FMBN): Mortgage House, Plot 266, Cadastral AO, Central Business District, PMB 2273, Garki, Abuja; tel. (9) 2920689; e-mail info@fmbn.gov.ng; internet www.fmbn.gov.ng; f. 1956 as Nigerian Building Society (NBS); Chair. AYODEJI ARIYO GBELEYI; Man. Dir HAMMAN MADU.

The Infrastructure Bank PLC (UDBN): Plot 977, Central Business Area, PMB 272, Garki, Abuja; tel. (9) 4604660; e-mail enquiries@tibplc.com; internet www.infrastructurebankplc.com; f. 1992; Chair. LAMIS DIKKO; Man. Dir ROSS OLUYEDE (acting).

The Nigerian Export-Import Bank (NEXIM): NEXIM House, Plot 975, Cadastral Zone AO, Central Business District, PMB 276, Garki, Abuja; tel. (9) 4603630; e-mail neximabj@neximbank.com.ng; internet www.neximbank.com.ng; f. 1991; Chair. Dr KINGSLEY OBIORA; Man. Dir ABUBAKAR A. BELLO.

Bankers' Association

Chartered Institute of Bankers of Nigeria: PC 19 Adeola Hopewell St, POB 72273, Victoria Island, Lagos; tel. 70034252426; e-mail cibn@cibng.org; internet www.cibng.org; Pres. BAYO WILLIAMS OLUGBEMI; Chief Exec. OLUSEYE AWOJOBI.

STOCK EXCHANGE

Securities and Exchange Commission (SEC): SEC Towers, Plot 272, Samuel Adesujo Ademulegun St, Central Business District, PMB 315, Garki, Abuja; tel. (9) 4621100; e-mail sec@sec.gov.ng; internet www.sec.gov.ng; f. 1979 as govt agency to regulate and develop capital market and to supervise stock exchange operations; Chair. OLUFEMI LIJADU; Dir-Gen. LAMIDO YUGUDA.

Nigerian Stock Exchange: Stock Exchange House, 2–4 Customs St, POB 2457, Lagos; tel. (1) 4638333; e-mail contactcenter@nse.com.ng; internet www.nse.com.ng; f. 1960; Pres. OTUNBA ABIMBOLA OGUNBANJO; CEO OSCAR N. ONYEMA.

INSURANCE

Regulatory Authority

National Insurance Commission (NAICOM): Plot 1239, Ladoke Akintola Blvd, PMB 457, Garki II, Abuja; tel. (9) 6733520; e-mail contact@naicom.gov.ng; internet www.naicom.gov.ng; f. 1992 as National Insurance Supervisory Board; present name adopted 1997; Chair. Chief EMMANUEL JIDEOFOR NWOSU; Commr for Insurance and CEO THOMAS OLORUNDARE SUNDAY.

Insurance Companies

African Alliance Insurance PLC: 54 Awolowo Rd, Ikoyi, Lagos; tel. 8066309476; e-mail customer@africanallianceplc.com; internet www.africanallianceplc.com; f. 1960; life assurance and pensions; Man. Dir and CEO JOYCE OJEMUDIA.

Aiico Insurance PLC (AIICO): AIICO Plaza, Plot PC 12, Churchgate St, Victoria Island, POB 2577, Lagos; tel. (1) 2792930; e-mail aiicare@aiicoplc.com; internet www.aiicoplc.com; f. 1963; Chair. KUNDAN SAINANI; Man. Dir and CEO BABATUNDE FAJEMIROKUN.

Ark Insurance Group: Glass House, 25 Karimu Kotun St, Victoria Island, POB 3771, Marina, Lagos; tel. 8090855551; e-mail enquiries@arkinsurancegroup.com; internet www.arkinsurancegroup.com; Chair. FRANCIS OLUWOLE AWOGBORO; Man. Dir and CEO OLUKAYODE AWOGBORO.

Continental Reinsurance Co Ltd: St. Nicholas House, 8th Floor, 6 Catholic Mission St, POB 2401, Lagos; tel. (1) 4622779; e-mail info@continental-re.com; internet www.continental-re.com; Chair. AJIBOLA OGUNSHOLA; CEO LAWRENCE MUTSUNGE NAZARE.

Cornerstone Insurance PLC: Cornerstone Complex 21, Water Corporation Dr., off Ligali Ayorinde St, POB 75370, Victoria Island, Lagos; tel. (1) 2806500; e-mail enquiries@cornerstone.com.ng; internet www.cornerstone.com.ng; f. 1991; Chair. SEGUN ADEBANJI; Group Man. Dir and CEO GANIYU MUSA.

Great Nigeria Insurance Co PLC: 8 Omo-Osaghie St, off Obafemi Awolono Rd, Ikoyi S/W, Ikoyi, POB 2314, Lagos; tel. (1) 3429161; e-mail info@greatnigeriaplc.com; internet www.greatnigeriaplc.com; f. 1960; all classes; Chair. BADE ALUKO; Man. Dir and CEO CECILIA OLAPEJU OSIPITAN.

Guinea Insurance PLC: Guinea Insurance House, 33 Ikorodu Rd, Jibowu, POB 1136, Lagos; tel. (1) 2934577; e-mail info@guineainsurance.com; internet www.guineainsurance.com; f. 1958; all classes; Chair. GODSON CHUKWUDI UGOCHUKWU; Man. Dir and CEO ADEMOLA ABIDOGUN.

Industrial and General Insurance Co Ltd: IGI House, 2 Agoro Odiyan St, off Adeola Odeku, Victoria Island, Victoria Island, Lagos; tel. (1) 2918853; e-mail info@iginigeria.com; internet www.iginigeria.com; f. 1992; Chair. Alhaji YAYALE AHMED; Man. Dir and CEO RACHEL VOKE EMENIKE.

Law Union and Rock Insurance PLC: 14 Hughes Ave, Alagomeji, Yaba, POB 944, Lagos; tel. (1) 8995010; internet lawunioninsurance.com; fire, accident and marine; Chair. REMI BABALOLA; Man. Dir and CEO ADEMAYOWA ADEDURO.

Leadway Assurance Co Ltd: 121/123 Funsho Williams Ave, Iponri, Lagos; tel. (1) 2700700; e-mail insure@leadway.com; internet www.leadway.com; f. 1970; all classes; CEO TUNDE HASSAN-ODUKALE.

National Insurance Corpn of Nigeria (NICON): NICON Plaza, Ground Floor, Plot 242, Muhammadu Buhari Way, Central Business District, Abuja; tel. 9087260168; internet niconinsurance.com.ng; f. 1969; all classes; Chair. OTUNBA YELE AKINROLABU; Man. Dir Alhaji MUHAMMAD BAGUDU HUSSAINI.

NEM Insurance Co (Nigeria) Ltd: 199 Ikorodu Rd, Obanikoro, POB 654, Lagos; tel. (1) 4489560; e-mail lagosnem@nem-Insurance.com; internet www.nem-insurance.com; all classes; Chair. Dr FIDELIS A. AYEBAE; Group Man. Dir and CEO TOPE SMART.

Niger Insurance PLC: 48/50 Odunlami St, POB 2718, Marina, Lagos; tel. 8133244981; e-mail info@nigerinsurance.com; internet www.nigerinsurance.com; f. 1962; all classes; Chair. Dr STEPHEN DIKE; Man. Dir EDWIN F. IGBITI.

Nigeria Reinsurance Corpn: 46 Marina, PMB 12766, Lagos; tel. (1) 2122086; e-mail contact@nigeriare.com.ng; internet nigeriare.com.ng; all classes of reinsurance; Chair. Chief Dr AMOS AKINGBA; CEO and Man. Dir AKINSOLA ALE.

Royal Exchange PLC: New Africa House, 31 Marina, POB 112, Lagos; tel. (1) 4606690; e-mail info@royalexchangeplc.com; internet www.royalexchangeplc.com; 1918; general and health insurance, life assurance, finance, asset management and microfinance banking; Chair. KENNETH EZENWANI ODOGWU; Group Man. Dir OLAWALE BANMORE.

SUNU Assurances Nigeria: Plot 1196, Bishop Oluwole St, Victoria Island, Lagos; tel. (1) 2802012; e-mail nigeria@sunu-group.com; internet sunuassurancesnigeria.com; f. 1991; fmrly Equity Assurance PLC; present name adopted 2018; general insurance; Chair. KYARI ABBA BUKAR; Man. Dir and CEO SAMUEL OGHENEBRUME OGBODU.

Tangerine Life Ltd: 22 Funsho Williams Ave, Alaka, Surulere, Lagos; tel. (1) 6309500; e-mail hello@tangerinelife.com; internet www.armlife.com.ng; f. 1994 as First Nigeria Life Insurance Co; subsequently CrystaLife and Arm Life; name changed as above in 2020; Chair. ERIC IDIAHI; Man. Dir LIVINGSTONE MAGORIMBO.

Veritas Kapital Assurance PLC: 497 Abogo Largema St, off Constitution Ave, Central Business District, POB 2044, Abuja; tel. (9) 4619900; e-mail info@veritaskapital.com; internet veritaskapital.com; f. 1973; fmrly UnityKapital Assurance PLC; present name adopted in 2018; Chair. NAHIM ABE IBRAHEEM; Man. Dir and CEO KENNETH EGBARAN.

Insurance Association

Nigerian Insurers' Association (NIA): 264 Ikorodu Rd, Savoil Bus Stop, POB 9551, Lagos; tel. 8170784444; e-mail info@nigeriainsurers.org; internet www.nigeriainsurers.org; f. 1971; Chair. GANIYU MUSA.

Trade and Industry

GOVERNMENT AGENCIES

Bureau of Public Enterprises: The Presidency, Bureau of Public Enterprises, 11 Osun Cres., off IBB Way, Maitama District, PMB 442, Garki, Abuja; tel. (9) 4604401; e-mail info@bpe.gov.ng; internet bpe.gov.ng; Dir-Gen. ALEXANDER AYOOLA OKOH.

Bureau of Public Procurement: 11 Suleiman Barau St, Presidential Villa, Abuja; tel. (9) 6252985; internet www.bpp.gov.ng; f. 2007; Dir-Gen. MAMMAN AMADU.

Corporate Affairs Commission: Plot 420, Tigris Cres., off Aguiyi Ironsi St, Maitama, PMB 198, Garki, Abuja; tel. 8182299016; e-mail cservice@cac.gov.ng; internet www.cac.gov.ng; Chair. ADEMOLA SERIKI; Registrar-Gen./CEO Alhaji GARBA ABUBAKAR.

National Council on Privatisation: Bureau of Public Enterprises, NDIC Bldg, Constitution Ave, Central Business District, PMB 442, Garki, Abuja; tel. (9) 5237405; internet bpe.gov.ng.

Nigeria Export Processing Zones Authority (NEPZA): 2 Zambezi Cres., Cadastral Zone A6, off Aguiyi Ironsi St, Maitama, PMB 037, Garki, Abuja; tel. 8024009408; e-mail enquiries@nepza.gov.ng; internet www.nepza.gov.ng; Chair. SEGUN ONI; Man. Dir/CEO ADESOJI ADESUGBA.

Nigeria Sovereign Investment Authority (NSIA): The Clan Place, 4th Floor, Plot 1386A, Tigris Crescent, Maitama, Abuja; tel. (9) 4610400; e-mail webmaster@nsia.com.ng; internet nsia.com.ng; f. 2011; manages 3 funds: the Stabilization Fund, the Future Generations Fund and the Nigeria Infrastructure Fund; Chair. OLAJIDE ZEITLIN; CEO/Man. Dir UCHE ORJI.

DEVELOPMENT ORGANIZATIONS

Chad Basin Development Authority (CBDA): Gamboru Rd, PMB 1130, Maiduguri; tel. 8082307243; e-mail info@chbda.com

.ng; internet www.chbda.com.ng; f. 1973; irrigation and agriculture-allied industries; Chair. ABBA GARBA.

Cross River Basin Development Authority (CRBDA): PMB 1249, Calabar; tel. 8185461116; e-mail crbdacal@yahoo.co.uk; internet crrbda.gov.ng; f. 1976; Gen. Man. Eng. BASSEY E. NKPOSONG.

Federal Institute of Industrial Research, Oshodi (FIIRO): 3 FIIRO Rd, by Cappa Bus Stop, off Agege Motor Rd, Oshodi, Ikeja, PMB 21023, Lagos; tel. 8023415016; e-mail info@fiiro.gov.ng; internet www.fiiro.gov.ng; f. 1956; plans and directs scientific research for industrial and technological development; provides tech. assistance and information to industry; specializes in foods, minerals, textiles, natural products and industrial intermediates; Chair. GAMBO MAGAJI; Dir-Gen./CEO Dr JUMMAI ADAMU TUTUWA.

Industrial Training Fund: 1 Kufang Village, Miango Rd, PMB 2199, Jos, Plateau; tel. 7031786065; internet www.itf.gov.ng; f. 1971 to promote and encourage skilled workers in trade and industry; Dir-Gen. Sir JOSEPH N. ARI.

Lagos State Development and Property Corpn: 2/4 Town Planning Way, Ilupeju Industrial Estate, PMB 21050, Lagos; tel. 8128839511; e-mail info@lsdpc.gov.ng; internet www.lsdpc.gov.ng; f. 1972; Man. Dir and CEO AYODEJI JOSEPH.

New Nigerian Development Co Ltd (NNDC): Ahmed Talib House, 18/19 Ahmadu Bello Way, PMB 2120, Kaduna; tel. 8127276497; e-mail nndc@nndcgroup.com.ng; internet www.nndcgroup.com.ng; f. 1949; owned by the govts of 19 northern states; investment finance; 8 subsidiaries, 83 assoc. cos; Chair. MALAM TANIMU YAKUBU; Group Man. Dir and CEO Dr SHEHU MAI-BORNU (acting).

Niger Delta Development Commission (NDDC): 167 Aba Rd, PMB 5253, Port Harcourt; e-mail info@nddc.gov.ng; tel. (8) 191941731; internet www.nddc.gov.ng; f. 2000; Interim Administrator EFFIONG OKON AKWA.

Odu'a Investment Co Ltd: Cocoa House Complex, 21st–23rd Floor, Oba Adebimpe Rd, PMB 5435, Ibadan; tel. 8151459359; e-mail info@oduainvestment.com.ng; internet oduainvestment.com.ng; f. 1976; jtly owned by Ogun, Ondo and Oyo States; Chair. OTUNBA BIMBO ASHIRU; Man. Dir ADEWALE ABIODUN RAJI.

Projects Development Institute (PRODA): Emene Industrial Layout, Proda Rd, off Enugu/Abakaliki Expressway, POB 01609, Enugu; tel. 8063392041; e-mail info@proda-ng.org; internet proda.gov.ng; f. 1970; promotes the establishment of new industries and develops industrial projects utilizing local raw materials; Dir-Gen. Eng. PETER OKWUDILICHUKWU OGBOBE.

Raw Materials Research and Development Council (RMRDC): Plot 17, Aguiyi Ironsi St, Maitama District, PMB 232, Garki, Abuja; tel. 9055556693; e-mail ceo@rmrdc.gov.ng; internet www.rmrdc.gov.ng; f. 1988; Chair. ABDULLAHI WAZIRI TAMBUWAL; Dir-Gen. Dr HUSSAINI DOKO IBRAHIM.

Rubber Research Institute of Nigeria (RRIN): off KM 19, Benin/Sapele Highway, Iyanomo, PMB 1049, Benin City; tel. 8168226594; e-mail info@rrin.gov.ng; internet www.rrin.gov.ng; f. 1961; conducts research into the production of rubber, gum arabic and other latex bearing plants of economic importance; Exec. Dir Prof. AIREGUAMEN I. AIGBODION.

Small And Medium Enterprises Development Agency of Nigeria (SMEDAN): 35 Port Harcourt Cres., Area 11, Garki, Abuja; e-mail info@smedan.gov.ng; internet www.smedan.gov.ng; Dir-Gen. Dr DIKKO UMARU RADDA.

CHAMBERS OF COMMERCE

Nigerian Association of Chambers of Commerce, Industry, Mines and Agriculture (NACCIMA): 8A Oba Akinjobi Way, PMB 12816, Lagos; tel. 8118877562; e-mail info@naccima.com; internet www.naccima.com; f. 1960; Pres. Chief JOHN CHINYELU UDEAGBALA; Dir-Gen. Ambassador AYOOLA OLUKANNI.

Enugu Chamber of Commerce, Industry, Mines and Agriculture (ECCIMA): Secretariat Complex, ECCIMA House, Old International Trade Fair Complex, Abakaliki Rd, POB 734, Enugu; tel. 7066944052; e-mail enuguchamber@yahoo.com; internet fb.com/enugu.eccima; f. 1963; Pres. JASPER NDUAGWUIKE; Dir-Gen. Eng. HENRY NDUKA AWUREGU.

Franco-Nigerian Chamber of Commerce and Industry (FNCCI): French Consulate, 1st Floor, 1 Oyinkan Abayomi Dr., 1st Floor, French Consulate, Ikoyi, POB 70001, Victoria Island, Lagos; tel. (1) 4545043; e-mail fncci@france-nigeria.fr; internet france-nigeria.org/home; f. 1985; Chair. OYE HASSAN ODUKALE; Gen. Man. and CEO MOSES UMORU.

Ibadan Chamber of Commerce and Industry: Commerce House, 1 Adeniran Oyinlola Ave, Ring Rd, Challenge, PMB 5168, Ibadan; tel. 7056778489; e-mail info@ibadanchamber.org.ng; internet ibadanchamber.org.ng; f. 1960; Pres. BAMIDELE SAMSON.

Kaduna Chamber of Commerce, Industry, Mines and Agriculture (KADCCIMA): Km 4, Zaria Rd, POB 728, Rigachikun, Kaduna; tel. (62) 290936; e-mail kadccima@gmail.com; internet kadccima.org.ng; f. 1973; Pres. Alhaji SULEIMAN ALIYU; Dir-Gen. Dr USMAN GARBA SAULAWA.

Kwara Chamber of Commerce, Industry, Mines and Agriculture: KWACCIMA House, Afon Junction, Along Ajase-Ipo Rd, Ganmo, POB 1634, Ilorin; tel. 8181793652; e-mail kwarachamber@gmail.com; internet kwarachamber.com; f. 1965; Pres. OLALEKAN FATAI AYODIMEJI.

Lagos Chamber of Commerce and Industry (LCCI): Commerce House, 1 Idowu Taylor St, Victoria Island, POB 109, Lagos; tel. (1) 2771557; e-mail lcci@lagoschamber.com; internet www.lagoschamber.com; f. 1888; 2,000 mems; Pres. Dr MICHAEL OLAWALE-COLE; Dir-Gen. CHIYENRE ALMONA.

INDUSTRIAL AND TRADE ASSOCIATIONS

Federation of Agriculture Commodity Associations of Nigeria (FACAN): Lagos; internet www.facan.org.ng; f. 2011; Pres. Dr VICTOR IYAMA; Sec.-Gen. AKIN GBADAMOSI.

National Cashew Association of Nigeria (NCAN): Plot No. 626, Ogwu James Onoja Cres., Wuye, Abuja; tel. 8033622074; e-mail info@ncan.org.ng; internet ncan.ng; Pres. OJO JOSEPH AJANAKU.

National Coffee and Tea Association of Nigeria: Old NRC Bldg, Gembu, Taraba; tel. 8033525482; Chair. IBRAHIM SADIQ.

National Cotton Association of Nigeria (NACOTAN): 48 Namagwatse House, 50 Ahmadu Bello Way, Kaduna; tel. 8035902208; e-mail info@nacotan.org.ng; internet nacotan.org.ng; Pres. ANIBE ACHIMUGU.

Nigerian Export Promotion Council (NEPC): Plot 424, Aguiyi Ironsi St, Maitama, Abuja; tel. (9) 2910966; e-mail info@nepc.gov.ng; internet nepc.gov.ng; f. 1977; Chair. MUSA IBRAHIM; Exec. Dir and CEO EZRA YAKUSAK.

Nigerian Investment Promotion Commission (NIPC): Plot 1181, Aguiyi Ironsi St, Maitama District, PMB 381, Garki, Abuja; tel. (9) 2900059; e-mail infodesk@nipc.gov.ng; internet www.nipc.gov.ng; Chair. BABANGIDA S. M. NGUROJE; Exec. Sec. and CEO SARATU A. UMAR.

EMPLOYERS' ORGANIZATIONS

Advertisers' Association of Nigeria (ADVAN): 17A, Salvation Rd, off Opebi Rd, Ikeja, Lagos; e-mail advansec2@yahoo.com; internet advertisersnigeria.com; f. 1992; Pres. FOLAKEMI ANI-MUMUNEY; 62 mems.

Association of Advertising Agencies of Nigeria (AAAN): Plot 8, Otunba Jobi Fele-Way, Central Business District, Alausa, Ikeja, Lagos; tel. (1) 4970842; e-mail info@aaan.org.ng; internet aaan.org.ng; f. 1971; Pres. STEVE BABAEKO; Dir KEMI FABUSORO.

Institute of Chartered Accountants of Nigeria (ICAN): Plot 16, Professional Layout Centre, Idowu Taylor St, Victoria Island, POB 1580, Lagos; tel. 8033886636; e-mail info.ican@ican.org.ng; internet www.icanig.org; f. 1965; Pres. Alhaji COMFORT OLU EYITAYO; CEO and Registrar AHMED MODU KUMSHE.

Nigeria Employers' Consultative Association (NECA): NECA House, Plot A2, Hakeem Balogun St, Central Business District, Alausa, Ikeja, POB 2231, Marina, Lagos; tel. (1) 3422356; e-mail neca@neca.org.ng; internet www.neca.org.ng; f. 1957; Pres. TAIWO ADENIYI; Dir-Gen. ADEWALE OYERINDE.

Nigerian Institute of Architects (NIA): 24 Magaji Muazu Cres., Katampe Extension, Abuja; tel. (9) 2900081; e-mail nia@niamails.com; internet www.nia.ng; f. 1960; Pres. ENYI BEN-EBOH.

Nigerian Institute of Building (NIOB): APDC Capital Estate, opp. Brick City, Kubwa Expressway, Kaba District, Abuja; tel. 8089248789; e-mail support@niobnat.org; internet niobnat.org; f. 1967; Pres. KUNLE AWOBODU.

Nigerian Institution of Estate Surveyors and Valuers (NIESV): Plot 759, BASSAN Plaza, Wing C, Last Floor, Central Business District, Independence Ave, PMB 5175, Wuse, Abuja; tel. 8078193014; e-mail info@niesv.org.ng; internet www.niesv.org.ng; f. 1969; Pres. JOHNBULL M. AMAYAEVBO; Nat. Sec. MONDAY N. AHIWE.

Nigerian Society of Engineers (NSE): National Engineering Centre, Plot 1035 Cadastral, off National Mosque-Labour House Rd, Central Business Area, PMB 13866, Abuja; tel. (9) 2917720; e-mail info@nse.org.ng; internet www.nse.org.ng; f. 1958; Pres. TASIU SAAD GIDARI-WUDIL.

UTILITIES

Electricity

Following the liberalization of the electricity sector in 2005, the Power Holding Company of Nigeria (PHCN), the national producer and distributor of electricity, was officially dissolved in early 2012, and its assets and responsibilities were transferred to 17 successor companies. The privatization process was completed in 2013.

Nigerian Electricity Management Services Agency (NEMSA): 4 Dar es Salaam Cres., off Aminu Kano Cres., Wuse 2, Abuja; tel. 7068681566; e-mail info@nemsa.gov.ng; internet nemsa.gov.ng; Man. Dir ALIYU TAHIR.

Nigerian Electricity Regulatory Commission (NERC): Plot 1387, Cadastral Zone A00, Central Business District, PMB 136, Garki, Abuja; tel. (9) 4621400; e-mail info@nerc.gov.ng; internet www.nerc.gov.ng; f. 2005; Chair. and CEO SANUSI GARBA.

Rural Electrification Agency (REA): 22 Freetown St, Wuse 2, Abuja; tel. 8107829134; e-mail info@rea.gov.ng; internet rea.gov.ng; Chair. UMARU MAZA MAZA; Man. Dir AHMAD SALIHIJO.

Gas

Nigeria Liquefied Natural Gas Co Ltd (NLNG): Intels Aba Rd Estate, KM 16 Port Harcourt-Aba Expressway, Port Harcourt; tel. 8039074000; internet www.nigerialng.com; f. 1989; Man. Dir and CEO PHILIP MSHELBILA.

MAJOR COMPANIES

The following are some of the largest companies in terms either of capital investment or employment.

Ardova PLC: Plot 89A, Ajose Adeogun St, Victoria Island, Lagos; tel. (1) 2784168; e-mail rc@ardovaplc.com; internet www.ardovaplc.com; fmrly BP Nigeria Ltd, subsequently African Petroleum Ltd and Forte Oil PLC; present name adopted 2020; markets lubricants, fuel oil, automotive gas oil, motor spirits, liquefied petroleum gas and kerosene; Chair. ABDULWASIU O. SOWAMI; CEO OLUMIDE ADEOSUN.

British American Tobacco Nigeria: 2 Olumegbon Rd, off Alfred Rewane Rd, Ikoyi, POB 137, Lagos; tel. 7046002511; e-mail batna_feedback@bat.com; internet www.batnigeria.com; f. 2000, merged with the Nigerian Tobacco Co the same year; mfrs of tobacco products; Man. Dir CHRIS MCALLISTER.

BUA Group: BUA Towers, 5th Floor, PC 32, Churchgate St, Victoria Island, Lagos; tel. (1) 4610669; e-mail info@buagroup.com; internet www.buagroup.com; f. 1988; conglomerate with interests in cement, edible oils, real estate, iron and steel, sugar, etc.; Chair. and CEO ABDUL SAMAD RABIU.

Camela Vegetable Oil Co Ltd: 126 Okigwe Road, POB 852, Owerri; tel. 803300089; e-mail info@camelaoil.com; internet fb.com/Camelaoil; f. 1960; production of vegetable oil products; Chair. and Man. Dir Chief OKEY IKORO.

Chellarams PLC: 110/114 Oshodi-Apapa Expressway, Isolo, Lagos; tel. (1) 7733838; e-mail info@chellaramsplc.com; internet www.chellaramsplc.com; f. 1923; conglomerate with interests in consumer goods, industrial chemicals and machinery; Chair. ASIWAJU SOLOMON KAYODE ONAFOWOKAN; Man. Dir Chief SURESH MURLI CHELLARAM.

Chemical and Allied Products PLC (CAP PLC): 2 Adeniyi Jones Ave, PMB 21072, Ikeja, Lagos; tel. 7027996860; e-mail careline@capplc.com; internet www.capplc.com; mfrs of paints, pesticides and pharmaceuticals, distributors of chemicals, dyestuffs, explosives, plastic raw materials and associated products; Chair. AWUNEBA AJUMOGOBIA; Man. Dir DAVID WRIGHT.

Coca-Cola Nigeria: 16 Gerrard Rd, Ikoyi, Lagos; tel. (1) 2709222; e-mail info_ng@coca-cola.com; internet www.coca-cola.com.ng; Man. Dir ALFRED OLAJIDE.

Conoil PLC: Mike Adenuga Towers, 1 Mike Adenuga Close, off Adeola Odeku, Victoria Island, PMB 2052, Lagos; tel. (1) 7037002; e-mail info@conoilproducing.com; internet www.conoilproducing.com; f. 1975; fmrly Shell Nigeria Ltd, subsequently National Oil and Chemical Marketing PLC; 74.4% owned by Conpetro Ltd; Chair. Dr MIKE ADENUGA, Jr; Man. Dir AKIN SEWEJE.

Dangote Group: Union Marble House, 1 Alfred Rewane Rd, PMB 40032, Falomo, Ikoyi, Lagos; tel. (1) 4480815; e-mail communications@dangote.com; internet www.dangote.com; conglomerate with interests in cement, sugar, flour, salt, fertilizers, etc.; Pres. Alhaji ALIKO ALIKO DANGOTE; Group Man. Dir OLAKUNLE ALAKE.

> **Dangote Cement:** Union Marble House, 1 Alfred Rewane Rd, Ikoyi, PMB 40032, Lagos; tel. (1) 4480815; e-mail cement-customercare@dangote.com; internet www.dangotecement.com; Chair. ALIKO DANGOTE; Group CEO MICHEL PUCHERCOS.

> **Dangote Fertiliser:** Dangote Free Trade Zone, Km 15, Lekki Coastal Rd, Okunraye, Ibeju Lekki Lekki, 105102, Lagos; tel. 8118484231; internet www.dangote.com/our-business/fertilizer; f. 2022; production of fertilizers.

> **Dangote Flour Mills:** Terminal E, Administrative Bldg, Apapa Port Complex, Lagos; tel. (1) 2712200; f. 1999; Group Man. Dir THABO MABE.

Dangote Sugar Refinery PLC: GDNL Administrative Bldg, 3rd Floor, Terminal E, Shed 20, NPA Wharf Complex, Apapa, Lagos; tel. 8150983259; e-mail srefinery@dangote.com; internet dangotesugar.com.ng; f. 2000; Man. Dir/CEO RAVINDRA SINGHVI.

National Salt Co of Nigeria PLC (NASCON): 15B Ikosi Rd, Oregun Industrial Estate, Oregun-Ikeja, Lagos; tel. 7008880888; e-mail nasconcare@dangote.com; internet www.nasconplc.com; f. 1973; Chair. YEMISI AYENI; Man. Dir THABO MABE (acting).

11PLC: 1 Mobil Rd, Apapa, Lagos; tel. (1) 2801600; e-mail info@11plc.com; internet 11plc.com; fmrly Mobil Oil Nigeria; distributor of Mobil fuel and lubricant brands; Chair. RAKESH KANSAGRA; Man. Dir ADETUNJI OYEBANJI.

Flour Mills of Nigeria PLC (FMN): 1 Golden Penny Pl., Wharf Rd, POB 341, Apapa, Lagos; tel. 7056891000; e-mail info@fmnplc.com; internet www.fmnplc.com; f. 1960; food and agro-based; Chair. JOHN G. COUMANTAROS; Group Man. Dir OMOBOYEDE OLUSANYA.

Guinness Nigeria PLC: 24 Oba Akran Ave, Ikeja, PMB 21071, Lagos State; tel. (1) 2709100; internet www.guinness-nigeria.com; f. 1950; brewers; breweries in Ogba, Benin and Aba; Chair. BABATUNDE ABAYOMI SAVAGE; Man. Dir and CEO JOHN MUSUNGA.

Ibeto Group: 60–61 Igwe Orizu Rd, PMB 50132, Nnewi; tel. 8148675041; e-mail sales@ibeto.com; internet ibeto.com; conglomerate with interests in lead acid battery manufacturing, petrochemicals, cement, hospitality, real estate, oil and gas; Chair. and CEO Dr CLETUS MADUBUGWU IBETO.

> **Eastern Bulkcem Co Ltd:** 11 Awolowo Rd, Flat 5, Block 2, Ikoyi, Lagos; tel. (1) 2691114; e-mail ebc@eaglecement.com; f. 1977.

Julius Berger Nigeria PLC: 10 Shettima A. Munguno Cres., Utako, Abuja; tel. (9) 6110000; e-mail info@julius-berger.com; internet www.julius-berger.com; construction and civil engineering; Chair. MUTIU SUNMONU; Man. Dir Dr LARS RICHTER.

Lafarge Africa PLC: 27B Gerrard Rd, Ikoyi, POB 1001, Lagos; tel. (1) 2713990; e-mail customerservice.ng@lafargeholcim.com; internet www.lafarge.com.ng; construction solutions co; Chair. ADEBODE ADEFIOYE; Group Man. Dir/CEO KHALED EL DOKANI.

A. G. Leventis Group: 2 Iddo House, Iddo, POB 159, Lagos; tel. (1) 7740844; e-mail info@agleventis.com; internet www.agleventis.com; activities include wholesale and retail distribution, vehicle assembly, food production and farming, manufacture of glass, plastics, beer, technical and electrical equipment, property investment and management; Chair. AHMED KAZALMA MANTEY; Group Man. Dir and CEO OLUWASEUN ABIMISOLA ONI.

Mandilas Group Ltd: 35 Simpson St, POB 35, Lagos; tel. 9093309918; e-mail mandilas@mandilasng.com; internet www.mandilasng.com; subsidiaries incl.: Mandilas Enterprises Ltd and Norman Industries Ltd; Group CEO OLA DEBAYO-DOHERTY.

Mobil Producing Nigeria: Mobil House, 1 Lekki Express Way, Victoria Island, PMB 12054, Lagos; tel. (1) 2621640; a subsidiary of ExxonMobil; offshore petroleum production; Chair. and Man. Dir RICHARD LAING.

Nautilus (Nigeria) Engineering and Construction Co Ltd (NNEC): 47A Itafaji St, Dolphin Estate, Ikoyi, Victoria Island, Lagos; tel. 9099330740; e-mail infonnec@nnecltd.com; internet www.nnecltd.com; engineering and construction.

Nigerian Breweries Ltd: Iganmu House, 1 Abebe Village Rd, Iganmu, POB 545, Lagos; tel. (1) 2717400; e-mail info@nbplc.com; internet www.nbplc.com; f. 1946; also facilities at Aba, Kaduna, Ibadan and Enugu; Chair. Chief KOLAWOLE B. JAMODU; Man. Dir and CEO HANS ESSAADI.

Nigerian National Petroleum Corpn Ltd (NNPC): NNPC Towers, Herbert Macauley Way, Central Business District, PMB 190, Garki, Abuja; tel. (9) 20081133; e-mail contactus@nnpcgroup.com; internet www.nnpcgroup.com; f. 1977; reorg. 1988; holding corpn for Fed. Govt's interests in petroleum cos; 11 operating subsidiaries; Chair MARGARET CHUBA OKADIGBO; CEO MELE KOLO KYARI.

> **Port Harcourt Refining Co Ltd:** Alesa Eleme, POB 585, Port Harcourt, Rivers State; tel. (84) 777848; e-mail phrc@nnpc-group.com; f. 1965; Man. Dir AHMED DIKKO.

> **Warri Petrochemical and Refining Co. (WRPC):** Refinery Rd, Ekpan, PMB 44, Effuron, Warri; tel. (53) 254161; e-mail press@wrpcnnpcng.com; internet www.wrpcnnpcng.com; f. 1978; Man. Dir P. OBELLEY.

Oando PLC: The Wings Complex, 17A Ozumba Mbadiwe, Victoria Island, Lagos; tel. (1) 2702400; e-mail info@oandoplc.com; internet www.oandoplc.com; f. 1956 as ESSO; rebranded in 1976 as Unipetrol Nigeria Ltd; merged with Agip Nigeria PLC in 2003 and assumed present name; Chair. OBA MICHAEL ADEDOTUN GBADEBO; Group CEO ADEWALE TINUBU.

Peugeot Automobile Nigeria Ltd: Plot 1144, Mallam Kulbi Rd, Kakuri Industrial Estate, PMB 2266, Kaduna; tel. 7055001000; e-mail customerservice@peugeotnigeria.com; internet www

.peugeotnigeria.com; f. 1972; engaged in the manufacture and marketing of fully built Peugeot automobiles through appointed network of distributors; 54.87% owned by ASD Motors-Nig, 10% owned by Automobiles Peugeot, Govt of Nigeria and Bank of India, Nigeria; Chair. MUNIR JA'AFARU; Man. Dir IBRAHIM TANKO MOHAMMED.

SCOA Nigeria PLC: 10 Creek Rd, Apapa, POB 2318, Lagos; tel. 8034027262; e-mail info@scoaplc.com; internet www.scoaplc.com; f. 1926; vehicle assembly and maintenance, distribution and maintenance of heavyweight engines, industrial air-conditioning and refrigeration, home and office equipment, textiles, tanning, general consumer goods, mechanized farming; Chair. HENRY H. AGBAMU; Man. Dir Dr MASSA F. BOULOS.

Shell Petroleum Development Company of Nigeria Ltd: Freeman House, 21–22 Marina, PMB 2418, Lagos; tel. 8070269999; e-mail shellnigeria@shell.com; internet www.shell.com.ng; the largest petroleum operation in Nigeria; carries out onshore and offshore exploration and production; 55% govt-owned; Man. Dir OSAGIE OKUNBOR.

Total Premier Services Nigeria Ltd (TPSNL): Plot 4 No. 16, Wole Ariyo St, Lekki Phase 1, Lagos; tel. (1) 4547222; e-mail info@tpsnl.com; internet www.tpsnl.com; supplier of oil country tubular goods (OCTGs); Chair. JAMES SIMMONS.

Triana Ltd: 18–20 Commercial Rd, PMB 1064, Apapa, Lagos; tel. 8113933193; e-mail trianaltd@yahoo.com; internet www.trianaltd.com; f. 1970; shipping, clearing and forwarding, warehousing, air freighting; Dir Alhaji R. A. O. MAJEKODUNMI.

UAC of Nigeria Ltd: Niger House, 1–5 Odunlami St, POB 9, Lagos; tel. (1) 2701879; e-mail info@uacnplc.com; internet www.uacnplc.com; fmrly United Africa Co; divisions include brewing, foods, electrical materials, packaging, business equipment, plant hire, timber; Chair. DANIEL OWOR AGBOR; Group Man. Dir and CEO FOLASOPE AIYESIMOJU.

Grand Cereals and Oil Mills Ltd: KM 17, Zawan Roundabout, POB 13462, Jos, Plateau; tel. (73) 290790; e-mail info@grandcereals.com; internet www.grandcereals.com; a subsidiary of UAC of Nigeria Ltd; Chair. JUSTIN OLABODE EMANUEL; Man. Dir ALEXANDER GOMA.

Unilever (Nigeria) PLC: 1 Billingsway, Oregun, POB 1063, Ikeja, Lagos; tel. (1) 2793000; internet www.unilevernigeria.com; f. 1923; mfrs of detergents, edible fats and toilet preparations; Chair. NNAEMEKA ALFRED ACHEBE; Man. Dir CARL CRUZ.

United Cement Company of Nigeria Ltd (UNICEM): Spring Rd, Diamond Hill, PMB 1017, Calabar; tel. 7034090955; e-mail customerservice.ng@lafargeholcim.com; internet www.lafarge.com.ng/unicem; f. 2002; Man. Dir OLIVIER LENOIR.

TRADE UNIONS

Federations

Nigeria Labour Congress (NLC): Labour House, Plot 820/821, Central Business District, Abuja; tel. 8033084549; e-mail gsec@nlcng.org; internet www.nlcng.org; f. 1978; comprised 50 affiliated industrial unions in 2022; Pres. AYUBA PHILIBUS WABBA; Gen. Sec. EMMANUEL UGBOAJA.

Trade Union Congress of Nigeria (TUC): Express House, 338 Ikorodu Rd, Maryland, Lagos; tel. (1) 7369896; e-mail admin@tucng.org; internet tucnigeria.org.ng; Nat. Pres. QUADRI A. OLALEYE; Sec.-Gen. MUSA-LAWAL OZIGI; 24 mem. orgs.

Principal Unions

Amalgamated Union of Public Corpns, Civil Service, and Technical and Recreational Services Employees (AUPC-TRE): 9 Aje St, PMB 1064, Yaba, Lagos; tel. 8033317436; internet aupctre.org.ng; Pres. BENJAMIN ANTHONY; Gen. Sec. WAHEED SIKIRU TOYIN.

Nigeria Union of Journalists (NUJ): 9A Lyalla St, off Kafi St, Alausa, Ikeja, Lagos; tel. 8065089917; e-mail nujlagos@gmail.com; internet nuj.org.ng; f. 1955; Chair. Dr QASIM AKINRETI; Sec. ODIFA ALFRED ADEBAYO.

Nigeria Union of Petroleum and Natural Gas Workers (NUPENG): 9 Jibowu St, off Ikorodu Rd, Yaba, Lagos; tel. 8134525338; e-mail headoffice@nupeng.org; internet nupeng.org; f. 1977; Pres. WILLIAMS AKPOREHA; Gen. Sec. OLAWALE AFOLABI.

Petroleum and Natural Gas Senior Staff Association of Nigeria (PENGASSAN): U. M. Okoro House, 288 Ikorodu Rd, Anthony, Lagos; tel. (1) 2790715; e-mail headoffice@pengassan.org; internet www.pengassan.org; f. 1978; Pres. FESTUS OSIFO; Gen. Sec. LUMUMBA OKUGBAWA.

Transport

RAILWAYS

In 2011 plans were announced for the construction of a 117-km monorail line in Enugu State at an estimated cost of US $1,600m. Construction of a 35-km light rail system was under way in Lagos in the early 2020s; the first section of the system was scheduled to commence operations in December 2022. Meanwhile, in July 2018 the first phase of a light rail transport system was officially inaugurated in Abuja, linking Nnamdi Azikiwe International Airport to the city centre.

Nigerian Railway Corpn: PMB 1037, Ebute-Metta, Lagos; tel. 9051902545; e-mail info@nrc.gov.ng; internet www.nrc.gov.ng; f. 1955; restructured in 1993 into 3 separate units: Nigerian Railway Track Authority; Nigerian Railways; and Nigerian Railway Engineering Ltd; Chair. IBRAHIM ALHASSAN; Man. Dir FREEBORN EDETAN-LAEN OKHIRIA.

ROADS

Bolloré Transport and Logistics Nigeria: Millenium Bldg, Plot No. 251, Herbert Macaulay Way, Central Business District, Abuja; tel. 8034023924; e-mail sade.akannishelle@bollore.com; internet www.bollore-logistics.com/en/country/nigeria; f. 1961; Dir-Gen. FOLASHADE AKANNI-SHELLE.

Federal Roads Maintenance Agency (FERMA): Plot 163, Aminu Kano Cres., Wuse II, Abuja; tel. 8129999936; e-mail info@ferma.gov.ng; internet www.ferma.gov.ng; f. 2002; Chair. Eng. LEMO BABATUNDE OLAKUNLE; Man. Dir and CEO Eng. NURUDEEN ABDURAHAMAN RAFINDADI.

Road Transport Employers' Association of Nigeria (RTEAN): Plot 2082, Harper Cres., Beside Police Officers Mess, Wuse Zone 7, FCT, Abuja; Pres. MUSA ISIWELE SHEHU; Sec.-Gen. YUSUF ADENIYI.

INLAND WATERWAYS

National Inland Waterways Authority (NIWA): Aliyu Obaje Rd, Via Hydro Junction, Adankolo, PMB 1004, Lokoja, Kogi State; tel. (81) 42660450; internet niwa.gov.ng; f. 1997; responsible for all navigable waterways; Man. Dir GEORGE MOGHALU.

SHIPPING

The principal ports are the Delta Port complex (including Warri, Koko, Burutu and Sapele ports), Port Harcourt and Calabar; other significant ports are situated at Apapa and Tin Can Island, near Lagos. The main petroleum ports are Bonny and Burutu.

Nigerian Maritime Administration and Safety Agency (NIMASA): 4 Burma Rd, Apapa, Lagos; tel. (1) 2713617; e-mail info@nimasa.gov.ng; internet nimasa.gov.ng; f. 2007 following merger of National Maritime Authority and Joint Maritime Labour Industrial Council; Dir-Gen. Dr BASHIR JAMOH.

Nigerian Ports Authority: 26/28 Marina, PMB 12588, Lagos; tel. (1) 4637496; e-mail info@nigerianports.org; internet www.nigerianports.org; f. 1955; Chair. AKIN RICKETTS; Man. Dir MOHAMMED BELLO-KOKO.

Association

Nigerian Shippers' Council: Shippers' Tower, 4 Otunba Ayodele Soyode Lane, Apapa, Lagos; tel. 7098767065; e-mail nsc@shipperscouncil.com; internet www.shipperscouncil.com; Chair. Lt-Gen. SALIHU IBRAHIM; Exec. Sec. and CEO EMMANUEL-LYAMBEE JIME.

CIVIL AVIATION

The principal international airports are at Lagos (Murtala Mohammed Airport), Kano, Port Harcourt and Abuja (Nnamdi Azikiwe International Airport). There are also 18 airports servicing domestic flights.

Federal Airports Authority of Nigeria (FAAN): Murtala Mohammed Airport, PMB 21607, Ikeja, Lagos; tel. (1) 4970335; e-mail contact@faan.gov.ng; internet www.faannigeria.org; Chair. Dr DAN KURE; Man. Dir and CEO Capt. RABIU HAMISU YADUDU.

Nigerian Civil Aviation Authority (NCAA): NCAA House, Murtala Mohammed Airport, PMB 21029, 21038 Ikeja, Lagos; tel. (1) 2790421; e-mail info@ncaa.gov.ng; internet www.ncaa.gov.ng; Dir-Gen. Capt. MUSA NUHU.

Principal Airlines

Aero Nigeria: Private Terminal, Domestic Wing, Murtala Mohammed Airport, Ikeja, Lagos; tel. (1) 6284140; e-mail customercare@acn.aero; internet www.flyaero.com; f. 1959; Assets Management Corpn of Nigeria acquired 60% equity stake in mid-2013; Man. Dir ADO SANUSI.

Arik Air: Murtala Mohammed Airport, POB 10468, Ikeja, Lagos; tel. (1) 2799999; e-mail talktous@arikair.com; internet www.arikair

.com; f. 2002; Chair. JOSEPH ARUMEMI-IKHIDE; Group CEO Dr MICHAEL ARUMEMI-IKHIDE.

Azman Air: 1 Zaria Rd, beside Federal Inland Revenue Services, Kano Line, Kano; tel. 9099800600; e-mail info@airazman.com; internet www.airazman.com; CEO Alhaji ABDULMUNAFI Y. SARINA.

Dana Air: Dana House, 116 Oshodi-Apapa Expressway, Isolo, Lagos; tel. (1) 2809888; e-mail contact@flydanaair.com; internet www.flydanaair.com; CEO JACKY HATHIRAMANI.

Overland Airways: 17 Simbiat Abiola Rd, POB 3165, Ikeja, Lagos; tel. 8035355000; internet www.overlandairways.com; f. 1998; CEO Capt. EDWARD BOYO.

Tourism

Federation of Tourism Associations of Nigeria (FTAN): 5 Lord Lugard St, behind Total Filling Station, Asokoro, Abuja; tel. 8065406678; e-mail info@ftan.org.ng; internet ftan.org.ng; f. 1997; Pres. NKEREUWEM ONUNG; 23 mems.

Hospitality and Tourism Management Association of Nigeria (HATMAN): Suite 99, Turaki Ali House, 5th Floor, NNDC, 3 Kanta Rd, Kaduna; tel. 8035991712; e-mail adminsec@hatman2010.org; internet hatman2010.org; f. 1996; Sec. MARTINS ALABI; c. 3,000 mems.

National Association of Nigeria Travel Agencies (NANTA): 84 Ikorodu Rd, Fadeyi, Lagos; tel. 8119041402; e-mail info@nanta.org .ng; internet www.nanta.org.ng; f. 1973; Pres. SUSAN AKPORIAYE.

National Commission for Museums and Monuments: Federal Secretariat Complex, Block C, 1st Floor, Shegu Shagari Way, PMB 171, Garki, Abuja; tel. 92920391; e-mail info@ncmm.gov.ng; internet www.ncmm.gov.ng; Dir-Gen. ISA TIJANI ABBA.

Nigerian Tourism Development Corpn: Old Federal Secretariat, Area 1, Garki, PMB 167, Abuja; tel. 7044960999; e-mail hello@ tournigeria.gov.ng; internet tournigeria.gov.ng; Dir-Gen. FOLORUNSHO COKER.

Defence

As assessed at November 2021, the total strength of the armed forces was 143,000: the army totalled 100,000 men, the navy 25,000 (including the coastguard) and the air force 18,000. There was also a paramilitary force of an estimated 80,000. Military service is voluntary. At November 2021 a total of 314 Nigerian troops were stationed abroad.

Defence Budget: ₦1,400,000m. in 2022.

Commander-in-Chief of the Armed Forces: Maj.-Gen. (retd) MUHAMMADU BUHARI.

Chief of Defence Staff: Maj.-Gen. LEO IRABOR.

Chief of Army Staff: Maj.-Gen. FAROUK YAHAYA.

Chief of Naval Staff: Vice-Adm. AWWAL ZUBAIRU GAMBO.

Chief of Air Staff: Air Marshal ISIAKA OLADAYO AMAO.

Education

Education is partly the responsibility of the state governments, although the Federal Government has played an increasingly important role since 1970. Primary education begins at six years of age and lasts for six years. Secondary education begins at 12 years of age and lasts for a further six years, comprising two three-year cycles. Education to junior secondary level (from six to 15 years of age) is free and compulsory. According to estimates by the United Nations Educational, Scientific and Cultural Organization (UNESCO), in 2015/16 primary enrolment was equivalent to 85% of children in the relevant age-group (males 87%; females 82%), while the comparable ratio for secondary enrolment was equivalent to 42% (males 44%; females 40%). Education was allocated ₦742,500m. in the federal budget for 2021, equivalent to around 5.7% of total projected expenditure.

Bibliography

Achebe, C. *There Was A Country: A Personal History of Biafra*. London, Penguin, 2012.

Adamokekun, L. *The Fall of the Second Republic*. Ibadan, Spectrum Books, 1985.

Adebanwi, W. *Yorùbá Elites and Ethnic Politics in Nigeria*. New York, Cambridge University Press, 2014.

Adibe, J. *Negotiating the Nigeria-Nation: Essays on State, Governance and Development*. London, Adonis & Abbey, 2012.

   Nigeria without Nigerians? Boko Haram and the Crisis in Nigeria's Nation-Building Project. London, Adonis & Abbey, 2012.

Adunbi, O. *Enclaves of Exception: Special Economic Zones and Extractive Practices in Nigeria*. Bloomington, IN, Indiana University Press, 2022.

Agbu, O. (Ed.). *Elections and Governance in Nigeria's Fourth Republic*. Dakar, CODESRIA, 2016.

Akinola, A. A. *Party Coalitions in Nigeria: History, Trends and Prospects*. Ibadan, Safari Books, 2014.

Ariweriokuma, S. *The Political Economy of Oil and Gas in Africa: The Case of Nigeria*. Abingdon, Routledge, 2008.

Ayoade, J., and Akinsanya, A. (Eds) *Nigeria's Critical Election: 2011*. Lanham, MD, Lexington Books, 2012.

Babawale, T. (Ed.). *Urban Violence, Ethnic Militias and the Challenge of Democratic Consolidation in Nigeria*. Lagos, Malthouse Press, 2003.

Bakarr Bah, A. *Breakdowns and Reconstitution: Democracy, the Nation-State, and Ethnicity in Nigeria*. Lanham, MD, Lexington Books, 2005.

Bergstresser, H. *A Decade of Nigeria*. Leiden, Brill, 2017.

Bourne, R. *Nigeria: A New History of a Turbulent Century*. London, Zed Books, 2015.

Campbell, J. *Nigeria: Dancing on the Brink*. Lanham, MD, Rowman and Littlefield, 2010.

Collier, P., Soludo, C. C., and Pattillo, C. (Eds) *How Economic Choices Will Determine Nigeria's Future*. Basingstoke, Palgrave Macmillan, 2007.

Comolli, V. *Boko Haram: Nigeria's Islamist Insurgency*. London, C. Hurst & Co., 2015.

Ejiogu, E. *The Roots of Political Instability in Nigeria*. Farnham, Ashgate, 2011.

Elaigwu, J. I. *The Politics of Federalism in Nigeria*. London, Adonis & Abbey, 2007.

Ellis, S. *This Present Darkness: A History of Nigerian Organised Crime Paperback*. London, C. Hurst & Co., 2018.

Eltantawi, S. *Shari'ah on Trial: Northern Nigeria's Islamic Revolution*. Oakland, CA, University of Califorña Press, 2017.

Falola, T., and, Heaton, M. *A History of Nigeria*. Cambridge, Cambridge University Press, 2008.

Falola, T., and Paddock, A. (Eds) *Environment and Economics in Nigeria*. Abingdon, Routledge, 2011.

Fawehinmi, F., and Fagbule, F. *Formation: The Making of Nigeria from Jihad to Amalgamation*. Abuja, Cassava Republic Press, 2020.

Gould, M. *The Struggle for Modern Nigeria: The Biafran War 1967–1970*. London, I.B. Tauris, 2011.

Hentz, J., and Solomon, H. (Eds) *Understanding Boko Haram: Terrorism and Insurgency in Africa*. Abingdon, Routledge, 2017.

Hill, J. *Nigeria Since Independence: Forever Fragile?* Basingstoke, Palgrave Macmillan, 2012.

Ikpuk, J. S. *Militarism of Politics and Neo-colonialism: The Nigerian Experience 1966–1990*. London, Janus Publishing Co, 1995.

Itugbu, S. *Foreign Policy and Leadership in Nigeria: Obasanjo and the Challenge of African Diplomacy*. London, I.B. Tauris, 2017.

Jeyifo, B. (Ed.). *Perspectives on Wole Soyinka: Freedom and Complexity*. Jackson, MS, University Press of Mississippi, 2001.

   Wole Soyinka: History, Politics and Colonialism. Cambridge, Cambridge University Press, 2003.

Kendhammer, B. *Muslims Talking Politics: Framing Islam, Democracy and Law in Northern Nigeria*. Chicago, IL, Chicago University Press, 2016.

Kilby, P. *Industrialization in an Open Economy: Nigeria 1945–1966*. Cambridge, Cambridge University Press, 2018.

LeVan, A. C. *Dictators and Democracy in African Development: The Political Economy of Good Governance in Nigeria*. Cambridge, Cambridge University Press, 2015.

   Contemporary Nigerian Politics: Competition in a Time of Transition and Terror. Cambridge, Cambridge University Press, 2019.

Mai-Bornu, Z. L. *Political Violence and Oil in Africa The Case of Nigeria*. Cham, Palgrave Macmillan, 2007.

Moses, D., and Heerten, L. (Eds). *Postcolonial Conflict and the Question of Genocide: The Nigeria-Biafra War, 1967–1970*. Abingdon, Routledge, 2017.

Mustapha, A. R., and Ehrhardt, D. (Eds). *Creed & Grievance. Muslim-Christian Relations & Conflict Resolution in Northern Nigeria*. Woodbridge, James Currey, 2018.

Mustapha, A. R., and Meagher, K. (Eds). *Overcoming Boko Haram: Faith, Society & Islamic Radicalization in Northern Nigeria*. Woodbridge, James Currey, 2020.

Nwabueze, B. O., and Akinola, A. (Eds). *Military Rule and Social Justice in Nigeria*. Ibadan, Spectrum Books, 1993.

Nwadiaru, R. *Nigeria: A Failed State? Profound Treatise on a Crippled Giant*. Herndon, VA, Mascot Books, 2018.

Nwankwo, A. A. *Nigeria: The Political Transition and the Future of Democracy*. Enugu, Fourth Dimension, 1993.

Obadare, E., and Adebanwi, W. *Nigeria at Fifty: The Nation in Narration*. Abingdon, Routledge, 2011.

Obasanjo, O. *My Command: An Account of the Nigerian Civil War 1967–1970*. London, Heinemann, 1981.

Obi, C., and Rustad, S. *Oil and Insurgency in the Niger Delta: Managing the Complex Politics of Petroviolence*. London, Zed Books, 2011.

Obulor, I. *Political Economy of Ethnic Militias and Political Violence in Nigeria*. Port Harcourt, Kemuela Publications, 2013.

Olaniyan, R. A. *The Amalgamation and its Enemies: An Interpretive History of Modern Nigeria*. Ile-Ife, Obafemi Awolowo University Press, 2003.

Olowu, D., and Soremekun, K. *Governance and Democratisation in Nigeria*. Ibadan, Spectrum Books, 1995.

Olutayo, A. O. et al. *Contemporary Development Issues in Nigeria*. Newcastle-upon-Tyne, Cambridge Scholars Publishing, 2015.

Omeje, K. *High Stakes and Stakeholders: Oil Conflict and Security in Nigeria*. Aldershot, Ashgate, 2006.

Omoweh, D. A. *Shell Petroleum Development Company, the State and Underdevelopment of Nigeria's Niger Delta: a Study in Environmental Degradation*. Lawrenceville, NJ, Africa World Press, 2005.

Oriola, T. B., Onuoha, F., and Oyewole, S. (Eds). *Boko Haram's Terrorist Campaign in Nigeria: Contexts, Dimensions and Emerging Trajectories*. Abingdon, Routledge, 2021.

Osaghae, E. E. *Crippled Giant: Nigeria Since Independence*. London, Hurst, 1998.

Paden, J. N. *Muhammadu Buhari: The Challenges of Leadership in Nigeria*. Berkeley, CA, Roaring Forties Press, 2016.

Peel, M. *A Swamp Full of Dollars: Pipelines and Paramilitaries at Nigeria's Oil Frontier*. London, I.B. Tauris, 2011.

Rotberg, R. I. *Crafting The New Nigeria: Confronting The Challenges*. Boulder, CO, Lynne Rienner Publications, 2004.

Schatz, S. P. *Nigerian Capitalism*. Berkeley, CA, University of California Press, 2019.

Siollun, M. *Soldiers of Fortune: Nigerian Politics Under Buhari and Babangida (1983–1993)*. Abuja, Cassava Republic Press, 2013.

Nigeria's Soldiers of Fortune: The Abacha and Obasanjo Years. London, C. Hurst & Co, 2019.

Smith, D. J. *A Culture of Corruption: Everyday Deception and Popular Discontent in Nigeria*. Princeton, NJ, Princeton University Press, 2007.

Smith, M. J. *Boko Haram: Inside Nigeria's Unholy War*. London, I.B. Tauris, 2015.

Soyinka, W. *The Open Sore of a Continent: a Personal Narrative of the Nigerian Crisis (W. E. B. Du Bois Institute Series)*. Oxford, Oxford University Press, 1998.

Thurston, A. *Salafism in Nigeria: Islam, Preaching, and Politics*. Cambridge, Cambridge University Press, 2016.

Udogu, E. I. *Nigeria in the Twenty-First Century: Strategies for Political Stability and Peaceful Coexistence*. Lawrenceville, NJ, Africa World Press, 2005.

Usman, Z. *Economic Diversification in Nigeria The Politics of Building a Post-Oil Economy*. London, Zed Books, 2022.

Venter, A. *Biafra's War 1967–1970: A Tribal Conflict in Nigeria That Left a Million Dead*. Solihull, Helion and Co., 2016.

Walker, A. *'Eat the Heart of the Infidel': The Harrowing of Nigeria and the Rise of Boko Haram*. London, C. Hurst & Co., 2016.

Watson, R. *Civil Disorder is the Disease of Ibadan: Chieftaincy and Civic Culture in a Colonial City (Western African Studies)*. Columbus, OH, Ohio University Press, 2002.

Williams, G. *State and Society in Nigeria*. Lagos, Malthouse Press, 2019.

RÉUNION

Physical and Social Geography

Réunion is a volcanic island in the Indian Ocean lying at the southern extremity of the Mascarene Plateau. Mauritius lies some 190 km to the north-east and Madagascar about 800 km to the west. The island is roughly oval in shape, being about 65 km long and up to 50 km wide; the total area is 2,507 sq km (968 sq miles). Volcanoes have developed along a north-west to south-east angled fault; Piton de la Fournaise (2,632 m) most recently erupted in September 2022. The other volcanoes are now extinct, although their cones rise to 3,000 m and dominate the island. The height of the volcanoes and the frequent summer cyclones help to create abundant rainfall, which averages 4,714 mm annually in the uplands, and 686 mm at sea level. Temperatures vary greatly according to altitude, being tropical at sea level, averaging between 20°C (68°F) and 28°C (82°F), but much cooler in the uplands, with average temperatures of between 8°C (46°F) and 19°C (66°F), owing to frequent winter frosts.

The population of Réunion has more than doubled since the 1940s, reaching 868,846 at 1 January 2022, giving a population density of 346.6 inhabitants per sq km. According to official figures, at 1 January 2021 29.6% of Réunion's population was under 20 years of age, while 51.1% of the population was aged between 20 and 59 years. The capital is Saint-Denis, with 153,810 inhabitants at the January 2019 census. Other major towns include Saint-Paul, with 103,208 inhabitants, and Saint-Pierre and Le Tampon, with 84,982 and 79,824 inhabitants, respectively, in January 2019. The population is of mixed origin, including people of European, African, Indian and Chinese descent.

History

Réunion (formerly known as Bourbon) was first occupied in 1642 by French settlers, and was governed as a colony until 1946, when it received full departmental status. In 1974 it became a Département d'Outre-mer (Overseas Department) with the status of a region. Réunion administered the small and uninhabited Indian Ocean islands of Bassas da India, Juan de Nova, Europa and the Iles Glorieuses, which are also claimed by Madagascar, and Tromelin, which is also claimed by both Madagascar and Mauritius, until January 2005 when they were placed under the authority of the Prefect, Chief Administrator of the French Southern and Antarctic Territories.

In January 1986 France was admitted to the Indian Ocean Commission (IOC), owing to its sovereignty over Réunion. Réunion was given the right to host ministerial meetings of the IOC, but, because of its non-sovereign status, is not eligible to occupy the presidency.

In the March 1986 elections to the French Assemblée Nationale (National Assembly), which took place under a system of proportional representation, the number of deputies from Réunion was increased from three to five. The Parti Communiste Réunionnais (PCR) won two seats, while the Union pour la Démocratie Française (UDF), the Rassemblement pour la République (RPR) and a newly formed right-wing party, France-Réunion-Avenir (FRA), each secured one seat. In the concurrent elections to the 45-seat Conseil Régional (Regional Council) the centre-right RPR-UDF alliance and FRA together received 54.1% of the votes cast, winning 18 and eight seats, respectively, while the PCR secured 13 seats.

The authorities ascribed violent protests in February 1991 to widespread discontent with the island's social and economic conditions. In March a parliamentary commission attributed the riots to the inflammatory nature of the television programmes that had been broadcast by Télé Free-DOM (a popular, but unlicensed, island television service) in the weeks preceding the disturbances, specifically blaming the station's director, Dr Camille Sudre, who was also a deputy mayor of the island's capital, Saint-Denis.

Sudre presented a list of independent candidates to contest the elections to the Regional Council in March 1992. Sudre's list of candidates secured 17 seats, while the Union pour la France (UPF) obtained 14 seats, the PCR nine and the Parti Socialiste (PS) five. In concurrent elections to the Conseil Général (General Council, which was enlarged from 44 to 47 seats), right-wing candidates secured 29 seats, the number of PCR deputies increased to 12, and the number of PS deputies to six; right-wing independent Eric Boyer retained the presidency of the General Council. In late March, with the support of the PCR, Sudre was elected as President of the Regional Council by a majority of 27 votes.

At the elections to the National Assembly in March 1993, Sudre was defeated by an incumbent right-wing deputy in the second round of voting, while the incumbent UPF deputy also retained his seat. The number of PCR deputies in the National Assembly was reduced from two to one, while the PS and RPR each secured one of the remaining seats.

In May 1993 the results of the regional elections of March 1992 were annulled following an appeal against them by the PS, and Sudre was prohibited from engaging in political activity for one year, on the grounds that programmes broadcast by his privately owned radio station, Radio Free-DOM, prior to the polls had contravened regulations by campaigning on his behalf. Sudre subsequently selected his wife, Margie, to assume his candidacy in fresh elections to the Regional Council. In the elections, which took place in June 1993, the Free-DOM list of candidates, headed by Margie Sudre, secured 12 seats, while the UDF obtained 10, the PCR nine, the RPR eight, and the PS six seats. Margie Sudre was subsequently elected as President of the Regional Council, with the support of the nine PCR deputies and three dissident members of the PS, by a majority of 24 votes.

At elections to the General Council in March 1994, the PCR retained 12 seats, while the number of PS deputies increased to 12. The representation of the RPR and UDF declined to five and 11 seats, respectively (compared with six and 14 in the previous Council). Despite longstanding inter-party dissension, the PCR and PS established a coalition within the General Council, thereby securing a majority of 24 of the 47 seats. In April Christophe Payet of the PS was elected President of the General Council by a majority of 26 votes, defeating Joseph Sinimalé; the right-wing parties (which had held the presidency of the General Council for more than 40 years) boycotted the poll. The PS and PCR agreed to control the administration of the General Council jointly.

Jacques Chirac, the official candidate of the RPR for the 1995 presidential election, visited Réunion in December 1994, when he was endorsed by the organ of the PCR, *Témoignages*, after declaring his commitment to social parity between the Overseas Departments and metropolitan France. In the second round of the French presidential election in May 1995, the socialist candidate, Lionel Jospin, secured 56% of votes cast on Réunion, while Chirac won 44% (although Chirac obtained the highest number of votes nationally); the PCR and Free-DOM had advised their supporters not to vote for Edouard Balladur of the RPR because of his opposition to the principle of social parity (he came in third place in the first round).

With effect from the beginning of 1996 the social security systems of the Overseas Departments were aligned with those of metropolitan France. In April Paul Vergès, a deputy in the National Assembly representing the PCR, was elected to the French Sénat (Senate, in which Réunion had three representatives) as a joint candidate of the PCR and the PS. In the by-election to replace Vergès in the National Assembly, which took place in September, the PCR candidate was elected as the new deputy with 56.0% of the votes cast, while Margie Sudre obtained 44.0%.

Four left-wing candidates were successful in elections to the National Assembly held in May and June 1997. The incumbent PCR deputy retained his seat and was joined by two fellow PCR members and by a representative of the PS; the deputy representing the RPR-UDF coalition was also re-elected.

In February 1998 the PCR (led by Vergès), the PS and several right-wing mayors presented a joint list of candidates, known as the Rassemblement, to contest forthcoming elections. In the elections to the Regional Council, which took place in March, the Rassemblement secured 19 seats, while the UDF obtained nine seats and the RPR eight, with various left-wing candidates representing Free-DOM winning five. Vergès was elected President of the Regional Council, with the support of the deputies belonging to the Rassemblement and Free-DOM groups. In concurrent elections to an expanded 49-member General Council, right-wing candidates (including those on the Rassemblement's list) secured 27 seats, while left-wing candidates obtained 22 seats, with the PCR and the PS each winning 10 seats. Jean-Luc Poudroux of the UDF was elected President of the General Council.

A proposal by the French Secretary of State for Overseas Departments and Territories to divide Réunion into two departments, Réunion South and Réunion North, was rejected by the Senate and the National Assembly in June 2000 and November 2000, respectively.

At municipal elections in March 2001, the left-wing parties experienced significant losses, notably including the defeat of the PS mayor of Saint-Denis, Michel Tamaya. At elections to the General Council, held concurrently, the right-wing parties also made substantial gains, obtaining 38 of the 49 seats; the UDF retained its majority and Poudroux was re-elected as President. In July Elie Hoarau of the PCR was forced to resign from his post as a deputy of the National Assembly, following his conviction on charges of electoral fraud; he received a one-year prison sentence and a three-year interdiction on holding public office.

In the first round of the 2002 French presidential election, held in April, Jospin secured 39.0% of the valid votes cast in the Department (although he was eliminated nationally), followed by Chirac, who received 37.1%. In the second round, in May, Chirac overwhelmingly defeated the candidate of the extreme right-wing Front National (FN), Jean-Marie Le Pen, with 91.9% of the vote. At legislative elections in June, the new Union pour la Majorité Présidentielle (UMP, which had recently been formed by the merger of the RPR, the Démocratie Libérale and elements of the UDF) won three of Réunion's seats in the National Assembly, while the PCR and the PS secured one apiece. In November the UMP was renamed the Union pour un Mouvement Populaire, retaining the same acronym.

In the elections to the Regional Council of March 2004, the Alliance, a joint list of candidates led by the PCR, secured 27 seats. The UMP won 11 seats, and an alliance of the PS and Les Verts Réunion obtained seven. Following concurrent elections to the General Council, to renew 25 of the 49 seats, right-wing representatives held 30 seats, while left-wing representatives held 19. On 1 April Nassimah Dindar of the UMP was elected to succeed Poudroux as President of the General Council. Vergès was re-elected as President of the Regional Council on the following day.

In May 2005 a national referendum on ratification of the proposed constitutional treaty of the European Union was held; 59.9% of those who voted in Réunion (on a turnout of around 53%) joined with a majority of French voters in rejecting the treaty.

In the first round of the 2007 French presidential election, held in April, Ségolène Royal of the PS secured 46.2% of the votes cast in Réunion, while Nicolas Sarkozy of the UMP received 25.1%. Sarkozy was elected to the presidency in the second round, in May; however, voting on Réunion again favoured Royal, who received 63.6% of the island vote. Legislative elections took place in June when the UMP retained two of its seats in the National Assembly, while the representation of the PS doubled to two and the remaining seat was again won by the PCR. In March 2008 Dindar was re-elected to the presidency of the General Council.

In January 2009 workers in Guadeloupe, a French overseas territory in the Caribbean, commenced industrial action in protest against rising fuel and food prices. The unrest soon spread to other Departments, including Réunion, where unemployment and living costs had increased significantly. In March protests staged in Saint-Denis to demand price reductions and a wage increase for low-paid workers degenerated into violence; police fired tear gas to disperse the crowds.

At elections to the Regional Council in March 2010, the La Réunion en Confiance alliance led by Didier Robert of the UMP won 27 seats. The Liste de l'Alliance, headed by Vergès' PCR, took 12 seats, while the PS-led Pour une Réunion plus Juste avec l'Union des Socialistes alliance secured six. Robert was elected to succeed Vergès as President of the Regional Council. In the elections to the Senate held in September 2011 the number of representatives from Réunion was increased from three to four.

In early 2012 further social unrest erupted, initially directed at the high cost of fuel, with transporters blocking fuel outlets; subsequently, protests against the generally high cost of living spread across the island and security forces were brought in from France to quell the violence. Following negotiations between local politicians, civil society representatives, transporters and petrol companies, an agreement was reached to lower prices of fuel and electricity for households on modest incomes and to freeze the prices of 60 staple products.

In the first round of the 2012 French presidential election, held in April, François Hollande (of the PS) secured 53.3% of the votes cast on Réunion, while the incumbent President Sarkozy won 18.0%. In the second ballot, in May, Hollande secured 71.5% of Réunion's ballot, comprehensively defeating Sarkozy, who won only 28.5%. Hollande also triumphed nationally and was sworn in as President later that month. In the legislative elections, which took place in June, Réunion's representation in the National Assembly was increased from five to seven seats. The PS secured five of the seats, with the two remaining mandates won, respectively, by Huguette Bello, the leader of the newly founded Pour La Réunion (PLR, a breakaway party from the PCR), and a representative of Le Centre pour la France (a coalition led by the Mouvement Démocrate—MoDem).

The French Minister of Overseas Territories, Victorin Lurel, visited Réunion in July 2012 to hold discussions with the local authorities regarding the high cost of living on the island. A bill to address the problem of inflated prices (and associated social unrest) in Réunion and other French Overseas Territories, drafted by Lurel, was promulgated in November. In November 2013 Lurel announced a decree (which entered into force on 1 January 2014) to regulate fuel prices in the Overseas Departments.

At the departmental elections held in March 2015, in accordance with national legislation adopted in May 2013, the General Council was renamed the Conseil Départemental (Departmental Council) and was expanded to comprise 50 members. Of these, 12 represented a grouping of right-wing parties, 10 were representatives of the UMP, eight were from the Union de la Droite, six were from the PS, and both the Union Démocrates et Indépendants and the Parti Communiste Français secured four representatives. Dindar was elected as President of the Departmental Council on 2 April 2015.

At regional elections, conducted in December 2015, the Union de la Droite's Réunionnous list, headed by Robert, won 52.7% of the second-round ballot and gained control of 29 of the 45 seats on the Regional Council. The left-wing Liste de Rassemblement Conduite par Bello, with 47.3% of the vote, secured the remaining 16 seats. Robert was re-elected as President of the Regional Council on 18 December.

In February 2016 President Hollande appointed Ericka Bareigts, one of Réunion's PS deputies in the National Assembly, to his cabinet to serve as Secretary of State responsible for equality, and in August she became Minister of Overseas Territories. Bareigts' many official visits to Réunion during 2016 largely focused on efforts to address housing shortages and the high rate of unemployment; to this end, the minister announced that the French Government would provide the territory with additional funding for various housing, education, training and job creation programmes.

In February 2017 the French parliament adopted further legislation (tabled by Bareigts) aimed at reducing the economic inequalities that still existed between mainland France and its overseas territories. The Loi Égalité Réelle Outre-mer (Real Overseas Equality Act) was intended to address the high cost of living and the lack of socioeconomic development in the territories.

In the first round of the French presidential election, held on 23 April 2017, Jean-Luc Mélenchon, representing a new left-wing parliamentary movement, La France Insoumise, secured 24.5% of the votes cast in Réunion, while Marine Le Pen of the FN received 23.5%. Le Pen was placed second nationally and contested the run-off on 7 May against Emmanuel Macron of the En Marche! movement, who decisively won the contest with 66.1% of the valid votes cast nationally (and 60.3% of the votes in Réunion). In the elections to the National Assembly, held on 11 and 18 June, Les Républicains (as the UMP had been renamed in May 2015) won three of Réunion's seven seats, while the left-wing Divers Gauche grouping won two seats, MoDem one seat and Bareigts of the PS obtained the remaining seat. Cyrille Melchior of Les Républicains was elected President of the Departmental Council in December 2017, succeeding Dindar, who had been legally obliged to relinquish the presidency after being elected to the Senate in September.

In July 2018 the Constitutional Council ruled that MoDem National Assembly deputy Thierry Robert had failed to comply with parliamentary tax regulations and ordered him to vacate his seat. The ensuing by-election, held in September, was won by the candidate of Les Républicains.

The anti-Government gilets jaunes ('yellow vests') protest movement, which had emerged in France during 2018 in response to increasing fuel prices, spread to Réunion in mid-November. Demonstrations were staged in protest against the high cost of living, rising taxes, persistent unemployment and the lack of transparency in local government. Demonstrators blockaded roads, the port and the main airport, precipitating violent clashes with the police; outbreaks of looting and rioting were also reported. In an attempt to restore order, the Prefect imposed a night-time curfew, while the French Government deployed security reinforcements to the island. Furthermore, the Minister of Overseas Territories, Annick Girardin, visited Réunion in late November and announced an increase in social spending and a package of measures to address the demonstrators' concerns. Although sporadic protest action continued, the movement appeared to have lost most of its momentum by early 2019.

In July 2019 Réunion concluded a 'convergence and transformation contract' with the French Government, which provided for €608m. of development financing for the territory in 2019–22. During a visit to Réunion by Macron in October 2019, he announced various initiatives to support the territory, including a new €700m. training and employment scheme and a €45m. agricultural production fund. Nevertheless, the President's visit was marked by several, at times violent, anti-Government protests.

Controversial plans by the Macron administration to restructure the French pension system prompted large demonstrations and strikes in France, Réunion and a number of the other overseas territories in late 2019. Trade unions claimed that the proposed reforms would result in lower pensions and a higher retirement age for many workers. Despite some concessions by the Government, further protests and industrial action took place in Réunion in early 2020.

In June 2020, in the second round of municipal elections, former Minister of Overseas Territories Ericka Bareigts (of the PS) defeated the long-serving President of the Regional Council, Didier Robert (of Les Républicains), to be elected as the first female mayor of Saint-Denis, with 58.9% of the vote. In September a by-election was held to elect a new representative from Réunion to the National Assembly, occasioned by Bello's departure from the legislature in July following her election as mayor of Saint-Paul; the PLR candidate was elected as the new deputy, securing 72.0% of the votes cast in the second round of voting.

Meanwhile, on 11 March 2020 Réunion reported its first confirmed case of COVID-19, which had first appeared in the People's Republic of China in late 2019 and subsequently escalated into a global pandemic. The French Government declared a state of health emergency on 23 March 2020, covering the mainland and overseas territories. Réunion's international airport was closed to commercial flights at the end of March, and various other measures were introduced in an effort to curb the spread of the virus, including the closure of schools and non-essential businesses, international and domestic travel restrictions, and a ban on social gatherings. Following a decrease in the number of confirmed cases, the restrictions were eased from April and schools reopened in August. However, a resurgence in the virus led to the French Government declaring a second state of health emergency in October. Strict lockdown measures were reimposed in Réunion in November, as the infection rate continued to escalate.

During a visit to Réunion in August 2020 the Minister of Overseas Territories, Sébastien Lecornu, announced an economic recovery plan for the island, involving some €2,000m. in allocated funds. A COVID-19 vaccination programme was launched in Réunion in mid-January 2021. At the end of that month travel restrictions between the territory and mainland France were reintroduced owing to renewed concerns about the virus. Between February and early March more than 60 health personnel were dispatched from France to Réunion to support the local health care teams. Although restrictions were eased in mid-2021, they were tightened again in December due to the spread of the highly contagious Omicron variant. According to World Health Organization figures, 474,623 confirmed cases of COVID-19 had been reported in Réunion by 21 September 2022, with 884 fatalities, a rate of around 90.8 per 100,000 of the population. By that date 66.6% of the population had received three doses of the vaccine.

At regional elections, conducted on 20 and 27 June 2021, the Union à Gauche, headed by Bello, won 51.9% of the second-round ballot and gained control of 29 of the 45 seats on the Regional Council. The Union au Centre et à Droite, headed by Didier Robert, with 48.1% of the vote in the second round, secured the remaining 16 seats. Bello was elected as President of the Regional Council on 2 July, replacing Robert. Following concurrent elections to the Departmental Council, the 50 seats were allocated as follows: 20 to various left-wing groups, 14 to various right-wing groups, 10 to various centrist groups, four to miscellaneous groups, and two to the Union au Centre et à Gauche. Melchior of Les Républicains was re-elected as President of the Departmental Council on 1 July, by 38 votes to 12.

The criminal trial of Dindar, the representative for Réunion in the French Senate and former President of the General/Departmental Council, finally commenced in Saint-Denis in March 2021. She was accused of exerting undue influence in the recruitment of two staff members while serving as President of the Departmental Fire and Rescue Service in 2015–18.

In the first round of the presidential election, held on 10 April 2022, Mélenchon, representing La France Insoumise, won 40.3% of the votes cast in Réunion, while Le Pen of the Rassemblement National (as the Front National had been restyled in 2018) received 24.7%. Le Pen was placed second nationally and contested the run-off poll on 24 April against Macron, who won the national contest decisively (although Le Pen secured 59.6% of votes in Réunion). In the elections to the National Assembly on 12 and 19 June, six of Réunion's seven seats were secured by Divers Gauche, with the remaining seat being won by Divers Droite.

Economy

Revised by the editorial staff

As a result of its connection with France, Réunion's economy is relatively developed, especially in comparison with its sub-Saharan African neighbours. During 2010–19 Réunion's population increased at an average annual rate of 0.5%, compared with 1.5% during 1999–2009. According to official estimates, the population at 1 January 2022 was 868,846. In 2020, according to official figures, Réunion's gross domestic product (GDP), measured at current prices, was €19,151m.; in that year GDP per head totalled €22,354. GDP increased, in real terms, at an average annual rate of 2.9% in 2014–18. According to the Institut d'Emission des Départements d'Outre-Mer (IEDOM), GDP increased by 3.2% in 2017, by 1.7% in 2018 and by 2.3% in 2019; although the economy contracted by 4.2% in 2020, it rebounded in 2021 (see below).

The economy has traditionally been based on agriculture, but in 2018 the sector directly contributed only 1.9% of GDP and in 2021, according to IEDOM, workers employed in agriculture, forestry and fishing accounted for a mere 1.2% of the salaried working population. The number of farms decreased from 9,300 in 2000 to 6,282 in 2020, while over the same period utilized agricultural land area decreased from 54,510 ha to 38,774 ha. In recent years some 19% of the total land area has been cultivated; around a further 21% of land is classified as agricultural but remains uncultivated, mainly because of the volcanic nature of the soil, but also owing to increasing urbanization. Sugar cane is the principal crop and has formed the basis of the economy for over a century; in 2019 22,700 ha were under sugar cane cultivation. According to IEDOM, in 2021 sugar and rum accounted for 23.6% of export earnings (sugar 17.9% and rum 5.7%). The cane is grown on nearly all the good cultivable land up to 800 m above sea level on the leeward side of the island, except in the relatively dry north-west, and up to 500 m on the windward side. According to estimates by the UN's Food and Agriculture Organization (FAO), 1.8m. metric tons of sugar cane were harvested in 2018. The secondary usage of agricultural land is for fodder, and this sector is growing, with relatively high yields. According to IEDOM, agricultural gross value added increased by 8.5% in 2019, by 0.1% in 2020 and by 0.9% in 2021.

Geraniums, vetiver and ylang ylang are grown for the production of aromatic essences. An agreement between Réunion, Madagascar and the Comoros concerning price and export quotas on vanilla ended in 1992, and production of vanilla on Réunion in that year reached 116.5 metric tons. However, between 1997 and 2003 annual production averaged just over 32 tons, and since then output has remained low (totalling just 4 tons in 2020, according to IEDOM). Tobacco cultivation (introduced at the beginning of the 20th century) produced a crop of 192.8 tons in 1988. Cyclone damage destroyed 115 of the island's 400 tobacco drying sheds in 1989/90, and production declined sharply, to 107.8 tons in 1990, and to just 22 tons in 1992; estimated annual production during 2000–17 remained at a constant of around 20 tons. A variety of tropical fruit is grown for export, including pineapples, lychees, bananas and mangoes, and the island is self-sufficient in cattle and pigs, and 80% self-sufficient in vegetables. Overall, however, substantial food imports are necessary to supply the dense population.

Although fish are not abundant off Réunion's coast, the commercial fishing industry is an important source of income and employment, especially in the deep-sea sector. According to FAO, the total catch in 2020 was an estimated 2,670 metric tons. In 2021 fishery products accounted for 23.1% of total export revenue.

In 2018 industry (including mining, manufacturing, construction and power) contributed 12.1% of GDP, and employed 12.3% of the salaried working population in 2020, according to provisional estimates. The principal branch of manufacturing is food processing, particularly the production of sugar and rum. Other significant sectors include the fabrication of construction materials, mechanics, printing, metalwork, textiles and garments, and electronics.

No mineral resources have been identified in Réunion, and imports of energy products comprised 9.6% of the value of total imports in 2021. Energy is derived principally from thermal and hydroelectric power. Power plants at Bois-Rouge and Le Gol produce around 45% of the island's total energy requirements; almost one-third of the electricity generated is produced using a mixture of coal and bagasse, a by-product of sugar cane. Total electricity production in 2021 was 3,088m. kWh. In recent years Réunion has made considerable investment in the development of renewable energy sources (particularly solar power), with the aim of becoming self-sufficient in energy by 2030. In 2020 renewable energy sources provided nearly 31% of total electricity produced.

Services (including transport, communications, trade and finance) contributed 86.0% of GDP in 2018, and employed an estimated 86.5% of the salaried working population in 2020. The public sector accounts for more than two-thirds of employment in the services sector. The development of tourism is actively being promoted, and it is hoped that increased investment in this sector will lead to higher receipts and will help to reduce the current account deficit, as well as provide new jobs. The COVID-19 pandemic had a drastic impact on the tourism industry in 2020; in that year tourist arrivals totalled 216,716 (the majority of whom were from metropolitan France), representing a 59.4% decrease from the 533,622 arrivals registered in 2019. According to IEDOM, tourism receipts fell from €410.0m. in 2019 to €158.3m. in 2020. However, a gradual recovery was evident in 2021, when tourist arrivals rose to 250,800 and receipts to €192.0m.

In 2021 Réunion recorded a trade deficit of €5,767m. The principal sources of imports in 2020 were France (58.7%) and other member states of the European Union (13.6%); Mauritius, Madagascar, the People's Republic of China and Singapore were also important suppliers. The principal markets for exports in 2020 were France (44.2%), Mayotte, Madagascar and India. The principal exports in 2021 were sugar, rum, fishery products and other non-durable consumer goods (together accounting for 55.3% of total exports), capital goods and intermediate goods. The principal imports in that year were non-durable consumer goods (accounting for 30.6% of total imports), capital goods (30.3%, with transport equipment constituting 14.6%) and intermediate goods. The contribution of exports to GDP declined from 12% at the beginning of the 1970s to 2% in 1992, owing partly to a decline in world sugar prices, and stood at only an estimated 1.7% in 2016. In 1998 the annual volume of goods passing through the island's ports increased, exceeding 3m. metric tons for the first time, principally as a result of a rise in imports. The figure has risen steadily since that time, reaching some 5.9m. tons in 2019 before declining to 5.3m. tons in 2020 as a result of the pandemic; however, it rose again to 6.0m. tons in 2021. Fuel imports have been boosted by the growing number of motor vehicles and a greater number of direct flights to Réunion.

The close connection with France protects the island from the dangers inherent in the narrowness of its economic base. Nevertheless, unemployment and inflation, compounded after 1974 by a number of bankruptcies among small sugar planters, have caused major social and economic problems. The annual rate of inflation averaged 0.8% in 2010–19; consumer prices increased by 0.4% in 2019 and remained stable in 2020. Although the level of unemployment remained worryingly high among Réunion's youth (aged 15–24 years), the overall unemployment rate decreased from 21% in 2019 to just over 18% in the third quarter of 2021. While the employment rate increased from 46% of the population aged 15 to 64 years in 2019 to 48% in 2020, it remained well below the employment rate of more than 65% in metropolitan France. Since 1980 the Government has invested significant sums in a series of public works projects in an effort to create jobs and to alleviate the high level of seasonal unemployment following the sugar cane harvest. However, large numbers of workers continue to emigrate in search of employment each year, principally to France.

Réunion has a relatively developed economy, but remains dependent on financial aid from France. The economy has traditionally been based on agriculture and is, therefore, vulnerable to poor climatic conditions. From the 1990s the production of sugar cane (the principal agricultural activity) was adversely affected by increasing urbanization, which resulted in a decline in agricultural land. Economic progress has been largely sustained by tourism and domestic consumption. Réunion's economy expanded by 3.1% in 2016, supported by increased domestic demand and investment, an upswing in tourist arrivals and positive developments in the agricultural sector. Growth of 3.2% was recorded in 2017. An outbreak of civil unrest in late 2018 caused widespread economic disruption, while poor weather conditions undermined sugar production, exports declined and unemployment rose. Although GDP growth decelerated to 1.7% in 2018, investment levels and construction activity both increased in that year and the tourism sector performed strongly. The economy recorded growth of 2.3% in 2019, as falling unemployment, lower inflation and an increase in the number of salaried jobs—particularly in the private sector—encouraged domestic consumption. In mid-April 2020, in response to the outbreak of COVID-19, French Prime Minister Edouard Philippe announced a series of social emergency measures for Réunion, including an exceptional benefit payment to families to cover increased food costs. The French Government also created a solidarity fund to provide financial support to companies affected by the crisis; additional measures were introduced to help self-employed workers. The 2020–25 investment plan announced by the Departmental Council in July 2020, in addition to providing €70m. of short-term assistance to the most vulnerable and disadvantaged households, envisaged the investment of €500m., primarily in housing, infrastructure, tourism, agriculture and food security. Construction of a new coastal road resumed in September, following a commitment by France to provide financial support for the project. The new road was scheduled for completion in 2023. Although the COVID-19 crisis had a seriously adverse effect on the tourism and construction sectors in 2020, Réunion's economy proved relatively resilient overall, buoyed by the authorities' swift and efficient implementation of support measures. The economy contracted by 4.2% in 2020, compounded by a poor sugar cane harvest as a result of drought conditions; however, it grew by an estimated 4.5% in 2021, amid higher rates of consumption and labour participation, as well as a successful COVID-19 vaccination campaign. In December the Departmental Council approved the budget for 2022: this included a 6% increase in expenditure, partly owing to higher welfare spending.

Statistical Survey

Source (unless otherwise indicated): Institut National de la Statistique et des Etudes Economiques, Service Régional de la Réunion, 15 rue de l'Ecole, 97490 Sainte-Clotilde; tel. 262-48-81-00; internet www.insee.fr.

AREA AND POPULATION

Area: 2,507 sq km (968 sq miles).

Population: 706,180 (males 347,076, females 359,104) at census of 8 March 1999; 861,210 at census of 1 January 2019. Note: According to new census methodology, data for 2019 refer to median figures based on the collection of raw data over a five-year period (2017–2021). *2022*(official estimate at 1 January): 868,846.

Density (at 1 January 2022): 346.6 per sq km.

Population by Age and Sex ('000, official estimates at 1 January 2022): *0–14 years:* 187.0 (males 93.8, females 93.2); *15–64 years:* 559.2 (males 263.7, females 295.5); *65 years and over:* 122.7 (males 53.7, females 69.0); *Total* 868.9 (males 411.2, females 457.7).

Principal Localities (census of 1 January 2019): Saint-Denis (capital) 153,810; Saint-Paul 103,208; Saint-Pierre 84,982; Le Tampon 79,824; Saint-André 56,902; Saint-Louis 53,120.

Births, Marriages and Deaths (2021 unless otherwise indicated): Registered live births 13,470 (birth rate 15.7 per 1,000); Registered marriages 1,921 (2020) (marriage rate 3.5 per 1,000 in 2017); Registered deaths 5,800 (death rate 6.8 per 1,000).

Life Expectancy (years at birth, 2021): Males 76.7; females 83.4.

Employment (persons aged 15 years and over, provisional estimates at 31 December 2020): Agriculture, forestry and fishing 3,141; Mining and quarrying 263; Electricity, gas and water supply 3,981; Manufacturing 13,887; Construction 14,674; Wholesale and retail trade; repair of motor vehicles, motorcycles, etc. 34,622; Transport 12,237; Hotels and restaurants 9,658; Information and communication 3,906; Financial activities and real estate 8,288; Private services 29,119; Public administration and defence; education, health and social work 111,689; Other community, social and personal service activities 20,966; *Total employed* 266,431. Note: Data exclude 38,320 persons employed without salary.

HEALTH AND WELFARE

Total Fertility Rate (children per woman, 2021): 2.5.

Physicians (per 1,000 head, 2012): 2.8.

Hospital Beds (per 1,000 head, 2000): 3.7.

Note: For sources and definitions, see Health and Welfare Statistics: Sources and Definitions section (europaworld.com/credits).

AGRICULTURE, ETC.

Principal Crops ('000 metric tons, 2018, FAO estimates): Aubergines (Eggplants) 1.0; Bananas 10.5; Beans, green 2.9; Cabbages and other brassicas 2.5; Carrots and turnips 1.1; Cauliflowers and broccoli 6.0; Lettuce and chicory 3.9; Maize 13.8; Mangoes, mangosteens and guavas 2.5; Onions and shallots, green 4.4; Potatoes 4.9; Pineapples 17.6; Pumpkins, squash and gourds 0.7; Sugar cane 1,789.3; Tangerines, mandarins, etc. 2.8; Tomatoes 6.4. *Aggregate Production* ('000 metric tons, may include official, semi-official or estimated data): Total fruits (excl. melons) 64.4; Total vegetables (incl. melons) 42.9.

Livestock ('000 head, 2018, FAO estimates): Cattle 31.0; Chickens 17,526; Goats 41.9; Pigs 68.8; Sheep 0.9.

Livestock Products ('000 metric tons, 2018, FAO estimates): Cattle meat 1.6; Cow's milk 21.5; Chicken meat 20.1; Pig meat 15.2; Rabbit meat 2.6; Hen eggs 7.3.

Forestry ('000 cu m, 2020, FAO estimates): *Roundwood Removals:* Sawlogs, veneer logs and logs for sleepers 10.6; Other industrial wood 0.9; Fuel wood 99.1; Total 110.5.

Fishing (metric tons, live weight, 2020): Capture 2,660 (Albacore 286; Yellowfin tuna 649; Bigeye tuna 164; Swordfish 898; Blue marlin 299); Aquaculture 10 (FAO estimate); *Total catch* (incl. others) 2,670 (FAO estimate).

Source: FAO.

INDUSTRY

Selected Products (metric tons, 2021 unless otherwise indicated): Sugar 159,600; Oil of geranium 2 (2007); Oil of vetiver root 0.4 (2002); Rum (hl) 113,425 (2020); Electrical energy (million kWh) 3,088 (Source: partly Institut d'Emission des Départements d'Outremer, *La Réunion: Rapport Annuel 2021*).

FINANCE

Currency and Exchange Rates: The French franc was used until the end of February 2002. Euro notes and coins were introduced on 1 January 2002, and the euro became the sole legal tender from 18 February. Some of the figures in this Survey are still in terms of francs. For details of exchange rates, see Mayotte.

Budgets (regional government, excl. debt rescheduling, € million, 2021): Total revenue 637.7 (Current 538.1, Capital 99.6); Total expenditure 812.6 (Current 414.4, Capital 398.2). Source: Observatoire des Finances et de la Gestion Publique Locales (OFGL), Paris.

Cost of Living (Consumer Price Index; base: 2015 = 100): All items 100.5 in 2017; 102.4 in 2018; 102.8 in 2019.

Expenditure on the Gross Domestic Product (€ million at current prices, 2021, estimates): Private final consumption expenditure 13,000; Government final consumption expenditure 8,300; Gross capital formation 4,600; *Total domestic expenditure* 25,900; Exports of goods 600; *Less* Imports of goods 6,400; Tourist expenditure 200; *GDP in market prices* 20,400.

Gross Domestic Product by Economic Activity (€ million at current prices, 2007): Agriculture, forestry and fishing 177; Mining, manufacturing, electricity, gas and water 917; Construction 1,274; Wholesale and retail trade 1,182; Transport and communications 820; Finance and insurance 704; Public administration 1,521; Education, health and social work 3,128; Other services (incl. hotels and restaurants) 3,472; *Sub-total* 13,196; *Less* Financial intermediation services indirectly measured 462; *Gross value-added at basic prices* 12,734; Taxes on products, *less* subsidies on products 1,235; *GDP in market prices* 13,969.

EXTERNAL TRADE

Principal Commodities (€ million, 2021): *Imports:* Capital goods 1,858.6 (Transport equipment 897.4); Durable consumer goods 392.5; Non-durable consumer goods 1,879.4; Intermediate goods 1,229.1; Energy products 589.4; Total (incl. others) 6,134.6. *Exports:* Capital goods 81.7; Non-durable consumer goods 203.5 (Sugar and rum 86.8; Fishery products 84.8); Intermediate goods 30.4; Total (incl. others) 367.8 (Source: Source: Institut d'Emission des Départements d'Outre-mer, *La Réunion: Rapport Annuel 2021*).

Principal Trading Partners (€ million, 2010): *Imports:* Belgium 52.1; China, People's Republic 287.5; France 2,312.8; Germany 200.6; Italy 89.8; Singapore 389.8; South Africa 100.0; Spain 62.0; Total (incl. others) 4,265.2. *Exports f.o.b.:* France 88.9; Hong Kong 13.4; Italy 6.7; Japan 10.5; Madagascar 15.1; Mauritius 7.4; Mayotte 26.5; Spain 18.0; USA 8.4; Total (incl. others) 281.5. *2021:* Total imports 6,134.6; Total exports 367.8 (Source: Institut d'Emission des Départements d'Outre-mer, *La Réunion: Rapport Annuel 2021*).

TRANSPORT

Road Traffic (new vehicle registrations, 2021): Private vehicles 26,660; Commercial vehicles 6,099; Other motor vehicles and public transport 404.

Shipping: *Flag Registered Fleet* (at 31 December 2021): Vessels 16; Total displacement 11,271 grt. Source: Lloyd's List Intelligence (www.bit.ly/LLintelligence). *Traffic* (2013 unless otherwise indicated): Passengers carried 41,883 (2014); Vessels entered 709 (2007); Freight unloaded 3,391,900 metric tons; Freight loaded 625,100 metric tons; Containers unloaded 111,952 TEUs (2007); Containers loaded 112,921 TEUs (2007).

Civil Aviation (2013): Passenger arrivals 1,030,000; Passenger departures 1,032,000; Freight unloaded 17,510 metric tons; Freight loaded 7,146 metric tons (Source: Institut d'Emission des Départements d'Outre-mer, *Rapport Annuel 2013*).

TOURISM

Tourist Arrivals: 533,622 in 2019; 216,716 in 2020; 250,800 in 2021 (Source: Institut d'Emission des Départements d'Outre-mer, *La Réunion: Rapport Annuel 2021*).

Arrivals by Country of Residence (2013): France (metropolitan) 337,200; Other EU 21,700; Total (incl. others) 416,000 (Source: Institut d'Emission des Départements d'Outre-mer, *La Réunion: Rapport Annuel 2013*).

Tourism Receipts (US $ million, excl. passenger transport): 427 in 2017; 511 in 2018; 459 in 2019 (provisional) (Source: World Tourism Organization).

COMMUNICATIONS MEDIA

Telephones ('000 main lines in use, 2010): 480.9.

Mobile Telephone Subscriptions ('000, 2008): 579.2.

Broadband Subscriptions ('000, 2009): 185.0.

Internet Users (2009): 300,000.

Source: International Telecommunication Union.

EDUCATION

Pre-primary and Primary (2020/21): Schools 539 (pre-primary 156, primary 383); pupils 114,667 (public sector pupils 104,323, private pupils 10,344).

Secondary (2020/21): Schools 137 (120 public sector, 17 private); pupils 101,862 (public sector 93,837, private 8,025).

University (2020/21): Institutions 1; students 17,495.

Other Higher (2011/12): Students 5,879.

Teaching Staff (2020/21 unless otherwise indicated, state schools): Pre-primary and primary 7,072; Secondary 9,312; University 421 (2012/13).

Directory

The Government

(October 2022)

HEAD OF STATE

President: EMMANUEL MACRON (took office 14 May 2017; re-elected 24 April 2022).

Prefect: JÉRÔME FILIPPINI, Préfecture, 6 rue des Messageries, CS 51079, 97404 Saint-Denis Cedex; tel. 262-40-77-77; e-mail courrier@reunion.pref.gouv.fr; internet www.reunion.gouv.fr.

DEPARTMENTAL ADMINISTRATION

President of the Departmental Council: CYRILLE MELCHIOR (Les Républicains), Hôtel du Département, 2 rue de la Source, 97488 Saint-Denis Cedex; tel. 262-90-30-30; e-mail accueil@cg974.fr; internet www.departement974.fr.

President of the Regional Council: HUGUETTE BELLO (Union à Gauche), Hôtel de Région Pierre Lagourgue, ave René Cassin, Moufia, BP 67190, 97801 Saint-Denis Cedex 9; tel. 262-48-70-00; e-mail region.reunion@cr-reunion.fr; internet regionreunion.com.

Elections, Departmental Council, 20 and 27 June 2021

Party	Seats
Divers Gauche	12
Divers Centre	10
Divers Droite	8
Parti Socialiste	6
Divers	4
Les Républicains	4
Parti Communiste Français	2
Union au Centre et à Gauche	2
Union à Droite	2
Total	**50**

Elections, Regional Council, 20 and 27 June 2021

Party	Seats
Union à Gauche	29
Union au Centre et à Droite	16
Total	**45**

REPRESENTATIVES TO THE FRENCH PARLIAMENT

Deputies to the French National Assembly: NATHALIE BASSIRE (Divers Droite), PERCIVAL GAILLARD (Divers Gauche), KARIN LEBON (Divers Gauche), FRÉDÉRIC MAILLOT (Divers Gauche), PHILIPPE NAILLET (Divers Gauche), EMELINE K/BIDI (Divers Gauche), JEAN-HUGUES RATENON (Divers Gauche).

Representatives to the French Senate: NASSIMAH DINDAR (Union Centriste), JEAN-LOUIS LAGOURGUE (Les Indépendants—République et Territoires), VIVIANE MALET (Les Républicains), MICHEL DENNEMONT (La République En Marche).

GOVERNMENT OFFICES

Department of the Economy, Employment, Labour and Solidarity: 112 rue de la République, 97488, Saint-Denis Cedex; tel. 262-94-07-07; internet reunion.deets.gouv.fr.

Department of the Environment, Planning and Housing: 2 rue Juliette Dodu, 97706 Saint-Denis Cedex; tel. 262-40-26-26; e-mail deal-reunion@developpement-durable.gouv.fr; internet www.reunion.developpement-durable.gouv.fr.

Department of Food, Agriculture and Forestry: blvd de la Providence, 97489 Saint-Denis Cedex; tel. 262-30-89-89; e-mail daaf974@agriculture.gouv.fr; internet daaf.reunion.agriculture.gouv.fr.

Department of Youth, Sports and Social Cohesion: 14 allée des Saphirs, 97487 Saint-Denis Cedex; tel. 262-20-54-54; e-mail ce .drajes@ac-reunion.fr; internet reunion.drjscs.gouv.fr.

Political Organizations

Mouvement Démocrate (MoDem): Saint-Denis; internet www .mouvementdemocrate.fr; f. 2007; fmrly Union pour la Démocratie Française (UDF); centrist.

Mouvement pour l'Indépendance de la Réunion (MIR): f. 1981 to succeed the fmr Mouvement pour la Libération de la Réunion; grouping of parties favouring autonomy; Leader ANSELME PAYET.

Parti Communiste Réunionnais (PCR): Saint-Denis; f. 1959; Nat. Sec. ELIE HOARAU.

> **Mouvement pour l'Egalité, la Démocratie, le Développement et la Nature:** affiliated to the PCR; advocates political unity; Leader RENÉ PAYET.

Parti Socialiste—Fédération de la Réunion (PS): Immeuble Futura, 190 route des Deux Canons, 97490 Sainte-Clotilde; tel. 262-28-53-03; e-mail psreunion@wanadoo.fr; internet www .parti-socialiste.fr/federation/la-reunion; left-wing; Sec. ANNETTE GILBERT.

Pour la Réunion: Saint-Paul; f. 2012; founded as a breakaway party from the Parti Communiste Réunionnais (q.v.); 3,000 mems (2014); Pres. HUGUETTE BELLO.

Rassemblement National (RN)—Fédération de la Réunion (RN): Saint-Denis; e-mail contact@rassemblement-national974.fr; internet rassemblement-national974.fr; f. 1972; extreme right-wing.

Renaissance: 25 rue Victor Schoelcher, 97419 La Possession; internet en-marche.fr/comites/en-marche-la-reunion; formerly known as La République En Marche; present name adopted in 2022.

Les Républicains: 66 rue Victor Le Vigoureux, BP 11, 97410 Saint-Pierre; tel. 262-20-21-18; e-mail michelfontaine@republicains974 .net; internet republicains.fr/federation/974-la-reunion; f. 2002; known as the Union pour un Mouvement Populaire until May 2015; centre-right; local branch of the metropolitan party; Pres. MICHEL FONTAINE.

Les Verts Réunion: Apt 30, Res ARIAL, 132 rue Général de Gaulle, 97400 Saint-Denis; tel. 262-55-73-52; internet lesverts.fr; ecologist; Regional Sec. JEAN ERPELDINGER.

Judicial System

Court of Appeal: Palais de Justice, 166 rue Juliette Dodu, 97488 Saint-Denis; tel. 262-40-58-58; First Pres. ALAIN CHATEAUNEUF.

Religion

A substantial majority of the population are adherents of the Roman Catholic Church. There is a small Muslim community.

CHRISTIANITY

The Roman Catholic Church

Réunion comprises a single diocese, directly responsible to the Holy See. The number of adherents is equivalent to around 80% of the population.

Bishop of Saint-Denis de la Réunion: Mgr GILBERT GUILLAUME MARIE-JEAN AUBRY, Evêché, 36 rue de Paris, BP 10055, 97461 Saint-Denis Cedex; tel. 262-94-85-70; e-mail eveche.lareunion@wanadoo .fr; internet www.diocese-reunion.org.

The Press

DAILIES

Journal de l'Ile de la Réunion: Centre d'affaires Cadjee, 62 blvd du Chaudron, BP 40019, 97491 Sainte-Clotilde Cedex; tel. 262-48-66-00; e-mail societe@jir.fr; internet www.clicanoo.re; f. 1951; CEO and Dir of Publication JACQUES TILLIER; Editor-in-Chief PHILIPPE LE CLAIRE.

Quotidien de la Réunion et de l'Océan Indien: BP 303, 97712 Saint-Denis Cedex 9; tel. 262-92-15-10; e-mail laredaction@ lequotidien.re; internet www.lequotidien.re; f. 1976; Dir of Publication CAROLE CHANE-KI-CHUNE.

Témoignages: 6 rue du Général Emile Rolland, BP 1016, 97828 Le Port Cedex; tel. 262-55-21-21; e-mail redaction@temoignages.re; internet www.temoignages.re; f. 1944; affiliated to the Parti Communiste Réunionnais; daily; Dir GINETTE SINAPIN; Editor-in-Chief MANUEL MARCHAL.

PERIODICALS

Al-Islam: Centre Islamique de la Réunion, BP 437, 97459 Saint-Pierre Cedex; tel. 262-25-45-43; e-mail centre-islamique-reunion@ wanadoo.fr; internet www.islam-reunion.fr; f. 1975; 4 a year; Dir ISSAC GANGAT.

L'Eco Austral: Technopole de la Réunion 2, rue Emile Hugot, BP 10003, 97801 Saint-Denis Cedex 9; tel. 262-41-51-41; internet www .ecoaustral.com; f. 1993; monthly; regional economic issues; Editor ALAIN FOULON.

L'Economie de la Réunion: c/o INSEE, Parc Technologique, 10 rue Demarne, BP 13, 97408 Saint-Denis Messag Cedex 9; tel. 262-48-89-00; e-mail bureau-de-presse@insee.fr; internet www.insee.fr/ reunion; 4 a year; Dir of Publication VALERIE ROUX; Editor-in-Chief CLAIRE GRANGE.

Leader Réunion: blvd du Chaudron, 97490 Sainte-Clotilde; tel. 692-28-71-13; e-mail infos@leaderreunionmagazine; internet www .leaderreunion.fr; Dir of Publication CAROLE MANOTE.

Lutte Ouvrière—Ile de la Réunion: BP 184, 97470 Saint-Benoît; internet www.lutte-ouvriere.org/en-regions/ile-de-la-reunion; monthly; communist; digital.

Le Mémento Industriel et Commercial Réunionnais: 80 rue Pasteur, BP 390, 97468 Saint-Denis; tel. 262-21-94-12; e-mail memento@memento.fr; internet www.memento.fr; f. 1970; monthly; Editor-in-Chief GEORGES-GUILLAUME LOUAPRE-POTTIER.

La Réunion Agricole: Chambre d'Agriculture, 24 rue de la Source, BP 134, 97463 Saint-Denis Cedex; tel. 262-94-25-94; e-mail herve .cailleaux@reunion.chambagri.fr; internet www.reunion.chambagri .fr; f. 2007; monthly; Dir JEAN-BERNARD GONTHIER; Chief Editor HERVÉ CAILLEAUX.

Visu: Immeuble Point Presse, 13 allée Bonnier, 97400 Saint-Denis; tel. 262-90-20-60; e-mail info@visu.re; f. 1982; weekly; Editor-in-Chief CHRISTIAN CHRISTIAN AH-SON.

NEWS AGENCY

Imaz Press Réunion: 12 rue Victor MacAuliffe, 97400 Saint-Denis; tel. 262-20-05-65; e-mail ipr@ipreunion.com; internet imazpress .com; f. 2000; photojournalism and news agency; Dir RICHARD BOUHET.

Broadcasting and Communications

TELECOMMUNICATIONS

Orange Réunion: 35 blvd du Chaudron, BP 7431, 97743 Saint-Denis Cedex 9; tel. 262-20-02-00; internet reunion.orange.fr; f. 2000; subsidiary of Orange France; mobile telephone operator; Dir JEAN-MARC ESCALETTES.

SFR Réunion: 21 rue Pierre Aubert, CS 62001 97743 Saint Denis Cedex 9; tel. 262-43-20-00; internet www.sfr.re; f. 1995; subsidiary of SFR Cegetel, France; mobile telephone operator; Deputy Dir-Gen. YVES GAUVIN.

Zeop: 39 rue Pierre Brossolette, 97420 Le Port; tel. 262-01-23-45; e-mail contact@zeop.re; internet www.zeop.re; f. 2008; Dir-Gen. XAVIER HERMESSE.

BROADCASTING

Réunion 1ère: 12 rue René Demarne, BP 47716, 97804 Saint-Denis Cedex 9; tel. 262-40-67-67; e-mail jttv@francetv.fr; internet la1ere .francetvinfo.fr/reunion; acquired by Groupe France Télévisions in 2004; fmrly Réseau France Outre-mer, present name adopted in 2010; radio and television relay services in French; Regional Dir (vacant).

Radio

Cherie FM Réunion: 1 rue Jean Chatel, 97400 Saint-Denis; tel. 262-97-32-00; e-mail contact@cheriefm.re; internet fb.com/ cheriereunion; Editor-in-Chief LEA BERTHAULT.

Kréol FM: 6 Ter route de Savanna, Local 2, 97460 Saint-Paul; tel. 262-22-61-76; e-mail contact@kreolfm.re; internet www.kreol.tv; Pres. THIERRY ARAYE.

NRJ Réunion: 1 rue de Kerveguen, 97490 Sainte-Clotilde; tel. 262-99-40-00; e-mail contact@nrj.re; internet www.nrj.re; commercial radio station; Station Man. THIERRY AUZOLE.

Radio Free-DOM: 131 rue Jules Auber, BP 666, 97400 Saint-Denis Cedex; tel. 262-41-51-51; e-mail web@freedom.fr; internet www

.freedom.fr; f. 1981; commercial radio station; Pres. Dr CAMILLE
SUDRE; Dir-Gen. MAYIA LE TEXIER.

RTL Réunion: 3 rue de Kerveguen, 97490 Sainte-Clotilde; tel. 262-
23-45-67; e-mail redaction@rtl.re; internet fb.com/RTLReunion;
f. 1995; commercial radio station; fmrly Radio Festival, present
name adopted in 2014; Editor-in-Chief GWEN BROT.

Television

Antenne Réunion: rue Emile Hugot, BP 80001, 97801 Saint-Denis
Cedex 9; tel. 262-48-28-28; e-mail contact@antennereunion.fr;
internet www.antennereunion.fr; f. 1991; broadcasts 10 hours daily;
Dir-Gen. MAYIA LE TEXIER.

Canal Réunion: 6 rue René Demarne, Technopole de la Réunion,
97490 Sainte-Clotilde; tel. 262-97-98-99; e-mail contact@
canalreunion.net; internet www.canalplus-reunion.com; f. 1991;
subscription television channel; broadcasts a minimum of 19 hours
daily; Dir AXEL GALLANT.

Télé Kréol: 6 Ter route de Savanna, Local 2, 97460 Saint-Paul; tel.
262-22-61-76; e-mail contact@telekreol.re; internet www.kreol.tv;
Pres. THIERRY ARAYE.

Other privately owned television services include TVB, TVE, RTV,
Télé-Réunion and TV-Run.

Finance
BANKING
Central Bank

Institut d'Emission des Départements d'Outre-mer: 4 rue
Etienne Regnault, 97400 Saint-Denis Cedex; tel. 262-90-71-00;
e-mail agence@iedom-reunion.fr; internet www.iedom.fr/
la-reunion; f. 1959; Dir PHILIPPE LA COGNATA.

Commercial Banks

Banque Française Commerciale Océan Indien (BFCOI): 58
rue Alexis de Villeneuve, BP 323, 97404 Saint-Denis Cedex; tel. 262-
40-99-00; internet www.bfcoi.com; f. 1976; Pres. PIERRE GUY-NOEL;
Gen. Man. RIDHA TEKAÏA.

Banque Publique d'Investissement: 15 rue Malartic, BP 980,
97400 Saint-Denis Cedex; tel. 262-20-93-47; e-mail reunion@
bpifrance.fr; internet www.bpifrance.fr; f. 2014; Regional Dir
CHRISTIAN QUÉRÉ.

BNP Paribas Réunion: 67 rue Juliette Dodu, BP 113, 97463 Saint-
Denis; tel. 262-40-30-02; e-mail contactreunion@bnpparibas.com;
internet www.bnpparibas.re; f. 1927; 100% owned by BNP Paribas;
Man. Dir JEAN-MARC DE COURSON.

BRED-Banque Populaire: 18 rue Jean Chatel, BP 60015, 97400
Saint-Denis; tel. 262-98-27-60; Dir STÉPHANE URBAIN.

**Caisse d'Epargne et de Prévoyance Provence-Alpes-Corse
(CEPAC):** 55 rue de Paris, 97711 Saint-Denis Cedex; tel. 262-94-
44-20; internet www.caisse-epargne.fr; f. 1853; formerly Banque de
la Réunion; Pres. JOËL CHASSARD; Gen. Man. ALAIN RIPERT.

**Caisse Régionale de Crédit Agricole Mutuel de la Réunion
(CRCAMR):** Parc Jean de Cambiaire, Cité des Lauriers, BP 84,
97462 Saint-Denis Cedex; tel. 262-40-81-81; internet www
.ca-reunion.fr; f. 1949; Chair. JOSEPH EMILE FONTAINE; Gen. Man.
FRÉDÉRIC BRETTE.

CASDEN Banque Populaire: 40 rue Juliette Dodu, 97400 Saint-
Denis; tel. 262-21-08-40; internet www.casden.fr.

Development Bank

**Société Financière pour le Développement Economique de la
Réunion (SOFIDER):** 3 rue Labourdonnais, BP 867, 97477 Saint-
Denis Cedex; tel. 262-40-32-32; internet www.sofider.re; part of the
Agence Française de Développement; Dir-Gen. FABIEN TOLEDO.

Trade and Industry
GOVERNMENT AGENCIES

**Agence de Gestion des Initiatives Locales en Matière Eur-
opéenne (AGILE)—Cellule Europe Réunion:** 3 rue Felix Guyon,
97400 Saint-Denis; tel. 262-90-10-80; e-mail celleurope@
agile-reunion.org; internet www.agile-reunion.org; responsible for
local application of EU structural funds; Dir SERGE JOSEPH.

Agence Régionale de Santé Océan Indien (ARS-OI): 2 bis ave
Georges Brassens, CS 60050, 97408 Saint-Denis Messag Cedex 9; tel.
262-97-90-00; e-mail ars-oi-delegation-reunion@ars.sante.fr; e-mail
ars-oi-delegation-reunion@ars.sante.fr; internet www.ocean-indien

.ars.sante.fr; f. 2010; responsible for implementation of health
policies in Réunion and Mayotte; Dir-Gen. MARTINE LADOUCETTE.

**Conseil Economique Social et Environnemental Régional
(CESER):** 10 rue du Béarn, BP 17191, 97804 Saint-Denis; tel.
262-97-96-30; e-mail ceser@cr-reunion.fr; internet www
.ceser-reunion.fr; f. 1984; Pres. DOMINIQUE VIENNE.

DEVELOPMENT ORGANIZATIONS

Agence Française de Développement (AFD): 44 rue Jean Cocteau, BP 20026, 97491 Sainte-Clotilde Cedex; tel. 262-90-00-90;
e-mail afdsaintdenis@afd.fr; internet www.afd.fr; Dir VIRGINIE
DELISÉE PIZZO.

**Association pour le Développement Industriel de la Réunion
(ADIR):** 30 rue Léon de Lepervanche, 97420 Le Port; tel. 262-94-43-
00; e-mail adir@adir.info; internet www.adir.info; f. 1975; Pres.
JÉRÔME ISAUTIER; Sec.-Gen. DANIEL MOREAU; 190 mems.

Chambre d'Agriculture de la Réunion: 24 rue de la Source,
97404 Saint-Denis Cedex; tel. 262-94-25-94; e-mail president@
reunion.chambagri.fr; internet www.reunion.chambagri.fr; Pres.
FRÉDERIC VIENNE; Sec. OLIVIER FONTAINE.

Jeune Chambre Economique de Saint-Denis de la Réunion:
23 rue Tourette, BP 1151, 97400 Saint-Denis; e-mail presidence
.saintdenis@jcer.fr; f. 1961; Pres. JEAN-MAX BOYER; Sec. JEAN CÉDRIC
MAILLOT.

CHAMBERS OF COMMERCE

Chambre de Commerce et d'Industrie de la Réunion (CCIR):
5B rue de Paris, BP 120, 97404 Saint-Denis Cedex; tel. 262-94-20-00;
e-mail sg.dir@reunion.cci.fr; internet reunion.cci.fr; f. 1830; Pres.
PIERRICK ROBERT; Sec. RICHARD BOQUI QUENI.

Chambre de Métiers et de l'Artisanat: 42 rue Jean Cocteau, BP
10034, 97491 Sainte-Clotilde Cedex; tel. 262-21-04-35; e-mail cdm@
cma-reunion.fr; internet www.artisanat974.fr; f. 1968; Pres. BER-
NARD PICARDO; Sec. JEAN-BERNARD DUGAIN; 14 mem. orgs.

EMPLOYERS' ASSOCIATIONS

Conseil de l'Ordre des Pharmaciens: 1 bis rue Sainte Anne,
Immeuble le Concorde, Appt. 26, 1er étage, 97400 Saint-Denis; tel.
262-41-85-51; e-mail delegation_reunion@ordre.pharmacien.fr;
Pres. CHRISTIANE VAN DE WALLE.

**Fédération Régionale des Coopératives Agricoles de la
Réunion (FRCA):** 8 bis, route de la Z.I. FRCA No. 2, 97410 Saint-Pierre;
tel. 262-96-24-40; internet www.frca-reunion.coop; f. 1979; Pres.
JOËL SORRES; Sec.-Gen. RITO FERRERE; 27 mem. orgs.

**Coopérative Agricole des Huiles Essentielles de Bourbon
(CAHEB):** 83 rue de Kerveguen, 97430 Le Tampon; BP 43, 97831
Le Tampon; tel. 262-27-02-27; f. 1963; represents producers of
essential oils; Pres. MARIE ROSE SEVERIN; Sec.-Gen. LAURENT JANCI.

Société Coopérative Agricole Fruits de la Réunion: 7 Chemin de l'Océan, 97450 Saint-Louis; e-mail scafruitsdelareunion@
gmail.com; f. 2002; Pres. CHRISTIAN BARRET.

**Union Réunionnaise des Coopératives Agricoles
(URCOOPA):** Z.I. Cambaie, BP 90, 97862 Saint-Paul Cedex;
tel. 262-45-37-10; e-mail urcoopa@urcoopa.fr; internet www
.urcoopa.fr; f. 1982; represents farmers; comprises Coop Avirons (f.
1967), Société Coopérative Agricole Nord-Est (CANE), SICA Lait
(f. 1961), and CPPR; Pres. PASCAL QUINEAU; Dir-Gen. PHILIPPE
PUISSEGUR.

Mouvement des Entreprises de France Réunion (MEDEF): 14
rampes Ozoux, BP 354, 97467 Saint-Denis; tel. 262-20-01-30; e-mail
medef.reunion@wanadoo.fr; Pres. FRANÇOIS CAILLÉ.

Ordre National de Médecins: 3 résidence Laura, 4 rue Milius,
97400 Saint-Denis; tel. 262-20-11-58; e-mail reunion@974.medecin
.fr; internet conseil974.ordre.medecin.fr; Pres. Dr BENJAMIN DUSANG;
Sec.-Gen. Dr FABRICE DARMON.

Syndicat des Pharmaciens de la Réunion: 28E ave Marcel
Hoarau, 97490 Sainte-Clotilde; tel. 262-50-56-17; e-mail synd974@
resopharma.fr; Pres. CYRIL APOSTOLOFF.

Syndicat des Producteurs de Rhum de la Réunion: chemin
Frédéline, BP 354, 97453 Saint-Pierre Cedex; tel. 262-25-84-27;
Chair. OLIVIER THIEBLIN.

Syndicat du Sucre de la Réunion: 33 rue d'Emmerez de Charmoy,
97495 Sainte-Clotilde, Cedex; tel. 262-47-76-76; internet sucre.re;
f. 1908; Pres. PHILIPPE LABRO.

UTILITIES
Electricity

EDF Réunion: 8 ave Georges Brassens, CS 62009, 97744 Saint-
Denis Cedex 9; tel. 262-28-98-00; internet reunion.edf.fr; Dir MICHEL
MAGNAN.

Water

CISE Réunion: 5 rue Camille Vergoz 97460 Saint-Denis; tel. 262-41-89-41; internet www.cise-reunion.re.

Runéo: 53 rue Sainte-Anne, CS 61011, 7743 Saint-Denis Cedex 9; tel. 262-90-25-25; e-mail contact974@veolia.com; internet www.runeo.re; f. 2017; subsidiary of Veolia Eau (France); Dir GEOFFROY MERCIER.

MAJOR COMPANIES

Brasseries de Bourbon: 60 Quai Ouest, BP 420, 97468 Saint-Denis; internet www.brasseriesdebourbon.fr; f. 1962; 85.6% owned by Heineken NV (Netherlands); brewery and distributor of alcoholic beverages and soft drinks; Pres. EDWIN BOTTERMAN; Man. WIJNSCHENK DORON.

Compagnie Laitière des Mascareignes (CILAM): 56 Quai Ouest, BP 264, 97400 Saint-Denis; tel. 262-90-27-27; f. 1965; 80% owned by mems of SICA Lait; dairy products; Pres. PAUL MARTINEL; Dir-Gen. GILLES ESPITALIER-NOËL.

Grands Travaux de l'Océan Indien (GTOI): Z.I. No. 2, BP 2016, 97824 Le Port Cedex; tel. 262-42-85-85; e-mail standard@gtoi.fr; internet www.gtoi.fr; construction and civil engineering; Dir-Gen. JEAN-MARIE MALLET.

Groupe Bernard Hayot:

Carrefour: tel. 262-29-09-09; internet www.carrefour-reunion.com; supermarkets at Sainte-Clotilde, Sainte-Suzanne and Saint-Pierre.

Cotrans Automobiles: 17 blvd du Chaudron 97490, Sainte-Clotilde; tel. 262-92-00-00; internet www.cotrans.re.

Société Réunionnaise Laitière: Le Port; e-mail contact-danone.reunion@gbh.fr; internet www.danonereunion.com; f. 1989; milk products.

Groupe Caillé: 31 rue Jean Chatel, 97400 Saint-Denis; tel. 262-94-00-44; internet groupe-caille.com; Pres. FRANÇOIS CAILLÉ.

Jules Caillé Auto: 1 rue Edouard Manès, Z.I. du Chaudron, BP 51, 97408 Saint-Denis Messagerie Cedex 9; tel. 262-48-86-00; internet www.peugeot.re; f. 1919; agent for Peugeot motor vehicles; Chair. FRANÇOIS CAILLÉ.

Groupe Marbour: Z.I. No. 1, 17 rue Armagnac, 97420 Le Port; tel. 262-42-15-24; internet www.marbour.eu; f. 1968; Dir-Gen. JEAN BOURDILLON; c. 140 employees (2017).

Cementis Réunion SA: Zone Industrielle No 1, rue Armagnac, CS61087, 97829 Le Port Cedex; tel. 262-42-58-00; e-mail commercial-reu@cementis.io; internet cementis-reunion.com; f. 1999; fmrly Holcim Réunion SA; name changed as above in 2021; operates the Centrale à Bétons de Saint-Pierre; construction materials; Dir THIERRY DESPERROIS.

Ravate Distribution: 131 rue Maréchal Leclerc, BP 450, 97400 Saint-Denis; tel. 262-90-40-40; internet www.ravate.com; f. 1939; retailers of construction materials, wood, hardware; Chair. ISSOP RAVATE; Dir ADAM RAVATE.

Société Bourbonnaise de Travaux Publics et de Constructions (SBTPC): 28 rue Jules Verne, BP 2013, 97824 Le Port; tel. 262-42-45-00; e-mail sbtpc@sbtpc.fr; internet www.sbtpc.re; subsidiary of Vinci Construction Filiales Int., France; construction and civil engineering; Pres. and Dir-Gen. ROGER GEORGES.

Société Réunionnaise de Produits Pétroliers (SRPP): Zone Industrielle No 1, CS 71169, 97829 Le Port cedex; tel. 262-42-77-77; e-mail contact@srpp.fr; internet srpp.re; storage and retail of petroleum products.

Teralta: 2 rue Amiral Bouvet, CS 91099, 97829 Le Port Cedex; tel. 262-42-69-69; e-mail teralta.contact@audemard.com; internet teralta-audemard.com; f. 2015 following acquisition of Lafarge Réunion by CRH; acquired by Groupe Audemard in 2020; construction materials; Dir-Gen. LAURENT LECOCQ.

Tereos Océan Indien: 23 rue Raymond Vergès, 97441 Sainte-Suzanne; tel. 262-58-82-82; e-mail communication-oi@tereos.com; internet www.tereos.re; f. 1923; fmrly Groupe Quartier Français; Pres. PHILIPPE LABRO; comprises:

Distillerie Rivière du Mât: chemin Manioc, Z. I. Beaufonds, 97470 Saint-Benoît; tel. 262-67-46-41; internet www.rivieredumat.com; f. 1886; Dir TEDDY BOYER.

Eurocanne: La Mare, 97438 Sainte-Marie; tel. 262-43-27-79; e-mail choarau@tereos.com; storage, packing and distribution; exports 85% of production; Dir JANICK SOUPRAYEN.

Mascarin: 1 rue Claude Chappe, ZAC 2000, BP 134, 97420 Le Port Cedex; tel. 262-55-10-20; e-mail mascarin@mascarin.fr; internet www.mascarin.fr; storage, packing and distribution; exports 90% of production; CEO FRÉDÉRIC AUCHÉ.

Sucrerie de Bois-Rouge: 2 chemin Bois-Rouge, BP 1017, Cambuston, 97440 Saint-André; tel. 262-58-83-30; e-mail clebon@tereos.com; f. 1817; 51% owned by Tereos, 39% owned by Groupe Quartier Français; produces, refines and exports sugar; fmrly Groupes Sucreries de Bourbon, acquired by Tereos in 2001; Dir JEAN CLAUDE PONY; processes c. 1m. metric tons of sugar cane per campaign; comprises:

Sucrerie du Gol: 23 rue Raymond Vergès, BP 95, 97441 Saint-Louis; tel. 262-91-29-70; e-mail communication-oi@tereos.com; internet www.tereos-oceanindien.com; Pres. PHILIPPE LABRO; processes c. 1.1m. metric tons of sugar cane per campaign.

TotalEnergies Réunion: 3 rue Jacques Prévert, Rivière des Galets, BP 286, 97827 Le Port Cedex; tel. 262-55-20-20; e-mail contact-clients@totalreunion.fr; internet services.totalenergies.re; retail and distribution of petroleum products; Dir-Gen. ELISA COEURU.

TRADE UNIONS

CFE-CGC de la Réunion: 1 Rampes Ozoux, Résidence de la Rivière, Appt 2A, BP 873, 97477 Saint-Denis Cedex; tel. 262-90-11-95; e-mail union@cfecgcreunion.com; internet www.cfecgcreunion.com; departmental br. of the Confédération Française de l'Encadrement-Confédération Générale des Cadres; represents engineers, teaching, managerial and professional staff and technicians; Pres. ALAIN IGLICKI; Sec.-Gen. DANIEL THIAW-WING-KAI.

Fédération Départementale des Syndicats d'Exploitants Agricoles de la Réunion (FDSEA): 105 rue Amiral Lacaze, Terre Sainte, 97410 Saint-Pierre; tel. 262-96-33-53; affiliated to the Fédération Nationale des Syndicats d'Exploitants; Sec.-Gen. JEAN-BERNARD HOARAU.

Fédération Réunionnaise du Bâtiment et des Travaux Publics: rue du Pont, CS 41051, BP 108, 97404 Saint-Denis Cedex; tel. 262-41-70-87; e-mail contact@frbtp.re; internet www.frbtp.re; Pres. ANTHONY ANTHONY LEBON.

Fédération Syndicale Unitaire Réunion (FSU): 4 rue de la Cure, BP 279, 97494 Sainte-Clotilde Cedex; tel. 262-86-29-46; e-mail fsu974@fsu.fr; internet sd974.fsu.fr; f. 1993; departmental br. of the Fédération Syndicale Unitaire; represents public sector employees in sectors incl. teaching, research and training, and also agriculture, justice, youth and sports, and culture; Sec. CHRISTIAN PICARD.

Union Départementale Confédération Française Démocratique du Travail (UD CFDT): Résidence Pointe des Jardins, 1 rue de l'Atillerie, 97400 Saint-Denis; tel. 262-41-22-85.

Union Départementale Force Ouvrière de la Réunion (FO): 81 rue Labourdonnais, BP 853, 97477 Saint-Denis Cedex; tel. 262-21-31-35; internet www.fo-reunion.net; Sec.-Gen. ERIC MARGUERITE.

Union Interprofessionnelle de la Réunion (UIR-CFDT): 58 rue Fénelon, 97400 Saint-Denis; tel. 262-90-27-67; e-mail uir.cfdt@wanadoo.fr; affiliated to the Confédération Française Démocratique du Travail; Sec.-Gen. JEAN-PIERRE RIVIERE.

Affiliated unions incl.:

FEP-CFDT Réunion: 58 rue Fénélon, 97400 Saint-Denis; tel. 262-90-27-67; e-mail jpmarchau@uir-cfdt.org; affiliated to the Fédération Formation et Enseignement Privés; represents private sector teaching staff.

SGEN-CFDT: 58 rue Fénélon, 97400 Saint-Denis; tel. 262-90-27-72; e-mail reunion@sgen.cfdt.fr; internet reunion.sgen-cfdt.fr; mem. of Union Interprofessionnelle de la Réunion; represents teaching staff; Sec.-Gen. DIDIER HOARAU.

Union Régionale UNSA-Education: BP 169, 97464 Saint-Denis Cedex; tel. 262-20-02-25; e-mail urreunio@unsa.org; represents teaching staff; Sec.-Gen. ERIC CHAVRIACOUTY.

Transport

ROADS

A route nationale circles the island, generally following the coast and linking the main towns. Another route nationale crosses the island from south-west to north-east linking Saint-Pierre and Saint-Benoît.

Société d'Economie Mixte des Transports, Tourisme, Equipements et Loisirs (SEMITTEL): 24 chemin Benoite-Boulard, 97410 Saint-Pierre; tel. 262-55-40-60; e-mail contact@semittel.re; f. 1984; bus service operator; Pres. and Dir-Gen. ALBERT PERIANAYAGOM.

SHIPPING

In 1986 work was completed on the expansion of the Port de la Pointe des Galets, which was divided into the former port in the west and a new port in the east (the port Ouest and the port Est), known together as Port Réunion. In 2012 legislation was adopted in France that transformed Port Réunion into the Grand Port Maritime de la Réunion (GPMR), a publicly owned entity administered by a supervisory board. In 2020 the GPMR handled freight totalling some 5.34m. metric tons, down from 5.92m. metric tons in 2019.

Grand Port Maritime de la Réunion: 2 rue Evariste de Parny, BP 18, 97821 Le Port Cedex; tel. 262-42-90-00; e-mail pr.com@reunion .port.fr; internet www.reunion.port.fr; Pres. ERIC LEGRIGEOIS.

CMA CGM Réunion: blvd des Mascareignes, CS 51041, 97829 Le Port Cedex; tel. 262-55-10-10; e-mail lar.genmbox@cma-cgm.com; internet www.cmacgm.com; f. 1996 by merger of Cie Générale Maritime and Cie Maritime d'Affrètement; shipping agents; Man. Dir EMMANUELLE HOAREAU.

MSC (Mediterranean Shipping Co): 1 bis, Gustave Eiffel, Z.A.C. 2000, BP 221, 97825 Le Port Cedex; tel. 262-42-78-00; e-mail msclareunion@mscfr.mscgva.ch; internet www.mscreunion.com.

Réunion Ships Agency (RSA): 17 rue R. Hoareau, BP 10186, 97825 Le Port Cedex; tel. 262-43-33-33; e-mail rsa@indoceanic.com; internet www.indoceanic.com; f. 1975; subsidiary of Indoceanic Services; Man. Dir HAROLD JOSÉ THOMSON.

Société d'Acconage et de Manutention de la Réunionnaise (SAMR): 3 ave Théodore Drouhet, Z.A.C. 2000, BP 40, 97821 Le Port Cedex; tel. 262-55-17-55; stevedoring; Pres. MARIE GUY STANISLAS DE SAINT-LOUVENT; Man. DANIEL MANTEUFFEL.

Société de Manutention et de Consignation Maritime (SOMA-COM): 3 rue Gustave Eiffel, Zac 2000, BP 97420, Le Port; tel. 262-42-60-00; stevedoring and shipping agents; Gen. Man. DANIEL RIGAT.

Société Réunionnaise de Services Maritimes (SRSM): 8 rue Gustave Eiffel, ZAC Ravine, 97419 La Possession; tel. 262-22-01-83; freight only; Dir-Gen. NATACHA DE PEINDRAY D'AMBELLE.

CIVIL AVIATION

Réunion's international airport, Roland Garros, is situated 8 km from Saint-Denis. The Pierrefonds airfield, 5 km from Saint-Pierre, commenced operating as an international airport in 1998. Air France, Corsair and Air Austral operate international services. In 2020 Roland Garros handled 1.04m. passengers (down from 2.49m. passengers in 2019), while Saint-Pierre Pierrefonds airport handled 99,120 passengers in 2019.

Air Austral: Zone Aéroportuaire, 97438 Sainte-Marie; tel. 262-93-10-10; e-mail reservation@air-austral.com; internet www.airaustral .com; f. 1975; subsidiary of Air France; CEO MARIE-JOSEPH MALÉ.

Tourism

L'Île de la Réunion Tourisme (IRT): pl. du 20 décembre 1848, BP 615, 97472 Saint-Denis Cedex; tel. 262-21-00-41; e-mail ctr@ la-reunion-tourisme.com; internet www.reunion.fr; fmrly Comité du Tourisme de la Réunion; name changed as above in 2009; Dir-Gen. WILLY EHTÈVE.

Defence

Réunion is the headquarters of French military forces in the Indian Ocean and French Southern and Antarctic Territories. As assessed at November 2021, there were 1,700 French troops stationed on Réunion and Mayotte, including a gendarmerie.

Commander of the French Armed Forces in Réunion and Mayotte: LAURENT CLUZEL.

Education

Education is modelled on the French system, and is compulsory for children between the ages of three and 16 years. Maternelle (early years) classes can begin at two years of age and attendance is compulsory from three years of age. Primary education lasts from the ages of six to 11. Secondary education, which begins at 11 years of age, lasts for up to seven years, comprising a first cycle of four years and a second of three years. From the 2020/21 academic year education or training (including apprenticeships and other vocational courses and activities) were to be compulsory up to the age of 18. The Université de la Réunion, which was established in 1982, comprises five faculties (providing higher education in law and economics, sciences and technology, arts and social sciences, human sciences and environment, and health), three institutes, an engineering school, a teacher training school, an observatory, a training centre and a language centre.

Bibliography

Boléguin, V. *La Réunion: une jeunesse tiraillée entre tradition et modernité. Les 16–30 ans au chômage.* Paris, L'Harmattan, 2011.

Dracius, S., Samlong, J.-F., and Theobald, G. *La crise de l'outre-mer français: Guadeloupe, Martinique, Réunion.* Paris, L'Harmattan, 2009.

Ho, H. Q. *La Réunion (1882–1960): Histoire économique Colonage, salariat et sous-développement.* Paris, L'Harmattan, 2008.

Maestri, E. *Les îles du sud-ouest de l'Océan Indien et la France de 1815 à nos jours.* Paris, L'Harmattan, 1994.

Martinez, E. *Le Département français de La Réunion et la coopération internationale dans l'Océan Indien.* Paris, L'Harmattan, 1988.

Médéa, L. *Reunion: an Island in Search of an Identity.* Pretoria, Unisa Press, 2010.

Payet, J. V. *Histoire de l'esclavage à l'île Bourbon (Réunion).* Paris, L'Harmattan, 2000.

RWANDA

Physical and Social Geography

PIERRE GOUROU

The Rwandan Republic, like the neighbouring Republic of Burundi, is distinctive both for the small size of its territory and for the density of its population. Covering an area of 26,338 sq km (10,169 sq miles), Rwanda had an enumerated population of 7,142,755 at the census of 15 August 1991, with a density of 271 inhabitants per sq km. However, political and ethnic violence during 1994 was estimated to have resulted in the death or external displacement of 35%–40% of the total population. Prior to these events, the population had been composed of Hutu (about 85%), Tutsi (about 14%) and Twa (1%). Rwanda's population was 10,515,973 at the census of August 2012, and was estimated by the United Nations (UN) to have risen to 13,600,466 by mid-2022, with a density of 516.4 inhabitants per sq km. The official languages are French, English (which is widely spoken by the Tutsi minority) and Kinyarwanda, a Bantu language with close similarities to Kirundi, the main vernacular language of Burundi.

It seems, at first sight, strange that Rwanda has not been absorbed into a wider political entity. Admittedly, the Rwandan nation has long been united by language and custom and was part of a state that won the respect of the east African slave-traders. However, other ethnic groups, such as the Kongo, Luba, Luo and Zande, which were well established in small territorial areas, have not been able to develop into national states. That Rwanda has been able to achieve this is partly the result of developments during the colonial period. While part of German East Africa, Rwanda (then known, with Burundi, as Ruanda-Urundi) was regarded as a peripheral colonial territory of little economic interest. After the First World War it was entrusted to Belgium under a mandate from the League of Nations. The territory was administered jointly with the Belgian Congo, but was not absorbed into the larger state. The historic separateness and national traditions of both Rwanda and Burundi have prevented their amalgamation.

Although the land supports a high population density, physical conditions are not very favourable. Rwanda's land mass is very rugged and fragmented. It is part of a Pre-Cambrian shelf from which, through erosion, the harder rocks have obtruded, leaving the softer ones submerged. Thus very ancient folds have been raised and a relief surface carved out with steep gradients covered with a soil poor in quality because of its fineness and fragility. Rwanda's physiognomy therefore consists of a series of sharply defined hills, with steep slopes and flat ridges, which are intersected by deep valleys, the bottoms of which are often formed by marshy plains. The north is dominated by the lofty and powerful chain of volcanoes, the Virunga, whose highest peak is Karisimbi (4,519 m) and whose lava, having scarcely cooled down, has not yet produced cultivable soil.

The climate is tropical, although tempered by altitude, with a daily temperature range of as much as 14°C. Kigali, the capital (1.2m. inhabitants at mid-2022, according to UN estimates), has an average temperature of 19°C and 1,000 mm of rain. Altitude is a factor that modifies the temperature (and prevents sleeping sickness above about 900 m), but such a factor is of debatable value for agriculture. Average annual rainfall (785 mm) is only barely sufficient for agricultural purposes, but two wet and two relatively dry seasons are experienced, making two harvests possible.

History

DUNCAN WOODSIDE

INTRODUCTION

A tiny, landlocked country of around 13.6m. people (at mid-2022) in central Africa, Rwanda is today one of the continent's most prominent sub-Saharan nations. Sadly, this familiarity stems largely from a genocide that took place over the course of just three months in 1994, which the United Nations (UN) estimated killed between 500,000 and 800,000 people, towards the end of a civil war that began in late 1990. Since then, the country has embarked on a remarkably strong economic growth trajectory, under the stewardship of a former guerrilla movement, which banished a short-lived extremist regime into exile. After the genocide Rwanda quickly became a favourite of donors, with the USA, the United Kingdom and the European Union (EU) all providing substantial funds for reconstruction. This recovery has been masterminded by President Paul Kagame, the former rebel leader, who has crafted a reputation for having zero tolerance of corruption. On the surface, modern-day Rwanda appears to be highly organized, efficient, peaceful and booming.

However, relations with donors cooled in the 2010s. The most prominent issue has centred on allegations that Kagame's regime has carried out repeated hostile military interventions in the Democratic Republic of the Congo (DRC), its large, mineral-rich neighbour. Seemingly emblematic of this military adventurism, near-palatial villas have sprung up to dot the skyline of Rwanda's capital, Kigali, on a hillside dubbed 'Merci Congo', a reference to the post-genocide regime's alleged systematic cross-border plunder of mineral wealth from the mid- to late 1990s. A total of 3.8m. people died in the DRC from conflict and war-related disease and hunger between 1998 and 2003, according to the International Rescue Committee; the new Rwandan army occupied swathes of its neighbour in 1996–97 and 1998–2002, ostensibly to hunt down exiled perpetrators of the 1994 genocide. Allegations of cross-border military activity to sustain illicit mineral networks continued for years after the Rwandan army's official withdrawal in the early 2000s, culminating in significant reductions in bilateral budgetary support by principal donors in the early 2010s.

Donors and other allies have also been embarrassed by repeated murders and apparent plots to kill dissidents exiled in their countries, allegedly masterminded by Rwanda's security services. Major incidents have taken place (or alleged plots have been uncovered) in Kenya, South Africa, the UK and Belgium. Elections in Rwanda resumed in 2003, but have consistently resulted in Kagame officially securing well over 90% of the vote. Recent constitutional changes have effectively cleared the way for the President to remain in power until at least 2034. It has long been evident that a facade of multi-party pluralism has been presented to the world by Kagame, in order to obscure what is a de facto one-party state. Increasingly, regional experts and disillusioned former supporters also view the country as a 'one-man system', where all institutions are subservient to the President.

HUTU ASCENDANCY REPLACES TUTSI DOMINANCE (1962–90)

Rwanda and its initial post-independence episodes of ethnic massacres and armed conflict are partially the creation of crude ethnic distinctions entrenched during colonial rule. When Rwanda and Burundi were absorbed by German East Africa in 1899, they had been established kingdoms for centuries. After Germany's defeat in the First World War, Rwanda formed part of Ruanda-Urundi from 1920, administered by Belgium under a League of Nations mandate and later as a UN Trust Territory. The Belgians viewed Tutsis, who formed a minority of the population, as superior to the majority Hutus. The colonizers measured the noses of people, to help distinguish whether they would be classified as Hutu or Tutsi. (A long, thin nose was thought to characterize a Tutsi and a short, wide nose a Hutu.) Tutsis took most of the attractive public sector jobs available to Rwandans, while the Belgians also allowed a Tutsi-dominated monarchy a say in governance. In both Rwanda and Burundi, the ethnic mix was estimated to be 14% Tutsi, 85% Hutu and 1% Twa, the latter being comprised of forest dwelling pygmies.

In the late 1950s elements within the Hutu majority began to organize and lobby for political reform. In 1957 newly formed Hutu political parties launched a manifesto, before Kigeli V, the Tutsi King, was forced into exile in 1959. In 1961 one of Belgium's final decisions in Rwanda was to support a demand for a referendum on whether to replace the monarchy with a republic. The referendum asked voters whether the monarchy should be preserved after independence was granted and whether Kigeli V should remain the King. Around 80% of voters rejected both propositions. That year the country was duly proclaimed a republic before full independence was granted on 1 July 1962. Political life in the new Government was dominated by Rwanda's first President, Grégoire Kayibanda, and the Mouvement Démocratique Républicain (MDR), also known as the Parti de l'Emancipation du Peuple Hutu (Parmehutu). Anti-Tutsi pogroms occurred repeatedly, in 1963–65, 1966–67, 1972–73 and 1993. These massacres sowed the seeds of the 1990–94 civil war and the genocide.

In July 1973 the Minister of Defence and head of the National Guard, Maj.-Gen. Juvénal Habyarimana, deposed Kayibanda, proclaimed a Second Republic and established a military Government under his leadership. A referendum in December 1978 approved a new Constitution, aimed at returning the country to civil government in accordance with an undertaking by Habyarimana in 1973 to end the military regime within five years. Habyarimana was elected President in the same month. Elections to the legislature, the Conseil National du Développement (CND), were held in December 1981 and in December 1983, in which month Habyarimana was re-elected President. In the presidential election of December 1988 Habyarimana, as the sole candidate, reportedly secured 99.98% of the votes cast.

CIVIL WAR AND PEACE INITIATIVES (OCTOBER 1990–APRIL 1994)

On 1 October 1990 an estimated force of 10,000 troops, comprising members of the exiled, Tutsi-dominated Rwandan Patriotic Front (RPF), crossed the border from Uganda into north-eastern Rwanda, where they swiftly occupied several towns. The invasion force was led by Maj.-Gen. Fred Rwigyema, a former Ugandan Deputy Minister of Defence. Rwigyema was killed on the second day of the conflict. He was replaced by Kagame who had previously served as a chief of military intelligence for Ugandan President Yoweri Museveni.

In response to a request for assistance from Habyarimana, Belgian and French paratroopers were dispatched to Kigali to protect foreign nationals and to secure evacuation routes. A contingent of troops sent by Zaire (as the DRC was then known) assisted the small Rwandan army in repelling the RPF some 70 km from the capital.

The RPF invasion accelerated a political reform process initiated in 1990. Following widespread public discussion of proposals suggested in December, a draft constitution was put forward in March 1991. The new Constitution, providing for the legalization of political parties, entered into force in June.

Full freedom of the press was declared, leading to the establishment of a number of magazines and newspapers critical of government policy. In April 1992 the composition of a broad-based coalition Government, incorporating four opposition parties—the revived MDR, the Parti Social-Démocrate (PSD), the Parti Libéral (PL) and the Parti Démocratique Chrétien (PDC)—together with the ruling Mouvement Républicain National pour la Démocratie et le Développement (MRNDD), was announced. The new administration was to be headed by Dismas Nsengiyaremye of the MDR as Prime Minister, a post established by the Constitution. In late April 1992, in compliance with a new constitutional prohibition of the armed forces' participation in the political process, Habyarimana relinquished his military title and functions.

The coalition Government and RPF representatives initiated dialogue in May 1992 and by July had reached an agreement on the implementation of a ceasefire; also agreed was the creation of a Neutral Military Observer Group (NMOG) sponsored by the Organization of African Unity (OAU, now the African Union—AU), to comprise representatives from both sides, together with officers drawn from the armed forces of Nigeria, Senegal, Zimbabwe and Mali. However, by October subsequent negotiations had failed to resolve outstanding problems concerning the creation of a 'neutral zone' between the Forces Armées Rwandaises (FAR) and the RPF (to be enforced by the NMOG), the incorporation of the RPF in a Rwandan national force, the repatriation of refugees, and the demands of the RPF for full participation in the transitional Government and legislature.

A resurgence in violence followed the breakdown of negotiations in early February 1993, resulting in hundreds of deaths on both sides. An estimated 1m. civilians fled southwards and to neighbouring Uganda and Tanzania, as the RPF advanced as far as Ruhengeri and seemed, for a time, on the verge of capturing Kigali. Belgium, France and the USA denounced the RPF's actions. In late February the Government accepted the RPF's terms for a ceasefire, including an end to attacks against RPF positions and on Tutsi communities, and the withdrawal of foreign troops.

In April 1993 the five participating parties in the ruling coalition agreed to a three-month extension of the Government's mandate in order to facilitate a peace accord. In June an agreed protocol outlined the repatriation of all Rwandan refugees resident in Uganda, Tanzania and Zaire, and the UN Security Council approved the creation of the UN Observer Mission Uganda-Rwanda (UNOMUR), to be deployed on the Ugandan side of the border for an initial period of six months, in order to block RPF military supply lines.

In July 1993 Habyarimana met representatives of the five parties represented in the coalition Government and sought a further extension to its mandate. However, Nsengiyaremye's insistence that the RPF should be represented in any new government exacerbated existing divisions within the MDR, prompting Habyarimana to conclude the agreement with a conciliatory group of MDR dissidents, including the Minister of Education, Agathe Uwilingiyimana, who was appointed as Rwanda's first female Prime Minister on 17 July. The Council of Ministers was reorganized to replace the disaffected MDR members.

Habyarimana and Col Alex Kanyarengwe of the RPF formally signed a peace accord in Arusha, Tanzania, on 4 August 1993. A new transitional government, to be headed by a mutually approved Prime Minister (later named as the MDR moderate faction leader, Faustin Twagiramungu), was to be installed by 10 September. By the end of August, however, there were reports of renewed outbreaks of violence in Kigali and Butare, Rwanda's second largest city. The Government and the RPF attributed the failure to establish a transitional government and legislature by the September deadline to the increasingly fragile security situation, and both sides urged the prompt dispatch of a neutral UN force to facilitate the implementation of the Arusha Accord.

On 5 October 1993 the UN Security Council adopted Resolution 872, endorsing the creation of the UN Assistance Mission for Rwanda (UNAMIR), under the leadership of Canadian Brig.-Gen. (later promoted to Maj.-Gen. and then Lt-Gen.) Roméo Dallaire, to be deployed in Rwanda for an initial period of six months. UNAMIR had a mandate to monitor observance of the ceasefire; contribute to the security of the capital; and facilitate the repatriation of refugees. Incorporating UNO-MUR and the NMOG, it was formally inaugurated on 1 November, and comprised some 2,500 personnel. In December the UN declared its satisfaction that conditions had been sufficiently fulfilled to allow for the introduction of the transitional institutions by the end of the month. In that month UNAMIR officials escorted a 600-strong RPF battalion to Kigali (as detailed in the Arusha Accord) to ensure the safety of RPF representatives selected to participate in the transitional government and legislature. On 5 January 1994 Habyarimana was invested as President of a transitional Government for a 22-month period, under the terms of the Arusha Accord.

Dallaire reported in early 1994 that the Habyarimana Government was increasing anti-Tutsi propaganda across Rwanda, stockpiling weapons and training youth militias, and that violence against Tutsi was likely in the coming months. In March the Prime Minister-designate, Twagiramungu, declared that he had fulfilled his consultative role as established by the Arusha Accord, and announced the composition of a transitional Government, in an attempt to accelerate the installation of the transitional bodies. However, political opposition to the proposed Council of Ministers persisted, and Habyarimana insisted that the list of proposed legislative deputies, newly presented by Uwilingiyimana, should be modified to include representatives of additional political parties, including the Coalition pour la Défense de la République (CDR). CDR participation was strongly opposed by the RPF, owing both to its alleged failure to accept the code of ethics for the behaviour of political parties, and to its strident anti-Tutsi rhetoric. The creation of a transitional administration was therefore again postponed.

In April 1994 the UN Security Council—which in February had warned that the UN presence in Rwanda might be withdrawn because of failure to make progress in implementing the Arusha Accord—agreed to extend UNAMIR's mandate for four months, pending a review of the Accord's implementation.

GENOCIDE AND RPF VICTORY (APRIL–JULY 1994)

On 6 April 1994 the presidential aircraft, returning from a regional summit in Dar es Salaam, Tanzania, was fired upon over Kigali, and exploded on landing. All 10 passengers were killed, including President Habyarimana, President Cyprien Ntaryamira of Burundi, two Burundian cabinet ministers and the Chief of Staff of the Rwandan armed forces. Although it was—and remains to this day—unclear who was responsible for the attack, in Kigali the presidential guard obstructed UNAMIR officials attempting to investigate the crash site, and immediately initiated a brutal, co-ordinated and extremely rapid campaign of retributive violence against political moderates. As politicians and civilians fled the capital, the brutality of the political assassinations was compounded by attacks on the clergy, UNAMIR personnel and Tutsi civilians. Hutu civilians were instructed to murder their Tutsi neighbours. The mobilization of the Interahamwe, a militia apparently committed to the massacre of government opponents and Tutsi civilians, was encouraged by the presidential guard (with support from some factions of the armed forces) and by inflammatory broadcasts from Radio-Télévision Libre des Mille Collines. Prime Minister Uwilingiyimana, the President of the Constitutional Court, the Ministers of Labour and Social Affairs and of Information, and the Chairman of the PSD were among the prominent politicians assassinated, or declared missing and presumed dead, within hours of Habyarimana's death.

The Speaker of the CND, Dr Théodore Sindikubwabo, announced on 8 April 1994 that he had assumed the office of interim President of the Republic, in accordance with the provisions of the 1991 Constitution. The five remaining participating political parties and factions of the Government selected a new Prime Minister, Jean Kambanda, and a new Council of Ministers (largely comprising MRNDD members). The RPF immediately challenged the legality of the new administration, claiming that the CND's constitutional right of succession to the presidency had been superseded by

Habyarimana's inauguration as President in January under the terms of the Arusha Accord. The legitimacy of the new Government, which had fled to Gitarama to escape escalating violence in the capital, was subsequently rejected by factions of the PL and MDR (led by Twagiramungu), and by the PDC and the PSD.

In mid-April 1994 the RPF resumed military operations from its northern stronghold, with the stated intention of relieving its beleaguered battalion in Kigali, restoring order to the capital and halting the massacre of Tutsi civilians. Grenade attacks and mortar fire intensified in the capital, prompting the UN to mediate a fragile 60-hour ceasefire, during which small evacuation forces from several countries escorted foreign nationals out of Rwanda. Belgium's UNAMIR contingent of more than 400 troops—potentially the most effective UN contingent on the ground—was also withdrawn, after Hutu militia killed and mutilated 10 Belgian peacekeepers.

As the political violence gathered momentum, the Interahamwe militia's identification of all Tutsis as political opponents of the state further inflamed decades-old ethnic polarization, resulting in a pogrom against Tutsis. Reports of mass Tutsi killings and unprovoked attacks on fleeing Tutsi refugees, and on those seeking refuge in schools, hospitals and churches, elicited unqualified international condemnation and outrage, and promises of financial and logistical aid for an estimated 2m. displaced Rwandans. By late May 1994 attempts to assess the full scale of the humanitarian catastrophe in Rwanda were complicated by unverified reports that the RPF, which claimed to control more than one-half of the country, was carrying out retaliatory atrocities against Hutu militias and civilians.

On 21 April 1994, with violence in Kigali intensifying, and the FAR refusing to agree to the neutral policing of the capital's airport (subsequently secured by the RPF), the UN Security Council resolved to reduce its force in Rwanda to 270 personnel. On 16 May, following intense international criticism and the disclosure of the vast scale of the humanitarian crisis in the region, the Security Council approved Resolution 917, providing for the eventual deployment of some 5,500 UN troops with a revised mandate, including the policing of Kigali's airport and the protection of refugees in designated 'safe areas'. However, further UN-sponsored attempts to negotiate a ceasefire failed, and the RPF made significant territorial gains in southern Rwanda, forcing the Government to flee Gitarama and seek refuge in the western town of Kibuye.

In early June 1994 the UN Security Council adopted Resolution 925, extending the mandate of the revised UN mission in Rwanda (UNAMIR II) until December. By mid-June confirmed reports of retributive murders committed by RPF members and the collapse of a fragile OAU-negotiated truce prompted the French Government to announce its willingness to lead an armed police action, endorsed by the UN, in Rwanda. Although France insisted that its military presence (expected to total 2,000 troops) would maintain strict political neutrality and operate from the border regions in a purely humanitarian capacity pending the arrival of a multinational UN force, the RPF contended that the French administration's maintenance of high-level contacts with representatives of the self-proclaimed Rwandan Government indicated political bias. On 23 June the first contingent of 150 French marine commandos launched Operation Turquoise, entering the western town of Cyangugu, in preparation for a large-scale operation to protect civilians in the area.

By mid-July 1994 the French initiative had successfully relieved several beleaguered Tutsi communities and had established a temporary 'safe haven' for the displaced population in the south-west, through which a mass exodus of Hutu refugees began to flow, amid reports that the advancing RPF forces were seeking violent retribution against Hutus. An estimated 1m. Rwandans sought refuge in the Zairian border town of Goma, while a similar number attempted to cross the border elsewhere in the south-west, along with the ex-FAR, interim government ministers and the Interahamwe. The RPF had swiftly secured all major cities and strategic territorial positions, but had halted its advance several kilometres from the boundaries of the French-controlled neutral zone, requesting the apprehension and return for trial of those responsible for the recent atrocities.

The first report of the UN Special Rapporteur on human rights in Rwanda confirmed at the end of June 1994 that at least 500,000 Rwandans had been killed since April, and urged the establishment of an international tribunal to investigate allegations of genocide. In early July the UN announced the creation of a commission of inquiry for this purpose.

On 19 July 1994 Pasteur Bizimungu, a Hutu moderate, was inaugurated as President for a five-year term, shortly after the RPF had secured control of Kigali. In November a multi-party protocol of understanding was concluded, providing for a number of amendments to the terms of the August 1993 Arusha Accord, relating to the establishment of a transitional legislature. Among the new provisions was the exclusion from the legislative process of members of those parties implicated in alleged acts of genocide during 1994. A 70-member National Transitional Assembly (TNA) was installed on 12 December. On 5 May 1995 the new legislature announced its adoption of a new Constitution based on selected articles of the 1991 Constitution, the terms of the Arusha Accord, the RPF's victory declaration of July 1994 and the November 1994 protocol of understanding.

KAGAME THE KINGPIN (1994–)

It was not until 2000 that Kagame became President of Rwanda, but he was the country's dominant political figure as soon as the RPF seized full control of Kigali in July 1994. Formally, Kagame was junior to Bizimungu, but his chairmanship of the RPF and control of the Ministry of Defence meant that the transitional Government, which remained in place until July 1999, did not constitute a progression to genuine civilian and multi-party rule. Indeed, power was very much vested in the new Tutsi-dominated military, with Kagame, also the country's Vice-President, controlling matters, just as he had through all but the first two days of the RPF's guerrilla and subsequent urban campaign between October 1990 and July 1994. Bizimungu, who was Vice-Chairman of the RPF, served as a convenient Hutu figurehead as head of state, in order to present an image of post-genocide Rwanda as pluralist and multi-ethnic.

One of the first significant casualties of the new regime was Prime Minister Twagiramungu, who fled into exile in late 1995, claiming that Kagame had made direct threats against him. A Hutu from the MDR's moderate wing, Twagiramungu had expected to be able to wield executive power in his role, but claimed that he was consistently undermined by Kagame. However, it was in the early stages of a second transitional administration—in place from July 1999 to September 2003 under a new interim constitution—that Kagame orchestrated his boldest consolidations of personal power. After an extensive replacement of non-RPF figures under an anti-corruption campaign, President Bizimungu resigned in March that year. Kagame was formally selected as the new head of state by the legislature on 17 April, becoming the country's first Tutsi President. Hutu politicians were not alone in claiming that they were victimized; in January 2000 Joseph Kabuye Sebarenzi, a former Tutsi speaker of the country's parliament, fled Rwanda, claiming that he feared for his life.

Some 93.4% of the electorate approved a new Rwandan Constitution on 26 May 2003. The new Constitution came into effect on 4 June and mandated a bicameral legislature, which would comprise an 80-member Chamber of Deputies and a 26-member Senate. On 25 August 2003 Kagame was the victor of the first presidential election to take place in Rwanda since the 1994 genocide, having officially received 95.1% of the valid votes cast. Former Prime Minister Twagiramungu (who returned briefly from exile to take part in the election, while most of his colleagues remained abroad) won 3.6% of the votes, and the only other opposition candidate, Jean-Népomuscène Nayinzira, 1.3%. Twagiramungu claimed that fraud had taken place and challenged the official results at the Supreme Court. EU monitors noted that irregularities had occurred.

The Constitution provided for legislative elections every five years and presidential polls every seven years. On 30 September 2003 some 218 candidates contested legislative elections

for 53 of 80 seats in the Chamber of Deputies. Official figures indicated that turnout was some 96%, although independent observers maintained that the number of voters was less than that for the presidential poll. The RPF won 33 seats; the PSD secured seven seats, the PL six, the Parti Démocrate Centriste three, the Parti Démocrate Idéal two, the Parti Socialiste Rwandais one and the Union Démocratique du Peuple Rwandais one. The new Constitution reserved the remaining seats in the Chamber of Deputies for 'special groups' (24 representatives of women, two of youth and one of disabled persons). The EU assessed that there had been serious irregularities in the legislative elections. In September 2008 the RPF maintained its parliamentary majority, winning 78.8% of the votes cast and 42 of the 53 directly elected seats. The PSD took seven seats and the PL four. For the first time, women outnumbered men in the legislature, occupying some 56% of the seats.

On 9 August 2010 Rwanda held its second presidential election since the genocide. Kagame once again secured an overwhelming victory, officially winning 93.1% of votes cast. His closest challenger, Dr Jean Damascène Ntawukuriryayo of the PSD, took just 5.2% of the votes, while Prosper Higiro of the PL secured 1.4%. Some 97.5% of the registered electorate participated in the poll, according to official figures. However, the biggest indication of the President's continued reluctance to expose himself to genuine competition was perhaps the way the authorities treated his principal potential challenger for the presidency. Victoire Ingabire Umuhoza, the leader of the Forces Démocratiques Unifiées—Inkingi (FDU—Inkingi) party, returned from exile intent on presenting a genuine alternative to Kagame, in contrast to Ntawukuriryayo and Higiro. However, Ingabire was prevented from taking part in the presidential poll, having been placed under house arrest.

Ingabire went on trial accused of six charges including genocide denial, involvement in terrorist activities, planning state insecurity and divisionism. In October 2012 the High Court sentenced her to eight years' imprisonment, having convicted her of conspiring to overthrow the Government through terrorist activities and of denying the 1994 genocide; she was acquitted of the four other charges. In December 2013 the Supreme Court rejected an appeal by Ingabire against her sentence, and increased her term of imprisonment to 15 years. After serving six years of her sentence, Ingabire was unexpectedly granted a presidential pardon on 15 September 2018 and was released from prison. Some 2,000 other prisoners were released at around the same time, just as the Rwandan Minister of Foreign Affairs and International Co-operation, Louise Mushikiwabo, was seeking to become the head of the Organisation Internationale de la Francophonie (OIF—see *World Power Relations (1994–)*).

The volume and details of cases where foreign governments and security forces have accused Kagame's regime of killing—or seeking to kill—its exiled opponents are overwhelming, making it difficult to believe that there is a credible alternative explanation (i.e. high incidences of intra-opposition conflict or business rivalry). Moreover, such allegations have come from within donor countries. In May 2011 British detectives warned two Rwandan exiles living in the UK that they had 'reliable intelligence' of an 'imminent threat' to their lives. One of the men, Jonathan Musonera, was a founding member of the Rwanda National Congress (RNC) opposition umbrella group, which draws on diaspora communities, since it is unable to operate inside Rwanda itself. The other, Rene Mugenzi, a genocide survivor, was not explicitly involved in exile politics, but stated that he had accused Kagame of being a despot during a British Broadcasting Corporation radio programme earlier that year, in which both the dissident and the President had participated.

Human Rights Watch (HRW) in January 2014 listed seven prominent Rwandans who had been murdered or disappeared abroad (apart from in the context of conflict in the neighbouring DRC) since the end of the civil war. Among the most high-profile were former Minister of the Interior Seth Sendashonga, who survived an assassination attempt in February 1996, only to be shot dead, along with his driver, in Nairobi, Kenya, in May 1998, and Patrick Karegeya, the head of Rwanda's external intelligence service between 1994 and 2004, who was strangled to death in a hotel room in Johannesburg, South Africa, on

31 December 2013. Former army Chief of Staff Faustin Kayumba Nyamwasa, meanwhile, has reportedly survived at least four assassination attempts in exile in South Africa.

Sendashonga had resigned and fled to Kenya in August 1995, after disagreeing with the policy direction of the first post-genocide Government and in protest at human rights abuses allegedly perpetrated by the RPF in the months after its July 1994 victory in the civil war. An employee at the Rwandan embassy in Nairobi was arrested in connection with the failed 1996 murder attempt, but was released without trial after the Rwandan Government refused to waive his diplomatic immunity. A case against three men, including two Rwandans, for the 1998 murder reached trial, but the defendants were acquitted. Karegeya was found dead on 1 January 2014, having fled Rwanda after being released in November 2007 from an 18-month sentence for insubordination. An inquest in South Africa into his death finally began some five years after the murder, during which Johannesburg magistrate Mashiane Mathopa revealed a letter dated 5 June 2018 from the Prosecutor's Office to the police unit that had investigated Karegeya's murder, declining to prosecute 'in this matter ... It appears that all the Rwandan suspects left the country in 2014 and returned to Rwanda. Furthermore, close links exist between the suspects and the current Rwandan government.' Gerrie Nel, an advocate representing Karegeya's family and formerly a public prosecutor in South Africa, named the perpetrators as Appollo Ismael Kiririsi, Alex Sugira, Samuel Niyoyita and Nshizrungu Vianney. The family and friends of Karegeya alleged that the first of these suspects had posed as a businessman and successfully befriended him, despite repeated warnings from other contacts that Rwandan military intelligence was attempting to hire contract killers in South Africa. Karegeya had also dismissed bodyguards that the South African Government had assigned to him after a June 2010 attempt to kill Nyamwasa, in which his fellow exile had been shot in the stomach as he returned to his Johannesburg home. Karegeya's family further alleged that 'Appollo' (also named as Apollo Kiririsi Gafaranga in a January 2019 article in *The Guardian* newspaper) had acted as a decoy, who was able to provide the other suspects with intelligence on Karegeya's whereabouts and eventual access to his hotel room. In a July 2013 interview with Radio France Internationale, Karegeya had reiterated an allegation that Kagame had ordered the April 1994 shooting down of Habyarimana's jet, explaining that Kagame believed that Habyarimana was, at that stage, 'his only obstacle' to power.

On 18 April 2019 Mathopa concluded that there appeared to be a case to answer and sent the matter to South Africa's National Prosecuting Authority, underlining the police's contention that the four suspects were 'directly linked' to the Rwandan Government. In September South Africa's National Prosecution Authority issued arrest warrants for two suspects. Although the presence of the suspects on Rwandan territory made a rapid conclusion to the Karegeya case highly improbable, in August 2014 a South African court had found four defendants guilty in connection with the June 2010 murder attempt against Nyamwasa, which the latter claimed to have been ordered by Kagame himself. The four, three Rwandans and a Tanzanian, were each sentenced to eight years in prison. In March 2014 armed men broke into Nyamwasa's home while he was away, prompting South Africa to expel three Rwandan diplomats; Rwanda responded by expelling six South African diplomats. In February 2021 an exiled Rwandan dissident, RNC official Seif Bamporiki, was shot dead while delivering furniture in Cape Town, South Africa. According to other RNC officials, Bamporiki had stopped outside a house at the behest of a purported customer, whereupon he was ambushed and killed by two men. Nyamwasa accused the Rwandan Government of responsibility for the murder.

In May 2015 an estimated 3.6m. voters—72% of the registered voting population—signed a petition requesting amendments to the Constitution to allow President Kagame to remain in office beyond a limit of two elected terms. (Kagame's final tenure was scheduled to end in August 2017.) The proposed changes would effectively allow Kagame to remain in office until at least 2034 and were put to a referendum on 18 December 2015. Officially, around 98% of those who voted supported

the amendments. The Democratic Green Party (DGP) opposed the changes, including through court proceedings, but claimed that it was blocked from campaigning by the regime, which continued to maintain firm control over every level of administration.

Despite the cautionary experience of Ingabire, another newcomer sought to challenge Kagame for the presidency. Diane Rwigara, the daughter of Tutsi businessman Assinapol Rwigara, who had died in a road accident in 2015, announced her candidature for the 2017 presidential election. The 35-year-old US-educated accountant publicly claimed that her father's death had been politically motivated. She based much of her campaign on pledges to eradicate poverty and injustice, alongside decrying Rwanda's human rights record under Kagame. In July the National Electoral Commission (NEC) disqualified her, alleging that she had been unable to gather 600 valid signatures in support of her candidacy from at least 12 of the country's 30 districts. Kagame therefore faced two challengers: Dr Frank Habineza, under the banner of his DGP, and Philippe Mpayimana, a former journalist who ran independently. Kagame expressed his confidence that he would triumph, in view of the resounding vote in favour of amending the Constitution two years earlier, and in the event he officially secured 98.8% of the valid votes cast in the election, which was held on 4 August. Turnout was recorded at 96.4%. Habineza, who won just 0.5% of the votes cast, stated that some of his observers had been shut out of counting premises, although he did not allege foul play over the counting and congratulated Kagame on his victory. The newly re-elected President pledged to maintain his focus on development, and in late August reorganized the Cabinet. Rwigara, her mother and her sister were repeatedly questioned in September over allegations of forgery and inciting insurrection; the family's assets were seized for forcible sale and charges were brought. Rwigara and her mother were acquitted on 6 December, amid pressure from several members of the US Congress.

Rwanda's parliamentary elections, held on 2–4 September 2018, produced no major surprises. The RPF took 74% of the vote and 36 out of 53 directly elected seats (the remaining 27 seats were decided by provincial councils, the National Youth Committee and the Federation of the Disabled). The ruling party's allies took a further 16%, in the shape of the PSD securing 9% of the vote (five seats) and the PL 7% (four seats). (Four other smaller parties allied to the RPF each secured one seat.) The Parti Social Imberakuri won 5%, giving it two seats, although its role as an opposition party had been long been neutered by its original leader, Bernard Ntaganda, receiving a four-year prison sentence in February 2011. Ntaganda's successor as party leader, Christine Mukabunani, described her organization as one 'that does not believe in confrontation'. For the first time, the DGP secured parliamentary representation, winning two seats, after also receiving 5% of the vote. Its leader, Habineza, claimed that the results were 'a sign that Rwanda is opening up its political spectrum'.

However, events during the remainder of 2018 and during 2019 continued to indicate that involvement in genuine opposition to the regime was a dangerous and unsustainable pursuit, highlighted by a growing list of deaths and disappearances maintained and investigated by Amnesty International. Between October 2018 and September 2019 three members of FDU—Inkingi went missing or were allegedly murdered: the party's Vice-President, Boniface Twagirimana, who disappeared in October 2018; Ingabire's assistant, Anselme Mutuyimana, who was found dead, having apparently been strangled, in March 2019; and the party's National Co-ordinator, Sylidio Dusabumuremyi, who was stabbed to death in September. In November Ingabire announced that she was to establish a new political party, Dalfa Umurunzi (Development and Liberty for All), declaring that she and her colleagues stood 'ready to fulfil all legal requirements for registration'. (FDU—Inkingi had never been granted official recognition by the Rwandan authorities.)

On 17 February 2020 the Rwanda National Police declared that gospel singer Kizito Mihigo had been found dead in custody after committing suicide. Mihigo survived the genocide when he was a young child, but lost both his parents, and went on to play a central role in composing Rwanda's national anthem, before eventually provoking the regime's displeasure. The police announced that Mihigo had hanged himself with bedsheets tied to a window, after he was taken into custody days earlier for allegedly attempting to cross into Burundi without the authorities' permission. Mihigo had angered the authorities in March 2014 by uploading a song in which he sought to reconcile the country's two main ethnic communities, and which referenced the genocide and those 'vanished in an accident'. Mihigo had also, in February 2015, been sentenced to 10 years' imprisonment after being convicted on charges of 'forming a criminal gang, conspiracy to murder and conspiracy against the established government or the president'; however, Kagame had pardoned him in September 2018.

Rwanda's tightly controlled political system and the culture of strong obedience helped the country to impose an effective lockdown in what appeared to be a successful initial suppression of the coronavirus disease (COVID-19) pandemic. Rwanda had, on 22 March 2020, been the first country in Africa to introduce a nationwide lockdown. It also closed its land borders except to cargo, after shutting down commercial airspace on 19 March. The Government began to ease restrictions from 4 May, but reinstated a lockdown in the capital in January 2021, in response to a rise in cases and deaths from late 2020. Workers in both the private and public sectors were ordered to operate from home, other than employees in essential services, while businesses were obliged to close, with a few exceptions, notably including essential medical, food and fuel outlets. Rwanda began its vaccination campaign against COVID-19 on 5 March 2021, using both the Oxford AstraZeneca and Pfizer vaccines (thereby becoming the first country in Africa to use the latter vaccine, which requires ultra-cold storage). In January 2022 the Minister of Local Government, Prof. Jean-Marie Vianney Gatabazi, announced that public sector workers who refused to be vaccinated would be forced to resign.

On 31 August 2020 Paul Rusesabagina—who had saved many Tutsi lives in the capital during the 1994 genocide in his role as the manager of a major hotel—was paraded in handcuffs by the Rwandan authorities in Kigali. The RIB announced that he faced charges including arson, kidnap, murder and the financing of terrorism. Rusesabagina had gained international fame after his depiction in the 2004 film Hotel Rwanda, and was awarded the Presidential Medal of Freedom by US President George W. Bush, subsequently becoming an increasingly vocal critic of the Kagame regime resident in the USA. Rusesabagina's daughter stated that he had last contacted relatives from Dubai, in the United Arab Emirates (UAE), a few days before his appearance in Rwanda. Kagame denied that Rusesabagina had been kidnapped, a claim that the latter maintained in pre-trial hearings, while HRW deplored the circumstances surrounding his apprehension as an 'enforced disappearance'. Rwandan officials preferred instead to term his arrival in Kigali, as opposed to his intended destination of Burundi, by a private jet and at the invitation of a pastor, as the result of an elaborate and entirely justified ruse. In reality, the Rwandan Government had organized and paid for the flight from the UAE—which it acknowledged—while the pastor had acted at the authorities' behest.

Rusesabagina told a pre-trial hearing in September 2020 that he had donated €20,000 to the National Liberation Front (NLF), purportedly the nascent military wing of his political party, the Rwandan Movement for Democratic Change (RMDC). He also appeared to speak in favour of military action to overthrow Kagame in a video released online in 2018, in which he expressed his 'unreserved support' for the NLF and declared that 'the time has come for us to use any means possible to bring about change in Rwanda'. The German magazine *Der Spiegel* reported that Rusesabagina's daughter, Anaïse Kanimba, contended that his words had been manipulated, and that he had been talking on the theme of conditions experienced by Rwandan refugees, rather than endorsing the overthrow of the Government by military means. However, *Der Spiegel* also reported that it had been privy to a confidential dossier written by European diplomats asserting that Rusesabagina had 'unapologetically' admitted to involvement from 2018 in starting an 'armed struggle' against the regime. In October 2020 two foreign lawyers acting for Rusesabagina, Vincent Lurquin and Philippe Larochelle, protested that they

had been denied access to their client during a visit to Rwanda, while his family alleged that he had been denied the right to choose his own lawyers, restricting the defence team to personnel appointed by the Rwandan state. Rusesabagina faced nine charges related to terrorism and the prosecution argued in court on 1 April 2021 that he had 'full knowledge' of a series of attacks launched on Rwandan territory in 2018–19, which had killed nine civilians. He was also accused of intending to travel to Burundi to co-ordinate rebel activities from that neighbouring country and from the DRC. By that time Rusesabagina was refusing to attend further proceedings, having complained at a hearing in March 2021 that he was being denied the right to a fair trial. In September Rusesabagina was convicted and sentenced to 25 years in prison; an appeal by the prosecution in favour of a life sentence was subsequently rejected. In the same month Yvonne Idamange, a Rwandan video blogger who had criticized Kagame's regime in content posted on YouTube, was sentenced to 15 years in prison upon her conviction on six charges, including inciting insurrection and obstructing the work of law enforcement organs. Idamange, a genocide survivor, had accused Kagame of being a dictator and of manipulating the genocide for political ends. Also in September, Joshua Tuyishime, a popular Rwandan rapper known as Jay Polly, died in hospital after being transferred in an unconscious state from Kigali's Nyarugene Prison, where he had been incarcerated since his arrest earlier in April for allegedly hosting a party in contravention of COVID-19 restrictions. The authorities announced that Tuyishime, whose lyrics indirectly accused the Government of human rights abuses and of stifling its critics, had died after consuming alcohol in haircare products, but some observers alleged that he had been poisoned by the authorities.

POST-GENOCIDE CRIMINAL JUSTICE

On 8 November 1994 the UN Security Council adopted Resolution 955, establishing the UN International Criminal Tribunal for Rwanda (ICTR), despite the negative vote of Rwanda, which held a non-permanent seat on the Council. Security Council Resolution 977 of 22 February 1995 established the ICTR's seat in Arusha. The ICTR, which was to investigate allegations made against individuals accused of direct involvement in the planning and execution of crimes against humanity perpetrated in Rwanda during 1994, began formal proceedings in November 1995, and the first trial commenced in January 1997.

Justice Richard J. Goldstone of South Africa served concurrently as Chief Prosecutor at the ICTR and the International Criminal Tribunal for former Yugoslavia (ICTY) between 15 August 1994 and September 1996. He was succeeded by Canadian appellate Louise Arbour, who took up her post on 1 October 1996. Arbour's tenure generated controversy, as investigators operating under her alleged that in early 1997 she blocked them from pursuing a line of inquiry against Kagame and the RPF as the orchestrators of the attack on Habyarimana's presidential aircraft. Responsibility for that attack has always been a deeply sensitive issue, since it was an indisputable trigger for the genocide that immediately followed. In a prepared statement on 6 April 2001, one of the investigators, James Lyons, a former supervisory special agent for the US Federal Bureau of Investigation, announced that three witnesses had come forward in February 1997. Lyons declared in his statement that the sources had furnished 'extremely detailed' information naming individuals responsible for carrying out the attack and alleging that 'General Paul Kagame ... had put into effect the plan to shoot down the Presidential aircraft as it approached Kigali Airport'. Lyons stated that he was present with fellow investigator Michael Hourigan, an Australian, when the latter had placed a telephone call on a secure line at the US embassy in Kigali to Arbour to report the development. Lyons also stated that the investigative team had been authorized to pursue three key channels of inquiry, one of which was 'the investigation and prosecution of persons responsible for the rocket attack on April 6, 1994'. Hourigan had travelled to The Hague, in the Netherlands, to discuss the evidence provided by the three informants who alleged that Kagame had ordered the plane attack. In a subsequent telephone conversation between the two investigators, Hourigan had told Lyons that Arbour had ordered him to shut down his investigation on the basis 'that 'the shooting down of the President's airplane was a crime outside the jurisdiction of the ICTR'. A year prior to Lyons' 2001 prepared statement, a memo written by Hourigan on 1 August 1997, during a new employment post at the UN's Office of Internal Oversight Services, was forwarded to the ICTR on the orders of UN Secretary-General Kofi Annan, according to Agence France-Presse (AFP). ICTR President Navanethem Pillay declared in April 2000 that she had directed the document to be placed under seal in the court's presidential chambers immediately upon receiving it, without her or the other judges reading it. On 10 February 2007 an Australian newspaper, *The Age*, published an article partly based on an interview with Hourigan and extracts from his two memos. The article corroborated the version of events put forward by Lyons in his prepared statement nearly six years earlier. Additional enquiries into who ordered and carried out the shooting down of Habyarimana's aircraft have also come in the form of two French judicial investigations (see *World Power Relations (1994–)*).

Arbour was succeeded in September 1999 as Prosecutor of the ICTR and the ICTY by Carla Del Ponte, who served on the Rwandan assignment until September 2003. Del Ponte complained that Kagame's opposition to her investigation of alleged RPF crimes, which she claimed included him successfully lobbying the UK and the USA, was the reason behind her mandate not being renewed. There have long been significant allegations of crimes committed by RPF forces, including systematic targeting of civilians that allegedly took place with near-total impunity. In August and September 1994 Robert Gersony, a consultant hired by the office of the UN High Commissioner for Refugees (UNHCR) to carry out a survey of refugees and displaced people, interviewed people in 41 out of 145 of Rwanda's communes, including in Gisenyi on the border with Zaire, Butare in the south of the country and Kibungo in the east, as well as in several refugee camps. A pattern allegedly became apparent; interviewees repeatedly testified that RPF soldiers had made contact with the local population, when they first arrived in newly won areas, initially reassuring people. However, within days soldiers would call people to a meeting, whereupon the assembled would allegedly be indiscriminately massacred. Gersony estimated that between 25,000 and 45,000 people had been killed by the RPF between early April and mid-September. While circulated to Rwanda's newly installed Government, the findings were suppressed by senior UN officials, who briefed Gersony never to speak publicly of his findings, according to Alison Des Forges and Gérard Prunier, two leading authorities on Rwanda during the 1990s. However, elements of the report were leaked to media outlets. The apparent suppression of Gersony's report was also referenced in a US diplomatic cable sent from Madrid, Spain, on 22 February 2008, published by WikiLeaks. It was alleged that in September 1994 UN Secretary-General Boutros Boutros-Ghali informed Rwanda's Minister of Foreign Affairs, Jean-Marie Vianney Ndagijimana, that if the killings stopped, this report would be 'swept under the rug'. Interviews and evaluation carried out by Prunier and HRW corroborated Gersony's conclusion that elements of the RPF had systematically targeted civilians both during the genocide and in the months that followed. In a more highly publicized incident, which was captured in part by a video journalist and witnessed by Australian peacekeepers and international aid workers, RPF troops repeatedly fired into a refugee camp at Kibeho on 22 April 1995. The RPF had been trying to disband the camp for months, amid concerns that it contained ex-FAR and Interahamwe elements. HRW estimated that 2,000 people were killed as a result of bullet wounds and a stampede, although other estimates put the death toll at up to 8,000. In December 1996 Col Fred Ibingira, the commanding officer at the time, was found guilty of failing 'to prevent criminal acts through immediate action', although he was acquitted of murder and the use of arms without orders. He was sentenced to 18 months in prison, but the presiding court stated that he had already spent this time in pre-trial detention, allowing his release. Seth Sendashonga, the post-genocide Minister of the Interior who was shot dead in exile in Nairobi in 1998, estimated that the RPF had killed a total of 60,000 people in Rwanda between April 1994 and August 1995.

However, the UN assessed that 500,000–800,000 Tutsis and moderate Hutus had been killed by the extremist Hutu regime, the Interahamwe and other militias between April and July 1994. The Rwandan Government, meanwhile, insists that it has identified by name 934,218 genocide victims, with help from survivor organizations, of whom 93.6% were Tutsi, while the others were categorized as Hutus who resembled Tutsis, were married to Tutsis, had hidden Tutsis or were opposed to the killings. On 28 August 2003 the UN Security Council called upon the ICTR to establish a 'Completion Strategy' to enable the conclusion of investigations by the end of 2004, of all trial activities at first instance by the end of 2008, and of all its work in 2010. In August 2004 Hassan Bubacar Jallow, who replaced Del Ponte at the ICTR, visited Rwanda to review the Government's proposal that at least some of those convicted by the ICTR of committing atrocities should serve their sentences in Rwandan prisons. The ICTR had initially opposed this strategy, as Rwanda at that time employed the death penalty, while the maximum ICTR sentence was life imprisonment. In June 2007 the Rwandan legislature removed the death penalty from all national statutes. In response, the ICTR commenced proceedings to transfer suspects from Arusha to the national courts in Kigali. The ICTR chambers initially denied some of the Prosecutor's requests for referral of cases to Rwanda for trial, noting concerns about obtaining witnesses, ensuring a fair trial and the risk of solitary confinement in Rwanda. More recently, however, the ICTR chambers have approved the referral of some suspects—the first being Jean-Bosco Uwinkindi, whose appeal against transfer was rejected in April 2012—to the Rwandan courts, which, in turn, instituted a special chamber in the High Court to handle the transfer and extradition of genocide suspects.

In mid-2005 the ICTR renewed its demand for prosecutions against members of the RPF for war crimes. Allegations that the RPF shot down President Habyarimana's aircraft in 1994 were of particular interest to the tribunal. In response, Aloys Mutabingwa, Rwanda's ICTR representative, demanded that the ICTR charge French government officials for their role in the events that precipitated the genocide. However, no prosecutions of RPF or French officials have occurred.

One of the ICTR's most significant convictions was that of Col Théoneste Bagosora, who was sentenced to life in prison in December 2008, having been convicted of genocide, war crimes and crimes against humanity. Bagosora was Cabinet Director in the Ministry of Defence, but assumed control of military and political affairs after Habyarimana's presidential aircraft was shot down. UNAMIR commander Dallaire described Bagosora as the 'kingpin' behind the genocide and alleged that the colonel had threatened to shoot him. Concluding that Bagosora had assumed authority over the military in the first days after the plane crash, the court found him responsible for the murder of five key moderate politicians, including Prime Minister Uwilingiyimana, as well as 10 Belgian peacekeepers assigned to protect her—a crime that had prompted the rapid decision of Belgium to withdraw its significant troop contingent—and of organized killings by troops under his command in Kigali and Gisenyi. He had been apprehended in Cameroon in 1996 and flown to the ICTR in 1997, prior to a trial that began in 2002 and continued until mid-2007. However, in December 2011 the Appeals Chamber overturned some of Bagosora's convictions, including responsibility for the murder of the peacekeepers and for ordering crimes committed at road blocks in the Kigali area, and reduced his sentence from life imprisonment to 35 years. Bagosora died at the age of 80 in Mali, where he had been serving his sentence, in September 2021.

By 15 May 2015 the ICTR had completed trial level work for all of its 93 accused individuals. It had delivered judgments at first instance for 75 defendants and appellate judgments for 55 defendants. The ICTR was the first international war crimes tribunal to: receive a guilty plea for genocide; convict an individual, a head of government, a woman and a clergyman for genocide; clarify the definition of rape in international law and hold that it could constitute genocide; and convict journalists for direct and public incitement to genocide.

Since the completion of trials at the ICTR, Rwanda has intensified efforts to extradite major alleged suspects to its own territory. Some countries refusing to extradite genocide suspects to Rwanda continued to cite concerns that the defendants would not receive a fair trial. In addition, by mid-2015 a number of countries—including Belgium, Canada, Denmark, Finland, France, Germany, the Netherlands, Norway, Sweden and Switzerland—had held, or were considering holding, trials of their own against suspected *génocidaires* on their territory.

The ICTR set out only to prosecute alleged major orchestrators of the crimes; anything else would be impossible, given the exhaustive procedures required to be observed by such international tribunals and the fact that tens of thousands—if not hundreds of thousands—of individuals took part in the genocide. It was always expected that Rwanda would organize its own parallel justice mechanism, which would concentrate on the numerous junior perpetrators. In February 1996 Rwanda announced the creation of special courts within the country's existing judicial system. Under these arrangements, the country's Supreme Court Chief Prosecutor began investigations in each of its 10 districts, and established three-member judicial panels in each district to consider cases. The panels were to comprise some 250 lay magistrates. In addition, 320 judicial police inspectors compiled dossiers on those detained for allegedly committing genocide. Newly established assessment commissions reviewed possible detentions on the basis of available evidence.

Despite significant reconstruction since then, the system had difficulties in dealing with the immense number of imprisoned genocide suspects awaiting trial. By late 2003 Rwandan courts had convicted approximately 6,500 suspects, of whom 600–700 received death sentences. To relieve the pressure on its courts and to facilitate a communal dialogue on the root causes of the genocide as a means to reconciliation, the Rwandan Government revived a long dormant entity, the so-called *gacaca* judicial system, whereby elders would deliberate and pass judgment. *Gacaca* thus represented a traditional, community-based model of participatory justice, to deal with the majority of genocide cases.

By June 2011 the *gacaca* courts had completed their backlog of genocide cases in all but a few jurisdictions. Rwanda's Government officially closed *gacaca* proceedings on 18 June 2012, exactly 10 years after the *gacaca* system's formal inauguration. A total of 1,958,000 suspects had been tried, of whom around 1,681,000 (86%) were convicted and some 277,000 (14%) acquitted. The *gacaca* courts reportedly heard appeals from 178,741 of those tried, affirming 132,902 and reversing 45,839.

In May 2020 Felicien Kabuga, a businessman who allegedly created and financed the Interahamwe, and was indicted by the ICTR in 1997 on seven counts, including genocide and incitement to commit genocide, was arrested by French agents. The 84-year-old Kabuga had been living under a false identity in a suburb of Paris, France, according to that country's Public Prosecutor and police, which issued a joint statement. In 2011 the ICTR, fearing that witnesses would die before Kabuga's arrest, had set up forums to gather and record witness testimonies ahead of any eventual trial. In October 2020 Kabuga was transferred from France to a UN detention facility in The Hague, where his trial was to be heard by the International Residual Mechanism for Criminal Tribunals, the ICTR having formally closed at the end of 2015. Kabuga avoided transfer to Tanzania after lawyers argued that his health was too poor and would be threatened further by the COVID-19 pandemic. A lawyer acting on his behalf entered a not guilty plea at a court hearing in The Hague in November, by which time the counts against him had been reduced to five. In June 2022 the UN Mechanism ruled that Kabuga was fit to stand trial, dismissing an argument presented by his defence to the contrary, and stipulated that proceedings should commence 'as soon as possible'. In December 2021 Rwanda's ambassador to the UN, Valentine Rugwabiza, complained that extended pre-trial hearings, reportedly centred on legal wranglings related to the seizure of assets, were further delaying victims' hopes of justice. In May 2022 UN prosecutors at the Mechanism announced that another alleged leader of the genocide and long-time fugitive, Protais Mpiranya, the former head of

Habyarimana's presidential guard, had in fact died in 2006 after contracting tuberculosis and been buried under a false name in Harare, Zimbabwe. He had long been accused of ordering or co-ordering the murder of Prime Minister Uwilingiyimana, the 10 Belgian peacekeepers assigned to protect her and other leading political moderates. His family was alleged by UN prosecutors to have repeatedly provided false statements to investigators, and to have urged those who knew of his presence and death in Harare to do likewise. A few days later the Mechanism announced that another high-profile fugitive, Pheneas Munyarugarama, was confirmed to have 'died of natural causes' in the DRC in 2002. He had been wanted on eight charges, including crimes of genocide and crimes against humanity.

Meanwhile, in November 2021 Claude Muhayimana, a Rwandan who had become a French national in 2010, went on trial in Paris on charges of complicity in the genocide. A hotel driver in 1994, he stood accused of driving Interahamwe and police personnel, in the knowledge that he was facilitating their efforts to massacre Tutsis, in Kibuye. Arrested in 2014 after an investigation by French prosecutors, Muhayimana was the first ordinary civilian to go on trial in France on charges pertaining to the Rwandan genocide, although a former intelligence officer and two Rwandan mayors had been convicted in France on genocide charges in March 2014 and July 2016, respectively. Complicating the Muhayimana case, investigators acknowledged that the driver had also hidden Tutsis and helped some to escape from militia. However, he was convicted of complicity in genocide and crimes against humanity in December 2021 and was sentenced to 14 years in prison.

In July 2022 Laurent Bucyibaruta, a former high-ranking Rwandan official, was convicted by a court in Paris of complicity in genocide and crimes against humanity during his prefecture of Gikongoro province in south-western Rwanda, where the Murambi Technical School, the site of one of the largest massacres of the genocide on 21 April 1994, was located. Bucyibaruta, who was acquitted of the more serious charge of genocide, was sentenced to 20 years' imprisonment.

RWANDA RECAST: A REGIONAL POWER (1994–)

When the RPF forced the short-lived extremist regime out of Rwanda in July 1994, it inherited little more than a graveyard full of unburied and mutilated bodies. The situation was worst in urban centres, while crops rotted in fields and most of the country's livestock had been slaughtered to feed the warring military factions and pro-Government militia. Not only had hundreds of thousands of civilians been killed, but millions more—some of whom were perpetrators of the genocide—had fled into exile in the neighbouring countries of Burundi, Tanzania and, above all, Zaire, where a well-armed rump of the FAR established itself as a regime-in-exile, launching cross-border attacks against the RPF.

In short, it was difficult to see how the country could be reassembled, and more difficult still to envisage that, in just a few years, Rwanda would become a regional military power with a strength far greater than had ever been believed possible by earlier governments. Yet, by the mid-2000s Rwanda's post-genocide Government had done much more than secure its own borders from the remnants of the FAR and the Interahamwe. It had established Kigali as one of the safest and fastest growing commercial centres in Africa; been instrumental in removing at least one President in the neighbouring DRC; and become a key contributor of troops to a UN peacekeeping mission in Sudan's Darfur provinces, intent—verbally, at least—on stemming an ethnic slaughter under way there.

Perhaps the biggest single factor in resurrecting Rwanda as a viable and coherent national entity has been the military discipline and aggression displayed by the country's new army, comprised overwhelmingly of the guerrilla fighters who had claimed victory in July 1994. This largely Tutsi force was spurred on initially by a desire to stem the murder of fellow Tutsi civilians. The rank and file displayed a formidable military coherence and willingness to die for their cause, under the stewardship of spectacularly effective senior leaders, including, but not limited to, Kagame.

When Rwanda invaded Zaire in October 1996, it was ostensibly to confront the remnants of the former national army, former presidential guard members and militia that had been responsible for the genocide. However, the invasion was about much more than hunting down and neutralizing the genocide perpetrators. The RPF had seized an opportunity to access the resources required to rebuild and rebrand Rwanda, becoming a major player in its giant eastern neighbour, which contains huge deposits of copper, gold, tin, coltan and wolframite. The RPF thus became a pivotal actor in the Alliance des Forces Démocratiques pour la Libération du Congo (AFDL), an armed coalition led by Congolese rebel Laurent-Désiré Kabila. In October the AFDL set out to oust the longstanding Congolese dictator Mobutu Sese Seko. An RPF leader, Gen. James Kabarebe, was the AFDL's chief military strategist. Battling cancer and unable to martial effective resistance, Mobutu and his national army crumbled, with many soldiers defecting, and he was duly removed from power in May 1997. After being welcomed by cheering crowds on the streets of Zaire's capital, Kinshasa, Kabila declared himself President and, at this point, renamed the country as the DRC. Kabarebe was appointed as head of the DRC's new national army, giving the Rwandan Government extraordinary regional influence. In the space of barely three years, the RPF had transformed from a largely untested guerrilla outfit fighting for recognition of an ethnic minority's rights in one of Africa's smallest countries, to a regional military player with largely unimpeded access to some of the world's most resource-rich territories.

While initially extremely grateful to the military guidance provided by Kabarebe, Kabila's relations with his RPF supporters soured quickly. Kabila ordered Rwandan troops to leave the DRC in July 1998, amid concerns that his initial popularity was being destroyed by the perception that the RPF was attempting to run the country as a client state and plundering its natural resources. This order precipitated a catastrophe; Rwanda and its close ally Uganda responded by going to war with Kabila's regime, which in turn requested military assistance from Angola. A five-year conflict ensued, also engaging Zimbabwe and Burundi in what became known as 'Africa's World War'.

So intense was the competition for control in the DRC—particularly in the eastern provinces, which hold the bulk of mineral wealth—that the Rwandan and Ugandan militaries clashed in Kisangani in August 1999, before further confrontations between the erstwhile allies in May 2000 and June 2002, when what was by then known as the Rwandan Patriotic Army finally dislodged the Ugandan People's Defence Forces from the city. Intense diplomatic engagement by world powers engineered a peace process, which required all foreign militaries to disengage from the DRC; Rwanda formally withdrew its forces in September 2002. In October 2010 a mapping report was published by the Office of the UN High Commissioner for Human Rights into atrocities committed in the DRC between March 1993 and March 2003. The report included details of grave human rights violations, largely allegedly committed in 1996–97 by the AFDL and the RPF, the latter standing accused of an 'apparently relentless pursuit and mass killing of Hutu refugees' resulting in the deaths of 'several tens of thousands'. The authors further stated that their findings revealed 'a number of inculpatory elements that, if proven before a competent court, could be characterized as crimes of possible genocide'. Kagame reacted with fury to the allegation of possible genocide by the RPF.

Allegations that Rwanda was continuing to deploy troops in the DRC, and support proxy forces, persisted for many years beyond the formal military withdrawal in 2002. In June 2004 a Congolese Tutsi faction briefly occupied Bukavu, the capital of Sud-Kivu province, before pulling out under heavy diplomatic pressure. Rwanda denied that it was supporting this faction, which was led by Laurent Nkunda, who in turn claimed to be protecting the Congolese Tutsi community from remnants of the extremist Hutu regime. By then, such remnants were down to a hardcore of a few thousand exiled fighters organized under the banner of the Forces Démocratiques pour la Libération du Rwanda (FDLR). Nkunda subsequently continued to expand

his sphere of influence, culminating in his rebel group, the Congrès National pour la Défense du Peuple (CNDP), nearly capturing Goma, the capital of Nord-Kivu province, in October 2008. The Kivu provinces border Rwanda and are two of the DRC's most mineral-rich areas.

There was a brief and highly unexpected rapprochement between Rwanda and the DRC in early 2009, when President Joseph Kabila (who had come to power after his father Laurent was assassinated in January 2001) invited Rwandan troops onto Congolese soil, for a six-week period, in a bid to strike a decisive blow against the FDLR. The logic in Kinshasa was that terminating the threat posed by the FDLR would remove any legitimate reason for Rwanda to have further involvement in the Kivu provinces, helping Kabila achieve his stated goal of pacifying this restive area ahead of presidential and legislative elections scheduled for 2011. However, Kabila was confounded by the emergence of a new Congolese Tutsi rebel group in April 2012, the Mouvement du 23 Mars (M23). The group's name was based upon the date of a 2009 peace deal between the CNDP and the DRC Government, and the rebel group claimed that Kabila had failed to honour that agreement, which was supposed to see the rebel outfit fully integrated into the Forces Armées de la République Démocratique du Congo (FARDC). This latest Tutsi-led insurgency in eastern DRC was orchestrated and controlled by Rwanda, according to a report by the UN Group of Experts. This accusation was strongly denied by the Rwandan Government, but it was unable to convince the majority of its donors of its innocence, resulting in suspensions of aid (see *World Power Relations (1994–)*). M23 seized control of much of Nord-Kivu between April and November 2012, culminating in it occupying Goma for a week, before intense international diplomatic pressure forced it to withdraw from the city.

The capture of Goma proved to be M23's peak; its influence waned thereafter, as its two main wings clashed militarily, while reports also indicated that they suffered a withdrawal of alleged Rwandan support, leaving them without international backing. In February 2013 11 countries—including Rwanda and the DRC—signed a new peace accord, the Great Lakes Agreement, which was fortified by a pledge of World Bank funding to the amount of US $1,000m. to be invested in infrastructure and cross-border trade. In early November the Congolese army scored a decisive and final victory against M23, as its remnants confirmed the end of their rebellion and sought sanctuary in Uganda.

While the border between Rwanda and the DRC has remained relatively calm subsequently, sporadic clashes or raids continued to occur, with Kigali periodically complaining of incursions by the FDLR. However, the election of a new President in the DRC in a long-delayed poll on 30 December 2018 spurred a dramatic improvement in relations between Kigali and Kinshasa. The incoming President, Félix Tshisekedi, a son of longstanding opposition figure Etienne Tshisekedi, embarked on new policy directions, including repairing relations with Rwanda. Tshisekedi laid a wreath at the genocide memorial in Kigali in March 2019 on the sidelines of an economic conference. He also held repeated consultations with Kagame on the DRC's potential entry to the East African Community (EAC), at a time when the Rwandan President was Chairman of that bloc. The DRC duly applied to join the EAC in June, in a formal letter dispatched by Tshisekedi to Kagame, who directed the Secretariat to submit the application for consideration at a heads of state summit in November. Relations were further bolstered by the Congolese army launching successful operations against the FDLR, which numbered between 500 and 600 active fighters in early 2019 according to UN estimates. In mid-September the FARDC launched an operation targeting Sylvestre Mudacumura, the military head of the FDLR, in Nord-Kivu. FARDC spokesperson Richard Kasonga announced that the operation had 'neutralized' Mudacumura (who had been sought since 2012 by the International Criminal Court (ICC) for war crimes committed during the joint DRC-Rwandan military campaign of 2009–10), along with 'all the elements accompanying him'. The news of the killing of Mudacumura, who had served as a deputy commander in Habyarimana's presidential guard and led a battalion in northern Rwanda during the genocide, was welcomed by Rwanda. In November 2019 the FARDC killed the leader of an FDLR offshoot, Juvenal Musabimana (also known by his nom de guerre, 'Jean-Michel Africa'), along with four bodyguards in a gun battle in Binza, Nord-Kivu. His splinter group was identified by Kigali as being responsible for a cross-border raid in the previous month that had killed eight people in north-western Rwanda's mountainous gorilla hotspot. Rwanda's Minister of State in charge of the East African Community, Olivier Nduhungirehe, described Musabimana's demise as 'confirmation of the resolve of President Félix Tshisekedi and the FARDC to eradicate armed groups and terrorist organizations in eastern Congo'. However, in an ominous sign of old military dynamics resurfacing on the DRC side of the border and generating renewed friction between the neighbouring states, the DRC army blamed M23 for a series of attacks against positions held by its troops in Rutshuru, Nord-Kivu, in November 2021. In January 2022 more than 20 DRC soldiers were killed during another ambush by this resurgent Tutsi rebel group, according to local authorities. In June Gen. Sylvain Ekenge, a spokesperson for the military governor of Nord-Kivu, claimed that Rwanda had covertly deployed 500 special forces personnel across the border, accusing the neighbouring country of changing the uniform of its soldiers 'to conceal its presence on Congolese territory alongside the terrorists of M23'. Rwanda repeatedly denied that it was backing the rebel group. In the same month the UN Group of Experts alleged that M23 was planning once again to seize the border town of Goma.

A Hutu-dominated administration came to power in Burundi with a landslide election victory in June 2005 and that country's new President, Pierre Nkurunziza, the leader of what had been a Hutu rebel group, maintained largely cordial relations with Kagame for the next decade. However, relations between Rwanda and Burundi deteriorated markedly in 2015–16. A political crisis erupted in Burundi in April 2015, when the ruling Conseil National pour la Défense de la Démocratie—Forces de Défense de la Démocratie selected Nkurunziza as its candidate for a presidential election scheduled to be held that year, contravening the terms of the peace accord that had ended the civil war (which stipulated a two-term limit for the presidency) and arguably also Burundi's Constitution. On 26 April street protests erupted in largely Tutsi opposition strongholds in Bujumbura, the capital, which were repeatedly suppressed by the police, including with gunfire. An unsuccessful coup attempt was launched on 13 May, and was subsequently used to justify a crackdown by Burundi's security forces; by the end of October UNHCR reported that over 200,000 people had fled the country, mainly to Tanzania and Rwanda. Meanwhile, armed elements emerged to begin fighting Nkurunziza's regime and reports indicated that Rwanda was providing military training to Burundian rebels on its territory. The Rwandan Government repeatedly denied the allegations. Nkurunziza died in June 2020, officially as a result of a heart attack, shortly after Evariste Ndayishimiye, the ruling party's former Secretary-General, had been elected as his successor. Under President Ndayishimiye, Burundi sought to repair relations with donors and also closer to home. The Rwandan and Burundian ministers responsible for foreign affairs, Vincent Biruta and Albert Shingiro, respectively, met in October at the Nemba-Gasenyi border post, in what Rwanda's Government described as 'a mutual effort to normalize bilateral relations', which it recognized as being damaged since the 2015 crisis in Burundi. Further tentative moves towards normalization came in 2021 and early 2022. In July 2021 Kagame dispatched Prime Minister Edouard Ngirente to attend celebrations held to commemorate Burundi's annual Independence Day, and in January 2022 he received a Burundian delegation led by the Minister for East African Community Affairs, Ezéchiel Nibigira, prompting the Rwandan President to declare in February that 'satisfying progress' was being made in rebuilding bilateral relations.

Kagame has long sought to improve Rwanda's credentials as both a significant diplomatic and military power continentally, by maintaining a high profile at the AU and through deployments to peacekeeping missions. In April 2004 Rwandan soldiers were the first foreign troops to arrive in the Darfur region of western Sudan, where they were to protect the AU observer mission and defend Sudanese civilians. By September 2010 a total of 3,300 Rwandan soldiers were serving with the AU/UN Hybrid operation in Darfur, the Force Commander of which, Lt-Gen. Patrick Nyamvumba, was a Rwandan. Rwanda contributed peacekeepers to the UN Mission in South Sudan, where a civil war broke out in December 2013. Rwanda has also deployed troops to the Central African Republic (CAR) to serve as part of a multilateral intervention, and in December 2020 the Rwandan Ministry of Defence confirmed that it had sent troops to support the once-more beleaguered CAR Government against various rebel groups. Kagame stated that the newly arrived personnel were bound by a bilateral agreement with the CAR, rather than by UN rules of engagement, informing journalists that the troops were instructed to contain 'any situation that is aimed at disrupting the elections and also protect Rwandan peacekeepers against being targeted by rebels'. The CAR Government was also receiving military support from the Russian Federation, amid efforts by the Russian Government to increase its influence in the mineral-rich region. Kagame assumed the one-year rotating chairmanship of the AU on 1 January 2018, during which he sought strongly to reduce the Union's dependence on foreign aid.

During his tenure as AU Chairman, Kagame worked hard to revive ties between Rwanda and South Africa, which had been severely strained by Karegeya's murder (see *Kagame the Kingpin (1994–)*) and the repeated attempts to assassinate Nyamwasa in South Africa. The Rwandan President met his new South African counterpart, Cyril Ramaphosa—who assumed office in February 2018, succeeding Jacob Zuma—on 20 March of that year, at a conference for the Africa Continental Free Trade Area. Following bilateral talks, South Africa's new head of state announced that he was working with President Kagame to 'put relations between Rwanda and South Africa on a much better footing'. However, those efforts encountered significant difficulties later in 2018, as South Africa's Minister of International Relations and Co-operation, Lindiwe Sisulu, came under fire from Rwanda for suggesting Nyamwasa was open to a rapprochement with Kigali. Sisulu had been tasked with handling the normalization process by Ramaphosa.

Further consolidating its continental political and military influence, Rwanda was the first African nation to send soldiers to reinforce Mozambique's army against Ahlu Sunna Wal Jama, a militant group that pledged allegiance to Islamic State's Wilayat Wasat Afriqiyya (Central Africa Province) in 2019. The rebel group's insurgency centred on Mozambique's gas-rich Cabo Delgado province, and it attacked the port city of Palma in March 2021. Rwanda dispatched the first of nearly 1,000 troops in July. Those soldiers worked closely with Mozambiquan government forces to push Ahlu Sunna Wal-Jama out of Mocímboa da Praia, another port city that had served as the rebels' headquarters. In September the Mozambiquan President, Filipe Jacinto Nyusi, received Kagame in Pemba, the capital of Cabo Delgado province, and told him that Mozambique would be 'forever grateful' for Rwanda's military assistance.

Relations between Rwanda and Uganda (which have been periodically strained) deteriorated afresh in 2019. In March the Rwandan Minister of Foreign Affairs and International Co-operation, Richard Sezibera, accused the Ugandan authorities of co-operating with the RNC, to the extent that the Rwandan opposition group (which also had significant elements in Belgium, South Africa and allegedly the DRC) had provided 'instructions on arresting Rwandans' in Uganda, and also of providing support to the FDLR. This came shortly after Rwanda had issued a travel advisory to its citizens, warning them against visiting Uganda for fear of arrest, torture and deportation. On 25 May Uganda's Ministry of Foreign Affairs released a statement to protest against a 'violation of its territorial integrity' by Rwandan soldiers, who were alleged to have fatally shot a Rwandan and a Ugandan in pursuit of a suspected smuggler. The key Gatuna border crossing, which had been temporarily closed, was reopened to cargo in June for a trial period of 12 days, but that period elapsed without the two sides making progress on the issues dividing them. Amid restrictions prompted by the COVID-19 pandemic, the border crossing did not fully reopen until March 2022, a few weeks after Museveni's son, Muhoozi Kainerugaba, who was widely regarded as the Ugandan President's chosen successor, travelled to Kigali to meet Kagame, in what was described by both sides as a cordial encounter.

WORLD POWER RELATIONS (1994–)

Rwanda's relations with the DRC have been key to the post-genocide narrative, not only in terms of Kigali's ties with the Great Lakes region, but also in the shape of alliances and tensions with major world powers. The spillover from the genocide is widely agreed to have been the main external stimulus for the DRC's repeated wars and instability over the last two decades, even if Mobutu's domestic mismanagement was bound to result in regime implosion at some stage. Rwanda has always sought to frame its interventions in the DRC as being motivated entirely by security concerns, emanating from the threat posed by the ex-FAR, the Interahamwe and the FDLR. At mid-2022 the FDLR maintained a foothold in the DRC, albeit a substantially diminished one.

Donors' responses to Rwanda's repeated interventions in the DRC were initially muted, but became increasingly strident from late 2004, when, more than two years after formally withdrawing its military, troops were allegedly again sent across the border. Rwanda's Government claimed that it had not acted on its threat to re-invade, but this was not sufficient to convince Sweden's Government, which suspended aid, while the UK and the USA also reportedly put pressure on Rwanda to withdraw. However, the most damaging episode came with the emergence of M23 some eight years later. The detailed allegations contained in the UN Group of Experts' report—particularly the charge that the rebellion was controlled by Gen. Kabarebe—were vehemently denied by Rwanda; however, the USA, the UK, Germany, the Netherlands and Sweden all suspended elements of their respective bilateral aid programmes to Rwanda in 2012 in response to the new crisis in eastern DRC, while, at the multilateral level, the EU—Rwanda's biggest donor—also partially froze its financial support. The US Department of State's Office of Global Criminal Justice warned Kagame in July that his Government's actions could leave him open to charges of 'aiding and abetting' crimes against humanity in a neighbouring country—charges similar to those that resulted in Liberia's former President Charles Taylor receiving a 50-year sentence in May that year.

Other factors were also increasingly undermining donor confidence, not least the multiple allegations that Kagame's regime was attempting to assassinate exiled dissidents in South Africa and the UK. In April 2011 Rwanda's High Commissioner to the UK, Ernest Rwamucyo, was warned by MI5, the British domestic intelligence and security agency, that a campaign of harassment and intimidation against Rwandan nationals in the country must cease if Kigali expected aid from the British Government to continue. (Rwanda had formally joined the Commonwealth in November 2009.) By 2016 the British Government's Department for International Development had become reluctant to furnish journalists with details of ongoing aid to Rwanda, beyond insisting that direct budgetary support had ceased. In April 2022 the British and Rwandan Governments concluded the UK-Rwanda Migration and Economic Development Partnership, under the terms of which Kigali agreed to receive asylum seekers in return for payment of £120m. (nearly US $160m.), as part of British efforts to discourage undocumented migrants from attempting to gain entry to the UK from France via the English Channel. Rwanda's Ministry of Foreign Affairs and International Co-operation stated that the agreement, which was widely condemned on humanitarian grounds, including by UNHCR, would involve migrants being 'integrated' into communities across Rwanda. A ruling by the European Court of Human Rights (ECHR) prevented the inaugural flight carrying asylum seekers from leaving the UK in June, shortly before it was due to take off for Rwanda. Both Rwanda and the UK defended the scheme, which was subsequently discussed between Kagame and the British Prime Minister, Boris Johnson, on the sidelines of the Commonwealth Heads of Government meeting in Kigali later that month, after the British Government had already pledged to introduce parliamentary legislation to nullify the ECHR ruling.

However, while the regime in Kigali accumulated diplomatic capital via its new arrangement with the UK, the continued resurgence of the M23 rebel group brought renewed friction with the USA as 2022 wore on. US Secretary of State Antony Blinken stated during a visit to the region in early August that Washington was 'very concerned' by 'credible' reports that Rwanda was backing the M23, referring to a report by the UN Group of Experts on the DRC which alleged, *inter alia*, that Rwandan troops had directly attacked the Congolese military across the border. Blinken's words came after the Chairman of the US Senate Foreign Relations Committee, Senator Robert Menendez, announced that Washington's security assistance to Kigali was being placed on hold.

Rwanda's post-genocide relationship with France, the West's other permanent member of the UN Security Council, was for a long time either tense or non-existent. Kagame and the RPF have viewed France with suspicion, due to its military intervention in support of Habyarimana in the early stages of the 1990–94 civil war and its intervention towards the end of the genocide, which perceived as an attempt to prevent a full military defeat for the extremist regime. Indeed, Operation Turquoise strongly facilitated the escape of the ex-FAR and Interahamwe to Zaire, contributing to the decades of crisis that followed across the border, even though the crisis was prolonged and severely exacerbated by the pursuit of mineral wealth by both Rwanda and Uganda. A commission appointed by the Rwandan Government to investigate France's alleged role in the Rwanda genocide published a report in August 2008, detailing the alleged involvement of senior French government and military officials in arming and training genocidal militias in 1994. The French Government maintained that French peacekeeping troops had saved 'several hundred thousand lives' during the genocide.

In November 2006 a French judge, Jean-Louis Bruguière, issued arrest warrants for nine of Kagame's aides, alleging their involvement in Habyarimana's assassination. Rwanda immediately severed relations with France, ordering the French ambassador and other diplomats in Rwanda to leave the country. However, in November 2009 it was announced that, following extensive dialogue between the two countries, Rwanda and France were to restore diplomatic relations. In January 2010 Laurent Contini, hitherto France's ambassador to Zimbabwe, was appointed to Rwanda, and Rwanda officially reopened its embassy in Paris in February, immediately prior to a visit to Kigali by French President Nicolas Sarkozy. During the visit, Sarkozy admitted that France had made a number of 'serious errors of judgement' (although without admitting responsibility) in the period following the assassination of Habyarimana, and pledged to bring to justice any person resident in France suspected of involvement in the genocide. The Rwandan Government welcomed a decision taken by the French authorities in the previous month to create a special investigative unit to expedite the prosecution of genocide crimes.

In December 2010 at least six of the arrest warrants issued against Kagame's aides were dropped by French investigative judges Marc Trevidic and Nathalie Poux, who took over the investigation from Bruguière. In January 2012 Poux and Trevidic presented their report to Kagame's lawyers, who told the media that the judges had concluded that the missiles could not have been fired from a base occupied by the RPF. Rwanda's Minister of Foreign Affairs and International Co-operation, Louise Mushikiwabo, asserted that 'it is now clear to all that the downing of the plane was a *coup d'état* carried by extremist Hutu elements and their advisers who controlled Kanombe barracks', referring to what was then the base of Habyarimana's presidential guard. The two judges relied heavily on ballistics experts during their investigation, and concluded that the Kanombe barracks was the 'most probable', albeit not proven, launch point for the missiles that had brought down the aircraft, based largely on analysis of wreckage distribution and firing trajectories. At the time of the attack, these barracks were accessible only to the FAR, the presidential guard, other high-ranking loyalist elements and foreign advisers to the Habyarimana regime. However, the French judges repeatedly reassessed the case in subsequent years. The investigative team had intended to hear testimony from a former soldier, Emmanuel Mughisa, in December 2014, according to his lawyer, but Mughisa was reportedly kidnapped close to his home in Nairobi in November and disappeared. The GlobalPost news service reported that he had claimed to possess evidence that Kagame had ordered Habyarimana's aircraft to be shot down. The case file in the French judicial investigation was closed again in January 2016, before being reopened later that year. According to French media, the new judicial move came after exiled former RDF Chief of Staff Gen. Nyamwasa provided a notarized deposition to the investigators in June, in which he claimed that Kagame had ordered the attack, while also asserting his own innocence. This resulted in France requesting help from South Africa in questioning Nyamwasa. In October 2017 AFP, citing a source close to the French investigation, reported that a new witness had claimed to have loaded two Russian-manufactured SA-16 surface-to-air missiles onto a truck that was headed for Kigali at RPF headquarters in Mulindi, northern Rwanda, in March 1994. The investigative judges had concluded in their report released in January 2012 that there was 'a very strong probability' that SA-16 missiles had been used in the attack.

A new diplomatic crisis had already erupted between France and Rwanda in April 2014, when Kagame reiterated allegations that France had played a direct role in the genocide. In June 2017 three non-governmental organizations filed a lawsuit in Paris against BNP Paribas, claiming that Banque Nationale de Paris (as it was known prior to merging with Paribas in 2000) knowingly facilitated a US $1.3m. transfer during the genocide from Banque Nationale du Rwanda to the account of an arms dealer, in contravention of an arms embargo. In May 2018 Kagame travelled to France and met French President Emmanuel Macron for talks, with both sides seeking yet again to improve ties and to draw a line under the post-genocide dispute. In a sign of potential rapprochement, Macron supported the candidature of Rwanda's Minister of Foreign Affairs and International Co-operation, Mushikiwabo, for the post of Secretary-General of the OIF, which comprised 58 full member states and brings together French-speaking nations across the globe. Mushikiwabo was duly confirmed in the post in October 2018, at an OIF conference in the Armenian capital, Yerevan. The appointment was highly symbolic after many years in which Rwanda had resolutely rejected its francophone past by promoting the English language and joining the British-led Commonwealth. France was reported to have ended the lengthy judicial investigation into the shooting down of President Habyarimana's aircraft in December 2018. The prosecutors had already requested in October that the case be abandoned, due to insufficient evidence. In February 2022 the Court of Cassation rejected an appeal seeking to overturn the closing of the case, which had been lodged by the families of those onboard the plane.

Meanwhile, in April 2019 President Macron announced the creation of a commission of historians and researchers who would be granted access to French government archives to evaluate the country's actions during the genocide. In March 2020 the commission, led by historian Vincent Duclert, presented a report of nearly 1,000 pages to Macron, which found that the French Government of the time bore 'heavy and overwhelming responsibilities' for the events that culminated in the genocide, notably including its long involvement 'with a regime that encouraged racist massacres'. The authors of the report did not accuse the Government of complicity in the ethnic slaughter, while describing it as having been 'blind to the preparation of a genocide by the most radical elements of this (Rwandan) regime'. However, they concluded that high-level perpetrators were granted safe haven by French troops during Operation Turquoise near the end of the civil war. Duclert told media that he believed France should apologize for its historical policies towards Rwanda, describing its approach of the time as violent and marked by 'a very colonialist superiority'. The report elicited mixed reactions from leading figures within the French Government of that time. While former Minister of Foreign Affairs Alain Juppé wrote in *Le Monde* that 'we did not act in the way we should have done', Edouard Balladur, Prime Minister between 1993 and 1995 in the Government of François Mitterrand, deplored the report's findings in an interview with news television network France 24. (Mitterrand himself had died in 1996.) Macron's Office of the President announced on 7 April 2021, the annual anniversary of the beginning of the genocide, that France would open state archives on Rwanda. During a visit to the Gisozi genocide memorial in Kigali in May, Macron declared: 'I hereby humbly and with respect ... come to recognize the extent of our responsibilities', and professed that 'only those who went through that night can perhaps forgive, and in doing so give the gift of forgiveness'. Kagame described his words as 'more powerful than an apology'.

Similar to most African nations, Rwanda has developed relations with the People's Republic of China, in a bid to spur its development and diversify dependence away from Western partners. Kagame has cautiously extolled the Chinese model of engagement, pointedly endorsing a preference for doing business on equal terms, rather than the West's tendency to use aid as a tool to influence governance. China is now Rwanda's leading non-African trade partner.

Economy

DUNCAN WOODSIDE

INTRODUCTION

Rwanda's economy has undergone significant development over the last two decades, despite the tiny country's landlocked status, extreme population density and the catastrophic legacy of the 1994 genocide. Real economic growth averaged 8% per year over the period 2001–15, according to the World Bank. For most of the post-genocide period, economic growth has been buoyed by high levels of donor engagement—in large part due to the international community seeking to make amends for standing aside during the genocide itself. Low levels of corruption have also spurred development, with Transparency International's 2021 Corruption Perceptions Index placing Rwanda 52nd out of 180 countries and territories, well above its regional peers. Indeed, neighbouring Burundi and the Democratic Republic of the Congo (DRC) were jointly ranked 169th, Somalia was ranked 178th and South Sudan was last, in 180th place.

The country's Vision 2020 development plan envisaged the transformation of the economy from one based largely on agriculture to a middle-income system predicated on knowledge, technology and services. To this end, a second Economic Development and Poverty Reduction Strategy (EDPRS) was announced, with steady progress made, and the Government drafted a new longer-term economic blueprint designed to help the country attain upper-middle income status by 2035. This new development strategy (provisionally entitled Vision 2050) included five priority goals: achieving high living standards, in part by improving infrastructure access and security; bolstering modern infrastructure and incomes through the development of more sustainable and sophisticated services; structurally overhauling the economy by boosting output and competitiveness in key fields; fostering social values such as gender equality, national unity, self-reliance and good governance; and increasing regional co-operation.

After several years of relatively slow expansion, Rwanda registered highly impressive gross domestic product (GDP) growth in 2018, at a rate of 8.6%, according to the International Monetary Fund (IMF). The rate of real GDP growth accelerated further to 9.5% in 2019. However, it quickly became clear in the early months of 2020 that the economy would be hit hard by the coronavirus (COVID-19) pandemic sweeping the world.

On 2 April 2020 the IMF's Executive Board approved the disbursement of US $109.4m. to Rwanda under a Rapid Credit Facility, in order to help the country tackle the economic impact of the COVID-19 crisis. The Fund also noted that the World Bank was expected to offer budget support of $59m. to the Government. Rwanda had, on 22 March, been the first country in Africa to impose a nationwide lockdown to stop the spread of COVID-19. It also closed its land borders to everything except cargo, after shutting down commercial airspace on 19 March. The Government eased the lockdown from 4 May, although some restrictions remained in place; schools partly reopened in November.

The IMF announced in a May 2021 press release, following a virtual mission review of performance under a Policy Co-ordination Instrument programme, that Rwanda's economy had contracted by 4.4% in real terms in the first half of 2020, before a partial stabilization in the second half of the year, resulting in a decline in GDP of 3.4% for that year overall. This represented the first year of recession since the 1994 genocide, according to the National Bank of Rwanda (NBR). However, the economy rebounded strongly in 2021, registering real GDP growth of 10.9%, thanks to a strong recovery by the industry and services sectors, alongside a robust performance by the agriculture sector, which was facilitated by favourable weather. This impressive economic growth rate was achieved even as consumer price inflation dropped into negative territory between May and September 2021, before increasing to a positive rate of 1.9% at the end of that year (and averaging 0.8% in 2021 overall).

The outlook for 2022 was clouded by the Russian Federation's invasion of Ukraine, which contributed to soaring global food and fuel prices, with resource-constrained developing countries that depend heavily on imports, such as Rwanda, particularly affected. The IMF forecast in May that Rwanda's real GDP growth would slow to 6.0% and raised concerns about the impact of the external headwinds on the country's fiscal deficit, which had already hovered at close to 9.0% of GDP in 2020 and 2021, due to increased expenditure as a result of the COVID-19 pandemic. Meanwhile, despite the implementation in February 2022 of a 50-basis-point increase in the benchmark rate, to 5.0%, consumer price inflation accelerated sharply, reaching an annualized rate of 13.7% in June, up from 5.8% in February and from just 1.9% in December 2021, according to official data.

AGRICULTURE

Agriculture remains by far the dominant economic activity in Rwanda, with the sector accounting for 24% of the country's GDP and 47.4% of the employed labour force in 2021, according to official figures. In 2018 arable land covered 46.7% of the country, while 10.1% of land nationwide was devoted to permanent crops and 17.4% to permanent pasture. Since the late 1970s the area of land annually made available for subsistence crops has increased only marginally, and crop yields have declined in many areas, owing to erosion and the traditional intensive cultivation methods used. The principal food crops are plantains, sweet potatoes, potatoes, cassava, beans, sorghum, rice, maize and peas. In general terms, production of cereals—particularly maize and sorghum—is strong. In 2005 the Government launched a 10-year rice development programme. Rice, then grown on approximately 7,455 ha, was selected as a 'priority crop' since it performs well in flood-prone valleys and eases pressure on hillside land for other crops, and also because domestic demand is high. It was planned to increase the cultivated area to 66,000 ha by 2016, through improved management of new areas in the marshlands, with the aim of meeting domestic requirements and generating export earnings. By 2019 estimated annual rice production shad risen to 131,600 metric tons; however, in 2020 output declined to 116,500 tons. Meanwhile, the Government was also attempting to bolster the potato industry, and in 2017 it concluded an agreement with Nigerian investors on a five-year project, worth US $120m., to boost the production and processing of Irish potatoes.

The IMF reported considerable success by Rwanda in tackling rural poverty, owing in large part, it claimed, to the implementation of its first EDPRS over the period 2007/08 to 2012/13. The Government published a second EDPRS, covering the period 2013/14 to 2017/18, which entailed an intensified drive to shift productive capacity away from agriculture and towards industry and services. The programme was guided by the Vision 2020 strategy, adopted in May 2012, which included targets to raise per capita GDP to US $1,240; attain average GDP growth of 11.5%; reduce poverty to 20% and eliminate extreme poverty; create 1.8m. off-farm jobs; increase exports by 28% a year; and establish the private sector as the dominant investor in the economy.

The UN's Food and Agriculture Organization (FAO) estimated that maize production in 2020 totalled 448,600 metric tons, compared with 421,200 tons in 2019. Production of sorghum increased from 159,600 tons in 2019 to 170,500 tons in 2020. The 2022/23 budget provided for a 65% increase in fertilizer subsidies across the fiscal year, amounting to additional support for the agriculture sector of 0.1% of GDP, according to the IMF. The extra funding was designed to boost domestic food production, amid the rising cost of imports owing to the Russian invasion of Ukraine (a major wheat producer) in February 2022. In May Prime Minister Edouard Ngirente noted that Rwanda had turned to Brazil and Australia as alternative sources of wheat, in a bid to mitigate the supply issues affecting wheat imports from Ukraine. The IMF was also seeking to boost credit to the agriculture sector, through a joint initiative with the World Bank, the US Agency for International Development and the African Development Bank (AfDB). In 2018 some 11.1% of the country was covered by forest, while forestry revenues accounted for 3.8% of GDP.

Coffee and Tea

Revenue from coffee fluctuates considerably from year to year, due to the effect of local weather patterns on output and quality and also price volatility in international markets. The principal destination for Rwanda's coffee, as reported in early 2017, was Switzerland, which received 42% of the crop, followed by the USA (21%) and the United Kingdom (12%). According to the National Agricultural Export Development Board (NAEB), coffee exports reached US $68.8m. in 2018/19, but declined to $60.4m. in 2019/20, before increasing to $61.5m. in 2020/21. The increase in receipts prior to 2019/20 came in a context where the country was increasingly focusing on producing premium coffee grades, with 60% of coffee exports falling into this category in 2018, up from 58% in 2017 and zero in 2000. Bill Kayonga, CEO of the NAEB, declared in September 2019 that the Board had set a target of 80% of coffee production falling into the premium category in 2020.

As with the coffee industry, the tea industry in Rwanda is notoriously volatile, owing to fluctuations in production and international prices. Green leaf production in 2016/17 reached 106,855 metric tons, down from 111,163 tons in 2015/16, according to the NAEB. Production of processed tea in 2016/17 totalled 25,565 tons, compared with 26,261 tons in the previous year. Rwanda's tea export earnings increased from US $83.6m. in 2018/19 to $93.7m. in 2019/20; despite increasing in volume terms in 2020/21, exports in revenue terms that year declined to $90.0m., owing to a decrease in average prices to $2.6 per kg, from $2.8 per kg in 2019/20.

INDUSTRY

The industrial sector has followed the usual pattern for less-developed African states. Food-based industries predominated, with the major companies prior to 1994 being BRALIRWA (the Rwandan subsidiary of the Dutch brewery Heineken), the Régie Sucrière de Kibuy (sugar processing) and the Office de la Valorisation Industrielle de la Banane du Rwanda, producing banana wine and liquors. In 2010 Skol Brewery Ltd, a competitor to BRALIRWA, began producing beer at its facility on the outskirts of Kigali. Owned by Belgian firm Unibra, it claims some 20% of the local beer market.

In April 2010 the Government announced that its remaining 30% stake in BRALIRWA would be sold before the end of the year: 5% would be sold to Heineken, which already held a 70% stake, and 25% to the public, in the first initial public offering

(IPO) on Rwanda's stock market. The IPO, which proceeded in November and December, was heavily oversubscribed, and when BRALIRWA commenced trading on the Rwanda Stock Exchange (RSE), on 31 January 2011, its share price surged in value by 62%, to 220 Rwanda francs. BRALIRWA announced in November 2018 that it would begin to brew Heineken locally, rather than importing it, allowing the firm to cut the retail price of the beer to 800 Rwanda francs per bottle, from 1,000 Rwanda francs. BRALIRWA reported a 15.4% increase in revenues, to 123,500m. Rwanda francs, in the 12 months to March 2022, with beer and soft drink sales increasing in volume terms by 7.5% and 17.7%, respectively.

German car manufacturer Volkswagen began assembly of three vehicle models at a new factory in Rwanda in June 2018, targeting both the local market and a ride-sharing initiative, as the company sought to expand across sub-Saharan Africa. The US $20m. investment was expected to create 1,000 jobs initially as Volkswagen attempted to convince consumers in the region to transition from purchasing second-hand imported vehicles to buying new locally built models.

Along with other countries in East Africa, Rwanda has sought to boost its domestic textile industry by restricting imports of used clothes and footwear, which have flooded the local market. In July 2016 the Government raised import duties on used clothes and footwear from US $0.20 to $2.50 per kg, while fellow East African Community (EAC) members Kenya, Tanzania and Uganda also hiked tariffs. The move brought criticism from citizens and traders in second-hand clothes in Rwanda, amid concerns that many people would be unable to afford adequate clothing, in a country where temperatures vary more substantially than elsewhere in the region. In March 2018 the USA, under protectionist President Donald Trump, announced that it would suspend duty-free imports of textiles from Rwanda.

SERVICES

A key emerging sector in Rwanda is the financial services industry, as the country integrates more closely with fellow EAC members and benefits from trade with the DRC. This has led to a rise in both commercial and personal incomes, which has in turn boosted bank deposits.

Bank of Kigali (BoK—Rwanda's largest commercial lender) has played a leading role in the expansion of the banking sector. By 2015 BoK maintained a network of 75 branches in Rwanda, supported by mobile vans, giving the bank a leading market share of 32.5% (in terms of total assets), in a sector comprising 12 players. The lender recorded a 25% increase in pre-tax profit to 42,600m. Rwanda francs in 2018, helped by higher interest income. By that time BoK had established a further four branches, increasing the total to 79. Also in 2018 the bank cross-listed on the stock exchange in Nairobi, Kenya, and announced that it would attempt to raise up to US $100m. through a share issuance, primarily to existing stakeholders, as it sought to expand, in part through online operations. BoK also announced in November that it would allocate around $40m. for loans to Rwandan firms, in a bid to stimulate the expansion of local commerce.

An additional factor helping the development of Rwanda's banking industry, and the country's private sector as a whole, was the approval of Kenya Commercial Bank's (KCB) application for a licence in the country. Rwanda's decision to grant market entry to the bank was interpreted as a positive development, which would help to intensify local competition and improve services for local entrepreneurs. By 2016 KCB Rwanda had built up an asset base of US $150m. in the country.

In March 2017 I&M Bank Rwanda became the eighth entity, and the third Rwandan firm after BoK and BRALIRWA, to be listed on the local stock market. The Government offered 99m. shares, translating into a privatization of 19.8% of the lender. Proceeds totalled 8,900m. Rwanda francs, or US $10.8m., which would be used to help fund the construction of the new international airport at Bugesera.

The IMF noted in its May 2022 report that the banking sector maintained a Capital Adequacy Ratio of 23.9%, well above minimum regulatory requirements. However, the Fund warned that, while 'resilient', the financial sector was 'exposed

to prolonged pandemic and geopolitical risks'. With regard to the former, there was clear concern about the health of corporate balance sheets once pandemic-related financial assistance and wider stimulus measures came to an end. In terms of geopolitical risks, one of the biggest policy consequences of the war in Ukraine, and its impact on energy and food prices, was to set in motion a global cycle of monetary policy tightening, which, if prolonged, would impair borrowers' ability to repay loans.

Rwanda has mooted plans to build a 'tech city' in a special economic zone, around 10 km east of Kigali's business district. The US $1,900m. project would seek to advance rapidly the country's plans to become a regional technology hub, and would include the construction of commercial office space, retail space, residential buildings and a health care centre. In December 2017 the RDB revealed that it was working with two unnamed investors as it sought to raise $200m. for the project. Progress was delayed by the COVID-19 pandemic, but the RDB and its partners unveiled an 'urban masterplan' for the so-called Kigali Innovation City in December 2021. Construction was scheduled to begin during the latter half of 2022.

Tourism is a significant foreign exchange earner for Rwanda's economy; it generates more revenue than the tea and coffee sectors combined. According to the RDB, receipts from the sector increased marginally to US $425m. in 2018, from $424m. in 2017, but rose substantially in 2019, to $498m. The Government had targeted $800m. in tourism receipts by 2024, but that campaign was at least temporarily interrupted by the extensive travel restrictions ensuing from policy responses to the COVID-19 pandemic, both domestically and in key source markets. The Minister of Finance and Economic Planning, Uzziel Ndagijimana, announced in March 2021 that the Government was providing $50m. in financial assistance to hotels. The Government also allowed banks to restructure loans, including by extending the duration of loans, reducing interest rates and providing grace periods. Tourism revenues in 2020 slumped to just $131m., before increasing by 25.2%, to $164m., in 2021.

Principal tourist attractions include silverback gorillas in the mountains of Ruhengeri and various animals in the Akagera National Park in the east. The eastern black rhino was reintroduced to the park in May 2017. Rangers and an electric fence would protect the new rhinoceroses, as poaching remains endemic in neighbouring Tanzania and in Kenya, with rhinoceros horn achieving around US $50,000 per kg on the black market. With the reintroduction of rhinoceroses, which had been wiped out in Rwanda around a decade before, the country reclaimed its status as a 'Big Five' player, since it is also home to buffalo, elephants, leopards and lions. Rwanda's Government has invested significantly in promoting the tourism sector in key European markets. After signing a £30m. ($39m.), three-year sponsorship deal with the English Premier League's Arsenal football club in 2018, Rwanda signed an agreement with French club Paris Saint Germain (PSG) the following year. Although the sum involved was undisclosed, PSG agreed to feature advertisements using the words 'Visit Rwanda' on advertising hoardings, as well as on the kits of its women's first team and the training ground jerseys of the men's team. The French daily newspaper *Le Monde* quoted sources indicating that the deal was worth €8m.–€10m. per year.

Rwanda also had ambitions of becoming a leader in the business tourism and conference sector, with the opening in July 2016 of the Kigali Convention Centre (KCC), which hosted the African Union's biannual summit. The country generated US $52m. by hosting international meetings and conferences between July 2018 and February 2019, according to the Rwanda Convention Bureau. However, the COVID-19 pandemic had a severe impact on conference hosting from 2020, including through postponements of the Commonwealth Heads of Government Meeting, which had originally been due to take place at the Convention Centre between in June 2020. The meeting was finally held at the KCC in June 2022.

MINING

Cassiterite (a tin-bearing ore) is Rwanda's principal mineral resource, followed by wolframite (a tungsten-bearing ore), columbo-tantalite (coltan) and gold. Rwanda's exports of minerals have regularly outstripped domestic production, reflecting the country's status as a conduit of its much larger neighbour, the DRC. However, Rwanda's domestic production prospects improved following the announcement of the discovery of gold deposits by TransAfrika Resources of Mauritius in February 2009.

In September 2010 the Rwandan Geology and Mines Authority announced that it would start tracing and certifying the sources of its cassiterite, in response to the Dodd-Frank Wall Street Reform and Consumer Protection Act, which was adopted in the USA in July. The US Congress gave the Securities and Exchange Commission (SEC), which regulates financial markets (and therefore the activity of listed firms) in the USA, nine months to design a certification scheme, in an effort to counteract the trade in 'conflict minerals'. In April 2011 Rwanda's Minister of Forestry and Mines announced that the country had banned the sale of minerals originating from conflict-affected parts of the DRC, in compliance with the Dodd-Frank Act. The SEC finally adopted a regulatory policy on 'conflict minerals' in August 2012. The legislation obliges US firms to certify whether minerals purchased from the DRC and nine neighbouring countries (including Rwanda) were sourced from areas of the DRC controlled by illegal armed groups. Companies using gold, tantalum, tin or tungsten in their products are required to investigate their supply chains, to ascertain where materials are sourced, and to disclose their conclusions (with an explanation of the investigatory process). In the event that a company verifiably concluded that a product did not contain 'conflict minerals', it would be permitted to label the relevant product 'DRC conflict-free'.

The construction of a US $20m. tantalum refinery in Rwanda, partly funded by a Macedonian firm, was originally scheduled for completion by the end of 2018, but was subject to delay. The facility would become the only functioning refinery in the country as a similar plant operated by local firm Phoenix Metals had entered into receivership in 2017.

NATURAL GAS AND ENERGY

Another important resource to be exploited is natural gas, which was discovered beneath Lake Kivu on the volatile border with the DRC. Reserves of an estimated 60,000m. cu m (about one-half of which are in the DRC) were believed to be among the largest in the world. In June 2008 the Minister of State in charge of Energy, Albert Butare, stated that the Government was poised to launch a 5-MW pilot project from the methane gas reserves. He claimed that the potential power generation from Lake Kivu stood at 350 MW, and the US firm Contour-Global subsequently signed an agreement with the Government to develop a US $325m. power project, which, according to the company, would involve extracting gas from a lake-based platform from a depth of 350 m. The gas would then be processed and carried through a pipeline to a proposed onshore plant, which would be situated close to the lake-shore, in the town of Kibuye. The first phase of the project involved powering three generators set to produce 26 MW for the local grid. This segment, at the KivuWatt plant, was completed in May 2016. Construction was under way on a second phase, which would deploy nine additional sets of generators of 75 MW.

At mid-2022 installed generating capacity in Rwanda stood at 276.1 MW and electricity was drawn from over 40 power plants across the country, according to the Rwanda Energy Group (REG), a body mandated by the Government to oversee energy development and utility service delivery. According to the REG, hydroelectric generation accounted for 45.2% of the country's power mix, diesel 26.8%, methane gas 13.9%, peat 6.9%, and solar 5.6%, while the remaining 1.6% of power requirement was imported from the DRC and Uganda. At mid-2022 a total of 34 hydroelectric power plants were connected to Rwanda's electricity grid, accounting for 122.4 MW of power capacity. One major hydropower project under construction is located at the Rusomo Falls on the border with Tanzania. The World Bank-funded project envisaged output of 80 MW to be shared equally between Rwanda, Tanzania and Burundi and was due for completion by the end of 2021; however, in late 2021 the project was reported to be only

81% complete, with completion expected in the second half of 2023. In September 2017 US firm Symbion Power secured US $100m. of investment from Highland Group Holdings Ltd of the UK as it sought to expand the capacity of Kibuye Power Plant 1 and to develop a second site into a 106-MW facility, requiring total funds of $370m.

Rosatom State Nuclear Energy Corporation (of Russia) announced in October 2019 that it had agreed to build a Centre for Nuclear Science and Technology in Rwanda. The Centre would focus on research into the use of nuclear technologies, including the production of radioisotopes that could be used in the industry, health and agriculture sectors. The site would also include a water-cooled reactor with a capacity of up to 10 MW.

In July 2019 the Rwandan, Burundian and DRC Governments signed a project agreement with a consortium comprising SN Power and Industrial Promotion Services for a 25-year concession to build, operate and transfer the 147-MW Rusizi III hydropower project. The power plant, to be built on the Rusizi River, was budgeted to cost between US $650m. and $700m., and was due to become operational by 2026. The three countries would each take a 10% stake in the project, which was 60% funded by multilateral institutions including the AfDB, the European Investment Bank, the Agence Française de Développement and the World Bank.

In February 2020 Rwanda secured a US $214m. loan from the People's Republic of China's Export-Import Bank that would be used to fund a 43.5-MW hydropower facility. The Nyabarongo II facility was to be completed by 2025, with part of the loan to go towards the construction of a substation and a 110-kV transmission line. The facility was also conceived to mitigate downstream flooding of the Nyabarongo River and to provide irrigation, according to the REG.

TRANSPORT AND COMMUNICATIONS

Internal communications in Rwanda are operated almost exclusively along the relatively well-developed road system, as there are no railways. Asphalted highways link Rwanda with Burundi, Uganda, the DRC and Tanzania. They also connect the principal towns. Paved roads extend to over 2,600 km, which, given the small size of the country, is one of the highest densities in Africa.

Rwanda's external trade is heavily dependent on the ports of Mombasa (Kenya), Dar es Salaam (Tanzania) and Matadi (the DRC), and about 80% of Rwandan exports and imports pass through Uganda and Kenya. Feasibility studies have been conducted for a railway network to link Uganda, Rwanda, Burundi and Tanzania. By mid-2016 discussions regarding the potential construction of a railway running to Dar es Salaam on Tanzania's coast had gained traction, with the projected cost of the proposed project totalling some US $900m. This was cheaper than the alternative of routing a railway through Kenya, which would cost about $1,000m. With Uganda reportedly prioritizing the development of a link to South Sudan, its neighbour to the north, it appeared that only three countries were likely to be involved in the Dar es Salaam link—namely Rwanda, Burundi and Tanzania. In January 2018 Rwanda and Tanzania agreed to fund and construct a standard gauge railway from Isaka to Kigali. However, given the history of delays, there remained major doubts that the estimated $2,500m. project would get under way before the early 2020s.

Rwanda's national carrier, RwandAir, offers daily services to Kenya, Uganda and Burundi, while also flying to the United Arab Emirates (UAE) and South Africa. Ambitious plans were announced in 2012 for a new international airport in Rwanda. A government document appealed for bids to construct, fund and operate the airport—to be located at Bugesera, about 25 km south-east of Kigali—on a 25-year lease. The Minister of Infrastructure announced in 2014 that the construction of the new airport would cost an estimated 197,000m. Rwanda francs (US $350m.) of both public and private financing. The airport would have an annual capacity of 1m. passengers and 15,500 metric tons of cargo. A subsequent expansion, with the aim of emulating Nairobi's status as a regional air traffic hub, would involve building a second runway and additional terminals, enabling the airport to accommodate 3m. passengers per year by 2030. Preparatory work finally got under way at the site in June 2017 and President Kagame laid a foundation stone in August of that year. The Government had signed a contract in September 2016 with a Portuguese company, Mota-Engil, to carry out the construction work and operate the airport for an initial 25-year period, extendable to 40 years. The cost of the project was revised upwards to $818m., with the first phase, costing $418m., initially planned for completion by December 2018. However, Kagame announced at a press conference in that month that the construction plans had been revised. In March 2022 it was announced that the first phase of the airport project was expected to be completed in December; by this time the total projected cost of the project had been further increased, to $1,300m.

RwandAir opened an office in Benin in 2017, and in that year also introduced direct flights to London (UK), Brussels (Belgium) and Mumbai (India). In February 2020 Qatar Airways CEO Akbar al-Baker announced that his firm was in talks to buy a 49% stake in Rwandair, which by that stage was flying to 29 destinations. The Doha-based carrier had agreed in December 2019 to take a 60% controlling stake in the under-construction Bugesera International Airport, with the Rwandan Government retaining a 40% stake. RwandAir halted all flights from 21 March 2020, initially for one month but subsequently extended, on the instructions of the Ministry of Health, in response to the spread of coronavirus disease. By November 70% of routes were operational once more, although flights were again briefly suspended during early 2021 in response to pandemic-related developments. In an interview with US broadcasting network CNN in March, the carrier's CEO, Yvonne Makolo, stated that the fleet and route network had been 'rationalized', together with 'right-sizing' of the company, amid the devastating effect on the pandemic on revenues. Minister of Finance and Economic Planning Ndagijimana announced later that month, as quoted in the *Jeune Afrique* periodical, that the prospective sale of a 49% stake to Qatar Airways had progressed as far as 'final talks'. In October RwandAir and Qatar Airways signed a codeshare agreement, under the terms of which the former commenced direct flights to Doha in December.

TELECOMMUNICATIONS

In March 2021 the mobile penetration rate in Rwanda stood at almost 83%, with MTN holding a 63% share of the market, ahead of Airtel with 37%. In 2018 MTN signed a loan agreement amounting to 50,000m. Rwanda francs to enable the overhaul of its network. The seven-year loan was provided by eight local and regional lenders, including BoK, KCB and Ecobank. MTN was also at that stage considering the flotation of shares in Rwanda, after it had earlier that year issued an IPO in Ghana. In 2014 MTN launched cloud computing services to its business customers and began a publicity campaign to promote internet usage in the country. It also announced a partnership with KCB, RSwitch and I&M Bank to develop its mobile money service in Rwanda, where it has 1.7m. customers. By March 2021 there were some 8.2m. internet subscribers in Rwanda.

In June 2013 the Rwandan Government concluded an agreement with the Republic of Korea (South Korea)'s KT Corpn to roll out 4G telecom services across the country. The deal involved the creation of a 25-year joint venture, which the South Korean firm would capitalize with an initial US $140m. in funds, as part of a strategy to ensure that 95% of Rwandans had access to broadband facilities. At that stage, however, the Government was still seeking additional sources of funding in order to complete its 4G programme. The Government is also making efforts to develop the country's information technology sector.

FOREIGN TRADE

Rwanda's principal export destination in 2020 was the UAE, accounting for 61.0% of the total US $1,095.3m., followed by the DRC (8.1%). Meanwhile, the largest source of imports was China, with a 18.5% share of a total $3,528.8m., followed by Tanzania (14.5%), Kenya (11.1%), India (8.1%) and the UAE (6.6%). During a visit to the UAE by Rwanda's President

Kagame in April 2022, the two countries signed an agreement aimed at boosting trade co-operation.

A customs union was established by the EAC in 2005, although Rwanda, which had long maintained high import tariffs on certain goods, in order to generate revenues and suppress the trade deficit, did not become a member until July 2007. With the entry into force of a full EAC customs union in January 2010, however, certain exemptions were granted to the common market (and the customs union) on an ad hoc basis. Rwanda, for example, received a six-month extension of a waiver on sugar duties in March 2012, having been unable, owing to supply constraints, to exploit fully an earlier allowance to import 50,000 metric tons of this commodity.

In mid-March 2019 Uganda (a significant trading partner) complained that all its exports of goods to Rwanda were being blocked at the border, amid an escalating political dispute between the two countries. At the heart of the issue were accusations by Rwanda that the Ugandan Government was supporting armed rebels based in its territory, notably the opposition umbrella grouping known as the Rwanda National Congress. In late February the Rwandan authorities had closed the Katuna border crossing—the busiest goods frontier between the two countries—to trucks, citing construction work, and instructing that commercial vehicles use a separate crossing some 100 km away, according to the Reuters news agency. However, Uganda's Minister of Foreign Affairs, Sam Kutesa, claimed in mid-March that while trucks carrying Ugandan goods continued to be blocked, those arriving from Kenya were being permitted to enter Rwanda, referring to the situation as an 'embargo on bilateral trade with Uganda'. Rwandan Minister of Foreign Affairs and International Co-operation Richard Sezibera, meanwhile, announced in early March that his Government was preventing its own citizens from crossing into Uganda, due to repeated cases of Rwandans being arrested on suspicion of spying in Ugandan territory. The border between Rwanda and Uganda was not fully reopened until March 2022.

Rwanda recorded a trade deficit of US $1,650m. in 2020, as exports of $1,408m. were dwarfed by imports totalling $3,058m., according to IMF figures published in January 2022. Net current transfers of $621m., including remittance inflows of $274m., helped to contain the current account deficit at $1,234m. in 2020, while a surplus of $1,166m. was recorded on the capital and financial account. According to data published by the IMF in June 2022, the trade deficit deteriorated slightly further in 2021, to $1,659m., based on exports of $1,531m. and imports of $3,190m. Net current transfers, however, rose to an estimated $756m. in 2021, boosted by a substantial rise in remittance inflows, to $379m., on the back of a strong global economic recovery following the previous year's pandemic-induced downturn. This all fed into a current account deficit of $1,209m. in 2021, which was more than financed by a capital and financial account surplus of an estimated $1,339m.

DEVELOPMENT PLANNING AND MACROECONOMIC POLICY

Rwanda has been a significant beneficiary of donor aid, in part due to the international community's desire to restore its credibility after failing to intervene during the 1994 genocide, and in part because the country has maintained a strong record on financial transparency under President Kagame. However, several important bilateral and multilateral donors suspended and/or reduced their financial assistance to Rwanda in 2012, following two reports by a UN Group of Experts alleging that the Government and military had played a major role in a new rebellion in eastern DRC. All these charges were vehemently denied by the Rwandan Government, but donors became increasingly sceptical from the second half of 2012, as the insurgents continued to achieve military successes against DRC government forces. After years of benefiting from favoured status, Rwanda's allegedly disruptive ongoing influence in the neighbouring country caused its traditional post-genocide Western donors to reconsider, with the UK at least briefly withholding direct budgetary support, in a context where cause for concern was also generated by repeated assassination attempts—some successful—against exiled Rwandan dissidents. However, amid a rapprochement with France, the two countries agreed a €60m. loan during a visit by President Emmanuel Macron in May 2021. The funds were largely to be spent on increasing the supply of COVID-19 vaccines to Rwanda.

The 2012 dispute with Western donors fuelled the regime's determination to diversify its dependence on traditional sources of aid. The country has since secured significant loans from other major economic powers. In July 2018 China's President, Xi Jinping, visited Rwanda, during which the Chinese Government agreed to provide a total of US $126m. for the construction of two roads, including an access road for Bugesera International Airport, according to Minister of Finance and Economic Planning Ndagijimana. In the same month India's Prime Minister, Narendra Modi, who also made a visit to Kigali, agreed to provide $200m. to develop three separate irrigation zones and create special economic zones.

A new source of funds from the West was secured in March 2018, when the Canada-based Mastercard Foundation announced that it would invest US $100m. in training young people in Rwanda. The Foundation announced that it would provide $50m. over five years to train 30,000 young Rwandans in digital and wider technological literacy in the tourism and hospitality markets. The other $50m. was designated for employing specialist teachers tasked with equipping young people with other skill-sets relevant to modern workplaces.

To coincide with the UK-Africa Investment Summit held in London, UK, in January 2020 Rwanda listed a 37,000m. Rwanda francs bond (equivalent to US $40m.) on the London Stock Exchange. The Rwandan franc-denominated bond allowed the Government to tap international players, rather than the limited pool of domestic investors, but without exposing itself to the exchange rate depreciation risks inherent in foreign currency borrowing. The three-year bond offered a coupon of 9.25%.

The IMF stated in its January 2021 review that the 2020/21 fiscal calculations incorporated pandemic-related spending needs of 2.9% of GDP, noting that the Government had set up a fiscal risk committee and compiled a comprehensive fiscal risk registry, with efforts particularly focused on the 'identification, quantification and mitigation' of risks generated by state-owned enterprises during the pandemic. At this stage, the IMF assessed that Rwanda's debt remained sustainable, but with a moderate risk of debt distress, while stressing that downside risks to the outlook were 'substantial', especially in the event of a protracted pandemic. Central government

revenues reached 2,605,000m. Rwanda francs in 2020/21, owing in large part to tax revenues of 1,659,000m. Rwanda francs and grants of 561,000m. Rwanda francs, according to preliminary data published by the IMF in May 2022. Central government expenses, meanwhile, reached 2,089,000m. Rwanda francs in 2020/21, while other items, including net liabilities totalling 911,000m. Rwanda francs, fed into an overall fiscal deficit (inclusive of grants and policy loans) of 850,000m. Rwanda francs (8.3% of GDP). In 2021/22 revenues were predicted by the IMF to climb to 2,992,000m. Rwanda francs, with tax revenues forecast to increase to 1,849,000m. Rwanda francs, while central government expenses were also projected to rise, to 2,427,000m. Rwanda francs. The IMF anticipated a further increase in incurred net liabilities, to 1,064,000m. Rwanda francs, contributing to the overall fiscal deficit increasing further, to 1,027,000m. Rwanda francs (8.7% of GDP).

In its May 2022 report, the IMF acknowledged the further fiscal strain precipitated by Russia's invasion of Ukraine, which led to global food and oil price increases, and thus also to increased spending on fuel subsidies by Rwanda's Government. While the IMF described the Government's plan to use 'existing social safety nets' as 'broadly appropriate', it also urged Rwanda to respond to the conflict in Ukraine with 'more targeted fiscal measures'. Ultimately, it called upon Rwanda to phase out fuel subsidies by the end of the 2022/23 fiscal year, which, it suggested, would create space for extending 'the coverage and benefits of existing social protection' programmes. In May Prime Minister Ngirente announced the allocation of an additional 250,000m. Rwanda francs (US $247m.) to the National Recovery Fund, which had been established to help businesses cope with the repercussions of the pandemic, notably in the travel, tourism and manufacturing sectors.

The NBR shifted its monetary policy framework from money supply targeting to inflation targeting in 2019. Compared with other central banks worldwide, it set a relatively wide target range of 2.0%–8.0%. The central bank cut its benchmark rate by 0.5% to 4.5% in April 2020 as it sought to ease liquidity conditions amid the COVID-19 crisis. That marked the first reduction in the benchmark rate since February 2019, when it was eased by a similar magnitude. In February 2022 the NBR raised the benchmark rate back to 5.0%, in the first increase in the cost of borrowing since May 2012. The NBR cautioned that inflation was likely to exceed the upper target of 8% by the end of 2022; indeed, by June the annualized rate of consumer price inflation had soared to 13.7%, compared with just 1.9% in December 2021.

Statistical Survey

Source (unless otherwise stated): National Institute of Statistics of Rwanda (NISR), POB 6139, Kigali; tel. 788383103; e-mail info@statistics.gov.rw; internet www.statistics.gov.rw.

Area and Population

AREA, POPULATION AND DENSITY

Area (sq km)	26,338*
Population (census results)	
16 August 2002	8,128,553
16 August 2012	
Males	5,064,868
Females	5,451,105
Total	10,515,973
Population (UN estimates at mid-year)†	
2020	12,952,209
2021‡	13,276,517
2022‡	13,600,466
Density (per sq km) at mid-2022‡	516.4

* 10,169 sq miles; includes approximately 2,120 sq km (820 sq miles) of inland water and land under swamp.

† Source: UN, *World Population Prospects: The 2019 Revision*.

‡ Projection.

POPULATION BY AGE AND SEX
('000, UN projections at mid-2022)

	Males	Females	Total
0–14 years	2,658.0	2,631.5	5,289.5
15–64 years	3,843.4	4,019.7	7,863.2
65 years and over	188.1	259.8	447.9
Total	6,689.5	6,910.9	13,600.5

Note: Totals may not be equal to sum of components, owing to rounding.

Source: UN, *World Population Prospects: The 2019 Revision*.

ADMINISTRATIVE DIVISIONS
(population at 2012 census)

	Population
Eastern Province	2,595,703
Bugesera	361,914
Gatsibo	433,020
Kayonza	344,157
Kirehe	340,368
Ngoma	336,928
Nyagatare	465,855
Rwamagana	313,461
Kigali City	1,132,686
Gasabo	529,561
Kicukiro	318,564
Nyarugenge	284,561
Northern Province	1,726,370
Burera	336,582
Gakenke	338,234
Gicumbi	395,606
Musanze	368,267
Rulindo	287,681
Southern Province	2,589,975
Gisagara	322,506
Huye	328,398
Kamonyi	340,501
Muhanga	319,141
Nyanza	323,719
Nyamagabe	341,491
Nyaruguru	294,334
Ruhango	319,885
Western Province	2,471,239
Karongi	331,808
Ngororero	333,713
Nyabihu	294,740
Nyamasheke	381,804
Rubavu	403,662
Rusizi	400,858
Rutsiro	324,654
Total	10,515,973

Principal Town (UN projection at mid-2022, incl. suburbs): Kigali 1,208,296 (Source: UN, *World Urbanization Prospects: The 2018 Revision*).

BIRTHS AND DEATHS
(annual averages, UN estimates)

	2005–10	2010–15	2015–20
Birth rate (per 1,000)	36.1	33.1	32.1
Death rate (per 1,000)	9.1	6.3	5.3

Source: UN, *World Population Prospects: The 2019 Revision*.

Life expectancy (years at birth, estimates): 69.3 (males 67.1; females 71.5) in 2020 (Source: World Bank, World Development Indicators database).

ECONOMICALLY ACTIVE POPULATION
('000 persons aged 16 years and above, annual labour force survey, 2021)

	Male	Female	Total
Agriculture, forestry and fishing	744.6	822.5	1,567.1
Mining and quarrying	26.1	3.8	29.9
Manufacturing	80.5	77.4	158.0
Electricity, gas and water supply	8.7	4.1	12.7
Construction	314.2	51.1	365.2
Wholesale, retail trade, repair of motor vehicles, motorcycles	155.0	196.0	351.0
Transportation, storage and communications	160.5	8.3	168.8
Restaurants and hotels	31.4	23.0	54.4
Financial intermediation	20.3	14.1	34.4
Real estate, renting and business activities	49.8	23.2	73.0
Public administration and defence	53.9	13.6	67.5
Education	63.4	60.9	124.3
Human health and social work activities	20.8	27.9	48.7

—continued	Male	Female	Total
Other community, social and personal service activities	53.2	45.1	98.3
Activities of households as employers	52.6	81.7	134.3
Total employed	1,835.0	1,452.7	3,287.7
Unemployed	417.0	461.9	878.9
Total labour force	2,252.0	1,914.6	4,166.6

Note: Totals may not be equal to sum of components, owing to rounding.

Health and Welfare

KEY INDICATORS

Total fertility rate (children per woman, 2020)	3.9
Under-5 mortality rate (per 1,000 live births, 2020)	40.5
HIV/AIDS (% of persons aged 15–49, 2020)	2.5
COVID-19: Cumulative confirmed deaths (per 100,000 persons at 31 August 2022)	10.9
COVID-19: Fully vaccinated population (% of total population at 7 August 2022)	77.9
Physicians (per 1,000 head, 2019)	0.1
Hospital beds (per 1,000 head, 2007)	1.6
Domestic health expenditure (2019): US $ per head (PPP)	58.2
Domestic health expenditure (2019): % of GDP	2.6
Domestic health expenditure (2019): public (% of total current expenditure)	39.9
Access to improved water resources (% of persons, 2020)	60
Access to improved sanitation facilities (% of persons, 2020)	69
Total carbon dioxide emissions ('000 metric tons, 2018)	1,080
Carbon dioxide emissions per head (metric tons, 2018)	0.1
Human Development Index (2021): ranking	165
Human Development Index (2021): value	0.534

Note: For data on COVID-19 vaccinations, 'fully vaccinated' denotes receipt of all doses specified by approved vaccination regime (Sources: Johns Hopkins University and Our World in Data). Data on health expenditure refer to current general government expenditure in each case. For more information on sources and further definitions for all indicators, see Health and Welfare Statistics: Sources and Definitions section (europaworld.com/credits).

Agriculture

PRINCIPAL CROPS
('000 metric tons)

	2018	2019	2020
Aubergines (eggplants)	79.5	77.5	83.2
Bananas	1,010.0	1,047.0	1,118.8
Beans, dry	485.8	484.3	438.7
Cabbages and other brassicas	95.0	58.5	61.2
Cassava (Manioc)	1,127.2	1,181.8	1,279.6
Coffee, green	38.6	29.4	20.5
Groundnuts, with shell	22.3	19.6	16.3
Maize	424.2	421.2	448.6
Peas, dry	14.8	15.4	14.0
Plantains and others	759.7	818.5	913.2
Potatoes	916.1	973.4	858.5
Pumpkins, squash and gourds*	258.7	257.2	258.1
Rice, paddy	113.9	131.6	116.5
Sorghum	154.7	159.6	170.5
Sugar cane*	113.3	109.6	111.9
Sweet potatoes	1,186.7	1,247.6	1,275.6
Taro (Cocoyam)	168.0	171.8	188.0
Tea	31.1	30.4	33.6
Tomatoes	107.7	105.8	90.5
Yams*	52.8	61.0	62.2

*FAO estimates.

Aggregate production ('000 metric tons, may include official, semi-official or estimated data): Total cereals 711.3 in 2018, 733.2 in 2019, 753.5 in 2020; Total fruit (primary) 1,919.3 in 2018, 2,030.5 in 2019, 2,176.9 in 2020; Total pulses 500.6 in 2018, 499.7 in 2019, 452.7 in 2020; Total roots and tubers 3,450.8 in 2018, 3,635.6 in 2019, 3,664.0 in 2020; Total vegetables (primary) 655.3 in 2018, 659.8 in 2019, 661.3 in 2020.

Source: FAO.

LIVESTOCK
('000 head, year ending September)

	2018	2019*	2020*
Cattle	1,293.8	1,325.5	1,333.2
Chickens	5,442	5,547	5,633
Goats	2,731.8	2,690.3	2,693.3
Pigs	1,330.5	1,577.2	1,541.4
Sheep	601.8	634.5	633.7

* FAO estimates.

Source: FAO.

LIVESTOCK PRODUCTS
('000 metric tons, FAO estimates)

	2018	2019	2020
Cattle hides, fresh	4.9	5.0	5.0
Cattle meat	33.7	34.6	34.8
Cows' milk	169.1	172.3	173.2
Chicken meat	18.7	19.1	19.3
Game meat	15.2	15.1	15.1
Goat meat	21.6	17.0	16.8
Goats' milk	72.3	71.6	71.7
Goats' skins, fresh	4.8	3.8	3.7
Pig meat	10.6	14.7	13.5
Sheep's (Ewes') milk	8.2	8.5	8.5
Hen eggs	7.8	7.8	7.7
Honey (natural)	5.0	5.0	5.8

Source: FAO.

Forestry

ROUNDWOOD REMOVALS
('000 cubic metres, excluding bark, FAO estimates)

	2007	2008	2009
Sawlogs, veneer logs and logs for sleepers	245	961	962
Other industrial wood	250	250	250
Fuel wood	5,000	5,000	5,000
Total	5,495	6,211	6,212

2010–20: Production assumed to be unchanged from 2009.

Source: FAO.

SAWNWOOD PRODUCTION
('000 cubic metres, including railway sleepers)

	2007	2008	2009
Coniferous (softwood)	22	40	50
Non-coniferous (hardwood) . .	57	81	85
Total	79	121	135

2010–20: Production assumed to be unchanged from 2009 (FAO estimates).

Source: FAO.

Fishing
(metric tons, live weight)

	2018	2019	2020
Capture	23,977	20,910	29,979
Nile tilapia	1,602	1,750	2,240
Mouthbrooding cichlids . . .	2,988	1,350	2,120
Lake Tanganyika sardine . .	16,604	14,800	19,560
North African catfish . . .	1,708	1,700	2,580
Aquaculture	3,357*	3,850	7,055
Nile tilapia	3,200*	3,450	6,500
Total catch	27,534*	24,760	37,034

* FAO estimate.

Source: FAO.

Mining
(metric tons, estimates)

	2016	2017	2018
Tin concentrates*	2,200	3,000	3,000
Tungsten concentrates* . . .	1,716	1,524	1,944
Columbo-tantalite†	1,270	1,725	1,641

* Figures refer to the metal content of ores and concentrates.
† Figures refer to the estimated production of mineral concentrates. The metal content (metric tons, estimates) was: Niobium (Columbium) 160 in 2016, 220 in 2017, 210 in 2018; Tantalum 270 in 2016, 370 in 2017, 350 in 2018.

Source: US Geological Survey.

Industry

SELECTED PRODUCTS

	2016	2017	2018
Cement ('000 metric tons)* . .	350	390	400
Electrical energy (million kWh) .	633	700	759

* Estimates.

Beer ('000 hectolitres): 1,293.5 in 2012.

Electrical energy (million kWh, estimate): 798 in 2019; 838 in 2020.

Sources: US Geological Survey; UN Energy Statistics Database.

2003: Cigarettes 402 million; Soap 4,456 metric tons (Source: IMF, *Rwanda: Selected Issues and Statistical Appendix*—December 2004).

Finance

CURRENCY AND EXCHANGE RATES

Monetary Units
100 centimes = 1 franc rwandais (Rwanda franc).

Sterling, Dollar and Euro Equivalents (31 May 2022)
£1 sterling = 1,286.81 Rwanda francs;
US $1 = 1,022.17 Rwanda francs;
€1 = 1,095.05 Rwanda francs;
10,000 Rwanda francs = £7.77 = $9.78 = €9.13.

Average Exchange Rate (Rwanda francs per US $)
2019   899.351
2020   943.278
2021   988.625

BUDGET
('000 million Rwanda francs)

Revenue*	2019/20	2020/21†	2021/22‡
Tax revenue	1,475.6	1,621.7	1,849.1
Direct taxes	646.1	721.3	856.3
Taxes on goods and services .	712.2	776.0	860.2
Taxes on international trade .	117.3	123.7	132.6
Non-tax revenue	279.8	385.4	442.5
Total	**1,755.4**	**2,007.1**	**2,291.6**

Expenditure§	2019/20	2020/21†	2021/22‡
Current expenditure	1,901.1	2,089.4	2,426.9
Wages and salaries . . .	266.3	302.3	313.4
Purchases of goods and services	572.3	624.0	663.4
Interest payments	139.1	180.7	241.2
Subsidies and 'grants . . .	752.3	809.1	1,033.5
Other expenditure	171.0	173.3	175.3
Capital expenditure	1,033.1	1,251.8	1,461.0
Domestic	485.3	569.5	769.9
External	547.8	682.3	691.1
Total	**2,934.2**	**3,341.2**	**3,887.9**

* Excluding grants received ('000 million Rwanda francs): 437.6 in 2019/20; 561.1 in 2020/21 (provisional); 700.3 in 2021/22 (projection).
† Provisional.
‡ Projections.
§ Excluding lending minus repayments ('000 million Rwanda francs): −741.3 in 2019/20; −773.0 in 2020/21 (provisional); −896.0 in 2021/22 (projection).

Source: Ministry of Finance and Economic Planning, Kigali.

INTERNATIONAL RESERVES
(US $ million at 31 December)

	2019	2020	2021
IMF special drawing rights . .	74.17	77.22	289.93
Reserve position in IMF . . .	27.70	28.85	28.04
Foreign exchange	1,363.00	1,700.00	1,577.00
Total	**1,464.87**	**1,806.07**	**1,894.96**

Source: IMF, *International Financial Statistics*.

MONEY SUPPLY
(million Rwanda francs at 31 December)

	2019	2020	2021
Currency outside depository corporations	209,207	237,188	262,164
Transferable deposits	1,194,468	1,399,910	1,689,419
Other deposits	672,302	880,211	1,027,207
Broad money	**2,075,977**	**2,517,310**	**2,978,789**

Source: IMF, *International Financial Statistics*.

COST OF LIVING
(Consumer Price Index; base: February 2014 = 100)

	2019	2020	2021
Food and non-alcoholic beverages .	130.7	150.8	144.6
Clothing and footwear	120.9	127.8	133.5
Housing, water, electricity, gas and other fuels	121.0	125.2	129.3
All items (incl. others) . . .	**124.8**	**137.1**	**136.6**

NATIONAL ACCOUNTS
('000 million Rwanda francs at current prices)

Expenditure on the Gross Domestic Product

	2019	2020	2021
Government final consumption expenditure	1,472	1,573	1,856
Private final consumption expenditure	6,988	7,205	7,933
Changes in inventories . . .	−317	−15	−38
Gross fixed capital formation . .	2,504	2,430	2,915
Total domestic expenditure .	**10,647**	**11,193**	**12,666**
Exports of goods and services . .	2,031	1,855	2,086
Less Imports of goods and services	3,365	3,442	3,807
GDP in purchasers' values .	**9,314**	**9,607**	**10,944**
GDP in constant 2017 prices .	**9,145**	**8,838**	**9,799**

Gross Domestic Product by Economic Activity

	2019	2020	2021
Agriculture, hunting, forestry and fishing	2,193	2,558	2,633
Mining and quarrying	135	121	307
Manufacturing	779	840	1,005
Electricity, gas and water . . .	145	151	157
Construction	698	679	758
Wholesale and retail trade, restaurants and hotels . . .	1,011	944	1,213
Finance, insurance, real estate and business services	1,390	1,397	1,547
Transport and communications .	758	742	822
Public administration and defence	523	562	591
Education	258	166	326
Health	157	185	193
Other personal services . . .	478	482	533
Sub-total	**8,525**	**8,827**	**10,085**
Indirect taxes (net)	789	780	858
GDP in purchasers' values .	**9,314**	**9,607**	**10,944**

Note: Totals may not be equal to the sum of components, owing to rounding.

BALANCE OF PAYMENTS
(US $ million)

	2018	2019	2020
Exports of goods	1,129.6	1,239.7	1,407.5
Imports of goods	−2,284.1	−2,704.6	−3,057.8
Balance on goods	**−1,154.5**	**−1,464.9**	**−1,650.3**
Exports of services	913.6	1,015.0	521.4
Imports of services	−1,057.2	−1,032.5	−519.8
Balance on goods and services	**−1,298.1**	**−1,482.5**	**−1,648.6**
Primary income received . . .	18.6	15.7	11.5
Primary income paid	−362.8	−345.5	−218.3
Balance on goods, services and primary income	**−1,642.3**	**−1,812.3**	**−1,855.3**
Secondary income received . .	752.1	657.7	683.3
Secondary income paid . . .	−84.6	−76.3	−62.6
Current balance	**−978.4**	**−1,230.9**	**−1,234.6**
Capital account (net)	244.5	260.2	312.5
Direct investment assets . . .	−18.0	−5.4	—
Direct investment liabilities . .	366.2	263.2	99.9
Portfolio investment assets . .	−16.5	−33.8	−10.4
Portfolio investment liabilities .	1.7	3.4	38.9
Other investment assets . . .	−106.0	71.4	−31.9
Other investment liabilities . .	558.4	627.5	785.2
Net errors and omissions . . .	15.3	156.7	176.5
Reserves and related items .	**70.7**	**112.3**	**136.1**

Source: IMF, *International Financial Statistics*.

External Trade

PRINCIPAL COMMODITIES
(US $ million)

Imports c.i.f.	2019	2020	2021
Food and live animals	391.5	422.1	513.3
Animals and vegetable oils, fats and waxes	101.5	110.6	178.0
Mineral fuels, lubricants and related materials	532.4	355.1	410.8
Chemicals and related products .	354.8	393.2	450.2
Manufactured goods classified chiefly by material	536.9	550.2	628.8
Machinery and transport equipment	647.9	649.3	779.1
Miscellaneous manufactured articles	236.4	234.3	310.6
Total (incl. others)	3,139.6	3,436.1	3,759.0

Exports f.o.b.*	2019	2020	2021
Food and live animals	270.8	241.8	337.2
Crude materials, inedible, except fuels	138.2	89.0	159.8
Manufactured goods classified chiefly by material	50.4	43.8	66.2
Machinery and transport equipment	13.3	11.3	15.1
Miscellaneous manufactured articles	14.8	15.9	22.0
Other commodities and transactions, n.e.s	276.4	646.2	363.2
Total (incl. others)	783.1	1,054.7	977.2

* Excluding re-exports.

PRINCIPAL TRADING PARTNERS
(US $ million)

Imports	2019	2020	2021
Belgium	43.7	75.4	69.1
China, People's Republic . .	628.0	651.8	725.6
Egypt	37.8	58.7	57.7
Germany	92.3	77.9	143.5
India	273.8	287.1	301.7
Indonesia	57.8	66.7	88.3
Kenya	277.6	382.8	283.5
Malaysia	28.7	26.8	56.6
Saudi Arabia	153.1	48.5	88.5
South Africa	120.8	133.6	136.9
Switzerland	114.1	79.4	78.0
Tanzania	268.6	476.3	510.8
Türkiye	75.0	54.3	93.4
United Arab Emirates . . .	244.5	232.2	307.5
USA	53.5	68.1	85.0
Total (incl. others)	3,139.6	3,436.1	3,759.0

Exports*	2019	2020	2021
Belgium	14.5	14.3	9.3
China, People's Republic . .	15.1	8.0	16.5
Congo, Democratic Republic .	62.1	88.4	118.4
Germany	3.3	3.5	11.1
Hong Kong	9.7	16.9	28.0
India	6.6	15.6	11.6
Kenya	20.7	9.4	24.0
Luxembourg	3.1	2.3	11.4
Pakistan	39.3	32.7	37.2
Singapore	29.8	18.3	25.6
South Sudan	20.0	12.3	7.2
Switzerland-Liechtenstein .	43.7	11.8	25.9
Uganda	28.6	19.2	22.3
United Arab Emirates . . .	332.2	627.6	434.2
United Kingdom	37.6	26.9	42.6
USA	12.4	19.1	28.6
Total (incl. others)	783.1	1,054.7	977.2

* Excluding re-exports.

Transport

ROAD TRAFFIC
(motor vehicles in use)

	2018	2019	2020
Passenger cars	36,951	34,555	38,938
Buses and coaches	1,576	1,706	1,965
Trucks and trailers	8,670	9,328	10,846
Motorcycles and mopeds . . .	112,404	117,199	130,326
Total (incl. others)	216,204	217,301	244,112

CIVIL AVIATION
(traffic on scheduled services)

	2017	2018	2019
Passengers carried	825,585	977,631	1,145,867
Freight carried (metric tons) . .	8,493	11,072	12,350

Tourism

FOREIGN VISITOR ARRIVALS*

	2017	2018	2019
Belgium	10,028	11,445	13,395
Burundi	253,170	302,499	255,065
Congo, Democratic Republic . .	16,471	1,286	1,419
India	13,547	13,987	14,690
Kenya	44,131	52,318	62,600
Tanzania	59,787	50,085	50,718
Uganda	227,989	272,314	181,620
United Kingdom	16,016	15,655	16,107
USA	33,230	38,294	40,167
Total (incl. others)	1,569,960	1,711,498	1,633,521

* Figures refer to total arrivals (including same-day visitors), excluding Rwandan nationals residing abroad.

Tourism receipts (US $ million, excl. passenger transport): 390 in 2016; 438 in 2017; 375 in 2018.

Source: World Tourism Organization.

Communications Media

	2018	2019	2020
Telephones ('000 main lines in use)	13.0	11.4	11.7
Mobile telephone subscriptions ('000)	9,700.6	9,658.5	10,614.4
Broadband subscriptions, fixed ('000)	7.5	8.9	17.7
Broadband subscriptions, mobile ('000)	4,799.1	5,341.7	5,548.6
Internet users (% of population) .	25.0	26.0	26.5

Source: International Telecommunication Union.

Education

(2020/21)

	Institutes	Teachers	Students		
			Males	Females	Total
Pre-primary . .	3,741	9,312	143,060	150,763	293,823
Primary . .	3,691	63,580	1,370,022	1,359,094	2,729,116
Secondary . .	2,213	36,286	363,214	419,632	782,846
Tertiary . . .	38	4,301	48,757	39,691	88,448

Source: Ministry of Education, Kigali.

Pupil-teacher ratio (qualified teaching staff, primary education, UNESCO estimate): 58.0 in 2018/19 (Source: UNESCO Institute for Statistics).

Adult literacy rate (UNESCO estimates): 73.2% (males 77.6%; females 69.4%) in 2018 (Source: UNESCO Institute for Statistics).

Directory

The Constitution

A new Constitution was approved at a national referendum on 26 May 2003 and entered into effect on 4 June. The main provisions, including amendments, the most recent of which were adopted in December 2015, are summarized below:

PREAMBLE

The state of Rwanda is an independent sovereign Republic. Fundamental principles are: the struggle against the ideology of genocide and all its manifestations; the eradication of all ethnic and regional divisions; the promotion of national unity; and the equal sharing of power. Human rights and personal liberties are protected. All forms of discrimination are prohibited and punishable by law. The state recognizes a multi-party political system. Political associations are established in accordance with legal requirements, and may operate freely, providing that they comply with democratic and constitutional principles, without harm to national unity, territorial integrity and state security. The formation of political associations on the basis of race, ethnicity, tribal or regional affiliation, sex, religion or any other grounds for discrimination is prohibited.

LEGISLATURE

Legislative power is vested in a bicameral Parliament, comprising a Chamber of Deputies and a Senate. The Chamber of Deputies has 80 deputies, who are elected for a five-year term. In addition to 53 directly elected deputies, 27 seats are allocated, respectively, to two youth representatives, one disabilities representative, and 24 female representatives, who are indirectly elected. The Senate comprises 26 members, of whom 12 are elected by local government councils in the 12 provinces, and two by academic institutions, while the remaining 12 are nominated (eight by the President and four by the National Consultative Forum of Political Organizations). Members of the Senate serve a five-year term, renewable once.

PRESIDENT

The President of the Republic is the Head of State, defender of the Constitution, and guarantor of national unity. He is the Commander-in-Chief of the armed forces. Presidential candidates are required to be of Rwandan nationality and aged a minimum of 35 years. The President is elected by universal suffrage for a five-year term, renewable once. He signs into law presidential decrees in consultation with the Cabinet.

GOVERNMENT

The President nominates the Prime Minister, who heads the Cabinet. Ministers are proposed by the Prime Minister and appointed by the President.

JUDICIARY

The judiciary is independent and separate from the legislative and executive organs of government. The judicial system is composed of the Supreme Court, the High Court, intermediate courts and primary courts. Military courts (the Military Tribunal and the High Military Court) have jurisdiction in military cases.

The Government

HEAD OF STATE

President: Maj.-Gen. PAUL KAGAME (took office 22 April 2000; re-elected 25 August 2003, 9 August 2010 and 4 August 2017).

THE CABINET
(October 2022)

Prime Minister: Dr EDOUARD NGIRENTE.

Minister of Local Government: Prof. JEAN-MARIE VIANNEY GATABAZI.

Minister of Foreign Affairs and International Co-operation: Dr VINCENT BIRUTA.

Minister of Trade and Industry: Dr JEAN CHRYSOSTOME NGABISINZE.

Minister of ICT and Innovation: PAULA INGABIRE.

Minister of Defence: Maj.-Gen. ALBERT MURASIRA.

Minister of Health: Dr DANIEL NGAMIJE.

Minister of Gender and Family Promotion: Dr JEANNETTE BAYISENGE.

Minister of Sports: AURORE MIMOSA MUNYANGAJU.

Minister in charge of Emergency Management: MARIE-SOLANGE KAYISIRE.

Minister in the Office of the President: JUDITH UWIZEYE.

Minister in the Office of the Prime Minister, in charge of Cabinet Affairs: INÈS MPAMBARA.

Minister of Finance and Economic Planning: Dr UZZIEL NDAGIJIMANA.

Minister of Infrastructure: Dr ERNEST NSABIMANA.

Minister of the Environment: Dr JEANNE D'ARC MUJAWAMARIYA.

Minister of Agriculture and Animal Resources: Dr GÉRARDINE MUKESHIMANA.

Minister of Education: Dr VALENTINE UWAMARIYA.

Minister of Youth and Culture: ROSEMARY MBABAZI.

Minister of Justice and Attorney-General: Dr EMMANUEL UGIRASHEBUJA.

Minister of Public Service and Labour: FANFAN RWANYINDO KAYIRANGWA.

Minister of National Unity and Civic Engagement: Dr JEAN DAMASCENE BIZIMANA.

Minister of Public Investments and Privatization: ERIC RWIGAMBA.

Minister of State in the Ministry of Local Government, in charge of Social Affairs: ASSUMPTA INGABIRE.

Minister of State in the Ministry of Justice, in charge of Constitutional and Legal Affairs: SOLINA NYIRAHABIMANA.

Minister of State in the Ministry of Finance and Economic Planning, in charge of Economic Planning: Dr CLAUDINE UWERA.

Minister of State in the Ministry of Finance and Economic Planning, in charge of the National Treasury: RICHARD TUSHABE.

Minister of State in the Ministry of Foreign Affairs, Co-operation and East African Affairs: Prof. NSHUTI MANASSEH.

Minister of State in the Ministry of Education, in charge of Primary and Secondary Education: GASPARD TWAGIRAYEZU.

Minister of State in the Ministry of Education, in charge of ICT and Technical and Vocational Education and Training: CLAUDETTE IRERE.

Minister of State in the Ministry of Health, in charge of Primary Health Care: Dr THARCISEE MPUNGA.

Minister of State in the Ministry of Youth and Culture, in charge of Youth and Culture: EDOUARD BAMPORIKI (suspended in May 2022).

Minister of State in the Ministry of Agriculture and Animal Resources: Dr ILDEPHONSE MUSAFIRI.

Minister of State in the Ministry of Infrastructure: PATRICIA UWASE.

The CEOs of the Rwanda Development Board and of the Rwanda Mines, Petroleum and Gas Board are also members of the Cabinet.

MINISTRIES

Office of the President: BP 15, Kigali; tel. 259062000; e-mail info@presidency.gov.rw; internet www.paulkagame.com.

Office of the Prime Minister: POB 1334, Kigali; tel. 788388499; e-mail info@primature.gov.rw; internet www.primature.gov.rw.

Ministry of Agriculture and Animal Resources: KG 569 St, POB 621, Kigali; tel. 788673779; e-mail info@minagri.gov.rw; internet www.minagri.gov.rw.

Ministry of Defence: POB 23, Kigali; tel. 788310178; e-mail info@mod.gov.rw; internet www.mod.gov.rw.

Ministry of Education: KG 7 Ave, Kacyiru, POB 622, Kigali; tel. 788388069; e-mail info@mineduc.gov.rw; internet mineduc.gov.rw.

Ministry of Emergency Management: Nyarugenge Pension Plaza, KN 3 Rd, POB 4386, Kacyiru, Kigali; e-mail info@midimar.gov.rw; internet minema.gov.rw.

Ministry of the Environment: Nyarugenge Pension Plaza, KN 3 Rd, POB 3052, Kigali; tel. 250582628; e-mail jumubyeyi@environment.gov.rw; internet environment.gov.rw.

Ministry of Finance and Economic Planning: blvd de la Révolution, opp. Kigali City Council, POB 158, Kigali; tel. 252577581; e-mail info@minecofin.gov.rw; internet www.minecofin.gov.rw.

Ministry of Foreign Affairs and International Co-operation: Kimihurura, 5th and 6th Floors, ave du lac Muhazi, POB 179, Kigali; tel. 252599128; e-mail info@minaffet.gov.rw; internet www.minaffet.gov.rw.

Ministry of Gender and Family Promotion: POB 969, Kigali; tel. 252587128; e-mail info@migeprof.gov.rw; internet www.migeprof .gov.rw.

Ministry of Health: KN 3 Rd, POB 84, Kigali; tel. 252577458; e-mail info@moh.gov.rw; internet www.moh.gov.rw.

Ministry of ICT and Innovation: KN 3 Rd, Sopetrad, BP 3882, Kigali; tel. 786791388; e-mail info@minict.gov.rw; internet minict .gov.rw.

Ministry of Infrastructure: KG 7 Ave, POB 24, Kigali; tel. 788387125; e-mail info@mininfra.gov.rw; internet www.mininfra .gov.rw.

Ministry of Justice: POB 160, Kigali; tel. 252586561; e-mail mjust@minijust.gov.rw; internet www.minijust.gov.rw.

Ministry of Local Government: KG 7 Ave, Kacyiru Sector, POB 3445, Kigali; tel. 788384081; e-mail webmaster@minaloc.gov.rw; internet www.minaloc.gov.rw.

Ministry of Public Service and Labour: POB 403, Kigali; tel. 785082849; e-mail info@mifotra.gov.rw; internet www.mifotra.gov .rw.

Ministry of Sports: KG 17 Ave, POB 1044, Kigali; tel. 788196300; e-mail info@minisports.gov.rw; internet minisports.gov.rw.

Ministry of Trade and Industry: KG 1 Roundabout, POB 73, Kigali; tel. 788488622; e-mail info@minicom.gov.rw; internet www .minicom.gov.rw.

Ministry of Youth and Culture: 21 KG 5 Ave, POB 6369, Kigali; tel. 785655755; e-mail info@myculture.gov.rw; internet www .myculture.gov.rw.

President

Presidential Election, 4 August 2017

Candidate	Valid votes	% of valid votes
Paul Kagame (Rwandan Patriotic Front)	6,675,472	98.79
Philippe Mpayimana (Ind.)	49,031	0.73
Frank Habineza (Democratic Green Party)	32,701	0.48
Total	**6,757,204***	**100.00**

* There were also 12,310 invalid votes.

Legislature

CHAMBER OF DEPUTIES

Chamber of Deputies: POB 352, Kigali; tel. 252594620; e-mail info@parliament.gov.rw; internet www.parliament.gov.rw.

Speaker: DONATILLE MUKABALISA.

General Election, 2–4 September 2018

Party	Seats
Rwandan Patriotic Front	36
Parti Social-Démocrate	5
Parti Libéral	4
Democratic Green Party	2
Parti Social Imberakuri	2
Parti Démocrate Centriste	1
Parti Démocrate Idéal	1
Parti du Progrès et de la Concorde . . .	1
Union Démocratique du Peuple Rwandais . .	1
Total	**80***

* In addition to the 53 directly elected deputies, 27 seats are allocated, respectively, to two youth representatives, one disabilities representative and 24 female representatives, who are indirectly elected.

SENATE

The Senate comprises 26 members, of whom 12 are elected by local government councils and two by academic institutions, while the remaining 12 are nominated (eight by the President and four by a regulatory body, the Parties' Forum).

Senate: POB 6729, Kigali; tel. 252594538; e-mail senate_rwanda@ parliament.gov.rw; internet www.parliament.gov.rw.

President: Dr AUGUSTIN IYAMUREMYE.

Election Commission

National Electoral Commission: BP 6449, Kigali; tel. 250597800; e-mail info@nec.gov.rw; internet www.nec.gov.rw; f. 2000; independent; Chair. Prof. KALISA MBANDA.

Political Organizations

Under legislation adopted in June 2003, the formation of any political organization based on ethnic groups, religion or sex was prohibited.

Democratic Green Party: BP 6334, Kigali; tel. 788563039; e-mail info@rwandagreendemocrats.org; internet www .rwandagreendemocrats.org; f. 2009; Pres. Dr FRANK HABINEZA; Sec.-Gen. JEAN-CLAUDE NTEZIMANA.

Forces Démocratiques Unifiées—Inkingi (FDU): Kigali; tel. 728636000; e-mail fdu.inkingi.rwa@gmail.com; internet www .fdu-rwanda.com; Chair. VICTOIRE INGABIRE UMUHOZA; Sec.-Gen. JEAN-BAPTISTE MBERABAHIZI.

Parti Démocrate Centriste (PDC): BP 2348, Kigali; tel. 250576542; internet www.pdc-rwanda.org; f. 1990; established as Parti Démocrate Chrétien, present name adopted in 2003; Chair. AGNES MUKABARANGA.

Parti Démocrate Idéal (PDI): Tresor Bldg, 2nd Floor, Kigali; internet www.pdi-rwanda.org; f. 1991; established as Parti Démocratique Islamique, renamed as above 2003; Leader SHEIKH MUSSA FAZIL HARERIMANA; Gen. Sec. FATOU HARERIMANA.

Parti Libéral (PL): BP 5434, Kigali; tel. 252577916; internet www .pl-rwanda.org; f. 1991; restructured 2003; Pres. DONATILLE MUKA-BALISA; Sec.-Gen. ODETTE NYIRAMILIMO.

Parti du Progrès et de la Concorde (PPC): internet ppc-rwanda .org; f. 2003; incl. fmr mems of Mouvement Démocratique Républicain; Leader Dr ALIVERA MUKABARAMBA; Sec.-Gen JEAN THIERRY KAREMERA.

Parti Social-Démocrate (PSD): Nyarugenge, Quartier Commercial, POB 6926, Kigali; tel. 252577452; e-mail psd200891@yahoo.fr; internet psd-rwanda.org; f. 1991 by a breakaway faction of fmr Mouvement Révolutionnaire National pour le Développement; Leader Dr VINCENT BIRUTA.

Parti Social Imberakuri (PS Imberakuri): Nyamirambo, Kigali; tel. 788307145; e-mail info@psimberakuri-rwanda.org; internet www.psimberakuri-rwanda.org; f. 2009; Pres. CHRISTINE MUKABU-NANI; Sec.-Gen. SCHOLASTICA NYIRAMAJYAMBERE.

Parti Socialiste Rwandais (PSR): BP 827, Kigali; tel. 252576658; internet psr-rwanda.org; f. 1991; workers' rights; Chair. JEAN-BAPTISTE RUCIBIGANGO; Sec.-Gen. EMILE MUNYEMANA.

Rwandan Patriotic Front (Front Patriotique Rwandais—RPF): BP 195, Kigali; tel. 788310075; e-mail info@rpfinkotanyi.rw; internet rpfinkotanyi.rw; f. 1990; also known as Inkotanyi; Chair. Maj.-Gen. PAUL KAGAME; Vice-Chair. CHRISTOPHE BAZIVAMO; Sec.-Gen. FRAN-ÇOIS NGARAMBE.

Diplomatic Representation

EMBASSIES AND HIGH COMMISSIONS IN RWANDA

Angola: 970 rue de la BRALIRWA, BP 3610, Kigali; tel. 250510820; Ambassador EDUARDO FILOMENO LEIRO OCTÁVIO.

Belgium: KN 3 Ave, BP 81, Kigali; tel. 252575551; e-mail kigali@ diplobel.fed.be; internet rwanda.diplomatie.belgium.be; Ambassador BERT VERSMESSEN.

Burundi: KG 7 Ave, Kacyiru, Kigali; tel. 252587940; e-mail ambabukgl1@yahoo.fr; Chargé d'affaires a.i. DOROTHEE NDAYIZIGA.

China, People's Republic: 34 KN 3 Ave, BP 1345, Kigali; tel. 252570843; e-mail chinaemb_rw@mfa.gov.cn; internet rw .china-embassy.gov.cn; Ambassador WANG XUEKUN.

Congo, Democratic Republic: 26 KN 16 Ave, Kiyovu, Kigali; tel. 252575999; e-mail ambardckigali@yahoo.fr; Ambassador JEAN DE DIEU MITIMA BULINZ.

Congo, Republic: 23 KG 230 St, Gasabo, Kigali; tel. 789920474; e-mail ambacokigali@gmail.com; Ambassador GUY NESTOR ITOU.

Egypt: KG 7 Ave, Kacyiru, Kigali; tel. 252587560; e-mail sec .egyptemb@gmail.com; Ambassador RANIA MAHMOUD MOHAMED EL-BANNA.

Ethiopia: cnr KG 303 and 305 Sts, Plot No. 600, Kimironko Sector, Kibagabaga Cell, Gasabo, POB 6575, Kigali; tel. 252601057; e-mail ethiopiaembrwa@gmail.com; internet www.kigali.mfa.gov.et; Ambassador DABA DEBELE HUNDE.

France: rue du Député Kamunzinzi, BP 441, Kigali; tel. 252551800; e-mail ambafrance.kigali-amba@diplomatie.gouv.fr; internet rw .ambafrance.org; Ambassador ANTOINE ANFRÉ.

Germany: 5 KN 27 St, BP 355, Kigali; tel. 280575141; e-mail info@ kigali.diplo.de; internet kigali.diplo.de; Ambassador THOMAS KURZ.

Holy See: KN 07 Ave, BP 261, Kigali (Apostolic Nunciature); tel. 252575293; e-mail na.rwanda@diplomat.va; Apostolic Nuncio ARNALDO CATALAN (Titular Archbishop of Apollonia).

India: Villa 67, KG 9 Ave, Nyarutarama, Kigali; tel. 737310017; e-mail hoc.kigali@mea.gov.in; internet hcikigali.gov.in; High Commissioner OSCAR KERKETTA.

Israel: Kigali; Ambassador RON ADAM.

Japan: 35 KG 7 Ave, Kacyiru, BP 3072, Kigali; tel. 252500884; e-mail rw.emb-japan@kq.mofa.go.jp; internet www.rw.emb-japan .go.jp; Ambassador MASAHIRO IMAI.

Kenya: 25 KG 7 Ave, BP 6159, Kigali; tel. 252583334; e-mail kigali@ mfa.go.ke; internet kigali.mfa.go.ke; High Commissioner DIANA KIAMBUTHI.

Korea, Republic: Plot No. 10050, Nyarutarama, POB 6404, Kigali; tel. 252577577; e-mail koremb-rwanda@hotmail.com; internet overseas.mofa.go.kr/rw-ko/index.do; Ambassador CHAE JIN-WEON.

Libya: 43 KG 7 Ave, Kacyiru, Kigali; tel. 784977782; e-mail libyanembassy2011@gmail.com; Ambassador IBRAHIM SIDY IBRAHIM MATTAR.

Mali: KG 627 Ave, Kigali; Ambassador YAYA DOUCOURE.

Morocco: 1 KG 416 St, Kinyinya, Kigali; Ambassador YOUSSEF IMANI.

The Netherlands: blvd de l'Umuganda, Kacyiru, BP 6613, Kigali; tel. 280280281; e-mail kig@minbuza.nl; internet www .nederlandwereldwijd.nl/landen/rwanda; Ambassador MATTHIJS CLEMENS WOLTERS.

Nigeria: 56 KG 13 Ave, Kagugu, Kigali; tel. 255119282; e-mail nigeriankigali@gmail.com; High Commissioner SANI SULEIMAN.

Pakistan: KG 676 St 44, Kamahwa, Kimihurura, Kigali; High Commissioner AMIR MOHAMMAD KHAN.

Qatar: Kigali; Ambassador MISFER FAISAL MUBARAK AL-AJAB AL-SHAHWANI.

Russian Federation: 19 KN 67 St, BP 40, Kigali; tel. 250575286; e-mail ambruss@rwanda1.rw; internet www.rwanda.mid.ru; Ambassador KARÉN DRASTAMATOVICH CHALYAN.

Senegal: Kigali; Ambassador DOUDOU SOW.

South Africa: 1370 blvd de l'Umuganda, Kacyiru-Sud, POB 6563, Kigali; tel. 252551300; e-mail kigali.admin@dirco.gov.za; High Commissioner MANDISI MPAHLWA.

Sudan: KG 9 Ave, Nyarutarama, Kigali; tel. 252575286; e-mail mwizasharifah@gmail.com; Ambassador ABDALLA HASSAN EISA BUSHARA.

Sweden: Aurore House, blvd de l'Umuganda, Kacyiru, POB 6387, Kigali; tel. 252597400; e-mail ambassaden.kigali@gov.se; internet www.swedenabroad.com/kigali; Ambassador. JOHANNA TEAGUE.

Tanzania: 15 KG 9 Ave, Nyarutarama, BP 3973, Kigali; tel. 252505400; e-mail kigali@nje.go.tz; internet rw.tzembassy.go.tz; High Commissioner Maj.-Gen. RICHARD MUTAYOBA MAKANZO.

Türkiye (Turkey): 25 KG 2 Ave, POB 7079, Kimihurura, Kigali; tel. 252600299; internet kigali.be.mfa.gov.tr; Ambassador BURCU ÇEVIK.

Uganda: 11 KG 569 St, Kigali; tel. 252503537; e-mail info@ ugandaembassy.rw; internet kigali.mofa.go.ug; High Commissioner Maj.-Gen. ROBERT RUSOKE.

United Arab Emirates: Kigali; Ambassador HAZZA MOHAMMED FALAH KHARSAN AL-QAHTANI.

United Kingdom: Parcelle 1131, blvd de l'Umuganda, Kacyiru-Sud, BP 576, Kigali; tel. 252556000; e-mail bhc.kigali@fco.gov.uk; internet www.gov.uk/world/organisations/british-high-commission -kigali; High Commissioner OMAR TALAL ALI DAAIR.

USA: 2657 ave de la Gendarmerie, Kacyiru, BP 28, Kigali; tel. 252596400; e-mail consularkigali@state.gov; internet rw .usembassy.gov; Chargé d'affaires a.i. DEB MACLEAN.

Zimbabwe: Kigali; Ambassador Prof. CHARITY MANYERUKE.

Judicial System

The judicial system is composed of the Supreme Court, the Court of Appeal, the High Court, intermediate courts and primary courts. In addition, there are specialized judicial organs, comprising commercial courts and military courts. The *gacaca* courts were established to try cases of genocide or other crimes against humanity committed between 1 October 1990 and 31 December 1994. Trials for categories of lesser genocide crimes were to be conducted by councils in the communities in which they were committed, with the aim of

alleviating pressure on the existing judicial system. Trials under the *gacaca* court system formally commenced on 25 November 2002 and the system closed in June 2012, having tried almost 2m. suspects. Military courts (the Military Tribunal and the High Military Court) have jurisdiction in military cases.

Supreme Court: BP 2197, Kigali; tel. 252517649; e-mail info@ judiciary.gov.rw; internet www.judiciary.gov.rw; the Supreme Court comprises 5 sections: the Department of Courts and Tribunals; the Court of Appeals; the Constitutional Court; the Council of State; and the Revenue Court; Pres. Dr FAUSTIN NTEZILYAYO; Vice-Pres. MARIE-THÉRÈSE MUKAMULISA.

Court of Appeal: Kigali; f. 2018; 13 judges; Pres. FRANÇOIS RÉGIS RUKUNDAKUVUGA.

High Court: Kigali; Pres. XAVIER NDAHAYO.

Prosecutor-General: AIMABLE HAVUGIYAREMYE.

Religion

According to the 2012 census, 93% of the total population are Christians (Roman Catholics 44%, Protestants 38% and Seventh-day Adventists 12%), while 2% are Muslims.

CHRISTIANITY

Union of Baptist Churches of Rwanda (UEBR): POB 896, Kigali; tel. 783452915; e-mail info@ubcr.org; internet www.ubcr .org; f. 1939; Legal Rep. THOMAS MURWANASHYAKA.

The Roman Catholic Church

Rwanda comprises one archdiocese and eight dioceses.

Bishops' Conference: Conférence Episcopale du Rwanda, KN 4 ave 36, BP 357, Kigali; tel. 252575439; e-mail eglisecatholiquerwanda@ gmail.com; internet eglisecatholiquerwanda.org; f. 1980; Pres. Rt Rev. PHILIPPE RUKAMBA (Bishop of Butare).

Archbishop of Kigali: Cardinal ANTOINE KAMBANDA, Archevêché, BP 715, Kigali; tel. 786123719; e-mail info@archidiocesekigali.org; internet archidiocesekigali.org.

The Anglican Communion

The Church of the Province of Rwanda, established in 1992, has 11 dioceses.

Archbishop of the Province of Rwanda and Bishop of Gasabo: Most Rev. Dr LAURENT MBANDA, BP 2487, Kigali; tel. 252576340; e-mail pearsecretariat@ear-acr.org; internet ear-acr.org.

Provincial Secretary: Rev. FRANCIS KAREMERA, BP 2487, Kigali; tel. 788590714; e-mail peer1925@yahoo.fr.

Protestant Church

Protestant Council of Rwanda (CPR): Amajyambere, Kimihur-ura, Gasabo, BP 79, Kigali; tel. 252583554; e-mail cpr@rwanda1.rw; internet cpr-rwanda.org; f. 1963

    Eglise Luthérienne du Rwanda: BP 3099, Kigali; tel. 755110035; e-mail luthchurchlcr@yahoo.com; Bishop EVALISTER MUGABO; 7,200 mems.

    Presbyterian Church in Rwanda: KN 35 St, BP 56, Kigali; tel. 252573789; e-mail epr@rwanda1.rw; internet epr.rw; Pres. Rev. Dr PASCAL BATARINGAYA.

BAHÁ'Í FAITH

National Spiritual Assembly: BP 652, Kigali; tel. 783458910; e-mail info@bahairwanda.org; internet www.bahairwanda.org.

ISLAM

Association des Musulmans au Rwanda (AMUR): POB 594, Kigali; tel. 252583271; e-mail islamour@yahoo.fr; f. 1964; Mufti SHEIKH SALIM HITIMANA.

The Press

REGULATORY AUTHORITY

Media High Council: Remera, Airport Rd, POB 6929, Kigali; tel. 788460385; e-mail info@mhc.gov.rw; internet www.mhc.gov.rw; f. 2002; Chair. ERIC NDUSHABANDI; Exec. Sec. PEACEMAKER MBUNGIRAMIHIGO.

DAILY NEWSPAPERS (PRINT AND ONLINE)

Imvaho Nshya: 6 KK Ave, opp. Magerwa Gikondo, Kigali; tel. 786686668; e-mail info@imvahonshya.rw; internet imvahonshya.co .rw.

The New Times: Immeuble Aigle Blanc, BP 4953, Kigali; tel. 788387760; e-mail editorial@newtimes.co.rw; internet www .newtimes.co.rw; f. 1995; daily; English; Man. Dir JAMES MUNYANEZA.

Nonaha: Kigali; tel. 788841249; e-mail contact@nonaha.com; internet www.nonaha.com; f. 2013; online-only; Kinyarwanda, English and French; business and agriculture.

PERIODICALS

La Nouvelle Relève: BP 6383, Kigali; tel. 788843863; e-mail info@ rppcmedia.co.rw; internet lanouvellereleve.co.rw; f. 1963; French; Dir GÉRARD RUGAMBWA.

Panorama: KG 6 Ave, POB 2136, Kigali; tel. 788300359; e-mail anthers2020@gmail.com; internet panorama.rw; f. 2015; Kinyarwandan, English and French; Chief Editor RENE ANTHERE RWANYANGE.

Rugali: Kigali; internet rugali.com.

Rushyashya: POB 4305, Kigali; tel. 788429205; e-mail info@ rushyashya.net; internet rushyashya.net.

Umuryango: Grand Pension Plaza, BP 3561, Kigali; tel. 788308594; e-mail info@umuryango.rw; internet umuryango.rw.

Umusingi: BP 4305, Kigali; tel. 788350847; e-mail umusingi@yahoo .com; Kinyarwandan; Editor STANLEY GATERA.

NEWS AGENCIES

Rwanda News Agency (RNA): BP 453, Kigali; tel. 250587215; internet www.rnanews.com; f. 1975.

PRESS ASSOCIATIONS

Association Rwandaise des Journalistes (ARJ): Plot No. 5856, Remera, opp. Amahoro Staduim Bldg, KG 17 Ave 37, POB 4305, Kigali; tel. 728251163; e-mail info@arj.org.rw; internet www.arj.org .rw; f. 1995; Pres. ALDO HAVUGIMANA; Exec. Sec. JANVIER POPOTE NSHIMYIYUMUKIZA; c. 800 mems (2019).

Rwanda Media Commission (RMC): POB 2136, Kigali; tel. 788316974; e-mail info@rmc.org.rw; internet rmc.org.rw; f. 2013; self-regulation; Chair. CLEOPHAS BARORE.

Publishers

Bakame Editions: Remera, BP 4281, Kigali; tel. 788422660; internet www.bakame.rw; children's literature.

Imprimerie de Kigali, SARL: 1 blvd de l'Umuganda, BP 956, Kigali; tel. 250582032; f. 1980; Dir LÉONCE NSENGIMANA.

Broadcasting and Communications

TELECOMMUNICATIONS

Airtel Rwanda: Airtel Head Office, nr Amahoro National Stadium, Kigali; tel. 733100100; e-mail customer.care@rw.airtel.com; internet airtel.co.rw; f. 2011; commenced operations in April 2012; provides mobile and fixed-line telephone services; Man. Dir AMIT CHAWLA; 4.0m. subscribers (Sept. 2021).

kt Rwanda Networks: Kigali Heights, 7th Floor, KG 7 Ave, POB 5440, Kigali; tel. 788318786; internet www.ktrn.rw; f. 2013; internet service provider; CEO AARON DAEHEAK AN.

Liquid Telecom Ltd: Ave de l'Armée and 3 KN 67 St, POB 6098, Kigali; tel. 252503571; internet liquid.tech; f. 2013; acquired the assets of former Rwandatel; provides fixed-line telephone and internet services; CEO ALEXIS KABEJA.

MTN Rwandacell: MTN Centre, Nyarutarama, BP 264, Kigali; tel. 280390000; e-mail pr2.rw@mtn.com; internet www.mtn.co.rw; f. 1998; provides mobile and fixed-line telephone services; CEO MITWA KAEMBA NG'AMBI; 6.9m. mobile subscribers (Sept. 2021).

REGULATORY AUTHORITY

Rwanda Utilities Regulatory Authority (RURA): POB 7289, Kigali; tel. 252584562; e-mail info@rura.rw; internet www.rura.rw; f. 2001; also responsible for regulation of electricity, water, sanitation, gas and transportation sectors; Dir-Gen. EMILE PATRICK BAGANIZI.

BROADCASTING

Radio

Flash FM: BP: 195, Kigali; tel. 788307863; e-mail info@flashfm.rw; internet flash.rw; Man. Dir LOUIS KAMANZI.

Isango Star: Kigali; tel. 788287900; e-mail info@isangostar.rw; internet isangostar.rw.

Kiss FM: Imela House, KK 10 Ave, Kicukiro, Gasharu, Kigali; e-mail info@kissfm.rw; internet kissfm.rw; Man. Dir JOHN WILKINS.

KT Radio: KN 2 Ave, BP 2229, Kigali; tel. 788351366; e-mail info@ kigalitoday.com; internet www.ktradio.rw; f. 2012; Dir PROSPER BITEMBEK.

90.7 Magic FM: Kigali; tel. 252576540; e-mail magicfm90.7@gmail .com; internet fb.com/pg/90.7MAGICFM.

Radio 10: blvd de l'aeroport Gishushu, Remera, POB 4307, Kigali; tel. 78444444; e-mail radiotv10rwanda@gmail.com; internet radiotv10.rw; f. 2004; Man. Dir AUGUSTIN MUHIRWA.

Radio Maria Rwanda: BP 52, Muhanga; tel. 784870045; e-mail radiomariarwanda@gmail.com; internet www.radiomaria.rw; Dir Fr CELSE NIYITEGEKA.

Radio Rwanda: blvd KG 7, Kacyiru, BP 83, Kigali; tel. 252576540; e-mail info@rba.co.rw; internet rba.co.rw/radio; f. 1961; state-controlled; daily broadcasts in Kinyarwanda, Swahili, French and English; Div. Man. of Radios ALDO HAVUGIMANA.

Television

Rwanda TV (RTV): blvd KG 7, Kacyiru, BP 83, Kigali; tel. 252576540; e-mail info@rba.co.rw; internet www.rba.co.rw/tv; f. 1992; broadcasts for 24 hours daily in Kinyarwanda, French and English; Dir INNOCENT NKURUNZIZA.

TV10: blvd de l'Aeroport Gishushu, POB 4307, Kigali; tel. 784444444; e-mail radiotv10rwanda@gmail.com; internet www .radiotv10.rw; f. 2012; privately owned commercial station; Man. Dir CEDRIC PIERRE-LOUIS.

Finance

BANKING

Central Bank

National Bank of Rwanda (BNR): 4 KN 6 Ave, POB 531, Kigali; tel. 788199000; e-mail info@bnr.rw; internet www.bnr.rw; f. 1964; bank of issue; Gov. JOHN RWANGOMBWA.

Commercial Banks

Access Bank (Rwanda) Ltd: UTC Bldg, 3rd Floor, ave de la Paix, BP 2059, Kigali; tel. 788145300; e-mail rwandacontactcenter@ accessbankplc.com; internet rwanda.accessbankplc.com; f. 1995 as Banque à la Confiance d'Or; fmrly Bancor SA; present name adopted in 2009; 75% owned by Access Bank (Nigeria); Country Man. Dir JEAN CLAUDE KARAYENZI.

Bank of Africa Rwanda Ltd (BOA Rwanda): POB 265, Kigali; tel. 788136205; e-mail info@boarwanda.com; internet www.boarwanda .com; f. 2015 following acquisition of Agaseke Bank; 89.4% owned by BOA Group; Chair. EMMANUEL NTAGANDA; Man. Dir ABDERRAHMANE BELBACHIR.

Bank of Kigali: 12 KN 4 Ave, Plot No. 790, POB 175, Kigali; tel. 788143000; e-mail info@bk.rw; internet www.bk.rw; f. 1966; Chair. ROD M. REYNOLDS; CEO Dr DIANE KARUSISI.

bpr Bank Rwanda PLC: KN 67 ST 2, BP 1348, Kigali; tel. 788187200; e-mail info@bpr.rw; internet bpr.rw; f. 1975; fmrly Banque Populaire du Rwanda; present name adopted in 2022 following the merger of Banque Populaire du Rwanda and KCB Bank Rwanda Ltd; Chair. GEORGE RUBAGUMYA; Man. Dir and CEO GEORGE ODHIAMBO.

Compagnie Générale de Banque (Cogebanque): KN 63 St, POB 5230, Kigali; tel. 788155500; e-mail customerservice@cogebank.com; internet www.cogebanque.co.rw; f. 1999; Chair. DÉSIRÉ MUSONI WA RWIHIMBA (acting); Man. Dir EMMANUEL MUGANDURA (acting).

Ecobank Rwanda: 314 KN4 Ave, BP 3268, Kigali; tel. 788161000; e-mail ecobankenquiries@ecobank.com; internet www.ecobank.com; Chair. Dr IVAN TWAGIRASHEMA; Man. Dir ALICE KILONZO-ZULU.

Equity Rwanda: Grand Pension Plaza Bldg, Ground Floor, POB 494, Kigali; tel. 788190000; e-mail info-rwanda@equitybank.co.rw; internet rw.equitybankgroup.com; f. 2011; Chair. EVELYN KAMAGAJU RUTAGWENDA; Man. Dir HANNINGTON NAMARA.

Guaranty Trust Bank Rwanda Ltd: MIC Bldg, First Floor, 1370 KN2 Ave, 20 BP 331, Kigali; tel. 788149600; e-mail inforw@gtbank .com; internet www.gtbank.co.rw; f. 1983 as Banque Continentale Africaine (Rwanda), subsequently became Fina Bank SA (2005);

name changed as above in 2014; Chair. PIPIAN HAKIZABERA; Man. Dir EMMANUEL EJIZU.

I&M Bank (Rwanda) PLC: 03 KN 9 Ave, POB 354, Kigali; tel. 788162006; e-mail info@imbank.co.rw; internet www.imbank.com/rwanda; f. 1963; privatized Sept. 2004; fmrly Banque Commerciale du Rwanda; name changed as above in 2013; Chair. WILLIAM C. IRWIN; Man. Dir ROBIN C. BAIRSTOW.

Development Bank

Banque Rwandaise de Développement, SA (BRD) (Development Bank of Rwanda): blvd de la Revolution, Kigali; tel. 250575079; e-mail brd@brd.rw; internet www.brd.rw; f. 1967; acquired the Banque de l'Habitat du Rwanda in 2011; 56% state-owned; Chair. BOBBY PITTMAN; CEO KAMPETA PITCHETTE SAYINZOGA.

Banking Association

Rwanda Bankers' Assocn: M. Peace Plaza, 5th Floor, KN 4 Ave, POB 2101, Kigali; e-mail info@rba.rw; internet rba.rw; f. 2000; Chair. ROBIN C. BAIRSTOW; Exec. Sec. TONY FRANCIS NTORE.

STOCK EXCHANGE

Rwanda Stock Exchange (RSE): Kigali City Tower (KCT), 1st Floor, KN 81 St, POB 5337, Kigali; tel. 788516021; e-mail info@rse.rw; internet www.rse.rw; f. 2005; Chair. BOB KARINA; CEO PIERRE CELESTIN RWABUKUMBA.

INSURANCE

BK Insurance: 12 KN 4 Ave, Plot No. 790, Nyarugenge, POB 724, Kigali; tel. 788143653; e-mail bkinsurance@bk.rw; internet www.bkinsurance.rw; f. 2015; owned by Bank of Kigali; Chair. SANDRA RWAMUSHAIJA; Man. Dir ALEX N. BAHIZI.

Britam: Union Trade Centre, 5th Floor, POB 913, Kigali; tel. 788198000; e-mail rwanda@britam.com; internet rw.britam.com; f. 2014; general insurance; Chair. SHELAGH KAHONDA; CEO JOHN BOSCO SEBABI.

MUA Rwanda Ltd: Grand Pension Plaza, Ground and 8th Floors, ave de la Paix, POB 82, Kigali; tel. 252570331; e-mail inforw@phoenix-assurance.com; internet www.mua.rw; f. 2006 as Phoenix of Rwanda Assurance Company Ltd; present name adopted 2018; Chair. ERNESTE GERALD LEMAIRE; Man. Dir GAUDENS KANAMUGIRE.

Prime Insurance Rwanda: MIC Bldg, KN2 Ave, Nyarugenge, Kigali; tel. 788150100; e-mail callcenter@prime.rw; internet prime.rw; f. 1995 as Cogear Ltd; acquired by Greenoaks Global Holdings in 2014 and renamed as above; life and general; Chair. FRANCIS NSENGIYUMVA; CEO JOHN MIRENGE.

Radiant: KN 2 Ave, Chic Bldg, Kigali; tel. 788381093; e-mail info@radiant.rw; internet radiant.rw; general; Chair. PROTAIS KARANGWA; Man. Dir MARC RUGENERA.

Sanlam General Insurance: cnr KN 3 Ave and KN 71 St, BP 942, Kigali; tel. 788185300; e-mail info@rw.sanlam.com; internet rw.sanlam.com; f. 1984; fmrly SORAS Group Ltd; name changed as above in 2019; Chair. VIANNEY RURANGIRWA SHUMBUSHO; CEO FIACRE G. BIRASA.

Sanlam Life Insurance: cnr KN 3 Ave and KN 71 St, BP 2616, Kigali; tel. 727555333; e-mail infovie@rw.sanlam.com; internet rw.sanlam.com; f. 1984; fmrly SORAS Group Ltd; name changed as above in 2019; life; Chair. ROBERT BAYIGAMBA; CEO JEAN CHRYSOSTOME HODARI.

SONARWA General Insurance Co. Ltd (SGICL): cnr KN 73 St and KN 3 Ave, BP 1035, Kigali; tel. 788225121; e-mail infos@sonarwa.co.rw; internet www.sonarwa.co.rw; f. 1975; 35% owned by Industrial and General Insurance Co Ltd (Nigeria); Chair. IZA IRAME; Man. Dir REES KINYANGI (acting).

SONARWA Life Assurance Co. Ltd: Kigali; tel. 788500144; e-mail info.life@sonarwa.co.rw; internet www.sonarwalife.co.rw; f. 2000; Chair. NICK BARIGYE; CEO ERIC KAMANZI (acting).

UAP Insurance Rwanda Ltd: Grand Pension Plaza, 7th Floor, ave de la Paix, BP 6644 Kigali; tel. 788168000; e-mail uapinsurancerw@uap-group.com; internet www.uaprwanda.rw; Man. Dir ANNIE NIBISHAKA.

Insurance Association

Rwanda Insurers Assocn (Association des Assureurs du Rwanda—ASSAR): Centenary House, 5th Floor, Kigali; tel. 788304577; e-mail info@assar.rw; internet assar.rw; f. 1992; Chair. JEAN CHRISOSTOME HODARI (acting); Exec. Sec. BEATRICE UWERA (acting).

Trade and Industry

GOVERNMENT AGENCIES

Capital Market Authority: RSSB Bldg, Tower 2, 5th Floor, KN3 Rd, African Union Blvd, POB 6136, Kigali; tel. 252500332; e-mail info@cma.rw; internet www.cma.rw; f. 2007; Chair. STACI WARDEN; Exec. Dir ERIC BUNDUGU (acting).

National Agricultural Export Development Board (NAEB): Magerwa St, Kigali; tel. 252575600; e-mail info@naeb.gov.rw; internet www.naeb.gov.rw; f. 2011; formulates policies and strategies for developing exports of agricultural and livestock products; JOSHUA RUGEMA (acting); CEO CLAUDE BIZIMANA.

Rwanda Agriculture and Animal Resources Development Board (RAB): BP 5016, Kigali; tel. 788385312; e-mail infos@rab.gov.rw; internet www.rab.gov.rw; f. 2006; contributes towards the growth of agricultural production through the development of appropriate technologies, providing advisory, outreach and extension services to stakeholders in agriculture; Chair. MAGNIFIC NDAMBE NZARAMBA; Dir-Gen. Dr PATRICK KARANGWA.

Rwanda Public Procurement Authority: Grand Pension Plaza, 10th Floor, Plot No. 2, KN 3 Ave, POB 4276, Kigali; tel. 786582957; e-mail info@rppa.gov.rw; internet rppa.gov.rw; f. 2008 to replace the Nat. Tender Bd (f. 1998); organizes and monitors general public procurement; Chair. HANNINGTON NAMARA; Dir-Gen. JOYEUSE UWINGENEYE.

Rwanda Revenue Authority (RRA): ave du Lac Muhazi, POB 3987, Kimihurura, Kigali; tel. 252595500; e-mail info@rra.gov.rw; internet www.rra.gov.rw; f. 1998 to maximize revenue collection; Commissioner-Gen. PASCAL BIZIMANA RUGANINTWALI.

DEVELOPMENT ORGANIZATIONS

Agaciro Development Fund: RSSB Bldgs, Tower II, 3rd Floor, African Union Blvd, Kiyovu-Nyarugenge, POB 674, Kigali; tel. 280832020; e-mail info@agaciro.rw; internet www.agaciro.rw; sovereign wealth fund; Chair. SCOTT T. FORD; CEO GILBERT NYATANYI.

Agence Française de Développement (AFD): PCD Tower, KN 67, St 2, POB 3845, Kigali; e-mail afdagencedekigali@afd.fr; internet www.afd.fr; closed 1994; re-established 2022; Dir ARTHUR GERMOND.

National Industrial Research and Development Agency (NIRDA): City Tower, 13th Floor, Kigali; tel. 782086953; e-mail info@nirda.gov.rw; internet www.nirda.gov.rw; f. 2012 to replace the Institut de Recherches Scientifiques et Technologiques; Chair. STEVE MUTABAZI; Dir-Gen. Dr CHRISTIAN SEKOMO BIRAME.

Rwanda Development Board: KN 5 Rd, KG 9 Ave, POB 6239, Kigali; tel. 727775170; e-mail info@rdb.rw; internet rdb.rw; f. 2008; Chair. ITZHAK FISHER; CEO CLARE AKAMANZI.

Rwanda Land Management and Use Authority: Basement 2, Sopetrade KN 3 Rd, POB 433, Kigali; e-mail info@rlma.rw; internet www.rlma.rw; f. 2017 following division of the Rwanda Natural Resources Authority; Dir-Gen. ESPERENCE MUKAMANA.

Rwanda Mines, Petroleum and Gas Board: KN 4 Ave, Kigali; tel. 788386220; e-mail info@rmb.gov.rw; internet www.rmb.gov.rw; f. 2017 following division of the Rwanda Natural Resources Authority; CEO YAMINA KARITANYI.

Rwanda Forestry Authority (RWFA): Blue House, Ngororero; e-mail info@rfa.rw; internet www.rfa.rw; f. 2020; Dir-Gen. SPIRIDO NSHIMIYIMANA.

INDUSTRIAL ASSOCIATIONS

Private Sector Federation (PSF): Gikonda Magerwa, POB 319, Kigali; tel. 252570650; e-mail info@psf.org.rw; internet www.psf.org.rw; f. 1999 to replace the Chambre de Commerce et d'Industrie de Rwanda; umbrella org. of 9 professional chambers; promotes and represents the interests of the Rwandan business community; Chair. ROBERT BAPFAKURERA; CEO STEPHEN RUZIBIZA.

Rwanda Association of Manufacturers: Inind House, Africa Union Rd, KN 3 Ave, Kicukiro Sonatubes, Kigali; tel. 783255622; e-mail info@ram.org.rw; internet www.ram.org.rw; f. 2013; fmrly Association des Industriels du Rwanda; Chair. FELICIEN MUTALIKANWA; Exec. Sec. ALPHONSE KWIZERA.

UTILITIES

Rwanda Utilities Regulatory Authority (RURA): see Telecommunications.

Rwanda Energy Group (REG): 3 KN 82 St, POB 537, Kigali; tel. 788181224; e-mail info@reg.rw; internet www.reg.rw; f. 2014 to replace Energy, Water and Sanitation Authority; produces and supplies electricity through its subsidiaries Energy Development Company Ltd and Energy Utility Company Ltd; state-owned; Chair. Dr DIDACIENNE MUKANYILIGIRA; CEO RON WEISS.

Water and Sanitation Corporation Ltd (WASAC): Centenary House, 8 KN 4 Ave, Nyarugenge District, POB 2331, Kigali; tel. 788181427; e-mail wasac@wasac.rw; internet www.wasac.rw; f. 2014; Chair. OMAR MUNYANEZA; Acting CEO GISELE UMUHUMUZA.

MAJOR COMPANIES

Ameki Color: Gikondo Industrial Park, Kigali; tel. 252500257; e-mail info@amekicolor.com; manufacturer of paints.

Barefoot Power Rwanda Ltd: Muhima Rd, Muhima, POB 2199, Kigali; tel. 786182281; internet www.barefootpower.com; Dir GEORG HEINEMANN.

BRALIRWA: BP 131, Kigali; tel. 252587200; e-mail bralirwa@heineken.com; internet www.bralirwa.com; f. 1959; 70% owned by Heineken NV, Netherlands; mfrs and bottlers of beer in Nyamyumba and soft drinks in Kigali; Chair. LIEVEN VAN DER BORGHT; Man. Dir ETIENNE SAADA.

Cimenterie du Rwanda (CIMERWA): CIMERWA House, Kimihurura, POB 644, Kigali; tel. 788194600; e-mail info@cimerwa.rw; internet www.cimerwa.rw; f. 1984; 51% owned by PPC; Chair. REGIS A. RUGEMANSHURO; Man. Dir ALBERT K. SIGEI.

East African Granite Industries (EAGI): POB 186, Nyagatare; tel. 788316073; e-mail info@eagi.rw; internet eagi.rw; f. 2009; granite processing; Dir-Gen. DIDACE MUGISHA.

Ecomake: Green House, Gitega, Hospital Rd, KN 75, POB 5560, Kigali; tel. 788301975; green energy; Dir PAULIN BUREGEYA.

Horizon Group Ltd: M&M Plaza, 4th Floor, KG 8 Ave, Gishushu, POB 6129, Kigali; tel. 252581221; e-mail info@horizongroup.rw; internet www.horizongroup.rw; f. 2007; govt-owned; holding co owning Horizon Construction, Horizon Sopyrwa and Horizon Logistics; Chair. REBECCA R. RUZIBUKA; CEO FRED MUZIRAGUHARARA.

Horizon SOPYRWA (SOPYRWA): BP 79, Ruhengeri; tel. 252546364; e-mail info@sopyrwa.com; internet sopyrwa.com; f. 1978 as Office du Pyrethre du Rwanda; owned by Horizon Group Ltd; cultivation and processing of pyrethrum; Dir-Gen. GABRIEL BIZIMUNGU.

Ikirezi Natural Products: POB 7446, Kigali; tel. 785489111; internet www.ikirezi.com; organic oils.

Inyange Industries: KN 3 Rd, Masaka, POB 4584, Kigali; tel. 788161900; e-mail info@inyangeindustries.com; internet www.inyangeindustries.com; organic juices, mineral water and dairy products.

Kabuye Sugar Works SARL: BP 373; Kigali; tel. 250575468; f. 1969; privatized 1997; owned by the Madhvani Group, Uganda; Gen. Man. THIRU NAVUKKARASU.

Kigali Cement Co.: ave de Poids Lourds, Kigali; tel. 788301985; f. 1998.

Minimex Ltd: Nyandungu/Nyarunga, Kicukiro, POB 277, Kigali; tel. 788304626; e-mail info@minimex.co.rw; internet www.minimex.co.rw; f. 2007; maize products; Chair. FELICIEN MUTALIKANWA; Gen. Man. TREVOR AUGUSTINE.

Mutara Enterprises Ltd: ave de la Justice, BP 1661, Kigali; tel. 252573530; e-mail marketing@mutaraenterprises.com; f. 1995; office furniture and partitioning, installation of vertical blinds, carpeting, air conditioning and carports.

Ngali Holdings: Bodifa House, 7th Floor, blvd de l'Umuganda, KG 624 St, Kimuhurura, Gasabo, POB 7189, Kigali; tel. 280305002; e-mail info@ngali.com; internet www.ngali.com; Chair. JEAN RUTAYISIRE MUSONI; CEO DIANE MUGISHA.

Papyrus Co Ltd: Gikondo Industrial Area, POB 5236, Kigali; tel. 252570500; interior design and furniture.

Phoenix Metal Ltd: Fonderie de Karuruma, route de Byumba, POB 3663, Kigali; tel. 788307235; e-mail contact@phoenix-metal.com; internet phoenix-metal.com; f. 2005; smelting and refining of tin; Man. Dir FRANÇOIS MUNYANKINDI.

Rwanda Foam Ltd (SAKIRWA): Industrial Park, Gikonda, POB 595, Kigali; tel. 788307532; e-mail info@rwandafoam.com; mfrs of mattresses, pillows and cushions; Man. Dir PATRICK MAKUZA; 100 employees.

Rwanda Investment Group Ltd (RIG): POB 2876, Kimihurura; tel. 252500288; e-mail rig@rig.co.rw; Chair. JACK KAYONGA; Exec. Dir Dr IVAN TWAGIRASHEMA.

Peat Energy Co Ltd (PEC): POB 2876, Kimihurura; tel. 252500288; a subsidiary of RIG; Dir PIERRE KALINGANIRE.

Rwanda Energy Co Ltd (REC): POB 2876, Kimihurura; tel. 252500288; Exec. Dir Dr IVAN TWAGIRASHEMA.

Safintra Rwanda Ltd: Prime Economic Zone, Plots 2156 and 2157, Phase 1, Masoro, Gasabo, POB 6959, Kigali; tel. 727888070; e-mail sales.safintrarwanda@safalgroup.com; internet www.safintra-rwanda.com; roofing sheets.

SHER Consult Ltd: rue de l'Akagera, Parcelle 3925, Nyarugenge, BP 1526, Kigali; tel. 788384648; e-mail info@sherconsult.com;

internet www.sherconsult.com; f. 1985; rural devt; Chair. and Man. Dir PAUL GATIN; Rwandan Rep. EGBERT HAMEL.

Société Petrolière SARL (SP): Petrocom Bldg, Ground Floor, ave des Poids Lourds, BP 144, Kigali; tel. 788306232; e-mail info@sp.co.rw; internet sp.co.rw; f. 1967 as Fina Rwanda; present name adopted 2007; import, distribution and marketing of petroleum products; Man. Dir CLAUDIEN HABIMANA.

Société Rwandaise pour la Production et la Commercialisation du Thé (SORWATHE), SARL: SOMECA Bldg, 1st Floor, blvd de la Révolution, POB 1136, Kigali; tel. 788302645; e-mail sorwathe@gmail.com; f. 1978; tea.

SOSOMA Industries Ltd: BP 441, Kigali; tel. 788617990; e-mail sosoma@sosoma.rw; internet www.sosoma.rw; flour and tea; Chair. GRACE NYINAWABAYIRU; Dir-Gen. DIANE NDAGIJIMANA.

Sulfo Rwanda Industries: 12 KN 82 St, POB 90, Kigali; tel. 252574556; e-mail info@sulfo.com; internet www.sulfo.com; 1962; mfrs and distributor of consumer goods; Chair. TAJDIN H. JAFFER; Man. Dir H. DHARMARAJAN.

Wolfram Mining and Processing Ltd: 428 Député Kayuku St, Kiyovu, POB 1856, Kigali; tel. 781270076; internet www.wmprwanda.com; Man. Dir JEAN MALIC KALIMA.

TRADE UNIONS

Centrale des Syndicats des Travailleurs du Rwanda (CESTRAR): BP 1645, Kigali; tel. 255106081; e-mail info@cestrar.rw; internet cestrar.rw; f. 1985; Sec.-Gen. BIRABONEYE AFRICAIN.

Congrès du Travail et de la Fraternité au Rwanda (COTRAF): ave Kimihurura, BP 1557, Kigali; tel. 788635536; e-mail cotraf_rw@yahoo.fr; internet www.cotraf.org; f. 2003; Pres. DOMINIQUE BICAMIMPAKA.

Conseil National des Organisations Syndicales Libres (COSYLI): BP 4866, Kigali; tel. 725102374; Pres. FLORIDA MUKARUGAMBWA.

Transport

Rwanda Transport Development Agency (RTDA): Queen's Land House, 1st Floor, KG 563 St, Kacyiru, POB 6674, Kigali; e-mail info@rtda.gov.rw; internet www.rtda.gov.rw; f. 2010; manages day-to-day aspects of the transport sector; Chair. Dr LEOPOLD MBEREYAHO; Dir-Gen. GUY M. KALISA.

RAILWAYS

There are no railways in Rwanda, although plans exist for the construction of a line linking Kigali and Isaka in Tanzania, with possible extensions to Bujumbura in Burundi and the DRC. Rwanda has access by road to the Tanzanian railways system. In 2011 the African Development Bank approved US $8.5m. in loans and grants to finance a multinational railway project study in Rwanda, Tanzania and Burundi.

ROADS

Rwanda Interlink Transport Corporation Ltd (RITCO): KN 119 St, Nyamirambo, BP 619, Kigali; tel. 788319333; internet www.ritco.rw; f. 2016 to replace the Office National des Transports en Commun; Man. Dir GODFREY NKUSI.

INLAND WATERWAYS

There are services on Lake Kivu between Cyangugu, Gisenyi and Kibuye, including two vessels operated by ONATRACOM.

CIVIL AVIATION

Kanombe International Airport (KIA) at Kigali can process up to 500,000 passengers annually. There is a second international airport at Kamembe, near the border with the DRC. Construction work began on Bugesera International Airport, which was intended to replace KIA, in mid-2017 and was scheduled to be completed in 2022. There are airfields at Butare, Gabiro, Nemba, Ruhengeri and Gisenyi, servicing internal flights.

Rwanda Civil Aviation Authority: BP 1122, Kigali; tel. 252505845; e-mail info@caa.gov.rw; internet www.caa.gov.rw; f. 2004 to replace the Rwanda Airport Authority; Dir-Gen. Col SILAS UDAHEMUK.

RwandAir: Kigali Int. Airport Bldg, Top Floor, BP 7275, Kigali; tel. 788177000; e-mail info@rwandair.com; internet www.rwandair.com; f. 2002 as Rwandair Express; renamed 2009; international services; CEO YVONNE MANZI MAKOLO.

Tourism

Office Rwandais du Tourisme et des Parcs Nationaux (ORTPN): blvd de la Révolution 1, BP 905, Kigali; tel. 250576514; e-mail reservation@rwandatourism.com; internet www .rwandatourism.com; f. 1973; govt agency; Dir-Gen. ROSETTE RUGAMBA.

Defence

As assessed at November 2021, the total strength of the Rwandan armed forces was estimated at 33,000, comprising an army of 32,000 and an air force of 1,000. In addition, there were an estimated 2,000 local defence forces. A programme to restructure the army, which was expected to be reduced in size to number about 25,000, was planned and a Rwanda Demobilization and Reintegration Commission was mandated to facilitate the reintegration of discharged military personnel into civilian life. In 2021 a total of 5,838 troops were stationed abroad.

Defence Budget: 178,000m. Rwanda francs in 2022.

Chief of Defence Staff: Gen. JEAN-BOSCO KAZURA.

Chief of Staff of the Army: Lt-Gen. MUBARAKH MUGANGA.

Chief of Staff of the Air Force: Lt-Gen. JEAN-JACQUES MUPENZI.

Education

Primary education, beginning at seven years of age and lasting for six years, is officially compulsory. Secondary education, which is not compulsory, begins at the age of 14 and lasts for a further six years, comprising two equal cycles of three years. In 2003, however, the Government announced plans to introduce a nine-year system of basic education, including three years of attendance at lower secondary schools. According to estimates by the United Nations Educational, Scientific and Cultural Organization (UNESCO), in 2018/19 enrolment at pre-primary level was equivalent to 28% of children in the relevant age-group (males 27%; females 28%). In that year 94% of children in the relevant age-group (males 94%; females 94%) were enrolled in primary schools, while secondary enrolment was equivalent to 44% of children in the appropriate age-group (males 42%; females 47%). Rwanda has a university, with campuses at Butare and Ruhengeri, and several other institutions of higher education, but some students attend universities abroad, particularly in Belgium, France or Germany. At the beginning of the 2011 school year English became the language of instruction in all public Rwandan educational establishments. In 2018 spending on education represented 10.8% of total budgetary expenditure.

Bibliography

Adelman, H., and Suhrke, A. (Eds). *The Path of a Genocide: The Rwanda Crisis from Uganda to Zaire.* Piscataway, NJ, Transaction Publishers, 2000.

Barnett, M. N. *Eyewitness to a Genocide: The United Nations and Rwanda.* Ithaca, NY, Cornell University Press, 2002.

Berry, J. A. (Ed.). *Genocide in Rwanda: A Collective Memory.* Washington, DC, Howard University Press, 1999.

Brauman, R. *Devant le mal. Rwanda, un génocide en direct.* Paris, Arléa, 1994.

Brown, S. E. *Gender and the Genocide in Rwanda: Women as Rescuers and Perpetrators.* Abingdon, Routledge, 2017.

Chrétien, J. P. *Rwanda, les Médias du génocide.* Paris, Editions Karthala, 1995.

Clark, P. *The Gacaca Courts, Post-Genocide Justice and Reconciliation in Rwanda: Justice without Lawyers.* Cambridge, Cambridge University Press, 2010.

Clark, P., and Kaufman Z. (Eds). *After Genocide: Transitional Justice, Post-Conflict Reconstruction and Reconciliation in Rwanda and Beyond.* New York, Columbia University Press and Hurst & Co, 2009.

Collins, B. *Rwanda 1994: The Myth of the Akazu Genocide Conspiracy and its Consequences.* Basingstoke, Palgrave Macmillan, 2014.

Crisafulli, P., and Redmond, A. *Rwanda, Inc.: How a Devastated Nation Became an Economic Model for the Developing World.* Basingstoke, Palgrave Macmillan, 2012.

Dallaire, R. *Shake Hands with the Devil: The Failure of Humanity in Rwanda.* Ontario, Random House of Canada Ltd, 2003.

Dorsey, L. *Historical Dictionary of Rwanda.* Lanham, MD, Scarecrow Press, 1999.

Eltringham, N. *Accounting for Horror: Post-Genocide Debates in Rwanda.* London, Pluto Press, 2004.

Gourevitch, P. *We Wish to Inform You That Tomorrow We Will Be Killed With Our Families: Stories from Rwanda.* New York, Picador, 1999.

Grayson, H., Hitchcott, N., Blackie, L., and Joseph, S. (Eds). *After the Genocide in Rwanda: Testimonies of Violence, Change and Reconciliation.* London, I. B. Tauris, 2019.

Grünfeld, F., and Huijboom, A. *The Failure to Prevent Genocide in Rwanda: The Role of Bystanders.* Boston, MA, Martinus Nijhoff, 2007.

Guichaoua, A. *From War to Genocide: Criminal Politics in Rwanda, 1990–1994.* Madison, WI, University of Wisconsin Press, 2015.

Guichaoua, A. (Ed.). *Les crises politiques au Burundi et au Rwanda (1993–1994).* Paris, Editions Karthala, 1995.

Harrell, P. E. *Rwanda's Gamble: Gacaca and a New Model of Transitional Justice.* Lincoln, NE, iUniverse, 2003.

Herr, A. *Rwandan Genocide: The Essential Reference Guide.* Santa Barbara, CA, ABC-CLIO, 2018.

Holmes, G. *Women and War in Rwanda: Gender, Media and the Representation of Genocide.* London, I. B. Tauris, 2014.

Huggins, S. *Agricultural Reform in Rwanda: Authoritarianism, Markets and Zones of Governance.* London, Zed Books, 2019.

Hunt, S. *Rwandan Women Rising.* Durham, NC, Duke University Press, 2017.

Jessee, E. *Negotiating Genocide in Rwanda: The Politics of History.* London, Palgrave Macmillan, 2017.

Jones, B. D. *Peacemaking in Rwanda: The Dynamics of Failure (Project of the International Peace Academy).* Boulder, CO, Lynne Rienner Publishers, 2001.

Kamukama, D. *Rwanda Conflict: Its Roots and Regional Implications.* Kampala, Fountain Publishers, 1993.

Khan, S. M., and Robinson, M. *The Shallow Graves of Rwanda.* London, I. B. Tauris & Co Ltd, 2001.

King, E. *From Classrooms to Conflict in Rwanda.* New York, Cambridge University Press, 2014.

Kinzer. S. *A Thousand Hills: Rwanda's Rebirth and the Man Who Dreamed It.* Hoboken, NJ, John Wiley & Sons, 2008.

Kuperman, A. J. *The Limits of Humanitarian Intervention: Genocide in Rwanda.* Washington, DC, Brookings Institution, 2001.

McDoom, O. *The Path to Genocide in Rwanda: Security, Opportunity, and Authority in an Ethnocratic State.* Cambridge, Cambridge University Press, 2020.

Mageza-Barthel, R. *Mobilizing Transnational Gender Politics in Post-Genocide Rwanda.* Farnham, Ashgate, 2015.

Mamdani, M. *When Victims Become Killers: Colonialism, Nativism and the Genocide in Rwanda.* Princeton, NJ, Princeton University Press, 2001.

Melvern, L. *A People Betrayed: The Role of the West in Rwanda's Genocide.* London, Zed Books, 2000.

   Conspiracy to Murder: The Rwandan Genocide. London, Verso, 2006.

Misser, F. *Vers un nouveau Rwanda?—Entretiens avec Paul Kagame.* Brussels, Editions Luc Pire, 1995.

Mitchell, S. *Institutional Legacies, Decision Frames and Political Violence in Rwanda and Burundi.* Abingdon, Routledge, 2018.

Mwakikagile, G. *Identity Politics and Ethnic Conflicts in Rwanda and Burundi: A Comparative Study.* Dar es Salaam, New Africa Press, 2012.

Mushikiwabo, L., and Kramer, J. *Rwanda Means the Universe: A Native's Memory of Blood and Bloodlines.* New York, St Martin's Press, 2006.

Palmer, N. F. *Courts in Conflict: Interpreting the Layers of Justice in Post-Genocide Rwanda.* New York, Oxford University Press, 2015.

Philpot, R. *Rwanda and the New Scramble for Africa: From Tragedy to Useful Imperial Fiction.* Montréal, QC, Baraka Books, 2013.

Pierce, J. R. *Speak Rwanda.* New York, Picador USA, 2000.

Prunier, G. *The Rwanda Crisis 1959–1964: History of a Genocide.* London, Hurst, 1995.

Rawson, D. *Prelude to Genocide: Arusha, Rwanda, and the Failure of Diplomacy*. Athens, OH, Ohio University Press, 2018.

Reyntjens, F. *Pouvoir et droit au Rwanda: droit public et évolution politique 1916–1973*. Tervuren, Musée royal de l'Afrique centrale, 1985.

    Political Governance in Post-Genocide Rwanda. New York, Cambridge University Press, 2013.

Rudakemwa, F. *Rwanda: à la recherche de la vérité historique pour une réconciliation nationale*. Paris, L'Harmattan, 2007.

Sabarenzi, J., and Mullane, L. *God Sleeps in Rwanda: A Personal Journey of Transformation*. New York, Atria, 2009.

Salton, H. *Dangerous Diplomacy: Bureaucracy, Power Politics, and the Role of the UN Secretariat in Rwanda*. Oxford, Oxford University Press, 2017.

Scherrer, C. P. *Genocide and Crisis in Central Africa: Conflict Roots, Mass Violence and Regional War*. Westport, CT, Praeger, 2001.

Sparrow, J. *Under the Volcanoes: Rwanda's Refugee Crisis*. Geneva, Federation of Red Cross and Red Crescent Societies, 1994.

Straus, S., and Waldorf, L. (Eds). *Remaking Rwanda: State Building and Human Rights after Mass Violence*. Madison, WI, University of Wisconsin Press, 2011.

Thomson, S. *Whispering Truth to Power: Everyday Resistance to Reconciliation in Postgenocide Rwanda*. Madison, WI, University of Wisconsin Press, 2013.

Twagilimana, A. *The Debris of Hate: Ethnicity, Regionalism, and the 1994 Genocide*. Lanham, MD, University Press of America, 2003.

Waugh, C. M. *Paul Kagame and Rwanda: Power, Genocide and the Rwandan Patriotic Front*. Jefferson, NC, McFarland & Co, 2004.

SAINT HELENA, ASCENSION AND TRISTAN DA CUNHA

Physical and Social Geography

Saint Helena, a rugged and mountainous island of volcanic origin, lies in the South Atlantic Ocean, latitude 16° S, longitude 5° 45' W, 1,131 km south-east of Ascension and about 1,930 km from the south-west coast of Africa. The island is 16.9 km long and 10.5 km broad, covering an area of 121 sq km (47 sq miles). The highest elevation, Diana's Peak, rises to 823 m above sea level. The only inland waters are small streams, few of them perennial, fed by springs in the central hills. These streams and rainwater are sufficient for domestic water supplies and a few small irrigation schemes.

The cool South Atlantic trade winds are continuous throughout the year. The climate is sub-tropical and mild: the temperature in Jamestown, on the sea-coast, 21°C–29°C in summer and 18°C–24°C in winter. Inland it is some 5°C cooler. Annual rainfall varies from 253 mm in Jamestown to 500 mm–1,100 mm elsewhere on the island.

According to the census of 7 February 2021, the population of Saint Helena was enumerated at 4,439, giving a density of 36.7 inhabitants per sq km. Jamestown, the capital, is the only town and had a population of 625 at the February 2021 census. The language of the island is English and the majority of the population (63.2%, according to the 2021 census) belong to the Anglican Communion.

Saint Helena has one of the world's most equable climates. Industrial pollution is absent from the atmosphere, and there are no endemic diseases of note. The island is of interest to naturalists for its rare flora and fauna; there are about 40 species of flora that are unique to Saint Helena.

The island of Ascension, with a population of 943 in December 2021, lies in the South Atlantic Ocean (7° 55' S, 14° 20' W), 1,131 km north-west of Saint Helena. The island, which covers an area of 88 sq km (34 sq miles), is a barren, rocky peak of purely volcanic origin, which was previously destitute of vegetation except above 450 m on Green Mountain (which rises to 875 m). The mountain supports a small farm producing vegetables and fruit. Since 1983 an alteration has taken place in the pattern of rainfall in Ascension. Total average annual rainfall has increased and the rain falls in heavy showers and is therefore less prone to evaporation. Grass, shrubs and flowers have grown in the valleys. Some topsoil has been produced by the decay of previous growth and root systems.

Tristan da Cunha, with a population of 238 in September 2022, lies in the South Atlantic Ocean, 2,800 km west of Cape Town, South Africa and 2,300 km south-west of Saint Helena. Also in the group are Inaccessible Island, 37 km west of Tristan; the three Nightingale Islands, 37 km south; and Gough Island (Diego Alvarez), 425 km south. Tristan is volcanic in origin and nearly circular in shape, covering an area of 98 sq km (38 sq miles) and rising in a cone to 2,060 m above sea level. The climate is typically oceanic and temperate. Rainfall averages 1,675 mm per year on the coast. The island group provides breeding grounds for albatrosses, rockhopper penguins and seals, and a number of endemic species, including the world's smallest flightless bird, the Inaccessible rail.

History

SAINT HELENA

The then uninhabited island of Saint Helena was discovered on 21 May 1502 by a Portuguese navigator, João da Nova, who named it in honour of St Helena, whose festival falls on that day. The British East India Co first established a settlement there in 1659 and in 1673 a charter to occupy and govern Saint Helena was issued by King Charles II to the East India Co. In this charter the King confirmed the status of the island as a British outpost, and bestowed full rights of British citizenship on all those who settled on the island and on their descendants in perpetuity (see below). In 1834 control over the island's affairs was transferred on a permanent basis from the East India Co to the British Government. Its importance as a port of call on the trade route between Europe and India ceased with the opening of the Suez Canal in 1869.

On 1 January 1989 a formal Constitution, replacing the Order in Council and Royal Instructions under which Saint Helena was governed, entered into force.

Owing to the limited range of economic activity on the island, Saint Helena is dependent on development and budgetary aid from the United Kingdom. From 1981, when the UK adopted the British Nationality Act, which effectively removed the islanders' traditional right of residence in the UK, opportunities for overseas employment were limited to contract work, principally in Ascension and the Falkland Islands. In July 1997 private legislation was introduced in the British Parliament to extend full British nationality to 'persons having connections with' Saint Helena. In the following month the British Government indicated that it was considering arrangements under which islanders would be granted employment and residence rights in the UK. In February 1998, following a conference held in London, UK, of representatives of the British Dependent Territories, it was announced that a review was to take place of the future constitutional status of these territories, and of means whereby their economies might be strengthened. It was subsequently agreed that the operation of the 1981 legislation in relation to Saint Helena would also be reviewed. As an immediate measure to ameliorate the isolation of Saint Helena, the British Government conceded permission for civilian air landing rights on Ascension Island, which, with the contemplated construction of a small airstrip on Saint Helena, could facilitate the future development of the island as a tourist destination.

On 21 May 2002 Saint Helenians celebrated both the 500th anniversary of the island's discovery and the restoration of British citizenship under the British Overseas Territories Act, which reinstated those rights removed in 1981.

On 4 February 2002 a referendum was held in Saint Helena, Ascension Island, the Falkland Islands and on RMS *St Helena* on future access to Saint Helena; 71.6% of votes cast were in favour of the construction of an airport. Tenders were invited for the construction of the airport; however, in February 2008 it was revealed that none of the shortlisted companies had provided an appropriate solution, and further negotiations would be necessary for the commencement of the project. Despite an initial commitment to bringing the airport into operation by 2012, in April 2009 the British Department for International Development (DfID) announced a further consultation on future access to Saint Helena. In December it was announced that as a result of 'current economic conditions' the British Government had decided that it would not be appropriate to proceed with the airport project 'at this time'. It was agreed, nevertheless, that a further analysis of potential cost savings to the airport contract which might be enabled by recent technological developments, and of options for funding the capital cost of the airport through a public-private partnership, would be carried out during 2010. In July it was decided that construction of the airport would go ahead, and in November 2011 a contract for the construction of the airport was signed with a South African company, Basil Read (Pty) Ltd. The total cost of the project was reported to be some £247m. In July 2012 the Government announced the first Variation Order under the airport construction project, which was to amend the runway design and allow for greater flexibility and the possibility of expanding the runway at a later date to accommodate larger aircraft. In August the new design for the terminal was unveiled. The airport was expected to commence operations on 21 May 2016, whereupon the RMS *St Helena* would be retired, and in March 2015 it was announced that Comair, a South African aviation and travel company, would operate a weekly flight between Johannesburg and Saint Helena. However, in late April 2016 the official opening of the airport was delayed on safety grounds. While some flights, including emergency medical evacuations and private charter jets, were able to arrive and depart, wind shear challenges meant that it was not initially possible for larger planes to land at the airport. Passenger and freight services were to be continued to be provided by RMS *St Helena* initially until July 2017, and then until February 2018, pending the commencement of full air services.

In December 2016 the Saint Helena Government released a tender which sought to award a contract for organizations to provide regular air services to Saint Helena for a three-year period. By this time 18 flights had successfully landed at the airport and in early May 2017 a charter plane carrying 60 passengers landed at the airport. The provider of that flight, SA Airlink of South Africa, was in June selected as the preferred bidder for the provision of a scheduled commercial air service to Saint Helena (and Ascension), and on 14 October the first commercial flight, which departed OR Tambo Airport in Johannesburg (South Africa), landed on Saint Helena. A weekly service was to operate between Saint Helena and South Africa (via Windhoek, Namibia), while a monthly service between Saint Helena and Ascension was introduced. (The frequency of the service to/from South Africa was subsequently increased to twice weekly and operated via Walvis Bay, also in Namibia.) RMS *St Helena* departed Saint Helena for the final time on 10 February 2018 and the Saint Helena Government confirmed the sale of the vessel in April.

Commercial flights between Saint Helena and South Africa were suspended in late March 2020 after lockdown measures were implemented in South Africa, in an attempt to counter the spread of the coronavirus (COVID-19) disease. However, charter (repatriation) flights from/to the UK (via Accra, Ghana) continued to take place during 2020 and 2021, although all arrivals to Saint Helena were required to quarantine for 14 days upon entering the island. By early September 2021 no cases of COVID-19 had been reported in the territory.

Meanwhile, a consultative poll on the draft for a new constitution, which, *inter alia*, proposed the creation of a ministerial form of government, took place on 25 May 2005. The draft document was rejected by 52.6% of voters. Concern was expressed at the low rate of voter participation, recorded at 43% of registered voters. The British Government subsequently stated that it wished to identify any possible improvements to the existing Constitution in conjunction with the new Executive Council, which took office following the elections held on 31 August. A new Governor, Andrew Gurr, was appointed in November 2007, and in April 2008 he outlined proposals for a new constitution that would be drafted following a full consultation process, which he envisaged would be completed by mid-2009.

On 1 September 2009 the Saint Helena, Ascension and Tristan da Cunha Constitution Order 2009 entered into force. Under the new Constitution, Ascension and Tristan da Cunha were no longer referred to as 'Dependencies' and the territory was henceforth to be known as Saint Helena, Ascension and Tristan da Cunha. The new Constitution also established fundamental rights and freedoms for each of the three islands,

which were to share the same Governor, Attorney-General, Supreme Court and Court of Appeal. Saint Helena was to be represented by a Legislative Council and an Executive Council, while Ascension and Tristan da Cunha were to be represented by Island Councils. Legislative elections were held in early November, following which the new councils were formed. The Legislative Council subsequently appointed chairmen to head the eight Council Committees responsible for overseeing policy formation. A new Governor, Mark Capes, took office in October 2011.

On 23 March 2013 a referendum, which attracted a turnout of just some 10%, was held on proposals to amend the Constitution whereby the members of the Legislative Council of Saint Helena would elect from among themselves a 'Chief Councillor' to head the Executive Council (a function currently performed by the Governor); the Chief Councillor would then nominate the other members of the Executive Council. The proposals, which were intended to improve democratic accountability, were defeated by 168 votes to 42. Governor Capes dissolved the Legislative Council in April 2013 pending the holding of a general election in July (shortly after the scheduled publication of a new and updated electoral register).

The general election took place on 17 July 2013, at which a total of 1,264 voters (some 55% of the eligible electorate) cast their ballots. Each eligible voter was to be permitted to select up to 12 (of a total of 20) candidates in the poll. The first formal meeting of the new Legislative Council was held on 24 July, at which the election of the five new Council Committee chairpersons also took place. In early July a new, five-member Executive Council was elected.

In January 2016 it was announced that Capes would be replaced as Governor in April by Lisa Phillips (known from February 2018 as Lisa Honan), who was duly sworn into office on 25 April. Meanwhile, in March a by-election was held at which Per Mikkel Olsson was elected to the Legislative Council. In April it was announced that Financial Secretary Colin Owen was to leave his post in July. Dax Richards was appointed to replace him. A further by-election to the Legislative Council was held in September, at which Cruyff Buckley was declared the winner of the seat.

In mid-January 2017 Governor Phillips announced her intention to dissolve the Legislative Council on 31 May in order that a general election be held in July. The date of dissolution was brought forward in February, to 20 May, with an election scheduled to take place on 26 July. Voting duly took place on that date and a total of 1,106 voters (49% of those eligible) cast their ballots. The new Legislative Council met for the first time on 2 August. Eric Benjamin was re-elected as Speaker and the five Committee chairpersons (and thus the members of the Executive Council) were also elected at that time. In March 2018 Sara O'Donnell was sworn in as the new Attorney-General and in April Susan O'Bey replaced Roy Burke as Chief Secretary.

Benjamin was succeeded as the Speaker of the Legislative Council by his hitherto deputy, John Cranfield, in March 2019, while in May Honan was replaced as Governor by Dr Philip Rushbrook. At a by-election to the Legislative Council in November Jeffrey Ellick was returned the victor.

In late June 2020 Buckley was elected to the Executive Council following the resignation of Russell Yon. Buckley was also elected as the new Chairperson of the Environment and Natural Resources Committee, while an additional (sixth) committee—Finance—was created. Clint Beard, the Chairperson of the Education Committee also headed the new committee.

In February 2021 the members of the Legislative Council agreed that a Consultative Poll on Governance Reform would take place on Saint Helena on 17 March. On that date voters were asked to decide whether the current governance system should be changed, and, if so, were given the option of choosing between a 'revised committee system' or a 'ministerial system'. According to official results, only 17.3% of the registered electorate cast their ballot; however, 79.2% of those who voted expressed their desire to change the system of governance, with 55.1% deciding in favour of a 'ministerial system'. The introduction of the new system would require amendments to be made to the Constitution of Saint Helena. The approval process, via an Order in Council laid before the UK Parliament, was completed in late July and the amendments entered into force after the general election, which took place on 13 October. A total of 12 candidates were elected to form the Legislative Council, and chose by secret ballot a Chief Minister from among their number. Julie Thomas was the sole, and therefore successful, candidate and subsequently selected four other elected members to serve as ministers. (Thomas also assumed the position of Minister of Education, Skills and Employment.) The Chief Minister and four other ministers replaced the committee chairpersons on the Executive Council, which henceforth comprised the Governor, the five ministers and the Attorney-General as an ex officio member. In August 2022 Rushbrook was replaced as Governor by Nigel Phillips, hitherto the Governor of the Falkland Islands and the Commissioner of South Georgia and the South Sandwich Islands.

ASCENSION

The island of Ascension was discovered by a Portuguese expedition on Ascension Day 1501. The island was uninhabited until the arrival of Napoleon Bonaparte, the exiled French Emperor, on Saint Helena in 1815, when a small British naval garrison was placed there. Ascension remained under the supervision of the British Admiralty until 1922, when it was made a dependency of Saint Helena. (This status was revoked under the new Constitution which entered into force on 1 September 2009.)

The island is famous for green turtles, which land there from December to May to lay their eggs in the sand. It is also a breeding ground of the sooty tern, or 'wideawake', vast numbers of which settle on the island every 10 months to lay and hatch their eggs. All wildlife, except rabbits and cats, is protected by law. Shark, barracuda, tuna, bonito, marlin and other game fish are plentiful in the surrounding ocean. Following the decision by the British Government in February 1998 to open airfield facilities on Ascension to civilian flights, a modest eco-tourism sector is being developed. A monthly flight from Saint Helena to Ascension was to be initiated as part of the SA Airlink agreement with the Saint Helena Government (see above).

Ascension does not raise its own finance; the costs of administering the island are borne collectively by the user organizations, supplemented by income from philatelic sales. Some revenue, which is remitted to the Saint Helena administration, is derived from fishing licences.

Dissent developed among the resident population in June 2002, following the decision of the Foreign and Commonwealth Office to impose taxes for the first time on the island. The primary objection of the population was that this was 'taxation without representation', as the islanders do not possess the right to vote, to own property or even to live on the island. (Protests took the form of a petition and the threat of legal action under the European Convention on Human Rights.) The Governor responded with plans to introduce a democratically elected council that would have a purely advisory function and no decision-making powers. On 22–23 August a vote on the democratic options took place on the island, with 95% of the votes cast being in favour of an Island Council; 50% of those eligible to vote did so. The Council was to be chaired by the Administrator, on behalf of the Governor. Elections for councillors took place in October, and the Island Council was inaugurated in the following month. A joint consultative council was also to be established, with representatives from both Ascension and Saint Helena, in order to formulate policy relating to economic development and tourism common to both islands.

In May 2007 the Island Council was suspended and the Ascension Island Advisory Group was established to provide advice to the Administrator on certain policy issues. It was anticipated that the Advisory Group would meet on a monthly basis, to be supplemented by informal meetings as necessary. Consultation papers were issued to encourage the people of Ascension to participate in the decision making process, such as that published by Governor Andrew Gurr in February 2008, which outlined the future responsibilities and operation of the Island Council. The suspension was initially expected to last until elections in May 2008, but after public consultation Gurr postponed the elections until later in that year; they were eventually held in October and a new Island Council was sworn in that month.

On 2 October 2013 the Island Council was dissolved, pending elections, which duly took place on 31 October. In August 2014 Marc Holland was sworn in as Administrator of Ascension Island.

On 14 July 2016 an early dissolution of the Island Council was announced by Governor Lisa Phillips. Elections took place on 1 September and on the following day a new Council took office. In November 2017 a new councillor, Terence Young, was elected to the four-member Island Council.

Also in November 2017 Nick Kennedy became Administrator of Ascension Island, but was replaced in March 2018 by Justine Allan. Steven Chandler was sworn in to replace Allan on 13 March 2019. On 15 March 2020 Sean Burns, a former Administrator of Tristan da Cunha, was sworn in to succeed Chandler.

Elections to the Island Council took place on 26 September 2019 and on the following day the new five-member Council was sworn into office.

TRISTAN DA CUNHA

The British navy took possession of Tristan da Cunha in 1816 during Napoleon's residence on Saint Helena, and a small garrison was stationed there. When the garrison was withdrawn, three men elected to remain and became the founders of the present settlement. Because of its position on a main sailing route the colony thrived until the 1880s, but with the replacement of sail by steam a period of decline set in. No regular shipping called and the islanders suffered at times from a shortage of food. Nevertheless, attempts to move the inhabitants to South Africa were unsuccessful. The islanders were engaged chiefly in fishing and agricultural pursuits.

The United Society for the Propagation of the Gospel has maintained an interest in the island since 1922, and in 1932 one of its missionary teachers was officially recognized as Honorary Commissioner and magistrate. In 1938 Tristan da Cunha and the neighbouring uninhabited islands of Nightingale, Inaccessible and Gough were made dependencies of Saint Helena. (This status was revoked under the new Constitution which entered into force on 1 September 2009.) In 1950 the office of Administrator was created. The Island Council was established in 1952.

The island is remote, and regular communications are restricted to about six calls each year by vessels from Cape Town, South Africa, (usually crayfish trawlers), an annual visit from a British vessel, the RMS *St Helena*, from Cape Town and the annual call by a South African vessel with supplies for the island and the weather station on Gough Island. There is, however, a wireless station on the island which is in daily contact with Cape Town. A satellite system, which provides direct dialling for telephone and fax facilities, was installed in 1992. The cost of international communications diminished greatly from mid-2006, with the installation of a satellite internet and telephone exchange, part of the British Foreign and Commonwealth Office telecommunications network.

An assessment was carried out on the island's harbour in 2006, as its location means that it is vulnerable to extreme weather conditions which threaten its structural integrity in the long term. Plans to relocate the harbour, however, proved too expensive and it was renovated early in 2008. This was paid for by the British Department for International Development and was completed in March with the help of Royal Engineers from the UK. The island is largely self-sufficient.

On 13 March 2013 a new 11-member Island Council was sworn in for a three-year term. No elections had been necessary as there had only been eight nominations for the eight vacant elective places on the Council. A further three members were appointed by the Administrator. Ian Lavarello, the only member of the outgoing Island Council to retain his position, was elected Chief Islander.

Lavarello was re-elected for a further three-year term as Chief Islander following local elections in early March 2016. A new, 11-member Island Council took office later that month. In

October Sean Burns, hitherto Head of the Saint Helena Governor's Office, replaced Alex Mitham as Administrator.

Local elections were held on 26 March 2019 (with a turnout of 76.4%), following which a new, 11-member Island Council was sworn in. James Glass, Tristan da Cunha's Director of Fisheries, was elected as Chief Islander and he was re-elected to this position in March 2022. (No local elections were necessary on this occasion as only eight candidates were nominated, and thus all were returned unopposed. A further three members were nominated by the joint Administrators.

Meanwhile, in January 2020 Steve Townsend and Fiona Kilpatrick were sworn in as the new joint Administrators of Tristan da Cunha. (The married couple were to occupy the post on a job share basis, with Kilpatrick assuming duties for an initial three-month period.) In September 2022 Jason Ivory was sworn in as the new Administrator of Tristan da Cunha.

Economy

SAINT HELENA

The economy of Saint Helena is heavily reliant on British aid. In 2021/22 total core budgetary support amounted to £30.8m. Local budget revenues totalled an estimated £16.5m. in that year. According to official figures, Saint Helena's gross domestic product (GDP) totalled £39.2m. in 2020/21; GDP per head was £8,690 in the same financial year. (Agriculture contributed 0.5% of GDP, while industry provided 11.0% and services 88.5%.) Overall GDP declined by 2.6% in 2019/20, but grew by 2.4% in 2020/21. The population increased by an average of 0.5% per year in 20011/12–2020/21/18, while GDP per capita increased by 0.3% per year in 2014/15–2020/21. The annual rate of inflation, according to retail prices, averaged 2.6% in 2011–21. The rate is influenced to a large extent by the prevailing rates in Saint Helena's two most important trading partners, South Africa and the UK. Retail prices increased by 2.6% in 2021, and were expected to rise further in 2022.

At the 2021 census 6.3% of the economically active population were engaged in agriculture and fishing, 16.7% in industry (predominantly construction) and 76.9% in services. The rate of unemployment was 3.6% of the active workforce.

There is a significant visible trade deficit (£19.4m. in 2019/20), and in 2021/22 the total value of imports amounted to £20.8m., while exports were reported to be of minimal value.

Fish of many kinds are plentiful in the waters around Saint Helena; however, the island's fisheries corporation operated at a significant and consistent loss, and was closed down December 2019. Preliminary discussions regarding the formation of a fish processing co-operative began in February 2020 and were successfully concluded in March 2021. Saints Tuna Corporation Limited (a collection of fishermen and vessel owners) agreed to lease the fish processing factory from the Saint Helena Government for a 10-year period from June, with the aim of establishing a sustainable and environmentally friendly fishing industry. No fish was exported in 2020/21, however, and the total catch was recorded at just 89 tons in 2020.

The only port in Saint Helena is Jamestown, which is an open roadstead with a good anchorage for ships of any size. In 1978, with the establishment of the Saint Helena Shipping Co, the Saint Helena Government assumed responsibility for the operation and maintenance of a charter vessel (known as the RMS *St Helena*, which entered operation in 1990), which carried cargo and passengers between Saint Helena and Cardiff, UK, via Vigo, Spain, and between Saint Helena and Cape Town, South Africa (with calls at the Canary Islands); in addition, there were also visits to Ascension Island and to Tristan da Cunha.

In April 2003 the Executive Council invited tenders for the construction of an airport, which was initially expected to be completed by 2012. This development represented the potential to expand significantly both the private sector and the economy as a whole, and plans included extensive infrastructural development to support the potential inflow of people and cargo. In July 2010 it was decided that construction of the airport would proceed and preparatory work began in early 2012 (see *History*). The airport was scheduled to be opened on 21 May 2016; however, safety concerns delayed the official opening of the airport to large commercial aircraft. SA Airlink of South Africa was subsequently selected as the provider of a scheduled commercial air service to Saint Helena (and Ascension) and on 14 October 2017 the first commercial flight, which departed OR Tambo Airport in Johannesburg (South Africa), landed on Saint Helena. A weekly service initially operated between Saint Helena and South Africa (at first via Windhoek, Namibia, and later via Walvis Bay), and this was increased to twice weekly from May 2018, while a monthly service between Saint Helena and Ascension was introduced.

RMS *St Helena* departed Saint Helena for the final time on 10 February 2018 and the Saint Helena Government confirmed the sale of the vessel in April. Meanwhile, AW Ship Management signed an agreement with the Saint Helena Government to provide a marine cargo service to Saint Helena which commenced in February 2018. The service connects Jamestown with Cape Town and also calls at Ascension Island four times per year.

New tourism and investment policies took effect in January 2007, aimed at increasing competitiveness and making Saint Helena an attractive option for international investment. A total of 3,103 tourists visited Saint Helena in 2015/16, although this number was expected to grow significantly following the opening of the airport. There are 118 km of all-weather roads, and a further 20 km of earth roads, which are used mainly by animal transport and are usable by motor vehicles only in dry weather. All roads have steep gradients and sharp curves.

In 2012 the Saint Helena authorities published a Sustainable Economic Development Plan (SEDP) for 2012/13–2021/22, which aimed to introduce a 'tourism driven economy' in conjunction with the construction of the airport. The SEDP stated that a 'relatively modest' number of visitors (totalling 30,000 per year) was required in order to make Saint Helena financially self-sustaining, and plans were already advanced with regard to the construction of a number of large tourism resorts on the island. In 2019 a total of 8,143 people (including day visitors from cruise ships) arrived on Saint Helena. However, the nascent tourism industry was adversely affected by the global COVID-19 pandemic, with restrictions placed on travel to and from the island (including the suspension of all flights to and from South Africa) from mid-2020, which were not repealed until early April 2021. In 2020 a total of just 2,806 people (including day visitors from cruise ships) arrived on Saint Helena and in 2021 this figure declined further to just 1,914.

In August 2011 the state-owned Saint Helena Broadcasting (Guarantee) Corporation Ltd (SHBC) was registered and in 2012 a new community-owned media services organization was established. SHBC (renamed South Atlantic Media Services—SAMS—in February 2013) broadcasts two radio stations. Existing radio station Saint FM was invited to join the corporation but declined. The final edition of *The Saint Helena Herald* was published in early March 2012, and was replaced by the SHBC's new weekly newspaper, *The Sentinel*, which published its first issue later that month. (Saint FM also publishes the weekly *Saint Helena Independent*, and this was to continue.) In August 2021 an undersea fibre optic cable was landed on Saint Helena and would provide vastly improved broadband internet connectivity.

ASCENSION

Ascension does not raise its own finance; the costs of administering the island are borne collectively by the user organizations, supplemented by income from philatelic sales. Government expenditure funds one school, one hospital (offering limited services), police and judicial services; these services are provided without charge to local taxpayers. The island is developing a modest eco-tourism sector. Some revenue, which is remitted to the Saint Helena administration, is derived from fishing licences. Facilities on Ascension underwent rapid development in 1982 to serve as a major staging post for British vessels and aircraft on their way to the Falkland Islands, and the island has continued to provide a key link in British supply lines to the South Atlantic.

TRISTAN DA CUNHA

The island's major source of revenue derives from a royalty for the crayfishing concession, supplemented by income from the sale of postage stamps and other philatelic items, and handicrafts. The fishing industry and the administration employ all of the working population. Some 20 power boats operating from the island land their catches to a fish-freezing factory built by the Atlantic Islands Development Corpn, the fishing concession of which was transferred in January 1997 to a new holder,

Premier Fishing (Pty) Ltd, of Cape Town, and later to another South African company, Ovenstone (Pty) Ltd. In February 2008, however, a fire destroyed the factory completely, along with the island's power plant. Ovenstone resumed operations in mid-2009 in a new factory built to European Union standards.

Development aid from the UK ceased in 1980, leaving the island financially self-sufficient. The UK, however, has continued to supply the cost of the salaries and passages of the Administrator, a doctor and visiting specialists (a dentist every two years and an optician every two years). In June 2008, prompted by concerns surrounding the island's dwindling capital reserves, an incremental system of income tax (with a maximum rate of 13%) was introduced. It was reported in May 2008 that the British Government had registered a claim with the United Nations Commission for the Limits of the Continental Shelf to extend its territorial waters around Tristan da Cunha. It was hoped that these areas of seabed could be secured with the possibility of drilling for petroleum, gas and mineral resources in future years.

Statistical Survey

Source (unless otherwise indicated): St Helena Statistics Office, Government of Saint Helena, The Castle, Jamestown, Saint Helena Island, STHL 1ZZ; tel. 22138; e-mail kelly.clingham@sainthelena.gov.sh; internet www.sainthelena.gov.sh/st-helena/statistics.

Note: Unless otherwise indicated, figures in this Statistical Survey relate only to the island of Saint Helena.

AREA AND POPULATION

Area: 411 sq km (159 sq miles). Saint Helena 121 sq km (47 sq miles); Ascension Island 88 sq km (34 sq miles); Tristan da Cunha 98 sq km (38 sq miles); Inaccessible Island 10 sq km (4 sq miles); Nightingale Islands 2 sq km (1 sq mile); Gough Island 91 sq km (35 sq miles).

Population: 4,802 at census of 7 February 2016 (enumerated total); 4,477 at census of 7 February 2021 (enumerated total), of whom 4,439 were normally resident. *Mid-2022:* 4,182 normally resident. *Tristan da Cunha* (at 15 September 2022): 238 normally resident. *Ascension Island* (at 31 December 2021): 943. Note: There are no indigenous inhabitants on Ascension Island, but several hundred personnel and employees and their families are normally resident (at 31 December 2021 these comprised Saint Helena 496, UK 138, USA 89 and others 220). There is a small weather station on Gough Island, staffed, under agreement, by personnel employed by the South African Government.

Density (normally resident population at mid-2022): 34.6 per sq km.

Population by Age and Sex (normally resident population at mid-2022): *0–14 years:* 579 (males 304, females 275); *15–64 years:* 2,505 (males 1,241, females 1,264); *65 years and over:* 1,098 (males 573, females 525); *Total* 4,182 (males 2,118, females 2,064).

Principal Town (at 2021 census): Jamestown (capital) 625 (although the adjoining suburb of Half Tree Hollow recorded a population of 1,034).

Births, Marriages and Deaths (2021): Registered live births 39 (9.4 per 1,000); Marriages 11; Registered deaths 68 (16.4 per 1,000).

Life Expectancy (years at birth, 2021): 77.5 (males 74.0; females 81.0).

Employment (2008 census): Agriculture, hunting and related activities 122; Fishing 33; Mining and quarrying 8; Manufacturing 115; Electricity, gas and water 113; Construction 190; Wholesale and retail trade, etc. 385; Hotels and restaurants 36; Transport, storage and communications 237; Financial intermediation 20; Real estate, renting and business activities 185; Public administration and defence 157; Education 157; Health and social work 178; Other community services 217; Private household 17; Extraterritorial organizations 5; *Total employed* 2,130 (males 1,174, females 956) (Source: ILO). *2021 Census* (normally resident population): Total employed 2,560; Total unemployed 94; Total labour force 2,654.

HEALTH AND WELFARE

COVID-19: Fully Vaccinated Population (% of total population at 5 May 2021): 65.3.

Human Development Index (official estimate, 2017): ranking: 83.

Human Development Index (official estimate, 2017): value: 0.756.

Note: For data on COVID-19 vaccinations, 'fully vaccinated' denotes receipt of all doses specified by approved vaccination regime (Sources: Johns Hopkins University and Our World in Data). For more information on sources and further definitions, see Health and Welfare Statistics: Sources and Definitions section (europaworld.com/credits).

AGRICULTURE, ETC.

Livestock (2020): Cattle 786; Chickens 6,790; Goats 847; Pigs 552; Sheep 1,223.

Livestock Products (metric tons, 2020): Cattle meat 32.9; Pig meat 73.4; Sheep meat 2.5.

Fishing (metric tons, live weight of capture, including Ascension and Tristan da Cunha, 2020): Yellowfin tuna 87; Tristan da Cunha rock lobster 410 (FAO estimate); Total catch (incl. others) 509 (FAO estimate). Figures include catches of rock lobster from Tristan da Cunha during the 12 months ending 30 April of the year stated. Source: FAO.

INDUSTRY

Electrical Energy (production, '000 kWh): 11,910 in 2019; 11,211 in 2020; 10,739 in 2021.

FINANCE

Currency, Exchange Rates and Fiscal Year: 100 pence (pennies) = 1 Saint Helena pound (£). *Sterling, Dollar and Euro Equivalents* (31 May 2022): £1 sterling = Saint Helena £1; US $1 = 79.43 pence; €1 = 85.10 pence; £10 = $12.59 = €11.75. *Average Exchange Rate* (£ per US dollar): 0.7834 in 2019; 0.7800 in 2020; 0.7271 in 2021. Note: The Saint Helena pound is at par with the pound sterling. *Fiscal Year:* The fiscal year ends on 31 March.

Budget (£ million, fiscal year ending March 2022, estimates): Total revenue 16.5 (excluding United Kingdom budgetary aid 30.8); Total expenditure 48.5. *Ascension Island* (£ million, year ending 31 March 2004, estimates): Total revenue 4.3; Total expenditure 4.0 (recurrent 3.3, capital 0.7). *Tristan da Cunha* (£ million, 2005/06, estimates): Total revenue 0.7; Expenditure 0.9 (with excess expenditure financed from capital reserves of 1.2).

Money Supply (£ '000, fiscal year ending March 2007): Currency in circulation 3,618 (excl. commemorative coins valued at 514).

Cost of Living (Retail Price Index; base: January–March 2018 = 100): 105.1 in 2019; 106.2 in 2020; 107.6 in 2021.

Gross Domestic Product (£ million at constant 2020/21 prices, fiscal year, estimates): 39.3 in 2018/19; 38.3 in 2019/20; 39.2 in 2020/21.

Gross Domestic Product by Economic Activity (£ million at current prices, fiscal year ending March 2021, estimates): Agriculture, forestry and fishing 0.2; Mining, manufacturing, power and utilities 2.7; Construction 1.4; Wholesale and retail trade, repair of motor vehicles and transportation 5.9; Accommodation and food service activities 0.5; Finance, insurance and real estate; information and communications 7.7; Government services 18.1; Other services 0.8; *Gross value added at basic prices* 37.3; Taxes, less subsidies, on products 1.9; *GDP in market prices* 39.2.

EXTERNAL TRADE

Principal Commodities (£ '000, fiscal year ending March 2022 unless otherwise indicated): *Imports:* Total 20,803 (Food and live animals 3,947; Beverages and tobacco 1,277; Mineral fuels, lubricants, etc. 2,486; Chemicals and related materials 1,664; Machinery and transport equipment 4,955; Manufactured goods and articles 6,082). *Exports* (2020/21): Total 24. Note: Trade is mainly with the United Kingdom (imports 8,930 in 2021/22) and South Africa (imports 9,061 in 2021/22).

TRANSPORT

Road Traffic (at December 2020): 3,276 licensed vehicles (incl. 1,499 passenger motor cars; 197 motorcycles and scooters; 106 buses; 1,231 vans and jeeps; and 67 lorries).

Shipping: *Vessels Entered* (incl. yachts and cruise ships, 2015/16) 232. *Flag Registered Fleet* (at 31 December 2021): Vessels 5; Total displacement 7,660 grt (Source: Lloyd's List Intelligence—www.bit.ly/LLintelligence).

TOURISM

Visitor Arrivals (excl. returning residents, fiscal year): 3,765 in 2019/20; 719 in 2020/21; 669 in 2021/22.

Cruise Ship Excursionists (fiscal year): 1,459 in 2017/18; 2,804 in 2018/19; 2,249 in 2019/20.

Receipts from Tourism (£ million, fiscal year, estimates): 0.8 in 2011/12–2014/15.

COMMUNICATIONS MEDIA

Television Subscribers (April 2007): 1,161.

Telephones (main lines in use, 2020): 4,000 (Source: International Telecommunication Union).

Mobile Telephones (2020): 4,000 (Source: International Telecommunication Union).

Broadband Subscriptions, Fixed (2017): 1,000 (Source: International Telecommunication Union)

Internet Users (% of population, 2012): 37.6 (Source: International Telecommunication Union).

EDUCATION

Primary (2013/14 unless otherwise indicated): 3 schools; 18 teachers (2010/11); 335 pupils (provisional).

Amalgamated School (2012/13): 3 school; 22 teachers (2010/11); 279 pupils (provisional).

Intermediate (2006/07): 2 schools; 17 teachers; 119 pupils.

Secondary (2013/14 unless otherwise indicated): 1 school; 30 teachers (2010/11); 236 pupils (provisional).

2012/13 (all levels): 4 schools; 82 teachers (2010/11); 524 enrolled pupils (provisional).

2014/15 (enrolment): Nursery 46; Primary 304; Secondary 207; Post-compulsory secondary 21; Apprenticeship schemes 45.

Directory

The Constitution

The Saint Helena, Ascension and Tristan da Cunha Constitution Order 2009, which entered into force on 1 September 2009, replaced the Saint Helena Constitution Order 1988 of 1 January 1989. While separate territories, Saint Helena, Ascension and Tristan da Cunha form a single territorial grouping under the British Crown and are represented by a single Governor. The Constitution order was amended in 2021 to permit the introduction of a ministerial system of government on Saint Helena.

Executive authority is reserved to the British Crown, but is exercised on behalf of His Majesty King Charles III by the Governor, either directly or through officers subordinate to him or her. Executive authority of Ascension is exercised by the Governor, either directly or through the Administrator of Ascension. Executive authority of Tristan da Cunha is exercised by the Governor, either directly or through the Administrator of Tristan da Cunha. The Executive Council for Saint Helena, which is chaired by the Governor, consists of the Chief Minister, four other ministers (as recommended for appointment by the Chief Minister) and the Attorney-General as an ex officio member without the right to vote.

Legislative authority for Saint Helena is vested in the Legislature, consisting of His Majesty King Charles III and the Legislative Council, which has the power to make laws for the peace, order and good government of Saint Helena. The Legislative Council consists of a Speaker and Deputy Speaker, 12 elected members, one of whom is elected from amongst their number as Chief Minister, and one ex officio member (the Attorney-General). Legislative authority on Ascension and on Tristan da Cunha is vested in the Governor, who acts after consultation with the respective Island Councils, although he or she is not obliged to act in accordance with this advice.

The Government

HEAD OF STATE

King: HM King CHARLES.

Governor: NIGEL PHILLIPS.

The Governor of Saint Helena, in their capacity as Governor of Ascension and Tristan da Cunha, is represented by an Administrator on those islands. The Governor, either directly, or through the Administrator, exercises executive authority on behalf of His Majesty King Charles III. The Governor, acting after consultation with the Island Councils, whose advice he or she is not obliged to follow, may make laws for the peace, order and good government of Ascension and Tristan da Cunha.

Administrator of Ascension: SEAN BURNS.

Administrator of Tristan da Cunha: JASON IVORY.

EXECUTIVE COUNCIL
(October 2022)

President: NIGEL PHILLIPS (Governor).

Chief Minister and Minister of Education, Skills and Employment: JULIE THOMAS.

Minister of Safety, Security and Home Affairs: JEFFREY ELLICK.

Minister of the Treasury, Infrastructure and Sustainable Development: MARK BROOKS.

Minister of the Environment, Natural Resources and Planning: CHRISTINE SCIPIO.

Minister of Health and Social Care: MARTIN HENRY.

Attorney-General: ALLEN CANSICK.

LEGISLATIVE COUNCIL
(October 2022)

The Legislative Council consists of the Speaker, the Deputy Speaker, 12 elected members, one of whom is elected from amongst their number as Chief Minister, and one ex officio member (the Attorney-General).

Speaker: CYRIL GUNNELL.

Deputy Speaker: CATHY CRANFIELD.

Chief Minister: JULIE THOMAS.

Elected Members: ROSEMARY BARGO, GILLIAN BROOKS, MARK BROOKS, RONALD COLEMAN, JEFFREY ELLICK, Dr CORINDA ESSEX, MARTIN HENRY, ROBERT MIDWINTER, CHRISTINE SCIPIO, KARL THROWER, ANDREW TURNER.

GOVERNMENT OFFICES

Office of the Governor: The Castle, Jamestown, STHL 1ZZ; tel. 22555; e-mail pagovernor@sainthelena.gov.sh; internet www.sainthelena.gov.sh.

Office of the Administrator of Ascension: The Residency, Georgetown, Ascension, ASCN 1ZZ; tel. 67000; e-mail aigenquiries@ascension.gov.ac; internet www.ascension.gov.ac.

Office of the Administrator of Tristan da Cunha: The Administrator's Office, Edinburgh of the Seven Seas, Tristan da Cunha, TDCU 1ZZ; tel. (20) 30142000; e-mail administrator@tdc-gov.com; internet www.tristandc.com/administrator.php.

Office of the Chief Minister: The Castle, Jamestown, STHL 1ZZ; tel. 22470; e-mail julie.thomas@helanta.co.sh.

Political Organizations

There are no political parties in Saint Helena. Elections to the Legislative Council, the latest of which took place on 13 October 2021, are conducted on a non-partisan basis.

Judicial System

The legal system is derived from English common law and statutes. There is a Supreme Court and a Court of Appeal, and provision was made in the 2009 Constitution for the establishment of other subordinate courts. The Supreme Court is presided over by a Chief Justice. The Court of Appeal consists of a President and two or more Justices of Appeal. There is also a four-member Judicial Services Commission, presided over by the Chief Justice.

The Attorney-General of Saint Helena is the principal legal adviser to the Government of Saint Helena. The Attorney-General of Ascension and of Tristan da Cunha is the principal legal adviser to the Government of Ascension and to the Government of Tristan da Cunha and is the person for the time being holding or acting in the office of Attorney-General of Saint Helena. The courts of Ascension and of Tristan da Cunha are the Supreme Court of Saint Helena, the Court of Appeal of Saint Helena, and such courts subordinate to the Supreme Court as may be established by law.

Chief Justice: RUPERT JONES.

President of the Court of Appeal: Sir JOHN HENRY BOULTON SAUNDERS.

Attorney-General: ALLEN CANSICK.

Sheriff: ETHEL YON.

Religion

The majority of the population (some 63.2%, according to the 2021 census) belong to the Anglican Communion. Ascension forms part of the Anglican diocese of Saint Helena, which normally provides a resident chaplain who is also available to minister to members of other denominations. There is a Roman Catholic chapel served by visiting priests, as well as a small mosque. Adherents of the Anglican church predominate on Tristan da Cunha, which is within the Anglican Church of Southern Africa, and is under the jurisdiction of the Archbishop of Cape Town, South Africa.

CHRISTIANITY

The Anglican Communion

Anglicans are adherents of the Anglican Church of Southern Africa (formerly the Church of the Province of Southern Africa). The Metropolitan of the Province is the Archbishop of Cape Town, South Africa. Saint Helena forms a single diocese.

Bishop of Saint Helena: Rt Rev. DALE BOWERS, Bishopsholme, POB 62, STHL 1ZZ; tel. 24471; e-mail bishop@helanta.co.sh; internet www.dioceseofsthelena.com; diocese f. 1859; has jurisdiction over the islands of Saint Helena and Ascension.

The Roman Catholic Church

The Church is represented in Saint Helena, Ascension and Tristan da Cunha by a Mission, established in August 1986.

Superior: Abbot HUGH ALLAN (also Prefect Apostolic of the Falkland Islands), Sacred Heart Church, Jamestown, STHL 1ZZ; tel. 22535; normally visits Tristan da Cunha once a year and Ascension Island two or three times a year.

Other Christian Churches

Jehovah's Witnesses, Baptists, Seventh-day Adventists, the Salvation Army, New Apostolics and the Rock Christian Fellowship are active on the island.

BAHÁ'Í FAITH

There is a small Bahá'í community on the island.

The Bahá'í Community of St Helena: Willowbough, POB 49, Jamestown, STHL 1ZZ; tel. 24525; e-mail busy.bee@helanta.co.sh; internet www.sthelenabahai.org; f. 1954; Chair. BASIL GEORGE.

The Press

The St Helena Independent: Livery Stables, Jamestown, STHL 1ZZ; tel. 22327; e-mail independent@helanta.co.sh; internet www.independent.sh; f. 2005; independent; weekly; Editor VINCE THOMPSON.

The Sentinel: The Media Centre, Castle Gdns, Jamestown, STHL 1ZZ; tel. 22727; e-mail news@sams.sh; internet sams.sh/archives.html; f. 2012.

Broadcasting and Communications

TELECOMMUNICATIONS

Sure South Atlantic: Bishop's Rooms, Jamestown, STHL 1ZZ; tel. 22222; e-mail service@sure.co.sh; internet www.sure.co.sh; f. 1899 as Cable and Wireless South Atlantic; present name adopted in 2013; provides national and international telecommunications; CEO CHRISTINE THOMAS.

BROADCASTING

The government-funded Saint Helena Broadcasting (Guarantee) Corporation (SHBC), which broadcasts two FM radio stations, became operational in December 2012 when Radio Saint Helena ceased broadcasting. SHBC also introduced a weekly newspaper; *The Sentinel* published its first edition in March 2012, replacing *The Saint Helena Herald*. SHBC was renamed South Atlantic Media Services in February 2013.

South Atlantic Media Services (SAMS): The Media Center, Castle Gdns, Jamestown, STHL 1ZZ; tel. 22727; e-mail news@sams.sh; internet www.sams.sh; f. 2011 as Saint Helena Broadcasting (Guarantee) Corporation; present name adopted in 2013; CEO EMMA WEAVER.

Saint FM Community Radio: Association Hall, Main St, Jamestown, STHL 1ZZ; tel. 22660; e-mail fm@helanta.co.sh; internet www.saint.fm; f. 2004; established as Saint FM; closed down Dec. 2012, but recommenced broadcasting, as Saint FM Community Radio, in March 2013; independent FM radio station; Station Man. TAMMY WILLIAMS.

Finance

BANK

Bank of Saint Helena Ltd: Market St, Jamestown, STHL 1ZZ; tel. 22390; e-mail info@sainthelenabank.com; internet www.sainthelenabank.com; f. 2004; Chair. GLENN OWEN; Man. Dir JOSEPHINE GEORGE.

Trade and Industry

CHAMBER OF COMMERCE

St Helena Chamber of Commerce: POB 34, Jamestown, STHL 1ZZ; tel. 22258; internet www.chamberofcommerce.org.sh; 60 mems; Pres. Dr CORINDA ESSEX.

UTILITIES

St Helena Utilities Regulatory Authority: The Castle, Jamestown; tel. 22340; e-mail judicial.manager@sainthelena.gov.sh; f. 2013; Chair. DUNCAN COOKE.

Connect Saint Helena Ltd: Seales Corner, Jamestown, STHL 1ZZ; tel. 22255; e-mail enquiries@connect.co.sh; internet www.connectsainthelena.com; f. 2012; 100% owned by Govt of Saint Helena; provision of electricity and water; Chair. ELIZABETH CLINGHAM; CEO JANET LAWRENCE.

MAJOR COMPANIES

Saint Tuna Corporation (STC): Rupert's Valley, STHL 1ZZ; internet www.sthelenatuna.co.uk; f. 2021.

Solomon & Co (St Helena) PLC: Main St, Jamestown, STHL 1ZZ; tel. 22380; e-mail generalenquiries@solomons.co.sh; internet solomons-sthelena.com; f. 1790; business operating units include: mercantile, procurement, shipping and travel agents, stevedoring, insurance, livestock and arable farming (including coffee production), bakery, butchery, bulk fuel management, autoshop, vehicle inspection service, construction works and information technology and administration services; CEO MANDY PETERS.

W. A. Thorpe & Sons: Market St, Jamestown, STHL 1ZZ; tel. 22781; e-mail office@thorpes.sh; internet www.thorpes.sh; f. 1865; imports groceries and hardware and maintains small cattle farm.

Transport

AIR

In July 2010 the British Government announced that construction of an airport on Saint Helena would proceed. In September 2015, as part of the calibration testing for the airport, an aircraft landed on Saint Helena for the first time. However, in late April 2016 the official opening of the airport (which had been scheduled for May) was delayed on safety grounds. SA Airlink of South Africa was subsequently selected to provide a scheduled commercial air service to Saint Helena (and Ascension), and on 14 October 2017 the first commercial flight, which departed OR Tambo Airport in Johannesburg (South Africa), landed on Saint Helena. A weekly service initially operated between Saint Helena and South Africa (via Windhoek, Namibia), although this was increased to twice weekly from May 2018, while a monthly service between Saint Helena and Ascension was introduced. In March 2019 Airlink announced that its service from Johannesburg to Saint Helena would henceforth operate via Walvis Bay (Namibia). There is a weekly US Air Force military service linking the Patrick Air Force Base in Florida, USA, with Ascension Island, via Antigua and Barbuda. There is no airfield on Tristan da Cunha.

St Helena Airport Ltd: Prosperous Bay Plain, STHL 1ZZ; tel. 25180; e-mail operations@sthelenaairport.aero; internet sthelenaairport.com; f. 2018; CEO GWYNETH HOWELL.

SHIPPING

RMS *St Helena* made its final voyage from Saint Helena to Cape Town on 10 February 2018. Prior to the airport becoming fully operational RMS *St Helena* provided a two-monthly passenger/cargo service from Cape Town, in South Africa, to Saint Helena and Ascension Island. A vessel under charter to the British Ministry of Defence visits the island monthly on its UK–Falkland Islands service. A US freighter from Cape Canaveral calls at three-monthly intervals. Occasional cruise ships also visit the island.

In February 2016 the Saint Helena Government announced that AW Ship Management Ltd (of the UK) had been contracted to provide a sea freight service (from the UK to Saint Helena via Cape Town), to replace that hitherto provided by RMS *St Helena*. The service commenced in February 2018.

AW Ship Management Ltd: The Loom, Suite 3.2, 14 Gowers Walk, London, E1 8PY; tel. (20) 7575-6000; e-mail shipman@awsml.co.uk; internet awshipmanagement.com/st-helena; operates a monthly marine cargo service between Saint Helena and Cape Town, South Africa; additionally calls at Ascension Island four times per year.

Tourism

St Helena Tourism: The Canister, Jamestown, STHL 1ZZ; tel. 22158; e-mail enquiries@tourism.gov.sh; internet www.sthelenatourism.com; f. 1998; Dir HELENA BENNETT.

Education

Education is compulsory and free for all children between the ages of five and 15 years, although power to exempt after the age of 14 years can be exercised by the Education Committee. The standard of work at the secondary comprehensive school is orientated towards the requirements of the General Certificate of Secondary Education and the General Certificate of Education Advanced Level of the UK.

There is a free public library in Jamestown, financed by the Government and managed by a committee, and a mobile library service in the country districts. There is also a Teacher Education Centre in Jamestown.

In 2020/21 a total of 270 children were enrolled in primary school education, while 203 children were enrolled in compulsory secondary school education.

Expenditure on education was budgeted to total £3.8m. in 2021/22, representing 8.1% of total recurrent government expenditure.

Bibliography

Ashmole, P., and Ashmole, M. *St Helena and Ascension Island: A Natural History*. Oswestry, Anthony Nelson, 2000.

Blackburn, J. *The Emperor's Last Island: A Journey to St Helena*. London, Secker & Warburg, 1992.

Day, A. (Ed.). *St Helena, Ascension and Tristan da Cunha* (World Bibliographical Series, Vol. 197). Santa Barbara, CA, ABC-Clio, 1997.

Eriksen, R. *St Helena Lifeline*. Coltishall, Mallett & Bell, 1999.

Hart-Davis, D. *Ascension: The Story of a South Atlantic Island*. London, Constable, 1972.

Johnston, Robert H. *Historic Saint Helena: Island Near the Sun*. Tunbridge Wells, Friends of St Helena, 2010.

Mabbett, B. J. *St Helena: The Postal, Instructional and Censor Markings, 1815–2000*. Reading, West Africa Study Circle, 2002.

Royle, S. A. *A Geography of Islands: Small Island Insularity*. London, Routledge, 2001.

The Company's Island: St Helena, Company Colonies and the Colonial Endeavour. London, I.B. Tauris, 2007.

Schreier, D., and Lavarello-Schreier, K. *Tristan da Cunha: History, People, Language*. London, Battlebridge Publishers, 2003.

Smallman D. L. *Quincentenary 1502-2002: A Governor's Story of St Helena*. Patten Press, Penzance, 2005.

SÃO TOMÉ AND PRÍNCIPE

Physical and Social Geography

RENÉ PÉLISSIER

The archipelago forming the Democratic Republic of São Tomé and Príncipe is, after the Republic of Seychelles, the smallest independent state in Africa. The two main islands, São Tomé and Príncipe, are in the Gulf of Guinea on a south-west/north-east axis of extinct volcanoes. The archipelago's boundaries take in the rocky islets of Caroço, Pedras and Tinhosas, off Príncipe, and, south of São Tomé, the Rôlas islet, which is bisected by the line of the Equator. The total area of the archipelago is 1,001 sq km (386.5 sq miles), of which São Tomé occupies an area of 859 sq km.

São Tomé is a former plantation island where the eastern slopes and coastal flatlands are covered by huge cocoa estates (roças) formerly controlled by Portuguese interests, alongside a large number of local smallholders. These plantations have been carved out of an extremely dense mountainous jungle, which dominates this equatorial island. The highest point is the Pico de São Tomé (2,024 m), surrounded by a dozen lesser cones above 1,000 m in height. Craggy and densely forested terrain is intersected by numerous streams. The coast of Príncipe is extremely jagged and indented by many bays. The highest elevation is the Pico de Príncipe (948 m). Both islands have a warm and moist climate, with a yearly average temperature of 25°C. Annual rainfall varies from over 5,100 mm on the south-western mountain slopes to under 1,020 mm in the northern lowlands. The dry season, known locally as gravana, lasts from June to September.

According to the census of May 2012, the total population was 178,739. By mid-2022, according to United Nations (UN) projections, the population had risen to 227,679, giving a density of 227.5 inhabitants per sq km. The capital city is São Tomé, with 80,099 inhabitants at mid-2018, according to UN estimates. It is the main export centre of the island. Inland villages on São Tomé are mere clusters of houses of native islanders. Príncipe has only one small town, Santo António, which had a population of 2,620 at the census of May 2012.

Portuguese is the official and national language, spoken by nearly all of the population. A number of native dialects are also widely spoken. Almost three-quarters of the inhabitants profess Christianity, and the majority (55.7% of the population, according to the 2012 census) are adherents of the Roman Catholic Church.

The native-born islanders (forros) are the descendants of imported slaves and southern Europeans who settled in the 16th and 17th centuries. Intermarriage was common, but subsequent influxes of Angolan and Mozambican contract workers until about 1950 re-Africanized the forros.

History

GERHARD SEIBERT

INTRODUCTION

São Tomé and Príncipe were colonized by Portugal in the 16th century. A nationalist group, the Comité de Libertação de São Tomé e Príncipe, was formed in 1960 and became the Movimento de Libertação de São Tomé e Príncipe (MLSTP) in 1972, under the leadership of Dr Manuel Pinto da Costa. Following the military coup in Portugal in April 1974, the Portuguese Government recognized the right of the islands to independence. In December Portugal appointed a transitional Government that included members of the MLSTP, which was recognized as the sole legitimate representative of the people. At elections for a Constituent Assembly in July 1975, the MLSTP won all 16 seats. Independence as the Democratic Republic of São Tomé and Príncipe took effect on 12 July, with Pinto da Costa as President and Miguel Trovoada as Prime Minister. The Constitution promulgated in November in effect vested absolute power in the President and the political bureau of the MLSTP.

MLSTP GOVERNMENT

During 1976–82 serious ideological as well as personal rifts developed within the MLSTP, and in March 1978 Angolan soldiers were dispatched to the islands, following an alleged attempt to overthrow the Government. In 1979 Trovoada was dismissed as Prime Minister, arrested and detained without trial until 1981, when he was permitted to leave the islands.

In its foreign relations, São Tomé and Príncipe avoided any formal commitment to the Eastern bloc, although close economic ties existed with the People's Republic of China and the German Democratic Republic. However, São Tomé and Príncipe extended the range of its international contacts by joining the International Monetary Fund (IMF) and the World Bank in 1977, acceding to the Lomé Convention in 1978, and participating in the foundation of the Communauté Economique des Etats de l'Afrique Centrale (CEEAC) in 1983. In 1985, confronted by the threat of complete economic collapse, Pinto da Costa began to abandon economic ties with the Eastern bloc in favour of capitalist strategies.

Political Change

In October 1987 the Central Committee of the MLSTP announced major political and constitutional changes, including that the head of state and members of the legislative Assembleia Popular Nacional (National People's Assembly) would henceforth be elected by universal suffrage. In January 1988 Celestino Rocha da Costa was appointed to the newly reintroduced post of Prime Minister. Carlos Monteiro Dias da Graça, who had been pardoned in 1985 for an alleged attempted coup in 1978, was appointed Minister of Foreign Affairs. By 1987 three small overseas opposition groups were already in existence.

Increasingly concerned by the country's economic problems, in late 1989 the MLSTP embarked on a transition to full multi-party democracy. In August 1990, in a national referendum, the electorate overwhelmingly approved the introduction of the new Constitution, proposed by the MLSTP, which provided for a multi-party political system with a semi-presidential regime. At the MLSTP party congress, held in October, da Graça succeeded Pinto da Costa as Secretary-General. In addition, the party's name was amended to the Movimento de Libertação de São Tomé e Príncipe—Partido Social Democrata (MLSTP—PSD). The major challenge to the ruling party came from the Partido de Convergência Democrática—Grupo de Reflexão (PCD—GR), a coalition of former MLSTP dissidents, independents and young professionals, which was founded in the same year.

At elections to the new National Assembly, held in January 1991, the MLSTP—PSD secured only 21 of the 55 seats in the legislature, while the PCD—GR obtained 33 seats; the Partido

Democrático de São Tomé e Príncipe—Coligação Democrática de Oposição (PDSTP—CODO, a merger of two opposition groups formerly in exile) took the one remaining seat. In March Trovoada, the sole candidate, was elected President, receiving 82% of the votes cast. Trovoada took office the following month and officially inaugurated a PCD—GR Government, led by Daniel Daio.

THE TROVOADA PRESIDENCY

In early 1992 co-operation between the Government and the presidency began to break down, after the PCD—GR attempted to introduce a constitutional amendment limiting presidential powers. Following two mass demonstrations held in April to protest against an economic austerity programme (which had been imposed by the IMF and the World Bank as preconditions for assistance), Trovoada dismissed the Daio Government. In May Norberto Costa Alegre of the PCD—GR (hitherto Minister of Economy and Finance) became Prime Minister and formed a new administration.

Following the National Assembly's approval in 1994 of a draft bill providing local autonomy for the island of Príncipe, in March 1995 the first elections to a new seven-member Assembleia Regional (Regional Assembly) and five-member Regional Government were conducted on Príncipe, resulting in victory for the MLSTP—PSD.

In early 1994 relations between the Government and the presidency again deteriorated. Trovoada dismissed the Alegre administration in July, appointing former defence minister Evaristo do Espírito Santo de Carvalho as Prime Minister later in that month. The PCD—GR, which refused to participate in the new Government, subsequently expelled Carvalho from the party. Trovoada dissolved the National Assembly and announced that legislative elections would be held in early October. These elections resulted in a decisive victory for the MLSTP—PSD, which secured 27 seats. The PCD—GR and the Acção Democrática Independente (ADI) each obtained 14 seats. In late October da Graça was appointed Prime Minister. The new Council of Ministers was composed almost entirely of members of the MLSTP—PSD.

On 15 August 1995, following a period of social unrest, a group of some 30 soldiers staged a coup and detained Trovoada. After negotiations, the military insurgents and the Government signed a memorandum of understanding (MOU), providing for the reinstatement of Trovoada and the restoration of constitutional order. In return, the Government gave an undertaking to restructure the armed forces, and the National Assembly granted a general amnesty to all those involved in the coup.

In December 1995 Armindo Vaz d'Almeida was appointed Prime Minister, at the head of a coalition Government of the MLSTP—PSD, the ADI and the PDSTP—CODO. The first round of a presidential election in June 1996 (rescheduled from March) was inconclusive. Consequently, a second ballot, between the two leading candidates, was conducted in July, at which Trovoada defeated Pinto da Costa, with 52.7% of the votes. In September the Vaz d'Almeida administration was dissolved, following its defeat in a confidence motion in the National Assembly. The motion was proposed by Vaz d'Almeida's own party, the MLSTP—PSD, which accused the Government of inefficiency and corruption, and was supported by the PCD—GR. In October the two parties signed an accord providing for the establishment of a coalition Government. In November the President appointed Raúl Wagner da Conceição Bragança Neto, the Assistant Secretary-General of the MLSTP—PSD, as Prime Minister of the new Government. The MLSTP—PSD secured an absolute majority in legislative elections held in November 1998. In the following month Guilherme Pósser da Costa was appointed Prime Minister, and a new Council of Ministers was installed in January 1999.

PRESIDENTIAL AND LEGISLATIVE ELECTIONS

At the presidential election in July 2001 Fradique de Menezes, a businessman standing for the ADI, was the winning candidate, with 56.3% of the votes cast, defeating Pinto da Costa of the MLSTP—PSD. In September de Menezes was inaugurated as President and appointed a Council of Ministers composed

entirely of members of the parliamentary opposition, including the ADI's Evaristo de Carvalho as Prime Minister.

In December 2001 Carlos Neves, hitherto the leader of the ADI, and several of his followers left the party, after the announcement by Patrice Trovoada (son of the former President Miguel Trovoada) of his candidacy for the party leadership. Later in that month the dissident ADI members joined a new party created by supporters of de Menezes, the Movimento Democrático Força da Mudança/Partido Liberal (MDFM/PL). Meanwhile, in an attempt to ensure political stability, the President and representatives of political parties signed a pact advocating the formation of an all-party government after legislative elections, which were scheduled for March 2002. At the elections, the MLSTP—PSD won 24 seats in the National Assembly and an alliance of the MDFM/PL and the PCD (the suffix Grupo de Reflexão had been dropped the previous year) secured 23, while Uê Kédadji (UK—an alliance comprising the ADI and four smaller parties) obtained eight seats. Following negotiations with the MLSTP—PSD, President de Menezes appointed Gabriel Costa, hitherto ambassador to Portugal, as Prime Minister. In April a Government of National Unity, including members of the MLSTP—PSD, the MDFM/PL-PCD alliance, UK and independents, was installed.

In September 2002 a member of the Supreme Defence Council accused de Menezes of having illegally promoted the Minister of Defence and Internal Affairs, Victor Monteiro, to the highest rank of Lt-Col, as the minister had not met the necessary legal requirements. This affair provoked an open conflict between Monteiro and Prime Minister Costa, who refused to continue working with the defence minister. Finally, on 27 September President de Menezes dismissed the Costa Government and in October appointed Maria das Neves de Souza of the MLSTP—PSD, hitherto the Minister of Trade, Industry and Tourism, as Prime Minister.

In December 2002 the National Assembly unanimously approved constitutional amendments significantly curbing the powers of the President and strengthening the mandate of government and the legislature; the changes were to come into effect after the expiry of the President's term in 2006. The National Assembly, although initially opposed to the idea of holding a referendum on the issue, subsequently agreed to submit the new Constitution to a popular vote at the end of de Menezes' mandate.

CIVIL UNREST AND MILITARY COUP

On 16 July 2003, while President de Menezes was on a visit to Nigeria, a group of military officers, led by Maj. Fernando Pereira ('Cobó'), together with a group of Santomean mercenaries, staged a bloodless coup and detained a number of government ministers in the military barracks. Pereira and the leaders of the mercenaries established a Military Junta of National Salvation (MJNS). The coup was quickly condemned by regional and international leaders, who demanded the restitution of constitutional order. On the fourth day of the rebellion the MJNS commenced negotiations with international mediators from the Comunidade dos Países de Língua Portuguesa, the CEEAC, the African Union, Nigeria, the USA and South Africa. On 22 July de Menezes returned to São Tomé and, together with Pereira, signed an MOU, which provided for, *inter alia*, a general amnesty for the coup leaders; the restoration of de Menezes to the presidency; the formation of a new Government; and the approval of a law on the proper use of petroleum revenue by the National Assembly. In March 2004, owing to a controversial petroleum agreement with Energem Petroleum the MDFM/PL resigned from the Government, and UK joined the coalition.

NEVES DISMISSED

In August 2004 the country's political elite were implicated in irregularities by an audit report of the accounts of the food aid agency Gabinete de Gestão das Ajudas (GGA), which had been created in 1993 to administer food aid counterpart funds. It was alleged that funds totalling US $1.9m. had been diverted to local politicians and officials, among them Prime Minister das Neves. Although she denied the allegations, in mid-September

2004 das Neves and her coalition Government were dismissed by President de Menezes, who subsequently asked the MLSTP—PSD to form a new government. The new Council of Ministers again comprised a coalition of the MLSTP—PSD, the ADI and independents. Damião Vaz d'Almeida, the former Minister of Labour, Employment and Solidarity, was appointed Prime Minister.

In May 2005 the public prosecutor formally charged das Neves and one other deputy with embezzlement. In October 2006 the Government dissolved the GGA. In April 2007 a judge dismissed the case against das Neves and the other deputy, owing to a lack of evidence. However, in March 2009 Diógenes Moniz, the former director of the GGA, and Aurélio Aguiar, the GGA treasurer, were sentenced to nine and seven years' imprisonment, respectively, after they were found guilty of forgery and harmful management as part of the embezzlement of funds.

Meanwhile, in February 2005 Pósser da Costa was elected as MLSTP—PSD President, replacing Manuel Pinto da Costa. In May trade unions representing public sector workers commenced a five-day general strike, demanding a more than threefold increase in the minimum salary. President de Menezes declared that the Government was responsible for the action, and on the fourth day of the strike Prime Minister Vaz d'Almeida abruptly resigned, accusing de Menezes of a lack of institutional solidarity with his administration. In June Maria do Carmo Silveira, hitherto the Governor of the central bank, was sworn in as Prime Minister, together with a new MLSTP—PSD Government.

THE 2006 ELECTIONS

At the legislative elections held in March 2006, the pro-de Menezes MDFM/PL-PCD alliance won 23 seats, the MLSTP—PSD and the ADI obtained 20 seats and 11 seats, respectively, while the newly established Novo Rumo took one seat. The MDFM/PL-PCD subsequently formed a minority Government led by Prime Minister Tomé Vera Cruz, the Secretary-General of the MDFM/PL.

At the presidential election, which took place in late July 2006, de Menezes secured 60.6% of the valid votes cast, while Patrice Trovoada of the ADI won 38.8%. In August, in the first local elections to be held on the islands since 1992, the MDFM/PL-PCD secured control of five of São Tomé's six district councils. In Príncipe, where regional elections had not been held since March 1995, the opposition União para a Mudança e Progresso do Príncipe (UMPP), led by José Cardoso Cassandra, gained an absolute majority.

Immediately after the local elections, MLSTP—PSD leader Pósser da Costa resigned from his post following the party's consecutive electoral defeats, and in February 2007 Joaquim Rafael Branco became its new President. At the MDFM/PL convention in May Prime Minister Vera Cruz was re-elected as the party's Secretary-General, and President de Menezes was elected as party President, despite the country's Constitution stipulating that the office of head of state was incompatible with any other public or private function. However, de Menezes opted not to assume the role publicly as long as he remained President of the country.

THE RESIGNATION OF VERA CRUZ

In January 2008 the Prime Minister withdrew the national budget for 2008 to avoid its rejection by the MLSTP—PSD and the ADI, which together held a legislative majority of 31 seats. On 7 February Vera Cruz resigned. On 13 February the MDFM/PL, the PCD and the ADI signed a coalition agreement which was valid until 2014. The following day the ADI leader, Patrice Trovoada, was sworn in as Prime Minister of a coalition Government of the MDFM/PL, the PCD and his own party, with a parliamentary majority of more than 30 seats.

Although a revised national budget for 2008 was eventually approved by the National Assembly, in May the MLSTP—PSD presented a motion of no confidence against Trovoada. The motion was carried, with the support of the MLSTP—PSD and the PCD, which accused Trovoada of lacking transparency in government affairs. Subsequently, the MDFM/PL denounced the party alliance with the PCD, making the MLSTP—PSD the majority party in the National Assembly. Following three days of talks, on 9 June the four major parties agreed to request that President de Menezes entrust the leader of the MLSTP—PSD, Rafael Branco, with the formation of a new government. Consequently, on 21 June President de Menezes appointed Branco at the head of a coalition Government composed of the MLSTP—PSD, the PCD and the MDFM/PL.

At an extraordinary congress of the MDFM/PL in December 2009, de Menezes was re-elected as party President. Although de Menezes declared that he would not officially assume this position until his term in the national presidency ended in September 2011, the other members of the coalition, the MLSTP—PSD and the PCD, accused him of violating the Constitution. In response, de Menezes ordered the withdrawal of the four MDFM/PL ministers from the Government. Although two of the ministers refused to accede to this demand, Branco's attempt to retain the two ministers in a reshuffled cabinet was vetoed by de Menezes. In January 2010 de Menezes inaugurated Branco's new Government, which comprised members of the MLSTP—PSD and the PCD, and publicly retracted his acceptance of the MDFM/PL leadership.

In March 2010 President de Menezes announced that local elections (which had reportedly been postponed owing to lack of funding) would be held in July and legislative elections in August. At the local elections the MLSTP—PSD obtained a majority in the four district councils of Lobata, Lembá, Cantagolo and Caué, while the ADI gained a majority in the two most populated districts of Agua Grande (with the capital São Tomé) and Mé-Zóchi. The UMPP won all seven seats in the Regional Assembly of Príncipe.

The ADI secured victory in the legislative elections of 1 August 2010, obtaining 26 seats in the National Assembly. The MLSTP—PSD of Prime Minister Branco won 21 seats, while its coalition partner, the PCD, secured only seven seats. Unexpectedly, the MDFM/PL received just one seat, down from 12 in the 2006 elections. Even combined with the MDFM/PL, the ADI remained one seat short of the total required for an absolute legislative majority. Later in August 2010 Trovoada was appointed Prime Minister and a new, minority Government, which included a number of independents in addition to ADI members, was installed.

At an extraordinary congress of the opposition MLSTP—PSD in January 2011, local businessman Aurélio Martins was elected as the new party leader. Xavier Mendes, a former Minister of Agriculture, became the new President of the PCD in the following month.

THE 2011 PRESIDENTIAL ELECTION

At the presidential election held on 17 July 2011, the country's first ever President, Manuel Pinto da Costa (standing as an independent), won 35.8% of the vote. His closest rivals were Evaristo de Carvalho (representing the ADI), who took 21.8%, Maria das Neves (running as an independent candidate) and Delfim Santiago das Neves (of the PCD), who secured 14.0% and 13.9%, respectively. Martins, the official candidate of the MLSTP—PSD, received only 4.2% of the votes. Pinto da Costa defeated Carvalho in a run-off ballot on 7 August, securing 52.9% of the votes cast, and was sworn in as President on 3 September.

In June 2012 the MLSTP—PSD elected Jorge Amado, São Tomé's ambassador to the Republic of China (Taiwan), as the new party leader, replacing Martins. In July the President of the National Assembly (Carvalho of the ADI) rejected, on procedural grounds, a censure motion against the Government, which had been submitted by the MLSTP—PSD. On 21 November the MLSTP—PSD, the PCD and the MDFM/PL presented another censure motion against Trovoada, whom they accused of irregularities and mismanagement. Carvalho resigned shortly thereafter, apparently in an attempt to impede the censure vote, and the ADI announced a parliamentary boycott. None the less, on 28 November the MLSTP—PSD, the PCD and the MDFM/PL used their combined legislative majority to elect Alcino Pinto of the MLSTP—PSD as the new President of the National Assembly and to approve the censure motion against the Trovoada administration.

On 4 December 2012 President Pinto da Costa formally dismissed Trovoada and six days later appointed former Prime Minister Gabriel Costa as the new premier. On 12 December Costa's coalition Government, comprising members of the MLSTP—PSD, the PCD and the MDFM/PL, was inaugurated. (Costa did not belong to any of the three parties, being a founder member of the União dos Democratas para a Cidadania e Desenvolvimento—UDD.)

In July 2013 a Swedish petroleum firm, Stena Oil, publicly accused São Tomé and Príncipe of state piracy after a local court confiscated two vessels that had been chartered by Stena Oil and sentenced the captains of the ships to three years' imprisonment, with a fine of €5m., for smuggling. The captains had been detained by the Santomean coastguard in March while allegedly conducting an unauthorized transshipment within the archipelago's territorial waters. Stena Oil denied the allegations and accused the local authorities of having staged a 'show trial' to enrich themselves. In September President Pinto da Costa pardoned the two captains, but insisted on the payment of the fine. In early October one of the ships was allowed to leave São Tomé and Príncipe after the shipowner had paid a fine of €28,000. In mid-October the Government unilaterally ceased negotiations with Stena Oil and sold the second ship's seized cargo of 8,000 metric tons of fuel (worth some US $7.5m.) to a Danish bunker company. The second ship was finally released in November, after its owner had also paid a fine of €28,000.

THE 2014 LEGISLATIVE ELECTIONS

In the legislative elections of 12 October 2014, which attracted a turnout of 74.4%, Trovoada's ADI unexpectedly won an absolute majority of 33 seats in the National Assembly, and the hitherto ruling parties all lost seats. The MLSTP—PSD received 16 seats, five fewer than in 2010, and the PCD retained only five of its seven seats. The MDFM/PL lost its single seat to the UDD. In concurrently held local elections (which had been postponed from July, on grounds of financial constraints), the ADI won a majority in all six districts in São Tomé, with the exception of Caué, where the MLSTP—PSD remained in power. In Príncipe the UMPP, led by José Cassandra, won the regional elections for the third consecutive time. In November 2014 Trovoada was sworn in as Prime Minister for a third term. Nine of the 13 members of his new cabinet had been ministers in his previous administration.

In March 2015 the Government decided to restore Santomean citizenship to all foreign nationals who had resided in the country at the time of independence in 1975, and to their descendants. The decision benefited mainly former plantation workers from Angola, Cabo Verde and Mozambique. These people had been granted citizenship at independence in 1975, but in 1996 this status had been withdrawn on electoral grounds.

In November 2015 Aurélio Martins was elected unopposed as the new leader of the MLSTP—PSD, replacing Jorge Amado. In February 2016 the PCD elected Arlindo Carvalho, a medical doctor and former health minister, as party leader for a four-year term, succeeding Xavier Mendes.

THE EVARISTO DE CARVALHO PRESIDENCY

Evaristo de Carvalho of the ruling ADI won the first round of the presidential election, held on 17 July 2016, with 49.9% of the votes cast. The incumbent President, Manuel Pinto da Costa, and Maria das Neves obtained 24.8% and 24.3% of the vote, respectively. They both ran as independents, although das Neves enjoyed the formal support of the MLSTP—PSD leadership. Voter turnout was 64.3%. Pinto da Costa and das Neves filed a legal appeal demanding the annulment of the election owing to alleged irregularities; the appeal was rejected as being groundless. Consequently, Pinto da Costa boycotted the second round of voting on 7 August, claiming electoral fraud on the part of the Comissão Eleitoral Nacional (CEN, National Electoral Commission). In the event, Carvalho won the run-off poll uncontested, with 82% of the votes cast, but with a turnout of only 46.1%. Carvalho took office as the country's new President on 3 September.

In April 2017 Manuel Silva Gomes Cravid, who was considered an opponent of Prime Minister Trovoada, was elected, with three votes in his favour, as the new President of the five-member Supreme Court. In mid-December opposition parliamentary deputies asked the Supreme Court to rule on the constitutionality of a proposed law on the establishment of a Constitutional Court, which had been approved by the ADI majority in August. (Although the 2003 Constitution had provided for the creation of a Constitutional Court, this body had never been officially instituted, and its functions had instead been performed by the Supreme Court of Justice.) None the less, in late December President Carvalho promulgated the controversial legislation. In response, Supreme Court President Gomes Cravid declared the President's action unconstitutional, on the grounds that he had ignored the legal term of 25 days for the preventive constitutionality check. President Carvalho rejected this assertion, claiming that the power of the Supreme Court to pass judgment on constitutional issues had ended with his promulgation of the Constitutional Court bill. The opposition also criticized the President's action as illegal, fearing that future election results might be manipulated by an ADI-controlled court, as the Constitutional Court was mandated to approve final election results. In early January 2018 the Supreme Court declared the law on the new Constitutional Court to be unconstitutional, as several provisions violated the constitutional principle of the election of its five judges by a qualified majority. In late January François Louncény Fall, the Special Representative of the United Nations General Secretary for Central Africa, undertook a five-day mediation mission to São Tomé, but the compromise proposal that he put forward was rejected by the opposition. Immediately after Fall's departure, the ADI parliamentary majority elected the five judges of the new Constitutional Court. The opposition parties boycotted their election and refused to recognize the new Court.

The political crisis worsened in May 2018 when 31 deputies approved a resolution to dismiss three Supreme Court judges, including Gomes Cravid, after the judges passed a ruling in a dispute over the ownership of the local brewery Rosema (see *Economy*). The opposition and international bodies considered the dismissal of the judges by the legislature to be unconstitutional, as it violated the independence of the judiciary. None the less, later in that month the ADI majority approved legislation that granted the National Assembly the authority to elect new judges to replace the dismissed Supreme Court members. Despite continued objections by the opposition parties, in early July the ADI majority in the National Assembly approved the appointment of five new Supreme Court judges. Raposo, the former Minister of Justice and Human Rights, subsequently became the new President of the Supreme Court.

The controversial dismissal of the Supreme Court judges also precipitated a major crisis within the MLSTP—PSD. In mid-May 2018 the party's National Council suspended six members, including party leader Aurélio Martins and three deputies, who had supported the resolution without party consent. The three suspended deputies responded by defecting from the MLSTP—PSD, reducing the party's representation in the National Assembly to only 13 seats. At an extraordinary MLSTP—PSD congress in late June, Jorge Bom Jesus, a former education minister, was elected to replace Martins as party leader. In early July President Carvalho announced that legislative and local elections were to be held on 7 October. Subsequently, brothers António and Domingos Monteiro, the owners of the Rosema brewery who had left the MLSTP—PSD in May, formed their own party, the Movimento Cidadão Independente de São Tomé e Príncipe (MCISTP). In August a merger between the MDFM/PL and the UDD (originally agreed in late 2017) was formalized, with the creation of the União MDFM-UDD (MDFM-UDD).

In August 2018 the authorities claimed to have discovered a conspiracy to overthrow the Trovoada Government. Five alleged plotters were detained, including Albertino Francisco, a former Minister of Youth and Sports and three Spanish former servicemen, who were reported to have been in the possession of weapons and other military equipment. The Spanish nationals denied all of the accusations, claiming that Francisco had invited them to establish a security service.

The 2018 Legislative Elections

In the legislative elections of 7 October 2018, the ADI lost its absolute majority of 33 seats, but remained the leading party in the National Assembly with 25 seats (43.7% of the votes). The MLSTP—PSD won 23 seats (42.1%), while an electoral coalition formed by the PCD and the MDFM-UDD secured five seats (9.9%) and the MCISTP obtained two seats (2.2%). Although the MLSTP—PSD and the PCD/MDFM-UDD alliance together had only a narrow majority of one seat, the two groups immediately declared their intention to form a government. After initial strong objections from the ADI, in early December MLSTP—PSD leader Bom Jesus was sworn in as Prime Minister and head of a new coalition Government.

Local elections were held concurrently with the legislative elections. In São Tomé, the ADI lost four of the five district assemblies that it had secured in 2014 to the MLSTP—PSD, retaining only Mé-Zóchí. The MLSTP—PSD won Cantagalo, Lembá, and Lobata, while in Caué, the MLSTP—PSD and the PCD/MDFM-UDD alliance obtained a majority. In the Regional Assembly of Príncipe, the UMPP won an absolute majority for the fourth consecutive time since 2006.

The Bom Jesus Government immediately revoked several controversial decisions taken by the Trovoada administration. In November 2018 the five suspected coup conspirators were released from detention, one week after Minister of Defence and Internal Administration Col Oscar Sousa had declared that the coup attempt in August had been fabricated by the former Government. In late December the four Supreme Court judges who had been dismissed or resigned in May were reinstated by the National Assembly with the support of the government parties, and their successors appointed by the ADI in July were removed, together with the five judges of the new Constitutional Court elected by the ADI majority in early 2018. In February 2019 the ruling parties in the National Assembly elected four new judges to the Constitutional Court, and one was reappointed. The appointments and dismissals were justified as a restitution of constitutional legality.

In April 2019 a former ADI Minister of Finance, Américo Ramos, was detained following accusations of his alleged involvement in irregularities relating to two loan agreements that he had signed on behalf of the Trovoada Government—one with the Hong Kong-based China International Fund, owned by controversial Chinese investment tycoon Sam Pa, in 2015 and the other with the Kuwait Fund for Arab Economic Development in 2016. In addition, Ramos was accused of having illegally withdrawn €624,000 from the local branch of the Gabonese BGFI Bank. In July 2019 Ramos was released from detention on bail of €100,000; he denied any wrongdoing.

In May 2019, at an extraordinary party congress, Agostinho Fernandes, a former minister in the Trovoada Government, was elected unopposed as the new President of the ADI. He replaced longstanding party leader Trovoada, who had resigned from the leadership after the legislative elections and left the country. Trovoada's followers had made unsuccessful efforts to impede the party congress. In the same month three of the five judges of the Constitutional Court were suspended by the Supreme Court, after they had taken a decision on the Rosema brewery that was considered illegal by the President of the Constitutional Court (see *Economy*). In August the three judges were definitively dismissed by the Superior Council of Judicial Magistrates, which found them guilty of insubordination. In the same month the National Assembly appointed three new judges to the Constitutional Court.

In September 2019, at an ADI congress, Trovoada was elected as ADI leader *in absentia*, which left the party with two leaders. In December the Constitutional Court unanimously refused to recognize Trovoada's election on the grounds that it had previously already approved as legitimate Fernandes's election as the ADI leader. Trovoada, who enjoyed the support of the majority ADI members, did not recognize the verdict.

On 19 March 2020 President Carvalho declared a state of emergency, including a ban on all flights and shipping entering or leaving the country, following the spread of the coronavirus disease (COVID-19) pandemic to West Africa, although at that time no cases of infection had been officially recorded in the country. The state of emergency was extended on five occasions until 15 June, when it was replaced by a less stringent state of public calamity until 31 July. From 15 June most restrictions were lifted, and the Santomean economy and airspace reopened. Between 6 April and 27 June 2021 the country's Ministry of Health reported 2,365 confirmed cases of COVID-19 and 37 deaths.

In August 2020 José Cassandra resigned as President of the Government of the Autonomous Region of Príncipe. He was replaced in that role by Filipe Nascimento, who had been elected to the leadership of the UMPP in November 2019.

In late September 2020 a government reorganization was effected. Most notably, Elsa Pinto was replaced as Minister of Foreign Affairs, Co-operation and Communities by Edite do Ramos da Costa Ten Jua.

At an extraordinary congress in October 2020, Patrice Trovoada was elected by acclamation, unopposed and *in absentia* as ADI leader, replacing Agostinho Fernandes, who had resigned from the post in July. However, the Constitutional Court refused to recognize the election, arguing that Trovoada had been elected by a simple show of hands instead of by secret ballot, as demanded by the ADI party statutes. In February 2021 the ADI agreed to hold another leadership election.

Also in February 2021, the ruling parties in the National Assembly adopted a revised electoral law, with alterations introduced due to a veto submitted by President Carvalho in late December 2020. The parliamentarians withdrew controversial provisions requiring permanent residence for presidential candidates and banning the participation of independent candidates in presidential elections, which had been criticized by Carvalho as being contrary to fundamental civil rights.

THE VILA NOVA PRESIDENCY

A total of 19 candidates contested the first round of the presidential election held on 18 July 2021. Only four of these were official party candidates, while the others were independents, most of them inexperienced newcomers who were not expected to secure any chance. Due to advanced age, the incumbent Carvalho did not run for a second term. According to results released by the CEN, Carlos Vila Nova, representing the opposition ADI, secured 43.7% of the valid votes cast, while Pósser da Costa (of the MLSTP—PSD) was placed second with 20.2%. Delfim Santiago das Neves took third place with 18.5%.

The run-off round was postponed twice, with the second postponement until 5 September 2021, meaning that the election took place after the expiry of Carvalho's term as President. In the second round Vila Nova defeated Pósser da Costa, securing 57.6% of the valid votes cast. Turnout was recorded at 65.4% of the eligible electorate.

In August 2021 the Minister of National Defence, Oscar Sousa, was dismissed for health reasons. His portfolio was temporarily assumed by Prime Minister Bom Jesus. In September Minister of Planning, Finance and the Blue Economy Osvaldo Vaz resigned and was replaced by Engrácio do Sacramento Soares da Graça, hitherto director of taxes in the finance ministry. In January 2022 Minister of Health Edgar Neves stepped down, following a dispute with the medical association. Finally, in February Bom Jesus carried out his long-expected government reshuffle. Jorge Amado, a former MLSTP—PSD leader, became national defence minister, while Filomena Santana Monteiro, a medical doctor, was appointed as the new health minister. Cilcio Pires dos Santos moved to the Ministry of Justice, Internal Administration and Human Rights, hitherto occupied by Ivete Lima Correia, who left the Government. (The public administration portfolio was renamed internal administration, which corresponded to the former portfolio in charge of the police that had been separated from defence.)

In March 2022 Bom Jesus was re-elected leader of the MLSTP—PSD, defeating two competitors at an extraordinary party congress. At an ADI congress held in São Tomé in April, Trovoada was elected party leader, for the third time since September 2019, unopposed and *in absentia*. On this occasion the Constitutional Court approved his election.

As widely expected, the ADI won the legislative elections of 25 September 2022, securing an absolute majority of 30 seats (compared with 25 in 2018). The MLSTP—PSD obtained 18 seats (down from 23), the Movimento de Cidadãos Independentes/Partido Socialista-Partido da Unidade Nacional (MCI/PS-PUN) took five seats and Movimento BASTA (only created in May) the remaining two, although with a higher vote share than MCI/PS-PUN. In Príncipe's regional elections the UMPP won for the fifth time consecutively, with six seats, while the Movimento Verde para o Desenvolvimento do Príncipe received three seats.

FOREIGN RELATIONS

In June 2006 the US Navy selected São Tomé to be the regional centre of its Marine Domain Awareness, a surveillance radar programme for the identification and monitoring of shipping traffic to be shared among the neighbouring countries in the Gulf of Guinea region. In January 2008 the Africa Partnership Station—a US initiative to promote maritime security in West and Central Africa, which included sailors from Africa, Europe and the USA aboard the amphibious dock landing ship USS *Fort McHenry*—made a 10-day visit to São Tomé. Furthermore, in the same month São Tomé and Príncipe became the first African country to receive global maritime traffic information from the US Navy's Regional Maritime Awareness Capability surface surveillance programme. In May 2012 President Pinto da Costa received the commander of the United States Africa Command (AFRICOM), Gen. Carter F. Ham, who emphasized the archipelago's strategic position as an important component for security in the Gulf of Guinea region. In September Prime Minister Trovoada became the first African head of government to visit the AFRICOM headquarters in Stuttgart, Germany. Trovoada emphasized his country's commitment to co-operate with the USA in upholding security in the Gulf of Guinea.

In June 2013 Minister of Defence and Internal Order Oscar Sousa and his Portuguese counterpart, José Pedro Aguiar Branco, signed an agreement providing for Portuguese military assistance in patrolling São Tomé's Exclusive Economic Zone (EEZ). In October Prime Minister Costa held talks with British officials regarding British support for the fight against piracy in São Tomé's territorial waters. In March 2014 a British frigate visited São Tomé to train the country's coastguard in maritime security. As part of the military assistance agreement signed with Portugal, in April a Portuguese frigate with members of São Tomé's coastguard on board carried out patrol operations in São Tomé's EEZ. In the same month a Brazilian navy vessel made a three-day visit to São Tomé to supply weapons, computer equipment and uniforms destined for the coastguard's first unit of marines, who were to be trained in São Tomé by Brazilian marines. In June the Brazilian navy donated three boats to the coastguard to strengthen its surveillance capacity. In March 2015 Portugal and São Tomé signed an amendment to their existing bilateral maritime security agreement, which permitted the Portuguese air force to monitor São Tomé's EEZ. In May the Brazilian navy established a Naval Mission Centre in São Tomé to oversee the further development of the country's coastguard.

In March 2016 the foreign ministers of the nine-member Comunidade dos Países de Língua Portuguesa (CPLP) agreed to split the next rotating four-year term of the organization's executive secretariat between São Tomé and Portugal. In July Prime Minister Trovoada nominated Maria do Carmo Silveira, the Governor of the central bank, to succeed Murade Murargy of Mozambique as Executive Secretary of the CPLP; in November, at the 11th biannual summit of the heads of state and government of the CPLP, Silveira was appointed to the post for a two-year period.

While São Tomé remained one of only three African countries to recognize Taiwan, in October 2013 a government delegation visited the Chinese capital, Beijing, to discuss the re-establishment of commercial relations with the People's Republic of China, reviving rumours that full diplomatic ties might soon be restored. In early November the Santomean Minister of Planning and Finance participated as an observer in the fourth ministerial conference of the Forum for Economic and Trade Co-operation between China and Portuguese-speaking Countries (Forum Macao) in Macao. In mid-November China inaugurated a trade mission in São Tomé, accommodated in its former embassy building. In an attempt to assuage Taiwanese concerns, later in that month a government delegation led by Prime Minister Gabriel Costa made a four-day official visit to Taipei to strengthen bilateral co-operation and attract Taiwanese private investment. In January 2014 Taiwan's President, Ma Ying-jeou, was warmly welcomed by President Pinto da Costa when he visited São Tomé for the first time. However, a visit to China by Pinto da Costa in early June, in search of private investment for a planned deep-sea harbour in São Tomé, prompted a formal expression of concern from Taiwan's Ministry of Foreign Affairs. In response, Pinto da Costa offered assurances to President Ma that his visit would not jeopardize relations with Taiwan.

In December 2016 the Trovoada Government unexpectedly severed diplomatic relations with Taiwan. (It was reported that the Taiwanese Government, which was highly critical of the decision, had denied requests by the Santomean authorities for assistance of some US $210m.) Diplomatic relations with China were re-established on 26 December. In March 2017 São Tomé was admitted as a full member of Forum Macao. In the following month, on his return from a visit to Beijing, Trovoada announced that China had pledged development assistance to São Tomé amounting to $146m. over a five-year period.

In December 2016 Prime Minister Trovoada visited Kigali, Rwanda, where he and the Rwandan President, Paul Kagame, agreed to engage in bilateral co-operation. In March 2017 the two countries signed agreements on co-operation in civil aviation and tourism, and on a mutual visa waiver, and MOUs on co-operation in agriculture, livestock and fishing, as well as a preferential trade agreement. The arrival of 20 Rwandan military instructors in São Tomé in May to train 90 local security personnel was fiercely contested by the parliamentary opposition, on the grounds that the Prime Minister had not concluded a relevant defence agreement during his visit to Rwanda.

Since 2010 São Tomé's coastguard has participated in Obangame Express, an annual military exercise of the US Navy in the Gulf of Guinea. Various other African navies, as well as those of Portugal and Brazil, take part in the exercise, which in March 2019 was co-ordinated from Lagos, Nigeria. In December 2017 the Brazilian navy concluded the military training of the fourth and final group of a total of 120 marines of São Tomé's coastguard.

In March 2020 São Tomé and Príncipe and Equatorial Guinea signed an agreement to create a Special Joint Exploration Zone for offshore oil and gas.

In June 2021 UN Secretary-General António Guterres stated that São Tomé and Príncipe was among five countries that were in arrears on paying their dues to the UN budget and would potentially lose its voting rights at the UN General Assembly. The country's minimum required payment was US $829,888 to reduce its arrears and avoid a possible loss of voting rights after September. In response, a Santomean foreign ministry spokesperson declared that it was the country's intention to settle at least part of the debt with the UN in the short term.

In December 2021 the Chinese ambassador, Xu Yingzhen, and São Tomé and Príncipe's Minister of Foreign Affairs, Co-operation and Communities, Edite do Ramos da Costa Ten Jua, signed a memorandum of understanding on co-operation as part of China's Belt and Road initiative.

Economy

GERHARD SEIBERT

INTRODUCTION

The economy of São Tomé and Príncipe, which until the 1990s was based almost exclusively on the export of cocoa, has experienced continuous setbacks since independence in 1975. The then socialist regime decided at independence to nationalize virtually all enterprises of any size. São Tomé became a member of the International Monetary Fund (IMF) and the World Bank in 1977 and introduced a new currency unit, the dobra, to replace the Portuguese escudo at par. The dobra became increasingly overvalued, placing considerable strain on the balance of payments.

In 1985, confronted by the threat of economic collapse, the socialist regime initiated a process of economic liberalization. Under a three-year Structural Adjustment Programme introduced in 1987, price controls were abolished or adjusted on many goods, trade was liberalized, wages, taxes and duties were increased, and the dobra was devalued. Since then the IMF has approved another seven economic reform arrangements for São Tomé, though without a great deal of success as far as economic recovery and debt reduction are concerned.

Nevertheless, in March 2007 the IMF and the World Bank announced that the country had now met the economic reform targets and was eligible for debt cancellation equivalent to US $317m. under the enhanced initiative for Heavily Indebted Poor Countries (HIPC). In May the Paris Club creditors agreed to write off bilateral debts of $24m. in nominal terms, and in 2008 Germany and France cancelled bilateral debts of €4.6m. and of €7.6m., respectively.

In 2019 the IMF approved a 40-month Extended Credit Facility (ECF) arrangement worth US $18.2m. The approval enabled the immediate first disbursement of $2.6m. to relieve the Government's desperate financial situation. As agreed with the IMF, in an attempt to increase government revenue, later in that month the National Assembly adopted a bill to introduce value-added tax (VAT) at a rate of 15% from March 2020, with a special rate of 7.5% VAT for certain essential goods. (However, in February 2020 the Government postponed the introduction of the 15% rate of VAT, claiming a lack of capacity for its implementation.) In December 2019 the National Assembly approved the national budget for the coming year, worth about $155m. The Government expected domestic revenue to finance 52.4% of the overall budget. A Public Investment Programme (PIP) was to be externally financed by about 90% and represented 44.5% of the total budget. The projected primary deficit was 1.9% of gross domestic product (GDP).

Although the Government had expected GDP growth of 4.0% in 2020, the coronavirus disease (COVID-19) pandemic rapidly altered the country's economic situation from early that year. In April the Government adopted a package of sectoral emergency economic and financial measures to combat the impact of the pandemic worth US $84.9m. In the same month the World Bank approved an International Development Association (IDA) grant of $2.5m. to assist the Government in fighting the pandemic, and the IMF cancelled six months of debt service payments of $151,500 each and approved a Rapid Credit Facility worth $12.3m.

In July 2020 the National Assembly approved the revised 2020 national budget of US $152.7m., which was 7.2% less in value than that adopted in December 2019. Current expenditure of $90.7m. accounted for 59.5% of the budget and $50.7m. (37.2%) was earmarked for the PIP. Expenditure on personnel represented 51.7% of total current expenditure, while education and health accounted for 16.1% and 12.9%, respectively, of total expenditure. Total revenue comprised current revenue of $63.3m., grants of $68.2m. and financing of $21.2m., of which $17.1m. stemmed from foreign donors.

In January 2021 the National Assembly approved the 2021 national budget of US $166m. The budget projected GDP growth of some 5%, mainly fostered by public investments in infrastructure and housing projects. On the income side, the budget expected $74m. of financial aid and $78m. from current revenue. Infrastructure and natural resource accounted for 27.8% of public investments, while 13% was allocated to health, 9.4% to education, and 7.9% to agriculture and fishing.

In February 2021 the Government reported an unexpected expansion in GDP for 2020 of 3.1%. In value terms it rose from US $427.4m. in 2019 to $472.9m. in 2020, whereas even as late as November the IMF had expected a decline of 6.0% due to weak external demand and pandemic containment measures. Mainly as a result of a 5.8% increase in the construction subsector, the secondary sector grew by 4.4%, while the tertiary sector increased by 2.6% due to growth in public administration and health services, by 13% and by 6.1%, respectively. The primary sector decreased by 1.1%, although extractive activities grew by 4%. As a result of improved economic performance, the primary domestic deficit in 2020 was 4.7%, significantly less than the 6.3% predicted by the IMF.

In December 2021 the National Assembly approved the 2022 national budget totalling €158m., of which 51% was to be financed externally. Current expenditure represented about 56.4% of total expenditure, while capital expenditure and debt service payments accounted for 38% and 5.3%, respectively. As far as public investments were concerned, infrastructure and health were each allocated 20% of the total, while 16% was designated for education. The Government projected economic growth of 2.8% and an average inflation rate of 7.5% for 2022.

In March 2022 the IMF completed the fourth review of the 40-month ECF arrangement approved in October 2019 and disbursed approximately US $2.7m., increasing total disbursements under the arrangement to about $15.2m.

AGRICULTURE

According to United Nations (UN) estimates, agriculture, hunting, forestry and fishing contributed 14.3% of GDP in 2020 and employed 27.9% of the employed labour force in 2015. At independence, São Tomé inherited a plantation economy owned by Portuguese companies, dominated by cocoa. In 1975 the Government nationalized all landholdings of over 200 ha and grouped them into state enterprises, which covered over 80% of the cultivable land area. The state farms incurred substantial deficits and, within a decade, were brought to the point of financial collapse.

Following the failure of initial efforts at privatization by the management of the estates in the second half of the 1980s, the end of the plantation economy was announced. At the instigation of the World Bank, which was providing finance of US $17.2m. towards land reform, the Government announced that more than 20,000 ha of former plantation lands would be transferred to smallholders between 1993 and 2000.

In July 2019 the Minister of Agriculture, Francisco dos Ramos, announced an evaluation of the use of 28,367 ha of arable former plantation lands that were distributed in the 1990s to small farmers (accounting for 69.7%), medium-sized enterprises (0.2%) and other citizens (30.3%) as part of agricultural reforms. Ramos claimed that most of the distributed lands had been abandoned by the concessionaries. The assessment aimed to make the lands profitable and transform the dominant subsistence agriculture into a commercial model to improve production for local consumption and export.

Following independence, cocoa regularly accounted for well over 90% of annual exports in goods by value. Annual production declined to about 4,000 metric tons in the 1980s, and export earnings from cocoa decreased by 67% between 1979 and 1988. As cocoa prices declined still further in the early 1990s, production fell to a low of 3,193 tons in 1991, and there has been no discernible recovery since, owing in part to recurrent insect infestations. According to estimates of the UN Food and Agriculture Organization (FAO), production of cocoa beans was 3,041 tons in 2020. The IMF estimated that revenue from cocoa exports increased from US $6.7m. (1.4% of GDP) in 2020 to $7.8m. (1.5% of GDP) in 2021.

The islands' principal secondary crops are coffee, palm oil and coconuts. Coffee output increased from 14 metric tons in 1992 to 36 tons in 1998, then declined to about 20 tons in 2006. According to FAO estimates, coffee production amounted to just 10 tons in 2018. Coconut production amounted to 750 tons in 2020.

Self-sufficiency in basic food crops has eluded São Tomé and Príncipe since independence, despite the high fertility of the islands' volcanic soils, the long growing season, the variety of micro-climates and abundant rainfall. The apportionment of centrally fixed planning targets for food production among the nationalized estates proved unsuccessful, and by the mid-1980s the country was estimated to be importing 90% of its food requirements. In July 2009 the Belgian consortium SOCFINCO (registered locally as Agripalma) signed an agreement with the Government to invest US $50m. in the rehabilitation of the state-owned palm oil manufacturer Empresa de Óleos Vegetais (EMOLVE), involving the establishment of 6,000 ha of palm oil plantations.

In December 2019 Agripalma inaugurated its new palm oil factory in São Tomé. The facility had an annual production capacity of 10,000 metric tons of palm oil produced on an area of 2,100 ha of oil palm plantations, where Agripalma employed about 850 workers, making it the country's largest private sector employer. Palm oil exports by Agripalma increased from 524 metric tons in 2019 to 4,883 tons in 2020, while cocoa exports decreased from 2,735 tons to 2,432 tons over the same period. Consequently, in terms of volume, in 2020 palm oil exports surpassed cocoa exports for the first time. However, in terms of value, in 2020 cocoa was still the main revenue generator with US $7m., while palm oil generated income of some $4m.

The livestock sector has been seriously affected by the decline in veterinary services since independence and by periodic outbreaks of swine fever. Goats are widely reared and sometimes exported to Gabon. In 2000 there were 26,253 head of goat and sheep, and 63 metric tons of goat and sheep meat were produced; however, according to FAO estimates, stocks in 2020 stood at only 3,348 sheep and 5,937 goats, and in that year goat and sheep meat production totalled just 11 tons. The islands are free of tsetse fly, but cattle have been badly affected by bovine tuberculosis. Production of cattle meat increased, however, from 12 tons in 1992 to an estimated 193 tons in 2020, according to FAO; the national cattle herd numbered 1,388 head in that year. According to FAO estimates, the national pig herd numbered 42,985 head in 2020. A consignment of 142 goats was shipped from Rwanda to São Tomé in an FAO-financed initiative in 2017, for cross-breeding with local species in order to boost goat meat and milk production.

The fishing sector has been identified as a priority area for economic diversification. The Government is basing its hopes for the fishing industry on the local tuna resources, and it is estimated that annual tuna catches could reach 17,000 metric tons without affecting stocks. In April 2019 the European Union (EU) and São Tomé signed a new, five-year protocol to renew a fisheries partnership agreement (concluded in 2007); the protocol would allow 34 Portuguese and Spanish trawlers to operate in the archipelago's waters. In exchange, the EU was to pay an annual €400,000 for access to these resources and another €440,000 annually to support sustainability in the local fisheries sector. In addition, shipowners were obliged to pay a fee of €70 per ton of fish caught; the annual reference tonnage was 1,000 tons. According to FAO estimates, the total fishing catch was 5,617 tons in 2020. According to a fishing sector survey financed by the World Bank, in 2019 some 4,150 artisan fishermen operated in the archipelago (using 2,600 canoes).

São Tomé and Príncipe's considerable forestry resources have been neglected. Colonial legislation for the protection of forests was replaced by a new law in 1979, but it was not enforced, and no barriers were imposed on the uncontrolled felling of trees. The programme of land distribution to small-holders led to increasing deforestation, with the new occupants arbitrarily felling trees. With the assistance of the UN Environment Programme, the Government formulated legislation, which was approved by the National Assembly in 1998,

concerning management of the environment in order to address this and other issues. Legislation approved by the National Assembly in 2004 led to the establishment, in August 2006, of the Obô Natural Park, covering some 235 sq km of São Tomé island and 65 sq km of Príncipe island.

INDUSTRY AND SERVICES

According to UN estimates, industry (including mining, manufacturing, construction and power) contributed an estimated 13.5% of GDP in 2020. The secondary sector comprises some 50 small and medium-sized enterprises and several hundred microenterprises. Many basic manufactured products are still imported, especially from Portugal. The Government aims to develop food processing and the production of construction materials. All industrial companies were originally scheduled for privatization by the end of 1993, but this target proved overambitious. Enterprises to remain under state control were the water and electricity utility Empresa de Agua e Electricidade (EMAE), the ports administration Empresa Nacional de Administração dos Portos (ENAPOR), the airport administration company Empresa Nacional de Aeroportos e Segurança Aérea (ENASA), the postal service Correios de São Tomé e Príncipe, the telecommunications company Companhia Santomense de Telecomunicações (CST) and the airline STP-Airways, of which the latter two have foreign shareholders.

In December 2020 the country's first mineral water factory (Bom Sucesso) located in the former Monte Café estate was inaugurated. Initiated by Libya in 2009, but interrupted for several years due to the political turmoil in that country, the plant was completed by a consortium of the Libyan Africa Investment and Trade Company and the Italian company Zarco with an investment of about US $2m. The factory has an average production capacity of 4,000 1.5-litre bottles per hour and employed 30 local people in the initial phase.

In March 2021 the Government signed a 90-year concession agreement on the construction of a US $1,300m. multisectoral free-trade zone in a 204-ha area in Malanza in the southern Caué district with the largely unknown Jordanian-born Canadian businessman Shanti Shebab.

In January 2018, as part of a currency reform, the central bank, the Banco Central de São Tomé e Príncipe (BCSTP), put into circulation six new bank notes and five new coins with three fewer zeros. The new bank notes of 5, 10, 20, 50, 100 and 200 dobras replaced the old notes of 5,000, 10,000, 20,000, 50,000, 100,000 dobras and coins of 2,000, 1,000, 500, 200 and 100 dobras. Consequently, the new fixed rate of exchange to the euro was 24.50 dobras = €1.00. In March 2019 the BCSTP decided to withdraw the new 200-dobra note from circulation, owing to inconsistencies in its printing and issue. In August 2021 the BCSTP put another 200-dobra note into circulation, together with new 5- and 10-dobra notes, all printed on improved secure paper.

In June 2018 the BCSTP launched the Payment System Infrastructure and Financial Inclusion Project. The project for the introduction of payments by international credit cards such as Visa and MasterCard—financed by a US $2.2m. loan from the African Development Bank (AfDB), $299,000 from the World Bank and €345,600 from the Portuguese Trust Fund—was intended to expand financial inclusion and boost tourism in the country. In the same month the BCSTP decided to close down the ailing Banco Privado—São Tomé e Príncipe, which since 2013 had suffered consecutive losses amounting to 36.9m. new dobras and had continuously violated banking regulations. The BCSTP promised that all affected deposits would be reimbursed to the holders without additional costs. The Banco Privado was the fourth local bank since 2011 to be closed, owing to bankruptcy, after the National Investment Bank, the Nigerian-owned Island Bank and Banco Equador, reducing to five the number of commercial banks still operating in São Tomé. In January 2019 the Government dismissed the Governor of the BCSTP, Hélio Silva Vaz Almeida, replacing him with economist Américo Barros, a former BCSTP board member. In August President Evaristo de Carvalho inaugurated the BCSTP's new headquarters in the capital. The building cost more than €17m.—equivalent to more than 20% of annual national budget expenditure.

In April 2021 Prime Minister Jorge Bom Jesus inaugurated the BCSTP's new digital instant payment processing platform SIBS. This allowed individuals to approve additional Point of Sale transactions, including the payment of taxes and payment for the services of a number of local companies (including EMAE, CST and Unitel), and for the first time the withdrawal of cash from ATMs with international Visa debit and credit cards. The entrance of Mastercard was expected in the second half of that year. The modernization of the banking and financial system was expected to boost tourism and attract foreign private investments. In January 2022 the BCSTP cancelled the licence of the Nigerian Energy Bank after attempts to recapitalize the ailing institution had failed.

ENERGY

There are no mineral resources on the islands, but offshore prospecting for hydrocarbons since the late 1980s has raised expectations for oil discoveries. In May 1997 the Government signed an accord with the Environmental Remedial Holding Corp (ERHC) of the USA and the South African Procura Financial Consultants (PFC) concerning the exploration and exploitation of petroleum, gas and mineral reserves in São Tomé's territorial waters. The agreement, which was valid for 25 years, provided for an initial payment to the Government of US $5m. ERHC and the PFC were to finance the evaluation of the petroleum reserves, and a petroleum company was to be established with the Government, from which the state would receive 40% of the revenue. In November the Government submitted details of the country's 370-km (200 nautical miles) Exclusive Economic Zone (EEZ), drafted by ERHC, to the UN and the Gulf of Guinea Commission. In March 1998 São Tomé approved a law establishing the boundaries of the EEZ, which was presented to the UN Law of the Sea Commission in May.

In October 1999 the Government rescinded its agreement with ERHC, on the grounds that the company had not met a number of contractual commitments. In May 2001, as part of an agreement brokered by the Nigerian Government, São Tomé settled the conflict with ERHC, which, in the meantime, had been taken over by a Nigerian company, Chrome Energy Corporation. In exchange for the settlement, the Government conceded to ERHC considerable financial advantages, including working interests in licences, a share in signature bonuses and profit oil and an overriding royalty in production.

In February 2001 Nigeria and São Tomé signed an agreement on the establishment of a Joint Development Zone (JDZ) in the waters disputed by the two countries. Nigeria was to receive 60% of the profits of the joint zone and São Tomé 40%. In January 2002 a Joint Development Authority (JDA), based in Abuja, Nigeria, was created to direct the affairs of the JDZ. In February 2001 the Government and the Norwegian company Petroleum Geo-Services (PGS) signed an agreement on the execution of seismic studies outside Blocks 1–22, which had been conceded by ExxonMobil of the USA; the studies commenced in November. In April 2002 PGS confirmed the country's oil potential and reported that the identified blocks were commercially viable. Following a critical assessment of São Tomé's oil agreements by US lawyers, conducted at the request of the IMF, in 2003 all oil contracts signed with ERHC/Chrome, ExxonMobil and PGS were renegotiated.

In October 2003 19 oil companies submitted 31 valid bids for seven of nine oil blocks in the JDZ that had been put out for public tender in April. In April 2004 the exploration rights for Block 1 were jointly awarded to ChevronTexaco of the USA (51%), ExxonMobil (40%) and Equity Energy Resources (9%). The sale of Block 1 entitled São Tomé to a signature bonus of US $49m.—much less than the $200m. expected from the auction. ChevronTexaco signed an eight-year product-sharing agreement with the JDA for Block 1 in February 2005.

In October 2004 the Agência Nacional de Petróleo de São Tomé e Príncipe (ANP—National Petroleum Agency of São Tomé and Príncipe) was established to act as the regulatory body of the petroleum sector.

In November 2004 the JDA organized a new licensing round for Blocks 2–6. In April 2005 five blocks were awarded to various companies. A consortium of ERHC and Devon Energy/Pioneer Natural Resources won a 65% stake of Block 2, and

Block 4 was awarded to a consortium of ERHC and Noble Energy. Anadarko Petroleum Corp received 51% of Block 3. An Iranian-Nigerian consortium was awarded the right to operate Block 5, and a Nigerian company became operator of Block 6. The five signature bonuses totalled US $283m. However, owing to ERHC's bonus-free options, São Tomé would receive only $57.2m.

In July 2005 Devon Energy withdrew from the consortium with ERHC. In November the Swiss-based Addax Petroleum replaced Noble Energy in the ERHC/Noble consortium of Block 4. In February 2006 Pioneer Natural Resources withdrew from the operatorship of Block 2 and was replaced by Addax and the Chinese state-owned China Petroleum and Chemical Corporation (Sinopec). Only in March did the JDA sign production-sharing contracts with Addax and other consortium winners for Block 4, with operator Anadarko and ERHC and other parties of Block 3, and with operators including Sinopec in Block 2. The signature bonuses for these blocks were US $90m., $40m. and $71m., respectively. As a result of ERHC's bonus-free options, São Tomé received only $28.6m. of the total amount.

In January 2006 ChevronTexaco started drilling the first exploration well in Block 1, but in May the enterprise announced that it had failed to discover oil and gas. Addax Petroleum announced in September 2007 that it had agreed to acquire ExxonMobil's 40% stake in Block 1 for US $77.6m. In October 2009 Sinopec became the largest stakeholder in the JDZ, after completing the takeover of Addax for $7,300m.

In February 2008 São Tomé was accepted as one of seven new applicant countries for the implementation of the Extractive Industries Transparency Initiative (EITI). However, in April 2010 the EITI board excluded São Tomé and Príncipe from the application process for failing to implement the established minimum requirements for candidate countries. In October 2012 the board approved the São Tomé Government's second application for candidate status. Although the Government did not provide data after 2017, in 2020 EITI classified São Tomé as having made 'meaningful progress' in implementing the 2016 EITI Standard. The next evaluation took place in July 2022.

In March 2010 the ANP launched the first licensing round for seven of 19 delineated blocks in the EEZ. In February ERHC and Equator Exploration, which had acquired PGS's pre-emption rights in 2004, had exercised their preferential options, obtaining Blocks 4 and 11 and Blocks 5 and 12, respectively. In November the French oil company Total acquired Chevron's 45.9% stake in Block 1 of the JDZ. In May 2011 the Government awarded the exploration licence for EEZ Block 3 to a Nigerian company, Oranto Petroleum; licences for the other six blocks were not allocated. In October the Government signed a 28-year production-sharing contract with Oranto, which included the payment of a signature bonus of US $2m.

In February 2012 the JDA signed a production-sharing contract with Iranian company ICC-EOC for Block 6 of the JDZ, which had been awarded in 2005. Following a lengthy dispute with other shareholders, ERHC transferred its 15% share in Block 5 to the Government. Consequently, São Tomé had to contribute 15% of the signature bonus of US $15m., of which it was entitled to receive 40%. In April 2012 the Government and Equator Exploration (since 2011 an 81.5% subsidiary of the Nigerian energy group Oando) signed a 28-year production-sharing contract for Block 5 of the EEZ, which included the payment of a signature bonus of $2m. In 2013, owing to inconclusive results, Sinopec, Addax, Equator Exploration and other stakeholders abandoned JDZ Blocks 2, 3 and 4 (ERHC being the only company that maintained its interests in the three blocks).

In October 2013 the ANP signed a production-sharing contract for Block 2 of the EEZ with the Hong Kong-registered Sinoangol STP, a joint venture between Sinopec and Angolan petroleum company SONANGOL. Under the agreement, Sinoangol STP paid a signature bonus of US $5m. and promised annual payments of $5m. to be disbursed on social projects and $250,000 for the training of local oil personnel. In 2014 Sinoangol STP sold 30% of its Block 2 stake to SONANGOL.

In June 2015 the JDA signed a new production-sharing contract for Block 1 with two Nigerian companies—Equator

Hydrocarbons (the operator, with a 56% share) and PAPIS Energy Solutions (35%)—and Dangote Energy Equity Resources (DEER) retained the 9% stake that it had been awarded in 2004. However, in July DEER abandoned the block.

In October 2015 the ANP signed a 28-year production-sharing contract for EEZ Block 6 with Galp Energia of Portugal and a US company, Kosmos Energy. The two firms, both of which paid a signature bonus of US $2m., were each awarded a 45% stake, with Galp as the operator, while the ANP retained a 10% stake. Simultaneously, the ANP approved the transfer to Kosmos of 100% of ERHC Energy's rights and interests in EEZ Block 11, which was adjacent to Block 6. Consequently, Kosmos became operator of Block 11, with a working interest of 85%, while the ANP kept the remaining 15%.

In February 2016 the ANP and Equator Exploration signed a 28-year production-sharing contract for EEZ Block 12. Equator paid a signature bonus of US $2.5m. as the operator, while the ANP held a 12.5% working interest. Under a second agreement signed at the same time, Equator awarded 65% of EEZ Block 5 to Kosmos Energy; Kosmos became operator, while Equator kept 20% of the interests and the ANP 15%. In March Equator sold 65% of its interest in EEZ Block 12 to Kosmos, retaining a 22.5% stake. In November Galp acquired from Kosmos an interest of 20% in each of the EEZ Blocks 5, 11 and 12. In December the ANP rescinded the licence of Sinoangol STP for EEZ Block 2, owing to the violation of the contract signed in October 2013.

Meanwhile, in August 2016 the JDA transferred the operatorship of Block 1 of the JDZ from Equator Hydrocarbons to PAPIS Energy Solutions, as the former had failed to fulfil its contractual obligations. In September the ownership of the block was restructured, and new investors were included. Under the new arrangement, PAPIS and Equator Hydrocarbons kept 32% and 10% of the acreage, respectively, while the Nakudu Group acquired 41% of the interests. The remaining 17% was transferred to the Joint Development Zone International Investment Ltd (JDZIIL), the business branch of the JDA.

Between January and August 2017 seismic surveys were carried out in EEZ Blocks 5, 6, 11 and 12, owned jointly by Kosmos Energy and Galp. In January 2018 the ANP awarded EEZ Blocks 10 and 13 to BP/Kosmos, and in March a 28-year production-sharing contract was signed. Under the agreement, the ANP held a 15% stake in each of the blocks, and the consortium paid a signature bonus of US $5m. for each of them.

In March 2019 Total signed a production-sharing contract with the JDA for JDZ Blocks 7, 8 and 11. After paying a signature bonus of US $5m. for the three blocks, Total announced that it would invest more than $10m. to carry out seismic surveys in the blocks during the four-year exploration period.

In January 2019 the consortium of BP Exploration and Kosmos Energy announced that a three-month seismic survey in EEZ Block 10 would be launched within two months. In March São Tomé's ANP signed production-sharing contracts with Total and SONANGOL for 55% and 30% of EEZ Block 1, respectively. As usual, the ANP held the remaining 15% of the block. Under the 28-year production-sharing contract, the companies paid a US $2.5m. signature bonus and promised $1m. annually for social projects during the first four years of the eight-year research phase.

At the start of 2019 Galp returned its 20% share in EEZ Block 5 to Kosmos Energy (14%) and Equator Exploration (6%). In November Royal Dutch Shell signed a farm-in agreement with Kosmos Energy for EEZ Blocks 6 and 11. Under the agreement, Shell took over from Kosmos 20% of its 45% stake in Block 6 and 30% of its 65% interest in EEZ Block 11. In January 2020 Galp announced that it would commence exploration drillings in EEZ Block 6 before the end of that year. However, owing to the COVID-19 pandemic, the drilling was postponed to the second quarter of 2021.

In September 2020 Kosmos Energy sold its interests in EEZ Blocks 6 (25%) and 10, 11 and 13 (35% each) to Royal Dutch Shell. Furthermore, earlier in 2020, prior to the outbreak of the pandemic, Kosmos had decided to exit Block 12. Consequently,

Kosmos' 45% stake in this block was proportionally awarded to the other two stakeholders Equator Exploration and Galp Energia, which increased their interests accordingly from 22.5% to 46.3% and from 20% to 41.2%, respectively, while the ANP kept its 12.5% interest. By mid-2021 Kosmos, once the major investor in the EEZ, retained only a 58.85% stake in Block 5. In April 2022 Galp and Royal Dutch Shell initiated three-month exploration drillings in EEZ Block 6.

In 1998, at the request of the World Bank, the Government sold a 49% share of the state fuel company, Empresa Nacional de Combustíveis e Oleos (ENCO), of which 40% was acquired by SONANGOL and 9% by local investors. In 2008 the Government sold 35% of its shares in ENCO to SONANGOL for US $32m., bringing SONANGOL's holding to 78% in total, following the purchase by the latter of a private shareholding of 3%. The Santomean state retained 16% of ENCO shares, with 6% remaining in private ownership.

In December 2009 the Government of the Republic of China (Taiwan) funded the construction of a new US $15m. thermal power station in Santo Amaro, with a total capacity of 8.5 MW; it was inaugurated in October 2010, under the management of Taiwan Electrical and Mechanical Engineering Services. Meanwhile, also in December 2009 Hidroeléctrica, a majority Portuguese-owned consortium, supplied six generators, which were installed in Bobô Fôrro and expected to produce 5 MW.

A World Bank document published in January 2018 revealed that although EMAE's revenue had increased over the previous six years, in 2016 electricity supplies generated an income of US $11.6m, and in that year the company's operational costs totalled $24.9m. It was estimated that to repair transmission and distribution networks and restore operational capacity to normal levels, EMAE would need to invest $67m. in the water sector and $61.2m. in electricity production and supply. In June 2018, according to the AfDB, the archipelago had an electricity access rate of 70%, and of the available capacity of 35 MW, only 58% was actually accessible, owing to losses caused by the ageing and lack of maintenance of the distribution network. In February 2019 the Government announced the rehabilitation and extension of the Contador hydroelectric power station, with funding of €14m. from the World Bank and the European Investment Bank (EIB). The project, which was expected to be completed in two years, aimed to double the dam's capacity from 2 MW to 4 MW.

At the instigation of the IMF, in order to settle its debts with EMAE, in July 2019 the Government began to regularly pay for supplies from the state-owned water and electricity supplier, while the latter pledged to transfer at least US $500,000 every month to the fuel company ENCO to settle an accumulated debt of $140m. In turn, ENCO would transfer the same amount to SONANGOL to reduce its own debts with the Angolan oil company, estimated at some $150m.

In August 2019 EMAE signed an agreement for the delivery of six new generators worth US $4.5m., financed by the consortium of Kosmos Energy and BP as part of their corporate social responsibility programme. Five generators with a total capacity of 9 MW were to be installed at the Santo Amaro thermoelectric power plant, and another, of 720 kW, was destined for Príncipe's thermoelectric power plant.

In June 2022 the foundation stone for the construction of EMAE's first solar power plant was laid in Santo Amaro. The project, which was financed jointly by the UN Development Programme (UNDP), the Global Environment Facility (GEF) and the AfDB, was expected to have a generation capacity of 2.2 MW after completion, contributing to a reduction of diesel consumption by the thermoelectric power plant in Santo Amaro.

TRANSPORT, TOURISM AND COMMUNICATIONS

In January 2008 the Government created a Maritime and Port Administration Institute to supervise navigation in the country's EEZ. The new institution was expected to regularize the activities of the 439 ships worldwide that were using the country's flag at that time. However, the country received only 10% of the potential registration fees.

Two agreements on the construction of a deep-sea container port in Fernão Dias, which had been signed by the Government with a French and a Chinese company in 2009 and 2015, respectively, failed due to a lack of funds. However, in May 2021 the project appeared to have been revived after the Government signed a memorandum of understanding (MOU) with the Ghanaian logistics services provider Safebond Africa Ltd. (SAL) for the construction of a deep-water port in Fernão Dias, and the modernization of the ports of Ana Chaves and of Santo António (Príncipe) as well as the management concessions for the three ports. The total investment was estimated at $250m.

Air São Tomé e Príncipe, which began operations in 1993, was dissolved in 2006 and replaced by STP-Airways, owned by the Government (35%) and private investors (65%). In May 2008 a Portuguese company, EuroAtlantic, announced that it had acquired a 37% stake in STP-Airways, while the Government retained 35%, and the local Banco Equador and the Grupo de Investimentos e de Apoio aos Serviços secured 14% each. EuroAtlantic assumed the management of STP-Airways. In November 2009 the European Commission included all airlines registered in São Tomé on a 'black list' of airlines banned from European airspace for safety reasons. Despite repeated warnings, São Tomé's Instituto Nacional de Aviação Civil (National Institute of Civil Aviation) had failed to fulfil the EU's international security standards.

In April 2011 the Government signed a 30-year concession agreement with SONANGOL on the management and exploitation of São Tomé's port of Ana Chaves and the country's international airport. The agreement included the establishment of a private management company, jointly owned by SONANGOL (80%) and the Santomean state (20%), to administer the two facilities. SONANGOL pledged to invest US $5m. in the port and another $7m. in the airport. In February 2020 the Santomean Government and the People's Republic of China signed an agreement to extend the runway of the international airport by 600 m and to modernize other infrastructure. In June 2022 China signed another agreement on the implementation of the project, which was budgeted at $100m., announcing that work would begin in 2023.

In 1990 the telecommunications company CST was established as a joint venture between the state (49%) and the Portuguese Rádio Marconi (51%). In March 1997 an internet service was officially launched. In February 2004 legislation was approved permitting the liberalization of the local telecommunications market, which had been a monopoly of CST. However, the implementation of this legislation was delayed, and it was not until 2006 that the Government set up the Autoridade Geral de Regulação (AGER), the communications regulatory authority. In July 2008 the Government and Portugal Telecom SGPS signed an agreement that allowed CST to participate with an investment of US $15m. in the international consortium West African Festoon System (WAFS), which constructed a fibre optic submarine cable link between Luanda, Angola, and Accra, Ghana. São Tomé e Príncipe would connect to the WAFS project through a ground station in Libreville, Gabon, and the SAT3 submarine cable.

In May 2011 the Government, CST and Africatel Holdings BV (until 2014 a subsidiary of Portugal Telecom, thereafter of Brazil's telecommunications company, Oi) signed an agreement on the archipelago's connection to another fibre optic submarine cable, which arrived on São Tomé island in November. In March 2012 CST commenced mobile broadband services. In October President Pinto da Costa inaugurated the African Coast to Europe fibre optic submarine cable station in São Gabriel, which would considerably increase internet speeds on the archipelago. In March 2013 the licence for a second telecommunications operator was awarded to Unitel International Holding, a Dutch-based company owned by Isabel dos Santos, the daughter of former Angolan President José Eduardo dos Santos. Unitel had offered immediate payment of US $7.5m. for the licence. Following an investment of an estimated $30m. in its network, Unitel São Tomé e Príncipe launched mobile services in the country in May 2014. In 2020 the International Telecommunications Union reported 2,790 fixed telephone lines, 174,203 mobile telephone subscribers and some 2,512 fixed broadband internet subscribers; around 33% of the population used the internet. In January 2020 the Government initiated the digitalization process of the state-

owned television and radio stations—TVS and Radio Nacional. In February 2022 the Portuguese Visabeira Group acquired a 51% stake in CST, hitherto held by Africatel Holdings BV (86% of which was owned by the loss-making Brazilian telecommunications operator Oi).

Tourism has long been identified as a growth sector; however, income from tourism has been variable in recent years. In 2017 tourist arrivals to the archipelago totalled 28,948. In that year there were 49 hotel units in São Tomé and Príncipe, with a total of 696 rooms and 1,454 available beds. In 2018 the number of foreign tourists increased to 33,424, according to the Direcção Geral de Turismo de São Tomé e Príncipe. A new Strategic and Marketing Plan for the country's tourism sector, which the Government launched in January 2018, aimed to increase the share of tourism to GDP by 73.4% and international tourist arrivals by 65.5% by 2025. In 2019 the number of tourist arrivals reached 34,918. The impact of COVID-19 on the tourism sector was, as for every country in the world, significant, and in 2020 the number of tourists dropped to just 10,718, of whom 51.3% were Portuguese. Consequently, according to the IMF, revenue from tourism dropped from US $66.6m. (15.5% of GDP) in 2019 to $16.4m. (3.4%) in 2020 but recovered to $30.7m. (5.9%) in 2021.

Meanwhile, in an attempt to encourage tourist arrivals, in August 2015 the Government exempted EU, US and Lusophone community citizens from visa requirements for stays of up to 15 days. According to the IMF, in 2015 the tourism sector accounted for an estimated 13% of overall formal employment and 66% of exports of goods and services.

In November 2016 a South African company, HBD (Here Be Dragons), a tourism developer, major investor and employer on the island of Príncipe, announced that it would halve its planned investment of US $11m. in 2017 and make 150 employees redundant. The company abandoned agricultural projects on two estates on the island, focusing instead on its core business of eco-tourism. In September 2017 HBD and the regional government of Príncipe commenced relocating 130 families, a total of 500 people (6.6% of the island's population), from their dilapidated accommodation in the Sundy estate in Príncipe to new homes elsewhere on the island. The resettlement project was conceived by UN Habitat and financed by HBD. In May 2020 HBD made 194 workers out of a total workforce of about 600 redundant, owing to financial losses suffered as a result of the COVID-19 pandemic.

FOREIGN TRADE, AID AND PAYMENTS

Owing to the importance of cocoa, palm oil and tourism, the islands' economic life is entirely dependent on external markets. For many years the country's trade balance has been negative since the value of imports far exceeds that of exports. Portugal is the country's principal supplier of goods, accounting for 52.7% of total imports in 2020; Angola is also an important supplier (particularly of fuel). In 2020 the main purchaser of São Tomé's exports was the Netherlands (49.6% of the total). According to IMF data, in 2020 the value of São Tomé's good exports was US $13.9m., while imports totalled $116.7m., resulting in a trade deficit of $102.8m. In 2020 exports of goods and services declined by 48.7% but they increased by 39.3% in 2021. Imports decreased by 11.4% in 2020 but recovered by 5.9% in 2021.

The UNDP, the World Bank, the AfDB, the EU, Portugal, France, Japan, China, Taiwan (1997–2016), Angola and Morocco have all been prominent as donors. However, the institutional weakness of São Tomé and the lack of co-ordination between donors have led to problems in aid utilization. The influx of aid has helped to contain the deficit on the current account, but has distorted prices.

In July 2009 São Tomé and Portugal concluded an exchange rate parity agreement which allowed the national currency to be pegged to the euro. The agreement, supported by a credit line of up to €25m. from Portugal to reinforce the archipelago's foreign exchange reserves, became effective in January 2010. The fixed exchange rate was expected to contribute to macroeconomic and financial stability in São Tomé and Príncipe by attracting foreign direct investment.

In December 2016 São Tomé and Príncipe (after severing relations with Taiwan) re-established diplomatic relations with mainland China (see *History*). In April 2017 the Chinese Government pledged aid of US $146m. over a five-year period and had waived São Tomé's bilateral debt of $18.4m.

In September 2017 the World Bank announced that it would provide São Tomé with an IDA grant of US $75m. over the period 2018–20 for the energy, environmental protection, education and institutional training sectors. In June 2018 the World Bank signed two agreements worth a total of $15m. with São Tomé—one concerning the strengthening of the institutional capacities of the finance ministry, the BCSTP and the National Institute of Statistics, and the other concerning budget support related to the PIP. In August Portugal granted €6m. for the Budu-Budu vocational training centre in São Tomé. In the same month the IMF provided direct budget support of $5m. In September China signed three agreements with São Tomé for a $29m. grant for the infrastructure and education sectors.

In January 2019 the World Bank donated US $10m. to São Tomé to finance social projects that would benefit at least 2,500 impoverished families. In February the EU and São Tomé signed an Indicative National Programme of €35m. to finance infrastructure, food security, agriculture and energy projects for 2019/20. In April the International Fund for Agricultural Development (IFAD) announced the provision of $25m. to finance agriculture, fishing, and rural development projects, as part of the Smallholder Commercial Agriculture Support Project. In the same month São Tomé and the World Bank signed an agreement on a grant of $29m. towards road repair works. In May the EU extended direct budget support to the São Tomé Government of €3m. In June the AfDB provided a $3.5m. grant towards the ongoing Infrastructure Rehabilitation for Food Security Support Project II.

In November 2019 the EIB approved a €12.5m. loan to finance the rehabilitation and modernization of 11 km of coastal road from Pantufo to the international airport. The Netherlands co-financed the project with a grant of €14.5m. In January 2020 the World Bank and the AfDB approved direct budget support of US $5m. and $7m., respectively. In the same month the Global Fund announced the disbursement of €11.6m. to finance São Tomé's programme to combat malaria, HIV/AIDS and tuberculosis in the period 2021–23. In February 2020 IFAD approved aid of €4.9m. to finance projects in agricultural productivity and nutrition.

In April 2020 the World Bank granted financing of $12m. for the Power Sector Recovery Project, the objective of which was to increase renewable energy generation and improve the reliability of the existing electricity supply. In July the IMF board completed the first review of the country's ECF and approved the immediate disbursement of US $4.8m. as part of the arrangement. In the same month the African Development Fund (ADF) approved a grant of $10.3m. for São Tomé as part of its Multi-Country COVID-19 Response Support Programme (MCRSP). In August the EU announced an increase in direct budget support for the year from initially promised €2m. to €5.3m. in order to finance the country's water supply and sanitation sectors. In October the Global Fund announced it would provide $15.1m. for the period 2021–23 towards the fight against malaria, HIV/AIDS, tuberculosis, as well as for use in strengthening the country's national health system.

In December 2020 the World Bank approved Development Policy Operation (DPO) funding of US $10m. to support São Tomé and Príncipe's response to COVID-19. In March 2021 an additional $6.5m. was approved as part of the DPO to prevent, detect and respond to the threat posed by COVID-19. Meanwhile, in February 2021 the IMF completed the second review of the ECF and disbursed another $2.7m. in the framework of this arrangement. In March the World Bank approved additional financing of $8m. for the Social Protection and Skills Development Project aimed at supporting the development of an effective national safety net system for poor households. In May the World Bank granted $7m. towards the modernization of São Tomé's banking system, including the expansion of the automatic payment systems. The grant increased to $19m. the Bank's total financing of the BCSTP's institutional capacity building project.

In June 2021 the GEF and the UNDP provided funds of around US $4m. for a national sustainable management of ecosystem and biodiversity project. Part of the project was the production of charcoal from coconut shells to replace the use of charcoal made of wood from the tropical forests. In June the Minister of Planning, Finance and the Blue Economy, Osvaldo Vaz, held talks with his Angolan counterpart, Vera Esperança dos Santos Daves, with a focus on finding a solution for São Tomé's huge bilateral debts of more than $200m. with Angola, which remained the country's major bilateral creditor. About one-half of the total debt stemmed from unpaid fuel supplies from SONANGOL. The two ministers agreed to make a thorough assessment of the debts that had accumulated over many years, and Vaz stated that he expected Angola to cancel or at least reschedule the debts, since São Tomé was unable to settle them. In December São Tomé and Portugal signed a new five-year Strategic Co-operation Programme worth €60m. for the period 2021–25.

São Tomé's total external debt was US $252m. at the end of 2019, of which $225m. was public and publicly guaranteed debt. In that year the cost of servicing long-term public and publicly guaranteed debt and repayments to the IMF was equivalent to 11.6% of the value of exports of goods, services and income (excluding workers' remittances). According to the World Bank, in 2020 total external debt amounted to $291.2m.

Statistical Survey

Sources (unless otherwise stated): Instituto Nacional de Estatística, CP 256, São Tomé; tel. 2221982; e-mail ine@ine.st; internet www.ine.st; Banco Central de São Tomé e Príncipe, Praça da Independência, CP 13, São Tomé; tel. 2243700; e-mail bcstp@bcstp.st; internet www.bcstp.st.

AREA AND POPULATION

Area: 1,001 sq km (386.5 sq miles); São Tomé 859 sq km (331.7 sq miles), Príncipe 142 sq km (54.8 sq miles).

Population: 137,599 at census of September 2001; 178,739 (males 88,867, females 89,872) at census of May 2012. *2020* (official projection): 210,240 (males 104,120, females 106,120). *Mid-2022* (UN projection): 227,679 (Source: UN, *World Population Prospects: The 2019 Revision*).

Density (at mid-2022): 227.5 per sq km.

Population by Age and Sex ('000, UN projections at mid-2022): *0–14 years:* 92.9 (males 47.0, females 45.9); *15–64 years:* 127.5 (males 63.8, females 63.7); *65 years and over:* 7.3 (males 3.1, females 4.2); *Total* 227.7 (males 113.9, females 113.8) (Source: UN, *World Population Prospects: The 2019 Revision*).

Population by District (official projections, 2020): Agua-Grande 80,908; Cantagolo 20,207; Caué 7,523; Lembá 16,940; Lobata 22,916; Mé-Zóchi 52,967; Pagué (Príncipe) 8,778; *Total* 210,240.

Principal Towns (population at 2012 census, preliminary): São Tomé (capital) 69,581; Trindade 19,659; Neves 12,205; Santana 11,551; Bombom 10,028; Santo Amaro 7,842. *2018* (UN estimate at mid-year): São Tomé (capital) 80,099 (Source: UN, *World Population Prospects: The 2018 Revision*).

Births, Marriages and Deaths (2021 unless otherwise indicated): Registered live births 5,544 (birth rate 25.8 per 1,000); Registered marriages 215 (marriage rate 1.1 per 1,000, 2017); Registered deaths 1,174 (death rate 5.5 per 1,000).

Life Expectancy (years at birth): 68.5 (males 65.3; females 71.6) in 2020.

Employment (2015): Agriculture and fishing 14,628; Mining 224; Manufacturing 4,861; Electricity, gas and water 315; Construction 3,596; Wholesale and retail trade 14,873; Hotels and restaurants 1,146; Transport, storage and communications 1,814; Finance, insurance and real estate 291; Public administration 2,634; Health 1,596; Education 1,395; Other activities 5,033; *Total employed* 52,406 (males 30,876, females 21,530).

HEALTH AND WELFARE

Total Fertility Rate (children per woman, 2020): 4.2.

Under-5 Mortality Rate (per 1,000 live births, 2020): 16.1.

HIV/AIDS (estimated % of persons aged 15–49, 2020): 0.3.

COVID-19: Cumulative Confirmed Deaths (per 100,000 persons at 31 August 2022): 34.1.

COVID-19: Fully Vaccinated Population (% of total population at 14 August 2022): 45.6.

Physicians (per 1,000 head, 2019): 0.5.

Hospital Beds (per 1,000 head, 2011): 2.9.

Domestic Health Expenditure (2019): US $ per head (PPP): 107.3.

Domestic Health Expenditure (2019): % of GDP: 2.6.

Domestic Health Expenditure (2019): public (% of total current expenditure): 47.3.

Access to Improved Water Resources (% of persons, 2020): 78.

Access to Improved Sanitation Facilities (% of persons, 2020): 48.

Total Carbon Dioxide Emissions ('000 metric tons, 2018): 140.

Carbon Dioxide Emissions Per Head (metric tons, 2018): 0.7.

Human Development Index (2021): ranking: 138.

Human Development Index (2021): value: 0.618.

Note: For data on COVID-19 vaccinations, 'fully vaccinated' denotes receipt of all doses specified by approved vaccination regime (Sources: Johns Hopkins University and Our World in Data). Data on health expenditure refer to current general government expenditure in each case. For more information on sources and further definitions for all indicators, see Health and Welfare Statistics: Sources and Definitions section (europaworld.com/credits).

AGRICULTURE, ETC.

Principal Crops (metric tons, 2020, FAO estimates): Bananas 5,078; Cabbages and other brassicas 848; Carrots and turnips 980; Cassava (Manioc) 1,422; Cinnamon 58; Cocoa beans 3,041; Coconuts 750; Lettuce and chicory 82; Maize 681; Onions, dry 361; Plantains and others 40,634; Taro 9,299; Yams 2,168. *Aggregated Production* (metric tons, may include official, semi-official or estimated data) Total fruit (primary) 50,601; Total oilcrops 17,632; Total vegetables (primary) 3,691.

Livestock (head, 2020, FAO estimates): Cattle 1,388; Chickens 299,000; Goats 5,937; Pigs 42,985; Sheep 3,348.

Livestock Products (metric tons, 2020, FAO estimates): Cattle hides, fresh 31; Cattle meat 193; Cattle offals, edible 27; Cows' milk 557; Chicken meat 575; Duck meat 38; Goat meat 8; Pig meat 515; Pig offals, edible 27; Sheep meat 3; Turkey meat 11; Hen eggs 186.

Forestry ('000 cubic metres, 2020, FAO estimates): Roundwood removals 142.2; Sawnwood production 12.0.

Fishing (metric tons, live weight, all capture, 2020): Total catch 5,617 (Golden African snapper 133; African forktail snapper 174; Atlantic emperor 142; Large-eye dentex 171; Flyingfishes 553; Scads 409; Jacks and crevalles 915; Amberjacks 88).

Source: FAO.

INDUSTRY

Production (metric tons, 2020 unless otherwise indicated): Coconut oil 459 (2019, FAO estimate); Palm oil 3,837 (2019, FAO estimate); Palm fruit oil 16,882 (FAO estimate); Palm kernel oil 459 (2019, FAO estimate); Electrical energy (million kWh) 91. Sources: UN Energy Statistics Database; FAO.

FINANCE

Currency and Exchange Rates: 100 cêntimos = 1 new dobra (Db). *Sterling, Dollar and Euro Equivalents* (26 February 2021): £1 sterling = 27.907 new dobras; US $1 = 20.041 new dobras; €1 = 24.292 new dobras; 10,000 new dobras = £3.58 = $4.99 = €4.12. *Average Exchange Rate* (new dobras per US $): 20.751 in 2018; 21.885 in 2019; 21.507 in 2020Note: A 2009 accord with Portugal effectively established a fixed exchange rate of 24,500 dobra to 1 euro. In August 2017 the Government announced a redenomination of the currency, with 1 new dobra becoming equivalent to 1,000 of the former iteration from the beginning of 2018.

Budget ('000 million dobras, 2022, estimates): *Revenue:* Current revenue 1,772.0 (Taxation 1,477.0, Non-tax revenue 295.0); Grants 1,643.0; Financing 456.0; Total 3,871.0. *Expenditure:* Current expenditure 2,182.8 (Personnel costs 1,165.0, Goods and services

274.8, Interest on external debt 74.2, Transfers 397.8, Other current expenditure 271.0); Capital expenditure 1,688.2; Total 3,871.0. Source: Ministry of Finance, Trade and the Blue Economy, São Tomé.

International Reserves (US $ million at 31 December 2020): IMF special drawing rights 1.15; Foreign exchange 74.14; *Total* 75.29. *2021:* IMF special drawing rights 1.11. Source: IMF, *International Financial Statistics*.

Money Supply ('000 million dobras at 31 December 2020): Currency outside depository corporations 347; Transferable deposits 2,537; Other deposits 480; *Broad money* 3,364. Source: IMF, *International Financial Statistics*.

Cost of Living (Consumer Price Index; base: December 2014 = 100): 127.9 in 2019; 140.6 in 2020; 152.0 in 2021.

Gross Domestic Product (million dobras at constant 2015): 7,829.2 in 2018; 8,002.2 in 2019; 8,249.5 in 2020. Source: UN National Accounts Main Aggregates Database.

Expenditure on the Gross Domestic Product (million dobras at current prices, 2020): Government final consumption expenditure 1,865.9; Private final consumption expenditure 9,288.4; Gross fixed capital formation 1,656.4; *Total domestic expenditure* 12,810.7; Exports of goods and services 1,109.2; *Less* Imports of goods and services 3,672.6; *GDP in purchasers' values* 10,247.3. Source: UN National Accounts Main Aggregates Database.

Gross Domestic Product by Economic Activity (million dobras at current prices, 2020): Agriculture, hunting, forestry and fishing 1,433.8; Mining and utilities 225.8; Manufacturing 570.5; Construction 560.3; Wholesale, retail trade, restaurants and hotels 2,972.7; Transport, storage and communications 1,125.1; Other activities 3,160.5; *Total gross value added* 10,048.7; Net taxes on products 198.6 (figure obtained as a residual); *GDP in purchasers' values* 10,247.3. Source: UN National Accounts Main Aggregates Database.

Balance of Payments (US $ million, 2020): Exports of goods 13.93; Imports of goods −116.72; *Balance on goods* −102.79; Exports of services 35.41; Imports of services −43.37; *Balance on goods and services* −110.76; Primary income received 6.41; Primary income paid −3.48; *Balance of goods, services and primary income* −107.83; Secondary income received 52.72; Secondary income paid −4.48; *Current balance* −59.60; Capital account (net) 16.90; Direct investment assets −0.85; Direct investment liabilities 47.11; Portfolio investment assets 0.50; Portfolio investment liabilities 0.01; Other investment assets −3.90; Other investment liabilities −1.69; Net errors and omissions −2.71; *Reserves and related items* −4.23. Source: IMF, *International Financial Statistics*.

EXTERNAL TRADE

Principal Commodities (US $ million, 2021): *Imports f.o.b.:* Foodstuffs 34.0; Beverages 11.9; Petroleum and petroleum products 34.1; Machinery 15.6; Transport equipment 6.8; Construction materials 16.4; Total (incl. others) 152.0. *Exports f.o.b.:* Cocoa 10.3; Total (incl. others) 18.8.

Principal Trading Partners (US $ million, 2021): *Imports c.i.f.:* Angola 20.7; Belgium 2.7; Brazil 2.6; China, People's Republic 9.5; France 0.9; Gabon 2.0; Netherlands 2.1; Portugal 72.9; Thailand 0.8; USA 1.5; Total (incl. others) 152.0. *Exports f.o.b.:* Angola 0.5; Belgium 3.6; Cameroon 0.4; France 0.2; Netherlands 8.8; Portugal 2.4; Total (incl. others) 18.8.

TRANSPORT

Shipping: *Flag Registered Fleet* (at 31 December 2021): Number of vessels 44; Total displacement 420,969 grt. Source: Lloyd's List Intelligence (www.bit.ly/LLintelligence).

Civil Aviation (traffic on scheduled services, 2009): Kilometres flown (million) 0.1; Passengers carried ('000) 51; Passenger-km (million) 20; Total ton-km (million) 2 (Source: UN, *Statistical Yearbook*). *2020* (domestic and international): Departures 366; Passengers carried 20,703; Freight carried 0.6m. ton-km (Source: World Bank, World Development Indicators database).

TOURISM

Foreign Tourist Arrivals: 28,919 in 2016; 28,948 in 2017; 33.424 in 2018.

Arrivals by Country of Residence (2010): Angola 1,105; Brazil 139; Cabo Verde 251; France 514; Gabon 144; Germany 193; Nigeria 198; Portugal 3,578; Spain 149; United Kingdom 229; USA 280; Total (incl. others) 7,963. *2018:* Africa 7,473; Americas 2,271; Europe 22,325; Total (incl. others) 33,424.

Tourism Receipts (US $ million, excl. passenger transport): 69 in 2016; 66 in 2017; 72 in 2018; 44 in 2019 (provisional).

Source: World Tourism Organization.

COMMUNICATIONS MEDIA

Telephones (2020): 2,790 main lines in use.

Mobile Telephone Subscriptions (2020): 174,203.

Broadband Subscriptions, Fixed (2020): 2,512.

Broadband Subscriptions, Mobile (2020): 78,382.

Internet Users (% of population, 2020): 33.0.

Source: International Telecommunication Union.

EDUCATION

Pre-primary (2015/16 unless otherwise indicated): 9,227 pupils (males 4,458, females 4,769); 662 teachers (2014/15).

Primary (2016/17): 37,172 pupils (males 19,079, females 18,093); 1,193 teachers.

Secondary (2016/17 unless otherwise indicated): 25,875 pupils (males 12,126, females 13,749); 936 teachers (2015/16).

Tertiary (2014/15): 2,336 pupils (males 1,158, females 1,178); 291 teachers.

Sources: UNESCO Institute for Statistics; *Carta Escolar de São Tomé e Príncipe,* Ministério de Educação de Portugal.

Pupil-teacher Ratio (primary education, UNESCO estimate): 31.2 in 2016/17. Source: UNESCO Institute for Statistics.

Adult Literacy Rate (UNESCO estimates): 92.8% (males 96.2; females 89.5) in 2018. Source: UNESCO Institute for Statistics.

Directory

The Constitution

A new Constitution came into force on 4 March 2003, after the promulgation by the President of a draft approved by the National Assembly in December 2002. A Memorandum of Understanding, which was signed in January 2003 by the President and the National Assembly, provided for the scheduling of a referendum on the system of governance in early 2006. However, the referendum did not take place. The following is a summary of the main provisions of the Constitution:

The Democratic Republic of São Tomé and Príncipe is a sovereign, independent, unitary and democratic state. Sovereignty resides in the people, who exercise it through universal, equal, direct and secret vote, according to the terms of the Constitution. There shall be complete separation between Church and State. There shall be freedom of thought, expression and information and a free and independent press, within the terms of the law.

Executive power is vested in the President of the Republic, who is elected for a period of five years by universal adult suffrage. The President's tenure of office is limited to two successive terms. He or she is the Supreme Commander of the Armed Forces and is accountable to the National Assembly. In the event of the President's death, permanent incapacity or resignation, his or her functions shall be assumed by the President of the National Assembly until a new President is elected.

The Council of State acts as an advisory body to the President and comprises the President of the National Assembly, the Prime Minister, the President of the Constitutional Court, the Attorney-General, the President of the Regional Government of Príncipe, former Presidents of the Republic who have not been dismissed from their positions, three citizens of merit nominated by the President and three elected by the National Assembly. Its meetings are closed and do not serve a legislative function.

Legislative power is vested in the National Assembly, which comprises 55 members elected by universal adult suffrage. The National Assembly is elected for four years and meets in ordinary session twice a year. It may meet in extraordinary session on the proposal of the President, the Council of Ministers or of two-thirds of its members. The National Assembly elects its own President. In the period between ordinary sessions of the National Assembly its functions are assumed by a permanent commission elected from among its members.

The Government is the executive and administrative organ of state. The Prime Minister is the head of government and is appointed by the President. Other ministers are appointed by the President on the proposal of the Prime Minister. The Government is responsible to the President and the National Assembly.

Judicial power is exercised by the Supreme Court of Justice and all other competent tribunals and courts. The Supreme Court of Justice is the supreme judicial authority and is accountable only to the National Assembly. Its members are appointed by the National Assembly. The right to a defence is guaranteed.

The Constitutional Court, comprising five judges with a mandate of five years, is responsible for jurisdiction on matters of constitutionality. During periods prior to, or between, the installation of the Constitutional Court, its function is assumed by the Supreme Court of Justice. The Constitution may be revised only by the National Assembly on the proposal of at least three-quarters of its members. Any amendment must be approved by a two-thirds' majority of the National Assembly. The President does not have right of veto over constitutional changes.

Note: In 1994 the National Assembly granted political and administrative autonomy to the island of Príncipe. Legislation was adopted establishing a seven-member Regional Assembly and a five-member Regional Government; both are accountable to the Government of São Tomé and Príncipe.

The Government

HEAD OF STATE

President and Commander-in-Chief of the Armed Forces: CARLOS VILA NOVA (took office 2 October 2021).

COUNCIL OF MINISTERS
(October 2022)

Prime Minister: JORGE BOM JESUS.

Minister of National Defence: JORGE AMADO.

Minister of Infrastructure and Natural Resources: OSVALDO VIEGAS D'ABREU.

Minister of Foreign Affairs, Co-operation and Communities: EDITE DO RAMOS DA COSTA TEN JUA.

Minister of Justice, Internal Administration and Human Rights: CILCIO PIRES DOS SANTOS.

Minister of Agriculture, Fisheries and Rural Development: FRANCISCO MARTINS DOS RAMOS.

Minister of the Presidency of the Council of Ministers, New Technologies and Parliamentary Affairs: WANDO BORGES CASTRO DE ANDRADE.

Minister of Planning, Finance and the Blue Economy: ENGRÁCIO DO SACRAMENTO SOARES DA GRAÇA.

Minister of Education and Higher Education: JULIETA IZIDRO RODRIGUES.

Minister of Tourism and Culture: AERTON DO ROSÁRIO CRISÓSTEMO.

Minister of Health: FILOMENA SANTANA MONTEIRO.

Minister of Labour, Solidarity, Families and Vocational Training: ADLANDER COSTA DE MATOS.

Minister of Youth, Sport and Entrepreneurship: VINICIUS XAVIER DE PINA.

Secretary of State for Social Communication: ADELINO LUCAS.

Secretary of State for Public Works, Environment: ERNESTINO JESUS DA COSTA GOMES.

Secretary of State for Trade and Industry: EUGÉNIO ANTÓNIO DA GRAÇA.

Government of the Autonomous Region of Príncipe
(October 2022)

President: FILIPE NASCIMENTO.

Regional Secretary for Finance and Administrative Modernization: Dr HÉLIO LAVRES.

Regional Secretary for the Environment and Energy Transition: ANA ALICE PINA.

Regional Secretary for Rural Development and Culture: FLASCOTER HUGO DE OLIVEIRA.

Regional Secretary for Social Affairs: HIGINO PEREIRA SANTIAGO.

MINISTRIES

Office of the President: Palácio Presidêncial, São Tomé; tel. 2223418; e-mail secretaria@presidencia.st; internet www.presidencia.st.

Office of the Prime Minister: Rua do Município, CP 302, São Tomé; tel. 2223913.

Ministry of Agriculture, Fisheries and Rural Development: São Tomé; internet dada.madr.gov.st.

Ministry of Defence and Internal Administration: Av. 12 de Julho, CP 427, São Tomé; tel. 2222041.

Ministry of Education and Higher Education: Rua Samora Machel, CP 41, São Tomé; tel. 2223366; internet www.mecc.gov.st.

Ministry of Foreign Affairs, Co-operation and Communities: Av. 12 de Julho, CP 111, São Tomé; tel. 2222309; e-mail info@mnec .gov.st; internet www.mnec.gov.st.

Ministry of Health: Rua Patrice Lumumba, CP 23, São Tomé; tel. 2226145; e-mail msaudestepgeral@gmail.com; internet fb.com/ MSaudeSTeP.

Ministry of Justice, Public Administration and Human Rights: Av. 12 de Julho, CP 4, São Tomé; tel. 2222256; internet www.justica.gov.st.

Ministry of Labour, Solidarity, Families and Vocational Training: São Tomé.

Ministry of Planning, Finance and the Blue Economy: Largo Alfândega, CP 168, São Tomé; tel. 2221083; internet www.financas .gov.st.

Ministry of the Presidency of the Council of Ministers and Parliamentary Affairs: São Tomé.

Ministry of Public Works, Infrastructure, Natural Resources and the Environment: Av. Marginal 12 de Julho, CP 130, São Tomé; tel. 2241750; e-mail mopirna17governo@gmail.com; internet fb.com/mirna.stp.

Ministry of Tourism, Culture, Commerce and Industry: São Tomé.

Ministry of Youth, Sport and Entrepreneurship: Av. Marginal 12 de Julho, CP 41, São Tomé; tel. 2224961; e-mail mjuventudeedesporto2016@gmail.com; internet fb.com/MJDESteP.

President

Presidential Election, First Round, 18 July 2021

Candidate	Valid votes	% of valid votes
Carlos Vila Nova	35,342	43.67
Guilherme Pósser da Costa	16,305	20.15
Delfim Santiago das Neves	14,941	18.46
Abel Bom Jesus	3,098	3.83
Maria das Neves	2,725	3.37
Others*	8,514	10.52
Total	80,925†	100.00

* There were 14 other candidates.
† Excluding 1,836 invalid votes and 650 blankvotes.

Presidential Election, Second Round, 5 September 2021

Candidate	Votes	% of votes
Carlos Vila Nova	45,534	57.55
Guilherme Pósser da Costa	33,585	42.45
Total	79,119*	100.00

* Excluding 1,158 invalid votes and 345 blank votes.

Legislature

National Assembly: Palácio dos Congressos, CP 181, São Tomé; tel. 2222986; e-mail ci@parlamento.st; internet www.parlamento.st.

President: DELFIM SANTIAGO DAS NEVES.

General Election, 25 September 2022

Party	Valid votes	% of valid votes	Seats
ADI	36,549	46.81	30
MLSTP—PSD	25,531	32.70	18
Movimento BASTA	6,874	8.80	2
MCI/PS-PUN	5,120	6.56	5
Others	4,011	5.14	—
Total	78,085*	100.00	55

* There were, in addition, 2,214 invalid votes and 675 blank votes.

Election Commission

Comissão Eleitoral Nacional (CEN): Av. Amílcar Cabral, CP 719, São Tomé; tel. 2225497; e-mail cen.geral@cen.st; internet www.cen .st; f. 1990; Pres. JOSÉ CARLOS BARREIROS MAQUENGO.

Political Organizations

Acção Democrática Independente (ADI): Av. Amílcar Cabral, São Tomé; tel. 2226566; internet fb.com/AccaoDemocratica Independente; f. 1992; Pres. PATRICE EMERY TROVOADA; Sec.-Gen. LEVY ESPÍRITO SANTO NAZARÉ.

Frente Democrata Cristã—Partido Social da Unidade (FDC—PSU): São Tomé; f. 1990; Pres. HAMILTON BARBOSA.

Movimento de Cidadãos Independentes/Partido Socialista (MCI/PS): São Tomé; f. 2018; established as Movimento de Cidadãos Independentes de São Tomé e Príncipe; present name adopted 2020; Pres. ANTÓNIO MONTEIRO.

Movimento de Libertação de São Tomé e Príncipe—Partido Social Democrata (MLSTP—PSD): Estrada Riboque, Edif. Sede do MLSTP, São Tomé; tel. 2221210; e-mail mlstppsd@cstome.net; internet fb.com/STP.MLSTP; f. 1972 as MLSTP; adopted present name in 1990; sole legal party 1972–90; Pres. JORGE BOM JESUS; Sec.-Gen. FILOMENA MONTEIRO.

Movimento Social Democrata—Partido Verde de São Tomé e Príncipe (MSD/PVSTP): Quinta de Santo António, São Tomé; tel. 9927271; e-mail geral@partidoverdestp.com; f. 2017; Pres. ELSA GARRIDO.

Movimento Socialista (MS): Pres. GILBERTO UMBELINA.

Partido de Convergência Democrática (PCD): Av. Marginal 12 de Julho, CP 519, São Tomé; tel. 2223257; f. 1990 as Partido de Convergência—Grupo de Reflexão; formed alliance with MDFM/PL to contest legislative elections during 2002–08; Pres. ARLINDO CARVALHO; Sec.-Gen. DELFIM SANTIAGO DAS NEVES.

Partido Força do Povo de São Tomé e Príncipe (PFPSTP): Rua Atanásio Gomes, São Tomé; tel. 9876969; f. 2019.

Partido de Todos os São-tomenses (PTS): São Tomé; f. 2019.

Partido Trabalhista Santomense (PTS): Bairro Quinta de Santo António, São Tomé; tel. 2223756; Leader ANACLETO EDMUNDO ROLIM; Sec.-Gen. MARIA TOMÉ BARROS DOS SANTOS VARELA.

Plataforma Nacional para o Desenvolvimento (PND): f. 2014; Leader ANTÓNIO QUINTAS AGUIAR; Sec.-Gen. LAILY GOMES PEREIRA.

União MDFM/UDD: São Tomé; f. 2018 following merger of Movimento Democrático Força da Mudança/Partido Liberal (f. 2001) and União dos Democratas para a Cidadania e Desenvolvimento (f. 2005 by breakaway group from ADI); Pres. CARLOS NEVES; Sec.-Gen. EUGÉNIO DA GRAÇA.

União para Mudança e Progresso do Príncipe (UMPP): Príncipe; internet fb.com/UMPP-União-para-Mudança-e -Progresso-do-Principe-130071637668843; Pres. FILIPE NASCIMENTO.

União Nacional para Democracia e Progresso (UNDP): São Tomé; f. 1998; Leader PAIXÃO LIMA.

Diplomatic Representation

EMBASSIES IN SÃO TOMÉ AND PRÍNCIPE

Angola: Av. Kwame Nkrumah 45, CP 133, São Tomé; tel. 2222376; e-mail benu25.nb@gmail.com; Ambassador JOAQUIM DUARTE POMBO.

Brazil: Av. Marginal 12 de Julho 20, CP 217, São Tomé; tel. 2226060; e-mail brasemb.saotome@itamaraty.gov.br; internet www.gov.br/ mre/pt-br/embaixada-sao-tome; Ambassador PEDRO LUIZ DALCERO (designate).

Cabo Verde: Rua Damão 10, CP 267, São Tomé; tel. 2222728; Ambassador JOSÉ MARIA SILVA.

China, People's Republic: Av. Kwame Nkrumah 24B, CP 176, São Tomé; tel. 2221798; e-mail sheng_pu@mfa.gov.cn; internet st .china-embassy.gov.cn; Ambassador XU YINGZHEN.

Equatorial Guinea: Av. Kwame Nkrumah, São Tomé; tel. 2225427; e-mail tctombada@yahoo.es; Ambassador PAULINO BOLOLO EKOBO.

Gabon: Rua Damão, CP 394, São Tomé; tel. 2224434; e-mail ambagabon@estome.net; Ambassador CORENTIN BERNARDIN MBOUROU HERVO AKENDENGUE.

India: Lote 41-B, 159 HF, Campo de Milho, São Tomé; tel. 2221184; e-mail admn.saotome@mea.gov.in; internet www.eoisaotome.gov.in; Ambassador RAGHU GURURAJ.

Nigeria: Av. Kwame Nkrumah, CP 1000, São Tomé; tel. 2225403; e-mail nigembstp@gmail.com; internet nigeriaembassysaotome.org; Ambassador (vacant).

Portugal: Av. Marginal 12 de Julho, CP 173, São Tomé; tel. 2221130; e-mail stome@mne.pt; internet saotome.embaixadaportugal.mne .gov.pt/pt; Ambassador RUI FERNANDO SUCENA DO CARMO.

South Africa: Campo de Milho, CP 555, São Tomé; tel. 2225733; e-mail saotome.dha@dirco.gov.za; Chargé d'affaires a.i. C. E. CASTLEMAN.

Judicial System

Judicial power is exercised by the Supreme Court of Justice and the Courts of Primary Instance. The Supreme Court is the ultimate judicial authority. The Constitutional Court rules on election matters. There is also an Audit Court and tribunals of first instance.

Supreme Court of Justice (Supremo Tribunal de Justiça): Av. Marginal de 12 de Julho, CP 04, São Tomé; tel. 2222615; internet www.stj.st; Pres. MANUEL SILVA GOMES CRAVID.

Constitutional Court (Tribunal Constitucional): Av. da Independência, São Tomé; e-mail 2226008; internet www .tribunalconstitucional.st; Pres. PASCOAL LIMA DOS SANTOS DAIO.

Audit Court (Tribunal de Contas): Praça da UCCLA, São Tomé; tel. 2242500; e-mail tribunal@tcontas.st; internet tcontas.st; Pres. JOSÉ ANTÓNIO MONTE CRISTO.

Attorney-General of the Republic: INALD KELVE NOBRE DE CARVALHO.

Religion

According to the 2012 census, almost three-quarters of the population were Christians, the majority of whom were Roman Catholics.

CHRISTIANITY

The Roman Catholic Church

São Tomé and Príncipe comprises a single diocese, directly responsible to the Holy See. The bishop participates in the Episcopal Conference of Angola and São Tomé (based in Luanda, Angola).

Bishop of São Tomé and Príncipe: Rt Rev. MANUEL ANTÓNIO MENDES DOS SANTOS, Centro Diocesano, CP 104, Rua P. Pinto da Rocha 1, São Tomé; tel. 2223455; e-mail diocese@cstome.net.

Other Churches

Igreja Adventista do 7° Dia (Seventh-Day Adventist Church): Rua Barão de Água Izé, São Tomé; tel. 2222270; e-mail sdastp@gmail .com; Pres. JOSÉ MARQUES.

Igreja Evangélica: Rua 3 de Fevereiro, São Tomé; tel. 2221350.

Igreja Evangélica Assembléia de Deus: Rua 3 de Fevereiro, São Tomé; tel. 2222442.

Igreja Maná: Av. Amílcar Cabral, São Tomé; tel. 2224654.

Igreja do Nazareno: Vila Dolores, São Tomé; tel. 2223943.

Igreja Nova Apostólica: CP 220, Vila Maria, São Tomé; tel. 2222797; e-mail j.cunha@ina-stp.org; internet fb.com/coroagostinho.

Igreja Universal do Reino de Deus: Travessa Imprensa, São Tomé; tel. 2224047.

The Press

Diário da República: Cooperativa de Artes Gráficas, Rua João Devs, CP 28, São Tomé; tel. 2222661; internet dre.pt/stp; f. 1975; official gazette; Dir OSCAR FERREIRA.

Jornal Kê-kuá: Vila Dolores 088, 265 São Tomé; tel. 2225814; weekly.

Jornal Transparência: Av. Marginal 12 de Julho, São Tomé; tel. 9936802; e-mail transparencia.st@hotmail.com; internet www .jornaltransparencia.st.

Jornal Tropical: Rua Padre Martinho Pinto da Rocha, São Tomé; tel. 9923140; e-mail jornaltropical05@hotmail.com; internet www .jornaltropical.st; Dir OCTÁVIO SOARES.

O Parvo: CP 535, São Tomé; tel. 2221031; f. 1994; weekly; Publr AMBRÓSIO QUARESMA; Editor ARMINDO CARDOSO.

Téla Nón: Largo Água Grande, Edif. Complexo Técnico da CST, São Tomé; tel. 9906263; e-mail contact@telanon.info; internet www .telanon.info; f. 2000; provides online daily news service; Chief Editor ABEL TAVARES DE VEIGA.

Online newspapers include **Duplo Insular** (duploinsular.info), **Jornal de São Tomé e Príncipe** (www.jornal.st), **Jornal Horizonte** (www.cstome.net/jhorizonte) and **Vitrina** (www.vitrina.st).

PRESS ASSOCIATIONS

Associação dos Jornalistas Santomenses (AJS): f. 2015; Pres. JUVENAL RODRIGUES.

Conselho Superior de Imprensa: Edifício Cinema Marcelo da Veiga, 1° piso, CP 1185, São Tomé; tel. 9060092; e-mail csimprensastp@hotmail.com; internet www.csi.st; Pres. JOSÉ CARLOS BARREIROS.

NEWS AGENCY

STP-Press: Av. Marginal de 12 de Julho, CP 12, São Tomé; tel. 2222087; e-mail info@stp-press.st; internet www.stp-press.st; f. 1985; Dir RICARDO NETO.

Broadcasting and Communications

TELECOMMUNICATIONS

Companhia Santomense de Telecomunicações, SARL (CST): Av. Marginal 12 de Julho, CP 141, São Tomé; tel. 2243900; e-mail geral@cst.st; internet cst.st; f. 1990; Pres. LUIZ HENRIQUE SOARES ROSA.

Unitel STP: Vila Maria, Edif. Equador 4 e 5, CP 85, São Tomé; tel. 9009500; e-mail apoio.cliente@unitel.st; internet www.unitel.st; f. 2014; Dir-Gen. SEGUNDO MANUEL LEMOS.

Regulatory Authority

Autoridade Geral de Regulação (AGER): Rua da Paz, CP 1047, São Tomé; tel. 2241500; internet www.ager-stp.org; f. 2005; also responsible for regulation of telecommunications, postal services, and water and electricity sectors; Pres. MARIA DA CONCEIÇÃO RAPOSO MENDES.

BROADCASTING

Radio

Rádio Jubilar: Av. Kwam Kruman-Edifício da Catequese, CP 104, São Tomé; tel. 2224930; internet www.rjemissora.caster.fm; f. 2005; operated by the Roman Catholic Church; Dir LEONEL PEREIRA.

Rádio Nacional de São Tomé e Príncipe: Av. Marginal de 12 de Julho, CP 44, São Tomé; tel. 2221342; e-mail atendimento@rnstp.st; internet www.rnstp.st; f. 1958; state-controlled; home service in Portuguese and Creole; Dir MANUEL BARROS.

Television

Televisão Santomense (TVS): Bairro Quinta de Santo António, CP 393, São Tomé; tel. 2221041; e-mail medeiros450@hotmail.com; internet tvs.st; state-controlled; Dir JOÃO BOUÇAS.

Finance

BANKING

Central Bank

Banco Central de São Tomé e Príncipe (BCSTP): Praça da Independência, Rua dos Martires da Liberdade, CP 13, São Tomé; tel. 2243700; e-mail bcstp@bcstp.st; internet www.bcstp.st; f. 1992 to succeed fmr Banco Nacional de São Tomé e Príncipe; bank of issue; Gov. AMÉRICO BARROS.

Commercial Banks

Afriland First Bank/STP: Av. Kwame Nkrumah, CP 202, São Tomé; tel. 2226749; internet www.afrilandfirstbankst.com; f. 2003; private bank; owned by Afriland First Bank, SA, Cameroon; Gen. Man. Dr ABUBAKAR MAYAKE.

Banco Internacional de São Tomé e Príncipe (BISTP) (International Bank of São Tomé and Príncipe): Praça da Independência 3, CP 536, São Tomé; tel. 2243105; e-mail sgeral@bistp.st; internet www.bistp.st; f. 1993; 48% govt-owned, 27% by Caixa Geral de Depósitos (Portugal), 25% by Banco Africano de Investimentos SARL (Angola); Pres. Dr NELSON LOMBÁ FERNANDES; CEO MIGUEL MALHEIRO REYMÃO.

BGFI Bank STP: Av. Marginal 12 de Julho, frente ao Museu Nacional, CP 744, São Tomé; tel. 2221603; e-mail bgfibankst@bgfi .com; internet sao.groupebgfibank.com; f. 2012; Gen. Man. Dr FELISBERTO CASTILHO.

Ecobank São Tomé: Edificio HB, Traversa de Pelorinho, CP 316, São Tomé; tel. 2222141; e-mail ecobankenquiries@ecobank.com; internet www.ecobank.com; f. 2007; Chair. CARLOS MANUEL VILA NOVA; Man. Dir DALTON COSTA DO ESPÍRITO SANTO GONÇALVES.

Energy Bank STP: 498 Rua da Guiné, CP 1175, São Tomé; tel. 2222689; e-mail info@energybanksaotome.com; internet www.energybanksaotome.com; f. 2008; established as Oceanic Bank STP; name changed as above in 2011; Chair. JIMOH IBRAHIM; Man. Dir and CEO KEHINDE OLATUNJI.

INSURANCE

NICON Seguros STP: Av. 12 de Julho 997, CP 556, São Tomé; tel. 2227057; e-mail info@niconseguros.st; internet niconseguros-stp.st; f. 2008; Dir ADESOLA MOROUNMUBO AHMED.

SAT INSURANCE: Av. Amílcar Cabral, CP 293, São Tomé; tel. 2226161; f. 2001; general insurance; Dir MÉDARD KENGNE KAMGA.

Trade and Industry

GOVERNMENT AGENCIES

Agência Nacional do Petróleo de São Tomé e Príncipe (ANP—STP): Bairro 3 de Fevereiro, Av. Nações Unidas, CP 1048, São Tomé; tel. 2243350; internet www.anp-stp.gov.st; f. 2004; manages and implements govt policies relating to the petroleum sector; Exec. Dir LUIZ MANUEL GAMBOA DA SILVA.

Agência de Promoção de Comercio e Investimento (APCI): Av. Marginal 12 de Julho, CP 168, São Tomé; tel. 2222642; e-mail apcistp@gmail.com; internet apcistp.com; Dir RAFAEL BRANCO.

Instituto de Inovação e Conhecimento (INIC): Rua Salustino da Graça, CP 302, São Tomé; tel. 2242650; e-mail inic@gov.st; internet fb.com/inicstp; f. 2008; Pres. CONSTÂNCIO ANDRADE.

Nigeria-São Tomé and Príncipe Joint Development Authority (JDA): 13 Audu Ogbe St, Abuja, Nigeria; Praça da UCCLA, São Tomé; tel. (234) 95241069; e-mail info@nstpjda.org; internet nstpjda.org; f. 2002; manages devt of petroleum and gas resources in Joint Development Zone; Exec. Dir ALMAJIRI GEIDAM.

CHAMBER OF COMMERCE

Câmara do Comércio, Indústria, Agricultura e Serviços (CCIAS): Av. Marginal de 12 de Julho, CP 527, São Tomé; tel. 2222723; e-mail cciasstp@gmail.com; internet ccias.st; Pres. JORGE CORREIA.

UTILITIES

Electricity and Water

Empresa de Agua e Electricidade (EMAE): Av. Água Grande, CP 46, São Tomé; tel. 2222096; e-mail geral@emae.st; internet www.emae.st; f. 1979; state electricity and water co; Dir-Gen. CELESTINO ANDRADE.

MAJOR COMPANIES

Agripalma: Av. Marginal 12 de Julho, São Tomé; tel. 2221551; internet www.socfin.com/en/locations/agripalma; f. ; palm oil producer, subsidiary of Luxembourg-based SOCFIN; Chair. LUC BOEDT; Dir-Gen. JOSÉ CORTEZ PEREIRA.

Diogo Vaz: Av. Marginal 12 de Julho, São Tomé; e-mail saotome_shop@diogovazchocolate.com; internet diogovazchocolate.com; f. ; cocoa plantation and chocolate factory; Dir-Gen. JEAN-RÉMY MARTIN.

Empresa Industrial de Madeiras (EIM): Fruta Fruta, CP 137, Água Grande; tel. 2222475; mfrs of wood products; Dir-Gen. HAMILTON CRUZ.

Empresa Nacional de Combustíveis e Óleos (ENCO): Rua da Guiné, CP 50, São Tomé; tel. 2241350; e-mail geral@enco.st; internet www.enco.st; Man. Dir MANUEL NAZARÉ AMADO.

Grupo HB: Praça da Independência, CP 15, São Tomé; tel. 22241100; e-mail comercial@grupohb.st; internet fb.com/grupohb; Dir JOÃO BRAGANÇA GOMES.

Rosema Brewery: Rua Cidade das Neves, CP 199, São Tomé; tel. 2243200; Dir-Gen. MÁRIO MELO XAVIER.

Sociedade Agrícola Santomense: Av. Marginal 12 de Julho, CP 678, São Tomé; tel. 2222336; e-mail ccoallo@cstome.net; coffee and cacao plantations, chocolate factory; Dir-Gen. CLAUDIO CORALLO.

Sociedade de Construção Civil, SA (CONSTROMÉ): Av. 12 de Julho, CP 551, São Tomé; tel. 2221775; construction.

TRADE UNIONS

Federação Nacional dos Pequenos Agricoltores (FENAPA): Rua Barão de Água Izé, São Tomé; tel. 2224741; Pres. COSME CABEÇA.

Organização Nacional de Trabalhadores de São Tomé e Príncipe (ONTSTP): Rua Cabo Verde, São Tomé; tel. 2222431; e-mail ontstpdis@cstome.net; Sec.-Gen. JOÃO TAVARES.

Sindicato de Jornalistas de São Tomé e Príncipe (SJS): Rua 3 de Fevereiro, São Tomé; Pres. HELDER BEXIGAS.

Sindicato dos Trabalhadores do Estado (STE): São Tomé; Sec.-Gen. AURÉLIO SILVA.

União Geral dos Trabalhadores de São Tomé e Príncipe (UGSTP): Av. Kwame Nkrumah, São Tomé; tel. 2222443; e-mail ugtdis@cstome.net; Sec.-Gen. COSTA CARLOS.

Transport

RAILWAYS

There are no railways in São Tomé and Príncipe.

ROADS

During 2005–14 the European Union (EU) granted €930,000 per year towards maintaining the road network. Part of the funding was used to pay 32 local Grupos de Interesse de Manutenção de Estradas (GIME), comprising a total of 1,600 people, to carry out basic maintenance and repair work. Although the EU road grants ceased in late 2014, the Government declared its intention independently to continue the road maintenance project.

SHIPPING

The principal ports are at São Tomé city and at Neves on São Tomé island. Plans were under way in early 2021 to construct a deep-water port at Fernão Dias, on the northern coast of São Tomé island.

Empresa Nacional de Administração dos Portos (ENAPORT): Largo Alfândega, CP 437, São Tomé; tel. 2221841; e-mail enaport@cstome.net; internet www.enaport.st; Pres. MANUEL DIOGO DO NASCIMENTO.

Instituto Marítimo Portuário de São Tomé e Príncipe (IMAP): Av. Marginal 12 de Julho, Largo das Alfândegas, São Tomé; tel. 2225688; e-mail imapstp@gmail.com; f. 2008; Dir-Gen. ALERES FRANK MENDES.

Navetur-Equatour: Rua Viriato da Cruz, CP 277, São Tomé; tel. 2223781; e-mail navetur@cstome.net; internet www.navetur-equatour.st; Dir-Gen. LUÍS BEIRÃO.

Transportes e Serviços, Lda (TURIMAR): Av. Marginal 12 de Julho, 2º Esq, CP 48, São Tomé; tel. 2221869; e-mail turimar@cstome.net; f. 1986; Man. LUÍS PEREIRA.

CIVIL AVIATION

There is an international airport at São Tomé. TAP Air Portugal and TAAG of Angola have local offices in São Tomé. In 2015 a new runway was brought into operation at Príncipe regional airport. Plans were under way in early 2021 to modernize and expand São Tomé international airport.

Empresa Nacional de Aeroportos e Segurança Aérea (ENASA): Aeroporto, CP 703, São Tomé; tel. 2221878; e-mail geral@enasa.st; Dir-Gen. GAUDÊNCIO COSTA.

Africa's Connection: Av. Marginal 12 de Julho, Chalet 6, São Tomé; tel. 2226983; e-mail reservations@africas-connection.com; internet africasconnection.net; offers scheduled and charter services; Flight Operations Man. Capt. FALKO HUB.

STP-Airways: Av. Marginal 12 de Julho, São Tomé; tel. 2221160; internet www.stpairways.st; f. 2006; 35% govt-owned; Dir FELISBERTO NETO.

Tourism

Direcção Geral de Turismo e Hotelaria: Av. Marginal 12 de Julho, CP 40, São Tomé; tel. 2221542; e-mail dturismostp@hotmail.com; internet fb.com/dgth.stp; Dir HUGO MENEZES.

Defence

In 2015 the armed forces were estimated to number some 800. Military service, which is compulsory, lasts for 30 months. There is also a presidential guard numbering some 160. In 2006 army recruitment was broadened to include women.

Defence Budget: 6,483m. dobras (excluding capital expenditure) in 2021.

Commander-in-Chief of the Armed Forces: CARLOS VILA NOVA.

Chief of Staff of the Armed Forces: Brig. IDALÉCIO CUSTÓDIO PACHIRE.

Army Commander: Col JOSÉ MARIA MENEZES.

Coastguard Commander: Capt. PEDRO AFONSO DE BARROS.

Education

Education is officially compulsory between six and 14 years of age. It starts at the age of six and lasts for six years, comprising a first cycle of four years and a second of two years. Secondary education lasts for a further six years, comprising two cycles of three years each. According to estimates by the United Nations Educational, Scientific and Cultural Organization (UNESCO), in 2015/16 enrolment at pre-primary level included 50% of children in the relevant age-group (males 48%; females 53%). In 2016/17 enrolment at primary schools included 93% of children in the relevant age-group (males 93%; females 93%), while the comparable ratio for secondary enrolment in 2014/15 was 65% (males 62%; females 69%). The country's first university, Universidade Lusíada, was inaugurated in 2006. In 2014 the Government transformed the Instituto Superior Politécnico and three other smaller institutions of higher education into the Universidade de São Tomé e Príncipe, the country's first public university. The budget for 2021 allocated 130,889m. dobras (excluding capital expenditure) to education, equivalent to 9.8% of total proposed current expenditure.

Bibliography

Bruzaca de Menezes, A. *Estado, Políticas Públicas e Desenvolvimento Cabo Verde e São Tomé e Príncipe*. Saarbrücken, Novas Edições Academicas, 2015.

Caldeira, A. M. *Mulheres, Sexualidade e Casamento no Arquipelago de São Tomé e Príncipe* (Seculos XV a XVII). Lisbon, Edições Cosmos, 1999.

    Viagens de um piloto português do século XVI à costa de África e á São Tomé. Lisbon, Comissão Nacional para as Comemorações dos Descobrimentos Portugueses, 2000.

Cardoso, M. *Cabo Verde e São Tomé e Príncipe. Educação e infra-estruturas como factores de desenvolvimento*. Oporto, Afrontamento, 2007.

Ceita, A. *Economia de S. Tomé e Príncipe. Entre o regime do partido único e o multipartidarismo*. Lisbon, Edições Colibri, 2008.

    S. Tomé e Príncipe. Problemas e Perspectivas para o seu Desenvolvimento. Lisbon, Edições Colibri, 2009.

    Cabo Verde e S. Tomé e Príncipe. Empresariado como Fator de Desenvolvimento e Transformação Social. Outros Olhares Sobre a Economia. Lisbon, Gradiva, 2013.

Chabal, P., Birmingham, D., Forrest, J., Newitt, M., Seibert, G., and Andrade, E. S. *History of Postcolonial Lusophone Africa*. Bloomington, IN, Indiana University Press, and London, Hurst, 2002.

Deus Lima, J. *História do Massacre de 1952 em São Tomé e Príncipe: Em Busca de Nossa Verdadeira História*. São Tomé, 2002.

Espírito Santo, C. *A Coroa do Mar*. Lisbon, Editorial Caminho, 1998.

    Enciclopédia Fundamental de São Tomé e Príncipe. Lisbon, Cooperação, 2001.

    A Guerra da Trindade. Lisbon, Cooperação, 2003.

    O Nacionalismo Político São-tomense. 2 vols. Lisbon, Edições Colibri, 2012.

    Alda Espírito Santos. Escritos. Lisbon, Edições Colibri, 2012.

    Mulheres Históricas de São Tomé e Príncipe. Lisbon, Edições Colibri, 2014.

    A Primeira República. Lisbon, Edições Colibri, 2015.

Forjaz, J. *Genealogias de São Tomé e Príncipe: Subsídios*. Lisbon, Dislivro Histórica, 2011.

Francisco, A., and Agostinho, N. *Exorcising Devils from the Throne. São Tomé and Príncipe in the Chaos of Democratization*. New York, Algora Publishing, 2011.

Gallet, D. *São Tomé et Príncipe: Les îles du milieu du monde*. Paris, Editions Karthala, 2001.

Graça, C. *Memórias Políticas de um Nacionalista Santomense Sui Generis*. São Tomé, UNEAS, 2011.

Guedes, A. M. *Litígios e Legitimação: Estado, Sociedade Civil e Direito em São Tomé e Príncipe*. Coimbra, Almedina, 2002.

Henriques, I. C. *São Tomé e Príncipe: A Invenção de uma Sociedade*. Lisbon, Vega Editora, 2000.

Higgs, C. *Chocolate Islands: Cocoa, Slavery and Colonial Africa*. Athens, OH, Ohio University Press, 2012.

Hodges, T., and Newitt, M. *São Tomé and Príncipe: From Plantation Colony to Microstate*. Boulder, CO, Westview Press, 1988.

Loude, J.-Y. *Coup de théâtre à São Tomé. Carnet d'énquête aux îles du milieu du monde*. Arles, Actes Sud, 2007.

Loureiro, J. *Postais Antigos de S. Tomé e Príncipe*. Lisbon, MaisImagem, 1999.

Mata, I. *Polifonias Insulares. Cultura e Literaturas de São Tomé e Príncipe*. Lisbon, Edições Colibri, 2010.

    Olhares Cruzados sobre a Economia de São Tomé e Príncipe. Lisbon, Edições Colibri, 2013

Mata, I., and Rodrigues da Silva, A. (Eds). *Trajetórias Culturais e Literárias das Ilhas do Equador: Estudos Sobre São Tomé e Príncipe*. Campinas, Pontes Editores, 2018.

Morais, J. S., and Malheiro, J. B. *São Tomé e Príncipe: As Cidades; Património Arquitetónico / The Cities; Architectural Heritage*. Casal de Cambra, Caleidoscópio, 2013.

Nascimento, A. *Poderes e Quotidiano nas Roças de São Tomé e Príncipe de finais de oitocentos a meados do novecentos*. Lisbon, 2002.

    Órfãos de Raça: Europeus Entre a Fortuna e a Desventura no São Tomé e Príncipe Colonial. São Tomé, Instituto Camões—Centro Cultural Português, 2002.

    O Sul da Diaspora: Cabo-Verdianos em Plantações de São Tomé e Príncipe e Moçambique. Praia, Presidência da República da Cabo Verde, 2003.

    Vidas de São Tomé segundo vozes de Soncente. Mindelo, Ilhéu Editora, 2008.

    São Tomé e Príncipe. Atlas da Lusofonia. Lisbon, Prefácio, 2008.

    Histórias da Ilha do Príncipe. Oeiras, Município de Oeiras, 2010.

Pape, D., and Andrade, R. R. de. *As roças de São Tomé e Príncipe*. Lisbon, Tinta-da-China, 2013.

Pereira, P. A. *Das Tchiloli von São Tomé: Die Wege des karolinischen Universums*. Frankfurt am Main, Iko Verlkag, 2002.

Pinto da Costa, M. *Terra Firme*. Porto, Afrontamento, 2011.

Ramos, J. *Quem é Quem em São Tomé e Príncipe. Who's Who*. 3rd edn. São Tomé, 2007.

Ratelband, K. *Nederlanders in West-Afrika 1600–1650: Angola, Kongo en São Tomé*. Walburg Pers, Zutphen, 2000.

Ribeiro, M. C., and Jorge, S. R. *Literaturas Insulares: Leituras e Escritas: Cabo Verde e S. Tomé e Príncipe*. Porto, Portugal, Edições Afrontamento, 2011.

Seibert, G. *Comrades, Clients and Cousins: Colonialism and Democratization in São Tomé and Príncipe*. 2nd edn. Leiden, Brill Academic Publishers, 2006.

Serafim, C. M. S. *As Ilhas de São Tomé no século XVII*. Centro de História de Além-mar, Universidade Nova de Lisboa, 2000.

Silva, O. *São Tomé et Príncipe: Ecos da Terra do Ossobó*. Lisbon, Colibri, 2004.

de Sousa Campos, F. R. *As Relações entre Portugal e São Tomé e Príncipe. Do Passado Colonial à Lusofonia*. Lisbon, Edições Colibri, 2011.

Tournadre, M. *São Tomé et Príncipe*. Aurillac, Editions Regads, 2000.

SENEGAL

Physical and Social Geography

R. J. HARRISON CHURCH

The Republic of Senegal, the most westerly state of mainland Africa, covers an area of 196,712 sq km (75,951 sq miles). The *de jure* population was 13,508,715, according to the census of November 2013, giving a population density of 76.1 per sq km. According to United Nations (UN) projections, by mid-2022 the population had risen to 17,738,795 (with a density of 90.2 per sq km). According to the 2013 census, the capital, Dakar, had a population of 1,146,053, while Pikine, near Dakar, had a population of 1,170,791. Other large cities included Rufisque (490,694) and Guediawaye (also near Dakar) 329,659. The population of Dakar (and its suburbs) was projected to have reached 3,229,800 by mid-2021, according to UN estimates. In July 2005 legislation was approved providing for the creation of a new administrative capital, near Kébémer, on the Atlantic littoral.

French is the official language, although use of Arabic has increased since the 1980s; the most widely spoken national languages at the time of the 2002 census were Wolof, Pulaar and Sérère. According to the 2002 census, almost 94% of the population were Muslims, and some 4% were Christians, mostly Roman Catholics; a small number followed traditional beliefs.

Senegal's southern border is with Guinea-Bissau, to the west, and with Guinea on the northern edge of the Primary sandstone outcrop of the Fouta Djallon. In the east the border is with Mali, in the only other area of bold relief in Senegal, where there are Pre-Cambrian rocks in the Bambouk mountains. The northern border with Mauritania lies along the Senegal river, navigable for small boats all year to Podor and for three months to Kayes (Mali). The river has a wide flood plain, annually cultivated as the waters retreat.

The Gambia forms a semi-enclave between part of southern Senegal and the sea, along the valley of the navigable Gambia river. This has meant that, since the colonial delimitation of the Gambia–Senegal borders in 1889, the river has played no positive role in Senegal's development and that the Casamance region, in the south, was isolated from the rest of Senegal until the opening of the Trans-Gambian Highway in 1958.

Apart from the high eastern and south-eastern borderlands most of the country has monotonous plains, which in an earlier period were drained by large rivers in the centre of the country. Relic valleys, now devoid of superficial water, occur in the Ferlo desert, and these built up the Sine Saloum delta north of The Gambia. In a later dry period north-east to south-west extensive sand dunes were formed, giving Senegal's plains their undulating and ribbed surfaces. These plains of Cayor, Baol and Nioro du Rip are inhabited by Wolof and Serer cultivators of groundnuts and millet. The coast between Saint-Louis and Dakar has a broad belt of live dunes. Behind them, near Thiès, calcium phosphates are quarried (aluminium phosphates are also present) and phosphatic fertilizer is produced.

Although Senegal's mineral resources are otherwise relatively sparse, there are potentially valuable reserves of gold, in the south-east, as well as deposits of high-grade iron ore, in considerable quantity, in the east. Reserves of natural gas are exploited offshore from Dakar, and there is petroleum off the Casamance coast.

Senegal's climate is widely varied, and the coast is remarkably cool for the latitude. The Cap Vert peninsula is particularly breezy, because it projects into the path of northerly marine trade winds. Average temperatures are in the range 18°C–31°C, and the rainy season is little more than three months in length. Inland, both temperatures and rainfall are higher, and the rainy season in comparable latitudes is somewhat longer. Casamance lies on the northern fringe of the monsoonal climate. Thus Ziguinchor has four to five months' rainy season, with average annual rainfall of 1,626 mm, nearly three times that received by Dakar. The natural vegetation ranges from Sahel savannah north of about 15° N, through Sudan savannah in south-central Senegal, to Guinea savannah in Casamance, where the oil palm is common.

History

KATHARINE MURISON

Revised for this edition by MARIE GIBERT

Following three centuries of French rule, Senegal became a self-governing member of the French Community in 1958. The Mali Federation, linking Senegal with Soudan (now Mali), was formed in April 1959 and became independent in June 1960, but collapsed two months later, when Senegal seceded. The Republic of Senegal was proclaimed on 5 September, with Léopold Sédar Senghor, the founder of the Union Progressiste Sénégalaise (UPS), as its first President. After his Prime Minister, Mamadou Dia, was convicted of plotting a coup, Senghor assumed the premiership himself in late 1962. A new Constitution, strengthening the powers of the President, was approved in a referendum in March 1963. In December the UPS won victory in elections to the Assemblée Nationale (National Assembly), and other parties were either outlawed or absorbed into the UPS, which by 1966 was the sole legal party.

In 1970 the office of Prime Minister was revived and assigned to a provincial administrator, Abdou Diouf. In 1976 Senghor announced the creation of a three-party system, comprising the UPS (later renamed the Parti Socialiste du Sénégal, PS), the Parti Démocratique Sénégalais (PDS) and a Marxist-Leninist party. At elections in February 1978 the PS won 83 of the 100 seats in the National Assembly, while Senghor defeated the PDS leader, Abdoulaye Wade, in the presidential election.

DIOUF'S PRESIDENCY, 1981–2000

Senghor resigned in December 1980 in favour of Diouf, who assumed the presidency in January 1981 and undertook to remove restrictions on political activity. Diouf retained the presidency at elections in February 1983, receiving 83.5% of the votes cast (to Wade's 14.8%), and the PS secured 111 of the 120 seats in the enlarged National Assembly. Diouf was re-elected as President in February 1988, securing 73.2% of the votes cast (to Wade's 25.8%), while the PS returned 103 deputies to the National Assembly and the PDS 17 in the legislative polls.

In September 1991 the National Assembly adopted amendments to the electoral code: the presidential election would, henceforth, take place every seven years, in two rounds if necessary, and an individual would be limited to a maximum of two terms of office.

Diouf was re-elected at the presidential election of February 1993, with 58.4% of the votes cast, while Wade secured 32.0%. The PS won 84 seats at elections to the National Assembly in May and the PDS 27. Shortly after the announcement of the results the Vice-President of the Constitutional Council, Babacar Sèye, was assassinated. Samuel Sarr, a close associate of Wade, a PDS deputy, Mody Sy, and two others were arrested in May on suspicion of involvement in Sèye's murder. In October Wade was charged with complicity in the assassination, and Wade's wife and a PDS deputy, Ousmane Ngom, were charged with complicity in a breach of state security, although none was detained. In November Ngom and Landing Savané, the leader of And Jëf—Parti Africain pour la Démocratie et le Socialisme (AJ—PADS), were among those arrested following a protest in Dakar. Ngom, Savané and more than 80 others were convicted of participating in an unauthorized demonstration and received six-month suspended prison sentences.

Diouf was regarded as a principal architect of the 50% devaluation, in January 1994, of the CFA franc, and the opposition accused the President of responsibility for resultant hardships. A demonstration in Dakar in February degenerated into serious rioting, as a result of which eight people were killed. Wade and Savané were among those charged with attacks on state security, but legal proceedings against them and 140 others implicated in the unrest were later dismissed. Charges against Wade and his associates in connection with Sèye's murder were also dismissed, and in October three people were convicted of the killing and sentenced to between 18 and 20 years' imprisonment, with hard labour. In March 1995 a newly appointed Council of Ministers included five PDS members, with Wade designated Minister of State at the Presidency.

In March 1998 the National Assembly voted to increase the number of deputies from 120 members to 140, despite opposition from the PDS, which withdrew from the Government. At legislative elections held in May the PS took 93 seats in the enlarged parliament and the PDS 23. The rate of voter participation was only 39%. Ngom resigned from the PDS in June 1998, and subsequently formed the Parti Libéral Sénégalais (PLS). In July Habib Thiam resigned as Prime Minister; he was replaced by Mamadou Lamine Loum, the Minister of the Economy, Finance and Planning.

In August 1998 the National Assembly voted to revise the Constitution to remove the clause restricting the President to a maximum of two terms of office and the requirement that a President be elected by more than 25% of all registered voters.

The PS won all 45 seats contested in indirect elections to a new, 60-member second legislative chamber, the Sénat (Senate), in January 1999; these 45 senators were elected by members of the National Assembly, together with local, municipal and regional councillors. In addition, 12 senators, including two opposition leaders, were chosen by President Diouf, and three were elected by Senegalese resident abroad. Only the PS, the PLS and a coalition of the Marxist-Leninist Parti de l'Indépendance et du Travail (PIT) and AJ—PADS participated in the elections. The main opposition parties described the new chamber as unnecessary and costly.

WADE'S PRESIDENCY, 2000–12

In the presidential election held on 27 February 2000, the three most successful candidates were Diouf with 41.3%, Wade with 31.0% and Moustapha Niasse, a former Minister of Foreign Affairs and Senegalese Abroad, with 16.8%. Wade had been nominated by a left-wing alliance of AJ—PADS, the PIT, the PDS and the Ligue Démocratique—Mouvement pour le Parti du Travail (LD—MPT), while Niasse, a founder member of the PS, had formed his own party, the Alliance des Forces de Progrès (AFP), prior to the election. Overall turnout was estimated at 61.0%. At the second round of voting on 19 March, Wade defeated Diouf, winning 58.5% of the vote. Turnout was estimated at 60.1%. Wade's Government included Niasse as Prime Minister. However, with the PS remaining the largest party in the legislature, an institutional crisis remained

possible. Wade therefore planned to call new legislative elections in 2001, after a constitutional referendum.

Approval of a New Constitution

The draft Constitution included the following revisions: a reduction in the presidential term of office from seven to five years; a transfer of some powers from the President to the Prime Minister; the abolition of the Senate; a reduction in the number of National Assembly seats (from 140 to 120); and the reintroduction of the requirement that a President be elected by more than 25% of all registered voters. At a national referendum on 7 January 2001, 94.0% of those voting (65.8% of the registered electorate) supported the changes.

In March 2001 Wade dismissed the AFP ministers from the Government. The non-partisan Mame Madior Boye, hitherto Minister of Justice, was appointed as Prime Minister. In the general election of 29 April the PDS-led Sopi (Change) Coalition won 89 of the 120 seats contested. The AFP and the PS won 11 and 10 seats, respectively. Turnout was 67.5%. Boye was reappointed as Prime Minister, leading a Government comprising 11 members of the PDS, nine representatives of civil society, and two members each of AJ—PADS and the LD—MPT.

The sinking of a state-owned passenger ferry, the MV *Joola*, in September 2002, en route from Ziguinchor, the principal city of Casamance, to Dakar, led to a political crisis, even before it was confirmed that 1,863 people had died. In October the Minister of Capital Works and Transport and the Minister of the Armed Forces resigned, as it became clear that the vessel had been severely overloaded (only 64 survivors were reported), and the head of the navy was dismissed. In November Wade dismissed Boye's Government. An inquiry found that safety regulations aboard had been violated, and that the dispatch of rescue equipment and staff by the armed forces had been delayed. Idrissa Seck, an ally of Wade, was appointed as the new Prime Minister. In August 2003 both the Chief of Staff of the Armed Forces and the Chief of Staff of the Air Force were dismissed as a result of the inadequate response to the disaster.

Wade dismissed Seck's Government in April 2004, appointing Macky Sall, hitherto Minister of State, Minister of the Interior and Local Communities, Government Spokesperson, as the new premier. The two LD—MPT members of the Council of Ministers were dismissed in March 2005, following the party's criticism of Wade's presidency. In August the National Assembly ruled that Seck, who had been accused by Wade of overspending on infrastructural works in Thiès (where Seck served as mayor), and the Minister of Property, Housing and Construction, Salif Bâ, should be tried on embezzlement charges. Bâ resigned from the Council of Ministers, while Seck was expelled from the PDS. Seck was released from prison in February 2006, after the charges were partly dismissed, and he formed a new party, Rewmi (Nation), in September. Bâ had been provisionally freed in January for health reasons. (The charges against Bâ were reportedly dismissed in January 2008.)

In December 2005 the National Assembly approved the extension of deputies' mandates until February 2007, to allow legislative and presidential elections to be held concurrently. In November 2006 the Assembly adopted a constitutional amendment abolishing the requirement that in order to be elected at a first round of voting presidential candidates receiving a majority of electoral votes should additionally secure the support of at least 25% of all registered voters. A few days later the legislature approved an increase in the number of deputies from 120 to 150. The legislative elections were further postponed in January 2007, until 3 June. In late January the National Assembly approved the re-establishment of the Senate; 65 of its 100 members were to be appointed by the President.

Presidential and Legislative Elections of 2007

The presidential election of 25 February 2007 was contested by 15 candidates and marked by a high turnout of 70.6%. Wade was re-elected with 55.9% of the valid votes. His closest rivals were Seck, with 14.9%, Ousmane Tanor Dieng, the First Secretary of the PS, with 13.6%, and the AFP's Niasse, with 5.9%. Wade was sworn in for a second term on 3 April.

The principal opposition parties boycotted the legislative elections. The PDS-led Sopi Coalition consequently secured 131 of the 150 seats in the National Assembly on 3 June 2007. None of the 12 other parties and coalitions that secured legislative representation took more than three seats. The lack of effective opposition and the extremely low turnout, of 34.7%, threatened to undermine the legitimacy of the new legislature. Cheikh Hadjibou Soumaré, who was not affiliated to any political party, was appointed as Prime Minister. Former premier Macky Sall was subsequently elected as President of the National Assembly.

Deputies and local, municipal and regional councillors elected 35 of the 100 members of the Senate on 19 August 2007. The polls were boycotted by the main opposition parties. The PDS secured 34 of the elective seats, while AJ—PADS took one. The Senate was installed in September, following Wade's nomination of the remaining 65 senators. In October Pape Diop, mayor of Dakar since 2002, was elected as the President of the Senate.

Wade's Second Term

In October 2008 Wade promulgated a constitutional amendment extending the presidential term of office from five years to seven (with effect from the next election). Opposition parties had denounced the revision, insisting that it should be subject to a popular referendum. A reduction in the mandates of the Presidents of the National Assembly and the Senate from five years to a renewable term of one year (which was to be applied to the incumbents) was also approved in a vote that was boycotted by opposition legislators and supporters of Macky Sall, who believed that the amendment was intended to marginalize the former Prime Minister. In the following month the National Assembly voted to remove Sall from his post. Sall resigned from the PDS and subsequently formed the Alliance pour la République (APR)—Yakaar (Hope). Mamadou Seck, a former minister reported to be close to Wade, was elected as the new President of the National Assembly.

The opposition performed well at local elections on 22 March 2009, gaining control of Dakar and several other major towns, while Sall was re-elected as mayor of Fatick. None the less, Wade's son, Karim, was elected to public office for the first time, winning a seat on the municipal council of Dakar. In April Soumaré was replaced as Prime Minister by Souleymane Ndéné Ndiaye, hitherto Minister of State, Minister of the Maritime Economy, Maritime Transport, Fisheries and Fishbreeding. Karim Wade was included in the new Council of Ministers. In May the legislature adopted a constitutional amendment providing for the creation of the post of Vice-President, to be appointed by the President.

In September 2009 President Wade declared his intention to seek a third term in office at the presidential election due in 2012. Although the 2001 Constitution had imposed a two-term limit, the PDS maintained that, as Wade had first been elected in 2000, under the previous Constitution (from which a clause restricting the President to a maximum of two terms of office had been removed in 1998), he was entitled to stand for a further presidential mandate. In November 2010 the management committee of the PDS endorsed Wade's candidacy for the presidential election scheduled for 26 February 2012. Former Prime Minister Idrissa Seck, who had rejoined the PDS in 2009, was one of three members of the committee to dissent and was expelled from the party in April 2011.

Two draft constitutional amendments creating an elected post of Vice-President and lowering the threshold required for an outright victory in the first round of a presidential election from 50% to 25% were withdrawn in June 2011, following violent protests outside the National Assembly. An opposition rally to protest against Wade's re-election bid took place in July, on the same day as a pro-Government demonstration. Wade was unanimously nominated as the PDS presidential candidate at a party conference in December 2011. His inclusion among the 14 presidential candidates approved by the Constitutional Council in January 2012 prompted further violent unrest in Dakar and elsewhere.

SALL'S PRESIDENCY, 2012–

Wade won the largest share of the valid votes cast at the first round of the presidential election on 26 February 2012, with 34.8%, followed by Macky Sall, representing the APR, who secured 26.6%, Moustapha Niasse (13.2%), Ousmane Tanor Dieng (11.3%) and Idrissa Seck (7.9%). A turnout of 51.6% was recorded. At a second round of polling on 25 March, Sall, having secured the support of the other main opposition candidates, defeated Wade, taking 65.8% of the valid votes cast. The turnout at the run-off vote was 55.0%.

Sall was inaugurated as President on 2 April 2012. Although elected to serve a seven-year term, he pledged to reduce the presidential term of office to five years and to maintain the two-term limit. He also promised to focus on poverty alleviation, vowing to lower the prices of basic goods by cutting public expenditure through measures such as halving the size of the Government and reducing Senegal's diplomatic representation. Sall appointed Abdoul Mbaye, a former banker without political affiliation, as his Prime Minister. The new Council of Ministers comprised 25 members, compared with 40 in the outgoing administration.

At elections to the National Assembly on 1 July 2012, a coalition of some 12 parties supporting President Sall, Benno Bokk Yaakaar (BBY—United in Hope), won 119 of the 150 seats; the PDS took 12 seats. The turnout was low, at 36.7%. Former Prime Minister Niasse was elected as President of the National Assembly. In September 2012, in order to reduce costs, the legislature voted to abolish the Senate (and the position of Vice-President of the Republic). Mbaye's Council of Ministers was expanded to 30 members in October.

In April 2013 Karim Wade was arrested and charged with illegal enrichment while serving as a government minister. A few days later a demonstration organized by the PDS in Dakar to demand Wade's release was attended by at least 2,500 people.

Sall dismissed Mbaye in September 2013, replacing him as Prime Minister with the hitherto Minister of Justice, Keeper of the Seals, Aminata Touré. A new, 32-member Government was installed.

In February 2014 a Commission Nationale pour la Réforme des Institutions (CNRI), which had been established by Sall to propose institutional reforms, presented its report, following nationwide public consultations. Proposals included requiring the President to stand down from the leadership of a political party following an election; limiting the President's capacity to dissolve the legislature; reducing the duration of the presidential mandate from seven to five years; and forbidding direct family members from succeeding an incumbent President.

A poor performance by Sall's APR at local elections on 29 June 2014 was attributed to voter dissatisfaction with the Government's economic achievements and led first to the resignation of the Minister of Communication and the Digital Economy and, in early July, to the dismissal of Prime Minister Touré, after they were defeated in polling in Saint-Louis and in Grand-Yoff (a suburb of Dakar), respectively. The BBY coalition had notably contested the elections divided, with the APR fielding separate lists of candidates in many towns and departments. Mahammed Boun Abdallah Dionne, hitherto in charge of implementing the Government's development plan (Plan Sénégal Emergent), replaced Touré as Prime Minister.

In March 2015 Karim Wade was convicted by the state anticorruption court, the Cour de Répression de l'Enrichissement Illicite, of illegal enrichment amounting to 69,119m. francs CFA and sentenced to six years' imprisonment and a fine of 138,000m. francs CFA. Seven co-defendants (four of whom were tried *in absentia*) were also found guilty. Two days earlier a PDS congress had selected Karim Wade as the party's presidential candidate at the next election in a move that reinforced divisions within the party between those loyal to Abdoulaye Wade, who remained PDS Secretary-General, and reformist members, who favoured a change in the party leadership. In June the working group on arbitrary detention of the Office of the United Nations (UN) High Commissioner for Human Rights opined that Karim Wade's detention was arbitrary, requesting that the Senegalese Government remedy the situation and provide compensation to Wade. The Government rejected UN interference in a domestic judicial matter. Wade's appeal against his conviction was rejected by the Supreme Court in August.

Constitutional Reform

In March 2015 President Sall announced plans to organize a referendum in 2016 on amending the Constitution to reduce the presidential mandate from seven to five years. The revision would apply retroactively to Sall's current term of office. In January 2016 the Government submitted 15 draft constitutional amendments to the Constitutional Council for its consideration. In addition to the reduction of the presidential mandate from seven to five years (renewable once), proposed changes included the imposition of an age limit of 75 years for presidential candidates; the strengthening of the rights of the opposition and the leader of the opposition; the expansion of the powers of the National Assembly and the Constitutional Council; and the creation of a High Council of Territorial Collectivities. In February Sall announced that he would complete his current seven-year term of office, on the advice of the Constitutional Council. At a referendum on 20 March, the introduction of a five-year presidential term from the 2019 election, as well as the other draft amendments to the Constitution, were approved by 62.7% of those who voted, although only 38.3% of the electorate participated.

A national dialogue was convened by President Sall in May 2016 and attended by religious leaders, representatives of civil society, trade unionists and politicians. Several opposition parties boycotted the forum, although the PDS agreed to participate. At the end of May the three men convicted alongside Karim Wade in March 2015 were freed from prison, and Wade was released in June 2016, after receiving a presidential pardon; he immediately left the country for Qatar.

Indirect elections in which departmental and municipal councillors voted to fill 80 of the 150 seats in the newly created High Council of Territorial Collectivities took place in September 2016, with the remaining 70 members to be appointed by the President.

In January 2017 the National Assembly approved an expansion in its members to 165, with the creation of 15 seats in eight new electoral regions for representatives of the diaspora. The new deputies would be required to return to Senegal to serve their five-year terms. Opposition deputies either abstained or voted against the measure, considering it unnecessary.

The mayor of Dakar, Khalifa Sall (a PS dissident), was arrested in March 2017, charged with fraud, corruption, criminal conspiracy and money laundering. Considered a potential presidential candidate, Khalifa Sall denied the charges, which he claimed were politically motivated. Anti-Government protests demanding his release took place in April and May.

The 2017 Legislative Elections

Legislative elections held on 30 July 2017 were contested by a record 47 lists or parties (compared with 24 in 2012). The BBY coalition of parties supportive of President Sall, led by Prime Minister Mahammed Dionne, secured a substantial majority, winning 125 of the 165 seats in the enlarged National Assembly. The Coalition Gagnante/Manko Wattu Sénégal (Winning Coalition), led by former President Abdoulaye Wade, who had returned from France (where he had been residing since his 2012 presidential election defeat), took 19 seats, while Manko Taxawu Sénégal (Coalition for the Revival of Senegal), an opposition coalition headed by Khalifa Sall, who remained in detention, secured seven; 11 other parties or groups also obtained legislative representation. Turnout was recorded at 53.7%. Wade subsequently announced that his coalition would not participate in any future elections organized by Sall's administration, denouncing the July polls as a 'masquerade', and resigned as a deputy shortly before the newly elected National Assembly convened in mid-September.

A new Government, again headed by Dionne, was formed in early September 2017; the post of Minister of Petroleum and Energy was created to oversee the development of recently discovered offshore reserves of petroleum and natural gas.

In November 2017 the Assembly voted to remove the immunity from prosecution of Khalifa Sall, who had been elected to the legislature in July. He was sentenced to five years' imprisonment and fined 5m. francs CFA in March 2018, having been convicted of the fraudulent use of public funds and forgery. Two

co-defendants also received five-year prison terms. Khalifa Sall appealed against his conviction, while his supporters continued to accuse President Macky Sall of orchestrating the legal proceedings in order to remove a rival from the 2019 presidential election.

The 2019 Presidential Election

In April 2018 the National Assembly approved a constitutional law on the sponsorship of candidates for elections, which required potential presidential contenders to collect the signatures of a minimum of 0.8% of registered voters (some 52,000 signatures), gathered in at least seven of the country's 14 regions, before being validated as candidates. The opposition claimed that the legislation was undemocratic and anti-constitutional, and protests were held in Dakar and elsewhere. Nevertheless, amendments to the electoral code were approved by the National Assembly in June.

The Court of Justice of the Economic Community of West African States (ECOWAS) ruled in June 2018 that Khalifa Sall's detention was arbitrary and that the right to presumption of innocence and to legal assistance had been infringed. None the less, the Court of Appeal upheld Sall's sentence in August, and he was removed from the mayorship of Dakar. In July it was confirmed that the electoral code precluded Karim Wade's inclusion on the register of voters (a requirement for presidential candidates) as he had been sentenced to more than five years in prison. Police fired tear gas to disperse an opposition rally held in Dakar in September to protest against the anticipated exclusion of Sall and Wade from the presidential election and to demand that an independent authority organize the poll instead of the Ministry of the Interior.

In December 2018 President Macky Sall confirmed that he would seek re-election. Although 87 people had initially sought to stand, in January 2019 only five presidential candidates were approved by the Constitutional Council, which had rejected the candidacies of Karim Wade and Khalifa Sall. The police blocked a planned opposition march against the Council's ruling. Tensions increased, and at least two people died in the eastern town of Tambacounda in February in clashes between rival supporters. Meanwhile, Abdoulaye Wade returned to Senegal, as he had done before the 2017 legislative elections, calling for the cancellation of the ballot and later urging 'peaceful resistance'.

Macky Sall won the presidential election in a first round of voting on 24 February 2019, securing 58.3% of the votes, while Idrissa Seck, who had been endorsed by Khalifa Sall, was placed second, with 20.5%; Ousmane Sonko (the leader of PASTEF—Les Patriotes) took 15.7% of the votes. Turnout was 66.3%. The four defeated candidates rejected the results, but they were confirmed by the Constitutional Council in March.

Sall's Second Term

President Sall was inaugurated for a second term on 2 April 2019. During his campaign he had pledged to continue implementing his Plan Sénégal Emergent, a long-term project aimed at boosting economic growth through the development of infrastructure. Mahammed Dionne was reappointed as Prime Minister, heading a 32-member Government, dominated by the APR. Dionne unexpectedly announced plans for constitutional revisions that included the establishment of a more presidential system of government, and the abolition of the post of Prime Minister. The changes, which were intended to accelerate the reform process, given the reduction in the presidential term to five years, were adopted by the National Assembly in May. As Minister of State, Secretary-General at the Presidency of the Republic, Dionne remained the most senior minister in Sall's administration.

A national dialogue was announced by President Sall in May 2019, in the presence of religious leaders, politicians and representatives of civil society. Defeated presidential contenders Ousmane Sonko and Idrissa Seck declined to participate in its launch, and Abdoulaye Wade ordered members of the PDS to boycott the event, but Oumar Sarr, the Deputy Secretary-General of the party, attended. Oumar Sarr was removed from his PDS post in August, amid continued internal divisions, with some members accusing Karim Wade (who remained exiled in Qatar) of seeking to take control of the party. The PDS dissidents subsequently created their own faction within the party, Suxxali Sopi. The steering committee of the national dialogue was installed in December and commenced work in the following month. As before, Ousmane Sonko, Idrissa Seck and the PDS were absent from proceedings, although Babacar Gaye of Suxxali Sopi was present.

A report by the British Broadcasting Corporation published in early June 2019 alleged that a company run by the President's brother, Aliou Sall, had received an undisclosed payment of US $250,000 in 2014 from an energy company, Timis Corporation, which had subsequently sold its stakes in two natural gas blocks off the Senegalese coast to UK-based multinational BP. The President and his brother denied any wrongdoing, and BP rejected any suggestion that it had acted improperly. Amid public discontent, an inquiry into the corruption claims was initiated by the Prosecutor-General of the Court of Appeal of Dakar, at the Government's request. In mid-June riot police fired tear gas and detained more than 20 people at a protest in the capital organized by opposition and civil society groups critical of the hydrocarbons contracts negotiated by the Government with foreign companies. A demonstration a week later was attended by thousands of people demanding the renegotiation of these contracts. In late June, while continuing to reject the bribery accusations, Aliou Sall resigned from his government post as head of the Caisse des Dépôts et Consignations (although he remained mayor of Guédiawaye). The allegations against Aliou Sall were dismissed by a judge in December 2020.

Having already been postponed from June 2019 to December, local elections were further delayed in August that year to allow the national dialogue to consider the introduction of measures aimed at reducing the number of candidates (and therefore reducing costs). In November the Ministry of the Interior announced that the elections would take place by 28 March 2021.

In September 2019 President Macky Sall pardoned Khalifa Sall, who later confirmed his intention to pursue his 'commitment to politics', although he remained ineligible to stand for public office. An unauthorized protest outside the presidential palace in November against a rise in electricity tariffs led to the arrest of nine demonstrators. Opposition leaders criticized their detention as disproportionate. Two weeks later several hundred people participated in a march in Dakar organized by the Noo Lank (We Refuse) movement, comprising more than 30 civil society organizations, in protest against the electricity price increase. Further demonstrations took place in January and February 2020 in the capital and other towns. Divisions within the APR emerged in January, when Moustapha Diakhaté, a former chief of staff and adviser to Sall, was expelled from the party after criticizing the President, supporting the anti-Government demonstrations and forming a new faction within the APR.

In early March 2020 Senegal recorded its first confirmed case of coronavirus disease (COVID-19). Measures undertaken from mid-March to contain the outbreak included the closure of schools and universities, a ban on public gatherings, the cancellation of celebrations planned for the 60th anniversary of independence on 4 April and the suspension of international passenger flights. President Sall declared a state of emergency on 23 March, imposing an overnight curfew and closing Senegal's borders. At the beginning of April, as part of the response to COVID-19, the National Assembly approved a law allowing the President to legislate for a three-month period by issuing ordinances (although only 33 of the 165 deputies were present at the vote). From 20 April the wearing of masks was mandated in a range of settings. Restrictions began to be eased slightly from mid-May, and the state of emergency and curfew ended on 30 June; international flights resumed on 15 July, but land and sea borders remained closed.

The national dialogue resumed in August 2020, following a five-month suspension. Already agreed was that an independent audit of the electoral register would be conducted before the local elections, that mayors would be elected by direct universal suffrage (rather than by municipal councillors) and that candidates in the local elections would not be required to secure sponsorship signatures. However, opposition parties were divided over who should be the official Leader of the Opposition: Abdoulaye Wade, as leader of the largest opposition bloc in the National Assembly, Manko Wattu Sénégal, although not a deputy himself, or Idrissa Seck, who came second in the last presidential election.

President Sall appointed an 'openness and unity' Government, incorporating several opposition members, on 1 November 2020, four days after dissolving the previous Council of Ministers. Oumar Sarr, who had formally left the PDS (together with Babacar Gaye and others), became Minister of Mining and Geology, Idrissa Seck was appointed as President of the Economic, Social and Environmental Council, and two others members of Rewmi were allocated ministerial portfolios. The exclusion from the new administration of former Prime Minister Dionne and other erstwhile APR ministers prompted speculation that Sall intended to seek a third presidential term and was sidelining potential rivals. A new political organization led by Sarr, the Parti des Libéraux et Démocrates—And Suqali, was launched later that month.

An increase in COVID-19 cases led to the declaration of a renewed state of emergency, together with the reimposition of an overnight curfew, in Dakar and Thiès on 6 January 2021, and restrictive measures were reintroduced nationwide. A few days later the National Assembly adopted legislation authorizing the President to establish a curfew without declaring a state of emergency and without having to submit such a decision to the Assembly; the new law was criticized by human rights organizations and the opposition. A vaccination programme against COVID-19 commenced in late February.

Meanwhile, in early February 2021 Ousmane Sonko, regarded by many as the most prominent opposition figure following Seck's move into government, was accused of rape and making death threats by an employee at a salon that he frequented. Sonko claimed the allegations to be politically motivated and orchestrated by Sall to prevent the PASTEF leader from contesting the presidency in 2024; Sall dismissed this claim. Later in February 2021 the National Assembly voted to remove Sonko's immunity from prosecution. On 3 March, while travelling to a court hearing, Sonko was arrested on charges of disturbing public disorder and participating in an unauthorized demonstration after he refused to comply with police demands to change his route and hundreds of supporters accompanying him clashed with the security forces. At least five people were killed in further clashes over the following few days, in Dakar and elsewhere, as demonstrators set fire to cars and erected barricades. Looting was reported, notably targeting French-owned businesses, with France considered an ally of the Sall administration. The authorities suspended the licences of two private television channels for 72 hours on the grounds that their coverage of the unrest had been excessive, restricted access to social media networks and messaging services, banned the use of motorcycles and mopeds in Dakar and closed schools for a week. Although sparked by Sonko's arrest, the protests, which were organized by the Mouvement de Défense de la Démocratie (M2D, a newly formed alliance of PASTEF, other opposition parties and civil society groups), reflected broader discontent over poverty, economic inequality and poor employment prospects for young people, as well as frustration with COVID-19 restrictions and their effect on the informal economy. Sonko appeared in court on 5 March on the charge of disrupting public order and was returned to custody. ECOWAS condemned the violence. Having been formally charged with rape and released on bail, on 8 March Sonko called for larger, but peaceful, anti-Government demonstrations. In a televised speech later that day, Sall promised to address youth unemployment and to shorten the overnight curfew. A day of national mourning was held on 11 March to commemorate those who had died in the violence. Tensions eased somewhat thereafter, as the M2D suspended further demonstrations after the intervention of religious leaders. However, the M2D issued 10 demands that it expected to be fulfilled in return, including an independent inquiry into recent events, the release of political activists, supporters of Sonko and protesters who had been detained during the preceding month, and official recognition of the 'constitutional and moral impossibility' of Sall contesting a third term of office. The alleged rape victim reiterated her claims on 17 March and denied Sall's involvement in the matter. The curfew and state of emergency ended on 20 March. Several political activists were provisionally released from detention later that month.

In early April 2021 the National Assembly approved a new deadline of the end of January 2022 for holding further postponed local elections; polling day was subsequently set for 23 January. Later in April 2021 the Minister of the Armed Forces, Sidiki Kaba, announced that an independent commission of inquiry into the March violence (in which the M2D claimed 13 people had died) would be appointed. In late April, in a case brought by the opposition Union Sociale Libérale, the ECOWAS Court of Justice ruled that the system of sponsorship of election candidates introduced under changes to the Constitution and electoral code adopted in 2018 (see *The 2019 Presidential Election*) violated the right to free participation in elections and ordered the Senegalese authorities to end sponsorship within six months. The report of a three-month audit of the electoral register by four international experts was released in early May 2021. Recommendations notably included restoring the civil rights of those convicted and then pardoned (such as Karim Wade and Khalifa Sall). However, the opposition largely rejected the findings, which concluded that there were few anomalies in the register, and expressed concern that only 53.8% of those aged 18–25 years were registered to vote. Sonko was barred from leaving Senegal in late May to attend a conference in Togo. At the end of the month the M2D accused Sall of failing to meet its demands, noting that young protesters remained in prison and that the commission of inquiry had yet to be established. The M2D organized a demonstration in mid-June to demand the release of detainees. Further protests took place later that month as the National Assembly adopted controversial anti-terrorism legislation, which opposition and human rights groups feared could be used to criminalize dissent.

In mid-July 2021, following two years of dialogue between President Sall and the opposition, the National Assembly approved a new electoral code. The new code's 25 clauses included provision for the direct election of mayors (instead of being chosen by the elected municipal councillors) and the creation of a new electoral commission, the Commission Nationale Electorale Autonome, and scrapped the system of sponsorship condemned by the ECOWAS Court of Justice. However, the clauses in the previous code banning individuals convicted of theft or corruption from voting or standing for elected office were retained.

November and December 2021 were marked by tensions linked to the campaign for the local elections due to take place on 23 January 2022. Violent protests broke out in Dakar, notably after Barthélémy Dias, a candidate for the capital's mayoralty, was arrested. In December the Groupe de Recherches et d'Appui à la Démocratie Participative et la Bonne Gouvernance (Gradec), a local non-governmental organization, launched a public campaign to encourage peaceful participation in the elections. The Cadre Unitaire de l'Islam du Sénégal, the collective voice of the religious brotherhoods that play an important role in Senegalese society, also pressed all political sides to adopt a charter of non-violence. Results of the local elections were released on 25 January, with Yewwi Askan Wi (YAW—Free the People), a new opposition alliance founded by Khalifa Sall and Ousmane Sonko, securing Dakar's mayoralty; Dias was formally appointed as Mayor in mid-February. YAW also secured Kaolack, Thiès, Casamance's Ziguinchor and other local positions in the capital and throughout the country, while President Sall's BBY retained most municipalities, including Saint Louis and Matam, as well as support in rural areas.

The 2022 Legislative Elections

The months following the local elections were dominated by the campaign for the legislative elections due to take place on 31 July. It was marked, in particular, by tensions and debates over the issue of inflation, with YAW promising to tackle the problem as a priority if elected. On 17 June, during protests in Dakar and the Casamance that had been banned by the authorities, three people were killed and about 200 arrested. In Dakar, at the end of June, a court dismissed all but one of the cases brought in relation to the protests and gave one deputy,

who admitted to having organized the protests, a suspended sentence of six months' imprisonment.

The elections took place peacefully, with a turnout of 47% (down from 54% in 2017). Provisional results were announced on 4 August, with President Sall's BYY seeing its seat count reduced to 82, one short of an absolute majority, while the opposition coalition YAW (with the allied Wallu Sénégal), claimed 80 seats. Although the opposition denounced alleged large-scale fraud and electoral irregularities and demanded the results be suspended, they were confirmed on 11 August by the Constitutional Court. The three remaining seats went to candidates of minority coalitions. One of them, Pape Diop, announced on 11 August that he was joining the ruling BYY, thereby giving it an absolute majority.

According to World Health Organization data, by mid-July 2022 86,594 confirmed cases of COVID-19 had been reported in Senegal, with 1,968 fatalities. By mid-August 2022 1,079,255 Senegalese (6.4% of the population) were fully vaccinated against COVID-19, while 1,460,773 (8.7%) had received at least one vaccine dose.

SEPARATISM IN CASAMANCE

The emergence in the early 1980s of the separatist Mouvement des Forces Démocratiques de la Casamance (MFDC) presented the Senegalese authorities with considerable security difficulties in the southern region of Casamance, which is virtually isolated from the rest of Senegal by The Gambia. Military reinforcements were dispatched to Casamance in 1990, following a series of MFDC attacks, and in September a military Governor was appointed for the region. By April 1991 at least 100 people had reportedly been killed as a result of violence in Casamance. The release of more than 340 detainees who had been arrested in connection with the unrest (including Fr Augustin Diamacouné Senghor, the Secretary-General and executive leader of the MFDC) facilitated the conclusion, at talks in Guinea-Bissau, of a ceasefire agreement by representatives of the Senegalese Government and the MFDC in May.

A resurgence of violence from July 1992 prompted the Government to redeploy armed forces in the region, giving rise to MFDC complaints of a 'remilitarization' of Casamance. Evidence emerged of a split within the MFDC: the 'Front Nord' and the MFDC Vice-President, Sidi Badji, appealed to the rebels to lay down their arms, while the other faction, the 'Front Sud', led by Senghor (himself now based in Guinea-Bissau), appeared determined to continue the armed struggle.

After an escalation of the conflict in late 1992 and early 1993, in which more than 500 people were killed and tens of thousands forced to leave their homes, negotiations resulted in the signing of a ceasefire agreement, known as the Ziguinchor Accord, in July 1993. Guinea-Bissau was to act as guarantor of the agreement, and the Government of France was asked to submit a historical arbitration regarding the Casamance issue. In December France issued its judgment that Casamance had not existed as an autonomous territory prior to the colonial period, and that independence for the region had been neither demanded nor considered at the time of decolonization.

From early 1995 renewed violence near the border with Guinea-Bissau indicated a re-emergence of divisions within the MFDC. Rebels in the south accused the Senegalese armed forces of violating the provisions of the Ziguinchor Accord. Senghor was placed under house arrest in Ziguinchor in April, and the other members of the MFDC political bureau were transported to Dakar and imprisoned. In June MFDC rebels announced an end to their ceasefire. Despite the establishment by the Government of a Commission Nationale de Paix (CNP) in September, violence intensified. In December Senghor made a televised appeal to the MFDC rebels to lay down their arms, and the members of the MFDC political bureau were released from house arrest. Salif Sadio, the MFDC military leader, confirmed observance of a truce in January 1996, and preliminary discussions between the MFDC and the CNP took place; however, negotiations broke down in April.

In January 1998 Senghor indicated that the MFDC would be prepared to abandon its demand for independence, on condition that the Government institute measures to ensure greater economic and social development in Casamance. However, from May 1999 dissident elements within the MFDC launched a series of mortar attacks near Ziguinchor. In June talks between various MFDC factions began in Banjul, the Gambian capital, although the leaders of several factions did not attend, claiming that Senghor was effectively a hostage of the Senegalese Government. At the meeting Léopold Sagna was confirmed as the head of the armed forces of the MFDC in place of Sadio, who was reportedly less prepared to compromise with government demands. The Senegalese authorities subsequently acceded to the MFDC's demand that Senghor be freed from house arrest, although his movements remained restricted.

At a meeting held in Banjul in December 1999, the Senegalese Government and the MFDC agreed to an immediate ceasefire and to create the conditions necessary to bring about lasting peace; the Governments of The Gambia and of Guinea-Bissau were to monitor the situation in the region. Following his election as President in March 2000, Abdoulaye Wade announced that he would continue negotiations and that Senghor would henceforth be permitted full freedom of movement. In November members of a peace commission, headed by the Minister of the Interior, Maj.-Gen. Mamadou Niang, and by Senghor, signed a joint statement that envisaged a series of meetings between the Senegalese Government and the MFDC. The first meeting, in December, was boycotted by the 'Front Sud' of the MFDC. The Senegalese Minister of the Armed Forces, Yoba Sambou, himself a native of Casamance, meanwhile stated that the Government preferred the rebels to unite into a single faction, so that more militant factions within the MFDC would not dispute the peace talks. In February 2001 Senghor announced that, in order to accelerate the peace process, several senior members of the MFDC, including Sidi Badji, had been removed from their positions. However, Badji rejected the legitimacy of his dismissal. In March, after Senghor accused Sadio of being implicated in the killing of 13 civilians in Casamance in February, the Senegalese Government issued an international arrest warrant for Sadio.

In mid-March 2001 Niang and Senghor signed a ceasefire agreement, which provided for the release of detainees, the return of refugees, the removal of landmines (which had been utilized in the region since 1998) and for economic aid to reintegrate rebels and to ameliorate the infrastructure of Casamance. Later that month Niang and Senghor signed a further agreement, which provided for the disarmament of rebel groups and the confinement to barracks of military forces in Casamance. In April Wade and Sambou participated in negotiations with Senghor, at which other MFDC leaders, including Badji, were also present.

Tensions between factions within the MFDC intensified in 2001. Senghor was removed from the position of Secretary-General of the MFDC in August, at a much-delayed reconciliation forum, and appointed as honorary President. Jean-Marie François Biagui, who had previously been involved in the French-based section of the MFDC, became Secretary-General and de facto leader. Badji, who continued to question Senghor's tactics, was appointed as the organization's head of military affairs and became the dominant force in the movement. A meeting between President Wade and Senghor in Dakar in September reportedly prompted the new leadership of the MFDC to suspend all further negotiations with the Government. Biagui resigned as Secretary-General in November. Badji was announced as Biagui's successor, in an acting capacity, although Senghor rejected this appointment.

In August 2002, following a joint declaration signed by Senghor and Badji urging the resumption of peace talks between the rebels and the Government, Wade appointed an official delegation to undertake negotiations with the MFDC. Meanwhile, the holding of an intra-Casamance conference, in early September, appeared to indicate a decline in support for separatist aspirations, as the conference produced a declaration, signed by representatives of 10 ethnic groups resident in the region, in favour of a 'definitive peace in Casamance', and which referred to the region as 'belonging to the great and single territory of Senegal'. However, the MFDC faction loyal to Badji was absent from the meeting. In late September five civilians were killed in an attack attributed to separatist rebels north of Ziguinchor. The internal disunity of the MFDC was emphasized in October, when Biagui publicly demanded forgiveness from the people of Casamance and Senegal for the actions of the organization in a statement that was emphatically rejected by Badji (who died from natural causes in May 2003).

In May 2003 President Wade, meeting with a delegation of MFDC leaders, including Senghor, in Dakar, announced that several substantive measures towards the normalization of the political and economic situation in Casamance were to be implemented, notably major infrastructural projects and the rehabilitation of damaged villages. An MFDC convention was held in Ziguinchor in October in the absence of hard-line factions. Both Senghor and Biagui issued statements confirming that the conflict had ended, and announced that what was termed the emancipation of Casamance did not necessarily entail its independence from Senegal. In March 2004 Senghor removed Biagui from the post of Secretary-General of the MFDC.

In April 2004, after many months of relative peace in Casamance, it was reported that three members of the armed forces had been killed while carrying out mine clearance operations in Guidel, 18 km south-east of Ziguinchor, in an attack attributed to the MFDC. The MFDC held a convention in Ziguinchor in May, at which it proposed the cantonment of its combatants while observing a unilateral one-month ceasefire, in return for the withdrawal of government troops deployed in Casamance since 1982. In July 2004 the National Assembly adopted legislation providing for an amnesty for all MFDC combatants; however, MFDC leaders claimed that their members had done nothing from which they required amnesty.

In September 2004 delegates at a general assembly of the MFDC dismissed Senghor as leader of the movement, designating him honorary President, as in 2001, and reappointed Biagui as Secretary-General and de facto leader. Biagui announced his intention to transform the MFDC into a political party, which would seek the establishment of a federal system of government, rather than full independence for Casamance. However, the MFDC remained divided. Its armed wing, known as Atika, rejected Biagui's proposals, insisting that independence remained the aim of the movement, with its head, Abdoulaye Diédhiou, claiming that he was the sole legitimate leader of the movement as he had the support of its fighters. Nevertheless, the Government continued to regard Senghor as the MFDC's leader.

On 30 December 2004 a general peace accord was signed at a ceremony in Ziguinchor by the Minister of the Interior, Ousmane Ngom, on behalf of the Government, and by Senghor, representing the MFDC. However, at least three factions of the MFDC—Atika, the 'Front Nord' and more hard-line elements of the diaspora based in France, led by Mamadou Nkrumah Sané—refused to sign the agreement, which provided for a ceasefire, to be followed by negotiations on political and economic development. Under the terms of the accord, the MFDC committed itself to disarming its fighters, who would be granted amnesty and integrated into paramilitary units on a voluntary basis. President Wade, who attended the ceremony, pledged that 80,000m. francs CFA from the Government and donor agencies would finance reconstruction and development programmes in Casamance. Negotiations aimed at achieving a definitive resolution of the conflict in Casamance were opened by Prime Minister Sall in February 2005, but were boycotted by Biagui and Diédhiou, who reportedly favoured further dialogue within the MFDC before engaging in talks with the Government. Both sides agreed to establish joint technical commissions to address reconstruction, economic and social development, as well as disarmament, demobilization and demining.

In mid-2005 a number of attacks in Casamance were variously attributed to dissident members of the MFDC or to bandits. In October Salif Sadio, who had not participated in the recent peace negotiations, stated his intention to continue fighting for Casamance's independence. Stalled talks between the MFDC and the Government scheduled to resume in December were postponed at the request of the movement, which was attempting to reconcile its various factions. One year after the signing of the peace accord, the number of armed attacks in Casamance was reported to be increasing. In March

2006 fierce fighting erupted in the border region with Guinea-Bissau between rival MFDC factions, with fighters led by Ismaïla Magne Dieme and César Badiate targeting territory held by Sadio and his supporters. The Guinea-Bissau armed forces subsequently intervened against Sadio's faction, which had established bases in northern Guinea-Bissau (see below), and by late April Sadio's forces had been expelled from that country. Factional fighting continued in Casamance, however, and in June it was reported that Sadio had seized control of several villages along the Gambian border from Dieme. An offensive by the Senegalese armed forces against Sadio's faction in August prompted some 4,500 Senegalese to cross into The Gambia to escape the unrest. The army took control of Sadio's main base in October, although further clashes followed. Senghor died in January 2007. Later in January, following clashes between Senegalese government troops and rebels belonging to Badiate's faction near the border with Guinea-Bissau, more than 100 Senegalese were reported to have fled to northern Guinea-Bissau. After several months of relative calm, in December a member of a government-appointed committee charged with bringing peace to Casamance was one of two people killed by unidentified armed men in the village of Mahmouda, some 70 km north-west of Ziguinchor. Biagui condemned the attack.

An upsurge in violent robberies in Casamance in early 2008 was attributed to MFDC dissidents. Meanwhile, the MFDC remained deeply divided following Senghor's death, undermining efforts to achieve a definitive peace. A further deterioration in the security situation in Casamance in mid-2009, again attributed to elements of the MFDC, prompted the Government to impose a night-time curfew on the region's two main highways. Clashes took place between government forces and MFDC dissidents in Casamance in August, and in September the military bombed MFDC bases in response to the killing of a soldier. The renewed violence prompted some 600 people to flee their homes on the outskirts of Ziguinchor. In October six soldiers were killed in a grenade attack near the border with Guinea-Bissau. Two leaders of dissident factions of the MFDC were arrested in mid-March 2010, shortly before the military initiated a further offensive against rebel bases. Later that month Badiate urged the Government to resume negotiations with the MFDC, while Wade stated his willingness to engage in talks with rebels seeking peace. None the less, the violence continued. In December seven soldiers were killed in clashes with MFDC rebels some 35 km from Ziguinchor. Further troops and rebels were killed in heavy fighting in early 2011, amid concerns that the MFDC had acquired more sophisticated weaponry.

Violence in Casamance increased in late 2011, with 10 civilians killed by rebels in November and some 30 soldiers killed in MFDC attacks on military positions in December. The disunity within the MFDC was apparent in December when separatists boycotted a conference at which Biagui announced plans to transform the MFDC into a political party. Further attacks on the security forces and civilians took place in early 2012. Two weeks before the presidential vote in February, President Wade visited Casamance, announcing a new peace plan. However, dissident MFDC leaders rejected Wade's proposal, and in the following days four soldiers were killed in clashes with MFDC fighters near Sindian, around 100 km north of Ziguinchor. A further three soldiers were killed in March by MFDC dissidents near the town of Sédhiou.

Following his inauguration as Wade's successor in April 2012, President Sall identified the peaceful resolution of the conflict in Casamance as a priority. In June Sall stated his readiness to open a dialogue with the MFDC factions that continued to fight, led by Sadio, Badiate and Ousmane Niantang Diatta, all three of whom responded positively. Badiate and Diatta reportedly reached agreement on reunification in September, while preliminary talks between representatives of the Government and Sadio's faction took place in Rome, Italy, in October, mediated by the Sant'Egidio Roman Catholic community. The release in December of eight captives who had been seized by Sadio's MFDC a year earlier was welcomed as a conciliatory move, as was government confirmation in April 2013 that no arrest warrant existed against Sadio. None the less, looting and attacks by MFDC rebels, as well as skirmishes

with the military, continued to occur sporadically. In May 12 employees from a South African company conducting demining operations were abducted in the village of Kailou, near Ziguinchor, by Badiate's faction, which claimed that an earlier agreement on demining limits had been violated. All 12 had been released by mid-July. A project for the development of Casamance, with a budget of some 23,000m. francs CFA, was officially launched during a visit to the region by President Sall in March 2014.

In April 2014, after engaging in further talks with Senegalese government officials in Italy, Sadio declared a unilateral ceasefire. Talks between representatives of the Government and Sadio's MFDC faction continued in Rome in July. In February 2015, during a six-day visit to Casamance, Sall attended the inauguration of the Ziguinchor electricity plant, the capacity of which had been doubled; other planned infrastructure projects included the construction of a railway linking Ziguinchor to Dakar. In July 12 forestry workers were abducted in Casamance; they were released following the payment of a ransom. Efforts were made in 2017 towards the reunification of the various factions of the MFDC, with an indirect dialogue being initiated between Badiate and Sadio, but were apparently unsuccessful. Meanwhile, dialogue between the Government and Sadio's MFDC faction reportedly recommenced in October, under the continued aegis of the Sant'Egidio Roman Catholic community, with Gambian President Adama Barrow allowing Sadio's representatives to travel to Rome via Banjul. In early January 2018 armed assailants killed 14 civilians in a protected area of forest in the region. Later that month 24 people, including an alleged member of the MFDC, were arrested in connection with the massacre. Sadio denied any involvement by the MFDC in the incident, which the organization attributed to rivalry between illegal loggers. In March the army announced that a Senegalese soldier had been killed during a military operation targeting 'criminal activities' by rebels in Casamance. Armed men attacked the Niambalang bridge near Zinguinchor in May, killing a fisherman. In April 2019 Sadio accused the Senegalese Government of reneging on its commitments. Demining operations in Casamance were temporarily suspended in May, after five deminers were kidnapped by two armed men and released the same day. In June the Senegalese army reinforced security measures around Diouloulou, near the border with The Gambia, where Sadio planned to hold an unauthorized public meeting; 13 members of Sadio's MFDC faction were reportedly arrested in Kagnobon in July for defying the ban on public meetings. Abdou Elinkine Diatta, who had declared himself Secretary-General of the political wing of the MFDC in March 2017, was killed with two others in October 2019 by unknown assailants in Mlomp, some 40 km from Ziguinchor; Diatta was reportedly replaced as MFDC Secretary-General by Edmond Bora in February 2020. Violent clashes erupted between Senegalese troops and MFDC rebels around Bissine, close to the border with Guinea-Bissau, in May.

With the stated aim of facilitating the return of those displaced by the conflict and ending the trafficking of wood and cannabis, the Senegalese army launched an offensive against the MFDC in Casamance in late January 2021, claiming to have captured three rebel bases, aided by the security forces of Guinea-Bissau, in early February. Representatives of the Government and a so-called Provisional Committee of the Unified Political and Combatant Wings of the MFDC held talks in Praia, Cabo Verde, in April, according to the Centre for Humanitarian Dialogue, a Swiss-based private diplomacy organization, which acted as facilitator, although it was not clear exactly who made up each delegation. A joint declaration adopted at the meeting included a proclamation of the willingness of both parties to resolve the conflict through dialogue, a commitment to full confidentiality on negotiations and a pledge to promote constructive behaviour and avoid any criminal action on the ground that could generate tension. A military offensive, targeting Badiate's MFDC faction, took place west of Cassolole, near the border with Guinea-Bissau, in late May, several days after a civilian was reportedly killed during an attack on an anti-trafficking patrol. In mid-June the army claimed to have seized several MFDC posts and camps in an offensive at the Guinea-Bissau border, around Badème and between Bagame and Bouniak. In late January 2022 deadly clashes broke out in The Gambia between the MFDC and Senegalese soldiers from the ECOWAS Mission in The Gambia, leaving as many as five dead and up to 10 prisoners captured. In March the Senegalese military launched a counter-insurgency operation against the MFDC along the border with The Gambia, with the stated aim of dismantling the group's bases and preserving the integrity of the national territory.

In August 2022 a disarmament deal was signed between an emissary for Senegal's President Sall and MFDC leaders César Atoute Badiate and Lansana Fabouré. Under this agreement, facilitated by ECOWAS Chairman and President of Guinea-Bissau Umaro Sissoco Embaló, the Southern wing of the MFDC agreed to lay down their weapons and contribute to a return to peace in the region. Salif Sadio, leader of the MFDC's northern factions, however, had not taken part in the talks or signing, thus potentially limiting the impact of the deal.

FOREIGN RELATIONS

Senegal maintains good relations with France, which retained a military presence in Senegal following Senegalese independence in 1960. In February 2010 it was announced that the Senegalese and French Governments had agreed to close the French military base in Dakar and gradually reduce the number of French troops based in Senegal from some 1,200 to around 300. A joint ceremony to mark the return of the base from French to Senegalese control took place in June. During a visit to France by President Macky Sall in April 2012 a new bilateral defence accord was signed (which confirmed the planned reduction in French troops in Senegal). French President François Hollande visited Senegal in October. The continued strength of Franco-Senegalese relations was reaffirmed during a two-day state visit to France by Sall in December 2016 and a three-day official visit to Senegal by Hollande's successor, Emmanuel Macron, in February 2018. Seven bilateral accords were signed during a visit to Dakar by French Prime Minister Edouard Philippe in November 2019.

A resurgence in 2020 of irregular migration by boat from Senegal to Europe, particularly to Spain's Canary Islands, prompted visits to Senegal in November that year by the Spanish Minister of Foreign Affairs, European Union and Co-operation, María Aránzazu González Laya, and in April 2021 by the President of the Spanish Government, Pedro Sánchez. The increase was attributed to a lack of prospects in Senegal for young people, particularly amid the COVID-19 pandemic, and the effect on coastal communities of severely depleted fish stocks in Senegalese waters due to overfishing, mainly by foreign vessels. Among the agreements signed by Sall and Sánchez in April was a memorandum of understanding on a policy of 'circular migration', whereby Senegalese citizens would be permitted to work in Spain for a fixed period before returning to Senegal.

Senegal hosts an annual high-level international forum on peace and security in Africa, the first taking place in Dakar in December 2014. In October 2015 the Senegalese security forces arrested five people on suspicion of links to Boko Haram, a militant Islamist group based in Nigeria. Security measures in Dakar were intensified following attacks by Islamist militants in Ouagadougou, the capital of Burkina Faso, in January 2016. In April, moreover, President Sall announced plans to reinforce Senegal's security forces in response to terrorist attacks on neighbouring countries, and in May the Senegalese and US Governments signed a defence accord allowing the permanent presence of US soldiers in Senegal in order to respond to security or health needs. The defence accord entered into force in August. Meanwhile, some 400 US and Senegalese troops participated in a two-week joint training exercise in Senegal in July. Senegal's largest ever terrorism-related trial concluded in July 2018 with the conviction of 14 defendants—who received prison sentences ranging from one month suspended to 20 years with hard labour for crimes including terrorism financing and criminal conspiracy—and the acquittal of 15 others. The group, which included those arrested in October 2015, had been accused of planning to establish a terrorist cell in Casamance and to foment terrorism in

neighbouring countries, as well as having links with Boko Haram. In February 2021 four alleged jihadists arrested the previous month in the Senegalese town of Kidira, on the border with Mali, were charged with criminal association and acts of support for terrorism.

In October 2005 Senegal severed diplomatic links with Taiwan, which had been maintained since 1996, in order to restore relations with the People's Republic of China. Senegal and China subsequently exchanged ambassadors, and ties were further strengthened during a six-day state visit by Wade to China in June 2006. Economic relations between the two countries were enhanced in 2008, with the signing of a free trade agreement in October and an economic and technical co-operation agreement in November. Further bilateral accords were concluded during visits to Senegal by Chinese President Hu Jintao in February 2009 and his successor, Xi Jinping, in July 2018.

Senegal is a significant contributor to peacekeeping activities in sub-Saharan Africa. Senegalese troops served in ECOWAS (and successor UN) missions in both Côte d'Ivoire and Liberia from 2003 and participated in the enhanced African Union (AU) Mission in Sudan from August 2005 and the replacement AU/UN hybrid operation in Darfur from December 2007. Senegal has also provided military personnel to successive UN missions in the Democratic Republic of the Congo (DRC). Following a coup in Guinea-Bissau in April 2012, Senegalese soldiers participated in the ECOWAS Mission in Guinea-Bissau established in May. The Senegalese Government contributed troops to the African-led International Support Mission in Mali (AFISMA), which commenced deployment in January 2013, shortly after a French military intervention began to assist Mali's armed forces to oust Islamist insurgents from the north of that country. AFISMA was reconstituted as the UN Multidimensional Integrated Stabilization Mission in Mali (MINUSMA) in July. Senegal also contributed troops and police to the UN Multidimensional Integrated Stabilization Mission in the Central African Republic (CAR), which succeeded an AU mission in that country in September 2014. The ECOWAS Mission in The Gambia, which was deployed in response to the dispute over the presidential election in that country in December 2016 and regularly extended thereafter, was led by Senegal (see *Relations with The Gambia*). At the end of March 2021 Senegal was contributing a total of 2,103 personnel to UN missions in the CAR, the DRC, Mali, the Darfur region of Sudan and South Sudan, its largest contribution being to MINUSMA (1,345, of whom 990 were troops).

In May 2015 the Senegalese Government announced that it was to deploy 2,100 troops to support a Saudi-led military intervention in Yemen, where al-Houthi rebels had seized the capital, San'a. Critics questioned the justification for Senegal's involvement, with some linking it to increased Saudi investment in Senegal, particularly in the Government's development plan. Senegal recalled its ambassador to Qatar for consultations between June and August 2017 in solidarity with Saudi Arabia and other Gulf countries that had severed their ties with Qatar on the grounds of its alleged support for Islamist groups.

Senegal recalled its ambassador to Iran in December 2010 in connection with the discovery in October of weapons at the Nigerian port of Lagos that were allegedly being transported from Iran to The Gambia, amid speculation that the arms were ultimately to have been smuggled to MFDC rebels in Casamance. The Senegalese Government decided to reinstate its envoy in January 2011, but severed bilateral relations again in the following month, citing further evidence that Iran was supplying weapons to MFDC rebels. Diplomatic relations were restored in February 2013.

In July 2006 the AU decided that Hissène Habré, President of Chad during 1982–90, should be prosecuted in Senegal (where he had fled after being deposed in 1990) over alleged human rights abuses committed during his presidency. In July 2012 the International Court of Justice (ICJ) in The Hague, Netherlands, issued its judgment in a case brought by Belgium in February 2009, ruling that Senegal should commence procedures to prosecute Habré 'without further delay' or, failing that, extradite him to Belgium. The Senegalese authorities accepted an AU proposal to try Habré before a special tribunal presided over by African judges appointed by the Union. In December 2012 the National Assembly approved the creation of the so-called African Extraordinary Chambers. Following his arrest in June 2013, in July Habré was charged with crimes against humanity, war crimes and torture. The former President's trial, before two Senegalese judges and a presiding judge from Burkina Faso, commenced in July 2015 and concluded in February 2016. In May Habré was convicted of crimes against humanity, war crimes and torture during his presidency in 1982–90 and sentenced to life imprisonment; this sentence was upheld on appeal in April 2017.

Following Senegal's co-sponsorship in December 2016 of UN Security Council Resolution 2334, which demanded an end to Israel's construction of Jewish settlements in East Jerusalem and the West Bank, the Israeli Government recalled its ambassador from Dakar and suspended its aid programmes to Senegal. However, full diplomatic relations were restored in June 2017, following talks between President Sall and the Israeli Prime Minister, Benjamin Netanyahu, on the sidelines of an ECOWAS summit in Monrovia, Liberia.

At an extraordinary AU summit in March 2018, Senegal was among 44 of the 55 member states to sign an agreement on the establishment of an African Continental Free Trade Area (AfCFTA), and also signed, together with 26 other member states, an agreement on the free movement of people across borders. The AfCFTA agreement entered into force in May 2019 for the 24 states (including Senegal) that had ratified it. Trading under the AfCFTA commenced on 1 January 2021, by which time the accord had been signed by 54 states and ratified by 34.

In February 2021 the Financial Action Task Force, an intergovernmental organization based in Paris, France, included Senegal on its list of jurisdictions under increased monitoring with regard to their systems for countering money laundering and the financing of terrorism.

Relations with Mauritania

In April 1989 the deaths of two Senegalese farmers, following a disagreement with Mauritanian livestock breeders regarding grazing rights in the border region between the two countries, precipitated a crisis that was fuelled by longstanding ethnic and economic rivalries. Mauritanian nationals residing in Senegal were attacked and their businesses ransacked, and Senegalese nationals in Mauritania suffered similar attacks. By early May it was believed that several hundred people, mostly Senegalese, had been killed. Operations to repatriate nationals of both countries were undertaken with international assistance. None the less, diplomatic relations were severed in August. Military engagements in the border region were reported in 1990, and in March 1991 several deaths were reported to have resulted from a clash, on Senegalese territory, between members of the two countries' armed forces, following an incursion by Senegalese troops into Mauritania.

Diplomatic links, at ambassadorial level, were restored in April 1992, and the process of reopening the border began in May. In December 1994 the Governments of Senegal and Mauritania agreed new co-operation measures, including efforts to facilitate the free movement of goods and people between the two countries. In October 1995, moreover, the Mauritanian authorities gave assurances that Mauritanian refugees in Senegal were free to return home. According to the office of the UN High Commissioner for Refugees (UNHCR), the number of Mauritanian refugees in Senegal declined from 65,485 in 1995 to 19,999 in 1999, although progress with repatriation subsequently stalled.

In June 2000 Mauritania accused Senegal of threatening its interests by relaunching an irrigation programme in the fossil valleys area of the River Senegal. Claiming that the project would deprive its own lands of water, Mauritania instructed Senegalese nationals to leave the country within 15 days. Of the 345,000 Senegalese resident in Mauritania, some 25,000 returned home before the order was rescinded on 10 June. Wade immediately visited Nouakchott, the Mauritanian capital, and announced the cancellation of the irrigation project.

A tripartite agreement on the voluntary repatriation and reintegration of Mauritanian refugees in Senegal was signed by UNHCR and the Mauritanian and Senegalese Governments in November 2007. The number of Mauritanian refugees in Senegal declined from 32,292 at the end of 2008 to 19,917 at the end of 2011, according to UNHCR. The repatriation programme ended in March 2012, with UNHCR reporting that some 14,000 Mauritanians had opted to remain in Senegal. The number of Mauritanian refugees registered in Senegal at mid-2021 was 14,195.

Meanwhile, after Mauritanian President Sidi Mohammed Ould Cheikh Abdellahi was overthrown in August 2008, President Wade opposed the imposition of sanctions against Mauritania's new military administration, headed by Gen. Mohamed Ould Abdel Aziz. In mid-2009 the Senegalese Government mediated in the Mauritanian political dispute regarding the restoration of constitutional order. In March 2010 the Senegalese and Mauritanian authorities agreed to reinforce security co-operation along the joint border. Wade's successor, Macky Sall, undertook his first official visit to Mauritania in September 2012. The Mauritanian and Senegalese armed forces commenced a joint awareness campaign on terrorism along their common border in December. A further strengthening of military co-operation, aimed at combating new cross-border security threats, was agreed in May 2013. In March 2014 a joint ministerial consultation commission on transport recommended the construction of a bridge across the River Senegal, which separates the two countries, at the Rosso border crossing; the bridge was expected to be completed in 2023. Following Mauritania's decision in 2016 not to renew an arrangement allowing Senegalese boats to fish in Mauritanian waters, several incidents involving Senegalese fishermen and the Mauritanian coast guard provoked tensions. Violent protests targeting Mauritanian businesses erupted in the northern Senegalese town of Saint-Louis in January and April 2018 after two incidents in which Senegalese fishermen were shot dead by members of the Mauritanian coast guard. Nevertheless, in February, during a state visit to Mauritania by the Senegalese President, Sall and Ould Abdel Aziz signed an inter-governmental agreement on the joint exploitation of a large offshore natural gas field straddling the maritime border between the two countries. Sall attended the inauguration of Ould Abdel Aziz's successor, Mohamed Ould Cheikh Mohamed Ahmed Ould Ghazouani, in Nouakchott in August 2019. Six bilateral agreements, most notably on fishing rights, were signed in February 2020, when Sall returned to the Mauritanian capital; he welcomed the annulment by Mauritania of fines imposed on Senegalese fishermen accused of operating in Mauritanian waters.

Relations with Guinea-Bissau

A dispute with Guinea-Bissau regarding the sovereignty of a maritime zone believed to contain reserves of petroleum, together with valuable fishing grounds, caused tensions between the two countries in the late 1980s and early 1990s. In July 1989 an international arbitration panel (to which the issue had been referred in 1985) judged the waters to be part of Senegalese territory. However, the Government of Guinea-Bissau referred the matter to the ICJ. In November 1991 the ICJ ruled that the existing delimitation of the maritime border remained valid, and Senegal and Guinea-Bissau signed a treaty recognizing this judgment in February 1993.

Although Guinea-Bissau played an important role in the formulation of the 1991 ceasefire agreement between the Senegalese Government and the MFDC, relations were again strained in late 1992. In December an offensive by the Senegalese armed forces against MFDC strongholds close to the border with Guinea-Bissau resulted in the deaths of two nationals of that country. The Guinea-Bissau Government formally protested against Senegalese violations of its airspace. None the less, Guinea-Bissau was again active in efforts to bring about a new ceasefire agreement between Senegal and the MFDC in mid-1993. In October of that year, moreover, the two countries signed a 20-year agreement regarding the joint exploitation and management of fishing and petroleum resources in their maritime zones.

Renewed operations by the Senegalese military against MFDC rebels in southern Casamance, from early 1995, again affected relations with Guinea-Bissau. In April Guinea-Bissau temporarily deployed as many as 500 troops near the border with Senegal, as part of attempts to locate four missing French tourists. The October 1993 treaty on the joint exploration of maritime wealth was ratified in December 1995: fishing resources were to be shared equally between the two countries, while Senegal was to benefit from a majority share (85%) of petroleum deposits.

In January 1998 it was announced that the authorities in Guinea-Bissau had intercepted a consignment of armaments destined for MFDC rebels and that some 15 officers of the Guinea-Bissau armed forces had been arrested and suspended from duty, including their leader, Brig. (later Gen.) Ansumane Mané. In June, however, troops loyal to Mané rebelled, and civil war broke out in Guinea-Bissau. Senegalese troops intervened in support of the forces loyal to the Government, and were subsequently reinforced to number more than 2,500. Senegal's involvement became the subject of controversy, with Guinea-Bissau refugees accusing Senegalese troops of brutality against civilians. In July the Guinea-Bissau insurgents signed a ceasefire agreement with their Government. Under the terms of an agreement brokered by ECOWAS in November 1998, the final 800 Senegalese soldiers withdrew from Guinea-Bissau in March 1999.

Tensions between the two countries resurfaced in April 2000, when an armed group, reportedly composed of members of the MFDC operating from within Guinea-Bissau, attacked a Senegalese border post. In late April the common border was temporarily closed. The Government of Guinea-Bissau continued to deny supporting the MFDC rebels. In August the revision was announced of the agreement on the joint exploitation of petroleum resources; henceforth Guinea-Bissau was to receive 20% rather than 15% of the revenue generated. Relations between Senegal and Guinea-Bissau improved significantly following the killing of Mané during a failed coup attempt in Guinea-Bissau in November 2000, and Guinea-Bissau forces launched a new offensive against MFDC rebel bases in early 2001.

In March 2006, following increasing instability along its border with Senegal, as rival factions of the MFDC clashed (see above), the Guinea-Bissau armed forces launched an offensive against bases established by Salif Sadio around the Guinea-Bissau town of São Domingos. Fighting between Guinea-Bissau troops and MFDC rebels continued until late April, leading to the displacement of several thousand Guinea-Bissau civilians, many of whom fled across the border to Ziguinchor. In January 2007 Guinea-Bissau deployed additional troops in its border area with Senegal, in response to reported clashes between Senegalese troops and forces belonging to César Badiate's MFDC faction. François Diatta, an alleged leader of the MFDC reported to be allied to Mamadou Nkrumah Sané, was arrested in Guinea-Bissau in July 2009. Tension arose in October when the Government of Guinea-Bissau placed its troops on alert along the border with Senegal, accusing the Senegalese authorities of having sold plots of land and removed border posts in a coastal border area claimed by Guinea-Bissau to be part of its territory. At a meeting held in Guinea-Bissau later that month, representatives of both countries agreed to revive a joint border commission that had not convened for 16 years. In December 2017 the Guinea-Bissau Government agreed to grant citizenship to all Senegalese refugees from the Casamance region (who numbered 10,061 at the end of that month, according to UNHCR). By the end of 2020 the number of Senegalese refugees in Guinea-Bissau had declined to 1,818, with more than 5,500 having been naturalized. In January 2020 Senegal was the first country visited by Umaro Sissoco Embaló following his (disputed) election as President of Guinea-Bissau in the previous month; he returned to Dakar in March. Bilateral relations were expected to be strong under Embaló's administration, owing to his long-standing relationship with President Macky Sall, with whose family he reportedly stayed for nine years after fleeing the civil war in Guinea-Bissau in 1998. The security forces of Guinea-Bissau reportedly assisted the Senegalese army in an offensive against the MFDC in Casamance, near the border with Guinea-Bissau, launched in late January 2021. In February Sall announced that Senegal would offer Guinea-Bissau 10,000 COVID-19 vaccines in a gesture of solidarity. As ECOWAS Chairman Embaló played an instrumental role in brokering a

disarmament deal between the MFDC's southern faction and the Senegalese Government in August 2022 (see *Separatism in Casamance*).

Relations with The Gambia

In August 1981, following a coup in The Gambia, President Diouf dispatched Senegalese troops to restore the deposed Gambian President, Sir Dawda Jawara, to power. Senegalese forces subsequently remained, and Diouf and Jawara established a confederation of the two states, with co-ordinated policies in defence, foreign affairs and economic and financial matters. The agreement establishing the Senegambian Confederation came into effect in February 1982. Diouf was designated permanent President of a Joint Council of Ministers, and a Confederal Assembly was established. In August 1989 the Diouf Government announced the withdrawal of 1,400 Senegalese troops from The Gambia, apparently in protest against a request by Jawara that his country be accorded more power within the Senegambian Confederation. The Confederation was dissolved in September, in view of The Gambia's reluctance to proceed towards full political and economic integration with Senegal. In January 1991 the ministers responsible for foreign affairs of the two countries signed a bilateral treaty of friendship and co-operation.

Following the coup in The Gambia in July 1994, and the assumption of power by Yahya A. J. J. Jammeh, Jawara was initially granted asylum in Senegal. Despite the presence in Senegal of prominent opponents of the Gambian military regime, in January 1996 the two countries signed an agreement aimed at increasing bilateral trade and at minimizing cross-border smuggling. A further accord, concluded in April 1997, was to facilitate the trans-border movement of goods destined for re-export. In June the two countries agreed to take joint measures to combat insecurity, illegal immigration and trafficking in arms and illegal drugs. In early 1998 President Jammeh offered to act as a mediator between the Senegalese Government and the MFDC (see *Separatism in Casamance*) and subsequently hosted regular meetings between the Government and the MFDC.

None the less, intermittent disputes relating to transportation issues between the two countries have occurred. Tensions arose in August 2005, for example, when The Gambia Ports Authority (GPA) doubled the cost of using the ferry across the Gambia river. Many Senegalese lorry drivers refused to pay the increased fare, while others blockaded the main border crossings between the two countries. The dispute was resolved in October, when Jammeh agreed to reverse the price increase, while Wade pledged to end the blockade of the border. Agreement was also reached on the construction of a bridge over the Gambia river and on the establishment of a permanent secretariat for bilateral co-operation.

In August 2006 UNHCR reported that more than 4,500 people had fled to The Gambia from Senegal that month, following renewed fighting in Casamance (see *Separatism in Casamance*); some 1,600 Senegalese had crossed into The Gambia earlier that year. Senegalese refugees registered with UNHCR in The Gambia numbered 4,019 at the end of 2020 (down from 7,557 at the end of 2017). A visit to The Gambia by President Wade in January 2010 followed claims made by Jammeh in the previous month that the Senegalese Government aided and hosted Gambian dissidents and allegations by the Gambian newspaper the *Daily Observer* that Senegal was seeking to destabilize The Gambia. Wade dismissed the accusations and signed a joint communiqué with Jammeh, in which they pledged to enhance peace and security and reaffirmed their commitment to implement the earlier agreements to construct a bridge over the Gambia river and to establish a permanent secretariat for bilateral co-operation. Tensions arose again in late 2010, however, amid Senegalese concerns that weapons allegedly being smuggled from Iran to The Gambia were intended for MFDC rebels in Casamance. Gambian-Senegalese relations had improved by February 2011, when The Gambia acknowledged having received weapons from Iran, but claimed that they were to be used to ensure Gambian national security. At the same time the Gambian and Senegalese Governments agreed to create the long-awaited permanent secretariat later that year and to organize joint military manoeuvres and border patrols. Nevertheless, a renewed dispute regarding the fees charged to Senegalese lorry drivers seeking to cross Gambian territory disrupted cross-border trade and movement for some three months from March.

President Macky Sall visited The Gambia shortly after his inauguration in April 2012, notably requesting Jammeh's assistance in resolving the conflict in Casamance. Relations were strained again in August, however, when two Senegalese nationals were among nine prisoners whose death sentences were controversially implemented by the Gambian authorities. The Senegalese Government summoned the Gambian ambassador formally to protest against the executions, about which it had not been informed. None the less, the permanent secretariat finally became operational in May 2013. Border issues continued to cause difficulties in early 2014, however, when the GPA's insistence that ferry tariffs be paid in foreign currency led to further restrictions on the cross-frontier movement of commercial and official vehicles. Amid tensions over the sovereignty of the border village of Tranquil, the joint border commission met in October 2015 in an effort to resolve the dispute. However, a standoff between troops from both countries continued in the following months, with the demarcation of the border unresolved. In February 2016 the Senegalese Transport Union again commenced a boycott of border crossing points in response to The Gambia's imposition of higher ferry tariffs, leading to a shortage of essential items in both countries. The border was fully reopened in May, following talks between the two sides; a principal Senegalese pre-condition for ending the blockade had been a resumption of construction work on the bridge over the Gambia river. In July the Gambia Revenue Authority and Senegal's Custom Administration signed a memorandum of understanding aimed at facilitating the movement of goods between the two countries.

Following Jammeh's refusal to relinquish office after his defeat in a presidential election in The Gambia on 1 December 2016, in January 2017 the victorious candidate, Adama Barrow, took refuge in Senegal, where he was sworn in as the new Gambian President on 19 January. On the same day Senegalese-led ECOWAS troops (numbering some 7,000) entered The Gambia with an initial mandate to ensure a peaceful transfer of power. Jammeh stood down on 21 January, and Barrow returned to The Gambia on 26 January. President Barrow undertook a three-day state visit to Senegal in March, his first foreign trip since taking office. He pledged to work with Senegal towards achieving peace in Casamance, and agreement on greater defence co-operation was also reached, with some 2,500 ECOWAS troops to remain in The Gambia to maintain stability. Moreover, Barrow and Sall agreed to raise bilateral relations to a strategic partnership and to establish a Presidential Council, which they would jointly chair. Having been recast as a peace support mission in June and extended several times, the ECOWAS mission remained in The Gambia at mid-2022; it was to be gradually transformed into a police mission. At the first meeting of the Presidential Council, which took place in Banjul in March 2018, Sall and Barrow signed various agreements, covering areas including trade, the extradition of fugitives, the transfer of already sentenced prisoners and the free movement of people across borders. The two countries also agreed to increase joint border patrols aimed at combating the trafficking of illegally logged timber. In January 2019 Barrow and Sall jointly inaugurated the long-awaited Senegambia Bridge across the Gambia river. The second meeting of the Presidential Council was held in Dakar in March 2020. In February 2021 Sall announced that Senegal would offer The Gambia 10,000 COVID-19 vaccines in a gesture of solidarity. More than 250 Senegalese nationals reportedly fled the Gambian fishing village of Sanyang in March, after the stabbing of a Gambian by a Senegalese fisherman provoked clashes and rioting. Fighting between Senegalese troops participating in the ECOWAS force and MDFC rebels in early 2022 in The Gambia caused an estimated 6,000 to flee their homes, but did not seem to threaten diplomatic relations between Senegal and its neighbour.

Economy

MARIE GIBERT

INTRODUCTION

Senegal retains some of the economic advantages derived from its leading position in pre-independence French West Africa. In 2021 its gross domestic product (GDP) was US $23,630m., or $1,607 per head. Its population was estimated at 17.7m. in 2022, and life expectancy stood at 68 years in 2020. Yet poverty remains widespread, especially in rural areas, and the adult literacy rate was only 51.9% in 2017. Senegal's ranking on the United Nations (UN) Development Programme's Human Development Index was 170th out of 189 countries in 2021.

As a former French colony and a member of the Union Economique et Monétaire Ouest-Africaine (UEMOA), since 1945 Senegal has shared the same currency as other UEMOA member states, the franc CFA, which was originally pegged to the French franc and then to the euro. The franc CFA was financially supported by France. In 2020 plans had been in progress to replace the franc CFA with a new currency, the eco, by the end of the year in at least eight countries (Benin, Burkina Faso, Guinea-Bissau, Côte d'Ivoire, Mali, Niger, Senegal and Togo). The eco would also be pegged to the euro, but France's financial support would be downgraded to an informal level. However, in light of dramatically higher levels of public spending by member states of the Franc Zone in 2020–21 as a result of the COVID-19 pandemic, the adoption of the eco was expected to be postponed by several years, as the convergence criteria for participation in the currency required limiting the budget deficit to below 3% of GDP, which few states appeared likely to achieve at that time.

Economic performance was strong for the decade spanning the turn of the 21st century. The economy responded positively to the major devaluation of the CFA franc in 1994, which, with the accompanying government reform programme, produced one of the best economic performances in sub-Saharan Africa between 1995 and 2005. Real growth in GDP averaged 4.5% per year during this period. The rate of poverty declined from 68% to 48% (although the level changed little subsequently), and Senegal registered progress in access to education. However, reflecting the economy's continuing vulnerability to internal constraints and difficult external circumstances, growth has been variable, owing to fluctuations in international prices for food and fuels, the global financial crisis and intermittent drought. GDP increased, in real terms, at an average annual rate of 4.1% per year in 2007–16. GDP growth of 6.7% was recorded in 2016 and of 7.2% in 2017, before dipping to 6.2% in 2018 and to 5.3% in 2019. It dropped sharply, to 1.3% in 2020, as a result of the global economic crisis related to the COVID-19 pandemic, but rebounded to 6.1% in 2021. Inflation remained below 2.0% between 2012 and 2019, but reached 2.5% in 2020 and 2.2% in 2021.

Although economic reforms under the guidance of the Bretton Woods institutions began in the 1980s, it was only after the 1994 devaluation that the programme of economic liberalization gained momentum. An ambitious privatization programme was adopted in the mid-1990s, with 20 state-owned companies offered for sale, including water and electricity services, telecommunications, the railways and the national airline, the groundnut and cotton sectors, and the port of Dakar. A further round of privatization commenced in 2003, under pressure from the International Monetary Fund (IMF), but advanced slowly.

Under President Abdoulaye Wade (2000–12) emphasis was placed on further liberalizing markets, transforming the peasant economy into a private sector-driven centre of agro-industry and services, and establishing Senegal as a regional trading centre. The Government embarked on an ambitious infrastructure programme, including a new international airport, road networks, port facilities and irrigation schemes. However, the economy remained dependent on public spending to provide growth momentum.

The administration of Macky Sall, which displaced the Wade regime at national elections in early 2012, initially sought to address popular discontent over jobs and the cost of living by lowering prices for certain essential goods, and in February 2013 took action to decrease rents while introducing the Bourse de Securité Familiale (Family Security Allowance), which was targeted to reach 250,000 low-income families by 2017, and a programme of universal health care. Sall's ambitious electoral promises to re-energize Senegal's development efforts were developed in November 2012 with the publication of the Stratégie Nationale de Développement Economique et Social. This envisaged an annual real growth rate of 7% by 2017 and to create 350,000 new jobs. In January 2014 the Government presented a large-scale development programme, aimed at transforming Senegal's economy by 2035. The Plan Sénégal Emergent (PSE) targeted 28 major projects in agriculture, infrastructure, transport and tourism. The second phase of the PSE, covering 2019–23, was intended to help Senegal to achieve emerging economy status, notably through rural infrastructure projects and social services. A donor summit held in Paris, France, in December 2018 raised more than €13,000m.—three times the amount expected.

AGRICULTURE AND FISHING

Some 49% of Senegal's population is now urban. However, agriculture continues to be the predominant sector for employment; the groundnut sector alone provides employment for around 500,000 (mostly small-scale) farmers. The agricultural sector's contribution to GDP declined steadily from the mid-1980s, from almost 25% in 1987, to 16.4% in 2021. The economy's agricultural base has been eroded by periodic droughts, gradual desertification and high levels of rural poverty, not least in the politically sensitive Casamance region in the south. Limited access to rural infrastructure and basic services has spurred migration to urban areas.

Groundnuts are the leading cash crop, but both the annual acreage planted and production have varied with external price fluctuations, drought and locust infestation. Severe drought in the early 2010s caused production to drop to just 525,528 tons in 2011, before progressively recovering and reaching a record 1.8m. tons in 2021, according to the Food and Agriculture Organization of the UN (FAO). Groundnuts are exported either as groundnut oil, groundnut cake for animal feed or shelled groundnuts.

The principal groundnut oil producer, the state-owned Société Nationale de Commercialisation des Oléagineux du Sénégal (SONACOS), was divested to the French company Advens in 2004; SONACOS was subsequently renamed SUNEOR ('Our Gold'). However, the Senegalese Government continued to intervene in the decisions of the Comité National Interprofessionnel de l'Arachide (CNIA), which fixes the producer price each season. In 2012 SUNEOR experienced a cash-flow crisis and was forced to seek government aid when buyers from the People's Republic of China purchased groundnuts direct from farmers above the official price, exporting the groundnuts direct to China. All three refining firms faced further financial difficulties in late 2013 when the CNIA announced a small increase in the official groundnut price, at a time when the international groundnut price had dropped by 40%. In October 2015 it was announced that Advens had withdrawn its capital and SUNEOR had returned to temporary state control. It was again named SONACOS in mid-2016, and reforms resulted in more successful commercialization campaigns. The company's financial future remained uncertain because of its accumulated debt, and some of its land was seized in June 2019 to cover debts owed to the Banking Company of West Africa. In that year the Government and

groundnut oil producers and sellers signed an agreement whereby sellers agreed to give priority to Senegalese groundnut oil before being authorized to import and sell oil produced abroad. Senegal produced 183,900 metric tons of groundnut oil in 2019.

The Government has attempted to reduce dependence on groundnuts, in particular by expanding output of cotton, rice, sugar and horticultural produce. Senegal's exports of cotton lint reached 8,860 metric tons in 2020, worth nearly US $16m. Cashew nut production was modest until 1998, when three successive seasons saw annual production reach 7,000 tons or more; in 2020 output amounted to an estimated 8,750 tons, according to FAO. Sugar is produced at the Richard Toll complex in the north, near Saint-Louis. Annual output of sugar cane reached an estimated 1.4m. tons in 2020. However, sugar output has increasingly failed to meet domestic needs, and imports of sugar totalled $90.6m. in 2021.

Output of rice has risen steadily over the past decade, from 405,824 metric tons in 2011 to 1,349,723 metric tons in 2020, according to FAO data. Domestic demand is far greater than output, and the shortfall is met through cheap imports of rice from the Far East—totalling 1,184,400 tons in 2021. Such imports seriously jeopardize local producers. With external support, boosted by the Manantali dam in Mali, and with renewed support from the Government, the area under irrigation for rice cultivation has been extended; some 403,700 ha were in production in 2021 (up from 135,000 ha in 2014).

Senegal's other principal food crops are millet, sorghum and maize. The traditional food sector has suffered reverses from recurring droughts and insufficient inputs. The combined harvest of millet and sorghum in 2020 was over 1.5m. metric tons, while cassava production reached 1.3m. Maize production increased dramatically following the introduction of hybrid seeds and an expansion of the area under cultivation during the early 2000s. However, having peaked at 453,678 tons in 2008, maize production fell to 178,732 tons by 2014, before rising again to a record 761,883 tons in 2020.

Livestock is a significant sector of the traditional economy, and is the basis of the dairy and meat processing industries. In 2020, according to FAO estimates, cattle totalled 3.7m. head, sheep 7.4m., goats 6.4m., pigs 478,100 and horses 578,800. Only 2%–3% of the country's meat requirements are currently imported.

Agricultural production is supplemented by output from fishing. This remains an important source of foreign exchange, despite ongoing political insecurity in the Casamance region (the main fishing area) and recurrent problems caused by overfishing. Annual catches averaged around 425,000 metric tons between 2003 and 2015, and amounted to 452,800 tons in 2020, according to FAO. While industrial fishing is practised by national and foreign operators, small-scale fishing, by some 85,400 fishermen, continues to predominate, providing a livelihood for as many as 600,000 people—including workers engaged in local canning factories. The development of large-scale aquaculture has been encouraged; some 1,000 tons were produced by such methods in 2019.

From 2001 Senegal had a special arrangement with Mauritania allowing Senegalese fishing boats to fish in Mauritanian waters. The two countries signed a protocol in December 2014 under which Mauritania was to receive an annual fee of US $925,000, one-third to be paid by the Senegalese Government and the remainder by the fishing boat owners. However, following a decision by the Mauritanian Government to boost local fishing, the agreement was not renewed in 2016. Fishing agreements with the European Community (now the European Union—EU) have been in place since 1979. Despite government concerns that industrial fishing was depleting stocks and undermining the artisanal fishing sector, a new agreement was signed with the EU in June 2002 enabling Senegal to receive financial compensation and incorporating several conditions intended to protect fish stocks. Negotiations for a successor accord stalled in June 2006, and EU vessels stopped fishing in Senegalese waters until a new agreement was reached in April 2014, covering November 2014–November 2019. In July 2019 the EU and Senegal concluded a new implementing protocol to the existing sustainable fisheries partnership agreement. The new protocol allowed EU vessels—a maximum of 28 tuna seiners, 10 pole and line vessels, five longliners and two trawlers—to fish tuna-like species and hake in Senegalese waters. In exchange for the fishing rights, the EU will offer Senegal a yearly financial contribution of €1.7m. Part of this contribution, €900,000 per year, has been earmarked to promote the sustainable management of fisheries in Senegal. In addition to this sum, ship owners are expected to contribute approximately €1.35m. per year.

MINING

The mining sector's contribution to GDP was only 3.6% in 2020. Mining in Senegal is dominated by phosphates, with reserves of calcium phosphates estimated at 100m. metric tons and deposits of aluminium phosphates at 50m.–70m. tons. Phosphate output reached 2.4m. tons in 2020.

Phosphate extraction is undertaken by several companies, including Industries Chimiques du Sénégal (ICS), which was acquired by Indonesia's Indorama in 2014 and exploits the Tobène deposit, Société Minière de la Vallée du Fleuve at the Matam deposit, the Baobab Mining and Chemicals Corporation, 80%-owned by Australian mining company Avenira, at the Bambey and Thiès (Ngakham-Chérif Lô) deposits and Société Sénégalaise des Phosphates at the Thiès (Lam-Lam) deposit.

Phosphate rock has been processed by ICS. The ICS complex produced 363,000 metric tons in 2012, with production increasing rapidly thereafter, reaching 1.8m. tons in 2018. ICS also produces fertilizer (with production amounting to 100,000 tons in 2016). As a result of declining market prices and rising costs of fuel and essential imports, ICS was declared bankrupt in 2006. An agreement was reached in 2008 whereby the Indian Farmers Fertiliser Co-operative (which purchased some 80% of ICS's phosphate and phosphoric acid output) would provide 91,000m. francs CFA (US $200m.) of new capital for ICS, in return for management control and a guaranteed 85% of the company's production; ICS subsequently reached an agreement with its creditors, allowing it to repay its debts over 12 years. In November 2016 an agreement was reached with ICS's creditors to restructure its considerable debt stock.

Deposits of an estimated 391m. metric tons of high-grade iron ore are located in the east, at Falémé, with an additional 250m. tons at Farangalia and Goto. In January 2006, with international demand for iron ore buoyant, Dutch-based Mittal Steel signed an agreement with the Senegalese authorities to develop the Falémé deposit. In July 2009, however, Arcelor-Mittal (as Mittal Steel had become) suspended the project. In May 2011, after conciliation efforts failed, the Senegalese Government submitted a case to the International Court of Arbitration of the International Chamber of Commerce, in Paris, demanding compensation of US $750m. In September 2013 the Court ruled in Senegal's favour, and the two parties subsequently agreed to settle the dispute, with the amount of the settlement being included within the financing cost. Finding a new owner for Falémé was among the priorities defined by President Sall in the PSE.

Exploration for diamonds is in progress, and significant gold deposits were discovered at Sabodala, in south-east Senegal, where artisanal production estimated at 600 kg annually had long taken place. Gold production reached 19,120 kg in 2021, compared with 4,089 kg in 2011. Canada-based Endeavour Mining has owned the Sabodala-Massawa gold mining complex since 2021, when it produced some 9,780 kg of gold. The British company Toro Gold began exploitation of a third mine in the Sabodala area in March 2018 and reported production of 245,230 troy oz in that year. Randgold Resources, a British-listed gold company, has made a large undeveloped discovery in the country, and Iamgold, a Canadian company, is exploring for more.

Commercially viable reserves of titanium were discovered in 1991. In 2007 the Government awarded a 25-year licence to the Australian company Mineral Deposits Ltd (MDL), for which MDL paid a fee of US $370m., to develop deposits of zircon and titanium-related minerals used in the paint, jewellery, ceramic and civil engineering industries, in the coastal area between Dakar and Saint-Louis. In July 2011 MDL combined with Eramet of France to form a new company, TiZir, to develop the Grande Côte mineral sands project. Construction work was completed in March 2014, costing $516m. In 2016 the TiZir project produced 416,349 tons of ilmenite, 52,627 tons of zircon and 9,664 tons of leuxocene. By 2020 production of zircon had increased to 85,000 tons and TiZir was planning to expand exploitation to the north by 2023.

Petroleum deposits, estimated at 100m. metric tons, were located in the Dôme Flore field, off the Casamance coast, but initially their development appeared uneconomical. Disagreement with Guinea-Bissau concerning sovereignty over the area was resolved by an agreement in 1993 providing for the joint management of the two countries' maritime zones for an initial 20-year period. The agreement provided for an 85%:15% division of petroleum resources between Senegal and Guinea-Bissau, respectively; this was altered to 80%:20% in August 2000. The Agence de Gestion et Coopération was created to administer petroleum and fishing activity in the 100,000-sq km joint area. All companies were expected to work in partnership with the majority state-owned Société Nationale des Pétroles du Sénégal (PETROSEN).

In 2014 the British firm Cairn Energy announced the discovery of two significant deep-water petroleum deposits, and in April 2016 it made a third exploitable find. By late 2017 Cairn Energy was drilling five wells off the coast and was expecting to begin extracting oil between 2021 and 2023. Further discoveries in 2018 confirmed large oil reserves. In May 2017 the French oil company Total signed two agreements with the Government for the exploration of the Rufisque Offshore Profond field and the assessment of Senegal's ultra-deep offshore acreage. Crude petroleum production, which commenced in 2006, amounted to 403,000 barrels in 2011, according to the US Geological Survey, but decreased 169,000 barrels in 2015 and to just 24,000 barrels in 2016 as international prices remained very low; it partially recovered to 95,000 barrels in 2017, remaining at that level in 2018. The value of petroleum exports increased from US $411m. in 2017 to reach a peak of $802m. in 2019; it receded slightly in the following two years, reaching $771m. in 2021, according to the International Trade Center. Commercial exploitation of the extended Sangomar oil field, in the Rufisque-Sangomar area, by Capricorn Senegal, comprising a subsidiary of Cairn Energy (36.4%), Australian companies Woodside Energy (31.9%) and FAR (13.7%), and PETROSEN (18%), was expected to begin in 2023.

In 1997 PETROSEN announced the discovery of a natural gas deposit, with reserves estimated at 10,000m. cu m, in the Thiès region. In April 2015 the US company Kosmos Energy claimed to have located a substantial gas deposit, called Greater Tortue, straddling the maritime frontier between Senegal and Mauritania. In December 2016 the British oil and gas company BP reached an agreement with Kosmos jointly to develop the deposit, the gross gas reserves of which were estimated at 15,000,000m. cu ft. In February 2018 Senegal and Mauritania signed a co-operation agreement for the exploitation of the deposit, giving an equal division of resources and revenue between both countries and a mechanism for future equity determination based on subsequent production. Following several postponements, production was expected to begin in 2023, with annual output projected at 2.5m. metric tons of liquefied natural gas for international export. In February 2020 BP signed a sales and purchase agreement for the project's entire first phase production. In September 2019 Kosmos announced positive results from its second appraisal well, Yakaar-2, on the Yakaar-Teranga offshore gas prospect, north-west of Dakar, estimating that it could contain as much as 20,000,000m. cu ft of gas.

POWER

Senegal is poor in indigenous resources for generating electricity. Most of Senegal's electric power comes from power stations dependent on expensive imported oil. From 2006, with ageing equipment and rising costs, frequent and extended power cuts began to affect urban centres; despite significant public investment from 2007, these were to become a highly charged political issue and contributed to serious rioting in major towns in 2011. Plan TAKKAL ('Light Yourself Up'), presented to the legislature in March, recommended expenditure of US $1,500m. on improving the power supply in 2011–15 and included a special Energy Support Fund to deal with short-term supply problems, together with substantial investments to enhance the performance of the Société Nationale d'Electricité (SENELEC). By September 2011 the mobilization of additional funds and the renting of two supplementary power stations (on barges) had stabilized the power supply.

In 2012 the administration of President Macky Sall confirmed that it would uphold the outgoing Government's commitments. A master plan for the electricity sector was finalized in February 2013. This envisaged the creation of additional production capacity; a major rehabilitation of SENELEC's production and distribution facilities; and a long overdue financial restructuring of the state company. There was also to be a greater reliance on solar energy and coal rather than oil for electricity generation, and the Government would draw up contracts with private companies to build and operate power stations. In February 2016 the new Tobène thermal plant, expected to provide 70 MW, was opened at Taiba Ndiaye. This was followed in October by the inauguration of the 20-MW Senergy II solar power plant. In February 2018 a new solar plant, known as Cheikh Anta Diop Park, was unveiled in Merina Dakhar, near Dakar, providing 30 MW of new energy. The plant was built by Solairedirect, a subsidiary of French energy company ENGIE, and its production was to be sold directly to SENELEC under a power purchase agreement. A 20-MW solar power plant was opened in Bokhol in late 2016, and further plants were to be built in Diourbel, Kaoack and Fatick (100 MW in total). In February 2020 Senegal inaugurated its first large commercial wind farm, the 159-MW Taïba Ndiaye project, which was expected to provide electricity to more than 2m. people. It was envisaged that the percentage of renewable energy in the country's energy mix would reach 15% by 2025. In June 2021 the National Assembly passed two bills allowing private investors to enter Senegal's electricity market and to thereby break the state monopoly. These bills provided for the restructuring of SENELEC into a holding company with several subsidiaries and the formation of a regulatory body for the energy sector.

Senegal's installed power capacity mainly services the urban centres, but solar power technology has allowed electricity to be extended to rural areas. Furthermore, in February 2017 the Government announced that electricity prices—among the highest in West Africa—would be reduced by 10% from March. In February 2018 the Government contracted the French company Vinci Energies to renovate parts of the electricity grid infrastructure, at a cost of €197m. (US $242m.) over three years. In 2021 the Government undertook, with the support of the World Bank and the African Development Bank (AfDB), to raise 732,000m. francs CFA ($1,300.) in order to achieve universal access to affordable electricity by 2025. In June 2021 the legislature adopted an electricity code that detailed the Senegalese electricity sector and its regulations for potential investors.

For the immediate future, Senegal's power needs are expected to grow by 10% annually, and SENELEC remains a heavy burden on government finances, with its electricity still among the most expensive in Africa. By 2020 an estimated 70.4% of Senegal's population (47.4% of the urban population) had access to electricity, according to the World Bank. In July 2021 the Government struck a deal with the EU, together with the USA and the World Bank, to finance the construction of a vaccine manufacturing plant in Senegal.

MANUFACTURING

After Côte d'Ivoire, Senegal has the most developed manufacturing sector in francophone West Africa; the sector accounted for 16.6% of GDP in 2021. Low labour productivity, infrastructural weaknesses and problems of access to credit have limited the competitiveness of Senegalese industry and constrained its potential as a growth stimulus. However, during the past decade its role has expanded considerably: in 2021 industry's value added amounted to US $6,810m. (compared with around $1,440m. in 2000). The main activity is light industry (mostly located in or near Dakar). The agro-industrial sector is dominated by fish canning and vegetable oil production, but also includes sugar refining, flour milling, tobacco, dairy products and drinks. Extractive industries (mainly the processing of phosphates) constitute a second important branch of activity. Leather goods production is also significant, as are paper and packaging, the manufacture of wood products and building materials, and the chemicals industry (including soap, paints, insecticides, plastics, pharmaceuticals and petroleum products). Senegal's first vehicle assembly plant, at Thiès—a joint venture between the Government and India's Tata International—started producing buses in 2003.

In 2013 combined output from Senegal's then two cement plants—one at Rufisque and the other at Kirène, near Thiès—was 5.9m. metric tons, of which 1.8m. tons were exported. The opening of a third plant, owned by Dangote Group of Nigeria, suffered an initial delay, after a dispute over ownership of the land that it occupied, but production began in December 2014. In 2019 Senegalese cement production amounted to 5.3m. tons, while exports had decreased to 1.5m. tons in 2017. In December 2021 the Rufisque plant announced that it was to construct a new production line that would use less power, in line with plans to reduce carbon emissions, and reach a capacity of some 10,000 tons of cement per day.

Senegal's only oil refinery is the Société Africaine de Raffinage (SAR), at M'Bao, near Dakar. In 2006 the Government had increased its stake in SAR to 57.2%, with the remainder being held by Total, Royal Dutch Shell and ExxonMobil. Although SAR is Senegal's largest enterprise, its debt overhang prompted the Government to invite the Saudi Binladin Group to acquire a 34% stake in May 2010, leaving the Government with 46% and Total with 20%. The energy sector remains critical to Senegal's development, but imposes heavy burdens on the balance of payments. Import spending on petroleum was partly offset by exports of refined petroleum to neighbouring countries in 2013–15; however, owing to falling petroleum exports in 2016–21, the net costs amounted to nearly US $1,575m. in 2021.

TRANSPORT INFRASTRUCTURE

Industrial development was stimulated by, and in turn boosted, the port of Dakar. With the completion of a new terminal in 1988, container handling facilities were increased from 29,000 metric tons to more than 100,000 tons. In 2007 the Government selected Dubai Ports World (DP World) of the United Arab Emirates (UAE) to develop and operate a terminal at Dakar's fishing port, which opened in November 2011. By 2021 Dakar was handling 769,400 containers annually, a nearly three-fold increase in capacity since 2008. Some 95% of the goods landed are destined for countries in the West African interior rather than the Senegalese market. In June 2018 the Government launched a strategic plan for 2019–23, with the objective of making the port of Dakar the most competitive in the Economic Community of West African States. In November 2017 DP World announced that the construction of a new port terminal (Port du Futur) would commence in 2018 next to the Blaise Diagne International Airport (BDIA—see below). DP World was also expected to design and build an adjacent logistics terminal with an annual handling capacity of 1.5m. containers and to continue upgrading the existing port facilities.

Air Sénégal, the national carrier, was partially privatized in 1999, with Royal Air Maroc (RAM) taking a 51% stake. Rising competition and fuel costs brought significant losses; in 2007 the Government retook control, increasing its share from 49% to 75% and providing €35m. in new capital. In May 2009, however, the Government and RAM agreed to close down the airline (by then technically bankrupt). The formation of its successor, Sénégal Airlines, was announced in November, with RAM replaced by Emirates Airline (of the UAE) as partner. Sénégal Airlines began operations in January 2011; however, in October 2013 with the airline suffering serious financial difficulties, the Government took 51% control and initiated a search for a new partner. After this search proved inconclusive, the Government announced in April 2016 that it was cancelling the airline's flying rights, thereby forcing it into liquidation. In April 2017 the new, entirely state-owned Air Sénégal

SA was launched; in 2019 it operated flights to Ziguinchor (Casamance), and to francophone West Africa's major cities, as well as Paris. As was the case with all international airlines, from March 2020 Air Sénégal was adversely affected by the temporary closure of borders as a result of the COVID-19 pandemic. With the removal of remaining restrictions on international flights in October 2021, by mid-2022 Air Sénégal flew to 24 destinations in Africa, Europe and North America.

After some years of delay, construction by the Saudi Binladin Group started in 2007 on the new BDIA, at Ndiass, 50 km east of Dakar, to replace the more central, former Léopold Sédar Senghor International Airport. However, its construction suffered multiple delays. In December 2015 the construction was taken over by Summa Limak of Turkey (now known as Türkiye) and made rapid progress thereafter. The new airport was inaugurated in December 2017 and had an initial capacity of 2m. passengers, which was initially expected to increase to 5m. with the opening of new terminals and a second runway. While air passenger traffic fell significantly, to 0.3m. in 2020, it increased again thereafter, reaching 1.9m. passengers in 2021.

Senegal has an extensive road network. In 2015 there were 16,495 km of classified roads, of which 5,956 km were surfaced. Construction of Senegal's first toll highway (the 25-km Dakar–Diamniadio route) by the French company Eiffage was completed in August 2013. In February 2014 the Government awarded Eiffage an additional contract to build a highway linking Dakar with the BDIA and the adjoining Dakar Integrated Special Economic Zone, under construction by the Dubai company Jebel Ali. Two further toll highways around Dakar—one linking Thiès, Diourbel and Touba and the other connecting the BDIA to Thiès and Mbour—were completed by early 2019, and by 2021 Senegal's highway network totalled 221 km, compared with 32 km in 2012. Work was also under way to build a highway connecting Mbour, Fatick and Kaolack, to be completed by mid-2025 and 85% funded by the Export-Import Bank of China and 15% by the Senegalese Government, similar to two previous highway projects. In April 2018 the Government announced that it was to receive US $56m. from the West African Development Bank to build 400 km of roads in order to open up the country's most remote regions. The Trans-Gambia Bridge was inaugurated in January 2019, facilitating travel between the Casamance region and The Gambia. In December 2021 the African Development Bank granted Senegal lending of more than US $160m. to build or reconstruct 483 km of roads in northern Senegal.

The rail infrastructure includes 922 km of track, although only 70 km of this is two-way. The two main lines run from Dakar to Kidira, and across the Malian border to Bamako; and from Dakar, via Thiès, to Saint-Louis in the north. In 1995 the Senegalese and Malian Governments established a joint company to operate the Dakar–Bamako line, with a 25-year concession granted in 2003 to a Canadian-French consortium, CANAC-Getma, which subsequently upgraded the line. Renewed work was under way in the early 2020s to rehabilitate the line, with the aim of offering two services a day between Dakar and Tambacounda, in the east. In December 2016 preparatory works were launched for the construction of a 55-km regional express railway to link Dakar with the BDIA. A 36-km stretch connecting Dakar to Damniado was inaugurated in early 2019. The works were completed by Eiffage, Yapi Merkezi (Turkey) and Compagnie Sahélienne d'Entreprises, the railway systems contractors were ENGIE Ineo and the Thales Group (both French), and the French railway companies SNCF and RATP were awarded the contract to operate the railway for the first five years. The project, costing 656,000m. francs CFA, was jointly funded by the AfDB, the Agence Française de Développement, the Islamic Development Bank and the Senegalese state. Works on the second stretch, to extend all the way to the BDIA, began in March 2022 and were expected to be completed by late 2023.

COMMUNICATIONS

With only three fixed-line telephones per 100 inhabitants in 2013 (and 1.37 in 2020), the installation of a national digital and fibre-optic network stimulated the rapid development of the telecommunications sector. According to the International Telecommunications Union, the penetration of mobile usage stood at 114% by the end of 2020. It was estimated that 42.6% of the population had access to the internet, notably by means of 4G technology, by the end of 2020.

In 1997 the national telecommunications company, Société Nationale des Télécommunications du Sénégal (SONATEL), was partially privatized. France Télécom subsidiary France Câbles et Radio acquired 33.3% of the company's capital (which it had increased to 52.2% by April 2009), and a further 10% of the shares went to SONATEL employees, with 18% being sold on the regional stock exchange in Abidjan, Côte d'Ivoire. SONATEL experienced strong growth after 1997 and, having moved into the mobile cellular telephone market, had 9.9m. subscribers in Senegal by early 2020. In terms of market share of mobile services, by mid-2021 SONATEL remained dominant, with 55% of the market; Free, formerly known as Tigo but rebranded in late 2019 to reflect its links to the French company of the same name, had 26.3%, and Expresso, a subsidiary of Sudan's Sudatel, 18.6%.

TOURISM

Beginning modestly, with a Club Med resort in Casamance in the 1970s, tourism has since developed to become a significant source of foreign exchange. Tourism receipts in 2018 were equivalent to 10% of GDP. Tourist arrivals steadily climbed during the 2000s and early 2010s to a record 1.1m. in 2012/13, and in 2017 this figure reached nearly 1.4m. Senegal has an estimated 45,000 hotel beds of international tourist standard, and Dakar is an important international conference centre. The tourism sector directly provided some 246,000 jobs prior to the COVID-19 pandemic. The Macky Sall administration raised the tourism target to 2m. arrivals by 2019 and provided significant further investment in the sector; however, the relatively high cost of holidaying in Senegal (compared with The Gambia and Cabo Verde) has limited the country's appeal to visitors. The COVID-19 pandemic had an adverse effect on the sector, despite the mitigating financial measures introduced by the state. An estimated 104,200 jobs were lost in the sector. The resumption of unrestricted international flights to Senegal from October 2021 raised hopes that the sector would recover rapidly.

INVESTMENT AND FINANCE

Private investment in industry and services rose vigorously after 2000. Although Senegalese private investment also played a significant role, the main growth was seen in foreign direct investment, which increased from US $45m. in 2005 to $398m. in 2008, before falling in subsequent years and rising again steadily from 2013; it amounted to $2,223m. in 2021, according to the UN Conference on Trade and Development. Despite the presence in Senegal of over 200 subsidiaries of French firms, investment from the Middle East has become prominent in sectors such as construction, tourism and communications, and Indian investments are significant in the mining sector. Chinese investment activity has also expanded. In the World Bank's 2020 *Doing Business* report Senegal was ranked 123rd out of 190 countries, 48 places higher than in 2013.

Since independence, Senegal has benefited from consistent support from Western donors keen to assist its relatively stable, conservative governments. In 2010–14 Senegal received an annual average of US $1,035m. in official aid; following a decrease to an average of $877m. per year in 2016–18, it received $1,444m. in 2019 and $1,611m. in 2020, according to the Organisation for Economic Co-operation and Development. Overwhelmingly, the aid that Senegal receives comes from donor countries rather than multilateral sources, although the International Development Association has systematically figured among the country's top three donors alongside France and the USA in 2016–20. Remittances from Senegalese working in Europe and North America remain important, and have a notable impact on local demand for housing construction; in 2020 remittances totalled $2,562m. (equivalent to 10.5% of GDP), according to the World Bank.

Considerable progress was made in the early 1980s in curbing Senegal's budget deficit, although prior to the major devaluation of the CFA franc in 1994, the currency's over-valuation had a negative effect on government revenues. More recently, revenue performance has improved, owing to tax reforms and more stringent financial management. Annual domestic tax revenue averaged 18.3% of GDP in 2011–18; it decreased to 16.7% in 2020 and 16.9% in 2021, due to the COVID-19 pandemic. Despite the impact of the 2011 drought, the energy sector's problems and increased security spending associated with the crisis in neighbouring Mali, the Government was able to reduce the fiscal deficit to 5.5% of GDP in 2013 (from 6.7% in 2011) and further in subsequent years, to an estimated 4.1% in 2019. It increased significantly in 2020 and 2021, however, to 6.4% and 6.3%, respectively, as a result of the COVID-19 pandemic, with the ensuing reduction in tax revenues and increase in (notably health) spending. Senegal nevertheless hoped to achieve the UEMOA convergence criteria of a budget deficit of no more than 3% of GDP by 2023. The private banking system remains burdened by non-performing loans; as of March 2022 these stood at 11.3% of total loan stock, although the banks did meet the higher minimum capital requirements introduced in 2010.

In 1994 Senegal was the first Franc Zone member to reach agreement with the IMF on new funding following the devaluation of the CFA franc. A new Enhanced Structural Adjustment Facility (ESAF) was approved in August. Senegal secured another three-year ESAF (later Poverty Reduction and Growth Facility—PRGF), equivalent to about US $144m., in 1998. A further PRGF, worth $33m., was granted in 2003 for the period to 2006. In 2007 the IMF awarded Senegal a three-year Policy Support Instrument (PSI). This did not include financial support, focusing rather on maintaining macroeconomic stability and enhancing fiscal governance. In 2008 the IMF approved further financial support worth around $112m., under the Exogenous Shocks Facility, to help the Government to cope with rising food and fuel prices. A second PSI was agreed in December 2010 and a third in June 2015. After negotiations on a follow-up arrangement, an unfunded Policy Coordination Instrument (PCI), which entailed further fiscal reforms and could unlock financing from other official creditors or private investors, was approved by the IMF executive board in January 2020. The IMF in April extended a $442m. disbursement in response to the challenges posed by the COVID-19 pandemic. During the third review of the PCI in April 2021, the Government and the IMF agreed on a new, 18-month financing arrangement under a Stand-By Credit Facility (SCF) and Stand-By Arrangement for a total amount of $650m., to run in conjunction with the PCI, and support the Government in its COVID-19 financial measures and post-pandemic recovery. Reviews under the PSI and SCF were conducted in January and June 2022, enabling the release of some $180m. and $216m., respectively. The IMF Executive Board noted that performance under the programmes had been satisfactory and that economic activity had remained robust in a challenging context compounded by the ongoing COVID-19 pandemic, the conflict in Ukraine and the impact of trade sanctions imposed by members of the Economic Community of West African States (ECOWAS) against neighbouring Mali from January 2022 (lifted in July).

FOREIGN TRADE AND PAYMENTS

Over the past 25 years Senegal's foreign trade and current account balance have remained in deficit. However, the fluctuations have tended to narrow, as exports of phosphates, minerals and fishery products have expanded alongside those of groundnuts. In nominal CFA franc terms, the value of both exports and imports increased substantially following the currency's 50% devaluation in 1994—exports by 119% and imports by 84%. Total exports rose from some 1,087,000m. francs CFA in 2010 to an estimated 3,047,000m. francs CFA in 2021. In 2007 the trade deficit amounted to 958,000m. francs CFA, widening thereafter to an estimated 2,038,000m. francs CFA in 2021, notably as a result of higher petroleum, cereals and machinery imports. In 2021 the five leading markets for Senegal's exports were Mali (20.2%), Switzerland (14.4%), India (9.8%), the People's Republic of China (6.6%) and Côte d'Ivoire (4.2%), and the country's main import providers were France (including Monaco—11.8%), China (9.7%), India (7.1%), the Russian Federation (5.7%) and Nigeria (5.3%).

Significant efforts to restructure and reduce Senegal's external debt were not made until after the devaluation of 1994. In 1996 commercial bank debt was considerably reduced following a World Bank-initiated 'buy-back' of 'London Club' debt at 16% of its face value. Substantial debt relief was approved by the 'Paris Club' of official creditors in 1994, and France cancelled one-half of Senegal's bilateral debt. The 'Paris Club' granted further concessionary relief in 1998. In 2000 Senegal became eligible for debt relief under the initiative for Heavily Indebted Poor Countries (HIPC). A debt relief programme for Senegal was subsequently announced, which, with the support of official creditors, was equivalent to some US $800m. Debt relief provided by the World Bank represented a 50% reduction in Senegal's obligations to the organization over the following nine years, and that given by the IMF represented 20% of obligations to the Fund over the following seven years. Senegal reached 'completion point' under its HIPC arrangements in 2004. Total debt relief was $488m. in net present value terms. In 2005 Senegal was among 18 countries to be granted substantial further debt relief under the Multilateral Debt Relief Initiative agreed by the Group of Eight (G8) leading industrialized nations. Following the debt write-offs, Senegal's total external debt stocks, according to the World Bank, fell from $3,860m. in 2005 to $2,150m. in 2006; it then rose again steadily, reaching $17,240m. in 2020. Senegal's major bilateral lenders include France, Kuwait, Spain, China and India. In 2016 a total of 73.5% of the country's external debt was owed on concessional terms to multilateral institutions. Since 2009 Senegal has used the Eurobond, Islamic and regional bond markets for sizeable bond issues on non-concessional terms.

Statistical Survey

Source (unless otherwise stated): Agence nationale de la Statistique et de la Démographie, blvd de l'Est, Point E, BP 116, Dakar; tel. 33-824-0301; e-mail statsenegal@yahoo.fr; internet www.ansd.sn.

Area and Population

AREA, POPULATION AND DENSITY

Area (sq km)	196,712*
Population (census results)†	
8 December 2002	9,858,482
19 November 2013	
Males	6,735,421
Females	6,773,294
Total	13,508,715
Population (official projections at mid-year)	
2020	16,705,608
2021	17,215,433
2022	17,738,795
Density (per sq km) at mid-2022‡	90.2

* 75,951 sq miles.
† Figures refer to the *de jure* population. The de facto population was 9,555,346 in 2002 and 13,281,722 in 2013.
‡ Projection.

POPULATION BY AGE AND SEX
('000, official projections at mid-2022)

	Males	Females	Total
0–14 years	3,739.8	3,629.1	7,368.9
15–64 years	4,775.5	4,946.9	9,722.4
65 years and over	309.9	337.6	647.5
Total	**8,825.2**	**8,913.6**	**17,738.8**

POPULATION BY ETHNIC GROUP
(at 1988 census)

Ethnic group	Number	%
Wolof	2,890,402	42.67
Serere	1,009,921	14.91
Peul	978,366	14.44
Toucouleur	631,892	9.33
Diola	357,672	5.28
Mandingue	245,651	3.63
Rural-Rurale	113,184	1.67
Bambara	91,071	1.34
Maure	67,726	1.00
Manjaag	66,605	0.98
Others	320,927	4.74
Total	**6,773,417**	**100.00**

Note: Classification of ethnicity reflects national census methodology.

Source: UN, *Demographic Yearbook*.

REGIONS
('000, official population projections, 2022)

	Area (sq km)	Population	Density (per sq km)
Dakar	547	4,042.2	7389.8
Diourbel	4,824	1,980.8	410.6
Fatick	6,849	965.9	141.0
Kaffrine	11,262	782.3	69.5
Kaolack	5,357	1,267.0	236.5
Kedougou	16,800	203.7	12.1
Kolda	13,771	875.7	63.6
Louga	24,889	1,121.6	45.1
Matam	29,445	789.2	26.8
Saint-Louis	19,241	1,150.1	59.8
Sedhiou	7,341	612.7	83.5
Tambacounda	42,364	937.2	22.1
Thiès	6,670	2,280.5	341.9
Ziguinchor	7,352	729.9	99.3
Total	**196,712**	**17,738.8**	**90.2**

PRINCIPAL TOWNS
(at 2013 census)

Pikine . . .	1,170,791		Saint-Louis . . .		209,752
Dakar (capital) . .	1,146,053		Diourbel . . .		133,705
Rufisque . .	490,694		Tambacounda . .		107,293
Guediawaye . .	329,659		Louga		104,349
Thiès . . .	317,763		Kolda		81,098
Kaolack . . .	233,708		Mbacké		77,255
Mbour	232,777				

Note: Data given pertain to communes, except for Dakar, Pikine, Rufisque and Guediawaye, where the figures given are for départements, all within Dakar region.

Mid-2021 (incl. suburbs, UN projection): Dakar 3,229,800 (Source: UN, *World Urbanization Prospects: The 2018 Revision*).

BIRTHS AND DEATHS
(annual averages, UN estimates)

	2005–10	2010–15	2015–20
Birth rate (per 1,000)	38.5	37.7	34.7
Death rate (per 1,000)	8.1	6.6	5.8

Source: UN, *World Population Prospects: The 2019 Revision*.

2018: Birth rate 36.8 per 1,000; Death rate 7.1 per 1,000 (Source: African Development Bank).

Life expectancy (years at birth, estimates): 68.2 (males 66.0; females 70.2) in 2020 (Source: World Bank, World Development Indicators database).

ECONOMICALLY ACTIVE POPULATION
(labour force survey, '000 persons aged 15 years and over, 2015)

	Males	Females	Total
Agriculture, hunting, fishing and forestry	742	393	1,135
Mining and quarrying	16	5	21
Electricity, gas and water . . .	17	1	18
Manufacturing	142	68	210
Construction	188	4	192
Wholesale and retail trade; repair of motor vehicles and motorcycles	316	375	691
Hotels and restaurants . . .	18	45	63
Transport, storage and communications	151	11	162
Financial intermediation . . .	12	7	19
Real estate, renting and business activities	18	8	26
Public administration and defence; compulsory social security . .	19	6	25
Education	98	43	141
Health and social work . . .	25	27	52
Other community, social and personal services	199	113	312
Private households with employed persons	68	255	323
Extraterritorial organizations and bodies	6	4	10
Sub-total	**2,035**	**1,364**	**3,400**
Not classified by economic activity	10	9	18
Total employed	**2,045**	**1,373**	**3,418**
Unemployed	140	108	248
Total labour force	**2,185**	**1,481**	**3,666**

Note: Totals may not be equal to the sum of components, owing to rounding.

2019: Agriculture 1,062; Mining and utilities 88; Manufacturing 594; Construction 295; Trade, transportation, accommodation and business and administrative services 1,655; Other services 925, Activities not classified 2; *Total employed* 4,621; Unemployed 136; *Total labour force* 4,757 (males 2,961, females 1,796).

Source: ILO.

Health and Welfare

KEY INDICATORS

Total fertility rate (children per woman, 2020) . . .	4.5
Under-5 mortality rate (per 1,000 live births, 2020) . . .	38.1
HIV/AIDS (% of persons aged 15–49, 2020)	0.3
COVID-19: Cumulative confirmed deaths (per 100,000 persons at 31 August 2022)	11.7
COVID-19: Fully vaccinated population (% of total population at 28 August 2022)	6.5
Physicians (per 1,000 head, 2019)	0.09
Hospitals (per 100,000 head, 2013)	0.2
Domestic health expenditure (2019): US $ per head (PPP) .	36.2
Domestic health expenditure (2019): % of GDP	1.0
Domestic health expenditure (2019): public (% of total current expenditure)	25.0
Access to improved water resources (% of persons, 2020) .	85
Access to improved sanitation facilities (% of persons, 2020) .	57
Total carbon dioxide emissions ('000 metric tons, 2018) . .	9,860
Carbon dioxide emissions per head (metric tons, 2018) . .	0.6
Human Development Index (2021): ranking	170
Human Development Index (2021): value	0.511

Note: For data on COVID-19 vaccinations, 'fully vaccinated' denotes receipt of all doses specified by approved vaccination regime (Sources: Johns Hopkins University and Our World in Data). Data on health expenditure refer to current general government expenditure in each case. For more information on sources and further definitions for all indicators, see Health and Welfare Statistics: Sources and Definitions section (europaworld.com/credits).

Agriculture

PRINCIPAL CROPS
('000 metric tons)

	2018	2019	2020
Bananas	30.0	31.4	36.5
Beans, green	18.7	18.8	18.8
Cabbages and other brassicas .	76.1	105.1	158.4
Cantaloupes and other melons* .	28.0	31.5	35.3
Carrots and turnips	16.0	17.1	22.3
Cashew nuts, with shell* . . .	8.7	8.6	8.8
Cassava (Manioc)	1,023.7	1,030.6	1,346.5
Cow peas, dry	152.8	184.1	253.9
Groundnuts, with shell . . .	1,500.6	1,421.3	1,797.5
Mangoes, mangosteens and guavas	128.5	130.0	121.0
Maize	485.7	530.7	761.9
Millet	897.6	807.0	1,144.9
Oil palm fruit*	125.6	124.4	124.8
Okra	41.2	35.2	23.1
Onions, dry	460.0	444.9	412.3
Oranges	45.0	48.5	56.8
Potatoes	118.8	140.0	148.0
Pumpkins, squash and gourds* .	16.7	17.1	17.0
Rice, paddy	1,206.6	1,155.7	1,349.7
Seed cotton	15.1	16.5	20.2
Sorghum	295.5	270.2	377.3
Sugar cane*	1,378.0	1,379.0	1,389.2
Sweet potatoes	72.0	89.4	89.7
Tomatoes	138.0	148.0	135.4
Watermelons	1,172.8	1,190.5	1,677.5
Yams*	70.0	77.5	95.3

* FAO estimates.

Aggregate production ('000 metric tons, may include official, semi-official or estimated data): Total cereals 2,889.2 in 2018, 2,768.8 in 2019, 3,640.5 in 2020; Total fruit (primary) 1,452.5 in 2018, 1,486.6 in 2019, 2,008.3 in 2020; Total oilcrops 1,664.7 in 2018, 1,592.1 in 2019, 1,984.1 in 2020; Total pulses 152.9 in 2018, 184.2 in 2019, 254.0 in 2020; Total roots and tubers 1,284.5 in 2018, 1,337.5 in 2019, 1,679.5 in 2020; Total vegetables (primary) 970.5 in 2018, 1,000.3 in 2019, 1,000.6 in 2020.

Source: FAO.

LIVESTOCK
('000 head, year ending September)

	2018	2019	2020*
Asses	478	483	488
Cattle	3,628	3,671	3,713
Chickens	72,523	81,419	88,495
Goats	6,051	6,232	6,405
Horses	568	575	579
Pigs	451	465	478
Sheep	7,132	7,382	7,426

* FAO estimates.

Source: FAO.

LIVESTOCK PRODUCTS
('000 metric tons)

	2018	2019	2020*
Cattle hides, fresh	15.3*	15.9*	15.4
Cattle meat	76.5	79.8	77.0
Cattle offals, edible	15.3*	15.9*	15.4
Cows' milk	221.0*	225.0*	220.7
Chicken meat	105.4	116.5	122.8
Goat meat	23.9	20.5	21.1
Goats' milk	16.0*	13.8*	14.0
Horse meat	7.2*	7.2*	7.2
Pig meat	17.9	18.8	19.5
Sheep meat	32.2	31.8	29.8
Sheep's (Ewe's) milk	13.1*	11.9*	11.9
Sheepskins, fresh	5.7*	4.9*	5.1
Hen eggs	36.8*	41.5*	41.5
Honey (natural)	3.7*	3.6*	3.6

* FAO estimate(s).

Source: FAO.

Forestry

ROUNDWOOD REMOVALS
('000 cubic metres, excl. bark, FAO estimates)

	2018	2019	2020
Sawlogs, veneer logs and logs for sleepers	62	62	62
Other industrial wood* . . .	754	754	754
Fuel wood	5,598	5,612	5,626
Total	6,414	6,428	6,442

* Annual output assumed to be unchanged since 1999.

Source: FAO.

SAWNWOOD PRODUCTION
('000 cubic metres, incl. railway sleepers, FAO estimates)

	2014	2015	2016
Total (all broadleaved) . . .	43	31	31

2017–20: Figure assumed to be unchanged from 2016.

Source: FAO.

Fishing

('000 metric tons, live weight)

	2018	2019	2020
Capture*	484.8	516.1	451.7
Freshwater fishes*	21.0	21.2	20.0
Largehead hairtail	9.2	4.9	3.9
Round sardinella . . .	88.4	121.3	65.6
Madeiran sardinella	81.6	96.3	100.9
Bonga shad	12.6	22.2	27.8
Aquaculture	0.8	1.0	1.1
Total catch*	485.6	517.1	452.8

* FAO estimates.

Source: FAO.

Mining

('000 metric tons unless otherwise stated)

	2016	2017	2018
Crude petroleum ('000 barrels) .	24	95	95*
Gold (kg)	6,874	6,732	7,628
Cement, hydraulic	5,149	5,197	5,412
Calcium phosphates . . .	1,610	1,385	1,649
Fuller's earth (attapulgite) . .	172	166	178
Salt (unrefined)	263	259	260*

* Estimate.

Aluminium phosphates: 4 in 2010 (estimate).

Source: US Geological Survey.

Industry

PETROLEUM PRODUCTS
('000 metric tons)

	2017	2018	2019
Motor gasoline (petrol) . . .	97	93	84
Naphthas	123	76	71
Gas-diesel (distillate fuel) oils .	679	576	522
Residual fuel oils (Mazout) . .	285	220	191
Liquefied petroleum gas . . .	3	3	3

Jet fuels ('000 metric tons): 19 in 2014; 18 in 2015.

Kerosene ('000 metric tons): 2 in 2014; 2 in 2015.

Source: UN Energy Statistics Database.

SELECTED OTHER PRODUCTS
('000 metric tons unless otherwise indicated)

	2017	2018	2019
Wheat flour	214.1	191.7	248.1
Sugar cubes	7.1	5.2	4.1
Salt	265.0	245.7	286.1
Phosphates	1,385.0	1,782.0	1,748.0
Fertilizers	200.0	143.6	162.1
Cement	5,196.6	5,412.0	5,283.2
Electrical energy (million kWh) .	3,866.6	4,033.1	4,004.0

Soap: 19.3 in 2011.

Finance

CURRENCY AND EXCHANGE RATES

Monetary Units
100 centimes = 1 franc de la Communauté Financière Africaine (CFA).

Sterling, Dollar and Euro Equivalents (31 May 2022)
£1 sterling = 770.824 francs CFA;
US $1 = 612.300 francs CFA;
€1 = 655.957 francs CFA;
10,000 francs CFA = £12.97 = $16.33 = €15.24.

Average Exchange Rate (francs CFA per US $)
2019   585.91
2020   575.59
2021   554.53

Note: An exchange rate of 1 French franc = 50 francs CFA, established in 1948, remained in force until January 1994, when the CFA franc was devalued by 50%, with the exchange rate adjusted to 1 French franc = 100 francs CFA. This relationship to French currency remained in effect with the introduction of the euro on 1 January 1999. From that date, accordingly, a fixed exchange rate of €1 = 655.957 francs CFA has been in operation.

BUDGET
('000 million francs CFA)

Revenue*	2020	2021	2022†
Tax revenue	2,368	2,691	3,025
Income tax	717	770	848
Taxes on goods and services .	1,228	1,410	1,591
Taxes on international trade and			
transactions	337	397	454
Other Taxes	86	114	132
Non-tax revenue	150	182	140
Other revenue	34	42	48
Total	2,552	2,915	3,213

Expenditure	2020	2021	2022†
Current expenditure	2,428	2,484	2,473
Wages and salaries	804	896	952
Interest payments	289	309	350
Other operational expenses . .	1,335	1,279	1,170
Transfers and subsidies . .	1,049	933	811
Goods and services . . .	285	346	359
Capital expenditure	1,317	1,591	1,772
Total	3,745	4,075	4,245

* Excluding grants received ('000 million francs CFA): 324 in 2020; 236 in 2021; 296 in 2022 (projection).
† Projections.

Source: Ministry of Finance and the Budget, Dakar.

INTERNATIONAL RESERVES
(excluding gold, US $ million at 31 December)

	2019	2020	2021
IMF special drawing rights . .	1.8	459.6	1,057.5
Reserve position in IMF . . .	59.0	61.4	59.7
Foreign exchange	3.2	5.0	4.7
Total	64.0	526.0	1,121.9

Source: IMF, *International Financial Statistics*.

MONEY SUPPLY
('000 million francs CFA at 31 December)

	2019	2020	2021
Currency outside depository			
corporations	1,302.37	1,529.48	1,964.37
Transferable deposits	2,666.28	2,984.18	3,311.88
Other deposits	1,718.47	1,875.76	2,040.07
Broad money	5,687.12	6,389.42	7,316.31

Source: IMF, *International Financial Statistics*.

COST OF LIVING
(Consumer Price Index; base: 2014 = 100)

	2020	2021
Food and non-alcoholic beverages	112.8	116.2
Clothing and footwear	102.2	103.0
Rent, fuel and energy	99.3	100.8
All items (incl. others)	107.4	109.7

NATIONAL ACCOUNTS
('000 million francs CFA at current prices)

Expenditure on the Gross Domestic Product

	2019	2020	2021
Final consumption expenditure .	11,286	11,775	12,551
Households	9,365	9,702	10,285
General government	1,921	2,073	2,266
Gross fixed capital formation . .	4,067	4,155	5,466
Changes in inventories, etc. . .	832	1,299	1,166
Total domestic expenditure .	16,185	17,229	19,183
Exports of goods and services . .	3,426	2,914	3,723
Less Imports of goods and services	5,898	6,042	8,156
GDP at purchasers' values .	13,713	14,101	14,751
GDP in constant 2014 prices .	13,197	13,372	14,162

Gross Domestic Product by Economic Activity

	2019	2020	2021
Agriculture, hunting, forestry and fishing	2,043	2,286	2,213
Mining and quarrying	520	595	689
Manufacturing	2,042	2,016	2,239
Electricity, gas and water . . .	278	299	322
Construction	392	365	400
Trade, restaurants and hotels .	1,997	1,871	1,971
Finance, insurance and real estate	2,109	2,248	2,450
Transport and communications .	1,053	1,010	1,056
Public administration and defence	736	821	893
Other services	1,093	1,134	1,230
Sub-total	12,262	12,646	13,463
Net taxes on products	1,450	1,455	1,288
GDP at purchasers' values .	13,713	14,101	14,751

BALANCE OF PAYMENTS
('000 million francs CFA)

	2020	2021*
Exports of goods	2,410	3,047
Imports of goods	−4,020	−4,753
Balance on goods	−1,610	−1,706
Services and incomes (net)	−1,358	−1,851
Balance on goods, services and primary income	−2,968	−3,557
Unrequited current transfers (net) . . .	1,435	1,519
Current balance	−1,532	−2,038
Capital account (net)	139	125
Direct investment (net)	1,005	1,379
Portfolio investment (net)	240	372
Other investment (net)	−250	268
Net errors and omissions	300	—
Overall balance	−97	105

* Preliminary.

Source: IMF, *Senegal: Fifth Review Under the Policy Coordination Instrument, Second Reviews Under the Stand-By Arrangement and the Arrangement Under the Standby Credit Facility, and Requests for Augmentation of Access, Waiver of the Nonobservance of a Performance Criterion, and Modification of a Performance Criterion and Quantitative Targets—Press Release; Staff Report; and Statement by the Executive Director for Senegal* (June 2022).

External Trade

PRINCIPAL COMMODITIES
('000 million francs CFA)

Imports c.i.f.	2019	2020	2021
Cereals	349.6	398.4	480.2
Animal and vegetable oils and fats	97.1	139.7	119.6
Mineral fuels, oil, waxes; bituminous materials	1,234.3	1,040.9	1,359.1
Pharmaceutical products . . .	155.4	161.7	188.0
Plastic materials and articles . .	131.5	134.0	176.6
Cast iron, iron and steel . . .	176.5	159.3	232.0
Articles of iron and steel . . .	153.0	114.7	167.6
Boilers and machines	429.3	382.6	487.1
Electrical machines, transmitting and receiving apparatus . .	318.4	309.1	313.0
Vehicles	290.6	255.5	302.1
Total (incl. others)	4,773.9	4,494.7	5,378.5

Exports f.o.b.	2019	2020	2021
Fish and crustaceans, molluscs and other shellfish	290.7	248.1	301.2
Miscellaneous food preparations .	84.8	85.4	95.3
Medicinal plants, grasses for commercial use	114.5	116.9	160.9
Mineral fuels, oil, waxes; bituminous materials . .	487.1	361.5	447.9
Inorganic chemicals; metal or radioactive compounds . . .	199.5	155.5	269.9
Sulphur; earth and stones; lime and cements	113.5	100.2	127.4
Ores, slag and ash	115.4	116.2	150.3
Pearls, gemstones, precious metals; costume jewellery; coins . .	376.2	423.1	540.5
Total (incl. others)	2,446.7	2,261.3	2,884.8

PRINCIPAL TRADING PARTNERS
('000 million francs CFA)

Imports c.i.f.	2019	2020	2021
Argentina	60.0	57.5	102.8
Belgium-Luxembourg	330.1	267.6	254.5
Brazil	72.2	98.4	88.8
China, People's Republic . . .	510.4	413.9	520.4
Côte d'Ivoire	55.2	58.7	58.2
Denmark	90.3	13.2	14.7
France (incl. Monaco)	801.1	704.0	632.8
Germany	93.1	85.7	96.5
Ghana	43.0	62.8	41.5
India	162.3	192.5	383.7
Italy	79.1	84.7	112.8
Japan	82.2	62.9	91.6
Malaysia	39.3	47.9	90.4
Morocco	74.8	84.6	91.5
Netherlands	322.8	277.3	260.0
Nigeria	245.6	257.2	287.6
Poland	47.6	52.6	53.9
Russian Federation	213.3	203.2	307.6
Singapore	85.5	11.1	24.0
South Africa	58.8	49.2	77.2
Spain	194.9	227.6	253.0
Switzerland	52.4	69.4	40.1
Thailand	68.9	42.7	46.7
Türkiye	177.7	160.0	229.4
Ukraine	84.7	62.1	72.7
United Arab Emirates	89.2	125.7	213.6
USA	93.6	117.6	150.4
Total (incl. others)	4,773.9	4,494.7	5,378.5

Exports f.o.b.	2019	2020	2021
Australia	1.6	123.1	120.4
Belgium-Luxembourg	28.3	27.9	12.1
Burkina Faso	38.0	30.0	36.8
China, People's Republic . . .	161.9	152.1	189.8
Congo, Republic	22.5	15.7	20.7
Côte d'Ivoire	91.9	110.3	120.6
France (incl. Monaco)	51.2	44.2	49.6
The Gambia	45.4	64.6	88.3
Guinea	78.8	85.4	80.5
Guinea-Bissau	38.4	32.9	41.4
India	211.9	172.0	282.4
Italy	59.6	31.1	60.7
Mali	562.1	474.8	582.6
Mauritania	39.7	40.8	51.5
Mexico	3.0	13.9	30.5
Netherlands	32.1	39.5	66.2
Norway	11.8	31.8	42.1
Spain	89.2	71.7	108.6
Switzerland	359.2	279.6	414.8
United Arab Emirates	34.1	25.4	34.4
United Kingdom	36.6	36.2	40.9
USA	77.5	67.5	69.4
Total (incl. others)	2,446.7	2,261.3	2,884.8

Transport

SHIPPING

Flag Registered Fleet
(at 31 December)

	2019	2020	2021
Number of vessels	121	129	140
Total displacement ('000 grt) . .	56.4	60.9	64.6

Source: Lloyd's List Intelligence (www.bit.ly/LLintelligence).

International Seaborne Freight Traffic
('000 metric tons)

	2019	2020	2021
Goods loaded	5,374	4,808	5,842
Goods unloaded	15,121	15,781	17,878

Source: Port Autonome de Dakar.

CIVIL AVIATION
(traffic on scheduled services)

	2013	2014	2015
Kilometres flown (million) . .	5	3	3
Passengers carried ('000) . . .	220	132	115
Passenger-km (million) . . .	384	222	192
Total ton-km (million)	4	4	3

Source: UN, *Statistical Yearbook*.

2020 (domestic and international): Departures 4,377; Passengers carried 0.3m.; Freight carried 3m. ton-km (Source: World Bank, World Development Indicators database).

Tourism

FOREIGN VISITORS BY COUNTRY OF ORIGIN*

	2015	2016	2017
Côte d'Ivoire	8,873	10,692	12,452
France	218,552	263,358	306,716
Germany	7,765	9,357	10,897
Guinea-Bissau	6,641	8,002	9,320
Italy	10,496	12,648	14,730
Mali	10,120	12,195	14,202
Spain	21,032	25,344	29,516
United Kingdom	8,543	10,294	11,989
USA	19,739	23,786	27,702
Total (incl. others)	680,491	820,000	955,000

* Arrivals at hotels and similar establishments.

Tourism receipts (US $ million, excl. passenger transport): 419 in 2017; 496 in 2018.

Source: World Tourism Organization.

Communications Media

	2018	2019	2020
Telephones ('000 main lines in use)	302.2	207.6	228.7
Mobile telephone subscriptions ('000)	16,559.9	17,880.6	19,078.9
Broadband subscriptions, fixed ('000)	129.8	152.0	177.4
Broadband subscriptions, mobile ('000)	6,678.4	8,840.1	11,168.8
Internet users (% of population) .	35.3	39.5	42.6

Source: International Telecommunication Union.

Education

(2019/20 unless otherwise indicated)

	Institutions	Teachers	Students ('000)		
			Males	Females	Total
Pre-primary .	3,152*	12,696	122.4	134.0	256.4
Primary . . .	9,827*	66,447	1,065.0	1,195.0	2,260.0
Secondary . .	1,122†	57,316‡	558.5	636.6	1,195.1
Tertiary . . .	n.a.	6,816	93.9	120.1	214.0

* 2015/16.
† 2008/09.
‡ 2016/17.

Sources: Ministry of National Education, Dakar; UNESCO Institute for Statistics.

Pupil-teacher ratio (qualified teaching staff, primary education, UNESCO estimate): 34.2 in 2019/20 (Source: UNESCO Institute for Statistics).

Adult literacy rate (UNESCO estimates): 51.9% (males 64.8%; females 39.8%) in 2017 (Source: UNESCO Institute for Statistics).

Directory

The Constitution

The Constitution of the Republic of Senegal was promulgated following its approval by popular referendum on 7 January 2001, and entered into force thereafter, with the exception of those sections relating to the National Assembly and the relations between the executive and legislative powers (articles 59–87), which took effect following legislative elections on 29 April 2001. The main provisions (including subsequent amendments, the most recent of which were promulgated in May 2019) are summarized below:

PREAMBLE

The people of Senegal, recognizing their common destiny, and aware of the need to consolidate the fundaments of the nation and the state, and supporting the ideals of African unity and human rights, proclaim the principle of national territorial integrity and a national unity respecting the diverse cultures of the nation, reject all forms of injustice, inequality and discrimination, and proclaim the will of Senegal to be a modern democratic state.

THE STATE AND SOVEREIGNTY

Articles 1–6: Senegal is a secular, democratic Republic, in which all people are equal before the law, without distinction of origin, race, sex or religion. The official language of the Republic is French; the national languages are Diola, Malinké, Pulaar, Sérère, Soninké, Wolof and any other national language that may be so defined. The principle of the Republic is 'government of the people, by the people and for the people'. National sovereignty belongs to the people who exercise it, through their representatives or in referenda. Suffrage may be direct or indirect, and is always universal, equal and secret. Political parties and coalitions of political parties are obliged to observe the Constitution and the principles of national sovereignty and democracy, and are forbidden from identifying with one race, one ethnic group, one sex, one religion, one sect, one language or one region. All political parties are guaranteed equal rights. All acts of racial, ethnic or religious discrimination, including regionalist propaganda liable to undermine the security or territorial integrity of the state are punishable by law. The institutions of the Republic are: the President of the Republic; the National Assembly; the Government; the High Council of the Territorial Collectivities; the Economic, Social and Environmental Council; and the Constitutional Council, the Supreme Court, the Revenue Court and Courts and Tribunals.

PUBLIC LIBERTIES AND THE HUMAN PERSON; ECONOMIC AND SOCIAL RIGHTS AND COLLECTIVE RIGHTS

Articles 7–25: The inviolable and inalienable rights of man are recognized as the base of all human communities, of peace and justice in the world, and are protected by the state. All humans are equal before the law. The Republic protects, within the rule of law, the right to free opinion, free expression, a free press, freedom of association and of movement, cultural, religious and philosophical freedoms, the right to organize trade unions and businesses, the right to education and literacy, the right to own property, to work, to health, to a clean environment, and to diverse sources of information. No prior authorization is required for the formation of an organ of the press. Men and women are guaranteed equal rights to possess property.

Marriage and the family constitute the natural and moral base of the human community, and are protected by the state. The state is obliged to protect the physical and moral health of the family, in particular of the elderly and the handicapped, and guarantees to alleviate the conditions of life of women, particularly in rural areas. Forced marriages are forbidden as a violation of individual liberty. The state protects youth from exploitation, from drugs, and from delinquency.

All children in the Republic have the right to receive schooling, from public schools, or from institutions of religious or non-religious communities. All national educational institutions, public or private, are obliged to participate in the growth of literacy in one of the national languages. Private schools may be opened with the authorization of, and under the control of, the state.

Freedom of conscience is guaranteed. Religious communities and institutions are separate from the state.

All discrimination against workers on grounds of origins, sex, political opinions or beliefs are forbidden. All workers have the right to join or form trade or professional associations. The right to strike is recognized, under legal conditions, as long as the freedom to work is not impeded, and the enterprise is not placed in peril. The state guarantees sanitary and human conditions in places of work.

THE PRESIDENT OF THE REPUBLIC

Articles 26–52: The President of the Republic is elected, for a term of five years, by universal direct suffrage. The mandate may be renewed once. Candidates for the presidency must be of solely Senegalese nationality, enjoy full civil and political rights, be aged between 35 and 75 years on the day of elections, and must be able to write, read and speak the official language fluently. If no candidate receives an absolute majority of votes cast in the first round, representing the support of at least one-quarter of the electorate, a second round of elections is held between the two highest-placed candidates in the first round. In the case of incapacity, death or resignation, the President's position is assumed by the President of the National Assembly, in all cases subject to the same terms of eligibility that apply to the President. The President presides over the Council of Ministers, the Higher Council of National Defence, and the National Security Council, and is the Supreme Chief of the Armed Forces.

THE OPPOSITION

Article 58: The Constitution guarantees the right to political parties that are opposed to Government policy to oppose, and recognizes the existence of a leader of the parliamentary opposition.

THE PARLIAMENT

Articles 59–66: Deputies of the National Assembly are elected by universal direct suffrage, for a five-year mandate, subject only to the dissolution of the National Assembly. Any serving deputy who resigns from his or her party shall have his or her mandate removed. Deputies enjoy immunity from criminal proceedings, except with the authorization of the bureau of the National Assembly. The National Assembly votes on the budget. Deputies vote as individuals and must not be obligated to vote in a certain way. Except in exceptional and limited circumstances, sessions of the National Assembly are public.

RELATIONS BETWEEN THE EXECUTIVE AND LEGISLATIVE POWERS

Articles 67–87: The Parliament is the sole holder of legislative power. The National Assembly votes on the budget and authorizes a declaration of war. The President of the Republic may pronounce by decree the dissolution of the National Assembly, except during the first two years of any Assembly.

JUDICIAL POWER

Articles 88–94: The judiciary is independent of the legislature and the executive power. The judiciary consists of the Constitutional Council, the Supreme Court, the Revenue Court and Courts and Tribunals. The Constitutional Council comprises seven members, including a President, a Vice-President and five judges. Each member serves for a mandate of six years (which may not be renewed) with partial renewals occurring every two years. The President of the Republic appoints members of the Constitutional Council, whose decisions are irreversible.

INTERNATIONAL TREATIES

Articles: 95–98: The President of the Republic negotiates international engagements, and ratifies or approves them with the authorization of the Parlement. The Republic of Senegal may conclude agreements with any African state that would comprise a partial or total abandonment of national sovereignty in order to achieve African unity.

THE HIGH COURT OF JUSTICE

Articles 99–101: A High Court of Justice, presided over by a magistrate and comprising members elected by the National Assembly, is instituted. The President of the Republic can only be brought to trial for acts accomplished in the exercise of his or her duties in the case of high treason. The High Court of Justice tries members of the Government for crimes committed in the exercise of their duties.

TERRITORIAL COLLECTIVITIES

Article 102: Local government bodies operate independently, by means of elective assemblies, in accordance with the law.

ON REVISION

Article 103: Amendments may be approved by referendum or, at the initiative of the President of the Republic, solely by approval by the Parliament, in which case a three-fifths' majority must be in favour.

The Government

HEAD OF STATE

President: MACKY SALL (took office 2 April 2012; re-elected 24 February 2019).

COUNCIL OF MINISTERS
(October 2022)

Prime Minister: AMADOU BA.

Minister of the Armed Forces: SIDIKI KABA.

Keeper of the Seals, Minister of Justice: ISMAÏLA MADIOR FALL.

Minister of Foreign Affairs and Senegalese Nationals Abroad: AÏSSATA TALL SALL.

Minister of the Interior: ANTOINE FÉLIX ABDOULAYE DIOME.

Minister of Finance and the Budget: AMADOU MOUSTAPHA BÂ.

Minister of Infrastructure, Land Transport and Improving Access to Isolated Regions: AMADOU MANSOUR FAYE.

Minister of Agriculture, Rural Equipment and Food Sovereignty: ALY NGOUILLE NDIAYE.

Minister of the Economy, Planning and Co-operation: OULIMATA SARR.

Minister of National Education: CHEIKH OUMAR ANNE.

Minister of Higher Education, Research and Innovation: MOUSSA BALDÉ.

Minister of Professional Training, Apprenticeship and Integration: MARIAMA SARR.

Minister of Water and Sanitation: SERIGNE MBAYE THIAM.

Minister of Women, Families and Child Welfare: FATOU DIANÉ.

Minister of Health and Social Action: MARIE KHEMESSE NGOM NDIAYE.

Minister of Mining and Geology: OUMAR SARR.

Minister of Petroleum and Energy: SOPHIE GLADIMA.

Minister of Air Transport and Development of Airport Infrastructure: DOUDOU KÂ.

Minister of the Environment, Sustainable Development and Ecological Transition: ALIOUNE NDOYE.

Minister of Fishing and the Maritime Economy: PAPA SAGNA MBAYE.

Minister of Labour, Social Dialogue and Relations with the Institutions: SAMBA SY.

Minister of Town Planning, Housing and Public Hygiene: ABDOULAYE SAYDOU SOW.

Minister of Trade, Consumer Affairs and Small and Medium-sized Enterprises, Government Spokesperson: ABDOU KARIM FOFANA.

Minister of Industrial Development and Small and Medium-sized Industry: MOUSTAPHA DIOP.

Minister of Community Development, National Solidarity and Social and Territorial Equity: SAMBA NDIOBÈNE KÂ.

Minister of Microfinance and the Social Solidarity Economy: VICTORINE NDÈYE.

Minister of Territorial Collectivities and Land Management and Development: MAMADOU TALLA.

Minister of Youth, Entrepreneurship and Employment: PAPE MALICK NDOUR.

Minister of Sport: YANKHOBA DIATTARA.

Minister of Tourism and Leisure: MAME MBAYE KA NIANG.

Minister of Culture and Historical Heritage: ALIOUNE SOW.

Minister of Communication, Telecommunications and the Digital Economy: MOUSSA BOCAR THIAM.

Minister of the Civil Service and Transformation of the Public Sector: GALLO BÂ.

Minister of Handicrafts and Transformation of the Informal Sector: PAPA AMADOU NDIAYE.

Minister of Stockbreeding and Animal Production: ALY SALEH DIOP.

Minister, Secretary-General to the Government: ABDOU LATIF COULIBALY.

Minister-delegate to the Minister of Foreign Affairs and Senegalese Nationals Abroad, in charge of Senegalese Nationals Abroad: ANNETTE SECK.

Minister-delegate to the Keeper of the Seals, Minister of Justice, in charge of the Promotion of Human Rights and Good Governance: MAMADOU SALIOU SOW.

Minister-delegate to the Minister of the Interior, in charge of Local Security and Civil Protection: BIRAME FAYE.

Minister-delegate to the Minister of Water and Sanitation, in charge of Flood Prevention and Management: YANKHOBA ISSA DIOP.

MINISTRIES

Office of the President: ave Léopold Sédar Senghor, BP 168, Dakar; tel. 33-880-8080; internet www.presidence.sn.

Ministry of Agriculture, Rural Equipment and Food Sovereignty: Bâtiment A Sénégal, Sphère Ministérielle du Premier Arrondissement de Diamniadio, BP 4005, Dakar; tel. 33-824-2580; internet www.maer.gouv.sn.

Ministry of Air Transport and Development of Airport Infrastructure: Dakar.

Ministry of the Armed Forces: Bldg Administratif, 8e étage, ave Léopold Sédar Senghor, BP 4041, Dakar; tel. 33-849-5032; internet www.forcesarmees.gouv.sn.

Ministry of the Civil Service and Transformation of the Public Sector: Immeuble Sokhna Mballo Asta Binta Kebe, 52 Vincens, angle Abdou Karim Bourgi, BP 4007, Dakar; tel. 33-839-6600; e-mail fonctionpublique@fonctionpublique.gouv.sn; internet www.fonctionpublique.gouv.sn.

Ministry of Communication, Telecommunications and the Digital Economy: Cité Keur Gorgui, Bâtiment Y21, BP 4027, Dakar; tel. 33-889-3779; internet www.numerique.gouv.sn.

Ministry of Community Development, National Solidarity and Social and Territorial Equity: Sphère Ministérielle de Diamniadio, Bâtiment B, Dakar; tel. 33-879-2960; e-mail mdcestsn@gmail.com; internet equite.sec.gouv.sn.

Ministry of Culture and Historical Heritage: Rond Point, pl. ONU, blvd Dial Diop, angle blvd du Canal 4, Dakar; tel. 33-849-0338; internet www.culture.gouv.sn.

Ministry of the Economy, Planning and Co-operation: rue René Ndiaye, angle ave Carde, BP 4017, Dakar; tel. 33-889-2100; e-mail infos@minfinances.sn; internet fb.com/minfinancessn.

Ministry of the Environment, Sustainable Development and Ecological Transition: Bldg Administratif, 2e étage, BP 4055, Dakar; tel. 33-889-0234; e-mail ministereenvironnement@gmail.com; internet www.environnement.gouv.sn.

Ministry of Finance and the Budget: rue René Ndiaye, angle ave Carde, BP 4017, Dakar; tel. 33-889-2100; e-mail infos@minfinances.sn; internet www.finances.gouv.sn.

Ministry of Fishing and the Maritime Economy: Point E, ave Cheikh Anta Diop, Dakar; tel. 33-849-8440; internet mpem.gouv.sn.

Ministry of Foreign Affairs and Senegalese Nationals Abroad: pl. de l'Indépendance, BP 4044, Dakar; tel. 33-889-1300; e-mail contact@diplomatie.gouv.sn; internet diplomatie.gouv.sn.

Ministry of Health and Social Action: Fann Résidence, rue Aimé Césaire, BP 4024, Dakar; tel. 33-869-4242; e-mail informatique@sante.gouv.sn; internet www.sante.gouv.sn.

Ministry of Higher Education, Research and Innovation: Sphère Ministérielle du Deuxieme Arrondissement de Diamniadio, BP 36005, Dakar; tel. 33-889-8131; internet mesr.gouv.sn.

Ministry of Handicrafts and Transformation of the Informal Sector: Sphères Ministérielles de Diamniadio, Arrondissement II, Bâtiment A, Dakar; internet fb.com/ministereartisanat secteurinformel.

Ministry of Industrial Development and Small and Medium-sized Industry: 122 bis, ave André Peytavin, BP 4037, Dakar; tel. 33-889-5757; e-mail mindpme@msn.com; internet industrie.gouv.sn.

Ministry of Infrastructure, Land Transport and Improving Access to Isolated Regions: Sphère Ministérielle 2, Diamniadio, BP 4014, Dakar; tel. 33-849-0760; e-mail mittdgouvsn@gmail.com; internet www.mittd.gouv.sn.

Ministry of the Interior: pl. Washington, BP 4002, Dakar; tel. 33-889-9100; internet interieur.sec.gouv.sn.

Ministry of Justice: Bldg Administratif, 7e étage, ave Léopold Sédar Senghor, BP 4030, Dakar; tel. 33-849-5362; internet justice.sec.gouv.sn.

Ministry of Labour, Social Dialogue and Relations with the Institutions: Immeuble Yoro Lam, 54 ave Georges Pompidou, Dakar; tel. 33-849-7000; internet www.travail.gouv.sn.

Ministry of Microfinance and the Social Solidarity Economy: Dakar; internet www.microfinance-ess.gouv.sn.

Ministry of Mining and Geology: Sphère Ministérielle Ousmane Tanor Dieng, Bâtiment B, Diamniadio, Dakar; tel. 33-889-0243; e-mail contact@minesgeologie.gouv.sn; internet www.minesgeologie.gouv.sn.

Ministry of National Education: Bâtiment B1, Sphère Ministérielle du 2ème Arrondissement de Diamniadio, BP 4025, Dakar;

tel. 33-849-5454; e-mail men@education.sn; internet www.education
.sn.

Ministry of Petroleum and Energy: Bldg Administratif Mamadou Dia, 3e et 4e étages, BP 4021, Dakar; tel. 33-889-2790; e-mail
contact@mpe.gouv.sn; internet energie.gouv.sn.

**Ministry of Professional Training, Apprenticeship and Inte-
gration:** Immeuble Y1D, Sicap Keur Gorgui, Dakar; tel. 33-865-
7070; e-mail mfpaa@mfpaa.gouv.sn; internet www.mfpaa.gouv.sn.

Ministry of Sport: rue G, angle rue 110, Zone B, BP 4019, Dakar;
tel. 33-859-3866; e-mail sports@gouv.sn; internet fb.com/
sportsgouvsn.

**Ministry of Territorial Collectivities and Land Management
and Development:** Dieuppeul-Derklé, Allées Khalifa Ababacar Sy,
angle rue DD 142, BP 10039, Dakar; tel. 33-869-4741; internet
decentralisation.gouv.sn.

Ministry of Tourism and Leisure: Sphère Ministèrielle 2, Bâtiment C, Diamniadio, BP 4049, Dakar; tel. 33-869-2690; e-mail
ministere@tourisme.gouv.sn; internet www.mtta.gouv.sn.

Ministry of Town Planning, Housing and Public Hygiene:
Immeuble B2, Sphère Ministérielle, 2e Arrondissement de Diamniadio, Dakar; tel. 33-869-1526; e-mail contacts@urbanisme.gouv.sn;
internet www.urbanisme.gouv.sn.

**Ministry of Trade, Consumer Affairs and Small and Medium-
sized Enterprises:** Bâtiment C, 1–6 Étages, Diamniadio Entrée
Principale, Sphère Ministérielle, BP 4037, Dakar; tel. 33-869-2120;
e-mail commerce@commerce.gouv.sn; internet commerce.gouv.sn.

Ministry of Water and Sanitation: Immeuble B2, Sphère Ministérielle, 2e Arrondissement de Diamniadio, BP 2373, Dakar; tel. 33-
869-6130; internet eau-assainissement.gouv.sn.

Ministry of Women, Families and Child Welfare: Immeuble
Adja Fatou Nourou Diop, 9e et 10e étages, Allées Papa Gueye Fall,
BP 4050, Dakar; tel. 33-822-9490; e-mail contact@famille.gouv.sn;
internet www.femme.gouv.sn.

Ministry of Youth, Entrepreneurship and Employment: Bldg
Administratif, 5e étage, Dakar; tel. 33-869-6065; e-mail
courrierjepvc@gmail.com; internet jeunesse.gouv.sn.

President

Presidential Election, 24 February 2019

Candidate	Valid votes	% of valid votes
Macky Sall	2,555,426	58.26
Idrissa Seck	899,556	20.51
Ousmane Sonko	687,523	15.67
Issa Sall	178,613	4.07
Madické Niang	65,021	1.48
Total	**4,386,139***	**100.00**

* In addition, there were 42,541 invalid votes.

Legislature

National Assembly: pl. Soweto, BP 86, Dakar; tel. 33-889-9900;
e-mail assnat@assemblee-nationale.sn; internet www.assemblee
-nationale.sn.

President: AMADOU MAME DIOP.
General Election, 31 July 2022

Party	Valid votes	% of valid votes	Seats
Benno Bokk Yaakaar	1,518,137	46.55	82
Yewwi Askan Wi	1,071,139	32.85	56
Wallu Sénégal	471,517	14.46	24
Les Serviteurs MPR	56,303	1.73	1
Alternative pour une Assemblée de Rupture	52,173	1.60	1
Bokk Gis-Gis	44,862	1.38	1
Naataangue Askan Wi	25,833	0.79	—
Bunt Bi	20,922	0.64	—
Total	**3,260,886***	**100.00**	**165**

* In addition, there were 18,224 invalid votes.

Election Commission

Commission Electorale Nationale Autonome (CENA): Immeuble Fonds de Garantie Automobile, ave Malick Sy, angle Impasse
Cosec, BP 28900, Dakar; tel. 33-889-6600; e-mail cena@cena.sn;
internet www.cena.sn; f. 2005; Pres. DOUDOU NDIR.

Political Organizations

Alliance des Forces de Progrès (AFP): rue 1, angle rue A, point E,
BP 5825, Dakar; tel. 33-869-7595; e-mail afp.net@yahoo.fr; internet
www.afp-senegal.org; f. 1999; Sec.-Gen. MOUSTAPHA NIASSE.

Alternative pour une Assemblée de Rupture: Dakar.

Alliance Jëf-Jël: Villa 5, rue 1, Castors Front de Terre, Dakar; tel.
77-652-2232; e-mail tallasylla@hotmail.com; f. 1997; Pres. MOUHA-
MADOU LAMINE BARA.

**And Jëf—Parti Africain pour la Démocratie et le Socialisme
(AJ—PADS):** Villa 1, Zone B, BP 12136, Dakar; tel. 33-864-4130;
f. 1992; Sec.-Gen. LANDING SAVANÉ.

Benno Bokk Yaakaar (BBY): Dakar; internet www.bby2022.com;
coalition comprising 80 political organizations.

Alliance pour la République (APR—Yaakaar): Dakar;
internet www.apronline.org; f. 2008; Leader MACKY SALL.

Bës du Niak: Leader SERIGNE MANSOUR MANSOUR SY DJAMIL.

Bokk Gis Gis (BGG): Dakar; coalition of political organizations.

Bloc des Centristes Gaïndé (BCG): Villa 734, Sicap Baobabs,
Dakar; tel. 33-825-3764; e-mail issa_dias@orange.sn; f. 1996; Pres.
and Sec.-Gen. JEAN-PAUL DIAS.

**Convergence Patriotique pour la Justice et l'Équité/Nay
Leer:** Dakar; Leader DEMBA DIOP.

Convergence pour le Renouveau et la Citoyenneté (CRC): 7
ave Bourguiba, Industrial Zone, Sodida, Dakar; tel. 33-824-4900;
Sec.-Gen. ALIOU DIA.

Deggo Soxali Transport Ak Commerce: Dakar; Leader ALASSANE
NDOYE.

Leeral: Dakar; Leader EL HADJI DIOUF.

**Ligue Démocratique—Mouvement pour le Parti du Travail
(LD—MPT):** ave Bourguiba, Dieuppeul 2, Villa 2566, BP 10172,
Dakar Liberté; tel. 33-825-6706; e-mail jallarbi@orange.sn; internet
www.ldmpt.sn; regd 1981; social-democrat; Sec.-Gen. ABDOULAYE
BATHILY.

**Mouvement pour la Démocratie et le Socialisme—Naxx Jar-
inu (MDS—NJ):** Unité 20, Parcelles Assainies, Villa 528, Dakar; tel.
33-869-5049; f. 2000; Leader OUMAR KHASSIMOU DAI.

Mouvement Patriotique du Sénégal/Faxas (MPS/Faxas):
Ouest Foire, en face du CICES, prés de la Station Shell, Dakar;
tel. 77-568-2787; internet www.mpsfaxas.com; Nat. Co-ordinator
GAOUSSOU KOMA.

**Mouvement de la Réforme pour le Développement Social
(MRDS):** HLM 4, Dakar, Villa 858, Dakar; internet www.mrds.sn;
f. 2000; Pres. IMAM MBAYE NIANG; Sec.-Gen. Imam IYANE SOW.

Mouvement Républicain Sénégalais (MRS): Résidence du Cap-
Vert, 10e étage, 5 pl. de l'Indépendance, BP 4193, Dakar; tel. 33-822-
0319; Sec.-Gen. DEMBA BA.

Parti Africain de l'Indépendance (PAI): Maison du Peuple,
Guediewaye, BP 820, Dakar; tel. 33-837-0136; f. 1957; reorg. 1976;
Marxist; Sec.-Gen. (vacant).

Parti Démocratique Sénégalais (PDS): blvd Dial Diop, Immeuble Serigne Mourtada Mbacké, Dakar; tel. 33-823-5027; e-mail
omasec@hotmail.com; internet fb.com/pdsonline.net; f. 1974; liberal
democratic; Sec.-Gen. Me ABDOULAYE WADE.

Parti de l'Indépendance et du Travail (PIT): route front de terre,
BP 10470, Dakar; tel. 33-827-2907; regd 1981; Marxist-Leninist;
Sec.-Gen. SAMBA SY.

Parti des Libéraux et Démocrates—And Suqali: 186 rue Lib, 50
Liberté 6 Extension, Dakar; tel. 33-848-9697; e-mail contact@pld.sn;
internet pld.sn; f. 2020; Pres. OUMAR SARR.

Parti Populaire Sénégalais (PPS): Quartier Escale, BP 212,
Diourbel; tel. 776588390; e-mail contact@pps-senegal.org; internet
www.pps-senegal.org; regd 1981; populist; Sec.-Gen. Dr OUMAR
WANE.

Parti pour le Progrès et la Citoyenneté (PPC): Quartier Merina,
Rufique; tel. 33-836-1868; Sec.-Gen. Me MBAYE JACQUES DIOP.

Parti pour la Renaissance Africaine—Sénégal (PARENA):
Sicap Dieuppeul, Villa 2685/B, Dakar; tel. 77-636-8788; e-mail
mariamwane@yahoo.fr; f. 2000; Sec.-Gen. MARIAM MAMADOU WANE
LY.

Parti de la Renaissance et de la Citoyenneté: Liberté 6, Villa 7909, Dakar; tel. 33-827-8568; f. 2000; Sec.-Gen. SAMBA DIOULDÉ THIAM.

Parti Social-Démocrate—Jant Bi (PSD—JB): HLM 2, Villa No 362, Dakar; tel. 33-824-25-59; e-mail psdjantbi@yahoo.fr; internet psd-jantbi.com; Leader MAMOUR CISSÉ.

Parti Socialiste Authentique (PSA): internet psa-senegal.org; Leader SOUTY TOURRE.

Parti Socialiste du Sénégal (PS): Maison du Parti Socialiste Léopold Sédar Senghor, Colobane, BP 12010, Dakar; tel. 33-824-7744; e-mail senegalpartisocialiste@gmail.com; internet www.ps-senegal.sn; f. 1958 as Union Progressiste Sénégalaise; Sec.-Gen. AMINATA MBENGUE NDIAYE.

Parti de l'Unité et du Rassemblement (PUR): Dakar; internet www.pur100.com; Pres. SERIGNE MOUSTAPHA SY; Leader Prof. El Hadji ISSA SALL.

Parti de la Vérité pour le Développement (PVD): Dakar; f. 2004; Leader SOKHNA DIENG MBACKÉ.

Rassemblement des Écologistes du Sénégal—Les Verts (RES): rue 67, angle rue 52, Gueule Tapée, BP 25226, Dakar-Fann; tel. 33-842-3442; f. 1999; Sec.-Gen. MAMADOU BERTHÉ.

Rassemblement National Démocratique (RND): Sacré Coeur III, Villa no. 9721, Dakar; tel. 76-580-8617; f. 1976; legalized 1981; mem. of opposition Bennoo Siggil Senegal (f. 2009); Sec.-Gen. MADIOR DIOUF.

Rassemblement Patriotique Sénégalais—Jammi Rewmi (RPS—JR): Leader ELY MADIODO FALL.

Rassemblement des Travailleurs Africains—Sénégal/Péncoo Réew (RTA—S/PENCOO REEW): Immeuble Seydou Nourou Tall, Apt. B6, 2e étage, 12 rue 14 angle P, BP 13725, Derklé, Grand-Yoff, Dakar; tel. 33-827-1579; e-mail rtas@rtasenegal.org; internet www.rtasenegal.org; f. 1997; Sec.-Gen. El Hadji MOMAR SAMBE.

Les Serviteurs MPR: Dakar; tel. 777543838; e-mail pendadieng1121@outlook.fr; internet fb.com/LesserviteursMPR; Leader PAPE DJIBRIL FALL.

Takku Defaraat Sénégal Coalition: VDN à côté de la Poste; tel. 33-860-5019; f. 2000; Leader ROBERT SAGNA.

Tekki 2012: Zone B, Villa 23A, Bis, Dakar; tel. 33-868-4333; e-mail tekki@orange.sn; Leader MAMADOU LAMINE DIALLO.

Union Nationale Patriotique (UNP): tel. 77-637-1017; e-mail unpsenegal@gmail.com; internet www.fb.com/UNPduSenegal; Leader MOCTAR SOURANG.

Union pour une Nouvelle République (UNR): Thiès; f. 2022; Leader MOUHAMADOU LAMINE MASSALY.

Union pour le Renouveau Démocratique (URD): Bopp Villa 234, rue 7, Dakar; tel. 33-864-7431; internet www.urdsenegal.sn; f. 1998 by breakaway faction of PS; Sec.-Gen. DJIBO LEÏTY KÂ.

Yewwi Askan Wi: Dakar; Leader OUSMANE SONKO.

Wallu Sénégal: Dakar.

The **Mouvement des Forces Démocratiques de la Casamance (MFDC)** was founded in 1947; it had paramilitary and political wings and formerly sought the independence of the Casamance region of southern Senegal. The MFDC is not officially recognized as a political party (the Constitution of 2001 forbids the formation of parties on a geographic basis), and it has waged a campaign of guerrilla warfare in the region since the early 1980s. Representatives of the MFDC have participated in extensive negotiations with the Senegalese Government on the restoration of peace and the granting of greater autonomy to Casamance, but no formal peace agreement has been concluded.

Diplomatic Representation

EMBASSIES IN SENEGAL

Algeria: 5 rue Mermoz, Plateau, POB 3233, Dakar; tel. 33-849-5700; e-mail ambalgdak@orange.sn; internet ambalgdakar.org; f. 1963; Ambassador BOUALEM CHEBIH.

Angola: Dakar; Ambassador ADÃO PINTO (designate).

Argentina: Dakar; Ambassador MARCIA ROSA LEVAGGI.

Austria: 18 rue Emile Zola, BP 3247, Dakar; tel. 33-849-4000; e-mail dakar-ob@bmaa.gv.at; internet www.bmeia.gv.at/oeb-dakar; Ambassador Dr URSULA FAHRINGER.

Belgium: ave des Jambaars, BP 524, Dakar; tel. 33-889-4390; e-mail dakar@diplobel.fed.be; internet diplomatie.belgium.be/senegal; Ambassador HUBERT ROISIN.

Brazil: Immeuble Abdoulaye Seck, 1er et 2e étages, rue de Fatick, Point E, BP 136, Dakar; tel. 33-825-9400; e-mail brasemb.dacar@itamaraty.gov.br; internet www.gov.br/mre/pt-br/embaixada-dacar; Ambassador FLAVIO HUGO LIMA ROCHA JÚNIOR.

Burkina Faso: Sicap Sacré Coeur III, Extension VDN No. 10628B, BP 11601, Dakar; tel. 33-864-5824; e-mail ambabf@orange.sn; internet ambaburkina-sn.org; Ambassador JACOB OUÉDRAOGO.

Cabo Verde: 3 blvd El-Hadji Djilly M'Baye, BP 11269, Dakar; tel. 33-822-4285; e-mail embcvsen@orange.sn; internet fb.com/Embaixada-da-República-de-Cabo-Verde-no-Senegal-1417364505186822; Ambassador HERMÍNIO MONIZ.

Cameroon: 157–159 rue Joseph Gomis, BP 4165, Dakar; tel. 33-849-0292; e-mail contact@ambacamdakar.org; internet www.ambacamdakar.org; Ambassador JEAN KOE NTONGA.

Canada: rue Galliéni, angle rue Amadou Cissé Dia, BP 3373, Dakar; tel. 33-889-4700; e-mail dakar@international.gc.ca; internet www.canadainternational.gc.ca/senegal; Ambassador MARIE-GENEVIÈVE MOUNIER (designate).

China, People's Republic: rue 18 prolongée, Fann Résidence, BP 342, Dakar; tel. 33-869-7701; e-mail chinaemb_sn@mfa.gov.cn; internet sn.china-embassy.gov.cn; Ambassador XIAO HAN.

Comoros: 9 rue Gallieni, angle 70 Foch, Dakar; tel. 33-889-8966; e-mail mariamasaidhalidi@gmail.com; Ambassador AHMED BEN SAÏD JAFFAR.

Congo, Democratic Republic: 16 rue Léo Frobénus, Fann Résidence, Dakar; tel. 33-824-6574; Chargé d'affaires a.i. FATAKI NICOLAS LUNGUELE MUSAMBYA.

Congo, Republic: Stèle Mermoz, Pyrotechnie, BP 5243, Fann Résidence, Dakar; tel. 33-824-8398; e-mail ambaco_sen@yahoo.fr; internet www.ambacongo-senegal.org; Ambassador JEAN-LUC AKA-EVY.

Côte d'Ivoire: ave Birago Diop, BP 359, Dakar; tel. 33-869-0270; internet senegal.diplomatie.gouv.ci; Ambassador SÉKOU TOURÉ.

Cuba: Fann Mermoz, Residence Ayola, Corniche Ouest, Dakar; tel. 33-869-8319; e-mail embacubasen@orange.sn; internet misiones.minrex.gob.cu/senegal; Ambassador SAYLÍN SÁNCHEZ PORTERO.

Czech Republic: 37 rue Jacques Bugnicourt, BP 6474, Dakar; tel. 33-821-4576; internet www.mzv.cz/dakar; Ambassador MAREK SKOLIL.

Egypt: 22 ave Brière de l'Isle, Plateau, BP 474, Dakar; tel. 33-889-2474; Ambassador NOHA AHMED MAHER KHEDR.

Ethiopia: Cite Keur Gorgui, Lot 19, BP 379, Dakar; tel. 33-864-9696; e-mail ethembas@orange.sn; internet www.dakar.mfa.gov.et; Ambassador MELAKU LEGESSE.

France: 1 rue El Hadj Amadou Assane Ndoye, BP 4035, Dakar; tel. 33-839-5100; internet sn.ambafrance.org; Ambassador PHILIPPE LALLIOT.

Gabon: rue 6, angle 16 Médina, BP 436, Dakar; tel. 33-865-2234; e-mail info@ambassadegabonsen.org; internet ambassadegabonsen.org; Ambassador MICHEL RÉGIS ONANGA MAMADOU NDIAYE.

The Gambia: 11 rue Elhadji Ismaïla Guèye (Thiong), BP 3248, Dakar; tel. 33-821-4416; Ambassador HADRAMMEH M. SIDIBEH.

Germany: 20 ave Pasteur, angle rue Mermoz, BP 2100, Dakar; tel. 33-889-4884; e-mail info@dakar.diplo.de; internet dakar.diplo.de; Ambassador SÖNKE SIEMON.

Ghana: Diari Bldg No. 7357, Sicap Mermoz, VDN, opp. PDS Headquarters, Dakar; tel. 33-869-1990; e-mail info@ghanaembdakar.org; internet dakar.mfa.gov.gh; Ambassador EMMA MENSAH.

Greece: rue de Diourbel, angle Rond Point de l'Ellipse, face à la Piscine Olympique, Point E, Dakar; tel. 778051702; e-mail gremb.dak@mfa.gr; internet www.mfa.gr/missionsabroad/fr/contact/senegal/senegal.html; Ambassador EFTHYMIOS GEORGES COSTOPOULOS.

Guinea: rue 7, angle B&D, point E, BP 7123, Dakar; tel. 33-824-8606; e-mail ambaguidak@gmail.com; internet ambaguidak.org; Ambassador Hadja AMINATA KOBÉLÉ KEITA.

Guinea-Bissau: rue 6, angle B, point E, BP 2319, Dakar; tel. 33-824-5922; e-mail ambgb@orange.sn; Ambassador IBRAHAIMA SANO.

Holy See: rue Aimé Césaire, angle Corniche-Ouest, Fann Résidence, BP 5076, Dakar; tel. 33-824-2674; e-mail na.senegal@diplomat.va; Apostolic Nuncio WALDEMAR STANISŁAW SOMMERTAG (Titular Archbishop of Traiectum ad Mosam).

India: 5 rue Carde, BP 398, Dakar; tel. 33-849-5875; e-mail hoc.dakar@mea.gov.in; internet embassyofindiadakar.gov.in; Ambassador DINKAR ASTHANA (designate).

Indonesia: ave Cheikh Anta Diop, BP 5859, Dakar; tel. 33-825-7316; e-mail kbri@orange.sn; internet kemlu.go.id/dakar; Ambassador DINDIN WAHYUDIN.

Iran: 17 ave des Ambassadeurs, Fann Résidence, BP 735, Dakar; tel. 33-825-2528; e-mail iranemb.dkr@mfa.gov.ir; internet senegal.mfa.gov.ir; Ambassador MOHAMMAD REZA DEHSHIRI.

Iraq: point E, rue 6, angle B, à côté de la Croix Rouge Internationale, BP 45448, Dakar; tel. 33-869-7799; e-mail dkremb@mofa.gov.iq;

internet www.mofa.gov.iq/dakar; Ambassador Ahmed Khalil Ahmed.

Israel: Immeuble SDIH, 3 pl. de l'Indépendance, BP 2096, Dakar; tel. 33-823-7965; e-mail info@dakar.mfa.gov.il; internet embassies .gov.il/dakar; Ambassador Ben Burgel.

Italy: rue Alpha Achamiyou Tall, BP 348, Dakar; tel. 33-889-2636; e-mail ambdakar.esteri.it/ambasciata_dakar/it; internet www .ambdakar.esteri.it; Ambassador Giovanni de Vito.

Japan: blvd Martin Luther King, Corniche-Ouest, BP 3140, Dakar; tel. 33-849-5500; internet www.sn.emb-japan.go.jp; Ambassador Osamu Izawa.

Kenya: Villa No. 16, Impasse FN 18, Fann Résidence, BP 1571, Dakar; tel. 33-864-4600; e-mail dakar@mfa.go.ke; internet fb.com/ Kenya-Embassy-Dakar-110295897256742; Ambassador Purity Muhindi.

Korea, Democratic People's Republic: Villa Hamoudy, rue Aimé Césaire, BP 58509, Dakar; tel. 33-824-06-72; e-mail coreamb@yahoo; Ambassador Hong Son Phyo.

Korea, Republic: Villa Hamoudy, rue Aime Cesaire, Fann Résidence, BP 5850, Dakar; tel. 33-824-0672; e-mail senegal@mofa.go.kr; internet overseas.mofa.go.kr/sn-ko/index.do; Ambassador Ji-Joon Kim.

Kosovo: Villa N° 145, Zone 08, Almadies, BP 29290, Dakar; tel. 33-820-2970; e-mail embassy.senegal@rks-gov.net; internet www .ambasada-ks.net/sg; Chargé d'affaires Sami Halili.

Kuwait: blvd Martin Luther King, Dakar; tel. 33-824-1723; e-mail q8embassydkr@orange.sn; Ambassador Adel Abdul Karim al-Amir.

Lebanon: 56 ave Jean XXIII, BP 6700 Dakar-Etoile, Dakar; tel. 33-822-0255; e-mail ambaliban@yahoo.com; internet www.ambaliban .sn; Ambassador Sami Haddad.

Liberia: 146 Ouest-Foire, BP 5845, Dakar-Fann; tel. 33-869-4019; e-mail libembdkr1@yahoo.com; Ambassador (vacant).

Libya: route de Ouakam, BP 16449, Dakar; tel. 33-824-5710; Ambassador Saleh Mohammed al-Makhzoum.

Luxembourg: Résidence Naja, Villa No 3, rue E, angle rue David Diop, Fann Résidence, BP 11750, Dakar; tel. 33-869-5959; e-mail dakar.amb@mae.etat.lu; internet dakar.mae.lu; Ambassador Georges Ternes.

Madagascar: Immeuble Royal Bldg, 2e Étage, Almadies Zone 16, BP 25395, Dakar; tel. 784276788; e-mail ambamaddakar@gmail .com; internet fb.com/mdg.dakar; Chargé d'affaires a.i. Misalintsoa Irodia.

Malaysia: Villa No 2, ave des Ambassades, Fann Résidence, Dakar; tel. 33-825-8935; e-mail mwdakar@orange.sn; internet www.kln.gov .my/web/sen_dakar/home; Ambassador (vacant).

Mali: Fann Résidence, Corniche-Ouest, rue 23, BP 478, Dakar; tel. 33-824-6250; e-mail ambamali@orange.sn; internet fb.com/ yaticko714; Ambassador Mohamed El-Moctar (designate).

Mauritania: 37 blvd Charles de Gaulle, Dakar; tel. 33-823-5344; e-mail ambarimdakar@gmail.com; Ambassador Mohamed Yahya Teiss.

Morocco: 73 ave Cheikh Anta Diop, BP 490, Dakar; tel. 33-824-6927; e-mail ambmadk@orange.sn; Ambassador Hassan Naciri.

Namibia: Lot No. 20, Zone 9, Route des Almadies, Dakar; tel. 33-859-2321; e-mail dakar@mirco.gov.na; Ambassador Elvis Toolouta Shiweda.

Netherlands: 37 rue Jaques Bugnicourt, BP 3262, Dakar; tel. 33-829-2121; e-mail dak@minbuza.nl; internet www .nederlandwereldwijd.nl/landen/senegal; Ambassador Joan Wiegman.

Nicaragua: Lot 148, NG-88, Ngor-Almadies, Dakar; tel. 77-356-0958; Ambassador Douglas Guerrero.

Niger: ave Cheikh Anta Diop, Dakar; tel. 33-824-1226; e-mail niger09@orange.sn; internet www.ambassadeniger-sn.org; Ambassador Abbami Ari.

Nigeria: 8 ave Cheikh Anta Diop, BP 3129, Dakar; tel. 33-869-8600; e-mail info@nigeriandakar.sn; internet www.nigeriandakar.sn; Ambassador Adamu Ibrahim Lamuwa.

Oman: Villa 7062, Stèle Mermoz, BP 2635, Dakar; tel. 33-824-6136; e-mail dakar@mofa.gov.om; Ambassador Abdulah bin Mohamed al-Amri.

Pakistan: rue FN 11, Fann Mermoze, BP 2635, Dakar; tel. 33-824-6135; e-mail parepdakar@gmail.com; internet mofa.gov.pk/ dakar-senegal; Ambassador Dr Ali Ahmed Arain.

Poland: App. 4/A, Les Jardins des Almadies, route des Almadies, BP 14419, Dakar; tel. 33-859-5770; e-mail dakar.amb.sekretariat@msz .gov.pl; internet www.gov.pl/web/senegal; Ambassador Pani Margareta Kassangana.

Portugal: Villa Martha, ave des Ambassadeurs 6, Fann Résidence, BP 281, Dakar; tel. 33-859-2662; e-mail dakar@mne.pt; internet dakar.embaixadaportugal.mne.pt; Ambassador Vítor Sereno.

Qatar: 1236 King Fahad Palace, Route des Almadies, BP 16259, Fann Résidence, Dakar; tel. 33-869-9000; e-mail dakar@mofa.gov .qa; internet dakar.embassy.qa; Ambassador Mohamed bin Kurdi Talib al-Mankhis al-Marri.

Romania: rue A prolongée, point E, BP 3171, Dakar; tel. 33-825-1913; e-mail romania.consul@orange.sn; internet dakar.mae.ro; Ambassador Nicolae Năstase.

Russian Federation: ave Jean Jaurès, angle rue Carnot, BP 3180, Dakar; tel. 33-822-4821; e-mail ambrus.senegal@gmail.com; internet senegal.mid.ru; Ambassador Dmitry V. Kurakov.

Rwanda: 2 Villa la Flèche des Almadies, Immeuble 2K Plaza, route du Méridien Président, Dakar; tel. 33-859-3949; e-mail ambadakar@ minaffet.gov.rw; internet www.rwandainsenegal.gov.rw; Ambassador Jean-Pierre Karabaranga.

Saudi Arabia: route Corniche Ouest, en face Olympique Club, BP 3109, Dakar; tel. 33-864-0140; internet embassies.mofa.gov.sa/sites/ senegal; Ambassador Saad al-Nufaiei.

Sierra Leone: Fenetre MERMOZ, 2éme Porte, Villa Yaye Dieynaba, BP 465 PR, Dakar; tel. 33-824-9595; e-mail sierraleoneembassydakar@yahoo.com; Ambassador Brima Elvis Koroma.

South Africa: Memoz SUD Lotissement, Ecole de Police, Lot No. 5, BP 21010, Dakar; tel. 33-865-1959; e-mail ambafsud@orange.sn; internet www.dirco.gov.za/dakar; Ambassador (vacant).

Spain: 18–20 ave Nelson Mandela, BP 2091, Dakar; tel. 33-889-6580; e-mail emb.dakar@maec.es; internet www.exteriores.gob.es/ embajadas/dakar; Ambassador Olga Cabarga Gómez.

Sudan: 31 route de la Pyrotechnie, Mermoz, Fann Résidence, BP 15033, Dakar; tel. 33-824-9853; e-mail sudembse@orange.sn; Ambassador Khalid Abdul-Gadir Shukri.

Switzerland: rue René N'Diaye, angle rue Seydou, BP 1772, Dakar; tel. 33-823-0590; e-mail dakar@eda.admin.ch; internet www.eda .admin.ch/dakar; Ambassador Andrea Semadeni.

Syrian Arab Republic: rue 1, point E, angle blvd de l'Est, BP 498, Dakar; tel. 33-824-6277; e-mail syrdak@orange.sn; Chargé d'affaires a.i. Dr Sawsan Alani.

Thailand: 10 rue Léon Gontran Damas, Angle F, Fann Résidence BP 3721, Dakar; tel. 33-869-3290; e-mail thaidkr@orange.sn; internet www.thaiembassy.org/dakar; Ambassador (vacant).

Tunisia: rue Alpha Hachamiyou Tall, BP 3127, Dakar; tel. 33-823-4747; e-mail at.dakar@orange.sn; Ambassador Mehdi Ferchichi.

Türkiye (Turkey): 7 rue Leo Frobenius, Fann Résidence, Dakar; tel. 33-869-7956; e-mail ambassade.dakar@mfa.gov.tr; internet dakar .be.mfa.gov.tr; Ambassador Nur Sağman.

Ukraine: route de l'Aéroport, Ngor-Almadies, BP 1148, Dakar; tel. 33-859-02-02; e-mail emb_sn@mfa.gov.ua; internet senegal.mfa.gov .ua; Ambassador Yurii Pyvovarov.

United Arab Emirates: Cabinet Atepa, Corniche Ouest Mermoz, Dakar; tel. 33-869-8390; e-mail dakar@mofa.gov.ae; Ambassador Sultan Ali al-Harbi.

United Kingdom: 20 rue du Dr Guillet, BP 6025, Dakar; tel. 33-823-7392; e-mail britembe@orange.sn; internet www.gov.uk/world/ senegal; Ambassador Juliette John.

USA: route des Almadies, BP 49, Dakar; tel. 33-879-4000; e-mail usadakar@state.gov; internet sn.usembassy.gov; Ambassador Michael A. Raynor.

Venezuela: Villa Khardiata, rue 11, angle 6, Fann Mermoz, BP 45287, Dakar; tel. 33-864-1515; e-mail embavenez_senegal@yahoo .com; Ambassador Eddy José Cordoba Corcega.

Zimbabwe: rue de Louga, angle rue 31, Point E, BP 25342, Fann, Dakar; tel. 33-825-4131; e-mail zimdakar@yahoo.com; Ambassador James Maridadi.

Judicial System

The Supreme Court was re-established in 2008, replacing the Court of Cassation and the Council of State. The Supreme Court is the highest court of appeal, and regulates the activities of subordinate courts and tribunals. It also judges complaints brought against the Executive and resolves electoral disputes. The Constitutional Council verifies that legislation and international agreements are in accordance with the Constitution, and decides disputes between the Executive and the Legislature. The Revenue Court supervises the public accounts.

Supreme Court (Cour Suprême): blvd Martin Luther King, BP 15184, Dakar; tel. 33-889-1025; e-mail sg@coursupreme.sn; internet www.coursupreme.gouv.sn; f. 2008; Pres. CHEIKH TIDIANE COULIBALY.

Constitutional Council (Conseil Constitutionnel): BP 45732, Dakar; tel. 33-859-7479; e-mail conseilconstitutionnel@conseilconstitutionnel.com; internet conseilconstitutionnel.sn; 7 mems; Pres. MAMADOU BADIO CAMARA.

Courts of Appeal (Cours d'Appel): Dakar: Pres. CIRÉ ALY BA; Kaolack: Pres. (vacant); Saint-Louis: Pres. CHEIKH NDIAYE; Tambacounda: Pres. WALY FAYE; Thiès: Pres. AMINATA LY; Ziguinchor: Pres. (vacant).

Revenue Court (Cour des Comptes): BP 9097, Dakar; tel. 33-859-9697; e-mail ccomptes@courdescomptes.sn; internet www.courdescomptes.sn; f. 1999; Pres. MAMADOU FAYE.

High Court of Justice (Haute Cour de Justice): Dakar; competent to try the Prime Minister and other members of the Government for crimes committed in the exercise of their duties; the President of the Republic may only be brought to trial in the case of high treason; mems elected by the National Assembly.

Religion

ISLAM

Around 95% of the population are Muslim. There are four main Islamic brotherhoods active in Senegal: the Tidjanes, the Mourides, the Layennes and the Qadiriyas.

Conseil Supérieur Islamique (CSI): SICAP Liberté/2, Villa No. 1688, BP 1341, Dakar; tel. 77-554-6791; e-mail csiahmediyane@yahoo.fr; internet csi-senegal.org; f. 2013; Pres. MOURCHID AHMED IYANE THIAM; Sec.-Gen. SERIGNE MAKIOU MOUNTAGA.

Grande Mosquée de Dakar: Dakar; tel. 33-822-5648; Grand Imam El Hadj ALIOUNE MOUSSA SAMB.

CHRISTIANITY

The Roman Catholic Church

Senegal comprises one archdiocese and six dioceses. Roman Catholics constitute about 4% of the total population.

Bishops' Conference: Conférence des Evêques du Sénégal, de la Mauritanie, du Cap-Vert et de Guinée-Bissau, BP 941, Dakar; tel. 33-836-3309; e-mail archevchedkr@orange.sn; f. 1973; Pres. Most Rev. JOSÉ CÂMNATE NA BISSIGN (Bishop of Bissau).

Archbishop of Dakar: Most Rev. BENJAMIN NDIAYE, Archevêché, ave Jean XXIII, BP 1908, Dakar; tel. 33-889-0600; e-mail archevechedkr@orange.sn.

The Anglican Communion

The Anglican diocese of The Gambia, part of the Church of the Province of West Africa, includes Senegal and Cabo Verde. The Bishop is resident in Banjul, The Gambia.

Protestant Church

Eglise Luthérienne du Sénégal: BP 9, Fatick, Niakhar; tel. 33-949-1171; e-mail elfsk1@orange.sn; internet egliselutherienne-senegal.org; Pres. Rev. MAMADOU THOMAS DIOUF.

Eglise Protestante du Sénégal: 65 rue Wagane Diouf, BP 22390, Dakar; tel. 33-821-5564; internet www.epsenegal.org; f. 1862; Pastor PHILIPPE JEAN-BAPTISTE MENDY; Sec.-Gen. SANDRA FONKUI.

BAHÁ'Í FAITH

National Spiritual Assembly: Point E, rue des Ecrivains, impasse 2 à droite après la Direction de la Statistique, BP 1662, Dakar; tel. 76-015-6503; e-mail asnsenegal@gmail.com; internet www.sn.bahai.org; regd 1975; Sec. CHEIKH TIDIANE.

The Press

DAILY NEWSPAPERS (PRINT AND ONLINE)

Les Echos: 118 ave Peytavin, Dakar; tel. 33-867-1375; e-mail lesechosdujour@gmail.com; internet fb.com/JournalLesEchos.

Enquête: blvd de l'Est, Point E, Dakar; tel. 33-825-0731; e-mail info@enqueteplus.com; internet www.enqueteplus.com; Editor-in-Chief GASTON COLY.

Le Quotidien: 269 Cité Djily Mbaye, Yoff Routes de Cimetières, BP 25221, Dakar; tel. 33-869-8484; e-mail lequotidien@lequotidien.sn; internet www.lequotidien.sn; f. 2003; Dir MOHAMED GUEYE.

Rewmi: SODIDA, Lot n°48 Bis, BP 16993, Dakar; tel. 33-867-6700; e-mail rewmiofficiel@gmail.com; internet www.rewmi.com; Dir of Publication ASSANE SAMB.

Le Soleil: Société Sénégalaise de Presse et de Publications, route du Service Géographique, Hann, BP 92, Dakar; tel. 33-859-5959; e-mail lesoleil@lesoleil.sn; internet www.lesoleil.sn; f. 1970; Dir of Publication YAKHAM MBAYE.

Sud Quotidien: Amitié II, angle blvd Bourguiba, BP 4130, Dakar; tel. 33-824-3306; e-mail contact@sudquotidien.sn; internet www.sudquotidien.sn; independent; Dir BAKARY DOMINGO.

Vox Populi: ave Bourguiba, Immeuble Baye Ndama, BP 11357, Dakar; tel. 77-138-3905; internet fb.com/Vox10; f. 2016; Dir of Publication DAOUDA DIARRA.

Walf Quotidien: 12 route du Front de Terre, BP 576, Dakar; tel. 33-869-1071; e-mail redaction@walf-groupe.com; internet www.walf-groupe.com; f. 1984; Dir of Publication ABDOURAHMANE CAMARA.

Zoom Infos: Dakar; internet zoominfos.net.

PERIODICALS

Dakar Life: Dakar; tel. 77-548-7506; internet fb.com/dakarmedia1; Dir of Publication MASSAMBA MBAYE.

Emergence Plus: Dakar; tel. 33-867-6705; e-mail emergencemag@orange.sn; Dir of Publication MOUMINA AÏDA KANE.

Ethiopiques: BP 2035, Dakar; tel. 33-849-1414; e-mail senghorf@orange.sn; internet www.refer.sn/ethiopiques; f. 1974; literary and philosophical review; publ. by Fondation Léopold Sédar Senghor; Editor AMADOU LY.

Journal Officiel de la République du Sénégal: Rufisque; tel. 33-849-1817; internet www.jo.gouv.sn; f. 1856; weekly; govt journal.

Réussir: Sicap Liberté 5, Villa No. 5492, Immeuble Microcred, 4e étage, BP 7064, Dakar; tel. 33-825-0506; e-mail k.ciss@reussirbusiness.com; internet www.reussirbusiness.com; f. 2006; business information; monthly; Dir of Publication BAYE DAME WADE.

Le Soleil Business: 21 Mermoz Pyrotechnie, VDN, Dakar; tel. 33-823-8983; internet www.lesoleil.sn; fortnightly.

Station One: Immeuble Cheikh Tall Dioum, 5e étage, 58 ave Bourguiba, Dakar; tel. 77-633-5040; f. 2008; monthly; Dir of Publication MOUSTAPHA SOW.

Weekend Magazine: 12 Cité Adama Diop, Yoff Routes de Cimetières, BP 25221, Dakar; tel. 33-869-8484; internet www.weekend.sn; f. 2007; publ. by Groupe Avenir Communication, which also publishes the daily *Le Quotidien*; Dir of Publication PAPA SAMBA DIARRA.

Le 221: BP 11600, Dakar; tel. 33-860-4515; internet agenda.au-senegal.com; Editor-in-Chief SELLY WANE.

NEWS AGENCIES

Agence Panafricaine d'Information—PANA-Presse SA: ave Bourguiba, BP 4056, Dakar; tel. 33-869-1234; e-mail marketing@panapress.com; internet www.panapress.com; f. 1979 as Pan-African News Agency (under the auspices of the Organization of African Unity), restructured as 75% privately owned co in 1997; Dir-Gen. BABACAR FALL.

Société Nationale Agence de Presse Sénégalaise (SN-APS): rue 5 Medina, BP 117, Dakar; tel. 33-821-1427; e-mail apscom.mark@gmail.com; internet www.aps.sn; f. 1959; govt-controlled; Pres. MOUSTAPHA SAMB; Dir-Gen. THIERNO BIRAHIM FALL.

PRESS ORGANIZATIONS

Syndicat des Professionnels de l'Information et de la Communication du Sénégal (SYNPICS): BP 21722, Dakar; tel. 33-842-4256; e-mail synpics@yahoo.fr; internet fb.com/synpics.senegal; Sec.-Gen. BAMBA KASSÉ.

Publishers

Agence de Distribution de Presse: km 2.5, blvd du Centenaire de la Commune de Dakar, BP 374, Dakar; tel. 33-832-0278; f. 1943; general, reference; Man. Dir PHILIPPE SCHORP.

Centre Africain d'Animation et d'Echanges Culturels Editions Khoudia: BP 5332, Dakar-Fann; tel. 33-821-1023; f. 1989; fiction, education, anthropology; Dir AISSATOU DIA.

Editions Clairafrique: BP 2005, Dakar; tel. 33-864-4429; e-mail clairaf@orange.sn; internet clairafrique.com; f. 1951; politics, law, sociology, anthropology, literature, economics, devt, religion, school books.

Editions des Ecoles Nouvelles Africaines: ave Cheikh Anta Diop, angle rue Pyrotechnie, Stèle Mermoz, BP 581, Dakar; tel. 33-864-0544; e-mail eenas@orange.sn; internet www.eenas.sn; youth and adult education, in French; Dir PAPA MADÉFALL GUÈYE.

Editions Juridiques Africaines (EDJA): 18 rue Raffenel, BP 22420, Dakar-Ponty; tel. 33-821-6689; e-mail edja.ed@orange.sn; internet www.edja.sn; f. 1987; law; Dir NDÉYE NGONÉ GUÈYE.

Editions des Trois Fleuves: blvd de l'Est, angle Cheikh Anta Diop, BP 123, Dakar; tel. 33-825-7923; f. 1972; general non-fiction; luxury edns; Dir GÉRARD RAZIMOWSKY; Gen. Man. BERTRAND DE BOISTEL.

Enda—Tiers Monde Editions (Environmental Development Action in the Third World): Bâtiment B, 1er étage, ave Cheikh Anta Diop, angle Canal IV, BP 3370, Dakar; tel. 33-869-9948; e-mail se@endatiersmonde.org; internet endatiersmonde.org; f. 1972; Third World environment and devt; Dir RAPHAËL NDIAYE; Exec. Sec. JOSÉPHINE OUÉDRAOGO.

Harmattan-Sénégal: BP 45034, Dakar; tel. 33-825-9858; internet harmattansenegal.com; Dir-Gen. ABDOULAYE DIALLO.

Institut Fondamental d'Afrique Noire (IFAN)—Cheikh Anta Diop: BP 206, Campus universitaire, Dakar; tel. 33-825-9890; internet www.afrique-ouest.auf.org; f. 1936; scientific and humanistic studies of Black Africa, for specialist and general public.

Nouvelles Editions Africaines du Sénégal (NEAS): 10 rue Amadou Assane Ndoye, BP 260, Dakar; tel. 33-822-1580; e-mail neas@orange.sn; f. 1972; literary fiction, school books; Dir-Gen. AMINATA SY.

Per Ankh: BP 2, Popenguine; e-mail perankheditions@arc.sn; internet www.perankhbooks.com; history.

Société Africaine d'Edition: 16 bis rue de Thiong, BP 1877, Dakar; tel. 33-821-7977; f. 1961; African politics and economics; Man. Dir PIERRE BIARNES.

Société d'Edition 'Afrique Nouvelle': 9 rue Paul Holle, BP 283, Dakar; tel. 33-822-3825; f. 1947; information, statistics and analyses of African affairs; Man. Dir ATHANASE NDONG.

GOVERNMENT PUBLISHING HOUSE

Société Sénégalaise de Presse et de Publications—Imprimerie Nationale (SSPP): route du service géographique, BP 92, Dakar; tel. 33-832-4692; f. 1970; 62% govt-owned; Dir MAMADOU AMADOU TAMIMOU WANE.

Broadcasting and Communications

TELECOMMUNICATIONS

In 2022 there were three providers of mobile telephone services and two providers of fixed-line telephone services in Senegal.

Arc Informatique: Point E, Impasse 29 PE-36, BP 3377, Dakar; tel. 33-859-8585; e-mail arc@arc.sn; internet www.arc.sn; f. 1993; internet service provider; Dir-Gen. MOHSEN CHIRARA.

Expresso Sénégal: Immeuble R+8, Sokhna Soda Cissé, Sacré Coeur 3, Lot N° 9476, VDN, BP 32454 Ponty, Dakar; tel. 30-100-0000; internet www.expressotelecom.sn; f. 2007; Dir-Gen. HANI OSMAN EL HASSAN.

Free Sénégal: 15 route de Ngor, BP 146, Dakar; tel. 33-824-70000; e-mail serviceclient@free.sn; internet www.free.sn; fmrly Sentel Sénégal GSM, subsequently Tigo; name changed as above in 2019; mobile telephone operator in Dakar, most western regions, and in selected localities nationwide; owned by Saga Africa Holdings Ltd; Dir-Gen. MAMADOU MBENGUE.

Société Nationale des Télécommunications du Sénégal (SONATEL): 46 blvd de la République, BP 64, Dakar; tel. 33-839-1118; e-mail servicepresse.sonatel@orange-sonatel.com; internet www.sonatel.sn; f. 1985; 42% owned by Orange SA (France), 27% owned by Govt; Man. Dir SÉKOU DRAMÉ.

Orange Sénégal: 46 blvd de la République, en face de la Cathédrale, BP 2352, Dakar; tel. 33-839-1771; internet www.orange.sn; f. 1996 as Sonatel Mobiles; fmrly known as Alizé.

WAW: 60 Route de Ngor, Dakar; tel. 33-860-1929; e-mail contact@wawtelecom.com; internet wawtelecom.com; Dir-Gen. ABDOU KANÉ.

Regulatory Authority

Autorité de Régulation des Télécommunications et des Postes (ARTP): Immeuble Thiargane, pl. OMVS, BP 14130, Dakar-Peytavin; tel. 33-869-0369; e-mail contact@artp.sn; internet www.artpsenegal.net; f. 2001; Dir-Gen. ABDOUL LY; Sec.-Gen. YELLAMINE GOUMBALA.

BROADCASTING

Regulatory Authority

Conseil National de Régulation de l'Audiovisuel (CNRA): Immeuble Tamaro, 10e étage, rue Mohamed V, angle Jules Ferry, BP 50059, Dakar; tel. 33-849-5252; e-mail contact@cnra.sn; internet www.cnra.sn; f. 2006 to replace Haut Conseil de l'Audiovisuel; Pres. BABACAR DIAGNÉ.

Radio

Radiodiffusion-Télévision Sénégalaise (RTS): Triangle sud, angle ave Malick Sy, BP 1765, Dakar; tel. 33-849-1212; e-mail rts@rts.sn; internet www.rts.sn; f. 1992; state broadcasting co; broadcasts Radio Sénégal Internationale, Chaîne Nationale and 10 other regional FM radio stations; Dir-Gen. RACINE TALLA.

Radio Sénégal Internationale: Triangle sud, angle ave El Hadj Malick Sy, BP 1765, Dakar; tel. 33-849-1212; f. 2001; broadcasts news and information programmes in French, English, Arabic, Portuguese, Spanish, Italian, Soninké, Pulaar and Wolof from 14 transmitters across Senegal and on cable.

iRADIO 90.3 FM: Dakar; internet emedia.sn; music.

Radio Futurs Médias (RFM): Dakar; internet www.rfm.sn; f. 2003.

Sud FM: Immeuble Fahd, 5e étage, BP 4130, Dakar; tel. 33-865-0888; e-mail info@sudonline.sn; internet sudfmsenradio.com; f. 1994; operated by Sud-Communication; regional stations in Saint-Louis, Kaolack, Louga, Thiès, Ziguinchor and Diourbel; Dir-Gen. BAYE OMAR GUÈYE.

Vibe Radio Sénégal (102.3 FM): Immeuble Clairafrique, pl. de l'Indépendance, rue Malenfant, Dakar; tel. 33-889-9291; e-mail communication@viberadio.sn; internet www.viberadio.sn.

Wal Fadjri FM: Sicap Sacré Coeur no. 8542, BP 576, Dakar; tel. 33-824-2343; e-mail redaction@walf-groupe.com; internet www.sunufm.com/walfadjri; f. 1997; Islamic broadcaster; Dir MOUSTAPHA DIOP.

Television

Radiodiffusion-Télévision Sénégálaise (RTS): see Radio; broadcasts four channels: RTS1, RTS2, RTS3 and RTS4; Dir of Television RACINE TALLA.

RTV: rue 14 Prolongée, HLM1 Domaine Sodida, BP 1656, Dakar; tel. 33-865-6801; e-mail contactrdv@gmail.com; internet rdvsenegal.com.

Finance

BANKING

Central Bank

Banque Centrale des Etats de l'Afrique de l'Ouest (BCEAO): blvd du Général de Gaulle, angle rue 11, BP 3159, Dakar; tel. 33-889-4545; e-mail mail.bceao@bceao.int; internet www.bceao.int; f. 1962; bank of issue for mem. states of the Union Economique et Monétaire Ouest-Africaine (UEMOA, comprising Benin, Burkina Faso, Côte d'Ivoire, Guinea-Bissau, Mali, Niger, Senegal and Togo); Gov. JEAN-CLAUDE KASSI BROU; Dir in Senegal AHMADOU AL AMINOU LO.

Commercial Banks

Bank of Africa—Sénégal: Immeuble Elan, Route de NGOR, Zone 12, Quartier des Almadies, BP 1992, Dakar; tel. 33-865-6444; e-mail information@boasenegal.com; internet www.boasenegal.com; f. 2001; Dir-Gen. ABDEL MUMIN ZAMPALEGRE.

Banque Atlantique Sénégal: 40 blvd de la République, Dakar; tel. 33-849-9292; e-mail infobasn@banqueatlantique.net; internet www.banqueatlantique.net/sen; f. 2005; Dir-Gen. ABDELMOUMEN NAJOUA.

Banque de Dakar: 7 ave Léopold Sédar Senghor, BP 32283, Dakar; tel. 33-849-8600; e-mail serviceclient@groupebdk.com; internet www.bdk.sn; f. 2015; Dir-Gen. MALÈYE FAYE.

Banque Internationale pour le Commerce et l'Industrie du Sénégal (BICIS): 2 ave Léopold Sédar Senghor, BP 392, Dakar; tel. 818040707; e-mail bicis@africa.bnpparibas.com; internet www.bicis.sn; f. 1962; 54.11% owned by Groupe BNP Paribas (France); Chair. MAMADOU LAMINE LOUM; Dir-Gen. PATRICK PITTON.

Banque Outarde (LBO): 20 blvd de la République, Dakar; tel. 33-889-4949; e-mail contact@labanqueoutarde.sn; internet www.labanqueoutarde.sn; f. 2018; Pres. ABDOULAYE DIAO; Dir-Gen. OLIVIER SANTI.

BGFIBank Sénégal: 122 rue Felix Faure, angle ave de la République, Dakar; tel. 33-839-9700; internet senegal.groupebgfibank.com; f. 2018; Pres. AMADOU KANÉ; Dir-Gen. MOHAMED KASIM YAYA.

CBAO Groupe Attijariwafa Bank: 1 pl. de l'Indépendance, BP 129, Dakar; tel. 33-849-6060; e-mail infocbao@cbao.sn; internet www.cbaobank.com/fr; fmrly Compagnie Bancaire de l'Afrique Occidentale (CBAO)l; present name adopted in 2008 following merger with Attijari bank Sénégal; 100% owned by Attijariwafa Bank Group (Morocco); Pres. BOUBKER JAÏ; Dir-Gen. MOUNIR OUDGHIRI.

Citibank Senegal SA: Immeuble SDIH, 4e étage, 2 pl. de l'Indépendance, BP 3391, Dakar; tel. 33-849-11114; f. 1975; wholly owned subsidiary of Citibank NA (USA); Dir-Gen. PAPE MASSAMBA SALL.

Coris Bank International: 26 ave Jean Jaures, angle Peytavin, Dakar; tel. 33-829-6666; e-mail corissn@coris-bank.sn; internet senegal.coris.bank; f. 2015; Dir-Gen. SOUKEYNA NIANG SAKHO.

Crédit du Sénégal (CLS): blvd El Hadji Djily Mbaye, angle rue Huart, BP 56, Dakar; tel. 33-849-0000; e-mail cl_senegal@creditdusenegal.com; internet www.creditdusenegal.com; f. 1989 by acquisition of USB by Crédit Lyonnais (France); name changed as above in 2007 following merger with Crédit Agricole (France); 95% owned by Attijariwafa Bank Group (Morocco); Pres. and Chair. BOUBKER JAÏ; Dir-Gen. FATOUMATA GUÈYE NDIAYE.

Ecobank Sénégal: km 5, ave Cheikh Anta Diop, BP 9095, Dakar; tel. 33-849-2300; e-mail ecobankenquiries@ecobank.com; internet www.ecobank.com; 41.45% owned by Ecobank Transnational Inc (Togo, operating under the auspices of the Economic Community of West African States), 17.0% by Ecobank Bénin, 12.43% by Ecobank Côte d'Ivoire, 4.56% by Ecobank Niger, 4.56% by Ecobank Togo; Chair. GABRIEL FAL; Dir-Gen. SAHID YALLOU.

FBN Bank Sénégal: route des Almadies, Zone 15, Lot D, Dakar; tel. 33-869-9269; e-mail complaints@fbnbanksenegal.com; internet www.fbnbanksenegal.com; f. 2006; fmrly International Commercial Bank (Senegal) SA; present name adopted in 2016; Pres. ADEREMI MUYINUDEEN MAKANJUOLA; CEO OLAWALE I. LATUNJI.

Société Générale Sénégal (SGBS): 19 ave Léopold Sédar Senghor, BP 323, Dakar; tel. 33-839-4242; e-mail sgbs@orange.sn; internet societegenerale.sn; f. 1962; 63.31% owned by Société Générale (France), 35.13% owned by private Senegalese investors; Pres. BASSIROU DIAGNE; Dir-Gen. JEAN-MARC MANCEL.

United Bank for Africa Senegal: Zone 12, Lot D, route des Almadies, BP 11476, Dakar; tel. 33-859-5100; e-mail cfcsenegal@ubagroup.com; internet www.ubasenegal.com; f. 2009; Pres. AMADOU DIAGNE THIOYE; Dir-Gen. BODE AREGBESOLA.

Development Banks

Banque Agricole: 31–33 rue Amadou Ndoye, BP 3890, Dakar; tel. 33-839-3636; e-mail cncas@cncas.sn; internet www.cncas.sn; f. 1984 as Caisse Nationale de Crédit Agricole du Sénégal; present name adopted 2019; 25.8% state-owned; Pres. BASSIROU FATY; Dir-Gen. MALICK NDIAYE.

Banque de l'Habitat du Sénégal (BHS): 69 blvd du Général de Gaulle, BP 229, Dakar; tel. 33-839-3333; e-mail contact@bhs.sn; internet www.bhs.sn; f. 1979; Dir-Gen. MAMADOU BOCAR SY.

Banque Nationale de Développement Economique (BNDE): Immeuble Rivonia, ave Lamine Gueye, angle Place Soweto, Dakar; tel. 33-829-2020; e-mail contact@bnde.sn; internet www.bnde.sn; f. 2014; Dir-Gen. THIERNO SEYDOU NOUROU SY.

Islamic Banks

Banque Islamique du Sénégal (BIS): Immeuble Abdallah Fayçal, rue Huart, angle rue Amadou Ndoye, BP 3381, 18524 Dakar; tel. 33-849-6262; e-mail contact@bis-bank.sn; internet www.ta-holding.com/fr/intl/senegal; f. 1983; 44.5% owned by Tamweel Africa Holding, 33.3% by Islamic Development Bank (Saudi Arabia), 16.2% by Société Générale d'Investissement, 6% state-owned; Pres. of Bd of Administration AMADOU THIERNO DIALLO; Dir-Gen. MOUHAMADOU MADANA KANE.

Financial Institutions

ALIOS Finance Senegal: blvd Djily Mbaye, angle rue de Thann, BP 23775, Dakar; tel. 33-859-0090; e-mail senegal@alios-finance.com; internet www.alios-finance.com; f. 2006; Dir HICHAM JAMIL.

Compagnie Ouest Africaine de Crédit Bail (LOCAFRIQUE): route de Ngor, angle route des Almadies, BP 292, Dakar; tel. 33-859-2760; e-mail contact@locafrique-sf.com; internet www.locafrique-sf.com; f. 1977; Pres. MAMADOU CAMARA; Dir-Gen. KHADIM BÂ.

Banking Associations

Association Professionnelle des Banques et des Etablissements Financiers du Sénégal (APBEF): 5 rue Calmette, angle ave Assane Ndoye, BP 6403, Dakar; tel. 33-823-6093; e-mail apbef@orange.sn; internet apbef.sn; Pres. MAMADOU BOCAR SY; 23 mems.

STOCK EXCHANGE

Bourse Régionale des Valeurs Mobilières (BRVM): 7 rue Jean Mermoz, BP 6956, Dakar; tel. 33-821-1518; e-mail oudeme@brvm.org; internet www.brvm.org; f. 1998; national branch of BRVM (regional stock exchange based in Abidjan, Côte d'Ivoire, serving the member states of UEMOA); Man. OUMAR DÈME.

INSURANCE

Allianz Sénégal Assurances: rue de Thann, angle ave Abdoulaye Fadiga, BP 2610, Dakar; tel. 33-849-4400; e-mail allianz.senegal@allianz.com; internet www.allianz.sn; present name adopted in 2009; Dir-Gen. ADJA SAMB; also **Allianz Sénégal Assurances Vie**; life insurance.

AMSA Assurances: 43 ave Hassan II, BP 225, Dakar; tel. 30-114-8081; internet www.amsaassurances.com; f. 1977; fmrly Assurances Générales Sénégalaises (AGS); Dir-Gen. FATOU QUINET DIENG; also **AMSA Assurances Vie**; life insurance.

Askia Assurances: 40 rue Carnot, angle Saint Michel, BP 14831, Dakar; tel. 33-889-4041; e-mail contact@askiassurances.com; internet www.askiaassurances.net; f. 2017; general; Dir-Gen. OUMOU NIANG TOURÉ.

Assurances la Providence: blvd Djily Mbaye, angle B. Feraud, Dakar; tel. 33-889-9077; e-mail assuranceslaprovidence@orange.sn; internet assuranceslaprovidence.com; f. 2016; Dir-Gen. NDÈYE KHADY DIOP.

Assurances la Sécurité Sénégalaise (ASS): BP 2623, Dakar; tel. 33-849-0599; e-mail ass.dk@orange.sn; f. 1984; Pres. MOUSSA SOW; Man. Dir MBACKÉ SENE.

AXA Sénégal: 5 pl. de l'Indépendance, BP 182, Dakar; tel. 33-849-1010; e-mail info@axa.sn; internet www.axa.sn; f. 1977; fmrly Csar Assurances; 51.5% owned by AXA (France); Dir-Gen. ALIOUNE DIAGNE.

Compagnie Nationale d'Assurance Agricole du Sénégal: BP 15297, Dakar; tel. 33-869-7800; e-mail cnaas@cnaas.sn; f. 2008; agricultural insurance; Dir-Gen. AMADOU NDIAYE.

Compagnie Nationale d'Assurance et de Réassurance des Transporteurs (CNART): Rocade Fann Bel-Air, pl. Bakou, BP 22545, Dakar; tel. 33-831-0606; internet www.cnart.sn; f. 2000; Dir-Gen. MOR ADJ.

Credit International: Immeuble le Geolan, blvd Djily Mbaye, angle Henri Dunan, Dakar; tel. 33-889-1818; e-mail info@cisenegal.com; internet www.cisenegal.com; f. 2009; 89.17% owned by Groupement Crédit Libanais (Lebanon); Pres. Dr JOSEPH TORBEY; Dir-Gen. CHRISTIAN KHALIFE.

Nouvelle Société Interafricaine d'Assurances Sénégal (NSIA): 18–20 ave Léopold Sédar Senghor, BP 18524, Dakar; tel. 33-889-6060; e-mail nsiasenegal@orange.sn; f. 2002; Dir-Gen. MAMADOU IBRA KANÉ; also **Nouvelle Société Interafricaine d'Assurances Vie Sénégal**; Dir-Gen. RAMATOULAYE NDIAYE.

SAAR Sénégal: Lot 265, Batrain, BP 1359, Mermoz, tel. 33-864-9451; e-mail contact@saar-assurances.com; internet www.saar-assurances.com/fr/senegal; f. 2014; Pres. PAUL KAMMOGNÉ FOKAM; Dir-Gen. MICHEL SOBGUI; also **SAAR Vie**.

Salama Assurances Sénégal: 67 blvd de la République, BP 21022, Dakar; tel. 33-849-4800; e-mail salama@salama.sn; f. 1987; fmrly Sosar al-amane, present name adopted in 2008; Dir-Gen. IBRAHIMA WANE.

Sanlam Assurance Sénégal: blvd de la Madeleine, angle rue Carnot, BP 21244, Dakar; tel. 33-849-6900; e-mail contact@sn.sanlam.com; internet sn.sanlam.com; f. 2008 as Colina Sénégal; name changed to Saham Assurance Sénégal in 2014; present name adopted 2021; general; Dir-Gen. MAJDI YASSINE; also **Sanlam Assurance Vie Sénégal**.

La Sénégalaise de l'Assurance Vie: 12 rue Félix Faure, BP 21381, Dakar; tel. 33-889-7389; e-mail senassurancevie@orange.sn; f. 2012; Dir-Gen. MAMADOU FAYE.

Société Nationale d'Assurances du Crédit et du Cautionnement (SONAC SA): Immeuble Trianon, 55 rue Wagane Diouf, BP 3939, Dakar; tel. 33-889-8210; e-mail sonacourrier@sonac.sn; internet www.sonacassurances.com; f. 1997; Dir-Gen. GORA MANGANE.

Société Sénégalaise de Réassurances SA (SENRE): 39 ave Georges Pompidou, BP 386, Dakar; tel. 33-822-8089; e-mail senre@senre.sn; internet www.senre.sn; Pres. OUMAR SARR; Dir-Gen. MOUSSA DIAW.

Sonam Assurances: 6 ave Léopold Sédar Senghor, angle Carnot, BP 210, Dakar; tel. 33-889-8900; e-mail sonam@sonam.sn; internet www.sonamassurances.sn; f. 1973; Dir-Gen. MAMADOU DIOP; also **Sonam Vie**.

Sunu Assurances IARD Sénégal: 1 rue Ramez Bourgi, BP 50184, Dakar; tel. 33-889-6200; e-mail senegal.iard@sunu-group.com; internet www.sunu-group.com; f. 2007; Pres. MAMADOU LAMINE LOUM; Dir-Gen. PAPA AMADOU NÉNÉ MBAYE.

Sunu Assurances Vie Sénégal: 1 rue Ramez Bourgi, BP 182, Dakar; tel. 33-889-0040; e-mail senegal.vie@sunu-group.com; internet www.sunu-group.com; f. 1986; fmrly Union des Assurances du Sénégal Vie; present name adopted in 2015; Dir-Gen. ADJARATOU KHADY N'DAW SY.

Willis Towers Watson Sénégal: Immeuble Isocèle au Point E, rue de Diourbel, angle Rond-Point de l'Ellipse, BP 9, Dakar; tel. 33-859-4051; fmrly Gras Savoye Sénégal; name changed as above in 2018; Man. CHRISTOPHE ROUDAUT.

Insurance Association

Association des Assureurs du Sénégal (AAS): 43 ave Hassan II, BP 1766, Dakar; tel. 33-889-4864; e-mail fssa@orange.sn; internet www.aas.sn; f. 1967; fmrly Comité des Sociétés d'Assurances du Sénégal, subsequently Fédération Sénégalaise des Sociétés d'Assurances; present name adopted 2018; Pres. MOUHAMADOU MOUSTAPHA NOBA; Exec. Dir MAKHTAR FAYE; 23 mems and 1 assoc. mem..

Trade and Industry

GOVERNMENT AGENCIES

Agence de Développement Local (ADL): Immeuble Nolvin, Lot No 23, Liberté VI, VDN, BP 38383, Dakar; tel. 33-869-3090; e-mail contact@adl.sn; internet www.adl.sn; f. 2010; Dir-Gen. ABDOULAYE NDAO.

Agence de Développement et d'Encadrement des Petites et Moyennes Entreprises (ADEPME): Immeuble Seydi Djamil, 8e étage, ave Cheikh Anta Diop, angle rue Léo Frobénius, BP 333, Dakar-Fann; tel. 33-869-7070; e-mail adepme@orange.sn; internet adepme.sn; f. 2001; assists in the formation and operation of small and medium-sized enterprises; Dir-Gen. IDRISSA DIABIRA.

Agence Nationale de l'Aménagement du Territoire (ANAT): Route du Service Géographique, Hann, BP 740, Dakar; tel. 33-832-1506; e-mail contact@anat.sn; internet www.anat.sn; f. 2009; Dir-Gen. MAMADOU DJIGO.

Agence Nationale Chargée de la Promotion de l'Investissement et des Grands Travaux (APIX): 52–54 rue Mohamed V, BP 430, 18524 Dakar; tel. 33-849-0555; e-mail contact@apix.sn; internet www.investinsenegal.com; f. 2000; promotes investment and major projects; Dir-Gen. ABDOULAYE BALDÉ.

Agence Sénégalaise de Promotion des Exportations (ASEPEX): Immeuble HDP, 2e étage, BP 14709, Dakar; tel. 33-869-2021; e-mail asepex@asepex.sn; internet www.asepex.sn; f. 2005; promotes exports; Dir-Gen. (vacant).

Fonds Souverain d'Investissements Stratégiques (FONSIS): Immeuble Elton, 3e étage, rond-point Stèle Mermoz, BP 50882, Dakar; tel. 33-889-63-69; e-mail contact@fonsis.org; internet www.fonsis.org; f. 2013; Dir-Gen. PAPA DEMBA DIALLO.

Société de Développement Agricole et Industriel (SODAGRI): Immeuble King Fahd, 9e étage, blvd Djily Mbaye, angle ave Macodou Ndiaye, BP 222, Dakar; tel. 33-821-0426; e-mail sodagri@orange.sn; internet www.sodagri.sn; f. 1974; agricultural and industrial projects; Dir-Gen. Dr ALPHA BOCAR BALDÉ.

Société de Gestion des Abattoirs du Sénégal (SOGAS): Km 9.5, blvd du Centenaire, Dakar; tel. 33-879-1879; e-mail contact@sogas.sn; internet www.sogas.sn; f. 1962; 28% state-owned; livestock farming; Dir-Gen. TALLA CISSÉ.

Société Internationale des Etudes de Développement en Afrique (SONED—AFRIQUE): Immeuble Ndiaga Diop, Parc à Mazout, Colobane, BP 2084, Dakar; tel. 33-825-8802; e-mail contact@soned-afrique.org; internet soned-afrique.org; f. 1974; Pres. ABDOUL EL MAZIDE NDIAYE.

Société Nationale d'Aménagement et d'Exploitation des Terres du Delta du Fleuve Sénégal et des Vallées du Fleuve Sénégal et de la Falémé (SAED): route de Rosso, BP 74, Saint-Louis; tel. 33-938-2200; e-mail saed@orange.sn; internet www.saed.sn; f. 1965; 100% state-owned; controls the agricultural devt of more than 40,000 ha around the Senegal river delta; Dir-Gen. SAMBA NDIOBÈNE KA.

DEVELOPMENT ORGANIZATIONS

Agence Française de Développement (AFD): 15 ave Nelson Mandela, BP 475, Dakar; tel. 33-849-1999; e-mail afddakar@afd.fr; internet www.afd.fr; Country Dir ALEXANDRE POINTIER.

Centre International du Commerce Extérieur du Sénégal (CICES): route de l'Aéroport, BP 8166, Dakar-Yoff; tel. 33-859-9600; e-mail cices@cices.sn; internet cices.sn; Dir-Gen. SALIOU KEÏTA.

Chambre des Investisseurs Européens au Sénégal (EUROCHAM): 3 pl. de l'Indépendance, BP 130, Dakar; tel. 33-823-6272; e-mail contact@eurocham.sn; internet www.eurocham.sn; f. 1993 as Club des Investisseurs Français au Sénégal; fmrly Conseil des Investisseurs Européens au Sénégal; name changed as above in 2020; Pres. GÉRARD SENAC.

France Volontaires: route de la VDN, Sacré Coeur 3, Villa no 8908, BP 1010, Dakar; tel. 33-824-5295; e-mail ev.senegal@france-volontaires.org; internet www.france-volontaires.org; f. 1972; name changed as above in 2009; Nat. Rep. GUY AHO TETE BENISSAN.

Service de Coopération et d'Action Culturelle: 1 rue El Hadji Amadou Assane Ndoye, BP 2014, Dakar; tel. 33-839-5100; e-mail cad.dakar-amba@diplomatie.gouv.fr; administers bilateral aid from France; fmrly Mission Française de Coopération et d'Action Culturelle; Dir LAURENT PEREZ-VIDAL.

CHAMBERS OF COMMERCE

Union Nationale des Chambres de Commerce, d'Industrie et d'Agriculture du Sénégal (UNCCIA): 1 pl. de l'Indépendance, BP 118, Dakar; tel. 33-822-4911; e-mail contact@unccias.sn; internet www.unccias.sn; f. 1888; restructured 2002; Pres. SÉRIGNE MBOUP.

Chambre de Commerce, d'Industrie et d'Agriculture de Dakar (CCIAD): 1 pl. de l'Indépendance, BP 118, Dakar; tel. 33-889-7680; e-mail cciad@orange.sn; internet www.cciad.sn; f. 1888; Pres. ABDOULAYE SOW; Sec.-Gen. SERIGNE NDIA NDONGO.

Chambre de Commerce, d'Industrie et d'Agriculture de Diourbel: 744 ave Léopold Sédar Senghor, BP 7, Diourbel; tel. 33-971-1203; e-mail mamandiaye@hotmail.com; f. 1969; Pres. MOUSTAPHA CISSÉ LO; Sec.-Gen. MAMADOU NDIAYE.

Chambre de Commerce, d'Industrie et d'Agriculture de Fatick: BP 66, Fatick; tel. 33-949-1425; Pres. BABOUCAR BOP; Sec.-Gen. SEYDOU NOUROU LY.

Chambre de Commerce, d'Industrie et d'Agriculture de Kaolack (CCIAK): BP 203, Kaolack; tel. 33-941-2052; internet www.cciak.sn; Pres. SERIGNE MBOUP.

Chambre de Commerce d'Industrie et d'Agriculture de Kolda: Quartier Escale, BP 23, Kolda; tel. 33-996-1230; e-mail cciakda@orange.sn; Pres. AMADOU MOUNIROU DIALLO; Sec.-Gen. YAYA CAMARA.

Chambre de Commerce, d'Industrie et d'Agriculture de Louga: Quartier Thiokhna, rue de Verdar, angle ave Lamine Gueye, BP 26, Louga; tel. 33-987-0385; e-mail ccialgbis@gmail.com; internet ccialouga.org; Pres. SEYNI NDIAYE SÈNE; Sec.-Gen. CHEIKH SENE.

Chambre de Commerce, d'Industrie et d'Agriculture de Matam: BP 95, Matam; tel. 33-966-6591; Pres. MAMADOU NDIADE; Sec.-Gen. BOCAR BA.

Chambre de Commerce, d'Industrie et d'Agriculture de Saint-Louis: 10 rue Blanchot, BP 19, Saint-Louis; tel. 33-961-1088; f. 1879; Pres. CHEIKH MOUHAMADOU SOURANG; Sec.-Gen. MOUSSA NDIAYE.

Chambre de Commerce, d'Industrie et d'Agriculture de Tambacounda: 120 blvd Diogoye, BP 127, Tambacounda; tel. 33-981-1014; Pres. DJIBY CISSÉ; Sec.-Gen. TENGUELLA BA.

Chambre de Commerce, d'Industrie et de Services de Thiès (CCIST): 96 ave Lamine Guèye, BP 3020, Thiès; tel. 33-951-1002; e-mail cciath@orange.sn; internet ccist.sn; f. 1883; 38 mems; Pres. MODOU DIOP; Sec.-Gen. ABDOULKHADRE CAMARA.

Chambre de Commerce, d'Industrie et d'Agriculture de Ziguinchor: rue du Gen. de Gaulle, BP 26, Ziguinchor; tel. 33-991-1310; internet fb.com/cciazig; f. 1908; Pres. JEAN PASCAL EHEMBA; Sec.-Gen. MAMADOU LAMINE SANE.

EMPLOYERS' ASSOCIATIONS

Chambre des Métiers de Dakar: route de la Corniche-Ouest, Soumbedioune, Dakar; tel. 33-821-7908; e-mail chambredemetiersdakar@gmail.com; internet fb.com/cmdakar1; Pres. MAGATTE MBOW; Sec.-Gen. SERIGNE MOR TALLA BABOU.

Confédération Nationale des Employeurs du Sénégal (CNES): 5 ave Carde, Rez de Chaussée, BP 3819, Dakar; tel. 33-823-0974; e-mail cnes@orange.sn; internet www.cnes.sn; Pres. ADAMA LAM.

Conseil National du Patronat du Sénégal (CNP): 7 rue Jean Mermoz, BP 3537, Dakar; tel. 33-889-6565; e-mail cnp@orange.sn; internet www.cnp.sn; Pres. BAÏDY AGNE; Sec.-Gen. HAMIDOU DIOP.

Groupement Professionnel de l'Industrie du Pétrole au Sénégal (GPP): rue 6, km 4.5, blvd du Centenaire de la Commune de Dakar, BP 479, Dakar; tel. 33-849-3115; e-mail noeljp@orange.sn; Pres. AHMEDINE SY.

Mouvement des Entreprises du Sénégal: Immeuble Horizon, 8e étage, Cité Keur Gorgui, BP 16993, Dakar; tel. 33-867-67-00; e-mail medssenegal@gmail.com; internet www.meds-senegal.org; development and promotion of enterprises; Pres. MBAGNICK DIOP.

Syndicat Professionnel des Entrepreneurs de Bâtiments et de Travaux Publics du Sénégal (SPEBTPS): Rocade Fann Bel Air, Pont Colobane, BP 1520, Dakar; tel. 33-859-0300; f. 1930; 130 mems; Pres. OUMAR SOW.

Syndicat Professionnel des Industries et des Mines du Sénégal (SPIDS): BP 593, Dakar; tel. 33-823-4324; f. 1944; 110 mems; Pres. CHRISTIAN BASSE.

Union des Entreprises du Domaine Industriel de Dakar: BP 10288, Dakar-Liberté; tel. 33-825-0786; e-mail snisa@orange.sn; Pres. ARISTIDE TINO ADEDIRAN.

Union Nationale des Chambres de Métiers (UNCM): Domaine Industriel SODIDA, ave Bourguiba, BP 30040, Dakar; tel. 33-825-0588; e-mail uncm@orange.sn; f. 1981; Pres. INSA DIÈYE; Sec.-Gen. BABOUCAR DIOUF.

Union Nationale des Commerçants et Industriels du Sénégal (UNACOIS): ave Cheikh Ahmadou Bamba 3780, face place de l'Obélisque, Colobane, BP 3698, Dakar; tel. 33-889-2970; e-mail unacois.as@orange.sn; internet www.unacois.org; Pres. IDY THIAM; Exec. Dir OUSMANE SY NDIAYE.

Union des Prestataires, des Industriels et des Commerçants du Sénégal (UPIC): rue A, angle 4 Point E, BP 806, Dakar; tel. 33-824-4424; e-mail upic@upic.sn; f. 1943; Pres. CHRISTIAN YVON BASS; Sec.-Gen. MAURICE SARR.

UTILITIES

Electricity

Commission de Régulation du Secteur de l'Electricité: Ex-Camp Lat Dior, BP 11701, Dakar; tel. 33-849-0459; e-mail crse@crse.sn; internet www.crse.sn; f. 1998; regulatory authority; Pres. IBRAHIMA AMADOU SARR.

Agence Sénégalaise d'Electrification Rurale (ASER): Ex-Camp Lat Dior, ave Peytavin, BP 11131, Dakar; tel. 33-849-4717; e-mail aser@aser.sn; internet www.aser.sn; Dir-Gen. BABA DIALLO.

Société Nationale d'Electricité (SENELEC): 28 rue Vincent, BP 93, Dakar; tel. 33-867-6666; e-mail webmaster@senelec.sn; internet www.senelec.sn; f. 1983; 100% state-owned; Pres. ABDOURAHMANE TOURÉ; Dir-Gen. PAPA MADEMBE BITEYE.

Water

Société Nationale des Eaux du Sénégal (SONES): route du Front de Terre, Hann, BP 400, Dakar; tel. 33-839-7800; e-mail sones@sones.sn; internet www.sones.sn; f. 1995; water works and supply; state-owned; Dir-Gen. CHARLES FALL.

Sénégalaise des Eaux (SDE): Centre de Hann-Route du Front de Terre, BP 224, Dakar; tel. 33-839-3737; e-mail eau@sde.sn; internet www.sde.sn; f. 1996; subsidiary of Groupe Saur International (France); water distribution services; Dir-Gen. ABDOUL BAAL.

MAJOR COMPANIES

The following are some of the largest companies in terms of either capital investment or employment.

Les Câbleries du Sénégal: Km 11, route de Rufisque, BP 3363, Dakar; tel. 33-879-1990; e-mail lcs@lcs.sn; internet www.lcs.sn; manufacture of cables; Dir-Gen. ADEL ATTIEH.

Compagnie Commerciale et Industrielle du Sénégal (CCIS): route de Petit Mbao, BP 137, Dakar; tel. 33-879-8484; e-mail ccis@ccis.sn; internet www.ccis.sn; f. 1972; mfrs of PVC piping and polyethylene; Man. Dir IMAD DERWICHE.

Compagnie Sucrière Sénégalaise (CSS): 49 Richard-Toll, BP 2031, Dakar; tel. 33-938-2323; e-mail info@css.sn; internet www.css.sn; f. 1970; growing of sugar cane and refining of cane sugar; Dir-Gen. ANDRÉ FROISSARD.

Elton Oil: rond-point Stèle Mermoz, route de Ouakam, BP 11325, Dakar; tel. 33-865-4200; e-mail contact@elton.sn; internet www.eltonoil.com; distribution of petroleum products.

Générale d'Entreprises: km 11, route de Rufisqaue, Dakar; tel. 33-839-8383; e-mail gesenegal@groupe-ge.sn; construction and civil engineering.

Grande Côte Operations: Immeuble Atryum Center, 2e étage, 6 route de Ouakam, BP 16844, Dakar; tel. 33-869-3181; internet www.tizir.co.uk; mining; Pres. BRUNO DELANOUE.

Les Grands Moulins de Dakar (GMD): ave Félix Eboué, BP 2068, Dakar; tel. 33-839-9797; e-mail gmd@gmd.sn; internet www.gmd.sn; f. 1946; production of wheat flour and animal food; Dir FRANCK BAVARD.

Groupe Diprom: km 10, blvd du Centenaire, Dakar; tel. 33-839-8201; conglomerate with interests in metal, gas distribution, logistics and industrial safety; subsidiary cos: DIPROM SA, Sitra, Touba Gaz, Touba Oil, Sarii SA, Senstock, Darou Khoudoss; Dir-Gen. MOUSTAPHA SEYE.

Industries Chimiques du Sénégal (ICS): km 18, Route de Rufisque, BP 3835, Dakar; tel. 33-879-1000; e-mail icssg@ics.sn; internet www.ics.sn; f. 1975; majority-owned by Govt of India, 10% state-owned; mining of high-grade calcium phosphates at Taïba,

production of sulphuric and phosphoric acid at 2 factories at Darou, fertilizer factory at M'Bao; Man. Dir ALASSANE DIALLO.

Libya Oil Sénégal: km 7.5, blvd du Centenaire de la Commune de Dakar, BP 227, Dakar; tel. 33-859-3125; internet www.oilibya.com; marketing and sale of petroleum and petroleum products; Pres. and Dir-Gen. IBRAHIM BUGAIGHIS.

Manufacture de Tabacs de l'Ouest Africain (MTOA): km 2.5, blvd du Centenaire de la Commune de Dakar, BP 76, Dakar; tel. 33-849-2500; f. 1951; mfrs of tobacco products; Dir-Gen. YANN FOUDRIGNEZ.

Mondial Paper: km 2.5, blvd du Centenaire de la Commune de Dakar, BP 29524, Dakar; tel. 33-889-7111; e-mail mondialpaper@mondialpaper.sn; internet www.mondialpaper.sn; paper; Dir-Gen. KRISTEL BOUGOUSSA.

Nestlé Senegal: km 14, route de Rufisque, BP 796, Dakar; tel. 77-672-0168; f. 1960; mfrs of sweetened and unsweetened condensed milk and culinary products; wholly owned by Nestlé (Switzerland); Dir-Gen. XAVIER BERAUD.

Rayon Vert Sarl: 34 Mermoz Pyrotechnique, ancienne piste, BP 11600, Dakar; tel. 33-860-1304; e-mail info@rayon-vert.pro; internet www.rayon-vert.pro; solar energy; Dir ROMUALD TAYLOR.

La Rochette Dakar (LRD): km 13.7, route de Rufisque, BP 891, Dakar; tel. 33-839-8282; e-mail larochette@larochettedakar.com; internet www.larochettedakar.com; f. 1946; mfrs of paper and cardboard packaging; Chair. and Man. Dir ADEL SALHAB.

Senbus Industries: 101 Sacré Coeur Extension, BP 45431, Dakar; tel. 33-869-3737; e-mail senbus@senbus.com; 93% owned by SIE—Société d'intervention financière, 7% state-owned; f. 2003; assembly of passenger coaches and buses; Dir-Gen. CHEIKH SADIBOUH DIOP.

Société Africaine de Raffinage (SAR): km 15, route de Rufisque, BP 203, Dakar; tel. 33-823-4684; e-mail sar@sar.sn; internet www.sar.sn; f. 1963; 46% owned by Petrosen, 34% by Locafrique, 8% by Sahara, 6% by Total and 5% by ITOC; petroleum refinery at M'Bao; Dir-Gen. SERIGNE MBOUP.

Société des Brasseries de l'Ouest Africain (SOBOA): route des Brasseries, BP 290, Dakar; tel. 33-859-2838; e-mail dga@soboa.sn; internet www.soboa.sn; f. 1928; mfrs of beer and soft drinks; Man. Dir DAMIEN BARON.

Société de Conserves Alimentaires du Sénégal (SOCAS): 50 ave Lamine Guèye, BP 451, Dakar; tel. 33-839-9000; e-mail socas@orange.sn; internet www.socas-senegal.com; f. 1969; mfrs of tomato concentrate, vegetable canning, export of fresh vegetables; Pres. DONALD BARON; Dir-Gen. ERIC BINSON.

Société de Développement et des Fibres Textiles (SODEFITEX): km 4.5, blvd du Centenaire de la Commune de Dakar, BP 3216, Dakar; tel. 33-889-7950; e-mail dg@sodefitex.sn; internet www.sodefitex.sn; f. 1974; 51.0% owned by Geocoton (France), 46.5% state-owned; responsible for planning and development of cotton industry and rural sustainable development; Dir-Gen. AHMED BACHIR DIOP.

Société Industrielle de Chocolat (SICO): Km 11, route de Rufisque, Dakar; tel. 33-879-1866; e-mail sico@orange.sn.

Société Industrielle Moderne des Plastiques Africains (SIMPA): km 18, route de Rufisque, BP 977, Dakar; tel. 33-879-0079; internet www.simpa.sn; f. 1958; mfrs of injection-moulded and extruded plastic articles; Dir-Gen. IBRAHIM HAWILI.

Sabodala Gold Operations (SGO): Immeuble 2K, Plaza Suite B4, route du Méridien Président, Almadies, BP 38385, Dakar; internet www.sabodalagold.com; 90% owned by Teranga Gold Corpn (Canada), 10% state-owned; Dir-Gen. ABDOUL AZIZ SY.

Société Nationale de Commercialisation des Oléagineux du Sénégal (SONACOS): 32–36 rue du Dr Calmette, BP 639, Dakar; tel. 33-849-1700; internet www.suneor.sn; f. 1975; name changed to SUNEOR in 2007 following privatization; reverted to its original name in 2015 following renationalization; comprises 5 factories, processing and export of edible oils, cattle feed, bleach and vinegar; Pres. YOUSSOU DIALLO; Dir-Gen. MAMADOU DIAGNE FADA.

Société Nationale des Pétroles du Sénégal (PETROSEN): route du Service Géographique, Hann, POB 2076, Dakar; tel. 33-839-9298; e-mail petrosen@petrosen.sn; internet www.petrosen.sn; f. 1981; 90% state-owned; exploration and exploitation of hydrocarbons; Pres. AYMÉROU GNINGUE; Dir-Gen. ADAMA DIALLO.

Société de Produits Industriels et Agricoles (SPIA): 56 ave Faidherbe, BP 3806, Dakar; tel. 33-869-3269; internet spia-sn.com; f. 1980; mfrs of plant-based medicines at Louga; Chair. DJILLY MBAYE; Dir-Gen. CHEIKH DEMBA KAMARA.

Société Sénégalaise des Phosphates de Thiès (SSPT): 39 ave Jean XXIII, BP 241, Dakar; tel. 33-823-3283; e-mail ssptdirect@orange.sn; f. 1948; owned by TOLSA SA (Spain); production of phosphates and attapulgite, mfrs of phosphate fertilizers; Man. FRANÇOIS CHERPION.

SOCOCIM Industries: km 33, ancienne route de Thiès, Rufisque, Dakar; tel. 33-839-8888; e-mail commercial@sococim.sn; internet www.sococim.com; production of cement; Dir-Gen. YOUBA SOW.

Tracto Service Equipement (TSE): 15 route des Brasseries, BP 8930 Dakar; tel. 33-832-9075; agricultural equipment; Dir CHEIKH AMAR.

Vivo Energy Sénégal: route des Hydrocarbures, BP 144, Dakar; tel. 33-849-3737; internet www.vivoenergy.com; f. 1961; a Shell licensee; jt venture between Vitol (40%), Helios Investment Partners (40%) and Shell (20%); marketing and distribution of petroleum and gas; Dir-Gen. KADER MAÏGA.

TRADE UNIONS

Confédération Nationale des Travailleurs du Sénégal (CNTS): Maison des Travailleurs Keur Madia, Quartier Cerf Volant, Dakar; tel. 33-825-4646; e-mail cnts@orange.sn; internet www.cnts.sn; f. 1969; Sec.-Gen. MODY GUIRO.

Confédération Nationale des Travailleurs du Sénégal—Forces de Changement (CNTS—FC): Dakar; f. 2002 following split from CNTS; Sec.-Gen CHEIKH DIOP; 31 affiliated asscns.

Confédération des Syndicats Autonomes (CSA): BP 10224, Dakar; tel. 33-835-0951; e-mail csasenegal@yahoo.com; organization of independent trade unions; Sec.-Gen. ELIMANE DIOUF.

Union Démocratique des Travailleurs du Sénégal (UDTS): BP 7124, Médina, Dakar; tel. 33-835-3897; 18 affiliated unions; Sec.-Gen. MARIAMA DIALLO.

Union Nationale des Syndicats Autonomes du Sénégal (UNSAS): BP 10841, HLM, Dakar; Sec.-Gen. MADEMBA SOCK.

Transport

RAILWAYS

One line runs from Dakar north to Saint-Louis, and the principal line runs to Bamako (Mali).

ROADS

Agence des Travaux et de Gestion des Routes (AGEROUTE): rue F, angle David Diop, Fann Résidence, BP 25242, Dakar-Fann; tel. 33-869-0751; e-mail ageroute@ageroute.sn; internet www.ageroute.sn; Pres. SOULEYMANE LY; Dir-Gen. IBRAHIMA NDIAYE.

Comité Executif des Transports Urbains de Dakar (CETUD): Fann Résidence, route du Front de Terre Hann, BP 17265 Dakar; tel. 33-859-4720; e-mail cetud@cetud.sn; internet www.cetud.sn; f. 1997; regulates the provision of urban transport in Dakar; Pres. AMADOU SAIDOU BA; Exec. Dir THIERNO BIRAHIM AW.

Dakar Dem Dikk: 101 Sacré-Cœur, 3 Pyrotechnie, angle VDN, BP 11725, Dakar; tel. 33-824-1010; e-mail commercial@demdikk.com; internet www.demdikk.com; f. 2001; 76.66% state-owned; Pres. MAHAM DIALLO; Dir-Gen. OUSMANE SYLLA.

Fonds d'Entretien Routier Autonome (FERA): Dakar; internet www.fera.sn; f. 2007; Pres. El Hadji SECK NDIAYE WADE; PAPA IBRAHIMA FAYE.

INLAND WATERWAYS

Senegal has three navigable rivers: the Senegal, navigable for three months of the year as far as Kayes (Mali), for six months as far as Kaédi (Mauritania) and all year as far as Rosso and Podor, and the Saloun and the Casamance. Senegal is a member of the Organisation pour la Mise en Valeur du Fleuve Gambie and of the Organisation pour la Mise en Valeur du Fleuve Sénégal, both based in Dakar. These organizations aim to develop navigational facilities, irrigation and hydroelectric power in the basins of the Gambia and Senegal rivers, respectively.

SHIPPING

The port of Dakar is the second largest in West Africa, after Abidjan (Côte d'Ivoire), and the largest deep-water port in the region, serving Senegal, Mauritania, The Gambia and Mali. The port's facilities include 40 berths, 10 km of quays, and also 53,000 sq m of warehousing and 65,000 sq m of open stocking areas. In addition, there is a container terminal with facilities for vessels with a draught of up to 11 m.

Conseil Sénégalais des Chargeurs (COSEC): ave Malick Sy, BP 1423, Dakar; tel. 33-849-0707; e-mail cosec@cosec.sn; internet www.cosec.sn; Dir-Gen. ABDOULAYE DIOP.

Dakarnave: blvd du Centenaire de la Commune, POB 438, Dakar; tel. 33-849-1001; e-mail commercial@dakarnave.sn; internet www.dakarnave.com; responsible for Senegalese shipyards; 50.99% owned by Lisnave International (Portugal), 48.99% owned by

NAVIVESSEL; Pres. FREDERICO JOSÉ FERREIRA DE MESQUITA SPRANGER; Dir-Gen. JOSÉ ANTONIO FERREIRA MENDES.

Maersk Sénégal: BP 3836, Dakar; tel. 33-859-1111; e-mail sensalmng@maersk.com; f. 1986; Dir-Gen. JORGEN HOLCK.

Société Maritime de l'Atlantique (SOMAT): c/o Port Autonome de Dakar, BP 3195, Dakar; internet www.somat.sn; f. 2005; 51% owned by Compagnie Marocaine de Navigation, COMANAV (Morocco), 24.5% by Conseil Sénégalais des Chargeurs, COSEC, 24.5% by Société Nationale de Port Autonome de Dakar, PAD; operates foot passenger and freight ferry service between Dakar and Ziguinchor (Casamance).

Société Nationale de Port Autonome de Dakar (PAD): 21 blvd de la Libération, BP 3195, Dakar; tel. 33-823-4545; e-mail pad@portdakar.sn; internet www.portdakar.sn; f. 1865; state-owned port authority; Pres. AMADOU KA; Dir-Gen. MOUNTAGA SY.

TransSene: 1 blvd de l'Arsenal, face à la gare ferroviaire, Dakar; tel. 33-823-0290; e-mail transsene@transsene.com; f. 1978; CEO ABDOURAHMANE DIOP.

CIVIL AVIATION

There are two international airports serving the capital. Dakar-Léopold Sédar Senghor and Blaise Diagne, near Ndiass, some 50 km east of Dakar, which was inaugurated in December 2017. There are other major airports at Saint-Louis, Ziguinchor and Tambacounda, in addition to about 15 smaller airfields.

Agence Nationale de l'Aviation Civile et de la Météorologie (ANACIM): BP 8184, Dakar; tel. 33-865-6000; e-mail anacim@anacim.sn; internet www.anacim.sn; f. 2011 following merger of the Agence Nationale de l'Aviation Civile du Sénégal (ANACS) and the Agence Nationale de la Météorologie du Sénégal (ANAMS); civil aviation authority; Dir-Gen. SIDY GUÈYE.

Air Sénégal SA: BP 099, Ndiass; tel. 33-959-26-16; internet flyairsenegal.com; f. 2016 to replace Sénégal Airlines; Pres. Gen. JOSEPH MAMADOU DIOP; Dir-Gen. EL HADJI ALIOUNE BADARA FALL.

Tourism

Agence Sénégalaise de Promotion Touristique (ASPT): Ngor Virage, route de l'aéroport, BP 29753, Dakar-Yoff; tel. 33-869-61-90; internet www.fb.com/ASPTOFFICIEL; f. 2014 to replace Agence Nationale de Promotion Touristique; Dir-Gen. MAHAWA DIOUF.

Société d'Aménagement et de Promotion des Côtes et Zones Touristiques du Sénégal (SAPCO): Sicap Liberté 3, Villa 2118, ave Bourguiba, Dakar; tel. 33-869-0888; e-mail contact@sapco.sn; internet www.sapco.sn; 98.75% state-owned; Dir-Gen. SOULEYMANE NDIAYE.

Defence

As assessed at November 2021, Senegal's active armed forces comprised a land army of 11,900, a navy of 950, and an air force of 750. There was also a 5,000-strong paramilitary gendarmerie. Military service is by selective conscription and lasts for two years. France and the USA provide technical and material aid. In April 2010 President Abdoulaye Wade announced that Senegal was to reclaim all military bases held by France and that 900 of the 1,200 French troops currently stationed in Senegal were to be withdrawn; the 300 troops who remained in the country were to comprise non-combat forces. The withdrawal of the French military finally commenced in June 2011. In 2021 a total of 1,270 Senegalese troops were deployed abroad.

Defence Budget: 263,000m. francs CFA in 2021.

Supreme Chief of the Armed Forces: MACKY SALL.

Chief of General Staff of the Armed Forces: Gen. CHEIKH WADE.

Chief of Staff of the Air Force: Gen. PAPA SOULEYMANE SARR.

Chief of Staff of the Army: Gen. SOULEYMANE KANDÉ.

Chief of Staff of the Navy: Rear-Adm. OUMAR WADE.

Education

Primary education, which usually begins at seven years of age, lasts for six years and is officially compulsory. Secondary education usually begins at the age of 13, and comprises a first cycle of four years (also referred to as 'middle school') and a further cycle of three years. According to estimates by the United Nations Educational, Scientific and Cultural Organization (UNESCO), in 2019/20 enrolment at pre-primary institutions was equivalent to 17% of children in the relevant age-group (males 16%; females 18%). In 2018/19 primary enrolment included 74% of children in the relevant age-group (males 70%; females 79%), while secondary enrolment was equivalent to 46% of children in the relevant age-group (males 43%; females 49%). There are 12 public universities in Senegal. Since 1981 the reading and writing of national languages has been actively promoted, and is expressly encouraged in the 2001 Constitution. In 2021 spending on education represented 21.1% of total government budgetary expenditure.

Bibliography

Barry, B. *Le royaume de Waalo: Le Sénégal avant la conquête*. Paris, Karthala, 2014.

Beck, L. *Brokering Democracy in Africa: The Rise of Clientelist Democracy in Senegal*. Basingstoke, Palgrave Macmillan, 2008.

Boubacar, B. *Agriculture et Sécurité Alimentaire au Sénégal*. Paris, L'Harmattan, 2008.

Coulibaly, A. L. *Le Sénégal à l'épreuve de la démocratie: Enquête sur 50 ans de lutte et de complots au sein de l'élite socialiste*. Paris, L'Harmattan, 1999.

Wade, un opposant au pouvoir: L'alternance piégée. Dakar, Editions Sentinelles, 2003.

Le Sénégal sous Macky Sall: De la vision à l'ambition, les réalisations à mi-mandat. Paris, L'Harmattan, 2015.

Cruise O'Brien, D. B., Diop, M. C., and Diouf, M. *La construction de l'Etat au Sénégal*. Paris, Éditions Karthala, 2002.

Diagne, A. *Abdou Diouf, le maître du jeu*. Dakar, Agence Less Com, 1996.

Diagne, A., and Daffé, G. (Eds). *Le Sénégal en quête d'une croissance durable*. Paris, Éditions Karthala, 2002.

Diallo, M. L. *Le Sénégal, un lion économique?* Paris, Éditions Karthala, 2004.

Diop, B. *Macky Sall: Du Plan Sénégal Emergent (PSE) au temps des actions d'un réformateur* Dakar, L'Harmattan-Sénégal, 2019.

Diop, M.- C. (Ed.).*La société sénégalaise entre le local et le global*. Paris, Éditions Karthala, 2002.

Le Sénégal contemporain. Paris, Éditions Karthala, 2003.

Gouverner le Sénégal: Entre ajustement structurel et développement durable. Paris, Éditions Karthala, 2004.

Le Sénégal sous Abdoulaye Wade. Le Sopi à l'épreuve du pouvoir. Paris, Éditions Karthala, 2013.

Dumont, G.-F., and Kanté, S. *La géopolitique du Sénégal: De Senghor à l'élection de Macky Sall*. Paris, L'Harmattan, 2018.

Gaye, M. *Le Sénégal sous Abdoulaye Wade: Banqueroute, corruption et liberticide*. Paris, L'Harmattan, 2011.

Gellar, S. *Senegal: An African Nation between Islam and the West*. 2nd edn. Boulder, CO, Westview Press, 1995.

Gueye, O. *Mai 1968 au Sénégal: Senghor face aux étudiants et au mouvement syndical*. Paris, Éditions Karthala, 2017.

Jus, C. *Soudan français–Mauritanie, une géopolitique coloniale (1880–1963): Tracer une ligne dans le désert*. Paris, L'Harmattan, 2003.

Kelly, C. L. *Party Proliferation and Political Contestation in Africa: Senegal in Comparative Perspective*. Washington, DC, Palgrave Macmillan, 2019.

Lambert, M. *Longing for Exile: Migration and the Making of a Translocal Community in Senegal, West Africa*. Westport, CT, Greenwood Press, 2002.

Loum, N. *Médias et l'état au Sénégal: L'impossible autonomie*. Paris, L'Harmattan, 2003.

Makédonsky, E. *Le Sénégal: La Sénégambie*. 2 vols. Paris, L'Harmattan, 1987.

Milcent, E., and Sordet, M. *Léopold Sédar Senghor et la naissance de l'Afrique moderne*. Paris, Editions Seghers, 1969.

Ngalane, A. *Sénégal. Une démocratie dans un chaos social*. Paris, L'Harmattan, 2018.

Parent, S. *Cultural Representations of Massacre: Reinterpretations of the Mutiny of Senegal*. New York, Palgrave Macmillan, 2014.

Robinson, D. *Sociétés musulmanes et pouvoir colonial français au Sénégal et en Mauritanie 1880–1920*. Paris, Éditions Karthala, 2004.

Roche, C. *Histoire de la Casamance: Conquête et résistance, 1850–1920*. Paris, Éditions Karthala, 1985.

Le Sénégal à la conquête de son indépendance: 1939–1960: Chronique de la vie politique et syndicale, de l'Empire français à l'indépendance. Paris, Éditions Karthala, 2001.

Saint-Martin, Y.-J. *Le Sénégal sous le second empire*. Paris, Éditions Karthala, 1989.

Sarr, P. *Le Sénégal: Des idées pour une nouvelle donne*. Paris, L'Harmattan, 2012.

Seck, A. *Sénégal émergence d'une démocratie moderne, 1945–2005: Un itinéraire politique*. Paris, Éditions Karthala, 2005.

Souane, L. *Sénégal: Histoire d'une démocratie confisquée*. Paris, L'Harmattan, 2012.

Sow, A. *Courage d'agir: Une nouvelle vision de la politique au Sénégal*. Paris, L'Harmattan, 2014.

Sy, B. *Macky Sall et le Sénégal: De la résilience à l'émergence*. Dakar, L'Harmattan-Sénégal, 2018.

Vaillant, J. G. *Vie de Léopold Sédar Senghor: Noir, Français et Africain*. Paris, Éditions Karthala, 2006.

Villalon, L. *Islamic Society and State Power in Senegal: Disciples and Citizens in Fatick*. Cambridge, Cambridge University Press, 1995.

Wade, A. *Un destin pour l'Afrique*. Paris, Éditions Karthala, 1992.

Wane, A. M. *Le Sénégal entre deux naufrages?: Le Joola et l'Alternance*. Paris, L'Harmattan, 2003.

SEYCHELLES

Physical and Social Geography

The Republic of Seychelles comprises a scattered archipelago of granitic and coralline islands, lying about 1,600 km east of continental Africa and ranging over some 1m. sq km of the western Indian Ocean. The exact number of islands is frequently given as 115, of which 41 are granitic and the remainder coralline. The group also includes numerous rocks and small cays. (However, the Constitution of Seychelles lists 155 islands.) At independence in June 1976, the Aldabra Islands, the Farquhar group and Desroches (combined area 28.5 sq km, or 11 sq miles), part of the British Indian Ocean Territory since 1965, were reunited with Seychelles, thus restoring the land area to 308 sq km (119 sq miles). Including the Aldabra lagoon, the country's area is 455.3 sq km (175.8 sq miles).

The islands take their name from the Vicomte Moreau de Séchelles, Controller-General of Finance in the reign of Louis XV of France. The largest of the group is Mahé, which has an area of about 148 sq km (57 sq miles) and is approximately 27 km long from north to south. Mahé lies 1,800 km due east of Mombasa, Kenya, 3,300 km south-west of Mumbai, India, and 1,100 km north of Madagascar. Victoria, the capital of Seychelles and the only port of the archipelago, is on Mahé. It is the only town in Seychelles of any size and had an estimated population of 28,091 (including suburbs) in mid-2018. The total population was enumerated at 90,945 at the August 2010 census, giving a density of 199.7 persons per sq km. By mid-2021 the total population was officially estimated to have risen to 99,202. The islanders have a variety of ethnic origins—African, European, Indian and Chinese. In 1981 Creole (Seselwa), the language spoken by virtually all Seychellois, replaced English and French as the official language.

The granitic islands, which are all of great scenic beauty, rise fairly steeply from the sea, and Mahé has a long central ridge, which at its highest point, Morne Seychellois, reaches 912 m. Praslin, the second largest island in the group, is 43 km from Mahé and the other granitic islands are within a radius of 56 km. The coral islands are reefs in different stages of formation, rising only marginally above sea level.

For islands so close to the Equator, the climate is surprisingly equable. Maximum shade temperature at sea level averages 29°C, but during the coolest months the temperature may fall to 24°C. There are two seasons, hot from December to May, and cooler from June to November while the south-east trade winds are blowing. Rainfall varies over the group; the greater part falls in the hot months during the north-west trade winds, and the climate then tends to be humid and somewhat enervating. The mean annual rainfall in Victoria is 2,360 mm and the mean average temperature nearly 27°C. All the granitic islands lie outside the cyclone belt.

History

KATHARINE MURISON

Revised for this edition by the editorial staff

The archipelago now forming the Republic of Seychelles was occupied by French settlers in 1770. Following its capture in 1811 by British naval forces, Seychelles was formally ceded by France to Britain in 1814. The islands were administered as a dependency of Mauritius until 1903, when Seychelles became a separate Crown Colony. The independent Republic of Seychelles was proclaimed on 29 June 1976, with James (later Sir James) Mancham of the Seychelles Democratic Party as President, and France Albert René of the Seychelles People's United Party (SPUP) as Prime Minister.

Supporters of the SPUP staged an armed coup in June 1977, while Mancham was in the United Kingdom, and installed René as President. A new Constitution was promulgated in 1979. The SPUP, redesignated the Seychelles People's Progressive Front (SPPF), was declared the sole legal party, and elections were held to legitimize the new political order. However, the Government's socialist programme led to discontent. Plots to overthrow René were suppressed in 1978, 1981, 1982 and 1983, and blamed by the Government on pro-Mancham exiled groups.

RESUMPTION OF MULTI-PARTY POLITICS

In December 1991 the SPPF conceded its political monopoly, agreeing that political groups numbering at least 100 members could be granted official registration. A draft Constitution was approved by 73.9% of voters at a referendum in June 1993. At a presidential election held in July, René received 59.5% of the vote and Mancham (who had returned from exile to lead the New Democratic Party, by now renamed the Democratic Party—DP) won 36.7%. In the concurrent legislative elections, the SPPF secured 28 of the 33 seats, while the DP took four and the Parti Seselwa (PS), led by Protestant clergyman Wavel Ramkalawan, one. The Government subsequently promoted a gradual transition from socialism to free-market policies, aimed at maximizing the country's potential as an offshore financial and business centre. In 1995 the PS merged with three other parties to form the United Opposition (UO).

James Michel, the Minister of Finance, Communications and Defence, was appointed to the newly created post of Vice-President in August 1996.

In elections held in March 1998, René obtained 66.7% of the presidential ballot. In the enlarged National Assembly, his SPPF won 30 of the 34 seats, while the UO won three and the DP only one.

At an early election held on 31 August–2 September 2001, René was re-elected with 54.2% of the valid votes cast, while Ramkalawan secured 45.0%. At legislative elections held in December 2002, the SPPF secured 23 of the 34 seats and the Seychelles National Party (SNP, as the UO had been renamed) 11.

THE MICHEL PRESIDENCY

On 14 April 2004 René resigned from the presidency and was succeeded by Vice-President Michel. Joseph Belmont was appointed as Vice-President. Michel secured his first elected term in office on 28–30 July 2006, with 53.7% of the valid votes cast, while Ramkalawan received 45.7%. At legislative elections held on 10–12 May 2007, the SPPF secured 23 of the 34 seats, while an SNP-DP alliance took 11.

In June 2009 the SPPF was restyled Parti Lepep (People's Party), while the DP reverted to the New Democratic Party (NDP). Michel was elected President of Parti Lepep (René being accorded the title Founding President). Belmont retired as Vice-President in July 2010, being succeeded by Danny Faure, the Minister of Finance.

Michel was re-elected as President on 19–21 May 2011, securing 55.5% of the valid votes cast, while Ramkalawan received 41.4%. Early legislative elections took place on 29 September–1 October, although these were boycotted by the SNP, which had disputed the result of the presidential vote. Parti Lepep secured 31 seats and the Popular Democratic Movement one.

The introduction of a continuous voters' registration system (whereby the roll could be amended at any time) and a requirement that political parties disclose all financing and donations were approved by the National Assembly in December 2014. The changes, which took effect in May 2015, also allowed Seychellois living abroad to register and to vote under certain conditions.

At an early presidential election held on 3–5 December 2015, Michel secured 47.8% of the valid votes cast, followed by Ramkalawan with 33.9%, and former government minister Patrick Pillay (the leader of a breakaway party from Parti Lepep, Lalyans Seselwa—Seychellois Alliance) with 14.2%. As none of the candidates won an absolute majority, the first ever run-off ballot in Seychelles was held, on 16–18 December: Michel narrowly defeated Ramkalawan, securing 50.2% of the valid votes cast. Turnouts of 87.4% and 90.1% were recorded at the first and second rounds, respectively. A petition by Ramkalawan against the results was rejected by the Constitutional Court in May 2016 and by the Court of Appeal in December. Meanwhile, a constitutional amendment reducing the number of consecutive terms a President could serve from three to two was adopted by the National Assembly in April (but was not to apply retroactively).

In April 2016 the SNP, the Seychelles Party for Social Justice and Democracy, the Seselwa United Party (formerly the NDP) and Lalyans Seselwa established Linyon Demokratik Seselwa (LDS—Seychellois Democratic Alliance). At legislative elections held on 8–10 September, the LDS won 19 of the 33 seats, while Parti Lepep, which had been in power since 1977 (first as the SPUP and then as the SPPF), secured 14. Voter turnout was 87.5%. On 27 September Michel announced his intention to resign from the presidency, and on 16 October, despite LDS demands for a fresh presidential election, he was succeeded by Vice-President Faure.

THE FAURE PRESIDENCY—POLITICAL COHABITATION

During his inaugural address President Faure expressed his willingness to work with the LDS-dominated National Assembly. Vincent Meriton, previously Minister of Community Development, Social Affairs and Sports (and Designated Minister), was sworn in as the new Vice-President on 28 October 2016.

A Committee on Truth, Reconciliation and National Unity (CTRNU) was established in 2017 to investigate events since the coup of 5 June 1977. The CTRNU, chaired by the Leader of the Opposition, Ramkalawan, submitted its final report to Faure in June 2018, having considered more than 300 complaints. Hearings on individual cases commenced before a seven-member Truth, Reconciliation and National Unity Commission (TRNUC) in August 2019. Following the expiry of the TRNUC's mandate in August 2022, the cabinet approved an extension until December, to allow the Committee sufficient time to complete its determinations. By that time the TRNUC was reported to have heard the testimony of more than 1,200 witnesses. In October 2021 the Government announced that it was to abolish a land compensation tribunal formed in July 2017 to address compensation claims related to illegal land acquisitions by the Government, with the tribunal's mandate to be transferred to the Ministry of Lands and Housing. At the beginning of October 2021 the Government had launched an initiative to return undeveloped land acquired by the state, with those wishing to lodge claims given three months within which to do so.

In January 2018 Patrick Pillay, Speaker of the National Assembly since 2016, resigned from the legislature, later claiming that cohabitation between the executive and legislative branches of government was not working. Pillay's Lalyans Seselwa withdrew from the LDS in February. Nicholas Prea of

the SNP was elected as Speaker in March. In November Parti Lepep was renamed United Seychelles.

In July 2018 seven appointed regional councils were established under a pilot project. The councils' membership reflected the political balance in the National Assembly.

The five members of a new Human Rights Commission were sworn into office in March and July 2019, and the director-general of the recently established Seychelles Intelligence Service was appointed in August.

In mid-March 2020 Seychelles recorded its first cases of COVID-19. In an attempt to prevent the virus entering Seychelles, the Government had implemented bans from late January 2020 on travel to/from the People's Republic of China and later other countries with high infection rates. In March–April Faure announced further measures aimed at curbing the transmission of COVID-19, including school closures, a ban on foreign travel, restrictions on assembly and the closure of non-essential services. The shutdown began to be eased from 4 May, and scheduled commercial passenger flights from countries deemed to be low- or medium-risk in terms of COVID-19 transmission were permitted from 1 August.

RAMKALAWAN ELECTED PRESIDENT

Legislative elections (which had been scheduled to take place in 2021) were held concurrently with the presidential election on 22–24 October 2020 in order to reduce costs. In the presidential ballot, Ramkalawan, standing for a sixth time, secured 54.9% of the valid votes cast, thereby becoming the first successful opposition candidate since independence in 1976. Faure of United Seychelles won 43.5% of the valid votes cast, and former Minister of Tourism and Culture Alain St Ange, representing One Seychelles (established in 2019), received only 1.6%. A turnout of 88.5% was recorded. In the legislative polls, Ramkalawan's LDS increased its majority, taking 25 of the 35 seats, while United Seychelles won 10. Upon his inauguration on 26 October 2020, President Ramkalawan called for national unity. His Vice-President, Ahmed Afif, took office on the following day. The new National Assembly elected Roger Mancienne, the LDS leader, as Speaker.

The new administration's immediate focus was recovery from a severe economic recession caused largely by the impact of the COVID-19 pandemic on Seychelles' vital tourism sector. In November 2020 Ramkalawan, who had assumed personal responsibility for the defence, legal affairs and public administration ministerial portfolios, announced measures aimed at cutting public expenditure, including the non-payment of the usual '13th month' salary (or bonus) to public and private sector employees and the cancellation of elections to district councils scheduled for January 2021. Plans for the restructuring of public institutions were announced in February 2021, with several to be merged or brought under the relevant government ministry, in a further attempt to reduce spending.

Former parliamentary Speaker Patrick Herminie was elected to succeed Vincent Meriton as leader of United Seychelles in January 2021. The Electoral Commission announced the deregistration of Lalyans Seselwa in May. Party leader Pillay, whose presidential candidacy had been rejected owing to his failure to collect the required 500 signatures from supportive registered voters, accepted the decision, and contended that his party's primary objectives had been achieved— namely, the removal of a corrupt administration and the forging of a stronger, more cohesive opposition.

New restrictions aimed at curbing the spread of COVID-19, including the closure of schools, bars, gyms and churches, were announced on 29 December 2020, following a rise in cases, and an overnight curfew was introduced on 25 January 2021. On 10 January, a week after recording its first death from COVID-19, Seychelles became the first African country to commence a vaccination programme against the virus, using 50,000 doses of China's Sinopharm vaccine donated by the United Arab Emirates (UAE); 50,000 doses of AstraZeneca's Covishield vaccine, donated by India, were received later that month, followed by 1,000 doses of the Russian Sputnik V vaccine, and 25,000 further Sinopharm doses donated by China, in mid-2021. Restrictions began to be eased from early March. Seychelles reopened its borders to nearly all visitors in late March, without the need to quarantine, but in late April banned travellers from several countries with high infection levels.

Some restrictions were reimposed in early May 2021, with schools closed again, amid a surge in transmissions fuelled by the Delta variant of the virus. Schools on Mahé reopened in June. The steep increase in the number of cases, despite more than 60% of the population having been fully vaccinated, prompted concerns over the efficacy of the Sinopharm vaccine. The first doses of the Sputnik V vaccine were administered in mid-May, and in September the USA donated 35,100 doses of the Pfizer vaccine via the COVID-19 Vaccines Global Access (COVAX) Facility.

In October 2021 the Government announced that the 13th month salary was to be withheld for the second consecutive year. Consultations on a proposed alternative, performance-based bonus scheme were held in February–March 2022; however, no decision had been announced as of late 2022. To address growing public discontent over economic conditions and the rising cost of living (which were exacerbated by the Russian invasion of Ukraine on 24 February), the Seychelles Government increased welfare assistance with effect from 1 May.

Meanwhile, further consternation was provoked in October 2021 by the publication of the Pandora Papers by the International Consortium of Investigative Journalists. The leaked documents, which revealed details of the clandestine financial activities of members of the global political and business elites, noted the prominence of Seychelles as a tax haven, owing to the country's weak tax regulations, with thousands of documents obtained from Seychelles-based offshore companies included within the release.

With the Seychelles authorities keen to appear committed to tackling financial impropriety, in November 2021 well-known business investor Mukesh Valabhji and his wife, Laura Valabhji, were arrested in connection with the alleged embezzlement of US $50m. of aid donated to Seychelles by the UAE in 2002. Mukesh Valabhji, who at the time of the alleged crime was an economic adviser to the then-President René, was said to have transferred the funds to a UK-based bank account of the Seychelles Marketing Board, before laundering it through a network of shell companies. Mukesh and Laura Valabhji, Sarah Zarqhani René (the widow of the former President, who had died in 2019), former cabinet minister Maurice Loustau-Lalanne, former director-general in the finance ministry Lekha Nair and senior military officer Leslie Benoiton were formally charged in connection with the case in December 2021, in the first major proceedings to be initiated by the Anti-Corruption Commission of Seychelles (ACCS), which had been established under legislation enacted in 2016.

Mukesh and Laura Valabhji were additionally charged with firearms and terrorism offences in February 2022, following the apparent discovery of arms and munitions during a police search of their residence. Fahreen Rajan (a business associate of Mukesh Valabhji) and René's son were charged in connection with the case in early 2022, while a third individual was arrested but subsequently released without charge. All eight facing charges denied any wrongdoing. In May the ACCS revised the charges against Mukesh Valabhji and Zarqhani René, after the National Assembly approved an amendment to the Anti-Money Laundering and Countering the Financing of Terrorism Act of 2020. A total of 10 charges relating to abuse of authority, corruption and money laundering were filed against Valabhji, while four money laundering charges were lodged against Zarqhani René. Both defendants entered formal not guilty pleas in mid-May; their trial was scheduled to commence in April 2023. All charges relating to the embezzlement scandal against Sarah Valabhji, Loustau-Lalanne and Nair were withdrawn by the ACCS in May 2022. However, the former remained in detention at late 2022, owing to the pending firearms and terrorism charges against her and her husband.

At an LDS convention in March 2022, the first to be held since its electoral victory in 2020, party members elected a new executive committee. Mancienne remained party leader and Chair of the committee, while Gervais Henrie was elected party Secretary-General.

At the end of May 2022 the National Assembly approved a bill providing for an amendment to the Constitution that endowed the Seychelles Defence Forces with the right to enforce domestic law outside of states of emergency. Assenting to the amendment in mid-June, Ramkalawan asserted that there was 'no need for the public to be fearful of these amendments', stressing that the military would not replace but merely provide 'support' to the police force and other public authorities in their handling of public security, maritime security and environmental protection issues.

The longstanding issue of water scarcity assumed greater prominence in 2021–22 owing to sustained periods of drought across Seychelles from April 2021, which prompted the authorities to restrict access to running water for households in most parts of Mahé from August, with the restrictions tightened from November. With climatic conditions causing renewed stress in mid-2022, water controls were reintroduced in southern Mahé in May between the hours of 10 p.m. and 4 a.m. Work to increase the capacity of La Gogue dam was nearing completion in late 2022, with the expanded facility expected to become operational in early 2023, while the rehabilitation of the Mare-aux-Cochons wetland—Seychelles' largest freshwater basin—was among a number of other ongoing projects designed to improve the country's water storage and supply facilities.

Meanwhile, the emergence of the highly transmissible Omicron variant precipitated another significant increase in the number of COVID-19 cases in Seychelles from late December 2021. However, with the Omicron variant typically leading to milder disease, and a steady decline in the rate of transmission evident from early February 2022, the authorities eased restrictions from March, including allowing fully vaccinated travellers to enter Seychelles without undertaking a COVID-19 test prior to travel. By 6 September the number of active cases had fallen to just 116 (of which the vast majority were on Mahé), with no patients admitted at any of the country's COVID-19 treatment facilities at that time. According to Johns Hopkins University, as of 6 September 46,175 confirmed cases of COVID-19 had been recorded in Seychelles, with 169 fatalities (a rate of 171.85 per 100,000 of the population). According to Our World in Data, 76.3% of the population had been fully vaccinated as of 28 August.

EXTERNAL RELATIONS

Seychelles, a member of the Commonwealth, the Common Market for Eastern and Southern Africa (COMESA), the African Union (AU) and the Southern African Development Community (SADC), has traditionally pursued a policy of non-alignment in international affairs. In April 2015 Seychelles was admitted to the World Trade Organization. In June the Seychelles Government signed the agreement establishing a COMESA-East African Community-SADC Tripartite Free Trade Area. In March 2018 Seychelles was among 44 of the 55 member states to sign an agreement on the establishment of an African Continental Free Trade Area (AfCFTA). The AfCFTA agreement entered into force in May 2019 in the 24 states that had ratified it, and trading under the AfCFTA commenced on 1 January 2021. The Seychelles National Assembly approved the ratification of the AfCFTA in June, by which time the accord had been signed by 54 states and ratified by 43.

In 1983 Seychelles, Madagascar and Mauritius agreed to form an Indian Ocean Commission (IOC) with the aim of increasing regional co-operation. The Comoros joined the IOC in 1985 and France (representing Réunion) in 1986.

During a visit to Seychelles by Indian Prime Minister Narendra Modi in March 2015 it was announced that a joint working group would be established to expand co-operation on the so-called 'blue economy' (the management of ocean resources), which had become a major focus of Seychelles government policy. Controversial plans for the establishment of a joint military facility on the remote Seychelles island of Assumption were abandoned in June 2018, following public protests. Nevertheless, six bilateral agreements were signed during a visit by President Faure to India later that month; Modi notably offered Seychelles credit worth US $100m. for defence and maritime security co-operation. Several Indian-funded projects, including a fast patrol vessel, a Magistrates'

Court building and a solar plant on Romainville Island, were officially handed over to Seychelles in April 2021. Defence relations were consolidated in March 2022 by the staging of a 10-day joint military exercise—the ninth iteration of the biennial event—at the Seychelles Defence Academy.

In July 2008 Seychelles and Mauritius signed a boundary agreement defining the areas of their two exclusive economic zones (EEZs), with that of Seychelles covering some 1.4m. sq km. In March 2011 the United Nations (UN) Commission on the Limits of the Continental Shelf confirmed the two countries' joint jurisdiction over an area extending approximately 396,000 sq km beyond their respective EEZs under the UN Convention on the Law of the Sea. In March 2012 two bilateral treaties were signed on the joint exercise of sovereign rights in the extended continental shelf and on a framework for the joint management of the area. In August 2018 a further UN ruling extended Seychelles' territorial waters by 14,840 sq km. In March 2020 President Faure announced the legal designation of 410,000 sq km of Seychelles' EEZ as a marine protected area, fulfilling a target set in 2012 to increase marine protection from 0.04% to 30% of the EEZ. During a visit to Mauritius by President Ramkalawan in November 2020, Seychelles and Mauritius signed two memorandums of understanding in the fields of security and combating crime and information and communication technology. Long-mooted plans to commence joint exploration hydrocarbons exploration in the extended continental shelf continued to be under consideration in late 2022.

Bilateral relations with the People's Republic of China were strengthened in December 2011 when the Seychelles Government announced that it was to provide facilities to resupply Chinese naval ships operating in the Indian Ocean. An agreement between China and Seychelles allowing mutual visa-free travel for up to 30 days for all passport holders came into force in June 2013, in the first such arrangement between China and an African country. President Faure visited China in September 2018, holding discussions with Chinese President Xi Jinping, following which memorandums of understanding were signed on co-operation within the framework of China's Belt and Road Initiative and co-operation in the marine sector through a 'blue partnership'. In January 2021 an agreement was signed on an $11m. grant from China to Seychelles, with $4.6m. allocated to renewable energy projects. A further $6.2m. was granted by China under an economic and technical co-operation agreement signed in February. A new purpose-made Chinese cultural centre was formally inaugurated in Victoria in June 2022.

Following a visit to Japan by President Faure in August 2019, in October an agreement was signed on the provision of a Japanese grant of US $7m. for maritime security projects in Seychelles, and in November Japan opened an embassy in Seychelles in Victoria. Attending the Eighth Tokyo International Conference on African Development, held in Tunis, Tunisia, in August 2022, Ramkalawan underscored the link between development, maritime security and climate change, and appealed for a more holistic approach to be adopted with regard to regional peace and security issues. Ramkalawan met with the Japanese Minister for Foreign Affairs, Yoshimasa Hayashi, on the sidelines of the conference, and were reported to have discussed expanding bilateral co-operation in, *inter alia*, maritime security, climate change, fisheries and wastewater treatment.

Seychelles has developed strong relations with the UAE, which is one of the country's most significant donors. A series of senior-level reciprocal visits in recent years has included a visit to the UAE by Ramkalawan in December 2020, when the UAE donated 50,000 doses of the Sinopharm COVID-19 vaccine to Seychelles, and a visit to Victoria by UAE President Sheikh Mohammed bin Zayed Al Nahyan in August 2022, when Sheikh Mohammed and Ramkalawan discussed strengthening bilateral co-operation in the fields of trade, investment and tourism. Meanwhile, during a visit by Ramkalawan to Qatar in March 2021, two agreements were signed on bilateral co-operation in military affairs, particularly maritime security,

and sports. Relations between Seychelles and Saudi Arabia have also increased in recent years. The two were reported to be negotiating on a visa waiver agreement in late 2022. In August Air Seychelles became the first airline to be granted permission by the Saudi authorities to fly over Saudi territory en route to Israel, allowing for a more direct route and thereby lessening both the duration and environmental impact of the journey.

Attacks by Somali pirates on ships off the coast of Seychelles became of increasing concern from 2009. In November 2009 Seychelles signed an agreement allowing the deployment of European Union (EU) troops on its territory to counter attacks. Amendments to the penal code adopted in March 2010 enabled the prosecution of suspected pirates, including those apprehended by foreign naval forces. By the end of 2015 Seychelles had convicted 138 pirates, most of whom had been repatriated to Somalia to serve their sentences. According to data compiled by EU NAVFOR, only one attempted Somali-based pirate attacks was reported in 2016, compared with 212 in 2011, the dramatic reduction being attributed to naval efforts. In December 2016 the North Atlantic Treaty Organization concluded its counter-piracy operation in the Indian Ocean, which had commenced in 2009. The number of Somali-based pirate attacks increased to nine in 2017, but declined to two in 2018 and just one in 2019, with no attacks reported in 2020. A thwarted pirate attack targeting a Turkish vessel off the coast of the Somali capital, Mogadishu, in August 2021 was the first Somali-based pirate attack to be reported since April 2019.

Meanwhile, two additional maritime security institutions were opened in Seychelles in July 2017: the National Information Sharing and Coordination Centre and the Regional Centre for Operations. In May 2021 the National Assembly approved the ratification of a bilateral agreement with the USA on co-operation in countering illicit transnational maritime activity. At a summit of SADC heads of state and government convened in Kinshasa, the Democratic Republic of the Congo, in August 2022, Ramkalawan called for enhanced maritime security co-operation among SADC members, noting the increasing threat posed to Seychelles and the wider region by drugs, human and weapons trafficking, and by marine pollution and poaching of maritime resources.

In December 2017 the EU included Seychelles on a 'grey list' of jurisdictions that it claimed were not fully compliant with EU standards on tax avoidance. Despite the adoption of amendments to Seychelles' preferential tax regimes in late 2018, Seychelles was moved to the EU's black list of non-co-operative tax jurisdictions in February 2020 after it failed promptly to implement agreed tax reforms. The EU announced the removal of Seychelles from its black list in October 2021, just two days after the Pandora Papers had identified Seychelles as a significant tax haven, eliciting widespread criticism. In the same month the eighth annual political dialogue between Seychelles and the EU was conducted in Victoria, following which the Seychelles Minister of Foreign Affairs and Tourism and the EU's ambassador to Seychelles pledged to continue co-operating actively to address post-pandemic challenges and to explore further co-operation opportunities in maritime and global security, climate change, sustainable fisheries management and the blue economy. Seychelles hosted the inaugural meeting of the EU's BlueInvest Africa initiative, which was convened on Mahé in September 2022. The two-day event brought African-based entrepreneurs, start-up companies and small-scale businesses together with investors from Africa and Europe, as well as representatives of international financial institutions, in order to generate business opportunities and promote the blue economy and sustainable development.

At the UN Climate Change Conference in Glasgow, UK, in October–November 2021, President Ramkalawan was a signatory to the Glasgow Leaders' Declaration on Forests and Land Use. The agreement pledged to halt and reverse forest loss and land degradation by 2030, as well as to promote sustainable development and 'inclusive rural transformation'.

Economy

ROBERT E. LOONEY

INTRODUCTION

By many measures, the Republic of Seychelles is sub-Saharan Africa's most prosperous economy. Per capita income (on a 2017 purchasing-power parity—PPP—basis) was US $29,128 in 2021, having been just $11,062 in 1980, $19,051 in 2000 and $21,111 in 2010. In current prices, per capita income in 2021 was $14,931, compared with $2,329 in 1980, $7,578 in 2000 and $10,805 in 2010. The average for the region in 2021 (by the 2017 PPP measure) was $3,879.

The country has had to overcome various obstacles to reach this level of prosperity. Geographically, it is an isolated island archipelago located north-east of Madagascar. There is little in the way of fertile agricultural soils, minerals or hydrocarbons. With a population of only 99,202 in 2021, the country mainly depends on developments in the global economy over which it has little or no control.

While the country has achieved much economic success, gross domestic product (GDP) growth has also been decelerating; it averaged 7.0% per year in the 1960s and 1970s, 3.8% during 1980–99 and 3.1% per year in 2000–21. Growth has largely occurred in the services area, with agriculture representing only 2.2% of GDP in 2021 (down from 6.8% in 1980), industry 14.4% (down from 15.6% in 1980) and services, particularly tourism, providing the remaining 83.4% (up from 77.6% in 1980).

Several structural vulnerabilities threaten future prosperity. The country remains heavily dependent on imported goods and foreign funding, particularly foreign direct investment (FDI). The country's tourism sector dominates the economy. However, the industry is highly vulnerable to adverse developments, such as the COVID-19 pandemic and the related drop in international tourism. Seychelles has a unique economy. Its sparse population, steep terrain, geographical remoteness, and few comparative advantages outside of tourism and fishing, mean that the country has had to create unique development and growth paths, such as its recent 'blue economy' initiative. The country's creativity will be sorely tested in future years if prosperity is to be maintained and growth sustained.

SOCIOECONOMIC DEVELOPMENT

As with per capita income, the country's socioeconomic development ranks relatively high. The United Nations (UN) Development Programme's 2020 *Human Development Report* (with data up to 2019) ranked Seychelles 67th out of 189 countries on its Human Development Index (HDI), the second-highest ranking (after Mauritius at 66th) in sub-Saharan Africa, but down from 62nd in 2018. The country's HDI ranking in 2018 was 15 places below its GNI per capita rank, suggesting that the country encountered difficulties translating economic success into broad-based prosperity. The country's HDI improvements have declined somewhat in recent years, averaging 0.68% per year in 2000–10 but 0.46% during 2010–19. In 2021 life expectancy in Seychelles was 73.5 years, and the mean years of schooling were 9.0 years in 2019. 100% of the rural population has access to electricity, with 100% using at least basic sanitation facilities. 97% of the country's secondary schools have access to the internet.

Using a broader measure of prosperity—the Legatum Prosperity Index for 2021—Seychelles ranked 50th (up from 51st in 2020) out of 167 countries. Of the Index's 12 dimensions, Seychelles performed best in health (37th), social capital (41st), governance (46th), natural environment (50th) and enterprise conditions (52nd). The country was weakest in economic quality (71st), personal freedom (70th) and investment environment (67th).

Offsetting these positive developments is the country's distribution of income. During 2010–18 the income share of the lowest 40% was only 15.2% of the total, while the wealthiest 10% took 39.9%, and the top 1% received 20.4%. The country's Gini coefficient (a standard measure of inequality, with high

numbers more unequal) stood at 46.8%, which is high for countries at its income level. According to the World Bank, 32% of the population suffered from multidimensional poverty in 2018. The relatively low standard of living for large segments of the population is perhaps the central failure of the country's vigorous growth over the last several decades.

As with GDP, Seychelles' population growth rate is gradually declining. The growth rate averaged 2.1% per year in the 1960s and 1970s, before falling to 1.2% in the 1980s and 1990s and reaching 1.0% in 2000–21. As a result of this decline, the country is experiencing a 'demographic dividend' where a growing percentage of the population will be of working age (15–64 years of age). During the 1960s and 1970s an average of 52.2% of the population was in this age group, increasing to 59.0% in the 1980s and 1990s and to 68.2% in 2000–21.

Most of the growth in the working-age population has come from reduced numbers of those 0–14 years of age. The population in this age group fell from 41.7% of the total in the 1960s and 1970s to 34.2% in the 1980s and 1990s. In 2000–21 this age group averaged just 24.4% of the population. These demographic patterns assure Seychelles the potential to attain high economic growth rates, providing the economy can diversify into new job-creating activities over the coming decades.

ECONOMIC GROWTH AND REFORMS

Following independence in 1976, the Seychelles Government established a socialist economic system that combined extensive state intervention and regulation with a comprehensive welfare system. The Government's macroeconomic disequilibrium strategy enabled it to channel resources to priority areas while suppressing activity in areas considered inessential. The Government restricted access to foreign exchange and created a captive market for its securities. This environment enabled the Government to borrow excessively from the banking system. Many state enterprises in the critical areas of production came into existence. Government expenditures increased rapidly, reaching 60.7% of GDP by 1998.

Although some privatization began in the 1990s, the disequilibrium system continued into the 2000s, with growth primarily supported by increased government borrowing and debt accumulation. Revenues remained constrained due to tax concessions to foreign investors, especially in the tourism industry. The country's development model finally hit constraints with the onset of the international financial crisis, the rise in commodity prices, particularly petroleum, and borrowing limits setting in as debt reached 192.1% of GDP in 2008, up from the already high level of 80.4% in 1990. By mid-2008 the country could no longer service its foreign debt, with the Standard & Poor's credit rating agency downgrading the country to selective default.

As part of an International Monetary Fund (IMF) programme, Seychelles began undertaking significant reforms to transition from a tightly regulated economy to one based on market mechanisms. The highly overvalued rupee was allowed to float with the Government removing all exchange controls, overhauling public spending, and tightening monetary policy. The switch from gradual to rapid reform was a precondition for IMF assistance. Adherence to the IMF programme enabled Seychelles to begin formal talks in 2009 with the 'Paris Club' of official creditors to reschedule foreign debt and negotiations with commercial lenders to get debt servicing back on track. In April Paris Club creditors reached an agreement reducing the country's debt by 45%.

The flotation of the rupee represented a critical step towards restoring macroeconomic equilibrium after years of imbalances. The Government accompanied it with comprehensive fiscal, monetary and structural reforms, particularly the reduction in the state's role and the facilitation of private sector expansion and privatization to absorb the cutbacks in the public sector workforce.

In further support of economic recovery and growth, the Government followed up its economic reforms with a series of improvements in its governance structures. In 2020, of the World Bank's Governance Indices (voice and accountability, political stability and absence of violence, government effectiveness, regulatory quality, the rule of law, and control of corruption), Seychelles scored highest in control of corruption at the 86th percentile, up from 61st in 2007.

Overall governance (an average of these six measures) declined from the 70th percentile in 1996 to the 53rd in 2007. However, the country has shown steady progress, rising to the 66th percentile in 2020. Government effectiveness increased from the 55th percentile in 2007 to the 71st by 2020. However, the chief weakness is regulatory quality, defined as the Government's ability to plan and implement sound policies and regulations that permit and promote private sector development. After reaching the 69th percentile in 1996, the country's ranking in this dimension fell to the 20th in 2007. Since then, improvements have brought the country to the 48th percentile by 2020.

Similar progress occurred in improved economic freedom. The Heritage Foundation's Index of Economic Freedom grouped Seychelles in its 'repressed' category in 2008 (the first year of data). However, liberalization lifted the economy into the Foundation's 'mostly free' group in 2010 and the 'moderately free' group in 2015. Progress continued and in 2020 the country was nearing the threshold for the 'mostly free' group. In the critical area of trade freedom, Seychelles moved from 'repressed' in 2014 to 'free' in 2015, and it remained there in 2021. In that year Seychelles ranked fifth among 47 countries in sub-Saharan Africa and was the world's 79th freest country.

TOURISM

Tourism began with the construction of an international airport on Mahé in 1971. Since then, the country has developed into one of the world's premier tourist destinations. Given its tropical location, Seychelles attracts visitors all year round, and its growth has resulted in the sector dominating the country's GDP, exports and employment.

In 1972 3,100 tourists arrived in Seychelles, but this number quickly rose to 79,000 by 1980. Arrivals contracted gradually from 142,000 in 1996 to 126,000 in 2004. From there, however, arrivals increased rapidly, reaching 239,000 in 2014. At that point, a further sharp upswing brought arrivals to 333,000 in 2016 and 428,000 by 2019. The number of hotels and similar establishments increased rapidly, from 487 in 2015 to 697 by 2019. The occupancy rate also increased steadily, from 62% in 2015 to 66% by 2019.

As in previous years, Europe accounted for the largest number of arrivals in 2019, with 69.0% of the total, followed by Asia with 17.4%. Germany accounted for Europe's largest share, with 18.9% of visitors. France accounted for 11%, followed by the United Kingdom at 8%, and Italy with 7%. The authorities' efforts to expand flight connections and market Seychelles aggressively as a tourist destination have also helped boost arrivals from newer markets, including the United Arab Emirates (UAE), South Africa and India. In 2019 the UAE accounted for 6% of tourist arrivals and was the fifth largest source of tourists.

In 2019 the industry contributed 26.4% of GDP. If the share of tourism activity in GDP captures vulnerability to tourism interruption, then Seychelles is the fifth most vulnerable, following the Maldives, the British Virgin Islands, Macao and Aruba. However, the tourism sector in Seychelles has significant 'positive spillovers' into the rest of the economy, boosting demand for ancillary services, including construction, banking, transportation and other services. Consequently, Seychelles is as dependent on tourism as any country worldwide.

Before the COVID-19 pandemic hit the country, Seychelles had developed an extensive network of international air links, and eight international airlines have direct service: Air Seychelles, Emirates Airlines, Etihad Airways (UAE), Austrian Airlines, Condor Flugdienst (Germany), Ethiopian Airlines, Qatar Airways and Turkish Airlines. In addition, charter flights, discouraged previously, were now welcome. Several cruise ships also visited the islands regularly.

However, the tourism situation changed dramatically. From March 2020, with the advent of the pandemic, almost everything related to the tourist sector shut down. Arrivals fell to 114,858 in 2020, and the sector's contribution to GDP declined by 46.4%. Similarly, its contrition to total employment declined by 28.5%, while visitor expenditures declined by 50.7%. Early indicators suggested that 2021 would also be a poor year for Seychelles tourism. However, by the end of the year tourist arrivals had increased to 177,504, with the sector's contribution to the economy increasing by 11%. In 2021 increased tourism caused a 5.9% rise in tourism-related employment and an 11.5% increase in foreign exchange earnings.

In 2021 Germany retained its position as the primary source of tourists, accounting for 18%. As in 2019, France was second, with its share expanding to 17%. The significant shift was the UAE, now third with 14%, up from 6% in 2019. Italy was fifth at 6%, followed by Switzerland at 5%.

AGRICULTURE

Before tourism dominated economic activity in Seychelles, agriculture played a vital role, accounting for 9.6% of GDP as late as 1976. Yet by 1990 its contribution had fallen to 4.8%, by 2000 it provided just 2.8%, and it had declined further, to 2.2%, by 2020. During 2010–21 the sector grew at an average annual rate of 2.8%. However, from 1980 to 2021 the average was only 0.3%. Growth has been volatile. In 2017 the sector expanded by 27.4%, but by just 1.3% in 2018. After recovering to grow by 10.5% in 2019, the industry contracted by 19.3% in 2020 and 1.2% in 2021. In 2021 the sector accounted for less than 1% of the country's workforce.

The principal crops include coconuts, cinnamon, vanilla, sweet potatoes, cassava (manioc, tapioca), copra and bananas. The sector has limited growth potential, with sparse cultivable land—around 6,000 ha—and the soil is often of poor quality on uneven terrain. Of the major crops, banana production increased from 900 metric tons in 1961 to 1,600 tons in 1990. However, after expanding to a high of 2,230 tons in 2004, production declined to 1,780 tons in 2010. Output averaged slightly less than 2,000 tons annually during 2012–20, with production of 1,995 tons recorded in 2020. Vegetable production increased gradually from 945 tons in 1961 to 2,051 tons in 2006. Production then increased rapidly, reaching 3,070 tons in 2017, before declining slightly to 3,001 tons in 2020.

Meat and poultry followed a distinct pattern. From an output of 282 metric tons in 1984, production increased reasonably rapidly to a high of 967 tons in 1996. However, production quickly declined to only 227 tons in 2013. Output recovered to 645 tons in 2017 before dropping to 500 tons in 2020. The falling output of meat and rising incomes have resulted in an acceleration in meat imports. While the data are not complete, a simple pattern emerges. In 2008 the value of meat imported was US $59,000, rising to a high of $1,381,000 in 2016 before falling off to $965,000 in 2020.

While the Government would like to increase the country's self-sufficiency in agricultural products, many constraints limit its efforts. Farmland is limited and shrinking, supporting infrastructure is aging, labour costs are high, and global warming has a reasonable chance of changing and destructive weather patterns.

FISHERIES

Fishing GDP contracted at an average annual rate of 4.6% in 2005–10 before increasing at an average rate of 5.4% per year in 2011–17 (last date of data). Relatively slow growth in the sector has reduced its share of GDP from 1.7% in 2005 to 0.9% by 2017. The production of canned tuna commenced in 1987, and by 2021 Seychelles had exported 47,385 metric tons, making tuna canning the second largest contributor to the country's GDP.

To curtail the activities of large foreign fleets (which until then had been freely catching almost 24,000 metric tons per year of deep-sea tuna), in 1978, Seychelles declared an exclusive economic zone (EEZ), extending 370 km (200 nautical miles) from the coast. Agreements after that were concluded with several foreign governments. A three-year fisheries agreement with the European Union (EU), which came into effect in January 2011 (and was renewed in 2014 and 2020), guaranteed Seychelles US $4m. annually for the tuna catch up to 52,000 tons, and an additional $93 per ton for catches above that amount. The latest agreement allowed 48 fishing vessels (40 purse seiners and eight surface longliners). Meanwhile, in 2018 the Seychelles Government committed to investing $600m. over the next 15 years to mitigate against climate change and to help maintain the sustainability of the country's fisheries.

Owing to concerns about overfishing, in mid-2016 the Indian Ocean Tuna Commission announced a reduction in the yellow-fin tuna catch allowance by 15%, introduced in 2017. Limiting skipjack tuna caught in the Indian Ocean will continue to weigh on the growth of canned tuna exports.

Given the likely importance of ocean resources to the future of Seychelles' economy, the country has been active in international movements to declare some waters off-limits to exploitation to protect oceanic biodiversity, that is, the creation of marine protected areas (MPAs). The UN Convention on the Law of the Sea (UNCLOS) provides states with a 200-nautical-mile EEZ from their coastline. Seychelles is taking full advantage of this provision to protect marine areas by initiating a 'blue economy' strategy of economic development and conservation. It will first develop a comprehensive marine spatial plan for its territory. As the first step in 2016, the country concluded a US $21m. 'debt-for-nature' swap with its Paris Club creditors. Its crucial undertaking is developing a marine spatial plan that anticipates designating around 30% of its EEZ as an MPA by 2020.

MANUFACTURING

Manufacturing in Seychelles includes a variety of small, light industries, including brewing, plastic goods, coconut oil, furniture, detergents, cigarettes, boat building, soap, printing, and steel products, as well as animal feed, meat and fish processing, dairy products, and handicrafts for the tourism industry.

The sector's growth has, however, been decelerating. After expanding at an average annual rate of 9.8% in the 1970s, growth fell to an average of 7.6% in the 1980s and 1990s and 2.2% in 2000–21. The sector's contribution to GDP fell from 19.2% in 2000 to 6.9% in 2021. The sector's growth has varied considerably in recent years, with an expansion of 14.8% in 2016, dropping to 1.5% in 2017 before expanding by 7.2% in 2018. The sector declined by 19.7% in 2019 but recovered to grow by 16.8% in 2020. In 2021 the industry contracted by 0.6%. In recent years manufacturing's main subcomponents have experienced irregular growth. Food production, which accounted for 37.0% of manufacturing in 2004, grew at an average annual rate of 4.5% in 2005–17. However, food production contracted at an average rate of 0.5% per year in 2005–10 before increasing at an average rate of 11.1% in 2011–17 and increasing its share of manufacturing to 42.5% in 2017 (last year of data). Beverages and tobacco produced 23.7% of manufacturing value-added in 2004. After contracting at an average annual rate of 0.4% in 2005–10, the sector grew at an average rate of 7.3% per year in 2011–17 to bring its share of manufacturing up to 31.7% by 2017.

The country's competitiveness will have to improve if manufacturing is to play a more significant role in the economy. The World Economic Forum's *Global Competitiveness Report 2019* ranked Seychelles 76th out of 141 countries. Of the 12 fundamental blocks of competitiveness, Seychelles ranks highest in skills (36th) and labour market (36th). The country's major handicap is market size, which ranks last at 141st. The country also ranks relatively low in infrastructure (87th), health (79th) and its financial system (84th). The country's transport infrastructure is also an impediment where the country ranks 96th overall, with airport connectivity at 100th and liner shipping connectivity at 95th. In the labour markets, the country ranks 109th in the flexibility of wage determination and 89th in internal labour mobility and ease of finding skilled employees (78th). In the financial area, the country ranks 108th in

domestic credit to the private sector and 90th in the soundness of banks (90th). In direct business activities, the country ranks (90th) in the cost of starting a business and 120th in the time to start a business.

TELECOMMUNICATIONS

Seychelles has a well-developed telecommunications infrastructure and is thus well-positioned to attract additional investment. In 2012 a 1,900-km submarine fibre-optic cable from Victoria to Dar es Salaam, Tanzania, was completed. The project increased broadband capacity and reduced costs (lessening the dependence on expensive satellite links). In May 2018 the Seychelles Cable System Company and the Government of Seychelles agreed to invest in a second submarine fibre-optic cable, costing US $20m. The landing of the second fibre-optic cable, the Pakistan East Africa Cable Express, is expected by 2023.

Seychelles' mobile services market has two licensed operators: incumbent CWS and Airtel Seychelles. CWS is part of the CWC Group acquired by Liberty Global Inc in May 2016. India-based Bharti Airtel owns Airtel. CWS operates a 2G voice service based on GSM technology and leveraging the 900 MHz band. CWS also operates 3G (UMTS/HSPA) and 4G (LTE/LTE-A) services in the 2,100 MHz band, with work having begun on the 4G rollout in November 2014. CWS has been improving its nationwide services, having enlisted TEOCO's ASSET system in 2016–17 to bolster its services further and improve 3G and 4G connections in the country. In June 2021 CWS launched a comprehensive 5G offering with over 1.2Gbps speeds.

The nation ranked highest in sub-Saharan Africa in terms of mobile telephone users in 2021: 185.9 per 100 people (equivalent to 183,498 subscribers). Seychelles ranked second highest for landline telephone usage, with 18 subscribers per 100 inhabitants. It was also the regional leader in personal internet usage: in 2020 79% of the country's population used the internet, compared with a regional average of around 29%. Fixed internet subscriptions increased from 3,417 in 2008 to 11,827 in 2014 and reached 34,966 in 2020. In 2021 there were 89,000 3G subscribers, 79,000 4G subscribers, and a small number of 5G subscribers. There were 56.2 broadband subscriptions per 100 inhabitants.

TRADE/BALANCE OF PAYMENTS

Given the size of its economy, Seychelles is very open to trade, with import and export share of GDP averaging 109.6% during 2018–20. The country's merchandise exports in 2019 comprised agricultural products (64.4%), fuels and mining products (17.3%) and manufactures (18.2%). Its principal trading partners in 2019 were the UAE (36.7%), followed by the EU (22.5%), the UK (14.8%) and the British Virgin Islands (12.6%).

The main service exports in 2020 were other (mainly tourism) commercial services (61.3%), followed by transport (16.1%), travel (17.7%) and transport (16.1%). The EU was the most significant service export destination (51.5%), followed by the USA (11.3%), the UK (8.5%), Switzerland (6.7%) and the Russian Federation (3.2%).

Between 1980 and 2007 the value of the imports of goods and services grew at an average annual rate of 7.0%, falling to 1.8% in 2008–21. Exports of goods and services grew at an average of 13.2% per year during 1980–2007, but the growth rate declined to 0.3% in 2008–2021. Consequently, the country's current account deficit proliferated, increasing from an average deficit of 10.4% of GDP in 1980–2007 to 18.9% in 2008–21, with the IMF projecting a deficit of 30.0% in 2021 and 23.5% in 2022. FDI has played a considerable role in financing the deficits, averaging 7.4% of GDP during 1980–2007, increasing to 15.4% in 2008–21. FDI flows remained strong during the COVID-19 pandemic, falling from 17.7% of GDP in 2019 to 10.1% in 2020, but recovering to 13.1% in 2021.

The country's massive current account deficits stem from a fundamental macroeconomic imbalance that has not corrected itself with time and reforms. Specifically, the country has a scant savings rate. Savings averaged only 15.6% of GDP per year in 1980–2007, falling to 12.4% in 2008–20. During these periods, investment averaged 26.9% of GDP in the first, rising to 31.3% in 2008–21. Capital inflows filled the gap between savings and investment, with capital inflows equal to the current account deficit. With a slowing world economy that may dampen tourism, the country will have to find ways of increasing FDI or raising savings if it is to maintain its investment rates. In 1993 Seychelles joined the Preferential Trade Area for Eastern and Southern Africa (which in 1994 became the Common Market for Eastern and Southern Africa—COMESA) and benefits from the clearinghouse function, which facilitates using member countries' currencies for regional transactions. This arrangement has reduced the pressure on foreign exchange resources, particularly from trade with Mauritius.

In late 2007 Seychelles signed an interim trade agreement with the EU (along with several other COMESA members), which guaranteed special trading privileges for Seychelles' exports into the EU, especially fisheries products. However, this also exposed Seychelles to greater competition from the EU, obliging the country to liberalize 62% of its imports. In 1995 Seychelles applied for full membership of the World Trade Organization (at which it previously had observer status), and it finally became a member in April 2015. Seychelles signed the African Continental Free Trade Area Agreement in 2018, a trade agreement between 49 African Union member states to create a single market followed by free movement and a currency union.

MONETARY POLICY

The Central Bank of Seychelles (CBS) conducts the country's monetary policy. As with most central banks, CBS has inflation control as one of its principal objectives.

Inflation in Seychelles has traditionally been relatively high for a small open economy, averaging 4% in the 1980s before dropping to 1.9% in the 1990s. However, in the 2000s inflation picked up to an average of 9.3% before falling off to 2.9% in 2010–21. In the late 2010s inflation remained low, with a rate of −1.0% recorded in 2016; the rate increased to 2.9% in 2017 and 3.7% in 2018

Due to increased inflationary pressures, CBS tightened its monetary policy at the end of 2018. However, CBS shifted to a proactive stance once the country recorded its first COVID-19 cases. On 30 June 2021 CBS lowered its primary policy rate by 100 basis points to 2%. The cut was the first since a reduction of 100 basis points in June 2020. The action intended to stimulate economic activity during a resurgence in COVID-19 cases in Seychelles. (GDP contracted by 24.6% year-on-year in the first quarter of 2021, mainly stemming from the reduction in tourism.) The rate cut came amid a spike in inflation; the consumer price index averaged 9.6% year on year in January–May 2021, compared with an average of 0.5% in the same period of 2020.

On 28 September 2021 CBS kept its benchmark interest rate on hold at 2%. The decision to keep the rate unchanged was aimed at supporting the country's economy, which contracted by 24.6% year on year in the first quarter of 2021. However, the

cost was inflation, which averaged 9.8% in 2021 (compared with just 1.3% in 2020).

FISCAL POLICY

The Government's finances have improved considerably since the initial round of liberalization in 2007. Although government revenues fell to an average of 36.2% of GDP per year during 2008–21 (from 47.9% in 1980–2007), expenditures also declined to an average of 36.4% of GDP. (This latter figure averaged 51.3% per year in 1980–2007.) These reduced revenues and expenditures resulted in the country maintaining an average budget surplus of 0.8% of GDP during 2008–20. During 1980–2007 the Government ran an average annual deficit of 3.3% of GDP.

In part, the revenue shift stemmed from tax reforms introduced in 2009. The Government intended to make taxation fairer and more transparent, broaden the tax base, and bring the tax system in line with international standards. It capped the top business tax rate at 33% (down from a high of 40%). In July 2010 it introduced a new personal income tax at a rate of 18.75%. Also initiated was an excise tax for four consumer categories—vehicles, fuel, cigarettes and alcohol. The Government also introduced a value-added tax of 15% in 2013, replacing the general sales tax. In the same year Seychelles also introduced a corporate social responsibility tax of 0.5% on business turnover above SR 1m. In 2015 the EU blacklisted Seychelles as a tax haven. However, the EU later shifted the country to the 'grey list' after it made some tax reform commitments.

Despite these reforms, the Government's response to the COVID-19 pandemic resulted in a budget deficit of 17.4% in 2020 and 5.8% in 2021. The surge in borrowing increased general government gross debt in 2020 to an unsustainable 89.1%, up from 54.2% in 2019. However, the Government's debt as a share of GDP fell to 72.5% in 2021, with the IMF anticipating a gradual decline to 57.5% by 2027.

ECONOMIC PROSPECTS

On 29 July 2021 the IMF approved a 32-month arrangement of US $105.63m. for Seychelles under its Extended Fund Facility (EFF). The programme's key objective was to support the authorities' efforts to restore macroeconomic stability and debt sustainability, while strengthening the country's post-COVID-19 recovery.

In the second review of its EFF on 29 June 2022, the IMF noted that the economy was outperforming expectations, with the Government's fiscal improvement at the point where it had the fiscal space to address current challenges. However, the Fund warned that: 'The economic outlook, while positive, remains subject to external risks, including from spillovers of the war in Ukraine, a further surge of commodity prices and fewer tourist arrivals.'

Statistical Survey

Sources (unless otherwise stated): Statistics and Database Administration Section, Management and Information Systems Division, POB 206, Victoria; tel. 4679400; e-mail stats@nbs.gov.sc; internet www.nbs.gov.sc; Central Bank of Seychelles, POB 701, Victoria; tel. 4282000; e-mail enquiries@cbs.sc; internet www.cbs.sc.

AREA AND POPULATION

Area: 455.3 sq km (175.8 sq miles), incl. Aldabra lagoon (145 sq km).

Population: 81,755 at census of 26 August 2002; 90,945 (males 46,912, females 44,033) at census of 26 August 2010. *Mid-2021* (official estimate): 99,202.

Density (at mid-2021): 217.9 per sq km.

Population by Age and Sex (official estimates at mid-2021): *0–14 years:* 21,430 (males 10,963, females 10,467); *15–64 years:* 65,855 (males 33,991, females 31,864); *65 years and over:* 11,917 (males 5,434, females 6,483); *Total* 99,202 (males 50,388, females 48,814).

Principal Town (incl. suburbs, UN estimate, mid-2018): Victoria (capital) 28,091. Source: UN, *World Urbanization Prospects: The 2018 Revision.*

Births, Marriages and Deaths (registrations, 2021): Live births 1,665 (birth rate 16.8 per 1,000); Marriages (of residents) 162 (marriage rate 1.6 per 1,000); Deaths 925 (death rate 9.3 per 1,000).

Life Expectancy (years at birth, official estimates): 73.5 (males 71.3; females 75.6) in 2021.

Employment (2021, averages): Agriculture, forestry and fishing 561; Manufacturing 3,859; Electricity and water 1,321; Construction 5,064; Wholesale and retail trade; repair of motor vehicles 4,361; Restaurants and hotels 7,895; Transport, storage and communications 4,926; Finance and real estate 8,654; Education 3,005; Health and social work 2,197; Public administration and defence; compulsory social security 6,078; Other services 1,566; Private households with employed persons 96; Activities of extraterritorial organizations and bodies 41; *Total* 49,623.

HEALTH AND WELFARE

Total Fertility Rate (children per woman, 2020): 2.3.

Under-5 Mortality Rate (per 1,000 live births, 2020): 13.9.

COVID-19: Cumulative Confirmed Deaths (per 100,000 persons at 31 August 2022): 158.7.

COVID-19: Fully Vaccinated Population (% of total population at 28 August 2022): 76.3.

Physicians (per 1,000 head, 2019): 2.1.

Hospital Beds (per 1,000 head, 2019): 3.5.

Domestic Health Expenditure (2019): US $ per head (PPP): 1,068.3.

Domestic Health Expenditure (2019): % of GDP: 3.8.

Domestic Health Expenditure (2019): public (% of total current expenditure): 72.7.

Access to Improved Water Resources (% of persons, 2019): 97.

Total Carbon Dioxide Emissions ('000 metric tons, 2018): 620.

Carbon Dioxide Emissions Per Head (metric tons, 2018): 6.4.

Human Development Index (2021): ranking: 72.

Human Development Index (2021): value: 0.785.

Note: For data on COVID-19 vaccinations, 'fully vaccinated' denotes receipt of all doses specified by approved vaccination regime (Sources: Johns Hopkins University and Our World in Data). Data on health expenditure refer to current general government expenditure in each case. For more information on sources and further definitions for all indicators, see Health and Welfare Statistics: Sources and Definitions section (europaworld.com/credits).

AGRICULTURE, ETC.

Principal Crops (metric tons, 2020, FAO estimates): Bananas 1,995; Cassava (Manioc) 230; Cinnamon 28; Coconuts 3,744; Tea 9; Tomatoes 433. *Aggregate Production* (metric tons, may include official, semi-official or estimated data): Total fruit (primary) 2,964; Total vegetables (primary) 3,001.

Livestock (head, 2020, FAO estimates): Cattle 282; Goats 5,771; Pigs 5,126.

Livestock Products (metric tons, 2020, FAO estimates): Chicken meat 494; Pig meat 447; Hen eggs 1,177.

Fishing (all capture, '000 metric tons, live weight, 2020): Skipjack tuna 75.5; Yellowfin tuna 38.3; Bigeye tuna 12.1; Total (incl. others) 132.4 (FAO estimate).

Source: FAO.

INDUSTRY

Selected Products (2021): Canned tuna 49,937 metric tons; Beer and stout ('000 litres) 5,446; Soft drinks ('000 litres) 7,036; Mineral water ('000 litres) 16,778; Cigarettes 57m.; Paint ('000 litres) 479.0; Construction blocks ('000) 3,299.1; Electrical energy 440m. kWh.

FINANCE

Currency and Exchange Rates: 100 cents = 1 Seychelles rupee (SR). *Sterling, Dollar and Euro Equivalents* (31 May 2022): £1 sterling = 17.810 rupees; US $1 = 14.147 rupees; €1 = 15.156 rupees; 1,000 Seychelles rupees = £56.15 = $70.69 = €65.98. *Average Exchange Rate* (Seychelles rupees per US $): 14.0333 in 2019; 17.6165 in 2020; 16.9205 in 2021. Note: In November 1979 the value of the Seychelles rupee was linked to the IMF's special drawing right (SDR). In March 1981 the mid-point exchange rate was set at SDR 1 = 7.2345 rupees. This remained in effect until February 1997, when the fixed link with the SDR was ended.

Budget (SR million, 2021): *Revenue:* Tax revenue 6,692.0 (Taxes on income, etc. 996.4; Domestic taxes on goods and services 2,316.9; Business tax 1,433.4; Excise tax 1,225.7); Non tax revenue 837.0; Total 7,529.0 (excl. grants received 563.3). *Expenditure:* Current expenditure 8,883.1 (Primary expenditure 8,217.6, Interest 665.5); Capital expenditure 129.2; Contingency 52.8; Total 9,065.0 (excl. lending minus repayments 222.1). Note: Figures represent the consolidated accounts of the central Government, covering the operations of the Recurrent and Capital Budgets and of the Social Security Fund (Source: Ministry of Finance, Trade and Economic Planning, Victoria).

International Reserves (US $ million at 31 December 2021): IMF special drawing rights 34.07; Reserve position in IMF 4.94; Foreign exchange 663.55; *Total* 702.56. Source: IMF, *International Financial Statistics*.

Money Supply (SR million at 31 December 2021): Currency outside depository corporations 1,499.6; Transferable deposits 18,393.5; Other deposits 6,735.7; *Broad money* 26,628.8. Source: IMF, *International Financial Statistics*.

Cost of Living (Consumer Price Index; base: 2014 = 100): All items 111.8 in 2019; 113.2 in 2020; 124.2 in 2021.

Gross Domestic Product (SR million at constant 2014 prices, provisional): 21,886.4 in 2019; 20,196.0 in 2020; 21,794.3 in 2021.

Expenditure on the Gross Domestic Product (SR million at current prices, 2020, provisional): Government final consumption expenditure 6,415.9; Private final consumption expenditure 14,344.1; Gross capital formation 5,357.2; *Total domestic expenditure* 26,117.2; Exports of goods and services 16,207.9; *Less* Imports of goods and services 21,174.1; *GDP in purchasers' values* 21,151.0.

Gross Domestic Product by Economic Activity (SR million at current prices, 2021, provisional): Agriculture, forestry and fishing 583.6; Manufacturing 1,436.6; Electricity and water 661.6; Construction 1,431.0; Wholesale and retail trade, and repair of motor vehicles and motorcycles 1,454.4; Restaurants and hotels 2,540.8; Transport, storage and communications 2,037.4; Finance, insurance, real estate and business services 5,986.0; Education 615.4; Public administration and defence, and social security 2,676.6; Other services 1,392.2; *Sub-total* 20,815.7; Taxes, less subsidies, on products 4,065.3; *GDP in purchasers' values* 24,881.0. Note: Financial services indirectly measured assumed to be distributed at origin.

Balance of Payments (US $ million, 2020): Exports of goods 419.79; Imports of goods −851.67; *Balance on goods* −431.88; Exports of services 682.89; Imports of services −482.84; *Balance on goods and services* −231.83; Primary income received 12.50; Primary income paid −79.19; *Balance on goods, services and primary income* −298.52; Secondary income received 27.34; Secondary income paid −40.60; *Current balance* −311.78; Capital account (net) 20.85; Direct investment assets 7.24; Direct investment liabilities 175.11; Portfolio investment assets −51.25; Portfolio investment liabilities −54.08; Other investment assets 131.00; Other investment liabilities 62.35; Net errors and omissions −30.97; *Reserves and related items* −51.52. Source: IMF, *International Financial Statistics*.

EXTERNAL TRADE

Principal Commodities (SR million, 2021, provisional): *Imports c.i.f.:* Food and live animals 4,810.2; Mineral fuels 3,777.1; Basic manufactures 4,205.3; Machinery and transport 4,195.0; Total (incl. others) 18,960.2. *Exports f.o.b.:* Canned tuna 4,676.2; Fish (fresh/frozen) 298.3; Fish meal 150.9; Fish oil and fats 69.0; Sea cucumber 91.6; Total (incl. others) 5,414.4 (excl. re-exports SR 2,368.7m.).

Principal Trading Partners (SR million, 2021, provisional): *Imports c.i.f.:* Belgium 155.6; China, People's Republic 594.8; France 2,065.6; Germany 213.3; India 832.6; Italy 1,566.1; Mauritius 554.1; Netherlands 277.3; Singapore 502.4; South Africa 1,532.1; Spain 1,532.5; Thailand 174.7; United Arab Emirates 5,774.6; United Kingdom 532.4; USA 196.3; Total (incl. others) 18,960.2. *Exports f.o.b.:* Australia 14.6; Denmark 99.0; France 2,173.7; Germany 318.0; Hong Kong 108.2; Italy 751.0; Netherlands 122.2; Taiwan 86.6; United Kingdom 1,129.1; USA 51.1; Total (incl. others) 5,414.4 (excl. re-exports SR 2,368.7m.).

TRANSPORT

Road Traffic (registered motor vehicles, 2020): Private 18,169; Commercial 4,590; Taxis 515; Self-drive 2,976; Motorcycles 1,411; Omnibuses 659; *Total* 28,320.

Shipping: *Flag Registered Fleet* (at 31 December 2021): Vessels 71; Total displacement 185,572 grt (Source: Lloyd's List Intelligence—www.bit.ly/LLintelligence); *International Seaborne Freight Traffic* (2020): Freight ('000 metric tons): Imports 24,019; Exports 20,208; Transshipment (of fish) 72.

Civil Aviation (traffic on scheduled services, 2015): Kilometres flown 10m.; Passengers carried 497,000; Passenger-km 1,157m.; Total ton-km 19m. (Source: UN, *Statistical Yearbook*). *2020:* Aircraft movements 3,374; Passengers embarked 136,000; Passengers disembarked 146,000; Freight embarked 5,244 metric tons; Freight disembarked 1,207 metric tons.

TOURISM

Foreign Tourist Arrivals: 384,204 in 2019; 114,858 in 2020; 182,849 in 2021.

Arrivals by Country of Residence (2021): Austria 4,068; France 18,425; Germany 17,673; Israel 10,551; Poland 5,100; Russian Federation 31,392; Saudi Arabia 4,327; Switzerland 8,486; Ukraine 5,526; United Arab Emirates 21,699; USA 5,551; Total (incl. others) 182,849.

Tourism Receipts (SR million, central bank estimates): 8,249 in 2019; 3,485 in 2020; 4,694 in 2021.

COMMUNICATIONS MEDIA

Telephones (2020): 18,882 main lines in use.

Mobile Telephones (2020): 183,498 subscribers.

Broadband Subscriptions, Fixed (2020): 34,966.

Broadband Subscriptions, Mobile (2020): 84,034.

Daily Newspapers (2020): 2.

Non-daily Newspapers (2020): 6.

Internet Users (% of population, 2020): 79.0. Source: International Telecommunication Union.

EDUCATION

Pre-primary (2020): 34 schools; 169 teachers; 3,108 pupils.

Primary (2020): 29 schools; 603 teachers (males 95, females 528); 9,509 pupils (males 4,784, females 4,725).

Secondary (2020): 15 schools; 653 teachers (males 286, females 287); 7,174 pupils (males 3,571, females 3,603).

Post-secondary (2020): 16 schools; 334 teachers; 3,136 pupils.

Special Education (2020): 1 institution; 24 teachers; 84 pupils.

Pupil-teacher Ratio (primary education): 15 in 2019.

Adult Literacy Rate (UNESCO estimate): 95.9% (males 95.4%; females 96.4%) in 2018 (Source: UNESCO Institute for Statistics).

Directory

The Constitution

The independence Constitution of 1976 was suspended after the coup in June 1977 but reintroduced in July with substantial modifications. A successor Constitution, which entered into force in March 1979, was superseded by a new Constitution, approved by national referendum on 18 June 1993. This document has since been amended on seven occasions, most recently in April 2017.

The President is elected by popular vote. The President fulfils the functions of head of state and Commander-in-Chief of the armed forces and may hold office for a maximum period of two consecutive five-year terms. The National Assembly is elected for a term of five years; 26 members are directly elected and a maximum of 10 seats are proportionally allocated. There is provision for an appointed Vice-President. The Council of Ministers is appointed by the President and acts in an advisory capacity to him. The President also appoints the holders of certain public offices and the judiciary.

The Government

HEAD OF STATE

President: Rev. WAVEL RAMKALAWAN (inaugurated 26 October 2020).

Vice-President: AHMED ABDULLAH AFIF.

COUNCIL OF MINISTERS
(October 2022)

President, Minister of Defence, of Legal Affairs and of Public Administration: Rev. WAVEL RAMKALAWAN.

Vice-President, Minister of Information Communications Technology and of Information: AHMED ABDULLAH AFIF.

Minister of Fisheries and the Blue Economy: JEAN-FRANCOIS FERRARI (Designated Minister).

Minister of Finance, Economic Planning and Trade: NAADIR HASSAN.

Minister of Foreign Affairs and Tourism: SYLVESTRE RADEGONDE.

Minister of Internal Affairs: ERROL FONSEKA.

Minister of Transport: ANTHONY DERJAQUES.

Minister of Health: PEGGY VIDOT.

Minister of Lands and Housing: BILLY RANGASAMY.

Minister of Family, Youth and Sports: MARIE-CÉINE ZIALOR.

Minister of Investment, Entrepreneurship and Industry: DEVIKA VIDOT.

Minister of Local Government and Community Affairs: ROSE MARIE HOAREAU.

Minister of Agriculture, Climate Change and the Environment: FLAVIEN JOUBERT.

Minister of Education: Dr JUSTIN VALENTIN.

Minister of Employment and Social Affairs: PATRICIA FRANCOURT.

MINISTRIES

Office of the President: State House, POB 55, Victoria; tel. 4295656; e-mail cps@statehouse.gov.sc; internet www.statehouse.gov.sc.

Office of the Vice-President: State House, POB 1303, Victoria; tel. 4295651; e-mail s.commettant@gov.sc; internet www.statehouse.gov.sc.

Ministry of Agriculture, Climate Change and Environment: Botanical Garden, POB 445, Mont Fleuri; tel. 4670500; e-mail info@env.gov.sc; internet www.meecc.gov.sc.

Ministry of Education: POB 48, Mont Fleuri; tel. 4283283; e-mail info@eduhq.edu.sc; internet edu.gov.sc.

Ministry of Employment and Social Affairs: Independence House Annex, 4th and 5th Floors, Victoria; tel. 4297200; e-mail contact@employment.gov.sc; internet www.employment.gov.sc.

Ministry of Family, Youth and Sports: Family House, French Chang-Him Rd, Victoria; tel. 4397979; e-mail info@gov.sc; internet fb.com/MinistryofYouthSportsandFamily.

Ministry of Finance, Economic Planning and Trade: Liberty House, Independence Ave, POB 313, Victoria; tel. 4382000; e-mail minister@finance.gov.sc; internet www.finance.gov.sc.

Ministry of Fisheries and the Blue Economy: Maison Collet, POB 408, Victoria; tel. 4672300; e-mail info@mofbe.gov.sc; internet www.mofbe.gov.sc.

Ministry of Foreign Affairs and Tourism: Maison Quéau de Quinssy, POB 656, Mont Fleuri; tel. 4283500; e-mail ps@mfa.gov.sc; internet www.mfa.gov.sc.

Ministry of Health: POB 52, Victoria; tel. 4388000; e-mail customerservice@health.gov.sc; internet www.health.gov.sc.

Ministry of Internal Affairs: Independence House, 3rd Floor, Victoria; tel. 4323205; e-mail mia@gov.sc.

Ministry of Investment, Entrepreneurship and Industry: Independence House Annex, 5th Floor, POB 1097, Victoria; tel. 4297216; e-mail industry.entrepreneurship@gov.sc; internet www.industry.gov.sc.

Ministry of Lands and Housing: Independence House, POB 1097, Victoria; tel. 4674444; internet www.luh.gov.sc.

Ministry of Local Government and Community Affairs: Ocean Gate House Annex, POB 731, Victoria; tel. 4297400; e-mail mlgca@gov.sc; internet www.localgovernment.gov.sc.

Ministry of Transport: Botanical House, 3rd Floor, POB 92, Mont Fleuri; tel. 4286500; internet transport.gov.sc.

President

Presidential Election, 22–24 October 2020

Candidate	Valid votes	% of valid votes
Rev. Wavel Ramkalawan (Linyon Demokratik Seselwa)	35,562	54.91
Danny Faure (United Seychelles) . .	28,178	43.51
Alain St Ange (One Seychelles) . .	1,021	1.58
Total	**64,761**	**100.00**

Legislature

National Assembly: Ile du Port, POB 734, Victoria; tel. 4285600; e-mail info@nationalassembly.sc; internet nationalassembly.sc.

Speaker: ROGER MANCIENNE.
Election, 22–24 October 2020

Party	Valid votes cast	% of valid votes	Seats*
Linyon Demokratik Seselwa (LDS)	35,202	54.83	25
United Seychelles	27,185	42.35	10
One Seychelles	1,420	2.21	—
Independents	317	0.49	—
Lalyans Seselwa	70	0.12	—
Total	64,194†	100.00	35

* Of the Assembly's 35 seats, 25 (including five nominated) were filled by the LDS and 10 (including four nominated) by United Seychelles.
† Excludes 1,784 invalid votes.

Election Commission

Electoral Commission: Suite 203, Aarti Bldg, Mont Fleuri, POB 741, Victoria; tel. 4295555; e-mail info@ecs.sc; internet www.ecs.sc; f. 1993; Chair. DANNY LUCAS.

Political Organizations

Independent Conservative Union of Seychelles (ICUS): La Retraite, Mahé; tel. 468322251; internet fb.com/groups/ICOSofseychelles; f. 2015; Pres. MIKE CHADSTONE; Sec.-Gen. ALIX LETOURDIE.

Linyon Demokratik Seselwa (LDS) (Seychellois Democratic Alliance): Lakaz Seselwa, Mont Fleuri; tel. 4321122; e-mail info@lds.sc; internet www.lds.sc; f. 2016 as a coalition of Lalyans Seselwa, the Seychelles National Party, the Seychelles Party for Social Justice and Democracy and the Seselwa United Party; Chair. ROGER MANCIENNE; Sec.-Gen. GERVAIS HENRIE.

Linyon Sanzman (Union for Change): Victoria; f. 2016; Leader MARTIN AGLAE.

One Seychelles: Victoria; internet fb.com/enselsesel; f. 2019; Interim Pres. and Sec.-Gen YVON ESTHER.

Seychelles National Party (SNP): Arpent Vert, Mont Fleuri, POB 81, Victoria; tel. 4224124; e-mail wavel24@hotmail.com; f. 1995 as the United Opposition, comprising the fmr mem. parties of a coalition formed to contest the 1993 elections; present name adopted in 1998; Leader Rev. WAVEL RAMKALAWAN.

Seychelles Party for Social Justice and Democracy (SPSJD): Suite 407, Premier Bldg, Victoria; tel. 4610414; f. 2015; Pres. ALEXIA G. AMESBURY; Sec. (vacant).

United Seychelles: POB 1242, Victoria; tel. 4284900; e-mail admin@partilepep.com; internet weareunitedseychelles.com; fmrly the Seychelles People's United Party (f. 1964), which assumed power in 1977; renamed Seychelles People's Progressive Front in 1978; sole legal party 1978–91; renamed Parti Lepep in 2009; present name adopted in 2018; Pres. PATRICK HERMINIE.

Diplomatic Representation

EMBASSIES AND HIGH COMMISSIONS IN SEYCHELLES

China, People's Republic: POB 680, St Louis; tel. 4671700; e-mail china@seychelles.net; internet sc.china-embassy.gov.cn; Ambassador GUO WEI.

Cuba: Bel Eau, POB 730, Victoria; tel. 4224094; e-mail cubasey@seychelles.net; internet misiones.minrex.gob.cu/es/seychelles; Ambassador MARTHA HERNÁNDEZ CANEIRO.

France: La Ciotat Bldg, Mont Fleuri, POB 478, Victoria; tel. 4225513; e-mail cad.victoria-amba@diplomatie.gouv.fr; internet sc.ambafrance.org; Ambassador (vacant).

India: Maison Esplanade, 3rd Floor, rue Pierre de Possession, POB 488, Victoria; tel. 4610301; e-mail hoc.mahe@mea.gov.in; internet www.hciseychelles.gov.in; High Commissioner KARTIK PANDE (designate).

Japan: Maison Esplanade, 5th Floor, rue Pierre de Possession, Victoria; tel. 4399900; internet www.sc.emb-japan.go.jp; Ambassador KEN OKANIWA (resident in Nairobi, Kenya); Chargé d'affaires KATO EIJI.

Russian Federation: Le Niol, POB 632, St Louis; tel. 4266590; e-mail rusemb.seychelles@mid.ru; internet seychelles.mid.ru; Ambassador ARTEM ALEXANDROVICH KOHZIN.

Sri Lanka: Suite 3-01, Capital City Bldg, Independence Ave, Victoria; tel. 4610590; e-mail srilanka@intelvision.net; High Commissioner SRIMAL WICKREMASINGHE.

United Kingdom: Oliaji Trade Centre, 3rd Floor, rue Pierre de Possession, Victoria; tel. 4283666; e-mail bhcvictoria@fco.gov.uk; internet www.gov.uk/world/seychelles; High Commissioner PATRICK LYNCH.

Judicial System

The legal system is derived from English Common Law and the French Code Napoléon. There are three main courts: the Court of Appeal, the Supreme Court and the Magistrates' Courts. The Court of Appeal has an appellate jurisdiction; it hears appeals from the Supreme Court in both civil and criminal cases. The Supreme Court hears appeals from lower and other subordinate courts while having its own jurisdiction. It attends to more complex matters that pertain to civil or criminal aspects as opposed to the Magistrates' Courts. The Constitutional Court, a division of the Supreme Court, determines matters of a constitutional nature, and considers cases bearing on civil liberties. It comes into force when two or more members of the Supreme Court hear an appeal. The Supreme Court can also refer a case to the Constitutional Court in case of any judgment related to the constitution arises. There is also a Family Tribunal, an Employment Tribunal, a Juvenile Court and a Rent Board.

Court of Appeal: Palais de Justice, 1st Floor, Ile Du Port, Victoria; tel. 4224078; internet www.judiciary.sc; Pres. ANTHONY FERNANDO.

Supreme Court: Palais de Justice, Ile Du Port, POB 157, Victoria; tel. 4285800; e-mail judiciary@seychelles.sc; internet www.judiciary.sc; Chief Justice RONNY GOVIDEN.

Attorney-General: FRANK ALLY; POB 118, Victoria; tel. 4383000; e-mail agoffice@seychelles.sc; internet www.attorneygeneraloffice.gov.sc.

Religion

The majority of the inhabitants are Christians. Hinduism, Islam, and the Bahá'í Faith are also practised.

CHRISTIANITY

The Anglican Communion

The Church of the Province of the Indian Ocean comprises eight dioceses: six in Madagascar, one in Mauritius and one in Seychelles. The Archbishop of the Province is the Bishop of Seychelles.

Bishop of Seychelles (and Archbishop of the Province of the Indian Ocean): Most Rev. JAMES RICHARD WONG YIN SONG, Bishop's House, Bel Eau, Victoria; tel. 2813377; e-mail angdio@seychelles.net.

The Roman Catholic Church

Seychelles comprises a single diocese, directly responsible to the Holy See.

Bishop of Port Victoria: ALAIN HAREL, Bishop's House, Olivier Maradan St, POB 43, Victoria; tel. 4322152; e-mail rcchurch@seychelles.net.

Other Christian Churches

Pentecostal Assemblies of Seychelles: POB 535, Riverside, Bel-Eau, Mahé; tel. 4226224; e-mail paos@seychelles.net; internet fb.com/PentecostalAssemblyOfSeychelles; Pastor HERMITTE FREMINOT; 1,333 mems.

The Press

L'Echo des Iles: POB 12, Victoria; tel. 4322262; e-mail echo@seychelles.net; bi-monthly; French, Creole and English; Roman Catholic; Editor Fr EDWIN MATHIOT.

The People: POB 1242, Victoria; tel. 4225859; e-mail editor@unitedseychelles.net; internet www.thepeopleonline.net; f. 1964; publ. by United Seychelles (fmrly Parti Lepep); weekly; Creole, French and English; Editor SHEILA LAFORTUNE.

Seychelles Nation: Laurier Rd, POB 800, Victoria; tel. 4385775; e-mail website@nisa.sc; internet nation.sc; f. 1976; fmrly Seychelles Bulletin; present name adopted 1984; govt-owned; daily; English, French and Creole; produced by National Information Services Agency Press; Chair. LUCY ATHANASIUS; Chief Editor MARIE-ANNE LEPATHY.

Seychelles Weekly: Progress House, Mont Fleuri; tel. 4611752; e-mail seychellesweekly@seyweekly.com; internet www.seyweekly.com; supports democracy in Seychelles; Editor ROBERT ERNESTA.

Le Seychellois Hebdo: Arpent Vert, Mont Fleuri; tel. 4325844; e-mail leseychellois@seychelles.net; internet fb.com/LeSeychellois; f. 2011; weekly; Editor (vacant).

Today in Seychelles: Today Publishers (Seychelles) Ltd, Le Chantier, POB 999, Victoria; tel. 4290999; e-mail info@today.sc; internet todayinseychelles.com; f. 2011; Mon.–Sat.; Chief Editor JENIFER BIPAT.

NEWS AGENCIES

Seychelles News Agency: Rm 106, Blk A, Unity House, Palm St, Victoria; tel. 2813627; internet www.seychellesnewsagency.com; f. 2014; Chief Editor RASSIN VANNIER.

Broadcasting and Communications

TELECOMMUNICATIONS

Airtel Seychelles Ltd: Emerald House, POB 1358, Providence; tel. 4600600; e-mail customerqueries@sc.airtel.com; internet www.airtel.sc; f. 1998 as Telecom Seychelles; present name adopted in 2010; 100% owned by Bharti Airtel (India); provides fixed-line, mobile and satellite telephone and internet services; Man. Dir AMADOU MAHAMAT DINA.

Cable and Wireless (Seychelles) Ltd: Mercury House, rue Pierre de Possession, POB 4, Victoria; tel. 4284000; e-mail cws@seychelles.net; internet www.cwseychelles.com; f. 1893; owned by CWS Investment Ltd; Interim Chief Exec. GEORGES D'OFFAY.

BROADCASTING

Seychelles Broadcasting Corpn (SBC): Hermitage, POB 321, Victoria; tel. 4289600; e-mail corporatecommunication@sbc.sc; internet www.sbc.sc; f. 1983 as Radio Television Seychelles; present name adopted in 1992; programmes in Creole, English and French; Chair. GERARD LAFORTUNE; CEO BÉRARD DUPRÈS.

Finance

BANKING

Central Bank

Central Bank of Seychelles (CBS): Independence Ave, POB 701, Victoria; tel. 4282000; e-mail enquiries@cbs.sc; internet www.cbs.sc; f. 1983; bank of issue; Gov. and Chair. CAROLINE ABEL.

National Banks

Development Bank of Seychelles: Independence Ave, POB 217, Victoria; tel. 4294400; e-mail devbank@dbs.sc; internet www.dbs.sc; f. 1977; 55.5% state-owned; Chair. NORMAN WEBER; CEO JEAN PREIRA.

Seychelles Commercial Bank Ltd (SCB): Orion Mall, POB 531, Victoria; tel. 4294000; e-mail ssb@savingsbank.sc; internet www.scb.sc; f. 1902; state-owned; fmrly Seychelles Savings Bank Ltd; present name adopted in 2013; term deposits, savings and current accounts; Chair. PATRICK PAYET; Man. Dir and CEO ANNIE VIDOT.

Seychelles International Mercantile Banking Corpn Ltd (SIMBC) (Nouvobanq): rue Pierre de Possession, POB 241, Victoria; tel. 4293000; e-mail nvb@nouvobanq.sc; internet www.nouvobanq.sc; f. 1991; 78% state-owned, 22% by Standard Chartered Bank (UK); Chair. JENNIFER MOREL; Man. Dir CHRISTOPHE EDMOND.

Foreign Banks

Absa Bank Seychelles Ltd (UK): Independence Ave, POB 167, Victoria; tel. 4383939; e-mail customerservices.sc@absa.africa; internet www.absa.sc; f. 1959fmrly Barclays Bank (Seychelles) Ltdpresent name adopted 2020; Chair. MARC HOUAREAU; Man. Dir JOHAN VAN SCHALKWYK.

Bank of Baroda (India): Trinity House, Albert St, POB 124, Victoria; tel. 4618000; e-mail customer@bankofbaroda.com; internet bankofbaroda.sc; f. 1978; CEO ASHOK KUMAR.

Mauritius Commercial Bank (Seychelles) Ltd (MCB Seychelles): POB 122, Manglier St, Victoria; tel. 4284555; e-mail contact@mcbseychelles.com; internet www.mcbseychelles.com; f. 1978 as Banque Française Commerciale (BFCOI); present name adopted in 2003; Man. Dir BERNARD JACKSON.

INSURANCE

H. Savy Insurance Co Ltd (HSI): Maison de la Rosière, Palm St, POB 887, Victoria; tel. 4280400; e-mail insurance@hsi.sc; internet www.hsi.sc; f. 1995; 50% owned by Corvina Investment Co Ltd; 50% owned by Mauritian Eagle Insurance Co Ltd, Harry Savy & Co (Seychelles) Ltd and Mahe Shipping Co Ltd; all classes; Chair. JEAN WEELING-LEE.

MUA (Seychelles) Co Ltd: Oliaji Trade Centre, 1st Floor, rue Pierre de Possession, Victoria; tel. 4322922; e-mail claims@muaseychelles.sc; internet www.muaseychelles.sc; f. 2011; CEO BERTRAND CASTERES.

Sacos Insurance Group (SACL): Maison Esplanade, rue Pierre de Possession, Victoria; tel. 4295000; e-mail info@sacos.sc; internet www.sacos.sc; f. 1980; fmrly State Assurance Corpn of Seychelles; all classes of insurance; Chair. LEKHA NAIR; CEO JENNIFER MOREL.

Trade and Industry

GOVERNMENT AGENCIES

Financial Services Authority (FSA): Industrial Trade Zone, Bois de Rose Ave, Roche Caiman, POB 991, Victoria; tel. 4380800; e-mail enquiries@fsaseychelles.sc; internet www.fsaseychelles.sc; f. 1995 to supervise registration of companies, transshipment and offshore financial services in an international free-trade zone covering an area of 23 ha near Mahé International Airport; fmrly Seychelles International Business Authority, present name adopted in 2014; Chair. PATRICK PAYET; CEO DAMIEN THESEE.

National Economic Council: Victoria; f. 2012; advisory body comprising the President as Chairman, the Vice-President as Vice-Chairman and also ministers, the Governor of the Central Bank and the CEOs of several banks and govt organizations.

Seychelles Agricultural Agency: Creole Spirit Bldg, 1st Floor, Quincy St, POB 166 Victoria; tel. 4676450; e-mail ceosecsaa@gov.sc; internet www.saa.gov.sc; f. 2009; CEO LINETTA ESTICO.

Seychelles Fishing Authority (SFA): Fishing Port, POB 449, Victoria; tel. 4670300; e-mail management@sfa.sc; internet www.sfa.sc; f. 1984; assessment and management of fisheries resources; Chair. RADLEY WEBER; CEO NICHOL JOHN ELIZABETH.

Seychelles Infrastructure Agency: Victoria; f. 2021; CEO JITESH SHAH.

Seychelles Planning Authority: Independence House, Independence Ave, Victoria; tel. 4674576; internet www.spa.gov.sc; Chair. CYRIL BONNELAME; CEO ANGELA SERVINA.

Seychelles Trading Co Ltd (STC): Latanier Rd, POB 634, Victoria; tel. 4285000; e-mail marketing@stcl.sc; internet stcl.sc; f. 2008 to replace import and distribution arm of the fmr Seychelles Marketing Board (SMB); manufacturing and marketing of products, retailing, trade; Chair. IMTIAZ UMARJI; CEO SIANA BISTOQUET.

Small Business Financing Agency (SBFA): Victoria; Chair. JOSEPHA ALBERT; CEO ROSANDA ALCINDOR.

DEVELOPMENT ORGANIZATIONS

Enterprise Seychelles Agency: Camion Hall, 1st Floor, POB 537, Victoria; tel. 4289050; e-mail info@esa.gov.sc; internet www.esa.gov.sc; f. 2018; fmrly the Seychelles Industrial Development Corpn (f. 1988), subsequently Small Enterprises Promotion Agency (2004); promotes and develops small enterprises, crafts and cottage industries; CEO ANGELIC APPOO.

Indian Ocean Tuna Commission (IOTC) (Commission de Thons de l'Océan Indien): Blend Seychelles Bldg, 2nd Floor, POB 1011, Victoria; tel. 4225494; e-mail IOTC-Secretariat@fao.org; internet www.iotc.org; f. 1996; an inter-governmental organization mandated to manage tuna and tuna-like species in the Indian Ocean and adjacent seas; Chair. JUNG-RE RILEY KIM; Exec. Sec. CHRISTOPHER O'BRIEN; 30 mems.

Islands Development Co Ltd: New Port, Latanier Rd, POB 638, Victoria; tel. 4384640; internet www.idcseychelles.com; f. 1980; Chair. PATRICK BERLOUIS; CEO GLENNY SAVY.

Seychelles Investment Board (SIB): Independence House Annex, 2nd Floor, POB 1167, Victoria; tel. 4295500; e-mail investinseychelles@sib.gov.sc; internet investinseychelles.com; f. 2004; Chair. GILBERT LEBON; CEO ANNE ROSETTE.

CHAMBERS OF COMMERCE

Seychelles Chamber of Commerce and Industry: HIS House, Providence Industrial Estate, Providence; tel. 4323812; e-mail admin@scci.sc; internet scci.sc; f. 1933; Chair. OLIVER BASTIENNE; Sec.-Gen. IOUANA PILLAY.

UTILITIES

Public Utilities Corpn: Electricity House, POB 174, Roche Caiman; tel. 4678000; e-mail customerservices@puc.sc; internet www.puc.sc; f. 1986; Chair. LEONARD ALVIS; CEO JOEL VALMONT.

Seychelles Energy Commission: Rm 307, Unity House, Blk B, POB 1488, Victoria; tel. 4610818; e-mail ceo@sec.sc; internet www.sec.sc; f. 2009; electricity regulator in Seychelles; Chair. YVES CHOPPY; CEO TONY IMADUWA.

MAJOR COMPANIES

Abhaye Valabhji (Pty) Ltd: Providence Industrial Estate, POB 175, Victoria; tel. 4434343; e-mail info@abhaye.com; internet www.abhaye.com; f. 1962; furniture, household appliances, marine engines and motor vehicles; Man. Dir ANIL VALABHJI.

Allied Builders (Seychelles) Ltd: Les Mamelles, POB 215, Victoria; tel. 4380700; e-mail allied@seychelles.net; internet www.alliedbuilders-seychelles.com; f. 1980; building and civil engineering construction; Chair. KALYAN KURJI PATEL.

JOUEL: Le Rocher, Mahe; tel. 4344551; e-mail marketing@jouel.sc; internet jouel.co; f. 2004; present name adopted in 2011; part of Diamond SA; Man. Dir ROD THORRINGTON.

Oceana Fisheries Co Ltd: Fishing Port, POB 71, Victoria; tel. 4224712; e-mail info@oceanafisheries.com; internet oceanafisheries.com; exports fish; Dir ANTOINE TIRANT.

Paradise Computer Services (Pty) Ltd: Victoria House, POB 847, Victoria; tel. 4289566; e-mail pcs@seychelles.net; internet www.paradisecomputer.sc; f. 1996; distributor of computers, laptops, printers, peripherals, accessories and cables, office equipment and supplies; Man. Dir N. RAMANI.

PetroSeychelles: Seypec Bldg, 1st Floor, New Port, Victoria; tel. 4324422; e-mail pr@petroseychelles.com; internet www.petroseychelles.com; f. 1984 as Seychelles National Oil Co Ltd; merged with Seychelles Petroleum Co (SEYPEC) in June 2005, retaining its own name; present name adopted in 2012; petroleum exploration in the exclusive economic zone; CEO PATRICK JOSEPH.

Seychelles Breweries Ltd (SeyBrew): O'Brien House, Le Rocher, POB 273, Victoria; tel. 4380600; e-mail seybrew@seychelles.net; f. 1973; sole producer of beer and soft drinks; Chair. ANTHONY SMITH; Man. Dir CONOR NEILAND.

Seychelles Petroleum Co Ltd (SEYPEC): New Port, POB 222, Victoria; tel. 4290600; e-mail enquiries@seypec.com; internet www.seypec.com; f. 1985; merged with Seychelles National Oil Co in June 2003, only to retain its name for international transactions; distributing fuel and lubricants; state-owned; Chair. JENNIFER MOREL; CEO SARAH ROMAIN (acting).

United Concrete Products (Seychelles) Ltd (UCPS): Anse Des Genets, Pointe Larue, POB 382, Victoria; tel. 4386000; e-mail info@ucps.sc; internet ucps.sc; f. 1970; manufactures concrete products; Chair. JOSEPH ALBERT; Gen. Man. GREGORY ALBERT.

TRADE UNIONS

Seychelles Federation of Workers' Unions (SFWU): Maison du Peuple, Latanier Rd, POB 154, Victoria; tel. 4224455; e-mail sfwu@seychelles.net; f. 1978 to amalgamate all existing trade unions; affiliated to Parti Lepep; Pres. EGBERT ROSALIE; Sec.-Gen. ANTOINE ROBINSON.

Transport

RAILWAYS

There are no railways in Seychelles.

ROADS

Seychelles Land Transport Agency (SLTA): Huteau Lane, Victoria; tel. 4224449; e-mail secretariat@slta.sc; internet slta.sc; f. 1974 as the Public Works Department; present name adopted in 2009; CEO PARINDA HERATH.

Seychelles Public Transport Corpn (SPTC): English River, POB 610, Victoria, Mahe; tel. 4280280; e-mail inquiry@sptc.sc; internet www.sptc.sc; f. 1977; covers 66 routes on Mahe; Chair. ANDY MONCHERRY; CEO PATRICK VEL.

SHIPPING

Privately owned ferry services connect Victoria, on Mahe, with the islands of Praslin and La Digue.

Seychelles Maritime Safety Authority (SMSA): Victoria; f. 2020 to replace Seychelles Maritime Safety Administration (f. 2004); regulates maritime affairs; Chair. VERONIQUE LAPORTE.

Seychelles Ports Authority (SPA): Commercial Port, New Port, Mahe Quay, POB 47, Victoria; tel. 4294700; e-mail enquiries@seyport.sc; internet www.seyport.sc; f. 2004; Chair. GILBERT FRICHOT; CEO RONNY BRUTUS.

Euro African Star Transport (EAST Services): A7-A8, Providence Complex, Providence; e-mail info@eastcargocompany.com; internet www.eastcargocompany.com; f. 2020; CEO CAROL NALLETAMBY.

Hunt, Deltel and Co Ltd: 3rd Floor, The Quadrant, Manglier St, Victoria, POB 14, Mahe; tel. 4380300; e-mail info@huntdeltel.com; internet www.huntdeltel.com; f. 1937; Man. Dir CHRISTOPHE HOUAREAU.

Mahe Shipping Co Ltd: Maritime House, POB 336, Victoria; tel. 4380500; e-mail mail@maheship.sc; internet www.maheship.com; f. 1969; shipping agents; CEOs MARK JEYASINGH, JOE MORIN.

CIVIL AVIATION

Seychelles International Airport is located at Pointe Larue, 10 km from Victoria. A new international passenger terminal and aircraft parking apron were constructed in the mid-2000s on land reclaimed in 1990. The airport also serves as a refuelling point for aircraft traversing the Indian Ocean. There are airstrips on 11 of the outlying islands.

Seychelles Civil Aviation Authority (SCAA): International Airport, POB 181, Victoria; tel. 4384011; e-mail secretariat@scaa.sc; internet www.scaa.sc; f. 1970; responsible for the Flight Information Region of 2.6m. sq km of Indian Ocean airspace; Chair. MARLON ORR; CEO GARRY ALBERT.

Air Seychelles: International Airport, POB 386, Victoria; tel. 4391000; e-mail callcenter@airseychelles.com; internet www.airseychelles.com; f. 1978; state-owned; Chair. JEAN WEELING-LEE; CEO SANDY BENOITON.

Tourism

Seychelles Parks and Gardens Authority (SPGA): Unit 5C–8C, Orion Mall, 2nd Floor, POB 1240, Victoria; tel. 4225114; internet www.spga.gov.sc; f. 2022 to replace the Seychelles National Parks Authority (SNPA) and the National Botanical Gardens Foundation (NBGF); Chair. LUCAS D'OFFAY; CEO ALLEN CEDRAS.

Seychelles Tourism Board (STB): Botanical House, Ground Floor, POB 1262, Victoria; tel. 4671300; e-mail info@seychelles.travel; internet seychellestourismboard.travel; f. 1998 as Seychelles Tourism Marketing Authority; merged with Seychelles Tourism Office in 2005; Chair. KATHLEEN MASON; CEO SHERIN FRANCIS.

Defence

As assessed at November 2021, the army numbered 200 men, the coast guard 200 men and the air force 20 men. Seychelles contributes servicemen to the East African Stand-by Brigade, a part of the African Union stand-by peacekeeping force.

Defence Expenditure: SR 155m. in 2014.

Commander-in-Chief of Seychelles Armed Forces: Rev. WAVEL RAMKALAWAN.

Chief of Defence Forces: Brig. MICHAEL ROSETTE.

Education

Education is free and compulsory for children between six and 16 years of age. A programme of educational reform, based on the British comprehensive schools system, was introduced in 1980. The language of instruction in primary schools is English. The duration of primary education is six years, while that of general secondary education is five years (of which the first four years are compulsory), beginning at 12 years of age. Pre-primary and special education facilities are also available. According to estimates by the United Nations Educational, Scientific and Cultural Organization (UNESCO), in 2018/19 enrolment at the pre-primary level was equivalent to 95% of children (males 95%; females 96%) in the relevant age-group, while enrolment at primary schools included 98% of children (males 95%; females 100%) in the relevant age-group. Secondary enrolment in 2018/19 was equivalent to 79% (males 76%; females 81%) of children in the relevant age-group. A number of students study abroad, principally in the United Kingdom. According to UNESCO estimates, government expenditure on education in 2021 was equivalent to about 10.5% of total spending.

Bibliography

Bennett, G., and Bennett, P. R. *Seychelles* (World Bibliographical Series). Santa Barbara, CA, ABC-Clio, 1993.

Bowden, A., et al. *The Economic Costs of Maritime Piracy.* One Earth Future Foundation Working Paper, December 2010.

Buttoud, G. *La colonisation française des Seychelles: (1742 - 1811).* Paris, L'Harmattan, 2017.

Central Bank of Seychelles. *Quarterly Review.* Victoria, Central Bank of Seychelles.

Durup, J. *The Seychelles Islands and Its First Landowners* Mahé, iMedia, 2016.

Gabby, R., and Ghosh, R. N. *Seychelles Marketing Board: Economic Development in a Small Island Economy.* Singapore, Academic Press International, 1992.

Lee, C. *Seychelles: Political Castaways.* London, Hamish Hamilton, 1976.

Mancham, Sir J. R. *Paradise Raped: Life, Love and Power in the Seychelles.* London, Methuen, 1983.

  Island Splendour. London, Methuen, 1984.

  The Saga of a Small Nation Navigating the Cross-Currents of a Big World. St Paul, MN, Paragon House Publishers, 2016.

Marsac, F., Fonteneau, A., and Michaud, P. *L'or bleu des Seychelles: Histoire de la pêche industrielle au thon dans l'océan Indien.* Bondy, IRD Editions, 2014

Nieuwkerk, A., and Bell, W. *Seychelles.* International Development Research Centre, 2007.

Payet, R. 'Climate Change and the Tourism-Dependent Economy of the Seychelles' in Leary, N., et al (Eds) *Climate Change and Vulnerability.* London, Earthscan, 2008.

Robinson, A. *René and Postcolonial Seychelles An African Chameleon in the Indian Ocean.* Abingdon, Routledge, 2022.

Scarr, D. *Seychelles since 1770: History of a Slave and Post-Slavery Society.* London, C. Hurst and Co., 2018.

Shillington, K. *Albert Rene: The Father of Modern Seychelles, a Biography.* Crawley, University of Western Australia Press, 2014.

Skerrett, J., and Skerrett, A. *Seychelles.* London, APA, 1994.

Toussaint, A. *History of the Indian Ocean.* London, Routledge and Kegan Paul, 1966.

Veenendaal, W. *Politics and Democracy in Microstates.* Abingdon, Routledge, 2015.

SIERRA LEONE

Physical and Social Geography

PETER K. MITCHELL

The Republic of Sierra Leone, which covers an area of 71,740 sq km (27,699 sq miles), rises from the beaches of the south-west to the broad plateaux of the Atlantic/Niger watershed at the north-eastern frontier. Despite the general horizontal aspect of the landscapes, developed over millennia upon largely Pre-Cambrian structures, there are a number of abrupt ascents to older uplifted erosion surfaces—most impressively along sections of a major escarpment, 130 km inland, separating a western lowland zone (c. 120 m above sea level) from the country's more elevated interior half (c. 500 m). Incised valleys, interspersed by minor waterfalls, carry drainage south-westwards; only locally or along a coastal sedimentary strip do rivers flow through open terrain.

A geologically recent submergence of major floodplains, particularly north of Cape St Ann, has brought tidewater into contact with the rocky margins of the ancient shield, impeding up-river navigation. Waterborne trade has found compensation in sheltered deep-water anchorages, notably off Freetown, the principal port and capital, where a line of coastal summits rising to almost 900 m above sea level facilitates an easy landfall.

Intrusive gabbros form the peninsular range; elsewhere, isolated blocks or hill groups consist of rock-bare granites or the metamorphic roots of long-vanished mountain chains, which provide mineral deposits: iron, chromite, gold, rutile and bauxite. Reserves of kimberlite in the southern high plateaux are approaching exhaustion. The pipes and dikes of kimberlite may provide the basis for future deep mining.

Differences in seasonal and regional incidence of humidity and rainfall are important. Prolonged rains (May to October, with heaviest rains from July to September) are bracketed by showery weather with many squally thunderstorms, such spells beginning earlier in the south-east. Consequently, the growing season is longest here (although total rainfall—over 5,000 mm locally—is greater along the coast) and the 'natural' vegetation is tropical evergreen forest; the cultivation of cash crops such as cocoa, coffee, kola and oil palm is successful in this area, and the more productive timber areas, although limited, are concentrated here. The savannah-woodlands of the north-east have less rain (1,900 mm–2,500 mm), a shorter period for plant growth and a dry season made harsh by harmattan winds, with cattle-rearing, groundnuts and tobacco as potential commercial resources. Semi-deciduous forest occupies most intervening areas, but long-term peasant occupation has created a mosaic of short-term cropland, fallow regrowth plots and occasional tracts of secondary forest.

Permanent rice-lands have been created from mangrove swamp in the north-west, and much encouragement is being given to the improvement of the many small tracts of inland valley swamp throughout the east. Such innovation contrasts with a widespread bush-fallowing technique, giving low yields of rain-fed staples, normally rice, but cassava (especially on degraded sandy soils) and millet in the north.

Sierra Leone's sixth national census, which was held in December 2021, provisionally enumerated 7,541,641 inhabitants, representing a population density of 105.1 inhabitants per sq km.

Traditional *mores* still dominate, in spite of the Westernizing influences of employment in mining, of education and of growing urbanization. A large proportion of the population follows animist beliefs, although there are significant Islamic and Christian communities. Extended family, exogamous kin-groups and the paramount chieftaincies form a social nexus closely mirrored by a hierarchy of hamlet, village and rural centre: some 29,000 non-urban settlements, including isolated impermanent homesteads. The towns, however, are expanding. Greater Freetown, which it was assumed was equivalent to the Western Area Urban District, had 1.06m. inhabitants at the 2015 census, while Port Loko included 615,376 inhabitants and Kenema included 609,891. Diamond mining has attracted settlers to many villages in the mining areas.

The official language of the country is English, while Krio (Creole), Mende, Limba and Temne are also widely spoken.

History

LEIGHANN SPENCER

ESTABLISHING FREETOWN AND BRITISH RULE (1787–1951)

Sierra Leone, as a state demarcated by borders with one overarching political system, began its existence with the 1787 settlement which would become known as Freetown. The settlement mainly consisted of blacks from England who had roots in the Atlantic slave trade, relocated under the auspices of the Committee for the Relief of the Black Poor and abolitionist Granville Sharp. The Committee had formed in 1786 with the intent to give charitable relief to the 'black poor' of London, and came to formulate the Sierra Leone Resettlement Scheme with Sharp as a way to 'repatriate' the former slaves. The scheme came to be funded by the British Treasury and Sharp, alongside abolitionists such as Henry Thornton, William Wilberforce and Thomas and John Clarkson.

In May 1787 the first shipment of approximately 300 blacks and 100 whites arrived on the West African coast, founding the Province of Freedom and settlement of Granville Town. The problem, as with any settler colonialism, was that the land was already occupied by indigenous people. In this case, the immediate area was that of the Temne, with various tribes such as the Mende and Sherbro in the nearby vicinity. A deal was brokered with Temne chief King Tom for the land. However, disputes broke out with other chiefs, and in 1789 Granville Town was burnt down by King Tom's successor, King Jimmy. Additionally, the settlers were unprepared for the living conditions, particularly as they arrived in the rainy season, and many succumbed to disease. Some joined the slave trade. This first settlement, therefore, was not overly successful.

Nonetheless, further shipments were sent to settle along the coast. In 1791 the Sierra Leone Company (SLC) was formed to take over the Province, with Thornton as Chairman. By early 1792 the SLC had gathered over 1,000 former African-American slaves who had originally been sent to Nova Scotia by the British following the American revolution. This group of settlers rebuilt on the site of Granville Town and coined the name Freetown, still the capital of Sierra Leone today. More Nova Scotians, this time of Jamaican heritage, arrived at the turn of the 19th century. They were followed by several thousand Africans, primarily from what is now southern Nigeria, who had been liberated from slave ships by the Royal British Navy's West African Squadron, the headquarters of which were at this point located in Freetown.

By the end of the 19th century black settlers had come to form the rather cohesive Krio identity. Although considered African, most had Western backgrounds in terms of language, education, religion and dress. This heightened the divide between the settlers and indigenous people, and, although they did not have the political might of white settlers in Africa, the Krio had relatively close links to the British administrators. Under the SLC, Clarkson had been the first Governor of the Freetown colony, being succeeded by Zachary Macaulay. From 1808 the British Crown assumed control, which marked expansion into the interior. This was supported by the Krio, who saw themselves as part of the 'civilizing' mission. They took positions in the administration, judiciary, health and education sectors, and as missionaries. In 1863 a Constitution establishing an Executive Council and Legislative Council, the latter including two Krio albeit appointed by the Governor, was introduced.

The infamous Berlin Conference of 1884–85, which split the African continent into arbitrary states allocated to European powers, saw the formal expansion of Sierra Leone to its current borders, with the interior declared a Protectorate in 1896. Consequently, more and more whites migrated to Sierra Leone and took up high-profile jobs, causing grievance among the now downgraded Krio. Despite still being held above the indigenous groups, the Krio took part in the Hut Tax War; an armed rebellion launched by Temne and Mende after the 1898 imposition of taxes based on the size of huts. The rebellion was ultimately unsuccessful but cemented the beginnings of resistance to white colonial rule. Furthermore, it resulted in increased tactics by the British to impose control, particularly the codifying and co-opting of chieftaincies and the fostering of ethnic divisions.

The largest indigenous ethnic groups in Sierra Leone are the Mende in the south and the Temne in the north, each constituting around 32% of the present-day population of Sierra Leone. Also in the north are the Limba, who constitute 8.4%. Then there are various smaller groups, such as the Koranko and Mandingo in the north, Kissi and Kono in the east, Sherbro in the south, and Fula in the west. Islam tends to be dominant in the north and Christianity in the south. However, there are no substantial religious divisions and adherents of both world religions share in local traditional beliefs. Core to these beliefs are 'secret societies', namely the Poro for men and Sande for women. Poro and Sande branches have long been responsible for regulating their communities. Nearly every Sierra Leonean belongs to one—the term 'secret society' reflects the sacred rituals and need for initiation rather than any conventional, conspiratorial meaning.

For the majority of British rule, the Freetown colony remained separate from the interior, where the various ethnic groups were, to an extent, allowed to regulate themselves. However, following the Hut Tax War, the colonial administration codified certain areas as chiefdoms and implemented Paramount Chiefs as a system of indirect rule. The Paramount Chiefs were then responsible for collecting taxes alongside more traditional duties. This system did see the Protectorate as comparatively underdeveloped to the colony in terms of education and infrastructure. In 1924 an attempt was made to merge the Freetown colony and the Protectorate with the expansion of the Legislative Council; in addition to 12 British officials and two members appointed from the colony, there were three members elected by colony voters and three Paramount Chiefs appointed from the Protectorate.

Further amalgamation was to occur in the following decades. Notably in 1930 diamonds were discovered in the east, joining the natural commodities such as iron ore for which Sierra Leone would subsequently be renowned. More importantly, this era saw agitation for African rights. The Krio initially dominated the unions and public movements fighting for enhanced enfranchisement and representation. However, later the post-Second World War sentiment saw countless others become politicized, and calls for self-determination grew. This was a time of shifting geopolitics and the British too recognized that independence for their colonies was imminent. In 1947 a new Constitution stipulated that Africans should hold the majority in both the Executive and Legislative Councils, paving the way for the formation of African political parties.

AN INDEPENDENT STATE (1951–67)

The 1947 Constitution came into force with the 1951 general elections. Two dominant political parties emerged: the Sierra Leone People's Party (SLPP) and the National Council of Sierra Leone (NCSL). The new structure of the Legislative Council was to be 14 Europeans and 21 Africans. Of the Africans, seven would be elected from the colony, and 14 from the Protectorate. However, the latter were indirectly elected via the Protectorate Assembly, which largely consisted of Paramount Chiefs. This marked the still differential treatment between the colony and Protectorate, between the elite Krio and other ethnic groups. Moreover, it marked the development of chiefly patronage and the breakdown of legitimate traditional systems.

The Legislative Council elections, in which five of the seven colony seats were contested, saw three seats go to the NCSL and two to the SLPP. Of the 14 Protectorate seats, every member subsequently declared support for the SLPP, and the Governor solely chose SLPP members as his appointments to the Executive Council. Prominent ministers included Milton Margai and his brother Albert Margai of the Mende, and Siaka Stevens of the Limba. When local ministerial responsibility was introduced in 1953, Milton Margai became the Chief Minister under the SLPP. The 1957 election would again result in an SLPP majority under Milton Margai, who would go on to negotiate successful constitutional talks in London and lead the way to Sierra Leone's independence.

Sierra Leone became independent on 27 April 1961. A new Constitution entered into force, establishing a parliamentary system with Queen Elizabeth II as sovereign, and elections were scheduled for the following year. The primary opposition to the SLPP was the All People's Congress (APC), which had formed in 1960. (The NCSL, having lost all its seats in the 1957 election, had ceased to exist.) There were two other parties in existence—the United Progressive Party and the Sierra Leone Progressive Independence Movement—but the SLPP and APC have dominated the political sphere since independence.

On 27 May 1962 Sierra Leone held its first general election under universal adult franchise. The SLPP secured a majority and Milton Margai became the first Prime Minister. He had the support of the Mende population, whereas the APC was backed by the northern Temne and Limba alongside the Krio. The old divisions between the Krio and other ethnic groups were henceforth sidelined by a new rivalry between the Mende and Temne. This was fortified as the Mende were encouraged into the civil service whereas APC seats in the legislature were reduced. For instance, five APC members were imprisoned for unlawful assembly and their seats declared vacant. Prime Minister Milton Margai did, however, attempt to nationalize the new country, and focused heavily on modernization while holding the admiration of chiefs who respected his role in gaining independence.

Milton Margai died in 1964 and was succeeded as Prime Minister by his brother Sir Albert Margai), again supported by—and supportive of—the Mende. Albert Margai, in an attempt to emulate President Kwame Nkrumah in Ghana, took to the idea of a one-party state. A committee was set up to oversee the introduction of such to Sierra Leone. This faced a considerable backlash, including a petition to declare the move unconstitutional, and the fall of Nkrumah in 1966, combined with popular opinion opposed to it, led Margai to relinquish the idea. However, the SLPP rushed through a new draft Constitution to establish Sierra Leone as a Republic. This too was unpopular and unsuccessful. Corruption and mismanagement of funds were other key concerns regarding the SLPP during this period, as was the introduction of the Public Order Act 1965, which would be used to silence critics.

Additionally, there was growing discontent within the armed forces, which were under the command of Brig. David Lansana, a Mende and ally of Margai. As in many areas of the civil service, Mende were favoured for military positions. Col

1079

John Bangura, a Temne and second-in-command of the armed forces, became distrusted for his alleged relations with the APC. On 8 February 1967 it was announced that Bangura and seven other officers (mainly Temne) had been arrested for plotting to murder Margai and Lansana. There is uncertainty as to whether such a plot existed. None the less, there were certainly factions in the armed forces, and the plot provided grounds for Margai to attack the opposition. He then bypassed Parliament to make an agreement with Guinea for mutual assistance should one country need help against internal subversion, adding to the continuing dissatisfaction with the SLPP.

COUPS, COUNTERCOUPS AND THE RISE OF STEVENS (1967–68)

This dissatisfaction came to a head with the general election held on 17 March 1967. Many citizens had become apprehensive of the SLPP due to over-representation of the Mende, attempts to turn Sierra Leone into a one-party state and ongoing corruption. Furthermore, the elections themselves were contentious, with the SLPP believed to have hampered nominations, campaigns and voting on the day itself.

As the votes began to be counted, news spread that the APC had been victorious. However, the dual system of rule—with Parliament and the chieftancies—caused confusion. The general election was to be followed by elections for Paramount Chiefs who would take the independent seats. Chiefs did not campaign under a particular party, being considered supportive of the ruling regime; this method had been shown useful under colonial rule to maintain chieftancy support. In the lead-up to the 1967 elections, it was debated whether such an assumption of support was best for the post-colonial political system. In the end, it was kept as was. However, confusion arose about whether the winner of the general election could be announced before the Paramount Chief election results.

On 21 March 1967 APC leader Stevens was sworn in as the new Prime Minister of Sierra Leone by the Krio Governor-General Henry Boston. This was before the Paramount Chiefs' elections, and, although within Boston's constitutional power, it was a move that caused grievance. Just hours later Lansana carried out a coup in which Stevens, Boston and a number of cabinet ministers were placed under house arrest (one of the arresters, Sam Hinga Norman, would come to play a significant role in Sierra Leonean history) and martial law was enacted. Lansana claimed that this was necessary to 'protect the constitution and maintain law and order' and that the country should wait for the Paramount Chief seats before deciding the election. However, it was widely perceived that he was taking advantage of the situation Lansana then unsuccessfully tried to gather all the elected deputies to form a 'constitutional' government under the SLPP.

Not only were Lansana's appeals ignored by parliamentary deputies, but his actions unpopular among colleagues in the armed forces. On 23 March 1967 a group of senior officers led by Maj. Charles Blake seized power, creating the National Reformation Council (NRC), with Andrew Juxon-Smith as its Chairman and the new head of state. The NRC suspended the Constitution, dissolved all political parties and arrested Lansana, who was later found guilty of treason. He, alongside his sister-in-law and Mende Paramount Chief Ella Koblo Gulama, was said to have conspired with Margai, and it has generally been concluded that elements of the SLPP did conspire to see the first coup take place. The charges against Gulama were eventually dropped, but in 1975 Lansana was hanged with other former officials in the notorious executions at Pademba Road Prison in Freetown.

During the 23 March 1967 broadcast by the NRC, Blake claimed that Lansana did not intend to create a legitimate government, but rather that Lansana simply wanted Margai reimposed. Blake also pointed to the 'tribalistic posture' and 'economic situation' of the country as justification for the creation of the NRC; interestingly, the constitutional legitimacy (or lack thereof) of Siaka's swearing in was not listed as a prominent reason. To its credit, the NRC did implement several austerity measures and anti-corruption initiatives. Nevertheless, there was still suspicion that the NRC was upholding

the SLPP, and Mende, supremacy. Others viewed the establishment and actions of the NRC as a means to resolve the tensions within the armed forces more than as a reform of politics.

Such a task was never realized. By April 1968 tensions remained in the armed forces, and grievances surrounding poor pay and living conditions had been exacerbated. On 18 April this culminated with the 'Sergeants Coup' undertaken by low-level officers led by Warrant Officer Patrick Conteh and Private Morlai Kamara under the Anti-Corruption Revolutionary Movement (ACRM). NRC members were imprisoned, and other military officers deposed. The ACRM was headed by Bangura, who had been arrested in 1967 for the alleged plot against Margai and Lansana, and had returned from exile in Guinea. Also returned from Guinea was Stevens, who had spent the time since his removal from the premiership raising a paramilitary organization with the intention to move in on Sierra Leone.

The paramilitary organization was now expendable. The ACRM restored constitutional rule, and Stevens was reinstated as Prime Minister of Sierra Leone one week later. These coups and countercoups, and the decades following them, would have disastrous consequences for the young country. The insecurity surrounding Prime Minister Stevens' hold on power led him to declare a state of emergency, crack down on any dissenting views and consolidate his power. When Bangura realized his mistake, he attempted another coup. However, he was unsuccessful, and was executed for treason in 1971.

A DISASTROUS DICTATORSHIP (1968–91)

The most immediate threat faced by Stevens when he came to power in 1968 was the armed forces, which were still largely Mende, and ethnic divisions remained salient. Moreover, it had been shown in Sierra Leone (and elsewhere over the continent during this period) that coups beget coups. The military had, and could, take power quite easily. To shore up support, Stevens appointed Bangura as head of the armed forces, and within months had the majority of Mende officers arrested and replaced with Temne. Stevens himself was of the Limba, but he made use of the pre-existing tensions with the APC base predominantly being from the north, inclusive of the Limba and Temne, alongside the Krio. Similarly, cabinet positions and the police force were filled with allies. Military spending was increased to quell tensions regarding conditions and pay.

In November 1968 unrest across the Southern and Eastern provinces resulted in Stevens implementing a state of emergency and deploying the military to restore calm. In October 1970 a new political party, the United Democratic Party (UDP), was founded by disaffected APC ministers and Temne. Clashes ensued and yet another state of emergency was declared. The UDP only lasted 18 days before it was banned and its members arrested. Stevens thus faced divisions in the armed forces along APC–UDP lines, which could not be subverted by purges along clear ethnic lines. None the less, he commenced dismissals of suspected UDP supporters within the military.

It was due to these reasons that on 23 March 1971 Bangura launched his coup attempt. This was held off by loyalists within the armed forces, and, to demonstrate his power, Stevens swiftly had Bangura and three co-conspirators executed. Others were imprisoned; significantly, their number included future Revolutionary United Front (RUF) leader Foday Sankoh, who was released in 1978. Col Joseph Saidu Momoh, a Limba and Stevens' eventual successor, took Bangura's place at the head of the armed forces. Temne were removed from political power and back-up was drawn from Guinea with a new defence pact, tactics that were reminiscent of the SLPP's under Margai.

Stevens began to rely heavily on obtaining a loyalist police force to mitigate the insecurities faced by the armed forces. He formed the Internal Security Unit (ISU—commonly referred to as 'I Shoot U'), which would later become the notorious Special Security Division (SSD—commonly referred to as 'Siaka Stevens' Dogs'). As signalled by the local nomenclature, this police unit was directly under Prime Minister Stevens' control and became a force of brutality and suppression. It was effectively a regime-aligned militia. In fact, its members were drawn from the paramilitary organization established during Stevens' time in exile. It was based purely on patronage, duplicating the regular Sierra Leone Police but with the mandate to carry firearms, and without training from a police academy. This demoralized the regular police, as well as the armed forces, which were now downgraded and treated with suspicion.

Opposition members, and anyone with dissenting views during this time, were arrested and often executed by the SSD. Parliament was reduced to simply passing laws desired by Stevens, and the judiciary was afraid to intervene. Press freedom was stifled via intimidation and the Public Order Act of 1965. Under these conditions, corruption reigned. The SSD, and the now demoralized regular police, were highly susceptible to bribery. Stevens used his position for his own wealth accumulation, particularly through Sierra Leone's diamond reserves. There were, on several occasions, mass protests, often with college students leading the way, but these were quelled by live bullets. Sierra Leone had become a police state, with Stevens as its dictator.

In addition to consolidating armed support, Stevens had set about consolidating his power. In April 1971 he oversaw the restructuring of Sierra Leone as a Republic, with himself as President. Although elections continued during this time, intimidation and violence kept the SLPP at bay and ethno-regional divisions remained. By 1978 Stevens had accomplished what leaders before him had been unable to achieve: Sierra Leone became a one-party state. A referendum was passed with a dubious 95% of voters in favour, and the new Constitution was signed off by a submissive Parliament. The threat of the SSD played its part, while another tactic was the use of inquiries, which would see an official dismissed or would ensure loyalty in return for a not guilty verdict. Primarily, however, it was the reign of neo-patrimony. Deputies, chiefs, judges and other civil servants and heads of government corporations all owed their position to the President. Stevens was framed as 'Pa Siakie', the father of Sierra Leone, and the APC became synonymous with the state.

Patronage was largely enabled by Stevens' links to the diamond trade. His expropriation of state resources, moreover, had immense effects on the economy. Diamonds had been Sierra Leone's main export since independence, accounting for about 70% of export revenue, and with the trade falling from formal control, revenue also fell. Other sectors were similarly politicized and privatized, such as banking, utilities and agriculture, with resources funnelled to President Stevens and his patronage networks. This resulted in shortages of essentials such as food and power. The remaining formal sectors began to collapse. Teachers went for months without pay and education facilities were minimal. The public health care system was also in ruins.

In 1985 the Commander of the Armed Forces, Momoh, was appointed successor to Stevens, with Stevens going into retirement and passing away in 1988. In 1986 general elections were held—elections still took place under one-party rule to decide seats—and surprisingly, President Momoh took steps to ensure a relatively peaceful and credible poll. However, peace was not going to last. Sierra Leone was still an APC state and patronage continued. Momoh oversaw an attempt at economic reform with credit from the International Monetary Fund (IMF) and the World Bank, but an economic state of emergency had to be declared in 1987 and credit ceased in 1990. Actions taken under Stevens were coming to a head, and would prove central to an insurgency by the RUF and the sustenance of an 11-year civil war.

THE CIVIL WAR (1991–95)

There are several factors which contributed to Sierra Leone's civil war. Although the country had been fraught with ethno-regional tensions and coerced rule since colonialism, it was the period under Stevens which cemented conditions for conflict. First was the protracted patronage, corruption and executive over-reach which resulted in the disaffection of much of the population, including some who fled across the border to Guinea and Liberia. In particular, there were disaffected youth who had faced brutality at the hands of the SSD, had seen their

education and other services dismantled, and were presented with ever-growing unemployment rates (and would become central to the RUF's recruitment base). Ethno-regionalism did play a role in terms of mounting resentment in the south-east. However, a significant growing divide was between the elite and non-elites, the latter inclusive of disaffected youth. The state, essentially in disarray, was not in a position to put down the insurgency. The armed forces were demoralized and largely ceremonial; those in positions of power occupied them due to patronage rather than expertise. The overall informalization of the state resulted in meagre available resources to direct into counterinsurgency.

The influence of the diamond sector is another often cited factor. It is debated how large a part diamonds played in causing the civil war; none the less, they were undoubtedly significant in incentivizing and funding the combatants. Diamonds, and particularly alluvial diamonds which are abundant in Sierra Leone, have been termed a 'guerrilla's best friend'. This is because they are diffuse, found remotely, easily mined, easily transported, are anonymous in nature and highly valuable. They are similar to timber, a diffuse and easily used resource of medium value, which played a part in neighbouring Liberia's civil war. This brings us to one more factor related to Sierra Leone's position: regional and international politics, primarily the influence of Charles Taylor and his National Patriotic Front of Liberia (NPFL).

Taylor and the RUF leader Sankoh had met in Libya, where they and other West Africans were given training and support by Muammar al-Qaddafi in his push against Western imperialism. Taylor would go on to launch an insurgency into Liberia from Côte d'Ivoire in December 1989, which was extremely brutal but also extremely successful, with his NPFL rebels having taken 95% of the country by 1991. As in Sierra Leone, the backdrop for the Liberian civil war was one of a dictatorship under President Samuel Doe which promoted ethno-regional tensions. Taylor would go on to become President of Liberia in August 1997. The period in between saw approximately 200,000 civilians killed, with the now infamous use of child soldiers and devastating plunder of the country's natural resources, including timber.

At the beginning of the Liberian civil war, the NPFL faced opposition from the APC Government of Sierra Leone. Furthermore, the diamond mines in the marginalized south-east appeared a lucrative asset which would be easy to commandeer. As such, Taylor backed Sankoh and his RUF, who on 23 March 1991 launched their own insurgency from Liberia, entering the Kailahun District of eastern Sierra Leone. Shortly after, they took other south-east districts such as Pujehun, Kono, and Bo. The RUF consisted of about 300 combatants in these early years, mostly drawn from the NPFL. They did not have substantive civilian support like the NPFL had in Liberia. They used brutal methods, including amputations and abductions. The RUF additionally lacked an overt political ideology and drive for permeation in taken territory compared with Taylor's 'Greater Liberia', which provided state-like services. Yet the RUF did, to an extent, promote Qaddafi-like egalitarianism with an anti-elite theme, providing free education and medical services.

Although brutalization and forced recruitment into the RUF was very real, many joined—or stayed—for economic, educational or sociopolitical reasons, particularly the youth. Interestingly, this played out against Sierra Leone's age-based social order. That is, the youth felt marginalized not only by the APC elite, but also by their local chiefs and other elders. The legitimacy of chiefs had been decreasing since colonial rule, and the subsequent patronage system reinforced this. Anti-chief sentiment was visible with the killings of chiefs throughout the war and their replacement with 'RUF chiefs', alongside the role of chiefs in the counterinsurgency. Despite the relative lack of RUF support in the early years, the ill-equipped Sierra Leone armed forces were unable to stop its expansion. By July 1991 the RUF had secured quite a stronghold. Facing widespread criticism, President Momoh led a return to multi-party politics. At a referendum in late August, 90% voted to end the one-party state, and elections were scheduled for June 1992.

However, the inability to overcome the rebels and the poor conditions of the armed forces resulted in a group of junior officers desposing President Momoh on 29 April 1992. He was exiled to Guinea and the legislature was dissolved. The National Provisional Ruling Council (NPRC) took control, with Capt. Valentin Strasser, a Krio, at its head. Civil defence units were used to provide security at a local capacity. These units were essentially vigilantes, that is, volunteer civilians, and consisted of pre-existing groups, primarily the Kamajor secret society of the Mende; they would come to form the Civil Defence Force (CDF). The civil defence units were largely formed under the auspices of local chiefs to uphold their legitimacy. Indeed, Hinga Norman, who would come to be the CDF leader, was the Mende chief of Bo District.

Bringing an end to more than two decades of APC rule, the NPRC was initially fairly popular and Sierra Leoneans were hopeful of change. There was also hope that the RUF insurgency would subside as their 'struggle' had been framed as being against the oppressive APC regime. However, this did not occur, with Sankoh claiming that the NPRC was also illegitimate. There are conflicting reports as to the extent of NPRC will and activity in defeating the rebels. Regardless, the war continued and in fact intensified. The RUF faced ongoing pressure from Taylor to obtain income from Sierra Leone's diamonds. Sierra Leone soldiers became involved in looting and other nefarious activities, including some collusion with the RUF. This was due to their ongoing poor working conditions and their recent history of being corrupt, untrained and unregulated. It created the 'sobel' phenomenon: state soldiers by day, rebels by night.

By 1994 the RUF had moved from their south-eastern hold and spread across the country. Collaboration between the RUF and the Sierra Leone armed forces (SLAF) also spread, particularly with regard to looting and illegal mining, and civilians could not always tell them apart. Strasser himself acknowledged that a great proportion of the SLAF was disloyal. As a result, CDF–SLAF relations soured. By 1995 the RUF had reached the outskirts of Freetown, and the NPRC called in the South African private military company Executive Outcomes to assist the counterinsurgency with the promise of future mining concessions. With the combined efforts of the CDF and Executive Outcomes, territory was regained. The NPRC saw a change in leadership to Brig.-Gen. Julius Maada Bio of the Mende, who was shortly afterwards forced to call elections. Bio did, however, commence peace negotiations with the rebels (and would go on to become a democratically elected President in 2018—see *Democracy (2007–21)*).

THE CIVIL WAR (1996–2001)

General elections took place on 26 February 1996, with a decent turnout and few irregularities considering the circumstances. The RUF increased their attacks in the lead-up to the polls, and conducted amputations as warnings to people not to vote. However, on election day itself poll security was successfully provided by the CDF. The main contenders were John Karefa-Smart of the newly formed United National People's Party (UNPP), a Sherbro from the north, and the SLPP's Ahmed Tejan Kabbah, a Mandingo from the Kailahun District in the east. The first round saw no victor—at least 55% of the vote was now required for a win—and thus a second round was held on 15 March. The SLPP won, and Kabbah was duly sworn in as President of Sierra Leone.

President Kabbah mainly received his votes from the south and east, whereas northerners tended to favour the UNPP. There were suspicions in regard to districts such as Kailahun and Bo, which recorded close to (or even over) 100% turnout for the second vote. Although internally displaced peoples in these areas likely played a part, it was agreed to subtract the additional votes from Kabbah's tally. Nevertheless, he still received 59% of the vote, and Kafera-Smart conceded defeat. The UNPP went on to be far less successful in future elections. Meanwhile, President Kabbah formed a coalition Government and appointed various allies to the cabinet. This included Bangura as Minister of Finance and the CDF leader, Hinga Norman, as Minister of Defence.

Shortly afterwards the CDF officially came into being (rather than operating as informal units), and large-scale initiation into the Kamajors took place. As a secret society, initiation was mandatory; one had to be endowed with the secret knowledge and ritual by the Kamajor High Priest Allieu Kondewa. This incorporated aspects of traditional magic and religion, becoming central to group cohesion and the ability to fight effectively. The CDF remained instrumental in regaining territory from the RUF.

At the same time, negotiations between the Government and the RUF continued, and the Abidjan Peace Accord was signed in Côte d'Ivoire in November 1996. This stipulated: a total cessation of hostilities; a blanket amnesty; a disarmament, demobilization and reintegration (DDR) process; monetary assistance for the RUF to transform into a political party; and the condition of Executive Outcomes' retreat from Sierra Leone. However, many have questioned Sankoh's commitment to this process and see the latter condition as the rebels' overarching goal. Indeed, this was the sole stipulation of the Abidjan Accord that would come into being in the following months. Violence did reach a comparatively low level, but continued none the less.

On 25 May 1997 another coup was undertaken by junior officers. This included a prison break and the release of inmates, in particular Maj. Johnny Paul Koroma, who had been imprisoned for coup-plotting the year before. The Armed Forces Revolutionary Council (AFRC) was established with Koroma at its head, and Kabbah fled to Guinea. A week of AFRC-led havoc ensued, dubbed 'operation pay yourself'. The junior officers had long felt neglected. However, the key justification for the coup was the collaboration with, and basically dependence on, the CDF, which soldiers saw as undermining the SLAF—and undermining their looting and other illegal activities. This was reflected in the Abidjan Peace Accord, which called for the demobilization of both the RUF and the SLAF, but failed to mention the CDF whatsoever. Instead, the CDF had been officiated under the SLPP. The AFRC thus demanded that the CDF demobilize and disarm, but to no avail; the CDF and now deposed Hinga Norman continued their counterinsurgency.

This further became a predicament as the AFRC called for a truce and collaboration with the RUF. Sankoh, recently arrested in Nigeria for arms importation, remained considered the RUF leader and was given the position of Vice-President of Sierra Leone *in absentia*. Maj.-Gen. Sam Bockarie took on-the-ground control of the RUF during Sankoh's two-year absence, and the group proceeded to Freetown to join the AFRC. This rebel-military junta regime, predictably brutal and arbitrary in rule, was illegitimate in the eyes of the international community and faced sanctions by the Economic Community of West African States (ECOWAS) and the United Nations (UN).

In October 1997 there was, however, an agreement reached in Guinea: the Conakry Peace Plan. This had similar stipulations to the Abidjan Accord, with an added focus on immunity for the May coup and the release of Sankoh in return for Kabbah's reinstatement within six months. The ECOWAS Ceasefire Monitoring Group (ECOMOG), comprising mainly of Nigerian troops, was deployed to Sierra Leone. Clashes then ensued, with the AFRC and the RUF on one side and ECOMOG and the CDF on the other. This escalated in February 1998, when ECOMOG and the CDF, backed by the likes of Nigeria and the United Kingdom, stormed Freetown. The AFRC and the RUF fled back east, and to the north, which had previously been relatively untouched by the war.

With Freetown recaptured, Kabbah was able to return from exile. He was reinstated as President of Sierra Leone on 10 March 1998. The CDF was placed under the control of ECOMOG, and the UN Observer Mission in Sierra Leone (UNOMSIL) commenced operations. Sankoh was extradited from Nigeria and sentenced to death for treason in Sierra Leone; he was imprisoned while awaiting an appeal.

Meanwhile, the rebels regrouped with considerable arms from their time in power. In January 1999 the RUF, in tandem with the AFRC, invaded Freetown and caused unprecedented and indiscriminate destruction. Sankoh openly called the offensive 'leave no living thing'. Over the course of two weeks more than 5,000 people were killed—mainly civilians, who were either burnt to death or executed—and many more were subjected to violence. This brought the Sierra Leone civil war into public view, with worldwide reports on events often depicting drugged and armed child soldiers.

Eventually the rebels were pushed back, and the main players forced into further negotiations. A ceasefire was agreed on 18 May 1999 and the Lomé Accord signed on 7 July in Togo. This third agreement granted the rebels an amnesty and their leaders senior government positions. Sankoh became Vice-President and was given control of Sierra Leone's diamond mines. ECOMOG withdrew, and the UN Mission in Sierra Leone (UNAMSIL), a peacekeeping operation, was deployed.

However, the Lomé agreement was tenuous. Many saw the granting of amnesty and political power to the rebels as scandalous, particularly after the Freetown catastrophe. As such, more violence broke out during the following year, including once again in Freetown. In May 1999 the RUF abducted several hundred UNAMSIL peacekeepers, leading to an intervention by British Special Forces and the bolstering of peacekeeper numbers. Guinea also intervened in 2000, claiming that the RUF had been launching cross-border attacks. This increase in reliable armed forces helped to restore peace, with disarmament commencing in 2001.

On 18 January 2002 President Kabbah declared Sierra Leone's civil war over. The 11-year war had devastated the country. It is estimated that 2.6m. Sierra Leoneans were displaced and over 50,000 killed. Others had been subjected to extensive injuries and trauma. The signature move of the RUF was amputation: the 'short sleeve' cut at the elbow, or the 'long sleeve' at the wrist. Another attribute was the use of child soldiers, with some 14,000 taking part in Sierra Leone's civil war. They eventually made up about one-half of the RUF, and significantly about one-quarter of the state forces. Children abducted into the RUF were sometimes forced to kill their parents as indoctrination, and were given drugs to enable violent acts.

The tactics used in Sierra Leone and Liberia were similar because of the link to Taylor's NPFL. Rape and other abuse towards civilians were also common, as was destruction of property and looting, particularly of the diamond mines. By the late 1990s diamonds earned the RUF between US $25m. and $125m. annually. However, it should be stressed that such actions were not constrained to the RUF, with state forces and even ECOMOG troops also committing crimes.

Although ethnicity has always played a prominent part in Sierra Leone's politics, its role in the civil war was not clear cut. Violence did tend play out along elite/non-elite lines, but even this division was not concrete. Indeed, people from all walks of life participated, and therefore the country's post-conflict reconstruction would be lengthy and demanding.

POST-CONFLICT RECONSTRUCTION (2002–07)

On 14 May 2002 general elections were held under the auspices of the UN. President Kabbah of the SLPP won a second term with 70% of the votes cast. The APC, under Ernest Bai Koroma from the Loko ethnic group, received 22%, showing lasting scepticism of the party linked to Steven's dictatorship and its contributions to the civil war. Similarly, the RUF's political party, the Revolutionary United Front Party, failed to take any seats, receiving less than 2% of the votes.

President Kabbah had to confront numerous challenges in this immediate post-conflict period. Sierra Leone's economic situation was dire, its infrastructure and public services were left derelict, the country's population was in much need of reconciliation and those responsible for war crimes had to be brought to justice. In late 2002 the Truth and Reconciliation Commission (TRC) began as mandated by the Lomé Accord. It was to provide a degree of accountability for human rights violations committed during the conflict: to investigate the causes, identify perpetrators and victims, promote healing and reconciliation, and effect change while acting as a historical record. Proceedings were finalized in 2004, with a report submitted to the UN Security Council. The report found that those most responsible for rights violations were the RUF, the AFRC, the SLAF and the CDF, in that order. While the majority of victims were found to be adult males, women

and children had too been targeted. The main causes of the war were executive over-reach and corruption, and the collapse of traditional systems since colonization. The legally binding recommendations of the TRC centred around eradicating corruption and decentralizing executive control. Additionally, a reparations programme was established, with victims receiving payouts from 2010. Yet the TRC has been criticized due to the inability and inaction of the Government to implement all of its recommendations.

Acting alongside the TRC was the Special Court for Sierra Leone (SCSL), which in 2003 indicted individuals for war crimes which were not covered for amnesty under the Lomé Accord. This intended to bring justice for the most serious of atrocities committed. However, former RUF leader Sankoh passed away in prison before his trial commenced, and Koroma of the AFRC had fled and was presumed dead. At this point, Taylor was President of Liberia and accordingly immune to prosecution—he subsequently fled into hiding in Nigeria, and was convicted at the SCSL in The Hague, Netherlands, in 2012. Taylor was given a 50-year prison sentence for aiding the RUF. In the mean time, the primary indictees to the SCSL were Hinga Norman, leader of the CDF, Moinina Fofana, the CDF's second-in-command, and the CDF/Kamajor High Priest, Allieu Kondewa, who was responsible for conducting initiations. This caused controversy as the CDF were considered heroes by many. None the less, Hinga Norman's trial went ahead, concluding in 2006; he passed away while awaiting the verdict. In 2007 Kondewa and Fofana were convicted of several war crimes, including murder, violence, pillage (looting) and the use of child soldiers. Kondewa was sentenced to 20 years' imprisonment, and Fofana to 15 years, served in Rwanda's Mpanga Prison until their recent conditional early release.

Another aspect of Sierra Leone's post-conflict reconstruction was the reintegration of ex-combatants, of which over 70,000 participated in the DDR programme. At a community level, this was quite successful with the efforts of healing and reconciliation. Still, there were issues particularly around socio-economic reintegration. Ex-combatants were provided with training in trades such as carpentry, mechanics and agriculture, but the flooding of the job market following the civil war left many unemployed. Some ex-combatants went on to fight in other wars across the region as a consequence of their financial situation and lack of renewed purpose. Furthermore, youth unemployment—important when reflecting on the number of child soldiers in the civil war—was roughly double that of the overall unemployment rate, and the DDR programme saw little emphasis on primary or secondary education. Some children, particularly girls, were left out of the process as they had played roles outside of combat. Women and girls were also most likely to face stigmatization.

President Kabbah did make some attempts to improve the country's infrastructure and public services. There was also security sector reform, including the restructuring of the SSD as the Operational Support Division. However, perceptions of government corruption and inadequacy grew in the reconstruction period. Of note, aid given by the World Bank and the IMF alongside countries such as the UK and the USA was often misappropriated by the SLPP and their networks of patronage. Media outlets which attempted to report on corruption were hit with charges under the Public Order Act 1965. None the less, peace has been kept. In 2005 the UN peacekeeping troops were withdrawn and the UN Integrated Office in Sierra Leone (UNIOSIL) was established.

DEMOCRACY (2007–22)

The 2007 general elections were highly competitive and considered an important test for Sierra Leonean democracy. The SLPP sought a third term under Solomon Ekuma Berewa. Given that Berewa had been hand-picked by President Kabbah as his successor, the new leadership hardly negated the reservations about the party. The APC was again the main opposition, with Koroma as leader. APC support was boosted with a new northern base, the party having formed a coalition with the UNPP and the People's Democratic Party. This election also saw a third significant player come onto the scene: the People's Movement for Democratic Change under Charles

Margai, son of Albert Maragi. Highlighting the competitiveness of the polls, both Berewa and Koroma faced petitions to disqualify them from running for the presidency. The Supreme Court did find them eligible, but only weeks before voting commenced.

There were some incidents of intimidation and violence during the election campaign. However, with plenty of external oversight, including by UNIOSIL, the elections ran smoothly, with a high turnout. Neither of the main parties received the necessary 55% of votes on 11 August 2007, and a second round was held on 7 September. The APC won this round, with 55% of the votes to the SLPP's 45%, and Koroma was installed as President. The win was attributed to the increased northern vote, as well as Sierra Leone's youth being largely anti-SLPP, having witnessed the effects of corruption and patronage. The SLPP blamed the external overseers for its defeat, but the democratic transfer of power was successful.

In 2012 another democratic election was held. President Koroma won a second term, receiving 58% of the votes to the SLPP's 37%. He promised zero tolerance towards corruption and passed the Anti-Corruption Act 2008. Koroma also oversaw the launch of an Independent Police Complaints Board (IPCB), and focused on rebuilding the country's infrastructure and boosting investments and tourism. Another positive policy was the restoration of pre-colonial chiefdoms, which had been codified by the British after the Hut Tax War and contributed to the collapse of Sierra Leone's traditional systems. However, despite the high hopes for the APC, President Koroma was far from eradicating corruption—a key concern. For instance, when Ebola Virus Disease spread to Sierra Leone from Guinea in 2014, millions of dollars allocated to fight the epidemic went missing. The virus had other detrimental effects on the country: the health care system was inundated, states of emergency declared, and lockdowns imposed. It is estimated that over 14,000 were killed before Sierra Leone was declared Ebola-free in March 2016. During this time, many journalists critical of President Koroma were detained.

At the March 2018 elections the SLPP was narrowly returned to power, with Julius Maada Bio, the 1996 military head of Sierra Leone and the son of a Sherbro Paramount Chief, securing 51.8% of the votes in the run-off contested against the APC's Samura Kamara. During his tenure, President Bio has overseen substantial reform including increasing educational funding, abolishing the death penalty, and repealing the section of the Public Order Act historically used to silence critics. He promised to tackle corruption, auditing ministry departments, governmental agencies and mining contracts. This process saw evidence of corruption in the prior regime come to light, as outlined above, with a commission of inquiry established to investigate further. In 2020 the inquiry's findings were published and Koroma, alongside another 126 former officials, were found culpable.

However, in 2021 it was reported that 85 of these officials had appealed the findings, with many being successful. This, alongside allegations of corruption in the current regime, does not bode well for the SLPP. Furthermore, in 2022 there were large scale protests regarding the country's ongoing economic difficulties. These were met with excessive force resulting in deaths, and hundreds of arrests. With the commencement of campaigning for the June 2023 elections commentators predict a close call between Sierra Leoneans giving the SLPP another chance or a return to APC rule. This tight competition has seen political violence at its highest level since the end of the war. The Armed Conflict Location and Event Data Project has reported between 10 to 30 incidents of political violence occurring per month, primarily being violence between APC and SLPP militias. Politicians also continue to draw upon ethnic-regional sentiments.

The situation in Sierra Leone is thus tentative. Many issues are a lingering presence of the civil war and a consequence of lasting corruption and patronage politics. Unemployment and a lack of access to public services continue to adversely affect the country, exacerbated by the COVID-19 pandemic, and are key contributors to crime and conflict. Despite the cessation of the SSD and the implementation of the IPCB, police brutality remains. In addition, executive over-reach has endured with interference in the judiciary and legislature, and a lack of accountability. The inefficiencies of the judicial system and police has seen a preference for traditional justice: from chiefs and other elders, including from societies such as the Poro, Sande and Kamajors. This rise in traditional legitimacy can, however, be considered a positive, and these actors should be prioritized in continued efforts to stabilize the country.

Given its chequered history, Sierra Leone has been considered something of a success story. A 2020 Afrobarometer survey showed that three-quarters of the population view the country as a 'full democracy' or a 'democracy with minor problems'. On the Vision of Humanity's 2021 Global Peace Index, Sierra Leone was ranked 50th out of 163 countries—the 4th best placing for sub-Saharan Africa. Yet worryingly, it had dropped globally by 13 places since 2018. This was specifically due to increasing militarization in combination with the potential for crime, conflict, and political insecurity. Indeed, with the general elections due in less than a year, Sierra Leone needs to sustain efforts for development and democracy, and to heed the lessons learnt from its past.

Economy

ROBERT E. LOONEY

INTRODUCTION

Sierra Leone is one of the poorest countries in the world. Decades of political instability, corruption and the mismanagement of its abundant natural resources have taken a heavy toll on economic activity. The civil war, which lasted from 1991 until 2002, destroyed or damaged much of the country's infrastructure and delayed the creation of vital human capital.

With a gross domestic product (GDP) in 2021 of approximately US $4,200m., Sierra Leone has one of the smallest economies in sub-Saharan Africa, smaller than South Sudan (some $4,400m.) but larger than Burundi (about $3,000m.) and Liberia (some $3,000m.). In 1980 the average per capita income in Sierra Leone in current US dollars was $480, dropping to $219 in 1990 and $205 in 2000. However, by 2010 it had risen to $402, increasing to $521 by 2021. On a purchasing-power parity (PPP) basis, per capita income dropped from $2,209 in 1980 to $1,959 in 1990 and $838 in 2000. By 2010 per capita income had risen to $1,406, increasing to $1,654 in 2021.

Sierra Leone's economic growth since 1980 falls into four distinct phases: pre-civil war (1980–90); the civil war years (1991–2002), the post-war period of recovery and buoyant commodity markets (2003–14); and the period since 2015, marked by the Ebola Virus Disease (EVD) epidemic, unstable commodity markets, the COVID-19 pandemic and, latterly, sharp rises in the prices of staple food items and energy. The outbreak of EVD in the country in May 2014 coincided with a steep decline in international iron ore prices, forcing the shutdown of two large iron ore mines. The consequent spread of EVD seriously disrupted economic activities across the country.

It was not until the post-civil war period that per capita incomes increased at a sustained rate, and average annual income per head actually fell by 1.1% in 1980–90 and by a further 3.5% during the civil war years, before increasing by 4.7% in the immediate post-war period of 2003–14. In 2015–21, annual per capita income growth again turned negative, averaging a contraction of 2.2%.

The growth patterns of the three main sectors—agriculture, industry and services—reflect these patterns. The agricultural sector expanded by an average annual rate of 7.4% in the pre-civil war period, dropping to a 0.3% during the war. Recovery during 2003–14 saw growth increasing to 6.1%, but dropping to 3.6% thereafter.

Industry, which includes mining, experienced average annual growth of 9.6% in the period leading up to the civil war but dropped to 0.5% during the war. In the post-war period, commodity prices boomed before and after the 2008–09 international financial crisis. During 2010–14 significant investments flowed into the country's mining sector, especially in developing two iron ore mines. The two mines entered production in 2011 and triggered a sharp rise in economic growth, with the industry expanding at an average annual rate of 24.3% during 2002–14. With the drop in commodity prices and the dislocations brought about by the EVD epidemic and the COVID-19 pandemic, industrial growth contracted at an average annual rate of 8.0% during 2015–21.

Considerable structural change has occurred, but not of the type usually associated with countries in Sierra Leone's income range. Instead of becoming more industrialized, more service-orientated and less dependent on agriculture, the reverse occurred. In 1980 World Bank data showed that the agriculture sector accounted for 30.4% of the country's GDP. By 2005 its share had increased to 49.4%, and in 2021 it stood at 60.9%. In 1980 industry (which includes mining, manufacturing, electricity and water and construction) accounted for 20.2% of GDP before falling to 11.3% in 2005. By 2020 industry accounted for only 6.3% of GDP. A similar pattern characterizes the country's manufacturing sector. In 1980 the sector accounted for 4.9% of GDP before falling to 2.5% in 2005 and just 2.0% in 2021. Finally, services accounted for 41.4% of GDP in 1980 before dropping to 36.2% in 2005 and 34.2% in 2021.

Successive governments have adopted ambitious policies to reverse these trends, hoping to transform the economy and support faster economic growth. The Government of President Ernest Bai Koroma (2007–18) launched a five-year plan—the Agenda for Prosperity—in 2013, which aimed to reduce the percentage of the population living below the poverty line to under 20%. The plan sought to draw on the country's natural resource endowment to drive the economy and invest in social and physical infrastructure. With the help of governance reforms, the strategy aimed to put Sierra Leone on the path toward middle-income country status by 2035.

After the Government led by President Julius Maada Bio assumed office in March 2018, it launched the US $8,000m. National Development Plan, which sought to diversify the economy, boost job creation and improve social outcomes. Key policies under this programme included the provision of free primary and secondary education, increased spending on a free health care initiative, the scaling-up of infrastructure spending and the implementation of pro-business reforms.

Despite these efforts, many problems remain. Besides the inability to expand the industrial and service sectors, male youth unemployment is high, at 15.8% in 2021. The Government is also highly dependent on foreign aid to fund its budget. In addition, poor infrastructure continues to impede the pace of economic growth and discourages investment. Less than 10% of Sierra Leone's roads are paved, and the country's socio-economic development lags behind that of other countries in the region.

The economy is experiencing a turbulent period. After declining by 2.0% at the height of the COVID-19 pandemic in 2020, GDP grew by 3.2% in 2021. However, growth is expected to dip below this rate in 2022, owing to a global economic slowdown and sharply rising inflation. The country's debt level rose considerably after significant falls in commodity prices in 2014 and the onset of the EVD epidemic and COVID-19 pandemic. The Government's budget will probably face severe constraints during a period of sharply higher costs of energy and food, combined with lower tax revenue.

SOCIOECONOMIC DEVELOPMENT

In view of the limited progress made in raising the level of per capita income, it is no surprise that Sierra Leone lags in many 'quality of life' measures. The country ranked 182nd out of 189 countries in the United Nations (UN) Development Programme's 2020 Human Development Index (HDI), placing the country in the Low Human Development category. In 2020 life expectancy at birth was just 55.1 years, and the mean years of schooling was only 3.7 years—both indicators among the lowest of any country in the world.

Between 2014 and 2019 the country dropped two places in its HDI ranking. During 1990–2000 the country's HDI score improved at an average rate of only 0.3% per year, increasing to 3.1% during 2000–10. However, the rate of improvement in the country's score dropped to 1.4% during 2010–19.

Progress in poverty reduction also lagged. By 2021 a total of 42.8% of the population lived in poverty (defined as income of less than US $1.90 income per day on a 2011 PPP basis). The recent COVID-19 pandemic and its effects on the economy no doubt increased the country's rate of poverty, although the rate in 2019 had fallen to 41.1%.

Significant progress has nonetheless been made in several areas. Sierra Leone's income distribution is one of the more equal in sub-Saharan Africa. The country's Gini coefficient (a measure of inequality) of 0.357 in 2018 represented a commendable improvement from 0.402 in 2003. During 2010–18 the poorest 40% of the population's income share was 19.6%, while the wealthiest 10% took 29.4%, and the top 1% took 10.5%. There are significant gender differences: the mean years of schooling are 4.5 years for males and just 2.9 for females. In 2019 the estimated per capita income (in US dollars at 2011 prices on a PPP basis) was $1,470 for females and $1,867 for males.

The Legatum Prosperity Index presents a broader picture of Sierra Leone's socioeconomic progress. The Index represents a composite of 12 aspects of prosperity/socioeconomic wellbeing. In the 2021 Index, Sierra Leone ranked 144th out of 167 countries. Since 2011 the country's ranking has risen by one place. The country ranked lowest (164th) in infrastructure and market access, followed by health (162nd), living conditions (155th), investment environment (151st) and education (150th). The country ranks most highly in social capital (66th), personal freedom (86th), natural environment (100th) and safety and security (106th).

While the country's progress in socioeconomic betterment is disappointing, the governance reform process that is currently under way has seen significant gains. Although still very low by international standards, Sierra Leone's standard of governance has been rising since the end of the civil war. As defined by the World Bank, the country's overall governance improved from the 19th percentile in 2003 to the 30th by 2020. The most extensive improvements were in several of the Bank's six governance dimensions. Control of corruption improved from the 18th percentile in 2003 to the 41st in 2020, political stability and the absence of violence rose from the 19th percentile to the 40th, while the rule of law improved from the 14th to the 24th percentile. However, progress lagged in several vital areas. Voice and accountability (a proxy for democracy) rose from the 39th percentile to only the 42nd, while government efficiency improved from the 10th to only the 13th percentile.

DEMOGRAPHY

As at mid-2022 Sierra Leone's population was estimated at 8.5m. Owing to the civil war, the country's population has not grown steadily over the past few decades. It increased at an average annual rate of 2.4% during 1980–90, before dropping to 1.2% during the civil war years of 1991–2002. As the country recovered during 2003–14, average annual population growth rose to 2.9%, but declined to 2.1% during 2015–21.

The population is young, and about 40% of Sierra Leoneans were aged under 14 years in 2021. Over time the share of the population in the working age group (15–64) has increased, from an average of 52.3% during 1991–2002 to 56.0% in 2015–21. Meanwhile, the share of the population aged 65 and older declined from 3.7% in 1980–90 to 2.1% in 2015–21. These patterns suggest that the country will probably benefit from the so-called 'demographic dividend', whereby an increasing share of the population is in the working-age group (aged 15–

64). Economists often cite a similar situation as one of the chief forces behind the rapid growth of the so-called 'miracle economies' of East Asia in the 1960s and 1970s, and some studies estimate that the demographic dividend has accounted for 40%–50% of India's per capita income growth since the 1970s.

However, a 'demographic dividend' does not automatically ensure higher economic growth rates. An acceleration in economic expansion will occur in Sierra Leone only if those entering the workforce have the appropriate education and training for the available jobs. The Government has acknowledged this problem and, in a significant step, initiated its Free Quality School Education (FQSE) programme in 2008. So far, the reforms under the FQSE programme are showing measurable results.

AGRICULTURE

Agriculture remains the dominant sector in Sierra Leone's economy, employing 54.5% of the labour force in 2019. Farmers in Sierra Leone cultivate about 70 different crops. However, most farmers are engaged in subsistence farming, producing food crops, such as the main staples—rice and cassava—and, to a lesser extent, sorghum and millet.

Cocoa and coffee are the principal cash crops and, together with a few other crops, such as palm kernels, groundnuts and piassava (a fibre crop), are primarily exported. Cocoa and cocoa preparations contributed 10.9% of export earnings in 2018.

The civil war devastated the sector. However, most refugees had returned to their land by 2003, and harvests consequently improved, although output growth has slowed in recent years. During 2002–14 the overall sector expanded at an average annual rate of 8.1%, and crop production increased by an average annual of 9.1%. Rice output was buoyant, growing at an average rate of 10.1%, and cassava averaged 10.5%, ground nuts 13.1%, maize 19.0% and sweet potatoes 16.2%. However, 2015–21 saw a marked drop in production, with growth in these segments declining to an average annual rate of 3.6% for crops, 4.2% for rice, 5.9% for cassava, 3.2% for ground nuts, 2.4% for maize and 3.7% for sweet potatoes.

The effects of the COVID-19 pandemic explain some of the recent slowdown in agricultural output. In an effort to contain the virus, the Government imposed lockdowns and curfews both at district level and nationwide, depending on the severity of the spread of local infections. The lack of government support for farmers during 2018 also dampened growth. However, in the longer term, the poor conditions for farming, including low levels of mechanization and training and poor access to fertilizers, enhanced seeds, credit and local markets, mean that productivity is low and that the country remains a net importer of staple foods. Furthermore, land degradation and deforestation have led to a decline in soil fertility, further affecting productivity for the worse.

In an effort to reverse these negative trends, the authorities have sought to boost commercial farming by attracting foreign investors, and several large investment deals involving palm oil, rubber, sugar cane and fruits have taken place in recent years.

The Bio Government has taken steps that have brought about a rise in agricultural output, including reaching self-sufficiency in rice production—a key policy aim. Rice production declined from 620,000 metric tons in 1978 to 503,700 tons in 1990 and to just 199,134 in 2000. Output then rose to reach a high of 1.3m. tons in 2013 and was recorded at more than 1m. tons in 2020. Rice imports accounted for 15.5% of the total cost of imports in 2018.

The country's food security was ranked 104th in the 2021 Corteva Agriscience/EIU Global Food Security Index. On the Index's three crucial dimensions, the country ranked 102nd for affordability, scoring 32.7% below the global average. Market access and agricultural financial services were of particular concern, where the country ranked about 50% below the global average. In terms of availability, the country ranked 108th, with its infrastructure 34.6% below the global average and access to policy commitments 43.8% below the global average. Finally, on the third measure (quality and safety) Sierra Lanka ranked 110th, with nutritional standards 35.6% below the global average and dietary diversity 31.9% below.

Following the onset of the COVID-19 pandemic, the International Monetary Fund (IMF) reported that the proportion of the food-insecure population in Sierra Leone had risen to 57% in 2020, some 10 percentage points higher than in 2010. In 2020 almost 4% of the population faced acute malnutrition.

The civil war severely affected the fisheries sector, but it recovered rapidly after peace returned, growing by an average annual of 9.5% in 2002–14. Although growth slowed to 1.6% in 2015–21, the sector still accounted for 14.9% of GDP in 2021 and employed about 500,000 people. Illegal and unregulated fishing by foreign vessels within Sierra Leone's coastal waters is a persistent problem. In April 2019 the Sierra Leonean authorities banned industrial fishing for one month, most of which is carried out by Asian-owned boats, in order to allow stocks of fish to be replenished amid widespread concerns about overfishing. Most official fishing is still artisanal and intended for the local market or neighbouring Guinea and Liberia. In May 2021 the Sierra Leonean Government and the People's Republic of China agreed to construct an industrial fishing harbour on 100 ha of beach and protected rainforest, prompting protests from conservationist campaign groups and affected landowners, who rejected a proposed compensation package of Le 13,760m. as inadequate.

The country's timber industry has grown steadily, averaging annual growth of 2.7% in 2002–14 and 2015–21. In 2021 the sector contributed 6.5% of the country's GDP. Sierra Leone's forested land has suffered significant losses in recent years, owing to widespread illegal logging. According to the World Bank, forests covered 35.1% of Sierra Leone's total land area in 2020, compared with 43% in 1990.

The Sierra Leonean authorities have issued temporary bans on the export of timber in order to curb the overuse of forest resources and in 2010 adopted guidelines on the forestry industry, which included requirements for the supervision of felling for logs. The uncontrolled illicit trade in timber with China has nonetheless continued. In April 2018 the new Government ordered the suspension of all timber exports, but in June President Bio announced the temporary lifting of the suspension, prompting renewed concerns about the impact of deforestation. A permanent ban would entail the loss of a significant source of government revenue. In 2018 wood and articles of wood provided 9.9% of Sierra Leone's officially recorded export earnings.

MINING

Mining sectors in developing economies are always volatile, subject to fluctuating global prices and frictions and disagreements between the government and local and foreign-based companies. Sierra Leone is no exception. Mining began in Sierra Leone in the 1930s. Mining operations generate the lion's share of Sierra Leone's foreign currency reserves, are a vital source of export revenue (usually over 80% of the country's export earnings) and create much-needed jobs. Like mining throughout Africa, growth is volatile, averaging 78.9% during 2002–14 but an average contraction of 2.6% in 2015–21. Mining and quarrying contributed 3.2% to GDP in 2021, with diamonds alone contributing 1.2% and iron ore 0.7%. Besides diamonds and iron ore, the country produces rutile and, to a lesser extent, ilmenite, bauxite, gold, zinc, tin and silver.

Sierra Leone has two major iron ore mines: Tonkolili and Marampa. In 2011 British firms African Minerals and London Mining invested in improving the mines' port, rail and road infrastructure. Iron ore production increased from. 1.3m. metric tons in 2011 to 6.7m. tons in 2012, 16.5m. tons in 2013 and to 21.4m. tons in 2014. However, in 2015, owing to rising international supplies and easing demand in China (the world's largest consumer of iron ore), production dropped by 88% to 2.6m. tons, after global prices for the commodity fell by some 50% during 2014. Eventually, with mining operations no longer profitable, production ceased at both Tonkolili, then owned by African Minerals, and Marampa, held by London Mining. By April 2015 both mines had new owners: Tonkolili was taken over by China's Shandong Iron and Steel Group (SISG), and Marampa was bought by Timis Mining Corporation (TMC), a British-based, privately held company.

The suspension of production at both mines caused a contraction of 20.5% in Sierra Leone's economy in 2015. Despite continuing low iron ore prices, SISG resumed operations at Tonkolili in February 2016. The mine can produce about 20m. metric tons per year, but output has remained well below that level, and the firm suspended operations again in November 2017 amid persistently low international iron ore prices and high operating costs.

Meanwhile, TMC failed to bring the Marampa mine back to production, and the British-based Gerald Group acquired the mining licence. Following a renovation, the mine entered production again in early 2019, and the first shipment of iron ore was made in June. However, in July the new Minister of Mines and Mineral Resources, Foday Rado Yokie, pledged to cancel all agreements that were not in the country's interest. In August the Government cancelled or suspended the licences for several large mining projects, including the Tonkolili and Marampa mines. SL Mining Ltd, a subsidiary of the Gerald Group, announced the suspension of operations in September.

The Sierra Leonean authorities claimed that the companies had failed to comply with the country's mining legislation and make royalty payments; however, in February 2020 the Government was ordered by the International Chamber of Commerce arbitration tribunal to rescind its decision to terminate SL Mining's licence and to lift any mineral export prohibition imposed on the company. President Bio replaced Yokie as Minister of Mines and Mineral Resources in July, after the latter was considered to have failed to improve the ministry's performance.

Iron ore output slumped to less than 1m. metric tons in 2020, following the suspension of operations at the Tonkolili and Marampa iron ore mines. Operations at Tonkolili resumed in March 2021, following its takeover by a Chinese-owned firm, Kingho Mining Company. After resolving a two-year royalty payment dispute, the Marampa mines resumed production in mid-2021. Output from Marampa will be boosted by signing a new 15-year large-scale mining licence with Marampa Mines, a West African subsidiary of the Gerald Group, with plans to ramp up production over 2022–23. The Marampa mine expansion project (commissioned in May 2022) seeks to boost annual output to at least 3.3m. tons by the end of 2022 and to some 7m. tons by 2023.

The diamond sector has been the most important source of export revenue for the past few decades. Production and exports fluctuate widely, but in 2020 output amounted to 641,469 carats, valued at US $119.4m.

Most diamond miners are artisanal, and the sector is a significant employer. During the civil war diamond smuggling escalated and the UN banned the export of diamonds to bring the problem under control. The embargo was lifted in 2003, when the country joined the Kimberley Process, an initiative to prevent the sale of 'blood diamonds' (proceeds from the sale of which are typically used to fund conflict and the purchase of armaments) on international markets. Nevertheless, diamond smuggling remains widespread, owing to the weak monitoring capacity of the Government and the small size of diamonds, which makes them easy to smuggle.

In 2020 Sierra Leone was the second-largest bauxite producer in sub-Saharan Africa, producing 1.3m. metric tons of bauxite, behind Guinea's 87.8m. tons and ahead of Ghana's 1.1m. tons. There are two main bauxite mining areas in Sierra Leone: Gondama, south-east of Freetown (the capital), and Port Loko, north-east of the capital.

Sierra Leone has one of the world's largest natural deposits of rutile, an essential ingredient of paint pigment. Before the disruption resulting from the civil conflict, Sierra Leone was, after Australia, the world's second largest producer of rutile, and the reserves at mines operated by Sierra Rutile, a subsidiary of Australian-based Iluka Resources, are reported to be the largest and highest-grade natural rutile resource in the world. In 2016 production capacity was about 175,000 metric tons per year, and rutile has in recent years become a significant source of export earnings. However, the owner of Sierra Rutile, Iluka Resources, notified the Government in May 2021 that it intended to suspend mining operations in six months, citing acute business challenges.

ENERGY

The lack of a reliable supply of electricity has been a significant constraint on growth in Sierra Leone. Even as late as 2020 a total of 68% of the population had no electric grid or connection, 22% had connections with the supply working most or all of the time, and only 11% had connections, but the supply worked only half the time. Most of those connected with a reliable supply are in Freetown. Many businesses and residences are therefore dependent on diesel generators for their electricity needs. In rural areas, connectivity to the grid is sporadic, and most of the population depends on biomass from fuelwood and charcoal to meet its energy needs.

The electricity sector grew at an average annual rate of 19.2% during 2002–14, dropping to 5.3% in 2015–21. In 2021 the industry accounted for just 0.1% of the country's GDP.

The total electricity generating capacity in Sierra Leone is just over 100 MW (compared with its pre-war level of some 120 MW), 86% of which is for Freetown. In addition, about 33,000 generators produce some 180 MW, and mining firms mostly have their own power sources. About one-half of the country's installed capacity is provided by the Bumbuna hydroelectric power station on the Seli river in Northern Province, which was finally completed in 2009, over 30 years after construction work began. It supplies 50 MW of power during the rainy season (supply falls below 15 MW during the dry season). However, weak maintenance and recurrent technical problems have meant that it has rarely operated at full capacity.

MANUFACTURING

Manufacturing has gradually declined in importance in Sierra Leone. The sector contracted at an average annual rate of 1.5% during the civil war (1991–2002). While the industry grew at an annual rate of 3.3% during the recovery period of 2003–14, expansion dropped to an average annual of just 2.2% between 2015 and 2021. In 2021 the sector accounted for 2.0% of GDP, down from 3.2% in 2000 and 4.3% in 1990. Supply-side constraints, such as poor infrastructure, weak access to credit and a lack of skilled labour (the adult literacy rate was just 43.2% in 2018), hinder the sector.

The Koroma Government aimed to make the business environment more attractive to investors. The Government's initial success appeared in the World Bank's annual Doing Business Index, in which the Bank ranked as one of the 12 leading reformers for 2012. Improvements in the ease of paying taxes, trading across borders and enforcing contracts moved Sierra Leone up to 137th place in the overall rankings of 185 countries in 2013; it ranked 160th five years earlier. The reform momentum has stalled since then, however, and Sierra Leone fell to 163rd out of 190 countries on the 2022 index.

A similar picture emerges from Sierra Leone's progress in improved economic freedom. The country's economic freedom improved steadily from 2003, when the Heritage House classified it as 'repressed', to 2013, when it entered the 'mostly unfree' group of countries. After falling back into the 'repressed' group in 2018, the country's ranking improved to the 'mostly unfree' group in 2020. Progress continued in 2021. Sierra Leone was 140th 'freest' country and ranked 30th among 47 sub-Saharan African countries. Its score is nonetheless below the regional and global averages.

Economic freedom has fluctuated over the past five years, and there have been falls in the scores for fiscal health and business freedom. These declines outpaced improvements in the rule of law. Business freedom began its decline from 'mostly unfree' in 2010 to 'repressed' in 2018. The descent continued in 2021, when the country received its lowest score for this measure. The country nonetheless scores highly in terms of trade freedom. Again, starting from 'repressed' in 2003, liberalization quickly brought the country into the 'moderately free' category in 2007. However, after improving to 'mostly free' in 2012, the country fell back to 'moderately free' in 2020.

Given the agriculture sector's central role in the economy, agro-processing is possibly the most promising sector to create jobs and build an industrial base. Foreign investment in the industry has risen over the past decade, and several large land-leasing deals with foreign investors have been undertaken.

The sector has significant potential, as some 75% of Sierra Leone's territory is arable, but only about 20% is cultivated.

TRANSPORT AND COMMUNICATIONS

Sierra Leone's state railway began operations in the late 1800s. The narrow-gauge line eventually had two branches: one from Freetown to Makeni in the north and one from Freetown to Daru in the east, but the last section of the network was closed in 1974. The prospect of iron ore production prompted the recent repair of the disused 74-km railway line from the port of Pepel to Lunsar. A further 126 km of a new line from Lunsar to the iron ore mine at Tonkolili is operational, and both are used exclusively for mining operations.

The country has 11,700 km of classified and unclassified roads, and road transport is the dominant mode of transport. However, only about 10% of the network is paved. Most roads between urban and rural areas, particularly productive agricultural regions, are unpaved and of poor quality, constituting a significant hindrance to boosting agricultural growth. It also renders regional trade difficult and costly. Rehabilitating Sierra Leone's road infrastructure is therefore a priority. Key road projects include reconstructing roads linking all major district towns and roads connecting to agricultural regions, as well as routes connecting Freetown and provincial capitals with neighbouring Guinea.

Freetown has one of Africa's largest natural harbours, but the port suffered damage during the civil war. In 2011 French company Bolloré won a tender to operate the container terminal in Freetown. Since then, it has invested about US $120m. in upgrading the terminal. This included a significant extension project, completed in August 2018, which has boosted the port's capacity to handle larger vessels. There is also a smaller port at Bonthe in the south, from where the country's bauxite and rutile exports are shipped. The country's third port, at Pepel, north-east of Freetown, was rehabilitated by African Minerals and is used to ship iron ore.

The services and facilities of the international airport at Lungi, north of Freetown, were improved once peace returned, but it remains relatively small. There are regular connections to a handful of European cities (Brussels, Paris and İstanbul) and several regional destinations. However, accessibility is a concern, as the mouth of the Rokel river separates it from Freetown, forcing passengers to take helicopters, ferries or small speedboats to reach the capital. China offered the Sierra Leonean Government a US $400m. loan in 2012 to finance the construction of a new international airport at Mamamah, nearer to Freetown, but the project was later put on hold, as the Government, in line with recommendations by the IMF, concluded that such a large loan would put the country at a high risk of debt distress.

The Koroma administration nevertheless considered the project to be a priority and signed a loan agreement with China shortly before the elections of March 2018. President Koroma lost the poll, and the new Government led by Bio later cancelled the project, choosing instead to focus on increasing the accessibility and utility of the Lungi airport. In June 2019 the Government opened a tender process for the construction of a 7-km bridge linking the airport with Freetown across the river, costing up to US $2,000m. However, the project was subsequently delayed amid the economic downturn in 2020 resulting from the COVID-19 pandemic. In December Parliament ratified the Lungi airport expansion project agreement between the Government and Russian-owned Summa Airports, which included the construction of a new passenger terminal. In May 2021 President Bio announced that construction work on the Lungi bridge would begin shortly after the projected cost had been reduced to $1,200m.

Sierra Leone's telecommunications market is still at a very early stage of development, and there is little publicly available data about its progress. From what is available, it is apparent that mobile penetration is relatively low, but subscriber numbers continue to grow. However, by mid-2022 the rollout of the 4G network appeared to be moving quickly.

Africell and Orange dominate the mobile telephone market in Sierra Leone. Wireline infrastructure is limited to major towns and cities, impeding the adoption of broadband. Several alternative licensees have failed to launch services. Returns on investment are slow to materialize, forcing some smaller operators to withdraw, and widespread poverty, unemployment and inequitable income distribution will continue to limit growth opportunities. Although 4G technology is being rolled out, operators are having difficulty weaning subscribers off low-cost voice and data packages.

TRADE

Sierra Leone's exports consist mainly of raw materials. In 2021 the country's major exports comprised mining products (80.5%) and food and agricultural products (15.4%). In that year the main food product was fish and shrimps (US $37m.), and cocoa and palm oil were also sizeable sources of revenue. The primary destinations for the country's exports in 2018 were the EU (29%), China (18.3%), Korea (14%), Somalia (10.8%) and Ghana (8%).

Sierra Leone's major imports in 2021 were agricultural products (26.0%), mineral fuels and lubricants, etc. (20.8%) and machinery and transport equipment (17.0%). In 2018 China supplied 20.1% of the country's imports, followed by the EU (18.5%), the United Arab Emirates (8.4%), India (7.2%), the USA (5.4%) and others (40.4%). In 2018 Sierra Leone imported US $153m. of rice, $21m. of wheat, $14m. of sugar and $13m of meat and poultry. The major non-agricultural imports in that year were motor cars ($45m.), followed by Portland cement ($41m.), structures of iron and steel ($25m.) and medicines ($21m.).

As with movements in GDP, Sierra Leone's exports and imports have varied considerably during the country's four recent stages of development. The significant difference was that the civil war period did not negatively affect exports or imports of goods and services. Exports of goods and services grew by an average annual rate of 5.4% during 1980–90, increasing to 8.7% in 1991–2002. During the 2003–14 period of post-war recovery and high commodity prices, exports averaged annual growth rates of 18.8%. However, as commodity prices declined and the EVD epidemic and COVID-19 pandemic took hold, export growth fell to an average annual rate of 1.0% in 2015–21. The pattern of imports differed somewhat, contracting by an average annual of 0.7% in 1980–90 but growing by 9.2% during the civil war years of 1991–2002. In the recovery phase in 2003–14 imports grew by an average annual of 17.0% but contracted by 3.7% per year in 2015–21.

These patterns of imports and exports produced chronic deficits in the country's current account. The deficit averaged 2.7% of GDP in 1980–90, increasing to 6.3% during the civil war and 16.5% in the period of recovery in 2003–14. More recently, in 2015–21, the current account recorded an average annual deficit of 13.7% of GDP. This widened to 20.0% in 2021, although the IMF predicted that this would narrow to 17.2% of GDP in 2022.

The country's current account deficits reflect a fundamental macroeconomic imbalance between savings and investment. Sierra Leone has one of the world's lowest savings rates. Countries in Sierra Leone's income range usually have savings of at least 15%–20% of GDP. Sierra Leone's averaged only about 1%–2% of GDP between 1980 and 2021. The average for sub-Saharan Africa during this period was 19.5% of GDP. Sierra Leone's stock of savings fell far short of the amount needed to finance the country's pattern of investment, which averaged 7.7% of GDP in 1980–90, 5.7% in 1991–2002, 16.6% in 2003–14 and 15.8% in 2015–21. While these investment rates were low by international standards, the inability to finance them out of domestic resources led to a large inflow of foreign capital, resulting in the extremely high current account deficits.

In part, the current account deficits after the civil war were financed by the inflow of foreign direct investment, which averaged 7.9% of GDP in 2002–14 and 6.7% in 2015–21. The other primary source of funding involved concessional loans from donors.

Besides being a member of the World Trade Organization, Sierra Leone belongs to several major trade bodies, including the Economic Community of West African States and the Mano River Union. The country also has a preferential trade agreement with the European Union (EU) under the Everything but Arms initiative (a scheme under which tariffs and quotas are removed for all imports of goods into the EU, except for arms and ammunition) and the USA's African Growth and Opportunity Act. The country is also a member of the African Continental Free Trade Area.

FISCAL POLICY

The civil war derailed Sierra Leone's attempts to maintain a prudent fiscal policy as public resources were redirected to the war effort, leading to the provision of public services collapsing. During this period (1991–2002), government revenue averaged 14.1% of GDP while government expenditure averaged 18.5%, producing an average annual deficit of 4.3% of GDP. Following the resumption of peace, the Government made progress in stabilizing its finances, helped by support from foreign donors, debt relief and the mining sector boom. In 2003–14 revenue increased to an average of 16.4% of GDP, while expenditure dropped to 17.8%, producing an average annual deficit of 1.4% of GDP, considerably below that during the civil war period.

However, following a drop in international commodity prices from 2014, the EVD epidemic and then the COVID-19 pandemic, in 2015–21 revenues averaged 17.1% of GDP, while expenditure increased to an average of 23.3%, producing an average deficit of 6.2% of GDP. As the budget deficit widened, the Government's stock of debt increased from 35.1% of GDP in 2014 to 60.7% in 2017, 72.5% in 2017 and to 76.2% in 2021.

The deterioration in the country's fiscal accounts after 2014 illustrated how vulnerable the country's public finances were to commodity price fluctuations and the demands arising from pandemics, placing an enormous strain on public expenditure. The deterioration in the public finances also underlined the detrimental impact of weak spending discipline and the failure to implement fiscal reforms.

The Government that took office in 2018 sought to improve the management of public finances and implemented measures on both the revenue and spending side. The most significant policy change was the removal of fuel subsidies in July of that year, necessitating a rise in the retail fuel price, to reflect prevailing market conditions. The IMF had repeatedly urged the Government to pass on the cost of global fuel prices to consumers in order to reduce the state's subsidy burden and allow for more targeted welfare provisions for the poorest segments of the population. The cost of subsidies and foregone revenues of the previous fuel pricing policy were equivalent to 2% of GDP.

The Bio administration also removed many tax and duty waivers, reviewed all tax concessions, fully operationalized the Treasury Single Account—which will help to improve oversight—and started collecting dividends from profitable state-owned enterprises, which have often operated in a non-transparent manner as near-independent entities. On the expenditure side, some capital spending projects were cancelled, and a wage reform plan was implemented, partly to reduce double payments in the wage bill.

PROSPECTS

In view of the country's high current level of debt and the slowing pace of economic reforms, Sierra Leone's growth will not recover to the post-war level of 2002–14 any time soon. Although there are encouraging signs, including rising iron ore export revenues, a series of harmful factors facing the economy might offset these. As the IMF summed up in an assessment in July 2022, 'The medium-term outlook remains challenging on account of the deteriorating terms of trade, more uncertain global prospects and remaining COVID-19 risks. A global supply shock resulting from the war in Ukraine is negatively impacting global growth and accentuating inflation, with spillovers to Sierra Leone. Further increases in already high global fuel and food prices could deteriorate budget and external balances, as well as development outcomes'.

Statistical Survey

Source (unless otherwise stated): Statistics Sierra Leone, PMB 595, Tower Hill, Freetown; tel. (22) 223287; e-mail statistics@statistics.sl; internet www.statistics.sl.

Area and Population

AREA, POPULATION AND DENSITY

Area (sq km)	71,740*
Population (census results)†	
5 December 2015	7,092,113
10 December 2021‡	
Males	3,716,263
Females	3,825,378
Total	7,541,641
Population (official projection at mid-year)§	
2022	8,494,260
Density (per sq km) at mid-2022	118.4

* 27,699 sq miles.
† Excluding adjustment for underenumeration.
‡ Provisional.
§ Projection not adjusted to take account of results of 2021 census.

POPULATION BY AGE AND SEX
('000, official projections at mid-2022)

	Males	Females	Total
0–14 years	1,731,132	1,785,757	3,516,889
15–64 years	2,316,913	2,390,015	4,706,928
65 years and over	133,122	137,321	270,443
Total	4,181,167	4,313,093	8,494,260

Note: Projections not adjusted to take account of results of 2021 census.

ADMINISTRATIVE DISTRICTS
(population at 2015 census)

	Population
Bo	575,478
Bombali	606,544
Bonthe	200,781
Kailahun	526,379
Kambia	345,474
Kenema	609,891
Koinadugu	409,372
Kono	506,100
Moyamba	318,588
Port Loko	615,376
Pujehun	346,461
Tonkolili	531,435
Western Area Rural District	444,270
Western Area Urban District	1,055,964
Total	7,092,113

PRINCIPAL TOWNS
(population at 2015 census)

Freetown (capital) .	1,055,964*	Koidu	128,030
Kenema	200,443	Makeni	125,970
Bo	174,369		

* Western Area Urban District.

BIRTHS AND DEATHS
(annual averages, UN estimates)

	2005–10	2010–15	2015–20
Birth rate (per 1,000)	40.7	36.6	33.7
Death rate (per 1,000)	17.1	13.7	11.9

Source: UN, *World Population Prospects: The 2019 Revision.*

Life expectancy (years at birth, estimates): 55.1 (males 54.2; females 55.9) in 2020 (Source: World Bank, World Development Indicators database).

EMPLOYMENT
(persons aged 10 years and over, 2015 census)

	Male	Female	Total
Agriculture, hunting and forestry .	775,216	856,274	1,631,490
Fishing	40,338	22,975	63,313
Mining and quarrying	63,583	18,669	82,252
Manufacturing	50,577	38,935	89,512
Electricity, gas and water supply .	21,989	6,084	28,073
Construction	49,929	4,128	54,057
Wholesale and retail trade; repair of motor vehicles, motorcycles, and personal and household goods	145,786	288,867	434,653
Hotels and restaurants . .	7,855	17,216	25,071
Transport, communications and storage	66,503	5,223	71,726
Financial intermediation . .	5,094	2,954	8,048
Real estate, renting and business activities	63,682	21,634	85,316
Public administration and defence; compulsory social security . .	27,677	8,364	36,041
Education	28,676	13,247	41,923
Health and social work . . .	11,861	14,984	26,845
Other community, social and personal service activities . .	27,703	19,270	46,973
Households with employed persons	10,802	18,538	29,340
Extraterritorial organizations and bodies	3,090	1,149	4,239
Total employed	**1,400,361**	**1,358,511**	**2,758,872**

Health and Welfare

KEY INDICATORS

Total fertility rate (children per woman, 2020)	4.1
Under-5 mortality rate (per 1,000 live births, 2020) . . .	107.8
HIV/AIDS (% of persons aged 15–49, 2020)	1.5
COVID-19: Cumulative confirmed deaths (per 100,000 persons at 31 August 2022)	1.5
COVID-19: Fully vaccinated population (% of total population at 28 August 2022)	26.0
Physicians (per 1,000 head, 2011)	0.03
Hospital beds (per 1,000 head, 2006)	0.4
Domestic health expenditure (2019): US $ per head (PPP) .	22.0
Domestic health expenditure (2019): % of GDP . . .	1.2
Domestic health expenditure (2019): public (% of total current expenditure)	14.0
Access to improved water resources (% of persons, 2020) .	64
Access to improved sanitation facilities (% of persons, 2020) .	17
Total carbon dioxide emissions ('000 metric tons, 2018) . .	1,020
Carbon dioxide emissions per head (metric tons, 2018) . .	0.1
Human Development Index (2021): ranking	181
Human Development Index (2021): value	0.477

Note: For data on COVID-19 vaccinations, 'fully vaccinated' denotes receipt of all doses specified by approved vaccination regime (Sources: Johns Hopkins University and Our World in Data). Data on health expenditure refer to current general government expenditure in each case. For more information on sources and further definitions for all indicators, see Health and Welfare Statistics: Sources and Definitions section (europaworld.com/credits).

Agriculture

PRINCIPAL CROPS
('000 metric tons)

	2018	2019	2020
Cassava (Manioc)	2,145.8	881.2	1,690.2
Cocoa beans	50.2	14.6	193.2
Coffee, green*	2.7	2.4	2.4
Groundnuts, with shell . . .	20.6	106.4	58.8
Kola nuts†	8.1	8.1	8.1
Maize	23.0	38.7	26.5
Mangoes, mangosteens, guavas† .	24.0	24.4	24.8
Millet*	38.0	38.0	32.0
Oil palm fruit†	315.7	272.9	272.4
Plantains and others†	44.8	45.0	45.0
Rice, paddy	918.7	947.5	1,049.8
Sorghum*	49.0	50.0	52.0
Sugar cane†	79.6	80.2	80.8
Sweet potatoes	157.0	178.8	195.0
Tomatoes†	19.6	19.9	19.7

* Unofficial figures.
† FAO estimates.

Aggregate production ('000 metric tons, may include official, semi-official or estimated data): Total cereals 1,038.7 in 2018, 1,084.1 in 2019, 1,170.3 in 2020; Total fruit (primary) 269.1 in 2018, 270.1 in 2019, 269.7 in 2020; Total oilcrops 344.0 in 2018, 386.9 in 2019, 338.9 in 2020; Total pulses 84.1 in 2018, 81.8 in 2019, 82.3 in 2020; Total roots and tubers 2,305.8 in 2018, 1,063.0 in 2019, 1,888.2 in 2020; Total vegetables (primary) 388.5 in 2018, 377.7 in 2019, 468.5 in 2020.

Source: FAO.

LIVESTOCK
('000 head, year ending September)

	2018	2019	2020*
Cattle	564.9	583.6	598.4
Chickens	22,599	23,729	25,032
Ducks	1,048	1,050	1,066
Goats	759.0*	815.7*	773.5
Horses	445.8*	448.9*	446.0
Pigs	233.8	251.3	268.7
Rabbits and hares	1,566*	1,571*	1,575
Sheep	927.6	981.0*	974.7

* FAO estimate(s).

Source: FAO.

LIVESTOCK PRODUCTS
('000 metric tons, FAO estimates)

	2018	2019	2020
Cattle hides, fresh	2.1	2.2	2.1
Cattle meat	9.7	10.1	9.4
Edible offals of cattle	2.9	3.0	2.8
Cows' milk	143.6	147.5	150.6
Chicken meat	15.6	18.2	19.9
Game meat	3.3	3.3	3.3
Rabbit meat	7.8	7.9	7.9
Hen eggs	11.5	11.6	11.6

Source: FAO.

Forestry

ROUNDWOOD REMOVALS
('000 cubic metres, excl. bark, FAO estimates)

	2018	2019	2020
Sawlogs, veneer logs and logs for sleepers	200.0	210.0	210.0
Other industrial wood* . . .	120.0	120.0	120.0
Fuel wood	5,926.6	5,974.4	6,024.8
Total	6,246.6	6,304.4	6,354.8

* Annual output assumed to be unchanged since 1980.

Source: FAO.

SAWNWOOD PRODUCTION
('000 cubic metres, incl. railway sleepers, FAO estimates)

	2016	2017	2018
Total (all broadleaved) . . .	20.0	30.0	30.0

2019–20: Figure assumed to be unchanged from 2018.

Source: FAO.

Fishing

('000 metric tons, live weight of capture, FAO estimates)

	2018	2019*	2020*
Marine fishes	11.3	11.3	11.5
West African ilisha	7.6	7.6	7.6
Bobo croaker	11.6	11.6	11.6
Sardinellas	26.0	26.0	26.0
Bonga shad	84.2	84.2	84.2
Total catch (incl. others) . .	202.2	202.2	200.7

* FAO estimates.

Source: FAO.

Mining

(metric tons unless otherwise indicated)

	2019	2020	2021
Cement (hydraulic)	346,190	349,010	340,940
Bauxite ('000 metric tons) . . .	1,963	1,442	1,456
Diamonds ('000 carats) . . .	812	686	829
Ilmenite	63,350	50,963	53,802
Rutile	136,190	166,569	131,311

Source: Bank of Sierra Leone, Freetown.

Industry

PETROLEUM PRODUCTS
('000 metric tons, estimates)

	2006	2007	2008
Jet fuels	22	22	22
Motor spirit (petrol)	33	33	33
Kerosene	11	11	12
Distillate fuel oils	60	60	60
Residual fuel oils	40	40	40

Source: UN Industrial Commodity Statistics Database.

SELECTED OTHER PRODUCTS
('000 metric tons unless otherwise indicated)

	2019	2020	2021
Beer, stout and malt drinks ('000 crates)	1,921.5	768.8	1,472.7
Confectionery ('000 kg) . . .	2,470.7	3,425.9	3,553.5
Soap (metric tons)	610.4	578.7	553.8
Paint ('000 litres)	730.5	735.0	690.0
Electrical energy (million kWh) .	260	n.a.	n.a.

Soft drinks ('000 crates): 1,085.9 in 2018.

Sources: Bank of Sierra Leone, Freetown; UN Energy Statistics Database.

Finance

CURRENCY AND EXCHANGE RATES

Monetary Units
    100 cents = 1 leone (Le).

Sterling, Dollar and Euro Equivalents (29 April 2022)
    £1 sterling = 15,832.83 leones;
    US $1 = 12,596.23 leones;
    €1 = 13,276.43 leones;
    10,000 leones = £0.63 = $0.79 = €0.75.

Average Exchange Rate (leones per US $)
    2019   9,010.22
    2020   9,829.93
    2021   10,439.43

CENTRAL GOVERNMENT BUDGET
(Le '000 million)

Revenue*	2020	2021†	2022‡
Tax revenue	5,388.1	6,588.4	7,356.2
Personal income tax . . .	1,665.3	1,752.0	1,904.0
Corporate income tax . . .	334.5	667.0	805.0
Goods and services tax . . .	1,033.4	1,262.8	1,464.0
Royalties and licences . . .	1,132.5	1,468.6	1,446.1
Mining	254.1	499.2	316.0
Import duties	643.2	853.1	950.1
Excise duties	514.3	520.1	706.0
Other excise duties . . .	64.9	64.8	80.9
Non-tax revenue	118.5	226.0	286.3
Total	5,506.7	6,814.5	7,642.5

Expenditure	2020	2021†	2022‡
Current expenditure	7,066.9	7,754.8	8,170.4
Wages and salaries . . .	3,263.5	3,756.8	3,898.0
Goods and services . . .	1,423.4	1,358.2	1,317.0
Transfer payments . . .	102.3	101.9	115.7
Interest	1,208.9	1,256.5	1,439.0
Domestic	1,088.5	1,129.9	1,402.0
Foreign	120.4	178.7	161.9
Grants to educational institutions	44.7	69.4	80.9
Other current expenditure . .	1,024.0	1,212.0	1,319.8
Capital expenditure	3,026.1	3,040.4	3,642.3
Total	10,093.1	10,795.2	11,812.6

* Excluding grants received (Le '000 million): 2,306.9 in 2020; 2,378.8 in 2021 (estimate); 2,300.5 in 2022 (budget figure).

† Estimates.

‡ Budget figures.

Source: Ministry of Finance and Economic Development, Freetown.

INTERNATIONAL RESERVES
(US $ million at 31 December)

	2019	2020	2021
IMF special drawing rights . .	145.2	224.7	496.6
Foreign exchange	384.9	483.0	449.3
Total	530.1	707.7	945.9

Source: IMF, *International Financial Statistics.*

MONEY SUPPLY
(Le million at 31 December)

	2019	2020	2021
Currency outside depository corporations	2,039,904	2,806,994	3,479,761
Transferable deposits . . .	4,000,432	5,734,179	7,439,786
Other deposits	2,492,685	3,249,750	3,471,512
Broad money	8,533,021	11,790,923	14,391,059

Source: IMF, *International Financial Statistics.*

COST OF LIVING
(Consumer Price Index; base: December 2021 = 100)

	2019	2020	2021
Food and non-alcoholic beverages .	72.3	82.3	96.3
Clothing and footwear	78.3	87.7	94.4
Housing, electricity, water, gas and other fuels	82.2	85.2	92.4
All items (incl. others) . . .	73.6	83.5	93.5

NATIONAL ACCOUNTS
(Le '000 million at current prices)

Expenditure on the Gross Domestic Product

	2019	2020	2021
Government final consumption expenditure	3,147	3,231	3,249
Private final consumption expenditure	36,216	40,411	47,040
Gross fixed capital formation . .	4,439	4,662	4,776
Changes in inventories . . .	164	171	177
Total domestic expenditure .	43,966	48,475	55,242
Exports of goods and services . .	6,702	6,027	7,509
Less Imports of goods and services	13,937	14,564	18,393
GDP in purchasers' values .	36,731	39,938	44,359
GDP at constant 2006 prices .	10,209	10,008	10,418

Gross Domestic Product by Economic Activity

	2019	2020	2021
Agriculture, hunting, forestry and fishing	21,361	23,758	25,484
Mining and quarrying	967	912	1,347
Manufacturing	717	753	833
Electricity, gas and water . . .	80	101	112
Construction	276	329	340
Wholesale and retail trade, restaurants and hotels . . .	3,215	2,309	2,601
Finance, insurance, real estate and business services	1,546	1,598	1,746
Transport and communications .	1,163	1,208	1,266
Public administration and defence	2,901	3,696	4,468
Education	890	905	938
Health and social work . . .	862	1,112	1,654
Other services	1,473	1,547	1,665
Sub-total	34,451	38,228	42,454
Less Imputed bank service charges	533	554	589
Indirect taxes, less subsidies . .	1,815	2,266	2,493
GDP in purchasers' values .	36,731	39,938	44,359

Note: Totals may not be equal to the sum of components, owing to rounding.

BALANCE OF PAYMENTS
(US $ million)

	2018	2019	2020
Exports of goods	884.8	985.4	648.0
Imports of goods	−1,209.8	−1,388.0	−1,221.0
Balance on goods	−325.0	−402.7	−573.0
Exports of services	79.2	74.6	53.0
Imports of services	−384.0	−430.0	−196.8
Balance on goods and services	−629.8	−758.0	−716.8
Primary income received . . .	18.5	19.8	15.2
Primary income paid	−87.3	−89.6	−41.8
Balance on goods, services and primary income . . .	−698.6	−827.8	−743.4
Secondary income received . .	200.8	249.1	476.2
Secondary income paid . . .	−7.1	−4.8	−8.4
Current balance	−504.9	−583.6	−275.6
Capital account (net) . . .	66.3	81.5	94.1
Direct investment (net) . . .	250.4	301.5	135.1
Other investment assets . . .	11.3	4.8	−51.6
Other investment liabilities . .	18.1	168.9	115.1
Net errors and omissions . .	144.6	54.8	11.3
Reserves and related items .	−14.2	27.9	28.4

Source: IMF, *International Financial Statistics.*

External Trade

PRINCIPAL COMMODITIES
(US $ '000)

Imports c.i.f.	2019	2020	2021
Animal and vegetable oils . . .	7,504	7,900	4,800
Food products	288,290	452,030	469,431
Rice	143,824	198,805	169,484
Beverages and tobacco	20,158	20,667	23,480
Crude materials, inedible (excl. fuels)	54,121	19,646	24,785
Mineral fuels, lubricants, etc. .	232,070	291,863	375,364
Fuels	209,621	204,479	283,768
Chemical products	119,759	115,370	206,279
Basic manufactures	229,549	162,440	190,344
Machinery and transport equipment	355,886	1,001,509	305,845
Miscellaneous manufactured articles	186,072	66,399	170,502
Other transactions and commodities	9,083	8,055	32,324
Total (incl. others)	1,502,492	2,145,878	1,803,153

Exports f.o.b.*	2019	2020	2021
Food and agricultural products .	83,376	77,958	107,457
Fish and shrimps	5,419	9,395	36,725
Minerals	399,813	312,159	560,760
Bauxite	63,738	43,778	47,614
Diamonds	167,646	119,452	160,819
Gem	162,597	117,347	151,657
Industrial	5,048	2,106	9,428
Gold	2,611	4,342	7,236
Total (incl. others)	634,928	422,994	697,023

* Including re-exports (US $ '000): 26,272 in 2019; 8,536 in 2020; 11,287 in 2021.

Source: Bank of Sierra Leone, Freetown.

PRINCIPAL TRADING PARTNERS
(US $'000)

Imports c.i.f.	2016	2017	2018
Belgium	58,262	69,103	74,612
Brazil	13,898	42,940	24,959
China, People's Republic	136,119	180,927	198,332
Denmark	25,774	13,474	11,217
Eswatini	645	1,001	11,124
France	23,025	36,317	16,944
Germany	17,868	21,665	13,946
Guinea	6,899	18,706	29,693
Hong Kong	26,696	26,854	21,152
India	82,714	83,757	71,209
Indonesia	5,660	12,343	6,421
Lebanon	11,443	20,946	8,527
Netherlands	38,754	40,862	28,476
Pakistan	41,331	50,489	36,531
South Africa	22,311	38,868	45,840
Spain	15,511	13,826	17,980
Thailand	12,321	14,902	10,082
Türkiye	60,804	77,254	51,084
United Arab Emirates	75,452	56,626	82,729
United Kingdom	49,658	32,720	33,058
USA	100,611	51,561	53,214
Uruguay	22,853	19,760	10,357
Viet Nam	12,169	11,047	9,974
Total (incl. others)	1,057,017	1,088,995	988,787

Exports f.o.b.	2016	2017	2018
Belgium	97,056	5,939	3,767
Benin	24	1,271	3,210
China, People's Republic	36,487	13,686	37,411
Côte d'Ivoire	171,402	15,657	3,920
Germany	2,348	312	10,839
Ghana	2,740	12,878	16,486
Guinea	1,424	11,137	9,217
India	2,361	2,211	3,299
Korea, Republic	2,867	2,403	28,623
Lebanon	53	5,582	199
Liberia	791	1,994	2,301
Netherlands	26,556	23,480	27,774
Romania	—	—	15,926
Senegal	491	856	6,128
Somalia	—	—	22,146
Switzerland	214	2,189	453
United Kingdom	4,046	8,518	1,885
USA	274,898	52,215	953
Total (incl. others)	630,094	167,880	204,991

Source: Trade Map—Trade Competitiveness Map, International Trade Centre, www.intracen.org/marketanalysis.

Transport

ROAD TRAFFIC
(new vehicle registrations)

	2011	2012	2013
Passenger cars	2,981	2,803	3,858
Buses and coaches	3,049	3,148	3,651
Vans and lorries	8,038	7,893	10,691
Motorcycles and mopeds	12,430	16,354	17,844

SHIPPING

Flag Registered Fleet
(at 31 December)

	2019	2020	2021
Number of vessels	684	697	686
Total displacement ('000 grt)	1,823.1	2,142.2	2,057.0

Source: Lloyd's List Intelligence (www.bit.ly/LLintelligence).

CIVIL AVIATION
(traffic on scheduled services)

	2007	2008	2009
Kilometres flown (million)	2	2	2
Passengers carried ('000)	20	21	22
Passenger-km (million)	108	110	107
Total ton-km (million)	19	19	18

Source: UN, *Statistical Yearbook*.

Passengers carried: 23,597 in 2010; 48,789 in 2011; 50,193 in 2012 (Source: World Bank, World Development Indicators database).

Tourism

TOURIST ARRIVALS BY COUNTRY OF RESIDENCE

	2018	2019	2020
Australia	1,896	2,244	660
Austria	1,754	84	56
Belgium	1,865	546	236
Canada	2,614	2,657	502
China, People's Republic	2,014	2,618	419
France	1,246	1,128	927
Germany	2,258	1,666	873
Ghana	2,457	1,694	963
India	1,110	3,646	969
Kenya	641	1,159	271
Lebanon	772	1,563	789
Morocco	1,204	92	36
Netherlands	1,357	1,498	1,184
Nigeria	3,114	2,398	2,195
South Africa	2,014	1,665	657
United Kingdom	2,101	8,921	2,924
USA	11,254	11,793	4,106
Total (incl. others)	56,500	63,090	24,456

Tourism receipts (US $ million, excl. passenger transport): 83 in 2017; 39 in 2018; n.a. in 2019.

Source: World Tourism Organization.

Communications Media

	2018	2019	2020
Telephones ('000 main lines in use)	4.4	0.5	0.2
Mobile telephone subscriptions ('000)	6,355.2	6,729.8	6,884.2
Broadband subscriptions, mobile ('000)	948.0	1,152.1	1,585.9
Internet users (% of population)	15.8	16.8	18.0

Source: International Telecommunication Union.

Education

(2018/19 unless otherwise indicated)

	Schools*	Teachers	Number of pupils		
			Males	Females	Total
Pre-primary	n.a.	5,957	65,756	72,414	138,170
Primary	2,704	46,677	866,227	893,546	1,759,773
Secondary	246	30,355†	250,581‡	241,559‡	492,140‡
Tertiary*	n.a.	1,198	6,439	2,602	9,041

* 2001/02.
† 2018/19.
‡ 2016/17.

Source: mainly UNESCO Institute for Statistics.

Pupil-teacher ratio (qualified teaching staff, primary education, UNESCO estimate): 58.3 in 2018/19 (Source: UNESCO Institute for Statistics).

Adult literacy rate (UNESCO estimates): 43.2% (males 51.6%; females 34.9%) in 2018 (Source: UNESCO Institute for Statistics).

Directory

The Constitution

Following the transfer of power to a democratically elected civilian administration on 29 March 1996, the Constitution of 1991 (which had been suspended since April 1992) was reinstated. The Constitution vests executive power in the President, who must be elected by the majority of votes cast nationally and by at least 25% of the votes cast in each of the four provinces. The maximum duration of the President's tenure of office is limited to two five-year terms. The President appoints the Cabinet, subject to approval by the Parliament. The Parliament is elected for a five-year term and comprises 146 members, 132 of whom are directly elected, while 14 Paramount Chiefs also represent the 14 provincial districts in the legislature. Members of the Parliament are not permitted concurrently to hold office in the Cabinet.

The Government

HEAD OF STATE

President and Commander-in-Chief of the Armed Forces: Brig. (retd) JULIUS MAADA BIO (inaugurated 4 April 2018).
Vice-President: Dr MOHAMED JULDEH JALLOH.

CABINET
(October 2022)

President: Brig. (retd) JULIUS MAADA BIO.
Vice-President: Dr MOHAMED JULDEH JALLOH.
Chief Minister and Minister of Finance: JACOB JUSU SAFFA.
Minister of Foreign Affairs and International Co-operation: Prof. DAVID J. FRANCIS.
Minister of Justice and Attorney-General: MOHAMED LAMIN TARAWALLEY.
Minister of Basic and Senior Secondary Education: Dr DAVID MOININA SENGEH.
Minister of Health and Sanitation: Dr AUSTIN DEMBY.
Minister of Internal Affairs: Dr DAVID MAURICE PANDA-NOAH.
Minister of Defence: Brig. (retd) KELLIE CONTEH.
Minister of Transport and Aviation: KABINEH M. KALLON.
Minister of Lands, Housing and Country Planning: Dr TURAD SENESIE.
Minister of Youth Affairs: MOHAMED BANGURA.
Minister of Agriculture, Forestry and Food Security: ABU BAKARR KARIM.
Minister of Political and Public Affairs: FODAY YUMKELLA.
Minister of the Environment: Prof. FODAY JAWARD.
Minister of Trade and Industry: Dr EDWARD HINGA SANDY.
Minister of Energy: Alhaji KANJA SESAY.
Minister of Information and Communications: MOHAMED SWARAY.
Minister of Marine Resources: EMMA KOWA-JALLOH.
Minister of Labour and Social Security: Alhaji ALPHA OSMAN TIMBO.
Minister of Water Resources: PHILIP KARIMU LANSANA.
Minister of Social Welfare: BAINDU DASSAMA.
Ministers of Gender and Children's Affairs: MANTI TARAWALLY.
Minister of Planning and Economic Development: Dr FRANCIS MUSTAPHA KAIKAI.
Minister of Technical and Higher Education: Prof. ALPHA TEJAN WURIE.
Minister of Works and Public Assets: PETER BAYUKU CONTEH.
Minister of Mines and Mineral Resources: MUSA TIMOTHY KABBA.
Minister of Local Government and Rural Development: TAMBA LAMINA.
Minister of Tourism and Culture: MEMUNATU B. PRATT.
Resident Minister, Southern Region: MOHAMED K. ALIE.
Resident Minister, Eastern Region: Brig.-Gen. (retd) K. E. S. BOYAH.
Resident Minister, Northern Region: ABU ABU KOROMA.
Resident Minister, Northwestern Region: Dr ALHAJI ALPHA BAKARR KANU.

Minister of State in the Vice-President's Office: FRANCESS PIAGIE ALGHALI.
In addition, there were 29 deputy ministers.

MINISTRIES

Office of the President: State Ave, Freetown; tel. 76277001; e-mail info@statehouse.gov.sl; internet www.statehouse.gov.sl.

Ministry of Agriculture, Forestry and Food Security: Youyi Bldg, 3rd Floor, Brookfields, Freetown; tel. 76601492; e-mail info@maf.gov.sl; internet www.maf.gov.sl.

Ministry of Basic and Senior Secondary Education: New England, Freetown; tel. 76604105; e-mail info@mbbse.gov.sl; internet www.education.gov.sl.

Ministry of Defence: Independence Ave, Tower Hill, Freetown; tel. 78750557; e-mail jas538@hotmail.com; internet fb.com/MinistryofDefenceSierraLeone.

Ministry of Energy: Stronge Tower, 3 and 3A Pademba Rd, Freetown; tel. 79328817; e-mail info@energy.gov.sl; internet www.energy.gov.sl.

Ministry of the Environment: Freetown.

Ministry of Finance: George St, Freetown; e-mail info@mof.gov.sl; internet mof.gov.sl.

Ministry of Foreign Affairs and International Co-operation: OAU Dr., Tower Hill, Freetown; tel. 75137028; e-mail info@mofaic.gov.sl; internet mofaic.gov.sl.

Ministry of Gender and Children's Affairs: Freetown.

Ministry of Health and Sanitation: Youyi Bldg, 4th and 5th Floors, Brookfields, Freetown; tel. 76460440; e-mail info@mohs.gov.sl; internet mohs.gov.sl.

Ministry of Information and Communications: Youyill Bldg, 8th Floor, Brookfields, Freetown; tel. 76613504; e-mail info@mic.gov.sl; internet mic.gov.sl.

Ministry of Internal Affairs: Liverpool St, Freetown; tel. (22) 226979.

Ministry of Justice: Guma Bldg, Lamina Sankoh St, Freetown.

Ministry of Labour and Social Security: New England Ville, Freetown; tel. 76709409.

Ministry of Lands, Housing and Country Planning: Youyi Bldg, 3rd Floor, Brookfields, Freetown; tel. 99605968; e-mail info@molhcp.gov.sl; internet molhcp.gov.sl.

Ministry of Local Government and Rural Development: Youyill Bldg, 6th Floor, Brookfields, Freetown; tel. (22) 226589; internet mlgrd.gov.sl.

Ministry of Marine Resources: Youyi Bldg, 7th Floor, Brookfields, Freetown; tel. (22) 242117; e-mail info@mfmr.gov.sl; internet www.mfmr.gov.sl.

Ministry of Mines and Mineral Resources: Youyi Bldg, 5th Floor, Brookfields, Freetown; tel. (22) 240467; internet slminerals.org.

Ministry of Planning and Economic Development: NAO Bldg, OAU Ave, Tower Hill, Freetown; tel. 76620679; e-mail info@moped.gov.sl.

Ministry of Political and Public Affairs: Youyi Bldg, 9th Floor, Freetown; e-mail info@moppa.gov.sl; internet moppa.gov.sl.

Ministry of Social Welfare: New England, Freetown; tel. 76268318; e-mail info@mswgca.gov.sl; internet mswgca.gov.sl.

Ministry of Technical and Higher Education: New England, Freetown; tel. 74210044; e-mail info@mthe.gov.sl; internet www.mthe.gov.sl.

Ministry of Tourism and Culture: 28B Kingharman Rd, Freetown; tel. 76704716; e-mail info@tourism.gov.sl; internet tourism.gov.sl.

Ministry of Trade and Industry: Youyi Bldg, 6th Floor, Brookfields, Freetown; tel. (22) 225127; internet trade.gov.sl.

Ministry of Transport and Aviation: Youyi Bldg, 7th Floor, George St, Freetown; tel. 30836464; e-mail info@mta.gov.sl; internet mota.gov.sl.

Ministry of Water Resources: 127 Kuku Dr., off Jomo Kenyatta Rd, Brookfields, Freetown; e-mail info@mwr.gov.sl; internet mwr.gov.sl.

Ministry of Works and Public Assets: New England, Freetown; tel. (22) 240937; internet fb.com/ministryofworksandpublicassetsSL.

Ministry of Youth Affairs: New England, Freetown; tel. 76617548; e-mail info@youthaffairs.gov.sl; internet youthaffairs.gov.sl.

President

Presidential Election, First Round, 7 March 2018

Candidate	Valid votes	% of valid votes
Julius Maada Bio (SLPP)	1,097,482	43.26
Samura Matthew Wilson Kamara (APC)	1,082,748	42.68
Kandeh Kolleh Yumkella (NGC) . . .	174,014	6.86
Samuel Sam-Sumana (C4C) . . .	87,720	3.45
Mohamed Kamarainba Mansaray (ADP) .	26,704	1.05
Others*	68,454	2.70
Total	**2,537,122†**	**100.00**

* There were 11 other candidates.
† Excluding 139,427 invalid votes.

Presidential Election, Second Round, 31 March 2018

Candidate	Valid votes	% of valid votes
Julius Maada Bio (SLPP)	1,319,406	51.81
Samura Matthew Wilson Kamara (APC)	1,227,171	48.19
Total	**2,546,577***	**100.00**

* Excluding 31,694 invalid votes.

Legislature

Parliament: OAU Dr., Tower Hill, Freetown; tel. 76256153; e-mail info@parliament.gov.sl; internet www.parliament.gov.sl.

Speaker: Dr ABASS CHERNOH BUNDU.

General Election, 7 March 2018

Party	Seats
All-People's Congress (APC)	68
Sierra Leone People's Party (SLPP)	49
Coalition for Change (C4C)	8
National Grand Coalition (NGC)	4
Independents	3
Total	**132***

* A further 14 seats were allocated to Paramount Chiefs, who represented the 14 provincial districts.

Election Commission

National Electoral Commission (NEC): OAU Dr., Tower Hill, Freetown; tel. 76647569; e-mail infor@necsl.org; internet necsl.org; f. 1991; Chair. MOHAMED KENEWUI KONNEH.

Political Organizations

In 2022 a total of 17 political parties were registered with the National Electoral Commission.

All-People's Congress (APC): 11 Old Railway Line, Brookfields, Freetown; tel. 76621919; internet fb.com/APC-All-Peoples-Congress-122456425777; f. 1960; sole authorized political party 1978–91; merged with the Democratic People's Party in 1992; reconstituted in 1995; Leader ERNEST BAI KOROMA; Sec.-Gen. OSMAN FODAY YANSANEH.

Alliance Democratic Party (ADP): 13 Rawdon St, Freetown; tel. 78747042; Chair. MOHAMED KAMARAINBA MANSARAY; Gen. Sec. ISATA ABDULAI KAMARA.

Citizens' Democratic Party (CDP): 55 Bye Pass Rd, Kissy, Freetown; tel. 78195663; f. 2012; Chair. GIBRIL THULLA; Gen. Sec. VICTOR KING.

Coalition for Change (C4C): 16 Main Motor Rd, Congo Town, Freetown; tel. 78376389; internet c4csalone.com; f. 2017; Chair. TAMBA R. SANDY; Sec.-Gen. ALOYSIOUS KOIGHOR FOH.

National Democratic Alliance (NDA): 15 Mountain Cut, Freetown; tel. 76637448; Chair. AUGUSTA JAMES-TEIMA; Gen. Sec. ABDULAIE BARRIE.

National Grand Coalition (NGC): 20 Nelson Lane, Freetown; tel. 30748961; internet fb.com/pg/National-Grand-Coalition-Sierra-Leone-2259802100731944; f. 2017; Chair. Dr DENIS BRIGHT; Sec.-Gen. FRANCIS HINDOWA.

National Progressive Democrats (NPD): 156 Bai BurehRd, Freetown; tel. 79725728; e-mail NPDMembershipDirector@gmail.com; internet npdsl.org; f. 2017; Chair. WADI WILLIAMS; Gen. Sec. SUSAN WILLIAMS.

Peace and Liberation Party (PLP): Freetown Central Lorry Park, Texaco, Kissy, Freetown; tel. 88909280; f. 2002; Leader Dr KANDEH BARBA CONTEH; Gen. Sec. THERESA FAYE.

People's Democratic Party (PDP): 7 Tejan Lane, Freetown; tel. 78345022; Chair. Dr PRINCE COKER; Gen. Sec. Alhaji BEN KAMARA.

People's Movement for Democratic Change (PMDC): 12 Prince St, off Circular Rd, Freetown; tel. 78501066; e-mail karamohslylhorg@aol.com; internet www.pmdcsl.net; f. April 2006 by fmr mems of Sierra Leone People's Party; Leader CHARLES F. MARGAI; Nat. Sec. Dr HABIB SESAY.

Revolutionary United Front Party (RUFP): 22 Antana St, Wellington, Freetown; tel. 76406283; Chair. KELFALA KOSIA; Gen. Sec. RAMOND KARTEWU.

Sierra Leone People's Party (SLPP): 15 Wallace Johnson St, Freetown; tel. 76661194; e-mail info@slpp.ws; internet slpp.sl; f. 1951; Chair. Dr PRINCE HARDING; Gen. Sec. UMARU NAPOLEON KOROMA.

United Democratic Movement (UDM): 112 Pademba Rd, Freetown; tel. 79492292; Chair. MOHAMED SOWA; Gen. Sec. ARNOLD BENDU.

United National People's Party (UNPP): 54 City Rd, Wellington, Freetown; tel. 76362962; Nat. Leader GABRIEL SAMUKA; Nat. Sec.-Gen. OSMAN KOROMA.

Diplomatic Representation

EMBASSIES AND HIGH COMMISSIONS IN SIERRA LEONE

Brazil: 58E Sir Samuel Lewis Rd, Aberdeen, Freetown; tel. 79626477; e-mail brasemb.freetown@itamaraty.gov.br; internet fb.com/BrazilFreetown; Chargé d'affaires a.i. KAISER PIMENTEL DE ARAÚJO.

China, People's Republic: 29 Wilberforce Loop, POB 778, Freetown; tel. (22) 231571; e-mail chinaemb_sl@mfa.gov.cn; internet sl.china-embassy.gov.cn; Ambassador (vacant).

Egypt: 174C Wilkinson Rd, POB 652, Freetown; tel. (22) 231245; internet www.mfa.gov.eg/english/embassies/egyptian_embassy_sierraleone; Ambassador SADIQ SILLA.

The Gambia: 6 Wilberforce St, Freetown; tel. (22) 225191; High Commissioner ALIEU K. JAMMEH.

Germany: 3 Middle Hill Station, POB 728, Freetown; tel. 78732120; internet freetown.diplo.de; Ambassador HORST GRUNER.

Ghana: 43 Spur Rd, Freetown; tel. 76100502; e-mail ghahicom@yahoo.com; internet ghanahighcommissionfreetown.sl; High Commissioner WORWORNYO AGYEMAN (designate).

Guinea: 111 Jomo Kenyatta Rd, New England Ville, Freetown; tel. 077834154; e-mail ambaguifreetown@mae.gov.gn; Ambassador TIDIANE CONDÉ.

India: 32B Wilkinson Rd, Freetown; tel. 73000000; e-mail ga.freetown@mea.gov.in; internet www.hcifreetown.gov.in; High Commissioner (vacant).

Iran: Freetown; Ambassador AKBAR KOSHRAWI NEJZHAD.

Ireland: 8 St Joseph's Ave, off Spur Rd, Freetown; tel. 79250623; internet www.dfa.ie/irish-embassy/sierra-leone; Ambassador CLAIRE BUCKLEY.

Lebanon: 22A Spur Rd, Wilberforce, POB 727, Freetown; tel. (22) 234677; e-mail embleb2006@yahoo.co.uk; Ambassador NIDAL YEHYA.

Liberia: 2 Spur Rd, Wilberforce, POB 276, Freetown; tel. (22) 230991; e-mail liberia_freetown@yahoo.com; Ambassador MUSU JATU RUHLE.

Libya: 1A and 1B P. Z. Compound, Wilberforce, Freetown; tel. (22) 235231; Chargé d'affaires a.i. Dr AHMED ABUDABBOUS.

Nigeria: Plot No. 1, Musa Yar'adua Cres., Hill Cot Junction, Freetown; tel. (22) 2224229; e-mail info@nigerianhighcommission-sle.org; internet nigerianhighcommission-sle.org; High Commissioner HENRY JOHN OMAKU.

Türkiye (Turkey): Freetown; Ambassador SIBEL ERKAN.

United Kingdom: 6 Spur Rd, Wilberforce, Freetown; tel. 78200190; e-mail freetown.general.enquiries@fco.gov.uk; internet www.gov.uk/government/world/sierra-leone; High Commissioner LISA CHESNEY.

USA: South Ridge, Hill Station, Freetown; tel. (99) 105000; e-mail consularfreetown@state.gov; internet sl.usembassy.gov; Ambassador DAVID D. REIMER.

Judicial System

The judicial system of Sierra Leone is composed of a Supreme Court, a Court of Appeal, a High Court and Magistrates' Courts. The Supreme Court is the ultimate court of appeal in both civil and criminal cases. In addition to its appellate jurisdiction, the Court has supervisory jurisdiction over all other courts and over any adjudicating authority in Sierra Leone, and also original jurisdiction in constitutional issues. The Court of Appeal has jurisdiction to hear and determine appeals from decisions of the High Court in both criminal and civil matters, and also from certain statutory tribunals. Appeals against its decisions may be made to the Supreme Court. The High Court has unlimited original jurisdiction in all criminal and civil matters. It also has appellate jurisdiction against the decisions of Magistrates' Courts. However, in the countryside where the majority of the population lives the informal judicial system—based on customary law and comprising local courts, district appeal courts and local chiefs—plays a significant role, although their jurisdiction is limited to matters of marriage, divorce, succession and land tenure.

Supreme Court: Law Courts Bldg, Siaka Stevens St, Freetown; tel. 76904134; e-mail cj@judiciary.gov.sl; internet www.judiciary.gov.sl; mainly consists of the Chief Justice and not fewer than 4 other judges; Chief Justice DESMOND BABATUNDE EDWARDS.

Court of Appeal: Freetown; mainly consists of the Chief Justice and not fewer than 7 other judges.

High Court: mainly consists of the Chief Justice and not fewer than 9 other judges; Master and Registrar ELAINE THOMAS-ARCHIBALD.

Magistrates' Courts: In criminal cases the jurisdiction of the Magistrates' Courts is limited to summary cases and to preliminary investigations to determine whether a person charged with an offence should be committed for trial.

Religion

It is estimated that some 60% of the total population are Muslims, 30% are Christians and the remaining 10% follow animist or traditional beliefs.

ISLAM

Ahmadiyya Muslim Mission: 15 Bath St, Brookfields, POB 353, Freetown; Emir and Chief Missionary SAID UR-RAHMAN.

Sierra Leone Muslim Congress: POB 875, Freetown; f. 1928; Pres. Alhaji MUHAMMAD SANUSI MUSTAPHA.

CHRISTIANITY

Council of Churches in Sierra Leone: 4A King Harman Rd, Brookfields, POB 404, Freetown; tel. 78987121; internet www.ccslaction.org; f. 1924; 24 mem. churches; Pres. Bishop JOHN K. YAMBASU; Gen. Sec. EBUN JAMES DEKAM.

The Anglican Communion

Anglicans in Sierra Leone are adherents of the Church of the Province of West Africa (CPWA). In September 2012 the CPWA was subdivided into two internal provinces: the Internal Province of Ghana, comprising the 10 (now 11) dioceses in Ghana, and the Internal Province of West Africa, comprising the remaining five (now six) dioceses, two of which are in Sierra Leone. The Archbishop of the CPWA is the Bishop of Liberia.

Bishop of Bo: Rt Rev. SOLOMAN SCOTT-MANGA, MacRobert St, POB 21, Bo, Southern Province; tel. 76677262.

Bishop of Freetown: Rt Rev. THOMAS ARNOLD IKUNIKA WILSON, Bishopscourt, 105 Fourah Bay Rd, POB 537, Freetown; tel. (22) 251307; e-mail vicnold2003@gmail.com.

Baptist Churches

Baptist Convention Sierra Leone: POB 64, Lunsar; 119 mem. churches; 994 mems; Exec. Pres. Rev. JOSEPH SAMUEL FORNAH; Gen. Sec. Rev. MOHAMED MANSARAY.

The Nigerian Baptist Convention is also active.

Methodist Churches

Methodist Church Sierra Leone: Wesley House, George St, POB 64, Freetown; tel. 76643037; e-mail mcsl@ymail.com; internet www.methodistchurchsierraleone.org; f. 1792; autonomous since 1967; Presiding Bishop Rt Rev. MARK K. NGOBEH; Sec. Rev. RONALD BOB-WILLIAMS; 26,421 mems.

United Methodist Church: Freetown; tel. 76444100; e-mail sierraleoneannualconference@yahoo.com; f. 1880; Presiding Bishop JOHN K. YAMBASU; 225,000 mems.

Other active Methodist bodies include the African Methodist Episcopal Church, the Wesleyan Church of Sierra Leone, the Countess of Huntingdon's Connexion and the West African Methodist Church.

The Roman Catholic Church

Sierra Leone comprises one archdiocese and three dioceses.

Inter-territorial Catholic Bishops' Conference of The Gambia and Sierra Leone (ITCABIC): Santanno House, POB 893, Freetown; tel. 79797066; e-mail itcabic71@yahoo.co.uk; internet catholicchurchsl.org; f. 1971; Pres. Rt Rev. CHARLES A. M. CAMPBELL (Bishop, of Bo); Sec.-Gen. Fr PAUL MORANA SANDI.

Archbishop of Freetown: Most Rev. EDWARD TAMBA CHARLES, Santanno House, 10 Howe St, POB 98, Freetown; tel. 76771165; e-mail jhg3271@sierratel.sl.

Other Christian Churches

The following are represented: the Christ Apostolic Church, the Church of the Lord (Aladura), the Evangelical Church, the Evangelical Lutheran Church in Sierra Leone, the Missionary Church of Africa, the Sierra Leone Church and the United Brethren in Christ.

AFRICAN RELIGIONS

There is a diverse range of beliefs, rites and practices, varying between ethnic and kinship groups.

The Press

DAILY NEWSPAPERS (PRINT AND ONLINE)

Awoko: Freetown; internet awoko.org; Man. Editor KEVIN LEWIS.

For di People: Freetown; independent; Editor PAUL KAMARA.

The Sierra Leone Daily Mail: 29–31 Rawdon St, POB 53, Freetown; tel. (22) 223191; internet www.sierraleonedailymail.com; f. 1931; state-owned; currently online only; Editor-in-Chief CHRISTIAN F. SESAY, Jr.

PERIODICALS

Concord Times: 51 Krootown Rd, Freetown; tel. (22) 229199; e-mail info@concordtimessl.com; internet www.concordtimessl.com; 3 a week; Editor DOROTHY GORDON.

The New Citizen: 7 Wellington St, Freetown; tel. (22) 228693; internet www.thenewcitizen-sl.com; f. 1982; Man. Editor SAMUEL B. CONTEH.

NEWS AGENCIES

Sierra Leone News Agency (SLENA): 15 Wallace Johnson St, PMB 445, Freetown; tel. (22) 224921; internet slena.gov.sl; f. 1980; Man. Dir AUGUSTUS KAMARA.

Broadcasting and Communications

TELECOMMUNICATIONS

Africell: 1 Pivot St, Wilberforce, Freetown; tel. 77777777; e-mail info@africell.sl; internet www.africell.sl; f. 2005; CEO SHADI AL-GERJAWI.

Orange Sierra Leone: 25 Main Rd, Hill Station, Regent, Freetown; tel. 76293444; e-mail customerservice@orange.sl; internet www.orange.sl; f. 2000; fmrly Airtel Sierra Leone, present name adopted in 2016; owned by Orange (France); CEO AMINATA KANE NDIAYE.

Sierra Leone Telecommunications Co (SIERRATEL): 7 Wallace Johnson St, POB 80, Freetown; tel. (22) 222801; e-mail sierratel-customercare@sierratel.sl; internet www.sierratel.sl; state-owned telecommunications operator; Chair. MOHAMED SHARKA KARGBO; Man. Dir FODAY SANKOH.

Regulatory Authority

National Telecommunications Commission (NATCOM): 13 Regent Rd, Hill Station, Freetown; tel. 76630640; e-mail info@natcom.gov.sl; internet www.natcom.gov.sl; f. 2006; regulates ICT services; Chair. JOSEPH CHRISTOPHER BLELL; Dir-Gen. DANIEL BOBSON KAITIBI.

BROADCASTING

Sierra Leone Broadcasting Corpn (SLBC): New England, Freetown; tel. 77577303; e-mail slbc.slnews@gmail.com; internet www.slbc.gov.sl; f. 1963; name changed as above in 2010 following merger of Sierra Leone Broadcasting Service and UN Radio in Sierra Leone; state-controlled; programmes mainly in English and the 4 main Sierra Leonean vernaculars: Mende, Limba, Temne and Krio; weekly broadcast in French; television service est. 1963; Dir-Gen. JOSEPH KAPUWA.

Capital Radio: Mammy Yoko Business Park, Aberdeen, Freetown; internet www.capitalradio.sl; f. 2006; privately owned.

Fountain of Peace Radio (FM 89.6): 1 Kondebotihun Rd, Mosoe Section, Salina, Moyamba; tel. 78896896; internet www.fopradio .org; religious broadcasts; Head of Broadcast THOMAS MATTHEW JOMBLA.

Radio Democracy (FM 98.1): New England Ville, Freetown; tel. 76603285; e-mail info@radiodemocracy.sl; internet radiodemocracy .sl; f. 1997; Station Man. ASMAA JAMES.

Star Radio (103.5 FM): 3 Mammah St, Brookfields, Freetown; tel. 88103500; internet fb.com/StarRadioSierraLeone; Gen. Man. YUSUF BANGURA.

Finance

BANKING

Central Bank

Bank of Sierra Leone: Siaka Stevens St, POB 30, Freetown; tel. (22) 226501; e-mail info@bsl.gov.sl; internet www.bsl.gov.sl; f. 1964; Gov. Prof. KELFALA MORANA KALLON.

Other Banks

Access Bank Sierra Leone Ltd: 30 Siaka Stevens St, Freetown; tel. 30969943; e-mail sierraleonecontactcenter@accessbankplc.com; internet sierraleone.accessbankplc.com; f. 2007; Chair. ALICE M. ONOMAKE; Man. Dir GANIYU SANNI.

Ecobank Sierra Leone Ltd: 7 Lightfoot-Boston St, POB 1007, Freetown; tel. (22) 221704; e-mail ecobankenquiries@ecobank.com; internet www.ecobank.com; Chair. CHRISTOPHER JOHN FORSTER; Man. Dir L. AINA MOORE.

First International Bank (SL) Ltd: 2 Charlotte St, PMB 450, Freetown; tel. (22) 292201; e-mail fib@sierratel.sl; f. 1998.

Guaranty Trust Bank: Sparta Bldg, 12 Wilberforce St, POB 1168, Freetown; tel. 99088888; e-mail complaints@gtbanksl.com; internet www.gtb.sl; f. 2002 through the acquisition of 90% of shareholding of First Merchant Bank of Sierra Leone by Guaranty Trust Bank of Nigeria; Chair. Dr GEORGE EMERSON TAYLOR-LEWIS; Man. Dir ADEKUNLE ADEBIYI.

Rokel Commercial Bank (Sierra Leone) Ltd: 25–27 Siaka Stevens St, POB 12, Freetown; tel. (22) 222501; e-mail info@ rokelbank.sl; internet www.rokelbank.sl; f. 1971; 51% govt-owned; Man. Dir WALTON EKUNDAYO GILPIN.

Sierra Leone Commercial Bank Ltd: Christian Smith Bldg, 29–31 Siaka Stevens St, Freetown; tel. (22) 225264; internet www.slcb .com; f. 1973; state-owned; Chair. Dr JAMES D. ROGERS; Man. Dir (vacant).

Skye Bank Sierra Leone Ltd: 31 Siaka Stevens St, Freetown; tel. (22) 220095; internet skyebanksl.net; a subsidiary of Sifax Group Nigeria; Chair. ABDUL RAHMAN TURAY; Man. Dir ABIOLA BOLAJI.

Standard Chartered Bank Sierra Leone Ltd: 9–11 Lightfoot-Boston St, POB 1155, Freetown; tel. 76505609; e-mail customerService.sl@sc.com; internet www.sc.com/sl; f. 1894; CEO and Man. Dir YETUNDE BOLANLE ONI.

Union Trust Bank Ltd: Lightfoot-Boston St, PMB 1237, Freetown; tel. (22) 226954; e-mail info@utb.sl; internet www.utb.sl; fmrly Meridien BIAO Bank Sierra Leone Ltd; adopted present name in 1995; Chair. MOHAMED S. FOFANA; Man. Dir and CEO JAMES SANPHA KOROMA.

United Bank For Africa Sierra Leone Ltd: 15 Charlotte St, Freetown; tel. 78200200; e-mail cfcsierra-leone@ubagroup.com; internet www.ubasierraleone.com; f. 2008; Chair. ABDUL SHEKU KARGBO; Man. Dir USMAN ISIAKA.

Zenith Bank Sierra Leone Ltd: 18–20 Rawdon St, Freetown; tel. 79370731; e-mail ibanksupport@zenithbank.com.sl; internet www .zenithbank.com.sl; f. 2007; Exec. Dir ADEWALE OLUKOYA.

INSURANCE

Aureol Insurance Co Ltd: Kissy House, 54 Siaka Stevens St, POB 647, Freetown; tel. 76175175; e-mail info@aureolinsurance.com; internet aureolinsurance.com; f. 1986; Chair. YASMIN FOFANAH; Gen. Man. RAYMOND MACAULEY.

National Insurance Co Ltd: 18–20 Walpole St, PMB 84, Freetown; tel. (22) 224328; e-mail info@nic-sl.sl; internet www.nic-sl.sl; f. 1972; state-owned; Chair. MARTHA CONSILLA KANAGBO; Man. Dir ABDUL KARGBO.

New India Assurance Co Ltd: 18 Wilberforce St, POB 340, Freetown; tel. (22) 226453; e-mail niasl@sierratel.sl.

Reliance Insurance Trust Corpn Ltd: 34 Percival St, Freetown; tel. (22) 220103; e-mail ritcorpltd@ritcorpltd.com; internet www .ritcorpltd.com; f. 1985; Chair. MOHAMED B. COLE; Man. Dir ALICE M. ONOMAKE.

Trade and Industry

GOVERNMENT AGENCIES

National Commission for Privatisation: Lotto House, OAU Dr., Tower Hill, POB 56, Freetown; tel. 76780008; e-mail info@ncpsl.gov .sl; internet www.ncpsl.gov.sl; f. 2001; Chair. Eng. HADJI DABO; Exec. Sec. JOSEPHINE ANSUMANA.

National Minerals Agency (NMA): New England Ville, Freetown; tel. 79250702; e-mail info@nma.gov.sl; internet www.nma.gov.sl; f. 2013; Chair. MICHAELA KADIJATU CONTEH; Dir-Gen. JULIUS DANIEL MATTAI.

Sierra Leone Extractive Industries Transparency Initiative (SLEITI): 17 Charles St, 2nd Floor, Freetown; tel. 79759547; e-mail info@sleiti.gov.sl; internet www.sleiti.gov.sl; f. 2006; govt regulatory agency for mining; Nat. Co-ordinator MOHAMED BAIMBA KOROMA.

CHAMBERS OF COMMERCE

Sierra Leone Chamber of Commerce, Industry and Agriculture (SLCCIA): Guma Bldg, 5th Floor, Lamina Sankoh St, POB 502, Freetown; tel. 76483017; e-mail info@slccia.sl; f. 1961; 300 mems; Pres. GLADYS STRASSER-KING.

TRADE AND INDUSTRIAL ASSOCIATIONS

Sierra Leone Investment and Export Promotion Agency (SLIEPA): OAU Dr., Tower Hill, Freetown; tel. (25) 332863; e-mail info@sliepa.org; internet sliepa.org; f. 2007; fmrly Sierra Leone Export Development and Investment Corporation; Chair. JONATHAN GEORGE; CEO SHEKU LEXMOND KOROMA.

EMPLOYERS' ORGANIZATIONS

Sierra Leone Chamber of Mines: POB 456, Freetown; tel. (22) 226082; f. 1965; mems comprise the principal mining concerns; Pres. JOHN SISAY; Exec. Officer N. H. T. BOSTON.

Sierra Leone Employers' Federation: POB 562, Freetown; Chair. AMADU B. NDOEKA; Exec. Sec. LESLIE THOMAS.

UTILITIES

Electricity

Electricity Distribution and Supply Authority (EDSA): Electricity House, 36 Siaka Stevens St, Freetown; tel. (22) 229868; e-mail customercare@edsa.sl; internet www.edsa.sl; f. 2015 following the dissolution of the National Power Authority; supplies all electricity in Sierra Leone; Dir-Gen. JAMES ROGERS (acting).

Electricity Generation and Transmission Co. (EGTC): Freetown; f. 2015 following the dissolution of the National Power Authority; Dir-Gen. DENNIS GARVIE.

Water

Guma Valley Water Co: Guma Bldg, 12/14 Lamina Sankoh St, POB 700, Freetown; tel. 79513400; e-mail gumasl@yahoo.co.uk; internet fb.com/GumaValleyWaterCompany; f. 1961; responsible for all existing water supplies in Freetown and surrounding villages, including the Guma dam and associated works; Gen. Man. MAADA S. KPENGE.

MAJOR COMPANIES

KPMG: KPMG House, 37 Siaka Stevens St, POB 100, Freetown; tel. (22) 222061; internet www.kpmg.com; f. 1987 following merger between KMG and Peat Marwick; accounting and consultancy services; CEO (West Africa) NII AMANOR DODOO.

Koidu Ltd: 84 Wilkinson Rd, Freetown; tel. 78874912; internet www .koiduholdings.com; f. 2003; privately owned by BSG Resources Ltd (BSGR) through its subsidiary OCTEA Ltd; diamond mining.

Sierra Leone Bottling Co. Ltd: George Brook, POB 412, Freetown; tel. 76315777; f. 2008; owned by Equatorial Coca-Cola Bottling Co; Country Man. ISRAEL OKUJAGU.

Sierra Leone Brewery Ltd: Wellington Industrial Estate, POB 721, Freetown; tel. (22) 263384; e-mail albert.collier@heineken.com; f. 1961; 45% owned by Heineken Technisch Beheer (Netherlands); brewing and marketing of Guinness stout and Star lager; Man. Dir V. L. THOMAS.

Sierra Leone National Petroleum Co: NP House, Cotton Tree, POB 277, Freetown; tel. 76602625; internet npgroupltd.com/ sierraleone; petroleum products; CEO KOBI WALKER.

Sierra Leone Produce Marketing Co (SLPMC): Freetown; tel. 78840903; f. 2013 to replace Sierra Leone Produce Marketing Board; marketing of agricultural produce; Man. Dir HENRY YAMBA KAMARA.

Sierra Mineral Holdings 1 Ltd (SMHL): 37 Wellington St, 3rd Floor, POB 59, Freetown; tel. 78883463; internet bauxite.vimetco.com; subsidiary of Vimetco N.V; bauxite mining.

Sierra Rutile Ltd: 30 Siaka Stevens St, 2nd Floor, Access Bank Bldg, Freetown; e-mail marketing@sierra-rutile.com; internet www.sierra-rutile.com; f. 1971; mining of rutile and ilmenite (titanium-bearing ores); Chair. ROBERT EDWARDS; CEO ROB HATTING.

TRADE UNIONS

Sierra Leone Labour Congress (SLLC): 35 Wallace Johnson St, POB 1333, Freetown; tel. 76511892; e-mail sierralabour@yahoo.com; internet fb.com/sierraleonelabourcongress; f. 1976; 32 affiliated unions; more than 140,000 mems; Pres. MOHAMED SALIEU BANGURA (acting); Sec.-Gen. MAX CONTEH.

Principal affiliated unions:

Sierra Leone Association of Journalists: 31 Garrison St, Freetown; tel. 76605811; e-mail slajalone@hotmail.com; Pres. KELVIN LEWIS; Sec.-Gen. NASRALLAH AHMED SAHID.

Sierra Leone Dockworkers' Union: 165 Fourah Bay Rd, Freetown; f. 1962; Pres. ALPHA SULAIMAN BUNDU; Gen. Sec. A. C. CONTEH.

Sierra Leone Motor Drivers' and General Transport Workers' Union: 10 Charlotte St, Freetown; f. 2001 following the merger of the Motor Drivers' Union and the Amalgamated Transport Workers' Union; Pres. ALPHA AMADU BAH; Gen. Sec. ALPHA KAMARA.

Sierra Leone Teachers' Union: Regaland House, Lowcost Step—Kissy, POB 477, Freetown; f. 1951; Pres. ABDULAI BRIMA KOROMA; Sec.-Gen. DAVIDSON KUYATEH.

Sierra Leone Traders Union: Freetown; Sec.-Gen. AARON A. BOIMA; 1,500 mems.

United Mineworkers' Union (UMU): 35 Wallace Johnson St, Freetown; f. 1944; Gen. Sec. EZEKIEL DYKE.

Also affiliated to the Sierra Leone Labour Congress: the **General Construction Workers' Union**, the **Municipal and Local Government Employees' Union** and the **Sierra Leone National Seamen's Union**.

Transport

RAILWAYS

There are no passenger railways in Sierra Leone.

ROADS

Sierra Leone Road Safety Authority (SLRSA): Kissy Rd, Freetown; tel. 76954803; e-mail info@slrsa.gov.sl; internet slrsa.gov.sl; f. 2014; Exec. Dir (vacant).

Sierra Leone Road Transport Corpn (SLRTC): Blackhall Rd, POB 1008, Freetown; tel. (22) 250442; internet fb.com/www.slrtc.org; f. 1965; state-owned; operates transport services throughout the country; Chair. MAYA KAIKAI; Gen. Man. BOCKARIE LEWIS KAMARA.

Sierra Leone Roads Authority (SLRA): Blackhall Rd, PMB 1324, Freetown; internet slra-gov.org; f. 1992; Chair. ARTHUR S. HARVEY; Dir-Gen. MEMUNA KOMBA JALLOH.

INLAND WATERWAYS

Established routes for launches, which include the coastal routes from Freetown northward to the Great and Little Scarcies rivers and southward to Bonthe, total almost 800 km. Although some of the upper reaches of the rivers are navigable only between July and September, there is a considerable volume of river traffic.

SHIPPING

Freetown, the principal port, has full facilities for ocean-going vessels.

Destiny Shipping Agencies Ltd: 211 Fourah Bay Rd, Freetown; tel. 76602813; internet www.destinyshipping-sl.com.

Sierra Leone National Shipping Co: 45 Cline St, Freetown; tel. 25255406; e-mail slnsc@gmail.com; internet www.slnsc.org; f. 1971 as Sierra Leone; Man. Dir AHMED SAYBOM KANU.

Sierra Leone Ports Authority: Queen Elizabeth II Quay, PMB 386, Cline Town, Freetown; tel. (22) 226480; e-mail sierraleoneports@yahoo.com; internet slpa.sl; f. 1965; parastatal body, supervised by the Ministry of Transport and Aviation; operates the port of Freetown; Chair. MANSO ABU DUMBUYA; Gen. Man. ABU BAKARR BANGURA.

Sierra Leone Shipping Agencies Ltd: Deep Water Quay, POB 74, Cline Town, Freetown; tel. (22) 221709; e-mail slsa@bollore.com; f. 1949; Man. Dir MICHEL MEYNARD.

CIVIL AVIATION

There is an international airport at Lungi.

Sierra Leone Civil Aviation Authority (SLCAA): NDB Bldg, 3rd Floor, 21–23 Siaka Stevens St, Freetown; tel. 76806885; e-mail info@slcaa.gov.sl; internet www.slcaa.gov.sl; f. 2008; Chair. PATRICK JAIAH KAIKAI; Dir-Gen. MOSES TIFFA BAIO.

Tourism

Sierra Leone National Tourist Board: Lumley Beach Rd, POB 1435, Freetown; tel. 88867663; e-mail info@ntb.gov.sl; internet ntb.gov.sl; f. 1990; Chair. TAMBA ALLIEU KOKOBAYE; Gen. Man. FATMATA KROMA.

Defence

As assessed at November 2021, the armed forces of the Republic of Sierra Leone numbered about 8,500, included in which was a maritime wing of 200.

Defence Budget: Le 124,000m. for 2022.

Commander-in-Chief of the Armed Forces: Brig. (retd) JULIUS MAADA BIO.

Chief of Defence Staff: Lt-Gen. SULLAY IBRAHIM SESAY.

Education

Primary education begins at five years of age and lasts for seven years. Secondary education, beginning at the age of 12, lasts for a further seven years, comprising a first cycle of five years and a second cycle of two years. In 1987 tuition fees for government-funded primary and secondary schools were abolished. In 2019/20 enrolment at the pre-primary level was equivalent to 21% of children in the relevant age-group (males 20%; females 22%). In 2018/19 primary enrolment included 99% of children (males 97%; females 100%) in the relevant age-group, while secondary enrolment in 2017/18 included 42% of children in the relevant age-group (males 43%; females 41%). There is one university, which comprises six colleges. Budgetary expenditure on education by the central Government in 2020 was equivalent to 20% of total government spending.

Bibliography

Abdullah, I. *Between Democracy and Terror: The Sierra Leone Civil War*. Muckleneuk, Unisa Press, 2004.

Ainley, K., Friedmann, R., and Mahony, C. (Eds). *Evaluating Transitional Justice: Accountability and Peacebuilding in Post-Conflict Sierra Leone*. New York, Palgrave Macmillan, 2015.

Albrecht, P. *Hybridization, Intervention and Authority: Security Beyond Conflict in Sierra Leone*. Abingdon, Routledge, 2019.

Beevers, M. *Peacebuilding and Natural Resource Governance After Armed Conflict: Sierra Leone and Liberia*. London, Palgrave Macmillan, 2018.

Bundu, A., and Karefa-Smart, J. *Democracy by Force? A Study of International Military Intervention in the Conflict in Sierra Leone from 1991–2000*. Parkland, FL, Universal Publishers, 2001.

Campbell, G. *Blood Diamonds: Tracing the Deadly Path of the World's Most Precious Stones*. Boulder, CO, Westview Press, 2003.

Châtaigner, J.-M. *L'ONU dans la crise en Sierra Leone : Les méandres d'une négociation*. Paris, Editions Karthala, 2005.

Conteh-Morgan, E., and Dixon-Fyle, M. *Sierra Leone at the End of the Twentieth Century: History, Politics and Society*. Bern, Peter Lang, 1999.

Cubitt, C. *Local and Global Dynamics of Peacebuilding: Post-conflict Reconstruction in Sierra Leone*. Abingdon, Routledge, 2011.

Denov, M. *Child Soldiers: Sierra Leone's Revolutionary United Front*. Cambridge, Cambridge University Press, 2010.

Enria, L. *The Politics of Work in a Post-Conflict State: Youth, Labour & Violence in Sierra Leone*. Woodbridge, James Currey, 2018.

Ferme, M. C. *Out of War: Violence, Trauma, and the Political Imagination in Sierra Leone*. Oakland, CA, University of California Press, 2018.

Francis, D. J. *The Politics of Economic Regionalism: Sierra Leone in ECOWAS (The International Political Economy of New Regionalisms)*. Burlington, VT, Ashgate Publishing Co, 2002.

Gberie, L. *A Dirty War in West Africa: The RUF and the Destruction of Sierra Leone*. London, Hurst & Co., 2005.

Rescuing a Fragile State: Sierra Leone 2002–2008. Waterloo, ON, Wilfrid Laurier University Press, 2009.

Harris, D. *Sierra Leone: A Political History*. London, C. Hurst & Co., 2013.

Kargbo, M. *British Foreign Policy and the Conflict in Sierra Leone, 1991–2001*. Oxford, Peter Lang, 2006.

Keen, D. *Conflict and Collusion in Sierra Leone*. New York, Palgrave Macmillan, 2005.

Kelsall, T. *Culture under Cross-Examination: International Justice and the Special Court for Sierra Leone*. Cambridge, Cambridge University Press, 2009.

Lahai, J. I. *The Ebola Pandemic in Sierra Leone: Representations, Actors, Interventions and the Path to Recovery*. London, Palgrave Macmillan, 2017.

Land, J. *Blood Diamonds*. New York, Tor Books, 2002.

Mitton, K. *Rebels in a Rotten State: Understanding Atrocity in the Sierra Leone Civil War*. Oxford, Oxford University Press, 2015.

Olonisakin, F. *Peacekeeping in Sierra Leone: The Story of UNAMSIL*. Boulder, CO, Lynne Rienner Publishers, 2007.

Peters, K. *War and the Crisis of Youth in Sierra Leone*. Cambridge, Cambridge University Press, 2011.

Reno, W. *Corruption and State Politics in Sierra Leone*. Cambridge, Cambridge University Press, 2008.

Turay, E. D. A., and Abraham, A. *The Sierra Leone Army: A Century of History*. London, Macmillan, 1988.

Wiafe-Amoako, F. *Human Security and Sierra Leone's Post-Conflict Development*. Lanham, MD, Lexington Books, 2014.

Wlodarczyk, N. *Magic and Warfare: Appearance and Reality in Contemporary African Conflict and Beyond*. New York, Palgrave Macmillan, 2009.

Wundah, M. *Sierra Leone's Corridors of Power*. New York, Strategic Book Publishing, 2009.

Wyse, A. *H. C. Bankole-Bright and Politics in Colonial Sierra Leone, 1919–1958*. Cambridge, Cambridge University Press, 2003.

SOMALIA

Physical and Social Geography

I. M. LEWIS

The Federal Republic of Somalia covers an area of 637,657 sq km (246,201 sq miles). It has a long coastline on the Indian Ocean and the Gulf of Aden, forming the 'Horn of Africa'. To the north, Somalia faces the Arabian peninsula, with which it has had centuries of commercial and cultural contact. To the north-west, it is bounded by the Republic of Djibouti, while its western and southern neighbours are Ethiopia and Kenya. The country takes its name from its population, the Somali, a Muslim Cushitic-speaking people who stretch into these neighbouring states.

Most of the terrain consists of dry savannah plains, with a high mountain escarpment in the north, facing the coast. The climate is hot and dry, with an annual average temperature of 27°C, although temperate at higher altitudes and along the coast during June–September, with annual rainfall rarely exceeding 500 mm in the most favourable regions. Only two permanent rivers—the Juba and Shabelle—water this arid land. Both rise in the Ethiopian highlands, but only the Juba regularly flows into the sea. The territory between these two rivers is agriculturally the richest part of Somalia, and constitutes a zone of mixed cultivation and pastoralism. Sorghum, millet and maize are grown here, while along the rivers, on irrigated plantations, bananas (traditionally the mainstay of Somalia's exports) and citrus fruits are produced. This potentially prosperous zone contains remnants of Bantu groups—partly of ex-slave origin—and is also the home of the Digil and Rahanweyne, who speak a distinctive dialect and are the least nomadic element in the population. Of the other Somali clans—the Dir, Isaak, Hawiye and Darod, primarily pastoral nomads who occupy the rest of the country—the Hawiye along the Shabelle valley are the most extensively engaged in cultivation. A small subsidiary area of cultivation (involving Dir and Isaak) also occurs in the north-west highlands.

In this predominantly pastoral country, permanent settlements are small and widely scattered, except in the agricultural regions, and for the most part are tiny trading centres built around wells. There are few large towns. Mogadishu, the capital, which dates from at least the 10th century as an Islamic trading post, had a population of 2,497,463 at mid-2022, according to United Nations (UN) projections. The other main centres are Merca (727,772), an ancient port town in the southern region of Lower Shabelle, and Berbera (545,378), the country's principal northern port. The northern town of Hargeysa was declared the capital of the secessionist 'Republic of Somaliland' in 1991, and had a projected population of 1,079,377 at mid-2022.

According to provisional results of the census of 1986/87, the population of Somalia was 7,114,431. According to UN estimates, at mid-2022 the population was 16,841,805, giving a density of 26.4 inhabitants per sq km. Important demographic changes took place from the later decades of the 20th century, beginning with the serious drought that affected the north of the country in 1974–75 and led to the resettlement of large numbers of people in the south. During 1980–88 successive influxes of refugees from Ethiopia created a serious refugee problem before repatriations began in 1990. Of greatest consequence, however, has been the dislocation of Somalia's population during the civil unrest that has raged since the late 1980s. At the end of February 2022, according to the office of the UN High Commissioner for Refugees, an estimated 2.97m. Somalis were internally displaced in Somalia, while at the end of August 660,935 were refugees in other countries in the near region.

History

DUNCAN WOODSIDE

Based on an earlier article by ANNA BRUZZONE

THE COLONIAL ERA

In the late 19th century Somali-populated territories were partitioned between three European colonial powers—the United Kingdom, France and Italy—and the Ethiopian Empire. British colonial possessions included British Somaliland, in the north-west, roughly corresponding to the present-day area of self-declared autonomous 'Republic of Somaliland', and a vast region in the south-west, which included present-day north-eastern Kenya and the Jubaland Province, extending from the right bank of the Juba river in Somalia to the eastern part of the Kenyan town of Wajir. In 1925 Jubaland was ceded to Italy and the international border was shifted to a line stretching from the confluence of the Ganale and Daua rivers, on the Anglo-Abyssinian frontier, to Ras Kamboni, on the Indian Ocean coast. Italian possessions comprised present-day north-eastern, central and southern Somalia. French Somaliland consisted of present-day Djibouti, while Abyssinia controlled the territory presently corresponding to Ethiopia's Ogaden region.

The Second World War temporarily reconfigured the region's political geography. Following Italy's defeat, British military administrations were established in former Italian Somaliland, the previously Ethiopian-ruled Somali territories and British Somaliland, bringing all Somali-inhabited regions, with the exception of French Somaliland (Djibouti), under British rule.

The transient prospect of creating a Greater Somalia, however, rapidly vanished. After the British withdrew in 1948, the Ethiopian Government resumed the administrative control of the Ogaden region. In November 1949 the United Nations (UN) General Assembly voted for the conditional return of Italian administration to south-central Somalia. The UN agreement established the Italian Trusteeship Administration for Somalia to prepare the former Italian colony for independence over a 10-year period. The trusteeship, however, was largely a failure, both politically and economically, as it resembled more an apparatus of control than a tool for gradual and effective decolonization. Political parties became a new way to articulate and express clan-based interests. The strength of clanship ties and their effectiveness in mobilizing lineage-based interest groups were revived during elections in 1956 and 1959. In the period prior to independence, the concept of clan balance was introduced in Somali politics as a synonym of democratic representation. British Somaliland and the UN Italian Trust Territory gained independence on 26 June and 1 July 1960, respectively, and united to form the Somali Republic.

THE SIAD BARRE REGIME, 1969–91

By the end of the 1960s the 'commercialized anarchy' into which the parliamentary system had degenerated since independence, compounded by the Government's inability to bring about economic improvement, fuelled popular discontent. In the legislative elections of March 1969 a total of 1,002 candidates, representing 62 parties, contested 123 seats. Following indecisive results, President Abdirashid Ali Sharmarke was assassinated by one of his own bodyguards on 15 October. A bloodless military coup, led by Maj.-Gen. Mohamed Siad Barre, overthrew the elected Government on 22 October, and the military junta suspended the Constitution and the Supreme Court, dissolved the legislature, and banned political parties. The Supreme Revolutionary Council (SRC), headed by Siad Barre and composed of 25 officers, became the main organ of political power. On 20 October 1970 the Somali Democratic Republic was officially proclaimed a 'socialist state' and the new regime presented socialism as an alternative to tribalism.

The choice of embracing socialism was not merely ideological: the Union of Soviet Socialist Republics (USSR) was the most significant provider of foreign aid to Somalia between 1963 and 1969. However, Somalia's strategic position in the confrontation between East and West determined the exponential growth of foreign aid. Development co-operation between Italy and Somalia resumed in 1971 and was significantly fostered. Bilateral funding for development programmes was agreed upon with the People's Republic of China, the Democratic People's Republic of Korea (North Korea) and Libya. Following its entry into the League of Arab States (the Arab League) in 1974, Somalia also became a recipient of aid from Kuwait and Saudi Arabia. The regime adopted socialist-inspired economic planning and used the foreign aid to fund development programmes.

Although the regime achieved limited results in the economic realm and institutionalized repression against political opponents, it made some progress towards social development. Somali became a written language in January 1973, replacing Italian and English as the country's official language. Profiting from political turmoil in Ethiopia, however, the regime increasingly focused on the liberation of the Ogaden region and moved its economic agenda to the background. In the mid-1970s the Somali state rested on a precarious balance, and the Ogaden war caused it to fail.

Following the 1974 revolution in Ethiopia, Siad Barre attempted to use pan-Somali nationalism and irredentist claims to consolidate his power base. The Ogaden campaign in 1977–78 structurally transformed the social dynamics of mobilization in Somalia. The clan system underwent a political revival. In 1975 Somali army officers began training Ogaden guerrilla groups, namely the Western Somalia Liberation Front (WSLF) and the Somali Abo Liberation Front. The Ogaden military campaign turned into a complete debacle for Somalia. Initially, the Somali national army together with WSLF fighters achieved several victories during mid-1977. However, the USSR's decision to abandon Somalia in favour of Ethiopia reversed the tide of war. Cuba and the People's Republic of South Yemen followed the Soviets, and, with assistance from Cuban forces, Ethiopia retook all of the Ogaden's major towns. On 9 March 1978 Siad Barre recalled the Somali army from Ethiopia.

In the aftermath of the chaotic withdrawal of the Somali troops, in April 1978 the regime foiled a coup attempt organized by Majerten army officers to overthrow Siad Barre. Military repression was not limited to the coup leaders; civilians who belonged to the Majerten clan were killed in the Mudug and Bari regions. These events led to the creation of the Somali Salvation Front (SSF) and marked the beginning of the armed opposition against the regime. The SSF, a Majerten-based group, became the Somali Salvation Democratic Front in 1981, while also in that year a group of Somali dissidents (largely Issak from Somaliland) living in London, UK, formed the Somali National Movement (SNM). Ethiopia subsequently became the sanctuary of Somali opposition groups.

In 1988 Siad Barre signed a deal with Lt-Col Mengistu Haile Mariam of Ethiopia in which the two regimes agreed to stop supporting each other's opposition groups. As a result, the SNM was ordered to vacate its bases in the Ogaden. The SNM subsequently captured Burao and occupied part of Hargeysa. Siad Barre responded by ordering retaliation, and South African mercenary pilots and heavy artillery were used to bombard Hargeysa. An estimated 40,000 people were killed and some 400,000 refugees fled to Ethiopia.

The Government's announcement, in October 1990, that a constitutional referendum and multi-party elections were to take place within 12 months failed to curb popular revolt. Meanwhile, armed opposition groups were growing in strength. The regime's massive crackdowns and subsequent reprisals by military factions precipitated a bloody civil war. In November the United Somali Congress (USC), a Hawiye-based paramilitary organization, marched south from Galkayo and initiated large-scale attacks on government installations and military facilities in and around the capital, Mogadishu. (The USC political wing was established in Rome, Italy, in January 1987, and the group's military wing was formed in Ethiopia a few months later, led by Gen. Mohamed Farah Aidid of the Hawiye/Habar Gidir clan.) On 1 January 1991 the forces of the USC entered Mogadishu, and Siad Barre left the capital on 27 January, fleeing south with the remnants of his army. The USC subsequently assumed power. The deposed President made an attempt to recapture Mogadishu in mid-1991, but was pushed back over the Kenyan border. Having failed to obtain political asylum in Kenya, Siad Barre fled to Nigeria, where he died in January 1995.

INTERNATIONAL MILITARY INTERVENTION, 1992–95

The civil war was not a political revolution. Although the Siad Barre regime had been overthrown, key actors of that period were still present in the inner circles of the warring factions throughout Somalia. In January 1991 the Manifesto Group appointed Ali Mahdi Mohamed, a Hawiye Abgal businessman and former government minister, as the interim President of Somalia. Ali Mahdi's appointment, however, was rejected by the USC faction led by Aidid. Heavy fighting between Aidid's forces and the militias allied to Ali Mahdi broke out in November, and consumed the Somali capital until March 1992. It was estimated that 35,000 civilians were killed and many more thousands displaced during the battle for Mogadishu. The capital was separated by a 'green line' demarcating the north–south boundary between the areas controlled by Ali Mahdi and Aidid. In southern Somalia fighting broke out between clan-based factions battling for control of the strategic port city of Kismayu. As a result of the combined effects of drought, factional struggle and poor aid politics, a severe famine broke out. Overall, an estimated 300,000 people died and a further 2m. were displaced.

In January 1992 the UN Security Council adopted a resolution imposing an arms embargo on Somalia. In April the Security Council authorized a very limited observation operation, the UN Operation in Somalia (UNOSOM). Lacking an effective mandate and adequate financial resources, UNOSOM failed to handle the humanitarian crisis (while the looting of humanitarian aid became systemic), and by September the political situation had worsened. In November, following an arrangement between the US Administration and the Security Council, a US-led UN peacekeeping operation was authorized to enter Somalia. The operation was mandated to create a secure environment for the delivery of humanitarian aid. In December the first US troops of the Unified Task Force (UNITAF) arrived in Mogadishu as part of Operation Restore Hope.

As a result of its shortcomings, the UN mission fell apart in 1993. UNITAF handed over the operation to a UN-led peacekeeping force (UNOSOM II) on 4 May. On 5 June a series of armed attacks against UNOSOM troops throughout south Mogadishu, in which 25 Pakistani soldiers were killed and 54 wounded, precipitated a crisis. Aidid, who had welcomed the US troops in Mogadishu in December 1992, became the most wanted man after the UN Security Council adopted a resolution providing for the arrest and prosecution of all those responsible for the attacks. The UN mission commander, retired US Navy Admiral Jonathan Howe, placed a US $20,000 bounty on Aidid's head. Lacking a clear political strategy, UNOSOM II turned into a military campaign against one section of the Somali population. The mission launched a series of air and ground operations in south Mogadishu on 12 June 1993, and US special forces were deployed in the Somali capital. On 3 October they instigated an operation in south Mogadishu aimed at capturing several of Aidid's key aides; however, during the operation, two US helicopters were shot down by Somali militiamen. In a two-day battle 18 US soldiers and about 1,000 Somalis were killed. The bodies of the US soldiers were dragged through the streets of Mogadishu, prompting a furious reaction from the US media and public. Four days later, US President Bill Clinton announced that US forces would be withdrawn from Somalia by 31 March 1994. All UN forces were eventually withdrawn by March 1995, leaving behind a ravaged country.

CIVIL WAR, GLOBALIZATION AND RECONCILIATION CONFERENCES, 1991–2000

Although the collapse of the Somali state had profound endogenous causes, it was also, in some ways, a consequence of globalization. In the early 1990s globalization resulted in the *détente* of the competition between East and West, and in Somalia's loss of strategic importance. The globalization trend that accompanied the international intervention after 1992 marked a shift in political culture from unity and nationalism to decentralization, regionalism and local governance. As these principles were encouraged by the international community, Somali leaders used the tactic of local governance and regional empowerment to build political entities; this was the case with Somaliland (established as a self-declared state in May 1991) and Puntland (declared an autonomous state in August 1998).

Following the withdrawal of UNOSOM II in 1995, the European Union (EU), which was the leading donor to Somalia at that time, attempted to bring recalcitrant interlocutors together using project funding and foreign aid conditionalities. Subsequently, Somalia's neighbouring states, namely Ethiopia and Djibouti, took the lead, thereby advancing their own agenda. From 1996 Ethiopia became a key player in the political management of the Somali crisis, directly or indirectly influencing the fate of reconciliation conferences. Ethiopian-sponsored meetings in Sodere in 1996 and 1997 were boycotted by Farah Aidid's son, Hussein Aidid. Farah Aidid had died a few months earlier, in August 1996, after a street battle in Mogadishu against forces loyal to Musa Sudi Yalahow, a minor warlord allied with Osman Hassan Ali Atto, Aidid's former financer, and Ali Mahdi Mohamed. The Sodere conference introduced the '4.5 formula', according to which a quota of representatives in the reconciliation process was allocated to each of Somalia's four major clan families (Darod, Dir, Hawiye and Digil-Mirifle) and one-half of a quota to the smaller clans or 'minorities' (grouped within the '0.5'). When the Somali groups attending the Egyptian-sponsored conference in December 1997 signed the Cairo Peace Accord, Ethiopia convinced two prominent warlords and close allies of the Ethiopian Government, Col Abdullahi Yussuf Ahmed (Darod/Majerten), one of the founders of the Somali Salvation Democratic Front (SSDF), who would become the first President of Puntland in 1998, and Gen. Abdullahi Nur Gabyow (Darod/Ogaden), a former Minister of Defence under Siad Barre and leader of the Somali Patriotic Movement (SPM), to withdraw from the conference and reject the accord.

In 2000 Ismaïl Omar Guelleh, the newly elected President of Djibouti, organized a major reconciliation conference in the village of Arta, west of Djibouti city, at the conclusion of which a Transitional National Charter and a power-sharing agreement based on the 4.5 formula were adopted. A Somali Transitional National Assembly (TNA) and a Transitional National Government (TNG) were subsequently formed; on 13 August the TNA held its inaugural session in Arta. On 26 August the TNA elected Abdulkasim Salad Hasan (Hawiye/Habar Gidir/Ayr), who had held several positions in the Siad Barre regime, as interim President of Somalia. In October President Hasan appointed Ali Khalif Galaydh, a Dulbahante from Somaliland, who was a former minister in the Siad Barre regime, as Prime Minister. Most faction leaders, however, did not participate in the talks, and Ethiopia maintained a hostile attitude towards the TNG. Within 12 months, internal conflict had undermined President Hasan's administration and led to the removal of Galaydh as premier.

THE ELDORET-MBAGATHI RECONCILIATION CONFERENCE, 2002–04

The international community organized a new national reconciliation conference, held under the auspices of the Intergovernmental Authority on Development (IGAD), which began in October 2002 in Eldoret, Kenya. Somali delegations in Eldoret included the TNG, representatives of Puntland, the Somalia Reconciliation and Restoration Council (SRRC), the Juba Valley Alliance and various Mogadishu-based faction leaders, with Somaliland intentionally excluded by the international community. The conference was moved from Eldoret to the Kenyan capital, Nairobi, in February 2003, but the change of locale did not solve the problems affecting the process, the issue of representation being the most serious challenge. However, in September the delegates at the conference adopted a Transitional Federal Charter (TFC), which would lead to the formation of a Transitional Federal Parliament (TFP) with a mandate of four years. However, in October President Hasan blamed the IGAD technical committee for what he termed 'the total breakdown' of the Nairobi conference. He claimed that the official delegates of the TNG had become a minority group in the face of a dozen factions created and supported by Ethiopia. An amended version of the TFC was signed in January 2004. The IGAD technical committee, under the aegis of Ethiopia, in effect selected most of the 275 members of the new parliament. In September Sharif Hassan Sheikh Adan, a businessman from the Rahanweyn clan, was elected Speaker of the TFP. The election for a new President was held in October in Nairobi. Abdullahi Yussuf Ahmed, a former commander of the Somali national army and a faction leader (who in 1998 had led the formation of the self-declared breakaway region of Puntland), as well as a longstanding ally of Ethiopia, secured victory in the third round of voting.

Shortly after his election, Abdullahi Yussuf requested that Ethiopia provide troops to ensure Somalia's security; the Ethiopian Prime Minister gave his assent. Pressure from Ethiopia led to the appointment of Ali Mohamed Ghedi as transitional Prime Minister in November 2004. Ghedi (Hawiye/Abgal/Harti/Warsangeli) was a close relative of a powerful faction leader, Mohamed Dhere, who was based in Jowhar, north of Mogadishu, and was rumoured to be an ally of Ethiopia. Approximately 80% of the Transitional Federal Government (TFG), which was announced in mid-January 2005 as the successor to the TNG, belonged to the SRRC, an alliance of factions that Ethiopia had supported against the TNG in 2001. Members of the TFP, however, were divided over the issue of Ethiopia providing troops to the TFG and the status of the capital. Following a scuffle initiated by supporters of Prime Minister Ghedi during a TFP meeting in March 2005, more than 100 deputies who supported parliamentary Speaker Sharif Hassan Sheikh Adan and a dozen ministers left Nairobi for Mogadishu. The remaining TFG faction left the Kenyan capital in June and established its residence in Jowhar. Abdullahi Yussuf and the TFP were eventually relocated to Baidoa in February 2006.

THE RISE OF THE ISLAMIC COURTS AND THE WAR IN MOGADISHU, 2002–06

The situation in Mogadishu worsened during the Eldoret-Mbagathi conference. In 2002 the various armed factions fought against each other to augment their bargaining power in the political process. Security deteriorated in the capital, and Mogadishu civilians and businessmen responded to the situation by creating neighbourhood militias. In 2002–04 a new set of Islamic courts was established in some zones in Mogadishu to cope with the insecurity. The courts progressively became an alternative to the TFG in exile. By early 2005 a total of 11 of these tribunals had united to form the Islamic Courts Union (ICU). As clan rules prevented full co-operation between the courts, the need for militia who would enforce

Shari'a and bypass clan controversies progressively emerged in 2004–05.

In January 2006 President Abdullahi Yussuf and Sharif Hassan Sheikh Adan, met in Aden, Yemen, and reached an agreement for the reunification of the transitional institutions in Baidoa. The faction leaders, who had proved unable to secure the capital, were politically marginalized. Against this background, a conflict erupted between the ICU and the Alliance for the Restoration of Peace and Counter-Terrorism (ARPCT), a US-backed counter-terrorism coalition. During the first half of the year tensions in Mogadishu escalated into extremely violent confrontations between the US-backed faction leaders and the ICU.

Although the population was not united, the fighting turned into a popular uprising. On 7 May 2006 heavy fighting broke out in north Mogadishu between ICU militia and loyalists of Nur Daqle, a businessman who supported the ARPCT. This fighting drew in both coalitions and led to a week of intensive battles; almost 200 people were killed in the unrest. The worsening violence prompted a large mobilization of militias, and a new round of fighting broke out on 24 May and quickly expanded to become a series of battles across Mogadishu, involving all of the main clan and court militias. In the following week the ARPCT lost ground, and the ICU took control of some of Mogadishu's most strategically important areas. The final battle took place in Bal'ad, north of Mogadishu, previously a stronghold of Yalahow, which fell to a local militia allied with the ICU. The ICU's victory in Mogadishu meant the end of the factions as structuring units of Somali politics.

The uncertain transition that followed the seizure of the capital marked a turning point in the radical transformation of the political arena in Mogadishu and elsewhere in Somalia, reshaping the relationship between the different groups that comprised the ICU. Al-Shabaab, 'the Youth', a radical Islamist populist group that had started organizing itself in 2003, progressively gained a degree of appeal and strength, while the ICU was confronted with many internal contradictions and external challenges. The precarious balance between the different groups within the ICU became increasingly unsteady after June 2006. Nevertheless, the influence of the ICU quickly spread beyond Mogadishu. The ICU's expansion took the form of military annexation in Lower Juba, with the capture of the city of Kismayu in September.

In June 2006 the TFG and the ICU met in Khartoum, Sudan, for talks. Although the two parties signed an accord in which they recognized each other and declared a ceasefire, the fragile agreement did not gain momentum. On 20 July US-backed Ethiopian troops entered Somalia to support the TFG in Baidoa. On 6 December the UN Security Council adopted a resolution authorizing IGAD and the African Union (AU) to establish a protection and training mission in Somalia. After vehemently criticizing the Security Council resolution, the Somali Supreme Islamic Courts Council (SSICC, as the ICU had been renamed) declared an ultimatum on 13 December, demanding the withdrawal of Ethiopian troops from the Baidoa area within one week. On 20 December skirmishes broke out near Baidoa, marking the beginning of a new war.

THE ETHIOPIAN INVASION AND THE DJIBOUTI ACCORDS, 2006–09

The US-backed Ethiopian military intervention in Somalia in December 2006 was based on international concerns related to the 'war on terror' and the hunt for members of the militant Islamist organization al-Qa'ida; it also advanced the interests of the Ethiopian regime, which was eager to prevent the emergence along its southern border of a new power sympathetic to Eritrea and armed Ethiopian opposition groups. After having defeated SSICC forces near Baidoa on 20 December, Ethiopian troops pressed southwards and eastwards, before marching into Mogadishu on 28 December. The Somali crisis entered a new cycle of violence. Under Ethiopian protection, the TFG moved to Mogadishu. By 13 January 2007 the Ethiopian army had driven most of the remnants of the SSICC forces into the southern tip of Somalia at Ras Kamboni, where the troops of the SSICC were attacked by US air and sea forces and Kenyan ground units. After Ethiopian and TFG forces defeated SSICC troops and allied militias in the town of Jilib at the beginning of January, Sheikh Sharif Sheikh Ahmed (the head of the SSICC's executive committee) fled towards the Kenyan border where he surrendered to the Kenyan authorities. However, on 1 February he was released from Kenyan custody and fled to Yemen, where he was granted political asylum.

On 21 February 2007 the UN Security Council adopted a resolution authorizing the AU to deploy up to 8,000 military personnel to assist the TFG. The first contingent of the AU Mission in Somalia (AMISOM) was deployed to Mogadishu in early March, but did little to stop the conflict. The SSICC's fight against Ethiopian forces and their TFG allies turned into an insurgency. By the end of March the fighting had intensified in Mogadishu, and more than 1,000 people had been killed. In July a fierce battle broke out in the Bakaraha market. Bloody armed confrontations continued over the following months.

The Ethiopian intervention and the following two years of fighting resulted in the reassertion of Salafi ideology and power. No longer a subordinate force within the SSICC, al-Shabaab became the symbol of resistance to the Ethiopian invasion. Recruitment rose, and al-Shabaab built paramilitary camps in areas that were beyond regular Ethiopian control. In July 2007 a reconciliation conference, chaired by Ali Mahdi Mohamed and boycotted by Hawiye elders, SSICC leaders and anti-Ethiopian militants, was held in Mogadishu, and a competing national reconciliation conference was organized in Asmara, Eritrea. After a week of talks, the conference participants announced the creation of a united opposition party, the Alliance for the Re-liberation of Somalia (ARS). A central committee of about 191 members, chaired by Sheikh Sharif Sheikh Ahmed, was established to lead the campaign against the TFG. Meanwhile, the conference in Mogadishu failed to stop the violence, with hundreds reported to have been killed in fighting during the talks. By October the TFG was beset by infighting, and on 11 October 22 ministers signed a letter requesting a vote of confidence; one week later Prime Minister Ali Mohamed Ghedi resigned. On 22 November Abdullahi Yussuf named Nur Hassan Hussein 'Adde' (Hawiye/Abgal), a former police chief and Secretary-General of the Somali Red Crescent Society, as Prime Minister.

By early 2008 it had become clear that Ethiopia could not win the war. In March negotiations between the TFG and the most moderate section of the opposition began in Djibouti (the so-called Djibouti Peace Process, which lasted until January 2009). As a result, the armed opposition started to fragment. In May 2008 the ARS split over the issue of rapprochement with the TFG. Hassan Dahir Aweys, a former senior commander of the ICU, established himself in Eritrea and committed his wing of the party, the ARS-Asmara, to a violent insurgency against the TFG and Ethiopian forces. Conversely, Sheikh Sharif Sheikh Ahmed adopted a conciliatory posture and his wing of the ARS, based in Djibouti, merged with the TFG. The Djibouti wing of the ARS also agreed to condemn violence and dissociate itself from those who broke the ceasefire, including al-Shabaab and the ARS-Asmara. Consequently, the UN Security Council recognized the Djibouti wing of the ARS.

Ethiopia withdrew its troops from Somalia in January 2009. Meanwhile, following the signing of a power-sharing agreement with his former opponents in the TFG on 26 November 2008 in Djibouti, Sheikh Sharif Sheikh Ahmed returned to Mogadishu. Ethiopia's withdrawal was intended to facilitate negotiations between Prime Minister Nur Hassan and Sheikh Sharif Sheikh Ahmed's faction of the ARS. However, personal rivalries between President Abdullahi Yussuf and the Prime Minister led to the dismissal of Nur Hassan in December. The TFP, instead of ratifying the President's action, voted overwhelmingly to reinstate the Prime Minister. As a result, Abdullahi Yussuf left office on 21 December and returned to Puntland. As Ethiopia began its withdrawal from Somalia, al-Shabaab troops entered Baidoa. In January 2009 members of the TFP relocated from Baidoa to Djibouti to elect a new President and also endorsed the power-sharing agreement that had been signed by Sheikh Sharif Sheikh Ahmed and the TFG in Djibouti in November 2008. This allocated 200 seats in the TFP to Sheikh Sharif Sheikh Ahmed's faction of the ARS and a further 75 to 'civil society' representatives and others. As a result, the TFP was expanded from 275 to 550 seats. On 31 January 2009 Sheikh Sharif Sheikh Ahmed was elected President of Somalia.

THE END OF THE TRANSITIONAL PERIOD, 2009–12

In February 2009 Sheikh Sharif Sheikh Ahmed appointed Omar Abdirashid Ali Sharmarke (Darod/Majerten/Osman Mahmud) as Prime Minister. A Canadian citizen, Ali Sharmarke was a son of former President Abdirashid Ali Sharmarke. Meanwhile, the TFG had lost most of the territory that it claimed to control a few days before Sheikh Sharif Sheikh Ahmed's election. Although a group of former SSICC cadres had defected to the TFG, the opposition had not disarmed; on the contrary, some former SSICC members had joined al-Shabaab, and in early February ARS remnants rallied in Afmadow under a new umbrella, Hizbul Islam ('Party of Islam'), led by Omar Imam Abubaker.

From the outset, the new TFG was tainted by corruption and badly managed. Moreover, the AU military intervention, in the form of about 3,500 Ugandan and Burundian soldiers receiving training from South African officers under the banner of AMISOM, was proving inadequate. Dahir Aweys returned to Mogadishu in late April 2009, with a view to rallying his Islamist troops on the ground, both from within the ARS-Asmara and from among supporters in his Hawiye/Habar Gidir/Ayr clan, and railed against the presence of AMISOM troops in Somalia. At the same time, President Sheikh Sharif Sheikh Ahmed endorsed the introduction of *Shari'a* in Somalia and convened a council of Somali clerics from all over the world in an attempt to rally Islamist elements around his own faction of the ARS. This tactic, however, failed to undermine al-Shabaab. Whereas Dahir Aweys endeavoured to unite Hizbul Islam against Sheikh Sharif Sheikh Ahmed, the latter gained support from Ahlu Sunna Wal Jama (ASWJ), a Sufi militia that had taken up arms against al-Shabaab and driven it out of most of the Galgaduud, Hiran and Middle Shabelle regions. Al-Shabaab responded to its loss of terrain by intensifying terror attacks. In May an insurgency front spearheaded by al-Shabaab and including fighters from various groups within Hizbul Islam conducted an offensive against Sheikh Sharif Sheikh Ahmed's regime in Mogadishu. The offensive failed, and the uneasy military co-operation between the two organizations collapsed a few months later as relations between al-Shabaab and Hizbul Islam dramatically deteriorated.

In August 2009 hostilities between the two groups erupted in southern Somalia, especially around Kismayu, after which al-Shabaab gained control of the city. Riven by internal divisions, Hizbul Islam was progressively defeated by its former ally during 2010. Al-Shabaab seized control of the Hiran and Bay regions and subsequently expelled Hizbul Islam from all the positions it held. In December Hizbul Islam's leadership was forced to merge with al-Shabaab.

Meanwhile, the TFG was blighted by a power struggle between Prime Minister Ali Sharmarke and President Sheikh Sharif Sheikh Ahmed. In September 2010 the Prime Minister announced his resignation and was replaced in November by Mohamed Abdullahi Mohamed 'Farmajo' (Darod/Marehan), a Somali-American who had lived outside Somalia for over 20 years. Growing enmity between the President and the TFP Speaker, Sharif Hassan Sheikh Adan, led to renewed external intervention, and, under pressure from the USA, the UN, Ethiopia and Uganda, a conference was held in the Ugandan capital, Kampala, on 9 June 2011 to discuss the modalities for completing the transition to a permanent government by the scheduled date—the TFG mandate was due to expire in August. It was agreed that this deadline would be impossible to meet and the planned completion date of the transition was postponed for one year, until August 2012.

Differences between President Sheikh Sharif Sheikh Ahmed and Sharif Hassan Sheikh Adan continued, however, mostly surrounding Abdullahi Mohamed 'Farmajo'. In order for the President to secure Sharif Hassan Sheikh Adan's agreement to the proposed extension of the transitional period, the Prime Minister was obliged to submit his resignation within 30 days. Abdiweli Mohamed Ali 'Gas' (Darod/Majerten), another Somali

from the diaspora with dual US nationality, was appointed Prime Minister on 23 June 2011. To ensure compliance with the Kampala agreement, the UN Special Representative for Somalia, Augustine Mahiga, a Tanzanian, negotiated a road map for completing the transition by 20 August 2012.

Although al-Shabaab retreated from Mogadishu on 7 August 2011, it was far from being defeated. The group had started recruiting members from Kenya and Uganda. Kenya intervened in Somalia on 16 October. Kenya's Chief of Defence Forces Gen. Julius Karangi declared that the intervention's aim was to oust al-Shabaab from southern Somalia and that the operation would continue until Kenya was safe. The operation, however, stalled because of the onset of the rainy season, and the Kenyan forces and their Raskamboni Movement Somali allies only captured Kismayu from al-Shabaab on 29 September 2012.

Instead of securing the Kenya–Somalia border region, Kenya's intervention led to an increasing number of terrorist attacks being carried out by al-Shabaab on Kenyan soil. It also created the conditions for a new intervention of the Ethiopian army, whose activities in the Bay and Bakool regions increased. However, the road map for the completion of the transition stayed on track, despite some political undercurrents, such as the parliamentary crisis that erupted in December 2011, leading to the eventual dismissal of Sharif Hassan Sheikh Adan, who was replaced as Speaker of the TFP in January 2012 by Madobe Nunow Mohamed.

Two conferences were held in Garowe, Puntland, on 15 December 2011 and on 15 February 2012. Six leaders from the TFG and the regional administrations of Puntland and Galmudug, under the auspices of the UN Political Office for Somalia, agreed on the 'end of the transition road map'. This included several provisions, among which were the creation of a bicameral federal legislature and the establishment of a National Constituent Assembly (NCA), which was to draw up and approve the draft of a new constitution. The NCA held its inaugural meeting on 25 July, and the text of the Provisional Constitution was approved by the NCA on 1 August. The Provisional Constitution provided for a bicameral Federal Parliament (replacing the TFP), which would comprise a 275-member House of the People and an Upper House, and which would elect a new President. A list of deputies was approved by the NCA (although the selection process was reportedly rife with corruption), and the Federal Parliament was officially inaugurated for a four-year term on 20 August. Mohamed Osman Jawari, a former minister of the Siad Barre regime, was elected as Speaker. The election of the new President by the Federal Parliament took place on 10 September. Sheikh Sharif Sheikh Ahmed narrowly won the first round, ahead of Hassan Sheikh Mohamud and Abdiweli Mohamed Ali. Abdiweli and a fourth candidate withdrew from the election prior to the second poll. In the second round of voting, which took place on the same day, Mohamud overwhelmingly defeated the outgoing President, Sheikh Sharif Sheikh Ahmed.

POST-TRANSITION SOMALIA, 2012–16

The end of the transition was internationally hailed as the beginning of a new era in Somalia's history. The election of Hassan Sheikh Mohamud (Hawiye/Abgal), a prominent civil society member, fostered this image of novelty. In early October 2012 President Mohamud appointed a relatively unknown political newcomer, Abdi Farah Shirdon Saaid (Darod/Marehan), a wealthy Kenyan businessman, as Prime Minister. On 4 November Shirdon announced a Government comprising just 10 ministers.

In January 2013 Mohamud visited the USA and met US Secretary of State Hillary Clinton, who announced formal US recognition of the Government of Somalia. This was the first time that the USA had recognized a Somali administration since 1991. A second London conference on Somalia was held in May 2013 (the first having taken place in February 2012), co-hosted by the UK and Somalia. The initial enthusiasm, however, progressively waned, as accusations of corruption multiplied and the Government's performance came under increasing criticism. Partly as a result of the pressure to meet external requirements and deadlines, and partly as a consequence of the ambiguous provisions contained in the Provisional Constitution, tensions within Somalia's ruling elite heightened. In December Abdi Farah Shirdon and Hassan Sheikh Mohamud failed to agree over the composition of a new Government, and the Prime Minister was removed following the passage of a parliamentary vote of no confidence.

Abdiweli Sheikh Ahmed (Darod/Marehan), an economist, was appointed as Prime Minister in December 2013. A new Government was formed in January 2014, but it was also relatively short-lived. A major political crisis erupted in October, resulting in a deterioration in relations between Hassan Sheikh Mohamud and Abdiweli Sheikh Ahmed. President Mohamud survived the crisis and Abdiweli was removed from his post following his defeat in a parliamentary vote of no confidence in early December. In mid-December Omar Abdirashid Ali Sharmarke (Prime Minister in 2009–10) again assumed the premiership, and in February 2015 a new Government was formed.

Al-Shabaab's terrorist activity also significantly increased in Kenya following the Kenya Defence Forces' intervention in Somalia. In September 2013 al-Shabaab staged a large-scale attack against the Westgate shopping mall in Nairobi, killing 67 people. In November 2014 al-Shabaab militants ambushed a bus in Mandera County, near the Kenya–Somalia border, killing 28 passengers, and 10 days later al-Shabaab attacked quarry workers in the same area, leaving 36 people dead. In April 2015 the Islamist movement launched a major onslaught against Garissa University College, in north-eastern Kenya, killing 147 people.

Following the Westgate attack, military action against al-Shabaab in Somalia intensified. Several counter-operations were conducted by US naval security forces in late 2013 and were followed by further US attacks by unmanned aerial vehicles (drones). In January 2014 Ethiopian troops were officially integrated into AMISOM, increasing its strength to more than 22,000. After the launch of Operation Indian Ocean in August, AMISOM and Somali government troops seized control of Barawa from al-Shabaab in October. Meanwhile, in early September al-Shabaab leader Ahmed Abdi Godane was killed in a US drone strike about 240 km south of Mogadishu. Sheikh Ahmad Umar 'Abu Ubaidah' was named as his successor.

The realities of Somalia's situation were in stark contrast to the goals of 'Vision 2016', the Government's 'blueprint for action'. This entailed: the democratic formation of regional interim administrations and federal states; the revision and adoption of the Constitution; and the holding of national elections in 2016. A cornerstone of both the road map for ending the transition and Vision 2016, the process of establishing a federal system precipitated repeated crises. After several months of political stalemate, the Interim Juba Administration (IJA) was established in August 2013 through an agreement signed in the Ethiopian capital, Addis Ababa, by the Government and the Kenyan-supported Raskamboni Movement and its leader, Ahmed Mohamed Islam Madobe. The IJA's Regional Assembly, the first regional parliament to be created in Somalia, was officially inaugurated in May 2015. Several clans, however, claimed that the selection process had been overly dominated by IJA President Madobe and that the number of assembly members had not been divided fairly between clans and districts. The Federal Parliament adopted a motion of no confidence in the Regional Assembly in June, and subsequently the IJA suspended relations with the Federal Government. In August Madobe was re-elected as President of the IJA.

The second step in the federation process was the creation of the South West Interim Administration, including Bay, Bakool and Lower Shabelle, and the election of its President, former parliamentary Speaker Sharif Hassan Sheikh Aden, in November 2014. Creating the Galmudug Interim Administration (GIA) proved more difficult, as Puntland's boundaries were affected by the idea of merging North Mudug with South Mudug to create a new federal entity. A regional assembly was finally inaugurated in the town of Adado in June 2015, and Abdikarim Hussein Guled, a former Minister of the Interior and Minister of National Security, was elected President of the

GIA in July. The contention with Puntland over borders, however, remained unresolved. In November clashes between clan militias erupted in the town of Galkayo, in the Mudug region, leaving at least 40 people dead and hundreds injured. These clashes followed tensions between the GIA and Puntland over disputed landing rights and the construction of a new road encroaching upon the line that demarcated clan-based zones on the town's north–south boundary. HirShabelle State, consisting of Hiran and Middle Shabelle regions, was established in October 2016.

In 2015–16 al-Shabaab suffered territorial losses, casualties among its senior commanders and defections. Together with the US campaign of drone strikes and Somali special forces operations, clan-based militias forced al-Shabaab out of several locations in the Middle Shabelle and Hiran regions in February 2016, as did the Sufi-inspired anti-al-Shabaab militia ASWJ, backed by Ethiopian forces, in Gedo. Furthermore, the Somali army, supported by AMISOM, recaptured several areas, particularly in the Bakool and Hiran regions. In the latter half of 2015 a split also emerged within al-Shabaab. As a result of ideological tensions and efforts by the militant Islamic State group to rally members of al-Shabaab to its cause, a prominent al-Shabaab leader, Sheikh Abdulqadir Mumin, pledged allegiance to Islamic State in October.

Despite the initial consensus that the 2012 election process should not be repeated, in 2015 it became clear that 'one person, one vote' elections would not be possible in the absence of a general census or a national electoral register. Elections for the Upper House and the House of the People were scheduled to take place in mid-2016, with a new President being elected in September, but they were postponed for several months. Moreover, the way in which Federal Member States had been created, without any popular consultation, had led to a situation where an arrangement between the country's main political players was needed to define the modalities of the electoral process. A National Consultative Forum, comprising the leaders of the Federal Government and the Federal Member States, was tasked with determining the electoral model.

THE 2016–17 ELECTION PROCESS

The electoral process began in October 2016 and ended on 8 February 2017 with the election of former Prime Minister Mohamed Abdullahi Mohamed 'Farmajo' as the new President of Somalia. An Upper House of Parliament was elected for the first time. Each new Federal Member State elected eight of its 54 members, while Somaliland and Puntland elected 11 senators each. However, the Parliament of Somaliland, which was supposed to choose the senators representing the self-proclaimed state, was strongly opposed to the electoral process. As a result, Somaliland's 11 representatives were selected by an assembly of customary chiefs. The President of each new Federal Member State was entrusted with presenting a list of candidates to the regional parliament, which would then elect the eight senators. However, some regional leaders presented a list of only eight candidates, thereby pre-determining the election outcome. This contributed to tensions between the Presidents of Jubaland, Galmudug and South West State and their regional parliaments after the elections. The President of Galmudug, Abdikarim Hussein Guled, a close ally of Hassan Sheikh Mohamud, resigned at the end of February, after the regional parliament approved a no-confidence motion against him in January. The members of the Galmudug state assembly elected Ahmed Duale Gelle 'Haaf', a well-known businessman, as President of Galmudug in May. Even more problematically, several former armed faction leaders, including Abdi Hassan Awale (Qeybdiid), Muse Sudi Yalahow and Abdirahman Mohamed Farole, were elected as Upper House representatives. The election of the representatives to the House of the People was even more controversial. As in 2012, the process began with the selection of 135 clan elders to represent the country's moral authority. The elders appointed a group of lower-ranking customary chiefs entrusted with the selection of an electoral body of 51 voters for each parliamentary seat. The selection of the 135 clan elders was reportedly influenced by political pressures, kinship considerations and group interests. The appointment of the 51 electors for each lower house seat was equally marred by irregularities.

The list of presidential candidates reflected the level of political fragmentation in the country. The incumbent President, Hassan Sheikh Mohamud (Hawiye/Abgal), former President Sheikh Sharif Sheikh Ahmed (Hawiye/Abgal), the incumbent Prime Minister, Omar Abdirashid Ali Sharmarke (Darod/Majerten) and former Prime Minister Mohamed Abdullahi Mohamed 'Farmajo' (Darod/Marehan) were among the 24 candidates contesting the presidency. For the first time, members of both houses of Parliament participated in the election. In the first round of voting, incumbent President Mohamud secured 88 votes, narrowly ahead of former Prime Minister Mohamed, with 72, while former President Sheikh Ahmed received 49 votes and incumbent premier Sharmarke 37. The last subsequently withdrew from the election, while the three other candidates contested a second round on the same day, at which Mohamed won 184 votes, Mohamud 97 and Sheikh Ahmed 46. Although a two-thirds' majority was constitutionally required to secure victory, Mohamud conceded the presidency to Mohamed, amid celebrations in Mogadishu. Mohamed was officially inaugurated as President on 22 February 2017. Hassan Ali Khayre (who, as prescribed by the 4.5 power-sharing formula, was Hawiye) was subsequently appointed as the new Prime Minister, and a new Government was formed.

RELATIONS WITH KEY EXTERNAL POWERS

After Saudi Arabia and its allies cut ties with Qatar in June 2017, President Mohamed, whose election campaign had been financially supported by Qatar, was put under pressure to sever Somalia's relations with Doha. None the less, he decided officially to maintain a neutral stance. Saudi Arabia remained Somalia's main trading partner, while the United Arab Emirates (UAE) had been providing financial assistance to the Federal Government, as well as equipment, funding and training to the Somali national army since 2014. In addition, earlier in 2017 the UAE had signed multi-million-US dollar port investment deals with Somaliland and Puntland (see *Economy*), and an agreement with Somaliland to lease a military base in Berbera for a 25-year period, with the intention of developing it into a military airport. Labelled as 'illegal' by the Somali Government, these deals had the effect of worsening the already complicated relations between Somalia, Somaliland and neighbouring Ethiopia, and between the Government and the Federal Member States. Meanwhile, Turkey finalized the construction of a US $40m. military training camp in Mogadishu in July.

Mounting tensions between the Federal Government and the UAE also complicated a crisis within the Somali Parliament. In late 2017 a dispute between Prime Minister Khayre and a pro-Government faction on the one side and a rival faction led by the Speaker of the House of the People, Mohamed Osman Jawari, on the other divided Parliament into two opposing blocs. The dispute, which had reportedly been prompted by the Prime Minister's frustration with Jawari's obstruction of government-sponsored bills, escalated in February 2018. No-confidence motions were tabled against the Prime Minister, while the Government accused its rivals of receiving financial backing from the UAE to orchestrate a parliamentary coup aimed at ousting President Mohamed and Prime Minister Khayre. Mohamed and Khayre gave their support to a large group of deputies who were demanding that the Speaker resign. Amid allegations of funding from Qatar and the UAE in support of the rival factions, a new crisis arose between the Federal Government on the one hand and Somaliland and the UAE on the other. In early March Somaliland finalized a contract with the Emirati-based port operator DP World for the development of Berbera port, allowing Ethiopia to take a 19% stake in the project for an undisclosed sum. The Somali Federal Government protested to the Arab League, arguing that the deal violated its sovereignty. At the same time, the Federal Parliament approved legislation banning DP World from operating in Somalia, thereby prohibiting other potential deals between the Emirati port operator and regional administrations. In response, Somaliland's newly

elected President, Muse Bihi Abdi (see *Somaliland*), labelled the Federal Government's attempt to block the Berbera contract as a 'declaration of war'. The new legislation, which was approved by a substantial majority, bolstered Jawari's political standing, strengthening him in his confrontation with the President and the Prime Minister. As a result, the dispute between the Government and the Speaker rapidly escalated. On 16 March, amid allegations that a group of 40 deputies was planning to introduce a no-confidence motion against the Prime Minister, the Government deployed army units outside the parliament building and throughout Mogadishu. Jawari urged deputies to protect the legislature, and some of them reportedly mobilized clan militias. However, on 9 April Jawari resigned, after realizing that he would lose a government-sponsored vote to oust him.

The Federal Government's relations with the UAE reached a new nadir on 8 April 2018, when Somali officials confiscated US $6m. in cash from an Emirati aeroplane at Mogadishu airport, on the grounds that it was evidence of the UAE's interference in Somali affairs. The UAE rejected this allegation, claiming that the money was to be used to pay the salaries of the Somali security forces, and halted its aid and military co-operation programmes in the Somali capital. As a result, the UAE continued to strengthen its relationships with the regional administrations and Somaliland. In late April a delegation from Puntland travelled to the UAE to meet with Emirati government officials and representatives of the state-owned firm P&O Ports, which had won a 30-year concession for the management and development of Bosaso port in 2017 (see *Economy*). Tensions between the Federal Government and the Federal Member States continued to mount, reaching a new peak in September 2018. Gathered in Kismayu for a meeting of the Council of Inter-State Co-operation, which had been established in October 2017, the regional leaders officially suspended working relations with the Federal Government, accusing it of interfering in regional issues, failing to manage the country's security, and neglecting to share national income and international aid.

Although he had repeatedly pledged to protect Somalia's sovereignty against foreign powers, especially Ethiopia, during his election campaign, President Mohamed promptly moved to reassure Ethiopia once in office. In June 2018 the President signed a co-operation agreement with the Ethiopian Prime Minister, Dr Abiy Ahmed Ali, securing Ethiopia's joint participation in the development of four of Somalia's most strategic ports. On 30 July, just weeks after Ethiopia and Eritrea had signed a peace agreement ending the 20-year conflict between the two countries, President Mohamed visited Asmara to meet with his Eritrean counterpart, President Issaias Afewerki, and restore diplomatic relations with Eritrea. Both sides also signed a co-operation agreement. The Presidents of Somalia and Eritrea and the Ethiopian Prime Minister gathered in Asmara for a tripartite meeting in September. The three leaders signed a joint co-operation agreement aimed at building closer ties in order to promote regional peace and stability.

Amid a fractured political landscape, al-Shabaab continued to attack civilian and military targets in Mogadishu and in rural areas across south-central Somalia. In January 2017, just over a year after the group had seized the Kenya Defence Forces' camp in El Adde, in the Gedo region, al-Shabaab temporarily captured a military base in Kolbiyow, 18 km from the Kenyan–Somali border, allegedly killing at least 57 Kenyan troops. During the first half of 2017 the usual pattern of conflict prevailed, with al-Shabaab and AMISOM alternatively gaining and losing territory in southern Somalia. On 14 October twin truck bombings in Mogadishu killed 512 people, the vast majority of whom were civilians, marking the deadliest attack in Somalia since 2007. Although al-Shabaab, confronted with unprecedented popular anger, neither denied nor claimed responsibility for the attack, it was established that the group was almost certainly culpable.

Only two days before the 14 October 2017 attack, the Chief of Staff of the Armed Forces, Ahmed Jimale Gedi, and the Minister of Defence, Abdirashid Abdullahi Mohamed, had resigned. Within weeks, the head of the National Intelligence and Security Agency and the Chief of the National Police had been dismissed for failing to prevent the 14 October bombings and an attack on the Nasa Hablod Hotel in Mogadishu on 28 October, which had left 23 people dead. In February 2018 twin car bombs exploded near the presidential residence, killing 45 people. In July 14 Somali security officers were arrested over alleged collusion with al-Shabaab following a deadly attack on the headquarters of the Ministry of the Interior, Federal Affairs and Reconciliation. Later that month President Mohamed announced a major reorganization of senior presidential and security personnel. Despite these measures, al-Shabaab continued to kill civilians, especially in Mogadishu, and to attack Somali soldiers and AMISOM troops in Lower Shabelle and Middle and Lower Juba during mid-2018. On 30 July the UN Security Council renewed AMISOM's mandate until 31 May 2019.

In October 2016 Ethiopia, concerned about domestic issues, began withdrawing troops from Bakool, Hiran and Galgadud regions, allowing al-Shabaab to fill the vacuum. The USA, meanwhile, was increasing its military engagement in Somalia. In September a US helicopter strike killed 22 GIA troops initially identified as al-Shabaab militants. Galmudug officials accused Puntland of giving the US military faulty intelligence. In March 2017 the new US President, Donald Trump, designated part of Somalia an 'area of active hostilities' and approved a proposal by the US Department of Defense to relax the rules of engagement for US air strikes and raids targeting suspected al-Shabaab militants. In May a member of a US Navy special operations group was killed (the first US casualty in Somalia since 1993) and at least two others were injured in a raid against al-Shabaab. US Africa Command (AFRICOM) increased air strikes and ground operations in 2018, particularly in Lower Shabelle and Juba. Although US attacks appeared to have damaged al-Shabaab's leadership and assets, these tactics failed to stop the insurgency.

Despite claims by the Federal Government and the US armed forces that the Islamist insurgency was on the wane, al-Shabaab remained in firm control of most rural areas, operating a parallel government that administered its own courts, road tolls and taxes, and continued to stage attacks across Somalia, ranging from kidnappings to major bomb attacks. Meanwhile, in January 2019 the Federal Government expelled UN Special Representative and Head of the UN Assistance Mission in Somalia (UNSOM) Nicholas Haysom from the country, after he denounced the federal authorities' arrest of the former deputy leader of al-Shabaab and candidate in the South West State presidential election, Sheikh Mukhtar Robow Ali (see *Recent Developments in the Federal Member States*). At the end of May the UN Secretary-General appointed a US diplomat, James Swan, to replace Haysom. At least 26 people, including several tribal leaders, regional politicians and foreign nationals, were killed and 56 injured during an attack by al-Shabaab gunmen and siege at the Asasey Hotel in Kismayu on 12 July. The Mayor of Mogadishu, Abdirahman Omar Osman, was seriously injured and six other officials killed in a suicide bombing at his offices in the capital on 24 July. Al-Shabaab stated that the attack had targeted Swan, who had visited the offices shortly before. Osman was taken to Qatar to receive medical treatment, where he died a week later. At the end of September al-Shabaab staged an offensive against a major launching site for drone operations, a US base at Baledogle, about 110 km north-west of Mogadishu; US military officials announced that the assailants had been repulsed rapidly. On the same day an AMISOM convoy of Italian peacekeepers was targeted in a car bomb attack in Mogadishu. Around 10 militants were reported to have been killed in two reprisal air strikes by US forces. However, the campaign of US air strikes in Somalia had become highly controversial following reports by human rights organization Amnesty International of civilian fatalities, and in April AFRICOM acknowledged for the first time that two civilians had been killed in an air strike one year earlier; some observers considered that the long-term impact of the operations was likely to exacerbate radicalization and violence. In the worst attack in Mogadishu since the truck bombings of October 2017, at least 79 people, principally university students and police officers, were killed and 125 injured in a truck bomb attack at a central security checkpoint on 28 December 2019.

As part of a decision by the outgoing US Administration of President Trump to reduce the number of US forces deployed globally, around 700 US military personnel based in Somalia had been withdrawn by mid-January 2021, despite the increasing number of attacks by al-Shabaab. (However, in June the head of AFRICOM announced that the US Department of Defense, under Trump's successor, President Joe Biden, was considering the return of troops to Somalia.) In July the first US air strike in Somalia since Biden came to office was conducted near Galkayo. The Biden Administration had initially suspended drone strikes to allow an investigation into their efficacy, in a context where human rights organizations had repeatedly drawn attention to the significant civilian casualties caused by drones.

Meanwhile, Somalia's politics were further polarized by the ongoing maritime border dispute between Somalia and Kenya. Somalia had brought a case against Kenya at the International Court of Justice (ICJ), at the Hague, the Netherlands, in August 2014, seeking to determine its maritime boundary with Kenya, following a long-term dispute over rights to the exploration and exploitation of offshore petroleum reserves. In early 2019 Kenya's diplomatic stance grew more assertive, notably after a document leaked from Somalia's Ministry of Petroleum and Mineral Resources suggested that five out of the 56 oil blocks that the ministry had unveiled in its inaugural offshore hydrocarbons licensing round in early February were located in the disputed maritime area. The Kenyan Government suspended diplomatic ties with Somalia later that month and expelled the Somali ambassador from Nairobi. Tensions rose further in May when the Kenyan Government hosted a delegation from Somaliland in Nairobi while on the same day denying transit through Kenya to several Somali federal government ministers. It was reported in March that Kenyan troops had begun to withdraw from Somalia, after abandoning a command centre in Jubaland. In mid-2019 Kenya sought to resolve the border dispute through political negotiations rather than through the ICJ, but Somalia insisted that the case be settled in court. On 3 September, shortly before proceedings were due to start, the Kenyan Government formally requested that the ICJ postpone the case in order to provide more time to recruit a new defence team. The ICJ accepted the request and delayed the public hearing of the case.

On 15 December 2020 the Somali Government severed diplomatic links with Kenya and deployed troops at the countries' joint border, in protest against perceived interference by Kenya in Somalia's internal affairs, after Somaliland President Bihi visited Kenya for co-operative discussions with Kenyan President Uhuru Kenyatta (see *Somaliland*); Kenya's ambassador in Mogadishu was ordered to leave the country. In early 2021 Somalia accused the Kenyan Government of equipping local militia in Jubaland's Gedo region. Proceedings on the maritime boundary dispute case commenced at the ICJ in mid-March, although Kenya had withdrawn participation in protest against perceived bias by the Court and its rejection of requests to delay hearings further. However, following mediation by Qatar, on 6 May the Somali Government announced the restoration of diplomatic relations with Kenya. In June Kenya accepted the invitation of Somalia to reopen its embassy in Mogadishu. In a further sign of improving ties, Kenyatta attended the inauguration of Somalia's new President, Hassan Sheikh Mohamud, in June 2022 (see below), and in the following month the two countries concluded a trade deal that provided for the resumption of qat imports from Kenya, after a two-year suspension.

On 12 March 2021 the UN Security Council extended the mandate of AMISOM (which had been due to expire on 28 February) to the end of December, maintaining its maximum strength of 19,626 uniformed personnel, prior to the planned transfer of responsibilities to the Somali security forces. On 31 March 2022 the UN Security Council unanimously adopted Resolution 2628, reconfiguring AMISOM into the AU Transition Mission in Somalia. In a significant reappraisal of its earlier ambitions regarding the Somali security forces, the UN Security Council expressed no more than the 'hope that the Government of Somalia will gradually assume greater security responsibilities', and 'underscored the need to continue countering al-Shabaab'. The mandated maximum force strength of this reconfigured military deployment was to remain at 19,626 until 31 December, and then be reduced to 17,626 during January–March 2023.

DELAYED ELECTIONS AND THE RETURN OF HASSAN SHEIKH MOHAMUD

On 19 December 2019 Somalia's 'international partners' (AMISOM, the UN, IGAD, the EU and international governments) issued a statement urging the Federal Government to fulfil its commitments to organize elections before the mandate of the current administration expired on 8 February 2021. Following nationwide consultative meetings, draft electoral legislation providing for a 'one person, one vote' system (replacing the 4.5 clan power-sharing formula) was overwhelmingly approved by the lower House of the People on 28 December 2019. Under the new system, Somali citizens were to vote directly for parties, with parliamentary seats being allocated according to the final tallies, following which the Federal Parliament would elect the President and Prime Minister. The Upper House approved the new legislation on 2 February 2020, and President Abdullahi Mohamed signed it into law on 20 February.

Somalia's political and security difficulties were compounded by the impact of the COVID-19 pandemic from March 2020. Measures introduced by the Government during March included the closure of borders, the prohibition of large gatherings and the suspension of international flights.

On 27 June 2020 the National Independent Electoral Commission (NIEC) announced that it would not be possible to hold the legislative elections on 27 November as provisionally scheduled, citing the COVID-19 pandemic, flooding, the ongoing insecurity and political differences, and informed the House of the People that elections based on a biometric system of voter registration would require a postponement to August 2021. Prime Minister Khayre maintained that there could be no delay in holding the elections, while President Abdullahi Mohamed favoured a postponement and the universal suffrage system. On 25 July 2020 Khayre was ousted by an overwhelming parliamentary vote of no confidence, with Speaker of the House of the People Mohamed Mursal Sheikh Abdirahman accusing the Federal Government of failing to fulfil its promises, including to hold 'one person, one vote' elections.

Meanwhile, al-Shabaab had increased its attacks across the country, and on 16 August 2020 staged an assault on the Elite Hotel in Mogadishu, in which at least 16 people were killed. Following a meeting on 19 August in Dhusamareb, the capital of Galmudug, between the leaders of Galmudug, South West State and HirShabelle, the Mayor of Mogadishu (representing the Benadir Regional Administration) and President Abdullahi Mohamed, it was announced that agreement had been reached on a new electoral model. On 17 September a new 15-point agreement was reached, according to which (similarly to the framework for the 2016–17 elections) clan elders would select a 101-delegate electoral college for each seat in the 275-member House of the People, while state assemblies would elect the Upper House; new federal and state-level electoral commissions would be appointed to supervise the voting processes. (The President was again to be elected by the Federal Parliament.) On the same day, President Mohamed appointed a hitherto UN official, Mohamed Hussein Roble, as the new Prime Minister. The new electoral model was ratified by both chambers of the Federal Parliament on 26 September. At the beginning of October it was further agreed that the parliamentary elections would be held in December, followed by a presidential election on 8 February 2021. A new transitional Government headed by Roble, which included many senior ministers from the previous administration, was approved by 188 deputies attending a session of the Federal Parliament on 24 October 2020.

However, the electoral preparations were soon beset by acrimony among the major players. Said Abdullahi Deni and Ahmed Mohamed Islam Madobe, the respective Presidents of Puntland and Jubaland, and a new grouping of 14 opposition presidential candidates led by former President Sheikh Ahmed, the Council of Presidential Candidates (CPC), claimed in November 2020 that President Mohamed had installed individuals loyal to him on the new electoral commissions. Tensions over the lack of progress in the electoral process increased significantly following the expiry of President Mohamed's mandate on 8 February 2021: Deni and Madobe announced that they no longer recognized his authority and, together with the CPC, demanded his resignation. The UN Secretary-General expressed strong concerns after a protest on 19 February escalated into armed clashes between government troops and opposition supporters. The CPC announced plans for a further rally; however, following a further surge in cases of COVID-19, restrictions, including a ban on public protests, were reinstated from 23 February.

At least 20 people were killed in an al-Shabaab car bomb attack at a popular restaurant in Mogadishu in early March 2021. On 12 April an emergency session of the House of the People voted overwhelmingly (by 149 of 153 votes cast) to extend the mandate of the Federal Parliament and of President Mohamed for a further two years, with the stated aim of allowing preparations for direct elections as originally planned. Despite widespread opposition and rejection of the 'Special Law' by the Upper House, Mohamed signed it into force on 13 April; the AU, the EU and the UN denounced the extension, while the USA indicated that it would 're-evaluate' relations with Somalia. On 25 April fighting erupted in Mogadishu between pro-Government forces and military units that supported the opposition, and a deterioration in security was reported in other parts of the country. After Mohamed announced that he would request the cancellation of the extension, on 1 May the House of the People voted unanimously to annul the new legislation and reinstate the electoral agreement of September 2020; the decision was welcomed by the UN Secretary-General. The dissident forces engaged in the capital subsequently returned to their barracks.

At the end of June 2021 the National Consultative Council, comprising Prime Minister Roble, the leaders of the Federal Member States and the Mayor of Mogadishu, released a new election timetable, according to which polls to the Upper House would begin on 25 July and polls to the House of the People on 10 August, to be followed by the indirect election of a President on 10 October. According to media reports, in early July the leader of al-Shabaab, Ahmad Umar 'Abu Ubaidah', warned politicians against participation in the planned elections in a recorded audio message. On 10 July a suicide car bomb targeting a government convoy transporting a senior police official exploded at a junction in Mogadishu, killing at least nine people. On 25 July the Federal Government announced without explanation the postponement of the elections, which had been due to begin on that day with voting for members of the Upper House. Delays by the federal regions in submitting candidate lists and in forming local committees to cast the ballots were unofficially cited. Nevertheless, by late August Puntland and South West State had elected their representatives to the Upper House, while the process had commenced in Jubaland and Galmudug.

In early September 2021 President Mohamed countermanded an order by Prime Minister Roble to suspend the Director-General of the National Intelligence and Security Agency (NISA), Fahad Yasin, over his failure to investigate the disappearance of a NISA agent who had allegedly been abducted and killed by al-Shabaab (although the jihadist group denied responsibility). Shortly afterwards, Mohamed appointed Yasin, who had resigned from the post, as his senior national security advisor. The dispute between the President and Prime Minister rapidly deteriorated, increasing fears of renewed turmoil, after the former also attempted to overrule Roble's appointment of an interim head of the NISA and his decision to replace Hassan Hundubey Jimale as Minister of Internal Security with Abdullahi Mohamed Nur (a former state finance minister) in order to 'revitalize' the ministry. On 16 September the Office of the President announced that the executive powers of the Prime Minister to appoint and dismiss officials had been suspended, on the grounds that Roble had issued decisions inconsistent with the Provisional Constitution. The dispute between Mohamed and Roble was finally resolved in the following month. However, by this point the 10 October deadline agreed in June for electing a new President had elapsed without any of the main prerequisites being fulfilled. The Upper House polls were still incomplete, while elections to the House of the People—which had been scheduled to conclude on 2 October, but had been postponed in early September to 25 November—were still not under way. Mohamed and Roble released a joint statement on 21 October in which they agreed to accelerate the process by calling on the Federal Member States to start the elections to the House of the People within two weeks. The electoral process for the lower house duly began on 1 November and was scheduled to conclude on 24 December. The Upper House elections were completed in November, although UNSOM noted that female representatives only received 14 of the 54 seats—four percentage points below the minimum quota of 30%. Only a few lower house deputies had been elected by the 24 December deadline. Moreover, another intragovernmental dispute erupted later that month when Mohamed suspended Roble as Prime Minister, after accusing him of stealing land belonging to the military. Roble responded by accusing Mohamed of seeking 'to derail the election and illegally remain in office'.

Further delays to the election of representatives to the House of the People followed, with three new deadlines in February and March 2022 all elapsing. Deputies were eventually sworn in on 14 April, even though approximately 20 out of the 275 seats had still to be determined by clan elders at that stage. Later that month the two houses of Parliament elected Speakers. The Upper House voted in favour of retaining the incumbent, Abdi Hashi Abdullahi, a longstanding critic of President Mohamed, while the House of the People elected Sheikh Adan Mohamed Nur, also known as Sheikh Adan Madobe, who had previously held the post between 2007 and 2010. Before the latter vote, Roble had requested that AU peacekeepers provide security for the process—a move opposed by the President, who asserted that the Somali police force should be responsible for security. Roble also warned of electoral 'irregularities'. Nevertheless, Nur's victory was accepted by both Roble and Mohamed, with the latter declaring that he hoped Nur's selection would represent 'the starting point for a greater change that saves this country'.

A total of 36 candidates participated in the presidential election, which was held on 15 May 2022. Alongside the incumbent, President Mohamed, key contenders included his two immediate predecessors, Hassan Sheikh Mohamud and Sheikh Sharif Sheikh Ahmed, as well as Puntland President Said Abdullahi Deni and former Prime Minister Hassan Ali Khayre. Prior to the vote, 30 multilateral bodies and numerous states, including the AU, the USA, the Russian Federation, Turkey, the UAE and Saudi Arabia, urged the relevant Somali parties 'to conclude this final stage of the electoral process swiftly, peacefully and credibly'. As a two-thirds' majority was needed for a presidential candidate to be declared the winner, the election required three rounds of voting by members of Parliament, culminating in a run-off between President Mohamed and Hassan Sheikh Mohamud. Mohamud emerged victorious, with 214 votes, while Mohamed secured 110 votes. While violence had erupted following the initial postponement of the electoral process, its ultimately successful completion maintained post-transition Somalia's track record of the peaceful transfer of presidential power through mandated channels. Analysts expressed hope that Mohamud's return to power would usher in a more consensual period for Somali politics, after the protracted disputes that had characterized much of the previous five years. However, the issue of government corruption continued to cause concern, in a context where the latter stages of Mohamud's 2012–17 presidency had been marred by multiple corruption scandals and large sums of money had again been reported to have changed hands during the recent selection of parliamentary deputies. In his inauguration speech in June 2022, Mohamud promised to foster 'consultation, mutual endorsement and unity' between the Federal Government and the Federal Member States, further bolstering hopes of a break from the conflicts between these entities under his predecessor. Also in June, Mohamud appointed Hamza Abdi Barre as Prime Minister, replacing Roble.

RECENT DEVELOPMENTS IN THE FEDERAL MEMBER STATES

Amid deepening tensions with the Federal Member States, President Abdullahi Mohamed faced overwhelming pressure to either unseat their leaders or bring them into line. The President of South West State, Sharif Hassan Sheikh Adan, resigned under duress in November 2018. Elections were subsequently called, and the Federal Government spent a considerable sum in support of its favoured candidate for the state presidency, Abdiaziz Hassan Mohamed. Sheikh Adan consequently withdrew from the electoral race, as he could not compete financially with Hassan Mohamed. On 25 November the electoral commission registered several candidates and cleared the former al-Shabaab leader Sheikh Mukhtar Robow Ali 'Abu Mansur' to contest the presidency of South West State. Robow Ali's candidacy raised the question of whether former al-Shabaab militants should be allowed to enter politics. Initially, the Federal Government and the international community were eager to support Robow Ali's participation in the state election. However, when Robow Ali emerged as a serious challenger to the Federal Government's preferred candidate, Hassan Mohamed, Mogadishu withdrew its support. Ethiopian armed forces arrested Robow Ali in Baidoa and took him to Mogadishu, ensuring victory for Hassan Mohamed, who was elected President of South West State in December. This prompted a major political crisis: riots broke out in Baidoa, during which at least 15 people, including two local government officials, were killed, and more than 200 civilians were arrested. Among Western donors, the EU, the UK and Germany criticized Robow Ali's arrest and suspended their financial support to the police force in South West State, citing their concerns about police conduct during the election period.

Elections were held in Jubaland in August 2019. A total of 18 candidates declared their intention to run for the Jubaland state presidency. However, the Jubaland Electoral Commission approved only eight candidates. The excluded candidates complained about unfair regulations, such as a US $30,000 non-refundable registration fee, which was apparently intended to give the incumbent President, Ahmed Mohamed Islam Madobe, an unfair advantage. The candidates who were barred from running boycotted the campaign and set about organizing rival parliamentary elections. Meanwhile, tensions grew between Kenya and Ethiopia, as the former supported the re-election of the incumbent President whereas the latter sided with Mogadishu. The ongoing maritime dispute between Kenya and Somalia made the electoral issue in Jubaland even more sensitive, as Kismayu's shoreline borders the disputed area. President Abdullahi Mohamed, for his part, was eager to exert greater control over Jubaland in order to increase his chances of winning the presidential election in 2021. The Federal Government sponsored candidates from Madobe's Ogaden clan to run against the incumbent. When President Abdullahi Mohamed's favoured candidates were barred from running, he accused Madobe of interfering in the electoral process. Meanwhile, the Head of UNSOM, Swan, was accused of actively assisting the Federal Government in its attempts to interfere in the elections in Jubaland. Swan harshly criticized the operations of the Jubaland Electoral Commission and on 17 August UNSOM imposed further measures to ensure that the electoral process be transparent and credible (and be recognized as the only legitimate poll, with reference to the rival parliamentary elections). On the same day, the opposition-backed self-styled parliament elected its own speaker. The Federal Government, however, declared the rival parliamentary elections to be null and void, stating that the process to select the state deputies had infringed electoral regulations. On 22 August Madobe was re-elected, garnering 56 out of the 74 votes cast by the Jubaland state deputies. On the same day, two former colleagues of Madobe—Abdinasir Seraar, a co-founder of the Ras Kamboni Brigade in Jubaland, and Abdirashid Mohamed Hidig, a former interior state minister—swore themselves in as presidents. The Federal Government declared that the re-election of Madobe was not free and fair and did not recognize either of the self-declared presidents.

Despite President Madobe's re-election for another four years, continued tensions between Jubaland and the Federal Government meant that his future and that of the regional administration were fraught with uncertainty. At the end of August 2019 the Federal Government imposed a ban on direct flights from Nairobi to Kismayu, requiring aircraft first to land in Mogadishu for clearance. Jubaland's security minister, Abdirashid Hassan Abdinur 'Janan', was arrested at Mogadishu airport on 31 August, on charges of serious human rights violations. The Jubaland administration repeatedly demanded the release of Abdirashid; in January 2020 the federal authorities reported that he had escaped after being placed on trial in Mogadishu. Meanwhile, Madobe's inauguration, scheduled for 26 September 2019, was postponed following efforts by the Federal Government to prevent prominent figures from attending, but finally took place on 13 October. A high-level parliamentary delegation took a direct flight from Nairobi to Kismayu, in contravention of the ban imposed by the Somali Government, to attend the inauguration. In March 2020 Kenyan President Uhuru Kenyatta accused the Somali army of violating Kenyan sovereignty during heavy fighting with Jubaland forces near the Kenyan border town of Mandera, in which at least one civilian was killed. Shortly afterwards, President Abdullahi Mohamed and Kenyatta agreed to establish joint committees in an effort to resolve tensions. The political impasse between Madobe and the opposition appeared to be resolved in late April, when the Jubaland President signed an agreement (under Kenyan mediation) with Abdirashid Hidig and two other opposition leaders. According to the agreement, the opposition recognized Madobe's election in 2019 and agreed to co-operate with his administration, while the Jubaland President pledged to include opposition members in a 'government of unity' and declared that he would not seek a third term in office. After further deployments by the Federal Government to the Gedo region, fighting between federal troops and Jubaland state forces near the border with Kenya, in which 11 people were killed, was reported in January 2021. Abdirashid, who had fled to Kenya following his escape, surrendered to the federal authorities following negotiations in March, and was formally dismissed by Madobe as Jubaland's security minister. It was later reported that the court in Mogadishu where he had been arraigned had shortly before withdrawn the charges against him of corruption and human rights violations, including torture.

Galmudug, the home state of President Abdullahi Mohamed, emerged as the scene of yet another tense state election from June 2019. With 11 feuding sub-clans, rival administrations, recurrent political crises and a protracted reconciliation process launched by Sheikh Sharif Sheikh Ahmed in 2010, Galmudug stood as an emblematic example of political fragmentation. Stretching over three months, the electoral process raised questions about the political viability of Galmudug as a state and of the federal project more broadly. Built on the ruins of city states run by sub-clans and various armed groups, chief among them being the Sufi group ASWJ, Galmudug has had two presidents since its establishment in 2015. The ASWJ had recognized the Galmudug administration only in December 2017. Most of the sub-clans inhabiting the state had been engaged in political or armed fighting against one another, and each successive federal government had added fuel to the fire, pitting one group against another to disempower its opponents. Al-Shabaab also continued to hold considerable sway over Galmudug's territory, controlling four of the regional administration's 10 districts. While the elders of the 11 sub-clans living in the region had contributed to the establishment of Galmudug state, the ASWJ, based in the state capital, Dhusamareb, had refused to join, claiming that its decade-long struggle against al-Shabaab in central Somalia had not been properly acknowledged.

Although the first President of Galmudug, Abdikarim Hussein Guled, had refused to cede significant political power to the ASWJ, Ahmed Duale Gelle 'Haaf', a powerful businessman and a former federal legislator who had succeeded Guled to the presidency after the latter's abrupt resignation in mid-2017, sought to bring the ASWJ into his administration. Following lengthy negotiations, the two sides had reached an agreement in Djibouti in January 2018. The ASWJ had obtained major concessions, including the creation of the post of head of cabinet for its leader, Sheikh Mohamed Shakir Ali Hassan. President Haaf had subsequently moved from Adado, the interim capital, to Dhusamareb. However, other issues continued to undermine the viability of the Galmudug administration. Power-sharing between clans remained a problem, as both Haaf and Sheikh Mohamed Shakir were from the Hawiye/Habar Gidir/Ayr clan. As Haaf had sided with the other Presidents of the Federal Member States in the power struggle with Mogadishu, President Abdullahi Mohamed sought to oust him. The Federal Government announced jointly with the ASWJ that the constitutional mandate of Haaf was to end in July 2019, although both Haaf and the ASWJ had previously maintained that they would stay in power until the end of his four-year term in January 2020. Haaf announced the nullification of the Djibouti agreement with the ASWJ, but also unexpectedly declared that he welcomed elections and that his dispute with the Federal Government was over, frustrating the latter's plans to hold elections in Dhusamareb without the Haaf administration. The ASWJ concluded a new agreement with the Federal Government on 4 July 2019, which provided for the incorporation of ASWJ forces into the national security forces. Following further negotiations, on 12 December the ASWJ was allocated a further 20 seats in Galmudug's new legislature (which was to be expanded to 89 members). The Galmudug Technical State Formation Committee appointed by the Federal Government selected the members of the Regional Assembly on 10 January 2020; however, the ASWJ announced its withdrawal from the process, accusing the Federal Government of interference. On 2 February Ahmed Abdi Kariye 'Qoor Qoor', a former state minister backed by the Federal Government, was elected as Galmudug President by the Regional Assembly, receiving 66 votes. ASWJ leader Sheikh Mohamed Shakir rejected the result and declared himself president, but ceded power after an armed confrontation in Dhusamareb at the end of the month, in which some 16 people were killed. Haaf also attempted to install himself as president in a parallel election organized by his supporters in Galkayo. However, following a protracted impasse, on 12 April Haaf officially relinquished power to Qoor Qoor, who formed a new cabinet later that month.

Following the creation of HirShabelle State on 4 October 2016, its new Regional Assembly, established by a State Formation Conference in Jowhar, on 17 October elected former federal legislator Ali Abdulahi Osoble as the President, by 61 votes to 36. A Council of Ministers appointed by Osoble in February 2017, as part of the HirShabelle Interim Administration, was approved by the Regional Assembly in early March. However, amid increasing dissent between Osoble and both the Assembly and his Government, a parliamentary no-confidence motion against him was overwhelmingly adopted in mid-August. Mohamed Abdi Ware (who had been defeated in the previous presidential poll) was elected as the new President the following month, securing 75 of 97 votes cast in a third round. Ware formed a new cabinet at the end of November. A new Regional Assembly, comprising 99 selected clan representatives, was formed at the end of October 2020. On 11 November Ali Abdullahi Hussein 'Gudlawe', hitherto the Vice-President of HirShabelle, was elected President, securing 86 votes in the Regional Assembly. Former President Ware accused the Federal Government of continued interference in the election process, and opposing clan factions contested the election outcome.

Puntland

The autonomous state of Puntland was established on 1 August 1998, following a decision by delegates from three northeastern regions of Somalia to establish a single administration for the area. Puntland was among the main beneficiaries of the US dual-track policy towards Somalia. Announced in October 2010, this policy provided diplomatic, financial and military support by the USA and other Western countries, which were seeking a local partner in the international struggle against maritime piracy and the increasing influence of jihadists.

The practice of postponing elections took root in Puntland as well. In late 2012 President Abdirahman Mohamed Farole, who had come to power in January 2009, announced his intention to extend his term for a further year. In April 2013 the Puntland Government postponed the first local elections, which were due to be held on 15 May, by two months. On 14 July, however, President Farole abruptly cancelled the elections, citing the risk of violence from unnamed parties. On 8 January 2014 the Puntland House of Representatives narrowly elected Abdiweli Mohamed Ali 'Gas', who had served as Prime Minister of Somalia from June 2011 to October 2012, as the new President of Puntland. In August 2018 the Puntland House of Representatives approved a law setting the date for the upcoming regional presidential election as 8 January 2019. Deputies also voted for the House to be dissolved by 31 September 2018.

From early 2015 there was an increase in attacks by al-Shabaab militants in the north-eastern region of Puntland. In 2016–18 Puntland's security forces found themselves engaged on multiple fronts: patrolling the border with south-central Somalia, dealing with rebellious clans in Sool and Sanaag, battling against GIA forces in Galkayo (see above), against al-Shabaab militants in the Galgala mountains and against a clan militia led by the Bari region's former Governor in the coastal town of Qandala. On 26 October 2016, one year after former al-Shabaab leader Sheikh Abdulqadir Mumin pledged his allegiance to Islamic State, about 50 Islamic State-aligned militants seized Qandala. The attack was rooted in a dispute that had broken out in June between Puntland President Abdiweli Mohamed Ali 'Gas' and Bari's former Governor Abdisamad Mohamed Galan (Majerten/Ali Saleban) over the distribution of revenue from the operations of the port. Mumin was able to exploit the stand-off between President 'Gas' and the former regional Governor, and to capitalize on the grievances of minority clans that felt marginalized by the largest Majerten sub-clans. Puntland security forces recaptured the town in early December. In July 2018 al-Shabaab temporarily seized Af Urur, a strategic town about 100 km south of Bosaso, in the Bari region, situated near the main road connecting Bosaso, Garowe and Mogadishu. Puntland security forces regained control of the town in August. None the less, peace in Puntland remained elusive.

On 8 January 2019 Puntland's parliament elected a new President, Said Abdullahi Deni, a former federal minister with strong ties to former President Mohamud. Deni won in the third round of voting, receiving 35 votes from the 66 deputies who participated in the election, just ahead of former intelligence chief Asad Osman Abdullahi. The incumbent President, 'Gas', had been eliminated in the first round of voting. Despite the election of a new state President, the leadership in Puntland remained in dispute with Mogadishu on several issues, primarily the Federal Government's reported failure to consult with Federal Member States on the sharing of power and resources. On 7 November the Puntland House of Representatives voted to remove its Speaker, Abdihakim Mohamed Ahmed, who was accused of violating the Constitution; the impeachment motion, which followed antagonism between the Speaker and President Deni, precipitated clashes between police and security guards at the parliamentary building in Garowe, in which four people were killed. Abwan Abdirashid Yusuf Jibril was elected as the new Speaker on 14 November. Deni, together with Jubaland's President Madobe, in August 2020 boycotted a meeting between the Federal Government and Federal Member States, at which a new model for the conduct of contentious national elections was agreed (see *Delayed Elections and the Return of Hassan Sheikh Mohamud*), and he was reported to have demanded the withdrawal of federal troops from the Gedo region before meeting President Abdullahi Mohamed in early September. Deni and Madobe denounced protracted delays to the national election process, and in February 2021 announced that they no longer recognized the authority of President Mohamed, following the official expiry of his mandate.

The Puntland administration announced in September 2021 that it had dispatched troops to assist the military in neighbouring Galmudug, where al-Shabaab forces had the previous month gained control of a military base in the strategic town of Amara.

SOMALILAND

The 'Republic of Somaliland' comprises the territory of the former British protectorate of the same name. It has a population of approximately 3.5m. and it has been self-governing since 1991. Although Somaliland has not succeeded in obtaining international recognition for its independence, from the 1990s it maintained good relations with several donors, given that progress was being made towards the creation of a formal democracy. None the less, Somaliland's desire to be recognized as a democratic model was negatively affected by President Dahir Riyale Kahin's various delays in holding a presidential election in 2008–09. In June 2010, when a presidential election was finally held, the incumbent President was defeated by the Peace, Unity and Development Party (known as Kulmiye) leader, Ahmad Muhammad Silanyo. In May 2015 the Somaliland National Electoral Commission (NEC) announced that elections scheduled for June would be postponed until June 2016 to allow for adequate preparation. The unelected elders who constituted the upper house of Somaliland's Parliament (the Guurti) subsequently further delayed the elections, extending the mandate of both President Silanyo and the Parliament until April 2017.

Somaliland's relatively successful state-building process, its special funding status with donors (namely the UK, the EU and Denmark), investment from the UAE and Turkey, and strong ties with Ethiopia and Djibouti raised the stakes of holding power. In October 2015 Kulmiye nominated Muse Bihi Abdi, a military officer and former warlord, as its presidential candidate. However, Bihi's nomination, which was strongly supported by President Silanyo, was vehemently criticized by two official opposition parties, the Waddani Somaliland National Party and the For Justice and Development Party (UCID).

The presidential election was held on 13 November 2017 and was contested by three parties: Kulmiye, Waddani and UCID. Kulmiye's candidate, Bihi, was elected President with 55.1% of the vote. Although the election was largely peaceful, except in six polling stations in the Sanaag region, where conflicts impeded proper voting procedures, the results were contested. High-ranking Waddani representatives alleged that the vote had been rigged in favour of Kulmiye. During 16–20 November demonstrations and riots occurred in several towns, leading to violent confrontations between Waddani supporters and government forces in which several protesters were killed. None the less, order was restored in late November and a new Government was formed in December. The presidential election marked an important step in the formal democratic process, but persistent challenges remained. There were ongoing conflicts in the far east of Somaliland, along the border with Puntland, where disputes between local clans continued to intermingle with sovereignty issues.

Tensions between Somaliland and the Federal Government over Somaliland's undecided status also complicated the situation in the disputed Sool and Sannag regions, which were claimed by both Somaliland and Puntland. In January 2018, ahead of a visit to Puntland by Somali President Abdullahi Mohamed, rumours spread that he would be meeting with Dulbahante and Warsangeli elders to discuss their position with regard to Somalia. In response to what Somaliland perceived as a provocation, President Bihi deployed Somaliland troops to Tukaraq, a tax station about 40 km to the west of Garowe (Puntland's administrative capital). Amid violent skirmishes, Puntland forces, which had controlled Tukaraq since 2004, retreated. After Somaliland troops seized Tukaraq in April 2018, the two sides engaged in fierce fighting for control of the village in May, causing dozens of deaths. In September more than 10 people were killed in clashes between clans in Dumay in the Sool region. Puntland regional deputies appealed for a ceasefire and accused the Somaliland Government of supplying the clan militias fighting in the area with weapons.

Frictions in Somaliland eased in the first half of 2019, and outside pressure created some momentum for resuming negotiations between Somalia and Somaliland. Nevertheless, efforts to restart dialogue continued to face opposition on both sides. With parliamentary elections approaching, President Abdullahi Mohamed was susceptible to pressure from his nationalist support base to avoid making any concessions, whereas Somaliland President Bihi, a former rebel commander who had fought against Siad Barre's regime in the late 1980s, appeared less inclined to compromise than his predecessor. External factors did not work in favour of a rapprochement either. In August 2019 Saudi Arabia recognized Somaliland as a de facto sovereign state. However, in September fissures in the Saudi-Emirati alliance in Yemen and the UAE's shift in strategy with regard to US-Iranian tensions triggered a new development, which some observers believed might help to ease frictions between the administration in Somaliland and the Federal Government in Mogadishu. In mid-September the UAE announced the termination of its lease on the Berbera military base. Although the Somaliland authorities thereby lost the revenue secured through leasing the facility, the region still stood to gain from Emirati investments, as a facility currently being built at Berbera was eventually to be transformed into a civilian airport. As the military base project had stirred up tensions with Somalia, its suspension removed a major impediment to improved dialogue between the authorities in Somaliland and Mogadishu.

Following continued dispute among the three main political parties (Kulmiye, Waddani and UCID), the Electoral Commission announced on 8 August 2019 that it had postponed local and parliamentary elections planned for 12 December. On 13 November Waddani and UCID parliamentary deputies boycotted a vote in the House of Representatives to approve a new electoral commission, claiming that the selection of its members had been unconstitutional. Police stormed Waddani party offices in the capital, Hargeysa, and arrested two senior party officials later that month, after the party leadership had organized banned protest rallies. Meanwhile, at the request of President Bihi, the House of Elders approved an extension of the mandate of the House of Representatives to January 2022, and that of the upper chamber to January 2023; the extension was rejected by the international community. At the end of February 2020 an internationally sponsored agreement was reached between Kulmiye, Waddani and UCID, providing for the establishment of a Technical Elections Management Unit which would organize the elections. Following further discussions, in August the three parties agreed that the delayed local and parliamentary elections would take place by May 2021.

Meanwhile, following a diplomatic initiative by Ethiopian Prime Minister Dr Abiy Ahmed Ali, he hosted a direct meeting between President Abdullahi Mohamed and Somaliland President Bihi in February 2020. Further mediation by Abiy Ahmed, together with US and EU officials, resulted in the resumption of dialogue between the two leaders in Djibouti on 14 June. While the discussions produced no significant progress on sovereignty, a final communiqué issued on 22 June proposed the creation of three sub-committees on humanitarian assistance and development aid, security, and the joint management of Somaliland's airspace. In the following month the Somaliland Government secured the establishment of new diplomatic engagements. On 1 July the Republic of China (Taiwan) announced that it had signed an agreement with Somaliland to establish reciprocal representative offices in order to strengthen co-operation. Later that month a high-level delegation from Egypt arrived in Hargeysa for talks with the Somaliland Government (with a senior Ethiopian delegation following soon afterwards, amid tensions between the two countries). President Bihi visited Kenya for discussions with President Uhuru Kenyatta in December, after which the Kenyan Government declared its intention to open a liaison office in Hargeysa (while Somaliland's liaison office in Nairobi was to be upgraded), and the proposed introduction of a visa regime for Somaliland citizens. (The Somali Government, in response, suspended diplomatic relations with Kenya until May 2021.)

In February 2021 the House of Elders approved a formal proposal by President Bihi that the parliamentary and local elections would take place on 31 May. Several UCID and Waddani candidates were arrested without explanation during the campaign period, and the harassment of local journalists was also reported. The parliamentary elections, the first to be held in Somaliland since 2005, proceeded on 31 May 2021. The NEC announced on 6 June that Waddani had received 31 of the 82 seats, Bihi's Kulmiye 30, and UCID 21. None of the 13 participating female candidates secured representation. In the concurrent local elections, Kulmiye secured 93 seats, Waddani 79 and UCID 48. Shortly afterwards, Waddani and UCID announced the formation of a political alliance. However, UCID subsequently divided, with a number of its members defecting to Kulmiye. On 3 August the Waddani candidate, Abdirizak Khalif Ahmed, was elected Speaker of the new House of Representatives, narrowly defeating the Kulmiye candidate by 42 votes to 39. Kenya's liaison office in Hargeysa was opened in early September.

Economy

DUNCAN WOODSIDE

Based on an earlier article by ANNA BRUZZONE

INTRODUCTION

The current state of Somalia's economy is influenced by three major components: persistent political and security challenges; an exceptionally resilient people who have long maintained an impressive scale of private economic activity despite extended state failure; and international re-engagement. Real gross domestic product (GDP) growth has, however, been far from robust in recent years, averaging just 1.7% during 2015–19. New businesses and the returning diaspora, although crucial drivers of activity, are unable to address the structural and infrastructural challenges that prevent Somalia's economy from growing in a steady and sustainable manner. Heavily dependent on a rudimentary agricultural sector prone to drought, the country has a massive debt burden, and public infrastructure remains extremely limited—even non-existent in some areas—due to a complete absence of central governance between the early 1990s and the early 2010s, and only a patchy emergence of federal authority since then. Much of the national budget remains concentrated on or otherwise constrained by persistent security challenges and institutional fragility. Those challenges range from a longstanding insurgency by the militant Islamist al-Shabaab group (linked to the al-Qa'ida network) on the one hand, to clan-related tensions between the presidency, national legislatures and Federal Member States on the other hand—tensions that once again threatened to spiral out of control in 2022, putting at risk the substantial investments made by both the international community and the returning diaspora over the last decade.

The International Monetary Fund (IMF) recognized the Federal Government of Somalia in April 2013, and has since been involved in the provision of policy advice and technical assistance. The World Bank resumed its engagement in the country in 2014, after a 23-year hiatus in relations. The re-engagement of the international financial institutions with Somalia was intended to establish a track record of co-operation that could help the country become eligible for borrowing from the IMF. Technical assistance has been provided in areas related to financial sector supervision, central banking, currency reform, banking operations, anti-money laundering and fiscal policy, but the limited nature of progress is highlighted by repeated corruption scandals and the continued dollarized status of much of the economy. With regards to fiscal policy and reforms, in 2016 the Somali authorities completed the installation of an electronic payment system for civil service wages and approved the 2016–20 public financial management reform action plan. In 2018 the World Bank approved US $80m. in grants to fund financial reforms—the first disbursement to Somalia in 30 years. The 'Paris Club' of creditors agreed in March 2020 to cancel $1,400m. of the country's debt, representing two-thirds of obligations to this group of creditors. This debt relief came days after the IMF and the World Bank declared that Somalia had become eligible for relief under the Highly Indebted Poor Countries (HIPC) initiative, a landmark moment that in effect restored the country's place in the international financial system after an absence of three decades. The HIPC programme envisaged the debt owed by Somalia to international creditors shrinking to $557m. over three years.

Somalia registered real GDP growth of 3.3% in 2019, according to the IMF, which also noted a 'relatively stable' inflation environment and improved fiscal data. The Fund announced in March 2020 that it had approved a three-year US $395m. financing mechanism for Somalia in the form of an Extended Credit Facility (ECF) and an Extended Fund Facility (EFF). Real GDP contracted by 0.3% in 2020, according to IMF data, owing to the effects of the COVID-19 pandemic. Global restrictions imposed in response to the COVID-19 crisis continued to undermine the economy in 2021. In particular, the *Hajj* (the annual Muslim pilgrimage to Mecca) in Saudi Arabia—a key destination for Somalia's livestock exports—was dramatically downscaled for a second consecutive year, although the overall impact of the pandemic was less severe than in 2020. An escalating political crisis, characterized by repeated postponements to the election timetable, which led to violent clashes between pro- and anti-presidential military factions in the capital, Mogadishu, in April, also had a negative impact on the economy in 2021. The mandate of President Mohamed Abdullahi Mohamed 'Farmajo' expired in February, and key donors suspended budget support in early 2021. Donor budget support during that year totalled just $147.0m., down from $285.6m. in 2020, according to government figures. Modest real GDP growth of 2.0% was achieved in 2021, according to IMF estimates, supported by a recovery in household consumption and exports.

The IMF warned in March 2022 that any further delays to the elections risked 'the automatic lapse' of the ECF. However, the long-delayed presidential election took place in May, resulting in the peaceful transfer of power from President Mohamed to Hassan Sheikh Mohamud. The successful election process prompted the IMF to complete its second and third reviews of the ECF in the following month, enabling the release of a further tranche of funding and encouraging a wider donor re-engagement with the country. The IMF forecast that real GDP growth would increase to 2.7% in 2022, driven by private consumption and remittances. While the domestic political normalization was expected to support the economy, the IMF noted that significant headwinds constrained the outlook in 2022, notably a protracted drought, which was affecting both crops and livestock, and rising global food and energy prices following the invasion of Ukraine by the Russian Federation. The Fund also cited a potential resurgence of desert locust infestations and security risks as further factors that could adversely affect economic growth in 2022.

MACROECONOMIC TRENDS

Mobilizing revenue remains a challenge, especially as the state-building process in Somalia has repeatedly largely failed to create a political economy that would enable the state to function. The politics of state formation requires the establishment of functional fiscal relations between the federal entities and the Federal Government of Somalia itself. The issue of resource sharing and redistribution needs to be dealt with in order to build a national economy where federal entities and the Government work together in the public interest, preserving a common economic space throughout the country and addressing inequalities across regions. However, the strategic (and highly sensitive) duties of managing international ports and airports, organizing the hydrocarbon sector, and building a national taxation system have long been neglected

in favour of hastening the establishment of federal administrations. None the less, the President's signing into law of the Petroleum Bill in early 2020 finally consolidated a revenue-sharing formula between the Federal Government and the Federal Member States.

According to World Bank estimates, taxes on international trade accounted for an average of 91% of total annual tax revenue between 2012 and 2014. Furthermore, in Puntland and Somaliland revenue collection essentially comprises solely customs and related taxes on international trade. Turnover taxes on businesses are a potential source of revenue, but the establishment of the relevant legal framework requires public-private dialogue. To date, attempts to develop public-private partnerships have repeatedly failed. Somali business people complain that international organizations maintain a 'traditional' approach to dealing with Somalia's economy by preferring to engage in short-term projects, while they themselves are interested in market expansion and profitability. Nevertheless, the Government, with the support of the World Bank and international partners, launched the country's first Public-Private Dialogue in July 2016. According to the World Bank's *Somalia Economic Update* report of July 2017, total Federal Government tax revenue represented just over 2% of GDP in 2016, which meant that the Government lacked the resources necessary to undertake any major development programme. However, a few positive steps towards domestic resource mobilization have recently been taken. In August 2017 Somalia's Federal Parliament unanimously approved the National Communications Act, and the Council of Ministers finally endorsed the long-awaited Public Financial Management Law.

The merchandise trade deficit widened slightly from US $3,003m. in 2018 to $3,060m. in 2019, driven largely by a rise in imports from $3,574m. to $3,614m., while exports fell marginally from $570m. to $554m., according to the IMF. Deficits on the services account took the overall trade deficit to $4,005m. in 2018 and to $4,104m. in 2019. However, these significant imbalances were largely offset by strong current transfers, amounting to $3,682m. in 2018 and $3,622m. in 2019, of which private flows, including remittances, accounted for $1,483m. and $1,578m., respectively, in these two years, while aid (overwhelmingly falling into the off-budget category) contributed $2,200m. and $2,043m., respectively. Together with moderate negative net income flows, these figures resulted in a widening of Somalia's current account deficit from $356m. in 2018 to a preliminary $518m. in 2019.

According to the IMF, the trade deficit fell slightly in 2020 to 63.4% of GDP, from 63.7% in 2019, despite a significant decline in exports of goods and services to 13.9% of GDP, from 17.3% in 2019. Livestock exports were particularly affected by the dramatically downscaled *Hajj* pilgrimage in Saudi Arabia. Imports declined to an estimated 77.3% of GDP in 2020, from 81.0% in 2019, as the pandemic depressed domestic demand. The current account deficit, meanwhile, rose from 10.4% of GDP in 2019 to an estimated 10.8% in 2020 and to an estimated 15.0% in 2021. This latter increase was largely driven by a rise in the trade deficit, which was estimated to have widened to 70.7% of GDP in 2021, as export growth was offset by an even greater expansion in imports. However, in a more positive development, remittances rose in 2021 to an estimated 28.2% of GDP, from an estimated 23.2% in 2020.

The 2022 budget projected expenditure of US $918.7m., almost double the $459.8m. programmed in the 2021 budget, owing to a substantial surge in donor support. Recurrent expenditures were set at $433.2m., while project expenditures were forecast at $485.5m. Total revenues and receipts in the 2022 budget were projected at $907.1m., compared with $376.5m. in 2021 and $496.6m. in 2020. Donor revenue was budgeted at $660.2m. in 2022, up from just $147.0m. in 2021 and $285.6m. in 2020. Tax revenue was also expected to rise, albeit at a much more modest rate than donor support; total tax receipts were projected at $173.7m. in 2022, up from $162.8m. in 2021 and $139.3m. in 2020. A budget deficit of $11.5m. was forecast for 2022, substantially lower than the $83.3m. deficit recorded in 2021 (which had represented a severe deterioration from a surplus of $23.6m. in 2020). The defence and security budget was set at $167.6m. in 2022, while $82.2m. was allocated to economic services and $323.6m. to social services. Spending on social services had totalled just $80.4m. in 2021.

The IMF noted in May 2022 that Somalia's planned budget for that year 'aligned' with the objectives of the ECF. With its completion of the second and third reviews of the ECF in June, the IMF made a tranche of US $18.8m. immediately available to the Somali Government, taking total disbursements under the ECF and the EFF to $384.3m.

INVESTMENT IN POST-TRANSITION SOMALIA

From 2012 the return of many individuals from the Somali diaspora and the relocation of several United Nations (UN) offices, embassies and non-governmental organizations to Mogadishu resulted in a minor economic boom, which saw rents in the capital's most prized locations increase threefold within a couple of months. Communal residential areas for the Somali diaspora returning to the country are being built in several zones around Mogadishu, and the influx of money related to the partial re-engagement of the international community in Somalia has stimulated private investment in certain sectors, such as real estate, the hotel industry and private security. Foreign investors have started to move into Somalia, with Turkey leading the way. According to Turkey's Ministry of Foreign Affairs, annual bilateral trade between Somalia and Turkey grew from US $6m. in 2010 to $72m. in 2015. A Turkish company, Albayrak, took over the management of Mogadishu seaport in September 2014, while another Turkish company, Favori LLC, operates the capital's Aden Adde International Airport (AAIA). The Turkish Cooperation and Coordination Agency constructed the Somalia-Turkey Training and Research Hospital in Mogadishu, which was officially inaugurated during a visit by Turkish President Recep Tayyip Erdoğan to Somalia in January 2015. Opened in June 2016, the Turkish embassy's new building complex in Mogadishu is Turkey's largest foreign mission. Somalia is, however, exposed to the effects of Turkey's political turmoil. Turkish charities operating in Somalia and believed to have links to the US-based cleric Fethullah Gülen, an adversary of President Erdoğan, have had their fundraising activities cut in recent years. Following the attempted military coup in Turkey on 15–16 July 2016, the Somali Government ordered Turkish citizens working in development organizations, schools and health care facilities linked to Gülen—the alleged mastermind behind the failed coup—to leave the country within seven days. Investment and funding support from the United Arab Emirates (UAE) and Saudi Arabia have also increased, as part of these countries' wider move towards East Africa to shore up support for their military operations in Yemen.

Although the regional governments are not officially mandated to make unilateral deals with foreign companies, Somaliland (which claims full independence from Somalia, a status recognized by neither the Federal Government nor the international community) and Puntland signed their largest ever investment agreements with UAE-based companies to develop Berbera and Bosaso ports, without the approval of the Federal Parliament. In September 2016 Somaliland's Government signed a US $442m. agreement with DP World (based in Dubai, UAE), permitting the latter to modernize and manage Berbera's cargo port for 30 years with an automatic 10-year extension. The deal also involved the construction of a highway linking Berbera's port to the town of Tog Wajaale on the Ethiopia–Somaliland border. Somaliland finalized the agreement with DP World in March 2018 and permitted Ethiopia to take a 19% stake in the Berbera port project, causing outrage in Mogadishu (see *History*). In response, the Somali Parliament adopted legislation that banned DP World from operating in Somalia and stipulated that any agreement signed with a foreign company would require parliamentary approval. The new law also targeted a 30-year concession concluded in April 2017 by Puntland's Government and Dubai-based P&O Ports for the management and development of a multi-purpose port project at Bosaso. The project, worth $336m., involved the construction of a 450-m quay and a 5-ha back-up area. The contract, however, raised concerns about land titles and financial transparency, to which Puntland's President, Abdiweli Mohamed Ali 'Gas', responded by accusing those who were

opposed to the project of accepting bribes from the Federal Government. Puntland's Government also approved a deal with China Civil Engineering Construction Corporation (CCECC) for the development of Galkayo airport and the construction of a paved road between Garowe and the coastal town of Eyl. It was believed that the deal with CCECC was signed in return for oil and gas exploration licences in Puntland. A Chinese construction firm was also awarded a multimillion-dollar contract for the development of a modern port facility in the coastal town of Hobyo in the Mudug region. The first phase of construction began in January 2018, and Somali President Mohamed Abdullahi Mohamed himself laid the foundation stone of what was the biggest project ever to be implemented in Galmudug. With a view to attracting further Chinese investment as part of the Chinese 'Belt and Road Initiative', President Mohamed attended the Forum on China-Africa Cooperation in the Chinese capital, Beijing, in September.

In March 2019 Somaliland President Muse Bihi Abdi signed an agreement with the UAE for the modernization of Berbera airport and for the construction of an electricity plant that would power Berbera city and of a cement plant. In a calculated bid to consolidate its influence in Somalia, rival Gulf state Qatar announced plans in August to construct a port in the coastal town of Hobyo in Galmudug. The new port was intended to increase aid deliveries to the region and to serve as a logistical hub for transshipment to Hamad Port (Qatar's main seaport).

The investment environment was adversely affected by the escalating political instability in late 2020 and early 2021, as the election timetable foundered and President Mohamed attempted to extend his mandate, resulting in armed clashes in the streets of Mogadishu in April. The violence and the political impasse threatened to cause the country to regress into clan-based civil conflict, potentially enabling al-Shabaab to capitalize on the security vacuum and re-establish itself in urban areas. Al-Shabaab has retained a revenue-generating system. A study by the Somalia-based Hiraal Institute in October 2020 found that the insurgent group was bringing in tax revenues of US $15m. per month, owing in part to taxing shipping containers at Mogadishu port, even though that entity was formally under the control of the Federal Government. Based on tax revenues for the Federal Government in 2019, which averaged $12.9m. per month, al-Shabaab was generating over 15% more each month through its own taxation, despite the dramatic curtailment of its territorial control during 2011–14.

TRANSPORT, TELECOMMUNICATIONS AND THE INTERNET

Albayrak has managed the Port of Mogadishu since September 2014, generating monthly revenue of US $4m., according to the company's manager; some 55% of this revenue is transferred to the Somali Government. Albayrak also has responsibility for rebuilding and modernizing the port, a project with estimated costs totalling around $80m. In October 2013 the Somali Government endorsed an agreement with the Turkish company to manage the Port of Mogadishu for a 20-year period. In April 2014, however, Parliament postponed the completion of the deal, pending the approval of new foreign investment legislation. In September the Somali Government officially delegated the management of the port to Albayrak. In August 2018 Mogadishu seaport began to operate 24 hours a day, with the aim of increasing revenue, reducing loading and unloading times, and making the port more competitive.

Favori LLC was responsible for the construction of a new terminal at AAIA, which opened in January 2015. Traffic through the airport has increased since 2013 when the International Civil Aviation Organization removed AAIA from the 'Zone 5' list of airports deemed to pose a security risk to aircraft, crew and passengers. The Kenya-based Jubba Airways, the unofficial national carrier of Somalia, has enlarged its fleet of leased Soviet Antonov propeller planes and old Boeing jets, and increased the number of its domestic and international flight routes. Competition from large international carriers such as Turkish Airlines, Ethiopian Airlines (EA) and Flydubai (of the

UAE) prompted the merger of Jubba Airways and Daallo Airlines, another regional carrier, in February 2015. Flydubai commenced operating flights from Dubai to Somaliland in December 2014, thereby becoming the largest carrier to fly to Hargeysa, Somaliland's capital. The UAE carrier has been flying between the two cities four times a week since March 2015. In July 2017 UAE-based budget carrier Air Arabia began operating flights to Hargeysa twice a week. In August 2018, amid a growing rapprochement between Somalia, Ethiopia and Eritrea, it was announced that EA would soon resume direct commercial flights between the Ethiopian capital, Addis Ababa, and Mogadishu. These had been stopped in 1977 due to the Ogaden war (see *History*). In July 2019 Qatar Airways began operating flights between the Qatari capital, Doha, and AAIA.

The telecommunications sector has boomed in Somalia in the last two decades. Prominent Somali telecommunications companies include Hormuud Telecom, Somtel, Nationlink Telecom, Golis Telecom, Somafone, Netco and Somali Telecom Group. Hormuud, one of the largest mobile operators, with a 60% share in national mobile and broadband services, introduced a 3G mobile internet service in Mogadishu in December 2012. By early January 2013 over 150,000 customers had signed up for the service. However, 3G mobile telephone services were cut off in early 2014 because of a threat from Islamist militants. In 2013 Somtel, in which the money transfer operator (MTO—see *Financial Services*) Dahabshiil acquired a majority stake in 2008, extended its services to south-central Somalia and Puntland.

In November 2012 the South Africa-based fibre optics company Liquid Telecom delivered a broadband internet cable to Somalia. This was the first terrestrial connection to the country, which for 20 years had had to rely on expensive satellite links. Liquid Telecom agreed a deal with Hormuud to connect the Somali mobile operator to its 17,000-km network of terrestrial cables. In February 2014 West Indian Ocean Cable Company, together with a local partner, Dalkom Somalia, brought the first broadband cable to Somalia via the East Africa submarine cable system. In April fibre optics services were launched in Mogadishu. Prior to this launch, access to the internet had been via dial-up or satellite links. Two new submarine cable projects are expected to improve Somalia's access to international bandwidth. The 1,500-km Gulf to Africa (G2A) cable, in operation since late 2016, connects Salalah, Oman, to Bosaso in Puntland and Berbera in Somaliland, with a terrestrial extension to Addis Ababa. The G2A consortium includes Omantel, Ethio Telecom, Golis Telecom (Puntland) and Telesom Company (Somaliland). The 5,500-km Djibouti-Africa Regional Express (DARE) cable project will connect Dar es Salaam (Tanzania), Mombasa (Kenya), Mogadishu, Bosaso, Berbera, Mocha (Yemen) and Djibouti. The agreement between the seven major carriers that comprise the DARE consortium (Djibouti Telecom, TeleYemen, Africa Marine Express, Telesom, Hormuud Telecom, Golis Telecom and Somtel) was signed in May 2016.

AGRICULTURE AND LIVESTOCK

There are four primary agricultural zones in Somalia: the Shabelle and Juba river valleys, in which rain-fed and irrigated maize is cultivated along with sesame and cash crops, namely bananas; a sorghum belt in the Bay and Bakool regions, with livestock production; a rain-fed area in the north-west, including parts of the Awdal and Galbeed regions, where maize and sorghum are cultivated and where there is some livestock farming; and a coastal cowpea (an African annual plant from the pea family) belt zone in central and southern Somalia. Despite the country's agricultural potential, nearly three decades of war, compounded by droughts and floods, have created a situation of protracted and complex emergency, which has eroded livelihoods and led to increased vulnerability to food insecurity.

Attempts are being made to rebuild the banana industry, once a leading export sector and one of the pillars of Somalia's economy. A group of farmers in the Afgoye area established FruitSome in 2013 to market and export their bananas, but multinationals remained cautious about committing to

Somalia. However, FruitSome, with assistance from the UN Food and Agriculture Organization (FAO), had some success in connecting with regional buyers. A conference was held in Dubai in 2014 at which Somali businesses exhibited their products to an international audience for the first time in years. By the end of 2014 FruitSome had exported five containers of bananas to markets in Saudi Arabia and the UAE. Nevertheless, with al-Shabaab still in control of the main plantation areas, banana exports are unlikely to recommence on a large scale in the immediate future.

Livestock is the mainstay of Somalia's economy, contributing some 40% of the country's annual GDP. In April 2015 the FAO-managed Food Security and Nutrition Analysis Unit revealed that in 2014 the country exported some 5m. head of livestock to markets in the Gulf. This was the highest number of live animals exported from the country in more than 20 years. According to FAO data, in 2014 Somalia exported 4.6m. goats and sheep, 340,000 cattle, and 77,000 camels, with a combined value of an estimated US $360m. Buyers of Somali livestock are mainly from Saudi Arabia, Yemen, the UAE, Qatar, Oman and Kuwait. However, the war in Yemen resulted in a decline in livestock exports. Moreover, Saudi Arabia, which had contributed steadily to increasing exports between 2009 and 2016, imposed a ban on the importation of livestock from Somalia and Somaliland in September 2016 following reports of an outbreak of Rift Valley fever in the Horn of Africa. The ban was eventually lifted in July 2018, but a few weeks later the Saudi Government sent a ship carrying 27,000 head of Somali livestock back to Bosaso port. According to FAO, in 2020 Somalia's livestock comprised 11.6m. goats, 12.1m. sheep, 4.8m. cattle and 7.3m. camels.

Due to the impact of a prolonged drought (which commenced in 2015) on the agricultural sector, overall economic growth decelerated to 1.4% in 2017. Food access has rapidly diminished as staple food prices have escalated substantially and livestock prices plummeted. Inflation, which had declined from 4.5% in 2013 to 1.2% in 2016, increased to an estimated 6.1% in 2017, according to the IMF. Although inflation was contained to some extent by subdued oil prices and dollarization, commodity prices were considerably higher than global market prices. As of mid-2017 an estimated 6.2m. people were in need of aid in Somalia. After slowly recovering from the drought of the mid-2010s, Somalia's economy rebounded in 2018. Better weather conditions enabled a 39% increase in maize and sorghum yields and revived animal production. Food prices subsequently stabilized and inflation decreased to an estimated 3.2% in 2018.

Somalia's agricultural sector suffered multiple adverse shocks in 2020, including flooding, the COVID-19 pandemic and an invasion of desert locusts. Flooding during the year overall was estimated by the UN Office for the Coordination of Humanitarian Affairs (OCHA) to have destroyed 144,000 ha of agricultural land and displaced 919,000 people in Somalia, nearly 6% of the country's total population. The plague of locusts arrived in Somalia in late 2019, but it was not until February 2020 that the Ministry of Agriculture declared a national emergency, noting that the swarms posed 'a major threat to Somalia's fragile food security situation'. By late May a second generation of mature adults was laying eggs, in a context where a previous batch had hatched in early April, according to the World Bank. At that stage, US $24.2m. had been donated to an FAO action plan to eliminate the insects, although a further $32.8m. was needed fully to implement the programme. The World Bank estimated that total losses to Somalia's agricultural sector as a result of the locust invasion and breeding could amount to $670m. if no efforts were made to eliminate the insects. The multilateral lender calculated that even in the event of countermeasures being successfully implemented, the sector's losses would exceed $200m. Alongside the complete eradication of crops in some areas, there was a risk of the locusts decimating livestock, which depend on vegetation as herds roam. A report by OCHA in March 2021 noted that 'tens of thousands of hectares' of cropland and pasture had been damaged by the desert locust invasion during 2020. In July 2021 FAO announced that it had increased aerial patrols to locate swarms in north-western Somalia, noting that the desert locust 'upsurge' was 'still underway' in the Greater Horn of Africa, despite the 'massive control operations' executed between May and July 2020 in Ethiopia, Kenya and Somalia. The 'Gu' rain season, which normally stretches from April to the harvest season in July, began late and heavy in early May, causing more floods, before ceasing earlier than normal, in late May. The erratic seasonal rains undermined yields of maize in Lower Shabelle, sorghum in the Bay region, and cowpeas in Middle Shabelle and beyond, according to FAO.

Meanwhile, the COVID-19 pandemic had a major impact on livestock exports to Saudi Arabia for the *Hajj*. Typically, some 2.5m. people converge annually on the city of Mecca for this event, but in July 2020 the Saudi authorities imposed a limit of 10,000 attendees, in an attempt to curb the spread of the virus. In 2018 revenue from Somalia's exports of sheep and goats totalled US \$176m., of which Saudi Arabia accounted for \$70.1m., largely for the *Hajj*. In a further setback for Somalia's livestock industry, Saudi Arabia announced in June 2021 that it would only allow 60,000 vaccinated residents of the kingdom to perform the *Hajj* that year, excluding all Muslims from abroad for a second consecutive year.

UN agencies, including the World Food Programme, FAO and OCHA, warned in June 2022 that the failure of four consecutive rain seasons, high levels of inflation and gaps in humanitarian funding had resulted in a 160% increase in the number of Somalis suffering from 'catastrophic levels of food insecurity, starvation and disease'. This analysis put the number of Somalis facing 'crisis-level food insecurity' by September at 7.1m., or nearly one-half of the country's population, of whom 210,000 faced 'catastrophic hunger and starvation'. The same analysis estimated the number of livestock in the country killed by drought at around 3m. since mid-2021. However, farmers who were able to sustain their herds were expected to benefit from a relatively normal *Hajj* in 2022. Saudi Arabia anticipated that 850,000 foreign pilgrims would participate in the event.

HYDROCARBON POTENTIAL

Somalia constitutes the latest 'frontier region' of hydrocarbon exploration in East Africa. Promising test wells, seismic surveys, actual oil seeps and the geological resemblance to Yemen indicate the presence of petroleum in commercial quantities in Somaliland, Puntland and Galmudug, and off the coast of south-central Somalia. However, the country presents numerous problems for hydrocarbon exploration, including political volatility, physical insecurity, institutional fragility, ambiguous property rights and scant infrastructure for transport and processing. Nevertheless, the mere indication of the existence of oil has resulted in a significant inflow of high-risk small exploration companies and oil-related investments, despite the volatile security situation in the country.

Most exploration efforts during the 2010s have been confined to Somalia's northern territories, Somaliland and Puntland, owing to security considerations. Since 2013, however, the Somali Federal Government has held discussions with previous concession holders, including ConocoPhillips, Royal Dutch Shell, Exxon Mobil, BP and Chevron, and in August of that year Soma Oil & Gas signed a contract with the Somali Government to collect data on onshore and offshore petroleum. In exchange for collecting data, Soma Oil & Gas was granted the right to apply for up to 12 oil blocks in an area viewed by the US 'oil majors' as one of the final frontiers for oil extraction. A seismic survey carried out by the company offshore and in certain limited onshore areas revealed encouraging results.

The Petroleum Bill was enacted in February 2020. This legislation enshrined a revenue-sharing agreement that stipulated how national oil revenues would be distributed among the Federal Government, Federal Member States and local communities; it also established the Somalia Petroleum Authority and the Somali National Oil Company The new law allocated 55% of potential offshore oil revenues to the Federal Government and 45% to the Federal Member States and local communities. Legal ownership of natural resources has been—and, despite the new legislation, in some cases remains—a highly contested and potentially dangerous issue in Somalia. According to local media, the federal states of Jubbaland and Puntland refused to recognize the legitimacy of the revenue-sharing law. Meanwhile, Somaliland has staked its own claims to hydrocarbon reserves. Furthermore, a number of major oil companies, including Eni (Italy) and Total (France), were involved in a legal dispute between Kenya and Somalia, which concerned the demarcation of the maritime border between the two countries and affected an offshore triangular area that was claimed by both Governments. The International Court of Justice (ICJ), in The Hague, the Netherlands, issued a final ruling on the case in October 2021, awarding the majority of the disputed maritime territory to Somalia, although the Kenyan Government, which had refused to recognize the ICJ's jurisdiction, rejected the decision.

In January 2020 President Erdoğan of Turkey announced that Somalia had invited Turkey to explore for oil and gas off shore in its exclusive economic zone. In May the Ministry of Petroleum and Mineral Resources announced a licensing round for up to seven offshore oil blocks, which it stated were 'estimated to be among the most prospective areas for hydrocarbon explorations and production in Somalia'. The bidding process commenced in August. The Ministry announced in March 2020 that it had concluded a preliminary agreement regarding a joint venture between Shell and Exxon Mobil for the exploration and exploitation of offshore hydrocarbon reserves. The two firms had arranged a joint venture covering five hydrocarbon blocks under Somali dictator Mohamed Siad Barre, before he was ousted in 1991, and in October 2019 they had agreed to pay the Federal Government US \$1.7m. in fees for that earlier leasehold tenure of the blocks.

Illustrating the extent to which the investment environment in Somalia remained highly volatile, in February 2022 Prime Minister Mohamed Hussein Roble and the Office of the President both declared a deal signed by the Ministry of Petroleum and Mineral Resources with a US-based firm, Coastline Exploration, to be invalid. The agreement, which involved seven production sharing agreements, covering two deep-water blocks, was described as 'illegal' by the Prime Minister within hours of it being signed. The Office of the President, meanwhile, claimed that the agreement had been nullified through an existing decree that banned such deals during elections.

FINANCIAL SERVICES

Confronted by the rapid modernization of the private financial sector, the Central Bank of Somalia (CBS) has attempted to strengthen its regulatory and supervisory capacity. In the absence of a national banking system linked to the global financial structure, an extensive and dynamic network of MTOs (see *Transport, Telecommunications and the Internet*) was developed to channel international remittance flows and operate domestic financial transactions. These MTOs began as *hawalas* (money remittance companies) and evolved into Somalia's de facto banking system. In late 2015 the CBS recognized 48 financial institutions in Somalia: four licensed and registered MTOs (Dahabshiil Money Transfer, Kaah Express, Tawakal Express and Juba Express), six licensed banks (Dahabshiil Bank International, Salaam Somali Bank, International Bank of Somalia, Trust African Bank, Premier Bank and Amal Bank—although the latter's licence had expired), and 38 MTOs or banks that had preliminarily been registered or had applied for a licence. Channelled through MTOs, remittances from the diaspora have played an essential role in sustaining Somalia's economy and supporting household income. According to IMF estimates, remittances amounted to more than US \$1,578m. in 2019, accounting for 31.9% of the country's GDP.

The CBS, however, does not have the capacity to conduct examinations of the banks that it recognizes in order to assess their financial soundness. There is no financial institution in Somalia that can issue letters of credit to banking institutions abroad. As a result, traders have no choice but to operate through banks in third countries, adding to the difficulties in regulating the financial sector. Oversight institutions are being established to enhance economic governance. The Financial Governance Committee (FGC), consisting of representatives from the Government and the international financial institutions, was set up in early 2014 to plan for, monitor and report on Somalia's public financial management systems. The Committee includes the Minister of Finance, the Governor of the CBS, representatives of the Office of the President, and two external appointees from the African Development Bank (AfDB) and the World Bank. With the help of the FGC, the Government has sought to renegotiate some of the 'stranglehold' public contracts that were previously signed. The review process began in February with a request by the Government to the AfDB and the World Bank to review a contract under negotiation with the British company Soma Oil & Gas Exploration Ltd covering seismic data processing and marketing. By August 2016 a total of 12 contracts had been placed under review, relating to: Mogadishu seaport development and operations; the development of Mogadishu's AAIA; Mogadishu

container port operations; oil and gas exploration and development; fisheries management and protection; and the construction of offshore patrol vessels. The CBS announced in July 2022 that it had for the first time awarded licences to two foreign banks, Egypt's Banque Misr and Turkey's Ziraat Katilim, enabling them to open branches in Somalia.

In February 2021 the CBS announced that it had granted the country's first mobile money licence to Hormuud, in a context where around 3m. people were already using that firm's EVC Plus mobile money platform, a substantial portion of its 3.6m. mobile telephone subscribers. CBS Governor Abdirahman Mohamed Abdullahi declared that granting the licence would help to integrate the sector into the international financial system, while also making this money market subject to regulation by the monetary authority for the first time.

Statistical Survey

Source (unless otherwise stated): National Bureau of Statistics, Federal Republic of Somalia, Afgooye Road, Wadajir District, Mogadishu; tel. (61) 3700080; e-mail snbs@nbs.gov.so; internet www.nbs.gov.so.

Area and Population

AREA, POPULATION AND DENSITY

Area (sq km)	637,657*
Population (census results)†	
7 February 1975	3,253,024
1986/1987 (provisional)	
Males	3,741,664
Females	3,372,767
Total	7,114,431
Population (UN estimates at mid-year)‡	
2020	15,893,219
2021§	16,359,500
2022§	16,841,805
Density (per sq km) at mid-2022§	26.4

* 246,201 sq miles.
† Excluding adjustment for underenumeration.
‡ Source: UN, *World Population Prospects: The 2019 Revision*.
§ Projection.

POPULATION BY AGE AND SEX
('000, UN projections at mid-2022)

	Males	Females	Total
0–14 years	3,880.6	3,828.6	7,709.2
15–64 years	4,277.5	4,361.6	8,639.2
65 years and over	237.6	255.8	493.4
Total	8,395.8	8,446.1	16,841.8

Note: Totals may not be equal to the sum of components, owing to rounding.

Source: UN, *World Population Prospects: The 2019 Revision*.

PRINCIPAL TOWNS
(incl. suburbs, UN projections at mid-2022)

Mogadishu (capital).	2,497,463		Berbera	545,378
Hargeysa . . .	1,079,377		Kismayu . . .	512,590
Merca	727,772			

Source: UN, *World Urbanization Prospects: The 2018 Revision*.

BIRTHS AND DEATHS
(annual averages, UN estimates)

	2005–10	2010–15	2015–20
Birth rate (per 1,000)	45.5	43.0	41.9
Death rate (per 1,000)	13.5	12.2	10.9

Source: UN, *World Population Prospects: The 2019 Revision*.

Life expectancy (years at birth, estimates): 57.7 (males 56.0; females 59.4) in 2020 (Source: World Bank, World Development Indicators database).

ECONOMICALLY ACTIVE POPULATION
('000, FAO estimates at mid-year)

	2013	2014	2015
Agriculture, etc.	2,720	2,794	2,870
Total labour force (incl. others) .	4,244	4,395	4,551

Source: FAO.

2019 (labour force survey, persons aged 15 years and over): Agriculture, forestry and fishing 128,941; Mining and quarrying 20,421; Manufacturing 108,679; Electricity, gas and water 12,966; Construction 29,900; Wholesale and retail trade, vehicle repairs 34,855; Hotels and restaurants 37,775; Transport, storage and communications 35,778; Financial intermediation 7,528; Real estate, renting and other business activities 69,973; Public administration and compulsory social security 15,905; Education 52,430; Health and social welfare 52,144; Other services 265,746; *Sub-total* 873,041; Activities not classified elsewhere 82,779; *Total employed* 955,820; Unemployed 259,652; *Total labour force* 1,215,472.

Health and Welfare

KEY INDICATORS

Total fertility rate (children per woman, 2020)	5.9
Under-5 mortality rate (per 1,000 live births, 2020) . . .	114.6
HIV/AIDS (% of persons aged 15–49, 2020)	<0.1
COVID-19: Cumulative confirmed deaths (per 100,000 persons at 31 August 2022)	8.0
COVID-19: Fully vaccinated population (% of total population at 29 August 2022)	14.3
Physicians (per 1,000 head, 2014)	0.02
Hospital beds (per 1,000 head, 2017)	0.9
Health expenditure (2001): US $ per head (PPP)	18
Health expenditure (2001): % of GDP	2.6
Health expenditure (2001): public (% of total)	44.6
Total carbon dioxide emissions ('000 metric tons, 2018) . .	690
Carbon dioxide emissions per head (metric tons, 2018) . .	0.0
Access to improved water resources (% of persons, 2020) .	56
Access to improved sanitation facilities (% of persons, 2020).	39

Note: For data on COVID-19 vaccinations, 'fully vaccinated' denotes receipt of all doses specified by approved vaccination regime (Sources: Johns Hopkins University and Our World in Data). Data on health expenditure refer to current general government expenditure in each case. For more information on sources and further definitions for all indicators, see Health and Welfare Statistics: Sources and Definitions section (europaworld.com/credits).

Agriculture

PRINCIPAL CROPS

('000 metric tons, FAO estimates unless otherwise indicated)

	2018	2019	2020
Bananas	23	23	23
Cassava (Manioc)	94	95	95
Dates	14	14	14
Grapefruit and pomelos . .	6	6	6
Groundnuts, with shell . .	8	8	8
Lemons and limes . .	8	8	8
Maize*	102	57	75
Oranges	11	11	11
Rice, paddy	1.5	1.3	1.2
Sesame seed	36*	36*	34
Sorghum*	130	125	100
Sugar cane	230	233	228
Sweet potatoes	8	8	8
Watermelons	7	7	6

* Unofficial figure(s).

Aggregate production ('000 metric tons, may include official, semi-official or estimated data): Total cereals 235 in 2018, 184 in 2019, 177 in 2020; Total fruit (primary) 213 in 2018, 214 in 2019, 214 in 2020; Total oilcrops 60 in 2018, 62 in 2019, 61 in 2020; Total roots and tubers 103 in 2018–20; Total vegetables (primary) 104 in 2018, 105 in 2019, 104 in 2020.

Source: FAO.

LIVESTOCK

('000 head, year ending September, FAO estimates)

	2018	2019	2020
Asses	22	23	23
Camels	7,295	7,319	7,337
Cattle	4,739	4,800	4,826
Chickens	3,717	3,744	3,771
Goats	11,641	11,599	11,587
Pigs	4	4	4
Sheep	10,635	12,116	12,064

Source: FAO.

LIVESTOCK PRODUCTS

('000 metric tons, FAO estimates)

	2018	2019	2020
Camel meat	48	48	48
Camel offals, edible	8	8	9
Camels' milk	963	966	969
Cattle hides, fresh	10	10	10
Cattle meat	56	56	55
Cattle offals, edible	11	11	11
Cows' milk	449	454	456
Goat meat	39	39	39
Goats' milk	379	378	378
Goats' skins, fresh	6	6	6
Sheep meat	41	47	48
Sheep's (Ewe's) milk	371	408	407
Sheepskins, fresh	8	9	9
Hen eggs	3	3	3

Source: FAO.

Forestry

ROUNDWOOD REMOVALS

('000 cubic metres, excl. bark, FAO estimates)

	2018	2019	2020
Sawlogs, veneer logs and logs for sleepers*	28	28	28
Other industrial wood	82	82	82
Fuel wood	15,604	16,013	16,435
Total	15,714	16,123	16,545

* Annual output assumed to be unchanged since 1975.

Source: FAO.

SAWNWOOD PRODUCTION

('000 cubic metres, incl. railway sleepers, FAO estimates)

	2018	2019	2020
Total (all broadleaved) . . .	14	14	14

Note: Annual production assumed to be unchanged since 1975.
Source: FAO.

Fishing

('000 metric tons, live weight, FAO estimates)

	2004	2005	2006
Marine fishes	28.7	23.9	28.7
Total catch (incl. others) . . .	30.0	25.0	30.0

2007–20: Figures assumed to be unchanged since 2006 (FAO estimates).
Source: FAO.

Mining

('000 metric tons, estimates)

	2002	2003	2004
Salt	1	1	1
Gypsum	2	2	2

Source: US Geological Survey.

Industry

SELECTED PRODUCTS

	2014	2015	2016
Raw sugar ('000 metric tons) . .	23	23	23
Electrical energy (million kWh) .	350	350	350

Electrical energy (million kWh, estimate): 367 in 2017–19; 391 in 2020.

Sources: UN Industrial Commodity Statistics Database; UN Energy Statistics Database.

Finance

CURRENCY AND EXCHANGE RATES

Monetary Units
100 cents = 1 Somali shilling.

Sterling, Dollar and Euro Equivalents (31 May 2022)
£1 sterling = 30,591.27 Somali shillings;
US $1 = 24,300.00 Somali shillings;
€1 = 26,032.59 Somali shillings;
100,000 Somali shillings = £3.27 = $4.12 = €3.84.

Average Exchange Rate (Somali shillings per US $, non-commercial rates derived from the Operational Rates of Exchange for United Nations Programmes)
2019   24,300.00
2020   24,300.00
2021   24,300.00

Note: A separate currency, the 'Somaliland shilling', was introduced in the 'Republic of Somaliland' in January 1995. The exchange rate was reported to be US $1 = 2,750 'Somaliland shillings' in March 2000.

BUDGET
(US $ million)

Revenue	2020	2021	2022*
Tax revenue	139.3	162.8	173.7
Non-tax revenue	71.7	66.8	73.3
Grants	285.6	147.0	660.2
Total	**496.6**	**376.5**	**907.1**

Expenditure	2020	2021	2022*
Current expenditure	354.3	330.8	433.2
Compensation of employees .	215.8	240.9	256.9
Use of goods and services . .	62.2	66.9	82.0
Consumption of fixed capital .	7.9	2.8	13.6
Interest	2.1	0.6	2.5
Grants	66.2	19.7	75.7
Contingency	—	—	2.5
Capital expenditure	118.7	129.0	485.5
Total	**473.0**	**459.8**	**918.7**

* Budget figures.

Source: Ministry of Finance, Mogadishu.

NATIONAL ACCOUNTS
('000 million Somali shillings at current prices, estimates)

Expenditure on the Gross Domestic Product

	2018	2019	2020
Government final consumption expenditure	3,545	3,883	3,971
Private final consumption expenditure	29,515	32,332	33,065
Gross fixed capital formation . .	8,106	8,880	9,081
Changes in inventories . . .	22	24	25
Total domestic expenditure .	**41,188**	**45,119**	**46,143**
Exports of goods and services . .	124	136	139
Less Imports of goods and services	683	748	765
GDP at purchasers' values .	**40,631**	**44,508**	**45,518**
GDP at constant 2015 prices .	**34,715**	**35,721**	**35,187**

Gross Domestic Product by Economic Activity

	2018	2019	2020
Agriculture, hunting, forestry and fishing	21,486	23,536	24,070
Mining, quarrying and utilities .	241	264	270
Manufacturing	887	972	994
Construction	1,499	1,642	1,679
Trade, restaurants and hotels .	3,791	4,153	4,247
Transport and communications .	3,351	3,671	3,754
Other activities	4,446	4,871	4,981
Sub-total	**35,701**	**39,108**	**39,995**
Indirect taxes (net)*	4,930	5,400	5,523
GDP at purchasers' values .	**40,631**	**44,508**	**45,518**

* Figures obtained as residuals.

Source: UN, National Accounts Main Aggregates Database.

BALANCE OF PAYMENTS
(US $ million, preliminary)

	2019	2020	2021
Exports of goods f.o.b.	554	545	693
Imports of goods f.o.b.	−3,622	−3,849	−4,610
Trade balance	**−3,068**	**−3,304**	**−3,917**
Exports of services	566	425	593
Imports of services	−1,623	−1,537	−1,886
Balance on goods and services	**−4,124**	**−4,416**	**−5,210**
Income (net)	−36	−38	−40
Balance on goods, services and income	**−4,160**	**−4,454**	**−5,250**
Current transfers (net) . . .	3,483	3,702	4,141
Current balance	**−676**	**−752**	**−1,109**
Investment liabilities . . .	672	784	1,284
Overall balance	**−5**	**32**	**175**

Source: IMF, *Somalia: Second and Third Reviews Under the Extended Credit Facility Arrangement and Request for Modification of Performance Criterion, Modification of Performance Criteria, Interim Assistance and Rephasing of Access and Extension of the Arrangement—Press Release; Staff Report; and Statement by the Executive Director for Somalia* (July 2022).

External Trade

SELECTED COMMODITIES
(US $ million)

Imports c.i.f.	2019	2020
Food	1,375	1,170
Beverages and tobacco	108	180
Petroleum products	111	345
Medical products	104	176
Personal care products	93	114
Clothing and footwear	451	569
Construction goods	364	414
Vehicles and spare parts	264	324
Total (incl. others)	3,204	3,759

Exports f.o.b.	2019	2020
Live animals	205	398
Animal skins and products thereof	35	30
Crops and vegetable oils	88	88
Forestry products	111	13
Total (incl. others)	445	545

SELECTED TRADING PARTNERS
(US $ million)

Imports c.i.f.	2014	2015	2016
Ethiopia	237	186	4
China, People's Republic . .	93	117	173
India	152	165	221
Oman	88	74	78
United Arab Emirates	379	318	346
Total (incl. others)	1,250	1,100	1,080

Exports f.o.b.	2014	2015	2016
India	42	11	24
Oman	105	88	190
Saudi Arabia	229	201	—
United Arab Emirates . . .	65	82	104
Yemen	19	13	—
Total (incl. others)	510	440	440

Source: African Development Bank.

2019: Total imports 3,204; Total exports 445.

2020: Total imports 3,759; Total exports 545.

Transport

SHIPPING
Flag Registered Fleet
(at 31 December)

	2019	2020	2021
Number of vessels	9	9	14
Total displacement ('000 grt) . .	5.0	5.0	5.0

Source: Lloyd's List Intelligence (www.bit.ly/LLintelligence).

CIVIL AVIATION
(traffic)

	2017	2018	2019
Departures	98	995	1,060
Passengers carried	4,486	33,729	34,066

Source: World Bank, World Development Indicators database.

Communications Media

(estimates)

	2018	2019	2020
Telephones ('000 main lines in use)	75	91	91
Mobile telephone subscriptions ('000)	7,653	8,227	8,844
Broadband subscriptions, fixed ('000)	—	98	119
Broadband subscriptions, mobile ('000)	—	414	445

Internet users (% of population): 1.9 in 2016; 2.0 in 2017.

Source: International Telecommunication Union.

Education

(2019/20 unless otherwise indicated)

	Institutions	Teachers	Pupils
Pre-primary*‡	16	133	1,558
Primary	773	10,017	317,881
Secondary	38	6,456	126,620
Higher‡	n.a.	817†	15,672†

* Figures refers to 1985.
† Figure refers to 1986.
‡ Source: UNESCO, *Statistical Yearbook*.

1991: University teachers 549; University students 4,640.

Pupil-teacher ratio (primary education, UNESCO estimate): 35.5 in 2006/07 (Source: UNESCO Institute for Statistics).

Adult literacy rate (UNESCO estimates): 24.0% in 2002 (Source: UN Development Programme, *Human Development Report*).

Directory

The Constitution

On 1 August 2012 a new Provisional Constitution was adopted by the National Constituent Assembly, a body comprising 825 elders drawn from traditional Somali clans. The main provisions are summarized below:

THE FEDERAL REPUBLIC OF SOMALIA

Somalia is a federal, sovereign and democratic republic founded on inclusive representation of the people, a multi-party system and social justice.

THE TERRITORY OF THE FEDERAL REPUBLIC OF SOMALIA

The boundaries of the Federal Republic of Somalia shall be those described in the 1960 Constitution of the Republic of Somalia and are to the north: The Gulf of Aden; to the north-west: Djibouti; to the west: Ethiopia; to the south-west: Kenya; to the east: the Indian Ocean.

STATE AND RELIGION

Islam is the religion of the state. No religion other than Islam can be propagated in the country. No law that is not compliant with the general principles of *Shari'a* (Islamic) law can be enacted. The official language of the Federal Republic of Somalia is Somali and Arabic is the second language.

THE STRUCTURE OF GOVERNMENT

The structure of the Government in the Federal Republic of Somalia is composed of two levels: the Federal Government level; and the Federal Member States level, which comprises the Federal Member State Government and the local governments. No single region can stand alone. Until such time as a region merges with another region (or other regions) to form a new Federal Member State, a region shall be directly administered by the Federal Government for a maximum period of two years.

THE FEDERAL PARLIAMENT

The Federal Parliament of the Federal Republic of Somalia consists of the House of the People and the Upper House. The term of office of the Federal Parliament is four years from the day of the announcement of the election results.

The members of the House of the People shall be elected by the citizens of the Federal Republic of Somalia in a direct, secret and free ballot. The number of ordinary members of the House of the People shall be 275. The House of the People is empowered to pass, amend or reject legislation tabled before it.

The members of the Upper House shall be elected through a direct, secret and free ballot by the people of the Federal Member States, and their number shall be no more than 54 members based on the 18 regions that existed in Somalia before 1991. All Federal Member States should have an equal number of representatives in the Upper House. The Upper House represents the Federal Member States, and its legislative duties include: participation in the process of amending the Constitution; and passing, amending, or rejecting the laws that are tabled before it.

THE PRESIDENT OF THE FEDERAL REPUBLIC OF SOMALIA

Any Somali citizen is eligible for the position of President of the Federal Republic of Somalia, as long as he or she is a Muslim and at least 40 years of age.

The Houses of the Federal Parliament shall elect the President of the Federal Republic of Somalia in a joint session. A minimum of two-thirds of the members of each House of the Federal Parliament must be present when electing the President. Candidatures must be proposed to the joint session of the Houses of the Federal Parliament by a minimum of 20 members of the House of the People, or a minimum of one Federal Member State.

The election of the President shall be conducted by secret ballot. Any candidate who gains a two-thirds' majority vote of the total membership of the two Houses of the Federal Parliament shall be elected President of the Federal Republic of Somalia. If no candidate gains the necessary two-thirds' majority in the first round, a second round of voting shall be conducted for the four candidates with the greatest number of votes from the first round, and any candidate who gains a two-thirds' majority vote of the total membership of the two Houses of the Federal Parliament in the second round shall be elected President of the Federal Republic of Somalia. If no candidate gains the necessary two-thirds' majority in the second round, a third round of voting shall be conducted between the two candidates with the greatest number of votes from the second round, and the candidate who gains the greatest number of votes in the third round shall be elected President of the Federal Republic of Somalia.

The President serves as Commander-in-Chief of the Armed Forces, appoints the Prime Minister, and dismisses ministers, state ministers and deputy ministers on the recommendation of the Prime Minister. The President shall hold office for a term of four years.

THE EXECUTIVE

The executive power of the Federal Government shall be vested in the Council of Ministers, which is the highest executive authority of the Federal Government and consists of the Prime Minister, the Deputy Prime Minister(s), ministers, state ministers and deputy ministers. The Prime Minister is the Head of the Federal Government and appoints the Deputy Prime Minister(s), ministers, state ministers, and deputy ministers. Those eligible for membership of the Council of Ministers may be, but shall not be limited to, members of the House of the People. Vacancy in the office of the Prime Minister caused by the resignation, dismissal, failure to fulfil responsibility, or death of the Prime Minister shall lead to the dissolution of the Council of Ministers.

The Council of Ministers has the power to: formulate the overall government policy and implement it; approve and implement administrative regulations, in accordance with the law; prepare draft laws, and table them before the House of the People of the Federal Parliament.

JUDICIAL AUTHORITY

The judiciary is independent of the legislative and executive branches of government while fulfilling its judicial functions. Members of the judiciary shall be subject only to the law. The national court structure shall be of three levels, which are: the Constitutional Court; the Federal Government level courts; and the Federal Member State level courts. The highest court at the Federal Government level shall be the Federal High Court, while the highest court at the Federal Member State level shall be the Federal Member State High Court.

The Government

HEAD OF STATE

President: HASSAN SHEIKH MOHAMUD (took office 23 May 2022).

COUNCIL OF MINISTERS
(October 2022)

Prime Minister: HAMZA ABDI BARRE.

Deputy Prime Minister: SALAH AHMED JAMA.

Minister of Religious Affairs and Endowments: SHEIKH MUKHTAR ROBOW ALI 'ABU MANSUR'.

Minister of Justice and Constitutional Affairs: HASSAN MOALIM.

Minister of the Interior, Federal Affairs and Reconciliation: AHMED MOALIM FIQI.

Minister of Finance: Dr ELMI MOHAMUD NUR.

Minister of Defence: ABDULKADIR MOHAMED NUR 'JAMA'.

Minister of Foreign Affairs and International Co-operation: ABSHIR OMAR HURUUSE.

Minister of Education and Training: FARAH SHEIKH ABDULQADIR.

Minister of Planning, Investment and Economic Development: MOHAMUD ABDIRAHMAN SHEIKH FARAH 'BEENE-BEENE'.

Minister of Ports and Maritime Transport: Gen. ABDULLAHI AHMED JAMA 'ILKAJIR'.

Minister of Air and Land Transport: FARDOWSA OSMAN IGAL DHORE.

Minister of Postal Services and Telecommunications: JAMA HASSAN KHALIF.

Minister of Animal Husbandry, Plantations and Pasture: HASSAN HUSSEIN MOHAMED 'HASSAN ELAAY'.

Minister of Trade and Industry: JIBRIL ABDIRASHID HAJI ABDI.

Minister of Public Works and Housing: ISMAIL ABDIRAHMAN SHEIKH BASHIR.

Minister of Women and Human Rights: KHADIJA MOHAMED DIRIYE.

Minister of Petroleum and Mineral Resources: Dr ABDIRIZAQ OMAR MOHAMED.

Minister of Internal Security: Dr MOHAMED AHMED SHEIKH ALI 'DOODISHE'.

Minister of Agriculture and Irrigation: AHMED MADOBE NUNOW.

Minister of Health and Social Care: Dr ALI HAJI ADEN.

Minister of Fisheries and Marine Resources: AHMED HASSAN ADAN.

Minister of Information and Tourism: DAOUD AWEYS JAMA.

Minister of Labour and Employment: BIHI IMAN EGEH.

Minister of Energy and Water: JAMA TAKHAL ABBAS.

Minister of Youth and Sport: MOHAMED BARRE MOHAMUD.

Minister of the Environment and Climate Change: KHADIJA MOHAMED ALMAKHZOUMI.

There were also 24 state ministers and 25 deputy ministers.

MINISTRIES

Office of the President: 1 Villa Somalia, 2525 Mogadishu; e-mail media@presidency.gov.so; internet villasomalia.gov.so.

Office of the Prime Minister: 1 Villa Somalia, 2525 Mogadishu; tel. (5) 543050; e-mail media@opm.gov.so; internet opm.gov.so.

Ministry of Agriculture and Irrigation: 1 Villa Somalia, 2525 Mogadishu; internet www.moa.gov.so.

Ministry of Air and Land Transport: Mogadishu.

Ministry of Animal Husbandry, Plantations and Pasture: Mogadishu.

Ministry of Defence: Mogadishu; internet mod.gov.so.

Ministry of Education and Training: Mogadishu.

Ministry of Energy and Water Resources: GPO Bldg, 3rd Floor, Corso Somalia Rd, Bondhere, Mogadishu; e-mail info@moewr.gov.so; internet moewr.gov.so.

Ministry of the Environment and Climate Change: Mogadishu.

Ministry of Finance: 1 Villa Somalia, 2525 Mogadishu; tel. (5) 404240; internet mof.gov.so.

Ministry of Fisheries and Marine Resources: Radio Mogadishu Rd, Wardhiigley, Mogadishu; e-mail dg@mfmr.gov.so; internet mfmr.gov.so/en.

Ministry of Foreign Affairs and International Co-operation: Afgooye Rd KM 5, 2525 Mogadishu; e-mail info@mfa.gov.so; internet www.mfa.gov.so.

Ministry of Health and Social Care: 1 Villa Somalia, 2525 Mogadishu; tel. (5) 424640; e-mail info@moh.gov.so; internet moh.gov.so.

Ministry of Information and Tourism: 1 Villa Somalia, 2525 Mogadishu; tel. 612111029; e-mail info@moi.gov.so; internet moi.gov.so.

Ministry of the Interior, Federal Affairs and Reconciliation: 1 Villa Somalia, 2525 Mogadishu; internet www.mois.somaligov.net.

Ministry of Internal Security: Mogadishu; tel. 610000001; e-mail info@mois.gov.so; internet www.mois.gov.so.

Ministry of Justice and Constitutional Affairs: Martine Hospital Rd, Hamar-Weine District, POB 629, Mogadishu; tel. (1) 865880; e-mail info@moj.gov.so; internet moj.gov.so.

Ministry of Labour and Employment: 1 Villa Somalia, 2525 Mogadishu; tel. 616666651; e-mail info@molgov.so; internet molgov.so.

Ministry of Petroleum and Mineral Resources: GPO Bldg, 3rd Floor, Corso, Bondhere, Mogadishu; tel. 619521111; e-mail info@mopmr.gov.so; internet mopmr.gov.so.

Ministry of Planning, Investment and Economic Development: Afgooye Rd, Mogadishu; tel. 615040610; e-mail info@mop.gov.so; internet mop.gov.so.

Ministry of Ports and Maritime Transport: Junction of Ex-Jubba Hotel, Corso Somalia Rd, POB 111, Mogadishu; e-mail min@malt.gov.so; internet mpmt.gov.so.

Ministry of Postal Services and Telecommunications: POB 66, Mogadishu; e-mail info@mptt.gov.so; internet moct.gov.so.

Ministry of Public Works, Reconstruction and Housing: 2nd Liido Rd, Shangani District, Mogadishu; tel. 618449370; e-mail planning@mpwr.gov.so; internet mpwr.gov.so.

Ministry of Religious Affairs and Endowments: Mogadishu; internet mera.gov.so.

Ministry of Trade and Industry: Mahmud Harbi Rd, Warta Nabada, Mogadishu; e-mail info@moci.gov.so; internet moci.gov.so.

Ministry of Women and Human Rights: 1 Villa Somalia, 2525 Mogadishu; internet mwhrd.gov.so.

Ministry of Youth and Sport: 1 Villa Somalia, 2525 Mogadishu; tel. 612222221; e-mail minister@moys.gov.so.

President

On 15 May 2022 Hassan Sheikh Mohamud was elected President of Somalia. A total of 36 candidates participated in the ballot, which was conducted on an electoral college basis with the 274 members of House of the People and the 54 members of the Upper House casting their votes. Following the first round of voting, incumbent President Mohamed Abdullahi Mohamed 'Farmajo', Mohamud, a former Prime Minister Hassan Ali Khayre and Puntland state's leader Said Abdullahi Deni proceeded to a second round in which none of the four candidates secured the required two-thirds majority. At a subsequent third round of voting, held between Mohamud and Mohamed 'Farmajo', the former received 214 votes, while the latter obtained 110 votes.

Legislature

FEDERAL PARLIAMENT

Federal Parliament: Mogadishue-mail info@parliament.gov.so; internet www.parliament.gov.so.

Speaker (House of the People): SHEIKH ADEN MOHAMED NUR 'MADOBE'.

Speaker (Upper House): ABDI HASHI ABDULLAHI.

According to the Provisional Constitution adopted on 1 August 2012, the Federal Parliament of the Federal Republic of Somalia consists of the House of the People and the Upper House (Aqalka Sare, sometimes referred to as the Senate). The term of office of the Federal Parliament is four years from the day of the announcement of the election results. The number of ordinary members of the House of the People shall be 275. The House of the People is empowered to pass, amend or reject legislation tabled before it. The members of the Upper House shall number no more than 54 members based on the 18 regions that existed in Somalia before 1991. All Federal Member States should have an equal number of representatives in the Upper House. The Upper House represents the Federal Member States, and its legislative duties include: participation in the process of amending the Constitution; and passing, amending, or rejecting the laws that are tabled before it.

Protracted indirect parliamentary elections were held from July 2021 and by mid-May 2022 all 54 members of the Upper House had been elected, while 274 members of the House of the People had been elected. (One seat remained vacant, following the annulment of the result.)

Election Commission

National Independent Election Commission: Villa Somalia, Mogadishu; tel. 613611116; e-mail contact@niec.so; internet niec.so; f. 2015; Chair. HALIMA ISMAIL IBRAHIM.

Political Organizations

According to legislation on political parties adopted by the Federal Parliament in September 2016, all registered political organization must have a national outlook, and represent at least two-thirds of the regions in the country, based on the regional boundaries that existed in 1991.

Cahdi Party: Km 4, Mogadishu; tel. 618558348; internet cahdiparty.com; Chair. Prof. ABDIRAHMAN IBRAHIM BILE.

Garsoor Party: Mogadishu; tel. 612944706; internet garsoor.org; Leader ZAKARIYE HAJI ABDI.

Gurmad: Airport Rd, Wadajir District, Mogadishu; tel. 614300900; internet gurmadparty.org; Leader Dr ABDINASIR MOHAMED.

National Democratic Party (NDP): Mogadishu; tel. 618092016; e-mail info@ndpsomalia.com; internet ndpsomalia.wordpress.com; Chair. FAWZIA YUSUF H. ADAM.

Peace and Development Party (PDP): Mogadishu; f. 2011; Chair. HASSAN SHEIKH MOHAMUD.

Al-Shabaab (The Youth): f. 2007 by fmr members of the Islamic Courts Union; Leader AHMAD UMAR.

Somali Democratic Alliance (SDA): f. 1989; represents the Gadabursi ethnic grouping in the north-west; opposes the declaration of an independent 'Republic of Somaliland'; Leader MOHAMED FARAH ABDULLAH.

Somali Justice and Peace Party (Tayo Political Party): Maka, al-Mukarrama, Mogadishu; f. 2012; Sec.-Gen. MOHAMED ABDULLAHI MOHAMED 'FARMAJO'.

Somali National Party (SNP): tel. 615795153; e-mail somalinp@hotmail.com; internet somalinp@hotmail.com; Chair. MOHAMMED AMEEN SAEED AHMED.

Wadajir Party: KM5, Zobe Bldg, Mogadishu; tel. 610000000; e-mail info@wadajirparty.org; internet xisbigawadajir.com; Chair. ABDIRAHMAN ABDISHAKUR WARSAME; Sec.-Gen. ABDIFITAH MOHAMED IBRAHIM GEESEY.

Diplomatic Representation

EMBASSIES IN SOMALIA

Burundi: former Somali National University, Jidka Afgooye Rd, Km 6, Mogadishu; tel. 617235670; e-mail emogadishu@yahoo.com; Ambassador REMY BARAMPAMA.

China, People's Republic: Halane, Mogadishu International Airport, Mogadishu; tel. 617023354; e-mail chinaemb_som@mfa.gov.cn; internet so.china-embassy.gov.cn; Ambassador FEI SHENGCHAO.

Djibouti: Abdi Aziz District, Mogadishu; tel. (1) 240347; e-mail ambassade-somalie@intnet.dj; Ambassador MOHAMED IBRAHIM YOUSSOUF.

Egypt: Mogadishu; e-mail egyptembassysomalia@yahoo.com; Ambassador MOHAMED EL-SAID AHMED AL-BAZ.

Ethiopia: POB 368, Mogadishu; Ambassador ABDULFATAH ABDULLAHI HASSAN.

Italy: Aden Adde International Airport, Mogadishu; tel. 205137500; e-mail somalia.ambasciata@esteri.it; internet ambmogadiscio.esteri.it/ambasciata_mogadiscio/it; Ambassador ALBERTO VECCHI.

Kenya: nr Aden Adde International Airport, Mogadishu; e-mail diaspora@kenyaembassysom.org; internet kenyaembassysom.org; Ambassador Maj.-Gen. (retd) THOMAS KIPKOSGEI CHEPKUTO.

Korea, Democratic People's Republic: Via Km 5, Mogadishu; Ambassador KIM RYONG SU.

Libya: Via Medina, POB 125, Mogadishu.

Nigeria: Via Km 5, POB 980, Mogadishu; tel. (5) 562233; Ambassador YUSUF YUNUSA.

Qatar: Hodan District, KM4 Square, Mogadishu; tel. (1) 856677; e-mail mogadishu@mofa.gov.qa; internet mogadishu.embassy.qa; Ambassador HASSAN HAMZA ASAD HASHEM.

Saudi Arabia: Via Benadir, POB 603, Mogadishu; Ambassador AHMED BIN MOHAMED AL-MUWALLAD.

Sudan: Via al-Mukarah, POB 552, Mogadishu; Ambassador KHALAFULAH MUSTAFA.

Türkiye (Turkey): Via Km 4, POB 2833, Mogadishu; tel. 618868491; internet mogadishu.be.mfa.gov.tr; Ambassador İBRAHIM METE YAĞLI.

Uganda: Mogadishu; tel. 612116639; e-mail sam.tulyamuhika@mofa.go.ug; internet mogadishu.mofa.go.ug; Ambassador Prof. SAM TULYA-MUHIKA.

United Arab Emirates: Lido St, Abelaziz Area (Old Port), Mogadishu; tel. 619777715; e-mail mogadishuemb@mofaic.gov.ae; internet www.mofaic.gov.ae/ar-ae/missions/mogadishu; Ambassador AHMAD JUMA AL-RUMAITHI.

United Kingdom: Aden Adde International Airport, Via Londra, POB 1036, Mogadishu; e-mail somalia.enquiries@fco.gov.uk; internet www.gov.uk/government/world/somalia; Ambassador KATE FOSTER.

USA: Mogadishu; e-mail somaliapublicaffairs@state.gov; internet so.usembassy.gov; Ambassador LARRY E. ANDRÉ, Jr.

Yemen: Km 4, Mogadishu; e-mail yemb-mogadishu@mofa.gov.ye; Ambassador AHMED HAMID ALI UMAR.

Judicial System

According to the Provisional Constitution adopted on 1 August 2012, the judiciary is independent of the legislative and executive branches of government. No law that is not compliant with the general principles of *Shari'a* (Islamic) law may be enacted. The national court structure shall be of three levels: the Constitutional Court; the Federal Government level courts; and the Federal Member State level courts. The highest court at the Federal Government level shall be the Federal Supreme Court, while the highest court at the Federal Member State level shall be the Federal Member State Supreme Court. If a case concerning the Federal Government is presented before a court, the court shall refer the case to a Federal Government

level court. If a case concerning a constitutional matter is presented before a court, the court may refer the case to the Constitutional Court. Any court with judicial powers can decide on whether a matter brought before it is a constitutional matter or not, if this does not contradict the exclusive powers of the Constitutional Court. The Constitutional Court is the final authority in constitutional matters and is composed of five judges, including the Chief Judge and the Deputy Chief Judge.

Supreme Court: Mogadishu; e-mail info@supremecourt.gov.so; internet supremecourt.gov.so; the court of final instance in civil, criminal, administrative and auditing matters; Chair. BASHE YUSUF AHMED.

Attorney-General: SULEIMAN MOHAMED MOHAMUD.

Religion

ISLAM

Islam is the state religion. Most Somalis are Sunni Muslims.

Imam: Gen. MOHAMED ABSHIR.

CHRISTIANITY

The Roman Catholic Church

Somalia comprises a single diocese, directly responsible to the Holy See.

Apostolic Administrator of Mogadishu: Mgr Dr GIORGIO BERTIN, POB 273, Ahmed bin Idris, Mogadishu; tel. (1) 20184.

The Anglican Communion

Within the Episcopal/Anglican Province of Alexandria (which was inaugurated in June 2020), the Bishop of the Horn of Africa has jurisdiction over Somalia.

The Press

New Dalka: Mogadishu; e-mail editor@dalka-magazine.com; internet www.dalka-magazine.com; f. 2017; monthly; online only; current affairs, culture, literature and arts; Editor HAROON MOHAMOUD.

Horseed: Horseed Bldg, nr former Five Star Hotel, Bosaso, Puntland State; tel. (90) 7729070; e-mail editor@horseedmedia.net; internet horseedmedia.net; online; in Somali and English; Editor MOHAMED ADAN DIRIR.

Jamhuuriya (The Republic): Hargeysa; independent; daily; Editor-in-Chief HASSAN SAÏD FAISAL ALI.

Mogadishu Times: Mogadishu; internet mogtimes.com; privately owned; Somali.

Sahan (Pioneer): Bosaso; e-mail contact@sahanjournal.com; Founder and Editor ABDI LATIF DAHIR.

Somali Magazine: Mogadishu; e-mail info@somalimagazine.so; internet somalimagazine.so; online-only.

Xog Doon: Mogadishu; internet xogdoonnews.net; daily; Somali.

Xog Ogaal: Mogadishu; internet xog-ogaal.net; daily; privately owned; Editor ABDI ADEN GULED.

Xushmo: Mogadishu; monthly.

NEWS AGENCIES

Somali National News Agency (SONNA): POB 1748, Mogadishu; tel. 615573627; e-mail info@sonna.so; internet sonna.so; Dir ABDULAHI SHEIKH ABDIRAHMAN.

Publisher

Government Printer: POB 1743, Mogadishu.

Broadcasting and Communications

National Communications Authority (NCA) (Hay'adda Isgaar): POB 55, Mogadishu; e-mail info@nca.gov.so; internet nca.gov.so; f. 2017; regulatory authority.

TELECOMMUNICATIONS

Following the collapse of the central Government in 1991 there was no authority in place to regulate the telecommunications sector. No licence was required to set up a telecommunications network or provide telephone services. However, in March 2012 the Government endorsed the National Communications Act, which provided for the establishment of a regulatory body for the broadcasting and communications sectors.

Amtelkom: Mogadishu; internet www.amtelkom.com; CEO ALI YASIN ALI.

Golis Telecom: Biyo Kulule Rd, Bosaso, Puntland; tel. (5) 822001; e-mail info@golistelecom.com; internet golistelecom.com; f. 2002.

Hormuud Telecom: Hormuud Tower, Howlwadaag St, Bakara Market, Mogadishu; tel. (1) 811200; e-mail info@hormuud.com; internet www.hormuud.com; f. 2002; fixed-line and mobile telecommunications operator; also operates mobile money service; 3.6m. mobile telephone subscribers (2021); Chair. and CEO AHMED MOHAMED YUUSUF.

Nationlink Telecom: Mogadishu; f. 1997; fixed-line and mobile telecommunications operator; Pres. ABDIRIZAK IDO.

SOMLINK: Mogadishu; f. 2021.

Somtel: 26 June Area, Hargeysa, Somaliland; tel. (7) 9888999; e-mail info@somtelnetwork.net; internet somtelnetwork.net; CEO NUH SAEED DUALEH.

Telecom Somalia (Olympic Telecommunications): Howlwadaag St, Bakara Market, Mogadishu; tel. 215000; tel. info@telcom-somalia.com; internet www.telcom-somalia.com.

Telesom: Hargeysa, Somaliland; tel. (2) 522008; e-mail info@telesom.com; internet telesom.com; CEO ABDIKARIM MOHAMED EID.

BROADCASTING

Radio

Mustaqbal Radio: Hodon District, KM4, Abdikasim Rd, Mogadishu; tel. 617549777; e-mail info@mustaqbalmedia.net; internet mustaqbalmedia.net/so.

Radio Banaadir: Tahlil Warsame Bldg, 4 Maka al-Mukarama Rd, Mogadishu; tel. (5) 960368; e-mail info@radiobanadir.com; internet radiobanadir.com; f. 2000; serves Mogadishu and its environs.

Radio Daljir 88.0 FM: Bosaso, Puntland; tel. 90743971; e-mail rdaljir@yahoo.com; internet www.radiodaljir.com; largest radio station in Puntland; Man. ABDIRAZAK HASSAN ABDI.

Radio Gaalkacyo: Galkayo, Puntland; tel. 907795004; e-mail radiogaalkacyo@hotmail.com; internet fb.com/radiogaalkacyo.

Radio Kulmiye: Hoyoyinka Bldg, Hawo-tako St, Hamarweine, Mogadishu; tel. (1) 85865666; e-mail knn@hotmail.com; internet radiokulmiye.com; f. 2011; Dir OSMAN ABDULLAHI GUURE.

Radio Mogadishu, Voice of the Somali Republic: Ministry of Information Bldg, nr Villa Somalia, 00252 Mogadishu; tel. 6699900376; e-mail radiomogadishu@gmail.com; internet radiomuqdisho.net; f. 1951; state-owned; Dir ABDIRAHIM ISSE ADOW.

Radio Risaala: Airport St, Bulo-Hubei, Wadajir, Mogadishu; tel. 615550138; e-mail info@radiorisaala.com; internet radiorisaala.com; Owner DAHIR MAHAMUD GEELLE.

Radio Shabelle: Maka al-Mukarama Rd, Next to Haji Basto, Mogadishu; tel. 619990006; e-mail info@radioshabelle.com; internet www.radioshabelle.com; f. 2002; Chair. and CEO ABDIMAALIK YUSUF.

Radio Simba 95.00 FM: Mogadishu; tel. 615591829; e-mail atoosh@live.com; internet www.simbanews.net; f. 2006; Dir ABDULLAHI ALI FARAH.

Radio Xamar (Voice of Democracy): Mogadishu; tel. (1) 620111; internet www.xamarradio.com; f. 2003; independent; Dir ABDIRAHMAN YASIN ALI.

Radio Xurmo 96.00 FM: Taleh Village, Hodan District, Mogadishu; tel. 615561892; e-mail xurmoradio1@yahoo.com; internet www.xurmo.net; f. 2006; Peace Human Rights Network (PHRN) Inxa; community radio station; Dir ABDIFITAH MO'ALLIM NOR.

Voice of Peace (Codka Nabada): Galkayo; tel. 90798171; e-mail cawkecc@yahoo.com; f. 2003; aims to promote peace and reconstruction in Somalia; receives support from UNICEF and the AU; Dir AHMED COWKE.

Television

Somali National Television (SNTV): Jamaal Abdinasir St, Mogadishu; e-mail sntvnews@gmail.com; internet sntv.so; re-launched 2011 after 20-year hiatus; state-owned; broadcasts 24 hrs a day; Dir SHARMAKE MOHAMED.

Finance

BANKING

Central Bank

Central Bank of Somalia: 55 Corso Somalia, POB 11, Mogadishu; tel. (1) 866131; e-mail info@centralbank.gov.so; internet centralbank.gov.so; f. 1960; Gov. ABDIRAHMAN MOHAMED ABDULLAHI.

Commercial Banks

Amal Bank: Garowe, Puntland; tel. (5) 843100; e-mail info@amalbankso.so; internet amalbankso.so; Chair. MOHAMED DALMAR AABDURAHMAN.

Dahabshiil Bank International: Km 4, Makka Al-Mukarama Rd, Hodan District, Mogadishu; tel. 2300001; e-mail info@dahabshilbank.com; internet dahabshilbank.com; f. 2012; CEO ABDIRASHED MOHAMED SAED.

International Bank of Somalia: Trepiano Bldg, POB 777, Waaberi, Mogadishu; tel. (1) 865999; e-mail info@ibsbank.so; internet ibosbank.com; f. 2013; Chair. MOHAMED WARSAME.

Premier Bank: KM 4, Makka Al-Makalmukarama St, Hodan District, POB 626, Mogadishu; tel. (61) 7771000; e-mail info@premierbank.so; internet www.premierbank.so; Chair. JIBRIL HASSAN MOHAMED; Man. Dir OSMAN DUALLE AHMED.

Salaam Somali Bank: Salaam Tower, KM 5, POB 626, Mogadishu; tel. (1) 658835; e-mail info@salaambank.so; internet www.salaamsombank.com; f. 2009; Man. Dir SHUAYB HAJI NUR MOHAMED.

Trust African Bank: Makka Al-Mukarama Rd, Taleh St, Mogadishu; tel. (61) 5377533; f. 2012; Man. Dir ABDI AHMED.

Development Bank

Somali Development and Reconstruction Bank: 11 Corso Somalia, POB 589, Mogadishu; tel. (1) 649004; e-mail info@sodevbank.so; internet www.sodevbank.so; f. 2012 to replace Somali Development Bank; Pres. Prof. ABDULLAHI AHMED AFRAH.

INSURANCE

First Takaful and Re-Takaful Insurance Co: POB 33, Shingani, Mogadishu; tel. 617747042; e-mail info@fisoinsurance.com; internet fisoinsurance.com; f. 2014; general insurance; Dir-Gen. MOHAMED ABDI MOHAMED.

Trade and Industry

GOVERNMENT AGENCIES

Somali Petroleum Authority: Mogadishu; e-mail info@hbs.gov.so; internet hbs.gov.so; f. 2020; Chair. and CEO ABDULKADIR ADEN MOHAMUD.

SOMINVEST: Hussein Elabe Fahie Bldg, Afgoye Rd, KM 5, Mogadishu; e-mail info@sominvest.gov.so; internet sominvest.gov.so; f. 2015; promotion of foreign investment; Dir MOHAMED DUBO.

DEVELOPMENT ORGANIZATIONS

Agency for Development and Environmental Care (ADEC): Bossaso, Puntland; tel. 907796178; e-mail info@adecsomalia.org; internet www.adecsomalia.org.

Somali Relief and Development Action (SRDA): Luug; tel. 615120787; e-mail management@srdaorganization.org; internet srdaorganization.org.

Somali Social Entrepreneurs Fund (SOMASEF): Garbolow, Gedo; tel. 615120229; e-mail info@ssef.org.so; internet ssef.org.so.

CHAMBER OF COMMERCE

Somali Chamber of Commerce and Industry (SCCI): Kamaludiin St, Bondere, Mogadishu; tel. (6) 15700948; e-mail info@somalichamber.so; internet www.somalichamber.so; f. 1970; Pres. MOHAMOUD ABDI ALI.

UTILITIES

Benadir Electric Company (BECO): Taleh Hodan, Mogadishu; tel. 619111114; e-mail info@beco.so; internet www.beco.so; f. 2014.

Blue Sky Energy: Eng. Yariisow Stadium, Abdiaziiz; tel. 619370091; e-mail info@blueskyenergy.so; internet blueskyenergy.so; f. 2015.

Mogadishu Power Supply: Mogadishu; tel. 621000111; e-mail info@muqdishupower.com; internet www.muqdishopower.com; f. 1994.

Water Development Agency: POB 525, Mogadishu; Dir-Gen. KHALIF HAJI FARAH.

MAJOR COMPANIES

FruitSome: Hotel Ambassador, opp. Tre Biano, Mogadishu; tel. 1851655; e-mail info@fruitsome.com; internet www.fruitsome.com.

Somali National Oil Co (SONOC): Mogadishu; f. 2020; Man. Dir HUSSEIN ALI AHMED.

TRADE UNION

National Union of Somali Journalists (NUSOJ): Tre Biano Bldg, Via al-Mukarah Km 4, Hodan, Mogadishu; tel. (61) 5889931; e-mail nusoj@nusoj.org; internet nusoj.org; f. 2002 as Somali Journalists' Network (SOJON); present name adopted in 2005; 6 brs across Somalia, 525 mems; Chair. BURHAN AHMED DAHIR; Sec.-Gen. OMAR FARUK OSMAN.

Transport

RAILWAYS

There are no railways in Somalia.

SHIPPING

Merca, Berbera, Bosaso, Mogadishu and Kismayu are the chief ports. There was a large increase in piracy off the coast of Somalia during the late 2000s, although a concerted response by multinational naval forces (including special maritime forces created by the European Union and NATO) led to a notable decline in piracy activity from the early 2010s.

Albayrak Group: Mogadishu; tel. 617976703; e-mail burak .sarikaya@alport.com.tr; internet www.portofmogadishu.com; 2014; to operate the Mogadishu port until 2044; Man. Dir BURAK SARIKAYA.

Berbera Port Authority: Berbera; tel. (2) 740224; e-mail info@ berberaseaport.net; internet www.berberaseaport.net; Gen. Man. SAID HASSAN ABDULLAHI.

CIVIL AVIATION

There are international airports at Mogadishu, Hargeysa and Bosaso, as well as some 20 smaller airfields throughout the country.

Somali Civil Aviation Authority: SCAA Bldg, Aden Adde International Airport, POB 1737, Mogadishu; tel. 1853675; e-mail info@ scaa.gov.so; internet scaa.gov.so; Dir-Gen. AHMED MOALLIM HASSAN.

Air Somalia: Mogadishu; f. 2001; operates internal passenger services and international services to destinations in Africa and the Middle East; Chair. ALI FARAH ABDULLEH.

Jubba Airways: 30th St, POB 6200, Mogadishu; tel. 61858777; e-mail info@jubbaairways.com; internet jubbaairways.com; f. 1998; merged with Daallo Airlines in 2015; operates domestic flights and flights to destinations in Djibouti, Saudi Arabia, the United Arab Emirates and Yemen; Man. Dir SAID QAILIE.

Defence

In November 2021 it was estimated that the armed forces of Somalia numbered around 13,900. The total armed forces of Somaliland numbered an estimated 12,500; there was also a coast guard of 600. The armed forces of Puntland were believed to number around 3,000, in addition to a maritime police force of around 1,000. The AU Mission in Somalia (AMISOM) was replaced in April 2022 by the African Union Transition Mission in Somalia (ATMIS). At the end of July 2021 the United Nations Assistance Mission in Somalia (UNSOM) comprised 644 personnel. On 26 May 2022 the UN Security Council extended UNSOM's mandate until 31 October 2022.

Defence Expenditure: Expenditure on defence in the budget for 2021 was projected at US $95.7m.

Chief of the Somali Armed Forces: Gen. ODOWAA YUSUF RAGEH.

Infantry Commander: Gen. ABBAS AMIN ALI.

Air Force Commander: Brig.-Gen. MOHAMED SHEIKH ALI.

Navy Commander: Brig.-Gen. ABDULHAMID MOHAMED DIRIR.

Education

Following the overthrow of Mohamed Siad Barre's Government in January 1991 and the ensuing internal disorder, Somalia's education system collapsed. In January 1993 a primary school was opened in the building of Somalia's only university, the Somali National University in Mogadishu (which had been closed in early 1991). A number of schools operating in the country were under the control of fundamentalist Islamist groups. According to a survey by the United Nations Children's Fund (UNICEF), there were 1,172 primary schools operating in 2003/04, with a total enrolment of 285,574 children, representing a 19.9% gross enrolment ratio (data from Lower Jubba Region, El Waq district of Gedo Region and Jilib district of Middle Jubba Region were not collected). In 2006/07, according to estimates by the United Nations Educational, Scientific and Cultural Organization (UNESCO), 457,132 children were enrolled at primary schools and 86,929 children at secondary schools. In the budget for 2021 the education sector was allocated US $29.1m. (equivalent to 4.3% of total projected expenditure).

Bibliography

Abdi Elmi, A. *Understanding the Somalia Conflagration: Identity, Political Islam and Peacebuilding.* London and New York and Oxford, Pluto Press and Pambazuka Press, 2010.

Ahmed, A. J. (Ed.). *The Invention of Somalia.* Lawrenceville, KS, Red Sea Press, 1995.

Bahadur, J. *The Pirates of Somalia: Inside their Hidden World.* New York, Pantheon Books, 2011.

Besteman, C., and Cassanelli, L. V. (Eds) *The Struggle for Land in Southern Somalia: The War Behind the War.* Boulder, CO, and Oxford, Westview Press, 1996.

Bongartz, M. *The Civil War in Somalia: Its Genesis and Dynamics.* Uppsala, Scandinavian Institute for African Studies, 1991.

Brown, D. E. *AFRICOM at 5 Years: The Maturation of a New U.S. Combatant Command.* Carlisle, PA, Strategic Studies Institute, 2013.

Cassanelli, L. V. *The Shaping of Somali Society: Reconstructing the History of a Pastoral People, 1600–1900.* Philadelphia, PA, Pennsylvania University Press, 1982.

Clarke, W., and Herbst, J. (Eds) *Learning from Somalia: The Lessons of Armed Humanitarian Intervention.* Boulder, CO, Westview Press, 1997.

DeLong, K., and Tuckey, S. *Mogadishu: Heroism and Tragedy.* Westport, CT, and London, Praeger, 1994.

Dualeh, H. A. *From Barre to Aidid: The Story of Somalia and the Agony of a Nation.* Nairobi, Stellagraphics, 1994.

Farah, A. O., Muchie, M., and Gundel, J. *Somalia: Diaspora and State Reconstitution in the Horn of Africa.* London, Adonis & Abbey Publishers, 2007.

Fitzgerald, N. J. *Somalia: History, Issues and Bibliography.* Hauppauge, NY, Nova Science Publishers, 2002.

Ghalib, J. M. *The Cost of Dictatorship. The Somali Experience.* New York, and Oxford, Lilian Barber Press, 1995.

Haji-Abdi, A. *Critical Realism, Somalia, and the Diaspora Community.* London, Routledge, 2014.

Hansen, S. J. *Al-Shabaab in Somalia: The History and Ideology of a Militant Islamist Group, 2005–2012.* London, C. Hurst & Co, 2013.

Harding, A. *The Mayor of Mogadishu: A Story of Chaos and Redemption in the Ruins of Somalia.* London, C. Hurst & Co, 2018.

Harper, M. *Getting Somalia Wrong? Faith, War and Hope in a Shattered State.* London and New York, Zed Books, 2012.

Hashim, A. B. *The Fallen State: Dissonance, Dictatorship and Death in Somalia.* Lanham, MD, University Press of America, 1997.

Hirsch, J. L., and Oakley, R. B. *Somalia and 'Operation Restore Hope': Reflections on Peacemaking and Peacekeeping.* Washington, DC, United States Institute of Peace Press, 1995.

Human Rights Watch. *Harsh War, Harsh Peace: Abuses by al-Shabaab, the Transitional Federal Government and AMISON in Somalia.* New York, 2010.

'You Don't Know Who to Blame'. War Crimes in Somalia. New York, 2011.

Issa-Salwe, A. M., and Cissa-Salwe, C. *The Collapse of the Somali State*. London, Haan Associates, 1994.

Kapteijns, L. *Clan Cleansing in Somalia: The Ruinous Legacy of 1991*. Philadelphia, PA, Pennsylvania University Press, 2012.

Kusow, A. (Ed.). *Putting the Cart before the Horse: Contested Nationalism and the Crisis of the Nation-state in Somalia*. Lawrenceville, NJ, Red Sea Press, 2005.

Laitin, D. D., and Saïd, S. S. *Somalia: Nation in Search of a State*. Boulder, CO, Westview Press, 1987.

Lewis, I. M. *A Modern History of Somalia: Nation and State in the Horn of Africa*. Boulder, CO, Westview Press, 1988.

    Blood and Bone: The Call of Kinship in Somali Society. Trenton, NJ, Red Sea Press, 1994.

    Saints and Somalis: Popular Islam in a Clan-Based Society. Lawrenceville, NJ, Red Sea Press, 1998.

    Understanding Somalia and Somaliland: Culture, History and Society. New York, Oxford University Press, 2018.

Little, P. D. *Somalia: Economy without State (African Issues)*. London, James Currey Publishers, 2003.

Lyons, T., and Samatar, A. I. *Somalia: State Collapse, Multilateral Intervention and Strategies for Political Reconstruction*. Washington, DC, Brookings Institution, 1995.

Mburu, N. *Bandits on the Border: The Last Frontier in the Search for Somali Unity*. Lawrenceville, NJ, Red Sea Press, 2005.

Menkhaus, K. *Somalia: State Collapse and the Threat of Terrorism*. Oxford, Oxford University Press, 2004.

Morin, D. *Littérature et politique en Somalie*. Talenco Cedex, Université Montesquieu—Bordeaux IV, 1997.

Mubarak, J. A. *From Bad Policy to Chaos in Somalia: How an Economy Fell Apart*. Westport, CT, and London, Praeger, 1996.

    An Economic Policy Agenda for Post-Civil War Somalia: How to Build a New Economy, Sustain Growth and Reduce Poverty. Lewiston, NY, The Edwin Mellen Press, 2006.

Mukhtar, M. H. *Historical Dictionary of Somalia: New Edition*. Metuchen, NJ, Scarecrow Press, 2003.

Njoku, R. C. *The History of Somalia*. Santa Barbara, CA, Greenwood Press, 2013.

Nenova, T., and Harford, T. 'Anarchy and Invention: How does Somalia's Private Sector Cope without Government?', in *Public Policy Journal*, Note No. 280. Washington, DC, World Bank, Nov. 2004.

Omar, M. O. *Somalia: A Nation Driven to Despair*. New Delhi, Somali Publications, 1996.

    Somalia: Past and Present. Mogadishu, Somali Publications, 2004.

Osman, A. A., and Souare, I. K. *Somalia at the Crossroads: Challenges and Perspectives in Reconstituting a Failed State*. London, Adonis & Abbey Publishers, 2007.

Phillips, S. G. *When There Was No Aid: War and Peace in Somaliland*. Ithaca, New York, Cornell University Press, 2020.

Rutherford, K. R. *Humanitarianism Under Fire: The US and UN Intervention in Somalia*. Sterling, VA, Kumarian Press, 2008.

Salih, M. A. M., and Wohlgemuth, L. (Eds). *Crisis Management and the Politics of Reconciliation in Somalia*. Uppsala, Scandinavian Institute for African Studies, 1994.

Samatar, A. I. (Ed.). *The Somali Challenge: From Catastrophe to Renewal?* Boulder, CO, Lynne Rienner Publishers, 1994.

Shay, S. *Somalia in Transition since 2006*. New Brunswick, Transaction Publishers, 2014.

Stevenson, J. *Losing Mogadishu: Testing US Policy in Somalia*. Annapolis, MD, Naval Institute Press, 1995.

Thompson, V. B. *Conflict in the Horn of Africa: The Kenya-Somalia Border Problem, 1941–2014*. Lanham, MD, Plymouth, University Press of America, 2015.

United Nations, Dept of Public Information. *The United Nations and Somalia 1992–1996*. New York, United Nations, 1996.

    Report of the Monitoring Group on Somalia and Eritrea Pursuant to Security Council Resolution 2002 (2011). New York, United Nations, 2012.

    Report of the Monitoring Group on Somalia and Eritrea Pursuant to Security Council Resolution 2060 (2012): Somalia. New York, United Nations, 2013.

Wam, P. E. *Conflict in Somalia: Drivers and Dynamics*. Herndon, VA, World Bank Publications, 2005.

Weldemichael, A. *Piracy in Somalia: Violence and Development in the Horn of Africa*. Cambridge, Cambridge University Press, 2019.

Williams, P. D. *Fighting for Peace in Somalia: A History and Analysis of the African Union Mission (AMISOM), 2007–2017*. Oxford, Oxford University Press, 2018.

World Bank. *Somalia: From Resilience Towards Recovery and Development. A Country Economic Memorandum for Somalia*. Report No. 34356. Washington, DC, World Bank, 2006.

SOUTH AFRICA

Physical and Social Geography

A. MacGREGOR HUTCHESON

The Republic of South Africa occupies the southern extremity of the African continent and, except for a relatively small area in the northern Transvaal, lies poleward of the Tropic of Capricorn, extending as far as latitude 34° 51' S. The republic covers a total area of 1,220,813 sq km (471,358 sq miles) and has common borders with Namibia to the north-west, with Botswana to the north, and with Zimbabwe, Mozambique and Eswatini (formerly known as Swaziland) to the north-east. Lesotho is entirely surrounded by South African territory, lying within the eastern part of the Republic.

PHYSICAL FEATURES

Most of South Africa consists of a vast plateau with upwarped rims, bounded by an escarpment. Framing the plateau is a narrow coastal belt. The surface of the plateau varies in altitude from 600 m to 2,000 m above sea level. It is highest in the east and south-east and dips fairly gently towards the Kalahari Basin in the north-west. The relief is generally monotonous, consisting of undulating to flat landscapes over wide areas. Variation is provided occasionally by low ridges and *inselberge* (or *kopjes*) made up of rock more resistant to erosion. There are three major subregions:

(i) the Highveld between 1,200 m and 1,800 m, forming a triangular area which occupies the southern Transvaal and most of the Free State;

(ii) a swell over 1,500 m high, aligned WNW–ESE, part of which is known as the Witwatersrand, rising gently from the plateau surface to the north of the Highveld and forming a major drainage divide; and

(iii) the Middleveld, generally between 600 m and 1,200 m, comprising the remaining part of the plateau.

The plateau's edges, upwarped during the Tertiary Period, are almost everywhere above 1,500 m. Maximum elevations of over 3,400 m occur in the south-east in Lesotho. From the crests the surface descends coastwards by means of the Great Escarpment, which gives the appearance of a mountain range when viewed from below, and which is known by distinctive names in its different sections. An erosional feature, dissected by seaward-flowing rivers, the nature of the Escarpment varies according to the type of rock that forms it. Along its eastern length it is known as the Drakensberg; in the section north of the Olifants river fairly soft granite gives rise to gentle slopes, but south of that river resistant quartzites are responsible for a more striking appearance. Further south again, along the KwaZulu/Natal–Lesotho border, basalts cause the Drakensberg to be at its most striking, rising up a sheer 1,800 m or more in places. Turning westwards the Great Escarpment is known successively as the Stormberg, Bamboes, Suurberg, Sneeuberg, Nieuwveld and Komsberg. The Great Escarpment then turns sharply northwards through the Roggeveld mountains, following which it is usually in the form of a simple step until the Kamiesberg are reached; owing to aridity and fewer rivers the dissection of this western part of the Escarpment is much less advanced than in the eastern (Drakensberg) section.

The Lowland margin that surrounds the South African plateau may be divided into four zones:

(i) the undulating to flat Transvaal Lowveld, between 150 m and 600 m above sea level, separated from the Mozambique coastal plain by the Lebombo mountains in the east, and including part of the Limpopo valley in the north;

(ii) the south-eastern coastal belt, a very broken region descending to the coast in a series of steps, into which the rivers have cut deep valleys. In northern KwaZulu/Natal the Republic possesses its only true coastal plain, some 65 km at its widest;

(iii) the Cape ranges, consisting of the remnants of mountains folded during the Carboniferous era, and flanking the plateau on the south and south-west. On the south the folds trend E–W and on the south-west they trend N–S, the two trends crossing in the south-western corner of the Cape to produce a rugged knot of mountains and the ranges' highest elevations (over 2,000 m). Otherwise, the Cape ranges are comparatively simple in structure, consisting of parallel anticlinal ridges and synclinal valleys. Narrow lowlands separate the mountains from the coast. Between the ridges and partially enclosed by them, e.g. the Little Karoo, is a series of steps rising to the foot of the Great Escarpment. The Great Karoo, the last of these steps, separates the escarpment from the Cape ranges; and

(iv) the western coastal belt is also characterized by a series of steps, but the slope from the foot of the Great Escarpment to the coast is more gentle and more uniform than in the south-eastern zone.

The greater part of the plateau is drained by the Orange river system. Rising in the Drakensberg within a short distance of the Escarpment the Orange flows westward for 1,900 km before entering the Atlantic Ocean. However, the western part of its basin is so dry that it is not unknown for the Orange to fail to reach its mouth during the dry season. The large-scale Orange River Project, a comprehensive scheme for water supply, irrigation and hydroelectric generation, aids water conservation in this western area and is making possible its development. The only other major system is that of the Limpopo, which rises on the northern slopes of the Witwatersrand and drains most of the Limpopo Province to the Indian Ocean. Apart from some interior drainage to a number of small basins in the north and north-west, the rest of the Republic's drainage is peripheral. Relatively short streams rise in the Great Escarpment, although some rise on the plateau itself, having cut through the escarpment, and drain directly to the coast. With the exception of riparian strips along perennial rivers, most of the country relies for water supplies on underground sources supplemented by dams.

CLIMATE AND NATURAL VEGETATION

Except for a small part of Limpopo Province the climate of South Africa is subtropical, although there are important regional variations within this general classification. Altitude and relief forms have an important influence on temperature and on both the amount and distribution of rainfall, and there is a strong correlation between the major physical and the major climatic regions. The altitude of the plateau modifies temperatures and because there is a general rise in elevation towards the Equator there is a corresponding decrease in temperature, resulting in a remarkable uniformity of temperature throughout the Republic from south to north (annual mean temperatures: Cape Town, 16.7°C; and Pretoria, 17.2°C). The greatest contrasts in temperature are, in fact, between the east coast, warmed by the Mozambique Current, and the west coast, cooled by the Benguela Current (respectively, monthly mean temperatures: Durban, January 24.4°C, July 17.8°C; and Port Nolloth, January 15.6°C, July 12.2°C). Daily and annual ranges in temperature increase with distance from the coast, being much greater on the plateau (mean annual temperature range: Cape Town, 8°C; and Pretoria, 11°C).

The areas of highest annual rainfall largely coincide with the outstanding relief features, over 650 mm being received only in the eastern third of South Africa and relatively small areas in the southern Cape. Parts of the Drakensberg and the seaward slopes of the Cape ranges experience over 1,500 mm. West of the Drakensberg and to the north of the Cape ranges there is a marked rain-shadow, and average annual rainfall decreases progressively westwards (Durban 1,140 mm, Bloemfontein 530 mm, Kimberley 400 mm, Upington 180 mm, Port Nolloth

50 mm). Virtually all the western half of the country, apart from the southern Cape, receives less than 250 mm and the western coastal belt's northern section forms a continuation of the Namib Desert. Most of the rain falls during the summer months (November to April) when evaporation losses are greatest, brought by tropical marine air masses moving in from the Indian Ocean on the east. However, the south-western Cape has a winter maximum of rainfall with dry summers. Only the narrow southern coastal belt between Cape Agulhas and East London has rainfall distributed uniformly throughout the year. Snow may fall occasionally over the higher parts of the plateau and the Cape ranges during winter, but frost occurs on average for 120 days each year over most of the interior plateau, and for shorter periods in the coastal lowlands, except in KwaZulu/Natal, where it is rare.

Variations in climate and particularly in annual rainfall are reflected in changes of vegetation, sometimes strikingly, as between the south-western Cape's Mediterranean shrub type, designed to withstand summer drought and of which the protea—the national plant—is characteristic, and the drought-resistant low Karoo bush immediately north of the Cape ranges and covering much of the semi-arid western half of the country. The only true areas of forest are found along the wetter south and east coasts—the temperate evergreen forests of the Knysna district and the largely evergreen subtropical bush, including palms and wild bananas, of Eastern Cape and KwaZulu/Natal, respectively. Grassland covers the rest of the Republic, merging into thornveld in the north-western Cape and into bushveld in Limpopo Province.

MINERAL RESOURCES

South Africa's mineral resources, outstanding in their variety, quality and quantity, overshadow all the country's other natural resources. They are found mainly in the ancient Pre-Cambrian foundation and associated intrusions and occur in a wide curving zone which stretches from Limpopo Province through the Free State and Northern Cape to the west coast. To the south of this mineralized zone the Pre-Cambrian rocks are covered by Karoo sedimentaries, which generally do not contain minerals, with the exception of extensive deposits of bituminous coal. These deposits occur mainly in the eastern Transvaal Highveld, the northern Free State and northern KwaZulu/Natal, mostly in thick, easily worked seams fairly near to the surface. Coal is of particular importance to South Africa because of relatively low production elsewhere in the continent south of the Equator, and South Africa's current dependence on imported petroleum.

The most important mineral regions are the Witwatersrand and the northern Free State, producing gold, silver and uranium; the diamond areas centred on Kimberley, Pretoria, Jagersfontein and Koffiefontein; and the Transvaal bushveld complex containing multiple occurrences of a large number of minerals, including asbestos, chrome, copper, iron, magnesium, nickel, platinum, tin, uranium and vanadium. In the Northern Cape important deposits of manganese, iron ore and asbestos occur in the Postmasburg, Sishen and Kuruman areas, while in the north-western Cape reserves of lead, zinc, silver and copper are being exploited. This list of occurrences and minerals is by no means exhaustive, and prospecting for new mineral resources is continuing. In 1988 exploitable petroleum deposits were discovered off the western Cape coast, and a substantial reserve of natural gas and petroleum was discovered south-west of Mossel Bay, off the south coast of the Cape.

ETHNIC GROUPS AND POPULATION

Five major ethnic groups make up South Africa's multiracial society. The 'Khoisan' peoples—Bushmen, Hottentots and Bergdamara—are survivors of the country's earliest inhabitants. The black Bantu-speaking peoples fall into a number of tribal groupings. The major groups are formed by the Nguni, comprising Zulu, Swazi, Ndebele, Pondo, Tembu and Xhosa on the one hand, and by the Sotho and Tswana on the other. The European or 'white' peoples, who once dominated the political and social organization of the Republic and continue to exercise considerable economic influence, are descended from the original 17th-century Dutch settlers in the Cape, refugee French Huguenots, British settlers from 1820 onwards, Germans, and more recent immigrants from Europe and ex-colonial African territories. The remainder of the population comprises so-called Coloureds (people of mixed race) and Asians, largely of Indian origin. At the October 2011 census the total population was 51,770,560, while the estimated ethnic composition of the total population at mid-2021 was: Africans (blacks) 80.9%; Coloureds 8.8%; Europeans (whites) 7.8%; and Asians/Indians 2.6%. The official languages are Afrikaans, English, isiNdebele, Sepedi, Sesotho, siSwati, Xitsonga, Setswana, Tshivenda, isiXhosa and isiZulu.

The overall density of the population was 42.4 inhabitants per sq km at the census of October 2011, but its distribution is extremely uneven. It is generally related to agricultural resources, more than two-thirds living in the wetter eastern third of the Republic and in the southern Cape. The heaviest concentrations are found in the Witwatersrand mining area—according to United Nations (UN) projections, the five cities in South Africa with the largest populations at mid-2022 (including suburbs) were Johannesburg (6.1m.), Cape Town (4.8m.), Ekurhuleni (4.0m.), Durban (3.2m.) and Pretoria (2.7m.). Cape Town is the legislative capital of the country, Pretoria the administrative capital and Bloemfontein the judicial capital. Europeans have a widespread geographical distribution, but more than 80% reside in towns. The majority of Africans live in the former tribal reserves, which extend in a great horseshoe along the south-eastern coast and up to Limpopo Province and then south-westwards to the north-eastern Cape. The Coloured population is resident mainly in the Cape, and the Asian population is concentrated largely in KwaZulu/Natal and the Witwatersrand. The total population, according to official estimates, was 60,142,978 at mid-2021, giving a population density of 49.3 per sq km.

History

CHRISTOPHER SAUNDERS

HISTORICAL BACKGROUND

Hunter-gatherers lived in many parts of South Africa for hundreds of thousands of years, leaving behind evidence of their activities in rock art. About 2,000 years ago descendants of the San (Bushman) people who had acquired sheep arrived from the north. These pastoralists, the Khoikhoi (Hottentot), were the first indigenous people to interact with European seafarers along the coast from the late 15th century. From about 1,500 years ago Bantu-speaking, iron-working farmers moved into the northern parts of South Africa and began to develop small kingdoms. Trading routes began to link the coastal areas with the interior. Over time these farmers spread southwards into what is now the Transkei in the Eastern Cape province and the Free State. In the early 19th century, a process of political centralization led to the emergence, in what is today KwaZulu/Natal, of the relatively large Zulu state. The Zulu and other black African peoples fought to resist white encroachment during much of the 19th century.

The Dutch East India Company established a settlement at the Cape in 1652. About 150 years later the British took over a sizeable white-ruled colony from the Dutch. Friction between the British authorities at the Cape and the Dutch (Afrikaner or Boer) frontier farmers led many of the latter, after the abolition of slavery in 1834, to embark upon a northward trek to establish an independent polity. The United Kingdom subsequently annexed the trekker Republic of Natalia (now part of the province of KwaZulu/Natal), but permitted the creation of two independent Boer republics, the Orange Free State (OFS), between the Orange and Vaal rivers, and the South African Republic or Transvaal. When a large diamond deposit was discovered at what became known as Kimberley in 1871, the British intervened to bring the contested diamond-rich territory under their rule. The rapid development of gold mining in the Transvaal after 1886, together with the emergence of the South African Republic as the most powerful state in the region, were perceived as a threat by British interests; the consequent exertion of pressure on the Transvaal and the OFS provoked the Anglo–Boer (or South African) war of 1899–1902. During the war the Boer republics passed under British control, and on 31 May 1910 the two conquered Boer republics and the two British colonies of the Cape and Natal were formally merged into the Union of South Africa, a dominion under the British crown.

The Constitution of the new Union gave the franchise to white males only, except in the Cape, where the existing non-racial voting rights, based on a qualified franchise, were protected. (However, in 1936 black Africans in the Cape were stripped of their right to vote, and only whites could be members of the Union Parliament.) The two Afrikaner parties in the ex-republics amalgamated with the Cape's South Africa Party to form the national South Africa Party (SAP). Led by two Boer generals, Louis Botha and Jan Smuts, the SAP formed the first Government of the new Union. In 1912 another general, J. B. M. Hertzog, broke away to found the National Party (NP), devoted to the exclusive interests of Afrikaners. In the same year members of the African elite, under the leadership of Pixley Seme, established the South African Native National Congress, soon renamed the African National Congress (ANC). The Congress protested in vain against the 1913 Land Act, which denied Africans the right to buy land outside the Native Reserves (which comprised only 13% of the national territory) or to lease white-owned land, and other legislation imposing racial segregation. As a consequence of the economic crisis of the early 1930s, Hertzog's NP, in power from 1924, entered a coalition with the SAP under Smuts, and the two parties subsequently merged to form the United Party. A small group of Afrikaner nationalists, under Daniel Malan, rejected the coalition and merger, and formed a 'purified' NP.

APARTHEID

Afrikaner farmers, who feared the loss of their low-wage African labour to the towns, and Afrikaner workers in the towns, who feared black competition for their jobs, supported the intensification of racial segregation, which the NP called 'apartheid'. In the 1948 general election the NP secured a narrow parliamentary majority. Malan formed a Government and began putting apartheid into practice. In 1954 he was replaced by the hard-line J. G. Strydom, who in 1958 was succeeded by Hendrik Verwoerd, apartheid's chief architect and leading ideologue. Verwoerd believed that each race should be kept apart (with each racial group having its own territorial areas), so that each could develop its unique cultural personality.

During 1948–59 a series of interrelated laws and measures were introduced that were aimed at restructuring South African society to conform to apartheid doctrine. The Population Registration Act provided for the classification of the entire population on the basis of race. Inter-racial marriages were forbidden, and the Immorality Act, banning sexual relations between whites and blacks, was extended to include relations between whites and so-called Coloureds (people of mixed race). The Group Areas Act of 1950 provided for the designation of particular residential areas for specific races. Existing provisions for the reservation of categories of employment for particular races were strengthened. Race segregation in public places was introduced wherever it had not been previously practised. The Extension of University Education Act removed the right of non-white students to attend the previously open universities of Cape Town and the Witwatersrand. To strengthen its hand against radical opposition, the

Government introduced the Suppression of Communism Act, which forced the Communist Party of South Africa to disband, only to regroup underground as the South African Communist Party (SACP).

The repressive policies of the NP prompted the ANC to embark on a programme of mass civil disobedience. After the Defiance Campaign of 1952, a Congress Alliance was formed, which drew together the ANC and other Congresses, including the South African Indian Congress. Some within the ANC did not approve of the Congress Alliance's assertion that South Africa belonged to all who lived in it, regardless of colour, and in 1959 Africanists formerly belonging to the ANC established the exclusively black Pan-Africanist Congress (PAC).

In March 1960 police in the township of Sharpeville, south of Johannesburg, opened fire on a crowd of unarmed black Africans who were surrounding the police station in response to a PAC demonstration, killing 69 people. The Sharpeville massacre aroused international indignation to an unprecedented degree, and appeals for military, economic and sporting boycotts began to receive serious attention. In 1961, following a referendum among white voters in October 1960, South Africa became a republic and left the Commonwealth.

In response to demonstrations within South Africa in protest against the Sharpeville massacre, the Government banned both the ANC and the PAC. In 1961 some within the ANC, together with white members of the SACP, formed a military organization, Umkhonto we Sizwe, which, under the leadership of Nelson Mandela, aimed to force the Government to negotiate by attacking white-owned property, while avoiding harm to people. Mandela was arrested in 1962 and, together with others, sentenced to life imprisonment on charges of sabotage in 1964. In the following decades the ANC in exile gradually organized a global campaign against apartheid.

Verwoerd argued that the Native Reserves constituted the historic 'homelands' (Bantustans) of different African nations. The homelands were to be led to self-government under constitutions giving scope to the elective principle, but with the balance of power in the hands of government-appointed chiefs. Transkei was accorded 'self-government' under such a system in 1963. Ciskei, Bophuthatswana, Lebowa, Venda, Gazankulu, Qwaqwa and KwaZulu followed in the early 1970s. Meanwhile, stricter controls were imposed to prevent Africans acquiring permanent residence in urban areas. Wherever possible, jobs were given to migrant labourers, and a massive campaign was launched to rid the white areas of 'surplus Bantu', who were to be forced into the overcrowded homelands. In the 1960s more than 1.5m. people were forcibly resettled. These measures were more drastic than those of the first phase of apartheid, and under John Vorster, the Minister of Justice, the powers of the security police were massively extended. Vorster succeeded Verwoerd as Prime Minister in 1966 when Verwoerd was assassinated.

South Africa took control of South West Africa (later to become Namibia) in 1915 and after the First World War ruled the territory as a mandate under the League of Nations. After the Second World War South Africa's application to annex the territory was rejected by the newly formed United Nations (UN), and in 1966 the UN General Assembly resolved to revoke South Africa's mandate and place the territory under direct UN administration. This was subsequently confirmed by the Security Council, but South Africa refused to co-operate. From 1966 South Africa fought a low-intensity war in northern Namibia against guerrillas of the South West Africa People's Organization (SWAPO, see Namibia).

INTERNAL PRESSURES FOR CHANGE

With violent resistance crushed, the most important internal opposition to apartheid from the late 1960s was the Black Consciousness Movement, founded by Steve Biko. A series of strikes by black workers in the Durban-Pinetown area from 1973 ultimately led to the formation of new trade unions. Meanwhile, formal independence was conferred on a number of the Bantustans: Transkei in 1976, Bophuthatswana in 1977, Venda in 1979 and Ciskei in 1981. All remained dependent on South African financial support and their 'independence' was not internationally recognized. The imposition of 'independence' was resisted by KwaNdebele and KwaZulu.

In June 1976 violent protests escalated into riots in Soweto (South-West Townships), an agglomeration of segregated African townships to the south-west of Johannesburg, rapidly spreading to other black townships and involving black, Coloured and Indian youths. Repeatedly and violently repressed, the uprisings were not brought under control until the end of the year. Several hundred people died in clashes with security forces; thousands of young people were arrested, while many others escaped across the borders to join the liberation movements. The ANC proved far more successful than the PAC in attracting this cadre of prospective freedom fighters, thus consolidating its political hold over the loyalties of the majority. Biko was arrested by the police and died in police custody in September 1977. At the subsequent inquest into his death, details were revealed of how he been had tortured, and the national and international outcry led the Government to ban the black consciousness organizations in October and the UN to impose a mandatory arms embargo on South Africa in November.

Pieter Willem (P. W.) Botha, a former Minister of Defence who took over from Vorster as Prime Minister in 1978, altered the balance of influence within the state security network in favour of the armed forces, as opposed to the police. The State Security Council (SSC), which brought together politicians and key officials in the security forces, became the main decision-making organ, with the roles of the NP and Parliament being progressively reduced. In the face of growing pressure on the apartheid regime, Botha introduced some reforms. Racial job restrictions were gradually abolished and trade union rights extended to black Africans. Restrictions on multi-racial sports were reduced, and the laws against inter-racial marriage and extra-marital sexual relations were repealed. However, any sharing of power with non-whites was rejected by the hard-liners in the NP, who broke away and formed the Conservative Party (CP). Nevertheless, in November 1983 white voters approved the creation of a tricameral legislature in a referendum. Elections for the Coloured House of Representatives and the Indian House of Delegates followed in August 1984, and in September Botha became the country's first executive President.

The introduction of the new Constitution was the catalyst for a large-scale rebellion in the black townships, which was supported by strikes, notably in the economically crucial mining industry. The Congress of South African Trade Unions (COSATU), a federation of black trade unions that were politically aligned with the ANC, was formed in December 1985 and demanded the abolition of pass restrictions (which required blacks by law to be in possession of special documentation in designated white urban areas), the withdrawal of foreign investment and the release of Mandela. The township rebellion escalated in March, when the police opened fire on an unarmed African procession in Uitenhage, killing 20 people. As internal demands for major reforms intensified, in June 1986 the Government extended the state of emergency to cover the whole country. This led European banks to suspend new lending to South Africa, and the European Community (EC, now the European Union—EU) and the USA introduced limited sanctions. On 1 July pass restrictions were officially removed and uniform identity documents introduced for all South African citizens.

At a general election to the white House of Assembly in 1987 the NP emerged with a secure majority but a considerably reduced vote. The CP obtained the second highest number of seats and became the official opposition, superseding the Progressive Federal Party (PFP) in that role. In 1989 the PFP was reconstituted as the Democratic Party (DP). In January that year, having suffered a stroke, Botha relinquished the NP leadership, while remaining as State President. He was succeeded as NP leader by Frederik Willem (F. W.) de Klerk. Botha met with Mandela—still serving a life sentence—in July, thus effectively recognizing the ANC leader's position as a potential alternative head of government. Botha's colleagues forced him to resign from the presidency in August. In parliamentary elections in September the opposition parties made considerable gains, although the NP retained a clear majority. Upon becoming State President, de Klerk downgraded the SSC and the role of the military, and ordered the country's nuclear weapons to be dismantled. He granted permission for the holding of a massive march in Cape Town and subsequently released key ANC leaders. De Klerk accepted that apartheid was unsustainable, and that the ANC must be accepted as a negotiating partner. The ANC, meanwhile, lost its military facilities in Angola as part of the agreement that brought Namibia its independence in March 1990, and had to move its camps even further away from South Africa.

THE NEGOTIATED SETTLEMENT

Addressing the three Houses of Parliament on 2 February 1990, President de Klerk made the dramatic announcement that Mandela would be released and that the ban had been lifted on the ANC, the PAC, the SACP and 33 other non-white organizations. It was the Government's intention to open negotiations with black leaders, with a view to devising a new constitution based on universal franchise. Equality of all citizens, regardless of race, was to be guaranteed by an independent judiciary, and protection for individual rights entrenched. On 11 February Mandela was freed, after 27 years in prison. ANC refugees soon began to return from exile. However, the ANC faced major problems in bringing the spontaneous loyalties of the great majority of the black population within a disciplined organizational framework.

In August 1990 the ANC agreed to the formal suspension of its guerrilla activities. In February 1991 de Klerk announced that all the remaining legislation enshrining apartheid was to be repealed; this was achieved by the end of June. The EC and the USA abandoned most sanctions, and contacts between South Africa and black African states expanded. In early July, at its national congress, the ANC elected a new National Executive. Mandela became its President, and the leader of the National Union of Mineworkers (NUM), Cyril Ramaphosa, became Secretary-General.

The main obstacle impeding constitutional negotiations was continuing violence between ANC supporters and adherents of the Inkatha Movement (reconstituted as the Inkatha Freedom Party—IFP—in July 1990), a Zulu organization led by Kwa-Zulu Chief Minister Mangosuthu Buthelezi. In July 1991, following ANC threats to withdraw from negotiations, it was admitted that secret payments had been made from government funds to Inkatha during 1989–90.

A multi-party conference, the Convention for a Democratic South Africa (CODESA), met in December 1991 to begin drafting a new constitution. However, the talks again came to an impasse, after which the ANC appealed for a campaign of non-violent mass action by its supporters to put pressure on the Government. In mid-June 1992, after a number of residents in the settlement of Boipatong, including women and children, were massacred by Inkatha supporters, the ANC broke off negotiations with the Government and demanded the disbandment of groups involved in covert operations.

The multi-party negotiating forum was reconvened in April 1993. Buthelezi, who protested vigorously against the bilateral agreements between the Government and the ANC, initiated meetings between representatives of Inkatha, a number of movements based in the homelands and the CP. By mid-year it had been decided that the elections would be held in April 1994. The interim Constitution was finalized in November 1993 and embodied major compromises by both the main negotiating partners. The regional proposals incorporated in the charter provided for some measure of federalism, but were insufficient to persuade Buthelezi to accept them. There were now to be nine provinces, each with their own legislature. The former homelands, including those purported to be 'independent', were absorbed into one or more of the new provinces. The national legislature, consisting of a 400-member National Assembly and a 90-member Senate, was also to act as a Constitutional Assembly charged with drafting the country's final Constitution within two years. Adoption of the Constitution required a two-thirds' majority of the Assembly.

Buthelezi was persuaded to register the IFP for the April 1994 general election, in return for the enhancement of the status of the Zulu monarchy by the transfer of extensive state lands to a trust in the name of the Zulu monarch, King Goodwill Zwelithini (who was Buthelezi's nephew). In the election, the ANC gained a majority at national level, although it fell short of the two-thirds' majority needed to write the final Constitution unilaterally. It also gained control of seven of the nine provinces. The NP—the only other grouping to secure more than 20% of the vote nationally—won control of Western Cape province. The IFP obtained 10% of the votes cast and was credited with a 51% victory in KwaZulu/Natal. The PAC, with its radical Africanist approach, and the white-led DP each received less than 2% of the vote. On 10 May Mandela was inaugurated as head of state, and a Government of National Unity (GNU) was formed, in which the ANC, NP and IFP were represented in proportion to the seats they had won. Thabo Mbeki of the ANC and de Klerk became Deputy Presidents.

THE MANDELA PRESIDENCY

Following the installation of a democratic Government, South Africa was admitted to the Organization of African Unity (OAU—subsequently the African Union—AU), the Commonwealth and the Southern African Development Community (SADC), and resumed its seat in the UN General Assembly. The arms embargo imposed by the UN in 1977 was finally removed.

Although the Government's schemes to provide electricity and clean water to all were initially successful, unemployment remained very high in the townships and many communities continued to refuse to pay for services and rents. A number of communities began to use vigilante methods in response to the police force's apparent inability to combat an increase in violent crime. Meanwhile, the new Constitutional Court abolished the death penalty in June 1995.

The Constitutional Assembly, comprising the two houses of Parliament, approved the final version of the Constitution in May 1996. This was ratified by the Constitutional Court and signed into law by President Mandela on 10 December. A National Council of Provinces replaced the Senate as the upper house of Parliament. Following the implementation of the new Constitution, the NP announced that it was to leave the GNU at the end of June to form a parliamentary opposition. A new political party, the United Democratic Movement (UDM), was founded in September 1997. In early 1998 Bantu Holomisa, the former ruler of Transkei, assumed leadership of the party, with the Government's former chief negotiator, Roelf Meyer, as his deputy. Meanwhile, in August 1997 De Klerk resigned as leader of the NP; the party continued to decline under its new leader Marthinus van Schalkwyk.

Mandela resigned as ANC President in December 1997 and was succeeded by Mbeki. Jacob Zuma was elected Deputy President of the party. Mandela remained active as head of state, and his personal stature enhanced South Africa's prestige internationally. South Africa's links with the USA, in particular, strengthened following the transition to democracy. In November 1996 Mandela announced that South Africa would transfer diplomatic recognition from Taiwan (Republic of China) to the People's Republic of China, with effect from the end of 1997. After becoming Chairman of SADC in September 1996, Mandela pursued a more active foreign policy, frequently engaging in diplomatic activity in an effort to resolve regional problems.

In 1995 Parliament finally approved the establishment of a Truth and Reconciliation Commission (TRC). President Mandela appointed Archbishop Desmond Tutu to head the TRC, and in October 1998 Tutu submitted to Mandela the TRC's interim report—after the ANC had failed in an attempt to delay publication of the report, on the grounds that it 'criminalized' the ANC's role in the struggle against apartheid. The work of the TRC's amnesty committee, which considered applications by perpetrators of human rights abuses and granted amnesty to those who gave a full account of their actions, finally came to an end in May 2001. Although the TRC's reparations committee recommended that R 3,000m. be granted to compensate victims, the Government made only about R 65m. available, which equated to a one-off payment of about R 30,000 to the 22,000 victims identified by the TRC. Mbeki rejected the suggestion of a wealth tax to pay for reparations and voiced strong disapproval of the cases being brought against multinational companies for their alleged complicity in apartheid, on the grounds that such cases would threaten future foreign investment. For many, the Government's response to the recommendations of the TRC was grossly inadequate.

THE MBEKI PRESIDENCY

In the later years of the Mandela presidency Mbeki increasingly assumed responsibility for government administration. One of his major achievements was to contribute to the restoration of relative peace in KwaZulu/Natal and to improve relations between the ANC and Inkatha. On 2 June 1999 almost 17m. voters participated in the general election, which was generally deemed to have been free and fair. The ANC obtained 266 seats, narrowly failing to secure a two-thirds' majority in the National Assembly. Support for the opposition fragmented, with the NP, reconstituted as the New National Party (NNP), winning only 28 seats. The DP, led by Tony Leon, increased its representation from seven to 38 seats, attracting white voters from the NP and becoming the official opposition. The IFP, which won 34 seats in the National Assembly, entered into a coalition with the ANC, and Buthelezi remained Minister of Home Affairs. The ANC secured a two-thirds' majority in the legislature, and Zuma became Deputy President.

On 16 June 1999 Mbeki was formally inaugurated as President. He signalled his intention to pursue the macroeconomic strategies that the Mandela Government had instigated, but pledged to accelerate the privatization of parastatal companies. One of Mbeki's main aims in foreign policy was to secure a peaceful settlement in the Democratic Republic of the Congo. He assisted in the arrangement of a ceasefire there in June, and South Africa agreed to contribute a small number of troops to the UN peacekeeping force. South African soldiers were also deployed in peacekeeping missions in Burundi and Sudan. In July 2002 Mbeki presided over a conference in Durban, at which the OAU was relaunched as the AU, of which he became the first Chairperson.

When the seizure of white-owned farms in neighbouring Zimbabwe began in 2000, Mbeki stated his preference for implementing a 'quiet diplomacy' with Zimbabwean President Robert Mugabe, in the hope of influencing him to hold a free and fair election and to deal with the land issue peacefully. Mbeki agreed reluctantly to recommend the suspension of Zimbabwe from the Commonwealth, but still refused to criticize Mugabe's increasingly authoritarian rule and the extreme measures taken against both white farmers and supporters of the Zimbabwean opposition Movement for Democratic Change. When the Mugabe regime destroyed homes and made hundreds of thousands homeless in 2005, Mbeki again offered no public criticism, despite the exodus of millions of refugees from Zimbabwe across the border into South Africa. In 2007, however, Mbeki was deputed by SADC to mediate in the crisis.

The programme for land restitution in South Africa proceeded slowly, owing mainly to a cumbersome bureaucratic process. By mid-2007 some 73,000 claims had been settled, most being resolved by monetary compensation rather than the return of land. Meanwhile, the Communal Land Rights Act of 2004 aimed to clarify the tenure rights of 15m. people in the former homelands.

Among other issues, Mbeki attracted criticism from the national and international media relating to his viewpoint on HIV/AIDS. He made statements in support of dissident scientists who questioned whether AIDS was caused by HIV, and promoted the idea that an indigenous cure might be found for the disease: these controversial views served to divert attention from the drive to combat the pandemic. By the end of 2001 an estimated 4.7m. South Africans were infected with HIV, which was responsible for some 40% of adult deaths. The lobby group Treatment Action Campaign won a court case in late 2001 in which the Government was ordered to provide antiretroviral drugs for all pregnant women infected with the virus. In 2003 the Government reluctantly accepted that it should make antiretrovirals freely available, but this proceeded slowly. It was not until 2006 that the Government committed itself to a new HIV/AIDS policy.

In June 2000 the NNP and DP established a new national coalition, the Democratic Alliance (DA), under the leadership of Leon, with the NNP leader van Schalkwyk as his deputy. The DA won control of the Cape Town municipality in the local elections of late 2000. In KwaZulu/Natal the loose alliance between the ANC and IFP brought relative stability, although the chiefs (*inkosi*), who were now paid by the Government, feared that the new local government system introduced with the elections (which replaced the more than 800 existing structures with 284 new municipalities) would reduce their powers, and sought unsuccessfully to challenge the demarcation of the new structures. In October 2001 the NNP faction of the DA, led by van Schalkwyk, suspended its participation in the alliance and formed a partnership with the ANC instead. In November the NNP and ANC entered into a power-sharing agreement in Western Cape, with van Schalkwyk as Premier. As a result of legislation adopted in June 2002 enabling elected members of the national and provincial assemblies to change party allegiance without being required to seek re-election, the UDM lost most of its members of Parliament to other parties, the DA gained members from the NNP, and the ANC was able to take power in Western Cape at local level. The IFP, however, managed to remain in power in KwaZulu/Natal until the 2004 elections.

In 2001 public hearings were held in Pretoria, under the auspices of the Auditor-General, the National Director of Public Prosecutions (NDPP) and the Public Protector, in relation to the purchase in 1999 by the Mbeki Government of a number of aircraft and vessels for the South African National Defence Force (SANDF) from the UK, Germany and Sweden. The ANC's chief whip, Tony Yengeni, was subsequently forced to resign, following allegations that he had received favours from one of the contractors in the arms deal while Chairman of the Parliamentary Defence Committee. He was sentenced to four years' imprisonment in March 2003 for defrauding the Government. In August the NDPP, Bulelani Ngcuka, announced that despite the existence of a *prima facie* case of corruption implicating Deputy President Zuma in the procurement deal, he would not be prosecuted, owing to insufficient evidence.

In 2004 celebrations around the 10th anniversary of South Africa's attaining democracy coincided with the holding in April of elections to the national and provincial legislatures. The ANC won 279 of the National Assembly's 400 seats, the DA 50 seats and the IFP 28. For the first time, the ANC won control of all nine provincial governments, although it failed to win outright majorities in KwaZulu/Natal and Western Cape. The new National Assembly voted unanimously to re-elect Mbeki to the presidency, and he was sworn in to serve a second term on 27 April. As part of a cabinet reorganization, van Schalkwyk was appointed as Minister of Environmental Affairs and Tourism, while Zuma remained Deputy President.

In the aftermath of the elections, the NNP, which won only 1.7% of the vote, disbanded: van Schalkwyk joined the ANC, but most NNP support was transferred to the DA. The loss of KwaZulu/Natal precipitated a major crisis in the IFP, which continued to be headed by the marginalized Buthelezi. In Western Cape the ANC had taken power before the elections after entering into an alliance with the NNP, and remained in control of the province. Holomisa's UDM, which had lost support to the ANC and other parties, emerged from the 2004 elections with nine seats and one deputy minister. Patricia de Lille, formerly a prominent member of the PAC, had broken away from that party to form the Independent Democrats (ID), which won seven seats, most of them in Western Cape. After the local government elections held in March 2006, no clear winner emerged in Cape Town; however, the DA and a coalition of small parties defeated the ANC, allied with the ID, by one vote. Helen Zille of the DA was elected mayor: she strengthened her position in January 2007 by forging a multi-party coalition with the ID. When Leon stepped down as DA leader in May, Zille was elected in his place.

Meanwhile, in May 2005 the Public Protector issued a report criticizing the NDPP for improperly prejudicing the Deputy President, whom many saw as the natural successor to Mbeki. The crisis over the corruption allegations involving Zuma culminated in June with his financial adviser, Schabir Shaik,

being found guilty of corruption and fraud and sentenced to 15 years' imprisonment by the Durban High Court, which found that a series of payments made by Shaik on behalf of Zuma were intended to influence Zuma to benefit Shaik's business. The trial revealed that Zuma had been party to a bid to solicit a bribe from the French defence company Thales, one of the contractors in the controversial arms deal (see above). On 14 June President Mbeki 'released' Zuma from his duties as Deputy President, replacing him with Phumzile Mlambo-Ngcuka, hitherto Minister of Energy and Mineral Affairs. Zuma retained the deputy premiership of the ANC.

Despite growing antagonism towards him, Mbeki insisted on standing for a third term as ANC President at the party's national conference in December 2007. However, Mbeki's secretive and remote leadership style was rejected, and the conference instead elected Zuma as the party's new President, along with many other controversial ANC figures with tainted records.

Mbeki remained in office as South African President, albeit as an increasingly isolated and discredited figure. He was slow to condemn the violence that erupted in a number of townships in May 2008, in which over 60 people were killed and tens of thousands were displaced by local mobs angry about the large influx of immigrants from neighbouring countries, such as Mozambique. It was widely accepted that, in the same way as lack of service delivery and a flawed immigration policy lay behind the violence, failures in government policy and lack of planning were at least partly to blame for the electricity crisis of early 2008, when the state-owned utility Electricity Supply Commission (ESKOM) was unable to meet the country's electricity requirements. Numerous scandals were exposed during Mbeki's second term. For example, it was discovered that a company that had obtained petroleum from Iraq had paid a large sum to the ANC before the 2004 elections, and South Africa's oil reserves had been rapidly divested under highly dubious circumstances. In September 2007 Mbeki had dismissed the NDPP, Vusi Pikoli, citing a breakdown in the relationship between Pikoli and the Minister of Justice, but the dismissal was ostensibly related to Pikoli having obtained an arrest warrant for the National Commissioner of Police, Jackie Selebi, who was to be found guilty of having entered into a corrupt relationship with a drug dealer.

When the National Prosecuting Authority (NPA) again charged Zuma (with fraud, corruption, tax evasion and money laundering) his lawyers argued that the NPA wanted to prevent him from becoming President and that he would not be granted a fair trial. In September 2008 a Pietermaritzburg court found that he should have been given the opportunity to make representations before being recharged, and the judge declared that there had been political interference in bringing the charges.

This caused the rift within the ANC to widen, and it was subsequently announced that Mbeki had relinquished the presidency at the party's request, effective from 25 September 2008. Kgalema Motlanthe, the Deputy President of the ANC, was sworn in as South Africa's new President later that day. Although the Supreme Court of Appeal overturned the September judgment and the charges against Zuma were reinstated, three weeks before the April 2009 elections the acting NDPP announced that new evidence showed that there had been interference in the process. All charges against Zuma were consequently dropped, allowing him to assume the national presidency after the elections.

THE ZUMA PRESIDENCY

In legislative elections held in April 2009, the ANC, as expected, won another overwhelming victory, securing 264 of the 400 seats in the National Assembly. The DA secured 67 seats and regained control of Western Cape from the ANC. Zille, who remained leader of the opposition, became Premier of Western Cape. She and others realized that only a coalition of opposition forces could threaten the ANC's majority, and in mid-2010 she announced that the ID, which now enjoyed little support, would join the DA. Although the DA presented itself as a genuinely multi-racial party, it did not enjoy the 'struggle credentials' of the ANC and attracted relatively little black African support.

Immediately after being inaugurated as President on 9 May 2009, Zuma announced his new Government and the reorganization of a number of ministries. A National Planning Commission (NPC) and a performance-monitoring and evaluation competency were created within the presidency, led by Trevor Manuel (hitherto Minister of Finance) and Collins Chabane, respectively. Appointments made to the enlarged administration included Motlanthe as Deputy President and Pravin Gordhan as Minister of Finance; Nkosazana Dlamini-Zuma (the former wife of President Zuma) was moved from Foreign Affairs to Home Affairs. The NPC finally began its work in 2010. In May 2011 it issued a report identifying the major challenges confronting South Africa and in November it presented a National Development Plan to President Zuma, which set out a vision of how the country could eliminate poverty and reduce inequality by 2030.

As the ANC continued to be wracked by infighting, tensions grew between the party and its alliance partners, COSATU and the SACP. Although Zuma succeeded in holding his party and the alliance together, he soon showed himself to be a weak and indecisive leader. Over a long period, the leader of the ANC Youth League, Julius Malema, was allowed to make highly provocative statements that increased racial tensions. In June 2010 South Africa's hosting of the International Federation of Association Football (Fédération Internationale de Football Association—FIFA) World Cup, which cost over R 40,000m. to stage, briefly improved the country's image abroad, although it did not produce the expected boom in tourism. Many argued that the World Cup distracted attention from the country's main problems—the lack of jobs and mass poverty. In May 2015 it emerged that South Africa had paid US $10m. to a FIFA official in the Caribbean in 2008 to win its bid to host the World Cup.

The Zuma Government acknowledged that unemployment was a key issue confronting the country, with over 1m. people losing their jobs as a result of the global economic slowdown from late 2008. A so-called New Growth Path was initiated in 2010 with the aim of creating 5m. new jobs within 10 years, largely in the public sector, and in 2012 the Government announced an extensive infrastructure building programme, but there was no subsequent decrease in unemployment. As joblessness and poverty continued to rise, so too did evidence of lavish spending by state officials, as well as massive wastage of public funds and gross mismanagement in parastatals and state departments. Corruption and misappropriation of funds became ever more blatant.

Although the media and civil society exposed many cases of corruption, leading figures in both the ANC and the SACP supported curbs on media freedom and the creation of a media appeals tribunal, both of which were widely seen as a response to press reports detailing incidents of self-enrichment by the new political class. When the Government's Protection of State Information Bill proposed harsh penalties for revealing classified information, a massive public campaign, led by the Right2Know coalition (a civil society campaign for freedom of information), was mounted against what was dubbed the Secrecy Bill. Many of the more draconian aspects of the proposed legislation were subsequently removed; however, critics continued to claim that the Bill would endanger freedom of expression and would, if President Zuma signed it into law, need to be challenged in the Constitutional Court.

South Africa's image within the international community was adversely affected by the Government's failure to act against oppression in Zimbabwe and Swaziland during its first tenure of a non-permanent seat on the UN Security Council, in 2007–08. Although Mbeki could take credit for persuading the parties in Zimbabwe to form a government of national unity in 2008, neither he nor Zuma, his successor as SADC mediator on Zimbabwe, openly criticized Mugabe when he continued to use violence against his political opponents and failed to honour the terms of the power-sharing agreement. In March 2011 Zuma prepared a slightly more critical report on Zimbabwe for SADC, but then approved the disbandment of the SADC tribunal after it ruled against the Zimbabwean Government. South Africa was elected for a second time as a

non-permanent member of the UN Security Council, for 2011–12, and in 2011 it was invited to join the Brazil-Russian Federation-India-China (BRIC) group of countries (subsequently known as BRICS), mainly because it was viewed as a gateway to the rest of Africa. Meanwhile, Zuma's mediation efforts on behalf of the AU during the crises in Côte d'Ivoire and Libya proved unsuccessful. South Africa caused further divisions on the continent when it nominated Dlamini-Zuma to be Chairperson of the AU Commission. In January 2012 she failed to attract sufficient votes to secure the post, but the Government refused to withdraw her candidacy and continued to lobby intensively on her behalf until she was eventually elected.

In mid-2011 Malema, who was re-elected as leader of the ANC Youth League after local government elections in May, demanded the nationalization of the mines and banks and the expropriation of white-owned property without compensation. While COSATU supported nationalization, the SACP did not, reflecting deep divisions within the alliance, which were linked to the succession battle in the ANC. In August Malema was charged with various violations of the ANC constitution, including bringing the party into disrepute, after stating that the Youth League would work to effect regime change in Botswana. Violent clashes between supporters of Malema and the security forces took place outside the ANC headquarters in Johannesburg. Eventually Malema was expelled from the ANC, as Zuma tried to consolidate his position ahead of the key ANC congress held at Mangaung (Bloemfontein) in December 2012. Malema's expulsion, and the subsequent virtual collapse of the ANC Youth League, represented a defeat for the more nationalist faction within the ANC. A fierce struggle ensued between those who supported Zuma and those who wished to see him replaced by Deputy President Motlanthe. At virtually the last moment, Motlanthe announced his candidacy, but Zuma was re-elected by a wide margin. To the surprise of many, Ramaphosa (now an extremely wealthy businessman) was elected Deputy President of the ANC. Although the outcome of the ANC congress strengthened Zuma's position within the party, he continued to be a consensus-seeking leader, and the tensions between the ANC and its alliance partners continued. The death of Mandela in December 2013, which prompted a vast outpouring of emotion, led many to contrast his leadership qualities with those of his successors.

Longstanding discontent among platinum miners in North-West province prompted many to switch allegiance from the NUM, an affiliate of COSATU, to the newly formed Association of Mineworkers and Construction Union (AMCU). Unrest culminated in August 2012 in unofficial industrial action by rock drill operators at the Lonmin mine near Marikana. After two police officers were killed, the police opened fire on the striking miners, 34 of whom died—many being shot in the back as they tried to flee. This event epitomized for many the fragility of South Africa's democracy. Industrial action at Marikana subsequently intensified and spread to other mines beyond those producing platinum. Malema, exploiting the situation, demanded Zuma's resignation; in retaliation, the Government accused Malema of inciting violence. Although Zuma appointed a judicial commission of inquiry to investigate the events at Marikana, many believed that the President failed to demonstrate decisive leadership in dealing with this and other crises affecting the country. In March 2015 the commission submitted its report, after hearing much conflicting evidence about the reasons for the violent response of the police to the striking miners in August 2012. The President initially refused to release the report, but, under pressure, did so in June 2015. Although critical of the police, the report did not attribute responsibility for the massacre to individuals. Ramaphosa, who had reportedly been asked by the managers of the Lonmin mine to co-ordinate 'concomitant action' against the striking miners, was therefore cleared of any wrongdoing, although the Economic Freedom Fighters (EFF), a new party formed by Malema in mid-2013, continued to demand that he be charged with inciting murder.

In the aftermath of the ANC congress at Mangaung in December 2012, a leading newspaper claimed that R 246m. (US $20m.) had been spent by the state on refurbishing Zuma's home at Nkandla, in KwaZulu/Natal province. In May 2013, in what was termed 'Guptagate', an aircraft bringing a wedding party from India to South Africa to attend the lavish nuptials of a relative of the wealthy Gupta brothers, who had close connections to Zuma and allegedly wielded considerable influence over the President, was allowed to land at a military airfield, in contravention of South African law. Meanwhile, a commission of inquiry into the controversial arms procurement deal made by the Government in 1999 (see above), which Zuma reluctantly agreed to establish in October 2011, failed to make any real progress. Amid continued concerns about executive interference in the judiciary, Zuma's appointee as NDPP, Menzi Simelane, was found in October 2012 to be unfit for office by the Constitutional Court, and his appointment was invalidated. In July 2015 Simelane's successor stood down from office after being refused security clearance for failing to disclose that he had been involved in a case of murder (for which he had been tried and acquitted on grounds of self-defence in 1985). After the Chairperson of the Independent Electoral Commission, Pansy Tlakula, was found guilty of misconduct with regard to the procurement of premises for the organization, she initially refused to resign but was also eventually persuaded to step down (in September 2014). Fears grew about political interference in state institutions such as the NPA and the South African Revenue Service (SARS). Meanwhile, in February 2015 the DA initiated legal proceedings to force the NPA to revisit its 2009 decision to drop the 783 corruption and other charges against President Zuma because of recorded conversations that suggested political interference in the process. The High Court in Pretoria subsequently ruled that the decision was irrational and that the charges against Zuma should be reinstated; the NPA appealed against the judgment.

In January 2014 some 70,000 platinum workers belonging to AMCU began a strike, which lasted for five months, becoming the longest and most costly strike action ever in South Africa's mining industry. The platinum producers—Lonmin, Impala Platinum and Anglo American Platinum—were able to draw on stockpiles, while the mineworkers remained adamant in their demand for a monthly basic salary of R 12,500 for the lowest-paid workers. Eventually this demand was met, with effect from 2017. In late June 2014, with the strike petering out (although with the AMCU pressing for additional demands), further electricity shortages and manufacturing job losses, the country's credit rating was downgraded by two agencies, amid general pessimism about the state of the economy. After the National Union of Metalworkers, which did not support the ANC in the 2014 elections, appealed for the formation of a workers' party, it was expelled from COSATU, as was its charismatic former General Secretary, Zwelinzima Vavi, who in 2017 emerged as head of a new South African Federation of Trade Unions (SAFTU).

From February 2014 the country entered a strenuously contested election campaign, in which one of the central issues was corruption—South Africa had dropped further on nongovernmental organization Transparency International's Corruption Perceptions Index—especially relating to the state spending on Zuma's Nkandla residence and to the benefits that had accrued to Zuma's family and business associates. None the less, when in April the country celebrated 20 years of democracy, the ANC was able to argue that the two decades had brought great improvements to the lives of most South Africans. In the general election, held in May, the ANC was returned with 62.2% of the valid votes cast and 249 seats in the National Assembly. The DA increased its share of the vote to 22.2% (compared with 16.7% in the previous election) and won 89 seats: it retained control of Western Cape, but failed to secure any other province. The EFF, under Malema, secured nearly 6.4% of the vote, taking 25 seats in the Assembly. After the election, Zuma reshuffled and enlarged his Cabinet, and Ramaphosa became the new Deputy President. Trevor Manuel retired from public office and Gordhan was replaced as Minister of Finance by Nhlanhla Nene. A few days after the election Lindiwe Mazibuko resigned as leader of the DA in Parliament. She was replaced by Mmusi Maimane, who in May 2015 succeeded Zille as party leader.

When Parliament convened in February 2015, EFF members staged a number of disruptive protests in the National Assembly referring to the Nkandla scandal, and Malema was temporarily suspended from the National Assembly after accusing the ANC of having been responsible for the violence at Marikana in 2012. Zuma continued to refuse to account for the spending on his private residence, and came under further criticism after a cabinet committee absolved him of having to pay anything to the state. Meanwhile, the country's image was damaged following another outbreak of xenophobic violence in April 2015: shops owned by Africans from other countries were looted, and eight people were killed.

Demands made in March 2015 for the removal of the statue of the imperialist politician Cecil Rhodes at the University of Cape Town sparked a new wave of student activism. The statue was removed, but protests continued over 'transformation', and in October protests over fee rises escalated until the Government agreed that no increases would be introduced in 2016. In that year a number of universities experienced incidents of violence and destruction of buildings and artefacts, and some were closed temporarily.

In December 2015 President Zuma abruptly dismissed Nene as Minister of Finance and appointed an inexperienced member of the National Assembly, David Van Rooyen, in his place, apparently without consulting the Cabinet or even senior members of the ANC. Some believed that Zuma wanted to gain control of the National Treasury, after Nene had refused to approve the restructuring of an agreement between South African Airways (SAA) and Airbus, angering the Chairperson of the SAA board, a close associate of Zuma. As huge sums of money subsequently poured out of the country, Zuma, responding to pressure from business leaders and senior ANC officials, replaced Van Rooyen with the respected former Minister of Finance Gordhan. The latter acted immediately to steady the economy and refused to allow SAA to restructure its agreement with Airbus.

The EFF had, meanwhile, taken the Nkandla issue to the Constitutional Court, which in March 2016 ruled that the President had in effect violated his oath of office and must repay some of the money spent on his residence. This ruling led to more demands for Zuma to be replaced as President. In another scandal, it was alleged that the Gupta family had attempted to offer the position of Minister of Finance to Nene's deputy. However, an attempt in April by the DA to have Zuma impeached by Parliament was quashed by the ANC majority. The finding by the Arms Procurement Commission that there was no evidence of any bribery on the part of the Government in securing its costly 1999 arms procurement deal was condemned by the opposition as a 'whitewash'. Zuma's weak leadership and his inability to deal with the massive rise in corruption, together with the slowing economy, led to concerns within the ANC that the party would suffer significant losses in the local government elections in August 2016. In the event, the ANC's share of the vote did indeed decrease, to 54%, despite the party's high level of expenditure on the campaign. The ANC lost control of three further metropolitan municipalities: Nelson Mandela Bay, in Eastern Cape; Tshwane, in Gauteng (which includes Pretoria) and Johannesburg. In these municipalities the DA was able to wrest control from the ANC by forming coalitions with the EFF. The new mayors in the three metropolitan areas found evidence of massive corruption by the former ANC authorities and took steps to improve the delivery of basic services. The DA increased its support in Western Cape and Cape Town, but in early 2017 its standing suffered some damage when Zille, the Premier of Western Cape, suggested in a message via social media that colonialism had not been wholly bad. Amid demands for her dismissal, the DA ordered an investigation. In June Zille apologized and was removed from all party positions, retaining her provincial premiership.

Meanwhile, in its foreign policy South Africa continued to emphasize its relationship with countries of the southern hemisphere and its membership of the BRICS group. A dispute arose with the USA in 2015 over whether South Africa would continue to benefit from the Africa Growth and Opportunity Act (AGOA), a trade and investment law approved by the US Congress in 2000. Agreement on the vexed issue of US meat imports into South Africa was finally reached in January 2016, allowing US meat imports, and South Africa remained a beneficiary of AGOA. In June 2015 South Africa hosted an AU summit in Johannesburg. One of the heads of state attending was Omar Hassan Ahmad al-Bashir, the President of Sudan and an alleged war criminal wanted by the International Criminal Court (ICC). As a signatory to the Rome Statute of the ICC, South Africa was legally obliged to arrest al-Bashir and transfer him to ICC custody. However, South Africa, which came under international criticism for its failure to arrest al-Bashir, asserted that diplomatic immunity had been applied. In October 2016 the South African Government announced its intention to withdraw the country from the ICC. After the High Court ruled, in February 2017, that such an action would be unconstitutional, the Government abandoned the withdrawal proceedings.

Immediately prior to leaving office at the end of her term in October 2016, the Public Protector, Thuli Madonsela, issued a damning 'State of Capture' report, which claimed that some state officials, influenced by considerations of personal interest or enrichment, had sought to control state institutions such as SARS, the NPA, the Directorate for Priority Crime Investigation (known as the Hawks), the South African Broadcasting Corporation and, most notably, the National Treasury, and that the Gupta family had influenced major policy decisions. In addition, the report alleged that Gupta-owned businesses had received government assistance in the purchase of mining interests. At a meeting of the ANC's National Executive Committee (NEC) in November there were demands for Zuma to resign, but he refused to do so, and later that month a parliamentary motion of no confidence was defeated.

During Gordhan's tenure as Minister of Finance, the National Treasury blocked unlawful transactions relating to contracts—especially those pertaining to the supply of coal to ESKOM—and attempted to exert greater control over certain state-owned enterprises (SOEs) that were making huge losses yet engaging in questionable transactions. In March 2017, as part of a wider cabinet reorganization, Zuma removed Gordhan from his post (against the background of the Ministry of Finance being involved in litigation against Oakbay Resources, a company controlled by Zuma's son and the Gupta family) and replaced him with the loyalist former Minister of Public Enterprises Malusi Gigaba. Three of the ANC's six most senior officials, including Deputy President Ramaphosa, made it clear that they disapproved of Zuma's cabinet reorganization, on the grounds that capable ministers had been removed from their posts, while others who were clearly incompetent remained in office. As an example of government incompetence, in late 2013 the Constitutional Court had ruled that a five-year contract awarded in 2012 by the South African Social Security Agency (SASSA) to a private company, Cash Paymaster Services (CPS), for the distribution of social grants to over 10m. South Africans was invalid because of the profits that CPS had made following the conclusion of the deal. However, SASSA failed to reassign the contract, and the Court was consequently forced to authorize the extension of CPS's invalid contract.

Gigaba had presided over the creation of a vast system of patronage in his previous ministerial position, and his appointment as Minister of Finance was regarded as a means of securing funding from the Treasury for the construction of new nuclear power stations. Under Gordhan, the Treasury had authorized only a relatively small amount of funding in support of a feasibility study for a proposed project, involving the construction of eight new nuclear plants with a combined capacity of 9,600 MW, for which Zuma had concluded a co-operation agreement in 2014 with Russian President Vladimir Putin. Most commentators accepted that the cost of the nuclear project, estimated at over R 1,000m., was unaffordable. Civil society groups appealed to the Western Cape High Court, which in April 2017 ruled the procurement process invalid. Meanwhile, in another highly controversial decision, the Government announced in March 2016 that licences were to be awarded for shale gas extraction in the Karoo, despite the environmental impact and the need for vast supplies of water to be made available for the process of hydraulic fracturing ('fracking'). From early 2016 the country suffered from the worst drought in living memory (linked to the El Niño climate phenomenon), which necessitated the importation of large amounts of maize. In early 2018 it was feared that Cape Town would exhaust its water supplies as the south-western Cape became increasingly dry as a result of climate change.

Gordhan's removal as Minister of Finance precipitated the long-feared downgrade, in April 2017, of South Africa's sovereign credit rating to sub-investment 'junk' status, first by Standard & Poor's and subsequently by Fitch. Opposition parties organized mass protest marches, while a number of prominent ANC members and the ANC's tripartite alliance partners—the SACP and COSATU—together with the newly formed SAFTU (see above), asked Zuma to step down as President. At a meeting of the ANC's NEC in May there were further demands for Zuma to resign, but again he refused to do so. By this time, he had made it clear that he favoured Dlamini-Zuma (who had returned to South Africa following the conclusion of her term as Chairperson of the AU Commission) to succeed him as ANC President, as she would help to shield him from the fraud and corruption charges pending against him. The other main candidate for the party presidency, Ramaphosa, began to campaign on an anti-corruption ticket and demanded a judicial inquiry into the accusations of state capture raised by the 2016 Public Protector's 'State of Capture' report.

Meanwhile, ongoing township protests reflected increasing discontent among the poor, who witnessed the new elite exploiting opportunities for personal enrichment and resented the continuing legacy of apartheid and the authorities' failure effectively to address the country's socioeconomic problems. As economic growth slowed, there were demands for labour market deregulation to create more jobs and at least the partial privatization of state assets, such as SAA and ESKOM, but these were rejected. Under Zuma, many key institutions had been weakened through corruption and gross mismanagement, with senior officials often appointed because of their loyalty to the ruling elite, while the President and his associates had benefited enormously from their collusion with the Gupta network. As these scandals began to be exposed in the media, the President and those loyal to him, including Dlamini-Zuma, increasingly used a populist rhetoric based on race and appealed for the Constitution to be amended so that land could be seized from whites and given to blacks without any compensation.

Although inequality between the races had lessened since 1994, with millions more South Africans living in permanent accommodation with access to electricity, economic growth had mainly benefited the better-educated and was in effect stagnant from 2009. South Africa remained one of the most unequal societies in the world; unemployment continued to grow, and rates of murder, rape, kidnapping and car hijacking were among the highest in the world. Despite the Minister of Health promoting a grandiose National Health Insurance Scheme, public health care facilities were often dire, with basic equipment frequently unavailable as a result of mismanagement and corruption. Although over 10% of black Africans had joined the middle class, and a few had become very wealthy indeed, the combined income of all black Africans (who comprised about 80% of the population) was only around 40% of the country's total. Social spending by the Government increased to over R 50,000m. per year, and there were more people receiving social grants than in formal employment. An estimated 25m. people lived in poverty—a greater number than had done so a decade earlier. Despite the construction by the state of over 3m. new houses since 1994, many millions continued to live in shack settlements. Although more than 2m. HIV-positive people were receiving antiretroviral drugs from the state, large numbers were still dying from HIV/AIDS. The country's land reform programme had stalled, owing partly to bureaucratic obstacles, and there were few examples of successful redistribution of land. The ANC promoted new legislation on the expropriation of land to replace the 'willing buyer, willing seller' policy and in 2013 (the centenary of the Land Act) announced that it would reopen the land claims process, despite a large existing backlog. A new deadline of the end of 2018 was set in legislation adopted by Parliament in February 2014. When the ANC proposed that 50% of all commercial farmland be allocated to farm workers, the DA and others perceived this as another example (in addition to the large amount of uncertainty surrounding other policies) of the ANC deterring much-needed foreign investment.

From May 2017 a collection of more than 100,000 e-mails indicating collusion between the Gupta family and state officials was slowly leaked to the media. Although the relevant state bodies—the dysfunctional Hawks and the NPA—failed to investigate the e-mails, Deputy President Ramaphosa increasingly spoke out against corruption and state capture, building support for his candidature for the presidency of the ANC. It was also revealed that Bell Pottinger, a British-based public relations firm retained by the Guptas, had deliberately stoked racial animosity in South Africa to divert attention from state capture by the Guptas and their allies, and had promoted the idea that 'white monopoly capital' posed a threat to the country. When the ANC held its elective conference in Johannesburg in December, Zuma unexpectedly announced that tertiary education would be made free for those who could not afford to pay, and the conference also voted to support a constitutional amendment to permit expropriation of land without compensation, which the EFF had repeatedly demanded, as well as the nationalization of the South African Reserve Bank. In the party leadership ballot, Ramaphosa gained the backing of the Premier of Mpumalanga, David Mabuza, who had been a Zuma supporter, and that secured Ramaphosa just enough votes—fewer than 200 out of almost 5,000—to defeat Dlamini-Zuma. Mabuza was elected as the ANC's Deputy President.

THE RAMAPHOSA PRESIDENCY

Once he became ANC President, Ramaphosa faced the difficult task of persuading Zuma, regarded by many in the ANC as an electoral liability, to stand down as national President. At the beginning of the new parliamentary session in February 2018 Zuma reluctantly agreed to step down, and on 15 February Ramaphosa was sworn in as national President. His Cabinet included Gordhan as Minister of Public Enterprises, and Nene was reappointed as Minister of Finance, but Ramaphosa was forced to include some ministers who had been tainted by corruption scandals under Zuma, including Mabuza, who became national Deputy President. In his first State of the Nation Address, Ramaphosa spoke of a new dawn and of 'nine lost [Zuma] years', and for a time there was a new spirit of confidence in the country, which some dubbed 'Ramaphoria'. In February Zuma finally appeared in court to face charges relating to the 1999 arms procurement deal; the case was swiftly adjourned.

Also in February 2018, pursuant to the Public Protector's report and on the advice of the Chief Justice, the Deputy Chief Justice, Raymond Zondo, was appointed to head a judicial commission of inquiry into allegations of state capture and to investigate fraud and corruption in the public sector. The Guptas, meanwhile, had left the country, taking several billion rand with them. Gordhan, who soon reported widespread corruption in the SOEs, appointed new boards to oversee those companies, but acknowledged that restoring ESKOM, SAA and others to financial health would be a lengthy and very difficult task. Ramaphosa appointed a team, which included Trevor Manuel, to try to attract US $100,000m. of new foreign investment, but Ramaphosa's embrace of the idea of land expropriation without compensation did not encourage investor confidence. A parliamentary committee then investigated whether the property clause in the Constitution should be changed to permit such expropriation. Ramaphosa made clear that his Government would not support land seizures and that whatever process of land reform was decided upon, it would adhere to the rule of law and would preserve food security. In July Ramaphosa reassured Zulu King Zwelithini that land held in trust under the monarch in KwaZulu/Natal would not be subject to expropriation.

From early 2018 protests over the lack of essential services escalated around the country. Extensive violence in North-West province resulted in the replacement of the Premier and the province being placed under the administration of the central Government. Zuma, who presented himself as a victim, did not hide his anger at the way in which he had been treated, and his supporters in KwaZulu/Natal rallied behind him. In May 2021 he finally pleaded not guilty to the charges brought

against him relating to the arms deal, but his trial was again postponed.

In the months leading up to the general election in May 2019, Ramaphosa appeared intent on preventing a split in the ANC, at the cost of failing to adopt the tough measures required to put the country's economy back on a growth path. He did, however, appoint several commissions of enquiry, including one into SARS, headed by a retired judge, Robert Nugent. After Lawrence Mrwebi, the NDPP, was removed from his post in April 2019, amid criticism of his poor performance in the role, Ramaphosa appointed Shamila Batohi as his replacement, tasking her with rebuilding the NPA and tackling corruption.

A total of 48 parties participated in the general election held on 8 May 2019. The polls were conducted peacefully and declared to be free and fair, although there were some logistical flaws, and a number of smaller parties called for the election to be re-run. The turnout of registered voters was the lowest since 1994, at 66%, and some 6m. people in the 18–29-year-old age group did not even register to vote. At the elections to the National Assembly, the ANC won 57.5% of the vote and 230 of the 400 seats. Ramaphosa gained new legitimacy from the result, even though the ANC's share of the vote was down from 2014. The DA, which some observers accused of inconsistency over whether or not it supported a form of black economic empowerment, retained its position as the official opposition, with 20.8% of the total votes cast and 84 seats, but it lost votes to the Afrikaner nationalist Vryheidsfront Plus party, which increased its support to 2.4% of the vote. The DA failed to gain significant new support from the black middle class; however, it retained its majority in the Western Cape provincial assembly, despite having forced out Patricia de Lille from her post as Mayor of Cape Town in October 2018, following a protracted dispute over her earlier decision to close the special investigations unit in that city, amid allegations that she had improperly benefited from security upgrades to her home at public expense. De Lille had founded a new party, Good, which won two seats in the National Assembly in May 2019. The biggest winner in the legislative elections was the EFF, which increased its share of the vote to 10.8%, taking 44 seats (up from 25 in 2014). It won almost 15% of the vote in Gauteng province, while becoming the main opposition party in North-West, Mpumalanga and Limpopo provinces. The ANC only just succeeded in retaining control of the Gauteng provincial assembly, while in KwaZulu/Natal the IFP again became the official opposition. Buthelezi announced shortly thereafter that he would resign as IFP leader, and the EFF announced that it would no longer remain in alliance with the DA to prevent provincial councils from being governed by the ANC.

Ramaphosa interpreted the ANC's performance in the general election as a mandate for pursuing an anti-corruption agenda. Although he removed Gigaba and several other under-performing ministers from his new Cabinet and reduced its size slightly, he retained Mabuza as Deputy President and appeared unable to deal decisively with ministers who were incompetent or corrupt (or both). De Lille was appointed as Minister of Public Works and Infrastructure. In the aftermath of the election, the Zuma faction in the ANC showed itself to be prepared to fight back against Ramaphosa's anti-corruption policies, and the EFF used ever more emotive language in demanding radical change. In July 2019 EFF deputies employed intimidatory tactics in the National Assembly to try to prevent Gordhan from speaking, and allied themselves with Madonsela's successor as Public Protector, Busisiwe Mkhwebane. The latter failed to tackle major cases of corruption and instead accused Ramaphosa of deliberately misleading Parliament and alleged—contrary to the findings of the Nugent Commission—that Gordhan had established an illegal unit during his term in office as Commissioner of SARS. When Mkhwebane called on the President to take action against Gordhan, Ramaphosa and Gordhan approached the courts, which ruled against her. In 2021 Parliament slowly began to consider whether a vote should be held on the possible impeachment and removal from office of Mkhwebane, who had attracted heavy criticism, including from the Constitutional Court, for her actions in other cases. However, in June 2022, before any such a vote had taken place, Ramaphosa suspended her from her duties.

Impeded by internal factional disputes within the ANC, Ramaphosa appeared unable to take the steps needed to arrest the growing economic and social decline. The economy continued to shed jobs at an alarming rate. By mid-2022 it was estimated that more than 50% of 15–34-year-olds were unemployed, which led to an increase in crime. Meanwhile, a new head of ESKOM worked to reduce the company's unsustainable debt and began the task of splitting it into three divisions (generation, transmission and distribution), in an attempt to make it more efficient, However, the company was forced from time to time to resort to load-shedding, sometimes owing to intentional sabotage or to illegal strike action, interrupting supply and thereby further damaging the economy.

Meanwhile, evidence of widespread and serious corruption and mismanagement, especially within SOEs, was revealed in testimony before the Zondo Commission into allegations of state capture. It was alleged, for example, that extensive bribes had been paid by Bosasa, a company headed by an ally of Zuma, in return for government tenders and favours. When Zuma gave evidence before the Commission in July 2019, he again presented himself as the victim of a conspiracy and refused to acknowledge that there had been any state capture or that the Gupta family had wielded undue influence over the appointment of ministers and other key officials. The Commission also heard evidence that some R 50,000m. had been misappropriated while Zuma was President. Zuma subsequently defied two summonses by the Commission to appear before it again. Accordingly, in June 2021 the Constitutional Court found him guilty of contempt of court and sentenced him to 15 months in prison, in a judgment that was widely considered to represent a major victory for the rule of law. Shortly after Zuma's imprisonment, in early July, his supporters set fire to lorries on the main road between Durban and Johannesburg, and property in KwaZulu/Natal was destroyed in what appeared to be a co-ordinated response. This sparked widespread, opportunistic looting, which soon spread to Gauteng. Denouncing the economic damage and the setback to the country's vaccination programme against COVID-19, President Ramaphosa deployed 25,000 members of the SANDF to quash the unrest in the two provinces. Property and goods worth several billion rand were destroyed and some 350 people were reported to have been killed before the security services were able to take control of the situation in mid-July. Zuma was released from prison on medical parole in September. As of August 2022, none of those responsible for instigating the riots had been convicted.

Factional battles within the ANC also contributed to the failure to convict any– major figures for crimes related to state capture, although the Asset Forfeiture Unit had seized a number of properties and assets that had been obtained illicitly. In June 2020 eight individuals were arrested in connection with the embezzlement of an estimated R 1,500m. from the VBS Mutual Bank prior to its collapse in 2018. Malema rejected accusations that he and other EFF leaders had received some of the fraudulently obtained funds from the bank. The most senior official to have been arrested and charged with corruption since Zuma was ANC Secretary-General Ace Magashule, who in November 2020 was charged with offences allegedly committed while he was Premier of Free State province, relating to a scheme for the eradication of asbestos from houses, which had become enmired in corruption. Magashule was suspended in April 2021 following a resolution adopted by the NEC stipulating that party officials facing criminal charges should 'step aside'. Although Magashule appealed against the ruling, his suspension was seen as a victory for Ramaphosa in the ongoing intra-party factional battles. Zuma and Magashule were leading members of a faction that opposed the anti-corruption measures adopted by Ramaphosa and hoped to topple him as ANC leader.

In October 2019 Zille was elected Chair of the DA's Federal Council. She had come to represent a wing of the party that was opposed to affirmative action and was considered by some to be lacking in sensitivity on racial issues. Her election prompted the resignation of two leading black DA politicians: Herman Mashaba, who stood down as Mayor of Johannesburg, and party leader Mmusi Maimane. Both subsequently launched new movements to test their political support. An outspoken white parliamentarian, John Steenhuisen, succeeded Maimane as DA leader and leader of the opposition in the National Assembly.

After some dispute as to whether the circumstances surrounding the COVID-19 pandemic would prevent the holding of a free and fair poll, local government elections went ahead on 1 November 2021. There was a record low voter turnout, with only 8m. voters casting their ballot. The ANC won 47.5% of the votes, while the DA secured just under 20% (retaining control of Western Cape province and the city of Cape Town) and the EFF won 10.5%.

Meanwhile, from January 2019 South Africa served another two-year term on the UN Security Council as a non-permanent member. President Ramaphosa was the only African head of state to attend the Group of 20 (G20) meeting of major economies in Osaka, Japan, in June 2019, and to be invited to the meetings of the Group of 7 (G7) group of countries in Cornwall, UK, in June 2021 and in Bavaria, Germany, in June 2022. As Chairman of the AU in 2020, Ramaphosa campaigned for the temporary waiver of certain provisions of the international Agreement on Trade-Related Intellectual Property Rights to allow more countries to produce vaccines against COVID-19 and for an increase in global access to vaccines.

On 17 March 2020 Ramaphosa announced the establishment of a National Coronavirus Command Council, in accordance with the Disaster Management Act of 2002, and nine days later he imposed a strict nationwide lockdown, which was initially to last for three weeks. These actions were at first widely welcomed as a bold approach towards combating the pandemic, despite the severe economic consequences of the lockdown measures. Almost all travel into and out of the country (and across provincial borders) was prohibited. A special Social Relief of Distress grant was to be paid to anyone without formal employment, the regular child support grant was increased, and grants were made to some South African-owned businesses. In late April 2020 Ramaphosa announced that the country would be subject to 'Alert Level Five'—the most stringent restrictions under a new five-level system. Having come under significant pressure, especially from the business community and the DA, to relax restrictions on economic activity in the interests of avoiding further devastation to the economy, from 1 June the alert level was lowered to Level Three, despite a growing number of infections. As the mines recommenced operations, there was a surge in the number of new cases. By this time there was much criticism of the authorities' mixed messages in relation to lockdown regulations and of the lack of any accountability to Parliament. Moreover, the security forces were frequently accused of using heavy-handed tactics in the townships. By late May almost 0.25m. people had been arrested for breaking lockdown regulations.

At the end of June 2020 some of the restrictions were relaxed further, despite South Africa having the continent's highest number of confirmed coronavirus cases, with Western Cape province, and especially the city of Cape Town, being an early focus of the epidemic. With relatively little testing being carried out, there were almost certainly far more cases than officially acknowledged. A new variant of the virus, first identified in South Africa, helped to fuel a second wave of infections in December, which peaked in early 2021. A third wave, which initially hit Gauteng province particularly hard, commenced in June and proved more severe than the first two, as the virus had mutated into the more infectious Delta variant. Meanwhile, the Government was slow to order vaccines, hoping to rely on the World Health Organization's COVAX Facility, and some 1m. vaccines that had been delivered were deemed unsuitable for South Africa and sold abroad. From February health care workers began to be vaccinated, and from May those over the age of 60 years. Amid a fourth wave of infections in mid-2021, Ramaphosa again increased restrictions on public gatherings and travel, reintroducing Level Four restrictions.

Meanwhile, investigative journalists reported evidence of corruption in respect of pandemic-related funding. The Minister of Health, Zweli Mkhize, was put on special leave by the President in June following allegations of his involvement with a communications company that had received a large amount of public funding to combat the pandemic, with little to show for it. Mkhize resigned from the Cabinet in early August and was replaced by Dr Mathume Phaahla. After another wave of infections had passed with relatively few hospitalizations and deaths, in June 2022 Ramaphosa dropped the last remaining restrictions on public activity, including the Government-mandated wearing of masks. By August there had been some 4m. confirmed cases of COVID-19 and over 100,000 deaths, and 32.5% of the population had been fully vaccinated.

The economy contracted by 6.4% in 2020 and, although there was a degree of economic recovery in early 2021 as lockdown restrictions were eased, the country remained in dire financial straits, with a sovereign debt crisis looming. Meanwhile, a new organization, the so-called Operation Dudula, stoked xenophobia. Public servants took strike action in protest against the Government's efforts to cut the public sector wage bill, which absorbed more than 40% of total revenue. In addition to continuing widespread corruption, there was much mismanagement and lack of coherence in government policies. For example, in March the Government selected a Turkish company, Karpowership, as the preferred bidder to supply electricity for 20 years from floating power plants at three ports, but in June the plan was rejected on environmental grounds by the Department of Forestry, Fisheries and the Environment. In the same month the Government finally approved the sale of its majority share in SAA and allowed much greater use of renewables for energy generation, but other unprofitable SOEs were not closed down, and most of the restrictions that hampered economic growth remained in place. The crisis within ESKOM continued unabated, and in June 2022 an illegal 'wildcat' strike added to the beleaguered parastatal's woes, and in that month and again in September South Africa suffered power outages lasting up to six hours a day. Ramaphosa hailed the Just Energy Transition Partnership at the UN Climate Change Conference of the Parties (COP26), in Glasgow, UK, in November 2021. The initiative provided for investment by Western countries to assist South Africa in moving away from its dependence on coal and decarbonizing its economy. However, floods in Durban in April 2022 that killed over 400 people suggested that the country would find it difficult to manage the impact of climate change.

The Zondo Commission was granted a further extension to complete its work, and its final report was handed over in June 2022, after a four-year investigation and at an estimated cost of more than R 1,000m. Spanning more than 5,000-pages, the report detailed the state capture project under Zuma and found the ANC and Ramaphosa to be politically responsible for not having taken a stand against it. The Commission condemned the ANC's policy of cadre deployment as unconstitutional and unlawful, recommended a directly elected President and called for the prosecution of a large number of former government officials. Some urged an amnesty process for lower-ranking officials, and it remained to be seen whether the NPA would charge the main offenders. Following the ratification of an extradition treaty between South Africa and the United Arab Emirates (UAE) in 2021, and after Interpol had called for their arrest, two of the Gupta brothers were arrested in Dubai, UAE, in June 2022, and negotiations got under way regarding their return to South Africa for trial.

By mid-2022 Ramaphosa seemed on the way to victory in his bid to secure re-election as ANC President at the party national congress scheduled to be held in December. However, in June, shortly prior to the release of the Zondo Commission's final report, the former head of the State Security Agency and Correctional Services, Arthur Fraser, lodged a criminal complaint against the President, alleging bribery and unlawful authorization of the pursuit of suspects relating to an alleged cover-up following the theft, in February 2020, of around US $4m. from Ramaphosa's private game farm in Limpopo province in what the media called the 'Farmgate' scandal. Supporters of the President contested that Fraser, an associate of Zuma, had fabricated the charges in order to prevent Ramaphosa from running for re-election as President of the ANC. If formally charged, Ramaphosa would be required to 'step aside' as ANC leader under the party rules that he himself had promoted. Opinion polls suggested that if Ramaphosa were not ANC leader, support for the party would decline further at the 2024 general election. Ramaphosa won the support of most of the provincial ANC congresses, although in KwaZulu-Natal he was challenged by Mkhize and in September Dlamini-Zuma made known that she would stand for ANC President. Meanwhile, the opposition parties remained deeply divided. The DA continued to lose leading black African members. With polls suggesting that the ANC had lost majority support in the country, meaning that a national coalition was likely, the EFF hinted that it be might be willing to join a coalition with the ANC to keep out other parties.

The Government's failure to condemn Russia for its invasion of Ukraine in February 2022 exacerbated the popular perception that South Africa had lost the moral authority that it had under Mandela. Given the scale of the economic, political and societal crises facing the country, and the possibility that populists on the right or the left might exploit them to gain power, fears were increasingly expressed that South Africa's fragile experiment in constitutional democracy that began in the mid-1990s was in jeopardy, while the collapse of state institutions and increasing lawlessness suggested to many that South Africa was on its way to becoming a failed state.

Economy

ROBERT E. LOONEY

INTRODUCTION

South Africa projects many contrasting images. On the one hand, the country represents one of Africa's rare economic success stories. The country has the most diversified and developed economy in sub-Saharan Africa. The economy's growth and development have been steady, if not spectacular, and its progress has been favourable enough to enable the country to join the group of rising emerging economies, the BRICS (Brazil, the Russian Federation, India, the People's Republic of China and South Africa), as Africa's only member. It is the second largest economy in sub-Saharan Africa (after Nigeria) and the fifth most populous country in the region.

Considerable progress has also been made in building democratic institutions anchored in one of the world's most progressive constitutions. On the other hand, the country has many long-term structural constraints, which have resulted in stunted growth in recent years, creating high levels of unemployment, declining productivity, growing inequality and sub-par educational levels. Although per capita gross domestic product (GDP) stood at US $6,950.4 in 2021, compared with $3,382.1 in 2000, it had declined markedly from a peak of $8,799.5 in 2011.

Since assuming the country's presidency in February 2018, Cyril Ramaphosa has contended that he can revive the country's struggling economy. However, to do so, he needs to remove a range of economic obstacles while addressing mismanagement and corruption in an environment where fiscal and monetary policy have little flexibility. From 2020 he made some progress in these areas while combating the debilitating domestic effects of the coronavirus disease (COVID-19) pandemic and associated global recession.

SOCIOECONOMIC DEVELOPMENTS

The South African economy exhibits remnants of its colonial past and the era of apartheid (1948–93). These historical relics persist in distributing assets, such as land and physical, human and financial capital. The country's unequal distribution of assets has made it difficult for successive governments to achieve their primary goal of inclusive growth with equity and equality of opportunity.

Since 1994 post-apartheid governments have faced the challenge of meeting often conflicting demands. On the one hand, there is an urgent need to improve the economic circumstances of the country's black population. On the other hand, relying on free markets is imperative to ensure a dynamic economy. Typically, the South African Government has taken an orthodox, conservative economic stance. However, it has come under criticism from populist constituencies in recent years, especially the Economic Freedom Fighters (EFF), a breakaway party from the dominant African National Congress (ANC). The installation of Ramaphosa as President in February 2018 and his election for a five-year term in May 2019 have had a generally positive effect on the country's economic policymaking. However, he governs under extreme pressure from various groups within the ANC to move in a more populist or radical direction.

Although South Africa's economy relies on private enterprise, there is also a considerable degree of state involvement. During the apartheid era, the Government established the Industrial Development Corporation, which, in turn, created and controlled a broad spectrum of state-owned enterprises (SOEs). Under post-apartheid governments, much privatization has taken place, despite strong objections from the trade unions. However, several strategic enterprises remain under public control, including the state-owned Electricity Supply Commission (ESKOM), the country's dominant electric utility.

The most significant economic challenge faced by the Government has been employment creation and poverty reduction. Unemployment in South Africa is pervasive, increasing from an average annual rate of 15.8% in 1980–93 (the final years of apartheid) to 23.6% in 1994–2008 (the beginning of the global financial crisis) and 26.7% in the post-financial crisis years of 2009–21. Unfortunately, unemployment continues to climb, steadily increasing from 24.7% in 2013 to 29.2% in 2020, before surging to 34.2% in 2021 as the country faced economic turmoil and restrictions on trade arising from the COVID-19 pandemic.

Unemployment in South Africa varies by ethnic group. Between the first quarter of 2019 and the first quarter of 2022 the unemployment rate among the black population increased from 31.1% to 38.6%. Among the so-called Coloured population (people of mixed race) unemployment increased from 22.2% to 25.9%. For the Indian population the corresponding increase was from 11.4% to 17.1%, while for whites unemployment increased from 6.6% to 10.0%.

Unemployment in South Africa is also age-specific. In the first quarter of 2022 some 63.9% of those aged 15–24 years were unemployed (up from 55.2% in the first quarter of 2019). Of those aged 25–34, 42.1% were unemployed (up from 34.2% in the first quarter of 2019). In the 35–44 age group, 29.4% were unemployed (up from 21.7% in the first quarter of 2019), while the unemployment rate for the upper age groups was 21.8% for those aged 45–54 and 12.2% for those aged 55–64.

In South Africa, unemployment translates directly into poverty. In 2020 the incidence of poverty, defined at US $1.90 a day (in 2011 purchasing power parity terms), was 21.4%, up from 19.4% in 2019. At $3.20 per day, poverty increased from 38.2% in 2019 to 40.8% in 2020. At $5.50 per day, the corresponding increase was from 57.7% to 59.8%.

As with unemployment, poverty still exists, mainly along racial lines. Between 1995 and 2008 the mean per capita income of the white population grew by over 80%, while the black population's income grew by less than 40%. Poverty remains overwhelmingly black: in the poorest 20% of households, 95% are black. Almost one-half of the wealthiest 20% of households are white, even though whites make up less than 10% of the total population.

Persistent poverty stems in part from the economy's inability to generate rates of growth capable of lifting the incomes of large segments of the population. Tellingly, the country's potential rate of economic growth has been declining in recent years. Potential growth averaged 4.0% per year in 2001–08 but decreased to 1.8% in 2009–20. Potential growth was only 1.9%

in 2016, 1.8% in 2017, 1.2% in 2018 and 1.7% in 2019, and a contraction of 5.7% occurred in 2020 following the onset of the COVID-19 pandemic. Growth in this range is considerably below the 5%–6% rate needed to reduce unemployment and poverty in the country.

In the 2020 Human Development Report of the United Nations (UN) Development Programme (a summary measure of well-being), the Human Development Index (HDI), based on data collected in 2019, ranked South Africa 114th (between Venezuela and Palestine) out of 189 countries. However, this ranking was 14 places lower than the country's ranking in terms of income per capita, suggesting a lower standard of living than one warranted by the country's overall level of prosperity. Life expectancy at birth in 2019 was 64.1 years, and citizens had an average of 10.2 years of schooling. However, the rate of improvement in the country's HDI score, while low, has been increasing over time, rising from an average annual rate of 0.06% in 1990–2000 to 0.51% in 2000–10 and 0.73% in 2010–18.

South Africa has one of the most unequal distributions of income globally and the most unequal in Africa, with a Gini coefficient (a measure of income inequality) of 0.630 in 2010–18. Also, in 2010–18 the wealthiest 10% of households received 50.5% of the country's national income, and the poorest 40% just 7.2%. The wealthiest 1% had 19.2% of the income. Income is also concentrated geographically, with 34.3% of GDP in 2018 generated in Gauteng province (South Africa's most urbanized province, containing the cities of Johannesburg and Pretoria), and the next largest province, KwaZulu/Natal, contributing only 16.0%. Per capita incomes are also much higher in Gauteng, at R 80,454 on average, with Western Cape province next, at R 69,058.

POPULATION

At 60,041,996 in 2021, according to UN data, South Africa was the sixth most populous nation in sub-Saharan Africa (after Nigeria, Ethiopia, Egypt, the Democratic Republic of the Congo and Tanzania). However, its population growth rate, at 1.2% in 2021, is significantly lower than its peers. In 2021 South Africa's urban population grew by 2.0% to reach 40,736,693 (68% of the total population), while the rural population contracted by 0.3%, numbering 19,305,303 (32% of the total).

South Africa's population in 2021 was still relatively young, with 29% aged 14 years and under and 66% aged 15–64 years. Among black South Africans, 69.0% were under the age of 35 years in 2020. In many developing countries, especially in East Asia, declining birth rates have created a similar 'demographic dividend'. This dividend has helped to accelerate economic growth by increasing the number of workers of a productive age relative to those who are too young or too old to work. These demographic patterns exist in South Africa, with the fertility rate declining steadily over the past 50 years—from 6.4 births per woman in 1950–60 to 2.4 births per woman in 2020. As a result, the working-age population was expected to increase from 66% of the total population in 2021 to 68% in 2030. However, the higher growth path facilitated by a demographic dividend depends on finding productive roles for the expanded working-age population. Unfortunately, in South Africa's case, this has not happened, and the country may miss its opportunity to utilize this mechanism for accelerated economic growth.

GROWTH DYNAMICS

After growing at an average annual rate of 1.4% during the latter years of apartheid (1980–93), the South African economy expanded at an average annual rate of 3.6% between 1994 and the international financial crisis in 2008. However, growth then decelerated to an average annual rate of 1.1% in 2009–21. Rates have remained low in recent years, with growth of 1.4% in 2014, 1.3% in 2015, 0.7% in 2016, 1.2% in 2017, 1.5% in 2018 and 0.1% in 2019, before a contraction of 6.4% in the pandemic year of 2020 and a partial recovery, with growth of 4.9%, in 2021. The economic slowdown is reflected in many of the country's key sectors. Given the relative labour intensity of several sectors, including agriculture and manufacturing, continued slow growth poses a significant obstacle to employment creation and poverty alleviation. It is also becoming a major political problem for the ruling ANC.

Slow growth is partly a consequence of South Africa's relatively low rates of investment. After declining at an average annual rate of 2.0% in 1980–93, the post-apartheid period witnessed a surge of investment, averaging 7.6% per year in 1994–2008. However, in the post-financial crisis years of 2009–21 investment contracted at an average rate of 1.4% per year. However, some of South Africa's difficulties stem from circumstances beyond its control: the end of the so-called 'commodity super-cycle', an increase in the frequency of drought, and an economic slowdown in key export markets in Western Europe and China.

While part of South Africa's rising unemployment stems from technological change, much of the problem stems from flawed labour market policies initially designed to address apartheid-era injustices. Chief among these policies are job and wage protection so extreme that in 2019 the World Economic Forum (WEF) ranked South Africa 139th out of 141 countries for co-operation in labour-employer relations in its Global Competitiveness Report. The country also ranked 134th in the flexibility of wage determination and 129th in hiring and firing practices. Minimum wages, which are among the highest in Southern Africa at US $282 per month, compared with Mauritius's at $247, combined with trade union rules that make it nearly impossible to dismiss unproductive workers, make South African firms understandably reluctant to hire additional workers.

Another factor in the country's declining growth trajectory is the pattern of overall productivity, known as total factor productivity (TFP). A significant source of growth in most advanced countries, TFP grew at a respectable average rate of 1.3% per year in 2001–08, but contracted at an average annual rate of 0.7% in 2009–20. The patterns of TFP suggest that the high investment rate in the post-apartheid era did not lead to improved overall productivity. A similar pattern exists for labour productivity. GDP per worker increased by an average of 2.4% per year in 2001–08, but by just 0.4% per year in 2009–20.

A lack of market competition is a common cause of declining TFP. The mechanism involves a misallocation of resources to less productive areas of the economy. Corruption may be a factor here. In South Africa's case, corruption hampers the functioning of government, often through state capture by powerful groups, and enforcement of anti-corruption statutes is inadequate. In 1996 South Africa ranked in the 76th percentile (where 100 is the highest) of the World Bank's corruption indices. By 2020 the country had fallen to the 59th percentile. Several other governance components deteriorated during this period, with government effectiveness declining from the 83rd percentile (1996) to the 63rd (2020), and regulatory quality from the 66th to the 60th. The country's ranking in the rule of law component fell from the 55th percentile to the 50th.

Correcting the situation will require significant economic reforms. As the World Bank notes, the growth, productivity and governance factors mentioned above have probably trapped the economy in a vicious circle of sluggish growth, low productivity, reduced investment, limited job creation, and depressed demand, resulting in further slow growth.

AGRICULTURE

South Africa has a diverse agricultural sector. The principal crops are maize, sugar cane, wheat, peanuts, tobacco and fruit. There are large stocks of sheep, goats, cattle and pigs. The production of milk, butter, cheese and eggs is also significant. Agriculture's share of GDP has contracted steadily since the mid-1900s; the sector accounted for 10.7% of GDP in 1960, declining to 6.8% in 1970 and 5.8% in 1980. In 2000 agriculture comprised only 2.6% of GDP, and its share was 2.7% in 2021. Although South Africa became a net food importer in 2007 for the first time, the agricultural sector is still significant, with the country ranking seventh globally in maize production and among the top 20 countries globally for many kinds of cereal, fruit and livestock. In the first quarter of 2022 the sector

employed 844,000 people, equivalent to 5.7% of the employed workforce.

The agricultural sector expanded at an average annual rate of 2.6% in 1980–93, increasing to 2.9% in 1994–2008 and 3.3% in 2009–21. In recent years, output has been relatively volatile. After expanding by 10.9% in 2014, a severe drought in 2015 caused the sector to contract by 3.6% that year and a further 5.2% in 2016. The most significant declines occurred in field crops and horticultural products. Rains in the second half of 2016 helped to increase yields and boost agricultural growth to 19.1% in 2017. In 2018 the sector expanded by only 0.4% and in 2019 it contracted by 6.3%, amid drought, policy uncertainty over land reform, and the generally weak expansion of the broader economy. Many farmers indicated that falling rates of investment in the sector stemmed from recent proposals by the ANC for land reform involving expropriation without compensation. The COVID-19 pandemic has had only a minimal impact on agricultural production in South Africa, with the sector remaining open after the Government designated agricultural employment as essential throughout the series of national lockdowns. In addition, highly favourable weather in 2020 and 2021 led to the agricultural sector expanding by 13.4% and 8.3%, respectively, with most sub-sectors experiencing significant increases in output.

Maize illustrates the volatility of agricultural production caused by changing weather conditions. In 2015 production declined by 22.7%, before increasing by 113.7% in 2016. Production contracted again in 2017 (by 25.3%) and 2018 (by 9.8%) but had expanded significantly by 2020.

Sugar producers have faced growing financial challenges in recent years, compounded by a decline in global demand during the COVID-19 pandemic. Difficulties occurred on two principal fronts. First, rising production costs, including increased fertilizer, electricity and fuel prices, have lowered profitability. Second, declining sugar prices further reduced profitability. Sugar prices fell from around US $0.20 per lb in 2009–13 to an average of $0.129 per lb in 2020. Consequently, some farmers in South Africa have diversified, increasing production of other crops, including macadamia nuts, avocados, citrus fruits and vegetables, as well as of poultry. Financial pressure has also affected mills. At the beginning of the 2021/22 season, two of South Africa's 14 sugar mills (the Darnall and Umzimkulu mills) remained closed.

Some of these challenges are addressed by the South African Sugarcane Value Chain Master Plan to 2030, the central aim of which is to improve the sugar industry's profitability and ensure its long-term sustainability. The first phase outlines immediate action to be taken to prevent the sector's collapse—for example, addressing the issue of mills being unable to open owing to financial pressures.

Land reform is an emotive issue for South Africans, given the large-scale dispossession of land from black Africans before and during the apartheid era. Since 1994 the ANC has championed a land reform programme, but it has failed to meet general expectations regarding land restitution, redistribution and tenure reform. According to the Constitution, land expropriation is possible if it is in the public interest or for a public purpose, 'subject to compensation', which should be 'just and equitable'.

None the less, in February 2018 Parliament endorsed proceeding with land expropriation without compensation. This contested policy had originated with the leftist EFF with support from the ANC. However, President Ramaphosa declared in March that South Africa could learn lessons from Zimbabwe's controversial land reform programme. Ramaphosa and moderate elements within the ANC have attempted to temper any potential constitutional amendments with stringent guidelines on maintaining food security and agricultural and economic stability.

Foreign investors and private sector companies remain very wary about the future of their involvement in South Africa, especially given the many details yet to be clarified, including the wording of any constitutional amendment.

While some legal experts argue that Section 25 of the existing Constitution technically allows for land expropriation without compensation in some circumstances, the ambiguity of the article's wording and the lack of a clear legal framework prompted the ANC, under pressure from internal populist factions and the EFF, to seek to amend the article explicitly to allow such expropriation. However, in December 2021 the ANC failed to secure the two-thirds' majority required to amend the Constitution.

Unless the ANC can reach a deal with the EFF, which seemed unlikely given the extent of the personal and ideological differences between the two, a renewed attempt at constitutional amendment to allow land expropriation was not expected to occur before the 2024 general elections. The ANC's declining vote share, as evidenced in the November 2021 municipal elections, was likely to translate into a smaller majority in the National Assembly, rendering future efforts to introduce an expropriation amendment even more difficult.

MINING

Mining has been a vital sector of the economy ever since diamonds were discovered in South Africa in 1867 and gold some 20 years later. South Africa's early industrialization was heavily based on mineral wealth and on supplying inputs to the mining industry. Minerals and ores dominated the country's exports for many years. However, the sector has not had high sustained rates of growth for several decades. During 1994–2008 growth declined at an average annual rate of 0.3% per year, and in 2009–21 it expanded at an average yearly rate of only 0.1%. As in most mining countries, the sector's growth has fluctuated widely with the rise and fall of global commodity prices. Strikes and other labour problems are other factors contributing to the sector's volatility. The industry expanded by 4.8% in 2015 but contracted by 3.4% in 2016. In 2017 the industry grew by 2.4%, only to contract by 0.8% in 2018 and by a further 0.6% in 2019 and 11.8% in 2020. However, with the rise in international mineral prices, the sector recovered in 2021.

Mining and quarrying employed 406,000 people in the first quarter of 2022, of which the majority worked in the platinum group of metals sub-sector, followed by gold and coal. The number of mining facilities declined from 285 facilities in 2000 to 127 in 2010, and to just 51 by 2019. However, the number of facilities subsequently increased, reaching 74 in 2021.

In the early 1970s, following the exhaustion of some of the original deposits, the mining sector contributed about 7.5% of GDP. However, rising gold prices in the 1970s caused a resurgence in mining activity, with the sector's share of GDP reaching 12.8% in 1980. A sharp decline in gold prices after 1980, falling ore grades, rising costs, and generally weaker global commodity prices led mining's share of GDP to decline to 6.1% in 2010, and it was 8.5% in 2021. However, the mining industry's (direct and indirect) contribution to GDP may be as high as 20% through its purchases from local suppliers in the steel, timber and rail sectors.

For around a decade, South Africa's mining industry has experienced policy instability and an increasingly acrimonious relationship between the industry, government and labour unions. Many South African platinum mines were registering losses even before 2014, when labour strikes affected the sector. This experience reflects rising costs in the mining industry globally, as well as rapidly increasing domestic electricity prices and surging labour costs. The mining sector's wage bill has increased threefold since 2002, mainly because of higher real wages. Earnings per employee increased by 179% during 2002–11, even as output fell. In that period, rising costs were initially more than offset by increasing commodity prices during the so-called 'commodities super-cycle'. However, subsequent price weaknesses (prior to 2021) meant that many higher-cost mines were operating at a loss.

The election of Ramaphosa as President in February 2018 led to a renewed impetus among the mining industry, government and community stakeholders to agree on drafting a new mining charter. In September the Government announced the introduction of the third version of the new Charter (Mining Charter III), which contains many provisions aimed at increasing local beneficiation, black ownership rates and community development. While the Charter will provide much-needed regulatory clarity and transparency, it remains more restrictive than the previous regulatory framework, and critics claim that companies will be challenged by the more stringent rules on black ownership and local beneficiation. As an added complication, in March 2019 the country's Minerals Council announced that it was to launch a legal challenge to the new Charter.

The coal sector is also facing uncertainty. In particular, ESKOM's insistence that coal producers have at least a 51% representation of black shareholders in their ownership structure will lead to some divestments. As an example, in February 2018 Anglo American confirmed that it had sold its three remaining ESKOM-tied South African operations—the New Vaal, New Denmark and Kriel mines—to a group of black-controlled companies. This move confirmed the company's complete exit from South African coal mining, following the sale of the New Largo mine to the same consortium in January. Also in February, the Australian mining company South32 announced that it was to spin off its South African coal assets within six months, as the company prepared to focus on base metals.

Such divestments will shake up the domestic coal sector, as it remains to be seen whether smaller domestic players will have the same operational capacity as the large, experienced mining companies. For instance, before the sale of its mines, Anglo American accounted for 21.5% of South Africa's total thermal coal production and employed 24,500 people in its coal assets.

Curbs on coal production are likely to occur as the Government ramps up its Renewable Energy Independent Power Producer Procurement Programme, launched in 2011. ESKOM has already announced the closure of various coal plants, with the industry standing to lose as many as 30,000 jobs. In a final blow to the coal industry, following parliamentary approval in February 2019, the Government implemented a new carbon tax in June. The legislation provided for a tax rate of R 120 per metric ton of carbon dioxide equivalent, with tax-free carbon allowances of between 60% and 95% of emissions applicable during the first phase (2019–22).

In response to COVID-19, the Government implemented a nationwide lockdown in March 2020. Opencast mines were permitted to resume operating at full capacity from 1 May 2020 and underground mines from 1 June. The platinum sub-sector registered the largest number of cases and deaths. Gold and platinum experienced the two largest contractions in annual production in 2020, falling by 14.5% and 9.8%, respectively. The pandemic hit these two sub-sectors particularly hard in 2020, owing to the difficulty of implementing social distancing measures in underground mines. However, coal producers were relatively unaffected by the COVID-19 lockdown in South Africa. Suppliers to state utility ESKOM were exempted from lockdown measures, with additional exemptions being made applicable to open-pit mines.

The platinum, chrome, iron ore and coal sub-sectors have been instrumental in driving South Africa's post-pandemic recovery, each posting vigorous growth in 2021, following sharp contractions in 2020 due to the imposition of strict measures to control the spread of COVID-19. From late 2021 high demand for metals led to a significant increase in South Africa's export revenues. This metal boom stemmed in part from broad supply chain disruptions, as well as from sanctions imposed on Russia following its invasion of Ukraine from February 2022—with South Africa, on account of its large coal reserves, well-placed to capitalize on the embargo on Russian energy supplies. South African coal exports to Europe and Japan soared in the first half of 2022, and the prospects for long-term sanctions on Russian coal will further expand export markets for coal from South Africa.

Sanctions on Russia and the growing transition to green energy will provide a further boost to the platinum metals group. South Africa is the world's largest exporter of platinum, which is needed to produce green hydrogen as well as for fuel cell electric vehicles. The imposition of sanctions on Russian palladium, which is widely used in vehicle manufacturing, has been encouraging producers increasingly to shift to platinum as an alternative.

The mining sector lacks accessible new deposits and is plagued by persistent labour, energy and transport issues. Any potential revival in South Africa's gold industry, once the world's largest by far, was likely to be modest. New mines would require enormous investment in order to access deposits at great depths. Historically, high gold prices in the 2000s slowed the industry's decline but did not lead to a revival. The industry's cost structure is even less favourable now than in the 2000s, as labour costs are higher.

Labour relations in South Africa's mining industry have typically been poor, and there is no indication that the situation will improve in the foreseeable future. Rapprochement between the National Union of Mineworkers (NUM) and the Association of Mineworkers and Construction Union (AMCU), the two largest mining unions in the country, could encourage more co-ordinated action over wages within the sector. The two unions have previously been adversarial, with the AMCU splintering from the NUM in 1998 and the two subsequently handling labour disputes separately. However, during a three-month strike at Sibanye Stillwater's gold mines in March–June 2022, the two unions collaborated closely to secure a favourable, three-year wage deal for miners.

Power remains one of the major issues afflicting the mining industry, with a shortage of generating capacity and frequent power outages leading to greater costs as mining and processing operations are curtailed. There is no resolution in sight amid the ongoing crisis at ESKOM (see *Power and Water*), which suffers from ageing generating and transmission infrastructure and a heavy debt burden that makes it impossible to rehabilitate its network. Alternatively, mining companies will have to consider generating their own power, to avoid the issues with the national electricity grid.

MANUFACTURING AND INDUSTRY

South African industry, particularly the manufacturing sector, has had a successful history. With a comparatively stable and transparent legal and regulatory environment and reliable infrastructure, South Africa's competitive advantages have traditionally offset the country's rising energy and labour costs. However, that trend is proving increasingly difficult to sustain, and manufacturing activity has slumped. The sector accounted for 15.9% of GDP in 1994, down from a peak of 21.3% in 1981. Although the industry grew at an average annual rate of 3.4% during 1994–2008, in 2009–21 it contracted at an average yearly rate of 0.3%.

Recent years have witnessed little or no growth, with the manufacturing sector growing by 0.4% in 2016, only to decline by 0.2% in 2017. Although growth resumed in 2018 at 1.6%, the sector contracted by 1.0% in 2019 and, owing to the pandemic, contracted sharply (by 12.5%) in 2020. Amid the general recovery in 2021, the sector grew by 6.6%. By that year, manufacturing's contribution to GDP had fallen to 11.5%. Manufacturing employment in the first quarter of 2022 was 1.58m. (10.6% of the employed workforce).

In the first quarter of 2022 the manufacturing sector's largest subcomponents were food and beverages (20.8% of total manufacturing), petroleum, chemical products, rubber and plastic products (25.0%), basic iron and steel and related products (19.7%), wood and wood products, paper, publishing and printing (10.6%), and motor vehicles, parts and accessories, and other transport equipment (8.9%). The Government is seeking a revival in manufacturing as part of its strategy to increase employment and revenue. However, in addition to the labour market problems noted above, business practices are also an area where considerable improvement is needed. According to the WEF, South Africa ranked 129th out of 141 countries in 2019 in terms of the time required to start a business. Education is another area in which South Africa has serious deficiencies. In 2019 the country ranked very low in many critical areas, including digital skills, where it ranked 126th, the pupil-to-teacher ratio in primary education (109th) and the quality of its vocational education (119th). Crime is another factor affecting the business climate, with the country ranking 128th in terms of the cost to business of organized crime and 121st in police service reliability.

Other problems that have undermined the competitiveness of South Africa's manufacturing sector in recent years include electricity shortages, rising power costs and weak links in the infrastructure chain, with the flow of raw materials or finished products at times interrupted or delayed. Although the

Government intends to support the manufacturing industry by expanding electricity generation capacity, improving distribution networks and upgrading transport infrastructure, these efforts will take time to make a difference. They also require investment levels that the budget-constrained Government cannot afford to undertake at present.

On a more positive note, South Africa is the second largest passenger car producer globally (after Morocco). Most multinational manufacturers, including General Motors (GM), Toyota, Ford, BMW and Volkswagen, have plants in South Africa, located mainly in Eastern Cape and Gauteng provinces. However, while export sales are rising, sales in the domestic market have been flat. In October 2019 Ford joined Volkswagen Group South Africa in announcing that it would take some of its plants off the national electricity grid and rely on its own power generation, in order to ensure a more stable electricity supply.

POWER AND WATER

South Africa's power sector (electricity, gas and water) accounted for 3.1% of GDP in 2021. The industry grew at an average annual rate of 2.5% from 1994 to 2008 but contracted by an average of 1.1% per year during 2009–21. The power sector contracted by 3.6% in 2016, before expanding by 0.3% in 2017 and 0.9% in 2018. The sector contracted by 3.3% in 2019 and by 5.9% in 2020, but recovered to grow by 2.2% in 2021. The industry employed 103,000 workers in the first quarter of 2022 (just 0.7% of the workforce). However, the sector's importance to the economy is far greater than these numbers suggest.

South Africa accounts for slightly less than two-thirds of Africa's total power generating capacity. The country possesses several energy resources, mainly coal. With its abundant coal reserves, South Africa has been able to take advantage of its comparative advantage in developing an energy-intensive mining sector by providing low-cost electricity. The resulting economic development model represents a powerful 'minerals-energy complex'. For many years, this model served the country well, generating relatively high economic growth rates, price stability, and more than adequate foreign exchange levels needed to supply essential imports.

However, in recent years, this energy-centred paradigm has come under increasing criticism for no longer being economically or environmentally sustainable. Growth in the power sector has stagnated. Electricity generation decreased from 256,064 GWh in 2018 to 239,459 GWh in 2020, although a modest increase to 244,322 GWh was recorded in 2021.

After many years of underinvestment in the nation's power supply, electricity demand began to outstrip supply from 2008. Since then, the country has experienced sharply rising power tariffs, frequent load-shedding, 'brownouts' (load reductions) and even complete blackouts.

Many of the problems experienced by ESKOM stem from a political directive issued in 2010 that 'the lights will not go off'. This policy forced the public utility to keep its plants running, to the detriment of required maintenance and the company's financial viability. Maintenance is now taking place, but the backlog has created a vicious cycle in which generation stoppages (for maintenance work) put pressure on other ageing plants, causing breakdowns and more outages. However, a new coal-fired plant, at Medupi, came online in August 2021 and another, at Kusile, was expected to be operational by 2023.

ESKOM's dire financial position has dramatically hampered its efforts to expand and improve the network. This reality was evident after load-shedding was once again implemented at the end of 2018, owing to a lack of maintenance at power plants. ESKOM had reportedly cut its maintenance budget to reduce costs, which resulted in a resumption of load-shedding in February 2019. As a possible solution to the company's financial problems, the Government announced in the same month that it would unbundle ESKOM into three separate entities, responsible for generation, transmission and distribution, respectively.

Load-shedding was persistent in 2022, with 40 days of load-shedding during the first five months of the year, compared with 54 days in 2020 as a whole and 75 days in the whole of

2021. If current trends are maintained, 2022 may emerge as the worst year on record for load-shedding.

In July 2022 President Ramaphosa announced an energy action plan to address the country's severe electricity shortages. The plan's objectives include improving ESKOM's existing production by funding accelerated maintenance, cutting red tape and local sourcing requirements complicating the ordering of parts, and importing additional electricity from neighbouring countries. The Government also plans to increase generating capacity by doubling the planned procurement of renewables. Furthermore, Ramaphosa is looking to the private sector for help with financing generation capacity, with the regulatory burden on private electricity providers, particularly in solar power generation, set to be loosened. ESKOM estimates that the sector will need to increase generating capacity by 50,000 MW by 2035 in order to offset reductions caused by scheduled closures of coal-fired plants and meet increased demand. In 2021 coal accounted for 84.4% of South Africa's total electricity generation. Other sources included nuclear (5.3%), wind (3.4%), hydro (2.8%) and solar (2.0%). South Africa has ambitious plans to expand renewable energy, and the wind and solar sectors have been experiencing significant growth. In April 2018 the Ministry of Energy signed contracts worth R 56,000m. (US $4,500m.) with 27 independent power producers, which were expected to add 2,300 MW of generation capacity to the national grid over the following five years.

South Africa is semi-arid and poorly endowed with groundwater: it lacks a principal aquifer and is subject to periodic droughts. The country receives less than 50 cm of rainfall in a typical year—less than one-half of the global average. In 2012 South Africa signed an agreement with Lesotho to begin the second phase of the Lesotho Highlands Water Project, Africa's most extensive water basin transfer scheme. However, phase two of the project did not commence until 2020, and new supply was not expected to arrive until 2026. Water demand is forecast to exceed supply in the early 2020s, owing mainly to underinvestment in existing and new water infrastructure, the post-apartheid priority of providing universal access to potable water, and the large-scale expansion of the extractive sector.

TRANSPORT AND COMMUNICATIONS

The transport, storage, and communications sector expanded rapidly between 1994 and 2008, with growth averaging 6.4% per year. Growth moderated to an average annual rate of 0.7% in 2009–21. In 2021 transport, storage and communications accounted for 7.1% of GDP, down from 8.1% in 2000. In the first quarter of 2022 the sector employed some 960,000 workers (6.4% of the employed workforce).

South Africa's transport system is by far the best in sub-Saharan Africa. However, much of the system is ageing, bottlenecks are developing, and companies' rising costs are causing them to lose their competitiveness. South Africa's road system is extensive, covering some 750,000 km. There are about 185,000 km of provincial roads, with the municipal total amounting to some 66,000 km. The rail network, comprising 22,387 km in 2017, is managed by the parastatal agency Transnet Ltd, which is responsible for ports, pipelines and other aspects of public infrastructure. The country has eight commercial ports under two Transnet divisions—Transnet National Ports Authority and Transnet Port Terminals.

Airports Company South Africa Ltd (ACSA) manages South Africa's nine major commercial airfields. Upgrades ahead of the 2010 International Federation of Association Football (Fédération Internationale de Football Association) World Cup left this market with soaring costs and excess capacity. This excess is particularly evident at Durban, where King Shaka International Airport can handle some 18m. passengers a year, but in mid-2019 was handling only about one-third of that amount, and even fewer than that in 2020 as a result of restrictions on movement owing to the COVID-19 pandemic. About 90% of the approximately 41m. passengers who normally use South African airports each year go through Johannesburg, Cape Town or Durban. Local government or private sector interests operate the airports outside the nine principal facilities owned by ACSA.

The country's national airline, South African Airways (SAA), entered bankruptcy protection proceedings in December 2019. In April 2020 the Government signalled that the current tranche of public funds would be the last available to the firm, which had not registered a profit since 2011. In June 2021 the Government announced that, in an attempt to revive the airline, it had entered into a partnership with the Takatso Consortium, which now held a 51% controlling stake in SAA.

South Africa has a well-developed telecommunications sector. Telkom, South Africa's former fixed-line monopoly holder, competes with many local mobile cellular telephone service providers. Internet connections are available in all major cities. Consolidation was the defining trend in the South African telecommunications market in 2017 and 2018, with Liquid Telecom acquiring Neotel and Blue Label Telecoms acquiring Cell C. Meanwhile, the Government's plans to sell some of its shares in Telkom were shelved in November 2018. In 2021 Mobile Telephone Networks (MTN) and Telkom continued to appeal for an auction of the digital dividend spectrum to aid their convergent service strategies. If this failed to transpire, the companies would either have to partner with wireline operators or make acquisitions.

TOURISM

South Africa offers a favourable climate, numerous natural and cultural attractions, and relatively well-developed transport and accommodation infrastructure. The spread of the COVID-19 virus from early 2020 had a devastating economic impact on South Africa's tourism industry, as countries worldwide implemented travel bans in an effort to curb contagion. On 15 March President Ramaphosa banned arrivals from countries where the virus was most prevalent. These countries included China, Italy, Iran, Spain, the Republic of Korea (South Korea), Germany, the USA and the United Kingdom, which account for many of South Africa's tourists, particularly to the Western Cape area. Owing to the pandemic, the share of tourism and travel in South Africa's GDP fell from 6.4% in 2019 to 3.1% in 2020, and the number of jobs associated with travel and tourism declined from 1.51m. to 1.06m. Similarly, tourism and international visitors' contribution to exports fell from 8.6% of total exports in 2019 to 2.9% in 2020. The tourism industry began to recover in 2021, with its share of GDP increasing to 3.2% and sectoral employment rising to 1.08m.; however, both of these values remained considerably below the corresponding figures for 2019.

The WEF ranked South Africa 61st out of the 136 markets assessed in its *Travel and Tourism Competitiveness Report 2019* (down from 48th in 2015). Aside from the COVID-19 pandemic, many long-term factors are constraining the sector's growth. Social inequality and poverty remain rife for investors and contribute to persistent security concerns, which will continue to deter holidaymakers and businesses. High levels of unemployment, a lack of skilled labour, weak electricity supply and general economic and political instability also present problems for the hotel sector and tour operators. On the demand side, the country still has to combat the negative perceptions widely held by tourists regarding cost and security. Recent attacks on citizens from neighbouring countries have reinforced these concerns.

BANKING AND FINANCE

South Africa's banking and financial services industry is the most developed in sub-Saharan Africa. The country is home to several major banks, multinational insurers, a significant stock exchange and a wide range of investment service providers. In recent years, the banking and finance sector has been one of the most prosperous areas of the national economy. South Africa has developed a robust financial system capable of serving a broad spectrum of borrowing needs. The country also has the continent's most comprehensive regulatory system to protect the soundness of the financial sector. However, the industry has not escaped the effects of the economic and political difficulties that South Africa currently faces.

In 2021 finance, real estate and business services accounted for 23.7% of GDP, up from 16.9% in 1994 and 22.4% in 2010. During 1994–2008 the sector averaged annual growth of 5.6%, falling to 2.3% in 2009–21. In recent years, the industry has expanded steadily, growing by 2.5% in 2017, 3.3% in 2018 and 2.5% in 2019; growth slowed to 0.7% in the pandemic year of 2020, before accelerating to 3.3% in 2021.

In 2022 the South African financial sector comprised 13 locally controlled banks, four foreign-controlled banks, 13 local branches of foreign banks, three mutual banks and 30 foreign banks with approved local representative offices. The top five banks—Standard Bank, FirstRand Bank, Absa Bank, Nedbank and Investec Bank—hold about 90% of total banking sector assets.

Most banks are well-capitalized and recording asset growth, despite high levels of household debt and elevated unemployment, which remain a drag on market potential. Regulatory oversight under the Prudential Authority and the Financial Sector Conduct Authority (FSCA) is extensive. The legislation is fragmented, and upcoming changes under the Competition Amendment Act, enacted in early 2019, together with the proposed Conduct of Financial Institutions Bill (the second draft of which was published in September 2020) could increase compliance costs. In March 2021 Deputy Minister of Finance David Masondo announced that the draft Conduct of Financial Institutions Bill would require financial institutions to draw up transformation plans to demonstrate their compliance with existing Black Economic Empowerment legislation. The FSCA was to enforce these criteria.

South Africa's insurance sector is enduring a difficult period. Many insurance products and services have increased in price significantly in recent years, owing in part to rising costs. There has been a substantial increase in the frequency and severity of losses, which has affected risk underwriting and insurance premiums. With loss ratios at about 90% in recent years, insurers struggle to maintain profitability and seek to raise premiums to remain in business.

The Johannesburg Stock Exchange (JSE) is the largest stock exchange in the region and among the top 20 worldwide. Four other stock exchanges in South Africa primarily offer secondary listing services; these are cheaper and more technologically advanced than the JSE, which may eventually spur change at the latter.

FOREIGN TRADE

Foreign trade is an increasingly important aspect of the South African economy. However, growth in the value of both exports and imports has decelerated in recent years. Exports of goods and services expanded at an average annual rate of 2.1% in 1980–93, increasing to 4.7% in 1994–2008 before slowing to an average of 0.2% per year in 2009–21. Meanwhile, imports of goods and services grew at an average annual rate of 2.6% in 1980–93, rising to 7.8% in 1994–2008 before decelerating to 0.8% in 2009–21. The South African economy is sub-Saharan Africa's seventh most open to trade, with imports and exports totalling 56.1% of GDP in 2021. The country's principal export items in 2020 included mineral products (23.4%), precious metals (23.0%), vehicles, aircraft and vessels (10.3%) and iron and steel products (8.9%). In 2021 China was the country's largest export destination, accounting for 11.0% of exports. The USA followed closely behind with 10.6%, ahead of Germany (8.5%), Japan (6.7%) and the UK (6.6%). China was also South Africa's largest source of imports in that year, accounting for 20.6% of the total, followed by Germany (8.1%), the USA (7.0%), India (5.7%) and Saudi Arabia (4.4%).

The South African Government has pursued several regional integration initiatives to expand regional trade, including the Southern African Customs Union and the Southern African Development Community. In March 2018 South Africa was one of 44 countries to establish the African Continental Free Trade Area, which entered into force in May 2019.

South Africa's current account on the country's balance of payments registered an average annual surplus of 0.95% of GDP in 1980–93, but an average annual deficit of 1.5% of GDP in 1994–2008, which expanded to an average annual deficit of 2.3% in 2009–21. Trends in the current account of the balance of payments reflect growing macroeconomic imbalances in South Africa. Since 1980 these imbalances have involved an

increasing relative share of consumption, declining rates of savings and low but expanding levels of investment. In 1980–93 investment accounted for an average of 14.1% of GDP, increasing to 16.8% in 1994–2008, before rising to 17.1% in 2009–21. By comparison, throughout much of this period, the average share of investment in GDP was 25%–27% for upper-middle-income countries and 22%–25% for lower-middle-income countries.

In contrast to investment, South Africa has experienced a dramatic decrease in its gross savings rate, from 30% of GDP in 1980 to 13% of GDP in 2019, before increasing to 18% in 2021. As a share of GDP, annual gross savings declined from an average of 19.9% in 1980–93 to 16.3% in 1994–2008 and 14.8% in 2009–21. Comparable figures for the World Bank's upper- and lower-income countries in this latter period—28.0% and 25.1%, respectively—suggest that South Africa's funding gap (the difference between capital formation and domestic savings) is increasing dramatically, relative to countries of similar income.

Owing to its low savings rate, South Africa has to rely on capital inflows to finance its domestic investment. Inflows of foreign direct investment (FDI) have varied widely since 1990, reaching a low of US $3.4m. in 1992 and rising to a peak of $9,890m. in 2008. However, FDI flows have generally been in decline since 2013, when inflows totalled $8,230m., falling to $2,060m. in 2017, before increasing to $5,570m. in 2018 and dipping to $5,120m. in 2019 and $3,150m. in 2020.

Capital flows remain problematic and highly dependent on global risk perceptions and on South Africa's bond ratings, which dropped to 'junk' status in March 2020. Moody's Investor Services' decision to downgrade South Africa's credit rating to sub-investment grade status came amid a debilitating nationwide lockdown introduced to combat the spread of the COVID-19 pandemic. The announcement of the downgrade put further pressure on South Africa's already stressed financial markets. In May 2021 Fitch and S&P both maintained their respective long-term sovereign credit ratings for South Africa in junk bond territory, at BB, which is three levels below investment grade.

By mid-2022, although all three ratings agencies had improved their respective outlooks for South Africa, the country remained two levels below investment grade according to Moody's, and three levels below according to Fitch and S&P.

MONETARY AND FISCAL POLICIES

Since the mid-1990s, South African governments have generally pursued conservative monetary and fiscal policies. Controlling inflation, maintaining a relatively stable rand exchange rate, and keeping the country's credit rating intact have been the main priorities of the South African Reserve Bank (SARB—the central bank). However, since the 2008–09 global financial crisis, monetary and fiscal policies have been subject to increasing stressors.

Specifically, the Government's ongoing efforts to deal with unemployment and its consequences have encountered some difficult trade-offs. At times, foreign exchange rate stability and inflation control have had to take priority over a fiscal stimulus and credit expansion that might have helped to reduce unemployment. An incidence of this quandary occurred in July 2014, when concerns about inflation forced the SARB, which aims to keep consumer price index growth within a targeted range of 3%–6%, to increase its key rate from 5.50% to 5.75%, while labour unrest threatened to tip the economy into recession.

The SARB responded to the COVID-19 crisis with a cut in the key rate by 100 basis points (one percentage point) in March and again in April 2020, followed by a further reduction, of 50 basis points, in May. Meanwhile, the SARB engaged in an aggressive programme of bond purchasing in early 2020, with an estimated R 11,000m. of government bonds purchased in April alone.

With the annualized rate of inflation exceeding the SARB's upper threshold of 6%, and expected to remain above target throughout 2022, in July of that year the central bank increased its repurchase rate by 75 basis points, to 5.50%. Monetary tightening should help to tackle broad price increases and remove possible currency depreciation pressures in the short term.

As with monetary policy, South Africa has traditionally pursued a sound orthodox fiscal policy, with budget deficits and government debt mainly remaining within safe ranges. However, there has been a deterioration in the Government's budgetary accounts in recent years, even though annual state revenue increased from an average of 23.2% of GDP from 1994–2008 to 25.4% in 2009–21. After averaging 23.7% of GDP during 1994–2008, annual government expenditure increased to an average of 30.1% in 2009–21. As a result, yearly government net borrowing rose from an average of 0.5% of GDP during 2000–2008 to 4.7% in 2009–21, according to the IMF. Increasing budgetary deficits resulted in government debt rising from 31.2% of GDP in 2010 to 45.2% in 2015 and 69.4% in 2020, before declining marginally, to 69.1%, in 2021, with the IMF forecasting 70.2% in 2022 and 80.1% in 2025.

The government funds the deficit principally through domestic borrowing. The principal instruments include treasury bills and inflation index bonds. However, reducing borrowing will be difficult and freeing up funding for necessary public investments. Part of the problem derives from the public sector wage bill, constituting the most significant component (some 35%) of public spending. Given the political difficulty of reducing public salaries or employment, the structure of government expenditure leaves little room for the significant increase in public investment needed to restore competitiveness in critical sectors such as agriculture, mining, and manufacturing.

In 2021 the Government's fiscal position improved due to a revenue windfall arising from higher commodity prices, as well as the rebasing of GDP in August, which increased the size of the economy in nominal terms by 10%–11%. As a result, the official budget deficit for 2020/21 was revised downwards to 10% of GDP (from 14% of GDP) while the expected shortfall in 2021/22 was revised to 7.8% of GDP (from 9.3% of GDP), leading to a slower rise in public debt. However, at mid-2022 the Government was facing mounting demands for wage increases and higher social outlays, alongside the financial demands of dysfunctional parastatal firms such as ESKOM.

ECONOMIC OUTLOOK

Economic prospects will remain dependent on global developments, especially regarding the terms of trade, the war in Ukraine and central bank policies in wealthy countries. The SARB faces the difficult task of striking the right balance between controlling inflation and potentially stifling growth.

Public service wage negotiations began in March 2022, with unions demanding a 10% wage increase plus expensive add-ons, while the Government committed to a mere 1.8% annual increase. At the beginning of June the Government offered various options for improved wages that it claimed were consistent with the fiscal framework. By August, there was no immediate threat of a strike, and talks remained ongoing.

According to the SARB, headline annual inflation stood at an estimated 5.9% in April 2022 and was expected to average 5.3% in the fourth quarter of that year, increasing to 6.2% in 2023. These forecasts, plus expectations of high government revenue due to strong commodity prices, were likely to encourage the unions to hold firm in wage negotiations.

The Government has made recent progress in delivering long-promised reforms, including opening up port and railway infrastructure to private sector involvement and granting permission to large industrial concerns for up to 100 MW of electricity self-generation.

Despite these encouraging assessments, the SARB anticipated GDP growth of just 1.7% in 2022 (revised downwards from an earlier projection of 2.0%), with ESKOM power outages and port and rail infrastructure constraints expected to hamper exporters' efforts fully to capitalize on higher commodity prices. Notwithstanding recent reform progress, securing tangible economic improvements will be a long-term process.

Statistical Survey

Source (unless otherwise indicated): Statistics South Africa, Private Bag X44, Pretoria 0001; tel. (12) 3108911; e-mail info@statssa.gov.za; internet www.statssa.gov.za.

Area and Population

AREA, POPULATION AND DENSITY

Area (sq km)	1,220,813*
Population (census results)	
9 October 2001	44,819,778
9 October 2011	
Males	25,188,791
Females	26,581,769
Total	51,770,560
Population (official estimates at mid-year)	
2019	58,775,022
2020	59,622,350
2021	60,142,978
Density (per sq km) at mid-2021	49.3

* 471,358 sq miles.

POPULATION BY AGE AND SEX
(official estimates at mid-2021)

	Males	Females	Total
0–14 years	8,625,386	8,417,889	17,043,275
15–64 years	19,369,289	20,040,877	39,410,166
65 years and over	1,393,372	2,296,165	3,689,537
Total	29,388,047	30,754,931	60,142,978

POPULATION BY ETHNIC GROUP
(official population estimates at mid-2021)

	Number	% of total
Africans (Blacks)	48,640,329	80.9
Coloureds	5,294,968	8.8
Europeans (Whites)	4,662,459	7.8
Asians/Indians	1,545,222	2.6
Total	60,142,978	100.0

Note: Classification of ethnicity reflects self-declaration and national census methodology.

PROVINCES
(official estimates at mid-2021)

	Area (sq km)	Population ('000)	Density (per sq km)	Capital
Eastern Cape .	168,966	6,676.6	39.5	Bisho
Free State* . .	129,825	2,932.4	22.6	Bloemfontein
Gauteng† . . .	18,178	15,810.4	869.8	Johannesburg
KwaZulu/Natal .	94,361	11,513.6	122.0	Pietermaritzburg
Limpopo‡ . . .	125,754	5,926.7	47.1	Pietersburg
Mpumalanga§ .	76,495	4,743.6	62.0	Nelspruit
Northern Cape .	372,889	1,303.0	3.5	Kimberley
North-West . .	104,882	4,122.9	39.3	Mmabatho
Western Cape .	129,462	7,113.8	54.9	Cape Town
Total	**1,220,813**	**60,143.0**	**49.3**	

* Formerly the Orange Free State.
† Formerly Pretoria-Witwatersrand-Vereeniging.
‡ Known as Northern Province (formerly Northern Transvaal) until February 2002.
§ Formerly Eastern Transvaal.

PRINCIPAL MUNICIPALITIES
(population at Community Survey 2016)

City of Johannesburg* .	4,949,347	Mbombela . . .	622,158
City of Cape Town†*	4,004,793	Madibeng . . .	537,516
eThekwini (incl. Durban)†* .	3,661,911	Emalahleni . . .	455,228
City of Ekurhuleni (incl. East Rand)*	3,379,104	Matjhabeng . .	428,843
City of Tshwane (incl. Pretoria)†* .	3,275,152	City of Matlosana .	417,282
Nelson Mandela Bay (incl. Port Elizabeth)*‡ .	1,263,051	Newcastle . . .	389,117
Buffalo City (incl. East London)*	810,528	Mogale City . .	383,864
Mangaung (incl. Bloemfontein)* .	759,693	uMhlathuze . .	370,579
Emfuleni . . .	733,445	Govan Mbeki . .	340,091
Polokwane . .	702,190	Drakenstein . .	280,195
The Msunduzi . .	679,766	Steve Tshwete . .	278,749
Rustenburg . . .	626,522	Sol Plaatjie . . .	255,351

* Metropolitan municipalities.
† Pretoria is the administrative capital, Cape Town the legislative capital and Bloemfontein the judicial capital.
‡ Port Elizabeth was renamed Gqeberha in 2021.

Note: Data cover metropolitan municipalities, secondary cities and local municipalities with sizeable budgets only.

Mid-2022 (incl. suburbs, UN projections): Johannesburg 6,065,354; Cape Town 4,800,954; Ekurhuleni 4,044,660; Durban 3,199,329; Pretoria 2,739,768; Gqeberha (Port Elizabeth) 1,280,550; West Rand 921,524; Soshanguve 878,960; Vereeniging 786,127; East London 726,091; Bloemfontein 588,013; Rustenburg 554,517; Pietermaritzburg 539,069; Witbank 485,280; Polokwane 462,843 (Source: UN, *World Urbanization Prospects: The 2018 Revision*).

BIRTHS AND DEATHS
(annual averages, UN estimates)

	2005–10	2010–15	2015–20
Birth rate (per 1,000)	23.5	22.6	20.7
Death rate (per 1,000)	13.6	10.5	9.5

Source: UN, *World Population Prospects: The 2019 Revision*.

Registered live births ('000): 927 in 2018; 955 in 2019; 899 in 2020.

Registered deaths: 471,955 in 2016; 459,083 in 2017; 454,014 in 2018.

Registered marriages: 131,240 in 2018; 129,597 in 2019; 89,338 in 2020.

Life expectancy (years at birth, estimates): 64.4 (males 61.0; females 67.9) in 2020 (Source: World Bank, World Development Indicators database).

NET INTERNATIONAL MIGRATION ASSUMPTIONS BY SELECTED GROUPS*

	2006–11	2011–16	2016–21
Africans	815,780	972,995	894,365
Asians/Indians	43,222	54,697	49,584
White (Europeans)	−106,787	−111,346	−90,957
Net migration	**752,215**	**916,346**	**852,992**

* Migration assumptions are modelled on 2011 South African census migration data, with inputs from the South African Department of Home Affairs (DHA), and relevant OECD and International Organization for Migration (IOM) resources, plus migration data from other countries. Reference period covers 1 July of first year to 30 June of last year in each case.

Note: Classification of migrant groups reflects national statistical methodology.

2015 (documented immigration): Permanent residence permits issued 6,397; Temporary residence permits issued 75,076.

ECONOMICALLY ACTIVE POPULATION
('000 persons aged 15 to 65 years, labour force survey, January-March)*

	2020	2021	2022
Agriculture, hunting, forestry and fishing	865	792	844
Mining and quarrying	436	395	406
Manufacturing	1,706	1,497	1,579
Electricity, gas and water . . .	116	115	103
Construction	1,343	1,079	1,073
Trade, restaurants and hotels .	3,320	2,979	2,994
Transport, storage and communications	995	903	960
Financing, insurance, real estate and business services . . .	2,517	2,527	2,332
Community, social and personal services	3,759	3,567	3,546
Private households	1,316	1,127	1,072
Other services	11	14	4
Total employed	**16,383**	**14,995**	**14,914**
Unemployed	7,070	7,242	7,862
Total labour force . . .	**23,452**	**22,237**	**22,776**
Males	12,755	12,245	12,544
Females	10,697	9,992	10,232

* Figures have been assessed independently, therefore totals are not always equal to the sum of component parts.

Health and Welfare

KEY INDICATORS

Total fertility rate (children per woman, 2020)	2.4
Under-5 mortality rate (per 1,000 live births, 2020) . . .	32.2
HIV/AIDS (% of persons aged 15–49, 2020)	19.1
COVID-19: Cumulative confirmed deaths (per 100,000 persons at 31 August 2022)	171.9
COVID-19: Fully vaccinated population (% of total population at 31 August 2022)	32.5
Physicians (per 1,000 head, 2019)	0.8
Hospitals (per 100,000 head, 2013)	0.7
Domestic health expenditure (2019): US $ per head (PPP) .	697.7
Domestic health expenditure (2019): % of GDP	5.4
Domestic health expenditure (2019): public (% of total current expenditure)	58.8
Access to improved water resources (% of persons, 2020) .	94
Access to improved sanitation facilities (% of persons, 2020) .	78
Total carbon dioxide emissions ('000 metric tons, 2018) . .	433,250
Carbon dioxide emissions per head (metric tons, 2018) . .	7.5
Human Development Index (2021): ranking	109
Human Development Index (2021): value	0.713

Note: For data on COVID-19 vaccinations, 'fully vaccinated' denotes receipt of all doses specified by approved vaccination regime (Sources: Johns Hopkins University and Our World in Data). Data on health expenditure refer to current general government expenditure in each case. For more information on sources and further definitions for all indicators, see Health and Welfare Statistics: Sources and Definitions section (europaworld.com/ credits).

Agriculture

PRINCIPAL CROPS
('000 metric tons)

	2018	2019	2020
Apples	829.6	892.0	993.0
Apricots	26.5	25.3	21.5
Avocados	127.6	89.1	98.0*
Bananas	444.9	405.1	402.0*
Barley	421.5	345.0	589.8
Beans, dry	69.4	66.4	64.8
Beans, green	24.0	21.0	19.8*
Cabbages and other brassicas	160.7	165.4	162.2*
Carrots and turnips	215.5	225.3	229.5*
Chillies and peppers, dry*	17.6	17.3	17.4
Cotton lint	28.8	24.0	n.a.
Cucumbers and gherkins	26.8	29.1	30.1*
Grapefruit and pomelos	445.4	378.6	416.1
Grapes	1,901.7	1,883.3	2,028.2
Groundnuts, with shell	57.0	19.4	50.1
Lemons and limes	474.1	510.5	667.2
Lettuce and chicory	33.1	32.0	32.5*
Maize	12,510.0	11,275.5	15,300.0
Maize, green	388.6	395.5	398.0*
Mangoes, mangosteens and guavas	91.3	112.5	115.3*
Mushrooms and truffles	21.1	22.9	24.3*
Oats	32.7	16.5	56.2
Onions, dry	726.8	707.2	735.8*
Oranges	1,775.8	1,686.5	1,555.1
Peaches and nectarines	152.4	144.3	172.3
Pears	397.6	407.2	431.0
Pineapples	112.4	115.1	112.4*
Plums and sloes	74.3	61.0	58.8
Potatoes	2,467.7	2,505.8	2,547.0*
Pumpkins, squash and gourds	266.7	270.5	266.2*
Rapeseed	104.0	95.0	167.0
Seed cotton	101.7	128.8	118.1
Sorghum	115.0	127.0	158.0
Soybeans (Soya beans)	1,540.0	1,170.3	1,245.5
Soybean oil	185.0†	n.a.	n.a.
Sugar cane	19,301.7	19,242.0	18,220.0
Sunflower oil	296.5	n.a.	n.a.
Sunflower seed	862.0	678.0	788.5
Sweet potatoes	86.2	88.7	82.5*
Tangerines, mandarins, etc.*	177.6	176.3	176.8
Tobacco, unmanufactured	15.6	15.0	13.1
Tomatoes	537.3	555.5	581.5*
Watermelons	75.2	76.0	78.9*
Wheat	1,868.0	1,535.0	2,109.1

* FAO estimate(s).
† Unofficial figure.

Aggregate production ('000 metric tons, may include official, semi-official or estimated data): Total cereals 14,971.8 in 2018, 13,323.7 in 2019, 18,237.2 in 2020; Total fruit (primary) 7,239.8 in 2018, 7,089.5 in 2019, 7,456.7 in 2020; Total oilcrops 2,686.1 in 2018, 2,113.1 in 2019, 2,390.6 in 2020; Total roots and tubers 2,553.9 in 2018, 2,594.5 in 2019, 2,629.5 in 2020; Total vegetables (primary) 2,573.3 in 2018, 2,593.4 in 2019, 2,636.2 in 2020.

Source: FAO.

LIVESTOCK
('000 head, year ending September)

	2018	2019	2020
Asses*	150	150	150
Cattle	12,790	12,589	12,298
Chickens*	176,078	177,548	179,017
Ducks*	412	415	417
Geese and guinea fowls*	142	143	144
Goats	5,405	5,251	5,170
Horses*	325	323	326
Pigs	1,454	1,390	1,357
Sheep	22,500	22,085	21,605
Turkeys*	542	545	547

* FAO estimates.

Source: FAO.

LIVESTOCK PRODUCTS
('000 metric tons)

	2018	2019	2020
Cattle hides, fresh*	125.9	130.1	130.3
Cattle meat	1,003.2	1,036.8	1,038.7
Cattle offals, edible*	291.8	301.6	302.2
Cows' milk	3,752.6	3,873.5	3,821.5
Chicken meat	1,754.6	1,808.2	1,873.2
Game meat*	48.5	47.5	47.8
Pig meat	265.5	279.8	302.0
Sheep meat	162.3	174.2	165.0
Sheep offals, edible*	56.3	60.4	57.2
Sheepskins, fresh*	23.5	25.2	23.9
Hen eggs*	475.6	564.7	593.5
Wool, greasy*	47.7	47.0	47.3

* FAO estimates.

Source: FAO.

Forestry

ROUNDWOOD REMOVALS
('000 cubic metres, excl. bark)

	2018	2019	2020
Sawlogs, veneer logs and logs for sleepers	4,702.4	2,786.5	5,309.7
Pulpwood	9,786.3	12,220.4	9,986.8
Other industrial wood	1,268.0*	1,290.5	1,365.2*
Fuel wood*	12,025.8	12,025.3	12,025.2
Total*	27,782.5	28,322.7	28,687.0

* FAO estimate(s).

Source: FAO.

SAWNWOOD PRODUCTION
('000 cubic metres, incl. railway sleepers, FAO estimates)

	2018	2019	2020
Coniferous (softwood)	2,000.0	2,000.0	2,000.0
Broadleaved (hardwood)	259.3	259.3	200.0
Total	2,259.3	2,259.3	2,200.0

Source: FAO.

Fishing

('000 metric tons, live weight)

	2018	2019	2020
Capture*	559.6	441.2	595.9
Cape hakes (Stokvisse)	125.7	128.6	142.7
Southern African pilchard	38.6	5.3	24.6
Whitehead's round herring	48.3	47.3	53.9
Southern African anchovy	253.2	164.7	285.0
Cape horse mackerel	23.6	28.0	28.8
Aquaculture	6.3	7.1	6.0
Total catch*†	565.9	448.3	601.9

* FAO estimates.
† Excluding seaweeds and other aquatic plants ('000 metric tons): 12.5 (capture 10.8, aquaculture 1.7) in 2018; 10.1 (capture 7.9, aquaculture 2.2) in 2019; 10.6 (capture 6.8, aquaculture 3.7) in 2020.

Note: Figures exclude aquatic animals, recorded by number rather than weight. The number of Nile crocodiles captured was: 55,076 in 2018; 68,820 in 2019; 43,407 in 2020.

Source: FAO.

Mining

('000 metric tons unless otherwise indicated)

	2016	2017	2018
Hard coal (anthracite)	2,635	2,886	3,317
Bituminous coal*	244,000	246,000	246,000
Natural gas	901	822	685
Iron ore†	43,000	47,600	47,200
Copper ore (metric tons)† . . .	65,300	65,500	48,100
Nickel ore (metric tons)† . . .	48,994	48,383	43,236
Lead concentrates (metric tons)† .	39,344	48,150	35,000*
Zinc ore (metric tons)† . .	26,695	30,778	28,129
Manganese ore and concentrates (metallurgical and chemical)‡ .	10,800	14,100	14,900
Chromium ore‡	14,700	16,500	17,600
Vanadium ore (metric tons)‡ . .	8,163	7,959	7,700
Zirconium concentrates (metric tons)	377,430	361,813	350,000*
Antimony concentrates (metric tons)†	350	n.a.	n.a.
Cobalt ore (metric tons)*† . .	2,300	2,300	2,300
Silver (kg)	55,622	62,536	46,467
Uranium oxide (metric tons) . .	382	310*	196
Gold (kg)	142,202	137,133	117,150
Platinum-group metals (kg) . .	264,000	260,000	271,000
Kaolin	21.1	31.3	23.7
Magnesite—crude*	60.0	80.0	90.0
Phosphate rock‡	1,697	2,079	2,058
Fluorspar	177	223	242
Salt	473.3	492.8	476.1
Diamonds ('000 carats) . . .	8,306	9,698	9,911
Gypsum—crude	262.4	320.7	313.9
Mica (metric tons)	8	21	32
Talc (metric tons)	4,462	3,728	3,897
Pyrophyllite (metric tons) . .	19,114	55,048	98,245

* Estimated figure(s).
† Figures refer to metal content of ores and concentrates.
‡ Gross weight.

Crude petroleum ('000 barrels): 139 in 2013.

Source: US Geological Survey.

Industry

SELECTED PRODUCTS
('000 metric tons unless otherwise indicated)

	2017	2018	2019
Chemical wood pulp	904	874	755
Newsprint	181	114	114
Motor spirit (petrol)	5,983	5,668	4,795
Kerosene	619	605	596
Jet fuel	2,062	2,019	2,100
Distillate fuel oils	5,861*	5,417	8,539
Petroleum bitumen—asphalt . .	475	n.a.	n.a.
Cement (sales)*	14,000	15,000	n.a.
Pig-iron	4,352	4,611	n.a.
Crude steel	6,301	6,327	n.a.
Refined copper—unwrought . .	65.5	48.1	n.a.
Electrical energy (million kWh) .	257,702	256,064	252,639

* Estimated figure.

Wheat flour (twelve months ending September): 2,527 in 2016.

2020: Chemical wood pulp 744; Newsprint 114.

Sources: FAO; UN Industrial Commodity Statistics Database; UN Energy Statistics Database; US Geological Survey.

Finance

CURRENCY, EXCHANGE RATES AND FISCAL YEAR

Monetary Units
100 cents = 1 rand (R).

Sterling, Dollar and Euro Equivalents (31 May 2022)
£1 sterling = 19.69 rand;
US $1 = 15.64 rand;
€1 = 16.75 rand;
100 rand = £5.08 = $6.39 = €5.97.

Average Exchange Rate (rand per US $)
2019   14.4484
2020   16.4591
2021   14.7787

Fiscal Year
The fiscal year ends on 31 March.

BUDGET
(million rand, fiscal year)

Revenue	2019/20	2020/21	2021/22*
Tax revenue (gross) . . .	1,355,766.3	1,249,711.2	1,547,070.5
Taxes on incomes and profits .	772,684.8	718,180.5	910,106.7
Individuals	527,632.5	487,011.1	553,529.2
Companies (including secondary tax)	240,048.6	227,459.1	351,042.4
Other	5,003.7	3,710.3	5,535.0
Taxes on payroll and workforce.	18,486.3	12,250.2	18,932.8
Taxes on property	15,979.9	15,946.6	19,693.3
Domestic taxes on goods and services	492,282.8	455,866.6	541,296.1
Value-added tax	346,760.8	331,196.8	383,723.9
Excise duties	53,397.0	37,704.7	54,698.8
Levies on fuel	80,175.2	75,502.8	89,883.8
Air departure tax	1,068.3	138.5	201.1
Other	10,881.6	11,323.8	12,788.4
State miscellaneous revenue .	10.0	11.9	—
Taxes on international trade and transactions	56,322.4	47,455.4	57,041.6
Departmental revenue . .	40,384.0	52,053.5	47,963.9
Sub-total	1,396,150.2	1,301,764.7	1,595,034.4
Less SACU payments† . .	50,280.3	63,395.2	45,966.2
Total	1,345,869.9	1,238,369.5	1,549,068.2

Expenditure	2019/20	2020/21	2021/22*
Central government administration	115,320.5	130,147.3	128,828.0
The Presidency	639.3	517.8	604.6
Parliament	1,993.5	2,015.8	2,144.1
Co-operative governance and traditional affairs	86,782.0	103,305.8	98,984.9
Foreign affairs	6,368.6	6,245.9	6,517.9
Home affairs	9,527.5	8,470.3	9,431.4
Planning, monitoring and evaluation	1,114.8	1,099.2	1,216.6
Public works	7,820.2	7,531.0	8,354.2
National school of government .	183.0	221.6	213.6
Traditional affairs . . .	160.7	137.5	165.2
Women, youth and persons with disabilities	730.9	602.4	1,195.5
Financial and administrative services	89,934.5	114,967.9	86,637.1
National treasury . . .	29,771.2	34,081.5	44,612.7
Public enterprises . . .	56,846.4	77,503.4	36,274.8
Public services and administration	763.4	691.7	818.0
Statistics South Africa . .	2,553.5	2,691.3	4,931.6
Social services	371,800.7	411,916.0	434,097.6
Arts and culture	5,468.5	5,175.5	5,728.3
Education	113,160.3	118,020.7	125,779.2
Health	50,772.8	58,116.6	65,108.7
Labour	3,215.9	3,103.1	3,783.5
Social development . . .	199,183.2	227,500.1	233,697.9
Justice and protection services .	191,617.6	194,455.5	197,076.3
Correctional services . .	25,184.8	25,027.1	25,943.3
Defence	50,229.7	54,086.2	48,796.4

Expenditure—*continued*	2019/20	2020/21	2021/22*
Independent complaints directorate	336.6	340.9	353.8
Justice and constitutional development	19,798.9	19,386.6	21,357.9
Safety and security . . .	96,067.6	95,614.7	100,624.9
Economic services and infrastructure	176,241.1	152,940.8	179,167.5
Communications	5,663.8	3,164.6	3,862.4
Environmental affairs . .	8,691.4	8,300.0	7,544.9
Human settlements . . .	33,345.6	28,775.5	31,624.8
Mineral resources and energy .	8,915.5	7,184.9	9,175.5
Rural development and land reform	16,948.1	14,093.0	18,023.3
Tourism	2,384.4	1,392.2	2,545.3
Science and technology . . .	8,081.4	7,165.3	9,005.6
Trade and industry . . .	13,104.7	11,288.9	14,364.1
Transport	63,888.6	57,073.8	65,286.5
Water affairs	15,217.6	14,502.6	17,735.1
Sub-total	944,857.1	1,004,428.1	1,025,806.5
State debt costs	204,769.4	232,595.7	268,306.2
Provincial equitable share .	505,553.8	520,717.0	544,834.9
Skills levy and SETAs . .	18,283.8	12,413.0	18,932.8
Members' remuneration . .	600.5	476.5	471.7
Judges' salaries	3,151.9	3,190.4	3,514.9
President and Deputy President salary	5.7	5.7	7.5
General fuel levy sharing with metros	13,166.8	14,026.9	14,617.3
National revenue fund payments .	468.5	588.3	2,008.5
Auditor-General of South Africa .	62.8	70.0	70.0
International oil pollution compensation fund (transport) .	2.6	—	11.6
Payments under section 70 and section 16 of the Public Management Finance Act (1999)	—	484.7	21,635.5
National government projected underspending	—	—	−4,263.0
Total	1,690,980.0	1,788,996.2	1,895,954.4

* Estimates.

† Payments to Botswana, Eswatini, Lesotho and Namibia, in accordance with Southern African Customs Union agreements.

Source: National Treasury, Pretoria.

INTERNATIONAL RESERVES
(US $ million at 31 December)

	2019	2020	2021
Gold (national valuation) . . .	6,140	7,626	7,327
IMF special drawing rights . .	2,069	2,157	6,189
Reserve position in IMF . . .	946	961	924
Foreign exchange	45,904	44,270	43,149
Total	55,060	55,013	57,589

Source: IMF, *International Financial Statistics.*

MONEY SUPPLY
(million rand at 31 December)

	2019	2020	2021
Currency outside depository corporations	127,072	139,569	144,403
Transferable deposits . . .	793,947	955,367	1,014,623
Other deposits	2,258,571	2,563,929	2,752,436
Securities other than shares . .	584,189	459,738	442,312
Broad money	3,763,779	4,118,602	4,353,774

Source: IMF, *International Financial Statistics.*

COST OF LIVING
(Consumer Price Index; base: December 2021 = 100)

	2019	2020	2021
Food and non-alcoholic beverages .	88.5	92.4	98.0
Clothing and footwear	97.1	97.9	99.3
Housing and utilities	91.1	94.5	97.6
All items (incl. others) . . .	90.3	93.2	97.5

NATIONAL ACCOUNTS
(million rand at current prices)

National Income and Product

	2019	2020	2021
Compensation of employees . .	2,732,292	2,678,050	2,861,309
Net operating surplus . . .	1,480,045	1,493,978	1,795,000
Consumption of fixed capital . .	726,169	752,613	797,230
Gross domestic product (GDP) at factor cost	4,938,506	4,924,641	5,453,539
Taxes on production	698,076	659,479	798,332
Less Subsidies	22,917	27,204	26,459
GDP at market prices . . .	5,613,665	5,556,916	6,225,412
Primary incomes received from abroad	123,324	128,789	167,431
Less Primary incomes paid abroad	263,240	221,488	286,029
Gross national income at market prices	5,473,749	5,464,217	6,106,814
Current transfers received from abroad	45,797	58,826	56,596
Less Current transfers paid abroad	80,367	101,022	92,360
Gross national disposable income at market prices .	5,439,179	5,422,021	6,071,050

Expenditure on the Gross Domestic Product

	2019	2020	2021
Government final consumption expenditure	1,104,496	1,155,421	1,216,650
Private final consumption expenditure	3,588,896	3,474,446	3,819,180
Increase in stocks	24,451	−75,671	−18,227
Gross fixed capital formation . .	865,499	764,731	810,714
Residual item	—	−6,495	15,040
Total domestic expenditure	5,583,341	5,312,433	5,843,357
Exports of goods and services . .	1,532,389	1,533,726	1,931,676
Less Imports of goods and services	1,502,065	1,289,242	1,549,621
GDP at market prices . . .	5,613,665	5,556,916	6,225,412
GDP at constant 2015 prices .	4,584,101	4,293,356	4,504,292

Gross Domestic Product by Economic Activity

	2019	2020	2021
Agriculture, forestry and fishing .	110,148	140,070	152,807
Mining and quarrying	314,382	351,790	474,946
Manufacturing	696,043	648,071	729,804
Electricity, gas and water . . .	151,136	157,151	171,651
Construction (contractors) . .	165,387	136,238	141,002
Wholesale and retail trade, catering and accommodation .	698,551	654,551	751,303
Transport, storage and communication	417,314	369,814	397,753
Finance, insurance, real estate and business services	1,206,927	1,229,160	1,320,471
Government services	438,690	474,647	498,256
Other community, social and personal services	846,349	868,084	934,615
Gross value added at basic prices	5,044,926	5,029,575	5,572,608
Taxes, less subsidies, on products .	568,739	527,341	652,804
GDP at market prices . . .	5,613,665	5,556,916	6,225,412

BALANCE OF PAYMENTS
(US $ million)

	2019	2020	2021
Exports of goods	90,095.7	85,464.0	121,708.9
Imports of goods	−87,473.6	−67,704.7	−91,196.9
Balance on goods . . .	**2,622.2**	**17,759.3**	**30,512.0**
Exports of services . . .	15,902.5	8,652.5	9,103.2
Imports of services	−16,484.9	−11,308.6	−13,586.7
Balance on goods and services	**2,039.8**	**15,103.2**	**26,028.4**
Primary income received . . .	8,541.1	7,892.1	11,347.1
Primary income paid . . .	−18,251.9	−13,611.7	−19,418.8
Balance on goods, services and primary income	**−7,671.0**	**9,383.6**	**17,956.7**
Secondary income received . .	3,168.4	3,587.8	3,819.1
Secondary income paid . . .	−5,562.5	−6,173.2	−6,247.1
Current balance	**−10,065.0**	**6,798.2**	**15,528.7**
Capital account (net) . . .	16.9	14.3	15.2
Direct investment assets . .	−3,140.9	1,935.9	6.4
Direct investment liabilities . .	5,116.1	3,153.6	41,289.1
Portfolio investment assets . .	2,841.7	2,922.6	−26,885.2
Portfolio investment liabilities .	6,076.6	−9,671.5	−28,302.3
Financial derivatives and employee stock options (net) . . .	−377.9	−654.8	−24.8
Other investment assets . . .	360.0	−10,469.3	176.6
Other investment liabilities . .	−2,072.0	−2,661.7	856.1
Net errors and omissions . . .	2,857.3	979.7	1,954.6
Reserves and related items .	**1,612.6**	**−7,653.2**	**4,614.4**

Source: IMF, *International Financial Statistics*.

External Trade

PRINCIPAL COMMODITIES
(distribution by HS, million rand)

Imports c.i.f.	2019	2020	2021
Prepared foodstuffs; beverages, spirits, vinegar; tobacco and articles thereof	29,250.9	38,120.7	41,847.8
Mineral products	159,225.7	160,260.7	233,510.7
Mineral fuels, oils, distillation products, etc.	155,270.0	156,842.5	228,264.5
Crude petroleum oils . .	88,178.6	82,962.5	80,083.3
Non-crude petroleum oils . .	51,170.2	58,056.7	123,327.8
Chemicals and related products	100,183.9	146,009.1	173,291.3
Pharmaceutical products . .	25,872.5	39,230.9	45,209.6
Plastics, rubber, and articles thereof	40,378.9	48,916.4	63,592.6
Textiles and textile articles .	35,578.9	50,640.6	51,127.4
Iron and steel; other base metals and articles of base metal	48,344.8	58,089.3	84,275.3
Machinery and mechanical appliances; electrical equipment; parts thereof .	215,591.9	263,513.6	293,847.4
Machinery, boilers, etc. . .	121,878.2	148,009.8	166,575.5
Electrical, electronic equipment .	93,713.7	115,503.7	127,271.9
Electric appliances for line telephony, etc. . .	33,113.2	40,174.3	45,528.9
Vehicles, aircraft, vessels and associated transport equipment	87,692.2	79,822.3	106,033.4
Vehicles other than railway, tramway	75,684.0	70,842.5	93,078.2
Cars (incl. station wagons) . .	41,528.5	33,674.3	45,980.7
Components and parts for motor vehicles	87,178.9	82,640.6	110,416.3
Total (incl. others)	**953,963.8**	**1,123,384.5**	**1,379,644.2**

Exports f.o.b.	2019	2020	2021
Vegetables and vegetable products	55,579.2	89,377.0	95,293.9
Edible fruit and nuts . . .	41,723.9	62,559.5	65,225.7
Prepared foodstuffs; beverages, spirits, vinegar; tobacco and articles thereof .	41,114.4	58,152.9	59,574.4
Mineral products	242,188.8	329,450.0	438,534.2
Ores, slag and ash	143,877.7	214,347.8	275,095.1
Iron ore and concentrates . .	62,274.2	107,247.4	145,381.5
Mineral fuels, oils, distillation products, etc.	92,287.6	108,223.4	155,780.2
Coal, briquettes, ovoids and similar solid fuels manufactured from coal . .	48,567.9	60,264.4	88,873.1
Non-crude petroleum oils . .	30,709.7	29,302.3	27,419.1
Chemicals and related products	59,495.6	90,640.7	113,011.7
Pearls, precious or semi-precious stones, precious metals, and articles thereof .	148,179.6	324,174.4	513,288.4
Gold, unwrought or in semi-manufactured forms . . .	43,987.7	108,307.8	107,996.7
Platinum, unwrought or in semi-manufactured forms	79,330.4	175,188.2	341,740.2
Iron and steel; other base metals and articles of base metal	106,720.3	126,060.6	169,985.6
Iron and steel	59,422.2	64,419.0	92,569.6
Ferro alloys	36,295.7	43,736.3	61,291.4
Machinery and mechanical appliances; electrical equipment; parts thereof .	77,191.7	105,119.2	123,024.5
Machinery, boilers, etc. . .	58,908.5	80,396.7	97,945.0
Vehicles, aircraft, vessels and associated transport equipment	134,323.9	144,843.3	167,782.9
Vehicles other than railway, tramway	125,382.5	135,437.3	157,254.1
Cars (incl. station wagons) . .	72,911.6	74,549.3	78,832.8
Trucks, motor vehicles for the transport of goods	39,731.3	44,798.0	59,062.7
Total (incl. others)	**953,392.2**	**1,394,959.4**	**1,820,394.6**

Source: Department of Trade and Industry, Pretoria.

PRINCIPAL TRADING PARTNERS
(million rand)*

Imports f.o.b.	2019	2020	2021
Australia	11,469.5	12,364.4	16,302.1
Belgium	10,127.3	14,526.2	20,230.5
Brazil	13,307.6	17,370.8	19,169.0
China, People's Republic . . .	176,546.1	232,958.5	283,865.0
Czech Republic	10,250.5	9,714.1	10,113.7
Eswatini	13,157.9	17,943.3	20,440.2
France (incl. Monaco)	21,538.9	25,517.7	29,018.5
Germany	98,714.7	102,162.6	111,429.4
India	46,150.1	58,491.7	78,911.7
Indonesia	7,483.9	10,258.8	14,644.3
Italy	24,701.0	28,724.9	37,982.9
Japan	31,145.3	31,270.5	38,427.4
Korea, Republic	9,394.4	11,079.6	16,257.8
Malaysia	10,169.7	12,468.3	14,918.3
Mozambique	9,665.6	10,753.6	11,592.7
Namibia	9,836.5	12,064.0	14,665.1
Netherlands	11,710.3	15,612.3	23,678.4
Nigeria	36,581.1	35,237.7	33,096.9
Oman	10,759.3	10,866.0	27,718.7
Poland	10,670.8	14,003.0	13,854.9
Saudi Arabia	37,967.7	43,846.4	60,613.9

Imports f.o.b.—*continued*	2019	2020	2021
Spain	17,138.9	24,190.7	23,211.5
Sweden	11,331.8	11,783.2	13,664.3
Switzerland	8,162.6	15,597.5	16,126.5
Thailand	29,939.2	34,933.9	43,920.6
Türkiye	6,712.5	9,058.1	13,808.4
United Arab Emirates	22,649.3	19,652.8	27,977.6
United Kingdom	30,497.9	27,652.5	27,675.1
USA	61,961.5	72,006.1	96,684.1
Viet Nam	10,799.0	14,338.5	15,708.7
Total (incl. others)	953,963.8	1,123,384.5	1,379,644.2

Exports f.o.b.	2019	2020	2021
Belgium	30,008.7	38,896.7	52,324.8
Botswana	40,952.9	53,183.4	64,661.7
China, People's Republic . .	103,404.6	164,205.7	200,653.1
Congo, Democratic Republic . .	11,147.0	12,715.9	15,898.6
Eswatini	13,859.8	18,906.2	22,305.3
Germany	79,314.0	113,523.5	155,066.6
Hong Kong	15,222.4	24,893.7	35,184.4
India	40,987.0	49,355.2	61,920.5
Japan	46,632.1	62,102.5	121,301.6
Korea, Republic	15,915.9	23,070.5	31,635.8
Lesotho	13,375.5	17,017.9	20,880.7
Mozambique	36,735.2	49,927.2	64,144.8
Namibia	37,555.6	43,510.1	50,759.6
Netherlands	32,841.1	54,480.8	60,670.9
Spain	12,557.8	14,909.8	28,470.9
United Arab Emirates	18,531.1	25,028.2	33,731.8
United Kingdom	48,678.7	68,862.7	120,702.3
USA	64,946.1	116,036.7	192,932.1
Zambia	22,794.9	27,931.8	34,445.8
Zimbabwe	21,074.7	36,202.2	43,088.0
Total (incl. others)	953,392.2	1,394,959.4	1,820,394.6

* Imports by country of origin; exports by country of destination.

Source: Department of Trade and Industry, Pretoria.

Transport

RAILWAYS
(traffic, preliminary)

	2019	2020	2021
Passengers ('000)	174,599	29,628	21,762
Total freight ('000 metric tons) .	215,740	191,847	178,795

ROAD TRAFFIC
(registered motor vehicles at 31 December)

	2016	2017
Passenger cars	6,996,599	7,172,283
Buses and coaches	369,586	381,682
Lorries and vans	2,806,086	2,871,280
Motorcycles and mopeds	358,351	351,756

Source: National Department of Transport, Pretoria.

SHIPPING
Flag Registered Fleet
(at 31 December)

	2019	2020	2021
Number of vessels	234	252	265
Total displacement ('000 grt) . .	402.0	329.1	436.8

Source: Lloyd's List Intelligence (www.bit.ly/LLintelligence).

International Seaborne Freight Traffic

	2010	2011	2012
Goods loaded ('000 metric tons) .	145,263.2	155,43.3	161,897.9
Goods unloaded ('000 metric tons)	48,066.7	48,965.2	48,059.2
Containers loaded (TEU) . . .	2,001,629	2,173,135	2,114,124
Containers unloaded (TEU) . .	2,010,846	2,219,656	2,194,945

Source: National Ports Authority of South Africa.

CIVIL AVIATION
(traffic on scheduled services)

	2013	2014	2015
Kilometres flown (million) . .	219	229	224
Passengers carried ('000) . . .	16,311	16,949	17,189
Passenger-km (million) . . .	32,259	31,603	31,075
Total ton-km (million)	1,123	1,043	885

Source: UN, *Statistical Yearbook*.

2019 (domestic and international): Departures 88,579; Passengers carried 8.3m.; Freight carried 102m. ton-km (Source: World Bank, World Development Indicators database).

Tourism

INTERNATIONAL TOURIST ARRIVALS*

Country of origin	2019	2020	2021
Botswana	668,315	129,467	103,158
Eswatini	917,631	214,947	177,650
Germany	322,720	106,092	44,388
Lesotho	1,563,448	448,745	355,255
Mozambique	1,333,195	422,537	522,866
Namibia	184,431	54,511	91,471
United Kingdom	436,559	132,384	45,777
USA	373,694	71,959	82,020
Zimbabwe	2,258,794	684,546	410,730
Total (incl. others and unspecified)	10,228,593	2,802,320	2,255,699

* Figures exclude same-day visitors (excursionists) and arrivals of South African nationals resident abroad. Border crossings by contract workers are also excluded.

Total visitor arrivals: 15,825,296 in 2019; 4,586,387 in 2020; 3,150,007 in 2021.

Tourism receipts (US $ million, excl. passenger transport): 8,818 in 2017; 8,944 in 2018; 8,384 in 2019 (provisional) (Source: World Tourism Organization).

Communications Media

	2018	2019	2020
Telephones ('000 main lines in use)	3,345	2,025	2,099
Mobile telephone subscriptions ('000)	92,428	96,972	95,959
Broadband subscriptions, fixed ('000)	1,107	1,250	1,303
Broadband subscriptions, mobile ('000)	44,781	59,859	65,628
Internet users (% of population)*	62.4	68.2	70.0

* Estimates.

Source: International Telecommunication Union.

Education

(2020 unless otherwise indicated)*

	Institutions	Teachers	Students
Primary†	14,795	203,139	6,929,834
Secondary†	6,186	140,532	3,989,236
Combined†	4,593	74,942	2,013,465
Intermediate†	497	6,495	208,521
Community education and training colleges	9	12,566	142,538
ELSEN centres†‡	455	9,972	119,403
TVET colleges§	50	n.a.	452,277
ECD†‖	3,896	11,980	267,694
Higher education¶	26	15,318	1,094,808

* Figures for public and independent institutions unless otherwise indicated.
† Figures for 2016.
‡ Education for learners with special needs.
§ Technical and vocational education and training.
‖ Early childhood development.
¶ Figures refer to public institutions only.

Source: Department of Education.

Pupil-teacher ratio (primary education, UNESCO estimate): 30.3 in 2014/15 (Source: UNESCO Institute for Statistics).

Adult literacy rate (UNESCO estimates): 87.0% (males 87.7%; females 86.5%) in 2017 (Source: UNESCO Institute for Statistics).

Directory

The Constitution

The Constitution was adopted by the Constitutional Assembly (comprising the National Assembly and the Senate) on 8 May 1996, and entered into force on 4 February 1997. Its main provisions are summarized below:

FOUNDING PROVISIONS

The Republic of South Africa is one sovereign democratic state founded on the following values: human dignity, the achievement of equality and advancement of human rights and freedoms; non-racialism and non-sexism; supremacy of the Constitution and the rule of law; universal adult suffrage, a national common voters' roll, regular elections, and a multi-party system of democratic government, to ensure accountability, responsiveness and openness. There is common South African citizenship, all citizens being equally entitled to the rights, privileges and benefits, and equally subject to the duties and responsibilities of citizenship.

BILL OF RIGHTS

Everyone is equal before the law and has the right to equal protection and benefit of the law. The state may not unfairly discriminate directly or indirectly against anyone on one or more grounds, including race, gender, sex, pregnancy, marital status, ethnic or social origin, colour, sexual orientation, age, disability, religion, conscience, belief, culture, language and birth. The rights that are enshrined include: protection against detention without trial, torture or any inhuman form of treatment or punishment; the right to privacy; freedom of conscience; freedom of expression; freedom of assembly; political freedom; freedom of movement and residence; the right to join or form a trade union or employers' organization; the right to a healthy and sustainable environment; the right to property, except in the case of the Government's programme of land reform and redistribution, and taking into account the claims of people who were dispossessed of property after 19 June 1913; the right to adequate housing; the right to health care, food and water and social security assistance, if needed; the rights of children; the right to education in the official language of one's choice, where this is reasonably practicable; the right to use the language and to participate in the cultural life of one's choice, but not in a manner inconsistent with any provision of this Bill of Rights; access to state information; access to the courts; the rights of people who have been arrested or detained; and the right to a fair trial.

CO-OPERATIVE GOVERNMENT

Government is constituted as national, provincial and local spheres of government, which are distinctive, interdependent and interrelated. All spheres of government and all organs of state within each sphere must preserve the peace, national unity and indivisibility of the Republic; secure the well-being of the people of the Republic; implement effective, transparent, accountable and coherent government for the Republic as a whole; respect the constitutional status, institutions, powers and functions of government in the other spheres; not assume any power or function except those conferred on them in terms of the Constitution.

PARLIAMENT

Legislative power is vested in a bicameral Parliament, comprising a National Assembly and a National Council of Provinces. The National Assembly has between 350 and 400 members and is elected, in general, by proportional representation. National and provincial legislatures are elected separately, under a 'double-ballot' electoral system. Each provincial legislature appoints six permanent delegates and nominates four special delegates to the 90-member National Council of Provinces, which is headed by a Chairperson, who is elected by the Council and has a five-year term of office. Parliamentary decisions are generally reached by a simple majority, although constitutional amendments require a majority of two-thirds.

THE NATIONAL EXECUTIVE

The head of state is the President, who is elected by the National Assembly from among its members, and exercises executive power in consultation with the other members of the Cabinet. No person may hold office as President for more than two terms. Any party that holds a minimum of 80 seats in the National Assembly (equivalent to 20% of the national vote) is entitled to nominate an Executive Deputy President. If no party, or only one party, secures 80 or more seats, the party holding the largest number of seats and the party holding the second largest number of seats in the National Assembly are each entitled to designate one Executive Deputy President from among the members of the Assembly. The President may be removed by a motion of no confidence or by impeachment. The Cabinet comprises a maximum of 27 ministers. Each party with a minimum of 20 seats in the National Assembly (equivalent to 5% of the national vote) is entitled to a proportional number of ministerial portfolios. The President allocates cabinet portfolios in consultation with party leaders, who are entitled to request the replacement of ministers. Cabinet decisions are reached by consensus.

JUDICIAL AUTHORITY

The judicial authority of the Republic is vested in the courts, which comprise the Constitutional Court; the Supreme Court of Appeal; the

High Courts; the Magistrates' Courts; and any other court established or recognized by an Act of Parliament. (See Judicial System)

PROVINCIAL GOVERNMENT

There are nine provinces: Eastern Cape, Free State (formerly Orange Free State), Gauteng (formerly Pretoria-Witwatersrand-Vereeniging), KwaZulu/Natal, Limpopo (formerly Northern Transvaal, subsequently Northern Province), Mpumalanga (formerly Eastern Transvaal), Northern Cape, North-West and Western Cape. Each province is entitled to determine its legislative and executive structure. Each province has a legislature, comprising between 30 and 80 members (depending on the size of the local electorate), who are elected by proportional representation. Each legislature is entitled to draft a constitution for the province, subject to the principles governing the national Constitution, and elects a Premier, who heads a Cabinet. Parties that hold a minimum of 10% of seats in the legislature are entitled to a proportional number of portfolios in the Cabinet. Provincial legislatures are allowed primary responsibility for a number of areas of government, and joint powers with central government in the principal administrative areas.

LOCAL GOVERNMENT

The local sphere of government consists of municipalities, with executive and legislative authority vested in the Municipal Council. The objectives of local government are to provide democratic and accountable government for local communities; to ensure the provision of services to communities; to promote social and economic development, and a safe and healthy environment; and to encourage the involvement of communities and community organizations in the matters of local government. The National Assembly is to determine the different categories of municipality that may be established, and appropriate fiscal powers and functions for each category. Provincial Governments have the task of establishing municipalities, and of providing for the monitoring and support of local government in each province.

STATE INSTITUTIONS SUPPORTING CONSTITUTIONAL DEMOCRACY

The following state institutions are designed to strengthen constitutional democracy: the Public Protector (whose task is to investigate any conduct in state affairs, or in the public administration in any sphere of government, that is alleged or suspected to be improper); the Human Rights Commission; the Commission for the Protection and Promotion of the Rights of Cultural, Religious and Linguistic Communities; the Commission for Gender Equality; the Auditor-General; and the Electoral Commission.

TRADITIONAL LEADERS

The institution, status and role of traditional leadership, according to customary law, are recognized, subject to the Constitution. A traditional authority that observes a system of customary law may function subject to any applicable legislation and customs. National and provincial legislation may provide for the establishment of local or provincial houses of traditional leaders; the National Assembly may establish a national council of traditional leaders.

The Government

HEAD OF STATE

President: CYRIL RAMAPHOSA (took office 15 February 2018; re-elected by vote of National Assembly 22 May 2019).
Deputy President: DAVID MABUZA.

THE CABINET
(October 2022)

President: CYRIL RAMAPHOSA.
Minister of Agriculture, Land Reform and Rural Development: ANGELA THOKO DIDIZA.
Minister of Basic Education: MATSIE ANGELINA MOTSHEKGA.
Minister of Communications and Digital Technologies: KHUMBUDZO NTSHAVHENI.
Minister of Co-operative Governance and Traditional Affairs: Dr NKOSAZANA DLAMINI-ZUMA.
Minister of Defence and Military Veterans: THANDI MODISE.
Minister of Employment and Labour and Acting Minister of Public Service and Administration: THEMBELANI WALTERMADE THULAS NXESI.
Minister of Finance: ENOCH GODONGWANA.
Minister of Forestry, Fisheries and the Environment: BARBARA DALLAS CREECY.

Minister of Health: Dr MATHUME JOSEPH 'JOE' PHAALA.
Minister of Higher Education, Science and Innovation: Dr BONGINKOSI EMMANUEL 'BLADE' NZIMANDE.
Minister of Home Affairs: Dr PAKISHE AARON MOTSOALEDI.
Minister of Human Settlements: MMAMOLOKO KUBAYI.
Minister of International Relations and Co-operation: Dr NALEDI PANDOR.
Minister of Justice and Correctional Services: RONALD OZZY LAMOLA.
Minister of Mineral Resources and Energy: SAMSON GWEDE MANTASHE.
Minister of Police: Gen. BHEKI CELE.
Minister in the Presidency: MONDLI GUNGUBELE.
Minister in the Presidency for Women, Youth and Persons with Disabilities: MAITE NKOANA-MASHABANE.
Minister of Public Enterprises: PRAVIN GORDHAN.
Minister of Public Works and Infrastructure: PATRICIA DE LILLE.
Minister of Small Business Development: STELLA NDABENI-ABRAHAMS.
Minister of Social Development: LINDIWE DAPHNE ZULU.
Minister of Sports, Arts and Culture: NKOSINATHI EMMANUEL 'NATHI' MTHETHWA.
Minister of Tourism: LINDIWE SISULU.
Minister of Trade and Industry: EBRAHIM PATEL.
Minister of Transport: FIKILE MBALULA.
Minister of Water and Sanitation: SENZO MCHUNU.

In addition, there were 35 deputy ministers.

MINISTRIES

The Presidency: Union Bldgs, West Wing, Government Ave, Pretoria 0001; Private Bag X1000, Pretoria 0001; tel. (12) 3005200; e-mail presidentrsa@presidency.gov.za; internet www.thepresidency.gov.za.
Ministry of Agriculture, Land Reform and Rural Development: Agriculture Bldg, 20 Steve Biko St, Arcadia, Pretoria 0002; Private Bag X250, Pretoria 0001; tel. (12) 3196000; e-mail info@dalrrd.gov.za; internet www.dalrrd.gov.za.
Ministry of Basic Education: 222 Struben St, Pretoria 0002; Private Bag X895, Pretoria 0001; tel. (12) 3573000; e-mail callcentre@dbe.gov.za; internet www.education.gov.za.
Ministry of Communications and Digital Technologies: Iparioli Office Park, 1166 Park St, Hatfield, Pretoria 0083; Private Bag X860, Pretoria 0001; tel. (12) 4278000; e-mail ministry@dtps.gov.za; internet www.doc.gov.za.
Ministry of Co-operative Governance and Traditional Affairs: 87 Hamilton St, Arcadia, Pretoria 0001; Private Bag X802, Pretoria 0001; tel. (12) 3340600; e-mail info@cogta.gov.za; internet www.cogta.gov.za.
Ministry of Defence and Military Veterans: Armscor Bldg, cnr Delmas Ave and Nossob Sts, Erasmuskloof 0181; Private Bag X427, Pretoria 0001; tel. (12) 3556999; e-mail info@dod.mil.za; internet www.dod.mil.za.
Ministry of Employment and Labour: Laboria House, 215 Francis Baard St, Pretoria 0001; Private Bag X117, Pretoria 0001; tel. (12) 3094000; e-mail cfcallcentre@labour.gov.za; internet www.labour.gov.za.
Ministry of Finance: 40 Church Sq., Pretoria 0002; Private Bag X115, Pretoria 0001; tel. (12) 3155046; e-mail media@treasury.gov.za; internet www.treasury.gov.za.
Ministry of Forestry, Fisheries and the Environment: Environment House, 473 Steve Biko St, cnr Soutpansberg Rd, Arcadia, Pretoria 0083; Private Bag X447, Pretoria 0001; tel. (12) 3999943; e-mail callcentre@environment.gov.za; internet www.environment.gov.za.
Ministry of Health: Dr AB Xuma Bldg, 1112 Voortrekker Rd, Pretoria Townlands 351-JR, Pretoria 0187; Private Bag X828, Pretoria 0001; tel. (12) 3958000; e-mail minister@health.gov.za; internet www.health.gov.za.
Ministry of Higher Education, Science and Innovation: 123 Francis Baard St, Pretoria 0001; Private Bag X174, Pretoria 0001; tel. (12) 3125911; e-mail callcentre@dhet.gov.za; internet www.dhet.gov.za.
Ministry of Home Affairs: Hallmark Bldg, 230 Johannes Ramokhoase St, Pretoria 0001; Private Bag X114, Pretoria 0001; tel. (12) 4062500; e-mail hacc@dha.gov.za; internet www.dha.gov.za.
Ministry of Human Settlements: Govan Mbeki House, 240 Justice Mahomed St, Sunnyside, Pretoria 0002; Private Bag X644,

Pretoria 0001; tel. (12) 4211311; e-mail info@dhs.gov.za; internet www.dhs.gov.za.

Ministry of International Relations and Co-operation: O. R. Tambo Bldg, 460 Soutpansberg Rd, Rietondale, Pretoria 0084; Private Bag X152, Pretoria 0001; tel. (12) 3511000; e-mail info@dirco .gov.za; internet www.dirco.gov.za.

Ministry of Justice and Correctional Services: Momentum Centre, 329 Pretorius St, cnr Sisulu St, Pretoria 0001; Private Bag X81, Pretoria 0001; tel. (12) 3151111; e-mail mediaenquiries@justice .gov.za; internet www.justice.gov.za.

Ministry of Mineral Resources and Energy: Trevenna Campus, Bldg 2c, Meintje and Francis Baard St, Sunnyside, Pretoria; Private Bag X59, Arcadia 0007, Pretoria; tel. (12) 4443000; e-mail enquiries@ dmr.gov.za; internet www.dmr.gov.za.

Ministry of Police: Koedoe Bldg, 236 Pretorius St, Pretoria; Private Bag X94, Pretoria 0001; tel. (12) 3931000; e-mail bloemb@saps.org .za; internet www.saps.gov.za.

Ministry of Public Enterprises: 80 Hamilton St, Arcadia, Pretoria 0007; Private Bag X15, Hatfield 0028; tel. (12) 4311000; e-mail info@ dpe.gov.za; internet www.dpe.gov.za.

Ministry of Public Service and Administration: Batho Pele House, 546 Edmond St, Arcadia; Private Bag X916, Pretoria 0001; tel. (12) 3361063; e-mail ministerinquiry@dpsa.gov.za; internet www.dpsa.gov.za.

Ministry of Public Works and Infrastructure: CGO Bldg, cnr Bosman and Madiba Sts, Pretoria 0001; Private Bag X65, Pretoria 0001; tel. (12) 4061000; e-mail dg.pa@dpw.gov.za; internet www .publicworks.gov.za.

Ministry of Small Business Development: 77 Meintjies St, Sunnyside, Pretoria 0002; Private Bag X672, Pretoria 0001; tel. (86) 1843384; e-mail info@dsbd.gov.za; internet www.dsbd.gov.za.

Ministry of Social Development: HSRC Bldg, 134 Pretorius St, Pretoria 0001; Private Bag X901, Pretoria 0001; tel. (12) 3127500; e-mail customercare@dsd.gov.za; internet www.dsd.gov.za.

Ministry of Sports, Arts and Culture: Sechaba House, 202 Madiba St, Pretoria; Private Bag X897, Pretoria 0001; tel. (12) 3045000; e-mail info@dac.gov.za; internet www.dac.gov.za.

Ministry of Tourism: Tourism House, 17 Trevenna St, Sunnyside, Pretoria 0001; Private Bag X424, Pretoria 0001; tel. (12) 4446000; e-mail callcentre@tourism.gov.za; internet www.tourism.gov.za.

Ministry of Trade, Industry and Competition: The dtic, 77 Meintjies St, Sunnyside, Pretoria 0002; Private Bag X84, Pretoria 0001; tel. (12) 3949500; internet www.thedtic.gov.za.

Ministry of Transport: Forum Bldg, 159 Struben St, Pretoria 0001; Private Bag X193, Pretoria 0001; tel. (12) 3093000; e-mail info@dot .gov.za; internet www.transport.gov.za.

Ministry of Water and Sanitation: Sedibang Bldg, 185 Frances Baard St, Pretoria; Private Bag X313, Pretoria 0001; tel. (12) 3367500; e-mail info@dws.gov.za; internet www.dws.gov.za.

Legislature

PARLIAMENT

National Council of Provinces

National Council of Provinces: Parliament St, Cape Town; POB 15, Cape Town 8000; tel. (21) 4032911; e-mail info@parliament.gov .za; internet www.parliament.gov.za.

Chairman: Amos Masondo.

The National Council of Provinces comprises 90 members, with six permanent delegates and four special delegates from each of the nine provinces.

National Assembly

National Assembly: Parliament Bldg, Room E118, Parliament St, Cape Town; POB 15, Cape Town 8000; tel. (21) 4032595; e-mail info@ parliament.gov.za; internet www.parliament.gov.za.

Speaker: Nosiviwe Mapisa-Nqakula.

General Election, 8 May 2019

Party	Valid votes	% of valid votes	Seats
African National Congress . . .	10,026,475	57.50	230
Democratic Alliance	3,621,188	20.77	84
Economic Freedom Fighters . . .	1,881,521	10.79	44
Inkatha Freedom Party	588,839	3.38	14
Vryheidsfront Plus	414,864	2.38	10
African Christian Democratic Party .	146,262	0.84	4
United Democratic Movement . .	78,030	0.45	2
African Transformation Movement .	76,830	0.44	2
Good	70,408	0.40	2
National Freedom Party	61,220	0.35	2
African Independent Congress . .	48,107	0.28	2
Congress of the People	47,461	0.27	2
Pan Africanist Congress of Azania .	32,677	0.19	1
Al Jama-ah	31,468	0.18	1
Others*	310,794	1.78	—
Total	**17,436,144†**	**100.00**	**400**

* A total of 34 other political parties contested the election.
† In addition, there were 235,472 spoiled votes.

Provincial Governments

(October 2022)

EASTERN CAPE

Premier: Oscar Mabuyane (ANC).

Speaker of the Legislature: Helen Sauls-August (ANC).

FREE STATE

Premier: Sefora Ntombela (ANC).

Speaker of the Legislature: Ntombizanele Beauty Sifuba (ANC).

GAUTENG

Premier: Panyaza Lesufi (ANC).

Speaker of the Legislature: Ntombi Mekgwe (ANC).

KWAZULU/NATAL

Premier: Nomusa Dube-Ncube (ANC).

Speaker of the Legislature: Nontembeko Nothemba Boyce (ANC).

LIMPOPO

Premier: Chupu Stanley Mathabatha (ANC).

Speaker of the Legislature: Rosemary Molapo (ANC).

MPUMALANGA

Premier: Refilwe Mtsweni-Tsipane (ANC).

Speaker of the Legislature: Makhosazane Masilela (ANC).

NORTHERN CAPE

Premier: Dr Zamani Saul (ANC).

Speaker of the Legislature: Newrene Klaaste (ANC).

NORTH-WEST

Premier: Bushy Maape.

Speaker of the Legislature: Sussana Rebecca Dantjie (ANC).

WESTERN CAPE

Premier: Alan Winde (DA).

Speaker of the Legislature: Masizole Mnqasela (DA).

Election Commission

Electoral Commission of South Africa (Independent Electoral Commission—IEC): Election House, Riverside Office Park, 1303 Heuwel Ave, Centurion, Pretoria; tel. (12) 6225700; e-mail info@ elections.org.za; internet www.elections.org.za; f. 1997; Chair. Mosotho Simon Moepya; Chief Electoral Officer Sy Mamabolo.

Political Organizations

A total of 304 political parties were registered at the national level in 2022. The 2019 general election was contested by some 48 political parties.

African Christian Democratic Party (ACDP): Stats Bldg, 2 Fore St, POB 1677, Alberton; tel. (11) 8693941; e-mail info@acdp.org.za; internet www.acdp.org.za; f. 1993; Leader Dr KENNETH MESHOE; Sec.-Gen. MOKHETHI RAYMOND TLAELI.

African Independent Congress (AIC): POB 352, Matatiele 4730; tel. (39) 7374045; f. 2005; Pres. MANDLA GALO.

African National Congress (ANC): 54 Pixley Seme St, Johannesburg 2001; POB 61884, Marshalltown 2107; tel. (11) 3761000; e-mail communications@anc.org.za; internet www.anc.org.za; f. 1912; in alliance with the South African Communist Party (SACP) and the Congress of South African Trade Unions (COSATU); governing party since April 1994; Pres. CYRIL RAMAPHOSA; Deputy Pres. DAVID MABUZA; Sec.-Gen. JESSIE DUARTE.

African People's Convention (APC): Dr Neil Aggett House, 4th Floor, 90 President St, Johannesburg 2001; tel. (11) 3331284; e-mail moshwadiba@webmail.co.za; internet www.theapc.org.za; f. 2007; Pres. THEMBA GODI; Sec.-Gen. PASEKA OA MOSHWADIBA.

African Transformation Movement (ATM): Fedsure House, 1st Floor, Church St, Pietermaritzburg 3201; e-mail info@atmovement .org; internet www.atmovement.org; f. 2018; Pres. VUYOLWETHU ZUNGULA.

Afrikaner Weerstandsbeweging (AWB) (Afrikaner Resistance Movement): POB 274, Ventersdorp 2710, Johannesburg; tel. (18) 2643669; e-mail awbhoofkantoor777@gmail.com; internet awb.co.za; f. 1973; Afrikaner (Boer) nationalist group seeking self-determination for the Afrikaner people in South Africa; Leader STEYN VAN RONGE.

Agang South Africa: 509 Van Erkom Bldg, Pretorius St, Pretoria 0001; tel. (12) 3210523; e-mail admin@agangsa.org.za; internet www .agangsa.org.za; f. 2013; Leader ANDRIES TLOUAMMA.

Al Jama-ah: 26 Voel St, Belgravia Estate, Athlone; tel. 827802573; e-mail info@aljama.co.za; internet www.aljama.co.za; f. 2007; Muslim party; Leader MOGAMAD GANIEF EBRAHIM HENDRICKS.

Azanian People's Organization (AZAPO): Investment Bldg, 4th Floor, 97 Commissioner St, Johannesburg 2001; POB 4230, Johannesburg 2000; tel. (11) 4436470; e-mail info@azapo.org.za; internet azapo.org.za; f. 1978; seeks establishment of a unitary, democratic, socialist republic; excludes white mems; Pres. NELVIS QEKEMA; Sec.-Gen. CHRIS SWEPU.

Boerestaat Party (Boer State Party): POB 4995, Luipaardsvlei 1743; tel. (11) 4116901; f. 1988; seeks the reinstatement of the Boer Republics in a consolidated Boerestaat; Leader COEN VERMAAK.

Congress of the People (COPE): Marks Bldg, 4th Floor, 90 Plein St, Cape Town; tel. (21) 4038915; e-mail copemedia2014@gmail.com; internet www.congressofthepeople.org.za; f. 2008 following split in the ANC; Pres. MOSIUOA LEKOTA; Sec.-Gen. LYNDALL SHOPE-MAFOLE.

Democratic Alliance (DA): Marks Bldg, 2nd and 3rd Floors, Parliament Plein St, Cape Town; POB 15, Cape Town 8000; tel. (21) 4651431; e-mail leader@da.org.za; internet www.da.org.za; f. 2000; Leader JOHN STEENHUISEN; Federal Chair. Dr IVAN MEYER.

Economic Freedom Fighters (EFF): 78 De Korte, Braamfontein, Johannesburg 2000; tel. (11) 4032313; e-mail communications@ effonline.org; internet www.effonline.org; f. 2013; Marxist-Leninist; supports Pan-Africanism; Pres. and Commander-in-Chief JULIUS SELLO MALEMA; Sec.-Gen. MARSHALL DLAMINI.

Good: 14 Kleinbosch St, Haasendal, Kuils River 7580; internet www .forgood.org.za; f. 2018; Leader PATRICIA DE LILLE.

Inkatha Freedom Party (IFP): 2 Durban Club Pl., Durban 4000; POB 4432, Durban 4000; tel. (31) 3651300; e-mail info@ifp.org.za; internet www.ifp.org.za; f. 1975 as Inkatha National Cultural Liberation Movement with mainly Zulu support; reorg. in 1990 as a multiracial political party; Pres. VELENKOSINI HLABISA; Sec.-Gen. SIPHOSETHU NGCOBO.

Minority Front: Rising Sun House, 13/15 Peak St, Arena Park, Chatsworth, Durban; tel. (31) 5007580; internet minorityfront.org; f. 1993; Indian support; Leader SHAMEEN THAKUR-RAJBANSI.

National Freedom Party: 7 Lenox Rd, Morningside, Durban; tel. (31) 3321228; e-mail info@nfp.org.za; internet www.nfp.org.za; f. 2011; Pres. JEREMIAH MAVUNDLA (acting); Sec.-Gen. CANAAN MDLETSHE.

Pan-Africanist Congress of Azania (PAC): Romi-Lee Bldg, 10th Floor, Office 1005, cnr Eloff and Marshall Sts, Marshall Town, Johannesburg 2001; POB 6010, Johannesburg 2000; tel. (11) 3313414; f. 1959 as a breakaway org. from the African National Congress; Pres. MZWANELE NYHONTSO; Sec.-Gen. PHILLIP DHALIMINI.

South African Communist Party (SACP): Cosatu House, 110 Jorissen St, Braamfontein 2017; POB 1027, Johannesburg 2000; tel.

(11) 3393621; e-mail info@sacp.org.za; internet www.sacp.org.za; f. 1921; reorg. 1953; supports the ANC; Nat. Chair. Dr BONGINKOSI EMMANUEL 'BLADE' NZIMANDE; Sec.-Gen. SOLLY MAPAILA.

United Christian Democratic Party (UCDP): POB 3010, Mmabatho; tel. (18) 3815691; internet www.ucdp.org.za; f. 1972 as the Bophuthatswana Nat. Party; name changed to Bophuthatswana Dem. Party in 1974; present name adopted in 1994; multiracial; Nat. Chair. IPUSENG CELIA DITSHETELO; Pres. MODIRI DESMOND SEHUME; Sec.-Gen. J. B. S. MOLOABI.

United Democratic Movement (UDM): C. P. A. House, 2nd Floor, 101 Du Toit St, Berea Park, Pretoria; POB 26290, Arcadia 0001; tel. (12) 3210010; e-mail reception@udm.org.za; internet udm.org.za; f. 1997; multiracial support; demands effective measures for enforcement of law and order; Pres. BANTU HOLOMISA; Sec.-Gen. BONGANI MSOMI.

Vryheidsfront Plus (Freedom Front Plus—VF Plus/FF Plus): Blk 8, Highveld Office Park, 11 Charles de Gaulle Cres., Highveld, Centurion, Pretoria; POB 67391, Highveld, 0169; tel. (12) 6650564; e-mail info@vf.co.za; internet www.vfplus.org.za; f. 1994 as Freedom Front; name changed after incorporating the Conservative Party and Afrikaner Eenheidsbeweging (Afrikaner Unity Movement) in Sept. 2003; right-wing electoral alliance; Leader Dr PIETER GROENEWALD; Gen. Sec. ANSIE DU PLOOY.

Diplomatic Representation

EMBASSIES AND HIGH COMMISSIONS IN SOUTH AFRICA

Algeria: 950 Arcadia St, Arcadia, Pretoria 0083; tel. (12) 3425074; e-mail algemb.pretoria@gmail.com; internet www .embassyofalgeria-rsa.org; Ambassador MOHAMED HACENE ECHARIF.

Angola: 1037 Pretorius St, Hatfield, Pretoria 0083; tel. (12) 3420049; internet angolanembassy-sa.ao; Ambassador MARIA FILOMENA LOBÃO TELO DELGADO.

Argentina: 200 Standard Plaza, 440 Hilda St, Hatfield, Pretoria 0083; tel. (12) 4303524; e-mail esafr@mrecic.gov.ar; internet esafr .mrecic.gov.ar; Ambassador CLAUDIO PEREZ PALADINO.

Australia: 292 Orient St, Arcadia, Pretoria 0083; Postnet Suite 493, Private Bag X15, Menlo Park, Pretoria 0102; tel. (12) 4236000; e-mail pretoria.info@dfat.gov.au; internet southafrica.embassy.gov.au; High Commissioner GITA KAMATH.

Austria: 454A Fehrsen St, Brooklyn, Pretoria 0181; POB 95572, Waterkloof 0145; tel. (12) 4529155; e-mail pretoria-ob@bmeia.gv.at; internet www.bmeia.gv.at/botschaft/pretoria; Ambassador JOHANN BRIEGER.

Azerbaijan: 302 Albert St, Waterkloof, Pretoria 0181; tel. (12) 3461018; e-mail pretoria.az@gmail.com; internet pretoria.mfa.gov .az; Chargé d'affaires a.i. YAMIN JAFAROV.

Bangladesh: 410 Farenden St, Sunnyside, Pretoria 0002; tel. (12) 3432105; e-mail mission.pretoria@mofa.gov.bd; High Commissioner NOOR EL-HELAL SAIFUR RAHMAN.

Belarus: 164 Orion Ave, Sterrewag, Pretoria 0181; POB 25763, Monument Park, Pretoria 0105; tel. (12) 4307709; e-mail rsa@mfa .gov.by; internet rsa.mfa.gov.by; Ambassador ALEXANDER D. SIDORUK.

Belgium: 625 Leyds St, Muckleneuk, Pretoria 0002; tel. (12) 4403201; e-mail pretoria@diplobel.fed.be; internet southafrica .diplomatie.belgium.be; Ambassador DIDIER VANDERHASSELT.

Benin: 900 Park St, cnr Orient and Park Sts, Arcadia, Pretoria 0083; POB 26484, Arcadia, Pretoria 0007; tel. (12) 3426978; e-mail pretoria@embbeninsa.org.za; internet www.embbeninsa.org.za; Ambassador ERIC FRANCK MICHEL A. SAIZONOU.

Botswana: 24 Amos St, Colbyn, Pretoria 0083; POB 57035, Arcadia, Pretoria 0007; tel. (12) 4309640; High Commissioner TSHENOLO MODISE.

Brazil: 152 Dallas Ave, Corobay Corner Bldg, 4th Floor, Waterkloof Glen, Pretoria 0181; tel. (12) 3665200; e-mail brasemb.pretoria@ itamaraty.gov.br; internet pretoria.itamaraty.gov.br; Ambassador SÉRGIO FRANÇA DANESE.

Bulgaria: 1071 Stanza Bopape St, Hatfield, Pretoria 0083; tel. (12) 3423720; e-mail embassy.pretoria@mfa.bg; internet www.mfa.bg/ embassies/southafrica; Ambassador MARIA PAVLOVA TZOTZORKOVA-KAYMAKTCHIEVA.

Burkina Faso: 767 Justice Mohamed St, Pretoria; POB 13710, Hatfield, Pretoria 0028; tel. (12) 3462704; e-mail ambabfpretoria07@ gmail.com; Ambassador OUMAROU MAIGA.

Burundi: 20 Glyn St, Colbyn, Pretoria 0083; POB 12914, Hatfield, Pretoria 0028; tel. (12) 3424881; Ambassador ALEXIS BUKURU.

Cameroon: 80 Marais St, Brooklyn, Pretoria 0181; POB 13790, Hatfield 0028; tel. (12) 4600341; e-mail info@camhicom.co.za;

internet www.camhicom.co.za; High Commissioner ANU'A-GHEYLE SOLOMON AZOH-MBI.

Canada: 1103 Arcadia St, cnr Hilda St, Hatfield, Pretoria 0083; Private Bag X13, Hatfield, Pretoria 0028; tel. (12) 4223000; e-mail pret@international.gc.ca; internet www.canadainternational.gc.ca/southafrica-afriquedusud; High Commissioner CHRISTOPHER COOTER.

Central African Republic: 209 Eastwood, opp. Eastwood Village, Stanza Bopape St, Arcadia, Pretoria 0083; tel. (12) 4302443; e-mail carembassysa@gmail.com; Ambassador ANDRÉ NZAPAYEKE.

Chad: 157 Banket St, cnr Dely Rd and Club Ave, Waterkloof, Pretoria 0181; POB 12648, Hatfield, Pretoria 0028; tel. (87) 8980032; e-mail info@chadembassy.co.za; internet www.chadembassy.co.za; Ambassador SAGOUR YOUSSOUF MAHAMAT ITNO.

Chile: 333 Main St, Pretoria; Waterkloof, Pretoria 0181; tel. (12) 4608090; e-mail esudafrica@minrel.gob.cl; internet chile.gob.cl/sudafrica; Ambassador JULIO FIOL ZÚÑIGA.

China, People's Republic: 972 Pretorius St, Arcadia, Pretoria 0083; POB 95764, Waterkloof, Pretoria 0145; tel. (12) 4316500; e-mail chineseembassysa@gmail.com; internet za.china-embassy.gov.cn; Ambassador CHEN XIAODONG.

Colombia: 177 Dyer Rd, Hillcrest Office Park, 2nd Floor, Woodpecker Pl., Hillcrest, Pretoria 0083; POB 12791, Hatfield, Pretoria 0028; tel. (12) 3623106; e-mail esudafrica@cancilleria.gov.co; internet sudafrica.embajada.gov.co; Ambassador CARLOS BARAHONA.

Comoros: 200 Beckett St, Eastclyffe, Arcadia, Pretoria 0083; tel. (12) 3438594; e-mail embassycomorospretoria@gmail.com; Ambassador CHAMSIDINE MHADJOU.

Congo, Democratic Republic: 791 Schoeman St, Arcadia, Pretoria 0083; POB 28795, Sunnyside 0132; tel. (12) 3446475; e-mail rdcongo@lantic.net; Ambassador FIDÈLE MULAJA (designate).

Congo, Republic: 960 Arcadia St, Arcadia, Pretoria 0083; POB 40427, Arcadia 0007; tel. (12) 3425508; e-mail pretoria@embassyofcongo.co.za; internet www.embassyofcongo.co.za; Ambassador CHANTAL MARYSE ITOUA-APOYOLO.

Côte d'Ivoire: 795 Government Ave, Arcadia, Pretoria 0083; POB 13510, Hatfield 0028; tel. (12) 3426913; e-mail ambaci.pretoria@gmail.com; internet afriquedusud.diplomatie.gouv.ci; Ambassador SAKARIA KONÉ.

Croatia: Omzik House, 165 Lynnwood Rd, Brooklyn, Pretoria 0181; POB 11335, Hatfield 0028; tel. (12) 3421206; e-mail croemb.pretoria@mvep.hr; internet mvep.gov.hr/za; Ambassador ANTE CICVARIĆ.

Cuba: 45 Mackenzie St, Brooklyn, Pretoria 0181; POB 11605, Hatfield 0028; tel. 878980018; e-mail embajada@za.embacuba.cu; internet misiones.minrex.gob.cu/es/sudafrica; Ambassador ENRIQUE ORTA GONZÁLEZ.

Cyprus: 375 Marais St, Brooklyn, Pretoria 0181; POB 36853, Menlo Park 0102; tel. (12) 3463298; e-mail pretoriahighcommission@mfa.gov.cy; internet www.mfa.gov.cy/mfa/highcom/highcom_pretoria.nsf; High Commissioner ANTONIS MANDRITIS.

Czech Republic: 936 Pretorius St, Arcadia, Pretoria 0083; POB 13671, Hatfield, Pretoria 0028; tel. (12) 4312380; e-mail pretoria@embassy.mzv.cz; internet www.mzv.cz/pretoria; Ambassador REYMUNDO ANTONIO GARRIDO LANTIGUA.

Denmark: iParioli Office Park, Blk B2, Ground Floor, 1166 Park St, Hatfield, Pretoria; POB 11439, Hatfield 0028; tel. (12) 4309340; e-mail pryamb@um.dk; internet sydafrika.um.dk; Ambassador TOBIAS ELLING REHFELD.

Dominican Republic: 252 Berea St, Muckleneuk, Pretoria 0181; POB 25897, Pretoria 0105; tel. (12) 3410177; e-mail dominicanembassy@gmail.com; Ambassador RAYMUNDO GARRIDO LANTIGUA.

Ecuador: Brookfield Court Bldg, 1st Floor, Bronkhorst St, Brooklyn, Pretoria; tel. (12) 3461662; Ambassador JUAN FRANCISCO LARREA MIÑO.

Egypt: 270 Bourke St, Muckleneuk, Pretoria 0002; POB 30025, Sunnyside 0132; tel. (12) 3431590; e-mail egyptembpa@gmail.com; Ambassador AHMED TAHER ELFADLY.

Equatorial Guinea: 48 Florence St, Colbyn, Pretoria; POB 12720, Hatfield 0028; tel. (12) 3429945; e-mail egembassy@mweb.co.za; Ambassador LIBRADA ELA ASUMU.

Eritrea: 1281 Cobham Rd, Queenswood, Pretoria 0186; POB 11371, Queenswood 0121; tel. (12) 3331302; e-mail eremb@lantic.net; Ambassador SALIH OMAR ABDU.

Eswatini: 715 Government Ave, Arcadia, Pretoria 0007; POB 14294, Hatfield 0028; tel. (12) 3441910; e-mail pretoria@swazihighcom.co.za; internet swazihighcom.co.za; High Commissioner LINDIWE CYNTHIA KUNENE.

Ethiopia: 763 Justice Mahomed St, Bailey's Muckleneuk, Brooklyn, Pretoria 0181; POB 11469, Hatfield 0028; tel. (12) 3464067; e-mail pretoria.embassy@mfa.gov.et; internet www.pretoria.mfa.gov.et; Ambassador MUKTAR KEDIR.

Finland: 628 Leyds St, Muckleneuk, Pretoria 0002; POB 443, Pretoria 0001; tel. (12) 3430276; e-mail sanomat.pre@formin.fi; internet finlandabroad.fi/web/zaf; Ambassador ANNE LAMMILA.

France: 250 Melk St, New Muckleneuk, Pretoria 0181; POB 4619, Pretoria 0001; tel. (12) 4251600; e-mail france@ambafrance-rsa.org; internet za.ambafrance.org; Ambassador AURÉLIEN LECHEVALLIER.

Gabon: 921 Schoeman St, Arcadia, Pretoria 0083; POB 9222, Pretoria 0001; tel. (12) 3424376; e-mail ambga.afriquedusud@diplomatie.gouv.ga; High Commissioner ANDRÉ WILLIAM ANGUILE.

The Gambia: Brookfield Office Park, 2nd Floor, North Block, 261 Middel St, Nieuw Muckleneuk, Pretoria 0181; tel. (12) 0040374; e-mail info@gambiahighcommissionsa.co.za; internet gambiahighcommissionsa.co.za; Acting High Commissioner BUBA AYI SANNEH.

Georgia: 270A Carina St, Waterkloof Ridge, Pretoria 0181; tel. (12) 3461831; e-mail pretoria.emb@mfa.gov.ge; internet www.rsa.mfa.gov.ge; Ambassador BEKA DVALI.

Germany: 201 Florence Ribeiro Ave, Groenkloof, Pretoria 0181; tel. (12) 4278900; e-mail info@pretoria.diplo.de; internet southafrica.diplo.de; Ambassador ANDREAS PESCHKE.

Ghana: 1038 Arcadia St, Hatfield, Pretoria 0083; POB 12537, Hatfield 0083; tel. (12) 3425847; e-mail headofmission@ghanahighcommission.co.za; internet ghanahighcommission-southafrica.com; High Commissioner CHARLES ASUAKO OWIREDU.

Greece: 323 Alpine Way and Village Rds, Lynwood, Pretoria 0081; tel. (12) 3482352; e-mail gremb.pre@mfa.gr; internet www.mfa.gr/pretoria; Ambassador GEORGIOS ARAVOSITAS.

Guatemala: Brooklyn Court, 1st Floor, 360 Veale St, E-2, Nieuw Muckleneuk, Pretoria 0181; tel. (12) 3463477; e-mail embsudafrica@minex.gob.gt; Ambassador Dr ERICK ESTUARDO ESCOBEDO AYALA.

Guinea: 336 Orient St, Arcadia, Pretoria 0083; POB 13523, Hatfield 0028; tel. (12) 3427348; e-mail embaguinea@iafrica.com; Ambassador KABA HAWA DIAKITÉ.

Guyana: Suite H, 3rd Floor, Grosvenor Pl., 235 Grosvenor St, POB 12238, Hatfield, Pretoria 0081; tel. (12) 9411694; e-mail ghcpretoria@hcguyana.co.za; internet www.guyana-hc-south-africa.co.za; High Commissioner CANDIDA DANIELS (acting).

Haiti: 826–830 Government Ave, Eastwood, Pretoria 0083; tel. (12) 3420192; internet fb.com/EmbassyofHaitiSA; Ambassador JACQUES JUNIOR BARIL.

Holy See: 4 Argo St, Waterkloof Ridge, Pretoria 0181; POB 95200, Waterkloof 0145; tel. (12) 3464235; e-mail nunziosa@nunciaturesa.co.za; Apostolic Nuncio PETER BRYAN WELLS (Titular Archbishop of Marcianopolis).

Hungary: 959 Arcadia St, Hatfield, Pretoria 0083; POB 13843, Hatfield 0028; tel. (12) 4303030; e-mail mission.prt@mfa.gov.hu; internet pretoria.mfa.gov.hu/eng; Ambassador ATTILA GYÖRGY HORVÁTH.

India: 852 Francis Baard St, Arcadia, Pretoria 0083; POB 40216, Arcadia 0007; tel. (12) 3425392; e-mail indiahc@hicomind.co.za; internet www.hcipretoria.gov.in; High Commissioner JAIDEEP SARKAR.

Indonesia: 949 Schoeman St, Arcadia, Pretoria 0082; POB 13155, Hatfield, Pretoria 0028; tel. (12) 3423350; e-mail info@indonesia-pretoria.org.za; internet www.kemlu.go.id/pretoria; Ambassador SALMAN AL-FARISI.

Iran: 245 Melk St, Middle St, Brooklyn, Pretoria 0181; POB 12546, Hatfield 0028; tel. (12) 3425880; e-mail iranemb.pry@mfa.gov.ir; internet southafrica.mfa.gov.ir; Ambassador MAHDI AGHA JAFARI.

Iraq: 803 Jan Shoba St, Brooklyn, Pretoria 0181; POB 11089, Hatfield 0028; tel. (12) 3622048; e-mail iraqiembassy5.pretoria@gmail.com; Ambassador ARSHAD OMAR ESMAEEL.

Ireland: Parkdev Bldg, 2nd Floor, 570 Fehrsen St, Brooklyn Bridge Office Park, Brooklyn 0181; POB 4174, Arcadia 0001; tel. (12) 4521000; e-mail pretoria@dfa.ie; internet dfa.ie/irish-embassy/south-africa; Ambassador FIONNUALA GILSENAN.

Israel: 428 King's Hwy, cnr Elizabeth Grove, Lynnwood, Pretoria; tel. (12) 4703500; e-mail consular@pretoria.mfa.gov.il; internet embassies.gov.il/pretoria; Ambassador ELIAV BELOTSERCOVSKY.

Italy: 796 George Ave, Arcadia, Pretoria 0083; tel. (12) 4230000; e-mail segreteria.pretoria@esteri.it; internet www.ambpretoria.esteri.it; Ambassador PAOLO CUCULI.

Jamaica: Brooklyn Court, 2nd Floor, 361 Veale St, Brooklyn, Pretoria 0181; Private Bag X5, Hatfield, Pretoria 0028; tel. (12) 3668500; e-mail info@jhcpretoria.co.za; internet www.jhcpretoria.co.za; High Commissioner ANGELLA VERONICA COMFORT.

Japan: 259 Baines St, cnr Frans Oerder St, Groenkloof, Pretoria 0181; Private Bag X999, Pretoria 0001; tel. (12) 4521500; e-mail info@pr.mofa.go.jp; internet www.za.emb-japan.go.jp; Ambassador NORIO MARUYAMA.

Jordan: 254 Crown Ave, Waterkloof, Pretoria; POB 14730, Hatfield 0028; tel. (12) 3468615; Ambassador IBRAHIM MOHAMMAD AWAWDEH.

Kazakhstan: 226 Aries St, Waterkloof Ridge, Pretoria 0181; tel. (12) 4600086; e-mail pretoria@kazembassy-sa.com; internet www.gov .kz/memleket/entities/mfa-pretoria; Ambassador KANAT TUMYSH.

Kenya: 302 Brooks St, Menlo Park, Pretoria 0081; POB 35954, Menlo Park 0012; tel. (12) 3622249; e-mail info@kenya.org.za; internet www.kenya.org.za; High Commissioner CATHERINE MUI-GAI-MWANGI.

Korea, Democratic People's Republic: 958 Waterpoort St, Faerie Glen, Pretoria; POB 1238, Garsfontein 0042; tel. (12) 9918661; e-mail dprkembassy@lantic.net; Ambassador JONG SONG IL.

Korea, Republic: 265 Melk St, Nieuw Muckleneuk, Pretoria 0081; POB 939, Groenkloof, Pretoria 0027; tel. (12) 4602508; e-mail embsa@mofa.go.kr; internet overseas.mofa.go.kr/za-en/index.do; Ambassador PARK CHULL-JOO.

Kuwait: 890 Arcadia St, Arcadia, Pretoria 0083; Private Bag X920, Pretoria 0001; tel. (12) 3420877; e-mail info@kuwaitembassy.co.za; internet www.kuwaitembassy.co.za; Chargé d'affaires SALEH AL-THUWAIKH.

Lebanon: 121 Muckleneuk St, Pretoria; tel. (12) 4302130; e-mail info@embassyoflebanon.co.za; internet fb.com/embassyoflebanon; Ambassador KABALAN FRANGIEH.

Lesotho: 391 Anderson St, Menlo Park, Pretoria 0081; POB 55817, Arcadia 0007; tel. (12) 4607648; e-mail lesothopretoria@yahoo.com; High Commissioner NEHEMIA SEKHONYANA BERENG.

Liberia: Suite 9, Forum Bldg, Section 7, 1157 Schoeman St, POB 14082, Hatfield, Pretoria 0028; tel. (12) 3422734; e-mail libempta@ pta.lia.net; Ambassador ETHEL DAVIS.

Libya: 900 Stanza Bopape St, Arcadia, Pretoria 0083; POB 40388, Arcadia 0007; tel. (12) 3423902; Ambassador ABDEL-QADER AL-NAZIF.

Lithuania: 235 Grosvenor St, Hatfield, Pretoria; tel. (12) 7609000; e-mail amb.za@urm.lt; internet za.mfa.lt; Ambassador DAINIUS JUNEVIČIUS.

Madagascar: 90B Tait St, Colbyn, Pretoria; POB 11722, Queens-wood 0120; tel. (12) 3420983; e-mail consul@infodoor.co.za; Chargé d'affaires a.i. VOLOLOMIORA LALANIRINA RABARIJAONA.

Malawi: 770 Government Ave, Arcadia, Pretoria 0083; POB 11172, Hatfield 0028; tel. (12) 3421759; Ambassador STELLA HAUYA NDAU.

Malaysia: 1007 Francis Baard St, Arcadia, Pretoria 0083; POB 11673, Hatfield 0028; tel. (12) 3425990; e-mail mwpretoria@kln.gov .my; internet www.kln.gov.my/web/zaf_pretoria; High Commissioner MOHAMAD NIZAN MOHAMAD.

Mali: 876 Pretorius St, Arcadia, Pretoria 0083; POB 12978, Hatfield, Pretoria 0028; tel. (12) 3427464; Ambassador BAKARY COULIBALY.

Mauritania: Lord Charles Office Park, Blk B, Ground Floor, 337 Brooklyn Rd, cnr Justice Mohamed Rd, Brooklyn, Pretoria 0181; tel. (12) 3623578; e-mail pretoria@mauritaniaembassy.co.za; internet mauritaniaembassy.co.za; Ambassador JARR OULD INALLA.

Mauritius: 97, 21st St, Menlo Park, Pretoria 0081; tel. (12) 3421283; e-mail pretoriahc@govmu.org; internet pretoria.mauritius.govmu .org; High Commissioner PRAKARAMAJIT VIJAYE LUTCHMUN.

Mexico: Parkdev Bldg, Ground Floor, 570 Fehrsen St, Brooklyn Bridge Office Park, Pretoria 0181; POB 9077, Pretoria 0001; tel. (12) 4601004; e-mail info@mexico.org.za; internet embamex.sre.gob.mx/ sudafrica; Ambassador SARA VALDES BOLAÑO.

Morocco: 799 Francis Baard St, cnr Farenden St, Arcadia, Pretoria 0083; tel. (12) 3430230; e-mail embassy.morocco.pretoria@gmail .com; internet www.moroccoembassy.co.za; Ambassador YOUSSEF EL AMRANI.

Mozambique: 529 Edmund St, Arcadia, Pretoria 0083; POB 57465, Pretoria 0001; tel. (12) 4010300; High Commissioner MARIA MANUELA DOS SANTOS LUCAS (designate).

Myanmar: 329 Julius Jeppe St, Waterkloof, Pretoria 0181; POB 12121, Queenswood 0121; tel. (12) 3412557; e-mail embmya@gmail .com; internet www.myanmarembassysa.com; Ambassador MYINT SWE.

Namibia: 197 Blackwood St, Arcadia, Pretoria 0083; POB 29806, Sunnyside 0132; tel. (12) 4819100; e-mail secretary@namibia.org.za; internet www.namibia.org.za; High Commissioner VEICCOH KAH-WADI NGHIWETE.

Nepal: 976 Frances Baard St, Arcadia, Pretoria 0083; tel. (12) 3427546; e-mail eonpretoria@mofa.gov.np; internet za .nepalembassy.gov.np; Ambassador DAN BAHADUR TAMANG (designate).

Netherlands: 210 Florence Ribeiro Ave/Queen Wilhelmina Ave, cnr Muckleneuk St, New Muckleneuk, Pretoria 0181; tel. (12) 4254500; e-mail pre@minbuza.nl; internet netherlandsworldwide.nl/ countries/south-africa; Ambassador HAN PETERS.

New Zealand: 125 Middel St, Muckleneuk, Pretoria 0181; tel. (12) 4359000; e-mail enquiries@nzhc.co.za; High Commissioner Dr EMMA REBECCA DUNLOP-BENNETT.

Niger: 821 Thomas Ave, Arcadia, Pretoria; tel. (12) 4302402; e-mail ambanigeras@gmail.com; Ambassador SEYDO MARIAMA.

Nigeria: 971 Francis Baard St, Arcadia, Pretoria 0083; POB 27332, Sunnyside 0132; tel. (12) 3420805; e-mail nhcp@telkomsa.net; internet nhcpsa.org; High Commissioner MUHAMMAD HARUNA MANTA.

Norway: Ozmik House, 165 Lynnwood Rd, Brooklyn 0181, Pretoria; POB 11612, Hatfield 0028; tel. (12) 3643700; e-mail emb.pretoria@ mfa.no; internet www.norway.no/south-africa; Ambassador (vacant).

Oman: 11 Anderson St, Brooklyn, Pretoria; POB 2650, Brooklyn 0075; tel. (12) 3628301; Ambassador (vacant).

Pakistan: 312 Brooks St, Menlo Park, Pretoria 0081; POB 11803, Hatfield 0028; tel. (12) 3624072; e-mail pareppretoria1@telkomsa .net; internet www.mofa.gov.pk/southafrica; High Commissioner AFTAB HASSAN KHAN (designate).

Panama: 141 Boshoff St, Bldg A, 1st Floor, Nieuw Muckleneuk, Pretoria 0181; tel. (12) 3467034; e-mail panamaembassy@gmail.com; internet panamaembassy-southafrica.co.za; Ambassador JORGE RICARDO SILEN SANTACOLOMA.

Paraguay: 189 Strelitzia Rd, Waterkloof Heights, Pretoria 0181; POB 95774, Waterkloof 0145; tel. (12) 3471047; e-mail embassy@ paraguayembassy.co.za; internet www.paraguayembassy.co.za; Ambassador JUAN IGNACIO LIVIERES OCAMPOS.

Peru: 200 Saint Patrick St, Muckleneuk Hill, Pretoria 0083; POB 907, Groenkloof 0027; tel. (12) 4401030; e-mail pa@embaperu.co.za; Ambassador JORGE FÉLIX RUBIO CORREA.

Philippines: 54 Nicholson St, Muckleneuk, Pretoria 0181; POB 2562, Brooklyn Sq., Pretoria 0075; tel. (12) 3462468; e-mail pretoria .pe@dfa.gov.ph; internet pretoriape.dfa.gov.ph; Ambassador NORA-LYN JUBAIRA-BAJA.

Poland: 14 Amos St, Colbyn, Pretoria 0083; POB 12277, Queens-wood 0121; tel. (12) 4302631; e-mail secretary.pretoria@msz.gov.pl; internet pretoria.mfa.gov.pl; Ambassador ANDRZEJ KANTHAK.

Portugal: 599 Leyds St, Muckleneuk, Pretoria 0002; POB 27102, Sunnyside 0132; tel. (12) 3412340; e-mail pretoria@mne.pt; internet www.embaixadaportugal.org.za; Ambassador MANUEL MARIA CARVALHO.

Qatar: 1077 Justice Mohamed St, Waterkloof, Pretoria 0181; Private Bag X13, Brooklyn Sq. 0075; tel. (12) 4521700; e-mail pretoria@mofa .gov.qa; internet pretoria.embassy.qa; Ambassador TARIQ ALI AL-ANSARI.

Romania: 877 Justice Mohamed St, Brooklyn Pretoria 0181; POB 11295, Hatfield 0028; tel. (12) 4606941; e-mail pretoria@mae.ro; internet pretoria.mae.ro; Ambassador MONICA-CECILIA SITARU.

Russian Federation: 316 Brooks St, Menlo Park, Pretoria 0081; POB 36034, Pretoria 0102; tel. (12) 3621337; e-mail ruspospr@mweb .co.za; internet russianembassyza.mid.ru; Ambassador ILYA ROGACHEV.

Rwanda: 983 Francis Baard St, Arcadia, Pretoria; POB 55224, Arcadia 0007; tel. (12) 3426536; e-mail ambapretoria@minaffet.gov .rw; internet www.southafrica.embassy.gov.rw; High Commissioner EUGENE KAYIHURA.

Saudi Arabia: 711 Jan Shoba St, cnr Lunnon St, Hatfield, Pretoria 0083; POB 13930, Hatfield 0028; tel. (12) 3624230; e-mail zaemb@ mofa.gov.sa; internet embassies.mofa.gov.sa/sites/southafrica; Ambassador SULTAN BIN ABDULLAH AL-ANQARI.

Senegal: 783 Justice Mahomed St, Baileys Muckleneuk, Pretoria 0181; POB 2948, Brooklyn Sq. 0075; tel. (12) 4605263; e-mail embasenegal@gmail.com; internet senegalembassy.co.za; Ambas-sador SAFIATOU NDIAYE.

Serbia: 163 Marais St, Brooklyn, Pretoria; POB 13026, Hatfield 0028; tel. (12) 4605626; e-mail info@srbembassy.org.za; internet www.pretoria.mfa.gov.rs; Ambassador GORAN VUJIČIĆ.

Seychelles: Delmondo Office Park, Blk C, 169 Garsfontein Rd, Ashlea Gardens, Pretoria; POB 697, Menlyn, Pretoria 0063; tel. (12) 3480270; e-mail sez@seychelleshc.co.za; High Commissioner CLAUDE MOREL.

Singapore: 980–982 Francis Baard St, Arcadia, Pretoria 0083; POB 11809, Hatfield 0028; tel. (12) 4306035; e-mail singhc_pry@sgmfa .gov.sg; internet www.mfa.gov.sg/pretoria; High Commissioner ZAINAL ARIF MANTAHA.

Slovakia: 930 Arcadia St, Pretoria 0083; POB 12736, Hatfield 0028; tel. (12) 3422051; e-mail emb.pretoria@mzv.sk; internet www.mzv .sk/pretoria; Ambassador VLADIMÍR GRÁCZ.

Somalia: 831 Arcadia St, Arcadia, Pretoria; tel. (12) 3433446; e-mail pretoriaembassy@mfa.gov.so; internet fb.com/SomaliainZA; Ambas-sador MOHAMED ALI MIRE.

South Sudan: 54 Amos St, Colbyn, Pretoria 0083; Postnet Suite 289, Private Bag X15, Menlo Park, Pretoria 0102; tel. (12) 3429754; Ambassador Simon Duku Michael.

Spain: Lord Charles Complex, 337 Brooklyn Rd, Brooklyn, Pretoria 0181; POB 35353, Menlo Park, Pretoria 0102; tel. (12) 4600123; e-mail emb.pretoria@maec.es; internet www.exteriores.gob.es/embajadas/pretoria; Ambassador Raimundo Robredo Rubio.

Sri Lanka: 410 Alexander St, Brooklyn, Pretoria 0181; tel. (12) 4607690; e-mail slhc@srilanka.co.za; internet www.srilanka.co.za; High Commissioner Sirisena Amarasekera.

Sudan: 1203 Pretorius St, Hatfield, Pretoria 0083; POB 25513, Monument Park 0105; tel. (12) 3424538; e-mail ambassadorsud@gmail.com; internet fb.com/SudanEmbassyPTA; Ambassador A. M. Hassan Dirar.

Sweden: iParioli Complex, 1166 Park St, Hatfield, Pretoria 0083; POB 27987, Sunny Side 0132; tel. (12) 4266400; e-mail ambassaden.pretoria@gov.se; internet www.swedenabroad.com/pretoria; Ambassador Håkan Juholt.

Switzerland: 225 Veale St, Parc Nouveau, New Muckleneuk, Pretoria 0181; POB 2508, Brooklyn Sq. 0075; tel. (12) 4520660; e-mail pretoria@eda.admin.ch; internet www.eda.admin.ch/pretoria; Ambassador Nicholas Brühl.

Syrian Arab Republic: 963 Francis Baard St, Arcadia, Pretoria 0083; POB 12830, Hatfield 0028; tel. (12) 3424701; Ambassador Mohammad Onfuan Naeb.

Tanzania: 822 George Ave, Arcadia, Pretoria 0007; POB 56572, Arcadia 0007; tel. (12) 3424393; e-mail pretoria@nje.go.tz; internet www.za.tzembassy.go.tz; High Commissioner Maj.-Gen. (retd) Gaudence Milanzi.

Thailand: 248 Hill St, cnr of Pretorius St, Arcadia, Pretoria 0028; POB 12080, Hatfield 0083; tel. (12) 3425470; e-mail info@thaiembassy.co.za; internet pretoria.thaiembassy.org; Ambassador Mungkorn Pratoomkaew.

Togo: 235 John St, Muckleneuk Hill, Pretoria; tel. (12) 3435939; e-mail ambatogopretoria@yahoo.fr; internet embassyoftogoza.com; Chargé d'affaires a.i. John D. Fintakpa Lamega.

Trinidad and Tobago: 258 Lawley St, Waterkloof, Pretoria 0181; POB 95872, Waterkloof, Pretoria 0145; tel. (12) 4609688; e-mail hcpretoria@foreign.gov.tt; internet foreign.gov.tt/hcpretoria; High Commissioner Dr Lovell Francis.

Tunisia: 850 Stanza Bopape St, Arcadia, Pretoria 0083; POB 56535, Arcadia 0007; tel. (12) 3426282; e-mail at.pretoria@diplomatie.gov.tn; internet fb.com/EmbassyOfTunisiaToPretoria; Ambassador Narjes Dridi.

Türkiye (Turkey): 573 Fehrsen St, Nieuw Mucklenuck, Pretoria; POB 36683, Menlo Park 0081; tel. (12) 3426055; e-mail embassy.pretoria@mfa.gov.tr; internet pretoria.emb.mfa.gov.tr; Ambassador Ayşegül Kandaş.

Uganda: 882 Stanza Bopape St, Pretoria 0083; POB 12442, Hatfield 0083; tel. (12) 3426031; e-mail ugacomer@mweb.co.za; internet pretoria.mofa.go.ug; High Commissioner Paul Amoru.

Ukraine: 398 Marais St, Brooklyn, Pretoria 0181; POB 36463, Menlo Park 0102; tel. (12) 4601943; e-mail emb_za@mfa.gov.ua; internet rsa.mfa.gov.ua; Ambassador Luibov Abravitova.

United Arab Emirates: 992 Arcadia St, Arcadia, POB 12612, Pretoria 0083; tel. (12) 3427736; e-mail pretoriaemb@mofaic.gov.ae; internet www.mofaic.gov.ae/Missions/Pretoria; Ambassador Mahash Saeed Salem Mahashal-Hameli.

United Kingdom: 255 Hill St, Arcadia, Pretoria 0002; tel. (12) 4217500; e-mail media.pretoria@fco.gov.uk; internet www.gov.uk/government/world/organisations/british-high-commission-pretoria; High Commissioner Antony Phillipson.

USA: 877 Pretorius St, Arcadia, Pretoria 0083; POB 9536, Pretoria 0001; tel. (12) 4314000; e-mail protocolpretoria@state.gov; internet za.usembassy.gov; Ambassador Reuben E. Brigety, II.

Uruguay: Office W3, Brooklyn Court, 361 Veale St, Nieuw Muckleneuk, Pretoria 0001; POB 14818, Pretoria 0028; tel. (12) 3626521; e-mail urusudafrica@mrree.gub.uy; Ambassador José Luis Rivas Lopez.

Venezuela: 230 Carina St, Waterkloof Ridge, Pretoria 0181; POB 11821, Hatfield 0028; tel. (12) 3465747; e-mail embavensudaf@yahoo.com; Ambassador Mairin Josefina Moreno-Mérida.

Viet Nam: 87 Brooks St, Brooklyn, Pretoria 0181; POB 13692, Hatfield 0028; tel. (12) 3628119; e-mail embassy@vietnam.co.za; internet www.vietnam.co.za; Ambassador Hoang Van Lol.

Yemen: 227 Murray St, Brooklyn, Pretoria 0181; tel. (12) 3460858; e-mail yemen.embassy.pta@gmail.com; internet yemenembassypretoria.com; Chargé d'affaires e.t. Ahmed Hassan Hassan Mohamed.

Zambia: 570 Ziervogel St, off Hamilton St, Arcadia, Pretoria 0083; POB 12234, Hatfield 0028; tel. (12) 3261847; e-mail press@zambiapretoria.net; internet www.zambiapretoria.net; High Commissioner Maj.-Gen. Jackson Miti.

Zimbabwe: Zimbabwe House, 798 Merton St, Arcadia, Pretoria 0083; POB 55140, Arcadia 0007; tel. (12) 3425125; e-mail zimpret@lantic.net; Ambassador David Douglas Hamadziripi.

Judicial System

The common law of the Republic of South Africa is the Roman-Dutch law, the uncodified law of Holland as it was at the time of the secession of the Cape of Good Hope in 1806. The law of England is not recognized as authoritative, although the principles of English law have been introduced in relation to civil and criminal procedure, evidence and mercantile matters.

The Constitutional Court, situated in Johannesburg, consists of a Chief Justice, a Deputy Chief Justice and nine other justices. Its task is to ensure that the executive, legislative and judicial organs of government adhere to the provisions of the Constitution. It has the power to reverse legislation that has been adopted by Parliament. The Supreme Court of Appeal, situated in Bloemfontein, comprises a President, a Deputy President and a number of judges of appeal, and is the highest court in all but constitutional matters. There are also High Courts and Magistrates' Courts. A National Director of Public Prosecutions is the head of the prosecuting authority and is appointed by the President of the Republic. A Judicial Service Commission makes recommendations regarding the appointment of judges and advises central and provincial government on all matters relating to the judiciary.

Constitutional Court: 1 Hospital St, Constitution Hill, Braamfontein, Johannesburg; Private Bag X1, Braamfontein, Johannesburg 2017; tel. (11) 3597400; e-mail info@concourt.org.za; internet www.constitutionalcourt.org.za; f. 1995; Chief Justice Raymond Zondo.

Supreme Court of Appeal: cnr Mirriam Makeba and President Brand Sts, Bloemfontein 9301; POB 258, Bloemfontein 9300; tel. (51) 4127400; e-mail ssteyn@sca.judiciary.org.za; internet www.supremecourtofappeal.org.za; f. 1910; Acting Pres. Xola Mlungisi Petse.

Religion

According to the 2015 General Household Survey, some 86.0% of the population professed the Christian faith. Other religions that are represented are Hinduism (0.9%), Islam (1.9%), Judaism (0.2%) and traditional African religions (5.4%).

CHRISTIANITY

South African Council of Churches: Khotso House, 62 Marshall St, Johannesburg; POB 62098, Marshalltown 2107; tel. (11) 2417800; e-mail support@sacc.org.za; internet sacc.org.za; f. 1968; 36 mem. churches; Pres. Bishop Ziphozihle Daniel Siwa; Gen. Sec. Bishop M. Malusi Mpumlwana.

The Anglican Communion

Most Anglicans in South Africa are adherents of the Anglican Church of Southern Africa (formerly the Church of the Province of Southern Africa), comprising 24 dioceses (including Lesotho, Namibia, St Helena and Eswatini—Swaziland). In November 2012 the Church consecrated the first ever woman bishop in Africa.

Archbishop of Cape Town and Metropolitan of the Province of Southern Africa: Most Rev. Thabo Cecil Makgoba, Bernard Mizeki Bldg, Zonnebloem Estate, 1 Cambridge St, Cape Town 8001; POB 1932, Cape Town 8000; tel. (21) 4693766; e-mail malambor@ctdiocese.org.za; internet www.ctdiocese.org.za.

The Dutch Reformed Church (Nederduitse Gereformeerde Kerk—NGK)

General Synod: c/o Jan Shoba (Duncan) and Pretorius Sts, Hatfield, Pretoria; POB 13528, Hatfield, Pretoria 0028; tel. 3420092; e-mail info@ngkerk.org.za; internet www.ngkerk.org.za; Moderator Rev. Nelis Janse van Rensburg; Gen. Sec. Gustav Claassen.

The Lutheran Churches

Lutheran Communion in Southern Africa (LUCSA): 24 Geldenhuys Rd, POB 7170, Bonaero Park 1622; tel. (11) 9797142; e-mail info@lucsa.org; internet www.lucsa.org; f. 1991; co-ordinating org. for the Lutheran churches in southern Africa, incl. Angola, Botswana, Malawi, Mozambique, Namibia, South Africa, Eswatini (Swaziland), Zambia and Zimbabwe; Exec. Dir Rev. Lilana Kasper.

Evangelical Lutheran Church in Southern Africa (Cape Church): 240 Long St, Cape Town 8001; POB 15528, Vlaeberg

8018; tel. (21) 4220592; e-mail office@elcsacape.co.za; internet www
.lutherancape.org.za; Pres. Bishop GILBERT FILTER.

Free Evangelical Lutheran Synod in South Africa (FELSISA):
156 Zwartkop Rd, Prestbury, Pietermaritzburg 3201; POB 21559,
Mayors Walk 3208; tel. 834409498; e-mail felsisamail@gmail.com;
internet www.felsisa.org.za; f. 1892; Bishop Dr DIETER REINSTORF.

Moravian Church in Southern Africa: POB 24111, Lansdowne
7779; tel. (21) 7614030; e-mail mcsa@iafrica.com; f. 1737; Pres. Rev.
MARTIN ABRAHAMS.

**Northeastern Evangelical Lutheran Church in South Africa
(NELCSA):** Church Council, 24 Savannah Rd, Bonaero Park 1622;
POB 7095, Bonaero Park 1622; tel. (11) 9797137; e-mail bishop@
elcsant.org.za; internet www.elcsant.org.za; f. 1981; fmrly Evangelical Lutheran Church in Southern Africa (N-T); present name
adopted 2019; Pres. Bishop HORST MÜLLER.

The Roman Catholic Church

For ecclesiastical purposes South Africa comprises five archdioceses,
20 dioceses, one apostolic vicariate and one military ordinariate.

Southern African Catholic Bishops' Conference (SACBC):
Khanya House, 129 Main St, Waterkloof, Pretoria 0001; tel. (12)
3236458; e-mail communication@sacbc.org.za; internet www.sacbc
.org.za; f. 1947; mems representing South Africa, Botswana and
Eswatini (Swaziland); Pres. Rt Rev. SITHEMBILE SIPUKA (Bishop of
Umtata); Sec.-Gen. Fr HUGH O'CONNOR.

Archbishop of Bloemfontein: Most Rev. ZOLILE PETER MPAMBANI,
Archbishop's House, 7A Whites Rd, POB 362, Bloemfontein 9300; tel.
(51) 4481658; e-mail bfnarch@mweb.co.za.

Archbishop of Cape Town: Most Rev. STEPHEN BRISLIN, Cathedral
Place, 12 Bouquet St, Cape Town; POB 2910, Cape Town 8000; tel.
(21) 4622417; e-mail info@adct.org.za; internet adct.org.za.

Archbishop of Durban: Most Rev. SIEGFRIED MANDLA JWARA,
Archbishop's House, 154 Gordon Rd, Morningside, Durban 4001;
POB 47489, Greyville 4023; tel. (31) 3031417; e-mail chancellor@
catholic-dbn.org.za; internet www.catholic-dbn.org.za.

Archbishop of Johannesburg: Most Rev. BUTI JOSEPH TLHAGALE,
Archbishop's House, 186 Nugget St, Berea, Johannesburg 2198;
PMB X10, Doornfontein 2028; tel. (11) 4026400; e-mail catholic@
icon.co.za; internet www.catholicjhb.org.za.

Archbishop of Pretoria: Most Rev. DABULA ANTHONY MPAKO,
Jolivet House, 140 Visagie St, Pretoria 0002; POB 8149, Pretoria
0001; tel. (12) 3265311; e-mail ptadiocese@absamail.co.za; internet
www.ptadiocese.org.za.

Other Christian Churches

In addition to the following Churches, there are a large number of
Pentecostalist groups, and more than 4,000 independent African
Churches.

Afrikaanse Protestantse Kerk (Afrikaans Protestant Church):
Makoustraat 516, Monumentpark X2, Pretoria; tel. (12) 3621390;
e-mail info@apk.co.za; internet apk.co.za; f. 1987 by fmr mems of the
Dutch Reformed Church (Nederduitse Gereformeerde Kerk) in
protest at the desegregation of church congregations; Dir DS. JOHAN
SCHÜTTE.

Apostolic Faith Mission of South Africa: Central Office Park,
Bldg No. 14, 257 Jean Ave, Centurion; POB 9450, Centurion 0046;
tel. (12) 6440490; e-mail info@afm-ags.org; internet www.afm-ags
.org; f. 1908; Pres. Pastor M. G. MAHLOBO; Gen. Sec. Dr H. J.
WEIDEMAN.

Assemblies of God Fellowship South Africa: POB 1679, Pretoria
0001; tel. (12) 3270094; e-mail info@agfsa.co.za; internet www.agfsa
.co.za; f. 1981; Pres. Rev. PHILIP DUNGULU; Gen. Sec. Rev. JULIO
DASILVA.

Baptist Union of Southern Africa: 44 Blende Ave, Roodekrans
1724; Private Bag X45, Wilropark 1731; tel. (11) 7685980; e-mail
secretary@baptistunion.org.za; internet www.baptistunion.org.za;
f. 1877; Pres. Rev. GREGORY MATTHEI; Admin. Rev. COLIN DIESEL.

Church of England in South Africa (CESA): POB 2180, Clar-
einch 7740; tel. (21) 6717070; e-mail melanie@reachsa.org.za;
internet reachsa.org.za; f. 1938; Presiding Bishop Rt Rev. GLENN
LYONS; Admin. Officer MELANIE BOTHA; 217 churches.

Evangelical Presbyterian Church in South Africa: POB 31961,
Braamfontein 2017; tel. (11) 3391044; e-mail headoffice@epcsa.org
.za; internet www.epcsa.org.za; f. 1875; Moderator Rev. G. S.
MOYANE; Gen. Sec. Rev. T. D. Y. SOMBHANE.

The Methodist Church of Southern Africa: 33 Ernest Oppenheimer Ave, Bruma Office Park, Bruma; Private Bag x11, Garden
View 2047; tel. (11) 6151616; e-mail gensec@mco.org.za; internet
www.methodist.org.za; f. 1883; Presiding Bishop Rev. PURITY
NOMTHANDAZO MALINGA; Gen. Sec. Rev. MICHEL HANSROD.

Nederduitsch Hervormde Kerk van Afrika: Derdepoort Congregation, 129 Swaan St, East Lynne, Pretoria; POB 2368, Pretoria

0001; tel. (12) 3228885; e-mail frikkie@nhk.co.za; internet www
.nhka.org; f. 1652; Gen. Sec. F. J. LABUSCHAGNE.

Nederduitse Gereformeerde Kerk in Afrika: 22 Badenhorst St,
Universitas, Bloemfontein 9301; Box 1004, Bloemfontein 9300; tel.
(51) 5220762; e-mail saakgelastigde@ngka.co.za; internet www
.ngka.co.za; Admin. Rev. J. C. BEZUIDENHOUT.

Presbyterian Church of Africa: 198 Botomane St, Skhosana
Section, Katlehong 1431; tel. (11) 9097474; e-mail gaclerk@
presbyterianchurchofafrica.com; internet www
.presbyterianchurchofafrica.co.za; f. 1898; 8 presbyteries (incl. 1 in
Malawi and 1 in Zimbabwe); Moderator Rt Rev. T. S. S. NKUMANDA;
Gen. Sec. MZUKISI FALENI.

Reformed Churches in South Africa (Die Gereformeerde Kerke):
POB 20004, North Bridge, Potchefstroom 2522; tel. (18) 2973986;
e-mail wymiedup@gksa.co.za; internet www.gksa.org.za; f. 1859;
Admin. Man. Dr WYMIE DU PLESSIS.

**Southern Africa Union Conference of the Seventh-day
Adventist Church:** 2 Fairview St, Bloemfontein; POB 468, Bloemfontein 9300; tel. (51) 4478271; e-mail info@sau.adventist.org;
internet www.adventist.org.za; Pres. Dr DAVID C. SPENCER; Exec.
Sec. Pastor TREVOR KUNENE.

United Congregational Church of Southern Africa (UCCSA):
5 Kurt St, Florida Glen 1709; POB 96014, Brixton 2019; tel. (11)
6730182; e-mail admin@uccsa.co.za; internet www
.unitedcongregational.org; f. 1967; Pres. Rev. SIKHALO CELE; Gen.
Sec. Rev. KUDZANI NDEBELE; 500,000 mems in 450 churches.

Uniting Presbyterian Church in Southern Africa: Plot 18, Tiyo
Soga House, Dann Rd, Glen Marais 1619; POB 12355, Aston Manor
1620; tel. (11) 7273500; e-mail gensec@unitingpresbyterian.org;
internet unitingpresbyterian.org; f. 1999; Moderator Rev. SIPHO J.
MTETWA; Gen. Sec. Rev. Dr LUNGILE MPETSHENI.

Zion Christian Church: Moria Zion City, Polokwane, Limpopo
0699; tel. (15) 2660073; e-mail office@zcc.za.org; f. 1910; South
Africa's largest black religious group; Leader Bishop BARNABAS
LEKGANYANE.

ISLAM

Islamic Council of South Africa: 14 Bellmore Ave, Mount View,
Athlone, Western Cape; tel. (21) 6912456; e-mail thaf@webmail.co
.za; internet www.islamiccouncilsa.co.za; f. 1975; umbrella body of
Muslim organizations in South Africa; CEO SHAIGH THAFIER
NAJJAAR.

JUDAISM

African Jewish Congress: POB 51663, Raedene 2124; tel. (82)
4402621; e-mail rabbiajc@gmail.com; internet www
.africanjewishcongress.com; f. 1994; co-ordinating body representing
Jewish communities in sub-Saharan Africa; Pres. ANN HARRIS;
Spiritual Leader and CEO Rabbi MOSHE SILBERHAFT.

South African Jewish Board of Deputies (SAJBD): POB 87557,
Houghton 2041; tel. (11) 6452523; e-mail sajbd@sajbd.org; internet
www.sajbd.org; f. 1904; the representative institution of South
African Jewry; Nat. Chair. SHAUN ZAGNOEV; Nat. Dir WENDY KAHN.

BAHÁ'Í FAITH

National Spiritual Assembly: 209 Bellairs Dr., North Riding
2169; POB 932, Banbury Cross 2164; tel. (11) 8013100; e-mail nsa
.sec@bahai.org.za; internet www.bahai.org.za; f. 1956; Gen. Sec.
CHARLOTTE MATDAT.

The Press

**Government Communication and Information System
(GCIS):** Tshedimosetso House, cnr 1035 Frances Baard and Festival
Sts, Hatfield, Pretoria; tel. (12) 4730000; e-mail information@gcis
.gov.za; internet www.gcis.gov.za; f. 1998; govt agency; Dir-Gen.
PHUMLA WILLIAMS.

Press Council of South Africa: 410 Jan Smuts Ave, Burnside
Island Office Park, Bldg 12, Craighall Park 2196; tel. (11) 4843612;
e-mail mobara@ombudsman.org.za; internet www.presscouncil.org
.za; Exec. Dir LATIEFA MOBARA.

DAILY NEWSPAPERS (PRINT AND ONLINE)

Eastern Cape

Die Burger (Oos-Kaap): Ivor-Benn Close, Fairview, POB 525,
Gqeberha 6000; tel. 873531300; e-mail diens@netwerk24.com;
internet www.netwerk24.com/dieburger-oos-kaap; f. 1914; daily
(online); weekly (print); Afrikaans; publ. by Media 24; Editor-in-
Chief ADRIAAN BASSON.

Daily Dispatch: cnr St Helena Rd and Quenera Dr., East London; POB 131, East London 5200; tel. (43) 7022000; e-mail news@dispatch .co.za; internet www.dispatchlive.co.za; f. 1872; publ. by Arena Holdings (Pty) Ltd; also publishes *Weekend Dispatch*; English; Editor CHERI-ANN JAMES; circ. 10,826 (2022).

The Herald: The Atrium Bldg, 24 Ring Rd, Greenacres, Gqeberha; Private Bag X6071, Gqeberha 1; tel. (41) 5047911; e-mail helpdesk@ heraldlive.co.za; internet www.heraldlive.co.za; f. 1845; fmrly *Eastern Province Herald*; also publishes weekly *Weekend Post* and online edn *HeraldLIVE*; publ. by Arena Holdings (Pty) Ltd; English; Editor ROCHELLE DE KOCK; circ. 11,481 (2022).

Free State

Die Volksblad: 79 Nelson Mandelaryln, POB 267, Bloemfontein 9300; tel. (51) 4047600; e-mail nuus@volksblad.com; internet www .netwerk24.com/volksblad; f. 1904; publ. by Media 24; Afrikaans; Editor-in-Chief HENRIETTE LOUBSER.

Gauteng

Beeld: Media Park, 69 Kingsway Ave, Auckland Park, Johannesburg; POB 333, Auckland Park 2006; tel. (11) 7139000; e-mail nuus@ beeld.com; internet www.netwerk24.com/beeld; f. 1974; publ. by Media 24; weekly: *Kampus-Beeld*, student news and information, and *JIP* youth supplement; Afrikaans; Editor-in-Chief HENRIETTE LOUBSER; Editor V. BARNARD BEUKMAN; circ. 21,596 (2022).

Business Day: Hill on Empire, 16 Empire Rd (cnr Empire and Hillside), Johannesburg; tel. (11) 2803000; e-mail feedback@ businesslive.co.za; internet www.businesslive.co.za; f. 1985; publ. by Arena Holdings (Pty) Ltd; English; financial; incl. *Wanted* arts and leisure magazine; Editor-in-Chief TIISETSO MOTSOENENG (acting); circ. 16,006 (2022).

The Citizen: 9 Wright St, Industria West, Johannesburg; tel. (10) 9764222; e-mail support@citizen.co.za; internet citizen.co.za; f. 1976; daily (Mon.–Fri.); weekly (Sat.); publ. by Caxton Publrs & Printers Ltd; supplements include: *Motoring*, *Hammer & Gavel*, *Phakaaathi* and *Racing Express*; English; Editor TREVOR STEVENS; circ. 27,097 (2022).

The Daily Sun: Media Park, 69 Kingsway Ave, Auckland Park; POB 121, Auckland Park 2006; tel. (11) 8776000; e-mail news@dailysun.co .za; internet www.dailysun.co.za; f. 2002; publ. by Media24; Editor-in-Chief (vacant); Editor PRINCE CHAUKE; circ. 35,085 (2022).

Pretoria News: 216 Vermeulen St, Pretoria 0002; POB 439, Pretoria 0001; tel. (12) 3002000; e-mail iolletters@inl.co.za; internet www.iol.co.za/pretoria-news; f. 1898; publ. by Independent Newspapers Gauteng Ltd; also publishes *Pretoria News Saturday*; English; Editor PIET RAMPEDI; circ. 2,372 (2022).

Sowetan: Hill on Empire, 16 Empire Rd, Johannesburg; POB 6663, Johannesburg 2000; tel. (11) 2803000; e-mail newsdesk@sowetan.co .za; internet www.sowetanlive.co.za; f. 1981; publ. by Arena Holdings (Pty) Ltd; English; Editor NWABISA MAKUNGA; circ. 29,263 (2022).

The Star: 47 Pixley ka Isaka Seme St, Johannesburg 2000; POB 1014, Johannesburg 2000; tel. (11) 6339111; e-mail starnews@inl.co .za; internet www.iol.co.za/the-star; f. 1886; publ. by Independent Newspapers Gauteng Ltd; English; also publishes *The Saturday Star*; Editor SIFISO MAHLANGU; circ. 27,984 (2022).

KwaZulu/Natal

Daily News: 18 Osborne St, Greyville, Durban 4001; POB 47549, Durban, Greyville 4023; tel. (31) 3082911; e-mail dnnews@inl.co.za; internet www.iol.co.za/dailynews; f. 1878; Mon.–Fri.; English; Editor AYANDA MDLULI; circ. 9,735 (2022).

Isolezwe: 18 Osborne St, Greyville, Durban 4001; POB 47549, Greyville, Durban 4023; tel. (31) 3082911; e-mail isolezwe@inl.co .za; internet www.isolezwe.co.za; f. 2002; Zulu; publ. by Independent Media; Editor KIKI NTULI; circ. 31,579 (2022).

The Mercury: 18 Osborne St, Greyville, Durban 4001; POB 47397, Greyville, Durban 4023; tel. (31) 3082911; e-mail mercnews@inl.co .za; internet www.iol.co.za/mercury; f. 1852; publ. by Independent Newspapers KZN; English; Editor PHILANI MAZIBUKO; circ. 11,719 (2022).

The Witness: 45 Willowton Rd, POB 362, Pietermaritzburg 3201; tel. (33) 3551111; e-mail letters@citypress.co.za; internet www .citizen.co.za/witness; f. 1846; Mon.–Fri.; English; also publishes *Weekend Witness* (Sat.); publ. by Media24; Editor STEPHANIE SAVILLE; circ. 7,183 (2022).

Northern Cape

Diamond Fields Advertiser (DFA): North Cape Hall, Kimberley 8301; tel. (53) 8326261; e-mail dfanewspaper@inl.co.za; internet www.dfa.co.za; f. 1878; publ. by Independent Newspapers Gauteng Ltd; English; Editor JOHAN DU PLESSIS; circ. 4,546 (2022).

Western Cape

Die Burger: 40 Heerengracht, POB 692, Cape Town 8000; tel. (21) 4062222; e-mail dieburger@dieburger.co.za; internet www .netwerk24.com/dieburger; f. 1915; Afrikaans; publ. by Media24; Editor WILLEM JORDAAN; circ. 29,120 (2022).

Cape Argus: 122 St George's St, Cape Town 8001; POB 56, Cape Town 8000; tel. (21) 4884911; e-mail argusnews@inl.co.za; internet www.iol.co.za/capeargus; f. 1857; publ. by Independent Newspapers Cape Ltd; Mon.–Fri.; English; also publishes *Weekend Argus*; Editor TAARIQ HALIM; circ. 10,834 (2022).

Cape Times: Newspaper House, 4th Floor, 122 St George's Mall, Cape Town; POB 56, Cape Town 8000; tel. (21) 4884911; e-mail ctletters@inl.co.za; internet www.iol.co.za/capetimes; f. 1876; publ. by Independent Newspapers Cape Ltd; English; Editor SIYAVUYA MZANTSI; circ. 11,829 (2022).

WEEKLIES AND FORTNIGHTLIES

Eastern Cape

Weekend Post: The Atrium Bldg, 24 Ring Rd, Greenacres, Gqeberha; Private Bag X6071, Gqeberha 6000; tel. (41) 5047911; e-mail helpdesk@heraldlive.co.za; internet www.heraldlive.co.za; publ. by Arena Holdings (Pty) Ltd; English; Editor ROCHELLE DE KOCK; circ. 9,410 (2022).

Free State

Vista: The Strip, 312 Stateway, Welkom 9459; tel. (82) 4665851; e-mail marti.will@media24.com; internet www.netwerk24.com/ netwerk24/za/vista; f. 1971; weekly; English and Afrikaans; Editor MARTI WILL; circ. 35,214 (2022).

Gauteng

City Press: 69 Media Park, Kingsway Auckland Park; POB 3413, Johannesburg 2000; tel. (11) 7139002; e-mail web@citypress.co.za; internet www.news24.com/citypress; f. 1983; weekly; English; publ. by RCP Media Bpk; CEO ISHMET DAVIDSON; Editor-in-Chief MONDLI MAKHANYA; circ. 21,026 (2022).

Engineering News: Bedford Centre, 4th Floor, cnr Smith and Bradford Rds, Bedfordview, Johannesburg; POB 785, Bedfordview 2008; tel. (11) 6223744; e-mail newsdesk@creamermedia.co.za; internet www.engineeringnews.co.za; f. 1981; Editor TERENCE CREAMER; circ. 13,428 (2022).

Financial Mail: Hill on Empire, 16 Empire Rd, Parktown 2193; tel. (11) 2805808; e-mail fmeditor@fm.co.za; internet www.businesslive .co.za; f. 1959; weekly; English; publ. by Arena Holdings (Pty) Ltd; Editor ROB ROSE; circ. 12,907 (2022).

Mail & Guardian: The Metal Box, 25 Owl St, Braamfontein Werf, Johannesburg 2001; POB 91667, Auckland Park, Johannesburg 2006; tel. (11) 2507300; e-mail newsdesk@mg.co.za; internet www .mg.co.za; f. 1985; weekly; English; publ. by M&G Media (Pty) Ltd; Editor-in-Chief RON DERBY; circ. 9,248 (2022).

Midweek Potchefstroom Herald: POB 515, Potchefstroom 2520; tel. (18) 2930750; e-mail potchherald@media24.com; internet www .potchefstroomherald.co.za; fmrly Noordwes Gazette; present name adopted in July 2015; weekly; English and Afrikaans; Editor HENNIE STANDER.

Mining Weekly: Bedford Centre, 4th Floor, cnr Smith and Bradford Rds, Bedfordview, Johannesburg; POB 785, Bedfordview 2008; tel. (11) 6223744; e-mail newsdesk@engineeringnews.co.za; internet www.miningweekly.com; f. 1981; weekly; publ. by Creamer Media; Editor MARTIN CREAMER; circ. 13,428 (2022).

Potchefstroom Herald: cnr Piet Uys St and Govin Mbeki St, Wilgepark Centre, Potchefstroom; POB 515, Potchefstroom 2520; tel. (18) 2930750; e-mail potchherald@media24.com; internet www .potchefstroomherald.co.za; f. 1908; weekly; English and Afrikaans; Editor DUSTIN WETDEWICH; circ. 16,938 (2022).

Rapport: 69 Kingsway, Auckland Park, Johannesburg; POB 8422, Johannesburg 2000; tel. (11) 7139633; e-mail nuus@rapport.co.za; internet www.netwerk24.com; f. 1970; weekly; Afrikaans; publ. by Media 24; Editor WALDIMAR PELSER; circ. 67,865 (2022).

South African Jewish Report: POB 84650, Greenside 2034; tel. (11) 4301980; e-mail editor@sajewishreport.co.za; internet www.sajr .co.za; f. 1998; weekly; publ. by SA Jewish Report (Pty) Ltd; Editor PETA KROST MAUNDER.

Springs Advertiser: 48 5th Ave, POB 761, Springs 1560; tel. (10) 9713300; e-mail springseditorial@caxton.co.za; internet springsadvertiser.co.za; f. 1916; English and Afrikaans; Editor SAMANTHA KEOGH; circ. 26,052 (2022).

Sunday Times: Hill on Empire, 16 Empire Rd, Parktown, Johannesburg; POB 1742, Saxonwold 2132; tel. (11) 2803000; e-mail helpdesk@timeslive.co.za; internet www.timeslive.co.za/

sundaytimes; f. 1906; weekly; English and Zulu; Editor S'THEMBISO MSOMI; circ. 116,295 (2022).

Vaalweekblad: Ekspa Bldg, 1st Floor, cnr Attie Fourie and DF Malan St, Vanderbijlpark 1900; tel. (16) 9507000; e-mail rfichat@media24.com; internet vaalweekblad.com; f. 1964; weekly; Afrikaans and English; Editor RETHA FICHAT; Man. Dir THYS FOORD; circ. 3,467 (2022).

KwaZulu/Natal

Farmers' Weekly: Caxton House, 368 Jan Smuts Ave, Craighall, Johannesburg 2196; tel. (10) 9713765; e-mail farmersweekly@caxton.co.za; internet www.farmersweekly.co.za; f. 1911; weekly; agriculture and horticulture; Editor JANINE RYAN; circ. 6,680 (2022).

Ilanga: 19 Timeball Blvd, The Point, Durban 4001; tel. (31) 3346700; e-mail info@ilanganews.co.za; internet www.ilanganews.co.za; f. 1903; biweekly; also publishes *Ilanga Lange Sonto*; Zulu; Editor ERIC NDIYANE; circ. 38,433 (2022).

Independent On Saturday: 18 Osborne St, Greyville, Durban 4001; POB 47397, Greyville, Durban 4023; tel. (31) 3082911; e-mail ios@inl.co.za; internet www.iol.co.za/ios; f. 1998; English; publ. by Independent Newspapers KZN; Editor ZOUBAIR AYOOB; circ. 14,176 (2022).

Ladysmith Gazette: 29B San Marco Centre, Ladysmith 3370; tel. (36) 6376801; e-mail ladysmith.gazette@caxton.co.za; internet fb.com/ladysmith.gazette; f. 1902; weekly; English, Afrikaans and Zulu; part of the Caxton Group of newspapers; Editor ROD SKINNER; circ. 1,297 (2022).

The Post: 18 Osborne St, Greyville, Durban 4000; POB 47397, Greyville, Durban 4023; tel. (31) 3082911; e-mail post@inl.co.za; internet www.iol.co.za/thepost; f. 1955 as *Golden City Post*; weekly; English; focus on the Indian community; publ. by Independent Newspapers KZN; Editor AAKASH BRAMDEO; circ. 19,373 (2022).

Sunday Tribune: 18 Osborne St, POB 47549, Greyville 4023; tel. (63) 8209897; e-mail tribuneletters@inl.co.za; internet www.iol.co.za/sunday-tribune; f. 1937; weekly; English; publ. by Independent Newspapers KZN; Editor SANDILE MDADANE; circ. 21,261 (2022).

North-West

Rustenburg Herald: 13 Coetzer St, POB 2043, Rustenburg 0299; tel. (14) 5928329; e-mail mailbag@rustenburgherald.co.za; internet fb.com/rustenburgherald; f. 1924; English and Afrikaans; Editor WALDIE WOLSCHENK.

Western Cape

Drum: Media Park, 69 Kingsway Rd, Johannesburg 2006; POB 7167, Roggebaai 8012; tel. (11) 7139140; e-mail letters@drum.co.za; internet www.news24.com/drum; f. 1951; English and Zulu; publ. by Media24; Editor-in-Chief THULANI GQIRANA.

Eikestadnuus: 44 Alexander St, Stellenbosch 7600; tel. (21) 8872840; e-mail eikestad@eikestadnuus.com; internet www.netwerk24.com/ZA/Eikestadnuus; weekly; English and Afrikaans; f. 1950; Editor ANGELO JULIES; circ. 23,850 (2022).

Fairlady: POB 1802, Cape Town 8000; tel. (21) 4081278; e-mail flmag@fairlady.com; internet fairlady.com; fortnightly; English; Editor SUZY BROKENSHA; circ. 38,698 (2022).

Huisgenoot: 40 Heerengracht, Cape Town 8001; POB 1802, Cape Town 8000; tel. (21) 4062115; e-mail hgnbrief@huisgenoot.com; internet www.netwerk24.com/huisgenoot; f. 1916; weekly; Afrikaans; Editor YVONNE BEYERS; circ. 126,659 (2022).

Move! Magazine: Media City, 10th Floor, 1 Heerengracht St, Foreshore, Cape Town 8001; tel. (21) 4461232; e-mail move@media24.com; internet www.news24.com/move; f. 2005; weekly; English; Editor-in-Chief CHARLENE ROLLS.

tvplus: Media City, 10th Floor, 1 Heerengracht St, Cape Town 8001; POB 7197, Roggebaai 8012; tel. (21) 4461222; e-mail tvplus@media24.com; internet fb.com/tvplus; f. 2000; biweekly; English and Afrikaans; Editor LUCIA SWART-WALTERS; circ. 4,000 (2021).

TygerBurger: Bloemhof Bldg, 112 Edward Rd, Bellville 7530; tel. (21) 9106500; e-mail cecilia@media24.com; internet www.netwerk24.com/ZA/Tygerburger; weekly; Afrikaans and English; Editor CECILIA HUME.

Weekend Argus: 122 St George's Mall, POB 56, Cape Town 8000; tel. (21) 4884528; e-mail wknews@inl.co.za; internet www.iol.co.za/weekend-argus; f. 1857; Sat. and Sun.; English; Editor MELANIE PETERS; circ. 13,230 (2022).

You Magazine: Naspers Bldg, 7th Floor, 40 Heerengracht St, Cape Town 8001; POB 7167, Roggebaai 8012; tel. (21) 4062506; e-mail news@you.co.za; internet www.news24.com/you; f. 1987; weekly; English; Editor CHARLENE ROLLS; circ. 67,392 (2022).

MONTHLIES

KwaZulu/Natal

Living and Loving: CTP Caxton Magazines, 4th Floor, Caxton House, 368 Jan Smuts Ave, Craighall Park, Johannesburg; tel. 870878823; e-mail livingandloving@caxton.co.za; internet fb.com/livingandlovingSA; f. 1970; English; parenting magazine; Editor SONYA NAUDÉ.

Rooi Rose: Caxton House, 368 Jan Smuts Ave, Craighall 2196; POB 412982, Craighall 2024; tel. (11) 8890665; e-mail rooirose@caxton.co.za; internet www.rooirose.co.za; f. 1942; Afrikaans; Editor MARTIE PANSEGROUW; circ. 25,964 (2022).

World Airnews: POB 35082, Northway 4065; tel. (31) 5641319; e-mail info@airnews.co.za; internet www.airnews.co.za; f. 1973; monthly; owned by TCE Publications; aviation news; Editor HEIDI GIBSON; Man. Editor JOAN CHALMERS.

Western Cape

Bona: Highbury Media, 36 Old Mill Rd, Ndabeni 7405; tel. (21) 5303300; e-mail bona@caxton.co.za; internet www.bona.co.za; f. 1956; English, Sotho, Xhosa and Zulu; Editor BONGIWE TSHIQI.

Car: 36 Old Mill Rd, Ndabeni, Maitland 7405; tel. (21) 5303300; e-mail admin@carmag.co.za; internet www.carmag.co.za; English; Editor STEVE SMITH; circ. 43,087 (2022).

Ideas/Idees: 6 Lismore Terrace, Green Point, POB 51083, Waterfront, Cape Town 8002; tel. 873531291; e-mail info@ideasfactory.co.za; internet fb.com/IdeesSA; f. 2017; English; Editor TERENA LE ROUX; circ. 15,915 (2021).

LiG: 69 Kerkstraat, Wellington; tel. (21) 8648202; e-mail lig@tydskrifte.co.za; internet lig.christians.co.za; f. 1937 as Die Voorligter; journal of the Dutch Reformed Church of South Africa; Editor FRANCINE PRINS; circ. 19,773 (2022).

Sarie: 5A Protea Park, Protea Place, Sandown; POB 785266, Sandton 2146; tel. (11) 3220745; e-mail sarie@sarie.com; internet www.netwerk24.com/sarie; f. 1949; monthly; Afrikaans; Editor MICHELLE VAN BREDA; circ. 62,348 (2022).

South African Medical Journal: Suite 11, Lonsdale Bldg, Gardener Way, Pinelands 7405; Private Bag X1, Pinelands 7430; tel. (21) 5321281; e-mail publishing@hmpg.co.za; internet www.samj.org.za; f. 1884; monthly; publ. by the South African Medical Asscn; Editor Dr BRIDGET FARHAM; circ. 9,297 (2022).

The Southern Cross: c/o The Chancery, 12 Bouquet St, Cape Town 8001; POB 2372, Cape Town 8000; tel. (83) 2331956; e-mail admin@scross.co.za; internet www.scross.co.za; f. 1920; monthly; English; Roman Catholic interest; publ. by Catholic Newspapers and Publishing Co Ltd; Editor GÜNTHER SIMMERMACHER; circ. 3,500 (2021).

WineLand Magazine: Vinpro, Picardi Farm, Cecilia St, Suider-Paarl 7624; tel. (21) 2760458; e-mail in@wineland.co.za; internet www.wineland.co.za; f. 1931; publ. by Vinpro wine producers' org.; viticulture and the wine and spirit industry; incorporates *Wynboer* technical guide for wine producers; Editor WANDA AUGUSTYN; circ. 3,200 (2022).

PERIODICALS

Eastern Cape

Africa Insight: 1 Whitnall St, Makhanda 6139; POB 420 Makhanda 6140; tel. (12) 3049700; e-mail info@ajol.info; internet www.ajol.info; f. 1960; quarterly; journal of the Africa Institute of South Africa; Editor SABELO J. NDLOVU-GATSHENI.

Gauteng

Historia: c/o Dept of Historical and Heritage Studies, Faculty of Humanities, Humanities Bldg (Main Campus), University of Pretoria, Pretoria 0028; tel. (12) 4202323; e-mail hasa@up.ac.za; internet hgsa.co.za; f. 1956; biannual; Journal of the Historical Asscn of South Africa; South African and African history; Editor-in-Chief Prof. JULIE PARLE.

The ScienceScope: Meiring Naudé Rd, Brummeria, Pretoria; POB 395, Pretoria 0001; tel. (12) 8412911; e-mail enquiries@csir.co.za; internet www.csir.co.za; f. 1991 as *Technobrief*; quarterly; publ. by the South African Council for Scientific and Industrial Research; CEO Dr THULANI DLAMINI.

South African Journal of Chemistry: University of University of the Witwatersrand, Private Bag X3, Braamfontein, Johannesburg 2050; tel. (11) 7176705; e-mail Cornie.VanSittert@nwu.ac.za; internet sajchem.co.za; f. 1921; publ. by the South African Chemical Institute; digital; Editor-in-Chief Prof. CORNIE VAN SITTERT.

South African Journal of Economics: Tukkiewerf 2/21, University of Pretoria, Lynwood Rd, Pretoria 0002; POB 73354, Lynnwood Ridge 0040; tel. (12) 4203525; e-mail saje@up.ac.za; internet www.essa.org.za; f. 1933; quarterly; English; journal of the Economic Soc.

of South Africa; publ. by Wiley-Blackwell; Man. Editor Prof. STEVE KOCH; Editorial Sec. TITIA ANTONITES.

Western Cape

Economic Prospects: Old Conservatorium, 10 Van Riebeeck St, Stellenbosch 7600; Private Bag 5050, Stellenbosch 7599; tel. (21) 8089755; e-mail hugop@sun.ac.za; internet www.ber.ac.za; quarterly; forecast of the South African economy for the coming 18–24 months; Editor HUGO PIENAAR.

NEWS AGENCIES

African News Agency (ANA): Newspaper House, 122 St George's Mall, Cape Town 8001; tel. (21) 4884001; e-mail hello@africannewsagency.com; internet www.africannewsagency.com; f. 2015 following the liquidation of South African Press Asscn (SAPA); CEO VASANTHA ANGAMUTHU.

South African Government News Agency (SAnews): Tshedimosetso House, 1035 cnr Frances Baard and Festival Sts, Hatfield, Pretoria 0083; tel. (12) 4730213; e-mail socialmedia@gcis.gov.za; internet www.sanews.gov.za; fmrly BuaNews; publ. by the Department of Communications, South African Government; Editor ROZE MOODLEY.

PRESS ASSOCIATIONS

Foreign Correspondents' Association of Southern Africa (FCA): POB 1136, Auckland Park, Johannesburg 2006; tel. 834420044; e-mail secretary@fcasa.net; internet www.fcasa.org; f. 1976; represents 285 int. journalists; Chair. GERSENDE RAMBOURG; Sec. STEVEN BRIMELOW.

Print and Digital Media South Africa: 410 Jan Smuts Ave, Burnside Office Park, Bldg 8, Craighall Park 2196; POB 47180, Parklands 2121; tel. (11) 3264041; e-mail administrator@pdmedia.org.za; internet www.pdmedia.org.za; f. 1995 following the restructuring of the Newspaper Press Union of Southern Africa; represents all aspects of the print media (newspapers and magazines); Pres NEO MOMODU.

Publishers

Bible Society of South Africa: Bible House, 134 Edward St, Bellville, POB 5500, Tyger Valley 7536; tel. (21) 9108777; e-mail biblia@biblesociety.co.za; internet www.biblesociety.co.za; f. 1820; bibles and religious material in 11 official languages; CEO Rev. DIRK GEVERS.

Brenthurst Press (Pty) Ltd: Federation Rd, Parktown, POB 87184, Houghton 2041; tel. (11) 5445400; e-mail info@brenthurst.co.za; internet www.brenthurst.org.za; f. 1974; Southern African history; Marketing Dir SALLY MACROBERTS.

Cambridge University Press SA (Pty) Ltd: Lower Ground Floor, Nautica Bldg, The Water Club Beach Rd, Granger Bay, Cape Town 8005; tel. (21) 4127800; e-mail capetown@cambridge.org; internet www.cambridge.org/africa; f. 1995; Dir COLLEEN McCALLUM.

Fisichem Uitgewers (Physichem Publishers): 19A Hofmeyer St, POB 3009, Matieland 7602; tel. (21) 8870900; e-mail info@fisichem.co.za; internet fisichem.co.za; f. 1985; owned by FRJ Trust; science and maths study guides; Man. RETHA JORDAAN.

Fortress Books: POB 2475, Knysna 6570; tel. (44) 3826805; e-mail fortress@iafrica.com; internet www.uys.com/fortress; f. 1973; military history, biographies, financial; Man. Dir I. UYS.

HSRC Press: 116–118 Merchant House, Buitengracht St, Private Bag X9182, Cape Town 8000; tel. (21) 4668000; e-mail jrwightman@hsrc.ac.za; internet www.hsrcpress.ac.za; Publishing Dir JEREMY WIGHTMAN.

Jonathan Ball Publishers: 66 Mimetes Rd, Denver Ext. 9, Johannesburg 2094; POB 33977, Jeppestown 2043; tel. (11) 6018000; e-mail services@jonathanball.co.za; internet www.jonathanball.co.za; f. 1976; acquired by Via Afrika (Naspers Group) in 1992; fiction, reference, bibles, textbooks, general; imprints incl. AD Donker (literature), Delta (general fiction and non-fiction) and Sunbird; CEO EUGENE ASHTON.

Juta and Co Ltd: Sunclare Bldg, 1st Floor, 21 Dreyer St, Claremont 7708; tel. (21) 6592300; e-mail cserv@juta.co.za; internet www.juta.co.za; f. 1853; academic and professional development, education, trade, law, electronics; imprints incl. UCT Press (scholarly and academic); CEO KAMAL PATEL.

LAPA Publishers (Lees Afrikaans Praat Afrikaans): Growth Point Business Park, 162 Tonetti St, Midrand; tel. (12) 4010700; e-mail lapa@lapa.co.za; internet www.lapa.co.za; f. 1996 as the publishing arm of the Afrikaans Language and Culture Asscn; present name adopted in 2000; acquired by Penguin Random House (SA) in 2020; Afrikaans; general fiction and non-fiction; CEO STEVE CONNOLLY.

Lemur Books (Pty) Ltd (Galago Publishing (1999) (Pty) Ltd): POB 1645, Alberton 1450; tel. (11) 8279418; e-mail lemur@mweb.co.za; internet www.galago.co.za; f. 1980; military, political, history, hunting, general; Man. Dir FRAN STIFF.

LexisNexis SA: Country Club Estate Office Park, Bldg 8, 21 Woodlands Dr., Woodmead, Johannesburg; tel. 860765432; e-mail customercare@lexisnexis.co.za; internet www.lexisnexis.co.za; f. 1948 as Butterworths; present name adopted in 2001; jtly owned by Reed Elsevier, USA, and Kagiso Media; law, tax, accountancy; Chair. W. ROGER JARDINE; Man. Dir VIDESHA PROOTHVEERAJH.

Lux Verbi: Naspers Centre, 12th Floor, 40 Heerengracht, Cape Town 8001; POB 879, Cape Town 8000; tel. (21) 4063033; e-mail nb@nb.co.za; internet www.nb.co.za/LuxVerbi; f. 1818 as the Dutch Reformed Church Publishing Co; merged with Bible Media in 1999, demerged in 2011; an imprint of NB publishers, a division of Media24 Boeke (Pty) Ltd; imprints incl. Hugenote, NG Kerk Uitgewers, Protea, and Waterkant; Christian media.

Macmillan South Africa: Hertford Office Park, Bldg G, 4th Floor, 90 Bekker Rd, Vorna Valley, Midrand 1685; tel. (11) 7313300; e-mail customerservices@macmillaneducation.co.za; internet www.macmillaneducation.co.za; f. 1994; Man. Dir PREGGY NAIDOO.

Methodist Publishing House: 16 Durham Ave, Salt River, 7925 Cape Town; POB 13128, Woodstock, Cape Town 7915; tel. (21) 4483640; e-mail retail@methbooks.co.za; internet methbooks.co.za; f. 1894; owned by Methodist Church of Southern Africa; Christian books and church supplies; Gen. Man. HYREATH ANDERSON.

NB Publishers: Naspers Center, 12th Floor, 40 Heerengracht, Cape Town 8001; POB 879, Cape Town 8000; tel. (21) 4063033; e-mail nb@nb.co.za; internet www.nb.co.za; English, Afrikaans, Xhosa and Zulu; Human & Rousseau (f. 1959; general, children's and youth literature, cookery and self-help), Kwela (f. 1994; fiction), Pharos (dictionaries), Tafelberg (f. 1950; fiction and non-fiction, politics, children's and youth literature) and Best Books (educational texts); CEO ELOISE WESSELS.

Oxford University Press: Vasco Blvd, N1 City, Goodwood Cape Town 7460; POB 12119, N1 City, Cape Town 7463; tel. (21) 5962300; e-mail oxford.za@oup.com; internet www.oxford.co.za; f. 1914; Man. Dir (Southern Africa) STEVE CILLIERS.

Pearson South Africa: Auto Atlantic, 4th Floor, cnr Hertzog Blvd and Heerengracht Blvd, Cape Town; POB 396, Cape Town 8000; tel. (21) 5326000; e-mail pearsonza.enquiries@pearson.com; internet za.pearson.com; f. 1893 as Miller Maskew; merged with Longman in 1983; owned by Pearson Education Group; educational and general; Man. Dir EBRAHIM MATTHEWS.

Penguin Random House South Africa: The Estuaries, No. 4, Oxbow Crescent, Century Ave, Century City, 7441; POB 1144, Cape Town 8001; tel. (21) 4605400; e-mail queries@penguinrandomhouse.co.za; internet www.penguinrandomhouse.co.za; f. 1966; fmrly Random House Struik; present name adopted in 2015 following merger with Penguin Books South Africa; general fiction and non-fiction (lifestyle, nature, sport, politics, general reference, travel and heritage); Man. Dir STEVE CONNOLLY.

Protea Book House: 8 Minnistraat, Clydesdale, Pretoria; POB 35110, Menlo Park, 0102 Pretoria; tel. (12) 3436279; e-mail martie@proteaboekhuis.co.za; internet www.proteaboekhuis.com; f. 1997; art and photography, Afrikaans fiction, South African history, spiritual, academic and general; Dir NICOL STASSEN.

Shuter & Shooter Publishers (Pty) Ltd: 110CB Downes Rd, Pietermaritzburg; POB 61, MKondeni 3212; tel. (33) 8468700; e-mail sylvie@shuter.co.za; internet www.shuters.co.za; f. 1921; educational, general and African languages and trade books; Man. Dir PRIMI CHETTY.

University of KwaZulu-Natal Press (UKZN Press): Private Bag X01, Scottsville 3209; tel. (33) 2605226; e-mail books@ukzn.ac.za; internet www.ukznpress.co.za; academic and scholarly; Dir PHINDILE DLAMINI.

Van Schaik Publishers: 1059 Francis Baard St, POB 12681, Hatfield 0028; tel. (12) 3422765; e-mail vanschaik@vanschaiknet.com; internet www.vanschaiknet.com; f. 1915; acquired by Nasionale Pers, latterly Via Afrika-Naspers Group in 1986; English and Afrikaans; academic and scholarly; CEO LEANNE MARTINI.

Via Afrika: Media24 Centre, 11th Floor, 40 Heerengracht, Cape Town; POB 5197, Cape Town 8000; tel. (21) 4063528; e-mail customerservices@viaafrika.com; internet viaafrika.com; f. 1963; educational; imprints incl. Action Publrs, Collegium, Nasou Via Afrika, Stimela, Via Afrika; subsidiary of Media24 (Naspers Group) and Thebe; CEO CHRISTINA WATSON.

Wits University Press: University of the Witwatersrand, 5th Floor, cnr Jan Smuts Ave and Jorissen St, Braamfontein, Johannesburg; PO Wits, Johannesburg 2050; tel. (11) 7178700; e-mail veronica.klipp@wits.ac.za; internet witspress.co.za; f. 1922; non-fiction and scholarly; Publr VERONICA KLIPP.

PUBLISHERS' ASSOCIATION

Publishers' Association of South Africa (PASA): PASA House, Vincent Wynberg Mews, 1st Floor, Unit 104, Brodie Rd, Wynberg, Cape Town; POB 18223, Wynberg 7824; tel. (21) 7629083; e-mail pasa@publishsa.co.za; internet www.publishsa.co.za; f. 1992; promotes and protects the rights and responsibilities of the independent publishing sector in South Africa; Chair. STEVE CILLIERS; Exec. Dir MPUKA RADINKU.

Broadcasting and Communications

REGULATORY AUTHORITY

Independent Communications Authority of South Africa (ICASA): 350 Witch-Hazel Ave, Eco-Park Estate, Centurion 0144; Private Bag X10, Highveld Park 0169; tel. (11) 5683000; e-mail info@icasa.org.za; internet www.icasa.org.za; f. 2000 as successor to the Independent Broadcasting Authority (f. 1993) and South African Telecommunications Regulatory Authority (f. 1996); regulates postal services, telecommunications and broadcasting; Chair. (vacant); CEO WILLINGTON NGWEPE.

TELECOMMUNICATIONS

Cell C (Pty) Ltd: Waterfall Campus, cnr Pretoria Main Rd and Maxwell Dr., Buccleuch, Midrand 2090; Private Bag X36, Benmore 2010, Johannesburg; tel. (84) 1744000; e-mail customerservice@cellc.co.za; internet www.cellc.co.za; f. 2001; 45% owned by Blue Label Telecoms, 30% by 3C Telecommunications, 15% by Net1 UEPS Technologies and 10% by Cell C management and staff; mobile telecommunications provider; Chair. J. S. MTHIMUNYE; CEO DOUGLAS CRAIGIE STEVENSON.

MTN SA: 3 Alice Lane, Ext. 38, PMB 9955, Sandton 2146; tel. (11) 9123000; e-mail customercare@mtn.com; internet www.mtn.co.za; f. 1994; mobile telecommunications provider; part of MTN Group (fmrly M-Cell); operations in 22 countries in Africa and the Middle East; CEO CHARLES MOLAPISI.

Telkom SA Ltd: Telkom Tower North, 152 Proes St, PMB X74, Pretoria 0001; tel. (12) 3111007; e-mail letlapll@telkom.co.za; internet www.telkom.co.za; f. 1991; 40.5% govt-owned; ICT solutions service provider; Chair. SELLO MOLOKO; Group CEO SERAME TAUKOBONG.

Vodacom Group Ltd (Vodacom): Vodacom Corporate Park, 082 Vodacom Blvd, Vodavalley, Midrand 1685; Private Bag X9904, Sandton 2146; tel. (11) 6535000; e-mail mediarelations@vodacom.co.za; internet www.vodacom.co.za; f. 1993; subsidiaries in the DRC (f. 2002), Lesotho (f. 1996), Mozambique (f. 2003) and Tanzania (f. 1999); CEO SHAMEEL AZIZ JOOSUB; Man. Dir SITHO MDLALOSE.

BROADCASTING

Radio

South African Broadcasting Corpn (SABC)—Radio: cnr Artillery and Henley Rds, Auckland Park, Johannesburg 2092; Private Bag X1, Auckland Park 2006, Johannesburg; tel. (11) 7149111; e-mail contactcentre@sabc.co.za; internet www.sabc.co.za; f. 1936; comprises 18 public radio stations and 5 television channels; Chair. BONGUMUSA MAKHATHINI; CEO MADODA MXAKWE.

Channel Africa Network: SABC Radio Park, 3rd Floor, Henley Rd, Auckland Park, Johannesburg; POB 91313, Auckland Park 2006; tel. (11) 7144832; e-mail info@channelafrica.org; internet www.channelafrica.co.za; f. 1966 as Radio RSA; merged with Global News Services in 1988; external service of SABC; broadcasts 217 hours per week in English, French, Portuguese, Kiswahili, Chinyanja and Silozi; Gen. Man. SOLLY PHETOE.

Domestic Services

SAfm; RSG (Radio Sonder Grense); 5 FM; Radio 2000; Good Hope FM; Lotus FM (Indian service in English); Metro FM (African service in English); Thobela FM; Ikwekwezi FM; Lesedi FM; Ligwalagwala FM; Munghana Lonene FM; Umhlobo Wenene FM; Ukhozi FM; Motsweding FM; Tru FMPhalaphala FM; X-K FM.

Privately-owned Radio Stations

567 CapeTalk: Suite 7D, Somerset Sq., Highfield Rd, Cape Town; Private Bag 567, Vlaeberg 8018; tel. (21) 4464700; e-mail chanelp@capetalk.co.za; internet www.capetalk.co.za; f. 1997; operated by Primedia Broadcasting; Public Relation Man. CHANEL PONTO.

947: Primedia Pl., 5 Gwen Lane, cnr Gwen Lane and Fredman Dr., Sandown, Gauteng; POB 3438, Rivonia 2128; tel. (11) 5063947; e-mail webmaster947@947.co.za; internet www.947.co.za; fmrly 94.7 Highveld Stereo; owned by Primedia Broadcasting; Station Man. RAVI NAIDOO.

Algoa FM: 5 Upper Valley Rd, Baakens Valley, Gqeberha 6001; tel. (41) 5059497; e-mail info@algoafm.co.za; internet www.algoafm.co.za; f. 1986; Man. Dir ALFIE JAY.

East Coast Radio: 313–315 Umhlanga Rocks Dr., Umhlanga Rocks, Durban; POB 25095, Gateway, Umhlanga Rocks 4321; tel. (31) 5709495; e-mail onair@ecr.co.za; internet www.ecr.co.za; f. 1967; owned by Kagiso Media Group; CEO BONI MCHUNU.

Hot 1027: Oxford Office Park 5, Blk A, 8th St, Houghton Estate, Johannesburg 2193; POB 782, Auckland Park 2006; tel. (10) 1571027; e-mail info@hot1027.co.za; internet hot1027.co.za; f. 1997; fmrly known as Classic FM and later as Classic 1027; present name adopted in 2021; Man. Dir LLOYD MADURAI.

Jacaranda FM: 89, 14th Rd, Erands Gardens, Midrand; POB 11961, Centurion 0046; tel. (11) 0635700; e-mail enquiries@jacarandafm.com; internet www.jacarandafm.com; owned by Kagiso Media Group; Man. Dir DEIRDRE KING; Programme Man. HENNIE MYBURGH.

Kaya FM 959: Kaya House, 195 Jan Smuts Rd, Parktown North 2193; POB 395, Parklands 2112; tel. (11) 6349500; e-mail pr@kayafm.co.za; internet www.kayafm.co.za; f. 1997; Man. Dir SIBONGILE MTYALI.

KFM 94.5: Suite 7D, Somerset Sq., Highfield Rd, PMB X945, Cape Town 8000; tel. (21) 4464700; e-mail kfm@kfm.co.za; internet www.kfm.co.za; f. 1994; part of the Primedia Broadcasting; Station Man. STEPHEN WERNER.

Mix 93.8 FM: 10 Zonnebloem Bldg, Constantia, Square Office Park, 16th Rd, Midrand; tel. (10) 5680871; e-mail info@mixfm.co.za; internet www.mixfm.co.za; community radio station; Station Man KUDZAYI TIRIBABI.

OFM: Central Media Park, 7 Christo Groenewald Ave, Wild Olive Estate, Bloemfontein; tel. (51) 5050900; e-mail info@ofm.co.za; internet www.ofm.co.za; f. 1996; fmrly Radio Oranje; managed by African Media Entertainment; CEO NICK EFSTATHIOU.

Talk Radio 702: Primedia House, 2nd Floor, 5 Gwen Lane, Sandown, Sandton; POB 5572, Rivonia 2128; tel. (11) 5063702; e-mail 702webmaster@702.co.za; internet www.702.co.za; owned by Primedia Broadcasting; Station Man. MZO JOJWANA.

YFM 99.2: 4 Albury Rd, Dunkeld Cres., Dunkeld (W), Ext. 8, Sandton 2196; tel. (11) 7596300; e-mail info@yfm.co.za; internet www.yfm.co.za; f. 1997; Man. Dir HASEENA CASSIM.

Television

In February 2007 the Government announced that the country would begin digital terrestrial broadcasting in November 2008 and that the country's analogue signal would be switched off by December 2013. However, the Government failed to meet this deadline and a subsequent deadline, of June 2015, was also not met. Commercial digital broadcasts finally commenced, in selected areas, in February 2016. The analogue signal was to be switched off in phases across the nine provinces, and commenced in Northern Cape in October 2016. In March 2022 it was announced that the analogue switch-off would be completed by the end of June.

e.tv: 4 Albury Rd, Dunkeld (W), Johannesburg 2196; Private Bag, X9944, Sandton 2146; tel. (11) 5379300; e-mail info@etv.co.za; internet www.etv.co.za; f. 1998; owned by E Media Holdings Ltd (itself a subsidiary of Hosken Consolidated Investments); CEO ANDRÉ VAN DER VEEN.

Naspers: 40 Heerengracht, Cape Town 8001; tel. (21) 4062121; e-mail communications@naspers.com; internet www.naspers.co.za; f. 1915; provides subscription television through Multichoice, M-Net and SuperSport packages; Chair. KOOS BEKKER; Chief Exec. BOB VAN DIJK.

South African Broadcasting Corpn (SABC)—Television: cnr Artillery and Henley Rds, Johannesburg 2092; Private Bag X1, Auckland Park 2006; tel. (11) 7149111; e-mail tvlic.info@sabc.co.za; internet www.sabc.co.za; transmissions began in 1976; broadcasts television services in 11 languages over 3 channels; SABC1 broadcasts in English, isiZulu, isiXhosa, isiNdebele and siSwati; SABC2 broadcasts in English, Afrikaans, Sesotho, Setswana, Sepedi, Xitsonga and Tshivendi; SABC3 broadcasts documentaries, educational programmes and sport in English; launched SABC Encore in 2015; Chair. BONGUMUSA MAKHATHINI; CEO MADODA MXAKWE.

Finance

BANKING

In 2022 the South African banking sector comprised 13 locally controlled banks, four foreign-controlled banks, three mutual banks, 13 local branches of foreign banks and 30 foreign banks with approved local representative offices.

Central Bank

South African Reserve Bank: 370 Helen Joseph St, Pretoria 0002; POB 427, Pretoria 0001; tel. (12) 3133911; e-mail media@resbank.co.za; internet www.resbank.co.za; f. 1921; Gov. LESETJA KGANYAGO.

Commercial Banks

Absa Bank Ltd: Absa Towers West, 7th Floor, 15 Troye St, Johannesburg; POB 7735, Johannesburg 2000; tel. (11) 3504000; e-mail absa@absa.co.za; internet www.absa.co.za; f. 1991; Group Chair. SELLO MOLOKO; CEO ARRIE RAUTENBACH.

African Bank Ltd: 59 16th Rd, Midrand, Johannesburg; Private Bag X170, Midrand 1685; tel. (11) 2569000; e-mail absocialmedia@africanbank.co.za; internet www.africanbank.co.za; f. 1975; Chair. THABO DLOTI; CEO KENNEDY BUNGANE.

Al Baraka Bank Ltd: 2 Kingsmead Blvd, Kingsmead Office Park, Stalwart Simelane St, Durban 4001; POB 4395, Durban 4000; tel. (31) 3649000; e-mail customerservices@albaraka.co.za; internet www.albaraka.co.za; f. 1989; 64.51% owned by Al Baraka Banking Group; operates according to Islamic principles; Chair. ADNAN AHMED YOUSIF; CEO SHABIR CHOHAN.

Bidvest Bank Ltd: 1 Park Lane, Wierda Valley, Sandton 2196; POB 185, Johannesburg 2000; tel. (11) 4073000; e-mail servicecentre@bidvestbank.co.za; internet www.bidvestbank.co.za; f. 1850 as Rennies Bank Ltd; present name adopted 2007; foreign exchange, trade finance and related activities; subsidiary of Bidvest Group Ltd; Chair. N. G. PAYNE; Man. Dir HANNAH SADIKI.

Capitec Bank: 1 Quantum St, Techno Park, Stellenbosch 7600; POB 12451, Die Board 7613; tel. (21) 9411377; e-mail clientcare@capitecbank.co.za; internet www.capitecbank.co.za; f. 2001; Chair. SANTIE BOTHA; CEO GERRIE FOURIE.

FirstRand Bank Ltd: 4 Merchant Pl., 4th Floor, cnr Fredman Dr. and Rivonia Rd, Bank City, Sandton 2196; POB 650149, Benmore 2010; tel. (11) 2821808; e-mail hr@firstrand.co.za; internet www.firstrand.co.za; f. 1971 as First National Bank of Southern Africa; merged with Rand Bank in 1998; 34.1% owned by RMB Holdings Ltd, 5.2% owned by BEE partners and 3.9% owned by Remgro Ltd; Chair. ROGER JARDINE; CEO ALAN PULLINGER.

GBS Mutual Bank: 18–20 Hill St, Grahamstown 6139; POB 114, Grahamstown 6140; tel. (46) 6227109; e-mail enquiries@gbsbank.co.za; internet www.gbsbank.co.za; f. 1877; fmrly Grahamstown Building Society; Chair. OWEN SKAE; Man. Dir A. M. VORSTER.

Grobank: Bldg 3, Inanda Greens Business Park, 54 Wierda Rd West, Wierda Valley, Sandton 2196; POB 784921, Sandton 2146; tel. (11) 6344300; e-mail info@grobank.co.za; internet grobank.co.za; f. 1947; fmrly South African Bank of Athens; present name adopted in 2019; owned by GroCapital Holdings Ltd; Chair. P. RANCHOD; CEO BENNIE VAN ROOY.

Habib Overseas Bank Ltd: N77 Oriental Plaza, Fordsburg, Johannesburg 2092; POB 62369, Marshalltown 2107; tel. (11) 8347441; e-mail habib@habiboverseas.co.za; internet www.habiboverseas.co.za; owned by Pitcairns Finance SA, Luxembourg; f. 1990; Chair. HABIB MOHAMED D. HABIB; Man. Dir S. MANZAR ABBAS KAZMI.

HBZ Bank Ltd: 135 Jan Hofmeyr Rd, Westville, Durban 3631; POB 1536, Wandsbeck 3631; tel. (31) 2674400; e-mail sazone@hbzbank.co.za; internet www.hbzbank.co.za; f. 1995; subsidiary of Habib Bank AG, Zurich; Chair. MUHAMMAD H. HABIB; CEO ZAFAR ALAM KHAN.

Nedbank Ltd: 135 Rivonia Rd, Sandown 2196, Johannesburg 2001; POB 1144, Johannesburg 2000; tel. (11) 2944444; e-mail contactcentre@nedbank.co.za; internet www.nedbankgroup.co.za; f. 1888; fmrly Nedcor Bank Ltd; present name adopted 2002; subsidiary of Nedbank Group Ltd; Acting Chair. MPHO MAKWANA; Group CEO MICHAEL WILLIAM THOMAS BROWN.

The Standard Bank of South Africa Ltd: 184 Hyde Park, Sandton 2196; tel. (11) 2831100; e-mail information@standardbank.co.za; internet www.standardbank.co.za; f. 1862; operations in 20 countries in sub-Saharan Africa; Chair. NONKULULEKO NYEMBEZI; CEO LUNGISA FUZILE.

Ubank Ltd: Ubank House, 10 Matuka Close, Erand Garden, Midrand; Private Bag X0030, Halfway House 1685; tel. (11) 5185863; e-mail customercare@ubank.co.za; internet www.ubank.co.za; f. 2000; fmrly Teba Bank Ltd, present named adopted 2010; specializes in microfinance and providing financial services to mining communities; Chair. KESHAN PILLAY; CEO LUTHANDO VUTULA.

Merchant Bank

Grindrod Bank Ltd: 5 Arundel Close, Kingsmead Office Park, Durban 4001; POB 3211, Durban 4000; tel. (31) 3336600; internet www.grindrodbank.co.za; f. 1994; present name adopted 2006; Chair. TYRONE SOONDARJEE; CEO DAVID POLKINGHORNE.

Investment Banks

Investec Bank Ltd: 100 Grayston Dr., Sandown, Sandton 2196; POB 785700, Sandton 2146; tel. (11) 2867000; e-mail investorrelations@investec.com; internet www.investec.co.za; f. 1974; CEO RICHARD WAINWRIGHT.

Sasfin Bank Ltd: 29 Scott St, Waverley 2090; POB 95104, Grant Park 2051; tel. (11) 8097500; e-mail info@sasfin.com; internet www.sasfin.com; f. 1951; subsidiary of Sasfin Holdings Ltd; Chair. ROY ANDERSEN; CEO MICHAEL SASSOON.

Development Bank

Development Bank of Southern Africa (DBSA): 1258 Lever Rd, Headway Hill; POB 1234, Halfway House, Midrand 1685; tel. (11) 3133911; e-mail webmaster@dbsa.org; internet www.dbsa.org; f. 1983; Chair. ENOCH GODONGWANA; CEO PATRICK DLAMINI.

Bankers' Association

Banking Association South Africa: Sunnyside Office Park, Bldg D, 3rd Floor, 32 Princess of Wales Terrace, Parktown 2193; POB 61674, Marshalltown; tel. (11) 6456700; e-mail webmaster@banking.org.za; internet www.banking.org.za; f. 1993; fmrly Banking Council of South Africa; present name adopted in 2005; 37 mem. banks (2019); Chair. RICHARD WAINWRIGHT; Man. Dir BONGIWE KUNENE.

STOCK EXCHANGES

JSE Ltd: One Exchange Sq., 2 Gwen Lane, Sandown, Sandton; Private Bag X991174, Sandton 2196; tel. (11) 5207000; e-mail info@jse.co.za; internet www.jse.co.za; f. 1887 as Johannesburg Stock Exchange; present name adopted in 2005; in late 1995 legislation was enacted providing for the deregulation of the Stock Exchange; automated trading commenced in June 1996; demutualized in July 2005 and became a listed co in June 2006; Chair NONKULULEKO NYEMBEZI-HEITA; Group CEO Dr LEILA FOURIE.

ZAR X: Jindal Africa Bldg, 2nd Floor, 22 Kildoon Rd, Bryanston, Johannesburg 2021; tel. (84) 5464048; e-mail info@zarx.co.za; internet www.zarx.co.za; f. 2016; CEO ETIENNE NEL.

INSURANCE

AIG South Africa Ltd: Sandown Mews West, 88 Stella St, Sandown 2196; POB 31983, Braamfontein 2017; tel. (11) 5518500; e-mail aigsafeedback@aig.com; internet www.aig.co.za; f. 1962; CEO WAYNE ABRAHAM.

Allianz Global Corporate & Specialty SA Ltd (AGCS SA Ltd): The Firs, 2nd Floor, 32A Cradock Ave, Rosebank 2196; tel. (11) 2147900; e-mail communicationsAfrica@allianz.com; internet www.agcs.allianz.com/global-offices/africa.html; CEO (AGCS Africa) THUSANG MAHLANGU.

Bryte Insurance Co South Africa Ltd: 15 Marshall St, Ferreirasdorp, Johannesburg 2001; POB 61489, Marshalltown 2107; tel. (11) 3709111; internet brytesa.com; fmrly Zurich Insurance Co South Africa Ltd; present name adopted in Feb. 2017 following acquisition by Fairfax Financial Holdings Ltd (Canada); Chair. MATTHEW WILSON; CEO EDWYN O'NEILL.

CFAO Motors Insurance Ltd: Hino Constantia Bldg, cnr Rhinoceros and Springhaas Sts, Weltevreden Park, Roodepoort; POB 69574, Bryanston 2021; tel. (11) 2888200; e-mail insure@cfaomotors.co.za; internet www.cfaomotorsinsurance.co.za; fmrly Unitrans Insurance; Chair. F. A. PATRIZI; CEO A. RHOODIE.

Clientèle Life Assurance Co: Bldg 1, Clientèle Office Park, cnr Rivonia and Alon Rds, Morningside, Johannesburg 2196; POB 1316, Rivonia 2128; tel. (11) 3203000; e-mail services@clientelelife.com; internet www.clientele.co.za; f. 1997; subsidiary of Hollard Insurance Group; Chair. GAVIN QUENTIN ROUTLEDGE; Group Man. Dir B. W. REEKIE.

Credit Guarantee Insurance Corpn of Africa Ltd: 1 Mutual Place, 107 Rivonia Rd, Sandton 2196; Private Bag 9908, Sandton 2146; tel. (11) 8897000; e-mail info@cgic.co.za; internet www.creditguarantee.co.za; f. 1956; part of Old Mutual Group; Chair. MELANIE BOSMAN; CEO CHARLES NORTJE.

Discovery Holdings Ltd: 1 Discovery Pl., Sandton 2146; POB 796722, Sandton 2146; tel. (11) 5292888; e-mail media_relations_team@discovery.co.za; internet www.discovery.co.za; f. 1992; health and life assurance; Chair. MARK TUCKER; CEO ADRIAN GORE.

Hollard Insurance Group: 22 Oxford Rd, Parktown, Johannesburg; POB 87419, Houghton, Johannesburg 2041; tel. (11) 3515000; internet hollard.co.za; f. 1980; Chief Exec. WILLIE LATEGAN.

Liberty Holdings Ltd: Liberty Life Centre, 1 Ameshoff St, Braamfontein, Johannesburg 2001; POB 10499, Johannesburg 2000; tel. (11) 5583911; e-mail info@liberty.co.za; internet www.liberty.co.za;

f. 1957; 53% stakes held by Standard Bank; Chair. Jacko Maree; CEO David Munro.

Old Mutual (Old Mutual Life Assurance Co (South Africa) Ltd): Mutualpark, Jan Smuts Dr., POB 66, Cape Town 8000; tel. (21) 5099111; e-mail contact@oldmutual.com; internet www.oldmutual.co.za; f. 1845; Chair. Trevor Manuel; CEO Iain Williamson.

Safire Insurance Co Ltd: Safire House, Redlands Estate, Pietermaritzburg 3201; POB 11475, Dorpspruit 3206; tel. (33) 2648500; e-mail admin@safireinsurance.com; internet safireinsurance.com; f. 1987; CEO Pierre Bekker.

Santam Ltd: 1 Sportica Cres., Bellville 7530; POB 3881, Tyger Valley 7536; tel. (21) 9157000; e-mail info@santam.co.za; internet www.santam.co.za; f. 1918; Chair. Vusi Khanyile; CEO Tavaziva Madzinga.

South African National Life Assurance Co Ltd (SANLAM): 2 Strand Rd, Bellville; POB 1, Sanlamhof 7532; tel. (21) 9479111; e-mail life@sanlam.co.za; internet www.sanlam.co.za; f. 1918; Chair. Elias Masilela; Group CEO Paul Hanratty.

Workeslife (Workeslife Assurance and Insurance): P. G. C. House, 273 Paul Kruger St, Pretoria 0001; tel. (86) 1520520; e-mail info@workerslife.co.za; internet www.workerslife.co.za; f. 1996; Chair. N. Ngcobo-Mthembu.

Association

South African Insurance Association (SAIA): Willowbrook House, Ground Floor, Constantia Office Park, cnr 14th Ave and Hendrik Potgieter St, Weltevreden Park; POB 30619, Braamfontein 2017; tel. (11) 7265381; e-mail info@saia.co.za; internet www.saia.co.za; f. 1973; represents short-term insurers; Chair. Cedric Masondo; CEO Viviene Pearson; 58 mems (2020).

Trade and Industry

GOVERNMENT AGENCIES

National Empowerment Fund: West Block, 187 Rivonia Rd, Morningside 2057; POB 31, Melrose Arch, Melrose North 2076; tel. (11) 3058000; e-mail info@nefcorp.co.za; internet www.nefcorp.co.za; f. 1998; Chair. Dr Nthabiseng Moleko; CEO Philisiwe Mthethwa.

Small Enterprise Development Agency (SEDA): The Fields, Office Block A, 1066 Burnett St, Hatfield 0833, Pretoria; POB 56714, Arcadia 0007; tel. (12) 4411000; e-mail info@seda.org.za; internet www.seda.org.za; f. 2004; Chair. M. Ndlovu; Acting CEO Nkosikhona Mbatha.

DEVELOPMENT ORGANIZATIONS

Business Partners Ltd: 37 West St, Houghton Estate, Johannesburg 2198; POB 7780, Johannesburg 2000; tel. (11) 7136600; e-mail enquiries@businesspartners.co.za; internet www.businesspartners.co.za; f. 1981 as Small Business Devt Corpn; present name adopted in 1998; invests in, and provides services to, small and medium-sized enterprises; Chair. Theo van Wyk; Man. Dir Ben D. Bierman.

Independent Development Trust: Glenwood Office Park, cnr Oberon and Sprite Sts, Faerie Glen, Pretoria 0043; POB 73000, Lynnwood Ridge 0040; tel. (12) 8452000; e-mail info@idt.org.za; internet www.idt.org.za; f. 1990; advances the national devt programme working with govt and communities in fields incl. poverty relief, infrastructure, empowerment, employment and capacity building; Acting CEO Tebogo Malaka.

Industrial Development Corpn of South Africa Ltd (IDC): 19 Fredman Dr., Sandown, POB 784055, Sandton 2146; tel. (11) 2693000; e-mail service@idc.co.za; internet www.idc.co.za; f. 1940; promotes entrepreneurship and competitiveness; Chair. Busi Mabuza; CEO Tshokolo Nchocho.

Productivity SA: International Business Gateway, cnr New and Sixth Rds, Midrand; tel. (11) 8485300; e-mail info@productivitysa.co.za; internet productivitysa.co.za; f. 1968; Chair. Prof. Mthunzi Mdwaba; CEO Dr Mothunye Mothiba.

CHAMBERS OF COMMERCE

Cape Chamber of Commerce and Industry: 1 Canal Close, Ground Floor, Century Falls Rd, Century City, Cape Town 7441; POB 204, Cape Town 8000; tel. (21) 4024300; e-mail info@capechamber.co.za; internet capechamber.co.za; f. 1804; Pres. Jacques Moolman; CEO John Lawson.

Durban Chamber of Commerce and Industry: 101 Isaiah Ntshangase Rd, Durban Country Club, Durban 4001; tel. (31) 3351000; e-mail info@durbanchamber.co.za; internet durbanchamber.co.za; f. 1856 as the Natal Chamber of Commerce; present name adopted in 1884; Pres. Nigel Ward; CEO Palesa Phili.

Johannesburg Chamber of Commerce and Industry (JCCI): JCC House, 6th Floor, 27 Owl St, cnr Empire Rd, Milpark; Private Bag 34, Auckland Park 2006; tel. (11) 7265300; e-mail denise@jcci.co.za; internet www.jcci.co.za; f. 1890; Pres. Shawn Theunissen; CEO Bernadette Zeiler.

Mangaung Chamber of Commerce and Industry (MCCI): 32 President Steyn St, Westdene, Bloemfontein 9301; tel. (51) 5221710; e-mail president@bcci.co.za; internet www.bcci.co.za; f. 2004; Pres. Nancy de Sousa.

National African Federated Chamber of Commerce and Industry (NAFCOC): Dr Richard Maponya House, 13 Summer St, Rivonia, Gauteng 2128; tel. (11) 8075063; e-mail info@nafcocnational.org.za; internet nafcocnational.org.za; f. 1964; Pres. Gilbert Mosena (acting); Sec.-Gen. Steve Skhosana.

Nelson Mandela Bay Business Chamber: 200 Norvic Dr., Greenacres, Gqeberha 6045; tel. (41) 3731122; e-mail info@nmbbusinesschamber.co.za; internet www.nmbbusinesschamber.co.za; f. 1994; fmrly Port Elizabeth Regional Chamber of Commerce and Industry, present name adopted 2011; Pres. Loyiso Dotwana; CEO Denise van Huyssteen.

Pietermaritzburg and Midlands Chamber of Business (PMCB): Shop No. 6A, Phase 3 Lifestyle Centre, Liberty Midlands Mall, 50 Sanctuary Rd, Chase Valley, Pietermaritzburg 3201; POB 11734, Dorpspruit, Pietermaritzburg 3206; tel. (33) 3452747; e-mail pmcb@pmcb.org.za; internet pmcb.org.za; f. 2002 following the merger of Midlands Black Business Chamber, the Pietermaritzburg Sakekamer and the Pietermaritzburg Chamber of Commerce & Industries; fmrly Pietermaritzburg Chamber of Business; present name adopted 2019; Pres. Bongi Mshengu; CEO Melanie Veness.

South African Chamber of Commerce and Industry (SACCI): 33 Fricker Rd, Illovo, Johannesburg 2196; tel. (11) 4463800; e-mail info@sacci.org.za; internet sacci.org.za; f. 1990 by merger of Asscn of Chambers of Commerce and Industry and South African Federated Chamber of Industries; fmrly known as South African Chamber of Business; Pres. Mtho Xulu; CEO Alan Mukoki.

Wesvaal Chamber of Business (WESCOB): 48 Buffeldoorn Ave, Klerksdorp 2571; POB 7167, Flamwood 2572; tel. (18) 4683750; e-mail kmmadi@wesvaalchamber.co.za; internet www.wesvaalchamber.co.za; f. 1898; Pres. Kgotso Mmadi.

INDUSTRIAL AND TRADE ORGANIZATIONS

Association of Cementitious Material Producers (ACMP): POB 168, Halfway House 1685; tel. (11) 3150300; e-mail dhirajr@acmp.co.za; internet www.acmp.co.za; f. 2005; Exec. Dir Dhiraj B. K. Rama.

Cape Wools SA: Wool Exchange of South Africa, 16 Grahamstown Rd, North End, Gqeberha 6001; tel. (41) 4844301; e-mail capewool@capewools.co.za; internet www.capewools.co.za; f. 1997; Chair. G. E. de Kock; CEO Deon Saayman.

Manufacturing Circle: tel. (11) 0615000; e-mail jo@manufacturingcircle.co.za; internet www.manufacturingcircle.co.za; f. 2008; corporate association of manufacturers; conducts research and engages with key stakeholders to promote the benefits of manufacturing growth; Chair. Ayanda Mngadi; Exec. Dir Philippa Rodseth.

Master Builders South Africa (MBSA): 1 Second Rd, Randjespark, Midrand; POB 1619, Halfway House 1685; tel. (11) 2059000; e-mail info@masterbuilders.org.za; internet www.masterbuilders.org.za; f. 1904; fmrly known as Building Industries Fed. South Africa; Pres. John Matthews.

Minerals Council South Africa: Rosebank Towers, 19 Biermann Ave, Rosebank, Johannesburg 2196; tel. (11) 4987100; e-mail info@mineralscouncil.org.za; internet www.mineralscouncil.org.za; f. 1889 as the Chamber of Mines; fmrly Chamber of Mines of South Africa; present name adopted 2018; Pres. Nolitha Fakude; CEO Roger Baxter.

Mining Industry Association of Southern Africa (MIASA): Rosebank Towers, 19 Biermann Ave, Rosebank, Johannesburg 2196; POB 61809, Marshalltown 2107; tel. (11) 4987100; e-mail vmabena@miasa.org.za; internet www.miasa.org.za; f. 1998; mems include chambers of mines body from Botswana, the DRC, Lesotho, Madagascar, Malawi, Namibia, South Africa, Tanzania, Zambia and Zimbabwe; Pres. Roger Baxter; Exec. Sec. Vusi Mabena.

National Association of Automobile Manufacturers of South Africa (NAAMSA): Alenti Office Park, Bldg F, Ground Floor, 457 Witherite Rd, The Willows X82, Pretoria; tel. (12) 8070152; e-mail info@naamsa.co.za; internet naamsa.co.za; f. 1935; Pres. Neale Hill; CEO Michael Mabasa.

National Chamber of Milling (NCM): Agri-Hub Office Park, Blk A, 477 Witherite St, The Willows, Pretoria 0081; Suite 211, Private Bag X025, Lynnwood Ridge 0040; tel. (12) 6631660; e-mail info@grainmilling.org.za; internet www.grainmilling.org.za; f. 1936; Exec. Dir Boikanyo Mokgatle.

Plastics Federation of South Africa: Corporate Park South, 18 Gazelle Ave, Old Pretoria Rd, Midrand; Private Bag X68, Halfway House 1685; tel. (11) 3144021; e-mail enquiries@plasticssa.co.za; internet www.plasticsinfo.co.za; f. 1979; Chair. JEREMY MACKINTOSH; Exec. Dir ANTON HANEKOM.

Printing Industries Federation of South Africa (PIFSA): Halfway House, 575 Lupton Dr., Midrand 1682; tel. (11) 2871160; e-mail info@printingsa.org; internet www.printingsa.org; f. 1916; CEO Dr ABDOOL MAJID MAHOMED; Pres. LEAL WRIGHT; 4 regional chambers.

Retail Motor Industry Org. (RMI): 330 Surrey Ave, Surrey Sq., Office Park, Ferndale, POB 2940, Randburg 2125; tel. (11) 8866300; e-mail rmi@rmi.org.za; internet www.rmi.org.za; f. 1908; affiliates throughout southern Africa; CEO JAKKIE OLIVIER.

SA Grain Milling Academy (SAGMA): Grain Bldg, AGRI-Hub Office Park, Blk A, 477 Witherite Rd, The Willows, Pretoria 0081; Suite 211, Private Bag X025, Lynnwood Ridge 0040; tel. (12) 6631660; e-mail info@sagma.co.za; internet www.sagma.co.za; f. 1944; fmrly Grain Milling Federation; Exec. Dir BOIKANYO MOKGATLE.

South African Federation of Civil Engineering Contractors (SAFCEC): SAFCEC House, 12 Skeen Blvd, Bedfordview, Johannesburg 2007; POB 644, Bedfordview 2008; tel. (11) 4090900; e-mail info@safcec.org.za; internet www.safcec.org.za; f. 1939; CEO WEBSTER MFEBE.

South African Paint Manufacturers' Asscn (SAPMA): 1 Casino Rd, Foundershill, Modderfontein, Johannesburg 1609; tel. (76) 7920048; e-mail sapma@sapma.org.za; internet www.sapma.org .za; Chair. SANJEEV BHATT; Exec. Dir TARA BENN.

South African Petroleum Industry Asscn (SAPIA): Grayston Ridge Office Park, Ground Floor, Blk B, 144 Katherine St, Sandton 2196; POB 783482, Sandton 2146; tel. (11) 7837664; e-mail info@ sapia.org.za; internet www.sapia.org.za; f. 1994; represents South Africa's principal petroleum cos; Chair. HLONIPHIZWE MTOLO; Exec. Dir AVHAPFANI TSHIFULARO.

South African Sugar Asscn (SASA): 170 Flanders Dr., Mount Edgecombe, POB 700, Durban 4300; tel. (31) 5087000; e-mail info@ sasa.org.za; internet www.sasa.org.za; Exec. Dir TRIX TRIKAM.

Includes:

> **South African Sugar Millers' Association NPC (SASMA):** Kwa-Shukela, 170 Flanders Dr., Mount Edgecombe POB 1000, Durban 4300; tel. (31) 5007000; e-mail sasmal@sasa.org.za; f. 1920 as Natal Sugar Millers' Asscn; present name adopted in 1964; represents interests of sugar millers and refiners within the operations of SASA; 6 sugar producer mems; Chair. MARTIN MOHALE; CEO DEANE ROSSLER.

Steel and Engineering Industries Federation of South Africa (SEIFSA): Metal Industries House, 6th Floor, 42 Anderson St, Marshalltown, Johannesburg 2001; tel. (11) 2989500; e-mail info@ seifsa.co.za; internet www.seifsa.co.za; f. 1943; Chair. and Pres. ELIAS MONAGE; CEO LUCIO TRENTINI.

VinPro NPC: Picardi Farm, Cecilia St, Suider-Paarl; POB 1411, Suider-Paarl 7624; tel. (21) 2760429; e-mail info@vinpro.co.za; internet vinpro.co.za; f. 2003; represents 2,600 wine producers and cellars; Chair. ANTON SMUTS; Man. Dir RICO BASSON.

UTILITIES

Electricity

Electricity Supply Commission (ESKOM): Megawatt Park, Maxwell Dr., Sunninghill, Sandton; POB 1091, Johannesburg 2001; tel. (11) 8008111; e-mail mediadesk@eskom.co.za; internet www.eskom.co.za; f. 1923; state-controlled; Chair. Prof. MALEGAPURU MAKGOBA; Group CEO ANDRE DE RUYTER.

Gas

SASOL Gas: 50 Katherine St, Sandton 2196; POB 5486, Johannesburg; tel. (10) 3445000; e-mail socialmedia@sasol.com; internet www .sasol.com; f. 1964; Exec. Dir, Pres. and CEO FLEETWOOD GROBLER.

Water

Umgeni Water: 310 Burger St, Pietermaritzburg 3201; POB 9, Pietermaritzburg 3200; tel. (33) 3411111; e-mail info@umgeni.co.za; internet www.umgeni.co.za; f. 1974; Chair. ZIPHOZETHU MATHENJWA; CEO MBONISENI DLAMINI (acting).

Water Research Commission: Lynnwood Bridge Office Park, Bloukrans Bldg, 4 Daventry St, Lynnwood Manor, Pretoria 0081; tel. (12) 7619300; e-mail info@wrc.org.za; internet www.wrc.org.za; Chair. NOZIBELE MJOLI; CEO Dr DHESIGEN NAIDOO.

MAJOR COMPANIES

The following are among the leading companies in South Africa:

AECI Ltd: AECI Pl., 24 Woodlands Dr., Woodmead, Sandton 2191; Private Bag X21, Gallo Manor 2052; tel. (11) 8068700; e-mail groupcommunications@aeciworld.com; internet www.aeciworld .com; f. 1924; mfrs of speciality chemicals for the mining and manufacturing sectors; large landholding for redevelopment; Chair. KHOTSO MOKHELE; CEO MARK DYTOR.

AfriSam: Holcim Bldg, Constantia Park, cnr 14th Ave and Hendrik Potgieter Rd, Roodepoort; POB 6367, Weltevredenpark 1715; tel. (11) 6705500; e-mail customer.service@za.afrisam.com; internet www .afrisam.co.za; f. 1934; fmrly Holcim (South Africa) (Pty) Ltd; present name adopted in 2008; major producer of cement, stone aggregates, lime, industrial minerals and ready-mixed concrete, with extensive interests in manufacture of paper sacks and fertilizers; Exec. Chair. and CEO ERIC DIACK.

ACTOM (Pty) Ltd: 2 Magnet Rd, Knights; POB 13024, Knights, 1413 Gauteng; tel. (11) 8205111; e-mail facebook@actom.co.za; internet www.actom.co.za; mfrs and suppliers of electro-mechanical equipments in Africa; Group CEO MERVYN NAIDOO.

Barloworld Ltd: 61 Katherine St, POB 782248, Sandton 2146; tel. (11) 4451000; e-mail groupmarcomms@barloworld.com; internet www.barloworld.com; f. 1902; conducts industrial brand management; represents principals incl. Caterpillar (machines and engines), Hyster (lift trucks), Freightliner (trucks) and other motor vehicle mfrs; Avis licensee for southern Africa; Chair. NOLULAMO (LULU) NOBAMBISWANO GWAGWA; Group CEO DOMINIC MALENTSHA SEWELA.

Carl Zeiss South Africa: 363 Oak Ave, Ferndale, Randburg, Johannesburg 2194; tel. (11) 8869510; e-mail info.za@zeiss.com; internet www.zeiss.co.za; f. 1939; mfr of optical and optoelectronic goods; Man. Dir SEYFI CEYHAN.

Denel SOC Ltd: Nellmapius Dr., Irene, Pretoria; POB 8322, Centurion 0046; tel. (12) 6712700; e-mail marketing@denel.co.za; internet www.denel.co.za; f. 1992; state-owned; mfr of defence equipment; Chair. (vacant); Group CEO MIKE KGOBE (acting).

Foskor (Pty) Ltd: Riverview Office Park, Blk G, Janadel Rd, Midrand; POB 2494, Halfway House, 1685; tel. (11) 3470600; internet www.foskor.co.za; f. 1951; phosphoric acid and fertiliser producer; 59% owned by IDC; Chair. ROBERT MICHAEL GODSELL; Interim CEO and Pres. JULIAN PALLIAM.

Frame Knitting Manufacturers (Pty) Ltd: 3 Nottingham Pl., Mobeni, Durban; tel. (31) 4509444; e-mail kerry.goodall@frame.co .za; internet www.frameknitting.co.za; f. 1928 as Consolidated Frame Textiles Ltd; mfrs of fabrics for clothing and textile industries; owned by Denel Group of cos.

Grinaker-LTA: 41 Jurgens St, Bramley, Johannesburg, Gauteng; POB 1517, Kempton Park 1620; tel. (11) 9235000; e-mail info@ grinaker-lta.com; internet www.grinaker-lta.com; f. 2000 by merger of LTA Ltd and Grinaker Holdings; multi-disciplinary construction and engineering group specializing in infrastructure, energy and mining; Chair. MLU CLIVE MANCI; Man. Dir BHEKANI MDLALOSE.

Illovo Sugar (South Africa) Ltd: 1 Nokwe Ave, Ridgeside, Umhlanga Rocks, POB 194, Durban 4000; tel. (31) 5084300; e-mail websa@illovo.co.za; internet www.illovosugar.com; f. 1891; Africa's largest sugar producer; downstream producer of syrup, furfural and its derivatives, ethyl alcohol and lactulose; agricultural, manufacturing and other interests in 6 southern African countries; wholly owned by Associated British Foods PLC, UK; Chair. MPHO MAKWANA; Man. Dir RICKY GOVENDER.

Irvin and Johnson Ltd: 1 Davidson St, Woodstock, Cape Town 7925; Private Bag X1, Lyndhurst 2106; tel. 800210279; e-mail talk2us@ij.co.za; internet www.ij.co.za; f. 1910; trawler operators; processors, distributors and exporters of frozen fish; subsidiary of food and beverage firm AVI Ltd (South Africa); Group Chair. and CEO GAVIN TIPPER.

Kutana Group: Monte Circle, 20 Monte Casino Blvd, Ground Floor, Blk B, Fourways, Johannesburg 2191; POB 71438, Bryanston 2021; tel. (86) 1112343; e-mail info@kutanagroup.co.za; internet www .kutanagroup.co.za; CEO THOKO MOKGOSI-MWANTEMBE.

Malesela Taihan Electric Cable (Pty) Ltd (M-Tec): 273 General Hertzog Rd, Vereeniging 1939; tel. (16) 4508000; e-mail info@m-tec .co.za; internet www.m-tec.co.za; f. 1911 as Union Steel Corpn of South Africa; mfr of copper and aluminium conductor and associated products; Chair. M. K. MADUNGANDABA; CEO J. M. CHO.

Nampak Ltd: Nampak House, Hampton Office Park, 20 Georgian Cres. (E), Bryanston, Sandton 2191; POB 69983, Bryanston 2021; tel. (11) 7196300; e-mail info@nampak.com; internet www.nampak.co .za; f. 1968; mfrs of packaging in various forms based on paper, paper board, metal, glass and plastics; has subsidiaries in the service area and fields allied to packaging; Chair. PETER SURGEY; CEO ERIC SMUTS; 4,252 employees (2022).

Petroleum, Oil and Gas Corporation of South Africa (Pty) Ltd (PetroSA): 151 Frans Conradie Dr., Parow 7500; Private Bag X5, Parow 7499; tel. (21) 9293000; e-mail media@petrosa.co.za; internet www.petrosa.co.za; f. 2002 by merger of Mossgas, Soekor and parts of the Strategic Fuel Fund Asscn; undertakes exploration and production of oil and natural gas off the coast of South Africa; Chair. FRANS BALENI; Group CEO PRAGASEN NAIDOO.

Premium Group: Premium House, Grey Owl Village, cnr Brakfontein and Erasmus Dr., Louwlardia, Centurion 0157; tel. (12) 0037000; e-mail info@premiumgroup.co.za; internet www .premiumgroup.co.za; f. 1972; importers and distributors of high-quality photographical and electronic brands; Group Chair. STEFAN VAN DER WALT; CEO GRANT NORTON.

Pretoria Portland Cement Co Ltd (PPC): PPC Bldg, 148 Katherine St, cnr Grayston Dr., Sandton; POB 787416, Sandton 2146; tel. (11) 3869000; e-mail contactus@ppc.co.za; internet www.ppc.co.za; f. 1892; mfrs and suppliers cement, lime and limestone products, paper sacks and other containers; also mines and markets gypsum; Chair. PHILLIP JABULANI MOLEKETI; CEO ROLAND VAN WIJNEN.

Protea Hospitality Corpn (Pty) Ltd: cnr Arthur's Rd and Main Rd, Sea Point; POB 75, Sea Point; tel. (21) 4305000; e-mail info@ proteahotels.com; internet protea.marriott.com; f. 1988; operates the largest hotel group in Africa; acquired by Marriott International in April 2014; Pres. (vacant).

Sappi Ltd: Sappi House, 48 Ameshoff St, Braamfontein, Johannesburg 2001; POB 31560, Braamfontein 2017; tel. (11) 4078111; internet www.sappi.com; f. 1936 as South African Pulp and Paper Industries Ltd; supplies coated fine paper and chemical cellulose; Chair. Sir ANTHONY NIGEL RUSSELL RUDD; Exec. Dir and CEO STEPHEN ROBERT BINNIE.

Sasol Ltd: Sasol Pl., 50 Katherine St, Sandton 2196; POB 5486, Johannesburg 2000; tel. (10) 3445000; e-mail sasolqueriesandenquiries@sasol.com; internet www.sasol.com; f. 1950; chemicals and energy co; group of cos operating the world's largest complex of oil-from-coal petrochemical installations; over 120 products related to fuels and oils, chemicals, polymers, explosives and gas; Chair. SIPHO NKOSI; Exec Dir., Pres. and CEO FLEETWOOD GROBLER.

South African Breweries Ltd (SAB): 56 Grosvenor Rd, Bryanston, Sandton; POB 782178, Sandton 2146; tel. (11) 8818111; e-mail media.relations@ab-inbev.com; internet www.sab.co.za; f. 1895; fmrly South African Breweries Ltd; largest non-mining industrial group in sub-Saharan Africa; brewing and marketing of beer; mfrs, wholesalers and retailers of furniture, footwear, domestic appliances, plate glass, textiles, natural fruit juices and soft drinks; discount department, food and fashion chain stores; also owns and operates hotels; acquired by Anheuser-Busch InBev SA, Belgium in 2016; CEO RICHARD RIVETT-CARNAC.

Stewarts & Lloyds Trading (Pty) Ltd: Eastgate Lane Office Park, Bldg D, Ground Floor, West Wing, 5 Iris Rd, Bedfordview, Gauteng 2007; POB 79458, Senderwood 2145; tel. (11) 5538500; e-mail info@ sltrading.co.za; internet www.stewartsandlloyds.co.za; f. 1898 as Lloyd & Lloyd; present name adopted in 1903; acquired by Stockwell in 2001; suppliers of metal products and services to the engineering, mining, water, chemical and petro-chemical, automotive, construction and agricultural industries.

Tongaat Hulett Ltd: Amanzimnyama Hill Rd, POB 3, Tongaat 4400; tel. (32) 4394000; e-mail info@tongaat.co.za; internet www .tongaat.com; f. 1892; subsidiaries incl. Tongaat Hulett Sugar (sugar milling and refining), Hippo Valley Estates Ltd (sugar cane farming, milling and sugar packing) and Tongaat Hulett Property (property devt); agri-processing business incl. integrated components of land management, property development and agriculture; Interim Chair. DAVID NOKO; CEO J. G. HUDSON.

Mining Companies

African Rainbow Minerals (ARM): ARM House, 29 Impala Rd, Chislehurston, Sandton 2196; POB 786136, Sandton 2146; tel. (11) 7791300; e-mail ir.admin@arm.co.za; internet www.arm.co.za; f. 2004; formed through merger of Ubuntu-Ubuntu Commercial Enterprises Ltd and Anglovaal Mining Ltd; interests in gold, copper, ferrous metals, platinum group metals and coal; Exec. Chair. PATRICE MOTSEPE; CEO MIKE SCHMIDT.

Anglo American Corpn of South Africa Ltd: 44 Main St, Johannesburg; POB 61587, Marshalltown 2107; tel. (11) 6389111; internet southafrica.angloamerican.com; f. 1917; mining and natural resource group; a world leader in gold, platinum group metals and diamonds, with significant interests in coal, base and ferrous metals, industrial minerals, forestry and financial services; wholly owned subsidiary of Anglo American PLC (UK); Chair. NOLITHA FAKUDE; CEO DUNCAN WANBLAD.

AngloGold Ashanti Ltd: 112 Oxford Rd, Houghton Estate 2198; Private Bag X20, Rosebank 2196, Johannesburg; tel. (11) 6376000; e-mail media@anglogoldashanti.com; internet www .anglogoldashanti.com; f. 1998 as AngloGold Ltd; present name adopted in 2004 following merger of AngloGold Ltd and Ashanti Goldfields Co Ltd; Chair. MARIO RAMOS; CEO ALBERTO CALDERON.

De Beers Consolidated Mines Ltd (De Beers Group): cnr Crownwood Rd and Diamond Dr., Theta/Booysens Reserve, Johannesburg; Private Bag X01, Southdale, Johannesburg 2193; tel. (11) 3747000; internet www.debeersgroup.com; f. 1888; reorg. 1990, when foreign interests were transferred to De Beers Centenary AG, Switzerland; group of diamond mining cos and allied interests; mining operations in Botswana, Canada, Namibia and South Africa; subsidiary of Anglo American PLC group; Group CEO BRUCE CLEAVER.

Gold Fields Ltd: 150 Helen Rd, Sandown, Sandton, Johannesburg 2196; tel. (11) 5629700; e-mail investors@goldfields.com; internet www.goldfields.com; f. 1887 as Gold Fields of South Africa Ltd; present name adopted in 1998 following merger with Gencor; 10 operating mines in Australia, Ghana, Peru, Chile and South Africa; Chair. CHERYL A. CAROLUS; CEO CHRIS GRIFFITH.

Kumba Iron Ore: Centurion Gate, 124 Akkerboom Rd, Centurion 0157; POB 9679, Centurion 0046; tel. (12) 6837000; internet www .angloamericankumba.com; f. 2005; division of Anglo American PLC; CEO MPUMI ZIKALALA.

MC Mining Ltd (MCM): Suite 7, Bldg 2, Waverley Office Park, 15 Forest Rd, Bramley Johannesburg 2090; tel. (10) 0038000; e-mail admin@mcmining.co.za; internet www.mcmining.co.za; fmrly Coal of Africa Ltd; present name adopted in 2017; Chair. NHLANHLA NENE; CEO GODFREY GOMWE.

Palabora Copper (Pty) Ltd: 1 Copper Rd, POB 65, Phalaborwa 1389; tel. (15) 7802911; e-mail abby.ledwaba@palabora.co.za; internet www.palabora.co.za; f. 1956; 74% owned by Palabora Mining Co; mining of copper, with by-products of magnetite, zirconia metals, uranium oxide, anode slimes, nickel sulphate, sulphuric acid and vermiculite; Chair. and CEO JINGHUA HAN.

Randgold & Exploration Co Ltd: Suite 25, Katherine and West Bldg, cnr Katherine and West Sts, Sandown, Sandton 2196; POB 202, Stellenbosch 7600; tel. (71) 5803739; e-mail info@randgoldexp .co.za; internet www.randgoldexp.co.za; f. 1992 to acquire gold mining interests of Rand Mines Ltd; mineral exploration and devt; Interim Chair. PATRICK ERNST BURTON; CEO MARAIS STEYN.

TRADE UNIONS

Trade Union Federations

Congress of South African Trade Unions (COSATU): COSATU House, 110 Jorissen St, cnr Simmonds St, Braamfontein 2017; POB 1019, Johannesburg 2000; tel. (11) 3394911; e-mail enquiries@cosatu .org.za; internet www.cosatu.org.za; f. 1985; 18 trade union affiliates representing c. 1.8m. paid-up mems; Pres. ZINGISWA LOSI; Gen. Sec. BHEKI NTSHALINTSHALI.

Affiliates with 20,000 or more mems include:

Chemical, Energy, Paper, Printing, Wood and Allied Workers' Union (CEPPWAWU): Renaissance Centre, 10th–11th Floors, 116–20 New St, South Gandhi Sq., Johannesburg 2001; tel. (10) 2066600; e-mail secretariat@ceppwawu.org.za; internet www.ceppwawu.org.za; f. 1999 by merger of the Chemical Workers' Industrial Union and Paper, Printing, Wood and the Allied Workers' Union; represents workers in the petrochemical, consumer chemical, rubber, plastics, glass and ceramics, printing, pulp and paper, furniture and woodworking industries; Admin. THULISILE NJAPA MASHANDA.

Communication Workers' Union (CWU): 222 Smit St, Braamfontein 2017; POB 10248, Johannesburg 2000; tel. (11) 7200360; e-mail membership@cwu.org.za; internet cwu.org.za; f. 1996 by merger of the Post Office Employees' Asscn, the Post and Telecommunication Workers' Asscn and the South African Post Telecommunication Employees' Asscn; Pres. CLYDE MERVIN; Gen. Sec. AUBREY TSHABALALA.

Democratic Nursing Organisation of South Africa (DENOSA): 605 Stanza Bopape St, POB 1280, Pretoria 0001; tel. (12) 3432315; e-mail info@denosa.org.za; internet www.denosa .org.za; f. 1996; Pres. SIMON HLUNGWANI; Gen. Sec. CASSIM LEKHOATHI (acting).

National Education, Health and Allied Workers' Union (NEHAWU): 33 Hoofd St, Braampark, Johannesburg 2001; tel. (11) 8332902; e-mail info@nehawu.org.za; internet www.nehawu .org.za; f. 1987; Pres. MICHAEL MADALA SHINGANGE; Gen. Sec. ZOLA SAPHETHA.

National Union of Mineworkers (NUM): 7 Rissik St, cnr Frederick St, Johannesburg 2000; POB 2424, Johannesburg 2000; tel. (11) 3772198; e-mail tphoko@num.org.za; internet num.org.za; f. 1982; represents workers in the mining, energy, construction, building material manufacturing, civil engineering and building industries; Pres. DANIEL BAIPILE; Gen. Sec. MAKGABO WILLIAM MABAPA.

Police and Prisons Civil Rights Union (POPCRU): 1 Marie Rd, Auckland Park 2006; tel. (11) 2424600; e-mail gs@popcru.org .za; internet popcru.org.za; f. 1989; Pres. ZIZAMELE CEBEKHULU; Gen. Sec. JEFF DLADLA.

SASBO: The Finance Union: Fourmall Office Park West, 1 Percy St, Fourways, Johannesburg 2191; Private Bag X84, Bryanston 2021; tel. (11) 4670192; e-mail reception@sasbo.org.za; internet www.sasbo.org.za; f. 1916 as the South African Soc. of Bank Officials; Pres. MOSES LEKOTA; Gen. Sec. JOE KOKELA.

Southern African Clothing and Textile Workers' Union (SACTWU): Industria House, 350 Victoria Rd, Salt River, Cape Town; POB 1194, Woodstock 7915; tel. (21) 4474570; e-mail headoffice@sactwu.org.za; internet www.sactwu.org.za; f. 1989 with the merger of Amalgamated Clothing and Textile Workers' Union and the Garment and Allied Workers Union; Pres. THEMBA KHUMALO; Gen. Sec. ANDRÉ KRIEL.

South African Commercial, Catering and Allied Workers' Union (SACCAWU): SACCAWU House, 11 Leyds St, Braamfontein; POB 10730, Johannesburg 2000; tel. (11) 4038333; e-mail secretariatadmin@saccawu.org.za; internet saccawu.org; f. 1975; represents workers in the service industry, commercial, catering, tourism, hospitality and finance sectors; Pres. LOUISE THIPE; Gen. Sec. BONES SKULU.

South African Democratic Teachers' Union (SADTU): SADTU Village, Portion 74, cnr Dann Rd and Loam St, Glen Marais, Ext. 144, Kempton Park 1619; Postnet Suite 106, Private Bag X5, Aston Manor 1630; tel. (11) 9712000; e-mail sadtu@sadtu.org.za; internet www.sadtu.org.za; f. 1990; Pres. MAGOPE MAPHILA; Gen. Sec. MUGWENA JOHN MALULEKE.

South African Municipal Workers' Union (SAMWU): 84 Fredericks St, Johannesburg 2001; Private Bag X9, Athlone 7760; tel. (11) 1002621; e-mail info@samwu.org.za; internet www.samwu.org.za; f. 1987; Pres. (vacant); Gen. Sec. DUMISANE MAGAGULA.

South African Transport and Allied Workers' Union (SATAWU): SATAWU House, 117 De Korte St, Braamfontein, POB 9451, Johannesburg 2001; tel. (11) 4032077; e-mail info@satawu.org.za; internet www.satawu.org.za; f. 2000; Pres. NTUTHUZELO MHLUBULWANA; Gen. Sec. JACK MAZIBUKO.

Other organizations affiliated to COSATU include: the Liberated Metalworkers Union of South Africa; the Creative Workers' Union of South Africa; the Public and Allied Workers' Union of South Africa; the South African Democratic Nurses' Union; the South African Football Players' Union; the South African Medical Association; and the South African State and Allied Workers' Union.

Federation of Unions of South Africa (FEDUSA): FEDUSA House, 10 Kingfisher St, Horizon Park, Roodepoort 1725; POB 7779, Westgate 1734; tel. (11) 2791800; e-mail dennis@fedusa.org.za; internet www.fedusa.org.za; f. 1997 by merger of the Fed. of South African Labour Unions (FEDAL) and Fed. of Orgs Representing Civil Employees (FORCE); 19 mem. unions; politically non-aligned; Pres. MASALE GODFREY SELEMATSELA; Gen. Sec. RIEFDAH AJAM.

Affiliated unions with 10,000 or more mems include:

Health and Other Services Personnel Trade Union of South Africa (HOSPERSA): Strangeways Office Park, 6 Delamore Rd, Hillcrest 3610; POB 231, Kloof 3640; tel. (31) 7654625; e-mail officegs@hospersa.co.za; internet www.hospersa.co.za; f. 1958; represents workers in the public and private health, welfare and services sectors, and the public safety and security and education sectors; Pres. GODFREY SELEMATSELA; Gen. Sec. NOEL DESFONTAINES.

National Union of Leather and Allied Workers (NULAW): 33 Selbourne Rd, Umbilo, Durban 4075; POB 59088, Durban 4075; tel. (31) 2060105; e-mail ashleybenjamin@nulaw.co.za; Gen. Sec. ASHLEY BENJAMIN.

Public Servants' Association of South Africa (PSA): 563 Belvedere St, Arcadia, Pretoria; POB 40404, Arcadia 0007; tel. (12) 3036500; e-mail ask@psa.co.za; internet www.psa.co.za; f. 1920; withdrew affiliation from FEDUSA in 2006; rejoined FEDUSA in May 2017; Pres. Dr LUFUNO MULAUDZI; Gen. Man. MARCUS RAMAKGALE.

South African Typographical Union (SATU): 4 Estcourt Ave, Centurion 0157; tel. (12) 3382021; e-mail admin@satu.co.za; internet www.satu.co.za; f. 1898; represents workers in the printing, newspaper and packaging industries; Gen. Sec. EDWARD DE KLERK.

Suid-Afrikaanse Onderwysersunie (SAOU) (South African Teachers' Union): SAOU Bldg, 278 Serene St, Garsfontein, Pretoria 0081; POB 90120, Garsfontein 0042; tel. (12) 4360900; e-mail saou@saou.co.za; internet www.saou.co.za; f. 1997; Pres. LOUIS SWANEPOEL; CEO CHRIS KLOPPER.

UASA—The Union: UASA Office Park, 42 Goldman St, Florida, Gauteng 1709; POB 565, Florida 1710; tel. (11) 4723600; e-mail pr@uasa.co.za; internet www.uasa.org.za; f. 1998 by merger of the Administrative, Technical and Electronic Asscn of South Africa and Officials' Asscn of South Africa; fed. of 31 unions incl. the fmr Nat. Employees' Trade Union; represents workers in the mining,

motor, transport, manufacturing and engineering industries; fmrly United Association of South Africa; Pres. PATIENCE MAPITSI; CEO JACQUES HUGO.

Other organizations affiliated to FEDUSA include: the Administrative Library and Technical Staff Association; the Hospitality Industry and Allied Workers' Union; the Insurance and Banking Staff Association; the Motor Industry Staff Association; the Motor Transport Workers' Union; the National Professional Teachers' Organisation of South Africa; the National Security and Unqualified Workers' Union; the National Union of Leather and Allied Workers; the National Tertiary Education Union; the South African Communications Union; the South African Parastatal and Tertiary Institutions Union; the Tertiary Education National Union of South Africa; the United National Public Servants' Association of South Africa and Allied Workers' Union; and the United Transport and Allied Trade Union.

National Council of Trade Unions (NACTU): Galleries, 3rd Floor, 72 Eloff St, Johannesburg; tel. (11) 3331800; e-mail info@nactu.org.za; internet nactu.org.za; f. 1986 by merger of the Council of Unions of South Africa and Azanian Confed. of Trade Unions; fed. of 22 African trade unions; aligned to the Pan-Africanist Congress of Azania party; Pres. PAT MPHELA; Gen. Sec. NARIUS MOLOTO.

Affiliates with 10,000 or more mems include:

Building, Construction and Allied Workers' Union (BCAWU): Standard Bank Galleries, 4th Floor, 81 Market St, Johannesburg 2001; POB 96, Johannesburg 2000; tel. (11) 3334898; e-mail bcawu@netactive.co.za; internet www.bcawu.co.za; f. 1974; Gen. Sec. NARIUS MOLOTO.

Metal and Electrical Workers' Union of South Africa (MEWUSA): Suit 401, Elephant House, 107 Albertina Sisulu St, Johannesburg 2000; tel. (11) 3316739; e-mail info@mewusa.org.za; internet www.mewusa.org.za; f. 1989; Pres. DANIEL LENGOABALA; Gen. Sec. EDWARD THOBEJANE.

National Union of Food, Beverages, Wine, Spirit and Allied Workers (NUFBWSAW): VUSA House, 4th Floor, 8 New St South, Johannesburg 2001; POB 5718, Johannesburg 2000; tel. (11) 8331140; e-mail generalsecretary@foodbev.org.za; f. 1977; Gen. Sec. NQOBILE N. TSHABANGU; Nat. Organizer JANE MUNYELA.

South African Chemical Workers' Union (SACWU): 1066 Bldg, 3rd Floor, 35 Pritchard St, cnr Harrison St, Johannesburg 2001; POB 236, Johannesburg 2000; tel. (11) 8386581; e-mail headoffice@sacwu.co.za; internet fb.com/revoltsacwu.

Other organizations affiliated to NACTU include: the Association of Mineworkers and Construction Union; the Banking, Insurance, Finance and Assurance Workers' Union; the Entertainment Catering Commercial and Allied Workers' Union of South Africa; the Hotel, Liquor, Catering, Commercial and Allied Workers' Union of South Africa; the Inqubela Phambili Trade Union; the Labour Equity General Workers' Union of South Africa; the National Public Service Workers' Union; the National Security Commercial and General Workers' Union; the National Services and Allied Workers' Union; the National Union of Food, Wine, Beverages, Spirits and Allied Workers; the Federal Council of Retail and Allied Workers; the Industrial Commercial and Allied Workers' Union; the Professional Educators' Union; the South African Private Security Workers' Union; the Transport and Allied Workers Union; and the Transport and Omnibus Workers' Union.

South African Federation of Trade Unions (SAFTU): 34 Ellof St, Johannesburg 2001; tel. (11) 3310124; e-mail info@saftu.org.za; internet saftu.org.za; f. 2017; Pres. RUTH NTLOKOTSE; Gen. Sec. ZWELINZIMA VAVI; 24 affiliates; represents c. 700,000 workers.

Major affiliated unions include:

Food and Allied Workers' Union (FAWU): 7 Steve Biko St, Guguletu, Cape Town 7750; tel. (21) 6379040; e-mail dominique.martin@fawu.org.za; internet www.fawu.org.za; f. 2007; fmrly affiliated to COSATU; joined SAFTU in 2017; Pres. ATWELL NAZO; Gen. Sec. MAYOYO MNGOMEZULU.

Media Workers' Association of South Africa (MWASA): 701, 83 Albertina Sisulu St, POB 11136, Johannesburg; tel. 827433867; e-mail tuwgum@yahoo.com; f. 1978 as the Writers' Asscn of South Africa, successor to the Union of Black Journalists; present name adopted in 1986; Gen. Sec. TUWANI GUMANI.

National Transport Movement (NTM): 23 Modderhill Rd, Edleen, Kempton Park 1625; tel. (86) 6092610; e-mail admin@ntmunion.org; internet www.ntmunion.org; Pres. MASHUDU RAPHETHA; Gen. Sec. EPHRAIM MPHAHLELE.

National Union of Metalworkers of South Africa (NUMSA): 153 Lilian Ngoyi St, cnr Gerard Sekoto St, Newtown Johannesburg 2001; POB 260483, Excom 2023; tel. (11) 6891700; e-mail info@numsa.org.za; internet numsa.org.za; f. 1987; fmrly affiliated to COSATU; Pres. ANDREW CHIRWA; Gen. Sec. IRVIN JIM.

National Union of Public Service and Allied Workers (NUPSAW): 17 Iris St, Heatherdale AH, Akasia 0182; POB 58481,

Karenpark 0118; tel. (12) 3421674; e-mail generalsecretary@nupsaw.co.za; internet nupsaw.org.za; f. 1998; fmrly affiliated with CONSAWU; Pres. TITUS DANISO; Gen. Sec. SOLLY MALEMA.

South African Police Union (SAPU): 85 Rauch Ave, Georgeville, Pretoria 0184; Private Bag X900, Pretoria 0001; tel. (12) 8042088; e-mail nationaloffice@sapu.org.za; internet www.sapu .org.za; f. 1993; Pres. THANDI MKHIZE (acting); Gen. Sec. TUMELO MOGODISENG.

Other affiliates of SAFTU include: the Academic and Professional Staff Association; the Chemical Wood and Allied Workers' Union; the Democratic Municipal and Allied Workers' Union of South Africa; the Democratic Postal and Communication Workers' Union; the Democratised Transport Logistics and Allied Workers' Union; the Finance Union of Workers; the Information Communication and Technology Union; the Municipal and Allied Trade Union of South Africa; the Private Schools and Allied Workers' Union; the South African Correctional Services Workers' Union; the South African Civil Servants Union; the South African Industrial Commercial and Allied Workers' Union; the South African Liberated Public Sector Workers' Union; the South African Security Workers' Union; the Tirisano Transport and Security Workers' Union; the Transport Action Retail and General Workers' Union; the Young Nurses Indaba Workers' Union and the Commercial, Stevedoring, Agricultural and Allied Workers' Union.

Non-affiliated Unions

National Teachers Union (NATU): 47–57 Biyela St, Empangeni 3880; tel. (35) 7721608; e-mail info@natu.org.za; internet natu.org .za; f. 1918 as Black Teachers' Trade Union; Acting Pres. SIBUSISO VICTOR MALINGA.

South African Forestry, Farming, Catering and Allied Workers Union (SAFFCAWU): Sanlam Park Bldg, 26 Bhimy Dhamane St, Middelburg; POB 1268, Middelburg 1050; tel. (72) 9428861; e-mail info@saffcawu.com; internet fb.com/saffcawu; f. 2015; Gen. Sec. JERRIE MAKANYA.

Transport

Most of South Africa's railway network, and the harbours and airways are administered by the state-owned Transnet Ltd. Private bus services are regulated to complement the railways.

Transnet Ltd: Waterfall Business Estate, 9 Country Estate Dr., Midrand 1662; POB 72501, Parkview 2122; tel. (11) 3083000; e-mail enquiries@transnet.net; internet www.transnet.net; divisions incl. Transnet Freight Rail (fmrly Spoornet), Transnet Rail Engineering (fmrly Transwerk), Transnet National Ports Authority (fmrly NPA), Transnet Port Terminals (fmrly SAPO) and Transnet Pipelines (fmrly Petronet); Chair. Dr POPO SIMON MOLEFE; CEO PORTIA DERBY.

RAILWAYS

With the exception of commuter services, the South African railways system is operated by Transnet Freight Rail Ltd (formerly Spoornet), the rail division of Transnet. Extensive rail links connect Transnet Freight Rail with the rail networks of neighbouring countries. Construction of the 80-km mass rapid transit railway system, Gautrain, was completed in 2012; the system links Johannesburg, Pretoria and O. R. Tambo International Airport.

Passenger Rail Agency of South Africa (PRASA): Prasa House, 1040 Burnett St, Hatfield, Pretoria; POB 101, Braamfontein 2017; tel. (12) 7487000; e-mail info@prasa.com; internet www.prasa.com; f. 1990 as South African Rail Commuter Corpn; state-owned; Chair. LEONARD RAMATLAKANE; CEO HISHAAM EMERAN (acting).

Transnet Freight Rail: 2 Inyanda House, 15 Girton Rd, Parktown 2193; Private Bag X47, Johannesburg 2000; tel. 860690730; e-mail TFR911@transnet.net; internet www.transnetfreightrail-tfr.net; fmrly Spoornet; present name adopted in 2007; division of Transnet; CEO SIZA MZIMELA.

ROADS

South African National Roads Agency Ltd (SANRAL): 48 Tambotie Ave, Val de Grace, Pretoria 0184; POB 415, Pretoria 0001; tel. (12) 8448000; e-mail info@nra.co.za; internet www.nra .co.za; f. 1998; responsible for design, construction, management and maintenance of 22,214 km of the national road network (2019); Chair. THEMBA BARRANGE MHAMBI; CEO SKHUMBUZO MACOZOMA.

SHIPPING

The principal harbours are at Richards Bay, Durban, Saldanha, Cape Town, Gqeberha (formerly Port Elizabeth), East London, Ngqura (Coega) and Mossel Bay. The deep-water port at Richards Bay has been extended and its facilities upgraded. Both Richards Bay and Saldanha Bay are major bulk-handling ports, while Saldanha

Bay also has an important fishing fleet. More than 30 shipping lines serve South African ports.

South African Maritime Safety Authority (SAMSA): 146 Lunnon Rd, cnr Jan Shoba St, Hillcrest, Pretoria 0083; POB 13186, Hatfield 0028; tel. (12) 3662600; e-mail info@samsa.org.za; internet www.samsa.org.za; f. 1998; advises the Govt on matters connected with sea transport to, from or between South Africa's ports, incl. safety at sea, and prevention of pollution by petroleum; Chair. MAVUSO MSIMANG; CEO TSEPISO TAOANA-MASHILOANE (acting).

Transnet National Ports Authority: 30 Wellington Rd, Johannesburg 2001; POB 32696, Braamfontein 2017; tel. (11) 3519001; e-mail transnet@tip-offs.com; internet www .transnetnationalportsauthority.net; f. 2000; fmrly part of Portnet; controls and manages 7 of the country's major seaports; division of Transnet; CEO PEPI SILINGA.

Transnet Port Terminals: Kingsmead Office Park, 4th Floor, Stalwart Simelane St, Durban; POB 10124, Durban 4005; tel. (31) 3088000; e-mail tptwebmaster@transnet.net; internet www .transnetportterminals.net; f. 2000 as South African Port Terminals; fmrly part of Portnet; present name adopted in 2008; operates 13 container, bulk, breakbulk and car terminals at 6 of the country's major ports; division of Transnet; CEO NOZIPHO SITHOLE.

CIVIL AVIATION

Civil aviation is controlled by the Minister of Transport. The Chief Directorate: Civil Aviation Authority at the Department of Transport is responsible for licensing and control of domestic and international air services.

Airports Company South Africa Ltd (ACSA): 24 Johnson Rd, The Maples Office Park, Bedfordview, Johannesburg; POB 75480, Gardenview 2047; tel. (11) 7231400; e-mail customercare@airports .co.za; internet www.airports.co.za; f. 1993; owns and operates South Africa's 9 principal airports, of which 4 (at Johannesburg, Cape Town, Durban and Pilanesburg) are classified as international airports; Chair. SANDILE NOGXINA; Man. Dir NOMPUMELELO MPOFU.

Civil Aviation Authority (CAA): 1 Ikhaya Lokundiza, Bldg 16, Treur Close, Waterfall Park, Bekker St, Midrand; Private Bag X73, Halfway House 1685; tel. (11) 5451000; e-mail mail@caa.co.za; internet www.caa.co.za; Chair. ERNEST KHOSA; CEO POPPY KHOZA.

Airlink (Pty) Ltd: No. 3, Greenstone Hill Office Park, Emerald Blvd, Greenstone Hill, Modderfontein; POB 7529, Bonaero Park 1622; tel. (11) 4517300; e-mail info@flyairlink.com; internet flyairlink.com; f. 1995; internal and external scheduled services and charters in Southern Africa; operates 2 subsidiaries: Swaziland Airlink, Airlink Cargo; Man. Dir RODGER FOSTER.

Interair South Africa: Voltex House, 1st Floor, 3 River Rd, Bedfordview, Johannesburg 2007; Private Bag 8, OR Tambo Int. Airport, Johannesburg 1627; tel. (11) 6160636; e-mail info@interair.co.za; internet www.interair.co.za; Exec. Chair. DAVID P. TOKOPH.

Mango Airlines: Mezzanine Level, Tambo Int. Airport, POB 1273, Kempton Park 1627; tel. (11) 8154100; e-mail enquiries@flymango .com; internet www.flymango.com; f. 2006; owned by South African Airways (itself govt-owned); CEO WILLIAM NDLOVU (acting).

Safair Operations (Pty) Ltd: Northern Perimeter Rd, Bonaero Park 1619; POB 938, Kempton Park 1620; tel. 9280000; e-mail marketing@safair.co.za; internet www.safairoperations.com; f. 1965 as Tropair (Pty) Ltd; launched FlySafair airline in 2014; aircraft leasing and full charter; part of the ASL Aviation Group, Ireland; CEO ELMAR CONRADIE.

South African Airways (SAA): Airways Park, 32 Jones Rd, Private Bag X13, Johannesburg 1627; tel. (11) 9781000; e-mail voyager@flysaa.com; internet www.flysaa.com; f. 1934; internal passenger services linking all the principal towns; international services to Africa, Europe, North and South America and Asia; 51% owned by the Takatso Consortium, 49% state-owned; Chair. GEOFF QHENA; CEO JOHN LAMOLA.

Tourism

South African Tourism: Bojanala House, 90 Protea Rd, Chislehurston, Johannesburg 2196; Private Bag X10012, Sandton 2146; tel. (11) 8953000; e-mail mediaq@southafrica.net; internet southafrica.net; f. 1947; 11 overseas brs; Chair. SIYABONGA DUBE; CEO STHEMBISO DLAMINI (acting).

Tourism Business Council of South Africa (TBCSA): Lyttleton Manor, 3 Amethyst St, cnr Lenchen Ave, Pretoria 0046; POB 11655, Centurion 0157; tel. 870490115; e-mail tourism@tbcsa.travel; internet tbcsa.travel; f. 1996; umbrella org of organized business in travel and tourism industry; Chair BLACKY KOMANI; CEO TSHIFHIWA TSHIVHENGWA.

Defence

As assessed at November 2021, the South African National Defence Force (SANDF) totalled 74,000: army 38,000, navy 6,650, air force 9,800, a medical corps numbering 7,300 and 12,250 others. There was also a reserve of 15,050 (army 12,250, navy 850, air 850, medical corps 1,100). The SANDF comprises members of the former South African armed forces, together with personnel from the former military wings of the African National Congress of South Africa and the Pan-Africanist Congress, and the former 'homelands' militias. At November 2021 a total of 1,211 South African troops were stationed abroad.

Estimated Defence Budget: R 46,300m. in 2021.

Chief of the South African National Defence Force: Gen. RUDZANI MAPHWANYA.

Chief of the South African Air Force: Lt-Gen. WISEMAN SIMO MBAMBO.

Chief of the South African Army: Lt-Gen. LAWRENCE KHULEKANI MBATHA.

Chief of the South African Navy: Rear-Adm. MONDE LOBESE (acting).

Education

School attendance is compulsory for children of all population groups between the ages of seven and 16 years. From 1991 state schools were permitted to admit pupils of all races, and in 1995 the right to free state education for all was introduced. According to estimates by the United Nations Educational, Scientific and Cultural Organization (UNESCO), pre-primary enrolment in 2017/18 was equivalent to 18% of children (males 18%; females 18%) in the relevant age-group. In that year enrolment at primary schools included 89% of children (males 88%; females 90%) in the relevant age-group, while enrolment at secondary schools included 72% of pupils (65% males; 79% females) in the relevant age-group. According to UNESCO estimates, government expenditure on education in 2021 was equivalent to about 18.4% of total spending.

Bibliography

Abel, R. L. *Politics by Other Means: Law in the Struggle Against Apartheid, 1980–1994.* London, Routledge, 1995.

Adam, H., et al. *Comrades in Business: Post-Liberation Politics in South Africa.* Cape Town, Tafelberg, 1997.

Adebajo, A., et al. (Eds). *South Africa in Africa: The Post-Apartheid Era.* Pietermaritzburg, University of KwaZulu-Natal Press, 2007.

Adebajo, A., and Virk, K. *Foreign Policy in Post-Apartheid South Africa: Security, Diplomacy and Trade.* London, I.B. Taurus, 2017.

Ajam, K., et al. (Eds). *The A–Z of South African Politics: People, Parties and Players.* Auckland Park, Jacana Media, 2019.

Alden, C., and Le Pere, G. *South Africa's post-apartheid Foreign Policy: From Reconciliation to Revival?* Oxford, Oxford University Press for the International Institute for Strategic Studies, 2003.

Bond, P. *Elite Transition: From Apartheid to Neoliberalism in South Africa.* London, Pluto Press, 2014.

Bhorat, H., Hirsch, A., Kanbur, R., and Ncube, M. (Eds). *The Oxford Companion to the Economics of South Africa.* Oxford, Oxford University Press, 2015.

Brown, J. *The Road to Soweto Resistance and the Uprising of 16 June 1976.* Woodbridge, James Currey, 2016.

Marikana: A People's History. Woodbridge, James Currey, 2022.

Bruggemans, C. *Change of Pace: South Africa's Economic Revival.* Johannesburg, University of the Witwatersrand Press, 2003.

Bundy, C. *Short-Changed?: South Africa Since Apartheid.* Athens, OH, Ohio University Press, 2015.

Burchardt, M. *Faith in the Time of AIDS: Religion, Biopolitics and Modernity in South Africa.* Basingstoke, Palgrave Macmillan, 2015.

Butler, A. *Contemporary South Africa.* 2nd edn. Basingstoke, Palgrave Macmillan, 2009.

Cyril Ramaphosa: The Path to Presidential Power. (3rd edn). Auckland Park, Jacana Media, 2019.

Callinicos, L. *People's History of South Africa.* 3 vols. Johannesburg, Ravan Press, 1981–93.

Carmichael, L. *Peacemaking and Peacebuilding in South Africa: The National Peace Accord, 1991–1994.* Woodbridge, James Currey, 2022.

Chan, S. *Southern Africa: Old Treacheries and New Deceits.* New Haven, CT, Yale University Press, 2011.

Davenport, R. and Saunders, C. *South Africa A Modern History.* 5th edn. London, Macmillan, 2000.

Davies, R. *Afrikaners in the New South Africa: Identity Politics in a Globalised Economy.* London and New York, I.B. Tauris, 2009.

Du Pre, R. H. *Separate but Unequal: The 'Coloured' People of South Africa: A Political History.* Johannesburg, Jonathan Ball, 1994.

Feinstein, C. *An Economic History of South Africa.* Cambridge, Cambridge University Press, 2005.

Forde, F. *An Inconvenient Youth: Julius Malema and the 'New' ANC.* Johannesburg, Picador, 2011.

Gevisser, M. *Thabo Mbeki. The Dream Deferred.* Johannesburg, Jonathan Ball, 2009.

Giliomee, H. *The Afrikaners: Biography of a People.* London, C. Hurst & Co, 2003.

The Rise and Demise of the Afrikaners. Cape Town, Tafelberg, 2019.

Giliomee, H. and Mbenga, B. (Eds). *New History of South Africa.* Cape Town, Tafelberg, 2007.

Gumede, V. *Political Economy of Post-Apartheid South Africa.* Dakar, CODESRIA, 2015.

Hentz, J. J. *South Africa and the Logic of Regional Co-operation.* Bloomington, IN, Indiana University Press, 2005.

Hickel, J. *Democracy as Death: The Moral Order of Anti-Liberal Politics in South Africa.* Berkeley, CA, University of California Press, 2015.

Holmes, C. *The Black and White Rainbow Reconciliation, Opposition, and Nation-Building in Democratic South Africa.* Ann Arbor, MI, University of Michigan Press, 2020.

Jeffrey, A. *People's War.* Johannesburg, Jonathan Ball, 2009.

Johnson, R. W. *South Africa: The First Man, the Last Nation.* London, Weidenfeld & Nicolson, 2004.

Fighting for the Dream. Johannesburg, Jonathan Ball, 2019.

Johnson, R. W., and Schlemmer, L. (Eds). *Launching Democracy in South Africa: The First Open Election, April 1994.* New Haven, CT, Yale University Press, 1996.

South Africa's Brave New World. London, Allen Lane, 2009.

Jolobe, Z. *International Mediation in the South African Transition: Brokering Power in Intractable Conflicts.* Abingdon, Routledge, 2019.

Klotz, A. *Migration and National Identity in South Africa, 1860–2010.* Cambridge, Cambridge University Press, 2013.

Koorts, L. *D. F. Malan and the Rise of Afrikaner Nationalism.* Cape Town, Tafelberg, 2014.

Laband, J. P. C. *Rope of Sand: The Rise and Fall of the Zulu Kingdom in the Nineteenth Century.* Johannesburg, Jonathan Ball, 1995.

Landsberg, C. *The Diplomacy of Transformation.* Johannesburg, Macmillan, 2010.

Lieberman, E. *Until We Have Won Our Liberty: South Africa after Apartheid.* Princeton, NJ, Princeton University Press, 2022.

Lodge, T. *Politics in South Africa: From Mandela to Mbeki.* Cape Town, David Philip; and Oxford, James Currey, 2003.

Sharpeville: An Apartheid Massacre and its Consequences. Oxford, Oxford University Press, 2011.

Macmillan, H. *The Lusaka Years: The ANC in Exile in Zambia, 1963 to 1994.* Auckland Park, Jacana, 2013.

Maharaj, B., Desai, A., and Bond, P. *Zuma's Own Goal: losing South Africa's 'War on Poverty'.* Trenton, NJ, Africa World Press, 2011.

Marais, H. *Pushed to the Limit.* Cape Town, University of Cape Town Press, 2010.

Marks, S., and Trapido, S. *The Politics of Race, Class and Nationalism in Twentieth Century South Africa.* London and New York, Longman, 1987.

Maylam, P. *History of the African People of South Africa.* Cape Town, David Philip, 1986.

Meli, F. *South Africa Belongs To Us: A History of the ANC.* London, James Currey; Cape Town, David Philip; and Bloomington, IN, Indiana University Press, 1989.

Newman, K. S. *After Freedom: The Rise of the Post-Apartheid Generation in Democratic South Africa*. Boston, MA, Beacon Press, 2014.

Oqubay, A., Tregenna, F., and Valodia, I. (Eds). *The Oxford Handbook of the South African Economy*. Oxford, Oxford University Press, 2021.

Picard, L. A. *The Limits of Democratic Governance in South Africa*. Boulder, CO, Lynne Rienner Publishers, 2015.

Renwick, R. *The End of Apartheid: Diary of a Revolution*. London, Biteback, 2015.

Russell, A. *After Mandela. The Battle for the Soul of South Africa*. London, Hutchinson, 2009.

Saul, S., and Bond, P. *South Africa—The Present as History: From Mrs Ples to Mandela and Marikana*. Woodbridge, James Currey, 2016.

Saunders, C., and Southey, N. *Dictionary of South African History*. Cape Town, David Philip, 1998.

Seegers, A. *The Military in the Making of Modern South Africa*. London, I.B. Tauris, 1997.

Seekings, J., and Nattrass, N. *Policy, Politics and Poverty in South Africa*. Basingstoke, Palgrave Macmillan, 2015.

Siko, J. *Inside South Africa's Foreign Policy: Diplomacy in Africa from Smuts to Mbeki*. London, I.B. Tauris, 2014.

South African Democracy Education Trust. *The Road to Democracy in South Africa*. 6 Vols. Cape Town and Pretoria, Zebra Press and UNISA Press, 2004–16.

Southall, R. and Daniel, J. (Eds). *Zunami! The 2009 South African Election*. Cape Town, Jacana Media, 2009.

Sparks, A. *Beyond the Miracle. Inside the New South Africa*. Johannesburg, Jonathan Ball, 2003.

Spence, J. and Welsh, D. *Ending Apartheid (Turning Points)*. London, Longman, 2010.

Terreblanche, S. *A History of Inequality in South Africa 1652–2002*. Scottsville, University of Natal Press, 2003.

Thompson, L. M. *A History of South Africa*. 4th edn. New Haven, CT, Yale University Press, 2014.

Tshitereke, C. *The Experience of Economic Redistribution: The Growth, Employment and Redistribution Strategy in South Africa*. Abingdon, Routledge, 2006.

Turner, R. *The Eye of the Needle: Towards Participatory Democracy in South Africa*. London, Seagull Books, 2015.

Venter, A., and Landsberg, C. *Government and Politics in South Africa*. 4th edn. Pretoria, Van Schaik, 2011.

Walker, C., et al. (Eds). *Land, Memory, Reconstruction and Justice: perspectives on land claims in South Africa*. Scottsville, University of KwaZulu-Natal Press, 2011.

Welsh, D. *The Rise and Fall of Apartheid*. Johannesburg, Jonathan Ball, 2009.

Wilson, R. *The Politics of Truth and Reconciliation in South Africa: Legitimizing the Post-Apartheid State*. Cambridge, Cambridge University Press, 2001.

SOUTH SUDAN

Physical and Social Geography

The territory of the Republic of South Sudan comprises all lands that constituted the three former Sudanese provinces of Bahr El-Ghazal, Equatoria and Upper Nile in their boundaries as they stood on 1 January 1956, and the Abyei Area, as defined by the Abyei Arbitration Tribunal Award of July 2009. South Sudan, which covers a total area of 644,329 sq km (248,777 sq miles), is bordered by Sudan to the north, by Ethiopia to the east, by Kenya and Uganda to the south, by the Democratic Republic of the Congo to the south-west, and by the Central African Republic to the west.

According to the Sudan Population and Housing Census of April 2008, the population of South Sudan was 8,260,490. At mid-2022, according to official projections, the population was estimated to have risen to 14,234,977, equating to a population density of 22.1 per sq km. The country is divided into 10 states; there are, additionally, two administrative areas (Greater Pibor and Ruweng) and one special administrative area (Abyei). The capital is Juba, which had an estimated population of 439,993 at mid-2022, according to United Nations projections. It was announced in September 2011 that the capital was to be relocated to Ramciel, in the centre of the country (although by mid-2022 the plan had not been implemented).

South Sudan is generally a flat, featureless plain reflecting the proximity to the surface of the ancient Basement rocks of the African continent. The Basement is overlain by the Umm Ruwaba formation which holds groundwater bodies of agricultural significance. No point in the country is very high above sea level, although elevations rise to 3,187 m on Mt Kinyeti, near the border with Uganda.

Average temperatures and rainfall change steadily from month to month, except where the effect of the Ethiopian highlands disturbs the east–west trend in the climatic belts in the south-east. Rainfall reaches over 1,000 mm per year at the southern border and generally occurs in the period April–October. Potential evaporation is always over 1,400 mm per year, even in the humid south.

The River Nile is the dominant geographic feature in South Sudan, flowing across the country. South Sudan is home to the world's largest swamp, the Sudd, which covers a total area of 30,000 sq km. The Nile and its many tributaries also provide access to almost unlimited sources of water which services the land, making it fertile to support diverse vegetation and crops. The flooded areas of the Sudd and the Machar, and their environs, support swamp vegetation and grassland. On the uplands of the southern border, rainfall is sufficient to support tropical rainforest.

South Sudan is predominantly Christian and this cultural difference from the largely Arab Sudan, added to the region's ethnic separateness and extreme remoteness, has been expressed in economic backwardness and a tendency to political distinctness. These factors have been the main causes of persistent unrest in southern Sudan and ultimately culminated in the secession of South Sudan from Sudan.

English is the official language, although Juba/South Sudanese Arabic (an Arabic pidgin) is the lingua franca around Juba. Other major languages are Dinka (spoken by 2m.–3m. people), Nuer, Bari, Zande and Shilluk.

History

DUNCAN WOODSIDE

INTRODUCTION

The Republic of South Sudan was created on 9 July 2011, when, following a referendum held between 9 January and 15 January, the semi-autonomous region of Southern Sudan seceded from Sudan. The referendum, in which 98.8% of those who voted (on a turnout of 97.6% of the electorate) opted in favour of independence, was the central pillar of a 2005 peace agreement that ended 22 unbroken years of civil war between Sudan's Arab-dominated central government and a guerrilla army in the largely Christian and animist south. Tens of thousands of people—many of them war veterans—observed the official secession proceedings in Juba, the southern capital, at which Lt-Gen. Salva Kiir Mayardit was inaugurated as President of the new state; the ceremonies were attended by United Nations (UN) Secretary-General Ban Ki-Moon, Sudanese President Lt-Gen. Omar Hassan Ahmad al-Bashir and about 30 other African heads of state. Kiir, hitherto the President of semi-autonomous Southern Sudan and the leader of its governing party, the Sudan People's Liberation Movement (SPLM), signed into force a new interim Constitution, under which the south's former guerrilla army—the Sudan People's Liberation Army (SPLA)—was formally reconstituted as the national army of the new country. South Sudan was immediately recognized by the principal world powers, including the USA, the United Kingdom and the People's Republic of China, and it became the 193rd member of the UN on 14 July 2011.

However, South Sudan was faced with multiple challenges. There were widespread concerns among informed observers that it could quickly degenerate into a failed state, because of an inability to fulfil the fundamental task of guaranteeing even a minimal level of security to its citizens. The new nation was bedevilled by multiple internal renegade movements, which had emerged in response to the SPLM's tendency to centralize power and its reluctance to work with opposition parties. In addition, despite Sudan's official recognition of the new nation's sovereignty, explosive bilateral disagreements threatened to provoke a return to a north–south war. The main points of disagreement were the failure to agree on the status of the disputed Abyei region; the lack of a mutually agreed wider border between the two sovereign territories; the absence of a deal on the sharing of the south's oil revenues; and the emergence of a new conflict in oil-rich Southern Kordofan State, in the southernmost part of Sudan.

The SPLA and the Sudan Armed Forces (SAF) came into renewed direct conflict in the Heglig oilfields in March–April 2012, causing a breakdown of negotiations under the auspices of the African Union High Implementation Panel in the Ethiopian capital, Addis Ababa. A threat of sanctions against both South Sudan and Sudan by the UN Security Council, in the form of the unanimously agreed Resolution 2046, was required in order to force the two sides back from the brink of renewed full-scale war. Meanwhile, each Government continued to accuse the other of supporting insurgent activity on each other's territory.

For much of 2013 there was no real progress in resolving outstanding disputes with Sudan, and there was a renewed deterioration in the internal politico-security situation, characterized by rising tensions between President Kiir, an ethnic Dinka, and his Nuer Vice-President, Dr Riek Machar Teny-Dhurgon. The President dismissed his deputy in July, and suspended and subsequently replaced his entire Cabinet. The rift between Kiir and Machar caused a descent into civil conflict in December. Kiir accused his former deputy of attempting to organize a coup—a charge denied by Machar, who accused the presidential guard of trying to assassinate him and of killing Nuer civilians in Juba. Journalists and the non-governmental organization (NGO) Human Rights Watch documented accounts of widespread ethnic killings of Nuer by Dinka elements of the security forces in Juba in that month, and fighting spread beyond the capital to engulf the oil-rich Upper Nile and Unity states. Both sides were accused of the widespread killing of civilians, as key towns—including Bentiu, the capital of Unity State and Malakal, the capital of Upper Nile—repeatedly changed hands. Several ceasefires were agreed between the two sides, and a peace agreement was concluded (with difficulty) in August 2015, but this collapsed, and fighting persisted into the first half of 2018 (see below). The signing of a renewed peace agreement in September led to a significant reduction in fighting between forces loyal to the main protagonists. Although conflicts persisted with other rebel groups, in February 2020 a transitional government of national unity was finally formed, after the Kiir and Machar camps reached agreement on security arrangements in Juba, a reduction in the number of states and the creation of three administrative areas.

THE FIRST NORTH–SOUTH CIVIL WAR

There is no consensus as to when Sudan's first north–south civil war began. Some observers date it from 1955, when southern soldiers rebelled against northern control in the garrison town of Torit. The administrative structure that was being established in advance of Sudan's independence from the UK (which was formalized on 1 January 1956) notably failed to take account of southern demands for federalism. It was 1964 before attacks by southern rebels against the northern army became anything more than sporadic. In 1970 Col Joseph Lagu brought together disparate factions with the formation of the Southern Sudan Liberation Front (SSLF). His authority was strengthened by military support from Israel.

The first civil war was brought to an end with the negotiation of the Addis Ababa Agreement of February 1972 between the Sudanese Government, under Col Gaafar Muhammad Nimeri, and the Southern Sudan Liberation Movement (previously the SSLF), which provided for regional autonomy in southern Sudan, allowing a tentative peace to prevail between north and south for the next 11 years.

THE 1983–2005 NORTH–SOUTH WAR

The political accommodation between Nimeri and the south's former rebels disintegrated during 1983. The creation of an Islamic state in Sudan in September of that year terminated the largely Christian and animist south's regional autonomy. A unified rebel politico-military command was established in the south, under the leadership of Col John Garang. The new rebel group became the SPLA, and its political wing the SPLM. The ultimate objective of the rebels at this time was to overthrow Nimeri and establish a secular state across the entire territory of Sudan.

The fortunes of the resulting conflict oscillated significantly for the two sides over the course of the next 20 years or so, not least because of a mismatch in the protagonists' external support. The SPLA (which had very limited external backing and depended overwhelmingly on the Soviet-backed regime of Ethiopian President Lt-Col Mengistu Haile Mariam) made significant gains at the end of the 1980s and in 1990. Meanwhile, following the end of the Cold War, the Sudanese Government (which had previously benefited from US support) became increasingly isolated internationally. President al-Bashir had assumed power in June 1989 by means of a military coup. The SPLA split into two rival factions in August 1991, when an influential southern rebel, Riek Machar (who was of Nuer descent) was among the leaders of a mutiny against the authority of Garang, an ethnic Dinka. In a clear policy of 'divide and rule', the Sudanese authorities supported the activities of the new grouping. (The split in the SPLA persisted until early

2002, while tensions between Machar's ethnic group, the Nuer, and the Dinka continued to simmer, even after southern independence in 2011.)

From 2000 the international community intensified efforts to mediate an end to the north–south civil war. Garang and Ali Osman Muhammad Taha, a key aide to al-Bashir, began direct talks in Kenya in September 2003, and a wealth-sharing protocol was signed in January 2004.

THE 2005 COMPREHENSIVE PEACE AGREEMENT

On 9 January 2005, in Nairobi, Kenya, the Sudanese Government and the SPLM signed a Comprehensive Peace Agreement (CPA), officially ending the civil war in the south, which had lasted for more than two decades—during which period at least 2m. people had been killed, and more than 4m. displaced. The accord comprised eight protocols, including agreements that political power and Sudan's national wealth would be shared between the national Government and the south; the SAF and the SPLA would remain separate forces within the national army, in addition to contributing equally to new Joint Integrated Units, which would be deployed on both sides of the north–south border; and all militias would be disbanded within a year. The south's oil revenues would be shared equally between the north and a semi-autonomous south; the SPLM and other southern groups would hold 30% of government positions in the north, while holding 70% in the south; and the contested provinces of the Blue Nile and the Nuba Mountains would be governed by an administration in which 55% of the seats would be held by northern government officials and the remainder by the SPLM. Meanwhile, the disputed, petroleum-rich Abyei region would be granted special status under the presidency. The application of *Shari'a* (Islamic) law would be limited to the north; and Garang would become Sudan's First Vice-President, President of the new Government of Southern Sudan (GOSS) and head of the SPLA forces during the six-year transition period, after which a referendum on secession would be held in the south.

An Interim National Constitution was promulgated on 9 July 2005, in accordance with the provisions of the CPA. On 1 August it was announced that Garang had been killed in a helicopter accident. Kiir, the Vice-President of the GOSS, succeeded Garang as leader of the SPLA/SPLM and subsequently as President of the GOSS and First Vice-President of Sudan. A Government of National Unity was established in September, dominated by al-Bashir's National Congress Party (NCP) and the SPLM.

THE NORTH–SOUTH POLITICAL TRANSITION

In addition to the GOSS, a new Transitional Southern Sudan Legislative Assembly was established, and regional administrations were created. In December 2005 a new transitional Constitution for the south was promulgated. Security remained a difficult issue, despite the conclusion of peace agreements with rebel groups after the signing of the CPA: concerns persisted about the capacity of the SPLA/SPLM to transform itself from an armed force into a solely political entity. The CPA provided for two secession referendums in 2011: a main plebiscite, covering all regions of southern Sudan except the disputed region of Abyei; and a second poll, to be held concurrently in Abyei, intended to give the people of that region the opportunity to decide whether to remain a part of Sudan or become part of an independent southern Sudan, in the event of a vote in favour of secession in the main referendum.

Disagreement over a number of issues in the CPA prompted the SPLM to withdraw temporarily from the Government of National Unity in late 2007. Its representation in the GOSS was increased in December. Major provisions of the CPA remained either unfulfilled or under dispute. One of the few achievements during 2008 in this regard was the selection of a nine-member National Elections Commission, which was approved in November by the National Assembly. This followed the adoption in July of an electoral law that guaranteed women 25% of seats in the legislature in a voting system based on proportional representation.

An interim administration was established in the Abyei region in August 2008, after a violent clash in April. In July, following a ruling by the Permanent Court of Arbitration in The Hague, Netherlands, a compromise agreement was reached concerning Abyei's boundaries; however, the status of the Heglig oilfield in Sudan's Southern Kordofan State remained unresolved, among other critical issues.

The first multi-party presidential, legislative and gubernatorial elections for more than two decades took place on 11–15 April 2010. As anticipated, incumbent President al-Bashir was re-elected, with 68.2% of the votes cast. In the south, Kiir retained the presidency, winning 93.0% of the vote and with only one opponent, Dr Lam Akol Ajawin of the Sudan People's Liberation Movement—Democratic Change (SPLM—DC). The SPLM secured 99 of the 450 seats in the National Assembly and 160 of the 170 seats in Southern Sudan's Legislative Assembly. Observer missions of the European Union (EU) and the US Carter Center refused to corroborate opposition allegations of widespread electoral malpractice but reported a high incidence of intimidation and a general failure to meet international electoral standards.

Kiir was inaugurated as President on 21 May 2010 and in June named a new GOSS Cabinet. Deng Alor Kuol was appointed as the Southern Sudan Minister of Regional Co-operation, while the Secretary-General of the SPLM, Pagan Amum, was named as Minister of Peace and CPA Implementation. Riek Machar remained as Vice-President.

THE JANUARY 2011 REFERENDUM

Under Kiir, the secessionist element within the SPLM gradually became politically ascendant. Voting in the main referendum on secession took place from 9–15 January 2011 and proceeded remarkably smoothly. Meanwhile, the parallel referendum to be held in the region of Abyei had been postponed after the SPLM and the NCP failed to agree on certain issues, including voter eligibility. According to the official results, announced on 7 February, 98.8% of participants in the referendum had opted in favour of secession on a turnout of 97.6% of the electorate.

POST-SECESSION NORTH–SOUTH TENSIONS

Barely one month before secession, in early June 2011 a new conflict broke out between the SAF and the SPLA/SPLA-aligned elements in the oil-rich Sudanese state of Southern Kordofan (home to a significant constituency of southerners) after a disputed election for the state governorship was won by the incumbent NCP candidate and the SPLM claimed fraudulent practices. The refusal of armed groups in Southern Kordofan to comply with government demands to disarm sparked fighting, which, according to the UN, caused more than 70,000 people to flee. Most of the displaced were ethnic Nubans, amid a bombing campaign by Sudan's air force, and South Sudan's Vice-President Riek Machar claimed that ethnic cleansing was taking place. The African Union (AU) brokered a preliminary agreement between the NCP and the SPLM over Southern Kordofan in late June, involving pledges to disarm non-SAF groups without the use of force.

While not as severe as the situation in Southern Kordofan, the Abyei region—officially a demilitarized zone, the future status of which was yet to be determined—remained tense in the immediate post-secession period. The SAF had occupied Abyei town in May 2011, after an attack on one of its military convoys outside the town by the SPLA, resulting in the displacement of some 50,000 inhabitants. Following AU-mediated negotiations, in June both the SPLM and the NCP accepted the planned deployment of up to 4,500 peacekeeping troops in Abyei, under the auspices of a new UN Interim Security Force for Abyei (UNISFA). On 8 July the UN Security Council adopted a resolution authorizing the establishment of the UN Mission in the Republic of South Sudan (UNMISS), which was mandated to support the southern authorities in peace consolidation and state building. However, the key issues of contention between the NCP and the SPLM over the future of the region remained unresolved. While the SPLM maintained (in accordance with the 2005 CPA) that a referendum must be held in Abyei, Sudan's President al-Bashir insisted immediately after South Sudan's independence that Abyei would remain part of Sudan.

The other main potential trigger for an escalation of north–south conflict was the expiry of an oil-sharing deal. Until 9 July 2011 revenues from the south's oilfields were shared equally between Sudan's central Government and the south. Following secession, the South Sudanese authorities took control of territory that had accounted for about three-quarters of Sudan's oil output. South Sudan's bargaining position was constrained by its dependence on Sudan's pipeline infrastructure. Juba investigated alternative export routes, culminating in January 2012 in the signing of a preliminary agreement with the Kenyan Government for a pipeline to the coastal town of Lamu. In March–April the SPLA occupied the town of Heglig and its surrounding oilfields, in Sudanese territory, triggering fierce fighting and the eventual withdrawal of the forces, under pressure from the UN. Two of the greatest impediments to a genuinely comprehensive settlement were the absence of an officially demarcated north–south border and the new conflict in Sudan's Southern Kordofan State, which spread to Blue Nile in September 2011. Upon South Sudan's secession, the SPLA units in Southern Kordofan officially became the SPLA—North (SPLA—N). Likewise, local SPLM members formally adopted a new political identity as the SPLM—North (SPLM—N).

In compliance with a deadline imposed by Resolution 2046 (which the UN Security Council passed in early May 2012, ordering the two sides to cease hostilities within 48 hours and urging both Governments to resume AU-mediated negotiations), South Sudan ordered its police force to withdraw from Abyei by 16 May. Subsequently all SAF forces were also withdrawn from Abyei town, in accordance with UNISFA's mandate to act as the sole provider of security in the disputed region. In August the two countries concluded an agreement on oil revenues and pipeline fees, which in effect provided for South Sudan to pay a form of compensation to Sudan for the loss of so much of its former oil reserves on South Sudan's secession. A further agreement was reached in September, whereby the two countries pledged to create a demilitarized zone (DMZ) along their common border. In March 2013 the two sides agreed to withdraw their forces from the DMZ and to implement the oil accord. Oil began flowing from the south in April.

Relations between Juba and Khartoum, the Sudanese capital, improved following the outbreak of civil conflict in the south in December 2013. President al-Bashir travelled to Juba to meet his South Sudanese counterpart in January 2014, backing Kiir in the dispute with his former deputy, Riek Machar (see *Civil War*). Sudan's Ministry of Foreign Affairs stated that there would be continued security co-operation in the border area and agreement on the potential deployment of 900 Sudanese oil workers to southern installations. As the conflict in the south persisted, unease rose in Juba about the stance of Sudan's Government. A visit by Machar to Khartoum in June—and a press conference held there by the rebel faction—prompted complaints by the South Sudan embassy, which stated that Sudan had violated the co-operation agreement signed by the two countries in September 2012.

INTERNAL POLITICAL TENSIONS

A major source of tensions between Sudan and newly independent South Sudan has been the existence of renegade movements in the south, several of which had splintered from the SPLA in the year or so prior to secession. The SPLM/SPLA consistently claimed that the NCP was supporting these movements in order to destabilize the south's ability to govern itself. However, no substantive evidence had been presented to confirm allegations of such tactics during and immediately after secession.

In the year after independence, there was an increase in the severity of inter-communal violence among ethnic militias. A violent cattle-raiding attack, by a Lou Nuer militia group against the Murle pastoralist community, took place in Pibor county, Jonglei State, in December 2011. The peacekeeping presence on the ground in Pibor—together with local detachments of the SPLA—proved powerless to intervene as hundreds of women and children were massacred. Nearly the entire cattle stock of the Murle was taken, and in early 2012 the Murle subsequently launched several retaliatory raids against Lou Nuer cattle encampments in Akobo county. Attempts by the SPLA to encourage the Murle and Lou Nuer communities to disarm met with reluctance, with the communities fearing that they would be left more vulnerable to attack both by local rivals and by cross-border raiders from Ethiopia, Kenya or Uganda. In March 2013 the SPLA stepped up anti-insurgency operations against the South Sudan Democratic Army (SSDA), which at this time was a largely Murle rebel group under the leadership of David Yau Yau, an ethnic Murle.

Beyond such inter-ethnic tensions and anti-Government insurgent activity, indications increased in 2013 of significant discord at the very heart of the regime, between President Kiir and Vice-President Riek Machar. Machar, a member of the influential Nuer community, was a divisive figure, having broken ranks from the SPLA rebellion during the north–south civil war and formed a Khartoum-backed splinter faction that fought against the independence movement in 1991–2002. In April 2013 Kiir disbanded an ethnic reconciliation programme led by Machar, amid perceptions that the Vice-President's initiative was raising his profile at the expense of the President. Further evidence of tensions between the two emerged in July, when Kiir dismissed Taban Deng Gai, the elected Governor of Unity State, replacing him, by presidential decree, with a caretaker Governor, Joseph Nguen Monytuil. The manner of Gai's dismissal and replacement suggested an increasingly authoritarian drift.

Kiir dismissed Machar in July 2013 and suspended the entire Council of Ministers, leading to fears of a political crisis. Machar nevertheless called for calm in the days following his dismissal, which initially served to assuage fears that he might mobilize Nuer elements of the national army to oppose Kiir. In August Kiir appointed a staunch ally, James Wani Igga (formerly the Speaker of the National Legislative Assembly), as the new Vice-President and reduced the number of ministers in a reorganized Government from 29 to 21.

CIVIL WAR

While internal tensions did increase significantly in the course of 2013, few observers predicted the ferocity of the conflict that broke out in December of that year, nor the speed at which the fighting spread. Hostilities began in Juba on 15 December; President Kiir claimed that the violence stemmed from a coup attempt by Machar, who countered that he and other opposition figures were the intended victims of a purge by Dinka elements within the security services. The fighting in the capital lasted for several days. Human Rights Watch corroborated reports that men from the Nuer ethnic group were being murdered by Dinka security forces; thousands of Nuer sought refuge at two UNMISS bases in Juba. Conflict spread rapidly, intensifying in violence, to Bentiu, Malakal and Bor, the capital of Jonglei State. The hostilities were characterized by a high number of civilian casualties.

A number of ceasefires were agreed in the first half of 2014, but each was swiftly violated. The first agreement came in January, when representatives of the Government and the rebels signed a deal in Addis Ababa, but this collapsed within hours as the rebels accused government forces of attacking them. A second ceasefire was signed by Kiir and Machar in May, after their first face-to-face meeting since the beginning of the conflict; this truce, like the first, ended swiftly. A third ceasefire arrangement entered into effect in June. Again signed by both Kiir and Machar, this was designed to pave the way for the formation of a government of national unity within 60 days; however, this deadline passed without any substantive progress. Meanwhile, Kiir elevated Paul Malong Awan to the post of SPLA Chief of General Staff in April. As Governor of Northern Bahr El-Ghazal, Malong had consolidated considerable power and influence, and he was the leader of a Dinka militia which had become dominant in the state security forces ahead of the outbreak of hostilities in December 2013.

In February 2015 the Government adopted a resolution postponing the elections that were scheduled for June and extending the presidential and legislative mandates in order to avoid the risk of a power vacuum, in the event of a continued failure of peace talks with the rebels. In response, Machar declared that Kiir, by staying in power beyond his democratic mandate, was no longer able to claim that he was an 'elected President'. Clashes broke out around oilfields in Unity State in June as fighting intensified in Upper Nile State; Malakal was once again seized by the rebels in late June. In July Machar reorganized his military leadership, giving rise to speculation that serious internal divisions were emerging within the rebel opposition forces.

Amid increasing international pressure on both the Government and the rebels to agree on some form of peace accord, on 17 August 2015, at a meeting in Addis Ababa overseen by various international mediators, Machar signed a document known as the Agreement on the Resolution of the Conflict in South Sudan (ARCSS). Although President Kiir eventually consented to sign the peace agreement on 26 August, he expressed 'serious reservations' to East African leaders who had gathered to witness him do so. South Sudan's National Legislative Assembly ratified the ARCSS unanimously in early September. Later in that month, the rebels' National Liberation Council formally approved Machar's signature of the deal and nominated him as their candidate for the post of Vice-President. The peace deal therefore presaged a deeply uneasy return to the pre-war status quo, with Kiir and Machar respectively resuming their positions as head of state and deputy head of state.

By October 2015 there had been over 50 ceasefire violations by the two sides since the first truce was signed in February 2014, according to mediators reporting to the Intergovernmental Authority on Development (IGAD). Conflict also began to flare up in states that had previously remained relatively unaffected by the violence. During late December 2015 and early January 2016 some 15,000 people were uprooted in Western Equatoria, largely from the towns of Yambio and Tambura, according to the UN High Commissioner for Refugees (UNHCR). A report by UN human rights investigators—the result of fieldwork carried out between October 2015 and January 2016—detailed horrendous abuses against civilians. The investigation found evidence that government-aligned militia had been given permission to steal cattle, rape women and abduct girls, as a substitute for wages.

Against this backdrop of largely unabated violence, President Kiir formally reinstated Machar as Vice-President in early February 2016 and called on him to return to Juba forthwith, to join the so-called Transitional Government of National Unity. Machar stated that he would not return until or unless Juba was demilitarized. Later in February it was agreed that troops loyal to Machar would return to the capital, to ensure his protection. Machar finally arrived in Juba on 26 April and was promptly sworn in as Vice-President. Within two days, Kiir named a 30-member Cabinet, with 10 positions filled by former rebels. Machar's arrival had been preceded by that of his Chief of Staff, Gen. Simon Gatwech Dual, who flew into the capital with the 195 men requested by the Vice-President, carrying weaponry.

The two protagonists co-existed in Juba for just over two months, before intense hostilities resumed in the capital in July 2016. An initial skirmish at a checkpoint on 7 July—in which five people were killed, according to the SPLA—was followed by heavy fighting at locations across the city the next day between troops loyal to Kiir and Machar. On 11 July both Kiir and Machar ordered ceasefires. By that stage, Machar's troops had fled Juba, after an onslaught by the SPLA. The UN described the initial death toll of 272 people, including 33 civilians (as disclosed by the Government) as likely to be 'only the tip of the iceberg'. As in December 2013, Machar's personal residence was attacked, according to his spokesman, Peter Gatkuoth, who stated that the Vice-President would not return to Juba, unless new international troops were deployed to the capital as a protection force, as well as the sizeable—but rather ineffective—presence provided by the existing UN peacekeeping mission.

Any hopes that the renewed gulf between Machar and Kiir would be bridged quickly were dashed when the President appointed Taban Deng Gai, formerly Machar's chief negotiator during peace talks, as Vice-President. Gai was sworn in on

26 July 2016. In addition, on 2 August Kiir dismissed six ministers loyal to the armed opposition, including the newly appointed Minister of Petroleum and Mining—a move that further narrowed power and control over the country's resources. Machar fled to the Democratic Republic of the Congo (DRC) later that month, then seeking medical treatment in Sudan, and in South Africa, where he was placed under effective house arrest. Meanwhile, in accordance with the August 2015 peace agreement, an expanded, 400-member Transitional National Legislative Assembly (TNLA) was inaugurated on 14 August 2016.

Following the clashes in Juba in July 2016, fighting spread rapidly to other areas of the country, in particular to Central Equatoria. Tensions in one of the state's major towns, Yei, had begun to heighten from late 2015. Conflicts over land proliferated between Equatorian communities and Dinka pastoralists, whose assertiveness was boosted by an increasingly ethnically homogenous SPLA. The situation was exacerbated when new SPLA troops from Dinka strongholds in Bahr El-Ghazal were deployed in the area under the command of Malong, according to the UN Panel of Experts on South Sudan. Fighting erupted in July–August 2016 between the SPLA and the rebel SPLA-in-Opposition (SPLA-IO) forces, leading loyalists to force civilians from surrounding villages into the centre of Yei, ostensibly in order to secure outlying areas from opposition forces. The UN Panel of Experts cited multiple reports of atrocities by the SPLA in Central Equatoria in its interim report to the Security Council in October. Between July and October some 200,000 people fled to Uganda, about 150,000 of whom had been displaced from the Equatoria states, according to UNHCR.

Alongside the violence in Central Equatoria, in late 2016 and early 2017 there was also significant fighting in Western and Eastern Equatoria, Western Bahr El-Ghazal and Jonglei, as well as in Machar's erstwhile strongholds in Unity State as new sources of rebellion materialized and the SPLA launched fresh large-scale offensives. The intensifying military reality on the ground stood in stark contrast to Kiir's unilateral launch of a 'national dialogue' in December 2016, designed, so he claimed, to 'end all violent conflicts in South Sudan, reconstitute national consensus and save the country from disintegration'. The Government suffered a setback following a series of new defections in early 2017, which drew further attention to—and in part appeared to be driven by—the increasingly mono-ethnic character of the military's highest de facto echelons and political decision making. Key among the resignations was that of a Deputy Chief of General Staff, Lt-Gen. Thomas Cirillo Swaka, a Bari from Equatoria who accused the regime of pursuing 'a tribally engineered war' and operating a parallel chain of command outside formal SPLA structures and centred on the Chief of General Staff.

In early March 2017 Lt-Gen. Cirillo announced the establishment of a new rebel group, the National Salvation Front (NSF). Later in that month Gen. Khalid Butrus Bora, the leader of the Murle-dominated SSDA, pledged loyalty to the NSF, apparently terminating his group's three-year alignment with the regime. In May an agreement was announced by seven groups, including the SPLA-IO, the NSF and members of the unarmed opposition, to co-ordinate diplomatic, military and political efforts against the regime.

In an unexpected development on 9 May 2017, Kiir abruptly dismissed Malong as SPLA Chief of General Staff. Explanations offered by analysts for Kiir's action ranged from a desire on the part of the President to relieve diplomatic pressure from Western powers, to the theory that Malong, who had always been extremely sceptical about the 2015 peace agreement, nurtured his own presidential ambitions and had thus become a threat to the incumbent. Malong was placed under house arrest and was officially replaced as Chief of General Staff by Gen. James Ajongo Mawut, who was described by the presidency as an ethnic Luo. Later in that month Kiir appointed Marial Chanuong as head of the SPLA's land forces, after promoting him to the rank of Lieutenant-General. Chanuong had been sanctioned by the UN Security Council in 2015 for orchestrating 'the slaughter of Nuer civilians in and around Juba' in his role as the head of the presidential guard, in the violence at the start of the civil war in December 2013.

Some of the worst fighting in 2017 took place in Upper Nile State, driven in part by divisions between the Dinka Padang and Shilluk groups. The SPLA took Lul in April, and by the end of May the Government controlled the entire stretch of the White Nile between Malakal and Renk. Government forces also made significant gains in the south-east of Upper Nile State during 2017, launching an offensive in June to expel Machar's SPLA-IO from its main headquarters in the town of Pagak on the Ethiopian border.

TOWARDS UNEASY CO-EXISTENCE

Regional powers revived efforts to secure a peace agreement between the civil war's two main protagonists during mid-2018. In June Machar was invited to talks in Addis Ababa hosted by Ethiopia's Prime Minister, Abiy Ahmed Ali, signalling an end to the apparent policy of keeping the linchpin of the rebel movement isolated in South Africa. After the Addis Ababa negotiations and the holding of a further round in Khartoum, on 27 June Kiir and Machar signed a declaration committing to a 'permanent ceasefire' to take effect within 72 hours, a 120-day 'pre-transitional period' and a 'transitional period' of 36 months, followed by national elections. However, the deal left many issues unresolved (including the sharing of power during the transitional period), which were to be agreed under a 'revised bridging proposal' in subsequent rounds of talks scheduled to take place in Nairobi and Addis Ababa.

Aside from the rebels' promptly voiced doubts, several other significant factors undermined the new ceasefire's chances of evolving into a durable peace settlement. While Machar's participation indicated a decision on the part of regional powers that the strategy of keeping him geographically and diplomatically isolated had not proved effective, it was not immediately clear where the rebel leader would reside. In March 2018, when IGAD recommended that Machar be freed from house arrest in South Africa, the regional body had initially recommended that he be 'allowed to relocate to any country outside the region and not neighbouring South Sudan'. However, Machar's signature of the Khartoum Declaration (and implicit recognition as the principal rebel leader) indicated that he would be central to renewed attempts to establish a power-sharing government.

Even in the event of Kiir and Machar making a serious attempt to conclude a new power-sharing deal, the fragmentation of the conflict meant that decisions by other major players could prolong the war. With regard to Dinka hardliners, the largest non-regime threat came from former SPLA Chief of General Staff Malong, who had been permitted to go into exile in Kenya and in April 2018 announced the foundation of his own group, the South Sudan United Front/Army (SSUF/A), claiming that it would 'struggle to [...] arrest the carnage' and shepherd the nation back to democratic rule. Meanwhile, the armed opposition was also fragmented, as not all groups maintained loyalty to Machar's SPLA-IO faction. The UN Commission on Human Rights in South Sudan estimated in February 2018 that there were about 40 armed factions in the country at that time, largely as a result of the spread of the conflict to the Equatoria states and the northern part of Upper Nile State in late 2016 and 2017, after a 'number of senior officers' defected from the SPLA, SPLA-IO and Gai's branch of the SPLA-IO 'to form and join these new groups'.

The permanent ceasefire signed in Khartoum was broken early on 30 June 2018, just hours after it came into effect; both sides blamed the other for the violation. However, on 7 July Kiir and Machar agreed the outlines of a power-sharing deal in the Ugandan capital of Kampala, according to Sudan's Minister of Foreign Affairs, Al-Dirdiri Ahmed, who stated that Machar would be appointed First Vice-President, ahead of three other Vice-Presidents. According to Ahmed, two of the other vice-presidencies would be occupied by the serving Vice-President Gai and by a female member of the opposition. A preliminary power-sharing deal, incorporating these provisions, was signed in Khartoum on 25 July. Meanwhile, on 12 July the TNLA voted to extend its own mandate, and that of President Kiir, the Vice-Presidents and the State Governors, for a further three years, until 2021.

The flurry of preliminary agreements on a ceasefire and power-sharing arrangements culminated in Kiir and Machar signing the Revitalized Agreement on the Resolution of the Conflict in South Sudan (R-ARCSS) in Addis Ababa on 12 September 2018, after its details had been finalized in Khartoum in August. However, in view of the events of the preceding five years, diplomats and powers outside the region expressed continued doubts about the ability of the two men and their armed supporters to co-exist and build peace in the country. A spate of clashes between forces loyal to Kiir and Machar in September did not, however, prefigure a return to intensive conflict. In October Kiir issued a presidential decree renaming the SPLA the South Sudan People's Defence Forces (SSPDF), and oil production began to ramp up, following repairs to damaged infrastructure. Lam Akol of the SPLM—DC returned to Juba in February 2019, having fled during the resurgence of violence in 2016. Akol claimed that he had come back in order to convey the message that political leaders were ready to progress and 'speed up' the peace plans. Nine days before the expiry of a deadline of 12 May 2019 to establish the new power-sharing Government, representatives of the two sides met in Addis Ababa and agreed to postpone setting up the administration by six months.

Quite apart from the slow progress in hammering out the pre-transition details—and the more fundamental concerns surrounding whether Machar and Kiir could ever restore enough mutual trust to co-exist in Juba—other significant factions did not relinquish their armed struggle. Malong remained outside the political system, and in early 2019 was reported to be living as a self-declared rebel leader in Nairobi. Meanwhile, fighting persisted between regime forces and non-core rebel groups in late 2018 and into 2019. The situation in the southern reaches of Central Equatoria, where Lt-Gen. Cirillo's NSF continued to oppose the R-ARCSS, remained especially volatile. In an indication of dramatically altered alliances on the ground, UNMISS in July 2019 noted increased co-operation between government forces and elements of the SPLA-IO against the other rebel groups. It also noted movement of some SPLA-IO forces towards cantonment sites, amid fragmentation and in order to seek protection from the remaining active insurgent factions.

The two sides repeatedly missed deadlines (including of 12 May and 12 November 2019) for the establishment of a new transitional administration under the power-sharing arrangements of the R-ARCSS. Just ahead of yet another deadline, of 22 February 2020, significant compromises were made by both sides. President Kiir agreed to reduce the number of states in the country from 32 back down to the original 10, while Machar took the risk of taking up position in Juba, even though the integrated force that was supposed to safeguard his security had still not graduated and begun service. Indeed, not a single integrated unit had been created at that time, with the training of an 83,000-strong national army still not under way. As a holding measure, the President stated that he would guarantee Machar's personal security, despite the fact that Kiir's men had twice driven Machar out of Juba under gunfire (in December 2013 and July 2016). On 20 February 2020, two days before the deadline, Machar announced that he and the President had agreed to form a Revitalized Transitional Government of Unity, despite his concerns about the Kiir camp's insistence on the creation of three new 'administrative areas': Abyei, Greater Pibor and Ruweng. Machar was duly sworn in as Kiir's First Vice-President on 22 February, a day after the President had dissolved his Cabinet. At the inauguration ceremony Machar swore the oath of office alongside his wife, Angelina Teny, before publicly embracing Kiir. The President's appointment of a new Cabinet by presidential decree on 12 March was broadcast live on state television. It had therefore taken just over 18 months since the agreement of September 2018 for a new power-sharing Government to be formed. Kiir notably appointed Machar's wife as Minister of Defence and Veteran Affairs. Minister of Information and Broadcasting Michael Makuei Lueth was retained in the Council of Ministers, as was Minister of Cabinet Affairs Martin Elia Lomuro, against whom the USA had imposed sanctions in December 2019 (see *External Relations and Intervention*). Paul Mayom Akec was named as the Minister of the Interior (a position that he had held in the GOSS) and Salvatore Garang Mabiordit Wol as Minister of Finance and Economic Planning. Puot Kang Chol of the SPLM-in-Opposition (SPLM-IO) was appointed to head the Ministry of Petroleum, while Deny Jock Chagor of the South Sudan Opposition Alliance (SSOA) became the Minister of Higher Education, Science and Technology.

A continued impasse over the allocation of state governorships in May 2020 heralded fresh tensions between Kiir and Machar, after the Office of the President announced on 7 May that six of the 10 state governorships would be allocated to Kiir loyalists, three to members of Machar's camp and one—that of the oil-rich Upper Nile State—to the SSOA, an arrangement that displeased Machar, as he himself coveted control of that state. After a meeting between the leaders in mid-June, the Minister of Presidential Affairs, Nhial Deng Nhial, declared that the dispute had been resolved, with the governorship of Upper Nile State reportedly allocated to the SPLM-IO, on the basis that the SPLM-IO would cede the governorship of Jonglei State to the SSOA. Kiir appointed eight state governors in late June, but the governorships of Upper Nile and Jonglei remained vacant, following renewed clashes at the inter-communal level in Jonglei State in which several hundred people were killed. Finally, on 15 July President Kiir named Deny Jock Chagor of the SSOA as the new Governor of Jonglei State; Chagor's erstwhile position as Minister of Higher Education, Science and Technology was allocated to Gabriel Changson Chang. The governorship of Upper Nile State, however, remained unfilled, as the President asserted that Machar's nominee for the post, Gen. Johnson Olony of the SPLM-IO, was not committed to the peace process. The Upper Nile governorship was eventually awarded to Budhok Ayang Kur in January 2021. Kiir's refusal to appoint Olony fuelled a resurgence of fighting in Upper Nile, briefly pitting the civil war's key protagonist forces—the SSPDF and the SPLA-IO—against each other again in December 2020 and January 2021, with the two sides receiving support from different local Maban militias, according to the UN Panel of Experts on South Sudan. The panel also reported that the National Security Service was exploiting internal disputes within the SPLM-IO to encourage defections to the presidential camp, while opposition within Kiir's core Dinka power base to the President's rule was voiced increasingly publicly.

Progress on the key transitional requirements remained slow. However, state television reported on 10 May 2021 that Kiir had dissolved the 400-member TNLA, and two days later the President announced that a new legislature had been formed, some 15 months after the February 2020 deadline. The new, 550-member TNLA comprised 332 deputies chosen by Kiir, 128 by Machar and 90 by other groups, in accordance with the R-ARCSS; their names were announced in a presidential decree broadcast on state television. The reconfigured upper house, known as the Council of States, now consisted of 100 seats—double the previous number—in an effort to appease restive factions. Later in that month the President oversaw a ceremony initiating the drafting of a new constitution—a challenging process that would involve figures outside the presidential camp seeking to revoke extraordinary powers, including Kiir's right to dismiss state governors and parliamentary deputies. The deputies of the two chambers were sworn in during early August 2021, although 62 of the 650 representatives boycotted the inauguration, amid continued wrangling over power-sharing privileges.

The NSF, meanwhile, remained outside the peace agreement, and negotiations organized by the Catholic Church's Sant'Egidio Community made little headway in late 2020, amid continued clashes involving the rebel group against both the SSPDF and the SPLA-IO. In February 2021 a report by the UN Commission on Human Rights in South Sudan found that, despite the fragile overall co-existence between the SSPDF and the SPLA-IO, localized violence among armed groups over the period February–November 2020 far exceeded that reported between 2013 and 2019, particularly in Central Equatoria, Warrap, Jonglei states and the Greater Pibor Administrative Area. The NSF was not the only 'hold-out' faction; among others, Malong's SSUF/A also remained absent from the new power-sharing arrangements. The Sant'Egidio process sought to reconcile these hold-out groups with those that had signed the 2018 transitional agreement, but that process was itself fraught with divisions among opposition figures. Notably, NSF leader Lt-Gen. Cirillo in September 2020 suspended Malong from a coalition of hold-out organizations, known as the South Sudan Opposition Movements Alliance (SSOMA), ostensibly because he had broken ranks to hold unilateral negotiations with Kiir's side. Amum, by then leader of a faction called the Real SPLM, was suspended from the SSOMA for similar reasons. (The SSOMA subsequently split into two factions, led, respectively, by Cirillo and by Malong and Amum.) This was followed by new fragmentation on Machar's side. In mid-August 2021 the Minister of Mining, Henry Dilang Odwar, resigned from his post in order reportedly to join a breakaway faction of the SPLM-IO led by Machar's former Chief of Staff, Gen. Simon Gatwech Dual. Odwar's resignation followed clashes earlier in the month at Magenis, near the border with Sudan, between troops loyal to Machar and supporters of Dual that left 34 soldiers dead.

Very little headway was made in the transitional process over the following seven months, before a renewed crisis between South Sudan's main protagonists arose on 22 March 2022, when Machar's SPLM-IO announced its withdrawal from participation in a range of transitional institutions, notably the Joint Transitional Security Committee (JTSC), the Joint Military Ceasefire Commission (JMCC) and the Reconstituted Joint Monitoring and Evaluation Commission (RJMEC). The SPLM-IO declared in a press release that its territory had repeatedly come 'under attack from our peace partner without action from those mandated to hold them accountable for such violations' and expressed frustration arising from 'non-productive meetings where issues are raised but not resolved'. On the following day the Governments of Norway, the UK and the USA—collectively known as the 'Troika' (the term dating back to the key role played by the three countries in promoting South Sudan's emergence as an independent state)—deplored 'reported attacks' by elements loyal to Kiir on SPLA-IO bases in both Unity State and Upper Nile State.

While the action of the SPLM-IO stoked fears that the precarious transition would collapse entirely, a few days later the two sides achieved a major breakthrough. On 3 April 2022 Kiir and Machar finally agreed on the establishment of a joint military command over their forces—a key provision of the transitional arrangements. A ceremony in the capital formalized the agreement, which provided for a 60:40 split of officer positions in the military, the police and other security organs. The SPLM-IO quickly rescinded its withdrawal from the JTSC, the JMCC and the RJMEC, in a declaration signed by Machar. However, on 8 April fresh clashes broke out between forces loyal to Kiir and Machar, when army-backed militia ambushed a garrison of SPLA-IO soldiers in Unity State. However, the military leadership of the two sides held a joint press conference in Juba, at which they urged restraint and calm. Kiir and Machar met on the same day, and the latter submitted a list of men loyal to him to be included in the new joint command structure. In mid-April the South Sudanese state broadcaster announced that the unified command of the armed forces had duly come into effect, after the President Kiir issued several decrees that obliged senior officers to relinquish their roles in favour of the SPLA-IO nominees.

Reports emerged in July 2022 that Kiir and Machar's camps were both seeking a substantial extension to the three-year transition period, beyond February 2023. Local media cited sources saying that an extension of 24 months, 28 months or 32 months had been proposed or even agreed in principle by the two sides. Meanwhile, the NSF accused South Sudan's military of attacking it in numerous locations in Central Equatoria State, and Malong criticized the moves towards extending the transition, even as he declared that holding elections in February 2023 would not be credible, owing to the continued prevalence of armed factions. In early August 2022, in an address to the nation, President Kiir confirmed an extension of 'the transition period as a pragmatic and realistic choice for 24 months of healing and consolidating'. Under a new roadmap signed by the parties to the September 2018 peace agreement, the period was extended to February 2025, with elections to take place in December 2024. The move was viewed unfavourably by the Troika, which expressed 'profound concern' and warned that to be legitimate, 'fully inclusive consultations' must take place with the full range of South Sudanese civilian actors, as well as international partners.

In common with most other countries around the world, in March 2020 South Sudan imposed lockdown measures and suspended all but essential public services, in an effort to prevent the spread of the coronavirus disease (COVID-19) pandemic. These measures included the imposition of a nighttime curfew, the closure of schools, non-essential businesses and land borders, the suspension of commercial flights and the banning of social gatherings. The restrictions were eased from May. Following a resurgence in cases of COVID-19 from January 2021, some lockdown measures were reinstated in February; these were lifted in April, after the number of cases stabilized. According to World Health Organization data, a total of 17,780 confirmed cases of COVID-19 had been reported in the country at 7 September 2022, with 138 fatalities. However, as the level of testing for the disease was very low, the actual number of infections was likely to be far higher. By that time only 15% if the population had been fully vaccinated against the disease—one of the lowest rates of any country.

EXTERNAL RELATIONS AND INTERVENTION

South Sudan has remained dependent on multilateral and bilateral assistance from the international community since independence. The country's most important bilateral ally has been the USA. At independence, South Sudan was confirmed to be no longer subject to the US Treasury Department's Sudanese Sanctions Regulations. The UK has been another key ally of South Sudan.

China, although a longstanding ally of Sudan, has also invested in its bilateral relationship with South Sudan. China, like the other permanent members of the UN Security Council, formally recognized South Sudan immediately on independence. After secession, however, South Sudan complained that it was still being treated as a province of Sudan, with most of China's diplomatic and commercial concessions being directed towards Sudan. Reflecting these anxieties, and in the context of the dispute between Juba and Khartoum over oil revenues, South Sudan expelled the Chinese head of the Petrodar oil consortium, Liu Yingcai, in February 2012 on grounds of 'non-co-operation'. (Unnamed oil companies were accused of colluding with Sudan in the alleged theft of southern oil in December 2011 and January 2012.) The state-owned China National Petroleum Corporation (CNPC) has long maintained a 41% stake in Petrodar, which operates in South Sudan's oilfields, and Liu's diplomatic rank equated to ministerial status in China.

The status of CNPC in South Sudan—and the supply of oil to China—was undermined by the South Sudan Government's decision to suspend oil production in January 2012. Chinese state interests were also affected by the impact on the Heglig oilfields of the fighting between the SPLA and the SAF in April. In order to protect its assets on both sides of the un-demarcated border, China used its status at the UN Security Council to assume an increasingly assertive multilateral role in 2012, agreeing to the wording of Resolution 2046 and the threat to consider the imposition of sanctions should South Sudan and Sudan fail to end hostilities or to resume dialogue. Previously, China had sought to influence South Sudan by offering the prospect of a huge bilateral economic package, including grants and a loan of US $1,000m. for infrastructure investment. Illustrating the apparent continued strength of the relationship between the two countries, in September the Government of South Sudan announced that China would provide $2,500m. in oil-backed funds in order to build new campuses for South Sudan's five public universities.

South Sudan's relations with its allies were severely affected by the civil conflict that broke out in December 2013, with rebel and government forces alike accused by human rights groups of perpetrating atrocities. The EU announced in July 2014 that it had imposed sanctions, including asset freezes and travel restrictions, on Maj.-Gen. Peter Gadet, a former SPLA general who was now the leader of the rebel militia accused of massacring 200 people at Bentiu in April, and SPLA commander Santino Deng. In May the USA had imposed sanctions against both Gadet and the head of the South Sudan presidential guard, Marial Chanuong, who had since been promoted to the rank of Major-General. These sanctions included the freezing of any assets held in the USA by the two men, and measures barring any US entity from dealing with them. The UN Security Council announced in mid-July that it was ready to consider what it termed 'appropriate measures' against the Government and opposition in South Sudan.

In terms of South Sudan's relations with its immediate neighbours, the most important of these relationships—that with Sudan—has been covered in detail above. Its relations with other neighbouring countries in the immediate post-secession period were cordial. Kenyan President Mwai Kibaki, Ethiopian Prime Minister Meles Zenawi and Ugandan President Yoweri Museveni all attended the independence celebrations in Juba in July 2011. Owing to low level of economic development, the new country was heavily reliant on imports and skilled labour from Uganda and Kenya in particular. President Museveni proved to be a key backer of the Juba Government during the civil conflict from December 2013. Ugandan troops, sent to support Kiir's SPLA forces, engaged in combat with the rebel faction loyal to Machar.

The new UNMISS peacekeeping force became operational on South Sudan's independence—replacing the UN Mission in Sudan (UNMIS), which had been mandated to operate in both the semi-autonomous Southern Sudan and in the north before secession and using the same personnel and structure. The new force received an initial one-year mandate, with the expectation that this mandate would be renewed for further periods as required. In mid-2013 UNMISS was criticized for its perceived inaction in protecting civilians under attack by ethnic militias in Jonglei State. Deflecting such criticisms, UN Security Council Resolution 2109 expressed 'grave concern' about the involvement of South Sudanese security services in 'human rights violations, including, *inter alia*, arbitrary arrests and detentions, torture, and incidences of extrajudicial killings' in Jonglei.

An emergency meeting of the UN Security Council in December 2013 authorized (in Resolution 2132) an increase in the number of UNMISS troops to a maximum strength of 12,500, from 7,000. The ceiling was further extended, to a maximum of 17,000 troops, at a meeting in March 2018. UNMISS maintains a Chapter VII mandate—giving it a responsibility forcefully to protect civilians—but it apparently struggled to cope with its duties as the new conflict unfolded, with human rights organizations documenting atrocities by both sides. By late April 2014 UNMISS stated that it was protecting more than 70,000 civilians at various locations in South Sudan; by July that figure had risen to about 100,000. There were repeated security breaches of UN compounds, especially during the early months of the conflict.

With elements on both sides associated with atrocities during the conflict, UNMISS struggled to balance the competing objectives of protecting civilians on the one hand and acting as a partner of the South Sudan Government on the other. In an interview with the Al Jazeera news service in January 2014, President Kiir accused elements of the UN in South Sudan of supporting the rebels, having earlier accused UNMISS of running a parallel government in the country. The relationship deteriorated further in March, when South Sudan's Government demanded that the UN leave the country, after claiming that arms found in a food convoy were destined for rebel fighters. Protesters gathered in Juba to demand the resignation of the Special Representative of the UN Secretary-General and Head of UNMISS, Hilde Johnson. Johnson stepped down at the end of her term in July; she was replaced by Ellen Margrethe Løj, of Denmark.

The UN Security Council in July 2015 imposed sanctions, including travel bans and the freezing of assets, against six South Sudanese military commanders: three from the side of the Government and three from the rebel side. These measures were taken despite a warning issued by South Sudan's Permanent Representative to the UN, Francis Deng, in November 2014 that sanctions would 'harden positions toward confrontation rather than co-operation'. Two of the commanders who

were sanctioned—Peter Gadet and Marial Chanuong—had already had similar restrictions placed on them, by the US Government, in April of that year. Gadet was accused of commanding rebel troops who reportedly committed atrocities during their capture of the town of Bentiu in that month, while Chanuong allegedly led attacks against civilian Nuer men by the presidential guard at the start of the war. The sanctions were supported by the US Government, the EU (notably the UK and France) and even by China, which has traditionally followed an official policy of non-interference in other countries' affairs. China's approval of the sanctions was crucial, owing to its power of veto as a permanent member of the UN Security Council.

China began deploying troops to South Sudan in January 2015, in an attempt to bolster the capabilities of UNMISS. By early April 700 Chinese troops were reportedly operating in the country. China's participation in UNMISS was the first time that it had deployed combat-ready troops to a peacekeeping mission, rather than non-combat contingents. There was speculation that the troop deployment was linked to China's significant interests in South Sudan's oil industry; in 2011 the East African nation accounted for 5% of China's oil imports, while China also has direct stakes in hydrocarbons operations on the ground.

In response to the fighting in July 2016, UN Secretary-General Ban made three recommendations to the UN Security Council, whose permanent members (China, France, the Russian Federation, the UK and the USA) were increasingly frustrated by the behaviour of South Sudan's leaders. The Secretary-General advocated sanctions against the country's leaders, an arms embargo on both sides and deploying new troops under a strengthened mandate. Having opposed an arms embargo in January, Russia indicated that it might not now block the measure. In July UN Secretary-General Ban participated in a meeting of regional mediators, under the auspices of IGAD, on the eve of the AU's biannual heads of state summit. The IGAD meeting was attended by nine African presidents and prime ministers, including al-Bashir, Museveni and South Africa's Jacob Zuma. Ban's recommendation to send new troops to South Sudan was endorsed by those present, and a communiqué requested that the UN Security Council 'extend the mission of UNMISS with a revised mandate including the deployment of a regional protection force to separate the warring parties, protect major installations (and) the civilian population of Juba'. This proposal—and the exact wording thereof—was formally ratified at the full heads of state meetings during the summit, according to Smail Chergui, the AU's Commissioner for Peace and Security, who told reporters that the new troops should be authorized to operate under a peace enforcement mandate, rather than a traditional peacekeeping mandate. The AU heads of states' backing for this proposal cleared the way for the UN Security Council to consider the deployment. The UN's Under-Secretary-General for Peacekeeping Operations, Hervé Ladsous, informed the UN Security Council that the aim of such a force should be to secure the city of Juba (and other key sites, including the international airport) through demilitarization.

The UN Security Council approved the deployment of a Regional Protection Force in August 2016, with the measure being endorsed by 11 member states. (Russia, China, Egypt and Venezuela abstained.) The new force would work within the UNMISS command structure and have an initial mandate until 15 December, with scope for renewal thereafter. President Kiir's stance then appeared to soften, as he consented, in principle, to the deployment after meeting a Security Council delegation, including US Permanent Representative to the UN Samantha Power, in September. However, the Government's rhetoric quickly stepped up again as government spokesman Michael Makuei Lueth warned that the country still needed to agree on who would contribute troops to the force, how it would be armed and when it would be deployed.

An improvement in ties with Sudan was the one positive development in South Sudan's otherwise unremittingly tense relations with regional and global powers in 2015–16. President al-Bashir's Government granted South Sudan a significant concession in early 2016 by agreeing to peg oil pipeline fees to prevailing prices, rather than keep them at a fixed rate, an arrangement that proved deeply unfavourable to South Sudan during declines in the oil market. Kiir then ordered his troops to retreat 5 km from the disputed border, according to a spokesman for the Sudanese Government, which encouraged al-Bashir to issue a decree reopening the border for the first time since 2011. A spokesman for South Sudan's Government expressed confidence that the developments would lead to a 'normalization' of relations between the two countries. However, tensions persisted over the two regimes' longstanding alleged support for rebel groups operating on one another's territory.

In September 2017 the US Treasury's Office of Foreign Assets Control (OFAC) announced sanctions against SPLA Chief of General Staff Paul Malong Awan, Minister of Information, Communication, Technology and Postal Services Michael Makuei Lueth and SPLA Deputy Chief of Defence Forces Malek Reuben Riak Rengu, freezing any personal and business assets they might have had in the USA and prohibiting US citizens from conducting business with them. Detailing the factors behind its decision to sanction Malong, OFAC cited allegations that he ordered his troops to disarm and subsequently attack Nuer soldiers in Juba at the start of the civil war in December 2013; his alleged blocking of humanitarian aid (and peacekeepers); and an order reportedly given by him to attack Machar's forces in Juba in July 2016. OFAC also cited reports that Malong was found with currency worth several million US dollars, allegedly taken from the SPLA's treasury, when he was stopped by other government troops outside Juba in May 2017. With regard to Makuei, OFAC referenced information that he was involved in co-ordinating an attack that took place in April 2014 against the UN compound in Bor, during which three UN guards and 140 civilians (mainly women and children) were killed. It also explicitly asserted that Makuei 'worked to obstruct and undermine' the August 2015 peace agreement. Finally, OFAC cited reports that Riak Rengu used his role as Deputy Chief of Staff for Logistics—an SPLA position that he held between 2013 and 2016—to 'issue contracts with inflated prices in order to receive extensive kickbacks'.

South Sudan's Government has generally shown contempt for multilateral sanctions. In December 2017 President Kiir allocated key roles to the three senior SPLA officers sanctioned by the UN Security Council in 2015. Marial Chanuong became Head of Army Operations, Training and Intelligence, Santino Deng Wol was appointed Head of Ground Forces and Gabriel Jok Riak became Deputy Chief of Defence. However, the threat of an arms embargo was one that arguably had the potential to influence Kiir's regime. In May 2018 the UN Security Council voted to maintain the sanctions regime introduced in 2015 for at least a further 45 days, with the option at the end of that period to impose an arms embargo and multilateral sanctions against six further individuals, in the event of continued fighting or a lack of a viable political agreement. The individuals in question were Malong, Makuei, Riak Rengu, rebel commander Koang Rambang Chol, Minister of Defence and Veteran Affairs Kuol Manyang Juuk and acting Minister of Foreign Affairs and International Co-operation Martin Elia Lomuro. Rambang Chol was identified by the Security Council as having led attacks in Bieh State and having been responsible for holding hostage two UN pilots who had been delivering aid, while Lomuro was cited as having threatened to eliminate members of the press and members of the Ceasefire and Transitional Security Arrangements Monitoring Mechanism.

Despite the signing of the Khartoum Declaration in June 2018, the UN Security Council in July approved the imposition of an arms embargo on South Sudan, which would remain in effect until at least 31 May 2019, under Resolution 2428 (2018). The resolution was passed with nine votes in favour and six nations abstaining; Russia, China and Ethiopia were again among those that abstained. Russia's First Deputy Permanent Representative to the UN, Dmitrii Polyanskii, spoke forcefully against the measure, but it was not immediately clear why he abstained, rather than voting to oppose the resolution. The measure committed member states to preventing 'arms and related material of all types, including weapons and ammunition, military vehicles and equipment, paramilitary

equipment, and spare parts' from entering South Sudan, with certain exceptions, mainly centring on the requirements of UNMISS and UNISFA. Resolution 2428 also incorporated a multilateral asset freeze and the imposition of a travel ban on two of the six individuals cited in the Security Council meeting held in May, namely Malong and Riak Rengu.

On 30 May 2019 the UN Security Council extended its arms embargo and sanctions regime on South Sudan by a further year, passing Resolution 2471 (2019) after 10 members voted in favour and five abstained. The USA again pushed hard in favour of the embargo, after arguing for its original imposition a year previously. China, Russia, Equatorial Guinea, Côte d'Ivoire and South Africa abstained. The embargo was extended by a further 12 months in the following year, and again in May 2021, when a Security Council resolution drafted by the USA, which strongly condemned 'past and ongoing human rights violations', was adopted with 13 votes in favour; Kenya was one of two states to abstain. The embargo was extended for a further 12 months in May 2022, with 10 votes in favour and five abstentions.

Several external factors—in part exacerbated by the enormous challenges on the ground—undermined the prospects for continued significant international engagement in propelling South Sudan's peace process forward. One of the major obstacles was the reluctance of the Troika to engage fully with the main South Sudanese protagonists, particularly in terms of their aversion to providing funds needed to fulfil key provisions of the R-ARCSS. Following the earlier wastage of billions of dollars between the 2005 CPA and the outbreak of war in December 2013—and the violent breakdown in July 2016 of the previous internationally funded attempt to cajole Machar and Kiir into working together again—these erstwhile crucial donors saw little point in putting significant funds on the table. Volatile political dynamics elsewhere in East Africa and the Horn of Africa also militated against continued external engagement in South Sudan's peace process, particularly by Sudan and Ethiopia. Sudanese President al-Bashir, one of the key architects of the R-ARCSS, was overthrown on 11 April 2019, in a coup triggered by months of street protests against his rule, and was replaced by a military council.

Under President Donald Trump, the USA remained a key player in cajoling the Machar and Kiir camps towards a second attempt at forming a unity government. In December 2019 OFAC imposed sanctions against Minister of Defence and Veteran Affairs Kuol Manyang Juuk and Martin Elia Lomuro, now Minister of Cabinet Affairs, for their roles in 'obstructing the reconciliation process or peace talks' and perpetuating the 'conflict for their own personal enrichment'. OFAC followed this with the imposition of further sanctions in January 2020 against First Vice-President Taban Deng Gai for serious human rights abuses, notably his involvement in the disappearance and reported deaths of two human rights activists in 2017. On 31 January 2020 the US Administration appointed Stuart Symington, a former US ambassador with longstanding diplomatic experience in sub-Saharan Africa, as Special Envoy for South Sudan. The US Department of State declared that Symington had been mandated to 'lead US efforts to support the peace process and a successful political transition' in the country, and in February it welcomed the agreement between the two hitherto opposing camps in South Sudan to form a Revitalized Transitional Government of National Unity. Pressure exerted by the US Department of State on South Sudanese politicians to adhere to commitments under the peace deal continued under the Administration of President Joe Biden. The Department of State in May 2021 made clear its 'particular concern' over the 'slow implementation' of the R-ARCSS and 'ongoing violence', in a statement one day before US Special Envoy Donald Booth visited South Sudan.

In June 2020 the Special Representative of the UN Secretary-General in South Sudan, David Shearer, warned that a continued 'political impasse, on top of the COVID-19 lockdown' had led to an escalation in conflict in South Sudan, particularly in Jonglei and Upper Nile states. However, this did not prevent UNMISS from announcing in September that it had begun to withdraw from Protection of Civilian sites, which had been established in the early stages of the civil war and still hosted about 180,000 people who had fled inter-ethnic massacres. The first such withdrawals were from Bor and Wau, to be followed by a gradual pullout of troops from other sites, according to UNMISS. A report submitted to the UN Security Council by the UN Panel of Experts on South Sudan in April 2021 warned that 'urgent engagement is needed to avert a return to large scale conflict'. It identified two key factors—concern among 'civil society, political leaders and military officials' surrounding the ability of the R-ARCSS to bring lasting peace to the country and 'nascent calls' within civil, political and military circles for both Kiir and Machar to resign. Earlier that month Shearer announced that UNMISS planned to reduce its military and police presence in South Sudan by about 7% in 2021, in view of a 'reduction in violence' since 2018. At that stage the mission maintained about 14,500 military peacekeepers and 2,000 police officers in the country. Noting, however, that the peace process remained fragile, Shearer also stated that the mission could be reinforced in the event of renewed large-scale conflict. In June 2021 the newly appointed head of UNMISS, Nicholas Haysom, told US broadcaster Voice of America that peacekeepers remained blocked from operating in Western Equatoria and Western Bahr El-Ghazal states, as the Government was refusing to allow patrols in those areas.

In a letter to the UN Security Council obtained by media outlets in April 2021, UN Secretary-General António Guterres expressed scepticism about a proposed drawdown of the UNISFA mission in Abyei, noting that agreement on the status of the region by Sudan and South Sudan was still necessary. The two countries enjoyed generally cordial relations by that stage, as the South Sudanese capital had hosted successful peace talks between Sudan's new Transitional Government and Sudanese rebel groups in 2020, although this new regime remained extremely fragile and beset by its own internal tensions. However, bilateral frictions between the two neighbouring states persisted over Abyei; although Guterres stated in his letter that Sudan believed an immediate drawdown of the 4,000 UNISFA troops might be viable, he noted South Sudan's insistence that security concerns remained too high for a withdrawal. The peacekeeping situation in Abyei was also complicated by rising tensions between Sudan and Ethiopia, including sporadic clashes in late 2020 in the disputed al-Fashqa area on the border between those countries, which motivated Sudan's demand that the largely Ethiopian UNISFA deployment be replaced by what it considered to be more neutral troops. Meanwhile, the internal situation in Ethiopia—where federal troops had seized Mekele, the capital of

Tigray state, from the Tigray People's Liberation Front (the country's former ruling party) in November 2020—diverted significant regional and wider international diplomatic attention away from South Sudan's fragile situation, increasing fears of a reopening of the country's main conflict fault line. Russia's invasion of Ukraine in February 2022 further reduced the scope for international engagement with South Sudan's faltering peace process.

However, the international community—led by the Administration of US President Biden—continued to exert periodic pressure on the leading players. In March 2022 a draft report to the US Congress by the US Department of State made clear its frustration with South Sudan's political leadership over continued delays in implementing key provisions of the transitional arrangements. The report, formally published about a month later, warned that the US Administration would 'continue to impose costs on those who perpetuate the conflict' and noted that the ongoing failure to integrate forces was a major driver of persisting violence. A few days after the draft report first emerged—and also after a tripartite declaration issued by the Troika condemning continued attacks by Kiir-aligned forces—the President and Machar finally agreed to integrate their forces under a unified command.

On 15 March 2022 the UN Security Council voted to extend the mandate of UNMISS by one year, under Resolution 2625. Three permanent members of the Council—the USA, France and the UK—voted in favour of this Resolution, together with all 10 non-permanent members, although Russia and China abstained. Reflecting the highly precarious security situation, the Resolution aimed explicitly to 'a prevent a return to civil war' by maintaining the maximum strength of the peacekeeping force at 17,000 troops and a police contingent of 2,100. At a Security Council meeting earlier in the month, the US ambassador to the UN, Linda Thomas-Greenfield, urged South Sudanese leaders to make progress on security sector reform, drafting a constitution and reforming public financial management in order to enable elections to take place. However, the UN's envoy to South Sudan, Nicholas Haysom, reiterated a previous conviction that 'elections have the potential to be a nation-building moment, or a catastrophe', in a context where even if the main protagonists were faithful to such a process, numerous armed factions continued to hold out and risk undermining the moves towards stabilizing the South Sudanese state.

Economy

DUNCAN WOODSIDE

INTRODUCTION

With the formal secession of the semi-autonomous region of Southern Sudan on 9 July 2011, a new country was created with considerable economic potential. The independent Republic of South Sudan possesses significant oil reserves, and at secession close to 370,000 barrels per day (b/d) of oil were being produced in southern territories, compared with just over 120,000 b/d in the remainder of Sudan. Based on prevailing prices for Sudan's Nile Blend oil in June 2011, South Sudan's potential gross annual revenue from oil output in the immediate post-secession period equated to an annual US $15,463m. The south had initially gained semi-autonomous status under the provisions of the 2005 Comprehensive Peace Agreement. However, even after six years of post-war reconstruction, basic infrastructure was severely lacking at independence. Paved roads did not exist outside the capital, Juba, making travel between it and the provincial capitals perilous. In the absence of even a basic manufacturing industry or organized agriculture, most goods and non-subsistence produce were imported from neighbouring Uganda and Kenya. The Government of independent South Sudan was thus faced with huge challenges in terms of attempting to meet the economic aspirations of a

population that fully expected an immediate peace and independence dividend after the end of what it regarded as exploitation by the Arab-dominated Government in the north. However, despite the high level of oil output per head, it was always difficult to see how the authorities in the south would be able to meet these expectations, especially in the absence of properly functioning institutions, and in view of the difficulties inherent in managing the transition from military to civilian rule.

Less than three years after independence, the descent into civil conflict in December 2013 saw the world's newest state implode. Fighting, demarcated partly along ethnic lines, spread quickly from Juba to other parts of the country, engulfing the oil-rich states of Upper Nile and Unity. After repeated attempts to bring the main protagonists in the conflict together, a Transitional Government of National Unity (TGoNU) came into being in April 2016. However, this fragile political edifice quickly crumbled. A fierce military confrontation erupted in Juba in July between troops loyal to President Salva Kiir Mayardit and newly reinstalled Vice-President Riek Machar Teny-Dhurgon, which resulted in the latter fleeing the country and precipitated further ethnically targeted killings. Any prospect of direct donor support being restored to the

Government appeared more remote than ever. A report by the International Monetary Fund (IMF) in March 2017 revealed the extent of the country's economic crisis. Inflation rose to 479% in December 2016, and the IMF estimated that the real (i.e. 'black market') value of the South Sudanese pound had fallen by 95% between December 2015 and March 2017. Another peace deal—the Revitalized Agreement on the Resolution of the Conflict in South Sudan—was signed by Machar and Kiir on 12 September 2018 in Addis Ababa, Ethiopia, in a bid to establish a new power-sharing administration, but it took another 18 months before the 'Revitalized Transitional Government of National Unity' was finally formed.

An absence of significant armed conflict—at least between forces loyal to the two key protagonists—helped further to alleviate the economic malaise as the two sides prolonged their already protracted negotiations throughout 2019. Gross domestic product (GDP) grew by 13.2% in the financial year 2019/20 (1 July 2019 to 30 June 2020), according to the IMF. This represented a substantial improvement compared with the growth rate of 3.4% in 2018/19 and a contraction of 2.4% in 2017/18. The performance in 2019/20 was buoyed by a strong recovery in the oil component of GDP, which rose by 26.4% amid a rebound in output, while non-oil GDP expanded by only 0.5%. However, the outlook was subsequently significantly undermined by the onset of the coronavirus disease (COVID-19) pandemic, mainly through the adverse impact on the demand for oil of economic lockdowns around the world, which sent prices for one key benchmark barrel of oil into negative territory at one stage in April 2020.

Acknowledging the adverse effects of the COVID-19 pandemic—and the related renewed damage to oil revenues—on South Sudan's fiscal and external accounts, the IMF in November 2020 approved the disbursement to the country of US $52.3m. under a Rapid Credit Facility (RCF). This financial assistance, the first provided by the IMF since South Sudan joined the multilateral lender in 2012, was forthcoming despite the country's extremely dubious record of financial management since seceding from Sudan. Moreover, the funding was provided at a time when the two key protagonists who tipped South Sudan into civil war were once again formally in government together, with little indication that their uneasy relationship would endure much longer than previous disastrous attempts to make them work together. The IMF approved the disbursement of a further $174.2m to South Sudan under the RCF on 30 March 2021, in order to help finance the country's 'urgent balance of payments needs and provide critical fiscal space to maintain poverty-reducing and growth-enhancing spending'. The substantial multilateral assistance followed the publication in September 2020 of a report by the United Nations (UN) Commission on Human Rights in South Sudan, which traced the alleged embezzlement of $36m. from accounts at the Ministry of Finance and Economic Planning and the National Revenue Authority from 2016 onwards.

An assessment of South Sudan's economy released by the IMF under its Staff-Monitored Programme (SMP) in July 2022 painted a bleak picture overall, despite some improvements in macroeconomic management and the boost to already high oil prices generated by the Russian Federation's invasion of Ukraine in February. After the strong rebound in real GDP growth to 13.2% in 2019/20, the economy underwent a contraction of 5.0% in 2020/21, according to final figures cited by the IMF. The multilateral lender estimated a further contraction, amounting to 2.8%, for 2021/22, even accounting for global oil benchmarks pricing close to—and at times substantially above—US $100 per barrel during the first half of 2022. The IMF noted that consecutive years of severe flooding in South Sudan were a key growth constraint—a phenomenon that disrupted oil output and crop cultivation, while also decimating hundreds of thousands of heads of livestock, according to UN agencies. However, the impact of flooding on the oil sector was much greater than on the non-oil sector, as the latter component of real GDP expanded at a rate of 6.3% in 2021/22, according to IMF estimates. The IMF further warned that the 'continuing fallout of flooding on oil production will cause a further contraction of output', while it also noted the adverse effects of the Ukraine war on global food prices.

However, despite the poor headline GDP data—and the IMF's downbeat overall outlook—trade and current account deficits turned into significant surpluses during 2021/22, and the fiscal deficit was nearly eliminated, thanks to the effect of high oil prices and significantly higher export revenue. For 2022/23, the Fund predicted a further, albeit modest, contraction in real GDP, amounting to 0.3%, before an eventual return to real GDP growth at a rate of 4.6% in 2023/24.

MINERAL RESOURCES

The oil industry has long been critical to South Sudan's economy, accounting for 98% of the semi-autonomous Government of Southern Sudan's revenues in 2010. Moreover, with the expiry, on the south's secession, of a transitional agreement whereby 50% of Southern Sudan's oil revenues were awarded to Sudan's central Government, the newly independent South Sudan's oil revenues were expected to grow significantly.

However, despite the six-year long political transition, a new oil deal between Sudan and South Sudan had not been reached by the time of independence. Such an agreement was crucial to both countries, as South Sudan was dependent on its northern counterpart's pipeline infrastructure in order to transport oil to Port Sudan on the Red Sea.

Despite the eventual conclusion of a deal on revenue sharing between South Sudan and Sudan in August 2012, the oil taps in South Sudan remained turned off for almost 15 months after output finally resumed in April 2013. The terms of the arrangement included South Sudan paying Sudan (in instalments) a sum of US $3,000m. (in effect, compensation for taking 75% of the north's oil reserves upon secession), in addition to a fee of $8.40 for each barrel of oil carried through pipelines in the north overseen by the Greater Nile Petroleum Operating Company and $6.50 for every barrel piped through the network of the oilfield operator Petrodar.

When oil production eventually did resume, the economies of both countries were near to collapse. South Sudan's output had not even recovered to one-half of its pre-shutdown level when it began to reduce production again: volumes peaked at 200,000 b/d in July 2013, compared with a maximum of 375,000 b/d in 2011. In March 2013, meanwhile, the Government of South Sudan signed a deal with the international commodities trading company Trafigura, whereby the latter was to export the Dar blend of oil via Port Sudan. However, oil output was then severely affected by the outbreak of civil conflict from the end of 2013. The ensuing shutdown mainly centred on the high-quality oilfields in Unity State, which, before the crisis, had accounted for about 20% of the country's output (some 100,000 b/d), rather than Upper Nile, which had provided the other 80%.

In early 2016 the oil industry was boosted by an agreement between the Governments of Sudan and South Sudan to revise the 2012 deal on pipeline fees, which had become extremely unfavourable to South Sudan. The price of Brent crude, an international benchmark for global oil, had declined from more than US $100 per barrel when the pipeline deal was signed, to just over $30 per barrel by January 2016. South Sudan was left with about $5 per barrel, before other costs were met. The new agreement, announced in February, provided for the replacement of the existing fixed-fee system with a sliding scale, so that South Sudan would pay Sudan on the basis of prevailing prices; this arrangement would give South Sudan some protection in times of depressed oil prices.

However, the prospects for the oil industry were further damaged by the fighting that broke out in Juba between forces loyal to President Kiir and Vice-President Machar in July 2016 and which once again prompted Machar to retreat from Juba to the bush. China National Petroleum Corporation announced that it had pulled out 191 staff working in the country, while it also helped to evacuate 157 Chinese people working for other organizations, in immediate response to the fighting in Juba. This left just 77 of the firm's employees at their stations, casting significant doubt on the sustainability of operations.

Despite the intensification of South Sudan's civil war, Nigeria's Oranto Petroleum International announced in March 2017 that it planned to invest US $500m. in the 25,150-sq-km Block B3, as the Government granted the firm a licence for the concession. In pledging the funds, Oranto pointed to reserve estimates of up to 3,000m. barrels and the block's status as a 'low risk, high reward' concession (political and security risks aside). Also in March 2017, three foreign oil workers (two Indian nationals and one Pakistani national) were kidnapped and temporarily detained in separate incidents by the main rebel faction in South Sudan, the Sudan People's Liberation Movement-in-Opposition (SPLM-IO).

Negotiations over rights to exploit Blocks B1 and B2 were opened to new potential bidders in late April 2017, according to Minister of Petroleum Ezekiel Lul Gatkuoth, after talks with the French company Total, Tullow Oil and Kuwait Foreign Petroleum Exploration Company broke down. Gatkuoth announced in June that the country aimed to ramp output back up to its pre-war level of 350,000 b/d by mid-2018. Production remained at about 130,000 b/d during the first nine months of 2017, owing to the continued dislocations generated by the country's civil war.

A significant decline in armed clashes between forces loyal to Kiir and Machar during the second half of 2018 and the first half of 2019 allowed a modest revival of South Sudan's oil industry. The level of oil output rose to 160,000 b/d in January 2019, up from 130,000 b/d in August 2018. By June 2019, according to official figures reported by the Reuters news agency, oil output had recovered further, to reach nearly 180,000 b/d. In August South Sudan announced its first discovery of oil since independence, in the Adar district in the north of Upper Nile State, near the substantial Paloch fields. The deposit contained an estimated 37m. barrels of oil, of which some 20% was extractable.

Under the terms for the establishment of the Revitalized Transitional Government of National Unity, the SPLM-IO was awarded control of the Ministry of Petroleum in the Council of Ministers that was formed in March 2020, with Puot Kang Chol receiving this portfolio. However, Chol was appointed at a time of plunging revenues. The devastating effect of worldwide lockdowns of national economies to combat the spread of the COVID-19 pandemic provoked a catastrophic fall in oil prices, which was compounded by a price war between Russia and Saudi Arabia. In April the price of a barrel of front-month West Texas Intermediate (WTI) crude briefly turned negative as storage space for inventories ran out. A deal reached that month by members of the Organization of the Petroleum Exporting Countries (OPEC) and other major oil producers, including Russia, collectively known as OPEC+, led to Russia and Saudi Arabia both agreeing to cut their respective production from 11m. b/d to 8.5m. b/d, while South Sudan pledged to reduce its output by 30,000 b/d.

International oil prices recovered thereafter. By mid-2021 both WTI and Brent crude were trading at more than US $70 per barrel. In June South Sudan's Ministry of Petroleum officially launched the country's first-ever hydrocarbons licensing round, with five exploration blocks on offer to foreign investors. Revenues from the hydrocarbons sector rose sharply through 2021, owing to benchmark oil prices gaining about $30 per barrel during the course of the year, before hydrocarbons revenues received a further boost in the first half of 2022 as the geopolitical impact of Russia's invasion of Ukraine drove oil prices even higher. However, flooding hit the oil sector over the same period, resulting in a contraction in output. Although not large enough to offset the positive effect on revenues of higher prices, the reduction in oil production did result in a 7.4% contraction in oil sector GDP in 2021/22, according to preliminary estimates by the IMF in July 2022, driving an estimated 2.8% contraction in overall GDP during the fiscal year.

AGRICULTURE AND FOOD SECURITY

At independence, agriculture in South Sudan remained drastically underdeveloped as a result of the long periods of civil war and the strong traditional preference for pastoralism, which further discouraged the emergence of a crop-based agricultural industry. As in neighbouring Kenya's Turkana region (and in Karamoja, in north-eastern Uganda), communities in southern Sudan have long depended on nomadic cattle and goat herding. About 75% of families in southern Sudan

owned livestock in 2009, according to a report by the US Agency for International Development (USAID).

What little crop-based agricultural activity that did exist in South Sudan in the initial post-secession period was largely centred on family-based subsistence farming, with negligible use of fertilizers or insecticides. In Juba the majority of fruit and vegetables on sale in the market was imported from Uganda, whence it was transported via a dirt track leading from the joint border.

South Sudan therefore remained dependent on food aid in order to supply part of its population. In 2010 and 2011 the UN Food and Agriculture Organization (FAO) distributed aid to 250,000 internally displaced people (IDPs) and returnees from the north who migrated south prior to independence. Approximately 2.5m. people were affected by food insecurity in southern Sudan in 2010, according to the USAID-funded Famine Early Warning Systems Network.

There is considerable long-term potential to develop South Sudan's agricultural sector. The south of the country is predominantly covered by savannah, wetlands and equatorial forests. South Sudan's three southernmost states—Western Equatoria, Central Equatoria and Eastern Equatoria—are the most fertile. The 2009 USAID report estimated that about 90% of land is suitable for agriculture, about one-half of which is of prime quality, with soil and climatic conditions suitable for the cultivation of groundnuts, sorghum, rice, cassava, maize and sesame. However, it claimed that no more than 2% of southern Sudan's land mass had ever been under cultivation at any one time. Much potentially cultivable land has remained unused, owing to the still-extensive presence of landmines laid during the recurrent periods of conflict.

As a result of the civil conflict that began in December 2013, some 1.5m people had been internally displaced and more than 7m. were estimated to be at risk of hunger and disease by August 2014. A report compiled jointly by the UN's World Food Programme (WFP), FAO and the UN Children's Fund (UNICEF) in mid-2016 estimated that 4.8m. people—about 45% of the population, using World Bank data for 2016—were in need of food aid. On 20 February 2017 the UN announced that a famine was under way in the counties of Leer and Mayendit in Unity State. A joint announcement, issued by FAO, WFP and UNICEF, estimated that 100,000 people were facing starvation, while a further 1m. were classified as being on the cusp of famine. An amelioration of the situation, helped by improved access to the affected areas, enabled the famine declaration to be lifted in May, but large swathes of the country's population remained in an extremely precarious situation.

Further undermining the country's already devastated agricultural sector, FAO identified an infestation by armyworm caterpillars in Equatoria in July 2017. Originating in West Africa, the outbreak had spread to Kenya, Rwanda and Uganda, before moving into South Sudan. Northern Bahr el-Ghazal and Jonglei states were also affected by the rampant pest. Tackling the infestation was expected to be harder than in other countries, owing to access being impeded by the fighting and by the Government's restrictions on movements.

In February 2020 the Minister of Agriculture and Food Security, Onyoti Adigo Nyikiwec, and FAO announced that a swarm of desert locusts originating from the Arabian peninsula and already highly active in northern Kenya, Ethiopia, Somalia and Uganda had crossed the border from Uganda into South Sudan, signifying the country's first such invasion by these insects in some 70 years. In the following month, WFP, which was supporting FAO's efforts to eradicate the insects, declared that the invasion would make for 'an incredibly difficult year' in South Sudan, in view of the fact that, in terms of food security, about 55% of the population was already deemed to be in the crisis categories.

Large parts of South Sudan suffered severe flooding in 2020, caused by the White Nile, Pibor, Sobat and other rivers overflowing. A particularly strong Indian Ocean Dipole (similar to the El Niño weather pattern) struck East Africa in 2019, feeding into unusually high river waters, which were then compounded by what the UN Office for the Coordination of Humanitarian Affairs (OCHA) described as abnormally heavy rainfall between July 2020 and October. The flooding affected nearly 1.7m. people in eight of the country's 10 states, including some 500,000 people who were displaced from their homes and land, according to OCHA. The flooding caused widespread crop destruction, particularly of sorghum, along with the displacement of cattle herds. The worst affected regions were Jonglei State and the Greater Pibor Administrative Area, followed by Lakes State and Unity State.

OCHA estimated in June 2022 that South Sudan's overall cereals deficit for the year as a whole was 541,000 metric tons—a rise of 16% from the level seen in 2021. At that time, OCHA forecast that about 7.7m. people in the country, amounting to 63% of the population, faced acute food insecurity, in a context where some 2m. people remained internally displaced. Adding to the strain on agriculture and food security generated by the repeated cycles of conflict, three consecutive years of heavy flooding between 2019 and 2021 further decimated resources and rural resilience. The 2020 floods affected about 700,000 people, many of whom saw their crops washed away or livestock drown, according to OCHA. In August 2021 OCHA reported that about 100,000 of those who had been displaced in the previous year were yet to return home, in a context where farmland in some areas remained submerged. The flooding during 2021 as a whole proved to be even more severe, reaching the 'worst on record', according to Andrew Harper, Special Advisor on Climate Action to the UN High Commissioner for Refugees. Eight of South Sudan's states were hit by the cumulative flooding, with Jonglei, Unity and Upper Nile bearing the brunt, and a total of 33 out of 79 counties badly affected. In total, UN agencies estimated that nearly 800,000 heads of livestock had perished as a direct result of the repeated flooding since 2019.

FOREIGN AID, TRADE AND DEVELOPMENT

In the immediate post-independence era, South Sudan relied heavily on international aid in order to provide food and shelter for IDPs. The USA was a particularly important bilateral donor, under the auspices of USAID. Another important donor was the United Kingdom, which announced that it would provide £90m. (US $150m.) in humanitarian and development aid in the year following independence.

According to the US Department of State, in the 2014 US fiscal year the USA provided more than US $456m. in humanitarian aid to refugees, IDPs and others affected by the conflict in South Sudan. By this stage, donors had become averse to providing direct bilateral aid to the South Sudan Government, because of widespread corruption problems and, from December 2013, the descent into civil conflict. As successive ceasefire agreements collapsed and fighting continued, the international community became increasingly impatient; the European Union and the USA imposed sanctions on individuals associated with both the government and opposition sides.

In December 2014 the USA announced that it was removing South Sudan from the African Growth and Opportunity Act—a programme that bestows trade favours upon participating nations across the continent. The decision to exclude South Sudan, with effect from January 2015, came at a time when the US Government was urging the UN Security Council to endorse the imposition of multilateral sanctions against the troubled young country. The UN's Humanitarian Coordinator for South Sudan announced in January 2016 that a sum of US $1,300m. would be the 'bare minimum needed' to support a total of about 5.1m. people in need in the country. At that time, about 20% of South Sudan's population was displaced.

Despite mounting evidence of ethnic cleansing being perpetrated by South Sudan's military, multilateral institutions reportedly continued to engage with the authorities in Juba. In April 2017 Reuters reported that the Government had secured US $106m. in funding from the World Bank and the African Development Bank (AfDB). According to the Minister of Finance and Economic Planning, Stephen Dhieu Dau, $50m. was provided by the World Bank 'to meet the food gaps' and $48m. by the AfDB towards other, undisclosed, economic priorities.

South Sudan's fiscal and external positions received significant support from the IMF in late 2020 and in 2021, as noted above (see *Introduction*). In its April 2021 report on the country's performance under the newly adopted SMP, the Fund stated that, after repeatedly resorting to monetary financing of the fiscal deficit, the South Sudanese authorities halted this damaging policy in October 2020. In its review of South Sudan's economic policy in July 2022, the IMF noted further progress in restraining inflation, even as the impact of Russia's invasion of Ukraine—and the consequent imposition of sanctions against Russia by Western powers—on global food, oil and gas supplies pushed inflation sharply higher in much of the rest of the world (see *Macroeconomic Policy and Corruption*). The Fund also noted that the South Sudanese Government was seeking to apply for an Extended Credit Facility, upon completion of the SMP, but that most IMF 'Directors agreed that discussions about such a programme would require satisfactory completion of the SMP'. It also noted that some directors emphasized 'the need for further progress on governance safeguards to monitor the use of funds'. In terms of the wider funding landscape, the IMF warned that crucial off-budget support from international donors was 'set to decline amid shrinking aid budgets and the rising cost of providing such aid'. Notably, the war in Ukraine would divert international donors' resources from the developing world towards eastern Europe, while soaring food prices arising from reduced wheat exports from the Black Sea region increased the cost of assistance.

The dramatic and sustained rise of oil prices throughout late 2021 and into the first half of 2022 fed into a substantial improvement in South Sudan's current account position. In 2019/20 South Sudan registered a final current account deficit of US $856m., owing in large part to a trade deficit of $606m., according to the IMF. However, preliminary data for 2020/21 showed a substantial narrowing of the current account deficit to $217m., partly owing to a reduction in the trade deficit to $408m., although this was also due to an increase in the surplus of current net transfers to $1,348m., from $957m. in 2019/20. For 2021/22, the IMF in July 2022 projected a current account surplus of $330m., owing to a dramatic turnaround in the trade account, to a surplus of $741m., as a result of a projected increase in oil exports to $4,810m., from a preliminary $3,440m. in 2020/21 and $3,061m. in 2019/20.

MACROECONOMIC POLICY AND CORRUPTION

Macroeconomic data has been limited since secession. Difficulty in collecting reliable data has been exacerbated by the civil war that began in December 2013. When South Sudan first became independent, in July 2011, the IMF, which was in the process of setting up a trust fund to help the new country establish a national financial architecture, envisaged that US $10.6m. would be required over nearly four years in order to ensure that South Sudan had a chance of building a system with statistical, analytical and policy-making capabilities sufficient to manage a national process of monetary, fiscal and regulatory decision-making. In April 2012 South Sudan became the IMF's 188th member, with an initial quota of 123m. in Special Drawing Rights (equivalent to $189.3m.).

A new currency, the South Sudanese pound, was released to banks on 18 July 2011, to replace the Sudanese pound. The South Sudanese pound came under significant pressure as a result of the shutdown of oil production in January 2012, which was instigated in response to new military tensions between the regimes in Khartoum and Juba. The black market exchange rate, which was 3.50 to the US dollar at secession, reached nearly 5.0 to the dollar before mid-2012. In 2012/13 a budgetary deficit of 5,400m. South Sudanese pounds was recorded, compared with a surplus of 1,600m. South Sudanese pounds in 2011/12, which was the country's first year of presenting its own budget. During a shutdown of oil production between January 2012 and April 2013, arising from tensions and military clashes with Sudan, South Sudan's Government sought ways to increase its non-oil revenues, including through customs duties and other taxes. The Government drafted the budget for 2014/15 under the most constrained circumstances yet, against a background of internal civil conflict and aversion on the part of donors. According to the IMF, expenditure in that year totalled 14,500m. South Sudanese pounds against revenue of 11,200m. South Sudanese pounds.

The onset of civil war in December 2013 resulted in a 12.8% contraction in real GDP in 2014/15, owing in large part to fresh disruptions to oil production, followed by a further decline, estimated by the IMF at 6.9%, in 2015/16. As the civil conflict persisted, GDP continued on a downward trajectory in 2016/17, contracting by 13.0%, before recording a smaller contraction of an estimated 2.4% in 2017/18. The outbreak of civil war choked off large parts of government revenue, while also threatening another precipitate fall in oil revenues—the mainstay of the budget. By January 2017 one US dollar was equivalent to about 105 South Sudanese pounds, compared with 3.5 South Sudanese pounds when the country gained independence less than six years earlier.

In its November 2016 report, the UN Panel of Experts on South Sudan highlighted the Government's use of forward oil sales to boost its income—a tactic that would deprive it of revenues later. In a submission to the UN Security Council in early 2017, the Panel estimated that forward oil sales leapt to US $243m. for the period between late March and late October 2016.

The Government announced in May 2018 that it would eliminate all remaining fuel subsidies. Fuel subsidies had cost the state budget US $183m. in 2017/18, but their removal would see the price of petrol for previously shielded users shoot up from 22 South Sudanese pounds per litre to nearly 300 per litre, according to the *Sudan Tribune*. The subsidies had been eliminated for the majority of consumers at the start of 2018, while certain privileged consumers—including government institutions, public transport and water tankers—had, during the first half of the year, been able to continue buying fuel at the subsidized rate, according to the same source.

The vulnerability of public funds to capture by individuals and groups driving South Sudan's conflict has been very high. In announcing sanctions against Paul Malong Awan, the former Chief of General Staff of the Sudan People's Liberation Army (SPLA), in September 2017 the US Treasury's Office of Foreign Assets Control cited an incident in early May where the former regime loyalist was reportedly stopped outside Juba with currency equivalent to millions of dollars 'allegedly stolen from the SPLA treasury'. The report published in March 2018 by The Sentry identified state oil company Nilepet as a key source of illicit funds, including for 'militias responsible for horrific acts of violence'. The report, entitled *Fueling Atrocities: Oil and War in South Sudan*, cited one key document that listed 84 transactions over a 15-month period to June 2015, involving US $80m. in payments to 'politicians, military officials, government agencies and companies owned by politicians and members of their families who were [...] paid for services such as military transport and logistics to forces implicated in atrocities'. The allegations in the report were denied by South Sudan's presidential spokesman Ateny Wek Ateny. Another report by The Sentry, entitled *Untapped & Unprepared: Dirty Deals Threaten South Sudan's Mining Sector*, which was published in April 2020, claimed that the chances of the state being able to garner meaningful revenues from the 'promising' gold sector were compromised by 'corruption involving President Salva Kiir's relatives and inner circle, military leaders, and other high-level officials'. The report pointed to illegal mining activity in Eastern Equatoria State, where the state Governor maintained 'ties to numerous mining businesses'. It also claimed that government ministers and close associates of President Kiir held stakes in a total of 32 firms that had been incorporated in order to extract minerals.

However, the World Bank was able to cite improvement in at least one economic indicator. Inflation fell from a peak of 550% in September 2016 to 118% for the period December 2016 to December 2017. The multilateral lender attributed this decrease to the central bank slowing the pace of printing money, after earlier falling into the trap of heavily monetizing the deficit. In March 2019 the IMF warned South Sudan against continuing to use future oil revenues as collateral for loans. In June legislators stormed out of a budget presentation in the Transitional National Legislative Assembly, in protest over unpaid salaries for civil servants and soldiers, which, according to a report by the Chinese news agency Xinhua, were six months overdue.

In its review of South Sudan's SMP in July 2022, the Fund pointed to tight control of the money supply and the removal of damaging restrictions on foreign exchange access as key factors in stabilizing the currency and bringing down inflation, from 43.5% in the 2020/21 fiscal year to an estimated 2.1% in 2021/22. This therefore represented one of the lowest rates in the world, in a context where inflation in developed markets—for so long anchored in the low single digits—approached, and in some cases exceeded, 10% year-on-year. After trading at an average of more than 520 to the US dollar on the parallel market in the 2020/21 fiscal year, the South Sudanese pound recovered to an average of 432 to the US dollar in 2021/22.

Following the dramatic improvement in the conduct of monetary policy in the late 2010s and early 2020s, the Government managed to bring the fiscal deficit under control, even before the dramatic surge in global oil prices. The fiscal deficit totalled 78,500m. South Sudanese pounds (some 10% of GDP) in cash terms in 2019/20, but fell to a preliminary 36,400m. South Sudanese pounds (3.7% of GDP) in 2020/21, due to a rise in revenues and grants to 341,500m. South Sudanese pounds in 2020/21 from 232,800m. in 2019/20, alongside a relatively small increase in expenditures to 378,000m. South Sudanese pounds from 311,400m. For 2021/22, the IMF projected a near three-fold surge in revenues and grants, to 907,700m. South Sudanese pounds, owing to high oil prices boosting oil revenues to 828,100m., from 294,100m. in the previous fiscal year. While spending was also projected to increase substantially in 2021/22, to 919,100m. South Sudanese pounds, the overall fiscal deficit in cash terms for that fiscal year was projected at a very modest 11,400m. South Sudanese pounds (just 0.4% of GDP).

INFRASTRUCTURE, INDUSTRY AND SERVICES

There were less than 100 km of paved roads in South Sudan upon independence. According to the World Bank, about 4,000 km of road were considered to be of all-weather quality, while an additional 13,000 km of tracks were largely impassable for parts of the year. The landlocked country did not possess its own oil pipeline infrastructure, and it depended heavily on imports by dirt road from neighbouring Kenya and Uganda.

A US $225m., USAID-funded project was inaugurated in February 2011 to tarmac the 192-km road between Juba and Nimule (on the Ugandan border). The World Bank provided a loan of $38m. in May 2012 in order to improve dirt roads in rural areas with high agricultural potential. By mid-2013, however, two years after independence, the paved road network still totalled only 300 km.

South Sudan's Minister of Transport, Kwong Danhier Gatluak, visited South Africa in August 2015, just as President Kiir signed a peace agreement with the rebels, which aimed to end the civil war. The visit centred on a deal that would see South Africa train South Sudanese road engineers and air traffic controllers. During the visit, Gatluak stated that his country required US $10,000m. for 10,000 km of roads, which needed either to be built from scratch or modernized. However, as the civil war continued to rage for several years after that—with significant outbreaks of fighting persisting well into the 2020s—the interest among foreign investors and donors in the rehabilitation of South Sudan's infrastructure remained deeply muted.

Airport infrastructure was relatively well developed at independence. It was possible to connect with regular commercial flights to Addis Ababa (Ethiopia), Entebbe (Uganda) and Jomo Kenyatta International Airport (Kenya) from Juba. Regional operators Fly 540, Kenya Airways, Air Uganda, Ethiopian Airlines and Jetlink all maintained regular services to and from Juba. Upgrading work at Juba International Airport, partly funded by means of a US $158m. loan from the People's Republic of China, began in early 2014, and a new terminal was inaugurated in October 2018. In the absence of adequate roads, it was also possible to connect to South Sudan's provincial capitals via landing strips; these were designed to accommodate UN humanitarian flights, including by WFP.

The principal telecommunications companies active in South Sudan at independence were Lebanon's Vivacell, South Africa's MTN, Kuwait's Zain and Libya's Gemtel. Network coverage was erratic outside provincial capitals, and many of those people who could afford mobile telephones kept SIM cards for two or more of these companies to allow for geographic variations in the quality of the different networks. The overall quality of South Sudan's networks deteriorated after independence, with complications arising from the adoption of a new dialling code (+211 instead of +249, which was retained by Sudan).

In July 2011 only 1m. of South Sudan's 9.9m. population had mobile telephones, although there were expectations of strong growth in the market following independence as a result of an influx of returnees and oil-led economic growth; Vivacell announced in April that it was targeting a subscriber base of 3m. by 2014. In July Zain announced that it would be willing to pay a fee in order to continue its services in the newly independent South Sudan, after it had earlier secured a licence from the Sudanese Government covering the whole country before secession. MTN South Sudan announced in March 2016 that it was abandoning plans to expand its services in the country through the construction of new transmission towers, citing a 10% drop in subscriptions to its services since October 2015. In 2021, pending approval for an operating licence for the country, Zain continued to provide services under a memorandum of understanding with the South Sudanese Government.

In March 2018 the South Sudanese Government suspended Vivacell's operating licence and shut down its service, leaving 900,000 subscribers—about one-quarter of the country's total—without coverage, after Vivacell had reportedly failed to meet undisclosed regulations and to pay overdue taxes and charges. These debts, according to the Minister of Information, Communication, Technology and Postal Services, Michael Makuei Lueth, amounted to US $66m. Mobile telephone subscriptions per 100 people in South Sudan peaked at 27.5 in 2013, before falling to 25.6 in 2017. Following the suspension of Vivacell's licence, a dramatic decline was recorded in 2018, with subscriptions per 100 people falling to 17.5, the lowest level since 2010, the year before South Sudan gained independence. By 2020 the ratio had partly rebounded to 20.1 per 100 people. In July 2021 Digitel South Sudan, the first locally owned mobile telecommunications company in South Sudan, commenced operations. In 2020 only 6.5% of the population used the internet, according to the International Telecommunication Union—one of the lowest rates in the world.

South Sudan lacks a developed power network, with little generation or transmission capacity beyond power lines—built before independence—extending from Sudan into southern territory in order to supply electricity to the oil industry. In 2020, according to the World Bank, only 7.2% of the population had access to electricity—again, among the lowest rates in the world. Even Juba remains woefully short of electricity to power businesses and homes, resulting in a very heavy reliance on expensive petrol-driven generators. The Government announced in June 2013 that it planned to construct a 60-

MW power plant in the form of a hydroelectric dam on a section of the White Nile that is 9 m–12 m wide.

The country's already weak infrastructure suffered further with the outbreak of the civil conflict from late 2013. The towns of Malakal and Bentiu—the respective capitals of Upper Nile and Unity states—were in effect razed to the ground, as both repeatedly changed hands between government and rebel forces during the early months of the fighting.

The beginnings of a retail sector had emerged in Juba by the time of independence. The Kenya-based conglomerate JIT Group was one of the first companies to become involved, establishing a moderate-sized retail outlet in Juba, in addition to its existing regional interests in food, consumer durables and jewellery. Compared with the subsequent destruction of other major towns, Juba was largely unaffected by the civil conflict that began there in late 2013, and many businesses continued operating after the brief outbreak of fighting in the capital at the start of the civil war.

The civil war that broke out in late 2013 had a dramatically negative effect on South Sudan's nascent industries and services sector. The banking sector, including KCB South Sudan (owned by Kenya Commercial Bank Group), was among the worst and most obviously affected. KCB closed its branches in Malakal, Bor and Bentiu in January 2014. However, restrictions on foreign exchange had a significant effect on many other businesses, especially owing to the fact that most depended heavily on supplies imported from abroad. Unable to source US dollars, businesses could not pay their suppliers, who, not surprisingly, refused to accept South Sudanese pounds.

Commercial banks recorded hefty hyperinflation-related losses in 2015 and 2016, owing in large part to restrictions on foreign exchange and a massive differential between the dollar rate offered by the central bank and the black market rate. The four Kenyan banks with operations in South Sudan—KCB, Equity Bank, Stanbic Bank and Co-operative Bank—were all left heavily exposed. KCB confirmed in May 2017 that it would close five more branches in South Sudan, at least on a 'temporary' basis. However, the lender expected to maintain a presence in the country. Also in May, Stanbic Bank informed Kenya's *Business Daily* newspaper that it too would continue operating in South Sudan. In August 2019 KCB announced plans to introduce mobile banking in South Sudan and to resume operations in the 12 branches that had been shut down during 2016–17, bringing the total number of operating branches in the country to 23.

South Sudan has moderate long-term potential for tourism, owing to its abundant wildlife, including antelopes, elephants, kob, giraffe and gazelles, some of which can be viewed by cruise along the Nile. However, the wildlife stock came under threat as a result of the civil war, and, in view of continued outbreaks of fighting, targeted attacks and kidnappings by armed groups and endemic violent crime, the authorities in many potential markets still advise their citizens against travel to the country.

Statistical Survey

Sources (unless otherwise stated): National Bureau of Statistics, P.O. Box 137, Near South Sudan High Court, May Street, Juba; e-mail contact.ssnbs@gmail.com; internet www.nbs.gov.ss; Bank of South Sudan, P.O. Box 136, Juba; tel. 920004100; e-mail info@boss.gov.ss; internet www.boss.gov.ss.

Note: The Republic of South Sudan achieved independence from Sudan on 9 July 2011 following a referendum held in January at which voters overwhelmingly approved the secession of South Sudan. More detailed statistical information on pre-secession Sudan can be found in that country's chapter.

Area and Population

AREA, POPULATION AND DENSITY

Area (sq km)	644,329*
Population (census results)	
22 April 2008	
Males	4,287,300
Females	3,973,190
Total	8,260,490
Population (official projections at mid-year)	
2020	13,249,924
2021	13,735,150
2022	14,234,977
Density (per sq km) at mid-2022	22.1

* 248,777 sq miles.

POPULATION BY AGE AND SEX
('000, official projections at mid-2022)

	Males	Females	Total
0–14 years	3,568.6	3,522.3	7,090.9
15–64 years	3,572.5	3,352.6	6,925.1
65 years and over	127.1	91.9	219.0
Total	7,268.3	6,966.7	14,235.0

Note: Totals may not be equal to the sum of components, owing to rounding.

STATES
(population at 2008 census)

	Area (sq km)	Population	Density (per sq km)
Central Equatoria	43,033	1,103,557	25.6
Eastern Equatoria	73,472	906,161	12.3
Jonglei	122,581	1,358,602	11.1
Lakes	43,595	695,730	16.0
Northern Bahr El-Ghazal . .	30,543	720,898	23.6
Unity	37,837	585,801	15.5
Upper Nile	77,283	964,353	12.5
Warrap	45,567	972,928	21.4
Western Bahr El-Ghazal . .	91,076	333,431	3.7
Western Equatoria	79,343	619,029	7.8
Total	644,329	8,260,490	12.8

PRINCIPAL TOWNS
(population at 2008 census)

Juba (capital) . .	368,436		Uror	178,519
Aweil East . . .	309,921		Magwi	169,826
Gogrial West . .	243,921		Aweil West . . .	166,217
Bor South . . .	221,106		Tonj North . . .	165,222
Luakpiny/Nasir .	210,002		Kapoeta East . .	163,997
Twic	204,905		Rumbek Centre . .	153,550
Yei	201,443		Yambio	152,257
Kajo-Keji . . .	196,387		Wau	151,320

Mid-2022 (incl. suburbs, UN projection): Juba (capital) 439,993 (Source: UN, *World Urbanization Prospects: The 2018 Revision*).

BIRTHS AND DEATHS
(annual averages, UN estimates)

	2005–10	2010–15	2015–20
Birth rate (per 1,000)	39.4	37.1	35.2
Death rate (per 1,000)	12.9	11.3	10.6

Source: UN, *World Population Prospects: The 2019 Revision*.

2019: Birth rate 60.0 per 1,000; Death rate 14.8 per 1,000 (Source: African Development Bank).

Life expectancy (years at birth, estimates): 58.1 (males 56.6; females 59.6) in 2020 (Source: World Bank, World Development Indicators database).

ECONOMICALLY ACTIVE POPULATION
('000, FAO estimates at mid-year)

	2013	2014	2015
Agriculture, etc.	1,792	1,843	1,887
Total labour force (incl. others) .	3,684	3,868	4,046

Source: FAO.

Health and Welfare

KEY INDICATORS

Total fertility rate (children per woman, 2020)	4.5
Under-5 mortality rate (per 1,000 live births, 2020) . . .	97.9
HIV/AIDS (% of persons aged 15–49, 2020)	2.3
COVID-19: Cumulative confirmed deaths (per 100,000 persons at 31 August 2022)	1.3
COVID-19: Fully vaccinated population (% of total population at 28 August 2022)	15.3
Domestic health expenditure (2019): US $ per head (PPP) .	10.3
Domestic health expenditure (2019): % of GDP	1.0
Domestic health expenditure (2019): public (% of total) . .	16.3
Access to improved water resources (% of persons, 2020) .	41
Access to improved sanitation facilities (% of persons, 2020) .	16
Total carbon dioxide emissions ('000 metric tons, 2018) . .	1,380
Carbon dioxide emissions per head (metric tons, 2018) . .	0.1
Human Development Index (2021): ranking	191
Human Development Index (2021): value	0.385

For data on COVID-19 vaccinations, 'fully vaccinated' denotes receipt of all doses specified by approved vaccination regime (Sources: Johns Hopkins University and Our World in Data). Data on health expenditure refer to current general government expenditure in each case. For more information on sources and further definitions for all indicators, see Health and Welfare Statistics: Sources and Definitions section (europaworld.com/credits).

Agriculture

PRINCIPAL CROPS
('000 metric tons)

	2018	2019	2020
Canteloupes (incl. other melons)*.	53.0	52.6	52.8
Cassava (Manioc)	544.5	563.4*	744.1*
Chillies and peppers, dry*	6.8	6.7	6.7
Groundnuts, with shell . .	68.7	70.1	64.2
Maize†	90.0	103.0	131.0
Melonseed*	22.5	22.5	22.7
Millet†	5.0	5.0	6.0
Pineapples*	4.2	4.1	4.2
Pumpkins, squash and gourds* .	68.3	66.9	67.6
Sesame seed*	191.8	190.8	189.7
Sorghum†	650.0	710.0	737.0
Sunflower seed*	52.7	51.6	52.1
Tangerines, mandarins, etc.* .	16.6	16.3	16.5
Yams*	52.1	51.7	51.9

* FAO estimate(s).
† Unofficial figures.

Aggregate production ('000 metric tons, may include official, semi-official or estimated data): Total cereals 745.0 in 2018, 818.0 in 2019, 874.0 in 2020; Total fruit (primary) 519.2 in 2018, 548.3 in 2019, 553.0 in 2020; Total oilcrops 385.7 in 2018, 385.0 in 2019, 378.9 in 2020; Total pulses 34.1 in 2018–20; Total roots and tubers 596.6 in 2018, 615.1 in 2019, 796.0 in 2020; Total vegetables (primary) 504.0 in 2018, 491.3 in 2019, 497.0 in 2020.

Source: FAO.

LIVESTOCK
('000 head, year ending September)

	2018	2019	2020
Asses*	336.0	333.8	334.8
Cattle	13,314.1	13,580.4	13,784.1
Chickens*	15,000	15,000	15,000
Goats*	16,990.6	17,330.4	17,590.3
Sheep*	14,449.2	14,738.2	14,959.2

* FAO estimates.

Source: FAO.

LIVESTOCK PRODUCTS
('000 metric tons, FAO estimates)

	2018	2019	2020
Cattle hides, fresh	27.1	29.6	28.1
Cattle meat	139.8	152.8	144.7
Cattle offals, edible	23.2	25.4	24.0
Cows' milk	2,369.1	2,416.5	2,452.7
Chicken meat	20.2	20.2	20.3
Goat meat	30.7	31.3	25.5
Goats' milk	525.5	533.4	467.1
Goat skins, fresh	5.9	6.1	4.9
Sheep meat	20.8	23.0	16.2
Sheep's (Ewe's) milk	134.2	136.1	137.5

Source: FAO.

Forestry

ROUNDWOOD REMOVALS
('000 cubic metres, excl. bark, FAO estimates)

	2018	2019	2020
Total (all broadleaved fuel wood) .	4,716	4,750	4,750

Source: FAO.

Fishing

('000 metric tons, live weight, FAO estimates)

	2018	2019	2020
Capture	32,000	32,000	30,000
Aquaculture	22	27	30
Total catch	32,022	32,027	30,030

Source: FAO.

Mining

Crude Petroleum ('000 metric tons): 8,448 in 2019; 8,126 in 2020; 7,516 in 2021 (Source: BP, *Statistical Review of World Energy*).

Industry

Electrical Energy (production, million kWh): 542 in 2017; 584 in 2018; 593 in 2019 (Source: UN Energy Statistics Database).

Finance

CURRENCY AND EXCHANGE RATES.

Monetary Units
100 piastres = 1 South Sudanese pound (SSP).

Sterling, Dollar and Euro Equivalents (31 December 2021)
£1 sterling = 580.394 South Sudanese pounds;
US $1 = 432.034 South Sudanese pounds;
€1 = 489.322 South Sudanese pounds;
1,000 South Sudanese pounds = £1.72 = $2.31 = €2.04.

Average Exchange Rate (South Sudanese pounds per US $)
2019   157.999
2020   165.907
2021   306.355

A new currency, the South Sudanese pound, was introduced, at par with the former new Sudanese pound (see the chapter on Sudan), in July 2011. An official exchange rate of 2.95 pounds to 1 US dollar was maintained by the central bank until late 2013, when it was reported that the currency had been devalued in order to allow the rate to become reconciled with the prevailing unofficial exchange rate of some 4.50 pounds per dollar; thereafter the value of the currency against the dollar weakened dramatically as central bank intervention was withdrawn and the currency floated freely on markets.

CENTRAL GOVERNMENT BUDGET
(million South Sudanese pounds)

Revenue*	2015/16	2016/17†	2017/18†
Petroleum reserves and borrowing	7,553	7,238	25,771
Non-petroleum revenue . . .	4,899	9,256	14,046
Total	12,452	16,494	39,817

Expenditure	2015/16	2016/17†	2017/18†
Current expenditure	11,695	19,454	28,303
Wages and salaries	7,487	14,358	22,405
Operating	4,208	5,096	5,898
Capital expenditure	2,099	1,588	3,232
Transfers	2,986	6,321	8,216
Other expenditure	965	6,026	3,940
Total	17,745	33,389	43,691

* Excluding grants (million South Sudanese pounds): 235 in 2015/16; 2,041 in 2016/17 (budget figure); 414 in 2017/18 (budget figure).
† Budget figures.

2019/20 (million South Sudanese pounds, budget figures): *Revenue:* Petroleum reserves and borrowing 151,631; Non-petroleum revenue 29,852; Total 181,483. *Expenditure:* Current expenditure 54,690 (Wages and salaries 26,899, Operating 27,791); Capital expenditure 122,428; Transfers 17,836; Other expenditure 13,202; Total 208,155.

2020/21 (million South Sudanese pounds, budget figures): *Revenue:* Petroleum reserves and borrowing 84,516; Non-petroleum revenue 44,409; Total 128,925. *Expenditure:* Current expenditure 75,274 (Wages and salaries 42,732, Operating 32,542); Capital expenditure 56,871; Transfers 23,811; Other expenditure 62,234; Total 218,191.

INTERNATIONAL RESERVES
(US $ million at 31 December)

	2018	2019	2020
IMF special drawing rights . .	0.98	0.47	0.01
Foreign exchange	35.41	377.81	183.60
Total	36.40	378.28	183.61

2021: IMF special drawing rights 120.24.

Source: IMF, *International Financial Statistics.*

MONEY SUPPLY
(million South Sudanese pounds at 31 December)

	2019	2020	2021
Currency outside depositary corporations	49,215.53	87,729.14	88,765.85
Transferable deposits	74,665.05	110,656.10	213,230,96
Other deposits	9,334.02	10,100.27	21,745.66
Broad money	133,214.60	208,485.51	323,742.47

Source: IMF, *International Financial Statistics.*

COST OF LIVING
(Consumer Price Index; base: June 2011 = 100)

	2018	2019	2020
Food and non-alcoholic beverages .	5,418.9	11,704.3	19,819.6
Clothing and footwear	9,447.0	10,156.6	11,767.2
Housing and fuels	6,229.5	10,658.9	12,701.0
All items (incl. others) . . .	6,255.1	11,511.4	19,185.7

NATIONAL ACCOUNTS
(million South Sudanese pounds in current prices)

Expenditure on the Gross Domestic Product

	2018	2019	2020
Government final consumption expenditure	147,111	231,683	387,743
Private final consumption expenditure	1,104,000	2,357,370	3,275,405
Gross fixed capital formation . .	156,482	210,646	420,621
Total domestic expenditure .	1,407,593	2,799,699	4,083,769
Exports of goods and services . .	454,751	541,097	924,361
Less Imports of goods and services	718,047	742,914	2,369,700
GDP in purchasers' values .	1,144,297	2,597,882	2,638,431
GDP in constant 2015 prices .	23,838	26,551	24,801

Gross Domestic Product by Economic Activity

	2018	2019	2020
Agriculture, forestry and fishing .	31,411	94,780	151,514
Mining and utilities	529,989	1,119,095	890,282
Manufacturing	22,667	53,739	77,444
Construction	51,613	169,113	88,636
Trade, restaurants and hotels .	101,637	217,491	247,680
Transport, storage and communications	105,641	218,826	254,260
Other services	285,677	689,511	892,778
Sub-total	1,128,633	2,562,556	2,602,595
Net taxes on products* . . .	15,664	35,326	35,836
GDP in purchasers' values .	1,144,297	2,597,882	2,638,431

* Figures obtained as residuals.

Source: UN National Accounts Main Aggregates Database.

Communications Media

	2018	2019	2020
Mobile telephone subscriptions ('000)	1,916.3	2,222.0	1,344.0
Broadband subscriptions, fixed .	200	200	n.a.
Broadband subscriptions, mobile .	658,147	658,150	550,000
Internet users (% of population) .	4.8	5.6	6.5

Telephones (main lines in use): 150 in 2012.

Source: International Telecommunication Union.

Education

	2008	2009	2010
Permanent schools	6,794	9,884	n.a.
Teachers	25,972	26,575	26,658
Pupil-teacher ratio	50	52	53

Student enrolment: *Primary:* 1,284,252 (males 809,519, females 474,733) in 2007/08; 1,380,580 (males 871,804, females 508,776) in 2008/09; 1,401,874 (males 880,208, females 521,666) in 2009/10. *Secondary:* 44,027 (males 31,977, females 12,050) in 2008/09; 34,487 (males 24,498, females 9,989) in 2009/10.

Students (2014/15): *Pre-primary:* 110,824 (males 57,677, females 53,147). *Primary:* 1,273,852 (males 753,113, females 520,739). *Secondary:* 164,135 (males 107,523, females 56,612) (Source: UNESCO Institute for Statistics).

Teachers (2014/15): *Pre-primary* 3,197; *Primary* 27,248; *Secondary* 5,974 (Source: UNESCO Institute for Statistics).

Pupil-teacher ratio (qualified teaching staff, primary education, UNESCO estimate): 55.4 in 2014/15 (Source: UNESCO Institute for Statistics).

Adult literacy rate (UNESCO estimate): 34.5% (males 40.3%; females 28.9%) in 2018 (Source: UNESCO Institute for Statistics).

Directory

The Constitution

The Transitional Constitution of the Republic of South Sudan was approved by the Southern Sudan Legislative Assembly on 7 July 2011 and entered into force on 9 July at South Sudan's formal secession from Sudan.

The President of the Republic of South Sudan is the head of state and of government, the Commander-in-Chief of the Sudan People's Liberation Army and the Supreme Commander of all the other regular forces.

Legislative authority is vested in and exercised by the National Legislature, which consists of the lower house, the National Legislative Assembly, and the upper house, the Council of States. The term of the National Legislature is five years.

The territory of South Sudan is divided into 10 states. (The number of states was increased from 10 to 28 by presidential decree in December 2015, and from 28 to 32 by a further presidential decree in January 2017, but was reduced back down to 10 in February 2020.) Each state has a State Government, consisting of a State Assembly and a State Executive. The latter is headed by a State Governor appointed by the President (prior to the passage of a constitutional amendment in November 2015, the State Governors were elected directly by popular vote). Additionally, there are two administrative areas and one special administrative area; each administrative area is headed by a Chief Administrator.

The Government

HEAD OF STATE

President: Lt-Gen. SALVA KIIR MAYARDIT (took office on 11 August 2005 as President of the Government of Southern Sudan).
First Vice-President: RIEK MACHAR TENY-DHURGON.
Second Vice-President: JAMES WANI IGGA.
Third Vice-President: TABAN DENG GAI.
Fourth Vice-President: REBECCA NYANDENG DE MABIOR.
Fifth Vice-President: Gen. HUSSEIN ABDELBAGI AKOL AGANY.

COUNCIL OF MINISTERS
(October 2022)

President: Lt-Gen. SALVA KIIR MAYARDIT.
Minister of Cabinet Affairs: MARTIN ELIA LOMURO.
Minister of Presidential Affairs: Dr BARNABA MARIAL BENJAMIN.
Minister of Foreign Affairs and International Co-operation: MAYIIK AYII DENG.
Minister of Defence and Veteran Affairs: ANGELINA TENY.
Minister of the Interior: MAHMOUD SOLOMON AGOK.
Minister for Peace Building: STEPHEN PAR KUOL.
Minister of Justice and Constitutional Affairs: Justice RUBEN MADOL AROI.
Minister of National Security: OBUTO MAMUR METE.
Minister of Parliamentary Affairs: MARY NAWAI MARTIN.
Minister of Information and Broadcasting: MICHAEL MAKUEI LUETH.
Minister of Federal Affairs: LASUBA L. WANGO.
Minister of East African Affairs: DENG ALOR KUOL.
Minister of Finance and Economic Planning: DIER TONG NGOR.
Minister of Petroleum: PUOT KANG CHOL.
Minister of Mining: Maj.-Gen. MARTIN GAMA ABUCHA.
Minister of Agriculture and Food Security: JOSEPHINE JOSEPH LAGU.
Minister of Livestock and Fisheries: ONYOTI ADIGO NYIKEC.
Minister of Trade and Industry: KUOL ATHIAN MAWIEN.
Minister of the Environment and Forestry: JOSEPHINE NAPWON COSMAS.
Minister of Water Resources and Irrigation: (vacant).
Minister of Lands, Housing and Urban Development: MICHAEL CHANJIEK GEAY.
Minister of Wildlife Conservation and Tourism: RIZIK ZAKARIA HASSAN.
Minister of Investment: DHIEU MATHOK DIING.
Minister of Higher Education, Science and Technology: GABRIEL CHANGSON CHANG.
Minister of General Education and Instructions: AWUT DENG ACHUIL.
Minister of Health: YOLANDA AWEL DENG JUACH.
Minister of Public Service and Human Resource Development: BABGASI JOSEPH BAKASORO.
Minister of Labour: JAMES HOTH MAI.
Minister of Energy and Dams: PETER MERCALLO NASIR.
Minister of Transport: MADUT BIAR YOL.
Minister of Roads and Bridges: SIMON MIJOK MIJAK.
Minister of Gender, Child and Social Welfare: AYAA BENJAMIN WARILLE.
Minister of Humanitarian Affairs and Disaster Management: PETER MAYEN.
Minister of Culture, Museums and National Heritage: NADIA AROP DUDI.
Minister of Youth and Sports: Dr ALBINO BOL DHIEU.
There were also 10 deputy ministers.

MINISTRIES

Office of the President: Juba; internet presidency.gov.ss.
Ministry of Agriculture and Food Security: Juba.
Ministry of Cabinet Affairs: Juba.
Ministry of Culture, Museums and National Heritage: Juba.
Ministry of Defence and Veteran Affairs: Juba; tel. 915485232; e-mail kdeimkuol@yahoo.com.
Ministry of East African Affairs: Juba.
Ministry of Energy and Dams: Juba; tel. 126298074; e-mail alieroka@yahoo.co.uk.
Ministry of the Environment and Forestry: Juba.
Ministry of Federal Affairs: Juba.
Ministry of Finance and Economic Planning: POB 80, Juba; tel. 122249178; internet www.mofep-grss.org.
Ministry of Foreign Affairs and International Co-operation: Juba.
Ministry of Gender, Child and Social Welfare: Juba; tel. 126925801; e-mail mgswragoss@gmail.com.
Ministry of General Education and Instructions: Juba; e-mail contact@mogei.org; internet mogei.org.
Ministry of Health: Ministries Complex, Juba; tel. 917036278; e-mail info@moh.gov.ss; internet moh.gov.ss.
Ministry of Higher Education, Science and Technology: Juba; tel. 955001002.
Ministry of Humanitarian Affairs and Disaster Management: Juba; tel. 915350540; e-mail contact@mhadm.gov.ss; internet www.mhadm.gov.ss.
Ministry of Information and Broadcasting: POB 33, Juba; tel. 977102623.
Ministry of the Interior: Juba; tel. 977103368; e-mail pmadol@yahoo.com.
Ministry of Investment: Juba.
Ministry of Justice and Constitutional Affairs: Airport Rd, opposite Juba Hotel, Juba; tel. 126310462; e-mail advgen2008@yahoo.com; internet mojss.org.
Ministry of Labour: Juba.
Ministry of Lands, Housing and Urban Development: Juba.
Ministry of Livestock and Fisheries: Juba.
Ministry of Mining: Nimra Talata, POB 376, Juba; tel. 915177771; e-mail info@mom-goss.org; internet mom-goss.org.
Ministry of Parliamentary Affairs: Juba; tel. 912339369; e-mail juliaduany@ymail.com.
Ministry of Peace Building: Juba.
Ministry of Petroleum: POB 376, Juba; tel. 915177770; e-mail info@mop.gov.ss; internet www.mop.gov.ss.
Ministry of Public Service and Human Resource Development: Juba; tel. 917259719; e-mail publicmirror2010@gmail.com.
Ministry of Roads and Bridges: Juba.
Ministry of Trade and Industry: Juba.
Ministry of Transport: Juba; tel. 129187774; e-mail airroadwater@yahoo.com; internet www.mtr-goss.org.
Ministry of Water Resources and Irrigation: Juba.
Ministry of Wildlife Conservation and Tourism: Juba.
Ministry of Youth and Sports: Juba.

STATE GOVERNORS
(October 2022)

Central Equatoria: EMMANUEL ADIL WANI ANTHONY.
Eastern Equatoria: LOUIS LOBONG LOJORE.
Jonglei: DENAY JOCK CHAGOR.
Lakes: Gen. RIN TUENY MABOR.
Northern Bahr El Ghazal: TONG AKEEN NGOR AKIECH.
Upper Nile: ABUDHOK AYANG KUR.
Unity: Dr JOSEPH NGUEN MONYTUIL WECJANG.
Warrap: ALEU AYIENY ALEU.
Western Bahr El Ghazal: SARAH CLETO HASSAN RIAL.
Western Equatoria: ALFRED FUTUYO K. K. ONYANGO.

CHIEF ADMINISTRATORS
(October 2022)

Abyei: KUOL DIM KUOL.
Greater Pibor: JOSHUA KONYI IRER ALAN.
Reweng: STEFANO WIEU MIALEK.

President

Election, 11–15 April 2010

Candidate	Votes	% of votes
Lt-Gen. Salva Kiir Mayardit (Sudan People's Liberation Movement) . . .	2,616,613	92.99
Dr Lam Akol Ajawin (Sudan People's Liberation Movement—Democratic Change)	197,217	7.01
Total	2,813,830	100.00

Legislature

Following the independence of South Sudan on 9 July 2011, the bicameral National Legislature was established. It was composed of a 332-member lower house, the National Legislative Assembly (NLA), and a 50-member upper house, the Council of States.

According to the terms of the Agreement on the Resolution of the Conflict in South Sudan, signed in August 2015, the NLA was to be expanded to 400 members and was to be known as the Transitional National Legislative Assembly (TNLA). The additional 68 members were selected to represent: the South Sudan armed opposition (50 members); former detainees (one member); other political parties (17 members). The TNLA was established on 4 August 2016 and was officially inaugurated on 14 August.

Amid persistent civil conflict, on 12 July 2018 the TNLA voted to extend its own mandate (and that of the President, the Vice-Presidents and the State Governors) for a further three years, until 2021.

On 8 May 2021 President Salva Kiir Mayardit announced the dissolution of the TNLA and of the Council of States. On 10 May he issued a decree reconstituting the TNLA, in accordance with a power–sharing agreement concluded in July 2018; of the 550 deputies in the new body, the former Transitional Government had nominated 332, the Sudan People's Liberation Movement-in-Opposition (SPLM-IO) 128, the South Sudan Opposition Alliance (SSOA) 50, the Other Political Parties 30, and the Former Detainees 10. According to the agreement, the Council of States was henceforth to comprise 100 members, and on 4 July 2021 a reconstituted Council of States, in which SPLM representatives held 46 seats, SPLM-IO 27, SSOA 10 and independents nine (with eight seats remaining vacant) was formed.

TRANSITIONAL NATIONAL LEGISLATIVE ASSEMBLY

Speaker: JEMMA NUNU KUMA.

COUNCIL OF STATES

Speaker: JOSEPH BOL CHAN.

Election Commission

National Elections Commission: Juba; f. 2012; Chair. Eng. ABEDNEGO AKOK KACUOL; Chief Electoral Officer MAC MAICA DENG.

Political Organizations

A Political Parties Council was established in 2013 to register and de-register political parties.

Democratic Change Party: Juba; internet democratic-change .com; f. 2009 as the Sudan People's Liberation Movement—Democratic Change; name changed as above in 2016; Chair. ONYOTI ADIGO NYIKWEC.

National Democratic Movement (NDM): internet fb.com/ The-National-Democratic-Movement-NDM-Public-Relationship -349389128844054; intends to work closely with the Sudan People's Liberation Movement-in-Opposition (q.v.) of former Vice-President Dr Riek Machar Teny-Dhurgon and other groups to take over the Government from President Salva Kiir Mayardit; f. 2016; Leader Dr LAM AKOL.

People's Liberal Party (PLP): Juba; internet fb.com/ PLPSouthSudan; f. 2015; Leader PETER MAYEN MAJONGDIT.

South Sudan United Front/Army (SSUF/SSUA): Juba; f. 2018; Chair. Gen. PAUL MALONG AWAN.

Sudan People's Liberation Movement (SPLM): Juba; e-mail info@splmtoday.com; internet www.splmtoday.com; Leader Lt-Gen. SALVA KIIR MAYARDIT; Sec.-Gen. PETER LAM BOTH (acting).

Sudan People's Liberation Movement-in-Opposition (SPLM-IO): Juba; Leader Dr RIEK MACHAR TENY-DHURGON; Sec.-Gen. DHIEU MATHOK.

United Democratic Party: Juba; Leader TONG LUAL AYAT.

Diplomatic Representation

EMBASSIES IN SOUTH SUDAN

Canada: Former JDO Compound, opp. New Sudan Palace Hotel, Airport Rd, Juba; tel. 916726304; e-mail juba-g@international.gc.ca; internet www.canadainternational.gc.ca/south_sudan-soudan_du _sud; Chargé d'affaires a.i. MARCELLO DIFRANCO.

China, People's Republic: POB 249, Juba; tel. 912386010; e-mail chinaemb_ss@mfa.gov.cn; internet ss.china-embassy.gov.cn; Ambassador MA QIANG.

Djibouti: Juba; tel. 956739316; Chargé d'affaires HASSAN ROBLEH MAHAMOUD.

Egypt: Iwzrat St, Plot No. J/119, Cinema Residential Area, Juba; tel. 955277596; internet fb.com/Egypt.SouthSudan; Ambassador MOHAMED EL-MOATEZ MOSTAFA.

Eritrea: Cemetry Rd, Malakia, Juba; tel. 926228425; e-mail eriembajuba@yahoo.com; Ambassador YOHANNES TEKLEMICHAEL.

Ethiopia: Hai Malakal, Juba; tel. 811823870; Ambassador NEBIL MAHDI ABDULLAHI.

France: EU Compound, Kololo Rd, Thomping, Juba; tel. 955999962; internet ssd.ambafrance.org; Ambassador CHRISTIAN BADER.

Germany: EU Compound, Kololo Rd, Thomping, Juba; tel. 916725693; internet dschuba.diplo.de; Ambassador TOBIAS EICHNER.

India: Plot No. 209–245, Block 3K (South), Juba; tel. 922458007; e-mail hoc.juba@mea.gov.in; internet www.indembjuba.gov.in/ index.php; Ambassador VISHNU KUMAR SHARMA.

Japan: Palm Tree Resort, No. 705, 3-K South Tongping 1st Class, POB 467, Juba; tel. 959003153; e-mail koji.ito-2@mofa.go.jp; internet www.ss.emb-japan.go.jp; Ambassador NAOHIRO TSUTSUMI.

Kenya: POB 208, Juba; tel. 959099900; e-mail kembaju@gmail.com; internet juba.mfa.go.ke; Ambassador Maj.-Gen. (retd) SAMUEL NANDWA.

Netherlands: Former JDO Compound, opp. New Sudan Palace Hotel, Juba; tel. 912117961; e-mail jba@minbuza.nl; internet www .netherlandsandyou.nl/your-country-and-the-netherlands/ south-sudan; Ambassador MARJAN SCHIPPERS.

Nigeria: Juba; e-mail nigeria.juba@foreignaffairs.gov.ng; Ambassador MUSA SABAN MAMMAN.

Norway: Airport Dr., opp. New Sudan Palace Hotel, Juba; tel. 920900530; e-mail emb.juba@mfa.no; internet www.norway.no/ south-sudan; Ambassador LINKEN NYMANN BERRYMAN (designate).

Qatar: Juba; e-mail juba@mofa.gov.qa; Ambassador ALI HAZZA AL-ATHBA.

Somalia: Hai Malakal, Hai Cinema Rd, opp. Oscar Hotel, Juba; tel. 956974010; e-mail jubbaembassy@mfa.gov.so; Ambassador ABDIHAKIM HAJI OMAR ABDULLAHI.

South Africa: House No. 28, DDR Ave, Tongping Area, Juba; tel. 922000440; e-mail juba.dha@dirco.gov.za; Ambassador MAHLODI SAM MUOFHE.

Sudan: off Ministries Rd, Juba; Ambassador (vacant).

Türkiye (Turkey): Block 3ᴋ South, Plot Nos 880-881, Hai Matar, POB 252, Juba; tel. 955721817; internet juba.be.mfa.gov.tr; Ambassador ERDEM MUTAF.

Uganda: Hai Amarat, Plot No. 254, Airport Rd, POB 66, Juba; tel. 955503330; e-mail juba@mofa.go.ug; internet juba.mofa.go.ug; Ambassador Brig.-Gen. RONNIE BALYA.

United Kingdom: EU Compound, Kololo Rd, Thomping, Juba; e-mail ukin.southsudan@fcdo.gov.uk; internet www.gov.uk/government/world/organisations/british-embassy-juba; Ambassador JONNY BAXTER.

USA: Kololo Rd, adjacent to EU Compound, Juba; tel. 912138622; e-mail usembassyjuba@state.gov; internet ss.usembassy.gov; Ambassador MICHAEL J. ADLER.

Zimbabwe: Juba; tel. 925618934; e-mail zimjuba@zimfa.gov.zw; Ambassador (vacant).

Judicial System

The judicial system of South Sudan comprises a Supreme Court, composed of a President, a Deputy President and five justices; three Courts of Appeal, located in Malakal, Juba and Rumbek, each consisting of a President and two justices; one High Court in each state, consisting of a President and one justice; county courts and other courts deemed necessary to be established; and town and rural courts. The President of the Supreme Court of South Sudan is the head of the judiciary and is answerable to the President of the Government of South Sudan for the administration of the judiciary. High Courts are the highest courts at the state level.

Supreme Court: Juba; Pres. CHAN REECH MADUT.

Courts of Appeal: located at Juba, Malakal and Rumbek.

Religion

The majority of the South Sudanese population are Christians or animists. There is a small Muslim minority.

CHRISTIANITY

South Sudan Council of Churches: May St, Juba; tel. 924043979; e-mail sscchurches@gmail.com; internet sscchurches.org; Chair. Bishop ARKANJELO WANI LEMI.

The Anglican Communion

Anglicans are adherents of the Province of the Episcopal Church of South Sudan (formerly the Episcopal Church of South Sudan and Sudan). The Primate of the Province of the Episcopal Church of South Sudan is the Bishop of Juba.

Archbishop of the Province of the Episcopal Church of South Sudan and Bishop of Maridi: Most Rev. JUSTIN BADI ARAMAinternet www.southsudan.anglican.org.

Roman Catholic Church

The Roman Catholic Church in Sudan officially remained unified after the secession of South Sudan, although some bishops desired division of the church and the formation of two conferences. For ecclesiastical purposes, South Sudan comprises one archdiocese and six dioceses.

Sudan Catholic Bishops' Conference: General Secretariat, POB 6011, Khartoum; tel. (183) 225075; f. 1971; Pres. Mgr EDUARDO HIIBORO KUSALA (Bishop of Tombura-Yambio); Sec.-Gen. PETER SULEIMAN.

Archbishop of Juba: Most Rev. STEPHEN AMEYU MARTIN MULLA, Catholic Church, POB 32, Juba; tel. 811820303; e-mail archbishopofjuba@hotmail.com.

ISLAM

South Sudan Islamic Council: Juba; Sec.-Gen. SHEIKH ABDULLAH BURJ RAWAL.

The Press

NEWSPAPERS (PRINT AND ONLINE)

Al-Isteqlal: Juba; f. 2011; daily; Arabic; Man. Editor GAMAL DALMAN.

Al-Maugif: Juba; tel. 929916555; e-mail almaugif@gmail.com; f. 2014; daily; Arabic.

The Citizen: Hai Amarat, Airport Rd, Juba; tel. 908760789; e-mail thecitizen2006@yahoo.com; f. 2005; daily; Editor-in-Chief NHIAL BOL AKEN.

This Day: Juba.

The Juba Monitor: Juba; e-mail info@jubamonitor.com; f. 2011; Editor-in-Chief ANNA NIMIRIANO NUNU SIYA.

The Juba Post: Juba; internet www.thejubapost.org; f. 2005; biweekly; owned by Juba Media Co; Editor-in-Chief MICHAEL KOMA.

Number One Citizen: Juba; internet onecitizendaily.com.

The Southern Eye: Tong Ping, Airport Rd, POB 243, Juba; tel. 977100072; e-mail southerneyegoss@yahoo.com.

Stance: Juba; daily; English; Editors ATEM SIMON, MICHAEL KOMA.

PERIODICAL

SHE: Juba; tel. 956922810; e-mail editor@SHEsouthsudan.com; internet www.shesouthsudan.org; f. 2012; publ. by Glocal Publishing Ltd; every 2 months; Man. Dir BRIGITTE SINS; Editor-in-Chief RACHEL ALEK AGUER.

Broadcasting and Communications

REGULATORY AUTHORITY

National Communication Authority (NCA): Juba; tel. 925258885; e-mail info@nca.gov.ss; internet nca.gov.ss; f. 2014; Chair. and Dir-Gen. Eng. NAPOLEON ADOK GAI.

TELECOMMUNICATIONS

Digitel South Sudan: 101 Hai Altala, Juba; tel. 980000100; e-mail info@digitelss.com; internet fb.com/DigitelSS; f. 2021; 100% owned by local investors; aims to extend mobile telecommunications services to remote rural areas; Exec. Vice-Pres. ATHIEI DE CHAN AWUOL.

MTN South Sudan: Hai Jerusalem, Residential Area, Hai Cinema, North East Juba, Basic School, POB 573, Juba; tel. 922333333; e-mail customercare.ss@mtn.com; internet fb.com/MTNSSD; CEO GORDIAN KYOMUKAMA.

Zain South Sudan: Mundri Rd, Hai Jebel, Gudele, Juba; tel. 912300000; e-mail info@ss.zain.com; internet fb.com/zainsouthsudan; CEO BASEL MANASRAH.

BROADCASTING

Radio

South Sudan Broadcasting Corpn (SSBC): Juba; Man. Dir JAMES MAGOG CHILIM.

Eye Radio: Plot 48, Block 1 Korok, POB 425, Juba; tel. 922486980; internet www.eyeradio.org; broadcasts in English, Arabic and in 7 local languages; Chair. Dr JOK MADUT JOK.

Grace FM: Kajo Keji; tel. 924167488; e-mail stevesok01@yahoo.com; f. 2008; broadcasts programmes on food security, water and sanitation, education, health democracy, good governance and religion in English and several local languages; Co-ordinator STEVE SOKIRI.

Liberty 89.0 FM: Juba; tel. 955214686; e-mail musa.david71@gmail.com; f. 2005; also operates another radio station in Yei; broadcasts in English, Juba Arabic and Bari from Juba, and in English, Kakwa, Kiswahili, Luganda and Arabic from Yei; News Editor MUSA DAVID.

Radio Miraya: Airport Rd, Juba; tel. 901239498; operated by the United Nations Mission in South Sudan in partnership with Fondation Hirondelle; Chief of Radio QUADE HERMANN.

Sudan Catholic Radio Network (SCRN): POB 258, Juba; tel. 924217188; e-mail crn.director@gmail.com; internet catholicradionetwork.org; nine FM radio stations, at Juba, Malakal, Rumbek, Torit, Yei, Tonj, Wau, Yambio and Nuba Mountains; Dir MARY AJITH.

Bakhita Radio 91 FM: St Joseph Parish, Juba; tel. 95155885; e-mail bakhitaradio@gmail.com; f. 2006; Catholic; Dir NOEL SANTO NYOMBE.

Television

South Sudan Broadcasting Corpn: see Radio.

Finance

BANKING

Established in 2005 as a branch of the Bank of Sudan, the Bank of Southern Sudan operated as the central bank of South Sudan until 9 July 2011. After secession it was formally transformed into the Bank of South Sudan. On 18 July the Bank of South Sudan introduced a new currency, the South Sudanese pound, which was to replace the Sudanese pound in South Sudan.

Central Bank

Bank of South Sudan (BOSS): Plot No. 1, Block D6, POB 136, Juba; tel. 920004100; e-mail info@bankofsouthsudan.org; internet bankofsouthsudan.org; f. 2011 to replace the Bank of Southern Sudan; Gov. JOHNNY OHISA DAMIAN.

Commercial Banks

Afriland First Bank South Sudan Cameroon: 3 Hai Cinema Rd, POB 640, Juba; tel. 959003555; f. 2012; Dir GILLES NZIE EDME.

Buffalo Commercial Bank PLC: BCB Junction, Juba; e-mail info@buffalocommercialbank.com; internet www .buffalocommercialbank.com; f. 2008; Chair. Dr LUAL ACUEK LUAL DENG; Man. Dir ALEMU ABERRA.

Charter One Bank Ltd USA: Kololo, Juba; tel. 92206666; e-mail info@charteronebankafrica.com; f. 2011; Chair. SALVATORE GARANG MABIORDIT; CEO JOHAN RHEEDER.

Ecobank South Sudan: Kolta Complex, POB 150, Juba; tel. 922018018; internet ecobank.com; f. 2013; Man. Dir (vacant).

Eden Commercial Bank: Malakia St, POB 384, Juba; tel. 921122224; e-mail info@edenbankplc.com; internet www .edenbankplc.com; f. 2012; Man. Dir FESTUS JOHN.

Equity Bank South Sudan Ltd (EBSSL): Equity Plaza, Ground Floor, BCB Junction, POB 349, Juba; tel. 916986000; e-mail info-southsudan@equitybank.co.ke; internet ss.equitybankgroup .com; f. 2008; privately owned; subsidiary of Equity Group Holdings Ltd; Non-Exec. Chair. SHEM E. MIGOT-ADHOLLA; Man. Dir ADDIS ABABA OTHOW.

International Commercial Bank Ltd (ICB): Airport Business Centre, Airport Rd, Tongping, POB 70, Juba; tel. 959777781; internet www.icb-ss.com; f. 2011; Chair. MARIANO AJUET AKUEI DENG; Man. Dir JOHNNY OHISA DAMIAN.

Ivory Bank: POB 11149, Juba; e-mail info@ivorybankss.com; internet www.ivorybankss.com; f. 1994; relocated from Khartoum, Sudan, to Juba in 2009; privately owned; Chair. Prof. ISAAC BIOR DENG; Man. Dir ERNEST WODERIF MARBAGA.

KCB South Sudan Ltd (Kenya): Buluk, Juba; internet ss .kcbgroup.com; f. 2005; 100% owned by Kenya Commercial Bank Group.

Liberty Commercial Bank (LCB): Liberty House, 2nd Floor, Ninra Talata, POB 549, POB 549, Juba; tel. 925695556; e-mail info@libertycombank.com; internet www.libertycommercialbank .com; f. 2012.

Mountain Trade and Development Bank (MTDB): POB 549, Juba; tel. 977130606; f. 2010; Chair. NEROUN PHILIP AJO.

Nile Commercial Bank: May St, POB 223, Juba; tel. 914111115; internet www.nilecommercialbankssd.com; f. 2006; Chair. LEONARD LOGO MALAWAT; Man. Dir MICHAEL MARINO WUSONG TONGUN.

Qatar National Bank: Plot No. 64, Port Rd, POB 587, Juba; tel. 912155822; e-mail qnbsouthsudan@qnb.com; f. 2011; Gen. Man. NADEEM BASHIR.

South Sudan Commercial Bank: Juba Market, Telecommunication Bldg, Juba; tel. 956600874; e-mail ssbak2012@gmail.com.

Stanbic Bank (South Africa): POB 630, Juba; tel. 912110004; e-mail customercaresouthsudan@stanbic.com; f. 2012.

Financial Institution

South Sudan Microfinance Development Facility: POB 73, Juba; tel. 919799905; internet www.ssmdf.net; Chair. ELIJAH CHOL YAK DIU YAK.

INSURANCE

Jamus International Insurance: Juba; tel. 954008119; e-mail jamusint-insujuba@yahoo.com.

National Insurance Corpn Ltd (NICL): Hai Suk Ra Office Complex No. 4, Haile Salassie, Juba; tel. 977104406.

New Sudan Insurance Co. Ltd: Nimra Talata, Block 1, POB 260, Juba; tel. 925955000; e-mail nesi@nesico.com; internet www.nesico .com; f. 2008; Chair. GHABRIEL ALAAK; Man. Dir ZERU W. MICHAEL.

Renaissance Insurance Co South Sudan Ltd: Hai Suk, POB 227, Juba.

Speed Insurance Ltd: Stanbic Bank Bldg, Juba; tel. 928508508; e-mail speedinsurancess@gmail.com; internet www .speedinsurancess.com; f. 2008; Man. Dir JIMMY OKELLO KOKOROM.

UAP Insurance South Sudan Ltd: POB 201, Juba; tel. 959000000; internet www.uap-group.com; f. 2006; general insurance.

Trade and Industry

CHAMBER OF COMMERCE

South Sudan Chamber of Commerce, Industry and Agriculture (SSCCIA): adjacent to Summer Palace Hotel, Juba; tel. 925096368; e-mail info@ssnccia.org; internet ssnccia.org; f. 2003; Chair. BENJAMIN BOL MELL; Sec.-Gen. SIMON AKUEI DENG.

MAJOR COMPANIES

GSM Ltd South Sudan: Tulip Inn Hotel, Office 404, TongPing, Juba; tel. 911100500; e-mail southsudan@geospatialminds.com; internet www.geospatialminds.com; f. 2014; geographical information systems and geospatial intelligence solutions.

Nature Valley Organic Farms Ltd: Tong Ping, off UNMIS Rd, POB 318, Juba; tel. 92165 4123; e-mail naturevalleyorganicfarms@ gmail.com; internet www.naturevalleyss.com; f. 2008; importer and distributor of meat, ice cream, assorted food products and cleaning supplies; Man. Dir VIKASH PATEL.

Nile Petroleum Corpn (Nilepet): Plot No. 496, Block No. 3K, opp. Arkel Restaurant, off Airport–Ministries Rd, POB 390, Juba; tel. 955668869; e-mail info@nilepet.com; internet nilepet.com; f. 2008; Chair. Dr BARNABA MARIAL BENJAMIN; Man. Dir Dr CHOL DENG THON ABEL.

PetroNile International: Juba; f. 2011; jt venture co; 51% owned by Nilepet (South Sudan) and 49% owned by Glencore International AG.

TRADE UNION

South Sudan Workers Trade Union Federation (SSWTUF): Juba; tel. 956193597; e-mail sswtuf@gmail.com; Pres. (vacant).

Transport

RAILWAYS

South Sudan's narrow-gauge railway line runs from the Sudanese border to Wau terminus. It has been proposed to extend the line from Wau to Juba. There are also plans to link Juba with the Kenyan and Ugandan railway networks.

ROADS

The road network in South Sudan is underdeveloped. Most roads are unpaved and in poor condition, and they become impassable during the rainy season.
South Sudan Road Authority: Juba; f. 2011.

CIVIL AVIATION

Juba Airport is the busiest and most developed international airport in South Sudan, with regular flights to Entebbe (Uganda), Nairobi (Kenya), Cairo (Egypt), Addis Ababa (Ethiopia) and Khartoum (Sudan). A new terminal at Juba Airport was opened in October 2018. Other international airports include Malakal, Wau and Rumbek.
South Sudan Civil Aviation Authority: Plot No. 90, Block A. Hai-Jalaba, Juba; e-mail info@sscaa.net; internet www.ssdcaa.com; f. 2013; CEO Capt. SUBEK DAVID DADA.

Interstate Airways Ltd: Crown Hotel, Juba; internet interstateairways.com; f. 2012; cargo and freight services.

Union Air: Juba; tel. 928000630; e-mail info@unionair.com; internet unionav.com; f. 2017; charter and cargo; CEO BUTRUS TOR KUOL.

Defence

As assessed at November 2021, the South Sudan People's Defence Forces (SSPDF, as the Sudan People's Liberation Army—SPLA—had officially been renamed by presidential decree in October 2018) numbered an estimated 185,000 personnel.
Expenditure of the SSPDF: Estimated at SS £14,300m. in 2021.
Chief of General Staff: Gen. SANTINO DENG WOL.

Education

In principle, basic education is free and compulsory in South Sudan. Primary education lasts for eight years and secondary education for four years. Following the implementation of the General Education Act in 2012, English became the language of instruction in South Sudanese schools. According to estimates by the United Nations

Educational, Scientific and Cultural Organization (UNESCO), in 2014/15 enrolment at pre-primary institutions was equivalent to 11% of children in the relevant age-group (males 12%; females 11%). In that year primary enrolment was equivalent to 73% of children in the relevant age-group (males 85%; females 60%), while secondary enrolment was equivalent to 11% of children in the relevant age-group (males 14%; females 8%). At independence in 2011 there were seven public universities and five officially recognized private universities in South Sudan. In the budget for 2018/19 the education sector was allocated 7,600m. South Sudanese pounds (equivalent to 9.4% of total projected budgetary expenditure).

Bibliography

Adar, K. G. *The Sudan Peace Process*. Pretoria, Africa Institute of South Africa, 2005.

Adwok Nyaba, P. *South Sudan: Elites, Ethnicity, Endless Wars and the Stunted State*. Dar es Salaam, Mkuki na Nyota Publishers, 2019.

Africa Watch. *War in South Sudan: The Civilian Toll*. New York, Africa Watch, 1993.

Alier, A. *Southern Sudan: Too Many Agreements Dishonoured*. Exeter, Ithaca Press, 1990.

Badiey, N. *The State of Post-conflict Reconstruction: Land, Urban Development and State-building in Juba, Southern Sudan*. Woodbridge, James Currey, 2014.

Beshir, M. O. *The Southern Sudan: Background to Conflict*. London, C. Hurst, and New York, Praeger, 1968.

Boggs, R. *Becoming Plural: A Tale of Two Sudans*. Reading, Garnet Publishing, 2012.

Butler, V., Carney, T., and Freeman, M. *Sudan: The Land and the People*. London, Thames & Hudson, 2005.

Collins, R. O. *Shadows in the Grass: Britain in the Southern Sudan 1918–1956*. New Haven, CT, Yale University Press, 1983.

   A History of Modern Sudan. Cambridge, Cambridge University Press, 2008.

Copnall, J. *A Poisonous Thorn in Our Hearts: Sudan and South Sudan's Bitter and Incomplete Divorce*. London, C. Hurst & Co., 2014.

Deng, F. M. *War of Visions: Conflict of Identities in the Sudan*. Washington, DC, Brookings Institution, 1995.

Deng, F. M., and Khalil, M. *Sudan's Civil War: The Peace Process Before and Since Machakos*. Pretoria, Africa Institute of South Africa, 2005.

Fluehr-Lobban, C., Fluehr-Lobban, R. A., and Voll, J. *Historical Dictionary of the Sudan*. 2nd edn. Metuchen, NJ, Scarecrow Press, 1992.

Holt, P. M., and Daly, M. W. *The History of the Sudan from the Coming of Islam to the Present Day*. 4th edn. London and New York, Longman, 1988.

Ibreck, R. *South Sudan's Injustice System: Law and Activism on the Frontline*. London, Zed Books, 2020.

Iyob, R., and Khadiagala, G. M. *Sudan: The Elusive Quest for Peace*. Boulder, CO, Lynne Rienner Publishers, 2006.

Johnson, D. H. *The Root Causes of Sudan's Civil Wars*. 3rd edn. Woodbridge, James Currey, 2016.

Keen, D. *The Benefits of Famine: A Political Economy of Famine and Relief in Southwestern Sudan, 1983–1989*. Princeton, NJ, Princeton University Press, 1994.

Khalid, M. *War and Peace in Sudan: A Tale of Two Countries*. London, Kegan Paul International, 2003.

Leonardi, C. *Dealing with Government in South Sudan: Histories of Chiefship, Community and State*. Woodbridge, James Currey, 2015.

LeRiche, M., and Arnold, M. *South Sudan: From Revolution to Independence*. London, C. Hurst & Co., 2012.

Malwal, B. *Sudan and South Sudan: From One to Two*. Basingstoke, Palgrave Macmillan, in association with St Antony's College, Oxford, 2015.

Natsios, A. *Sudan, South Sudan, and Darfur: What Everyone Needs to Know*. New York, Oxford University Press, 2012.

Nouwen, S., James, L., and Srinivasan, S. (Eds). *Making and breaking Peace in Sudan and South Sudan: The Comprehensive Peace Agreement and Beyond*. Oxford, Oxford University Press, 2021.

Nyaba, P. A. *The Politics of Liberation in South Sudan: An Insider's View*. Kampala, Fountain Publishers, 1997.

O'Ballance, E. *The Secret War in the Sudan 1955–1972*. London, Faber and Faber, 1977.

Oduho, J., and Deng, W. *The Problem of the Southern Sudan*. Oxford, Oxford University Press, 1963.

Petterson, D. *Inside Sudan: Political Islam, Conflict, and Catastrophe*. Philadelphia, PA, Westview, 1999.

Pinaud, C. *War and Genocide in South Sudan*. Ithaca, NY, Cornell University Press, 2021.

Prunier, G. *From Peace to War: The Southern Sudan (1972–1984)*. Hull, University of Hull, 1986.

Rolandsen, O. H. *Guerrilla Government: Political Changes in the Southern Sudan during the 1990s*. Uppsala, Nordic Africa Institute, 2005.

   A History of South Sudan: From Slavery to Independence. Cambridge, Cambridge University Press, 2016.

Rone, J., et al. (Eds). *Civilian Devastation: Abuses by the Parties in the War in Southern Sudan*. New York, Human Rights Watch, 1994.

Ruay, D. D. A. *The Politics of Two Sudans: The South and the North, 1921–1969*. Uppsala, Nordic Africa Institute, 1994.

Sidahmed, A. S. *Politics and Islam in Contemporary Sudan*. Richmond, Curzon Press, 1996.

Sidahmed, A. S., and Sidahmed, A. *Sudan*. Abingdon, Routledge, 2004.

Srinivasan, S. *When Peace Kills Politics: International Intervention and Unending Wars in the Sudans*. London, C. Hurst & Co., 2021.

Sylvester, A. *Sudan under Nimeri*. London, Bodley Head, 1977.

Thomas, E. *South Sudan: A Slow Liberation*. London, Zed Books, 2015.

Thomas, G. F. *Sudan: Struggle for Survival, 1984–1993*. London, Darf, 1993.

Tounsel, C. *Chosen Peoples: Christianity and Political Imagination in South Sudan*. Durham, NC, Duke University Press, 2021.

Vaughan, C, Schomerus, M., and de Vries, L. *The Borderlands of South Sudan: Authority and Identity in Contemporary and Historical Perspectives*. Basingstoke, Palgrave Macmillan, 2013.

Vertin, Z. *A Rope from the Sky: The Making and Unmaking of the World's Newest State*. Stroud, Amberley Publishing, 2018.

Woodward, P. *Sudan 1898–1989: The Unstable State*. Boulder, CO, Lynne Rienner Publishers, 1990.

Young, J. *South Sudan's Civil War: Violence, Insurgency and Failed Peacemaking*. London, Zed Books, 2019.

SUDAN

Physical and Social Geography

J. A. ALLAN

THE NILE

The River Nile and its tributaries form the basis of much of the economic activity of Sudan, and of most of the future activity that is now envisaged. The river largely traverses arid deserts and the Nile waters either evaporate or flow until they reach Lake Nubia on the Egyptian border. Prior to the secession of South Sudan in 2011, the Republic of Sudan had a total area of 2,505,813 sq km (967,500 sq miles). The area was estimated to have been reduced to 1,861,484 sq km, based upon South Sudan's declaration of its total area. The distances are vast, and the remoteness of places on the Nile system, and those of the rest of the country, explains much of the character of Sudan's land use. The other important factor is climate, which influences vegetation and, more significantly, affects the seasonal flow of the Nile tributaries.

The Blue Nile is the main tributary, both in the volume of water that it carries (four-sevenths of the total average flow of the system) as well as in the area of irrigated land, of which it supports over 40% of the present area and 70% of potential irrigable land. The Blue Nile and other east-bank tributaries are sustained by monsoon rains over the Ethiopian highlands, which cause the river to flood at the end of July, reach a peak in August and remain high through September and the first half of October. The Atbara, another seasonal east-bank tributary, provides a further one-seventh of the flow in the system, and the remaining two-sevenths come from the White Nile. (These figures relate to pre-secession Sudan.) The sustained flow of the White Nile arises first because its main source is Lake Victoria, which regulates the flow, and secondly because the swamps of the Sudd and Machar (in South Sudan) act as a reservoir, absorbing the irregular stream flow while discharging a regular flow, much reduced by evaporation, in the north.

The River Nile is an international river system, and Sudan depends on river flows from eight other states. In 1959 Sudan concluded an agreement with Egypt according to which it was allotted 18,500m. cu m of the total average flow at Aswan of 84,000m. cu m. (Egypt was to receive 55,500m. cu m, while 10,000m. cu m was assumed to evaporate annually from Lake Nasser/Nubia.)

PHYSICAL FEATURES AND CLIMATE

Sudan is generally a flat, featureless plain reflecting the proximity to the surface of the ancient Basement rocks of the African continent. The Basement is overlain by the Nubian Sandstone formation in the centre and north-west of the country. These formations hold groundwater bodies of agricultural significance. No point in the country is very high above sea level. Elevations rise to 3,071 m on Jebel Marra, an extinct volcano, in south-west Sudan near the frontier with Chad. Some idea of the level character of the landscape is provided by the small amount of the fall in the Blue Nile, which starts its 2,000-km flow through Sudan at 500 m above sea level at the Ethiopian border and formerly flowed past Wadi Halfa (now flooded) at an elevation of 156 m. It now flows into Lake Nubia at 180 m above sea level. The White Nile, as it emerges from Uganda, falls some 600 m between the border of South Sudan and Uganda and the Sudanese capital, Khartoum, a distance of 1,700 km, but falls only 17 m in the last 700 km from entering the southern clay plains.

Average temperatures and rainfall change steadily from month to month, except where the effect of the Ethiopian highlands disturbs the east–west trend in the climatic belts in the south-east. The north of Sudan is a desert, with negligible rainfall and high daily average temperatures (summer 35°C, winter 20°C). Low temperatures occur only in winter. Rainfall increases steadily south of Khartoum (200 mm per year), but varies from year to year, especially in the north, and is seasonal. The rainy season is progressively shorter towards the north, where it lasts only from July until August. Potential evaporation approaches 3,000 mm per year in the north and is always over 1,400 mm per year.

VEGETATION AND SOILS

The soil resources of Sudan are rich in agricultural potential. Their exploitation, however, depends on the availability of the limiting factor, water, and only a small proportion of the clay plains of central and east Sudan are currently farmed intensively. Recent alluvium provides a basis for productive agriculture in the narrow Nile valley north of Khartoum. Elsewhere, in the west and north the soils are sandy, with little agricultural potential, except in the dry valleys, which generally contain some soil moisture.

Vegetation is closely related to the climatic zones. From the desert in the north, vegetation gradually improves through semi-arid shrub to low woodland savannah characterized by acacia and short grasses. Progressively higher rainfall towards the south promotes trees and shrubs as well as herbs, while the more reliably watered rangeland of the Bahr al-Arab, in the south-west border area of the country, provides an important seasonal resource for the graziers from the poor pastures of Darfur and Kordofan.

Much of Sudan is so dry for part of each year that the only possible way to use the land and vegetation resources is by grazing, and tribes such as the Baggara traverse the plains and plateaux of Darfur and Kordofan in response to the availability of fodder.

POPULATION

The population of Sudan was enumerated at 39,154,490 at the census held in April 2008; of this total, 30,894,000 were estimated to be resident in areas not part of the secession state of South Sudan. According to United Nations (UN) projections, the population of Sudan was 45,992,018 at mid-2022, giving a population density of 24.7 per sq km. Much of the population is concentrated in Khartoum state, the population of which totalled an estimated 8,697,162 at mid-2021, according to official projections. As communications are very poor and since Khartoum is a huge distance away from most other parts of the country, the influence that the capital exerts on the rest of the country is small.

The ethnic origin of the people of Sudan is mixed, and the country is still subject to significant immigration by groups from Nigeria and Chad, such as the Fulani. Arab culture and language predominate. The official languages of Sudan are Arabic and English; there are also more than 100 indigenous languages. The vast majority of the population (some 97%) are Muslims, while there are small minorities of animists and Christians.

History

DUNCAN WOODSIDE

The territory known as the Sudan achieved independence as a parliamentary republic on 1 January 1956; the first Sudanese Prime Minister was Ismail al-Azhari of the National Unionist Party (NUP). Shortly after independence, al-Azhari's Government was replaced by an unstable coalition of the Mahdist-supported Umma Party (UP) and the People's Democratic Party (PDP), with Abdallah Khalil, the UP Secretary-General, as Prime Minister. A military coup in November 1958, led by Gen. Ibrahim Abboud, won the support of civilian politicians with assurances by the junta that it aimed merely to restore stability. After a period of increasing discontent prompted by growing military involvement in government and allegations of corruption, in 1964 Abboud transferred power to a transitional Government, which comprised representatives of all parties, including, for the first time, the Communist Party of Sudan (CPS) and the Muslim Brotherhood. Following elections held in June 1965, a coalition Government was formed by the UP and the NUP, with the UP's Muhammad Ahmad Mahgoub as Prime Minister and al-Azhari as permanent President of the committee that acted as collective head of state.

The CPS was banned in late 1965 by the increasingly right-wing Government. A split meanwhile developed within the UP, and Prime Minister Mahgoub resigned in July 1966, with the party President, Sadiq al-Mahdi, being elected to replace him at the head of another UP-NUP coalition, which collapsed in May 1967. Mahgoub again became Prime Minister. Challenged by worsening violence in the south and growing divisions within the coalition, the Government was overthrown in a bloodless coup, led by Col Gaafar Muhammad Nimeri, in May 1969.

THE NIMERI REGIME, 1969–85

Nimeri's first two years in power were characterized by the adoption of socialist policies and the forging of an alliance between the new military leadership and the CPS. The foundations of a one-party state were laid with the formation of the Sudanese Socialist Union (SSU), and the country was renamed the Democratic Republic of the Sudan. Internal opposition was ruthlessly suppressed. The Government declared its commitment to regional administrative autonomy for the south, and created a Ministry for Southern Affairs.

Nimeri won Sudan's first presidential election in October 1971. The SSU became the sole legal political party. The Addis Ababa Agreement, signed in the Ethiopian capital in February 1972 between the Government and southern rebels (and ratified the following month), appeared to establish the basis for a settlement by introducing regional autonomy for the three predominantly Christian and animist southern provinces of Bahr El-Ghazal, Equatoria and Upper Nile.

In May 1983 a decision to divide the south into three sub-regions, to avoid the domination of one ethnic group (the Dinka), was implemented. However, the division met with opposition from many southerners, which escalated into armed insurrection following the Nimeri regime's adoption in September of certain aspects of Islamic *Shari'a* law and the imposition of martial law between April and October 1984. The Sudan People's Liberation Movement (SPLM) was established in the south; during 1983–84 its military wing, the Sudan People's Liberation Army (SPLA), engaged government forces in a series of battles in the southern provinces.

Public discontent with Nimeri's regime was exacerbated by substantial increases in the price of food and fuel, and the capital, Khartoum, was immobilized by a general strike in March 1985.

MILITARY COUP AND MULTI-PARTY ELECTIONS

On 6 April 1985, while Nimeri was visiting the USA, he was deposed in a bloodless military coup led by Lt-Gen. Abd al-Rahman Swar al-Dahab, the Minister of Defence and Commander-in-Chief of the armed forces. A state of emergency was declared, and a Transitional Military Council (TMC) was appointed to govern the country. The SSU was dissolved following the coup, and hundreds of Nimeri's officials arrested. A 15-member Council of Ministers was to be responsible to the TMC during a 12-month transitional period prior to the holding of free elections, scheduled for April 1986. A transitional Constitution was signed in October 1985, which allowed the emergence of new political groupings. In December the country reverted to its pre-1969 name as the Republic of Sudan. The TMC adopted a foreign policy which sought to improve relations with Ethiopia, Libya and the Union of Soviet Socialist Republics (USSR), in contrast to Nimeri's strongly pro-Western stance.

More than 40 political parties participated in the general election held in April 1986. The UP, led by Sadiq al-Mahdi (who had strongly criticized the Islamization policies of the Nimeri regime) won 99 of the 264 seats in the National Assembly, followed by Osman al-Mirghani's Democratic Unionist Party (DUP—the successor to the PDP and NUP), with 63 seats, and Hassan al-Turabi's National Islamic Front (NIF, a faction of the Muslim Brotherhood), with 51. The new Council of Ministers was a coalition of the UP and the DUP, with four portfolios also allocated to southern parties. Al-Mahdi became Prime Minister and Minister of Defence. The TMC was dissolved in preparation for the return to civilian rule, and Swar al-Dahab relinquished the posts of head of state (being replaced by a six-member Supreme Council) and military Commander-in-Chief.

In April 1988, following a vote by the National Assembly in favour of the formation of a national unity administration, the coalition Government was dissolved. In May al-Mahdi was reappointed as Prime Minister at the head of a Government of National Unity, comprising members of the UP, the DUP, the NIF and a number of southern Sudanese political parties. Al-Turabi was appointed Deputy Prime Minister in February 1989 and a new, broadly based Government was appointed in March. Peace negotiations between a government delegation and the SPLM commenced in Ethiopia in April.

AL-BASHIR SEIZES POWER

The al-Mahdi Government was deposed on 30 June 1989, in a bloodless coup led by Brig. (later Lt-Gen.) Omar Hassan Ahmad al-Bashir. A 15-member Revolutionary Command Council for National Salvation (RCC) was formed, declaring its primary aim to be the resolution of the southern conflict. The Constitution and National Assembly were dissolved, all political parties and trade unions were abolished, and a state of emergency was declared. About 30 members of the former Government were detained, including al-Mahdi.

In February 1991 the RCC enacted a decree instituting a new, federal system of government. Sudan was divided into nine states, each of which had its own governor and cabinet of ministers, and assumed responsibility for local administration. In the same month al-Bashir signed a decree introducing a new penal code, again based on *Shari'a* law. The code was stated not to apply in the three southern states of Equatoria, Upper Nile and Bahr El-Ghazal. Proposals for constitutional reform were announced by al-Bashir in January 1992. A 300-member transitional National Assembly was to be appointed, with full legislative functions and the power to veto decisions of the RCC. The Assembly, which convened for the first time in February, included, *inter alia*, all members of the RCC (excluding al-Bashir), state governors and representatives of the army. In October 1993 al-Bashir announced political reforms in preparation for presidential and legislative elections, initially scheduled to be held in 1994 and 1995, respectively, but subsequently postponed. Having appointed al-Bashir as President and as head of a new civilian administration, the RCC was dissolved.

POST-ELECTION DOMESTIC ISSUES

Legislative and presidential elections eventually took place in March 1996. Some 55% of Sudan's eligible voters were reported to have participated in the election of 275 deputies to a new, 400-seat National Assembly. The remaining 125 deputies had been appointed at a national conference in January. In the presidential election al-Bashir obtained 75.7% of the valid votes cast, and he formally commenced a five-year term of office on 1 April. On the same day al-Turabi was unanimously elected President of the National Assembly.

A 277-member constitutional committee was formed in October 1997 to draft a new Constitution. Having been approved by 96.7% of those who voted in a national referendum held in May 1998, according to official figures, the new Constitution came into force in July. New legislation approved in November provided for the establishment of an independent election commission and a Constitutional Court, and for the legalization of political associations. In January 1999 the age of eligibility to vote was reduced to 17 years. In May former President Nimeri returned to Khartoum from exile in Egypt.

AL-BASHIR EXERTS GREATER CONTROL

In December 1999 President al-Bashir declared a three-month state of emergency and suspended the National Assembly, and in January 2000 he formed a new Government. In May al-Bashir suspended al-Turabi, who had become increasingly vocal in his criticism of the Government and demands for a more open political system, as Secretary-General of the governing National Congress Party (NCP); al-Turabi subsequently established a new political party, the Popular Congress Party (PCP). Presidential and legislative elections took place over 10 days in December; they were boycotted by the main opposition parties, and voting did not take place in three southern states. Al-Bashir was re-elected President with 86.5% of the votes cast, according to the official results, while his nearest rival, Nimeri, obtained just 9.6%. The NCP secured 355 seats in the new, 360-member National Assembly.

In January 2002 talks sponsored jointly by the USA and Switzerland commenced in Bürgenstock, Switzerland, following which the Sudanese Government and the SPLM agreed to observe a six-month ceasefire, to be supervised by a joint military commission, in the central Nuba region in order to facilitate the delivery of vital aid supplies to the area. A series of resolutions adopted in April granted al-Bashir the right to appoint provincial governors and abolished the two-term limit on the presidential mandate. In September Dr Lam Akol Ajawin, the Minister of Transport and former commander of the breakaway SPLA—United, established a new political party, the Justice Party; he was subsequently dismissed from his ministerial post. Having been placed under a detention order the previous year, in September al-Turabi was removed from house arrest and transferred to prison. In December Parliament approved al-Bashir's request to extend the state of emergency (twice extended in 2001) for another year.

THE COMPREHENSIVE PEACE AGREEMENT AND 2005–11 TRANSITION

On 9 January 2005 the Government and the SPLM signed a Comprehensive Peace Agreement (CPA) in Nairobi, Kenya, officially ending the civil war in the south, during which at least 2m. people had been killed and more than 4m. displaced. The accord comprised eight protocols, including agreements that political power and Sudan's national wealth would be shared between the national Government and the south; that the SAF and the SPLA would remain separate forces within the national army, in addition to contributing equally to new Joint Integrated Units that would be deployed on both sides of the north–south border, and that all militias would be disbanded within a year; that oil revenues would be shared equally between the north and the south; that the SPLA and other southern groups would hold 30% of government positions in the north, while holding 70% in the south; that the contested regions of the Blue Nile and the Nuba Mountains would be governed by an administration in which 55% of the seats would

be taken by government officials and 45% by the SPLM, while the petroleum-rich region of Abyei would be granted special status under the presidency; that the application of *Shari'a* law would be limited to the north; and that Col John Garang, the leader of the SPLM, would become Sudan's First Vice-President and would act as President of Southern Sudan and head of the SPLA forces during a six-year period of autonomy, after which a referendum on secession would be held.

The groundwork for the deal had been established during the preceding two years. In September 2003 the Sudanese Government and the SPLM signed an accord in Naivasha, Kenya, which provided for the withdrawal from southern Sudan of 100,000 government troops within two-and-a-half years, in addition to the withdrawal of rebel forces from eastern Sudan within a year. Government and rebel troops were to be integrated as the Sudan Armed Forces (SAF), which was to be deployed in southern Sudan. In January 2004 the two sides signed a further accord, on wealth- and revenue-sharing, ahead of the conclusion in May of three protocols detailing power-sharing arrangements.

The Interim National Constitution was promulgated on 9 July 2005, in accordance with the terms stipulated in the CPA. On 1 August, however, it was announced that Garang had been killed in a helicopter accident while en route to Rumbek, in southern Sudan, from Uganda. Garang was replaced as leader of the SPLA/SPLM by Commdr (later Lt-Gen.) Salva Kiir Mayardit, hitherto deputy leader of the organization. Salva Kiir was later appointed First Vice-President in the national Government and assumed the presidency of the new Government of Southern Sudan (GOSS). In September a Government of National Unity was established, which was dominated by the NCP and the SPLM.

In addition to the GOSS, a new Transitional Southern Sudan Legislative Assembly was established and regional administrations were created. In December 2005 a new Constitution for the south was promulgated. However, as well as the forces of the SPLA, a number of other rebel groups remained active in the south, including the Southern Sudan Defence Force, drawn mostly from the Nuer people of Upper Nile region. The Ugandan Lord's Resistance Army (LRA) had also carried out attacks in the south. Also in December the Office of the United Nations High Commissioner for Refugees (UNHCR) announced that it would begin to repatriate some 500,000 refugees from neighbouring countries. Furthermore, many southerners who were displaced to the north of the country began to return to their homes in the south.

The Abyei Borders Commission, established in accordance with the CPA in July 2005, presented al-Bashir with its final recommendations, which were, however, firmly rejected both by the Government and by the Misseriya ethnic Arab group, despite the fact that all parties had promised to honour the agreement. In June 2008 further violent clashes in Abyei were followed by a compromise agreement that the issue of Abyei's boundaries be referred to the Permanent Court of Arbitration in The Hague, Netherlands.

The first multi-party elections for more than two decades took place on 11–15 April 2010. In the weeks immediately preceding the polls the Government extended national security laws, which drastically restricted the freedom of opposition parties to assemble and campaign. In response, and amid concerns about the impartiality of a new National Electoral Commission (NEC), the two main opposition challengers for the presidency—Yasir Saeed Arman of the SPLM and al-Mahdi, leader of the Umma National Party, as the UP had been renamed—withdrew their candidacies just days before the polls. Several smaller parties also boycotted the elections. The electorate voted in concurrent presidential, legislative and gubernatorial ballots. As anticipated, incumbent President al-Bashir was re-elected with 68.2% of the vote. In the south, Salva Kiir retained the presidency, securing 93.0% of the ballot. The NCP secured 312 of the 450 legislative seats, while the SPLM won 99 seats.

In June 2010 al-Bashir announced a new coalition cabinet, which included nine members of the SPLM. In an appointment intended to ensure high-level SPLM engagement in negotiations on a post-secession oil revenue-sharing agreement, Lual

Achwel Deng of the SPLM, Minister of Foreign Affairs in the previous Government, was appointed as Minister of Petroleum. Meanwhile, President Salva Kiir appointed a new GOSS cabinet. The Secretary-General of the SPLM, Pagan Amum, was named as South Sudan's Minister of Peace and CPA Implementation, while Riek Machar Teny-Dhurgon continued as Vice-President.

The strength of al-Bashir's hold on power became increasingly questionable during 2009–11. The issuance, in March 2009, of an arrest warrant by the International Criminal Court (ICC), based in The Hague, against the President for alleged war crimes and crimes against humanity in Darfur further isolated his regime diplomatically. Furthermore, the secession of South Sudan in 2011, while welcomed by the wider international community, angered government hardliners in Sudan.

THE 2011 REFERENDUM AND SECESSION OF SOUTH SUDAN

Al-Bashir's Government sought to delay preparations for the 2011 secession referendum, with many of the crucial prerequisites stipulated by the CPA still not in place by mid-2010. These included the demarcation of the North–South border; the post-referendum status of Southern Kordofan and Blue Nile; the formation of referendum commissions for South Sudan and Abyei; and the negotiation of a post-secession oil-sharing agreement. Meanwhile, the stability of southern territories was undermined by the emergence of new militias opposed to the GOSS, which, the SPLM claimed, were being supported by the NCP as a means of destabilizing the southern Government.

By early 2011 the GOSS was being forced into compromise over the planned simultaneous plebiscite in the disputed Abyei region. First Vice-President Ali Osman Muhammad Taha asserted in October 2010 that it would not be possible to hold the vote in Abyei, in the event that the main referendum took place on schedule. This decision generated significant new tensions, with fighting taking place in Abyei in early January 2011 between Ngok Dinka militias and the Misseriya.

Despite the events in Abyei, voting in the referendum in Southern Sudan itself took place during 9–15 January 2011, as scheduled. In early February it was confirmed by the newly established Southern Sudan referendum commission that 98.8% of those who had participated in the poll (some 97.6% of registered voters) had chosen independence.

The semi-autonomous region of Southern Sudan officially seceded from Sudan as a whole on 9 July 2011, creating a new nation state, the Republic of South Sudan. President al-Bashir became the first head of state to recognize the new country, formally acknowledging South Sudan's right to exist as a sovereign entity on 8 July.

POST-SECESSION NEGOTIATIONS AND CONFLICT

Despite South Sudan's achievement of independence—and the acceptance of this outcome by Sudan's President al-Bashir—this occurred in a context where the two Governments had failed to agree on almost all outstanding issues, including the status of the disputed Abyei region, the wider demarcation of a border, the sharing of oil revenues and the status of citizens living in one another's territories. Most portentously of all, however, the long-planned (but loosely defined) popular consultations on the governance of the disputed states of Southern Kordofan and Blue Nile had yet to yield results. The situation in these two states, which remained part of Sudan, was particularly volatile because of a high preponderance of SPLM-aligned citizens and former SPLA combatants, who had never been fully integrated into the SAF.

A new conflict broke out between the SAF and armed elements in Southern Kordofan's Nuba Mountains in early June 2011, after a dispute about the results of a state governorship election. The authorities demanded that all non-SAF military units disarm. The refusal of the thousands of SPLA soldiers and aligned militia in the state to demobilize precipitated fighting, which, according to the UN, caused more than 70,000 people (mostly ethnic Nubans) to flee over the next

month, amid a bombing campaign by Sudan's air force. Despite a preliminary agreement mediated by the African Union (AU) between the NCP and the SPLM in late June, hostilities continued to escalate in Southern Kordofan.

The armed rebels in Southern Kordofan officially became known as the Sudan People's Liberation Army North (SPLA-N), while their political wing was named the Sudan People's Liberation Movement North (SPLM-N). Sudan's Government accused South Sudan of providing material support to the rebels, while the South Sudanese Government insisted that it had no contact with the SPLM-N or the SPLA-N in the post-independence era. Fighting spread from Southern Kordofan to neighbouring Blue Nile State in early September 2011 after the removal by the Sudanese Government of the Governor of Blue Nile, Malik Agar, who was also Chairman of the SPLM-N. Hostilities quickly escalated, resulting in a large-scale cross-state insurgency under the auspices of the SPLA-N. Furthermore, the leaders of this growing rebellion sought support from Darfur's main rebel groups, including the Justice and Equality Movement (JEM), and factions of the Sudan Liberation Army (SLA) led, respectively, by Minni Minawi (SLA-MM) and Abd al-Wahid Muhammad al-Nur (SLA-AW). In November the SPLA-N signed an agreement with these three Darfur factions, thereby forming the Sudan Revolutionary Front (SRF). Agar was appointed as head of the joint rebel command. The movement's stated objective was to overthrow al-Bashir's Government and establish a democratic, secular republic.

While not as severe as the situation in Southern Kordofan and Blue Nile, the Abyei region (officially a demilitarized zone—DMZ) remained tense in the immediate post-secession period. Despite the successful conclusion of South Sudan's main independence referendum, the plebiscite in Abyei was postponed indefinitely, owing to the ongoing failure of the SPLM and the NCP to agree on who would be eligible to vote.

Following AU-mediated negotiations, both the SPLM and the NCP accepted in June 2011 the planned deployment of 4,200 peacekeepers to Abyei, under the auspices of a new UN mission, the UN Interim Security Force for Abyei (UNISFA). While the SPLM maintained (in line with the 2005 CPA) that a referendum must be held in Abyei, al-Bashir insisted two days after South Sudan's secession that Abyei must remain part of Sudan.

In addition to the failure of the SPLM and NCP to agree on the demarcation of a wider border, the other main potential trigger for an eruption of direct north–south conflict was the expiry of the previous oil-sharing deal, under which until 9 July 2011 revenues from the south's oilfields had been shared equally between Sudan's central Government and the south. Negotiations aimed at securing a new agreement continued during the second half of 2011, with both sides adopting entrenched positions. At the end of 2011 Sudan was demanding that South Sudan pay US $32.20 for each barrel of southern oil piped through the north's infrastructure to Port Sudan, while also demanding the payment of a cash grant to guarantee pipeline access to the south and offset the effect of lost oil revenues on its budget.

The oil impasse reached crisis point in December 2011, when Sudan began to impound southern oil. In January 2012 South Sudan shut down its oil production, claiming that Sudan had stolen oil worth US $815m. Sudan counter-claimed that it was merely extracting redress for South Sudan's alleged non-payment of pipeline fees. The bilateral crisis escalated when South Sudan's Government deployed its military in the northern reaches of the Heglig oilfields in late March and early April, causing substantial damage to infrastructure which led to the suspension of approximately one-half of Sudan's (already diminished) oil production. Sudan denounced this action as a flagrant breach of its sovereignty and a territorial infringement into Southern Kordofan. The international community concurred; UN Resolution 2046 (2012), which was agreed on 2 May, condemned South Sudan's occupation of Heglig. However, it also condemned Sudan for launching bombing raids against targets in South Sudan's oil-rich Unity State, which borders Southern Kordofan. The Resolution impelled the two sides to cease fighting within 48 hours and resume AU-sponsored negotiations within two weeks, or face an imposition of multilateral sanctions.

A breakthrough was eventually achieved in August 2012, when Sudan and South Sudan agreed a formula for oil revenue-sharing. The arrangement entailed South Sudan paying Sudan a sum (albeit in instalments) of US \$3,000m. in order to guarantee pipeline access. This fee effectively amounted to compensation to Sudan for the loss of oil infrastructure, and reserves, incurred after South Sudan seceded. Additionally, South Sudan would be required to pay a fee for each barrel of oil transported through the north's pipelines, totalling either \$6.50 per barrel or \$8.40 per barrel, depending on the route used. However, despite the fact that the two countries' economies were being crippled by the shutdown of oil production in the south, it was a further eight months before oil began to flow again.

The suspension of output in the south was prolonged, even though the bilateral arrangement was being finalized in September 2012, when the two countries also reached agreement on issues including banking co-operation and the establishment of a DMZ. Both sides remained suspicious that insurgency on its territory was being covertly fuelled by the other. The impasse was ended, largely through economic necessity it appeared, since each country's treasury by early 2013 appeared to be on the brink of bankruptcy. Hence, the flow of oil resumed from the south in early April.

Post-secession relations between Sudan and South Sudan were further complicated when the latter became mired in a new conflict in late 2013. A political dispute that began in July that year when President Salva Kiir dismissed his Vice-President, Riek Machar, escalated into a military confrontation as soldiers loyal to the two men clashed in Juba in December. Salva Kiir accused Machar of plotting to orchestrate a coup, while the former Vice-President accused the President of attempting to purge the opposition. The fighting quickly spread to the country's two most oil-rich states, Upper Nile and Unity, and severely reduced oil production, with negative implications for Sudan, given that it relied on pipeline fees paid by the south. Moreover, with South Sudan's Government focused on its worsening internal crisis, key post-secession bilateral issues—notably, the status of Abyei and the demarcation of a border—remained unaddressed.

Relations between Sudan and South Sudan improved in early 2016. The Sudanese Government agreed to South Sudan's request for an alteration to the oil pipeline agreement in January, after a sharp fall in global oil prices meant that the terms originally agreed between the two countries were highly unfavourable to South Sudan. The two Governments therefore agreed a deal 'in principle' in February, under which the fixed-price arrangements would be replaced by a sliding scale, with the pipeline fees paid by South Sudan to Sudan tracking the price of oil on international markets. The agreement was sufficient to ensure that the SPLA moved its troops 5 km back from the disputed frontier, a move that prompted Sudan to reopen the border, for the first time since 2011.

In June 2016 the Government of Sudan announced a unilateral ceasefire in Blue Nile and Southern Kordofan, for an initial four months. The ceasefire was extended regularly thereafter. However, the civil war in South Sudan intensified in the second half of 2016 and into 2017, as the latest power-sharing arrangement between Salva Kiir and Machar collapsed, following the onset of heavy fighting between their respective military guards in Juba in July 2016. After finding sanctuary in the Democratic Republic of the Congo, Machar flew to Khartoum to seek medical treatment for an injury that he had suffered as he fled with his forces from Juba. By the end of 2016 Machar was reported to be under virtual house arrest in South Africa, as a result of co-operation between mediators from the Intergovernmental Authority on Development, notably including Sudan and Ethiopia. The renewed fighting in South Sudan, which was especially heavy in Unity State and Northern Bahr El-Ghazal, risked further destabilizing Sudan itself as increasing numbers of South Sudanese citizens fled northward to escape both the war and famine.

Fresh attempts were made to mediate an end to South Sudan's civil war in 2018, with Sudan playing a leading role in regional efforts to negotiate a lasting peace deal. At negotiations in the Sudanese capital in July, the two warring factions agreed to a 'preliminary' power-sharing pact, under

which Machar would return as First Vice-President in an interim government.

RISING UNREST AND THE DOWNFALL OF AL-BASHIR

In addition to rising inter-ethnic tensions and the growing SRF insurgency, Sudan's Government was faced with escalating protests from 2013, in the context of stringent austerity measures. Anti-Government protests grew steadily larger in June, with several thousand demonstrators gathering in Omdurman to demand al-Bashir's resignation. Further protests, precipitated by reductions in gas and fuel subsidies, took place in September. In the ensuing response by security forces, large numbers of protesters were shot dead: it was subsequently estimated by the international non-governmental organization Human Rights Watch that at least 170 people had been killed. Sudan's Government announced a death toll of 34 and stated that it had detained 700 people in connection with the protests. The NEC announced in August 2014 that the next presidential and parliamentary elections would take place in April 2015. Al-Bashir was retained as the NCP's leader and formally selected (reportedly by a narrow majority over four other candidates) as the ruling party's presidential candidate during its convention in October 2014.

Predictably, al-Bashir, at the age of 71 years, successfully secured another presidential mandate, after officially winning 94% of the vote in the election held on 2 April 2015. Al-Bashir's key campaign theme had been his success in maintaining Sudan as a viable entity, in a context of the chaos experienced by neighbouring countries—especially Libya and the Syrian Arab Republic—following intervention by the West and populist revolution or revolt. In the legislative elections, which were held on 13–16 April, the NCP secured 323 of the 426 parliamentary seats, with a voter turnout of 46.4%, according to the NEC. AU monitors estimated that voter turnout was between 30% and 35%. Most of the significant opposition groups boycotted the poll.

In April 2016 al-Bashir insisted that he would step down when his mandate ended in 2020, although intense scepticism persisted over whether he would honour the pledge. Despite an improvement in ties with the USA, which led to the US President, Donald Trump, lifting key sanctions against Sudan in October 2017 (see *Foreign Relations*), the Sudanese economy remained in a dire condition and the political situation unstable. Amid a severe lack of foreign currency, in the first two months of 2018 the authorities twice devalued the Sudanese pound, but the 'black market' price continued far to exceed the official rate. The removal of subsidies for wheat imports, which caused bread prices to double, sparked popular protests against the Government. In a bid to tackle the instability, al-Bashir instituted a senior-level reorganization in February 2018, replacing his intelligence, security and military chiefs in quick succession. In April the President dismissed the Minister of Foreign Affairs, Ibrahim Ghandour, and in the following month he appointed seven new ministers. In September al-Bashir dismissed the entire cabinet, with a view to reducing the number of ministers from 32 to 21.

On 19 December 2018 protests erupted in the town of Atbara, in River Nile State, in response to a threefold increase in the price of bread, as, amid an increasing economic crisis, the Government dramatically curtailed subsidies for the staple commodity. With organization led by a banned grouping of unions, the Sudanese Professionals Associations (SPA), the protests quickly spread to other towns and cities, including Khartoum. Protesters called openly for al-Bashir's downfall, and demonstrations quickly became a daily occurrence, especially on Fridays, when huge numbers would mobilize. Although the state suppression of the protests was less deadly than in September 2013, security forces used tear gas and live ammunition to disperse demonstrators.

On 27 December 2018 the Government acknowledged on state television that 19 people had been killed during the demonstrations, including two security personnel, while 219 had been wounded. The regime appeared unsure of how to respond, vacillating between a reactionary stance and concessions. One initial tactic was to organize rallies in support of al-

Bashir, but the numbers attending were dwarfed by the anti-regime demonstrations. On 29 January 2019 the head of the NISS, Salah Gosh, ordered the release of all protesters who had been arrested over the previous six weeks, estimated to number over 1,000.

An increasingly desperate al-Bashir made one final significant attempt to reassert control through repressive means. In an address on state television on 22 February 2019, he declared a 12-month state of emergency across the country. He also dissolved the Government, for the second time in just over five months. Three days later, al-Bashir banned all gatherings in public places and ordered the security forces to carry out raids against premises suspected of harbouring activists. Special emergency courts were established to judge those arrested for breaching the state of emergency. However, on 11 March Parliament voted to reduce the duration of the state of emergency to six months. Meanwhile, al-Bashir relinquished the NCP leadership to his deputy (and fellow ICC indictee), Ahmed Mohamed Haroun, who assumed the post on an interim basis, ahead of the party's general convention (although this was subsequently postponed indefinitely). Protests continued, and on 21 March al-Bashir reduced the maximum prison term for those caught violating the state of emergency from 10 years to six months. While six protesters had been sentenced to the new maximum term three days after al-Bashir's concession, on 1 April the increasingly beleaguered President acknowledged the protesters' demands, referring to the impact of the economic crisis on the population.

Emboldened, on 6 April 2019 protesters converged on military headquarters in Khartoum, gathering in hitherto unprecedented numbers and encamping near the compound. Soldiers mixed with the demonstrators in an atmosphere that was at times convivial, and at others deadly; on 9 April longstanding opposition leader al-Mahdi announced that 20 people had been killed by armed and masked men during the first few days of the sit-in. On the same day Sudan's police force effectively declared its support for the protest movement, calling for a 'peaceful transition of power' and ordering its personnel not to 'intervene against citizens or peaceful rallies', according to a spokesman.

The final downfall of al-Bashir came two days later. Minister of Defence Lt-Gen. Awad Mohamed Ahmed Ibn Auf announced on state television on 11 April 2019 that the President had been removed and detained 'in a secure place'. Ibn Auf announced a new state of emergency (this time for three months), the temporary closure of the country's borders and airspace, the creation of a Transitional Military Council (TMC), which was to oversee a transitional period of two years, and the suspension of the 2005 Constitution. He also declared nationwide ceasefires, to take effect in South Kordofan, Blue Nile and Darfur. The state Sudan News Agency announced that the NISS was 'releasing all political detainees across the country'. The following day Lt-Gen. Omar Zain al-Abdin, head of the TMC's political committee, stated that al-Bashir would not be extradited to face the ICC. A newly formed protest umbrella group, the Forces of Freedom and Change (FFC), quickly denounced the newly formed TMC, declaring that it too closely resembled the previous leadership. One day after taking power, Ibn Auf resigned and Lt-Gen. Abdel Fattah al-Burhan Abdelrahman, a veteran officer who had been further from the centre of power, replaced him as head of the TMC.

On 31 August 2019 al-Bashir was charged in court with the illegal acquisition and use of foreign funds, following the seizure of millions of euros, US dollars and local currency at his residence shortly after he was deposed. Al-Bashir told the court that the foreign currencies had been part of a private donation totalling US $25m. from Saudi Arabia's Crown Prince Mohammed bin Salman, claiming that the latter had wished to remain anonymous as the donor and that some of the funds had been spent on wheat imports, the education sector and a hospital. On 14 December al-Bashir was convicted of corruption and illegal possession of foreign currency. He was sentenced to two years in a reform institution for the elderly. Eight days later Prosecutor-General Tagelsir al-Heber announced that al-Bashir would be investigated alongside 50 other regime officials, including Haroun, for alleged crimes committed during the Darfur conflict. The prosecutor at al-Bashir's initial

corruption trial also noted that the ousted President was being investigated in relation to the 1989 coup that had installed him in power. The transitional authorities, however, appeared to give conflicting signals as to whether the former President would be sent to face trial at the ICC. While Human Rights Watch suggested in February 2020 that al-Burhan had indicated his willingness to hand over al-Bashir to stand trial, other reports suggested that there was resistance to this among Sudan's transitional authorities, amid the ongoing domestic investigations against him. During a visit to Sudan in early June 2021, the ICC's outgoing Chief Prosecutor, Fatou Bensouda, stated that the court was willing to negotiate with the Sudanese authorities on where al-Bashir's trial should be held.

CIVILIAN-MILITARY NEGOTIATIONS AND TRANSITION

While al-Burhan was a more acceptable figurehead than former Minister of Defence Ibn Auf to the protesters, thousands remained massed outside army headquarters throughout April 2019 and for several weeks thereafter, fearing that if they dispersed, the opportunity for a more extensive reorganization of the state would be lost. On 13 April the TMC announced that Salah Gosh had resigned as head of the NISS, in what amounted to another victory for the protesters. On 17 April the Agence France-Presse news agency quoted a 'family source' stating that al-Bashir had been transferred to the notorious Kober prison in Khartoum the previous evening. On the same day Abd al-Aziz al-Hilu, the leader of the SPLM-N rebel group, announced a three-month suspension of hostilities, 'as a goodwill gesture'.

During May 2019 the TMC and the FFC held sporadic negotiations, but without any significant progress. The key point of contention was the generals' refusal to meet the protesters' principal demand—for a transfer to civilian authority. While the army insisted that a military figure preside over a transition, the protest movement demanded that any interim governing apparatus have a civilian majority and be overseen by a civilian. A hardline influence was exerted by Lt-Gen. Mohamed Hamdan Dagalo, officially the deputy head of the TMC, but also the head of the much-feared Rapid Support Forces (RSF) militia, which had been deployed in Darfur (see *The Conflict in Darfur and Peace Agreement with the SRF*). In an interview with Agence France-Presse on 1 May, al-Mahdi warned the protest movement against provoking the generals, stressing that 'we must not challenge them in a way that makes it necessary for them to assert themselves in a different way'. Tensions between protesters and elements of the security forces heightened during May, even as many soldiers and junior officers in the army continued to demonstrate solidarity with the civilians. Meanwhile, Islamists counter-rallied against the FFC's ambivalent attitude towards a continuation of *Shari'a* law. In a reflection of the struggles occurring within Sudan's political and security apparatus, prosecutors announced on 21 May that agents protecting Salah Gosh had thwarted an attempt to arrest him and allegedly drawn their guns on police accompanying the prosecutors.

In a major escalation, paramilitary forces raided the sit-in on 3 June 2019, beating and shooting protesters as they were dispersed. A total of 128 demonstrators were killed in the violent operation, according to Human Rights Watch, quoting the figure given by local monitors. The Ministry of Health, however, acknowledged fatalities totalling 'no more than 46', claiming that the figure included those killed on 3 June and over several subsequent days. The protest movement was for a time significantly weakened, but the TMC officially distanced itself from the violence. Human Rights Watch accused the RSF of being responsible, alleging that these forces had 'raided the Khartoum sit-in site, burned down tents, and shot and beat protesters'.

Amid widespread international condemnation of the violence, a tense period of heightened uncertainty followed, as the TMC and the FFC tested one another's resolve. A week after the raid on the protest site, Yasir Saeed Arman, the deputy head of the SPLM-N, announced that he had been 'deported' by military helicopter from Khartoum to Juba, along with two other rebel leaders. The protest movement organized a national civil disobedience campaign that took place during 9–11 June 2019, followed by a huge protest on 30 June (which was opposed by al-Mahdi, indicating his increasing lack of influence in attempting to shape political change). Together with intensive efforts by mediators (see *Foreign Relations*), the success of these fresh initiatives by the protest organizers gave impetus to resumed negotiations.

On 5 July 2019 the TMC and the FFC reached a framework agreement, under which an interim executive body, the Sovereign Council, would be created as the highest authority in the land, to be headed by a military figure for the first 21 months of its existence and a civilian for the remaining 18 months, as part of a transitional period of three years and three months prior to elections. The framework agreement stipulated that the new governing body would be composed of six civilians (five chosen by the protest movement, together with one civilian jointly selected by the two sides) and five military representatives. The 11-member executive organ would in turn appoint a wider, predominantly civilian administration. However, the agreement depended heavily on the TMC, including the powerful and hardline Dagalo, meeting these commitments. Dagalo and key protest leader Ahmed al-Rabie, representing the FFC, on 17 July initialled a political declaration formalizing in principle the agreement that had been reached earlier that month. Further talks were expected to address issues including a demand by the TMC's generals for 'absolute immunity' in relation to the violence against protesters. Al-Rabie was adamant that the protest movement would 'totally reject' any such immunity. Yet, despite al-Rabie's vehement rejection of impunity on behalf of the FFC, he co-initialled an expanded deal—known as the Constitutional Declaration—with the RSF leader himself on 4 August, before the two leaders signed a final version of that document on 17 August, on the authority of the FFC and the Military Council, respectively.

This document formalized the transition process, setting in motion a timetable that included confirmation of the 11-member Sovereign Council, the inauguration of a Prime Minister, to be selected by the FFC, and the appointment by the new premier of a cabinet. All these measures were scheduled to be effected by the end of August 2019, ahead of a planned first meeting between the Sovereign Council and the cabinet scheduled for 1 September. The Constitutional Declaration also stipulated that a 300-member legislative assembly be installed within 90 days. The new assembly was to comprise 201 legislators selected by the FFC, with the remainder of seats being allocated to other political groups (none with links to al-Bashir).

The FFC chose as Prime Minister a respected economist, Abdalla Hamdok, who had refused al-Bashir's offer of the finance portfolio in the September 2018 reorganization. Hamdok was duly inaugurated on 21 August 2019. Al-Burhan was sworn in as head of the new joint civilian-military Sovereign Council on the same day, when the composition of that body was finally confirmed, after differences within the FFC over civilian candidates had delayed the appointments for two days. The newly established Sovereign Council superseded the TMC, which was dissolved. Dagalo, widely regarded as the most powerful individual during the military transition, predictably became one of the military's representatives in the joint Council. A Christian, Raja Nicola Abdel Maseeh, received the position in the Sovereign Council reserved for a civilian selected jointly by the military and civilian factions. However, appointment of a cabinet was delayed by further differences within the FFC, which on 27 August submitted a list of 49 candidates for 14 positions, with the nominees for the defence and interior portfolios to be decided by the military representatives of the Sovereign Council. Prime Minister Hamdok had still not revised that list sufficiently to announce his new ministers on 1 September, when the Sovereign Council and his administration had been due to meet for the first time. On 5 September Hamdok finally announced 18 members of a new Transitional Government, which was inaugurated three days later; they included Asmaa Mohamed Abdallah, who became the country's first female Minister of Foreign Affairs, and former World Bank economist Dr Ibrahim Ahmed al-Badawi as Minister of Finance and Economic Planning.

The Transitional Government and the Sovereign Council in November 2019 presided over the establishment of a new body, the Empowerment Removal Committee (ERC), which was mandated to dismantle institutions and dismiss individuals associated with the former al-Bashir regime. A decree on 29 November cancelled the NCP's registration as a political party and dissolved the entity. On the same day the new authorities formally abolished Sudan's longstanding Public Order Law, under which women considered to have deviated from *Shari'a* expectations had been flogged, fined and imprisoned. In early January 2020 the ERC announced that it had seized NCP assets, including the infrastructure and equipment of four media outlets. However, the joint civilian-military Sovereign Council faced its first significant domestic threat in that month, in the shape of a mutiny by former NISS personnel, who clashed with troops loyal to the new Transitional Government at several locations in Khartoum amid dissatisfaction over severance pay. The mutiny, which broke out on 14 January and also included the seizure of two small oilfields in Darfur, was quelled within hours, although the country's airspace was briefly closed, according to the Civil Aviation Authority. Dagalo alleged that Gosh was behind the violence, which al-Burhan alluded to as a coup attempt.

This incident was followed by an attempt on Hamdok's life on 9 March 2020, when his convoy was targeted near his office in Khartoum; the Prime Minister escaped unharmed and subsequently pledged to redouble his reform efforts. The Ministry of the Interior later announced that initial investigations into the attack indicated the deployment of a roadside device, while the Ministry of Culture and Information declared that several people had been arrested, including a number of foreigners, without giving details. Both episodes illustrated the fragility of the interim administration, and the Sovereign Council announced that it would step up its campaign to remove al-Bashir loyalists from institutions. On 29 February 2020 Mohamed al-Faki Suleiman, the deputy head of the ERC and a spokesman for the Sovereign Council, announced that the Ministry of Foreign Affairs had dismissed 109 employees (including ambassadors and diplomats), who had originally been appointed by the NCP or directly by al-Bashir.

Early 2020 also witnessed indications of heightened discord between the civilian and military elements of the transitional administration. In February the military dismissed army officers who had refused to obey orders in 2019 to crack down on civilians protesting against al-Bashir's regime. The Sudanese Professionals Association asserted that the officers should be reinstated, and organized a demonstration on 20 February that was met with the deployment of truncheons and tear gas by the security services. Hamdok ordered an investigation into the violence.

Fearing further precarious power struggles between the civilian and military elements of the transitional authorities, the Ministry of Finance and Economic Planning announced on 28 June 2020 that it would assume control of all state firms, including those owned by the security services. The move was part of a Staff Monitored Programme (SMP) agreed with the International Monetary Fund (IMF), which also required subsidy reform—a path that could lead to significant popular unrest. Embarking on the SMP, therefore, entailed significant risks for the stability and viability of the Transitional Government. In mid-June a panel chaired by Prime Minister Hamdok had approved a plan to liquidate or privatize 650 state-owned entities.

Meanwhile, on 3 June 2020—the first anniversary of the massacre at the protest sit-in—Hamdok promised justice for those killed, pledging that 'all those found guilty of participating in the massacre' would be processed through 'fair and public trials'. This pledge sat rather uneasily alongside persistent allegations that RSF personnel had been heavily involved in the killings, and in a context where Dagalo was arguably the most powerful figure within the transitional power structures. There were also increasing signs of tensions among the civilian elements of the transitional authorities, according to a report published by the European Council on Foreign Relations in June. Al-Tijani Hussein, a key FFC member of the transition administration's Economic Committee, lambasted al-Badawi's policies as 'ready-made prescriptions . . . by the IMF". On 30 June tens of thousands of people took part in a demonstration in the capital, in a bid to maintain pressure on the authorities to provide accountable governance and justice for the families of those killed during earlier protests. On 9 July Hamdok's office announced that six ministers—including al-Badawi—had resigned, and that the Minister of Health, Dr Akram Ali al-Tom, had been dismissed, citing a need to 'satisfy public opinion following calls for a government reshuffle'.

While disputes among the civilian elements of the country's new political leadership undermined the transition's credibility, persistent and rising tensions between the civilian and military leadership were of greater concern as 2020 came to a close. Prime Minister Hamdok and head of the Sovereign Council al-Burhan differed significantly over the case for normalizing ties with Israel, with the former much more reluctant than the latter (see *Foreign Relations*). When US Secretary of State Mike Pompeo visited Khartoum in late August, Hamdok told him that his Government did not 'have a mandate' to make a decision on the matter, which would be deferred to elected bodies created after the country's three-year transition was completed. Differences between the two leaders intensified further towards the end of the year, as al-Burhan declared in a speech to a military unit near the capital on 9 December that the Sovereign Council had 'failed', while he simultaneously pledged that the army would remain at the forefront of efforts to defend the people and protect the 'revolution'. The speech came shortly after his establishment by decree of a new political body, in addition to the plethora of decision-making institutions already created since al-Bashir's fall from power. The Sudan News Agency (SUNA) described the new body as a Council of Transitional Partners (CTP), with responsibility for leading the transition with all 'necessary prerogatives' for exercising power, especially within the context of any political dispute. These reported broad-ranging powers heightened concerns that al-Burhan was intent on bypassing his civilian colleagues in key decision making, and appeared at variance with his claim that the new body would never interfere in the work of the other transitional institutions. Hamdok, for his part, was widely reported to oppose the creation of this new body.

Popular discontent, spurred also by worsening economic hardship—itself exacerbated by the global COVID-19 pandemic, in addition to the country's existing domestic privations, led to street protests on 19 December 2020, the two-year anniversary of the uprising against al-Bashir. Thousands took to the streets of the capital and its twin city of Omdurman to decry rocketing prices and the lack of discernible political progress, including the failure—nearly half way through the three-year transition—to establish a promised interim parliament. The domestic political situation remained highly precarious during the first half of 2021, as socioeconomic grievances escalated, driven by inflation reaching 379% year-on-year in May, power cuts, water supply interruptions and the abolition of fuel subsidies in June, even although the latter was offset by new welfare payments. Popular resentment also continued to build over the slow progress of the investigation into the June 2019 massacre. Although the investigative panel in December 2020 summoned all members of the disbanded TMC—implicitly including both al-Burhan and RSF head Dagalo—for questioning on the matter, the Sovereign Council in May 2021 accepted the resignation of Prosecutor-General Tagelsir al-Hebr, and dismissed Chief Justice Nemat Abdullah Mohamed Khair. Both had been appointed in October 2019, a month before the investigation into the June massacre. A statement by the Sovereign Council noted that al-Hebr had tried to resign several times before, but that 'this time he was more insistent', in a context of diminishing prospects of senior RSF suspects being held to account.

In mid-June 2021 the Sovereign Council announced that a joint force would be established immediately with a mandate to tackle insecurity. The declaration cited an order by Dagalo, whose RSF would contribute personnel to this force, together with the police, the military, the General Intelligence Service (GIS) and former rebel groups. Hamdok acknowledged tensions between the civilian and military members of the transitional authorities and also warned of inter-military tensions,

nevertheless calling for the RSF to be integrated into the military. This stance put the Prime Minister in conflict with Dagalo, who warned that 'talk of RSF integration into the army could break up the country'. Appearing to endorse the legitimacy of at least the legislative branch of the former regime, Dagalo also noted that his militia had been 'established under a law passed by an elected parliament'.

THE OCTOBER 2021 MILITARY TAKEOVER

Hamdok's concerns about the commitment of the various elements of the security forces to the political transition proved justified. On 21 September 2021 the army announced that a failed coup attempt by dissident officers had resulted in the arrest of 21 officers and an undisclosed number of soldiers. The Prime Minister said that the attempted coup was 'orchestrated. . . by factions inside and outside the armed forces' driven by elements of al-Bashir's former regime who remained determined to 'abort the civilian democratic transition'. Minister of Defence Lt-Gen. Yasin Ibrahim identified the coup leader as Abdalbagi Alhassan Othman Bakrawi. Al-Burhan, meanwhile, declared that the coup, if successful, would have set in motion 'catastrophic consequences' for the unity of the military and the country.

Yet, a little over a month later, al-Burhan himself led a military takeover. On 25 October 2021 he announced that the Transitional Government had been dissolved, and declared a state of emergency. The Ministry of Information announced that civilian members of the Sovereign Council and a number of ministers had been detained, in events that amounted to a coup. The Office of the Prime Minister, who was among those detained, urged citizens to protest using all peaceful means possible. As people took to the streets in defiance of the military and to demand the restoration of the transition to civilian rule, al-Burhan defended his actions, maintaining that he had intervened to avoid a potential descent into civil war, in an apparent reference to the emergence of rival protest camps just ahead of the coup. In one these demonstrations—limited in scale and discernibly orchestrated—apparently pro-military crowds decried alleged incompetence on the part of the civilian element of the transition, in keeping with the army increasingly presenting itself as the guardian of the 2019 revolution. Larger pro-civilian counter-protests took place in response, culminating in a demonstration by tens of thousands of people on 21 October, just four days before the takeover.

In the wake of the military seizure of power, pro-democracy protests, along with co-ordinated pressure by key Western donors (see *Foreign Relations*), generated pressure on al-Burhan to return to the power-sharing arrangements stipulated by the transitional framework agreement. The protests continued even as security forces repeatedly fired live rounds at demonstrators, killing 40 by 20 November 2021, according to the monitoring Sudanese Doctors' Committee. On 21 November Hamdok formally agreed to resume his role as Prime Minister, in order to 'stop the bloodshed'. Under a 14-point agreement signed with al-Burhan, the military released Hamdok from house arrest, and pledged to free all those detained since the coup and restore power sharing with civilian figures ahead of elections in 2023. Hamdok announced that, reinstated as premier, he would have a free hand in appointing a cabinet of technocrats that would supervise the transition to the planned elections. While some civilian figures were quickly released, protesters accused Hamdok of betraying them to become a puppet of the 'coup regime'. The agreement between al-Burhan and Hamdok made no mention of the FFC, which remained the main civilian political grouping, and elements of which described the deal as illegitimate and unconstitutional. In late November Hamdok did, however, dismiss the head of police, Lt-Gen. Khaled Mahdi Ibrahim al-Emam, along with his deputy, Ali Ibrahim.

The pro-democracy protests continued, together with the exercise of lethal force by the security forces. Frustrated in his efforts to form a technocratic government, Hamdok's return to the premiership proved short-lived. He resigned on 2 January 2022, declaring in a televised address that he had attempted to stop the country descending into disaster, and that its existence was now under serious threat. His move made it clear once more that the military remained very much in charge.

Under pressure from Western powers, the military regime appeared to make several concessions in May 2022, releasing a number of detained opposition figures and lifting the state of emergency that had been in place since the takeover of the previous October. A new round of UN-facilitated talks began in June, but the FFC continued to refuse to participate and the initiative once more collapsed within days. On 30 June protesters staged one of the largest demonstrations since the initial mobilization against al-Burhan's takeover. Security forces again fired live rounds; at least nine protesters were killed, taking the total number of fatalities since the coup to 112. On 4 July, as sit-in protests continued in the wake of this rally, al-Burhan declared that the military would no longer make itself available for talks and suggested that civilian factions negotiate among themselves to form a new civilian Government. He announced that the existing Sovereign Council would be dissolved to make way for such an administration. However, he also announced plans for the creation of a new Supreme Council of the Armed Forces, without clarifying as to how executive powers would be divided between any new civilian administration and this new security body. The FFC rejected the proposal, amid widespread suspicions that al-Burhan envisaged the new council as a means to ensure that any civilian Government would in effect be without authority.

THE CONFLICT IN DARFUR AND PEACE AGREEMENT WITH THE SRF

In February 2003 two rebel groups, the Sudan Liberation Movement (SLM), which reportedly comprised up to 2,500 armed troops, and the JEM, estimated to number several hundred, organized a rebellion against the Government in an attempt to end political oppression and economic neglect in the Darfur region of western Sudan. The authorities responded by employing pro-Government ethnic Arab militias—the *Janjaweed*—to suppress the revolt; these militias were widely reported to have engaged in targeted killings, mass rapes, the burning of villages and food stocks, and the contamination of water supplies. By 2006 estimates indicated that up to 200,000 people had died directly or indirectly as a result of the conflict. Another 250,000 had sought refuge in neighbouring Chad, with a further 2m. displaced in Darfur.

International pressure on the Sudanese Government to take measures to halt the atrocities in Darfur continued in 2004. In July the US House of Representatives approved a resolution declaring the human rights abuses in Darfur a 'genocide'. In March 2005 the UN Security Council adopted Resolution 1593, referring the situation in Darfur to the Prosecutor of the ICC. Al-Bashir subsequently vowed not to send any Sudanese national to The Hague for trial, and mass demonstrations were held in the capital against the ICC. In January 2007 the ICC issued indictments against Ahmed Haroun, a Minister of State, and Ali Muhammad Ali Abdul al-Rahman (known as Ali Kushayb), a *Janjaweed* leader. However, al-Bashir repeated his refusal to co-operate. Shortly after being indicted, Haroun was appointed as Sudan's Minister of State for Humanitarian Affairs, subsequently becoming the Governor of Southern Kordofan State in May 2009.

The AU announced in April 2005 that it was to increase its African Mission in Sudan (AMIS) to an authorized strength of 7,731 troops, and in June further talks between the Government and rebels commenced in Abuja, Nigeria, in which a declaration of principles was signed. Violence continued to escalate, however. Efforts to reach a negotiated peace settlement continued in late April 2006 under AU auspices in Abuja. AU mediators submitted a peace proposal on 30 April, and finally the Government and one of the SLM factions, led by Minni Minawi, agreed to accept the proposal, although the other main SLM leader, al-Nur, and the JEM leader, Khalil Ibrahim, refused to sign the agreement, known as the Darfur Peace Agreement (DPA). Rebel negotiators had insisted on the creation of a national Vice-President's position, but eventually agreed to accept the role of Senior Assistant to the President on Darfur (to be included in the presidency). The Senior Assistant would chair a new Transitional Darfur Regional Authority.

The DPA also provided for the holding of a referendum in 2008 to decide upon the issue of the recognition of Darfur as a region rather than three separate states—another demand made by the rebels.

With the situation in Darfur deteriorating, and increasing fragmentation among rebel groups, in mid-2007 the Government finally agreed to the establishment of a joint AU-UN hybrid peacekeeping operation in Darfur (UNAMID), which would be composed of 26,000 troops. Disagreements threatened to disrupt the process when, in August, the AU announced that UNAMID peacekeeping forces would comprise only African personnel, safeguarding the AU's lead role in Sudan. UNAMID assumed peacekeeping operations on 31 December but remained severely under-resourced.

In September 2008, under heavy pressure from the international community, the Sudanese Government launched a peace initiative for Darfur, the Sudan People's Initiative, to be hosted by Qatar. However, many opposition groups refused to participate. Only the JEM attended discussions, which took place in February 2009 in the Qatari capital, Doha, and it withdrew from the talks following the Sudanese Government's decision in March to expel 13 aid agencies which it claimed had provided evidence to the ICC. The expulsion of the agencies led to a significant reduction in international humanitarian aid to Sudan.

Periodic attempts continued to be made to persuade the various rebel factions to enter into negotiations in the later part of 2010 and in 2011, and a peace agreement was signed in Doha between the Government and the Liberation and Justice Movement faction in July 2011. However, this represented only a small component of Darfur's rebels, and conflict with the main factions—particularly the JEM—continued. Furthermore, rebel forces apparently combined their efforts with the establishment in November of the SRF, an alliance between the principal Darfur factions and insurgents in Southern Kordofan and Blue Nile (see *Post-secession Negotiations and Conflict*).

The establishment of the SRF enabled the various rebel factions operating under its umbrella to extend their operations and seize towns beyond their respective original zones of the three Darfur states and the Southern Kordofan/Blue Nile states. Perhaps of even greater concern to the Sudanese Government, there was significant inter-ethnic conflict from the first half of 2013 between Arab groups that had traditionally been allied with the Government, suggesting a possible fragmentation of its core sources of support. These included large-scale clashes in the Jebel Amer region of North Darfur between the Beni Hussein and Rizeigat in January, in which more than 500 people were reportedly killed.

The situation in Darfur continued to fragment in 2014. The JEM was drawn into neighbouring South Sudan's new conflict, leaving something of a security vacuum in parts of Darfur. Government militia, led by the RSF, sought to exploit this, attacking on multiple fronts, and attracting fresh criticism from human rights groups. Fresh allegations of mass rape by government-backed forces in Darfur emerged in 2014–15. Human Rights Watch accused SAF troops of raping at least 221 women and girls in the village of Tabit over three days in late October/early November 2014, while the UN complained that its own investigators were repeatedly denied access to the site of the alleged atrocities. Another alleged case of mass rape was reported in the town of Golo, where forces loyal to the Government intensified a military campaign in early 2015. Sudan's Government claimed that the reports of mass rape were fabricated by rebel elements, in an attempt to discredit Sudan.

The Assistant Secretary-General for Peacekeeping Operations at the UN, Edmond Mulet, quoted new displacement figures to the Security Council in June 2015, including a confirmed 78,000 people displaced in Darfur since the start of that year, and another, unverified, estimate of an additional 130,000, as a result, he stated, of the Government launching the second stage of an offensive called 'Decisive Summer'. Sudan's acting permanent representative at the UN, Hassan Hamid Hassan, countered that the violence was attributable to rebel groups, rather than government forces. Despite the demands by Sudan's Government that UNAMID terminate its mission, in late June the UN Security Council extended its mandate for a further 12 months.

The unilateral ceasefire announced in June 2016 by the Government of Sudan for Blue Nile and Southern Kordofan was extended to Darfur, although fighting persisted there in the second half of that year. In October the official unilateral ceasefire was extended for all areas, before a further extension in December. However, in that month Gibril Ibrahim, the leader of the JEM since January 2012 (following the death of his brother Khalil Ibrahim in an SAF airstrike in Northern Kordofan in December 2011), dismissed the Sudanese Government's invitations to engage in dialogue.

In November 2017 al-Bashir argued for the closure of 60 camps housing around 1.6m. displaced people in Darfur, claiming that the crisis in the region had ended. However, the Office of the UN High Commissioner for Human Rights rejected al-Bashir's call to close down the facilities, insisting that the Government first needed 'to carry out a prompt and comprehensive disarmament of armed militias' to create a stable enough security situation to allow people to return to their homes. The Government appeared to tighten its control over Darfur in late November when its forces arrested powerful Arab militia chief Musa Hilal, an erstwhile staunch ally of al-Bashir who had rejected disarmament. The detention of Hilal, who was put on trial by a military tribunal in May 2018, represented a new dynamic in the Darfur crisis and threatened to provoke greater intra-Arab fighting. However, Hilal was eventually released in March 2021, following a pardon issued by the Sovereign Council installed following the removal of al-Bashir. It came as Hilal's supporters had become increasingly restive in the Jebel Marra area of Darfur, but the move was deplored by rights organizations, including Human Rights Watch, which cited his longstanding role in leading the *Janjaweed*.

In June 2019 the UN Security Council unanimously voted to extend UNAMID's mandate by four months to the end of October, maintaining the mission's existing troop and police levels and pausing a drawdown that had been intended to bring the long-serving mission to a close in 2020. By mid-2019 the mission had been reduced to around 7,200 troops and police officers, from a peak of more than 16,000. The Security Council in early June 2020 approved a six-month extension of UNAMID's mandate to the end of 2020, leaving its troop and police levels unchanged. It also established the UN Integrated Transition Assistance Mission in Sudan (UNITAMS), mandated to assist the country's political transition towards democracy, support peace building and help in 'civilian protection and (the) rule of law'. The new mission would focus largely on Darfur, Blue Nile and South Kordofan, and would have an initial 12-month mandate, eventually taking over the responsibilities of UNAMID in a 'phased' manner.

On 31 August 2020 the Transitional Government and the SRF rebel umbrella group, representing the JEM and SLA-MM rebel factions from Darfur, and the Agar-led faction of the SPLM-N from Blue Nile and South Kordofan, initialled a peace deal in Juba. The accord covered areas including the return of displaced people, justice mechanisms, security provisions and the eventual integration of rebel forces into a reformed national army. It also envisaged key government positions being allocated to rebel leaders and legislative representation in the yet to be established parliament. Four days later, al-Hilu, since 2017 the leader of a splinter faction of the SPLM-N, signed a separate agreement with Hamdok in Ethiopia for a 'cessation of hostilities', allowing the group to retain its weapons until the country's Constitution was amended to separate religion and the state. This left al-Nur's SLA-AW faction as the only major group resisting a political settlement with the new administration.

On 3 October 2020 the SRF factions and the Transitional Government signed the peace deal in full, at a ceremony in Juba. A few days beforehand, the SLA-AW faction reaffirmed its resistance to the agreement and launched an attack, according to Sudan's military. Key SRF leaders were greeted in the capital by Hamdok in mid-November, as part of an organized welcome event, shortly after an amnesty was granted to many thousands of former combatants in Sudan's conflicts (but excluding those accused of war crimes and other

indictable charges). The rebel leaders also met al-Burhan, who hailed them as 'partners', while Minawi, who was among the attendees, declared 'we have come to put the peace agreement into effect'. In February 2021 Hamdok appointed JEM leader Ibrahim—an Islamist and Japanese-educated economist—as Minister of Finance and Economic Planning, in a government reorganization, while six other former rebel leaders likewise received cabinet portfolios, including those of education, urban development, roads and bridges, livestock and minerals. However, a 25 February deadline for establishing a transitional parliament came and went, with no further progress having been made towards that benchmark by the end of August. In late March al-Hilu's SPLM-N faction signed a further agreement with al-Burhan (representing the Sudanese Government), known as the Declaration of Principles, which offered a guarantee of religious freedom, and was regarded as paving the way for a final peace agreement with the group. However, subsequent talks to achieve a lasting settlement with this SPLM-N faction foundered, and in June chief rebel negotiator Amar Amon, in an interview with Agence France-Presse, cited continued disagreements over the devolution of power from the central Government to the regions sought by the SPLM-N. In accordance with the Juba Peace Agreement of October 2020, on 10 August 2021 Minawi was sworn in as Governor of the Darfur region (having been appointed to the post by presidential decree on 29 April).

UNAMID's mandate ended as planned on 31 December 2020, with plans to complete a full withdrawal during subsequent months, even as displaced people in Darfur expressed fears that they would be exposed to fresh violence. The end of the mission's operations came four days after state news agency SUNA reported that the country's military was to dispatch reinforcements to South Darfur, after 15 people were killed in clashes between the Massalit and Fallata ethnic groups. The deployment of government forces to stabilize the situation was to include police, army, the GIS and the RSF. There was a significant upsurge in violence in Darfur in mid-January 2021; 159 people were killed in clashes in Western Darfur's state capital, El-Geneina, between Arab pastoralists and the Massalit, according to a doctors' committee, while fighting between the Fallata and Arab Rizeigat in South Darfur resulted in at least 55 deaths. Jan Egeland, Secretary-General of the Norwegian Refugee Council, urged greater protection of civilians in the immediate aftermath of the deadly clashes, which were followed in April by renewed fighting between the Arab and Massalit groups that killed at least 132, according to the local authorities. However, the violence was consistent with an overall pattern of localized clashes, rather than signifying a return to conflict between marginalized ethnic groups and government-aligned forces. The trial of *Janjaweed* leader Ali Kushayb, on a various war crimes and crimes against humanity charges, began in The Hague in April 2022. He had surrendered to authorities in the Central African Republic and been deported to the ICC in June 2020. More than 200 people were killed in further clashes near El-Geneina in April, in fighting between the Massalit and the Rizeigat communities that began around the Krink district. Further clashes involving the Rizeigat, this time in conflict with the Gimir in Kolbus district, around 100 km to the north of El-Geneina, erupted in the first half of June 2022, killing more than 125 people, according to the UN Office for the Coordination of Humanitarian Affairs.

Fierce fighting broke out in July 2022 in Blue Nile, near the border with Ethiopia, between members of the Hausa and Berti ethnic groups; 105 people were killed, according to the state government. However, the rebel factions that signed the 2020 peace deal largely continued to co-operate with Sudan's military in the wake of the October 2021 military takeover, unlike most of the civilian factions that had been part of the Transitional Government formed in 2019.

FOREIGN RELATIONS

Since al-Bashir seized power in 1989 Sudan's foreign policy has passed through several phases. Initially, the new regime sought to preserve relations with the West, but its active policy of support for radical Islamism contributed to the deterioration of relations with neighbouring countries. The Government fostered new links with Middle Eastern countries, including Iraq (which supplied arms to Sudan and received reciprocal support for its invasion of Kuwait in 1990) and Iran. Meanwhile, the USA condemned the Sudanese Government for its alleged role in the organization of international terrorism, and sought to isolate the country—especially after Sudan was implicated in the attempted assassination of President Muhammad Hosni Mubarak of Egypt in 1995. The USA imposed sanctions on Sudan from November 1997, banning imports of Sudanese goods to the USA and preventing US firms from exporting goods to Sudan.

In May 2004 the US Administration of President George W. Bush removed Sudan from a blacklist of countries deemed not to be co-operating with US anti-terrorism efforts, but it remained on the Department of State's list of 'state sponsors of terrorism'. US-Sudanese relations continued to focus on the implementation of the CPA and attempts to end the fighting in Darfur. With frustration growing in the USA over Darfur, in May 2007 President Bush announced new sanctions against Sudan which aimed to increase the pressure to reach agreement with the UN.

In March 2005 the UN resolved to refer allegations of human rights abuses in Darfur to the ICC, and investigations began later that year; two indictments were issued in 2007 (see *The Conflict in Darfur and Peace Agreement with the SRF*). However, the Sudanese Government refused to co-operate with ICC investigators. In July 2008 Chief Prosecutor of the ICC Luis Moreno Ocampo presented evidence against President al-Bashir in respect of war crimes committed in Darfur from March 2003, and requested the issuance of a warrant for his arrest. Accordingly, a warrant against al-Bashir, on seven counts of war crimes and crimes against humanity, was issued by the ICC in March 2009. However, the Sudanese Government continued to reject the legitimacy of the ICC and its charges. In July 2010 the ICC issued a second arrest warrant against President al-Bashir—this time on charges of genocide in connection with crimes committed in Darfur.

The structural underpinnings of relations between Sudan and the USA initially appeared to shift with the inauguration of Barack Obama as US President in January 2009. The new US Permanent Representative to the UN, Susan Rice, quickly voiced support for the ICC's investigation into alleged war crimes in Darfur. This marked a break with the policy of the Bush Administration, which had distanced itself from the ICC. None the less, and although the Obama Administration had previously adopted a number of hardline positions—advocating, for example, the aggressive enforcement of a 'no-fly zone' over the Darfur provinces—from mid-2009 it demonstrated an increasing willingness to engage with the Sudanese Government. In June the USA hosted a conference, attended by members of al-Bashir's NCP and the SPLM, with the aim of addressing divisive issues in the CPA.

Speaking in Juba in July 2011, when the Republic of South Sudan was declared a sovereign nation state, President al-Bashir publicly urged President Obama to end US sanctions against Sudan, claiming that Sudan had fulfilled its undertaking to honour the CPA. However, the sanctions remained in place, as many north–south issues (including a post-secession sharing of oil revenues, the status of Abyei and the demarcation of a wider border) remained unresolved. Moreover, the USA remained concerned about the new conflict in Southern Kordofan, and in November 2012 the Obama Administration renewed sanctions against al-Bashir's Government.

In January 2017, in one of the final policy measures implemented by the Obama Administration, the USA announced an easing of its sanctions on Sudan. The new policy suspended elements of the trade embargo, unfroze assets of senior officials and loosened financial restrictions, all for an initial period of 180 days. The US Administration attributed the move to the co-operation of the Sudanese Government in counter-terrorism operations, including the fight against the militant organization Islamic State. Among other reasons given for the partial suspension of the sanctions regime, the US Department of State cited Sudan's commitments to 'ceasing hostilities' in Darfur, Southern Kordofan and Blue Nile; improving humanitarian access; co-operating in the fight against the LRA (see

The Comprehensive Peace Agreement and 2005–11 Transition); and ending interference in South Sudanese affairs. However, the policy change did not apply to sanctions pertaining to the Darfur conflict, which were separate and included multiple legal authorities, including presidential executive orders; these sanctions remained in place. The decision by the Obama Administration drew criticism, including from Human Rights Watch and from the Enough Project, a US anti-genocide non-governmental organization, which described the move as 'premature'. However, in response to the US measure, Sudan once again extended a unilateral ceasefire in the conflict-ravaged areas of Blue Nile, Southern Kordofan and Darfur, by six months. As the end of the 180-day trial period of the partial suspension of sanctions approached, the new US Administration, under President Trump, considered a permanent termination of the main sanctions regime against Sudan. In an executive order issued in July 2017, the Trump Administration extended the suspension by a further three months. The US Department of State emphasized the continued progress made by Sudan, including counter-terror co-operation, improved humanitarian access, and respect for ceasefires in conflict areas. Another factor likely to have contributed to the strengthening of bilateral relations between the USA and Sudan was the latter's burgeoning alliance with Saudi Arabia, a key US ally, after al-Bashir had severed diplomatic relations with Iran in January 2016.

In October 2017 President Trump finally lifted the main US sanctions against Sudan, ending an economic embargo and freeze of government assets that had cut Sudan's access to the global economy for two decades. The move was justified by the US Department of State on the grounds that the Sudanese Government had made sustained efforts to 'maintain a cessation of hostilities in conflict areas in Sudan [and to] improve humanitarian access throughout Sudan', while co-operating with the USA on improving regional security and counter-terrorism measures. Central to the decision to lift the sanctions definitively was, reportedly, the Sudanese Government's agreement to sever ties with the Democratic People's Republic of Korea (North Korea) and cease buying arms from the North Korean Government, as part of President Trump's broad campaign to increase pressure on the North Korean regime. However, Sudan remained on the US list of 'state sponsors of terrorism' and sanctions imposed in response to the Darfur conflict also stayed in place.

Since the oil industry began to be developed in the 1990s, the People's Republic of China has been a close commercial partner of Sudan, and an opponent in the UN Security Council of sanctions over Darfur. Given China's leverage over the NCP, its support for the referendum was crucial to a successful vote in January 2011 and to the subsequent secession of South Sudan in July. President al-Bashir was received by President Hu Jintao in China shortly before secession occurred. During the visit, the state-owned China National Petroleum Corporation signed a co-operation agreement with Sudan's Ministry of Petroleum. China's bilateral dealings with Sudan and South Sudan continued to shift subtly after independence, not only as it was more dependent on the south than the north for its oil supply, but also since southern territories hosted the larger share of Chinese state-owned commercial assets. In September 2015 China's President, Xi Jinping, welcomed al-Bashir in the Chinese capital, Beijing. During al-Bashir's visit, the two leaders signed a bilateral strategic partnership, including an agreement granting China concessions for the production of natural gas in eastern Sennar State, in addition to the expansion of its petroleum operations in Sudan.

Sudan's relations with Eritrea have been marred by repeated cross-border incidents involving clashes with the Sudanese-supported Eritrean Islamic Jihad, which reportedly aims to overthrow the Eritrean Government. Eritrea's hosting of and support for the Sudanese opposition coalition the National Democratic Alliance (NDA) also contributed to the severe tensions between the two countries. Nevertheless, Sudan maintained diplomatic relations with Eritrea and allowed the repatriation of tens of thousands of Eritrean refugees from camps in Sudan to continue. In October 2002 Sudanese-Eritrean relations were further strained after the Sudanese Government accused Eritrea of participating in the

NDA offensive in north-eastern Sudan and of providing support to the SLM/JEM campaign in Darfur. Following these developments, the border was closed and Sudan rejected offers of AU mediation.

Sudanese-Egyptian relations historically have vacillated between confrontation and co-operation. In June 1995 the Egyptian Government accused Sudan of involvement in an unsuccessful assassination attempt against President Mubarak in Addis Ababa, and relations quickly deteriorated. After a number of conciliatory measures, the bilateral relationship had improved markedly by late 1999, when al-Bashir visited Egypt and the two countries agreed to normalize diplomatic relations. In 2016 tensions rose when Egypt rejected a request by Sudan to negotiate the sovereignty of the disputed so-called Halaib triangle, located in the two countries' borderlands, or to seek international arbitration over its status. In May 2017 al-Bashir accused Egypt of backing Sudanese rebels, after Egyptian armoured vehicles were allegedly seized from insurgents in Darfur. The allegation was rejected by Egyptian President Abd al-Fatah al-Sisi. Later that month the Sudanese Government banned agricultural imports from Egypt, following the imposition, in April, of a requirement that Egyptian men travelling to Sudan secure a visa prior to their journey, in an effort to reduce the passage of terrorists between the two countries. In June Sudan proposed the establishment of joint border patrols by the SAF and Egyptian troops, to help secure the porous 1,200 km-long frontier; Sudan's military already had similar arrangements in place with the armed forces of Chad and Ethiopia. Tensions persisted into 2018 and Sudan recalled its ambassador to Egypt in January for consultations. The Sudanese envoy eventually returned to Egypt in March, after a meeting in the Egyptian capital, Cairo, of senior officials from the two countries, including their respective foreign ministers and intelligence chiefs. Al-Bashir himself visited Cairo in March, declaring support for his Egyptian counterpart's bid for re-election. Al-Sisi made a reciprocal visit to Khartoum in July in an attempt further to improve relations, when a joint committee to strengthen ties was established.

A trilateral agreement signed by Egypt, Ethiopia and Sudan in March 2015 set out a co-operative framework for issues arising from the construction of the Grand Ethiopian Renaissance Dam, situated close to the source of the Blue Nile. (The proposed dam had caused significant concerns in Egypt and Sudan, as these two countries are downstream and rely heavily on Nile waters.) However, the Egyptian Government remained deeply concerned. While Sudan claimed neutrality in negotiations over the dam, in reality it irked Egypt by shifting its longstanding stance to favour Ethiopia, with the project set to bolster its energy supply and increase water for irrigation. Further discussions between the foreign ministers and other officials of Egypt, Ethiopia and Sudan were convened in Khartoum in April 2018; however, efforts to reach an agreement on outstanding issues of contention regarding the ongoing construction of the dam proved unsuccessful.

Tensions between Sudan and Eritrea emerged in early 2018, following reports that Egypt had deployed troops to Eritrea. Sudan closed its border with Eritrea in January and massed troops in the frontier region. In March the Eritrean Government issued accusations (which were strongly refuted by the Sudanese Ministry of Foreign Affairs) that Sudan, with assistance from Qatar, was providing support to an Eritrean militant opposition group, including the establishment of a military training camp near the border.

During the 2000s the Libyan leader, Col Muammar al-Qaddafi, was involved in mediation initiatives in Sudan, focusing on the conflict in Darfur in the middle of the decade. Relations between Sudan and Libya deteriorated in 2014, as the latter's NATO-backed administration (which took power following the ousting of al-Qaddafi in 2011) accused the Sudanese Government of attempting to arm a rival faction, which was claiming to be the legitimate government. In September the regime of Libyan Prime Minister Abdallah al-Thani, which had in the previous month been forced to relocate from Libya's capital, Tripoli, to the eastern cities of Tobruk and al-Bayda under military pressure from an Islamist militia, accused Sudan of attempting to transport air consignments of weapons and ammunition to the rival administration in the

capital. Sudan claimed that the weapons were merely for use by a joint border patrol, comprising troops from the militaries of both countries, under the terms of a bilateral security agreement. Relations remained tense during 2015. In April a Sudanese consul in the eastern Libyan town of Benghazi was arrested, allegedly on the grounds that he had visited Sudanese detainees in a military prison without first seeking permission from the relevant Libyan authorities. Sudan summoned Libya's ambassador to protest against the arrest and the consul was promptly released. As conflict continued in Libya, the Sudanese authorities became increasingly concerned about Darfur rebels who had moved to the south of the country. In 2017 Sudan warned the Libyan military commander Gen. Khalifa Haftar—who controlled much of the east of his homeland—not to support the rebels.

The crisis in Darfur has long affected Sudan's relations with its western neighbour Chad. Darfur, which borders on Chad, has longstanding links with the country, and both Hissène Habré and the current President, Idriss Deby Itno, launched coups with Sudanese assistance from bases in Darfur. Deby's seizure of power was supported by both Libya and Sudan, but relations with the latter deteriorated sharply from late 2005 as the Chadian Government expressed fears that the conflict in Darfur could spread across the border. In December Chad declared 'a state of belligerence' with Sudan, and, in response, Sudan subsequently supported opposition movements operating both within Chad and in Darfur that sought to overthrow Deby. In April 2006 Deby severed relations with Sudan, accusing the Sudanese Government of supporting an attempted coup. However, relations improved from July when the two Governments agreed to withdraw support for rebel groups on both sides of the border.

Sudan and Chad officially restored diplomatic ties in November 2008. However, in May 2009 Chad again accused Sudan of supporting a rebel attack, while Chad admitted launching air attacks on the Sudanese side of the border, in a bid to neutralize Chadian rebels operating from bases in Darfur. When Chad announced that it was sending ground troops into Sudan to confront these rebels, Sudan stated that it would eliminate any Chadian forces found on its territory. Nevertheless, al-Bashir held talks with Deby in Khartoum in February 2010, and the two Presidents agreed not to support rebel groups as proxy forces. The decision to deny entry to JEM leader Khalil Ibrahim and his entourage at N'Djamena international airport in May underlined Deby's commitment to the new agreement. At the first Sudanese–Chadian border development conference, held in El-Geneina (Western Darfur) in April 2018, al-Bashir and Deby signed a communiqué agreeing to strengthen judicial, police and customs co-operation on their countries' joint borders to combat terrorism, organized crime and all forms of illegal trade.

There was a sharp escalation in tensions between Sudan and Israel in late 2012. Sudan accused the latter of being responsible for an air strike against a munitions factory near Khartoum in October, while the Israeli military accused Sudan of facilitating the smuggling of weapons to Hamas in the Palestinian territories. In this context, Sudan allowed two warships belonging to Iran to dock at Port Sudan. The enhancement of ties with Iran was viewed with unease not only by Israel, but also by Sudan's partners (and key donors) in the Persian (Arabian) Gulf. However, Sudan's transition after the removal of al-Bashir raised the prospect of the restoration of formal ties between Khartoum and the Jewish state, particularly in view of Sudan's desire that the USA—a key ally of Israel—remove it from the 'state sponsors of terrorism' blacklist. Israeli Prime Minister Benjamin Netanyahu confirmed on 3 February 2020 that he had met al-Burhan in Uganda's capital, Kampala, announcing that the two of them had agreed to 'start co-operation leading to normalization of the relationship between the two countries'. The announcement came amid Israel's establishment in recent years of increasingly significant informal ties with key Arab powers, most notably Saudi Arabia and the United Arab Emirates (UAE), although Jordan and Egypt remained the only Arab countries to have concluded bilateral peace agreements with Israel. Notably, on 2 February US Secretary of State Mike Pompeo had invited al-Burhan to Washington, DC, for talks later in the year, according to the

Sovereign Council. However, Sudanese officials subsequently sought to downplay the prospects for any rapid restoration of ties between Sudan and Israel. In a sign of internal dissension over the issue, Sudan's cabinet announced that it had not been informed in advance that the meeting between al-Burhan and Netanyahu was to take place. Pompeo then increased pressure on Sudan to normalize relations with Israel by visiting Khartoum as part of a tour of Arab countries in late August 2020 (see below).

Al-Bashir's regime engineered a significant reorientation of foreign policy away from Iran and towards Saudi Arabia in 2015, as it supported a military operation by Gulf state forces, led by Saudi Arabia, against Iran-aligned al-Houthi rebels in Yemen. This reorientation appeared designed to elicit financial assistance from Saudi Arabia, whose ambassador to Sudan pledged 'huge' investment in the agriculture sector, in the context of continued economic stagnation. However, al-Bashir was faced with a difficult choice; Iran had been a major investor in Sudan's arms industry, including through the provision of technical expertise, and alienating one of the country's key powers could prove costly. None the less, in January 2016 Sudan terminated diplomatic ties with Iran, ostensibly in protest at the attack that month on the Saudi embassy in the Iranian capital, Tehran, which was set on fire by protesters after Saudi Arabia executed dissident Shi'a cleric Sheikh Nimr Baqr al-Nimr. Sudan expelled Iran's diplomatic representatives and recalled its own staff from Tehran. The move helped to cement Sudan's ties with Saudi Arabia, as illustrated by Sudan's hosting of a joint air force exercise with Saudi Arabia in April 2017. In April 2018 Sudan vowed to remain in the Saudi-led coalition force fighting in Yemen, despite the reported deaths of dozens of Sudanese soldiers in a rebel ambush in the northern Yemeni province of Hajjah. A month later the Saudi Government agreed to provide Sudan with up to 1.8m. barrels of oil per year to assist in fuel shortages.

In June 2017 Saudi Arabia severed ties with Qatar, as did Egypt, Bahrain and the UAE shortly thereafter. This concerted action against Qatar centred on the latter's relationship with Iran and its alleged financial dealings with hardline Iranian officials and Shi'a militia, which were viewed highly unfavourably by the Saudi regime. Despite pressure from Saudi Arabia, Sudan refrained from taking sides in the diplomatic crisis, and indeed offered to act as a mediator between Qatar and those countries that had cut ties with Doha. While the Gulf diplomatic crisis persisted, the Sudanese Government managed to avoid much of its impact, and continued to receive support from all sides. In March Qatar and Sudan reached agreement on a US $4,000m. project jointly to develop and manage the Red Sea port of Suakin, and in June a subsidiary of Qatar's sovereign wealth fund announced that it would invest $500m. in Sudan's agriculture sector.

As the street protests against President al-Bashir gathered pace (see *Rising Unrest and the Downfall of al-Bashir*), the key geopolitical players attempted to maintain or extend their influence. On 9 March 2019 a Turkish military ship docked at Port Sudan to enhance 'security and safety' in the Red Sea, according to Sudan's military. However, after al-Bashir's removal from office on 11 April, Turkey's newly won influence waned, as the UAE and Saudi Arabia aggressively sought to ensure the new TMC's loyalty to their regional policy priorities. Indeed, the new rulers appeared to diverge from al-Bashir's policy of attempting to maintain favour with both the Saudi Government and its allies on one side, and the Qatar axis of Muslim powers on the other side. Qatar's Al Jazeera television channel was forced to close its Khartoum bureau on 30 May. On 21 April the UAE and Saudi Arabia announced that they had pledged total support of US $3,000m. for Sudan, involving each depositing an initial US $250m. at the central bank. The size of the funding on offer would clearly exert a substantial influence on the policy of the TMC, making it very difficult to heed calls from the protest movement for the withdrawal of all Sudanese troops from Yemen. Ten days before the violent operation against protesters outside army headquarters in Khartoum on 3 June, RSF commander Dagalo visited Saudi Arabia's Deputy Prime Minister and Minister of Defence, Crown Prince Mohammed bin Salman, while TMC head al-Burhan was hosted by the powerful Crown Prince of the Emirate of Abu Dhabi, Sheikh Mohammed bin Zayed Al Nahyan, and also visited Saudi Arabia, shortly before the attack.

However, other governments and multilateral bodies had much less cordial relations with the immediate post al-Bashir regime. The AU's Peace and Security Council on 15 April 2019 condemned the TMC's seizure of power as a coup and initially threatened to suspend Sudan's membership unless the council transferred power to a civilian administration within a 15-day deadline. Meanwhile, the US Department of State announced on 23 April that it supported the 'legitimate demand of the people of Sudan for a civilian-led government'. On 30 April the AU moderated its position, extending its deadline for a transfer to civilian rule to 60 days. Egyptian President al-Sisi—who at that time held the AU's presidency—was widely regarded as being favourable towards Sudan's new army rulers. Al-Burhan visited Cairo for talks with al-Sisi in late May, just before his trip to the Gulf. Protesters had rallied outside Egypt's Khartoum embassy in April, accusing al-Sisi of interference in favour of Sudan's ruling generals.

On 6 June 2019 the AU member states acted decisively through the Peace and Security Council, which suspended Sudan's membership. In explaining its decision, the AU declared that the transfer of power to a civilian administration was 'the only way to allow the Sudan to exit the current crisis'. The day after the attack on protesters, the USA, the United Kingdom and Norway had called for an 'orderly transition' to civilian government, while directly accusing the army rulers of orchestrating the killings. On 6 July the US Department of State welcomed the outline deal reached the previous day by the TMC and protest movement, describing it as 'an important step forwards' and noting that mediation by both Ethiopia and the AU had been crucial in drawing up the accord. The office of the EU's foreign policy chief, Federica Mogherini, described the agreement as a 'breakthrough', and lauded the 'civilian-led' nature of the planned three-year transition. However, the EU also urged a continuation of 'talks on outstanding issues'. The USA, the UK and Norway, in a tripartite statement, welcomed the inauguration of Prime Minister Hamdok on 21 August. Hamdok subsequently announced that he intended to prioritize Sudan's rapid removal from the USA's 'state sponsors of terrorism' list.

This goal did indeed prove to be a significant focus over subsequent months, at least for Sudan. Hamdok undertook a visit to the USA in early December 2019, when Secretary of State Pompeo announced that the two nations would exchange ambassadors for the first time in over 20 years. Sudan's Ministry of Foreign Affairs announced in early May 2020 that it had appointed Noureldin Sati, a veteran diplomat, as Sudan's ambassador to Washington, DC, although the new US ambassador, John Godfrey, did not arrive in Khartoum until August 2022. Meanwhile, on 20 December 2019 the US Department of State removed Sudan from its blacklist for religious freedom violations. Saudi state television reported in late January 2020 that the Saudi Government had requested that the USA remove Sudan from its 'state sponsors of terrorism' list. The following month, according to state news agency SUNA, Sudan agreed to pay compensation to the families of 17 US sailors who were killed in an al-Qa'ida bomb attack on the USS *Cole* warship in October 2000 when it was refuelling in the Yemeni port of Aden; a US court had ruled in 2014 that Sudanese aid to the jihadist group 'led to the murders' of the sailors and had awarded their families US $35m. However, Sudan faced a substantially larger liability—and an essentially unpayable one, given the current condition of the Government's finances—related to the 1998 al-Qa'ida bomb attacks on the US embassies in Kenya and Tanzania. A ruling by the US Supreme Court in May 2020 unanimously reinstated around $826m. of $4,300m. in punitive damages that had previously been struck down by a lower court.

In the final months of the Trump Administration, the US State Department and Sudan engaged in extended negotiations, which were to yield a substantial move beyond the extended period of deadlock. Pompeo visited Khartoum in late August 2020, during a tour of several Arab capitals, in the wake of landmark initial agreements by the UAE and Bahrain to normalize ties with Israel. Hamdok insisted during Pompeo's visit that the Transitional Government had no mandate to decide on any potential normalization of relations with Israel. Despite Hamdok's objections, however, the Trump Administration remained determined to secure Sudanese recognition of Israel's legitimacy in exchange for removing Sudan from the US 'state sponsors of terrorism' list. In Khartoum, there was growing resentment in governing circles—among the civilian component, at least—at the Trump Administration's commitment to this condition, especially since bilateral intelligence co-operation over jihadism long pre-dated even al-Bashir's removal from office. Yet, given a worsening economic crisis in Sudan—and the fact that its listing excluded it from debt forgiveness and new funding by the IMF and World Bank— Hamdok was unable to maintain his bargaining stance, particularly with the military's more pliable positioning. Delicate diplomatic negotiations between the USA and Sudan thus produced a series of major announcements between late October 2020 and early January 2021. On 21 October 2020 Pompeo announced that the USA was initiating the process of removing Sudan from its 'state sponsors of terrorism' list, after Sudan transferred payments totalling US $335m. as compensation for the relatives of victims of the 1998 al-Qa'ida bombings of US embassies in Kenya and Tanzania. Two days later, the USA, Sudan and Israel released a tripartite statement stating that 'the leaders agreed to the normalization of relations between Sudan and Israel and to end the state of belligerence between their nations'. These two key developments were followed by several smaller trust-building steps, including an announcement by Sudan's Ministry of Foreign Affairs that it would discuss trade and migration deals with Israel, and by its Ministry of Justice on 30 October that an agreement had been signed with the USA to restore Sudan's sovereign immunity, protecting the country against further terrorism-related compensation claims in US courts. On 14 December the USA confirmed that it had completed Sudan's removal from its 'state sponsors of terrorism' list, following a 45-day period allowing the US Congress to review the process. On 6 January 2021 US Secretary of the Treasury Steven Mnuchin and Sudan's Minister of Justice, Nasr el-Din Abdul-Bari, signed the Abraham Accords—the name given to the range of Arab-Israeli normalization agreements of late 2020 and early 2021—in Khartoum. In view of the unpopularity of normalization in many circles in Sudan, the signing was finalized without any fanfare exactly two weeks before Trump left office. Furthermore, the signature of any full diplomatic recognition agreement by Israel and Sudan was still to come, as acknowledged by Israel's Minister of Intelligence Eli Cohen in late January. On 6 April Sudan's Transitional Government approved a bill that repealed a law prohibiting diplomatic and business relations with Israel, which had been in place since 1958.

The repaired relationship between Sudan and the USA initially continued to evolve under the Administration of President Joe Biden. The naval destroyer USS *Winston Churchill* docked at Port Sudan in early March 2021, reported to be the first visit by a US naval vessel in 'over three decades'. The visit came one day after a Russian frigate entered Port Sudan, and amid plans by the Russian Federation to establish a naval base there. However, Chief of General Staff of the Sudanese Armed Forces Lt-Gen. Mohamed Othman al-Hussein announced in June that the contract with Russia, which had been agreed by the previous regime, was under review, containing clauses found to be 'somewhat harmful'. Russia backed al-Burhan after his October 2021 takeover, and the military leader announced in early November, referring to the contract for the Russian base, that Sudan remained committed to international agreements and would continue to implement them. A delegation of senior Sudanese officials, including the Vice-Chairman of the Sovereign Council, Dagalo, and Minister of Finance and Economic Planning Gibril Ibrahim Muhammad, visited the Russian capital, Moscow, in late

February 2022, meeting Russian Minister of Foreign Affairs Sergei Lavrov on the same day that Russia's invasion of Ukraine began. Dagalo announced that the two nations had agreed to strengthen co-operation in various economic sectors, notably energy. In early March Sudan abstained from voting on a UN General Assembly resolution condemning the invasion and demanding an immediate withdrawal of Russia's military from Ukraine. Later that month the USA, the UK and Sweden alleged that the Wagner Group, a private military organization linked to the Russian Government, was engaged in illicit activities connected to gold mining in Sudan, an allegation denied by the Sudanese foreign ministry.

Relations with the USA and other Western powers deteriorated significantly after the October 2021 military takeover. The US Department of State announced that the US Special Envoy for the Horn of Africa, Jeffrey Feltman—who visited Khartoum just ahead of the coup, amid tensions between the military and civilian leaders—had warned al-Burhan and others that a termination of the power-sharing arrangement would have consequences. The USA announced its condemnation of the coup and duly suspended US $700m. in direct financial support to Sudan, warning that additional assistance could also be withdrawn. UN Secretary-General António Guterres, the EU, the UK and Norway were among other multilateral figures and key donor nations to condemn the coup. The UN High Commissioner for Human Rights, Michelle Bachelet, designated Adama Dieng, a Senegalese national, as a human rights expert for Sudan in November 2021, amid repeated instances of lethal force being used by security forces against pro-democracy protesters.

While the US Department of State welcomed Hamdok's reinstatement as Prime Minister in late November 2021, calling it a 'first step', it made clear that a return to a meaningful transition would have to be evident before financial assistance resumed. Hamdok's resignation in January 2022, in frustration at the military's continued monopolization of power, dashed any hopes of a restoration of direct aid from major Western powers. During a visit to Sudan in late February 2022, Dieng urged the authorities to stop using live ammunition against protesters, who continued to demand that the military return to barracks and hand over power to civilians. In early April al-Burhan threatened to deport Volker Perthes, the Special Representative of the UN Secretary-General for Sudan, accusing him of interference in the country's affairs.

Relations with neighbouring Ethiopia deteriorated significantly from late 2020. The crisis in Ethiopia's Tigray region, which involved a federal offensive against the country's former ruling party and the once-dominant Tigray ethnic group, led to an influx of some 25,000 refugees into eastern Sudan in November. The Ethiopian Government accused Sudan of exploiting the situation by invading its territory that month, as tensions heightened over the long-disputed al-Fashqa area, consisting of agricultural lands bordering Tigray. Sudan announced on 31 December that it had taken control of all Sudanese territory in the area, with the Ministry of Foreign Affairs later stating that the Sudanese military had acted against insecurity generated by Ethiopian 'gangs'. These tensions were accompanied by rising concerns about the implications of Ethiopia's ongoing construction of the Grand Ethiopian Renaissance Dam for downstream Sudan and Egypt, despite substantial and multiple international initiatives to mediate on the matter. In April 2021 Sudan's Minister of Irrigation and Water Resources, Yaser Abbas Mohammed Ali, threatened legal action against the Ethiopian Government if it proceeded to fill the dam, and in the same month Egyptian President al-Sisi warned Ethiopia against the consequences of touching a single 'drop of Egypt's water'.

Economy

DUNCAN WOODSIDE

INTRODUCTION

Sudan's economy has long been drained by corruption, multiple armed conflicts and restricted access to world markets, due in large part to poor governance by the narrowly based regime of President Lt-Gen. Omar Hassan Ahmad al-Bashir, which replaced an elected government in a 1989 Islamist-backed coup. The protracted war with the Sudan People's Liberation Army in the south from 1983 to 2005, heavy military spending, sanctions imposed by the USA from 1998, conflict in the Darfur provinces from 2003 and patronage dispensed to a range of competing security organs—the latter designed to sustain al-Bashir in power and play potential challengers off against one another—have all combined to keep productivity well below its potential. In the 2019 Corruption Perceptions Index of non-governmental organization Transparency International (the last one using data compiled when al-Bashir was in power), only Yemen, the Syrian Arab Republic, South Sudan and Somalia ranked below Sudan.

Perhaps ironically, however, it was al-Bashir's peaceful acquiescence to the south's independence referendum in January 2011—which resulted in an overwhelming vote in favour of 'separation'—and the subsequent creation of the Republic of South Sudan in July that dealt one of the greatest blows to Sudan's economy. The economic ramifications of secession by the southern territories persisted for many years, as Sudan sought to adjust to a massive loss of hydrocarbon reserves and a host of related difficulties. At independence, South Sudan assumed control of around 75% of Sudan's oil production. Real economic output contracted by 17.0% in 2012. The fiscal accounts never recovered from that hammer blow during the remainder of al-Bashir's years in power, during which he became locked in an increasingly tortuous dance with rival external benefactors—notably Saudi Arabia and its allies on one side, and Turkey and Qatar on the other—ahead of huge popular protests provoked by a tripling of bread prices from December 2018. The economy underwent a renewed recession in that year, and al-Bashir's 30-year grip on power finally came to an end in April 2019, as the army stepped in to remove him. An ensuing four months of further protests and stand-offs, ahead of the establishment in August of a highly precarious transitional power-sharing Government between the military and civilians, did little to ease Sudan's economic malaise, with gross domestic product (GDP) contracting by a further 2.2% in 2019.

The newly appointed Prime Minister, Abdalla Hamdok, announced in late August 2019 that he would prioritize efforts to persuade the USA to remove Sudan from its list of 'state sponsors of terrorism', a long-sought outcome since al-Bashir's later years in power. However, this would prove a delicate and protracted task, and was only achieved in mid-December 2020, by which time Sudan was contending with the extended global and domestic economic effects of the coronavirus (COVID-19) pandemic. Over a period of a week from 16 March that year, Sudan shut its airspace, closed its land and sea borders, banned mass gatherings and then imposed a 10-hour night-time curfew, in a bid to forestall the spread of the enormous virus domestically. In an attempt to mitigate some of the enormous economic pressures caused by these restrictions, the Government eased some measures in early July, including shortening the nocturnal curfew in Khartoum State by three hours and allowing restaurants and shops to reopen. Real GDP decreased by 3.6% in 2020, representing a third consecutive year of contraction. Like many other developing countries, Sudan was unable to make significant progress with its COVID-19 vaccination programme in the first half of 2021, with some developed nations even hoarding stocks of vaccines. Hyperinflation became a real risk, as the inflation rate reached 379% year-on-year in May.

An international donors' conference, held in Berlin, Germany, in June 2020, resulted in a total of US $1,800m. in pledges for Sudan. However, the funds fell far short of the $8,000m. that Hamdok had in August 2019 estimated would be required for economic recovery—an estimate that, of course, came before the additional blow dealt by the COVID-19 pandemic. While the USA's removal of Sudan from its 'state sponsors of terrorism' list was a prerequisite for debt relief, it took a further six months before the International Monetary Fund (IMF) and the World Bank announced that the Sudanese authorities had achieved the economic policy benchmarks required for such relief. Key policy changes included the unification of various official and black market exchange rates and the removal of subsidies, both long-term practices regarded as highly distortionary and wasteful. Together with forgiveness on Sudan's unsustainable external debt burden, this envisaged the release of $2,472.7m. in IMF funding over three years in late June 2021, in addition to a World Bank commitment grant of $2,000m. and another grant of $207m. from the African Development Bank (AfDB), going some way towards meeting the country's enormous funding needs.

Sudan's intensifying economic crisis in the two years after al-Bashir's fall from power brought with it an ever-heightening risk that the transitional arrangements would crumble, a scenario that could herald state failure and the collapse of all remaining facets of formal economic activity. Inflation reached 422.8% year-on-year in July 2021, driven higher in large part by the removal of subsidies and exchange rate devaluation required by the IMF's reform programme. Anticipated higher revenues from custom reforms were then interrupted by a blockade of Port Sudan for six weeks in September and October. The economic crisis fuelled significant discontent, including divisions within the civilian component of the transitional Government, which helped enable Lt-Gen. Abdel Fattah al-Burhan Abdelrahman to seize power on 25 October 2021. The military takeover was swiftly condemned by key donors, many of which suspended funding. The US Administration of President Joe Biden led the way, immediately freezing US $700m. in support, while the World Bank likewise declared that it had suspended disbursements. In December Gibril Ibrahim Muhammad—who remained Minister of Finance and Economic Planning after al-Burhan's takeover—told news agency Reuters that during November the country had been unable to access a total of $650m. in multilateral funding alone, consisting of $500m. in direct budgetary support from the World Bank and $150m. from the IMF.

The year 2021 therefore proved another poor one for Sudan's economy, with the impact first of stringent multilateral reforms, and then of the suspension of funding by traditional donors in the wake of the military takeover. While other countries in the region were helped by both sustained multilateral support and a recovery in global aggregate demand stemming from accommodative fiscal policies in developed markets in response to the pandemic, Sudan's economy grew in real terms by just 0.1% in 2021, following the 3.6% contraction in 2020, according to preliminary figures from the World Bank. In his December 2021 interview with Reuters, Ibrahim expected that the Government's forecast for real GDP growth in 2022 would fall to 1.5%–2.0%, from an initial forecast of 3.0%. In August the IMF predicted that Sudan's economy would expand by just 0.3% in real terms in 2022, while it forecast that consumer price inflation in the year overall would average 245.1%. The renewed international isolation of Sudan otherwise resulted in a lack of reliable economic data for the country in 2020 and 2021. One positive development for the beleaguered economy came in the shape of growing investment pledges from the Middle East, notably the United Arab Emirates (UAE—see *Foreign Aid and Sanctions*), but it remained unclear how far such funding would meet the huge gap left by Western donors.

AGRICULTURE

Approximately one-third of Sudan's pre-secession total area of about 2.5m. sq km is considered to be suitable for some form of agriculture. Of this, about 84m. ha is potential arable land and the remainder pastoral. Only about 15%, however, of the available arable area is cropped, reflecting the critical role of water availability in the development of the sector. The vast majority of settled cultivation has, until recently, been limited to the permanent watercourses of the Blue and White Niles and their tributaries in north-central Sudan. It is these areas which, within the framework of Sudan's 2m. ha of irrigation schemes, have been the focus of modern, commercial agriculture—producing the major export crop, cotton, as well as vital import substitutes such as sugar and wheat. As oil income has plummeted since the secession of South Sudan in 2011, agriculture and livestock have become increasingly important for Sudan's economic diversification. Agriculture (including forestry and fishing) contributed 21.4% of GDP in 2020, according to United Nations (UN) estimates.

The rainlands account for virtually all output of the staple grains—sorghum, millet and wheat—as well as of meat, milk and some vegetable products, and output in normal rainfall years has usually been enough to achieve self-sufficiency. Livestock has also been an important export, as have other rain-fed products such as sesame seed. According to figures from the UN Food and Agriculture Organization (FAO), sorghum production increased from 4.2m. metric tons in 2017 to 5.4m. tons in 2018, but then fell to 3.7m. tons in 2019 and 2.5m. tons in 2020.

The development of sugar production began in the 1960s, in an effort to reduce the cost of what was at that time Sudan's second most expensive import commodity, after petroleum. The White Nile region is the centre of Sudan's sugar industry. Development of the sugar sector received even higher priority after South Sudan seceded in 2011, as a means of diversifying the economy beyond dependence on oil. Production of sugar in 2012 was estimated at 600,000–800,000m. metric tons, but this level was not sufficient to meet domestic demand, as consumption amounted to 1.2m. tons. In 2013 the Ministry of Industry targeted an increase in annual sugar production to at least 1.5m. tons, which would enable the country to become self-sufficient. The planned increase in output was expected to be driven by expansion of the Kenana Sugar Co, owned jointly by the Governments of Sudan, Kuwait and Saudi Arabia, with funding by the latter two states. However, according to UN figures, raw sugar production totalled only 601,000 tons in 2016.

Parts of Sudan have relied heavily on food assistance from the World Food Programme (WFP) and FAO well into the 21st century, due to multiple conflicts and the prolonged displacement of people away from their familial lands and other economic dislocations caused by war, particularly in the Darfur states. Out of a total population of some 43m., 1.9m. remained internally displaced in 2020, according to the WFP. Further waves of displacement came in 2021 and 2022, driven by renewed conflict in outlying regions amid the disintegration of power sharing between civilian and military leaders in Khartoum. In May 2022 the WFP assisted 1.6m. people in the country, including 129,000 who were newly displaced in late April by intercommunal violence in the Kereinik region of Western Darfur. The UN agency delivered 8,700 metric tons of food and nutrition assistance that month. The war in Ukraine from February had a major adverse effect on Sudan and other North African nations that rely heavily on wheat imports from the Black Sea region due to the under-development of their domestic agriculture sectors. This supply interruption—together with the depreciation of the Sudanese pound and elevated transport costs, due to high fuel prices—caused wheat prices in Sudan to rise by 176% year-on-year by May, according to the WFP. Also citing poor local harvests, the WFP noted that the number of people classified as 'food insecure' in Sudan could rise from 15m. to 18m. (39% of the population) by September.

Farmers protested in Northern State in May 2022, after the government-controlled Agricultural Bank of Sudan reneged on a commitment to buy their wheat. The bank did not have enough liquidity to fulfil its commitment, claiming a lack of funding provided by the Ministry of Finance and Economic Planning and the Central Bank of Sudan (CBS). The following month the ministry committed to building a strategic wheat reserve of 300,000 metric tons, without elaborating on how this would be achieved. Sudan's annual wheat consumption needs at that stage amounted to an estimated 2.2m. tons.

INDUSTRY AND MINERALS

Beyond petroleum, Sudan's industrial sector remains underdeveloped. In 2000 the Sudanese authorities officially established the Red Sea Free Trade Zone between Port Sudan and the port of Suakin, encompassing warehouse, industrial and commercial areas. However, reports in 2002 indicated that just seven of the factories in the Red Sea Free Trade Zone were still functioning, and since then the Zone has collapsed. Also in 2000, President al-Bashir opened the US $450m. industrial town of Jiad, south of Khartoum, which included factories for manufacturing cables, cars, electrical wires, steel, trucks and pipeline products, together with housing, health and education facilities. Egypt's Asec Cement started production at a $250m. plant in Al-Takamul in July 2010, with annual capacity of 1.6m. metric tons of cement and 1.5m. tons of clinker. In May 2010 Asec inaugurated a 42-MW power plant to supply the cement factory.

While the overall industrial sector (both heavy and light manufacturing) was still largely underdeveloped by the second decade of the 21st century, the oil sector provided a significant exception. According to the BP *Statistical Review of World Energy*, Sudan's proven reserves of petroleum were equivalent to 1,500m. barrels at the end of 2020. However, Sudan's oil industry had been dealt a colossal blow by the secession of South Sudan in July 2011, since the new state hosted the bulk of hydrocarbon deposits. Before secession, Sudan and the then semi-autonomous region of Southern Sudan had shared revenues from southern oilfields equally. With the south dependent on Sudan's pipeline infrastructure to deliver its oil to the coast for shipping on to the global market, a new oil agreement would need to involve South Sudan paying transit fees to Sudan. The oil-rich states of Unity, Upper Nile and Jonglei all became part of South Sudan, leaving Sudan with only one major oil-producing state, Southern Kordofan. With the secession of South Sudan in 2011, Sudan's own oil exports decreased from 415,000 barrels per day (b/d) in 2010 to 51,000 b/d in 2012, according to an IMF report published in October 2013. Oil revenue fell from 11.3% of GDP in 2010 to about 3.5% in 2012.

The two countries eventually came to an agreement on oil revenues in August 2012. The key details included South Sudan paying a grant of US $3,000m. (in instalments) to guarantee pipeline access, partly in order to compensate Sudan for the oil infrastructure in the south that it had lost as a result of secession. South Sudan would also pay Sudan a fee for each barrel of oil exported through the north's pipeline network. For every barrel of oil transported through pipelines operated by Greater Nile Petroleum Operating Co, South Sudan would pay Sudan $8.40; and for use of the oilfield operator Petrodar's network, the fee would be $6.50 per barrel. Oil exports by South Sudan eventually resumed in April 2013, but were dealt a further blow by the outbreak of civil war in the world's newest nation state in December, which severely curtailed output. Total oil production in South Sudan in early 2017 was estimated at 130,000 b/d, compared with 350,000 b/d in the immediate post-independence era. By early 2019 production had only partially recovered to 175,000 b/d.

According to the BP *Statistical Review of World Energy*, published in July 2021, Sudan's own oil production in 2020 declined to 86,000 b/d, from 98,000 b/d in the previous year. The Government has also undertaken work to increase refined products output in an effort to address its fiscal deficit. However, Sudan's oil revenue was adversely affected by a further plunge in prices in the first quarter of 2020, caused by the global societal lockdowns to curb the spread of COVID-19, and by a price war between two of the world's major oil producers, Saudi Arabia and the Russian Federation. On 12 April the Organization of the Petroleum Exporting Countries Plus (OPEC+) grouping of oil producers reached an agreement to restrict global supply, thereby effectively ending the damaging price war. Sudan pledged to reduce its output of oil by 17,000 b/d, while South Sudan promised to scale back production by 30,000 b/d. By early June the price of Brent crude had partially recovered to approximately US $43 per barrel, and it continued to trade at that level into September. However, prices continued to rise as the economic impact of the pandemic began to moderate and mass vaccination campaigns against COVID-19 were instigated around the world; by mid-2021 Brent crude was trading at more than $70 per barrel.

It is clear that Sudan needs to diversify its economy beyond its dependence on oil. The principal means by which the Government has thus far sought to do so is through the gold sector. According to figures from the CBS, gold exports increased from US $989.1m. in 2019 to a provisional $1,480.4m., although this was still considerably less than the export revenue of $2,158m. achieved in 2012, when very high global prices buoyed receipts. The share of gold in the country's export earnings increased from 1.0% in 2008 to an estimated 38.9% in 2020, and was expected to account for about one-third of exports in the medium term, according to the IMF. Production rose steadily from 34.0 metric tons in 2010 to 107.3 tons in 2017 (according to the Geological Research Authority of Sudan). This confirmed a clear upward trend, when set against figures for earlier years collated by the British-based consultancy GFMS Ltd, which estimated that Sudan produced just 2.7 tons in 2008. In 2017 the country ranked second in Africa in terms of gold production, behind South Africa and overtaking Ghana; output reached 63.3 tons in the first six months of 2018.

There was a noticeable increase in international interest in the gold sector after the USA lifted economic sanctions in late 2017. According to the Government, 13 companies signed contracts relating to the mining of gold and other minerals in the first quarter of 2018, and in May the Australian company Resolute Mining announced a US $22.5m. deal to buy a 15% stake in Canada-based Orca, whose major asset was a 70% interest in Sudan's oil exploration Block 14. However, revenues from gold exports almost halved from $1,558.5m. in 2017 to $832m. in 2018, before rising to $989.1m. in 2019 and further to $1,480.4m. in 2020, according to preliminary data. Lt-Gen. Mohamed Hamdan Dagalo—the leader of the much-feared Rapid Support Forces (RSF) militia and the second in command in Sudan's Government—has major interests in Sudan's gold industry, which he has allegedly used to consolidate his already considerable influence. The Sudanese gold company Algunade, which an investigation by the Reuters news agency found was linked to Dagalo's brother, donated $100m. to a planned $2,000m. trade financing fund that the Ministry of Finance and Economic Planning began to establish in June 2020. According to the Ministry, the aim of the fund was to help facilitate the import and export of food commodities.

Sudan's other known mineral resources include marble, mica, chromite and gypsum. There are uranium reserves on the western borders with Chad and the Central African Republic. Until recently, only the chromite deposits in the Ingessana Hills near the Ethiopian border were exploited on a substantial scale, by the state-owned Sudan Mining Co, which produces 10,000–15,000 metric tons per year for export. The known reserves exceed 1m. tons of high-quality chromite.

BALANCE OF PAYMENTS, FISCAL POLICY AND THE EXCHANGE RATE

According to provisional figures from the CBS, Sudan's main export partners in 2021 were the UAE, which received an estimated 51.5% of the total, the People's Republic of China (14.4%), Egypt (11.6%) and Saudi Arabia (8.5%). The principal sources of imports in that year were China, which provided an estimated 24.1% of the country's imports, the UAE (17.9%), India (8.8%) and Saudi Arabia (5.3%).

In 2010, the last full year before South Sudan seceded, oil exports had totalled US $9,433m. (although revenues were split between the central Government and the then semi-autonomous Government of South Sudan). Exports of crude petroleum in 2016 totalled just $271m., down from $1,719m. in 2013, although they rallied slightly over the next three years to reach $474m. in 2019, before recording a sharp decrease, to only $44.9m. in 2020, according to provisional figures, as a result of the impact of the pandemic. In a bid to curb the major imbalances created by the secession of South Sudan and the loss of oil revenue, the authorities intensified austerity measures from 2016, including restricting imports. For the first year

since 2011, according to the IMF, Sudan recorded a rise in exports in 2017, of 32.5%, partly as a result of increased gold output. The trade deficit in that year was $4,120m., while the current account deficit was $4,611m. In 2018, when a considerable reduction in imports more than compensated for a further decline in exports, the trade deficit fell to $3,580m., while the current account deficit rose slightly to $4,679m. In 2019, however, the trade deficit increased to $4,627m., with a surge in imports, while the current account deficit amounted to $4,780m. In 2020, amid the COVID-19 pandemic, the trade deficit widened to $5,051m. and the current account deficit to $5,841m.

In December 2018 street protests broke out in Atbara and two other cities, initially against a threefold rise in the price of a small loaf of bread, from 1.00 new Sudanese pounds to 3.00 new Sudanese pounds, caused by the decision of the cash-depleted Government to reduce flour subsidies. However, even in January 2019—by which time the protests had escalated into mass rallies demanding the 'fall of the regime'—the Government continued to subsidize the price of bread heavily, according to sources quoted by Reuters. In a report on 17 January, the news agency noted that the Government was funding private traders at 680 new Sudanese pounds per 150-kg sack of imported flour, equivalent to more than one-half of the cost of each sack (1,230 new Sudanese pounds). Al-Bashir dismissed Moataz Moussa as both Prime Minister and Minister of Finance in late February, and assigned the finance portfolio to Mustafa Youssef.

Following the overthrow of President al-Bashir, on 23 September 2019 Sudan's new Minister of Finance and Economic Planning, Ibrahim Elbadawi, unveiled a nine-month emergency rescue plan to cover the period from October 2019 to June 2020. Under the plan, food and fuel subsidies—the fuel component alone being equivalent to 8% of GDP—were to remain in place until mid-2020, when such subsidies would purportedly be progressively replaced by direct cash transfers to poor families. The plan ambitiously also sought to reduce tax exemptions, in a context where around 60% of economic activity fell into the untaxed category, and to align the official and black market exchange rates, which stood at 45 new Sudanese pounds per US dollar and 69 new Sudanese pounds per US dollar, respectively, in late September 2019. Elbadawi told Reuters in November 2019 that Sudan needed at least US $3,000m.–$4,000m. (and possibly up to $5,000m.) in budget support in order to avoid economic collapse. Some funding was forthcoming from Saudi Arabia and the UAE (see *Foreign Aid and Sanctions*), but it was clear that significantly more would be required.

The overall fiscal balance registered a deficit of 220,500m. new Sudanese pounds in 2019, according to IMF estimates released in March 2020, compared with a deficit of 107,900m. new Sudanese pounds in 2018. While revenues and grants rose from a total of 121,400m. new Sudanese pounds in 2018 to 159,200m. new Sudanese pounds in 2019, this increase was more than offset by a rise in expenditure from 229,300m. new Sudanese pounds in 2018 to 379,700m. new Sudanese pounds in 2019. The 2020 budget targeted revenues and grants of 568,300m. new Sudanese pounds and expenditure of 642,400m., which would have resulted in the overall deficit decreasing to 74,100m. new Sudanese pounds, but the onset of the chaos induced by the COVID-19 pandemic rendered these figures overly ambitious. In its October 2020 report issued as part of an Article IV consultation, the Fund predicted that revenues and grants would total just 304,700m. new Sudanese pounds in 2020, and that expenditure would increase to 612,700m. new Sudanese pounds, resulting in a forecast overall fiscal deficit of 308,000m. new Sudanese pounds. According to the IMF projections, the budget deficit (including grants) was expected to rise further to 367,200m. new Sudanese pounds in 2021.

A major part of the Government's fiscal policy from 2021 was the removal of the substantial subsidies, a measure that had cost around US $1,000m. in state funds per year. The subsidies were eventually removed in June, allowing, together with other reforms, relief on the country's enormous debt burden later that month and immediate IMF financial support (see *Foreign Aid and Sanctions*). This major policy measure involved the termination of all subsidies on fuel pump prices, which raised the price of petrol to 290 new Sudanese pounds per litre from 150 new Sudanese pounds (while the price of diesel fuel rocketed to 285 new Sudanese pounds per litre, up from 125 new Sudanese pounds). However, this was a deeply socially contentious development and precipitated protests. The rationale behind the reform was that it removed a key economic distortion that had long favoured wealthier elements of society, but some took the opposite view, arguing that the higher fuel prices would adversely affect the poor through the higher cost of transporting food to market. Seeking to ease the impact—but also risking some of the fiscal gains—the Ministry of Finance and Economic Planning announced that it would consider the provision of direct subsidies to the agriculture, power and transport sectors in order to mitigate 'the burden of rationalized fuel prices'.

The reform programme agreed with the IMF sought to offer some protection to the poor against the effects of subsidy removal—and also against the COVID-19 pandemic—by introducing the Sudan Family Support Programme, which was launched in July 2020. The assistance amounted to 500 new Sudanese pounds per eligible person per month and was targeted to reach 80% of the population. Costing US $820m. and financed by grants through the International Development Association (IDA) of the World Bank, the initiative was slow to gain traction, according to a report by Reuters in April 2021. The IMF programme envisaged the withdrawal of the support in 2022, on the basis of an anticipated exit from the worst phase of economic transition and crisis.

Another important aspect of the reform programme was exchange rate rationalization, focused on eliminating the gap between various privileged official rates and the black market rate. In late February 2021 the CBS abandoned the main official fixed exchange rate of 55 new Sudanese pounds to the US dollar and introduced a managed floating system, which immediately took the official rate to 375 new Sudanese pounds to the dollar, close to the black market level. In late June, just a week before the IMF and the World Bank declared that Sudan had qualified for debt relief, the Ministry of Finance and Economic Planning announced that the customs exchange rate, long fixed at 20 new Sudanese pounds to the dollar, had been abolished, a final major step in the unification of exchange rates.

FOREIGN AID AND SANCTIONS

Throughout the post-independence period, Sudan's economic wellbeing depended on ever-increasing amounts of foreign aid. During the Cold War the USA became Sudan's largest single donor; other important bilateral donors included Egypt, Libya, the United Kingdom, Kuwait, China and Saudi Arabia. The principal multilateral donors included the World Bank, the European Community (now the European Union—EU) and the IMF. The end of the Cold War coincided with the rise of the al-Bashir regime, and Sudan's economic performance for much of the subsequent period was increasingly poor, resulting in international sanctions and isolation, and difficulties with the World Bank and IMF.

The conflict in Sudan's western Darfur states, which began in 2003 and intensified once again in 2014, meant that many countries denied Sudan bilateral assistance. China remained Sudan's primary source of bilateral assistance. According to the Minister of State for Finance and National Economy in May 2009, Sudan was relying on China for some US $4,300m. in loans for infrastructure development (with a focus on roads and railways). The Organization of the Islamic Conference announced in March 2010 that it had raised $850m. for reconstruction and development projects in Sudan's Darfur states, focusing on basic infrastructure requirements, including housing, water and agricultural modernization.

Enhanced ties with Saudi Arabia led to a significant aid boost from the oil-rich Arab kingdom in 2015, following the dispatch of Sudanese troops to support the Saudi-led coalition force fighting in Yemen against the Iranian-backed al-Houthi rebel movement. This policy realignment—Sudan had historically fostered close ties with Iran and there had been past tensions in its relationship with Saudi Arabia—was followed by Saudi Arabia's ambassador to Sudan pledging 'huge' investment in the latter's agriculture sector. In April 2015 Sudan's Minister of Agriculture and Irrigation met with a technical delegation from Saudi Arabia to discuss modalities for trade co-operation. In July the Minister of State for Finance and National Economy announced that Sudan had received a total of around US $2,000m. in loans from Arab states of the Persian (Arabian) Gulf, at concessional rates. The following month the Ministry of Finance and National Economy clarified that it had received $1,000m. in deposits from Saudi Arabia, in two equal tranches, since the beginning of July. Another welcome source of support has been the UAE, a key Saudi ally. The Governor of the CBS signed an agreement in January 2017 with the Abu Dhabi Fund for Development, under which the latter would deposit $500m. in the CBS, in order to assist monetary and fiscal stability in Sudan, and encourage foreign investment. In March 2018 the Abu Dhabi Fund made a further deposit, of $1,400m.

The reorientation away from Iran and towards Saudi Arabia—a key US ally—also related to the drive to end US sanctions. Al-Bashir's regime had expected that its assent to the secession of South Sudan would pave the way for immediate sanctions relief, but the Administration of US President Barack Obama expressed deep concerns about the Sudanese regime's conduct in Darfur and the outbreak of new conflict in 2011 in the Southern Kordofan and Blue Nile states. Eventually, however, the USA—in the context of Sudan's dramatic Middle East policy shift, which better reflected its own geopolitical allegiances—began to implement sanctions relief. One of the final acts of the second Obama Administration, in January 2017, was to suspend the Sudan sanctions regime for 180 days, pending a full termination of the package of measures. Crucially, this allowed US citizens and entities to engage in transactions involving persons in Sudan; to import goods and services from the country; to export goods, technology and services; and to carry out transactions involving property owned (or part-owned) by the Sudanese Government.

A further sign of the regime's desire for economic normalization was its bid to join the World Trade Organization (WTO). In early 2017 negotiations between the Sudanese Government and the WTO reopened for the first time since 2004. In October 2017 the Administration of US President Donald Trump continued the process begun under Obama and lifted key sanctions that for some two decades had prohibited US citizens and entities from 'engaging in transactions with Sudan and the Government of Sudan'. However, Sudan's inclusion on the USA's list of 'state sponsors of terrorism'—a crucial additional impediment to restoring Sudan's access to the global financial system—remained in place. Private investors therefore remained reluctant to engage in the country, and the USA's designation of Sudan as a 'state sponsor of terrorism' persisted throughout the remainder of al-Bashir's increasingly tenuous hold on power and beyond. The designation also prevented the Sudanese Government from accessing IMF and World Bank funding.

Qatar became a major source of assistance during the latter years of al-Bashir's rule. In March 2012 the Qatar Government announced that it would invest up to US $2,000m. in Sudan, particularly in the oil, mining and agriculture sectors. In March 2018 Qatar announced the provision of funding for a $4,000m. project to rehabilitate the Red Sea port of Suakin, and a $500m. agricultural investment project. Turkey also emerged as an important source of support in 2017, with the Turkish President, Recep Tayyip Erdoğan, overseeing the conclusion of several deals during a visit to Khartoum in December. In March 2018 the CBS announced that it had accepted a $2,000m. loan from an unnamed Turkish company towards the costs of petroleum and wheat imports.

In the immediate post al-Bashir period, the danger to Sudan of economic collapse was averted by Saudi Arabia and the UAE, which each provided an initial US $250m. in direct assistance deposited in the CBS in May 2019, pending the provision of a wider package totalling $3,000m. In early October Sudan's new Minister of Finance and Economic Planning, Ibrahim Elbadawi, told Reuters that $1,500m. promised by Saudi Arabia and the UAE had thus far materialized, in the shape of the $500m. received by the CBS in May and $1,000m. worth of commodities, notably agriculture inputs, petroleum products and wheat, while the remaining $1,500m. was due to be disbursed by the end of 2020.

The IMF announced in late June 2020 that it had agreed a Staff-Monitored Programme (SMP) with Sudan, subject to approval by the multilateral lender's management. The programme envisaged energy subsidy reforms to fund higher social spending, including direct cash transfers to families. The agreement to reduce fuel subsidies represented a step forward, since the Ministry of Finance and Economic Planning estimated that this category of subsidies alone was equivalent to 8% of GDP.

Sudan's subsidy system is widely considered to be deeply inefficient and vulnerable to significant abuse, which has resulted in unearned income for firms operating in subsidized sectors, to the detriment of the state and citizens. In order to offset the impact of subsidy phase-outs, the Ministry of Finance and Economic Planning announced in mid-June 2020 that it was set to launch a pilot of a cash transfer scheme, initially involving monthly payments of 500 new Sudanese pounds (just under US $10) per recipient in the West Soba district of Khartoum. The ministry planned subsequently to extend the scheme to provide a total of $1,900m. to needy citizens. The direct cash transfers to families would initially be funded partly through the proceeds from a donor conference hosted by Germany in late June 2020. A total of $1,800m. was pledged at the conference, with the EU promising $350m., the USA $356m., the UK $186m., Germany $168m., France $112m., the UAE $50m. and Saudi Arabia $10m.

The USA eventually confirmed that it had completed the process of removing Sudan from its 'state sponsors of terrorism' list on 14 December 2020. This followed a 45-day congressional review period after Sudan had paid US $335m. in compensation to families of victims of the 1998 al-Qa'ida bombings of the US embassies in Tanzania and Kenya, in a context where the al-Bashir regime was believed to have offered sanctuary to the jihadist network's leader, Osama bin Laden, in the 1990s. This step paid much-needed dividends for the increasingly financially desperate Government. In the immediate aftermath of the country's formal de-listing, Sudan's acting Minister of Finance and Economic Planning, Heba Ahmed, stated that the US Administration had pledged aid over the next four years in the form of wheat and other commodities. His ministry also announced that a delegation comprising representatives of the USA's 10 largest agricultural companies would visit Sudan, with a view to investing in the agriculture sector. Crucially, Steven Mnuchin, Secretary of the Treasury in the outgoing Trump Administration, on 6 January 2021 signed an agreement to provide Sudan with a $1,200m. bridging loan to cover the country's arrears at the World Bank, thereby allowing the release of nearly $2,000m. in new grants through the IDA.

At that stage, Sudan also maintained arrears of around US $1,300m. at the IMF. In early March 2021 the IMF approved its first review of progress under Sudan's SMP, citing 'tangible progress toward establishing a strong track record of policy and reform implementation', notably including the long-prescribed unification of the main official exchange rate with the black market rate. In mid-May France hosted a conference designed to support Sudan's political and economic transition, during which President Emmanuel Macron announced that IMF member states had agreed to clear Sudan's accumulated arrears, again through a bridging loan, this time totalling $1,500m. Following the removal of fuel subsidies and the elimination of the customs exchange rate in June (see *Balance of Payments, Fiscal Policy and the Exchange Rate*), together with the pledge by member states to cover Sudan's arrears, the IMF and the World Bank announced jointly on 29 June that Sudan had finally qualified for debt relief under the Highly Indebted Poor Countries (HIPC) initiative, a programme launched jointly by the two multilateral lenders in 1996. They declared that Sudan would be eligible for total debt relief of $23,300m. in present value terms, equivalent to over one-third of the value of such relief previously granted to a total of 37 qualifying nations. In addition to this major development, the IMF announced that its Executive Board had approved an Extended Credit Facility (ECF), advancing Sudan beyond its credit-less SMP to a funding facility. The 39-month ECF

amounted to $2,472.7m., of which $1,414.7m. would be made available immediately.

The formal qualification for debt relief involved multilateral, bilateral and commercial loans; taking into account all forgiveness indirectly 'anchored' to, as well as directly stemming from, the HIPC initiative, Sudan would be eligible for more than US $50,000m. in relief in net present value terms, according to the IMF, representing over 90% of the country's external debt burden. This would bring Sudan's external debt burden down from $56,600m. (equivalent to 163% of GDP) to around $6,000m. over approximately three years. France was at the forefront of countries pledging bilateral debt forgiveness; Macron announced at the Paris Conference in May that France was in favour of cancelling the entire $5,000m. in debt owed to it by Sudan. France was among the top three bilateral creditors grouped under the Paris Club, a grouping to which Sudan owed a total of some $19,000m., while around $9,800m. was owed to non-Paris Club bilateral creditors (including China, Kuwait and Saudi Arabia) and nearly $6,000m. to commercial lenders.

World Bank President David Malpass met Prime Minister Hamdok in Khartoum in September 2021, in a context where the adverse effects of the measures prescribed by the IMF and World Bank—notably subsidy removal and a devaluation of the official exchange rate—appeared to be starting to abate slightly, as inflation eased in August to 388% year-on-year, from 423% year-on-year in July. Malpass noted that 'Sudan is making a transition from a ... situation of shortages to a situation that is gradually improving'. However, as noted above, much of the financial support from Western donors came to a halt as a result of the October 2021 military takeover. One of the biggest blows in this respect was the suspension of US $2,000m. in grants that had been on offer from the World Bank. Withholding funds was central to the bargaining power of Western nations, led by the US Administration of President Biden, as they sought to persuade al-Burhan to reverse his coup and cede power to civilian leaders. Nominally, leading Gulf states supported the drive to restore civilian rule. However, in reality, they appeared to undermine the policy stance of the USA and the EU by continuing to engage with a view to providing additional direct funding to the military regime. In late March 2022 al-Burhan travelled to Saudi Arabia, where he met both King Salman bin Abdulaziz Al Sa'ud and the effective political leader, Crown Prince Mohammed bin Salman. Soon afterwards, in early April, Sudan's Ministry of Finance and Economic Planning released a statement noting that Ibrahim would shortly visit the Saudi city of Jeddah to 'discuss co-operation and arrangements' for a $1,000m. deposit by Saudi Arabia at the CBS. In late June Reuters quoted a Sudanese official on a planned deal that would reportedly bring $6,000m. of UAE investment to Sudan, including $4,000m. for the construction of a new port around 200 km north of Port Sudan. The deal would also include a $300m. deposit by the UAE at the CBS, according to the same official. Reuters noted that this would be the first such deposit by the UAE since the military takeover, and it cited two 'high-level current Sudanese officials' as corroborating the form of this deal. Abu Dhabi Ports, the key prospective partner in the port construction, told Reuters at that stage it had not signed any agreements regarding this venture, but confirmed that preliminary discussions were ongoing with the Sudanese authorities. The military regime in Khartoum also sought assistance from Russia to stem the shortfall from Western powers. Visiting the Russian capital, Moscow, in late February as Russia launched its invasion of Ukraine, Dagalo and Ibrahim reportedly received assurances of increased co-operation in the oil and gas, mining, manufacturing and agriculture sectors.

POWER, TRANSPORT AND COMMUNICATIONS

Sudan's electricity sector has been beset by poor infrastructure, frequent outages and a small customer base. In 2019, according to the World Bank, 53.8% of the population had access to electricity. The Government has sought to increase capacity through various projects. The Merowe hydroelectric facility, with a generating capacity of 1,250 MW—far surpassing the total capacity previously recorded for the whole country—was inaugurated in 2009 and is located 250 miles north of

Khartoum at the River Nile's Fourth Cataract. In April 2010 a US $838m. contract was awarded to the China International Water and Electric Corpn and China Three Gorges Corpn for the construction of the Upper Atbara and Setit Dam Complex in eastern Sudan. Twin dams—the Rumela and the Burdana, both utilizing the Atbara river—with a combined generating capacity of 320 MW were inaugurated in February 2017; by this time the construction cost of the project had risen to $1,900m. Long-term plans by the Government to construct further large-scale dams, including the Kajbar, Dal and Shireik dams at cataracts of the River Nile, for which President al-Bashir secured Saudi funding in 2015, have not been realized. Environmental groups have protested strongly against the proposed projects, citing potential damage to the Nile's ecosystem and to the culture of the displaced Nubian residents of the area. In mid-October 2020 the Government signed a memorandum of understanding with General Electric to increase the country's power generation by 470 MW, which, according to the US firm, would deliver electricity to approximately another 600,000 households. According to Reuters, the project would entail the refurbishment of three existing power facilities and the installation of new mobile turbines, although financial details were not disclosed.

In late 2014 President al-Bashir announced plans to increase exploitation of Sudan's natural gas reserves, as well as incorporating a state-owned gas company, which would import supplies of gas, in part to boost power generation in the country. The move would help to reduce dependence on hydropower (which accounted for 78.3% of total output in 2014). At that stage, Sudan possessed gas reserves of 3,000,0000m. cu ft, but these were largely unexploited.

Although Sudan still depends heavily on railways for transport, the road network has played an increasingly important role since 1980. In 2000 there were some 11,900 km of roads and more than 48,000 km of tracks are classed as 'motorable'. In 2014 the total length of railways was 7,251 route-km. The main line runs from Wadi Halfa, on the Egyptian border, to al-Obeid, via Khartoum. Lines from Atbara and Sinnar connect with Port Sudan. There are lines from Sinnar to Damazin on the Blue Nile (227 km) and from Aradeiba to Nyala, in Darfur (689 km), with a 446-km branch line from Babanousa to Wau in Bahr El-Ghazal. In 2009 plans were announced for the construction of a 10,000-km transcontinental railway project linking Port Sudan with Dakar, Senegal.

Although Sudan has 4,068 km of navigable river, with 1,723 km open throughout the year, river transport has, until recently, been minimal. The most frequently used waterway is the 1,435-km section of the White Nile route between Karima and Dongola. Sudan Airways, the national carrier, is under the control of the Ministry of Transport and Infrastructure. In June 2005 the Government announced that the initial stages of construction work had been completed for a new international airport, 40 km south-west of the capital. The airport, the construction of which was to be funded through a preferential loan from the Export-Import Bank of China (according to a contract signed in July 2013), was to have the capacity eventually to receive 12m. passengers per year. In March 2018 the Turkish construction company Summa signed a US $1,150m. deal to build the airport, the first phase of which was scheduled to be completed by the end of 2022.

According to the International Telecommunication Union, there were 35.2m. mobile telephone subscribers in 2020. The market leader is the local subsidiary of Kuwait's Zain, while other operators include South Africa's MTN and the mobile telephone branch of local firm Sudatel (operating under the name Sudani). In 2020 Zain's revenue reached $416m., a rise of 37% year-on-year, and in that year the number of subscribers increased to 16.6m. In a bid significantly to bolster its fixed access and mobile services by 2020, Sudatel launched a trial in July 2018 with the Finnish telecommunications company Nokia of the provision of 4.5G, 4.9G and 5G technologies, initially focusing on Khartoum.

Statistical Survey

Sources (unless otherwise stated): Department of Statistics, Ministry of Finance and National Economy, POB 735, Khartoum; tel. (183) 777563; internet www.mof.gov.sd; Central Bureau of Statistics, POB 700, Khartoum; tel. (183) 777255; e-mail info@cbs.gov.sd; internet www.cbs.gov.sd; Central Bank of Sudan, Gamhoria St, POB 313, Khartoum; tel. (187) 056000; e-mail info@cbos.gov.sd; internet cbos.gov.sd.

Note: The Republic of South Sudan achieved independence from Sudan on 9 July 2011, following a referendum held in January at which voters overwhelmingly approved the secession of South Sudan. Unless otherwise indicated, data in this survey refer to pre-secession Sudan. For detailed statistical information on South Sudan, see separate chapter on that country.

Note: Data for South Sudan published by the Republic of South Sudan's National Bureau of Statistics (NBS) in 2011 indicated a residual post-secession total area of 1,861,484 sq km (718,724 sq miles) for Sudan (previously 2,505,813 sq km, equivalent to 967,500 sq miles). Of the total enumerated population of 39,154,490 at the time of the 2008 census, according to NBS estimates, 30,894,000 were estimated to be resident in areas not part of the secession state of South Sudan.

Mid–2022 (UN population projection): 45,992,018 (Source: UN, *World Population Prospects: The 2019 Revision*).

Area and Population

AREA, POPULATION AND DENSITY

Area (sq km)	1,861,484*
Population (census results)†	
1 February 1993	24,940,683
22 April 2008	
Males	20,073,977
Females	19,080,513
Total	39,154,490
Population (official projections at mid-year)	
2019	43,201,816
2020	44,433,485
2021	45,678,376
Density (per sq km) at mid-2021	24.5

* 718,723 sq miles; approximate figure (see Note).

† Figures for pre-secession Sudan; excluding adjustments for underenumeration, estimated to have been 6.7% in 1993.

POPULATION BY AGE AND SEX
('000, UN projections at mid-2022)

	Males	Females	Total
0–14 years	9,119.3	8,871.4	17,990.8
15–64 years	13,057.3	13,211.6	26,268.9
65 years and over	804.7	927.6	1,732.3
Total	22,981.4	23,010.7	45,992.0

Note: Totals may not be equal to the sum of components, owing to rounding.

Source: UN, *World Population Prospects: The 2019 Revision*.

STATES
(official projections at mid-2021)*

	Population
Blue Nile	1,205,908
Central Darfur	826,736
Eastern Darfur	1,570,210
Gadarif (Al-Qadarif)	2,402,682
Gezira (Al-Jazirah)	5,545,355
Kassala	2,740,702
Khartoum	8,697,162
Northern	1,018,628
Northern Darfur	2,507,743
Northern Kordofan	2,703,439
Red Sea	1,612,446
River Nile	1,644,421
Sennar (Sinnar)	2,087,501
Southern Darfur	4,253,782
Southern Kordofan	1,166,253
Western Darfur	1,105,458
Western Kordofan	1,876,655
White Nile	2,713,295
Total	45,678,376

* Population of states forming the Republic of Sudan following the secession of South Sudan in 2011. New states of Central Darfur and Eastern Darfur were created in 2012, and the state of Western Kordofan, abolished in 2005, was re-established in 2013, bringing the total to 18.

PRINCIPAL TOWNS
(population at 2008 census)

Omdurman	1,849,659	Kassala	298,529
Khartoum (capital)	1,410,858	Wad Madani	289,482
Khartoum North	1,012,211	Gedaref (El-Gadarif)	269,395
Nyala	492,984	El-Fasher	217,827
Port Sudan	394,561	Kosti	213,080
El-Obeid	345,126		

Mid-2021 (including suburbs, UN projections): Khartoum 5,989,024; Nyala 967,430; El-Obeid 495,283; Port Sudan 493,366; Wad Madani 383,456; Kassala 371,326; Gedaref (El–Gadarif) 365,632 (Source: UN, *World Urbanization Prospects: The 2018 Revision*).

BIRTHS AND DEATHS
(annual averages, UN estimates)

	2005–10	2010–15	2015–20
Birth rate (per 1,000)	36.6	34.4	32.4
Death rate (per 1,000)	8.6	7.7	7.2

Source: UN, *World Population Prospects: The 2019 Revision*.

Registered live births: 1,668,517 in 2015; 2,404,577 in 2016; 2,188,528 in 2017.

Registered deaths: 179,941 in 2016; 103,542 in 2017.

Life expectancy (years at birth, estimates): 65.5 (males 63.7; females 67.4) in 2020 (Source: World Bank, World Development Indicators database).

ECONOMICALLY ACTIVE POPULATION
('000, FAO estimates at mid-year)

	2013	2014	2015
Agriculture, etc.	6,025	6,088	6,153
Total labour force (incl. others)	12,394	12,785	13,200

Source: FAO.

Health and Welfare

KEY INDICATORS

Total fertility rate (children per woman, 2020)	4.3
Under-5 mortality rate (per 1,000 live births, 2020)	56.6
HIV/AIDS (% of persons aged 15–49, 2020)	0.2
COVID-19: Cumulative confirmed deaths (per 100,000 persons at 31 August 2022)	10.9
COVID-19: Fully vaccinated population (% of total population at 30 May 2022)	9.9
Physicians (per 1,000 head, 2017)	0.3
Hospital beds (per 1,000 head, 2017)	0.7
Domestic health expenditure (2019): US $ per head (PPP)	46.4
Domestic health expenditure (2019): % of GDP	1.0
Domestic health expenditure (2019): public (% of total current expenditure)	22.7
Access to improved water resources (% of persons, 2020)	60
Access to improved sanitation facilities (% of persons, 2020)	37
Total carbon dioxide emissions ('000 metric tons, 2020)	20,200
Carbon dioxide emissions per head (metric tons, 2020)	0.5
Human Development Index (2021): ranking	172
Human Development Index (2021): value	0.508

Note: For data on COVID-19 vaccinations, 'fully vaccinated' denotes receipt of all doses specified by approved vaccination regime (Sources: Johns Hopkins University and Our World in Data). Data on health expenditure refer to current general government expenditure in each case. For more information on sources and further definitions for all indicators, see Health and Welfare Statistics: Sources and Definitions section (europaworld.com/credits).

Agriculture

PRINCIPAL CROPS
(excl. South Sudan, '000 metric tons)

	2018	2019	2020
Aubergines (Eggplants)*	92	95	97
Bananas	913	919	924
Broad beans, dry	157	165	473
Canteloupes (incl. other melons)*	41	40	40
Carrots and turnips*	53	72	67
Chick peas	64	73	84
Cow peas, dry	175	161	148
Cucumbers and gherkins*	226	293	307
Dates	414	439	465
Garlic*	11	43	44
Grapefruits and pomelos	238	252	268
Groundnuts, with shell	2,884	2,828	2,773
Lemons and limes	309	324	341
Maize	46	25	14
Mangoes, mangosteens and guavas	656	663	670
Melonseed	129	93	71
Millet	2,647	1,133	485
Onions, dry*	1,717	1,919	1,950
Okra*	302	309	316
Oranges	160	166	173
Potatoes	440	466	494
Pumpkins, squash and gourds*	34	33	33
Rice, paddy	30	32	34
Seed cotton*	353	282	321
Sesame seed	960	1,210	1,525
Sorghum	5,435	3,714	2,538
Sugar cane	6,084†	5,449†	5,192*
Sunflower seed	108	107	106
Tomatoes*	648	677	692
Watermelons*	117	78	70
Wheat	702	726	751
Yams*	167	166	167

* FAO estimate(s).
† Unofficial figure.

Aggregate production ('000 metric tons, may include official, semi-official or estimated data): Total cereals 8,860 in 2018, 5,630 in 2019, 3,821 in 2020; Total fruit (primary) 3,163 in 2018, 3,192 in 2019, 3,263 in 2020; Total roots and tubers 851 in 2018, 886 in 2019, 924 in 2020; Total vegetables (primary) 3,435 in 2018, 3,799 in 2019, 3,868 in 2020.

Source: FAO.

LIVESTOCK

(excl. South Sudan, '000 head, year ending September)

	2018	2019	2020
Asses	7,609	7,620	7,632
Camels	4,872	4,895	4,918
Cattle	31,223	31,489	31,757
Chickens	49,294	50,015	50,747
Goats	31,837	32,032	32,228
Horses	792	792	793
Sheep	40,846	40,896	40,946

Source: FAO.

LIVESTOCK PRODUCTS

('000 metric tons)

	2018	2019	2020
Camel meat	145	146	147
Camels' milk	61	62	63
Cattle hides, fresh*	75	75	75
Cattle meat*	387	388	389
Cattle offals, edible* . . .	64	64	65
Cows' milk	2,965	2,988	3,011
Chicken meat	70	75	80
Goat meat	119	120	121
Goats' milk	1,151	1,158	1,165
Sheep meat	264	265	266
Sheep's (Ewe's) milk . . .	414	415	416
Sheepskins, fresh*	40	40	40
Hen eggs	65	70	75

* FAO estimates.

Source: FAO.

Forestry

ROUNDWOOD REMOVALS

('000 cubic metres, FAO estimates)

	2017	2018	2019
Sawlogs, veneer logs and logs for sleepers	360	360	360
Pulpwood	301	301	301
Other industrial wood	496	496	496
Fuel wood	15,417	15,526	15,583
Total	16,574	16,683	16,740

2020: Production assumed to be unchanged from 2019 (FAO estimates).
Source: FAO.

SAWNWOOD PRODUCTION

(cubic metres, incl. railway sleepers)

	2012	2013	2014
Total (all broadleaved) . . .	32,000	28,000	11,000

2015–20: Production assumed to be unchanged from 2014 (FAO estimates).
Source: FAO.

Fishing

('000 metric tons, live weight)

	2018	2019*	2020*
Capture	41.0	40.7	37.7
Nile tilapia	25.0	25.0	23.0
Other freshwater fishes . .	13.0	13.0	12.0
Marine fishes	2.9	2.6	2.5
Aquaculture	10.0	10.1	9.9
Total catch	51.0	50.8	47.5

* FAO estimates.

Source: FAO.

Mining

('000 metric tons unless otherwise stated)

	2016	2017	2018
Crude petroleum ('000 barrels) .	37,960	34,675	36,500
Salt (unrefined)	223.4	235.0	267.0
Chromite	15.0	32.0	27.0
Gold ore (kilograms)*	93,400	107,300	93,600

* Figures refer to the metal content of ores.

Source: US Geological Survey.

Industry

PETROLEUM PRODUCTS

(metric tons)

	2016	2017	2018
Motor spirit (petrol)	16,660	9,037	7,865
Naphtha	94	33	75
Jet fuels	1,247	658	304
Kerosene	85	57	78
Gas-diesel (distillate fuel) oils .	10,168	11,517	12,810
Residual fuel oils	1,957	1,753	1,848

Source: US Geological Survey.

SELECTED OTHER PRODUCTS

('000 metric tons unless otherwise stated)

	2014	2015	2016
Wheat flour	1,957	2,000	2,126
Raw sugar	n.a.	591	601
Cement	3,478	3,708	4,013
Electrical energy (million kWh) .	11,505	13,171	14,558

Electrical energy (million kWh): 15,679 in 2017; 16,395 in 2018; 17,024 in 2019.

Sources: UN Industrial Commodity Statistics Database; UN Energy Statistics Database.

Finance

CURRENCY AND EXCHANGE RATES

Monetary Units
100 piastres = 1 new Sudanese pound (SDG).

Sterling, Dollar and Euro Equivalents (31 May 2021)
£1 sterling = 595.152 new Sudanese pounds;
US $1 = 421.347 new Sudanese pounds;
€1 = 514.085 new Sudanese pounds;
1,000 new Sudanese pounds = £1.68 = $2.37 = €1.95.

Average Exchange Rate (new Sudanese pounds per US $)
2018   24.3289
2019   45.7670
2020   53.9960

Note: On 1 March 1999 the Sudanese pound (£S) was replaced by the Sudanese dinar (SDD), equivalent to £S10. The pound was withdrawn from circulation on 31 July 1999. A new Sudanese pound (SDG), equivalent to 100 dinars (and 1,000 old pounds) was introduced on 10 January 2007. The new currency was to circulate along with previous currencies (the old pound had continued to circulate in some regions) for a transitional period, but became the sole legal tender on 1 July 2007.

CENTRAL GOVERNMENT BUDGET
('000 million new Sudanese pounds)

Revenue*	2019	2020†	2021†
Oil revenue	26.7	59.7	184.0
Non-oil revenue	123.1	178.6	978.2
Taxes	110.5	157.8	925.3
Other revenue	12.7	20.8	52.9
Total	149.8	238.3	1,162.2

Expenditure	2019	2020†	2021†
Current expenditure	375.9	596.7	1,710.1
Wages	58.4	226.8	527.2
Goods and services	20.7	45.0	104.6
Interest	3.6	0.4	3.8
Subsidies	239.9	168.2	222.9
Fuel	214.0	100.6	69.3
Transfers	35.1	55.6	444.2
Other current expenditure . .	18.3	100.7	407.3
Capital expenditure	2.9	16.0	104.8
Total	378.8	612.7	1,814.9

*Excluding grants totalling ('000 million new Sudanese pounds): 9.4 in 2019; 66.4 in 2020 (projection); 285.5 in 2021 (projection).
† Projections.

Source: IMF, *Sudan: Staff-Monitored Program—Press Release; Staff Report; and Statement by the Executive Director for Sudan* (October 2020).

INTERNATIONAL RESERVES
(US $ million at 31 December)

	2008	2009	2010
IMF special drawing rights . .	—	197.2	193.5
Foreign exchange	1,399.0	897.0	842.8
Total	1,399.0	1,094.2	1,036.2

IMF special drawing rights: 171.3 in 2019; 178.2 in 2020; 1,080.5 in 2021.

Source: IMF, *International Financial Statistics.*

MONEY SUPPLY
(million new Sudanese pounds at 31 December)

	2019	2020	2021
Currency outside depository corporations	281,336	556,672	905,706
Transferable deposits	192,053	352,592	1,142,273
Other deposits	216,209	387,120	1,249,642
Broad money	689,598	1,296,384	3,297,620

Source: IMF, *International Financial Statistics.*

COST OF LIVING
(Consumer Price Index for middle income group; base: 2007 = 100)

	2016	2017	2018
Food and beverages	570.6	770.5	1,310.7
Clothing and footwear	808.5	952.0	1,393.2
Housing	357.9	413.3	500.5
All items (incl. others) . . .	591.7	783.2	1,278.8

All items: 2,339.2 in 2019; 8,639.4 in 2020; 36,131.1 in 2021.

NATIONAL ACCOUNTS
(million new Sudanese pounds at current prices)

Expenditure on the Gross Domestic Product

	2018	2019	2020
Government final consumption expenditure	91,159	127,626	620,891
Private final consumption expenditure	1,010,751	1,427,665	2,666,661
Gross capital formation . .	185,581	200,406	168,476
Total domestic expenditure	1,287,491	1,755,696	3,456,028
Exports of goods and services . .	71,182	136,149	171,563
Less Imports of goods and services	182,043	284,550	161,672
GDP in purchasers' values .	1,176,630	1,607,295	3,350,851
GDP at constant 2015 prices	563,775	570,953	562,034

Gross Domestic Product by Economic Activity

	2018	2019	2020
Agriculture, hunting, forestry and fishing	252,975	324,774	717,098
Mining, quarrying and utilities .	113,277	160,261	303,215
Manufacturing	128,846	134,026	287,877
Construction	39,127	57,484	110,218
Wholesale and retail trade, restaurants and hotels . . .	191,277	265,403	592,293
Transport, storage and communication	105,624	142,033	291,499
Other services	345,503	523,313	1,033,812
GDP in purchasers' values .	1,176,630	1,607,295	3,350,851

Source: UN National Accounts Main Aggregates Database.

BALANCE OF PAYMENTS
(US $ million)

	2018	2019	2020
Exports of goods	3,484.7	3,734.7	3,802.6
Imports of goods	−7,065.1	−8,361.5	−8,853.9
Balance on goods	−3,580.4	−4,626.8	−5,051.3
Exports of services	1,511.0	1,366.6	1,262.9
Imports of services	−1,172.2	−1,425.4	−1,665.7
Balance on goods and services	−3,241.6	−4,685.6	−5,454.2
Other income received	127.1	101.9	61.3
Other income paid	−1,939.5	−1,722.0	−1,534.5
Balance on goods, services and primary income	−5,053.9	−6,305.7	−6,927.4
Secondary income received . .	890.5	2,001.9	1,511.6
Secondary income paid . . .	−515.1	−476.0	−425.4
Current balance	−4,678.5	−4,779.8	−5,841.2
Capital account (net)	162.9	188.2	143.6
Direct investment liabilities . .	1,135.8	825.4	716.9
Portfolio investment assets . .	1.0	−36.4	−13.9
Other investment assets . . .	−395.2	−736.2	−911.4
Other investment liabilities . .	305.8	2,115.9	2,712.8
Net errors and omissions . . .	1,547.4	642.7	1,211.4
Reserves and related items .	−1,920.8	−1,780.2	−1,979.2

Source: IMF, *International Financial Statistics.*

External Trade

PRINCIPAL COMMODITIES
(US $ million)

Imports c.i.f.	2019	2020	2021*
Foodstuffs	2,141.4	2,685.7	1,924.7
Wheat	1,085.8	916.9	542.0
Sugar	335.1	749.4	486.2
Raw materials	1,997.1	1,482.9	1,812.4
Petroleum products	1,791.7	1,250.3	1,626.5
Chemicals and related products	969.0	883.4	1,006.9
Medicinal and pharmaceutical products	367.2	339.9	489.3
Textiles and related products .	389.3	500.8	468.0
Basic manufactures . . .	1,550.1	1,904.0	1,546.2
Iron and steel	534.0	728.1	333.9
Machinery and electrical equipment	1,398.8	1,518.6	1,602.1
Non-electrical appliances . . .	340.8	353.4	386.8
Electrical appliances . . .	281.1	322.3	351.6
Spare parts for machinery . .	83.3	51.1	48.2
Transport equipment . . .	752.0	744.5	715.0
Motor cars	145.6	122.5	140.1
Trucks and lorries	188.8	108.9	110.6
Total (incl. others)	9,290.5	9,837.7	9,237.9

Exports f.o.b.	2019	2020	2021*
Sesame products	771.6	788.7	508.6
Cotton	160.8	168.0	164.9
Gum Arabic	109.5	104.3	110.6
Crude petroleum	474.1	44.9	—
Benzene	44.8	9.8	—
Gold	989.1	1,480.4	2,063.2
Total (incl. others)	3,734.7	3,802.6	4,279.0

* Provisional.

Source: Central Bank of Sudan, Khartoum.

PRINCIPAL TRADING PARTNERS
(US $ million)

Imports c.i.f.	2019	2020	2021*
China, People's Republic . . .	1,801.6	2,317.4	2,226.8
Egypt	496.3	535.2	810.6
Germany	231.3	225.1	141.5
India	682.4	985.9	813.3
Indonesia	139.7	155.6	112.2
Japan	157.0	192.1	177.8
Jordan	106.2	63.8	101.8
Korea, Republic	114.3	138.2	131.1
Oman	64.4	21.2	38.8
Russian Federation	809.7	733.0	220.4
Saudi Arabia	1,000.5	910.8	491.6
Thailand	202.6	182.0	44.7
Türkiye	291.4	362.3	315.1
Ukraine	160.2	108.3	37.6
United Arab Emirates	1,441.0	1,061.6	1,657.9
United Kingdom	75.2	86.8	94.4
Total (incl. others)	9,290.5	9,837.7	9,237.9

Exports f.o.b.	2019	2020	2021*
China, People's Republic . . .	747.7	752.3	614.9
Egypt	366.2	363.8	496.4
Ethiopia	53.1	36.2	43.8
France	56.7	52.7	47.2
India	682.4	158.7	87.0
Pakistan	43.1	49.2	39.5
Saudi Arabia	510.1	284.9	365.3
Türkiye	291.4	93.6	86.7
United Arab Emirates	1,067.0	1,637.5	2,203.1
Total (incl. others)	3,734.7	3,802.6	4,279.0

* Provisional.

Source: Central Bank of Sudan, Khartoum.

Transport

RAILWAY TRAFFIC

	2007	2008	2009
Passengers carried ('000) . . .	51	91	87
Passenger-km (million) . . .	50	67	62
Freight carried ('000 metric tons) .	1,091	1,033	907
Freight ton-km (million) . . .	781	919	800

Passengers carried ('000): 188.0 in 2014; 179.4 in 2015; 210.9 in 2016.

SHIPPING
Flag Registered Fleet
(at 31 December)

	2019	2020	2021
Number of vessels	12	12	14
Total displacement (grt) . . .	12,802	12,802	12,927

Source: Lloyd's List Intelligence (www.bit.ly/LLintelligence).

CIVIL AVIATION
(traffic on scheduled services)

	2013	2014	2015
Kilometres flown (million) . .	13	10	9
Passengers carried ('000) . . .	542	502	496
Passenger-km (million) . .	931	888	887
Total ton-km (million)	12	12	13

Source: UN, *Statistical Yearbook*.

2020 (domestic and international): Departures 2,261; Passengers carried 386,838 (Source: World Bank, World Development Indicators database).

Tourism

	2017	2018	2019
Foreign visitor arrivals . . .	812,000	836,000	n.a.
Tourism receipts (US $ million, excl. passenger transport) . .	1,029	1,043	821*

* Provisional.

Source: World Tourism Organization.

Communications Media

	2018	2019	2020
Telephones (main lines in use) .	136,923	137,842	129,408
Mobile telephone subscriptions ('000)	30,100.4	33,014.2	35,195.2
Broadband subscriptions, fixed .	31,352	32,762	28,782
Broadband subscriptions, mobile ('000)	13,557.4	16,241.1	18,565.7
Internet users (% of population)* .	24.6	25.9	28.4

* Estimates.

Source: International Telecommunication Union.

Education

(2017/18 unless otherwise stated)

			Students		
	Institutions*	Teachers	Males	Females	Total
Pre-primary .	5,984	38,046	557,387	542,266	1,099,653
Primary . .	11,982	169,408†	2,684,198	2,433,942	5,118,140
Secondary . .	3,512	50,632†	1,110,665	1,105,597	2,216,262
Universities, etc‡. . .	n.a.	13,102	327,599	325,489	653,088

* Figures refer to 1998.
† Figure refer to 2012/13.
‡ Figures refer to 2014/15.

Source: UNESCO Institute for Statistics.

Pupil-teacher ratio (primary education, UNESCO estimate): 25.3 in 2012/13 (Source: UNESCO Institute for Statistics).

Adult literacy rate (UNESCO estimates): 60.7% (males 65.4%; females 56.1%) in 2018 (Source: UNESCO Institute for Statistics).

Directory

The Constitution

Following the removal from power of President Omar Hassan Ahmad al-Bashir in April 2019, the Constitution of Sudan was suspended by the Transitional Military Council (TMC), which initially assumed power. The TMC was replaced by a Sovereign Council on 20 August, prior to which, on 17 August, a Constitutional Declaration had been signed. This document formalized the transition process and also stipulated that a 300-member legislative assembly, comprising 201 lawmakers selected by the Forces of Freedom and Change (FFC), with the remainder allocated to other political groups (none with links to al-Bashir), be installed within 90 days. The Sovereign Council comprised five members from the military nominated by the TMC, five civilian members nominated by the FFC and one other civilian member jointly chosen by the TMC and the FFC. In July 2020 Prime Minister Abdalla Hamdok appointed 18 civilian state governors. Following the signing of the Juba Peace Agreement by the Transitional Government and the Darfur rebel groups in October, the Sovereign Council was expanded to 14 members in March 2021 through the allocation of three new posts to representatives of the rebel groups.

The Government

HEAD OF STATE

Chairman of the Sovereign Council: Gen. ABDEL FATTAH AL-BURHAN ABDELRAHMAN (sworn in 21 August 2019).

SOVEREIGN COUNCIL
(October 2022)

On 11 April 2019 President Field Marshall Omar Hassan Ahmad al-Bashir was deposed in a military coup. A Transitional Military Council (TMC), initially led by Lt-Gen. Awad Mohamed Ahmed Ibn Auf, assumed power and dissolved the Council of Ministers and dismissed the State Governors. On 12 April Ibn Auf resigned as Chairman of the TMC and on the following day he was replaced by Gen. Abdel Fattah al-Burhan Abdelrahman. Following the signing of a power-sharing agreement between the TMC and the Forces of Freedom and Change (FFC, an alliance of protest groups and opposition parties), the former was replaced by a new, 11-member Sovereign Council on 20 August. The Sovereign Council comprised five members from the military nominated by the TMC, five civilian members nominated by the FFC and one other civilian member jointly chosen by the TMC and the FFC. Abdelrahman was to hold the chairmanship of the Sovereign Council for the first 21 months of a 39-month transitional period, following which a civilian member was to hold the chairmanship for the remaining 18 months. A Transitional Government was sworn in on 8 September. Following the conclusion of a peace agreement in October 2020 between the Transitional Government and the Darfur rebel groups, on 7 March 2021 a further three individuals, representing the rebel groups, were sworn in to the Sovereign Council, increasing its size to 14 members. On 25 October

Abdelrahman announced the dissolution of the Transitional Government and it was reported that the Prime Minister, Abdalla Hamdok, had been detained, along with the civilian members of the Sovereign Council. On 11 November Abdelrahman reformed the Sovereign Council, replacing all but one of the previous civilian members, and on 21 November Adelrahman and Hamdok signed an agreement which provided for the latter's reinstatement as Prime Minister. Representatives from the FFC who had served as ministers in the outgoing Transitional Government formally resigned their posts on 23 November stating that the agreement 'legitimized and perpetuated the military coup regime'. On 2 January 2022 Hamdok announced his resignation.

Chairman of the Sovereign Council: Lt-Gen. ABDEL FATTAH AL-BURHAN ABDELRAHMAN.

Additional Members: Gen. MOHAMED HAMDAN DAGALO (Vice-Chairman), Gen. SHAMS AL-DIN KHABBASHI, Lt-Gen. YASSER ABDEL-RAHMAN AL-ATTA, Lt-Gen. IBRAHIM JABIR IBRAHIM, MALIK AGAR EYRE, AL-TAHIR ABUBAKR HAJAR, AL-HADI IDRISS YAHYA, RAJA NICOLA ABDELMASIH, YUSUF GAD-KARIM MOHAMED ALI, ABDULGASSIM MOHAMED MOHAMED AHMED, ABDELBAGI ABDELGADIR AL-ZUBAIR, SALMA ABDELJABBAR AL-MUBARAK MUSA.

TRANSITIONAL GOVERNMENT
(October 2022)

Prime Minister: (vacant).

Minister of Cabinet Affairs: OSMAN HUSSEIN OSMAN (acting).

Minister of Defence: Lt.-Gen. (retd) YASSIN IBRAHIM YASSIN.

Minister of the Interior: Lt-Gen. EZZ EL-DIN AL-SHEIKH.

Minister of Foreign Affairs: ALI SADIQ ALI (acting).

Minister of Justice: (vacant).

Minister of Federal Government: Dr BUTHAINA IBRAHIM DINAR.

Minister of Finance and Economic Planning: Dr GIBRIL IBRAHIM MUHAMMAD.

Minister of Agriculture and Forestry: Dr ABU-BAKR OMER AL-BUSHRA (acting).

Minister of Trade and Supply: Dr AMAL SALEH SAAD (acting).

Minister of Industry: BATUL ABBAS ALLAM AWAD (acting).

Minister of Energy and Petroleum: MOHAMMED ABDULLAH MAHMOUD (acting).

Minister of Minerals: Dr MOHAMED BASHIR ABUNMO.

Minister of Irrigation and Water Resources: DHU AL-BAYT ABDUL RAHMAN MANSOUR (acting).

Minister of Livestock: HAFEZ IBRAHIM ABDEL NABI.

Minister of Transport: (vacant).

Minister of Urban Development, Roads and Bridges: ABU-BAKR ABU AL-QASIM ABDULLAH (acting).

Minister of Communication and Digital Transformation: ADEL HASSAN MOHAMMED HUSSEIN (acting).

SUDAN

Minister of Investment and International Co-operation: AHLAM MADANI MAHDI (acting).

Minister of Education: MAHMOUD SIR AL-KHATIM AL-HOURI (acting).

Minister of Higher Education and Scientific Research: Prof. MOHAMMED HASSAN DAHB (acting).

Minister of Health: HAITHAM MOHAMMED IBRAHIM (acting).

Minister of Labour and Administrative Reform: SUAD TAYEB HASSAN (acting).

Minister of Social Development: AHMED ADAM BAKHEET.

Minister of Religious Affairs and Endowments: BDEL ATI AHMED ABBAS (acting).

Minister of Culture and Information: GARAM ADBEL KADER (acting).

Minister of Youth and Sports: AYMAN SAYED SALIM (acting).

MINISTRIES

Office of the President: Khartoum; internet www.presidency.gov.sd.

Ministry of Agriculture and Natural Resources: University St, POB 285, Khartoum; tel. (183) 780951; e-mail info@moaf.gov.sd; internet moaf.gov.sd.

Ministry of Cabinet Affairs: POB 931, Khartoum; tel. (183) 784205; e-mail info@sudan.gov.sd; internet www.sudan.gov.sd/index.php/ar.

Ministry of Culture and Information: Algamaa St, Khartoum; tel. 120340075; e-mail culturesudan59@gmail.com; internet moc.gov.sd.

Ministry of Defence: POB 371, Khartoum; tel. (183) 774910; internet fb.com/sudanese.ministry.of.defence.

Ministry of Education: Nile St, Khartoum; tel. 913118982; e-mail info@moe.gov.sd; internet moe.gov.sd.

Ministry of Energy and Petroleum: Africa St, POB 2087, Khartoum; tel. (183) 776684; e-mail info@mopg.gov.sd; internet mop.gov.sd.

Ministry of Federal Government: Khartoum.

Ministry of Finance and Economic Planning: POB 735, Khartoum; tel. (183) 777672; e-mail info@mof.gov.sd; internet www.mof.gov.sd.

Ministry of Foreign Affairs: University St, POB 873, Khartoum; tel. (183) 772756; e-mail mfaweb@mofa.gov.sd.

Ministry of Health: Nile St, POB 303, Khartoum; tel. 917047000; e-mail info@fmoh.gov.sd; internet www.fmoh.gov.sd.

Ministry of Higher Education and Scientific Research: POB 2081, Khartoum; tel. (183) 779312; e-mail info@mohe.gov.sd; internet mohe.gov.sd.

Ministry of Industry: Khartoum; internet fb.com/SudanMOI.

Ministry of the Interior: POB 2793, Khartoum; tel. (183) 776554; internet www.moi.gov.sd.

Ministry of Irrigation and Water Resources: Nile St, POB 878, Khartoum; tel. (183) 773838; e-mail info@wre.gov.sd; internet wre.gov.sd.

Ministry of Justice: Tower of Justice, Al-Gomhoria St, POB 302, Khartoum; tel. (183) 4567890; internet www.moj.gov.sd.

Ministry of Labour and Administrative Reform: Khartoum.

Ministry of Livestock: Kalakleh St, POB 293, Khartoum; tel. (155) 660723; e-mail info@mar.gov.sd; internet mar.gov.sd.

Ministry of Religious Affairs and Endowments: Khartoum; e-mail info@mraa.gov.sd; internet mraa.gov.sd.

Ministry of Social Development: Khartoum.

Ministry of Trade and Supply: Khartoum.

Ministry of Transport and Infrastructure: Khartoum.

Ministry of Youth and Sports: Khartoum.

STATE GOVERNORS
(October 2022)

Blue Nile: AHMED AL-OMDA.

Central Darfur: SAAD BABIKIR.

East Darfur: MOHAMED ADAM.

Gadarif: MOHAMED ABDELRAHMAN MAHGOUB.

Gezira: ISMAIL AWADALLA AL-AGEEB (acting).

Kassala: KHOGALI HAMAD ABDALLA.

Khartoum: AHMED OSMAN HAMZA (acting).

Northern: AL-BAQIR AHMED ALI (acting).

North Darfur: HAFEZ BAKHEET (acting).

North Kordofan: FADLALLAH EL-TOM.

Red Sea: ALI ABDALLA ADAROB.

River Nile: MUHAMMAD AL-BADAWI ABU GUROON.

Sennar: IBRAHIM AL-NOUR.

South Darfur: HAMID EL-TIJANI HANOON.

South Kordofan: MOUSA JABUR.

West Darfur: KHAMIS ABDALLA ABAKAR.

West Kordofan: KHALED JEILI.

White Nile: OMER AL-KHALIFA.

In accordance with the Juba Peace Agreement of 3 October 2020, on 10 August 2021 Minni Minawi was sworn in as Governor of the Darfur region (having been appointed to the post by presidential decree on 29 April).

President

Election, 13–16 April 2015

Candidate	Votes	% of votes
Omar Hassan Ahmad al-Bashir (National Congress Party)	5,252,478	94.05
Fadul Al Sayed Isa Shuaib (Federal Truth Party)	79,779	1.43
Prof. Fatima Abdul Mahmoud (Sudanese Socialist Party)	47,653	0.85
Mohamed Al Hassan Mohamed (National Reform Party)	42,399	0.76
Abdul Mahmoud Abdul Jabar Rahamtalla (Union of the Nation's Forces)	41,134	0.74
Others*	121,420	2.17
Total	5,584,863	100.00

* There were 11 other candidates.

National Legislature

NATIONAL ASSEMBLY

National Assembly: POB 14416, Khartoum; tel. (187) 558537; e-mail info@parliament.gov.sd; internet www.parliament.gov.sd.

Speaker: Prof. IBRAHIM AHMED OMER.

Election, 13–16 April 2015

Party	Seats*
National Congress Party	323
Democratic Unionist Party—Original	25
Independents	19
Democratic Unionist Party—Jalal al-Digair	15
Federal Umma Party	7
Umma Party—Collective Leadership	6
Hizb ut-Tahrir	5
Umma Reform and Renewal Party	5
Others	21
Total	426

* 213 of the 426 members of the National Assembly were directly elected in single-seat constituencies; 85 'party members' were elected on the basis of proportional representation at the state level from separate and closed party lists; and a further 128 women members were elected on the basis of proportional representation at the state level from separate and closed party lists.

COUNCIL OF STATES

Council of States: Khartoum; tel. (187) 577931; e-mail info@councils.gov.sd; internet www.councilofstates.gov.sd.

Speaker: Dr OMER SULEIMAN ADAM.

Election Commission

National Election Commission (NEC): Al-Taef, Al-Nakhel St, Khartoum; tel. (183) 520282; internet nec.org.sd; Chair. Prof. MUKHTAR MUHAMMAD MUKHTAR AL-ASAM; Sec.-Gen. Dr JALAL MOHAMED AHMED.

Political Organizations

Democratic Unionist Party (DUP): Khartoum; Leader MUHAMMAD OSMAN AL-MIRGHANI.

Moderate Trend Party: Khartoum; Leader MAHMUD JIHA.

Muslim Brotherhood: Khartoum; Islamist fundamentalist; Leader Dr HABIR NUR AL-DIN.

New National Democratic Party: Leader MUNEER SHEIKH EL-DIN JALAB.

Popular Congress Party (PCP): Khartoum; internet fb.com/popularcongress; f. 2000; Sec.-Gen. Dr BASHIR ADAM RAHMA (acting).

Sudanese Communist Party (SCP): Khartoum; tel. 121058001; e-mail almidan@sudancp.com; internet sudancp.com; f. 1946; Political Sec. MOHAMED ELKHATIB.

Sudanese Socialist Democratic Union (SSDU): Leader (vacant).

Umma National Party (UNP): internet www.umma.org; f. 1945; Mahdist party based on the Koran and Islamic traditions; Chair. Dr UMAR NUR AL-DA'IM; Interim Leader FADLALLAH BURMA NASSER.

Umma Reform and Development Party: Khartoum; f. 2002; Chair. IBRAHIM ADAM IBRAHIM.

Union of Sudan African Parties (USAP): f. 1987; Chair. JOSEPH OKELLO; Sec.-Gen. Prof. AJANG BIOR.

United Democratic Salvation Front (UDSF): Khartoum; political wing of the Sudan People's Defence Force; Chair. Dr GABRIEL CHANGSON CHANG.

Diplomatic Representation

EMBASSIES IN SUDAN

Algeria: Blvd El-Mechtel Eriad, POB 80, Khartoum; tel. (183) 234773; Ambassador MUNAWAR RABEI.

Bahrain: Khartoum; tel. (155) 159895; e-mail khartoum.mission@mofa.gov.bh; internet mofa.gov.bh/Khartoum; Ambassador ABDULLAH RABIA SAEED RABIA.

Brazil: St 57, Block 40, Sq 11/F East, New Extension, al-Amarat, POB 8255, 12217 Khartoum; tel. (183) 217079; e-mail brasemb.cartum@itamaraty.gov.br; internet www.gov.br/mre/pt-br/embaixada-cartum; Ambassador PATRÍCIA MARIA OLIVEIRA LIMA DO NASCIMENTO PEDRO.

Canada: 29 Africa Rd, Block 56, POB 10503, Khartoum; tel. (156) 550500; e-mail khrtm@international.gc.ca; internet www.canadainternational.gc.ca/sudan-soudan; Ambassador PHILIP LUPUL.

Central African Republic: House No. 69, Block 344, El Maamura, Khartoum; tel. (183) 259003; e-mail carembassy.sd@yahoo.fr; Ambassador ABDUL RAHIM ABDALLA.

Chad: St 57, al-Amarat, POB 1514, Khartoum; tel. (183) 471084; Ambassador ABDELKERIM KOIBORO ONY.

China, People's Republic: Doha St, Al-Manshia, POB 1425, Khartoum; tel. (183) 272730; e-mail chinaemb_sd@mfa.gov.cn; internet sd.china-embassy.gov.cn; Ambassador MA XINMIN.

Congo, Democratic Republic: Riyadh Mashtal, Block 8, Salaam St 145, POB 10300, Khartoum; tel. (183) 471125; e-mail ambardc_khartoum@yahoo.fr; Chargé d'affaires a.i. BAWAN MUZURI.

Djibouti: Block 22, Bldg 493, Al-Salaam, Khartoum; tel. (183) 251950; Ambassador ISSA KHAIREH ROBLEH.

Egypt: al-Mugran, University St, POB 1126, Khartoum; tel. (183) 777646; internet www.mfa.gov.eg/khartoum_emb; Ambassador HOSSAM ISSA.

Eritrea: St 39, House No. 26, Riyadh District, POB 11618, Khartoum 2; tel. (183) 521000; e-mail erenainsudan@yahoo.com; Ambassador ISA AHMED ISA.

Ethiopia: Amarat Mohamed Nejib St 11, Block 9/10G, POB 844, Khartoum South; tel. (123) 177522; e-mail ethioembassysudan@gmail.com; internet fb.com/ethioembassysudan; Ambassador YIBELTAL AEMERO.

France: al-Amarat, St 13, Plot No. 11, Block 12, POB 377, 11111 Khartoum; tel. (183) 471082; e-mail cad.khartoum-amba@diplomatie.gouv.fr; internet sd.ambafrance.org; Ambassador RAJA RABIA.

Germany: Riverside Apartment C7, Plot No. 12/13, Bahri, Helat Hamad Kafouri Estate, POB 970, Khartoum; tel. 912301115; e-mail info@khartum.diplo.de; internet khartum.diplo.de; Ambassador THOMAS TERSTEGEN.

Holy See: Kafouri Belgravia, POB 623, Khartoum (Apostolic Nunciature); tel. (183) 330037; e-mail kanuap@yahoo.it; Apostolic Nuncio LUÍS MIGUEL MUÑOZ CÁRDABA (Titular Archbishop of Nasai).

India: Plot No. 2, al-Amarat St 01, Block 12DH, Eastern Extension, POB 707, Khartoum 2; tel. (183) 574001; e-mail amb.khartoum@mea.gov.in; internet www.eoikhartoum.gov.in/index.php; Ambassador B. S. MUBARAK.

Indonesia: Plot No. 14, St 60, Block No. 12, Al Riyadh Area, POB 13374, Khartoum; tel. (183) 527417; e-mail khartoum.kbri@kemlu.go.id; internet www.kemlu.go.id/khartoum; Ambassador SUNARKO.

Iran: Sq. 15, House No. 4, Moghren, POB 10229, Khartoum; tel. (183) 781490; Ambassador SHABIB JURIJARI (expelled Jan. 2016).

Iraq: Sharia al-Shareef al-Hindi, POB 1969, Khartoum; tel. (183) 271866; internet www.mofa.gov.iq/khartoum; Ambassador HUSSEIN AL-AMIRI.

Italy: St 39, Block 61, Khartoum 2, POB 793, Khartoum; tel. (183) 471615; e-mail ambasciata.khartoum@esteri.it; internet ambkhartoum.esteri.it/ambasciata_khartoum/it; Ambassador MICHELE TOMMASI (designate).

Japan: St 43, House No. 67, POB 1649, Khartoum; tel. (183) 471601; e-mail contact@kt.mofa.go.jp; internet www.sdn.emb-japan.go.jp; Ambassador TAKASHI HATTORI.

Jordan: Block 117, Home No. 40, Jazar St, al-Riyadh, POB 1379, Khartoum; tel. (183) 522290; e-mail khartoum@fm.gov.jo; internet mfa.jo/Khartoum/contents/Embassy; Ambassador Dr SAYID KHALID AL-RADAIDA.

Kenya: Plot No. 516, Block 1, West Giraif, St 60, POB 8242, Khartoum; tel. (155) 772800; e-mail kenemb@yahoo.com; internet khartoum.mfa.go.ke; Ambassador Maj.-Gen. (retd) NGEWA MUKALA.

Korea, Republic: House No. 55, Al-Jazira St 56, POB 2414, Khartoum; tel. (183) 580031; e-mail sudan@mofa.go.kr; internet overseas.mofa.go.kr/sd-ko/index.do; Ambassador LEE SANG-JEONG.

Kuwait: Riyadh District, Omak St, No. 94, Block 9, POB 1457, Khartoum; tel. (183) 773184; e-mail alkhartoum@mofa.gov.kw; Ambassador Dr FAHAD AL-DHAFIRI.

Lebanon: St 5, Al-Amarat, Block 11, POB 1407, Khartoum; tel. (183) 461320; e-mail amlebanonsoudan@gmail.com; Ambassador DEEMA HADAD.

Libya: Riyadh District, Block 18, POB 1526, Khartoum; tel. (183) 222457; Chargé d'affaires ALI MUFTAH MAHROUG.

Malaysia: Petronas Sudan Complex, Plot No. 13, Block 7, Nile Ave, POB 11150, Khartoum; tel. (156) 556400; e-mail mwkhartoum@kln.gov.my; internet www.kln.gov.my/web/sdn_khartoum/home; Ambassador MOHAMAD RAZDAN JAMIL.

Mauritania: House No. 4/75, Block 1, West Gereif, Khartoum; tel. (183) 269128; Ambassador MOHAMED MAHFOUDH OULD YAHYA OULD CHEIKH EL-GHADI.

Morocco: St 19, House No. 32, New Extension, POB 2042, Khartoum; tel. (183) 473068; Ambassador MOHAMED MAA AL-AINAIN.

Netherlands: St 47, House No. 76, Khartoum; tel. (156) 559990; e-mail kha-ca@minbuza.nl; internet www.netherlandsworldwide.nl/countries/sudan; Ambassador IRMA VAN DUEREN.

Nigeria: St 17, Sharia al-Mek Nimr, POB 1538, Khartoum; tel. (183) 770148; e-mail nigeriankhartoum@yahoo.com; internet nigeriaembassysudan.com; Ambassador SAFIU OLUKAYODE OLANIYAN.

Norway: St 49, House No. 63, POB 13096, Khartoum; tel. (183) 188100; e-mail emb.khartoum@mfa.no; internet www.norway.no/sudan; Ambassador THERESA LØKEN GHEZIEL.

Oman: St 1, New Extension, POB 2839, Khartoum; tel. (183) 471606; e-mail khartoum@mofa.gov.om; Ambassador ALI BIN SULAIMAN BIN SAID AL-DARMAKI.

Pakistan: Building No. 108, Block No. 1/E, East Khartoum, Doha Road, Al Manshiya, POB 1178, Khartoum; tel. 999818440; e-mail pakembkhartoum@gmail.com; internet fb.com/PakinSudan; Ambassador MEER BEHROSE REGI.

Qatar: Al-Manshia Block 92H, POB 223, Khartoum; tel. (183) 261113; e-mail khartoum@mofa.gov.qa; internet khartoum.embassy.qa; Ambassador ABDULRAHMAN ALI RABIAH AL-AJAJ AL-KUBAISI.

Romania: Kassala Rd, Plot No. 172–173, Kafouri Area, POB 1494, Khartoum North; tel. (185) 338114; e-mail khartoum@mae.ro; internet khartoum.mae.ro; Chargé d'affaires a.i. Dr MARIUS NICOLESCU.

Russian Federation: St 5, Block 10A, al-Amarat, POB 1161, Khartoum; tel. (183) 471239; e-mail rfsudan@mid.ru; internet sudan.mid.ru; Ambassador VLADIMIR FILIPPOVICH ZHELTOV.

Rwanda: Al Amarat St, 7 African Rd, Khartoum; tel. (155) 174662; e-mail rwandainsudan@minaffet.gov.rw; internet www.rwandainsudan.gov.rw; Chargé d'affaires ABEL BUHUNGU.

Saudi Arabia: 29 King Abdulaziz St, POB 852, Khartoum; tel. (183) 471121; internet embassies.mofa.gov.sa/sites/sudan; Ambassador ALI BIN HASSAN JAAFAR.

Somalia: Al-Manshia, Siteen St, POB 1857, Khartoum; tel. (183) 283558; e-mail khartoumembassy@gmail.com; Ambassador MOHAMED SHEIKH ISAK.

South Africa: St 11, House No. 16, Block B9, al-Amarat, POB 12137, Khartoum; tel. (183) 585301; e-mail khartoum@foreign.gov.za; internet www.dirco.gov.za/Khartoum; Ambassador CASSANDRA MBUYANE-MOKONE.

South Sudan: Elriyadh St, No. 279, Block 10, opp. Egyptian House, Khartoum; tel. 926289590; e-mail southsudanembassykh@yahoo .com; Ambassador KAU NAK MAPER.

Spain: Sharia'al-maraad 1, Block 7/A, Burri El Daraisa, POB 274, Khartoum; tel. (183) 763639; e-mail emb.jartum@maec.es; internet www.exteriores.gob.es/embajadas/jartum; Ambassador ISIDRO ANTONIO GONZÁLEZ AFONSO.

Sweden: House 70, St 43, POB 2206, Khartoum; tel. (187) 188700; e-mail ambassaden.khartoum@gov.se; internet www.swedenabroad .se/sv/utlandsmyndigheter/sudan-khartoum; Ambassador SIGNE BURGSTALLER.

Switzerland: St 15, House No. 7, al-Amarat, POB 1707, Khartoum; tel. (183) 471010; e-mail khartoum@eda.admin.ch; internet www .eda.admin.ch/khartoum; Ambassador CHRISTIAN WINTER.

Syrian Arab Republic: St 3, New Extension, POB 1139, Khartoum; tel. (183) 471152; e-mail syrianembassy.khartoum@yahoo.com; Ambassador HABIB ALI ABBAS.

Tanzania: Amarat St 33, Plot No. 12, Block No. 12K, POB 7268, Khartoum; tel. (183) 564384; e-mail khartoum@nje.go.tz; internet www.sd.tzembassy.go.tz; Ambassador SALEEM KOMBO HAJ.

Tunisia: St 15, House No. 35, al-Amarat, Khartoum; tel. (183) 487947; e-mail at.khartoum@diplomatie.gov.tn; Ambassador CHAFIK HAJJI.

Türkiye (Turkey): Baladia St, House No. 21, Block 8H, POB 771, Khartoum; tel. (183) 794210; internet hartum.be.mfa.gov.tr; Ambassador İRFAN NEZIROĞLU.

Uganda: Block 18, House No. 64, Khalid Ebn Alwaleed St, off Mecca St, al-Riyadh, POB 2676, Khartoum; tel. (156) 544440; e-mail khartoum@mofa.go.ug; internet khartoum.mofa.go.ug; Ambassador Dr YAHYA RASHID SSEMUDU (designate).

United Arab Emirates: St 9, POB 1225, Khartoum; tel. (155) 888888; e-mail khartoum@mofa.gov.ae; internet uae-embassy.ae/ Embassies/kh; Ambassador HAMAD MOHAMMED AL-JUNAIBI.

United Kingdom: off Sharia al-Baladia, Khartoum East, POB 801, Khartoum; tel. (156) 775500; e-mail information.khartoum@fco.gov .uk; internet www.gov.uk/world/organisations/british-embassy -khartoum; Ambassador GILES LEVER.

USA: Kilo 10, Soba, off Wad Medani Highway, POB 699, Khartoum; tel. (187) 022000; internet sd.usembassy.gov; Ambassador JOHN T. GODFREY.

Venezuela: St 15, Amarat, House No. 4, Khartoum; tel. (183) 563944; e-mail embve.sdjar@mppre.gob.ve; internet sudan .embajada.gob.ve; Ambassador DEIBY COLMANARES BOULLON.

Yemen: al-Amarat, St 11, New Extension, Bldg 94/89, POB 1010, Khartoum; tel. (183) 471623; e-mail yemb-khartoum@mofa.gov.ye; Ambassador OMER ABDALLA AL-MADAWI.

Zimbabwe: House No. 20, Block B, Amarat Rd, Khartoum; tel. (183) 472254; e-mail zimkhartoum@zimfa.gov.zw; Ambassador Dr EMMANUEL B. RUNGANGA GUMBO.

Judicial System

The Supreme Court is the highest court of justice in the country. There is also a Constitutional Court, as well as Courts of Appeal, district courts, urban and rural courts and various other courts.

Supreme Court: Khartoum; Chief Justice ABDEL AZIZ FATTAH AL-RAHMAN ABDEEN.

Constitutional Court: Khartoum; Chair. Dr WAHBI MOHAMED MUKHTAR.

Attorney-General: (vacant).

Religion

The majority of the population of post-secession Sudan are Muslims.

ISLAM

Islam is the state religion. Sudanese Islam has a strong Sufi element, and is estimated to have more than 15m. adherents.

CHRISTIANITY

Sudan Council of Churches: Inter-Church House, St 35, New Extension, POB 469, Khartoum; tel. 912377854; e-mail williamdeng452@yahoo.com; f. 1967; 12 mem. churches; Chair. Fr ANTHONIO; Gen. Sec. Rev. Fr WILLIAM DENG MIAN.

Roman Catholic Church

Latin Rite

The Roman Catholic Church officially remained undivided following the secession of South Sudan. For ecclesiastical purposes Sudan comprises one archdiocese and one diocese.

Sudan Catholic Bishops' Conference: General Secretariat, POB 6011, Khartoum; tel. (183) 225075; f. 1971; Pres. Mgr EDUARDO HIIBORO KUSALA (Bishop of Tombura-Yambio); Sec.-Gen. PETER SULEIMAN.

Archbishop of Khartoum: Most Rev. MICHAEL DIDI ADGUM MANGORIA, Catholic Church, POB 49, Khartoum; tel. 915716321.

Maronite Rite

Maronite Church in Sudan: POB 244, Khartoum; Rev. Fr YOUSEPH NEAMA.

Melkite Rite

Patriarchal Vicariate of Egypt and Sudan: Greek Melkite Catholic Patriarchate, 16 Sharia Daher, 11271 Cairo, Egypt; tel. (2) 5905790; e-mail grecmelkitecath_egy@hotmail.com; General Patriarchal Vicar in Egypt and Sudan Mgr (JOSEP) JULES ZEREY (Titular Archbishop of Damietta); Patriarchal Vicar in Sudan Mgr Exarkhos GEORGE BANNA; , POB 766, Khartoum; tel. (183) 777910.

Syrian Rite

Syrian Church in Sudan and South Sudan: Under the jurisdiction of the Patriarch of Antioch; Patriarchal Administrator Rt Rev. CAMIL AFRAM ANTOINE SEMAAN (Titular Bishop of Hierapolis in Syria dei Siri).

Orthodox Churches

Coptic Orthodox Church

Metropolitan of Khartoum, Southern Sudan and Uganda: Rt Rev. ANBA DANIAL, POB 4, Khartoum; tel. (183) 770646; e-mail metaous@email-sudan.net.

Bishop of Atbara, Omdurman and Northern Sudan: Rt Rev. ANBA SARABAMON, POB 628, Omdurman; tel. (183) 550423.

Greek Orthodox Church

Metropolitan of Nubia: POB 47, Khartoum; tel. (183) 772973; Archbishop DIONYSSIOS HADZIVASSILIOU.

The Ethiopian Orthodox Church is also active.

The Anglican Communion

Anglicans are adherents of the Province of the Episcopal Church of Sudan, which was inaugurated in July 2017 following the separation of the Episcopal Church of South Sudan and Sudan. The Primate of the Province of Sudan is the Bishop of Khartoum.

Archbishop of the Province of the Episcopal Church of Sudan and Bishop of Khartoum: Most Rev. EZEKIEL KUMIR KONDO, POB 65, Omdurman; e-mail bishop@khartoum.anglican.org; internet sudan.anglican.org.

Other Christian Churches

Evangelical Church: POB 57, Khartoum; c. 1,500 mems; administers schools, literature centre and training centre; Chair. Rev. RADI ELIAS.

The Lutheran Church of Sudan: Omdurman Elarda-Markh Studo, POB 12354, Omdurman, Khartoum; tel. 912972828; e-mail rev_yousifkh@hotmail.com; Bishop AKILLA YOUSIF ELTAHIR.

Presbyterian Church: POB 40, Malakal; autonomous since 1956; 67,000 mems (1985); Gen. Sec. Rev. THOMAS MALUIT.

The Africa Inland Church, the Sudan Interior Church and the Sudanese Church of Christ are also active.

The Press

Following the secession of South Sudan, the licences of six newspapers, partially or wholly owned by South Sudanese nationals, were revoked by the Sudanese National Council for Press and Publications, citing a law that bars foreigners from owning newspapers. The six newspapers were: *Ajras Al-Hurriya, Khartoum Monitor, Juba Post, Sudan Tribune, Advocate* and *The Democrat.*

DAILIES (PRINT AND ONLINE)

Abbar al-Youm: Khartoum; tel. (183) 779396; daily; Editor AHMED AL-BALAL AL-TAYEB.

Akhir Lahza: Khartoum; tel. (183) 741730; internet akhirlahza-sd.com; Editor SALEH ABDELAZIM.

Al-Dar: Khartoum; Editor AHMED AL-BALAL AL-TAYEB.

Al-Intibaha: Khartoum; tel. (183) 747878; e-mail alintibaha@yahoo.com; internet www.alintibaha.net; f. 2006.

Al-Mijhar al-Siyasi: Khartoum; internet www.almeghar.com; f. 2012; daily.

Al-Rai al-Amm: Khartoum; tel. (183) 778182; e-mail info@rayaam.net; f. 1945; daily; Editor SALAH MUHAMMAD IBRAHIM.

Al-Sudani: Khartoum; f. 1985; Editor DIA AL-DIN BILAL.

Al-Tayyar: Khartoum; e-mail altayar.sd@gmail.com; tel. 912356175; internet al-tayar.net; f. 2009; privately-owned; Editor-in-Chief OSMAN SAEED.

Al-Wan: Khartoum; tel. (183) 775036; internet www.alwandaily.com; f. 1985; daily; independent; pro-Govt; Editor HOUSSEN KHOGALI.

PERIODICALS

Al-Guwwat al-Musallaha (The Armed Forces): Khartoum; f. 1969; publs a weekly newspaper and monthly magazine for the armed forces; Editor-in-Chief Maj. MAHMOUD GALANDER.

New Horizon: POB 2651, Khartoum; tel. (183) 777913; f. 1976; publ. by the Sudan House for Printing and Publishing; weekly; English; political and economic affairs, devt, home and international news; Editor AL-SIR HASSAN FADL.

Sudanow: SUNA Bldg, Gamhoria St, Khartoum; tel. 909220011; e-mail info@sudanow-magazine.net; internet sudanow-magazine.net; publ. by the Sudan News Agency (SUNA); weekly; English; Editor-in-Chief AISHA SULIEMAN BRAIMA.

NEWS AGENCY

Sudan News Agency (SUNA): Gamhoria St, POB 1506, Khartoum; tel. (183) 776013; e-mail suna@sudanet.net; internet www.suna-sd.net; Dir-Gen. AWAD JADAIN MOHI-EDDIN.

PRESS ASSOCIATION

Sudanese Media Center (SMC): Al-Gomhouria St, Khartoum East, Khartoum; tel. (183) 787604; e-mail smcnews@hotmail.com; internet smc.sd; f. 2002.

REGULATORY AUTHORITY

National Council for Press and Journalistic Publications: Khartoum; tel. (183) 772519; e-mail ncpp.sd@gmail.com; internet ncpp.sd; f. 1999; Chair. A. FADLALLAH MOHAMMED; Sec.-Gen. ABDEL AZIM AWAD.

Publishers

Al-Ayyam Press Co Ltd: Aboulela Bldg, POB 363, United Nations Sq., Khartoum; f. 1953; general fiction and non-fiction, arts, poetry, reference, newspapers, magazines; Man. Dir BESHIR MUHAMMAD SAID.

Al-Sahafa Publishing and Printing House: POB 1228, Khartoum; f. 1961; newspapers, pamphlets, fiction and govt publs.

Khartoum University Press: POB 321, Khartoum; tel. (183) 776653; f. 1964; academic, general and educational in Arabic and English; Man. Dir ALI EL-MAK.

GOVERNMENT PUBLISHING HOUSE

El-Asma Printing Press: POB 38, Khartoum.

Broadcasting and Communications

TELECOMMUNICATIONS

Sudan Telecom (Sudatel) provides both fixed-line telephone services and mobile telephone services. In addition, there is one other fixed-line operator and two other mobile operators in the country.

Canar Telecommunication (Canartel): Al-Qibla Centre, Block 37, cnr Al-Sahafa and Madani Rds, POB 8182, Khartoum; tel. (15) 5550000; internet canar.sd; f. 2005; operates fixed-line telephone and internet services; CEO ABDULLAH SAEED ABDULLAH MOHAMED (acting).

MTN-Sudan: Manchiya East 60th Ave, Block 64, District 1, Khartoum; tel. 921111111; e-mail customercare@mtn.sd; internet www.mtn.sd; f. 2005; mobile telephone provider; CEO MALIK K. MELAMO.

Sudan Telecom Co (Sudatel): Sudatel Tower, Sinkat St, POB 11155, Khartoum; tel. (183) 797725; e-mail stginfo@sudatel.sd; internet www.sudatel.sd; f. 1993; mobile telephone branch operates under the name Sudani; Pres. and CEO MAGDI MOHAMMAD ABDALLA TAHA.

Zain: Al-Mogran, ACOLID Bldg, al-Ghaba St, POB 13588, Khartoum; tel. 91230000; e-mail info@sd.zain.com; internet www.sd.zain.com; f. 1997 as MobiTel; name changed as above in 2007; provides mobile telephone services; Man. Dir ELFATIH M. ERWA; 16.6m. subscribers (2020).

Regulatory Authority

Telecommunications and Post Regulatory Authority: Buri, North to Manshya Bridge, POB 2869, Khartoum; tel. (187) 171144; e-mail itisalat@tpra.gov.sd; internet tpra.gov.sd; f. 2018 to replace National Telecommunication Corpn; Dir-Gen. AL-SADIQ JAMAL AL-DEEN.

BROADCASTING

Radio

Sudanese Radio and Television Corporation: POB 572, Omdurman; tel. (187) 559315; e-mail info@sudanradio.info; internet www.sudanradio.sd/ar; f. 1940; state-controlled service broadcasting daily in Arabic, English, French and Swahili; Dir-Gen. IBRAHIM AL-BUZAI.

Sudan Radio Service (SRS): Umeme Plaza, Old Naivasha Rd, off Ngong Rd, Dagoretti, POB 4392, 00100 Nairobi, Kenya; tel. (20) 2346218; f. 2003 by the Education Development Center with support from the United States Agency for International Development; broadcasts in 10 languages including Dinka, Bari, Nuer, Zande, Shilluk, Arabic, Juba-Arabic and English; Chief of Party CHARLES NORTHRIP.

Alrabaa 94 FM: Airport Rd, Khartoum; tel. (183) 527794; e-mail info@alrabaa94fm.sd; internet www.alrabaafm.com; f. 2013.

Beladi FM (96.6 FM): Amarat St 29, Khartoum; tel. (183) 470678; e-mail info@beladifm.com; internet beladifm.com; f. 2016.

Capital Radio (91.6 FM): Khartoum; tel. 999809160; f. 2012; est. by Taha Al Roubi; culture, art and music.

Television

Sudanese Radio and Television Corporation: see Radio.

Finance

BANKING

Central Bank

Central Bank of Sudan: Gamhoria St, POB 313, Khartoum; tel. (183) 782246; internet www.cbos.gov.sd; f. 1960; bank of issue; Gov. HUSSEIN YAHYA JUNGOUL.

Commercial Banks

Al-Baraka Bank: Baraka Tower, Zubeir Pasha St, POB 3583, Khartoum; tel. (187) 112140; e-mail info@albaraka.com.sd; internet www.albaraka.com.sd; f. 1984; 75.7% owned by Al-Baraka Banking Group (Bahrain); Chair. ADNAN AHMED YOUSIF; Gen. Man. EL RASHEED ABDEL RAHMAN ALI.

Animal Resources Bank: Obeid Khatim St, Khartoum; tel. (183) 471534; e-mail info@ar-bank.sd; internet www.ar-bank.sd.

Balad Bank: Republic St, POB 10036, 11111 Khartoum; tel. (183) 779078; e-mail bab@baladbank.com; internet baladbank.com; f. 1990; Chair. ABDULLATIF OSMAN MOHAMED SALEH.

Bank of Khartoum: Intersection Gamhoria St and El-Gaser St, POB 1008, Khartoum; tel. (156) 661000; e-mail info@bok.sd; internet bankofkhartoum.com/sudan; f. 1913; 81% owned by Dubai Islamic Bank PJSC (United Arab Emirates); absorbed National Export/Import Bank and Unity Bank in 1993; Chair. MOHAMED SAEED AHMED ABDULLA AL-SHARIF; CEO Dr MUSTAFA EL HASSAN.

Blue Nile Mashreg Bank: Barlaman St, POB 984, Khartoum; tel. (183) 764490; e-mail info@bluemashreg.com; internet www.bluemashreg.com; f. 1983; Chair. MUHAMMAD ISMAIL MOHAMMAD; CEO Dr MAHMOUD HASSAN.

Farmers Commercial Bank: Al-Qasr Ave, POB 1116, Khartoum; tel. (183) 778507; e-mail info@fcbsudan.com; internet www.fcbsudan.com; f. 1960 as Sudan Commercial Bank; name changed as above in 1999 following merger with Farmers Bank for Investment and Rural

Development; Chair. SAMIA AHMED MOHAMED HASSAN; Pres. SULIMAN HASHIM MOHAMED TOUM.

National Bank of Sudan: Block 1, Kasr Ave, POB 1183, Khartoum; tel. (183) 778154; e-mail info@nbs.com.sd; internet www.nbs.sd; f. 1982; Chair. MATAR HAMDAN SULTAN HAMAD AL-AMERI; Gen. Man. MOHAMED AHMED ABDUL MAJED.

Omdurman National Bank: Al-Qaser Ave, POB 11522, Khartoum; tel. (183) 777225; e-mail info@onb.com.sd; internet onb-sd .com/index.php/ar; f. 1993; Chair. MOHAMED SAMIR MUSTAFA KHALIL; Gen. Man. ABDELHAMID MOHAMED JAMEEL.

Sudanese French Bank: Plot No. 6, Block A, Al-Qasr St, POB 2775, Khartoum; tel. (183) 787868; internet sfbank-sd.com; f. 1978 as Sudanese Investment Bank; name changed as above in 1993; Chair. TAHA ALI AL-BASHIR; Gen. Man. ABDEL KHALEQ AL-SAMMANI ABDUL RAZEK.

Tadamon Islamic Bank: Baladia St, POB 3154, Khartoum; tel. (183) 771505; e-mail info@tadamonbank-sd.com; internet tadamonbank-sd.com; f. 1981; Chair. Dr HASSAN OSMAN SAKOTA; Gen. Man. ABBAS ABDALLA ABBAS.

Foreign Banks

Byblos Bank Africa Ltd: 21 Al-Amarat St, POB 8121, Khartoum; tel. (156) 552222; e-mail byblosbankafrica@byblosbank.com; internet www.byblosbankafrica.com; 56.86% owned by Byblos Bank SAL (Lebanon); f. 2003; Chair. Dr FRANÇOIS S. BASSIL; Gen. Man. AMIN SHIBEIKA.

Faisal Islamic Bank (Sudan) (Saudi Arabia): Faih'a Bldg, Ali al-Latif St, POB 10143, Khartoum; tel. (183) 741326; e-mail info@fib-sd .com; internet fib-sd.com/ar; f. 1977; Chair. Prince MUHAMMAD AL-FAISAL AL-SA'UD; CEO MOAWIA AHMED ELAMIN.

Saudi Sudanese Bank: Al-Muk Nemer St, POB 1773, Khartoum; tel. (183) 485675; e-mail ssb@saudisb.sd; internet saudisb.sd; f. 1986; Chair. AL-FAKI MOHAMMED JIBALLAH MOHAMMED SALEH; Gen. Man. HASSAN MOHAMED AL-HASSAN.

Sudanese Egyptian Bank (SEB): Bldg 17, St 61, Alamarat, Khartoum; tel. (183) 250000; e-mail info@sebank.sd; internet www .sebank.sd; f. 2005; Chair. MOHAMMED KHAIR OMAR AWAD MPIOA; Gen. Man. ABO-OBAIDA ELHAG.

Development Banks

Agricultural Bank of Sudan: Gamhoria St, POB 1263, Khartoum; tel. (183) 779410; e-mail agribank@yahoo.com; internet www.abs.sd; f. 1957; provides finance for agricultural projects; Chair. MOHAMMED KHAIR AHMED AL-ZUBAYR; Dir-Gen. ABDELMAJID KHOJALI MOHAMED.

Al-Nile Bank: Al-Nile Tower, cnr Hashim Baeh St and Kolyat Eltib St, POB 62, Khartoum; tel. (183) 777789; e-mail info@alnilebank .com; internet fb.com/AlNileBank3838; f. 1983; fmrly Islamic Co-operative Development Bank; Chair. El-Haj ATTA EL-MANAN IDRIS; Gen. Man. AHMED ABDELRAHMAN AL-HOURI.

El-Nilein Bank: United Nations Sq., POB 1722, Khartoum; tel. (183) 771984; f. 1993 by merger of En-Nilein Bank and Industrial Bank of Sudan; name changed as above in 2007; 99% owned by Bank of Sudan; provides tech. and financial assistance for private sector industrial projects and acquires shares in industrial enterprises; Man. Dir MOHAMED ABBAS AGAB.

Industrial Development Bank: Amarat, 21 Sudan St, POB 710, Khartoum; tel. (183) 472157; e-mail info@idb.sd; f. 2005.

Real Estates Commercial Bank: Al-Baladia St, POB 309, Khartoum; tel. (183) 777917; e-mail info@rcb-sd.com; internet rcb-sd.com/index.php/ar; f. 1967; mortgage bank financing private sector urban housing devt; Chair. GILI MOHAMMED BASHIR; Man. Dir OSMAN ABDUL AZIM MOHAMMED HUSSEIN.

STOCK EXCHANGE

Khartoum Stock Exchange: Al-Baraka Tower, 5th Floor, POB 10835, Khartoum; tel. (183) 782450; internet www.kse.com.sd; f. 1995; Man. Dir Dr ALI KHALED MOHAMMED AHMED AL-FUWAIL; 27 mems.

INSURANCE

Al Baraka Insurance Co (Sudan) Ltd: Al Baraka Tower, 2nd Floor, Flat Nos 507–508, POB 3877, Khartoum; tel. (183) 770713; e-mail info@albaraka-ins.com; internet www.albaraka-ins.com; f. 1985; Chair. ABDALLA KHAIRY HAMED; Gen. Man. ADAM AHMED HASSAN.

Al Salama Insurance Co Ltd: Alsheikh Mustafa Alamin St, Khartoum; tel. (183) 772862; e-mail info@alsalama.sd; internet alsalama.sd/home; f. 1992; Chair. ALI MOHAMED EL HASSAN ABARSI; Gen. Man. TAMADOR ABU ELGASIM A. RAHIM.

Blue Nile Insurance Co (Sudan) Ltd: Al-Qasr Ave, Blue Nile Insurance Bldg, POB 2215, Khartoum; tel. (183) 780580; e-mail bluenile@bluenileins.net; internet bluenileins.com; f. 1965; Chair. SADIK MUHAMMAD AHMED AL-JACK; Gen. Man. SALAH EL-DIN MUSA MUHAMMAD SULIEMAN.

General Insurance Co (Sudan) Ltd: Plot No. 2/8, Block H/5, Mak Nimir St, POB 1555, Khartoum; tel. (183) 777838; e-mail generalinsurance@hotmail.com; internet www.fb.com/general.insu; f. 1961; Chair. NADIR HASSAN IBRAHIM MALIK; Gen. Man. MOHAMMED HASSAN IDRIS.

Islamic Insurance Co Ltd: Islamic Insurance Tower, Ali Abdulla-tif St, POB 2776, Khartoum; tel. (183) 771189; e-mail info@ islamicinsur.com; internet www.islamicinsur.com; f. 1979; all classes; Chair. MUAWIYA AHMED AL-AMIN ABDUL RAHMAN; CEO ABDULLAHI AHMED ABDULLAHI.

Middle East Insurance Co Ltd: Kuwaiti Sudanese Bldg, 1st Tower, Mezzanine Floor, Nile Ave, POB 3070, Khartoum; tel. (183) 772202; e-mail info@middleeast-ins.com; internet middleeast-ins.com; f. 1981; fire, marine, motor and general liability; Chair. SAMIR AHMED GASIM; Gen. Dir MUAWIA MIRGHANI ABBASHER.

Shiekan Insurance and Reinsurance Co Ltd: Shiekan Bldg, 10037 Khartoum; tel. (183) 781656; e-mail info@shiekanins.sd; internet www.shiekanins.sd; f. 1983; Gen. Man. SALAH EL DIN MUSA MOHAMED.

Sudanese Insurance and Reinsurance Co Ltd: North Bank Bldg, First Floor, Arab Market, POB 2332, Khartoum; tel. (183) 777796; e-mail info@sudinre.com; internet www.sudinre.com; f. 1967; Chair. MOHAMMED JAFAR SAYED AHMED QURAISH; Gen. Man. ADEL EZZEDINE EL-SAYED.

United Insurance Co (Sudan) Ltd: United Insurance Tower, 9th and 10th Floors, Parliament St, POB 318, Khartoum; tel. (183) 776630; e-mail info@unitedinsurance.ws; internet www .unitedinsurance.ws; f. 1968; Chair. TAREK KHALIL OSMAN; Gen. Man. ABDEL KHALIQ ABDALLAH.

Regulatory Authority

National Insurance Regulatory Authority Sudan: Al-Muqrin, Al-Ghaba St, Khartoum; e-mail insurance.authority1@gmail.com; internet fb.com/InsuranceSudan.

Trade and Industry

GOVERNMENT AGENCIES

Agricultural Research Corpn (ARC): POB 126, Wadi Medani; tel. (51) 1842226; e-mail info@arc.gov.sd; internet arc.gov.sd; f. 1967; Dir-Gen. Prof. ABDELMONEIM TAHA AHMED.

Gum Arabic Co Ltd: POB 857, Khartoum; tel. (183) 462111; f. 1969; Chair. ABD EL-HAMID MUSA KASHA; Gen. Man. HASSAN SAAD AHMED.

Sudan Cotton Co Ltd: POB 1672, Khartoum; tel. (183) 775755; e-mail sccl@sudan-cotton.com; internet www.sudan-cotton.com; f. 1970; exports and markets cotton; Chair. SALAM MOHAMED EL-BASHIR; Dir-Gen. MOHI EL-DEEN MOHAMED ALI.

Sudan Petroleum Corpn Ltd (Sudapet): Block 9/10, Resident No. 22/1, Africa St, POB 13188, Khartoum 11111; tel. (156) 557777; internet www.sudapet.sd; f. 1998; Chair. Dr AWAD AHMED AL-JAZZ; Sec.-Gen. Dr NURELDIN SAADELDIN.

DEVELOPMENT COMPANY

Sudan Rural Development Co Ltd (SRDC): POB 2190, Khartoum; tel. (183) 773855; e-mail srdc.hq@gmail.com; internet srdc.sd; f. 1980; SDC has 27% shareholding; Gen. Man. KAMAL EL DIN HASSAN HILALI.

CHAMBER OF COMMERCE

Union of Sudanese Chambers of Commerce: cnr al-Gomhouria St and al-Hurriya St, POB 81, Khartoum; tel. (183) 772346; e-mail info@sudanchamber.org.sd; internet www.sudanchamber.org.sd; f. 1908; Pres. YUSUF AHMED YUSUF; Sec.-Gen. IBRAHIM MUHAMMAD OSMAN.

INDUSTRIAL ASSOCIATION

Sudanese Chambers of Industries Association: Africa St, POB 2565, Khartoum; tel. (183) 471717; e-mail info@sudanindustry.com; internet sudanindustry.com; f. 1976; comprises 14 industrial chambers and some 3,000 industrial establishments in the private sector; Chair. NOUR ELDIN SAEED AL-SAID; Sec.-Gen. Dr ABBAS ALI ALSAYID.

UTILITIES

Public Water Corpn: POB 381, Khartoum 11111; tel. (183) 416799; Dir-Gen. MOHAMED HASSAN AMAR.

Sudanese Electricity Distribution Co Ltd: 99 Gama'a Ave, POB 1380, Khartoum; e-mail info@sedc.com.sd; internet www.sedc.com.sd; f. 2010; fmrly National Electricity Corpn; Dir KHALED MUSTAFA MUHAMMAD FADLALLAH.

MAJOR COMPANIES

The following are among the larger companies, either in terms of capital investment or employment.

Elnefeidi Group: cnr Abusin and Parlaman Sts, POB 1222, Khartoum; tel. (183) 762013; e-mail info@elnefeidigroup.com; internet elnefeidi.com; conglomerate with interests in agriculture, logistics, mining and real estate; Chair. AMIN BASHIR ELNEFEIDI.

Greater Nile Petroleum Operating Co Ltd (GNPOC): Block No. 4, Plot No. 91, GNPOC Tower, POB 12527, al Mugran District, Khartoum; tel. (187) 0370000; internet www.gnpoc.com; f. 1997; jt venture co 40% owned by CNPC (China), 30% by PETRONAS (Malaysia), 25% by ONGC of India and 5% by Sudapet (Sudan); Pres. CHEN HUANLONG.

HAFAST: Khartoum-Omdurman Industrial Area, Khartoum; tel. 912287606; e-mail hafast@hafast.com.sd; internet www.hafast.com.sd; export and import; Gen. Man. HANE SAEED.

Kenana Sugar Co Ltd: POB 2632, Khartoum; tel. (183) 152000; e-mail info@kenana.com; internet www.kenanasugarcompany.com; f. 1971; financed by Sudanese Govt and other Arab nations; Chair. GABRIEL IBRAHIM; Man. Dir ABDEL RAOUF MERGANI ABDURAHMEN.

Libya Oil Sudan Co. Ltd (Oilibya): Shell House, Aboullela Bldg, Parliament Ave, POB 320, Khartoum; tel. (187) 014114; marketing of petroleum products; Gen. Man. LAMINE KABA.

Petrodar Operating Co (PDOC): Petrodar Tower, al Mugran District, POB 11778, Khartoum; tel. (187) 008000; internet www.petrodar.com; f. 2000; joint venture co 41% owned by CNPC, 40% by Petronas, 8% owned by Sudapet, 6% by Sinopec and 5% by Tri-ocean; Pres. AZHAN ALI.

PROTECH Engineering Co: Salam St, Bldg 241, Block 22, Taief, POB 7468, Khartoum 11123; tel. (120) 609940; e-mail info@protech.sd; internet www.protech.sd; f. 2005; chemicals, interior and exterior coatings and lining products; Gen. Man. Eng. MOSAB ADAM MOHAMMED.

Salfi Co Ltd: Mohamed Nageeb St, Khartoum; tel. 967663832; internet www.salfiltd.com; f. 2001; mining and general trading; Chair. M. A. SUHAIL.

White Nile (5B) Petroleum Operating Co Ltd: PETRONAS Complex Nile Ave, POB 8207, Khartoum; tel. (187) 091000; internet www.wnpoc.com.sd; f. 2001; jt venture co 50% owned by PETRONAS (Malaysia) and 50% owned by Sudapet (Sudan).

TRADE UNIONS

Federation

Sudan Workers Trade Unions Federation (SWTUF): POB 2258, Khartoum; tel. (183) 777463; includes 42 trade unions representing c. 1.75m. public service and private sector workers; affiliated to the Int. Confed. of Arab Trade Unions and the Org. of African Trade Union Unity; Pres. YOUSIF ALI ABDEL KARIM YOUSIF; Gen. Sec. YOUSUF ABU SHAMA HAMED.

Transport

RAILWAYS

The main railway line runs from Wadi Halfa, on the Egyptian border, to al-Obeid, via Khartoum. Lines from Atbara and Sinnar connect with Port Sudan. There are lines from Sinnar to Damazin on the Blue Nile and from Aradeiba to Nyala in Southern Darfur, with a branch line from Babanousa to Wau in Western Bahr El-Ghazal state in South Sudan.

Sudan Railways Corpn (SRC): Sudan Railways Corpn Bldg, al-Tabia St, POB 1812, Khartoum; tel. (183) 770652; e-mail info@sudanrailways.gov.sd; internet www.sudanrailways.gov.sd; f. 1875; operates 4,725 km of narrow-gauge, single-track railways that serve the northern and central parts of the country; Gen. Man. MOHAMMED TAHA AHMED.

INLAND WATERWAYS

The total length of navigable waterways served by passenger and freight services is 4,068 km, of which approximately 1,723 km are open all year. From the Egyptian border to Wadi Halfa and Khartoum navigation is limited by cataracts to short stretches, but the White Nile from Khartoum to Juba, in South Sudan, is almost always navigable.

Nile River Transport Co/Sudan River Transport Co (NRTC/SRTC): al-Amarat St 25, Block 9, Bldg No. 5, Khartoum; tel. (183) 560034; fmrly River Transport Corpn.

River Navigation Corpn: Khartoum; f. 1970; jtly owned by Govts of Egypt and Sudan; operates services between Aswan and Wadi Halfa.

SHIPPING

Port Sudan, on the Red Sea, 784 km from Khartoum, and Suakin are the only commercial seaports.

Red Sea Shipping and Services Co: POB 308, Khartoum; tel. (183) 580933; e-mail redseaco@redsea-sd.com; internet www.redsea-sd.com; Gen. Man. AWAD HAG ALI HAMED.

Sea Ports Corpn: Port Sudan; tel. (311) 822061; e-mail info@sudanports.gov.sd; internet sudanports.gov.sd; f. 1906; Gen. Man. OMER AHMED MOHAMED ALI.

Sea Pride Enterprise: POB 76, Port Sudan; tel. (311) 820583; e-mail info@spesudan.com; internet www.spesudan.com; f. 1932; fmrly Sea Prince Enterprise; Man. Dir ALNASSER SIDKI.

Sudan Shipping Line Ltd: POB 426, Port Sudan; POB 1731, Khartoum; tel. (183) 780017; f. 1960; 10 vessels totalling 54,277 dwt operating between the Red Sea and western Mediterranean, northern Europe and the UK; Chair. ISMAIL BAKHEIT; Gen. Man. SALAH AL-DIN OMER AL-AZIZ.

CIVIL AVIATION

In early 2019 construction work commenced on a new international airport at a site 40 km south-west of Khartoum. The airport, the construction of which was to be funded through a preferential loan from the Export—Import Bank of China, was to have the capacity eventually to receive 12m. passengers per year. The first phase of the construction of the new airport was scheduled to be completed by the end of 2022.

Civil Aviation Authority: Sharia Sayed Abd al-Rahman, POB 430, Khartoum; tel. (183) 787757; internet scaa.gov.sd; f. 1936; Dir-Gen. IBRAHIM ADLAN IBRAHIM.

Badr Airlines: Arkaweet Block 65, Bldg No. 393, Mamon Behari St, POB 6899, Khartoum; tel. 901230002; e-mail info@badrairlines.com; internet www.badrairlines.com; operates cargo and passenger air services for humanitarian aid; CEO Eng. AHMED ABU SHAIRA.

Nova Airways: Kuwait Bldg, Gamhoria St, Khartoum; tel. (183) 744744; e-mail info@novaairways.com; internet www.novaairways.com; f. 2000.

Sudan Airways Co Ltd: Sudan Airways Complex, 161 Obeid Khatim St, Riyadh Block No. 10, POB 253, Khartoum; tel. (183) 243738; e-mail customerinfo@sudanair.com; internet www.sudanair.com; f. 1947; internal flights and international services to Africa, the Middle East and Europe; Man. Dir ABDUL MAHMOUD SULIMAN.

Tourism

Public Corpn of Tourism and Hotels: POB 7104, Khartoum; tel. (183) 781764; f. 1977; Dir-Gen. Maj.-Gen. EL-KHATIM MUHAMMAD FADL.

Defence

As assessed at November 2021, the armed forces comprised: army an estimated 100,000; navy an estimated 1,300; air force 3,000. Gendarmerie and paramilitary forces included 40,000 personnel. Military service is compulsory for males aged 18–30 years and lasts for two years.

Defence Budget: 89,820m. new Sudanese pounds in 2021.

Chief of General Staff of the Sudanese Armed Forces: Gen. MOHAMED OTHMAN AL-HUSSEIN.

Commander of the Air Force: Lt-Gen. ESSAM AL-DIN SAEED KOKO ABDALRRAHMAN.

Commander of the Land Forces: Gen. ESSAM MOHAMED-HASSAN KARAR.

Commander of the Navy: Rear-Adm. MAHJOUB BUSHRA AHMED RAHMA.

Education

The Government provides free primary education from the ages of six to 13 years. Secondary education begins at 14 years of age and lasts for up to three years. According to estimates by the United Nations Educational, Scientific and Cultural Organization (UNESCO), in

2016/17 pre-primary enrolment was equivalent to 47% of children in the relevant age-group (males 46%; females 47%). Enrolment at primary schools in that year included 62% of children in the relevant age-group (boys 62%; girls 61%), while enrolment at secondary schools was equivalent to 47% of children in the relevant age-group (boys 46%; girls 47%). The budget for 2021 allocated some 137,000m. new Sudanese pounds to education (equivalent to about 12.4% of total projected expenditure).

Bibliography

Adar, K. G. *The Sudan Peace Process*. Pretoria, Africa Institute of South Africa, 2005.

Ali, H. E. (Ed.). *Darfur's Political Economy: A Quest for Development.* Abingdon, Routledge, 2014.

Alier, A. *Southern Sudan: Too Many Agreements Dishonoured.* Exeter, Ithaca Press, 1990.

Asher, M. *Khartoum: The Ultimate Imperial Adventure*. London, Viking, 2005.

Berridge, W., Lynch, J. Makawi, R., and de Waal, A. *Sudan's Unfinished Democracy The Promise and Betrayal of a People's Revolution*. London, C. Hurst & Co., 2022.

Bassil, N. *The Post-Colonial State and Civil War in Sudan: The Origins of Conflict in Darfur*. London, I. B. Tauris, 2013.

Boggs, R. *Becoming Plural: A Tale of Two Sudans*. Reading, Garnet Publishing, 2012.

Brosché, J. and Rothbart, D. *Violent Conflict and Peacebuilding: The Continuing Crisis in Darfur*. Abingdon, Routledge, 2012.

Burr, J. M., and Collins, R. O. *Requiem for the Sudan: War, Drought and Disaster Relief on the Nile*. Boulder, CO, Westview Press, 1995.

   Revolutionary Sudan: Hassan al-Turabi and the Islamist State, 1989–2000. Leiden, Brill, 2003.

   Darfur: The Long Road to Disaster. Princeton, NJ, Markus Wiener Publishers, 2006.

Cockett, R. *Sudan: Darfur, Islamism and the World: Darfur and the Failure of an African State*. New Haven, CT, Yale University Press, 2010.

Collins, R. O. *A History of Modern Sudan*. Cambridge, Cambridge University Press, 2008.

Copnall, J. *A Poisonous Thorn in Our Hearts: Sudan and South Sudan's Bitter and Incomplete Divorce*. London, C. Hurst & Co., 2014.

Daly, M. W. *Imperial Sudan*. New York, Cambridge University Press, 1991.

   Darfur's Sorrow: The Forgotten History of a Humanitarian Disaster. Cambridge, Cambridge University Press, 2010.

Deng, F. M. *War of Visions: Conflict of Identities in the Sudan*. Washington, DC, Brookings Institution, 1995.

Deng, F. M., and Khalil, M. *Sudan's Civil War: The Peace Process Before and Since Machakos*. Pretoria, Africa Institute of South Africa, 2005.

Elnur, I. *Contested Sudan: The Political Economy of War and Reconstruction*. Abingdon, Routledge, 2009.

Flint, J., and de Waal, A. *Darfur: A Short History of a Long War*. London, Zed Books, 2005.

Fukui, K., and Markakis, J. (Eds) *Ethnicity and Conflict in the Horn of Africa*. London, James Currey, 1994.

Gabriel, W. *Islam, Sectarianism and Politics in Sudan since Mahdiyya*. London, C. Hurst & Co., 2003.

Garang, J. *The Call for Democracy in Sudan* (Ed. Khalid, M.). 2nd edn. London, Kegan Paul International, 1992.

Holt, P. M., and Daly, M. W. *The History of the Sudan from the Coming of Islam to the Present Day*. 6th edn. London, Routledge, 2014.

Iyob, R., and Khadiagala, G. M. *Sudan: The Elusive Quest for Peace*. Boulder, CO, Lynne Rienner Publishers, 2006.

Jaspars, S. *Food Aid in Sudan*. London, Zed Books, 2018.

Johnson, D. H. *The Root Causes of Sudan's Civil Wars*. 3rd edn. Woodbridge, James Currey, 2016.

Katsuyoshi, F., and Markakis, J. *Ethnicity and Conflict in the Horn of Africa*. London, James Currey, 1994.

Keen, D. *The Benefits of Famine: A Political Economy of Famine and Relief in Southwestern Sudan, 1983–1989*. Princeton, NJ, Princeton University Press, 1994.

Khalid, M. *War and Peace in Sudan: A Tale of Two Countries*. London, Kegan Paul International, 2003.

Lanz, D. *The Responsibility to Protect in Darfur: From Forgotten Conflict to Global Cause and Back*. Abingdon, Routledge, 2019.

Mamdani, M. *Saviors and Survivors: Darfur, Politics, and the War on Terror*. New York, Pantheon, 2009.

Niblock, T. *Class and Power in Sudan: The Dynamics of Sudanese Politics 1898–1985*. Albany, NY, State University Press of New York, 1987.

Nouwen, S., James, L., and Srinivasan, S. (Eds). *Making and breaking Peace in Sudan and South Sudan: The Comprehensive Peace Agreement and Beyond*. Oxford, Oxford University Press, 2021.

Nyaba, P. A. *The Politics of Liberation in South Sudan: An Insider's View*. Kampala, Fountain Publishers, 1997.

O'Fahey, R. S. *Darfur: A History*. London, C. Hurst & Co., 2007.

Patey, L. *The New Kings of Crude: China, India, and the Global Struggle for Oil in Sudan and South Sudan*. London, C. Hurst & Co., 2014.

Petterson, D. *Inside Sudan: Political Islam, Conflict, and Catastrophe*. Philadelphia, PA, Westview, 1999.

Prendergast, J. *Sudanese Rebels at a Crossroads: Opportunities for Building Peace in a Shattered Land*. Washington, DC, Center of Concern, 1994.

Prunier, G. *From Peace to War: The Southern Sudan (1972–1984)*. Hull, University of Hull, 1986.

   Darfur: The Ambiguous Genocide. London, C. Hurst & Co., 2005.

Reeves, E. *A Long Day's Dying: Critical Moments in the Darfur Genocide*. Toronto, The Key Publishing House, 2007.

Reilly, H. *Seeking Sanctuary: Journeys to Sudan*. Bridgnorth, Eye Books, 2005.

Rolandsen, O. H. *Guerrilla Government: Political Changes in the Southern Sudan during the 1990s*. Uppsala, Nordic Africa Institute, 2005.

Rone, J., et al. (Eds). *Civilian Devastation: Abuses by the Parties in the War in Southern Sudan*. New York, Human Rights Watch, 1994.

Ruay, D. D. A. *The Politics of Two Sudans: The South and the North, 1921–1969*. Uppsala, Nordic Africa Institute, 1994.

Santi, P., and Hill, R. (Eds). *The Europeans in the Sudan 1834–1878*. Oxford, Oxford University Press, 1980.

Sharfi, M. H. *Islamist Foreign Policy in Sudan: Between Radicalism and the Search for Survival*. Abingdon, Routledge, 2019

Sidahmed, A. S. *Politics and Islam in Contemporary Sudan*. Richmond, Curzon Press, 1996.

Sidahmed, A. S., and Sidahmed, A. *Sudan*. Abingdon, Routledge, 2004.

Suliman, O. *The Darfur Conflict: Geography or Institutions?* Abingdon, Routledge, 2011.

Srinivasan, S. *When Peace Kills Politics: International Intervention and Unending Wars in the Sudans*. Oxford, Oxford University Press, 2021.

Vaughan, C. *Darfur: Colonial Violence, Sultanic Legacies and Local Politics, 1916–1956*. Woodbridge, James Currey, 2015.

Verhoeven, H. *Water, Power and Civilization in Sudan: The Political Economy of Military-Islamist Statebuilding*. Cambridge, Cambridge University Press, 2015.

Vezzadini, E. *Lost Nationalism: Revolution, Memory and Anticolonial Resistance in Sudan*. Woodbridge, James Currey, 2015.

Voll, J. O. (Ed.). *Sudan: State and Society in Crisis*. Bloomington, IN, Indiana State University Press, 1991.

Woodward, P. *Sudan 1898–1989: The Unstable State*. Boulder, CO, Lynne Rienner Publishers, 1990.

TANZANIA

Physical and Social Geography

L. BERRY

PHYSICAL FEATURES AND CLIMATE

The 947,300 sq km (365,755 sq miles) of the United Republic of Tanzania (incorporating mainland Tanganyika and a number of offshore islands, including Zanzibar, Pemba, Latham and Mafia) have a wide variety of land forms, climates and peoples. The country includes the highest and lowest points in Africa—the summit of Mt Kilimanjaro (5,892 m above sea level) and the floor of Lake Tanganyika (358 m below sea level). The main upland areas occur in a northern belt—the Usambara, Pare, Kilimanjaro and Meru mountains; a central and southern belt—the Southern highlands, the Ugurus and the Ulugurus; and a north–south trending belt, which runs southwards from the Ngorongoro Crater. The highest peaks are volcanic, although block faulting has been responsible for the uplift of the plateau areas. Other fault movements have resulted in the depressed areas of the rift valleys; Lakes Tanganyika, Malawi, Rukwa, Manyara and Eyasi occupy part of the floor of these depressions. Much of the rest of the interior comprises gently sloping plains and plateaux, broken by low hill ranges and scattered isolated hills. The coast includes areas with wide sandy beaches and with developed coral reefs, but these are broken by extensive growth of mangroves, particularly near the mouths of the larger rivers.

With the exception of the high mountain areas, temperatures in Tanzania are not a major limiting factor for crop growth, although the range of altitude produces a corresponding range of temperature regimes from tropical to temperate. Rainfall is variable and is generally lower than might be expected for the latitude. About one-fifth of Tanzania can expect with 90% probability more than 750 mm of rainfall annually, and only about 3% normally receives more than 1,250 mm. The central third of the country is semi-arid (with less than 500 mm of rainfall per year), with evaporation exceeding rainfall in nine months of the year. For much of Tanzania most rain falls in one rainy season, December–May, although two peaks of rainfall, in October–November and April–May, are found in some areas. Apart from the problem of the long dry season over most parts of the country, there is also a marked fluctuation in annual rainfall from one year to the next, and this may be reflected in the crop production and livestock figures.

The surplus water from the wetter areas drains into the few large perennial rivers. The largest of these, the Rufiji, drains the Southern highlands and much of southern Tanzania. With an average discharge of 1,133 cu m per second, it is one of the largest rivers in Africa, and has major potential for irrigation and hydroelectric power development. The Ruvu, Wami and Pangani also drain to the Indian Ocean. The Pangani has already been developed for hydroelectric power, which supplies Arusha, Moshi, Tanga, Morogoro and Dar es Salaam. Apart from the Ruvuma, which forms the southern frontier, most other drainage is to the interior basins, or to the Lakes Tanganyika, Victoria and Malawi.

The most fertile soils in Tanzania are the reddish-brown soils derived from the volcanic rocks, although elsewhere *mbuga* and other alluvial soils have good potential. The interior plateaux are covered with tropical loams of moderate fertility. The natural vegetation of the country has been considerably modified by human occupation. In the south and west-central areas there are large tracts of woodland covering about 30% of the country, while on the uplands are small but important areas of tropical rainforest. Clearly marked altitudinal variations in vegetation occur around the upland areas and some distinctive mountain flora is found. Tanzania has set aside about one-third of its land for national parks and game and forest reserves.

POPULATION AND RESOURCES

According to the census of 26 August 2012, Tanzania had a population of 44,928,923, resulting in a population density of 47.5 people per sq km. Of that number 1,303,569 people resided in the autonomous Zanzibar region (the islands of Pemba and Zanzibar). By mid-2022, according to United Nations projections, Tanzania's population had risen to 63,298,542, giving a population density of 71.6 people per sq km. The highest population densities, reaching over 250 per sq km, occur on the fertile lower slopes of Mt Kilimanjaro and on the shores of Lake Malawi. Most other upland areas have relatively high densities. Most of the country's inhabitants are of African origin, although people of Indian and Pakistani ancestry comprise a significant component of the urban population. There are more than 120 distinct ethnic groups and tribes in Tanzania, of which the largest are the Sukuma and the Nyamwezi. The official languages are Swahili and English and there are numerous tribal languages. There are Muslim, Christian and Hindu communities, while many Tanzanians follow traditional beliefs.

Tanzania's mineral resources include diamonds, other gemstones, gold, salt, phosphates, coal, gypsum, kaolin, tin, limestone and graphite, all of which are exploited. There are also reserves of nickel, silver, copper, cobalt, lead, soda ash, iron ore, tungsten, pyrochlore, magnesite, niobium, titanium, vanadium, uranium and natural gas.

Dar es Salaam is the main port, the dominant industrial centre, and the focus of commercial activity. Dar es Salaam has been growing at a substantial rate and attempts are being made to decentralize industrial development to other centres. Arusha has also been growing rapidly in recent years, partly because of its importance to tourism. The administrative capital is Dodoma, to which most government offices had transferred (from Dar es Salaam) by late 2018.

History

MICHAEL JENNINGS

Prior to the onset of European interest in the 17th century, the area that now comprises the United Republic of Tanzania was embedded in regional trade networks focusing on the Indian Ocean and the Omani-controlled caravan trade that extended outwards from Zanzibar into the eastern Congo and Buganda. Zanzibar declared its independence from Oman in 1856, and its mainland areas were acquired by the United Kingdom and Germany in 1886–90, when a British protectorate was established over the islands of Zanzibar and Pemba.

Mainland Tanganyika was declared a German protectorate in 1885. In 1920, following the defeat of Germany in the First World War, Tanganyika was placed under a League of Nations mandate, with the UK as the administering power, and in 1946 it became a United Nations (UN) trust territory, still under British administration. The politicization of indigenous Africans began in 1929, with the formation of the Tanganyika African Association, which evolved in 1954 into the Tanganyika African National Union (TANU), under the leadership of Julius Nyerere.

THE NYERERE PERIOD, 1959–85

TANU won decisive victories in general elections held in Tanganyika in 1959 and 1960, when Nyerere became Chief Minister. Nyerere became Prime Minister when internal self-government was granted in May 1961. Full independence followed on 9 December. In December 1962 Tanganyika became a republic, with Nyerere (having been elected in the previous month) as the country's first President. Rashidi Kawawa became Vice-President.

Zanzibar (together with the neighbouring island of Pemba and several smaller islets) became an independent sultanate in December 1963. The Sultan was overthrown in an armed uprising in January 1964, following which a republic was declared and the Afro-Shirazi Party (ASP) took power. In April an Act of Union between Tanganyika and Zanzibar was signed. The leader of the ASP, Abeid Karume, became the United Republic's First Vice-President, as well as being Chairman of the ruling Supreme Revolutionary Council of Zanzibar. The Union was named Tanzania in October.

A new Constitution, introduced in July 1965, provided for a one-party state (although until 1977 TANU and the ASP remained the respective official parties of mainland Tanzania and of Zanzibar, and co-operated in affairs of state). Nyerere was re-elected as President in 1965, and subsequently in the 1970, 1975 and 1980 elections. Early in 1967 TANU adopted a programme of socialism and self-reliance, termed the Arusha Declaration. National development was to be based on that of the rural sector via community (*ujamaa*) villages. Commercial banks and many industries were nationalized. However, the programme ran into difficulties in the 1970s, faced with increased resistance from those being forced into *ujamaa* villages and worsening economic problems.

In Zanzibar, Karume was assassinated in April 1972. His successor, Aboud Jumbe, reorganized the islands' Government by extending the powers of the ASP. Despite its incorporation into Tanzania, Zanzibar retained a separate administration, and ruthlessly suppressed all opposition. In 1977 TANU and the ASP merged to form the Chama Cha Mapinduzi (CCM—Revolutionary Party).

In 1985 Nyerere resigned and Ali Hassan Mwinyi was elected as President of Tanzania. Idris Abdul Wakil was elected President of Zanzibar in succession to Mwinyi. The change of President coincided with a deterioration in the economic crisis. The new administration was forced to implement a range of policy proposals by the International Monetary Fund (IMF), including greater encouragement to the private sector, and policies on budgeting, agricultural reform and currency valuation, in order to ensure continued aid flows from key donors. Mwinyi (the sole candidate) was re-elected to the presidency in 1990, and in Zanzibar Dr Salmin Amour was elected as Wakil's successor.

THE 'THIRD PHASE' GOVERNMENT

Following a constitutional amendment in May 1992, which introduced a plural political system, Tanzania's first multi-party legislative and presidential elections were held in October 1995. The CCM won with a large majority, and Benjamin Mkapa was elected national President, with 61.8% of the votes cast. Omar Ali Juma (hitherto Chief Minister of Zanzibar) was appointed Vice-President.

Mkapa was re-elected President in October 2000, winning 71.7% of the votes cast. The polls on the mainland were declared by international observers to have been free and fair, in marked contrast to the controversial events in Zanzibar (see *Developments in Zanzibar*).

Jakaya Mrisho Kikwete was appointed as the CCM candidate to succeed Mkapa in the 2005 elections, amid signs of serious internal tensions within the party. The opposition remained divided and unable to present a serious challenge to the dominance of the CCM (except in Zanzibar, where the Civic United Front—CUF—which advocated Zanzibari autonomy, maintained a strong presence).

THE KIKWETE PRESIDENCY

Kikwete won the (delayed) presidential election in December 2005 with 80.3% of the votes cast. The CCM still dominated the National Assembly with 266 seats. The CUF held 28, and Chama Cha Demokrasia na Maendeleo (Chadema) 11. Kikwete appointed Edward Lowassa as Prime Minister. Internal disputes continued to undermine unity within the CCM, which was in effect split between a 'reformist', anti-corruption group—led by National Assembly Speaker Samuel Sitta—and a 'traditionalist' faction—led by Lowassa. Chadema had also suffered internal divisions, leading party Deputy Secretary-General Freeman Mbowe to announce that he would not stand as Chadema's presidential candidate in the forthcoming election.

Corruption appeared to be a worsening problem under Kikwete's administration. A series of scandals led to the departure of a number of high-profile officials, including the Governor of the Bank of Tanzania in January 2008. In the following month Prime Minister Lowassa resigned after being implicated in an energy contract scandal. In April the Minister of Infrastructure Development, Andrew Chenge, was implicated in a scandal involving the purchase of radar equipment from British firm BAE Systems.

Nevertheless, in the legislative and presidential elections held in October 2010, Kikwete was re-elected as President with 62.8% of the votes cast (on a turnout of 43%), although this was the lowest percentage ever received by a CCM presidential candidate. The CCM's support in rural areas appeared strong, while the level of support for Chadema was high in urban centres including Arusha and Mwanza (where the party's Secretary-General, Willibrod Peter Slaa, received more votes than Kikwete).

The CCM secured a total of 254 seats in the National Assembly. Chadema replaced the CUF as the official opposition party, winning 46 seats to the CUF's 36. The National Convention for Construction and Reform (NCCR—Mageuzi) won four seats, and the Tanzania Labour Party and the United Democratic Party one each. Following the elections, opposition parties organized protests against the Government, with demonstrations being staged in Dar es Salaam, Mwanza and Zanzibar. Protests in early 2011 led to violent clashes with the security forces, and two Chadema supporters were killed by police in Arusha.

Although discoveries of onshore and offshore gas deposits in Tanzania and the concomitant rapid growth of the extractive industries sector promised significant potential for exploitation, the question of how to divide prospective gas revenues within Tanzania generated considerable tensions. Riots erupted in Mwanza in May 2013 after the Government confirmed that a gas processing plant would instead be built in Dar es Salaam, and that a gas pipeline would be constructed to transport gas from Mwanza to the plant. Chadema used the protests to continue to build its strength in opposing the Government's energy and extractive industry policies. Religious tensions also led to violence in Dar es Salaam in 2012, and some 1,200 people were arrested after rioting in the city over the alleged desecration of a copy of the Koran.

Chadema presented a growing challenge to CCM dominance and to the Government, and in April 2012 the opposition party won a surprise victory at a by-election in Arumeru East. In the same month Chadema legislator Zitto Kabwe, who was the Chairman of the parliamentary Public Accounts Committee, forced the dismissal of six government ministers who were implicated in a corruption scandal. However, Chadema suffered an internal crisis towards the end of 2013, when Kabwe and two other prominent party members were dismissed in an internecine power struggle. After losing a legal appeal against his dismissal, in March 2015 Kabwe was appointed leader of the newly established Alliance for Change and Transparency (ACT Wazalendo).

The Government sought to manage information about its performance in the public arena. Attacks on print and other media continued, with journalists being accused of publishing articles that could undermine confidence in the Government. In March 2015 a controversial law was approved banning the publication of data not provided by the National Bureau of Statistics, and the publication of false or misleading data.

CONSTITUTIONAL REFORM

In March 2011 the National Assembly adopted the Constitutional Review Act, providing for consultation on a new draft constitution. The Tanzania Constitutional Review Commission published its first draft for public consultation in June 2013. The key recommendation was for the establishment of a federal system of government, in which both Zanzibar and the mainland would have their own administrations.

In February 2014 a Constituent Assembly began working on finalizing the draft Constitution which was to be put to a referendum in October. The work of the Assembly was repeatedly delayed by disputes and walkouts by opposition and independent members, concerned over attempts by the ruling CCM to push through a version that suited its own interests. To little surprise, the Government announced in September that the referendum would be delayed until April 2015. As disagreements continued over the draft charter, at the start of April 2015 the Government again delayed the planned referendum.

The issue of constitutional reform appeared to be shelved following the 2015 elections. However, in April 2017 the new Minister of Justice and Constitutional Affairs and former member of the Constitutional Review Commission, Prof. Palamagamba Kabudi, announced that the Government would now resume consideration of constitutional reform, although he gave no further details about what this would entail, nor of any timetable.

THE 2015 ELECTIONS AND THE FIRST MAGUFULI ADMINISTRATION

Voting in the presidential and parliamentary elections took place on 25 October 2015, with a turnout of 67.3%. The polling was generally peaceful and considered free and fair. Dr John Pombe Magufuli of the CCM (hitherto the Minister of Works, Transportation and Communications) was declared the victor of the presidential election, with 58.5% of the vote, while Lowassa, who had defected to Chadema and stood as its candidate, performed more strongly than previous opposition candidates, taking 40.0%.

In the parliamentary elections, the CCM secured 189 of the elective seats. Chadema won 34 seats, the CUF 31, and ACT Wazalendo and NCCR—Mageuzi each obtained one seat. The CCM's share of the vote fell from 60% to 55%, while that of the opposition rose from 24% to 32%. The opposition was able to establish its dominance in major urban areas such as Dar es Salaam and Tanga; it also performed strongly in Mbeya and

Iringa towns, and in the regions of Arusha and Kilimanjaro. The CCM continued to dominate in rural areas.

President Magufuli initially adopted a dynamic style of governance, winning plaudits for quick and decisive action in campaigns against wasteful expenditure, improving public services, ensuring that private companies paid their taxes and tackling corruption. However, raise soon turned to criticism as it became apparent that Magufuli was making decisions based on discussions with a small group of loyal advisers and was becoming increasingly intolerant of public criticism. In July 2016 Magufuli decreed that all political rallies would be banned until at least 2020. Demonstrations against the presidential decree were forcibly dispersed by police officers, and a number of opposition leaders, including Lowassa, were detained for organizing protests. New cybercrimes legislation sought to limit criticism of the President and Government on social media, and other media outlets faced repeated attacks in the following years, including the arrest of a number of journalists and the closure of several newspapers.

In November 2017 Azory Gwanda, a journalist for the Swahili-language newspaper *Mwananchi*, disappeared after investigating police violence against protesters, and a number of individuals were arrested for criticizing the Government on online social media.

International commercial companies also faced the ire of the Government, especially the mining sector. In late 2016 President Magufuli launched a prolonged campaign to revise contracts that he criticized as being unfair to Tanzania. Mining companies were forced to negotiate new terms, and British-based Acacia Mining became a primary target.

In September 2017 Tundu Lissu, a politician for the opposition Chadema party, was shot by unknown gunmen in Dodoma. He was flown out of Tanzania for treatment. Before the shooting, Lissu had been arrested six times in 2017 and had faced a charge of sedition for criticizing Magufuli. By-elections held in November reflected the growing tensions between government and opposition, with violence breaking out and accusations emerging of abductions, arrests and torture of opposition supporters and leaders, as well as the removal of opposition agents from polling stations. On the eve of the poll, police used live ammunition against opposition demonstrators, injuring three and killing a passer-by. Despite growing criticism of the Government's increasingly authoritarian stance, the CCM won all but one of 47 by-elections. European Union (EU) and US diplomats criticized the Government for its heavy-handed response to opposition protests and called for transparent investigations into allegations of police brutality and the murder of the opposition campaigner.

Opposition leaders continued to be harassed: Chadema's party Chairman Mbowe and Secretary-General Vincent Mashinji were arrested; and members of the party (including Mbowe) were frequently detained for organizing illegal protests in the following months.

Internal security continued to cause local problems. During 2017 armed groups attacked ruling CCM and state officials in a series of attacks in Pwani Region in response to a state security crackdown. Attacks in February, April and June left at least 16 people dead, including police officers and local village leaders. The police stepped up operations, killing suspected members of the groups in raids in June and August, during which they reported finding large numbers of weapons. Some of the groups were alleged to have links to the jihadist fundamentalist group al-Shabaab, although a government report in March 2018 sought to link the attacks to anti-Magufuli activists, seemingly in an attempt to justify the authorities' crackdown on opposition leaders.

In November 2018 Mbowe and fellow Chadema legislator Esther Matiko were denied bail after failing to attend a court hearing related to the opposition protests held in February in which a student had been killed by the police. Mbowe and seven other opposition leaders were facing charges of sedition, incitement to violence and holding an illegal rally. Mbowe and Matiko were released in March 2019, with the judge condemning the decision to detain them. A ruling in a separate court on the same day saw the release of two other Chadema legislators and a number of party members facing charges related to their political activities.

By the end of 2018 the CCM appeared to be resurgent following a string of high-profile defections from opposition parties: seven legislators defected from Chadema, a further three from the CUF, and some 70 councillors and other party officials. Although the CCM claimed that this was due to its economic management, infrastructure development and growing popularity, opposition parties attributed the defections to government efforts to undermine opposition politics and media freedom in order to maintain its authority.

New legislation introduced in January 2019 gave new powers to the Registrar of Political Parties, including the authority to intervene in internal party decision-making processes, and to suspend registration. The law also included measures to limit opportunities for mergers and coalitions. Opposition politicians condemned this as an attempt to undermine challenges to the Government in the 2020 elections, noting that the Registrar is a government appointee. Despite claims by the Government that the new powers were designed to protect against fraud and increase transparency, in February 2019 the Registrar began moves to deregister the opposition ACT Wazalendo party, led by Kabwe, over its failure five years previously to submit its financial records. Opposition parties launched a legal challenge to the legislation in April, bringing a case to the East African Court of Justice (EACJ).

In March 2019 former Prime Minister Lowassa resigned from Chadema and rejoined the CCM. Lowassa had been facing investigations into his businesses, and his son-in-law had been charged with bank fraud. Rumours circulated that either, or both, could have been the motivation for Lowassa's surprise defection back to his original party. Others suggested that it was linked to internal CCM politics, with Magufuli hoping that his erstwhile rival would now bolster his support against internal rivals, especially in the run-up to the 2020 elections.

The EACJ ruled against part of another piece of controversial government legislation in April 2019. The Court declared that sections of the Media Services Act, which had been criticized by opposition politicians, civil society organizations and journalists as an attempt to stifle freedom of speech, were too broadly defined.

In June 2019 a former aide to Kabwe, Raphael Ongangi, was reportedly abducted in Dar es Salaam by unidentified kidnappers, before reappearing in Mombasa just over one week later. During his disappearance, Kabwe's social media account appeared to have been hacked, with posts expressing support for Magufuli. This was one of three high-profile kidnappings in Tanzania during the previous seven months. In October 2018 Mohamed Dewji was kidnapped and released after 10 days. The former politician had been in dispute with the Government over a business issue when he was seized. In May 2019 Mdude Nyagali, a social media activist who had been critical of government policies, was abducted from outside his office in southern Tanzania, and was found five days later in the countryside, having apparently suffered a physical beating. The absence of suspects or arrests fuelled suspicion that the Government was using such tactics further to undermine the opposition.

Local elections held in Tanzania in November 2019 were boycotted by the main opposition parties, which accused the Government of interfering in the polls in order to undermine the opposition. The Chairman of Chadema, Mbowe, accused election officials of unfairly disqualifying over 90% of the party's candidates for minor infractions. As a result of the boycott, the CCM won a landslide victory, securing 99% of the contested seats at the lowest tier of local government positions. In the previous local elections, in December 2014, Chadema had secured 16% of the total seats, and the CCM had taken about 75%.

Meanwhile, the Government stepped up its attempts to undermine the opposition through targeted attacks on opposition leaders. In April 2020 a warrant for the arrest of Kabwe was issued by a court in Dar es Salaam after he failed to appear in court to face a charge of sedition. Kabwe was found guilty of sedition in May and ordered by the court not to write seditious statements for a period of 12 months, before being released on a conditional discharge. In June Kabwe was arrested again as he was about to leave Tanzania, on suspicion of violating the Media Services Act after he and other opposition leaders had publicly criticized the Government and Prime Minister Magufuli. He was banned from leaving the country.

Mbowe was attacked in Dodoma in June 2020, sustaining a broken leg after he was ambushed by unknown assailants. Chadema claimed that it was politically motivated; Lissu, the Deputy Chair of the party, had been due to announce his candidacy for the presidency on the same day as the attack. The EU and the USA both condemned the attack and called on the Government to ensure free and fair elections. On the same day, an investigation into corruption in Chadema was announced.

In July 2020, after three years of living in exile in Belgium, Lissu returned to Tanzania to launch his presidential bid. He was met by a large number of supporters as he left the airport in Dar es Salaam. Police had threatened to disperse them and cancel a rally for Lissu, but in the event, the rally went ahead.

With legislative elections due in October 2020, the opposition parties began to negotiate a new coalition in order to challenge the CCM. By June of that year the main opposition leaders, including Kabwe, had agreed to work together during the election campaign.

THE COVID-19 PANDEMIC IN TANZANIA

Tanzania recorded its first positive case of infection from the coronavirus disease (COVID-19) on 16 March 2020. The Government initially responded quickly as the pandemic spread, closing schools and universities and suspending sporting events. The first death from the disease in Tanzania was recorded on 31 March, and on 9 April the Government announced the first case of local transmission.

Despite an encouraging early start to controlling the spread of COVID-19, the Tanzanian Government soon gained a reputation for using only limited measures to control the virus, for giving poor and misleading advice and for refusing to acknowledge the scale of the problem. From the end of April 2020 the Government refused to publish new data on infections and deaths from the virus, with the result that official figures remained static for many weeks, at a reported 509 cases and 21 deaths. Rumours nevertheless spread in urban areas of large-scale burials of those who had died from the spread of the virus. Magufuli was accused of giving misleading official advice about how to protect against infection from COVID-19, after he claimed that traditional herbal remedies could be beneficial. Citizens were encouraged to continue to attend places of worship and advised that prayers were more effective at protection than face masks. Concerned about the Tanzanian Government's poor handling of the pandemic, Kenya and Zambia closed their borders with Tanzania in late May. Earlier in that month, despite public fears that cases of infection from COVID-19 were significantly higher than being officially reported, it was announced that schools and universities would reopen.

THE 2020 ELECTIONS AND A RENEWED MANDATE FOR THE CCM

In September 2020 Lissu of Chadema was accused of sedition and promoting violence during his campaigning and was hauled before the National Election Commission (NEC) ethics committee. He was then suspended from campaigning for a week. Chadema accused the Government of attacking supporters and party offices in northern Tanzania as part of a campaign of intimidation. It also accused the NEC of systematically disqualifying about one-quarter of its candidates, as well as candidates from other opposition parties.

Despite a prohibition on formal opposition coalitions, discussions between ACT Wazalendo and Chadema established an informal alliance to challenge the CCM. ACT Wazalendo announced in September 2020 that it would be backing Lissu as the main opposition candidate. In return, Chadema announced it would withdraw its candidate from the Zanzibar presidential election and ask its supporters to vote for the ACT Wazalendo candidate, Seif Sharif Hamad.

Opposition politicians continued to accuse the Government of restricting and undermining their campaign efforts. On Zanzibar, police were accused of detaining and killing ACT

Wazalendo supporters, and the opposition party accused armed forces of distributing pre-marked ballot papers in favour of the CCM. On the mainland, Chadema accused CCM officials of orchestrating the shooting of two of its supporters. Access to the internet, including social media, appeared to be being restricted as the elections drew close. On the day of the poll Hamad was arrested and detained.

The presidential elections were held on 28 October 2020 and resulted in a significant victory for Magufuli and the ruling CCM. Magufuli won 84.4% of the vote—a significant improvement from his 58.5% share in the 2015 elections. Lissu, the main opposition candidate, won 13.0% of the vote. A turnout of 50.7% (a total of 14.8m. votes were cast) was recorded. On Zanzibar the CCM's Dr Hussein Ali Mwinyi (son of the former President) won with 76.3% of the vote, while Hamad secured 19.3%.

In the concurrent parliamentary elections, the CCM increased its dominance, securing 256 of the 264 constituency seats. ACT Wazalendo secured four seats, the CUF three, and Chadema just one. Several key opposition figures, including Mbowe and Zitto Kabwe, lost their seats. After the allocation of the seats reserved for women, the CCM was left with 93% of all seats. The opposition, which in 2015 had secured 114 seats, was now left with just 27.

Opposition parties dismissed the result, claiming that it had been rigged. ACT Wazalendo and Chadema demanded new elections and called for mass protests. The NEC denied accusations of electoral fraud, but international election missions (of which there were fewer in number, owing to the COVID-19 pandemic) criticized the conduct of the elections and raised serious doubts over their credibility.

Fearing large-scale protests, the Government immediately launched a crackdown on opposition leaders. Mbowe and two other Chadema leaders were arrested within days of the result, accused of planning violent protests. Lissu was also detained and claimed to have received death threats. He then sought refuge in the German embassy before leaving the country again for Belgium. Kabwe was forced into hiding to evade the crackdown. Hundreds of opposition workers and activists were also detained. Opposition legislators initially announced they would not take up their seats in protest, but later reversed that position. On Zanzibar the ACT Wazalendo leadership agreed to join a national unity government (as required under the terms of the Constitution) with the CCM.

The Hassan Administration

Despite clear signs of a new wave of infections from COVID-19 at the start of 2021, the Government continued to deny the scale of the problem, and Minister of Health Dorothy Gwajima confirmed that Tanzania would not be participating in the COVID-19 Vaccines Global Access (COVAX) Facility for securing vaccines. In mid-February Hamad, who had been appointed First Vice-President of Zanzibar only two months earlier, died from suspected COVID-19 infection. Minister of Finance and Planning Philip Mpango gave a public address confirming that he had been seriously ill, although he did not mention COVID-19 by name. The Government responded by advocating the use of face masks, hand washing and sanitizers, and recommended shielding for vulnerable people, in addition to its previous advice for people to pray.

On 27 February 2021 President Magufuli made what was to be his last public appearance. His death was announced by Vice-President Samia Suluhu Hassan on 17 March. Announcing two weeks of national mourning, Hassan was sworn in as President on 19 March.

Although the Government continued to deny that Magufuli had been infected with COVID-19, Hassan quickly changed the tone of its response to the pandemic and immediately established a committee of medical experts to advise on the issue. In May 2021 Hassan revealed that nationally about 100 people were in hospital with COVID-19, but no other data were given. In July Tanzania formally applied to join the COVAX Facility.

The need to appoint a new Vice-President led to a government reorganization. Mpango was appointed as the new Vice-President; his replacement as Minister of Finance and Planning was Mwigulu Nchemba; Liberata Mulamula became the new Minister of Foreign Affairs and East African Co-operation;

and Prof. Kabudi took on the role of Minister of Justice and Constitutional Affairs. In what might have been a signal of intent, Bashiru Ally, a close ally of Magufuli, was replaced as Chief Secretary.

In August 2021 four people, including three police officers, were killed and six injured in an attack by a gunman near the French embassy in Dar es Salaam. The attacker was eventually killed by the police. Although initial speculation suggested the incident could have been a terrorist attack linked to the presence of Tanzanian armed forces in the Mozambican province of Cabo Delgado, in support of local troops combating a separatist insurgency led by Islamic State-affiliated militant, the police later announced that they did not know what the motive was for the incident.

Meanwhile, despite a weakened opposition following the elections, the Government was still concerned about the possibility of opposition-led protests, possibly reflecting the continuing influence of unpopular Magufuli loyalists in the cabinet. In July 2021 Mbowe was arrested and charged, together with three alleged co-conspirators, with terrorism and economic sabotage. He was accused of plotting to blow up petrol stations in order to create political instability. The opposition denounced the charges as politically motivated, and one of the co-accused, Adamu Hassan Kasekwa, alleged that he had been tortured until he made a false confession. In September the judge hearing the cases recused himself, after it was reported that he had close links to the Tanzanian intelligence services. The new judge, Mustapha Siyani, left the trial within a few weeks after being appointed as Principal Judge of the High Court of Tanzania. Opposition leaders continued to push for Mbowe's release; and Lissu called for opposition parties to refuse to engage with the Government and its agencies until the release of the four men.

In October 2021 Zanzibari-born author Abdulrazakh Gurnah was awarded the Nobel Prize for Literature, although amid the celebrations, questions were asked about Tanzania's refusal to allow dual citizenship (Gurnah is a British citizen, having left Zanzibar during the uprising of 1964).

Meanwhile, President Hassan sought to stamp her authority on her new Government. In October 2021, following a limited cabinet reshuffle, she presented an economic recovery plan, which reinforced her administration's focus on health care and education as key priorities. She also announced an ambitious timeline for getting negotiations back on track to exploit Tanzania's offshore gas reserves. The appointment of a key ally, January Yusuf Makamba, as Minister of Energy was regarded as critical in achieving progress in this area. In a further signal of a shift away from the Magufuli era, the Government announced an end to the controversial ban on pregnant girls from attending school. The move was welcomed by women's rights groups and by foreign donors who had strongly criticized Magufuli over the law.

In January 2022 Job Ndugai resigned as Speaker of the National Assembly after a public clash with President Hassan. A video recording of Ndugai criticizing the high level of government debt had been publicized in December 2021, and despite Ndugai's apology and claims that his comments had been selectively edited, Hassan called on all those in her administration who disagreed with the direction that her Government was taking to step down. Hassan's growing confidence in exerting her authority was reinforced by a more substantial cabinet reshuffle later that month. Several Magufuli loyalists were dismissed, including Prof. Kabudi (Minister of Justice and Constitutional Affairs), Prof. Kitila Mkumbo (Minister of Industry and Trade) and Geoffrey Mwambe (Minister of Investment). Dotto James, also seen as close to Magufuli, was also replaced as permanent secretary in the Ministry of Finance. Hassan also merged the Ministry of Investment with the Ministry of Industry and Trade and divided the Ministry of Health and Social Welfare into the Ministry of Health and a new Ministry of Community Development, Gender, Women and Special Groups. Former President Kikwete's son, Ridhiwan Kikwete, was given a ministerial role as Deputy Minister of Land, Housing and Human Settlement.

At the start of 2022 Hassan's position within the CCM and the Government was strengthening and ignited debate about her ambition to continue as head of state following the end of her shortened presidential term in 2025. As several senior members of the CCM were by that time quite open about their own ambitions to contest the next presidential election, by asserting her control over her administration, Hassan was sending a message about her possible intention to be more than a caretaker President.

Feeling more secure, President Hassan made a series of overtures to the opposition. In February 2022 Magufuli-era official bans on four newspapers (including one owned by Mbowe) were lifted This followed similar reversals of the ban on a number of online television channels. Despite imposing bans herself in mid-2021 on two newspapers that had criticized the Government, the move was presented as a shift away from Magufuli-era authoritarianism.

Also in February 2022 President Hassan made overtures to the opposition. She met Lissu, who was still living in exile in Brussels, Belgium, during an EU-AU summit. In March Mbowe was released, after the Director of Public Prosecutions dropped the charges against him. Within hours of his release, Hassan held a private meeting with Lissu, who consequently announced that he would return to Tanzania and stated that he had encouraged Hassan to resume efforts to reform the Constitution. In June Hassan announced that she would indeed focus on constitutional reform as a priority.

In April 2022 Abdulrahman Kinana was elected as the Vice-Chairman of the CCM by the party's National Executive Committee. Kinana, an ally of Hassan, had fallen out with Magufuli, who he had helped to secure the nomination as the party's presidential candidate in 2015, and resigned in 2018. His return was seen as further reinforcing Hassan's position within the CCM and increasing the likelihood of her seeking the nomination as the CCM's candidate in the presidential election in 2025. The efforts to break with the recent past—and in particular to be seen to be moving away from the authoritarianism of the Magufuli era—reflected her success in establishing her own authority within government and her own party.

Tanzania signed a major agreement with energy companies in June 2022 for the exploitation of the country's offshore gas reserves, fulfilling Hassan's pledge for rapid progress and opening up space for the final negotiations to take place. The Government also announced a fuel subsidy programme worth US \$43m. (about 100,000m. shillings) to help to address the growing cost of living in the country amid soaring prices for energy and food.

DEVELOPMENTS IN ZANZIBAR

Opposition in Zanzibar coalesced around the newly established CUF in 1992. However, the CCM defeated the CUF in elections to both the presidency and the House of Representatives in October 1995.

There were widespread accusations of electoral fraud following the presidential and legislative elections held in Zanzibar and Pemba in October 2000. Re-run elections in 16 constituencies saw violent clashes in advance of the poll, in which the CCM defeated the CUF in what were widely viewed as rigged elections. The CUF refused to recognize the results; two days of clashes between police and demonstrators in January 2001 left at least 40 people dead (including six members of the security forces) and 100 injured.

Voting proceeded in Zanzibar at the end of October 2005 in comparative calm, and international observers noted that the poll was generally free and fair. Amani Abeid Karume (son of Karume) was re-elected as President of Zanzibar, with 53.2% of the votes cast. The CCM won 31 seats in the House of Representatives, and the CUF 18. The CUF rejected the result and there were violent clashes over several days between the police and CUF supporters in Stone Town. Renewed talks on ending the political crisis repeatedly stalled until an agreement was reached in November 2009 on the establishment of a unity government. The creation of the Government of National Unity (GNU) was supported by 66.4% of those who voted at a referendum held in July.

At the presidential poll held in Zanzibar in October 2010, the CCM candidate, Ali Mohamed Shein, secured victory over

former Chief Minister Hamad (of the CUF) by fewer than 4,000 votes, winning 50.1% of votes cast. The election was regarded by observers as generally free and fair. A GNU was formed, in accordance with the power-sharing agreement signed in July, with Shein as Zanzibar President and Hamad as First Vice-President. Despite this, there were signs of growing tensions between Zanzibaris and mainland Tanzanians living on the islands, with several houses belonging to the latter being burned down in May 2011. In June two churches were also burned down, and pamphlets were circulated protesting against the presence of Christian churches in the area. In December a Roman Catholic priest was shot and killed on Christmas Day. An Islamist group called Uamsho (Awakening) was implicated in many of the protests and attacks on police and churches in 2012–14, in which several people were killed.

The October 2015 elections in Zanzibar did not proceed as smoothly as those on the mainland. Amid a prolonged period of vote counting, on 16 October Hamad (of the CUF) announced that he had won the presidential election on the island. On the morning of 28 October journalists and election observers were ejected from a vote-counting centre, and later that morning the Zanzibar Electoral Commission nullified the results, citing vote-rigging and malpractice. This decision was denounced by the CUF and by observers from Europe and North America, who viewed it as an attempt by the CCM to retain power in Zanzibar.

Despite CUF protests, a new poll was announced for March 2016. The CUF boycotted the elections, and Shein was re-elected as President with a large majority (91.4% of votes cast). He was inaugurated for a second term on 24 March. Following the elections, Shein included in his cabinet three members of a number of small opposition parties that had not boycotted the vote but refused to reinstate the GNU.

In August 2016 former CUF Chairman Lipumba announced that he would seek to be restored as party leader. His decision led to a political split within the CUF, between supporters of Lipumba and Hamad. In March 2019, when the High Court ruled that Lipumba was the legitimate Chairman of the CUF, Hamad resigned from the party and joined ACT Wazalendo, taking with him a significant number of former CUF supporters.

On 27 October 2020 (the day before elections took place) Hamad was reportedly detained. As mentioned above, the CCM's Hussein Ali Mwinyi won the presidential election with 76.3% of the vote, with Hamad securing just 19.3%. Despite concerns about the conduct of the election, ACT Wazalendo agreed to join the GNU, and Hamad took on the role of First Vice-President. Following Hamad's death in February, Othman Masoud Othman Sharif was appointed to replace him.

FOREIGN RELATIONS

The East African Community (EAC) was established by the Governments of Kenya, Tanzania and Uganda in July 2000. It would eventually encompass the East African Legislative Assembly and the EACJ (both created in 2001), the East African Customs Union (2005) and the Common Market (2010). South Sudan acceded to the EAC in April 2016.

In October 2008 the three main African trading blocs—the EAC, the Southern African Development Community (SADC) and the Common Market for Eastern and Southern Africa, signed an agreement in Kampala, Uganda, to create a single free trade zone of 26 countries.

Instability in Burundi in 2015 and 2016 saw renewed waves of refugees entering Tanzania. The UN High Commissioner for Refugees reported that there were 126,497 Burundian refugees in Tanzania on 31 August 2022. In March 2016 an agreement was signed between President Magufuli and his Ugandan counterpart, President Yoweri Museveni, for the construction of an oil pipeline running between Hoima in Uganda and the Tanzanian port of Tanga.

In October 2018 the Tanzanian security forces arrested more than 100 alleged Islamist militants. The detainees were accused of attempting to cross into neighbouring Mozambique to join an extremist Islamist group, which had carried out numerous deadly attacks in the north of that country since late 2017, killing dozens of people. The Mozambican authorities suspected that some of the raids had been launched from Tanzania. Nearly 500 people, including about 50 Tanzanian nationals, had been detained by the Mozambican police in June in connection with the attacks. In response to growing violence led by Islamist insurgents in the Mozambican province of Cabo Delgado, Tanzanian armed forces were sent to the border with Mozambique in March 2020. In May two leaders of the insurgency killed by Mozambican forces were declared to be Tanzanian nationals.

In October 2020 up to 300 Mozambican fighters attacked the Tanzanian town of Kitaya. Just before the Tanzanian elections, fighters again struck within Tanzania, kidnapping Tanzanian nationals from villages in Tandahimba district. In response, the Government stepped up operations against suspected supporters of the Mozambican insurgency and arrested over 500 people suspected of having links to the insurgents, most from among the Mozambican refugee population in the region. In November the Tanzanian and Mozambican Governments signed another memorandum of understanding to create systems for intelligence-sharing and joint operations.

In May 2021 President Hassan conducted an official visit to Kenya. Hassan and the Kenyan President, Uhuru Kenyatta, announced several measures to strengthen relations, including waivers of work and business permits, and the acceleration of work on the gas pipeline linking the ports of Dar es Salaam and Mombasa.

Meanwhile, in the immediate aftermath of the elections in October 2015, donors expressed concern over the emerging political crisis in Zanzibar. EU and North American donors criticized the Government for its suspected influence in the cancellation of the Zanzibar poll and called upon Magufuli personally to intervene in order to resolve the issue. In March 2016, following the re-holding of elections in Zanzibar, the US Government's Millennium Challenge Corporation suspended US $472.8m. of aid. However, at the same time donors expressed their support for President Magufuli's actions against corruption in the first months of his term in office, tempering criticism over events in Zanzibar. Tanzania's relations with international donors began to improve under newly appointed President Hassan, and in July 2022 the Government and the IMF concluded an agreement for a Extended Credit Facility worth $1,046m., including the immediate disbursement of $151.7m. to the Tanzanian Treasury (see Economy).

Economy

JÖRG WIEGRATZ

INTRODUCTION

Tanzania is one of sub-Saharan Africa's fastest growing economies, with an average annual rate of gross domestic product (GDP) growth of 6.5%, in real terms, in 2012–20. Growth dipped to an average of 5.8% per year in 2008–10, when the global financial crisis affected foreign direct investment (FDI) and foreign demand. The shock was mitigated by the low interconnectedness of Tanzania's banking system with global markets and the country's gold exports, which were in global demand as a safe haven asset. The Tanzanian economy benefits from a good standard of public policy, a healthy financial sector, high international reserves and favourable international prices for its major export commodities.

At mid-2022 the United Nations (UN) estimated Tanzania's population at 63.3m. During 2011–20, according to estimates by the World Bank, the population increased at an average annual rate of 3.0%, while GDP per head grew, in real terms, by an average of 2.6% per year. GDP per head on an international purchasing-power parity basis was US $2,760 in 2020.

According to the 2012 census, 28% of Tanzanians lived in extreme poverty. This proportion decreased to an estimated 24.5% in 2015 but increased to 26.4% in 2017/18 and has been further affected by the effects of the COVID-19 pandemic that began in 2020. Generally, poverty reduction occurs mostly in urban areas, and some rural districts still have poverty rates of up to 60%. Low skill levels and productivity, as well as adverse employment conditions, are major barriers to poverty alleviation. According to the 2014 Integrated Labour Force Survey, more than 18m. people (92% of those surveyed) worked informally without any legal protection and benefits, and, of these, some 10m. were young workers aged 15–37 years. About 7m. of these young workers were employed in agriculture, generally a 'low tech, low returns' sector. Furthermore, between 2011 and 2018 total real consumption grew by less (0%–1%) for people in the bottom half of the population in terms of wealth than among the better-off half (1%–3%). Consumption growth was generally higher in urban areas than in rural areas.

THE ECONOMY UNTIL EARLY 2020

As external conditions continued to be favourable, Tanzania's economic growth remained solid in 2019. According to World Bank data, GDP growth was 7.0% (the same level as in 2018). The leading sectors in terms of growth were mining, construction, transport, communications and financial services. The growth in mining production (12.6%) was driven by a surge in gold output, which rose by 11.6% (28.3 metric tons in 2018 to 31.6 tons in 2019). Growth in construction (14.8%) was driven by work on public infrastructure projects (notably, roads, bridges, water supply facilities and buildings) and residential projects. There was a corresponding rise in production of construction materials (mainly cement, iron and steel). In the 2018/19 financial year and the first half of 2019/20 there was growth in public consumption, gross fixed capital formation and exports, as well as recurrent and development spending and tax revenue, credit to the private sector, imports of capital goods and raw materials. Tourism has become a key sector; it contributed about 1% to total GDP growth and constituted more than 26% of total exports in 2019. However, the COVID-19 pandemic, which spread to East Africa in early 2020, has affected the economy highly negatively, and Tanzania's recent robust economic growth slowed sharply (see below).

Agriculture

In 2019 the agricultural sector grew by 4.4%, in real terms. The sector continues to be a significant contributor to the economy, accounting for 28.9% of total GDP in 2019. However, during 2011–19 the agricultural sector's contribution to GDP grew much more slowly than the rest of the economy, averaging 4.4% per annum (and only about 1.5% on a per capita basis). As more than two-thirds of the population who live in poverty are dependent on agriculture for their livelihoods, agricultural sector growth is crucial in order to achieve poverty reduction. In 2019 agricultural GDP per capita was about 10% higher than in 2011, but lower than in other sectors that employ smaller sections of the poor (industry employs 7.0% of the population in poverty, and services employs 17.5%).

Crop production is the main sub-sector. Important food crops include maize, rice, sorghum, cassava, legumes, bananas and potatoes. The major cash crops are coffee, tobacco, cashew nuts, cotton, sugar, tea and sisal. Volatile and falling global coffee prices in recent years have led to declining coffee production—one of Tanzania's most well-known export goods—from a bumper harvest of 71,200 metric tons in 2013, down to 42,700 tons in 2015, according to the UN's Food and Agriculture Organization (FAO). However, output of coffee rose substantially in 2016, to an estimated 52,700 tons, and it totalled some 68,100 tons in 2019. In the same year, about 225,100 tons of cashew nuts, 264,500 tons of seed cotton, 90,700 tons of tobacco, 61,700 tons of tea and 8,500 tons of cloves were produced.

Agriculture is of high importance to the Government's development strategies for three major reasons. First, about 65% of Tanzania's working-age population are estimated to work in the sector. Therefore, agricultural growth substantially affects a large proportion of household incomes. Second, agriculture is viewed as instrumental to initiating the country's industrialization by domestically providing the necessary inputs for the first stage, which is focused on low-technology agro-processing. Finally, the sector is crucial to food security, which in turn affects social stability and economic growth. Consequently, many policies, pieces of legislation and strategies actively target agricultural growth and modernization.

A major constraint to agricultural development is the low level of technology application. According to the first Five-Year Development Plan (FYDP I), covering the period 2011/12–2015/16, of a total of 44m. ha of arable land, about 29.4m. ha were suitable for irrigation systems. However, only 461,326 ha were irrigated in 2014. The remainder relied exclusively on rain-fed irrigation, exposing crop production to considerable climatic risks. Nonetheless, government efforts have achieved some progress, as the total size of irrigated cultivated land has increased by 41.3% since 2009.

Land and trade policies are another factor affecting agricultural investment. In response to concerns about the welfare of smallholder households, land grabbing, and domestic food supply, the Government has introduced restrictive and partly adverse legislation on land ownership and trade. Examples of such measures include restricting sugar exports while subsidizing sugar imports, and limiting the amount of land that investors can acquire for rice and sugar production. A substantial obstacle to investment originates, however, from the 1999 Land Act. This legislation states that all land belongs to Tanzania's people, administrated by the Government on their behalf, and divides land into three categories which determine its potential uses. The categories are: Village Land—public land owned by villages and administrated by local and central government agencies such as village councils or the Prime Minister's Office; Reserved Land—areas that include national parks and military installations; and General Land—land that can be 'occupied', i.e. leased and economically developed under an official right of occupancy. Village and Reserved Land can be transformed into General Land for economic development through application and various bureaucratic procedures depending on its current categorization, location, size and development plans. Rights of occupancy are usually temporary and thus subject to renewals, but can still be bought, sold or transferred. However, inadequate land governance systems, combined with the convoluted bureaucratic procedures required to recategorize land and/or obtain right of occupancy, have led to a very low degree of formal land ownership, especially among farmers. Apart from creating various direct disincentives for investment in agriculture, the low degree of official land ownership also renders access to formal investment finance very difficult, as land cannot be used as collateral. As a result, only about 10% of private sector credit is extended to agriculture each year. In 2015 the Government established the Tanzania Agricultural Development Bank to deal exclusively with agricultural loans.

Industry

Industry is Tanzania's key to middle-income status, as stated in the Tanzania Development Vision 2025 (comprising three FYDPs covering 2011–25). Accordingly, the past, current and upcoming FYDPs all focus on preparing and initializing Tanzania's industrialization. To reach middle-income country status by 2025, the industry sector would need to grow at an annual rate of 10%. Various initiatives and bodies, as well as several export processing zones and special economic zones, have been established to stimulate small- and large-scale industrial development. However, in the World Bank's 2020 *Doing Business* report, which provides data for 2019, Tanzania ranked 141st out of 190 countries—behind many other countries in the region, although three places higher than in the previous year.

The contribution of industry to real GDP increased from 19.4% in 2005 to 31.1% in 2019. The sector grew by 11.8% in 2019. The largest sub-sectors and growth drivers are construction and manufacturing, with shares of 15.5% and 9.2% of GDP, respectively, in 2019.

Manufacturing in Tanzania revolves mostly around agro-processing. Important agricultural manufactured goods include flour, beer and other beverages, sisal-based products such as ropes and twines, sugar, as well as plywood, paper and other wood products. More sophisticated, non-agricultural manufactured goods include paints, rolled steel, iron and aluminium sheets, dry cells, batteries and cement. Cement is of particular significance to Tanzania's economy as domestic cement companies such as Tanzania Portland Cement Company Ltd and Tanga Cement plc are important employers and major companies listed on the Dar es Salaam Stock Exchange (DSE). Total cement production amounted to a provisional 6.5m. metric tons in 2019, up from 3.1m. tons in 2015. Manufacturing GDP grew by 5.8% in 2019 (down from 8.3% in 2018).

Owing to the discovery of natural resources, strong economic growth and Tanzania's strategic business location in East Africa, the construction sector has expanded strongly in recent years, especially in the commercial capital, Dar es Salaam. It grew by 14.1% in 2019.

Power, Natural Gas and Petroleum

Tanzania's main producer and supplier of electricity is the Tanzania Electric Supply Company Ltd (TANESCO), a state-owned company supervised by the Ministry of Energy, and the Electricity and Water Utilities Regulatory Authority. There are three categories of power supply: the national grid, independent producers and isolated stations. Independent producers are private companies that sell their electricity to the national grid.

In 2019 Tanzania produced 7,616m. kWh of electric energy. Fossil fuels supplied about two-thirds of Tanzania's electricity, while hydroelectric power contributed about one-third. In addition, Tanzania imported electricity supplies from Uganda, Kenya and Zambia. Only about one-third of Tanzanians had access to electricity in the late 2010s, and rural access was particularly low. Electricity supply is a major issue for Tanzania's global competitiveness and its appeal to investors.

The country's reliance on hydroelectricity has been a problem for Tanzania, owing to its dependence on seasonal rains to feed reservoirs. Irregular rains frequently lead to electricity rationing, which adversely affects business activities.

The Government plans to expand thermal electricity generation using Tanzania's gas and coal reserves to provide a more reliable energy supply. Coal reserves are estimated at some 1,900m. metric tons, of which about 25% are proven. According to the Electricity Supply Industry Reform Strategy and Roadmap (2014–25), the Government aims to invest over US $1,150m. by 2025 to restructure and liberalize the energy sector. In particular, TANESCO will be split into three separate companies responsible for generation, transmission and distribution, in order to improve efficiency and quality. Overall, the Government plans to increase electricity capacity by 500% during 2014–25, to meet growing demand.

Hopes are high for Tanzania's gas sector. Following significant discoveries of offshore natural gas deposits since 2010, in 2017 the country's total natural gas reserves were estimated at 57,000,000m. cu ft. Apart from becoming an important generator of employment, skills transfer and revenue, the sector is also viewed as being pivotal to ending energy supply problems through the construction of gas-fired power plants. Since 2004 there has been a 214-km pipeline network connecting gasfields near Songo Songo island with the Ubungo power plant in Dar es Salaam. To expand gas-fuelled energy generation, the Government has built further processing stations and a new 532-km pipeline to connect the ports of Mtwara and Lindi with gas-fired power stations at Kinyerezi, near Dar es Salaam. The pipeline's capacity is 784m. cu ft per day, sufficient to generate 3,900 MW of electricity. The costs of about US $1,200m. were covered by a loan from the People's Republic of China's Export and Import (Exim) Bank. The Kinyerezi I power station began full production of 150 MW of electricity in March 2016. In April

2018 the Government inaugurated the $334m. Kinyerezi II plant, which had an initial generation capacity of 167.8 MW and was expected eventually to reach full capacity of 240 MW. The construction of a further two new gas-fuelled plants; Kinyerezi III (600 MW) and Kinyerezi IV (450 MW), was planned. Gas-fuelled power plant capacity was targeted to grow from 1,501 MW in 2015 to 4,915 MW in 2040. Under an initiative announced in June 2018, US companies were to invest a total of $175,000m. in gas power projects in Tanzania and eight other African countries. Construction work on the 2,115-MW hydroelectric Julius Nyerere Hydropower Station, at Stiegler's Gorge in the Morogoro Region, commenced in 2019.

The volume of Tanzania's gas reserves and the country's strategic proximity to Asia's emerging economies has attracted the attention of global oil and gas companies such as Statoil (of Norway), ExxonMobil (USA), BG Group (United Kingdom), which was acquired by Royal Dutch Shell in 2016, Ophir Energy (UK) and Halliburton (USA.) Other entrants include the Russian Federation's Gazprom, China National Offshore Oil Corpn and the Abu Dhabi state-owned investment fund Mubadala. Companies interested in operating in Tanzania's gas sector have to negotiate production-sharing agreements (PSA) with the Government; all financial charges, including profit-sharing rates, are established under these agreements. Negotiations are led by the Tanzania Petroleum Development Corporation (TPDC), the Government's representative in the gas sector and currently a hybrid between a regulatory agency and a national oil company supervised by the Ministry of Energy. In August 2016 the Government announced plans to construct a liquefied natural gas plant and export terminal at Likong'o in Lindi region, at a cost of US $30,000m. In 2017 Tanzania received a $29.8m. loan from the African Development Bank (AfDB) to develop the project, and construction of the plant was due to begin by the end of 2022.

The long-awaited Petroleum Act was approved by the National Assembly in July 2015. The new legislation aimed to mitigate the high degree of bureaucratic inefficiency and clashes between different government agents caused by over-lapping and inadequately defined areas of responsibility. The TPDC would lose all of its regulatory functions and become a fully commercially operating national oil company, with the Government as the majority stakeholder. Furthermore, the then Ministry of Energy and Minerals would take charge of PSA negotiations and a Petroleum Upstream Regulatory Authority would be created to assume the TPDC's upstream regulatory tasks.

Geological data have revealed the existence of an active petroleum system. However, to date the results of oil exploration have been disappointing, although several international companies have been active, both in on- and offshore areas. There has been considerable interest in exploring the waters off Zanzibar. Following an initial agreement in October 2012 which granted resource ownership to Zanzibar, a memorandum of understanding was signed by Royal Dutch Shell and the Zanzibari Government regarding initial activities and co-operation. As a result, the latter is also considering the foundation of its own national hydrocarbons company.

Mining and Quarrying

Despite being crucial for Tanzania's exports, mining and quarrying accounted for just 5.6% of GDP in 2019, according to provisional figures. Annual mining growth accelerated from 3.9% in 2013 to 17.5% in 2017 but slowed to just 1.5% in 2018. In 2019 it expanded by 17.7%. The importance of gold has exposed sectoral growth to the high volatility of global gold prices; for example, the mining sector expanded by 18.7% in 2009 when the global financial crisis pushed up international gold prices. Growing demand for building materials has improved the sector's prospects.

Gold remains an important export commodity, and in 2020 gold exports amounted to US $2,186m. Production of gold ores and concentrates rose from 43,293 kg in 2015 to 45,155 kg in 2016 but declined to 43,171 kg in 2017 and 39,300 kg in 2018, before reaching 48,400 kg in 2019. According to the Tanzania Minerals Audit Agency (TMAA), in 2016 a total of 98.6% of the total gold output was produced in Tanzania's five largest mines. Geita Gold Mine, operated by AngloGold Ashanti, produced 34.4%, followed by North Mara (26.6%) and Bulyanhulu (20.1%), both of which are owned by Acacia Mining. Acacia's Bulyanhulu and Buzwagi mines produce about 50,000 metric tons of gold/copper concentrate a year. All major mines are located around Lake Victoria, but there are also smaller, locally operated artisanal mines.

Other valuable minerals extracted in Tanzania include diamonds, phosphate, coal, silver, tin, gypsum, copper and bauxite, as well as various gemstones, most notably tanzanite, a gemstone found only in Tanzania. Diamond production amounted to 416,000 carats in 2019.

Coal is widely viewed as a complementary energy source to the Government's energy strategy, which is focused on natural gas. There are very large deposits of coal in the south-western regions of Mbeya and Songwe. Total coal production in Tanzania amounted to 257,300 metric tons in 2015, rising to 712,100 tons in 2019.

Stone quarrying for building materials and cement inputs, as well as industrial minerals mining are rapidly expanding, driven by Tanzania's construction sub-sector. According to the TMAA, in 2016 15.5m. metric tons of building materials and industrial minerals were produced by licensed miners and sold at a value of 230,811.9m. shillings. In 2014 salt production and sales increased by 60.9% and 124.3% year on year (to 54,757 tons and US $5.27m.), respectively, as Tanzanian salt producers entered new central African markets. Salt production reached 36,400 tons in 2018, representing a 63.6% decrease from 2017, but recovered to 99,500 tons in 2019.

In recent years large uranium deposits have been discovered, raising hopes of potentially applying nuclear technology to the country's energy mix. Two exploration projects are still under way: the Manyoni uranium project being undertaken by Magnis Resources Ltd (formerly known as Uranex) in the Manyoni district of central Tanzania, and the Mkuju River project being undertaken by Mantra Resources Ltd in south-western Tanzania.

As part of President John Pombe Magufuli's plans to tighten state control over Tanzania's mining sector, in March 2017 the Government banned the export of mineral concentrates and metallic ores, to ensure that the country would also process mined raw materials. In May Magufuli announced the findings of a recent investigation: that Acacia Mining export containers of mineral sands held as much as 15.5 metric tons of gold, rather than the 1.1 tons declared, and that the presence of other precious metals in the consignments had not been declared. In response to these findings, the President dismissed the Minister of Energy and Minerals, together with the TMAA board. By mid-2017 two government commissions had issued reports concluding that Acacia Mining, majority-owned by Barrick Gold Corporation of Canada, had over many years under-reported the percentage of gold and copper in mineral sand concentrates that it exported from Tanzania, with a potential undervaluation amounting to about 10% of the country's GDP. In July 2017 Acacia Mining received a US $190,000m. fine from the Government for unpaid taxes, penalties and interest accrued during 2000–17. This was part of a longstanding dispute between the Government and Acacia over tax evasion, breach of environmental regulations and other issues. The mining company denied any wrongdoing.

In July 2017 the National Assembly adopted three new laws which substantially changed the regulatory framework of Tanzania's extractive industry, with the stated aim of improving transparency, as well as increasing the state's share of revenue. The new legislation increased royalty taxes on both uranium and gold, allowed the Government to cancel and renegotiate existing contracts for both mining and energy companies if the terms were deemed unfavourable, and removed the right for companies operating in Tanzania to seek international arbitration. Furthermore, the Government was henceforth to hold at least a 16% equity in all mining operations and was empowered to enforce new regulations requiring mining companies to list 30% of their equity on the DSE.

Despite the new regulations, Acacia Mining reportedly served arbitration notices against the Tanzanian Government in London, UK, after operating contracts for its mines had been abandoned. At the end of July 2017, however, it was announced that the Government and majority owner Barrick Gold had begun negotiations (from which Acacia officials were excluded), in an effort to resolve the dispute.

As reported in detail in 2019, negotiations between the Government and Barrick Gold resulted in a deal being reached in October 2017 according to which: (i) the Government would receive a 16% stake in the three gold mines operated by Acacia Mining; and (ii) the company would pay US $300m. to the Government (over seven years) as a gesture of good faith. To facilitate this arrangement, a new company based in Tanzania would be formed to replace British-based Acacia Mining. According to the agreement, the 2017 ban on mineral concentrate exports that affected Acacia's subsidiaries would be lifted. (Tanzania imposed an export ban on gold and copper concentrates to curb smuggling and tax evasion.) However, in May 2019 the Government announced that it wanted to cut ties with Acacia entirely and have a deal only with Barrick; the latter proposed that it purchase the shares of Acacia's minority stakeholders in order fully to take over the company, but this was rejected. In September Barrick Gold acquired Acacia Mining in a deal worth $1,200m., and in October Barrick Gold agreed to pay the Tanzanian Government $300m. to end the dispute. Furthermore, Barrick agreed to share the future economic benefits from the mines equally. The Tanzanian state was to receive a 16% stake in each of the Bulyanhulu, North Mara and Buzwagi mines, to be managed by a new operating company, called Twiga Minerals; in addition, a ban on concentrate exports was lifted.

The Government is advancing efforts towards the construction of a smelter to boost the benefits accruing to Tanzania from its natural resources. According to reports, the Government has issued a licence to several Chinese companies to build the smelter. However, to operate the smelter sufficient concentrates are needed, which makes the lifting of the export ban contested.

The Financial Sector

In 2019 there were 39 commercial banks, six community banks, five microfinance banks, two development financial institutions and three financial leasing companies operating in Tanzania's financial sector, according to the Bank of Tanzania (BoT).

The financial sector has grown rapidly in recent years, with an average annual growth rate of 10.2% in 2010–15. Banks drive growth and dominate the financial sector, holding 70% of the sector's total assets as of March 2017, according to the BoT. With shares of about 50%, commercial banks have also been the largest holders of domestic government debt. The financial sector's contribution to GDP has nevertheless remained low, amounting to just 3.8% of total GDP in 2019.

The level of financial development has been subdued, and uncertainty and low profitability are persistent problems. Despite two credit reference bureaus already operating, their databases covered less than 1% of adults in 2014. The high geographical dispersion of Tanzania's population is a further factor constraining banks' ability to expand their services profitably. Only about 30% of Tanzanians lived within 5 km of an access point to formal finance in 2012. Rapidly growing mobile money services have, however, significantly expanded the population share, with access to payment services reaching 56% in 2013, from 13% in 2009. Vodacom Tanzania launched the M-Pesa mobile money service in 2008. Several other mobile network operators subsequently introduced micro-lending services using a mobile platform: Airtel Tanzania set up the Timiza service in 2015 and Tigo Tanzania introduced the Tigo Nivushe service in 2016. The value of mobile money transactions was equal to 52% of GDP in 2015. Access to loans and other more sophisticated financial products is also improving; in 2014 Vodacom Tanzania and the Commercial Bank of Africa introduced a service to M-Pesa customers to open mobile savings accounts, earn interest and take out micro-loans.

The quality of the banking sector's assets has improved, as reflected by the ratio of non-performing loans (NPLs) to gross loans, which declined to 10.2% at the end of June 2018, compared with 10.6% at the end of 2016/17. Improvement in the ratio of NPLs is partly explained by the BoT's directives to banks with a high NPL ratio to formulate and implement strategies to lower the ratio to a maximum of 5.0%. The measures include: improvement of credit issuance; management and recovery of loans; and mandatory usage of credit reference bureau reports during the loan appraisal process. In January 2018 the BoT revoked the banking business licences of five undercapitalized banks that had failed to raise capital to conform to the legal minimum requirement after the five-year moratorium lapsed.

Domestic credit issued by the Tanzanian banking sector (loans extended to the central government and the private sector) grew by 3.5% in the year ending May 2020. The sectoral breakdown of credit indicated the rapid growth of loans extended to building, construction, transport, communications and private consumption-related economic activities (mostly small and medium-sized enterprises—SME). The profile of loans outstanding indicates that much of the credit was extended to private consumption-related activities, trade and manufacturing, of which the loans outstanding as a share of the total were 31.7%, 17.3% and 11.5%, respectively.

A stock exchange has been operating in Dar es Salaam since 2008. In September 2019 a total of 27 companies were listed on the DSE. The exchange also lists international companies operating in Tanzania; the number of such firms listing is rising, as the Government intends to make listing at the DSE a requirement for all foreign oil and gas companies operating in Tanzania. In June 2015 the DSE self-listed and became a public limited company.

Between January 2019 and January 2020 the Tanzanian shilling depreciated by 0.7% against the US dollar and by 2.2% against the Kenyan shilling, but it appreciated by 1.1% against the Chinese yuan and by 2.1% against the euro. This low level of volatility was in part the result of interventions by the BoT in the foreign exchange market; to keep the shilling stable the BoT has taken measures to minimize fluctuations and to keep the interbank foreign exchange market orderly.

Money supply expanded by 9.6% in December 2019 (up from 4.5% in December 2018), owing to credit to the private sector increasing (to 11.1% compared with 4.9% in 2018), with loans to the agriculture, construction and transportation sectors markedly higher, and also to the monetary policy pursued by the BoT. Lending to SMEs was restricted, owing to especially risky premiums in the context of a high level of NPLs, which in February 2020 stood at 10%—far above the BoT's target of less than 5%. The commercial lending rate stood at 16.8% in December 2019. The Government's clearance of about 1,000,000m. shillings in verified payment arrears in 2020/21 in April 2020, together with other measures, was intended to address the NPL issue.

In the first half of 2019/20 the budget deficit stood at 0.4% of GDP, in line with the Government's target of 0.5% for the period. Tax revenue fell only about 4% short of target (compared with more than 10% in previous years) in the first half of 2019/20, although non-tax revenue fell well short of budget projections. Domestic revenue stood at 7.0% of GDP (compared with 6.9% in the first half of 2018/19). Spending pressure was heightened in advance of the general election in October 2020. In the first half of 2019/20 public spending was much higher than in the first half of the previous fiscal year, largely because more funding was allocated to capital projects. Development spending in the first half of 2019/20 amounted to 3.3% of GDP; much of it was allocated to large infrastructure projects in the transport and energy sectors, including roads, standard gauge railways and the Julius Nyerere Hydropower Station project. The Government financed the budget deficit mainly through external borrowing and used some of this funding to expedite planned repayments to domestic creditors. Commercial financing of the budget, which stood at just 4% in 2010/11, reached 25% in December 2019. In 2019/20 debt servicing was expected to consume 40% of domestic revenues. In November 2017 the Government conducted an annual debt sustainability analysis, which indicated that all indicators of the stock of debt were below the recommended thresholds; the Government thus maintained that Tanzania's debt level outlook in the short, medium and long term is sustainable.

Information and Communications Technology (ICT)

During 2010–15 ICT was the fastest-growing sector, with an average annual growth rate of 14.7%, according to the *National Plan for Development 2016/2017*. Mobile telephony and internet services are the drivers of the ICT sector, with 47.7m. mobile subscriptions in the country by 2019, while the number of fixed-line subscriptions steadily declined. The rate of increase in mobile telephone subscriptions slowed in the late 2010s as markets for standard services reached saturation. Yet only about 25% of Tanzanians are currently internet users, and therefore there exists huge potential for further expansion.

The ICT sector is dominated by four major companies, Vodacom Tanzania (a subsidiary of Vodacom South Africa), Airtel Tanzania (a subsidiary of Bharti Airtel), MIC Tanzania Ltd—Tigo (owned by Millicom International Cellular of Luxembourg) and Zantel (owned by Etisalat of the United Arab Emirates—UAE).

In 2008 Tanzania's larger mobile telephone companies began moving into financial service provision when Vodacom introduced its M-Pesa mobile payment service. Several other companies subsequently followed suit, and the number of active mobile money accounts had grown to 10.7m. by 2015. Airtel introduced its Timiza financial service in 2015, and in March 2016 Tigo introduced its new service, Tigo Nivushe, offering loans that required no collateral and averaged US $5. In 2017 Vodacom had 54% of the mobile money market share in Tanzania, while Tigo had 29% and Airtel 13%. In 2015 there were over 69,000 official mobile money agents and other third parties offering mobile money services. In comparison, there were only 1,094 automated teller machines. Providers have now also moved on to offering cross-border mobile money transfers and even currency exchange services such as Tigo's services between Tanzania and Rwanda, and M-Pesa's links with Safaricom in Kenya; about 500,000 Kenyans in Tanzania send remittances home. Mobile money services are instrumental in extending financial services to remote populations. Since February 2016 the four main mobile financial service providers in Tanzania have been interoperable, enabling users to perform person-to-person payments between accounts operated by different service providers, albeit with some limitations.

The output of the ICT sector, which has grown by an annual average of 13% since 2010, can play a key role in driving the recovery and future growth of the post-COVID-19 pandemic economy.

Tourism

Tanzania is a leading tourist destination for wildlife watching (with 28% of its vast area protected), beaches, water sports and marine wildlife sites. Kilimanjaro, Serengeti and Zanzibar continue to be the main attractions, but the Tanzania Tourist Board has also aimed to encourage more people to visit the country's cultural and historical heritage sites such as the ancient ruins of Kilwa Kisiwani and Songo Mnara. Tourism continues to be Tanzania's leading service export. The sector has attracted new private investment in infrastructure and brought in US $247m. of FDI inflows (about one-quarter of the total) in 2017. Exports of tourism services are considerably higher than in other member states of the East African Community (EAC). Between 2014 and 2018 the number of non-African tourist arrivals increased by 31.1%. In 2019 Tanzania attracted more than 1.5m. visitors (compared with 1.1m. in 2015); tourism revenue totalled $2,605m. in that year. The main visitor origin countries were Kenya, the USA and the UK.

In order fully to utilize its tourism potential, Tanzania will have to invest in improving its infrastructure (such as safe roads) and tourism facilities, as well as the quality of service. The Government is also trying to improve employment opportunities through the National College of Tourism. In mid-2018 the Government announced further initiatives designed to stimulate the tourism sector, including the planned establishment of a beach management authority.

Transport

The transport and communications sector contributed 9.1% of GDP in 2019 and is the country's second largest source of service receipts after tourism. Transport plays a crucial part in the Government's plans to make Tanzania East Africa's logistics hub, thus tapping into the highly lucrative business of functioning as its landlocked neighbours' gateway to global trade. Tanzania has an 86,472-km road network, a 3,676-km railway network, 58 airports and three ocean ports.

Road transportation is currently the dominant mode of transport, accounting for an estimated 90% of all passenger and about 75% of all freight traffic. The road network remains in dire need of repairs and investment, hence its prioritization in the Tanzania Development Vision 2025; however, significant progress has been made. Commuting times in Dar es Salaam improved significantly in 2016 with the opening of the World Bank-funded Bus Rapid Transit service, which aims to alleviate congestion in the city with high-capacity, environmentally friendly buses, and the opening of the Chinese-funded US $140m. Kigamboni Bridge. In addition, a 251-km road between the administrative capital, Dodoma, and north-central Babati, which was co-funded by the AfDB, was inaugurated in April 2018, as part of a Trans-Africa Highway to link Cape Town in South Africa to Cairo in Egypt.

Rail transport is the second most important mode of transport. The network is run by two companies, the Tanzania-Zambia Railway Authority (Tazara) and the Tanzania Railways Corpn (TRC). Tazara operates a 1,869-km Chinese-built line linking Dar es Salaam with copper mining regions in Zambia. TRC operates the central and northern lines, with a total length of about 2,600 km linking Dar es Salaam with urban centres in central and northern Tanzania.

Overall, both railway companies have seen passenger and cargo numbers dwindle. Nevertheless, the Government views the railways as the cargo transportation of the future. Accordingly, in 2015 the Government announced plans to invest US $14,200m. in modernizing and extending the rail network over the next five years. As part of these plans, the construction of a 521-km line connecting the town of Isaka in Tanzania to the Rwandan capital, Kigali, was envisaged. The first phase, consisting of a 205-km standard gauge railway (SGR) line from Dar es Salaam to Morogoro, in central Tanzania, officially began in May 2017 and was completed by Turkish firm Yapi Merkezi and Portuguese firm Mota-Engil Africa in April 2020. In January 2018 President Magufuli and his Rwandan counterpart agreed jointly to fund an Isaka–Rusumo (Rwanda) section, with construction scheduled to begin in December (although by mid-2021 construction work had not yet commenced on the Tanzania side). The Government subsequently sought funding from South Africa and the World Bank for the project, which was projected to cost some $2,500m.

Strategically, the most important location for Tanzania's logistics ambitions is Dar es Salaam port. The port accounted for 92% of all Tanzanian naval cargo traffic in 2015. The port handled 16.4m. metric tons of goods in 2019, compared with 10.4m. tons in 2011. The authorities aimed to raise the port's capacity to 28m. tons a year by 2025. Demand to use Dar es Salaam port for transit goods is also growing. Despite investment in increasing handling capacity and speed, the rapid growth of cargo volume has led to long waiting times. Average container and conventional cargo waiting times are about four and six days, respectively, while international standards are about three days.

Aviation is the major means of transportation for tourism. In 2015 Tanzania had 58 airports and more than 300 private airstrips, owned by mining companies and tour operators, and 21 airlines were in operation. In that year Julius Nyerere International Airport in Dar es Salaam accounted for about 70% of Tanzania's air passengers; other major airports are located in Zanzibar, Mwanza and Kilimanjaro. Dar es Salaam and Kilimanjaro airports have been operated by Swissport since 2005. The Government attempted to attract further business through completion of a new cargo facility at Julius Nyerere International Airport in mid-2016. Domestic demand for air transport has also been growing since the expansion of flight routes and the entry onto the market of Fastjet, Africa's first low-cost airline. Fastjet expanded from two domestic routes in 2012 to 11 destinations in six African countries in 2016. Consequently, the Government is currently increasing capacity at regional airports in Tabora, Arusha and Bukoba.

Public Finances

Tanzania benefited from large-scale debt-forgiveness programmes under the Heavily Indebted Poor Countries initiative in 2001 and 2006. In 2006 lenders forgave US $3,800m. worth of loans, reducing the country's external debt from $8,400m. (59% of GDP) in 2005 to $4,100m. (29% of GDP) in 2006. Nevertheless, total debt has since risen rapidly. At the end of May 2020 external debt amounted to $22,503.2m., representing a decrease of $54.4m. from the end of April but an increase of $867.1m. year on year. Recent inflows of debt are lower than historical averages, and external concessional borrowing is below the average of the past five years. Much of the external debt stock was central government at 78.2%. The profile of external debt by creditor remained dominated by multilateral institutions, which normally provide concessional loans, followed by commercial debt. In terms of the use of funds, much of the debt contracted was allocated to transport and telecommunication activity, which accounted for 26.6% of the total, followed by social welfare and education (17.7%). The domestic debt stock was 15,069,700m. shillings at the end of May 2020—an increase of 216,500m. shillings compared with the end of April and a decrease of 443,600m. shillings year on year. The profile of domestic debt by creditor category remained largely unchanged, dominated by commercial banks with a share of 38.1% of the debt, followed by pension funds (29.4%).

Initial plans by the Government to issue its first Eurobond in the 2012/13 financial year were abandoned owing to the negative impact of the global financial crisis, and the launch was subsequently delayed several times as the Government sought to obtain a sovereign credit rating. In May 2017 the Government initiated a further process to issue a Eurobond of US $700m. However, in March 2018 ratings agency Moody's issued Tanzania's first international credit rating, of B1 with a negative outlook (on grounds of the issues affecting investment in the country).

In recent years the Government has invested substantially in public infrastructure, education and water projects, with a continued focus on industrialization of the economy. The Government pursued a policy of tax reforms designed to strengthen domestic revenue collection and also ease strains on SMEs. In July 2018 it was announced that the Trade and Development Bank of the Common Market for Eastern and Southern Africa was to provide US $660m. in financing to boost Tanzania's economic growth.

The overall inflation rate was contained at an average of averaged 7.2% in 2010-19, this being primarily attributed to improved availability of food and stable energy prices. Inflation in 2019 was low and stable, standing at 3.8% at the end of the year—well below the target of 5%, the lowest rate since 2000 and one of the lowest rates among members of the EAC.

International Trade and External Balances

A treaty for the re-establishment of the EAC, which was dissolved in 1977, providing for the creation of a free trade area, was formally ratified by Tanzania, Kenya and Uganda in November 1999. In March 2004 the Presidents of the three countries signed a protocol on the creation of a customs union (eliminating most duties on goods within the EAC), which entered effect on 1 January 2005. The EAC was expanded to include Rwanda and Burundi in 2007. A common market protocol, allowing the free movement of goods, services, people and capital within the EAC came into force in July 2010. Despite major differences between Tanzania and the other EAC members about the speed and nature of the organization's integration efforts, in November 2013 the EAC heads of state signed a monetary union protocol, which was to enter effect within a decade, with the final phase being the introduction of a single currency for the bloc. In mid-2014 Tanzania and Burundi joined an incipient EAC Single Customs Territory, which had been initiated by Kenya, Rwanda and Uganda in late 2013. South Sudan acceded to the EAC in April 2016. None the less, in 2017 a trade dispute between Tanzania and Kenya, in which both parties imposed bans on several the other's import commodities, resulted in a sharp reduction in the volume of bilateral trade.

In 2019 Tanzania's total exports grew by 15.7%, driven by higher sales of gold, manufactured goods and tourism. The value of exports reached almost US $6,000m., after a period of export stagnation since 2013. Revenue was driven by exports of cashew nuts, cotton, cloves and sisal. In the 12-month period ending May 2020 exports of gold rose by nearly 50% to $2,522.1m., owing to an increase in both output and international prices, and accounted for about 55% of non-traditional exports. The price of gold in the global market remained high as investors sought a safe-haven asset amid financial market volatility as a result of the outbreak of the COVID-19 pandemic.

Higher exports helped to reduce the current account deficit from 3.8% of GDP in 2018 to 3.0% in 2019. Imports rose more slowly (by 7.7%); the growth in imports of intermediate goods was the highest, owing especially to an increase in the oil import bill (38.3%) and capital goods (6.6%). The principal imports are mineral fuels (mainly petroleum), machinery and electrical equipment, vehicles and chemical products. The current account deficit was funded mostly by external borrowing. Tanzania has traditionally recorded substantial current account deficits (including a recent high of 10.7% of GDP in 2013/14), as imports have generally far exceeded exports.

In December 2019 Tanzania's official gross reserves stood at US $5,600m., covering 6.4 months of imports of goods and services and thus above the Government's target of 4 months' coverage, as well as those of the EAC and of the Southern African Development Community (SADC), of 4.5 and 6 months, respectively.

Further Developments under the Magufuli Government

There was friction between the Government and some international donors over their assessment of Tanzania's economic development. For example, in April 2019 the Government reportedly blocked from publication an International Monetary Fund (IMF) report that was critical of certain new economic policies and initiatives, and included growth projections that were lower than the Government's (4%–5% against 7%). The World Bank has also expressed concerns regarding, *inter alia*, the implementation of public development projects, new laws regarding mining and public-private partnerships, extended government control over the economy, levels of domestic revenue, the current account deficit, falling reserves and the Government's outstanding arrears (to suppliers, contractors and pension funds, etc.).

THE COVID-19 PANDEMIC AND THE ECONOMY SINCE 2020

In 2020, despite the economic disruption caused by the COVID-19 pandemic, GDP growth of 4.8% was achieved. This was a very strong performance by regional and international standards. Although the construction and manufacturing sectors registered growth in that year, there was a decline in tourism activity and foreign investment, and private consumption rates were subdued. In June, to alleviate the impact of the COVID-19 crisis, the IMF granted Tanzania US $14m. of emergency debt relief under the Catastrophe Containment and Relief Trust, while the African Development Bank authorized the disbursement of $51m. of financial assistance in October.

According to the Government, Tanzania recorded GDP growth of 4.9% in 2021. The main drivers of growth were: infrastructure investments (particularly in energy, water, health care, education, roads, railways and airports), minerals production (chiefly gas and coal) and credit provision to the private sector. The highest levels of growth year on year were recorded in the sectors of arts and entertainment (19.4%), electricity (10%), mining and quarrying (9.6%) and information and communication (9.1%). The revival of tourist activity spurred particular growth in sectors that had been hit hard by the pandemic in the previous year, namely accommodation, food and the arts and entertainment, although the last constitutes only a small share (0.3%) of total GDP. The leading GDP contributors in 2021 were agriculture (26.1%), construction (13.8%), trade (8.7%), manufacturing (7.8%) and transport (7.1%).

In 2021/22 headline inflation averaged 4%, an increase from 3.3% in the previous fiscal year. Inflation in Tanzania has picked up since early 2022, owing primarily to the effects of the Russian Federation's invasion of Ukraine on supplies of fuel and food globally. It stood at 4.4% year on year in June. Food inflation increased in 2021/22 an average of 5.9%, from 4.7% in 2020/21, owing to a surge in prices for staple goods, especially maize grain and flour, wheat flour, sweet potatoes, fresh cassava and rice. Core inflation fell to 3.4% year on year in June 2022 (from 4.0% year on year in June 2021). This was due to lower prices for accommodation, recreation, sports and culture, garments and information and communication.

The current account recorded a deficit US $3,766.9m. in 2021/22, a significant rise from the $1,789.5m. shortfall recorded in 2020/21. A rise in the import bill drove this trend. However, the overall balance of payments recorded a surplus of $75.6m. (owing to higher receipts of loans and grants). The balance of payments had recorded a deficit of $132.7m. in 2020/21.

Tanzania recorded growth in the export of goods and services from US $8,848.4m. in 2020/21 to $11,098.6m. in 2021/22. Non-traditional exports experienced very high growth over that period (27.6%). Growth was pronounced in manufactured goods (particularly iron and steel), textiles, horticultural products, fish and fish products and cereals (notably maize and rice). Cashew nuts and cloves were also in high demand in external market. Imports amounted to $14,135m. in 2021/22, up from $9,841.4m. in 2021/21. Imports of petroleum, iron, steel and plastic products all rose significantly. The war in Ukraine has led to higher prices of petroleum, edible oil, wheat grain and fertilizers.

The Tanzanian Government is currently operating under the third FYDP (covering the period 2021/22–2025/26), under which the Development Vision 2025 will be implemented. The latest FYDP, based on the theme of 'realising competitiveness and industrialisation for human development', aims to increase productivity and efficiency in manufacturing, making use of Tanzania's abundant land resources. By late 2022 construction of the Central Corridor SGR for major routes was near completion, including the Dar es Salaam–Morogoro section (some 300 km) and the Morogoro–Makutupora section (422 km). Furthermore, the Government has signed contracts for the construction of more than 1,000 km of new railway lines across the country (including a line that links the country to the DRC), worth over US $4,000m. The Government's focus is on industrialization, particularly in sectors that add value to crops, livestock and fisheries products. For this purpose, the Government plans to invest in irrigation and crop storage infrastructure; research centres and extension services; value-addition activities regarding crops, livestock, fish and fisheries products; the improvement of artificial insemination services for livestock; and the construction of modern abattoirs and livestock markets. Furthermore, it is seeking to invest in the value-addition of minerals and to promote the development and growth of sectors including tourism, financial and insurance services and pharmaceuticals and medical equipment. The country's dairy processing sector has expanded from 99 businesses in 2020/21 to 105 in 2021/22, and output of dairy goods increased from 75.9m. litres to 77.6m. during that period.

Tanzania's foreign reserves as at 30 June 2022 stood at US $5,110.3m. (or 4.6 months' worth of imports of goods and services). This level was above the EAC's convergence criteria (of at least 4.5 months). Credit to the private sector increased by 9.9% in 2021/22. This is a significant expansion from 4.3% in 2020/21. The average policy interest rate of the BoT was at 16.4% in 2021/22, a small decrease from the previous fiscal year, owing to the accommodative monetary policy of the Government. The exchange rate remained broadly stable in 2021/22, at an average of 2,298 shillings = US $1. This can be attributed to a modest and manageable current account deficit and low inflation, as well as prudent fiscal and monetary policies. As at March 2022 non-performing loans as a proportion of total loans stood at 8.1%, which was higher than the BoT's recommended upper limit. The Government attributed this to lending practices by banks that in some cases do not comply with regulations and are the result of poor practice on the part of some bankers.

The Government collected domestic revenue of 24,395,800m. shillings in 2021/22. This constituted a an increase of 18.6% from 2020/21. It received 708,500m. shillings in grants (a combination of budget support, basket funds and especially project grants). Government expenditure in 2021/22 amounted to 36,292,100m. shillings, of which 62% was allocated to recurrent activities and the remainder to development projects, including work on the SGR, the Julius Nyerere Hydropower Station and support for Air Tanzania (all domestically financed). Only 55.4% of the foreign development budget was disbursed, owing to donors not fulfilling commitments and/or implementation delays in a number of projects. The Government also used substantial resources (772,870m. shillings) to pay domestic arrears. Financing for 2021/22 amounted to 5,960,300m. shillings (of which net foreign financing comprised 52%). The Government's stock of debt stock stood at 71,559,020m. shillings as at 30 June 2022, constituting a 11.3% increase from 30 June 2021. A total of 33.6% of the stock was domestic debt. External debt was acquired mostly on concessional terms: 61% of came from multilateral creditors, followed by commercial banks and export credit agencies, as well as bilateral creditors. The Government conducted a debt sustainability analysis in November 2021, concluding that the country's debt remained sustainable in foreseeable future. The debt to GDP ratio stood at 31% in 2021/22 and was expected to rise to 33% in 2021/32 respectively (against a threshold of 70%). By late 2022 the Government was in the final stage of negotiations concerning concessional loans—with the World Bank (for US $500m.) and with the IMF (for $1,100m. for the period 2022–25). The funding is expected to be allocated to increasing industrial production, improving business and investment conditions and strengthening support to sectors of the economy that have been negatively affected by the Ukraine war, as well as social services.

The Government has reduced levies that affect the price of petroleum products and allocated 100,000m. shillings to fund subsidies to offset the effects of rising fuel prices. It plans to establish a Fuel Price Stabilization Fund in the near future and focus on the establishment of a National Strategic Petroleum Reserve and Single Receiving Terminal. It also intends to prioritize an increase in the production of edible oils by investing in the sunflower cultivation segment and the production of pre-geminated palm seeds. The Government is aiming to subsidize agricultural input, including fertilizers, farming equipment, pesticides, high-quality seeds, as well as enhancing irrigation of farmland and giving preference to the local fertilizer industry. For respective locally used and locally produced products, such as fertilizers and edible oil, it has set the rate of VAT at 0%.

OUTLOOK

In its budget for 2022/23 budget the Government has focused on five priority areas: agriculture, livestock, fishing, energy and developing the business and investment environment. The real GDP growth rate is projected to be 4.7% in 2022 and 5.3% in 2023. The Government aims to keep inflation between 3% and 7% in the medium term and to achieve domestic revenue collection of 14.9% of GDP in 2022/23 (with tax revenue collection at 11.7% of GDP). It wants increasingly to use ICT to estimate the tax liabilities of SMEs that might have problems in keeping records and preparing reliable accounts. The use of modern technology is expected to help to collect taxes. Notably, the Government plans to put in place price ceilings for goods and services that it purchases (via the Tanzania National e-Procurement System) in order to contain rising prices of certain government transactions. In 2022/23 the Government plans to spend 41,480,000m. shillings (63.8% of which will be recurrent expenditure), with 5,700,000m. shillings allocated to education, 2,100,000m. shillings to health care, 9,100,000m. shillings to servicing debt, 1,200,000m. shillings to agriculture (notably irrigation, fertilizer subsidies and the construction of fisheries facilities), 1,400,000m. shillings to railway projects and 83,300m. shillings to mining. Government expenditure will be funded by domestic revenue (67.5% of the total), external grants and concessional loans (11.2%) and domestic and external non-concessional loans (21%).

The Government aims to increase the value of exports of agricultural produce from about US $1,200m. per year currently to more than $5,000m. by 2030, with sales of horticulture produce alone projected to increase from some $750m. per year today to $2,000m. per year by 2030. Irrigation is central to this ambition: the Government plans to increase the area of irrigated land to some 8.5m. ha, equivalent to 50% of the total area cultivated in the country by 2030. This is being done via the construction of dams to harvest rainwater and the maximum use of available sources of water. The number of large-scale commercial farms is expected to increase from just 110 in 2020 to some 10,000 in 2030, with a focus on commercializing the cultivation of palms and sunflowers for oil.

CONCLUSION

Tanzania has enjoyed relative stability and favourable economic prospects in recent years, with very strong GDP growth and impressive performances in the tourism and construction sectors. The country's natural gas reserves offer great opportunities to attract significant foreign investment, and also to bring an end to an unreliable and inadequate energy supply. Furthermore, agriculture could become a driving force for poverty alleviation and industrial development. Following his inauguration as President in October 2015, Magufuli effected many high-profile corruption-related dismissals in the government administration, but the radical nature of his actions to combat malpractice became a source of concern. During 2017 the President's wide-ranging anti-corruption measures focused on the mining sector (see *Mining and Quarrying*), resulting in a dispute with one of the largest international gold mining companies operating in Tanzania, Acacia Mining, although the dispute was finally resolved in late 2019. In 2018 and 2019 GDP growth remained at a high level, and the country began to benefit from a recovery in the international prices of gold and other export commodities. The effect of the COVID-19 pandemic on the economy was a setback for the country, with tourism particularly adversely affected, but by late 2022 Tanzania was on a strong recovery path with a rebound in growth in several sectors, continued infrastructure development and strong gold exports. There has also been a slight change in the economic policy mix under the new President, Samia Suluhu Hassan, who took office after the death of Magufuli in March 2021. She has recalibrated some of the foreign economic relations of the country—notably in May she signed a preliminary agreement with her Kenyan counterpart, Uhuru Kenyatta, for the construction of an ambitious gas pipeline costing US $1,100m. between Dar es Salaam and Mombasa, Kenya—and by late 2022 the economic outlook for the country looked to be broadly positive.

Statistical Survey

Sources (unless otherwise stated): Economic and Research Policy Dept, Bank of Tanzania, POB 2939, Dar es Salaam; tel. (22) 2233328; e-mail info@bot.go.tz; internet www.bot.go.tz; National Bureau of Statistics, POB 796, Dar es Salaam; tel. (22) 2122722; e-mail dg@nbs.go.tz; internet www.nbs.go.tz.

Area and Population

AREA, POPULATION AND DENSITY

Area (sq km)	
Land	884,000*
Inland water	61,500
Total	945,500†
Population (census results)	
25 August 2002	34,443,603
26 August 2012	
Males	21,869,990
Females	23,058,933
Total	44,928,923‡
Population (UN estimates at mid-year)§	
2020	59,734,213
2021¶	61,498,438
2022¶	63,298,542
Density (per sq km) at mid-2022¶	71.6‖

* Of this total, Tanganyika (mainland) is 881,300 sq km (340,182 sq miles), and Zanzibar 2,700 sq km (1,042 sq miles).
† 364,963 sq miles.
‡ Tanganyika (mainland) 43,625,354, Zanzibar 1,303,569.
§ Source: UN, *World Population Prospects: The 2019 Revision*.
‖ Land area only.
¶ Projection.

POPULATION BY AGE AND SEX
('000, UN projections at mid-2022)

	Males	Females	Total
0–14 years	13,759.0	13,453.5	27,212.5
15–64 years	17,152.1	17,224.8	34,376.9
65 years and over	732.5	976.6	1,709.1
Total	**31,643.7**	**31,654.8**	**63,298.5**

Note: Totals may not be equal to the sum of components, owing to rounding.

Source: UN, *World Population Prospects: The 2019 Revision*.

REGIONS
(population at 2019, official projections)

	Area ('000 sq km)*	Population	Density (per sq km)
Arusha	37.6	2,051,852	54.6
Dar es Salaam	1.4	5,275,315	3,768.1
Dodoma	41.3	2,568,514	62.2
Geita	20.1	2,335,134	116.2
Iringa	35.5	1,122,131	31.6
Kagera	25.3	3,127,908	123.6
Katavi	45.8	771,287	16.8
Kigoma	37.0	2,706,831	73.2
Kilimanjaro	13.3	1,906,978	143.4
Lindi	66.0	1,004,439	15.2
Manyara	44.5	1,810,929	40.7
Mara	21.8	2,298,317	105.4
Mbeya	37.7	2,136,614	56.7
Morogoro	70.6	2,662,468	37.7
Mtwara	16.7	1,451,078	86.9
Mwanza	9.5	3,676,300	387.0
Njombe	21.3	820,355	38.5
Pwani	32.5	1,295,267	39.9
North Pemba†	0.6	282,716	471.2
North Unguja†	0.5	227,317	454.6
Rukwa	22.8	1,231,959	54.0
Ruvuma	63.7	1,616,991	25.4
Shinyanga	18.9	1,933,768	102.3
Simiyu	25.2	2,196,449	87.2
Singida	49.3	1,658,086	33.6
Songwe	22.6	1,239,970	54.9
South Pemba†	0.3	261,853	872.8
South Unguja†	0.9	136,235	151.4
Urban West†	0.2	717,468	3,587.3
Tabora	76.2	2,974,427	39.0
Tanga	26.7	2,391,791	89.6
Total	**885.8**	**55,890,747**	**63.1**

* Land area only, at 2019 (total was revised to 884.0 in 2021), excluding inland water.
† Part of the autonomous territory of Zanzibar.

PRINCIPAL TOWNS
(population at 2012 census)

Dar es Salaam*	4,364,541	Zanzibar	. . .	223,033
Mwanza	706,453	Sumbawanga	. .	209,793
Arusha	416,442	Songea		203,309
Dodoma (capital)* .	410,956	Moshi		184,292
Shinyanga . . .	403,599	Iringa		151,345
Mbeya	385,279	Singida		150,379
Morogoro . . .	315,866	Musoma		134,327
Tanga	273,332	Bukoba		128,796
Tabora	226,999	Mtwara		108,299

* Although Dodoma is officially the administrative capital, Dar es Salaam is still considered the commercial capital, and a number of government offices remain there.

Mid-2018 ('000, incl. suburbs, UN estimates): Dar es Salaam 6,048; Mwanza 1,003; Zanzibar 650; Mbeya 516; Arusha 473; Morogoro 381; Dodoma (capital) 262 (Source: UN, *World Urbanization Prospects: The 2018 Revision*).

BIRTHS AND DEATHS
(annual averages, UN estimates)

	2005–10	2010–15	2015–20
Birth rate (per 1,000)	41.3	38.9	36.9
Death rate (per 1,000)	10.4	8.1	6.5

Source: UN, *World Population Prospects: The 2019 Revision*.

Life expectancy (years at birth, estimates): 65.8 (males 64.0; females 67.6) in 2020 (Source: World Bank, World Development Indicators database.).

ECONOMICALLY ACTIVE POPULATION
(labour force survey, '000 persons aged 15 years and over, 2014)

	Males	Females	Total
Agriculture, hunting, forestry and fishing	6,485.8	6,913.2	13,399.0
Mining and quarrying . . .	173.9	44.1	218.0
Manufacturing	366.3	252.6	618.8
Electricity, gas and water supply .	27.1	5.9	33.0
Construction	408.7	13.7	422.4
Wholesale and retail trade . .	1,263.1	1,271.1	2,534.2
Hotels and restaurants . . .	143.7	645.7	789.4
Transport, storage and communications	526.4	26.0	552.4
Financial intermediation . .	27.4	33.2	60.6
Real estate, renting and business activities	134.6	35.1	169.7
Public administration and defence; compulsory social security . .	153.3	38.6	192.0
Education	209.3	204.4	413.7
Health and social work . . .	71.8	95.4	167.2
Community, social and personal services	117.7	111.6	229.3
Households with employed persons	32.6	196.1	228.7
Activities of extraterritorial organizations	1.7	—	1.7
Total employed	10,143.4	9,886.7	20,030.1
Unemployed	903.0	1,388.7	2,291.7
Total labour force	11,046.4	11,275.4	22,321.8

2020 ('000 persons aged 15 years and over): Agriculture 16,376.9; Manufacturing 1,111.6; Construction 598.9; Mining and utilities 276.3; Trade, transportation, accommodation and food, and business and administrative services 5,055.9; Public administration, community, social and other services and activities 1,471.6; Activities not adequately specified 127.6; *Total employed* 25,018.7; Unemployed 715.6; *Total labour force* 25,734.3 (males 12,995.3, females 12,739.0) (Source: ILO).

Health and Welfare

KEY INDICATORS

Total fertility rate (children per woman, 2020) . . .	4.8
Under-5 mortality rate (per 1,000 live births, 2020) . . .	48.9
HIV/AIDS (% of persons aged 15–49, 2020)	4.7
COVID-19: Cumulative confirmed deaths (per 100,000 persons at 31 August 2022)	1.3
COVID-19: Fully vaccinated population (% of total population at 28 August 2022)	27.3
Physicians (per 1,000 head, 2018)	0.05
Hospital beds (per 1,000 head, 2010)	0.7
Domestic health expenditure (2019): US $ per head (PPP) .	40.6
Domestic health expenditure (2019): % of GDP	1.6
Domestic health expenditure (2019): public (% of total current expenditure)	40.9
Access to improved water resources (% of persons, 2020) .	61
Access to improved sanitation facilities (% of persons, 2020).	32
Total carbon dioxide emissions ('000 metric tons, 2018) . .	11,580
Carbon dioxide emissions per head (metric tons, 2018) . .	0.2
Human Development Index (2021): ranking	160
Human Development Index (2021): value	0.549

Note: For data on COVID-19 vaccinations, 'fully vaccinated' denotes receipt of all doses specified by approved vaccination regime (Sources: Johns Hopkins University and Our World in Data). Data on health expenditure refer to current general government expenditure in each case. For more information on sources and further definitions for all indicators, see Health and Welfare Statistics: Sources and Definitions section (europaworld.com/credits).

Agriculture

PRINCIPAL CROPS
('000 metric tons)

	2018	2019	2020
Bananas	3,395.5	3,406.9	3,419.4*
Beans, dry	1,096.9	1,197.5	1,267.7*
Cabbages and other brassicas* .	84.0	86.0	84.0
Cashew nuts, with shell . . .	313.8	225.1	232.7
Cassava (Manioc)	8,372.2	8,184.1	7,549.9*
Chick peas	66.8	42.2	47.1*
Chillies and peppers, green* . .	15.4	15.2	15.3
Cloves*	8.6	8.5	8.6
Cocoa beans†	15.0	7.0	7.0
Coconuts	436.8†	419.9*	382.2*
Coffee, green	45.3	68.1	60.7
Cow peas, dry	121.8	127.9	139.6*
Garlic*	6.0	6.2	6.3
Groundnuts, with shell† . . .	670.0	680.0	690.0
Maize	6,273.2	5,652.0	6,711.0
Maize, green*	51.7	51.0	51.2
Mangoes, mangosteens and guavas*	436.4	439.4	437.7
Millet	316.2	386.0	325.0†
Oil palm fruit*	75.9	76.5	76.0
Onions, dry*	198.8	199.0	200.2
Oranges*	466.0	541.4	497.2
Pigeon peas	101.4	90.1	136.3*
Pineapples*	369.1	369.5	368.8
Plantains and others*	580.0	579.8	579.6
Potatoes	1,080.1	1,013.4	1,078.3*
Pyrethrum, dried*	6.4	6.5	6.5
Rice, paddy	3,414.8	3,474.8	4,528.0†
Seed cotton	269.4	264.5*	301.7*
Sesame seed†	640.0	680.0	710.0
Sorghum	672.2	731.9	750.0†

—continued	2018	2019	2020
Sugar cane	3,117.8	3,589.5	3,619.6*
Sunflower seed†	1,000.0	1,040.0	1,075.0
Sweet potatoes	3,744.1	3,921.6	4,435.1*
Tea	55.4	61.7*	46.1*
Tobacco, unmanufactured . .	93.1	90.7	91.2
Tomatoes*	466.5	461.5	464.0
Wheat	56.7	63.4	77.0

* FAO estimate(s).
† Unofficial figure(s).

Aggregate production ('000 metric tons, may include official, semi-official or estimated data): Total cereals 10,826.6 in 2018, 10,404.9 in 2019, 12,492.6 in 2020; Total fruit (primary) 5,606.2 in 2018, 5,697.9 in 2019, 5,664.2 in 2020; Total oilcrops 3,178.0 in 2018, 3,247.8 in 2019, 3,322.9 in 2020; Total pulses 1,536.4 in 2018, 1,555.4 in 2019, 1,675.4 in 2020; Total roots and tubers 13,208.2 in 2018, 13,130.8 in 2019, 13,075.0 in 2020; Total treenuts 342.9 in 2018, 253.9 in 2019, 261.6 in 2020; Total vegetables (primary) 2,788.2 in 2018, 2,761.2 in 2019, 2,772.5 in 2020.

Source: FAO.

LIVESTOCK
('000 head, year ending September, FAO estimates)

	2018	2019	2020
Asses	188.3	188.7	189.0
Cattle	27,298.6	27,816.8	28,335.0
Chickens	37,924	38,369	37,995
Goats	17,968.8	18,387.6	18,618.7
Pigs	517.5	519.3	520.9
Sheep	7,369.0	7,322.0	7,854.8

Source: FAO.

LIVESTOCK PRODUCTS
('000 metric tons)

	2018	2019	2020
Cattle hides, fresh*	90.7	97.5	93.6
Cattle meat	471.7	506.8	486.7
Cattle offals, edible*	70.8	76.0	73.0
Cows' milk	2,400.1	2,678.5	3,010.0
Chicken meat	78.1	79.3	86.6*
Goat meat*	41.7	42.4	43.1
Goats' milk*	206.1	209.4	211.2
Goats' skins, fresh*	8.3	8.5	8.6
Pig meat*	14.9	14.9	15.0
Sheep meat*	26.6	27.8	29.1
Sheepskins, fresh*	6.4	6.7	7.0
Hen eggs*	83.3	83.3	91.8
Honey (natural)*	30.9	31.1	31.4
Wool, greasy*	7.5	7.3	7.4

* FAO estimate(s).

Source: FAO.

Forestry

ROUNDWOOD REMOVALS
('000 cubic metres, excluding bark, FAO estimates)

	2018	2019	2020
Sawlogs, veneer logs and logs for sleepers*	785.1	785.1	785.1
Pulpwood*	209.0	209.0	209.0
Other industrial wood† . . .	1,844.0	1,844.0	1,844.0
Fuel wood	24,816.4	25,072.3	25,340.2
Total	27,654.5	27,910.3	28,178.3

* Figures assumed to have been unchanged since 2013.
† Figures assumed to be unchanged since 1998.

Source: FAO.

SAWNWOOD PRODUCTION
('000 cubic metres, including railway sleepers, FAO estimates)

	2013	2014	2015
Coniferous (softwood) . . .	13	13	13
Broadleaved (hardwood) . . .	35	35	60
Total	48	48	73

2016–20: Production assumed to be unchanged from 2015.

Source: FAO.

Fishing

('000 metric tons, live weight)

	2018	2019	2020
Capture	374.5	469.7	468.3
Tilapias	13.7	27.7	15.9
Nile perch	79.6	91.7	93.0
Dagaas	31.1	31.9	55.4
Other freshwater fishes . . .	26.5	45.6	43.7
Sardinellas	6.7	7.7	8.0
Aquaculture	15.5	16.6	17.5
Total catch	390.0	486.3	485.8

Note: Figures exclude aquatic plants ('000 metric tons): 1.9 (capture 0.6, aquaculture 1.3) in 2018; 2.0 (capture 0.6, aquaculture 1.4) in 2019–20. Also excluded are crocodiles, recorded by number rather than by weight; the number of Nile crocodiles caught was: 1,291 in 2018; 1,328 in 2019; 1,243 in 2020.

Source: FAO.

Mining

('000 metric tons unless otherwise indicated)

	2019	2020	2021
Coal (bituminous)	712.1	690.0	976.3
Diamonds ('000 carats)* . . .	416.8	147.2	62.5
Gold (refined, kilograms) . .	48.4	55.5	59.6
Salt	99.5	84.0	113.0
Gypsum and anhydrite . . .	256.5	443.9	598.0
Gemstone ('000, kilograms) . .	1,929.7	23,564.5	3,851.8
Pozzolanic materials	263.1	160.1	216.9
Bauxite	0	26	38

* Estimated at 85% gem-quality and 15% industrial-quality stones. Excluding smuggled artisanal production.

Industry

SELECTED PRODUCTS
(Tanganyika, '000 metric tons unless otherwise indicated)

	2019	2020	2021*
Refined sugar	359.2	311.2	367.7
Cigarettes (million)	8,369	7,320	7,021
Beer (million litres)	391	386	380
Textiles (million sq m) . . .	45	53	65
Cement	6,514	6,496	6,531
Rolled steel	273	278	291
Iron sheets	101	108	114
Paints ('000 litres)	58,024	48,261	64,614
Electrical energy (million kWh) .	7,616.4	7,677.2	8,356.5

* Provisional.

Selected Products for Zanzibar (2021, provisional): Beverages (incl. mineral water and juices, million litres) 22; Noodles (metric tons) 380; Garments (dish dash, pieces) 4,125; Bread ('000 loaves) 239; Jewellery (gold and silver, kg) 20.4.

Finance

CURRENCY, EXCHANGE RATES AND FISCAL YEAR

Monetary Units
100 cents = 1 Tanzanian shilling.

Sterling, Dollar and Euro Equivalents (31 May 2022)
£1 sterling = 2,896.51 Tanzanian shillings;
US $1 =2,300.82 Tanzanian shillings;
€1 = 2,464.87 Tanzanian shillings;
10,000 Tanzanian shillings = £3.45 = $4.35= €4.06.

Average Exchange Rate (Tanzanian shillings per US $)
2019   2,288.21
2020   2,294.15
2021   2,297.76.

Fiscal Year
The fiscal year ends on 30 June.

BUDGET
('000 million shillings, fiscal year)*

Revenue†	2018/19	2019/20
Tax revenue	15,387	17,472
Taxes on imports	5,668	5,994
Value-added tax	3,710	3,841
Income tax	5,072	6,490
Other taxes	937	1,147
Non-tax revenue	3,140	3,579
Total	18,527	21,052

Expenditure	2018/19	2019/20
Recurrent expenditure	13,807	14,201
Wages	6,660	7,006
Interest	2,409	2,299
Internal	1,623	1,459
External	786	841
Goods, services and transfers	4,739	4,895
Development expenditure and net lending	8,573	9,301
Local	6,615	6,833
Foreign	1,958	2,468
Total	22,380	23,502

*Figures refer to the Tanzania Government, excluding the revenue and expenditure of the separate Zanzibar Government.
†Excluding grants received ('000 million shillings): 931 in 2017/18; 461 in 2018/19; 928 in 2019/20.

2020/21 ('000 million shillings, fiscal year, budget forecasts): *Revenue:* Tax revenue 20,136 (Taxes on imports 7,169, Value-added tax 4,473, Income tax 7,174, Other taxes 1,320); Non-tax revenue 3,114; Total 23,250 (excluding grants 949). *Expenditure:* Recurrent expenditure 16,321 (Wages and salaries 7,762, Interest payments 2,870, Goods, services and transfers 5,688); Development expenditure and net lending 12,779 (Local 10,043, Foreign 2,736); Total 29,100.

2021/22 ('000 million shillings, fiscal year, budget forecasts): *Revenue:* Tax revenue 20,738 (Taxes on imports 7,787, Value-added tax 4,677, Income tax 7,018, Other taxes 1,254); Non-tax revenue 4,782; Total 25,521 (excluding grants 1,138). *Expenditure:* Recurrent expenditure 16,801 (Wages and salaries 8,150, Interest payments 2,677, Goods, services and transfers 5,974); Development expenditure and net lending 13,679 (Local 10,723, Foreign 2,956); Total 30,480.

INTERNATIONAL RESERVES
(excl. gold, US $ million at 31 December)

	2016	2017	2018
IMF special drawing rights	25.7	1.3	26.7
Reserve position in IMF	80.3	85.1	83.1
Foreign exchange	4,244.7	5,801.5	4,939.8
Total	4,350.7	5,887.9	5,049.6

2019: IMF special drawing rights 9.0; Reserve position in IMF 82.6.

2020: IMF special drawing rights 9.1; Reserve position in IMF 86.0.

2021: IMF special drawing rights 543.1; Reserve position in IMF 83.6.

Source: IMF, *International Financial Statistics.*

MONEY SUPPLY
('000 million shillings at 31 December)

	2018	2019	2020
Currency outside depository corporations	3,866.67	4,221.83	4,500.53
Transferable deposits	11,835.78	13,322.31	14,029.40
Other deposits	10,121.00	10,769.01	11,390.64
Broad money	25,823.45	28,313.15	29,920.57

Source: IMF, *International Financial Statistics.*

COST OF LIVING
(National Consumer Price Index; base December 2015 = 100)

	2018	2019	2020
Food and non-alcoholic beverages	116.6	120.0	124.9
Clothing and footwear	108.9	112.1	114.5
Housing, water, electricity, gas and other fuels	129.2	139.4	150.0
All items (incl. others)	112.2	116.1	119.9

All items (National Consumer Price Index; base 2020 = 100): 103.7 in 2021.

NATIONAL ACCOUNTS
(mainland only, '000 million shillings at current prices)

Expenditure on the Gross Domestic Product

	2019	2020	2021
Government final consumption expenditure	10,978.6	11,115.2	11,864.5
Private final consumption expenditure	82,023.7	89,528.9	95,855.9
Changes in inventories	−4,951.5	−6,234.6	−5,882.8
Gross fixed capital formation	60,713.9	65,886.8	71,005.1
Total domestic expenditure	148,764.7	160,296.3	172,842.7
Exports of goods and services	22,160.0	20,028.4	23,166.0
Less Imports of goods and services	24,152.3	21,051.4	26,957.3
Statistical discrepancy	−7,130.6	−8,106.9	−7,525.7
GDP in purchasers' values	139,641.9	151,166.4	161,525.8
GDP at constant 2015 prices	123,196.7	129,130.2	135,517.8

Gross Domestic Product by Economic Activity

	2019	2020	2021
Agriculture, hunting, forestry and fishing	37,192.5	39,965.6	42,233.2
Mining and quarrying	7,213.4	9,948.0	11,587.5
Manufacturing	11,860.4	12,531.0	12,635.2
Electricity, gas and water . . .	998.1	1,143.3	1,257.0
Construction	19,872.3	21,328.1	22,364.8
Wholesale and retail trade, hotels and restaurants	14,029.4	14,441.9	15,771.9
Transport and communications .	11,675.0	13,369.5	13,902.9
Financial intermediation . . .	4,927.6	5,259.8	5,414.8
Real estate, renting and business activities	8,378.0	9,231.6	10,021.2
Public administration and defence	5,354.9	5,530.7	5,876.7
Education	3,322.0	3,440.5	3,649.8
Health and social work . . .	1,921.0	2,060.6	2,213.8
Other community, social and personal service activities . .	1,809.6	1,884.9	2,168.3
Sub-total	128,554.3	140,135.4	149,096.9
Indirect taxes, less subsidies .	11,087.6	11,031.0	12,428.9
GDP in purchasers' values .	139,641.9	151,166.4	161,525.8

Zanzibar ('000 million shillings): *GDP in purchasers' values:* 4,137 in 2019; 3,954 in 2020; 4,780 in 2021 (preliminary). *GDP at constant 2015 prices:* 2,876 in 2019; 3,116 in 2020; 3,275 in 2021 (preliminary).

BALANCE OF PAYMENTS
(US $ million)

	2018	2019	2020*
Exports of goods	4,292.7	5,377.6	6,371.7
Imports of goods	−8,483.1	−8,793.1	−7,889.0
Balance on goods	−4,190.4	−3,415.5	−1,517.2
Exports of services	4,014.7	4,281.	2,183.8
Imports of services	−1,915.9	−1,782.5	−1,239.1
Balance on goods and services	−2,091.6	−917.0	−572.6
Primary income received . . .	155.9	212.4	111.2
Primary income paid	−781.1	−1,204.9	−966.0
Balance on goods, services and primary income . . .	−2,716.8	−1,909.5	−1,427.4
Secondary income received . .	535.8	474.9	452.6
Secondary income paid . . .	−67.3	−56.4	−52.7
Current balance	−2,248.3	−1,490.9	−1,027.5
Capital account (net)	464.1	481.2	342.9
Direct investment liabilities . .	971.6	1,217.2	684.9
Portfolio investment (net) . . .	−3.7	36.8	−2.1
Other investment assets . . .	−149.8	−31.8	−24.4
Other investment liabilities . .	792.4	1,120.9	128.3
Net errors and omissions . . .	−610.4	−746.4	−866.9
Reserves and related items .	−784.0	587.0	−764.9

* Provisional.

External Trade

PRINCIPAL COMMODITIES
(distribution by HS, US $ million)

Imports c.i.f.	2019	2020	2021
Vegetables and vegetable products	102.2	264.4	322.3
Mineral products	1,967.1	1,438.7	2,339.3
Mineral fuels, oils, distillation products, etc.	1,918.4	1,377.2	2,268.0
Non-crude petroleum oils . .	1,798.7	1,227.6	2,113.7
Chemicals and related products	1,150.1	1,349.7	1,560.6
Pharmaceutical products . . .	339.1	437.2	458.8
Medicaments consisting of mixed or unmixed products for therapeutic or prophylactic uses	249.9	371.6	357.4
Plastics, rubber and articles thereof	665.7	642.6	891.4
Plastics and articles thereof . .	489.6	469.5	670.4
Textiles and textile articles .	336.7	320.7	363.6
Iron and steel, other base metals and articles of base metal	1,026.0	964.8	1,226.8
Iron and steel	493.1	411.8	706.9
Flat-rolled products of iron or non-alloy steel	187.1	155.1	335.8
Articles of iron and steel . . .	356.5	362.5	291.2
Machinery and mechanical appliances; electrical equipment; parts thereof .	1,723.0	1,613.7	1,857.9
Machinery, boilers, etc. . . .	1,142.5	947.5	1,189.7
Electrical, electronic equipment .	580.5	666.2	668.1
Vehicles, aircraft, vessels and associated transport equipment	1,055.6	841.4	1,061.2
Vehicles other than railway, tramway	930.2	749.5	953.0
Motor cars and other motor vehicles	279.6	216.1	241.7
Total (incl. others)	9,077.1	8,477.7	10,873.3

Exports f.o.b.	2019	2020	2021
Live animals and animal products	191.2	155.4	210.4
Fish, crustaceans, molluscs, aquatic invertebrates, etc. . .	165.8	137.5	164.3
Vegetables and vegetable products	1,043.9	1,206.4	1,475.7
Edible vegetables and certain roots and tubers	141.4	221.0	310.8
Dried vegetables, shelled . .	119.0	193.1	269.0
Edible fruit, nuts, peel of citrus fruit, melons	368.4	376.8	179.4
Brazil nuts, cashew nuts and coconuts	356.3	364.2	163.9
Coffee, tea, mate and spices . .	208.9	200.9	261.8
Coffee	151.5	148.2	171.5
Oil seed, oleagic fruits, grain, seed, fruit, etc.	196.1	196.3	269.0
Prepared foodstuffs; beverages, spirits, vinegar; tobacco and articles thereof .	302.1	310.5	316.6

Exports f.o.b.—*continued*	2019	2020	2021
Tobacco and manufactured tobacco			
substitutes	168.8	164.6	159.5
Unmanufactured tobacco and			
tobacco refuse	144.6	146.6	127.5
Mineral products	197.4	514.7	315.8
Ores, slag and ash . . .	0.5	356.8	132.6
Precious-metal ores and			
concentrates	—	352.8	100.9
Chemicals and related			
products	146.7	192.1	213.7
Textiles and textile articles .	263.3	220.9	248.5
Pearls, precious or semi-			
precious stones, precious			
metals and articles thereof .	2,295.8	2,964.7	2,970.6
Gold, incl. gold plated with			
platinum, unwrought . . .	2,186.2	2,915.9	2,743.1
Total (incl. others)	4,932.7	5,984.8	6,390.9

Source: Trade Map-Trade Competitiveness Map, International Trade Centre, marketanalysis.intracen.org.

PRINCIPAL TRADING PARTNERS
(US $ million)

Imports c.i.f.	2019	2020	2021
Australia	153.1	46.8	87.8
China, People's Republic . . .	1,992.5	2,146.9	2,696.1
France	85.8	80.6	63.5
Germany	230.3	238.3	243.8
India	1,262.3	1,084.5	1,209.5
Indonesia	169.7	130.7	220.0
Italy	115.4	176.4	105.1
Japan	488.8	374.5	469.0
Kenya	266.3	246.6	410.8
Korea, Republic	109.8	125.4	137.3
Malaysia	103.0	114.4	111.7
Netherlands	84.6	133.7	94.3
Oman	152.2	93.0	221.1
Russian Federation . . .	48.2	170.5	150.5
Saudi Arabia	428.4	341.8	674.1
South Africa	440.5	344.2	432.3
Switzerland-Liechtenstein . .	163.8	99.6	77.0
Thailand	110.1	84.3	110.5
Türkiye	167.4	223.1	237.4
Uganda	60.1	73.6	109.6
United Arab Emirates . . .	951.6	820.7	1,359.5
United Kingdom . . .	140.2	117.8	133.7
USA	323.7	240.1	261.3
Total (incl. others)	9,077.1	8,477.7	10,873.2

Exports f.o.b.	2019	2020	2021
Belgium	184.3	122.8	101.4
Bulgaria	1.4	91.3	6.8
Burundi	86.8	177.0	163.2
China, People's Republic . . .	230.7	235.6	273.1
Congo, Democratic Republic . .	162.6	142.2	207.2
Germany	41.5	50.3	39.9
Hong Kong	49.0	126.4	61.3
India	856.5	521.0	1,008.7
Japan	63.3	55.0	67.4
Kenya	266.6	227.3	397.2
Malawi	56.7	46.5	64.0
Netherlands	78.0	63.6	78.8
Pakistan	48.4	80.1	62.1
Rwanda	188.5	205.3	277.8
Singapore	7.4	43.0	139.2
South Africa	958.9	1,145.5	916.6
Spain	14.3	192.0	16.9
Switzerland-Liechtenstein . .	322.3	858.7	526.9
Uganda	122.1	188.7	314.0
United Arab Emirates . . .	390.0	744.3	1,051.7
USA	51.7	46.4	39.0
Viet Nam	304.3	226.6	102.0
Zambia	56.5	53.7	68.6
Total (incl. others)	4,932.7	5,984.8	6,390.8

Source: Trade Map-Trade Competitiveness Map, International Trade Centre, marketanalysis.intracen.org.

Transport

RAILWAYS

	2019	2020	2021
Passengers ('000)	3,449	3,069	1,958
Freight ('000 metric tons) . . .	374	340	380

SHIPPING

Flag Registered Fleet
(at 31 December)

	2019	2020	2021
Number of vessels	424	426	422
Displacement ('000 grt) . . .	681.1	1,333.6	1,225.7

Source: Lloyd's List Intelligence (www.bit.ly/LLintelligence).

International Seaborne Traffic
(port of Dar es Salaam only)

	2019	2020	2021
Vessels docked	1,516	1,407	1,610
Cargo ('000 metric tons) . . .	16,405	15,365	17,038
Passengers ('000)	2,035	1,307	1,610

CIVIL AVIATION
(traffic on scheduled services)

	2013	2014	2015
Kilometres flown (million) . .	22	18	17
Passengers carried ('000) . . .	1,174	1,073	1,240
Passenger-km (million) . . .	911	884	964
Total ton-km (million)	—	1	2

Source: UN, *Statistical Yearbook*.

2020 (domestic and international): Departures 53,848; Passengers carried 0.9m.; Freight carried 1.8m. ton-km (Source: World Bank, World Development Indicators database).

Tourism

FOREIGN VISITOR ARRIVALS
(by country of residence)

	2018	2019	2020
Burundi	76,445	107,440	77,212
China, People's Republic . . .	32,773	33,541	7,989
France	41,330	56,297	25,366
Germany	62,346	67,284	23,615
India	48,127	36,161	12,393
Italy	61,670	74,835	14,938
Kenya	238,642	254,291	84,871
Malawi	45,560	46,243	16,200
Mozambique	39,841	30,205	9,631
Netherlands	26,951	26,161	9,311
Russian Federation	18,762	12,965	48,985
Rwanda	61,231	79,821	28,274
South Africa	54,107	44,795	13,352
Uganda	43,394	42,877	16,860
United Kingdom	77,199	77,082	27,667
USA	94,876	101,556	31,211
Zambia	30,845	32,473	13,107
Zimbabwe	46,542	23,997	9,524
Total (incl. others)	1,505,720	1,527,230	620,867

Tourism receipts (US $ million, excl. passenger transport) 2,250 in 2017; 2,449 in 2018; 2,605 in 2019 (provisional).

Source: World Tourism Organization.

Communications Media

	2018	2019	2020
Telephones ('000 main lines in use)	124.2	76.3	72.5
Mobile telephone subscriptions ('000)	43,497.3	47,685.2	51,220.2
Broadband subscriptions, fixed ('000)	861.2	1,039.7	1,084.7
Broadband subscriptions, mobile ('000)	5,124.8	5,679.7	8,546.9
Internet users (% of population) .	19.0	20.0	22.0

Source: International Telecommunication Union.

Education

(2021 unless otherwise indicated)

	Institutions	Teachers	Students
Pre-primary (state) . . .	15,802*	7,549†	1,291,868
Pre-primary (private) . .	1,055*	5,678†	98,957
Primary (state)	16,656	171,993	10,687,593
Primary (private) . . .	1,890	25,926	509,195
Secondary (state) . . .	4,002	87,992	2,379,945
Secondary (private) . . .	1,287	21,343	291,982
Higher (state)	51‡	n.a.	140,293§
Higher (private)	80‖	n.a.	68,851§

* 2016 figures.
† 2020 figures.
‡ Comprising 35 teacher training colleges, 12 full universities and 4 university colleges.
§ 2019 figures.
‖ Comprising 53 teacher training colleges, 18 full universities and 9 university colleges.

Pupil-teacher ratio (qualified teaching staff, primary education, UNESCO estimate): 57.0 in 2019/20 (Source: UNESCO Institute for Statistics) (Source:).

Adult literacy rate (UNESCO estimates): 77.9% (males 83.2%; females 73.1%) in 2015 (Source: UNESCO Institute for Statistics) (Source:).

Directory

The Constitution

The United Republic of Tanzania was established on 26 April 1964, when Tanganyika and Zanzibar, hitherto separate independent countries, merged. An interim Constitution of 1965 was replaced, on 25 April 1977, by a permanent Constitution for the United Republic. In October 1979 the Revolutionary Council of Zanzibar adopted a separate Constitution, governing Zanzibar's internal administration, with provisions for a popularly elected President and a legislative House of Representatives elected by delegates of the then ruling party. A new Constitution for Zanzibar, which came into force in January 1985, provided for direct elections to the Zanzibar House of Representatives. The provisions below relate to the 1977 Constitution of the United Republic, as subsequently amended.

GOVERNMENT

Legislative power is exercised by the Parliament of the United Republic, which is vested by the Constitution with complete sovereign power, and of which the present National Assembly is the legislative house. The Assembly also enacts all legislation concerning the mainland. Internal matters in Zanzibar are the exclusive jurisdiction of the Zanzibar executive, the Supreme Revolutionary Council of Zanzibar, and the Zanzibar legislature, the House of Representatives.

National Assembly

The National Assembly comprises both directly elected members (chosen by universal adult suffrage) and nominated members (including five members elected from the Zanzibar House of Representatives). The number of directly elected members exceeds the number of nominated members. The Electoral Commission may review and, if necessary, increase the number of electoral constituencies before every general election. The National Assembly has a term of five years.

President

The President is the head of state, head of government and Commander-in-Chief of the Armed Forces. The President has no power to legislate without recourse to Parliament. The assent of the President is required before any bill passed by the National Assembly becomes law. Should the President withhold his or her assent and the bill be re-passed by the National Assembly by a two-thirds' majority, the President is required by law to give his or her assent within 21 days unless, before that time, he or she has dissolved the National Assembly, in which case he or she must stand for re-election.

The President appoints a Vice-President to assist him or her in carrying out his or her functions. The President presides over the Cabinet, which comprises a Prime Minister and other ministers who are appointed from among the members of the National Assembly.

JUDICIARY

The independence of the judges is secured by provisions that prevent their removal, except on account of misbehaviour or incapacity when they may be dismissed at the discretion of the President. The Constitution also makes provision for a Permanent Commission of Enquiry, which has wide powers to investigate any abuses of authority.

CONSTITUTIONAL AMENDMENTS

The Constitution can be amended by an act of the Parliament of the United Republic, when the proposed amendment is supported by the votes of not fewer than two-thirds of all of the members of the National Assembly.

The Government

HEAD OF STATE

President: SAMIA SULUHU HASSAN (took office 19 March 2021).
Vice-President: Dr PHILIP ISDOR MPANGO.

CABINET
(October 2022)

President and Commander-in-Chief of the Armed Forces: SAMIA SULUHU HASSAN.

Prime Minister: MAJALIWA KASSIM MAJALIWA.

Minister of State in the President's Office, responsible for Special Functions: Capt. GEORGE HURUMA MKUCHIKA.

Minister of State in the President's Office, responsible for Personnel Management and Good Governance: Dr JENISTER JOACKIM MHAGAMA.

Minister of State in the President's Office, responsible for Regional Administration and Local Government: ANGELLAH JASMINE KAIRUKI.

Minister of State in the Vice-President's Office, responsible for Union Affairs and the Environment: SELEMAN JAFFO.

Minister of State in the Prime Minister's Office, responsible for Labour, Youth, Employment and the Disabled: Prof. JOYCE LAZARO NDALICHAKO.

Minister of State in the Prime Minister's Office, responsible for Policy and Parliamentary Affairs: PINDI H. CHANA.

Minister of Finance and Planning: Dr MWIGULU NCHEMBA MADELU.

Minister of Defence and National Service: INNOCENT LUGHA BASHUNGWA.

Minister of Home Affairs: HAMAD Y. MASAUNI.

Minister of Justice and Constitutional Affairs: GEORGE BONIFACE SIMBACHAWENE.

Minister of Foreign Affairs and East African Co-operation: Dr STERGOMENA LAWRENCE TAX.

Minister of Agriculture, Food and Co-operatives: HUSSEIN BASHE.

Minister of Livestock and Fisheries: MASHIMBA MASHAURI NDAKI.

Minister of Lands, Housing and Human Settlements Development: Dr ANGELINA S. MABULA.

Minister of Natural Resources and Tourism: Dr DAMAS NDUMBARO.

Minister of Energy: JANUARY YUSUF MAKAMBA.

Minister of Minerals: DOTTO MASHAKA BITEKO.

Minister of Works and Transport: Prof. MAKAME MNYAA MBARAWA.

Minister of Investment, Industry and Trade: Dr ASHATU KACHWAMBA KIJAJI.

Minister of Health: UMMY A. MWALIMU.

Minister of Education, Science and Technology: Prof. ADOLF F. MKENDA.

Minister of Community Development, Gender, Women and Special Groups: Dr DOROTHY ONESPHORO GWAJIMA.

Minister of Water: JUMA HAMIDU AWESU.

Minister of Culture, Arts and Sports: MOHAMMED OMAR MCHENGERWA.

Minister of Information, Communications and Information Communication Technology: NAPE M. NNAUYE.

There were also 25 deputy ministers.

MINISTRIES

Office of the President: State House, 1 Julius Nyerere Rd, 40400 Dodoma; tel. (26) 2961500; e-mail press@ikulu.go.tz; internet www.ikulu.go.tz.

Office of the Vice-President: LAPF Bldg, 7th Floor, Makole St, POB 2502, 40406 Dodoma; tel. (22) 2329006; e-mail ps@vpo.go.tz; internet www.vpo.go.tz.

Office of the Prime Minister: 2 Railway St, POB 980, 40480 Dodoma; tel. (26) 2322480; e-mail ps@pmo.go.tz; internet www.pmo.go.tz.

Ministry of Agriculture: POB 2182, Dodoma; tel. (26) 2321407; e-mail ps@kilimo.go.tz; internet www.kilimo.go.tz.

Ministry of Community Development, Gender, Women and Special Groups: POB 573, 40478 Dodoma; tel. (26) 2963341; e-mail ps@communitydevelopment.go.tz; internet www.mcdgc.go.tz.

Ministry of Culture, Arts and Sports: Mji wa Serikali Mtumba, POB 25, Dodoma; tel. 262322129; e-mail km@michezo.go.tz; internet www.michezo.go.tz.

Ministry of Defence and National Service: Area D, Plot J, House Nos 18 and 19, POB 2924, Dodoma; tel. (26) 2350762; e-mail ps@modans.go.tz; internet www.modans.go.tz.

Ministry of Education, Science and Technology: POB 10, Dodoma; tel. (26) 2963533; e-mail info@moe.go.tz; internet www.moe.go.tz.

Ministry of Energy: Kikuyu Ave, POB 422, 40474 Dodoma; tel. (26) 2322018; e-mail ps@nishati.go.tz; internet www.nishati.go.tz.

Ministry of Finance and Planning: 18 Jakaya Kikwete Rd, POB 2802, 40468 Dodoma; tel. (26) 2963101; internet www.mof.go.tz.

Ministry of Health: Dodoma.

Ministry of Foreign Affairs and East African Co-operation: LAPF Bldg, 6th Floor, Makole Rd, POB 2933, 40466 Dodoma; tel. (26) 2323201; e-mail nje@nje.go.tz; internet www.foreign.go.tz.

Ministry of Home Affairs: POB 2916, 40483 Dodoma; tel. (26) 2323189; e-mail ps@moha.go.tz; internet www.moha.go.tz.

Ministry of Information, Communications and Information Communication Technology: POB 677, 40470 Government City, Dodoma; tel. (26) 2963470; e-mail ps@mawasiliano.go.tz; internet www.mawasiliano.go.tz.

Ministry of Investment, Industry and Trade: POB 2996, Dodoma; tel. (26) 2963117; e-mail dawatilamsaada@mit.go.tz; internet www.mit.go.tz.

Ministry of Justice and Constitutional Affairs: POB 315, Dodoma; tel. (26) 2321680; e-mail km@sheria.go.tz; internet www.sheria.go.tz.

Ministry of Labour, Youth, Employment and the Disabled: POB 2890, Dodoma; tel. (26) 2963450; e-mail ps@kazi.go.tz; internet www.kazi.go.tz.

Ministry of Lands, Housing and Human Settlements Development: National Audit Office, 6th Floor, University of Dodoma Rd, POB 2908, Dodoma; tel. (26) 2963313; e-mail ps@lands.go.tz; internet lands.go.tz.

Ministry of Livestock and Fisheries: POB 2870, Dodoma; tel. (22) 2861910; e-mail ps@mifugo.go.tz; internet www.mifugouvuvi.go.tz.

Ministry of Minerals: Kikuyu Ave, POB 422, 40474 Dodoma; tel. (26) 230051; e-mail ps@madini.go.tz; internet www.madini.go.tz.

Ministry of Natural Resources and Tourism: Government City, Mtumba, Prime Ministers St, POB 1351, Dodoma; tel. (26) 2321514; e-mail ps@maliasili.go.tz; internet www.maliasili.go.tz.

Ministry of Water: NBC Mazengo Branch Bldg, Kuu St, POB 456, 40473 Dodoma; tel. (26) 2324634; e-mail ps@maji.go.tz; internet www.maji.go.tz.

Ministry of Works and Transport: 3 Moshi St, POB 677, 40470 Dodoma; tel. (22) 2123936; e-mail ps@mow.go.tz; internet www.mow.go.tz.

ZANZIBAR GOVERNMENT OF NATIONAL UNITY
(October 2022)

President: Dr HUSSEIN ALI MWINYI (took office 2 November 2020).

First Vice-President: OTHMAN MASOUD OTHMAN.

Second Vice-President: HEMED SULEIMAN ABDULLA.

Minister of State in the President's Office, in charge of the State House: JAMAL KASSIM ALI.

Minister of State in the President's Office, in charge of Regional Administration, Local Government and Special Departments of the Revolutionary Government of Zanzibar: MASOUD ALI MOHAMMED.

Minister of State in the President's Office, in charge of Constitutional Affairs, Law, Personnel and Good Governance: HAROUN ALI SULEIMAN.

Minister of State in the President's Office, in charge of Labour, the Economy and Investment: MUDRIK RAMADHAN SORAGA.

Minister of State in the President's Office, in charge of Finance and Planning: Dr SAADA MKUYA SALUM.

Minister of State in the First Vice-President's Office: HARUSI SAID SULEIMAN.

Minister of State in the Second Vice-President's Office, in charge of Policy and Co-ordination with the House of Representatives: HAMZA HASSAN JUMA.

Minister of Construction, Communications and Transport: Dr KHALID SALUM MOHAMED.

Minister of Agriculture, Irrigation, Natural Resources and Livestock: SHAMATA SHAAME KHAMIS.

Minister of Education and Vocational Training: LELA MUHAMED MUSSA.

Minister of Information, Youth, Culture and Sports: TABIA MAULID MWITA.

Minister of Land and Housing Development: RAHMA KASSIM ALI.

Minister of Water, Energy and Minerals: SHAIB HASSAN KADUARA.

Minister of the Ocean Economy and Fisheries: SULEIMAN MASOUD MAKAME.

Minister of Tourism and Historical Affairs: SIMAI MOHAMED SAID.

Minister of Health: NASSOR AHMED MAZRUI.

Minister of Social Welfare, Gender, the Elderly, and Children: RIZIKI PEMBE JUMA.

Minister of Trade and Industrial Development: OMAR SAID SHAABAN.

There were also seven deputy ministers. The Attorney-General is also an ex officio member of the Cabinet.

MINISTRIES

Office of the President: POB 2422, Zanzibar; tel. (24) 2230814; e-mail info@ikuluzanzibar.go.tz; internet www.ikuluzanzibar.go.tz.

Ministry of Agriculture, Irrigation, Natural Resources and Livestock: POB 159, Pemba, Zanzibar; tel. (24) 2233320; e-mail info@kilimoznz.go.tz; internet kilimoznz.go.tz.

Ministry of Constitutional Affairs and Justice: POB 772, Zanzibar; tel. (24) 2234683; e-mail info@sheriasmz.go.tz; internet sheriasmz.go.tz.

Ministry of Construction, Communications and Transport: 190 Fumba Rd, POB 266, Zanzibar; tel. (24) 2231391; e-mail info@moic.go.tz; internet moic.go.tz.

Ministry of Education and Vocational Training: POB 394, Zanzibar; tel. (24) 2232827; e-mail info@moez.go.tz; internet www.moez.go.tz.

Ministry of Finance and Planning: Vuga St, POB 1154, Zanzibar; tel. (24) 2231169; e-mail info@mofeaznz.org; internet mofzanzibar.go.tz/pofp.

Ministry of Health: Mtoro Rd, POB 236, Zanzibar; tel. (24) 2231614; e-mail info@mohz.go.tz; internet mohz.go.tz.

Ministry of Labour, the Economy and Investment: POB 884, Zanzibar; tel. (24) 2223664; e-mail uchumi@kaziuwekezajismz.go.tz; internet fb.com/kaziuwekezaji.

Ministry of Information, Youth, Culture and Sports: POB 394, Zanzibar.

Ministry of Land and Housing Development: POB 238, Zanzibar; tel. (24) 2941193; e-mail info@ardhismz.go.tz; internet ardhismz.go.tz.

Ministry of the Ocean Economy and Fisheries: Zanzibar.

Ministry of Social Welfare, Gender, the Elderly, and Children: Zanzibar.

Ministry of Tourism and Historical Affairs: POB 2277, Zanzibar; e-mail info@utaliismz.go.tz; internet utaliismz.go.tz.

Ministry of Trade and Industrial Development: POB 772, Zanzibar; tel. (24) 232321.

Ministry of Water, Energy and Minerals: Mwanakwerekwe, Zanzibar; tel. (24) 2232702; e-mail zanzibarenergy@hotmail.com; internet www.zanzibar-energy.com.

President

PRESIDENT

Election, 28 October 2020

Candidate	Valid votes	% of valid votes
Dr John Pombe Magufuli (CCM) . . .	12,516,252	84.40
Tundu Antiphas Mughwai Lissu (Chadema)	1,933,271	13.04
Bernard Kamillius Membe (ACT-Wazalendo)	81,129	0.55
Leopold Lucas Marshalla Mahona (NRA) .	80,787	0.54
Ibrahim Haruna Lipumba (CUF) . .	72,885	0.49
John Paul Shibuda (ADA-TADEA) . .	33,086	0.22
Hashim Spunda Rungwe (Chaumma) . .	32,878	0.22
Others*	79,907	0.54
Total	14,830,195†	100.00

* There were eight other candidates.
† Excluding 261,755 invalid votes.

ZANZIBAR PRESIDENT

Election, 28 October 2020

Candidate	Valid votes	% of valid votes
Dr Hussein Mwinyi	380,402	76.27
Seif Sharif Hamad	96,103	19.27
Others*	22,281	4.47
Total	498,786†	100.00

* There were 15 other candidates.
† Excluding 10,944 invalid votes.

Legislature

NATIONAL ASSEMBLY

National Assembly: POB 941, Dodoma; tel. (26) 2322761; e-mail cna@bunge.go.tz; internet www.parliament.go.tz.

Speaker: Dr TULIA ACKSON.

Elections, 28 October 2020

Party	Elective seats	Special seats	Total seats
Chama Cha Mapinduzi (CCM) . .	256	94	350
Chama Cha Demokrasia na Maendeleo (Chadema) . . .	1	19	20
Alliance for Change and Transparency (ACT)	4	—	4
Civic United Front (CUF) . . .	3	—	3
Total	264	113	377*

* In addition to the 264 elective seats and 113 special seats, 10 seats are reserved for presidential nominees and five for members of the Zanzibar House of Representatives; the Attorney-General is also an ex officio member of the National Assembly as is the Speaker of Parliament, should they be elected from without the National Assembly.

ZANZIBAR HOUSE OF REPRESENTATIVES

House of Representatives: POB 902, Zanzibar; tel. (24) 2242000; e-mail zahore@zanlink.com; internet zanzibarassembly.go.tz.

Speaker: ZUBEIR ALI MAULID.

Elections, 28 October 2020

Party	Elective seats	Special seats reserved for women	Presidential nominees	Total seats
Chama Cha Mapinduzi (CCM)	46	18	4	68
Alliance for Change and Transparency (ACT)	4	—	2	6
Tanzania Democratic Alliance Party (TADEA)	—	—	1	1
Total	50	18	7	75*

* In addition, one seat is reserved for the Speaker (of the CCM) and one for the Attorney-General (as an ex officio member).

Election Commissions

National Election Commission of Tanzania (NEC): Uchaguzi House, Njedengwa Investment Area, Block D, Plot No. 4, POB 358, Dodoma; tel. (26) 2962345; e-mail uchaguzi@nec.go.tz; internet www.nec.go.tz; f. 1993; Chair. JACOBS MWAMBEGELE; Dir of Elections WILSON M. CHARLES.

Zanzibar Electoral Commission (ZEC): POB 1001, Zanzibar; tel. (24) 2231489; e-mail election@zec.go.tz; internet www.zec.go.tz; f. 2007; Chair. HAMID MAHMOUD HAMID; Dir of Elections KHAMIS KONA KHAMIS.

Political Organizations

Alliance for Change and Transparency (ACT) (Chama Cha Wazalendo): POB 105043, Dar es Salaam; tel. 719847032; internet www.actwazalendo.or.tz; f. 2014; Chair. JUMA DUNI HAJI; Leader ZITTO ZUBERI RUYAGWA KABWE.

Chama Cha Demokrasia na Maendeleo (Chadema—Party for Democracy and Progress): House No. 170 Ufipa St, POB 31191, Dar es Salaam; tel. (22) 2668866; e-mail info@chadema.or.tz; internet www.chadema.or.tz; supports democracy and social development; Chair. FREEMAN MBOWE; Sec.-Gen. JOHN MNYIKA.

Chama Cha Kijamii (CCK): Kinondoni, Dar es Salaam; f. 2010; Chair. CONSTANTINE AKITANDA; Sec.-Gen. RENATUS MUHABHI.

Chama Cha Mapinduzi (CCM) (Revolutionary Party of Tanzania): Kuu St, POB 50, Dodoma; tel. (26) 2180575; internet www.ccmtz.org; f. 1977 by merger of the mainland-based Tanganyika African National Union (TANU) with the Afro-Shirazi Party, which operated on Zanzibar and Pemba; sole legal party 1977–92; socialist orientation; Chair. SAMIA SULUHU HASSAN; Sec.-Gen. DANIEL CHONGOLO.

Civic United Front (CUF): Mtendeni St at Malindi, POB 3637, Zanzibar; tel. (24) 2237446; e-mail headquarters@cuftz.org; internet www.cuf.or.tz; f. 1992 by merger of Zanzibar opposition party Kamahuru and the mainland-based Chama Cha Wananchi;

commands substantial support in Zanzibar and Pemba, for which it demands increased autonomy; Pres. Prof. IBRAHIM LIPUMBA.

National Convention for Construction and Reform (NCCR—Mageuzi): Plot No. 2 Kilosa St, Ilala, POB 72444, Dar es Salaam; tel. (22) 2111484; internet nccrmageuzi.or.tz; f. 1992; Chair. JAMES F. MBATIA; Sec.-Gen. JUJU NDADA.

National League for Democracy (NLD): Plot No. D/73 Sinza, POB 352, Dar es Salaam; tel. 714259442; f. 1993; Chair. EMMANUEL J. E. MAKAIDI; Sec.-Gen. FERUZI MSAMBICHAKA.

National Reconstruction Alliance (NRA): Bububu St, Tandika Kilimahewa, POB 100125, Dar es Salaam; tel. 754496724; f. 1993; Chair. RASHID MTUTA; Sec.-Gen. MARSHEED H. HEMED.

Tanzania Democratic Alliance Party (TADEA): Buguruni Malapa, POB 482, Dar es Salaam; tel. (22) 2865244; f. 1993; Pres. JOHN D. LIFA-CHIPAKA; Sec.-Gen. JUMA ALI KHATIB.

Tanzania Labour Party (TLP): Argentina Manzese, POB 7273, Dar es Salaam; tel. (22) 2443237; f. 1993; Chair. AUGUSTINE MREMA; Sec.-Gen. JOHN KOMBA.

United Democratic Party (UDP): Plot No. 34, Block 28, Ilemela St, Mwananyamala, Kinondoni, POB 5918, Dar es Salaam; tel. 784613723; f. 1994; Chair. JOHN MOMOSE CHEYO.

Union for Multi-Party Democracy (UMD): House No. 84, Plot No. 630, Block No. 5, Kagera St. Magomeni, POB 2985, Dar es Salaam; tel. 744478153; f. 1993; Chair. SALUM S. ALLI; Sec.-Gen. ALI MSHANGAMA ABDALLAH.

United People's Democratic Party (UPDP): 46 Kagera St, POB 11746, Dar es Salaam; tel. 754753075; e-mail opodsm@yahoo.com; f. 1993; Chair. YAHMI NASSORO DOVUTWA; Sec.-Gen. ABDALLAH NASSORO ALLY.

Diplomatic Representation

EMBASSIES AND HIGH COMMISSIONS IN TANZANIA

Algeria: 34 Ali Hassan Mwinyi Rd, POB 2963, Dar es Salaam; tel. (22) 2117619; e-mail algembdar@yahoo.com; Ambassador AHMED DJELLAL.

Angola: Plot No. 1016, Buzwagi St, Chole Rd, Msasani Penisula, POB 20793, Dar es Salaam; tel. (22) 2602683; Ambassador SANDRO RENATO AGOSTINHO DE OLIVEIRA.

Belgium: 5 Barack Obama Rd, POB 9210, Dar es Salaam; tel. (22) 2112688; e-mail daressalaam@diplobel.fed.be; internet tanzania.diplomatie.belgium.be; Ambassador PETER VAN ACKER.

Brazil: Coco Plaza Office Complex, 2nd Floor, Rooms 201/202, Plot No. 254, Toure Dr., Msasani Peninsula, POB 105818–14111, Dar es Salaam; tel. (22) 2602660; e-mail brasemb.dar@itamaraty.gov.br; internet www.gov.br/mre/pt-br/embaixada-dar-es-salaam; Ambassador ANTONIO AUGUSTO MARTINS CESAR.

Burundi: 1007 Lugalo Rd, POB 2752, Upanga, Dar es Salaam; tel. (22) 2127008; e-mail burundiembassydar@yahoo.com; Ambassador GERVAIS ABAYEHO.

Canada: 38 Mirambo St, Garden Ave, POB 1022, Dar es Salaam; tel. (22) 2163300; e-mail dslam@international.gc.ca; internet www.canadainternational.gc.ca/tanzania-tanzanie; High Commissioner PAMELA O'DONNELL.

China, People's Republic: 2 Kajificheni Close at Toure Dr., POB 1649, Dar es Salaam; tel. (22) 2668064; e-mail chinaemb_tz@mfa.gov.cn; internet tz.china-embassy.gov.cn; Ambassador CHEN MINGJIAN.

Comoros: 967 Mawaziri Rd, Mikocheni B, Dar es Salaam; tel. (22) 2221204; Ambassador ELBADAOUI ALLAOUI.

Congo, Democratic Republic: 20 Malik Rd, Upanga, Dar es Salaam; tel. (22) 2152388; e-mail drcembatz@yahoo.com; Ambassador JEAN-PIERRE MUTAMBA.

Cuba: Plot 313, Lugalo Rd, POB 9282, Upanga, Dar es Salaam; tel. 75358173; e-mail embajada@tz.embacuba.cu; internet misiones.minrex.gob.cu/es/tanzania; Ambassador YORDENIS DESPAIGNE VERA.

Denmark: Ghana Ave 1, POB 9171, Dar es Salaam; tel. (22) 2165200; e-mail daramb@um.dk; internet tanzania.um.dk; Ambassador METTE NORGAARD DISSING-SPANDET.

Egypt: 24 Garden Ave, POB 1668, Dar es Salaam; tel. (22) 2113591; e-mail embassy.daressalaam@mfa.gov.eg; Ambassador MOHAMMED GABER ABULWAFA.

Ethiopia: Plot No. 230, Yasser Arafat Rd, Oysterbay, Dar es Salaam; tel. (22) 2668991; e-mail daressalaam.embassy@mfa.gov.et; internet www.daressalaam.mfa.gov.et; Ambassador YONAS YOSEF SANBE.

Finland: Mirambo St and Garden Ave, POB 2455, Dar es Salaam; tel. (22) 2212400; e-mail sanomat.dar@formin.fi; internet finlandabroad.fi/web/tza; Ambassador THERESA ZITTING.

France: 7 Ali Hassan Mwinyi Rd, POB 2349, Dar es Salaam; tel. (22) 2198800; e-mail contact@ambafrance-tz.org; internet tz.ambafrance.org; Ambassador NABIL HAJLAOUI.

Germany: Umoja House, Mirambo St/Hamburg Ave, 2nd Floor, POB 9541, Dar es Salaam; tel. (22) 2212300; internet daressalam.diplo.de; Ambassador REGINE HESS.

Holy See: Plot 146, Haile Selassie Rd, Oyster Bay, POB 480, Dar es Salaam; tel. (22) 2666422; Apostolic Nuncio (vacant).

India: Plot No. 213/51, Shaaban Robert St, POB 2684, Dar es Salaam; tel. (22) 2113094; e-mail hoc.desalaam@mea.gov.in; internet hcindiatz.gov.in; High Commissioner BINAYA SRIKANTA PRADHAN.

Indonesia: 299 Ali Hassan Mwinyi Rd, POB 572, Dar es Salaam; tel. (22) 2119119; e-mail daressalaam.kbri@kemlu.go.id; internet www.kemlu.go.id/daressalaam; Ambassador TRI YOGO JATMIKO.

Iran: Plot 581, Chole Rd, Haile Selassie Rd, Lincoln St, POB 5802, Dar es Salaam; tel. (22) 2600335; e-mail iranemb.dar@mfa.gov.ir; internet tanzania.mfa.gov.ir; Ambassador HOSSEIN ALVANDI BEHINEH.

Ireland: 353 Touré Dr., Masaki, Dar es Salaam; tel. (22) 2213800; internet www.dfa.ie/irish-embassy/tanzania; Ambassador MARY O'NEILL.

Italy: Plot 316, Lugalo Rd, Upanga, POB 2106, Dar es Salaam; tel. (22) 2115935; e-mail amb.daressalaam@cert.esteri.it; internet ambdaressalaam.esteri.it; Ambassador MARCO LOMBARDI.

Japan: 1018 Ali Hassan Mwinyi Rd, POB 2577, Dar es Salaam; tel. (22) 2115827; e-mail embassyofjapan_tz@dr.mofa.go.jp; internet www.tz.emb-japan.go.jp; Ambassador SHINICHI GOTO.

Kenya: Harambee Plaza, 2nd Floor, cnr Ali Hassan Mwinyi Rd and Kaunda Dr., Oysterbay, POB 5231, Dar es Salaam; tel. (22) 2668285; e-mail info@kenyahighcomtz.org; internet dar.mfa.go.ke; High Commissioner ISAAC NJENGA (designate).

Korea, Democratic People's Republic: Plot 5, Ursino Estate, Kawawa Rd, Msasani, POB 2690, Dar es Salaam; tel. (22) 2771923; Ambassador KIM YONG SU.

Korea, Republic: Golden Jubilee Towers, 19th Floor, Ohio St, City Centre, POB 1154, Dar es Salaam; tel. (22) 2116086; e-mail embassy-tz@mofa.go.kr; internet overseas.mofa.go.kr/tz-ko/index.do; Ambassador KIM SUN-PYO.

Kuwait: Tour Dr., Plot No. 92, Oysterbay, POB 9610, Dar es Salaam; tel. (22) 2923451; e-mail kuwait.tanzania@gmail.com; internet kuwaitembassy.or.tz; Ambassador MUBARAK MUHAMMAD AL-SAHEGAN.

Libya: 386 Mtitu St, POB 9413, Dar es Salaam; tel. (22) 2150188; e-mail libymbt@gmail.com; Ambassador (vacant).

Malawi: Rose Garden Rd, Gamshard Circle St, Mikocheni A, POB 7616, Dar es Salaam; tel. (22) 2774220; e-mail malawihctz@malawihctz.org; internet www.malawihctz.org; High Commissioner ANDREW P. E. Z. KUMWENDA.

Morocco: House No. 11, Mkwawa Rd, Oyster Bay, Dar es Salaam; tel. (22) 2666443; e-mail moroccoembassy.dsm@gmail.com; Ambassador ZAKARIA EL KOUMIRI.

Mozambique: 25 Garden Ave, POB 9370, Dar es Salaam; tel. (22) 2124673; e-mail embamoc.tanzania@minec.gov.mz; High Commissioner RICARDO MTUMBULDA.

Namibia: 3 Rufiji St, Masaki, Msasani Peninsula, POB 80211, Dar es Salaam; tel. (22) 2601903; e-mail info@namibiahc.or.tz; internet namibiahc.or.tz; High Commissioner LEBBIUS TANGENI TOBIAS.

Netherlands: Umoja House, 4th Floor, Garden Ave, POB 9534, Dar es Salaam; tel. (22) 2194000; e-mail dar@minbuza.nl; internet www.netherlandsworldwide.nl/countries/tanzania; Ambassador WIEBE DE BOER.

Nigeria: 83 Haile Selassie Rd, POB 9214, Oyster Bay, Dar es Salaam; tel. (22) 2666001; e-mail info@nhcdsm.or.tz; internet nhcdsm.or.tz; High Commissioner HAMISU UMAR TAKALMAWA.

Norway: cnr Garden Ave, Mirambo St, POB 2646, Dar es Salaam; tel. (22) 2163100; e-mail emb.daressalaam@mfa.no; internet www.norway.no/tanzania; Ambassador ELISABETH JACOBSEN.

Oman: Plot No. 810, Mwai Kibaki Rd, Mikocheni Area, POB 34741, Dar es Salaam; tel. (22) 2773104; e-mail daressalaam@mofa.gov.om; Ambassador SAUD HILAL AL-SHIDANI.

Pakistan: Plot No. 338, House No. MKC/1259, Maziede, Garden Rd, Mikocheni-B, POB 61336, Dar es Salaam; tel. (22) 2773658; e-mail pahictanzania@mofa.gov.pk; internet fb.com/PakistanHighCommissionTanzania; High Commissioner MUHAMMAD SALEEM.

Poland: 15 Mtwara Rd, Oysterbay, POB 249, Dar es Salaam; tel. (22) 2221050; e-mail daressalaam.amb.sekretariat@msz.gov.pl; internet www.gov.pl/web/tanzania; Ambassador KRZYSZTOF BUZALSKI.

Qatar: Msasani Rd 6, Oysterbay, Dar es Salaam; tel. (22) 2664713; e-mail daressalaam@mofa.gov.qa; internet dar-es-salaam.embassy .qa/en; Ambassador HUSSAIN BIN AHMED AL-HOMADI.

Russian Federation: Ali Hassan Mwinyi Rd, POB 1905, Dar es Salaam; tel. (22) 2666006; e-mail embrusstanz@mid.ru; internet tanzania.mid.ru; Ambassador ANDREI L. AVETISYAN (designate).

Rwanda: 452 Haile Selasie Rd, POB 2918, Dar es Salaam; tel. (22) 2600500; tel. ambadsm@minaffet.gov.rw; internet www .rwandaintanzania.gov.rw; High Commissioner Maj.-Gen. CHARLES KARAMBA.

Saudi Arabia: Oyster Bay, 113, Ali Bin Said Rd, POB 238, Dar es Salaam; tel. (22) 2667833; internet embassies.mofa.gov.sa/sites/ Tanzania; Ambassador ABDULLAH AL-SHORAYAN.

Somalia: Plot No. 333A, Msasani Rd, Oysterbay, POB 10191, Dar es Salaam; tel. (22) 2668655; e-mail somaliembassydar@yahoo.com; Ambassador ZAHRA ALI HASSAN.

South Africa: Plot Nos 218/50 and 219/50, cnr Garden Avenue and Shabani Robert St, Ilala District, POB 10723, Dar es Salaam; tel. (22) 2218500; e-mail sahc.tanzania@dirco.gov.za; High Commissioner (vacant).

Spain: 99B Kinondoni Rd, POB 842, Dar es Salaam; tel. (22) 2666936; e-mail emb.daressalaam@maec.es; internet www .exteriores.gob.es/embajadas/daressalaam; Ambassador FRANCISCA MARÍA PEDRÓS CARRETERO.

Sudan: 'Albaraka', 64 Ali Hassan Mwinyi Rd, POB 2266, Dar es Salaam; tel. (22) 2117641; e-mail sudan.emb_dar@yahoo.com; Ambassador MAHJOUB AHMED SHARFI.

Sweden: Mirambo St and Garden Ave, POB 9274, Dar es Salaam; tel. (22) 2196500; e-mail ambassaden.dar-es-salaam@gov.se; internet www.swedenabroad.se/en/embassies/tanzania-dar-es -salaam; Ambassador ANDERS SJÖBERG.

Switzerland: Plot 79 Kinondoni Rd/, POB 2454, Dar es Salaam; tel. (22) 2666008; e-mail daressalaam@eda.admin.ch; internet www.eda .admin.ch/daressalaam; Ambassador DIDIER CHASSOT.

Syrian Arab Republic: 49 Laibon Rd, Upanga East, POB 2442, Dar es Salaam; tel. (22) 2664655; e-mail syrianembassy.dsm@hotmail .com; Ambassador SAWSAN ADNAN AL-ANI.

Türkiye (Turkey): Toure Dr. 8, Plot No. 97, Oysterbay, POB 21761, Dar es Salaam; tel. (22) 2923413; internet darusselam.be.mfa.gov.tr; Ambassador MEHMET GÜLLÜOĞLU.

Uganda: Oysterbay, 25 Msasani Rd, POB 6237, Dar es Salaam; tel. (22) 2667391; e-mail daressalaam@mofa.go.ug; internet www .daressalaam.mofa.go.ug; High Commissioner Col (Retd) FRED MWESIGYE (designate).

United Arab Emirates: 375 Toure Dr., Oysterbay, Dar es Salaam; tel. (22) 5522222; e-mail daralsalamemb@mofaic.gov.ae; internet www.mofaic.gov.ae/en/missions/dar-es-salaam; Ambassador KHA-LIFA ABDULRAHAMAN MOHAMED AL-MARZOOQI.

United Kingdom: Umoja House, Garden Ave, POB 9200, Dar es Salaam; tel. (22) 2290000; e-mail bhc.dar@fco.gov.uk; internet www .gov.uk/world/organisations/british-high-commission-dar-es -salaam; High Commissioner DAVID CONCAR.

USA: 686 Old Bagamoyo Rd, Msasani, POB 9123, Dar es Salaam; tel. (22) 2294000; internet tz.usembassy.gov; Ambassador Dr DONALD J. WRIGHT.

Viet Nam: Plot No. 11, Bongoyo Rd, Oysterbay, POB 9724, Dar es Salaam; tel. (22) 2664535; e-mail vnemb.tz@mofa.gov.vn; internet vnembassy-daressalaam.mofa.gov.vn; Ambassador NGUYEN NAM TIEN.

Yemen: 804 Mwai Kibaki Rd, Mikocheni Area, POB 349, Dar es Salaam; tel. (22) 2775316; e-mail yembdsm@hotmail.com; Ambassador (vacant).

Zambia: 5–6 Ohio St/Sokoine Dr. Junction, POB 2525, Dar es Salaam; tel. (22) 2125529; e-mail zambia@tanz.net; High Commissioner (vacant).

Zimbabwe: Plot No. 298, Chake chake St, POB 20762, Dar es Salaam; tel. (22) 2602930; e-mail info@zimembassytanzania.com; Ambassador Lt-Gen. (retd) ANSELEM SANYATWE.

Judicial System

The judicial system of Tanzania is composed of a Court of Appeal, a High Court, Magistrates' and District Courts, and Primary Courts. The Court of Appeal is the highest court of the country (including Zanzibar) and hears appeals from the lower courts. The High Court comprises 15 zones, with three specialized divisions—Commercial Division, Land Division and Labour Division. There are 22 Resident Magistrates' Courts and 109 District Courts, in addition to 1,105 Primary Courts. There are also several specialized quasi-judicial tribunals, including the District Land and Housing Tribunal, the Tax Tribunal and the Tax Appeals Tribunal. Zanzibar has a separate judicial system headed by the Chief Justice of Zanzibar, comprising a High Court, Regional Magistrates' Courts, District Magistrates' Courts and Primary Courts. There is also a Labour Court, Juvenile Courts and Kadhis' Courts (with exclusive jurisdiction over matters of Islamic law) in Zanzibar.

Court of Appeal: POB 9004, Dar es Salaam; tel. (22) 2116654; internet judiciary.go.tz/web; f. 1979; consists of the Chief Justice and 15 Justices of Appeal; Chief Justice Prof. IBRAHIM HAMIS JUMA.

High Court: POB 9004, Dar es Salaam; tel. (22) 2116654; internet www.judiciary.go.tz; Principal Judge MUSTAPHER MOHAMED SIYANI.

High Court of Zanzibar: Kaunda Rd, near Victoria Gardens, Stone Town, POB 160, Zanzibar; internet judiciaryzanzibar.go.tz/web; Chief Justice of Zanzibar KHAMIS RAMADHAN ABDALLA.

District Courts: situated in each district and presided over by either a Resident Magistrate or District Magistrate; limited jurisdiction, with a right of appeal to the High Court.

Primary Courts: established in every district and presided over by Primary Court Magistrates; limited jurisdiction, with a right of appeal to the District Courts and then to the High Court.

Attorney-General: Dr ELIEZER MBUKI FELESHI.

Attorney-General of Zanzibar: Dr MWINYI TALIB HAJI.

Director of Public Prosecutions: BISWALO MGANGA.

Director of Public Prosecutions of Zanzibar: SALMA ALI HASSAN.

Religion

Religious surveys were eliminated from all government census reports after 1967. However, religious leaders and sociologists generally believe that the country's population is 30%–40% Christian and 30%–40% Muslim, with the remainder consisting of practitioners of other faiths, traditional indigenous religions and atheists. Foreign missionaries operate in the country, including Roman Catholics, Lutherans, Baptists, Seventh-day Adventists, Mormons, Anglicans and Muslims.

ISLAM

The Muslim population is most heavily concentrated on the Zanzibar archipelago and in the coastal areas of the mainland. There are also large Muslim minorities in inland urban areas. Some 99% of the population of Zanzibar is estimated to be Muslim. Between 80% and 90% of the country's Muslim population is Sunni; the remainder consists of several Shi'a groups, mostly of Asian descent. A large proportion of the Asian community is Isma'ili.

National Muslim Council of Tanzania (Baraza Kuu la Waislamu Tanzania—BAKWATA): Togo St, Kinondoni Manyanya, Dar es Salaam; tel. 888000000; e-mail info@bakwata.or.tz; internet bakwata.or.tz; f. 1969; supervises Islamic affairs on the mainland only; Chair. Sheikh ABUBAKAR ZUBERI.

Supreme Muslim Council: Zanzibar; f. 1991; supervises Islamic affairs in Zanzibar; Mufti SHEIKH SALEH OMAR KABI.

Wakf and Trust Commission: Sheria House, POB 4092, Zanzibar; tel. (24) 2238186; e-mail ceo@wakf.go.tz; internet www.wakf.go.tz; f. 1905; Islamic affairs; Chair. Prof. HAMED RASHID HIKMANY; Exec. Sec. SHEIKH ABDULLA TALIB ABDULLA.

CHRISTIANITY

The Christian population is composed of Roman Catholics, Protestants, Pentecostals, Seventh-day Adventists, members of the Church of Jesus Christ of Latter-day Saints (Mormons) and Jehovah's Witnesses.

Christian Council of Tanzania (Jumuiya ya Kikristo Tanzania): Church House, POB 1454, Dodoma; tel. (26) 2324445; internet cct.or .tz; f. 1934; Chair. Rt Rev. Dr ALINIKISA CHEYO (Bishop of South West Tanzania Province—Moravian Church of Tanzania); Gen. Sec. Rev. Dr MOSES MATONYA.

The Anglican Communion

Anglicans are adherents of the Church of the Province of Tanzania, comprising 28 dioceses.

Archbishop and Primate of the Province of Tanzania and Bishop of Tanga: Most Rev. Dr MAIMBO WILLIAM MNDOLWA, POB 35, Korogwe; tel. (27) 2640568; e-mail imba612@yahoo.com; internet www.anglican.or.tz.

Provincial Secretary: Rev. Canon Dr MECKA OGUNDE, POB 899, Dodoma; tel. (26) 2324574; e-mail act@anglican.or.tz.

Lutheran

Evangelical Lutheran Church in Tanzania: Boma Rd, POB 3033, Arusha; tel. (27) 2508856; e-mail elcthq@elct.or.tz; Presiding Bishop Rt Rev. Dr FREDRICK ONAEL SHOO; Sec.-Gen. BRIGHTON L. KILLEWA.

The Roman Catholic Church

Tanzania comprises seven archdioceses and 27 dioceses.

Tanzania Episcopal Conference: Catholic Secretariat, Mandela Rd, Kurasini, POB 2133, Dar es Salaam; tel. (22) 2851075; e-mail info@tec.or.tz; internet www.tec.or.tz; f. 1980; Pres. Rev. GERVAS JOHN MWASIKWABHILA NYAISONGA (Archbishop of Mbeya); Sec. Gen. Rev. Dr CHARLES KITIM.

Archbishop of Arusha: Most Rev. ISAAC AMANI MASSAWE, Archbishop's House, POB 3044, Arusha; tel. (27) 2544361; e-mail idr0@habari.co.tz.

Archbishop of Dar es Salaam: Most Rev. JUDE THADDEUS RUWA'ICHI, Archbishop's House, POB 167, Dar es Salaam; tel. (22) 2113223.

Archbishop of Dodoma: Most Rev. BEATUS KINYAIYA, Archbishop's House, POB 922, Dodoma; tel. (26) 2394462.

Archbishop of Mbeya: Most Rev. GERVAS JOHN MWASIKWABHILA NYAISONGA, Archbishop's House, POB 179, Mbeya; tel. (25) 2502250.

Archbishop of Mwanza: Most Rev. RENATUS LEONARD NKWANDE, Archbishop's House, POB 1421, Mwanza; tel. (28) 2501029; e-mail archmwz@gmail.com.

Archbishop of Songea: Most Rev. DAMIAN DENIS DALLU, Archbishop's House, POB 152, Songea; tel. (25) 2602004; e-mail bishop@songea.org; internet www.songea.org.

Archbishop of Tabora: PAUL R. RUZOKA, Archbishop's House, Private Bag, Tabora; tel. 786521904; e-mail archbishops_office@yahoo.co.uk; internet catbr.or.tz.

Other Christian Churches

Moravian Church in Tanzania (MCT): Dar es Salaam.

Pentecostal Missionary Church: POB 9848, Dar es Salaam; internet pmc-ministries.com; Pastor GERVASE MARTIN MASANJA.

Presbyterian Church: POB 2510, Dar es Salaam; tel. (22) 229075.

BAHÁ'Í FAITH

National Spiritual Assembly: POB 585, Dar es Salaam; tel. (22) 2152766; internet www.bahai.org; f. 1950; mems resident in 3,000 localities.

OTHER RELIGIONS

Many people follow traditional beliefs. There are also some Hindu communities.

The Press

NEWSPAPERS (PRINT AND ONLINE)

Daily

The Citizen: Plot No. 34/35, Mandela Rd, POB 19754, Dar es Salaam; tel. 76918198; e-mail online@thecitizen.co.tz; internet www.thecitizen.co.tz; f. 2004; Man. Editor BAKARI MACHUMU.

Daily News: Samora Ave, POB 9033, Dar es Salaam; tel. (22) 2110595; e-mail info@tsn.go.tz; internet dailynews.co.tz; f. 1972; govt-owned; Man. Editor TUMA ABDALLAH.

Majira: POB 71439, Dar es Salaam; tel. (22) 2113693; independent; Swahili; Editor IMMA MBUGHUNI.

Mwananchi: Plot No. 34/35, Mandela Rd, POB 19754, Dar es Salaam; tel. (22) 2450311; e-mail msackyd@yahoo.com; internet www.mwananchi.co.tz; f. 2000; Swahili; Man. Editor FRANK SANGA.

Tanzania Times: e-mail timesoftanzania@gmail.com; internet tanzaniatimes.net.

Weekly

Business Times: 11286 Samora Ave, POB 71439, Dar es Salaam; tel. 777733999; independent; English; Editor ALLI MWAMBOLA.

The Express: POB 20588, Dar es Salaam; tel. (22) 2180058; e-mail express@raha.com; independent; English; Editor FAYAZ BHOJANI.

Kiongozi (The Leader): POB 9400, Dar es Salaam; tel. (22) 2851075; e-mail kiongozinews@yahoo.com; f. 1950; owned by Catholic Publishers Ltd; weekly; Swahili; Roman Catholic; Dir JOSEPH MATUMAINI.

Mwanaspoti: Plot No. 34/35, Mandela Rd, POB 19754, Dar es Salaam; tel. 713471195; e-mail mwanaspoti@mwanaspoti.co.tz; internet www.mwanaspoti.co.tz.

PERIODICALS

Nuru: POB 1893, Zanzibar; f. 1992; bi-monthly; official publ. of Zanzibar Govt.

Ukulima wa Kisasa (Modern Farming): Farmers' Education and Publicity Unit, POB 2308, Dar es Salaam; tel. (22) 2866424; e-mail fepu@hotmail.co.uk; internet www.kilimo.go.tz; f. 1955; bi-monthly; Swahili; Editor LUCAS NYANGI.

PRESS ORGANIZATIONS

Media Council of Tanzania (MCT): Bagamoyo Rd, POB 10160, Dar es Salaam; tel. 719494640; e-mail media@mct.or.tz; internet mct .or.tz; f. 1995; self-regulation; Pres. Justice THOMAS BASHITE MIHAYO; Exec. Sec. KAJUBI DIOCLES MUKAJANGA.

Union of Tanzania Press Clubs (UTPC): Isamilo Rd, Isamilo, POB 314, Mwanza; tel. (28) 2540243; e-mail info@utpc.or.tz; internet www.utpc.or.tz; f. 1996; 23 mem. clubs; Pres. DEOGRATIOUS NSOKOLO; Exec. Dir ABUBAKAR KARSAN.

Tanzania Editors' Forum: POB 10160, Dar es Salaam; tel. 715369090; Chair. DEODATUS BALILE.

Publishers

Central Tanganyika Press: POB 1129, Dodoma; tel. (26) 2390015; e-mail ctp@anglican.or.tz; internet www.anglican.or.tz/ctp.htm; f. 1954; religious; Man. PETER MANG'ATI MAKASSI.

Mkuki na Nyota Publishers Ltd: 24 Samora Machel Ave, Dar es Salaam; tel. 787558448; e-mail publishing@mkukinanyota.com; internet www.mkukinanyota.com; f. 1991; educational, academic and children's books in Swahili and English; Man. Dir WALTER BGOYA.

Mture Educational Publishers Ltd: POB 75610, Mwanza; tel. (22) 2775577; e-mail mturepublishers@yahoo.com; internet mturepublishers.com; school books; Man. Dir ELIBARIKI A. MOSHI.

Oxford University Press: Maktaba Rd, POB 5299, Dar es Salaam; tel. (22) 229209; f. 1969; literature, literary criticism, essays, poetry; Man. SALIM SHAABAN SALIM.

Tanzania Publishing House: 47 Samora Machel Ave, POB 2138, Dar es Salaam; tel. (22) 2137402; e-mail tphhouse@yahoo.com; f. 1966; educational and general books in Swahili and English; Gen. Man. PRIMUS ISIDOR KARUGENDO.

GOVERNMENT PUBLISHING HOUSE

Government Printer: Office of the Prime Minister, POB 3021, Dar es Salaam; tel. (22) 2860900; Dir KASSIAN C. CHIBOGOYO.

Broadcasting and Communications

REGULATORY AUTHORITY

Tanzania Communications Regulatory Authority (TCRA): Mawasiliano Towers, Plot 2005/5/1, Block C, 20 Sam Nujoma Rd, POB 474, Dar es Salaam; tel. (22) 2199760; internet www.tcra.go.tz; f. 1993; licenses postal and telecommunications service operators; manages radio spectrum; acts as ombudsman; Chair. JONES A. KILLIMBE; Dir-Gen. Dr JABIR BAKARI KUWE.

TELECOMMUNICATIONS

Airtel Tanzania: Airtel House, cnr Ali Hassan Mwinyi and Kawawa Rds, POB 9623, Dar es Salaam; tel. 784103001; e-mail helpdesk@tz .airtel.com; internet airtel.co.tz; f. 2001; 51% owned by Bharti Airtel (India); 49% state-owned; fmrly Zain Tanzania, present name adopted 2010; Man. Dir DINESH BALSINGH; 13.8m. subscribers (March 2021).

Halotel Tanzania: Tropical Centre, 4th Floor, Plot 30 (A and B), New Bagamoyo Rd, POB 34716, Dar es Salaam; tel. 620100100; e-mail info@halotel.co.tz; internet and mobile services provider; owned by Viettel (Viet Nam); Man. Dir DO MANH HUNG; 7.4m. subscribers (March 2021).

MIC Tanzania (Mobitel) Ltd: New Bagamoyo Rd, POB 2929, Dar es Salaam; tel. 716123103; e-mail customercare@tigo.co.tz; internet www.tigo.co.tz; operates mobile services through Mobitel network; brand name Tigo; 100% owned by Millicom International Cellular (Luxembourg); Man. Dir (vacant); 13.5m. subscribers (March 2021).

Tanzania Telecommunications Co Ltd (TTCL): Extelcoms House, Samora Ave, POB 9070, Dar es Salaam; tel. (22) 2142000; internet www.ttcl.co.tz; operates fixed-line and CDMA network; Chair. ZUHURA SINARE MURO; Dir-Gen. WAZIRI KINDAMBA; 1.0m. subscribers (March 2021).

Vodacom (Tanzania) Ltd: Vodacom Tower, 15th Floor, Ursino Estate, Plot No. 23, Old Bagamoyo Rd, POB 2369, Dar es Salaam; tel. 754705000; e-mail feedback@vodacom.co.tz; internet vodacom.co.tz; mobile telephone operator; Man. Dir Sitholizwe Mdlalose; 15.9m. subscribers (March 2021).

Zanzibar Telecom (Zantel): POB 3459, Zanzibar; tel. 775000001; e-mail info@zantel.co.tz; internet www.zantel.co.tz; f. 1999; mobile telephone operator for Zanzibar; 18% state-owned, 65% owned by Emirates Telecommunications Corpn (Etisalat, United Arab Emirates) and 17% owned by Meeco International; Chair. Essa al-Haddad; CEO Benoit Janin; 1.0m. subscribers (March 2021).

BROADCASTING

Radio

Clouds FM: POB 31513, Dar es Salaam; tel. (22) 2781445; internet cloudsmedia.com; CEO Joseph Kusaga.

Parapanda Radio Tanzania: POB 9191, Dar es Salaam; tel. (22) 2860760; state-run FM station.

Radio 5 Arusha: POB 11843, Arusha; tel. (27) 2503622; e-mail sikutegemea@yahoo.com.

Radio Kwizera: POB 154, N'Gara; tel. (28) 2226079; internet www .radiokwizera.com; f. 1995; station's objective is to educate, entertain and inform refugee and local communities, with the aim of bringing about peace and reconciliation; Dir Damas S. J. Missanga.

Radio One: Mikocheni Light Industrial Area, POB 4374, Dar es Salaam; tel. (22) 2775916; e-mail info@radio1.co.tz; internet www .radio1.co.tz; wholly owned by IPP Ltd; Man. Dir Joyce Mhaville.

Radio Tumaini (Hope): 1 Bridge St, POB 9916, Dar es Salaam; tel. (22) 2117307; internet radiotumaini.tripod.com; broadcasts in Swahili within Dar es Salaam; operated by the Roman Catholic Church; broadcasts on religious, social and economic issues; Dir Esther Chilambo.

Tanzania Broadcasting Corporation (TBC): Broadcasting House, Nyerere Rd, POB 9191, Dar es Salaam; tel. (22) 2860760; e-mail info@tbc.go.tz; internet www.tbc.go.tz; f. 2008; incorporates Radio Tanzania Dar es Salaam and the national TV network, Televisheni ya Taifa; Dir-Gen. Dr Ayub Rioba.

    TBC Taifa (RTD): POB 9191, Dar es Salaam; tel. (22) 2860760; e-mail info@tbcorp.org; internet www.tbc.go.tz; f. 1951; state-owned; subsidiary of TBC; domestic services in Swahili; external services in English; Gen. Man. Edda Sanga.

Television

Channel Ten: POB 19045, Jamhuri/Zaramo St, Dar es Salaam; tel. (22) 2113112; e-mail info@channelten.co.tz; internet www .channelten.co.tz.

Dar es Salaam Television (DTV): POB 19045, Dar es Salaam; tel. (22) 2116341; f. 1994; Man. Dir Franco Tramontano.

East Africa Television: Mikocheni Light Industrial Area, POB 4374, Dar es Salaam; tel. (22) 2775914; e-mail info@eatv.tv; internet www.eatv.tv.

Independent Television (ITV): Mikocheni Light Industrial Area, Plot No. 130, POB 4374, Dar es Salaam; tel. (22) 2775914; e-mail itv@ ipp.co.tz; internet www.itv.co.tz; f. 1994; wholly owned by IPP Ltd; 65% of programmes are locally produced and in Kiswahili; Man. Dir Joyce Mhaville.

Star TV: Post Rd, POB 1732, Mwanza; tel. (28) 2503262; e-mail marketing@startvtz.com; internet www.startvtz.com; f. 2000.

Tanzania Broadcasting Corporation (TBC): see Radio

    Televisheni ya Taifa (TVT): POB 31519, Dar es Salaam; tel. (22) 2700011; internet www.tbc.go.tz; f. 2000; state-owned; subsidiary of TBC since 2008; Gen. Man. Clement Mshana.

Zanzibar Broadcasting Corporation (ZBC): Karume House, POB 314, Zanzibar; tel. (24) 2330000; e-mail info@zbc.co.tz; internet www.zbc.co.tz; f. 2013; Chair. Dr Ali Ahmed Uki; Man. Dir Imane Duwe.

Finance

BANKING

In 2022 there were 34 commercial banks, four microfinance banks, two development finance institutions and three financial leasing companies.

Central Bank

Bank of Tanzania (Benki Kuu Ya Tanzania): 16 Jakaya Kikwete Rd, POB 2303, 40184 Dodoma; tel. (26) 2963183; e-mail info@hq .bot-tz.org; internet www.bot.go.tz; f. 1966; bank of issue; Gov. and Chair. Prof. Florens Luoga.

Principal Banks

Absa Bank Tanzania: Absa House, Ohio St, POB 5137, Dar es Salaam; tel. 746882000; e-mail talktous.tz@absa.africa; internet www.absa.co.tz/personal; f. 1925; fmrly Barclays Bank Tanzania; present name adopted 2020; part of Absa Group Ltd; Chair. Simon Mponji; Man. Dir Abdi Mohamed.

Akiba Commercial Bank Ltd (ACB): Amani Pl., 3rd Floor, Ohio St, POB 669, Dar es Salaam; tel. (22) 2118340; e-mail info@acbtz .com; internet www.acbbank.co.tz; f. 1997; 51% owned by the National Bank of Malawi; Chair. Ernest Masawe; Man. Dir Augustine Akowuah.

Azania Bank Ltd: Mawasiliano Towers, Sam Nujoma Rd, POB 32089, Dar es Salaam; tel. (22) 2412025; e-mail customercare@ azaniabank.co.tz; internet azaniabank.co.tz; f. 1995; 51.95% owned by Parastatal Public Servant Service Fund, 27.99% owned by National Social Security Fund; Chair. Julius Ndyamukama; Man. Dir (vacant).

BancABC (Tanzania) Ltd: 5th and 6th Floors, Uhuru Heights, Bibi Titi Mohammed Rd, POB 31, Dar es Salaam; tel. (22) 2111990; internet www.bancabc.co.tz; f. 1996; Chair. Protase Ishengoma; Man. Dir Imani John Bgoya.

Bank of Africa—Tanzania (BOA—Tanzania): NDC Development House, cnr Kivukoni Front and Ohio St, POB 3054, Dar es Salaam; tel. (22) 2110104; e-mail info@boatanzania.com; internet www.boatanzania.com; f. 1994 as Eurafrican Bank (Tanzania) Ltd, name changed as above in 2007; 72.85% owned by BMCE Bank; Chair. Mwanaidi Sinare Maajar; Man. Dir Wasia Issa Mushi.

Citibank Tanzania Ltd: Citibank House, Plot 1962, Toure Dr., Oyster Bay, POB 71625, Dar es Salaam; tel. (22) 2211226; 99.98% owned by Citibank Overseas Investment Corpn; CEO Geofrey Daniel Mchangila.

CRDB Bank: Azikiwe St, POB 268, Dar es Salaam; tel. (22) 2197700; e-mail info@crdbbank.com; internet crdbbank.co.tz; f. as Co-operative and Rural Development Bank in 1947, transferred to private ownership and current name adopted 1996; 21.0% owned by DANIDA Investment Fund, 13.3% owned by PSSSF Pension Fund; Chair Ally Hussein Laay; CEO and Man. Dir Abdulmajid Mussa Nsekela.

DCB Commercial Bank PLC (DCB): DCB House, Magomeni Mwembechai, Morogoro Rd, POB 19798, Dar es Salaam; tel. (22) 2172201; e-mail info@dcb.co.tz; internet www.dcb.co.tz; f. 2001 as Dar es Salaam Community Bank Ltd; name changed as above in 2012; Chair. Prof. Lucian A. Msambichaka; Man. Dir Godfrey Ndalahwa.

Diamond Trust Bank Tanzania Ltd: Jamat/Mosque St, POB 115, Dar es Salaam; tel. (22) 2114888; e-mail customercare@ diamondtrust.co.tz; internet diamondtrust.co.tz; f. 1946 as Diamond Jubilee Investment Trust; converted to bank and adopted current name in 1996; 55% owned by Diamond Trust Bank Kenya Ltd, 23% owned by Aga Khan Fund for Economic Development SA (Switzerland); Chair. Karim Wissanji; CEO Ravneet Chowdhury.

EXIM Bank (Tanzania) Ltd: Exim Tower, Ghana Ave, POB 1431, Dar es Salaam; tel. (22) 2113091; e-mail customercare@eximbank.co .tz; internet www.eximbank.co.tz; Chair. Yogesh Manek; Man. Dir Jaffari Matundu.

Habib African Bank Ltd: Indira Gandhi/Zanaki St, POB 70086, Dar es Salaam; tel. (22) 2111107; e-mail hasanrizvi@ habibafricanbank.co.tz; internet www.habibafricanbank.co.tz; f. 1998; Chair. Zain Habib; Man. Dir Syed Hasan Rizvi.

I & M Tanzania Ltd Bank Ltd: Maktaba Sq., Maktaba St, POB 1509, Dar es Salaam; tel. (22) 2127330; internet www.imbank.com; f. 2002 by merger of Furaha Finance Ltd and Crown Finance & Leasing Ltd; present name adopted 2010; Chair. Sarit S. Raja Shah; CEO Mohammed Baseer.

International Commercial Bank (Tanzania) Ltd: Vijana Towers, 2nd Floor, Plot No. 1081/2/2, Fire Station Rd, POB 9362, Dar es Salaam; tel. (22) 2134989; e-mail enquiry@icbank.co.tz; internet icbank.co.tz; f. 1998; 75.08% owned by ICB Financial Group Holding AG; CEO Villy Vellayappan.

Kenya Commercial Bank (Tanzania) Ltd: Harambee Plaza, 1st Floor, POB 804, Dar es Salaam; tel. (22) 2664388; e-mail customercare@tz.kcbbankgroup.com; internet tz.kcbgroup.com; Chair. John Ulanga; Man. Dir Cosmas Kimario.

MUCOBA Bank PLC (MuCoBa): Iringa/Mbeya Rd, POB 147, Mafinga, Iringa; tel. (26) 2772165; e-mail mucoba@mucobatz.com; internet www.mucobatz.com; Chair. Prof. Dominicus Kasilo; Gen. Man. Philip Raymond Phanuel (acting).

Mwanga Hakika Microfinance Bank Ltd (MHB): Sky Tower, Plot Nos 1 and 50, Block No. 45A, Kijitonyama, New Bagamoyo Rd, POB 11735, Dar es Salaam; tel. 747666511; e-mail info@mhbbank.co .tz; internet mhbbank.co.tz; f. 2020 following merger of Mwanga Community Bank Ltd, Hakika Microfinance Bank Ltd and EFC

Tanzania Microfinance Bank; Chair. RIDHIWANI MRINGO; Man. Dir JAGJIT SINGH.

NMB Bank: cnr Ohio St and Ali Hassan Mwinyi Rd, POB 9213, Dar es Salaam; tel. (22) 2322000; e-mail info@nmbtz.com; internet www.nmbbank.co.tz; f. 1997 following disbandment of the National Bank of Commerce; 49% owned by a consortium led by Rabobank Group, 30% state-owned; Chair. Dr EDWIN P. MHEDE; Man. Dir RUTH ZAIPUNA.

NBC Ltd (National Bank of Commerce Ltd): NBC House, Sokoine Dr., POB 1863, Dar es Salaam; tel. (22) 2193000; e-mail contact .centre@nbctz.com; internet www.nbc.co.tz/en/personal; f. 1997; 55% owned by Absa Group Ltd (South Africa), 30% by Govt and 15% by International Finance Corpn; Man. Dir THEOBALD M. SABI.

NCBA Bank Tanzania: Amani Place Bldg, 1st, 2nd and 10th Floors, Ohio St, POB 20268, Dar es Salaam; tel. (22) 2130113; internet ncbagroup.co.tz; f. 2020 following merger of NIC Bank Tanzania and CBA Tanzania; Chair. SHARMAPAL AGGARWAL; CEO MARGARET KARUME.

People's Bank of Zanzibar Ltd (PBZ): ZIC Bldg, 2nd Floor, Mpirani, POB 1173, Stone Town, Zanzibar; tel. (24) 2234571; e-mail info@pbzbank.co.tz; internet pbzbank.co.tz; f. 1966; controlled by Zanzibar Govt; Exec. Dir Dr MUHSIN SALUM MASOUD.

Stanbic Bank Tanzania Ltd: Sukari House, cnr AH Mwinyi/Kinondoni Rd, POB 72647, Dar es Salaam; tel. 800751111; e-mail tanzaniaccc@stanbic.com; internet www.stanbicbank.co.tz; f. 1993; wholly owned by Standard Africa Holdings Ltd; Chair MARK MWANDOSYA; Chief Exec. KEVIN WINGFIELD.

Standard Chartered Bank Tanzania Ltd: International House, 1st Floor, cnr Shaaban Robert St and Garden Ave, POB 9011, Dar es Salaam; tel. (22) 2122160; e-mail callcentre@sc.com; internet www.sc.com/tz; f. 1992; wholly owned by Standard Chartered Holdings (Africa) BV, Netherlands; Man. Dir SANJAY CHAMANLAL RUGHANI.

Tanzania Postal Bank (TPB): 10th LAPF Towers, Bagamoyo Rd, Kijitonyama, POB 9300, Dar es Salaam; tel. (22) 2162940; e-mail info@tpbbank.co.tz; internet www.tpbbank.co.tz; f. 1991; state-owned; CEO SABASABA KITEWITA MOSHINGI.

TIB Development Bank: Bldg No. 3, Mlimani City Office Park, Sam Nujoma Rd, POB 9373, Dar es Salaam; tel. (22) 2163600; e-mail md@tib.co.tz; internet www.tib.co.tz; f. 1970 as Tanzania Investment Bank; govt-owned; Chair. Dr MARY SALOME MASHINGO; Man. Dir CHARLES G. SINGILI.

United Bank for Africa Tanzania Ltd: 30C/30D Nyerere Rd, POB 80514, Dar es Salaam; tel. (22) 2864468; e-mail customerservicetz@ubagroup.com; internet www.ubatanzania.co.tz; Chair. TUVAKO MANONGI; Man. Dir KINGSLEY ULINFUN.

Development Bank

Tanzania Agricultural Development Bank (TADB): Acacia Estate, 4th Floor, 84 Kinondoni Rd, POB 63372, Dar es Salaam; tel. (22) 2923500; e-mail info@tadb.co.tz; internet www.tadb.co.tz; f. 2015; state-owned; Chair. ROSEBUD V. KURWIJILA; Man. Dir JAPHET JUSTINE.

BANKING ASSOCIATION

Tanzania Bankers Association: Faykat Tower, 1st Floor, Plot No. 236, Ali Hassan Mwinyi Rd, POB 70925, Dar es Salaam; tel. (22) 2668221; e-mail info@tanzaniabankers.org; internet www.tanzaniabankers.org; f. 1995; Chair. ABDULMAJID MUSA NSEKELA.

STOCK EXCHANGE

Dar es Salaam Stock Exchange: NHC Corporate Office, Kambarage House, 3rd Floor, 6 Ufukoni St, POB 70081, Dar es Salaam; tel. (22) 2123983; e-mail info@dse.co.tz; internet www.dse.co.tz; f. 1998; 28 listed cos (2020); Chair. JONATHAN A. NJAU; Chief Exec. MOREMI MARWA.

INSURANCE

Alliance Insurance Corpn Ltd: 7th Floor, Exim Tower, Ghana Ave, POB 9942, Dar es Salaam; tel. (22) 2139104; e-mail admin@alliance.co.tz; internet alliance.co.tz; Chair. SHAFFIN JAMAL; CEO K. V. A. KRISHNAN.

Jubilee Insurance Co of Tanzania Ltd (JICT): Amani Plaza, 6th Floor, Ohio St, POB 20524, Dar es Salaam; tel. 800780066; e-mail enquiry@jubileetanzania.co.tz; internet jubileeinsurance.com/tz/general; 40% owned by Jubilee Insurance Kenya, 24% by local investors, 15% by the IFC, 15% by the Aga Khan Fund for Economic Devt, 6% by others; Chair. NIZAR JUMA; CEO DIPANKAR ACHARYA.

National Insurance Corporation of Tanzania Ltd (NIC): NIC Bldg, cnr Samora Ave and Pamba Rd, POB 9264, Dar es Salaam; tel. (22) 2113823; e-mail info-nic@nictanzania.com; internet nictanzania .co.tz; f. 1963; state-owned; all classes of insurance; Man. Dir Dr ELIREHEMA DORIYE.

Sanlam General Insurance: Amani Pl., 4th Floor, Ohio St, POB 21228, Dar es Salaam; tel. (22) 2120188; e-mail info@sanlamgeneralinsurance.co.tz; internet www.sanlam.com/tanzania; f. 1998; fmrly Niko Insurance (Tanzania) Ltd; name changed as above in 2015; Chair. ARNOLD KILEWO; CEO KHAMIS SULEIMAN.

Sanlam Life Insurance: Amani Place, 9th Floor, Ohio St, POB 22229, Dar es Salaam; tel. (22) 2127151; e-mail info@sanlam.co.tz; internet www.sanlam.com/tanzania; f. 2005; Chair. Dr MATERN Y. C. LUMBANGA; CEO JULIUS MAGABE.

REGULATORY AUTHORITY

Tanzania Insurance Regulatory Authority (TIRA): LAPF Bldg, 5th Floor, Plot No. 4/5, Makole St, POB 2987, Dodoma; tel. (26) 2321180; e-mail coi@tira.go.tz; internet www.tira.go.tz; f. 2009; Commr of Insurance Dr BAGHAYO SAQWARE.

Trade and Industry

GOVERNMENT AGENCIES

Business Registrations and Licensing Agency (BRELA): BRELA House, House No. 11, Plot No. 20, Block No. 23, cnr Shaban Robert St and Sokoine Dr., POB 9393, Dar es Salaam; tel. (22) 2212800; e-mail maoni@brela.go.tz; internet www.brela.go.tz; f. 1999; registration of companies, business names and trade and service marks registration, granting of patents and issuing of industrial licences; CEO GODFREY NYAISA.

Tanzania Investment Centre (TIC): Shaaban Robert St, POB 938, Dar es Salaam; tel. (22) 2116328; e-mail info@tic.go.tz; internet www.tic.go.tz; f. 1997; promotes and facilitates investment in Tanzania; Chair. Prof. LONGNUS K. RUTASITARA; Exec. Dir JOHN MATHEW MNALI (acting).

Tanzania Minerals Audit Agency: Plot No. 1129, Chole Rd, Masaki, POB 23400, Dar es Salaam; tel. (22) 2601819.

Tanzania Revenue Authority: 28 Edward Sokoine Dr., 11105 Mchafukoge, Ilala CBD, POB 11491, Dar es Salaam; tel. (22) 2119343; e-mail services@tra.go.tz; internet www.tra.go.tz; f. 1995; Commr-Gen. ALPHAYO KIDATA.

Tanzania Trade Development Authority (TanTrade): Mwl J. K. Nyerere Fair Grounds, Plot No. 436, Block A, Kilwa Rd, POB 5402, Dar es Salaam; tel. (22) 2850238; e-mail info@tantrade.go .tz; internet www.tantrade.go.tz; f. 2009 to replace the Board of Internal Trade and the Board of External Trade; aims to develop and promote internal and external trade; Chair. Prof. ULINGETA MBAMBA; Dir-Gen. LATIFA MOHAMED KHAMISI.

CHAMBERS OF COMMERCE

Tanzania Chamber of Commerce, Industry and Agriculture (TCCIA): PPF House, cnr Morogoro Rd and Samora Ave, POB 9713, Dar es Salaam; tel. (22) 2119437; e-mail hq@tccia.com; internet www.tccia.or.tz; f. 1988; Pres. PAUL F. KOYI; Exec. Dir NEBART MWAPWELE.

Zanzibar National Chamber of Commerce (ZNCC): Livingstone House, Kinazini, POB 1407, Zanzibar; tel. 778344003; e-mail info@zncc.or.tz; internet zncc.or.tz; Pres. TOUFIQ SALIM TURKY; Exec. Dir HAMAD HAMAD.

DEVELOPMENT CORPORATIONS

Deep Sea Fishing Authority (DSFA): DSFA Bldg, POB 56, Zanzibar; tel. 779888215; e-mail info@dsfa.go.tz; internet www .dsfa.go.tz; to regulate and control fishing in the Exclusive Economic Zone; Dr EMMANUEL SWEKE.

National Development Corporation: Development House, Kivukoni Front, Ohio St, POB 2669, Dar es Salaam; tel. (22) 2112893; e-mail info@ndc.go.tz; internet ndc.go.tz; f. 1965; state-owned; promotes progress and expansion in production and investment; Chair. Dr YAMUNGU KAYANDABILA; Man. Dir Prof. DAMIAN GABAGAMBI.

National Housing Corpn: Plot No. 1, Ufukoni St/Ally Hassan Mwinyi Rd, Upanga, POB 2977, Dar es Salaam; tel. (22) 2105002; e-mail dg@nhc.co.tz; internet nhc.co.tz; provision of housing; Chair. Dr SOPHIA KONGELA; Dir-Gen. Dr MAULID BANYANI.

Small Industries Development Organization (SIDO): Mfaume/Fire Rd, Upanga, POB 2476, Dar es Salaam; tel. (22) 2151948; e-mail dg@sido.go.tz; internet www.sido.go.tz; f. 1973; parastatal; promotes and assists development of small-scale enterprises in public, co-operative and private sectors, aims to increase the involvement of women in small businesses; Chair. WILFRED NYACHIA; Dir-Gen. OMARI J. BAKARI.

State Mining Corpn (STAMICO): United Nations Rd, Upanga, Plot No. 417/418, POB 4958, Dar es Salaam; tel. (22) 2150029; e-mail info@stamico.co.tz; internet www.stamico.co.tz; Chair. Maj.-Gen. (retd) MICHAEL J. ISAMUHYO; Man. Dir Dr VENANCE MWASSE (acting).

Tanzania Petroleum Development Corpn (TPDC): PSSF Kambarage Tower, 8th Floor, Jakaya Kikwete Rd, POB 1191, Dodoma; tel. (22) 2200103; e-mail info@tpdc.co.tz; internet tpdc.co.tz; f. 1969; state-owned; oversees petroleum exploration and undertakes autonomous exploration, imports crude petroleum and distributes refined products; Chair. OMBENI SEFUE; Man. Dir Dr JAMES P. MATARAGIO.

INDUSTRIAL AND TRADE ASSOCIATIONS

Cashewnut Board of Tanzania (CBT): POB 533, Mtwara; tel. (23) 2333303; e-mail info@cashew.go.tz; internet www.cashew.go.tz; f. 2009; govt-owned; regulates the marketing, processing and export of cashews; Chair. Brig.-Gen. MSTAAFU ALOYCE DAMIAN MWANJILE; Dir-Gen. FRANCIS ALFRED (acting).

Confederation of Tanzania Industries (CTI): NIC Investment House, 9th Floor, Samora Ave, POB 71783, Dar es Salaam; tel. (22) 2114954; internet www.cti.co.tz; f. 1991; Chair. PAUL MAKANZA; Exec. Dir LEODEGAR C. TENGA.

Sugar Board of Tanzania: Sukari House, 6th Floor, cnr Ohio St and Sokoine Dr., POB 4355, Dar es Salaam; tel. (22) 2111523; e-mail info@sbt.go.tz; internet www.sbt.go.tz; f. 2001; Chair. Dr ASHURA LUZI-KIHUPI; Dir-Gen. Prof. KENNETH BENGESI.

Tanzania Coffee Board (TCB): Kahawa House, POB 732, Moshi; tel. (27) 2752324; e-mail info@coffeeboard.or.tz; internet www.coffeeboard.or.tz; Chair. Dr AURELIA KAMUZORA; Dir-Gen. PRIMUS KIMARYO (acting).

Tanzania Cotton Board (TCB): Regional Dr., POB 61, Mwanza; tel. (28) 2500528; e-mail info@tcb.go.tz; internet www.tcb.go.tz; f. 2004 replacing Tanzania Cotton Marketing Board (1984); regulates, develops and promotes the Tanzanian cotton industry; Chair. Dr JOEL KABISA (acting); Dir-Gen. MARCO CHARLES MTUNGA.

Tanzania Exporters' Association: NIC Investment House, 6th Floor, Wing A, Samora Ave, POB 1175, Dar es Salaam; tel. 732924564; e-mail tanexa.exporters@yahoo.com; f. 1994; Chair. ISSAC DALLUSHI; Exec. Dir MTEMI LAWRENCE NALUYAGA.

Tanzania Horticultural Association (TAHA): Kanisa Rd, House No. 49, POB 16520, Arusha; tel. (27) 2544568; e-mail info@taha.or.tz; internet taha.or.tz; f. 2004; Chair. ERIC NG'IMARYO; Exec. Dir JACQUELINE MKINDI.

Tanzania Sisal Board: 1 Tasma Rd, POB 277, Tanga; tel. (27) 2645060; internet www.tsbtz.org; f. 1997; Chair. Prof. JOSEPH SEMBOJA; Dir-Gen. YUNUS MSSIKA.

Tanzania Smallholder Tea Development Agency (TSTDA): Tetex House, 1st Floor, Pamba Rd, POB 5815, Dar es Salaam; tel. (22) 2127860; Chair. Dr NICODEMUS P. SICILIMA; Man. Dir MUSTAFA HAMISI UMANDE.

Tanzania Tobacco Board: Plot No. 375, Bima St, POB 227, Kihonda 67128, Maghorofani, Morogoro; tel. (26) 2604417; e-mail info@tobaccoboard.go.tz; internet www.tobaccoboard.go.tz; Dir-Gen. STANLEY NELSON MNOZYA.

Tea Board of Tanzania: TETEX House, 1st Floor, Pamba Rd, POB 2663, Dar es Salaam; tel. (22) 2114400; e-mail info@teaboard.go.tz; internet teaboard.go.tz; Chair. Eng. STEVEN D. M. MLOTE; Dir-Gen. Eng. NICHOLAUS W. MAUYA.

Zanzibar State Trading Corporation: Maisara St, POB 26, Zanzibar; tel. (24) 2230271; e-mail info@zstcznz.org; internet www.zstcznz.org; govt-controlled since 1964; sole exporter of cloves, clove stem oil, chillies, copra, copra cake, lime oil and lime juice; Chair. KASSIM MAALIM SULEIMAN; Dir SULEIMAN JONGO.

UTILITIES

Regulatory Authority

Energy and Water Utilities Regulatory Authority (EWURA): EWURA House, Plot No. 3, Block AD, Medeli West, POB 2857, Dodoma; tel. (26) 2329003; e-mail info@ewura.go.tz; internet www.ewura.go.tz; f. 2001; technical and economic regulation of the electricity, petroleum, natural gas and water sectors; Chair. Prof. JAMIDU KATIMA; Dir-Gen. Eng. GODFREY CHIBULUNJE.

Zanzibar Utilities Regulatory Authority (ZURA): ZURA House, POB 2238, Maisara, Zanzibar; tel. (24) 2941190; e-mail info@zura.go.tz; internet www.zura.go.tz; f. 2013; Dir-Gen. OMAR ALI YUSSUF.

Electricity

Songas Ltd: Cape Town Fish Market, 4th Floor, 179/180 Msasani Bay, Msasani Village, Block B, Kinondoni District, POB 6342, Dar es Salaam; tel. 764701001; e-mail songas.info@songas.com; internet www.songas.com; f. 1998; generates electricity using gas from the Songo Songo Island gas fields; Man. Dir ANAEL SAMUEL.

Tanzania Electric Supply Co Ltd (TANESCO): Plot No. 114, Block G, Dar es Salaam Rd, POB 453, Dodoma; tel. 768985100; e-mail communications.manager@tanesco.co.tz; internet www.tanesco.co.tz; state-owned; Chair. Dr OMARI ISSA; Man. Dir MR. MAHARAGE CHANDE.

Zanzibar Electricity Corpn (ZECO): Gulioni St, POB 235, Zanzibar; tel. (24) 52255; internet zeco.co.tz; f. 2006; Chair. Maj.-Gen. (retd) SHARIF SHEHE OTHMAN.

Gas

Lake Gas Ltd: Plot No. 49, Mikocheni Light Industrial Area, POB 5055, Dar es Salaam; tel. (22) 2780510; e-mail admin@lakeoilgroup.com; internet lakeoilgroup.com; CEO ALLY EDHA AWADH.

Oryx Energies: Plot No. 34/1, Tan House, Bagamoyo Rd, Victoria Area, Kinondoni, POB 9540, Dar es Salaam; tel. (22) 5514000; e-mail oryx.tanzania@oryxenergies.com; internet www.oryxeveryday.com.

Water

Dar es Salaam Water Supply and Sanitation Authority: DAWASA House, cnr Dunga and Malanga Sts, Mwananyamala, POB 1573, Dar es Salaam; tel. (22) 2760006; e-mail info@dawasa.go.tz; internet www.dawasa.go.tz/en; following merger in 2018 of DAWASA and DAWASCO; sole provider of water supply and sewerage services in Dar es Salaam and parts of the coastal region; Chair. DAVIS MWAMUNYANGE; CEO Eng. CYPRIAN LUHEMEJA.

Zanzibar Water Authority (ZAWA): POB 460, Mabluu, Zanzibar; tel. (24) 2231151; e-mail info@zawa.go.tz; internet zawa.go.tz; f. 2006; Chair. Maj.-Gen. (retd) ISSA SLEIMAN NASSOR; Dir-Gen. Dr SALHA MOHAMMED KASSIM.

MAJOR COMPANIES

The following are some of the largest companies in terms either of capital investment or employment.

A to Z Textile Mills Ltd: Dodoma Rd, Networld Area, Kisongo, Matevesi, POB 945, Arusha; tel. 788808534; e-mail info@azpfl.com; internet www.azpfl.com; f. 1966; CEO KALPESH SHAH.

ACACIA Mining PLC Tanzania: Tanhouse Tower, Plot No. 34/1, Ursino South, New Bagamoyo Rd, POB 1081, Dar es Salaam; tel. (22) 2164200; internet www.acaciamining.com; operates gold mines at Bulyanhulu, Buzwagi and North Mara; Pres. and CEO MARK BRISTOW.

Afri Tea and Coffee Blenders: Bandari Rd, nr Gate No. 4 of DSM Port, Kurasini, POB 747, Dar es Salaam; tel. (22) 2112430; e-mail sales@ttb.co.tz; internet atcb.co.tz; f. 1963 as Brookebond Tanganyika Ltd; present name adopted 2008; owned by Lushoto Tea Co; blending and packing of teas, packing of instant coffee powder and roasting, grinding and packing of coffee beans.

Aluminium Africa Ltd (ALAF): Nyerere Rd, Area Plot No. 18, POB 2070, Dar es Salaam; tel. 768555560; e-mail sales.alaf@safalgroup.com; internet alaf.co.tz; f. 1960; mfrs of aluminium circles, corrugated and plain sheets, galvanized corrugated iron sheets, furniture tubes, steel billets, galvanized pipes, cold-rolled steel sheets and coils; Chair. M. P. CHANDARIA; CEO SHARAD N. SALGAR.

Azania Group of Companies: Nyerere Rd, Industrial Area, Opposite Quality Centre, POB 5055, Dar es Salaam; tel. (22) 2861235; e-mail info@azaniawheatflour.com; internet www.azaniawheatflour.com; production of wheat flour.

Bakhresa Group: POB 2517, Dar es Salaam; tel. (22) 2861116; internet bakhresa.com; flour-milling, bakeries, bottled water, fruit juice and polypropylene woven sacks; Chair. SAID SALIM BAKHRESA.

IPP Ltd: POB 163, Dar es Salaam; tel. (22) 2119349; internet www.ippmedia.com; f. 1978; holding co; Exec. Chair. REGINALD A. MENGI.

Kamal Group: Plot No. 188/2, Chang'ombe Rd, POB 10392, Dar es Salaam; tel. (22) 2862975; e-mail info@kamal-group.com; internet kamal-group.co.tz; f. 2004; conglomerate with interests in steel, alloy, mining, agriculture, construction and medical and industrial gases; Chair. and Man. Dir GAGAN SANTOSH GUPTA.

Katani Ltd: 1 Tasma Rd, Bombo Area, POB 123, Tanga; tel. (27) 2644401; e-mail info@katanitz.com; f. 1997; mfrs of sisal products; Man. Dir SALUM SHAMTE.

LafargeHolcim Tanzania (Mbeya Cement Co Ltd): Oyster Plaza, 3rd Floor, Plot 1196 Haile Selassie Rd, POB 46452, Dar es Salaam; tel. (22) 2923300; e-mail customercare.mcc@lafargeholcim.com; internet lafargeholcim.co.tz; manufacturer of cement; CEO KHALED GHAREIB.

MAC Group: 439 Mahando St, Masasani Penisula, POB 2552, Dar es Salaam; tel. (22) 2600000; e-mail operations@mactz.com; internet www.mactz.com; f. early 1980s; business conglomerate with interests in banking, insurance, consumer products, real estate and logistics; Chair. YOGESH MANEK.

ChemiCotex Industries Ltd: 88–89 Mbezi Beach, New Bagamoyo Rd, POB 347, Dar es Salaam; tel. (22) 2628014; e-mail sect@ cciltz.com; f. 1975; consumer goods.

Minjingu Mines and Fertiliser Ltd: Old Moshi Rd, POB 912, Arusha; tel. (27) 2545047; e-mail sales@minjingumines.com; internet minjingumines.com; f. 2001; extraction of phosphate ore and production of fertilizers; Gen. Man. ANUP MODHA.

Mohammed Enterprises Tanzania Ltd (MeTL): Golden Jubilee Towers, 20th Floor, Ohio St and Garden Ave, Dar es Salaam; tel. (22) 2122830; e-mail info@metl.net; internet www.metl.net; f. 1970; conglomerate with interests in trading, agriculture, manufacturing, energy and petroleum, financial services, mobile telephony, infrastructure and real estate, transport and logistics and distribution; CEO MOHAMMED DEWJI.

Mount Meru Group: Plot No. 77, Block EE, Ngarenaro, POB 7094, Arusha; tel. 715696969; e-mail energy.tz@mountmerugroup.com; internet www.mountmerugroup.com; f. 1978; import and distribution of petroleum products (Mount Meru Petroleum Ltd), production of cooking oil (Mount Meru Millers Ltd) and logistics (Mount Meru Logistics Ltd); Group Exec. Dir ATUL MITTAL.

Murzah Oil Mills Ltd: Kipawa, Nyerere Road Industrial Area, POB 2339, Dar es Salaam; tel. (22) 2843288; Gen. Man. LAKSHMI NARAYANA CHUNDURI.

New World Furniture: Kwa Iddi, opp. Njake Petrol Station, POB 8154, Arusha; tel. (73) 2971787; e-mail newage_nwg@yahoo.com; f. 2004; CEO BENSON NGOMUO.

PanAfrican Energy Tanzania Ltd: Oyster Plaza Bldg, 5th Floor, Haile Selassie Rd, POB 80139, Dar es Salaam; tel. (22) 2138737; e-mail info@panafricanenergy.com; internet www.panafricanenergy .com; Country Chair. PATRICK RUTABANZIBWA; Man. Dir ANDREW HANNA.

Sagera Estates Ltd: POB 117, Tanga; tel. (27) 2646847; internet www.agriafrica.co.tz; sisal fibre and yarn.

SBC Tanzania Ltd: 54/57 Nyerere Rd, POB 4162, Dar es Salaam; tel. (22) 2860780; e-mail pepsi@sbctz.com; internet www .sbctanzania.com; f. 2001; Chair. FAYSAL M. EL-KHALIL; Exec. Dir ZIAD EL-KHALIL.

Serengeti Breweries Ltd: Plot No 117/2 Access Rd, Nelson Mandela Expressway, Chang'ombe Industrial Area, POB 41080, Dar es Salaam; tel. 784104100; Man. Dir MARK OCITTI ONGOM.

Sunflag (Tanzania) Ltd: Themi Industrial Area, POB 3123, Arusha; tel. (27) 2549268; e-mail info@sunflag-tz.com; internet www.sunflag-tz.com; f. 1965; mfrs of textiles and clothing; Chair. SATYA DEV BHARDWAJ.

Swala Oil and Gas (Tanzania) PLC: Oyster Plaza, 2nd Floor, Plot No. 1196, Oysterbay Haile Selassie Rd, POB 105266, Dar es Salaam; tel. 755687785; e-mail info@swalaoilandgas.com; internet www .swalaoilandgas.com; Chair. ABDULLAH MWINYI; CEO Dr DAVID MESTRES RIDGE.

Tanga Cement Co Ltd: Coco Plaza, 3rd Floor, Toure Dr., POB 78478, Dar es Salaam; tel. (22) 2602784; e-mail info@simbacement.co .tz; internet simbacement.co.tz; subsidiary of Holcim Ltd (Switzerland); mfrs of Portland cement; Chair. LAWRENCE KEGO MASHA; Man. Dir REINHART SWART.

Tanganyika Instant Coffee Co Ltd (TANICA): Custom Rd, POB 410, Bukoba; tel. 734251456; e-mail info@tanicacafe.co.tz; internet tanicacafe.co.tz; f. 1963; production of coffee; Chair. FRANK MUGANYIZI; Gen. Man. Eng. RODNESS MILTON.

Tanpack Tissues Ltd: POB 21359, Dar es Salaam; tel. (22) 2773901; e-mail info@tanpack.com; internet fb.com/ tanpacktissues; f. 1996; wholly owned by Chandaria Industries Ltd; mfrs of paper and tissue; Man. Dir MAHESH M. CHANDARIA; Gen. Man. RAJESH SHA.

Tanzania Breweries Ltd (TBL): Plot 79, Uhuru St, Block AA, Mchikichini, Ilala, POB 9013, Dar es Salaam; tel. (22) 2182780; internet tanzaniabreweries.co.tz; f. 1960; subsidiary of South African Breweries International; manufacture, bottling and distribution of malt beer; Chair. CLEOPA MSUYA; Man. Dir PHILIP REDMAN.

Tanzania China Friendship Textile Co.: POB 20842, Dar es Salaam; tel. (22) 2189841; f. 1966; wholly owned by National Textile Corpn; dyed and printed fabric mfrs.

Tanzania Cigarette Co (TCC): POB 40114, Dar es Salaam; tel. (22) 2166217; e-mail emma.oriyo@jti.com; internet www.jti.com/ africa/tanzania; f. 1965; 75% owned by JT International; manufacture and marketing of cigarettes; CEO MAJD ABDOU.

Tanzania Portland Cement Co Ltd (Twiga Cement): Wazo Hill, Bagamoyo Rd, POB 1950, Dar es Salaam; tel. 746810930; e-mail info@twigacement.com; internet www.twigacement.com; f. 1959; 69.3% owned by HeidelbergCement Group, Germany; mfrs of ordinary Portland cement; Man. Dir ALFONSO VELEZ MARTINEZ.

TanzaniteOne Mining Ltd: Block C, Merelani Simanjiro District, POB 15237, Arusha; internet www.tanzaniteone.com; mining of tanzanite; Man. Dir FAISAL JUMA.

TOL Gases Ltd: 4B Nyerere Rd, POB 911, Dar es Salaam; tel. (22) 2863838; internet tolgases.com; f. 1950; 11.4% owned by Govt; manufacture and distribution of industrial and chemical gases; Chair. HAROLD TEMU.

Toyota Tanzania Ltd: 5 Nyerere Rd, POB 9060, Dar es Salaam; tel. (22) 2866352; e-mail sales@toyotatz.com; internet www.toyotatz .com; f. 1825; wholly owned by Karimjee Jivanjee Ltd; distribution of Toyota motor vehicles; Man. Dir VINOD RUSTAGI.

Unilever Tea Tanzania Ltd: POB 40, Iringa, Mufindi; subsidiary of Unilever; grows and processes black and green tea; Man. Dir NICHOLAOS YIANNAKIS.

CO-OPERATIVES

Tanzania Federation of Co-operatives Ltd: Ushirika Bldg, 16th Floor, Lumumba St, POB 2567, Dar es Salaam; tel. (22) 2184084; e-mail ushirika@ushirika.co.tz; internet ushirika.co.tz; f. 1962; Exec. Sec. ABERHARD J. MBEPERA.

Principal Societies

Kagera Co-operative Union Ltd: POB 5, Bukoba; tel. (28) 2220229; e-mail kcubukoba@gmail.com; internet kcu.or.tz; 125 affiliated societies.

Kilimanjaro Native Co-operative Union (1984) Ltd (KNCU): KNCU Bldg, 1st Floor, Plot No. 33-34-1, Old Moshi Rd, POB 3032, Moshi; tel. (27) 2752785; e-mail info@kncutanzania.com; internet kncutanzania.com; f. 1984; represents smallholder farmers and coffee producers; 68 regd co-operative societies; Gen. Man. TOBIA MASAKI.

TRADE UNIONS

Trade Union Congress of Tanzania (TUCTA): Bibi Titi/Sophia Kawawa Rd, POB 15359, Dar es Salaam; tel. (22) 2127281; e-mail tucta2012@yahoo.com; internet www.tucta.or.tz; f. 2000; Pres. TUMAINI NYAMHOKYA; Sec.-Gen. HERY H. MKUNDA.

Zanzibar Trade Union Congress (ZATUC): POB 667, Zanzibar; tel. 777776400; e-mail zatuc_congress@yahoo.com; f. 2002; Sec.-Gen. KHAMIS MWINYI MOHAMMED.

Transport

RAILWAYS

Some 2,600 km of 1,000-mm-gauge railway track is operated by Tanzania Railways Ltd through Reli Assets Holding Co Ltd, which develops, promotes and manages rail infrastructure assets. Plans were under way in 2018 to construct new railway lines linking Tanga with Musoma on Lake Victoria. The 1,067-mm-gauge Tazara railway line linking Dar es Salaam with New Kapiri Mposhi, Zambia, has a total length of 1,860 km, of which 969 km are within Tanzania.

Tanzania Railways Corpn (TRC): Sokoine Dr., POB 76959, Dar es Salaam; tel. (22) 21334028; e-mail info@trl.co.tz; internet www.trc .co.tz; f. 2017 following the merger of Tanzania Railways Ltd and the Rail Assets Holding Company; state-owned; operates about 2,700 km of lines within Tanzania; Chair. Prof. JOHN WAJANGA KONDORO.

Tanzania-Zambia Railway Authority (Tazara): Nyerere Rd, POB 2834, Dar es Salaam; tel. 732998855; e-mail mdhq@ tazarasite.com; internet www.tazarasite.com; jtly owned and administered by the Tanzanian and Zambian Govts; operates a 1,860-km railway link between Dar es Salaam and New Kapiri Mposhi, Zambia, of which 975 km are within Tanzania; Man. Dir BRUNO TANDEO CHING'ANDU.

ROADS

Tanzania National Roads Agency (TANROADS): Airtel House, 3rd Floor, Ali Hassan Mwinyi/Kawawa Rd Junction, POB 11364, Dar es Salaam; tel. (22) 2926001; e-mail tanroadshq@tanroads.org; internet tanroads.go.tz; f. 2000; responsible for the maintenance and development of the trunk and regional road network; Chair. HAWA M. MMANGA; Chief Exec. ROGATUS HUSSEIN MATIVILA.

INLAND WATERWAYS

Steamers connect with Kenya, Uganda, the Democratic Republic of the Congo, Burundi, Zambia and Malawi. A rail ferry service operates on Lake Victoria between Mwanza and Port Bell.

SHIPPING

Tanzania's major harbours are at Dar es Salaam (with 11 deep-water berths, a grain terminal and an oil jetty) and Mtwara. There are also ports at Tanga, Bagamoyo, Zanzibar and Pemba.

Tanzania Ports Authority (TPA): POB 9184, Dar es Salaam; tel. (22) 2117816; e-mail dg@ports.go.tz; internet ports.go.tz; f. 2005 to replace the Tanzania Harbours Authority, in preparation for privatization; Chair. Prof. IGNAS A. RUBARATUKA; Dir-Gen. PLASDUCE MBOSSA.

Chinese-Tanzanian Joint Shipping Co: 31 Kisutu Rd, POB 696, Dar es Salaam; tel. (22) 2131165; e-mail admin@sinotaship.com; f. 1967; services to People's Republic of China, South-East Asia, Eastern and Southern Africa, Red Sea and Mediterranean ports.

Shipping Management Services (SHMASE): POB 5480, Dar es Salaam; tel. (22) 2123796; e-mail info@shmase.com; internet www.shmase.com; Man. Dir HASHIM MASHELLE.

CIVIL AVIATION

There are more than 100 airports and landing strips in Tanzania. The major international airport is at Dar es Salaam, 13 km from the city centre, and there are also international airports at Kilimanjaro, Mwanza and Zanzibar.

Tanzania Civil Aviation Authority (TCAA): Aviation House, Nyerere/Kitunda Rd Junction, POB 2819, Dar es Salaam; tel. (22) 2198196; e-mail tcaa@tcaa.go.tz; internet www.tcaa.go.tz; f. 2003; replaced Directorate of Civil Aviation (f. 1977); ensures aviation safety and security, provides air navigation services; Dir-Gen. HAMZA S. JOHARI.

Air Tanzania: ATC House, 2nd Floor, Ohio St/Garden Ave, POB 543, Dar es Salaam; tel. (22) 2113248; e-mail info@airtanzania.co.tz; internet www.airtanzania.co.tz; f. 1977; grounded in 2011; revived in 2016; Chair. Eng. EMMANUEL KOROSSO; CEO Eng. LADISLAUS MATINDI.

Precision Air Services Ltd: Diamond Plaza, 1st Floor, Plot No. 162/38, Mirambo St/Samora Ave, POB 70770, Dar es Salaam; tel. (22) 2191000; e-mail pwreservations@precisionairtz.com; internet www.precisionairtz.com; f. 1993; operates scheduled and charter domestic and regional services; Chair. MICHAEL N. SHIRIMA; Group Man. Dir and CEO SAUDA S. RAJAB.

Tanzania Air Services Ltd (TANZANAIR): Julius Nyerere Int. Airport, POB 364, Dar es Salaam; tel. (22) 2843131; e-mail info@tanzanair.com; internet www.tanzanair.com; f. 1969; operates domestic and regional charter services, offers full engineering and maintenance services for general aviation aircraft; agent for sales of Cessna aircraft; Man. Dir JOHN SAMARAS.

Tourism

Tanzania Tourist Board: Utalii House, Laibon St, POB 2485, Dar es Salaam; tel. (22) 2664878; e-mail info@tanzaniatourism.go.tz; internet www.tanzaniatourism.go.tz; f. 1993; state-owned; supervises the development and promotion of tourism; Chair. THOMAS MIHAYO; Dir-Gen. BETRITA JAMES (acting).

Tanzania National Parks (TANAPA): J. K. Nyerere Conservation Centre, Burka Estate, Dodoma Rd, POB 3134, Arusha; tel. (27) 2503471; e-mail info@tanzaniaparks.go.tz; internet www.tanzaniaparks.go.tz; f. 1959; conservation of 16 national parks; Chair. Gen. (retd) GEORGE MARWA WAITARA.

Tourism Confederation of Tanzania (TCT): Dar es Salaam; tel. (22) 2136177; e-mail info@tct.co.tz; internet www.tct.co.tz; f. 2000; Exec. Sec. RICHARD O. RUGIMBANA.

Zanzibar Commission for Tourism: POB 1410, Amani; tel. (24) 2233485; e-mail marketing@zanzibartourism.go.tz; internet www.zanzibartourism.go.tz; f. 1992; Chair. RAHIM MOHAMMED BHALOO; Exec. Sec. Dr ABDULLA JUMA.

Defence

As assessed at November 2021, total armed forces numbered 27,000, of whom an estimated 23,000 were in the army, 1,000 in the navy and 3,000 in the air force. Paramilitary forces comprised a 1,400-strong Police Field Force and an 80,000-strong reservist Citizens' Militia. In 2021 a total of 1,722 Tanzanian troops were stationed abroad.

Defence Budget: 1,920,000m. shillings in 2021.

Commander-in-Chief of the Armed Forces: President SAMIA SULUHU HASSAN.

Chief of Defence Forces: Gen. JACOB JOHN MKUNDA.

Chief of Staff of Tanzania People's Defence Force: Lt-Gen. SALUM HAJI OTHMAN.

Commander of Land Forces: Maj.-Gen. GEORGE THOMAS MSONGOLE.

Commander of Air Force: Maj.-Gen. WILLIAM INGRAM.

Commander of Naval Force: Rear Admiral RAMSON GODWIN MWAISAKA.

Education

Education at primary level is officially compulsory and is provided free of charge. In secondary schools a government-stipulated fee is paid. Villages and districts are encouraged to construct their own schools with government assistance. Almost all primary schools are government-owned. Primary education begins at seven years of age and lasts for seven years. Secondary education, beginning at the age of 14, lasts for a further six years, comprising a first cycle of four years and a second of two years. According to estimates by the United Nations Educational, Scientific and Cultural Organization (UNESCO), in 2019/20 enrolment at pre-primary level was equivalent to 78% of children in the relevant age-group (males 78%; females 78%). In 2018/19 enrolment at primary level included 87% of pupils in the appropriate age-group (85% of boys; 88% of girls), while secondary enrolment in that year was equivalent to 32% of children in the appropriate age-group (males 31%; females 33%). According to UNESCO, in 2019/20 spending on education constituted 13.6% of total government expenditure in that year.

Bibliography

Admassu Kebede, J. *The Changing Face of Rural Policy in Tanzania.* London, Minerva Press, 2000.

Bagachwa, M. S. D., and Mbelle, A. V. Y. (Eds). *Economic Policy under a Multiparty System in Tanzania.* Dar es Salaam, Dar es Salaam University Press, 1993.

Bjerk, P. *Building a Peaceful Nation. Julius Nyerere and the establishment of Sovereignty in Tanzania, 1960–1964.* Rochester, NY, University of Rochester Press, 2015.

Brennan, J., Burton, A., and Lawi, Y. (Eds). *Dar es Salaam. Histories from an Emerging African Metropolis.* Dar es Salaam, Mkuki na Nyota Publishers, 2007.

Buchert, L. *Education in the Development of Tanzania, 1919–1990.* London, James Currey Publishers, 1994.

Campbell, H., and Stein, H. *Tanzania and the IMF: The Dynamics of Liberalization.* Boulder, CO, Westview Press, 1990.

Edwards, S. *Toxic Aid: Economic Collapse and Recovery in Tanzania.* Oxford, Oxford University Press, 2014.

Giblin, J. L., et al. (Eds). *In Search of a Nation: Histories of Authority and Dissidence in Tanzania (Eastern African Studies).* Oxford, James Currey Publishers, 2003.

Glassman, J. *War of Words, War of Stones: Racial Thought and Violence in Colonial Zanzibar.* Bloomington, IN, Indiana University Press, 2011.

Havenik, K. J. and Isinika, A. (Eds). *Tanzania in Transition: From Nyerere to Mkapa.* Dar es Salaam, Mkuki na Nyota Publishers, 2010.

Hyden, G., and Mukandala, R. (Eds). *Agencies in Foreign Aid.* London and Basingstoke, Palgrave, 2000.

Kaijage, F., and Tibaijuka, A. *Poverty and Social Exclusion in Tanzania.* Geneva, International Labour Organisation, 1996.

Lange, S. *From Nation-Building to Popular Culture: The Modernization of Performance in Tanzania.* Bergen, CMI, 1995.

Lapperre, P., and Szirmai, A. (Eds). *The Industrial Experience of Tanzania.* London and Basingstoke, Palgrave, 2001.

Legum, C., and Mmari, G. (Eds). *Mwalimu: The Influence of Nyerere.* London, James Currey Publishers, 1995.

Lofchie, M. *The Political Economy of Tanzania: Decline and Recovery.* Philadelphia, PA, University of Pennsylvania Press, 2014.

Lovejoy, P. E. *Slavery and the Muslim Diaspora: African Slaves in Dar Es-Salaam.* Princeton, NJ, Markus Wiener Publishers, 2003.

Luvanga, N. and Shitundu, J. *The Role of Tourism in Poverty Alleviation in Tanzania*. Dar es Salaam, Mkuki na Nyota Publishers, 2005.

Maddox, G., Giblin, J. L., and Kimambo, I. N. (Eds). *Custodians of the Land: Environment and Hunger in Tanzanian History*. London, James Currey Publishers, 1995; Athens, OH, Ohio University Press, 1996.

Markle, S. *A Motorcycle on Hell Run: Tanzania, Black Power, and the Uncertain Future of Pan-Africanism, 1964–1974*. East Lansing, MI, Michigan University Press, 2017.

Martin, D. *Serengetu Tanzania: Land, People, History*. Harare, APG, 1997.

Mbelle, A., and Mjema, G. D. (Eds). *The Nyerere Legacy and Economic Policy Making in Tanzania*. (2nd edn). Dar es Salaam, Dar es Salaam University Press, 2004.

Mbogoni, L. E. Y. *The Cross Versus the Crescent: Religion and Politics in Tanzania from the 1880s to the 1990s*. Dar es Salaam, Mkuki na Nyota Publishers, 2005.

McHenry, D. E., Jr. *Limited Choices: The Political Struggle for Socialism in Tanzania*. Boulder, CO, Lynne Rienner Publishers, 1994.

Mhando, P. C., *Corporate Governance in Tanzania: Ethics and Accountability at the Crossroads*. Abingdon, Routledge, 2019.

Mkapa, B. *My Life, My Purpose: A Tanzanian President Remembers*. Dar es Salaam, Mkuki na Nyota Publishers, 2019.

Mmuya, M. (Ed). *Functional Dimensions of the Democratization Process: Tanzania and Kenya*. Dar es Salaam, Dar es Salaam University Press, 1994.

Molony, T. *Nyere: The Early Years*. Woodbridge, James Currey, 2016.

Monson, J. *Africa's Freedom Railway: How a Chinese Development Project Changed Lives and Livelihoods in Tanzania*. Bloomington, IN, Indiana University Press, 2011.

Mukandala, R., and Othman, H. *Liberalization and Politics: The 1990 Election in Tanzania*. Dar es Salaam, Dar es Salaam University Press, 1994.

Mwakikagile, G. *Nyerere and Africa: End of an Era*. Atlanta, GA, Protea Publishing, 2002.

Nyang'oro, J. *JK: A Political Biography of Jakaya Mrisho Kikwete*. Trenton, NJ, Africa World Press, 2011.

Othman, H. I. B., and Okema, M. *Tanzania: Democracy in Transition*. Dar es Salaam, Dar es Salaam University Press, 1990.

Potts, D. *Tanzanian Development: A Comparative Perspective*. Woodbridge, James Currey, 2019.

Pratt, C. *The Critical Phase in Tanzania: Nyerere and the Emergence of a Socialist Strategy*. Cambridge, Cambridge University Press, 2009.

Rosch, P. G. *Der Prozess der Strukturanpassung in Tanzania*. Hamburg, Institut für Afrika-Kunde, 1995.

Sheriff, A. *Slaves, Spices and Ivory in Zanzibar: Integration of an East African Commercial Empire into the World Economy, 1770–1873*. London, James Currey Publishers, 1987.

Shivji, I. G. *Tanzania: the Legal Foundations of the Union*. Dar es Salaam, Dar es Salaam University Press, 1999.

Wange, S. M., et al. (Eds). *Traditional Economic Policy and Policy Options in Tanzania*. Dar es Salaam, Mkuki na Nyota Publishers, 1998.

TOGO

Physical and Social Geography

R. J. HARRISON CHURCH

The Togolese Republic, a small state in West Africa (bordered to the west by Ghana, to the east by Benin and to the north by Burkina Faso), covers an area of 56,600 sq km (21,853 sq miles), and comprises the eastern two-thirds of the former German protectorate of Togoland. From a coastline of 56 km on the Gulf of Guinea, Togo extends inland for about 540 km. According to the census of November 2010, the population numbered 6,191,155, giving a density of 109.4 persons per sq km (higher than the average for West Africa). United Nations (UN) projections recorded the population at 8,680,832 in mid-2022, with a density of 153.4 per sq km. Northern Togo is more ethnically diverse than the south, where the Ewe predominate. The most numerous ethnic group in 1995 was the Kabré, who represented an estimated 23.7% of the population, while the Ewe accounted for 21.9%. The official languages are French, Ewe and Kabiye. According to UN projections, the population of the capital, Lomé, located on the coast, amounted to 1,925,517 in mid-2022.

The coast, lagoons, blocked estuaries and Terre de Barre regions are identical to those of Benin, but calcium phosphate, the only commercially exploited mineral resource, is quarried north-east of Lake Togo. Pre-Cambrian rocks with rather siliceous soils occur northward, in the Mono tableland and in the Togo-Atacora mountains. The latter are, however, still well wooded and planted with coffee and cocoa. To the north is the Oti plateau, with infertile Primary sandstones, in which water is rare and deep down. On the northern border are granite areas, remote but densely inhabited, as in neighbouring Ghana and Burkina Faso. Togo's climate is similar to that of Benin, except that Togo's coastal area is even drier: Lomé had an average annual rainfall of 734 mm in 1999–2000, around one-half of the rainfall recorded in northern regions. Thus Togo, although smaller in area than Benin, is physically, as well as economically, more varied than its eastern neighbour.

History

KATHARINE MURISON

Revised for this edition by the editorial staff

Togoland, of which the Togolese Republic was formerly a part, became a German protectorate in 1894. The territory was occupied by Anglo-French forces after the outbreak of the First World War in 1914. A League of Nations mandate in 1919 awarded France the larger eastern section and the United Kingdom the west. This partition divided the homeland of the Ewe people of the southern part of the territory. Ewe demands for reunification intensified during the United Nations (UN) trusteeship system that followed the Second World War. In May 1956 a UN-supervised plebiscite in British Togoland produced, despite Ewe opposition, majority support for a merger with the neighbouring territory of the Gold Coast, then a British colony. The region was transferred to the independent state of Ghana in the following year. In October 1956, in a further plebiscite, French Togoland voted to become an autonomous republic within the French Community.

Political life in French Togoland was dominated by the Comité de l'Unité Togolaise, led by Sylvanus Olympio, and the Parti Togolais du Progrès, led by Nicolas Grunitzky. Following independence on 27 April 1960, Olympio, a campaigner for Ewe reunification, became President.

In January 1963 Olympio was killed in a military coup led by Sgt (later Gen.) Etienne (Gnassingbé) Eyadéma, a Kabiye from the north of the country, who invited Grunitzky to return from exile as head of state. Following unsuccessful efforts by Grunitzky to achieve constitutional multi-party government, in January 1967 Eyadéma, by then army Chief of Staff, assumed power. Political activity remained suspended until the creation in 1969 of the Rassemblement du Peuple Togolais (RPT). Plots to overthrow Eyadéma were suppressed in 1970 and 1977. Eyadéma was elected unopposed as President of the Republic in December 1979, when a new Constitution was also endorsed. In 1985 the Constitution was amended to allow candidates for election to the Assemblée Nationale (National Assembly) to be adopted without prior approval by the RPT, which remained the only legal political party.

In December 1986 Eyadéma was re-elected as President. In the same month 13 people were sentenced to death, and 14 to life imprisonment, for complicity in an apparent coup attempt in September, in which 13 people were killed. Gilchrist Olympio, son of the former President, was one of three people sentenced to death *in absentia*. Most of the death sentences were later commuted.

In April 1991, following a campaign for the introduction of a multi-party political system, Eyadéma agreed to an amnesty for political dissidents, the legalization of political parties and the organization of a national forum. Numerous political movements subsequently obtained official status. Opposition allegations that 26 bodies discovered in a lagoon in Lomé later in April were those of demonstrators who had been beaten to death by the security forces were denied by the Government. Fearing a conflict between the Kabiye and Ewe ethnic groups, Eyadéma announced that a new constitution would be introduced within one year, and that multi-party legislative elections would be organized. In July the national human rights commission, the Commission Nationale des Droits de l'Homme (CNDH), concluded that the security forces had been responsible for the deaths of at least 20 of those whose bodies had been discovered.

A national conference was opened in July 1991, attended by some 1,000 delegates, and resolved to declare itself sovereign, to suspend the Constitution and to dissolve the National Assembly. In August Eyadéma suspended the conference, which had deprived him of most of his powers. Opposition delegates responded by proclaiming a provisional Government under the leadership of Joseph Kokou Koffigoh, the head of the independent Ligue Togolaise des Droits de l'Homme (LTDH). The conference also voted to dissolve the RPT and to form an interim legislature, the Haut Conseil de la République (High Council of the Republic—HCR). Fearing renewed unrest, Eyadéma confirmed Koffigoh as transitional Prime Minister. Although Koffigoh assumed personal responsibility for defence, the Kabiye-dominated armed forces looked to Eyadéma for their command. In December the military captured the Prime Minister. Following negotiations between Eyadéma and Koffigoh, a 'Government of National Unity', including two close associates of Eyadéma, was formed. The HCR also restored legal status to the RPT.

The HCR returned some powers to the President in August 1992, notably empowering Eyadéma to preside over the Council of Ministers. Koffigoh remained Prime Minister in a new transitional Government appointed in September, but the most influential posts were allocated to RPT members. On 27 September a new Constitution was approved in a referendum by 98.1% of the votes cast.

In January 1993 Eyadéma dissolved the Government, but reappointed Koffigoh as Prime Minister. At least 20 people were killed that month when police opened fire on anti-Government protesters. The formation of a 'Crisis Government' was announced shortly afterwards; supporters of Eyadéma retained the principal posts.

THE FOURTH REPUBLIC

At a presidential election held on 25 August 1993, Eyadéma was re-elected by 96.5% of voters. Only about 36% of the electorate voted. Eyadéma was sworn in as President of the Fourth Republic on 24 September.

At elections to the National Assembly conducted on 6 and 20 February 1994, the opposition won a narrow victory, with the Comité d'Action pour le Renouveau (CAR) securing 36 of the 81 seats and the Union Togolaise pour la Démocratie (UTD) seven; the RPT obtained 35 seats and two smaller pro-Eyadéma parties won three. In March and April the Supreme Court declared the results of the legislative elections invalid in three constituencies (in which the CAR had won two seats and the UTD one) and ordered by-elections. The UTD leader, Edem Kodjo, took office as Prime Minister on 25 April, having been nominated by Eyadéma, despite objections by the CAR.

The RPT and its allies won the three seats contested at by-elections in August 1996, thus securing a legislative majority and forcing the resignation of the Kodjo administration. Eyadéma appointed Kwassi Klutse, hitherto Minister of Planning and Territorial Development, as Prime Minister. The new Council of Ministers comprised almost exclusively supporters of Eyadéma.

Electoral Controversies

A presidential election took place on 21 June 1998. On the following day, as early voting figures indicated that Eyadéma might lose the election, the vote count was suspended. On 23 June five of the nine members of the electoral commission resigned, reportedly as a result of intimidation. On 24 June the Minister of the Interior and Security declared Eyadéma to have won the election with 52.1% of the vote. European Union (EU) observers expressed serious concern at the suspension of the vote count. Monitors reported that all indications were of a victory for Gilchrist Olympio, the leader of the Union des Forces de Changement (UFC), who was living in exile in Ghana.

Elections to the National Assembly held on 21 March 1999 were boycotted by the main opposition parties. The RPT won 77 seats and independent candidates two, with fresh elections scheduled in two constituencies. In May Eugène Koffi Adoboli, a former UN official, was appointed Prime Minister.

Discussions took place in Lomé in July 1999 between the Government, the opposition and four international facilitators, representing France, Germany, the EU and La Francophonie. After Eyadéma announced that he would not stand for re-election, and that new legislative elections would be held in 2000, the opposition agreed to accept Eyadéma's victory in the presidential election, and an accord was signed on 29 July. In December agreement was reached on a revised electoral code, which was approved by the National Assembly in April 2000.

In August 2000 Adoboli was defeated in a vote of no confidence; Eyadéma appointed Agbéyomé Kodjo, hitherto President of the National Assembly, as Prime Minister. Kodjo announced in August 2001 that legislative elections scheduled for October would be postponed until 2002. In February 2002 the National Assembly approved amendments to electoral legislation; henceforth all candidates for legislative elections were required to have been continuously resident in Togo for six months prior to elections and presidential candidates for 12 months, while the Commission Electorale Nationale

Indépendante (CENI) was to be reduced in size from 20 to 10 members. In March five opposition parties that accused the Government of violating the July 1999 accord refused to nominate representatives to the CENI. In May 2002 a committee of seven judges (the Comité de Sept Magistrats—C-7) was appointed to monitor the electoral process in the absence of a CENI.

Eyadéma dismissed Kodjo as Prime Minister in June 2002, replacing him with Koffi Sama, hitherto Minister of National Education and Research. Kodjo subsequently criticized the 'monarchic, despotic' regime of Eyadéma. He was charged with disseminating false information and demeaning the honour of the President, and later took up residence in France.

In September 2002 the authorities announced that the legislative elections would be held on 27 October. In late October nine opposition parties that had declined to participate in the elections formed a new alliance, the Coalition des Forces Démocrates (CFD); members included the Convergence Patriotique Panafricaine (CPP—formed in 1999 by a merger of the UTD and three other parties), the CAR, the UFC and a faction of 'renovators' within the RPT (which subsequently became the Pacte Socialiste pour le Renouveau—PSR). Meanwhile, a group of 'constructive' opposition parties (including the Rassemblement pour le Soutien de la Démocratie et du Développement—RSDD, led by Harry Octavianus Olympio, a cousin of Gilchrist Olympio), which were prepared to participate in the electoral process, formed the Coordination des Partis Politiques de l'Opposition Constructive (CPOC). The RPT won 72 of the 81 seats (46 unopposed) and the RSDD three, while three other parties won a total of five seats, and one independent candidate was elected. Turnout was estimated at 67.4% by the C-7, but at no more than 10% by the CFD. Eyadéma reappointed Sama as Prime Minister in November. The only non-RPT minister was Harry Octavianus Olympio, who was appointed Minister responsible for Relations with Parliament.

In December 2002 the National Assembly approved the removal of the constitutional restriction that had limited the President to serving two terms of office and a reduction in the age of eligibility from 45 to 35 years. (It was widely believed that these measures were intended to permit Eyadéma to serve a further term of office, and also to permit the possible candidacy of Eyadéma's son, Faure Gnassingbé.) Candidates were henceforth to be required to hold solely Togolese citizenship. In February 2003 the UFC withdrew from the CFD, after other parties within the grouping agreed to appoint representatives to the CENI.

Eyadéma was returned to office in a presidential election held on 1 June 2003, receiving 57.8% of the votes cast. His nearest rival was Emmanuel Bob Akitani, the First Vice-President of the UFC, with 33.7% of the votes; Gilchrist Olympio's candidacy had been rejected as he did not meet residency requirements. Several of the six defeated candidates alleged electoral fraud, although observers from the Economic Community of West African States (ECOWAS) and the African Union (AU stated that only minor irregularities had been witnessed. Eyadéma was inaugurated on 20 June. Sama was reappointed as premier on 1 July. His new Government included two representatives of the CPOC. Faure Gnassingbé received his first ministerial posting.

Discussions between the Government and the EU on the conditions for a resumption of economic co-operation commenced in April 2004; the government delegation pledged to implement 22 measures, including the revision of the press code, the introduction of more transparent conditions for fair elections and a guarantee that political parties would be free to conduct their activities without fear of harassment. In November the EU partially resumed economic co-operation with Togo. In January 2005 the National Assembly amended the electoral code, notably strengthening the powers of the CENI and increasing its membership to include two representatives of civil society.

Presidential Succession

On 5 February 2005 Prime Minister Sama announced that President Eyadéma had died while being transported to France for medical treatment. Although the Constitution provided for the assumption of the functions of head of state by the President of the National Assembly, Ouattara Fambaré Natchaba, pending an election, the closure by the military of Togo's borders prevented Natchaba from returning to the country from a visit to Europe. The Chief of General Staff of the armed forces, Gen. Zakari Nandja, declared that the Constitution had been suspended and named Faure Gnassingbé as his father's successor. The AU denounced the installation of Gnassingbé as President as a coup. On the following day, in an attempt to legitimize Gnassingbé's assumption of power, the National Assembly abolished the constitutional provision requiring an election to take place within 60 days of the death of the President, instead authorizing the new head of state to serve the remainder of his predecessor's term, and removed Natchaba from the presidency of the legislature, electing Gnassingbé in his place.

Gnassingbé was sworn in as President of the Republic on 7 February 2005. Opposition parties called a strike in protest. La Francophonie suspended Togo's membership of the organization, while ECOWAS threatened to impose sanctions against the new regime if it did not apply the Constitution as it stood before Eyadéma's death. On 18 February Gnassingbé pledged to hold an election within 60 days, but stated his intention to remain in power in the mean time. The National Assembly subsequently reversed the constitutional changes adopted following Eyadéma's death. Nevertheless, ECOWAS suspended Togo's membership of the Community, imposed an arms embargo on the country, banned its government ministers from travelling in the region and ordered the recall of ambassadors of member states from Lomé. On 25 February, following the imposition of sanctions against Togo by the AU, Gnassingbé resigned from the presidency of the National Assembly, and therefore from the presidency of the Republic. He was replaced by the Vice-President of the legislature, Abass Bonfoh. Earlier that day Gnassingbé had been acclaimed President of the RPT and endorsed as the party's candidate for the forthcoming presidential election. ECOWAS rescinded its sanctions against Togo.

The presidential election took place on 24 April 2005 in relatively peaceful conditions. However, the announcement by the CENI, on 26 April, that preliminary results indicated a clear victory for Gnassingbé provoked widespread rioting, particularly in Lomé and Aného, east of the capital. The security forces quelled the unrest after two days. A six-party radical opposition coalition, which had fielded Bob Akitani, of the UFC, as its sole candidate, later stated that 106 people had been killed in the violence, although the Government estimated the death toll at 22, while thousands fled the country for neighbouring Benin and Ghana. On 3 May the Constitutional Court proclaimed Gnassingbé's election as President, with 60.2% of the votes cast, followed by Bob Akitani, with 38.3%. A turnout of 63.6% of the electorate was recorded. Gnassingbé was inaugurated on the following day.

In mid-May 2005 the LTDH claimed that 790 people had been killed between 28 March (when the authorities began updating the electoral register) and 5 May, far more than previous estimates. Gnassingbé later appointed a national commission of inquiry into the violence. In late May the AU removed sanctions against Togo. Meanwhile, refugees continued to flee Togo, amid reports that opposition supporters were being arrested or kidnapped by the security forces.

Gnassingbé designated Edem Kodjo, the leader of the moderate opposition CPP, as Prime Minister on 8 June 2005. The new Government was dominated by the RPT, although some members of the opposition and civil society received posts. The appointment of Tchessa Abi of the PSR as Keeper of the Seals, Minister of Justice led to the party's expulsion from the radical opposition coalition. Zarifou Ayéva, the leader of the moderate opposition Parti pour la Démocratie et le Renouveau (PDR), became Minister of State, Minister of Foreign Affairs and African Integration, while a younger half-brother of the President, Kpatcha Gnassingbé, joined the Government as Minister-delegate at the Presidency of the Republic, responsible for Defence and Veterans.

Reconciliation Efforts

Efforts to promote national reconciliation and to encourage the return of refugees dominated the new Government's agenda. At a meeting in Rome, Italy, in July 2005, Gnassingbé and Gilchrist Olympio agreed that political prisoners arrested during the electoral process should be released. Earlier that month the Government had announced that some 170 prisoners were to be released, including 48 opposition supporters who had been detained following the electoral violence.

In September 2005 the office of the UN High Commissioner for Human Rights (OHCHR) released a report stating that 400–500 people had been killed in Togo between 5 February and 5 May and that responsibility for the political violence and human rights violations that occurred during this period lay principally with the security forces. The Togolese Government disputed OHCHR's findings, and in November the national commission of inquiry into the violence reported that 154 people had died.

Representatives of Gnassingbé and Olympio held further talks in Rome in November 2005. Some 460 prisoners were released in that month; many of those freed were opposition supporters. In March 2006 the Government abandoned judicial proceedings against alleged perpetrators of acts of violence related to the 2005 election, with the exception of those accused of 'bloody crimes'.

Following talks chaired by the President of Burkina Faso, Blaise Compaoré, on 20 August 2006 the Government and opposition parties signed a comprehensive political accord, which provided, *inter alia*, for the formation of a government of national unity, pending legislative elections, the re-establishment of the CENI, the revision of the electoral register, the creation of a commission of inquiry into past political violence and the establishment of a committee charged with accelerating the return of refugees. In September Yawovi Agboyibo, the leader of the CAR, was designated Prime Minister.

Legislative Elections of 2007

Legislative elections were held on 14 October 2007, with the participation of all the main opposition parties. The RPT secured 50 of the National Assembly's 81 seats, while the UFC won 27 and the CAR four. International observers declared themselves satisfied with the conduct of the elections, welcoming the high turnout (84.9%). In November the EU resumed full co-operation with Togo. Komlan Mally, hitherto Minister of Towns and Town Planning and a member of the RPT, was appointed Prime Minister in December. The President assumed responsibility for the defence portfolio from Kpatcha Gnassingbé. Mally resigned in September 2008. Gnassingbé appointed Gilbert Houngbo, hitherto director of the UN Development Programme's Bureau for Africa, to the premiership.

Kpatcha Gnassingbé was arrested in April 2009 and charged with plotting to overthrow the President. In September 2011 Kpatcha Gnassingbé, the former armed forces Chief of General Staff, Gen. Assani Tidjani, and the former head of the gendarmerie special forces, Commdt Abi Atti, were convicted of orchestrating the purported coup attempt and each sentenced to 20 years' imprisonment.

Meanwhile, a permanent forum for discussions on constitutional, political and electoral issues was created in February 2009: the Cadre Permanent de Dialogue et de Concertation (CPDC) comprised representatives of the Government and parties that either held seats in the National Assembly or had secured at least 5% of the votes cast in the last legislative elections (i.e. the RPT, the UFC and the CAR). However, participants struggled to reach a consensus on matters of institutional reform, and the UFC and the CAR withdrew from the CPDC in mid-June. Later that month, in the absence of UFC and CAR deputies, the National Assembly adopted CPDC-proposed amendments to the electoral code. Following negotiations in early August, mediated by Compaoré, the RPT, the UFC and the CAR reached agreement on matters concerning the CENI and the eligibility of presidential candidates (Gilchrist Olympio having been barred from contesting the 2003 and 2005 elections owing to residency requirements). Later in August 2009 the National Assembly elected the new

CENI's 17 members. However, the UFC and the CAR boycotted the election, in September, of Henri Kolani of the PDR as President of the Commission, accusing the PDR of being manipulated by the RPT. In October Kolani was replaced by a representative of civil society. In February 2010 the UFC and the CAR suspended their participation in the CENI, citing concerns regarding the accuracy of the voters' register.

Gnassingbé Re-elected

Seven candidates contested a presidential election held on 4 March 2010. Faure Gnassingbé was re-elected, winning 60.9% of the valid votes cast. His closest challenger, receiving 33.9% of the votes, was Jean-Pierre Fabre, the Secretary-General of the UFC (Gilchrist Olympio having been forced to withdraw his candidacy for medical reasons). A turnout of 65.7% was recorded. (In February 2021, in a long-running corruption case in France, the French company Bolloré admitted having contributed to Gnassingbé's communication costs for his 2010 presidential election campaign in exchange for a contract to manage the port of Lomé.)

Gnassingbé was sworn in on 3 May 2010. Houngbo was subsequently reappointed as Prime Minister. In late May Gilchrist Olympio signed an accord with the RPT on the UFC's participation in Houngbo's administration. The UFC received seven of the 32 ministerial posts. However, Fabre denounced the accord, and the UFC national bureau suspended Olympio and the seven ministers from the party. The split in the UFC was confirmed in August, when the two factions of the party held separate congresses, electing Fabre and Olympio as their respective Presidents. The Government stated that it recognized Olympio as the leader of the UFC. In October Fabre formed a new party, the Alliance Nationale pour le Changement (ANC).

The RPT was dissolved in April 2012, and replaced by the Union pour la République (UNIR), a new organization supportive of President Gnassingbé, who was to be its leader. In May the National Assembly adopted legislation increasing the number of seats in the legislature from 81 to 91 (with effect from the next elections) and amending the boundaries of the electoral constituencies. In June the Collectif Sauvons le Togo (CST), comprising seven opposition movements, including the ANC, and nine civil society groups, organized protests against the reforms, on the grounds that they favoured the ruling party, and in support of demands for the reintroduction of a two-term limit on the presidential mandate. Violent clashes broke out during the three days of protests. Several CST leaders, including former Prime Minister Agbéyomé Kodjo, the President of the Organisation pour Bâtir dans l'Union un Togo Solidaire (OBUTS), were briefly detained. In July 2012 the security forces raided Fabre's home, prompting several thousand people to participate in a protest in Lomé a week later to denounce what they claimed to be a government crackdown on dissent. Prime Minister Houngbo resigned from office that month, being replaced by CPP member Arthème Kwesi Séléagodji Ahoomey-Zunu, hitherto Minister of Trade and the Promotion of the Private Sector.

Amid ongoing anti-Government protests, legislative elections did not take place, as had been anticipated, in October 2012, with the UFC, the CAR, the OBUTS, the CST and another opposition coalition, Arc-en-Ciel (Rainbow), all insisting on the introduction of reforms (most significantly, a two-term limit on the presidential mandate) prior to polling. In December President Gnassingbé announced that the elections would be held in March 2013. However, they were subsequently further postponed, owing to delays in the registration of voters.

Legislative Elections of 2013

Elections to the National Assembly were finally conducted on 25 July 2013. Having earlier threatened a boycott, the principal opposition parties, grouped in the CST and Arc-en-Ciel coalition, chose to participate, following an agreement with the Government under which several opposition members charged with involvement in alleged arson attacks on markets in January were provisionally released. UNIR secured an absolute majority, winning 62 of the 91 seats, while the CST and Arc-en-Ciel took 19 and six seats, respectively, and UNIR's coalition partner, the UFC, only three (compared with 27 at the

2007 elections); the remaining seat was obtained by an independent. A turnout of 66.1% was recorded. The opposition parties alleged irregularities, but AU and ECOWAS observers declared themselves satisfied overall with the transparency and credibility of the elections. Ahoomey-Zunu was reappointed to the premiership in September; the number of posts in the Council of Ministers awarded to members of the UFC was reduced from seven to three.

Discussions on institutional and constitutional reform resumed in March 2014. A formal inter-party dialogue took place between mid-May and early June, but participants failed to reach agreement, with UNIR rejecting opposition proposals for a two-term limit on the President's mandate and a two-round presidential voting system. At the end of June a government-sponsored bill introducing many of the changes sought by the opposition, including those related to the presidential term and method of election, was rejected by the National Assembly. (Opposition deputies voted in favour of the bill, despite their dissatisfaction that the presidential term limit would not have been applied retrospectively, thereby preventing Gnassingbé from seeking re-election.)

Gnassingbé's Third Term

Fabre was nominated as the ANC's presidential candidate in October 2014, and eight of the 12 parties comprising the CST and Arc-en-Ciel coalition subsequently formed an electoral alliance, Combat pour l'Alternance Politique en 2015 (CAP 2015), in support of his candidacy. In November CAP 2015 and human rights organizations organized two demonstrations in support of continued demands for institutional and constitutional reforms, notably a two-term limit on the presidential mandate, and the parliamentary opposition submitted draft legislation on such reforms to the National Assembly. In early January 2015 a further demonstration was postponed pending the outcome of discussions on the proposals by the parliamentary law commission. On 9 January President Gnassingbé signed a decree establishing a commission on political, institutional and constitutional reforms, chaired by Amadou Abdou-Nana Awa-Daboya, the recently appointed Mediator of the Republic (see *Human Rights Issues*). However, lacking confidence in this process and following the apparent failure of the law commission to reach agreement on reform, CAP 2015 and human rights organizations called a protest march for 13 January. On 24 February it was announced that the presidential election would take place on 15 April. On 25 February a UNIR congress selected Gnassingbé as the party's candidate. In March, at the recommendation of ECOWAS, the election was postponed until 25 April to allow the resolution of organizational issues, particularly complaints regarding the voter register.

At the election on 25 April 2015, Gnassingbé was re-elected President, with 58.8% of the valid votes cast, while Fabre won 35.2% and Aimé Tchabouré Gogué (of the opposition Alliance des Démocrates pour le Développement Intégral—ADDI) 4.0%, with the other two opposition candidates receiving only 1.0% of the vote each. A turnout of 60.9% was recorded. Fabre rejected the results, claiming fraud, although ECOWAS and AU observers deemed the ballot to have been conducted transparently. Gnassingbé was sworn in to serve a third term of office on 4 May. In mid-May opposition supporters demonstrated in Lomé against the results. Prime Minister Ahoomey-Zunu and his Government resigned on 22 May. The First Vice-President of the National Assembly, Komi Sélom Klassou of UNIR, was appointed as the new Prime Minister in June.

The introduction of prison terms (of between six months and two years) for those found guilty of contravening the country's media regulations, as part of amendments to the penal code approved in November 2015, was condemned as being draconian by eight media organizations.

Continued Demands for Reform

A demonstration by CAP 2015 took place in Lomé in May 2016 in support of its demands for the implementation of the constitutional, institutional and electoral reforms that remained outstanding from the comprehensive political accord signed in August 2006 (see *Reconciliation Efforts*) and for the organization of local elections (last held in 1987). In June 2016 deputies of the ANC and the ADDI presented to the National Assembly several draft constitutional amendments (similar to those that had been rejected in 2014), including the introduction of a two-term limit on the President's mandate and a two-round presidential voting system. Although the authorities organized a national dialogue on reforms in July 2016, opposition parties boycotted the discussions. In August a parliamentary committee began examining the draft constitutional revisions proposed by the ANC and the ADDI, but this process subsequently stalled.

In January 2017 Gnassingbé established a commission charged with considering institutional and constitutional reforms; however, there were no opposition representatives on the commission. Shortly afterwards the ADDI and five other parties formed a new opposition alliance with the aim of continuing to campaign for the introduction of political reforms. In June, as part of a process of decentralization, the National Assembly adopted legislation on the creation of 116 communes (municipalities) in Togo; this was increased to 117 in December 2018. The opposition condemned the legislation, claiming that the ruling party had divided the country with a view to securing control over the maximum number of municipalities at the next local elections, rather than taking into account the number of inhabitants. In July the commission appointed by the President in January initiated nationwide consultations on reforms.

In early August 2017 several thousand opposition supporters participated in a march organized by CAP 2015 in Lomé in support of its continued demands for the introduction of a two-term limit on the President's mandate and a two-round voting system. Further protests took place on 19 August in the capital and other towns, led this time by the Parti National Panafricain (PNP, established in 2014 by Tikpi Atchadam). Amid the forceful suppression of these demonstrations by the security forces, at least two people were killed in Sokodé, some 325 km north of the capital. CAP 2015 and the PNP subsequently agreed to work together in opposition to the Government as part of a coalition of 14 parties (C14), which comprised CAP 2015's five members (including the ANC and the PSR), the six-party group formed by the ADDI and five others in early 2017, as well as the PNP, the CAR and Santé du Peuple. Tikpi Atchadam fled to Ghana later in August, and at the end of the month 15 PNP supporters who were arrested during the 19 August demonstrations were sentenced to prison terms.

Mass protests continued in the following months, with the opposition demanding Gnassingbé's departure from office, in addition to constitutional and institutional reforms. A further three people were reportedly killed during demonstrations in September 2017. On 15 September the law commission of the National Assembly endorsed a government-proposed constitutional amendment bill, which introduced the presidential term limit but not its retroactive application, thus leaving Gnassingbé free to stand for re-election in the 2020 and 2025 presidential elections. The C14 boycotted the parliamentary vote on it on 19 September, thus making parliamentary approval impossible (a four-fifths' majority being required for the adoption of constitutional changes) and allowing for a national referendum on the issue. Violence erupted at nationwide anti-Government protests on 20 September, particularly in several northern towns.

On 10 October 2017 the Government announced a ban on weekday political marches, but protests continued. The arrest of a prominent imam associated with the PNP in Sokodé a week later prompted significant unrest, with three further deaths reported there and one in Lomé. In mid-October the National Assembly approved the appointment of new members of the CENI, although the opposition refused to nominate members or to participate in the vote.

The Government sought to defuse tensions in November 2017, lifting the ban on weekday marches and releasing 42 protesters who had been detained during the previous few months. Ghanaian President Nana Akufo-Addo and Guinean President Alpha Condé subsequently commenced mediation efforts. Further protesters were released from prison in December, and the Government invited political parties to engage in preliminary consultations on the format of a planned dialogue, but the C14 declined to participate (only five of its 14 constituent parties having been invited), insisting that any

consultation process should be led by Akufo-Addo and Condé. Talks aimed at resolving the deadlock between the Government and the opposition finally began in Lomé on 19 February 2018, facilitated by Akufo-Addo. A suspension of protests for the duration of the dialogue was agreed, and a presidential pardon was announced for 45 of the 92 people detained for participating in the demonstrations. Further negotiations on 23 February were swiftly adjourned, not resuming until a month later, when they again stalled amid continued disagreement over whether Gnassingbé should be permitted to stand for re-election. Further anti-Government protests were staged by the C14 in April, while ECOWAS formally designated Akufo-Addo and Condé as its mediators in the Togo crisis.

As the political stalemate persisted, in June 2018 the Constitutional Court urged the Government and the CENI to organize legislative elections (which were constitutionally due to be held in July) by the end of the year. Opposition parties criticized the Court's intervention, noting that they had not yet nominated representatives to the CENI owing to their belief that the composition of the electoral commission should be revised under the stalled institutional reform process. Following talks in Lomé on 27 June with representatives of the opposition, the Government and the ruling UNIR, Akufo-Addo and Condé presented recommendations on resolving Togo's political crisis to ECOWAS, which were adopted at a summit of the organization held in the Togolese capital on 31 July. Among these recommendations were the organization of legislative elections for 20 December, the introduction of a two-term limit on presidential mandates and a two-round system of presidential election, the revision of the electoral register, the appointment of new members of the Constitutional Court and the extension of the right to vote to Togolese living abroad. However, the issue of Gnassingbé's potential candidacy at the 2020 presidential election was not addressed, to the dissatisfaction of the C14.

2018 Legislative Elections and Constitutional Revision

In September 2018 the CENI announced that a constitutional referendum would take place concurrently with local elections on 16 December, followed by legislative polls on 20 December. Continuing to demand a delay in the electoral process, pending the implementation of constitutional and institutional reforms, opposition parties urged their supporters to boycott a voter census conducted in October. In early November several thousand people participated in a protest organized in Lomé by a coalition of civil society organizations, the Front Citoyen Togo Debout, to demand reforms, as well as the release of some 50 people who remained in detention following their arrest during recent demonstrations. On 9 November the Government approved a constitutional reform bill, which, as with that proposed in September 2017, introduced a two-round system of presidential election and a presidential two-term limit (but not its retroactive application), the plan to organize a referendum and local polls prior to the elections to the National Assembly having been abandoned. Although the C14's demand that it be granted eight, rather than four, of the 17 seats in the CENI was met, the C14 representatives refused to take up their posts when the new commission was inaugurated on 13 November 2018. On 26 November, moreover, the C14 announced that it would boycott the forthcoming elections to the National Assembly. The C14 subsequently organized protests against alleged irregularities in the electoral process, which continued during the campaign period, in defiance of a ban imposed by the authorities. At least two people died in Lomé on 8 December and two in Sokodé on 10 December, when protesters clashed with the security forces.

The legislative elections took place, as scheduled, on 20 December 2018, amid a heavy military presence. The ruling UNIR retained its majority, winning 59 of the 91 seats, while the UFC took seven, the Nouvel Engagement Togolais (NET) three, the Mouvement Patriotique pour la Démocratie et le Développement (MPDD, as the OBUTS had been renamed in October 2018) two and the Mouvement des Républicains Centristes and the Parti Démocratique Panafricain one each; 18 independents were also elected. The turnout was 59.2%. Klassou was reappointed Prime Minister on 24 January

2019. On the same day Yawa Djigbodi Tségan of UNIR was elected President of the National Assembly, becoming the first woman to hold this office. The C14 organized demonstrations on 26 January to protest against the election results. At the end of January, in a stated effort to calm sociopolitical tensions, President Gnassingbé ordered the release of 44 people accused of participating in the demonstrations that began in August 2017.

Members of the C14 met with Gnassingbé in late March 2019. However, internal divisions within the opposition coalition prompted several constituent parties, including the ANC, the CAR and the PNP, to suspend their participation in the C14 that month. Meanwhile, representatives of the ADDI and the CAR accepted two of the three seats reserved for extra-parliamentary parties in the CENI. The PNP decided to resume nationwide protests in April in support of continued demands for a presidential two-term limit. One demonstrator died on 13 April at an unauthorized PNP rally dispersed by the security forces in Bafilo, northern Togo. Some 30 PNP members were reportedly detained, and two PNP leaders were arrested a few days later.

On 8 May 2019 the National Assembly approved constitutional reforms introducing the two-round system of presidential election and the two-term limit on presidential mandates (but not retroactively, allowing Gnassingbé potentially to stand in 2020 and 2025). The C14 denounced the changes. Also amended was the mandate for deputies, which was increased from five years to six, but also limited to two terms, while immunity for life was guaranteed for all former Presidents. The revised Constitution also provided for the future election of a second legislative chamber, the Sénat (Senate), the members of which would also serve for a maximum of two six-year terms; two-thirds of senators would be elected by local representatives and one-third would be designated by the President.

Local elections (the first since 1987) were conducted on 30 June 2019, with the participation of the main opposition groups, including the C14 (now comprising seven parties), although notably not the PNP. Campaigning and polling took place in largely peaceful conditions, although opposition parties complained of organizational problems, notably with voter registration. Voting was postponed in three communes, owing to technical concerns in two communes and inter-communal violence in the other. Following the release of the provisional results, the C14 alleged that fraud had taken place. According to final results released by the Supreme Court, UNIR secured 878 of the 1,464 municipal councillor seats filled, the ANC 132, the C14 129, the UFC 42, the NET 31 and the MPDD 25. The participation rate was 52.5%. The ballot was invalidated in two communes owing to serious irregularities, but 39 challenges, mostly lodged by the opposition, were rejected.

A Fourth Term for Gnassingbé

On 8 August 2019 the National Assembly modified legislation governing the organization of protests, notably prohibiting demonstrations on national roads, in certain urban centres and near government institutions. In November the National Assembly amended the electoral code to permit the diaspora to vote in Togolese elections, and an elected consultative body for Togolese living abroad, the Haut Conseil des Togolais de l'Extérieur, was established. However, in the same month a number of opposition and civil society organizations, including the remaining members of the C14, united with former Archbishop of Lomé Mgr Philippe Kpodzro, to demand the suspension of the forthcoming presidential election pending the introduction of various reforms, including the reorganization of the CENI and the Constitutional Court and a commitment to publish the election results by polling station to enhance transparency. A new Constitutional Court was officially installed in December.

With the opposition divided, Gnassingbé comfortably secured a fourth term in office in a first round of voting at the presidential election on 22 February 2020, winning 70.8% of the valid votes cast, according to the final official results, and defeating six challengers, his nearest rivals being former Prime Minister Agbéyomé Kodjo, the leader of the MPDD, who took 19.5%, and Fabre (4.7%). A turnout of 92.3% was recorded. Polling took place peacefully, although the residences of Kodjo and Kpodzro (who had endorsed the former's candidacy) were surrounded by the security forces for several hours after voting had ended, purportedly to ensure their safety amid an alleged security threat. Kodjo rejected the results, claiming victory and denouncing alleged electoral irregularities, although observers from ECOWAS and the AU declared their satisfaction with the conduct of the election. An unauthorized demonstration organized by Kpodzro for 28 February was largely thwarted when the security forces again surrounded both his and Kodjo's residences, and tear gas was used to disperse protesters. In mid-March the National Assembly voted to revoke Kodjo's immunity from prosecution, and he was arrested on 21 April (together with a number of family members and supporters) in relation to his claim to be the legitimate President. After being charged with disturbing public order, undermining state security and disseminating false news, Kodjo was released under judicial supervision on 24 April, as were three other leading members of the Dynamique Monseigneur Kpodzro (DMK), an alliance of opposition and civil society organizations that had supported Kodjo's candidacy. On the following day 18 of the 34 people arrested with Kodjo (who remained in detention) were reportedly freed; the 16 others were subsequently convicted of rebellion and sentenced to one year in prison with eight months suspended. Gnassingbé was sworn in to serve his fourth term of office on 3 May.

Meanwhile, on 6 March 2020 Togo confirmed its first case of COVID-19, amid the onset of the global pandemic. Action taken later in March in an effort to curb the transmission of the disease included the closure of schools, universities and land borders, the suspension of flights from countries with high rates of infection, and restrictions on domestic travel and large gatherings. On 27 March the National Assembly authorized the Government to adopt measures to combat COVID-19 by decree for a six-month period, and on 1 April President Gnassingbé declared a state of health emergency and an overnight curfew. Also announced was the creation of a 5,000-member force to ensure compliance with the measures and a national solidarity fund to mitigate the socioeconomic effects of the crisis. Togo subsequently received pandemic-related financial support from donors including France, the World Bank and the EU, as well as debt service relief from the Paris Club of creditor nations. The authorities revoked the curfew on 9 June, while the state of health emergency was regularly extended, despite opposition and civil society leaders questioning the justification for its renewal. International flights resumed in August (although land borders remained closed), and schools reopened in November.

Prime Minister Klassou presented his Government's resignation on 25 September 2020. Three days later President Gnassingbé appointed Togo's first female Prime Minister, Victoire Sidémého Tomégah-Dogbé, hitherto the Minister of Basic Development, Handicrafts, Youth and Youth Employment. Several senior ministers were retained in the new Council of Ministers formed at the beginning of October, including those responsible for the economy and finance, foreign affairs and security portfolios, but Essozimna Marguerite Gnakadè, a sister-in-law of the President, notably joined the Government as Minister of the Armed Forces, the first woman to hold this post.

Two DMK leaders, Brigitte Kafui Adjamagbo-Johnson and Gérard Yaovi Djossou, were arrested in late November 2020, after the authorities banned a demonstration planned by the movement to protest against the results of the presidential election and the harassment of government opponents. They were charged with criminal conspiracy and undermining state security and released under judicial supervision later that month. Adjamagbo-Johnson, the DMK co-ordinator, was already under judicial supervision, having been charged along with Kodjo and two others in April with disturbing public order, undermining state security and disseminating false news.

Cases of COVID-19 rose significantly from January 2021. A vaccination programme against COVID-19 commenced in March, using vaccine doses provided under the World Health Organization's COVAX initiative. The National Assembly further extended the state of health emergency that month, until mid-September (when it was extended for a further year), and further restrictions, including a ban on mass gatherings, were announced. After a further wave of cases in December and January 2022 stabilized, pandemic-related travel restrictions were eased from late April. (A total of 39,053 confirmed COVID-19 cases, with 285 deaths, had been reported in Togo by the end of September.)

Meanwhile, talks between the Ministry of Territorial Administration, Decentralization and Territorial Development and political parties, under the framework of a Concertation Nationale des Acteurs Politiques (CNAP), on matters including the organization of regional elections commenced in January 2021. Only parties that contested at least one of the previous three elections were permitted to take part in the discussions; of the 21 parties thus eligible, 17 participated (notably not the DMK). The CAR officially suspended its participation in the CNAP in February, claiming that the ministry had refused to include on the agenda any of the party's concerns, and urged the authorities to end legal proceedings against Kodjo and other political figures in order to allow the dialogue to be inclusive.

Djimon Oré, the President of the opposition Front des Patriotes pour la Démocratie and Minister of Communication in 2010–13 (when a member of the UFC), was sentenced to two years' imprisonment in May 2021, having been convicted of insulting public officials and spreading false news in relation to his criticism of the Gnassingbé regime in a radio broadcast on 27 April marking the 61st anniversary of Togo's independence. The CNAP concluded its work in mid-July, and in August submitted a total of 52 recommendations for political reform to the Government, which included the reconstitution of the CENI, the organization of a new electoral census and revision of the electoral code and the charter of political parties.

On 1 October 2021 the National Assembly adopted three laws based on the CNAP's recommendations, which, respectively, amended the electoral code, provided for increased decentralization and eased the measures regulating assembly and peaceful public demonstrations which had been imposed in 2019. Legislation proposed by the Government that provided for the creation of local authorities at regional level as part of the decentralization process was adopted by the National Assembly on 2 March. The National Assembly also, on 24 March, approved the formation of a new CENI, comprising seven representatives of the parliamentary majority, seven of the opposition, two of civil society and one of the government administration, prior to the organization of the regional elections which were planned for 2023.

However, in January 2022 the Council of Ministers approved a decree, which was to enter into force in April 2023, requiring non-governmental organizations (NGOs) to align their activities to governmental development priorities by that time, including by notifying regional officials beforehand of operations. Any foreign or international association established in Togo was also obliged to submit a request for NGO status. On 24 June the Minister of Security and Civil Protection, Gen. Damehame Yark, banned on grounds of security a public meeting which had been planned by the DMK to protest against the high cost of living and bad governance.

Jihadist Attacks

The Government announced in early May 2022 that eight soldiers had been killed and 13 injured in fighting following a jihadist attack against a military border post at Kpékpakandi; a total of 15 militants had also been killed. The Mali-based Jama'at Nusrat al-Islam wal-Muslimeen (Group for Support of Islam and Muslims) subsequently claimed responsibility for the attack, which was the first in the country to have resulted in fatalities and increased fears of an expansion in jihadist operations from neighbouring Burkina Faso, and Mali and Niger southwards in the region. A three-month state of security emergency was declared by the Government in the northern border region of Savanes on 13 June. A few days later, militants clashed with Togolese troops outside a military post in the north-western Goulingoushi area. In the most severe eruption of jihadist violence recorded in the country, simultaneous attacks were staged against four villages near the border

with Burkina Faso on 14 July, killing up to 30 civilians. Shortly afterwards, a local official who was travelling to the area was killed by an explosive device. Meanwhile, the Government admitted to having mistakenly killed seven civilians in an air strike intended to target jihadists on 9 July. After the Togolese military announced on 23 August that it had repelled a 'terrorist' attack in the far northern village of Blamonga on the border with Burkina Faso, the National Assembly on 6 September extended the state of emergency in the Savanes region for a further six months.

HUMAN RIGHTS ISSUES

In May 1999 Amnesty International published a report detailing numerous abuses of human rights allegedly committed by the security forces in Togo, claiming that hundreds of political opponents of Eyadéma had been killed following the previous year's presidential election. Eyadéma agreed to the establishment of an international commission of inquiry into the allegations. A UN-OAU joint commission of inquiry concluded in February 2001 that 'systematic violations of human rights' had occurred in Togo in 1998, and that allegations of extrajudicial executions, particularly of opposition activists, could not be refuted. The commission stated that individuals linked to the security forces appeared to be responsible for the killings, and recommended that the authorities punish those responsible, and that a special rapporteur be appointed to monitor human rights in Togo. However, the Government dismissed the inquiry's conclusions.

During discussions with the EU in April 2004, the Government pledged to release all political prisoners and guarantee the absence in Togo of extrajudicial executions, torture and other inhumane and degrading acts. The International Federation of Human Rights Leagues (FIDH) released a report severely criticizing the Government's human rights record in June. Seven UFC militants were among 494 prisoners released in August, having been pardoned by the President, although the authorities denied that they had been political detainees.

Following the presidential election in April 2005, human rights groups claimed that the thousands of people leaving the country for Benin and Ghana were fleeing severe harassment by the security forces. The Government dismissed allegations of human rights abuses. However, in July Amnesty International issued a report denouncing human rights violations allegedly perpetrated by the Togolese security forces and pro-Government militias before and after the presidential election. A report by OHCHR on pre- and post-election violence and alleged human rights violations, which was published in September (see *Reconciliation Efforts*), stated that torture and inhumane treatment had been widely used by the security forces during the unrest. Amnesty International released a further report in April 2006 that criticized the Government for failing to prosecute those responsible for crimes committed during the 2005 election period and claiming that a culture of impunity had existed in Togo for more than 30 years. Following the signature of a memorandum of understanding with the Togolese Government in July 2006, OHCHR opened an office in Lomé.

In January 2008 the UN Human Rights Council's special rapporteur on torture and other cruel, inhuman or degrading treatment or punishment issued a report on a visit to Togo made in April 2007, in which he commended the Government for its commitment to combating torture and ill-treatment, but recommended the implementation of further measures against impunity, including the establishment of effective mechanisms to investigate incidents of torture and to conduct unannounced inspections of places of detention.

In accordance with the commitments made in the political accord of August 2006, an 11-member Truth, Justice and Reconciliation Commission (Commission Vérité, Justice et Réconciliation—CVJR), comprising religious leaders, academics and traditional chiefs, was inaugurated in May 2009, charged with investigating political violence between 1958 and 2005. In June 2009 the National Assembly unanimously approved the abolition of the death penalty. In February 2011 the EU granted €6m. in support of the development of Togo's civil society organizations and the ongoing activities of the

CVJR, which had recorded more than 20,000 cases of alleged political violence by June that year. Hearings, at which 523 witnesses gave testimony, were conducted later that year, and the CVJR submitted its report in April 2012, making 68 recommendations aimed at creating a culture of human rights in Togo, consolidating the rule of law, reconciling Togolese citizens and preventing future conflict. The CVJR also proposed the establishment of a new body to implement such reforms and the instigation of further investigations with a view to prosecuting perpetrators of the most serious human rights violations.

Meanwhile, in February 2012 the national human rights commission, the CNDH, issued a report on torture allegations made by several of those accused of involvement in a coup plot in 2009 (see *Legislative Elections of 2007*), concluding that the suspects had indeed been subjected to 'acts of physical violence, and inhuman and degrading treatment' by members of the national intelligence agency. In response, the Government announced that it had requested that the military leadership take disciplinary action against intelligence agents implicated in perpetrating the violence. Following a visit to Togo in February 2014, the UN Deputy High Commissioner for Human Rights, Flavia Pansieri, praised the country's progress on human rights issues and the Togolese Government's co-operation with OHCHR, while acknowledging that challenges remained, noting, in particular, the need to establish mechanisms to prevent torture and to address prison conditions and overcrowding. In December Amadou Abdou-Nana Awa-Daboya was nominated as Mediator of the Republic and President of the High Council for Reconciliation and Strengthening of National Unity (Haut Conseil à la Réconciliation et au Renforcement de l'Unité Nationale—HCRRUN), the establishment of both institutions having been proposed by the CVJR. In January 2017 the Government announced that it had allocated some 2,000m. francs CFA to begin compensating victims of political violence from 1958–2005. However, the level of force used to suppress anti-Government protests from August that year was condemned by international and local human rights organizations. Amnesty International criticized a new cyber-security law adopted in December 2018, citing significant restrictions on freedom of expression and a concern that 'vague' provisions related to terrorism and treason could be misused. In a report released in May 2019 the LTDH accused the Togolese authorities of numerous human rights abuses, particularly in the repression of political demonstrations, noting that at least five people had been killed in such circumstances since August 2018. Restrictions on public demonstrations imposed in August 2019 (see *A Fourth Term for Gnassingbé*), which the Government claimed were intended to ensure the public's safety, were criticized by the LTDH and other human rights groups, and in September four special rapporteurs of the UN Human Rights Council requested that the Government review the legislation. In June 2020, in its judgment on a case filed by seven NGOs, the ECOWAS Court of Justice ruled that the Togolese authorities' decision to block internet access in September 2017, amid widespread anti-Government protests, was unlawful, violating the right to freedom of expression.

In January 2021 the Haute Autorité de l'Audiovisuel et de la Communication regulatory authority closed down the newspaper *L'Indépendant Express* for publishing an article about four government ministers who were accused of theft. The editors of newspapers *L'Alternative* and *Fraternité*, Ferdinand Ayité and Joël Egah, respectively, were arrested and transferred to prison in early December 2021 for contempt of authority and spreading false statements, after they had made comments during an online broadcast suggesting that two unnamed ministers were connected with the misuse of government funds. Following protests from Amnesty International and NGO Reporters Without Borders, they were provisionally released at the end of that month, but subject to stringent conditions, including a bar on leaving the country. (Ayité reported that his passport had been retained by the authorities until June 2022, while Egah died of a heart attack in March.)

At the end of March 2022 the Government dismissed 137 teachers who had participated in a two-day strike organized by the teachers' union, Syndicat des Enseignants du Togo (SET),

to demand a monthly housing allowance and other benefits for teachers. A further seven teachers were dismissed in early April, following further strike action. Meanwhile, students in several regions began to stage protests, some of which escalated into violence, to demand the return of teachers. Civil society organizations condemned the arrest on 8 April of three leading members of the SET, who were accused of incitement to revolt. The three SET members and five students, who had been detained for involvement in violence during the protests, remained imprisoned in September.

FOREIGN RELATIONS

The issue of Ewe reunification has at times led to difficult relations with Ghana. Diplomatic relations were suspended in 1982, but were formally resumed in November 1994. Thousands of Togolese sought refuge in Benin and Ghana from late April 2005, fleeing the violence that followed the presidential election (see *Presidential Succession*). Following the restoration of stability, many refugees returned to Togo. (According to the office of the UN High Commissioner for Refugees, at the end of August 2022 3,394 Toglese refugees remained in Ghana.) During a visit to Ghana by President Gnassingbé in August 2009, it was agreed to increase co-operation in combating cross-border crime and to reconstitute the Ghana-Togo Border Demarcation Commission. Relations between Togo and Ghana were strengthened following the inauguration of Nana Akufo-Addo as Ghanaian President in January 2017. Tensions over the delimitation of the maritime boundary arose from late 2017, when the Togolese navy prevented two Ghanaian vessels from conducting oil exploration activities in a disputed area. Akufo-Addo was central in mediating a resolution in the crisis between the Government and opposition in Togo during 2018, while in that year a joint technical committee began to hold meetings on delimitation of the joint maritime boundary. The 10th meeting of the maritime technical committee was conducted in Lomé in early September 2022.

In May 2017 the security forces of Togo and Benin conducted their first joint operation at their shared border, arresting 185 people. Under the framework of the Accra Initiative, which was launched in September by Benin, Burkina Faso, Côte d'Ivoire, Ghana and Togo to combat increasing insecurity, a similar joint security operation (Koudanlgou I) took place in May 2018, involving Benin, Burkina Faso, Ghana and Togo; some 202 people were arrested, including 95 in Togo. (Only Burkina Faso, Côte d'Ivoire and Ghana participated in Koudanlgou II in November.) Amid rising concerns regarding frequent Islamist militant attacks in Burkina Faso, further regional security co-operation was discussed in October at meetings of the ministers responsible for defence, security and foreign affairs of Benin, Burkina Faso, Niger and Togo and of the chiefs of the armed forces of Benin, Burkina Faso, Niger, Nigeria and Togo. In April 2019, moreover, representatives from Benin, Burkina Faso, Côte d'Ivoire, Ghana, Mali, Niger and Togo met in Lomé to plan the deployment of joint forces along Burkina Faso's borders. Earlier that month the Togolese security forces, acting on information from the Burkinabè intelligence services, had reportedly arrested more than 20 suspected jihadists from Burkina Faso in northern Togo and transferred them to Burkina Faso. The Togolese Government established a 15-member ministerial committee in May to address security threats related to terrorism and cross-border crime.

Relations with France improved following the resumption of civil co-operation with Togo in June 1994, and were further strengthened with the election in 1995 of Jacques Chirac as French President. Following Eyadéma's re-election in June 2003, Chirac attempted to persuade his European counterparts to resume co-operation with Togo. Chirac urged the Togolese authorities to respect the Constitution following Faure Gnassingbé's installation as President in February 2005, and welcomed Gnassingbé's subsequent decision to stand down. Chirac congratulated Gnassingbé on his victory in the presidential election in April. In November 2008 President Gnassingbé made his second visit to France since taking office, holding talks with his French counterpart, Nicolas Sarkozy. Following the suppression of protests against electoral reforms in Togo in June 2012 (see *Gnassingbé Re-*

elected), the French Government called for civil liberties to be respected and urged dialogue. President Gnassingbé held cordial talks with his French counterpart, François Hollande, in November 2013, during his first visit to France since the latter's election. French Prime Minister Manuel Valls visited Togo in October 2016 (the first French premier to visit Togo in 27 years). In December 2018 the Togolese security forces took part in a joint military exercise with French forces aimed at combating terrorism. In April 2021 Gnassingbé made his first visit to France since his re-election in February 2020; talks with French President Emmanuel Macron reportedly focused on economic developments in Togo and the threat from jihadist groups in the Sahel.

President Gnassingbé visited the People's Republic of China in May 2016, at the invitation of his Chinese counterpart, Xi Jinping; the two leaders agreed to strengthen bilateral co-operation in various fields, with the Togolese delegation securing pledges of substantial investment in infrastructure projects. A new Chinese-funded parliamentary building was officially opened in Lomé in June 2018.

Togolese troops have participated in a number of peacekeeping operations. In particular, Togo contributed troops to the African-led International Support Mission in Mali (AFISMA), which commenced deployment in January 2013 to assist Mali's armed forces in combating an insurgency in the north of that country. AFISMA was reconstituted as the UN Multidimensional Integrated Stabilization Mission in Mali (MINUSMA) in July. Togo contributed a contingent of 1,024 personnel to MINUSMA at June 2022. In May of that year it was announced that President Gnassingbé had agreed to act as a mediator in a worsening political crisis in Mali (following a military takeover there in August 2020 and extension of the transitional period).

Amid mounting concern regarding piracy in the Gulf of Guinea, in September 2011, while addressing the UN General Assembly, the Togolese Prime Minister, Gilbert Houngbo, called for closer international co-operation to combat the problem. Following a UN assessment mission, in February 2012 the Security Council adopted a resolution (No. 2039) on piracy in the Gulf of Guinea, in which it encouraged the development of national and regional maritime security strategies, including a legal framework for the prosecution of persons engaged in piracy. During a visit to Lomé in August, the US Secretary of the Navy, Ray Mabus, pledged US assistance in combating maritime piracy, subsequently dispatching a US naval ship and personnel to provide training to Togolese soldiers. At an AU extraordinary summit held in Lomé in October 2016, heads of state and government adopted a charter on maritime security, safety and development, which was intended to increase co-operation between member states in addressing issues such as piracy, trafficking (of drugs, arms and people), illegal fishing and pollution. According to the International Maritime Bureau, attacks off Togo's coast rose to 15 in 2012, but activity had decreased sharply by 2015. Three tankers were attacked in Togolese waters in 2019, with a total of seven crew members kidnapped, the motivation for piracy in the Gulf of Guinea having reportedly shifted from cargo theft to hostage-taking for ransom. Two actual attacks were reported in 2020, in one of which three crew members were kidnapped. Reported maritime crime and piracy incidents, including in the Gulf of Guinea, declined significantly during 2021 and the first half of 2022. In the first trial for maritime piracy to be conducted in Togo, in July 2021 seven Nigerians and one Togolese national were found guilty of involvement in the attempted hijacking of a tanker in Togolese waters in May 2019 and sentenced to prison terms ranging from 12 to 15 years; a Ghanaian, for whom an international arrest warrant had been issued, was sentenced *in absentia* to 20 years' imprisonment.

At an extraordinary AU summit held in March 2018, Togo was among 44 of the 55 member states to sign an agreement on the establishment of an African Continental Free Trade Area (AfCFTA), and also signed, together with 26 other member states, an agreement on the free movement of people across borders. The AfCFTA agreement entered into force in May 2019 for the 24 states (including Togo) that had ratified it. Trading under the AfCFTA officially commenced on 1 January 2021.

Togo has developed strong relations with Israel, and Gnassingbé made a five-day visit to that country in August 2016. Lomé was due to host an Israel-Africa summit in October 2017, but this was postponed indefinitely in September, following the domestic unrest experienced in Togo and amid threats to boycott the event by several African countries. Togo's relations with Turkey were strengthened by a visit by the Turkish Minister of Foreign Affairs, Mevlüt Çavuşoğlu, in July 2020 and by the opening of a Turkish embassy in Lomé in April 2021.

The Togolese Government conducted the first Togo-EU economic forum in Lomé in June 2019, seeking investment for its National Development Plan for 2018–22. In June 2021, during a visit to Lomé by the German Minister for Economic Co-operation and Development, Gerd Müller, the Togolese and German Governments signed an agreement for a 'reform partnership'. Also in June, a delegation from the Commonwealth reportedly visited Lomé to conduct an evaluation mission on Togo's desire to apply for membership of the organization. The National Assembly on 22 April 2022 approved a resolution requesting that the Government officially apply for Togo to join the Commonwealth. At the Commonwealth Heads of Government Meeting held in Rwanda on 25 June, Togo, together with Gabon, was formally admitted as a member state. Togo's Minister of Foreign Affairs, Regional Integration and Togolese Abroad Prof. Robert Dussey confirmed that the country sought to develop closer ties with anglophone countries (in a move away from France's sphere of influence).

Economy

PAUL MELLY

INTRODUCTION

Weathering the global financial crisis and, a decade later, the economic impact of the COVID-19 pandemic, Togo has continued steadily to reinforce its role as a financial services centre and regional transport gateway. However, in 2022 this country of just 8.7m. people was presented with severe new challenges, with the rise in international food and fuel prices that followed the Russian Federation's invasion of Ukraine in February, and the spread of jihadist violence from Burkina Faso into the northernmost reaches of national territory. Hitherto spared the terrorist activity so widespread across the Sahel, Togo now finds itself directly affected by a destabilizing phenomenon that threatens the security of community and economic life in some of its poorest areas and that could have a broader impact on investor confidence and the smooth operation of the logistics corridors carrying merchandise to and from Lomé port.

The southward spread of the violence that has wrought such havoc across large parts of the inland Sahel could have a more fundamentally disruptive impact on economic stability than the political tensions around constitutional change, the contentious 2020 presidential election and subsequent government attempts to curb opposition activism. Periodic episodes of political pressure and the sporadic detention of critics are nothing new in Togo and international partners have factored these into their planning: for example, the USA provides significant development support but denies Togo full access to its Millennium Challenge aid facility, which is subject to democratic governance conditions. In contrast, terrorism risk can significantly influence how commercial investors perceive countries as potential project locations.

These new challenges have come after a period that saw Togo, under the leadership of President Faure Gnassingbé, make significant progress in sustained economic growth and diversification, and steady advances in social development and public service provision. Although the country's political model still falls well short of a genuine democracy of citizen choice, it has moved a long way from the brutally repressive rule of the President's father and predecessor, Gnassingbé Eyadéma, whose regime was largely shunned by international donors during the 1990s, a period when development stagnated. Faure, in power since 2005, oversaw a steady process of recovery and re-engagement with key international partners such as the International Monetary Fund (IMF), laying the foundations for a renewed effort to tackle deep-seated poverty and an ambitious drive to establish Lomé, the capital, as a trade gateway and transport hub for larger and more populous regional neighbours. The city has a massively expanded container port, a new airport terminal, an upgraded highway route to Burkina Faso and an integrated joint border control post where West Africa's main coastal highway crosses into Ghana. Activity in financial services is also significant, although Lomé must also compete with other regional centres such as the Nigerian capital, Lagos, and Abidjan, the capital of Côte d'Ivoire. A longstanding reputation for efficiency and pragmatism has also helped Togo's efforts to expand its role as a business hub.

However, Togo's long-term economic recovery only gathered momentum over time, and growth in gross domestic product (GDP), in real terms, stagnated for much of the 2004–08 period. Between 2009 and 2016 growth was more consistent, at between 5.0% and 7.0% per year, and as this outpaced the steady rise in population the foundations were laid for a gradual improvement in living standards. The Government played a central driving role through heavy public spending, only part-financed by donor grants: in 2016 the fiscal deficit was 9.6% of GDP, and 12.4% excluding the impact of grants.

As in many other countries, the COVID-19 pandemic applied a sharp brake to economic activity, with real GDP growth plunging from 5.5% in 2019 to just 1.8% in 2020, thanks largely to the disruption of the transport and commercial activity that plays such a major role in Lomé. But 2021 brought an impressive rebound in GDP growth to 5.3%, before the surge in world food and fuel prices after the Russian invasion of Ukraine cast uncertainty over projections for 2022.

However, imbalances in the geographical and sectoral distribution of economic growth remain. Despite the important contributions of phosphates mining, cement production, port operations and transport services, and trading, the majority of Togolese still make a living from smallholder farming and, in northern areas, some pastoralism.

ECONOMIC FUNDAMENTALS

Non-commercial services accounted for an average 18% of GDP per year in 2015–19, with banking, insurance and other commercial services generating a further 15%. The largest contribution to economic output still comes from agriculture, livestock husbandry, fisheries, hunting and forestry, which accounted for 22% of GDP in 2020. The largest exports include phosphates, cotton and gold. However, trade, transport and related activity is a cornerstone of the Lomé urban economy, a major employer and a crucial source of government revenue: even in 2015, before it was fully expanded, the capital's port generated 57% of Togo's entire fiscal receipts.

The dynamism of such activity in the coastal south can distract from the continuing fragility of conditions in central and northern rural communities. By 2020 the proportion of Togolese living below the poverty line had edged below 50%, substantially down on the incidence of deprivation just a few years earlier, but it remains to be seen whether this positive trend will be confirmed over succeeding years. Real GDP per capita reached US $992 in 2021, but still lagged well behind neighbouring Benin ($1,428).

The Government acknowledges the need for sustained efforts to strengthen the agricultural value chain—the processing of farm output—to generate high incomes and more livelihoods in the rural economy upon which so many Togolese

still depend. It is hoped that a new multi-sector industrial park being developed by ARISE Integrated Industrial Platforms at Adétikopé, 15 km outside Lomé, will attract textiles manufacturing investors, who will then use locally grown cotton. Meanwhile, phosphate mines and limestone quarries are islands of industrial activity in rural areas.

Because of its regional trade gateway, Togo has a major stake in the progress of West African economic and infrastructure integration and thus in the role of the regional structures to which it belongs—of which the most important are the 15-member Economic Community of West African States (ECOWAS), the eight-member Union Economique et Monétaire Ouest-Africaine (UEMOA) single currency bloc and the Comité Permanent Inter-Etats de Lutte Contre la Sécheresse dans le Sahel (CILSS). All member states in UEMOA belong to ECOWAS.

Although ECOWAS plays a prominent role in co-ordinating a united regional response to political and security crises, it also has a major economic agenda in leading the gradual progress towards trade integration and the development of shared infrastructure networks. For decades progress on this agenda was slow, but a significant breakthrough came with the 2015 adoption of a Common External Tariff, harmonizing import tariffs across West Africa. By gradually eliminating tariff competition between ports in the region this reform has enabled Lomé port to make the most of its extensive modern container handling capacity and reputation for efficiency and thus attract business far beyond the needs of the small Togolese national market.

ECOWAS has also set up a region-wide market for trading in electricity and, supported by the European Union (EU), it has encouraged member states to build modern 'one-stop' frontier posts on principal land border crossings. One such facility was opened in 2018 by the Togolese and Ghanaian authorities at Noépé-Akanu, 30 km north-east of Lomé. The bloc has also drawn up a detailed timetable for preparing the introduction of a long-discussed single regional currency, the eco. In June 2021 the leaders of all ECOWAS states agreed a new timetable for convergence to be monitored through until 2026, prior to the launch of the eco in 2027. However, many technical and institutional arrangements remain to be resolved, a task complicated by the fact that the region has two strong and self-confident central banks—the Central Bank of Nigeria in Abuja and the UEMOA central bank, the Banque Centrale des Etats de l'Afrique de l'Ouest (BCEAO), headquartered in the Senegalese capital, Dakar—the roles of which will have to be merged, while also combining with the other national central banks. A further complication is the still uncompleted reform of the West African CFA franc.

Togo is one of eight members of UEMOA, the bloc of countries that use the West African version of the CFA franc common currency. The other seven members—Côte d'Ivoire, Senegal, Guinea-Bissau, Mali, Burkina Faso, Benin and Niger—include many of Togo's regional neighbours and trading partners. UEMOA provides a framework for monetary stability: the CFA franc has been devalued only once, in 1994, and it has a fixed rate of exchange against the euro, guaranteed by the French treasury. Monetary affairs are governed by the BCEAO, the bloc's independent central bank, which maintains a conservative monetary stance. UEMOA also operates a common system of bank regulation, a regional capital market and a shared electronic stock exchange (based in Abidjan). The bloc is run by a central administrative commission, based in Ouagadougou, Burkina Faso, which pursues regional integration and is a major voice on development issues.

Since 1994 the CFA exchange rate has remained broadly viable and competitive for West African economies such as Togo and the BCEAO's close alignment with the conservative stance of the European Central Bank has kept inflation low. However, the sustainability of the current arrangements has been coming under political and policy pressure over recent years. A growing slice of urban and youth opinion regards the system as a tool for perpetuating French post-colonial influence, while some prominent West African economists argue that the peg to the euro keeps the CFA artificially strong, hindering the competitiveness of local exporters while enabling the affluent elite to deploy comfortable spending power in Europe.

In 2017 President Emmanuel Macron said France would support any reform model chosen by UEMOA leaders and they then chose Côte d'Ivoire's President, Alassane Ouattara—a former deputy managing director of the IMF—to develop a plan. Announced in December 2019, this comprised three elements: renaming the CFA franc as the eco, France's withdrawal from its seats in the oversight of BCEAO and UEMOA institutions and the abolition of the longstanding requirement for UEMOA countries to keep one-half of their foreign exchange reserves in an official bank account in France, to underpin the fixed parity. France rapidly gave formal approval to these changes, dropping the reserve requirement almost immediately. But amid the disruption caused by the COVID-19 pandemic UEMOA countries were slower to ratify the reforms. Moreover, Nigeria and some other West African states outside UEMOA were angered by Ouattara's proposal that the bloc should maintain its peg to the euro and yet adopt the eco currency name that all West African countries had already approved as the future name of the planned common currency. By mid-2022 the politically sensitive name issue had still not been resolved, and with just five years remaining until the planned launch of the all-ECOWAS eco (which would replace the CFA franc anyway) it seemed possible that UEMOA might quietly abandon plans to rename the CFA franc in the interim.

CILSS was originally set up to monitor the risks of drought and food insecurity and co-ordinate strategies for rural resilience and emergency reserves and supplies across the drought-prone Sahel (which includes the far north of Togo). However, there are close food supply links between the Sahel and coastal economies and CILSS has therefore been extending its purview to encompass much of coastal West Africa too.

Like most francophone African countries, Togo belongs to the OHADA regime of harmonized business law, with a supranational appeals tribunal to rule on disputes. Meanwhile, Lomé hosts the headquarters of the West African Development Bank (BOAD).

SOCIETY

The United Nations estimated Togo's population at 8.7m. in 2022, increasing by 2.3% per year—a rate of growth that is steadily contracting. However, the country is still far from demographic stability, with an average fertility rate of 4.2 children per woman. While 22% of women aged 15–49 years use a modern form of contraception, just as many would like to do so but do not yet have access to the necessary family planning services; around 25% of Togolese marry by the age of 18.

With the population still rising quite rapidly, some 40% of Togolese are aged under 15 years, which presents the state with a massive challenge to provide basic child health services and places in school; and with 23% of Togolese in the 10–19 year age-group, every year brings further growth in the number of young people entering the labour market. That trend, and the high levels of poverty in many rural areas, which can only be exacerbated by the destabilizing impact of terrorist attacks in the far north, fuels continuing migration to Lomé, which is now home to some 1.9m. people.

The sustained development efforts of the past 15 years have enabled Togo to recoup much of the social ground lost during the 1990s crisis decade, and average life expectancy in 2020 was 62 years for women and 60 for men—only slightly lower than in Burkina Faso and Benin. The same applies to aspects of health service provision: 69% of births are attended by trained personnel and the rate of maternal mortality, at 396 deaths per 100,000 live births is now slightly lower than Benin's, although still worse than the rate in Burkina Faso (320). At 82%, the proportion of children aged 12–23 months vaccinated against diphtheria, pertussis and tetanus has dropped slightly, but this slight decline is in line with international trends and may reflect the disruptive impact of COVID-19 on health service provision. Nevertheless, health indicators that are more greatly influenced by poverty and broad development shortcomings remain troubling: 23.8% of children under the age of five suffer from stunting, while some 20% of all Togolese are undernourished. Meanwhile, the education system has been extending its reach: 90% of boys and 86% of girls now complete primary school and 79% of children enrol in lower secondary education.

ECONOMIC POLICY AND PUBLIC FINANCE

Togo's economic strategy is underpinned by its membership of the UEMOA single currency bloc and its policy partnership with the IMF, which approved a three-year Extended Credit Facility (ECF) programme in May 2017. With the Government under pressure to increase spending in response to the COVID-19 pandemic, the Fund massively boosted its support in April 2020: after completing the scheduled sixth review of Togo's performance under the ECF arrangement, it approved a disbursement of US $131.3m., almost four times larger than had originally been planned. During the following year the IMF held fresh talks with the Government about the principal features of a successor ECF programme, with a focus on strengthening the socially inclusive nature of private sector-led growth and reinforcing development initiatives. In January 2022 the Togolese media reported that agreement on a programme and funding had already been reached, but such optimism proved premature: negotiations continued during an IMF mission to Lomé in March, and no final agreement of Fund approval had yet been announced by the second half of 2022.

Despite the absence of an IMF programme during much of 2021 and 2022, the Government has stuck to its strategic fundamentals: strengthening fiscal revenue and administration and tightening public finance management, while sustaining investment in core services and development. This approach appears to have been vindicated by Togo's capacity to withstand periods of economic stress: real GDP growth remained resilient, at 5.6% in 2016 and 4.3% the following year, despite an upsurge in domestic political tension, and then 5.0% in 2018 and 5.5% in 2019. Even in 2020, the most intense year of the pandemic—and with both port activity and local farm exports at risk of disruption from Nigeria's closure of its western land border—growth remained significantly positive, at 1.8%, and it rebounded strongly to 5.3% in 2021.

However, the authorities have struggled to bolster tax and customs revenues, despite the efforts of the consolidated Office Togolais des Recettes, which tries to induce citizens and businesses to paying tax through the banking system. Indeed, measured as a proportion of economic output, revenues actually fell from 24.6% of real GDP in 2016 to just 21.7% in 2019. Trends in both total government revenue—excluding grant aid—and fiscal revenue have not consistently followed the upward trend in growth. Budget receipts reached 637,400m. francs CFA in 2016, but then slipped back to 621,400m. francs CFA the following year, before recovering to 659,400m. francs CFA in 2018 and 699,300m. francs CFA in 2019. Within this overall total, fiscal revenues totalled 575,000m. francs CFA in 2016, before sinking back to 563,200m. francs CFA in 2017 and 546,900m. francs CFA the following year; however, 2019 brought a rebound to 626,200m. francs CFA. Donor grant support has partly compensated for the fluctuations in domestic revenue, growing steadily, from just 57,200m. francs CFA in 2015 to 122,400m. francs CFA in 2019.

Current expenditure amounted to 562,100m. francs CFA in 2016, but in 2017—a politically troubled year—it fell back to just 545,800m. francs CFA. Current outlays resumed their upward track in 2018, reaching 586,700m. francs CFA, and rose again the following year, to 623,700m. francs CFA. Within this overall total, spending on public service salaries and other staff benefits increased steadily, in part because of the recruitment of additional health, education and security service personnel, rising from 171,700m. francs CFA in 2015 to 214,600m. francs CFA in 2019. Capital expenditure was reduced after heavy development outlays in the middle of the last decade: it totalled 322,200m. francs CFA in 2016, but was then cut back to just 174,500m. francs CFA in 2017 before gradually recovering to 234,700m. francs CFA in 2019. The fluctuations in capital investment impacted on the overall spending total, which surged from 636,400m. francs CFA in 2014 to 884,400m. francs CFA in 2016, but then fell back to 720,300m. francs CFA in 2017, amid political tensions; however, 2018 brought a resurgence to 788,400m. francs CFA, followed by a further rise the year after, to 858,500m. francs CFA. With Togo having benefited from international debt forgiveness, government interest payments on external debt amounted to only 8,900m. francs CFA in 2019, whereas interest payments to domestic creditors that year were 77,000m. francs CFA.

Overall, Togo managed to contain its primary fiscal deficit (excluding grants) to an affordable level, at only 49,100m. francs CFA in 2019. The IMF reported that the overall cash deficit, including grant aid, averaged 4.2% of GDP over 2010–18; a surplus of 1.6% of GDP was achieved in 2019 but as Togo felt the impact of the pandemic public finances were pushed back into the red, recording deficits of 6.9% of GDP in 2020 and 6.5% of GDP the following year. The deficit was initially projected to shrink in 2022, but the global surge in fuel and food prices could impact the final out-turn.

The IMF is encouraging Togo to develop a more socially inclusive growth model. That could present challenges for a political and economic system that tends to favour those with connections to the inner circles of a regime that has been in power, albeit in an evolving form, since the 1960s.

AGRICULTURE

The foundation of the domestic Togolese economy is small-holder agriculture, on which most families depend, and livestock husbandry also makes an important contribution, particularly in the more arid northern areas. In the more humid tropical climate of the south, farmers produce cocoa and coffee for export sale, while cassava and yams are among the principal food crops. In the drier climate of the savannah and Sahel areas further north the main food crops are maize, sorghum, millet and legumes, including cowpeas (*niébé*), groundnuts and soya, while cotton is the main export cash crop. Cotton is an annual rain-fed crop and can therefore be grown in rotation with cereals, which benefit from the residues of fertilizer applied for the cotton produced on the same patch of ground the previous year. Rice is produced in low-lying fields that can be irrigated. Only one-half of Togo's 3.4m. ha of cultivable land is currently farmed, so there is scope to expand out, but resources of land, water and grazing will have to be carefully managed to avoid the risks of soil exhaustion and erosion, desertification through loss of plant cover or the emergence of tensions between herders and farmers competing for water and land.

The Government has developed various initiatives for the growth of the sector, such as co-operatives and other tools for providing credit and technical advice, a risk-sharing scheme to incentivize banks to finance agriculture, the subsidized distribution of fertilizer, the supply of improved seed varieties, the improvement of rural roads, the creation of hubs for crop processing ('agropôles') and measures to strengthen the downstream farm products' value chain. Measures to improve water supply and foster mechanization are under way.

Annual harvests for key crops have been rising steadily. Production of cassava climbed from 1.04m. metric tons in the 2015/16 season to 1.05m. tons the next year, 1.09m. tons in 2018/19, then 1.12m. tons in 2019/20 and 1.15m. tons in 2020/21. Output of yams climbed from 781,400 tons in 2015/16 to 858,800 tons in 2018/19, then 874,300 tons in 2019/20 and 868,700 tons in 2020/21. Cereal production is always vulnerable to the risk of drought, but has in fact been rising: the maize harvest did slip from 833,200 tons in 2014/15 to 794,700 tons in 2015/16, but rebounded to 826,900 tons in 2016/17, some 854,700 tons the year after, then 886,600 tons in 2018/19 and 912,100 tons in 2019/20, before reaching 885,000 tons in 2020/21. Although millet and sorghum are more drought-resistant, output still fell from 332,300 tons in 2014/15 to 297,800 tons in 2015/16, before slowly recovering to 299,300 tons in 2016/17 and 302,200 tons the next year, then 303,300 tons in 2018/19, some 309,400 tons in 2019/20 and 309,000 tons in 2020/21. Paddy rice is obviously vulnerable to low rainfall without supplementary water supply from a river or lake and output plunged from 140,500 tons in 2014/15 to just 97,500 tons the following year; however, it rebounded to 137,100 tons in 2016/17 and 140,500 tons in the year after, and edged up to 145,500 tons in 2018/19, some 147,100 tons in 2019/20 and

160,000 tons in 2020/21. Groundnut output has not substantially progressed, slipping from 43,200 tons in 2013/14 to 40,700 tons in 2014/15 and to 40,900 tons in 2015/16; it reached 43,500 tons in 2017/18 and 43,800 tons the following season, before edging up to 44,600 tons in 2019/20 and then slipping back slightly to 44,500 tons in 2020/21. Most villagers also grow vegetables and fruit; they tend to grow their own food and sell the surplus for cash, locally or further afield, as there is substantial trade in food crops across West Africa: for example, Togolese farmers export tomatoes to Nigeria.

Cotton, cocoa, coffee are the main crops produced for the international export market, so the viability of these sectors is strongly influenced by global demand and price levels. Cotton is an annual crop, which means farmers can adjust the proportion of their land that they allocate to it from year to year, in response to global price and demand signals. However, cocoa and coffee are tree or bush crops planted for the long term, so the Government provides support to these sectors, to help them to make the most of Togo's distinct high-quality market niche; this also helps to sustain sales, even when Togolese production has to compete with cheaper lower quality output from other countries.

The Government has been supporting the replanting of the ageing cocoa plantations of the 27,000-ha Kpalimé plateau, which had suffered from declining soil fertility and diseases such as swollen shoot; old bushes have been replaced with more resilient varieties and this investment has underpinned a recovery in output, from a mere 6,500 metric tons in 2012/13 to 11,600 tons 2017/18, 12,700 tons in 2018/19, a strong 14,300 tons in 2019/20 and 15,700 tons in 2020/21; growers have been incentivized by rises in the producer price to 965 francs CFA per kg in 2018/19, 1,051 francs CFA in 2019/20 and 1,088 francs CFA in 2020/21. Coffee saw a large rise in the national harvest, from just 8,000 tons in 2013/14 to 18,500 tons in 2017/18, then 19,100 tons in 2018/19 and 21,300 tons in 2019/20, before declining to 17,400 francs CFA in 2020/21. The production surge was achieved despite a cut in the producer price, from 815 francs CFA per kg in 2018/19 to a mere 600 francs CFA in 2019/20, followed by a gentle increase, to 623 francs CFA, in 2020/21.

Togo has to compete with cheap US and Asian competition on the international market and, indirectly, in the home market, with imports of cheap Chinese-produced cotton textiles. The volumes of cotton planted are also influenced by the relative attractiveness of alternative annual cash crops such as maize. The parastatal Nouvelle Société Cotonnière du Togo (NSCT), 40% owned by producers and 60% owned by the state, provides a supportive framework for the sector and over recent years it has gradually increased the producer price from 230 francs CFA per kg previously to 250 francs CFA in 2018/19, then 265 francs CFA in 2019/20 and 271 francs CFA in 2020/21. This supportive stance encouraged farmers to plant more cotton, with output climbing from 80,000 metric tons in 2015/16 to 110,000 tons in 2016/17, 117,200 tons in 2017/18 and 137,300 tons in 2018/19. Production subsequently suffered a slight decline to 116,600 tons in 2019/20 and 102,500 tons in 2020/21, because of bad weather, problems with seed and the impact of COVID-19. In November 2020 the Government sold majority control of the NSCT to Singaporean group Olam, which had already taken on a similar role in Chad, and which now faces the challenge of restoring long-term trend growth. Initial indications suggest that the 2021/22 harvest has been impacted by both unseasonal rainfall and some localized droughts.

In drier northern regions livestock husbandry plays a major role: the activity is the second largest source of income for rural communities, where at least one-half of all households own some sheep or goats. Coastal urban centres are a significant market for northern cattle herders, who have seen their incomes rise substantially over the past decade, in part thanks to a campaign to improve animal health. In 2021 the Government launched a campaign to bolster domestic meat production and reduce reliance on imports.

The country has only 96 km of coastline, but fish is an important component of diet in the south and the national catch meets only 30% of consumer demand, with the rest imported (at a cost of US $32m. in 2017). The maritime catch was 18,800 metric tons in 2020. About 5,400 tons annually is caught in lagoons, lakes and rivers, and fish farms produce about 130 tons a year, mostly tilapia and catfish. Some large vessels based in Lomé fish deep-sea for the export market, and total fish exports were worth $4m. in 2017. Altogether, around 10,000 people are largely dependent on fishing for their livelihood.

MINING, INDUSTRY AND ENERGY

Limestone and phosphates are Togo's main mineral products. Unlike neighbouring Ghana, it is not a hydrocarbons exporter, although the Government did sign up for the Extractive Industries Transparency Initiative (EITI) in the hope that this might stimulate exploration interest; the country has been compliant with EITI standards since 2013. Italy's Eni and Oranto Petroleum (Nigeria) have been active offshore, but have not so far found commercially viable deposits.

Deposits of phosphates deposits were found in 1952 and by the 1980s Togo was producing 3m. metric tons a year. But output later halved, undermined by a shortage of investment, poor management, concern over high levels of cadmium and the gradual exhaustion of the upper layer of high grade reserves. But some 2,000m. tons of carbonated phosphate— lower grade but also with a far lower incidence of cadmium— lay beneath the remaining 260m. tons of high quality deposits. To revive the sector the Government set up International Fertilizers Group-Togo to rehabilitate production facilities and in 2007 this was followed by the creation of a new operating venture, Société Nouvelle des Phosphates du Togo. More than €134m. was invested in modernizing production, opening up the carbonated phosphate deposits and developing downstream value-added processing. These efforts have had mixed results, with large fluctuations in output, which rose from 695,200 tons in 2010 to 1.2m. tons in 2015/16, but slipped to 843,500 tons the next year and only 732,500 tons in 2017/18. There was a rebound to an estimated 800,000 tons in 2018/19 and 2019/20, but production surged back to 1.3m. tons in 2021/21.

The Kpémé deposit, one of the largest in Africa, is sited conveniently for export trade, just 30 km from the coast. In 2015 a development licence to was awarded to Elenilto-Wengfu, a Chinese-Israeli consortium, which drafted plans for a US $1,000m. project, to produce 3m. metric tons of concentrated phosphate rock and use gas imported from Nigeria through the West Africa Gas Pipeline (WAGP) to fuel a processing plant that would produce 500,000 tons of phosphoric acid and 1.3m. tons of fertilizer.

With 175m. metric tons of limestone deposits, Togo is a major producer of clinker, a key component of cement. Two offshoots of the German group Heidelberg are active: Cimtogo operates plants in Lomé and Dapaong, with annual production capacity of 750,000 tons and 250,000 tons, respectively, while Scantogo-Mines exploits the Sika-Kondji limestone deposit and produces up to 5,000 tons a day of clinker, taking total national clinker output to 1.5m. tons per year. Diamond Cement Togo, part of the West African Cement (Wacem) group, is also present. But all Togo's producers face stiff competitive pressure from imports sold into Togo by the Nigeria-based Dangote group.

Togo has 20m. tons of marble deposits at Gnaoulou and Pagala and the Société des Pierres Ornementales et de Marbre was awarded a contract to develop Pagala. India's MM Mining has looked at developing the 500m.-ton Bandjéli iron ore deposit, which has an average 45% metal content; however, this could necessitate the construction of a rail link to a maritime export terminal. There are also deposits of manganese in Togo.

From 1968 onwards Togo and neighbouring Benin organized power generation and transmission through a joint parastatal entity, the CEB. They eventually decided to dissolve this arrangement, a move that was formalized by the CEB board in March 2021. This did not bring an end to their co-operation, because they developed power infrastructure in partnership: the 66-MW Nangbeto hydro power station, two 20-MW thermal plants, a 1,763-km high tension distribution network, two cross-border interconnectors and a supply link from Nigeria.

By 2019 some 52.4% of Togolese had access to electricity but demand, already far beyond what the CEB could generate, had continued to increase, forcing both Togo and Benin to rely substantially on imports of electricity from Nigeria, the Azito gas-fired plant in Côte d'Ivoire and the Akosombo dam in Ghana, although generating capacity at Akosombo is vulnerable to episodes of low rainfall.

Supply security was reinforced by the 2021 inauguration of the 65-MW Kékéli thermal plant in Lomé, operated by the French group Eranove and a 50-MW solar power plant at Blitta, in central Togo, established by the Emirati group Amea; these two installations have provided sufficient additional power to supply 850,000 households.

Moreover, over time the security of supply should be enhanced by the strengthening of transmission links across West Africa and the 2018 creation of a structured regional market, overseen by the ECOWAS Regional Electricity Regulatory Authority. Togo's power utility, the Compagnie Energie Electrique du Togo (CEET), has begun to upgrade the domestic transmission network, with World Bank support; and in April 2021 the Agence Française de Développement, the EU and Germany's KfW approved a €70m. package of funding to extend power supply to more than 100,000 urban households.

Cotton ginning and cement production are Togo's major industries; the sector also encompasses agricultural processing activities, such as cassava milling, palm oil extraction and coffee roasting, import substitution manufacturers of footwear, textiles, salt, beverages, confectionery and tyres, the Danone offshoot Fan Milk and the Geocoton subsidiary Nioto, which produces cooking oil and shea butter from cotton, soya and shea nuts. With cheap Chinese textiles imports flooding the market, the Government shut the local wax print producer Togotex, but it hopes that the new Arise industrial site near Lomé will attract investors to revive textiles manufacturing using locally grown cotton.

FINANCIAL SERVICES

Lomé remains a niche regional financial hub, despite strong competition from Lagos and Abidjan, offering much larger volumes of local economic activity. The city hosts the head office of UEMOA's Banque Ouest-Africaine de Développement and the ECOWAS Bank for Investment and Development. It is also the seat of Ecobank Transnational Inc., the largest independent regional banking group in West Africa and Central Africa, with operations in 36 countries in sub-Saharan Africa. Many banks from other African countries are also present, among them Orabank, Banque Atlantique, Bank of Africa, Diamond Bank, the International Bank of Africa in Togo (BIAT) and Coris Bank. Moreover, the local financial sector has extended deeper roots than in some neighbouring countries, with bank lending to clients equal to 40% of GDP at the end of 2017 (compared with a 28% average for UEMOA). The 13 banks and two regulated financial institutions suffered a difficult 2018, with net profits slumping by 81.7%, before a modest recovery the following year. Performance during 2020, amid the COVID-19 pandemic, was mixed: solvability slipped to just 7.4%, well below the 9.5% regulatory minimum, yet the proportion of non-performing loans dropped to 15.9%, from 16.5% the previous year, and average provisioning levels against bad debt rose to 69%. After a delay because of COVID-19-related disruption, in August 2021 the Government completed the sale of the state-owned Banque Togolaise pour le Commerce et l'Industrie (BTCI) to IB Holding, a financial services and banking group owned by the Burkinabè construction tycoon Mahamadou Bonkoungou; the state retains a 10% share. The IMF had long been pressing the Government to privatize BTCI and Union Togolaise de Banque (UTB).

Togo's 190 microfinance institutions play a crucial role in the grassroots economy, with 795 service points, but only about 20 satisfy all the regulatory prudential ratios and 140 operate entirely without a licence.

TRANSPORT, COMMUNICATIONS AND TOURISM

Lomé's role as a regional trade gateway is partly founded on its location, midway along West Africa's key Abidjan–Lagos coastal corridor and at the start of a key northbound trunk route to Sinkassé on the border with Burkina Faso. The coastal highway enters Togo from Benin at the Sanvee–Condji–Hillacondji border post and then skirts the northern fringes of Lomé before crossing into Ghana at the new Noépé-Akanu integrated frontier post, where officials from both countries work alongside each other to process the formalities efficiently and transparently. There is a similar integrated post at the Sinkassé crossing into Burkina Faso and another has been under construction at the Sanvee–Condji–Hillacondji border with Benin. An integrated post also exists on the highway between Cotonou (Benin) and Lagos, smoothing the transit of goods from Lomé port to the vast Nigerian market. The EU and the African Development Bank are funding the establishment of such modern 'one-stop' frontier posts at major border crossings right across West Africa, to enhance trade and travel efficiency and reduce the risks of hassle and corruption. Much traffic also still passes through the Aflao border post on the Lomé seafront, where the capital runs right up to the boundary with Ghanaian territory. The Société d'Exploitation du Guichet Unique du Commerce Extérieur operates a one-stop shop system for trade formalities at Lomé port and airport and Noépé-Akanu.

Within Togo, the domestic road network is an essential support for domestic agriculture and commerce and the transport of farm produce from rural areas to urban markets and export traders.

Togo's 519 km of railway track is mostly in poor condition and passenger services have not run since the 1990s. Cement producer Wacem acquired the national rail company Société Nationale des Chemins de Fer du Togo in 2003 and uses a 40-km stretch of track from Tabligbo to Dalavé to transport clinker. The Government hopes that the People's Republic of China will help build a new line to the Burkina Faso border, but the project would have to compete with the existing line from Abidjan port to the Burkinabè capital Ouagadougou, which has been undergoing an upgrade, and the new line being developed from the Ghanaian port Tema to Ouagadougou.

Lomé has one of the few natural deep-water harbours on the West African coast, with a 14-m draught, and the past 15 years have seen the Government oversee a major port expansion in partnership with the French group Bolloré, one of the main container terminal operators in the region, and the Swiss-based shipping giant MSC and China Merchant Holding. In 2009 Bolloré was awarded a 35-year concession to operate Lomé's existing container terminal (Togo Terminal), replacing the Franco-Spanish group Progosa, and in 2014 it added a third quay equipped with modern gantry cranes; the facility remains the trade gateway serving Togo and neighbouring land transit destinations, of which Burkina Faso is much the largest. Meanwhile, the Government chose Swiss-based shipping giant MSC and China Merchant Holding to develop and operate a new maritime transshipment hub, the Lomé Container Terminal (LCT), under a 35-year concession. The terminal, which also opened in 2014, can accommodate some of the world's largest container vessels, from which cargo is then transferred to smaller ships that operate feeder lines to other West African ports that are too shallow to welcome the largest deep-sea ships. The opening of the LCT produced an immediate upsurge in container freight flows through Lomé and this transshipment business soon came to account for the large majority of total container volumes and became the principal driver behind the growth in traffic. Of the 380,798 containers handled in 2014, some 132,946 were in transhipment; by 2021 the total number of containers handled by the port had risen to 1.9m., of which more than 1.5m. was transhipment business. Lomé also has quays for handling conventional and bulk cargo, oil and minerals.

Lomé's Tokoin airport is the home base of ASKY Airlines, an Ethiopian Airlines subsidiary that operates one of the most extensive short-haul networks in West Africa. A new terminal opened in April 2016. The airport is served by Ethiopian and several other sub-Saharan carriers, Air France, Brussels Airlines, Royal Air Maroc and Turkish Airlines.

Mobile telecommunications grew more slowly in Togo than in many other African countries and there were still only 79 subscribers for every 100 people in 2020; the three operators are state-owned Togocel, Togo Télécom and Moov, a subsidiary of Maroc Télécom that has been building a 910-km fibre-optic spine network. Togo is linked to international fibre-optic networks through West Africa Cable Systems.

The Government is trying to encourage diversification of the tourism sector away from a reliance on the beach holiday market by expanding conference business and eco-tourism. In 2019 some 876,000 tourists were recorded as staying at least one night, a figure that plunged to 482,000 in 2020 as the COVID-19 pandemic forced a major clampdown on travel. However, official tourism visitor figures should be treated with caution as government data may not fully distinguish between those coming on holiday, short-term business and other work visitors and West Africans visiting for family, work or informal commercial reasons.

PAYMENTS AND FOREIGN TRADE

After its re-engagement with the international community Togo was allocated €216m. in EU support under its 11th European Development Fund (2014–20), while the IMF and the World Bank approved debt relief under the Heavily Indebted Poor Countries initiative and Multilateral Debt Relief Initiative in 2011, almost halving the country's external debt to just $629.4m., before France cancelled the entire $101m. owed to it in 2012. Consequently, official external debt fell from 52.6% of GDP in 2009 to just 12.9% in 2012. However, with the Government subsequently taking on new development loans to catch up on the backlog of long-neglected capital spending, debt rose to 23.5% by 2018. Although this was affordable, the IMF pressed the Government to pursue a more strategic approach to debt management and it expressed concern over the high levels of government domestic debt, which risked 'crowding out' the local private sector securing adequate local credit.

Togo's current account deficit shrank from 258,700m. francs CFA in 2016 to just 56,100m. francs CFA the next year, rebounded to 102,700m. francs CFA in 2018 and fell back to 32,500m. francs CFA the following year, before ballooning to 172,600m. in 2020. The country has consistently recorded a large deficit in merchandise trade: this totalled 571,700m. francs CFA in 2016, contracting to 373,800m. francs CFA the year after, but then rebounding to 434,600m. in 2018; there was fresh shrinkage, to 398,500m. francs CFA, in 2019, before the deficit grew again, to 499,900m. in 2020.

The value of imports—measured in cost, insurance and freight value terms—has remained fairly stable, and totalled 1,340,500m. francs CFA in 2016 and 1,091,000m. francs CFA in 2017. It reached 1,176,000m. francs CFA in 2018, then 1,225,100m. francs CFA in 2019 and 1,246,500m. in 2020. Within this overall total, the value of imports of petroleum products—hugely influenced by fluctuating world oil prices—rose from 130,500m. francs CFA in 2017 to 166,900m. francs CFA the following year, yet by 2020 it had contracted to 139,900m. Imports of food have also been on a steady upward track, climbing from 142,300m. francs CFA in 2016 to 162,100m. francs CFA in 2019, but they dropped to 152,600m. the following year. Capital equipment imports can fluctuate, reflecting the episodic nature of procurement for major mining and development projects. Their value amounted to 323,300m. francs CFA in 2016, but then declined to 202,500m. francs CFA in 2017 and to 209,600m. francs CFA in 2018, before recovering to 287,000m. the year after, only to decline again, to 214,100m. francs CFA, in 2020.

Officially recorded exports from Togo, reached some 614,200m. francs CFA in 2016, then slipped back to 591,500m. francs CFA in 2017, recovered to 600,400m. francs CFA in 2018 and to 618,200m. francs CFA in 2019, and fell again, to 580,400m. in 2020. However, the value of the main exports actually produced in Togo is far short of the headline export totals, which include large volumes of cargo brought into the country but then re-exported. The main home-produced exports are phosphates, cotton and cocoa; gold is also exported, much having probably arrived in Togo informally from mine sites in neighbouring countries. Exports of phosphates fell from 59,200m. francs CFA in 2015 to just 39,600m. francs CFA in 2017; the value recovered to 46,200m. francs CFA the next year but declined to just 37,400m. francs CFA in 2019 and fell further, to 35,200m., in 2020. Exports of cotton declined from 37,400m. francs CFA in 2015 to 30,200m. francs CFA in 2016, before recovering to 42,300m. francs CFA in 2017, 49,100m. francs CFA in 2018 and 57,300m. francs CFA in 2019, before falling back to 46,500m. in 2020. Fluctuations in the value of cocoa exports may reflect the challenges the sector has faced, the impact on production of clearing old plants and, finally, a resurgence as improved varieties have begun to produce results: they sank from 14,600m. francs CFA in 2015 to 8,100m. francs CFA the following year and then to just 3,100m. francs CFA in 2017, before recovering to 5,100m. francs CFA in 2018, 5,900m. francs CFA in 2019 and 11,700m. francs CFA in 2020. Gold worth 14,600m. francs CFA was exported in 2016 and the value increased dramatically to 20,100m. francs CFA in 2017, before slumping to 10,200m. francs CFA the following year. No exports were recorded in 2019, but shipments reached 15,500m. in 2020. Cement is also exported, and shipments were worth 29,100m. francs CFA in 2016. Unusually for a West African country, on average, over the period 2015–19, Togo sent much of its exports to (48.1%) to sub-Saharan markets, which may partly reflect deliveries of phosphates for use in agricultural fertilizer; its largest individual markets were the United Arab Emirates (13.4%), Benin (9.8%) and India (8.5%). Only 7.6% of exports went to Europe.

Remittances from the Togolese diaspora make an important contribution to the balance of payments, rising from 86,600m. francs CFA in 2012 to 192,600m. francs CFA in 2016 and to 271,000m. francs CFA in 2020, despite the impact of the pandemic on economic activity in countries with large Togolese diaspora communities such as France and Benin. Fluctuations in the volume of foreign direct investment result from the one-off nature of projects, business launches, disposals and privatization acquisitions, and the net inflow declined from 150,600m. francs CFA in 2014 to just 53,700m. francs CFA in 2015, before rebounding to 179,700m. francs CFA in 2016; a net outflow of 70,300m. francs CFA followed in 2017 before a fresh net inflow of 139,500m. francs CFA the year after that; then came a fresh net outflow, of 177,400m. francs CFA in 2019, before a net surplus of 168,000m. francs CFA in 2020. Portfolio investment saw a net outflow of 160,500m. francs CFA in 2016 followed by inflows of 176,600m. francs CFA in 2017, then 91,900m. francs CFA in 2018, some 239,000m. francs CFA the year after and 168,000m. francs CFA in 2020.

Budget aid makes a small positive contribution to the balance of payments, with inflows of 11,300m. francs CFA in both 2016 and 2017, then 32,200m. francs CFA in 2018 and 20,400m. francs CFA in 2019.

Statistical Survey

Source (except where otherwise indicated): Institut national de la statistique et des études économiques et démographiques, BP 118, Lomé; tel. 22-21-62-24; e-mail inseed@inseed.tg; internet www.inseed.tg.

Area and Population

AREA, POPULATION AND DENSITY

Area (sq km)		56,600*
Population (census results)		
22 November 1981		2,719,567
19 November 2010		
Males		3,009,095
Females		3,182,060
Total		6,191,155
Population (UN estimates at mid-year)†		
2020		8,278,737
2021‡		8,478,242
2022‡		8,680,832
Density (per sq km) at mid-2022‡		153.4

* 21,853 sq miles.
† Source: UN, *World Population Prospects: The 2019 Revision*.
‡ Projection.

POPULATION BY AGE AND SEX
('000, UN projections at mid-2022)

	Males	Females	Total
0–14 years	1,739.3	1,728.6	3,468.0
15–64 years	2,464.4	2,491.1	4,955.5
65 years and over	117.7	139.7	257.4
Total	**4,321.4**	**4,359.4**	**8,680.8**

Note: Totals may not be equal to the sum of components, owing to rounding.

Source: UN, *World Population Prospects: The 2019 Revision*.

ADMINISTRATIVE DIVISIONS
(population estimates, 2013)

Region	Area (sq km)	Population	Density (per sq km)	Principal city
Centrale . .	13,317	647,300	48.6	Sokodé
Kara . . .	11,738	811,800	69.2	Kara
Maritime .	6,100	2,860,500	468.9	Lomé
Plateaux .	16,975	1,442,900	85.0	Atakpamé
Savanes . .	8,470	885,600	104.6	Dapaong
Total . .	**56,600**	**6,648,100**	**117.5**	

PRINCIPAL TOWNS
('000, official population projections, 2020 unless otherwise indicated)

Lomé (capital)* .	837.4	Atakpamé . . .	81.1
Kara	115.4	Dapaong . . .	69.9
Sokodé	109.2	Tsevie	56.2
Kpalimé	89.7		

* Figure as at 2010 census.

Mid-2022 (incl. suburbs, UN projection): Lomé (capital) 1,925,517 (Source: UN, *World Urbanization Prospects: The 2018 Revision*).

BIRTHS AND DEATHS
(annual averages, UN estimates)

	2005–10	2010–15	2015–20
Birth rate (per 1,000)	38.4	35.8	33.3
Death rate (per 1,000)	11.1	9.3	8.6

Source: UN, *World Population Prospects: The 2019 Revision*.

Life expectancy (years at birth, estimates): 61.3 (males 60.4; females 62.2) in 2020 (Source: World Bank, World Development Indicators database).

EMPLOYMENT

(persons aged 15 years and over, 2010 census)

	Males	Females	Total
Agriculture, hunting, forestry and fishing	520,470	487,868	1,008,338
Mining and quarrying	2,568	1,412	3,980
Manufacturing	131,082	167,266	298,348
Electricity, gas and water . . .	2,902	436	3,338
Construction	78,453	1,029	79,482
Trade, restaurants and hotels .	148,241	452,986	601,227
Transport, storage and communications	103,105	3,994	107,099
Financing, insurance, real estate and business services	28,411	8,490	36,901
Public administration	29,316	5,828	35,144
Education	48,901	10,397	59,298
Health and social work . . .	15,069	11,373	26,442
Community, social and personal services	27,669	60,842	88,511
Other services	3,004	18,700	21,704
Activities of extraterritorial organizations	1,566	411	1,977
Total employed	**1,140,757**	**1,231,032**	**2,371,789**

Mid-2015 (estimates in '000): Agriculture, etc. 1,488; Total labour force 2,960 (Source: FAO).

Health and Welfare

KEY INDICATORS

Total fertility rate (children per woman, 2020)	4.2
Under-5 mortality rate (per 1,000 live births, 2020) . . .	64.4
HIV/AIDS (% of persons aged 15–49, 2020)	2.0
COVID-19: Cumulative confirmed deaths (per 100,000 persons at 31 August 2022)	3.3
COVID-19: Fully vaccinated population (% of total population at 28 August 2022)	16.6
Physicians (per 1,000 head, 2019)	0.1
Hospitals (per 100,000 head, 2013)	0.6
Domestic health expenditure (2019): US $ per head (PPP) .	18.9
Domestic health expenditure (2019): % of GDP . . .	0.9
Domestic health expenditure (2019): public (% of total current expenditure)	15.1
Access to improved water resources (% of persons, 2020) .	69
Access to improved sanitation facilities (% of persons, 2020) .	19
Total carbon dioxide emissions ('000 metric tons, 2018) . .	2,260
Carbon dioxide emissions per head (metric tons, 2018) . .	0.3
Human Development Index (2021): ranking	162
Human Development Index (2021): value	0.539

Note: For data on COVID-19 vaccinations, 'fully vaccinated' denotes receipt of all doses specified by approved vaccination regime (Sources: Johns Hopkins University and Our World in Data). Data on health expenditure refer to current general government expenditure in each case. For more information on sources and further definitions for all indicators, see Health and Welfare Statistics: Sources and Definitions section (europaworld.com/credits).

Agriculture

PRINCIPAL CROPS

('000 metric tons)

	2018	2019	2020
Bambara beans	20.2	20.2	19.9
Bananas*	24.3	24.4	24.4
Beans, dry	207.6	202.7	217.6
Cashew nuts, with shell* . . .	8.3	8.0	8.1
Cassava (Manioc)	1,089.5	1,117.9	1,154.3
Cocoa beans†	7.5	10.6	10.0
Coconuts	11.2†	11.2*	10.9*
Coffee, green	19.1	21.3	17.4
Cotton lint*	45.6	58.5	n.a.
Groundnuts, with shell . . .	43.8	44.6	44.5
Karité nuts (Sheanuts)* . . .	13.3	13.0	13.0

—*continued*	2018	2019	2020
Maize	886.6	912.1	885.0
Millet	26.1	26.8	30.0
Oil palm fruit*	533.7	560.4	585.7
Oranges*	15.0	14.9	14.9
Rice, paddy	145.5	147.1	160.0
Seed cotton	137.3	116.6	102.5
Sorghum	277.2	282.6	279.0
Sweet potatoes	8.6	8.7	7.4
Taro (Cocoyam)	16.4	17.3	17.5
Yams	858.8	874.3	868.7

* FAO estimate(s).
† Unofficial figure(s).

Aggregate production ('000 metric tons, may include official, semi-official or estimated data): Total cereals 1,339.1 in 2018, 1,372.4 in 2019, 1,357.5 in 2020; Total fruit (primary) 66.9 in 2018, 66.9 in 2019, 66.8 in 2020; Total oilcrops 743.0 in 2018, 749.5 in 2019, 760.3 in 2020; Total pulses 229.2 in 2018, 224.4 in 2019, 239.0 in 2020; Total roots and tubers 1,979.5 in 2018, 2,024.7 in 2019, 2,054.1 in 2020; Total vegetables (primary) 148.5 in 2018, 149.0 in 2019, 149.5 in 2020.

Source: FAO.

LIVESTOCK

('000 head, year ending September)

	2018	2019	2020
Cattle	453.1	459.7	469.3
Chickens*	27,877	29,209	30,534
Goats	3,945.0	4,329.2	4,661.5
Pigs	1,057.1	1,085.5	1,120.8
Sheep	1,552.1	1,672.0	1,785.9

* FAO estimates.

Source: FAO.

LIVESTOCK PRODUCTS

('000 metric tons, FAO estimates unless otherwise indicated)

	2018	2019	2020
Cattle meat	5.7	5.7	6.4
Cows' milk*	11.5	11.6	11.5
Chicken meat	40.0	41.7	43.4
Game meat	6.0	6.1	6.0
Goat meat	7.7	8.6	9.7
Pig meat	19.0	19.5	20.4
Sheep meat	3.8	4.0	4.3
Hen eggs	24.3	24.3	23.7

* Official figures.

Source: FAO.

Forestry

ROUNDWOOD REMOVALS

('000 cubic metres, excluding bark, FAO estimates)

	2017	2018	2019
Sawlogs, veneer logs and logs for sleepers	166.0	166.0	166.0
Other industrial wood	80.0	18.1	21.9
Fuel wood*	4,424.0	4,424.0	4,424.0
Total	**4,670.0**	**4,608.1**	**4,611.9**

* Figure assumed to be unchanged since 2004.

2020: Production assumed to be unchanged from 2019 (FAO estimates).

Source: FAO.

SAWNWOOD PRODUCTION
('000 cubic metres, incl. railway sleepers, FAO estimates)

	2018	2019	2020
Total (all broadleaved) . . .	67.4	67.4	67.4

Note: Figures assumed to be unchanged from 2016.

Fishing

('000 metric tons, live weight)

	2018	2019	2020
Capture	24.6	25.5	18.0
Tilapias	4.5	4.5	4.3
Other freshwater fishes . . .	1.4	1.4	1.5
Round sardinella	1.8	1.9	2.7
European anchovy	10.6	10.6	4.6
Little tunny	1.0	1.0	0.3
Jacks, crevalles	0.3	0.3	0.4
Aquaculture	0.3	1.0	0.7
Total catch	24.9	26.5	18.8

Source: FAO.

Mining

('000 metric tons unless otherwise indicated)

	2017	2018	2019
Diamonds (carats)	2	—	—
Limestone*	1,800	1,800	1,800
Phosphate rock (gross weight) .	733	800*	800*
Phosphate content*	220	240	240

* Estimated production.

Source: US Geological Survey.

Industry

SELECTED PRODUCTS
('000 metric tons unless otherwise indicated)

	2017	2018	2019
Palm oil*	96.0	100.0	105.0
Cement†	2,400	2,570	2,570
Electrical energy (million kWh) .	690	589	723

* Unofficial figures.
† Estimated production.

Sources: FAO; US Geological Survey; UN Energy Statistics Database.

Finance

CURRENCY AND EXCHANGE RATES

Monetary Units
100 centimes = 1 franc de la Communauté Financière Africaine (CFA).

Sterling, Dollar and Euro Equivalents (31 May 2022)
£1 sterling = 770.824 francs CFA;
US $1 = 612.300 francs CFA;
€1 = 655.957 francs CFA;
10,000 francs CFA = £12.97 = $16.33 = €15.24.

Average Exchange Rate (francs CFA per US $)
2019   585.91
2020   575.59
2021   554.53

Note: An exchange rate of 1 French franc = 50 francs CFA, established in 1948, remained in force until January 1994, when the CFA franc was devalued by 50%, with the exchange rate adjusted to 1 French franc = 100 francs CFA. This relationship to French currency remained in effect with the introduction of the euro on 1 January 1999. From that date, accordingly, a fixed exchange rate of €1 = 655.957 francs CFA has been in operation.

BUDGET
('000 million francs CFA)

Revenue*	2018	2019†	2020‡
Tax revenue	491.9	551.4	603.0
Tax administration	259.8	292.5	327.2
Customs administration . .	232.1	258.9	275.8
Non-tax revenue	113.0	73.1	76.8
Total	604.9	624.5	679.9

Expenditure§	2018	2019†	2020‡
Current expenditure	532.2	548.9	614.2
Salaries and wages	200.4	214.6	239.1
Goods and services	144.9	125.9	143.9
Transfers and subsidies . .	116.5	122.6	131.3
Capital expenditure	201.7	129.7	329.4
Externally financed	130.9	122.5	194.5
Total	733.8	678.8	943.5

* Excluding grants received ('000 million francs CFA): 105.9 in 2018; 122.4 in 2019 (estimate); 138.6 in 2020 (projection).
† Estimates.
‡ Projections.
§ Including lending minus repayments.

Source: IMF, *Togo: Sixth Review under the Extended Credit Facility Arrangement and Request for Augmentation of Access—Press Release; Staff Report; and Statement by the Executive Director for Togo* (April 2020).

INTERNATIONAL RESERVES
(excluding gold, US $ million at 31 December)

	2019	2020	2021
IMF special drawing rights . .	159.1	301.9	490.4
Reserve position in IMF . . .	26.7	28.1	27.3
Foreign exchange	2.3	2.6	2.3
Total	188.1	332.6	519.9

Source: IMF, *International Financial Statistics.*

MONEY SUPPLY
('000 million francs CFA at 31 December)

	2019	2020	2021
Currency outside depository corporations	339.2	328.0	321.3
Transferable deposits	597.9	725.6	884.4
Other deposits	841.3	927.2	1,013.1
Broad money	1,778.4	1,980.8	2,218.9

Source: IMF, *International Financial Statistics.*

COST OF LIVING
(Consumer Price Index; base: 2014 = 100)

	2019	2020	2021
Food and non-alcoholic beverages .	106.1	111.2	122.1
Clothing and footwear	105.4	107.1	107.7
Housing, water, electricity, gas and other fuels	98.7	99.5	100.4
All items (incl. others) . . .	104.1	106.0	110.8

NATIONAL ACCOUNTS
(million francs CFA at current prices)

Expenditure on the Gross Domestic Product

	2018	2019	2020
Government final consumption expenditure	515,483	475,715	535,255
Private final consumption expenditure	2,986,766	3,130,465	3,172,289
Gross capital formation . . .	719,183	744,264	769,462
Total domestic expenditure	4,221,432	4,350,444	4,477,006
Exports of goods and services . .	949,931	1,021,947	909,046
Less Imports of goods and services	1,297,951	1,332,926	1,285,698
Statistical discrepancy	—	—	12,633
GDP in purchasers' values	3,873,412	4,039,465	4,112,986
GDP at constant 2015 prices .	3,816,981	3,954,392	3,982,073

Gross Domestic Product by Economic Activity

	2018	2019	2020
Agriculture, hunting, forestry and fishing	766,918	794,360	819,572
Mining, quarrying and utilities .	196,829	192,631	198,441
Manufacturing	516,685	542,005	545,201
Construction	106,679	105,150	111,395
Wholesale and retail trade, restaurants and hotels . . .	327,030	343,856	349,132
Transport, storage and communication	471,213	488,500	487,177
Other services	1,144,918	1,160,870	1,220,974
GDP at factor cost	3,530,272	3,627,372	3,731,892
Indirect taxes (net)*	343,140	412,093	381,094
GDP in purchasers' values .	3,873,412	4,039,465	4,112,986

* Figures obtained as a residual.

Source: UN National Accounts Main Aggregates Database.

BALANCE OF PAYMENTS
(US $ million)

	2018	2019	2020
Exports of goods	1,081.0	1,055.1	1,207.4
Imports of goods	−1,863.5	−1,812.0	−1,951.3
Balance on goods	−782.5	−756.9	−743.9
Exports of services	621.9	610.0	514.1
Imports of services	−465.4	−448.8	−437.9
Balance on goods and services	−626.0	−595.6	−667.6
Primary income received . . .	251.6	258.6	283.8
Primary income paid	−232.3	−236.5	−241.1
Balance on goods, services and primary income	−606.7	−573.5	−624.9
Secondary income received . .	561.9	657.7	710.2
Secondary income paid . . .	−140.0	−139.7	−106.0
Current balance	−184.9	−55.4	−20.7
Capital account (net)	316.4	289.9	372.8
Direct investment assets . . .	−70.2	−42.8	112.3
Direct investment liabilities . .	−181.0	345.7	−59.2
Portfolio investment assets . .	−89.5	−181.8	−485.0
Portfolio investment liabilities .	−80.5	−327.0	17.6
Other investment assets . . .	−56.9	−55.3	−265.4
Other investment liabilities . .	122.1	572.6	388.0
Net errors and omissions . . .	−8.2	9.0	14.6
Reserves and related items .	−232.6	554.8	74.9

Source: IMF, *International Financial Statistics.*

External Trade

PRINCIPAL COMMODITIES
(distribution by HS, US $ million)

Imports c.i.f.	2019	2020	2021
Live animals and animal products	82.2	74.0	83.8
Vegetables and vegetable products	86.0	109.9	100.4
Cereals	51.9	78.4	70.9
Animal or vegetable fats and oils, and product thereof .	62.9	74.3	77.7
Palm oil and its fractions . . .	59.5	68.0	70.8
Prepared foodstuffs; beverages, spirits, vinegars; tobacco and articles thereof .	133.0	124.6	164.4
Mineral products	275.2	281.1	279.5
Salt; sulphur; earths and stone; plastering materials, lime and cement	30.6	42.6	78.8
Mineral fuels, oils, distillation products, etc.	244.6	235.4	198.9
Non-crude petroleum oils . .	65.5	70.1	90.7
Petroleum coke, petroleum bitumen, etc.	31.5	28.1	75.0
Chemicals and related products	248.8	260.9	268.7
Pharmaceutical products . . .	132.8	121.2	143.9
Medicament mixtures put in dosage	119.5	110.6	103.3
Plastics, rubber, and articles thereof	166.7	165.0	206.0
Plastics and articles thereof . .	152.6	147.1	183.8
Polymers of ethylene in primary forms	83.6	73.1	92.2
Textiles and textile articles	173.9	183.4	220.6
Cotton	64.7	47.3	47.9
Iron and steel; other base metals and articles of base metal	147.0	142.0	203.4
Iron and steel	91.1	59.0	97.7
Machinery and mechanical appliances; electrical equipment; parts thereof	271.5	305.4	327.3
Machinery and boilers, etc. . .	148.8	180.1	191.8
Electrical, electronic equipment .	122.7	125.3	135.6
Vehicles, aircraft, vessels and associated transport equipment	182.0	279.1	361.8
Vehicles other than railway, tramway	179.6	275.6	354.5
Motor cars and other motor vehicles	58.1	84.3	113.1
Motorcycles	58.4	72.9	133.0
Total (incl. others)	1,964.4	2,160.2	2,493.1

Exports f.o.b.	2019	2020	2021
Vegetables and vegetable products	46.6	58.1	52.7
Oil seeds and oleaginous fruits; miscellaneous grains, seeds and fruit	21.5	34.0	29.9
Animal or vegetable fats and oils, and products thereof	42.6	75.1	64.7
Palm oil	36.2	63.8	56.8
Prepared foodstuffs; beverages, spirits, vinegars; tobacco and articles thereof	68.3	88.4	97.9
Beverages, spirits and vinegar	31.9	43.8	54.9
Waters, incl. mineral waters	7.5	12.0	14.5
Mineral products	347.9	233.4	277.6
Salt, sulphur, earth, stone, plaster, lime and cement	175.4	173.1	205.3
Calcium and aluminium calcium phosphates, natural and phosphatic chalk, etc.	78.3	86.0	129.2
Cements, portland, aluminous, slag, supersulphate, etc.	93.8	81.5	69.3
Mineral fuels, oils, distillation products, etc.	172.5	60.3	72.3
Non-crude petroleum oils	50.1	52.4	64.9
Chemicals and related products	87.1	97.9	81.8
Essential oils, perfumes, cosmetics and toiletries	75.1	82.1	71.0
Beauty, make-up and skin-care preparations, sunscreen, etc.	73.1	81.2	69.9
Plastics, rubber, and articles thereof	105.6	127.1	125.2
Plastics and articles thereof	105.0	125.9	124.0
Plastic packing goods or closures, stoppers, lids, caps, etc.	73.5	87.6	82.6
Textiles and textile articles	144.7	100.1	108.3
Cotton	125.1	83.7	91.0
Cotton, not carded or combed	97.8	63.5	65.1
Footwear, headgear, umbrellas, walking sticks, etc.	24.6	32.9	56.9
Vehicles, aircraft, vessels and associated transport equipment	66.7	82.6	101.7
Vehicles other than railway or tramway rolling stock	61.7	76.0	94.0
Total (incl. others)	1,025.3	980.1	1,069.3

Source: Trade Map-Trade Competitiveness Map, International Trade Centre, marketanalysis.intracen.org.

PRINCIPAL TRADING PARTNERS
(US $ million)

Imports c.i.f.	2019	2020	2021
Belgium	35.6	49.8	54.6
Brazil	25.6	34.7	37.3
China, People's Republic	403.1	439.9	556.5
Côte d'Ivoire	34.3	33.6	31.2
Denmark	6.9	23.6	14.6
Egypt	20.3	12.9	47.3
France (incl. Monaco)	150.2	185.2	216.5
Germany	54.3	76.3	82.7
Ghana	117.7	121.7	72.7
Greece	19.4	28.9	62.3
India	88.9	162.3	175.4
Indonesia	38.0	37.9	38.4
Italy	30.7	34.1	32.2
Japan	77.9	93.7	108.6
Korea, Republic	20.1	22.1	23.1
Malaysia	49.7	57.9	71.9
Mauritania	20.7	18.9	11.5
Morocco	23.9	20.5	37.2
Netherlands	86.6	56.7	61.4
Nigeria	100.9	77.4	52.2

Imports c.i.f.—*continued*	2019	2020	2021
Russian Federation	16.9	29.0	40.7
Saudi Arabia	51.8	49.5	57.8
Singapore	4.9	25.9	1.4
South Africa	22.9	23.1	35.5
Spain	28.5	37.1	84.1
Türkiye	41.2	70.8	71.9
Ukraine	29.2	9.7	34.5
United Arab Emirates	25.5	48.5	41.2
USA	121.5	58.0	60.4
Total (incl. others)	1,964.4	2,160.2	2,493.1

Exports f.o.b.	2019	2020	2021
Australia	12.1	11.7	32.0
Bangladesh	1.8	3.5	11.7
Belgium	9.5	11.4	6.5
Benin	218.2	97.9	116.2
Burkina Faso	132.6	134.9	153.4
China, People's Republic	9.3	24.2	8.2
Côte d'Ivoire	74.0	62.1	84.7
France (incl. Monaco)	53.9	55.8	61.5
Ghana	79.5	79.5	93.9
India	107.0	73.4	78.2
Malaysia	26.7	21.8	7.3
Mali	74.8	127.3	118.9
Niger	81.9	83.5	87.0
Nigeria	35.1	39.3	30.7
Pakistan	7.7	6.9	31.2
Senegal	13.3	48.6	46.7
Türkiye	4.6	3.8	12.0
USA	4.7	11.6	10.7
Viet Nam	11.6	8.1	3.5
Total (incl. others)	1,025.3	980.1	1,069.3

Source: Trade Map-Trade Competitiveness Map, International Trade Centre, marketanalysis.intracen.org.

Transport

RAILWAYS
(traffic)

	1997	1998	1999
Passengers carried ('000)	152.0	35.0	4.4
Freight carried ('000 metric tons)	250	759	1,090
Passenger-km (million)	12.7	3.4	0.4
Freight ton-km (million)	28.8	70.6	92.4

Source: Société Nationale des Chemins de Fer du Togo, Lomé.

SHIPPING

Flag Registered Fleet
(at 31 December)

	2019	2020	2021
Number of vessels	517	496	487
Total displacement ('000 grt)	1,264.4	1,559.9	1,848.1

Source: Lloyd's List Intelligence (www.bit.ly/LLintelligence).

CIVIL AVIATION
(traffic on scheduled services)

	2013	2014	2015
Kilometres flown (million)	9	8	7
Passengers carried ('000)	841	779	770
Passenger-km (million)	696	645	655
Total ton-km (million)	32	34	n.a.

Source: UN, *Statistical Yearbook*.

2020 (domestic and international): Departures 6,191; Passengers carried 320,806; Freight carried 9.83m. ton-km (Source: World Bank, World Development Indicators database).

Tourism

FOREIGN TOURIST ARRIVALS*

	2018	2019	2020
Belgium	19,830	26,145	2,363
Benin	36,469	65,753	28,914
Burkina Faso	16,788	31,643	12,619
Cameroon	10,163	14,693	8,157
Côte d'Ivoire	37,404	55,478	25,560
Ethiopia	46,445	39,848	43,031
France	91,582	132,630	48,708
Germany	9,216	19,568	13,038
Ghana	18,244	30,720	7,681
India	11,787	18,728	25,968
Morocco	18,547	27,495	9,003
Nigeria	17,548	40,785	9,722
Senegal	18,109	25,305	14,165
South Africa	4,234	10,320	12,163
USA	26,532	38,708	15,449
Total (incl. others)	573,136	876,326	481,769

* Arrivals at hotels and similar establishments, by country of residence.

Receipts from tourism (US $ million, excl. passenger transport): 119 in 2016; 138 in 2017; 153 in 2018.

Source: World Tourism Organization.

Communications Media

	2018	2019	2020
Telephones (main lines in use)	37,691	43,605	46,499
Mobile telephone subscriptions ('000)	6,144.5	6,239.2	6,516.5
Broadband subscriptions, fixed .	26,156	31,899	52,706
Broadband subscriptions, mobile ('000)	2,524.3	3,322.2	2,591.7
Internet users (% of population) .	15.5	19.3	24.0

Source: International Telecommunication Union.

Education

(2019/20 unless otherwise indicated)

	Institutions*	Teachers	Students		
			Males	Females	Total
Pre-primary .	3,120	7,598	102,228	105,275	207,503
Primary . . .	7,662	41,685	831,635	802,806	1,634,441
Secondary . .	2,385	30,494	422,540†	305,409†	727,949†
Tertiary . . .	83	5,361	73,821	41,135	114,956

* 2018/19 figures.
† 2016/17 figure.

Source: mostly UNESCO Institute for Statistics.

Pupil-teacher ratio (qualified teaching staff, primary education, UNESCO estimate): 90.7 in 2019/20 (Source: UNESCO Institute for Statistics).

Adult literacy rate (UNESCO estimates): 66.5% (males 80.0%; females 55.1%) in 2019 (Source: UNESCO Institute for Statistics).

Directory

The Constitution

The Constitution that was approved in a national referendum on 27 September 1992, and subsequently amended (most recently in May 2019), defines the rights, freedoms and obligations of Togolese citizens, and defines the separation of powers among the executive, legislative and judicial organs of state.

Executive power is vested in the President of the Republic, who is elected, by direct universal adult suffrage, with a five-year mandate, renewable once. The legislature, the National Assembly, is similarly elected for a period of six years, its 91 members being directly elected by universal suffrage. The President of the Republic appoints a Prime Minister who is able to command a majority in the legislature, and the Prime Minister, in consultation with the President, appoints other government ministers. A Constitutional Court is designated as the highest court of jurisdiction in constitutional matters.

The Government

HEAD OF STATE

President: FAURE ESSOZIMNA GNASSINGBÉ (inaugurated 4 May 2005; re-elected 4 March 2010, 25 April 2015 and 22 February 2020).

COUNCIL OF MINISTERS
(October 2022)

Prime Minister: VICTOIRE SIDÉMÉHO TOMÉGAH-DOGBÉ.

Minister of State, Minister of Territorial Administration, Decentralization and Territorial Development: PAYADOWA BOUKPESSI.

Minister of Trade, Industry and Local Consumption: KODJO SÉVON-TÉPÉ ADÉDZÉ.

Minister of the Civil Service, Labour and Social Dialogue: GILBERT BAWARA.

Minister of the Digital Economy and Digital Transformation: CINA LAWSON.

Minister of Security and Civil Protection: Gen. DAMEHAME YARK.

Minister of Road, Rail and Air Transport: AFFOH ATCHA-DÉDJI.

Minister, Secretary-General of the Presidency: ABLAMBA AHOÉ-FAVI JOHNSON.

Minister of the Environment and Forestry Resources: KATARI FOLI-BAZI.

Minister of Water and Village Water Supply: BOLIDJA TIEM.

Minister of the Economy and Finance: SANI YAYA.

Minister of Primary, Secondary and Technical Education and of Handicrafts: Prof. KOMLA DODZI KOKOROKO.

Minister of Foreign Affairs, Regional Integration and Togolese Abroad: Prof. ROBERT DUSSEY.

Minister of Agriculture, Stockbreeding and Rural Development: ANTOINE LÉKPA GBEGBENI.

Minister of the Armed Forces: ESSOSSIMNA MARGUERITE GNAKADÈ.

Minister, Secretary-General of the Government: KANKA-MALICK NATCHABA.

Keeper of the Seals, Minister of Justice and Legislation: PIUS AGBÉTOMEY.

Minister of Public Works: ZOURÉHATOU TCHA-KONDO KASSA-TRAORÉ.

Minister of Health, Public Hygiene and Universal Access to Health Care: Prof. MOUSTAFA MIJIYAWA.

Minister of Human Rights, Citizenship Training and Relations with the Institutions, Government Spokesperson: Dr ENINAM MASSIA CHRISTIAN TRIMUA.

Minister responsible for Financial Inclusion and the Organization of the Informal Sector: MAZAMESSO ASSIH.

Minister of Improving Access to Isolated Regions and of Rural Tracks: BOURAÏMA KANFITINE TCHÉDÉ-ISSA.

Minister of Higher Education and Research: Prof. MAJESTÉ IHOU WATÉBA.

Minister of Basic Development, Youth and Youth Employment: MYRIAM DOSSOU-D'ALMEIDA.

Minister of the Maritime Economy, Fisheries and Coastal Protection: EDEM KOKOU TENGUÉ.

Minister of Social Action, the Promotion of Women and Literacy: ADJOVI LONLONGNO APEDO-ANAKOMA.

Minister of Investment Promotion: KAYI MIVEDOR.

Minister of Urban Planning, Housing and Land Reform: KOFFI TSOLENYANOU.

Minister of Communication and Media, Government Spokesperson: Prof. AKODAH AYÉWOUADAN.

Minister of Sport and Leisure: LIDI KEDEKA BESSI-KAMA.

Minister of Culture and Tourism: KOSSI GBÉNYO LAMADOKOU.

Minister-delegate to the Minister of Territorial Administration, Decentralization and Territorial Development, responsible for Territorial Development: ESSOMANAM EDJÉBA.

Minister-delegate to the Minister of Health, Public Hygiene and Universal Access to Health Care, responsible for Universal Access to Health Care: Dr MAMESSILÉ AKLAH AGBA-ASSIH.

Minister-delegate to the President, responsible for Energy and Mining: MAWOUNYO MILA AZIABLÉ.

Minister-delegate to the Minister of Primary, Secondary and Technical Education and Handicrafts, responsible for Technical Education and Handicrafts: KOKOU EKÉ HODIN.

MINISTRIES

Office of the President: Palais Présidentiel, ave de la Marina, Lomé; tel. 22-21-27-01; internet presidence.gouv.tg.

Office of the Prime Minister: Palais de la Primature, Cité OUA, BP 1161, Lomé; tel. 22-61-06-05; internet primature.gouv.tg.

Ministry of the Armed Forces: Lomé; internet defense.gouv.tg.

Ministry of Agriculture, Stockbreeding and Rural Development: 5 ave de Duisburg, BP 385, Lomé; tel. 22-20-54-73; e-mail presse@agriculture.gouv.tg; internet agriculture.gouv.tg.

Ministry of Basic Development, Youth and Youth Employment: 37 Cité OUA, BP 1299, Lomé; tel. 22-31-37-44; e-mail mindevbasemarche@outlook.fr; internet devbase.gouv.tg.

Ministry of the Civil Service, Labour and Social Dialogue: angle de la Marina et rue Kpalimé, BP 372, Lomé; tel. 22-21-41-83; internet fonctionpublique.gouv.tg.

Ministry of Communication and Media: 26 ave de Nangbéto, BP 40, Lomé; tel. 22-21-29-30; internet communication.gouv.tg.

Ministry of Culture and Tourism: Lomé; internet tourisme.gouv.tg.

Ministry of the Digital Economy and Digital Transformation: ave de Sarakawa, BP 389, Lomé; tel. 22-23-14-00; internet numerique.gouv.tg.

Ministry of the Economy and Finance: CASEF, ave Sarakawa, BP 387, Lomé; tel. 22-21-35-54; e-mail minifin@yahoo.fr; internet www.finances.gouv.tg.

Ministry of the Environment and Forestry Resources: 590 ave Sarakawa, BP 4825, Lomé; tel. 22-21-28-97; e-mail merf-togo@yahoo.fr; internet environnement.gouv.tg.

Ministry of Foreign Affairs, Regional Integration and Togolese Abroad: pl. du Monument aux Morts, ave Georges Pompidou, BP 900, Lomé; tel. 22-21-29-10; e-mail maeirtgce@yahoo.fr; internet diplomatie.gouv.tg.

Ministry of Health, Public Hygiene and Universal Access to Health Care: rue Branly, BP 386, Lomé; tel. 22-21-35-24; internet sante.gouv.tg.

Ministry of Higher Education and Research: angle rue 2 février, ave Sarakawa, BP 12175, Lomé; tel. 22-22-09-83; e-mail mesrtogo@yahoo.fr; internet edusup.gouv.tg.

Ministry of Human Rights, Citizenship Training and Relations with the Institutions: Lomé; internet droitsdelhomme.gouv.tg.

Ministry of Improving Access to Isolated Regions and of Rural Tracks: Lomé.

Ministry of Investment Promotion: 2564 ave de la Chance, Bè Klikamé, BP 3250, Lomé; e-mail contact@investissement.gouv.tg; tel. 22-53-53-72; internet investissement.gouv.tg.

Ministry of Justice and Legislation: 3 rue de l'Ocam, BP 121, Lomé; tel. 22-21-26-53; internet justice.gouv.tg.

Ministry of the Maritime Economy, Fisheries and Coastal Protection: Lomé; internet maritime.gouv.tg.

Ministry of Mining and Energy: rue des Hydrocarbures, BP 4227, Lomé; tel. 22-21-20-04; internet www.mines.gouv.tg.

Ministry of Primary, Secondary and Technical Education and of Handicrafts: ave de Sarakawa, BP 398, Lomé; internet education.gouv.tg.

Ministry of Public Works: Lomé.

Ministry of Road, Rail and Air Transport: Lomé; internet transports.gouv.tg.

Ministry of Security and Civil Protection: rue Albert Sarraut, Lomé; tel. 22-22-57-12; internet securite.gouv.tg.

Ministry of Social Action, the Promotion of Women and Literacy: face ave de la Présidence, Ancien Immeuble de la Direction des Impôts, 1e étage, BP 369, Lomé; tel. 22-21-68-79; internet actionsociale.gouv.tg.

Ministry of Sport and Leisure: rue Yoti, BP 3193, Lomé; tel. 22-22-10-53; e-mail secretariat.ministre@sports.gouv.tg; internet sports.gouv.tg.

Ministry of Territorial Administration, Decentralization and Territorial Development: ave de la Présidence, BP 390, Lomé; tel. 22-22-57-16; internet territoire.gouv.tg.

Ministry of Trade, Industry and Local Consumption: 1 ave de Sarakawa, face au Monument aux Morts, BP 383, Lomé; tel. 22-21-20-25; e-mail ministereducommercetogo@yahoo.fr; internet commerce.gouv.tg.

Ministry of Urban Planning, Housing and Land Reform: BP 14182, Lomé; tel. 22-22-55-94; internet urbanisme.gouv.tg.

Ministry of Water and Village Water Supply: Lomé; internet eau.gouv.tg.

President

Presidential Election, 22 February 2020

Candidate	Valid votes	% of valid votes
Faure Gnassingbé (UNIR)	1,760,309	70.78
Agbéyomé Gabriel Kodjo (MPDD)	483,926	19.46
Jean-Pierre Fabre (ANC)	116,336	4.68
Aimé Tchabouré Gogué (ADDI)	59,777	2.40
Komi Wolou (PSR)	29,791	1.20
Georges-William Assiongbon Kouessan (SP)	19,923	0.80
Mouhamed Tchassona Traoré (MCD)	16,814	0.68
Total	**2,486,876**	**100.00**

Legislature

National Assembly: Palais des Congrès, BP 327, Lomé; tel. 22-22-57-91; e-mail asnato@tg.refer.org; internet assemblee-nationale.tg.

President: YAWA DJIGBODI TSÉGAN.

General Election, 20 December 2018

Party	Seats
Union pour la République (UNIR)	59
Union des Forces du Changement (UFC)	7
Nouvel Engagement Togolais (NET)	3
Mouvement Patriotique pour la Démocratie et le Développement (MPDD)	2
Mouvement des Républicains Centristes (MRC)	1
Parti Démocratique Panafricain (PDP)	1
Ind.*	18
Total	**91**

* Comprising the following independent groups: Cercle de Réflexion et d'Action pour le Développement—CRAD (three seats); Duanényo (two seats); ISOPE (two seats); Liste des Indépendants pour la République—LIR (two seats); Pour Construire (two seats); Bâtir (two seats); Allolédou Vo (two seats); Avé en Marche (one seat); Conscience Patriotique (one seat); and Nouvelle Vision (one seat).

Election Commission

Commission Electorale Nationale Indépendante (CENI): blvd Eyadema, Cité OUA, BP 7005, Lomé; tel. 22-53-61-00; e-mail info@

ceni-tg.org; internet www.ceni-tg.org; 17 mems; Pres. TCHAMBAKOU AYASSOR.

Political Organizations

Alliance des Démocrates pour le Développement Intégral (ADDI): Lomé; tel. 22-21-47-90; Leader Prof. AIMÉ TCHABOURÉ GOGUÉ.

Alliance Nationale pour le Changement (ANC): Lomé; e-mail sncom@anctogo.com; internet www.anctogo.com; f. 2010; Pres. JEAN-PIERRE FABRE; Sec.-Gen. CODJO DELAVA KOMLAN.

Comité d'Action pour le Renouveau (CAR): 58 ave du 24 janvier, BP 06, Lomé; tel. 22-22-05-66; moderately conservative; Pres. (vacant).

Convention Démocratique des Peuples Africains—Branche Togolaise (CDPA—BT): 5 rue Djidjollé, BP 13963, Lomé; tel. 22-25-38-46; e-mail cdpa-bt.cdpa-bt@orange.fr; f. 1991; pan-Africanist; First Sec. Prof. EMMANUEL Y. GU-KONU.

Convergence Patriotique Panafricaine (CPP): BP 12703, Lomé; tel. 22-21-58-43; f. 1999; Pres. EMMANUEL ANANI AKOLI.

Front des Patriotes pour la Démocratie (FPD): Lomé; f. 2014; Pres. DJIMON ORÉ.

Mouvement Citoyen pour la Démocratie et le Développement (MCD): Lomé; f. 2007; Founding Pres. MOUHAMED TCHASSONA TRAORÉ.

Mouvement Patriotique pour la Démocratie et le Développement (MPDD): Quartier Djidjole, 688 rue 129 Aflao Gakli, Lomé; tel. 22-51-95-95; internet fb.com/MPDD.LesPatriotes; f. 2008 as the Organisation pour Bâtir dans l'Union un Togo Solidaire; present name adopted in 2018; Pres. AGBÉYOMÉ MESSAN KODJO; Sec.-Gen. COMBÉTÉ PASCAL COMBEY.

Nouvel Engagement Togolais (NET): Lomé; tel. 91815052; internet fb.com/Nouvel.Engagement.Togolais; Pres. GERRY TAAMA.

Pacte Socialiste pour le Renouveau (PSR): Quartier Agbalé-pédogan, BP 8520, Lomé; tel. 90-03-38-05; e-mail kwoloup@gmail.com; internet www.psr-togo.org; Sec.-Gen. KOMI WOLOU.

Parti Démocratique Panafricain (PDP): Lomé; f. 2005; Leader INNOCENT KAGBARA.

Parti National Panafricain (PNP): Lomé; f. 2014; Leader TIKPI ATCHADAM.

Parti du Renouveau et de la Rédemption (PRR): Quartier Kodjoviakopé, 34 rue Alédjo, Lomé; tel. 22-32-98-49; e-mail lerenouveau2003@yahoo.fr; internet www.prr-togo.com; Pres. JEAN NICOLAS MESSAN LAWSON.

Parti Social Démocrate du Togo (PSDT): Lomé; e-mail info@psdt-info.org; internet psdt-info.org; 2014; First Sec. LAURENT LATÉ DANKOU LAWSON.

Parti des Togolais: BP 665, Lomé; tel. 97348214; e-mail info@partidestogolais.org; internet fb.com/partidestogolais; Pres. NATHANIEL OLYMPIO.

Parti des Travailleurs (PT): 49 ave de Calais, BP 13974, Nyékonakpoé, Lomé; tel. 90136554; socialist; Co-ordinating Sec. CLAUDE AMEGANVI.

Santé du Peuple (SP): Lomé; Pres. GEORGES-WILLIAM ASSIONGBON KOUESSAN.

Union des Forces de Changement (UFC): 59 rue Koudadzé, Lom-Nava, BP 62168, Lomé; tel. 22-21-33-32; e-mail contact-togo@ufctogo.com; internet www.ufctogo.com; f. 1992; social-democratic; Pres. GILCHRIST OLYMPIO; Sec.-Gen. TEDDY EDWARDS MENSAH.

Union des Libéraux Indépendants (ULI): f. 1993 to succeed Union des Démocrates pour le Renouveau; Leader KWAMI MENSAN JACQUES AMOUZOU.

Union pour la République (UNIR): 572 rue Pydal Tokoin Wuiti, BP 1208, Lomé; tel. 22-26-04-95; e-mail unir.tgofficiel@gmail.com; internet www.unir.tg; f. 1969 as Rassemblement du Peuple Togolais; sole legal party 1969–91; present name adopted in 2012; Pres. FAURE GNASSINGBÉ; Exec. Sec. AKLESSO ATCHOLI.

Diplomatic Representation

EMBASSIES IN TOGO

Angola: blvd du 13 janvier, Lomé; tel. 221-72-11; Ambassador (vacant).

Brazil: rue 125, Maison 35, Cité OUA, près de la Primature, BP 916, Lomé; tel. 22-61-56-59; e-mail brasemb.lome@itamaraty.gov.br; internet www.gov.br/mre/pt-br/embaixada-lome; Ambassador NEI FUTURO BITENCOURT.

China, People's Republic: 2000 Cité OUA, BP 2690, Lomé; tel. 22-61-40-88; e-mail chinaemb_tg@mfa.gov.cn; internet tg.china-embassy.gov.cn; Ambassador CHAO WEIDONG.

Congo, Democratic Republic: Lomé; tel. 22-21-51-55; Ambassador LOKOKA IKUKELE BOMOLO.

Egypt: Cité OUA, rue 168, BP 8, Lomé; tel. 22-26-24-43; e-mail embassy.lome@mfa.gov.eg; Ambassador AHMED ADEL AHMED EL-SAMARI.

France: 13 ave Mama Fousséni, BP 337, Lomé; tel. 22-23-46-00; internet tg.ambafrance.org; Ambassador JOCELYNE CABALLERO.

Gabon: blvd Jean Paul II, BP 12025, Lomé; tel. 22-26-75-63; e-mail ambagabontbg@yahoo.fr; internet ambagabon-togo.com; High Commissioner SAYID ABELOKO.

Germany: blvd de la République, BP 1175, Lomé; tel. 22-23-32-32; e-mail amballtogo@cafe.tg; internet lome.diplo.de; Ambassador MATTHIAS VELTIN.

Ghana: 38 rue Moyama, BP 92, Lomé; tel. 22-21-31-94; e-mail lome@mfa.gov.gh; internet ghanaembassy-togo.com; High Commissioner KOFI DEMETIA.

Holy See: BP 20790, Lomé; tel. 22-26-03-06; e-mail noncia.tg@gmail.com; Apostolic Nuncio MARK GERARD MILES (Titular Archbishop of Città Ducale).

India: 92 rue de la Primature, Cité OUA, Lomé; tel. 22-60-85-50; e-mail hoc.lome@mea.gov.in; internet www.embassyofindialome.gov.in; High Commissioner SANJIV TANDON.

Libya: Cité OUA, BP 4872, Lomé; tel. 22-61-47-08; Ambassador AHMED BALLUZ.

Niger: Lomé; tel. 22-21-63-73; Ambassador SIDI ZAKARI.

Nigeria: 311 blvd du 13 janvier, BP 1189, Lomé; tel. 22-21-34-55; High Commissioner JULIUS ADESINA.

Senegal: 1391 blvd de la Kara, Lomé; tel. 22-22-98-35; e-mail ambassenelome@yahoo.fr; Ambassador ROKHAYA BÂ.

Türkiye (Turkey): 02 BP 20308, Lomé; tel. 705689141; e-mail ambassade.lome@mfa.gov.tr; internet lome.be.mfa.gov.tr/Mission; Ambassador ESRA DEMIR.

USA: blvd Eyadéma, BP 852, Lomé; tel. 22-61-54-70; internet tg.usembassy.gov; Ambassador ELIZABETH ANNE NOSEWORTHY FITZSIMMONS.

Judicial System

Justice is administered by the Constitutional Court, the Supreme Court, two Courts of Appeal and the Tribunaux de Première Instance, which hear civil, commercial and criminal cases. There is a labour tribunal and a tribunal for children's rights.

Constitutional Court: Cité OUA, Villa No. 15, BP 1331, Lomé; tel. 22-61-06-40; internet courconstitutionnelle.tg; f. 1997; 9 mems; Pres. ABOUDOU ASSOUMA.

Supreme Court: BP 906, Lomé; tel. 22-21-22-58; e-mail coursupremeto@yahoo.fr; f. 1961; consists of 2 chambers (judicial and administrative); Pres. ABDOULAYE YAYA.

Courts of Appeal: located at Lomé (lacourdappeldelome.com) and Kara; Pres. (Lomé) DINDANGUE KOMINTE; Pres. (Kara) NTIFAFATO MOTI.

Audit Court (Cour des Comptes): Quartier Wuiti, blvd Léopold Sedar Senghor, BP 1336, Lomé; tel. 22-61-05-10; e-mail cour_descomptes@yahoo.fr; internet www.courdescomptes.tg; f. 2009; Pres. JEAN KOFFI EDOH.

State Attorney: MAWAMA TALAKA.

Religion

It is estimated that about 50% of the population follow traditional animist beliefs, some 35% are Christians and 15% are Muslims.

CHRISTIANITY

The Roman Catholic Church

Togo comprises one archdiocese and six dioceses.

Bishops' Conference: Conférence des Evêques du Togo, 561 rue Aniko Palako, BP 348, Lomé; tel. 22-61-36-29; e-mail cetogo2013@yahoo.com; internet www.cet.tg; statutes approved 1979; Pres. Most Rev. BENOÎT COMLAN MESSAN ALOWONOU (Bishop of Kpalimé).

Archbishop of Lomé: Most Rev. NICODÈME BARRIGAH BÉNISSAN, Archevêché, 561 rue Aniko Palako, BP 348, Lomé; tel. 22-22-26-10; e-mail archlom@yahoo.cfr; internet www.archidiocesedelome.org.

Protestant Churches

L'Eglise des Assemblées de Dieu du Togo: 173 ave Duisburg, BP 2527, Lomé; tel. 98095895; e-mail contact@eadtogo.tg; internet fb .com/eadtogo; Nat. Pres. DJAKOUTI MITRÉ; Sec.-Gen. AYI ADADE.

Eglise Evangélique Luthérienne au Togo: POB 80780, Lomé; tel. 22-25-23-51; Pres. Rev. KOFFI GAWU SALLAH HUKPORTI.

Eglise Evangélique Presbytérienne du Togo (EEPT): 1 rue Tokmake, BP 2, Lomé; tel. 22-21-46-69; e-mail blocsynodal@ eept-online.net; internet www.eept-online.net; Moderator Rev. Dr DANIEL MAWUSSI AKOTIA.

Fédération des Evangéliques du Togo: Lomé; Co-ordinator HAPPY AZIADEKEY.

BAHÁ'Í FAITH

Assemblée Spirituelle Nationale: BP 1659, Lomé; tel. 22-21-21-99; e-mail asnbaha@yahoo.fr; Sec. BOUROGOUTAMA TARENOA.

The Press

DAILY NEWSPAPERS (PRINT AND ONLINE)

Le Clik: Lomé; tel. 93152916; e-mail leclikinfo@gmail.com; internet leclik.com; Online-only.

Forum de la Semaine: BP 81129, Lomé; tel. 22-61-36-32; e-mail forumhebdo7@yahoo.fr; internet forumdelasemaine.tg; Dir DIMAS DZIKODO.

Liberté: 21 rue des Ormes-Hanoukopé, 08 BP 80744, Lomé; tel. 90335380; e-mail libertehebdo2@gmail.com; internet libertetogo .info; Dir of Publication MÉDARD AMETÉPÉ.

Nouvelle Expression: blvd du 30 Août, Soviépé, BP 2587, Lomé; tel. 22-36-05-12; e-mail expression@yahoo.com; Dir of Publication RAPHAËL H. TOMEGAH.

Togo-Presse: BP 891, Lomé; tel. 22-21-37-18; e-mail info@ togopresse.tg; internet togopresse.tg; f. 1961; official govt publ; French, Kabiyé and Ewe; political, economic and cultural.

La Voix de la Nation: Lomé; tel. 90116133; e-mail contact@ lavoixdelanation.info; internet lavoixdelanation.info; Online-only.

PERIODICALS

L'Alternative: BP 41632, Lomé; tel. 90094133; bi-weekly; Dir of Publication FERDINAND MENSAH AYITE; Editor-in-Chief ISIDORE KOUWONOU.

Le Canard Indépendant: 63 rue Bèkpo Tokoin Ouest, Lomé; tel. 99472410; weekly; Dir of Publication AUGUSTIN KOFFI AMEGA.

Carrefour: 596 rue Ablogame, BP 6125, Lomé; tel. 99444543; f. 1991; pro-opposition; weekly; Dir HOLONOU HOUKPATI.

Le Combat du Peuple: 62 rue Blagogee, BP 4682, Lomé; tel. 90045383; f. 1994; pro-opposition weekly; Editor LUCIEN DJOSSOU MESSAN.

Le Correcteur: Casier 23, Lomé; tel. 98050958; e-mail honoson84@ yahoo.fr; internet www.lecorrecteur.info; Dir of Publication OLIVIER K. GLAKPE.

Courrier de la République: 179 rue Agbalépédogan, Quartier Djidjolé, Lomé; tel. 90089060; e-mail courrierdelarepublique@yahoo .fr; weekly; Editor-in-Chief DERMAN SALIFOU SONGOI.

Echos du Pays: BP 507, Lomé; tel. 90031824; e-mail augustin .sizing@yahoo.fr; weekly; Dir of Publication AUGUSTIN M. SIZING.

Etudes Togolaises (Revue Togolaise des Sciences): Institut National de la Recherche Scientifique, BP 2240, Lomé; tel. 22-21-01-39; e-mail inrstogo@yahoo.fr; f. 1965; 2 a year; scientific review, mainly anthropology; Dir of Publication MESSANVI GBEASSOR.

Flambeau des Démocrates: blvd du 13 Janvier, Nyékonakpoè, 06 BP 60364, Lomé; tel. 90346325; e-mail loiclate@gmail.com; internet flambeaudesdemocrates.com; weekly; Dir of Publication LOÏC LAWSON; Editor ISAAC T. AGBESSI.

Focus Infos: BP 431, Lomé; tel. 22-50-91-01; e-mail focusinfos@ focusinfos.net; internet www.focusinfos.net; fortnightly; Dir of Publication EKPÉ K. AGBOH AHOUELETE; Editor-in-Chief FRANCK NONNKPO.

Golfe Infos: Immeuble ICI, Route d'Adidogomé, 57 rue 248, Quartier Soviépé, 08 BP 81104, Lomé; tel. 22-50-50-27; e-mail golfe_info@ yahoo.fr; internet golfe-info.com; 3 a week; Dir of Publication KOUANVI K. SODJI.

L'Indépendant Express: Nyékonakpoè, Lomé; tel. 23-20-41-66; internet www.independantexpress.net; f. 2007; weekly; Dir of Publication CARLOS K. KETOHOU.

Journal Officiel de la République du Togo (JORT): BP 891, Lomé; tel. 22-21-37-18; e-mail jo@jo.gouv.tg; internet jo.gouv.tg; govt acts, laws, decrees and decisions.

Le Messager: Kégué, Lomé; tel. 90047159; internet lemessager-actu.com; Dir of Publication BOURAÏMA TCHABORE.

Le Medium: 893 rue 19 Saint Joseph, 01 BP 450, Lomé; tel. 99520515; e-mail lemedium2013@yahoo.fr; internet lemedium .info; weekly; Dir of Publication CRÉDO ADJÉ K. TETTEH; Editor ALI SAMBA.

Nouvel Echo: BP 3681, Lomé; tel. 99477240; f. 1997; pro-opposition; weekly; Dir ALPHONSE NEVAME KLU; Editor CLAUDE AMEGANVI.

Nouvelle Opinion: Adidoadin, Pavée prolongé, 2ème carré après Pharmacie Le Galien, Lomé; tel. 91363755; weekly; Dir of Publication El Hadj ARIMIYAO TCHAGNAO.

Plume Libre: Avédji, Lomé; tel. 90234095; Dir of Publication TOMI E. VIVIEN.

Présence Chrétienne: Foyer Pie XII, Lomé; tel. 22-22-38-84; e-mail presencechretienne@yahoo.fr; f. 1960; monthly; Dir of Publication AMÉVI DABLA.

Le Regard: BP 81213, Lomé; tel. 90040909; f. 1996; weekly; pro-opposition; supports promotion of human rights; Editor ABASS DURMAN MIKAÏLA.

L'Union: Wuiti Nkafu, 1165 blvd Jean-Paul II, Lomé; tel. 22-61-35-29; e-mail patrie006@yahoo.fr; internet www.pa-lunion.com; biweekly; Dir of Publication HUGUE ERIC JOHNSON; Editor JEAN AFOLABI.

Warra—Les Vainqueurs: derrière EPP Kélégougan, 13 BP 152, Lomé; tel. 90025245; e-mail micheltchadja@yahoo.fr; weekly; Dir of Publication MICHEL YAO TCHADJA.

PRESS ASSOCIATIONS

Conseil National des Patrons de Presse du Togo (CONAPP): Maison de la Presse, Tokoin Trésor, BP 81213, Lomé; tel. 90110506; Pres. TCHAGNAO ARIMIYAO; Sec.-Gen. MARC ABOFLAN.

Observatoire Togolais des Médias: rue Sovegan, BP 30277, Lomé; tel. 22-36-25-35; Pres. AIMÉ DODZI KOMLA EKPÉ.

Patronat de la Presse Togolaise (PPT): Lomé; tel. 99407733; internet www.patronatpressetogo.org; f. 2014; Pres. ISIDORE AKOLLOR.

Syndicat National des Journalistes Indépendants du Togo (SYNJIT): Lomé; tel. 90240375; f. 2011; Sec.-Gen. ISIDORE KOUWONOU.

Union des Journalistes Indépendants du Togo: BP 81213, Lomé; tel. 22-26-13-00; e-mail maison-du-journalisme@ids.tg; also operates Maison de Presse; Sec.-Gen. PIERRE AKILISSO.

NEWS AGENCIES

AfreePress: blvd de la Kara, angle rue de la Paroisse, Saint Kizito, Tokoin Doumassesse, BP 20752, Lomé; tel. 90004762; e-mail afreepresstg@yahoo.fr; internet afreepress.tg.

Agence Togolaise de Presse (ATOP): 35 rue des Medias, BP 2327, Lomé; tel. 22-21-43-39; e-mail info@atop.com; internet atoptg.com; f. 1975; Dir-Gen. JEAN-BAPTISSE EYEBIYI.

Savoir News: Lomé; tel. 99352923; e-mail info@savoirnews.net; internet www.savoirnews.net; f. 2009; private; Gen. Co-ordinator EMILE KOUTON.

Publishers

Les Nouvelles Editions Africaines du Togo (NEA-TOGO): BP 60335, Lomé; tel. 90037336; e-mail neatogo@yahoo.fr; general fiction, non-fiction and textbooks; Dir-Gen. KOKOU A. KALIPE; Editorial Dir TCHOTCHO CHRISTIANE EKUE.

Société Nationale des Editions du Togo (EDITOGO): 5 Ave Leopold Sedar Senghor, BP 891, Lomé; tel. 22-21-37-18; internet www.editogo.tg; f. 1961; govt-owned; general and educational; Pres. BIOSSEY KOKOU TOZOUN; Man. Dir WIYAO DADJA POUWI.

Broadcasting and Communications

TELECOMMUNICATIONS

Moov Africa Togo: blvd de la Paix, BP 14511, Lomé; tel. 99997777; e-mail moovcontact@moov.tg; internet moov-africa.tg; operates mobile telecommunications in 80 localities; Dir-Gen. ABDELLAH TABHIRET.

Togocom: pl. de la Réconciliation, Quartier Atchante, BP 333, Lomé; tel. 22-21-44-01; e-mail contact@togotelecom.tg; internet togocom.tg; f. 2017 following merger of Togo Télécom and Togo Cellulaire—Togocel; 51% owned by Agou Holding; Dir-Gen. (vacant).

Regulatory Authority

Autorité de Régulation des Communications Électroniques et des Postes (ARCEP): Immeuble ARCEP, Cité OUA, 4638 blvd Eyadema, BP: 358 Lomé; tel. 22-23-63-80; internet www.arcep.tg; f. 2012; Dir-Gen. MICHEL YAOVI GALLEY.

BROADCASTING

Haute Autorité de l'Audiovisuel et de la Communication (HAAC): BP 8697, Lomé, tel. 22-50-16-78; e-mail infos@haactogo.tg; internet www.haactogo.tg; Pres. PITALOUNANI TÉLOU.

Radio

Radiodiffusion du Togo (Internationale)—Radio Lomé: BP 434, Lomé; tel. 22-21-24-93; e-mail radiolome@yahoo.fr; internet www.radiolome.tg; f. 1953; state-controlled; radio programmes in French, English and vernacular languages; Dir-Gen. TAKOUDA A. KOMLA TAKOU.

Pyramide FM: Lomé; tel. 70430970; e-mail pierrotfidel16@gmail.com; internet fb.com/PyramideFm; Dir PIERROT KOSSI ATTIOGBÉ.

Radio Frequence 1: Immeuble Golfe-Immobilier, 57 rue 248, 08 BP 81104, Lomé; tel. 22-50-50-27; internet frequence1.com; f. 2002; Dir KOUANVI SODJI.

Radio Kanal FM: Immeuble de CAMPOS, ave Champs de Course, BP 61554, Lomé; tel. 22-21-33-74; internet kanalfm.com; f. 1997; broadcasts in French and Mina; independent; Dir MODESTE MESSAVUSSU-AKUE.

Radio Maria Togo: BP 30162, 155 de la rue 158, Hédzranawoé, Lomé; tel. 22-26-11-31; e-mail info.tog@radiomaria.org; internet www.radiomaria.tg; f. 1997; Roman Catholic; broadcasts in French, English and 6 local languages; Dir BENU EFOEVI PENOUKOU.

Radio Nana FM: 29 rue Béeniglato, BP 6212, Lomé; tel. 22-20-12-02; e-mail nanafm_tg@yahoo.fr; internet nanafm.tg; f. 1999; broadcasts in French and Mina; community station; political, economic and cultural information; Dir FERDINAND AFFOGNON.

Radio Sport FM: Tokoin, Lomé; tel. 9002601; internet radiosportfmtg.com; f. 2001.

Radio X-Solaire: Kodjoviakopé; tel. 22-22-30-48; f. 2000; Dir MIWONOVI AKUÉ.

Victoire FM: Quartier Tokoin Habitat, rue des Hirondelles, 01 BP 80195, Lomé; tel. 22-21-80-99; e-mail info@victoirefm.com; internet victoirefm.com.

Zéphyr FM: 143 rue des Sureaux Hédzranawoé, BP, 20017, Lomé; tel. 22-26-50-36; Dir GONDOHU MARTIN N'BATOU.

Television

Télévision Togolaise: rue des Médias, BP 3286, Lomé; tel. 22-21-53-57; e-mail televisiontogolaise@yahoo.fr; internet www.tvt.tg; f. 1973; state-controlled; 3 stations; programmes in French and vernacular languages; Dir-Gen. DOTSE DAMIEN EPEY.

Direct 7: 05 BP 63 Lomé, Lomé; tel. 90999464; e-mail direct7tv@gmail.com; internet direct7.tg; f. 2015; Dir AYI SAMSON KOUEVI.

TV2: BP 13100, Agoe; tel. 90332383; e-mail tv2tg@yahoo.fr; internet tv2tg.tv; f. 2001; Dir EUDOXIE THEOPHANE.

Other television channels include TV Jabal Nour al-Islamia and Télé Sport. Many foreign channels, such as TV 5, France 2, France 3, France 24, France 5/Arte, RTI, ORTB, RTS, ORTM, Canal Horizons, Direct 8 and Télésud, are also broadcast to Togo.

Finance

BANKING

Central Bank

Banque Centrale des Etats de l'Afrique de l'Ouest (BCEAO): rue Abdoulaye Fadiga, BP 120, Lomé; tel. 22-21-53-84; internet www.bceao.int; HQ in Dakar, Senegal; f. 1962; bank of issue for the mem. states of the Union Economique et Monétaire Ouest-Africaine (UEMOA, comprising Benin, Burkina Faso, Côte d'Ivoire, Guinea-Bissau, Mali, Niger, Senegal and Togo); Gov. JEAN-CLAUDE KASSI BROU; Dir in Togo KOSSI TÉNOU.

Commercial Banks

Bank of Africa—Togo: 22 blvd de la République, BP 229, Lomé; tel. 22-53-62-62; e-mail information@boatogo.com; internet www.boatogo.com; f. 2013; Dir-Gen. BAHAA EL YAMAMI ALAMI.

Banque Internationale pour l'Afrique au Togo (BIA—Togo): 13 ave Sylvanus Olympio, BP 346, Lomé; tel. 22-21-32-86; internet www.attijariwafabank.com/fr/filiale-internationale/bia-togo;

f. 1965; fmrly Meridien BIAO—Togo; owned by Attijariwafa Bank (Morocco); Gen. Man. FAISAL CHAHROUR.

Banque Sahélo-Saharienne pour l'Investissement et le Commerce—Togo (BSIC—Togo): 3802 blvd du 13 janvier, BP 3296, Lomé; tel. 22-20-21-98; internet www.bsicbank.com/togo; Pres. MAMADOU PONA; Dir-Gen. KADIDIATOU JOSIANE KOSSOMI.

Coris Bank International: Quartier Béniglato, blvd du 13 Janvier, BP 4032, Lomé; tel. 22-20-82-82; e-mail corisbank-tg@coris-bank.com; internet togo.coris.bank; f. 2014; Pres. TALKAYE ROMBA; Dir-Gen. ALASSANE KABORÉ.

Ecobank Togo (EBT): 20 ave Sylvanus Olympio, BP 3302, Lomé; tel. 22-21-72-14; e-mail ecobanktg@ecobank.com; internet www.ecobank.com; f. 1988; 81.8% owned by Ecobank Transnational Inc (operating under the auspices of the Economic Community of West African States), 12.7% by Togolese private investors; Chair. AYÉWANOU AGBÉTOHO GBEASOR; Man. Dir MAMADY DIAKITÉ.

Ecobank Transnational Inc: 2365 blvd du Mono, BP 3261, Lomé; tel. 22-21-03-03; e-mail info@ecobank.com; internet www.ecobank.com; f. 1985; holding co for banking cos in Benin, Burkina Faso, Cameroon, Côte d'Ivoire, Ghana, Guinea, Liberia, Mali, Niger, Nigeria, Senegal and Togo, Ecobank Development Corpn and EIC Bourse; Chair. ALAIN FRANCIS NKONTCHOU; Group CEO ADE AYEYEMI.

IB Bank Togo (BTCI): 169 blvd du 13 janvier, BP 363, Lomé; tel. 22-23-55-00; internet www.btci.net; f. 1974; fmrly Banque Togolaise pour le Commerce et l'Industrie; 10% state-owned; remainder sold to IB Holding in Aug. 2021 and name changed as above; Pres. AGBENOXEVI K. PANIAH; Dir-Gen. KADÉVI AKAKPO.

Orabank Bank Togo: 11 ave du 24 janvier, BP 325, Lomé; tel. 22-21-62-21; e-mail info-tg@orabank.net; internet www.orabank.net; f. 2004; fmrly Financial Bank Togo, present name adopted 2012; 83.67% owned by Oragroup SA; Dir-Gen. GUY-MARTIAL AWONA.

Société Générale Togo: 2983 ave de la Libération, Tokoin-Gbadago, 01 BP 5012, Lomé; tel. 22-53-75-00; e-mail banque.sgtg@socgen.com; internet societegenerale.tg; Dir-Gen. JOCELYNE N'GUESSAN.

Société Interafricaine de Banque (SIAB): 14 ave Sylvanus Olympio, BP 4874, Lomé; tel. 22-21-28-30; e-mail info@siabtogo.com; internet www.siabtogo.com; f. 1975; fmrly Banque Arabe Libyenne-Togolaise du Commerce Extérieur; 94.1% owned by Libyan Arab Foreign Bank, 5.9% state-owned; CEO VICTOR N'SOUWODJI EHE.

Sunu Bank: Immeuble SUNU Bank, 23 ave Kleber Dadjo, Hanoukopé, BP 904, Lomé; tel. 22-53-47-00; e-mail togo.bank@sunu-group.com; internet sunu-group.com/en/notrereseau/filiales/tg; fmrly Caisse d'Epargne du Togo, subsequently Banque Populaire pour l'Epargne et le Crédit; present name adopted 2020; Pres. MOHAMED BAH; Dir-Gen. MYRIAM ADOTEVI.

Union Togolaise de Banque (UTB): UTB Circulaire, blvd du 13 janvier, Nyékonakpoè, BP 359, Lomé; tel. 22-23-43-00; internet www.utb.tg; f. 1964; state-owned; Chair. EKPAO ADJABO; Dir-Gen. ZAKARI DAROU-SALIM.

Financial Institutions

Africa Guarantee Fund—West Africa (AFG): Immeuble BOAD, 1er étage, 68 ave de la Libération, BP 985, Lomé; tel. 22-21-06-05; e-mail agfwestafrica@agf.africa; internet africanguaranteefund.com; 80.55% owned by AFG; fmrly Fonds de Garantie des Investissements Privés en Afrique de l'Ouest; present name adopted 2017; Pres. FÉLIX ADAHI BIKPO; Dir-Gen. ADIDJA HASSAN ZANOUVI.

Caisse Régionale de Refinancement Hypothécaire (CRRH): Immeuble BOAD, 68 ave de la Libération, BP 1172, Lomé; tel. 22-23-27-22; e-mail infos@crrhuemoa.org; internet crrhuemoa.org; Pres. PAUL DERREUMAUX.

Bankers' Association

Association Professionnelle des Banques et Etablissements Financiers du Togo (APBEF): rue Docteur Kaolo-Tokoin Tamé, près de la Résidence du Bénin, BP 4863, Lomé; tel. 22-26-69-13; e-mail info@apbeftogo.com; internet apbef-togo.org; Pres. MICHEL KOFI DORKENOO; Exec. Dir KOFFI EZA.

STOCK EXCHANGE

Bourse Régionale des Valeurs Mobilières (BRVM): Immeuble SGI Togo, 2e Etage, 4691, blvd Gnassingbé Eyadéma, BP 3263, Lomé; tel. 22-61-2316; e-mail bbodet@brvm.org; internet www.brvm.org; f. 1998; national branch of BRVM (regional stock exchange based in Abidjan, Côte d'Ivoire, serving the member states of UEMOA); Man. in Togo BERTRAND BODET.

INSURANCE

CIF Assurances-Vie: Immeuble CIF Vie Togo, Quartier Attikoumé, 08 BP 8715 Lomé Togo, 08 BP 8715, Lomé; tel. 22-20-52-94; e-mail contact@cifvietogo.com; internet www.cifvietogo.com; f. 2018; Dir-Gen. FEDY KOKOUMEH.

Compagnie Commune de Réassurance des Etats Membres de la CICA (CICA—RE): 43 ave du 24 janvier, 07 BP 12410, Lomé; tel. 22-23-62-69; e-mail cica-re@cica-re.com; internet www.cica-re.com; f. 1981; reinsurance co-operating in 12 West and Central African states; Dir-Gen. KARIM DIARASSOUBA.

Fidelia Assurances: 93 blvd du 13 janvier, 01 BP 1679, Lomé; tel. 22-20-74-94; e-mail contact@fideliaassurances.com; internet fideliaassurances.com; f. 2004; Dir-Gen. AYOKO KUEVIAKOE BONOU.

Gras Savoye Togo: 140 blvd du 13 janvier, BP 2932, Lomé; tel. 22-21-35-38; internet www.grassavoye.com; affiliated to Gras Savoye (France); Dir BABACAR M. GUEYE.

GTA Assurance: route d'Atakpamé, BP 3298, Lomé; tel. 22-25-60-75; f. 1974; fmrly GTAC2A; name changed as above in 2019; non-life insurance; Man. Dir JEAN-MARIE KOFFI E. TESSI; also **GTA Assurance-Vie**, life insurance; Man. Dir DATÉ YAO GBIKPI.

Nouvelle Société Interafricaine d'Assurances Togo (NSIA Togo): rue Brazza, BP 1120, Lomé; tel. 22-20-81-50; e-mail nsia.tg@groupensia.com; f. 2005; Dir-Gen. CONSTANT DJEKET; also **NSIA Vie Togo**; acquired Sanlam Assurance Togo in 2022.

Prudential Beneficial Life Insurance Togo: 2963 rue de la chance, Quartier Agbalépédogan, BP 1115, Lomé; tel. 22-22-06-07; e-mail infos@prubeneficial.tg; internet prubeneficial.tg; f. 2000; fmrly Beneficial Life Insurance Togo; name changed as above in 2019; Dir-Gen. JUSTIN GBADAGO.

Sanlam Assurance Togo: 10 ave Sylvanus Olympio, BP 1349, Lomé; tel. 22-21-59-58; internet tg.sanlam.com; fmrly Colina Togo, subsequently Saham Assurance Togo; name changed as above in 2021; general; Dir-Gen. SIMON PIERRE GOUEM.

Sunu Assurances IARD Togo: Immeuble Sunu, 812 blvd du 13 janvier, BP 495, Lomé; tel. 22-21-10-34; e-mail togo.iard@sunu-group.com; internet www.sunu-group.com; Dir-Gen. HEMNIA AKUVIE ADJAMAGBO; also **Sunu Assurances Vie Togo**; Dir-Gen. CHARLES ALAIN CISSÉ.

Insurance Association

Comité des Assureurs du Togo: 7 blvd de la Paix, 01 BP 2689, Lomé; tel. 22-21-70-92; e-mail cat@ca-togo.org; internet www.ca-togo.org; Pres. DATÉ YAO GBIKPI.

Trade and Industry

GOVERNMENT AGENCIES

Agence de Promotion des Investissements et de la Zone Franche (API-ZF): 2564 ave de la Chance, Bè-Klikamé, BP 3250, Lomé; tel. 22-53-53-53; e-mail info@apizf.org; internet www.apizf.org; promotion of investment and implementation of the Investment Code, the Free Zone Status, and any other special economic regime; Dir-Gen. ATSOUVI YAWO SIKPA (acting).

Autorité de Régulation des Marchés Publics (ARMP): Immeuble Saham Assurances, 6e et 7e étages, blvd Gnassingbe Eyadema, BP 12484, Lomé; tel. 22-23-06-80; e-mail armptogo@yahoo.fr; internet armp.tg; Dir-Gen. AFTAR TOURÉ MOROU.

Centre de Formalités des Entreprises: angle ave de la Présidence et ave Georges Pompidou, BP 360, Lomé; tel. 22-20-63-60; e-mail cfe@cfetogo.org; internet www.cfetogo.tg.

Direction Générale des Mines et de la Géologie: 6, Av. de Sarakawa BP 356, Lomé; tel. 22-21-30-01; e-mail info@togo-mines.com; internet www.togo-mines.com; organization and administration of mining in Togo; Dir-Gen. MARCEL D. SOGLE.

Initiative pour la Transparence des Industries Extractives (ITIE): 4412 blvd Jean Paul II, 08 BP 8288, Lomé; tel. 22-26-89-90; e-mail itietogo@ itietogo.org; internet itietogo.org; Nat. Co-ordinator DIDIER KOKOU AGBEMADON.

Office Togolais des Recettes: 1 rue des Impôts, 02 BP 20823, Lomé; tel. 22-53-14-00; e-mail otr@otr.tg; internet www.otr.tg; f. 2012; Commr Gen. PHILIPPE KOKOU TCHODIÈ.

DEVELOPMENT ORGANIZATIONS

Agence Française de Développement (AFD): 437 ave de Sarakawa, BP 33, Lomé; tel. 22-23-07-30; e-mail afdlome@afd.fr; internet www.afd.fr; Country Dir (vacant).

France Volontaires: Quartier Nyekonakpoe, 364 rue Soreda, BP 1511, Lomé; tel. 22-21-09-45; e-mail ev.togo@france-volontaires.org; internet www.france-volontaires.org; f. 1965; fmrly Association Française des Volontaires du Progrès; present name adopted in 2009; Nat. Rep. BAH MOUSSA.

Office de Développement et d'Exploitation des Forêts (ODEF): 20 rue des Evala, Agbalépédogan, face à l'Hôtel les Palmiers, BP 334, Lomé; tel. 22-51-42-17; e-mail info@odeftg.com; internet www.odef.tg; f. 1971; develops and manages forest resources; Man. Dir EDJIDOMÉLÉ GBADOE.

Service de Coopération et d'Action Culturelle: ave du Général de Gaulle, BP 91, Lomé; tel. 22-53-58-60; e-mail scac-lome@tg.refer.org; administers bilateral aid from the French Ministry of Foreign Affairs; Dir YANNICK LE ROUX.

CHAMBERS OF COMMERCE

Chambre de Commerce et d'Industrie du Togo (CCIT): ave de la Présidence, angle ave Georges Pompidou, 01 BP 360, Lomé; tel. 22-23-29-00; e-mail ccit@ccit.tg; internet www.ccit.tg; f. 1921; Pres. GERMAIN ESSOHOUNA MEBA; br. at Kara.

EMPLOYERS' ORGANIZATIONS

Association des Grandes Entreprises du Togo (AGET): Immeuble SUNU, 3e étage, 812 blvd du 13 janvier, 01 BP 2407, Lomé; tel. 22-21-95-85; e-mail contact@aget-togo.org; internet aget-togo.org; f. 2007; Pres. JONAS AKLÉSSO DAOU; Sec.-Gen. JEAN-MARIE TESSI.

Conseil National du Patronat du Togo: 60 blvd du Mono, BP 12429, Lomé; tel. 22-21-08-30; e-mail cnptogo@gmail.com; internet www.cnp-togo.org; f. 1963 as Groupement Interprofessionnel des Entreprises du Togo; present name adopted in 1990; Pres. COAMI LAURENT TAMÉGNON; Exec. Dir TÉVI TETE-BENISSAN.

Syndicat des Commerçants, Industriels, Importateur et Exportateurs du Togo: BP 1166, Lomé; tel. 22-22-59-86; Pres. AMA JUSTIN D'ALMEIDA.

Syndicat des Entrepreneurs de Travaux Publics, Bâtiments et Mines du Togo: BP 12429, Lomé; tel. 22-21-19-06; Pres. JOSÈPHE NAKU.

UTILITIES

Electricity

Autorité de Réglementation du Secteur de l'Electricité (ARSE): rue des Hydrocarbures, face Air Liquide (ex-TOGOGAZ), BP 3489, Lomé; tel. 22-20-70-78; e-mail arse@arse.tg; internet www.arse.tg; f. 2000; Dir-Gen. THÉOPHILE ATSITSOGBOE KOMLA NYAKU.

Compagnie Energie Electrique du Togo (CEET): 426 ave Mama Fousséni, BP 42, Lomé; tel. 22-21-27-43; e-mail ceet@ceet.tg; internet www.ceet.tg; f. 1963; production, transportation and distribution of electricity; Dir-Gen. BARANDAO DÉBO-K'MBA.

ContourGlobal Togo SA: Centrale Thermique de Lomé, Zone Industrielle, route d'Aneho, 01 BP 3662, Lomé; tel. 22-23-74-00; e-mail africa.inquiry@contourglobal.com.

Water

Société Togolaise des Eaux (TdE): 53 ave de la Libération, BP 1301, Lomé; tel. 22-21-34-81; e-mail contact@tde.tg; internet tde.tg; f. 2003 to replace Régie Nationale des Eaux du Togo; production and distribution of drinking water; Dir-Gen. GBATI YAWANKE WAKE.

MAJOR COMPANIES

The following are among the country's largest companies in terms of either capital investment or employment:

Afrique Audit and Consulting: Immeuble AAC, 63 blvd du 13 Janvier, BP 61825, Lomé; tel. 22-23-21-00; e-mail aac.togo@gha-exco.com.

Amexfield Togo Steel SA (ATS): BP 9159, Lomé; tel. 22-27-90-59; steel production; Dir-Gen. MAWULÉ AHIALEY CLÉMENT.

Amina Togo SA: 32 blvd de la Paix, BP 10230, Lomé; tel. 22-26-84-04; e-mail aminatogo@hotmail.com; production of synthetic hair; operates in the Export Processing Zone; South Korean-owned; Man. LEE DAE.

Atlantic Produce Togo SA: Plantes ornamentales, route de Kegue, BP 3170, Lomé; tel. 22-26-31-64; internet atlanticproduce.tg; exporter of tropical houseplants; Danish-owned; operates in the Export Processing Zone; Pres. and Dir-Gen. ANTHONY AHIABA.

Brasserie BB Lomé: 169 Agoenyivé route d'Atakpamé, PK 10, BP 896, Lomé; tel. 22-25-39-04; e-mail bblome@castel-afrique.com; internet www.bblome.com; f. 1964 as Brasserie du Bénin; 25% owned by Castel, France; mfrs of beer and soft drinks at Lomé and Kara; Man. Dir THIERRY FÉRAUD.

Cajou Espoir Tchamba SARL: BP 298, Lomé; tel. 90-04-59-14; e-mail amedorh@gmail.com; internet www.cajouespoir.com; Dir-Gen. MAURICE EDORH.

Heavymat Industry SA: BP 1409, Lomé; tel. 22-71-22-78; e-mail contact.group@heavymat.com; internet www.heavymat-industry.com; f. 2008; assembly of heavy vehicles imported from China.

Nouvelle Industrie des Oléagineux du Togo (NIOTO): Zone Industrielle du Port, BP 3086, Lomé; tel. 22-27-23-79; e-mail nioto@nioto-togo.com; internet www.nioto-togo.com; f. 1976; affiliate of Groupe Dagris (France); production and marketing of edible plant oils; Man. Dir THIERRY AWESSO.

Nouvelle Société Cotonnière du Togo (NSCT): BP 219, Atakpamé; tel. 24-40-01-53; e-mail nsct@nsct.tg; internet www.nsct.tg; f. 2009 to replace the Société Togolaise du Coton (SOTOCO), f. 1974 to promote and develop cotton cultivation; absorbed cotton production and marketing activities of fmr Office des Produits Agricoles du Togo in 2001; 60% state-owned; Dir-Gen. NANA ADAM NANFAMÉ.

Ramco SA: Immeuble Ramco, ave du 24 Janvier, BP 3467, Lomé; tel. 22-21-40-78; e-mail contact@ramco.tg; internet ramco.tg; supermarkets.

Société des Ciments du Togo (CIMTOGO): Zone Industrielle Portuaire PK 12, BP 1687, Lomé; tel. 22-27-08-59; internet www.heidelbergcement.tg/fr/cimtogo; f. 1969; owned by HeidelbergCement Group (Norway); production and marketing of cement and clinker; Dir-Gen. ÉRIC GOULIGNAC.

Société Générale des Moulins du Togo (SGMT): Zone Industrielle Portuaire, BP 9098, Lomé; tel. 22-27-43-77; e-mail sgmtsa@yahoo.fr; f. 1971; flour-milling at Lomé; Chair. KOUDJOLOU DOGO; CEO VILGRAIN VILGRAIN.

Société Nouvelle des Phosphates du Togo (SNPT): BP 379, Lomé; tel. 23-31-80-13; e-mail info@snptogo.com; internet www.snptogo.com; f. 2007 to replace the International Fertilizers Group-Togo (f. 2002); production and marketing of phosphates; Dir-Gen. MICHEL KÉZIÉ.

Société Togolaise de Stockage de Lomé (STSL): BP 3283, Lomé; tel. 22-27-50-64; f. 1976; exploitation and commercialization of hydrocarbons; Dir-Gen. M. BLAZJENVICZ.

TRADE UNIONS

Confédération Générale des Cadres du Togo (CGCT): BP 12837, Lomé; tel. 22-23-13-09; Sec.-Gen. MOLI EPHREM TSIKPLONOU.

Confédération Nationale des Travailleurs du Togo (CNTT): Bourse du Travail, BP 163, 160 blvd du 13 janvier, Lomé; tel. 22-22-02-55; e-mail boursecntt@yahoo.fr; f. 1973; Sec.-Gen. AGUI YVES PALANGA.

Confédération Syndicale des Travailleurs du Togo (CSTT): 14 rue Van Lare, BP 3058, Lomé; tel. 22-22-11-17; e-mail cstt_cstt@yahoo.fr; internet www.cstt-togo.org; f. 1949, dissolved 1972, re-established 1991; comprises 80 unions and 8 professional federations; Sec.-Gen. KOMLAN EMMANUEL AGBENOU.

Groupe des Syndicats Autonomes (GSA): BP 1728, Lomé; f. 1991; Sec.-Gen. (vacant).

Union Générale des Syndicats Libre du Togo (UGSL): BP 30137, Lomé; tel. 22-25-32-28; e-mail usycort@yahoo.fr; Sec.-Gen. (vacant).

Union Nationale des Syndicats Indépendants du Togo (UNSIT): Tokoin-Wuiti, BP 30082, Lomé; tel. 22-21-32-88; f. 1991; Sec.-Gen. TÉTÉVI GBIKPI-BENISSAN; 17 affiliated unions.

Transport

RAILWAYS

Société Nationale des Chemins de Fer du Togo (SNCT): BP 340, Lomé; tel. 22-22-42-06; e-mail togorail@yahoo.com; f. 1900; under concession with Togorail since 2003; total length 519 km, incl. lines running inland from Lomé to Atakpamé and Blitta (276 km), and Lomé to Tabligbo (77 km); Gen. Man. M. M. REDDY.

SHIPPING

The major port, at Lomé, generally handles a substantial volume of transit trade for the landlocked countries of Mali, Niger and Burkina Faso. There is another port at Kpémé for the export of phosphates.

Conseil National des Chargeurs du Togo (CNCT): BP 2991, Lomé; tel. 22-23-71-00; e-mail cnct@cnct.tg; internet www.cnct.tg; f. 1980; restructured 2001; Dir-Gen. TOÏ GNASSINGBÉ.

Ecomarine International (Togo): Immeuble Ecomarine, Zone Portuaire, BP 6014, Lomé; tel. 22-27-48-04; f. 2001 to develop

container-handling facility at Lomé Port; operates maritime transport between Togo, Senegal and Angola; Chair. Alhaji BAMANGA TUKUR.

Port Autonome de Lomé: BP 1225, Lomé; tel. 22-27-47-42; e-mail togoport@togoport.tg; internet www.togo-port.net; f. 1968; transferred to private management in 2002; Man. Dir Adm. FOGAN KODJO ADEGNON.

Togolaise d'Affrètements et d'Agence de Lignes SA (TAAL): 21 blvd du Mono, BP 9089, Lomé; tel. 22-23-19-00; e-mail taalmanagement@taal-sa.com; internet www.taal-sa.com; f. 1992; shipping agents, haulage management, crewing agency, forwarding agents; Dir-Gen. DANI ABLA AKAKPO.

CIVIL AVIATION

There are international airports at Tokoin, near Lomé (Gnassingbé Eyadéma International Airport), and at Niamtougou. In addition, there are smaller airfields at Sokodé, Sansanné-Mango, Dapaong and Atakpamé.

Agence Nationale de l'Aviation Civile du Togo: BP 2699, Lomé; tel. 22-26-37-40; e-mail anac@anactogo.fr; internet www.anac-togo.tg; Dir-Gen. LATTA GNAMA.

ASKY Airlines: BP 2988, Lomé; tel. 22-23-05-10; e-mail headoffice@flyasky.com; internet www.flyasky.com; f. 2008; commenced operations in 2010; 25% owned by Ethiopian Airlines; regional services; CEO (vacant).

Société Aéroportuaire de Lomé-Tokoin (SALT): Aéroport International Gnassingbé Eyadéma, BP 10112, Lomé; tel. 22-23-60-60; e-mail salttogo1@gmail.com; internet aeroportdelome.com; f. 1987; Dir-Gen. LATTA GNAMA.

Tourism

Office National Togolais du Tourisme (ONTT): BP 1289, Lomé; tel. 22-21-43-13; e-mail angelodjiss@yahoo.fr; internet www.togo-tourisme.com; f. 1963; Dir ANGELO DJISSODEY.

Defence

As assessed at November 2021, Togo's armed forces officially numbered about 8,550 (army 8,100, air force 250, naval force 200). Paramilitary forces comprised a 750-strong gendarmerie. Military service is by selective conscription and lasts for two years. Togo receives assistance with training and equipment from France. In 2021 a total of 945 Togolese troops were stationed abroad.

Defence Budget: 65,600m. francs CFA in 2021.

Chief of General Staff: Gen. DADJA MAGANAWÉ.

Chief of Staff of the Land Army: Col KASSAWA KOLEMAGA.

Chief of Staff of the Navy: Capt. KOSSI MAYO.

Chief of Staff of the Air Force: Col TASSOUNTI DJATO.

Education

Education is officially compulsory between the ages of six and 15 years. Primary education is free, begins at six years of age and lasts for six years. It is divided into three cycles, each of two years. Secondary education, beginning at the age of 12, lasts for a further seven years, comprising a first cycle of four years and a second of three years. According to estimates by the United Nations Educational, Scientific and Cultural Organization (UNESCO), in 2019/20 enrolment at pre-primary level was equivalent to 30% of children in the relevant age-group (males 29%; females 30%), while enrolment at primary schools in 2018/19 included 97% of children in the relevant age-group (males 98%; females 96%). In 2016/17 secondary enrolment was equivalent to 62% of the relevant age-group (males 72%; females 52%). Proficiency in the two national languages, Ewe and Kabiyé, is compulsory. Mission schools are important, educating almost one-half of all pupils. In 2018 spending on education represented 21.8% of total budgetary expenditure.

Bibliography

Agboyibo, Y. *Combat pour un Togo démocratique: une méthode politique*. Paris, Editions Karthala, 1999.

Ameagbleame, S. *Histoire, littérature et société au Togo*. Frankfurt, IKO Verlag, 1997.

Amenumey, D. *The Ewe Unification Movement: A Political History*. Accra, Ghana University Press, 1989.

Amouzou, E. *Gilchrist Olympio et la lutte pour la libération du Togo*. Paris, L'Harmattan, 2010.

Atisso, F. S. *Le Togo sous la dynastie des Gnassingbé*. Paris, L'Harmattan, 2012.

Cornevin, R. *Le Togo: des origines à nos jours*. Paris, Académie des sciences d'outre-mer, 1987.

Decalo, S. *Togo*. Paris, ABC-Clio, 1995.

   Historical Dictionary of Togo. 3rd edn. Metuchen, NJ, Scarecrow Press, 1996.

Degli, J. Y. *Togo: La Tragédie Africaine*. Ivry-sur-Seine, Editions Nouvelles du Sud, 1996.

   Togo: À quand l'alternance politique. Paris, L'Harmattan, 2007.

Dossouvi Logo, H. *Lutter pour ses droits au Togo*. Paris, L'Harmattan, 2004.

Feuillet, C. *Le Togo 'en général': La Longue Marche de Gnassingbé Eyadéma*. Paris, Afrique Biblio Club, 1976.

Gayibor, N. L. and Marguerat, Y. (eds) *Territoires et Administrateurs du Togo* Paris, L'Harmattan, 2019.

Houngnikpo, M. C. *Determinants of Democratization in Africa: A Comparative Study of Benin and Togo*. Lanham, MD, University Press of America, 2001.

Napo Kakaye, L. *Histoire politique et administrative du Togo: Regard sur un nationaliste de la première heure*. Paris, L'Harmattan, 2010.

Nugent, P. *Smugglers, Secessionists and Loyal Citizens on the Ghana–Togo Frontier: The Lie of the Borderlands since 1914*. Oxford, James Currey, 2002.

Schuerkens, U. *Du Togo allemand aux Togo et Ghana indépendants: Changement social sous régime colonial*. Paris, L'Harmattan, 2001.

Scrive, S. *La crise de la démocratie en Afrique: L'exemple du Togo*. Pars, L'Harmattan, 2009.

Stoecker, H. (Ed.). *German Imperialism in Africa*. London, Hurst Humanities, 1987.

Tété-Adjalogo, T. G. *De la colonisation allemande au Deutsche-Togo Bund*. Paris, L'Harmattan, 1998.

   Démocratisation à la togolaise. Paris, L'Harmattan, 1998.

   Histoire du Togo: Le coup de force permanent (2006–2011). Paris, L'Harmattan, 2012.

Verdier, R. *Le pays kabiyé Togo*. Paris, Editions Karthala, 1983.

UGANDA

Physical and Social Geography

B. W. LANGLANDS

PHYSICAL FEATURES AND CLIMATE

The Republic of Uganda is located on the eastern African plateau, at least 800 km inland from the Indian Ocean, and has a total area of 241,551 sq km (93,263 sq miles), including 41,028 sq km of inland water and swamp. There are several large freshwater lakes, of which Lakes Victoria, Edward and Albert are shared with neighbouring states. These lakes and most of the rivers form part of the basin of the upper (White) Nile, which has its origin in Uganda. At the point where the upper Nile leaves Lake Victoria, it is harnessed for hydroelectricity by the Owen Falls dam.

Of the land area (excluding open water), 84% forms a plateau at 900 m–1,500 m above sea level, with a gentle downwarp to the centre to form Lake Kyoga. The western arm of the east African rift system accounts for the 9% of the land area at less than 900 m. Some 5% of the land area lies at an altitude of 1,500 m–2,100 m, including (in the eastern and western extremities) the shoulders of rift valley structures, and also the foothills of the mountains referred to below. Mountains of over 2,100 m occupy the remaining 2% of the land area and these lands are above the limit of cultivation. The highest point is Mt Stanley, 5,109 m, in the Rwenzori group on the border with the Democratic Republic of the Congo.

Geologically, the great proportion of the country is made up of Pre-Cambrian material, largely of gneisses and schists into which granites have been intruded. In the west, distinct series of metamorphosed rocks occur, mainly of phyllites and shales, in which mineralized zones contain small quantities of copper, tin, tungsten and beryllium. Deposits of cobalt and nickel have also been identified, as well as potentially substantial reserves of gold-bearing ores. Small quantities of gold, tungsten and tin concentrates are currently mined. In the east of the country there are extensive reserves of magnetite, apatite and crystalline limestone. The apatite provides the basis for a superphosphate industry and the limestone for a cement industry.

NATURAL RESOURCES

The economy of Uganda has traditionally depended upon agriculture and this, in turn, is affected by climate. The country's location gives little variation in temperature throughout the year, affording an equatorial climate modified by altitude. Rainfall is greatest bordering Lake Victoria and on the mountains, where small areas have over 2,000 mm per year. The high ground of the west, the rest of the Lake Victoria zone, and the eastern and north-central interior all have more than 1,250 mm annually. Only the north-east (Karamoja) and parts of the south (east Ankole) have less than 750 mm. However, total amounts of rain are less significant agriculturally than the length of the dry season. For much of the centre and west there is no more than one month with less than 50 mm and this zone is characterized by permanent cropping of bananas for food, and coffee and tea for cash crops. To the south the dry season increases to three months (June–August); in the north it rises to four months (December–March) and in the north-east the dry season begins in October.

Western Uganda, where there is a greater range of different physical conditions, and where population densities are generally below average, shows a diversity of land use, with tropical rainforest, two game parks, ranch lands, fishing, mining and the cultivation of coffee and tea. The north and east is more monotonous, savannah-covered plain with annually sown fields of grain and cotton. Most of the country's coffee comes from the Lake Victoria zone (*Coffea robusta*) and Mt Elgon (*Coffea arabica*). The economy relies heavily upon smallholding peasant production of basic cash crops; however, the discovery of petroleum reserves in the 2000s was expected to result in significant changes to the Ugandan economy.

POPULATION

The most recent census, conducted in August 2014, enumerated a population of 34,634,650, giving a density of about 143.4 inhabitants per sq km. This was officially projected to have risen to 44,212,800 by mid-2022 (220.5 inhabitants per sq km). The population is predominantly rural; in 2019, according to the World Bank, only about 24% of the populace resided in urban centres. At mid-2016 the population of Kampala, the capital, was estimated at 1,568,900. The annual birth rate was 46.3 per 1,000 of the population in 2017, while average life expectancy at birth in 2020 was 63.7 years. Demographic patterns have been significantly affected by the high rate of incidence of HIV/AIDS, which, by the early 1990s, had reportedly reached epidemic proportions in parts of Uganda. According to estimates by the World Bank, almost 10% of the adult population were infected with HIV in 1997. By 2020, however, following mass education and prevention campaigns, the percentage of adults (persons aged 15–49) living with HIV/AIDS had been reduced to 5.4%.

History

MICHAEL JENNINGS

INTRODUCTION

British colonial activity in Uganda, which commenced after 1860, was consolidated in 1891 by a treaty with the Kabaka (King) of Buganda, the dominant kingdom. In 1954 the Democratic Party (DP) was formed, favouring a unitary independent state of Uganda and opposing the ambitions of the Baganda people, who did not wish Buganda's influence to be diminished after independence. The Uganda National Congress (UNC), meanwhile, advocated greater African control of the economy in a federal independent state. In 1958 seven African members of the protectorate's Legislative Council, including two members of the UNC, joined another faction, led by Dr Milton Obote,

to form the Uganda People's Congress (UPC). By 1960 the UPC, the DP (led by Benedicto Kiwanuka) and the Lukiiko (legislature) of Buganda were the principal political forces in Uganda.

In 1961, at the first countrywide elections to the Legislative Council, the DP won a majority of the seats. The Kabaka Yekka (KY, or King Alone), a political party representing the interests of the Bugandan Lukiiko, was formed to ally with the UPC against the DP. Uganda was granted self-government in 1962, with Kiwanuka as Prime Minister. The new Constitution provided for a federation of four regions—Buganda, Ankole, Bunyoro and Toro—each with considerable autonomy. In October Uganda became independent, within the

Commonwealth, and one year later, on 9 October 1963, the country became a republic, with Mutesa II, the Kabaka of Buganda, as non-executive President.

OBOTE AND THE UPC

During the first years of independence the UPC-KY alliance was placed under increasing strain. Defections allowed the UPC to rule without the alliance, and it also gained control of all district councils and kingdom legislatures, except in Buganda. However, the UPC was itself split between conservative, centrist and radical elements. In February 1966 the National Assembly approved a motion demanding an investigation into gold smuggling, in which Obote, the Minister of Defence, and the second-in-command of the army, Col Idi Amin Dada, were alleged to be involved. Later in that month Obote led a pre-emptive coup against his opponents within the UPC. The Constitution was suspended, the President was deposed, and all executive powers were transferred to Obote. A new Constitution was adopted in September 1967, establishing a unitary republic, and abolishing traditional rulers and legislatures. National elections were postponed until 1971.

During the late 1960s the Obote regime came to rely increasingly on detention and armed repression by the paramilitary and intelligence services. Estrangement began to develop, however, between Obote and the army, and in December 1969 Obote was wounded in an assassination attempt in the capital, Kampala.

THE AMIN REGIME

Amin seized power in January 1971, while Obote was out of the country. In February Amin declared himself head of state and consolidated his military position by the massacre of troops and police (particularly those of the Langi and Acholi tribes) who had supported the Obote regime. Soon after taking power, he suspended political activity and most civil rights. The National Assembly was dissolved, and Amin ruled by decree. In August 1972 he announced the expulsion of all non-citizen Asians (who comprised the majority of the resident Asian population). The order was subsequently extended to include all Asians (thought to number some 80,000 people), and although this was later rescinded, under internal and external pressure, all but 4,000 Ugandan Asians left the country. Most went to the United Kingdom, which severed diplomatic relations and imposed a trade embargo against Uganda. By the end of 1972 virtually all Western aid to Uganda had ceased. No coherent economic development policy existed, and the country's infrastructure deteriorated.

In October 1978 Ugandan forces invaded Tanzania. In response, President Julius Nyerere of Tanzania encouraged political exiles to form a united political front to remove Amin. In January 1979 the Tanzanian armed forces invaded Uganda, assisted by the Uganda National Liberation Army (UNLA) under the command of David Oyite-Ojok and Yoweri Museveni. They met little resistance, and captured Kampala in April. Amin fled the country, eventually taking refuge in Saudi Arabia, where he remained until his death in 2003.

TRANSITIONAL GOVERNMENT

A provisional government, the National Executive Council, was established in April 1979 from the ranks of the Uganda National Liberation Front (UNLF, a coalition of 18 previously exiled groups), with Dr Yusuf Lule, a former Vice-Chancellor of Makerere University, as President. Lule was succeeded by Godfrey Binaisa (a former Attorney-General), who was, in turn, overthrown by the Military Commission of the UNLF in May 1980. The Military Commission was chaired by Paulo Muwanga (an associate of Obote), supported by Oyite-Ojok and with Museveni as Vice-Chairman.

OBOTE AND OKELLO

Elections held in December 1980 were won by the UPC, and Obote was proclaimed President for a second time. However, the losing candidates (including Museveni) rejected the outcome of the poll, and turned to guerrilla warfare. Museveni and

Lule (now in exile) led one of three armed movements, the National Resistance Movement (NRM), with Museveni becoming sole leader after Lule's death in 1985.

In July 1985 Obote (a Langi) was overthrown in an Acholi military coup, led by Brig. (later Lt-Gen.) Basilio Okello. A Military Council, led by Lt-Gen. (later Gen.) Tito Okello, the Commander-in-Chief of the army, was established to govern the country pending elections to be held a year later. With the NRM controlling much of southern Uganda, Museveni refused to join the Military Council and continued his offensive.

THE MUSEVENI PRESIDENCY

National Resistance Army (NRA—the military wing of the NRM) troops took control of Kampala in January 1986. Museveni was sworn in as President, and formed a National Resistance Council (NRC) with both civilian and military members drawn from across the political spectrum. Elections were postponed for at least three years and the activities of political parties were officially suspended in March. In that month an armed movement seeking the overthrow of Museveni, the Uganda People's Democratic Movement (UPDM), was formed, with Obote's former premier, Eric Otema Allimadi, as leader. This, together with raids by remnants of the UNLA, chronic problems with armed cattle rustlers in the north-east and the lack of any basic infrastructure of law and order, prevented President Museveni from consolidating his control over Uganda. Museveni refused to restore Uganda's traditional monarchies until stability had returned to the country.

The largest uprising in the period immediately following Museveni's accession to power was led by a charismatic cult leader, Alice Lakwena, whose religious sect attracted both peasant farmers from the Acholi tribe and former soldiers of the UNLA. The rebel Holy Spirit Movement, as it became known, was crushed in late 1987 and Lakwena fled to Kenya. However, remaining members of the movement subsequently regrouped as the Lord's Resistance Army (LRA), under the leadership of Lakwena's nephew, Joseph Kony.

In June 1987 an amnesty was declared for insurgents (except those accused of murder or rape); this was subsequently extended at repeated intervals, and by April 1988 Ugandan officials reported that almost 30,000 rebels had surrendered. Peace talks with the armed wing of the UPDM led to agreement in June under the leadership of Lt-Col John Angelo Okello. However, a faction of the Uganda People's Democratic Army regrouped, led by Odong Latek, and continued to oppose the Government.

Post-election Reforms

The first national elections since 1980 took place in February 1989. In October the NRC approved draft legislation to extend the Government's term of office by five years from January 1990. In May 1991 President Museveni formally invited all Ugandan Asians who had been expelled during the Amin regime to return.

In December 1992 the Constitutional Commission recommended continuing the non-party democracy system. In April 1993 the NRC adopted legislation authorizing the establishment of a Constituent Assembly. Legislation was approved in July for the restoration of each of Uganda's traditional monarchies; these were to be limited to ceremonial and cultural functions.

Political and Constitutional Changes

Museveni and the NRM won overwhelming support in the March 1994 elections for the Constituent Assembly. Officially, all candidates were required to stand on a non-party basis. However, tacit official tolerance of party campaigning was reflected in the leaders of three parties—the DP, the Conservative Party (CP) and the UPC—being given access to national radio and television during the weeks prior to the elections.

In May 1996 Museveni convincingly won the presidential election, with 74.2% of the votes cast; his principal challenger, Paul Ssemogerere of the DP, took 23.7%. Museveni immediately declared that he would not restore multi-party democracy for at least five years. Elections to the Parliament (as the NRC had been restyled under the 1995 Constitution), which now consisted of 276 seats, comprising 214 elected and 62 nominated representatives, took place in June 1996.

A referendum on Uganda's non-party system took place in June 2000, and was declared by external electoral monitors to be free and fair. However, opposition parties boycotted the poll, and the participation rate was only around 45%. The existing system was supported by 90.7% of those who voted.

Museveni Re-elected

In the March 2001 presidential election Museveni's main challenger was Dr Kizza Besigye, a former ally who commanded significant support within the Uganda People's Defence Forces (UPDF—the country's armed forces). The election campaign period was characterized by violence, and opposition groups complained that state security services were intimidating their members and supporters. Museveni was re-elected President with a decisive 69.3% of the votes cast, against Besigye's 27.8%. There were reports of electoral malpractice and intimidation during the poll, but international observers concluded that the voting was conducted in a generally free and fair manner. There were a number of bombings in the immediate aftermath of the election, including one in Kampala just after the results were announced. The Government accused Besigye of being linked to the attacks and barred him from leaving the country. Museveni subsequently purged the UPDF of Besigye supporters, and Besigye fled to the USA in August. The NRM secured more than 70% of seats at the legislative elections held in June.

In February 2004 the seven main opposition parties—the DP, the UPC, the CP, the Justice Forum, the National Democratic Forum, the Free Movement and the Reform Agenda—established a coalition termed the Group of Seven (G7). Throughout 2004 and 2005 opposition politicians regularly denounced the Government for banning rallies and undermining their campaigns. In November 2004 the Constitutional Court overturned legislation preventing parties other than the NRM from contesting elections, and upheld a ruling allowing candidates who lived abroad to lead political parties.

In April 2004 Museveni formally retired from the UPDF (having been promoted to the rank of General), in order to comply with legislation barring serving members of the armed forces from active membership of a political party. In June 2005 Parliament approved legislation officially restoring multiparty democracy and removing restrictions on the renewal of the presidential mandate. In the following month the changes were ratified by 92.5% of those who voted at a national referendum, albeit on a relatively low turnout of 47%.

The 2006 Elections

Besigye returned from his self-imposed exile in October 2005 in order to contest the 2006 elections. Three weeks later he was arrested and imprisoned on charges of treason and rape. His arrest provoked two days of rioting in Kampala, in which one opposition supporter was shot dead by police. In December 2005, despite his detention, Besigye was permitted by the Electoral Commission to file his nomination papers as a presidential candidate. The country's external donors raised concerns over government efforts to intimidate the opposition, and several reduced or postponed aid payments, or diverted payments away from government agencies.

At the presidential election, held on 23 February 2006, Museveni was re-elected with 59.3% of the votes cast; Besigye, who had been released on bail by the High Court, won 37.4% as the candidate of the Forum for Democratic Change (FDC). In the concurrent parliamentary elections, the NRM secured 202 seats, and the FDC 40. The remaining seats were split between the DP (10 seats), the UPC (nine seats), the CP (one seat), the Justice Forum (one seat) and 28 independents.

Museveni's Third Term

Although Besigye was acquitted of rape in March 2006, his trial for treason continued. After a ruling in January that he and his co-defendants could not be tried before a court martial, the trial was moved to the High Court.

Throughout 2006 and 2007 opposition politicians continued to make allegations of intimidation by the Government and the security apparatus, and restrictions were placed on opposition rallies and demonstrations. Questions were also asked about the Government's perceived lack of willingness to ensure the independence of the judiciary. In March 2007, in a repetition of events of late 2005, police and prison guards stormed the High Court to re-arrest nine individuals linked to Besigye (who had been granted bail on charges of treason). The judiciary observed a three-day strike in protest at what it deemed government interference in the legal system, and opposition activists marched in Kampala in support of the strike. Museveni wrote to the Chief Justice, Benjamin Odoki, to apologize for the confrontation and offered the Government's assurances that such action would not be repeated.

Concerns over growing anti-Asian feelings in Uganda were heightened following riots in April 2007, in which one Asian Ugandan was stoned to death and a Hindu temple was attacked. The riots followed protests organized against the Ugandan Asian-owned Sugar Corporation of Uganda, which had been awarded substantial areas of forest by the Government for cultivating sugar. Police were required to protect more than 100 individuals from being attacked by protesters in Kampala, and two opposition members of Parliament, Beatrice Atim and Hussein Kyanjo, who had organized the protests, were arrested, together with 26 others, on charges of inciting anti-Asian violence. The arrests provoked further demonstrations in Kampala, and police used water cannons, tear gas and live ammunition against protesters.

In April 2008 concerns over government attempts to limit the freedom of the press were revived when three journalists from *The Independent* magazine were arrested after publishing articles alleging corruption within the armed forces, and accusing the UPDF of committing atrocities in northern Uganda as part of the military campaign against the LRA.

Museveni reorganized the Cabinet in February 2009, appointing Syda Bbumba as Minister of Finance, Planning and Economic Development. The Government tabled a bill in March that sought to authorize telephone tapping by the security services. Opposition deputies criticized the proposed legislation, claiming that the Government would use it to undermine the political opposition. Later in that month Museveni was forced to defend his decision to appoint his wife to a cabinet post, as Minister of State for Karamoja, amid concerns over nepotism within the Government; Museveni's son and brother also held senior government positions.

Tensions between the Kabaka of Buganda, Ronald Muwenda Mutebi, and the Government intensified from mid-2009, with the Kabaka seeking to have more powers restored. The Government's barring of Mutebi from visiting a district within the Bugandan Kingdom prompted riots in Kampala; more than 20 people died in the ensuing unrest. Museveni and Mutebi met following the violence, but little progress was made in resolving underlying antagonisms. In March 2010 police opened fire on protesters at the Bugandan royal mausoleum at Kasubi, killing two people. Demonstrators had sought to prevent Museveni from making an official visit following a fire that had destroyed the tombs. Another person died in the crowds of mourners who came to visit the mausoleum.

During 2009–10 the issue of rising homophobia in Uganda caused consternation among donor governments. In October 2009 a private member's bill was introduced in Parliament that sought to increase punishments for homosexuality, the definition of which was also broadened to include lesbianism. Most controversially, the proposed legislation included provision for the death penalty for the offence of 'aggravated homosexuality'. The 'promotion' of homosexuality was also criminalized; this was interpreted by non-governmental organizations (NGOs) as an attack on organizations campaigning for gay rights. The Government was equivocal in its support for the bill: torn between supporting legislation with widespread popular appeal and the demands of donors that the bill be moderated or abandoned.

In April 2010 Besigye accused the Government of continuing its campaign to undermine him, after he was questioned by police over allegations of inciting violence against government supporters, and of complicity in a corruption scandal. In June Besigye was physically attacked during an opposition rally. The FDC accused the Government of covertly supporting private groups seeking to sabotage opposition rallies with violence. In October treason charges against Besigye, long seen as politically motivated, were finally rejected by the Constitutional Court.

Within the governing NRM, factional struggles abated in 2010 as the party sought to ensure victory in the 2011 elections. No action was taken against several ministers implicated in corruption scandals. A parliamentary report leaked in April 2010 appealed for Vice-President Gilbert Bukenya (who had been removed from the Cabinet in the previous month) and Minister of Foreign Affairs Sam Kutesa to be prosecuted over a scandal involving the procurement of luxury vehicles for the 2007 Commonwealth Heads of Government Meeting (CHOGM), held in Uganda.

The 2011 Elections and Museveni's Fourth Term

Museveni was re-elected for a fourth term at the presidential election held on 18 February 2011, increasing his share of the vote to 68.4% (from 59.3% in 2006). Besigye, again representing the FDC, received 26.0%. In the concurrent parliamentary elections, the NRM won 164 of the directly elected seats; the FDC took 24 directly elected seats, the DP 11, the UPC seven, and the CP and the Justice Forum one each.

Despite victory in the elections, the Government cracked down on all signs of dissent and opposition. Protests were met with police violence and arrests of opposition leaders. Besigye was detained in April 2011, provoking violent demonstrations in Kampala in which two people were killed by police. Besigye was repeatedly detained during 2011–13, together with other opposition leaders, as the Government sought to quell opposition protests. Some of those detained alleged that they had suffered police brutality and torture while being held.

Meanwhile, in October 2011 Kutesa, government Chief Whip John Nasasira and a junior minister appeared in court on charges of corruption in connection with the 2007 CHOGM. (All charges against former Vice-President Bukenya were abandoned just days before his trial was due to begin.) Allegations were also made against Prime Minister John Patrick Amama Mbabazi and former energy minister Hilary Onek in relation to contracts awarded to Tullow Oil. In February 2012 the Minister of Gender, Bbumba, and the Minister of General Duties, Khiddu Makubuya, both resigned following allegations of corruption.

In August 2013 Parliament approved the controversial Public Order Management Bill, despite criticism from opposition deputies and other groups. The legislation required police approval for any gathering of more than three people to discuss political issues. It also authorized police use of firearms in self-defence, or against persons resisting arrest.

Museveni also signed a new Anti-Homosexuality Bill into law in February 2014, despite widespread international condemnation and criticism. Major donors such as the USA, the European Union (EU) and the World Bank reduced or withheld aid to Uganda in response. However, in August the Constitutional Court struck down the new legislation as unconstitutional.

In September 2014 Museveni dismissed Prime Minister Amama Mbabazi. Mbabazi was seen as a potential challenger to Museveni for the NRM candidature for the presidency in the 2016 election, and it was widely believed that Museveni had removed him from office to prevent such a challenge. Museveni also sought to head off challenges from potential opposition candidates.

In February 2015 the police sought an international arrest warrant to detain Dr Aggrey Kiyingi, an Australian-based Ugandan cardiologist. Kiyingi, who had announced his intention to stand in the 2016 presidential election, was accused of funding the Allied Democratic Forces (ADF)—a long-favoured tactic of the Government in seeking to undermine opposition figures—and of supporting the assassination of several Muslim clerics in Uganda over the previous few months. Kiyingi denied having any dealings with the ADF.

The main opposition parties sought to form a coalition around a single candidate for the 2016 elections, establishing The Democratic Alliance (TDA), a group consisting of the FDC, the DP and several other opposition parties. Efforts to unite all the main opposition parties were hampered when the UPC announced in June 2015 that it was still unsure as to whether to join the TDA. Besigye had previously announced that he

would not contest the election; however, in July he confirmed that he would stand for nomination as the FDC presidential candidate, leading to divisions within the party, with FDC President Maj.-Gen. Gregory Mugisha Muntu also announcing his candidacy for the FDC nomination.

In June 2015 the Government pushed forward an NGO bill, which sought to increase government oversight over the country's large NGO sector. The bill proposed that NGOs would be required to declare all income sources, and would need permits from local authorities in order to operate. Furthermore, NGOs deemed to be operating in ways that could undermine security could be closed down.

The 2016 Elections

In September 2015 Besigye was formally adopted as the FDC's candidate in the 2016 presidential election. He was placed under house arrest soon afterwards, in an attempt to bring to an end the opposition rallies that he had been organizing.

Uganda's presidential and parliamentary elections were held on 18 February 2016. Museveni secured victory in the presidential ballot, gaining 60.8% of the votes cast. His main rival, Besigye, took 35.4% of the vote. The third-placed candidate, Mbabazi, standing as an independent, won just 1.4%. Turnout was 68%. In the parliamentary elections, the NRM secured 199 of the directly elected seats (30 seats more than in 2011). The FDC won 29 seats, the DP 13 and the UPC four. The remaining 44 seats were obtained by candidates registered as independents. Besigye was repeatedly detained following the elections, after claiming that the polls had been fraudulent and refusing to accept the results.

International observers criticized the Electoral Commission, claiming that it lacked transparency and independence. However, in late March 2016 Uganda's Supreme Court rejected an opposition challenge to the election results, citing insufficient evidence of vote rigging. The Government continued to suppress protests heavily, and to detain and charge opposition leaders, including Besigye.

Political Developments During Museveni's Fifth Term

In May 2016 Museveni promoted his son, Muhoozi Kainerugaba, to the rank of Major-General. In January 2017 Kainerugaba was appointed as a special presidential adviser during a reorganization of senior army commanders, further reinforcing his status as the heir apparent to Museveni.

The Government instituted measures to impose tighter control on media reporting. Media outlets were frequently threatened, and journalists detained. A number of editors faced legal sanctions after publishing pieces critical of the Government, and newspapers and other media outlets were threatened with closure during Museveni's fifth term.

In November 2016 members of the armed forces and police officers stormed the administrative offices of the Rwenzururu Kingdom, in Kasese. The resultant shoot-out between Ugandan security forces and royal guards inside the building left more than 80 people dead, including at least one member of the Ugandan army and 14 police officers; hundreds of people were arrested during and after the military operation. The Government accused the Kingdom of training and arming a group of fighters in a bid to secede from Uganda. Local leaders, for their part, cited anger over unfulfilled government promises as the cause of the tensions, denying that the group was a secessionist rebel force, and rejecting army claims that the movement was linked to the rebel ADF. Charles Wesley Mumbere, the King of Rwenzururu, was charged with terrorism, aggravated robbery and attempted murder in December, although he was granted bail in February 2017.

During 2018 opposition to President Museveni was increasingly focused around musician-turned-politician Robert Kyagulanyi Ssentamu (popularly known as Bobi Wine), who represented a generational shift in opposition leadership. Entering Parliament after winning a by-election in Kyadondo in 2017, Wine became a vocal critic of Museveni and his Government, leading campaigns against removing the presidential age limit and against the social media tax, and using his broad popularity among Ugandan youth to support opposition candidates in local and by-elections. In August 2018 Wine was detained and accused of treason, together with over 30 opposition politicians, after stones were allegedly thrown at

Museveni's convoy following a political rally during a by-election campaign. The campaign had been characterized by tension and violence, and Wine's driver had been shot and killed after police raided a hotel where Wine was staying. Journalists covering the protests against Wine's arrest were attacked by soldiers, with one such incident being caught on film and leading to a rare apology from the army. One person was killed in the protests and many others (including journalists) were arrested. Wine alleged that he had been tortured and beaten while in detention.

Following a spate of crime in Kampala, at the end of 2018 the Government increased police patrols, installed more surveillance cameras, and created a controversial new civilian militia, the Local Defence Units (LDUs), to help to reduce crime. By mid-2019 around 6,000 people had been trained to carry out patrols and gather intelligence on crime as part of these units, although there were some fears that the low salaries paid to members of the LDUs, whose members would be armed, could actually increase crime and instability.

After parliamentary approval was secured in December 2018, the Constitution was amended in early 2019 to remove the presidential age limit, to extend the term of office for holders of the presidency and parliamentary seats from five to seven years (with effect from 2016, meaning that the next elections would be pushed back to 2023) and to restore the two-term limit from after the next elections. The opposition opposed the amendments, which were unpopular among certain sections of the public, and made an appeal to the Constitutional Court to overturn the changes. As the judges of the Constitutional Court gathered to give their ruling in July 2019, the opposition organized protests against the amendments, and some 50 demonstrators were arrested. The Court approved the removal of the presidential age limit (thereby allowing Museveni to stand once more for re-election), but rejected the extension of tenures for the President and parliamentary deputies; as a result, the next elections were due to take place in 2021.

Wine was detained by police in his own home again in April 2019. Although released, he was detained once more the following week, and criminal charges were laid against him for his role in protests against the social media tax the previous year. After his court appearance, Wine was refused bail and remanded to a maximum security prison.

In July 2019 Wine was again arrested, after failing to appear in court to hear the treason charges against him. Later in that month Wine announced the long-expected news that he would stand as a presidential candidate in the 2021 election. However, if found guilty of either of the charges that he faced—treason or holding an unauthorized public meeting—he would not be eligible to stand.

In August 2019 Stella Nyanzi, a prominent critic of President Museveni and the Government, was convicted on charges of cyber-harassment and sentenced to 18 months in prison, after publishing a poem critical of Museveni and his late mother on Facebook. The conviction was overturned on appeal in February 2020, and Nyanzi was released. Police fired live rounds into the air to disperse a crowd of her supporters who had gathered outside the court in Kampala.

The Government faced further criticism in November 2019 over efforts to de-register a large number of NGOs, after the removal of about 12,000 mostly local organizations and charities from the official register by a government review. Critics argued that the Government was targeting organizations that had criticized it, as part of efforts to undermine the opposition.

In March 2020 Wine, together with several other activists, challenged the legality of the Public Order Management Act, under which Wine had been charged for protesting against the social media tax in 2018, in the Constitutional Court. The Court ruled that the legislation was indeed unconstitutional; the Government announced that it would appeal against the ruling.

In June 2020 Wine and Besigye formed an alliance, the United Forces of Change, to contest the elections. Several days later, Wine announced that he would represent the alliance as its presidential nominee, and Besigye agreed to support him to this end; the latter continued to be a frequent target of police action in early 2020.

The COVID-19 Pandemic in Uganda

Uganda undertook one of the earliest responses to the COVID-19 pandemic that spread across the world in early 2020, as well as one of the strictest series of measures to limit the spread of the virus. In mid-February the Minister of Health, Dr Jane Ruth Aceng, warned the country to be vigilant about the growing threat of COVID-19 and called on health care workers to be ready to respond to cases of infection. The Government began screening arrivals at the international airport in Kampala, with teams monitoring for symptoms of the virus in nationals who had returned to Uganda. Meanwhile, stocks of testing kit at the country's virus-testing laboratory were strengthened. Uganda recorded its first confirmed case of COVID-19 on 15 March. The response of the Government was swift: schools and universities were closed, and large public gatherings were prohibited. The Government closed all bars, ended public court hearings, and individuals entering Uganda from countries deemed to be at high risk for the virus were required to self-quarantine in designated hotels, initially at their own expense. On 25 March the Government closed public transport and non-food markets. On 30 March new restrictions were announced, including a dusk-to-dawn curfew, a ban on making journeys in privately owned vehicles and the closure of all shopping malls and non-food stores for 14 days.

The police took action against individuals who issued false information about the virus. A Christian pastor was arrested in Kampala in late March 2020 for claiming that the virus was not present in Uganda, and at the end of the month at least three Roman Catholic priests were arrested for holding religious services and contravening the regulation against holding large gatherings.

In April 2020 the Government announced a major package of economic support to help businesses and individuals through the COVID-19 crisis. The package immediately became subject to wrangling between Parliament and the Government over whether the spending should be controlled by Parliament or the executive. Parliament voted to allocate 20m. new Uganda shillings (about US $4,000) to each parliamentary deputy, which President Museveni immediately condemned. At the end of April the High Court in Kampala ordered that the funding should be allocated to official COVID-19 taskforces. The Speaker of Parliament, Rebecca Kadaga, directed deputies to ignore the ruling; observers suggested that she was seeking to please deputies as part of her campaign for re-election as Speaker. In May it emerged that several NRM deputies who had publicly praised Museveni for his leadership during the crisis had each been allocated 40m. new Uganda shillings to spend on COVID-19 support programmes in their own constituencies. Opposition politicians condemned this measure as a bribe to deputies in return for their support for the Government.

In early May 2020 the Government eased the lockdown restrictions. The rapid and comprehensive response of the Government and the use of digital technology, such as the Health Management Information System, to report on suspected cases of infection and organize sample testing across the country appeared to have ensured that Uganda had the smallest number of confirmed cases in the East African region: 97 recorded infections at 5 May, when the restrictions were lifted, with no deaths. However, despite receiving praise for taking the COVID-19 threat seriously and responding quickly, the Government was criticized for not providing enough support to those individuals most affected by the impact of the lockdown. The promised food supplies and a financial package for the most vulnerable were insufficient, and opposition politicians, including the Mayor of Kampala, Erias Lukwago Ssalongo, as well as Besigye and Wine, demanded that the Government introduce further measures.

The Government was also criticized for encouraging a heavy-handed response from police and security forces. At the end of March 2020 the army had announced that it would co-ordinate the enforcement of the lockdown. From the start of the lockdown the police were accused of reacting with excessive force to apparent contraventions of the regulations. In Mukono, two people were shot by police in late March for using a motorcycle taxi after the use of these had been banned, and police opened fire on a group of people in Budada, accusing them of breaking the ban on public gatherings. Members of LDUs were accused of beating market vendors and motorcycle riders in Kampala for disobeying the lockdown, and a motorcycle taxi driver died after setting himself on fire outside a police station in Masaka in June, after officers allegedly demanded a bribe that he could not afford to pay in order to release his vehicle.

The Government was also accused of using the lockdown restrictions to silence the opposition, with bans on public gatherings rigorously enforced, and efforts made to limit criticism of the Government's record. In mid-May 2020 activists organized a march, demanding that the Government provide more support for poor Ugandans, including food and face-mask distribution, as well as releasing individuals who had been detained for violating the lockdown restrictions. Nyanzi, who organized the protest, was arrested with several other activists; the police claimed that she was exploiting the pandemic for political reasons. Following an announcement that the distribution of food would be considered a breach of the restrictions, Francis Zaake, an independent politician and a supporter of Wine's People Power movement, was arrested after distributing food. Zaake later claimed that he had been tortured in police custody. The police were criticized for arresting opposition politicians who distributed relief, but they did not act against officials from the ruling NRM for doing the same.

In June 2020 Museveni criticized the World Health Organization (WHO), claiming that it had been inconsistent in its response and had issued impractical guidelines for dealing with COVID-19. He argued that those who had been infected outside of Uganda and consequently returned to the country should not be included in the data for the prevalence of the virus in Uganda, as this falsely inflated Uganda's infection rate. Later in June the World Bank provided a US $300m. package to support Uganda's efforts in containing the virus and to help those affected by the restrictions.

The 2021 Election Campaign

Wine announced the creation of his new political party, the National Unity Platform (NUP), in July 2020, for which he would stand as presidential candidate. His candidacy was given a boost in the following month when Besigye announced that he would not stand as the FDC candidate.

Throughout the election campaign COVID-19 laws to limit large public gatherings were used as a tool to undermine opposition efforts to campaign. Opposition leaders, especially Wine, were repeatedly targeted for detention for allegedly breaking the laws. On 18–19 November 2020 there were large-scale protests against the Government in Kampala and several other cities, following the arrest of Wine for allegedly breaching COVID-19 restrictions. Around 50 people were killed and many more injured after police used live bullets to try to disperse the crowds A report into the incident published in May 2021 showed evidence of shots being fired by police and undercover officers. However, the authorities continued to deny that the deaths were the result of deliberate action.

Later in November 2020 the EU announced that it would not deploy an election observer mission to Uganda due to the failure of the Government to respond to previous concerns. Shortly before the elections in January 2021, the USA also cancelled its planned observer mission after the Government had failed to provide accreditation on time.

Meanwhile, in early December 2020 Wine alleged that security forces had opened fire on his convoy, injuring several of his team. Wine announced he would temporarily suspend campaigning in the face of this kind of intimidation. At the end of that month there was another attack on Wine that left his bodyguard dead and two journalists accompanying the campaign were injured. Wine accused the police of deliberately running over his security official in a military police truck. FDC presidential candidate Patrick Amuriat was also repeatedly detained and his campaign meetings broken up by police.

The 2021 Elections and Their Aftermath

Uganda's parliamentary and presidential elections were held on 14 January 2021. Museveni won the presidential poll, securing 58.4% of the votes cast; Wine took 35.1% of the vote

and Patrick Oboi Amuriat secured 3.3%, with none of the other candidates reaching 1%. Museveni's NRM won a majority in the National Assembly elections, with 337 of the parliament's 529 seats. However, around 30 of its deputies, including cabinet ministers and the Vice-President, lost their seats—mostly to Wine's NUP, which secured 57 seats. The NUP overtook the FDC in parliamentary seats, becoming the new main opposition party. There were 73 independent deputies in the assembly, although many of these would be likely to support the Government's legislative agenda. Turnout, at 59%, was the lowest since Museveni became head of state.

Opposition parties claimed that the elections were fraudulent, and contested the results. The EU announced that it was gravely concerned over the conduct of the election campaigns. In mid-April 2021 the USA issued visa restrictions against Ugandan officials it claimed had been 'responsible for, or complicit in, undermining the democratic process in Uganda'; and the US Secretary of State accused security forces of responsibility for the deaths and injuries of significant numbers of innocent bystanders and opposition supporters.

After the elections Wine was placed under house arrest, as the Government sought to quash protests against the result. The US ambassador was prevented by security forces from visiting Wine at his home during his detention. The Government then accused the USA of trying to subvert the election process.

In May 2021, as Museveni was preparing to be sworn into office once more, security forces were accused of arresting hundreds of opposition supporters in an attempt to clamp down on any protests against the contested election results. Wine alleged that one of his security team had been tortured and killed by security forces in Kampala, after the body of Daniel Apedel was fund dumped in a Kampala mortuary. Police denied complicity in the death, claiming he had been killed by a mob. The detentions continued after the inauguration ceremony on 12 May. Museveni admitted that around 200 opposition activists, described as criminals, were in detention, although Wine claimed that the true figure was over 700.

Political tensions continued to rise, and in early June 2021 an assassination attempt on Gen. Edward Katumba Wamala, Minister of Works and Transport and a close ally of the President, resulted in the death of Wamala's daughter and their driver. The Government blamed terrorist groups operating in the Democratic Republic of the Congo (DRC) for the attack on Katumba's car. By July eight men had been detained in connection with the incident; a further four suspects had earlier been shot dead by the investigating security team.

By late May–early June 2021 Uganda was in the middle of its second wave of the COVID-19 pandemic, with infection numbers increasingly driven by the rapid spread of the Delta variant of the virus. In mid-June President Museveni ordered new lockdown measures, which would last for 42 days. Schools and businesses were closed, all non-essential activity stopped and people were required to remain at home. By June stocks of COVID-19 vaccine had run out and oxygen supplies were also depleted as the number of people admitted to hospital increased rapidly. At the end of July Museveni announced the lifting of some of the lockdown restrictions, although schools remained closed pending the vaccination of essential workers.

Uganda's schools were only reopened in January 2022, representing—at 22 months—one of the longest school closures due to COVID-19 in the world. Over one-half of the country's 15m. school-age children had received no education during this period. In secondary schools, there was a significant problem of school-age children failing to attend classes. The United Nations Children's Fund (UNICEF) reported that one in 10 children failed to return when schools opened in January, and an official government report estimated that up to 30% of children could drop out of formal education after the long gap. At 13 October, according to WHO, 169,274 confirmed cases of COVID-19, with 3,630 deaths, had been reported in Uganda.

In August 2021 a 2014 anti-pornography law, which had been criticized for potentially leading to women being harassed for wearing certain clothes, was annulled by the Constitutional Court. Following a crime wave in Masaka in September, in which 28 people were killed by assailants with machetes, the police operation arrested two opposition deputies from Wine's NUP. The Government alleged that the NUP had been involved in orchestrating the violence, but the NUP described the arrests as politically motivated and designed to undermine the opposition.

Besigye announced the formation of a new opposition coalition, the People's Front for Transition (known as the Front), in October 2021. The announcement was seen by many as an attempt by Besigye to restore his position as the country's most prominent opposition leader, instead of Wine.

In March 2022 speculation over plans for a succession of power from Museveni to his son, Kainerugaba, were reignited during expansive celebrations for Kainerugaba's birthday. He announced his retirement from the army on social media network Twitter, opening the way for his entry into politics. The army subsequently denied that Kainerugaba had retired, however, and he then appeared to reverse that decision. This came after a number of high-profile meetings and negotiations, including a meeting with the South African President, Cyril Ramaphosa, and discussions in Rwanda prior to the reopening of the Rwanda–Uganda border in January.

Others interpreted Kainerugaba's birthday celebrations as part of government attempts to distract the population from rapidly increasing inflation. The Government was also accused of inflating COVID-19 infection data in order to divert criticism away from Uganda's growing economic woes. The Government appeared to be concerned about the impact of rising prices, and security officials were increasingly visible in urban areas, probably in order to repress emerging protests. In May 2022 Museveni gave a televised address, during which he ruled out cutting taxes or increasing subsidies for basic commodities.

Also in May 2022, Besigye organized a protest against rising prices in Kampala, where he was arrested and charged with inciting violence by police. Released in early June, Besigye organized a second protest, and was arrested and detained again, but denied bail by the court. Other opposition leaders also voiced their own concerns over the rising cost of living, but did not offer their full support for Besigye in his protests against the Government.

INTERNAL SECURITY CONCERNS

From the mid-1990s rebel groups in northern and western Uganda challenged the Museveni administration. The ADF carried out several attacks on targets in western Uganda. In the north, meanwhile, the LRA (backed by Sudan) became increasingly disruptive, killing as many as 10,000 people during 1993–98, and displacing around 220,000, who sought refuge in protected camps.

In December 1999 Parliament approved a bill granting a general amnesty to all rebels who were prepared to renounce rebellion. During the early 2000s the Government stepped up its military offensives against the LRA, with increased co-operation from the Sudanese Government. The LRA responded with its own attacks in the north. By the mid-2000s the LRA began to move its military bases from southern Sudan to the DRC, and later the Central African Republic (CAR), establishing camps in Garamba National Park.

In October 2005 the International Criminal Court (ICC) in The Hague, Netherlands, issued arrest warrants for Kony and four other LRA commanders (deputy leader Vincent Otti, Raska Lukwiya, Okot Odhiambo and Dominic Ongwen). From 2005 a series of peace talks repeatedly stalled, then broke down, before being reinstated. Despite a lack of progress in the talks, violence within Uganda declined, and by January 2007 some 230,000 people had returned to their villages as security conditions in the north improved. However, an estimated 1.2m. people remained in the camps.

In 2007 the LRA moved its main base from the DRC to the CAR, carrying out attacks against civilians in both countries. In December 2009 the UN High Commissioner for Human Rights, Navanethem Pillay, accused the LRA of having killed at least 1,200 civilians between September 2008 and June 2009, mostly in the CAR and southern Sudan. However, the group's leadership was reduced through a series of captures, surrenders and deaths of senior LRA commanders. From 2010

the USA increased its support for the defeat of the LRA in the DRC and the CAR, dispatching troops to the region to participate in the military campaign. Amid continued defections and killings of senior LRA commanders, the group's strength declined further, although it retained the capacity to perpetrate sporadic attacks and abductions in eastern DRC and the CAR.

From 2010 Uganda was faced with a new internal security threat arising from its involvement in the African Union (AU) military operation in Somalia. In July 2010 two bombs killed at least 74 people in Kampala, and injured some 70 others. The Somali militant Islamist organization al-Shabaab claimed responsibility. In September 2011 two Ugandans who admitted involvement in the Kampala bombings received prison sentences.

A bomb attack on a bar in Kampala in October 2021 killed one person and left three people injured. The ADF later claimed responsibility for the attack, which came after the UK Government had warned of an increased risk of a terrorist incident in Uganda. Within a few days, a suicide bomber blew himself up on a bus near Kampala, injuring several people. On 16 November a series of suicide bombings occurred across the capital, killing four people and injuring over 30. The ADF was blamed for these attacks, and in the following days police arrested 21 people accused of being involved in ADF terrorist cells, while security forces shot and killed a Muslim cleric accused of recruiting members for ADF. Security forces also clashed with ADF forces near the DRC border, killing four. The bombings represented a significant escalation in ADF activity since its formal affiliation to the Islamic State militant organization in 2019.

In November 2021 the UPDF launched an offensive against ADF forces in the eastern DRC, in response to the bomb attacks. The operation was sanctioned by the DRC's President, Felix Tshisekedi, who may have seen it as helping to secure his authority in the increasingly unsettled area of the DRC. In January 2022 Ugandan forces announced the capture of a senior ADF leader, Benjamin Kisokoranio.

During 2022 protests and armed violence intensified in the Karamoja region. The rapid expansion of formal and informal mining had pushed up land prices, and local communities were being forced from their lands. Pastoralist communities were finding it harder to access water points and pasture land, fuelling the violence. However, the Government was accused of making the situation worse through its heavy-handed response. A security operation launched in mid-2021 had, by the following year, killed more than 300 people, and UPDF leaders were accused of the forced displacement and execution of protest leaders.

REGIONAL RELATIONS

The East African Community (EAC) was established by the Governments of Kenya, Tanzania and Uganda in 2000. In January 2005 the East African Customs Union came into effect, and the EAC was expanded to include Burundi and Rwanda in December 2006.

In October 2008, in Kampala, the three main African trading blocs (the EAC, the Southern African Development Community and the Common Market for Eastern and Southern Africa), signed an agreement to create a single free trade zone of 26 countries.

In March 2007 Uganda sent 1,700 troops to Somalia as part of an AU peacekeeping force, known as AMISOM (African Union Mission in Somalia), where Uganda remained as one of the largest foreign troop presences until it began to withdraw its forces from the end of 2017. Following an attack on a UPDF military base by al-Shabaab fighters in April 2018, which left 46 Ugandan soldiers dead, in July the Government announced a small increase in the number of soldiers based in Somalia.

During the early 1990s Uganda provided support for Laurent-Désiré Kabila, leader of the Alliance des Forces Démocratiques pour la Libération du Congo-Zaïre, which overthrew the Government of President Mobutu Sese Seko in May 1997. However, Kabila's failure to tackle Ugandan rebels in the renamed DRC led to renewed tensions, and Uganda subsequently backed anti-Kabila rebels in 1998 in co-operation with the Rwandan Government, with whom relations became increasingly tense. In April 2002 Uganda and Rwanda signed a peace treaty, and both withdrew their troops.

Throughout early 2019 the Ugandan and Rwandan governments exchanged criticisms of alleged interference by the other in their respective domestic politics. In January the Ugandan security services alleged that they had arrested a Rwandan spy. In the following month Rwanda closed the main border crossing into Uganda and advised against Rwandans travelling to Uganda, accusing the Ugandan Government of having illegally deported almost 1,000 Rwandan nationals since 2017, and having detained and tortured nearly 200 more. In March 2019 the leaders of both countries exchanged accusations of seeking to destabilize each other.

In January 2022 Rwanda reopened its border with Uganda. The move came after Museveni replaced the chief of Ugandan intelligence, Maj.-Gen. Abel Kandiho, who was believed by the Rwandan Government to have been behind efforts to undermine it. Museveni's son, Muhoozi Kainerugaba, played a critical role in leading the discussions with Rwandan officials and in helping to soften the still icy relations between the two Presidents.

Relations improved between Sudan and Uganda after Museveni and his Sudanese counterpart, President Omar al-Bashir, signed a peace agreement in December 1999. Each country undertook to stop hosting guerrilla groups directed against each other.

During the conflict in South Sudan between supporters of President Salva Kiir Mayardit and his former Vice-President Dr Riek Machar Teny Dhurgon, from late 2013, Uganda was accused of providing the Government of South Sudan with military assistance.

Some 340,000 refugees from South Sudan fled the conflict there into Uganda during 2016, making Uganda the world's largest recipient of refugees of any country in that year. By the end of 2016 Uganda was host to an estimated total of 940,800 refugees. In August 2017 the number of refugees who had entered Uganda from South Sudan surpassed 1m., with the Ugandan Government receiving praise from international organizations and donors for its policy of accepting and supporting refugees.

In March 2020 the Ugandan Government closed its border crossings in response to the spread of the COVID-19 pandemic, which prevented refugees fleeing the conflict in the DRC from entering the country. After an estimated 10,000 refugees from neighbouring countries were left stranded on Uganda's frontiers, the Government reopened its border crossings in mid-June, with Museveni ordering that all refugees be allowed to cross into the country. The Office of the UN High Commissioner for Refugees set up a testing facility in Uganda to undertake random testing of refugees for COVID-19.

In May 2016 President Museveni was criticized by donors for inviting Sudanese President al-Bashir (who had been indicted by the ICC on charges of genocide) to his inauguration. He caused further controversy by using his speech at the event to criticize the ICC and to announce that Uganda no longer supported it (despite being a signatory to the Court). A number of European, US and Canadian diplomats walked out of the ceremony in protest at Museveni's remarks.

In August 2021, following the fall of the Afghan Government and the Taliban takeover in Kabul, Uganda agreed to host up to 2,000 Afghan refugees who were fleeing the conflict. The US Government was to meet the costs of hosting these refugees.

In February 2022 the International Court of Justice ordered the Ugandan Government to pay US $325m. to the DRC, in a ruling which found that Uganda had violated its international obligations while acting as an occupying force in the DRC during the 1998–2003 conflict. The reparations were to cover the violence to people and property, and compensate for the Ugandan military's role in looting resources during the conflict. However, the Government dismissed the verdict, and refused to confirm whether it would pay the reparations, the payments of which were to be spread over five years.

In July 2022 a leaked document alleged that the Ugandan Government was providing training for insurgent troops in Ethiopia's Tigray region. Museveni's son, Kainerugaba, had previously expressed support on social media for the Tigray People's Liberation Front, which was in conflict with Ethiopian government forces in the region, and the report suggested that the Ugandan army was training up to 4,600 soldiers in four facilities. However, the UPDF denied the allegations, claiming that the report was a fabrication.

Economy

JÖRG WIEGRATZ

INTRODUCTION

Since the accession to power of the National Resistance Movement (NRM) Government of President Yoweri Museveni in 1986, Uganda has undergone a significant neoliberal restructuring. During the 2000s Uganda was considered the star economic reformer and the example that other African countries should emulate. The 2010s were turbulent in economic terms, with a mixed economic growth record. The early 2020s are now being shaped by major trends, many related to the economic impact of the coronavirus disease (COVID-19) pandemic and the war in Ukraine: preparing the country for oil production in western Uganda; national debt and fiscal revenue challenges; the increasing role in the country of non-Western actors, such as the People's Republic of China; the urbanization, digitization and diversification (also in terms of export destinations) of the economy; foreign direct investment (FDI); regional economic integration; the intensification of labour migration; rising inflation (driven by an increase in fuel prices); the impact of climate change; and the governance of President Museveni, who secured re-election for a sixth term in January 2021.

Notably, the country was in lockdown or under restrictive measures for long periods between March 2020 and July 2021, and the economy only reopened fully in January 2022. In this context, the Government's aims are: (i) economic recovery through increased production, enhancing supply, as well as boosting demand and external market access (particularly via regional integration); (ii) supporting livelihoods and household incomes by addressing poverty, vulnerability and regional inequalities, and sustaining job creation; and (iii) continued investment infrastructure and workforce training, which promote growth.

Uganda remains a major hub of liberal economic policy-making in the region and is a key partner for both Western and non-Western actors. The role of the international financial institutions (IFIs) and the international donor community in pushing for structural adjustment policies in the 1980s was key, as was the support lent by international non-governmental organizations and bilateral donors. By building a closer relationship with the IFIs and international donors, the Government has secured continued financial support while consolidating the neoliberal architecture of post-1986 Uganda. This relationship is built on matters concerning not just the economy but also, for example, security and refugee politics.

Neoliberal reforms were proposed as domestic policies aimed at transforming Uganda into a modern industrial economy, away from peasant-based agriculture and towards a society with sustained employment and a growing middle class. The reforms included a swift liberalization of the foreign exchange markets and of the export crop sectors, including coffee and cotton, on which the economy depended heavily.

The reforms entailed the dismantling and privatization of the respective marketing boards, the liberalization of trade and active promotion of FDI. The agricultural extension service was dismantled and turned into a private-led, demand-driven service that could not cater to most farmers. These reforms were complemented by an extensive reconstruction and downsizing of the civil service. The neoliberal reform package also introduced business-friendly legislation, privatized state-owned property and companies and established public bodies charged with promoting investment (such as the Uganda Investment Authority) and increasing fiscal revenue (such as the Uganda Revenue Authority—URA). The deregulation of the economy took its toll on Ugandan society, since protective buffers for the most vulnerable in society were removed and social services, such as health care and education, were privatized, as was land. These reforms gradually led to a shift in power and assets towards capital—especially foreign—and away from most working people.

The significant economic, political and social changes brought about by the neoliberal reform package have resulted in a contradictory combination of poverty reduction and poverty creation. The past three decades have seen a relatively stable country, with sustained rates of poverty reduction and growth and an expansion of the private sector. The physical infrastructure of Uganda has been substantially enlarged, and both public and private investment has increased, as signalled by a steady inflow of FDI. The country continues to be attractive to local and foreign investors in various sectors (banking, agriculture, telecommunications, real estate, tourism and, recently, oil). Meanwhile, inequality has increased, and unemployment—and underemployment—characterize a society that is marked by economic insecurity and pressure. This is compounded by waves of dispossession of sections of the population, who are increasingly excluded from access to land and water. There has also been an increase in widespread fraud and corruption, starting from the notorious privatization sagas of the 1990s, to the corruption involved in many programmes designed to assist the poor and to deliver basic services such as education and health care or post-conflict reconstruction in northern Uganda. The money gained from large-scale corruption fuels various economic activities, for example in the real-estate sector.

Since the dismantling of state boards and co-operatives, the rural economy has become dominated by numerous private intermediaries, brokers and traders, alongside a few large (and often foreign) agribusinesses. These economic actors have a disproportionate bargaining power *vis-à-vis* a large, but fragmented and impoverished peasantry, which often receives little support in terms of production and marketing of agricultural products.

Current public and policy debate have focused on the issue of foreign dominance and control of the economy, as key sectors, notably banking, are to a very significant extent in the hands of foreign firms. The Government has not altered its stance over FDI, arguing that it is a key pillar in advancing the industrialization of the country, but qualifying that with an emphasis on giving policy attention to domestic actors as well (via, for example, local purchase campaigns such as 'Buy Uganda Build Uganda').

Finally, Uganda has started to develop its oil sector, after the discovery of significant reserves since 2006. Although the start of production was postponed for several years, owing partly to disputes over taxation between the Government and oil companies, important agreements were signed in April 2021 regarding the construction of the East African Crude Oil Pipeline (EACOP—see *Petroleum and Energy*). Reaping more and sustained benefits of closer economic integration with neighbouring Democratic Republic of the Congo, Rwanda and Kenya are major priorities too, as are the expansion of the manufacturing and services (including real estate) sectors, and the digitization of the economy.

THE CURRENT ECONOMIC SITUATION

Key Macroeconomic Indicators

Uganda, like other East African Community (EAC) economies such as Kenya and Tanzania, rebased its gross domestic product (GDP) in 2014 better to reflect the recent structure of the economy, and the base year was adjusted from 2002 to 2009/10. The rebasing showed that the Ugandan economy was 13% larger than previously indicated.

Before the COVID-19 pandemic, Uganda's growth performance compared positively with that of the region and continent at large. The services sector dominates the economy (accounting for 44.9% of GDP in 2021/22), followed by industry and agriculture (29.0% and 26.1% of GDP, respectively). The Greater Kampala Metropolitan Area, which hosts about 10% of Uganda's population and 70% of its manufacturing plants, alone contributes more than 30% of GDP. Urban expansion is estimated at 6% per year, which is much faster than the global rate. The area covered by Kampala City has grown from 0.7 sq km in 1902 to the current estimated 839 sq km. More than 20m. people (about one-third of Uganda's forecast population) were expected to live in cities by 2040. Between 2002 and 2010 the urban population grew by 5.6%—about twice as fast as the rural population.

The diversification of incomes away from agriculture has been a key trend of the post-1986 economy, and although the 2012/13 Uganda National Household Survey data suggested that 76% of households earned income from agricultural production, it was the most important source of income for only 42% of households, and just 26% of households relied on agriculture exclusively.

The Government forecasts that Uganda will transition from the status of a least developed country to that of a lower-middle income country with a GDP per capita of over US $1,039 in the coming years, and to that of an upper-middle income country with a GDP per capita of $9,500 by 2040. To achieve this goal, the Government has focused on improving Uganda's competitiveness. The Second National Development Plan (NDPII) identified three key sectors with strong growth potential (agriculture, tourism, and minerals, oil and gas) and two economic fundamentals (infrastructure and human capital development). Investment in these priority areas was expected to have the greatest multiplier effect on the economy. In 2018/19 some of the completed NDPII core projects included the Isimba hydroelectric plant, the Source of the Nile Bridge (or New Jinja Bridge), the Masaka–Mbarara transmission line and the revival of Uganda Airlines. By mid-2022 the first phase of construction of the Kiira Vehicle Plant, at the Jinja Industrial and Business Park, was almost complete, while two Kayoola Electric Buses have since been produced and tested under a technology transfer project with the China High-Tech Corporation. Uganda is now in the NDPIII phase (2020/21–2024/25), which aims to enhance value added in the three key growth sectors mentioned above; to consolidate and increase the stock and quality of productive infrastructure; to increase the stock of a skilled, innovative and healthy population; and to strengthen the private sector to drive growth.

Since 2021 the economy has been shaped, *inter alia*, by climate change (floods), the reopening of the border with Rwanda (after a year of closure), the reopening and gradual recovery of the economy after the end of the COVID-19 pandemic, and the effects of the war in Ukraine following the invasion by the Russian Federation in February 2022, which has driven up the costs of energy and food.

The Uganda Business Impact Survey 2020 showed the most affected sectors to be heavy and light manufacturing, services, food processing and transport. The lockdown ban on public transport and movement restrictions rendered many workers unable to reach the plants; almost three-quarters of the companies surveyed were estimated to have lost more than 30% of their employees. The increased revenue losses, high unemployment levels and rising loan defaults made the future of micro- and small and medium-sized enterprises (SMEs) and their contribution to economic growth uncertain. Inflows of FDI and remittances of Ugandans in the diaspora have also declined sharply. Consumer-facing sectors were severely affected by social distancing measures imposed by the Government and heightened uncertainty, while the manufacturing sector has declined, owing to disruptions to the inflow of raw materials.

All of this has had profound effects, especially on the informal sector, which employs many urban poor people, mostly women and youths. Before the COVID-19 pandemic, 85% of people employed in the informal sector were already operating below the poverty line; many were at high risk of slipping into poverty in the current crisis. According to the Government, because of the lockdown and mobility restrictions, many urban poor lost their sources of regular income, creating financial instability as they have little or no savings. There has been a decline in the quantity of work, hence a decline in wages/income, as economic activity is predicated on daily customer flow and face-to-face interactions. Surveys indicated that micro- and small businesses, which employ most of the urban poor, experienced the most severe effects compared with medium and large businesses. This might be due to the fact that 47% of informal business in Kampala alone sell directly to individuals/households. This exacerbated pre-existing credit constraints as 69% of the businesses surveyed reported a decline in credit (34% experienced a severe decline). This led to many micro- and small business owners failing to meet their loan obligations. The lockdowns also caused a surge in unemployment. An estimated 100,000 jobs have been lost since the start of the pandemic.

The number of formal jobs, as recorded by the Pay As You Earn (PAYE) register, declined from 1,336,234 jobs in 2017/18 to 1,210,450 jobs in 2020/21 as the pandemic took hold. In the manufacturing sector, where there was no full lockdown, the number of jobs increased by 8,943 in 2020/21, and the education sector registered the highest number of losses (40,590). Many Ugandans who lost jobs in the formal and informal sectors sought employment abroad, particularly in the Middle East. The number of Ugandan migrant workers—the majority employed as maids, cleaners and security guards—increased from 11,009 in 2019/20 to 28,235 in 2020/21, and to 88,553 in 2021/22 as restrictions on global travel were lifted. There is concern about the conditions of Ugandans working abroad, and the Government has responded with initiatives, including helplines for workers (especially domestic household staff) suffering abuse by their employers.

Overall, poverty has remained relatively unchanged in the last decade. The poverty rate stood at 19.7% in 2012/13, before increasing to 21.4% in 2016/17 and falling to 20.3% in 2019/20. Income inequality declined from 21.4% in 2016/17 to 20.3% in 2019/20. Of the approximately 8.3m. persons registered as poor in 2019/20, the majority resided in rural areas, and only about 1.3m. poor persons lived in urban areas. The incidence in income poverty increased during the COVID-19 pandemic, from a pre-pandemic 19% to 22% at mid-2021. The Government reported a decline in income inequality as measured by the Gini coefficient of 1.4% (0.419 to 0.413) between 2016/17 and 2019/20.

Uganda's GDP per capita has continued to improve, rising from US $916 in 2019/20 to $1,046 in 2021/22, in a context of high population growth, and Uganda's eventual transition to a middle-income country appears to be under way.

The Uganda Bureau of Statistics (UBOS) estimated that the size of the economy in 2020/21 was 148,278,000m. shillings in nominal terms (an increase from 139,711,000m. shillings in 2019/20).

In 2021/22 there was a gradual recovery in economic activity: in real terms, the economy grew by 4.6%, up from 3.5% in 2020/21. The growth was driven by a significant recovery of the service sector (after the reopening of the leisure and entertainment industry, accommodation and food services), and a dynamic information and communications sector. The services sector expanded by 3.8% in 2021/22 (compared with 2.8% in 2020/21); industry by 5.4% (from 3.5%), driven by manufacturing (particularly processing of meat, grain milling, pharmaceuticals, and edible oils and fats production), with a rise of 3.9% (compared with 2.2% in 2020/21); and agriculture, forestry and fisheries by 4.3% (unchanged from 2020/21). Food crops (particularly bananas, vegetables and sweet potatoes) and cash crops (particularly robusta coffee) grew by 3.5% in 2021/22 (from 4.1% in 2020/21) and 7.1% (from 12.5%), respectively; livestock grew by 8.3% (from 7.8%). Construction grew by 5.3% (from 3.6%), mining and quarrying by 21.8% (from 6.9%), information and communication by 7.3% (from 11.8%) and real estate by 9.4% (from 3.9%).

The agricultural sector, which accounts for about 45% of exports and employs around 65% of working-age Ugandans (72% of youths), is of vital importance for household incomes. In a context of climate change, it is notable that the threat of

drought comprised 72.6% of all insurable risk in the agriculture insurance business sector (at September 2021). This led to increased promotion of the weather/drought index insurance service for farmers based on satellite data, and the Government has put in place regulatory provision for this new, fast-growing scheme which by the end of 2021 had been taken up by over 300,000 farmers.

The Government continues to offer post-pandemic recovery support: notably, together with financial institutions, it has provided an agricultural credit facility since 2010. The portfolio was valued at 669,900m. shillings, across 2,063 projects, at March 2022. The scheme brought together various public and private sector institutions and supports agro-industrialization in the country. In November 2021 the Government and private sector actors launched a small business recovery fund—a risk-sharing instrument to support businesses that had suffered owing to the COVID-19 pandemic yet showed potential for recovery if loans and liquidity were provided. By the end of March 2022 some 359m. shillings had been disbursed to 14 successful applicants, and a further 1,120m. shillings had been approved for 71 other projects.

Financial Inclusion and Personal Finance

Financial inclusion (access to and usage of appropriate financial services) continues to constitute a major government priority. In 2017 the Ministry of Finance, Planning and Economic Development, in conjunction with the central bank, the Bank of Uganda (BoU) and various stakeholders, developed and launched the National Financial Inclusion Strategy (NFIS) 2017–22. According to the Government, the NFIS aimed to reduce economic insecurity by facilitating greater access to affordable financial services.

About 78% of all Ugandan adults had access to financial inclusion by 2018, and 58% of adults used formal financial services. Much of the inclusion is driven by the use of payment services via mobile telephones, which are being used by 57% of the adult population to save, access credit and send and receive money. However, formal inclusion is more limited: 18% of the adult population saves in formal institutions, while 5% use formal credit, and just 1% have a formal insurance policy.

Mobile money services entered the Ugandan market in March 2009, and by March 2018 such services were available to 23m. users. By April 2021 the total number of registered mobile money users had grown to an all-time high of 36.9m., with 60% of those registered also being active users of the service. The value of mobile money transactions increased from 3,400,000m. shillings in 2016 to 12,500,000m. shillings in April 2022.

Mobile money service providers include MTN, Airtel, Uganda Telecom, Orange, M-cash and Eeezy Money. The first four of these providers are mobile network operators (MNOs), and the last two are independent third-party providers that use the telecommunications platform provided by the MNOs. Both in terms of registered and active users, mobile money has surpassed the number of people holding 'traditional' accounts (5.6m.) with the financial institutions that are supervised by the BoU—commercial banks, credit institutions and microfinance deposit-taking institutions (collectively known as supervised financial institutions). This indicates the scale of the potential offered by mobile money.

The mobile money service offering has expanded from person-to-person transfers to bill payment and loan repayments. There are also increasing linkages to the 'traditional' financial sector, including mapped accounts. It is expected that these linkages will proliferate by offering mobile money account holders the opportunity to save in formal bank accounts and accrue interest (paid into the mobile money account). Mobile money is already being used by microfinance institutions to facilitate loan (re)payments. This reduces transaction costs, enabling service delivery to remote rural areas. In 2020/21 users diversified their use of mobile money as a result of the pandemic-related lockdown, leading to growth in the value of many subsectors of mobile money. This trend has continued. Users increasingly pay their commercial bills for goods and services via mobile money services: person to business value increased from 2,500,000m. to 8,800,000m. shillings in the year to April 2022. The Government has taken regulatory measures that aim to advance financial consumer empowerment and protection. An administrative unit handles information requests and complaints from customers about the services.

Formal saving and investment products/services remain in relatively low demand, particularly among the rural population, and only about 25% of adults use banks. Uganda's level of domestic savings has fluctuated in the recent past, from 19.7% in 2019 of GDP in 2019 to 18.2% in 2020. This performance was expected to improve to 21.4% in 2022 (although this is well below the NDPIII target of 35%). The Government aims to increase financial access and encourage a savings culture by strengthening savings and credit co-operatives and developing and advancing the supervisory and regulatory framework for the financial sector overall (including non-bank institutions). The financial sector (including money-lending services) has a mixed reputation because of the harsh practices of debt collection of some operators and the very high formal and informal interest rates.

In an effort to increase financial inclusion and enable the spread and penetration of banking services, in December 2017 the BoU approved the Shared Agent Banking System, which was launched by the Uganda Bankers Association in April 2018. An agent could be a petrol station, a supermarket, a permanent mobile money agent, a pharmacy or a retail shop that is fully licensed and has been in existence for one year. The system allows connectivity between member banks, enabling agents to serve customers of any other member bank, thereby minimizing duplication of agency networks and increasing and maximizing points of presence. Moreover, the Inter-Institutional Committee on Financial Inclusion has been implementing the NFIS, with a view to harmonizing all efforts by different ministries, departments and agencies and other stakeholders in the pursuit of financial inclusion.

Trade, Manufacturing and Tourism

Uganda's formal exports to other EAC partner states increased from US $425.2m. in 2010 to $1,255.28m. in 2018; exports to Kenya and South Sudan registered the fastest growth. EAC partner states are committed to establishing a single currency by 2024. In order to promote and enhance industrialization, EAC partner states operate under the Regional Industrialisation Strategy (2012–32). The strategy aims to enhance industrial production and productivity and accelerate the structural transformation of the EAC economies. The EAC has identified investment opportunities covering a wide range of sectors. The six key and strategic regional industries identified as having a huge potential comparative advantage are: iron-ore and other mineral processing; fertilizers and agro-chemicals; pharmaceuticals; petrochemicals and gas processing; agro-processing; and energy and bio-fuels.

EAC countries expect intra-EAC trade to be a main source of growth, employment and income (and thus poverty reduction) for their economies. The infrastructure and border administration systems—e.g., via the establishment of One Stop Border Posts (OSBP)—are being improved for the purpose of trade facilitation. For example, the implementation in 2014 of a single customs union reduced the turnaround time from 18 days to four for cargo being transported from Mombasa (Kenya) to Kampala. Following the introduction of the OSBPs, clearance for large consignments now takes about 20–30 minutes, compared with the three hours previously.

During 2018/19 the Common Market for Eastern and Southern Africa launched the Digital Free Trade Area (DGFTA) programme, which aims to use information and communications technology to improve efficiency in cross-border trade between member states by minimizing physical barriers. DGFTA incorporates e-trade, e-logistics, e-legislation and an electronic Certificate of Origin.

Uganda has significant deposits of iron ore, and reserves total some 580m. metric tons. These remain unexploited, however, and in 2018/19 Uganda registered a large trade deficit, of US $194m., in its iron and steel sector. The Government's ban on exports of unprocessed iron ore in 2011 aimed to promote value-added in raw iron ore in order to produce sponge or pig iron for iron and steel production. The country currently has 24 steel facilities with an annual installed capacity of 1.7m. tons.

The textiles, clothing and footwear products subsector registered the highest annual growth in the manufacturing sector in both 2016 and 2017, followed by the saw-milling, paper and printing subsector. The Government is supporting vertically integrated industries in the textile sector by subsidizing power to reduce production costs. Uganda has 10 operational tanneries, two of which process a small proportion of their hides and skins to produce finished leather. The installed tanning capacity amounts to 1.1m. hides and 2.0m. skins per year. The Government is also encouraging the growth of assembling plants. Saachi Technologies' assembly plant, for example, was commissioned in 2018 to assemble domestic home appliances, including flat irons, televisions and refrigerators, which were originally imported by the company in 2014. The Government has also earmarked 7 ha of land for the development of an information technology business process outsourcing park at Lunyo, in Entebbe.

Uganda is increasingly recognized as a leading global tourism destination, attracting well over 1m. international tourists each year, up from 600,000 in 2006. The number of tourists in 2018 totalled 1.8m. In 2017 Uganda's annual earnings from tourism totalled almost US $1,500m. However, the COVID-19 pandemic had a significant adverse effect on tourist arrivals and revenue. A total of 448,996 hotel room bookings were cancelled between March and June 2020, and the Government estimated a loss of almost $1,000m. from the decline in foreign tourist arrivals in that year, to only 473,085. Since the reopening of the economy, tourism has rebounded significantly (owing in part to the new sports and cycling tourism segments). Tourism was boosted by the official launch of the new 'Explore Uganda' brand that is being used to promote the country as a travel destination, and domestic tourism is also growing, although an Ebola virus disease outbreak in the country in September 2021 further affected tourism in the short term. Uganda is part of the Northern Corridor Integration Projects (NCIP) with Kenya, Rwanda and South Sudan. In February 2017 the NCIP launched the East African Tourism portal—an online platform marketing the region as a single tourism destination.

Petroleum and Energy

Commercially viable petroleum was discovered in Uganda's Albertine Rift region in 2006, and reserves are estimated at 3,500m. barrels of crude. There are high expectations of significant benefits accruing from the exploitation of oil. For instance, the objective of Uganda Vision 2040 to transform Ugandan society 'from a peasant to a modern and prosperous country within 30 years' is to a large extent based on expected revenues from oil and gas.

The commercialization of the country's oil resources has been a relatively slow process since then, but in April 2021 three key agreements were signed relating to the EACOP—a 1,443-km crude oil pipeline to run from Kabaale in Uganda to near the port of Tanga in Tanzania. At a meeting in Kampala, President Museveni and Tanzanian President Samia Suluhu Hassan signed the Host Government Agreement, the Shareholders Agreement (for the pipeline company in which TotalEnergies SE and China National Offshore Oil Corporation were partners) and the Tariff and Transportation Agreement. It was hoped that these developments would unlock about US $20,000m. in investment, with a view to starting production in the mid-2020s and that there would be economy-wide benefits. TotalEnergies stated that it expected to begin commercial oil production from the Uganda oilfields in early 2025. The final investment decision was signed in February 2022, and construction of the pipeline was expected to begin in the 2022/23 financial year. However, the European Parliament, among other bodies, has expressed concerns about the environmental and social impact of the project and its contribution to climate change and the displacement of many communities along the planned route of the line. The Ugandan and Tanzanian Governments have rejected these concerns.

The share of the population with access to the national electricity grid increased from 10% in 2009 to 14% in 2013, with access in rural areas rising from 1% to 7%. Access to electricity increased to 28% in 2021, up from 23% in 2017. Of the country's 122 districts, 98 are connected to the national grid. The Government aims to increase access by implementing the Electricity Access Scale-up Project to boost access to 60% by 2027 for households, industrial parks, commercial enterprises and health care and education facilities.

Electricity generation capacity was estimated to have reached 1,868 MW by the end of 2021, with the completion of the 600-MW Karuma Power Project. The Karuma–Kawanda Transmission Line was complete in early 2022, while construction of the Nyagak III Power Project resumed in May 2019. The electrification of industrial parks has advanced with the commissioning of the Mukono and Iganga Industrial Parks substations. Under the Rural Electrification programme, 14,820 km of medium-voltage power lines and 10,280 km of low-voltage distribution power lines have been constructed. Since the Government launched the free Electricity Connections Policy in November 2018, 277,500 rural households have been connected, and in the first half of 2019/20 1,859 km of medium- and low-voltage lines were constructed and added to the grid. However, operating costs for companies in the sector increased during the COVID-19 pandemic, and subsequent connection targets were missed.

Poverty Reduction and Employment

The country's Vision 2040 set a target of reducing the poverty rate to 5% by 2040. However, the slowdown in economic growth and climatic shocks experienced in recent years (notably floods) and the COVID-19 crisis affected the income-generating potential of Ugandans. The number of registered poor persons increased from 6.6m. at the time of the 2012/13 Uganda National Household Survey (UNHS) to 8.0m. in the 2016/17 survey, and to 8.3m. in 2019/20 (a poverty rate of 20.3%). The UNHS 2019/20 showed that in subregions with poverty rates above the national average of 20.3%, such as Acholi (67.7%) and Karamoja (65.7%), there was an upsurge in poverty between the two survey periods. However, rural poverty in northern Uganda has fallen, owing to increased agricultural production (especially of cassava, sorghum and maize) and government and donor spending on development programmes following the end of years of severe armed conflict and insecurity there.

Nevertheless, poverty remains widespread in rural areas, and the level of deprivation of basic services—water, education, health care and electricity—is still very high, alongside child malnutrition. Regional differences, with higher poverty rates in the Northern and Eastern regions, also indicate the need for a regional approach to poverty reduction policies. The usefulness and accuracy of the official poverty data are contested. The 2019 Human Development Index (HDI), published by the United Nations Development Programme (UNDP), placed Uganda in the 'low human development' category, with a value of 0.544 (159th out of 189 countries), representing a small improvement from 0.528 in 2018; however, inequality has increased.

By 2021 life expectancy in Uganda had improved to 63.7 years (up from 59 years in 2015). The literacy rate of Ugandans in 2018 increased to 76.5% of all adults (from 72% in 2014). In 2020 the child mortality rate (of children under five years old) had declined to 43.3 per 1,000 births (from 137 in 2011). The share of the population with no access to water has fallen from about 8.5m. in 2016 to some 7m. in 2022.

Uganda has one of the fastest-growing populations in the world, totalling an estimated 44.2m. at mid-2022. As the country has a very young population, dependency ratios remain very high, and as the rate of population growth is higher than the rate of productive employment growth, there is significant unemployment and underemployment.

Uganda's total formal labour force increased from about 8.8m. people in 2012/13 to some 10.0m. people in 2016/17, and the working-age population also rose during that time, from 16.5m. people to 19.1m. However, according to the National Labour Force Survey of 2016/17, Uganda's working population was estimated at 15.3m. people, of which 16% were enrolled under the existing formal retirement benefit arrangements, which doubles as the retirement benefits sector coverage (up

from 6% in 2014). The employment to population ratio stood at 39% in 2020.

One major problem is the fact that the formal sector provides only limited employment opportunities. For instance, the manufacturing sector currently accounts for only about 3%–4% of all workforce jobs, and the deceleration in that sector's growth has been considerable (from 13.8% in the 1990s to 6.6% in the 2000s). In the post-pandemic economy, the major sectors driving formal employment are manufacturing, education, human health and social work, public administration and defence. The Government reported an increase of 12.5% in registered formal sector jobs between 2019/20 and 2020/21 (to 1,448,144 employees).

According to the UNHS, employment fell from 60% of the working population in 2016/17 to 52% in 2019/20. The agricultural sector in Uganda remains the main employer: the working population in subsistence agriculture increased from 36% in 2016/17 to 47% in 2019/20. This suggests that people who lost their jobs resorted to subsistence agriculture, leading to an increase in the subsistence economy from 3.3m. people in 2016/17 to 3.5m. in 2019/20. This was due to a contraction of employment opportunities as household enterprises' employment share fell from 38% in 2016/17 to 31% in 2019/20, owing largely to the COVID-19 pandemic. The entire agricultural sector employed 65.1% of the labour force in 2016/17 (compared with industry at just 8.6%).

The non-agricultural informal sector employs 14% of the labour force (some 2.1m. people), and 86% of these jobs are household-based. The manufacturing sector is dominated by informal activities, with three informal jobs for every one formal position in that sector. However, with regard to overall employment in formal enterprises, the manufacturing sector has the largest share of jobs (21,000), followed by administrative services (15,700), finance and insurance (8,200) and trade (6,500). Most new formal jobs are service-based, and some 75% are created in the most urbanized districts, namely Kampala, Wakiso, Mukono, Mbarara, Jinja and Arua.

An estimated 80% of the labour force are self-employed or employed as unpaid family workers in the agricultural sector. Informal employment constitutes 67% of total employment outside agriculture. Most of the jobs (60%) are in micro-enterprises (employing less than five people), while small enterprises (between five and 20 people) and large enterprises (more than 20 people) account for a significantly smaller number of jobs (18% and 12%, respectively).

A challenge facing the development of the private sector in Uganda is the large informal sector and activities in the SMEs. These comprise about 1.1m. businesses and employ some 2.5m. people, across all economic sectors, with 49% in the services sector, 33% in commerce and trade, 10% in manufacturing and 8% in other sectors. The informal sector provided 43% of GDP in 2014/15, reflecting its very high potential, when formalized, in terms of contribution to the country's GDP. The large informal sector regularly exhibits low quality of labour, poor productivity and high mortality rates. However, it still accommodates the majority of the labour force, employing 93.5% of the total. The number of large enterprises in the economy grew at an annual average rate of 15% between 2012/13 and 2017/18, from 799 to 1,594. This growth trend is mirrored in the annual increase in the number of active industrial consumers of electricity, which grew by an average of 4.1% per year between 2014 and 2018.

The Government is concerned about the economy being dominated by very small firms for various reasons. One of them is the pressing issue of high unemployment, particularly in urban areas and among the young. Hundreds of thousands of graduates struggle to find employment, and many remain unemployed for several years. There is a considerable gap between the number of new jobs created in the formal economy (estimated at less than 40,000) and the number of new labour force entrants (about 400,000). There has been considerable public debate about the 'jobless growth' problem that Uganda (and many other countries) has experienced and about ways to address it. Moreover, pressure on the labour market will intensify, as the workforce is expected to rise from an estimated 15m. in 2014 to about 36m. by 2040. Another concern is the limited contribution that small and informal businesses and casual labourers make to tax revenues.

Finally, data from the 2014 Population and Housing Census showed that household reliance on subsistence farming has stagnated, with the share of households reporting subsistence agriculture as their main source of livelihood rising only marginally, from 68% in 2002 to 69% in 2014. The share of households relying on employment income as the main source of livelihood decreased, from 22% to 16%, over the 12-year period (representing an overall decline of 27%).

Employment income is particularly significant in urban areas, where more than two out of every five households rely on it as their main source of livelihood. The decline in the share of households primarily engaged in employment was coupled with a rise in the share of the working population that was neither employed nor in education/training from 4.6% to 5.4% over the same period. This reflects the inability of economic growth, which has been driven mainly by the services sector over the past decade, to translate into significant job opportunities. Commercial activity is the other notable source of livelihood for households, with one in 10 households reporting it as their main livelihood source. Meanwhile, according to the 2014 census, 4% of households (about 255,500) relied on social support systems for their livelihood. Agricultural land remains the dominant production asset for most households, especially in rural areas, where more than 70% of households reported ownership of agricultural land. Of the 5.2m. farming households in the country in 2014, only 119,209 (2.3%) were engaged in commercial farming, and they were almost evenly distributed between rural and urban areas. The Government's efforts to encourage farming households to practise agriculture as a business through various programmes have yet to bear substantial results. The latest programme to this effect was launched in February 2022: the Parish-Development model, intended to integrate some 3.5m. households from the subsistence economy into the formal economy. Each of the over 10,000 parishes across Uganda was to receive 100m. shillings (involving over 1,059,000m. shillings in total) from a revolving fund in 2022/23 through the Parish Savings and Credit Co-operative. However, so far cash flow problems have undermined the disbursement of funding.

Public Debt Stock

The country's public debt stood at US $19,540m. at 30 June 2021 (63% of this was external debt); the debt-to-GDP ratio was 47%. Debt is increasing, and the ratio was estimated at 52.7% at 30 June 2022. The major risks to the external debt position are poor performance in exports and an increased rate of debt accumulation, particularly on non-concessional terms, and the impact of the COVID-19 pandemic on state finances. There is ongoing public discussion about the country's indebtedness and the burden of loan repayments on the national budget. There are also frequent media reports about delays to salary payments to government workers, owing to a shortage of government funding.

FURTHER CONTEMPORARY POLICY ISSUES

A key economic aim remains the reduction of costs of production and transport and the increase in connectivity between production areas and markets. Joint infrastructure programmes with EAC partner states are expected to improve connectivity and integration across the region and enhance Uganda's export potential. For instance, the Governments of Uganda, Kenya and Rwanda have agreed to prioritize the development of a standard-gauge railway, which will run from Mombasa to Kampala and on to Kigali (Rwanda). The new railway will probably reduce transport costs and increase business efficiency and thus spur investment. Further reforms related to reducing the cost of business licensing and expediting commercial laws and regulations are envisioned.

The Ugandan authorities are increasingly combating the proliferation of substandard and counterfeit goods, as well as fuel adulteration, the sale of expired food and animal and human medicines, money laundering and non-transparent bank fees, all of which have negatively affected consumers and businesses. There is also a growing public outcry about widespread corruption, fraud and poor service delivery in the public sector, as well as malfeasance in the private sector. Initially, the Government responded by attempting to curb critical debate, especially about large-scale corruption, but subsequently sought to enhance its legitimacy and renewed its appeal for modernization and development, and the ruling NRM has been designated to act as the guarantor for Uganda becoming a middle-income country. The Government has also advanced a programme of zero-tolerance for corruption, while advocating integrity, transparency, accountability, service delivery and wealth for all.

There is increased recognition of the role of more advanced regulatory systems, greater consumer protection and standard adherence in developing the economy and ensuring growth of production and trade (i.e. via sales of certified quality goods to neighbouring markets). To compete in these regional markets (for example with Kenyan counterparts), Ugandan firms will have to be able to produce quality products in order to gain consumer trust and confidence. Standards-related scandals therefore constitute potential hazards to Ugandan consumer brands and their exports to these growing markets.

The Uganda National Bureau of Standards (UNBS) is playing an increasing role in this regard, as is the URA, and local authorities have also been involved, in addressing some of these shortcomings in the private sector. A key driver for some of the standard initiatives is the incentive pressure structure of the EAC market integration project. The UNBS is co-operating with its counterparts in neighbouring countries to improve and harmonize standards, checks and enforcement systems.

Renewed efforts are under way to address regional trade barriers, including non-tariff barriers. Several measures in recent years have contributed to a significant reduction in trade costs. Government interventions in the road sector led to an increase in the share of paved national roads from 4% in 2008/09 to 19% (or more than 4,000 km) in March 2015. The stock of the paved national road network had increased to 5,419 km by 2021. An increasing number of national roads are now in fair to good condition, and the total road network amounts to more than 35,000 km. Notably, the EAC has identified five major corridors in Uganda—totalling about 12,000 km—for rehabilitation and upgrading and plans for the country to have a paved road network of 35,250 km by 2030 and 65,700 km by 2050. Furthermore, the standard-gauge railway network is being rehabilitated. The railway currently facilitates transportation of some 18,000 metric tons of cargo monthly and 2,000 passengers daily in order to support decongestion in Greater Kampala. In the air transport sector, 13 aerodromes have been rehabilitated countrywide, and the expansion of Entebbe International Airport and construction of Kabaale International Airport are under way. Uganda Airlines resumed operations in August 2019, but since 2021 former and current members of its senior management team have been under investigation for alleged corruption and mismanagement. The performance of public corporations and state enterprises remains mixed. In 2020/21, out of 26 public enterprises, 17 made profits, including Uganda Electricity Transmission Company (112,000m. shillings of profits), Uganda Electricity Generation Company (91,900m. shillings) and National Water and Sewerage Corporation (47,800m. shillings). However, Uganda Railways Corporation, Kilembe Mines, Uganda Civil Aviation Authority and Uganda National Airlines Company all recorded losses in 2020/21.

The insurance sector has also been the target if regulatory measures, in line with the Insurance Act of 2017, with the aim of making the sector more focused on risk management. In 2021 gross written premium income grew by 7.9%. Non-life insurance dominates the sector in that year (61.4% of total business). Uganda has a growing retirement benefits sector: at December 2021 there were 65 schemes and 258 service providers catering to the sector, the assets of which had grown by an annual average of 20% in the previous six years, reaching over 18,000,000m. shillings (11.3% of GDP), up from 15,400,000. shillings in 2020, across some 2.8m. accounts (18% of the total working population). The sector's investment portfolio totalled 18,900,000m. shillings at 31 December 2021, up from 8,040,000m. five years earlier. The sector's investments were diversified across the East Africa region (with

Uganda accounting for 67.6% of the total, Kenya 22%, Tanzania 10% and Rwanda 0.4%).

Notably, Uganda's capital market industry was boosted by the initial public offering of MTN in late 2021 (4,500m. ordinary shares at 200 shillings a share). A total of 535,900m. shillings were raised, and MTN joined the Uganda Securities Exchange (USE) in December. This led to the ratio of domestic market capitalization to GDP rising to 5.6%.

THE EFFECTS OF COVID-19 ON THE ECONOMY

The manufacturing sector has been hugely affected by the COVID-19 pandemic, and cargo movements at border points (especially Malaba, Busia, Elegu and Mutukula) were subject to severe delays during the lockdowns to contain the virus, and the flow of goods to and from the country slowed sharply. This undermined output and delivery, especially where imports of raw materials were required. A recent survey suggested that 75% of manufacturing firms experienced disruption in the supply of raw materials during the lockdowns. Furthermore, restrictions on the movement of people led to the temporary or part-closure of factories, while a recent fall in demand for goods has been attributed to the loss of income opportunities for most people in the informal sector. Restrictions on movement also disrupted the role of intermediaries, who collect various goods or products from different manufacturers for resale to retailers and through informal cross-border trade. Moreover, the closure of bars and other entertainment venues reduced demand for alcoholic and non-alcoholic beverages, and the closure of educational institutions reduced the market stationery and food served in school.

Meanwhile, manufacturing SMEs suffered from restricted access to working capital. As SMEs have limited cash reserves, they operate mostly on liquidity from sales as capital. Owing to restrictions to contain the pandemics, SMEs were hit by a liquidity shock. Owing to fear of the virus, consumer priorities also changed, and essential items were prioritized, to the detriment of discretionary purchases. This situation made many SMEs vulnerable to bankruptcy. Furthermore, as many manufacturing sector SMEs do not employ full-time maintenance engineers and rely on service providers in the case of emergencies, access to these essential service providers was limited, making operations more challenging and costly.

Given the size of certain larger factories (with more than 200 workers), social distancing measures were difficult to implement (e.g. in some agro-processing industries). This forced most factories to temporarily lay off some workers, while others suspended production. However, given the import problems (and the Government's heightened emphasis on import substitution), some sectors have benefited. For example, textile industries have boosted their capacity to produce face masks, and over 40 companies were certified by the UNBS to produce hand sanitizers (up from just two, pre-pandemic). The information and communications technology sector also boomed, owing to an unprecedented adaptation of digital systems in business processes. There was reportedly a 40% increase in the use of digital solutions in procurement/supply delivery channels by Ugandan organizations in March–April 2020.

Given that the manufacturing sector accounts for almost 80% of all electricity sales, the reduced production activity in the sector led to a fall in demand and sales. This put financial pressure on the Government to pay deemed electricity for the available generation capacity that is not being utilized. The reduction in revenue inflows for electricity suppliers was aggravated by the Government's directive to halt disconnection of customers in default. There was also a reduction in demand for petroleum products during the lockdown, owing to the ban on the movement of most private vehicles.

Following the onset of the pandemic, the agriculture sector reportedly struggled with wastage of produce, owing to the inaccessibility to markets and falling farm prices (especially in remote areas); inadequate farm labour and extension services, owing to social distancing measures, leading to poor management of pests and diseases; and shortages of feed, drugs, good quality seed and chemicals, owing to disruption in the transport system. Consequently, food insecurity is estimated to be at an all-time high.

MONETARY POLICY FRAMEWORK

In 2021/22 the BoU maintained an accommodative monetary policy stance to support economic recovery. It kept the Central Bank Rate at 6.5%. The BoU also continued to provide targeted credit relief measures until September 2022 for sectors particularly heavily affected by the pandemic, for example education and hospitality. The BoU established the COVID-19 Liquidity Assistance programme to manage liquidity risks until the disruptive effects of the pandemic had abated and the economy returned to normal. The BoU also cleared a significant section of its domestic arrears with businesses (around 526,000m. shillings) and settled court awards (57,000m. shillings).

During 2020/21 the UBOS rebased the Consumer Price Index (CPI) using enhanced methodology and ensuring the representativeness of the Index. The new CPI basket, with a base year of 2016/17, had 344 items (compared with 274 items in the previous basket, set in 2009/10), in line with international practice. Until recently inflation had remained low, with both annual headline and core inflation averaging 2.8% in the 10 months to April 2022. However, since October 2021 inflation has risen sharply, increasing year-on-year from 2.7% in January 2022 to 6.3% in May, driven by higher prices for fuel, cooking oil and soap owing to various supply chain disruptions ensuing from the war in Ukraine. Headline and core inflation were expected to rise to 8% by early 2023, owing to high prices for energy and food (which are affected by the weather and the depreciating shilling, among other factors).

PRIVATE SECTOR CREDIT

In 2021/22 growth in private sector credit increased modestly year-on-year but was still relatively low in historical terms, owing to heightened risk-aversion by commercial banks in the aftermath of the pandemic and fear of risk arising from borrowers' ability to pay, and the recovery in economic activity was weak. Private sector credit grew by 9% in the nine months to March 2022 (compared with 8.1%). Credit growth was strongest in the agriculture, trade, construction and real estate sectors.

The ratio of non-performing loans (NPL) to total loans rose to 5.8% in the first quarter of 2022 (from 5.4% in the same period of the previous year). NPLs rose most in the construction and the real estate and business services sectors (from 5.7% and 5.2% to 10.1% and 9.8%, respectively).

DEVELOPMENTS IN THE FINANCIAL SECTOR

The financial services sector, which is shaped increasingly by electronic and agent banking platforms, comprises banking, insurance, capital markets, pensions, microfinance and money laundering and combating of financial terrorism, as well as financial inclusion. In 2020/21 the Government undertook several reforms in the financial sector to stimulate economic activity and moderate the impact of the COVID-19 pandemic on the performance of the financial system. It permitted credit relief via the restructuring of loans extended to borrowers for a period of 12 months from 1 April 2020 (at the discretion of the respective credit-providing financial institutions). At a meeting of the BoU's Monetary Policy Committee in February 2021 these measures were extended for six months with effect from April. Between the inception of the credit relief measures and December 2020, the cumulative total credit relief applied for by borrowers amounted to 7,900,000m. shillings.

According to the Government's *Background to the Budget Fiscal Year 2022/23*, the banking sector in Uganda experienced growth in the year to March 2022, and an expansion in total assets of 10.8%. The sector remained well capitalized. Commercial banks' net profit after tax increased from some 900,000m. shillings to about 1,000,000m.

In December 2021 the BoU raised the core and total capital-to-risk-weighted assets ratios from 10% to 12.5% and 12% to 14.5%, respectively, following the issuance of new regulations in 2020. The rates stood at 13.4% and 14.3%, respectively, at 31 March 2022 (down from 16.6% and 17.8% at 31 March 2021). Two of Uganda's four credit institutions needed to recapitalize, as they did not meet the required minimum rates. Total assets held by credit institutions fell by 63% (amounting to 424,700m. shillings at March 2022). This trend was due mostly to the change of one bank to a now Tier 1 institution; this affected the respective level of liabilities, deposits and borrowings in this subsector.

In deposit-taking microfinance institutions, total assets rose by 1.1% year-on-year at 31 March 2022 (to 740,900m. shillings), owing mainly to the purchase of government securities. However, total liabilities fell by 1.4% (7,200m. shillings) to 521,800m. shillings (at 31 March 2022), owing to a decrease in long-term borrowing. The Government is working on provisions to allow these institutions to offer Islamic banking, agent banking and bancassurance services. By May the Government had licensed 1,396 institutions to operate in the country (up from just 239 in 2018).

Equity turnover on the USE fell by about 90%, to just 11,300m. shillings, in 2020/21. Average turnover per trading day also decreased, to 60.1m. shillings in 2020/21 (from 609.1m. shillings in 2019/20). The decline in market activity was attributed to limited participation from domestic and offshore investors (who account for over 70% of turnover at the USE), owing to the perception of pandemic-related risk.

THE CURRENT ACCOUNT AND TRADE BALANCE

The current account deficit in Uganda widened by US $992.6m. to $3,614.1m., in the year to March 2021, owing largely to the effect of the pandemic on tourism inflows. (Travel receipts fell by 78.7%.) However, the merchandise trade deficit narrowed from $2,811.5m. in 2019/20 to $2,531.1m., in 2020/21. This was due to a 20.3% increase in exports, offsetting the 7.7% increase in imports during that financial year.

The growth in exports and imports can be attributed largely to an expansion in the trading of gold. In 2020/21 exports of the commodity rose by US $1,046.6m. to $2,066.0m., while the value of imports grew by $809.4m. to $1,856.5m. Uganda has increased its refining capacity significantly, which has led to the country's emergence as a regional processing hub for gold. Other sectors also remained resilient amid the pandemic, maintaining, or indeed bettering, pre-COVID-19 levels. There was also an increase in the volume of coffee exported (offsetting a decline in international coffee prices), and higher earnings were also recorded for cocoa, tea, cement, beans and exports of flowers. Lower imports of oil and a decline in government project-related imports contributed to the fall in formal import costs.

However, the pandemic had a substantial adverse impact on informal cross border trade in 2020/21, resulting in a decline in informal exports and imports by 47.8% (to US $280m.) and by 48.2% (to $32.6m.), respectively. Border closures implemented both by neighbouring countries and domestically at the height of the pandemic slowed trade dramatically.

Total export of goods and services stood at US $5,740m. in the year to April 2022, constituting a decline from some $6,200m. in the previous 12-month period. Merchandise exports declined by $858m. overall, although revenue from coffee rose by $279.5m. to $811m. Private sector imports of goods increased sharply, to some $6,400m., from about $5,000m. in the previous 12-month period. Greater imports for investments in the oil and gas sector contributed to this trend. Notably, gold trade was suspended for much of 2021/22, owing to a dispute between the Government and gold traders relating to a new levy on gold exports from July 2021.

The Balance of Payments

In the year to February 2022 Uganda achieved a balance-of-payments surplus of US $642.2m. (about four months' worth of imports of goods and services), from a deficit of $74.9m. in the year to February 2021, owing largely to an increasing surplus on the financial account (which rose by 43.8%, to $3,878.5m.). The current account balance widened by 3.3% (owing mainly to a deteriorating trade deficit) and stood at $3,647m. in the year to February 2022. The remittances inflow increased by 8.3% (or $83.8m.). This came after BoU data indicated that remittances fell by 14.7% in 2020/21, due to the effect of the pandemic on the incomes of Ugandans working abroad. Remittances contributed about 10% of income for the rural poor and urban households and accounted for 4.5% of GDP in 2018/19.

The currency appreciated by 3.1% in the 10 months to April 2022, to an average rate of 3,548.8 shillings = US $1, owing to a strong performance in the coffee sector, tourism, FDI and significant loan disbursements to the Government. The BoU's reserves increased by $353.1m. in the first 10 months of 2021/22. However, in the three months to June 2022 the shilling depreciated by 1.7%, owing to the effects of the war in Ukraine, among other factors.

FOREIGN DIRECT INVESTMENT

FDI inflows to Uganda have remained strong, owing mainly to a robust recovery since the reopening of the economy and positive prospects in the oil and gas sector (after major agreements have been signed in recent months). Inflows amounted to US $1,324.7m. in the year to February 2022—an increase of 51.2% from the previous year.

In terms of sectoral contribution to FDI, in 2019 manufacturing accounted for 37% of total inflows, while the major source of FDI inflows was China, which provided 35% of the total. In 2020 China reportedly invested in 55 projects (worth US $234.5m.). Madagascar, India and Sri Lanka were also major sources of FDI in that year. Investment inflows were allocated to capital infrastructure projects (e.g. related to power generation and its supporting industries), manufacturing and construction in the oil and gas sector. In terms of investors from the East Africa region, Kenya is the main cross-border investor in Uganda (accounting for $20.3m. in 2020). There has been a recent increase in domestic direct investment (DDI), owing partly to the effect of restrictions on movement during the pandemic: domestic investors expanded production, for example, of food, medicine and sanitizers. This trend was also driven by the Government's agenda of export promotion and import replacement. The contribution of DDI to GDP stood at 20% in 2020, up from 13% in 2019.

CENTRAL GOVERNMENT FISCAL OPERATIONS

Between July 2021 and April 2022 total tax collection increased by 6.9% (349,110m. shillings) to 16,248,810m. shillings, compared with the same period in the 2020/21 financial year. The Government nevertheless collected less than expected, owing mainly to shortfalls in corporate income tax (as a result of a decline in firms' profitability, lower consumer demand, restrictions on transport the closure of educational institutions, all owing to the pandemic), as well as withholding tax and rental income tax. However, inflows of revenue from pay-as-you-earn tax and gaming tax were higher than budgeted. The Government increasingly obtains financing from domestic sources (6,465,200m. shillings over that period), but external financing is still significant (9,027,000m. shillings). The overall fiscal deficit (including grants) stood at 7.3% of GDP in 2021/22 (compared with 9% in 2020/21).

OUTLOOK

Real GDP growth of 5.5% is expected in 2022/23, according to official figures, driven by government support for economic development, regional integration and a positive outlook for the nascent oil and gas sector. The Government also forecasts robust expansion in the agriculture, agro-processing and manufacturing sectors, owing in part to more industrial parks, better infrastructure, more and less costly electricity and access to cheaper long-term capital. Inflation in 2022/23 is expected to average 7.2%. The Government forecasts that by 2025/26 real GDP growth will reach 6.5% and that public debt will fall to below 50% of GDP.

The World Bank forecasts real GDP growth of 3.7% in 2022, 5.1% in 2023 and 6% in 2024, and highlights the following challenges to the Ugandan economy, in particular: higher commodity prices, the rising cost of living and the threat of a significant section of the population falling into poverty, the need to offer support to vulnerable sections of population as well as to local businesses, while containing the levels of public debt and inflation. The World Bank also urges the Government to increase domestic revenue, better manage public investment and expenditure, improve public project management and enhance the environment for trade and industry, while greening the economy.

CONCLUSION

Uganda's economy has undergone substantial restructuring, following the implementation of all-encompassing neoliberal reforms. The regional and global factors that affect the national dynamics are not only of an economic nature, but also of a political character. Neoliberal reforms have nevertheless generated a severe and ongoing social crisis, and multidimensional poverty and dependence on agriculture are the norm for the majority of the population. Whether the current 'jobless growth' structure will be challenged by the ambitious fiscal interventions related to the emerging oil industry, the investment in infrastructure and the business environment remains to be seen. How the country will fare in the coming years also depends on how the actors involved respond to the political-economic tensions and conflicts that the neoliberal reform process and the current economic order have aggravated, such as increasing inequality, high structural unemployment and a surge in dispossession. Low wages and a lack of employment security for workers, widespread

poverty, political corruption and economic fraud are major features of contemporary Uganda. Recent political campaigns have highlighted the pressures under which policymakers find themselves when promising voters that the jobless growth model will start to change into a model that delivers employment and decent living standards for the majority of Ugandans.

What will be achievable within a short-term framework depends on how the Government manages both this complex scenario of conflicting, and all equally pressing, social, economic and political demands, and its relationship with the major opposition forces and their supporters (see *History*). Issues that will remain on the agenda of public discussion include: public infrastructure projects, public indebtedness, fiscal (in)stability, public sector performance, fraud, corruption and everyday crime, industrialization, the commercialization of agriculture, FDI (and the role of foreign companies), the oil sector, political uncertainty (a possible successor to President Museveni), and poverty, inequality and (un)employment, all of which are now shaped by the health and economic dynamics and recovery from the COVID-19 pandemic.

Statistical Survey

Sources (unless otherwise stated): Uganda Bureau of Statistics, POB 7186, Kampala; tel. (41) 706000; e-mail ubos@ubos.org; internet www.ubos.org; Statistics Department, Ministry of Finance, Planning and Economic Development, POB 8147, Kampala.

Area and Population

AREA, POPULATION AND DENSITY

Area (sq km)	
Land	200,523
Inland water and swamp	41,028
Total	241,551*
Population (census results)	
12 September 2002	24,442,084
28 August 2014	
Males	17,060,832
Females	17,573,818
Total	34,634,650
Population (official projections at mid-year)	
2020	41,583,600
2021	42,885,900
2022	44,212,800
Density (per sq km) at mid-2022†	220.5

* 93,263 sq miles.
† Land area only.

POPULATION BY AGE AND SEX
('000, official projections at mid-2022)

	Males	Females	Total
0–14 years	10,008.2	9,599.7	19,607.9
15–64 years	11,294.6	12,250.8	23,545.4
65 years and over	459.0	600.5	1,059.5
Total	**21,761.8**	**22,451.0**	**44,212.8**

PRINCIPAL ETHNIC GROUPS
(at census of 28 August 2014)*

Baganda . .	5,555,319	Langi	2,131,495
Banyakole . .	3,216,332	Bagisu	1,646,904
Basoga . .	2,960,890	Acholi	1,470,554
Bakiga . . .	2,390,446	Lugbara	1,099,733
Iteso	2,364,569		

* Ethnic groups numbering more than 1m. persons, excluding population enumerated in hotels.

SUBREGIONS
(official population projections at mid-2021)

Region	Area (sq km)	Population ('000)	Density (per sq km)*
Central	61,403	11,952.6	194.7
Western	55,277	10,898.3	197.2
Northern	85,392	8,870.2	103.9
Eastern	39,479	11,164.8	282.8
Total	**241,551**	**42,885.9**	**177.5**

* Total area, including inland water and swamp.

PRINCIPAL TOWNS
('000, official population estimates at mid-2016)

Kampala (capital) .	1,568.9	Lira	104.2
Mbarara . .	202.8	Njeru . . .	84.3
Mukono . . .	170.2	Entebbe . . .	78.9
Nansana . .	162.7	Jinja . . .	74.8
Gulu . . .	161.2	Arua . . .	65.8
Masaka . . .	107.7	Kabale . . .	50.8
Kasese . . .	106.3	Kitgum . . .	45.9

BIRTHS AND DEATHS
(annual averages, UN estimates)

	2005–10	2010–15	2015–20
Birth rate (per 1,000) . . .	46.1	42.9	38.4
Death rate (per 1,000) . . .	11.2	8.4	6.7

Source: UN, *World Population Prospects: The 2019 Revision.*

2015: Birth rate 42.5 per 1,000; Death rate 9.3 per 1,000 (Source: African Development Bank).

2016: Birth rate 38.7 per 1,000 (Source: African Development Bank).

2017: Birth rate 46.3 per 1,000; Death rate 13.1 per 1,000 (Source: African Development Bank).

Life expectancy (years at birth, estimates): 63.7 (males 61.3; females 66.0) in 2020 (Source: World Bank, World Development Indicators database).

EMPLOYMENT

(persons aged 10 years and over, census of 12 September 2002)*

	Males	Females	Total
Agriculture, hunting and forestry.	2,545,962	2,649,779	5,195,741
Fishing	102,043	16,743	118,786
Mining and quarrying . . .	13,613	6,127	19,740
Manufacturing	108,653	45,594	154,247
Electricity, gas and water supply	12,860	1,509	14,369
Construction	105,769	2,939	108,708
Wholesale and retail trade, repair of motor vehicles, motorcycles and personal and household goods	191,191	143,145	334,336
Hotels and restaurants . . .	23,741	64,099	87,840
Transport, storage and communications . . .	119,437	5,798	125,235
Financial intermediation . .			
Real estate, renting and business activities	14,539	7,562	22,101
Public administration and defence, compulsory social security	146,319	27,278	173,597
Education	124,167	85,015	209,182
Health and social work . . .	54,327	53,108	107,435
Other community, social and personal service activities .	22,736	26,734	49,470
Private households with employed persons	14,019	19,115	33,134
Not classifiable by economic activity	120,219	76,167	196,386
Total employed	3,719,595	3,230,712	6,950,307

* Excluding population enumerated at hotels.

2016/2017 ('000 persons aged 14–64 years, national household survey, year ending 30 June): Agriculture, hunting and forestry 9,015; Mining and utilities 130; Manufacturing 730; Construction 337; Trade, transportation and accommodation 2,325; Public administration, community, social and other services 1,311; Not classifiable by economic activity 9; *Total employed* 13,857; Unemployed 524; *Total labour force* 14,381 (Source: ILO).

2019/20 ('000 persons aged 14–64 years, national household survey, year ending 30 June): Total labour force 15,904 (7,991 males, 7,913 females).

Health and Welfare

KEY INDICATORS

Total fertility rate (children per woman, 2020)	4.7
Under-5 mortality rate (per 1,000 live births, 2020) . . .	43.3
HIV/AIDS (% of persons aged 15–49, 2020)	5.4
COVID-19: Cumulative confirmed deaths (per 100,000 persons at 31 August 2022)	7.9
COVID-19: Fully vaccinated population (% of total population at 21 August 2022)	27.3
Physicians (per 1,000 head, 2020)	0.1
Hospitals (per 100,000 head, 2013)	0.4
Domestic health expenditure (2019): US $ per head (PPP) .	14.0
Domestic health expenditure (2019): % of GDP	0.6
Domestic health expenditure (2019): public (% of total current expenditure)	15.1
Access to improved water resources (% of persons, 2020) .	56
Access to improved sanitation facilities (% of persons, 2020) .	20
Total carbon dioxide emissions ('000 metric tons, 2018) . .	6,130
Carbon dioxide emissions per head (metric tons, 2018) . .	0.1
Human Development Index (2021): ranking	166
Human Development Index (2021): value	0.525

Note: For data on COVID-19 vaccinations, 'fully vaccinated' denotes receipt of all doses specified by approved vaccination regime (Sources: Johns Hopkins University and Our World in Data). Data on health expenditure refer to current general government expenditure in each case. For more information on sources and further definitions for all indicators, see Health and Welfare Statistics: Sources and Definitions section (europaworld.com/credits).

Agriculture

PRINCIPAL CROPS

('000 metric tons)

	2018	2019	2020
Bananas*	549.5	544.6	n.a.
Beans, dry	940.3	627.0	609.0*
Cassava (Manioc)	4,390.2	6,983.0	4,207.9*
Cocoa beans†	35.0	35.0	35.0
Coffee, green	284.2	312.6	290.7*
Cow peas, dry	12.4	13.0*	13.7*
Groundnuts, with shell . . .	193.2	302.0	336.0*
Maize	2,772.7	3,588.0	2,750.0†
Millet	142.0	196.0	209.7*
Onions, dry*	319.8	316.3	317.7
Pigeon peas	13.7	15.1*	17.9*
Plantains and others . . .	3,450.0	8,326.0	7,401.6*
Potatoes	327.3	326.0	309.3*
Rice, paddy	199.3	255.0	200.0*
Seed cotton*	110.0	120.0	127.8
Sesame seed†	144.0	144.0	146.0
Sorghum	268.5	211.0	251.6*
Soybeans (Soya beans) . . .	107.6	117.0	75.1*
Sugar cane*	5,503.0	5,500.0	5,778.2
Sunflower seed	272.3	260.0†	275.0†
Sweet potatoes	1,484.2	1,485.0	1,536.1*
Tea	74.2	60.3	63.4*
Tobacco, unmanufactured* . .	32.1	32.3	32.1
Tomatoes*	37.4	37.0	37.2

* FAO estimate(s).
† Unofficial figure(s).

Aggregate production ('000 metric tons, may include official, semi-official or estimated data): Total cereals 4,075.4 in 2018, 4,274.0 in 2019, 3,436.3 in 2020; Total fruit (primary) 3,506.2 in 2018, 8,382.2 in 2019, 7,457.8 in 2020; Total oilcrops 874.7 in 2018, 990.7 in 2019, 1,007.4 in 2020; Total pulses 983.5 in 2018, 673.2 in 2019, 659.1 in 2020; Total roots and tubers 6,201.7 in 2018, 8,794.0 in 2019, 6,053.3 in 2020; Total vegetables (primary) 1,384.7 in 2018, 1,375.3 in 2019, 1,380.5 in 2020.

Source: FAO.

LIVESTOCK

('000 head, year ending September, FAO estimates)

	2018	2019	2020
Cattle	14,617.9	15,092.7	15,541.3
Chickens	34,589	35,452	36,263
Goats	14,660.3	15,022.9	15,430.0
Pigs	2,530.9	2,582.7	2,638.3
Sheep	1,958.7	1,986.4	2,024.2

Source: FAO.

LIVESTOCK PRODUCTS

('000 metric tons, FAO estimates unless otherwise indicated)

	2018	2019	2020
Cattle hides, fresh	24.0	23.6	23.2
Cattle meat	169.5	166.5	163.9
Cattle offals, edible	28.6	28.1	27.7
Cows' milk	2,040.0*	1,724.7*	1,766.4
Chicken meat	67.0	68.5	70.0
Goat meat	35.8	35.5	35.2
Goat offals, edible	11.0	10.9	10.8
Goats' skins, fresh	7.3	7.2	7.2
Pig fat	10.7	10.8	11.0
Pig meat	127.5	129.4	131.2
Pig offals, edible	10.7	10.8	11.0
Sheep meat	9.9	10.0	10.1
Hen eggs	45.0	45.0	44.7

* Official figure.

Source: FAO.

Forestry

ROUNDWOOD REMOVALS
('000 cubic metres, excl. bark, FAO estimates)

	2018	2019	2020
Sawlogs, veneer logs and logs for sleepers*	3,553.0	3,553.0	3,553.0
Other industrial wood* . . .	1,777.0	1,777.0	1,777.0
Fuel wood	43,731.0	44,177.1	44,630.9
Total	49,061.0	49,507.1	49,960.9

*Figures assumed to be unchanged since 2016.

Source: FAO.

SAWNWOOD PRODUCTION
('000 cubic metres, incl. railway sleepers)

	2011	2012	2013
Coniferous (softwood)	70	80	132
Broadleaved (hardwood) . . .	280	320	308
Total	350	400	440

2014–20: Production assumed to be unchanged from 2013 (FAO estimates).
Source: FAO.

Fishing

('000 metric tons, live weight)

	2018	2019	2020
Capture	439.4	603.2	566.3
Cyprinids	201.4	253.1	255.7
Tilapias	47.3	49.1	52.8
Nurse tetra	59.1	67.5	92.4
African lungfishes . . .	7.2	9.7	10.6
Characins	15.3	30.6	19.6
Nile perch	80.8	109.7	88.5
Aquaculture	103.7	102.9	123.9
Total catch	543.1	706.2	690.2

Note: Figures exclude aquatic animals, recorded by number rather than weight. The number of Nile crocodiles captured was 500 in 2018–2019; n.a. in 2020.
Source: FAO.

Mining

('000 metric tons unless otherwise indicated)

	2016	2017	2018
Cement (hydraulic)	2,494	2,511	2,200*
Limestone	1,203.1	1,231.9	810.0*
Salt (unrefined)*	15	15	15

*Estimate(s).

Cobalt (metric tons): 376 in 2013.

Source: partly US Geological Survey.

Limestone ('000 metric tons): 942.5 in 2019; 705.1 in 2020.

Industry

SELECTED PRODUCTS
('000 metric tons unless otherwise indicated)

	2003	2004	2005
Soft drinks (million litres) . . .	78.5	111.5	163.5
Sugar	139.5	189.5	182.9
Soap	101.3	93.4	127.6
Cement	507.1	559.0	692.7
Paint (million litres)	1.9	2.2	8.2
Edible oil and fat	56.0	58.1	43.3
Animal feed	20.9	19.6	17.3
Footwear (million pairs) . . .	3.4	3.6	46.3
Wheat flour	42.2	25.7	20.3
Processed milk (million litres) .	14.9	19.6	18.5
Cotton and rayon fabrics (million sq m)	11.1	10.1	13.6
Clay bricks, tiles, etc. . . .	33.3	15.4	36.2
Corrugated iron sheets . . .	39.2	48.8	61.6

Cement ('000 metric tons): 1,780 in 2012; 2,023 in 2013; 2,141 in 2014.

Processed milk (million litres): 1,461 in 2012; 1,504 in 2013; 1,550 in 2014.

Source: Bank of Uganda.

Electrical energy (million kWh): 3,854 in 2017; 4,040 in 2018; 4,364 in 2019 (Source: UN Energy Statistics Database).

Finance

CURRENCY, EXCHANGE RATES AND FISCAL YEAR

Monetary Units
100 cents = 1 new Uganda shilling.

Sterling, Dollar and Euro Equivalents (31 May 2022)
£1 sterling = 4,753 new Uganda shillings;
US $1 = 3,776 new Uganda shillings;
€1 = 4,045 new Uganda shillings;
10,000 new Uganda shillings = £2.10 = $2.65 = €2.47.

Average Exchange Rate (new Uganda shillings per US $)
2019   3,704.0
2020   3,718.2
2021   3,587.1

Note: Between December 1985 and May 1987 the official exchange rate was fixed at US $1 = 1,400 shillings. In May 1987 a new shilling, equivalent to 100 of the former units, was introduced. At the same time, the currency was devalued by 76.7%, with the exchange rate set at $1 = 60 new shillings. Further adjustments were implemented in subsequent years. Foreign exchange controls were mostly abolished in 1993.

Fiscal Year
The fiscal year ends on 30 June.

BUDGET
('000 million new shillings, fiscal year)

Revenue*	2019/20	2020/21	2021/22†
Taxes	15,912	18,337	20,305
Taxes on income and profits .	6,045	6,805	7,298
Taxes on goods and services .	4,732	5,439	5,579
Taxes on international trade .	1,209	1,403	1,873
Excise duty	3,462	4,119	4,476
International levy	82	95	97
Other taxes	382	476	980
Non-tax revenue	1,374	1,502	1,196
Petroleum revenue	0	141	0
Total	17,286	19,839	21,501

Expenditure‡	2019/20	2020/21	2021/22†
Current expenditure . . .	15,103	18,165	20,088
Wages and salaries . . .	4,861	5,180	5,625
Interest payments . . .	2,932	3,990	4,947
Other current revenue . . .	7,310	8,995	9,516
Development expenditure . .	12,064	15,085	14,276
Externally-financed projects .	3,967	5,479	5,712
Government investment . .	8,097	9,606	8,564
Other expenses	405	794	603
Total	27,572	34,044	34,967

* Excluding grants received ('000 million new shillings): 1,156 in 2019/20; 1,400 in 2020/21; 1,794 in 2021/22 (revised).
† Revised.
‡ Excluding net lending ('000 million new shillings): 831 in 2019/20; 1,096 in 2020/21; 147 in 2021/22 (revised).

Source: IMF, *Uganda: 2021 Article IV Consultation and First Review under the Extended Credit Facility Arrangement and Requests for Modifications of Performance Criteria—Press Release; Staff Report; and Statement by the Executive Director for Uganda* (March 2022).

INTERNATIONAL RESERVES
(US $ million at 31 December)

	2016	2017	2018
IMF special drawing rights . .	63.5	66.4	63.3
Foreign exchange	3,034.4	3,654.5	3,295.2
Total	3,097.9	3,720.9	3,358.5

2019: IMF special drawing rights 61.1.
2020: IMF special drawing rights 63.1.
2021: IMF special drawing rights 545.2.

Source: IMF, *International Financial Statistics.*

MONEY SUPPLY
('000 million new shillings at 31 December)

	2019	2020	2021
Currency outside depository corporations	4,688.70	5,435.85	5,792.86
Transferable deposits . . .	11,826.41	14,147.64	15,337.66
Other deposits	10,593.75	12,169.75	12,221.62
Broad money	27,108.86	31,753.24	33,352.15

Source: IMF, *International Financial Statistics.*

COST OF LIVING
(Consumer Price Index; base: 2016/17 = 100)

	2019	2020	2021
Food and non-alcoholic beverages .	104.3	106.9	107.4
Clothing and footwear	110.9	113.4	115.0
Housing and utilities . . .	109.8	112.3	111.4
All items (incl. others) . . .	107.6	110.6	113.0

NATIONAL ACCOUNTS
('000 million new shillings at current prices, fiscal year)

Expenditure on the Gross Domestic Product

	2019/20	2020/21	2021/22
Government final consumption expenditure	13,286	14,730	15,776
Private final consumption expenditure	99,531	106,953	115,095
Increase in stocks	975	1,108	1,226
Gross fixed capital formation . .	32,852	34,615	38,108
Total domestic expenditure .	146,645	157,405	170,205
Exports of goods and services . .	21,533	23,405	19,121
Less Imports of goods and services	30,153	38,461	35,629
Statistical discrepancy	1,665	5,961	8,426
GDP in purchasers' values .	139,689	148,310	162,123
GDP at constant 2016/17 prices	126,410	130,881	136,871

Gross Domestic Product by Economic Activity

	2019/20	2020/21	2021/22
Agriculture, hunting, forestry and fishing	33,426	35,360	39,028
Mining and quarrying	2,266	2,796	2,314
Manufacturing	22,064	24,373	26,661
Electricity and water	5,051	5,392	5,687
Construction	7,623	7,704	8,730
Wholesale and retail trade . .	11,758	11,739	13,374
Hotels and restaurants . . .	3,645	3,549	3,568
Transport, storage and communications	7,347	7,483	7,941
Financial intermediation . . .	3,816	4,103	4,637
Real estate	8,907	9,273	10,265
Business services	5,479	5,803	6,284
Public administration and defence	3,865	4,455	4,778
Education	5,767	5,565	5,874
Health	4,496	5,078	5,505
Other services	4,760	5,015	5,045
Gross value added at basic prices	130,271	137,688	149,691
Net taxes on products	9,418	10,623	12,432
GDP at market prices . . .	139,689	148,310	162,123

BALANCE OF PAYMENTS
(US $ million)

	2018	2019	2020
Exports of goods	3,636.2	4,095.6	4,461.3
Imports of goods	−6,098.1	−6,850.2	−7,103.2
Balance on goods	−2,462.0	−2,754.6	−2,641.9
Exports of services	2,446.7	2,207.8	1,217.0
Imports of services	−2,631.7	−2,911.1	−3,148.1
Balance on goods and services	−2,647.0	−3,457.8	−4,573.0
Primary income received . . .	43.5	58.0	41.5
Primary income paid	−1,005.0	−789.2	−700.5
Balance on goods, services and primary income	−3,608.5	−4,189.1	−5,232.0
Secondary income received . .	1,882.0	2,032.3	1,831.0
Secondary income paid . . .	−209.4	−185.2	−87.3
Current balance	−1,935.9	−2,341.9	−3,488.3
Capital account (net)	144.7	134.0	194.4
Direct investment assets . . .	−0.3	−0.3	−0.3
Direct investment liabilities . .	1,055.4	1,273.9	873.8
Portfolio investment assets . .	−165.2	−356.3	−166.0
Portfolio investment liabilities .	85.0	−3.6	34.3
Financial derivatives and employee stock options (net) . . .	3.1	3.1	9.0
Other investment assets . . .	−349.6	−204.8	−476.2
Other investment liabilities . .	1,039.6	975.6	2,285.9
Net errors and omissions . . .	−165.3	502.4	999.9
Reserves and related items .	−288.6	−18.1	266.5

Source: IMF, *International Financial Statistics.*

External Trade

PRINCIPAL COMMODITIES
(distribution by SITC, US $ million)

Imports c.i.f.	2018	2019	2020
Food and live animals . . .	548.7	609.6	623.5
Cereals and cereal preparations .	276.4	302.3	295.1
Mineral fuels, lubricants etc. .	1,317.9	1,250.0	975.5
Petroleum, petroleum products and related materials	1,291.7	1,228.3	951.0
Animal and vegetable oils, fats and waxes	244.0	202.4	277.2
Fixed vegetable fats and oils . .	243.4	201.6	275.3
Chemicals and related products	1,141.6	1,141.2	1,256.4
Medicinal and pharmaceutical products	284.1	278.4	293.4
Basic manufactures . . .	1,046.8	1,035.4	1,028.9
Iron and steel	367.5	356.2	341.1
Machinery and transport equipment	1,514.3	1,502.3	1,564.4
Electrical machinery, apparatus, etc.	221.1	188.9	196.1
Road vehicles (incl. air-cushion vehicles) and parts (excl. tyres, engines and electrical parts) .	497.1	514.8	513.4
Miscellaneous manufactured articles	403.5	422.3	421.2
Total (incl. others)	6,789.4	7,753.8	8,267.7

Exports f.o.b.	2018	2019	2020
Food and live animals . . .	1,670.4	1,451.3	1,376.3
Fish, crustaceans, molluscs and preparations thereof	211.7	227.0	137.9
Cereals and cereal preparations .	321.8	232.8	197.9
Vegetables and fruits . . .	221.3	146.7	111.1
Sugar, sugar preparations and honey	111.6	86.6	76.8
Coffee, tea, cocoa, spices and manufactures	605.0	603.9	701.5
Beverages and tobacco . . .	146.6	147.3	111.4
Crude materials (inedible) except fuels	172.1	182.4	156.8
Mineral fuels, lubricants and related materials	171.8	182.7	98.8
Petroleum, petroleum products and related materials	135.4	138.2	78.7
Basic manufactures . . .	380.1	328.3	296.9
Iron and steel	111.3	90.3	89.0
Miscellaneous manufactured articles	187.3	181.8	74.6
Total (incl. others)	3,633.9	4,095.7	4,286.8

2021: *Imports:* Cereals and cereal preparations 487.3; Petroleum, petroleum products 1,260.8; Fixed vegetable fats and oils 371.0; Medicinal and pharmaceutical products 376.9; Iron and steel 578.6; Electrical machinery, apparatus, etc. 224.7; Road vehicles 636.1; Total (incl. others) 9,154.1. *Exports:* Fish, crustaceans, molluscs 150.0; Cereals and cereal preparations 175.0; Vegetables and fruits 241.4; Sugar, sugar preparations and honey 114.4; Coffee, tea, cocoa, spices and manufactures 929.9; Petroleum, petroleum products 104.1; Iron and steel 130.9; Total (incl. others) 4,494.2.

PRINCIPAL TRADING PARTNERS
(US $ million)

Imports c.i.f.	2018	2019	2020
Belgium	55.0	31.5	52.7
China, People's Republic . . .	1,184.4	1,256.6	1,352.0
Egypt	106.7	112.0	101.1
Germany	122.0	114.0	142.2
India	816.9	855.1	959.1
Indonesia	210.5	184.5	191.2
Japan	316.9	306.8	342.9
Kenya	540.8	792.0	780.4
Malaysia	66.7	99.4	134.3
Netherlands	77.9	66.9	200.5
Pakistan	58.8	49.8	34.8
Russian Federation	111.0	81.6	78.7
Saudi Arabia	605.3	429.1	274.5
South Africa	311.9	385.9	220.9
Tanzania	262.4	476.2	746.8
Thailand	70.1	71.9	47.9
United Arab Emirates . . .	784.1	822.4	495.9
United Kingdom	81.1	71.8	76.4
USA	116.7	133.0	143.2
Total (incl. others)	6,789.4	7,753.8	8,267.7

Exports f.o.b.	2018	2019	2020
Belgium	75.3	81.9	72.5
Burundi	40.7	51.4	58.5
Congo, Democratic Republic . .	474.1	578.9	344.2
Germany	94.6	79.7	93.8
Italy	132.4	141.8	138.1
Kenya	730.1	539.9	489.5
Netherlands	114.5	99.4	78.1
Rwanda	261.1	52.9	2.6
South Sudan	406.1	413.2	379.3
Sudan	55.4	62.1	89.9
Tanzania	93.2	100.8	109.6
United Arab Emirates	562.4	1,196.0	1,844.8
Total (incl. others)	3,633.9	4,095.7	4,286.8

2021: Total imports 9,154.1; Total exports 4,494.2.

Transport

ROAD TRAFFIC
(new registrations, private)

	2018	2019	2020
Passenger cars	43,764	38,182	42,284
Motorcycles	93,213	107,273	102,848

CIVIL AVIATION
(traffic on scheduled services)

	2013	2014	2015
Kilometres flown (million) . .	6	4	1
Passengers carried ('000) . .	199	164	42
Passenger-km (million) . . .	125	101	5
Total ton-km (million) . . .	1	1	n.a.

Source: UN, *Statistical Yearbook*.

Passengers carried ('000, Entebbe international airport): 1,645 in 2017; 1,697 in 2018; 1,829 in 2019.

Tourism

FOREIGN TOURIST ARRIVALS

Country of residence	2017	2019*	2020
Congo, Democratic Republic . .	99,096	9,645	3,644
India	35,676	34,066	10,223
Kenya	334,788	243,479	321,770
Rwanda	441,994	60,006	22,660
Sudan	36,062	2,866	985
Tanzania	89,253	29,463	21,878
United Kingdom	33,564	18,940	5,481
USA	61,775	25,427	7,100
Total (incl. others)	1,402,409	657,037	473,085

* Figures for 2018 were not available.

2021: Total tourist arrivals 512,945.

Tourism receipts (US $ million): 1,069 in 2015; 1,154 in 2016; 1,453 in 2017.

Communications Media

	2018	2019	2020
Telephones ('000 main lines in use)	82.1	85.7	90.8
Mobile telephone subscriptions ('000)	24,472.0	25,395.5	27,689.0
Broadband subscriptions, fixed .	n.a.	32,370	58,594
Broadband subscriptions, mobile ('000)	14,360.8	16,971.6	20,117.0
Internet users (% of population) .	10.9	14.7	19.9

Source: International Telecommunication Union.

Education

(2017 unless otherwise indicated)

	Institutions	Teachers	Students
Pre-primary	7,210	27,641	608,973
Primary	20,305	207,238	8,840,589
Secondary	2,995	64,966	1,370,583
Tertiary	201*	9,282*	258,866†

* 2014.
† 2016.

Source: Ministry of Education and Sports, Kampala.

Pupil-teacher ratio (primary education, UNESCO estimate): 42.7 in 2016/17.

Adult literacy rate (UNESCO estimates): 76.5% (males 82.7%; females 70.8%) in 2018 (Source: UNESCO Institute for Statistics).

Directory

The Constitution

In September 1995 a Constituent Assembly (comprising 214 elected and 74 nominated members) enacted a draft Constitution, which was promulgated on 8 October. Amendments to the Constitution, introducing a multi-party political system and removing the two-term limit on the President, were endorsed at a national referendum held on 28 July 2005. Under the amended Constitution, the President (who had an unlimited number of mandates) and the unicameral legislature, the Parliament, were directly elected for a five-year term.

The Government

HEAD OF STATE

President: Gen. (retd) YOWERI KAGUTA MUSEVENI (took office 29 January 1986; elected 9 May 1996; re-elected 12 March 2001, 23 February 2006, 18 February 2011, 18 February 2016 and 14 January 2021).

Vice-President: Maj. (retd) JESSICA ROSE EPEL ALUPO.

THE CABINET
(October 2022)

Prime Minister and Leader of Government Business in Parliament: ROBINAH NABBANJA.

First Deputy Prime Minister and Minister of East African Community Affairs: REBECCA ALITWALA KADAGA.

Second Deputy Prime Minister and Deputy Leader of Government Business in Parliament: Gen. (retd) MOSES ALI.

Third Deputy Prime Minister and Minister without Portfolio: LUKIA ISANGA NAKADAMA.

Minister of Education and Sports: JANET KATAAHA MUSEVENI.

Ministers in the Office of the President: BABIRYE MILLY BABALANDA (Presidency), JIM KATUGUGU MUHWEZI (Security), Dr MUSENERO MONICA MASANZA (Science, Technology and Innovation), Dr HAJJAT MINSA KABANDA (Kampala Capital City and Metropolitan Affairs).

Ministers in the Office of the Prime Minister: JUSTINE KASULE LUMUMBA (General Duties), HILARY ONEK (Relief, Disaster Preparedness and Refugees), Dr MARY GORETTI KITUTU (Karamoja Affairs).

Government Chief Whip: HAMSON OBUAS.

Minister of Agriculture, Animal Industry and Fisheries: FRANK KAGYIGYI TUMWEBAZE.

Attorney-General: KIRYOWA KIWANUKA.

Minister of Defence and Veteran Affairs: VINCENT BAMULANGAKI SSEMPIJJA.

Minister of Energy and Minerals Development: RUTH NANKABIRWA SSENTAMU.

Minister of Finance, Planning and Economic Development: MATIA KASAIJA.

Minister of Foreign Affairs: Gen. ODONGO JEJE ABUBAKER.

Minister of Gender, Labour and Social Development: AMONGI BETTY AKENA.

Minister of Health: Dr JANE RUTH ACENG OCERO.

Minister of Information, Communications Technology and National Guidance: Dr CHRIS BARYOMUNSI.

Minister of Internal Affairs: Maj.-Gen. KAHINDA OTAFIIRE.

Minister of Justice and Constitutional Affairs: NORBERT MAU.

Minister of Lands, Housing and Urban Development: JUDITH NALULE NABAKOOBA.

Minister of Local Government: RAPHAEL MAGYEZI.

Minister of Public Service: WILSON MURULI MUKASA.

Minister of Tourism, Wildlife and Antiquities: Col TOM BUTIME.

Minister of Trade, Industry and Co-operatives: FRANCIS MWEBESA.

Minister of Water and Environment: SAM MANGUSHO CHEPTORIS.

Minister of Works and Transport: Gen. EDWARD KATUMBA WAMALA.

There were also 50 ministers of state.

MINISTRIES

Office of the President: Parliament Bldg, POB 7168, Kampala; tel. (41) 4258441; e-mail info@statehouse.go.ug; internet www .statehouse.go.ug.

Office of the Prime Minister: Plot 9–11, Apollo Kaggwa Rd, POB 341, Kampala; tel. (41) 7770500; e-mail ps@opm.go.ug; internet www .opm.go.ug.

Ministry of Agriculture, Animal Industry and Fisheries: Plot 16–18, Lugard Ave, POB 102, Entebbe; tel. (41) 4320004; e-mail info@agriculture.go.ug; internet www.agriculture.go.ug.

Ministry of Defence and Veteran Affairs: Chwa II Rd, Mbuya, POB 3798, Kampala; tel. (41) 4565100; e-mail mod.ps@defence.go .ug; internet www.defence.go.ug.

Ministry of Disaster Preparedness and Refugees: Twin Towers, Apollo Kaggwa Rd, Kampala.

Ministry of East African Community Affairs: Postel Bldg, 2nd Floor, 67/75 Yusuf Lule Rd, POB 7343, Kampala; tel. 716159418; e-mail meaca@meaca.go.ug; internet www.meaca.go.ug.

Ministry of Education and Sports: POB 7063, Kampala; tel. (41) 7893600; e-mail permasec@education.go.ug; internet www .education.go.ug.

Ministry of Energy and Minerals Development: Amber House, Kampala Rd, POB 7270, Kampala; tel. (41) 4344414; e-mail psmemd@energy.go.ug; internet www.energyandminerals.go.ug.

Ministry of Finance, Planning and Economic Development: Plot 2/12, Apollo Kaggwa Rd, POB 8147, Kampala; tel. (41) 4707000; e-mail finance@finance.go.ug; internet finance.go.ug.

Ministry of Foreign Affairs: 2A/B Apollo Kaggwa Rd, POB 7048, Kampala; tel. (41) 4345661; e-mail info@mofa.go.ug; internet www .mofa.go.ug.

Ministry of Gender, Labour and Social Affairs: Plot 2, Lumumba Ave, Simbamanyo House, POB 7136, Kampala; tel. (41) 4347854; e-mail ps@mglsd.go.ug; internet mglsd.go.ug.

Ministry of Health: Plot 6, Lourdel Rd, Nakasero, POB 7272, Kampala; tel. (41) 7712260; e-mail info@health.go.ug; internet www.health.go.ug.

Ministry of Information, Communications Technology and National Guidance: ICT House, Plot 10/12, Parliamentary Ave, POB 7817, Kampala; tel. (41) 4236262; e-mail ictinfo@ict.go.ug; internet ict.go.ug.

Ministry of Internal Affairs: Plot 75, Jinja Rd, POB 7191, Kampala; tel. (41) 4595945; e-mail info@mia.go.ug; internet www .mia.go.ug.

Ministry of Justice and Constitutional Affairs: Bauman Hse, Plot 7, Parliament Ave, POB 7183, Kampala; tel. (41) 4230537; e-mail info@justice.go.ug; internet justice.go.ug.

Ministry of Lands, Housing and Urban Development: Plot 13–15, Parliament Ave, POB 7096, Kampala; tel. (41) 4373511; e-mail mlhud@mlhud.go.ug; internet mlhud.go.ug.

Ministry of Local Government: Workers' House, Southern Wing, 5th Floor, Plot 1, Pilkington Rd, POB 7037, Kampala; tel. (41) 4341224; e-mail ps@molg.go.ug; internet molg.go.ug.

Ministry of Public Service: Plot 12, Nakasero Hill Rd, POB 7003, Kampala; tel. (41) 4250534; e-mail ps@publicservice.go.ug; internet publicservice.go.ug.

Ministry of Science, Technology and Innovation: Rumee Bldg, Plot 19, Lumumba Ave, POB 7466, Kampala; tel. (41) 47888200; e-mail info@mosti.go.ug; internet mosti.go.ug.

Ministry of Security: Kampala; internet security.go.ug.

Ministry of Tourism, Wildlife and Antiquities: Rwenzori Towers, 2nd Floor, Plot 6, Nakasero Rd, POB 4241, Kampala; tel. (41) 4561700; e-mail info@tourism.go.ug; internet tourism.go.ug.

Ministry of Trade, Industry and Co-operatives: Plot 6/8, Parliament Ave, POB 7103, Kampala; tel. (31) 2324000; e-mail mintrade@mtic.go.ug; internet www.mtic.go.ug.

Ministry of Water and Environment: Plot 21/28, Port Bell Rd, Luzira; POB 20026, Kampala; tel. (41) 4505942; e-mail mwe@mwe.go .ug; internet www.mwe.go.ug.

Ministry of Works and Transport: off Jinja Rd, POB 7174, Kampala; tel. (41) 4320135; e-mail mowt@works.go.ug; internet www.works.go.ug.

President

Presidential Election, 14 January 2021

Candidate	Valid votes	% of valid votes
Gen. (retd) Yoweri Kaguta Museveni (NRM)	6,042,898	58.38
Robert Kyagulanyi Ssentamu 'Bobi Wine' (NUP)	3,631,437	35.08
Patrick Oboi Amuriat (FDC)	337,589	3.26
Gregory Mugisha Muntuyera (ANT)	67,574	0.65
Nobert Mao (DP)	57,682	0.56
Henry K. Tumukunde (Ind.)	51,392	0.50
Others*	162,247	1.57
Total	10,350,819†	100.00

* There were five other candidates.
† In addition, there were 393,500 invalid votes and 29,913 spoiled ballots.

Legislature

Parliament: Plot 16–18, Parliament Ave, POB 7178, Kampala; tel. (41) 4377000; e-mail cpa@parliament.go.ug; internet www .parliament.go.ug.

Speaker: ANITA ANNET AMONG.

Deputy Speaker: THOMAS TAYEBWA.

General Election, 14 January 2021

Party/Group	Directly elected seats	Women members	Special seats*	Total seats
NRM	219	101	17	337
NUP	43	14	—	57
FDC	24	8	—	32
DP	8	1	—	9
UPC	7	2	—	9
JEEMA	1	—	—	1
PPP	1	—	—	1
Ind.	50	20	3	73
Uganda People's Defence Forces	—	—	10	10
Total	353	146	30	529

* Comprising 10 nominated representatives from the Uganda People's Defence Forces, five nominated representatives for young people, five nominated representatives for people with disabilities, five nominated representatives for senior citizens and five nominated representatives for workers.

Election Commission

Electoral Commission: 55 Jinja Rd, POB 22678, Kampala; tel. (41) 4337500; e-mail info@ec.or.ug; internet ec.or.ug; f. 1997; independent; Chair. SIMON MUGENYI BYABAKAMA.

Political Organizations

Alliance for National Transformation (ANT): Plot 87, Buganda Rd, Nakasero, Kampala; tel. 786931773; e-mail info@theallianceug .com; internet theallianceug.com; Leader Maj.-Gen. GREGORY MUGISHA MUNTUYERA.

Conservative Party (CP): POB 5145, Kampala; tel. 751971928; internet fb.com/Conservative-Party-Uganda-196729223853846; f. 1979; Leader KEN LUKYAMUZI.

Democratic Party (DP): City House, Plot 2/3, William St, POB 7098, Kampala; tel. (41) 4236010; internet fb.com/ DemocraticPartyU; f. 1954; main support in southern Uganda; Pres. NORBERT MAO.

Forum for Democratic Change (FDC): Plot 1164, Najjankumbi, Entebbe Rd, POB 26928, Kampala; tel. 706396051; e-mail info@fdc .ug; internet fdc.ug; f. 2004 by a merger of the Reform Agenda, the Parliamentary Advocacy Forum and the National Democratic Forum; Pres. Maj.-Gen. PATRICK OBOI AMURIAT; Sec.-Gen. NANDALA NATHAN MAFABI.

Forum for Integrity in Leadership (FIL): Carol House, Bombo Rd, POB 7606, Kampala; tel. 772628786; Chair. EMMANUEL TUMUSIIME.

Justice Forum (JEEMA): POB 3999, Kampala; internet fb.com/jeema.uganda; Leader MUHAMMAD KIBIRIGE MAYANJA; Sec.-Gen. HUSSEIN KYANJO.

National Unity Platform (NUP): Kampala; e-mail info@yoursite.com; internet nupuganda.org; Leader ROBERT KYAGULANYI 'BOBI WINE' SSENTAMU; Sec.-Gen. DAVID LEWIS RUBONGOYA.

National Resistance Movement (NRM): Plot 10, Kyadondo Rd, POB 7778, Kampala; tel. (41) 4346295; e-mail communications@nrm.ug; internet www.nrm.ug; Chair. YOWERI MUSEVENI; Sec.-Gen. RICHARD TODWONG.

People's Development Party (PDP): Makerere Hill Rd, Relief Bldg (opp. LDC), POB 25765, Kampala; f. 2007; Pres. Dr ABED BWANIKA.

People's Progressive Party (PPP): POB 9252, Kampala; tel. (41) 4505178; internet www.ppp.ug; f. 2004; Chair. JABERI BIDANDI SSALI.

Uganda Federal Alliance (UFA): POB 14196, Kampala; tel. 783438201; f. 2010; Pres. (vacant).

Uganda Patriotic Movement (UPM): POB 2083, Kampala; tel. 752654524; e-mail lubegabyayida@yahoo.com; f. 1980; Nat. Chair. D. A. LUBEGA BYAY; Sec.-Gen. MARIAM SSEMPIJJA.

Uganda People's Congress (UPC): Uganda House, Plot 8–10, Kampala Rd, POB 37047, Kampala; tel. (41) 4236748; e-mail upcsecretariat@upcparty.net; internet www.upcparty.net; f. 1960; socialist-based philosophy; ruling party 1962–71 and 1980–85, sole legal political party 1969–71; Pres. JIMMY AKENA; Sec.-Gen. FRED EBIL.

Diplomatic Representation

EMBASSIES AND HIGH COMMISSIONS IN UGANDA

Algeria: Plot 14, John Babiha Ave, Kololo, Kampala; tel. (41) 4343886; e-mail ambalgka@mtninternet.co.ug; Ambassador CHÉRIF OUALID.

Belgium: Rwenzori Towers, 6th Floor, Plot 6, Nakasero Rd, POB 7043, Kampala; tel. (41) 4349559; e-mail kampala@diplobel.fed.be; internet uganda.diplomatie.belgium.be; Ambassador RUDI VEESTRAETEN.

Burundi: Plot 12A York Terrace, Kololo, POB 29214, Kampala; tel. (41) 4235850; e-mail ambabukpl@utlonline.co.ug; Ambassador EPIPHANIE NTAMWANA KABUSHEBEYE.

China, People's Republic: 37 Malcolm X Ave, Kololo, POB 4106, Kampala; tel. (41) 4259881; e-mail chinaemb_ug@mfa.gov.cn; internet ug.china-embassy.gov.cn; Ambassador ZHANG LIZHONG.

Congo, Democratic Republic: 20 Philip Rd, Kololo, POB 4972, Kampala; tel. (41) 4250099; e-mail missionrdckampala@gmail.com; Chargé d'affaires a.i. JEAN PIERRE MASSALA.

Cuba: Plot 7A, Serumkuma Rd, Upper Mbuya, Kampala; tel. (41) 4233742; internet misiones.minrex.gob.cu/es/uganda; Ambassador TANYA PÉRES XIQUÉS.

Denmark: Plot 3, Lumumba Ave, POB 11243, Kampala; tel. (31) 2363000; e-mail kmtamb@um.dk; internet uganda.um.dk; Ambassador SIGNE WINDING ALBJERG.

Egypt: 24 Kololo Elizabeth Lane, Kampala; tel. (41) 4254525; e-mail embegyug@hotmail.com; internet www.mfa.gov.eg/kampala_emb; Ambassador ASHRAF MOHAMED NABHAN SWELAM.

Equatorial Guinea: Kampala; tel. (14) 237006; Ambassador CARMELO MICHA NGUEMA.

Eritrea: Plot 49B, Upper Kololo Terrace, POB 35417, Kampala; tel. (41) 4342625; e-mail emba.eri.kamp@gmail.com; Ambassador MOHAMMED SULEIMAN AHMED.

Ethiopia: Plot 3L, off Kira Rd, Kitante Close, POB 7745, Kampala; tel. (41) 4348340; e-mail ethiokam@utlonline.co.ug; Ambassador ALEMTSEHAY MESERET.

France: 16 Lumumba Ave, Nakasero, POB 7212, Kampala; tel. (41) 4304500; e-mail scg.kampala-amba@diplomatie.gouv.fr; internet ug.ambafrance.org; Ambassador XAVIER STICKER (designate).

Germany: 15 Philip Rd, Kololo, POB 7016, Kampala; tel. (41) 4501111; e-mail info@kampala.diplo.de; internet kampala.diplo.de; Ambassador MATTHIAS SCHAUER.

Holy See: Chwa II Rd, Mbuya Hill, POB 7177, Kampala; tel. (41) 4505619; e-mail sphorgan@hotmail.com; Apostolic Nuncio LUIGI BIANCO (Titular Archbishop of Falerone).

Iceland: Plot 3, Lumumba Ave, Nakasero, POB 7592, Kampala; tel. (31) 2531100; e-mail kampala@utn.is; internet www.stjornarradid.is/sendiskrifstofur/sendirad-islands-i-kampala; Ambassador UNNUR ORRADOTTIR RAMETTE.

India: 11 Kyadondo Rd, Nakasero, POB 7040, Kampala; tel. (41) 4344631; e-mail hc.kampala@mea.gov.in; internet hci.gov.in/kampala; High Commissioner A. AJAY KUMAR.

Iran: Plot 8, Moyo Close, Kololo Hill Lane, POB 24529, Kampala; tel. (41) 4505886; e-mail iranemb.kpl@mfa.gov.ir; internet uganda.mfa.gov.ir; Ambassador SEYED MORTEZA MORTAZAVI.

Ireland: 25 Yusuf Lule Rd, Nakasero, POB 7791, Kampala; tel. (41) 7713000; e-mail kampalaembassy@dfa.ie; internet www.dfa.ie/irish-embassy/uganda; Ambassador KEVIN COLGAN.

Italy: 11 Lourdel Rd, Nakasero, POB 4646, Kampala; tel. (31) 2188000; e-mail segreteria.kampala@esteri.it; internet www.ambkampala.esteri.it; Ambassador MASSIMILIANO MAZZANTI.

Japan: Plot 8, Kyadondo Rd, Nakasero, POB 23553, Kampala; tel. (31) 2261564; e-mail jp-embassy@kp.mofa.go.jp; internet www.ug.emb-japan.go.jp; Ambassador HIDEMOTO FUKUZAWA.

Kenya: Plot 3, Upper Kololo Terrace, POB 5220, Kampala; tel. (41) 4258235; e-mail info@kenyamissionkampala.ug; internet kampala.mfa.go.ke; High Commissioner Maj.-Gen. (retd) GEORGE OWINOW.

Korea, Democratic People's Republic: 10 Prince Charles Dr., Kololo, POB 5885, Kampala; tel. (41) 4254603; Ambassador JONG TONG HAK.

Korea, Republic: Plot 14, Ternan Rd, Nakasero, POB 27278, Kampala; tel. (41) 4500197; e-mail emb.kampala@mofa.go.kr; internet overseas.mofa.go.kr/ug-ko/index.do; Ambassador PARK SUNG-SOO.

Libya: Plot No. 26, Hill Dr., Kololo, POB 6079, Kampala; tel. (41) 7700700; e-mail libyaembassy172@yahoo.com; Ambassador IBRAHIM AHMED SULTAN.

Netherlands: DFCU Towers, 6th Floor, 26 Kyadondo Rd, Nakasero, POB 7728, Kampala; tel. (20) 4346000; e-mail kam@minbuza.nl; internet www.netherlandsworldwide.nl/countries/uganda; Ambassador KARIN BOVEN.

Nigeria: 33 Nakasero Rd, POB 4338, Kampala; tel. (41) 4233691; e-mail nighicom-sgu@africaonline.co.ug; High Commissioner ISMAIL AYOBAMI ALATISE.

Norway: Plot 18B, Akii-Bua Rd, POB 22770, Kampala; tel. (31) 2246000; e-mail emb.kampala@mfa.no; internet www.norway.no/uganda; Ambassador ELIN ØSTEBØ JOHANSEN.

Russian Federation: 28 Malcolm X Ave, Kololo, POB 7022, Kampala; tel. (41) 4345698; e-mail rusemb.uganda@mid.ru; internet uganda.mid.ru; Ambassador VLADLEN S. SEMIVOLOS.

Rwanda: 2 Nakayima Rd, Kitante, POB 2468, Kampala; tel. (41) 4344045; e-mail ambakampala@minaffet.gov.rw; internet www.rwandainuganda.gov.rw; High Commissioner Col JOSEPH RUTABANA.

Saudi Arabia: 25A Elizabeth Ave, Kololo, Kampala; tel. (31) 3340616; e-mail ugemb@mofa.gov.sa; internet embassies.mofa.gov.sa/sites/uganda; Ambassador Dr JAMAL BIN MUHAMMAD AL-MADANI.

Somalia: Plot No. 16, Nile Ave, Shimon Rd, POB 569, Kampala; tel. 753081558; e-mail kampalaembassy@mfa.gov.so; internet fb.com/SomaliainUganda; Ambassador ALI MOHAMED MOHAMUD AGABARUR.

South Africa: Plot 15A, Nakasero Rd, POB 22667, Kampala; tel. (41) 7702100; e-mail sahc@kampala.gov.za; internet www.dirco.gov.za/uganda; High Commissioner LULAMA MARYTHERESA XINGWANA.

South Sudan: Plot 2B, Nakasero Hill Lane, POB 22667, Kampala; tel. (31) 220006; internet embrssug.org; Ambassador SIMON JAUCH (designate).

Sudan: 21 Nakasero Rd, POB 3200, Kampala; tel. (41) 4230001; e-mail sudanikampala@utlonline.co.ug; Ambassador AHMED IBRAHIM AWADELSEED.

Sweden: 24 Lumumba Ave, Nakasero, POB 22669, Kampala; tel. (41) 7700800; e-mail ambassaden.kampala@gov.se; internet www.swedenabroad.se/kampala; Ambassador MARIA HÅKANSSON.

Tanzania: 6 Kagera Rd, POB 5750, Kampala; tel. (41) 4256272; e-mail kampala@nje.go.tz; internet ug.tzembassy.go.tz; High Commissioner Dr AZIZ PONARY MLIMA.

Türkiye (Turkey): 23 Prince Charles Dr., Ibis Vale, Kololo, POB 34718, Kampala; tel. (41) 4500182; e-mail embassy.kampala@mfa.gov.tr; internet kampala.be.mfa.gov.tr; Ambassador FIKRET KEREM ALP.

United Arab Emirates: 39 Kitante Rd, Nakasero, Kampala; tel. (31) 2203119; e-mail KampalaEMB@mofaic.gov.ae; Ambassador ABDULLAH HUSSAIN OBAID HASSAN AL-SHAMSI.

United Kingdom: Plot 4, Windsor Loop, POB 7070, Kampala; tel. (31) 2312000; e-mail kampala.bhcinfo@fco.gov.uk; internet www.gov.uk/world/uganda; High Commissioner KATE AIREY.

USA: 1577 Ggaba Rd, Kampala; tel. (31) 2306001; e-mail kampalawebcontact@state.gov; internet ug.usembassy.gov; Ambassador NATALIE BROWN.

Judicial System

The judicial system comprises a Supreme Court, a Court of Appeal, a High Court and Magistrates' Courts. The Court of Appeal sits, whenever necessary, as a Constitutional Court to determine matters of a constitutional nature. There are also quasi-judicial institutions, such as Local Council Courts, Family and Children Courts and Land Courts. The Chief Justice is the head of the judiciary and is responsible for the administration and supervision of all courts in Uganda; he may issue orders and directions to the courts necessary for proper and efficient administration of justice.

Supreme Court: Plot 10, Upper Koloko, Seenu Awasthi Terrace, Mengo, Kampala; internet www.judiciary.go.ug; hears appeals from the Court of Appeal and the Constitutional Court; consists of the Chief Justice and 8 other judges; Chief Justice ALFONSE CHIGAMOY OWINY-DOLLO.

Court of Appeal: 5 Parliament Ave, Kampala; hears appeals from the High Court; acts as a Constitutional Court; consists of the Deputy Chief Justice and no fewer than 7 Justices of Appeal, the number thereof being prescribed by Parliament; Deputy Chief Justice RICHARD BUTEERA.

High Court: Plot 1, The Square, POB 7085, Kampala; tel. (41) 4233422; the court's services are also available from 11 High Court circuits, located at Fort Portal, Mbarara, Masaka, Masindi, Jinja, Soroti, Mbale, Gulu, Lira, Arua and Kabale; has full criminal and civil jurisdiction; Principal Judge Dr FLAVIAN ZEIJA.

Magistrates' Courts: These were established under the Magistrates' Courts Act of 1970 and exercise limited jurisdiction in criminal and civil matters. The country is divided into magisterial areas, presided over by a Chief Magistrate. Under the Chief Magistrate there are two categories of Magistrates. The Magistrates preside alone over their courts. Appeals from the first category of Magistrates' Court lie directly to the High Court, while appeals from the second categories of Magistrates' Court lie to the Chief Magistrate's Court, and from there to the High Court. There are 27 Chief Magistrates' Courts, 52 Magistrates' Grade I Courts and 428 Magistrates' Grade II Courts.

Attorney-General: KIRYOWA KIWANUKA.

Religion

Christianity is the majority religion—at the time of the 2014 census, its adherents constituted around 84.5% of the population. Muslims accounted for some 13.7% of the population. A variety of other religions, including traditional indigenous religions, several branches of Hinduism, the Bahá'í Faith and Judaism, are practised freely. There are few atheists in the country. In many areas, particularly in rural settings, some religions tend to be syncretistic: deeply held traditional indigenous beliefs are blended into or observed alongside the rites of recognized religions, particularly in areas that are predominantly Christian.

CHRISTIANITY

According to the 2014 census, 39.3% of the population were members of the Roman Catholic Church, while 32.0% were members of the Anglican Church. The Seventh-day Adventist Church, the Church of Jesus Christ of Latter-day Saints (Mormons), the Orthodox Church, Jehovah's Witnesses, the Baptist Church, the Unification Church and the Pentecostal Church, among others, are also active.

The Anglican Communion

Anglicans are adherents of the Church of the Province of Uganda, comprising 34 dioceses.

Archbishop of Uganda and Bishop of Mityana: Most Rev. STEPHEN SAMUEL KAZIIMBA MUGALU, POB 102, Mityana; tel. 772512175; e-mail couoffice@gmail.com; internet churchofuganda .org.

Greek Orthodox Church

Metropolitan of Kampala and All Uganda: JERONYMOS MUZEEYI, POB 3970, Kampala; tel. (41) 4542461; e-mail info@uganda orthodoxchurch.co.ug; internet www.ugandaorthodoxchurch.co.ug.

The Roman Catholic Church

Uganda comprises four archdioceses, 15 dioceses and one military ordinariate.

Uganda Episcopal Conference: Uganda Catholic Secretariat, Plot No. 672, Hanlon Rd, Nsambya Hill, POB 2886, Kampala; tel. (41) 4510398; e-mail info@uecon.org; internet www.uecon.org; f. 1974; Chair. Rev. JOSEPH ANTHONY ZZIWA (Bishop of Kiyinda-Mityana).

Archbishop of Gulu: Most Rev. JOHN BAPTIST ODAMA, Archbishop's House, POB 200, Gulu; tel. (47) 4132026; e-mail metrog@ archdioceseofgulu.org.

Archbishop of Kampala: Most Rev. PAUL SSEMOGERERE, Archbishop's House, POB 14125, Mengo, Kampala; tel. (41) 4270183; e-mail klarchdioc@infocom.co.ug; internet klarchdiocese.org.ug.

Archbishop of Mbarara: Most Rev. LAMBERT BAINOMUGISHA, POB 184, Mbarara; tel. 778532926; e-mail archdiocesembarara@gmail .com; internet www.archdioceseofmbarara.org.ug.

Archbishop of Tororo: Most Rev. EMMANUEL OBBO, Archbishop's House, POB 632, Tororo; tel. 753603635; e-mail tororoad@ africaonline.co.ug; internet tororoarchdiocese.org.

ISLAM

Muslims are mainly Sunni, although there are Shi'a followers of the Aga Khan among the Asian community.

The Uganda Muslim Supreme Council: National Mosque, Old Kampala Hill, POB 1146, Kampala; tel. 772853077; e-mail pro_umsc@yahoo.com; Mufti of Uganda Sheikh SHABAN RAMADHAN MUBAJJE; Chief Kadi and Pres. of Council HUSAYN RAJAB KAKOOZA.

BAHÁ'Í FAITH

National Spiritual Assembly: POB 2662, Kampala; tel. (41) 4540511; e-mail ugandabahai@gmail.com; f. 1951; mems resident in more than 2,800 localities.

JUDAISM

There is a small Jewish community, the Abayudaya, based near the town of Mbale in eastern Uganda, with some 2,000–3,000 members and seven synagogues.

The Press

DAILY AND OTHER NEWSPAPERS (PRESS AND ONLINE)

The Daily Monitor: Plot 29–35, 8th St, POB 12141, Kampala; tel. (31) 312301212; e-mail editorial@ug.nationmedia.com; internet www.monitor.co.ug; f. 1994; daily; English; Gen. Man. DANIEL KALINAKI.

Munno: POB 4027, Kampala; f. 1911 as a daily newspaper; Luganda; closed in the 1990s, relaunched as a weekly newspaper in 2014; publ. by the Roman Catholic Church; Editor ISAIAH RWANYEKIRO.

New Vision: Plot 19–21, First St Industrial Area, POB 9815, Kampala; tel. (41) 4337000; e-mail website@newvision.co.ug; internet www.newvision.co.ug; f. 1986; official govt newspaper; daily; English; Editor-in-Chief BARBARA KAIJA.

Bukedde: Kampala; tel. (41) 4337000; e-mail digital@newvision .co.ug; internet www.bukedde.co.ug; daily; Luganda; Editor PAUL KADDU.

Etop: Plot 14 Engwau Rd, Soroti; e-mail etop@newvision.co.ug; weekly; vernacular; Editor KENNETH OLUKA.

The Kampala Sun: Kampala; internet kampalasun.co.ug; weekly; English; Editor EMMANUEL SEJJENGO; Chief Sub-Editor REBECCA RUGYENDO.

The Observer: Kampala; tel. (41) 4230433; internet www .observer.ug; f. 2004; English; 3 a week; Chief Sub-Editor DAVID LUMU.

Orumuri: Plot 4, Stanley Rd, Boma Mbarara; tel. 759585424; e-mail editors@newvision.co.ug; internet www.fb.com/orumuri; biweekly; vernacular.

The Red Pepper: Namanve Industrial Area, POB 7335, Kampala; tel. 782377584; e-mail admin@redpepper.co.ug; internet www.redpepper.co.ug; f. 2001; CEO RICHARD TUSIIME.

Rupiny: 256 Lira, Lira Town; tel. (41) 4337000; e-mail rupiny@ newvision.co.ug; internet fb.com/rupiny.newspaper.7; weekly; vernacular; Editor ROBERT OKWIR.

Uganda Today: Kampala; tel. 712172005; internet www .theugandatoday.com.

PERIODICALS

Bride and Groom: Pika House, 1st St, Industrial Area, Kampala; tel. (41) 4337000; e-mail brideandgroom@newvision.co.ug; internet brideandgroomexpo.co.ug; f. 2004; 4 a year; publ. by New Vision Group; Editor LUCY PARWOT.

The CEO Magazine: Akamwesi Complex, 2nd Floor, Plot 112, New Portbell Rd, Nakawa, Kampala; tel. 759800326; e-mail ceomagazine@gmail.com; internet www.ceo.co.ug; f. 2007; monthly; business; Chief Editor MUHEREZA KYAMUTETERA.

The Eye: Plot 2489, off Kamuli Rd, Naalya, Kampala; tel. 782947882; e-mail info@theeye.ug; internet theeye.ug; f. 1990; 6 a year; travel; Editor SHAZ DUNBAR.

Flair for Her: Plot 19/21, 1st St, Industrial Area, POB 9815, Kampala; tel. (41) 4337000; e-mail flair@newvision.co.ug; internet fb.com/flairforher; f. 2007; 4 a year; publ. by New Vision Group; Editor EVA NABAGESERA KIRUNDA.

The Independent: Kampala; tel. (31) 2637391; e-mail info@independent.co.ug; internet www.independent.co.ug; f. 2007; weekly; Editor ANDREW MWENDA.

Leadership: POB 2522, Kampala; tel. (41) 4422407; f. 1956; 11 a year; English; Roman Catholic; Editor BEATRICE AKITE (acting).

REGULATORY AUTHORITY

Media Council of Uganda: Communications House, Rm 305, 3rd Floor, Colville St, POB 23780, Kampala; tel. (41) 4254908; e-mail secretary@mediacouncil.ug; internet mediacouncil.go.ug; Chair. PAULO EKOCHU; Sec. DAVID KYETUME KASANGA.

NEWS AGENCIES

Uganda Radio Network (URN): Plot 823, Mawana Rd, Kamwokya, POB 7584, Kampala; tel. (41) 4530777; e-mail sgummah@ugandaradionetwork.com; internet ugandaradionetwork.com; f. 2005; Exec. Dir SAMUEL GUMMAH.

Publishers

Centenary Publishing House Ltd: POB 6246, Kampala; tel. (41) 4241599; f. 1977; religious (Anglican); Man. Dir Rev. SAM KAKIZA.

Fountain Publishers Ltd: Plot No. 55, Nkrumah Rd, POB 488, Kampala; tel. (41) 4259163; e-mail publishing@fountainpublishers.co.ug; internet www.fountainpublishers.co.ug; f. 1989; general, school textbooks, children's books, academic, scholarly; Man. Dir JAMES TUMUSIIME.

GW Publishing Co: Raja Chambers, 4th Floor, POB 2726, Kampala; tel. (41) 4388179; internet www.gwpc.ug.

MK Publishers: Plot No. 1187, Kibuye Entebbe Rd, Kampala; tel. 707999044; e-mail info@mkpublishers.com; internet mkpublishers.com; f. 1995; primary and secondary school books.

Moran Publishers Uganda Ltd: Freedom City Mall Basement, Entebbe Rd, POB 2762, Kampala; tel. (41) 4236111; internet moranpublishers.com; a subsidiary of Moran Publishers (Kenya).

Pearson Longman Uganda Ltd: Plot 8, Berkeley Rd, POB 3409, Kampala; tel. (41) 4242940; f. 1965; Man. Dir M. K. L. MUTYABA.

Uganda Printing and Publishing Corporation (UPPC): Plot No. 8–12, Airport Rd, POB 33, Entebbe; tel. (41) 4220639; e-mail info@uppc.co.ug; internet www.uppc.co.ug; f. 1993; Man. Dir TOM DAVIS WASSWA.

Broadcasting and Communications

REGULATORY AUTHORITY

Uganda Communications Commission: UCC House, 42–44 Spring Rd, Bugolobi, POB 7376, Kampala; tel. (41) 4339000; e-mail ucc@ucc.co.ug; internet www.ucc.co.ug; f. 1998; regulatory body; Chair. Eng. Dr DOROTHY OKELLO; Exec. Dir IRENE KAGGWA SEWANKAMBO (acting).

TELECOMMUNICATIONS

Airtel Uganda Ltd: Airtel House, 40 Jinja Rd, POB 6771, Kampala; tel. 752230110; e-mail customerservice@ug.airtel.com; internet www.airtel.co.ug; f. 1995; fmrly Celtel Uganda, subsequently Zain Uganda, present name adopted in 2010; acquired Warid Telecom (f. 2006) in 2013; Man. Dir MANOJ MURALI.

Datanet: Crested Towers, Short Wing, Ground Floor, Suite 1, 22 Hannington Rd, Kampala; tel. (41) 4255520; e-mail info@data.co.ug; internet datanet.ug; f. 1999; internet service provider.

K2 Telecom: Muganzirwazza Commercial Plaza, Kibuye Ring Rd, POB 4722, Kampala; tel. 730730001; e-mail info@k2telecom.ug; internet www.k2telecom.ug; f. 2013; mobile virtual network operator; CEO JESSICA NANYONGA.

MTN Uganda Ltd: Plot 69–71, Jinja Rd, POB 24624, Kampala; tel. (31) 2120011; e-mail customerservice@mtn.co.ug; internet www.mtn.co.ug; f. 1998; CEO WIM VANHELLEPUTTE.

Smile Communications Uganda Ltd: Plot 10–12, Corporation Rise, Bukoto, Kampala; tel. 720100100; e-mail info@smile.co.ug; internet smile.co.ug; internet service provider; Country Man. STEVE BANNON.

TruIT: Plot 218, Kiwanuka Musoke Close, off Wavamuno Rd, POB 8370, Kampala; tel. (31) 3222444; e-mail support@truit.ug; internet www.truit.ug; f. 2012.

Uganda Telecom Ltd (UTL): Plot 2A–4A, Telephone House, Speke Rd, POB 7171, Kampala; tel. (41) 4333200; e-mail customercare.info@utl.co.ug; internet www.utl.co.ug; f. 1998; state-owned; Chair. STEPHEN KABOYO; Man. Dir MARK SHOEBRIDGE.

BROADCASTING

Radio

91.3 Capital FM: Plot 1A, Cooper Rd, Kisementi, Kololo, POB 7638, Kampala; tel. (41) 4235092; internet capitalradio.co.ug; f. 1993; independent music station broadcasting from Kampala, Mbarara and Mbale; Chief Officers WILLIAM PIKE, PATRICK QUARCOO.

Central Broadcasting Service (CBS): Mengo Bulange House, Kabaka Anjagala Rd, POB 12760, Kampala; tel. (31) 2333100; internet www.cbsfm.ug; f. 1996; independent station broadcasting in local languages and English to most of Uganda; Chair. MATHIAS KATAMBA.

Metro FM 90.8: Plot 16B Martin Rd, POB 946, Kampala; tel. (39) 3908908; e-mail metro90.8@gmail.com; internet fb.com/metrofm90.8.

Radio One: Duster St, POB 4589, Kampala; tel. (41) 43235324; e-mail info@radioonefm90.com; internet www.radioonefm90.com.

Sanyu Radio: Plot 38, Crane Chambers, 6th Floor, Kampala Rd, Kampala; tel. (41) 4343663; internet www.sanyufm.com; f. 1993; independent station broadcasting to Kampala and its environs.

UBC Radio: Plot 17–19, Nile Ave, POB 2038, Kampala; tel. (41) 4257257; internet ubc.go.ug/ubc-radios; f. 1954; state-controlled; under Uganda Broadcasting Corpn (UBC), formed by merger of Radio Uganda and Uganda Television in 2005; broadcasts in 23 languages, including English and Ugandan vernacular languages, through 10 stations, Mega, UBC West, Ngeya, West Nile, Voice of Burundi, Buruli, Butebo, Magic 100, Totoore, and Star FM; Man. Dir DOREEN NDEEZI.

Television

NTV-Uganda: Serena Conference Centre, 1 Simoni Rd, POB 35933, Kampala; tel. (41) 4563400; e-mail newsdesk@ntv.co.ug; internet www.ntv.co.ug; f. 2006; Man. Dir JOHNSON OMOLLO.

UBC TV: Plot 17–19, Nile Ave, POB 2038, Kampala; tel. (41) 4257034; internet www.ubc.go.ug/tv; f. 1962; state-controlled commercial service; under Uganda Broadcasting Corpn (UBC), formed by merger of Radio Uganda and Uganda Television in 2005; programmes mainly in English, also in Swahili and Luganda; transmits over a radius of 320 km from Kampala; 5 relay stations are in operation, others are under construction; Chair. JAMES RWEHABURA; Man. Dir WINSTON ABAGA.

Finance

BANKING

At July 2020 there were 25 commercial banks, five credit institutions and four microfinance deposit-taking institutions licensed to operate in Uganda.

Central Bank

Bank of Uganda: 37–45 Kampala Rd, POB 7120, Kampala; tel. (41) 4258441; e-mail info@bou.or.ug; internet www.bou.or.ug; f. 1966; bank of issue; Gov. (vacant); Dep. Gov. Dr MICHAEL ATINGI-EGO.

State Bank

Uganda Development Bank Ltd (UDBL): Rwenzori Towers, 1st Floor, Wing B, Plot 6, Nakasero Rd, POB 7210, Kampala; tel. (31) 2355555; e-mail info@udbl.co.ug; internet www.udbl.co.ug; f. 1972; state-owned; Chair. FELIX OKOBOI; Man. Dir PATRICIA ADONGO OJANGOLE.

Commercial Banks

ABC Capital Bank (U) Ltd: Colline House, Plot 4, Pilkington Rd, POB 21091, Kampala; tel. (20) 0516600; e-mail customerservice@abccapitalbank.co.ug; internet www.abccapitalbank.co.ug; f. 1993 as Capital Finance Corpn Ltd; present name adopted in 2010; Chair. Dr JAMES WILSON MUWANGA; CEO JESSE TIMBWA.

Absa Bank Uganda Ltd: Plot 2, Hannington Rd, POB 7101, Kampala; tel. (31) 2218348; e-mail absa.uganda@absa.africa; internet www.absa.co.ug; f. 1969 as Barclays Bank of Uganda Ltd; present name adopted 2019; Chair. NADINE BYARUGABA; Man. Dir MUMBA KALIFUNGWA.

Bank of Africa—Uganda Ltd: Plot 45, Jinja Rd, POB 2750, Kampala; tel. (41) 4302001; e-mail feedback@boauganda.com; internet boauganda.com; f. 1986 as Allied Bank International (Uganda); present name adopted in 2005; 47.7% owned by Bank of Africa—Kenya, 21.9% by Aureos East Africa Fund, 19.8% by The Netherlands Development Finance Co, 10.6% by Central Holdings Ltd; Chair. GEORGE EGADDU; Man. Dir ARTHUR ISIKO.

Cairo Bank Uganda Ltd: Lotis Towers, Plot 16, Mackinnon Rd, Nakasero, Kampala; tel. (41) (41) 7230105; e-mail feedback@cbu.co.ug; internet cbu.co.ug; fmrly Cairo International Bank; present name adopted 2020; subsidiary of Banque du Caire; Chair. CHARLES BYARUHANGA; Man. Dir AHMAD MAHER.

Centenary Rural Development Bank: Plot 44–46, Kampala Rd, POB 1892, Kampala; tel. (41) 7202002; e-mail info@centenarybank.co.ug; internet www.centenarybank.co.ug; Chair. BWOCH GUSTAVIO ORACH LUJWERO; Man. Dir FABIAN KASI.

DFCU Bank Ltd: Plot 26, Kyadondo Rd, POB 70, Kampala; tel. (41) 4351000; e-mail customercare@dfcugroup.com; internet www.dfcugroup.com; f. 1984 as Gold Trust Bank Ltd; current name adopted 2000; Chair. JIMMY D. MUGERWA; CEO MATHIAS KATAMBA.

Diamond Trust Bank (Uganda) Ltd: Diamond Trust Bldg, Plot 17–19, Kampala Rd, POB 7155, Kampala; tel. (31) 4387387; e-mail info@dtbuganda.co.ug; internet www.dtbafrica.com; f. 1995; 40% owned by The Diamond Jubilee Investment Trust, 33.3% owned by Aga Khan Fund for Economic Development, 26.7% owned by Diamond Trust Bank Kenya Ltd; Chair. AZIM KASSAM; CEO VARGESE THAMBI.

Ecobank Uganda Ltd: Plot 4, Parliament Ave, POB 7368, Kampala; tel. (41) 7700100; e-mail ecobankug@ecobank.com; internet www.ecobank.com; f. 2008; Chair. KIN KARIISA; Man. Dir CLEMENT DODOO.

Equity Bank Uganda Ltd: Church House, Plot 34, Kampala Rd, POB 10184, Kampala; tel. (31) 2327000; e-mail info@equitybank.co.ug; internet equitygroupholdings.com/ug; Chair. APOLLO MAKU-BUYA; Man. Dir SAMUEL KIRUBI.

Finance Trust Bank: Plots 121 and 115, Block 6, Finance Trust Bldg, Katwe, POB 6972, Kampala; tel. 751932900; e-mail customercare@financetrust.co.ug; internet www.financetrust.co.ug; f. 1984 as Uganda Finance Trust Ltd MDI; present name adopted in 2013; Chair. Dr EVELYN KIGOZI KAHIIGI; Man. Dir ANNET NAKAWUNDE MULINDWA.

Guaranty Trust Bank Uganda Ltd: Plot 56, Kiira Rd, POB 7323, Kampala; tel. (20) 0710500; e-mail bankingug@gtbank.com; internet www.gtbank.co.ug; f. 2008; fmrly Fina Bank Uganda Ltd; present name adopted in 2014; Chair. B. S. RAMESH BABU; Man. Dir OLALEKAN SANUSI.

Housing Finance Bank Ltd: Investment House, Plot 4, Wampewo Ave, Kololo, POB 1539, Kampala; tel. (41) 4803000; e-mail info@housingfinance.co.ug; internet www.housingfinance.co.ug; f. 1967; 49.18% owned by Govt, 50% owned by National Social Security Fund, 0.82% owned by National Housing and Construction Corpn; Chair. DAVID G. OPIOKELLO; Man. Dir MICHAEL MUGABI.

Opportunity Bank Ltd (UCBL): Plot 1259, Old Kiira Rd, POB 33513, Kampala; tel. (41) 4236724; e-mail customerservice@opportunitybank.co.ug; internet www.opportunitybank.co.ug; f. 1995 as Faulu Uganda; 49% owned by MyBucks SA; Chair. PHILLIP KARUGABA; CEO ROBERT ONGODIA.

Orient Bank Ltd: Orient Plaza, Plot 6/6A, Kampala Rd, POB 3072, Kampala; tel. (41) 7719101; e-mail mail@orient-bank.com; internet www.orient-bank.com; f. 1993; Chair. SULEIMAN I. KIGGUNDU, Jr; CEO/Man. Dir KUMARAN PATHER.

Development Bank

East African Development Bank (EADB): Plot 4, EADB Bldg, Nile Ave, POB 7128, Kampala; tel. (41) 7112900; e-mail enquiry@eadb.org; internet www.eadb.org; f. 1967; majority stake held by the Govts of Kenya, Tanzania and Uganda; provides financial and tech. assistance to promote industrial development within Uganda, Kenya, Rwanda and Tanzania; regional offices in Nairobi (Kenya), Kigali (Rwanda) and Dar es Salaam (Tanzania); Dir-Gen. VIVIENNE YEDA.

Foreign Banks

Bank of Baroda (Uganda) Ltd (India): 18 Kampala Rd, POB 7197, Kampala; tel. (41) 4233680; e-mail md.uganda@bankofbaroda.com; internet www.bankofbaroda.ug; f. 1953; 80% owned by Bank of Baroda (India); Chair. VASTINA RUKIMIRANA NSANZE; Man. Dir RAJ KUMAR MEENA.

Citibank (Uganda) Ltd (USA): Plot 4, Ternan Ave, Nakasero, POB 7505, Kampala; tel. (41) 4305500; internet www.citigroup.com/citi/about/countries-and-jurisdictions/uganda.html; 99.9% owned by Citicorp Overseas Investment Corpn, 0.1% owned by Foremost Investment; Man. Dir SARAH ARAPTA WOJEGA.

KCB Bank Uganda Ltd (Kenya): Commercial Plaza, Plot 7, Kampala Rd, POB 7399, Kampala; e-mail contactcenterug@ug.kcbbankgroup.com; internet ug.kcbgroup.com; Chair. CONSTANT OTHIENO MAYENDE.

Stanbic Bank Uganda Ltd (UK): Crested Towers, Plot 17, Hannington Rd, POB 7131, Kampala; tel. (31) 2224900; e-mail cccug@stanbic.com; internet www.stanbicbank.co.ug; f. 1906 as National Bank of India Uganda present name adopted in 199380% owned by Stanbic Africa Holdings Ltd (UK); merged with Uganda Commercial Bank Ltd 2002; Chair. JAPHETH KATTO; CEO ANNE JUUKO.

Standard Chartered Bank Uganda Ltd (UK): Plot 5, Speke Rd, POB 7111, Kampala; tel. (31) 3294100; e-mail ug.service@sc.com; internet www.sc.com/ug; f. 1912; wholly owned by Standard Chartered Bank PLC; Chair. ROBIN KIBUKA; Man. Dir ALBERT RICHARD SALTSON.

Tropical Bank (Libya): Plot 54, Lugogo Bypass Rotary Ave, POB 9485/7292, Kampala; tel. (41) 4313100; e-mail admin@trobank.com; internet www.trobank.com; f. 1973; 99.99% owned by Libyan Foreign Bank; Chair. MOSES KIWE SEBUNYA; Man. Dir ABDULAZIZ M. A. MANSUR.

United Bank for Africa (Uganda) Ltd (Nigeria): Plot 2, Jinja Rd, POB 7396, Kampala; tel. (41) 7715100; e-mail cfcuganda@ubagroup.com; internet www.ubauganda.com; f. 2008; Chair MARIA KIWA-NUKA; Man. Dir and CEO CHIOMA MANG.

Credit Institutions

Mercantile Credit Bank Ltd: 8 Old Port Bell Rd, POB 620, Kampala; tel. (41) 4235967; e-mail info@mcb.co.ug; internet mcb.co.ug; CEO PAUL SENYOMO.

Post Bank Uganda Ltd: Plot 4/6, Nkrumah Rd, POB 7189, Kampala; tel. (41) 4258551; e-mail info@postbank.co.ug; internet www.postbank.co.ug; wholly state-owned; Chair. GRACE BAKUNDA; Man. Dir JULIUS KAKEETO.

Top Finance Bank Uganda Ltd: Plot 53, Kampala Rd, POB 33913, Kampala; tel. 702363167; e-mail info@topfinancebank.co.ug; internet www.topfinancebank.co.ug; f. 2012; Chair. DAMIEN KATO TAMALE; Man. Dir DENIS KIBUKAMUSOKE.

Banking Association

Uganda Bankers' Association: Plot 2702, Block 244, Nyangweso Rd, Muyenga, Kampala; tel. (41) 4343199; e-mail secretariat@ugandabankers.org; internet ugandabankers.org; f. 1981; Chair. MATHIAS KATAMBA; Exec. Sec. WILBROD HUMPHREY OWOR.

STOCK EXCHANGE

Uganda Securities Exchange: UAP Nakawa Business Park, Block A, 4th Floor, Plot 3–5, New Port-Bell Rd, POB 23552, Kampala; tel. (31) 2370815; e-mail info@use.or.ug; internet www.use.or.ug; f. 1997; Chair. CHARLES MAGEZI MBIRE; CEO PAUL BWISO.

INSURANCE

At April 2022 there were 29 insurance companies licensed to operate in Uganda, of which 21 provided non-life insurance and eight provided life insurance. There were also two micro insurance companies.

APA Insurance (Uganda) Ltd: AHA Towers, 7 Lourdel Rd, POB 7651, Kampala; tel. (20) 0907004; e-mail apa.uganda@apainsurance.org; internet apainsuranceuganda.com; f. 2003 following the merger of Pan Africa General (1946) and Apollo Insurance Co (1997); CEO MANAN DESAI.

Jubilee Insurance Co. of Uganda Ltd: Parliament Ave, POB 10234, Kampala; tel. (41) 4311701; e-mail jicug@jubileeuganda.com; internet jubileeinsurance.com/ug; 66% owned by Allianz (Germany); CEO PAUL KAVUMA.

Excel Insurance Co Ltd: Crest House, 1st–3rd Floors, Plot 2D, Nkurumah Rd, POB 7213, Kampala; tel. (41) 4348595; e-mail excelins@infocom.co.ug; internet exico.co.ug; f. 1997; Man. Dir PAUL MUWANGA.

First Insurance Co Ltd: Plot 21, Luthuli Ave, Bugolobi, POB 5254, Kampala; tel. (41) 4342863; e-mail fico@fico.co.ug; internet www.fico.co.ug; f. 1962; Chair. SAM JOHN KIBUUKA; CEO BURUGUPALLI VYASA KRISHNA.

GoldStar Insurance Co Ltd: Plot 38, Kampala Rd, Crane Chambers, POB 7781, Kampala; tel. (41) 4250110; e-mail goldstar@goldstarinsurance.com; internet www.goldstarinsurance.com; f. 1996; Chair. Dr SUDHIR RUPARELIA; Man. Dir AZIM THARANI.

MUA Insurance Co Uganda Ltd: Redstone House, 3rd Floor, Bandali Rise, POB 70149, Kampala; tel. (41) 4349659; e-mail infoug@mua.co.ug; internet www.mua.co.ug; f. 2018 following acquisition of Phoenix of Uganda Assurance Co Ltd; Chair. BERTRAND CASTERES; Man. Dir LATIMER KAGIMU MUKASA.

National Insurance Corporation: Plot 3, Pilkington Rd, POB 7134, Kampala; tel. (41) 7119900; e-mail nic@nic.co.ug; internet www.nic.co.ug; f. 1964; 60% owned by IGI PLC, Nigeria; general and life; Chair. MARTIN ALIKER; Man. Dir BAYO FOLAYAN.

Pax Insurance Co Ltd: Platinum Jubilee House, Plot 3, Colville St, POB 7030, Kampala; tel. (41) 4233096; e-mail info@paxinsurance.co .ug; internet www.paxinsurance.co.ug; f. 2008; owned by the Catholic Church; Chair. KASOZI MULINDWA SATURNINUS.

Sanlam Uganda General Insurance: Plot No. 18B, Clement Hill Rd, Shimoni Office Village, POB 24256, Kampala; tel. (31) 2264720; e-mail info@sanlam.co.ug; internet www.sanlam.com/uganda; f. 1992; fmrly NIKO Insurance; CEO GARY CORBIT; also **Sanlam Uganda Life Insurance**.

Statewide Insurance Co Ltd (SWICO): Sure House, Plot 1, Bombo Rd, POB 9393, Kampala; tel. (41) 4345996; e-mail swico@ swico.co.ug; internet www.swico.co.ug; f. 1982; Chair. JOSEPH MUBIRU KIZITO; Man. Dir JOSEPH WILLIAM KIWANUKA.

TransAfrica Assurance Co Ltd: Impala House, 2nd Floor, Plot 13–15, Kimathi Ave, POB 7601, Kampala; tel. (41) 4251411; e-mail taacl@transafricaassurance.com; internet www .transafricaassurance.com; f. 1992; Chair. MAHENDRA N. MEHTA; CEO MADHAV S. KUMAR.

UAP Old Mutual General Insurance Uganda: Block D, 6th Floor, UAP Nakawa Business Park, Plot 3–5, New PortBell Rd, POB 7185, Kampala; tel. (41) 4332700; e-mail uapuganda@uap-group.com; internet www.uap-group.com; Chair. Dr JOSEPH BARRAGE WANJUI; Group CEO ARTHUR OGINGA; also **UAP Old Mutual Life Assurance Uganda**.

Regulatory Authority

Insurance Regulatory Authority of Uganda: Legacy Towers, Block B, 2nd Floor, Plot 5, Kyadondo Rd, Nakasero, POB 22855, Kampala; tel. (41) 7425500; e-mail ira@ira.go.ug; internet www.ira .go.ug; Chair. Dr ISAAC NKOTE NABETA; CEO Alhaj KADDUNABBI IBRAHIM LUBEGA.

Insurance Association

Uganda Insurers' Association: Plot 24A, John Babiha (Acacia) Ave, Kololo, POB 8912, Kampala; tel. 800105050; e-mail info@uia.co .ug; internet www.uia.co.ug; f. 1965; CEO IBRAHIM LUBEGA KADDUNABBI.

Trade and Industry

GOVERNMENT AGENCIES

Capital Markets Authority (CMA): Jubilee Insurance Centre, 8th Floor, 14 Parliament Ave, POB 24565, Kampala; tel. (41) 4342788; e-mail info@cmauganda.co.ug; internet cmauganda.co.ug; f. 1996 to develop, promote and regulate capital markets sector; Chair. JACQUELINE KOBUSINGYE OPONDO; CEO KEITH KALYEGIRA.

Enterprise Uganda: 38 Lumumba Ave, Nakasero, POB 24581, Kampala; tel. (31) 2382100; e-mail info@enterprise.co.ug; internet enterprise.co.ug; f. 2001; Exec. Dir CHARLES OCICI.

Privatization Unit: Communications House, 2nd and 11th Floors, 1 Colville St, POB 10944, Kampala; tel. (41) 4705600; e-mail info@ perds.go.ug; internet www.perds.go.ug; f. 2001; oversees privatization programme and public-private partnerships; Exec. Dir MOSES MWASE.

Uganda Export Promotion Board: UEDCL Tower, 2nd Floor, 37 Nakasero Rd, POB 5045, Kampala; tel. (41) 4230250; e-mail info@ ugandaexports.go.ug; internet ugandaexports.go.ug; f. 1983; provides market intelligence, organizes training, trade exhibitions, etc.; Exec. Dir ELLY TWINEYO KAMUGISHA.

Uganda Investment Authority (UIA): Investment Centre, TWED Plaza, Plot 22B, Lumumba Ave, POB 7418, Kampala; tel. (41) 4301000; e-mail info@ugandainvest.go.ug; internet www .ugandainvest.go.ug; f. 1991; promotes foreign and local investment, assists investors, provides business information, issues investment licences; Chair. MORRIS RWAKAKAMBA; Dir-Gen. ROBERT MUKIZA.

Uganda Revenue Authority: Plot No. M193/M194, Nakawa Industrial Area, POB 7279, Kampala; tel. (41) 7440000; e-mail services@ura.go.ug; internet www.ura.go.ug; f. 1991; Commr Gen. JOHN MUSINGUZI RUJOKI.

DEVELOPMENT ORGANIZATIONS

Dairy Development Authority (DDA): Plot 1, Kafu Rd, POB 34006, Kampala; tel. (41) 4343901; internet dda.go.ug; f. 2000; development and regulation of the dairy industry in a sustainable manner; Exec. Dir Dr MICHAEL KANSIIME.

National Agricultural Research Organisation (NARO): Plot 3, Lugard Ave, POB 295, Entebbe; tel. (41) 320512; e-mail dgnaro@naro .go.ug; internet naro.go.ug; f. 2005; Dir-Gen. Dr AMBROSE AGONA.

National Housing and Construction Corpn (NHCC): Plot 3/5, 7th St Industrial Area, POB 659, Kampala; tel. (31) 2119300; e-mail sales@nhcc.co.ug; internet nhcc.co.ug; f. 1964; govt agent for building works; also develops residential housing; Chair. SYLVESTER WANJUSI WASIEBA; CEO Eng. KENNETH KAIJUKA.

Uganda Development Corpn (UDC): Soliz House, 5th Floor, 23 Lumumba Ave, POB 7042, Kampala; tel. (41) 4258204; e-mail info@ vitaco-demo.com; internet www.udc.co.ug; f. 1952; facilitates industrial and economic development; Exec. Dir PATRICK BITONDER BIRUNGI.

CHAMBER OF COMMERCE

Uganda National Chamber of Commerce and Industry: Plot 1A, Kira Rd, POB 3809, Kampala; tel. 753503035; e-mail info@ chamberuganda.go.ug; internet www.chamberuganda.go.ug; f. 1933; Pres. OLIVE Z. KIGONGO; Sec.-Gen. BRENDA TIBAMWENDA.

INDUSTRIAL AND TRADE ASSOCIATIONS

Cotton Development Organization: Plot 15, Clement Hill Rd, POB 7018, Kampala; tel. (41) 4232968; e-mail cdo@africaonline.co .ug; internet www.cdouga.org; monitors the production, processing and marketing of cotton in Uganda; Chair. BEN ANYAMA; Man. Dir JOLLY SABUNE.

Horticultural Exporters' Association of Uganda (HORTEXA): POB 29392, Kampala; tel. (77) 2419357; e-mail hortexa@yahoo.com; f. 1990; Chair. DAVID LULE.

Uganda Coffee Development Authority (UCDA): Coffee House, Plot 35, Jinja Rd, POB 7267, Kampala; tel. (31) 2260470; e-mail info@ ugandacoffee.go.ug; internet www.ugandacoffee.go.ug; f. 1991; enforces quality control and promotes coffee exports, maintains statistical data, advises Govt on local and world prices and trains processors and quality controllers; Chair. Dr CHARLES FRANCIS MUGOYA; Man. Dir EMMANUEL NIYIBIGIRA IYAMULEMYE.

Uganda Manufacturers' Association (UMA): Lugogo Show Grounds, POB 6966, Kampala; tel. (41) 4221034; e-mail administration@uma.or.ug; internet uma.or.ug; f. 1988; promotes mfrs' interests; Chair. DEO KAYEMBA.

Uganda National Farmers' Federation: Plot 27, Nakasero Rd, POB 6213, Kampala; tel. (41) 4230705; e-mail info@unffe.org.ug; internet unffe.org.ug; f. 1992 as Uganda National Farmers' Association; Pres. Dr DICK NUWAMANYA KAMUGANGA; CEO KATUNGISA KENNETH.

Uganda Tea Development Agency Ltd (UTDAL): Plot 821 Rubaga Rd, POB 6204, Kampala; tel. (41) 4343633; e-mail marketing@ugatea.com; internet ugatea.com; f. 2001; Chair. JOHN MUBANGIZI; CEO ROBERT EJIKU.

EMPLOYERS' ORGANIZATION

Federation of Uganda Employers (FUE): Plot 1207, Kiwanga Rd, Namanve, POB 3820, Kampala; tel. (39) 2777410; e-mail info@ fuemployers.org; internet www.fuemployers.org; f. 1958; Chair. Dr Eng. SILVER MUGISHA; Exec. Dir DOUGLAS OPIO.

Private Sector Foundation Uganda: Plot 43, Nakasero Rd, POB 7683, Kampala; tel. (31) 2263850; e-mail psfu@psfuganda.org.ug; internet www.psfuganda.org; f. 1995; comprised of 190 business assocns, corporate bodies and major public sector agencies; Chair. ELLY KARUHANGA; Exec. Dir STEPHEN ASIIMWE.

UTILITIES

Electricity

Bujagali Energy Ltd: 8km, off Kayunga Rd, POB 186, Kikubamutwe; tel. 752120122; e-mail info@bujagali-energy.com; internet www.bujagali-energy.com; f. 2012.

Electricity Regulatory Authority (ERA): ERA House, Plot 15, Shimon Rd, Nakasero, POB 10332, Kampala; tel. (41) 4341852; e-mail info@era.or.ug; internet www.era.or.ug; f. 2000; Chair. Dr SARAH WASAGALI KANAABI; CEO Eng. ZIRIA TIBALWA WAAKO.

Eskom Uganda Ltd: 5 Bandali Rise, Bugolobi, POB 942, Jinja; tel. (33) 2240400; internet www.eskom.co.ug; f. 2002; manages and maintains 2 government hydroelectricity power plants at Nalubaale and Kiira; Chair. NARESH SINGH; Man. Dir THOZAMA GANGI.

Rural Electrification Agency: House of Hope, 2nd Floor, Plot 10, Windsor Loop, Kololo, POB 7317, Kampala; tel. (31) 2318100; e-mail rea@rea.or.ug; internet www.rea.or.ug; f. 2001; Chair. KASANDE ROBERT; CEO Eng. JOAN KAYANGA MUTIIBWA (acting).

Uganda Electricity Distribution Co Ltd (UEDCL): UEDCL Towers, 6th Floor, 37 Nakasero Rd, Kampala; tel. (31) 2330300; e-mail contact@uedcl.co.ug; internet www.uedcl.co.ug; f. 2001 as one of the successor bodies of the Uganda Electricity Board; privatized and operations handed over to UMEME Uganda Ltd in 2005 under a 20-year concession agreement; functions as a statutory body overseeing the operations of UMEME Uganda Ltd; Chair. FRANCIS TUMUHEIRWE; Man. Dir PAUL MWESIGWA.

UMEME Uganda Ltd: Rwenzori House, Plot 1, 2nd Floor, Lumumba Ave, POB 23841, Kampala; tel. (41) 4185185; e-mail info@umeme.co.ug; internet www.umeme.co.ug; f. 2005; develops, operates and maintains the electricity distribution network on behalf of UEDCL; Chair. PATRICK BITATURE; Man. Dir SELESTINO BABUNGI.

Uganda Electricity Generation Co Ltd: Plot Nos 6–9, Okot Close, Bukoto Victoria Office, Blk C, POB 75831, Kampala; tel. (31) 2372165; e-mail info@uegcl.co.ug; internet www.uegcl.com; f. 2001 as one of the successor bodies of the Uganda Electricity Board; Chair. Eng. PROSCOVIA MARGARET NJUKI; CEO Eng. HARRISON E. MUTIKANGA.

Uganda Electricity Transmission Co Ltd (UETCL): Plot 10, Hannington Rd, POB 7625, Kampala; tel. (41) 7802000; e-mail transco@uetcl.com; internet uetcl.go.ug; f. 2001 as one of the successor bodies of the Uganda Electricity Board; Chair. (vacant); Man. Dir MICHAEL TAREMWA KANANURA (acting).

Gas

Homegas (U) Ltd: Plot 77, 1st St, Kampala; tel. (39) 2889254; e-mail info@homegas.ltd.ug; internet www.homegas.ltd.ug; supplies piped LPG.

RamcoGas: Plot 735, Block 111, Namanve, Mukono; tel. 772728089; e-mail info@ramcogas.com; internet ramcogas.com; import and distribution of LPG.

Water

National Water & Sewerage Corpn (NWSC): Plot 3, Nakasero, POB 7053, Kampala; tel. (41) 4315100; e-mail info@nwsc.co.ug; internet www.nwsc.co.ug; f. 1972; state-owned; serves 162 towns; Chair. Eng. Dr Prof. BADRU. M. KIGGUNDU; Man. Dir Dr Eng. SILVER MUGISHA.

STATE PETROLEUM COMPANIES

Petroleum Authority of Uganda: 34–36 Lugard Ave, POB 833, Entebbe; tel. (41) 4320423; e-mail ed@pau.go.ug; internet www.pau.go.ug; f. 2014; Chair. Dr JANE NAMBAKIRE MULEMWA; Exec. Dir ERNEST N. T. RUBONDO.

Uganda National Oil Co (UNOC): Plot 15, Yusuf Lule Rd, POB 36316, Kampala; tel. (41) 444600; e-mail info@unoc.co.ug; internet unoc.co.ug; f. 2014; Chair. EMMANUEL KATONGOLE; CEO PROSCOVIA NABBANJA.

MAJOR COMPANIES

The following are some of the largest companies in terms either of capital investment or employment.

Aarcee Distilleries (U) Ltd: Plot 774/5, Blk 208, Bombo Rd, Kawempe, Kampala; tel. (41) 4568568; producer of red wine, brandy, gin and vodka.

Africa Polysack Industries Ltd: Plot 171–172, Blk 106, Nvumwa, Seeta, Mukono, POB 4886, Kampala; tel. (41) 4290087; e-mail info@africapolysack.com; internet www.africapolysack.com; f. 1999.

Agro Ways (U) Ltd: Plot 34–60, Kyabazinga Way, POB 1924, Jinja, Kampala; tel. (45) 4479381; internet www.agroways.ug; f. 2005; corn products and ware housing.

Alam Group of Cos: Casements Complex, 5th St, Plot No. 86/90, Industrial Area, POB 4641, Kampala; tel. (41) 4234001; internet www.alam-group.com; subsidiaries include: Casements Africa Ltd, Rhino Footwear Ltd, Roofclad Ltd, Steel Rolling Mills Ltd and Sugar and Allied Industries Ltd; Chair. MANZUR ALAM; Group Man. Dir ABID ALAM.

Aya Group of Companies: Plot 62, Kawempe Bombo Rd, Kampala; tel. (31) 2318888; conglomerate with interests in food processing, transport and logistics, real estate, investment and development, hotel development and hospitality industry and mining; constituent cos include Aya Biscuits Ltd, Aya Mining (U) Ltd, Aya Investment (U) Ltd, Fifi Transportation, Pan Afric Commodities, Aya Mills (U) Ltd and Aya Bakery (U) Ltd; Chair. and Man. Dir MOHAMMED HAMID.

Bakhresa Grain Milling (U) Ltd: Bweyogerere, Jinja Rd, POB 22844, Kampala; tel. (41) 4286398; internet bakhresa.com; owned by Bakhresa Group (Tanzania); production of superfine bakers flour, home baking flour and biscuit flour.

Bee Natural Uganda Ltd: Pan Africa House, Plot No. 3, Kimathi Ave, POB 5318, Kampala; tel. (41) 4232679; e-mail info@beenaturalproducts.com; internet www.beenaturalproducts.com; f. 2008; honey producer; Man. Dir MARIA ODIDO.

Bidco Uganda Ltd (BUL): Plot No. 152/M, Massese Industrial Area, POB 1136, Masese, Jinja; tel. (43) 4124200; e-mail info@bul.co.ug; internet www.bul.co.ug; producer of vegetable fats, vegetable oils, soaps, margarines and baking powder; also owns oil palm plantations through its subsidiary Oil Palm Uganda Ltd; Man. Dir DANIEL KER.

BPC Chemicals Ltd: Plot M/264, Ntinda Industrial Area, POB 10356, Kampala; tel. (41) 4221118; e-mail kplbpc@utlonline.co.ug; internet www.bpcuganda.com; f. 1990; Man. Dir PANKAJ PATELHE.

Busoga Forestry Co: 9B Kyagwe Ave, POB 1900, Jinja; tel. (43) 4121835; e-mail bfc@greenresources.no; internet www.busoga-forestry.com; Man. Dir JOHN FERGUSON.

Cipla Quality Chemicals Ltd: Plot No. 1–7, 1st Ring Rd, Luzira Industrial Park, POB 34871, Kampala; tel. (31) 2341100; e-mail info@ciplaqcil.co.ug; internet www.ciplaqcil.co.ug; f. 2005; jt venture co between Cipla Ltd (India) and Quality Chemicals Ltd (Uganda); manufactures antiretroviral and antimalarial medicines; Exec. Chair. EMMANUEL KATONGOLE; CEO AJAY KUMAR PAL.

Crown Beverages Ltd: Plot M214, Nakawa Industrial Area, POB 20021, Kampala; tel. (31) 2343100; e-mail info@pepsi-cola.co.ug; internet www.pepsi-cola.co.ug; CEO PADDY MURAMIIRAH.

Hima Cement: Plot 838, Namanve Industrial Park, POB 7230, Kampala; tel. (31) 2213200; e-mail hima.kampala@lafargeholcim.com; internet www.lafarge.co.ug; f. 1994; subsidiary of Bamburi Cement and a member of the Lafarge Group; Chair. BARBARA MULWANA; Country CEO JEAN-MICHEL PONS; Man. AHMED MEBASHER.

Kinyara Sugar Works Ltd: Plot 91, 1st Street, Industrial Area, POB 7474, Kampala; tel. (41) 4236382; f. 1990; sugar production; 51% owned by Rai Group; Gen. Man. RAVI RAMALINGHAM.

Madhvani International, SA: Plot 96–98, Madhvani Industrial Park, POB 33479, Kampala; tel. (41) 4259390; e-mail info@madhvanifoundation.com; f. 1979; involved in the tea, plant-extracts, sugar and chemicals industries; infrastructure devt; maintains interests in East Africa, Europe and India; Pres. NITIN MADHVANI.

Kakira Sugar Works Ltd: Kakira Estate, POB 121, Jinja; tel. (41) 4444000; e-mail kakira@kakirasugar.com; internet www.kakirasugar.com; f. 1985; also operates sugar mills in Rwanda; mfrs of some 100,000 metric tons of sugar annually; Man. Dirs KAMLESH MADHVANI, MAYUR MADHVANI.

The Mehta Group: Kampala; internet www.mehtagroup.com.

Sugar Corpn of Uganda Ltd: Plot No. 135, 6th St, Industrial Area, POB 1185, Kampala; tel. (41) 4255036; e-mail scoul@mehtagroup.com; f. 1924.

TransAfrica Commerce Ltd: Plot No. 133–135, 6th St, Industrial Area, POB 25900, Kampala; tel. (41) 4255036; e-mail tac@mehtagroup.com; f. 1992; trade.

Movit Products Ltd: Plot No. 4454–4455, Zana, Bunamwaya, off Entebbe Rd, POB 27109, Kampala; tel. (39) 2736801; e-mail info@movit.co.ug; internet movit.co.ug; f. 1999; cosmetic products; Chair. SIMPSON BIRUNGI.

Mpanga Growers' Tea Factory Ltd: POB 585, Fort Portal; tel. (392) 722441; e-mail mpangatea@iwayafrica.com; internet www.mpangatea.com; Gen. Man. KUSEMERERWA SAUL BALISIMA.

Mukwano Industries (Uganda) Ltd: Plot No. 30 Mukwano Rd, POB 2671, Kampala; tel. (41) 4313200; e-mail customercare@mukwano.com; internet www.mukwano.com; f. 1984; refining of crude palm and sunflower oils, mfrs of vegetable cooking oils, beverages, soaps, detergents, personal hygiene products and plastics; Man. Dir ALYKHAN KARMALI.

Multiple Industries Ltd: Plot No. 714/715, 8th St, Industrial Area, POB 20166, Kampala; tel. (41) 4236021; e-mail response@multipleindustries.com; internet www.multipleindustries.com; f. 1991; manufacturing and trading of domestic and industrial building materials.

Nile Breweries Ltd: M90, Yusuf Lule Rd, Njeru, POB 762, Njeru; tel. (33) 2210009; internet www.nilebreweries.com; Dir THOMAS KAMPHUIS.

Ntake Group: Plot 26/28 Nalukolongo, POB 15207, Kampala; tel. (41) 4272960; e-mail ntakegroup@gmail.com; internet www.ntakegroup.co; conglomerate with interests in bread and confectionary, real estate, paper recycling, animal and crop husbandry, purified drinking water, transport and haulage, food and outside catering, bridal wear and general hardware; Dir GASTER LULE.

Quality Chemicals Ltd: Plot No. 64/65, Katwe Rd, POB 3381, Kampala; tel. (41) 4347611; e-mail qcl@quality-chemicals.co.ug; internet www.quality-chemicals.co.ug; f. 1997; pest control solutions; Chair. EDWARD MARTIN; CEO ROBERT KAKANDE.

Roko Construction Ltd: Plot 160A-B, Bombo Rd, Kawempe, POB 172, Kampala; tel. (31) 2203110; internet www.roko.com; f. 1969; civil engineering and construction; affiliated cos in Rep. of the Congo, Rwanda and Sudan; Man. Dir MARK KOEHLER.

Roofing Group: Plot No. 126, Lubowa Estate, Entebbe Rd, POB 7196, Kampala; tel. (31) 2340100; e-mail roofings@roofings.co.ug; internet www.roofingsgroup.com; f. 1994; comprised of three subsidiaries: Roofings Ltd, Roofings Rolling Mills and Roofings Polypipes; galvanized and pre-painted roofing sheets, eco tiles, hollow sections, mild steel plates and open profiles; Exec. Dir NASHILA LALANI.

Shumuk Group of Companies: Plot 24 Mukabya Rd, Nakawa Industrial Area, POB 6552, Kampala; tel. (41) 4286282; e-mail shumuk@shumukgroup.net; internet www.shumukgroup.net; conglomerate with interests in steel and aluminium works, real estate, dairy products and tourism; constituent cos include: Shumuk Aluminium Industries Ltd, Shumuk Dairy Products (U) Ltd, and Shumuk Properties Ltd; Chair. MUKESH SHUKLA.

Southern Range Nyanza Ltd: Plot 8–10, Kampala-Jinja Rd, POB 1025, Jinja; tel. 707309154; e-mail sales@nytil.co.ug; internet www.nytil.com; f. 1949 as Nyanza Textile Industries Ltd (NYTIL); textile mfrs; Chair. KISHOR JOBANPUTRA.

Sybyl Ltd: Plot 1A, Kafu Rd, POB 7585, Kampala; tel. (41) 4305400; e-mail sales@computerpointuganda.com; internet sybyl.com; ICT solutions; f. 1991; Chair. P. K. KURUVILLA; Man. Dir ANIL KURUVILLA.

Tibet Hima Co: POB 1, Kilembe; tel. (41) 4234909; f. 1950; operates the Kilembe mines (fmrly operated by Kilembe Mines); mining of cobalt and copper, generation of hydroelectric power, production of lime, foundry production; Gen. Man. ALEX KWATAMPORA.

Tororo Cement Ltd: Jinja-Malaba Rd, POB 74, Tororo; tel. (35) 2512500; e-mail tcl@tororocement.com; internet www.tororocement.com; f. 1952 as Uganda Cement Industry Ltd; privatized and renamed in 1995; mfrs of cement, construction steel, wire products and iron sheets; Man. Dir B. M. GAGRANI.

Total E&P Uganda B.V.: Course View Towers, Plot No. 21, Yusuf Lule Rd, POB 34867, Kampala; tel. (20) 4916000; e-mail ep.tepuinfo@total.com; internet ug.total.com; Gen. Man. PIERRE JESSUA.

Uganda Breweries Ltd: Plot 3–17, Port Bell, POB 7130, Kampala; tel. (31) 2210011; e-mail contact@ugandabreweries.com; internet www.ugandabreweries.com; f. 1964 as International Distilleries Uganda Ltd; subsidiary of East African Breweries Ltd (Kenya); production of potable spirits; Man. Dir ALVIN MBUGUA.

Uganda Clays Ltd: Km 14, Entebbe Rd, POB 3188, Kampala; tel. (31) 2305403; e-mail uclays@ugandaclays.co.ug; internet www.ugandaclays.co.ug; f. 1950; mfrs of bldg and roofing materials; Chair. MARTIN KASEKENDE; Man. Dir JACQUELINE KIWANUKA (acting).

Unilever (U) Ltd: 10/12 Nyondo Close, Bugolobi, POB 3515, Kampala; tel. (41) 4343547; internet www.unilever-ewa.com.

Vivo Energy Uganda: Plot Nos 9 and 11, 7th St, Industrial Area, POB 7082, Kampala; tel. (31) 2210010; internet www.vivoenergy.com; f. 1953; fuels and lubricants; a Shell licensee; Man. Dir GILBERT ASSI.

CO-OPERATIVES

Uganda Co-operative Alliance Ltd: Plot 47–49, Nkurumah Rd, POB 2215, Kampala; tel. (41) 4258898; internet www.uca.co.ug; f. 1961; co-ordinating body for co-operative unions; Chair. JONAS TWEYAMBE.

TRADE UNIONS

National Organization of Trade Unions (NOTU): Plot 64, Ntinda Rd, POB 2150, Kampala; tel. (41) 4256295; internet www.notu.or.ug; f. 1973; Chair. OWERE USHER WILSON; Sec.-Gen. PETER CHRISTOPHER WERIKHE.

Amalgamated Transport and General Workers' Union (ATGWU): POB 30407, Kampala; tel. (41) 232508; internet www.atgwu.or.ug; f. 1938; Chair. OWERE USHER WILSON; Gen. Sec. AZIZ KIRYA.

Transport

RAILWAYS

Uganda Railways Corporation (URC): Plot 46 Nasser Rd, Kampala; tel. (41) 4254961; e-mail info@urc.go.ug; internet urc.go.ug; f. 1977 following the dissolution of East African Railways; management of operations assumed by Rift Valley Railways consortium in Nov. 2006; CEO CHARLES KATEEBA.

ROADS

Road transport remains the dominant mode of transport in terms of scale of infrastructure and the volume of freight and passenger movement. The National (Trunk) Road Network carries 80% of Uganda's passenger and freight traffic and includes international routes linking Uganda to neighbouring countries and to the sea (via Kenya and Tanzania), and internal roads linking areas of high population and large administrative and commercial centres. It provides the only form of access to most rural communities. The

Government is implementing a programme of continuous upgrading of key gravel roads to bitumen standard.

Uganda National Roads Authority (UNRA): Blocks C and D, UAP Nakawa Business Park, Plot 3–5, New Port Bell Rd, POB 28487, Kampala; tel. (41) 4318111; e-mail info@unra.go.ug; internet www.unra.go.ug; f. 2006; Chair. FRED JACHAN OMACH; Exec. Dir ALLEN KAGINA.

Uganda Road Fund: Twed Towers, 5th Floor, 10 Kafu Rd, Nakasero, POB 7501, Kampala; tel. (31) 2178250; e-mail info@roadfund.ug; internet www.roadfund.ug; f. 2008; Chair. MERIAN SEBUNYA; Exec. Dir Eng. Dr MICHAEL M. ODONGO.

INLAND WATERWAYS

A rail wagon ferry service connecting Jinja with the Tanzanian port of Tanga, via Mwanza, was inaugurated in 1983, thus reducing Uganda's dependence on the Kenyan port of Mombasa. In 1986 the Uganda and Kenya Railways Corporations began the joint operation of Lake Victoria Marine Services, to ferry goods between the two countries via Lake Victoria.

CIVIL AVIATION

There is an international airport at Entebbe, on Lake Victoria, some 40 km from Kampala. There are also several small airfields providing domestic services.

Uganda Civil Aviation Authority (UCAA): Airport Rd, Entebbe International Airport, POB 5536, Kampala; tel. (31) 2352000; e-mail aviation@caa.co.ug; internet caa.go.ug; f. 1991; Chair. Justice STEVEN KAVUMA; Dir-Gen. FRED BAMWESIGYE.

Principal Airlines

AeroLink Uganda Ltd: POB 689, Entebbe; tel. (31) 7333000; e-mail info@aerolinkuganda.com; internet www.aerolinkuganda.com; f. 2012; domestic services, charter flights; Country Man. ANTHONY NJOROGE.

Eagle Air Ltd: Adam House, Plot 11, Portal Ave, POB 7392, Kampala; tel. (41) 4344292; e-mail admin@eagleair-ug.com; internet www.eagleair-ug.com; f. 1994; domestic services, charter flights to neighbouring countries; CEO Capt. ANTHONY RUBOMBORA.

Uganda Airlines Corpn: Eagle House, Tunnel Rd, Entebbe Airport, POB 431, Entebbe; tel. (20) 0406400; e-mail info@ugandaairlines.com; internet ugandaairlines.com; f. 1976; liquidated 2001; relaunched 2019; state-owned; CEO JENNIFER BAMUTURAKI.

Tourism

Uganda Tourism Board: 42 Windsor Crescent, Kololo, POB 7211, Kampala; tel. (41) 4342197; e-mail website@utb.go.ug; internet utb.go.ug; Chair. DAUDI MIGEREKO; CEO LILLY AJAROVA.

Uganda Wildlife Authority: Plot No. 7, Kira Rd, Kamwokya, POB 3530, Kampala; tel. (41) 4355000; internet www.ugandawildlife.org; f. 1996 following the merger of Uganda National Parks and the Game Department; Chair. Dr PANTALEON KASOMA MUKASA BANDA.

Defence

As assessed at November 2021, the Uganda People's Defence Forces (UPDF, formerly the National Resistance Army) was estimated to number 45,000 troops, including an estimated 400 marines. There was also a border defence unit of about 600 men. In 2021 more than 6,400 Ugandan troops were stationed abroad.

Defence Budget: 3,870,000m. shillings in 2022.

Chief of Defence Forces: Gen. WILSON MBASU MBADI.

Commander of the Air Force: Lt-Gen. CHARLES LWANGA LUTAAYA.

Commander of the Land Forces: Lt-Gen. KAYANJA MUHANGA.

Education

Most schools are supported by the Government, although a small proportion are sponsored by missions. Traditionally, all schools have charged fees. In 1997, however, the Government introduced an initiative known as Universal Primary Education (UPE), whereby free primary education was phased in for up to four children per family. In January 2007 the Government initiated free secondary school education in 700 public schools as part of a phased programme to introduce universal free education. Primary education, which is in principle free and compulsory, begins at six years of age and lasts for seven years. Secondary education, beginning at the age of 13, lasts for a further six years, comprising a first cycle of four years and a second of two years. In 2016/17, according to the United Nations Educational, Scientific and Cultural Organization (UNESCO), enrolment at pre-primary level was equivalent to 14% of children in the relevant age-group (males 14%; females 15%). In 2012/13 enrolment at primary level included 96% (males 94%; females 97%) of children in the relevant age-group, while in 2009/10 enrolment at secondary schools included 23% (males 24%; females 22%) of children in the relevant age-group. In the budget for 2020/21 education was allocated 3,286,500m. shillings, representing 10.9% of total forecast budgetary expenditure.

Bibliography

Ahluwalia, D. P. S. *Plantations and the Politics of Sugar in Uganda.* Kampala, Fountain Publishers, 1995.

Allen, T., and Vlassenroot, K. (Eds). *The Lord's Resistance Army: Myth and Reality.* London, Zed Books, 2010.

Armstrong, J. *Uganda's AIDS Crisis: Its Implications for Development.* Washington, DC, World Bank, 1995.

Barter, J. *Idi Amin (Heroes & Villains).* San Diego, CA, Lucent Books, 2005.

Bigsten, A., and Kayizzi-Mugerwa, S. *Is Uganda an Emerging Economy?* Uppsala, Nordiska Afrikainstitutet, 2001.

Eichstaedt, P. *First Kill Your Family: Child Soldiers of Uganda and the Lord's Resistance Army.* Chicago, IL, Chicago Review Press, 2009.

Hansen, H. B., and Twaddle, M. (Eds). *Uganda Now.* London, James Currey, 1988.

   Changing Uganda: The Dilemmas of Structural Management Adjustment and Revolutionary Change. London, James Currey, 1991.

   Developing Uganda. Oxford, James Currey, 1998.

Ingham, K. *Obote.* London, Routledge, 1994.

Jones, B. *Beyond the State in Rural Uganda: Development in Rural Uganda.* Edinburgh, Edinburgh University Press, 2011.

Karugire, S. R. *A Political History of Uganda.* London, Heinemann, 1980.

   Roots of Instability in Uganda. Kampala, Fountain Publrs, 1996.

Kasozi, A. B. K. *Social Origins of Violence in Uganda, 1964–1985.* London, University College London Press, 1995.

Kuteesa, F., Tumusiime-Mutebile, E., Whitworth, A., and Williamson, T. (Eds). *Uganda's Economic Reforms: Insider Accounts.* Oxford, Oxford University Press, 2009.

Langer, A., Ukiwo, U., and Mbabazi, P. (Eds). *Oil Wealth and Development in Uganda and Beyond: Prospects, Opportunities, and Challenges.* Leuven, Leuven University Press, 2020.

Langseth, P., and Katotobo, J. (Eds). *Uganda: Landmarks in Rebuilding a Nation.* Kampala, Fountain Publrs, 1993.

Lubanga, F., and Villadsen, S. (Eds). *Democratic Decentralisation in Uganda.* Kampala, Fountain Publrs, 1997.

Mamdani, M. *Imperialism and Fascism in Uganda.* London, Heinemann Educational, 1983.

Measures, R., and Walker, T. *Amin's Uganda.* Whitstable, Oyster Press, 2002.

Mwakikagile, G. *Uganda: A Nation in Transition: Post-Colonial Analysis.* Dar es Salaam, New Africa Press, 2013.

Mukholi, D. *A Complete Guide to Uganda's Fourth Constitution: History, Politics and the Law.* Kampala, Fountain Publrs, 1995.

Museveni, Y. K. *Sowing the Mustard Seed: The Struggle for Freedom and Democracy in Uganda.* London, Macmillan, 1997.

Mutibwa, P. *Uganda since Independence: A Story of Unfulfilled Hopes.* London, C. Hurst & Co., 1992.

Mwakikagile, G. *Uganda: A Nation in Transition: Post-colonial Analysis.* Dar es Salaam, New Africa Press, 2012.

Nzita, R., and Mbaga-Niwampa. *Peoples and Cultures of Uganda.* 2nd edn. Kampala, Fountain Publrs, 1995.

Oghojafor, K. *Uganda (Countries of the World).* Milwaukee, WI, Gareth Stevens Publishing, 2004.

Okoth, G. P., and Muranga, M. (Eds). *Uganda: A Century of Existence.* Kampala, Fountain Publrs, 1995.

Pirouet, M. L. *Historical Dictionary of Uganda.* Metuchen, NJ, Scarecrow Press, 1995.

Reid, R. J. *Political Power in Pre-Colonial Buganda.* Athens, OH, Ohio University Press, 2003.

   A History of Modern Uganda Cambridge, Cambridge University Press, 2017.

Rotberg, R. I. (Ed.). *Uganda (Africa: Continent in the Balance).* Broomall, PA, Mason Crest Publishers, 2005.

Rubongoya, J. B. *Regime Hegemony in Museveni's Uganda: Pax Musevenica.* Basingstoke, Palgrave Macmillan, 2007.

Ruzindana, A., et al. (Eds). *Fighting Corruption in Uganda.* Kampala, Fountain Publrs, 1998.

Soghayroun, I. E.-Z. *The Sudanese Muslim Factor in Uganda.* Khartoum, Khartoum University Press, 1981.

Ssekamnsa, I. C. *History and Development of Education in Uganda.* Kampala, Fountain Publrs, 1997.

Suruma, E. S. *Advancing the Ugandan Economy: A Personal Account.* New York, Brookings Institution, 2014.

Tangri, R., and Mwenda, A. *The Politics of Elite Corruption in Africa: Uganda in Comparative African Perspective.* Abingdon, Routledge, 2013.

Tapscott, R. *Social Control and Modern Authoritarianism in Museveni's Uganda.* Oxford, Oxford University Press, 2021.

Tripp, A. M. *Women and Politics in Uganda.* Madison, WI, University of Wisconsin Press, 2000.

   Museveni's Uganda: Paradoxes of Power in a Hybrid Regime. Boulder, CO, Lynne Rienner Publishers, 2010.

Whyte, S. R. *Questioning Misfortune.* Cambridge, Cambridge University Press, 1998.

Wiegratz, J. *Uganda's Human Resource Challenge: Training, Business Culture and Economic Development.* Kampala, Fountain Publishers, 2009.

ZAMBIA

Physical and Social Geography

GEOFFREY J. WILLIAMS

PHYSICAL FEATURES

The Republic of Zambia is a landlocked state occupying elevated plateau country in south-central Africa. Zambia has an area of 752,612 sq km (290,585 sq miles). The country is irregularly shaped, and shares a boundary with eight other countries.

The topography of Zambia is dominated by the even skylines of uplifted plantation surfaces. Highest elevations are reached on the Nyika plateau on the Malawi border (2,164 m). Elevations decline westward, where the country extends into the fringe of the vast Kalahari basin. The plateau surfaces are interrupted by localized downwarps (occupied by lakes and swamp areas, such as in the Bangweulu and Lukanga basins) and by the rifted troughs of the mid-Zambezi and Luangwa rivers.

Katangan rocks of upper-Pre-Cambrian age yield the copper ores exploited on the Copperbelt. Younger Karoo sedimentaries floor the rift troughs of the Luangwa and the mid-Zambezi rivers, while a basalt flow of this age has been incised by the Zambezi below the Victoria Falls to form spectacular gorges. Coal-bearing rocks in the Zambezi trough are of this same system. Over the western third of the country there are extensive and deep wind-deposited sands.

The continental divide separating Atlantic from Indian Ocean drainage forms the frontier with the Democratic Republic of the Congo, then traverses north-east Zambia to the Tanzanian border. Some 77% of the country is drained to the Indian Ocean by the Zambezi river and its two main tributaries, the Kafue and Luangwa, with the remainder being drained principally by the Chambeshi and Luapula via the River Congo to the Atlantic. Rapids occur along most river courses, so the rivers are of little use for transportation.

Zambia's climatic year can be divided into three seasons: a cool dry season (April–August), a hot dry season (August–November) and a warm wet season (November–April). Temperatures are generally moderate. Mean maximum temperatures exceed 35°C only in southern low-lying areas in October, most of the country being in the range 30°C–35°C. July, the coldest month, has mean minima of 5°C–10°C over most of the country, but shows considerable variability. Rainfall is highest on the high plateau of the Northern Province and on the intercontinental divide west of the Copperbelt (exceeding 1,200 mm per year).

The eastern two-thirds of the country has generally poor soils. Soils on the Kalahari Sands of the west are exceptionally infertile, while seasonal waterlogging of soils in basin and riverine flats makes them difficult to use. Savannah vegetation dominates, with miombo woodland extensive over the plateau, and mopane woodland in the low-lying areas. Small areas of dry evergreen forest occur in the north, while treeless grasslands characterize the flats of the river basins.

RESOURCES AND POPULATION

Zambia's main resource is its land, which, in general, is underutilized. Although soils are generally poor, altitudinal modifications of the climate make possible the cultivation of a wide range of crops. Cattle numbers are greatest in the southern and central areas. In the Western Province their numbers are fewer, but their importance to the local economy is even greater. Subsistence farming characterizes most of the country, with commercial farming focusing along the 'line of rail', which extends south from the Copperbelt, through Lusaka, to the Victoria Falls, and forms the major focus of Zambia's economic activity. Commercial forestry is important on the Copperbelt, where there are extensive softwood plantations, and in the south-west, where hardwoods are exploited. The main fisheries are located on the lakes and rivers of the Northern Province, with the Kafue Flats, Lukanga and Lake Kariba also contributing significantly. Zambia's 20 national parks and 34 game management areas together covered some 30% of the country's total land area.

For many years, the mining of copper has been the mainstay of Zambia's economy, although its contribution has fluctuated in line with prices on international commodity markets. In 2021 the country was Africa's second largest producer of copper (after the Democratic Republic of the Congo), and the seventh largest in terms of copper output worldwide. Cobalt, a by-product of copper mining, has recently gained in significance, and Zambia has been steadily expanding its cobalt production in an attempt to offset falls in copper output. Coal is mined in the Zambezi valley, although this industry is in need of re-equipment and modernization. Deposits of uranium and iron ore have been located; the country's first commercial iron ore mine, at Sanje Hill in Lusaka Province commenced production in 2015. To date, no petroleum deposits have been located. However, Zambia is rich in hydropower, both developed and potential.

According to the census of October 2010, Zambia's population was 13,092,666, equivalent to 17.4 inhabitants per sq km (rising to 18,926,743 by mid-2022, giving a density of 25.1 inhabitants per sq km, according to official projections). In 2017 some 73.5% of Zambia's population was classified as urban by the African Development Bank; the vast majority of the urban population live in urban areas situated on the 'line of rail'. Lusaka, with a projected population of 2.84m. at mid-2022, is the largest single urban centre, but the Copperbelt towns together constitute the largest concentration of urban population. While the high rate of population growth for the country as a whole (averaging 3.1% per year in 2011–20) is a problem, the sustained influx to urban areas is even more acute as this growth has not been matched by employment and formal housing provision.

There are around 73 different ethnic groups among Zambia's indigenous population. Major groups are: the Bemba of the north-east, who are also dominant on the Copperbelt; the Nyanja of the Eastern Province, also numerous in Lusaka; the Tonga of the Southern Province; and the Lozi of the west. Over 70 languages have been identified (although many of these might better be regarded as dialects), of which seven are recognized as 'official' vernaculars. English, the official language, is the language of government and the main language of business and education.

History

SISHUWA SISHUWA

Zambia's colonial history began in the 1890s, when British troops forced African leaders to accept treaties ceding large tracts of land north of the Zambezi river, enabling the British to extend the territory they had earlier annexed south of the river. The first captured territory became known as Southern Rhodesia (now Zimbabwe) and the second as Northern Rhodesia (now Zambia). By the mid-1930s, following earlier discoveries of vast copper deposits, large-scale mining in the northern region of Northern Rhodesia, soon known as the Copperbelt, was firmly established. The British colonial authorities granted Northern Rhodesia's prime agricultural land to white farmers, removing Africans to 'native reserves' on inferior land, thus inhibiting the development of African farming—a legacy that affects Zambia to this day.

Mining helped foster an industrial class-consciousness among Northern Rhodesians, which was both hindered and radicalized by the prohibition of African trade unions. Miners, and later other African workers, instead formed 'welfare societies', which by 1951 had emerged as an anti-colonial political force, the Northern Rhodesia African National Congress. The Congress unsuccessfully opposed federation with Southern Rhodesia, and in 1953 the colony became part of the Central African Federation (CAF) with Southern Rhodesia and Nyasaland (now Malawi). In 1958 leadership of the Congress passed to Kenneth Kaunda, whose demands for the CAF's dissolution and the independence of Northern Rhodesia, under the name of Zambia, led to his imprisonment and the banning of the Congress in 1959. On his release a few months later, Kaunda became leader of the newly formed United National Independence Party (UNIP). In 1962, following a civil disobedience campaign led by UNIP, the British Government agreed to introduce a more democratic Constitution for Northern Rhodesia. UNIP participated in the ensuing elections, and formed a coalition Government with the remaining Congress supporters. The CAF was dissolved in December 1963, and Northern Rhodesia became independent as the Republic of Zambia on 24 October 1964, with Kaunda as President.

UNIP was returned to power at the general election in 1968, but popular support for the party was in decline. Sensing an opportunity, Simon Kapwepwe, a former Vice-President of Zambia, left UNIP in 1971 and formed the rival United People's Party (UPP). However, the Government banned the UPP, and in December 1972 Zambia was declared a one-party state. Legislative elections took place in December 1973, and Kaunda was re-elected as President.

In January 1973 the Government of Rhodesia (formerly Southern Rhodesia) closed the border to all Zambian exports except copper, with serious consequences for the Zambian economy. The Zambian Government's subsequent decision to divert copper exports using routes to Tanzania and Angola led to lower mineral volumes being exported at greater cost, resulting in further economic deterioration; this was compounded, following the outbreak of civil war in Angola in late 1975, by the closure of the Benguela railway, which had provided access to the Atlantic. By the end of 1975 there was widespread domestic discontent at high food prices, import restrictions and increasing unemployment. Prompted by his apparent belief that external forces were exploiting this unrest, Kaunda declared a state of emergency in January 1976.

In 1978 Kapwepwe rejoined UNIP after being courted by Kaunda, who wanted a recognized Bemba leader at a time of acute internal instability. In October rail links with Rhodesia were restored, and an agreement was reached on the shipping of exports via South Africa. From 1977, however, Zambia had openly harboured members of the Zimbabwe African People's Union (ZAPU) wing of the Patriotic Front, and in 1978–79 Rhodesian forces attacked ZAPU bases in Zambia and carried out air raids on the Zambian capital of Lusaka. In December 1979 an agreement was finally implemented providing for the internationally recognized independence of Rhodesia as Zimbabwe; this entered effect in April 1980.

ECONOMIC PROBLEMS AND POLITICAL UNREST

Political dissent increased in late 1980, amid worsening economic conditions. However, despite his increasing unpopularity, Kaunda (the sole candidate) won 93% of the votes cast in the presidential election of October 1983. In May 1987 Kaunda announced that the economic programme previously agreed with the International Monetary Fund (IMF) was to be replaced by a government-devised strategy involving greater state controls.

In the October 1988 presidential election, Kaunda, again the only candidate, received 95.5% of all votes cast. There followed unrest among workers and students, and in June 1990 a drastic increase in the price of maize meal led to severe rioting in Lusaka, in which at least 30 people reportedly died.

In May 1990 Kaunda announced that a referendum on the introduction of a multi-party political system would be conducted in October. In July the Movement for Multi-party Democracy (MMD), an informal opposition alliance, was formed under the leadership of former finance minister Arthur Wina and the Chairman of the Zambia Congress of Trade Unions (ZCTU), Frederick Chiluba. In September, however, Kaunda proposed abandoning the referendum and instead pressing ahead with organizing multi-party elections (later scheduled for October 1991) and appointing a commission to revise the Constitution. UNIP endorsed the new proposals.

CONSTITUTIONAL TRANSITION

In December 1990 Kaunda formally adopted constitutional amendments, approved by the National Assembly, providing for a multi-party system. Shortly afterwards, the MMD was officially recognized as a political organization; a further 11 opposition movements were soon established. In early 1991 several prominent members of UNIP defected from the party to join the MMD, while the ZCTU formally transferred its allegiance to the MMD.

The constitutional commission presented its recommendations in June 1991, but they were rejected by the MMD, which threatened to boycott the elections if the National Assembly accepted the proposals. In July Kaunda conceded to opposition demands that ministers be appointed only from members of the legislature and that the proposed establishment of a constitutional court be abandoned; presidential powers to impose martial law were also to be rescinded. On 2 August the National Assembly formally adopted the new draft Constitution, which included these amendments. In September 1991 Kaunda formally announced the disassociation of UNIP from the state and banned public-sector workers from engaging in party-political activity.

THE CHILUBA PRESIDENCY

International observers described the elections of October 1991 as free and fair. In the presidential election, Chiluba, who received 75.8% of the valid votes cast, defeated Kaunda, who obtained 24.2%. In the legislative elections, the MMD triumphed, securing 125 of the 150 contested seats in the National Assembly, while UNIP won just 25. Chiluba was inaugurated as President in early November; he appointed Levy Mwanawasa, a lawyer, as Vice-President and Leader of the National Assembly, and formed a new Cabinet. In addition, a minister was appointed to each of Zambia's nine provinces. Two days later the Government allowed the state of emergency to lapse. Chiluba subsequently began a major restructuring of the civil service and parastatal organizations, replacing Kaunda's appointees with his own supporters.

Political Realignments and Electoral Controversies

Amid persistent divisions, 15 prominent members left the MMD in August 1993, accusing the Government of protecting corrupt cabinet ministers. Their opposition to Chiluba's

Government was consolidated later in August by the formation of a new political group, the National Party (NP).

In July 1994 Mwanawasa resigned as Vice-President, citing longstanding differences with Chiluba, and was replaced by Brig.-Gen. Godfrey Miyanda. In June 1995 Kaunda, who had announced that he might contest the 1996 presidential poll, was elected UNIP President by a large majority.

On 28 May 1996 a new Constitution—which contained a clause banning any President from seeking a third term, thereby precluding any future Kaunda candidacy—was officially adopted by Chiluba, the Government having ignored opposition demands that it negotiate with them on its proposed constitutional changes. Donors reduced aid in protest, while Kaunda announced that he would contest the presidency despite the ban. In August Chiluba and Kaunda met for discussions in Lusaka, following which the Government made minor concessions regarding the conduct of forthcoming elections, while rejecting UNIP's central demand that the polls be conducted according to the 1991 Constitution.

Elections took place in mid-November 1996, with a boycott of the proceedings by UNIP and other opposition parties ensuring that Chiluba and the MMD were easily returned to power. In the presidential election Chiluba secured 72.5% of the valid votes cast. His nearest of four rivals (with only 12.5%) was Dean Mung'omba of the Zambia Democratic Congress (ZADECO). The MMD secured 131 of the 150 legislative seats. Of the eight other participating parties, only the NP (five seats), ZADECO (two seats) and Agenda for Zambia (two seats) won representation, with independent candidates taking the remaining 10 seats. Chiluba was inaugurated for a second presidential term in late November.

Internal Tensions

In August 1997 Kaunda and Dr Rodger Chongwe, leader of the Liberal Progressive Front, were shot and wounded when security forces opened fire on an opposition gathering in Kabwe, north of Lusaka. Kaunda's allegation that the shooting was an assassination attempt orchestrated by the Government was strongly denied by Chiluba.

On 28 October 1997 rebel officers, led by Capt. Stephen Lungu, briefly captured the national television and radio station, from where they proclaimed the formation of a military regime. The attempted coup was suppressed within a few hours by regular military units; 15 people, including Lungu, were arrested during the operation and one man was killed. Chiluba declared a state of emergency on 29 October, allowing the detention for 28 days without trial of people suspected of involvement in the attempted coup; Mung'omba was among 84 people subsequently arrested.

In December 1997 Kaunda was arrested under emergency powers and imprisoned, prompting widespread international condemnation. The former President was subsequently transferred to house arrest, and then in January 1998 arraigned in court. At the end of that month the National Assembly voted to extend the state of emergency for a further three months; however, it was revoked in March following pressure from external donors. Kaunda was released from detention in June, after charges against him were withdrawn, apparently owing to lack of evidence. His resignation as UNIP President in July created a split within the party over the nomination of a replacement.

In March 1999 the High Court ruled on the issue of Kaunda's citizenship, declaring him to be stateless; he appealed to the Supreme Court. In November Kaunda's son, Maj. Wezi Kaunda, who had been groomed by his father to succeed him as UNIP President, was shot dead outside his Lusaka home. Kaunda alleged that the murder had been politically motivated, while police sources described it as an attempted car hijack.

Kenneth Kaunda resigned again as UNIP President in March 2000, and Francis Nkhoma was elected as the new party leader in May. Another of Kaunda's sons, Tilyenji, was appointed as UNIP Secretary-General. Nkhoma was suspended as President by senior UNIP officials in November, and in January 2001 Tilyenji Kaunda was named as his replacement.

At a special party convention held in April 2001 to decide the MMD's position on whether to push for a further constitutional amendment to allow Chiluba to seek a third presidential term, party members opposed to a third term were physically prevented from attending, while pro-third term delegates proceeded to nominate Chiluba as the MMD's presidential candidate. On 2 May Chiluba dismissed 21 cabinet members who had signed a petition against his re-election bid, and they were expelled from the MMD. The former ministers established their own political party, the Forum for Democracy and Development (FDD). On 3 May 65 deputies signed a motion to impeach Chiluba for allegedly violating the Constitution. (After the Speaker of the National Assembly, Amusaa Mwanamwambwa, prevented a legislative debate on the motion, the National Assembly failed to convene for five months.) Several days later Chiluba finally ceded to pressure, and stated that he would not seek a third term in office.

THE MWANAWASA PRESIDENCY

In July 2001 Chiluba selected Levy Mwanawasa as the MMD's presidential candidate; the party endorsed his candidature in August. The FDD held its first national convention in October, electing Christon Tembo as party President. However, Tembo and other opposition party leaders failed to agree on a single candidate from among their number to oppose Mwanawasa.

The elections took place in December 2001. According to the Electoral Commission of Zambia (ECZ), Mwanawasa narrowly won the presidential election—with 29.2% of the votes cast, defeating his closest rival, Anderson Mazoka of the United Party for National Development (UPND), who won 27.2%. In the National Assembly elections, the MMD secured 69 seats and opposition parties 80, of which the UPND took 49; one independent was elected. The Constitution allowed Mwanawasa to appoint eight additional deputies, who were then brought into the Government, but—in a first for Zambia— his party still lacked a legislative majority. In February 2002 an European Union (EU) monitoring team alleged electoral malpractice, including state media bias and the deliberate failure to supply ballot boxes in marginal constituencies.

Nevertheless, Mwanawasa was sworn in as President in early January 2002, and a new Government was announced shortly afterwards. A rift with Chiluba soon became evident. Later in January Mwanawasa removed senior Chiluba appointees in the army, intelligence services and civil service, replacing them with his own. Chiluba stood down as MMD President in March, following a legal ruling that his continuation in active politics would disqualify him from receiving the benefits package to which he was entitled as a former head of state. In July 2002 Mwanawasa called a special session of the National Assembly and implicated Chiluba in several major corruption scandals. Mwanawasa also established a new anti-corruption task force. At the request of the President, the Assembly lifted Chiluba's immunity from prosecution. In February 2003 Chiluba was arrested and charged with over 200 counts of corruption and embezzlement.

Inclusive Politics

UNIP formed an alliance with the MMD in May 2003. At the end of the month Mwanawasa reorganized his Cabinet, appointing Nevers Mumba, an evangelical pastor who had previously led the opposition National Citizens' Coalition, as Vice-President. In August, despite several influential MMD members supporting the motion, Mwanawasa survived an attempt by opposition members of the National Assembly to impeach him over the manner of Mumba's appointment and the President's alleged corruption. Mwanawasa removed those implicated from the MMD's National Executive Committee (NEC) soon afterwards. As a consequence of its success in 12 legislative by-elections, by the end of 2003 the MMD held its first legislative majority since Mwanawasa became President. Several of the by-elections had been necessitated by the defection of UPND incumbents to the MMD. Mwanawasa dismissed Vice-President Mumba in October, replacing him with Lupando Mwape, a former transport minister.

In November 2005 opposition parties and civil society activists grouped together as the Oasis Forum protested in Lusaka to demand the adoption of a new constitution before the 2006 elections. Mwanawasa reversed his longstanding opposition to the reform, but insisted that the change could only be introduced after the elections, subject to approval by a national referendum.

Mwanawasa Secures a Second Term

In March 2006 Zambia's three main opposition parties—the UPND, the FDD and UNIP—announced that they would endorse a single presidential candidate under the new United Democratic Alliance (UDA). Mwanawasa was rushed to London, United Kingdom, for medical treatment at the end of March, after suffering a stroke; however, he soon returned to Zambia. In June the UPND selected Hakainde Hichilema as its new leader, after the death in May of Anderson Mazoka.

The presidential election took place in late September 2006, attracting a turnout of over 70%. Mwanawasa took 43% of the votes cast, enough to secure a comfortable victory. Michael Sata of the Patriotic Front (PF), who alleged electoral fraud, was his nearest opponent with 29.4%, while Hichilema secured 25.3%, suggesting that a united opposition might have defeated Mwanawasa. In the legislative elections, the MMD secured 75 seats, to which were added eight nominated seats. The PF took 43 seats, the UDA 26, and smaller parties and independents secured the remaining six elective seats, leaving the MMD with an overall majority of five seats. Most electoral observers judged the polls to have been free and fair, although the EU observer group stated that Mwanawasa and the MMD had benefited from insufficient regulation of campaign spending. Mwanawasa was sworn in as President in early October. In the largely unchanged Cabinet, Lupando Mwape, who lost his legislative seat, was replaced as Vice-President by veteran politician Rupiah Banda (a former Minister of Foreign Affairs under Kaunda).

In May 2007 the British High Court found Chiluba guilty of conspiring to defraud Zambia of US $46m. via a London account of the Zambia National Commercial Bank, and ordered the former President and his co-conspirators to repay 85% of the money. Zambia's Attorney-General had decided in 2006 to launch a civil prosecution case against Chiluba in the UK, since the Zambian criminal trial against him had stalled. Chiluba, who had refused to testify, denounced the verdict as a conspiracy between Mwanawasa and the British Government.

Despite PF opposition, in August 2007 the National Assembly approved legislation providing for a broadly constituted National Constitutional Conference (NCC) to make recommendations on a new constitution, which would then require legislative approval. The PF and Oasis Forum reiterated previous demands that a new constitution should be adopted by a specially convened constituent assembly. Of the PF's 43 deputies, 27 signalled their intention to participate in the NCC against Sata's wishes. The dissident deputies subsequently secured an injunction preventing Sata from carrying out his threat to expel them from the party if they took part in the NCC.

MWANAWASA'S DEATH AND BANDA'S SUCCESSION

Mwanawasa suffered another stroke while attending the 11th African Union (AU) summit in Egypt in July 2008, and was taken to France to receive treatment. He died there on 19 August, and Vice-President Banda became acting head of government. In October Banda, Sata, Miyanda and Hichilema contested a presidential election, in which Banda received 40.6% of the votes cast. Sata was again placed second, with 38.6% of the total; Hichilema took 20% and Miyanda 0.8%. Turnout was just 45%.

Banda reorganized the Government in November 2008, removing several ministers. George Kunda, the former Minister of Justice, was appointed to the vice-presidency. In March 2009 the Minister of Communications and Transport, Dora Siliya, a close ally of the President, resigned after months of corruption allegations against her in the local press. Banda had staunchly defended Siliya, but an independent tribunal ruled that she had broken the law in awarding a US $2m. contract without following correct tender procedures. In July George Mpombo, the Minister of Defence and an influential member of the MMD, resigned from the Government and the NEC, in protest against the NEC's endorsement, in February

of Banda as party leader; he subsequently became an outspoken critic of the President. In October Mpombo publicly accused Banda of being dictatorial, prompting the MMD to suspend his party membership.

In August 2009 the High Court acquitted former President Chiluba of all the corruption charges against him. Controversially, Chalwe Muchenga, the Director of Public Prosecutions, elected not to appeal against the verdict, prompting allegations from civil society organizations and donors that Banda had lost interest in the struggle against corruption. However, in February 2010 the Supreme Court upheld the 2007 British High Court decision that had found Chiluba and his close allies guilty of stealing US $46m. from the Zambian state. However, in August 2010 the Lusaka High Court ruled that the London verdict could not be enforced, and the Government announced that it would not appeal against this decision. Chiluba died of a heart attack in June 2011.

SATA'S PRESIDENCY

On 23 September 2011 Sata was declared the winner of the presidential election (which had been contested three days earlier by 10 candidates), despite the ECZ not having released full results; he was sworn in later that day. Election monitors from the EU and the Southern African Development Community (SADC) declared the vote to have been free and fair. On 28 September the ECZ confirmed that Sata had won 42.9% of the valid votes cast, while Banda had received 36.2%. Of the eight other candidates, only Hichilema (with 18.5%) secured more than 1% of the vote. At the concurrent legislative elections, the PF won 60 of the 150 elective seats; the MMD took 55 and the UPND 28. Among the notable appointments to the new Government was that of Guy Scott as Vice-President, the first white person to hold that position since independence.

In May 2012 the Government sought the extradition from South Africa of Henry Banda, the son of the former President, on suspicion of fraud. The Government refuted criticism from some civil society groups that Sata was using his anti-corruption policy to target political opponents. Later that month former Vice-President Mumba was elected as the new MMD President, following Rupiah Banda's retirement from active politics. In June, amid growing public demands for their resignation and for judicial reforms, Zambia's Chief Justice and his deputy were replaced. However, the opposition complained that the new Chief Justice, Lombe Chibesakunda, was related to Sata and had passed the retirement age.

In January 2013 Mumba and Hichilema were arrested for alleged corruption and defamation of the President, respectively. The MMD and UPND leaders both accused the Government of intimidation and of seeking to create a one-party state. In February the main opposition leaders held a press conference in South Africa, at which they urged the Commonwealth to suspend Zambia's membership for alleged human rights violations and democratic infringements. A Commonwealth fact-finding team subsequently arrived in Zambia to investigate the allegations.

Former President Banda's immunity from prosecution was removed by the National Assembly in March 2013, in response to a motion from Minister of Justice Wynter Kabimba, implicating Banda in several cases of corruption and the misappropriation of public funds. In June the Chief Immigration Officer revoked Banda's diplomatic passport, a move described by opposition parties and civil society groups as illegal. However, Vice-President Scott defended the decision, claiming that there was a real threat that Banda would attempt to flee the country.

In August 2013 Sata dismissed the Minister of Foreign Affairs, Effron Lungu, following allegations that he had divulged confidential information to the opposition MMD. Tensions within the ruling party became evident later in the month, when Minister of Defence Geoffrey Mwamba launched a campaign to endorse Sata as the PF's presidential candidate for the 2016 election. In an apparently veiled reference to Kabimba, Mwamba explained that he was protecting the PF from the secret agendas of 'riffraffs' who were seeking to succeed Sata. However, Scott, Kabimba and other PF leaders accused Mwamba of using Sata to advance his own presidential ambitions.

In December 2013 Mwamba, hitherto regarded as one of the President's principal allies, resigned as Minister of Defence in protest against Sata's refusal to recognize Henry Sosala (Mwamba's grandfather) as the next *Chitimukulu*—the paramount chief of the Bemba-speaking people. Earlier that month Sata had ordered the deployment of more than 200 armed paramilitary police to the Bemba sovereign's palace to prevent his installation, arguing that the manner in which Sosala had ascended to the throne contravened Bemba traditions and customs. As well as dismissing the President's claim, the *Bashilubemba* (Bemba regents who oversee succession) accused him of interfering in Bemba chiefly politics.

In January 2014 President Sata's eldest son, Mulenga, was appointed as the ruling PF's chairperson for Lusaka after the other candidates withdrew from the contest. Speculation that Sata was grooming his son as his successor intensified in April, when Mulenga was elected unopposed as Mayor of Lusaka, and further, in June, when he assumed the presidency of the Local Government Association of Zambia.

Mwamba was expelled from the ruling party in February 2014, an action that he subsequently challenged in court (he continued to sit in the National Assembly as a PF legislator). The dismissal in March of Alfredah Kansembe, the Deputy Minister of Home Affairs, for associating with Mwamba (her brother-in-law) highlighted the growing factionalization within the PF. Later that month Sata dismissed Minister of Tourism and the Arts Sylvia Tembo Masebo, also hitherto a key ally.

In March 2014 several senior members of the MMD, including the two Vice-Presidents, demanded the resignation of party President Mumba. Mumba claimed that the revolt against him had been instigated by Sata and was aimed at weakening the opposition. The dispute continued until June, when the dissenting group were removed from their party positions by the MMD NEC.

Police brutality and suppression of freedoms, such as the right of assembly, continued to characterize the Government's relationship with its political opponents. In April 2014 Mumba was arrested (and briefly imprisoned) for holding a meeting without a permit in the Copperbelt with MMD members. In the same month Hichilema and over 30 of his supporters were physically attacked by ruling party activists in the Copperbelt for criticizing PF policies.

In June 2014 Sata left Zambia for Israel on a visit described as a working holiday, although the opposition claimed that the President was in ill health and had travelled for specialist medical treatment. Sata returned to Zambia in July, but did not appear in public until September, further fuelling speculation and reactivating succession-driven disputes within the PF. Meanwhile, in August Sata dismissed Kabimba (who had widely been regarded as a potential successor of the President) from his posts as Minister of Justice and PF Secretary-General; Kabimba was replaced in both positions by Minister of Defence Edgar Lungu.

SATA'S DEATH AND LUNGU'S SUCCESSION

On 28 October 2014 Sata died at a hospital in London, where he was being treated for an undisclosed ailment. Edgar Lungu had been appointed acting President and attempted to retain that position. However, Attorney-General Musa Mwenye upheld the Constitution in transferring power to Vice-President Scott, who assumed the presidency for an interim period of three months, during which he was to oversee a political transition. Barred from running himself by a constitutional provision that required a presidential candidate's parents to be Zambian by birth or descent—his parents being from Scotland—Scott announced that the presidential election would be held on 20 January 2015.

In early November 2014 Scott, who also became interim PF President, dismissed Lungu as PF Secretary-General for alleged indiscipline, but was forced quickly to reinstate him following protests in Lusaka. A tumultuous PF conference in early December saw both Lungu and Sata's nephew and Deputy Minister of Commerce, Trade and Industry, Miles Sampa, claim victory as the party's candidate for the presidential election, splitting the party into two factions. After a

series of lawsuits, the two groups reached a truce later in the month and resolved to field Lungu in the national election. Lungu, who thereby became the PF President, endeavoured to exert his hold on the party by removing Scott from his position as party Vice-President and appointing Davies Chama as the new Secretary-General. Meanwhile, Kabimba resigned from the PF, citing intolerable violence and corruption, and founded the Rainbow Party.

Also in December 2014 several members of the MMD's NEC nominated former President Banda, who had earlier retired from politics, as the party's candidate for the national presidency. Banda launched his campaign in the face of a legal challenge from MMD President Mumba, who contended that he was the rightful candidate. In early January 2015 Banda endorsed the PF presidential candidate in protest against a Supreme Court ruling that confirmed Mumba as the official MMD candidate. Amid media reports that he had struck a deal with Lungu that would result in the termination of his court cases, Banda began campaigning on behalf of the ruling party candidate, causing confusion within the MMD, which subsequently split into three factions, supporting either Lungu, Mumba or the UPND's Hichilema.

On 20 January 2015, in a presidential election marked by a record low turnout of 32.4%, Lungu secured 48.8% of the valid votes cast, narrowly defeating Hichilema, who won 47.2%. The appointments made by Lungu to his transitional Cabinet in late January and early February reflected his reluctance to undertake any policy changes that might affect his electability in the forthcoming presidential election, scheduled for 2016. The ministerial positions were largely unchanged, apart from those who had not supported Lungu's candidacy, including Vice-President Scott. Lozi-speaking Inonge Wina was named as the new Vice-President, and five other women were assigned cabinet positions. The inclusion of two MMD members reflected Banda's influence over Lungu, who credited his victory to the former President.

The governing PF won all three legislative by-elections held in April 2015 in the Copperbelt, Lusaka and Northern Provinces. One notable aspect of the election results was that two of the winning candidates were previously MMD members whose victories for that party had been overturned by the courts after the PF petitioned the results. Another was the fact that the MMD, which enjoyed diminishing support, chose not to field candidates in any of the three constituencies.

In May 2015 police detained Hichilema for alleged breach of the Public Order Act, after the opposition leader held a series of unauthorized campaign meetings. In June former President Banda was acquitted of corruption charges against him, prompting further opposition claims of a pre-election deal between Banda and Lungu. At the end of the month the PF won three legislative by-elections in which two of the victorious candidates were close associates of Banda and former MMD members who had earlier lost their seats after the ruling party had successfully petitioned the courts to nullify their mandates on the grounds of electoral corruption. As in April, the MMD chose not to contest the polls.

PF legislator and former Minister of Defence Geoffrey Mwamba endorsed the opposition UPND in July 2015. He was subsequently appointed Vice-President of the party in an attempt by Hichilema to improve the UPND's electoral showing in Bemba-speaking Northern, Luapula and Muchinga provinces. Mwamba refused to relinquish his legislative seat on the grounds that he had not resigned from the PF but had merely accepted a position of service in the opposition party. When the Speaker of the National Assembly, Patrick Matibini, declared Mwamba's seat to be vacant, Mwamba challenged the decision in the High Court, which eventually ruled in his favour a few months before the 2016 elections.

In August 2015 President Lungu appointed Richwell Siamunene of the UPND as Minister of Defence. Siamunene, hitherto Deputy Minister of Transport and Communication, was one of the several opposition legislators who were earlier co-opted into the Cabinet by Sata to create a working majority in the National Assembly. The promotion to more senior ministerial posts of legislators such as Siamunene from the Southern Province, a key power base for the UPND, signified an attempt by Lungu to increase the PF's electoral appeal in that part of Zambia.

A slump in world copper prices and severe power cuts prompted several mining companies on the industrial Copperbelt to suspend (and, in some cases, shut down) operations in September 2015. Nearly 10,000 mineworkers lost their jobs over the following three months as production declined and firms struggled to survive, leading to widespread social unrest and clashes between the police and former mineworkers. While the Government variously blamed the economic challenges on adverse climatic conditions, such as poor rainfall, and on external factors, such as the slowdown of the Chinese economy, the opposition blamed Lungu's incompetence. Meanwhile, in late September the PF won a legislative by-election in the Northern Province.

In October 2015 Lungu appointed Dora Siliya, a virulent critic of the PF under Sata's rule, as Minister of Energy. Her appointment was strongly opposed by a Sata-aligned faction within the PF, which argued that Lungu was promoting Banda's allies and overlooking PF loyalists.

In November 2015 Lungu introduced a series of policy interventions and austerity measures aimed at reinvigorating the economy. As well as cutting down on foreign trips to reduce government expenditure, the President removed subsidies on electricity and fuel, stressing that he was not afraid to take unpopular decisions in order to stabilize the economy. However, a public outcry forced Lungu to reverse the measures within weeks, highlighting the President's fear of losing support in urban Lusaka and the Copperbelt, the PF's core constituencies.

Also in November 2015, as part of apparent ongoing government efforts to suppress press freedom, the Zambia Revenue Authority (ZRA) attempted to shut down *The Post* newspaper—the country's leading independent daily since 1991—on the grounds of alleged tax evasion. The High Court halted the move, albeit temporarily. A few weeks later a team of armed state police, intelligence officers and revenue collectors raided the newspaper's head office and seized company computers and documents. Again, the High Court declared the move illegal and ordered the return of the items. The incidents were widely interpreted as evidence of Lungu's fears that *The Post* could potentially damage his chances of re-election. *The Post* reported in December that ruling party officials were recruiting foreign nationals in the border areas of Eastern and Luapula Provinces—both PF strongholds—to register as voters in Zambia. The Eastern Province borders Malawi, while Luapula shares a border with the Democratic Republic of the Congo (DRC). Later in December the journalist who exposed the story was seriously assaulted by supporters of the ruling party.

Also in December 2015 the National Assembly approved the Constitution of Zambia Amendment Bill, which stipulated that a winning presidential candidate should secure a minimum of '50% + 1' of valid votes cast and that the Vice-President should be elected alongside the President as a running mate. In addition, with effect from the next legislative elections, the maximum number of National Assembly members was to be increased from 158 (150 directly elected and up to eight appointed) to 168 (156 directly elected and up to eight appointed by the President, plus the Vice-President, the Speaker and the First and Second Deputy Speakers). The legislation came into effect in early January 2016. Eager to reap any electoral benefits, Lungu emphasized that the revision of the Constitution represented the fulfilment of one of the PF's key pledges made during the election campaign.

In February 2016 Lungu appointed six nominees to serve as judges on the newly created Constitutional Court. Despite criticism from civil society groups that none of the appointees met the constitutional requirements for the role—namely, specialist training or experience in human rights or constitutional law, as well as 15 years' experience as a legal practitioner—the PF's legislative majority meant that all six appointments were subsequently ratified. The Constitutional Court, which ranked equal with the Supreme Court and had the final jurisdiction on all matters relating to the interpretation of the Constitution, including the election of the President, had the authority, in the event of an election

petition being filed against a President-elect, to dismiss the petition or to call a fresh poll. Opposition parties argued that the appointment of unqualified judges to the Constitutional Court was part of a calculated strategy aimed at ensuring that Lungu received a favourable hearing should the election results be contested.

In mid-January 2016 Sampa resigned from the PF to become the leader of a recently formed opposition party, the Democratic Front (DF). Former Vice-President Scott subsequently also joined the new party. In March two cabinet ministers, Obvious Mwaliteta of the PF and Keith Mukata of the MMD, resigned from the Government to join the opposition UPND. Twelve serving MMD legislators endorsed the presidential candidature of Hichilema, as the opposition began to coalesce around the UPND leader. Following the dissolution of the National Assembly in May, these legislators formally joined the UPND.

The National Assembly was dissolved on 11 May 2016, three months prior to the scheduled election date of 11 August, in accordance with the revised Constitution. President Lungu, however, ignored the constitutional requirement that he also dissolve the Cabinet (although some observers claimed that the ministers were constitutionally entitled to remain in office pending the election). In August the Constitutional Court upheld a petition lodged by the UPND and Law Association of Zambia to declare Lungu's actions unconstitutional.

Meanwhile, Felix Mutati was elected MMD President at a party convention in May 2016. However, the incumbent party leader, Mumba, dismissed the appointment as illegal. In February Mumba had expelled Mutati from the party and announced that the MMD had entered into negotiations regarding a possible electoral alliance with the PF. When the government-run Registrar of Societies proceeded to recognize Mutati as the new MMD leader, Mumba's faction endorsed Hichilema's presidential candidature, while Mutati's faction pledged to back the PF's Lungu, further illustrating the ongoing disintegration of the former ruling party.

Nine presidential candidates successfully filed their nominations for the forthcoming election. Joining the two front runners, Lungu and Hichilema, were the FDD's Edith Nawakwi, UNIP's Tilyenji Kaunda, Rainbow's Wynter Kabimba and four other contestants from lesser-known parties. Notable absentees included the MMD, which did not field a candidate.

In June 2016 the ZRA shut down *The Post*, alleging unpaid taxes totalling some K53m. The newspaper accused the authorities of trying to silence it ahead of a crucial election, claiming that the actual outstanding bill was much smaller than the quoted figure. Despite a court order demanding the reopening of *The Post* prior to the determination of the case, the newspaper remained closed.

LUNGU RE-ELECTED

On 15 August 2016 the ECZ announced that Lungu had won the presidential election, held as scheduled on 11 August, with 50.4% of the valid votes cast, defeating Hichilema who obtained 47.6%. The seven other contenders each received less than 1%. At 56%, the turnout was considerably higher than in 2015. In the elections to the enlarged National Assembly, the PF secured 80 of the 156 directly elective seats, followed by the UPND, which won 58. Independent candidates obtained 14 seats, while the deeply fractured MMD won only three and the FDD one. Although voting generally passed off peacefully, accounts of a number of irregularities emerged before and during the official count.

Since the new electoral legislation required that a winning presidential candidate should secure 50% + 1 of the total votes cast, Lungu's narrow margin of victory, by only 13,021 votes, left him vulnerable to a legal challenge. Hichilema presented a petition to the Constitutional Court on 19 August 2016, seeking the nullification of Lungu's victory on charges of electoral fraud. Under the terms of the amended Constitution, Lungu was prevented from being inaugurated, opening the National Assembly or making any appointments, pending a ruling by the Constitutional Court.

According to the Constitution, the Speaker of the National Assembly could assume presidential powers when an electoral petition had been filed against a President-elect who was also the sitting President. The Speaker was legally mandated to exercise executive functions until the case was dismissed, or until after a fresh presidential election had been held within 30 days from the date of the nullification. However, against the advice of the Attorney-General, Lungu refused to step aside for the Speaker, Patrick Matibini. On 26 August 2016 the UPND requested that the Constitutional Court declare Lungu's move unconstitutional and order him to step down. On 5 September the Constitutional Court and the High Court both ruled against the electoral petition and Lungu was inaugurated as President on 13 September. A new Cabinet was sworn in during September; among the notable appointees were MMD leader Mutati as Minister of Finance and former PF Secretary-General Chama as Minister of Defence (who was replaced in the party role by former home affairs minister Davies Mwila). Arguing that the Constitutional Court had infringed upon his constitutional right to be heard, Hichilema announced that the UPND would not recognize Lungu's presidency. Political uncertainty persisted in the months after the elections. Meanwhile, a record 84 legislative election petitions were filed in the High Court, prompting opposition supporters to claim that this was evidence of the serious irregularities that had marred the general election.

Meanwhile, the suppression of media freedom continued in late August 2016, when the government-controlled Independent Broadcasting Authority (IBA) shut down the country's largest private television station, Muvi TV, which had provided an important platform for opposition parties denied coverage in state-owned media, and had uncovered many of the irregularities that took place during the presidential election. Two independent radio stations were also closed, with the IBA claiming that the activities of all three outlets 'posed a risk to national peace and security'.

In November 2016 Lungu dismissed Chishimba Kambwili as Minister of Information and Broadcasting Services. Although no official reasons were given, Kambwili's dismissal was widely viewed as part of an attempt by Lungu to consolidate his hold on power. Kambwili, a former Chief Government Spokesperson and a PF legislator representing the Roan constituency on the Copperbelt, had been a leading opponent of Lungu's decision to incorporate several former MMD figures in the Cabinet. He was expelled from the PF in July 2017, following allegations that he was destabilizing the party. Kambwili, who had founded the PF alongside the late President Sata in 2001, had earlier indicated that he planned to challenge Lungu for the party leadership at the 2020 elective conference.

In November 2016 *The Post* was placed under compulsory liquidation in a controversial decision at the High Court. However, owner Fred M'membe announced the rebranding of *The Post* as a new independent newspaper, *The Mast*, which appeared on the market shortly afterwards. Also in November the High Court annulled the election of two PF legislators and prominent cabinet ministers representing urban Lusaka constituencies: Nkandu Luo, the Minister of Higher Education, and Margaret Mwanakatwe, the Minister of Commerce, Trade and Industry. The electoral victories of the two politicians were invalidated after the defeated UPND candidates successfully challenged their election. Luo and Mwanakatwe subsequently appealed to the Constitutional Court, while remaining in their ministerial posts.

Lungu's announcement in January 2017 that he would consider standing for a third term in the 2021 presidential election attracted a mixed reaction. Lungu argued that, according to his interpretation of the amended Constitution, he considered himself eligible to seek another term of office. He challenged opponents to his position to seek the official opinion of the Constitutional Court on the matter; four small opposition parties subsequently presented a petition to the Court requesting a declaration of Lungu's eligibility. The Law Association of Zambia (LAZ) and the opposition UPND, which argued that the four opposition parties were acting on behalf of Lungu, sought a declaration from the Court that Lungu was not eligible to stand for a third presidential term.

LUNGU'S SECOND TERM AND DEMOCRATIC DETERIORATION

UPND legislators, unwilling to recognize Lungu as the legitimate President, boycotted his State of the Nation address to the National Assembly in March 2017. In June the Speaker, Matibini, suspended the 48 dissident legislators from the National Assembly for 30 days and challenged them to resign if they did not recognize Lungu as President. On 10 April police officers raided the home of UPND leader Hichilema in Lusaka and arrested him on treason charges, following the apparent obstruction, two days earlier, of Lungu's motorcade by Hichilema's own convoy as the two leaders were travelling to attend a traditional ceremony of the Lozi-speaking people in Western Province. Hichilema's arrest drew widespread criticism, most notably from the influential Zambia Conference of Catholic Bishops, which, on 23 April, stated that the country was now essentially 'a dictatorship'. Beyond Zambia's borders, outrage against Hichilema's arrest and calls for his release came from many quarters, including from Kenya's former Prime Minister Raila Odinga, former Nigerian President Olusegun Obasanjo, and South African opposition leaders Julius Malema and Mmusi Maimane. In late May Maimane was deported from Zambia following his arrival at the Kenneth Kaunda International Airport to attend Hichilema's trial.

Lungu added to concerns over his increasing authoritarianism on 5 July 2017 when he declared a week-long state of emergency, citing a spate of suspicious fires targeting public buildings and stalls at Lusaka City Market. The PF-dominated National Assembly approved the measure for a period of 90 days. Lungu stated that the action was necessary to forestall chaos, while the opposition claimed that it exemplified the President's attempt to quash dissent.

Hichilema was discharged from prison in mid-August 2017, after four months in detention. His release on a *nolle prosequi* followed high-level diplomatic negotiations between him and Lungu, mediated by Zambia's Catholic bishops and Commonwealth Secretary-General Patricia Scotland. In a bid to diffuse the heightened political tension that had gripped the country since the disputed elections of August 2016, the two leaders committed themselves to participating in a political dialogue supervised by the Commonwealth in a bid to reach agreement on a number of institutional electoral reforms.

Lungu warned in November 2017 that protests and chaos would follow if the judges of the Constitutional Court ruled that he was ineligible to seek a third term. Lungu's comments came in the wake of the decision by Kenya's Supreme Court to invalidate the election of Uhuru Kenyatta in that country's presidential poll in August—a verdict that attracted plaudits across Africa. PF Secretary-General Mwila announced in November that the party had adopted Lungu as its presidential candidate for the 2021 elections. Mwila's remarks, in advance of a ruling by the Constitutional Court, met with strong criticism from the political opposition, which accused him of undermining judicial independence.

In December 2017 Lungu dismissed Minister of National Development Planning Lucky Mulusa, who had publicly attributed a wave of power shortages in 2016–17 to the Government's energy policy and the incompetence of public servants, instead of low water levels as a result of scarce rainfall (the official explanation). The resignation, in January 2018, of Minister of Foreign Affairs Harry Kalaba exposed sharp divisions within the Government. Kalaba cited 'swelling levels of greed and corruption' during Lungu's tenure and the Government's preference for outsiders, particularly from the People's Republic of China, over Zambians in relation to business opportunities as the key reasons for his decision. Lungu appointed Joseph Malanji as Kalaba's successor. Also in January, a devastating cholera outbreak in Lusaka led to several deaths, the closure of schools nationwide, a ban on street vending and the deployment of the military to enforce the ban, which remained in effect for nearly two months. In a government reshuffle in February, Mwanakatwe was appointed as Minister of Finance, replacing Mutati, who became Minister of Works and Supply.

In April 2018 the UPND filed a motion seeking the impeachment of Lungu for alleged constitutional breaches and gross misconduct. Since the opposition lacked the requisite two-thirds' legislative majority for the motion to pass, political commentators interpreted the move as part of the UPND's wider strategy of delegitimizing Lungu's administration. The motion failed to advance further in the National Assembly, as a result of court challenges to its legality and the Speaker's reluctance to table it for debate. Meanwhile, Fresher Siwale, leader of a small opposition party, New Labour, was arrested in April for alleged defamation of the President. Siwale had earlier claimed that Lungu's real identity was Jonathan Mutaware, born in 1956 to Malawian parents working on the Copperbelt mines. Siwale insisted that Lungu was not eligible to seek presidential office in 2015 when he was first elected, since the Constitution at the time stipulated that an individual could only stand for election as President if both of their parents were Zambian by birth or descent. Differences within the UPND came to the surface in May 2018, when the party's Vice-President, Mwamba, left the main political opposition, citing differences with UPND leader Hichilema. Mwamba subsequently rejoined the ruling PF, which he had left in July 2015.

The growing influence of China in Zambia was underlined in June 2018, when StarTimes, a private media corporation with close ties to the Chinese Government, acquired a 60% stake in the state-owned Zambia National Broadcasting Corporation (ZNBC) before the Zambian Government sanctioned a joint venture enterprise between the two companies. StarTimes obtained a US $273m. loan from the Exim Bank of China on behalf of ZNBC, which sought the funds to switch from analogue to digital broadcasting. In return, the Chinese company would be in charge of signal transmission throughout Zambia and collect all advertising revenue and tower rental fees generated by ZNBC for the next 25 years. Despite criticism from the Zambian opposition that China was taking control of the country's state media, the Government defended the move as irreversible.

In November 2018 residents on the industrial Copperbelt took to the streets in protest against the rumoured sale of state-owned timber company Zambia Forestry and Forest Industries Corporation to China. The Government swiftly denied the reports and accused Hichilema of having incited the marchers. The protests underlined growing public concerns that Zambia's sovereignty was under threat from China. Meanwhile, President Lungu dismissed Minister of Works and Supply Mutati and revoked his nomination as a legislator.

Reports that the Government had procured a US $68m. aeroplane for Lungu emerged in December 2018, sparking a public backlash and strong criticism of official extravagance amid an economic downturn and spiralling public debt. Sturdy Mwale, Permanent Secretary of the Ministry of Defence, confirmed and defended the purchase of the presidential aircraft, which was delivered in early 2019.

On 7 December 2018 the Constitutional Court ruled unanimously that Lungu was free to seek a third presidential term in 2021 without breaching the two-term limit, thereby discounting the one-and-a-half years that he had spent in office prior to being elected to his first full term in 2016. The unanimous decision was preceded by strong threats from the President that an unfavourable verdict would be met with chaos.

In February 2019 parliamentary Speaker Matibini declared vacant the Roan constituency seat held by expelled PF deputy Kambwili. Kambwili had challenged his expulsion from the ruling party in court, but Matibini argued that the former Minister of Information and Broadcasting Services had taken up a leadership position in the recently formed opposition National Democratic Congress (NDC). On 11 April the NDC, supported by the UPND, defeated the ruling party in the ensuing by-election—the PF's first loss to another political party at legislative level on the urban Copperbelt since the 2001 election. In what was widely seen as a retaliation, the Government deregistered the NDC in August 2019 for alleged undemocratic tendencies and for having an 'inoperative constitution'. Kambwili's party filed a legal challenge against the move. Meanwhile, Prime TV, a leading private television station, was suspended for 30 days in March for allegedly broadcasting anti-Government rhetoric that had contributed

to the PF's by-election defeat, underlining the Government's continued crackdown on media freedom.

In May 2019 Lungu announced the Government's decision to place into liquidation Konkola Copper Mines, which played a crucial role in Zambia's copper-dominated economy and was majority-owned by Vedanta Resources. The decision, which came into effect a few days later, provoked concern among foreign investors. Lungu claimed that the London-based Indian multinational corporation was underinvesting in the mine and underpaying taxes to Zambia; Vedanta denied the accusations and launched a legal challenge against the takeover. (However, a Zambian court ruling on 1 February 2021 allowed the asset sales of Konkola Copper Mines to proceed.)

In June 2019 the Government published the controversial Constitution of Zambia Amendment Bill Number 10, which sought, *inter alia*, to reduce the oversight role of the judiciary and legislature on the executive. Ignoring criticism from both local and international actors that the proposed new legislation would undermine key democratic principles, the Government presented it to the National Assembly for its first reading in July. In the same month Lungu dismissed Minister of Finance Mwanakatwe, choosing as her replacement the Deputy Governor of the Bank of Zambia, Bwalya Ng'andu, who thus became the fourth Minister of Finance since January 2015, when Lungu came to power.

Official intolerance of sexual minorities (same-sex sexual relations being illegal in Zambia) resurfaced in July 2019 when the openly gay South African media personality Somizi Mhlongo was prevented from travelling to Zambia for an official engagement. The sentencing in November of a gay couple to 15 years in prison for contravening anti-homosexuality laws prompted stark criticism from the US ambassador to Zambia, Daniel Foote, who also rebuked the Zambian Government for failing to tackle corruption and for the lack of accountability in Zambian politics. After the Zambian Government announced in December that Foote's position was 'no longer tenable', the US Administration recalled the ambassador and installed a chargé d'affaires in March 2020. Meanwhile, in August 2019 the LAZ, together with a human rights organization, Chapter One Foundation, launched an action at the Constitutional Court to challenge the constitutionality of the proposed Bill 10. The draft legislation was deferred in December after the PF failed to obtain the support of at least two-thirds of deputies in the National Assembly, as required by the Constitution for it to be approved. In July 2020 the Constitutional Court dismissed the petition brought by the LAZ and the Chapter One Foundation on the grounds of it being premature.

In September 2019 students at the University of Zambia took to the streets of Lusaka to protest against a series of xenophobic attacks directed at African foreign nationals in South Africa. The students attacked South African-owned stores, forcing them to close, and marched to the South African high commission, where they unsuccessfully demanded to speak with officials. Police fired tear gas to disperse the demonstrating students. The High Court ruled in November that Mumba was the legitimate President of the MMD, invalidating the party convention that had elected Mutati as party President in May 2016 and thus ending a three-year battle for the leadership of the former ruling party.

In the first three months of 2020 several of Zambia's urban centres—mainly Lusaka and the cities on the Copperbelt—were hit by a spate of incidents in which unknown assailants sprayed unidentified chemical substances on citizens. The 'gassing attacks', as the incidents became known, killed at least 50 people. The authorities deployed the military to quell the attacks, which only ceased upon the outbreak of coronavirus disease (COVID-19) in March 2020. The Government accused the opposition of being behind the attacks, while the opposition alleged that the ruling party had staged them as a pretext for arresting major political opponents ahead of the 2021 general election.

Zambia's first case of COVID-19 was confirmed on 18 March 2020. In an effort to prevent a wider outbreak of the disease, the Government introduced various travel restrictions, placed limitations on large public gatherings, and ordered the closure of all schools and universities, as well as some non-essential businesses. The Government began to ease the pandemic restrictions in May, following the apparent success of its campaign to curb the spread of the disease. Zambia's international airports, most of which had been closed since March, were reopened in June.

Meanwhile, in April 2020 the IBA cancelled the broadcasting licence of Prime TV, stating that its decision had been taken in the 'public interest'. The station, arguing that it had been denied its legal right to be heard, unsuccessfully appealed for redress to the Minister of Information and Broadcasting Services, who stated that the licence had already expired when the IBA took the decision. The authorities' actions highlighted the curtailment of media freedom in Zambia in advance of the 2021 general election.

The shrinking democratic space was further highlighted in June 2020 when several youths took to the bush on the outskirts of Lusaka to protest against the escalating erosion of civil liberties and rising levels of corruption in government. The youth activists, whose action followed the refusal of the police to sanction their application to stage a peaceful march, then live-streamed video of themselves to an audience of at least 30,000 people on social media. Also in June, the Minister of Health, Dr Chitalu Chilufya, was arrested for suspected corruption and charged with possession of property suspected of being the proceeds of crime. However, Lungu refused to dismiss Chilufya from the Cabinet, and he was acquitted of all charges in August. In the same month Lungu abruptly removed the Governor of the Bank of Zambia, Denny Kalyalya, for undisclosed reasons, replacing him with Christopher Mvunga, hitherto Deputy Secretary to the Cabinet. The dismissal of Kalyalya, a widely respected figure, attracted local and international criticism.

In a victory for the NDC, the High Court in August 2020 overturned the deregistration of the party one year earlier. However, in October the NDC leader, Kambwili, was found guilty on forgery and false information charges and received a one-year prison sentence. Kambwili was released on bail later that month pending an appeal against his sentence. In December UPND leader Hichilema was summoned by the police for questioning in connection with an allegedly fraudulent real estate purchase. A demonstration staged outside the police station by Hichilema's supporters was violently suppressed by the security forces, resulting in the deaths of two people. Kambwili resigned from the NDC in April 2021, following an internal dispute with the party's Vice-President, and rejoined the PF the following month, having reconciled with Lungu.

Meanwhile, in October 2020 the PF failed to secure the passage at the second reading of Bill 10, which would have increased executive control over the judiciary and monetary policy, and potentially enabled the Government to rearrange electoral constituencies. The Bill received 105 votes in its favour in the National Assembly, six fewer than the required two-thirds' of deputies, with most UPND deputies observing a boycott of the session instructed by the party leadership.

ELECTION OF PRESIDENT HAKAINDE HICHILEMA

In a second wave of the COVID-19 pandemic, recorded cases rose sharply from 20,725 at the end of 2020 to 84,950 by mid-March 2021. A third wave began at the end of May, when cases numbered 95,263. In June the Government reinstated the closure of schools, universities, bars and nightclubs; intercity travel was prohibited and a night curfew was introduced. Stricter lockdown measures were implemented in some districts where cases were concentrated. (Cases began to level off in August, but reached 208,599 by 21 September, with 3,639 related deaths.) Meanwhile, Lungu dismissed Chilufya as Minister of Health in January, after it was revealed that the Ministry of Health had distributed substandard medical supplies under a contract with an unqualified company.

Lungu was re-elected leader of the PF at the party's national congress in April 2021, and on 3 May he was officially confirmed as its presidential candidate in the forthcoming general election, which was scheduled to be held on 12 August. The National Assembly was dissolved on 12 May, in accordance with the Constitution. On 19 May Hichilema was officially nominated as the presidential candidate of the UPND; by late

June a further 14 opposition candidates had also registered to contest the election. The President instructed that the police enforce the pandemic-related restrictions and that opposition parties avoid holding large public gatherings. As COVID-19 cases continued to surge, on 3 June the ECZ suspended campaign rallies. In late July the UPND Secretary-General, Batuke Imenda, issued a statement complaining that Lungu was using government institutions such as the ECZ to prevent Hichilema from campaigning. Shortly afterwards, Hichilema and his campaign team were prevented by police from entering the major towns of Mbala, in Northern Province, and Chipata, the main city of Eastern Province, where he was temporarily detained at the airport, on the grounds that he lacked required permits. At the beginning of August Lungu ordered the deployment of armed forces personnel to quell increasing political violence, following clashes between rival party supporters, in which two PF activists were killed in Lusaka.

A further two prominent members of the PF were killed in North-Western Province during violence accompanying the polling on 12 August 2021. Shortly afterwards, Lungu protested that the elections were not free or fair, and demanded that the results be annulled, due to the violence reported in three provinces, claiming that PF polling officials had been harassed. However, AU and EU observer missions endorsed the conduct of the election (although the EU monitors noted the misuse of state resources and biased media reporting during the campaign). On 16 August the ECZ declared Hichilema President-elect, after he secured 59.0% of votes cast, with a voter turnout of 70.6%; Lungu, who had received 38.7% of the vote, conceded defeat in a television address on the same day, as Hichilema's supporters celebrated in the streets. Hichilema's decisive victory (after he had contested five previous presidential elections unsuccessfully) reflected the extent of voter dissatisfaction with Lungu's regime. The annual summit of SADC leaders hosted in Malawi shortly afterwards acclaimed the peaceful transition of power in Zambia. In the elections to the National Assembly, the UPND was first-placed, with 82 seats, while the PF received 59 seats; the only other party to secure representation, the newly relaunched Party of National Unity and Progress, obtained one seat and 13 independent candidates were elected. (Voting in one constituency was postponed until 21 October, following the death of the UPND candidate.) A voter turnout of 70.4% was recorded. Hichilema was inaugurated as President on 24 August, with his running mate, Mutale Nalumango, becoming Vice-President.

By the end of August 2021 Hichilema had replaced the heads of the armed and security forces. Hichilema began to appoint the members of his new UPND Cabinet, which was complete by mid-September. The new ministers included Situmbeko Musokotwane as Minister of Finance and National Planning, Jacob Jack Mwiimbu as Minister of Home Affairs and Stanley Kakubo as Minister of Foreign Affairs and International Co-operation. Two former PF ministers who had left the party, Sylvia Tembo Masebo and Felix Mutati, became Minister of Health and Minister of Technology and Science, respectively. On 3 September lawyer Nelly Butete Kashumba Mutti of the UPND was elected unopposed as the new Speaker of the National Assembly, becoming the first woman to hold the post. Mvunga resigned as Governor of the Bank of Zambia on 7 September and later that month Klayalya was reappointed to that position. Musokotwane (who had previously held the finance portfolio in 2008–11) was tasked with concluding negotiations with the IMF on a lending programme, after Hichilema pledged to restore macroeconomic stability. Supreme Court judge Mumba Malila was appointed Chief Justice in December 2021, replacing Irene Mambilima, who had died in June.

In January 2022 opposition parties questioned the nature of the relationship between Hichilema and the Johannesburg-based Brenthurst Foundation after the President travelled to the South African capital to launch a book authored by the Foundation's director, Greg Mills. Fred M'membe, now leader of the Socialist Party, which he had formed as a breakaway group from the Rainbow Party in 2018, accused Mills of having financed Hichilema's election campaign in return for influence on the President and on direction of policy, especially in mining.

On 4 February 2022 the governing UPND retained the Kabwata parliamentary seat at a by-election caused by the death of incumbent deputy Levy Mkandawire. UPND candidate Andrew Tayengwa polled 13,574 votes, defeating eight other contenders including Clement Tembo of the PF, who finished in second place with 11,192 votes. Also in February, the Supreme Court ruled that the 2016 liquidation of *The Post* was null and void, as the publication was denied the opportunity to be heard. The appellant court ordered a retrial of the case in the High Court.

The death of 85-year-old Rupiah Banda on 11 March 2022 left Edgar Lungu as Zambia's only surviving former President, following the death of founding President Kenneth Kaunda, at the age of 97, in June 2021. On 15 March 2022 the Deputy Speaker of the National Assembly suspended 30 opposition PF lawmakers from parliament for 30 days for peacefully protesting against a decision they deemed unfavourable. This action highlighted a new attack on democratic rights under Hichilema, one that has seen the arrest and conviction of several ordinary people on charges of insulting the President. In the same month Hichilema co-opted into government bodies some of the leading voices from civil society who had spoken out against attacks on democracy under Lungu. Former Attorney-General Musa Mwenye was appointed Chairperson of the Anti-Corruption Commission, while civil society leader Laura Miti was appointed as a Commissioner at the Human Rights Commission.

In May 2022 Hichilema removed High Court judge Joshua Banda from office and suspended another High Court judge, Sunday Nkonde. No official explanations were provided for the actions, although the President stated that he was acting on the recommendation of the Judicial Complaints Commission. Kelvin Bwalya Fube, popularly known as KBF, launched a new political party, Zambia Must Prosper, in August. Fube had been a key member of a small cluster of opposition parties that supported Hichilema in the 2021 election. He was arrested by the Drug Enforcement Commission in September 2022 on money laundering charges that were dismissed by his supporters as being politically motivated.

Meanwhile, Hichilema's refusal to state the value of his assets and liabilities prior to the election in August 2021 continued to feed criticism from civil society and opposition parties, on the grounds that it undermined the fight against corruption and the need for government transparency. It also added to growing suspicion over the extent of the President's involvement in Zambia's economy and whether his policies were deliberately designed to benefit companies in which he has an interest. Sean Tembo, leader of the opposition Patriots for Economic Progress party, brought a legal suit against Hichilema for his refusal to publish his net worth, but the Constitutional Court dismissed the matter in March 2022, saying that Tembo should have sued all 16 presidential candidates who took part in the 2021 election, including himself, and not just Hichilema. On 31 August 2022 the IMF Executive Board finally approved a US $1,300m., 38-month extended credit facility for Zambia to 'help restore macroeconomic stability and foster higher, more resilient, and more inclusive growth'.

In September 2022 Hichilema suspended Director of Public Prosecutions Lilian Siyunyi from office. Siyunyi, a Lungu-era appointee, had earlier been reported to the Judicial Complaints Commission by several individuals and organizations for alleged incompetence and gross misconduct. Later in September Lungu publicly challenged Hichilema to initiate the process of lifting his immunity from prosecution, asserting that he was ready to defend himself in court and that he had had enough of Hichilema's constant accusations that he ran a corrupt administration, and stating: 'we in the PF have been called criminals, looters ... may the President start the process of removing my immunity so that I have my day in court.'

REGIONAL RELATIONS

Relations between Zambia and newly independent Zimbabwe were initially tense, owing to Kaunda's longstanding support for Robert Mugabe's political rival, Joshua Nkomo, although the two countries' shared experience as 'front-line' states opposed to apartheid South Africa did much to improve relations. Nevertheless, President Mwanawasa became increasingly agitated by developments in Zimbabwe, and in 2006 he publicly compared Zimbabwe to the sinking ship *Titanic*. Prior to his appointment as SADC Chairman in August 2007, he attempted to heal the rift with Mugabe, dispatching Vice-President Banda to Harare, Zimbabwe, for talks. However, following the controversial presidential election in Zimbabwe in June 2008, which was contested solely by Mugabe, Mwanawasa denounced the outcome as undemocratic. Banda, by contrast, was supportive of Mugabe, as was Sata.

The deportation from Zambia of Zimbabwean opposition leader Tendai Biti in August 2018 attracted local and international condemnation, most notably from the Zambian political opposition and from the USA. Biti, who entered Zambia through the border town of Chirundu, requested asylum following threats on his life in Zimbabwe. The Zambian Government rejected his application and handed him back to Zimbabwean authorities immediately. Rights group Amnesty International and civil society organizations condemned the move, stating that it demonstrated Zambia's lack of adherence to norms of international law. The UPND claimed that Biti was being penalized for his open support for Hakainde Hichilema in 2017, when the UPND leader was facing a treason charge.

Kaunda assumed a leading role in peace initiatives in Southern Africa and supported both the South West Africa People's Organisation of Namibia (SWAPO), allowing it to operate from Zambian territory, and the African National Congress of South Africa, which, until its return to South Africa in mid-1990, maintained its headquarters in Lusaka. Zambia was frequently subjected to military reprisals from South Africa, but South African political reforms from 1990 onwards eased relations, and in mid-1993 President F. W. de Klerk made the first official visit to Zambia by a South African head of state. The South African Government endorsed Mwanawasa's controversial first election victory, and, in return, Mwanawasa supported Thabo Mbeki's proposal for the New Partnership for Africa's Development.

Zambia's support for the Governments of Angola and Mozambique during the Kaunda era resulted in retaliatory attacks by União Nacional para a Independência Total de Angola (UNITA) rebels and by Mozambican guerrillas of the Resistência Nacional Moçambicana (Renamo). Renamo attacks ceased after a peace agreement was reached in October 1992. During the Chiluba presidency, the Angolan Government frequently alleged that senior members of the Zambian Government were supporting UNITA. Chiluba denied the charges, but it was widely suspected that covert Zambian assistance for UNITA was taking place, even though in early 1996 Zambia contributed some 1,000 troops to the United Nations (UN) Angola Verification Mission. In early 1999 bilateral tensions peaked when the Angolan Government accused Chiluba's administration of complicity in a mysterious bomb blast that severely damaged the Angolan embassy in Lusaka. The two Governments later signed an agreement aimed at resolving their differences, but Angola was angered that Chiluba refused to allow its troops to pursue UNITA forces onto Zambian territory, and in December Angolan military aircraft bombed border areas of Zambia's North-Western Province. Following the end of the Angolan war in 2001, relations eased considerably as peace largely returned to the border region and refugees began to go home. According to the office of the UN High Commissioner for Refugees (UNHCR), the number of Angolan refugees in Zambia declined from 218,154 in January 2002 to 20,970 in January 2012. Due to the improved security environment in Angola, the refugee status of Angolans in Zambia was rescinded in June. At the end of August 2022 UNHCR reported that 18,829 Angolan former refugees remained in Zambia.

A longstanding border dispute between Zambia and the DRC was rekindled in March 2020 when Zambian troops seized control of several villages in the DRC's Tanganyika Province. Subsequent clashes between Zambian and Congolese forces in the region left at least two soldiers dead. (Similar border incursions had been reported sporadically since the

1990s.) High-level discussions between Zambian and Congolese officials later in March appeared to alleviate tensions, with both sides committing to a peaceful resolution. The Zambian military withdrew from the villages in August following diplomatic intervention by SADC. On 20 August 2021 demarcation work resumed in an effort to resolve the border

dispute between the two countries. Zambia continues to host thousands of Congolese refugees who fled the DRC during or after the conflict, most of whom live in UNHCR camps. Amid persistent volatility in the DRC, at the end of August 2022 the number of UNHCR-registered refugees from the DRC in Zambia totalled 56,535.

Economy

DUNCAN WOODSIDE

Revised for this edition by the editorial staff

INTRODUCTION

Despite its landlocked status, Zambia's economy is one of the most developed in sub-Saharan Africa. However, the economy—and particularly financial stability—remains subject to the vagaries of commodity prices, particularly that of copper, the country's principal export. This commodity accounts for around 80% of foreign exchange earnings, making it the key determinant of Zambia's economic growth rate, trade balance and exchange rate. In recent years the international copper price has been particularly volatile. According to figures from the International Monetary Fund (IMF), real gross domestic product (GDP) grew by 7.6% in 2012, owing to strong performances in agriculture, construction and communications, but most of all the elevated price of copper. The rate of economic growth decelerated to 5.1% in 2013 and 4.7% in 2014, with commodity prices falling substantially in the second half of the latter year.

The economy deteriorated sharply in 2015 and 2016, largely due to an economic slowdown in the People's Republic of China (which accounts for more than one-half of global copper consumption), resulting in a further drop in global copper prices. Real GDP growth fell to 2.9% in 2015. In March 2016 the IMF warned that the Government's finances were suffering 'immense stress', with expenditure running significantly above target, partly due to fuel subsidies and electricity imports, which were costing the Government US $660m. per year (3.2% of GDP). Adding to the instability, President Edgar Lungu won a controversial presidential election in August 2016, with his closest challenger, Hakainde Hichilema, claiming that the election had been rigged. While external trends—notably higher copper prices—helped to ease the crisis during the second half of 2016 and 2017, hefty capital expenditure placed further pressure on the fiscal situation. GDP growth was 3.8% in 2016 and 3.5% in 2017. In September 2018 the Government declared that it would add $3,500m. to Zambia's external debt in 2019–21 to finance the capital expenditure budget. However, in its budget for 2019 the Government sought to raise revenues by replacing value-added tax with a non-refundable sales tax and increasing royalties on copper mining.

According to official figures, GDP growth in 2018 was 4.0%, aided by higher copper prices, good rains and strong services growth, before a significant slowdown in 2019, with GDP registering just 1.4% growth and inflation increasing to 9.2%. Copper production declined by around 100,000 metric tons, owing to new taxes on the sector, according to the Zambia Chamber of Mines (ZCM), although power outages also affected smelter output. The GDP growth rate represented a damning indictment of successive Patriotic Front Governments that had borrowed heavily in a bid to boost the economy since the party came to power in 2011. The budget deficit reached 10.9% of GDP in 2019, while general government gross debt reached 91.9% of GDP. The surging level of national debt significantly raised the risk of default, even before the COVID-19 pandemic struck in early 2020. Zambia's mineral-dependent economy was highly exposed to the global policy responses to the pandemic, as global lockdowns sent demand for raw materials crashing and copper prices sank considerably lower. Unsustainable fiscal policies meant that Zambia did not

appear among the 25 countries initially approved by the IMF in April 2020 for immediate debt service relief under its Catastrophe Containment and Relief Trust. In mid-June the IMF confirmed that it had agreed a 'consultative exchange mission' to examine a request by the Government for emergency assistance. However, as a precursor to the provision of financial assistance, the IMF re-emphasized that 'steps would need to be taken to restore debt sustainability'. Later in June the Cabinet approved a K8,000m. (US $439m.) stimulus package, which was to be funded through a 'COVID-19 bond', with the proceeds being used to pay pensions and contractors to the public sector.

The economy contracted by 2.8% in 2020, while the exchange rate depreciated significantly, and the rate of inflation increased sharply, reaching 15.7% in that year overall. The fiscal deficit widened to a projected 11.7% of GDP and the debt-to-GDP ratio exceeded 100% as a result of the Government's expansionary spending and the pandemic-related decline in revenues. In November Zambia defaulted on a US $43m. debt payment on a Eurobond, becoming the first country in Africa to suffer a pandemic-era sovereign default. The Government in the following month opened negotiations with the IMF with the aim of securing a credit arrangement, also announcing an economic recovery programme. However, Zambia defaulted on an additional $56m. of debt in late January. In February the country applied for a debt-restructuring arrangement under the Common Framework established by the Group of 20 (G20) leading economies. Prospects for economic recovery improved hugely with a rebound in global copper prices (see *Mining*), and with the victory of hitherto opposition figure Hichilema at the presidential election on 12 August 2021. President Hichilema immediately pledged to address the inherited unsustainable debt burden, reduce the fiscal deficit, tackle corruption, and implement reforms necessary to secure the long-awaited loan agreement with the IMF. Two of his principal aims were to bolster investor confidence (especially in mining) and to increase economic growth. In December the Government reached a preliminary agreement with the IMF on a three-year reform programme, underpinned by US $1,400m. of financing under the Fund's Extended Credit Facility. The programme was approved by the IMF board on 31 August 2022, allowing an immediate payment to Zambia of $185m. The Fund described its aims as to 'restore debt sustainability, create fiscal space for essential social spending and strengthen economic governance'. Meanwhile, debt-restructuring negotiations under the G20 Common Framework were continuing.

GDP growth was an estimated 4.6% in 2021, with Zambia's principal industries starting to recover from the COVID-19 pandemic as the economy gradually reopened. High copper prices assisted this growth, and favourable weather conditions also benefited the agricultural sector. However, inflation again rose sharply in 2021, to 22.0%, while preliminary figures suggested that the country maintained a large fiscal deficit, of some 9.0% of GDP.

AGRICULTURE

Agriculture is an important sector of the economy. According to the Central Statistical Office of Zambia, agriculture (including hunting, forestry and fishing) accounted for only 2.9% of GDP in 2020. However, the sector engaged 22.5% of the employed labour force in that year. Zambia's topography, with its varied elevation, enables a variety of crops to be grown, although only about 7% of the surface area is under cultivation, while some 40% serves as permanent pasture and 43% is under forest. The Government estimates that, of the country's 60m. ha of arable land, only about 15% is currently being exploited. Maize is the staple food crop, consumed in the form of nshima, a porridge-like dish. In August 2019 the Government intervened to cap maize prices, sparking concerns among farmers and raising memories of a previous era of price controls. The Ministry of Agriculture announced that stakeholders—including millers and traders—had agreed to a price cap of K2,600 per metric ton, (just below US $200 per ton). The move came in a context where the cost of a 25-kg bag of maize meal had doubled in some areas since the start of the year, from K75 to K150, amid shortages caused by drought.

Besides maize, Zambia also produces cassava, wheat, millet, vegetables, sugar cane, groundnuts, sweet potatoes, melons, fruits, cotton, sorghum, barley, pulses, soya beans, tobacco, sunflower seeds and paddy rice. Zambia has several hundred large commercial farms, which account for about 45% of its agricultural output. Wheat is grown almost exclusively on these farms, usually under irrigation. The country's flour mills require some 140,000 metric tons per year to keep the nation supplied with bread; thus, even in very productive seasons, wheat has to be imported.

Sugar represents an important cash crop for Zambia. Production reached 380,000 metric tons in the 12 months to the end of March 2016, before declining to 359,000 tons over the same period of 2016/17. Zambia Sugar attributed the decline in part to low domestic consumer demand, alongside strong competition in the European Union market. However, a new refinery, built at a cost of US $80m., saw Zambia Sugar record a 47% increase in output of refined sugar in 2016/17, with total production rising to 65,000 tons. Externally, Zambia Sugar focused on Burundi, the Democratic Republic of the Congo (DRC), Kenya and South Africa, all of which were considered strong export customers. Zambia and Kenya signed a bilateral deal in July 2017 under which the former would export 40,000 tons of sugar and 100,000 tons of maize to the latter, since Kenya was suffering from drought-related shortages. Zambia maintained a maize surplus of 1.4m. tons, thanks to a very good harvest in 2016. Sugar production was 413,142 tons in 2020/21, and Zambia Sugar achieved record annual revenues of K4,989m.

Maize production rose to a record 3.6m. metric tons in 2017, according to the Food and Agriculture Organization of the United Nations (FAO), due to good rains. However, following a prolonged drought, maize output in 2018 dropped to 2.4m. tons in 2018 and 2.0m. tons in 2019. An outbreak of fall armyworm also undermined production, affecting more than 215,000 ha of maize fields. Maize output recovered in 2020, reaching 3.4m. tons. Meanwhile, soya bean output followed a similar pattern, declining from 351,400 tons in 2017 to 302,700 tons in 2018 and 281,400 tons in 2019, then rising to about 296,900 tons in 2020.

The horticultural sector has experienced strong growth, with the export of fruits, vegetables and flowers to Europe. The sector's interests are overseen by the Zambia Export Growers' Association, which, among other things, lobbies for affordable air freight charges. Zambia has more than 30 flower farms, covering 135 ha, growing more than 50 varieties of roses and some 20 kinds of summer flowers for export. The flower markets of the Netherlands are the most significant purchasers of these exports.

About 70% of livestock is owned by traditional farmers. The national cattle herd numbered 3.7m. head in 2020, according to FAO, while goats totalled 2.9m. and pigs 1.1m. A small amount of beef is generally exported each year. Zambeef Products PLC, the largest meat company in Zambia, employs over 7,000 workers. The company also grows maize, wheat, barley, lucerne (alfalfa) and soya beans on 16,594 ha of land, of which 7,971 ha are under irrigation. After witnessing a downturn due to two years of economic turmoil in Zambia, in 2018 Zambeef posted an increase in pre-tax profits to US $2.8m., up from $572,000, as revenue grew by 9.6% to $280.3m.

In light of Zimbabwe's economic collapse during the early 21st century—and the loss of its status as Southern Africa's 'food basket'—Zambia has tentative plans to fill the production vacuum. In some ways, this process was already under way, through, for example, the export of refined sugar by Zambia Sugar. However, in May 2017 the UN's Special Rapporteur on the Right to Food, Hilal Elver, warned that expanding commercial farming by encouraging multinational participation risked forcing indigenous farmers to become 'squatters on their own land'. She pointed to the fact that around 40% of under-fives in Zambia suffered from stunting as a result of malnutrition, despite the ongoing recovery in economic growth. She also voiced concern that evicted farmers were working in poor conditions on industrial farms, while remaining smallholders were subject to the mercy of anti-competitive buying practices by export oligopolies. The UN estimates that around 60% of Zambians are small-scale farmers, while 85% of agricultural land is held under customary tenure, which provides little protection against eviction.

As a landlocked country, Zambia has a number of important lakes and rivers, particularly Lake Kariba on the southern border with Zimbabwe and those in the Northern Province; these all offer considerable potential for fishing. The total catch in 2020 was 152,500 metric tons, according to FAO.

Zambia has 323,000 sq km of forested land, 265,000 sq km of which is open to exploitation. Commercial forestry is important on the Copperbelt, where there are numerous softwood tree plantations, and in the hardwood areas of the south-west, which are rich in African teak. Total roundwood removals amount to an estimated 25m. cu m per year, according to FAO, but around 23m. cu m is consumed locally in the form of fuel wood. In 2016 Zambia banned the felling and sale of the Pterocarpus chrysothrix tree, a relative of rosewood, in an attempt to end the rapid depletion of the species caused by growing demand from Asia. Under a scheme to bolster foreign currency reserves, the authorities in 2018 then began to sell off confiscated stocks to Asia through South Africa, with the Zambia Revenue Authority stating that over 250 trucks full of the illegal timber had been confiscated since the ban came into force. Zambian conservationists have estimated that the country loses between 100m. and 280m. trees each year to illegal logging.

MINING

According to the Central Statistical Office, the mining sector contributed 22.3% of GDP in 2020. The sector engaged 2.0% of the employed labour force in that year. Zambia has some 3% of the world's copper reserves. In 2021, according to estimates by the US Geological Survey (USGS), the country was Africa's second largest producer of copper (after the DRC), and the seventh largest in terms of copper output worldwide. An estimated 656,000 metric tons of copper ore were produced in 2019. Zambia was also a significant producer of cobalt, with output of cobalt ore totalling an estimated 835 tons in 2018, although output declined to 420 tons in 2019. According to official figures, copper production was recorded at 837,996 tons in 2020, declining to 800,696 tons in 2021. Meanwhile, cobalt output was 316 tons in 2020, owing partly to reduced cobalt mineralization; it fell further, to 247 tons, in 2021. The ZCM attributed the decline in minerals output in 2021 to 'operational challenges' linked to the country's mining tax regime. Other minerals exploited included zinc, lead, gold, silver, selenium, marble, emeralds, amethysts, aquamarines, tourmalines and garnets.

Konkola is potentially the richest of Zambia's copper mines, possessing reserves of 44.3m. metric tons, with a copper content of 3.9%, while reserves at Nchanga have a copper content of 3.8% and those at Mufulira have a content of 3.2%; Nkana is the largest mine, with 108.1m. tons of reserves, but with a copper content of only 1.8%. Konkola Copper Mines PLC (KCM), 51% of which is owned by Vedanta Resources of India, was already the largest mining company in Zambia when, in 2007, it announced plans to mine even deeper. Vedanta also owns two mines at Nchanga and one at Nampundwe, as well as smelters at Nkana and Nchanga. The Konkola Deep Mining Project (KDMP), the largest-ever single mining investment in Zambia, was expected to cost around US $1,500m. and was to take the mine down to a depth of 1,505 m. KDMP was to extend the life of the mine to 2035 and intended to increase its throughput from 2m. tons of copper ore per year to 7.5m. tons.

Zambia's Kansanshi mine, situated near Solwezi, in North-Western Province, was the 13th largest copper mine in the world in 2015. The mine commenced production in 2004 and was expected to have a lifespan of 17 years. Following several expansions, in 2018 the mine produced 251,522 metric tons of copper and a by-product of 130,019 oz of gold. Also in North-Western Province, the 1,355-sq km open-pit Lumwana copper mine, acquired by Equinox Minerals Ltd of Canada and Australia, was expected to produce 172,000 tons of copper per year during the first six years of its projected 37-year life. Production began in 2009 and in 2010 totalled some 146,690 tons. In 2011 Equinox Minerals was bought by the Canadian company Barrick Gold Corporation. Output from the Lumwana mine totalled some 101,605 tons in 2018. Meanwhile, in June 2013 Mopani Copper Mines (MCM), the majority of which was owned by Glencore PLC, announced that it aimed to increase annual copper output from 120,000 tons to more than 170,000 tons over the next five years. To achieve this target, the venture was to invest US $323m. in a new shaft, while also upgrading a copper smelter, at an estimated cost of $145m. In March 2013 Anglo American resumed copper exploration in Zambia at two locations in the north-west, after an 11-year absence from the country. The firm had decided to sell KCM in 2002, prior to its eventual purchase by Vedanta Resources in 2004.

Glencore announced in March 2016 that it would invest US $1,100m. in Zambia to develop MCM's three mine shafts. Using new technology, Glencore planned to turn MCM into a 'world class' operation by 2023 and extend the longevity of the mining project by 25 years. The planned closure of two of Mopani's old mine shafts, in stages between June and October 2019, was likely to affect 600 workers and 1,500 contractors employed at the site. The COVID-19 pandemic and associated economic crisis severely affected global copper prices in early 2020, with a fall from $2.85 per lb in mid-January 2020 to a low of $2.17 per lb in mid-March. On 7 April MCM announced that it was temporarily suspending activities in Zambia, with the shutdown scheduled to take effect on the following day. The Government complained that it had not been given sufficient notice of the move, and threatened to revoke MCM's licence. MCM announced in early May that it would resume mining for 90 days, but with a view to suspending production again at the end of that period. However, a sharp recovery in the copper market subsequently began, amid a rebound in demand from China together with supply disruptions at mines in Central America, with the copper price increasing progressively to $3.52 per lb by the end of 2020. Despite Zambia's debt position, the Government in January 2021 controversially purchased a 90% stake in MCM, principally from Glencore, for $1,500m., subsequently controlling 100% of the venture. The international price of copper continued to rise to an all-time high of $4.75 per lb in early May, with the resumption of global industrial activity, moderating to $4.11 at 20 September. The high global demand for copper was expected to persist, especially due to its use in renewable energy systems. The new Government of President Hichilema in September announced its intention to repair the mining investment climate, which had deteriorated under the Lungu regime, and expand the industry, including plans to raise annual copper output to 2m. tons by 2026.

In May 2016 the High Court in London, United Kingdom, authorized the initiation of legal proceedings by 1,826 Zambian villagers against Vedanta Resources and KCM. The villagers sought damages for environmental pollution. The Court ruled that the villagers had a right to have their case heard under English law, stating that they would be unlikely to secure a fair trial in Zambia. However, lawyers for Vedanta appealed against this judgment, the hearings for which commenced in July 2017. In October London's Court of Appeal rejected Vedanta's attempt to block the case, upholding the rights of the Zambian villagers to sue the mining firm in a London court. A further appeal by Vedanta was similarly rejected by the UK's Supreme Court in April 2019.

Vedanta announced in March 2017 that it would once again increase its investment in Zambia's mining sector, after the cutbacks of the preceding years. The firm pledged to invest US $1,000m. in the KCM project and to create 7,000 new jobs, adding to the near $4,000m. that it had already reportedly invested in upgrading and expanding the project since 2004. In June 2018 Vedanta announced that it planned to double production at its Konkola copper mine to 200,000 metric tons during the year. The company also announced that it had begun feasibility studies on a $300m., 300-MW coal-fired power plant in Zambia. However, in May 2019 President Lungu announced the Government's decision to place KCM into liquidation, claiming that Vedanta was under-investing in the mine and underpaying taxes to Zambia. Vedanta denied the accusations and launched a legal challenge against the takeover. A Zambian court ruling on 1 February 2021 allowed the asset sales of KCM to proceed, after it was divided by the state-appointed liquidator into two units, KCM SmelterCo Limited and Konkola Mineral Resources Ltd. However, in September the new Minister of Mines and Minerals Development, Paul Chanda Kabuswe, strongly criticized the strategy of the previous administration, indicating the Government's intention to reduce state involvement in the mining sector.

The Canadian company First Quantum Minerals (FQM), which invested over US $3,000m. in two Zambian units in the three years to 2015, announced in August that it was poised to shed about 1,480 jobs, owing to ongoing power shortages in the country. In February 2017 Zambia's High Commissioner to South Africa, Emmanuel Mwamba, told Reuters news agency that FQM was, like Vedanta, planning to resume significant investment in its mining operations in Zambia, involving more than US $1,000m. to be spent on a new smelter and on modernizing the Kansanshi copper mine. However, FQM President Clive Newall told Reuters that any new investment in Zambia would be 'very conditional'. At that time, significant tensions existed between FQM and Zambia, as a result of a $1,400m. legal claim made by Zambia Consolidated Copper Mines-Investment Holdings (ZCCM-IH—see below) against the Canadian company in relation to alleged fraudulent loans made by Kansanshi Mining to FQM. In July 2021 FQM announced that it had suspended previous plans to sell part of its stake in its Kansanshi and Sentinel copper mines, but cited continued concerns at rising costs due to higher royalty rates following the increase in the copper price, and limited progress in talks with the Lungu Government for terms that would allow an expansion of ore processing at Kansanshi.

The main risk to the mining sector has often been the paucity of energy supply; planned growth in mining could still be hampered in the near term by production stoppages, despite significant planned investment in Zambia's generating capacity. Demand for power looks set to exceed supply over the next few years, as more households are connected to the power grid and more mining projects get under way. This is despite priority of energy supply already being granted to mining companies. In August 2017 a dispute between the authorities and FQM over higher electricity prices led to supply being reduced to mines run by the company. Power was fully restored after several days of negotiation that saw FQM agree to pay the new tariff of US $0.09 per kWh, with the firm deemed to have migrated to the new plan in January 2018.

While electricity supply is a major concern, other infrastructural issues have also impeded the mining sector. In January 2018 the ZCM complained about a new law that required companies in the sector to transport at least 30% of their freight by rail. Industry representatives claimed that the legislation, which the Government hoped would revive the railway network and lower business costs, would hamper the mining sector, given the poor state of the country's rail infrastructure.

ZCCM-IH is the government-owned operator of mines, and owns between 10% and 20% of virtually all copper mines in the country. Until mid-2015 the Government controlled 87.6% of the company, and 12.4% of the shares were traded on the Lusaka, Euronext and London stock exchanges. In June 2015 a stake in ZCCM-IH was sold to the National Pension Scheme Authority for K571m., representing the first stage of the Government's plan to reduce its stake in ZCCM-IH to 60%. This left the Government in control of 77.7% of the company.

Marble deposits in Lusaka Province and elsewhere in Zambia range from pure white to pale pink, deep salmon pink and dark green in colour, and some varieties are hard-wearing enough for use in flooring. Zambian granite tends to be dark and suitable for kitchen counters in homes. A rare blue granite has been found near Solwezi. Metorex owns a marble-processing plant in Kabwe. Lafarge Zambia, which is owned by the Lafarge Group of France, has cement plants in Chilanga and Ndola.

Petroleum exploration has been carried out since 2000, and in 2006 traces of oil were found in several locations, leading the Government to promulgate a Petroleum Act in 2007 and to offer concessions for exploration. Tenders were invited in June 2009 for 23 blocks; bidding closed in November and concessions were awarded for 11 of the 23 blocks, to eight companies: four of them being Zambian, two from the UK, one from the USA and one from Canada. A second round of bidding was opened in December, and a total of 23 blocks were again offered, comprising 12 that had not been sold in the first round plus 11 new blocks. In December 2013 Australia's Swala Energy announced that it had been awarded nine exploration blocks from a bid launched in June. In August 2017 Anglo-Irish firm Tullow Oil began exploring for oil and gas as part of the latest drive by the Zambian authorities to diversify the economy away from copper. Tullow stated that exploration activities in the north of the country would last between two and 10 years, and that production could potentially take place over 20 to 50 years. In a bid to bolster the country's refinery capacity to match future demand, in April 2018 Zambia shortlisted five bidders—Glencore Energy and Sahara Energy Resources from the UK, Global Security of the Russian Federation, China's Petroleum Technology and Development and a consortium of Beijing Huiersanji Green Chem Tech and Avic International Holding Corporation—to buy a majority stake in the Indeni oil refinery.

INDUSTRY

Manufacturing's share of GDP has changed little over the years. While developing nations typically experience an increase in the contribution of this sector to the economy over time, in Zambia there has been a slight decline, signalling the country's failure to diversify substantially beyond mineral extraction. The manufacturing sector contributed 7.7% of GDP in 2020, compared with 9.1% in 1990. Annual growth in the manufacturing sector was for many years very modest, rarely amounting to a whole percentage point.

In August 2014 it was reported that Zimbabwe-owned Green Fuel had invested US $500m. in a planned ethanol project in Zambia, with the acquisition of 30,000 ha of land for a sugar cane plantation in Luapula Province. The investment was to cover the construction of a sugar, ethanol and molasses processing plant. A partnership of the local Mahtani Group and the UK's Sunbird Group also planned to construct a $150m. ethanol plant in the same province; the plant, which was to be fuelled by cassava, was expected to produce 120m. litres of bioethanol per year.

In July 2017 President Lungu unveiled ambitious plans to build a US $548m. cement plant in the Copperbelt region. The initiative would be jointly undertaken by ZCCM-IH and SinoConst, a Chinese firm, with funding to be raised in local and international markets. Located in Ndola, the plant would produce 5,000 metric tons of cement per day and would be served by two new 20-MW coal-fired power stations. The construction phase of the project would provide 1,000 jobs, according to Lungu, who explicitly framed the initiative as a bid to diversify Zambia's copper-dependent economy.

ENERGY

More than 99% of Zambia's electricity is generated by hydro-electric installations. The Zambia Electricity Supply Corporation (ZESCO) oversees the country's power generation and distribution. Maximum generating capacity increased to 2,000 MW in 2013, which was still some 180 MW short of demand. In this context, ZESCO planned to spend US $5,000m. to increase capacity.

Major investment was planned by Zambia-registered Kalahari GeoEnergy with the aim of generating geothermal energy in the country's Southern Province. Exploratory drilling began

in August 2013. Output was expected to be in the range of 100 MW–1,000 MW. Another major initiative was undertaken by Nava Bharat Singapore Pte, which invested US $750m. in a 300-MW, coal-fired plant, also in Southern Province, at a site near Lake Kariba. Maamba Collieries Ltd, a joint venture which was owned 65% by Nava Bharat Singapore and 35% by the Zambian Government, oversaw the project and sought $550m. in debt-financing from a combination of multilateral and private lending institutions. Unit 1 of the plant (with a capacity of 150 MW) began operations in July 2016. Zambia's electricity generation rose significantly from 11.7m. MWh in 2016 to 16.2m. MWh in 2018, but declined to 15.0m. MWh in 2019.

Although rural electrification is a stated priority, many areas of rural Zambia still do not have access to mains power supply. Charcoal and fuel wood remain the main sources of energy supply for cooking and heating purposes for most people. Zambia's sole remaining colliery, at Maamba, has coal reserves of 78m. metric tons and a life span of more than 70 years.

ZESCO announced in May 2020 that it had concluded agreements worth US $548m. with the Chinese state-owned renewable energy developer Power China for the latter to install three 200-MW photovoltaic power plants, in the districts of Chibombo, Chirundu and Siavonga, and connect them to the national power network. At that stage, Zambia's installed power generation capacity stood at 2,800 MW, meaning that the new photovoltaic initiatives equated to 21.4% of existing capacity.

Power consumption in Zambia is dominated by mining companies, with the Government prioritizing their operations above all other industries, and even household consumption, resulting in frequent blackouts.

Fears over power supply took centre stage in 2015 as low water levels in Zambia's hydroelectric dams created nationwide electricity shortages. Cuts by state-owned ZESCO had already resulted in power shortages for First Quantum Minerals and Barrick Gold (see *Mining*, above), while private generator Copperbelt Energy Corpn (CEC) was in discussions with its main clients in the mining sector—the local units of Vedanta Resources and Glencore—over how it would ration electricity.

In an attempt to alleviate the electricity shortages, negotiations between CEC and the international banking group Old Mutual took place in June 2015, geared towards the latter providing US $205m. towards the construction of a new hydropower station, which would have a generating capacity of 40 MW. The Kabompo Gorge hydropower project was expected to cost more than $220m. and was scheduled for completion in 2018, although in April CEC announced that it was redesigning the hydropower station to reduce its overall cost. Zambia was forced to increase electricity imports in order to address the power crisis. The Government also increased electricity tariffs in December 2018, from an average of 6 US cents per KWh to 10.4 cents per KWh. However, following considerable public opposition, in May 2019 President Lungu ordered the Ministry of Energy to postpone any further tariff increases.

In June 2018 the authorities announced that they were carrying out a cost of service study across the electricity sector and planned to replace a flat tariff with a payment plan by the end of the year which better reflected the price of production. The shift could see power costs rise for mining firms, which at that stage paid a flat tariff of just over US $0.09 per kWh. Despite the potential for increased expenditure, the cost of service study was supported by FQM, which argued that it could help attract foreign investors into the electricity sector and bolster supplies. However, the mining company insisted that energy prices remained too high due to wastage at the state-run power firm. In a bid to help diversify its power sources away from hydroelectric power, in October 2017 the Zambian Government launched a Renewable Energy Feed-in Tariff Strategy, which aimed to generate up to 200 MW of capacity from small and medium-scale private sector projects. As part of the programme, in July 2018 the African Development Bank approved a $50m. financing framework.

TRANSPORT

Zambia's transport network is moderately developed. The road system is better than in many other countries in the region, with over 20,000 km of paved roads. In September 2017 Lungu announced that Zambia had awarded a US $1,200m. contract to Chinese firm Jiangxi Corporation to expand a vital stretch of road running to the DRC and other neighbouring countries. In a bid to bolster safety—after 2,206 road deaths in 2016—the country hired Austrian firm Kapsch TrafficCom in October 2017 to establish and operate a surveillance system to reduce the number of accidents. By 2019 the number of road deaths had declined to 1,746, according to Zambia Police; however, the figure had increased to 2,163 by 2021.

The railway system was also in significant need of repair, with much of the 2,139 km of tracks unusable. State-owned Zambia Railways announced in January 2013 that it intended to draw on US $500m. from international debt markets, as part of a funding effort designed to raise up to $1,500m. The Government announced plans in July 2014 to build five new railway lines over the next three years to help improve infrastructure and link Zambia's mining provinces to trading corridors across the continent. In 2012 China provided a $42.6m. interest-free loan and a $23.5m. grant to the Tanzania-Zambia Railway authority to support the rehabilitation of railway lines and infrastructure. The Governments of Zambia and Tanzania announced plans in August 2014 to spend $80m. on the rail link between the two countries over the coming year. In August 2017 the authorities introduced a law obliging mining companies to transport at least 30% of their freight by rail. However, the industry objected to the legislation due to concerns over capacity in the rail sector. In July 2018 a senior Tanzanian official announced that the two countries would review legislation potentially to allow private investors to operate the joint Tanzania-Zambia Railway Authority (TAZARA) line, which was constructed by China in the 1970s and comprises 1,860 km of track running from Dar es Salaam, Tanzania, to New Kapiri Mposhi.

At 2011 Proflight Zambia operated domestic flights to 11 destinations. After the demise of Zambezi Airlines in 2012, in 2013 Proflight Zambia began regional services to Lilongwe, Malawi, and Dar es Salaam. Zambia Airports Corpn Ltd operates Lusaka International Airport, in addition to the Ndola, Livingstone and Mfuwe airports. Government plans to re-establish a state-owned, national airline led to the planned relaunch of Zambia Airways, which would be 45% owned by Ethiopian Airlines. The relaunch, initially scheduled for October 2018, was delayed repeatedly even before the COVID-19 pandemic wreaked unprecedented damage on the global aviation industry from early 2020. However, the new Zambia Airways finally launched commercial operations on 1 December 2021, initially on domestic routes and then on regional routes to South Africa and Zimbabwe from early 2022. Zambia's international travel restrictions imposed during the pandemic began to be eased in March 2022.

TOURISM AND SERVICES

Zimbabwe and Zambia share one of the great tourist attractions of the world in the form of the Victoria Falls, on the Zambezi river. Prior to the crisis in Zimbabwe, that country attracted a far larger share of the tourists visiting the Falls and had the more highly developed tourism infrastructure. On the Zambian side of the river, the town of Livingstone is the focus of renewed tourism development. Tourist interest in Zambia has expanded beyond Victoria Falls to the country's game parks. According to the Ministry of Tourism and the Arts, Zambia received 956,332 tourist arrivals in 2016. In a bid to boost tourism numbers further, in 2017 Zambia and Zimbabwe relaunched a single Kavango Zambezi Trans-frontier Conservation Area visa to allow tourists to visit both countries. Zambia's state budget for 2017 also allocated K15.6m. for tourism marketing. Tourist arrivals reached around 1.0m. in 2017, 1.1m. in 2018 and a record 1.3m. in 2019, when receipts from tourism amounted to an estimated US 819m. However, there were just 501,606 tourist arrivals in 2020, a decline of 60.4%.

One of Zambia's largest service industries is its telecommunications market. The telecommunications sector received a boost in August 2014, when China announced a US $280m. loan that would see Huawei erect over 800 towers and construct additional infrastructure to expand voice service reach across Zambia to almost 100% and data service to 40%, as part of a plan aimed at increasing mobile users over the next three years. In November the state-owned Zambia Telecommunications Co Ltd (ZAMTEL) announced that it expected to double its number of mobile subscribers to 5m. over the same period, after significantly increasing the number of its transmission sites under a $300 investment scheme. In June 2017 Zambia's National Assembly passed a law lifting the ceiling on the number of mobile telephone service providers in order to boost competition. The legislation introduced a new licensing framework and enabled Vodafone Zambia to become active in the mobile telephone market; in 2015 Vodafone had been granted a licence to operate in the data segment of the industry. In March 2018 the authorities chose Unitel International Holdings of the Netherlands as Zambia's fourth mobile voice service provider, after the company promised to invest over $350m. and create almost 450 jobs. Meanwhile, Vodafone announced that it too would begin offering voice service later that year after being granted a licence allowing it to expand its services. In 2020 there were 19.1m. mobile cellular telephone subscribers in Zambia, according to the International Telecommunication Union, while telephone main lines in use had fallen to 71,800.

MACROECONOMIC POLICY

According to IMF figures, the value of total merchandise exports increased to a high of US $9,029.4m. in 2018, before falling to $7,246.1m. in 2019. Imports of goods, meanwhile, increased to $8,515.5m. in 2018, before declining to $6,501.7m. in 2019, producing a visible trade surplus of $744.3m. Despite the pandemic, exports benefited from strong copper output and recovered international copper prices during the second half of 2020, rising to $8,002.9m. in that year, while imports fell further to $4,786.8m., amid decreased economic activity. Consequently, the trade surplus expanded to $3,216.0m., and the surplus on the current account widened dramatically from $140.7m. in 2019 to $2,253.8m. in 2020. The surplus on the current account was only marginally lower in 2021, at $2,351.7m., while the visible trade surplus increased to $4,730.6m. (with goods exports of $11,114.6m. and imports of $6,384.0m.). The principal export, copper, accounted for 75.8% of the total in 2021. The principal imports in that year were chemicals, machinery and electrical equipment, mineral products and mineral fuels. In 2021 Switzerland-Liechtenstein was Zambia's most significant export destination, receiving 42.1% of its exports, followed by China with 18.7%, Singapore (13.4%) and the DRC (10.0%). South Africa was Zambia's most important source of imports in that year, supplying 31.6% of all imports; it was followed by China (12.6%) and the United Arab Emirates (11.3%).

In June 2014 the IMF reported that expansionary fiscal policy, along with currency depreciation, had created large budget imbalances and that spending over-runs would require adjustments to meet the targeted budget deficit. The Government had, in April, launched a 10-year Eurobond worth US $1,000m., with a yield of 8.63%. Zambia offered a further $1,250m. of new Eurobonds in July 2015, with maturities of between 10 and 12 years. The instruments carried a coupon of 8.97%, reflecting the rising concerns about the Government's credit. Such concerns were encapsulated in the downgrading by rating agency Standard & Poor's (S&P) of Zambia's credit rating from B+ to B. The one-notch downgrade left Zambia five notches below investment grade. While giving the country something of a liquidity buffer against its intensifying fiscal difficulties, the Eurobond offering in July 2015 was not considered a success, with the market's reception of the deal understandably sceptical. The bonds were marketed below face value, trading initially at $97.26—representing an immediate price loss of $2.74—resulting in a debut yield of 9.38%, the highest dollar-denominated yield that any African issuer had ever offered. Reflecting the deep concerns about Zambia's fiscal position, the yield quickly increased by a further 29 basis points, to reach 9.67%.

Zambia's financial difficulties worsened in the second half of 2015. Ratings agency Moody's downgraded the country's long-term foreign currency sovereign debt rating in September from B1 to B2. The budget deficit widened to 8.1% of GDP in 2015 (against a target of 6.9%), a level acknowledged in March 2016 to be 'unsustainable', in the words of the Secretary to the Treasury, Fredson Yamba. One month earlier, the Minister of Finance, Alexander Chikwanda, announced that the 2016 budget deficit would be contained at approximately 3.9% of GDP, through the implementation of austerity measures. However, the holding of presidential and legislative elections in August meant that this pledge was always likely to be over-optimistic. Also in February 2016, rating agency Fitch revised its projection for Zambia's long-term 'B' foreign currency rating from stable to negative.

Despite an improvement in economic growth, Zambia again struggled to contain its fiscal deficit in 2016, failing to achieve the fiscal deficit target of 3.8% of GDP. Instead, the deficit was equivalent to 5.7% of GDP on a cash basis. This led to a total estimated debt stock of US \$7,900m. by the end of 2016, up from \$5,300m. at the end of 2014. Therefore, the cost of servicing Zambia's debt rose from 8% of domestic revenues in 2012 to 20% in 2017. Economic performance improved for a period, due largely to a continued recovery in copper prices during 2017, which allowed GDP growth to recover to 4.1%. A fall in inflation allowed the central bank (the Bank of Zambia) to cut its key rate further, by 0.50 percentage points to 9.75%, in February 2018 as it sought to prioritize economic expansion. However, the scale of Zambia's public debt—over 61% of GDP by March 2018—had by then become the major concern for the IMF, with the multilateral lender placing a US \$1,300m. loan deal on hold after stating that the country was at 'high risk of debt distress'. As investor risk aversion drove yields on Zambia's 2027 Euro-bonds to 10.0% in May 2018, and with the value of the kwacha slipping against the US dollar, the authorities announced that they were suspending all planned borrowing in a bid to reassure the IMF. However, while the fiscal deficit for 2018 was initially projected at a substantial 6.1% of GDP, central bank officials conceded in December that the deficit was actually 7.6%, as a result of ongoing spending pressures.

In May 2019 Zambia's central bank raised its benchmark lending rate from 9.75% to 10.25%—the first such increase since 2015—in an attempt to stabilize the kwacha, which had lost 13% of its value against the US dollar since the start of 2019. The Bank of Zambia increased the key rate by a further 1.25 percentage points in November 2019, to a two-and-a-half year high of 11.5%, as it continued to struggle to stem a weak currency and rising inflation, which reached 10.7% year on year in October that year. The increase went against the global trend, as much of the world was in a cycle of monetary easing, but the central bank warned that inflation would likely remain above target—the ceiling for its preferred rate band being 8%—until some time in 2021. However, the COVID-19 pandemic brought a change of priorities for Zambia, as the central bank sought to ease the pain of its beleaguered commercial sector, in common with monetary authorities around the world. It slashed its key rate by 2.25 percentage points, to 9.25%, on 20 May 2020. The key rate stood at 9.0% in September 2022.

The kwacha surged to its highest level since November 2015, after Hichilema was declared President-elect on 16 August 2021. However, Hichilema's new Government, formed in mid-September, inherited at least US \$12,700m. in external debt, according to reported official figures, of which about \$3,000m. was in the form of Eurobonds, \$3,500m. was bilateral debt, \$2,100m. was owed to multilateral lending agencies and \$2,900m. was commercial bank debt. The Government was reported to have initiated talks to restructure debt held by the Chinese Government or Chinese entities under sometimes undisclosed agreements, which was believed to account for around one-third of the total. Zambia attracted bids for more than eight times the amount of domestic currency bonds offered at an auction at the end of August, when the Bank of Zambia was reported to have raised K2,500m. (\$157m.). Nevertheless, other essential debt-restructuring with external creditors was contingent on the successful conclusion of a new loan agreement with the IMF, which the Government had pledged to secure by the end of 2021, requiring the implementation of agreed reforms. A \$1,300m. loan was finally concluded with the Fund on 31 August 2022 (see *Introduction*).

Statistical Survey

Source (unless otherwise indicated): Central Statistical Office, Nationalist Road, POB 31908, Lusaka; tel. (211) 251377; internet www.zamstats.gov.zm.

Area and Population

AREA, POPULATION AND DENSITY

Area (sq km)	752,612*
Population (census results)	
25 October 2000	9,885,591
15 October 2010	
Males	6,454,647
Females	6,638,019
Total	13,092,666
Population (official projections at mid-year)	
2020	17,885,422
2021	18,400,556
2022	18,926,743
Density (per sq km) at mid-2022	25.1

* 290,585 sq miles.

POPULATION BY AGE AND SEX
(official projections at mid-2022)

	Males	Females	Total
0–14 years	4,298,091	4,251,267	8,549,358
15–64 years	4,844,727	5,038,323	9,883,050
65 years and over	225,480	268,855	494,335
Total	9,368,298	9,558,445	18,926,743

PROVINCES
(official projections at mid-2022)

	Area	Population	Density
Central	94,394	1,829,283	19.4
Copperbelt	31,328	2,803,519	89.5
Eastern	69,106	2,174,115	31.5
Luapula	50,567	1,340,032	26.5
Lusaka	21,896	3,610,977	164.9
Northern*	147,826	2,798,101	18.9
North-Western	125,826	1,000,815	8.0
Southern	85,283	2,256,160	26.5
Western	126,386	1,113,741	8.8
Total	752,612	18,926,743	25.1

* Including 1,184,232 persons enumerated in districts that were separated into the new province of Muchinga in 2011.

PRINCIPAL TOWNS
(official projections at mid-2022)

Lusaka (capital) .	2,838,001	Kalomo	428,182
Kitwe	814,457	Petauke	423,931
Ndola	609,623	Solwezi	350,021
Chipata . . .	590,463	Choma	314,057
Lundazi	470,383	Chingola	308,617

BIRTHS AND DEATHS
(annual averages, UN estimates)

	2005–10	2010–15	2015–20
Birth rate (per 1,000)	42.4	39.8	36.3
Death rate (per 1,000)	12.2	8.3	6.6

Source: UN, *World Population Prospects: The 2019 Revision*.

2020 (estimates): Births 721,993; deaths 212,364.

Life expectancy (years at birth, estimates): 64.2 (males 61.1; females 67.2) in 2020 (Source: World Bank, World Development Indicators database).

ECONOMICALLY ACTIVE POPULATION
(population aged 15 years and over)

	2018	2019	2020
Agriculture, hunting, forestry and fishing	830,858	664,539	671,761
Mining and quarrying . . .	85,111	79,933	59,371
Manufacturing	242,779	236,858	252,075
Electricity, gas and water . . .	21,890	44,863	19,075
Construction	174,009	147,168	160,762
Wholesale and retail trade . .	690,666	836,443	780,950
Hotels and restaurants . . .	67,887	80,538	74,071
Transport, storage and communications	129,860	143,520	189,273
Financial, insurance, real estate and business services . . .	163,031	174,068	193,115
Public administration	61,023	65,393	89,876
Education	166,024	152,269	170,447
Health and social work . . .	79,073	86,590	82,809
Other community, social and personal services	134,706	138,428	141,910
Households with employed persons	92,659	131,612	98,835
Extraterritorial organizations and bodies	9,395	12,882	4,048
Total employed	2,948,971	2,995,103	2,988,379
Unemployed	380,176	428,383	477,147
Total labour force	3,329,147	3,423,486	3,465,526
Males	2,040,649	2,059,965	2,042,680
Females	1,288,498	1,363,521	1,422,846

Health and Welfare

KEY INDICATORS

Total fertility rate (children per woman, 2020)	4.5
Under-5 mortality rate (per 1,000 live births, 2020) . . .	61.4
HIV/AIDS (% of persons aged 15–49, 2020)	11.1
COVID-19: Cumulative confirmed deaths (per 100,000 persons at 31 August 2022)	20.6
COVID-19: Fully vaccinated population (% of total population at 29 August 2022)	29.3
Physicians (per 1,000 head, 2018)	0.1
Hospitals (per 100,000 head, 2013)	0.5
Domestic health expenditure (2019): US $ per head (PPP) .	77.2
Domestic health expenditure (2019): % of GDP	2.1
Domestic health expenditure (2019): public (% of total current expenditure)	40.1
Access to improved water resources (% of persons, 2020) .	65
Access to improved sanitation facilities (% of persons, 2020) .	32
Total carbon dioxide emissions ('000 metric tons, 2018) . .	7,740
Carbon dioxide emissions per head (metric tons, 2018) . .	0.4
Human Development Index (2021): ranking	154
Human Development Index (2021): value	0.565

Note: For data on COVID-19 vaccinations, 'fully vaccinated' denotes receipt of all doses specified by approved vaccination regime (Sources: Johns Hopkins University and Our World in Data). Data on health expenditure refer to current general government expenditure in each case. For more information on sources and further definitions for all indicators, see Health and Welfare Statistics: Sources and Definitions section (europaworld.com/credits).

Agriculture

PRINCIPAL CROPS
('000 metric tons)

	2018	2019	2020
Barley*	5.1	5.8	6.7
Cassava (Manioc)	4,102.3	4,036.6	3,931.9*
Coffee, green*	6.5	6.6	6.5
Groundnuts, with shell . . .	181.8	130.8	127.2
Maize	2,394.9	2,004.4	3,387.5
Millet	32.3	24.8	45.0
Onions, dry*	39.8	40.3	40.8
Potatoes	13.5	38.8	80.0
Rice, paddy	43.1	29.6	34.6
Seed cotton	88.2	72.5	41.4
Sorghum	13.1	6.7	20.0
Soybeans (Soya beans) . . .	302.7	281.4	296.9
Sugar cane*	4,630.0	4,682.0	4,827.1
Sunflower seed	47.6	34.2	50.5
Sweet potatoes	183.3	109.3	144.7
Tobacco, unmanufactured* . .	24.9	29.6	25.8
Tomatoes*	25.9	25.9	26.0
Wheat	114.5	151.9	191.6

* FAO estimate(s).

Aggregate production ('000 metric tons, may include official, semi-official or estimated data): Total cereals 2,602.9 in 2018, 2,223.1 in 2019, 3,685.5 in 2020; Total fruit (primary) 115.3 in 2018, 115.8 in 2019, 116.3 in 2020; Total oilcrops 620.3 in 2018, 518.9 in 2019, 515.9 in 2020; Total roots and tubers 4,299.1 in 2018, 4,184.7 in 2019, 4,156.6 in 2020; Total vegetables (primary) 435.5 in 2018, 434.6 in 2019, 434.8 in 2020.

Source: FAO.

LIVESTOCK
('000 head, year ending September, FAO estimates)

	2018	2019	2020
Cattle	3,714.7	3,696.0	3,740.5
Chickens	39,399	40,200	41,085
Goats	2,777.5	2,857.8	2,932.3
Pigs	1,082.8	1,062.5	1,066.4
Sheep	248.0	252.7	257.9

Source: FAO.

LIVESTOCK PRODUCTS
('000 metric tons, FAO estimates)

	2018	2019	2020
Cattle hides, fresh	23.8	26.0	27.1
Cattle meat	175.2	191.0	199.0
Cattle offals, edible	28.4	30.9	32.2
Cows' milk	384.9	385.7	389.1
Chicken meat	49.8	50.7	51.6
Game meat	40.8	40.3	40.5
Goat meat	10.6	10.8	11.0
Pig meat	28.4	28.0	29.2
Hen eggs	n.a.	65.7	66.2

Source: FAO.

Forestry

ROUNDWOOD REMOVALS
('000 cubic metres, FAO estimates unless otherwise indicated)

	2016	2017	2018
Sawlogs, veneer logs and logs for sleepers	475	1,441*	1,345*
Pulpwood	—	119*	267*
Other industrial wood	1,080	1,080	1,080
Fuel wood	23,033	23,033	23,033
Total	24,588	25,673	25,725

* Official figure.

2019–20: Figures assumed to be unchanged from 2018 (FAO estimates).

Source: FAO.

SAWNWOOD PRODUCTION
('000 cubic metres, incl. railway sleepers, FAO estimates)

	2017	2018	2019
Coniferous (softwood) . . .	145	145	145
Broadleaved (hardwood) . . .	12	25	45
Total	157	170	190

2020: Figures assumed to be unchanged from 2019 (FAO estimates).

Source: FAO.

Fishing

('000 metric tons, live weight)

	2018	2019	2020
Capture	98.5	97.5	106.8
Dagaas	9.3	6.1	11.9
Other freshwater fishes . . .	89.2	91.3	94.9
Aquaculture	29.6*	38.5*	45.7
Nile tilapia	22.8*	28.2	30.6
Three-spotted tilapia . . .	2.1*	4.7	4.3
Total catch	128.1*	135.9*	152.5

* FAO estimate.

Note: Figures exclude crocodiles, recorded by number rather than weight. The number of Nile crocodiles caught was: 8,913 in 2018; 27,519 in 2019; 22,767 in 2020.

Source: FAO.

Mining

(estimates)

	2017	2018	2019
Coal ('000 metric tons)	209	345	335
Copper ore ('000 metric tons)* .	628	677	656
Cobalt ore (metric tons)* . . .	990	835	420
Amethysts ('000 kg) . . .	749	547	1,104

* Figures refer to the metal content of the ore.

Source: US Geological Survey.

Industry

SELECTED PRODUCTS
('000 metric tons unless otherwise indicated)

	2017	2018	2019
Cement	2,210	2,751	2,480*
Copper (unwrought): smelter .	788	829	639
Copper (unwrought): refined .	431	425	262
Cobalt (refined, metric tons) . .	2,520	1,613	1,500
Electrical energy (million kWh) .	14,185	16,191	15,041

* Estimate.

Raw sugar ('000 metric tons): 359 in 2016.

Sources: US Geological Survey; UN Industrial Commodity Statistics Database; UN Energy Statistics Database.

Finance

CURRENCY AND EXCHANGE RATES

Monetary Units
100 ngwee = 1 Zambian kwacha (K).

Sterling, Dollar and Euro Equivalents (29 April 2022)
£1 sterling = 21.400 kwacha;
US $1 = 17.025 kwacha;
€1 = 17.945 kwacha;
100 Zambian kwacha = £4.67 = $5.87 = €5.57.

Average Exchange Rate (Zambian kwacha per US $)
2019   12.890
2020   18.344
2021   20.019

Note: On 23 January 2012 it was announced that the kwacha was to be rebased, with existing currency denominations divided by 1,000; the newly redenominated currency was formally introduced on 1 January 2013, and both old and new denominations circulated during a transitional period until 30 June 2013, after which the old currency ceased to be legal tender.

CENTRAL GOVERNMENT BUDGET
(K million)

Revenue	2017	2018*	2019†
Tax revenue	36,490	44,240	49,228
Non-tax revenue	6,076	8,563	10,884
Total‡	42,566	52,802	60,112

Expenditure	2017	2018*	2019†
Expense	47,842	52,569	52,756
Compensation of employees .	19,995	21,856	23,992
Goods and services	5,930	7,944	5,120
Interest payments	9,826	12,988	15,477
Subsidies	4,666	3,136	1,876
Intergovernmental transfers .	5,506	5,631	4,910
Social benefits	1,919	1,015	1,381
Net acquisition of non-financial			
assets	13,658	23,936	23,006
Total	**61,500**	**76,505**	**75,762**

* Preliminary.

† Projections.

‡ Excluding grants received (K million): 467 in 2017; 647 in 2018 (preliminary); 694 in 2019 (projection).

Source: IMF, *Zambia: 2019 Article IV Consultation—Press Release; Staff Report; and Statement by the Executive Director for Zambia* (August 2019).

2021 (K million, budget proposals): Total revenue 65,983 (Tax revenue 53,273, Non-tax revenue 12,709); Total expenditure 119,616 (General public services 57,819—Debt repayments 46,083; Defence 5,642; Public order and safety 3,079; Economic affairs 21,500; Health 9,653; Education 13,773; Social protection 4,821). Note: Revenue figures exclude domestic financing 17,430, and foreign financing and grants 36,203 (Source: Ministry of Finance, Lusaka).

2022 (K million, budget proposals): Total revenue 98,859 (Tax revenue 77,852, Non-tax revenue 21,007); Total expenditure 119,616 (General public services 86,370—Debt repayments 78,680; Defence 7,634; Public order and safety 3,493; Economic affairs 33,706; Health 13,912; Education 18,073; Social protection 6,294). Note: Revenue figures exclude domestic financing 24,459, and foreign financing and grants 49,669 (Source: Ministry of Finance, Lusaka).

INTERNATIONAL RESERVES
(excl. gold, US $ million at 31 December)

	2019	2020	2021
IMF special drawing rights . .	189.6	180.1	1,493.4
Foreign exchange	1,259.0	1,023.3	1,260.4
Total	**1,448.6**	**1,203.4**	**2,753.9**

Source: IMF, *International Financial Statistics*.

MONEY SUPPLY
(K million at 31 December)

	2019	2020	2021
Currency outside depository			
corporations	6,791.1	9,838.2	9,231.0
Transferable deposits . . .	38,261.5	61,663.1	64,150.5
Other deposits	25,847.5	32,327.5	34,244.4
Broad money	**70,900.2**	**103,828.7**	**107,625.8**

Source: IMF, *International Financial Statistics*.

COST OF LIVING
(Consumer Price Index; base: 2009 = 100)

	2019	2020	2021
Food and non-alcoholic beverages .	229.4	266.7	340.6
Clothing and footwear	232.4	251.1	287.4
Housing and utilities	244.2	290.2	343.8
All items (incl. others) . . .	**229.7**	**265.8**	**324.3**

NATIONAL ACCOUNTS
(K million at current prices)

Expenditure on the Gross Domestic Product

	2018	2019	2020
Government final consumption			
expenditure	34,971.0	53,132.1	48,875.5
Private final consumption			
expenditure	123,740.7	126,936.4	127,844.8
Changes in inventories . . .	9,716.3	10,531.6	8,058.5
Gross fixed capital formation . .	96,614.1	107,430.3	99,226.8
Total domestic expenditure .	**265,042.1**	**298,030.4**	**284,005.6**
Exports of goods and services . .	104,449.1	104,064.0	155,447.8
Less Imports of goods and services	101,624.6	102,618.3	108,089.9
Statistical discrepancy	7,307.9	972.5	859.7
GDP in purchasers' values .	**275,174.5**	**300,448.7**	**332,223.2**
GDP at constant 2015 prices .	**201,213.8**	**204,113.9**	**198,429.2**

Source: UN National Accounts Main Aggregates Database.

Gross Domestic Product by Economic Activity

	2018	2019*	2020*
Agriculture, hunting, forestry and			
fishing	9,193.9	8,595.2	9,684.0
Mining and quarrying . . .	40,942.6	42,643.2	74,246.4
Manufacturing	18,843.3	20,397.4	25,684.4
Electricity, gas and water . .	8,786.9	8,939.5	12,153.0
Construction	26,322.0	33,002.8	39,377.1
Wholesale and retail trade; repair			
of motor vehicles and			
motorcycles	59,298.0	60,418.7	57,832.5
Restaurants and hotels . . .	3,353.8	3,503.4	2,434.6
Transport and communications .	26,048.3	32,708.8	33,774.0
Financial intermediation . . .	15,430.8	21,324.2	28,714.8
Real estate, renting and business			
services	13,221.1	14,614.9	16,390.2
Public administration and defence;			
compulsory social security . .	10,133.7	12,779.5	14,100.0
Education	13,643.1	11,147.8	11,012.9
Health and social work . . .	4,407.9	5,440.5	6,055.0
Other services	3,730.5	2,118.4	938.2
Sub-total	**253,355.9**	**277,634.2**	**332,397.1**
Indirect taxes, less subsidies . .	21,818.6	22,814.5	22,012.5
GDP in purchasers' values .	**275,174.5**	**300,448.8**	**354,409.7**

* Preliminary.

BALANCE OF PAYMENTS
(US $ million)

	2019	2020	2021
Exports of goods	7,246.1	8,002.9	11,114.6
Imports of goods	−6,501.7	−4,786.8	−6,384.0
Balance on goods	**744.3**	**3,216.0**	**4,730.6**
Export of services	1,011.8	555.6	501.4
Import of services	−1,534.0	−1,049.4	−1,277.6
Balance on goods and services	**222.2**	**2,722.2**	**3,954.4**
Primary income received . . .	45.2	35.3	9.9
Primary income paid	−449.1	−546.0	−1,931.6
Balance on goods, services and			
primary income	**−181.7**	**2,211.5**	**2,032.7**
Secondary income received . .	389.1	285.2	406.0
Secondary income paid . . .	−66.6	−63.9	−87.0
Current account	**140.7**	**2,432.8**	**2,351.7**
Capital account (net)	96.6	79.8	77.1
Direct investment assets . . .	−696.2	−35.4	453.4
Direct investment liabilities . .	548.0	−172.8	−456.7
Portfolio investment assets . .	—	−38.1	−134.2
Portfolio investment liabilities .	−53.0	232.5	2,106.5
Financial derivatives and employee			
stock options (net)	83.9	−10.4	−30.1
Other investment assets . . .	−531.2	−2,940.8	−6,082.9
Other investment liabilities . .	413.4	144.5	3,223.0
Net errors and omissions . . .	−101.3	−119.1	23.5
Reserves and related items .	**−99.3**	**−426.9**	**1,531.3**

Source: IMF, *International Financial Statistics*.

External Trade

PRINCIPAL COMMODITIES
(distribution by HS, US $ million)

Imports c.i.f.	2019	2020	2021
Mineral products	1,596.8	688.7	1,081.8
Ores, slag and ash	159.6	74.8	211.4
Copper ores and concentrates .	154.0	61.0	206.0
Mineral fuels, oils, distillation			
products, etc.	1,256.6	503.9	722.7
Petroleum, crude	504.7	229.9	464.7
Petroleum, non-crude	701.5	215.9	610.4
Chemicals and related			
products	1,195.4	1,239.6	1,554.1
Pharmaceutical products . . .	205.7	270.8	362.8
Medicaments for therapeutic or			
prophylactic uses	150.1	213.6	229.9
Fertilizers	343.9	415.7	438.4
Mineral or chemical fertilisers			
containing nitrogen elements .	170.1	243.2	135.0
Miscellaneous chemical products .	228.0	250.6	298.5
Plastics, rubber, and articles			
thereof	441.2	428.0	592.7
Plastics and articles thereof . .	305.2	291.2	402.8
Textiles and textile articles .	149.5	189.9	159.2
Iron and steel; other base			
metals and articles of base			
metal	609.2	398.7	575.2
Articles of iron or steel . . .	293.0	144.5	191.5
Machinery and mechanical			
appliances; electrical			
equipment; parts thereof .	1,572.8	1,053.2	1,305.4
Machinery, appliances, nuclear			
reactors, boilers, and parts			
thereof	1,132.7	780.4	994.8
Electrical, electronic equipment .	440.1	272.8	310.5
Vehicles, aircraft, vessels and			
associated transport			
equipment	605.9	466.2	719.0
Vehicles other than railway,			
tramway	583.3	458.3	707.4
Total (incl. others)	7,226.9	5,378.3	7,111.5

Exports f.o.b.	2019	2020	2021
Prepared foodstuffs;			
beverages, spirits, vinegars;			
tobacco and articles thereof .	392.6	433.2	626.3
Mineral products	276.8	649.1	633.4
Salt; sulphur; earths and stone;			
plastering materials, lime and			
cement	233.7	257.7	303.8
Ores, slag and ash	35.5	253.9	143.4
Chemicals and related			
products	340.2	266.3	299.0
Pearls, precious or semi-			
precious stones, precious			
metals, and articles thereof .	234.1	158.1	189.0
Iron and steel; other base			
metals and articles of base			
metal	5,220.8	6,076.3	8,813.6
Copper and articles thereof . .	5,040.9	5,924.2	8,498.7
Unrefined copper and copper			
anodes for electrolytic refining	3,771.2	4,329.8	6,225.2
Refined copper and copper alloys,			
unwrought	1,132.1	1,475.3	2,167.3
Total (incl. others)	6,962.5	8,060.5	11,217.5

Source: Trade Map-Trade Competitiveness Map, International Trade Centre, marketanalysis.intracen.orgs.

PRINCIPAL TRADING PARTNERS
(US $ million)

Imports c.i.f.	2019	2020	2021
China, People's Republic . . .	1,020.0	885.9	896.3
Congo, Democratic Republic . .	231.7	71.5	315.0
Germany	112.5	73.7	93.2
India	348.0	290.4	441.7
Ireland	52.4	47.5	99.1
Japan	222.7	115.8	250.9
Malaysia	41.5	44.9	91.4
Mauritius	201.6	109.2	113.2
Mozambique	82.7	49.4	59.4
Namibia	106.1	87.0	130.4
Netherlands	56.5	68.9	62.8
South Africa	2,226.1	1,802.9	2,243.9
Tanzania	206.0	69.9	56.1
United Arab Emirates	745.5	464.9	802.4
United Kingdom	130.9	98.9	110.5
USA	185.8	121.4	214.4
Zimbabwe	62.0	63.4	80.2
Total (incl. others)	7,226.9	5,378.3	7,111.5

Exports f.o.b.	2019	2020	2021
China, People's Republic . . .	1,506.0	1,492.5	2,099.0
Congo, Democratic Republic . .	866.1	995.0	1,121.6
Hong Kong	76.5	51.6	106.8
India	55.9	39.0	98.6
Luxembourg	64.9	110.4	244.8
Malawi	99.8	108.4	125.4
Singapore	589.7	935.5	1,505.9
South Africa	298.5	203.5	288.8
Switzerland-Liechtenstein . .	2,899.6	3,589.6	4,723.5
Zimbabwe	98.3	105.7	198.6
Total (incl. others)	6,962.5	8,060.5	11,217.5

Source: Trade Map-Trade Competitiveness Map, International Trade Centre, marketanalysis.intracen.org.

Transport

CIVIL AVIATION
(traffic on scheduled services)

	2013	2014	2015
Kilometres flown (million) . .	5	5	5
Passengers carried ('000) . . .	10	9	12
Passenger-km (million) . . .	4	3	4
Total ton-km (million)	93	83	79

Source: UN, *Statistical Yearbook*.

2020 (domestic and international): Departures 777; Passengers carried 8,717; Freight carried 70m. ton-km (Source: World Bank, World Development Indicators database).

Tourism

TOURIST ARRIVALS BY NATIONALITY

	2018	2019	2020
China, People's Republic . . .	27,796	34,400	7,870
India	25,505	30,789	10,963
South Africa	94,170	92,033	28,437
Tanzania	161,990	206,771	118,708
United Kingdom	34,789	27,019	8,502
USA	41,390	39,930	39,930
Zimbabwe	340,263	424,921	184,477
Total (incl. others)	1,072,012	1,266,427	501,606

Tourism receipts (US $ million, excl. passenger transport): 653 in 2017; 742 in 2018; 819 in 2019 (provisional).
Source: World Tourism Organization.

Communications Media

	2018	2019	2020
Telephones ('000 main lines in use)	100.4	96.7	71.8
Mobile telephone subscriptions ('000)	15,470.3	17,220.6	19,104.2
Broadband subscriptions, fixed ('000)	72.2	88.9	82.3
Broadband subscriptions, mobile ('000)	9,825.7	9,121.9	10,220.0
Internet users (% of population) .	14.3	16.8	19.8

Source: International Telecommunication Union.

Education

(2017)

	Institutions	Teachers	Students
Primary	8,843	78,099	3,287,907
Secondary	1,009	28,171	851,483
Tertiary	n.a.	1,246	48,782

Source: Ministry of General Education, Lusaka.

Pupil-teacher ratio (primary education): 42.1 in 2017 (Source: Ministry of General Education, Lusaka).

Adult literacy rate (UNESCO estimates): 86.7% (males 90.6%; females 83.1%) in 2018 (Source: UNESCO Institute for Statistics).

Directory

The Constitution

The Constitution of the Republic of Zambia, which was formally adopted on 28 May 1996 (and amended on 5 January 2016), declares Zambia to be a unitary, multi-party and democratic sovereign state.

The head of state and of government is the President of the Republic, who is elected (along with a Vice-President) by popular vote at the same time as elections to the National Assembly. If no presidential candidate secures 50% of the valid votes cast, a second ballot shall be held within 37 days of the initial ballot, between the first and second placed candidates. The President's tenure of office is limited to two five-year terms.

The legislature comprises a National Assembly of a maximum of 168 members: 156 members are elected by universal adult suffrage on a first-past-the-post basis, while no more than eight are nominated by the President. In addition the Vice-President, the Speaker and the First and Second Deputy Speakers are ex officio members of the National Assembly.

The Constitution also provides for a government advisory body—the House of Chiefs—comprising five members from each of the provinces. Members of the House of Chiefs, who serve five-year terms, consider and discuss legislation relating to custom or tradition referred to it by the President, before the legislation is introduced into the National Assembly

The Supreme Court and the Constitutional Court rank equivalently. The Supreme Court is the final Court of Appeal. The Constitutional Court has the final jurisdiction in all matters relating to the interpretation of the Constitution.

The Government

HEAD OF STATE

President: HAKAINDE HICHILEMA (inaugurated 24 August 2021).
Vice-President: MUTALE NALUMANGO.

THE CABINET
(October 2022)

President: HAKAINDE HICHILEMA.
Vice-President: MUTALE NALUMANGO.
Minister of Finance and National Planning: Dr SITUMBEKO MUSOKOTWANE.
Minister of Defence: AMBROSE LWIJI LUFUMA.
Minister of Home Affairs: JACOB JACK MWIIMBU.
Minister of Foreign Affairs and International Co-operation: STANLEY KAKUBO.
Minister of Energy: PETER CHIBWE KAPALA.
Minister of Water Development and Sanitation: MIKE ELTON MPOSHA.
Minister of Health: SYLVIA TEMBO MASEBO.
Minister of Education: DOUGLAS SIAKALIMA.
Minister of Community Development and Social Services: DOREEN MWAMBA.
Minister of Labour and Social Security: BRENDA MWIKA TAMBATAMBA.
Minister of Justice: MULAMBO HAIMBE.

Minister of Lands and Natural Resources: ELIJAH MUCHIMA.
Minister of Transport and Logistics: FRANK TAYALI.
Minister of Infrastructure, Housing and Urban Development: CHARLES LUBASI MILUPI.
Minister of Technology and Science: FELIX MUTATI.
Minister of Local Government and Rural Development: GARY NKOMBO.
Minister of Tourism: RODNEY SIKUMBA.
Minister of Small and Medium Enterprises Development: ELIAS MUBANGA.
Minister of Information and Media: CHUSHI KASANDA.
Minister of the Green Economy and the Environment: COLLINS NZOVU.
Minister of Fisheries and Livestock: MAKOZO CHIKOTE.
Minister of Mines and Minerals Development: PAUL CHANDA KABUSWE.
Minister of Agriculture: MTOLO PHIRI.
Minister of Commerce, Trade and Industry: CHIPOKO MULENGA.
Minister of Youth, Sports and Arts: ELVIS NKANDU.
Minister of Central Province: CREDO NANJUWA.
Minister of Copperbelt Province: ELISHA MATAMBO.
Minister of Eastern Province: PETER PHIRI.
Minister of Luapula Province: DERRICK CHILUNDIKA.
Minister of Lusaka Province: SHEAL SHACHOLI MULYATA.
Minister of Muchinga Province: HENRY SIKAZWE.
Minister of Northern Province: LEONARD MBAO.
Minister of North-Western Province: ROBERT LIEFU.
Minister of Southern Province: CORNELIUS MWEETWA.
Minister of Western Province: KAPELWA MBANGWETA.

The Attorney-General is also a member of the Cabinet.

MINISTRIES

Office of the President: POB 30135, Lusaka 10101; tel. (211) 260211; e-mail info@sh.gov.zm; internet www.sh.gov.zm.
Office of the Vice-President: Cabinet Office, 4th Floor, Independence Ave, POB 50773, Lusaka; tel. (211) 250827; internet www.ovp.gov.zm.
Ministry of Agriculture: Mulungushi House, Independence Ave, Nationalist Rd, POB 50197, Lusaka; tel. (211) 253933; e-mail pcd@maff.gov.zm; internet www.agriculture.gov.zm.
Ministry of Commerce, Trade and Industry: New Government Complex, 8th–10th Floors, Nasser Rd, POB 31968, Lusaka 10101; tel. (211) 228301; e-mail info@mcti.gov.zm; internet www.mcti.gov.zm.
Ministry of Community Development and Social Services: Community House, Sadzu Rd, Private Bag W252, Lusaka; tel. (211) 225327; e-mail info@mcdss.gov.zm; internet www.mcdss.gov.zm.
Ministry of Defence: Independence Ave, POB RW 17X, Lusaka; tel. (211) 251211; e-mail info@mod.gov.zm; internet www.mod.gov.zm.
Ministry of Education: 89 cnr Mogadishu and Chimanga Rds, POB 50093, Lusaka 10101; tel. (211) 250855; e-mail moge.information@moge.gov.zm; internet fb.com/www.moge.gov.zm.

Ministry of Energy: Government Complex, 14th Floor, Lusaka; tel. (211) 230840; e-mail info@moe.gov.zm; internet www.moe.gov.zm.

Ministry of Finance and National Planning: Chimanga Rd, POB 50062, Lusaka; tel. (211) 253512; internet www.mofnp.gov.zm.

Ministry of Fisheries and Livestock: Mulungushi House, POB 50060, Lusaka; e-mail info@mfl.gov.zm; internet www.mfl.gov.zm.

Ministry of Foreign Affairs and International Co-operation: Charter House, Independence Ave, POB 50069, Lusaka; tel. (211) 252666; e-mail pro.mfa@grz.gov.zm; internet www.mofaic.gov.zm.

Ministry of the Green Economy and the Environment: Lusaka; e-mail info@mgee.gov.zm; internet www.mgee.gov.zm.

Ministry of Health: Ndeke House, Haile Selassie Ave, POB 30205, Lusaka; tel. (211) 253040; e-mail info@moh.gov.zm; internet www.moh.gov.zm.

Ministry of Home Affairs: Independence Ave, POB 50997, Lusaka; tel. (211) 254336; e-mail info@moha.gov.zm; internet www.moha.gov.zm.

Ministry of Housing, Infrastructure and Urban Development: Stand No. 28, UN Ave, POB 50235, Ridgeway, Lusaka; tel. (211) 259342; e-mail info@mhid.gov.zm; internet fb.com/MIHUD.Zambia.

Ministry of Information and Media: New Government Complex, 5th and 6th Floors, Nassar Rd, POB 51025, Lusaka; tel. (211) 237150; e-mail info@mim.gov.zm; internet www.mim.gov.zm.

Ministry of Justice: Fairley Rd, POB 50106, Lusaka; tel. (211) 251588; e-mail info@moj.gov.zm; internet www.moj.gov.zm.

Ministry of Labour and Social Security: New Government Complex, Independence Ave, POB 32186, Lusaka; tel. (211) 221432; e-mail info@mlss.gov.zm; internet www.mlss.gov.zm.

Ministry of Lands and Natural Resources: Mulungushi House, Independence Ave, POB 50694, Lusaka; tel. (211) 252323; e-mail info@mlnr.gov.zm; internet www.mlnr.gov.zm.

Ministry of Local Government and Rural Development: cnr Pandit Nehru, POB 50027, Lusaka; tel. (211) 250528; e-mail controlling.officer@mlgrd.gov.zm; internet www.mlgrd.gov.zm.

Ministry of Mines and Minerals Development: New Government Complex, 12th and 14th Floors, Naseer Rd, POB 31969, Lusaka; tel. (211) 235329; e-mail info@mmmd.gov.zm; internet www.mmmd.gov.zm.

Ministry of Small and Medium Enterprise Development: Lusaka.

Ministry of Technology and Science: Maxwell House, Los Angeles Blvd, POB 50464, Lusaka; tel. (211) 252082; internet www.mots.gov.zm.

Ministry of Tourism: POB 30055, Lusaka; tel. (211) 223930; e-mail info@mota.gov.zm; internet www.mota.gov.zm.

Ministry of Transport and Logistics: 5199 United Nations Ave, Lusaka; tel. (211) 251444; e-mail info@mtc.gov.zm; internet www.motl.gov.zm.

Ministry of Water Development and Sanitation: Independence Ave, 4th Floor, POB 50773, Lusaka; tel. (211) 250827; e-mail info@mwds.gov.zm; internet www.mwds.gov.zm.

Ministry of Youth, Sports and Arts: New Government Complex, 11th Floor, Independence Ave, Kamwala, POB 50195, Lusaka; tel. (211) 224011; e-mail info@mysa.gov.zm; internet www.mysa.gov.zm.

President

Presidential Election, 12 August 2021

Candidate	Valid votes	% of valid votes
Hakainde Hichilema (UPND) . . .	2,852,348	59.02
Edgar C. Lungu (PF)	1,870,780	38.71
Harry Kalaba (DP)	25,231	0.52
Andyford M. Banda (PAC) . . .	19,937	0.41
Fred M'membe (SP)	16,644	0.34
Highvie H. Hamududu (PNUP) . .	10,480	0.22
Others*	37,343	0.77
Total	**4,832,763†**	**100.00**

* There were 10 other candidates.
† In addition, there were 126,569 invalid votes.

Legislature

National Assembly: Parliament Rd, POB 31299, Lusaka 10101; tel. (211) 292425; e-mail info@parliament.gov.zm; internet www.parliament.gov.zm.

Speaker: NELLY BUTETE KASHUMBA MUTTI.

General Election, 12 August 2021

Party	Elective Seats*
United Party for National Development . .	82
Patriotic Front	59
Party of National Unity and Progress . . .	1
Independents	13
Total	**155†**

* According to constitutional amendments introduced in 2016, the statutory maximum membership of the National Assembly is 168; in addition to the 156 directly elected deputies, there are up to eight presidential nominees and the Vice-President, the Speaker and the First and Second Deputy Speakers are ex officio members.
† Voting in one constituency did not take place owing to the death of a candidate. The election took place in October 2021 at which the seat was won by the PF.

House of Chiefs

The House of Chiefs is an advisory body that may submit resolutions for debate by the National Assembly. There are 50 Chiefs, with five Chiefs elected in each of the 10 provinces.

Chairman: Chief CHIKWANDA.

Election Commission

Electoral Commission of Zambia (ECZ): Elections House, Haile Selassie Ave, POB 50274, Longacres, Lusaka; tel. (211) 253155; e-mail elections@elections.org.zm; internet www.elections.org.zm; f. 1996; independent; Chair. ESAU CHULU; Chief Electoral Officer (vacant).

Political Organizations

Alliance for Democracy and Development (ADD): Plot 6592, Nationalist Rd, opp. UTH Filter Clinic, POB 36792, Lusaka; tel. 977822902; f. 2009; Pres. CHARLES MILUPI.

Citizens Democratic Party (CDP): POB 37277, Lusaka; tel. 955600674; Pres. ROBERT MWANZA.

Democratic Party (DP): Plot C4, President Ave (N), POB 71628, Ndola; f. 1991; Pres. (vacant).

Forum for Democracy and Development (FDD): 48 Independence Ave, POB 37838, Lusaka; tel. (211) 257090; internet www.fddzambia.org.zm; f. 2001 by expelled mems of the MMD; Pres. EDITH NAWAKWI; Nat. Sec. NATHAN MULONGA.

Green Party of Zambia: 18 Chishimba Cres., POB 23202, Kitwe; tel. 955887514; e-mail secretariat@zambiagreens.org; internet fb.com/ZambiaGreens; f. 2013; Pres. and Leader PETER SINKAMBA.

Movement for Multi-party Democracy (MMD): POB 30708, Lusaka; tel. (211) 268670; internet fb.com/mmdzambia; f. 1990; Pres. NEVERS MUMBA.

National Democratic Congress (NDC): Lusaka; f. 2016; rival faction led by SABOI IMBOELA; Pres. GEORGE SICHULA.

National Restoration Party (NAREP): Plot 2386, Tuleteka Rd, off Makishi Rd, Fairview, Lusaka; tel. 966102016; internet fb.com/NAREPZambia; f. 2009; Pres. CHARLES MABOSHE; Sec.-Gen. Bishop EZRA NGULUBE.

National Revolution Party (NRP): Lusaka; Pres. COSMO MUMBA.

New Heritage Party (NHP): 53 Cedar Rd, Woodlands, Lusaka; tel. 977529250; e-mail info@newheritageparty.org; internet newheritageparty.org; f. 2001 by expelled mems of the MMD; de-registered in 2019 by founder Brig.-Gen. Godfrey Miyanda; fmrly known as Heritage Party; present name adopted in 2020 following its revival; Pres. CHISHALA KATEKA.

Party for National Unity and Progress (PNUP): Lusaka; tel. 763564782; internet fb.com/PNUP2021; f. 2017 as Party of National Unity; present name adopted in 2021; Pres. HIGHVIE H. HAMUDUDU.

Patriotic Front (PF): Farmers House, POB 320015, Lusaka; tel. 96768080; internet fb.com/patrioticfrontzambia; f. 2001 by expelled mems of the MMD; Acting Pres. GIVEN LUBINDA; Sec.-Gen. DAVIES MWILA.

People's Alliance for Change (PAC): Lusaka; e-mail info@paczambia.org; internet www.paczambia.org; Chair. and Leader ANDYFORD MAYELE BANDA.

Socialist Party (SP): internet socialistpartyzambia.com; f. 2018; Leader FRED M'MEMBE.

United National Independence Party (UNIP): POB 30302, Lusaka; tel. (211) 221197; f. 1959; sole legal party 1972–90; Pres. Rev. TREVOR MWAMBA; Sec.-Gen. MULENGA MWICHE.

United Party for National Development (UPND): 83A Provident St, POB 38032, Lusaka; tel. (211) 238625; internet upnd-zambia .org; f. 1998; incl. fmr mems of the Progressive People's Party and Zambia Democratic Party; Nat. Chair. STEPHEN KATUKA; Pres. HAKAINDE HICHILEMA.

Zambia Republican Party (ZRP): Cairo Rd, POB 37348, Lusaka; tel. 955625748; e-mail info@zrp.org.uk; internet www.zrp.org.uk; f. 2001 by merger of the Republican Party (f. 2000) and the Zambia Alliance for Progress (f. 1999); Pres. WRIGHT MUSOMA.

Diplomatic Representation

EMBASSIES AND HIGH COMMISSIONS IN ZAMBIA

Algeria: 4A/45 Warthog Rd, Kabulonga, Lusaka; e-mail alglusaka@yahoo.fr; Ambassador AHMED SAADI.

Angola: Plot 6660, Olympia Extension, Mumana Rd, POB 31595, 10101 Lusaka; tel. (211) 292277; e-mail embaixada.zambia@mirex .gov.ao; internet angolanembassy.org.zm; Ambassador AZEVEDO XAVIER FRANCISCO.

Botswana: 5201 Pandit Nehru Rd, Diplomatic Triangle, POB 31910, 10101 Lusaka; tel. (211) 250555; High Commissioner ALPHEUS MATLHAKU.

Brazil: 4 Manenekela Rd, Woodlands, POB 33737, Lusaka; tel. (211) 252171; e-mail lusaka@itamaraty.gov.br; internet www.gov.br/mre/pt-br/embaixada-lusaca; Ambassador ARTHUR HENRIQUE VILLANOVA NOGUEIRA.

Burundi: 6 United Nations Ave, Longacres, Lusaka; tel. (211) 258810; e-mail ambabulska2012@yahoo.com; Ambassador PASCAL RUHOMVYUMWORO.

China, People's Republic: Plot 7430, United Nations Ave, Longacres, POB 31975, 10101 Lusaka; tel. (211) 256144; e-mail chinaemb_zm@mfa.gov.cn; internet zm.china-embassy.gov.cn; Ambassador DU XIAOHUI.

Congo, Democratic Republic: Plot 1124, Parirenyatwa Rd, POB 31287, 10101 Lusaka; tel. (211) 235679; e-mail congodr@zamnet.zm; Ambassador KONJI MALOBA CHANTAL.

Cuba: Plot 5574 Mogoye Rd, Kalundu, POB 33132, 10101 Lusaka; tel. (211) 291308; e-mail ambassador@iconnect.zm; internet misiones.minrex.gob.cu/es/zambia; Chargé d'affaires a.i. FRANCISCO JAVIER VIAMONTES CORREA.

Czech Republic: 4 Twin Palm Rd, Kabulonga, Lusaka; tel. (211) 269878; e-mail lusaka@embassy.mzv.cz; internet www.mzv.cz/lusaka/en/kontakty.html; Ambassador PAVEL PROCHAZKA.

Egypt: Plot 5206, United Nations Ave, Longacres, POB 32428, 10101 Lusaka; tel. (211) 250229; e-mail embassy.lusaka@mfa.gov.eg; internet www.mfa.gov.eg/lusaka_emb; Ambassador (vacant).

Finland: Haile Selassie Ave, opp. Ndeke House, Longacres, POB 50819, 15101 Lusaka; tel. (211) 251234; e-mail sanomat.lus@formin .fi; internet finlandabroad.fi/web/zmb/frontpage; Ambassador PIRJO SUOMELA-CHOWDHURY.

France: 31F Leopard's Hill Close, POB 30062, 10101 Lusaka; tel. (211) 251322; e-mail lusaka@ambafrance-zm.org; internet zm .ambafrance.org; Ambassador FRANÇOIS GOLDBLATT.

Germany: Plot 5219 Haile Selassie Ave, POB 50120, 5219 Lusaka; tel. (211) 250644; e-mail info@lusaka.diplo.de; internet www.lusaka .diplo.de; Ambassador ANNE WAGNER-MITCHELL.

Ghana: 326 Independence Ave, POB RW 50515, Lusaka; tel. (211) 238128; e-mail ghcomlsk@gmail.com; internet ghanahigh commission-zambia.com; High Commissioner KHADIJA IDDRISU.

Holy See: 283 Los Angeles Blvd, POB 31445, 10101 Lusaka; tel. (211) 251033; Apostolic Nuncio Most Rev. GIANFRANCO GALLONE (Titular Archbishop of Mottola).

India: 1 Pandit Nehru Rd, Longacres, POB 32111, 10101 Lusaka; tel. (211) 253159; e-mail hc.lusaka@mea.gov.in; internet www .hcizambia.gov.in; High Commissioner ASHOK KUMAR.

Ireland: 6663 Katima Mulilo Rd, Olympia Park, POB 34923, Lusaka; tel. (211) 426900; internet www.dfa.ie/irish-embassy/zambia; Ambassador BRONAGH CARR.

Italy: Plot 5211, Embassy Park, Diplomatic Triangle, POB 50497, Lusaka; tel. (211) 250781; e-mail ambasciata.lusaka@esteri.it; internet amblusaka.esteri.it; Ambassador ANTONINO MAGGIORE.

Japan: Plot 5218, Haile Selassie Ave, POB 34190, 10101 Lusaka; tel. (211) 251555; e-mail jez@lu.mofa.go.jp; internet www.zm.emb-japan .go.jp; Ambassador RYUTA MIZUUCHI.

Kenya: 5207 United Nations Ave, POB 50298, 10101 Lusaka; tel. (211) 250722; e-mail highcommissioner@kenyamission.org.zm; internet www.kenyamission.org.zm; High Commissioner FLORA KARUGU.

Libya: Plot 4900 Los Angeles Blvd, POB 35319, Lusaka; tel. (211) 253055; e-mail libya-zambia@yahoo.com; Chargé d'affaires a.i. OMAR B. A. ABDULKARIM.

Malawi: Plot 5202 Pandit Nehru Rd, Diplomatic Triangle, Longacres, POB 50425, Lusaka; tel. (211) 265768; e-mail lusaka .malawimission@foreignaffairs.gov.mw; internet www.lusakamhc .gov.mw; High Commissioner WARREN GUNDA.

Morocco: Plot No. 20, Milima Rd, Woodlands, Lusaka; Chargé d'affaires a.i. MOHAMED KALAKHI.

Mozambique: Plot 9592, Kacha Rd, POB 34877, 10101 Lusaka; tel. (211) 220333; e-mail embamoc.zambia@gmail.com; High Commissioner MÓNICA PATRÍCIO MUSSA.

Namibia: 30B Mutende Rd, Woodlands, POB 30577, 10101 Lusaka; tel. (211) 260407; e-mail lusaka@mirco.gov.na; High Commissioner HAINDONGO SIYAVE.

Nigeria: 5203 Haile Selassie Ave, Diplomatic Triangle, Longacres, POB 32598, Lusaka; tel. (211) 253177; e-mail megnigerialusaka@yahoo.com; High Commissioner OMINIYI EZE.

Russian Federation: Plot 6407, Diplomatic Triangle, POB 32355, 10101 Lusaka; tel. (211) 252120; e-mail rusembzambia@mid.ru; internet zambia.mid.ru; Ambassador AZIM ALAUDINOVICH YARAKHMEDOV.

Rwanda: Plot 10818, Kabulonga Lake Rd, Lusaka; tel. (21) 1269320; e-mail ambalusaka@minaffet.gov.rw; internet www .rwandainzambia.gov.rw; Ambassador AMANDIN RUGIRA.

Saudi Arabia: 27BC Leopards Hill Rd, Kabulonga, POB 34411, 10101 Lusaka; tel. (211) 266861; e-mail zmemb@mofa.gov.sa; internet embassies.mofa.gov.sa/sites/Zambia; Ambassador OSAMA BIN MOHAMMED KRANCHI.

Serbia: Plot 5216 Diplomatic Triangle, Embassy Park, POB 33379, 10101 Lusaka; tel. (211) 250235; e-mail serbianemb.lusaka@gmail .com; internet lusaka.mfa.gov.rs; Chargé d'affaires a.i. VLADIMIR ODAVIĆ.

Somalia: G3/377A Kabulonga Rd, POB 34051, Lusaka; tel. (211) 263944; e-mail lusakaembassy@mfa.gov.so; internet fb.com/SomaliainZambia; Ambassador HAWA HASSAN MOHAMED.

South Africa: 26D, Cheetah Rd, Kabulonga, Private Bag W369, Lusaka; tel. (211) 260497; e-mail lusaka.admin@dirco.gov.za; internet www.dirco.gov.za/zambia; High Commissioner GEORGE NKOSINATI TWALA.

Sudan: 31 Ng'umbo Rd, Longacres, POB RW179X, 15200 Lusaka; tel. (211) 252116; e-mail sudemblsk@hotmail.com; Chargé d'affaires MOHAMED AHMED MOHAMED.

Sweden: Haile Selassie Ave, POB 50264, 10101 Lusaka; tel. (211) 426100; e-mail ambassaden.lusaka@gov.se; internet www .swedenabroad.com/lusaka; Ambassador ANNA MAJ HULTGÅRD.

Tanzania: Ujamaa House, Plot 5200, United Nations Ave, POB 31219, 10101 Lusaka; tel. (211) 253323; e-mail lusaka@nje.go.tz; internet www.zm.tzembassy.go.tz; High Commissioner Lt-Gen. MATHEW EDWARD MKINGULE.

Türkiye (Turkey): 5208 United Nations Ave, Longacres, Lusaka; tel. (211) 258341; e-mail embassy.lusaka@mfa.gov.tr; internet lusaka.be.mfa.gov.tr; Ambassador İSTEM CIRCIROĞLU.

United Kingdom: Plot 5210, Independence Ave, POB 50050, 15101 Ridgeway, Lusaka; tel. (211) 423200; e-mail lusakageneralenquiries@fco.gov.uk; internet www.gov.uk/world/zambia; High Commissioner NICHOLAS WOOLLEY.

USA: Eastern end of Kabulonga Rd, Ibex Hill, POB 320065, Lusaka; tel. (211) 357000; e-mail irclusaka@state.gov; internet zm .usembassy.gov; Ambassador MICHAEL GONZALES.

Zimbabwe: 11058 Haile Selassie Ave, Longacres, POB 33491, 10101 Lusaka; tel. (211) 254012; e-mail zimlusaka@zimfa.gov.zw; internet zimlusaka.org; Ambassador CHARITY ANGELINE CHARAMBA.

Judicial System

The judicial system of Zambia comprises superior and lower courts. The superior courts include a Supreme Court and a Constitutional Court (which rank equivalently), a Court of Appeal, and a High Court. On the other hand, the lower courts comprise Subordinate

Courts, Small Claims Courts, Local Courts and other courts as prescribed. The Supreme Court, consisting of a Chief Justice, a Deputy Chief Justice and 11 other judges (or any such number of judges as may be prescribed by an Act of Parliament), is the final court of appeal. The Constitutional Court, consisting of a President, a Deputy President and 11 other judges (or any such number of judges as may be prescribed by an Act of Parliament), has the final jurisdiction in all matters relating to the interpretation of the Constitution. The Court of Appeal is composed of a Judge President, a Deputy Judge President and 17 other judges. The High Court has unlimited and original jurisdiction in civil and criminal matters.

Supreme Court: Independence Ave, POB 50067, Ridgeway, Lusaka; tel. (211) 251330; e-mail info@judiciaryzambia.com; internet www.judiciaryzambia.com/supreme-court; Chief Justice MUMBA MALILA.

High Court: Lusaka; internet www.judiciaryzambia.com/high-court; consists of the Chief Justice and 19 other judges.

Attorney-General: MULILO DIMAS KABESHA.

Religion

CHRISTIANITY

Council of Churches in Zambia: CCZ Ecumenical Centre, Plot 377A, Bishops Rd, Kabulonga, POB 30315, Lusaka; tel. (211) 267744; e-mail info@ccz.org.zm; internet www.ccz.org.zm; f. 1914; Pres. Rev. SAUROS PHAIKA (Uniting Presbyterian Church); Gen. Sec. Rev. EMMANUEL YONA CHIKOYA; 22 mem. churches and 19 affiliate mem. orgs.

The Anglican Communion

Anglicans are adherents of the Church of the Province of Central Africa, covering Botswana, Malawi, Zambia and Zimbabwe. The Church comprises 15 dioceses, including five in Zambia.

Archbishop of the Province of Central Africa and Bishop of Northern Zambia: Most Rev. ALBERT CHAMA, POB 22137, Kitwe; tel. (212) 223264.

Bishop of Central Zambia: Rt Rev. DEREK GARY KAMUKWAMBA, POB 70172, Ndola; tel. (212) 612431.

Bishop of Eastern Zambia: Rt Rev. WILLIAM MCHOMBO, POB 510154, Chipata; tel. (216) 221294; e-mail dioeastzm@zamnet.zm.

Bishop of Luapula: Rt Rev. ROBERT MUMBI, POB 710210, Mansa, Luapula.

Bishop of Lusaka: Rt Rev. DAVID NJOVU, Bishop's Lodge, POB 30183, Lusaka; tel. (211) 254789; e-mail bishop@lusakadiocese.org.

Protestant Churches

African Methodist Episcopal Church: Carousel Bldg, Lumumba Rd, POB 36628, Lusaka; tel. 955708031; Presiding Elder Rev. PAUL KAWIMBE.

Brethren in Christ Church: POB 630115, Choma; tel. (213) 320228; e-mail biccz@zamtel.zm; internet www.bic-church.org; f. 1906; Bishop Rev. THUMA HAMUKANG'ANDU.

Evangelical Lutheran Church in Zambia: Plot No. 58, Lukanga Rd, POB 37701, 10101 Lusaka; tel. 978288979; e-mail elczaheadoffice@gmail.com; Senior Pastor Rev. ELIPHAS RUGOWO.

Reformed Church in Zambia: Plot 3695, Mwaleshi Rd, POB 38255, Lusaka; tel. (211) 295369; f. 1899; African successor to the Dutch Reformed Church mission; Synod Moderator Rev. EDWIN ZULU; Gen. Sec. Rev. ISAIAH MUNALI.

Seventh-day Adventist Church: Plot 9221, cnr Burma Rd and Independence Ave, POB 36010, Lusaka; tel. (211) 254036; e-mail church@lcsda.org; internet www.lcsda.org; f. 1905; Pastor A. MUKWAKWA.

United Church of Zambia: Nationalist Rd, off Burma Rd, POB 50122, Lusaka; tel. (211) 250641; e-mail info@uczsynod.org; internet www.uczsynod.org; f. 1965; Synod Bishop Rev. SYDNEY SICHILIMA; Gen. Sec. Rev. CHIPASHA MUSABA.

The Roman Catholic Church

Zambia comprises two archdioceses and nine dioceses.

Bishops' Conference: Catholic Secretariat, Kapingila House, Kabulonga, Lusaka; tel. (211) 262641; e-mail zec@zamnet.zm; f. 1965; Pres. Most Rev. IGNATIUS CHAMA (Archbishop of Kasama).

Archbishop of Kasama: Most Rev. IGNATIUS CHAMA, Archbishop's House, Plot 935/936 Mpika Rd, POB 410143, Kasama; tel. (214) 221248.

Archbishop of Lusaka: Most Rev. ALICK BANDA, 41 Wamulwa Rd, POB 32754, 10101 Lusaka; tel. (211) 255973.

ISLAM

Islamic Supreme Council of Zambia (ISCZ): Plot 12394, off Buluwe Rd, Woodlands Extension, Lusaka; POB 37412, Lusaka; tel. (211) 267750; e-mail islamicsupreme.c.zm@gmail.com; internet iscz.webs.com; f. 1987; Pres. BILAL KAWANDAMA.

BAHÁ'Í FAITH

National Spiritual Assembly: 1502 Ridgeway, Private Bag RW227X, Lusaka; tel. 976746655; e-mail externalaffairs@nsazambia.org; internet www.bahaizambia.org; f. 1952; Sec.-Gen. HOLDEN SAMBOKO.

The Press

DAILY NEWSPAPERS (PRINT AND ONLINE)

Daily Nation: POB 34553, Lusaka; tel. (211) 243527; e-mail dailynation@ymail.com; internet dailynationzambia.com; f. 2012; Editor-in-Chief RICHARD L. SAKALA.

The Mast: Plot 37666, off Twin Palm Rd, Ibex Hill, Lusaka; tel. (211) 264454; e-mail editorial@themastonline.com; internet fb.com/themastzambia; f. 1991; fmrly known as *The Post*; forcibly closed by the Government in June 2016; present name adopted in Nov. 2016; privately owned; Editor-in-Chief LARRY MOONZE.

Rainbow Newspaper: Stand No. 459613/3, 641 New Chilenje, POB 31765, Lusaka 10101; tel. (211) 266789; e-mail rainbownewszambia2012@gmail.com; internet rainbownewszambia.com; Editor-in-Chief DERRICK SINJELA.

The Times of Zambia: Kabelenga Ave, POB 70069, Ndola; tel. (212) 621305; e-mail advertising@times.co.zm; internet www.times.co.zm; f. 1943; English; govt-owned; Man. Dir NEBAT MBEWE.

Zambia Daily Mail: POB 31421, Longolongo Rd, Lusaka; tel. (211) 227793; e-mail adverts@daily-mail.co.zm; internet www.daily-mail.co.zm; f. 1968; English; govt-owned; Man. Editor NEBAT MBEWE.

PERIODICALS

Chipembele Magazine: Plot 4435, Kumoyo Rd, Longacres POB 30255, Lusaka; tel. (211) 251630; e-mail wecsz@microlink.zm; internet www.conservationzambia.org; f. 1953; 6 a year; publ. by Wildlife and Environmental Conservation Society of Zambia; environmental magazine for children and youth; Editor ADAM GOULDING.

Icengelo: Lusaka; tel. 979700700; e-mail icengelomag@gmail.com; internet fb.com/Icengelo; Bemba language.

Lusaka Times: Lusaka; e-mail editor@lusakatimes.com; internet www.lusakatimes.com; f. 1999 as Lusaka Information Dispatch; suspended operations in 2002; revived in 2007.

Speak Out!: POB 70244, Ndola; tel. 955761459; e-mail 4speakout1984@gmail.com; f. 1984; 6 a year; Christian; aimed at youth readership up to 35 years; Man. Editor CONSTANTIA TREPPE.

Zambia Government Gazette: POB 30136, Lusaka; tel. (211) 228724; f. 1911; weekly; English; official notices.

NEWS AGENCY

Zambia News and Information Services (ZANIS): Mass Media Complex, 2nd Floor, Alick Nkhata Rd, POB 50020, Lusaka; tel. (211) 255255; e-mail zana@zamnet.zm; internet www.zanis.com.zm; f. 2005 through merger of Zambia News Agency (ZANA) and Zambia Information Services (ZIS); Dir LOYCE SAILI.

PRESS ASSOCIATIONS

Media Institute of Southern Africa—Zambia (MISA—Zambia): Plot 3814, Martin Mwamba Rd, Olympia Park, POB 32295, Lusaka; tel. (211) 294285; e-mail info@misazambia.org.zm; internet zambia.misa.org; Chair. Fr BARNABAS SIMATENDE; Nat. Dir AUSTIN KAYANDA.

Press Association of Zambia (PAZA): Bishops Rd, Multi-Media Centre, POB 37065, Lusaka; tel. (211) 263595; f. 1983; Pres. ANDREW SAKALA.

Zambia Media Council (ZAMEC): Lusaka; f. 2012; Chair. PAUL MUSUSU.

Zambia Union of Journalists: POB 30394, Lusaka; tel. (211) 227348; e-mail zambiaunionofjournalits@gmail.com; internet fb.com/vivazuj; Pres. SAMUEL LUKHANDA; Sec.-Gen. ANGELA CHISHIMBA-NDUBA.

Publishers

African Social Research: Institute of Economic and Social Research, University of Zambia, POB 32379, Lusaka; tel. (211) 294131; Editor MUBANGA E. KASHOKI.

Bookworld Ltd: Plot 10552, off Lumumba Rd, POB 31838, Lusaka; tel. (211) 230606; e-mail info@bookworldzambia.com; internet www.bookworldzambia.com; f. 1991.

University of Zambia Press (UNZA Press): POB 32379, 10101 Lusaka; tel. (211) 292269; e-mail press@unza.zm; internet www.unza.zm/unzapress; f. 1989; academic books, papers and journals; Editor ALEX MWAMBA NG'OMA.

Zambia Educational Publishing House: Chishango Rd, POB 32708, 10101 Lusaka; tel. (211) 222324; e-mail zeph.marketing@gmail.com; internet fb.com/Zambiaeducationalpublishinghouse; f. 1967; educational and general; Man. Dir JOHN NYANYU.

GOVERNMENT PUBLISHING HOUSE

Government Printer: POB 30136, Lusaka; tel. (211) 228724; official documents and statistical bulletins.

Broadcasting and Communications

TELECOMMUNICATIONS

Airtel Zambia Ltd: Nyerere Rd, Woodlands, POB 320001, Lusaka; tel. (211) 250707; e-mail customerservice@zm.airtel.com; internet www.airtel.co.zm; f. 1998 as ZamCell Ltd; fmrly Celtel Zambia, subsequently Zain Zambia, present name adopted 2010; mobile telephone operator; Chair. MONICA MUSONDA; Man. Dir and CEO APOORVA MEHROTRA.

MTN (Zambia) Ltd: 4647 Beit Rd, Addis Ababa Roundabout, Rhodespark, POB 35464, Lusaka; tel. 966750750; e-mail mtn@mtnzambia.co.zm; internet mtnzambia.com; f. 1997 as Telecel (Zambia) Ltd; acquired by MTN Group, South Africa, in 2005; mobile telecommunications provider; CEO BART HOFKER.

Zambia Telecommunications Co Ltd (ZAMTEL): Zamtel House, POB 37000, Lusaka; tel. (211) 333152; e-mail customercare@zamtel.co.zm; internet www.zamtel.zm; f. 1994 following split from Post and Telecommunications Corpn (f. 1975); operates fixed-line network and Cell-Z mobile network; state-owned; CEO (vacant).

Regulatory Authority

Zambia Information and Communications Technology Authority (ZICTA): Plot 4909, cnr Independence Ave and United Nations Rd, POB 36871, Lusaka; tel. (211) 244424; internet www.zicta.zm; f. 1994; fmrly Zambian Communications Authority, present name adopted 2009; Dir-Gen. MILENGA CHISANGA (acting).

BROADCASTING

Zambia National Broadcasting Corpn: Mass Media Complex, Alick Nkhata Rd, POB 50015, Lusaka; tel. (211) 252005; e-mail sales2@znbc.co.zm; internet www.znbc.co.zm; f. 1988; state-owned; services in English and 7 Zambian languages; Chair. JACK KALALA; Dir-Gen. (vacant).

Radio

Breeze FM: Plot 21/22 Parirenyatwa Rd, POB 511178, Chipata; tel. (216) 221893; e-mail info@breezefmchipata.com; internet breezefmchipata.com; f. 2002; Nyanja and English; community-based commercial radio; broadcasts to the Eastern Province; signal is also received in parts of north-west Malawi and border areas of Tete Province in Mozambique; Man. Dir MIKE DAKA; Station Man. SAMUEL NDHLOVU.

Hot 87.7 FM: Plot 2658, Los Angeles Blvd, Longacres, Lusaka 10101; tel. (211) 258948; e-mail info@hot877.com; internet fb.com/HotFmZambia; commercial radio station; CEO (vacant).

Phoenix FM: 6025 Chigwilizano Rd, Northmead, Private Bag E702, Lusaka; tel. (211) 226292; e-mail info@phoenixfm.co.zm; internet www.phoenixfm.co.zm; f. 1996; commercial radio station; broadcasts sponsored programmes, incl. news bulletins, musical shows and commercials; Chair. (vacant).

Q FM: Plot 1198A, 16 Addis Ababa Dr., POB 30896, Lusaka; tel. (211) 252235; e-mail qfmmarketing@qfmzambia.com; internet qfmzambia.com; Man. Dir ASAN NYAMA.

Radio Chikaya: POB 530290, Lundazi; tel. 979137800; e-mail chikayafm.985@gmail.com; community radio station; Station Man. RABSON MUMBA.

Radio Chikuni: POB 660239, Monze; tel. (21) 3255708; e-mail chikuniradio@gmail.com; internet www.chikuniradiozm.org; Man. Dir Fr ANDREW LESNIARA.

Radio Icengelo: Plot 5282, Mwandi Cres., Riverside, POB 20694, Kitwe; tel. 968536010; e-mail radioice@radioicengelo.org; internet www.radioicengelo.org; f. 1996; run by diocese of Ndola; Station Man. LEWIS MUTACHILA.

Radio Maria Zambia: Leopards Hill Rd, Bauleni, POB 320147, Lusaka; tel. (216) 221655; e-mail coordinator.zam@radiomaria.org; internet www.radiomaria.org.zm; f. 1999; Priest Dir Fr JAMES DAKA.

Zambezi FM: Tunya Bldg, 6th Floor, Livingstone; tel. (211) 228674; internet fb.com/zambezifm94.1; f. 2006; news, talk shows and music; covers Livingstone, Kazungula, Zimba and parts of Kalomo, incl. Victoria Falls in Zimbabwe; Man. Dir SWITHIN HAANGALA; Gen. Man. ERNEST PHIRI.

Television

Muvi Television: Plot 17734, Nangwenya Rd, POB 33932, Lusaka; tel. (211) 377611; e-mail frontoffice@muvitv.com; internet fb.com/askmuvi; f. 2005; CEO STEVE NYIRENDA.

REGULATORY AUTHORITY

Independent Broadcasting Authority (IBA): cnr Thabo Mbeki Rd and Alick Nkhata Rd, Mass Media Complex, POB 32475, Lusaka; tel. (211) 250589; e-mail info@iba.org.zm; internet www.iba.org.zm; f. 2013; Chair. (vacant); Dir-Gen. JOSEPHINE MAPOMA.

Finance

BANKING

Central Bank

Bank of Zambia: Bank Sq., Cairo Rd, POB 30080, 10101 Lusaka; tel. (211) 399300; e-mail info@boz.zm; internet www.boz.zm; f. 1964; bank of issue; Gov. DENNY KALYALYA.

Commercial Banks

AB Bank Zambia Ltd: 7393 Chainda Pl., off Cairo Rd, POB 38173, Lusaka; e-mail contact@abbank.co.zm; internet www.abbank.co.zm; 51% owned by Access Microfinance Holding AG (Germany); CEO COSMIN OLTEANU.

Access Bank Zambia Ltd: Plot 683, Cairo Rd, POB 35273, Lusaka; tel. (211) 227941; internet zambia.accessbankplc.com; f. 2008; Group Chair. CALEB AMOS MULENGA; Man. Dir JOANA BANNERMAN.

Atlas Mara Zambia: Finance House, Cairo Rd, POB 37102, 10101 Lusaka; tel. (211) 233585; internet atlasmarazambia.com; f. 2016 following the acquisition of Finance Bank Zambia Ltd and consolidation with BancABC Zambia; Man. Dir JAMES KONI.

Cavmont Bank Ltd: Plot 2374, Cavmont House, Thabo Mbeki Rd, Lusaka; tel. (211) 360023; internet www.cavmont.com.zm; f. 2004 after merger between Cavmont Merchant Bank Ltd and New Capital Bank PLC; 100% owned by Cavmont Capital Holdings Zambia PLC; Chair. GUY D. Z. PHIRI; Man. Dir PETRUS VAN DER WALT.

First Alliance Bank Zambia Ltd: Plot 627, Alliance House, Cairo Rd, POB 33959, Lusaka; tel. (211) 229303; internet www.firstalliancebankzambia.com; f. 1994; Chair. SANMUKH R. PATEL; Man. Dir KULDIP PALIWAL.

First National Bank Zambia Ltd: Stand No. 22768, Acacia Office Park, cnr Thabo Mbeki and Great East Rds, POB 36187, Lusaka; tel. (211) 366800; e-mail fnb@fnbzambia.co.zm; internet www.fnbzambia.co.zm; f. 2009; Chair. RENATUS MUSHINGE; CEO BYDON LONGWE.

Zambia Industrial Commercial Bank (ZICB): Central Park, cnr of Church and Cairo Rds, Lusaka; tel. (211) 428700; e-mail info@zicb.co.zm; internet www.zicb.co.zm; f. 2018; fmrly Intermarket Banking Corporation Zambia Ltd; CEO IGNATIUS MWANZA.

Zambia National Commercial Bank PLC (ZANACO): Plot 33454, Cairo Rd, POB 33611, Lusaka; tel. (211) 228979; e-mail customerservice@zanaco.co.zm; internet www.zanaco.co.zm; f. 1969; 50.8% govt-owned; Chair. CHARITY CHANDA LUMPA; Man. Dir HENK GEZIENUS MULDER.

Foreign Banks

Absa Bank Zambia PLC (UK): Elunda Office Park, Plot 4643/4644, Private Bag E308, Addis Ababa Roundabout, Rhodespark, Lusaka; tel. (211) 366150; internet www.absa.co.zm; f. 1971fmrly Barclays Bank Zambia PLCpresent name adopted in 2019; Chair. CHISHALA KATEKA; Man. Dir MIZINGA MELU.

Bank of China (Zambia) Ltd (China): Plot 2339, Kabelenga Rd, POB 34550, Lusaka; tel. (211) 238686; internet www.bankofchina.com/zm; f. 1997; Gen. Man. WANG QI.

Citibank Zambia Ltd (USA): Stand 4646, Addis Ababa Roundabout, Lusaka; tel. (211) 444492; e-mail zambia.citidirect@citi.com;

f. 1979; Regional CEO MARTIN MUGAMBI; Man. Dir and CEO LOWANI CHIBESAKUNDA.

Ecobank Zambia: Plot 22768, Thabo Mbeki Rd, POB 30705, Lusaka; tel. (211) 250056; e-mail ecobankzm@ecobank.com; internet www.ecobank.com/zm/personal-banking/countries; f. 2009; Chair. CHILESHE KAPWEPWE; Man. Dir KOLA ADELEKE.

Indo-Zambia Bank (IZB): Plot 6907, Cairo Rd, POB 35411, Lusaka; tel. (211) 224653; e-mail izb@izb.co.zm; internet www.izb .co.zm; f. 1984; Chair. ORLEAN Y. MOYO; Man. Dir K. SHASHIDHAR.

Stanbic Bank Zambia Ltd: Plot 2375, Addis Ababa Dr., POB 31955, Lusaka; tel. (211) 370000; e-mail zambiacallcentre@stanbic .com; internet www.stanbicbank.co.zm; f. 1971; wholly owned by Standard Bank Investment Corpn; Chair. ABRAHAM MWENDA; CEO LEINA GABARAANE.

Standard Chartered Bank Zambia PLC: Standard House, Cairo Rd, POB 32238, Lusaka; tel. (211) 229242; internet www.sc.com/zm; f. 1906; 90% owned by Standard Chartered Holdings (Africa) BV, Netherlands; 10% state-owned; Chair. Dr CALEB M. FUNDANGA; CEO and Man. Dir SONNY ZULU.

Other Financial Institutions

Development Bank of Zambia: cnr Katondo and Chachaha Rds, Lusaka; tel. (211) 425501; e-mail dbzmail@dbz.co.zm; internet www .dbz.co.zm; f. 1972; Chair. Prof. PINALO CHIFWANAKENI; Man. Dir Dr SAMUEL MULENGA BWALYA.

National Savings and Credit Bank (NATSAVE): Savers House, Plot 248B, Cairo Rd, POB 30067, Lusaka; tel. (211) 226834; e-mail natsave@zamnet.zm; internet www.natsave.co.zm; f. 1972; state-owned; savings bank; Chair. GEORGE MWAMBAZI; CEO MUKWANDI CHIBESAKUNDA.

Banking Association

Bankers' Association of Zambia: Mukuba Pension House, 2nd Floor, Dedani Kimathi Rd, POB 34810, Lusaka; tel. (211) 234255; e-mail bazsecretariat@baz.co.zm; internet www.baz.org.zm; 18 mems (2017); Chair. HERMAN KASEKENDE; CEO LEONARD MWANZA.

STOCK EXCHANGE

Lusaka Securities Exchange PLC (LuSE): MAMCo House, Plot 316B, 2nd Floor, Independence Ave, POB 34523, Lusaka; tel. (211) 228537; e-mail info@luse.co.zm; internet www.luse.co.zm; f. 1994; Chair. ALFRED JACK LUNGU.

INSURANCE

Goldman Insurance Ltd: Goldman Insurance House, 3rd Floor, Great East Rd, Arcades, Lusaka; tel. 968325169; e-mail goldman@ zamnet.zm; internet www.goldman.co.zm; f. 1992; CEO MUPPALA N. RAJU.

Madison General Insurance Co Zambia Ltd (MGen): Plot 318, Independence Ave, Lusaka; tel. (211) 378700; e-mail insure@ madison.co.zm; internet www.madison.co.zm; f. 1992; general and micro-insurance; Chair. ROBIN MILLER; Man. Dir CHABALA LUMBWE.

NICO Insurance Zambia Ltd (NIZA): Plot Nos 6106 & 6107, Great East Rd, Northmead, POB 32825, Lusaka; tel. (211) 222862; e-mail info@nicoinsurance.co.zm; internet www.nicoinsurance.co.zm; f. 1997; subsidiary of NICO Group, Malawi; general insurance; Chair. VIZENGE KUMWENDA; CEO GEOFFREY CHIRWA.

Professional Insurance Corpn Zambia PLC (PICZ): Finsbury Park, Kabwe Roundabout, POB 34264, Lusaka; tel. (211) 366703; e-mail customerservice@picz.co.zm; internet www.picz.co.zm; f. 1992; Chair. I. S. WAMBULAWAE-MSONI; Man. Dir and CEO MOSES SIAME.

ZSIC Ltd: Premium House, Independence Ave, POB 30894, Lusaka; tel. (211) 229345; e-mail info@zsicgi.co.zm; internet zsicgi.co.zm; f. 1968; fmrly Zambia State Insurance Corpn Ltd; comprises ZSIC Life Co and ZSIC General Insurance; acquired by Industrial Development Corpn in March 2017; Man. Dirs CHRISTABEL BANDA (life), CHARLES NAKHOZE (general).

Association

Insurers Association of Zambia (IAZ): Finsbury Park, 3rd Floor, Kabwe Roundabout, POB 95, Lusaka; tel. 960705768; e-mail iazsecretariat@iaz.org.zm; internet www.iaz.org.zm; f. 1997; Exec. Dir Dr NKAKA MWASHIKA.

Regulatory Authority

Pensions and Insurance Authority (PIA): 4618 Lubwa Rd, off Church Rd, Rhodespark, Lusaka; tel. (211) 251401; e-mail pia@pia .org.zm; internet www.pia.org.zm; f. 2005; regulatory body for

pensions and insurance industry in Zambia; Registrar and CEO CHRISTOPHER MAPANI.

Trade and Industry

GOVERNMENT AGENCIES

Food Reserve Agency (FRA): Manda Rd Light Industrial Area, Lusaka; POB 34054, Lusaka; tel. (211) 286113; e-mail fra@fra.org .zm; internet fra.org.zm; f. 1995; Chair. KELWIN HAMBWEZYA; Exec. Dir CHOLA KAFWABULULA.

Zambezi River Authority: Kariba House, 32 Cha Cha Cha Rd POB 30233, Lusaka; tel. (211) 226950; e-mail info@zambezira.org; internet www.zambezira.org; f. 1987; jtly owned and administered by the Govts of Zambia and Zimbabwe; Chair. (Zimbabwe) Dr GLORIA S. MAGOMBO; Co-Chair. (Zambia) FRANCESCA CHISANGANO-ZYAMBO; CEO MUNYARADZI MUNODAWAFA.

Zambia Development Agency (ZDA): Privatisation House, Nasser Rd; POB 30819, Lusaka; tel. (211) 220177; e-mail info@zda.org .zm; internet www.zda.org.zm; f. 2006 by merger of the Zambia Privatization Agency, the Zambia Investment Centre, the Export Board of Zambia, the Zambia Export Processing Zones Authority and the Small Enterprises Development Board; Chair. DAVID M. MASUPA; Acting Dir-Gen. ALBERT HALWAMPA.

Zambia Environmental Management Agency (ZEMA): Plot 6975, cnr Church and Suez Rds, POB 35131, Lusaka; tel. (211) 254023; e-mail info@zema.org.zm; internet www.zema.org.zm; f. 2011 as Zambia Environmental Council; Chair. Dr Brig-Gen. (retd) DANI ELIYA BANDA; Dir-Gen. DOUTY CHIBAMBA.

Zambia Revenue Authority (ZRA): Revenue House, Kabwe Roundabout, Kalambo Rd, POB 35710, Lusaka; tel. (211) 382831; e-mail advice@zra.org.zm; internet www.zra.org.zm; f. 1994; Chair. Dr CALEB FUNDANGA; Commr-Gen. DINGANI BANDA (acting).

DEVELOPMENT ORGANIZATION

Industrial Development Corpn (Zambia) Ltd (IDC): 61 Independence Ave, Prospect Hill, POB 37232, Lusaka; tel. (211) 427000; e-mail info@idc.co.zm; internet idc.co.zm; Group CEO MATEYO C. KALUBA.

CHAMBERS OF COMMERCE

Zambia Chamber of Commerce and Industry: Great East Rd, Showgrounds, POB 30844, Lusaka; tel. (211) 252483; e-mail secretariat@zacci.co.zm; internet zambiachamber.org; f. 1933; Pres. CHABUKA KAWESHA; CEO PHIL E. DAKA.

Member chambers and associations include:

Zambia Association of Manufacturers (ZAM): Plot 6438, Mungwi Rd, Heavy Industrial Area, Lusaka; tel. (211) 253696; e-mail info@zam.co.zm; internet zam.co.zm; f. 1985; Pres. ASHU SAGAR; CEO FLORENCE MULEYA; 250 mems (2021).

Zambia Chamber of Mines (ZCM): Mpile Office Park, Cathedral Hill, 74 Independence Ave, POB 51393 RW, Lusaka; tel. (211) 258383; e-mail info@mines.org.zm; internet mines.org.zm; f. 1942 as Northern Rhodesia Chamber of Mines; replaced by the Copper Industry Service Bureau 1965; present name adopted in 2000; represents mining employers; 30 mems; Pres. Dr GODWIN BEENE; CEO SOKWANI CHILEMBO.

INDUSTRIAL AND TRADE ASSOCIATIONS

Tobacco Board of Zambia (TBZ): Plot 19288, Mungwi Rd, Industrial Area, Lusaka; tel. (211) 847714; e-mail tbz@tbz.co.zm; internet www.tbz.co.zm; f. 1964; promotes, monitors and controls tobacco production; CEO RHIDAH MUNG'OMBA.

Other associations include: the Cotton Asscn of Zambia; the Environmental Conservation Asscn of Zambia; the Kapenta Fishermen Asscn; the National Aquaculture Asscn of Zambia; the National Council for Construction; the Tobacco Asscn of Zambia; the Wildlife Producers' Asscn of Zambia; the Zambia Asscn of Manufacturers; the Zambia Coffee Growers' Asscn; the Zambia Export Growers' Asscn; and Zambian Women in Agriculture.

EMPLOYERS' ORGANIZATIONS

Zambia Federation of Employers (ZFE): Plot 6662, Mberere Rd, Olympia Park, POB 31941, Lusaka; tel. (211) 295969; e-mail zfe@ zamnet.zm; internet www.zfe.co.zm; f. 1966; Exec. Dir HARRINGTON CHIBANDA.

UTILITIES

Regulatory Authority

Energy Regulation Board (ERB): Plot 9330, off Alick Nkhata Rd, POB 37631, Lusaka; tel. (211) 258844; e-mail erb@erb.org.zm; internet www.erb.org.zm; f. 1998; Chair. REYNOLDS BOWA; Dir-Gen. YOHANE MUKABE.

Electricity and Water

Copperbelt Energy Corpn PLC (CEC): Green City, 2nd Floor, Stand No. 2374, Kelvin Siwale Rd, Lusaka; tel. (212) 244956; e-mail facebook@cecinvestor.com; internet cecinvestor.com; f. 1997 upon privatization of the power div. of Zambia Consolidated Copper Mines; privately owned co supplying power generated by ZESCO to mining cos in the Copperbelt; Chair. LONDON MWAFULILWA; Man. Dir OWEN I. SILAVWE.

Lusaka Water Supply and Sanitation Co: Stand No. 871 Katemo Rd, Rhodes Park, POB 50198, Lusaka; tel. (211) 251571; e-mail customerservice@lwsc.com.zm; internet www.lwsc.com.zm; f. 1990; Man. Dir JONATHAN KAMPATA.

ZESCO: Stand No. 6949, Old Bldg, Ground Floor, Great East Rd, POB 33304, Lusaka; tel. (211) 361111; e-mail zesco@zesco.co.zm; internet www.zesco.co.zm; f. 1970; fmrly Zambia Electricity Supply Corpn Ltd; present name adopted in 1994; state-owned; Chair. VICKSON NCUBE; Man. Dir Eng. VICTOR B. MAPANI.

MAJOR COMPANIES

The following are among the largest companies in terms either of capital investment or employment.

Afrox Zambia Ltd: Chisokone Ave, POB 70252, Ndola; tel. (212) 611801; e-mail afrox.afroxzambia@afroxzambia.com.zm; internet www.afrox-zambia.com; f. 1929 as Allen Liversidge Ltd; present name adopted in 2008; part of the Linde Group (Germany); manufacturer and supplier of industrial, medical and special gases, welding equipment accessories, and bulk gas tank and gas pipeline installations.

Alliance One Zambia Ltd: 3140 Buyantanshi Rd, Industrial Area, POB 30994, Lusaka; tel. (211) 266799; internet www.aointl.com; subsidiary of Alliance One International (USA); tobacco; Pres. ALEX STROHSCHOEN.

British American Tobacco (Zambia) PLC: Plot F10723, Chifwema Rd, off Leopards Hill Rd, POB 31062, Lusaka; tel. 965450784; internet www.bat.com; Regional Dir LUCIANO COMIN; Man. Dir SIVENASEN MOODLEY.

Chilanga Cement PLC: Farm No. 1880 Kafue Rd, POB 32639, Lusaka; tel. (211) 367415; e-mail enquiries.zambia@huaxincem.com; internet chilangacement.co.zm; f. 1949 as Chilanga Cement; privatized in 1994; name changed to Lafarge Cement Zambia PLC in 2007; adopted former name again in 2022; former subsidiary of LafargeHolcim; acquired by Huaxin Cement Co Ltd in 2021; cement plants at Chilanga and Ndola; manufacture and marketing of cement; Chair. MUNA HANTUBA; CEO and Man. Dir JIANPING CHAI.

Good Time Steel Co Ltd: Plot 33811, Mungwi Rd, Heavy Industrial Area, Lusaka; POB 309, Private Bag E10, Lusaka; tel. (211) 241437; e-mail goodtimesteel888@gmail.com; internet www.gtsteel.co.zm; mfrs of reinforcing bar; f. 2005; Gen. Man. JACKY HUANG.

Konkola Copper Mines PLC (KCM): Stand M/1408, Fern Ave, Private Bag KCM (C) 2000, Chingola; tel. (212) 350604; e-mail corporate.communications@kcm.co.zm; internet kcm.co.zm; f. 2000; 79.4% owned by Vedanta Resources, India; 20.6% by Zambia Copper Investments Ltd; acquired ZCCM mining operations in 2000; mines at Chingola (Nchanga), Chililabombwe (Konkola) and Nampundwe; smelter and refinery at Kitwe; produces around one-half of Zambia copper output; Chair. TOM ALBANESE; Acting CEO ENOCK MPONDA.

ZCCM-Investment Holdings PLC (ZCCM-IH): Stand No. 16806, Alick Nkhata Rd, Mass Media Complex Area, POB 30048, Lusaka 10101; tel. (211) 388000; e-mail corporate@zccm-ih.com.zm; internet www.zccm-ih.com.zm; f. 1982 pursuant to privatization of Consolidated Copper Mines and Roan Consolidated Mines Ltd; Chair. DOLIKA E. S. BANDA; CEO TISA REUBEN CHAMA (acting).

Lactalis Zambia: Mungwi Rd, Industrial Area, POB 34930, Lusaka; tel. (211) 286855; internet lactalis.co.za; f. 1964 as Dairy Produce Board of Zambia; fmrly Parmalat Zambia; producers of milk and mfrs of dairy products and fruit juices; Man. Dir RAKESH SHARMA.

Lamasat International Zambia Ltd: Plot 397/01, Chipwenupwenu Rd, off Kafue Rd, Makeni, Lusaka; tel. 954848450; e-mail sales@lamasat.co.zm; internet www.lamasatinternational.com; f. 2002; mfrs of pipes and fittings, water tanks, polypropylene bags, etc.; Chair. MOHAMMED AHMAD.

Metal Fabricators of Zambia Ltd (ZAMEFA): 20996 Kafue Rd, Makeni, Lusaka; tel. (211) 274300; e-mail lusaka.sales@zamefa.com; internet www.zamefa.com; f. 1968; privatized in 1996; a subsidiary of

Circuit Breaker Industries Ltd (CBI), South Africa; mfrs of copper rods, and copper and aluminium wire and cables; Man. Dir KANGWA DAVID BWALYA.

Mopani Copper Mines PLC (MCM): Nkana West, cnr Central St and 5th Ave, POB 22000, Kitwe; tel. (212) 247000; e-mail public.relations@mopani.com.zm; internet mopani.com.zm; f. 1932; copper mine, smelter and refinery at Mufulira; copper mine and cobalt plant at Nkana; Chair. HASTING MTINE; CEO CHARLES P. SAKANYA.

Nampak Zambia Plastics: Plot 8214, Mungwi Rd, Heavy Industrial Area, Lusaka; tel. (211) 242753; e-mail info@nampakzambia.com; internet www.nampak.com; f. 1963; packaging products (paper, plastic and metal); CEO ANDRÉ DE RUYTER.

Nitrogen Chemicals of Zambia Ltd (NCZ): Kafue Industrial Estates, POB 360226, Kafue; tel. (211) 312258; e-mail nitrochem@yahoo.com; f. 1967; govt-owned; production of ammonium nitrate for fertilizer and explosives, nitric acid, ammonium sulphate, sulphuric acid, methanol, compound fertilizers, and liquid carbon dioxide; Chair. CHRISTABEL BANDA; CEO WILLIAM MWALE.

NWK Agri-Services: Plot 397A, Kafue Rd, Makeni Lusaka; tel. (211) 259200; e-mail info@nwkzambia.com; internet nwkzambia.com; f. 2000 as Dunavant; present name adopted in 2013; CEO PIERRE LOMBARD.

Puma Energy Zambia PLC: Stand No. 1710 Mungwi Rd, POB 31999, Lusaka; tel. (211) 376100; e-mail zambia@pumaenergy.com; internet www.pumaenergy.com; f. 1963; privatized in 1996; fmrly BP Zambia PLC; present name adopted 2011; 75% owned by Puma Energy (Switzerland); retail and distribution of petroleum products; Man. Dir PATRICIO CHABABO.

Shoprite Zambia: Manda Hill Shopping Centre, Plot 19255, cnr Great East/Manchinchi Rds, POB 37226, Lusaka; tel. (211) 255710; internet www.shoprite.co.zm; f. 1995; wholly owned subsidiary of Shoprite Group, South Africa; supermarket retail and distribution; Gen. Man. CHARLES BOTA.

Universal Mining and Chemical Industries Ltd (UMCIL): POB 30824, Lusaka; tel. (211) 289735; e-mail sales@umcil.co.zm; internet www.umcil.co.zm; f. 1989; a subsidiary of Trade Kings Group; a major producer of steel in Zambia; Exec. Dir Dr JULIUS KAOMA.

Zambeef Products PLC: Plot 4970, Manda Rd, Industrial Area, Private Bag 17, Woodlands, Lusaka; tel. (211) 369000; internet www.zambeefplc.com; interests in arable and livestock farming and processing, feedlotting, and retail; group comprises Zamleather Ltd and Zambeef Retailing Ltd subsidiaries; Chair. MICHAEL MUNDASHI; CEO FAITH MISOZI MUKUTU.

Zambia Bata Shoe Company PLC: Marketing Dept, Mukwa Rd, Industrial Area, POB 30479, Lusaka; tel. (211) 244397; e-mail zambia.ecommerce@bata.com; internet www.bata.co.zm; f. 1937; a subsidiary of Bata Ltd; Man. Dir BENSON OKUMU.

Zambia Forestry and Forest Industries Corpn PLC (ZAFFICO): POB 71566, Dola Hill, Ndola; tel. (211) 628300; e-mail info@zaffico.co.zm; internet www.zaffico.co.zm; f. 1982; Chair. ANNE DOMA GRAY-KUNDA; Man. Dir MUNDIA MUNDIA.

Zambia Sugar PLC: Nakambala Sugar Estate, Plot 118A, Lubombo Rd, off Great North Rd, POB 270240, Mazabuka; tel. (213) 230144; e-mail corporate@zamsugar.zm; internet www.illovosugar.co.za; f. 1968; Chair. NORMAN MBAZIMA; Man. Dir OSWALD MAGWENZI.

Zambian Breweries PLC: Plot 6438, Mungwi Rd, Heavy Industrial Area, POB 35135, Lusaka; tel. (211) 244501; e-mail info.zambrew@zm.sabmiller.com; internet www.ab-inbev.com; f. 1952; opened in Lusaka 1968; privatized 1994; subsidiary of Anheuser-Busch InBev NV; brewing, bottling and distribution of beers and soft drinks; major bottler of Coca-Cola in Zambia; Exec. Dir OBED SOMALI.

CO-OPERATIVE

Zambia Co-operative Federation Ltd: Co-operative House, Plot 692, Cha Cha Cha Rd, POB 33579, Lusaka; tel. (211) 238902; e-mail zambiacooperativefederation@gmail.com; internet www.zcf.org.zm; f. 1973; agricultural marketing; supply of agricultural chemicals and implements; cargo haulage; insurance; agricultural credit; auditing and accounting; property and co-operative devt; Dir-Gen. JAMES EMMANUEL CHIRWA.

TRADE UNIONS

Zambia Congress of Trade Unions (ZCTU): National Centre, Solidarity House Pl. 9026, Buluwe Rd, Lusaka; tel. (211) 260016; e-mail zctu@microlink.zm; internet www.zctu.org; f. 1965; sole umbrella org. of trade unions in Zambia; unified with Federation of Free Trade Unions of Zambia in April 2017; Pres. CHISHIMBA NKOLE; Sec.-Gen. COSMAS MUKUKA.

Affiliated Unions

Basic Education Teachers Union of Zambia (BETUZ): Paddy House, Plot 40, Mpulungu Rd, Olympia Park, Lusaka,; tel. (211)

255362; e-mail info@betuz.org.zm; internet www.betuz.org.zm; f. 1997 as Primary Teacher's Education Union of Zambia; present name adopted in 2004; Pres. (vacant).

Civil Servants' & Allied Workers' Union of Zambia (CSAWUZ): Plot 5045A, Mumbwa Rd, POB 50160, Lusaka; tel. (211) 287106; e-mail info@csawuz.org.zm; internet www.csawuz.org.zm; f. 1975; Pres. DAVY CHIYOBE; Gen. Sec. MAKAI MAKAI.

Mineworkers' Union of Zambia (MUZ): Katilungu House, Plot 27, Obote Ave, POB 20448, Kitwe; tel. (212) 214022; f. 1967; Pres. JOSEPH CHEWE; Gen. Sec. GEORGE S. MUMBA.

Railway Workers' Union of Zambia: POB 80302, Kabwe; tel. (21) 5221685; Pres. NATHAN ZULU.

Zambia National Farmers' Union: Tiyende Pamodzi Rd, Show Grounds, POB 30395, Lusaka; tel. (211) 252649; e-mail president1@znfu.org.zm; internet www.znfu.org.zm; f. 1905; fmrly Rhodesia National Farmers Union, subsequently Commercial Farmers Bureau; present name adopted in 1992; Pres. JERVIS ZIMBA.

Zambia United Local Authorities Workers' Union (ZULAWU): Mugala House, POB 70575, Ndola; tel. (212) 615022; e-mail zauthoritiesworkersunion@yahoo.com; internet fb.com/www.zauthoritiesworkersunion.com.zm; Pres. EMMANUEL MWINSA; Gen. Sec. MACHUSHI MULENGA.

Principal Non-affiliated Union

Zambia Union of Financial Institutions and Allied Workers (ZUFIAW): Plot 6579, Chainama Rd, Olympia Park, POB 31174, Lusaka; tel. (211) 296052; e-mail mw@zufiaw.org; internet www.zufiaw.org; affiliated to the Union Network Int; f. 1961 as Rhodesian Society of Bank Officials; Pres. ALFRED CHIFOTA; Gen. Sec. KASAPO KABENDE.

Transport

RAILWAYS

There are two major railway networks: the Zambia Railways network, which traverses the country from the Copperbelt in northern Zambia and links with the National Railways of Zimbabwe to provide access to South African ports, and the Tanzania–Zambia Railway (Tazara) network, linking New Kapiri-Mposhi in Zambia with Dar es Salaam in Tanzania. In August 2010 a 27-km railway line linking Chipata with Mchinji, Malawi, was inaugurated. Construction work was expected to commence in 2021 on the first section of a railway line connecting Chingola and Benguela, Angola, via the Angolan border crossing of Jimbe; the first section (166 km in length) would link Chingola with Solvíz in North-Western Province.

Tanzania–Zambia Railway Authority (Tazara): POB T01, Mpika; Head Office: POB 2834, Dar es Salaam, Tanzania; tel. (214) 370684; e-mail info@tazarasite.com; internet tazarasite.com; f. 1975; operates passenger and freight services linking New Kapiri-Mposhi, north of Lusaka, with Dar es Salaam in Tanzania, a distance of 1,860 km, of which 891 km is in Zambia; jtly owned and administered by the Govts of Tanzania and Zambia; Chair. (Tanzania) Dr LEONARD CHAMURIHO; Co-Chair. (Zambia) Eng. MISHECK LUNGU; Man. Dir Eng. BRUNO TANDEO CHING'ANDU.

Zambia Railways Ltd (ZRL): Kafue River Ave, POB 80935, Kabwe; tel. (215) 555500; e-mail info@zrl.com.zm; internet zrl.com.zm; f. 1967; 100% state-owned; Chair. (vacant); Man. Dir CHRISTOPHER MUSONDA.

ROADS

The main arterial roads run from Beitbridge (Zimbabwe) to Tunduma (the Great North Road), through the copper mining area to Chingola and Chililabombwe (hitherto the Zaire Border Road), from Livingstone to the junction of the Kafue river and the Great North Road, and from Lusaka to the Malawi border (the Great East Road). The 300-km BotZam highway links Kazungula with Nata, in Botswana. A 1,930-km main road (the TanZam highway) links Zambia and Tanzania.

Road Development Agency: Government Rd, POB 50003, Lusaka; tel. (211) 253801; e-mail rda_hq@roads.gov.zm; internet www.rda.org.zm; f. 2002; fmrly Dept of Roads; Chair. MULCHAND Y. KUNTAWALA; CEO Eng. GRACE MUTEMBO (acting).

Road Transport and Safety Agency (RSTA): Premium House, Lusaka; e-mail info@rtsa.org.zm; internet www.rtsa.org.zm; tel.

(211) 222222; f. 2002; Chair. Dr CORNELIUS CHIPOMA; CEO GLADWELL BANDA.

CIVIL AVIATION

There are four designated international airports in Zambia, at Lusaka, Ndola, Livingstone and Mfuwe.

Civil Aviation Authority: fmr Zambia Airways Technical Base, Hangar 38/947M, Kenneth Kaunda International Airport, POB 50137, Lusaka; tel. (211) 251861; internet www.caa.co.zm; f. 2014 to replace the Department of Civil Aviation; Chair. Gen. KAYUMBA; Dir-Gen. GABRIEL LESA.

Mahogany Air: New Wing East Park Mall, 1st Floor, cnr Great East and Thabo Mbeki Rd, Lusaka; tel. 968786614; e-mail sales@mahoganyair.com; internet www.mahoganyair.com; f. 2014; domestic and air charter services; CEO JIM BELEMU.

Proflight Zambia: 13396 Kamloops Ave, Munali Roundabout, POB 30536, Lusaka; tel. (211) 252452; e-mail reservations@proflight-zambia.com; internet www.proflight-zambia.com; f. 1991; Man. Dir TONY IRWIN.

Staravia: Hangar 15D, Kenneth Kaunda International Airport, Lusaka; tel. 966750800; e-mail staravia@staravialimited.com; internet www.staraviazambia.com; air charter service within Zambia and Southern Africa; Dir WAYNE GROVE.

Zambia Airports Corpn Ltd (ZACL): Airport Rd, POB 30175, 10101 Lusaka; tel. (211) 271313; e-mail zacl@zacl.aero; internet www.zacl.co.zm; f. 1989 as National Airports Corpn Ltd; present name adopted 2014; state-owned; provides air cargo services; also responsible for development and maintenance of the country's designated international airports; Chair. (vacant); Man. Dir FUMU MONDOLOKA.

Zambia Airways: Haile Selassie Ave, POB 30272, Lusaka; internet fb.com/ZambiaAirways; f. 1964 as a subsidiary of Central African Airways; ceased operations in 1994; re-launched in 2021; Chair. BONAVENTURE MUTALE; CEO ABIY ASRAT JIRU.

Tourism

Tourism Council of Zambia: 55–56 Mulungushi International Conference Centre, POB 36561, Lusaka; tel. (211) 291788; f. 1997.

Zambia Tourism Agency: Petroda House, 1st Floor, Great East Rd, POB 30017, Lusaka; tel. (211) 229087; e-mail info@zambia.travel; internet www.zambia.travel; f. 2015; CEO FELIX CHAILA.

Defence

As assessed at November 2021, Zambia's armed forces officially numbered about 15,100 (army 13,500 and air force 1,600). Paramilitary forces numbered 1,400. There was also a reserve of 3,000. Military service is voluntary. At November 2021 a total of 960 South African troops were stationed abroad.

Defence Budget: K3,250m. in 2022.

Commander-in-Chief of the Armed Forces: HAKAINDE HICHILEMA.

Commander of the Army: Lt-Gen. DENNIS ALIBUZWI.

Commander of the Air Force: Lt-Gen. COLLINS BARRY.

Education

Primary education, which is compulsory, begins at seven years of age and lasts for seven years. Secondary education, beginning at the age of 14, lasts for a further five years, comprising a first cycle of two years and a second of three years. According to estimates by the United Nations Educational, Scientific and Cultural Organization (UNESCO), in 2016/17 85% of children (83% of boys; 87% of girls) in the relevant age group attended primary schools. There are three main public universities: the University of Zambia at Lusaka, Mulungushi University at Kabwe and the Copperbelt University at Kitwe. There are also 14 teacher training colleges. The allocation for the education sector in the budget for 2022 was K18,073.3m., equivalent to some 10.4% of total projected expenditure.

Bibliography

Adam, C., Collier, P., and Gondwe, M. (Eds). *Zambia: Building Prosperity from Resource Wealth*. Oxford, OUP, 2014.

Akashambatwa, M. *Milk in a Basket: The Political-Economic Malaise in Zambia*. Lusaka, Zambia Research Foundation, 1990.

Andersson, P., Bigsten, A., and Persson, H. *Foreign Aid, Debt and Growth in Zambia*. Uppsala, Nordiska Africainstitutet, 2001.

Banda, T., Kaaba, O., Hinfelaar, M., and Ndulo, M. (Eds). *Democracy and Electoral Politics in Zambia*. Leiden, Brill, 2020.

Carmody, B. P. *The Evolution of Education in Zambia*. Lusaka, Bookworld Publrs, 2004.

Chan, S. *Zambia and the Decline of Kaunda 1984–1998*. Lewiston, NY, Edward Mellen Press, 2000.

Ferguson, J. *Expectations of Modernity*. Berkeley, CA, University of California Press, 1999.

Fraser, A., and Larmer, M. (Eds). *Zambia, Mining, and Neoliberalism: Boom and Bust on the Globalized Copperbelt*. Basingstoke, Palgrave Macmillan, 2011.

Gewald, J-B., Hinfelaar, M., and Macola, G. (Eds). *Living the End of Empire: Politics and Society in Late Colonial Zambia*. Leiden, Brill, 2011.

Grotpeter, J. J., Siegel, B. V., and Pletcher, J. R. *Historical Dictionary of Zambia*. Lanham, MD, Scarecrow Press, 1998.

Hamalengwa, M. *Class Struggle in Zambia, 1884–1989, and the Fall of Kenneth Kaunda, 1990–1991*. Lanham, MD, University Press of America, 1992.

Hill, C. B., and McPherson, M. F. *Promoting and Sustaining Economic Reform in Zambia*. Cambridge, MA, Harvard University Press, 2003.

Ihonvbere, J. O. *Economic Crisis, Civil Society and Democratization: The Case of Zambia*. Trenton, NJ, Africa World Press, 1996.

Larmer, M. *Mineworkers in Zambia: Labour and Political Change in Post-colonial Africa*. London, Tauris Academic Studies, 2006.

Macmillan, H. *The Lusaka Years: The ANC in Exile in Zambia, 1963 to 1994*. Auckland Park, Jacana, 2013.

Macmillan, H., and Shapiro, F. *Zion in Africa—The Jews of Zambia*. London and New York, I. B. Tauris, 1999.

Makungu, K. *The State of the Media in Zambia: From the Colonial Era to December 2003*. Lusaka, Media Institute of Southern Africa, Zambian Chapter, 2004.

Meebelo, H. S. *Reaction to Colonialism: A Prelude to the Politics of Independence in Northern Zambia, 1839–1939*. International Academic Publrs, 2001.

Moore, H., and Vaughan, M. *Cutting Down Trees: Gender, Nutrition and Agricultural Change in Northern Province, Zambia, 1890–1990*. Zambia, University of Zambia Press, 1994.

Moore, R. C. *The Political Reality of Freedom of the Press in Zambia*. Lanham, MD, University Press of America, 1992.

Mutale, E. *The Management of Urban Development in Zambia*. Aldershot, Ashgate, 2004.

Mwanakatwe, J. M. *End of Kaunda Era*. Lusaka, Multimedia, 1994.

Mwanza, A. M. (Ed.). *The Structural Adjustment Programme in Zambia: Lessons from Experience*. Harare, SAPES Books, 1992.

Noyoo, N. *Social Policy and Human Development in Zambia*. London, Adonis & Abbey Publishers, 2010.

Puta-Chekwe, C. *Getting Zambia to Work*. London, Adonis & Abbey Publishers, 2011.

Rakner, L. *Trade Unions in Processes of Democratisation: A Study of Party Labour Relations in Zambia*. Bergen, Michelsen Institute, 1992.

Saasa, O., and Carlsson, J. *The Aid Relationship in Zambia: A Conflict Scenario*. Uppsala, Nordiska Afrikainstitutet, 1996.

Saasa, O., Wilson, F., and Chingambo, L. *The Zambian Economy in Post-Apartheid Southern Africa: A Critical Analysis of Policy Options*. Lusaka, IAS Consultancy Services, 1992.

Sichone, O., and Chikulo, B. *Democracy in Zambia*. Aldershot, Avebury, 1997.

ZIMBABWE

Physical and Social Geography

GEORGE KAY

The Republic of Zimbabwe, covering an area of 390,757 sq km (150,872 sq miles), is landlocked and is bounded on the north and north-west by Zambia, on the south-west by Botswana, by Mozambique on the east and on the south by South Africa. The census of August 2012 enumerated 13,061,239 persons, giving an average density of 33.4 inhabitants per sq km. According to official figures, the population was projected to have risen to 15,790,716 in 2021, giving an average density of 40.4 inhabitants per sq km.

The population of Zimbabwe has altered considerably in recent years. At mid-1980 it was estimated to include some 223,000 persons of European descent and some 37,000 Asians and Coloureds, all of them a legacy of the colonial era. However, the census of 2002 recorded the number of Europeans (whites) at just 46,743 and, according to the 2012 census, the total had declined further to 28,732 by that year (while Asians numbered 10,155 and Coloureds 17,923). The indigenous inhabitants broadly comprise two ethnic or linguistic groups, the Ndebele and the Shona. The Shona, with whom political power now rests, outnumber the Ndebele by 4:1. There are, in addition, several minor ethnic groups, such as the Tonga, Sena, Hlengwe, Venda and Sotho. There are 16 official languages, of which the most commonly spoken are English, ChiShona and SiNdebele. According to official figures, in 2017 around 84% of the population professed to be Christian (predominantly Protestant), although most people also practice, to varying degrees, elements of the indigenous religions.

From the late 20th century urban growth proceeded rapidly. The urban poor, operating within the highly competitive 'informal economy', are now a large and increasing part of the urban social structure. According to the 2012 census, the population of Harare (including suburbs) was 1,485,231 and that of Bulawayo 653,337. The population of Harare (including suburbs) was projected by the UN to be 1,557,740 at mid-2022.

Zimbabwe lies astride the high plateaux between the Zambezi and Limpopo rivers. It consists of four relief regions. The Highveld, comprising land more than 1,200 m above sea level, extends across the country from south-west to north-east; it is most extensive in the north-east. The Middleveld, land of 900 m–1,200 m above sea level, flanks the Highveld; it is most extensive in the north-west. The Lowveld, land below 900 m, occupies the Zambezi basin in the north and the more extensive Limpopo and Sabi-Lundi basins in the south and south-east. These three regions consist predominantly of gently undulating plateaux, except for the narrow belt of rugged, escarpment hills associated with faults along the Zambezi trough. The fourth physical region, the eastern highlands, is distinctive because of its mountainous character. Inyangani rises to 2,594 m and many hills exceed 1,800 m.

Temperatures vary by altitude. Monthly average temperatures range from 22°C in October and 13°C in July on the Highveld to 30°C and 20°C in the low-lying Zambezi valley. Winters are noted for a wide diurnal range; night frosts can occur on the high plateaux and can occasionally be very destructive.

Rainfall is largely restricted to the period November–March and, except on the eastern highlands, is extremely variable; in many regions it is too low for commercial crop production. Mean annual rainfall ranges from 1,400 mm on the eastern highlands, to 800 mm on the north-eastern Highveld and to less than 400 mm in the Limpopo valley. The development of water resources for economic uses is a continually pressing need which, to date, has been met by a major dam building programme. Underground water resources are limited.

Soils vary considerably. Granite occurs over more than one-half of the country and mostly gives rise to infertile sandy soils; these are, however, amenable to improvement. Kalahari sands are also extensive and provide poor soils. Soil forming processes are limited in the Lowveld and, except on basalt, soils there are generally immature. Rich, red clays and loams occur on the limited outcrops of Basement Schists, which are also among the most highly mineralized areas of Zimbabwe.

Zimbabwe possesses a wide variety of workable mineral deposits, including gold, platinum, asbestos, copper, chrome, nickel, palladium, cobalt, tin, iron ore, limestone, iron pyrites, phosphates and coal. Most mineralization occurs on the Highveld and adjacent parts of the Middleveld.

The socioeconomic difficulties of rural African society are compounded by ecological problems. While some extensive areas (notably in remote northern parts of the country) remain sparsely populated, the greater part of the communal lands suffers from overpopulation and overstocking. Deforestation, soil erosion and a deterioration of wildlife and water resources are widespread, and in some areas they have reached critical dimensions. Desertification is a real danger in the semi-arid regions of the country.

History

CHRISTOPHER SAUNDERS

The boundaries of modern Zimbabwe were demarcated after Cecil Rhodes, mine magnate and then Prime Minister of the British Cape Colony, sent whites to settle north of the Limpopo River in 1890. The mineral deposits found there proved much more limited than Rhodes had hoped, but within a decade large areas of land had been seized from the Shona and Ndebele people and occupied by white farmers, mainly from Britain and South Africa. In 1923 the small white population of Southern Rhodesia, as the territory was then known, was accorded self-government. In 1953 Southern Rhodesia was united by the British Government with Northern Rhodesia and Nyasaland (now Zambia and Malawi, respectively) in a Central African Federation, which was opposed by Africans in all three territories. The British Government eventually recognized the strength of African hostility in Northern Rhodesia and Nyasaland, and conceded independence to those territories, breaking up the federation in 1963. Whites in Southern Rhodesia viewed these developments as the outcome of British appeasement, and in 1962 voted into office the newly formed Rhodesian Front (RF), which under Prime Minister Ian Smith in November 1965 declared unilateral independence from Britain. Repressive measures preceding this had seriously weakened the black African nationalist opposition, which in 1963 had split into the Zimbabwe African People's Union (ZAPU), led by Joshua Nkomo, and the breakaway Zimbabwe African National Union (ZANU), led by Rev. Ndabaningi Sithole and subsequently Robert Mugabe. These nationalists embarked upon a 'people's war' to overthrow the Smith regime. ZAPU, based mainly in Zambia, received training and armaments from the Union of Soviet Socialist Republics (USSR).

ZANU developed strong links with the Frente de Libertação de Moçambique (FRELIMO) movement fighting the Portuguese in Mozambique, and with the People's Republic of China.

From 1976 a combined struggle was waged in the name of the Patriotic Front (PF), an uneasy alliance formed by ZAPU and ZANU. In that year Smith was pressured by South Africa to concede the principle of majority rule. Smith and the South African Government then hoped that they could arrange for a moderate black party to take over, with the white minority retaining ultimate control. Such an 'internal settlement' was put in place in early 1979, but, with the nationalists excluded from it, the war continued. All parties were then persuaded by the British Government to attend a conference at Lancaster House in London, United Kingdom, to reach an inclusive settlement. At this conference it was agreed that the UK would again take control of the country for a short period, during which an election would take place, monitored by the UK and the Commonwealth; the country would subsequently move to independence. The small white minority was given 20 of the 100 seats in the House of Assembly and the UK gave only vague assurances of a fund to assist in the redistribution of land. Mugabe was reluctant to sign the agreement, but was pressured to do so by Samora Machel of Mozambique, in whose country ZANU—PF had its military bases. Mugabe, however, correctly anticipated that his party, which had taken the lead in fighting the liberation war, would triumph in the election, held in February 1980. ZANU—PF won 57 of the 80 African seats, taking 63% of the votes, while Nkomo's ZAPU won 20 seats. On 18 April Mugabe became the first Prime Minister of independent Zimbabwe.

Mugabe initially adopted a conciliatory stance. To restore stability, he quickly stressed the need for reconciliation; disavowed rapid change towards his stated socialist goals; emphasized non-alignment in foreign affairs; and included two whites in his Cabinet. Nevertheless, the new Government was faced with formidable problems and the South African Government, which regarded Mugabe as a dangerous radical, waged a campaign of destabilization. Nkomo, who rejected Mugabe's offer of the ceremonial presidency, was soon ousted from the Cabinet, and dissident members of ZAPU's guerrilla army began to perpetrate minor acts of violence in Matabeleland. In response Mugabe used an army brigade to unleash a massive wave of terror in that province, in which perhaps 15,000 people were killed. Despite this, Nkomo was persuaded to enter into negotiations for a merger with ZANU—PF, and a unity accord was eventually signed in December 1987. Nkomo became one of two Vice-Presidents, but ZAPU was effectively subsumed by ZANU—PF. After an amnesty was proclaimed in April 1988, there was a rapid improvement in political and security conditions in Matabeleland.

By then, constitutional changes had moved Zimbabwe closer to becoming a one-party state. The reservation of 20 seats for whites in the House of Assembly and 10 seats in the Senate was abolished in September 1987, and in the following month the 80 remaining members of the Assembly elected 20 candidates, all nominated by ZANU—PF, to fill the vacant seats. Parliament also replaced the ceremonial presidency with an executive presidency incorporating the post of Prime Minister. On 31 December Mugabe was inaugurated as Zimbabwe's first executive President, the Senate was abolished, and the House of Assembly enlarged to 150 seats, some filled by presidential nominees.

As unemployment and prices rose, open public and parliamentary criticism of corrupt government officials mounted. In October 1988 a former Secretary-General of ZANU—PF, Edgar Tekere, was expelled from the party for his persistent denunciation of its leadership and policies, including the plans to introduce a one-party state. He then founded the Zimbabwe Unity Movement (ZUM). In the general election of March 1990 ZANU—PF secured 117 of the 120 elective seats, and ZUM two, while in the presidential election, Mugabe received 2.03m. votes and Tekere 413,840.

Vigorous debate followed the expiry of the remaining restrictions of the Lancaster House agreement in April 1990. Amid rising urban discontent fuelled by corruption scandals and declining real wages, the Government was increasingly preoccupied by the land issue, which it considered the key to

retaining power. A Land Acquisition Act (LAA), adopted in 1992, provided for the compulsory acquisition of land by the state. This brought the Government into conflict with the powerful, white-dominated Commercial Farmers' Union (CFU) and Western aid donors. Both groups were angered by the decision in April 1993 to designate 70 commercial white-owned farms for purchase. Many of them were productive holdings, which, it had been understood, were to be exempt from compulsory purchase. In 1994 it emerged that most of the farms acquired by compulsory purchase had been leased to prominent party figures and civil servants, and were not being used for peasant resettlement.

In the general election of April 1995 ZANU—PF received around 82% of the votes and secured 118 of the 120 elective seats (55 of them uncontested), as well as control of 30 nominated and reserved seats. In the presidential election of March 1996, Mugabe won 93% of the votes cast, although only 32% of the eligible electorate voted.

LAND INVASIONS AND ELECTION FRAUD

During 1997 and 1998 the Mugabe administration was increasingly criticized for corruption, arrogance and maladministration. In August 1997 so-called 'war veterans', many too young to have taken part in the liberation war, were awarded substantial benefits that had not been included in the budget. In October, in an attempt to revive his declining popularity, Mugabe announced that the hitherto slow pace of the national land resettlement programme would be accelerated, and white commercial farmers would not receive compensation for confiscated land. He challenged the UK, in its role as former colonial power, to take responsibility for assisting them.

Following a Southern African Development Community (SADC) summit in the Zimbabwean capital of Harare in August 1998, the Zimbabwe Government dispatched troops and arms to the Democratic Republic of the Congo (DRC) to support the regime of President Laurent-Désiré Kabila against advancing rebel forces. The action was domestically unpopular and placed Zimbabwe's financial and military resources under considerable strain. A ceasefire agreement was signed in Lusaka, Zambia, in July 1999, and troop withdrawals were scheduled to take place over the following months. However, within a few days both the rebels and the allies of the DRC were accused of violating the accord, and the Zimbabwean troops remained in the DRC in support of Kabila. This enabled the Mugabe Government to benefit economically from exploiting the DRC's natural resources, especially diamonds. In October 2002 Zimbabwean troops finally completed their withdrawal.

In October 1998 the Government embarked on discussions with a National Constitutional Assembly of opposition interests on proposed changes to the country's Constitution, but Mugabe then unilaterally appointed a commission to make recommendations. The new Constitution put to the voters in a referendum in February 2000 was essentially a ZANU—PF document, but 55% of those who took part in the poll voted to reject it (although only 26% of registered voters participated). The level of participation was highest in urban areas, where support for the Movement for Democratic Change (MDC), which had been formed in September 1999 under the leadership of Morgan Tsvangirai, was strong. Mugabe accepted the referendum result, but a state-sponsored campaign of occupations of white-owned farms began, carried out by 'war veterans', and which turned increasingly violent. In parliamentary elections in June 2000, which most international observers concluded had not been free and fair, ZANU—PF won 62 of the 120 contested seats in the House of Assembly. The MDC secured 57 seats and subsequently challenged the results in 37 constituencies, citing voter intimidation or electoral irregularities.

By mid-2001 the Government claimed to have little foreign currency, and there was a severe fuel crisis. Some 400 manufacturers were forced to close their businesses within one year. With an estimated 60% of the workforce unemployed, an estimated 80% of the population now lived below the poverty line. When the Supreme Court ruled that the fast-track land reform programme could continue only if the Government presented a clear plan of action, Mugabe chose to interpret this as an invitation to continue to pursue the policy of seizing commercial farmland, much of which was taken over by members of the ruling elite.

Violence increased significantly before the presidential election in March 2002, and land owned by white commercial farmers (12 of whom had been killed by mid-2002) continued to be seized. As many of the previously landless people who occupied the land of commercial farmers had no expertise in farming, production declined dramatically, and at least 70,000 farm workers lost their jobs as a consequence of the land reform programme. Torture and intimidation of opposition supporters was now widespread.

According to official results of the March 2002 presidential election, Mugabe won 56.2% of the votes, and Tsvangirai 42.0%. Most observer groups, including that of the Commonwealth, found that the poll was neither free nor fair, while the South African observer mission gained notoriety for declaring the election 'legitimate'. After the election another 2,900 white farmers were given a deadline by which to vacate their farms under the LAA. About one-half left their properties, but the rest remained on their farms and awaited the outcome of legal challenges to the legislation. In September the House of Assembly adopted an amendment to the LAA, which provided for the eviction of farmers within seven days of being served notice, rather than the 90-day deadline hitherto in force.

Following a new wave of demonstrations in 2003, more MDC supporters were arrested, and Tsvangirai was charged with treason for seeking to overthrow the Mugabe regime. While the MDC continued to express its willingness to enter into discussions with ZANU—PF, Mugabe insisted that it must first recognize that his re-election as President was legitimate and withdraw its legal challenge to the 2002 election. As the crisis intensified, Zimbabwe's position on the UN Human Development Index plummeted. Life expectancy, which had been 61 years in 1991, declined to 36 years in 2004, and by then an estimated 6,000 people were dying each week from AIDS-related diseases. Meanwhile, the country's economy contracted at an alarming rate. Inflation soared to over 600%, and an estimated 75% of the population were unemployed. Many industries were forced to close, and agricultural production continued to decline. Shortages of foreign currency, fuel, power, basic commodities and food became commonplace. Although the Government blamed drought and even economic sabotage by the opposition, its land redistribution policies were largely responsible for the massive decrease of 67% in cereal production since 1999. Stocks of maize held by some commercial farmers were seized, and all maize producers had to sell their grain to the state-owned Grain Marketing Board; maize meal, cooking oil, salt and sugar became increasingly scarce. In mid-2003 Mugabe announced plans to extend his land policy to the seizure of white-owned mines and industries, and to introduce legislation to force companies to offer one-fifth of their shares to local black investors. By then an estimated 500,000 Zimbabweans had left the country, mostly to settle in the UK, Botswana and South Africa, often illegally in the case of the latter.

In late 2004 internecine conflict within ZANU—PF came to a head over the appointment of a new Vice-President to fill the vacancy created by the death of Simon Muzenda. A group led by Emmerson Mnangagwa, whom many saw as the heir apparent, and Jonathan Moyo met to try to prevent the elevation of Joice Mujuru, who had been in the Cabinet since independence and was Mugabe's choice for the post. Moyo was removed from the party's politburo and the Cabinet, however, and Mujuru was appointed Vice-President.

Prior to the March 2005 parliamentary elections the Government excluded foreign observers considered unsympathetic to its cause, and delayed accrediting other observers until one month before the poll. SADC and South African observers reported a credible process that 'reflected the will of the Zimbabwean people', but the USA and the European Union (EU), among others, condemned the elections as 'phony'. Many potential voters had been turned away from the polls, and there were gross discrepancies between official figures for the numbers of voters and the results. According to official results, the MDC won 41 of the 120 contested seats (39.5% of the votes

cast), 16 fewer than in 2000, but it alleged widespread electoral fraud and filed petitions at the Electoral Court challenging the results in 13 constituencies. Nevertheless, MDC members took up their seats in the House of Assembly, and the party welcomed the election of the relatively conciliatory John Nkomo as the new Speaker. ZANU—PF won 78 of the contested seats (59.6% of the vote), but the President was able to allocate 12 seats in the House of Assembly to candidates of his choosing. Other seats were reserved for tribal chiefs, also loyal to Mugabe, and thus ZANU—PF gained the two-thirds' majority necessary to approve constitutional reforms. When Parliament convened in June 2005 the Government introduced legislation providing for the reintroduction of a second chamber. Meanwhile, it was announced that white farmers who had lost their farms during the resettlement programme would be compensated for the value of assets and improvements, but not for the land itself, which the Government maintained was the responsibility of the UK. The country's white population had declined from 200,000 in 2000 to around 25,000 at March 2005; of these, some 500 were farmers.

After the elections the economic situation deteriorated further: fuel was again in very short supply, and a devaluation of the currency did not improve matters. However, the MDC proved unable to capitalize on the ongoing crisis. Its appeal for a national strike at the time of the opening of Parliament in June 2005 was not widely observed. Mugabe continued to accuse the MDC of being in league with foreign enemies of the country, and to claim that Zimbabwe's economic problems were a result of sabotage by Western governments opposed to the seizure of white land.

In late 2005 the MDC split over the question of participating in the election of members of the new Senate. In the elections to the upper house, held in November, turnout was very low, and ZANU—PF won 43 of the 50 directly elected seats. Although most members of the MDC, led by Tsvangirai, rejected the idea of participating in the poll, a faction led by Gibson Sibanda, the party Vice-President, and Welshman Ncube, the Secretary-General, insisted on doing so. Arthur Mutambara, a scientist who had returned from exile, took over leadership of the breakaway group. Tsvangirai was able to reassert his leadership over the main body of MDC supporters, and demanded that a commission be established to investigate political and human rights abuses and corruption.

THE CRISIS DEEPENS

By 2006 commercial agricultural production had contracted by 60%–70% since the land redistribution exercise began in 2000. The commercial herd had decreased from 1.2m. cattle to 150,000, and milk production had halved. In March 2007 Tsvangirai and other leading MDC figures were savagely beaten by the police when attempting to hold a prayer rally in Harare; one MDC activist was killed in the incident. Mugabe claimed that the MDC was responsible for a spate of petrol bombings earlier in the month aimed at bringing about regime change. President Thabo Mbeki of South Africa, appointed by SADC as mediator, continued to engage in 'quiet diplomacy' to try to ensure that the harmonized presidential and parliamentary elections scheduled to be held in March 2008 were at least relatively free and fair.

Following the elections, the Zimbabwe Electoral Commission (ZEC) delayed announcing the official results, but eventually conceded that the faction of the MDC led by Tsvangirai (MDC—T) had secured 99 of the 210 seats in the House of Assembly, ZANU—PF 97 seats and the MDC faction led by Mutambara (MDC—M) 10 seats. However, no immediate announcement was made regarding the outcome of the presidential poll. Widespread irregularities were reported, and observers expressed concern that the delay in releasing official results was enabling the ruling party to manipulate ballot papers. Furthermore, no monitors from Western countries were allowed, and Zimbabweans in exile had not been permitted to vote. In early May 2008 the ZEC announced that in the presidential election Tsvangirai had secured 47.9% of the votes and Mugabe 43.2%, which meant that a second round of voting would have to be conducted. The date for a run-off was eventually set for 27 June. Tsvangirai remained outside the country, fearing for his safety if he returned, and established a number of conditions for his participation in the run-off, including the presence of international peacekeepers, election monitors, free media and an end to violence. He subsequently agreed to take part even though these conditions were not met and returned to Zimbabwe in mid-May, despite a systematic campaign of retributive violence and terror against MDC supporters by state agents and their allies.

On 22 June 2008 Tsvangirai withdrew from the run-off, citing the continued violence against his supporters. SADC later claimed that conditions did not exist for a free and fair election, and similar statements were made by a number of regional heads of state and by the Pan-African Parliament election observer mission. Despite increasing international condemnation of events in Zimbabwe and the reported killing of up to 200 MDC members, the election proceeded as scheduled and Mugabe secured 90.2% of the valid votes cast, although, according to some reports, only around 20% of the electorate voted. Mugabe was sworn in for a sixth term as President on 29 June, amid appeals for international intervention. The USA and the UK announced that they would tighten the targeted sanctions they had imposed since 2003 and promised financial aid if democracy was restored. Whereas in 2000 Zimbabwe had exported tobacco, sugar and maize, it was now the largest beneficiary of food aid in the world.

THE POWER-SHARING EXPERIMENT

Mbeki's continued mediation produced a memorandum of understanding, outlining a framework for formal talks aimed at ending the political crisis. Although Mugabe and Tsvangirai signed the memorandum on 21 July 2008, they failed to reach agreement on the composition of a government of national unity. Representatives of ZANU—PF and the two MDC factions met in South Africa later that month to begin negotiations. Talks continued regarding a power-sharing deal until, on 15 September, what was termed the Global Political Agreement (GPA) was signed by Mugabe, Tsvangirai and Mutambara, under which Mugabe would remain President with executive authority and chair a 31-member Cabinet and the National Security Council. Tsvangirai would become Prime Minister, also with executive authority, and would chair a council of ministers. The Cabinet was to comprise 15 members of ZANU—PF, 13 members of Tsvangirai's MDC faction and three members of Mutambara's faction.

The process of setting up the unity Government proved problematic, while farm invasions continued, and the MDC appeared powerless to prevent them. On 11 February 2009 Tsvangirai was inaugurated as Prime Minister, and Thokozani Khupe and Mutambara were sworn in as First and Second Deputy Prime Ministers, respectively. The original agreement, providing for a 31-member Cabinet, was amended to allow ZANU—PF and the MDC—T to share responsibility for the Ministry of Home Affairs. Eventually, 35 ministers were sworn in on 13 February, with ZANU—PF allocated a total of 17 ministers in the new Cabinet. The MDC—T had 15 representatives in the Government, most notably Tendai Biti as Minister of Finance, and the MDC—M three portfolios. Shortly before the inauguration ceremony, the designated Deputy Minister of Agriculture, Roy Bennett, of the MDC—T, was arrested and charged with treason. His detention threatened to undermine the projected image of unity within the Government, which was already viewed by many analysts with extreme suspicion.

African leaders failed to criticize Mugabe's lawless and authoritarian rule, although he had been removed as chair of the SADC organ on politics, defence and security in 2001. Zimbabwe had been suspended from the Commonwealth in March 2002, and targeted sanctions were imposed by the EU and the USA on Mugabe and other leading government figures. However, Mugabe continued to travel abroad and attend meetings with other African leaders. While continuing to insist that there was no alternative to 'quiet diplomacy', Mbeki frequently showed his partisanship to Mugabe and failed in his statements to distinguish between the principle of land redistribution and the violent means used in Zimbabwe to seize land.

Once the unity Government was in place, and the Zimbabwe dollar was replaced by the use of the US dollar and the South African rand, inflation decreased to normal levels and the shops filled with goods, but the hoped-for investment from abroad did not materialize because Mugabe continued to hold power. The exodus of Zimbabweans continued, with South Africa absorbing most of the refugees, thought to number one-quarter of Zimbabwe's population. In January 2011 Mutumbara was replaced by Ncube as leader of the MDC—M faction, but refused to resign as Second Deputy Prime Minister.

As the harassment of political opponents increased the process of consulting the people over a new constitution began. Although commissions were appointed to run elections, monitor human rights and open up the media, the MDC could do nothing to stop the political violence directed against it, as Mugabe retained control of most of the levers of state power, and his dictatorial instincts were deeply ingrained. In May 2010 the High Court had dismissed charges against Bennett, but the state subsequently appealed to the Supreme Court, and Mugabe continued to refuse to swear him in as a deputy minister. (In March 2011 the Supreme Court upheld the High Court's judgment.) The likelihood of another rigged election and increased violence seemed high, unless SADC was able to insist that its election guidelines were followed. To Mugabe's chagrin, President Zuma of South Africa, who had taken over from Mbeki as the SADC facilitator on Zimbabwe, informed a SADC summit meeting in Livingstone, Zambia, in March 2011 that a new constitution must be put in place before any election was held; this 'roadmap' was approved by the SADC heads of state when they met in Sandton, South Africa, in June.

Meanwhile, the Indigenization and Economic Empowerment Act, which was adopted in 2008, required all foreign and white-owned companies worth more than US $500,000 to cede at least 51% of their holdings to black Zimbabweans within five years. As the MDC pointed out, this not only severely discouraged any possible foreign direct investment, but led some foreign firms to sell their assets in Zimbabwe. In March 2012 the world's second largest platinum mining company, Impala, agreed to cede 51% of its Zimbabwean business, Zimplats, in accordance with government policy. In 2013 the Government announced that it would extend the indigenization process to other sectors of the economy, including banking.

In July 2012 the Constitution Committee of Parliament, comprising representatives from the three coalition parties, finally agreed on a draft Constitution, and in February 2013 Parliament finally approved the draft, ending a three-year process. The new Constitution retained stringent laws against homosexuality and the death penalty for certain murders, but it limited presidential powers in relation to the right to veto legislation and appoint provincial governors. However, a two-term limit for Presidents would not be applied retroactively. A national referendum on the new Constitution, held in March, resulted in its overwhelming endorsement. Despite continuing allegations of human rights abuses being perpetrated by the police, the EU acknowledged progress, and, in order to encourage further reforms, it removed some individuals and entities from its sanctions list. Other sanctions were to remain in place until 'peaceful, transparent and credible' elections took place. The International Monetary Fund (IMF) relaxed most of its restrictions on assistance to Zimbabwe, despite its concerns about the size of the public sector wage bill and allegations that revenues from diamonds were going to ZANU—PF.

FROM THE JULY 2013 ELECTIONS TO THE FALL OF MUGABE

In the run-up to the concurrent presidential, parliamentary and local elections, Tsvangirai repeatedly accused ZANU—PF of trying to manipulate the conduct of the polls and demanded, in vain, the implementation of all the agreed reforms, especially in the security sector and in the media, where the bias in favour of ZANU—PF was blatant. It was alleged that the electoral register included the names of several thousand dead people, and large numbers of potential voters in urban areas were unable to register. High-ranking members of the security forces continued to indicate that they would not accept an MDC victory. The MDC—T entered an electoral pact with Mugabe's former Minister of Finance, Simba Makoni, and another small party to form a 'coalition for change' supporting Tsvangirai's campaign, while the MDC—M faction led by Ncube formed a pact with ZAPU. Although the MDC could point to some successes in government, many saw the party as being tainted by power and lacking vision. Western European countries and the USA were not permitted to monitor the elections; however, former Nigerian President Olusegun Obasanjo headed an African Union (AU) team of election observers and SADC sent a large observer mission.

After Mugabe unilaterally chose 31 July 2013 as polling day, both the MDC and SADC called for a postponement of the elections until reforms had been introduced to enable a free and fair process, but the country's Constitutional Court confirmed the date. With funding for the ZEC inadequate, the necessary reforms for free and fair elections lacking, millions of Zimbabweans abroad unable to vote, and voters mindful of what had taken place in 2008, ZANU—PF was able to secure a large majority without large-scale intimidation or violence. Only after the voting had proceeded peacefully but chaotically on 31 July did Tsvangirai claim electoral malpractice. Mugabe was then declared the winner of the presidential election with 61.9% of the vote; Tsvangirai secured 34.4%. ZANU—PF won 160 seats in the House of Assembly and 30 in the Senate. The MDC—T obtained 49 seats in the House of Assembly and 21 in the Senate. Mugabe was again able to rule without recourse to a government of national unity, but although the extent of the ZANU—PF victory suggested that there was widespread support for its indigenization policy, his re-election meant that the Zimbabwe crisis continued. While Western governments expressed their grave concerns regarding the credibility of the election, SADC and South Africa were quick to accept the results, despite SADC's electoral guidelines having been violated. After Mugabe was sworn in to serve a seventh term of office in August, he announced the formation of a new, 26-member Cabinet. There was soon widespread acceptance of the outcome of the election, which ended SADC mediation. That body elected Mugabe as its deputy chairman in August, and he was appointed to the chairmanship of the bloc in August 2014. In February of that year the EU lifted most of the restrictions that it had imposed, retaining only those on Mugabe and his wife, as well as the arms embargo; the USA retained sanctions on 113 individuals and 70 entities.

In the aftermath of the election, the struggle over the succession to Mugabe, who celebrated his 90th birthday in early 2014, intensified and led to major disputes within ZANU—PF over corruption and aspects of policy. In what was dubbed the 'salarygate' scandal, the controversial Minister of Information and Broadcasting, Jonathan Moyo, confirmed media reports that vast salaries were being paid to heads of certain parastatal bodies. Although Mugabe attacked factionalism in his party and called Moyo 'a weevil in our midst', the Government and the private sector issued a National Code of Corporate Governance that imposed maximum salaries for high earners in state enterprises and local authorities. There were many other instances of policy incoherence. On the one hand, the Government's indigenization policy was modified, with the threshold of indigenous ownership thenceforward being decided on a sector-by-sector basis; less radical nationalist language was used; and some argued that Zimbabwe should re-engage with Western countries and normalize relations with them. (In May 2014, for example, the Minister of Finance announced that 'systematic engagement with all nations' was the 'key to unlocking funding' and necessary for the country to overcome its liquidity problem, while another minister asserted that the state would no longer seize white-owned farms.) On the other hand, repression continued and in July 2014 Mugabe demanded that the few remaining white commercial farmers leave their lands.

With much of the 2013 Constitution not implemented, Zimbabwe effectively again became a de facto one-party state, with key state institutions, including the army, the police and much of the judiciary, openly aligned with ZANU—PF. There was widespread corruption and mismanagement of state resources, but the opposition was unable to capitalize on this, as it became even more demoralized and divided after

the 2013 elections. Biti, the Secretary-General of the MDC—T, convened a national council, which in April 2014 voted for the suspension of Tsvangirai and others. In response, Tsvangirai used his party's youth militia to intimidate his opponents, insisted he could be removed only at a national party congress, and expelled Biti and his allies from the MDC—T.

With the opposition in disarray, factionalism in ZANU—PF increased. In August 2014 Mugabe's wife, Grace, was nominated by the ZANU—PF Women's League to serve as its President. She began to criticize Mujuru for incompetence, disloyalty and plotting to assassinate the President, and speculation mounted in the run-up to the ZANU—PF congress in December that she fostered ambitions to succeed her husband. After the congress, President Mugabe used his executive powers to remove Mujuru from both the vice-presidency of the party and of the country, and dismissed other ministers whose loyalty he questioned. ZANU—PF declared that Mugabe would be its candidate in the 2018 presidential election. Mujuru formed a group that claimed to be the 'original' ZANU—PF and announced that she would contest the presidential election in 2018 as head of a new party, Zimbabwe People First, subsequently the National People's Party, which in April 2017 entered into an agreement with the MDC—T.

In 2016 Zimbabwe suffered a major drought, more than 90% of the population were unemployed, and the Government was unable to find the funds to pay civil servants' salaries. Government ministers began to promise reforms, including revision of the indigenization policy and compensation for white farmers ousted from their land, in an attempt to gain financial support from abroad; discussions were held with the IMF, the World Bank and the African Development Bank (AfDB) on possible bailouts, but Zimbabwe remained unable to repay its debts. Facing a severe shortage of US dollars, the Government introduced 'bond notes' to help restore liquidity in November 2016, and the issuance of more of these in July 2017 led to fears of a new era of hyperinflation.

In May 2016 a Baptist pastor in Harare, Evan Mawarire, had recorded himself lamenting the state of the nation with a Zimbabwean flag over his shoulders, and the footage was distributed around the world. His #ThisFlag social media movement—critical of the ruling party for failing Zimbabwe and urging citizens to speak out—generated a new wave of protests and calls for the country to be 'shut down'. Although Mawarire fled the country in the face of threats against him and his family, he returned to Zimbabwe as Mugabe celebrated his 93rd birthday in February 2017. While Mugabe at times showed signs of physical decline, he continued to travel extensively on official engagements, and for medical attention in Singapore.

Infighting in the ZANU—PF leadership reached a crescendo in the second week of November 2017. Acting, it was rumoured, on the advice of his wife Grace, Mugabe dismissed Mnangagwa as Vice-President. Mnangagwa fled into exile, and tanks appeared on the streets of Harare and elsewhere. Although the military denied that what they called Operation Restore Legacy was a coup, the Constitution stated that the armed forces could be deployed only with the authority of the President. As there was virtually no loss of life, most urban Zimbabweans accepted the de facto coup. During ensuing negotiations with army generals, Mugabe resisted demands for his resignation, but ZANU—PF promptly removed Grace Mugabe from the party and informed Mugabe that if he did not resign he would be impeached in Parliament. Following Mugabe's subsequent resignation on 21 November, Mnangagwa returned to Zimbabwe from South Africa and was sworn in as the new President on 24 November.

THE MNANGAGWA PRESIDENCY

Mnangagwa included in his Government the three military officers behind the de facto coup. Dr Gen. Constantino Chiwenga, the army commander, was appointed Vice-President and Minister of Defence and War Veterans, while Air Chief Marshal Perrance Shiri, the air force chief who, like Mnangagwa, was deeply implicated in the Matabeleland massacres of the early 1980s, was appointed Minister of Lands, Agriculture and Rural Resettlement. Kembo Mohadi, a former ZAPU member who had been Minister of Defence and Security, was appointed Vice-President and Minister for National Peace and Reconciliation. The death of Tsvangirai in February 2018 left the opposition in further disarray, although the 40-year-old Nelson Chamisa, a lawyer, quickly assumed leadership of what was now called the MDC Alliance.

In the run-up to the July 2018 presidential, parliamentary and local government elections, Mugabe's diehard supporters, who were angered by the way in which he had been forced out of office, campaigned against Mnangagwa. (On the eve of the elections Mugabe himself came out in support of Chamisa.) During the campaign Mnangagwa pledged to tackle corruption and improve the efficiency of government. The Indigenization Act was amended to rescind the requirement of majority local ownership in all but the platinum industry. Some white farmers were allowed back to their farms, while farms were confiscated from those with multiple properties. Although a number of former cabinet ministers were arrested on corruption charges, most corruption continued to go unpunished, and Mugabe was allowed to retain his presidential perks.

Mnangagwa was aware that without foreign investment he would not be able to deliver on his promises, particularly to urban workers and the business sector, and so he kept repeating the mantra that Zimbabwe was 'open for business' and sought to project Zimbabwe as a stable country where investments would be protected. He promised free and fair presidential and parliamentary elections and allowed international observers to monitor them. A new climate of openness allowed for discussion, and the MDC Alliance was able to campaign in rural areas, where more than 70% of the electorate—and 60% of the country's youth—lived. The IMF and most European governments stated that they would grant new credit only if Zimbabwe's debts were paid, but the British Government indicated that it was keen to re-engage and granted its first direct commercial loan to Zimbabwe in more than two decades. Other claims of new foreign investment were met with scepticism, and the economy remained in dire straits. ZANU—PF continued to control many aspects of rural life, including the distribution of food aid.

The decision of the Constitutional Court in May 2018 to deny the vote to Zimbabweans in the diaspora was a setback for the opposition, which objected when the Government announced that a further 1,500 polling stations were to be added to the previously agreed total of 10,000. The MDC Alliance also demanded that all participating political parties should be given equal coverage on state media. Efforts to bring Mugabe before Parliament to answer questions over his claim that Zimbabwe had lost US $15,000m. in revenue owing to corruption in the diamond industry came to nothing. Ahead of the elections, Mnangagwa agreed to award pay rises to the country's 350,000 public service workers and increased benefits for war veterans. While his supporters suggested that his administration was legitimate, stable and reformist, his critics described it as a military junta. As the elections approached, Chamisa increasingly accused the ruling party of intending to rig the results, and the ZEC of being biased. Although voting itself proceeded peacefully, when the ZEC announced in early August 2018 that ZANU—PF had won over two-thirds of the parliamentary seats protests erupted in Harare and the army intervened, killing six unarmed protesters. After a further delay, and with Chamisa declaring that he had won the popular vote, the ZEC announced that Mnangagwa had secured 2.45m. votes and Chamisa 2.14m., with Mnangagwa's 50.8% share of the vote obviating the need for a run-off round.

Mnangagwa's hopes that his election would give him new legitimacy and lead to the return of the donor funding and foreign investment that was required to revive Zimbabwe's shattered economy were not realized. Following the security forces' violent quashing of protests in Harare in early August 2018, the Government appointed a commission of inquiry, led by a former South African President, Kgalema Motlanthe. When the commission reported in December it blamed the army, but no action was taken against the individuals responsible. Meanwhile, the MDC Alliance lodged an appeal against the result of the presidential election with the Constitutional Court, which on 24 August ruled that the evidence of irregularities was not 'sufficient and credible'. On 26 August Mnangagwa was inaugurated again as President.

State-orchestrated violence broke out again in January 2019 after the Government unexpectedly allowed the price of petrol to more than double, prompting large-scale nationwide protests. In February Mnangagwa invited the leaders of 20 political parties, including the opposition, to begin a process of national dialogue; the MDC Alliance and five smaller opposition parties rejected the invitation, stating that they would only participate in a dialogue overseen by a neutral entity. In March US President Donald Trump, citing the violence and flawed elections, extended sanctions against Zimbabwe, despite calls by South Africa and other African countries for all sanctions to be lifted.

The Minister of Finance and Economic Development, Mthuli Ncube, a former chief economist at the AfDB, sought to re-engage with international financial institutions, and the Government announced that it would start paying compensation to the white farmers who had lost their land since 2000. In May 2019 Zimbabwe reached an agreement with the IMF, and in late June the Zimbabwe dollar was reintroduced, replacing the interim Real Time Gross Settlement dollar that had been introduced in February to take the place of a basket of international currencies. The Zimbabwe dollar rapidly depreciated against the US dollar and by June year-on-year inflation had soared to 176%. Although the prices of some commodities decreased, salaries fell far short of inflation, many goods were in short supply, if available at all, and the supply of electricity was limited and erratic. Zimbabweans applying for passports were informed that the backlog of applications would not be cleared for several years. While over 90% of Zimbabweans continued to make a living in the informal sector, public sector employees threatened to strike unless their salaries were raised. An estimated one-third of the population needed food aid. Eastern areas of Zimbabwe were hit hard by Cyclone Idai in March, while by July very severe drought conditions meant that the maize produced in a country once described as the 'breadbasket of southern Africa' met only about 20% of domestic requirements.

Following the death of the 95-year-old Mugabe on 6 September 2019 in Singapore, where he had been undergoing medical treatment, Mnangagwa declared the former President a national hero and indicated that he would be interred at the National Heroes Acre burial ground in Harare. After a state funeral held on 14 September, however, the Government agreed with the wishes of his family that Mugabe should be buried in his home village of Kutama. In May 2021 a traditional court ordered that his remains be exhumed and reburied at the Heroes Acre, although three of his children subsequently appealed against that decision.

Zimbabwe entered 2020 with inflation over 300% and one-half of the population food insecure. At the end of March, in response to the coronavirus (COVID-19) pandemic, the Government announced a strict lockdown, initially for three weeks. With the closing of the borders, it was more difficult for people to leave the country, although a fence that the South African Government quickly erected on either side of the Beitbridge border crossing proved inadequate in preventing people crossing there illegally. Ncube appealed to the World Bank, the IMF and the AfDB for assistance to deal with Zimbabwe's dire economic and humanitarian situation, but his request for rescheduling or cancelling all of Zimbabwe's foreign bilateral debt was rejected and the Government resorted to printing money, further stoking inflation. Ongoing negotiations, designed to gain international favour, on compensation for expropriated white farmers remained inconclusive, with uncertainty over how it would be financed. Celebrations on 18 April marking the 40th anniversary of independence were muted because of the pandemic. On 1 May the lockdown was slightly relaxed but extended indefinitely. A US $430m. economic rescue and stimulus package announced by President Mnangagwa did little to address the negative impact of the pandemic on the economy.

ZANU—PF took advantage of the situation to further harass the opposition, now divided between the MDC Alliance and a small MDC—T faction led by Thokozani Khupe, which allied itself with the ruling party. After the Supreme Court ruled in late March 2020 that Chamisa had not been legitimately elected as MDC Alliance leader, Khupe's faction was allocated all the party funds due to the MDC. Although on social media there was widespread support for the hashtags #ZanuPF-MustGo and #ZanuPFMustFall, the opposition was prevented by the lockdown from organizing street protests. In early June police ejected the MDC Alliance from its headquarters in central Harare and the party's Vice-President, Tendai Biti, was arrested and briefly detained, reportedly in horrific conditions. Other MDC Alliance deputies, opposition politicians and journalists were harassed, detained and sometimes tortured. In early May the MDC—T requested the removal of several MDC Alliance deputies, as part of the ongoing dispute regarding Chamisa's presidency. By-elections were not held because of the pandemic. As the military increased its presence and involvement in political and social affairs, the Minister of State for National Security accused the MDC Alliance of planning an armed uprising. Hopewell Chin'ono, an investigative journalist and filmmaker who had reported extensively on official corruption, including in the National Prosecuting Authority, was arrested for a second time in November and briefly imprisoned. In December Biti was again arrested on the charge of assault, which was denounced by the MDC Alliance as spurious, after he had reportedly tried to expose government corruption involving a land procurement agreement. In early 2021 Chin'ono was again one of those detained, until the charges against him were quashed in April, while in March Biti was expelled from Parliament, together with a further five MDC Alliance deputies. As reports of human rights abuses in Zimbabwe mounted, South Africa's ruling African National Congress and the South African Government both sent delegations to Harare in 2020, but these were not permitted to meet opposition leaders and achieved nothing.

Meanwhile, widespread and endemic corruption, benefiting especially the military elite, also surrounded the COVID-19 crisis. In 2020 President Mnangagwa's son was alleged to have links with a company that had supplied the Government with personal protective equipment (PPE) at grossly inflated prices. The Minister of Health and Child Care, Obediah Moyo, was dismissed by the President after being arrested for corruption in the procurement of PPE and COVID-19 test equipment from a company based in the United Arab Emirates. Nurses and doctors in state hospitals staged strike action in protest at low wages in a situation of high inflation and the lack of PPE. The Government did raise the salaries of public sector workers by 50% and offered a one-off COVID-19 payment of US $75, but funded this by printing more money, and inflation soared to almost 840% in August. The pandemic increased joblessness and contributed to ever-declining social services. COVID-19 cases surged in December, with the arrival of a more contagious variant of the disease. Restrictions on gatherings were tightened. Some prominent members of the ruling elite, including three cabinet ministers, reportedly died as a result of COVID-19. Vaccines from China began to be administered on a large scale from April 2021 and by June over 700,000 people had been vaccinated, but supply, especially in the rural areas, was limited. A further, much larger, wave of COVID-19 cases began in late June, prompting the reinstatement of more stringent restrictions on movement and gatherings.

From early 2021 ZANU—PF and President Mnangagwa sought to consolidate their power in anticipation of the presidential and legislative elections in 2023, when it was expected that Mnangagwa would be returned for a final five-year term. There was a reported increase in violence against opponents of the Government. Controversial amendments to the 2013 Constitution received approval in Parliament, with the aid of the MDC—T opposition. Critics claimed that these entrenched the powers of the executive and threatened judicial independence by considerably strengthening the authorities of the President. Notably, the President was henceforth empowered to appoint without consultation senior judges, including the Chief Justice and the Deputy Chief Justice, and to extend their term in office beyond the retirement age of 70. When President Mnangagwa then extended the term of the Chief Justice, Luke Malaba, who was regarded as his ally, by five years, this was ruled invalid by the High Court. Malaba returned to the post after the Government appealed against the judgment and the High Court

upheld his right to return to work. With Mnangagwa ruling in an increasingly authoritarian manner, reminiscent of that of Mugabe, few saw any escape for Zimbabwe from an ever-deepening social, economic and political crisis.

The COVID-19 pandemic not only increased unemployment and contributed to ever-declining social services, it also aggravated a severe agricultural crisis in the rural areas, where, according to a report issued by the Global Network Against Food Crises (comprising the EU, the UN World Food Programme and other partners) in April 2020, over 4m. Zimbabweans were food insecure. The restrictions imposed in 2020 to deal with the pandemic were continued into 2022, as the Omicron variant led to a sharp rise in cases in late 2021. By 7 September 2022, according to the World Health Organization, 256,825 confirmed cases of COVID-19 had been reported in Zimbabwe, with 5,596 deaths; by that time only 31.8% of the population were fully vaccinated.

With the ruling ZANU—PF party taking advantage of the COVID-19 restrictions to undermine the MDC Alliance further, its leader, Nelson Chamisa, called for a broad alliance for change and embarked on a number of 'meet the people' tours to rally support ahead of by-elections in March 2022 and the general election due in 2023. His campaign to mobilize students, women, community leaders, traditional leaders and workers took him into the rural areas. In October 2021 the MDC Alliance accused ZANU—PF of trying to assassinate Chamisa, after his convoy was attacked on a number of occasions.

Meanwhile, a ZANU—PF faction that was opposed to President Mnangagwa seeking a second term rallied behind Vice-President Constantino Chiwenga. Those loyal to Mnangagwa, including the leadership of the influential Zimbabwe National Liberation War Veterans Association, pushed for the removal of Chiwenga, who had become the sole Vice-President when his counterpart, Kembo Mohadi, resigned over a sex scandal in early March 2021. When independence war veterans held a series of protests in 2021 over their pensions, both the ZANU—PF faction known as Generation 40 and the MDC Alliance were accused of inciting them in order to embarrass Mnangagwa, whose ties to the military remained strong.

Although the closing of the country's borders during the pandemic made it more difficult for Zimbabweans to cross illegally into South Africa in search of jobs, many continued to do so, despite xenophobic attacks on Zimbabweans in that country. Traffic between Zimbabwe and South Africa at Beitbridge continued to be subject to long delays. Bilateral relations became strained as Zimbabweans in South Africa suffered from xenophobic attacks and South Africa's Ministry of Home Affairs announced in November 2021 that it would not extend the Zimbabwean Exemption Permits which allowed up to 182,000 Zimbabweans to continue living and working in South Africa. Those who wished to remain in South Africa after December 2022 would have to obtain a visa. Challenges to this decision continued in the South African courts during 2022 and in September these Zimbabweans were given another six-month reprieve.

From early 2022 both the ruling ZANU—PF and the opposition actively campaigned for the forthcoming elections. Chamisa in late January announced the creation of a new party, the Citizens Coalition for Change (CCC), to replace the MDC Alliance, which was greeted with excitement in opposition circles. After not much more than a month of campaigning, the CCC performed well in the by-elections held on 26 March, winning 19 of the 28 parliamentary seats it contested. However, the political and electoral playing field remained deeply uneven and stacked in favour of the ruling party, which used the law and security institutions against its opponents, and conflated party and state resources to boost its position. Mnangagwa who criticized what he called 'foreign interference' ahead of the 2023 election, publicly vowed that no opposition political party would ever rule Zimbabwe. Among the opposition figures imprisoned on spurious charges was Job Sikhala, the CCC Vice-Chairperson, human rights lawyer and deputy. Those appointed to the ZEC were ZANU—PF supporters; traditional leaders were in the pay of the ruling party; and the media, including the public broadcaster, was controlled by the ruling party. The military remained the final arbiter of the country's political future. There was no sign that South Africa or SADC would pressure Zimbabwe to implement the letter and spirit of its electoral guidelines.

Zimbabwe's macroeconomic crisis continued, with the consumer price index measuring year-on-year inflation for all items estimated at 260% in July 2022 and unemployment in the formal sector at over 90%. In June health care workers were among those who staged strike action, demanding that the Government pay their salaries in US dollars as spiralling inflation had eroded the purchasing power of their pay.

In March 2022 US President Joe Biden extended the sanctions imposed on Zimbabwe for another year, while it seemed unlikely that the country would be readmitted to the Commonwealth, following a meeting of the Commonwealth Heads of Government in June in Kigali, Rwanda. The Russian Federation and China eyed Zimbabwe's mineral resources, as Zimbabwe refused to condemn the Russian invasion of Ukraine in February. China's growing influence in Zimbabwe was evident in mid-2022 with the completion of an imposing new parliament building, some 18 km north-west of central Harare, which had been constructed and funded by the Chinese Government at an estimated cost of US \$140m. This was at a time when an increasing number of Zimbabweans had lost faith in the electoral process, citing, in particular, the violent nature of the country's politics in the run-up to the 2023 elections.

Economy

ALBERT MAKOCHEKANWA

INTRODUCTION

Since the beginning of the 21st century the Government of Zimbabwe has guided the country's economy mainly by introducing a number of policy frameworks. These have included, *inter alia*, the Zimbabwe Millennium Economic Recovery Programme (MERP, 2000–02), the National Economic Recovery Programme (NERP, 2003), the Macroeconomic Policy Framework (2005–06), the Short Term Economic Recovery Programme (STERP I, February–December 2009), STERP II (2010–12) and the Medium Term Plan (2011–15). Following the July 2013 elections, an urgently needed new policy framework, aptly named the Zimbabwe Agenda for Sustainable Socio-Economic Transformation (Zim Asset), was drawn up to cover the period 2013–18. Over the plan period the economy was projected to grow by an average annual rate of 7.3%, with strong performances expected in the mining and agricultural sectors. The economy was forecast to grow by 6.1% in 2014 and thereafter to follow an upward growth trajectory to 9.9% by 2018. In August 2015 the Government adopted a 10-point plan that cut across all economic sectors and was expected to maintain economic growth and create employment. Following the legislative and presidential elections of 2018, the Government launched the Transitional Stabilization Programme (TSP), which was themed 'Towards a Prosperous and Empowered Upper Middle Income Society by 2030'. The TSP was expected to stabilize the macroeconomy and the financial sector, and to introduce necessary policies and institutional reforms, in order to transform Zimbabwe to a private sector-led model, and launch 'quick wins' to stimulate growth over the period between October 2018 and December 2020. Another policy document, the National Development Strategy (NDS) 1 (2021–25), was launched in November 2020 as the successor to the TSP and was the first five-year Medium Term Plan aimed at realizing the country's Vision 2030. The Strategy was to build on the success of the TSP, notably by entrenching the macroeconomic stability necessary for economic recovery and growth, and creating new opportunities for wealth creation, innovation and enterprise development.

RECENT ECONOMIC DEVELOPMENTS

The Government has continued to implement economic policy changes, with the introduction of one key Statutory Instrument (SI) in the first half of 2021. In May the Government issued SI 127, which was intended to curb the abuse of foreign currency obtained at the Foreign Currency Auction Trading System of the Reserve Bank of Zimbabwe (RBZ—the central bank). Under the SI, substantial penalties were introduced for individuals and businesses found to be in violation of the official foreign exchange auction system. However, some retailers responded by suspending the use of US dollar payments for purchases. One of the biggest retail shops in the country, OK Zimbabwe, announced shortly afterwards that it would no longer accept foreign currency as payment, but that those intending to use foreign currency had to exchange it in-store.

Previously, two other SIs had been issued in 2019, principally SI 142, which was introduced on 25 June and brought the reintroduction of the Zimbabwean dollar and an abrupt end to the multi-currency regime—just over a decade after the Zimbabwean dollar was made almost worthless by hyperinflation. The RBZ declared that, effective immediately, currencies including the US dollar and the South African rand—in use in Zimbabwe since 2009—were no longer accepted as legal tender. A local quasi-currency, a bond note, which had been introduced in 2016 and replaced in February 2019 by the Real Time Gross Settlement (RTGS) dollar, was replaced in June by the new Zimbabwean dollar. The authorities had abandoned the Zimbabwean dollar after inflation reached an estimated 500,000m.% in 2008, according to the International Monetary Fund (IMF). While the country has since used a basket of currencies from the African continent and abroad as well as bond notes and the RTGS dollar, some government departments and agencies have, until recently, demanded payment in US dollars. The central bank made it clear in its announcement that money held in foreign currency accounts was not affected, but the step was greeted with alarm and memories of the lives wrecked and the pensions and savings lost in 2008. Recollections of what effectively became a barter economy, in a country where a suitcase full of banknotes was needed to purchase a pair of jeans, will be hard to erase.

To buttress the local currency, the RBZ responded by outlining six measures. First, banks were directed to transfer to the RBZ the RTGS dollars that they were holding as counterpart funds for the foreign currency historical or legacy debt that the Government, through the RBZ, was assuming at the rate of 1:1 between the RTGS dollar and the US dollar. This measure was expected to mop up around Z.\$1,200m. from the market by the end of the week following the announcement. Second, it adjusted the interest rate on the RBZ overnight window upwards from 15% per annum to 50%, in line with inflation trends. Third, it removed administrative limits on the operation of bureaux de change and the cap on margins for banks for interbank foreign exchange transactions. Fourth, it put a vesting period of 90 days on the disposal of dual-listed securities or shares purchased by investors on the Zimbabwe Stock Exchange (ZSE). Fifth, it increased the supply of foreign currency into interbank foreign exchange markets by ensuring that at least 50% of the surrender portion of foreign currency was sold to the interbank market. This was supplemented by the use of Letters of Credit (LC) for the import of essential commodities that include fuel, cooking oil and wheat. The RBZ put in place LCs amounting to US \$330m. for this purpose. Sixth, it printed Z.\$400m. to increase the supply of paper money and bridge the gap created by the non-usage of foreign currency. Under SI 145 of 28 June 2019 the Government also imposed strict controls on the sale and transportation of maize. Among other things, SI 145 makes it illegal for individuals and companies to buy maize directly from farmers, as they must now go through the Grain Marketing Board.

However, the RTGS dollar and the Zimbabwean dollar introduced by the RBZ have continued to weaken against major currencies, as exporters continue to hold on to their US dollar earnings waiting for the exchange rate to slide further. The RBZ had already scrapped its 1:1 parity policy between local bond notes and electronic dollars, and it introduced an interbank foreign exchange market which, however, saw the rate remaining at 2.5 RTGS dollars to US $1 for only one week or so before the RTGS dollar gradually started losing value. By June 2020 the RTGS dollar was trading at 25 to the US dollar on the interbank market and 110 to the US dollar on the black market. Meanwhile, local companies with significant foreign debts were sinking deeper into financial trouble, due to currency volatility and exchange rate fluctuations, with their balance sheets being increasingly eroded and foreign currency liabilities ballooning. This has left some companies technically insolvent and facing bankruptcy.

However, recovery in line with these policy framework growth targets will require significant investment in both foreign and domestic infrastructure, new equipment, machinery and more modern technologies. Despite the above economic policies, the economy of Zimbabwe continues to be constrained in performing to its full potential and faces a number of challenges in order to do so. Among the most serious are: liquidity constraints; erratic and inadequate water and power supplies; obsolete infrastructure; a lack of credit lines for recapitalization by industries; high external debt overhang; and a lack of medium- to long-term finance.

To worsen the situation, the period before 2009 was characterized by unprecedented levels of hyperinflation, which led to the massive devaluation and subsequent abandonment of the domestic currency, a sustained period of negative gross domestic product (GDP) growth rates, low productive capacity, job losses, food shortages, poverty, massive de-industrialization and general despondency. Specifically, the country was characterized by: a cumulative economic contraction in excess of 40% in 2000–08; a resultant drastic fall in per capita GDP, from US $700 in 1997 to about $290 by 2008; a hyperinflationary environment, with a recorded inflation rate of over 231m.% in 2008, which wiped out savings in financial instruments, including pension and insurance products; a widespread rejection of the domestic currency by the public; and the collapse of industry as a result of a massive business regulatory regime of controls, lack of re-investment, obsolete equipment, and shortages of raw materials, all of which contributed to a reduction in average capacity utilization to below 10% by the end of 2008. The negative consequences of this economic meltdown included, *inter alia*, high formal unemployment levels (estimated to be higher than 80% by the end of 2008), the disappearance of basic consumer goods and services amid price controls and other distortions unrelated to cost of production and replacement, the accumulation of external payment arrears totalling US $3,007m. at December 2008, and the depletion of external reserves, leading to total absence of import cover. It was, therefore, fundamental that a government of national unity was formed in 2009 to address the above and to resuscitate and rehabilitate the economy. In addition, the Government had to attend to the major imperative of nation building and national healing.

In introducing STERP I in 2009 and STERP II in 2010, the Ministry of Finance was able to achieve the broad objective of ensuring economic recovery. Indeed, according to the IMF, GDP growth of 7.5% was recorded in 2009, increasing to 11.4% in 2010. During the early 2010s the macroeconomic environment remained stable, with strong GDP growth rates of 11.9% in 2011 and 10.6% in 2012. Growth then decelerated to 5.3% in 2013, to 2.8% in 2014 and to 1.4% in 2015. In 2016 GDP was estimated to have grown by 0.6%. The inflation rate remained below 1% in the early 2010s, largely as a result of the multi-currency regime introduced in 2009, and negative inflation occurred between 2014 and 2016, dipping as low as –2.4% in 2015, according to the IMF. This was attributed to a decline in health care prices and global prices for fuel. However, the year-on-year inflation rate accelerated to 0.5% in April 2017, from –0.7% in January 2017, before, as noted above, a return to significant levels of inflation was recorded. The annual inflation rate in Zimbabwe soared to 176% in June 2019 from 97.85% in the previous month. Headline inflation has been on an upward trend since October 2018, amid worsening economic conditions characterized by shortages of fuel, power and foreign currency. The reading reflected a generalized rise in prices, as a weakening local currency motivates retailers to peg prices in line with parallel market rates.

The economic recovery of 2009–12 was not accompanied by a commensurate rise in employment and job creation, nor by a decline in poverty. Therefore, despite a few years of positive economic performances, the economy remains fragile. This is due mainly to political challenges, poor social and economic infrastructure, and very low levels of official development assistance and low inflows of foreign direct investment (FDI). The latter totalled just an estimated US $387m. in 2011; the annual total in 2016 was below this level, at some $385m. These low levels of investment are below thresholds consistent with rapid and sustainable rates of economic growth.

In addition to the above challenges, the coronavirus disease (COVID-19) pandemic that originated in the People's Republic of China in December 2019 also caught Zimbabwe unaware. In March 2020 the RBZ suspended the managed float foreign currency trading system and lifted controls on free funds to make it easier for the public to transact in the wake of the COVID-19 pandemic. In line with similar swift responses by global economies, the central bank introduced measures to boost the domestic economy, by reducing statutory reserve requirements from 5% to 4.5% and cutting the bank's policy rate from 30% to 25%, to promote lending by banks. Furthermore, the Ministry of Finance and Economic Development introduced mitigatory interventions covering both prevention and support to Zimbabwe's productive sectors. First, the Treasury made available more than Z.$100m. to fight COVID-19. Second, resources designated for mitigating the effects of the pandemic were ring-fenced to ensure the achievement of planned activities. The Treasury directed the utilization of the existing National Disasters Accounts to serve this purpose. Third, the Treasury also agreed to the unfreezing of over 4,000 health sector posts and the creation of an additional 200 medical posts, with a view to scaling up the response to the COVID-19 pandemic. Fourth, it suspended duty and tax on various goods and services related to testing, protection, sterilization, and other medical consumables.

The COVID-19 pandemic forced the Government to announce a nationwide 21-day lockdown on 30 March 2020 to control the spread of the disease. (The manufacturing, mining, public and health sectors were exempt from the measures.) In mid-May the lockdown was extended indefinitely, with the country remaining under lockdown, and the Government was to assess the situation at two-week intervals. Despite the extension, the Government announced some relaxation of measures, including the extension of shop opening hours, in early May. Most other measures remained in place, however. Under the lockdown measures, citizens were expected to stay at home, except to seek medical assistance, buy food and receive other essential services. All public transportation services, except bus routes operated by the Zimbabwe United Passenger Co, were suspended. Security personnel were deployed across the country to ensure that the public complied with the lockdown measures. A further severe surge of COVID-19 cases from June 2021 prompted the reinstatement of more stringent restrictions. The Government started to ease the various travel and quarantine restrictions in early 2022.

In June 2022 SI 118A was introduced by the Government, entrenching the multi-currency system in an effort to control further hyperinflation (see *Inflation*). The SI was to run from January 2021 to December 2025—the same duration as NDS 1. At the same time, the RBZ raised its main policy interest rate from 80% to 200% (following smaller increases in 2021 and in April 2022), in an attempt to prevent cheaper speculative borrowing, which has adverse effects on exchange rates. The developments came after investigations by the central bank's Financial Intelligence Unit revealed that some businesses were manipulating the loans system, obtaining foreign currency via the official foreign exchange auction system to raise money for restocking and later selling goods at prices far above the official rate.

NATIONAL INCOME

In late July 2022 Zimbabwe's Ministry of Finance and Economic Development lowered its growth forecast for 2022 to 4.6%, from the 5.5% that had been predicted in the budget statement of November 2021. The earlier forecast, which was slightly below the 5.8% growth in 2021, had been based on higher output in the mining, manufacturing, agriculture and construction sectors, as well as in accommodation and food services (tourism). The 2022 growth projection was, however, subject to risks relating to the future course of the pandemic and its impact on key sectors of the economy. At mid-2022 the country continued to be constrained by many challenges, notably the considerable power outages, huge external debt and financial constraints, severe shortages of credit and cash, and inadequate infrastructure. The IMF expected the recovery in output to continue, though at a slower pace, with GDP projected to grow by 3.5% in 2022 and 3,0% in the medium term, while the World Bank forecast GDP growth of 3.7% in 2022.

MINING

Mining is one of the sectors that has the potential to propel the economy of Zimbabwe to greater levels, as the country is endowed with a diversity of minerals that offer prospects of substantial revenue. Mining (including utilities) accounted for 8.8% of GDP in 2020, according to UN estimates, and the sector's GDP increased at an average annual rate of 1.8% during 2011–20. The mining sector is now the main source of export revenue for the country, accounting for more than 60% of total exports. Zimbabwe produced 29,429 kg of gold in 2019, with output spurred by small-scale miners. However, output fell to 20,873 kg in 2020, amid the pandemic. Growth of about 8.0% in the sector was projected for 2022, based largely on the realization of projects like the opening of new mines, the reopening of closed mines and the expansion of existing ones. As part of the Mines and Minerals Amendment Bill, which was approved by the Cabinet in July, an automated information management system was expected to rationalize the way mining claims were allocated and prevent the illicit extraction and smuggling of minerals that cost the country billions of dollars in potential revenue. The country's 800 mines have the capacity to earn US $18,000m. per annum, but they have only generated about $2,000m. annually since 2009. This represents about one-10th of the sector's full potential and translates to an incredible opportunity for investors, for whom the Government is fully committed to creating an enabling environment. The mining sector is also encountering difficulties in raising the requisite capital to ramp up production, challenges the Government of President Emmerson Mnangagwa is working hard to address. In order to ensure that mining contributes significantly to the economic recovery, it is necessary that the Government supports investment in the industry and implements the following policy measures: increase investment in mineral exploration; address electricity supply problems; ensure the availability of long-term capital to mining companies; expedite the finalization of amendments to mining laws; and improve infrastructure to support investment.

AGRICULTURE

Agriculture remains the backbone of Zimbabwe's economy. There is a strong relationship between the performance of the economy and that of the agricultural sector. If output in the agricultural sector increases, this will result in a resurgence in the economy, as the latter depends heavily on farm output for production purposes. Agriculture's contribution to GDP was generally in decline between 1996 and 2002, but increased during 2003–07. Between 2008 and 2010 output in the agricultural sector declined dramatically due to a number of factors, including the apparent change in the pattern of the rainy season and difficulties in acquiring farming inputs. According to UN estimates, agriculture (including forestry

and fishing) contributed 9.2% of GDP in 2020, and agricultural GDP increased by an average of 3.1% per year during 2011–20. In 2022 the sector had been projected to grow by a modest 5.1%, based on an expected favourable rainfall season and the implementation of government support programmes. However, rain in March and April arrived too late, with poor yields for 2022 being forecast by early May, a situation exacerbated by the increasing cost of inputs.

MANUFACTURING

The manufacturing sector remains constrained as a result of the following main factors: liquidity challenges leading to high borrowing costs; lack of competitiveness due to antiquated machinery; the interrupted supply of key enablers (power and water); and competition from cheap imports. There has been a general decline in the contribution of manufacturing to GDP, from around 25% in 1993 to a low of around 10% in 2008. According to UN estimates, manufacturing accounted for 12.1% of GDP in 2020, and the sector's GDP decreased by an average of 0.3% per year during 2011–20. According to the budget statement of November 2021, growth in manufacturing output of 5.5% was projected for 2022, compared with a growth forecast of 6.2% in the sector for 2021. Since the introduction of the multi-currency regime in 2009, capacity utilization improved, to around 57% in 2012 from a low of 10% in 2008. However, capacity utilization experienced a further decline from 2013, and in late 2014 it was estimated at 36%; it rose slightly, to about 37%, by the end of 2016. The Confederation of Zimbabwe Industries (CZI) reported capacity utilization to have increased to 50% in May 2018, from 45% in January 2018. According to the CZI, capacity utilization rose by 11 percentage points to 47% in 2020 from 36.4% in 2019, due to improved foreign currency availability, increased sales and retooling. The current low levels of capacity utilization can be largely attributed to a number of reasons that are similar, but are not limited, to those that explain the poor performance of the agricultural sector, namely: inconsistent electricity supply; lack of foreign currency; obsolete industrial equipment; and the mass exodus of professionals from the sector. These have resulted in the de-industrialization that has occurred across Zimbabwe, with firms located in the country's second largest city, Bulawayo, being the worst affected.

TOURISM

Tourism has been recognized as one of the pillars anchoring Zimbabwe's economic growth and job creation strategies, alongside agriculture, mining and manufacturing. The sector had continued on a positive trajectory, with a rise in the number of tourist arrivals from 1.8m. in 2013 to 2.6m. in 2018. However, tourist arrivals fell in 2019, to 2.3m., which was attributed to the prevailing macroeconomic environment. The travel restrictions imposed in response to the global COVID-19 pandemic had a severe impact on tourist flows from all markets, with the total number of arrivals falling to 639,356 in 2020 and then to 380,820 in 2021. Tourists remained wary of travelling for fear of contracting the virus at airports and other ports of entry. The airline industry faced significant financial losses after dozens of carriers cancelled or reduced flights because of the pandemic. The sector was projected to grow by 18.8% in 2022, as a result of the full resumption of domestic and international travel.

ENERGY

Net production of electricity was 7,536.0m. kWh in 2019. In 2022 electricity generation was projected to grow by 5.4%, reinforced by ongoing rehabilitation and expansion projects, as well as the engagement of new independent power producers. There are 20 independent power projects to produce solar energy already lined up for implementation. However, electricity generation continues to be hampered by the existence of obsolete equipment, which often results in long periods of power outages (load shedding) sometimes for up to 18 hours a day. For Zimbabwe, electricity generation and distribution has become one of the greatest challenges of recent years. All sectors of the economy have highlighted that intermittent supply of electricity is stalling production. As a consequence, many of the country's economic activities rely on the use of expensive energy supply alternatives—for example, the use of generators.

The national average daily demand (domestic and industrial) for electricity is approximately 2,200 MW per hour; however, the current installed capacity is 1,960 MW per hour. This has resulted in Zimbabwe importing around 35% of its electricity from neighbouring countries, including the Democratic Republic of the Congo, Mozambique and Zambia. Furthermore, since 2006 there has been a decline in both production of electricity and the amount of electricity Zimbabwe has imported. This is manifested by the intermittent supply of electricity the country is currently experiencing. The Government's Zim Asset policy framework for 2013–18 emphasized that electricity provision was one of the chief enablers to be addressed during the planning period. Accordingly, numerous mini hydro projects were identified and the expansion of the Kariba power station was just one of many proposed projects that were intended to ease the problem.

INFLATION

Prior to 2009 the country was characterized by hyperinflation, which most financial experts pinpointed to have been caused by governmental actions. The Government attempted to fix the economic crisis by simply printing more money. This had the effect of decreasing the value of the currency. The hyperinflation of 2008 was brought to a halt in 2009, reflecting the dollarization of the economy, the end of monetary injections by the authorities, and the increase in food crops and in the supply of goods in the shops. Year-on-year inflation fell to –7.7% in December 2009 (i.e., the cost of goods declined), but picked up during the first quarter of 2010, reaching 6.1% by May 2010, due to rising prices of food and non-alcoholic beverages, significant wage increases awarded to both public and private sector employees, and the appreciation of the South African rand against the US dollar. It also reflected tariff adjustments for public utilities. Annual inflation, however, registered a downward trend from June 2010, easing to 3.6% in October. The country continued to score positively in maintaining stable price levels, with annual inflation for the greater part of 2011 remaining in the 3.0%–4.5% band. Stability in price levels was the result of the containment of costs, particularly with regards to the wage bill, depressed demand under tight liquidity conditions, and decreasing international oil prices. Furthermore, there had been a tightening of market competition and a depreciation of the rand against the US dollar. The rate of inflation fell to 1.6% in 2013, according to Zimbabwe National Statistics Agency (ZIMSTAT), and remained very low during 2014, with ZIMSTAT registering price declines as low as –0.1% as the continuing liquidity crunch depressed consumer spending. This was in line with the Southern African Development Community (SADC) prevailing macroeconomic convergence target of gradually reducing inflation to single digit levels of between 3% and 7%.

However, 2019 was marked by sharp increases in consumer prices. Inflationary pressures mainly arose from the depreciating exchange rate of the local currency, further fuelled by adverse market expectations and increases in money supply. Month-on-month inflation started the year at 10.8% in January, slowed down to 1.7% in February, before moderately picking up in March and April. In June it hit a peak of 39.3%. With the adoption of a mono currency regime, in combination with corrective measures on the foreign exchange market, month-on-month inflation slowed down during the second half of the year. It ended 2019 at 16.6%. Monthly inflation had been expected to fall to single digit figures from the first quarter of 2020, to close the year at around 2%, on the strength of a commitment by the central bank to fight inflation through implementing an active reserve money targeting programme. However, these figures proved to be significantly incorrect.

ZIMSTAT began to release the country's year-on-year inflation figures in March 2020, after the Government had suspended the publication of data following the adoption of a new currency. The consumer price index measured year-on-year inflation for all items at 191% in June 2022, compared with 5.4% in June 2021. Following the Russian Federation's invasion of Ukraine in February 2022, Zimbabwe's inflation rate rose sharply from 66% in that month to more than 130% in May, before it increased again to 191% in June, causing the RBZ to introduce new measures (see *Recent Economic Developments*).

PERFORMANCE OF THE ZSE

The market capitalization of the shares of companies listed on the ZSE grew by 314.4%, from Z.$317,880m. in December 2020 to Z.$1,317,210m. at the end of December 2021, amid the post-pandemic recovery. Foreign investor participation in the ZSE was reported to be minimal since 2015, but foreign investor net inflows increased from Z.$5,010m. to Z.$9,740m. over that period. Market capitalization then rose further to a record high of Z.$3,547,350m. at 29 April 2022. However, after the Zimbabwe authorities in mid-2022 increased taxes on equity transactions and took other measures, including the introduction of gold bullion, to support the devaluating currency and curb hyperinflation, market capitalization dropped by more than 50% from the end of April to August. The market capitalization of the ZSE at 9 September was Z.$1,552,018m.

BALANCE OF PAYMENTS

During the 1990s there were huge discrepancies between the value of exports and that of imports. Between 1993 and 1995 exports marginally outweighed imports, resulting in a favourable trade balance. However, from 2003–13 the cost of imports far exceeded the value of exports, resulting in an unfavourable trade balance. This was due particularly to over-reliance on imports for food sustenance and other commodities to cushion Zimbabwean citizens from the effects of chronic shortages of basic goods. This period saw the country importing basic groceries such as cooking oil, mealie meal, flour and soap, as local industries had lost capacity owing to a number of bottlenecks. Generally, lack of competitiveness in the economy due to the use of antiquated machinery and old technology has constrained domestic growth. As a result, imports of consumer goods remain unsustainably high.

The growth of exports has generally been on the negative side, with the exception of 2010 when there was a high growth rate of exports. This could have been caused by the stabilization of the economy and the subsequent increase in industry capacity utilization, as well as mining sector growth. There was a deficit on the overall balance of payments in each year between 1990 and 2015, with only a few exceptions. Poor export performance and lack of balance of payments support from international institutions such as the World Bank and the IMF have been held responsible for the poor performance in the balance of payments for most of the years under review, and for the low import coverage ratios (the share or percentage of a country's own imports that is subject to non-tariff barriers) that the country experienced from 2009 to 2015. Zimbabwe's external sector position was expected to remain under pressure over the coming years. The balance of payments deficit is traditionally financed through accumulation of external payment arrears, which increased significantly in the mid-2010s.

According to the RBZ monetary policy statement published in February 2022, Zimbabwe's external sector position remained strong following growth in exports, with preliminary estimates showing that the current account surplus was US $926.8m. in 2021, which represented an increase of 36.6% compared with a surplus of $678.3m. in 2020. Strong global commodity prices supported export performance during the greater part of 2021, while relatively subdued petroleum prices in that year moderated the import bill during the first four months of the year. None the less, the continued softening of prices for some key export commodities presents a potential risk to the outlook for exports in the medium term.

REVENUE AND EXPENDITURE

According to IMF estimates, total revenue recovered from Z.$183,039m. in 2020 to Z.$495,035m. in 2021, while total expenditure increased, respectively, from Z.$177,111m. to

Z.\$539,460m. In his budget statement of November 2021, the Minister of Finance and Economic Development presented a budget for 2022 based on revenue collection of Z.\$850,700m. and expenditure of Z.\$927,300m., with a target budget deficit of Z.\$76,500m. (1.5% of GDP), which was to be funded through the issuance of treasury bills, utilization of the country's allocation of IMF special drawing rights funds and domestic loans. The health sector, agriculture and infrastructure were to receive the greatest share of expenditure.

However, following the onset of hyperinflation, in July 2022, together with the mid-term fiscal policy statement, the minister presented a supplementary budget requesting additional spending of Z.\$929,300m. which would double the initially approved expenditure for 2022. The largest part of the supplementary budget (53%) was allocated to large salary increments for civil servants to compensate for the increasing cost of living (amid growing labour unrest in the public sector). Despite strong criticism from opposition deputies, the supplementary budget was approved by the National Assembly in early September.

DEBT

The country's creditworthiness and its ability to secure new financing from both bilateral and multilateral sources continue to be seriously undermined by the accumulation of external debt payment arrears. In November 2010 the Government approved the Zimbabwe Accelerated Arrears Clearance, Debt and Development Strategy (ZAADDS) in its quest to clear arrears and obtain debt relief for the country. The following plans were incorporated, *inter alia*, in the ZAADDS: the finance ministry was to establish a debt management office; Zimbabwe's public and publicly guaranteed debt database with all creditors was to be validated and reconciled; the removal of sanctions was to be realized through re-engagement with the international community; the clearance of arrears, debt relief and acquisition of new finance were to be effected through negotiation with creditors and development partners; and the pursuit of debt relief was to be undertaken through the leverage of Zimbabwe's natural resources. Progress was subsequently made in the implementation of these plans; an Aid and Debt Management Office was established within the Ministry of Finance in December 2010, highlighting the importance of prudent management to the country's sustained economic development. Moreover, by mid-2014 the validation and reconciliation of the external debt data had been completed (having been commenced in 2011). The reforms in external debt management were based on best international practices, taking into account the relevant experiences of other countries. In the short term, the Government planned to review the existing External Loans Coordinating Committee, and external borrowing criteria and guidelines. This was to allow for the development of an explicit Debt Management Policy that would form the basis of all future debt management strategy formulation.

At independence in 1980, Zimbabwe inherited US \$700m. of debt from the Rhodesian Government (largely the result of United Nations—UN—sanction-busting loans to the white regime to buy arms during the civil war). This inherited debt was short-term and high-interest, imposing a large repayment burden in the early 1980s just as drought struck. In the absence of significant grant aid to deal with the drought and fund post-civil war reconstruction, Zimbabwe relied on loans to buy imports. The country's large debt burden was thereby created. Throughout the 1980s Zimbabwe borrowed from foreign governments and international lenders such as the World Bank, supposedly to invest in productive activities. Many of these projects were of dubious benefit, such as World Bank loans to plant trees in areas where local people already had enough wood for their energy needs. Loans from foreign governments, including many counted as 'aid', tended to be tied to using that country's companies. The most expensive project in the 1980s was the development of Hwange power station, funded by lenders including the World Bank, the European Investment Bank and the British Government (again, tied to the use of British companies). However, devaluation of the Zimbabwean dollar meant the power station was far too expensive ever to generate the resources to repay the debt that the loans had created.

The level of poverty declined through the 1980s. None the less, by the end of the decade the cost of debt repayments was equivalent to the value of 25% of Zimbabwe's total exports, and 25% of government revenue. In reality, the only way Zimbabwe could keep paying was to receive new loans to pay old debts. With private banks less willing to lend to the country, the country was effectively bailed out by new loans from international financial institutions, particularly the World Bank, the African Development Bank and the IMF. These structural adjustment loans were not for investment in any particular project, but were used to repay existing debts, and were linked to Zimbabwe introducing policies such as reductions in government spending, trade liberalization, deregulation of prices, devaluation of the exchange rate and removal of labour laws. Such policies certainly enjoyed support within government, and were presented as home grown, but they were also a requirement of the lending needed to pay old debts. In 1991 and 1992 Zimbabwe was hit by a major drought, which led to rapid rises in poverty and inequality, while the debt burden continued to grow. This trend continued until Zimbabwe's external debt became highly unsustainable and continued to grow owing to accrual of arrears and new payments of interest and penalty charges on existing payment arrears. The above resulted in the country's external debt reaching some US \$10,770m. (equivalent to 76% of GDP) as of December 2015, according to IMF figures, of which just over one-half was contributed by the stock of accumulated arrears. The country is actually in debt distress, as characterized by large external payment arrears against the background of limited fiscal space and rising domestic debt.

Further exacerbating the situation is the prevailing large external account deficit, at a time when the country has no reserves to withstand any shocks. This has seriously affected the country's creditworthiness, thus constraining access to concessional financing and to the international capital markets. This presents an impediment to the capital flows and poses serious difficulties to Zimbabwe attaining its own development objectives. On the positive side, efforts are being made through the adoption by the Government of the ZAADDS, which is aimed at dealing with the debt issue and providing access to new financing for broad-based economic development.

Total public and publicly guaranteed debt remains unsustainably high, due to the continuous accumulation of arrears, as well as expansion in domestic debt. The Government has, in recent years, been relying on the domestic financial markets to meet its budget financing needs. This has resulted in a huge increase in domestic debt since 2017. However, since the end of 2018 domestic debt has been stabilizing, reflecting improved management, together with some increased debt service repayments. External debt stood at US \$8,000m. at the end of September 2019. The external arrears prevent Zimbabwe from accessing new financing from international financial institutions, and traditional bilateral and commercial creditors. As a signal of its commitment to the re-engagement process, the Government resumed token payments to international financial institutions in April 2019, and these continued in 2020.

According to government estimates, Zimbabwe's total public debt at the end of September 2021 amounted to US \$13,732m., a figure which comprised public external debt of \$13,200m. and domestic debt of \$532m. The total public debt stock excluded contingent liabilities of \$3,500m. for the compensation of former farm owners, which were to be incorporated on the completion of cession agreements with those owners.

LITERACY RATES AND EDUCATION

In the mid-2010s Zimbabwe had the highest adult literacy rate in Africa. According to estimates by the UN Educational, Scientific and Cultural Organization, in 2015 Zimbabwe's literacy rate stood at 86.9%, up from 77.8% in 1982. However, more recent data (from 2018), in which there was no figure given for Zimbabwe, indicated that Seychelles, São Tomé and Príncipe, Namibia and Mauritius had moved ahead of

Zimbabwe. The majority of the Zimbabwean labour force is educated to at least four years of secondary school. Labour rates are very competitive in comparison with the rest of the world, and due to a high unemployment rate, skilled, semi-skilled and unskilled labour is readily available. Most of the labour force is English-speaking.

ECONOMIC OUTLOOK

According to the World Bank, the economy of Zimbabwe was expected to continue to recover in the medium term, amid downside risks. GDP is projected to grow by 3.7% in 2022 but to slow down in the medium term as the positive base effects diminish. The rise in global commodity prices due to the impact of the war in Ukraine has exacerbated Zimbabwe's long-standing structural issues, which are characterized by rapidly rising inflation and the sharp depreciation of the Zimbabwean dollar, and continue to undermine economic recovery from the COVID-19 pandemic and weather shocks. Despite headline growth having rebounded in 2021, high poverty rates and youth unemployment persist. Protests over high fuel prices, high levels of food insecurity and endemic corruption, as well as declining real wages as inflation soars, highlight the risk of wider political instability.

Statistical Survey

Source (unless otherwise stated): Zimbabwe National Statistics Agency, 20th Floor Kaguvi Building, Cnr Fourth St/Central Ave, PO Box CY 342, Causeway, Harare; tel. (4) 706681; internet www.zimstat.co.zw.

Area and Population

AREA, POPULATION AND DENSITY

Area (sq km)	390,757*
Population (census results)	
17 August 2002	11,631,657
18 August 2012	
Males	6,280,539
Females	6,780,700
Total	13,061,239
Population (official projections)	
2019	15,159,624
2020	15,473,818
2021	15,790,716
Density (per sq km) at 2021	40.4

* 150,872 sq miles.

POPULATION BY AGE AND SEX
('000 official projections at 2021)

	Males	Females	Total
0–14 years	2,868.0	2,954.1	5,822.1
15–64 years	4,479.7	4,898.0	9,377.7
65 years and over	244.1	346.8	590.9
Total	7,591.9	8,198.8	15,790.7

Note: Totals may not be equal to the sum of components, owing to rounding.

PROVINCES
(demographic survey results, population at 2017)

	Area (sq km)	Population	Density (per sq km)
Bulawayo	479	738,600	1,542.0
Harare	872	1,973,906	2,263.7
Manicaland	36,459	1,861,755	51.1
Mashonaland Central .	28,347	1,441,944	50.9
Mashonaland East . .	32,230	1,366,522	42.4
Mashonaland West . .	57,441	1,567,449	27.3
Masvingo	56,566	1,553,145	27.5
Matabeleland North .	75,025	744,841	9.9
Matabeleland South .	54,172	810,074	15.0
Midlands	49,166	1,514,325	30.8
Total	390,757	13,572,560	34.7

PRINCIPAL TOWNS
(population at 2012 census)

Harare (capital) .	1,485,231	Chinhoyi (Sinoia) .	77,929
Bulawayo . . .	653,337	Marondera	
Chitungwiza . .	356,840	(Marandellas) .	61,998
Mutare (Umtali) .	187,621	Zvishavane	
Gweru (Gwelo) . .	157,865	(Shabani) . . .	45,230
Kwekwe (Que Que) .	100,900	Hwange (Wankie) .	37,522
Kadoma (Gatooma) .	92,469	Redcliff	35,929
Masvingo . . .	87,886		

Mid-2022 (incl. suburbs, UN projection): Harare (capital) 1,557,740 (Source: UN, *World Urbanization Prospects: The 2018 Revision*).

BIRTHS AND DEATHS
(annual averages, UN estimates)

	2005–10	2010–15	2015–20
Birth rate (per 1,000)	35.2	36.4	30.8
Death rate (per 1,000)	16.9	10.2	8.1

Source: UN, *World Population Prospects: The 2019 Revision*.

2017: Birth rate 29.8 per 1,000; Death rate 10.2 per 1,000 (Source: African Development Bank).

Life expectancy (years at birth, estimates): 61.7 (males 60.0; females 63.2) in 2020 (Source: World Bank, World Development Indicators database).

ECONOMICALLY ACTIVE POPULATION
(labour force and child labour survey, persons aged 15 years and over, 2019)

	Males	Females	Total
Agriculture, hunting, forestry and fishing	609,083	432,424	1,041,507
Mining and quarrying	174,566	34,413	208,979
Manufacturing	153,735	64,242	217,977
Electricity, gas and water . . .	17,540	3,848	21,388
Construction	94,793	9,352	104,145
Trade, restaurants and hotels .	203,749	337,694	541,443
Transport, storage and communications	87,175	10,391	97,565
Financing, insurance, real estate and business services . . .	62,023	28,313	90,336
Public administration and defence; compulsory social security . .	42,212	27,421	69,633
Education	76,547	119,174	195,721
Human health and social work activities	21,707	35,768	57,475

—continued	Males	Females	Total
Arts, entertainment and recreation and other service activities . .	50,245	33,247	83,491
Activities of households as employers of domestic personnel	46,494	119,138	165,632
Activities of extraterritorial organizations and bodies . .	1,132	640	1,772
Total employed	1,641,001	1,256,063	2,897,064
Unemployed	305,034	261,415	566,448
Total labour force	1,946,035	1,517,478	3,463,512

Note: Totals may not be equal to the sum of components, owing to rounding. Methodologies differ from previous labour force surveys, as persons engaged wholly or mainly in subsistence foodstuff production are excluded for the first time.

Health and Welfare

KEY INDICATORS

Total fertility rate (children per woman, 2020)	3.5
Under-5 mortality rate (per 1,000 live births, 2020) . . .	53.9
HIV/AIDS (% of persons aged 15–49, 2020)	11.9
COVID-19: Cumulative confirmed deaths (per 100,000 persons at 31 August 2022)	35.0
COVID-19: Fully vaccinated population (% of total population at 27 August 2022)	29.5
Physicians (per 1,000 head, 2018)	0.2
Hospitals beds (per 1,000 head, 2011)	1.7
Domestic health expenditure (2019): US $ per head (PPP) .	36.7
Domestic health expenditure (2019): % of GDP	1.4
Domestic health expenditure (2019): public (% of total current expenditure)	17.6
Access to improved water resources (% of persons, 2020) .	63
Access to improved sanitation facilities (% of persons, 2020) .	35
Total carbon dioxide emissions ('000 metric tons, 2018) . .	12,270
Carbon dioxide emissions per head (metric tons, 2018) . .	0.8
Human Development Index (2021): ranking	146
Human Development Index (2021): value	0.593

Note: For data on COVID-19 vaccinations, 'fully vaccinated' denotes receipt of all doses specified by approved vaccination regime (Sources: Johns Hopkins University and Our World in Data). Data on health expenditure refer to current general government expenditure in each case. For more information on sources and further definitions for all indicators, see Health and Welfare Statistics: Sources and Definitions section (europaworld.com/credits).

Agriculture

PRINCIPAL CROPS
('000 metric tons)

	2018	2019	2020
Bananas*	180.0	143.6	196.8
Barley*	53.8	54.4	55.0
Beans, dry	22.1	5.2	15.9
Cassava (Manioc)*	250.0	254.1	263.8
Grapefruit and pomelos* . . .	9.4	9.4	9.5
Groundnuts, with shell . . .	103.0	16.8	77.0
Lemons and limes* . . .	17.1	17.1	17.1
Maize	1,560.1	509.3	1,202.3
Millet	39.0	6.8	43.4
Oranges*	97.1	97.5	97.9
Potatoes*	15.0	15.3	15.2
Seed cotton	105.9	100.0*	93.4
Sorghum	75.3	10.9	143.1

—continued	2018	2019	2020
Soybeans (Soya beans) . . .	69.7	23.5	59.7
Sugar cane	3,583.0	3,562.0†	3,589.9*
Sweet potatoes*	27.0	27.1	27.1
Tangerines, mandarins, etc.* .	13.2	13.1	13.2
Tobacco, unmanufactured . .	239.9	184.6	203.5
Tomatoes*	25.2	25.2	25.1
Wheat	45.0*	80.0†	150.0†

* FAO estimate(s).
† Unofficial figure.

Aggregate production ('000 metric tons, may include official, semi-official or estimated data): Total cereals 1,777.3 in 2018, 665.6 in 2019, 1,598.0 in 2020; Total fruit (primary) 342.2 in 2018, 304.2 in 2019, 358.6 in 2020; Total oilcrops 297.0 in 2018, 157.5 in 2019, 256.9 in 2020; Total roots and tubers 293.2 in 2018, 297.6 in 2019, 307.3 in 2020; Total vegetables (primary) 184.8 in 2018, 229.0 in 2019, 228.5 in 2020.

Source: FAO.

LIVESTOCK
('000 head, year ending September, FAO estimates)

	2018	2019	2020
Asses	563.2	575.3	575.5
Cattle	5,415.1	5,521.9	5,513.4
Chickens	7,690	7,083	7,579
Goats	4,872.8	4,744.3	4,773.5
Horses	28.2	28.3	28.3
Pigs	230.4	279.5	272.2
Sheep	277.0	370.4	375.9

Source: FAO.

LIVESTOCK PRODUCTS
('000 metric tons, FAO estimates)

	2018	2019	2020
Cattle hides, fresh	6.9	6.0	6.0
Cattle meat	60.6	53.6	52.7
Cattle offals, edible	8.7	7.7	7.5
Cows' milk	420.5	427.0	426.8
Chicken meat	65.6	67.1	67.2
Game meat	36.4	36.6	36.8
Goat meat	25.2	24.7	36.8
Goats' skins, fresh	4.2	4.1	4.2
Pig meat	9.6	10.7	10.1
Hen eggs	24.5	24.5	24.3
Wool, greasy	2.5	2.5	2.5

Source: FAO.

Forestry

ROUNDWOOD REMOVALS
('000 cubic metres, excl. bark, FAO estimates)

	2018	2019	2020
Sawlogs, veneer logs and logs for sleepers	549.7	549.7	549.7
Pulpwood	27.6	27.6	27.6
Other industrial wood	45.9	45.9	45.9
Fuel wood	9,296.8	9,360.2	9,424.0
Total	9,920.0	9,983.4	10,047.1

Source: FAO.

SAWNWOOD PRODUCTION

('000 cubic metres, incl. railway sleepers, FAO estimates unless otherwise indicated)

	2011	2012	2013
Coniferous (softwood) . . .	163.0	184.3*	184.3
Broadleaved (hardwood) . . .	14.0	14.0	14.0
Total	177.0	198.3	198.3

* Unofficial figure.

2014–20: Figures assumed to be unchanged from 2013 (FAO estimates).

Source: FAO.

Fishing

('000 metric tons, live weight)

	2018	2019	2020
Capture	21.3	16.7	18.7
Tilapias	5.6	5.3	5.9
Dagaas	9.5	5.8	6.5
Other freshwater fishes . . .	6.3	5.7	6.4
Aquaculture	11.0	12.5	15.4
Tilapias	10.9	12.4	15.4
Total catch	32.3	29.2	34.2

Note: Figures exclude aquatic animals, recorded by number rather than weight. The number of Nile crocodiles caught was: 98,797 in 2018; 85,148 in 2019; 213,063 in 2020.

Source: FAO.

Mining

('000 metric tons unless otherwise indicated)

	2019	2020
Gold (kg)	29,428.6	20,873.2
Platinum (kg)	13,856.8	15,003.9
Palladium (kg)	11,639.6	12,889.9
Rhodium (kg)	1,224.2	1,367.5
Ruthenium (kg)	791.6	1,026.3
Diamond ('000 carats)	2,119.2	2,670.5
Chrome	1,550.1	1,272.1
Nickel (metric tons)	16,277.6	16,336.3
Copper (metric tons)	8,678.0	7,932.8
Cobalt (metric tons)	401.8	955.9
Coal	2,729.9	2,750.9
Lithium (metric tons)	62,622.8	20,858.9
Phosphate (metric tons)	27,148.0	45,083.5
Granite (metric tons)	154,884.5	644,715.1
Vermiculite (metric tons)	25,523.5	26,387.9

Source: Reserve Bank of Zimbabwe, *Annual Report.*

Industry

SELECTED PRODUCTS

('000 metric tons)

	2016	2017	2018
Coke (metallurgical)	51	90	103
Cement	1,650*	1,750	1,800
Ferro-chromium	78.2	142.8	365.0

* Estimate.

Refined copper (unwrought, metric tons, estimate): 1,500 in 2014.

Refined nickel (unwrought, metric tons): 2,915 in 2014; 617 in 2015.

Source: US Geological Survey.

Raw sugar ('000 metric tons): 455 in 2014; 410 in 2015; 450 in 2016 (Source: UN Industrial Commodity Statistics Database).

Electricity (net production, million kWh): 7,396.1 in 2017; 9,172.8 in 2018; 7,536.0 in 2019.

Finance

CURRENCY AND EXCHANGE RATES

Monetary Units
100 cents = 1 new Zimbabwe dollar (Z.$).

Sterling, US Dollar and Euro Equivalents (31 May 2022)
£1 sterling = Z.$366.198;
US $1 = Z.$290.888;
€1 = Z.$311.628;
Z.$1,000 = £2.73 = US $3.44 = €3.21.

Average Exchange Rate (new Zimbabwe dollar per US dollar)
2020   51.329
2021   88.552

Note: On 1 August 2008 a redenomination of the Zimbabwe dollar was introduced whereby 10,000m. of the former currency was revalued at 1 dollar. In January 2009, in order to address the diminishing value of the national currency, a number of foreign currencies (including the US dollar, the euro, the British pound sterling, the South African rand and the Botswana pula), were also declared legal tender in Zimbabwe. A further massive redenomination of the Zimbabwe dollar was announced in February (whereby 1,000,000m. of the former currency was to be revalued at 1 dollar), but in April of the same year legal use of the national currency was effectively suspended. In 2015 it was announced that the practically worthless Zimbabwe dollar was to be decommissioned completely by September of that year, with extravagant-sounding private savings converted into just a few US dollars. A number of foreign currencies (specifically those of Australia, Botswana, the People's Republic of China, the eurozone, India, Japan, South Africa, the United Kingdom and the USA) were all in regular use in the following years, but shortages of US dollars in particular prompted the central bank to issue bond notes as a 'surrogate' currency in 2016. In February 2019 physical and electronic bond notes were merged to form the Real Time Gross Settlement (RTGS) dollar (or 'Zimdollar') with an initial market rate of 2.5 per US dollar, but the rate had fallen to 10.7 per US dollar by the end of August, and the rate against the dollar continue to fall thereafter. In June 2019 the Government had banned the use of foreign currencies in local transactions (until March 2020), and in November 2019 the central bank issued new Zimbabwe dollars (ZWL) for the first time since 2009 to circulate in parity with existing bond notes and RTGS dollars.

BUDGET

(million new Zimbabwe dollars)

Revenue	2020	2021*	2022†
Tax revenue	176,499	474,264	810,186
Personal income tax . . .	28,509	78,356	156,695
Corporate income tax . . .	33,869	124,986	195,607
Other direct taxes	12,270	26,317	48,052
Customs	14,572	28,228	44,178
Excise	25,824	51,736	85,467
Value-added tax	43,797	112,854	199,139
Other taxes	17,659	51,788	81,050
Non-tax revenue	6,540	20,771	40,092
Total	183,039	495,035	850,278

Expenditure	2020	2021*	2022†
Current expenditure . . .	106,364	375,235	695,964
Salaries and wages . . .	64,596	193,261	340,000
Pensions and benefits . .	9,785	30,399	58,853
Interest payments . . .	3,129	12,551	34,249
Foreign	2,802	11,714	23,835
Goods and services . . .	20,013	99,469	171,559
Current transfers . . .	18,626	69,954	150,156
Capital expenditure‡ . . .	70,747	164,224	251,165
Total	177,111	539,460	947,130

* Estimates.
† Projections.
‡ Including net lending.

Source: IMF, *Zimbabwe: 2022 Article IV Consultation—Press Release; Staff Report; and Statement by the Executive Director for Zimbabwe* (April 2022).

INTERNATIONAL RESERVES
(US $ million at 31 December)

	2019	2020	2021
Gold (national valuation) . . .	0.6	2.1	2.1
IMF special drawing rights . .	3.2	1.9	669.7
Reserve position in IMF . . .	0.5	0.5	0.5
Foreign exchange	146.9	29.6	166.6
Total	151.2	34.1	838.9

Source: IMF, *International Financial Statistics*.

MONEY SUPPLY
(million new Zimbabwe dollars at 31 December)

	2019	2020	2021
Currency outside depository corporations	907.6	1,198.1	2,313.8
Transferable deposits . . .	31,978.7	192,383.7	431,948.4
Other deposits	1,887.9	9,906.8	37,403.0
Securities other than shares .	244.0	1,436.2	3,696.3
Broad money	35,018.2	204,924.9	475,361.5

Source: Reserve Bank of Zimbabwe, Harare.

COST OF LIVING
(Consumer Price Index; base: February 2019 = 100)

	2019	2020	2021
Food and non-alcoholic beverages .	295.7	2,072.8	4,265.8
Alcoholic beverages and tobacco .	293.6	2,185.2	4,412.9
Clothing and footwear	269.5	2,015.1	3,632.6
Housing, water electricity, gas and other fuels	163.1	663.0	1,125.9
Health	300.5	2,345.5	4,614.7
Transport	252.1	1,481.0	2,931.1
All items (incl. others) . . .	240.3	1,579.1	3,135.2

Source: Reserve Bank of Zimbabwe, Harare.

NATIONAL ACCOUNTS
(US $ million at current prices, estimates)

Expenditure on the Gross Domestic Product

	2018	2019	2020
Government final consumption expenditure	6,228	4,781	5,016
Private final consumption expenditure	18,729	17,529	17,161
Gross capital formation . . .	2,272	2,114	2,083
Total domestic expenditure .	27,230	24,425	24,261
Exports of goods and services . .	4,619	4,285	4,226
Less Imports of goods and services	7,538	6,774	6,700
GDP in purchasers' values .	24,312	21,935	21,787

Gross Domestic Product by Economic Activity

	2018	2019	2020
Agriculture, hunting, forestry and fishing	2,019	1,793	1,802
Mining and utilities	1,881	1,772	1,739
Manufacturing	2,575	2,428	2,373
Construction	563	491	495
Trade, restaurants and hotels .	4,931	4,452	4,436
Transport, storage and communications	2,533	2,255	2,247
Other services	7,434	6,622	6,580
Sub-total	21,936	19,812	19,672
Net taxes on products*	2,376	2,123	2,114
GDP in purchasers' values .	24,312	21,935	21,787

* Figures obtained as residuals.

Source: UN National Accounts Main Aggregates Database.

BALANCE OF PAYMENTS
(US $ million)

	2018	2019	2020*
Exports of goods	5,178.2	5,266.9	5,263.3
Imports of goods	−7,642.2	−5,398.4	−5,489.5
Balance on goods	−2,464.0	−131.4	−226.2
Exports of services	500.5	603.2	331.4
Imports of services	−1,026.2	−909.1	−769.6
Balance on goods and services	−2,989.70	−437.3	−664.4
Primary income received . . .	7.9	15.4	7.6
Primary income paid	−319.1	−354.2	−480.5
Balance on goods, services and income	−3,300.9	−776.1	−1,137.3
Secondary income received . .	1,424.2	1,413.4	1,828.3
Secondary income paid . . .	−28.6	−22.7	−33.1
Current balance	−1,379.6	920.5	1,096.0
Capital account (net)	308.8	52.8	243.3
Direct investment assets . . .	−0.8	−2.4	3.5
Direct investment liabilities . .	717.9	249.5	150.4
Portfolio investment liabilities .	54.7	3.7	−81.6
Other investment assets . . .	−149.7	−366.1	−321.8
Other investment liabilities . .	262.1	−228.5	−710.8
Net errors and omissions . . .	92.9	−664.7	−466.6
Overall balance	−93.7	−35.3	−87.6

* Preliminary estimates.

Source: Reserve Bank of Zimbabwe, Harare.

External Trade

PRINCIPAL COMMODITIES
(US $ million)

Imports c.i.f.	2018	2019	2020*
Food products	451.2	194.3	591.6
Rice	125.4	50.5	106.1
Wheat	117.2	51.6	102.2
Animal, vegetable fats and oils .	174.0	92.5	165.8
Mineral fuels, oils and distillation products	1,770.6	1,311.6	608.0
Chemicals and related products .	662.1	356.4	489.7
Raw materials	1,229.6	662.0	909.5
Manufactured goods	574.8	381.4	392.9
Machinery, etc.	1,026.8	835.1	971.9
Transport equipment and motor vehicles	641.6	347.9	264.6
Total (incl. others)	7,067.0	4,817.2	4,982.4

Exports	2018	2019	2020*
Animal hides	35.1	30.9	29.6
Sugar, refined	23.4	51.4	65.1
Macadamia nuts	16.8	20.7	13.7
Tobacco and manufactures . .	934.4	818.1	795.0
Gold	1,245.4	1,063.9	982.3
Platinum group metals (PGMs) .	1,037.3	1,264.0	1,964.4
High carbon ferrochrome . . .	272.0	280.9	129.3
Diamonds	98.2	166.1	150.7
Chrome ores (chromite) and concentrates	118.9	70.3	54.2
Electrical machinery, equipment, parts and appliances . . .	34.8	41.2	24.5
Jewellry	73.7	160.8	84.7
Total (incl. others)	4,654.1	4,663.7	4,931.9

* Preliminary estimates.

Source: Reserve Bank of Zimbabwe, Harare.

PRINCIPAL TRADING PARTNERS
(US $ million)

Imports f.o.b.	2014	2015	2016
Botswana	148.0	55.0	39.5
China, People's Republic . . .	398.8	458.2	365.5
Hong Kong	53.9	90.1	47.3
India	131.7	237.7	166.0
Japan	154.8	129.8	99.6
Mauritius	53.6	47.9	72.2
Mozambique	148.4	169.0	162.4
Singapore	1,168.0	1,338.2	1,117.9
South Africa	2,735.5	2,305.2	2,152.8
United Arab Emirates . .	106.9	79.7	61.7
United Kingdom	208.4	98.0	91.4
USA	76.8	69.7	67.1
Zambia	179.7	277.5	182.4
Total (incl. others)	6,379.8	6,001.1	5,212.1

Exports f.o.b.*	2014	2015	2016
Belgium	125.0	18.8	45.7
Botswana	27.5	30.7	28.8
China, People's Republic . . .	12.4	4.4	0.8
Israel	9.6	13.7	1.2
Mozambique	574.1	407.6	265.8
South Africa	2,014.9	1,908.7	2,245.5
United Arab Emirates . . .	96.0	147.8	116.7
Zambia	95.1	86.3	69.4
Total (incl. others)	3,009.0	3,225.3	3,308.5

* Excluding re-exports 55.6 in 2014; 23.0 in 2015; 10.3 in 2016.

Transport

ROAD TRAFFIC
(new vehicle registrations)

	2012	2013	2014
Passenger cars	57,380	68,159	58,242
Heavy motor vehicles . . .	4,509	5,441	3,703
Trailers, tractors and construction vehicles	1,494	1,616	1,095
Motorcycles and mopeds . .	2,316	1,882	1,926

CIVIL AVIATION
(traffic on scheduled services)

	2013	2014	2015
Kilometres flown (million) . .	21	20	19
Passengers carried ('000) . .	352	301	370
Passenger-km (million) . .	682	662	808
Total ton-km (million) . .	33	33	1

Source: UN, *Statistical Yearbook*.

2020 (domestic and international): Departures 3,450; Passengers carried 324,227; Freight carried 10m. ton-km (Source: World Bank, World Development Indicators database).

Tourism

VISITOR ARRIVALS BY NATIONALITY

	2019	2020	2021
Australia and New Zealand . .	34,972	4,444	5,731
Botswana	69,095	15,974	5,218
Malawi	454,888	127,349	61,567
Mozambique	213,913	80,458	27,734
South Africa	562,643	152,845	71,884
USA	73,987	12,183	18,756
Zambia	409,672	137,940	69,608
Total (incl. others)	2,294,259	639,356	380,820

Tourism receipts (US $ million, excl. passenger transport): 1,247 in 2019; 360 in 2020; 397 in 2021.

Source: Zimbabwe Tourism Authority, Harare.

Communications Media

	2018	2019	2020
Telephones ('000 main lines in use)	268.8	265.7	252.1
Mobile telephone subscriptions ('000)	12,909.0	13,195.9	13,191.7
Broadband subscriptions, fixed ('000)	203.1	204.4	203.5
Broadband subscriptions, mobile ('000)	7,460.2	7,569.9	8,695.2
Internet users (% of population) .	25.0	25.1	29.3

Source: International Telecommunication Union.

Education

(2017 unless otherwise indicated)

	Institutions	Teachers	Students
Primary	6,123	71,242	2,676,485
Secondary	2,830	45,780	1,075,325
Technical colleges	n.a.	2,279*	19,600†
Teacher training colleges‡ .	n.a.	1,175*	28,610
Other vocational colleges . .	n.a.	113§	1,527*

* 2014.
† 2016.
‡ Excludes Zimbabwe integrated teacher education course.
§ 2011.

Pupil-teacher ratio (qualified teaching staff, primary education, UNESCO estimate): 38.3 in 2019/20 (Source: UNESCO Institute for Statistics).

Adult literacy rate (UNESCO estimates): 86.9% (males 88.5%; females 85.3%) in 2015 (Source: UNESCO Institute for Statistics).

Directory

The Constitution

A new Constitution replacing that introduced at independence on 18 April 1980 (and as subsequently amended) was approved at a national referendum on 16 March 2013 and was signed into law on 22 May. Its main provisions, including subsequent amendments, are summarized below.

FOUNDING PROVISIONS

Zimbabwe is a unitary, democratic and sovereign republic and the Constitution is the supreme law.

DECLARATION OF RIGHTS

The declaration of rights guarantees the fundamental rights and freedoms of the individual, regardless of race, tribe, place of origin, political opinions, colour, creed or sex.

THE PRESIDENT

Executive power is vested in the President, and is exercised by him/her through the Cabinet. The President is head of state, head of government and Commander-in-Chief of the Defence Forces. The President is elected by direct universal suffrage and must be a Zimbabwean citizen of at least 40 years of age. Upon assuming office, the President appoints up to two Vice-Presidents. The President appoints ministers and deputy ministers from among the senators and the members of the National Assembly, to be members of the Cabinet; he/she may also appoint up to seven members of the Cabinet from outside Parliament, on the basis of their skills and competence. The President and Vice-Presidents hold office for five years. The President is eligible for re-election for one further term.

PARLIAMENT

Legislative power is vested in the legislature, which consists of the President and a bicameral Parliament, comprising the Senate and the National Assembly. The Senate comprises 80 members, of whom 60 are elected by a proportional representation system (six are elected in each of the 10 provinces by voters registered in the 60 senatorial constituencies), 16 are Chiefs, two are the President and the Deputy President of the National Council of Chiefs and two are elected to represent persons with disabilities. The life of the Senate is ordinarily to be five years. The National Assembly comprises 210 members, all of whom are directly elected by universal adult suffrage, as well as an additional 60 women members, six from each province, elected through a proportional representation system. (However, the quota system for additional women members is scheduled to end in 2033.) From 2023 10 new seats in the National Assembly were to be reserved for individuals aged between 21 and 35 years and awarded on the basis of proportional representation. The life of the National Assembly is ordinarily to be five years.

OTHER PROVISIONS

There is an independent Zimbabwe Human Rights Commission (ZHRC), comprising a chairperson and eight other members, to promote the protection, development and attainment of human rights and freedoms and to investigate the conduct of any authority or person, where it is alleged that any of the human rights and freedoms set out in the Declaration of Rights has been violated by that authority or person. (However, according to constitutional amendments introduced in May 2021, certain functions of the ZHRC, concerning public maladministration etc., were to be transferred to the holder of the new office of Public Protector.) Among other independent commissions are: the Zimbabwe Electoral Commission, the Zimbabwe Gender Commission, the Zimbabwe Media Commission and the National Peace and Reconciliation Commission.

Chiefs shall be appointed by the President on the recommendation of the Provincial Assembly of Chiefs through the National Council of Chiefs and the minister responsible for traditional leaders.

The Government

HEAD OF STATE

President: EMMERSON MNANGAGWA (inaugurated 24 November 2017; elected 30 July 2018).
First Vice-President: Dr Gen. (retd) CONSTANTINO CHIWENGA.
Second Vice-President: (vacant).

THE CABINET
(October 2022)

The Cabinet is composed of representatives of the Zimbabwe African National Union—Patriotic Front.

President: EMMERSON MNANGAGWA.

First Vice-President and Minister of Health and Child Care: Dr Gen. (retd) CONSTANTINO CHIWENGA.

Second Vice-President: (vacant).

Minister of Defence and War Veterans: OPPAH ZVIPANGE MUCHINGURI-KASHIRI.

Minister of Finance and Economic Development: Prof. MTHULI NCUBE.

Minister of Energy and Power Development: SODA ZHEMU.

Minister of Women Affairs, Community, Small and Medium Enterprises Development: SITHEMBISO G. G. NYONI.

Minister of Home Affairs and Cultural Heritage: KAZEMBE KAZEMBE.

Minister of Transport and Infrastructural Development: FELIX MHONA.

Minister of Local Government, Public Works and National Housing: JULY G. MOYO.

Minister of Higher and Tertiary Education, Science and Technology: Prof. AMON MURWIRA.

Minister of Lands, Agriculture, Fisheries, Water and Rural Resettlement: Dr ANXIOUS JONGWE MASUKA.

Minister of Industry and Commerce: Dr SEKESAI IRENE NZENZA.

Minister of the Environment, Climate Change, Tourism and Hospitality Industry: MANGALISO NDLOVU.

Minister of Public Service, Labour and Social Welfare: Prof. PAUL MAVIMA.

Minister of Foreign Affairs and International Trade: Dr FREDERICK SHAVA.

Minister of Primary and Secondary Education: Dr EVELYN NDLOVU.

Minister of Mines and Mining Development: WINSTON CHITANDO.

Minister of Information, Publicity and Broadcasting Services: MONICA MUTSVANGWA.

Minister of Information Communication Technology, and Postal and Courier Services: JENFAN MUSWERE.

Minister of Youth, Sport, Arts and Recreation: KIRSTY COVENTRY.

Minister of Justice, Legal and Parliamentary Affairs: ZIYAMBI ZIYAMBI.

Minister of National Housing and Social Amenities: DANIEL GARWE.

Minister without Portfolio in the Office of the President and Cabinet: CAIN MATHEMA.

Minister of State for Presidential Affairs in charge of Implementation and Monitoring: JORAM GUMBO.

Ministers of State in the Office of the Vice-President: DAVIS MARAPIRA, SIBANGUMUZI SIXTONE KHUMALO.

Minister of State for National Security: (vacant).

Ministers of State for Provincial Affairs: JUDITH MKWANDA (Bulawayo), NOKUTHULA MATSIKENYERI (Manicaland), MONICA MAVHUNGA (Mashonaland Central), APOLLONIA MUNZVERENGI (Mashonaland East), MARY MLISWA (Mashonaland West), EZRA CHADZAMIRA (Masvingo), LARRY MAVIMA (Midlands), RICHARD MOYO (Matabeleland North), ABEDNICO NCUBE (Matabeleland South).

In addition, there were 20 deputy ministers. The Attorney-General is also a member of the Cabinet.

MINISTRIES

Office of the President and Cabinet: Munhumutapa Bldg, cnr Samora Machel Ave and Sam Nujoma St, Private Bag 7700, Causeway, Harare; tel. (24) 2707091; e-mail info@opc.gov.zw; internet www.theopc.gov.zw.

Ministry of Defence and War Veterans: Defence House, cnr Kwame Nkuruma Ave and Third St, Harare; tel. (24) 2700055; internet www.defence.gov.zw.

Ministry of Energy and Power Development: John Boyne Bldg, 2nd Floor, cnr Speke Ave and Inez Terrace, Private Bag 7758, Causeway, Harare; tel. (24) 2791760; e-mail moepd@energy.gov.zw; internet www.energy.gov.zw.

Ministry of the Environment, Climate Change, Tourism and Hospitality Industry: Kaguvi Bldg, 11th Floor, cnr 4th St and Central Ave, Private Bag 7753, Causeway, Harare; tel. (24) 2750401; e-mail info@environment.gov.zw; internet fb.com/METHIZimbabwe.

Ministry of Finance and Economic Development: Dlodlo Bldg (New Govt Complex), 3rd Floor, cnr Samora Machel Ave and Fourth St, Private Bag 7705, Causeway, Harare; tel. (24) 2794571; e-mail feedback@zimtreasury.gov.zw; internet www.zimtreasury.gov.zw.

Ministry of Foreign Affairs and International Trade: Munhu-mutapa Bldg, cnr Samora Machel Ave and Sam Nujoma St, POB 4240, Causeway, Harare; tel. (24) 2794681; e-mail mfa@zimfa.gov.zw; internet www.zimfa.gov.zw.

Ministry of Health and Child Care: Kaguvi Bldg, 4th Floor, Central Ave, POB CY198, Causeway, Harare; tel. (24) 2798555; e-mail pr@mohcc.gov.zw; internet www.mohcc.gov.zw.

Ministry of Higher and Tertiary Education, Science and Technology: Govt Composite Bldg, Blks F and G, 5th Floor, cnr Samora Machel Ave and Simon Muzenda St, POB CY7732, Causeway, Harare; tel. (24) 2796440; e-mail admin@mhtestd.gov.zw; internet www.mhtestd.gov.zw.

Ministry of Home Affairs and Cultural Heritage: Mukwati Bldg, 11th Floor, cnr Fourth St and Livingstone Ave, POB CY7703, Causeway, Harare; tel. (24) 2703641; e-mail thesecretary@moha.gov.zw; internet www.moha.gov.zw.

Ministry of Industry and Commerce: Mukwati Bldg, 13th Floor, cnr Fourth St and Livingstone Ave, Private Bag 7708, Causeway, Harare; tel. (24) 2707540; e-mail mic@mic.gov.zw; internet www.mic.gov.zw.

Ministry of Information Communication Technology and Courier Services: 76 Samora Machel Ave, 7th Floor, Bank Chambers, Harare; tel. (24) 2707347; e-mail info@ictministry.gov.zw; internet www.ictministry.gov.zw.

Ministry of Information, Publicity and Broadcasting Services: Bank Chambers Bldg, 1st Floor, 76 Samora Machel Ave, POB CY1176, Harare; tel. (24) 2795807; e-mail info@informin.org.zw; internet www.infomin.org.zw.

Ministry of Justice, Legal and Parliamentary Affairs: New Govt Complex, 6th Floor, Blk C, cnr S. V. Muzenda St and Samora Machel Ave, Private Bag 7751, Causeway, Harare; tel. (24) 2774620; e-mail justice@justice.gov.zw; internet justice.gov.zw.

Ministry of Lands, Agriculture, Fisheries, Water and Rural Resettlement: Ngungunyana Bldg, 1 Borrowdale Rd, Harare; tel. (24) 2797400; e-mail infor@moa.gov.zw; internet www.moa.gov.zw.

Ministry of Local Government, Public Works and National Housing: Makombe Bldg, cnr Leopold Takawira St and Herbert Chitepo Ave, Private Bag 7706, Causeway, Harare; tel. (24) 2756521; e-mail communications@mlg.gov.zw; internet www.mlg.gov.zw.

Ministry of Mines and Mining Development: ZIMRE Centre, 6th Floor, cnr Leopold Takawira St and Kwame Nkrumah Ave, Private Bag 7709, Causeway, Harare; tel. (24) 2777022; e-mail mmmd@mines.gov.zw; internet www.mines.gov.zw.

Ministry of Primary and Secondary Education: Ambassador House, 88 Kwame Nkrumah Ave, cnr Second St, POB CY121, Causeway, Harare; tel. (24) 2705153; e-mail admin@mopse.gov.zw; internet www.mopse.co.zw.

Ministry of Public Service, Labour and Social Welfare: Kaguvi Bldg, 9th Floor, cnr S. V. Muzenda St and Central Ave, POB CY17, Causeway, Harare; tel. (24) 2790871; e-mail mpslswzim@gmail.com; internet www.mpslsw.gov.zw.

Ministry of Transport and Infrastructural Development: Kaguvi Bldg, 13th Floor, cnr S. V. Muzenda St and Central Ave, POB CY595, Causeway, Harare; tel. (24) 2700991; e-mail info@transcom.gov.zw; internet www.transcom.gov.zw.

Ministry of Women Affairs, Community, Small and Medium Enterprises Development: Kaguvi Bldg, 8th Floor, cnr Fourth St and Central Ave, Harare; tel. (24) 2708389; internet fb.com/ZWwomensmed.

Ministry of Youth, Sport, Arts and Recreation: Chinengundu Mashayamombe Bldg, cnr 4th and Nelson Mandela Ave, Harare; tel. (24) 2708373; e-mail info@moysar.gov.zw; internet fb.com/moysarzim.

President

Presidential Election, 30 July 2018

Candidate	Valid votes	% of valid votes
Emmerson Mnangagwa (ZANU—PF) . .	2,456,010	51.43
Nelson Chamisa (MDC Alliance) . . .	2,151,927	45.07
Thokozani Khupe (MDC—T) . . .	45,626	0.95
Joseph Makamba Busha (FZC) . . .	17,540	0.37
Nkosana Donald Moyo (APA) . . .	15,172	0.31
Evaristo Washington Chikanga (RZP) .	13,132	0.28
Joice Teurai Ropa Mujuru (PRC) . . .	12,853	0.27
Others*	62,657	1.31
Total	**4,774,917†**	**100.00**

* There were 16 other candidates.
† In addition, there were 72,340 invalid votes.

Legislature

NATIONAL ASSEMBLY

National Assembly: cnr Kwame Nkrumah and Third Sts, Box CY 298, Causeway, Harare; tel. (24) 2700181; e-mail clerk@parlzim.gov.zw; internet www.parlzim.gov.zw.

Speaker: Jacob Mudenda.

General Election, 30 July 2018

Party	Seats
ZANU—PF	145
MDC Alliance	63
NPF	1
Independent	1
Total	**210***

* In addition to the 210 directly elected members, an additional 60 women members, six from each province, were elected under a proportional representation system. Of these, 35 represented ZANU—PF, 24 represented the MDC Alliance and one represented the MDC—T.

SENATE

Speaker: Mabel M. Chinomona.

General Election, 30 July 2018

Party	Seats
ZANU—PF	35
MDC Alliance	24
MDC—T	1
Total	**60***

* In addition to the 60 members elected under a proportional representation system (six are elected in each of the 10 provinces), there are a further 20 members in the Senate. These additional members include 16 tribal Chiefs, the President and the Deputy President of the National Council of Chiefs, and two individuals elected to represent persons with disabilities.

Election Commission

Zimbabwe Electoral Commission (ZEC): Mahachi Quantum Bldg, 1 Nelson Mandela Ave, PMB 7782, Causeway, Harare; tel. (24) 2781903; e-mail inquiries@zec.org.zw; internet www.zec.gov.zw; f. 2005; Chair. Priscilla Chigumba; Chief Elections Officer Utoile Silaigwana.

Political Organizations

Alliance for the People's Agenda (APA): Harare; tel. 772766654; e-mail voteapa@gmail.com; internet fb.com/APAZimbabwe; Pres. Albert Gumbo (acting).

Citizens Coalition for Change (CCC): Harare; internet ccczimbabwe.com; f. 2022 following spilt from Movement for Democratic Change Alliance (MDC Alliance); Leader Nelson Chamisa.

Free Zimbabwe Congress (FZC): Masvingo; e-mail admin@freezimcongress.org; internet www.freezimcongress.com; f. 1986; Leader JOSEPH MAKAMBA BUSHA.

Mavambo Kusile Dawn (MKD): 72 George Silundika Ave, opp. Raylton Club, Harare; tel. (24) 2795266; internet www.mavambokusiledawn.org; f. 2009; Leader SIMBA MAKONI.

Movement for Democratic Change Alliance (MDC Alliance): 44 Nelson Mandela Ave, Harare; tel. 772233872; e-mail info@mdcallianceparty.org; internet www.mdcallianceparty.org; f. 1999; established as the Movement for Democratic Change—Tsvangirai (MDC—T); present name adopted in 2018; breakaway faction led by Douglas Mwonzora continues to use the name MDC—T; breakaway faction led by former leader, Nelson Chamisa, operates under the name Citizens Coalition for Change (CCC); Pres. DOUGLAS MWONZORA; Sec.-Gen. PAURINA MPARIWA.

Mthwakazi Liberation Front (MLF): Office 9, Solomon Bldg, cnr Raymond and Rockey Sts, Yeoville, Johannesburg, South Africa; f. 2010; secessionist movement; Pres. MPIYESIZWE GUDUZA; Sec.-Gen. ANDREA SIBANDA.

National People's Party (NPP): Harare; f. 2016; Leader JOICE TEURAI ROPA MUJURU; Sec.-Gen. LLOYD MSIPA.

Rebuilding Zimbabwe Party (RZP): Harare; internet fb.com/rebuildingzimparty; Pres. EVARISTO WASHINGTON CHIKANGA.

Zimbabwe African National Union—Patriotic Front (ZANU—PF): cnr Rotten Row St and Samora Machel Ave, Harare; tel. (24) 2750697; e-mail info@zanupf.org.zw; internet www.zanupf.org.zw; f. 1989 by merger of ZAPU and ZANU; Pres. EMMERSON MNANGAGWA; Vice-Pres CONSTANTINO CHIWENGA, KEMBO MOHADI.

Zimbabwe African People's Union (ZAPU): 8 Rudd Ave, North-end, Bulawayo; tel. (29) 2888850; e-mail zmazibuko@aol.com; internet www.zapu.org; f. 1961; merged into ZANU—PF in 1989; re-established 2008; Pres. SIBANGILIZWE NKOMO; Sec.-Gen. Dr STRIKE MKANDLA.

Zimbabwe Development Party: Harare; tel. (24) 2777777; f. 2008; Leader (vacant).

Diplomatic Representation

EMBASSIES IN ZIMBABWE

Algeria: 8 Pascoe Ave, Belgravia, Harare; tel. (24) 2791773; e-mail offambalch@utande.co.zw; Ambassador NOUREDDINE YAZID.

Angola: Doncaster House, 26 Speke Ave, POB 3590, Harare; tel. (24) 2770075; Ambassador AGOSTINHO TAVARES DA SILVA NETO.

Australia: 1 Green Close, Borrowdale, Harare; tel. (24) 2853235; e-mail zimbabwe.embassy@dfat.gov.au; internet zimbabwe.embassy.gov.au; Ambassador BRONTE MOULES.

Botswana: 22 Phillips Ave, Belgravia, POB 563, Harare; tel. (24) 2794647; e-mail botzim@gov.bw; internet botswanaembassy.co.zw; Ambassador SARAH SITHABILE MOLOZIWA.

Brazil: 16 Prestwood Lane, Borrowdale, POB 2530, Harare; tel. (24) 2862269; e-mail brasemb.harare@itamaraty.gov.br; internet www.gov.br/mre/pt-br/embaixada-harare; Ambassador VILMAR ROGEIRO COUTINHO JUNIOR.

Canada: 45 Baines Ave, POB 1430, Harare; tel. 8677008600; e-mail hrare@international.gc.ca; internet www.canadainternational.gc.ca/zimbabwe; Ambassador CHRISTINA BUCHAN.

China, People's Republic: 58 Golden Stairs Rd, Mount Pleasant, POB 4749, Harare; tel. (24) 2332760; e-mail chinaemb_zw@mfa.gov.cn; internet zw.china-embassy.gov.cn; Ambassador GUO SHAOCHUN.

Congo, Democratic Republic: 5 Pevensey Rd, Highlands, POB 2446, Harare; tel. (24) 2496421; Ambassador MAWAMPANGA MWANA NANGA.

Cuba: 5 Phillips Ave, Belgravia, POB A1196, Harare; tel. (24) 2790126; e-mail embajada@zw.embacuba.cu; internet misiones.minrex.gob.cu/es/zimbabwe; Ambassador (vacant).

Egypt: 7 Aberdeen Rd, Avondale, POB A433, Harare; tel. (24) 2303445; e-mail egyptianembassy@live.com; internet fb.com/EmbassyofEgyptinHarareZimbabwe; Ambassador SALWA MOWAFI.

Equatorial Guinea: 3 Phillips Ave, Harare; tel. (24) 2791913; e-mail embarege.harare@hotmail.com; Ambassador JOSÉ ELA EBANG.

Ethiopia: 14 Lanark Rd, Belgravia, POB 2745, Harare; tel. (24) 2701514; Ambassador RASHID MOHAMMED ABDUL WAHID.

France: 3 Princess Dr., Newlands, POB 1378, Harare; tel. 8677007154; e-mail web.harare@diplomatie.gouv.fr; internet zw.ambafrance.org; Ambassador LAURENT CHEVALLIER.

Germany: 30 Ceres Rd, Avondale, POB A1475, Harare; tel. (24) 2308655; e-mail info@harare.diplo.de; internet www.harare.diplo.de; Ambassador UDO VOLZ.

Ghana: 11 Downie Ave, Belgravia, POB 4445, Harare; tel. (24) 2701014; e-mail harare@mfa.gov.gh; internet ghanaembassy-zimbabwe.com; Ambassador ALEXANDER NTRAKWA.

Greece: 8 Deary Ave, Belgravia, POB 4809, Harare; tel. (24) 2793208; e-mail gremb.har@mfa.gr; internet www.mfa.gr/harare; Ambassador LOUKAS KARATSOLIS.

Holy See: 5 St Kilda Rd, Mount Pleasant, POB MP191, Harare; tel. (24) 2744547; Apostolic Nuncio PAOLO RUDELLI (Titular Archbishop of Mesembria).

India: 12 Natal Rd, Belgravia, POB 4620, Harare; tel. (24) 2795955; e-mail ambassadoroffice@embindia.org.zw; internet eoi.gov.in/harare; Ambassador VIJAY KHANDUJA.

Indonesia: 3 Duthie Ave, Belgravia, POB CY69, Causeway, Harare; tel. (24) 2251799; e-mail harare.kbri@kemlu.go.id; internet www.kemlu.go.id/harare; Ambassador DEWA MADE SASTRAWAN.

Iran: 8 Allan Wilson Ave, Avondale, POB A293, Harare; tel. (24) 2250286; e-mail iranemb.hre@mfa.gov.ir; internet zimbabwe.mfa.gov.ir; Ambassador ABBAS NAVAZANI.

Italy: 7 Bartholomew Close, Greendale North, POB 1062, Harare; tel. (24) 2497373; e-mail ambasciata.harare@esteri.it; internet www.ambharare.esteri.it; Ambassador UMBERTO MALNATI.

Japan: Social Security Centre, 4th Floor, cnr Julius Nyerere Way and Sam Nujoma St, POB 2710, Harare; tel. (24) 2250025; e-mail info.emb-japan@hz.mofa.go.jp; internet www.zw.emb-japan.go.jp; Ambassador SATOSHI TANAKA.

Kenya: 95 Park Lane, POB 4069, Harare; tel. (24) 2704820; e-mail harare@kenyaembassy.co.zw; internet harare.mfa.go.ke; Ambassador STELLA MUNYI.

Korea, Republic: 1 Phillips Ave, Belgravia, POB 4970, Harare; tel. (24) 2756542; e-mail zim@mofa.go.kr; internet overseas.mofa.go.kr/zw-en/index.do; Ambassador DO BONG-KAE.

Kuwait: 1 Bath Rd, Avondale, POB A485, Harare; tel. (24) 2251584; e-mail kuwait@mweb.co.zw; Ambassador SALEM SHIBEEB HAMAD ALKALEDI.

Malawi: 9–11 Duthie Rd, Alexandra Park, POB 321, Harare; tel. (24) 2798584; e-mail malahigh@africaonline.co.zw; Ambassador MWAYIWAWO MCLLOYD POLEPOLE.

Malaysia: 40 Downie, Avondale, POB 5570, Harare; tel. (24) 2334413; e-mail mwharare@kln.gov.my; internet www.kln.gov.my/web/zwe_harare; Chargé d'affaires TAN TSIU YIN.

Mozambique: 152 cnr Herbert Chitepo Ave and Leopold Takawira St, POB 4608, Harare; tel. (24) 2253871; Ambassador FRANCISCO ELIAS PAULO CIGARRO.

Namibia: Lot 1, 7A Borrowdale Estates, 69 Borrowdale Rd, Harare; tel. (24) 2885841; e-mail secretary@namibianembassy.co.zw; Ambassador NICKLAAS KANDJII.

Netherlands: 2 Arden Rd, Highlands, Harare; tel. 772236151; e-mail har@minbuza.nl; internet www.netherlandsworldwide.nl/countries/zimbabwe; Ambassador Dr MARGARET VERWIJK.

Nigeria: 36 Samora Machel Ave, POB 4742, Harare; tel. (24) 2253900; e-mail info@nigeriaembassy.co.zw; internet www.nigerianembassy.co.zw; Ambassador ZACHARIA IFU.

Pakistan: 11 Van Praagh Ave, Milton Park, POB 3050, Harare; tel. (24) 2762018; e-mail parepharare@mofa.gov.pk; internet mofa.gov.pk/zimbabwe; Ambassador MURAD BASEER.

Portugal: 5 Wadham Lane, Borrowdale, Harare; tel. 772318441; e-mail harare@mne.pt; internet fb.com/EmbPortugalHarare; Ambassador MIGUEL DE MASCARENHAS DE CALHEIROS VELOZO.

Romania: 105 Fourth St, cnr Chinamano Ave, POB 4797, Harare; tel. (24) 2700853; e-mail romemb@comone.co.zw; internet harare.mae.ro; Chargé d'affaires ALEXANDRU IRIMIA.

Russian Federation: 70 Leonid Brezhnev St, POB 4250, Harare; tel. (24) 2701957; e-mail zimbabwe@mid.ru; internet zimbabwe.mid.ru; Ambassador NIKOLAI KRASILNIKOV.

Rwanda: 22 Cambridge Rd, Avondale, Harare; tel. 8677008344; e-mail inforwandainharare@minaffet.gov.rw; internet www.rwandainzimbabwe.gov.rw; Ambassador JAMES MUSONI.

South Africa: 7 Elcombe Rd, Belgravia, POB A1654, Avondale, Harare; tel. (24) 2251843; e-mail harare.consular@dirco.gov.za; Ambassador REJOICE THIZWILONDI MABUDAFHASI.

South Sudan: 14 Phillips Ave, Belgravia, Harare; tel. (24) 2794634; e-mail thokbeng1@yahoo.co.uk; Ambassador Lt-Gen. MALEK REUBEN RIAK (designate).

Spain: 16 Phillips Ave, Belgravia, POB 3300, Harare; tel. (24) 2250740; e-mail emb.harare@maec.es; internet www.exteriores.gob.es/embajadas/harare; Ambassador (vacant).

Sudan: 4 Pascoe Ave, Belgravia, POB A1706, Harare; tel. 776878623; e-mail sudan@africaonline.co.zw; Chargé d'affaires a.i. KHALID MOHAMED OSMAN.

Sweden: 32 Aberdeen Rd, Avondale, POB 4110, Harare; tel. (24) 2302636; e-mail ambassaden.harare@gov.se; internet www .swedenabroad.com/harare; Ambassador ASA PEHRSON.

Switzerland: 9 Lanark Rd, Belgravia, POB 3440, Harare; tel. (24) 2703997; e-mail harare@eda.admin.ch; internet www.eda.admin.ch/ harare; Ambassador STÉPHANE REY.

Tanzania: Ujamaa House, 23 Baines Ave, POB 4841, Harare; tel. (24) 2792714; e-mail harare@nje.go.tz; internet www.zw.tzembassy .go.tz; Ambassador Prof. SIMON SIRRO (designate).

Türkiye (Turkey): 15 Maasdorp Ave, Alexandra Park, Harare; tel. (24) 2799761; e-mail embassy.harare@mfa.gov.tr; internet harare .emb.mfa.gov.tr; Ambassador BERNA KASNAKLI VRESTEDEN.

United Kingdom: 3 Norfolk Rd, Mount Pleasant, POB 4490, Harare; tel. (24) 285855200; e-mail ukinfo.harare@fco.gov.uk; internet www.gov.uk/world/zimbabwe; Ambassador MELANIE ROBINSON.

USA: 172 Herbert Chitepo Ave, POB 3340, Harare; tel. (24) 2250593; e-mail hararepas@state.gov; internet zw.usembassy.gov; Chargé d'affaires a.i. ELAINE M. FRENCH.

Zambia: Zambia House, 48 Kwame Bkrumah Ave, POB 4698, Harare; tel. (24) 2773777; e-mail zambiae@mweb.co.zw; Ambassador DERICK LIVUNE (designate).

Judicial System

The legal system is Roman-Dutch, based on the system that was in force in the Cape of Good Hope on 10 June 1891, as modified by subsequent legislation. The court system comprises a Supreme Court, a High Court, an Administrative Court, Magistrates' Courts and Labour Courts. The Supreme Court is the final court of appeal and hears appeals from the High Court, the Labour Courts and the Administrative Court. It sits as a court of first instance in constitutional cases. As well as hearing appeals from the subordinate courts, the High Court has full, original and unlimited jurisdiction over all persons and matters in Zimbabwe. Below the High Court are Magistrates' Courts with both civil and criminal jurisdiction presided over by full-time professional magistrates. The Customary Law and Local Courts Act, adopted in 1990, abolished the village and community courts and replaced them with customary law and local courts, presided over by chiefs and headmen. Appeals from the Chiefs' Courts are heard in Magistrates' Courts and, ultimately, the Supreme Court. All magistrates now have jurisdiction to try cases determinable by customary law. A Constitutional Court was established in 2013, according to the provisions of the new Constitution. It is the highest court in all matters related to the constitution. There is also a Labour Court and an Administrative Court with jursidictions limited to labour disputes and civil cases of administrative nature, respectively.

Supreme Court: Supreme Court Bldg, cnr Third St and Kwame Nkrumah Ave, Harare; tel. (24) 2703501; internet www.jsc.org.zw; has original jurisdiction in matters in which an infringement of Chapter III of the Constitution defining fundamental rights is alleged; consists of the Chief Justice, the Deputy Chief Justice and such other judges of the Supreme Court, being not less than 2, as the President may deem necessary; Chief Justice LUKE MALABA.

High Court: Harare; internet www.jsc.org.zw; consists of the Chief Justice, the Judge President, and such other judges of the High Court as may from time to time be appointed; Judge Pres. MARY ZIMBA-DUBE.

Constitutional Court: Mashonganyika Bldg, cnr Third St and Samora Michel Ave, Harare; f. 2013; consists of the Chief Justice, the Deputy Chief Justice and five other judges; the final court of appeal for all matters relating to the Constitution; its decisions are binding on all other courts.

Attorney-General: PRINCE MACHAYA.

Religion

AFRICAN RELIGIONS

Many Zimbabweans follow traditional beliefs.

CHRISTIANITY

According to official figures, in 2017 around 84% of the population professed to be Christian (predominantly Protestant).

Zimbabwe Council of Churches: 27 St Patrick's Rd, Hatfield, POB 3566, Harare; tel. (24) 2572122; e-mail opa@zcc-eco.org; internet www.zcc-eco.org; f. 1964; Pres. Rev. L. KHANYE; Gen. Sec. Dr KENNETH MTATA; 26 mem. churches, 9 assoc. mems.

The Anglican Communion

Anglicans are adherents of the Church of the Province of Central Africa, covering Botswana, Malawi, Zambia and Zimbabwe. The Church comprises 15 dioceses, including five in Zimbabwe. The current Archbishop of the Province is the Bishop of Northern Zambia.

Bishop of Central Zimbabwe: Rt Rev. Dr IGNATIUS MAKUMBE, POB 25, Gweru; tel. (54) 221030.

Bishop of Harare: Rt Rev. Dr FARAI MUTAMIRI, Paget House, 2nd Floor, 87 Kwame Nkurumah Ave, Harare; tel. (24) 2702253; e-mail bishop@angdiohrecpca.co.zw; internet hreanglicancpca.org.zw.

Bishop of Manicaland: Rt Rev. ERICK RUWONA, 113 Herbert Chitepo St, Mutare; tel. (20) 2064194; e-mail info@manicaland .anglican.org; internet fb.com/Anglicandomcpca.

Bishop of Masvingo: Rt Rev. GODFREY TAWONEZVI, POB 1421, Masvingo; tel. (39) 2362536; e-mail anglicandiomsv@gmail.com; internet masvingo.anglican.org.

Bishop of Matabeleland: Rt Rev. CLEOPHAS LUNGA, POB 2422, Bulawayo; tel. (29) 261370; e-mail clunga@aol.com.

The Roman Catholic Church

For ecclesiastical purposes, Zimbabwe comprises two archdioceses and six dioceses.

Zimbabwe Catholic Bishops' Conference: Africa Synod House, 29/31 Selous Ave, POB CY738, Causeway, Harare; tel. (24) 2705368; e-mail gensec@zcbc.co.zw; internet www.zcbc.co.zw; f. 1969; Pres. Rt Rev. PAUL HORAN (Bishop of Mutare); Sec.-Gen. Fr FRADERECK CHIROMBA.

Archbishop of Bulawayo: Most Rev. ALEX THOMAS KALIYANIL, cnr Lobengula St and 9th Ave, POB 837, Bulawayo; tel. (29) 263590; e-mail archdbyo@mweb.co.zw; internet www.bulawayoarchdiocese .org.

Archbishop of Harare: Most Rev. ROBERT CHRISTOPHER NDLOVU, Archbishop's House, 66 Fifth St, POB CY330, Causeway, Harare; tel. (24) 2727386; e-mail hrearch@zol.co.zw.

Other Christian Churches

Dutch Reformed Church in Zimbabwe (Nederduitse Gereformeerde Kerk): 35 Samora Machel Ave, POB 503, Harare; tel. 772361850; e-mail johanhaasbroek24@gmail.com; f. 1895; 8 congregations in Zimbabwe and 2 in Zambia; Chair. DIRK ODENDAAL; Sec. Rev. JOHAN HAASBROEK.

Evangelical Lutheran Church: 7 Lawley Rd, POB 2175, Bulawayo; tel. (29) 2254991; e-mail elczhead@elcz.co.zw; internet www .elcz.co.zw; f. 1903; Presiding Bishop Rt Rev. C. FAINDI; Gen. Sec. Rev. M. M. DUBE.

Greek Orthodox Church: POB 2832, Harare; tel. (24) 2744991; e-mail zimbabwe@greekorthodox-zimbabwe.org; f. 1968; Archbishop SERAPHIM KYKKOTIS.

Methodist Church in Zimbabwe: Wesley House, 17 Selous Ave, POB CY71, Causeway, Harare; tel. (24) 2250523; e-mail methodist@ mczconnexional.co.zw; internet www.methodistchurchinzimbabwe .org; f. 1891; Presiding Bishop Rev. Dr SOLMON ZWANA; Gen. Sec. Rev. Dr JIMMY DUBE.

United Methodist Church: 10 Harvey Brown Ave, Milton Park, Harare; tel. (24) 2751509; e-mail info@umczea.org; internet umczea .org; f. 1890; Bishop EBEN NHIWATIWA.

Among other denominations active in Zimbabwe are the African Methodist Church, the African Methodist Episcopal Church, the African Reformed Church, the Christian Marching Church, the Church of Christ in Zimbabwe, the Independent African Church, the Presbyterian Church (and the City Presbyterian Church), the United Church of Christ, the Zimbabwe Assemblies of God and the Ziwezano Church.

JUDAISM

The Jewish community numbered 897 members at 31 December 1997; by 2020 that number had fallen to around 400.

Zimbabwe Jewish Board of Deputies: 54 Josiah Chinamano Ave, POB 342, Harare; tel. (24) 2723647; Pres. (vacant); Sec. E. ALHADEFF.

BAHÁ'Í FAITH

National Spiritual Assembly: 80 Greendale Ave, POB GD380, Greendale, Harare; tel. (24) 2495945; Nat. Sec. DEREK SITHOLE; f. 1970; mems resident in 57 clusters.

The Press

DAILY NEWSPAPERS (PRINT AND ONLINE)

The Chronicle: George Silundika St and 9th Ave, POB 585, Bulawayo; tel. (29) 2888871; e-mail editor@chronicle.co.zw; internet www.chronicle.co.zw; f. 1894; publ. by govt-controlled co Zimpapers; circulates throughout south-western Zimbabwe; English; Editor LAWSON MABHENA.

The Daily News: 18 Sam Nujoma St and cnr Speke Ave, Harare; tel. (24) 2753027; e-mail news@dailynews.co.zw; internet dailynews.co.zw; f. 1999; publ. by Associated Newspapers of Zimbabwe (ANZ); English; Editor GUTHRIE MUNYUKI.

The Herald: Herald House, cnr George Silundika and Sam Nujoma Sts, Harare; tel. (24) 2795771; internet www.herald.co.zw; f. 1891; publ. by govt-controlled co Zimpapers; English; Editor-in-Chief HATRED ZENENGA.

The Insider: 12 Penwith Court, Jason Moyo St, Bulawayo; tel. 712789739; e-mail charlesrukuni@insiderzim.com; internet www.insiderzim.com; f. 1990; digital newsletter; news and current affairs; Editor and Publr CHARLES RUKUNI.

NewsDay: 1 Kwame Nkrumah Ave, Harare; tel. (24) 2773839; e-mail feedback@newsday.co.zw; internet www.newsday.co.zw; f. 2009; publ. by Alpha Media Holdings; Chair. TREVOR NCUBE; Editor-in-Chief WISDOM MDZUNGAIRI.

The Zimbabwe Mail: e-mail editor@thezimbabwemail.com; internet www.thezimbabwemail.com; f. 2011; Man. Editor NKULU-LEKO NDLOVU.

WEEKLY NEWSPAPERS (PRINT AND ONLINE)

Financial Gazette: Fingaz House, 2nd Floor, Green Bridge South, Eastgate Complex, POB 66070, Kopje, Harare; tel. (24) 2781571; e-mail newsdesk@fingaz.co.zw; internet www.fingaz.co.zw; f. 1969; a publ. of Associated Newspapers of Zimbabwe (ANZ); affiliated to the ZANU—PF party; Editor-in-Chief (vacant).

Kwayedza: Herald House, cnr George Silundika and Sam Nujoma Sts, Harare; tel. (24) 2795771; e-mail kwayedzazimpapers@gmail.com; internet www.kwayedza.co.zw; publ. by govt-controlled co Zimpapers; f. 1986; ChiShona.

Manicaland Post: Herald House, cnr George Silundika and Sam Nujoma Sts, Harare; tel. (24) 2795771; internet manicapost.co.zw; f. 1893; publ. by govt-controlled co Zimpapers; English; Editor WENDY NYAKURERWA-MATINDE.

Masvingo Mirror: 265 Hofmeyer St, POB 1214, Masvingo; tel. (39) 2264372; e-mail marketing@masvingomirror.com; internet masvingomirror.com; f. 1992; independent; Editor NKULUMANI MLAMBO.

Masvingo Star: 49 S. Muzenda St, POB 138, Masvingo; tel. (39) 263978; e-mail masvingostar@gmail.com; internet newziana.co.zw/masvingo-star; f. 1984; English; distributed in Masvingo province; Editor HERBERT MUTUGWI.

Midlands Observer: 34 Nelson Mandela Way, POB 533, Kwekwe; tel. (55) 2522248; e-mail midprint2013@gmail.com; internet www.themidlandsobserver.co.zw; f. 1953; English; Editor CHIPO GUDHE.

The Standard: Ernst and Young Bldg, 1st Blk, 3rd Floor, 1 Kwame Nkrumah Ave, POB 661730, Kopje, Harare; tel. (24) 2773930; e-mail feedback@newsday.co.zw; internet www.thestandard.co.zw; f. 1997; a part of the Alpha Media Holdings group; Sun.; Chair. TREVOR NCUBE; Editor WISDOM MDZUNGAIRI.

The Sunday Mail: Herald House, cnr George Silundika and Sam Nujoma Sts, POB 396, Harare; tel. (24) 2795771; e-mail sundaymail@zimpapers.co.zw; internet www.sundaymail.co.zw; f. 1935; publ. by govt-controlled co Zimpapers; English; Editor VICTORIA RUZVIDZO.

The Sunday News: cnr George Silundika and Sam Nujoma Sts, Harare; tel. (24) 2795771; e-mail editor@sundaynews.co.zw; internet www.sundaynews.co.zw; f. 1930; publ. by govt-controlled co Zimpapers; English; News Editor DARLINGTON MUSARURWA.

uMthunywa (The Messenger): Herald House, cnr George Silundika and Sam Nujoma Sts, Harare; tel. (24) 2795771; e-mail advertising@chronicle.co.zw; internet www.umthunywa.co.zw; f. 2004; SiNdebele; publ. by govt-controlled co Zimpapers; Editor GUGU NCUBE.

Zimbabwe Independent: cnr Bessemer and Strand Multiprint Rds, Graniteside, Harare; tel. (24) 2773934; e-mail subscriptions@alphamedia.co.zw; internet www.theindependent.co.zw; f. 1996; publ. by Alpha Media Holdings; English; Chair. TREVOR NCUBE; Editor FAITH ZABA.

Zimbabwean Government Gazette: POB 8062, Causeway, Harare; official notices; Editor L. TAKAWIRA.

PERIODICALS

African Fisherman Magazine: POB 6204, Harare; tel. (24) 2572786; e-mail africanfisherman@mag-set.com; internet www.africanfishermanonline.com; Editor-in-Chief ANT WILLIAMS.

Moto (Fire): POB 890, Gweru; tel. (54) 224886; e-mail moto@telco.co.zw; internet www.motonews.co.zw; f. 1959; monthly; editor of moto magazine zimpapers; banned in 1974; relaunched in 1980 as a weekly newspaper, then in magazine format in 1982; Roman Catholic.

Mukai-Vukani Jesuit Journal for Zimbabwe: Jesuit Communications, 37 Admiral Tait Rd, Malborough, POB A949, Avondale, Harare; tel. (24) 2309623; e-mail jescomzim@gmail.com; internet www.jesuitszimbabwe.co.zw; 4–6 a year; Catholic; Editors Fr EMMANUEL GURUMOMBE, KUDAKWASHE MARTIN MATAMBO.

The Outpost: cnr 7th St and J. Chinamano Ave, Harare; tel. (24) 2700171; e-mail feedback@zrp.gov.zw; internet www.zrp.gov.zw; f. 1911; publ. of the Zimbabwe Republic Police; monthly; English; Dep. Editor RESISTANT NCUBE.

Southern African Political and Economic Monthly (SAPEM): Southern Africa Political Economy Series Trust, 4 Deary Ave, Belgravia, POB MP111, Mount Pleasant, Harare; tel. (24) 2252962; e-mail info@sapestrust.org.zw; internet sapes.org.zw; f. 1987; monthly; publ. by the SAPES Trust; incorporates *Southern African Economist*; Publr and Editor IBBO MANDAZA.

The Worker: ZCTU, 9th Floor, Chester House, 9th Floor, Speke Ave and Third St, POB 3549, Harare; tel. (24) 2794742; e-mail info@zctu.co.zw; internet www.theworkerzimbabwe.co.zw; f. 1988; publ. by the Zimbabwe Congress of Trade Unions.

Zambezia: University of Zimbabwe Publications, POB MP203, Mount Pleasant, Harare; tel. (24) 2303211; e-mail publications@uzlib.uz.ac.zw; internet www.uz.ac.zw/publications; f. 1969; biannual; humanities and general interest; Editor Prof. R. MAGOSVONGWE.

PRESS ORGANIZATION

Voluntary Media Council Zimbabwe (VMCZ): 34 Colenbrander Rd, Bishop Gaul Dr., Milton Park, Harare; tel. (24) 2708035; e-mail director@vmcz.co.zw; internet vmcz.co.zw; f. 2007; Chair. ALEC MUCHADEHAMA; Exec. Dir LOUGHTY DUBE.

REGULATORY AUTHORITY

Zimbabwe Media Commission: 108 Swan Dr., Alexndra Park, Parallel Borrowdale Rd, opp. The National Archives of Zimbabwe, Harare; tel. (24) 2253509; e-mail information@mediacommission.co.zw; internet fb.com/zimbabwemediacommission; f. 2009 to introduce media reforms; Chair. Prof. RUBY MAGOSVONGWE; Sec. BVUMAYI CHINAMORA (acting).

Publishers

Baobab Books (Pvt) Ltd: 4 Conald Rd, Graniteside, POB 567, Harare; tel. (24) 2665187; general, literature, children's.

College Press Publishers (Pvt) Ltd: 1 Giraffe Cres., cnr Teviotdale/Alpes Rd and Giraffe Cres., Borrowdale West, POB 3041, Workington, Harare; tel. (24) 2754145; e-mail zw.customerservice@collegepress.co.zw; internet www.collegepress.co.zw; f. 1967; educational and general.

Gramsol Books: The Law Society House, 46 Kwame Nkrumah Ave, Harare; tel. 773779034; e-mail sales@gramsol.com; internet gramsol.com; f. 2010; Man. COURAGE MABHODYERA.

Pearson Africa (Pvt) Ltd: 19 Glenara Ave, Eastleas, Harare; tel. (24) 2621661; e-mail fiona.macgregor@pearson.com; internet www.pearson.com/africa/countries/zimbabwe.html; f. 1964; general and educational; Man. Dir FIONA MACGREGOR.

Southern African Printing and Publishing House (SAPPHO): 109 Coventry Rd, Workington, POB MP1005, Mount Pleasant, Harare; tel. (24) 2621681; internet www.zimmirror.co.zw; Editor-in-Chief Dr IBBO MANDAZA.

University of Zimbabwe Publications: University of Zimbabwe, 630 Churchill Ave, POB MP203, Mount Pleasant, Harare; tel. (24) 2303211; e-mail infor@admin.uz.ac.zw; internet www.uz.ac.zw; f. 1969; Chair. CHARLES F. B. NHACHI.

Weaver Press: 38 Broadlands Rd, Emerald Hill, POB A1922, Avondale, Harare; tel. (24) 2308330; e-mail weaveradmin@mango.zw; internet www.weaverpresszimbabwe.com; f. 1998; Dir MURRAY MCCARTNEY; Publr IRENE STAUNTON.

Zimbabwe Newspapers (1980) Ltd (Zimpapers): cnr George Silundika and Sam Nujoma, Harare; tel. (24) 2795771; e-mail theherald@zimpapers.co.zw; internet www.herald.co.zw; f. 1981; 51% state-owned; publ. the newspapers *The Herald, The Sunday Mail, The Manica Post, The Chronicle, The Sunday News, Kwayedza,* uMthunywa and *The Southern Times* (based in Namibia); and magazines incl. *Zimbabwean Travel, Trends Magazine* and *New Farmer Magazine*; Chair. DELMA LUPEPE; Group CEO PIKIRAYI DEKETEKE.

ZPH Publishers (Pvt) Ltd: 183 Arcturus Rd, Kamfinsa, GD510, Greendale, Harare; tel. (24) 2497258; e-mail munyaradzie@zph.co.zw; f. 1981 as Zimbabwe Publishing House Ltd; CEO BLAZIO GINIO TAFIREYI.

Broadcasting and Communications

TELECOMMUNICATIONS

Econet Wireless Zimbabwe: 2 Old Mutare Rd, Msasa, POB BE1298, Belvedere, Harare; tel. (24) 2486121; e-mail enquiry@econet.co.zw; internet www.econet.co.zw; f. 1998; mobile telecommunications operator; Chair. Dr JAMES MYERS; CEO DOUGLAS MBOWENI.

NetOne Ltd: Kopje Plaza Bldg, 16th Floor, 1 Jason Moyo Ave, POB CY579, Causeway, Harare; tel. 712980795; e-mail customercare@netone.co.zw; internet www.netone.co.zw; f. 1996; state-owned; mobile telecommunications operator; Chair. SUSAN MUTANGADURA (acting); CEO LAZARUS MUCHENJE.

Telecel Zimbabwe: 148 Seke Rd, Graniteside, POB CY232, Causeway, Harare; tel. (24) 2748321; e-mail info@telecelzim.co.zw; internet www.telecel.co.zw; f. 1998; mobile telecommunications operator; Chair. JAMES MAKAMBA; CEO ANGELINE VERE.

TelOne: Runhare House, 107 Kwame Nkrumah Ave, POB CY331, Causeway, Harare; tel. (24) 2798111; e-mail clientservices@telone.co.zw; internet www.telone.co.zw; state-owned; sole fixed-line telecommunications operator; Chair. JAMES MUTIZWA; Man. Dir CHIPO MTASA.

Regulatory Authority

Postal and Telecommunication Regulatory Authority (POTRAZ): 1008 Performance Close, Mount Pleasant Business Park, POB MP843, Mount Pleasant, Harare; tel. (24) 2333032; e-mail the.regulator@potraz.gov.zw; internet www.potraz.gov.zw; fmrly Post and Telecommunications Corpn; Chair. OZIAS BVUTE; Dir-Gen. GIFT KALLISTO MACHENGETE.

BROADCASTING

Regulatory Authority

Broadcasting Authority of Zimbabwe: 27 Boscobel Dr. West, Highlands, Causeway, POB CY496, Belvedere, Harare; tel. (24) 4434657; e-mail info@baz.co.zw; internet www.baz.co.zw; Chair. CHARLES SIBANDA; CEO OBERT MUGANYURA.

Radio

Diamond FM: Manica Post Bldg, Herbet Chitepo, Mutare; tel. (20) 2061212; e-mail info@diamondfm.co.zw; internet diamondfm.co.zw; f. 2016; Station Man. JABULANI MANGEZI.

Feba Radio: 69 Books Drive Hillside, Harare; tel. (24) 2543553; e-mail radiofebazim@gmail.com; internet febaradiozim.org.

Star FM: 102 Simon Mazorodze Rd, Southerton, Harare; tel. (24) 2663663; internet starfm.co.zw; f. 2012; broadcasts in Harare and Bulawayo; Gen. Man. COMFORT MBOFANA.

YAFM: 797 Grosvener Rd, Highlands, Harare; tel. 8644203360; e-mail info@yafm.co.zw; internet www.yafm.co.zw; f. 2015; Chair. and CEO MUNYARADZI HWENGWERE.

ZiFM Stereo: 7 Kenilworth Rd, Newlands, Harare; tel. (24) 2746668; e-mail feedback@zifmstereo.co.zw; internet zifmstereo.co.zw; f. 2012; music station; transmission across all major towns; Owner SUPA MANDIWANZIRA.

Zimbabwe Broadcasting Corpn: 1 Northend Rd, Pocket Hill, POB HG444, Highlands, Harare; tel. (24) 2498641; e-mail pr@zbc.co.zw; internet www.zbc.co.zw; f. 1963 as Rhodesian Broadcasting Corpn; present name adopted in 1980; programmes in English, ChiShona, SiNdebele and 14 minority languages, incl. Chichewa, Venda and Xhosa; broadcasts a general service (mainly in English), vernacular languages service, light entertainment, and educational programmes; Chair. JOSIAH TAYI; CEO ADELAIDE CHIKUNGURU; Radio stations operated by Zimbabwe Broadcasting Corpn are:

Classic 263: 1 Northend Rd, Highlands, Harare; tel. (24) 2498651; e-mail pr@zbc.co.zw; internet classic263.co.zw; fmrly SFM, present name adopted in 2018; Station Man. TERRENCE MAPURISANA.

National FM: S. Mazorodze Rd/Remembrance Dr., POB 9048, Harare; tel. (24) 2774488; e-mail info@nationalfm.co.zw; internet www.nationalfm.co.zw.

Power FM: 1 Northend Rd, Highlands, Harare; tel. (24) 2498670; e-mail powerfm@zbc.co.zw; internet www.powerfm.co.zw; f. 2002 as Radio 3; 24 hour music channel; Station Man. RUMBIDZAI MOYO.

Radio Zimbabwe: S. Mazorodze/Rememberance Dr., Harare; tel. (24) 2774488; internet www.radiozim.co.zw; Station Man. ALBERT CHEKAYI.

Television

Zimbabwe Broadcasting Corpn: (see Radio).

Ke Yona TV: Harare; f. 2020; owned by Fairtalk Communications; Chair. CONT MHLANGA; Man. Dir QHUBANI MOYO.

The main broadcasting centre is in Harare, with a second studio in Bulawayo. ZBC-TV is broadcast 24 hours per day, while a second channel (ZBC Channel 2) was launched in 2010.

Finance

BANKING

Central Bank

Reserve Bank of Zimbabwe: 80 Samora Machel Ave, POB 1283, Harare; tel. (24) 2703000; e-mail info@rbz.co.zw; internet www.rbz.co.zw; f. 1964 as Reserve Bank of Rhodesia; bank of issue; Gov. Dr JOHN MANGUDYA.

Commercial Banks

CBZ Bank Ltd (CBZ): Union House, 5th Floor, 60 Kwame Nkrumah Ave, POB 3313, Harare; tel. (24) 2748050; e-mail info@cbz.co.zw; internet www.cbz.co.zw; state-owned; f. 1980 as Bank of Credit and Commerce Zimbabwe Ltd; renamed Commercial Bank of Zimbabwe Ltd in 1991; present name adopted 2005; Chair. MARC HOLTZMAN; Man. Dir LAWRENCE NYAZEMA.

FBC Bank Ltd: FBC Centre, 6th Floor, Marketing and Public Relations Division, 45 Nelson Mandela Ave, POB 1227, Harare; tel. (24) 2783204; e-mail help@fbc.co.zw; internet www.fbc.co.zw/banking; f. 1997; Group Chair. HERBERT NKALA; Man. Dir WEBSTER RUSERE.

First Capital Bank Ltd (FCAZW): Barclays House, cnr First St and Jason Moyo Ave, POB 1279, Harare; tel. (24) 2250579; e-mail customer-service@barclays.com; internet zw.barclays.com; f. 1912 as Barclays Bank of Zimbabwe Ltd; current name adopted in 2018; commercial and merchant banking; Chair. PATRICK DEVENISH; Man. Dir CIARAN MCSHARRY.

Stanbic Bank Zimbabwe Ltd: Stanbic Centre, 59 Samora Machel Ave, POB 300, Harare; tel. (24) 2759471; e-mail zimccc@stanbic.com; internet www.stanbicbank.co.zw; f. 1990 as ANZ Grindlays Bank; acquired by Standard Bank Investment Corpn in 1992; Chair. GREGORY SEBBORN; CEO SOLOMON NYANHONGO.

Standard Chartered Bank Zimbabwe Ltd: Africa Unity Square Bldg, 1st Floor, 68 Nelson Mandela Ave, POB 373, Harare; tel. (24) 253801; e-mail contactus.zw@sc.com; internet www.sc.com/zw; f. 1892; incorporated in 1983; Chair. L. T. MANATSA; CEO RALPH WATUNGWA.

ZB Bank Ltd: 21 Natal Rd, Avondale, Harare; tel. (24) 2304044; e-mail info@zb.co.zw; internet www.zb.co.zw; f. 1951; Chair. STANFORD A. SIBANDA.

Development Banks

African Export-Import Bank (Afreximbank): Eastgate Bldg, 3rd Floor, Gold Bridge (North Wing), Second St, POB 1600, Causeway, Harare; tel. (24) 2700941; e-mail info@afreximbank.com; internet www.afreximbank.com; f. 1993; Pres. and Chair. Dr BENEDICT ORAMAH.

Infrastructure Development Bank of Zimbabwe (IDBZ): IDBZ House 99 Rotten Row, Harare; tel. (24) 2750171; e-mail management@idbz.co.zw; internet www.idbz.co.zw; f. 2005; to replace Zimbabwe Development Bank; Chair JOE MUTIZWA; CEO THOMAS ZONDO SAKALA.

Merchant Banks

BancABC Zimbabwe: 1 Endeavour Cres., Mount Pleasant Business Park, Mount Pleasant, POB 2786, Harare; tel. (24) 2369701; internet www.bancabc.co.zw; f. 1956 as Rhodesian Acceptances Ltd; name changed to First Merchant Bank of Zimbabwe Ltd in 1990; merged with Heritage Investment Bank in 1997; present name adopted in 2001; part of Atlasmara Group; Chair. ALVORD MABENA; Man. Dir and CEO LANCE MAMBONDIANI.

Nedbank Zimbabwe Ltd: Old Mutual Centre, 14th Floor, cnr Third St and Jason Moyo Ave, POB 3200, Harare; tel. (24) 2254800; e-mail contactcenter@nedbank.co.zw; internet nedbank

.co.zw; f. 1956 as Merchant Bank of Central Africa Ltd; present name adopted in 2004; a mem of the Nedbank Group; Chair. SHEPHERD SHONHIWA; Man. Dir SIBONGILE MOYO.

NMB Bank Ltd: Unity Court, 4th Floor, cnr Union Ave and First St, POB 2564, Harare; tel. (24) 2759651; e-mail enquiries@nmbz.co.zw; internet www.nmbz.co.zw; f. 1993; fmrly Nat. Merchant Bank of Zimbabwe; Chair. BENEDICT CHIKWANHA; Group CEO GERALD GORE.

Banking Organization

Bankers' Association of Zimbabwe (BAZ): 14177 Gunhill Ave, Gunhill, Harare; tel. (24) 2744987; e-mail info@baz.org.zw; internet www.baz.org.zw; f. 1992; Pres. RALPH WATUNGWA; Exec. Dir SIJABULISO T. BIYAM.

STOCK EXCHANGE

Securities and Exchange Commission of Zimbabwe: Smatsatsa Office Park, Blk C, Ground Floor, Borrowdale Rd, Harare; tel. (24) 2870042; e-mail seczim@seczim.co.zw; internet seczim.co.zw; f. 2009; CEO ANYMORE TARUVINGA.

Zimbabwe Stock Exchange: 44 Ridgeway North, Highlands, Harare; tel. (24) 2886830; e-mail info@zse.co.zw; internet www.zse.co.zw; f. 1894; Chair. CAROLINE SANDURA; CEO JUSTIN BGONI.

INSURANCE

Export Credit Guarantee Corpn of Zimbabwe (Pvt) Ltd: 6 Earles Rd, Alexandra Park, POB CY2995, Causeway, Harare; tel. (24) 2745452; e-mail info@ecgc.co.zw; internet www.ecgc.co.zw; f. 1999 as national export credit insurance agency; also provides export finance guarantee facilities; 100% owned by Reserve Bank of Zimbabwe; Chair. P. MASVIKENI; Man. Dir S. CHIRUME.

Fidelity Life Assurance of Zimbabwe (Pvt) Ltd: Fidelity House, 7th Floor, 66 Julius Nyerere Way, POB 435, Harare; tel. (24) 2750927; e-mail marketing@fidelitylife.co.zw; internet www.fidelitylife.co.zw; f. 1936 as Legal and General; present name adopted in 1989; 52% owned by Zimre Holdings Ltd; pensions and life assurance; Chair. CHIPO MATONGO; CEO LIVINGSTONE GWATA.

NICOZ Diamond: Insurance Centre, 30 Samora Machel Ave, POB 1256, Harare; tel. (24) 2251015; e-mail info@nicozdiamond.co.zw; internet www.nicozdiamond.co.zw; f. 2002 by merger of National Insurance Co of Zimbabwe and Diamond Insurance of Zimbabwe; Chair. ELISHA MOYO; Man. Dir DAVID NYABADZA.

Old Mutual Zimbabwe: 100 The Chase West, Emerald Hill, POB 70, Highlands, Harare; tel. (24) 2308400; e-mail contactus@oldmutual.co.zw; internet www.oldmutual.co.zw; f. 1845; life and general insurance, asset management and banking services; Chair. J. !GAWAXAB; Group CEO SAMUEL MATSEKETE.

ZB Life Assurance Ltd: 21 Natal Rd, Avondale, Harare; tel. (24) 2708801; e-mail info@zblife.co.zw; internet www.zb.co.zw; f. 1964 as Intermarket Life Assurance; subsidiary of ZB Financial Holdings Ltd, which also owns ZB Reinsurance; Exec. Chair. EDWIN T. CHIDZONGA; Man. Dir LETWIN MAWIRE.

Zimnat Lion Insurance Co Ltd: Zimnat House, cnr Nelson Mandela Ave and Third St, POB 2417, Causeway, Harare; tel. (24) 2701179; e-mail customercare@zimnat.co.zw; internet zimnat.co.zw; f. 1999 by merger of Zimnat Insurance Co Ltd and Lion of Zimbabwe Insurance; merged with AIG Zimbabwe in 2005; part of Sanlam group; short-term insurance; Chair. BOTHWELL NYAJEKA; Man. Dir STANLEY MAZORODZE.

Trade and Industry

GOVERNMENT AGENCIES

Industrial Development Corpn of Zimbabwe Ltd (IDCZ): 93 Park Lane, POB CY1431, Causeway, Harare; tel. (24) 2706971; e-mail administrator@idc.co.zw; internet www.idc.co.zw; f. 1963; state investment agency; Chair WINSTON MAKAMURE; CEO (vacant).

Procurement Regulatory Authority of Zimbabwe (PRAZ): Pearl House, 9th Floor, 61 Samora Machel Ave, Harare; tel. 715429774; e-mail feedback@praz.gov.zw; internet www.praz.gov.zw; f. 2018 to replace State Procurement Board; Chair VIMBAI NYEMBA; CEO CLEVER RUSWA.

State Enterprises Restructuring Agency (SERA): Cecil House, 1st Floor, cnr Third St and Jason Moyo Ave, Harare; tel. (24) 2762594; e-mail imawoko@sera.co.zw; internet sera.co.zw; f. 1999 as Privatisation Agency of Zimbabwe; present name adopted in 2004; Exec. Dir EDGAR NYONI.

Zambezi River Authority: Club Chambers, 4th Floor, Nelson Mandela Ave, POB 630, Harare; tel. (24) 2704031; e-mail info@zambezira.org; internet www.zambezira.org; f. 1987; jtly owned and administered by the Govts of Zimbabwe and Zambia; operates and

maintains the Kariba Dam on the Zambezi River; Chair. (Zimbabwe) Dr GLORIA S. MAGOMBO; Co-Chair. (Zambia) FRANCESCA CHISANGANO-ZYAMBO; CEO MUNYARADZI C. MUNODAWAFA.

Zimbabwe Investment and Development Agency (ZIDA): ZB Life Towers, 1st Floor, cnr Jason Moyo and Sam Nujoma Sts, Harare; tel. 8688002639; e-mail info@zidainvest.com; internet www.zidainvest.com; f. 2020 following the dissolution of Zimbabwe Investment Authority, Joint Venture Unit and Zimbabwe Special Economic Zones Authority; CEO TAFADZWA CHINAMO.

Zimbabwe Revenue Authority (ZIMRA): ZB Centre, cnr Nkwame Nkrumah Ave, First St, POB 4360, Harare; tel. (24) 2795720; internet www.zimra.co.zw; Chair. ANTHONY MANDIWANZA; Commr-Gen. REGINA CHINAMASA.

ZimTrade: 188 Sam Nujoma St, Avondale, Harare; tel. (24) 2369330; e-mail info@zimtrade.co.zw; internet www.tradezimbabwe.com; f. 1991; national trade development and promotion org.; jt venture between the private sector and the Govt; Chair. CLARA MLAMBO; CEO ALLAN MAJURU.

DEVELOPMENT ORGANIZATIONS

Indigenous Business Women's Organisation (IBWO): 73B Central Ave, POB 3710, Harare; tel. (24) 2702076; f. 1994; Pres. JANE MUTASA.

Zimbabwe Women's Bureau: 43 Hillside Rd, POB CR120, Cranborne, Harare; tel. (24) 2747809; e-mail director@zwbonline.org; internet www.zwbonline.org; f. 1978; promotes entrepreneurial and rural community devt; Chair. SITHABILE MANGWENGWENDE; Exec. Dir RONIKA MUMBIRE.

CHAMBERS OF COMMERCE

Chamber of Mines of Zimbabwe: 20 Mount Pleasant Dr., Mount Pleasant, POB 712, Harare; tel. (24) 2334517; internet www.chamberofminesofzimbabwe.com; f. 1939 by merger of the Rhodesian Chamber of Mines (Bulawayo) and Salisbury Chamber of Mines; Pres. COLIN CHIBAFA; CEO ISAAC KWESU.

Confederation of Zimbabwe Industries (CZI): 31 Josiah Chinamano Ave, Harare; tel. (24) 2251490; e-mail membership@czi.co.zw; internet www.czi.co.zw; f. 1923; Pres. KURAI MATSHEZA; regional chamber offices, in Matebeleland, Midlands and Manicaland.

CZI Manicaland Chamber of Industries: 3 Durban Rd, Mutare; tel. (20) 2164909; e-mail smuteva@czi.co.zw; internet www.czi.co.zw; f. 1923; Pres. JOSEPH MAVU.

CZI Matabeleland Chamber of Industries: 104 S. Parirenyatwa St, POB 2317, Bulawayo; tel. (29) 260642; e-mail czibyo@czi.co.zw; f. 1931; Pres. RAYMOND SHONHIWA.

Midlands Chamber of Industries: POB 213, Gweru; tel. (29) 60642; e-mail helpdesk@czi.co.zw; Pres. AGATHA GANDIDZE.

Zimbabwe National Chamber of Commerce (ZNCC): 5 Orkney Rd, Eastlea, Harare; tel. (24) 2770244; e-mail info@zncc.co.zw; internet www.zncc.co.zw; f. 1983; represents small and medium-sized businesses; Pres. MIKE KAMUNGEREMU; CEO CHRISTOPHER TAKUNDA MUGAGA.

INDUSTRIAL AND TRADE ASSOCIATIONS

Construction Industry Federation of Zimbabwe (CIFOZ): Conquenar, 256 Samora Machel Ave East, POB 1502, Harare; tel. (24) 2746661; e-mail infor@cifozzim.co.zw; internet www.cifoz.co.zw; f. 1915; Pres. EMMANUEL CHIMEDZA; CEO MARTIN CHINGAIRA.

CropLife Zimbabwe: POB BW 577, Borrowdale, Harare; tel. (77) 2307660; internet www.croplife.co.zw; fmrly Agricultural Chemical Industry Asscn; Chair. MAZVITA SHUMBA.

Grain Marketing Board (GMB): 179–187 Samora Machel Ave, Eastlea, POB CY77, Causeway, Harare; tel. (24) 2701870; e-mail publicrelations@gmbdura.co.zw; internet gmbdura.com; f. 1931 as the Maize Control Board; responsible for maintaining national grain reserves and ensuring food security; Chair. JOYLYN NDORO; Chief Exec. ROCKIE MUTENHA.

Grain Millers Association of Zimbabwe (GMAZ): 13 Bodle Ave, Eastlea, Harare; tel. 8644255873; internet grainmillers.co.zw; Nat. Chair. TAFADZWA MSARARA.

Marketers Association of Zimbabwe (MAZ): 21 Lezard Ave, cnr Prince Edward St, Harare; tel. (24) 2795764; e-mail mazmembership@mazim.co.zw; internet www.maz.co.zw; f. 2007; Pres. Prof. ZORORO MURANDA; Exec. Sec. GILLIAN RUSIKE.

Minerals Marketing Corpn of Zimbabwe (MMCZ): 90 Mutare Rd, Msasa, POB 2628, Harare; tel. (24) 2487200; e-mail info@mmcz.co.zw; internet mmcz.co.zw; f. 1982; sole authority for marketing of mineral production (except gold); state-owned; Chair. JEMISTER CHININGA; Gen. Man. TONGAI MATTHEW MUZENDA.

Tobacco Industry and Marketing Board: 429 Glen Eagles Rd, Southerton, Harare; tel. (77) 2145166; e-mail info@timb.co.zw;

internet www.timb.co.zw; f. 1936 as Tobacco Marketing Board; Chair. PATRICK DEVENISH; CEO MEANWELL GUDU.

Zimbabwe National Traditional Healers' Association (ZINATHA): Red Cross House, 2nd Floor, Rm 202, 98 Cameron St, POB 1116, Harare; tel. (24) 2751902; e-mail zinatha@mweb.co.zw; f. 1980; certifies and oversees traditional healers and practitioners of herbal medicine through the Traditional Medical Practitioners Council; promotes indigenous methods of prevention and treatment of HIV/AIDS; Pres. GEORGE KANDIERO.

Zimbabwe Seed Association (ZSA): Harare; fmrly known as Zimbabwe Seed Trade Association; present name adopted in 2020; Chair. JOHN MAKONI.

Zimbabwe Tobacco Association (ZTA): 108 Prince Edward St, Milton Park, POB 1781, Harare; tel. (24) 2797010; internet fb.com/Zimbabwe-Tobacco-Association-703616106734234; f. 1928; represents growers; Pres. GRANT GARDNER; CEO RODNEY AMBROSE.

EMPLOYERS' ASSOCIATIONS

Commercial Farmers' Union of Zimbabwe (CFU): Harare Show Grounds, Belvedere, POB WGT390, Westgate, Harare; tel. (24) 2770029; internet www.cfuzim.org; f. 1942; Pres. ANDREW PASCOE; CEO BENJAMIN PURCELL-GILPIN.

Zimbabwe Association of Dairy Farmers (ZADF): 46 Lawson Ave, Milton Park, POB WGT390, Westgate, Harare; tel. (24) 2251848; e-mail admin@zadf.co.zw; internet www.zadf.co.zw; f. 2013; Chair. ERNEST MUZOREWA.

Zimbabwe Poultry Association (Commercial Poultry Producers' Association): Old Show Office, Exhibition Park, Samora Machel Ave, POB BE209, Belvedere, Harare; tel. (24) 2756600; e-mail admin@lit.co.zw; Chair. SOLOMON ZAWE; represents c. 200 producers.

Employers' Confederation of Zimbabwe (EMCOZ): 21 Smit Cres., Eastlea, POB 158, Harare; tel. (24) 2739649; e-mail emcoz@emcoz.co.zw; internet www.emcoz.co.zw; f. 1980; Pres. DEMOS MBAUYA; Exec. Dir NESTER MUKWEHWA.

Timber Producers' Federation (TPF): Fidelity Life Centre, 4th Floor, H. Chitepo St, POB 1736, Mutare; tel. (20) 2067482; e-mail timberpf@gmail.com; Chair. DANIEL SITHOLE; CEO DARLINGTON DUWA.

Zimbabwe Building Contractors' Association (ZBCA): Office 202, St Barbara House, 2nd Floor, 115 Takawira St and Nelson Mandela Ave, Harare; tel. (24) 2779283; e-mail zbcaoffice@gmail.com; internet zimbca.co.zw; f. 1985; represents small-scale building contractors; Pres. PETROS KAGWERE.

Zimbabwe Commercial Farmers' Union (ZCFU): Harare Agricultural Showgrounds, Samora Machel Ave, West Belvedere, POB CY610, Causeway, Harare; tel. (24) 2773062; e-mail info@zcfu.org.zw; internet zcfu.org.zw; f. 1990; fmrly Indigenous Commercial Farmers' Union; Pres. Dr SHADRECK P. MAKOMBE; Chief Exec. HENDRIEK OLIVIER.

Zimbabwe Farmers' Union (ZFU): 5 Van Praagh Ave, Milton Park, Harare; tel. (24) 2252474; e-mail info@zfu.org.zw; internet zfu.org.zw; f. 1991 following the merger of the Zimbabwe National Farmers' Union of Zimbabwe and the National Farmers' Association of Zimbabwe; Pres. Maj. (retd) ABDUL CREDIT NYATHI; Exec. Dir PAUL ZAKARIYA.

UTILITIES

Zimbabwe Energy Regulatory Authority (ZERA): Century Towers, 14th Floor, 45 Samora Machel Ave, POB CY308, Causeway, Harare; tel. (24) 2780010; e-mail admin@zera.co.zw; internet www.zera.co.zw; f. 2011; Chair. Dr DAVID MADZIKANDA; CEO EDDINGTON MAZAMBANI.

Electricity

Rural Electrification Agency (REA): Megawatt House, 44 Samora Machel Ave, POB 250A, Harare; tel. (24) 2708110; e-mail info@rea.co.zw; internet rea.co.zw; f. 2002; manages the Rural Electrification Fund to expand and accelerate the electrification of rural areas; Chair. WILLARD CHIWEWE; CEO GEOFFREY MUSONDA.

ZESA Holdings (Pvt) Ltd: 25 Samora Machel Ave, POB 377TA, Harare; tel. (24) 2774508; e-mail pr@zesa.net; internet www.zesa.co.zw; f. 2002 following restructure of Zimbabwe Electricity Supply Authority; operates 1 hydroelectric and 4 thermal power stations; Exec. Chair Dr SYDNEY ZUKUZO GATA.

Zimbabwe Electricity Transmission and Distribution Co (ZETDC): Electricity Centre, 25 Samora Machel Ave, POB 377, Harare; tel. (24) 2774508; e-mail pr@zedc.co.zw; internet zetdc.co.zw; f. 2010; established following merger of Zimbabwe Electricity Transmission Co (ZETCO, f. 2002) and Zimbabwe Electricity Distribution Co (ZEDC); develops, operates and maintains

transmission infrastructure; a subsidiary of ZESA Holdings; Man. Dir LOVEMORE CHINAKA.

Oil

National Oil Infrastructure Co of Zimbabwe (Pvt) Ltd (NOICZ): 100 Leopold Takawira St, cnr J. Moyo, POB CY223, Causeway Harare; tel. (24) 2748518; e-mail info@noic.co.zw; internet www.noic.co.zw; f. 2011; state-owned; receipts, storage and quality control of liquid fuel; Chair. Eng. MACKENZIE NCUBE; CEO WILFRED MATUKENI.

Petrotrade (Pvt) Ltd: NOCZIM House, 100 Leopold Takawira St, POB CY223, Causeway, Harare; tel. (24) 2748512; internet www.petrotrade.co.zw; f. 2010; state-owned; fmrly National Oil Company of Zimbabwe (NOCZIM); responsible for marketing and distributing petroleum products; Chair. (vacant); Acting CEO GODFREY NCUBE.

Water

Zimbabwe National Water Authority (ZINWA): Celestial Park, Blk 4 (E), Borrowdale Rd, POB CY617 Causeway, Harare; tel. 774674333; e-mail callcentre@zinwa.co.zw; internet www.zinwa.co.zw; f. 2000; fmrly Dept of Water, privatized in 2001; construction of dams, water supply, resources planning and protection; Chair. Eng. BONGILE NDIWENI; Chief Exec. Eng. TAURAYI MAURUKIRA.

MAJOR COMPANIES

African Distillers Ltd (AFDIS): 22km Peg Lomagundi Rd, POB WGT900, Westgate, Harare; tel. 773156547; e-mail customercomplaints@afdis.co.zw; internet www.africandistillers.co.zw; f. 1944; mfrs and importers of wines and spirits; Chair. PEARSON GOWERO; Man. Dir STANLEY MUCHENJE.

Almin Metal Industries Ltd: cnr Willowvale/Dagenham Rds, Willowvale, POB ST394, Southerton, Harare; tel. (24) 2620110; e-mail sales@almin.co.zw; internet www.almin.co.zw; f. 1969; semi-fabricators in non-ferrous metals; Man. Dir DAVID STALLY.

British American Tobacco Zimbabwe (Holdings) Ltd (BAT Zimbabwe): 1 Manchester Rd, Southerton, POB ST98, Harare; tel. 772131883; internet www.batzimbabwe.com; Man. Dir SIVENASEN MOODLEY.

Border Timbers Ltd: 1 Aberdeen Rd, POB 458, Mutare; tel. (20) 2064224; e-mail btlinfo@bordertimbers.com; internet www.bordertimbers.com; f. 1979 following the amalgamation of Border Eastern Forest Estates, Renfee Timbers (Pvt) Ltd and Forestry Management Services.

Bindura Nickel Corpn Ltd: 1 Trojan Mine Rd, Bindura; tel. 772100506; e-mail info@bnc.co.zw; internet www.binduranickel.co.zw; f. 1966; 75.4% owned by Mwana Africa Holdings (pvt) Ltd (part of Asa Resource group); mining, smelting and refining of nickel; Chair. M. A. MASUNDA; Man. Dir THOMAS LUSIYANO.

Cotton Co of Zimbabwe Ltd (COTTCO): 1 Lytton Rd, Workington, POB 2697, Harare; tel. (24) 2771981; e-mail info@cottco.co.zw; internet cottco.co.zw; f. 1994; provides services to cotton growers at every stage of the production and sales process; Chair. SIFELANI JABANGWE; Man. Dir PIOUS MANAMIKE.

Dairibord Zimbabwe Ltd (DZL): 1225 Rekayi Tangwena Rd, POB 2512, Harare; tel. (24) 2790801; e-mail marketing@dairibord.co.zw; internet www.dairibord.com; f. 1952 as Dairy Marketing Board; present name adopted in 1994; milk processors and mfrs of dairy products and beverages; factories at Harare, Chitungwiza and Chipinge; privatized in 1997; incorporates Lyons, NFB Logistics, and Dairibord Malawi; Group Chief Exec. MERCY RUFARO NDORO; Man. Dir TATENDA NAPATA.

Delta Corpn Ltd: Sable House, Northridge Close, Northridge Park, Borrowdale, Harare; tel. (24) 2883865; e-mail info@delta.co.zw; internet www.delta.co.zw; f. 1898; brewers and mfrs of soft drinks and agro-industrial products; Chair. STERNFORD MOYO; CEO MATLHOGONOLO VALELA.

First Mutual Properties: First Mutual Park, 100 Borrowdale Rd, Borrowdale, POB MP 373, Harare; tel. (24) 2886000; e-mail info@firstmutual.co.zw; internet www.firstmutual.co.zw; f. 2006; Chair. ELISHA MOYO; Man. Dir CHRISTOPHER KUDAKWASHE MANYOWA.

Hippo Valley Estates Ltd: POB 1, Chiredzi; tel. (31) 2315151; e-mail hve.companysecretary@tongaat.com; internet www.tongaat.com/hippo-valley-estates; f. 1956; part of Tongaat Hulett Group (South Africa); production and milling of sugar from cane and other farming operations; Chair. CANAAN DUBE; CEO AIDEN MHERE.

Hwange Colliery Co Ltd (Wankie Colliery Co Ltd): Coal House, 7th Floor, 17 Nelson Mandela Ave, Harare; tel. (24) 2781985; e-mail marketing@hwangecolliery.co.zw; internet hwangecolliery.co.zw; f. 1925; 51% state-owned; coal mining and production of coke and by-products; Chair. WINSTON CHITANDO; Acting Man. Dir Eng. BLAKE MHATIWA.

Lafarge Cement Zimbabwe Ltd: Limited Manresa Plant, Arcturus Rd, Manresa, Harare; tel. 8677215000; e-mail zim.sales@lafarge.com; internet www.lafarge.co.zw; f. 1954 as Circle Cement Ltd; present name adopted in 2007; 74.5% stake acquired by Fossil Mines (Pvt) Ltd in 2022; mfrs and distributors of cement and allied products; Chair. KUMBIRAI KATSANDE; CEO GEOFFREY NDUGWA.

OK Zimbabwe Ltd: OK House, 7 Ramon Rd, Graniteside, POB 3081, Harare; tel. (24) 2757311; e-mail info@okziminvestor.com; internet okziminvestor.com; f. 1953 as Springmaster Corpn; fmrly Deltrade Ltd; present name adopted in 2001; retailers of groceries, clothing, houseware and furniture; Chair. HERBERT NKALA; CEO MAXEN KAROMBO.

RioZim Ltd (RioZim): 1 Kenworth Rd, Newlands, Harare; tel. (24) 2776085; e-mail info@riozim.co.zw; internet www.riozim.co.zw; f. 1956 as Rio Tinto Southern Rhodesia Ltd; nickel and copper refining; gold mining; also diamond and coal prospecting; Chair. SALEEM RASHID BEEBEEJAUN; CEO MANIT MUKESH SHAH.

> **Murowa Diamonds:** 1 Kenilworth Rd, Harare; tel. (24) 2746614; e-mail info@murowadiamonds.com; internet murowadiamonds.com; commenced operations in 2004; 77.8% owned by RZ Murowa Holdings Ltd, 22.2% owned by Riozim Ltd; CEO MANIT M. SHAH; Gen. Man. ISLAM CHIPANGO.

Schweppes Zimbabwe Ltd: 67A Woolwich Rd, Willovale, Harare; tel. (24) 2620232; e-mail feedback@schweppes.co.zw; internet www.schweppes.co.zw; manufacturer and distributor of non-carbonated, still beverages; Group Man. Dir CHARLES MSIPA.

Seed Co Zimbabwe: Shamwari Rd, Stapleford, POB WGT 64, Westgate, Harare; tel. (24) 2308881; e-mail seedco@seedcogroup.com; internet seedcogroup.com; Chair. MICHAEL S. NDORO; Man. Dir TERRENCE CHIMANAYA.

Starafricacorporation Ltd: 45 Douglas Rd, Workington, POB 396, Southerton, Harare; tel. (24) 2666636; e-mail marketing@starafrica.co.zw; internet www.starafricacorporation.com; f. 1935 as Rhodesia Sugar Refinery; present name adopted in 2006; conglomerate with interests in food products, logistics and real estate; Chair. Dr RUNGANO J. MBIRE; CEO Eng. ROBSON NYABADZA.

Tanganda Tea Co Ltd: 194 Mutare Rd, Msasa, Harare; tel. (24) 2447525; e-mail letstalktea@tangandatea.com; internet tangandatea.com; f. 1924; tea growing, processing and blending; Chair. JAMES M. WARD; CEO TIMOTHY FENNELL.

Turnall Holdings Ltd: 5 Glasgow Rd, Workington, POB 3985, Harare; tel. (24) 2754625; e-mail customercare@turnall.co.zw; internet turnall.co.zw; f. 1943; manufacturer and supplier of asbestos-cement roofing and water and sewerage conveyance products; Chair. BOTHWELL PATRICK NYAJEKA; Man. Dir ZVIDZAYI BIKWA.

Willdale Ltd: 19.5 km Peg Lomagundi Rd, Mount Hampden, POB MR 93, Marlborough, Harare; tel. (24) 2777199; e-mail marketing@willdale.co.zw; internet www.willdale.co.zw; f. 1957; bricks and related products; Chair. WASHINGTON CHIDZIWO; CEO NYASHA MATONDA.

Zimbabwe Mining and Alloy Smelting Co Pvt Ltd (ZIMASCO): Pegasus House, 6th Floor, 52–54 Samora Machel Ave, Harare; tel. (24) 2251823; e-mail info@zimasco.co.zw; internet zimasco.co.zw; f. 1926; chromite mines at Shurugwi and Mutorashanga, smelter at Kwekwe; holding Co Zimasco Consolidated Enterprises (ZCE) is 86.3% owned by Sinosteel Corpn (People's Republic of China) and 13.7% owned by China-Africa Development Fund; Chair. LI JINQIAN; Gen. Man. CLARA SADOMBA.

Zimbabwe Fertilizer Co Ltd: 35 Coventry Rd, Workington, POB 385, Harare; tel. (24) 2753882; e-mail zfc@zfc.co.zw; internet www.zfc.co.zw; Man. Dir RICHARD DAFANA.

Zimplow Holdings Ltd: 36 Birmingham Rd, Southerton, POB HG 298, Highlands, Harare; tel. (24) 2754613; e-mail powermec@powermec.co.zw; internet www.zimplow.com; f. 1939; agro-industrial group; mfrs of farm equipment; Chair. GODFREY TSIKAYI MANHAMBARA; CEO VIMBAYI NYAKUDYA.

TRADE UNIONS

Trade Union Congress of Zimbabwe (TUCZ): Harare; f. 2017 by group of fmr Zimbabwe Congress of Trade Unions (ZCTU) affiliates; fmrly known as Congress of Zimbabwe Trade Unions; Interim Pres. ANGELINE CHITAMBO; Sec.-Gen. RAYMOND MAJONGWE.

Affiliated unions incl. the following:

Civil Service Employees' Association (CSEA): PSA House, 3rd Floor, 9 Livingstone Ave, POB CY202, Causeway, Harare; tel. (24) 2701123; e-mail nashowilson@yahoo.com; internet www.csea.co.zw; f. 1966; represents public sector employees; Pres. EVELYN D. DEMBETEMBE (acting); Gen. Sec. EMELDA MHURIRO.

Commercial Workers' Union of Zimbabwe (CWUZ): CWUZ House, 15 Sixth Ave, Parktown, POB 3922 Harare; tel. (24) 2664701; internet fb.com/REALCWUZINTELLIGENCE; f. 1980; Pres. BARBARA TANYANYIWA; Gen. Sec. GILBERT KARIKUIMBA.

Communication and Allied Services Workers' Union of Zimbabwe (CASWUZ): Morgan House, 4th Floor, G. Silundika Ave, POB 739, Harare; tel. (24) 2794763; e-mail caswuz@africaonline.co.zw; f. 1970; fmrly Rhodesia Posts and Telecommunications Workers Union and later (1983) the Zimbabwe Post and Telecommunication Workers' Union; present name adopted 2002; Pres. TAURAI MEREKI (acting).

National Airways Workers' Union: POB AP1, Harare; tel. (24) 2737011; affiliated to the Int. Transport Workers' Fed; Vice-Pres. (vacant).

Progressive Teachers' Union of Zimbabwe (PTUZ): 14 McLaren Rd, Milton Park, POB CR620, Cranborne, Harare; tel. (24) 2741937; e-mail admin@ptuz.org; internet www.ptuz.org.zw; f. 1997; Pres. TAKAVAFIREI ZHOU; Sec.-Gen. RAYMOND MAJONGWE.

Zimbabwe Energy Workers' Union (ZEWU): Construction House, 6th Floor, 110 Leopold Takawira St, West Wing, Harare; tel. (24)2754438; e-mail stembidube@yahoo.com; internet www.zewu.org.zw; f. 1987 as Zimbabwe Electricity and Energy Workers Union; present name adopted in 2006; Pres. ANGELINE CHITAMBO; Gen. Sec. MARTIN CHIKUNI.

Zimbabwe Congress of Trade Unions (ZCTU): Gorlon House, 7 Jason Moyo Ave, Harare; tel. (24) 2794742; e-mail info@zctu.co.zw; internet www.zctu.co.zw; f. 1981 by merger of the African Trade Union Congress, the Nat. African Trade Union Congress, the Trade Union Congress of Zimbabwe, the United Trade Unions of Zimbabwe, the Zimbabwe Fed. of Labour and the Zimbabwe Trade Union Congress; co-ordinating org. for trade unions; Pres. FLORENCE MUCHA TARUVINGA; Sec.-Gen. JAPHET MOYO.

In 2022 there were 41 affiliated unions. These included:

Energy Sector Workers' Union of Zimbabwe (ESWUZ): Construction House, Suite 306, 3rd Floor, 110 L Takawira St, Harare; tel. (24) 2774789; f. 2014; Sec.-Gen. GIBSON MUSHUNJE.

Food Federation and Allied Workers Union of Zimbabwe (FFAWUZ): Gorlon House, 1st Floor, Eastwing, 7 Jason Moyo Ave, Harare; tel. (24) 2757600; e-mail ffawuz@gmail.com; internet www.ffawuz.co.zw; f. 1995; Gen. Sec. RUNESU DZIMIRI.

General Agricultural and Plantation Workers' Union (GAPWUZ): cnr Jason Moyo and First Sts, POB 1952, Harare; tel. (24) 2762896; e-mail gapwuzinfo@gmail.com; f. 1982; Gen. Sec. GOLDEN MAGWAZA.

National Union of Clothing Industry Workers (NUCI): 13th Ave, Lobengula St, POB RY28, Raylton, Bulawayo; tel. (29) 264432; Gen. Sec. JOSEPH TANYANYIWA.

Zimbabwe Amalgamated Railway Workers' Union (ZARU): Unity House, 13th Ave, Herbert Chitepo St, POB 556, Bulawayo 10; tel. (29) 260948; e-mail zarwubyo@mweb.co.zw; fmrly Railway African Workers' Union; Pres. KAMURAI MOYO; Gen. Sec. KENNETH NHEMACHENA.

Zimbabwe Banks and Allied Workers' Union (ZIBAWU): 1 Meredith Dr., Eastlea, POB 966, Harare; tel. (24) 2703744; e-mail bankunion@zibawu.co.zw; internet www.zibawu.co.zw; f. 1961; aims to promote interest of workers in Zimbabwe's banking and financial sector; Pres. TAWANDA MUTEMI; Gen. Sec. PETER MUTASA.

Zimbabwe Construction and Allied Trades Workers' Union (ZCATWU): Office 305–313, St Barbara House, 3rd Floor, cnr Leopold Takawira St and Nelson Mandela Ave, POB 1291, Harare; tel. (24) 2750159; e-mail zcatwu@ecoweb.co.zw; internet zcatwu.co.zw; Gen. Sec. NICHOLAS MAZARURA.

Zimbabwe Teachers' Association (ZIMTA): ZIMTA House, 190 Herbert Chitepo Ave, POB 1440, Harare; tel. (24) 2706441; e-mail zimta@telco.co.zw; internet fb.com/zimbabweteachersassociation; f. 1942; Pres. RICHARD GUNDANE; Sec.-Gen. GOODWILL TADERERA.

Zimbabwe Textile Workers' Union (ZTWU): Gowero House, 1st Floor, 148 Mbuya Nehanda St, POB 10245, Harare; tel. (24) 2758333; e-mail zim.textile.union@gmail.com; Gen. Sec. NORMAN.

Zimbabwe Union of Journalists: 42 Dan Judson Ave, New Milton Park, Harare; tel. (24) 2741413; e-mail admin@zuj.org.zw; internet zuj.org.zw; f. 1985; Pres. GEORGE MAPONGA; Sec.-Gen. PERFECT HLONGWANE.

Zimbabwe Urban Councils Workers' Union (ZUCWU): 26 Airport Rd, Hatfield, POB CY 1859, Causeway, Harare; tel. 712868826; e-mail mosietshimu@gmail.com; f. 1990; represents workers in engineering, housing and community services, health and emergency services, and clerical and treasury services; Pres. MAXWELL TAKAVINGOFA KIMBINI; Gen. Sec. KUDAKWASHE MUNENGIWA.

Zimbabwe Federation of Trade Unions (ZFTU): Makombe Complex, Causeway, Harare; tel. (24) 2756493; f. 1996 as alternative to ZCTU; aligned to ZANU—PF; Pres. ALFRED MAKWARIMBA; Gen. Sec. KENIAS SHAMUYARIRA.

Non-affiliated Unions

Amalgamated Rural Teachers Union of Zimbabwe: Bard House, 10th Floor, 69 Samora Machel Ave, Harare; tel. 775643192; e-mail info@ruralteachers.co.zw; internet ruralteachers.co.zw; f. 2013; Pres. OBERT MASARAURE; Sec.-Gen. ROBSON NIKITA CHERE.

Zimbabwe National Students' Union (ZINASU): 7 Capri Rd, Highlands, Harare; tel. 776835596; e-mail info@zinasu.co.zw; internet www.zinasu.co.zw; f. 1986; represents students in over 60 higher learning institutions; Pres. BENON NCUBE; Sec. Gen. JOSEPH NYAMAYARO.

Zimbabwe Nurses' Association (ZINA): 47 Livingstone Ave, POB 2610, Harare; tel. (24) 2700479; e-mail zimnurse@mweb.co.zw; f. 1980; Pres. ENOCH DONGO.

Transport

RAILWAYS

Trunk lines run from Bulawayo south to the border with Botswana, connecting with the Botswana railways system, which, in turn, connects with the South African railways system; north-west to the Victoria Falls, where there is a connection with Zambia Railways; and north-east to Harare and Mutare connecting with the Mozambique Railways' line from Beira. From a point near Gweru, a line runs to the south-east, making a connection with the Mozambique Railways' Limpopo line and with the Mozambican port of Maputo. A connection runs from Rutenga to the South African railways system at Beitbridge. In January 2018 the Government announced that it was reviving plans (originally mooted in 1980) to construct a railway line from the small town of Lion's Den in northern Zimbabwe to the border with Zambia, which would eventually be linked with the southern Zambian town of Kafue.

National Railways of Zimbabwe (NRZ): NRZ Parkade Centre, 6th Floor, cnr Ninth Ave and Fife St, POB 596, Bulawayo; tel. (29) 2363522; e-mail pubreloffice@nrz.co.zw; internet www.nrz.co.zw; f. 1897; Chair. MARTIN DINHA; Gen. Man. RESPINA ZINYANDUKO.

ROADS

Zimbabwe National Road Administration (ZINARA): ZINARA House, Stand No. 389 Runville, Glenroy Cres., Highlands, Harare; tel. (24) 2442711; e-mail info@zinara.co.zw; internet www.zinara.co .zw; f. 2002; Chair. Dr GEORGE MANYAYA; CEO NKOSINATHI NCUBE.

Zimbabwe United Passenger Co (ZUPCO): 109 Belvedere Rd, POB 3298, Harare; tel. 8688002886; e-mail safetravel@zupco.co.zw; internet www.zupco.co.zw; provides rural, urban and regional bus services; Zimbabwe's largest bus operator; state-owned; Chair. Eng. QUINTON KANHUKAMWE; CEO EVERISTO MADANGWA.

CIVIL AVIATION

AirZim operates an effective monopoly over air travel and transport within Zimbabwe. International and domestic air services connect most of the larger towns.

Civil Aviation Authority of Zimbabwe (CAAZ): Harare Int. Airport Terminal, Level 3, New Terminal Bldg, Private Bag CY7716, Causeway, Harare; tel. (24) 2585073; e-mail pr@caaz.co .zw; internet www.caaz.co.zw; f. 1999; regulates aircraft operations; Chair. THEOPHILUS GAMBE; Dir-Gen. Dr ELIJAH CHINGOSHO.

Air Zimbabwe (Pvt) Ltd (AirZim): POB AP1, Harare Airport, Harare; tel. (24) 2575111; e-mail reservations@airzimbabwe.aero; internet www.airzimbabwe.aero; f. 1967 as Air Rhodesia Corpn; placed into administration in October 2018; Chair Dr SILVANO GWARINDA; CEO EDMUND MURAMBIWA MAKONA.

Tourism

Zimbabwe Parks and Wildlife Management Authority (ZIM-PARKS): cnr Sandringham and Borrowdale Rds, Botanical Gardens, Harare; POB CY140, Causeway, Harare; tel. (24) 2706077; e-mail bookings@zimparks.org.zw; internet zimparks.org; Dir-Gen. FULTON UPENYU MANGWANYA.

Zimbabwe Tourism Authority (ZTA): Tourism House, 55 Samora Machel Ave, POB CY286, Causeway, Harare; tel. (24) 2758712; e-mail info@ztazim.co.zw; internet www.zimbabwetourism.net; f. 1984; promotes tourism domestically and from abroad; Chair. RAYNOLD MAWERERA; CEO WINNIE MUCHANYUKA.

Associations licensed by the ZTA include:

Hospitality Asscn of Zimbabwe: 129 Baines Ave, POB CY 398, Harare; tel. (24) 2708872; e-mail hazimsec@gmail.com; internet www.haz.co.zw; f. 1963; Pres. CLIVE CHINWADA.

Safari Operators Association of Zimbabwe (SOAZ): Muku-visi Woodlands, Hillside Rd/Glenara Ave South, Hillside, Harare; tel. (24) 2779792; e-mail soaz@mweb.co.zw; internet www.soaz .net; f. 1973 as Zimbabwe Association of Tourist and Safari Operators; present name adopted 2006; Pres. EMMANUEL FUNDIRA.

Zimbabwe Council for Tourism: 129 Baines Ave, POB 7240, Harare; tel. (24) 2250246; e-mail ceozct@gmail.com; internet zct.co .zw; f. 1988; Pres. WINNIE MUCHANYUKA; CEO PAUL N. MATAMISA.

Defence

As assessed at November 2021, total armed forces numbered about 29,000: 25,000 in the army and 4,000 in the air force. Paramilitary forces comprised a police force of 21,800 and a police support unit of 2,300.

Defence Budget: Z.$23,300m. in 2021.

Commander-in-Chief of the Armed Forces: Pres. EMMERSON MNANGAGWA.

Commander of the Zimbabwe Defence Forces: Gen. PHILIP VALERIO SIBANDA.

Commander of the Zimbabwe National Army: Lt-Gen. DAVID SIGAUKE.

Commander of the Air Force of Zimbabwe: Air Marshal ELSON MOYO.

Education

Primary education, which begins at six years of age and lasts for seven years, is free and has been compulsory since 1987. Secondary education begins at the age of 13 and lasts for six years, comprising a first cycle of four years and a second cycle of two years. According to estimates by the UN Educational, Scientific and Cultural Organization (UNESCO), in 2012/13 enrolment at pre-primary schools included 28% of children (males 27%; females 29%) in the relevant age-group. The enrolment in the same school year at primary schools included 100% of children (males 99%; females 100%) in the relevant age-group, while the comparable ratio for secondary enrolment was just 52% of children (males 53%; females 51%) in the relevant age-group. In 2021 there were 18 universities in Zimbabwe, including the state-run University of Zimbabwe, in Harare, and the National University of Science and Technology, in Bulawayo. Primary and secondary education was allocated Z.$124,070m. by the central Government in the budget for 2022, equivalent to 12.8% of total projected expenditure and net lending in that year, while higher and tertiary education and science and technology development were allocated Z.$35,457m. (3.7%).

Bibliography

Alexander, J. *The Unsettled Land: State-Making and the Politics of Land in Zimbabwe 1893–2003*. Oxford, James Currey, 2006.

Barclay, P. *Zimbabwe: Years of Hope and Despair*. London, Bloomsbury, 2010.

Bhebe, N., and Ranger, T. (Eds). *Society in Zimbabwe's Liberation War*. Portsmouth, NH, Heinemann, 1993.

   Soldiers in Zimbabwe's Liberation War. Portsmouth, NH, Heinemann, 1993.

Bond, P., and Manyanya, M. *Zimbabwe's Plunge: Exhausted Nationalism, Neoliberalism and the Struggle for Social Justice*. Scottsville, University of Natal Press; London, Merlin; Harare, Weaver Press, 2002.

Bourne, R. *Catastrophe: What Went Wrong in Zimbabwe?* London, Zed Books, 2011.

Bowyer-Bower, T. A. S., and Stoneman, C. (Eds). *Land Reform in Zimbabwe: Constraints and Prospects*. Aldershot, Ashgate Publishing Ltd, 2000.

Brownell, J. *The Collapse of Rhodesia: Population Demographics and the Politics of Race*. London, I.B. Tauris, 2011.

Chan, S. *Southern Africa: Old Treacheries and New Deceits*. New Haven, CT, Yale University Press, 2011.

   Mugabe: A Life of Power and Violence. London, I.B. Tauris, 2018.

Chan, S., and Primorac, R. (Eds). *Zimbabwe since the Unity Government*. Abingdon, Routledge, 2012.

Chigudu, S. *The Political Life of an Epidemic: Cholera, Crisis and Citizenship in Zimbabwe*. Cambridge, Cambridge University Press, 2020.

Chikuhwa, J. W. *Zimbabwe at the Crossroads*. Bloomington, IN; Milton Keynes, Authorhouse, 2006.

Cliffe, L., Alexander, J., Cousins, B., and Gaidzanwa, R. (Eds). *Outcomes of Post-2000 Fast Track Land Reform in Zimbabwe*. Abingdon, Routledge, 2012.

Coltart, D. *The Struggle Continues: 50 Years of Tyranny in Zimbabwe*. Auckland Park, Jacana Media, 2016.

Compagnon, D. *A Predictable Tragedy: Robert Mugabe and the Collapse of Zimbabwe*. Philadelphia, PA, University of Pennsylvania Press, 2011.

Dashwood, H. S. *Zimbabwe: the Political Economy of Transformation*. Toronto, ON, University of Toronto Press, 2000.

De Waal, V. *The Politics of Reconciliation: Zimbabwe's First Decade*. London, Hurst, 1990; Harare, Longman Zimbabwe, 1992.

Duri, F. P. T., Marongwe, N., Mawere, M. (Eds). *Mugabeism After Mugabe? Rethinking Legacies and the New Dispensation in Zimbabwe's 'Second Republic'*. Masvingo, Africa Talent Publishers, 2019.

Ellert, H., and Anderson, D. *A Brutal State of Affairs: The Rise and Fall of Rhodesia*. Harare, Weaver Press, 2020.

Gallagher, J. *Zimbabwe's International Relations: Fantasy, Reality and the Making of the State*. Cambridge, Cambridge University Press, 2017.

Goebel, A. *Gender and Land Reform: The Zimbabwe Experience*. Montréal, QC, McGill-Queen's University Press, 2005.

Hammar, A., Raftopolous, B., and Jensen, S. (Eds). *Zimbabwe's Unfinished Business: Rethinking Land, State and Nation in the Context of Crisis*. Harare, Weaver Press, 2003.

Harold-Barry, D. (Ed.). *Zimbabwe: The Past is the Future*. Harare, Weaver Press, 2004.

Herbst, J. *State Politics in Zimbabwe*. Berkeley, CA, University of California Press; Harare, University of Zimbabwe Publications, 1990.

Kriger, N. *Guerrilla Veterans in Post-war Zimbabwe: Symbolic and Violent Politics, 1980–1987*. Cambridge, Cambridge University Press, 2003.

Laurie, C. *The Land Reform Deception: Political Opportunism in Zimbabwe's Land Seizure Era*. New York, Oxford University Press, 2016.

Meredith, M. *Mugabe: Power, Plunder, and the Struggle for Zimbabwe's Future*. New York, Public Affairs, 2007.

Moore, D. B. *Mugabe's Legacy: Coups, Conspiracies, and the Conceits of Power in Zimbabwe*. London, Hurst, 2021.

Moore, D. S. *Suffering for Territory: Race, Place, and Power in Zimbabwe*. Durham, NC, Duke University Press, 2005.

Moyo, J. N. *Voting for Democracy: A Study of Electoral Politics in Zimbabwe*. Harare, University of Zimbabwe Publications, 1992.

Moyo, S. *Economic Nationalism and Land Reform in Zimbabwe*. Harare, Southern African Printing and Publishing House, 1994.

   The Land Question in Zimbabwe. Harare, Southern African Printing and Publishing House, 1995.

Ndhlovu, F. *The Politics of Language and Nation Building in Zimbabwe*. New York, Peter Lang, 2009.

Ndlovu, R. *In the Jaws of the Crocodile: Emmerson Mnangagwa's Rise to Power in Zimbabwe*. Cape Town, Penguin, 2018.

Ndlovu-Gatsheni, S. (Ed.) *Joshua Mqabuko Nkomo of Zimbabwe: Politics, Power, and Memory*. London, Palgrave Macmillan, 2017.

Nklwane, S. M. (Ed.). *Zimbabwe's International Borders: A Study in National and Regional Development in Southern Africa*. Harare, University of Zimbabwe Publications, 1997.

Nyarota, G. *The Graceless Fall of Robert Mugabe: The End of a Dictator's Reign*. Cape Town, Penguin, 2018.

Pikirayi, I. *The Zimbabwe Culture: Origins and Decline of Southern Zambezian States*. Walnut Creek, CA, AltaMira Press, 2002.

Raftopoulos, B., and Mlambo, A. (Eds). *Becoming Zimbabwe: A History from the Pre-colonial Period to 2008*. Harare, Weaver Press, 2009.

Raftopoulos, B., and Savage, T. (Eds). *Zimbabwe: Injustice and Political Reconciliation*. Cape Town, Institute for Justice and Reconciliation, 2004.

Ranger, T. *The Historical Dimensions of Democracy and Human Rights in Zimbabwe, Vol. 2*. Harare, Zimbabwe University Publications, 2003.

Rasmussen, R. K., and Rubert, S. C. *Historical Dictionary of Zimbabwe*. 2nd edn. Metuchen, NJ, Scarecrow Press, 1991.

Rich Dorman, S. *Understanding Zimbabwe: From Liberation to Authoritarianism*. New York, Oxford University Press, 2016.

Rogers, D. *Two Weeks in November: The Astonishing Untold Story of the Operation that Toppled Mugabe*. London, Short Books, 2019.

Schmidt, H. *Colonialism and Violence in Zimbabwe: A History of Suffering*. Woodbridge, James Currey, 2013.

Scoones, I. *Zimbabwe's Land Reform: Myths and Realities*. Woodbridge, James Currey, 2010.

Shumba, J. M. *Zimbabwe's Predatory State*. Pietermaritzburg, University of KwaZulu-Natal Press, 2018.

Sibanda, E. M. *The Zimbabwe African People's Union, 1961–87: A Political History of Insurgency in Southern Rhodesia*. Trenton, NJ, Africa World Press, 2005.

Simon, D., Gaitskell, D., and Schumaker, L. (Eds). *Zimbabwe's Crisis*. Abingdon, Routledge, 2006.

Stiff, P. *Cry Zimbabwe: Independence—Twenty Years On*. Johannesburg, Galago Publishing Co, 2002.

Tendi. B-M. *Making History in Mugabe's Zimbabwe: Politics, Intellectuals and the Media*. Oxford, Peter Lang, 2010.

   The Army and Politics in Zimbabwe: Mujuru, the Liberation Fighter and Kingmaker. Cambridge, Cambridge University, 2020.

PART THREE

Regional Information

REGIONAL ORGANIZATIONS

UNITED NATIONS

Address: 405 East 42nd St, New York, NY 10017, USA.

Telephone: (212) 963-1234; **fax:** (212) 963-4879; **internet:** www.un.org.

The United Nations (UN) was founded in 1945 to maintain international peace and security and to develop global co-operation in addressing economic, social, cultural and humanitarian problems. Its principal organs are the General Assembly, the Security Council, the Economic and Social Council, the International Court of Justice and the Secretariat.

The UN's chief administrative officer is the Secretary-General, elected for a five-year term. The General Assembly comprises representatives of all 193 UN member states. The Security Council investigates disputes between member countries, and may recommend ways and means of peaceful settlement: it comprises five permanent members (the People's Republic of China, France, the Russian Federation, the United Kingdom and the USA) and 10 other members elected by the General Assembly for a two-year period. The Economic and Social Council comprises representatives of 54 member states, elected by the General Assembly for a three-year period: it promotes co-operation on economic, social, cultural and humanitarian matters, acting as a central policy-making body and co-ordinating the activities of the UN's specialized agencies. The International Court of Justice, mandated to adjudicate in legal disputes between UN member states, comprises 15 judges of different nationalities, elected for nine-year terms by the General Assembly and the Security Council.

Secretary-General: ANTÓNIO MANUEL DE OLIVEIRA GUTERRES (Portugal) (2017–26).

MEMBER STATES IN AFRICA SOUTH OF THE SAHARA
(with assessments for percentage contributions to UN budget in 2022, and year of admission)

Angola	0.010	1976
Benin	0.005	1960
Botswana	0.015	1966
Burkina Faso	0.004	1960
Burundi	0.001	1962
Cabo Verde	0.001	1975
Cameroon	0.013	1960
Central African Republic	0.001	1960
Chad	0.003	1960
Comoros	0.001	1975
Congo, Democratic Republic	0.010	1960
Congo, Republic	0.005	1960
Côte d'Ivoire	0.022	1960
Djibouti	0.001	1977
Equatorial Guinea	0.012	1968
Eritrea	0.001	1993
Eswatini	0.002	1968
Ethiopia	0.010	1945
Gabon	0.013	1960
The Gambia	0.001	1965
Ghana	0.024	1957
Guinea	0.003	1958
Guinea-Bissau	0.001	1974
Kenya	0.030	1963
Lesotho	0.001	1966
Liberia	0.001	1945
Madagascar	0.004	1960
Malawi	0.002	1964
Mali	0.005	1960
Mauritania	0.002	1961
Mauritius	0.019	1968
Mozambique	0.004	1975
Namibia	0.009	1990
Niger	0.003	1960
Nigeria	0.182	1960
Rwanda	0.003	1962
São Tomé and Príncipe	0.001	1975
Senegal	0.007	1960
Seychelles	0.002	1976
Sierra Leone	0.001	1961
Somalia	0.001	1960
South Africa	0.244	1945
South Sudan	0.002	2011
Sudan	0.010	1956
Tanzania	0.010	1961
Togo	0.002	1960
Uganda	0.010	1962
Zambia	0.008	1964
Zimbabwe	0.007	1980

Diplomatic Representation

All member states co-ordinate their representation at the UN through an appointed Permanent Representative, and diplomatic mission staff.

PERMANENT MISSIONS TO THE UNITED NATIONS
(October 2022)

Angola: 820 Second Ave, 12th Floor, New York, NY 10017; tel. (212) 861-5656; fax (212) 861-9295; e-mail theangolamission@angolaun.org; internet www.un.int/angola; Permanent Representative MARIA DE JESUS DOS REIS FERREIRA.

Benin: 355 Lexington Ave, Unit 14B, New York, NY 10017; tel. (212) 684-1339; fax (646) 790-3556; e-mail onu.newyork@gouv.bj; internet www.un.int/benin; Permanent Representative MARC HERMANNE G. ARABA.

Botswana: 154 East 46th St, New York, NY 10017; tel. (212) 889-2277; fax (212) 725-5061; e-mail botswana@un.int; Permanent Representative COLLEN VIXEN KELAPILE.

Burkina Faso: 633 Third Ave, Suite 31A, 31st Floor, New York, NY 10017; tel. (212) 308-4720; fax (212) 308-4690; e-mail bfapm@un.int; internet www.un.int/burkinafaso; Permanent Representative SEYDOU SINKA.

Burundi: 336 East 45th St, 12th Floor, New York, NY 10017; tel. (212) 499-0001; fax (212) 499-0006; e-mail ambabunewyork@yahoo.fr; internet www.burundimission.org; Permanent Representative ZÉPHYRIN MANIRATANGA.

Cabo Verde: 27 East 69th St, New York, NY 10021; tel. (212) 472-0333; e-mail capeverde@un.int; internet www.un.int/capeverde; Permanent Representative JÚLIO CÉSAR FREIRE DE MORAIS.

Cameroon: 22 East 73rd St, New York, NY 10021; tel. (646) 850-1827; fax (646) 850-1820; e-mail cameroon.mission@yahoo.com; Permanent Representative MICHEL TOMMO MONTHE.

Central African Republic: 369 Lexington Ave, Apt 7A, New York, NY 10017; tel. (646) 833-7937; fax (646) 833-7289; e-mail repercaf.ny@gmail.com; internet www.pmcar.org; Permanent Representative (vacant).

Chad: 129 East 36th St, New York, NY 10016; tel. (212) 986-0980; fax (212) 986-0152; e-mail chadmission.un@gmail.com; Permanent Representative MOUCTAR ABAKAR.

Comoros: 866 UN Plaza, Suite 495, New York, NY 10017; tel. (212) 750-1637; fax (212) 750-1657; e-mail comoros@un.int; internet www.un.int/comoros; Permanent Representative ISSIMAIL CHANFI.

Congo, Democratic Republic: 866 UN Plaza, Suite 511, New York, NY 10017; tel. (212) 319-8061; e-mail missiondrc@gmail.com; internet www.un.int/drcongo; Permanent Representative GEORGES NZONGOLA-NTALAJA.

Congo, Republic: 14 East 65th St, New York, NY 10065; tel. (212) 744-7840; fax (212) 744-7975; e-mail congo@un.int; internet www.un.int/congo; Permanent Representative LAZARE MAKAYAT SAFOUESSE.

Côte d'Ivoire: 800 Second Ave, 5th Floor, New York, NY 10017; tel. (646) 649-5986; fax (646) 781-9974; e-mail cotedivoiremission@yahoo.com; Permanent Representative KACOU HOUADJA LÉON ADOM.

Djibouti: 866 UN Plaza, Suite 4011, New York, NY 10017; tel. (212) 753-3163; fax (212) 223-1276; e-mail djibouti@nyct.net; internet www.un.int/djibouti; Permanent Representative MOHAMED SIAD DOUALEH.

Equatorial Guinea: 800 Second Ave, Suite 305, New York, NY 10017; tel. (212) 223-2324; fax (212) 223-2366; e-mail info@equatorialguineaun.org; internet equatorialguineaun.org; Permanent Representative ANATOLIO NDONG MBA.

Eritrea: 800 Second Ave, 18th Floor, New York, NY 10017; tel. (212) 687-3390; fax (212) 687-3138; e-mail general@eritrea-unmission.org; internet www.eritrea-unmission.org; Permanent Representative SOPHIA TESFAMARIAM YOHANNES.

Eswatini: 408 East 50th St, New York, NY 10022; tel. (212) 371-8910; fax (212) 754-2755; e-mail eswatini@un.int; Permanent Representative MELUSI MARTIN MASUKU.

Ethiopia: 866 Second Ave, 3rd Floor, New York, NY 10017; tel. (212) 421-1830; fax (212) 756-4690; e-mail ethiopia@un.int; Permanent Representative TAYE ATSKE-SELASSIE AMDE.

Gabon: 244 East 58th St, New York, NY 10022; tel. (212) 686-9720; fax (917) 675-7485; e-mail info@gabonmission.com; internet gabonconsulate-nyc.com; Permanent Representative MICHEL XAVIER BIANG.

The Gambia: 336 East 45th St, 7th Floor, New York, NY 10017; tel. (212) 949-6640; fax (212) 856-9820; e-mail gambia_un@hotmail.com; internet www.un.int/gambia; Permanent Representative LAMIN B. DIBBA.

Ghana: 19 East 47th St, New York, NY 10017; tel. (212) 832-1302; fax (212) 751-6743; e-mail ghanaperm@aol.com; internet www.un.int/ghana; Permanent Representative HAROLD ADLAI AGYEMAN.

Guinea: 140 East 39th St, New York, NY 10016; tel. (212) 687-8115; fax (212) 687-8248; e-mail missionofguinea@aol.com; Permanent Representative ALY DIANE.

Guinea-Bissau: 336 East 45th St, 13th Floor, New York, NY 10017; tel. (212) 896-8311; fax (212) 896-8313; e-mail guinea-bissau@un.int; Permanent Representative SAMBA SANE.

Kenya: 767 Third Ave, 33rd Floor, New York, NY 10017; tel. (212) 421-4740; fax (212) 486-1985; e-mail info@kenyaun.org; internet www.un.int/kenya; Permanent Representative MARTIN KIMANI MBUGUA.

Lesotho: 210 East 39th St, New York, NY 10016; tel. (212) 661-1690; fax (212) 682-4388; e-mail lesothonewyork@gmail.com; Permanent Representative NKOPANE RASEENG MONYANE.

Liberia: 228 East 45th St, 6th Floor, Suite 600A, New York, NY 10017; tel. (917) 261-6056; fax (917) 261-6086; e-mail liberia@un.int; Permanent Representative MAGGIE GIBSON-GLAY (acting).

Madagascar: 820 Second Ave, Suite 800, New York, NY 10017; tel. (646) 933-1028; fax (212) 986-6271; e-mail repermad.ny@gmail.com; internet www.un.int/madagascar; Permanent Representative (vacant).

Malawi: 866 UN Plaza, Suite 486, New York, NY 10017; tel. (212) 317-8738; fax (212) 317-8729; e-mail malawinewyork@aol.com; Permanent Representative AGNES CHIMBIRI-MOLANDE.

Mali: 111 East 69th St, New York, NY 10021; tel. (212) 737-4150; fax (212) 472-3778; e-mail miperma@malionu.com; internet www.un.int/mali; Permanent Representative ISSA KONFOUROU.

Mauritania: 820 Second Ave, Suite 17A, New York, NY 10017; tel. (212) 252-0113; fax (212) 252-0175; e-mail mauritaniamission@gmail.com; internet www.un.int/mauritania; Permanent Representative SIDI MOHAMED LAGHDAF.

Mauritius: 211 East 43rd St, 22nd Floor, Suite 1502, New York, NY 10017; tel. (212) 949-0190; fax (212) 697-3829; e-mail mauritius@un.int; internet newyork.mauritius.govmu.org; Permanent Representative JAGDISH DHARAMCHAND KOONJUL.

Mozambique: 420 East 50th St, New York, NY 10022; tel. (212) 644-5965; fax (212) 644-5972; e-mail mozambique@un.int; internet www.un.int/mozambique; Permanent Representative PEDRO COMISSÁRIO AFONSO.

Namibia: 135 East 36th St, New York, NY 10016; tel. (212) 685-2003; fax (212) 685-1561; e-mail info@namibiaunmission.org; internet www.un.int/namibia; Permanent Representative NEVILLE MELVIN GERTZE.

Niger: 417 East 50th St, New York, NY 10022; tel. (212) 421-3260; fax (212) 753-6931; e-mail nigermission@ymail.com; internet www.un.int/niger; Permanent Representative ABDOU ABARRY.

Nigeria: 828 Second Ave, New York, NY 10017; tel. (212) 953-9130; fax (212) 697-1970; e-mail permny@nigeriaunmission.org; internet nigeriaunmission.org; Permanent Representative Prof. TIJJANI MUHAMMAD-BANDE.

Rwanda: 124 East 39th St, New York, NY 10016; tel. (212) 679-9010; fax (917) 591-9279; e-mail ambanewyork@minaffet.gov.rw; Permanent Representative CLAVER GATETE.

São Tomé and Príncipe: 336 East 45th St, 13th Floor, New York, NY 10017; tel. (212) 651-8116; fax (212) 651-8117; e-mail rdstppmun@gmail.com; internet www.un.int/saotomeandprincipe; Permanent Representative (vacant).

Senegal: 229 East 44th St, New York, NY 10017; tel. (212) 517-9030; fax (212) 517-3032; e-mail senegal.mission@yahoo.fr; internet www.un.int/senegal; Permanent Representative CHEIKH NIANG.

Seychelles: 685 Third Ave, Suite 1107, 11th Floor, New York, NY 10017; tel. (212) 972-1785; fax (212) 972-1786; e-mail seychellesmissionun@gmail.com; Permanent Representative IAN DERECK JOSEPH MADELEINE.

Sierra Leone: 336 East 45th St, 6th Floor, New York, NY 10017; tel. (212) 688-1656; fax (212) 688-4924; e-mail sierraleone@un.int; Permanent Representative ALHAJI FANDAY TURAY.

Somalia: 425 East 61st St, Suite 702, New York, NY 10021; tel. (212) 688-9410; fax (212) 759-0651; e-mail somalia@un.int; internet www.un.int/somalia; Permanent Representative ABUKAR DAHIR OSMAN.

South Africa: 845 Third Ave, 9th Floor, New York, NY 10022; tel. (212) 213-5583; fax (212) 692-2498; e-mail pmun.newyork@dirco.gov.za; internet southafrica-usa.net/pmun; Permanent Representative MATHU JOYINI.

South Sudan: 336 East 45th St, 5th Floor, New York, NY 10017; tel. (646) 362-1668; fax (212) 697-1353; e-mail info@rssun-nyc.org; Permanent Representative AKUEI BONA MALWAL.

Sudan: 305 East 47th St, 3 Dag Hammarskjöld Plaza, 4th Floor, New York, NY 10017; tel. (212) 573-6033; fax (212) 573-6160; e-mail sudan@sudanmission.org; Permanent Representative AL-HARITH IDRISS AL-HARITH MOHAMED.

Tanzania: 307 East 53rd St, 5th Floor, New York, NY 10022; tel. (212) 697-3612; fax (212) 697-3618; e-mail newyork@nje.go.tz; internet www.un.int/tanzania; Permanent Representative KENNEDY GODFREY GASTORN.

Togo: 600 Third Ave, 2nd Floor, New York, NY 10016; tel. (212) 490-3455; fax (212) 983-6684; e-mail togo.mission@togounmission.org; internet www.missiontogo-onu-newyork.com; Permanent Representative (vacant).

Uganda: 336 East 45th St, New York, NY 10017; tel. (212) 949-0110; fax (212) 687-4517; e-mail admin@ugandaunny.com; internet newyork.mofa.go.ug; Permanent Representative ADONIA AYEBARE.

Zambia: 237 East 52nd St, New York, NY 10022; tel. (212) 888-5770; fax (212) 888-5213; e-mail zambia@un.int; Permanent Representative CHOLA MILAMBO.

Zimbabwe: 228 East 45 St, Third Floor, New York, NY 10022; tel. (212) 980-9511; fax (212) 308-6705; e-mail zimnewyork@gmail.com; Permanent Representative ALBERT RANGANAI CHIMBINDI.

OBSERVERS

Intergovernmental organizations and non-member states active in the region that participate in the sessions and the work of the UN General Assembly as Observers, maintaining permanent offices at the UN.

African Union: 305 East 47th St, 5th Floor, 3 Dag Hammarskjöld Plaza, New York, NY 10017; tel. (212) 319-5490; fax (212) 319-7135; e-mail au-newyork@africa-union.org; internet www.africanunion-un.org; Permanent Observer FATIMA KYARI MOHAMMED.

Asian-African Legal Consultative Organization: 275 West 10th St, New York, NY 10014; tel. (917) 623-2861; fax (206) 426-5442; e-mail aalco@un.int; internet www.aalco.int; Permanent Observer ROY S. LEE.

Commonwealth Secretariat: 685 Third Ave, 11th Floor, New York, NY 10017; tel. (212) 599-6190; fax (212) 808-4975; e-mail newyork@commonwealth.int.

Economic Community of Central African States (Communauté Economique des Etats de l'Afrique Centrale): 311-315 37th St, Suite 203, Union City, NJ 07087; tel. (201) 453-3842; fax (201) 472-9807; e-mail ceeaceccasom@gmail.com.

Economic Community of West African States: 828 Second Ave, 15th Floor, New York, NY 10017; tel. (914) 738-0430; e-mail ecowasmission.ny@gmail.com; Permanent Observer MAHAMA MUMUNI KAPPIAH.

International Committee of the Red Cross: 801 Second Ave, 18th Floor, New York, NY 10017; tel. (212) 599-6021; fax (212) 599-6009; e-mail newyork@icrc.org; Head of Delegation LAETITIA COURTOIS.

International Criminal Court: 866 UN Plaza, Suite 566, New York, NY 10017; tel. (212) 486-1362; fax (212) 486-1361; e-mail liaisonofficeny@icc-cpi.int; internet www.icc-cpi.int; Head of Liaison Office KAREN RENEE ODABA MOSOTI.

International Institute for Democracy and Electoral Assistance: 336 East 45th St, 14th Floor, New York, NY 10017; tel. (212) 286-1084; fax (212) 286-0260; e-mail unobserver@idea.int; Permanent Observer MASSIMO TOMMASOLI (Italy).

International Olympic Committee: 708 Third Ave, 6th Floor, New York, NY 10017; tel. (212) 209-3952; fax (212) 209-7100; e-mail IOC-UNObserver@olympic.org; Permanent Observer (vacant).

International Organization of La Francophonie (Organisation Internationale de la Francophonie): 801 Second Ave, Suite 605, New

York, NY 10017; tel. (212) 867-6771; fax (212) 867-3840; e-mail reper .new-york@francophonie.org; internet www.francophonie.org; Permanent Observer IFIGENEIA KONTOLEONTOS.

Inter-Parliamentary Union: 336 East 45th St, 10th Floor, New York, NY 10017; tel. (212) 557-5880; e-mail ny-office@mail.ipu.org; internet www.ipu.org/Un-e/un-opo.htm; Permanent Observer PATRICIA (PADDY) TORSNEY (Canada).

Organization of Islamic Cooperation: 320 East 51st St, New York, NY 10022; tel. (212) 883-0140; fax (212) 883-0143; e-mail oicny@un.int; internet www.oicun.org; Permanent Observer HAMEED AJIBAIYE OPELOYERU (Nigeria).

South Centre: 1102 Round Tree Pl., Lawrenceville, NJ 08648; e-mail south@southcentre.int; internet www.southcentre.int.

The following are among several intergovernmental organizations that have a standing invitation to participate as Observers in the sessions and work of the General Assembly, but do not maintain permanent offices at the UN: African Development Bank; Asian Infrastructure Investment Bank; Indian Ocean Commission; Indian Ocean Rim Association; Intergovernmental Authority on Development; International Conference on the Great Lakes Region of Africa; International Network for Bamboo and Rattan; New Development Bank; Organisation of African, Caribbean and Pacific States; Regional Centre on Small Arms and Light Weapons in the Great Lakes Region, Horn of Africa and Bordering States; Pan African Intergovernmental Agency for Water and Sanitation for Africa; Southern African Development Community.

United Nations Information Centres/Services

A network of Information Centres and Services aims to communicate UN policies, programmes and activities at a local or regional level.

Burkina Faso: BP 135, 14 ave de la Grande Chancellerie, Secteur 4, Ouagadougou; tel. 25-30-60-76; fax 25-31-13-22; e-mail unic .ouagadougou@unic.org; internet ouagadougou.unic.org; also covers Chad, Mali and Niger.

Burundi: BP 2160, ave de la Révolution 13, Bujumbura; tel. (2) 225018; fax (2) 241798; e-mail unic.bujumbura@unic.org; internet bujumbura.sites.unicnetwork.org.

Cameroon: BP 836, Immeuble Tchinda, rue 2044, Yaoundé; tel. 222-21-23-67; fax 222-21-23-68; e-mail unic.yaounde@unic.org; internet cameroon.un.org; also covers the Central African Republic and Gabon.

Congo, Republic: POB 13210, ave Foch, Case ORTF 15, Brazzaville; tel. 661-20-68; e-mail unic.brazzaville@unic.org; internet brazzaville.sites.unicnetwork.org.

Eritrea: Hiday St, Airport Rd, Asmara; tel. (1) 151166; fax (1) 151081; e-mail dpi.er@undp.org; internet asmara.unic.org.

Ghana: POB GP 2339, Fao Bldg 2, Gamel Abdul Nassar/Liberia Rds, Accra; tel. (2) 665511; e-mail unic.accra@unic.org; internet ghana.un .org.

Kenya: POB 67578-00200, United Nations Office, Gigiri, Nairobi; tel. (20) 76225421; fax (20) 7624349; e-mail unon-nairobiunic@un .org; internet www.unicnairobi.org; also covers Seychelles and Uganda.

Lesotho: POB 301, Maseru 100; tel. (22) 313790; fax (22) 310042.

Madagascar: 159 rue Damantsoa Ankorahotra, Antananarivo; tel. (20) 2233050; fax (20) 2236794; e-mail unic.antananarivo@unic.org; internet madagascar.un.org.

Namibia: Private Bag 13351, UN House, 38–44 Stein St, Klein Windhoek; tel. (61) 2046367; e-mail unic.windhoek@unic.org; internet namibia.un.org.

Nigeria: POB 1068, 17 Alfred Rewane (formerly Kingsway) Rd, Ikoyi, Lagos; tel. (1) 4630915; fax (1) 4630916; e-mail lagos@unic.org; internet nigeria.un.org.

Senegal: Parcelle N°20, route du King Fahd, Almadies, Dakar; tel. 33-869-99-11; fax 33-820-30-46; e-mail unic.dakar@unic.org; internet dakar.sites.unicnetwork.org; also covers Cabo Verde, Côte d'Ivoire, The Gambia, Guinea, Guinea-Bissau and Mauritania.

South Africa: Metro Park Bldg, 351 Francis Baard St, POB 12677, Pretoria 0126; tel. (12) 354-8507; fax (12) 354-8501; e-mail unic .pretoria@unic.org; internet unicpretoria.org.za.

Sudan: POB 1992, UN Compound, House No. 7, Blk 5, Gamma'a Ave, Khartoum; tel. (187) 121404; fax (183) 773772; e-mail unic.sd@ undp.org; internet sudan.un.org; also covers Somalia.

Tanzania: POB 9224, 182 Mzinga Way, Oysterbay, Dar es Salaam; tel. (22) 2199200; e-mail unic.daressalaam@unic.org; internet tanzania.un.org.

Togo: 468 angle rue Atimé et ave de la Libération, BP 911, Lomé; tel. 221-23-06; fax 221-11-65; e-mail unic.lome@unic.org; internet togo .un.org; also covers Benin.

Zambia: POB 32905, Revenue House, Ground Floor, Kalambo Rd, Lusaka; tel. (21) 1228487; fax (21) 1222958; e-mail unic.lusaka@unic .org; internet lusaka.sites.unicnetwork.org.

Zimbabwe: POB 4408, Sanders House, 2nd Floor, First St/Jason Moyo Ave, Harare; tel. (4) 777060; fax (4) 750476; e-mail unic .harare@unic.org; internet zimbabwe.un.org.

Economic Commission for Africa—ECA

Address: Menelik II Ave, POB 3001, Addis Ababa, Ethiopia.

Telephone: (11) 5445000; **fax:** (11) 5514416; **e-mail:** ecainfo@uneca .org; **internet:** www.uneca.org.

ECA, established in 1958, promotes sustainable socioeconomic development in Africa and aims to advance economic integration among African countries. It provides a forum for international co-operation in support of these aims.

MEMBERS

Algeria	Eritrea	Namibia
Angola	Eswatini	Niger
Benin	Ethiopia	Nigeria
Botswana	Gabon	Rwanda
Burkina Faso	The Gambia	São Tomé and
Burundi	Ghana	Príncipe
Cabo Verde	Guinea	Senegal
Cameroon	Guinea-Bissau	Seychelles
Central African	Kenya	Sierra Leone
Republic	Lesotho	Somalia
Chad	Liberia	South Africa
Comoros	Libya	South Sudan
Congo, Democratic	Madagascar	Sudan
Republic	Malawi	Tanzania
Congo, Republic	Mali	Togo
Côte d'Ivoire	Mauritania	Tunisia
Djibouti	Mauritius	Uganda
Egypt	Morocco	Zambia
Equatorial Guinea	Mozambique	Zimbabwe

Organization

(October 2022)

COMMISSION

The Commission is empowered to make recommendations on any matter within its competence directly to governments of members or associate members, to governments admitted in a consultative capacity, and to the UN specialized agencies.

CONFERENCE OF AFRICAN MINISTERS

The Conference of African Ministers of Finance, Planning and Economic Development, which meets every year, is attended by ministers responsible for finance, planning and economic development, and is the main deliberative body of the Commission. The Commission's responsibility to promote concerted action for the economic and social development of Africa is vested primarily in the Conference, which addresses matters of general policy, considers inter-African and international economic policy, and makes recommendations to member states in connection with such matters. The 54th session was held in May 2022, in Dakar, Senegal.

SECRETARIAT

The secretariat implements the resolutions and programmes adopted by the Conference and the meetings of the Commission's subsidiary bodies. It is headed by an Executive Secretary, who is supported by two Deputy Executive Secretaries. A Partnerships Office includes teams from the African Union (AU) and the AU Development Agency (AUDA-NEPAD).

Executive Secretary: ANTONIO PEDRO (acting).

AFRICAN POLICY CENTRES

The following are focal points for continental policymaking and programming:

African Centre for Statistics;

African Climate Policy Centre;

African Institute for Economic Development and Planning;

African Land Policy Centre;

African Minerals Development Centre;

African Trade Policy Centre.

SUBREGIONAL OFFICES

The Subregional Offices (SROs) provide advisory services to member states, regional economic communities and subregional development stakeholders, in support of economic and social transformation. Regional observatories have been established in each of the SROs, to provide localized information and data relating to the continental integration agenda.

Central Africa: POB 14935, Yaoundé, Cameroon; tel. 222-50-43-30; internet www.uneca.org/central-africa; Subregional Officer JEAN-LUC NAMEGABE MASTAKI.

East Africa: POB 4654, Kigali, Rwanda; tel. 252586549; fax 252586546; e-mail eca-sro-ea-srdc@un.org; internet www.uneca.org/sro-ea; Dir MAMA KEITA.

Southern Africa: Lusaka, Zambia; e-mail director@uneca.org; internet www.uneca.org/southern-africa; Dir ISATOU GAYE.

West Africa: POB 744, Niamey, Niger; tel. 20-72-73-00; fax 20-72-28-94; internet www.uneca.org/west-africa; Dir NGONE DIOP.

Activities

The Commission's activities are focused on two 'pillars': on promoting regional integration in support of the visions and priorities of the African Union (AU), through research and policy analysis, capacity building, and the provision of technical assistance to relevant institutions; and on meeting emerging global challenges and the special needs of Africa, with particular emphasis on achieving the Sustainable Development Goals (SDGs) that were adopted in September 2015 by UN heads of state and government. The secretariat's work is guided by major regional strategies, including the Abuja Treaty on the establishment of an African Economic Community, Agenda 2063 (the AU's long-term framework for economic and social transformation of the continent), AUDA-NEPAD, the UN's 2030 Agenda for Sustainable Development, and the Agreement Establishing the African Continental Free Trade Area (AfCFTA), adopted by an extraordinary summit of AU heads of state and of government in March 2018. In early March 2021 the inaugural meeting took place of a new Regional Collaborative Platform: Africa (RCP: Africa), which aimed to enhance the effectiveness and co-ordination of UN development entities. The Platform is chaired by the UN Deputy Secretary-General, with ECA's Executive Secretary and the Director of the UNDP Regional Bureau for Africa acting as Vice-Chairs.

ECA supports the independent, Kigali, Rwanda-based Sustainable Development Goals Center for Africa, which was inaugurated in July 2016 to promote a continental vision for the attainment of the SDGs, and to extend technical support to assist in their implementation.

ECA participates in the annual Africa Regional Forum on Sustainable Development (ARFSD), which addresses progress being made towards achieving the SDGs. The eighth ARFSD, hosted from Kigali, Rwanda, in March 2022, in a partly virtual format, was themed 'Building forward better: a green, inclusive and resilient Africa poised to achieve the 2030 Agenda and the AU Agenda 2063'.

Joint meetings of ECA ministers responsible for economic affairs, planning and economic development and AU ministers responsible for the economy and finance are convened annually. In January 2018 the UN Secretary-General and AU Chairperson signed an AU-UN Framework for the Implementation of Agenda 2063 and the 2030 Agenda for Sustainable Development.

ECA hosts the secretariat of an independent Coalition for Dialogue on Africa (CoDA), which was founded in 2009, with the support of ECA, the AU and the African Development Bank (AfDB), and evolved from the other high-level consultative processes, including an African Development Forum.

During 2022 ECA's work programme focused on the following five strategic directions: Build ECA analytical capabilities; Formulate macroeconomic and structural policy; Design innovative financing models; Integrate regional and subregional transboundary initiatives; and Advocate continental ideas at the global level.

ECONOMIC POLICY AND DEVELOPMENT

ECA advocates for a sound regional macroeconomic policy framework, with the aim of promoting inclusive growth. The Commission aims to assist the economic development of member states through the collection and analysis of data; the preparation of annual economic surveys; the compilation of reports on regional economic conditions, governance and development management; the production of regional and national policy studies covering economic reforms, international and illicit financial flows, domestic resource mobilization, external debt, and exchange rate management; and the dissemination of best practices relating to specific aspects of economic management. In March 2021 ECA initiated a Liquidity and Sustainability Facility (LSF) to support the issuance by member state governments of sovereign bonds.

ECA's African Institute for Economic Development and Planning (UNIDEP), founded in 1962, undertakes pan-African capacity development and training programmes, and also conducts policy research and dialogue initiatives.

Since 2006 ECA, with the AfDB and UNDP, has organized an annual African Economic Conference (AEC) to promote an exchange of ideas among economists and policymakers on development policy. The 2022 AEC was to be hosted from Port Louis, Mauritius as a virtual event in December, focusing on the theme 'Supporting climate-smart development in Africa'. In July 2016 the UN designated 2016–25 as the Third Industrial Development Decade for Africa.

In April 2020 ECA established a multi-agency Africa Knowledge Hub for COVID-19, which includes data on and analysis of sectoral impacts of the pandemic—covering economy, private sector, supply chains, agriculture, trade, transport, tourism, the social sphere, and environment—and also collates related policy papers, research, resources and best practices. In mid-2020 ECA and partner agencies initiated an Africa Communication and Information Platform, which aimed to provide national and regional COVID-19 governmental task forces with data on survey responses, and actionable economic and health findings. At that time ECA became part of the Access to COVID-19 Tools (ACT) Accelerator partnership, focused on expediting the development and production of, and promoting equitable global access to, new health diagnostics, therapeutics and vaccines, to combat the pandemic and its onwards economic and social impacts. In August ECA joined the African Vaccine Acquisition Task Team. A decline of around 2% in African continental GDP was recorded in 2020, followed by a return to growth of 3.3% in 2021 (partly assisted by a rise in commodity prices). In 2022 ECA was implementing (in 10 member states) a pilot AfCFTA-anchored Pharmaceutical Initiative, which aimed to scale up the expansion of local pharmaceutical production, and to promote continental pooled procurement and harmonized regulatory standards.

The 2021 edition of the *Economic Report on Africa*, released in May 2022, estimated that 55m. people across the continent had been tipped into extreme poverty in 2020, through job losses and shrinking income, reversing more than two decades of poverty reduction progress. The report emphasized the importance of placing risk and vulnerability to shocks at the centre of poverty reduction strategies in the region, and the need for policies and social safety nets that would protect vulnerable populations. Also in that month, the 54th session of the Conference of African Ministers of Finance, Planning and Economic Development—emphasizing the adverse economic impacts of the COVID-19 crisis, the war in Ukraine, and deteriorating climatic condition—urged the ECA to advocate for the continuation of debt suspension support to member states.

GOVERNANCE

ECA aims to improve member states' capacity for good governance and development management. The Commission provides support for the African Peer Review Mechanism, an AUDA-NEPAD initiative whereby participating member governments mutually assess compliance with a number of codes, standards and commitments that uphold good governance and sustainable development. In January 2017 ECA and the Mechanism signed a Memorandum of Understanding (MOU) establishing a continuous partnership in support of the goals of the AU and the UN. ECA assists civil society organizations to participate in governance; supports the development of private sector enterprises; and helps to improve public administration in member states. To achieve these aims the Commission provides technical assistance and advisory services, conducts studies, and organizes training workshops, seminars and conferences at national, subregional and regional level for ministers, public administrators and senior policymakers, as well as for private and non-governmental organizations (NGOs).

The sixth edition of the *African Governance Report*, on the theme 'African Governance Futures to 2063', was finalized in 2021.

In November 2018, jointly with UNDP and other partners, the Commission issued the second edition of an *Africa Data Revolution Report*, with a focus on open government data.

REGIONAL INTEGRATION, TRADE AND INVESTMENT

ECA supports the implementation of the AU's regional integration agenda, through research; policy analysis; strengthening capacity and the provision of technical assistance to the regional economic communities; and through working on transboundary initiatives and undertaking activities across a variety of sectors. ECA promotes best practice in trade policy development, and undertakes research and dissemination activities on bilateral and international trade negotiations, with a view to helping African countries to benefit from globalization through trade. Projects are undertaken to support governments' strategies on implementing the AfCFTA. The African Trade Policy Centre (ATPC), established in 2003, aims to strengthen the human, institutional and policy capacities of African governments to formulate and implement sound trade policies and to participate more effectively in international trade negotiations.

In December 2021 ECA, AU, AfDB and UN Conference on Trade and Development issued their 10th joint *Assessing Regional Integration in Africa* report (*ARIA X*); this addressed the liberalization and integration of continental trade in services under the AfCFTA.

In April 2016 an ECA-AU-AfDB Africa Regional Integration Index (ARII) was launched. Using 16 indicators, the Index systematically measured progress in regional integration across areas including governance; investment; trade; infrastructure; industry; the free movement of persons; energy; culture; and macroeconomic policy convergence. An updated version of ARII was released in 2019. In February 2022 ECA issued an AfCFTA Country Business Index (ACBI) Report aimed at linking businesses and policymakers.

ECA organized the fifth African Business Forum in February 2022, in Addis Ababa.

In April 2021 ECA, the AU, the AfDB and Afreximbank issued an *African Trade Finance Survey Report,* which surveyed 185 banks from across the continent in the context of the COVID-19 crisis. The report noted that in the first quarter of 2020 there had been a massive outflow of capital from Africa, that exceeded US $5,000m. and placed strain on the net foreign assets of African banks.

ECA acts as the secretariat for the AUDA-NEPAD-co-ordinated (2021–30) Programme for Infrastructure Development in Africa Priority Action Plan (PIDA-PAP II), which covers infrastructure development in transport, energy, ICT, and transboundary water resources.

ECA and the World Bank jointly co-ordinate the sub-Saharan Africa Transport Programme (SSATP), established in 1987, which aims to facilitate policy development and related capacity building in the continent's transport sector. The regional Road Management Initiative under the SSATP seeks to encourage a partnership between the public and private sectors to manage and maintain road infrastructure more efficiently. An interconnected Trans-African Highways scheme, initiated by ECA in 1981, is focused on nine designated principal axes of roads across the continent. An Urban Mobility component aims to improve sub-Saharan African urban transport services, while a Trade and Transport component aims to enhance the international competitiveness of regional economies through the establishment of more cost-effective services for shippers. The Railway Restructuring element focuses on the provision of financially sustainable railway enterprises.

The eighth Forum on China-Africa Cooperation (FOCAC) ministerial summit, held in November 2021, in Dakar, adopted a China-Africa Cooperation Vision 2035; the Dakar Action Plan covering 2022–24 (the first phase of Vision 2035); the Sino-African Declaration on Climate Change; and a general Declaration. Nine programmes were to be implemented under the Dakar Action Plan. These included a medical and health programme, under which, *inter alia,* China was to donate 600m. further COVID-19 vaccine doses to Africa, and to provide 400m. doses through joint Chinese-African production; poverty reduction, agricultural, and trade and investment programmes; a digital innovation programme; green initiatives; capacity building support; cultural initiatives; and a peace and security programme (which was to include military assistance to the AU). Addressing the conference by videolink, China's President Xi Jinping pledged continued support for expanding Africa's local capacity for COVID-19 vaccine production, and to promote vaccine waiver exemptions. A reduced Chinese financial commitment, totalling US $40,000m., was made for 2022–24, compared with $60,000m. in 2019–21. The eighth Tokyo International Conference on African Development (TICAD-8) was held in August 2022. A third Japan-Africa Business Forum was organized in July 2021.

TECHNOLOGY

ECA supports member states in drafting and implementing national policies on innovation and technology, and undertakes relevant research, for example on emerging technologies that might facilitate economic development, and on technology transfer. It also has a focus on measuring the social, economic and other outcomes of policies on innovation and technology. ECA helps to organize the (normally) annual African Science, Technology and Innovation Forum, which was established in 2018 as a multi-stakeholder event to promote debate and the exchange of knowledge in all aspects of science, technology and innovation, and in particular their contribution to the pursuit of the SDGs.

ECA hosts the secretariat of the African Internet Governance Forum (AfIGF), which it established in 2011, jointly with the AU. The 11th Forum was convened in July 2022 in Lilongwe, Malawi, on the theme 'Digital inclusion and trust in Africa'.

In September 2012 ECA launched an African Forum for Geospatial Information Systems (GIS), aimed at enhancing the capacity of African media professionals to promote GIS.

ECA provided technical support to the AU in developing a Convention on Cyber Security and Personal Data Protection, which was adopted in 2014. An annual ECA Cybersecurity Week is held (in 2021: in early September).

In February 2022 ECA inaugurated an African Research Centre on Artificial Intelligence (ARCAI), in Brazzaville, Republic of the Congo.

CLIMATE CHANGE AND NATURAL RESOURCE MANAGEMENT

ECA conducts research in support of policy, legal and regulatory frameworks underpinning the management of natural resources in Africa. It also works to strengthen regional and national human and institutional capacities and to widen stakeholder participation in the protection of Africa's environment and in the management of the continent's mineral resources.

The African Climate Policy Centre (ACPC), launched by the ECA in December 2007, helps member states to incorporate climate-related concerns in their development policies. In 2006, with the AU and the AfDB, the Commission initiated a Climate for Development in Africa Programme (ClimDev-Africa) to improve the collection of climate-related data and assist in forecasting and risk management. ECA provides the technical secretariat for ClimDev-Africa. Since 2011 ClimDev-Africa has organized (normally) annual Climate Change and Development in Africa Conferences (CCDAs). CCDA-IX, themed 'Towards a just transition that delivers jobs, prosperity and climate resilience in Africa: Leveraging the green and blue economy' was held in September 2021, on the island of Sal, Cabo Verde. In June ECA and the AU jointly organized the fifth Africa Climate Resilient Investment Summit (ACRIS-5). The first session of the fourth edition of a series of Africa Climate Talks ('ACTs!-4'), co-hosted by the ACPC in July 2022, addressed the theme 'Ensuring a just and equitable transition and human security in Africa: Building resilience'.

ECA assists member states in the assessment and use of water resources and the development of river and lake basins common to more than one country. ECA encourages co-operation between countries with regard to water issues and collaborates with other UN agencies and regional organizations to promote technical and economic co-operation in this area.

ECA has been particularly active in efforts to promote the integrated development of the water resources of the Zambezi river basin and of Lake Victoria.

ECA aims to advance the development of Africa's extensive mineral and energy resources, focusing on promoting co-operation, integration and public-private sector partnerships; facilitating policy and dissemination of best practices; and supporting capacity building. A joint ECA-AU-AfDB multilateral Working Group on Infrastructure and Energy was established in November 2019.

In April 2016 ECA issued *Africa's Blue Economy Policy Handbook*, which noted that 38 member countries were coastal states, that in excess of 90% of Africa's trade is conducted by sea, and that marine and freshwater fisheries contribute significantly to the continent's food and nutritional security. In November 2018 ECA's Executive Secretary, attending a sustainable blue economy conference held in Nairobi, announced the development of a joint ECA-AU Regional Blue Economy Framework.

ECA, the AU and the AfDB jointly co-ordinate the Addis Ababa-located African Land Policy Centre (ALPC), which—based on the former joint Land Policy Initiative (LPI, formed in 2006)—was inaugurated in November 2017, during the second Conference on Land Policy in Africa (CLPA-2). The ALPC promotes equitable access to, and the efficient and sustainable utilization of land. It aims to advance women's secure access to land, and the recognition of African customary land rights. The former LPI finalized guidelines on land policy in Africa in 2009 and in July 2015 it established, with the German Government, a Network of Excellence on Land Governance in Africa. In July 2016 the LPI initiated a campaign that aimed to ensure the allocation of 30% of documented land holdings on the African continent to African women by 2025. CLPA-4 was hosted by Rwanda in November 2021, in a hybrid format, on the theme 'Land governance for safeguarding art, culture and heritage towards the Africa we want'.

GENDER, POVERTY AND SOCIAL POLICY

ECA aims to improve the socioeconomic prospects of women through the promotion of equal access to resources and opportunities, and equal participation in decision making. An African Centre for Gender and Development was established in 1975 to service all national, subregional and regional bodies involved in development issues relating to gender and the advancement of women. The Centre manages the African Women's Development Fund, which was established in June 2000. An African Gender and Development Index, measuring the extent to which member states meet their commitments towards international agreements on gender equality and women's advancement, was inaugurated in January 2005; the fifth phase of the Index was initiated in 2019. In April 2019 ECA launched an African Women Leadership Fund, which was to provide sustainable investment capital to businesses owned and led by African women.

The Commission provides information on global processes on social policy, including on the International Conference on Population and Development and the UN's 2030 Agenda for Sustainable Development. ECA maintains an African Social Development Index, which measures degrees of social exclusion. In November 2014 an African Disability Forum was established under the auspices of the Commission.

DATA AND STATISTICS

The African Centre for Statistics was established in 2006 to encourage the use of statistics in national planning, to provide training and technical assistance for the compilation, analysis and dissemination of statistics, and to assist member states with the compilation of population censuses. ECA assists its member states in population data collection and data processing; analysis of demographic data obtained from censuses or surveys; formulation of population policies; and integrating population variables in development planning. The 14th meeting of African Directors-General of Statistics was held online in December 2020 (the first having taken place in December 2014). In October 2019 the fifth conference of African ministers responsible for civil registration was convened, in Lusaka, Zambia. (The first was held in August 2010, in Addis Ababa.) In September 2021 an online Africa UN Data for Development Platform was initiated. In July 2022 the African Centre for Statistics launched an Africa SDGs Progress Dashboard.

Finance

ECA's regular budget for 2022, an appropriation from the UN budget, was US $78.5m.

Publications

Africa Statistical Flash (monthly).
Africa Sustainable Development Report (every 2 years).
African Governance Report.
African Statistical Yearbook.
Assessing Regional Integration in Africa (with the AU and the AfDB).
Country Profiles.
Economic Report on Africa (annually).
Subregional reports, policy and discussion papers, reports of conferences and meetings, training series, working paper series.

United Nations Children's Fund—UNICEF

Address: 3 United Nations Plaza, New York, NY 10017, USA.
Telephone: (212) 326-7000; **fax:** (212) 326-7096; **internet:** www .unicef.org.

UNICEF was established in 1946 as the UN International Children's Emergency Fund, with an initial focus on post-war Europe. In 1953 the General Assembly extended indefinitely UNICEF's mandate, which had expanded to cover children in developing countries, and revised its name (retaining the same acronym). UNICEF works to promote the rights and wellbeing of all children, adolescents and women, and places particular emphasis on assisting the most vulnerable and disadvantaged.

Organization
(October 2022)

EXECUTIVE BOARD

UNICEF reports on its activities to UN member states meeting in the General Assembly through its Executive Board, which is accountable to the UN Economic and Social Council (ECOSOC).

The Executive Board comprises 36 member governments from all regions, elected in rotation for a three-year term by ECOSOC. As UNICEF's governing body, the Board establishes policy, reviews programmes and approves expenditure. A Bureau is elected by the Board each year, comprising a President and four Vice-Presidents, representing five regional groupings. The Office of the Secretary of the Executive Board services the Board's work and liaises with the Secretariat.

SECRETARIAT

UNICEF's Executive Director is appointed by the UN Secretary-General in consultation with the Executive Board.

Around 85% of UNICEF staff positions are based in field offices. Divisions and programme groups cover education; child protection; early childhood development; adolescent development; nutrition and child development; social policy and social protection; health; HIV/AIDS; water, sanitation, hygiene and climate, environment and energy, and disaster risk reduction; gender and development; private fundraising and partnerships; public partnerships; information and communication technology for development; programmes; global communications and advocacy; field results and innovation evaluation; global insight and policy; internal audit and investigations; and financial and administrative management.

Executive Director: Catherine M. Russell (USA).

UNICEF REGIONAL AND OTHER OFFICES

The UNICEF Office of Emergency Programmes co-ordinates support for humanitarian action, and has a subsidiary Operations Centre.

Regional Office for Eastern and Southern Africa: POB 44145, Nairobi, Kenya 00100; e-mail unicefesaro@unicef.org; internet www .unicef.org/esaro; co-ordinates and supervises UNICEF's work in 21 countries; Dir Mohamed M. Malick Fall.

Regional Office for West and Central Africa: POB 29720, Dakar-Yoff, Senegal; tel. 33-831-02-00; fax 33-820-89-64; e-mail wcaro@ unicef.org; internet www.unicef.org/wcaro; co-ordinates and supervises UNICEF's work in 24 countries; Dir Marie-Pierre Poirier.

UNICEF Office of Research—Innocenti: Piazza della Santissima Annunziata 12, 50121 Florence, Italy; tel. (055) 20330; fax (055) 2033220; e-mail florence@unicef.org; internet www.unicef-irc.org; f. 1988; undertakes focused research to support UNICEF and other orgs to deliver results to children; works closely with all Fund offices as well as external academic and research institutions; examples of ongoing research projects include child rights in the digital age, multidimensional child poverty, and adolescent wellbeing; hosts the Global Longitudinal Researchers Initiative (GLORI, which surveys demographic groups periodically over a long time frame); Dir Gunilla Olsson (Sweden).

UNICEF Supply Division: Oceanvej 10–12, 2150 Nordhavn, Copenhagen, Denmark; tel. 45-33-55-00; fax 35-26-94-21; e-mail supply@unicef.org; internet www.unicef.org/supply; responsible for overseeing UNICEF's global procurement and logistics operations; there is a Supply Centre in New York, USA; further strategic supply hubs are located in Dubai, United Arab Emirates; Douala, Cameroon; Colón, Panama; and Shanghai, People's Republic of China; Dir Etleva Kadilli.

NATIONAL COMMITTEES

UNICEF is supported by a network of 33 independent National Committees (structured as non-governmental organizations), which are mostly based in developed countries. The Committees undertake advocacy and awareness campaigns, raise funds, and liaise with the general public.

Activities

UNICEF is dedicated to the wellbeing of children, adolescents and women and works for the realization and protection of their rights within the frameworks of the Convention on the Elimination of All

Forms of Discrimination Against Women (adopted by the UN General Assembly in 1979) and the Convention on the Rights of the Child (adopted by the UN General Assembly in 1989, and monitored by the 18-member UN Committee on the Rights of the Child). Promoting the full implementation of the Conventions, UNICEF aims to ensure that children worldwide are given the best possible start in life and the opportunity to attain a good level of basic education, and that adolescents are enabled to develop their capabilities and to participate successfully in society. The Fund also provides relief and rehabilitation assistance in emergencies. Through its extensive field network UNICEF undertakes, in co-ordination with governments, local communities and other aid organizations, programmes (that are preferably community-based and low-cost) in health, nutrition, education, the environment, gender issues, development, and water and sanitation.

UNICEF was a lead organization in consultations on the development of the Sustainable Development Goals (SDGs), adopted in September 2015 by UN heads of state and of government, as part of the UN's 2030 Agenda for Sustainable Development. The SDGs included new goals and targets aimed at improving the lives of children by 2030, such as: ending all forms of malnutrition, including achieving (by 2025) internationally agreed targets on stunting and wasting in children under five years of age, and addressing the nutritional needs of adolescent girls, pregnant and lactating women and older persons (SDG 2, Target 2.2); ending preventable deaths of newborn babies and children under five years of age, with all countries to reduce neonatal mortality to at least as low as 12 per 1,000 live births, and the under-five mortality rate to at least as low as 25 per 1,000 live births (SDG 3, Target 3.2); ensuring that all girls and boys have access to quality early childhood development, care and pre-primary education (SDG 4, Target 4.2); eliminating gender disparities in, and inequities in access to, education (Target 4.5); eliminating harmful practices, such as child, early and forced marriage, and female genital mutilation (SDG 5, Target 5.3); ending, by 2025, child labour in all its forms, including securing the prohibition and elimination of its worst forms, such as the recruitment and use of child soldiers (SDG 8, Target 8.7); and ending the abuse, exploitation, trafficking, and all forms of violence against and torture of children (SDG 16, Target 16.2). In May 2015 UNICEF inaugurated an Innovation Fund and a Global Innovation Centre, based in Nairobi, Kenya, which aimed to support the development of creative and cost-effective means of improving the situation of children in poverty.

From March 2020 UNICEF's COVID-19-related emergency response activities—which prioritized countries that were already challenged by humanitarian crises—included prevention and hygiene messaging, the provision of WASH (i.e. safe water, sanitation and hygiene) supplies and healthcare services, support for distanced learning, nutrition assistance, and the extension of social and gender-based violence protection services. During 2020 COVID-19-related emergency operations undertaken by the Fund and its partners supported 261m. children. Furthermore, they trained some 3.3m. health workers in infection prevention and control and provided 1.8m. health workers with personal protective equipment. In March 2021 UNICEF's Executive Director warned that progress on almost every key indicator measuring childhood had regressed during the first year of the pandemic, and that the numbers of children who were isolated, hungry, living below the poverty line, abused, stressed and vulnerable had increased. Access to education, health and other essential services, and protection had declined. She urged that children should be placed at the core of recovery planning. It was reported in January 2022 that more than 6.7m. children globally had lost a parent or caregiver as a result of the COVID-19 pandemic.

Strategic Plan: UNICEF's strategic plan for 2022–25 (endorsed by the Executive Board in September 2021) took into account the challenges posed by the COVID-19 public health crisis and socio-economic emergency, which, it noted, disproportionately disadvantaged children and women. It had the following cross-cutting themes: gender equality; disability inclusion; climate action and environmental sustainability; peacebuilding; and building resilience.

CHILD PROTECTION AND INCLUSION

UNICEF affirms that every child has a right to grow up in a safe and inclusive environment.

The Fund is actively involved in several global child protection partnerships, including the Inter-Agency Working Group on Unaccompanied and Separated Children; the Inter-Agency Co-ordination Panel on Juvenile Justice; the Donors' Working Group on Female Genital Mutilation/Cutting; and the Better Care Network (aiming to facilitate support for children without adequate family care). UNICEF works with the International Labour Organization and other partners to promote an end to exploitative and hazardous child labour, and supports special projects to provide education, counselling and care in developing countries.

With a view to incorporating provisions for the protection of migrant children, UNICEF actively participated in the intergovernmental discussions to formulate a Global Compact on Safe, Orderly and Regular Migration, which was adopted in December 2018. In the field, UNICEF helps to supply humanitarian assistance to displaced children, works to promote their rights, and often establishes child-friendly spaces within refugee camps. In May 2022 UNICEF and the International Organization on Migration agreed a new Strategic Collaboration Framework aimed at protecting the rights of migrant children. In June UNICEF reported that 36.5m. children worldwide were displaced: 22.8m. internally, and 13.7m. as refugees and asylum seekers. UNICEF estimates that some 1.2m. children worldwide are trafficked each year. It promotes ratification of the Optional Protocol to the Convention on the Rights of the Child on the sale of children, child prostitution and child pornography. In June 2016 a Global Interagency Working Group issued a set of Terminology Guidelines for the Protection of Children from Sexual Exploitation and Sexual Abuse (the 'Luxembourg Guidelines'). More generally, the Fund supports initiatives to promote the rights of adolescents and their healthy development.

During 2021 the UN secured the release of, and organized after-care and reintegration support for 12,214 children who had been recruited into armed groups and forces. In December 2021 the UNICEF Executive Director noted that during that year the UN had verified 22,645 incidents of grave violations perpetrated against children in conflict situations—including killing and maiming. Most cases of verified grave violations were reported in Afghanistan, the Democratic Republic of the Congo—DRC, Israel and the Palestinian Territories, Somalia, the Syrian Arab Republic, and Yemen. The number of attacks on schools and hospitals was reported to have increased by 5% in 2021, compared with the previous year.

In June 2010 representatives of six central African states, Cameroon, Chad, the Central African Republic, Niger, Nigeria and Sudan, adopted the N'Djamena Declaration, in which they made a commitment to ending the recruitment of child soldiers in the region.

It is estimated that landmines kill and maim between 8,000 and 10,000 children every year. UNICEF supports mine awareness campaigns, and promotes the full ratification of the Convention on the Prohibition of the Use, Stockpiling, Production and Transfer of Anti-Personnel Mines and on their Destruction, which was adopted in December 1997 and entered into force in March 1999.

In March 2016 UNICEF and UNFPA jointly initiated a Global Programme to Accelerate Action to End Child Marriage, with a focus on providing education and health services to adolescent girls and their wider communities in 12 countries in the Middle East, Africa and South Asia; the Programme was renewed for a further four years in March 2020. In March 2018 UNICEF reported that around one-fifth of women globally had become married during childhood, compared with one-quarter a decade earlier. In March 2021 UNICEF warned that school closures, economic stress and parental deaths arising from the COVID-19 pandemic risked placing 10m. additional girls at risk of child marriage over the next decade.

An UNFPA-UNICEF Joint Programme on Female Genital Mutilation aims to eliminate that practice, with a focus on 17 countries in Africa and the Middle East.

UNICEF works to ensure that children live in a safe and clean environment, in particular advocating for improved air quality, and supports the active involvement of youth in the implementation of climate adaptation strategies and response plans.

The right to a name and nationality is enshrined in the Convention on the Rights of the Child. UNICEF promotes universal registration of births in order to prevent the abuse of children without proof of age and nationality, for example through trafficking, forced labour, early marriage and military recruitment. The Fund provides support for the enactment of legislation, and policies and standards that advance free and universal birth registration. It has facilitated the organization of birth registration data in rural areas of developing countries through text messaging. In May 2022 UNICEF estimated that, globally, 75% of children below the age of five were registered (compared with 63% in 2009). UNICEF has stated concern that significant numbers of registered children nevertheless lack a certificate or formal proof of registration.

UNICEF estimated in May 2022 that 61% of children aged under five in Eastern and South Africa and 47% in West and Central Africa were unregistered. In June 2020, in co-operation with the African Union, UNICEF initiated a No Name Campaign, promoting children's right to a legal identity.

CHILD SURVIVAL

SDG Target 3.2 requires a reduction by 2030 in the neonatal mortality rate to at least as low as 12 per 1,000 live births, globally, and of the under-five mortality to at least as low as 25 per 1,000 live births. Updated child mortality data is provided on an annual basis by the Inter-agency Group for Child Mortality Estimation, established in 2004 by UNICEF, the World Health Organization (WHO), the World Bank and the UN Population Division. The 2021 edition of the Group's *Levels and Trends in Child Mortality,* released in December, estimated that 7.2m. children, adolescents and youth aged under 25 (including more than 5m. children under the age of five, of whom

2.4m. were newborn infants) died in 2020, largely of preventable or treatable causes. By comparison, some 12.5m. children under the age of five died in 1990. It reported that, by 2020, more than 50 countries were deemed to be at risk of missing the under-five mortality target set for 2030, and more than 60 states (two-thirds of which were in Africa) were deemed to be at risk of missing the 2030 neonatal mortality rate target. Nearly two-thirds of low and middle income countries were reported to have no reliable mortality data over the past three years.

Under the Global Partnership for Maternal, Newborn and Child Health, established in 2005, UNICEF works with WHO, the UN Population Fund (UNFPA) and other partners in countries with high maternal mortality to improve maternal health and prevent maternal and newborn deaths through the integration of a continuum of home, community, outreach and facility-based care, embracing every stage of maternal, newborn and child health.

UNICEF is a founding partner of Gavi, the Vaccine Alliance, which works to protect all children against vaccine-preventable diseases. In April 2019 UNICEF launched a global campaign, #vaccineswork, to promote the use of and confidence in vaccines, with a particular focus on the recent global acceleration in the incidence of cases of measles. UNICEF is a key implementing partner of the COVID-19 Vaccines Global Access (COVAX) Facility, one of four pillars of the Access to COVID-19 Tools Accelerator, which was launched in April 2020 by WHO, the European Commission and France, to generate equitable access to COVID-19 diagnostics, therapeutics and vaccines. On behalf of the COVAX Facility UNICEF leads end-to-end procurement and supply of COVID-19 vaccines, testing kits, personal protective equipment and treatments. In December 2020 UNICEF launched an online COVID-19 Vaccine Market Dashboard to track developments in the COVID-19 vaccine market.

UNICEF, WHO, the UN Development Programme and the World Bank inaugurated 'Roll Back Malaria' in October 1998—a global campaign to combat the disease, which killed an estimated 1m. people each year at that time, the majority of whom were children in sub-Saharan Africa. UNICEF facilitates the distribution of highly subsidized insecticide-treated mosquito nets at community level, thereby increasing the proportion of children and pregnant women who use them. Four-fifths of malaria deaths in Africa in 2020 were reported to be in children aged under five.

UNICEF works to improve safe water supply, sanitation and hygiene, 'WASH', and thereby reduce the risk of diarrhoea and other waterborne diseases, such as cholera, dysentery, Hepatitis A, and typhoid. It places great emphasis on increasing the testing and protection of drinking water, and on promoting the practice of thoroughly washing hands with soap. In March 2021 UNICEF estimated that 3,000m. people worldwide lacked basic hand washing facilities, such as soap and clean water, at home. UNICEF-assisted programmes for the control of diarrhoeal diseases promote the low-cost manufacture and distribution of prepackaged salts. In July 2022 UNICEF reported that each year the deaths of around 484,000 children under five years of age (primarily in sub-Saharan Africa and South Asia) were caused by diarrhoea attributed to poor sanitation and to contaminated drinking water. UNICEF hosts the secretariat of a multi-stakeholder partnership, Sanitation and Water for All, which promotes, co-ordinates and monitors efforts to achieve SDG targets relating to WASH.

UNICEF participates (with FAO, IFAD, WFP and WHO) in the Steering Committee of UN Nutrition, which was initiated in early 2021 to co-ordinate UN agencies in advancing nutrition and eliminating hunger, malnutrition and obesity. According to UNICEF estimates, one-quarter of children under five years of age are underweight, while each year malnutrition contributes to more than one-third of child deaths in that age group and leaves millions of others with physical and mental disabilities. UNICEF supports national efforts to reduce malnutrition, for example, fortifying staple foods with micronutrients, widening women's access to education, improving the nutritional status of pregnant women, strengthening household food security and basic health services, providing food supplies in emergencies, and promoting sound childcare and feeding practices. By 2022 more than 20,000 hospitals in 152 countries had been designated 'baby-friendly', having implemented a set of UNICEF and WHO recommendations. A Baby-Friendly Hospital Initiative Congress was convened in October 2016, in Geneva, under the joint auspices of UNICEF and WHO. In April 2015 UNICEF, the World Bank and other partners launched the Power of Nutrition, an independent fund that aimed to raise US $200m., initially, towards ending child undernutrition.

In 2021 it was estimated that, worldwide, 1.7m. children aged under 15 were living with HIV/AIDS (around 90% of whom were in Africa). Some 160,000 children were estimated to have been newly infected with HIV during that year. Only 52% of children who were living with HIV in 2021 had access to life-saving treatments. In 2020 an estimated 99,000 children died of AIDS-related causes.

As a result of HIV/AIDS—which had deprived an estimated 14.9m. children in 2021 of one or both of their parents—UNICEF is concerned that many children have suffered poverty, homelessness, discrimination, exploitation, and loss of education and other life opportunities. The Fund aims to provide expertise, support, logistical co-ordination and innovation towards ending the epidemic and limiting its impact on children and their mothers. Its priorities in this area include prevention of mother-to-child transmission ('PMCTC'); prevention of infection among young people (through, for example, support for education programmes and media campaigns); care and protection of orphans and other vulnerable children; and care and support for children, young people and parents living with HIV/AIDS. UNICEF works closely in this field with governments and co-operates with other UN agencies in the Joint UN Programme on HIV/AIDS (UNAIDS).

During 2016–21 UNICEF implemented a Last Mile to Elimination of Mother-To-Child Transmission (EMTCT) framework in localities with high prevalence of HIV; by December 2021 an end to mother-to-child HIV transmission had been certified in 15 countries, including Botswana—the first country with a severe HIV epidemic to end mother-to-child transmission.

Despite representing one-tenth of the population of sub-Saharan Africa, adolescent girls and young women aged 15–24 accounted for one-quarter of new HIV infections there in 2020. In 2021 an estimated 250,000 adolescent girls and young women aged 15–24 globally were newly infected with HIV, of whom 82% were in sub-Saharan Africa. In 2020 Eswatini (with a score of 98%-98%-91%) was the only country globally to have achieved, with regard to children aged 0–14, the 90-90-90 target (set by UNAIDS in 2014) of at least 90% of people living with HIV being aware of their serostatus; at least 90% of these taking ART; and at least 90% being virally suppressed.

In August 2022 UNICEF, UNAIDS, WHO and other partners established a Global Alliance for Ending AIDS in Children by 2030.

EDUCATION

UNICEF works to ensure that all children receive equal access to quality education, which it identifies as a fundamental human right. UNICEF is the agency assigned formal responsibility within the initiative for education in emergencies, early childhood care and technical and policy support. UNICEF advocates the implementation of the Child Friendly School model, designed to facilitate the delivery of safe, quality education. In September 2019 UNICEF and the International Telecommunication Union initiated a new Giga initiative, which aimed to ensure internet connectivity for every school and thus facilitate online access to information and opportunities for all young people. In March 2020 UNICEF, with WHO and the International Committee of the Red Cross, issued guidance to support schools in dealing with the COVID-19 pandemic, in particular to protect children from transmission and to implement educational strategies to maintain learning in the event of school closures. *The State of Global Learning Poverty: 2022 Update,* issued in June of that year by UNICEF, the World Bank and other partners, warned that disruptions arising from the COVID-19 pandemic—which had caused an average global loss of 141 in-person schooling days during February 2020–February 2022—had significantly worsened (already widespread) learning poverty (measured as the number of children who have not acquired a minimal level of proficiency in literacy by age 10). The report observed that in 2019 the average global learning poverty rate in low- and middle-income countries had been 57% (with a peak of 86% in sub-Saharan Africa). Lack of internet access and connectivity were reported to have widely increased reliance on television and radio as learning sources during school closures. The report recommended a RAPID framework of policy interventions, devised with input from UNICEF, to accelerate learning: Reach every child and keep them in school; Assess learning levels regularly; Prioritize teaching the fundamentals; Increase the efficiency of instruction, including through catch-up learning; Develop psychosocial health and wellbeing.

In May 2016 UNICEF released a report which found that—although one-quarter of school-age children globally (some 462m. children) were living in humanitarian emergency-affected countries—education accounted for a negligible proportion (2%) of funds requested under humanitarian appeals. A new fund, Education Cannot Wait (ECW), was launched at the inaugural World Humanitarian Summit, held later in May, in Istanbul, Türkiye, with a view to increasing access to learning opportunities for children living through emergencies. The fund, which aimed to support 75m. children by 2030, has a First Emergency-Response Window, a Multi-Year Resilience Window, and an Acceleration Facility (which supports activities and research to improve crisis preparedness and response). By January 2022 the fund had mobilized resources totalling US $1,100m.

UNICEF also advocates Life Skills-Based Education as a means of empowering young people to cope with challenging situations and to adopt healthy patterns of behaviour.

UNICEF leads and acts as the secretariat of the UN Girls' Education Initiative (UNGEI), which aims to increase the enrolment of girls in primary schools in more than 100 countries. In May 2010

UNGEI participants unanimously adopted the Dakar Declaration on Accelerating Girls' Education and Gender Equality.

SOCIAL POLICY

UNICEF seeks to work with governments and other external partners to strengthen capacities to design and implement cross-sectoral social and economic policies, child-focused legislative measures and increased focus on children in national budgets. UNICEF has identified the following priority areas of support to 'upstream' policy work: child poverty and disparities; social budgeting; decentralization; social security and social protection; and the impact of migration on children. It supports cash transfer programmes to help to address child poverty, and works to identify the impact of social and economic vulnerabilities on children.

UNICEF works with other agencies to advance universal social protection by 2030 (USP2030), with guaranteed equitable access for all to social mechanisms to counter poverty. UNICEF, UNDP, ILO and WHO co-chair the UN Issue-Based Coalition on Social Protection, which serves as a platform for advocacy, policy advice and exchange of information on the creation of sustainable, holistic and integrated social protection systems.

EMERGENCIES AND HUMANITARIAN RESPONSE

UNICEF's activities aimed at providing emergency relief assistance to children and young people affected by conflict, natural disasters and food crises are co-ordinated through its Office of Emergency Programmes and subsidiary Operations Centre (OPSCEN). In situations of violence and social disintegration the Fund provides support in the areas of education, health, mine-awareness and psychosocial assistance, and helps to demobilize and rehabilitate child soldiers. In December 2021 UNICEF launched a humanitarian appeal for US $9,395m. to meet the urgent requirements of more than 300m. children and their families and other caregivers during 2022. Some $933m. was requested under the appeal to fund operations undertaken in the framework of the collaborative Access to COVID-19 Tools Accelerator (q.v.), and $69.6m. was allocated to global support for UNICEF's humanitarian action.

Since 1998 UNICEF's humanitarian response has been structured within a framework of identified Core Commitments for Children in Humanitarian Action (CCCs), which reflect optimum humanitarian structures, principles and best practices to ensure that every child is protected, their dignity respected and that no child is left behind during humanitarian crises. Revised CCCs were issued in October 2020 to incorporate best practices in providing quality, prompt humanitarian support during fast-moving emergency situations. Within the UN system's 'Cluster Approach', developed to co-ordinate the international response to humanitarian disasters, UNICEF is the lead agency for Education (jointly with Save The Children); Nutrition; and WASH.

UNICEF aims to ensure the uninterrupted provision of education in emergencies. The Fund works to secure (and where necessary to reconstruct) safe learning spaces that are equipped with WASH facilities, to procure learning materials, to train teachers, and to support governments in the use of disaster risk reduction strategies. Emergency education assistance provided by UNICEF includes the provision of 'school-in-a-box' kits in refugee camps, the supply of flashlights to protect girls and women at night, and the organization, in co-operation with WHO, of outreach campaigns to enable the immunization of children in conflict zones. Through the Giga initiative (q.v.) the Office supports distance learning during emergencies. Psychosocial assistance activities include special programmes to support traumatized children, and the provision of 'child-friendly spaces'. UNICEF helps unaccompanied children to reunite with parents or extended families.

Sub-Saharan Africa: Under UNICEF's 2022 humanitarian appeal, US $1,356m. was allocated to West and Central Africa. Some $356m. was requested to fund UNICEF's emergency humanitarian operations in the DRC in that year, including the provision of safe water for 1.5m. people; the vaccination of 1.1m. children against measles; and treating nearly 538,500 children with severe acute malnutrition. For 2022 UNICEF also requested, *inter alia,* $231m. to provide assistance in Nigeria, in particular in northern areas affected by Boko Haram and inter-communal violence, $181m. to fund operations in Burkina Faso, and $119m. for Mali.

The Eastern and Southern Africa region was allocated US $1,092m. in the 2022 humanitarian appeal. UNICEF requested $351m. to fund its emergency humanitarian operations in Ethiopia, which were to include enabling 3.5m. people to access a sufficient quantity of safe drinking water, ensuring that 3m. children were vaccinated against measles, and treating nearly 619,500 children for severe acute malnutrition. Some $270m. was requested to fund operations in Sudan (which UNICEF classifies as part of its Middle East and North Africa region), $184m. for activities in South Sudan, and $177m. for Somalia.

RESEARCH AND ANALYSIS

The Fund promotes the collection and analysis of statistical data relating to the wellbeing of children and women. UNICEF's Multiple Indicator Cluster Survey (MICS) method of household data collection, initiated in 1995, analyses data on child protection, education (including remote learning), health (including HIV/AIDS and COVID-19), nutrition, and water and sanitation. By September 2022 349 MICS surveys had been completed in 118 countries. The seventh MICS round was scheduled to begin in 2023. A MICS Plus initiative, which uses mobile phones to supplement existing household data, was launched in October 2018. During 2012 UNICEF developed a Multiple Overlapping Deprivation Analysis tool to assess poverty and inequalities within countries.

The theme in 2022 of UNICEF's flagship *The State of the World's Children* report was 'immunization'.

Finance

UNICEF is funded by voluntary contributions from governments and non-governmental and private sector sources. UNICEF's income is divided into contributions for 'regular resources' and for 'other resources' (for special purposes, including expanding the outreach of country programmes of co-operation, and ensuring capacity to deliver critical assistance to women and children, for example during humanitarian crises). UNICEF's integrated budget for the period 2022–25 amounted to US $26,942m., and included proposed expenditure of $23,259m. for programme activities; the institutional budget amounted to $2,738m. during that period.

Publications

Progress for Every Child in the SDG Era.

The State of Food Security and Nutrition in the World (with FAO, WFP, IFAD and WHO).

The State of Global Learning Poverty.

The State of the World's Children (annually).

UNICEF Annual Report.

UNICEF Humanitarian Action for Children Report (annually).

Reports and studies; analyses of the situation of children and women by country or region.

United Nations Development Coordination Office

Address: One United Nations Plaza, DC1-1600, New York, NY 10017, USA.

Telephone: (212) 906-5500; **e-mail:** dcocommunications@un.org; **internet:** unsdg.un.org/about/development-coordination-office.

The Office was established in 1997, as the UN Development Operations Coordination Office (UN DOCO), along with a UN Development Group to enhance the UN's co-ordinated delivery of development assistance. In 2018, as part of extensive reforms to the UN development system, UN DOCO became a subsidiary office of the UN Secretariat, and was renamed the UN Development Coordination Office (DCO) with an enhanced role within the system. In particular, the DCO assumed managerial and supervisory functions in respect of the UN Resident Coordinator system.

Organization

(October 2022)

The DCO serves as the secretariat of the UN Sustainable Development Group, at the regional and global levels. At the regional level five DCO Regional Directors provide region-specific support to Resident Coordinators from offices based in Addis Ababa, Ethiopia; Amman, Jordan; Bangkok, Thailand; Panama City, Panama; and İstanbul, Türkiye.

Assistant Secretary-General: Oscar Fernández-Taranco (Argentina) (acting).

UN Development System

The UN's principal organ for intergovernmental policy review, dialogue, and overseeing the implementation of internationally agreed sustainable development objectives is the UN Economic and Social Council (ECOSOC). In June 2017 the UN Secretary-General issued a series of proposals outlining major changes that were required to realign the UN development system in order to maximize the delivery of the 2030 Agenda (see below), and in December he proposed improvements to the UN Country Team and Resident Coordinator (RC) system. In May 2018 the General Assembly adopted a landmark resolution on repositioning the UN development system.

The UN Sustainable Development Group (UNSDG), established as the UN Development Group in 2007 and renamed in 2018, provides strategic direction for the UN development system. Chaired by the UN's Deputy Secretary-General, the UNSDG serves as a high-level forum for inter-agency policy formation, operating through a Core Group and four Strategic Results Groups. The UNSDG Core Group consists of the heads of the UN Department of Economic and Social Affairs, the Food and Agriculture Organization of the UN, the International Labour Organization, the International Organization for Migration, the Office of the UN High Commissioner for Human Rights, the Office of the UN High Commissioner for Refugees, the UN Children's Fund, the UN Development Programme (UNDP), the UN Educational, Scientific and Cultural Organization, the UN Environment Programme, the UN Population Fund, UN Women, the World Food Programme, the World Health Organization, as well as the rotating Chair of the UN Regional Economic Commissions. The UNSDG also promotes the implementation of coherent policy at regional and country level, and supports, guides and tracks the local co-ordination of UN development operations. Its regional teams, *inter alia,* provide strategic guidance and support to the RC system, UN Country Teams and the Common Country Assessment mechanism (CCA, a process for evaluating national development needs). Based on the CCA, and in full consultation with national governments, the UN formulates a specific framework for development operations at country level, known as the UN Sustainable Development Cooperation Framework.

In accordance with the 2018 reforms of the UN development system, the DCO was repositioned as a stand-alone office within the UN Secretariat, and assumed managerial and oversight functions of the RC system, under UNSDG supervision. The office reports directly to the UNSDG's Chair, and services and facilitates its work, providing technical and advisory support to its members. The DCO's critical functions for the UNSDG and the RC system are defined as: providing focused policy co-ordination and technical support to the Group's global work; supporting the UNSDG regional teams, the RCs and UN Country Teams; and gathering evidence and data on activities in programme countries to inform the UNSDG's analytical work and decision making.

From 2020, with a view to streamlining co-ordination, five Regional Collaborative Platforms (RCPs) were initiated, with participation by all development-focused UN agencies working within each region. Each RCP is chaired by the UN Deputy Secretary-General. The heads of the relevant UNDP Regional Bureau and UN Regional Economic Commission act as Vice-Chairs.

2030 Agenda for Sustainable Development

In September 2015 UN heads of state and government, gathered in New York, USA, at a high-level plenary meeting of the UN General Assembly, adopted an outcome document known as the '2030 Agenda for Sustainable Development'. This had been drafted during an intensive, inclusive three-year collaborative process aimed at designing a new forward-looking global framework for the pursuit of sustainable development and the eradication of extreme poverty. It incorporated the following 17 Sustainable Development Goals (SDGs)—reinforced by 169 specific targets—which were to be pursued during the period 2016–30:

1. End poverty in all its forms everywhere;

2. End hunger, achieve food security and improved nutrition and promote sustainable agriculture;

3. Ensure healthy lives and promote well-being for all at all ages;

4. Ensure inclusive and equitable quality education and promote lifelong learning opportunities for all;

5. Achieve gender equality and empower all women and girls;

6. Ensure availability and sustainable management of water and sanitation for all;

7. Ensure access to affordable, reliable, sustainable and modern energy for all;

8. Promote sustained, inclusive and sustainable economic growth, full and productive employment and decent work for all;

9. Build resilient infrastructure, promote inclusive and sustainable industrialization and foster innovation;

10. Reduce inequality within and among countries;

11. Make cities and human settlements inclusive, safe, resilient and sustainable;

12. Ensure sustainable consumption and production patterns;

13. Take urgent action to combat climate change and its impacts;

14. Conserve and sustainably use the oceans, seas and marine resources for sustainable development;

15. Protect, restore and promote sustainable use of terrestrial ecosystems, sustainably manage forests, combat desertification, and halt and reverse land degradation and halt biodiversity loss;

16. Promote peaceful and inclusive societies for sustainable development, provide access to justice for all and build effective, accountable and inclusive institutions at all levels;

17. Strengthen the means of implementation and revitalize the Global Partnership for Sustainable Development.

The UN High-Level Political Forum (HLPF) on Sustainable Development, convened annually in July under the auspices of ECOSOC, is the focus for the system-wide follow up and review of the 2030 Agenda and the SDGs; as the principal UN intergovernmental platform on sustainable development, the Forum adopts negotiated political declarations. An independently produced annual *Sustainable Development Report,* incorporating SDG-tracking progress charts, is presented to the HLPF. The report is compiled with data from national statistical offices, from international organizations, and from non-official sources, including research centres. The UN Office of Intergovernmental Support and Coordination for Sustainable Development, part of the UN Department of Economic and Social Affairs, supports the HLPF and relevant work of the UN General Assembly and ECOSOC. A voluntary national review (VNR) mechanism is used to report on countries' progress in implementing the 2030 Agenda.

The 2022 regular HLPF, held in July, addressed 'Building back better from COVID-19 while advancing the full implementation of the 2030 Agenda for Sustainable Development', and reviewed progress achieved in the pursuit of SDGs 4 (on quality education), 5 (gender equality), 14 (life below water), 15 (life on land), and 17 (on partnerships). A series of VNR Labs was convened on the sidelines of HLPF 2022 to share country-level information and experiences in implementing the 2030 Agenda. The 2022 *Sustainable Development Report,* issued in advance of the Forum, warned that a confluence of 'cascading and intersecting crises' (notably climate change, conflicts and COVID-19—impacting the environment, peace and security, food, nutrition, health and education) was reversing development gains and jeopardizing the achievement of the 2030 Agenda as well as the very survival of humanity. The report emphasized that the SDGs represented a roadmap for survival, and also stressed the necessity of (i) ending armed conflicts and embarking on a path of diplomacy and peace, as an essential precondition for sustainable development; (ii) adopting low-carbon, resilient, inclusive development pathways aimed at conserving natural resources, transforming food systems, creating better jobs, and facilitating the transition to a greener and more inclusive economy; and (iii) implementing a comprehensive transformation of the international financial and debt architecture.

UN Resident Coordinators

Resident Coordinators have an independent, sustainable development-focused co-ordination function, and act as the designated representative of the UN Secretary-General in a country, with respect to its development operations. They lead the UN Country Team to support co-ordinated, inter-agency activities, as well as other national strategies and development priorities. RCs report both to the UN Secretary-General (through the Chair of the UNSDG) and to the host government on the implementation of a country's UN Sustainable Development Coordination Framework. In 2022 UN Country Teams—including UN agencies, funds and specialized programmes—were based in 132 countries, covering the 162 states and territories in which UN development activities were being undertaken.

OFFICES OF UN RESIDENT COORDINATORS IN AFRICA SOUTH OF THE SAHARA

Angola: Edifício ONU, Estrada Direita da Samba, Condomínio Rosalinda, Futungo de Belas, Luanda; tel. 226430880; e-mail onu.angola@one.un.org; internet onuangola.org; Resident Coordinator ZAHIRA VIRANI.

Benin: Lot 111, Zone Residentielle, BP 506, Cotonou; tel. 21-31-30-45; fax 21-31-57-86; e-mail rcs-onubeninregistry@un.org; internet benin.un.org; Resident Coordinator SALVATOR NIYONZIMA.

Botswana: UN Bldg, Khama Cres., Government Enclave, Gaborone; tel. 74217118; e-mail zia.choudhury@un.org; internet botswana.un.org; Resident Coordinator ZIA CHOUDHURY.

Burkina Faso: Immeuble des Nations Unies, 34 ave CES, secteur 401, 01 BP 575, Ouagadougou 01; tel. 25-31-04-70; e-mail burkina@onubf; internet onubf.org; Resident Coordinator BARBARA MANZI.

Burundi: Rohero I-Ave des Patriotes N° 10, BP 1490, Bujumbura; tel. 22301100; e-mail nicole.kouassi@undp.org; internet burundi.un.org; Resident Coordinator DAMIEN MAMA.

Cabo Verde: Maison des Nations Unies, Avda OUA, Achada de Santo António, CP 62, Praia; tel. 260-06-00; fax 262-14-04; e-mail unoffice.cv@one.un.org; internet www.un.cv; Resident Coordinator ANA PATRICIA GRAÇA.

Cameroon: 1232 Immeuble Mellopolis, rue 1794, Ekoudou, Bastos, Yaoundé; tel. 222-20-08-00; e-mail info.cameroon@un.org; internet cameroon.un.org; Resident Coordinator MATTHIAS Z. NAAB.

Central African Republic: PK4, ave Boganda, BP 3338, Bangui; tel. 75-89-72; e-mail denise.brown@un.org; internet republiquecentrafricaine.un.org; Resident Coordinator DENISE L. BROWN.

Chad: Rondpoint de la Francophonie, BP 906, N'Djamena; tel. 63-90-09-64; e-mail coodination.chad@one.un.org; internet chad.un.org; Resident Coordinator VIOLET KAKYOMYA.

Comoros: Hamramba, BP 648, Moroni; tel. 763-1089; e-mail registry.km@undp.org; internet comoros.un.org; Resident Coordinator FRANÇOIS BATALINGAYA.

Congo, Democratic Republic: ave Colonel Mondjiba, Concession Utex, Kinshasa; tel. 81890-7128; e-mail ndeye.lo@un.org; internet drcongo.un.org; Resident Coordinator BRUNO LEMARQUIS.

Congo, Republic: ave du Maréchal Foch, BP 465, Brazzaville; tel. 67-75-99; e-mail joanne.pindera@un.org; Resident Coordinator CHRIS MBURU.

Côte d'Ivoire: angle rue Gourgas et ave Marchand, Abidjan-Plateau, 01 BP 1747, Abidjan 01; tel. 20-31-74-03; e-mail snud.ci@one.un.org; internet cotedivoire.un.org; Resident Coordinator PHILIPPE POINSOT.

Djibouti: Tour Mezz, 8e étage, route de Venise, Djibouti; tel. 21353371; fax 21350587; e-mail jose.barahona@un.org; internet djibouti.un.org; Resident Coordinator JOSÉ BARAHONA.

Equatorial Guinea: UNDP Compound, POB 339, Malabo; e-mail pont1@un.org; Resident Coordinator ANNA MARTTINEN-PONT.

Eritrea: UN Offices, Hday St, POB 5366, Asmara; tel. (1) 151166; fax (1) 151081; e-mail yohanes.tesfay@un.org; internet eritrea.un.org; Resident Coordinator AMAKOBE SANDE.

Eswatini: Lilunga House, 5th Floor, Somhlolo St, POB 261, Mbabane; tel. 24096600; fax 24045341; e-mail registry.un.sz@one.un.org; internet eswatini.un.org; Resident Coordinator GEORGE WACHIRA.

Ethiopia: Congo Bldg, Addis Ababa; tel. (11) 5444386; e-mail uncommunication.et@un.org; internet ethiopia.un.org; Resident Coordinator CATHERINE SOZI.

Gabon: Maison des Nations Unies, Près du Pont de Gué-Gué, BP 2183, Libreville; tel. 74-82-69-77; internet gabon.un.org; Resident Coordinator SAVINA AMMASSARI.

The Gambia: 5 ave Kofi Annan, Cape Point, POB 553, Banjul; tel. 4494760; e-mail rco.gm@one.un.org; internet gambia.un.org; Resident Coordinator SERAPHINE WAKANA.

Ghana: Ring Rd Dual Carriage, nr Police HQ, POB 1423, Accra; tel. (21) 56709; fax (21) 773899; e-mail rcs-unrcoghana@un.org; internet ghana.un.org; Resident Coordinator CHARLES ABANI.

Guinea: Maison Commune, rue MA 002, Coléah Corniche Sud, Commune de Matam, BP 222, Conakry; tel. 24-40-49; e-mail coordination.gn@one.un.org; internet guinee.un.org; Resident Coordinator VINCENT MARTIN.

Guinea-Bissau: CP 179, 1011 Bissau Codex Bissau; e-mail un-gb@un.org; internet guineabissau.un.org; Resident Coordinator ANTHONY OHEMENG-BOAMAH.

Kenya: United Nations Ave, Gigiri, POB 30218, 00100 Nairobi; e-mail mwendwa.kiogora@un.org; internet kenya.un.org; Resident Coordinator STEPHEN JACKSON.

Lesotho: UN House, 13 United Nations Rd, Maseru; tel. 2222800; fax 22310042; e-mail un.lesotho@one.un.org; internet lesotho.un.org; Resident Coordinator AMANDA KHOZI MUKWASHI.

Liberia: One UN House, 1st and 2nd Sts, Tubman Blvd, Sinkor, Monrovia; e-mail rco.lr@one.un.org; internet liberia.un.org; Resident Coordinator NIELS SCOTT.

Madagascar: Maison Commune des Nations Unies, Zone Galaxy, rue du Dr Raseta, Andraharo, Antananarivo 101; tel. (20) 2330092;

e-mail issa.sanogo@un.org; internet madagascar.un.org; Resident Coordinator ISSA SANOGO.

Malawi: Plot No 7, Area 40, POB 30135, Lilongwe 3; tel. (1) 773500; e-mail rcs-malawi@un.org; internet malawi.un.org; Resident Coordinator a.i. MARIA DO VALLE RIBEIRO.

Mali: Maison Commune des Nations Unies, rue 39, Lot 2704 Badalabougou Est, Bamako; e-mail un_rco_ml@one.un.org; internet mali.un.org; Resident Coordinator MBARANGA GASARABWE.

Mauritania: Corniche Rd No. 159–161, Tevragh Zeina, BP 620, Nouakchott; tel. (45) 25-24-09; internet mauritania.un.org; Resident Coordinator ANTHONY OHEMENG-BOAMAH.

Mauritius: Anglo-Mauritius House, 6th Floor, Intendance St, POB 253, Port Louis; tel. 212-3726; e-mail robert.banamwana@un.org; Resident Coordinator CHRISTINE N. UMUTONI.

Mozambique: Avda Kenneth Kaunda 931, POB 4595, Maputo; tel. (21) 481404; e-mail myrta.kaulard@un.org; internet mozambique.un.org; Resident Coordinator MYRTA KAULARD.

Namibia: UN House, 38–44 Stein St, PMB 13329, Windhoek; tel. (61) 2046111; fax (61) 2046203; e-mail namibia.rco@one.un.org; internet namibia.un.org; Resident Coordinator SEN PANG.

Niger: Maison des Nations Unies, ave du Fleuve 428, BP 11207, Niamey; tel. 20-73-13-00; e-mail registry.ne@undp.org; internet niger.un.org; Resident Coordinator LOUISE AUBIN.

Nigeria: UN House, Plot 617/618, Central Area District, Diplomatic Zone, Abuja; e-mail rc.office.nigeria@one.un.org; internet nigeria.un.org; Resident Coordinator a.i. MATTHIAS SCHMALE.

Rwanda: 4 KN 67 St, BP 455, Kigali; tel. 788122416; e-mail rcoffice.rw@one.un.org; internet rwanda.un.org; Resident Coordinator OZONNIA OJIELO.

São Tomé and Príncipe: Avda das Naçoes Unidas, CP 109, São Tomé; tel. 221123; fax 222198; internet unstp.org; Resident Coordinator ERIC JAN OVERVEST.

Senegal: Immeuble Wolle Ndiaye, route du Meridien President, BP 154, Dakar; tel. 33-859-67-67; internet senegal.un.org; Resident Coordinator COULIBALY SIAKA.

Seychelles: Maison de Mahé, State House Ave, Victoria, Mahé; e-mail christine.umutoni@un.org; internet seychelles.un.org; Resident Coordinator CHRISTINE N. UMUTONI.

Sierra Leone: Fourah Bay Close, off Main Motor Rd, POB 1011, Freetown; e-mail babatunde.ahonsi@un.org; internet sierraleone.un.org; Resident Coordinator BABATUNDE AHONSI.

Somalia: e-mail unsom-odsrsg-rc-hc@un.org; internet somalia.un.org; Resident Coordinator ADAM ABELMOULA.

South Africa: Metropark Bldg, 351 Francis Baard St, Pretoria 0001; internet southafrica.un.org; Resident Coordinator a.i. Dr AYODELE ODUSOLA.

South Sudan: UNDP Compound, Plot 21, Ministries Rd, POB 410, Juba; e-mail info.unct.ss@one.un.org; internet southsudan.un.org; Resident Coordinator SARA BEYSOLOW NYANTI.

Sudan: House No 7, Block 5, Gama'a Ave, 11111 Khartoum; tel. (187) 120-000; e-mail khardiata.londiaye1@un.org; internet sudan.un.org; Resident Coordinator KHARDIATA LO N'DIAYE.

Tanzania: 182 Mzinga Way, off Msasani Rd, Oysterbay, Dar es Salaam; tel. (22) 2199200; e-mail info.untz@one.un.org; internet tanzania.un.org; Resident Coordinator ZLATAN MILIŠIĆ.

Togo: 40 ave des Nations Unies, le étage, BP 911, Lomé; tel. 22-21-20-08; fax 22-21-19-16; e-mail contact@tg.undp.org; internet togo.un.org; Resident Coordinator a.i. ALIOU MAMADOU DIA.

Uganda: UN Offices, Plot 11, Yusuf Lule Rd, Nakasero, Kampala; e-mail unrcs.uganda@un.org; internet uganda.un.org; Resident Coordinator SUSAN NGONGI NAMONDO.

Zambia: UN House, Alice Nkhata Rd, Longacres, POB 31966, Lusaka; tel. (21) 1386200; e-mail rcs.zambia@un.org; internet zambia.un.org; Resident Coordinator BEATRICE MUTALI.

Zimbabwe: Block 10, Arundel Office Park, Norfolk Rd, Mt Pleasant, POB 4775, Harare; tel. (4) 338836; e-mail sirak.gebrehiwot@one.un.org; internet zimbabwe.un.org; Resident Coordinator EDWARD KALLON.

Finance

With a view to securing consistent funding for the RC system, from 1 January 2019 member states' contributions under the UNSDG's existing cost-sharing mechanism were doubled. Furthermore, in July 2018 a dedicated Special Purpose Trust Fund was established, to which all member states were urged to contribute. Its requirements in 2022 totalled US $281m. UN member states were invited to provide voluntary contributions of $35m. to support the RC system, and $295m. annually to the Joint Fund for the 2030 Agenda for Sustainable Development (which was established in 2018).

United Nations Development Programme—UNDP

Address: One United Nations Plaza, New York, NY 10017, USA.
Telephone: (212) 906-5300; **fax:** (212) 906-5364; **e-mail:** hq@undp.org; **internet:** www.undp.org.

UNDP was established in 1965 by the UN General Assembly. Its central mission is to help countries to eradicate poverty and achieve a sustainable level of human development, an approach to economic growth that encompasses individual wellbeing and choice, equitable distribution of the benefits of development, and conservation of the environment.

Organization

(October 2022)

UNDP is responsible to the UN General Assembly, to which it reports through the Economic and Social Council (ECOSOC).

EXECUTIVE BOARD

The Executive Board is responsible for providing intergovernmental support to, and supervising the activities of UNDP, the UN Population Fund (UNFPA) and the UN Office for Project Services. It comprises 36 members, elected by ECOSOC for a three-year term: eight from Africa, seven from Asia and the Pacific, four from Eastern Europe, five from Latin America and the Caribbean and 12 from Western Europe and other countries.

SECRETARIAT

The Administrator is supported by one Associate Administrator and nine Assistant Secretaries-General. Offices and divisions at the secretariat include Offices of the Human Development Report, Audit and Investigations, Ethics, and Independent Evaluation; Global Services Solution and Global Policy Centres; and Bureaux for Policy and Programme Support, External Relations and Advocacy, Management Services, and Crisis. Five Regional Bureaux cover Africa; Asia and the Pacific; the Arab states; Latin America and the Caribbean; and Europe and the Commonwealth of Independent States.

Administrator: ACHIM STEINER (Germany).

Assistant Administrator: USHA RAO-MONARI (India).

Director, Regional Bureau for Africa: AHUNNA EZIAKONWA-ONOCHIE (Nigeria).

With a view to streamlining co-ordination, five Regional Collaborative Platforms (RCPs) were initiated from 2020, with participation by all development-focused UN agencies working within each region. Each RCP is chaired by the UN Deputy Secretary-General. The heads of the relevant UNDP Regional Bureau and UN Regional Economic Commission act as Vice-Chairs.

COUNTRY OFFICES

In almost every country receiving UN assistance there is an office, headed by a UNDP Resident Representative. UNDP maintains a regional hub for Africa in Addis Ababa, Ethiopia.

GLOBAL CENTRES

UNDP supports a network of global centres that undertake specialized research and advance sustainable development-related solutions and policy design.

Global Centre for Technology, Innovation and Sustainable Development: Block A, 29 Heng Mui Keng Terrace, Singapore 119620; tel. 69081063; fax 67744571; e-mail registry.SG@undp.org; internet sgtechcentre.undp.org; f. 2019; administered jointly by UNDP and the Singapore Government, the Centre aims to identify and promote innovative and technological solutions to sustainable devt challenges; the Centre's focal areas in 2022 included digital solutions for COVID-19, sustainable and digital agriculture, smart cities, and sustainable finance.

Global Policy Centre for Resilient Ecosystems and Desertification (GC-RED): UN Gigiri Compound, Block M, Middle Level, United Nations Ave, POB 30218, 00100 Nairobi, Kenya; tel. (20) 7624640; e-mail gc-red@undp.org; f. 2015; aims to promote knowledge sharing on and solutions for inclusive sustainable devt in drylands and other fragile ecosystems; focuses on building ecological and social resistance and on the sustainable management of renewable natural capital to improve livelihoods. The Centre is the managing agent for a jt UNDP-UNEP project, Poverty-Environment Action for the SDGs, which aims to integrate programmes that mainstream poverty-environment linkages into national devt planning processes; Dir ANNE JUEPNER (Germany).

International Policy Centre for Inclusive Growth (IPC-IG): Setor Bancário Sul, Quadra 1, Bloco J, Ed. BNDES, 13°, Brasília 70076-900, Brazil; e-mail ipc@ipc-undp.org; internet ipcig.org; f. 2002, became operational in 2004; IPC-IG promotes the exchange of knowledge, technical capabilities, and institutional capacity building expertise to advance policymaking that reduces inequalities and fosters human devt; encourages South-South collaboration; provides advisory services, training, organizes confs; in 2022 had a principal thematic focus on inclusive growth; poverty reduction policy design; social protection; technological innovation; and sustainable devt; Dir KATYNA ARGUETA (Honduras).

Istanbul International Centre for Private Sector in Development (IICPSD): İstiklal Sk, 34381 İstanbul, Türkiye; tel. (850) 288-2534; e-mail iicpsd@undp.org; internet www.iicpsd.undp.org; f. 2011; managed jtly by UNDP and the Turkish Govt, the Centre supports the devt of inclusive and competitive markets and aims to promote economic devt by engaging people in value chains in production and entrepreneurial roles; Dir SAHBA SOBHANI.

Oslo Governance Centre (OGC): Kongens Gate 12, 0153 Oslo, Norway; tel. (2) 212-1600; e-mail oslo.governance.centre@undp.org; internet www.undp.org/oslocentre; f. 2002, relaunched in June 2015, at the same time as the inaugural edition of a series of Oslo Governance and Peacebuilding Dialogues; the Centre aims to support the devt of more effective and inclusive forms of governance in UNDP member states and to prevent violent extremism; Dir ARVINN GADGIL.

United Nations Office for South-South Cooperation (UNOSSC): 304 East 45th St, 12th Floor, New York, NY 11017, USA; tel. (212) 906-6392; fax (212) 906-6352; internet www.unsouthsouth.org; f. 1978 as the Special Unit for Technical Cooperation among Developing Countries (present name adopted in 2012); aims to co-ordinate and support South-South and triangular co-operation in the political, economic, social, environmental and technical areas, to facilitate relevant intergovernmental processes, and to support 'triangular' collaboration on a UN system-wide and global basis (in 2022 a new South-South and triangular co-operation solution lab was under devt); organizes the annual UN Day for South-South Cooperation (12 Sept.), and manages the UN Trust Fund for South-South Cooperation (UNFSC), the India-UN Development Partnership Fund, and the Perez-Guerrero Trust Fund for Economic and Technical Co-operation among Developing Countries (PGTF); heads of state and of government attending the Second High-level UN Conference on South-South Cooperation (BAPA+40), held in Buenos Aires, Argentina, in March 2019, issued the Buenos Aires Outcome Document, which urged that South-South collaboration be strengthened, to take into account a shifting geopolitical landscape and increasing constraints on resources, while noting that North-South co-operation continued to be the main devt co-operation framework; the BAPA+40 Outcome Document was endorsed by the UN General Assembly in April; regular resources for 2022–25 (allocated under the broader UNDP integrated budget), amounted to US $30.7m., of which $21m. was for programme activities; Dir a.i. ADEL ABDELLATIF (Egypt).

Activities

UNDP works as the UN's global development network, advocating for change and connecting countries to knowledge, experience and resources to help people to build a better life. UNDP's Administrator serves as the Vice-Chair of the UN Sustainable Development Group, which aims to co-ordinate and enhance the efforts of some 36 UN offices and programmes to deliver the UN's 2030 Agenda for Sustainable Development.

UNDP's Strategic Plan for 2022–25 was focused on supporting countries to work towards building resilience, structural transformation and 'leaving no one behind' in order to help achieve the UN Sustainable Development Goals (SDGs) by 2030. Within this framework, UNDP identified the following six 'signature solutions': tackling poverty and inequality; future-proofing governance systems; building resilience; putting the natural environment at the heart of economies and planning; increasing access to energy and accelerating the transition to renewable sources of energy; and combating structural challenges to gender equality. In order to maximize its impact and enhance the development activities of recipient countries, UNDP aimed to promote digitalization, strategic innovation and development financing.

In 2022 UNDP was implementing development activities in 162 countries and territories. It provides advisory and support services to governments and UN teams with the aim of advancing sustainable human development and building national development capabilities.

Assistance is mostly non-monetary, comprising the provision of experts' services, consultancies, equipment and training for local workers. Developing countries themselves contribute significantly to the total project costs in terms of personnel, facilities, equipment and supplies. UNDP also supports programme countries in attracting aid and utilizing it efficiently. UNDP's development activities place particular emphasis on people living in poverty—as defined by the global (in purchasing power parity) US $1.90 per day poverty line, national poverty lines, and by UNDP's *Global Multidimensional Poverty Index,* which includes indicators such as access to education, food, safe water and electricity. Groups experiencing the greatest social inequalities and exclusion, especially women, female-headed households and youth, are a particular focus of attention.

UNDP aims to catalyse a South-South or triangular (i.e. engaging additional partners) model of co-operation, and to utilize its knowledge base in assisting developing countries' efforts to achieve the SDGs.

In 2021 UNDP implemented 1,270 projects in sub-Saharan Africa, of which 975 were focused on ending poverty in all its forms and dimensions.

COVID-19 RESPONSE

From early 2020 UNDP provided technical leadership to the UN system's COVID-19 crisis recovery efforts. The UN development system adopted a UN Framework for the Immediate Socio-economic Response to COVID-19, which focused on strengthening health systems' capacities; enhancing social protection and basic services; initiating economic recovery programmes to save livelihoods and small businesses and to protect informal sector workers (it was noted that developing countries would disproportionately suffer devastating economic and social impacts from the crisis); guiding multilateral and regional responses, and fiscal and financial stimulus initiatives, to help the most vulnerable; and promoting social cohesion and community-led resilience and response mechanisms. In April a UNDP-led inter-agency UN COVID-19 Response and Recovery Fund was established to support low- and middle-income countries' efforts to build back better (by March 2022 the Fund had received donations of US $86.3m.). In July 2020 UNDP, WHO and the Joint UN Programme on HIV/AIDS (UNAIDS) established a COVID-19 Law Lab, to enable the implementation of robust legal frameworks to manage the coronavirus situation. In September UNDP and partners initiated a COVID-19 Private Sector Global Facility, which aimed to promote public-private collaboration on recovery initiatives. In December UNDP launched an online COVID-19 Data Futures Platform, which aggregated diverse information sources to enable policymakers to cost and to visualize the impacts of various socioeconomic intervention options. By that time UNDP and partners had compiled 128 rapid Digital Socio-Economic Impact Assessments (Digital SEIAs) in 93 countries, providing detailed reviews of the impacts of the pandemic crisis on specific population groups and economic sectors. In 2022 UNDP was maintaining a Global Dashboard for Vaccine Equity, to track developments in access to and affordability of COVID-19 vaccines. In April UNDP launched a new Tax for SDGs initiative, which aimed to support recovery from the pandemic through combating tax evasion and aligning tax and fiscal policies with the SDGs. Also in that month, UNDP and partners initiated an Integrated National Financing Framework, which aimed to channel investment to assist the implementation of the SDGs.

HUMAN DEVELOPMENT REPORTS

UNDP's annually updated global *Human Development Report* ranks countries in accordance with three key indicators: life expectancy; adult literacy; and basic income required for a decent standard of living. The 2022 edition was subtitled *Uncertain Times, Unsettled Lives: Shaping our Future in a World in Transformation.* A special human development study titled *New Threats to Human Security in the Anthropocene* was published in February. UNDP country offices support the formulation of national human development reports, which aim to facilitate policymaking, guide the allocation of resources, and monitor progress towards poverty eradication and sustainable development. In addition, UNDP prepares Advisory Notes and bespoke Cooperation Frameworks to highlight country-specific priorities. Regional human development reports are also prepared intermittently.

In August 2021 a national human development report was issued for Rwanda (the third for that country).

UNDP's Human Development Report Office also releases annually five updated composite indices: the *Global Multidimensional Poverty Index* (produced jointly with the United Kingdom-based Oxford Poverty and Human Development Initiative), a *Human Development Index,* an *Inequality-Adjusted Human Development Index, Gender Inequality Index,* and a *Gender Development Index.*

TACKLING POVERTY AND INEQUALITY

UNDP's *2021 Global Multidimensional Poverty Index,* issued in October, monitored progress towards the achievement of SDG 1, relating to the elimination of poverty in all its forms, using data for 109 countries. It found that 1,300m. people globally (644m. of whom were children under the age of 18) were living in multidimensional poverty. Some 1,000m. multidimensionally poor people did not have access to clean cooking fuel, while a similar number were housed with substandard materials and/or were deprived of adequate sanitation. Some 788m. people reportedly lived in a household where someone was undernourished, 588m. lacked improved drinking water and 836m. resided in households where no woman or girl had completed at least six years of education. About two-thirds of multidimensionally poor people resided in middle-income countries. The report disaggregated data on ethnicity, race or caste for 41 countries, finding significant disparities in multidimensional poverty between such groups.

UNDP assists member countries to maximize the use of domestic capabilities and institutional and policy mechanisms towards the elimination of poverty and the realization of national development goals. Through its support for the multi-stakeholder Global Partnership for Effective Development Cooperation (established in 2011), and by means of Development Finance Assessments, UNDP aims to maximize the development impact of collaboration. It is also the custodian agency of SDG 17 (Strengthen the means of implementation and revitalize the global partnership for sustainable development). In January 2017 the Cape Town Global Action Plan for Sustainable Development Data was launched at the inaugural UN World Data Forum. (The fourth UN World Data Forum was to be held in April 2023, in Hangzhou, People's Republic of China.) In July 2019 UNDP, with the Governments of Germany and Qatar, launched a series of Accelerator Labs, tasked with identifying and analysing specific local development challenges, and pursuing solutions for these. As at mid-2022 there were 91 Labs that were supporting 115 countries. The Accelerator Labs represent a key component of an evolving Global Policy Network, which aims to enhance policy and knowledge capabilities and to connect experts across the organization, in collective pursuit of integrated development solutions. UNDP hosts Global Dev Hub, an online network of international development practitioners and professionals.

UNDP's Administrator is Co-Chairperson of a global Task Force on Digital Financing that was launched in November 2018 by the UN Secretary-General to support the implementation of the SDGs. In November 2020 UNDP and the Organisation for Economic Co-operation and Development (OECD) jointly launched a UNDP-OECD Framework for SDG Aligned Finance, with the aim of promoting investment in developing countries that would support the pursuit of the SDGs. The UN Secretary-General issued a report in August of that year that addressed the empowerment potential arising from transformative advances in financial technologies ('fintech'), such as mobile payment technologies, crowdfunding platforms, peer-to-peer lending, online marketplaces, and cryptocurrencies and assets. A Tech Access Partnership was initiated in May of that year by UNDP, the UN Conference on Trade and Development (UNCTAD) and partners. UNDP, UNICEF and other partners co-host the Digital Public Goods Alliance, which facilitates investment in digital public goods to accelerate the attainment of the SDGs in low- and middle-income countries. UNDP's Digital Strategy (2022–25), launched in February 2022, aimed to embed a digital focus into all dimensions of the Programme's work; to support governments to establish more inclusive and resilient digital ecosystems; and to continue to upgrade and transform the scope of digital skills to meet present and future technological challenges.

In May 2022—within the framework of the Essential Digital Infrastructure and Services Network (EDISON) Alliance that was initiated by the World Economic Forum in February 2021—UNDP launched a Lighthouse Countries Network aimed at accelerating digital inclusion in the education, health and finance sectors.

UNDP is committed to ensuring that the process of economic and financial globalization, including national and global trade, debt and capital flow policies, incorporates human development concerns. UNDP is a partner—with the IMF, the International Trade Centre, UNCTAD, the World Bank and the World Trade Organization (WTO)—in the Enhanced Integrated Framework (EIF) for trade-related assistance to LDCs, a multi-donor programme which aims to support greater participation by least developed countries (LDCs) in the global trading system. EIF funds are channelled through a dedicated EIF Trust Fund that was initiated in 2009. A second phase of the EIF, supporting 51 beneficiaries, was being implemented during 2016–22.

In April 2016 a Global Platform on Inclusive Business was launched, as an initiative of the G20 to be implemented by UNDP and the World Bank, with a mandate to support policymakers and to promote inclusive business practices and policies. UNDP hosts the secretariat of the Business Call to Action multilateral grouping, which assists private organizations to promote the SDGs and inclusive development. UNDP supports a regular Responsible Business Forum.

The 2030 Agenda and SDGs recognize the linkages between health and poverty reduction and development. UNDP promotes universal health coverage, and helps to strengthen national capacities at all levels to combat HIV/AIDS. The agency places a particular focus on combating the spread of HIV/AIDS through the promotion of women's rights. UNDP is a co-sponsor of UNAIDS. UNAIDS co-ordinates UNDP's HIV and Development Programme. UNDP works in partnership with the Global Fund to Fight HIV/AIDS, Tuberculosis and Malaria, in particular to support the local principal recipient of grant financing and to help to manage fund projects.

GOVERNANCE

Around one-third of UNDP's expenditure is focused on SDG 16: Promote peaceful and inclusive societies for sustainable development, provide access to justice for all and build effective, accountable and inclusive institutions at all levels. UNDP supports national efforts to ensure efficient and accountable governance, to improve the quality of institutions and democratic processes, to foster the rights of Indigenous peoples and other marginalized communities, and to build effective relations between the state, the private sector and civil society, in order to underpin sustainable development.

UNDP is mandated to assist developing countries to fight corruption and improve accountability, transparency and integrity. It has helped to establish national and international partnerships in support of its anti-corruption efforts, and assists governments to conduct self-assessments of their public financial management systems. UNDP co-ordinates the secretariat of the International Aid Transparency Initiative, which was inaugurated in September 2008.

UNDP works to strengthen parliaments and other legislative bodies as institutions of democratic participation. The Programme assists with constitutional reviews and reform, training of parliamentary staff, and capacity building of political parties and civil organizations. It also supports the establishment of electoral commissions, as well as voter registration and education, undertakes missions to help to prepare for and ensure the conduct of free and fair elections, and provides training to journalists to provide impartial election coverage.

UNDP supports projects to improve access to justice, in particular for marginalized populations, and to promote judicial independence, legal reform and understanding of the legal system. UNDP also promotes support for the international human rights system and advocates for the integration of human rights issues into activities concerned with sustainable human development.

Within the context of the Plan of Action to Prevent Violent Extremism launched in 2015 by the UN Secretary-General, and of SDG 16, UNDP has developed a strategic framework: Preventing Violent Extremism through Inclusive Development and the Promotion of Tolerance and Respect for Diversity. In March 2018 UNDP, with International Alert, issued a 'toolkit' to help to improve the design, implementation and monitoring of Prevention of Violent Extremism (PVE) programmes. In May UNDP signed an MOU with the UN Office of Counter-Terrorism to strengthen collaborative PVE efforts. UNDP's Oslo Governance Centre focuses on fostering more effective and inclusive forms of governance and on PVE.

UNDP collaborates with other UN agencies to promote relief and development efforts in countries in crisis, in order to secure reconciliation, reconstruction and the foundations for sustainable human development, and to increase national capabilities to prevent or mitigate future crises.

Special development initiatives undertaken by UNDP in post-conflict countries include the demobilization of former combatants and destruction of illicit small armaments, the rehabilitation of communities for the sustainable reintegration of returning populations, and the restoration and strengthening of democratic institutions and rule of law. The latter is achieved through UNDP's Global Programme on Strengthening the Rule of Law and Human Rights for Sustaining Peace and Fostering Development. UNDP assists the establishment of regulatory frameworks and mechanisms aimed at conflict prevention and consensus building, and promotes conflict analysis and assessments. It supports the UN Global Focal Point (GFP) arrangement for Police, Justice and Corrections Areas in the Rule of Law in Post-Conflict and other Crisis Situations, which co-ordinates and represents a single entry point for UN system-wide rule of law assistance.

UNDP manages a trust to support the African Union Development Agency's African Peer Review Mechanism, under which member countries evaluate standards of governance in other participating states. UNDP co-organized an International Conference on the Emergence of Africa in January 2019, in Dakar, Senegal.

UNDP's Regional Stabilization Facility for the Lake Chad Basin, which was initiated in 2019, aims to build resilience against the Boko Haram militant insurgency in Cameroon, Chad, Niger and Nigeria, by strengthening civilian security, improving basic services, and enhancing local livelihoods.

The Programme supports the strengthening of national capacities and institutions with a view to improving security and controlling the proliferation and use of small arms in, *inter alia,* Burundi, the DRC, Liberia, and northern Uganda.

UNDP helps to organize the (normally) annual Africa Regional Judges Forum, which in 2021 was held in July, in a virtual format.

UNDP supported a High-level Global Conference on Youth-Inclusive Peace Processes that was convened online in January 2022.

RESILIENCE

UNDP supports countries and communities in building resilience to potential crises and shocks (such as natural disasters, conflict, impacts of climate change, and public health epidemics and pandemics). UNDP is the focal point within the UN system for strengthening national capacities for natural disaster reduction. UNDP's Crisis Bureau, in conjunction with the Office for the Coordination of Humanitarian Affairs and UN Office for for Disaster Risk Reduction, oversees the system-wide Capacity for Disaster Reduction Initiative (inaugurated in 2007). In March 2015, at the Third UN World Conference on Disaster Risk Reduction, UNDP initiated '5-10-50', a global programme to support, over a 10-year period, the disaster reduction efforts of some 50 member states, with a focus on the following five areas: preparedness; risk awareness and early warning; risk governance and mainstreaming; resilient recovery; and local and urban risk reduction.

UNDP established a mine action unit within its Crisis Bureau in order to strengthen national and local demining capabilities including surveying, mapping and clearance of anti-personnel landmines. UNDP works closely with UNICEF to raise awareness and implement risk reduction education programmes, and manages global partnership projects concerned with training, legislation and the socioeconomic impact of anti-personnel devices. In July 2016 UNDP initiated a Development and Mine Action Support Framework.

NATURAL ENVIRONMENT AND ENERGY

UNDP aims to strengthen national capacities to implement effective and sustainable environmental management policies and practices, including addressing the challenges of climate change. Together with the UN Environment Programme (UNEP) and the World Bank, UNDP is an implementing agency of the Global Environment Facility (GEF), which was established in 1991 to finance international co-operation in projects to benefit the environment.

Community-based initiatives worldwide concerned with climate change mitigation and adaptation, reversal of land degradation, biodiversity conservation, sustainable forestry and water management, and chemicals management including the elimination of persistent organic pollutants, are supported through a Small Grants Programme, administered by UNDP and funded by the GEF.

The Equator Initiative—a UNDP-initiated multi-stakeholder project that since 2002 has focused on communities in the equatorial belt—fosters local partnerships and 'Equator dialogues', addressing local knowledge and conservation and sustainable practices. It awards an annual Equator Prize that recognizes innovative initiatives from local communities and Indigenous peoples.

In August 2021 the Coordinator of the Equator Initiative issued a statement that called for a new global social contract. He emphasized that the modern social contract had failed to recognize the contribution of Indigenous peoples as custodians of a large proportion of the Earth's lands, water and biodiversity, which, while under their care, had remained overall more ecologically intact than modern developed areas, and remain of critical importance for the planet's water security, biodiversity conservation, and attainment of climate goals. He noted, furthermore, that Indigenous peoples had retained traditional sustainable food systems and resourceful safety nets (such as emergency bartering models for basic supplies), as well as ancestral knowledge of traditional medicines, land management, and sustainable agricultural practices.

UNDP recognizes that in parts of the world land degradation, desertification and drought are major causes of rural poverty, and promotes sustainable land management, reform of land tenure, drought preparedness, and the implementation of conventions that aim to protect the environment. UNDP is a partner agency of the Climate and Clean Air Coalition to Reduce Short Lived Climate Pollutants (SLCPs), which was launched in February 2012 with the aim of combating SLCPs, including methane, black carbon and certain hydrofluorocarbons. UNDP also implements projects funded by the International Climate Initiative (launched in 2008 by the German Government). In March 2015 the Green Climate Fund, established by the UNFCCC to support developing countries with implementing emissions mitigation and climate change adaptation policies, approved UNDP as an implementing agency. In October 2021 UNDP and partners launched the online UN Biodiversity Lab, as a resource for governments, policymakers and other stakeholders.

UNDP works to ensure the effective governance of freshwater and aquatic resources, and promotes co-operation in transboundary water management, ocean and coastal management, and efforts to promote safe sanitation and community water supplies. UNDP, with the GEF, supports a range of projects that incorporate development and ecological requirements in the sustainable management of international waters, within the following framework: global programmes; large marine ecosystems; transboundary lakes, rivers and aquifers; and integrated water resources and coastal area management. Projects being implemented in 2022 focused, *inter alia,* on eliminating plastic pollution from water reserves, enhancing local knowledge of threatened ecosystems, and developing community-based climate adaptation models. UNDP-GEF manages the International Waters Learning Exchange and Resources Network. In December 2016 UNDP established an Ocean Action Hub, which acts as a focal point of information resources concerning SDG 14 (on oceans). In June 2022, at the Second UN Oceans Conference, co-hosted by Portugal and Kenya in the Portuguese capital Lisbon, UNDP launched an Ocean Promise initiative, through which it pledged to support 100 coastal countries to develop, by 2030, sustainable, low-emission, climate-resilient blue economies.

UNDP was actively involved in the development of the Strategic Approach to International Chemicals Management policy framework, that was launched in February 2006. UNDP assists countries to integrate the 'sound management of chemicals' into national development planning.

In September 2021 the UN Secretary-General convened a landmark High-level Dialogue on Energy (the first UN summit-level meeting on energy in four decades) to address means of achieving the goals of the 2015 Paris Agreement on climate change, and, simultaneously, of attaining SDG 7 (affordable, reliable, sustainable energy for all). The meeting adopted a roadmap to support the achievement of clean energy access for all by 2030 and net-zero emissions by 2050, and resulted in the conclusion by stakeholders of more than 150 'Energy Compacts' reflecting actions and financial commitments to be achieved by 2030. In this context, a UNDP Energy Compact was pledged, in accordance with which the Programme was to mobilize partners to facilitate the supply of clean and affordable energy to 500m. people by 2030, with a focus on very vulnerable communities.

UNDP, with the GEF and the International Maritime Organization, implements the Global Maritime Energy Efficiency Project (GloMEEP), which supports energy efficiency measures in the shipping sector.

GENDER

UNDP's annual *Gender Inequality Index* and *Gender Development Index* assess gender equality on the basis of life expectancy, education and income.

In March 2021 UNDP established a Gender and Crisis Engagement Facility, which aimed to strengthen women's leadership and participation in crisis contexts, and to target response initiatives specifically to the needs of women and girls. A UNDP report issued in that month called for the implementation of a temporary basic income to support women in crisis-affected developing countries, noting that during the COVID-19 emergency women were more likely to lose paid work and assume caring duties. In September 2020 UNDP and UN Women introduced a COVID-19 Global Gender Response Tracker, to monitor the inclusion of gender-sensitive measures in social protection and labour policy responses to the pandemic crisis.

In March 2022 UNDP and UN Women jointly launched a new Gender Justice Platform, which was to support transformational change to ensure the empowerment of women in justice and transitional justice frameworks.

CRISIS RESPONSE

UNDP's 'SURGE' Immediate Crisis Response programme aims to strengthen the agency's capacity to respond quickly and effectively in the recovery phase following a conflict or natural disaster. Under the programme Immediate Crisis Response Advisers UNDP staff with special expertise in at least one of 14 identified areas, including early recovery, operational support and resource mobilization, are swiftly deployed to UNDP country offices dealing with crises. UNDP is the lead agency for the Early Recovery cluster response to a humanitarian disaster, linking the immediate needs with medium- and long-term recovery efforts. UNDP 'crisis response packages' aim to restore core government functions; to stabilize livelihoods; to manage debris and the rehabilitation of core infrastructure; and to plan for crisis recovery.

Finance

UNDP's Integrated Budget for 2022–25, underpinning its Strategic Plan covering that period, projected resources amounting to US $28,265m.; 91% of the total resources were to be allocated to development activities. Programmatic expenditure during 2022 was projected at $483.8m.

Publications

Annual Report of the Administrator.
Human Development Report (annually).
Impact Series.
South-South Quarterly.
Other reports, strategy papers, policy briefings, factsheets.

Funds and Programmes

A number of associated funds and programmes, financed separately by means of voluntary contributions, provide specific services through the UNDP network.

GEF Small Grants Programme (SGP): 304 East 45th St, 9th Floor, New York, NY 10017, USA; tel. (646) 781-4385; fax (646) 781-4075; e-mail sgp.info@undp.org; internet sgp.undp.org; f. 1992, becoming operational in 1996; UNDP (also responsible for the capacity building, targeted research, pre-investment activities and technical assistance areas of GEF activity, and for managing the GEF Country Dialogue Workshop Programme) administers the SGP, which provides grants of up to US $50,000; by July 2022 the SGP had supported 27,187 community-based projects in more than 130 countries, implemented by local NGOs, addressing biodiversity, climate change mitigation and adaptation, land degradation and sustainable forest management, international waters, and chemicals; initial funding of $128m. had been pledged for the SGP's 7th operational phase covering 2020–24; maintains an 'innovation library'; SGP Global Man. YOKO WATANABE.

Joint SDG Fund: SDG-F Secretariat, c/o UNDP, One United Nations Plaza, New York, NY 10017, USA; tel. (646) 781-4255; e-mail admin@sdgfund.org; internet jointsdgfund.org; f. 2017, superseding a previous SDG Achievement Fund (f. 2014); the Joint SDG Fund is a pooled inter-agency mechanism that provides integrated policy support and strategic financing to assist the design and implementation of joint programmes—under the co-ordination of UN Resident Coordinators and Country Teams—that aim to accelerate progress towards achieving the UN's 2030 Agenda and SDGs; by March 2022 the Fund had received contributions amounting to US $276m.; during 2020–22 (at a cost of $72m.) the Joint SDG Fund was implementing 36 country projects that were supporting policies aimed at accelerating the SDGs, with a focus on integrated social protection, particularly for very marginalized and vulnerable communities, and SDG finance; leadership and strategic guidance is provided by a Strategic Advisory Group that is co-chaired by the UN Deputy Sec.-Gen. and the UNSDG Chair., and comprises (on a rotational basis) representatives of 15 UN mem. states; UNDP chairs an Operational Steering Cttee.

Multi-Partner Trust Fund Office: 304 East 45th St, 11th Floor, New York, NY 10017, USA; tel. (212) 906-6355; fax (212) 906-6705; e-mail executivecoordinator.mptfo@undp.org; internet mptf.undp.org; f. 2003, initially as the International Reconstruction Fund Facility for Iraq, later the Iraq Trust Fund Office, then, in 2006, the Multi-Donor Trust Fund Office; present name adopted in 2011; engages in collaborative activities to address pandemics, climate change and the conservation of biodiversity, and facilitates UN coherence and devt effectiveness in addressing complex challenges, such as humanitarian crises and peacebuilding; assists the UN system and national govts in managing pooled financing mechanisms: mainly UN Multi-Donor Trust Funds (MDTFs—which are often thematic, and can be established at global, regional or national level), National MDTFs (at times complementing a UN MDTF), and stand-alone Joint Programmes (established by UN agencies in support of a strategic vision); Exec. Co-ordinator JENNIFER TOPPING (Canada).

UNDP Montreal Protocol/Chemicals Unit: through its Montreal Protocol/Chemicals Unit UNDP collaborates with public and private partners in developing countries to assist them in eliminating the use of ozone-depleting substances (ODS), in accordance with the Montreal Protocol to the Vienna Convention for the Protection of the Ozone Layer, through the design, monitoring and evaluation of ODS phase-out projects and progs; in particular, UNDP provides technical assistance and training, national capacity building and demonstration projects and technology transfer investment projects.

United Nations Capital Development Fund (UNCDF): Two United Nations Plaza, 26th Floor, New York, NY 10017, USA; tel. (212) 906-6565; fax (212) 906-6479; e-mail info@uncdf.org; internet www.uncdf.org; f. 1966; UNCDF facilitates the use of public and private finance to support the poor in LDCs; offers 'last mile' finance models aimed at unlocking public and private resources, in particular at the domestic level, with the goal of reducing poverty and supporting local economic devt; promotes the expansion of inclusive digital local economies, with participation by individuals, households and small businesses; in May 2020 UNCDF and UNDP announced jt support for a new mem. state-led initiative, Remittances in Crisis, that aimed to ensure migrants' means of sending and receiving remittances, and to reduce relevant costs, in view of the widespread restrictions imposed to contain the COVID-19 pandemic; in Jan. 2021 co-launched a Women Enterprise Recovery Fund; UNDP's Administrator serves as the Man. Dir of UNCDF; Exec. Sec. PREETI SINHA.

United Nations Volunteers (UNV): POB 260111, 53153 Bonn, Germany; tel. (228) 8152000; fax (228) 8152001; e-mail unv.media@unv.org; internet www.unv.org; f. 1970; supports sustainable devt, and in particular the attainment of the SDGs; works to mobilize volunteers to serve UNDP initiatives and also to support the activities of other partner UN agencies and bodies; advocates the use of volunteers and the integration of volunteerism and civic engagement into sustainable devt, humanitarian and peace projects worldwide; UNV focuses participation on the following areas: peacebuilding; community resilience for environment and disaster risk reduction; securing access to basic social services; youth; and national capacity devt; a Plan of Action to Integrate Volunteering into the 2030 Agenda was being implemented during 2016–30; in July 2020 UNV hosted a global meeting on Re-imagining Volunteering for the 2030 Agenda; by 2022 the number of people who had served on the ground as UNVs exceeded 70,000; during 2021 10,921 UNVs were deployed in 160 countries, working with some 56 UN entities; an additional 2,546 online volunteering projects were carried out; Exec. Co-ordinator TOILY KURBANOV (Russia); publ. *State of the World's Volunteerism Report* (every 3–4 years).

United Nations Environment Programme—UNEP

Address: POB 30552, Nairobi 00100, Kenya.

Telephone: (20) 7621234; **fax:** (20) 7623927; **e-mail:** unepinfo@unep.org; **internet:** www.unenvironment.org.

UNEP (commonly referred to as UN Environment) was established in 1972, following recommendations of the 1972 UN Conference on the Human Environment, in Stockholm, Sweden, to facilitate international co-operation on the environment. It has become the lead UN agency for formulating the global environment agenda and promoting sound environmental management in support of sustainable development.

Organization
(October 2022)

UN ENVIRONMENT ASSEMBLY

The Assembly—at which all UN member states are represented—was established in accordance with a resolution adopted in December 2012 by the UN General Assembly; its inaugural meeting was convened in June 2014. The fifth meeting (UNEA-5)—themed 'Strengthening Actions for Nature to Achieve the Sustainable Development Goals'—was convened in two parts, as a result of the COVID-19 emergency. The first session of the meeting was held in February 2021, in a virtual format; the Assembly was then resumed, in-person and virtually, in late February–early March 2022.

COMMITTEE OF PERMANENT REPRESENTATIVES

The Committee, comprising all accredited permanent representatives of member states to UNEP, meets at least four times each year. It prepares the meetings of the Assembly and helps to oversee implementation of Assembly decisions. It is led by a five-member Bureau, elected for a two-year period.

EXECUTIVE OFFICE

Offices and divisions at UNEP headquarters include the Offices of the Executive Director and Deputy Executive Director; the Governance Affairs Office (which also serves as the Secretariat of Governing Bodies); and Divisions of Communications, Economy, Ecosystems, Law, Science, Corporate Services, and Policy and Programmes.

Executive Director: INGER ANDERSEN (Denmark).

REGIONAL OFFICES

UNEP's regional offices provide a focal point for building national, subregional and regional partnerships and enhancing local participation in UNEP initiatives. A co-ordination office has been established at headquarters to promote regional policy integration, to co-ordinate programme planning, and to provide necessary services to the regional offices.

Africa: NOF Block 2, Level 1, South-Wing POB 30552, Nairobi, Kenya; tel. (20) 7624235; e-mail communication.roa@unep.org; internet www.unenvironment.org/regions/africa; hosts the Secretariat of the African Ministerial Conference on the Environment and the Secretariat of the Bamako Convention on hazardous waste; subsidiary entities incl. an Abidjan, Côte d'Ivoire-based Sub-Regional Office for West Africa, an Addis-Ababa, Ethiopia-based liaison office, and country offices in South Africa and Tanzania; Dir a.i. FRANK TURYATUNGA.

OTHER OFFICES AND RELATED SECRETARIATS

UNEP administers, or provides secretarial functions for, several multilateral environmental agreements.

Basel, Rotterdam and Stockholm Conventions, Secretariat: 11–13 chemin des Anémones, 1219 Châtelaine, Geneva, Switzerland; tel. 229178271; fax 229178098; e-mail brs@un.org; internet www.basel.int; www.pic.int; chm.pops.int; Exec. Sec. Dr ROLPH PAYET (Seychelles).

Convention for Cooperation in the Protection and Development of the Marine and Coastal Environment of the West and Central African Region (Abidjan Convention), Secretariat: II Plateaux-Vallon, rue Harris Memel Foteh, Abidjan, Côte d'Ivoire; tel. 22-514-600; e-mail unenvironment-abidjan-convention@un.org; internet www.abidjanconvention.org; entered into force 1984.

Green Climate Fund, Secretariat: 175 Art Center-Daero, Yeonsu-gu, Incheon 22004, Seoul, Republic of Korea; tel. (2) 458-6059; e-mail info@gcfund.org; internet www.greenclimate.fund/home; f. 2010; acts as the financial mechanism under the UNFCCC and the 2015 Paris Agreement; supports projects investing in low emission and climate resilient devt; offers a wide range of financial products tailored to specific project needs; states may access the Fund through multiple entities simultaneously; Exec. Dir YANNICK GLEMAREC (France).

Minamata Convention on Mercury, Secretariat: 11–13 chemin des Anémones, 1219 Châtelaine, Geneva, Switzerland; fax 227973460; e-mail mea-minamatasecretariat@un.org; internet mercuryconvention.org; Exec. Sec. MONIKA STANKIEWICZ (Poland).

Multilateral Fund for the Implementation of the Montreal Protocol, Secretariat: 1000 De La Gauchetière St West, Suite 4100, Montréal, QC H3B 4W5, Canada; tel. (514) 282-1122; fax (514) 282-0068; e-mail secretariat@unmfs.org; internet www.multilateralfund.org.

Nairobi Convention for the Protection, Management and Development of the Marine and Coastal Environment of the Western Indian Ocean, Secretariat: c/o UNEP, POB 30552, Nairobi 00100, Kenya; tel. (20) 7622022; e-mail unep-nairobiconvention@un.org; internet www.nairobiconvention.org; entered into force in 1996.

UNEP International Environmental Technology Centre (IETC): 2–110 Ryokuchi koen, Tsurumi-ku, Osaka 538-0036, Japan; tel. (6) 6915-4581; e-mail ietc@un.org; internet www.unep.org/ietc; Dir KEITH ALVERSON.

UNEP Ozone Secretariat: POB 30552, Nairobi, Kenya; tel. (20) 7623851; fax (20) 7620335; e-mail mea-ozoneinfo@un.org; internet ozone.unep.org; services both the 1985 Vienna Convention for the Protection of the Ozone Layer and its 1987 Montreal Protocol; Exec. Sec. MEGUMI SEKI (Japan).

United Nations Scientific Committee on the Effects of Atomic Radiation (UNSCEAR): Vienna International Centre, Wagramerstr. 5, POB 500, 1400 Vienna, Austria; tel. (1) 26060-4360; fax (1) 26060-5902; internet www.unscear.org; f. 1955; secretariat provided by UNEP; convenes annually (69th session: May 2022); Sec. BORISLAVA BATANDJIEVA-METCALF (Slovakia).

Activities

UNEP aims to maintain a constant watch on the changing state of the environment; to analyse trends; to assess problems using a wide range of data and techniques; and to undertake or support projects leading to environmentally sound development. UNEP helps to define and oversee the global environmental agenda, sponsoring international conferences, programmes, plans and agreements regarding all aspects of the environment. It aims to promote its mission through active engagement with the private sector, civil society and other stakeholders.

In June 2022 an international conference titled 'Stockholm+50' was co-hosted by Kenya and Sweden in Stockholm, Sweden, to commemorate the 1972 UN Conference on the Human Environment; this urged genuine commitment to realizing a just transition to sustainable economies. The fourth global session of the UN Science-Policy-Business Forum on the Environment (a biennial series) was convened on the sidelines of Stockholm+50.

In July 2022 the UN General Assembly adopted a landmark resolution that declared the human right to a clean, healthy and sustainable environment. Eight states abstained: Belarus, Cambodia, Ethiopia, the People's Republic of China, Iran, Kyrgyzstan, the Russian Federation and the Syrian Arab Republic.

Medium-Term Strategy: UNEP's Medium-Term Strategy for the period 2022–25, approved by the Assembly in February 2021, aimed to strengthen UNEP's contribution to addressing global environmental and societal challenges and to achieving the UN's 2030 Agenda for Sustainable Development, and its related Sustainable Development Goals (SDGs). It identified climate action, natural action, and chemicals and pollution waste as the key thematic sub-programmes. The Strategy also recognized the need for robust economic governance and innovative science policy, and incorporated these as foundational sub-programmes. In order to deliver on the actions required, the Strategy identified two enabling sub-programmes: finance and economic transformation, and digital transformation. The following were identified as key targets: supporting countries to pursue decarbonization processes, to implement dematerialization practices (limiting the environmental impact of products or services), and to strengthen resilience to climate change; ensuring that states and other stakeholders have increased capacity, finance and access to sustainable technologies to deliver on the adaptation and mitigation commitments of the Paris Agreement; and supporting countries to meet their reporting obligations and implement required transparency framework arrangements.

CLIMATE ACTION

UNEP worked in collaboration with the World Meteorological Organization (WMO) to formulate the 1992 UN Framework Convention on Climate Change (UNFCCC), with the aim of reducing the emission of gases that have a warming effect on the atmosphere (known as greenhouse gases). In 1998 UNEP and WMO established the Intergovernmental Panel on Climate Change (IPCC), as an objective source of scientific information about the warming of the earth's atmosphere.

UNEP's climate action sub-programme aims to achieve long-term climate stability, working in alignment with the emissions reduction targets and climate resilience goals of the Paris Agreement, adopted at the 21st UNFCCC Conference of the Parties (COP) in November 2015.

UNEP, with the UN Industrial Development Organization (UNIDO), hosts a Climate Technology Centre and Network (CTCN) which operates as a part of UNFCCC's Technology Mechanism to accelerate the transfer of climate-related technology and expertise to developing nations. By the end of 2021 the CTCN had completed 320 technology transfer projects. UNEP's Technology Needs Assessment Project aims to support the formulation and implementation of national Technology Needs Assessments (TNAs), within the framework of the UNFCCC, involving, *inter alia*, detailed analysis of mitigation and adaptation technologies. A Facilitating Implementation and Readiness for Mitigation (FIRM) project works at a national level to develop low carbon strategies, and contributes to the formulation and implementation of National Adaptation Programmes of Action (NAPAs) for addressing climate change.

UNEP's climate change-related activities have a particular focus on strengthening the capabilities of countries to integrate climate change responses into their national development processes, including through adaptation and mitigation initiatives. The latter includes a collaborative programme, the UN Reduced Emissions from Deforestation and Forest Degradation (UN-REDD), which was launched in September 2008 by UNEP, the UN Development Programme (UNDP) and Food and Agriculture Organization of the UN (FAO) to promote a transformation of forest and land use patterns through the implementation at national level of so-called REDD+ strategies.

UNEP encourages the development of and investment in alternative and renewable sources of energy. By mid-2022 the UNEP-supported Powering Past Coal Alliance, which had been established in November 2017 to promote renewable energies, comprised 48 national governments, 48 subnational regions, and 70 private corporations. UNEP also supports REN21, a global community representing governments, academia, industry and non-governmental

organizations that aims to promote the use of renewable energy sources. UNEP is a member of the Global Bioenergy Partnership to support the sustainable use of biofuels.

A UNEP report on *Global Trends in Renewable Energy Investment 2020*, issued in September of that year, estimated that global capacity of new renewable energy (excluding large hydro) sources had increased by a record 184 GW in 2019. The development of new technologies was reported to be driving down the cost of solar and wind power.

Through its Transport Programme UNEP promotes the use of renewable fuels. It also supports the integration of environmental factors into transport planning, leading a worldwide Partnership for Clean Fuels and Vehicles, a Global Fuel Economy Initiative, and a Non-Motorized Transport 'Share the Road' scheme.

UNEP is a founding member of the Climate and Clean Air Coalition (CCAC) to Reduce Short Lived Climate Pollutants (SLCPs), which was launched in February 2012 as an international partnership, with the aim of reducing SLCPs, including methane and black carbon, to counter their negative impact on human health, crop yields and global warming. By mid-2022 the partnership comprised 73 governments, 78 non-state partners, and 192 other actors. In October 2021 UNEP launched, with EU support, an International Methane Emissions Observatory to enhance global monitoring and reporting of methane emissions.

UNEP leads a GEF-funded scheme, Sustainable Cities Impact Program (also named UrbanShift), which promotes integrated approaches to urban development. By 2022 some 23 primary cities and 16 additional cities in nine countries (Argentina, Brazil, China, Costa Rica, India, Indonesia, Morocco, Rwanda, Sierra Leone) were participating in the initiative.

NATURE ACTION

UNEP recognizes the urgent need to conserve healthy ecosystems and to prevent further biodiversity loss in order to meet future ecological needs, to enhance human wellbeing and to advance climate change resilience. It supports integrated ecosystem management and the mainstreaming of biodiversity for sustainable development.

UNEP was instrumental in the drafting of the Convention on Biological Diversity (CBD). In June 2018 UNEP, UNDP and the CBD Secretariat collectively initiated the UN Biodiversity Lab, an open source interactive mapping platform which was designed to support policymakers in addressing conservation and development challenges. A Global Biodiversity Information Facility (GBIF) was established in 2001, to provide open and free access to data on biodiversity. By mid-2022 this comprised nearly 2,180m. records and 69,694 data sets. The GBIF has also contributed to the development of a Biodiversity Habitat Index. A new Post-2020 Global Biodiversity Framework was to be finalized at the second part of the 15th Conference of the Parties (COP) of the CBD, to be hosted by the People's Republic of China in Montreal, Canada in December 2022. The Framework was to set out 10 collective goals in areas including the removal of harmful environmental subsidies; significantly lowering the rate of extinctions of species; enhancing the integrity of ecosystems; pesticide reduction; eliminating plastic pollution; and halving the rate of introduction of invasive species.

In January 2020 UNEP and the IUCN initiated a €20m. Global Fund for Ecosystem-based Adaptation, to provide seed capital for rapid targeted support mechanisms promoting innovative approaches to ecosystem-based adaptation strategies. In March 2019 the UN General Assembly designated UNEP and FAO as the lead agencies of the UN Decade on Ecosystem Restoration (2021–30). At the launch of the Decade, in June 2021, UNEP published a synthesis report, *Ecosystem Restoration for People, Nature and Climate*, to demonstrate the urgent need for active engagement in re-establishing healthy ecosystems.

UNEP supports an international Global Peatlands Initiative. It was established at the 2016 UNFCCC COP in order to conserve and restore peatland regions which provide immense natural carbon storage, with the potential to emit damaging levels of gases if destroyed (through drainage or burning). The Republic of the Congo, the Democratic Republic of the Congo (DRC), Indonesia and Peru are the initial partner countries of the Initiative. In March 2018 UNEP welcomed the conclusion, at the third partners meeting, of the Brazzaville Declaration on protecting the Cuvette Centrale region of the Congo Basin (the world's largest tropical peatland) from unregulated land use and on preventing its degradation. A UN Global Fund for Coral Reefs, initiated in September 2020, aimed to raise some US $500m. over 10 years to support coral reef conservation.

In November 2018 the 16th session of the normally biennial African Ministerial Conference on the Environment (AMCEN) adopted a Pan-African Action Agenda on Ecosystem Restoration for Increased Resilience. The eighth special session of AMCEN, convened in December 2020, determined to support a new African-led African Green Stimulus Programme, with a focus on 'building back better' from the COVID-19 crisis by reinvigorating economies and social protection systems, and by accelerating the protection and restoration of biodiversity and ecosystems.

In accordance with its medium-term strategy, from 2022 UNEP was committed to increasing its collaboration with international partners to strengthen the linkages between biodiversity and health and to implement biosecurity measures. In April 2022 UNEP, the World Health Organization (WHO), FAO and the World Organisation for Animal Health (OIE) concluded a Memorandum of Understanding that provided for the establishment of a Quadripartite Collaboration for One Health, which was collectively to address challenges at the human-animal-plant-ecosystem interface.

UNEP promotes international co-operation in the management of river basins and coastal areas and for the development of tools and guidelines to achieve the sustainable management of freshwater and coastal resources. UNEP's Regional Seas Programme, incorporating relevant conventions and action plans, promotes the sustainable management and use of marine and coastal ecosystems.

UNEP supports the Convention for the Protection, Management and Development of the Marine and Coastal Environment of the Western Indian Ocean (Nairobi Convention), and the Convention for Cooperation in the Protection and Development of the Marine and Coastal Environment of the West and Central African Region (Abidjan Convention).

RESOURCE EFFICIENCY

UNEP encourages governments and the private sector to develop and adopt policies and practices that are cleaner and safer, make efficient use of natural resources, ensure the environmentally sound management of chemicals, and reduce pollution and risks to human health and the environment. UNEP also promotes the transfer of appropriate technologies, and organizes conferences and training workshops to support sustainable production and consumption practices.

In November 2011, under the auspices of UNEP and UNIDO, the global network for Resource Efficient and Cleaner Production (RECPnet) was launched, with a focus on developing and transition countries (by 2022 it was active in more than 70 states). In February 2021 UNEP, with UNIDO and the European Commission, initiated a Global Alliance on Circular Economy and Resource Efficiency to promote broad collaboration on initiatives relating to the circular economy and sustainable consumption and production.

The International Resource Panel (q.v.) works, under UNEP auspices, to address over-consumption, wastage and ecological harm. A 10-Year Framework of Programmes (10YFP) on Sustainable Consumption and Production Patterns was initiated in 2012, hosted by UNEP. A progress report on 10YFP, released in July 2022, emphasized the programme's contribution to global sustainability and to recovery from the COVID-19 pandemic.

Prior to the first session of UNEA-5, in February 2021, UNEP published *Making Peace with Nature*, drawing together findings of its recent major studies and presenting a transformative approach to addressing biodiversity loss, waste and pollution, and climate change—described as the interconnected planetary crises. The Assembly called for greater multilateral co-operation and the urgent adoption of sustainable consumption and production patterns.

CHEMICALS AND POLLUTION ACTION

UNEP aims to provide leadership in the sound management of chemicals and waste, in order to address the wide-ranging related human health and environmental concerns. It supports the objectives of various multilateral environmental agreements, and is resolved to implementing strong regulatory frameworks.

UNEP administers the Basel Convention on the Control of Transboundary Movements of Hazardous Wastes and their Disposal, which entered into force in 1992 with the aim of preventing the uncontrolled movement and disposal of toxic and other hazardous wastes, particularly the illegal dumping of waste in developing countries by companies from industrialized countries. At mid-2022 there were 189 parties to the Convention. In August 2016 the inaugural meeting of an Informal Group on Household Waste was held, in Montevideo, Uruguay, under the auspices of the Convention. In February 2004 the Rotterdam Convention on the Prior Informed Consent Procedure for Certain Hazardous Chemicals and Pesticides in International Trade entered into force, having been formulated and promoted by UNEP, in collaboration with FAO. The Convention (which had 165 parties by mid-2022) aims to reduce risks to human health and the environment by restricting the production, export and use of hazardous substances and by enhancing information exchange procedures. UNEP played a leading role in formulating, and provides technical support to, the 2004 Stockholm Convention on Persistent Organic Pollutants (POPs), addressing particularly hazardous pollutants: pesticides, industrial chemicals and harmful substances that are not produced intentionally. By 2022 some 26 POPs were listed under Annex A of the Convention, which requires their elimination; two were listed under Annex B (requiring restrictions on their production and use); and seven unintentionally produced

substances were listed under Annex C (they were to be minimized). At mid-2022 the Stockholm Convention had 185 parties.

UNEP promotes environmentally sustainable water management, regards the unsustainable use of water as one of the most urgent environmental issues, and places a particular focus on shared transboundary waters. The Global Programme of Action for the Protection of the Marine Environment from Land-based Activities (the GPA, adopted in November 1995) focuses on the effects of pollution on freshwater resources, marine biodiversity and the coastal ecosystems of small island developing states (SIDS). A Global Wastewater Initiative (GW2I) was established in 2013 within the framework of the GPA. The third target of SDG 6: Ensure access to water and sanitation for all includes 'halving the proportion of untreated wastewater by 2030 and substantially increasing recycling and safe reuse globally'. A Global Partnership on Marine Litter was established in 2012. In early 2017 UNEP launched a UN Clean Seas campaign to address the issue that 80% of all marine litter, some 8m. metric tons collected each year, consists of single-use or non-recoverable plastic; this generally has a slow rate of degradation, and has been identified as entering the human food chain, and killing marine life. In September 2019 the Mississippi River Basin became the first river system member of UN Clean Seas.

A joint meeting of the COPs of the Basel, Rotterdam and Stockholm (BRS) Conventions that was held in late April–early May 2019, agreed to put in place a legally binding global framework on monitoring, tracking and managing plastic waste, with a view to restricting dumping in developing nations (countries proposing to export plastic waste were to be required to receive explicit prior consent from the governments of receiving states) and to prompting countries to manage their own plastic waste at the point of generation. In mid-May, accordingly, the parties to the Basel Convention determined to categorize plastic waste of a mixed, contaminated, non-hazardous, non-recyclable, or difficult-to-recycle nature under that Convention's Annex II, i.e. as waste that requires special consideration and transboundary movement restrictions. The parties to the Basel Convention also established a Plastic Waste Partnership, tasked with collecting information and undertaking analysis of the environmental, economic and social impacts of plastics-related policies.

In March 2022 the second session of the fifth UNEA (UNEA-5.2) resolved to establish an intergovernmental negotiating committee to draft a legally-binding multilateral instrument to address plastic pollution, including production, design and disposal.

In June 2013 the first COP took place, in Bamako, Mali, of the Bamako Convention on the Ban of the Import into Africa and the Control of Transboundary Movement and Management of Hazardous Wastes within Africa—which had entered into force in 1998. The meeting agreed that UNEP should provide secretariat services for the Convention, and that designated centres in Africa serving the Basel and Stockholm conventions would also serve the Bamako Convention (which, unlike the Basel Convention, also covers radioactive wastes). COP3, organized in February 2020, in Brazzaville, Republic of the Congo, determined to intensify synergies between the Bamako Convention and the Secretariat of the BRS Conventions. By mid-2022 29 states had ratified the Bamako Convention.

UNEP's OzonAction branch supports governments and industry in developing countries to undertake measures promoting the cost-effective phasing-out of ozone-depleting substances. UNEP was the principal agency in formulating the 1987 Montreal Protocol to the Vienna Convention for the Protection of the Ozone Layer (1985), which provided for a 50% reduction by 2000 in the production of chlorofluorocarbons (CFCs). An amendment to the Protocol was adopted in 1990, which required complete cessation of the production of CFCs by 2000 in industrialized countries and by 2010 in developing countries. The Copenhagen Amendment, adopted in 1992, stipulated the phasing out of production of hydrochlorofluorocarbons (HCFCs) by 2030 in developed countries and by 2040 in developing nations. Subsequent amendments aimed to introduce a licensing system for all controlled substances, and imposed stricter controls on the import and export of HCFCs, and on the production and consumption of bromochloromethane (Halon-1011, an industrial solvent and fire extinguisher). In September 2007 the states parties to the Vienna Convention agreed to advance the deadline for the elimination of HCFCs to 2020 in developed countries and to 2030 in developing countries. In September 2009 the Vienna Convention and Montreal Protocol became the first agreements on the global environment to attain universal ratification; universal ratification of amendments to the Montreal Protocol was achieved in December 2014. UNEP is the implementing agency of the Multilateral Fund for the Implementation of the Montreal Protocol, which supports compliance by developing states parties with relevant control measures. (By 2022 147 of the 197 Parties to the Protocol—known as Article 5 countries—were in compliance.) UNEP, UNDP, the World Bank and UNIDO are the sponsors of the Fund. In November 2019 the states parties to the Montreal Protocol agreed terms of reference for negotiations on an 11th replenishment of the Fund, to cover 2021–23. The process of replenishment was delayed, however, by the onset of the COVID-19 pandemic crisis. In October 2016 the states parties, gathered in

Kigali, Rwanda, adopted the Kigali Amendment to the Montreal Protocol, in accordance with which a phased reduction by more than 80% in the production and consumption of hydrofluorocarbon (HFC) gases—substances used increasingly in air conditioners and refrigerators—was to be implemented over 30 years. (HFC consumption levels were to be frozen from 2024 in most developing countries or, exceptionally, from 2028.) The Kigali Amendment entered into force on 1 January 2019; it had received 137 ratifications by August 2022.

In February 2006 an International Conference on Chemicals Management (ICCM) adopted a Strategic Approach to International Chemicals Management (SAICM), which aimed to minimize significant adverse impacts of chemicals on the environment and human health. The fourth ICCM session, convened in September–October 2015, addressed issues relating to environmentally persistent pharmaceutical pollutants and highly hazardous pesticides, and agreed a process aimed at ensuring the sound management of chemicals beyond 2020. ICCM5 was scheduled to be held in 2023, having been postponed twice as a result of the COVID-19 pandemic.

In October 2013 an intergovernmental meeting in Minamata, Japan, adopted the Minamata Convention on Mercury, which provides for controls relating to the usage, release, mining, import and export, and safe storage of mercury (which acts in humans as a neurotoxin), and for the phasing-out of the production of several mercury-containing products. The Convention entered into force on 16 August 2017, and by mid-2022 had been ratified by 136 states and the EU. The fourth Minamata COP—convened in two segments, in November 2021 (online) and in late March 2022 (in-person, in Bali, Indonesia)—extended the list of mercury-containing products that were to be phased out. It was envisaged that a deadline of 2025 set by the meeting for the phasing-out of compact fluorescent lamps (in favour of non-toxic and more energy-efficient and cost-effective Light Emitting Diode—LED lighting) would save 26.2m. metric tons of mercury pollution over the period 2025–50. The phasing-out of linear fluorescent lamps (fluorescent tube lighting commonly used in shops and offices) was to be addressed by COP5, to be held in November 2023.

SCIENCE POLICY

UNEP is mandated to analyse the world environment, to provide early warning information, to assess global and regional trends, and to equip policymakers with data to underpin planning. It is determined to make that data widely available, in order both to broaden societal engagement with environmental challenges and to place science at the centre of transformative decision making. Annual flagship reports produced by UNEP include the *Emissions Gap Report* (assessing progress made to meet commitments under the Paris Agreement on climate change); the *Adaptation Gap Report* (the fifth edition, released in January 2021, highlighted large gaps in developing countries' access to climate finance, and a general failure to advance adaptation projects to the point where they would be effective in bringing about real reductions in climate risks); the *Production Gap Report*; and the biennial *Inclusive Wealth Report*, which evaluates the sustainability of economies and wellbeing of citizens (with inclusive wealth defined as the social value of all a country's assets, including natural resources, production, and human capital). UNEP's *Frontiers* report series identifies emerging issues of environmental concern. Furthermore, with UNEP support, the Intergovernmental Panel on Climate Change and Intergovernmental Science-Policy Platform on Biodiversity and Ecosystem Services issue systematic assessments in their respective areas of interest.

UNEP's Global Environment Outlook (GEO) process of environmental analysis and assessment, launched in 1995, is supported by an extensive network of collaborating centres. The sixth 'umbrella' report on the GEO process (*GEO-6*) was endorsed by UNEA-4 in March 2019. It emphasized that technology and finance should be mobilized to support environmental protections, sustainable development, and a near zero-waste economy—warning that, otherwise, progressive damage to the Earth would have dire impacts on human health and lead to numerous premature deaths, particularly in Africa, Asia and the Middle East. The report also warned, *inter alia,* that children's neurodevelopment and adult fertility were being put at risk by endocrine disruptors (found in many products, such as some plastic containers, detergents and cosmetics), and that pollutants in freshwater systems risked accelerating antimicrobial resistance (AMR).

During 2020 UNEP developed a World Environment Situation Room, which was to serve as its online platform for sharing data, information and knowledge. It aimed to use geospatial technologies and other real-time monitoring to highlight environmental threats, health risks, and policy priorities.

UNEP is a sponsoring agency of the Joint Group of Experts on the Scientific Aspects of Marine Environmental Pollution (GESAMP) and contributes to the preparation of reports on the state of the marine environment and on the impact on it of land-based activities. In March 2019 GESAMP issued *Guidelines for the Monitoring and Assessment of Plastic Litter in the Ocean*. In 2020 UNEP established an International Seagrass Experts Network to support research and the exchange of knowledge.

In November 2020 a China-Africa Environmental Cooperation Center was inaugurated in Beijing, People's Republic of China; the Centre promotes Sino-African co-operation on environmental matters and promotes green development and investment.

ENVIRONMENTAL GOVERNANCE

UNEP promotes international environmental legislation and the development of policy tools and guidelines aimed at achieving the sustainable management of the world environment and the objectives of the Paris Agreement and the 2030 Agenda. Through its regional offices, and working with other UN agencies, UNEP helps governments to implement multilateral environmental agreements, and to report on their results. At national level it assists governments to develop and implement appropriate environmental instruments, in particular through its so-called Montevideo Programme for the Development and Periodic Review of Environmental Law. UNEP also aims to co-ordinate policy initiatives, and provides training in various aspects of environmental law and its applications.

UNEP hosts the secretariats of a number of global and regional environmental conventions. It also works closely with other mechanisms, such as the Global Environment Facility and the Green Climate Fund, to support countries to meet their environmental obligations. UNEP co-Chairs (with CITES) the InforMEA initiative, which collates comprehensive information on multilateral global and regional, and bilateral environmental instruments. Additionally, InforMEA provides relevant introductory courses and case studies, and information on environmental events. Jointly with FAO and the International Union for the Conservation of Nature (IUCN), UNEP maintains ECOLEX, an internet-based resource for biodiversity-related international and national legislation and policy.

UNEP endorsed the decision of the UN General Assembly in May 2018 to open negotiations on the development of a Global Pact for the Environment, that was to harmonize existing environmental legislation into one document with the aim of assisting governments to formulate and implement localized environmental rules.

A new Strategy on South-South and Triangular Co-operation was adopted in March 2020 to guide UNEP's activities to promote greater collaboration among developing countries, as well as partnerships with developed countries or multilateral agencies.

UNEP supports member states in combating environmental degradation and natural resources mismanagement, and promotes the integration of environmental concerns into risk reduction policy and practices. A UNEP-UN Office for the Coordination of Humanitarian Affairs Joint Environment Unit identifies acute environmental risks, and co-ordinates and mobilizes appropriate emergency responses to emergencies (including natural disasters, industrial accidents and conflicts). It uses a Flash Environmental Assessment Tool (FEAT) to assess risks from such sites. The Unit hosts an Environmental Emergencies Centre. Impact assessments have been conducted in recent years in Afghanistan, Colombia, the DRC, Iraq, Kosovo, Lebanon, the Palestinian territories, Somalia, South Sudan, Sudan, Ukraine and the Western Balkans. UNEP evaluates the risks posed by environmental impacts on human health, security and livelihoods, and provides field-based capacity building and technical support, in affected countries. It collaborates with the World Bank, UN agencies and other partners to compile Post-Disaster Needs Assessments.

FINANCIAL AND ECONOMIC TRANSFORMATIONS

UNEP recognizes that a transformation of financial and business practices, while promoting more sustainable patterns of consumption or production, is required to achieve the 2030 Agenda and long-term environmental stability. Its activities include promoting environmentally sound technologies; 'green' subsidies; more efficient or circular global value chains; and reducing the environmental footprint of trade.

UNEP is a founding member of the Partnership for Action on Green Economy (PAGE), initiated in February 2013 collectively with the ILO, UNIDO and the UN Institute for Training and Research. During 2021–30 PAGE aimed to support 30 countries in developing green economy strategies in order to generate employment, promote social equity, strengthen livelihoods, enhance environmental stewardship, and ensure sustained growth aligned with the SDGs, the Paris Agreement and the Post-2020 Global Biodiversity Framework. The Green Growth Knowledge Platform, launched in January 2012 by UNEP, the World Bank and other partners, aims to advance efforts to identify and address major knowledge gaps in green growth theory and practice, and to support countries in formulating and implementing policies aimed at developing a green economy. The Economics of Ecosystems and Biodiversity global initiative aims, under the auspices of UNEP, to highlight the values of biodiversity and ecosystem services in economic terms and translate these into decision making.

The UNEP Finance Initiative (UNEP FI), established in 1992 as a partnership between UNEP and the global financial sector, encourages banks, insurance companies and other financial institutions to invest in an environmentally responsible way. A biennial UNEP FI Global Roundtable meeting is held (the 17th was to take place in October 2022, as a virtual event). UNEP FI regional roundtables are also convened.

In June 2019 UNEP and the AU jointly organized Africa's inaugural Wildlife Economy Summit, held at Victoria Falls, Zimbabwe, with participation by African heads of state, government ministers, academics, business people and other representatives of civil society.

DIGITAL TRANSFORMATION

In March 2019 UNEA-4 mandated UNEP with an institutional responsibility to integrate environmental and sustainability values and goals into the global digital economy, as well as to support the harmonization and greater accessibility of relevant data.

In March 2021 UNEP, UNDP and partners established the global Coalition for Digital Environmental Sustainability (CODES), which aimed to anchor environmental sustainability concerns in the Roadmap for Digital Cooperation—an initiative of the UN Secretary-General that was launched in June 2020.

Finance

UNEP's budget for 2022–23 totalled US $200m. UNEP is allocated a contribution from the UN regular budget, and derives most of its finances from voluntary contributions to the Environment Fund and to trust funds.

Publications

Annual Report.

Adaptation Gap Report.

Emissions Gap Report (annually).

Frontiers (normally annually, addresses emerging environmental issues).

Global Chemicals Outlook.

Green Economy Report.

Inclusive Wealth Report.

Our Planet (quarterly).

Ozonaction Newsletter (quarterly).

Planet in Peril: Atlas of Current Threats to People and the Environment.

Production Gap Report (every 2 years).

Sustainable Finance Progress Report.

UNEP Year Book (annually).

Studies, reports (including the *Global Environment Outlook* series), regional and thematic updates, atlases, legal texts, technical guidelines.

Associated Bodies

Global Environment Facility (GEF): c/o United Nations Development Programme, 304 East 45th St, 9th Floor, New York, NY 10017, USA; e-mail gefinfo@undp.org; internet www.thegef.org; f. 1991, by UNEP, the World Bank and UNDP; aims to support the implementation in developing countries of projects in the six thematic areas of climate change; the conservation of biological diversity; the protection of international waters; forests; arresting land degradation; and addressing harmful chemicals and waste. Capacity building to allow countries to meet their obligations under international environmental agreements, and adaptation to climate change, are priority cross-cutting components of these projects. UNEP services the Scientific and Technical Advisory Panel, which provides expert advice on GEF programmes and operational strategies. Funding is channelled through a GEF Trust Fund, a GEF Least Developed Countries Fund (LDC-F—established to address the special needs of the LDCs in relation to the UN Framework Convention on Climate Change, with a particular emphasis on financing the preparation and implementation of NAPAs), and a Special Climate Change Fund (SCCF, established in 2001). In April 2022 29 donor countries pledged US $5,250m. for the 8th periodic replenishment of GEF funds (GEF-8), covering the period July 2022–June 2026; by 2022 the programme, since its inception, had supported more than 20,000 community-based projects worldwide; it acts as the financial mechanism for the following major international environmental conventions: the Minamata Convention on Mercury, Stockholm Convention on Persistent Organic Pollutants, UN Convention on Biological Diversity, UN Convention to Combat Desertification, and the UN Framework Convention on Climate Change; the GEF has 18 partner agencies; Chair. and CEO Dr CARLOS MANUEL RODRIGUEZ (Costa Rica).

Intergovernmental Panel on Climate Change (IPCC): c/o WMO, 7 bis, ave de la Paix, 1211 Geneva 2, Switzerland; tel. 227308208; fax 227308025; e-mail ipcc-sec@wmo.int; internet www.ipcc.ch; f. 1988 by the World Meteorological Organization (WMO) and UNEP; comprises some 3,000 scientists as well as other experts and representatives of all UN mem. govts. Approximately every 5 years the IPCC assesses all available scientific, technical and socioeconomic information on anthropogenic climate change. The IPCC provides, on request, scientific, technical and socioeconomic advice to the COP to the UN Framework Convention on Climate Change and to its subsidiary bodies, and compiles reports on specialized topics, such as *Aviation and the Global Atmosphere*, *Regional Impacts of Climate Change*, and *Managing the Risks of Extreme Events and Disasters to Advance Climate Change Adaptation*. The IPCC informs and guides, but does not prescribe, policy. On 1 Nov. 2014 the IPCC released a *Synthesis Report*, concluding its Fifth Assessment process; it emphasized that the immediate introduction of new policies and forms of international co-operation was required to achieve necessary reductions in greenhouse gas emissions (of some 40%–70% globally by 2050) at a manageable cost. The 47th session of the IPCC, convened in March 2018, established new task groups on gender, and on the implications for the Panel's future work of the 2015 Paris Agreement on climate change. In April 2016 the IPCC agreed—at the request of the UNFCCC—to produce a special report on the impact of global warming at 1.5°C above pre-industrial levels, and on related global greenhouse gas emission pathways: this was issued in Oct. 2018, and concluded that global warming of even 0.5°C in excess of 1.5°C would expose a significantly higher proportion of the global population to water stress and food scarcity, would increase the incidence and severity of extremely hot weather, would exacerbate sea level rises and almost eradicate ocean corals, and would render insects more than two times as likely to lose one-half of their habitat (with an onwards impact on crop pollination); an IPCC special report on *Climate change, desertification, land degradation, sustainable land management, food security, and greenhouse gas fluxes in terrestrial ecosystems* was considered by the 50th IPCC session in Aug. 2019; in Sept. a further special report, *Ocean and Cryosphere in a Changing Climate*, was presented to the 51st session; a second *Synthesis Report* was to be released in late 2022 or early 2023 (concluding the Sixth Assessment—'AR6' process, which was initiated in Oct. 2015); 3 instalments, each compiled by a dedicated working group, were published in advance of the full AR6 *Synthesis Report*: the first instalment, *AR6 Climate Change 2021: The Physical Science Basis*, released in Aug. 2021, emphasized that it was unequivocal that the warming consequences of human influence had caused rapid and unprecedented changes to the Earth's atmosphere, oceans, cryosphere and biosphere, and noted that evidence of changes in extremes—e.g. in relation to heavy precipitation, tropical cyclones, heatwaves and droughts—had strengthened since AR5 (2013); and now envisaged global warming in excess of 2°C during the 21st century, unless 'deep reductions' in CO_2 were implemented (it was noted that many changes attributed to greenhouse gas emissions, particularly concerning the ocean, global sea level and ice sheets, were irreversible over a very long term); *AR6 Climate Change 2022: Impacts, Adaptation and Vulnerability*, released in Feb. 2022, placed an increased focus on the integration of natural, social and economic sciences—acknowledging the interdependence of humans, biodiversity and climate, and the interaction between climate change and global trends such as mounting (particularly poorly planned) urbanization, the unsustainable use of natural resources, and damage caused by extreme events; it emphasized the need to restore degraded ecosystems and to conserve up to one-half of the Earth's land, freshwater and ocean habitats, and called for urgent, ambitious, accelerated action on climate change adaptation, combined with simultaneous rapid, deep reductions in greenhouse gas emissions; finally, *AR6 Climate Change 2022: Mitigation of Climate Change,* which was issued in April, emphasized that developing appropriate policy measures, technologies and infrastructures to bring about major energy sector and lifestyle transitions could lead by 2050 to a 40%–70% reduction in global greenhouse gas emissions: fossil fuel use would need to be replaced by alternatives such as hydrogen and by widespread electrification, while more effective energy efficiency would be required, involving, *inter alia*, lower consumption, a more efficient use of materials, advancing carbon capture and storage policies on land use, and measures such as promoting 'walkable' cities and zero carbon buildings; the report emphasized the need to address continuing investment gaps; Chair. Dr HOESUNG LEE (Republic of Korea); Sec. ABDALAH MOKSSIT (Morocco).

Intergovernmental Science-Policy Platform on Biodiversity and Ecosystem Services (IPBES): UN Campus, Platz der Vereinten Nationen 1, 53113 Bonn, Germany; e-mail secretariat@ipbes.net; internet www.ipbes.net; f. 2012; administered by UNEP; undertakes, periodically, scientific assessments of biodiversity and ecosystems, with a focus on outputs beneficial to humans, including timber, fresh water, fish and climatic stability. IPBES issued a *Thematic Assessment of Pollinators, Pollination and Food Production* in Feb. 2016, and an *Assessment Report on Land Degradation and Restoration* as well as related regional assessment reports (covering Africa, the Americas, Asia and the Pacific, and Europe and Central Asia) in March 2018; the final draft of an *IPBES Global Assessment Report on Biodiversity and Ecosystem Services*—the culmination of a scientific assessment process formally launched in Feb. 2016—was released in May 2019. With a view to enhancing policymaking, the *Global Assessment Report* aimed to provide an overview of the state of global nature and ecosystems, evaluating changes undergone during the previous 5 decades, and including a systematic examination of local and indigenous knowledge; it also considered progress achieved in implementing relevant SDGs, targets, and the Paris Agreement on climate change, and implications for economies, food security, livelihoods, and quality of life of the unprecedented rate of erosion of biodiversity; it noted that up to 1m. species were threatened with extinction and that populations of mammals, fish, birds, reptiles and amphibians had decreased by 60% in the preceding 40 years; the report strongly emphasized the interrelationship between climate change, biodiversity loss and human wellbeing and stated that urgent global action, such as a redirection of government subsidies towards regenerative agriculture, was required to maintain sustainable natural support systems for humanity; mems: 132 states; Chair. ANA MARÍA HERNANDEZ SALGAR (Colombia); Exec. Sec. ANNA LARIGAUDERIE (France).

International Resource Panel (IRP): c/o UNEP Division of Technology, Industry and Economics, 15 rue de Milan, 75441 Paris, Cedex 09, France; tel. 1-44-37-14-50; fax 1-44-37-14-74; internet resourcepanel.org; f. 2007; aims to build knowledge with a view to improving the local/global use of resources and thus reduce overconsumption, wastage and ecological harm; participating scientists report on technical, scientific and socioeconomic findings relating to resources use; the IRP provides advice to, and fosters linkages between, policymakers, industry stakeholders, and communities; issues assessment reports on, *inter alia,* urbanization, decoupling economic growth from adverse environmental impacts, resource efficiency and governance, pollution reduction, water, land and soils, metals, and food. The IRP's *Global Resources Outlook 2019,* published during UNEA-4 in March, observed that rapid growth in the extraction of minerals represented the principal cause of biodiversity loss and climate change; the report noted that since 1970 resource extraction had increased from 27,000m. metric tons to 92,000m. metric tons in 1997, and stated that the extraction and processing of materials, food and fuels accounted for more than 90% of biodiversity loss and water stress, and for one-half of total global greenhouse gas emissions; meanwhile, the global population had doubled over that period; the report called for urgent systemic reform of resource use. Steering Cttee comprises representatives of UNEP, the European Commission and 27 govts; Co-Chair. IZABELLA MÔNICA VIEIRA TEIXEIRA (Brazil), JANEZ POTOČNIK (Slovenia); Head of Secretariat MERLYN VAN VOORE (South Africa).

The Rio Conventions

The following three Conventions arose from the UN Conference on Environment and Development (known as the Earth Summit), that was convened in Rio de Janeiro, Brazil, in June 1992. They aim to combat the triple planetary crisis that has arisen from escalating biodiversity loss, land degradation, and climate change.

Convention on Biological Diversity: 413 St Jacques St, Suite 800, Montréal, QC H2Y 1N9, Canada; tel. (514) 288-2220; fax (514) 288-6588; e-mail secretariat@cbd.int; internet www.cbd.int; the CBD entered into force at the end of 1993, and is focused on the preservation of the Earth's immense variety of plant and animal species, in particular those threatened with extinction; a Cartagena Protocol on Biosafety regulates the transboundary movement and use of living modified organisms (LMOs) resulting from biotechnology: it entered into force in Sept. 2003, and had been ratified by 173 states parties by mid-2022. An Advanced Informed Agreement procedure to govern the import of LMOs and a Biosafety Clearing-House mechanism to facilitate information sharing on LMOs have been established under the Cartagena Protocol. In Oct. 2010 the 10th Conf. of the Parties (COP) to the CBD, meeting in Nagoya, Japan, approved the Nagoya Protocol to the CBD, focused on establishing an international regime on access to and benefit sharing of genetic resources; this entered into force in Oct. 2014 and had 137 ratifications at mid-2022. The meeting also adopted a supplementary

agreement to the Cartagena Protocol (the so-called Nagoya-Kuala Lumpur Supplementary Protocol) concerned with liability and redress; it entered into force in March 2018, and had received 49 notifications by mid-2022. The 12th COP to the CBD, convened in Oct. 2012, in Hyderabad, India, determined formally to classify marine areas of ecological or biological significance. In July 2018 an MOU was concluded between the CBD and FAO's International Treaty on Plant Genetic Resources for Food and Agriculture. The 5th edition of the CBD's *Global Biodiversity Outlook,* issued in Sept. 2020, recommended 8 transformative actions for reversing the degradation of the natural world: conserving land and forest ecosystems; designing sustainable agriculture systems; enabling sustainable (and more plant-based) food systems; ensuring sustainable fisheries and oceans; creating green cities and infrastructure; ensuring sustainable freshwater systems; undertaking sustainable climate action; and implementing an integrated 'One Health' approach to promote healthy ecosystems and healthy people. The first phase of the 15th CBD COP, held in Oct. 2021, in a hybrid in-person and virtual format hosted from Kunming, People's Rep. of China, adopted the Kunming Declaration (themed 'Ecological Civilization: Building a Shared Future for All Life on Earth'), in which more than 100 states committed to mainstreaming biodiversity in decision making and to adopting an effective Post-2020 Global Biodiversity Framework; the meeting also established a US $223.4m. Kunming Biodiversity Fund, which was to support biodiversity conservation in developing states; the detail of the new Framework was to be finalized during the second phase of the COP, to be hosted by China from Montreal, Canada in Dec. 2022; by mid-2022 195 states and the EU were parties to the CBD; Exec. Sec. ELIZABETH MARUMA MREMA (Tanzania).

United Nations Convention to Combat Desertification in Those Countries Experiencing Serious Drought and/or Desertification, Particularly in Africa (UNCCD): UN Campus, Platz der Vereinten Nationen 1, 53113 Bonn, Germany; tel. (228) 815-2800; fax (228) 815-2898; e-mail secretariat@unccd.int; internet www.unccd.int; UNCCD entered into force in Dec. 1996. In Oct. 1998 a Global Mechanism was established under UNCCD, to provide strategic advisory services to developing countries on means of attracting and increasing investments in sustainable land management, for example through microfinance and climate change funds. COP11, held in Windhoek, Namibia, in Sept.–Oct. 2013 agreed to establish a Science Policy Interface to facilitate the communication of scientific findings to policymakers. A Land Degradation Neutrality (LDN) Fund was established during COP13, held in Ordos, People's Republic of China, in Sept. 2017; the Fund, under private management, was to finance projects designed to rehabilitate degraded land. A 12-year strategy aimed at halting the spread of land degradation, and an inaugural gender action plan were adopted by COP13. In Sept. 2017 UNCCD issued the first edition of the *Global Land Outlook (GLO),* which stated that consumption of the Earth's natural reserves had doubled over the previous 30 years and that some 15,000,000m. trees were being felled annually; the 2017 *GLO* emphasized the linkages between drought and land degradation and food security, migration and employment. COP14, held in Sept. 2019, in New Delhi, India, introduced a UNCCD Drought Toolbox (aimed at strengthening states' preparedness and resilience), and established an international coalition to co-ordinate action on sand and dust storms; *GLO2,* released in April 2022, in advance of COP15 (held in May, in Abidjan, Côte d'Ivoire), reported that up to 40% of land on Earth was already degraded, and that funding of US $1,600,000m. would be required to support the restoration of 1,000m. ha of degraded land by 2030. The report stressed that present mismanagement of land resources (i.e. of biodiversity, soil and water) threatened the health (incl. through a higher risk of transmission of zoonotic diseases) and the onwards survival of many species, including humankind, and that maintaining the present trajectory would prompt further land degradation and increased disruptions to food supplies, forced migration and land resource conflicts; modern agriculture was cited as the cause of 80% of deforestation and of most biodiversity loss, and was reported to account for 70% of freshwater use—requiring a revision of global food systems; the report emphasized that the traditional and local knowledge of Indigenous peoples and local communities could be used to protect and regenerate natural capital; the participants at COP15 established a $2,500m. Abidjan Legacy Programme that aimed to address deforestation and to future-proof supply chains, and committed to improve data gathering and monitoring relating to the goal of restoring 1,000m. ha of degraded land by 2030; COP15 also created a new Intergovernmental Working Group on Drought to consider global policy instruments and regional policy frameworks; by mid-2022 UNCCD had been ratified by 196 states and the EU; Exec. Sec. IBRAHIM THIAW (Mauritania).

United Nations Framework Convention on Climate Change (UNFCCC): UN Campus, Platz der Vereinten Nationen 1, 53113 Bonn, Germany; tel. (228) 8151000; fax (228) 815-1999; e-mail secretariat@unfccc.int; internet unfccc.int; WMO and UNEP worked together to formulate the UNFCCC, in response to the first report of the IPCC, issued in Aug. 1990, which predicted an increase in the concentration of greenhouse gases (i.e. carbon dioxide and other gases that have a warming effect on the atmosphere) owing to human activity. The Convention was signed in May 1992 and entered into force in March 1994, committing countries to submitting reports on measures being taken to reduce the emission of greenhouse gases and recommending the stabilization of these emissions at 1990 levels by 2000; however, this was not legally binding. Following the 2nd session of the COP of the Convention, held in July 1996, multilateral negotiations ensued to formulate legally binding objectives for emission limitations. At the 3rd COP, held in Kyoto, Japan, in Dec. 1997, 38 industrial nations endorsed mandatory reductions of combined emissions of the 6 major gases by an average of 5.2% during the period 2008–12, to pre-1990 levels. The so-called Kyoto Protocol was to enter into force on being ratified by at least 55 countries party to the UNFCCC, including industrialized countries with combined emissions of carbon dioxide in 1990 accounting for at least 55% of the total global greenhouse gas emissions by developed nations. The 4th COP, convened in Buenos Aires, Argentina, in Nov. 1998, adopted a plan of action to promote implementation of the UNFCCC and to finalize the operational details of the Kyoto Protocol. These included the Clean Development Mechanism, by which industrialized countries may obtain credits towards achieving their reduction targets by assisting developing countries to implement emission-reducing measures, and a system of trading emission quotas. In March 2002 the USA (then the most prolific national producer of harmful gas emissions) announced that it would not ratify the Kyoto Protocol. The Protocol eventually entered into force on 16 Feb. 2005. The UN Climate Change Conference (COP14), convened in Poznań, Poland, in Dec. 2008, finalized the Kyoto Protocol's Adaptation Fund, which was to finance projects and programmes in developing signatory states that were particularly vulnerable to the adverse effects of climate change. The Copenhagen Accord, agreed at COP15, held in Dec. 2009, determined that international co-operative action should be taken to reduce global greenhouse gas emissions so as to hold the ongoing increase in global temperature below 2°C; it was agreed that enhanced efforts should be undertaken to reduce vulnerability to climate change in developing countries, with special reference to LDCs, SIDS and Africa; developed countries agreed to pursue strengthened carbon emissions targets, while developing nations were to implement actions to slow down growth in emissions. A Green Climate Fund was to be established to support climate change mitigation actions in developing countries, and a Technology Mechanism was also to be established, with the aim of accelerating technology devt and transfer in support of climate change adaptation and mitigation activities. COP16, convened in Cancún, Mexico, in Nov.–Dec. 2010, approved the establishment of a Cancún Adaptation Framework and associated Adaptation Committee. COP17, held in Durban, South Africa, in Nov.–Dec. 2011 concluded with an agreement on a Durban Platform for Enhanced Action. The Platform incorporated agreements to extend the Kyoto provisions regarding emissions reductions by industrialized nations beyond the expiry at the end of 2012 of the initial commitment phase, and to commence negotiations on a new, inclusive global emissions arrangement (to be concluded by 2015). During the conference sufficient funds were committed to enable the inauguration of the Green Climate Fund. In Dec. 2012 COP18, convened in Doha, Qatar, approved an amendment of the Kyoto Protocol to initiate a 2nd commitment period of 8 years. States parties committed to reducing greenhouse gas emissions by at least 18% below 1990 levels during 2013–20. COP18 also secured a commitment by developed nations to mobilize US $100,000m. to support climate change adaptation and mitigation initiatives in affected developing countries. A pledging conference for the (Sondgo, South Korea-based) Green Climate Fund was convened in Berlin, Germany, in Nov. 2014. In July 2015 the Green Climate Fund accredited UNEP as one of the entities through which it was to channel funding; by Jan. 2022 the Fund had committed $10,000m. towards 190 projectsi. In Dec. a plenary meeting of COP21, convened in Paris, France, established the Comité de Paris (superseding the Durban Platform) to facilitate and co-ordinate negotiations in order to secure a new climate agreement. The so-called Paris Agreement was adopted on 12 Dec. and incorporated commitments to reduce emissions and to strengthen, through increased financing, the ability of developing countries to adapt to climate change and to recover from the impact of climate-related shocks; a multilateral stocktaking review was to be convened every 5 years, while national action plans, in the form of voluntary national determined contributions (NDCs), were to be submitted for review and updated every 5 years; significantly, states parties agreed to include in the agreement a declared aim to pursue efforts to limit the rise in global temperatures by 2100 to 1.5°C (over pre-industrial levels), alongside the main objective of limiting the rise to 2°C. At a ceremony held in April 2016 175 states parties signed the Paris Agreement and 15 also deposited their instruments of ratification; the accord was to enter into effect 30 days following ratification by at least 55 nations responsible for 55%

of man-made greenhouse gas emissions. In early Sept. the People's Republic of China and the USA (together responsible for some 38% of global carbon emissions) both ratified the Convention during the summit of G20 states; the required ratification thresholds were achieved on 5 Oct., enabling the Agreement to enter into force on 4 Nov. COP22 and the first meeting of the parties to the Paris Agreement were convened in Marrakesh, Morocco, in Nov.; COP22 adopted the Marrakech Action Proclamation, which called for the highest level of political commitment to combat climate change, as a matter of urgent priority. In Jan. 2017 the outgoing US Pres. Barack Obama authorized a second payment of $500m. to the Green Climate Fund (a first $500m. instalment by the USA having been paid in March 2016); the incoming US Administration of Pres. Donald Trump had declared that it would not pursue a commitment previously made by the USA to transfer in total $3,000m. to the Fund; COP23 was organized by Fiji and convened in Bonn, in Nov. 2017; it initiated a facilitative process, the 'Talanoa dialogue', to reflect upon and discuss climate action during 2018. A Netherlands-based Global Centre of Excellence on Climate Adaptation—a collaboration between UNEP, the Netherlands and Japan—was established in late 2017. COP24, held in Katowice, Poland, in Dec. 2018, secured an initial agreement on a so-called rulebook on implementation of the Paris Agreement, which was to address the measurement and reporting of emission-reducing efforts; signatory countries also agreed in principle on the need for more ambitious limitations of greenhouse gas emissions, in accordance with the most recent IPCC special report. At COP25, convened in Madrid, Spain, in Dec. 2019, no consensus was reached on the substantial issues of carbon trading, or on addressing effectively the climate change-derived so-called 'loss and damage' increasingly borne by some poorer countries (i.e. irreversible harm caused by extreme weather events); a technical assistance initiative, the Santiago Network, was established in 2019 to support the minimization of loss and damage; COP26, held in Glasgow, Scotland, UK, in Nov. 2021, adopted the Glasgow Climate Pact, which, for the first time, called for the 'phase-down of unabated coal power and inefficient fossil fuel subsidies'. (India had declined to accept a proposed text that alluded to ending their use.) Under the Pact the developed parties to the UNFCCC were urged at least to double by 2025, over 2019 levels, the collective provision of climate finance to support developing members' adaptation activities, and multilateral development banks, etc., were also encouraged to scale up climate finance provision; a new Climate Finance Delivery Plan: Meeting the US $100 Billion Goal (focused on the annual mobilization of $100,000m. in climate finance during 2021–25) was welcomed. While the UNFCCC's developed states parties were urged to provide financial support for the Santiago Network, and a Glasgow Dialogue was initiated, wherein, until mid-2024, states parties and other stakeholders were to discuss arrangements for the funding of activities aimed at countering loss and damage, the long-proposed establishment of a formal funding mechanism dedicated to loss and damage was not substantively addressed. 'Climate justice' was acknowledged by the Pact—i.e. consideration of social equality and human rights in tandem with action on climate change. During COP26 technical negotiations on the rulebook for Article 6 of the Paris Agreement were finalized, establishing detailed reporting requirements (to be obligatory by 2024) on emissions targets, and mechanisms governing the functioning of international carbon markets (for example on the taxation of bilateral trades). Declarations and agreements reached on the sidelines of COP26 included a Global Methane Pledge, according to which more than 100 states resolved to lower global methane emissions by 30% by 2030; the Glasgow Leaders' Declaration on Forests and Land Use (a collective commitment to reverse forest loss and land degradation by 2030); a US-China Joint Glasgow Declaration on Enhancing Climate Action in the 2020s; and the establishment of a Champions Group on Adaptation Finance, of an Infrastructure for Resilient Island States funding mechanism, and of a Just Energy Transition Partnership to support South Africa's decarbonization activities; COP27 was to be convened in Sharm el-Sheikh, Egypt, in Nov. 2022; UNFCCC's Global Climate Action portal had 29,550 stakeholders at mid-2022; at mid-2022 the UNFCCC had been ratified by 197 parties (196 countries and the EU); the Kyoto Protocol had 192 states parties (191 countries and the EU); and the Paris Agreement had 193 states parties (192 countries and the EU) (during the period 4 Nov. 2020–18 Feb. 2021 the USA temporarily withdrew from the Paris Agreement); Exec. Sec. SIMON STIELL (Grenada).

Other Biodiversity-related Conventions

In addition to the CBD, several other global conventions have been negotiated on biodiversity-related issues, of which UNEP hosts the secretariats of the Convention on International Trade in Endangered Species of Wild Flora and Fauna (CITES) and the Convention on the Conservation of Migratory Species of Wild Animals (CMS). A Liaison Group of Biodiversity-related Conventions (BLG) was established by the states parties to the CBD to enhance synergies and collaborative action between its secretariat and related conventions and bodies. The BLG comprises the heads of the secretariats of the CBD, CITES, the CMS, the International Treaty on Plant Genetic Resources for Food and Agriculture, the Ramsar Convention on Wetlands, the World Heritage Convention, the International Plant Protection Convention, and the International Whaling Commission.

Convention on International Trade in Endangered Species of Wild Flora and Fauna (CITES): 11–13 chemin des Anémones, 1219 Châtelaine, Geneva, Switzerland; tel. 229178139; fax 227973417; e-mail cites.info-cites@un.org; internet cites.org/eng; entered into force in 1975; regulates international trade in more than 35,000 species of plants and animals, as well as products and derivatives therefrom; species addressed by the Convention are listed in three appendices: Appendix I, which covers 1,082 species and 36 sub-species that are critically threatened with extinction, in which (except in exceptional circumstances) trade is prohibited; Appendix II, covering 37,420 universally vulnerable species (and 15 sub-species), in which trade is permitted, conditionally; and Appendix III, comprising 211 species and 14 sub-species that are protected in at least one mem. country; CITES has special programmes on the protection of, *inter alia,* elephants (including an African Elephant Action Plan and, jtly with the CMS, Monitoring the Illegal Killing of Elephants—MIKE), falcons, great apes, hawksbill turtles, sturgeons, tropical timber (jtly with the International Tropical Timber Organization), shark and manta ray, and big leaf mahogany; states parties meet in conference every 3 years; in Aug. 2019 the 18th CITES COP (also referred to as the World Wildlife Conference), held in Geneva, Switzerland, amended rules and quotas governing trade in numerous wildlife species placed at risk by overhunting, overfishing or overharvesting; the conference added to Appendix II, *inter alia,* giraffes, 18 further shark species (including sharpnose and blacknose guitarfishes that are hunted for their fins), sea cucumbers, eels, marine turtles, queen conches, sturgeons, seahorses and precious corals; tighter rules were imposed on trade in African teak and in cedar from Latin America; Asian small-clawed and smooth-coated otters—at risk of habitat loss and possible trade in live specimens—were transferred to Appendix I; the conference mandated the establishment of a CITES Big Cat Task Force, which was to promote the conservation of and combat illegal trade in cheetahs, jaguars, leopards, lions and tigers; a CITES Strategic Vision Post-2020 was endorsed, with a focus on strengthening environmental, economic and social sustainability and on promoting the achievement of the SDGs; the 19th CITES COP was to be hosted by Panama, in Nov. 2022. The CITES Secretariat contributes to the World Wildlife Seizure ('World WISE') database, which is maintained by the UN Office on Drugs and Crime (UNODC); it supports the International Consortium on Combating Wildlife Crime (ICCWC), which aims to end the poaching of wild animals and illegal trade in wild animals and wild animal products, and in 2014, with UNEP, UNDP and UNODC, launched a #WildforLife campaign against illegal trade in wildlife; the CITES Secretariat is the facilitating body for observance of World Wildlife Day, held annually on 3 March; 183 states and the EU (at mid-2022); Sec.-Gen. Ivonne Higuero (Panama).

Convention on the Conservation of Migratory Species of Wild Animals (CMS): UN Campus, Platz der Vereinten Nationen 1, 53113 Bonn, Germany; tel. (228) 8152401; fax (228) 8152449; e-mail cms.secretariat@cms.int; internet www.cms.int; concluded under UNEP auspices in 1979, aims to conserve avian, marine and terrestrial species throughout the range of their migration. Memorandums of Understanding concluded under the CMS include conservation measures for the West African Elephant (2005), the Saiga Antelope (2006), Atlantic Populations of the Mediterranean Monk Seal (2007), Dugongs (2007), Migratory Birds of Prey in Africa and Eurasia (2008), High Andean Flamingos and their Habitats (2008) and Migratory Sharks (2010). Other multilateral agreements negotiated under CMS auspices include: the Agreement on the Conservation of Populations of European Bats (adopted in 1991 and entered into force in 1994); the Agreement on Cetaceans of the Black Seas, Mediterranean, and Contiguous Atlantic Area (ACCOBAMS—adopted in 1996, entered into force in 2001); the African-Eurasian Migratory Waterbird Agreement (AEWA—entered into force in Nov. 1999) which focuses on the conservation of waterbirds that migrate along the so-called 'African Eurasian Flyway'; the Agreement on the Conservation of Albatrosses and Petrels (ACAP—signed in 2001, entered into force in 2004); and the Agreement on the Conservation of Gorillas and Their Habitats (concluded in 2007, covering 10 range states, and entered into force in 2008). In Nov. 2014 the COP to the CMS adopted a strategic plan to guide the Convention during the period 2015–23, which was, *inter alia,* to address underlying causes of the decline of migratory species; to reduce direct pressures on migratory species and their habitats; and to enhance the conservation status of migratory species and the resilience of their habitats. A Multi-Stakeholder Energy Task Force, established in 2016, is tasked with reconciling renewable energy developments with the conservation of migratory species. In Feb. 2020 the 13th CMS COP, held in Gandhinagar, India, assigned the strictest level of protection to 7 further species: the Asian elephant, jaguar, great Indian bustard, little bustard, Bengal florican, Oceanic white-tip shark, and Antipodean albatross. The meeting adopted the Gandhinagar Declaration, which advocated for the concept of 'ecological connectivity' to be prioritized in the draft Post-2020 Global Biodiversity Framework (q.v.); 133 states parties (as at mid-2022); Exec. Sec. Amy Fraenkel.

United Nations High Commissioner for Refugees—UNHCR

Address: CP 2500, 1211 Geneva 2 dépôt, Switzerland.

Telephone: 227398111; **fax:** 227397377; **e-mail:** unhcr@unhcr.org; **internet:** www.unhcr.org.

The Office of the High Commissioner, established by the UN General Assembly in December 1950 (initially with a three-year mandate to address the needs of refugees in Europe displaced by the Second World War), provides assistance and international protection to refugees and to internally displaced persons, and seeks durable solutions to their problems.

Organization
(October 2022)

The High Commissioner is elected by the UN General Assembly, and is responsible to the General Assembly and to the UN Economic and Social Council (ECOSOC). The High Commissioner is supported by a Deputy High Commissioner; an Assistant High Commissioner for Protection (who manages the division on International Protection, and a co-ordination team and a multi-stakeholder engagement team supporting the Global Compact on Refugees); and an Assistant High Commissioner for Operations (who oversees divisions of Emergency, Security and Supply; and Resilience and Solutions).

High Commissioner: Filippo Grandi (Italy).

Deputy High Commissioner: Kelly T. Clements (USA).

Assistant High Commissioner, Operations: Raouf Mazou (Republic of the Congo).

Assistant High Commissioner, Protection: Gillian Triggs (Australia).

EXECUTIVE COMMITTEE

The Executive Committee of the High Commissioner's Programme (ExCom), established by ECOSOC, meets once a year, and during the period October 2021–October 2022 comprised representatives of 107 states. ExCom gives the High Commissioner policy directives regarding material assistance programmes and advice on international protection. In addition, it oversees UNHCR's general policies and use of funds. A Standing Committee meets throughout the year to support ExCom's activities.

ADMINISTRATION

A Special Envoy for the Horn of Africa is attached to the Executive Office.

At 31 December 2021 UNHCR was active in 133 countries, and employed 13,908 permanent staff and 4,977 affiliates (including UN Volunteers and individual contractors and consultants). Of the total workforce, some 91% were field-based. UNHCR Global Service

Centres, based in Budapest, Hungary, and in Copenhagen, Denmark, provide administrative support to the headquarters.

OFFICES IN AFRICA

Regional Office for Central Africa: BP 7248, Kinshasa, Democratic Republic of the Congo; e-mail codki@unhcr.ch.

Regional Office for West Africa: BP 3125, Dakar, Senegal; e-mail senda@unhcr.ch.

Regional Office for Southern Africa: BP 12506, Pretoria 0001, South Africa; e-mail rsapr@unhcr.ch.

Activities

The competence of the High Commissioner extends to any person who, owing to well-founded fear of war, violence or persecution, is outside the country of his or her nationality; to stateless people; and to internally displaced persons (IDPs—with similar needs to those of refugees but who have not crossed an international border) or those who are threatened with displacement. IDPs include—in addition to conflict-affected populations—people displaced by situations of general violence, human rights violations, natural or human-made disasters or environmental degradation. UNHCR aims to address the fundamental causes of refugee flows, and has urged recognition and comprehension of the broad patterns of global displacement and migration, and of the mixed nature of many 21st century population flows, which often comprise economic migrants, refugees, asylum seekers and victims of trafficking requiring detection and support.

In the UN system UNHCR is lead co-ordinator in refugee emergencies. Within the UN's overall Cluster Approach to co-ordinate an international response to humanitarian disasters, UNHCR is the lead agency for Protection, and in conflict situations the Office leads the clusters on Camp Co-ordination and Camp Management (CCCM) (the International Organization for Migration—IOM—leads that cluster in natural disaster situations), and on Shelter (with the International Federation of Red Cross and Red Crescent Societies leading in natural disaster situations).

At 31 December 2021 the total population of concern to UNHCR, based on provisional figures, amounted to 94.7m., compared with 91.9m. in the previous year, and with 33.9m. in 2010. The total number of people forcibly displaced as a result of persecution, conflict or other violence amounted to 89.3m. by the end of 2021, including 27.1m. refugees and people in refugee-like situations (of whom 21.3m. came under UNHCR's mandate, and 5.8m. Palestinians under the mandate of the UN Relief and Works Agency), 53.2m. IDPs, 4.6m. asylum seekers and 4.4m. Venezuelans displaced abroad (designated as a discrete category). UNHCR was also concerned with 5.7m. recently returned refugees and IDPs, 4.3m. stateless persons, and 4.2m. others deemed to require the Office's protection or assistance.

The states hosting the most refugees at 31 December 2021 were Turkey (now known as Türkiye—3.8m.), Colombia (1.8m.), Uganda (1.5m.), Pakistan (1.5m.), and Germany (1.3m.). At that time Aruba was hosting the largest number of refugees relative to their national populations (one in six), owing to an influx of people fleeing socio-economic turmoil in Venezuela, followed by Lebanon (one in eight, mainly Syrian, refugees), Curaçao (one in 10, mainly Venezuelans) and Jordan (one in 14).

In September 2016 a UN high-level Summit on Addressing Large Movements of Refugees and Migrants adopted the New York Declaration for Refugees and Migrants. Several commitments were made therein that aimed to ensure the rights and safety of refugees, acknowledging in particular the vulnerability of women and children, and the risks posed by trafficking and forced labour. The Office was tasked with leading a broad consultative process to formulate a Global Compact on Refugees. This was eventually adopted by the UN General Assembly in December 2018, and had four principal objectives: to relieve the pressure on refugee hosting countries; to enhance refugee self-reliance; to expand access to third-country solutions; and to support conditions in refugees' countries of origin to enable safe, dignified returns. It incorporated a Comprehensive Refugee Response Framework, already approved as an annex to the New York Declaration, which aimed to strengthen the resilience of host communities. It also defined a Programme of Action to support host countries and refugees, determined that a ministerial Global Refugee Forum (GRF) would be convened periodically, and proposed the establishment of multi-stakeholder Support Platforms to address specific refugee situations.

The Office maintains an online population statistics database. World Refugee Day, sponsored by UNHCR, is held annually on 20 June.

INTERNATIONAL PROTECTION

In the exercise of its mandate UNHCR seeks to ensure that refugees and asylum seekers are protected against *refoulement* (forcible return); that they receive asylum; and that they are treated according to internationally recognized standards. The Office discourages the detention and encampment of refugees and asylum seekers, as this restricts their freedom of movement and opportunities to become self-reliant. UNHCR supervises the application of, and actively encourages states to accede to, the 1951 UN Convention relating to the Status of Refugees (with 146 parties at mid-2022) and its 1967 Protocol (which had 147 parties at that time). These define the rights as well as the duties of refugees and contain provisions that address a variety of matters that affect their day-to-day lives. The treatment of refugees is also guided by a number of instruments adopted at regional level. UNHCR works in countries of origin and of asylum to ensure that policies, laws and practices comply with international commitments, and seeks to facilitate swift, just asylum procedure systems.

UNHCR prioritizes the specific needs of refugee women, children, and elderly refugees in its programme planning and implementation. The Office actively seeks solutions to support refugees residing in urban areas (who by 2022 represented more than three-fifths of all refugees). In June 2011 UNHCR issued an updated strategy on Action against Sexual and Gender-Based Violence. A UNHCR Framework for the Protection of Children was adopted in 2012. Since 2017 UNHCR has reported on the number of unaccompanied and separated children in refugee populations, and from 2018 the Office urged national governments to follow suit. In 2021 there were 27,000 new asylum applications from unaccompanied or separated children (compared with 21,000 in the previous year).

UNHCR has attempted to address the issue of military attacks on refugee camps through the promotion of a set of principles aimed at ensuring refugee safety.

As one of the 10 co-sponsors of the Joint UN Programme on HIV/AIDS (UNAIDS), UNHCR promotes access for displaced populations to HIV/AIDS prevention services, treatment and care.

In November 2014 UNHCR initiated a global action plan aimed at ending statelessness (lack of legal nationality) by 2024. The Office promotes new accessions to the 1951 Convention Relating to the Status of Stateless Persons (which had 96 states parties at mid-2022) and to the 1961 Convention on the Reduction of Statelessness (with 78 states parties at that time).

ASSISTANCE ACTIVITIES

In the early stages of a crisis UNHCR conducts an initial assessment to ascertain the scale of response required and immediate critical requirements. Rapid assessments are undertaken next to identify key priorities for intervention and to estimate total resource requirements. UNHCR uses existing data to accelerate its crisis assessments. The subsequent pattern of operations is as follows: emergency planning (in complex emergencies a UNHCR-led inter-agency Refugee Response Plan is organized); implementation; monitoring; reporting; and evaluation. The Office's assistance can take various forms, including the provision of shelter/non-food items (NFIs—for example household goods, jerry cans, sleeping mats and blankets; also referred to as core relief items—CRIs), clean water, sanitation, medical care, education, and counselling; supporting asylum applications; and facilitating refugee registration. UNHCR has developed a Biometric Identity Management System (BIMS), which swiftly registers and verifies refugees' identities, using iris scans, fingerprints and digital photographs, and gathers detailed social background information on education, skills, etc.

As far as possible, assistance is geared towards the identification and implementation of durable solutions to refugee problems. These generally take one of three forms: voluntary repatriation; local integration; or resettlement onwards to a third country. Where voluntary repatriation, generally the preferred solution, is feasible, the Office assists refugees to overcome obstacles preventing their return to their country of origin. This may be done through negotiations with governments involved, and by arranging transport for and providing basic assistance packages to repatriating refugees, and also by implementing or supporting local integration or reintegration programmes in their home countries, including Quick Impact Projects (QIPs) aimed at income generation and at the restoration of local infrastructures. Similarly, the Office works to enable local communities to support returned IDPs. Some 429,300 refugees repatriated voluntarily to their home countries in 2021. When voluntary repatriation is not an option, efforts are made to assist refugees to integrate locally and to become self-supporting in their countries of asylum. Assistance in procuring accommodation may be offered, as well as the provision of skills training, or of loans. In cases where resettlement through emigration is the only viable solution to a refugee problem, UNHCR negotiates with governments to obtain suitable resettlement opportunities, to encourage liberalization of admission criteria, and to draft special immigration schemes. During 2020, owing to restrictions imposed on international travel as a consequence of the COVID-19 pandemic crisis, only 34,400 refugees were resettled to third countries (compared with nearly 107,800 in 2019); 57,500 were resettled in 2021.

During 2022, in response to the COVID-19 pandemic, UNHCR and other agencies were continuing to provide additional hygiene measures and quarantine facilities at camps. In co-operation with the World Health Organization (WHO) and with Gavi, the Vaccine Alliance, UNHCR was working to ensure that populations of concern were reached by COVID-19 risk communication activities and vaccination campaigns.

SUB-SAHARAN AFRICA

UNHCR has provided assistance to refugees and IDPs in many parts of the continent where civil conflict, violations of human rights, drought, famine or environmental degradation have forced people to flee their home regions. The majority of African refugees and returnees are located in countries that are themselves suffering major economic problems, and often complex, multidimensional emergencies, and are thus unable to provide the basic requirements of the uprooted people. At the end of 2021 there were an estimated 39.2m. people of concern to UNHCR in Africa.

In August 2017 the French, German, Italian and Spanish Governments determined to support Chad and Niger with strengthening their border control capabilities, with a view to stemming the influx of migrants from sub-Saharan Africa into Libya—which is both a destination country for economic migrants (who may find informal employment there) and also a principal country of transit for mixed migration flows of refugees and economic migrants attempting to travel to European destinations. Nearly 650,000 migrants, the majority of whom originated from African countries, were reported in April 2022 to be in Libya; the top five countries of origin of the migrant population were: Niger (25%), Egypt (19%), Sudan (18%), Chad (13%), and Nigeria (5%). UNHCR works within Libya as well as in neighbouring countries to provide durable solutions and find credible alternatives for refugees and asylum seekers, including resettlement to third countries.

Persistent severe food insecurity in southern areas of Somalia has exacerbated the longstanding humanitarian crisis in that country. In 2022 UNHCR was attempting to find durable solutions for a Somali IDP population totalling nearly 3m., of whom 2m. were in south-central Somalia. There were also (as at 31 January) 134,276 refugee returnees; some 92,444 of the total voluntary repatriations had been assisted by UNHCR, including (during 2014–21) 85,465 from Kenya. UNHCR had also, during 2015–21, monitored the arrival of 46,740 Somalis from conflict-affected Yemen, and had during 2017–21 assisted 5,416 Somali refugee returns from that country. (In 2017 UNHCR launched a campaign aimed at deterring people from the Horn of Africa from migrating to Yemen.) Furthermore, at 31 July 2022 Somalia was hosting 15,170 registered refugees and 18,217 asylum seekers. UNHCR promotes the assisted voluntary return of IDPs and Somali refugees to their communities of origin, or to other selected integration areas, and the implementation of community-based projects to benefit both returnees and their host communities. The Office has continued to provide protection and supply basic services to populations of concern; to extend technical support to the federal authorities on the development of a national policy framework for people of concern; to advocate for equal access to justice; to offer return and reintegration support to Somali returnees from Kenya; to foster local integration, community empowerment, economic inclusion and self-reliance; to promote legislation on citizenship; and to provide protection from sexual and gender-based violence and exploitation.

At 31 January 2022 there was an estimated total Somali refugee population of 633,921 sheltering in nearby countries, principally Kenya (hosting 278,657), Ethiopia (225,877), Yemen (75,315), and Uganda (53,992). Meanwhile UNHCR has assisted the Kenyan authorities with strengthening the response capacity of national and local institutions and with finding durable solutions for refugees. Following an al-Shabaab terrorist attack against Garissa University, Kenya, in April 2015, the Kenyan Government announced that the north-eastern Dadaab complex of camps—suspected of harbouring militants—must be removed. In February 2016 the Kenyan authorities ordered UNHCR to close the Dadaab complex within three months; in May this deadline was extended until May 2017, and the Kenyan Government disbanded its Department of Refugee Affairs and suspended registration of new Somali refugees. Consequently, UNHCR, which urged Kenya to reconsider its intention to cease hosting refugees, determined to accelerate a voluntary returns programme to Somalia that had been initiated in 2013 (based on a tripartite agreement concluded in November of that year by the Office, Kenya and Somalia). The Office declined, however, actively to promote repatriation, on the grounds that conditions in south-central Somalia were not suitable for mass returns. In February 2017 the High Court of Kenya overturned the Government's decision to close Dadaab and forcibly to repatriate the Somali refugees, deeming it to be discriminatory. UNHCR and partner agencies

provided repatriating Somali refugees with an assistance package comprising a cash grant in addition to some NFIs, and vouchers for—where available—limited food assistance. UNHCR and partners were not, however, able to follow up the situation of returnees to areas of Somalia where the agencies' access was restricted by security concerns. In late March 2021, once again accusing elements of the refugee population of having connections to al-Shabaab, the Kenyan authorities gave UNHCR an ultimatum to draw up a plan to guide the repatriation of all the Somali refugees from Dadaab and from Kakuma. A repatriation roadmap, providing for voluntary safe returns, departures to third countries and some alternative remain options, was formulated by UNHCR and Kenyan Government representatives and concluded by the Kenyan President and the High Commissioner meeting in Nairobi at the end of April, at which time the Kenyan authorities stated that the two camps would be closed down in 2022. As at 30 June 2022 some 226,031 Somali refugees were still accommodated under UNHCR protection in Garissa (at Dadaab and also at the Fafi complex)—representing the majority of the total of 233,805 refugees there. At that time a further 23,335 Somali refugees were living in and near Nairobi, the Kenyan capital, and 38,389 Somali refugees were accommodated at the Kakuma camp and nearby smaller Kalobeyei settlement, in Turkana, north-western Kenya. From 2012 the Turkana area had received a sharply increased inflow of new refugees, predominantly originating from South Sudan; the outbreak of violent conflict in that country from mid-December 2013, in particular, had prompted an escalation in new arrivals. As at 30 June 2022 there were an estimated 134,359 South Sudanese refugees at the Kakuma camp and Kalobeyei settlement. A further 8,535 South Sudanese refugees were residing in and near Nairobi. At that time Kenya was also hosting some 31,342 refugees from the Democratic Republic of the Congo (DRC) and 21,066 from Ethiopia.

At 31 July 2022 871,910 registered refugees and asylum seekers were sheltering in Ethiopia, including 403,802 from South Sudan. UNHCR has supported the Ethiopian authorities in implementing the advanced BIMS biometric refugee registration system. Long-term persistent intercommunal violence, the onset in November 2020 of devastating full-scale civil conflict in and beyond the country's northern Tigray region, and episodes of drought and flooding had resulted in an Ethiopian IDP population that totalled 4.5m. by mid-2022. Those conditions had also prompted an exodus of Tigrayans seeking shelter in Sudan (which by 31 July 2022 was hosting 73,880 Ethiopian asylum seekers and refugees), as well as to Djibouti and Eritrea. In September 2021 UNHCR rejected allegations by the Ethiopian Government that Tigrayan People's Liberation Front (TPLF) militants were using refugee camps in Sudan as hideouts, following the reported discovery of UNHCR-issued refugee identification cards in the possession of TPLF members. The Office requested US $335m. to fund its operations in Ethiopia during 2022, which were to include registration and protection and the provision of shelter, latrines, water, and of NFIs—such as blankets, sleeping mats, bedsheets, mosquito nets, jerricans, cooking utensils and firewood. During 2021–25 UNHCR was implementing a protection strategy in Ethiopia that aimed to support the high proportion of children aged 0–14 years of age in the refugee population (accounting for 58% in 2021, including nearly 42,000 highly vulnerable unaccompanied and separated children), and youth aged 15–24 years.

At 31 December 2021 an estimated 825,290 Sudanese were exiled as refugees, mainly in South Sudan, Chad, Ethiopia, Kenya and Uganda, owing in part to the conflict that had emerged in 2003 in the western Sudanese province of Darfur. In August 2011 the Sudanese Government amended legislation to deprive of Sudanese citizenship all individuals who acquired the nationality of newly independent South Sudan. UNHCR repeatedly expressed concern over the implications of this for significant numbers of people of mixed origin living in border areas. In September 2012 the South Sudanese and Sudanese authorities concluded a 'Four Freedoms' agreement, permitting citizens of each state to enjoy freedom of residence, movement, property ownership and economic activity on either side of the border; however this was not subsequently fully implemented. A UNHCR-Sudanese Government initiative was launched on 1 February 2015 to facilitate the registration of and issuance of identity cards to South Sudanese people living in Sudan, to enable them to access basic services and employment. South Sudan acceded to the 1951 UN Convention relating to the Status of Refugees in December 2018, and at 31 January 2022 was accommodating—mainly in the Upper Nile and Unity regions—334,568 registered refugees, of whom the majority were from Sudan. Insecurity within South Sudan, including persistent inter-ethnic clashes, has caused significant population displacement. As at 31 January 2022 there were more than 2m. South Sudanese IDPs; of these, nearly 1.6m. were sheltering in host communities and 440,299 were accommodated at designated displacement sites. From late 2018 (when a peace agreement was concluded in South Sudan)–January 2022 UNHCR assisted in facilitating 18,690 spontaneous IDP returns to home communities. Meanwhile, at 31 July 2022 some 2,339,429 South Sudanese refugees were sheltering in neighbouring countries, including 920,768 in Uganda,

814,127 in Sudan, and 403,802 in Ethiopia. UNHCR has supported the construction of new camps and the expansion of existing ones in the countries that have received significant inflows of South Sudanese refugees. A formal UNHCR non-return advisory remained in place for South Sudan in 2022, aimed at preventing forced repatriations, pending an improvement in local conditions (relating to human rights, security and rule of law). At the same time, however, the Office was offering support to refugees who had returned independently.

From January 2021, almost immediately following the termination of the UN-AU Hybrid Operation in Darfur (active from July 2007–end-2020), intercommunal violence escalated in El Geneina (West Darfur), as well as in Tawila (North Darfur) and East Jebel Marra (South Darfur), generating new waves of population displacement in the region. Some 183,000 new IDPs were reported in mid-January 2021. At the end of February 2022 there were more than 3m. UNHCR-registered IDPs in Sudan, of whom nearly 2.6m. were reported to be in Darfur, 364,124 in Sudan's two Kordofan states (that border South Sudan), and nearly 82,000 in Blue Nile state (bordering Ethiopia). Around 1.8m. IDPs were living in camps. Sudan was also hosting a large refugee and asylum seeker population, totalling (as at 31 July 2022) 1,146,999, of whom nearly two-fifths were accommodated in 24 camps and at other designated settlements. During 2022 UNHCR's activities in Sudan included facilitating refugee status determination and registration; voluntary returns and resettlement; and access to NFIs. At 31 July 2022 some 391,601 Sudanese refugees, mainly originating in Darfur, were still residing in 12 camps and one village site in eastern Chad, near the Sudan border.

In response to a severe breakdown in law and order in the Central African Republic (CAR) from December 2012 that culminated in the overturning of the legitimately elected Government in March 2013, large numbers of people became displaced from their homes. Intense violent conflict that had erupted in the CAR capital, Bangui, from early December 2013 had by January 2014 temporarily displaced up to two-thirds of Bangui's population. Meanwhile, refugees from the CAR fled to Cameroon, Chad, the Republic of the Congo and DRC. An intensification of violent insecurity in the CAR from May 2017 prompted a new wave of internal displacement and refugee outflows. In addition to its leadership of the inter-agency Protection, Shelter and CCCM cluster activities, UNHCR has registered the CAR refugees in nearby countries, facilitating their transferral to camps, providing them with documentation, and distributing basic assistance. A democratically elected Government took power in April 2016, and a Political Agreement for Peace and Reconciliation in the CAR was achieved in February 2019. A general election held in the CAR during December 2020–March 2021, against a background of escalating violent unrest, prompted significant new population displacement (some temporary) of more than 210,000. At 31 July 2022 610,265 people were displaced within that country, of whom 456,290 were sheltering informally with families. During December 2020–31 July 2021 some 131,275 people were reported to have fled the CAR. By 31 July 2022 the registered CAR refugee population in neighbouring countries totalled 734,923, including 347,575 in Cameroon, 206,967 in the DRC, and 124,488 in Chad.

Since the 1990s the Great Lakes region of central Africa has experienced massive population displacement, causing immense operational challenges and demands on the resources of international humanitarian and relief agencies. From late 1998 substantial numbers of DRC nationals fled escalating civil conflict to neighbouring countries (mainly Tanzania and Zambia) or were displaced within the DRC. In view of the conclusion, in December 2002, of a peace agreement, UNHCR planned for eventual mass refugee returns. Owing to incessant rebel activity, insecurity continued to prevail, however, during 2003–22, in north-eastern areas of the DRC, resulting in further population displacements; by 2022 it was estimated that the DRC had 5.2m. IDPs. Many IDPs were reportedly living with host families or in spontaneous settlements. Meanwhile, at 31 January 2022, the DRC was hosting 524,125 refugees and asylum seekers, principally from the CAR and Rwanda; 232,366 had been registered biometrically. UNHCR was working to provide protection assistance and long-term solutions for affected populations. At 31 July 2022 there were 1,042,573 DRC refugees in neighbouring countries, of whom 440,365 were accommodated in Uganda, 84,961 (at 31 January) in Burundi, 80,826 in Tanzania, and 76,847 in Rwanda. From April 2015 violent unrest in Burundi prompted a new wave of refugees seeking shelter in surrounding countries. A tripartite meeting of UNHCR with government officials of Burundi and Tanzania was convened in September 2017 to discuss the voluntary repatriation of refugees given the more stable environment in Burundi. Further political and social unrest ensued, however, and at 31 July 2022 the Burundian regional refugee population still totalled 257,974.

At December 2021 Côte d'Ivoire was hosting an estimated 931,166 people who were stateless or of undetermined nationality. This was attributed to longstanding legislation preventing the descendants of immigrants from acquiring Ivorian citizenship; unregistered births; and the destruction of civil registries and loss of documentation during the 2002 and 2010–11 civil conflicts in that country, rendering it impossible for many people to prove their citizenship. UNHCR has worked to support the modernization of Côte d'Ivoire's civil registration processes, facilitating the issuance of birth certificates, passports and refugee identity cards. In February 2015 UNHCR and the Economic Community of West African States organized a high-level meeting, hosted by Côte d'Ivoire, on statelessness in West Africa. UNHCR commended the adoption by the Ivorian authorities in September 2020 of a formal statelessness determination procedure (Africa's first).

At 31 January 2022 UNHCR reported that there were 2,200,357 IDPs in Nigeria (particularly in the northeastern states of Adamawa, Borno and Yobe) owing to great instability caused by the longstanding militant Islamist insurgency in that region. Meanwhile, some 187,145 Nigerian refugees were sheltering in Niger, 121,539 in Cameroon, and 19,321 in Chad. UNHCR has focused on the protection requirements of refugees under its mandate in Nigeria, and has aimed to strengthen its presence and enhance its capacity in that country, as well as to provide training to national agencies on protection and CCCM. By 30 June UNHCR and the Nigerian authorities had registered an influx into Nigerian border areas (Akwa-Ibom, Anambra, Benue, Cross River, Enugu, and Taraba states) of 73,000 asylum seekers fleeing violent insecurity in English-speaking areas of Cameroon. UNHCR was providing protection, settlement management and shelter/NFIs, and was assisting the local Nigerian authorities with the issuance of birth registration certificates for children born to refugees, and with maintaining a COVID-19 testing system. Cameroon itself, at 22 January 2022, had an internally displaced population totalling 936,767, and 518,853 IDP returnees. Cameroon was also hosting 467,550 refugees, principally from the CAR, at that time. In early 2021 UNHCR, Nigeria and Cameroon concluded a tripartite agreement establishing a refugee repatriation framework. A significant deterioration of the security situation in Burkina Faso from the first half of 2019 prompted a massive increase in the number of Burkinabè IDPs, to 1,579,976 by 31 January 2022. UNHCR provided protection monitoring and assistance to the newly displaced. There were also, at 31 January 2022, 406,573 IDPs in Chad, 264,257 in Niger, and (as at 31 December 2021) 350,110 IDPs, and 659,005 IDP returnees, in Mali.

Finance

The regular budget of the UN provides limited finance for UNHCR's administrative expenditure. The majority of UNHCR's programme expenditure is funded by voluntary contributions; around 87% of this from governments and the EU, 9% from private sector sources, and 3% from other intergovernmental organizations as well as from pooled funding mechanisms. UNHCR's projected funding requirements for 2022 totalled US $8,994m. UNHCR also accepts in-kind contributions, such as medicines, tents and vehicles. The proposed budget for Africa in that year was $2,740m.

Publications

Global Appeal (annually).
Global Report (annually).
Global Trends (annually).
Refworld.
The State of the World's Refugees (every 2 years).
UNHCR Statistical Yearbook (annually).
UNHCR Handbook for Emergencies.
Country reports, analyses, handbooks.

Statistics

POPULATIONS OF CONCERN TO UNHCR BY SUB-REGION
('000 persons, at 31 December 2021, provisional figures)

	Refugees*	Asylum seekers	Returned refugees and IDPs†	IDPs*	Stateless persons	Others of concern‡
East Africa, Horn of Africa and the Great Lakes . .	4,717.5	195.8	2,437.6	11,686.8	103.3	23.8
Southern Africa	783.2	289.1	1,042.3	6,287.2	—	36.5
West and Central Africa .	1,488.4	57.7	753.3	7,270.5	931.3	158.8
Total	6,989.1	542.5	4,233.1	25,244.5	1,034.6	219.2

* Includes persons recognized as refugees under international law, and also people receiving temporary protection and assistance outside their country but who have not been formally recognized as refugees.
† Refugees and IDPS who returned to their place of origin during 2021.
‡ Non-categorized persons of concern to UNHCR.
Source: UNHCR, *Global Trends, Forced Displacement in 2021.*

MAJOR POPULATIONS OF CONCERN TO UNHCR ORIGINATING IN SUB-SAHARAN AFRICA
('000 persons, at 31 December 2021, provisional figures)

Origin	Population of concern to UNHCR
Congo, Democratic Republic	7,521.8
South Sudan	4,655.3
Somalia	4,350.9
Sudan	3,937.4
Nigeria	3,773.9
Ethiopia	5,488.0
CAR	1,822.9
Burkina Faso	1,618.8

Source: UNHCR, *Global Trends, Forced Displacement in 2021.*

PERSONS OF CONCERN TO UNHCR IN AFRICA SOUTH OF THE SAHARA*
('000 persons, at 31 December 2021, provisional figures)

Host Country	Refugees†	Asylum seekers	Returned refugees and IDPs	IDPs	Stateless persons	Others of concern‡
Angola	26.0	30.3	0.0	—	—	0.2
Burkina Faso	25.0	9.4	—	1,580.0	—	—
Burundi	81.5	4.3	68.8	19.2	—	2.2
Cameroon	457.7	8.0	53.1	933.1	—	1.2
CAR	9.3	0.8	376.9	691.8	—	—
Chad	555.8	4.7	0.0	406.6	—	106.9
Congo, Democratic Rep. . .	524.1	2.2	1,042.1	5,407.8	—	—
Congo, Rep.	40.8	13.7	0.0	134.4	—	10.2
Côte d'Ivoire	4.3	0.1	22.5	—	931.2	0.1
Djibouti	23.2	11.5	—	—	—	—
Ethiopia	821.3	2.3	1,549.5	3,646.3	—	0.4
Ghana	11.9	1.9	—	—	—	—
Kenya	481.0	59.0	—	—	16.8	—
Liberia	8.2	9.8	—	—	—	—
Malawi	21.5	30.9	—	—	—	0.2
Mali	50.0	0.8	78.7	350.1	—	—
Mauritania	101.9	3.4	—	—	—	—
Mozambique	4.8	24.4	—	744.9	—	0.0
Niger	249.9	16.5	—	224.0	—	50.4
Nigeria	77.1	1.7	222.2	3,084.9	—	—
Rwanda	121.9	0.4	2.0	—	9.5	5.5
Senegal	14.5	2.0	—	—	—	—
Somalia	13.8	16.3	547.0	2,967.5	—	0.0
South Africa	75.5	167.4	—	—	—	—
South Sudan	333.7	4.3	270.2	2,017.2	10.0	—
Sudan	1,103.9	26.6	0.0	3,036.6	—	3.9
Tanzania	207.1	27.8	—	—	—	11.8
Togo	10.7	0.8	0.0	—	—	—
Uganda	1,529.9	43.4	0.0	—	67.0	—
Zambia	75.2	4.4	—	—	—	24.9
Zimbabwe	9.5	12.0	0.2	—	—	0.9

* Figures are provided mostly by governments, based on their own records and methods of estimations. Countries with fewer than 10,000 persons of concern to UNHCR are not listed.
† Includes persons in refugee-like and IDP-like situations.
‡ Non-categorized persons of concern to UNHCR.
Source: UNHCR, *Global Trends, Forced Displacement in 2021.*

United Nations Peacekeeping

Address: Department of Peace Operations, Room S-3727B, United Nations, New York, NY 10017, USA.

Telephone: (212) 963-8077; **fax:** (212) 963-9222; **internet:** peacekeeping.un.org.

The UN undertakes impartial peacekeeping operations (deploying either peacekeeping forces or observer missions), with the consent of the principal parties involved, and without prejudice to their positions or claims, in order to maintain international peace and security and to facilitate the search for political settlements through peaceful means. Each peacekeeping operation is established with a specific mandate, which requires periodic review by the UN Security Council.

Peacekeeping forces—composed of contingents of military personnel, experts and other civilian staff, made available by member states—assist in preventing the recurrence of fighting, restoring and maintaining peace, and promoting a return to normal conditions. To this end, they are authorized, as necessary, to undertake negotiations, persuasion, observation and fact-finding. They conduct patrols and interpose physically between the opposing parties. Peacekeeping forces are permitted to use their weapons only in self-defence. Military observer missions—comprising officers who are made available by member states—monitor and report to the UN Secretary-General on the maintenance of a ceasefire.

The Department of Peace Operations, which replaced the Department of Peacekeeping Operations on 1 January 2019, provides political support and executive direction. It incorporates an Office for the Rule of Law and Security Institutions, an Office of Military Affairs, and a Policy, Evaluation and Training Division. A regional structure of oversight is shared with the Department of Political and Peacebuilding Affairs.

The UN's peacekeeping forces and observer missions are financed, in most cases, by assessed contributions from member states. The approved budget for all operations during 1 July 2022–30 June 2023 totalled US $6,450m. At 30 April 2022 outstanding assessed contributions to the peacekeeping budget were reported to amount to $2,800m. Many countries also voluntarily, on a non-reimbursable basis, offer additional resources to operations, such as material items and transportation.

A Regional Services Centre in Entebbe (Uganda) provides logistical, administrative and communications support to missions in Africa.

By October 2022 the UN had deployed a total of 71 peacekeeping operations, of which 13 were authorized during the period 1948–88 and 58 since 1988. As at 30 June 2022 121 countries were contributing 73,603 uniformed personnel to the ongoing 12 UN operations. Of these, 62,936 were troops, 2,040 were staff officers, 7,263 police officers, and 1,004 were military observers. During 1948–mid-2022 4,210 people died while serving in UN peacekeeping missions.

United Nations Interim Security Force for Abyei—UNISFA

Address: Abyei Town, Sudan.

Head of Mission, and Force Commander: Maj.-Gen. BENJAMIN OLUFEMI SAWYERR (Nigeria).

Establishment and Mandate: UNISFA was established by UN Security Resolution 1990 on 27 June 2011, and is mandated to protect civilians and humanitarian personnel in the disputed oil-rich Abyei Area (located at the Sudan–South Sudan border); to facilitate the free movement of humanitarian aid; to monitor and verify the redeployment of government and rebel forces from the Abyei Area; to participate in relevant Abyei Area bodies; to provide demining assistance and advice on technical matters; to strengthen the capacity of the Abyei Police Service; and, as necessary, to provide—in co-operation with the Abyei Police Service—security for the regional oil infrastructure. In December the UN Security Council expanded UNISFA's mandate to include assisting all parties in ensuring the observance of the Safe Demilitarized Border Zone, and supporting the Joint Border Verification and Monitoring Mechanism (the creation of the Zone and Mechanism having been outlined in Agreements concluded in June 2011); facilitating liaison between the parties; and supporting the parties, when requested, in developing effective bilateral management mechanisms along the border. UNISFA pursues contact with local community leaderships, and promotes intercommunity dialogue.

Activities, 2011–13: In June 2011 the parties to the conflict in Abyei signed an Agreement on Border Security, in which they reaffirmed commitment to a Joint Political and Security Mechanism and agreed to establish a Safe Demilitarized Border Zone (SDBZ) and Joint Border Verification and Monitoring Mechanism, pending the resolution of the status of disputed areas; UNISFA was mandated from December to provide protection for the Monitoring Mechanism. Since its inauguration UNISFA has conducted regular air and ground patrols, and has established permanent operating bases in Abyei Town, Agok and Diffra. In March 2012 the UN Secretary-General reported that the security situation in Abyei remained tense, owing to the continued presence of unauthorized Sudanese armed forces, South Sudanese police, and rebels in the area, as well as ongoing large-scale nomadic migration and returns of internally displaced persons. In April the UN Security Council demanded that Sudan and South Sudan redeploy their forces from Abyei; that the two sides withdraw forces from their joint border and cease escalating cross-border violence with immediate effect, with the support of UNISFA and through the establishment of a demilitarized border zone; that Sudanese rebels should vacate oilfields in Heglig (Sudan); that Sudan should cease aerial bombardments of South Sudan; and that a summit should be convened between the two states to resolve outstanding concerns. By early May South Sudan and Sudan had agreed to abide by a seven-point Roadmap for Action, approved in late April by the AU Peace and Security Council. Accordingly, South Sudan withdrew its forces from Abyei, with logistical support and protection from UNISFA; and, also with UNISFA assistance, Sudan withdrew its military and most police from the area by early June. (However, the UN Security Council has persistently condemned the continuing deployment of a Sudanese police presence in Abyei—the so-called 'Diffra Oil Police'—to guard infrastructures at the Diffra oilfields, in contravention of the June 2011 Agreement.) In March 2013, in accordance with a co-operation agreement concluded in the previous September by the Sudan and South Sudan Governments, UNISFA monitored the withdrawal of forces from the SDBZ; violations of the bilateral agreement by both countries were, however, subsequently reported. In mid-March Sudan and South Sudan reached agreement on restarting South Sudanese petroleum exports through Sudan. In May the UN Security Council authorized an increase in UNISFA's strength; the additional peacekeepers were to be tasked with providing protection for border patrols by the Joint Border Verification and Monitoring Mechanism. A referendum on the future status of Abyei was held at the end of October, but—against the wishes of the AU—was organized and conducted on a unilateral basis by an Abyei Referendum Task Force comprising only members of the Ngok Dinka community. Following the referendum the Task Force unilaterally declared that 99.99% of eligible voters had elected for Abyei to be a part of South Sudan, and declared that this was to be the case with immediate effect. The unilateral referendum heightened intercommunity tensions, and a seasonal migration from Sudan of nomadic Misseriya pastoralists into the area, as well as a disorganized influx of 6,000 people from South Sudan, contributed to the increasing volatility of the security situation. UNISFA worked to ensure that the Misseriya migration was conducted calmly, and pursued a dialogue with the Ngok Dinka and Misseriya communities on establishing strategies and monitoring procedures aimed at eliminating weaponry from Abyei. In November South Sudan suspended its co-operation with the Joint Border Verification and Monitoring Mechanism, owing to disagreement on the location of the centre line in two areas of the SDBZ, and its link to proposed border corridors.

2014–20: From early 2014 a series of grave security incidents erupted between South Sudanese military and police units and Sudanese armed militias illegally deployed in the Abyei Area. In late February UNISFA's Head of Mission, accompanied by the Special Envoy of the UN Secretary-General for South Sudan, met with the South Sudanese President, Salva Kiir, with the aim of securing the withdrawal of that country's military from Abyei. Although a near-complete withdrawal was effected in late March, a residual South Sudanese military and police presence remained, illegally, in the Awang Thou area. In late May the South Sudanese Government informed UNISFA that it would resume its co-operation with the Joint Border Verification and Monitoring Mechanism. Although the Mechanism was consequently reactivated in mid-June, its activities were hampered at that time by insufficient equipment and restrictions on movement. At the end of May, and again in October, the Security Council demanded that South Sudan and Sudan immediately resume the work of the Abyei Joint Oversight Committee, and also—as provided for under the June 2011 Agreement—initiate the establishment of an Abyei Area Administration and Council (which had been deadlocked owing to disagreements over their composition); and establish an Abyei Police Service. UNISFA was requested to observe, note and report on the presence of weaponry in Abyei. Meanwhile, South Sudan and Sudan were urged to implement confidence-building measures among the local communities. In March 2015 the Abyei Joint Oversight Committee reconvened—under new leadership—after a suspension of activities that had lasted nearly two years. Meeting in October—for the first time since May 2013—the Joint Political and Security Mechanism adopted a map of the SDBZ, the centre line of which was defined as the separation line between the armed forces of the Sudan and South Sudan Governments. Furthermore, the parties to the conflict determined to activate, in co-operation with UNISFA, all mechanisms relating to the Joint Political and Security Mechanism, including the Joint Border Verification and Monitoring Mechanism. During late 2015—guarded by around 30 armed police, in violation of the June 2011 Agreement—the Sudanese authorities undertook excavation work in Diffra (also a violation), that was aimed at fortifying the local oil installations. UNISFA requested, without success, that the construction activities cease. In May 2017 the UN Security Council reduced the mission's authorized troop ceiling to 4,791, urged that the Abyei Joint Oversight Committee should meet in regular sessions, and reiterated the need to establish promptly the planned Abyei Area Administration and Council and Abyei Police Service. Pending the full operationalization of the latter, UNISFA's police component has continued to conduct community-based patrols, and to help build the capacity of community protection committees.

Meeting in February 2018, under AU auspices with UNISFA participation, the Joint Political and Security Mechanism agreed to finalize forthwith the activation of the SDBZ. The UN Secretary-General reported in August that a recent review of UNISFA's mandate had found that—notwithstanding the lack of progress achieved in the implementation of new security arrangements or on determining the final status of Abyei—the mission had demonstrably had a stabilizing role in the Abyei area. He proposed that, additionally to its focus on maintaining security and stability in Abyei, and monitoring the Sudan–South Sudan border, the role of the mission should be expanded to foster day-to-day solutions in support of the relevant commitments agreed by the two countries. In November 2018 the UN Security Council determined to reduce the mission's authorized troop ceiling to 4,140; by a further 295 troops following the deployment of increased police personnel (to a ceiling of 345); and then by a further 557 troops from April 2019—unless sufficient progress was achieved towards, *inter alia,* demarcating the South Sudan–Sudan border; ensuring full freedom of movement for UNISFA ground and air patrols; developing Joint Border Verification and Monitoring Mechanism local team sites; and the withdrawal of both parties from the SDBZ. In mid-May 2019 the Security Council authorized a reduced troop ceiling of 3,550 and an increased police ceiling of 640. In mid-July the Head of Mission deplored an unprovoked armed attack on UNISFA peacekeepers who had been providing security at Amiet Market, Abyei, resulting in several deaths. By October 2020 the Secretary-General reported that the security situation in Abyei remained tense, and that attacks on UNISFA personnel and incidents of intercommunal violence were continuing.

2021–22: In mid-August 2021 protesters gathered in two locations in Northern Bahr el-Ghazal state, South Sudan—in 'Sector 1' covered by the Joint Political and Security Mechanism—to demand the withdrawal of both the Joint Border Verification and Monitoring Mechanism and of UNISFA, which was reportedly accused of patrolling in a manner that was biased towards Sudan; looting ensued, and mission troops were forced to relocate. In early September UNISFA stated grave concern at the recent developments. Shortly afterwards a meeting of the Joint Political and Security Mechanism (the first since October 2020) requested South Sudan urgently to address the continuing restrictions that were being imposed by local communities in Northern Bahr el Ghazal on the Joint Border Verification and Monitoring Mechanism, and to reactivate the temporarily vacated team sites. In renewing UNISFA's mandate in December 2021, the Security Council reduced its authorized troop ceiling to 3,250; the police strength was to be reduced only as the Abyei Police Service became better established with enhanced law enforcing capabilities. As at mid-2022 UNISFA was supporting two Joint Political and Security Mechanism team sites, at Tishwin and Abu Qussa/Wunkur (in the Mechanism's Sector 2). Some local opposition had also been encountered there. In March UNISFA stated deep concern at a recent escalation of violence in southern Abyei, particularly in Abyei Town and Agok/Anet, that had resulted in fatalities and in the displacement of several thousand civilians. The mission had intensified patrols in the most affected areas and had offered protection and shelter to local civilians.

In August 2021 the UN Security Council agreed to a request made in April by Sudan—in view of mounting tensions in the Sudan–Ethiopia border area—that Ethiopia (then the sole troop provider) should withdraw its military from UNISFA. Most of the Ethiopian troop contingent withdrew in April 2022; UNISFA's reconfiguration as a multinational force was ongoing.

UNISFA maintains a weapons and ammunition management facility at Dokura, central Abyei, where confiscated ordnance is destroyed. The mission has undertaken demining operations and conducted mine risk education activities, distributed educational kits, supported basic health promotion and provision and drilled bore holes to facilitate access to water, and promoted the rule of law, traditional justice, social and community development, and women's empowerment. Several cycles of Quick Impact Projects have been

implemented. In 2021 the mission implemented an initiative aimed at supporting local journalists.

The Security Council has repeatedly condemned the continuing deployment of the Diffra Oil Police units in the Abyei Area (in continuing violation of the June 2011 Agreement), as well as the intermittent presence there of South Sudan security personnel.

UNISFA has continued to implement a conflict prevention and mitigation strategy in Abyei, involving regular patrols, monitoring and early warning assessments.

Community Liaison: UNISFA maintains a disengagement area between the local Misseriya and Ngok Dinka communities, and liaises with the Misseriya and Ngok Dinka on means of ensuring full compliance with Abyei's status as a weapons-free area. The mission's Community Liaison Office supports dialogue and initiatives conducted by the two traditional groups, particularly in the context of a Joint Peace Committee that was established in February 2016. A four-day Misseriya-Nkok Dinka peace conference took place in February 2021. A co-ordinated Misseriya armed attack against a Ngok Dinka village was strongly condemned by UNISFA in January 2022. In April the UN Secretary-General stated deep concern at levels of community unrest. In May, however, a UNISFA-mediated Misseriya-Ngok Dinka peace accord was signed, in which local leaders committed to advancing inter-community dialogue.

Operational Strength: At 30 June 2022 UNISFA comprised 2,134 troops, 94 military observers, 81 staff officers, and 42 police officers.

Finance: The approved budget for the operation for the period 1 July 2022–30 June 2023 was US $280.3m.

United Nations Mission in South Sudan—UNMISS

Address: Juba, South Sudan.

Special Representative of the Secretary-General: NICOLAS HAYSOM (South Africa).

Force Commander: Lt-Gen. MOHAN SUBRAMANIAN (India).

Establishment and Mandate: UNMISS was established in July 2011 upon the independence of South Sudan, succeeding a former UN Mission in the Sudan (UNMIS). UNMISS is mandated to support the consolidation of peace, thereby fostering longer-term state building and economic development; to assist the South Sudan authorities in conflict prevention, mitigation and the protection of civilians; and to develop the South Sudan Government's capacity to establish the rule of law and to strengthen the security and justice sectors. In May 2014 the UN Security Council restructured the mission's mandate, with the aim of strengthening its capability to protect civilians and to support the implementation of a ceasefire agreement concluded earlier in that year.

Activities, 2011–12: From July 2011 UNMISS liaised with the South Sudan Government and provided good offices to facilitate inclusive consultative processes involving all the stakeholders invested in nation building. The mission responded to a request by the South Sudan authorities to support the development of a national security strategy; demined (through its Mine Action Service) and opened roads; and assisted in preparing a disarmament, demobilization and reintegration (DDR) policy, as well as contributing to the construction of a DDR transitional facility in Wau, South Sudan. UNMISS supported the new Government's ratification of principal international human rights treaties, and monitored the harmonization of the national legislative framework with international human rights standards. From the inception of UNMISS its forces were deployed in response to violent unrest in the politically volatile Jonglei State. Further deployments from 2011 included deterrence operations in Western Equatoria, and a mission to support the integration of rebel forces in Pibor (in eastern South Sudan, adjacent to Jonglei). UNMISS police activities focused on training and advising the new South Sudan Police Service.

From January 2012 relations between South Sudan and Sudan deteriorated, owing to factors including the disputed delineation of the joint border; control over the territory of Abyei; mutual accusations of support for anti-government rebel militia groups; and the dependence at that time of landlocked South Sudan on the use of Sudanese infrastructure for the export of its petroleum. In April the African Union (AU) Peace and Security Council approved a seven-point Roadmap for Action by Sudan and South Sudan (see under the UN Interim Security Force for Abyei); accordingly, both countries withdrew their forces from Abyei. In September the Presidents of South Sudan and Sudan signed a co-operation agreement, which included activating agreed security mechanisms, finalizing both sides' full withdrawal from the border area, as well as covering other issues including the status of nationals resident in each country, banking, and oil and transitional financial arrangements.

2013–15: An implementation matrix for the September 2012 co-operation agreement was concluded in March 2013. At that time

South Sudan and Sudan also reached agreement on reinstating South Sudanese petroleum exports through Sudan, and, in early April, oil production was restarted in South Sudan, albeit not at full output.

In mid-December 2013 political unrest in Juba, the South Sudanese capital, spread, almost immediately, to Jonglei, and the crisis soon escalated into full-scale conflict between forces loyal to the President, Salva Kiir, and those supportive of the Vice-President, Riek Machar. An attack against an UNMISS camp in Akobo, eastern Jonglei, caused a number of casualties, including the deaths of two mission peacekeepers. In late December the UN Security Council—condemning reported violations of human rights by all parties to the conflict, as well as threats made to and attacks upon UNMISS personnel and UN facilities—demanded an immediate cessation of hostilities and initiation of dialogue; insisted that all parties co-operate with UNMISS, in particular with respect to its mandate to protect civilians; and determined, as an urgent temporary measure, to increase the mission's overall force strength to up to 12,500 troops and 1,323 police officers. Agreements on Cessation of Hostilities and on the Status of Detainees were concluded on 23 January 2014, and from mid-February the rebels and government pursued a dialogue aimed at resolving the situation; each side accused the other, meanwhile, of violating the ceasefire. UNMISS conducted numerous military and police patrols and worked closely with the Intergovernmental Authority on Development (IGAD), providing logistical support for the deployment of IGAD monitoring and verification teams (MVTs) that were deployed in South Sudan from 1 April to observe the ceasefire. In May a new political agreement was signed. The Security Council subsequently authorized an increase in the troop and police strength of UNMISS, and refocused its mandate towards protecting civilians; monitoring and investigating violations of human rights; creating the necessary conditions for the delivery of humanitarian assistance; and supporting the implementation of the January ceasefire agreement. The Council expressed deep concern at persistent restrictions placed upon the mission's movement and operations, and strongly condemned attacks perpetrated by both government and opposition forces, and other groups, on UN personnel and facilities. In August 2015 the parties to the conflict adopted the Agreement on the Resolution of the Conflict in the Republic of South Sudan. UNMISS continued to pursue its mandate to protect civilians, and to engage local stakeholders in support of the conflict resolution process, and co-operated with the IGAD Ceasefire and Transitional Security Arrangements Monitoring Mechanism that was established at that time. Despite the declaration of a permanent ceasefire, armed clashes persisted.

2016–18: The Transitional Government of National Unity of South Sudan was appointed in April 2016—with Kiir remaining as President and Machar returning to Juba as First Vice-President (a newly established post). In July violent unrest erupted once again in Juba, prompting Machar to flee the South Sudanese capital. In mid-August the UN Security Council—expressing grave alarm and concern at the country's ongoing humanitarian, security, political and economic crisis—authorized the deployment of a 4,000-strong Regional Protection Force within UNMISS. Reporting to the mission's Force Commander, the Protection Force was tasked with advancing co-operation with the Transitional Government and creating a secure environment in and around Juba, and—in response to extreme circumstances—elsewhere in South Sudan. Having initially rejected the immediate deployment of the Force, the South Sudanese authorities eventually gave consent in early September, during a visit to the country by a UN Security Council delegation. In October the mission urged the immediate cessation of hostilities in Yei, Central Equatoria, where an estimated 100,000 people had become trapped by a severe deterioration in the security situation.

In November 2016 the final report was published of a special investigation (authorized by the UN Secretary-General) into the violent unrest in Juba in July. It found that an overall lack of leadership, preparedness and organizational integration had prevented UNMISS from responding effectively to the uprising. Consequently, the UN Secretary-General dismissed the UNMISS Force Commander. In January 2017 UNMISS and the Office of the UN High Commissioner for Human Rights (OHCHR) issued a joint report on the July 2016 atrocities which found that both government and opposition troops had showed a complete disregard for civilians, and had routinely targeted women and children, in particular those of the Nuer ethnicity. Hundreds of killings were reported to have occurred, as well as 217 rapes, and such violations were also reported to be ongoing. UNMISS and OHCHR urged the Transitional Government to remedy the pattern of violence and impunity, and stated support for the proposed establishment by the AU of a Hybrid Court for South Sudan.

Also in November 2016 the UN Secretary-General reported that, as a result of Machar's flight from Juba in July and replacement as First Vice-President, the opposition to Kiir was split, and that leadership and representation in the institutions of transition had become disputed. The Secretary-General noted that the priority

objectives of UNMISS should include support for the implementation of the peace agreement; improvement of the security situation; protection of civilians; support for human rights; establishing conditions favourable for the delivery of humanitarian assistance; and the development of the rule of law and security institutions. He recommended that the Security Council impose an arms embargo on South Sudan. (This was effected in July 2018.) The Council adopted a Resolution in December 2016 which increased the ceiling for mission police personnel and authorized the Regional Protection Force to use all necessary means to accomplish its mandate. (The phased deployment of the Force—following logistical preparations undertaken in April–May by a 60-strong advance party—began in August 2017.) In February 2017 the Security Council stated deep concern that UNMISS was not being supported by the Transitional Government of National Unity in implementing its mandated task to protect civilians and establish conditions enabling the delivery of humanitarian assistance. A national dialogue process, with a focus on forgiveness, commenced in May. On 21 December, at an IGAD-sponsored High-Level Revitalization Forum of the parties to the August 2015 Agreement on the Resolution of the Conflict in South Sudan, a new Agreement on Cessation of Hostilities, Protection of Civilians, and Humanitarian Access was adopted. However, in January 2018 the UN Secretary-General and the Chairperson of the AU Commission strongly condemned violations of the 21 December 2017 accord. In May 2018 the SRSG visited Unity State in response to an intensification of violence there. Violent clashes had also escalated in Central Equatoria and Jonglei. On 12 September 2018 the SRSG welcomed the adoption by the parties to the conflict, gathered in Addis Ababa, of a new Revitalized Agreement on the Resolution of the Conflict in South Sudan (R-ARCSS).

2019–22: In February 2019 the UN Secretary-General reported that the parties to the R-ARCSS had made modest progress in the implementation of clauses relating to procedural matters, with the permanent ceasefire having been upheld in most areas of the country and confidence-building measures ongoing. In early May the parties to the R-ARCSS extended the pre-transition stage of the agreement (which was to have imminently ended) by six months, until November, at which time a transition period was to commence, in advance of national elections. Several pre-transition stage tasks, including the cantonment, screening, training and unification of forces, and the determination of the number and borders of states, remained to be finalized. In early June UNMISS commended the South Sudanese legislature for ratifying two international covenants relating to civil and political rights and economic, social and cultural rights. In July more than 100 civilians were killed and around 100 incidents of rape and sexual violence were reported in Central Equatoria region. Militant groupings that were not signatories to the R-ARCSS reportedly remained active there, in particular in the Yei area. Some 150 troops were sent to reinforce the mission's presence around Yei in early 2019. In November, the parties to the R-ARCSS agreed to extend the pre-transition stage of the process for a further 100 days. On 22 February 2020 (100 days later) Kiir and Machar concluded a power-sharing agreement, formally ending the civil war. In accordance with the accord, a new Revitalized Transitional Government of National Unity (RTGoNU) was established, including Machar and other opposition leaders as Vice-Presidents.

In June 2020 the SRSG stated concern that the RTGoNU, and civilians' lives and livelihoods, were being jeopardized by an intensifying spiral of intercommunal fighting in Jonglei (in which members of the Nuer, Dinka and Murle communities were engaged), as well as by clashes in Central Equatoria, and armed attacks in northern Unity state and in Warrap and Lakes states. The SRSG indicated that failure by political parties to agree hitherto on the appointment of governors at state level had caused a vacuum that was accommodating the lawlessness. It was reported in late July that thousands of people uprooted by the renewed conflict had sought sanctuary at an UNMISS base in Pibor. At the beginning of September UNMISS established a temporary base at Lobonok, Central Equatoria, with a view to deterring armed road ambushes of civilians and humanitarian convoys. The SRSG reported in that month that at least 600 people had been killed in Jonglei since March. He noted that UNMISS was organizing meetings with the Dinka, Murle and Nuer communities aimed at resolving grievances, emphasized the need to address contributory underlying factors (such as access to water, education and markets), and stressed the communities' own responsibility to pursue a peaceful agenda. In December, responding to a request made in March by the UN Security Council, the Secretary-General released the results of an independent strategic review that had been conducted into challenges to peace and security in South Sudan and into UNMISS's effectiveness. The report noted that, while the R-ARCSS had been effective in curbing major violent conflict, the implementation of reforms envisaged by the Agreement had been slow, small arms and light weapons abounded, the national security sector remained underdeveloped, and, owing to a paucity of diverse employment opportunities, young people were at risk of recruitment by armed groups. In February 2021 the UN Secretary-General reported that some progress had been achieved in making regional gubernatorial appointments. At the beginning of June a joint delegation that included representatives of UNMISS, the AU and IGAD visited Pibor (eastern South Sudan), where intercommunal violence had recently escalated. UNMISS's response activities in Pibor had included intensifying patrols, guarding humanitarian food supplies, and engaging with local leaders to foster dialogue and reconciliation. In mid-September a peace mission comprising delegates from UNMISS, IGAD and other partners visited Tambura, in Western Equatoria, where since June some 440 people had been killed and 80,000 displaced by conflict. UNMISS had established a temporary base in the locality from which to co-ordinate its efforts to protect civilians. In August UNMISS and IGAD stated concern at splits that had emerged within Machar's Sudan People's Liberation Movement/ Army-in-Opposition (SPLM/A-IO), that had led to unrest in Magenis, Upper Nile. The mission welcomed the inauguration in that month of a (reconstituted) Revitalized Transitional National Legislative Assembly and Council of States. The SRSG reported in December that nine state assemblies had been reconstituted. In that month the UN Secretary-General reiterated that deadlines and benchmarks relating to the implementation of the R-ARCSS were being missed. In late February 2022 UNMISS condemned and urged an end to escalating violence in Unity State. In March the SRSG stated deep concern over a decision by the SPLM/A-IO to suspend participation in the security structures of the R-ARCSS. In mid-April the SRSG convened a press conference at which he strongly condemned violent attacks being perpetrated against civilians and humanitarian workers, and emphasized the urgent need for all parties (including also non-signatories) fully to implement the R-ARCSS. In August the RTGoNU adopted an Agreement on the Roadmap to a Peaceful and Democratic End to the Transitional Period in South Sudan; this extended the end of the ongoing transitional period by 24 months, to 22 February 2025. In early October 2022 UNMISS condemned and stated deep concern over violent clashes in Fashoda (Upper Nile), which thus far had caused numerous fatalities and had displaced more than 8,000 people.

UNMISS (despite restrictions imposed in the context of the COVID-19 pandemic) has continued to conduct peacekeeping patrols aimed at deterring intercommunal violence, and to mediate with local traditional leaders. The mission has also organized workshops that engage youth and local leaders; training projects (for example on livelihoods skills such as computing and tailoring); and management of a peace dialogue between local farmers and migrant pastoralists.

During 2013–20 South Sudanese internally displaced persons (IDPs) sought shelter inside several so-called Protection of Civilian (PoC) sites attached to UNMISS bases. During 2019–20 most were transformed into regular IDP sites, no longer under the mission's jurisdiction. In 2022 a PoC site at Malakal (Upper Nile) remained under UNMISS control.

The mission operates a radio station (Radio Mireya), providing news and public service announcements.

The UNMISS Human Rights Division (HRD), which represents locally the Office of the UN High Commissioner for Human Rights, monitors the observance of human rights, undertakes capacity-building initiatives in collaboration with the Southern Sudan Human Rights Commission and other partners, and reports on potential threats against the civilian population and violations of international humanitarian law. The UNMISS Child Protection Unit monitors and reports on the perpetration of Grave Violations against Children in Situations of Armed Conflict (for detail on the Grave Violations see under UNICEF). In June 2014 the Special Representative of the UN Secretary-General for Children and Armed Conflict secured a commitment from President Kiir to issue a presidential decree criminalizing the recruitment and deployment of children by all parties to the conflict. In July 2021 UNMISS urged local and national authorities to end a wave of extrajudicial executions. Through 10 field offices and two team sites, the UNMISS Civil Affairs Division links the mission to local communities and authorities. The Political Affairs Division supports the implementation of the peace process. There is also an Office of the Gender Adviser, an HIV/AIDS Unit, and a Relief, Reintegration, and Protection Section, with a humanitarian focus.

Operational Strength: At 30 June 2022 UNMISS comprised 13,221 troops, 389 staff officers, 200 military observers, and 1,468 police.

Finance: The approved budget for the mission amounted to US $1,205.5m. for the period 1 July 2022–30 June 2023, funded from a Special Account comprising assessed contributions from UN member states.

United Nations Multidimensional Integrated Stabilization Mission in the Central African Republic—MINUSCA

Address: Bangui, Central African Republic.

Special Representative of the Secretary-General and Head of Mission: VALENTINE RUGWABIZA (Rwanda).

Force Commander: Lt-Gen. DANIEL SIDIKI TRAORÉ (Burkina Faso).

Establishment and Mandate: MINUSCA was authorized in April 2014 by UN Security Council Resolution 2149, in response to the ongoing security, humanitarian and political crisis in the Central African Republic (CAR—where, in March 2013, the administration of President François Bozizé had been overturned). MINUSCA immediately subsumed the responsibilities of the former UN Integrated Peacebuilding Office in the CAR (BINUCA), and in September the mission took over the military and policing functions of the former African Union (AU)-led International Support Mission to the CAR (MISCA). MINUSCA was mandated, as its first priority, to protect civilians, as well as to support the transition process in the CAR (which ended at the end of March 2016), to facilitate humanitarian assistance, to promote and protect human rights, justice and the rule of law, and to support disarmament, demobilization, reintegration and repatriation processes. The French military 'Opération Sangaris' (deployed to the CAR during 2013–16) was instructed to use all necessary means to support MINUSCA, and the Council authorized MINUSCA—under limited circumstances and exceptionally—to adopt urgent temporary measures to maintain law and order and combat impunity. In July 2016 the Security Council amended MINUSCA's mandate to focus on the strategic objective of supporting conditions conducive to a sustainable reduction in the threat to peace and security posed by armed groups.

Activities, 2014–17: In September 2014, marking the transfer of responsibility to MINUSCA from MISCA, the UN Secretary-General expressed deep concern over continuing violence in the CAR, in particular in northern areas, in spite of the conclusion of a ceasefire accord between the parties in July. He reiterated demands that all parties to the conflict halt attacks against civilians. In February 2015 MINUSCA expressed concern at widespread renewed outbreaks of communal violence since the start of that year, including within the capital, Bangui. During late 2014–early 2015 the mission captured and detained two prominent rebel leaders. In late March 2015 the UN Security Council authorized an increase in MINUSCA's military and police personnel. MINUSCA co-chaired (with the UN Development Programme) local consultations in advance of, and helped to organize and provided logistical and political support to, the Bangui Forum on National Reconciliation, which took place in May, with participation by around 600 national stakeholders. The Forum, chaired by the Special Representative of the UN Secretary-General (SRSG), addressed issues relating to governance, peace and security, justice and reconciliation, and economic and social development. MINUSCA deployed experts to advise on the operationalization of a Special Criminal Court in the CAR, which was established in June to hold accountable those guilty of grave crimes against humanity committed since 2003 that were not already under the jurisdiction of the International Criminal Court.

During 2015 MINUSCA initiated patrols of areas under threat from the militant Lord's Resistance Army, including Bangassou, Obo, Rafai and Yalinga. The mission provided technical, logistical and security support to the transitional authorities in advance of and during the national elections that were organized at the end of December (these having been postponed from October, owing to a renewed escalation of violent unrest). In mid-December the mission furthermore provided support to facilitate the successful organization of a referendum at which the electorate approved a new national Constitution. In view of the annulment in January 2016 of the results of the legislative elections, these were repeated in mid-February, alongside a second round of presidential elections; a further round of legislative elections was held in late March. A new President, Faustin Archange Touadéra, was inaugurated at the end of March, marking the end of the period of transitional governance. In July MINUSCA's mandate was adapted to focus on achieving a sustainable reduction in the threat to peace and security posed by armed groups. MINUSCA was to assist with the design and implementation of security sector reforms, to support the independence of the judiciary, and to seize arms and related materiel illegally smuggled into the CAR. From 2016, with the aim of promoting peaceful co-existence, MINUSCA increased its use of strategic communications, such as its nationwide 'Guira FM' radio station, and the organization of public information events. In July the EU deployed the EUTM-RCA mission in the CAR, tasked with providing strategic advice and training support to the CAR armed forces. Following the termination in October of Opération Sangaris a contingent of 350 French troops remained deployed in the country. Later in the month violent demonstrations took place in Bangui demanding the withdrawal of MINUSCA.

In February 2017 the SRSG called for the immediate cessation of hostilities in Ouaka (central CAR) and Haute Kotto (in the east) between militants of the rival groupings Front Populaire pour la Renaissance de Centrafrique (FPRC) and the Mouvement pour l'Unité et la Paix en Centrafrique (UPC), which were causing civilian fatalities and significant displacement. In that month the UN Secretary-General noted that recent rising tensions and renewed outbreaks of violence were exacerbated, *inter alia*, by lack of sufficient progress in addressing the root causes of insecurity. The international human rights organization Amnesty International reported in September that MINUSCA did not have the capacity to curb systematic atrocities against civilians allegedly being perpetrated by UPC combatants.

2018–22: In January 2018 MINUSCA, the AU and the CAR Government condemned ongoing violence being perpetrated by Revolution et Justice (RJ) and Mouvement national pour la libération de la Centrafrique (MNLC) militants in the Paoua area, in northeastern CAR, near the border with Chad. MINUSCA was attempting at that time to remove armed combatants from Paoua to enable IDP returns. In early 2018 a first round of consultations was convened with 14 rebel groupings within the context of an African Initiative for Peace and Reconciliation in the CAR, led jointly by the AU, CEEAC and the International Conference on the Great Lakes Region (ICGLR). In mid-June the UN Secretary-General noted a deterioration since April in the security situation in Bangui, and also noted increased political polarization, including a trend towards undermining the authority of the President and the credibility of MINUSCA. (A joint operation undertaken in April by the mission and the security forces to restore order in Bangui had led to significant popular criticism.) In late July the UN, AU, CEEAC, EU, World Bank, France and the USA jointly issued a statement that condemned in the strongest terms the recent violence that had erupted in Bambari, Bria, Kaga-Bandoro and Ndele, leading to significant civilian fatalities. In late January–early February 2019, in Khartoum, Sudan, representatives of the CAR Government, leaders of 14 armed groups, and delegates of political parties, religious bodies and civil society, eventually participated in direct talks within the framework of the ongoing African initiative. On 6 February they formally signed, in Bangui, a Political Agreement for Peace and Reconciliation in the CAR, which covered, *inter alia*, more transparent and inclusive governance, justice and transitional security arrangements; a follow up mechanism was to oversee its implementation. In late March President Touadéra appointed a new government, with more representation of former militant groupings. A Memorandum of Understanding (MOU) was concluded in mid-2020 between MINUSCA and a new AU Military Observers Mission to the CAR (MOUACA). In July the Security Council strongly condemned an armed attack against a MINUSCA convoy in Gedze, in which one peacekeeper was killed. In November the Council tasked MINUSCA with supporting the CAR national authorities in promoting inclusive dialogue among all political stakeholders during the course of a general election, which was initiated in December. In January 2021 the Constitutional Court confirmed the re-election of the incumbent President Touadéra, validating that he had won an outright majority at the first round of the presidential poll; the results of the first round of the legislative election were proclaimed in early February. Opposition leaders rejected the official results. The election was marred by violence by armed factions, which escalated in early 2021. The Security Council strongly condemned the killings of three MINUSCA peacekeepers on 25 December 2020, and of a further two peacekeepers, who died in attacks near Bangui and near Grimari (central CAR), in mid-January 2021. The SRSG and other international partners engaged with national stakeholders throughout the electoral process. Although it had been envisaged that the CAR security forces would assume the role of first responders to electoral security threats, they were deployed in insufficient numbers, and MINUSCA assumed most security responsibilities. In view of the election violence and deteriorating security situation, on 23 December 2020, and again on 10 February 2021, the Security Council authorized an exceptional reinforcement of MINUSCA, in a framework of inter-mission collaboration with UNMISS. In mid-February the UN Secretary-General recommended that MINUSCA's military and police ceilings should be strengthened to 14,400 and 3,020, respectively, in order to enable it to fulfil its mandate as conditions evolved, and to pre-empt any further deterioration in the security situation; this was authorized by the Security Council on 12 March. A second round of the legislative election took place in mid-March. MINUSCA provided logistical support in late May to a final round of legislative elections that were held in 50 remaining constituencies. In June the UN Secretary-General commended public condemnation by the CAR President of misinformation campaigns that were seeking to incite hatred against MINUSCA and other international agencies; these, however, reportedly continued into 2022. In September 2021 the ICGLR adopted a roadmap to reinvigorate the February 2019

Political Agreement for Peace and Reconciliation; the roadmap was supported by a unilateral ceasefire announced in October by President Touadera, and the first follow-up meeting on its implementation was held in January 2022. In November 2021 the UN Security Council renewed MINUSCA's mandate until 15 November 2022, and tasked the mission, *inter alia*, with supporting local elections initially scheduled to be held in September 2022 but subsequently postponed to January 2023, and a planned Republican Dialogue. The latter took place in March 2022, although with minimal opposition representation. During 2022 MINUSCA was, accordingly, conducting outreach and civic education sessions in support of the planned elections. The mission was also providing related training to local authority and administrative officials, and other national stakeholders.

MINUSCA has undertaken efforts to facilitate intracommunity dialogue, and, in support of the African Initiative, it provides assistance to government-led local peace and reconciliation activities, and advocates for the participation of women in the process. The mission's Human Rights Division documents violations of human rights and international humanitarian law committed in the CAR. MINUSCA has also implemented several Quick Impact Projects, including on the rehabilitation of damaged civic infrastructure, and has supported an International Organization for Migration project aimed at relocating former rebel combatants.

Operational Strength: At 30 June 2022 MINUSCA comprised 11,629 troops, 416 staff officers, 152 military observers, and 2,629 police officers.

Finance: MINUSCA's approved budget for the period 1 July 2022–30 June 2023 amounted to US $1,159.9m., funded from a Special Account comprising assessed contributions from UN member states.

United Nations Multidimensional Integrated Stabilization Mission in Mali—MINUSMA

Address: Bamako, Mali.

Special Representative of the Secretary-General and Head of Mission: EL-GHASSIM WANE (Mauritania).

Force Commander: Lt.-Gen. CORNELIS JOHANNES MATTHIJSSEN (Netherlands).

Establishment and Mandate: On 1 July 2013 MINUSMA—authorized in April by the UN Security Council—assumed the authority of the former African Union (AU)-led International Support Mission in Mali (AFISMA, authorized by the Council in December 2012). MINUSMA was mandated to support the re-establishment of state authority in Mali (a ceasefire accord having been concluded between warring parties there in June 2013) and to stabilize key population centres, especially in northern areas; to support the Mali transitional authorities in implementing a transitional roadmap towards the full restoration of constitutional order, democratic processes and national unity; to protect civilians and UN personnel; to promote and protect human rights; to help to create a suitable environment for the civilian-led delivery of humanitarian assistance; to support the transitional authorities in protecting Mali's cultural sites; and to provide support in bringing to justice individuals accused of serious violations of international humanitarian law. MINUSMA was mandated to use all necessary means to address threats to the implementation of its mandate, acting either alone or in co-operation with the Malian security forces. Its initial authorized strength was 11,200 military and 1,440 police personnel. On several occasions French troops deployed to the Chad-based Opération Barkhane—initiated in 2014, and in early 2022 in the process of being withdrawn from Mali—intervened to assist MINUSMA personnel. The mandate of MINUSMA was extended in June 2022 by a further year, until 30 June 2023.

Activities, 2013–16: MINUSMA provided security and logistical support during the presidential elections that were held in July–August 2013, and during the two rounds of legislative elections that were held in November and December (resulting in the inauguration, in January 2014, of a new National Assembly). From late 2013 the security situation in northern areas of the country deteriorated, with militant Islamist groupings increasingly launching asymmetric attacks against the Malian security forces, MINUSMA, and locally deployed French forces. Inter-faction fighting, and harassment and banditry by armed elements (including by self-defence militias), were also reported in northern areas and the Niger Delta region. MINUSMA assisted the Malian authorities with the design of a strategy for the cantonment of armed groups, which was finalized in February 2014, and the mission provided logistical support to the pre-cantonment and cantonment process. On 23 May the Special Representative of the UN Secretary-General (SRSG), the Mauritanian President and the AU Chairperson jointly mediated a ceasefire agreement between Malian security forces and militants of the Mouvement national pour la libération de l'Azawad and associated armed groupings, following the eruption of intense conflict in mid-May in the northern Kidal region. In June the Security Council urged the mission to expand its presence in northern Mali 'beyond key population centres', particularly to areas where civilians were at risk; furthermore, the mission was requested to support the activities of a planned commission of inquiry into violence perpetrated since 2012 in northern areas. In July the SRSG commended the recent decision to establish, with MINUSMA's support, a joint commission to oversee the cessation of hostilities in the northern Tabankort oilfield area. In January 2015 the first meeting was held of an expanded Mixed Technical Commission on Security (established—under MINUSMA's chairmanship—with a ceasefire monitoring mandate).

MINUSMA, with the AU, the Economic Community of West African States, the European Union (EU), the Organization of Islamic Cooperation, and regional governments, participated in the Algerian-led mediation process that culminated in the opening for signature, on 1 March 2015, of the Algiers Agreement for Peace and Reconciliation in Mali; the accord was signed by further opposition groupings in May and June. Meetings of an Agreement Monitoring Committee, established in June to oversee the implementation of the accord, were subsequently held. In May 2016 two UN sites in northern Mali were attacked by separatist militants. In the following month the UN Security Council voted to reinforce MINUSMA by an additional 2,049 military personnel and 480 police officers, and authorized it to adopt a more 'proactive and robust posture', including with regard to protecting civilians from asymmetric threats. The Council authorized the transfer to MINUSMA of a rapid reaction force that had been jointly developed under the auspices of the (former) UN Operation in Côte d'Ivoire and UN Mission in Liberia. Previously postponed local elections were eventually held, with logistical, security and technical support from MINUSMA, in November 2016. In view of violent confrontations from July between armed groups that were signatories to the May 2014 ceasefire, the Mixed Technical Commission on Security determined in late September 2016 that from mid-October convoys comprising five or more vehicles would require prior consent from MINUSMA, and that—where it had not been informed of movements of armaments—the mission would confiscate these.

2017–19: In March 2017 several terrorist entities merged to form the multi-ethnic al-Qaʻida-affiliated Jamaʼa Nusrat ul-Islam wa al-Muslimin (JNIM: Group for the Support of Islam and Muslims). Attacks were perpetrated during 2017 against MINUSMA and the Malian security forces by the new grouping as well as by Islamic State in the Greater Sahara. In early September the UN Security Council imposed a sanctions regime, comprising a travel ban and freezing of assets, against individuals and entities implementing policies and activities identified as undermining the ongoing peace process in Mali. In early November MINUSMA and the Mali Government concluded an MOU on procedures governing the mission's support to the Malian military—covering logistics, co-ordinated operations, information and intelligence sharing, explosive ordnance disposal, medical evacuations, transport, training and planning.

In December 2017 the UN Security Council (acting on a proposal drafted by France) authorized MINUSMA to provide logistical and operational support—such as fuel, water, food rations, medical evacuations and engineering assistance—to the counter-terrorism force of the G5 Sahel: the Force conjointe du G5 Sahel (FC-G5S). (The FC-G5S comprised at that time troops from Burkina Faso, Chad, Mali, Mauritania and Niger, and was tasked with combating violent extremist groups operating in the G5 common space.) MINUSMA established a forward command post in Sévaré, central Mali, to co-ordinate action between mission units, the FC-G5S, the French-led Opération Barkhane and the EU-Training Mission in Mali (established in February 2013). In January 2020, at a summit attended in Pau, France, by the G5 Sahel heads of state, President Emmanuel Macron of France and the UN Secretary-General, a Niamey, Niger-based joint command mechanism was established for the FC-G5S and Opération Barkhane. The strategic concept of operations of the FC-G5S was revised at that time. MINUSMA has provided planning support to the G5 Sahel force, and has continued to facilitate closer co-ordination at Sévaré headquarters. All international and Malian forces meet quarterly to determine common strategic objectives and co-ordination measures.

The UN Secretary-General reported in January 2018 that many of the provisions of the Agreement on Peace and Reconciliation in Mali remained only partially implemented. In mid-January the parties to the Agreement endorsed a roadmap detailing a schedule for the implementation of prioritized provisions. In June the UN Secretary-General reported a renewed momentum in the peace process and implementation of the Agreement on Peace and Reconciliation in Mali, facilitated by the Malian Prime Minister, the recently established sanctions regime, and by the appointment of an independent observer to the process. MINUSMA provided advisory, technical, logistical and advisory support to electoral management bodies in advance of presidential elections that were held at the end of July. In

August 2019, however, the UN Panel of Experts on Mali reported that, in the aftermath of the 2018 election, the signatory parties to the Agreement had failed to maintain efforts to accelerate its implementation. A high-level meeting on Mali and the Sahel organized in September on the sidelines of the UN General Assembly reaffirmed that the Algiers Agreement remained the cornerstone of resolving the crisis in Mali. In December 2019 Malian stakeholders, meeting in Bamako, adopted four resolutions—including to hold legislative elections before May 2020, and to follow those with a constitutional referendum.

2020–22: A workshop convened in January 2020, with support by MINUSMA and by UN Women, adopted the following measures aimed at increasing the participation of women in the political and peace processes: the proportion of women working in follow-up mechanisms to the Algiers Agreement was to be increased from 3% to 30%; and an autonomous women's observatory would be established to monitor the peace process. Neither objective had been achieved by 2022.

Legislative elections were held in two rounds, on 29 March and 19 April 2020, with the final outcome confirmed on 30 April by Mali's Constitutional Court—which had overturned the results for 31 seats, resulting in the re-election of the political party associated with Mali's President Ibrahim Boubacar Keïta. Subsequently tensions over the validity of the election results, dangerous national security situation, and growing economic uncertainty (exacerbated by the COVID-19 situation) erupted into large-scale and increasingly violent protests in Bamako, resulting in 11 fatalities in early July. A newly formed opposition alliance known as the June 5 Movement demanded the resignation of President Keïta. On 18 August Keïta—who was forced to announce his resignation and the dissolution of the Malian Government—as well as Prime Minister Boubou Cisse, and other senior government figures, were detained by members of the Mali military, and were removed from Bamako to a military base in the nearby settlement of Kati. The UN Secretary-General and Security Council condemned the coup, calling for the urgent restoration of constitutional order and the rule of law. During late August–October Keïta left Mali to receive medical treatment in the United Arab Emirates. In mid-September the new military leadership determined that an 18-month transitional administration would be established pending new national elections. The inaugural meeting of a Transition Support Group on Mali (GST-Mali)—with participation by MINUSMA, ECOWAS, the AU, and other partners—was convened at the end of November, in Bamako. A programme of action, providing for reforms and the organization of a general election at the end of the transition period, was presented to the meeting by the Prime Minister of the transitional administration. The SRSG continued to engage with President N'Daou and other members of the transitional administration, while MINUSMA continued to exercise good offices to help prepare an environment conducive to holding the planned elections. Consultations were organized by the mission with worker's, women's and youth groupings and with traditional and religious leaders. A second GST-Mali meeting took place in March 2021.

In February 2020 the SRSG strongly condemned an attack on Ogossagou village, in the Mopti region of central Mali, which resulted in numerous fatalities and injuries, and the destruction of homes. A MINUSMA quick reaction force was sent to Ogossagou, and the SRSG noted that the mission would support the Malian Government in investigating and following up the atrocity. (In October 2021 a reconciliation accord, mediated with support from MINUSMA, was signed by representatives of Ogossagou and several other local villages.) In June 2020 Abdelmalek Droukdel, the leader of al-Qaʻida in the Islamic Maghreb, was killed in Mali by French forces participating in Opération Barkhane, and in November Ba Ag Moussa, a principal JNIM military commander, was also killed during an Opération Barkhane sortie. Nonetheless, the UN Secretary-General reported at the end of 2020 that JNIM and Islamic State in the Greater Sahara were establishing a threatening presence in central Mali, and that clashes between terrorist groupings and local communities had led to several blockades that had had a dire impact on many civilians. The Mopti region was a focus of violence driven by extremists and self-defence militias. Meanwhile, in northern Mali, terrorist clashes persisted, including in the tri-border zone neighbouring Burkina Faso and Niger (particularly in the Gao area). MINUSMA strengthened its presence in conflict-affected areas, and assisted efforts to reduce the community violence and to advance social cohesion, intercommunity reconciliation and mediation skills. Furthermore, the mission worked to strengthen local land commissions (land-related issues being a driver of the ongoing tensions). In early April 2021 the UN Security Council condemned an attack against a MINUSMA camp, in Aguelhok (Kidal region), that resulted in the deaths of four peacekeepers and injured nineteen others. The Council urged that the perpetrators be held to account by the transitional administration, and emphasized that attacks on peacekeepers might, under international law, constitute war crimes. On 24 May MINURSO and the other participants in the Follow-Up and

Support Committee for the Transition stated deep concern at the recent arrest by the Malian military of members of the transitional authorities—including President N'Daou and the interim Prime Minister—and demanded their immediate release. Shortly afterwards both men were forced to resign their posts (while continuing to be detained under house arrest). In late June the UN Security Council renewed MINUSMA's mandate until 30 June 2022, and tasked the mission with supporting the political transition in advance of a general election that was (then) scheduled to take place in Mali on 27 February 2022. In August the UN Secretary-General strongly condemned attacks recently committed against civilians in the Gao area, which had resulted in at least 50 fatalities. MINUSMA was reported to have enhanced its presence and the frequency of its patrols in that area. The Malian authorities were called on to ensure accountability for the atrocities. In October a peacekeeper was killed in an attack on a MINUSMA convoy near Tissalit; seven peacekeepers died in a convoy attack in December, in the Bandiagara region.

During October–December 2021 French troops withdrew from bases in Tessalit, Kidal and Tombouctou, and in mid-February 2022 the French Government confirmed that more than 2,000 French troops deployed to Mali in the framework of the (4,500-strong) Chad-based Opération Barkhane were to be withdrawn—citing significant obstructions imposed on their activities by the military junta (which, meanwhile, had reneged on its previous pledge to hold democratic legislative and presidential elections in early 2022). In January MINUSMA concluded an agreement with the Malian authorities to resume air operations. In June the UN Secretary-General expressed outrage at the recent murder of numerous civilians by extremists in Mali's Bandiagara region and in Gao. Mali's military regime withdrew from all organs of the G5 Sahel in mid-2022. At that time a new Malian transition timetable was announced under which a referendum on a proposed new Constitution would be organized in March 2023, local elections in June, legislative elections during October–November, and a presidential poll would be held in February 2024. In August 2022 the UN Secretary-General strongly condemned a terrorist assault perpetrated against the Malian military in the town of Tessit (Gao). A third meeting of the GST-Mali was held in early September.

MINUSMA has continued to monitor checkpoints, and to conduct medium- and long-range patrols and reconnaissance flights, as well as to support operations of the Malian security forces. The mission has assisted the Malian Government in developing a specialized unit on terrorism and transnational organized crime. It has also provided training in human rights and international law for the Mali national police, and has implemented Quick Impact Projects to enable the operationalization of judicial courts in northern areas. The mission has systematically documented violations of human rights perpetrated by the security forces and militant groupings, and has developed an integrated strategy aimed at the protection of civilians, involving the deployment of joint protection teams, and establishment of co-ordination mechanisms, aimed at interlinking all local UN protection actors. MINUSMA supports the Government in convening intercommunal dialogues and has organized local information sessions and in establishing reconciliation fora. The mission operates the local 'Mikado FM' radio station. The UN Secretary-General reported in June 2022 that MINUSMA had recently observed, and was attempting to counter, a significant increase in orchestrated disinformation campaigns.

Operational Strength: At 30 June 2022 MINUSMA comprised 11,726 troops, 506 staff officers, and 1,744 police officers.

Finance: The approved budget for the mission amounted to US $1,344.1m. for the period 1 July 2022–30 June 2023.

United Nations Organization Stabilization Mission in the Democratic Republic of the Congo—MONUSCO

Address: Kinshasa, Democratic Republic of the Congo.

Liaison offices are situated in Kampala (Uganda), Kigali (Rwanda) and Pretoria (South Africa). A logistics base is located in Entebbe, Uganda.

Special Representative of the UN Secretary-General and Chief of Mission: BINTOU KEITA (Guinea).

Force Commander: Lt-Gen. MARCOS DE SÁ AFFONSO DA COSTA (Brazil).

Establishment and Mandate: MONUSCO's deployment was authorized in May 2010, under UN Security Council Resolution 1925, to reflect a new phase in the ongoing peace process in the Democratic Republic of the Congo (DRC). MONUSCO was inaugurated on 1 July, succeeding the former UN Mission in the DRC (MONUC), which had been active since August 1999. MONUSCO

was to use all necessary means to carry out its mandate, which focused on protecting civilians and humanitarian personnel, as well as safeguarding UN staff, facilities, installations and equipment; assisting the DRC regime in efforts towards stabilizing the country and consolidating peace, including supporting its International Security and Stabilization Support Strategy (ISSSS); helping with strengthening the capacity of the military and with police reforms; supporting disarmament, demobilization and rehabilitation (DDR) activities; developing and implementing a multi-year joint UN justice support programme; consolidating state authority in areas freed from the control of armed militia; providing technical and logistics support for local and national elections at the request of the Government; monitoring the arms embargo against rebel militia active in the DRC; providing human rights training to DRC government officials, security service personnel, journalists and civil society organizations; advancing child protection; combating sexual violence; and promoting the representation of women in decision-making roles. MONUSCO was to focus its military forces in mineral-rich insecure eastern areas of the DRC, while maintaining a reserve force that could be deployed elsewhere at short notice. Prior to the provision of logistical and other support, the mission screens DRC military commanders for human rights violations.

2012–13: MONUSCO undertook several military operations in 2012 to protect civilians in Lord's Resistance Army (LRA)-affected areas, and—including through its regional radio network 'Radio Okapi'—supported an initiative of the national armed forces to encourage LRA members to enter a disarmament, demobilization, repatriation, resettlement and reintegration process. The mission was tasked with assisting the African Union (AU) Regional Task Force, which was mandated to combat the LRA, through the provision of logistical support to the Force's Dungu (Haut-Uele) Joint Intelligence and Operations Centre. Militants of the newly formed Kivu-based 23 March Movement (known as M23) became increasingly active from May 2012, clashing with government forces and causing mass population displacement. In late August the Special Representative of the UN Secretary-General (SRSG) expressed deep concern over continued reports of systematic massacres of civilians in North Kivu. In September three UN integrated offices were launched, under the authority of UN Area Co-ordinators, in Matadi (Bas-Congo), Mbuji-Mayi (Kasaï Oriental) and Kananga (Kasaï Occidental), in place of previous MONUSCO offices, signifying the first phase of the transition process towards an emphasis on peacebuilding. In November MONUSCO deployed attack helicopters and ground infantry support vehicles in order to assist the Congolese army and to protect civilians against an escalation of fighting by M23 in North Kivu. The UN Security Council, meeting in emergency session, condemned the resumption of violence and consequent displacement of the civilian population. At the end of November MONUSCO mobilized 17 rapid reaction units with the intent of monitoring the withdrawal of M23 troops to an internationally agreed Neutral Zone some 20 km outside of Goma. MONUSCO troops also escorted national police forces to key locations within that city with a view to restoring lawful control. In early December, in accordance with the terms of a 24 November communiqué of the International Conference of the Great Lakes Region (ICGLR), representatives of M23 and the DRC Government initiated a dialogue, mediated by the Ugandan Minister for Defence. By early 2013 police numbers in Goma had been restored, with support from MONUSCO, to the pre-M23-occupation level of around 3,500. In February the leaders of 11 African countries, meeting in Addis Ababa, Ethiopia, signed the Peace, Security and Cooperation Framework for the DRC and the Region, which aimed to protect and stabilize the Great Lakes region; the UN, the AU, the ICGLR and Southern African Development Community (SADC) were to act as guarantors of the Framework.

In March 2013, at the request of the UN Secretary-General, the Security Council authorized the establishment of a Force Intervention Brigade (FIB), to be deployed under the umbrella of MONUSCO's operations, and under the direct command of the MONUSCO Force Commander, with a mandate to confront urgent threats to security by conducting targeted offensive operations against any armed militia perpetrating violence in eastern areas of that country, including foreign armed groups active in the region; and to disable and disarm such militia and reduce the threat posed by them to state authority and civilian security. Based in North Kivu, the FIB was to comprise a total of 3,069 peacekeeping troops. From May the new Force was deployed, in the form of a brigade from SADCBRIG, the SADC's regional standby force, comprising troops from Malawi, South Africa and Tanzania. The FIB was activated for the first time in July to enforce a security zone around Goma. In September the ICGLR granted MONUSCO permanent representation on its Expanded Joint Verification Mechanism (a military monitoring team) and appealed to MONUSCO to provide logistical support to the Mechanism. The full deployment of the FIB was completed in early October. Towards the end of that month the Brigade assisted the DRC security forces in a robust action against M23 rebels, starting in the Kibumba area, to the north of Goma. On 5 November the M23 declared the end of its rebellion in eastern DRC. Subsequently, a so-called Kampala dialogue took place between the DRC Government and the M23 leadership, culminating, in December, in the signing of final declarations by the parties, representing a political resolution to issues including the cantonment and DDR of former combatants. MONUSCO was to assist efforts to restore state authority in areas that had been destabilized by the rebel grouping, to support the DDR process, and to undertake extensive patrols, including jointly with the DRC armed forces, throughout the Kivus, and Orientale, Maniema and Katanga provinces.

2014–17: From 2014 MONUSCO undertook to strengthen its active presence in eastern DRC, while maintaining an antenna presence in areas not affected by armed conflict. The transfer of certain tasks from the mission's remit to the scope of the UN's DRC Country Team was envisaged, in areas including humanitarian demining, technical elections support, capacity building, and justice and corrections. In July, under the ISSSS, 13 'Priority Zones' were formally designated by national and international stakeholders. In March 2015 the Security Council authorized a reduction, by 2,000 personnel, in the mission's actual troop strength, while maintaining the previously authorized troop ceiling.

During 2016–17, in accordance with a request by the Security Council in March 2016, MONUSCO was restructured around four 'Pillars', to enhance implementation of its mandate to protect civilians from violence by armed groups. Under Pillar (i) capability development, training, equipment and other resources were to be improved; under Pillar (ii) troops and assets were to be deployed with optimum accuracy; under Pillar (iii) the command, control, logistics support, and other capabilities of the DRC armed forces were to be developed, to enable the transfer of security responsibilities upon the eventual withdrawal of MONUSCO; and under Pillar (iv) military engineering was to be developed to contribute more effectively towards the neutralization of armed groups.

In mid-September 2016 President Joseph Kabila of the DRC (whose second and final term of office was constitutionally mandated to end on 19 December) postponed a general election that had been scheduled for November, thereby prompting widespread protests and violent unrest in Kinshasa. MONUSCO strengthened its presence and undertook robust patrolling in the DRC capital. In late October MONUSCO and the Office of the UN High Commissioner for Human Rights released the preliminary report of a joint investigation into the human rights violations perpetrated during the September unrest. Meanwhile, in late 2016, in support of a mediation initiative being led by the National Episcopal Conference of Congo, the SRSG and the Special Envoy of the UN Secretary-General for the Great Lakes Region held consultations in Kinshasa with principal DRC political stakeholders. Eventually, on 31 December, a political compromise was reached, whereby Kabila was to remain head of state pending a general election to be held before the end of 2017. In January 2017 the UN Secretary-General noted mounting political tensions in the DRC. He reported that joint operations conducted by the FIB and the national Forces armées de la République démocratique du Congo (FARDC), focused on the Beni area of North Kivu (and assisted by MONUSCO during May–September 2016), had significantly disrupted armed rebel activity in that province. He determined to deploy a strategic assessment mission to review the UN's engagement in the DRC. A new Prime Minister was appointed in April 2017, and in May a transitional administration was inaugurated. In August the UN Secretary-General reported that a deepening rift between the DRC Government and opposition platforms was impeding the implementation of the political process. In November the long-awaited general election was further postponed, until December 2018.

2018–22: In January 2018 the UN Security Council strongly condemned the continuing political stalemate and also recent violence perpetrated against protesters. The Council urged all DRC stakeholders to remain committed to the agreement made on 31 December 2016. In July 2018 the UN Secretary-General reported a recent significant deterioration in the security situation in North and South Kivu provinces, owing to a resurgence of activities by the rebel Mai-Mai and Allied Democratic Forces (ADF). He noted resultant popular discontent with the national security forces and with MONUSCO, and that, in response, the mission had increased its presence and community outreach activities. MONUSCO's Community Alert Network was reportedly transmitting more than 500 alerts per month at that time, mainly in North and South Kivu and in Tanganyika. During 2018, in the context of the ISSSS, MONUSCO supported the implementation of six targeted stabilization interventions which aimed to address the root causes of conflicts in Ituri, North Kivu and South Kivu.

In August 2018 MONUSCO, the AU, the EU and other international stakeholders issued a joint statement welcoming Kabila's withdrawal from the presidential contest. Later in that month the UN Secretary-General also urged the Independent National Electoral Commission to submit necessary details to enable MONUSCO to provide timely and efficient technical and logistical support to the

electoral process, as mandated by the UN Security Council (the DRC Government was at that time refusing all external electoral assistance). In early September DRC opposition leaders issued a joint statement urging the Government to abide by the constitutional process, and for MONUSCO to be able, unhindered, to provide assistance. The long-awaited general election was postponed from 23 to 30 December, following an allegedly deliberately caused fire earlier in that month at the central warehouse of the Independent National Electoral Commission, which destroyed a significant amount of electoral equipment, including nearly 8,000 voting machines. On 24 January 2019, in a controversial outcome of the presidential poll, Félix Tshisekedi was inaugurated as the new DRC president. In March the UN Security Council welcomed initial actions taken by President Tshisekedi to remove restrictions on the political space in the DRC. The Council called for an independent strategic review of MONUSCO, which was to include a comprehensive exit strategy for the mission. The mission subsequently discussed this with the DRC authorities. On 30 December a DRC-UN Sustainable Development Cooperation Framework was adopted, to cover the period 2020–24; MONUSCO was to be closely engaged with implementing the Framework.

An independent assessment report was issued in January 2020 on MONUSCO's response to a high number of attacks allegedly perpetrated by the ADF, that resulted in the deaths of more than 260 civilians during the final two months of 2019, in Beni (North Kivu). In late November 2019, in this respect, a MONUSCO local office had been attacked by hostile residents. The report also addressed attacks against Ebola crisis responders in Mambasa (Ituri). It was noted that, since 2014, the ADF had systematically attacked civilians as a means of deterring the DRC military. The report recommended a comprehensive response to civilian protection, from MONUSCO, the UN DRC Country Team, and other partners. In March 2020 the UN Secretary-General observed that armed attacks against civilians had been increasing in North Kivu and Ituri, and that elements of the local population were increasingly protesting MONUSCO's and the armed forces' perceived lack of decisive, effective action against the militia. In August a unilateral UN decision to reconfigure the FIB was protested by the SADC; subsequently, however, it was agreed that non-SADC forces should be included in the format.

In early December 2020 President Tshisekedi announced the establishment of a new ruling coalition, the Union sacrée de la nation. A new Prime Minister was appointed in February 2021, and a new government was to be formed subsequently. (The SRSG urged the Prime Minister to ensure true representation of women in the formation of the administration.) At the beginning of April the UN Secretary-General reported that the security situation in Ituri and North Kivu had recently deteriorated, characterized by an intensification of attacks by the ADF and other armed militants. Meanwhile, numerous human rights violations were attributed to both state and non-state actors, and intercommunal violence was persisting in Ituri, the Kivus and in Tanganyika. At the beginning of May the national Government imposed a 'state of seige' in North Kivu and Ituri, entailing martial law; MONUSCO offered its support to the DRC military in this context. A volcanic eruption at Mount Nyiragongo, near Goma (North Kivu), later in May, which caused several fatalities and displaced 20,000 people, complicated the security and humanitarian situation. In December the UN Secretary-General reported that high numbers of civilians were continuing to be killed, injured and displaced as a consequence of ongoing insecurity in Ituri; North Kivu also remained volatile, with an intensification of attacks against civilians by armed groups ongoing; and violence had escalated in South Kivu—where Mai Mai elements had targeted local communities in tandem with an increase in illegal mining there.

MONUSCO has implemented local strategies aimed at protecting civilians and promoting reconciliation and reducing community violence, has implemented projects aimed at supporting communities and reintegration, and has extended logistical, technical and financial assistance to support the efforts of the DRC authorities to bring those accused of war crimes to accountability. The mission regularly destroys small arms ammunition and remnants of war. It has supported the operationalization of a new disarmament, demobilization, community reintegration and stabilization programme that was initiated by the DRC authorities in July 2021. In December of that year the UN Security Council determined that MONUSCO's troop ceiling should comprise 13,500 military personnel, 660 military observers and staff officers, 591 police and 1,050 personnel of formed police units, and agreed to the temporary deployment of up to 360 formed police unit personnel, as long as they were replacing military personnel. The mission was requested fully to account for child protection and gender considerations as cross-cutting dimensions across its mandate. In 2022 MONUSCO and the UN DRC Country Team were formulating detailed plans for scaling up the Team's presence and programme activities in areas that were to be vacated by the mission during its drawdown. On 30 June 2022 the mission withdrew from most of Tanganyika (where, notwithstanding some persistent Mai Mai activity, the security situation had reportedly improved; a small presence was to remain in the northern Nyunzu and Kalemie areas of the province). It was reported in late July that three MONUSCO peacekeepers had been killed during anti-UN protests in Butembo, North Kivu; the protesters accused the mission of failing to protect local communities from escalating violence between armed militias. In the following month MONUSCO strongly condemned an attack against mission premises in Goma, and urged restraint.

Operational Strength: At 30 June 2022 MONUSCO comprised 12,840 troops, 166 military observers, 325 staff officers, and 1,665 police.

Finance: The authorized budget for the mission amounted to US \$1,112m., for the period 1 July 2022–30 June 2023, funded from a Special Account comprising assessed contributions from UN member states.

United Nations Political Missions and Peacebuilding

Address: Department of Political and Peacebuilding Affairs, United Nations, New York, NY 10017, USA.

Telephone: (212) 963-1234; **fax:** (212) 963-4879; **internet:** www.un .org/Depts/dpa.

UN political missions and peacebuilding operations work in the field to prevent and resolve conflicts or to promote enduring peace in post-conflict societies. They are supported by the Department of Political and Peacebuilding Affairs (DPPA), which was established on 1 January 2019. The Department assists envoys and advisers bearing the UN Secretary-General's 'good offices' for the resolution of conflicts or implementation of other UN mandates.

United Nations Office for West Africa and the Sahel—UNOWAS

Address: BP 23851 Dakar-Ponty, Dakar, Senegal.

Telephone: 33-849-07-29; **fax:** 33-842-50-95; **internet:** unowas .unmissions.org.

Special Representative of the UN Secretary-General for West Africa and the Sahel: ANNADIF KHATAR MAHAMAT SALEH (Chad).

Establishment and Mandate: UNOWAS was established in January 2016 through a merger of the former UN Office for West Africa (UNOWA, established in 2002) and the Office of the Special Envoy for the Sahel, to provide preventive diplomacy, good offices, and political mediation and facilitation efforts in the combined region. UNOWAS is also mandated to support the implementation of the October 2002 ruling of the International Court of Justice relating to land and maritime boundaries between Cameroon and Nigeria; the Cameroon-Nigeria Mixed Commission, chaired by the Special Representative of the Secretary-General (SRSG) meets regularly in this respect.

Activities: UNOWAS supports regional institutions and member states to enhance their capacities to promote good governance, respect for the rule of law, human rights and the mainstreaming of gender in conflict prevention. It also assists the consolidation of democratic governance, stability and development in post-crisis countries in the region, and provides support to strategies aimed at resolving cross-cutting security threats—such as violent extremism, terrorism, transnational organized crime, and maritime piracy.

UNOWAS co-operates closely on security matters with, *inter alia,* the African Union (AU), the Economic Community of West African States (ECOWAS), the Lake Chad Basin Commission (LCBC), the Mano River Union (comprising Guinea, Liberia and Sierra Leone), G5 Sahel, and the Gulf of Guinea Commission. A trilateral partnership is pursued between UNOWAS, the European Union and ECOWAS. UNOWAS chairs regular high-level meetings of the heads of UN missions in West Africa. A UNOWAS-UN Office for Central Africa co-ordination meeting is held annually. In mid-March 2022 the Deputy SRSG chaired the inaugural annual Women's Forum for Peace and Security in West Africa and the Sahel, organized under UNOWAS-ECOWAS auspices in Nouakchott, Mauritania.

UNOWAS supports the implementation of the Code of Conduct concerning the Prevention and Repression of Piracy, Armed Robbery against Ships, and Illegal Maritime Activities in West and Central Africa, which was opened for signature at a regional summit held in Yaoundé, Cameroon, in June 2013 (and is thus referred to as the Yaoundé Code of Conduct).

The SRSG chairs the steering committee of, and UNOWAS is the implementing agency of the UN Integrated Strategy for the Sahel (UNISS—endorsed in June 2013 by the UN Security Council), which aims to enhance governance, resilience and security in that sub-region, where, from 2016, conflict that had originated in 2012 in Mali spilled over into Burkina Faso and Niger. A UNISS Support Plan being implemented during 2018–22 aligned assistance to the region with the UN's 2030 Agenda, the AU's Agenda 2063, and with national and regional priorities. In mid-2022 a regional platform for regional youth was initiated under UNISS.

In June 2017 the UN Security Council endorsed the deployment of a joint counter-terrorism force of the G5 Sahel grouping—the Force conjointe du G5 Sahel (FC-G5S), which was to combat violent extremist groups operating in the common space of the G5 Sahel member states. UNOWAS has provided technical support to the G5 Secretariat. In October 2018 UNOWAS, UN Women, the AU and the G5 Sahel collectively established a G5 Sahel Women's Platform. UNOWAS and the UN Department of Political and Peacebuilding Affairs jointly recruit specialists to strengthen the implementation of G5 Sahel action plans. UNOWAS also supports the G5 Sahel Sahelian Threat Analysis and Early Warning Centre, which was inaugurated in the Mauritanian capital Nouakchott in June 2018.

UNOWAS and the UN Multidimensional Integrated Stabilization Mission in Mali jointly undertake reviews of developing trends in the dynamics among terrorist groupings in the Sahel. The two UN entities liaised closely to assess regional implications following the overthrow of the Malian Government in mid-August 2020, and second military coup that took place in May 2021. In June 2022 the UN Secretary-General reported that confrontations were intensifying in the Liptako-Gourma region between militants from the terrorist groupings Jama'a Nusrat ul-Islam wa al-Muslimin and Islamic State in the Greater Sahara.

In September 2021 the SRSG conducted a good offices mission to Guinea following the overthrow in a military coup of that country's longstanding President Alpha Condé and the dissolution of the Guinean Government and of the national Constitution. The SRSG met the coup leader, Col Mamady Doumbouya, and the leaders of the principal political parties at that time, and urged that respect for the rule of law and human rights, and the security of citizens, should be maintained. In November the SRSG helped to launch a new Promotion of Inclusiveness and Social Cohesion in Guinea initiative, aimed at supporting a peaceful and inclusive period of transition. In February 2022 a joint SRSG-ECOWAS mission to Guinea assessed progress made thus far in the transition. In January 2022 the SRSG and an ECOWAS delegation undertook a joint assessment mission to Burkina Faso, in the wake of the overthrow of that country's democratically elected Government in a military coup. The SRSG returned in April and engaged in further consultations with stakeholders, following the adoption by the military regime on 1 March of a Transition Charter. (A revised timetable to guide the Burkinabè transition back to constitutional rule was agreed in mid-2022. On 30 September a new seizure of power took place in Burkina Faso.)

In April 2018 UNOWAS, the LCBC and the AU organized a workshop aimed at developing a Regional Stabilization, Recovery and Resilience Strategy for Areas Affected by Boko Haram in the Lake Chad Basin; the Strategy was adopted in August by an AU-LCBC ministerial conference held in Abuja, Nigeria (with participation by UNOWAS and other stakeholders). (In August 2020 UNOWAS and UNOCA were designated as co-leaders of the governance cluster of the regional task force guiding the implementation of the Strategy.) Addressing the root causes of the presence of Boko Haram in the Lake Chad Basin had been a focus of UN Security Council 2347, adopted in March 2017. The SRSG supported the organization in July 2018 of a joint summit meeting of ECOWAS and the Communauté Economique des Etats de l'Afrique Centrale—CEEAC (Economic Community of Central African States) that focused on the root causes—including local socioeconomic grievances—of the Boko Haram insurgency. It was reported in late April 2021 that Boko Haram factions had taken control of some territory in the north of Nigeria's Niger state, representing an extension of operations into central Nigeria. In mid-October the SRSG and his counterpart for Central Africa undertook a joint tour of Lake Chad Basin countries impacted by Boko Haram, to assess means by which UN and partner agencies might better support efforts to stabilize the area and promote sustainable development for local civilian communities. In late June 2022 the UN Secretary-General reported that during January–May violence perpetrated by Boko Haram-connected and splinter groupings in northeastern Nigeria had caused more than 700 casualities (including civilians). Some 2,472 Boko Haram elements were reported to have surrendered during January–March.

UNOWAS, ECOWAS and the Mano River Union co-operate in reviewing the implementation of the latter's Strategy for Cross-Border Security in the Mano River Union. In February 2020

UNOWAS and the Mano River Union adopted a framework of co-operation with a focus on peace and security and on supporting young people and women in the sub-region.

By mid-2022 the Cameroon-Nigeria Mixed Commission had endorsed the completion of around three-quarters of an estimated total of 2,696 new border pillars.

In June 2021 UNOWAS, the United Nations Environment Programme and partners inaugurated a UN Regional Working Group to address the environment, climate change, security and development in West Africa.

United Nations Assistance Mission in Somalia—UNSOM

Address: Mogadishu, Somalia.

Internet: www.unsom.org.

Special Representative of the UN Secretary-General and Head of Mission: JAMES CHRISTOPHER SWAN (USA).

Establishment and Mandate: The UN Assistance Mission in Somalia (UNSOM) was authorized by the UN Security Council in May 2013, under Resolution 2102, to supersede the former Political Office for Somalia (established in 1995). UNSOM was mandated to provide UN good offices functions in support of the peace and reconciliation process of the Federal Government of Somalia (inaugurated in August 2012); to monitor and help to prevent abuses of human rights and of humanitarian law; and to support the Federal Government and the African Union (AU) Mission in Somalia (AMISOM; on 31 March 2022 AMISOM was superseded by the AU Transition Mission in Somalia). UNSOM was requested by the Federal Government to deploy across Somalia, and by 2022 was maintaining presences in Mogadishu (the Somali capital), Baidoa, Baidoa, Beledweyne, Berbera, Boosaaso, Dhooble, Dhuusamarreeb, Doolow, Gaalkacyo, Garoowe (Puntland), Hargeisa (Somaliland), Jawhar and Kismaayo. In May UNSOM's mandate was extended until 31 October.

The Mogadishu-based UN Support Office in Somalia (UNSOS), established in November 2015, extends critical logistics assistance to UNSOM, and generally in support of peacebuilding activities.

Activities: From mid-2013 the Special Representative of the UN Secretary-General (SRSG) undertook mediation and good offices activities aimed at promoting reconciliation and dialogue, engaging with local leaders, the Federal Government, and with international partners. In September an integrated UN constitutional support team was established, comprising UNSOM, the UN Development Programme (UNDP) and other UN bodies involved in assisting the ongoing constitution-making process in Somalia. UNSOM assisted the Federal Government with the development of a human rights roadmap, and has provided training for police and law enforcement officers, and human rights and humanitarian law guidance for personnel from the national armed forces. The mission has worked to eliminate the recruitment of children into the national military and into militias. The SRSG has repeatedly condemned atrocities by the terrorist organization al-Shabaab, and the serial targeting of members of the Somali Federal Parliament for assassination.

In late 2014 the SRSG worked with Somali political leaders and with representatives of the AU, the Intergovernmental Authority on Development (IGAD), the European Union (EU), and other organizations, to mediate a political dispute that arose in October between the Federal Prime Minister and Federal President. Following a vote of no confidence in the Prime Minister (upheld) and the appointment of a new premier in December, the SRSG urged the prompt formation of a new inclusive administration. In July 2015 UNSOM and the Federal Government of Somalia jointly convened, in Mogadishu, the inaugural ministerial High-level Partnership Forum (HLPF). The HLPF welcomed the recent establishment of three constitutionally mandated Commissions, the Boundaries and Federalism Commission, the National Independent Electoral Commission, and the Independent Commission for the Review and Implementation of the Constitution. In January 2016 the UN Secretary-General welcomed the adoption by the Federal Government of Somalia—following a four-month national consultation process—of a model for the electoral process to establish a new, bicameral Federal Parliament in 2016, including a commitment to ensure representation by women and minority groups. Meanwhile, electoral advisers from UNSOM and UNDP (co-operating as the Integrated Electoral Support Group) assisted the electoral process, including through the procurement and delivery to polling sites of necessary equipment, and through capacity-building training. The legislative elections were held in October–November 2016 and a new Somali Federal Parliament was inaugurated in late December. Following the presidential poll, held in early February 2017 (with live stream coverage provided by UNSOM, to promote transparency), the mission congratulated Mohamed Abdullahi 'Farmajo' on his election as Somalia's new President, and emphasized the preparedness of the UN and the

wider international community to support his administration. From 2017 UNSOM assisted the Federal Government in the implementation of pilot community reintegration projects for 1,000 demobilized al-Shabaab combatants, which aimed to provide short-term employment opportunities as well as training in practical skills. The SRSG held regular meetings with Somali leaders, international partners, and other stakeholders, with a view to ensuring support for building peace and national institutions.

In August 2018 UNSOM and the Office of the UN High Commissioner for Human Rights (OHCHR) issued a report, *Securing Political Participation: Human Rights in Somalia's Electoral Processes*, which detailed allegations of violations of human rights and abuses perpetrated by the state security forces, and by al-Shabaab and other non-state actors, before, during and after the elections held in 2016–17. The report noted that, hitherto, only two of the 44 documented killings had been investigated and prosecuted, and observed that human rights activists, journalists and political leaders had been harassed and attacked. It demanded prompt and impartial investigations into all related human rights violations and abuses, and urged the Somali Government to ensure the enactment of national electoral legislation prior to planned elections; and to ensure the application of international human rights standards as well as vetting of the human rights records of candidates (to eliminate candidatures by, for example, former warlords).

In early January 2019 the Government ordered the SRSG to leave the country as a result of his perceived interference in domestic affairs, which included raising concerns at the detention of a former al-Shabaab member who was a candidate in regional elections and at the response by local police to the ensuing civil unrest. At the end of January the UN Under-Secretary-General for Political and Peace-building Affairs, Rosemary DiCarlo, met the country's leaders to discuss means of strengthening co-operation between the Somali authorities and the UN.

In June 2020 it was announced that Somali legislative and presidential elections would be held in February 2021. In August 2020 the SRSG noted that the legal framework underpinning the pending elections had not been completed and that the necessary security arrangements were not yet in place. He urged broad-based co-operation among national stakeholders. In mid-September the UN, AMISOM and other international partners welcomed ongoing dialogue between the Federal Government and five Somalian Federal States on the development of a credible electoral model. On 17 September a model was broadly agreed, providing for an indirect voting format. (The SRSG subsequently urged that a one-person-one-vote universal suffrage model should be developed by 2024.) The 2020 Somalia Partnership Forum, held in Mogadishu, in December, with participation by representatives of the Somali Government, UN, other multilateral organizations, and partner governments, addressed the impacts of COVID-19, other political, economic development and humanitarian issues, and the pending Federal election. (The inaugural Somalia Partnership Forum had been held in December 2017.) In December 2020 UNSOM police assumed responsibility for the co-ordination of election security training.

During 2021 UNSOM and UNDP jointly undertook to support the electoral process, in collaboration with UNSOS, UN-Women, and the UN Office for Project Services, through the extension of good offices and of technical, operational and logistical assistance. Owing to contention concerning the composition of the electoral management bodies and certain outstanding regional electoral issues, the planned elections were further postponed, from February, prompting violent unrest in Mogadishu. The UN Secretary-General stated grave concern over the violence, urging all parties to exercise restraint and calm. He called on the Federal Government and leaders of the Federal States urgently to reach consensus on a means of proceeding with the planned elections, on the basis of the so-called 17 September electoral model. He also urged respect for the right to peaceful assembly. Several rounds of Somali political consultations were subsequently held, seeking a resolution of the impasse. In early March the UN Secretary-General deplored a terrorist attack that was perpetrated in Mogadishu. On 9 March the SRSG condemned an al-Shabaab mortar attack that targeted the international airport in Mogadishu. Later in that month the Secretary-General reiterated his deep concern over the delayed election schedule, and over the risk this posed to national stability. In mid-April UN and international partners collectively stated deep concern over a recent decision by the Somali legislature to replace the '17 September' agreement with a different electoral process that entailed a lengthy extension to the current presidential and parliamentary mandates. Later in the month they strongly condemned an eruption of violence in Mogadishu, reiterating that adherence to the 17 September arrangement should represent the only model for the electoral process, and that an extension of government mandates would cause a destabilizing political crisis. They stated particular concern over emerging fragmentation of the Somali National Army into clan-based factions. In late May they welcomed the decision made by a Federal Government of Somalia-Federal Member States summit, held on 27 May, to hold presidential and parliamentary elections promptly (within two months; this schedule was not, however, met), and thanked President Farmajo for having appealed at the beginning of the month for a reversion to the consensus-based 17 September electoral model. In mid-2021 the SRSG and representatives of AMISOM, IGAD and the EU visited Somalia's federal member states with the aim of fostering constructive engagement in the electoral preparations. In mid-September the UN Security Council emphasized its deep concern at persisting discord within the Somali Government and the ensuing negative impact on the electoral process and schedule. Legislative elections were initiated in November and were scheduled to be completed on 15 March 2022; by that time, however, 40 of the 275 seats in the lower house remained unelected. The UN, AU, and other international partners issued a collective statement in mid-March that urged the prompt completion of the electoral process, and emphasized the need to adhere to a 30% quota of female parliamentarians. In late March the UN Security Council condemned a series of deadly terrorist attacks mounted by al-Shabaab with the stated intent of destabilizing the process. On 31 March the UN Security Council endorsed the new AU Transition Mission in Somalia (ATMIS), that replaced AMISOM. ATMIS was tasked with reducing the threat posed by al-Shabaab, assisting efforts to build the capacity of the Somali security and police forces, supporting national peacebuilding and reconciliation activities, and with undertaking a phased transfer of security responsibilities to Somalia. Senators and members of parliament were eventually inaugurated in mid-April (women having secured only 21% of the seats), and preparations for a presidential poll ensued. In early May 2022 the Security Council strongly condemned an al-Shabaab terrorist attack against an ATMIS operating base that caused the deaths of 10 Burundian troops. The SRSG welcomed the decisive election on 15 May of a new Somalian President, Hassan Sheikh Mohamud (marking the completion of the lengthy electoral process). He observed, however, that the earlier phase of the electoral process had been characterized by delays and shortcomings. Mohamud was inaugurated in early June. The SRSG subsequently continued to engage with regional leaders. In mid-August he deplored a terrorist atrocity perpetrated against a hotel in Mogadishu, and in early October he strongly condemned al-Shabaab attacks against targets in Beledweyne (near the border with Ethiopia).

United Nations Integrated Transition Assistance Mission in Sudan—UNITAMS

Address: Khartoum, Sudan.

Internet: unitams.unmissions.org.

Special Representative of the UN Secretary-General: VOLKER PERTHES (Germany).

Establishment and Mandate: UNITAMS was established on 4 June 2020 by UN Security Council Resolution 2524. The activities of the mission—which is headquartered in the Sudanese capital, Khartoum—extend across the entire country, including the Darfur region, where the mandate and operational phase of the long-term AU/UN Hybrid Operation in Darfur (UNAMID) ended on 31 December. (UNAMID then entered a six-month final drawdown phase and was fully withdrawn from Sudan by 30 June 2021.) UNITAMS was mandated to co-operate closely with the Sudanese Transitional Government, Sudanese people, and UN entities to assist Sudan's democratic transition. It was also to support, as required, the implementation of peace agreements in conflict-affected areas; to assist government-led peacebuilding activities and the strengthening of human rights and rule of law institutions; and to support the mobilization of economic and development assistance, and the co-ordination of humanitarian assistance.

In January 2021 the UN Secretary-General stated deep concern over a recent rapid escalation of intercommunal violent clashes in the vicinity of El Geneina, West Darfur, which had caused 162 fatalities, numerous injuries, and large-scale displacement and destruction of property. He called on all militant groupings that remained outside the peace process to commit to peace negotiations. In early February the Special Representative of the UN Secretary-General (SRSG) welcomed the formation by Prime Minister Abdalla Hamdok of an expanded transitional Cabinet, incorporating representation of signatories of the Juba Agreement that had been concluded in October 2020 between the transitional administration and rebel movements. In March 2021 the UN Secretary-General reported that UNITAMS had reached its full operational capacity in mid-February. He urged the Sudanese transitional authorities swiftly to deploy a joint security-keeping force comprising government forces and armed movements that were signatories to the Juba Agreement. In June the UN Security Council extended the mission's mandate until 3 June 2022, and requested the Sudanese Government promptly to sign a status of mission agreement to enable its full and effective functioning. The Council mandated UNITAMS to refocus its efforts towards promoting peace talks, ceasefire monitoring, and supporting the national plan for the protection of civilians. In June 2021 UNITAMS

facilitated negotiations between the Sudanese Government and the al-Hilu faction of the Sudan People's Liberation Movement-North. In mid-September the UN Secretary-General condemned an attempt by the military to seize power in Sudan. On 25 October the Transitional Government of Sudan was overthrown in a military coup, the transitional institutions dissolved and the civilian leadership detained. The UN Secretary-General called for the immediate release of the detained government members. In November UNITAMS welcomed an agreement concluded between Hamdok and the military Commander-in-Chief Gen. Abdel Fattah al-Burhan to establish a new civilian transitional administration, but urged the immediate release of all those arrested during the coup. Hamdok resigned at the start of 2022. During January–February 2022 UNITAMS convened the first phase of UN-Facilitated Consultations for a Political Process, with diverse participation, including representatives of civil society, women's organizations, political parties, and academics and experts. Addressing the UN Security Council in March the SRSG noted continuing protests against the October 2021 coup and continuing violent repression of the protesters (including sexual violence). At the end of March 2022 UNITAMS welcomed a statement by the international Friends of Sudan Group (including Canada, France, Germany, Italy, the Netherlands, Norway, Saudi Arabia, Sweden, the United Arab Emirates and the United Kingdom) which welcomed ongoing efforts by UNITAMS, the AU and the Intergovernmental Authority on Development (IGAD) to facilitate a political process aimed at resolving the political crisis in Sudan. From April UNITAMS, IGAD and the AU initiated a new phase of the process, convening discussions with stakeholders to the Juba Peace Agreement in order to advance more formal political dialogue. They issued a joint statement, as the Trilateral Mechanism, in mid-May urging a lifting of the country's state of emergency and an end to violence on the part of the authorities, and reiterated their support to restoring constitutional order. At the end of May Sudan's military regime issued a decree ending the state of emergency. In early September the SRSG stated deep concern over a recent resurgence of violence in the Blue Nile Region, which had caused numerous deaths and significant displacement. Reporting to the UN Security Council in mid-September he noted a deterioration in Sudan's socioeconomic and human rights landscape and ongoing political stalemate, while emphasizing that the Trilateral Mechanism remained ready to mediate a resolution between the Sudanese stakeholders. The surge of violence in the Blue Nile Region, and also in Darfur, was highlighted (during May–August UNITAMS had confirmed 40 incidents of intercommunal violence, that had led to more than 300 civilian fatalities).

United Nations Office to the African Union—UNOAU

Address: Menelik II Ave, POB 3001, Addis Ababa, Ethiopia.

Telephone: (11) 5442275; **e-mail:** unoau-public-information@un.org; **internet:** unoau.unmissions.org.

Special Representative of the UN Secretary-General to the African Union and Head of Office: PARFAIT ONANGA-ANYANGA (Gabon).

Establishment and Mandate: UNOAU was established by Resolution 64/288 of the UN General Assembly, on 1 July 2010, with a mandate to enhance the partnership between the UN and African Union (AU) with respect to peace and security; to provide co-ordinated and consistent UN advice to the AU on short-term operational support matters and on long-term capacity building; and to render the UN presence in Addis Ababa more efficient in delivering support to the AU.

Activities: UNOAU's Division of Political Affairs promotes the strategic partnerships between the two organizations, in support of regional security mechanisms. The second principal Division, of Peacekeeping, Planning and Management, provides technical, logistical and administrative assistance to AU peace support operations. In particular, it focuses on child protection, counter-terrorism, mine action, small and light weapons, and disarmament, demobilization and reintegration programmes. A UN-AU Joint Task Force on Peace and Security, and a UN-AU 'Desk to Desk' consultative meeting on the prevention and management of conflict, convene regular consultations.

In April 2017 the inaugural UN-AU Annual Conference was convened, at which the UN Secretary-General and the Chairperson of the AU Commission endorsed a Joint UN-AU Framework for Enhanced Partnerships in Peace and Security. The second annual UN-AU Conference, held in July 2018, endorsed an Action Plan on the AU-UN Framework for the Implementation of the AU's Agenda 2063 and UN 2030 Agenda for Sustainable Development. The fifth session of the Conference, convened in December 2021, in New York, USA, urged the international community to accelerate the supply of COVID-19 vaccines in Africa.

United Nations Regional Office for Central Africa—UNOCA

Address: BP 23773, Cité de la Démocratie, Villas 55–57, Libreville, Gabon.

Telephone: 01-74-14-01; **internet:** unoca.unmissions.org.

Special Representative of the UN Secretary-General: ABDOU ABARRY (Niger).

Establishment and Mandate: UNOCA—covering the 10 member states of the Communauté Economique des Etats de l'Afrique Centrale (CEEAC)—was inaugurated in March 2011, with a mandate to extend the UN's good offices and other assistance to regional states and organizations in support of preventive diplomacy and the consolidation of peace. It is also mandated to work closely with UN and other entities to address cross-border challenges, such as organized crime, trafficking in arms, and the activities of armed groups. In August 2021 the Security Council extended UNOCA's mandate until 31 August 2023.

Activities: UNOCA's priority areas of activity include supporting conflict mediation, and, where requested, assisting with the peaceful conduct of elections in the region; facilitating cohesion in the general regional work of the UN, including in partnership with other agencies; promoting activities in partnership with the private sector and civil society networks; co-ordinating UN efforts in the region against armed groups; undertaking studies on regional challenges and threats; providing technical assistance aimed at advancing early warning and mediation capabilities; helping to build the capacity of CEEAC; promoting the formulation of a regional integrated approach to addressing cross-border insecurity; and combating maritime insecurity in the Gulf of Guinea. UNOCA has focused on the threats to regional stability caused by illicit cross-border movements, poaching and illegal trade in wildlife, and the Special Representative of the UN Secretary-General (SRSG) has promoted the development of an integrated regional anti-poaching approach. UNOCA acts as the secretariat of the UN Standing Advisory Committee on Security Questions in Central Africa, through which several regional arms control and confidence-building measures have been adopted, such as the 2010 Central African Convention for the Control of Small Arms and Light Weapons, their Ammunition, and All Parts and Components for their Manufacture, Repair and Assembly (Kinshasa Convention), which entered into force in March 2017. In October 2020 the UN Secretary-General approved a UN Strategy for Peace Consolidation, Conflict Prevention and Conflict Resolution in the Great Lakes region.

In June 2022 UNOCA and partners issued *Sustaining Peace in Central Africa through Addressing the Adverse Impact of Climate Change on Peace and Security,* which addressed six linkages between climate change and peace and security in the region: increased human mobility; increased intercommunal violence (particularly between herders and farmers); increased organized crime, and activities by non-state armed groups; a rise in maritime crime and piracy; a rise in land conflicts and food insecurity; and increased risk to the Congo Basin rainforest.

In June 2012 a Regional Strategy to Address the Threat and Impact of the Activities of the Lord's Resistance Army (LRA)—developed by UNOCA to address the challenges posed by the armed grouping to civilians in the Central African Republic (CAR), the Democratic Republic of the Congo (DRC), South Sudan, and in Uganda—was endorsed by the UN Security Council. The SRSG and African Union (AU) Special Envoy on the LRA have undertaken joint diplomatic missions to areas affected by the LRA. A UNOCA-AU workshop to promote co-ordination between AU-RTF, CAR and DRC military sector commanders that was convened in March 2018 established common practices to guide the repatriation of LRA defectors. In December 2019 UNOCA convened the 11th meeting of LRA 'focal points', with participation by representatives of CEEAC, LRA-affected countries, and other partners. In June 2021 the SRSG noted a pattern that during 2019–21 LRA attacks and abductions in Haut-Uélé and Bas-Uélé (DRC) had intensified over the period March–May (the last phase of the dry season, at which time movement is less hindered). During January–May 2021, meanwhile, some 60 people were reported to have defected from LRA splinter factions.

UNOCA has reported regularly to the UN Security Council on the activities of the terrorist grouping Boko Haram in the Lake Chad Basin area and northern Nigeria. (In March 2015 Boko Haram had pledged allegiance to Islamic State, formally becoming Islamic State's West Africa Province—ISWAP. However, a splinter faction subsequently re-identified as Boko Haram.) UNOCA has conducted regular missions to investigate the impact of Boko Haram's atrocities on the region, and to explore ways in which the UN might provide support to local communities. In mid-August 2018 the UN team monitoring the imposition of sanctions against Boko Haram presented to the UN Security Council a list of alleged financial sponsors

of the grouping, which—with ISWAP—was believed to benefit from the regional prevalence of an uncontrolled cash economy. In that month the Security Council issued a Presidential Statement that condemned the devastating impacts of ongoing terrorist activity in Central Africa and requested the UN Secretary-General to implement a review of UNOCA's work. UN sanctions were imposed on ISWAP in February 2020. In August 2020 UNOCA and UNOWAS were designated as co-leaders of the governance cluster of the regional task force guiding the Regional Stabilization, Recovery and Resilience Strategy for Areas Affected by Boko Haram in the Lake Chad Basin Region (adopted in August 2018 by the Lake Chad Basin Commission—LCBC). The inaugural meeting of the governance cluster was convened in March 2021. Also in that month, UNOCA engaged in a regional expert consultation on the gender dimensions of the prosecution, rehabilitation and reintegration of former Boko Haram members. In June the SRSG reported an intensification of Boko Haram-related activity in Cameroon and Chad during the period 1 December 2020–30 April 2021 (this having caused 145 civilian fatalities in Cameroon and 199 in Chad). In October the SRSG undertook a joint visit with his UNOWAS counterpart to Lake Chad Basin countries impacted by the Boko Haram insurgency. UNOCA participated in a workshop in March 2022 that addressed the preparation of a regional action plan (that was adopted later in the month by the LCBC) to support the implementation of the Regional Stabilization, Recovery and Resilience Strategy during 2022–24.

In November 2017 the SRSG expressed concern at an escalation of violent unrest in the anglophone western areas of Cameroon, and reiterated that UNOCA was ready to provide support towards achieving a peaceful resolution of the ongoing crisis. Visiting Cameroon in late February–early March 2018 the SRSG emphasized the UN's support for dialogue and readiness to assist national decentralization efforts within the framework of the Cameroonian Constitution. In June the UN Secretary-General noted continuing reports of alleged human rights violations in anglophone and Boko Haram-impacted areas of Cameroon. In late January 2020 the SRSG and the Secretary-General of CEEAC conducted a joint mission to Cameroon, in advance of legislative and municipal elections that were held in early February. In February the SRSG called on armed militants in that country to cease all attacks against civilians and to uphold international humanitarian and human rights legislation. In July the SRSG called for increased international engagement and co-ordination on resolving the situation in Cameroon. UNOCA and partner agencies organized two workshops in September, in Douala and Krabi, that addressed the protection of media workers. At the request of the Cameroonian authorities the SRSG visited Cameroon in March 2021. Meanwhile, in that year he was also maintaining lines of communication with leaders of Cameroonian armed groups who were based outside that country.

Special Appointments of the UN Secretary-General Concerned with His Good Offices and with Peacebuilding

SPECIAL ADVISERS

Special Adviser on Africa: CRISTINA DUARTE (Cabo Verde).

Special Adviser on the Prevention of Genocide: ALICE WAIRIMU NDERITU (Kenya).

Special Adviser on the Responsibility to Protect: GEORGE OKOTH-OBBO (Uganda).

SPECIAL ENVOYS

Special Envoy for the Great Lakes Region of Africa: HUANG XIA (People's Republic of China).

Special Envoy for the Horn of Africa: HANNA SERWAA TETTEH (Ghana).

SPECIAL REPRESENTATIVES

Special Representative on Sexual Violence in Conflict: PRAMILA PATTEN (Mauritius).

Special Representative on Violence against Children: Dr NAJAT MAALLA M'JID (Morocco).

Further high-level appointees of the UN Secretary-General are listed under Peacekeeping and Other UN Organizations Active in the Region.

World Food Programme—WFP

Address: Via Cesare Giulio Viola 68, Parco dei Medici, 00148 Rome, Italy.

Telephone: (06) 65131; **fax:** (06) 6590632; **e-mail:** wfpinfo@wfp.org; **internet:** www.wfp.org.

WFP became operational in 1962 as the UN's principal food assistance agency. It aims to alleviate acute hunger by providing emergency relief in humanitarian disaster situations. It also assists vulnerable populations in developing countries to improve nutrition, to eradicate chronic undernourishment, and to further social advancement by developing assets and promoting self-reliance. WFP was awarded the 2020 Nobel Peace Prize.

Organization

(October 2022)

The governing body of WFP is the Executive Board. An Executive Director is appointed jointly by the UN Secretary-General and the Director-General of FAO and is responsible for the management and administration of the Programme.

EXECUTIVE BOARD

The Board comprises 36 members, 18 of whom are elected by the UN Economic and Social Council and 18 by the Council of the Food and Agriculture Organization (FAO). The Board meets four times a year.

SECRETARIAT

Around 90% of WFP staff members work in the field. WFP administers some 88 country offices, and maintains six regional bureaux, located in Bangkok, Thailand (for Asia); Cairo, Egypt (for the Middle East, Central Asia and Eastern Europe); Panama City, Panama (for Latin America and the Caribbean); Johannesburg, South Africa (for southern Africa); Kampala, Uganda (for Central and Eastern Africa); and Dakar, Senegal (for West Africa).

Executive Director: DAVID MULDROW BEASLEY (USA).

Activities

WFP is the frontline UN agency in combating hunger. It focuses its efforts on the world's poorest countries, and aims to provide at least 90% of its total assistance to those designated as 'low-income food-deficit'. WFP has a particular focus on UN Sustainable Development Goal (SDG) 2 (Zero Hunger), which in 2022 was the focus of around 78% of the Programme's operational requirements; and SDG 17 (on achieving the Goals through strategic partnerships). A Country Strategic Plan (CSP) framework initiated by WFP in 2016 introduced a system of (standard) CSPs and (interim) ICSPs that were to be aligned flexibly to national priorities. WFP's Strategic Plan for 2022–26 focused on achieving the following five outcomes: People are better able to meet their urgent food and nutrition needs; People have better nutrition, health and education outcomes; People have improved and sustainable livelihoods; National programmes and systems are strengthened; and Humanitarian and development actors are more efficient and effective. A WFP management plan for 2022–24, approved by the Executive Board in November 2021, envisaged that in 2022 77% of resources would be allocated to crisis response operations, 19% to resilience-building activities, and 4% to addressing the root causes of food insecurity. In-kind food transfers were to account for 63% of WFP assistance in 2022, cash-based transfers for 35%, and commodity vouchers (redeemable against fixed quantities of specific foods) for less than 2%. During 2022 (as updated in September) WFP aimed to extend support to 152m. people.

WFP manages active trust funds for special purposes outside its regular operational programmes, with a view to supporting CSPs, in areas such as enhancing food security and nutrition, the development of supply chains, innovation acceleration, strengthening government capacities, and improving climate change and disaster risk resilience.

WFP aims to combat poverty in developing countries by promoting self-reliant families and communities. It emphasizes training and capacity-building elements within relief operations, such as income-generating activities and environmental protection measures; and seeks to integrate elements that strengthen disaster mitigation into development projects, including soil conservation, reafforestation, irrigation infrastructure, and transport construction and rehabilitation. No individual country is permitted to receive more than 10% of the Programme's available development resources.

WFP, FAO, IFAD and the UN Secretary-General collectively undertook preparations for a Food Systems Summit (FSS) that was held in September 2021, with a view to raising global awareness of challenges related to the production, processing and consumption of food, and to improving the output of safe, nutritious food. In January 2022, to support the follow-up to the FSS, a co-ordination hub was launched, under the joint leadership of WFP, FAO and IFAD, and assisted by a Champions Advisory Group comprising stakeholder representation by, *inter alia,* producers, the private sector, Indigenous peoples, youth and women.

Emergency Preparedness and Response: WFP uses geographic information systems to manage and visualize incoming data on crisis situations. Through its Vulnerability Analysis and Mapping (VAM) initiative the agency aims to identify potentially vulnerable groups of people, and efficiently to focus emergency contingency-planning and long-term assistance activities.

WFP co-sponsors, with FAO and the International Food Policy Research Institute, the Food Security Information Network, which compiles a *Global Report on Food Crises*. The 2022 edition of the report, published in May, found that 193m. people in 53 countries and territories were affected by episodes of acute food insecurity during 2021.

The UN Humanitarian Response Depot—a network of depots, based in Accra, Ghana; Dubai, United Arab Emirates; Subang, Malaysia; Panama City, Panama; Las Palmas, Spain; and Brindisi, Italy—stores essential rapid response equipment. Within the UN's 'Cluster Approach' to co-ordinating the international response to humanitarian disasters, WFP is a joint lead agency for the clusters on Emergency Telecommunications, and Logistics and Food Security, and is also actively involved in the Nutrition Cluster. WFP also manages the UN Humanitarian Air Service (UNHAS). When engaging in a crisis WFP dispatches an emergency preparedness team to quantify the amount and type of food assistance required, and to identify the beneficiaries, timescale and logistics underpinning the ensuing assistance programme. Emergency Food Security Assessments, either prompt or in-depth, analyse the impact of a crisis on households and community food security.

A UN policy brief on *The Impact of COVID-19 on Food Security and Nutrition,* issued in June 2020, outlined a series of recommended actions including: declaring food production, marketing and distribution to be an essential service everywhere; placing food and nutrition assistance at the core of social protection systems; and accelerating investment in both the immediate response and in developing long-term inclusive, resilient, environmentally sustainable food systems.

In November 2020 the joint WFP-FAO *Early Warning Analysis of Acute Food Insecurity Hotspots* reiterated the risk posed by the combination of the COVID-19 emergency (restricting employment and access to food) and conflict, and warned that precarious conditions might tip communities into catastrophic famine in Burkina Faso, north-eastern Nigeria, South Sudan and Yemen. During 2020–23 WFP, FAO and OCHA were to implement an extraordinary resource mobilization strategy aimed at preventing famine.

The inaugural meeting was convened in April 2021 of a High-Level Task Force on Preventing Famine, created in March by the UN Secretary-General.

In February 2022 WFP's Executive Director warned that the interaction of climate shocks and conflict, compounded by the COVID-19 pandemic and rising prices for food and essential supplies, was causing mounting starvation, mass migration, and destabilization. He estimated that at that time 45m. people were close to famine, that the numbers of food-insecure people had soared to 283m. (from 235m. in early 2020), and forecast that the consequence of not addressing the crisis immediately would be further famine and deeper destabilization and insecurity. In March 2022 WFP emphasized the need to find solutions to the further shock to global food and energy prices prompted by the Russian Federation's invasion of Ukraine. (Russia and Ukraine were major exporters of cereals to the global markets, Ukraine also of sunflower oil, and Russia of crude and processed petroleum.) WFP was invited to engage with a joint G7-World Bank Global Alliance for Food Security that was launched in May at a meeting of G7 ministers responsible for development. In that month WFP urged the prompt opening of ports in Ukraine's Odesa area, to enable imports and exports of grain (Ukraine's silos of grain awaiting export were reported to be full at that time). Rising food and fuel prices were reported to be driving up WFP's operational costs significantly. Meanwhile, WFP emphasized the urgent need to address the root causes of food crises and to build people-focused resilient food systems. In July negotiations held in İstanbul, Türkiye, under the auspices of the UN and Türkiye, culminated in the conclusion by Russia and Ukraine, in the presence of the UN Secretary-General and the President of Türkiye, of a UN-backed agreement aimed at alleviating global food insecurity by enabling the resumption of exports of grain, sunflower oil and other essential goods from Odesa and two other Ukrainian Black Sea ports (that had hitherto been blockaded by Russia), and at facilitating fertilizer and grain exports from Russia (which had been subjected to punitive sanctions).

Food Security and Nutrition: WFP is a participant in the long-standing intergovernmental Committee on World Food Security (CFS), which develops and endorses policy guidance and recommendations that are based on work undertaken by WFP, IFAD and FAO, and also on scientific evidence-based reports produced regularly by a UN High Level Panel of Experts (HLPE) on Food Security and Nutrition (established in 2009). An HLPE report titled *Food Security and Nutrition: Building a Global Narrative towards 2030* was published in July 2020.

Jointly with 12 other partners WFP participates in the Integrated Food Security Phase Classification (IPC) partnership, which aims to analyse and address the multidimensional characteristics of food security issues. The IPC classifies crises under the following categories: acute food security, chronic food security, or acute malnutrition. The severity of acute food insecurity is categorized in accordance with the following scale: minimal, stressed, crisis, emergency, famine (catastrophe).

WFP recognizes that undernutrition—the insufficient intake of nutrients—undermines energy and health, that poor nutrition can also lead to obesity and be a contributory factor in a variety of non-communicable diseases, and that extreme malnutrition can, as well as being potentially fatal, cause stunting and impaired development in children. The impacts of malnutrition can also have the onwards consequences of undermining economies and impeding sustainable development. WFP implements targeted programmes that prevent and treat malnutrition in high-risk groups such as young children, pregnant and breastfeeding women, and people who are living with HIV or tuberculosis. WFP contributes to the implementation of the Decade of Action on Nutrition (2016–25), declared in April 2016 by the UN General Assembly.

Where used, full WFP rations comprise essential food items (staple foods such as wheat flour or rice; pulses such as lentils and chickpeas; vegetable oil fortified with vitamins A and D; sugar; and iodized salt). Supplementary rations (such as fortified blended foods) are designed to improve the nutritional intake of beneficiaries who have access to some food supplies.

The Centre of Excellence Against Hunger, in Brasília, Brazil, inaugurated by WFP and the Brazilian authorities in 2011, utilizes techniques used in a long-term Brazilian initiative known as Fome Zero (Zero Hunger) to support other countries in ending malnutrition and hunger. The Centre is a global reference point on school meals, nutrition and food security.

An African School Feeding Network was founded by 20 African countries in 2015.

WFP is a co-sponsor of the Joint UN Programme on HIV/AIDS (UNAIDS). It focuses resources on supporting the nutrition and food security of households and communities affected by HIV/AIDS, and on promoting food security as a means of mitigating extreme poverty and vulnerability and thereby combating the spread and impact of HIV/AIDS.

Climate Action: WFP aims to enable farmers to protect their enterprises from the impacts of climatic shocks—such as droughts, floods and tropical storms—noting that, after conflict situations, climate extremes represent the next major threat to food security and livelihoods, having the capacity to destroy crop production and local infrastructures, and to disrupt markets. WFP (including through the Weather Risk Management Facility, a joint initiative with IFAD) promotes access to climate information services and forecast-based financing systems, and also facilitates access to agriculture output index-based macro- and microinsurance schemes. Such activities are increasingly supported by funding mechanisms such as the Green Climate Fund (see UNEP). WFP also supports governments with incorporating climate risk assessments into their planning, and with accessing funding for priority climate risk management activities.

Food for Assets (FFA): WFP's FFA projects focus on enhancing long-term food security by meeting the immediate nourishment requirements of food-insecure people (through food rations or cash-based transfers), thereby providing them with more energy and time to work on building lasting sustainable community assets, and to undertake livelihood and self sufficiency enhancing activities. FFA projects include, for example, building new irrigation or terracing infrastructures; soil and water conservation activities; and constructing schools and health clinics. The implementation, where possible, of targeted cash assistance (including mobile and e-money, physical cash, debit cards, and e- or else card vouchers) to buy food, including fresh produce, boosts local output as well as retail activities, and simultaneously reduces the Programme's food transportation and storage costs. The value of virtual money and vouchers can be increased or reduced depending upon the severity of an emergency situation. WFP's SCOPE digital platform stores data on individual and household beneficiaries and facilitates the management of WFP

transfers. WFP continues to provide basic rations in emergency situations, and special nutrition support where needed. It is WFP policy to buy food as near as possible to the communities that require it. In more than 40 developing countries WFP works to build the capacity of smallholder and low-income farmers to compete competitively in the market place.

RECENT OPERATIONS

Sub-Saharan Africa: In 2016 WFP designated Boko Haram-affected areas of north-eastern Nigeria as a Level 3 Emergency (the highest level). A US $1,436m. CSP for Nigeria, covering 2019–22, was focused on the transfer of expertise to the national and local authorities and to communities. During February–July 2022 WFP's funding requirements for operations to support around 2.6m. food-insecure people in the Central Sahel region (Burkina Faso, Mali and Niger)—which, undermined by climatic shocks, insecurity, displacement and poverty, was declared a WFP Level 3 Emergency in September 2019—amounted to $174m. WFP's European Union-co-funded CRIALCES (Réponse à la Crise Alimentaire au Centre Sahel) initiative, launched in July 2020 and ongoing in 2022, aimed to strengthen national food systems, improve children's and women's nutritional status, and support livelihoods in the region. An ICSP for South Sudan, covering the period 1 January 2018–31 December 2022, at a cost of $5,044m., was designed to support 6.4m. beneficiaries. In March 2022 WFP warned that more than 70% of the South Sudanese population would struggle to survive at the impending peak of the lean season (March–August, the interim phase between harvests)—with unprecedented levels of food insecurity attributed to the impacts of conflict, the COVID-19 pandemic, price rises, and climatic shocks.

In January 2022 WFP issued a Regional Drought Response Plan for the Horn of Africa, with a particular focus on southern and south-eastern parts of Ethiopia, semi-arid and arid zones of Kenya, and a large area of south-central Somalia, all affected by the impacts of three consecutive poor rainy seasons, compounded by conflict, flash floods, high food prices, desert locust swarms, and effects of the COVID-19 pandemic, that had caused widespread hardship, and emaciation and death of livestock. Local food security was subsequently exacerbated by repercussions of the war in Ukraine. In May WFP issued a revision of the Plan, covering the period May–December, and requiring funding of US $982m.; some 7.8m. people were to be supported through, *inter alia*, the provision of food and cash assistance, fortified foods for young children and for pregnant or nursing mothers, and cash grants for sustaining livestock. A CSP being undertaken in Ethiopia during 1 July 2020–30 June 2025, at a cost of $3,938m., aimed to ensure that 20.3m. beneficiaries in crisis-affected populations (including refugees) met their basic food and nutrition requirements. In particular, the Plan was to support vulnerable and food-insecure populations to establish shock-resilient livelihoods and increase consumption of nutritious foods; to strengthen the capacity of emergency preparedness systems; to improve safety nets and supply chains management; and to facilitate cost-effective logistics services. In February 2021 WFP emphasized the urgent need to scale up a collective response in Ethiopia's Tigray region (where in November 2020 the federal Ethiopian Government had launched a military offensive, prompting the withdrawal of humanitarian agency personnel): 9.4m. people overall in northern Ethiopia were deemed to require food assistance as at January 2022. WFP provided high energy biscuits and hot meals to refugees who fled from Tigray into neighbouring Sudan. Meanwhile, a $1,941m. Somalia CSP, covering the period January 2022–December 2025, was focused on both crisis response and building resilience. In September 2022 WFP reported that more than 7m. people in Somalia were acutely food insecure, and that 213,000 were suffering famine conditions. A $1,100m. CSP was being implemented in Kenya during 2018–23 in support of a national strategy aimed at achieving 100% food and nutrition security.

In October 2017 WFP declared a Level 3 Emergency in response to food insecurity in the DRC. By March 2022 WFP reported that 25.9m. people in that country were highly food-insecure (10m. more than at the start of 2020), with emergency levels of malnutrition reportedly affecting 5.4m.; the scope of the food insecurity covered the conflict-affected regions of North Kivu, South Kivu, Ituri, Kasaï and Tanganyika. A US $1,674m. CSP for the DRC, was approved by the Executive Board in November 2020, covering the period 1 January 2021–31 December 2024. A $926m. ICSP was aiming to support 1.7m. critically food-insecure people in the Central African Republic during 2018–22. In March 2019 WFP declared a Level 3 Emergency in Mozambique; a CSP that was being implemented by WFP in that country during 2017–22, at a cost of $1,092m., aimed to assist 6.3m. beneficiaries. During 2019–23 WFP was implementing a $364m. CSP to support 3.8m. beneficiaries in the drought-affected Grand Sud area of Madagascar.

Finance

The Programme is funded by voluntary contributions from donor countries, intergovernmental bodies such as the European Commission, and the private sector. Contributions are made in the form of commodities, finance and services (particularly shipping). Commitments to the International Emergency Food Reserve (IEFR), from which WFP provides the majority of its food supplies, and to the Immediate Response Account of the IEFR, are also made on a voluntary basis by donors. WFP's estimated operational requirements for 2022 (as forecast in September) totalled some US $22,200m.

Publications

Food and Nutrition Handbook.

State of Food Security and Nutrition in the World (annually, with FAO, IFAD, UNICEF and WHO).

World Hunger (series).

Other papers, situation reports, brochures.

WFP supports an African Union-led *Cost of Hunger in Africa* series.

WFP maintains an online *HungerMap LIVE*.

Food and Agriculture Organization of the United Nations—FAO

Address: Viale delle Terme di Caracalla, 00153 Rome, Italy.
Telephone: (06) 57051; **e-mail:** fao-hq@fao.org; **internet:** www.fao.org.

FAO, the first specialized agency of the UN to be founded after the Second World War, aims to eradicate hunger and malnutrition and achieve food security for all; to eliminate poverty and facilitate economic and social progress for all; and to promote the sustainable management and utilization of natural resources (land, water, air, climate and genetic) for the benefit of present and future generations. FAO serves as a co-ordinating agency for development programmes in the whole range of food and agriculture, including forestry and fisheries.

Organization

(October 2022)

CONFERENCE

The governing body is the FAO Conference of member nations. It meets every two years, formulates policy, determines the organization's programme and budget on a biennial basis, and elects new members. It also elects the Director-General and the Independent Chairman of the Council.

COUNCIL

The FAO Council is composed of representatives of 49 member nations, elected by the Conference for rotating three-year terms. It is the interim governing body of FAO between sessions of the Conference, and normally holds at least five sessions in each biennium. The main Governing Committees of the Council are: the Finance, Programme, and Constitutional and Legal Matters Committees, and the Technical Committees on Agriculture, Commodity Problems, Fisheries and Forestry.

SECRETARIAT

The Director-General is supported by three Deputy Directors-General, a Chief Scientist, a Chief Economist and two Assistant Directors-General. Principal divisions, each headed by a Director, align under Partnership and Outreach; Natural Resources and Sustainable Production; and Economic and Social Development.
Director-General: Qu Dongyu (People's Republic of China).

REGIONAL OFFICES

FAO maintains five regional offices, 11 subregional offices, five liaison offices (in Yokohama, Japan; Washington, DC, USA; Geneva, Switzerland, and New York, USA: liaison with the UN; and Brussels, Belgium: liaison with the EU), and more than 130 country offices.
Africa: POB 1628, Accra, Ghana; tel. (30) 2610930; fax (30) 2668427; e-mail fao-ro-africa@fao.org; internet www.fao.org/africa; a Regional Conference for Africa is normally convened every 2 years; Regional Rep. Abebe Haile Gabriel.
Subregional Office for Central Africa: POB 2643, Libreville, Gabon; tel. 01-44-33-09; fax 01-74-00-35; e-mail fao-sfc@fao.org; internet www.fao.org/africa/central-africa; Co-ordinator Hélder Muteia.
Subregional Office for Eastern Africa: CMC Rd, nr ILRI, Kebele 12/13, Bole Sub City, Gurd Shola, Addis Ababa, Ethiopia; tel. (11) 6478888; fax (11) 6478800; e-mail fao-sfe@fao.org; internet www.fao.org/africa/eastern-africa; Co-ordinator Chimimba David Phiri.
Subregional Office for Southern Africa: POB 3730, Harare, Zimbabwe; tel. (4) 253655; e-mail fao-sfs@fao.org; internet www.fao.org/africa/southern-africa; Co-ordinator Patrice Talla Takoukam.
Subregional Office for West Africa: BP 3300, Dakar, Senegal; tel. 33-889-16-59; internet www.fao.org/africa/west-africa/en; Regional Rep. Gouantoueu Robert Guei (Côte d'Ivoire).

Activities

FAO's Strategic Framework for 2022–31, endorsed by the Conference in June 2021, aimed to support the UN's 2030 Agenda for Sustainable Development by guiding a global transformation to more resilient, inclusive, efficient and sustainable agrifood systems, characterized by four guiding aspirations: Better Production, Better Nutrition, Better Environment, and Better Life, with a strong focus on leaving no one behind. The Framework placed a particular focus on the achievement of Sustainable Development Goal (SDG) 1: End poverty in all its forms everywhere; SDG 2: End hunger, to achieve food security and improved nutrition, and to promote sustainable agriculture; and SDG 10: Reduce inequalities in and among countries. It included four cross-cutting 'accelerators'—innovation, technology, data, and 'complements' (i.e. human capital, governance and institutions)—to be prioritized in all of its programme interventions. The Framework had 20 inter-disciplinary programme priority areas ('PPAs'), grouped under each of the four aspirations. The PPAs for Better Production were: green innovation, blue (i.e. marine) transformation, one health, small-scale producers' equitable access to resources, and digital agriculture; for Better Nutrition: healthy diets for all, nutrition for the most vulnerable, safe food for everyone, reducing food loss and waste, and transparent markets and trade; for Better Environment: climate change mitigating and adapted agrifood systems, bioeconomy for sustainable food and agriculture, and biodiversity and ecosystem services for food and agriculture; and for Better Life: gender equality and rural women's empowerment, inclusive rural transformation, achieving sustainable urban food systems, agriculture and food emergencies, resilient agrifood systems, FAO's Hand-in-Hand initiative (q.v.), and scaling up investment. A Medium-Term Plan aligned with the 2022–31 Strategic Framework, was being implemented during 2022–25.

FAO aims to serve as a knowledge network in support of development, as well as to provide a neutral forum to enhance public-private collaboration and to bring knowledge directly to the field. In February 2020 FAO was a founding signatory of the Rome Call for Artificial Intelligence Ethics, which outlined fundamental principles to ensure that technological advances serve all of humanity and contribute to protection of the global environment. FAO has aimed to lead efforts to transform food systems on the basis of a digital, data and scientific approach. In December 2020 the FAO Council approved a new Strategy for Private Sector Engagement.

The FAO Director-General assists the UN Secretary-General's chairmanship of a High-Level Task Force (HLTF) on Global Food and Nutrition Security that was established in 2008 and has 22 member (mainly UN) agencies. FAO hosts at its headquarters the intergovernmental Committee on World Food Security (CFS: established in 1974 and reformed in 2009), which is tasked with influencing hunger elimination programmes at global, regional and national level, taking into account that food security relates not just to agriculture but also to economic access to food, adequate nutrition, social safety nets and human rights. FAO, WFP and IFAD, and science-based reports produced regularly by a UN High Level Panel of Experts (HLPE) on Food Security and Nutrition (established in 2009), support the policy work of the CFS.

In March 2022, in an address to an extraordinary meeting of the ministers responsible for agriculture of the Group of Seven (G7) advanced economies, the FAO Director-General stated great concern at the level of food prices in the context of the Russian Federation's military invasion of Ukraine in late February, noting that prices had already been at a record high (attributed to market conditions, and high prices for energy and agricultural services and fertilizers). The Director-General warned that the international food price and food security outlook remained very uncertain, given that Russia and Ukraine had accounted for around 30% of wheat exports and 55% of sunflower oil to global markets in 2021, and were also major exporters of barley, maize and rapeseed oil; in addition, Russia was a significant exporter of fertilizers. Also in March 2022, the G7 leaders emphasized the role of the Agricultural Market Information System (q.v.) in sharing information and exploring options to keep food prices under control. FAO was invited to engage with a new G7-World Bank Global Alliance for Food Security that was launched in May at a meeting of G7 ministers responsible for development. In July negotiations held in İstanbul, Türkiye, under the auspices of the UN and Türkiye, culminated in the conclusion by Russia and Ukraine, in the presence of the UN Secretary-General and the President of Türkiye, of a UN-backed agreement aimed at alleviating global food insecurity by enabling the resumption of exports of grain, sunflower oil and other essential goods from Odesa and two other Ukrainian Black Sea ports (that had hitherto been blockaded by Russia), and at facilitating fertilizer and grain exports from Russia (which had been subjected to punitive sanctions).

In 2022 FAO was implementing the following principal regional initiatives in Africa: Africa's commitment to end hunger by 2025; Pursuing an inclusive agricultural transformation agenda to reduce poverty; and Enhancing the resilience of livelihoods and production systems.

The first meeting of a youth-led World Food Forum, held in October 2021, focused on the transformation of food systems to achieve the SDGs, and in particular on eliminating hunger.

World Food Day, commemorating the foundation of FAO, is held annually on 16 October.

Food Systems Summit (FSS): In September 2021, at the start of the 76th UN General Assembly, FAO, WFP, IFAD and the UN Secretary-General collectively hosted the FSS (from New York, USA, in a virtual format), with a view to raising global awareness of challenges related to the production, processing, distribution and consumption of food, and to improving the output of safe, nutritious food. A multi-stakeholder Advisory Committee had been established in June 2020 to provide strategic guidance on the summit. This was supported by an independent Scientific Group, a system-wide UN Task Force, and a Champions Network comprising stakeholders in food systems from around the world. A high-level Pre-Summit gathering was held in July 2021, in Rome, with in-person participation by more than 500 people from more than 130 countries, and 22,000 'virtual' delegates from 183 countries. National dialogues on food systems were convened across 148 countries. The FSS focused on the following five 'Action Tracks': (1) Ensure access to safe and nutritious food for all (1.1: Promote food security and reduce hunger; 1.2: Improve access to nutritious foods; and 1.3: Make food safer); (2) Shift to sustainable consumption patterns (2.1: Enable, inspire and motivate people to enjoy healthy and sustainable options; and 2.2: Slash food loss and waste and transition to a circular economy); (3) Boost nature-positive production (3.1: Protect natural ecosystems from new deforestation and from being converted into sources of food and feed production; 3.2: Manage, sustainably, existing food production systems; and 3.3: Restore degraded ecosystems and rehabilitate soil function for sustainable food production); (4) Advance equitable livelihoods (4.1: Rebalance agency within food systems—including a greater focus on the rights of and participation by often excluded groups; 4.2: Eliminate worker exploitation and ensure decent work in food systems; and 4.3: Localize food systems—including prioritizing short food chains and local markets); and (5) Build resilience to vulnerabilities, shocks and stress (5.1: Build food systems resilience; 5.2: Ensure universal food access to build resilience—i.e. reframe food as a public common good and human right, rather than as a commodity; and 5.3: Develop climate-resilient development pathways for the transformation of food systems and achievement of the UN SDGs). Governance—i.e. both FSS governance and broader food systems governance—was identified as a cross-cutting action area. A co-ordination hub, jointly led by FAO, WFP and IFAD, was established in January 2022 to support the follow-up to the summit, by collaborating with the intergovernmental CFS and the UN High Level Panel of Experts on Food Security and Nutrition (q.v.), and by strengthening synergies with the UN High-Level Political Forum (HLPF) on Sustainable Development, financing for development, and other intergovernmental processes relating to the environment, biodiversity, climate, food security, health and nutrition. The hub

was to be assisted by a Champions Advisory Group comprising strong stakeholder representation by, *inter alia,* producers, the private sector, Indigenous peoples, youth and women. Until 2030 the UN Secretary-General was to submit an annual report to the HLPF on progress in following up the FSS, and was to convene a biennial global post-FSS stocktaking meeting.

In May 2022 FAO helped to launch, as a core group member, a Coalition of Action for Healthy Diets from Sustainable Food Systems.

BETTER PRODUCTION

FAO promotes innovation, technologies and policies to promote green business opportunities across sustainable crop, livestock and forestry production systems, as well as a transformation to efficient, resilient 'blue' food systems.

FAO promotes an integrated One Health approach to the pursuit of safe and resilient agrifood systems and the protection of the environment and biodiversity, working closely with WHO, UNEP and the World Organisation for Animal Health (OIE).

FAO promotes equitable access to land and water resources and supports integrated land and water management, including river basin management and improved irrigation systems. In May 2012 the CFS endorsed a set of landmark Voluntary Guidelines on the Responsible Governance of Tenure of Land, Fisheries and Forests in the Context of National Food Security, with the aim of supporting governments in safeguarding the rights of citizens to own or have access to natural resources.

FAO's Agro-Ecological Zoning (AEZ) methodology, developed jointly with the International Institute for Applied Systems Analysis, is used for land resources assessment, identifying homogenous and contiguous areas possessing similar soil, land and climate characteristics. FAO's database of Global Agro-Ecological Zones (GAEZ) is updated periodically. FAO has developed AQUASTAT as a global information system concerned with global water issues, and comprising databases, country and regional profiles, surveys and maps. AquaCrop, CropWat and ClimWat are further productivity models and databases which have been developed to help to assess crop requirements and potential yields.

FAO promotes the equitable access of small-scale producers and family farmers to economic and natural resources, markets, services, education, information and technologies. Accessible digital technologies are also promoted, in agrifood systems, to enhance resilience, productivity and market opportunities. A 1,000 Digital Village Initiative was being piloted in 2022 to advance the digitalization of rural areas.

Through its Progressive Management Pathway for Antimicrobial Resistance (FAO-PMP-AMR) FAO supports countries to develop national action plans to guide the prudent use of antimicrobials in agriculture and food production and the prevention and control of antimicrobial resistance (AMR) in food systems. In June 2019 FAO, the OIE and WHO collectively established an AMR Multi Partner Trust Fund, with initial funding of US $5m. FAO, the OIE and WHO maintain an online Global Database for Antimicrobial Resistance Country Self Assessment. FAO also helped to formulate a Progressive Control Pathway for Foot and Mouth Disease (PCP-FMD).

FAO works with regional and international associations to develop seed networks, to encourage the use of improved seed production systems, to elaborate quality control and certification mechanisms and to co-ordinate seed security activities, in particular in areas prone to natural or man-made disasters. In November 2011 the FAO Council adopted the Second Global Plan of Action for Plant Genetic Resources for Food and Agriculture (updating the first, 1996 Global Plan). The International Treaty on Plant Genetic Resources for Food and Agriculture, which was adopted by the FAO Conference in 2001 and entered into force in June 2004, provides a framework to ensure access to plant genetic resources and to related knowledge and technologies. The Treaty's Benefit-sharing Fund (BSF) provides finance to enable small-scale farmers in developing countries to conserve principal food crops and build resilience to impacts of climate change. By 2022 around 1,750 gene banks had been established worldwide, storing more than 7m. plant samples, covering both food crops and related wild variants.

FAO hosts the secretariat of the International Plant Protection Convention. Other Regional Plant Protection Organizations (RPPOs) and National Plant Protection Organizations (NPPOs) work to promote harmonized phytosanitary standards and measures in the context of the IPPC. Common global challenges and collective strategies are discussed at an annual RPPO Technical Consultation.

Through the Food Chain Crisis (FCC) Management Framework FAO addresses, by means of a comprehensive, multidisciplinary approach, risks posed to the human food chain, human health, food security, local livelihoods and national economies by threats such as food-borne pathogens, mycotoxins, locust and other insect infestations, avian influenza, peste des petits ruminants (PPR), fall armyworm (FAW), and wheat rust and banana diseases. The Framework integrates prevention, early warning, preparedness, and response to food chain emergencies, from food production to food consumption.

The FCC operates through an Intelligence and Coordination Unit, an Emergency and Resilience Division, and the Emergency Prevention Systems (EMPRES)—which has three thematic divisions: EMPRES Plant Protection, EMPRES Animal Health, and EMPRES Food Safety. In November 2021 FAO launched a global information system, EMPRES-i+.

In October 2016 FAO and the OIE launched an initiative aimed at eradicating by 2030 PPR, a highly contagious viral disease affecting goats and sheep in around 70 countries in Africa, the Middle East and Asia. At a global ministerial conference on Partnering and Investing for a PPR-Free World, jointly organized by FAO and the OIE in September 2018, 45 states pledged renewed commitment to the eradication of PPR. It was estimated at that time that PPR caused annual economic losses in excess of US $2,100m., globally, and that, in developing and emerging economies, small ruminants represented the principal livestock resource of around 300m. poor rural families.

FAO was implementing a Global Action for Fall Armyworm Control initiative during 2020–23, which aimed to mobilize some US $500m. to co-ordinate global and regional monitoring and control of FAW (a pest that has spread rapidly in recent years and increasingly poses a threat to smallholders' crops in Africa, the Middle East and Asia and the Pacific; in November 2021 FAO reported that more than 70 countries in those regions were combating FAW).

FAO's global Desert Locust Information Service (DLIS) monitors and issues early warning alerts on invasions of desert locusts, swarms of which have the capacity to breed and migrate rapidly, posing a significant threat to food security. FAO also undertakes national capacity-building activities and training on locust control, carries out field assessment missions, co-ordinates locust control operations, and extends emergency assistance during upsurges in locust populations (i.e. when uncontrolled breeding occurs for successive seasons, leading to the formation of 'hopper bands' of flightless juveniles and to adult swarms; in the most extreme scenario widespread intense infestations are referred to as a 'plague'). Three specialized FAO locust commissions cover arid and semi-arid areas of Africa and Asia where desert locusts are particularly prevalent. (In times of plague the scope of desert locusts can spread from their usual habitat, covering around 16m. square km and including around 30 countries, to an area of up to 29m. square km, affecting twice as many countries.) Main responsibility for local survey and control activities lies with national ministries responsible for agriculture. Control methods include aerial, vehicle-mounted or manual spraying of affected areas with conventional chemical pesticides (of which 10 have been approved by an advisory body of experts: the Pesticide Referee Group); biopesticides; or insect control regulators. FAO promotes the use of biopesticides during control operations. During 2020–21 FAO supported a series of emergency locust control operations in East Africa, Yemen, Iran and Pakistan (see under *Emergency Preparedness and Response*).

The Joint FAO/International Atomic Energy Agency Division maintains a network of agriculture and biotechnology laboratories. Through its Animal Production and Health Laboratory, an OIE collaborating centre, the Division works to detect and control transboundary animal and zoonotic diseases. It manages a veterinary diagnostic laboratory network (VETLAB) and an iVetNet Information Platform. In 2020 the Division formulated standard operating procedures to detect and monitor the SARS-CoV-2 virus that causes COVID-19, and provided technical guidance on COVID-19 at the animal-human interface to veterinary diagnostic laboratories in more than 100 FAO member states.

FAO hosts the secretariat of the Global Forum on Agricultural Research, which was established in 1996 as a collaboration of research centres, non-governmental and private sector organizations and development agencies. The Forum aims to strengthen research and promote knowledge partnerships concerned with the alleviation of poverty, the enhancement of food security and the sustainable use of natural resources. Furthermore, FAO hosts the secretariat of the Science Council of the Consultative Group on International Agricultural Research (CGIAR), which aims to mobilize global scientific expertise.

FAO aims to facilitate and secure the long-term sustainable development of capture fisheries and aquaculture, in both inland and marine waters, and to promote their contribution to world food security. It plays a leading role in working towards attainment of SDG 14: To conserve and sustainably use the oceans, seas and marine resources for sustainable development. In February 2021 FAO's Committee on Fisheries acknowledged the role of sustainable managed aquatic food systems in combating poverty and malnutrition, leading to the incorporation of a Blue Transformation concept as a priority area in FAO's new Strategic Framework.

FAO collates statistics on global capture and aquaculture production, publishing *The State of World Fisheries and Aquaculture* every two years, while a GLOBEFISH network focuses on market trends, tariffs and other industry issues. FAO extends technical support to improve the management and conservation of aquatic resources, trade of products, preservation, marketing and quality assurance. FAO works to ensure that small-scale fishing communities

(accounting for around 90% of the sector's work force) reap equitable benefits from the international trade in fish (including crustaceans and molluscs), fish products and fish by-products (such as fish heads, backbones and viscera). The agency led an initiative in 1999 to establish the Regional Fishery Body Secretariat Network (RSN) as a mechanism to facilitate the exchange of information, data and best practices among FAO and non-FAO regional fishery bodies or arrangements. FAO hosted the eighth meeting of the RSN, as a virtual event, in February 2021.

In February 1999 the FAO Committee on Fisheries adopted voluntary international measures, within the framework of a 1995 Code of Conduct for Responsible Fishing (CCRF), in order to reduce over-exploitation of the world's fish resources. Voluntary guidelines concerning the so-called eco-labelling and certification of fish and fish products were adopted in March 2005. FAO's FishCode programme supports developing countries in implementing the CCRF. Several international plans of action (IPOA) have been elaborated within the context of the Code, including the IPOA to Prevent, Deter and Eliminate Illegal, Unreported and Unregulated Fishing (IPOA-IUU, 2001). In June 2014 FAO endorsed a series of Voluntary Guidelines for Securing Sustainable Small-Scale Fisheries (SSF).

In 2017 FAO initiated a Global Programme to Support the Implementation of the 2009 Agreement on Port State Measures to Prevent, Deter and Eliminate Illegal, Unreported and Unregulated Fishing (which had been endorsed by the FAO Conference in November 2009 and entered into force in June 2016), and complementary international instruments. The Global Programme had a particular focus on assisting developing states to formulate related national strategies, policy and legislation.

FAO promotes preventive measures to reduce marine litter and microplastics, including the development of biodegradable materials for fishing gear. In July 2018 the Committee on Fisheries endorsed a series of FAO Voluntary Guidelines for the Marking of Fishing Gear, with a view to reducing the level of discarded so-called 'ghost gear' that represents a significant proportion of marine plastic pollution, putting marine species at risk.

More than 600 fish species are produced in aquaculture, with a particular focus on salmonids, carps, tilapias and shrimps. The establishment of a Global Aquaculture Advancement Partnership (GAAP), conceptualized by FAO, and comprising governments, UN agencies, non-governmental organizations and private sector interests, was approved by more than 50 states in October 2013; GAAP was tasked with pursuing sustainable solutions to meeting the growing global demand for fish products, over a 10–15-year time period. In December 2021 the FAO Council adopted a Global Action Plan on AqGR, and FAO has developed an Aquatic Genetic Resources (AqGR) Monitoring System, with a view to promoting the sustainable conservation of genetic diversity in aquaculture production.

FAO was designated as the lead agency supporting the International Year of Artisanal Fisheries and Aquaculture, which was observed during 2022.

BETTER NUTRITION

FAO, the World Food Programme (WFP), the International Fund for Agricultural Development (IFAD) and the World Health Organization (WHO) participate in the Steering Committee of UN Nutrition, which was initiated in early 2021 to co-ordinate UN agencies in advancing nutrition and eliminating hunger, malnutrition and obesity.

In November 2014 FAO, WFP and WHO, in co-operation with the HLTF, and other partners, organized the Second International Conference on Nutrition (ICN2, ICN1 having been convened in December 1992). ICN2 reviewed progress achieved since 1992 towards improving nutrition, and—taking into account subsequent advances in science and technology and changes to food systems—endorsed the Rome Declaration on Nutrition and Framework for Action, aimed at eradicating malnutrition and ensuring that nutritious diets become available for all. In April 2016 FAO welcomed the designation by the UN General Assembly of 2016–25 as the UN Decade of Action on Nutrition; implementation of the Decade was led by FAO and WHO, in co-ordination with WFP, IFAD and the UN Children's Fund. A new Framework for the Urban Food Agenda, which aimed to promote issues of nutrition and food systems in urban planning and policymaking, was launched in March 2019.

In the UN's flagship annual *State of Food Security and Nutrition in the World* report, jointly prepared by FAO, IFAD, WFP, UNICEF and WHO, food security is defined as adequate access to food in both quality and quantity. The principal indicator used for ascertaining progress towards the eradication of hunger is SDG 2, Indicator 2.1.1: 'Prevalence of Undernourishment' (PoU—i.e. the estimated proportion of people with habitual food consumption that is insufficient to provide sufficient dietary energy levels to maintain a normal active and healthy life). In 2017 estimates derived from FAO's Food Insecurity Experience Scale (FIES) that related to the prevalence of severe food insecurity were incorporated for the first time into the *State of Food Security and Nutrition in the World*, to supplement the metrics on PoU. (The FIES—initiated by FAO during 2014—provides internationally comparable measurements of the difficulty of accessing food, using data gathered in response to direct interviews with households or individuals.) Severe food insecurity refers to the exhaustion of food supplies, and to resulting hunger and grave impacts on health, wellbeing and ability to function. In 2019 *State of Food Security and Nutrition in the World* included, for the first time, FIES estimates of the prevalence of moderate as well as severe food insecurity, to address progress made towards achieving SDG 2, Indicator 2.1.2, relating to the ability to access nutritious and sufficient food, beyond the more extreme focus of 2.1.1 on the elimination of hunger. Moderate food insecurity is defined as a lack of assured, consistent access to food, involving the need at certain times to reduce the quality and/or the quantity of food intake.

The 2022 edition of *State of Food Security and Nutrition in the World,* issued in July, reported that the rate of PoU globally had risen significantly during 2019–21, and that, in 2021, some 702m.–828m. people had suffered hunger and around 2,300m. had been moderately or severely food-insecure. Nearly 30% of women of childbearing age were reported to have suffered from anaemia in 2019, an upwards trend in levels of adult obesity was observed, and (in 2020) 5.7% of children worldwide were reportedly clinically overweight, 22% were suffering from stunting, and 6.7% were acutely affected by wasting. Some 43.8% of infants aged under six months were reported to have been exclusively breast-fed in 2020, respresenting an advancement over 37.1% in 2012. In 2020 almost 3,100m. people worldwide reportedly were unable to afford a healthy diet (with a deterioration of conditions particularly notable in Asia, followed by Africa). The report emphasized the role of government policies—such as trade and market interventions, fiscal subsidies, and general services support—in influencing the food availability environment, and recommended means of repurposing existing support to enhance the availability to consumers of nutritious foods.

The Codex Alimentarius Commission sets standards for food products and issues guidelines and codes of practice on food safety and quality and on trade in food. The FAO Organic Agriculture Programme helps to build the capacities of member states in the areas of organic food production, processing, certification and marketing. In February 2019 FAO organized, with the African Union and WHO, in Addis Ababa, Ethiopia, the inaugural International Food Safety Conference, addressing the human health and economic challenges posed by unsafe food. An International Forum on Food Safety and Trade, following on from the Conference, was organized by FAO, WHO and the World Trade Organization in April.

Within the context of the G20 Action Plan on Food Price Volatility, adopted in June 2011 by ministers responsible for agriculture from G20 countries, an Agricultural Market Information System (AMIS) was established, under FAO auspices, with a view to improving market transparency and stabilizing food price volatility. The Group on Earth Observations Global Agricultural Monitoring (GEOGLAM) initiative was launched at that time, to strengthen international capacity to produce and disseminate efficient forecasts of agricultural production. The monthly *AMIS Market Monitor* collates data on crop growing conditions recorded in GEOGLAM's regularly updated *Crop Monitor*. GEOGLAM became a full member of the AMIS Secretariat in June 2016 (in 2022 the Secretariat had 10 members).

The FAO Food Price Monitoring and Analysis mechanism issues warnings for countries where the cost of one or more basic food commodity is trending towards an abnormally high level. In February 2011 FAO's Food Price Index recorded the highest levels of global food prices since 1990. In 2021 the Index averaged 125.7 points (compared with 97.9 points in the previous year), and in March 2022 it reached a new all-time high, for the third consecutive month: of 159.3 points (a significant rise over 140.7 points in February). Small consecutive decreases were reported in April–August: in the latter month the Index stood at 138.0 points (10.1 points higher than the August 2021 level). In addition to the Food Price Index, FAO maintains price indices for cereal, dairy, oils and fats, meat, and sugar.

BETTER ENVIRONMENT

FAO hosts the Facilitation Unit of the multi-stakeholder Global Alliance for Climate-Smart Agriculture (GACSA), initiated in September 2014. GACSA develops policy briefs and fosters partnerships to promote climate-smart agricultural practices. FAO's multi-partner Energy-Smart Food Programme promotes energy efficiency and renewable energy in agrifood systems. A Globally Important Agricultural Heritage programme aims to identify and protect traditional agricultural systems that represent models of sustainable agricultural production.

FAO offers policy guidance and technical support to policymakers regarding the development of a sustainable, circular bioeconomy, i.e. harnessing bioscience and biotechnology to provide food, animal feed, paper, bio-based textiles, wood products, bioplastics, biochemicals, biopharmaceuticals and bioenergy.

FAO hosts the Global Soil Partnership, an alliance that promotes sustainable soil management (SSM), with a view to fostering productive, healthy soils and maintaining essential ecoystems. In June 2019 the FAO Conference mandated the development of an FAO Strategy on Mainstreaming Biodiversity across Agricultural Sectors. FAO's inaugural *The State of the World's Biodiversity for Food and Agriculture,* issued in February of that year, emphasized that biodiversity losses are unrecoverable, and that numerous species underpinning food systems are under threat—including plants, animals, insects and micro-organisms ('associated biodiversity') that support food production through ecosystem services, such as maintaining soil fertility, purifying air and water, pollinating plants, and countering livestock and crop diseases and pests. Changes in land and water use and management, overexploitation, overharvesting, pollution, climate change, deforestation, population growth and urbanization were reported to be key drivers of biodiversity loss. The report urged governments and other stakeholders to strengthen frameworks and incentives aimed at reversing the biodiversity crisis. In December 2021 FAO and the International Fertilizer Association concluded a Memorandum of Understanding (MOU) on future co-operation in promoting sustainable fertilizer use and healthy soils. In January 2022 the FAO Executive Director called for a reversal of soil degradation, caused by unsustainable agricultural practices.

FAO was designated the lead agency in managing a seven-year EU-funded Sustainable Wildlife Management programme, which was initiated in October 2017 with the aim of supporting the conservation and sustainable use of wildlife in forests, wetlands and savannas. Focal areas of the programme were to be the regulation of hunting, strengthening the management capacities of Indigenous and rural communities, and augmenting the supply of sustainably produced farmed fish and meat products to provide an alternative to the consumption of meat sourced from the wild. Participating countries included Chad, Republic of the Congo, the Democratic Republic of the Congo (DRC), Gabon, Guyana, Madagascar, Mali, Papua New Guinea, Senegal, Sudan, Zambia and Zimbabwe.

FAO aims to ensure the conservation of forests and forestry resources while maximizing their potential to contribute to food security and to social and economic development. It assists member countries to formulate, implement and monitor national forestry programmes, and encourages the participation of all stakeholders in developing plans for the sustainable management of tree and forest resources. FAO voluntary guidelines aimed at supporting states to develop mechanisms for monitoring national forest resources were issued in July 2017. FAO's Forest Resources Long-Term Strategy, supporting sustainable forest management over the period 2012–30, aimed to strengthen the quality, harmonizing and sharing of multi-country forest resource information used in policy reviews. A Global Plan of Action for the Conservation, Sustainable Use and Development of Forest Genetic Resources, adopted by the FAO Conference in June 2013, detailed 27 strategic priorities for action. FAO maintains an online Forestry Information System (FORIS).

FAO's first UN Strategic Plan for Forestry, covering the period 2017–30, aimed to reverse the trend of deforestation and to expand global forest coverage by 120m. ha by 2030. At global level FAO undertakes surveillance of forestry related issues; the 2020 edition of a *Forest Resources Assessment* (issued every five years) was published in May 2020. At that time FAO estimated that 420m. ha of forest had been lost as a result of deforestation during the period 1990–2020. It was noted that, globally, forests provide habitat for 68% of terrestrial mammals, 75% of bird species, and 80% of species of amphibians. The 2022 edition of FAO's biennial report *The State of the World's Forests* focused on the potential contribution of three interrelated forestry pathways to the broader goals of a green recovery and more efficient, resilient and sustainable agrifood systems. FAO aimed to support member states to implement the pathways: Halting deforestation and maintaining forests; Restoring degraded lands and expanding agroforestry; and Sustainably using forests and building green value chains.

In September 2008 FAO, with UNEP and the UN Development Programme, launched the UN Collaborative Programme on Reducing Emissions from Deforestation and Forest Degradation in Developing Countries (UN-REDD), with the aim of enabling donors to pool resources (through a trust fund established for that purpose) to promote a transformation of forest resource use patterns.

FAO is a member of the Collaborative Partnership on Forests, an informal voluntary arrangement among 14 agencies with significant forestry programmes, which was established in April 2004. FAO organizes a World Forestry Congress, generally held every six years. World Forestry Congress XV, co-organized by FAO and South Korea in that country's capital, Seoul, in May 2022, adopted the Seoul Forest Declaration, which addressed the role of forests in combating global challenges including land degradation, biodiversity loss, climate change, hunger, and poverty.

World Forest Day, sponsored by FAO and the UN Forum on Forests, is observed on 21 March.

In September 2020 FAO launched a Green Cities initiative, which aimed to strengthen urban-rural linkages and improve the resilience of urban environments.

BETTER LIFE

FAO promotes women's equal rights and control over decision making, resources, technologies, services, economic opportunities and institutions, and works to ensure the inclusive transformation and revitalization of rural areas to ensure equal participation by, and benefits to marginalized groups.

During 2020 FAO undertook to roll out a new flagship initiative, Hand-in-Hand, to support the efforts of member countries to eradicate poverty and end hunger (SDGs 1 and 2). With a focus on data and evidence and the use of new technologies, the initiative aimed to accelerate agricultural transformations and sustainable rural development in countries with limited national capacities or with the greatest operational challenges. As part of the approach countries were to be matched to work in close partnership with other organizations, financial institutions, research bodies and donors. In July FAO launched a new Hand-in-Hand Geospatial Platform, comprising data on food, agriculture, fisheries, forestry, markets, animal health, natural resources and socioeconomics, to support evidence-based decision making within the scheme. The initiative aimed to facilitate partnerships and donor 'matchmaking', in particular in countries facing challenges to sustainable development.

As a means of addressing urban poverty, malnutrition and food security, FAO works towards transforming urban and peri-urban agrifood systems, through the adoption of supportive policies and initiatives, and by scaling up investments.

FAO and IFAD were mandated to support the UN Decade of Family Farming (2019–28), which aimed to position small-scale family farming at the centre of national agricultural, environmental and social policies. FAO welcomed the adoption by the UN General Assembly in December 2018 of a landmark Declaration on the Rights of Peasants and Other People Working in Rural Areas; this aimed to protect the rights of rural workers and Indigenous peoples and also to recognize their contribution to sustainable development and to preserving biodiversity.

In 1999 FAO signed an MOU with UNAIDS on strengthening co-operation to combat the threat posed by the HIV/AIDS epidemic to food security, nutrition and rural livelihoods. FAO is committed to incorporating HIV/AIDS into food security and livelihood projects, to strengthening community care and to highlighting the importance of nutrition in the care of those living with HIV/AIDS.

In October 2015 the CFS adopted a Framework for Action on Food Security and Nutrition in Protracted Crises, which took into account the disruptive impact of long-term crises on food production systems and livelihoods, on illness and mortality rates, and in relation to the incidence of hunger and severe undernutrition in affected communities. The Framework placed a particular focus on the need for strengthening resilience, on integrating efforts to address both immediate and longer-term challenges, and on promoting the empowerment of women and the productivity of smallholders. In August 2017 the FAO Director-General welcomed a statement by the President of the UN Security Council that recognized conflict as a major source of famine. The *Global Report on Food Crises*, issued annually by the Global Network Against Food Crises, comprising FAO, WFP, the EU and other partners, addresses hunger prompted by conflict, insecurity, economic turbulence and climate shocks.

FAO and WFP co-lead the inter-agency Food Security and Livelihoods Cluster during humanitarian crises.

TECHNICAL CO-OPERATION

FAO provides policy advice to support the formulation, implementation and evaluation of agriculture, rural development and food security strategies in member countries. It supports developing countries to strengthen their agricultural trade technical negotiating skills. FAO also co-ordinates and facilitates the mobilization of extrabudgetary funds from donors. It administers a range of trust funds, including a Trust Fund for Food Security and Food Safety, established in 2002 to generate resources for projects to combat hunger, and the Government Co-operative Programme. FAO's Investment Centre, established in 1964, assists member countries to formulate effective projects and programmes to attract rural development investment. The Centre administers cost-sharing arrangements, with, typically, FAO funding 40% of a project.

FAO assembles, analyses and disseminates statistical data on world food and agriculture. FAOSTAT serves as a core database of statistical information relating to nutrition, fisheries, forestry, food production, land use, population, etc. FAO compiles and co-ordinates an extensive range of international databases on agriculture, fisheries, forestry, food and statistics, the most important of these being AGRIS (the International Information System for the Agricultural Sciences and Technology). FAO's Gender and Land Rights Database breaks down land-related statistics by gender. In June 2015 FAO inaugurated a digital platform on family farming, providing data, legislation, and other relevant information.

In February 2013 an Africa Solidarity Trust Fund (ASTF) was inaugurated, which aimed to mobilize Africa-to-Africa financial resources in support of strengthening regional food security. In February 2020 the ASTF donated US $1m. to support FAO's efforts to eradicate the upsurge of desert locusts in the Horn of Africa.

EMERGENCY PREPAREDNESS AND RESPONSE

FAO's emergency operations are concerned with all aspects of disaster and risk prevention, mitigation, reduction and emergency relief and rehabilitation, with a particular emphasis on food security and rural populations. FAO works with governments to develop and implement disaster prevention policies and practices; it disseminates information from the various early warning systems and supports adaptation to climate variability and change, for example through the use of drought-resistant crops or the adoption of conservation agriculture techniques. Following an emergency, FAO works with governments and other development and humanitarian partners to assess the immediate and longer-term agriculture and food security needs of the affected population. It determines the appropriate response to a disaster situation through the Integrated Food Security Phase Classification (IPC) scheme. Emergency co-ordination units may be established to manage the local response to an emergency and to facilitate and co-ordinate the delivery of inter-agency assistance. In order to rehabilitate agricultural production following a natural or man-made disaster FAO provides emergency seeds, tools, other materials and technical and training assistance. FAO aims to strengthen the capacity of local institutions to manage and mitigate risk and provides technical assistance to improve access to land for displaced populations in countries following conflict or a natural disaster. Under the UN's Cluster Approach to co-ordinating the international response to humanitarian disasters, FAO and WFP jointly lead the Food Security Cluster, which aims to combine expertise in agricultural assistance and food aid to improve the resilience of food-insecure disaster-affected communities.

FAO's Global Information and Early Warning System (GIEWS), which become operational in 1975, monitors and maintains a database on the crop and food outlook at global, regional, national and subnational level in order to detect emerging food supply difficulties and disasters, and to ensure rapid intervention in countries experiencing food supply shortages. It publishes regular updates, highlighting countries in crisis requiring external assistance for food; countries with unfavourable prospects for current crops; and domestic price warnings (for countries where abnormally high prices are being reported in main markets for one or more basic food commodities). An appropriate international response is then recommended. FAO's Agricultural Stress Index System (ASIS), initiated in 2015, uses earth observation technologies to identify agricultural areas at risk of 'water stress' (drought).

The monthly *FAO Cereal Supply and Demand Brief* provides a detailed assessment of cereal production and of supply and demand conditions. The quarterly publication *Crop Prospects and Food Situation* reviews the global food production situation, and provides regional updates and a special focus on countries experiencing food crises and requiring external assistance. In September 2022 it reported that 45 countries (of which 33 were in Africa) required external food assistance.

In July 2022 FAO's *Crop Prospects and Food Situation* reported exceptional shortfalls in aggregate food production and supplies in the Central African Republic, Kenya, Niger and Somalia, and widespread lack of access to food in Burundi, Chad, Djibouti, Eritrea, Ethiopia, Nigeria, South Sudan and Zimbabwe.

Food Outlook, issued in June and November, analyses developments in global food and animal feed markets.

FAO-led Food Security Information System (FSIS) projects monitor national and broader food security situations.

FAO's Emergency Management Centre for Animal Health (EMC-AH) extends training in Good Emergency Management Practice (GEMP) to veterinary services, to support the building of national animal health emergency management capabilities. EMC-AH deploys (at the request of governments) rapid response missions to support preparedness and response activities to prevent and control outbreaks of animal diseases, including zoonotic diseases. EMC-AH collaborates with EMPRES and with FAO's Emergency Centre for Transboundary Animal Diseases (ECTAD). ECTAD facilitates FAO's Global Health Security Agenda (GHSA) and Emerging Pandemic Threats (EPT) programmes: GHSA aims to strengthen the capacity of states to prevent, and works to control outbreaks of, zoonotic and non-zoonotic diseases, while the EPT enhances national capacity to pre-empt the emergence or re-emergence of zoonotic diseases, with a focus on, *inter alia,* avian influenza and (believed to be transmissible to humans via camels) Middle East Respiratory Syndrome.

An FAO Special Fund for Emergency and Rehabilitation Activities was established in 2004. FAO contributes the agricultural relief and rehabilitation component of joint UN humanitarian appeals, which aim to co-ordinate and enhance the effectiveness of the international community's response to an emergency. In December 2021 FAO appealed for US $1,500m. to assist 50m. people during 2022.

FAO publishes an annual *African Regional Overview of Food Security and Nutrition*. The 2020 report, issued in June 2021, estimated that some 250.3m. people across the continent (one-fifth of the total population) were suffering from chronic malnutrition.

The food security situation in Somalia—a drought-prone low production, food-deficit country—has been exacerbated by the inaccessibility of extensive rebel-controlled areas, as well as high staple food prices and low purchasing power. An FAO-EU joint Information for Nutrition, Food Security and Resilience for Decision Making (INFORMED) programme is implemented in Somalia. Rapid food security assessments and household surveys are regularly conducted through FAO's Food Security and Nutrition Analysis Unit for Somalia (FSNAU). A national emergency was declared in Somalia in May 2021 in view of protracted drought. In April 2022 the IPC warned that more than 6m. people in Somalia were at risk of acute food insecurity, and that up to 81,000 were in danger of starvation. In June FAO issued a revised Rapid Response and Mitigation Plan for Djibouti, Ethiopia, Kenya and Somalia, the worst drought-affected countries, which required funding of US $219m., of which $47m. had been mobilized at that time. Under the UN's 2022 Global Humanitarian Appeal FAO requested, *inter alia,* $114m. to assist 913,000 people in Chad, $70m. for the DRC (to assist 1.2m. people), $55m. for northeastern Nigeria (for 1.8m. beneficiaries), 40m. for Burkina Faso (1.2m. beneficiaries), $30m. for Mali (to assist 990,900 people), $26.7m. for Mozambique (666,680 beneficiaries), and $20.6m. for Niger (1.1m. beneficiaries).

From January 2020 FAO worked intensively to survey and combat the risk posed to crops and livestock by a proliferation of desert locust swarms in East Africa. Environmental impact assessments of damaged pastures and croplands were conducted in the worst affected countries (notably Ethiopia, Somalia and—experiencing locust infestation for the first time in 70 years—Kenya). During January–June FAO and partners significantly reduced the scope of the initial locust infestation, particularly in Kenya. Throughout the region they eradicated more than 400,000m. individual locusts and cleared 600,000 ha from locust swarms, preventing them from causing catastrophic damage to crops. The swift mobility of the swarms, their tendency to spread out in remote areas, rendering surveillance more difficult, and the appearance of a second generation of juvenile locusts remained challenges at that time. A joint statement issued in late July by FAO, WFP and the Intergovernmental Authority on Development, emphasized the triple risk to regional food security arising from the combined impact of the desert locust and COVID-19 crises, compounded by climatic shocks. FAO appealed for US $230.5m., in a series of appeals, to support its locust surveillance and control operations and safeguard livelihoods during the period January 2020–December 2021. In March 2022 FAO concluded that the two-year upsurge of desert locusts in East Africa had ended, in part owing to low seasonal rainfall. In mid-2020 large-scale control operations prevented a potential spread of the desert locust infestation to West Africa.

FAO Statutory Bodies and Associated Entities

(based at the Rome headquarters, unless otherwise indicated)

African Commission on Agricultural Statistics: c/o FAO Regional Office for Africa, POB 1628, Accra, Ghana; tel. (30) 2610930; fax (30) 2668427; e-mail Paul.NGomaKimbatsa@fao.org; internet www.fao.org/africa/afcas; f. 1961; aims to advise mem. countries on the devt and standardization of food and agricultural statistics; 26th session: Nov. 2019, in Libreville, Gabon; 37 mem. states.

African Forestry and Wildlife Commission: c/o FAO Regional Office for Africa, POB 1628, Accra, Ghana; tel. (30) 2675000; e-mail nora.berrahmouni@fao.org; internet www.fao.org/africa/afwc; f. 1959; aims to advise on the formulation of forest policy and to review and co-ordinate its implementation at regional level; to exchange information and advise on technical problems; meets every two years; 23rd session: Aug. 2022, Kinshasa, Democratic Rep. of the Congo; 53 mem. states.

Codex Alimentarius Commission (Joint FAO/WHO Food Standards Programme): e-mail codex@fao.org; internet www.fao.org/fao-who-codexalimentarius; f. 1963; supports the co-ordination of all international food standards work and publishes a code of international food standards; a Codex Trust Fund (CTF) was inaugurated in 2003; in June 2016 this was superseded by the CTF2, which aimed to support participation by more than 100 developing countries over a 12-year period; there are numerous specialized Codex committees, on e.g. contaminants in foods, food additives, food hygiene, food import and export inspection and certification systems, food labelling, nutrition and foods for special dietary uses, methods of analysis and sampling, and pesticide and veterinary drug residues,

fresh fruits and vegetables, fish and fishery products, fats and oils, and spices and culinary herbs; intergovernmental task forces may be appointed; FAO/WHO Codex co-ordinating committees cover Africa, Asia, Europe, Latin America and the Caribbean, the Near East, and North America and the South West Pacific; the Commission had established by 2022 378 food standards guidelines, codes of practice, limits and principles relating to food production and processing (including Maximum Residue Limits and Risk Management Recommendations for Residues of Veterinary Drugs in Foods); in Nov. 2021 new standards were adopted (online) by the Commission for, *inter alia,* dried basil, cloves and dried or dehydrated ginger; 188 mem. states and the EU; 240 observers; Sec. TOM HEILANDT.

Commission for Controlling the Desert Locust in the Central Region: c/o FAO Regional Office for the Near East, POB 2223, Cairo, Egypt; tel. (2) 33316000; fax (2) 37495981; e-mail Mamoon.AlAlawi@fao.org; internet desertlocust-crc.org; f. 1967; covers the Middle East, Near East and the Horn of Africa; 32nd session: June 2022, in Jeddah, Saudi Arabia; 16 mem. states; Exec. Sec. MAMOON AL SARAI ALALAWI.

Commission for Controlling the Desert Locust in the Western Region: 30 rue Asselah Hocine, BP 270, Algiers, Algeria; tel. (21) 73-33-54; e-mail clcpro@fao.org; internet www.fao.org/clcpro/fr; f. 2002; implements preventive locust surveillance and control measures in mem. countries and conducts training for novice and master locust field 'prospectors' (Oct. 2020: on the use of Metarhizium in locust spraying); 10th session: late Nov.–early Dec. 2022; 10 mem. states.

Committee for Inland Fisheries and Aquaculture of Africa (CIFAA): c/o FAO Regional Office for Africa, POB 1628, Accra, Ghana; tel. (30) 2610930; e-mail Ndiaga.Gueye@fao.org; internet www.fao.org/fishery/rfb/cifaa; f. 1971; works to improve inland fisheries and aquaculture in Africa; 37 mem. states; Sec. NDIAGA GUEYE.

FAO Desert Locust Control Committee: e-mail Annie.Monard@fao.org; f. 1955; serves as a primary forum bringing together locust-affected countries, international donors and other agencies, to advise FAO on the management of desert locusts; 41st session: Dec. 2019, in Addis Ababa, Ethiopia.

Fishery Committee for the Eastern Central Atlantic: c/o FAO Regional Office for Africa; tel. (06) 57052019; e-mail Ndiaga.Gueye@fao.org; internet www.fao.org/cecaf/en; f. 1967; promotes improvements in inland fisheries in the Eastern Central Atlantic area between Cape Spartel (Morocco) and the Congo River; 22nd session: Sept. 2019, in Libreville, Gabon; 23rd session scheduled for March 2023; 33 mem. states and the EU; Sec. NDIAGA GUEYE.

South West Indian Ocean Fisheries Commission: 347 rua Consiglieri Pedroso, Maputo, Mozambique; tel. (21) 080489; e-mail SWIOFC-Secretariat@fao.org; internet www.fao.org/fishery/rfb/swiofc; f. 2004; promotes the sustainable devt and utilization, through proper management, of living marine resources; 11th session: Aug. 2021, held in a virtual format; 12 mem. states; Sec. VASCO SCHMIDT.

Finance

FAO's Regular Programme, which is financed by contributions from member governments, covers the cost of FAO's Secretariat, its Technical Co-operation Programme and part of the cost of several special action programmes. In June 2021 the FAO Conference endorsed a budget totalling US $1,005.6m. to fund its activities during 2022–23. Much of FAO's technical assistance programme and emergency relief and rehabilitation activities are funded from extrabudgetary sources, predominantly by trust funds that come mainly from donor countries and international financing institutions.

Publications

Crop Prospects and Food Situation (5/6 a year).

Food Outlook (2 a year).

Global Report on Food Crises (annually, with the EU and WFP).

The State of Agricultural Commodity Markets (every 2 years).

The State of Food and Agriculture (annually).

The State of Food Security and Nutrition in the World (annually, with IFAD, UNICEF, WFP and WHO).

The State of World Fisheries and Aquaculture (every 2 years).

The State of the World's Forests (every 2 years).

Unasylva (2 a year).

Other major reports, commodity reviews, statistical pocketbooks, atlases, studies, manuals.

International Bank for Reconstruction and Development— IBRD—World Bank

Address: 1818 H St, NW, Washington, DC 20433, USA.

Telephone: (202) 473-1000; **fax:** (202) 477-6391; **e-mail:** pic@worldbank.org; **internet:** www.worldbank.org.

The IBRD was established in December 1945. Initially, it was concerned with post-war reconstruction in Europe; since then its aim has been to assist the economic development of members by making loans where private capital is not available on reasonable terms to finance productive investments. The World Bank, as it is commonly known, comprises the IBRD and the International Development Association (IDA). The affiliated group of institutions, comprising the IBRD, IDA, the International Finance Corporation (IFC), the Multilateral Investment Guarantee Agency (MIGA) and the International Centre for Settlement of Investment Disputes (ICSID), is referred to as the World Bank Group (WBG), and aims to eradicate extreme poverty, and pursue shared prosperity, while promoting environmentally sustainable development.

Organization

(October 2022)

Officers and staff of the IBRD serve concurrently as officers and staff in IDA. The World Bank has offices in New York, USA; Brussels, Belgium; Paris, France (for Europe); Frankfurt, Germany; London, United Kingdom; Geneva, Switzerland; and Tokyo, Japan; and in some 130 countries of operation. There are also two shared services offices, based in Chennai, India, covering accounting, human resources and information technology support; and in Sofia, Bulgaria, providing corporate and technology support to the WBG's global business operations. The World Bank employed 12,528 staff members and 5,944 consultants at 30 June 2021.

BOARDS OF GOVERNORS AND BOARDS OF DIRECTORS OF THE WBG

The WBG Boards of Governors and WBG Boards of Directors refer to the separate Boards of Governors and Boards of Directors of the IBRD, IDA, IFC and MIGA. When a country is a member of the IBRD and simultaneously of the IDA or IFC, Governors and Alternates, and Executive Directors and Alternates, serve ex officio in those roles on (respectively) the IDA and IFC Boards of Governors and the IDA and IFC Boards of Directors. MIGA Governors and Alternates and Executive Directors and Alternates are appointed separately.

The Development Committee of the WBG and IMF (established in 1974 as the Joint Ministerial Committee of the Boards of Governors of the Bank and the Fund on the Transfer of Real Resources to Developing Countries) reviews development policy issues and financing requirements.

BOARD OF GOVERNORS

The IBRD's Board of Governors consists of one Governor appointed by each member nation. Typically, a Governor is the country's minister responsible for finance, central bank governor, or a minister or an official of comparable rank. The Board normally meets once a year.

EXECUTIVE DIRECTORS

There are 25 Executive Directors and each Director selects an Alternate. Six Directors are appointed by the six members having the largest number of shares of capital stock, and the rest are elected by the Governors representing the other members. The President of the Bank is Chairman of the Board.

PRINCIPAL OFFICERS

The principal officers of the Bank are the President of the Bank, four Managing Directors, three Senior Vice-Presidents and 25 Vice-Presidents.

President and Chairman of Executive Directors: DAVID R. MALPASS (USA).

Vice-President, Eastern and Southern Africa: HAFEZ GHANEM (Egypt/France).

Vice President, Western and Central Africa: OUSMANE DIAGANA (Mauritania).

Activities

The World Bank's primary objectives are the achievement of sustainable economic growth and prosperity, and the reduction of extreme poverty in developing countries. Extreme poverty is defined by the Bank through its Multidimensional Poverty Measure (MPM), which takes into account monetary poverty: living on less than US $1.90 per day, and also deprivations in access to basic infrastructure (sanitation, drinking water and electricity) and to education. From 2014/15, in order to support individual countries in pursuing the 'twin objectives' by 2030, the Bank introduced a new country engagement model with a focus on tailoring and targeting support selectively through newly established Country Partnership Frameworks. Jointly with the IMF the Bank undertakes national financial sector assessment reviews, aimed at identifying and rectifying vulnerabilities in financial systems.

DEVELOPMENT

The Bank's annual *World Development Report* presents policy recommendations on and analysis of various specific aspects of development. The 2022 edition, issued in February, assessed means of addressing the economic and financial risks that had been aggravated by the COVID-19 pandemic, with a focus on over-indebtedness and increased financial fragility. The need for early detection of emerging risks, for proactive management of sovereign debt burdens, and for ensuring continued access to credit was emphasized.

In July 2015 the Third International Conference on Financing for Development, convened in Addis Ababa, Ethiopia, approved an Action Agenda in which governments expressed their commitment to strengthen the framework to finance sustainable development activities, in particular the UN's post-2015 development agenda, and global climate action. The Conference determined that a new Technology Facilitation Mechanism would be established as a collaborative effort between member states, civil society, the private sector and several UN entities, including the World Bank, in order to promote science, technology and innovation. An Inter-Agency Task Force on Financing for Development—with participation by more than 60 UN and other entities—was established by the UN Secretary-General to follow up the implementation of the Addis Ababa Action Agenda. At the December UN Climate Change Conference, held in Paris, France, the Bank and other multilateral development banks issued a collective statement in which they committed to taking urgent action to support clients in adapting to and mitigating risks associated with climate change and, in particular, in implementing the goals of the Paris Agreement and in ending the use of fossil fuels.

The Bank supports sessions of the Small States Forum (SSF), which represent a platform for high-level dialogue on the particular development needs of 42 micro and small states and eight larger countries that were deemed to be addressing similar challenges (Botswana, Gabon, The Gambia, Jamaica, Guinea-Bissau, Lesotho, Namibia and Qatar). Meeting in April 2022, in a virtual format, the SSF noted that small economies—already very vulnerable to impacts of climate change, and having been disproportionately adversely impacted by the economic fallout of the COVID-19 pandemic (their economies had contracted, on average by more than 8% in 2020, and had subsequently rebounded relatively slowly, with increased debt burdens)—were being confronted in 2022 by global impacts of the ongoing war in Ukraine, such as escalating food and fuel price inflation, rising interest rates and borrowing costs, and outflows of capital, representing an exceptional convergence of hardships.

In October 2016 the Bank, with public and private sector stakeholders, initiated a Digital Development Partnership, tasked with working towards ending the global digital divide, with a view to ensuring that the economic and social benefits of digital connectivity would be universally available. A report titled *People's Money: Harnessing Digitalization to Finance a Sustainable Future* that was issued by the UN Secretary-General in August 2020 addressed the empowerment potential arising from transformative advances in 'fintech' (financial technology), such as mobile payment technologies, crowdfunding platforms, peer-to-peer lending, online marketplaces, and cryptocurrencies and crypto-assets. It was noted that in 2018 fintech investment had reached US $120,000m., representing one-third of global venture capital funding.

In May 2018 the WBG and the UN Secretary-General (on behalf of the wider UN system) concluded a Strategic Partnership Framework (SPF) governing future co-operation in supporting states to implement the UN's 2030 Agenda for Sustainable Development and set of Sustainable Development Goals (SDGs, adopted by UN heads of state and of government in September 2015). The SPF provided for the following four priority areas of collaboration: finance and implementation support; global action on climate change; activities in humanitarian and post-crisis settings; and harnessing data to enhance development outcomes.

ENVIRONMENT AND SOCIAL POLICIES

Concerned that cities are expanding at an unprecedented rate, the Bank undertakes Urbanization Reviews, providing diagnostic tools and a framework to guide city authorities in decision making. The Bank's urban agenda is aligned to its twin objectives on poverty reduction and boosting shared prosperity by 2030. The Bank has initiated the following programmes in support of urban development: Low Carbon, Liveable Cities; Resilient Cities; Competitive Cities; and Inclusive Cities. The Bank also convenes periodically a Global Lab on Metropolitan Strategic Planning (MetroLab), to facilitate knowledge sharing on urban development, and co-ordinates the Global Platform for Sustainable Cities, a Global Environment Facility (GEF) initiative that was launched in March 2016 to develop urban sustainability programmes in 11 developing countries.

Since 2017 all Bank operations have been assessed for climate and disaster risk. In January 2019 the Bank determined promptly to end financial support for oil and gas extraction (other than in exceptional circumstances involving very poor countries). In accordance with the WBG's Climate Change Action Plan for the period 2021–25 climate financing was to represent 35% of its portfolio by 2025.

COVID-19 PANDEMIC RESPONSE

In early March 2020 the Executive Board approved an emergency initial US $12,000m. package comprising fast-track low-cost loans, grants and technical assistance, to support at-risk developing countries in containing and combating COVID-19 contagion. The mechanism was to assist member states with the implementation of prevention, detection and response programmes and to alleviate the impacts of the crisis on businesses and the labour force. On 17 March the IBRD's and IFC's Boards of Directors augmented the total to $14,000m., of which $6,000m. was to be made available in the near term by the IBRD and IDA to support health care activities, and $8,000m. was to be channelled through the IFC to support private businesses (with a view to protecting vulnerable economies and jobs). In April the steering body of the World Bank's Pandemic Emergency Financing Facility (PEF, an insurance window that was inaugurated in July 2017) allocated $195.8m. to assist 64 developing countries' efforts to combat and contain COVID-19. Also in April 2020 the WBG, IMF and the Group of 20 (G20) leading economies agreed a Debt Service Suspension Initiative (DSSI), under which, from 1 May, the debt service payments of up to 73 eligible countries (40 in Africa) were to be temporarily frozen. In July, addressing a (virtual) meeting of G20 finance ministers and central bank governors, the World Bank's President emphasized that the COVID-19 pandemic had prompted the worst economic recession in decades, and that developing countries (with relatively fragile social safety nets) were particularly severely affected by outflows of capital, the collapse of informal labour markets, declines in remittances, and weak investment prospects. Addressing the UN General Assembly in September 2020 the World Bank's President observed that the DSSI was proving to be inadequate, as the moratorium that was being provided by multilateral lending institutions was not supported by non-participant commercial creditors, or, fully, by some official bilateral creditors. Under a Common Framework for Debt Treatment, endorsed in November by the G20 and by the so-called Paris Club of sovereign creditors (which seeks to find co-ordinated solutions for debtor states), DSSI-eligible countries with particularly challenging debt burdens were, upon their own request, to be given special support. The amount of debt service suspended through the DSSI during May 2020–December 2021 (when it expired, having twice been extended, in November 2020 and in April 2021) totalled $12,900m.; 48 of the 73 eligible countries participated in the initiative. During 1 April 2020–30 June 2021 the WBG mobilized or committed $157,100m. in new financing to counter the economic, health and social impacts of the pandemic. In January 2022 the WBG President prioritized vaccines, climate, and debt transparency and sustainability as urgent challenges. An edition released at that time of the Bank's *Global Economic Prospects* listed recommendations on means of enhancing the effectiveness of the new G20 Common Framework for Debt Treatment. The report addressed three major challenges facing the recovery of developing countries: unprecedented macroeconomic imbalances; rising income inequality; and mounting global uncertainty, relating, *inter alia,* to the continuing COVID-19 pandemic, supply bottlenecks, volatile commodity prices and the risk of extreme weather events. In early June *Global Economic Prospects* forecast global economic growth in 2022 of only 2.9%, depressed by spillover effects of the ongoing war in Ukraine, including higher commodity prices, disruptions to supplies and mounting food insecurity.

The Bank has collaborated with the World Health Organization (WHO) and other agencies to strengthen health and vaccination systems, to enable the procurement and distribution of vaccines, and advance treatments and tests in low- and middle-income countries. (See WHO for details on the Access to COVID-19 Tools Accelerator, which was initiated, with participation by the WBG, in April 2020. From June 2021 the WBG President participated in a Multilateral Leaders Taskforce on vaccines access.) In mid-October 2020 the Executive Board approved additional financing totalling US $12,000m. to support developing countries' COVID-19 vaccine programmes. At the end of June 2021 the total available financing for COVID-19 vaccines was expanded to $20,000m., until the end of 2022. In April G20 finance ministers reached a provisional consensus on establishing, under World Bank auspices, a new Financial Intermediary Fund for Pandemic Prevention, Preparedness and Response. As at 30 June 2022 the Bank had approved operations totalling $10,100m. to support the COVID-19 vaccine rollouts in 78 countries.

OTHER PRIORITIES

Human Capital: The Bank's Social Protection and Labour Strategy, covering the period 2012–22, aims to assist countries with the development of affordable social protection systems; to enable individuals to manage risk; and to improve resilience through investment in human capital (including in education, health, nutrition and jobs). In April 2014—estimating that 2,500m. adults worldwide were 'unbanked', i.e. excluded from access to formal banking or financial services—the Bank initiated a Financial Inclusion Support Framework. In July 2017 the Bank, ITU and the Committee on Payments and Market Infrastructures jointly launched a Financial Inclusion Global Initiative (FIGI), which aimed to advance research in and to formulate policy recommendations for digital financial inclusion. The third FIGI Symposium was convened in May–June 2021, in a virtual format. In September 2016 the WBG and the International Labour Organization initiated a Global Partnership for Universal Social Protection to Achieve the SDGs (USP2030). The WBG and WHO issue a biennial *Tracking Universal Health Coverage: Global Monitoring Report*.

The Bank participates in the multi-stakeholder Partnership for Economic Inclusion (PEI), a platform that aims to establish a global network of formalized partnerships between governments, policymakers, development partners, research organizations and NGOs, with a focus on developing economic inclusion programmes and building a knowledge base of related good practices. In January 2021 the PEI issued *State of Economic Inclusion (SEI) Report 2021: The Potential to Scale*, which reviewed the state of financial inclusion, jobs and social protection, in the context of the ongoing pandemic crisis.

The Bank's Women Entrepreneurs Finance Initiative, endorsed by the G20 in July 2017, aimed to support women-led business development by facilitating access to equity and insurance services and mobilizing up to US $1,000m. in institutional financing.

People, Peace and Prosperity: In February 2020 the WBG finalized its first strategy to address—through expertise and financing—the underlying causes of Fragility, Conflict and Violence (FCV) during the period 2020–25. The UN-World Bank Fragility and Conflict Partnership Trust Fund, established in 2010, is funded by Switzerland and Norway.

The WBG compiles an annual list of fragile and conflict-affected situations (FCS), which in 2022/23 comprised 37 countries and territories, of which 19 were in sub-Saharan Africa (including Burkina Faso, Cameroon, the Central African Republic, the Democratic Republic of the Congo, Ethiopia, Mali, Mozambique, Niger, Nigeria, Somalia and South Sudan designated as 'conflict states'), and—listed as states experiencing 'institutional and social fragility'—Burundi, Chad, Comoros, Republic of the Congo, Eritrea, Guinea-Bissau, Sudan and Zimbabwe. The UN-World Bank Fragility and Conflict Partnership Trust Fund, established in 2010, is funded by Switzerland and Norway.

The Bank is a co-sponsor of the Joint UN Programme on HIV/AIDS (UNAIDS), and is the UNAIDS lead agency for support to strategic planning and for conducting analysis to underpin evidence-informed policies. The Bank also co-leads (with UNFPA) UNAIDS support relating to combating the sexual transmission of HIV, and co-leads (with UNICEF) activities relating to social protection. The WBG co-sponsored the fifth Universal Health Care Financing Forum, which was held, in a virtual format, in two parts, in July and November–December 2020.

FINANCIAL OPERATIONS

IBRD capital is derived from members' subscriptions to capital shares, the calculation of which is based on their quotas in the IMF. At 30 June 2021 the total subscribed capital of the IBRD was US $297,856m., of which the paid-in portion was $19,244m. (6.5%); the remainder was subject to call if required. In April 2018 the Development Committee endorsed a package of measures that included a series of internal organizational reforms within the

WBG, and new policies aimed at strengthening the Group's operational effectiveness (including a shift in the focus of lending to poorer member states). In October the Board of Governors endorsed an increase of $52,600m. in the IBRD's callable capital and of $7,500m. in the paid-in portion. A temporary expansion of IBRD lending at times of global financial crisis was agreed. It was envisaged that the financing capacity of the WBG would increase from around $60,000m. annually to $100,000m. by 2030. Most of the IBRD's lendable funds come from its borrowing, on commercial terms, in world capital markets, and also from its retained earnings and the flow of repayments on its loans. IBRD loans carry a variable interest rate, rather than a rate fixed at the time of borrowing.

IBRD loans usually have a 'grace period' of five years and are repayable over 15 years or fewer. Loans are made to governments, or must be guaranteed by the government concerned, and are normally made for projects likely to offer a commercially viable rate of return. In 1980 the World Bank introduced structural adjustment lending, which (instead of financing specific projects) supports programmes and changes necessary to modify the structure of an economy so that it can restore or maintain its growth and viability in its balance of payments over the medium term.

The IBRD made 125 new lending and investment commitments totalling US $30,523m. during the financial year ending 30 June 2021 (compared with $27,976m. for 152 operations in the previous year). Total disbursements by the IBRD in the year ending 30 June 2021 amounted to $20,238m. Total WBG (i.e. combined IBRD, IDA, IFC, MIGA and recipient-executed trust fund) commitments in 2020/21 amounted to $98,830m., and disbursements to $60,956m.

Of total IBRD lending for 2020/21 US $2,025m. (7%) was allocated to projects in Africa.

In January 2012 the Bank launched the Program for Results (PforR), a lending instrument that links the disbursement of funds to the delivery of predefined results. By 30 September 2021 121 PforR projects were active, requiring funding of US $38,200m.

A trust fund was established in April 2010 to support a Global Agriculture and Food Security Programme (GAFSP), with total donations amounting to US $900m. In October 2020 the GAFSP Replenishment Period 2020–25 was initiated, during which it was envisaged that $1,500m. would be raised. In May 2022, in response to the wider global impacts of the Russian Federation's invasion of Ukraine, the World Bank, IMF and other international financial institutions collectively issued the Joint International Financial Institution Plan to Address Food Insecurity, with a focus on the following six objectives: (i) support vulnerable people; (ii) promote open trade; (iii) mitigate fertilizer shortages; (iv) support food production now; (v) invest in climate-resilient agriculture for the future; and (vi) co-ordinate for maximum impact. At a meeting of G7 ministers responsible for development held in that month a joint G7-World Bank Global Alliance for Food Security was created, with the aim of promptly catalyzing a concerted response to the global hunger crisis. Other international partners were invited to participate. Also in that month the World Bank announced that it would invest up to $30,000m. in new and existing projects in areas that included agriculture, fertilizer production, nutrition, social protection, water and irrigation.

In May 2020 the Bank's Board of Executive Directors approved a new Emergency Locust Response Programme, costing US $500m., which was to provide urgent financing to countries in eastern Africa and the Middle East to eliminate locust swarms that were placing crop production and food security at risk.

A joint World Bank/IMF initiative to assist heavily indebted poor countries (HIPCs) to reduce their debt burden to a sustainable level, in order to make more resources available for poverty reduction and economic growth, was established in 1996. An enhanced HIPC scheme was approved in September 1999, incorporating the requirement for applicant countries to formulate, in consultation with external partners and other stakeholders, a results-oriented national strategy to promote growth and reduce poverty, to be presented in the form of a Poverty Reduction Strategy Paper (PRSP). At a pivotal 'decision point' of the process, having developed and successfully applied, for at least one year, a PRSP, applicant countries still deemed to have an unsustainable level of debt qualified for interim debt relief from the IDA and IMF, as well as relief on highly concessional terms from other official bilateral creditors and multilateral institutions. During the ensuing 'interim period' countries were required successfully to implement further economic and social development reforms, as a final demonstration of suitability for securing full debt relief at the 'completion point' of the scheme. In the majority of cases a sustainable level of debt was targeted at 150% of the net present value (NPV) of the debt in relation to total annual exports. Other countries with lower debt-to-export ratios were to be eligible for assistance under the scheme, providing that their export earnings were at least 30% of gross domestic product (GDP), and government revenue at least 15% of GDP. In 2001 the Bank introduced a Poverty Reduction Support Credit to help low-income countries to implement the policy and institutional reforms outlined in their PRSP. In September 2005 the Bank's Development Committee

and the International Monetary and Financial Committee of the IMF endorsed a G8 proposal—subsequently referred to as the Multilateral Debt Relief Initiative (MDRI)—to provide additional resources to achieve the cancellation of debts owed by eligible HIPCs; countries that had reached their completion point qualified for immediate assistance.

By 2022 36 countries, including Benin, Burkina Faso, Burundi, Cameroon, the Central African Republic, Chad, Comoros, Côte d'Ivoire, the Democratic Republic of the Congo, the Republic of Congo, Ethiopia, The Gambia, Ghana, Guinea, Guinea-Bissau, Liberia, Madagascar, Malawi, Mali, Mauritania, Mozambique, Niger, Rwanda, São Tomé and Príncipe, Senegal, Sierra Leone, Tanzania, Togo, Uganda and Zambia, had reached completion point under the enhanced HIPC initiative. In March 2020 Somalia was deemed to have reached decision point, and thus eligible for initial debt reduction, while Sudan was declared to have reached decision point in late June 2021. Eritrea remained under consideration as potentially eligible for the initiative at that time.

TECHNICAL ASSISTANCE AND KNOWLEDGE

The Bank's Advisory Services and Analytics (ASA) products include reports, policy notes, workshops, and technical action plans. Highly flexible Reimbursable Advisory Services (RAS)—paid for by clients—represent around 10% of ASA support. The Bank encourages the use of local consultants to assist with projects and to strengthen institutional capability. Annually the Bank issues around 400 working papers, with the aim of catalysing research and stimulating debate. Through its Development Research Group the Bank conducts its own research into a broad range of topics. The Bank supports learning and capacity building, in particular through the Open Learning Campus and knowledge sharing initiatives. The Bank has supported efforts, such as the Development Gateway, to disseminate information on development issues and programmes, and, since 1988, has organized the Annual Bank Conference on Development Economics (ABCDE) to provide a forum for the exchange and discussion of development-related ideas and research. The 2022 ABCDE was held in a virtual format in June, on the theme 'Recovery, Reform, and Business Environment'. In March 2016 the WBG inaugurated a Global Knowledge and Research Hub in Kuala Lumpur, Malaysia.

The İstanbul, Türkiye-based Global Centre for Islamic Finance, inaugurated by the Bank in October 2013, acts as a knowledge hub, to conduct research and training, and to provide technical assistance and advisory services to interested client countries on the development of Islamic financial institutions and markets.

The Bank's Office of the Chief Economist in the Africa Region (AFRCE) guides the Bank's strategic engagement with Africa. AFRCE activities include fostering a community of economists with an interest in sub-Saharan Africa; organizing research on regional development issues; producing *Africa's Pulse,* which offers analysis of the continent's development challenges and short-term economic prospects; and organizing the Annual Bank Conference on Africa (ABCA). The first Investing in Africa Forum (IAF) was convened in June 2015 by the WBG and partners. At the second IAF, held in September 2016, in Guangzhou, China, the World Bank, Chinese Ministry of Finance and Chinese National Energy Administration signed a Memorandum of Understanding aimed at strengthening co-operation on the promotion of clean and renewable power in Africa, including through geothermal, hydro, solar, wind, and natural gas technologies. A new Africa Think Tank Alliance was launched at the 2016 IAF. The fifth IAF, held in September 2019, in Brazzaville, Republic of the Congo, focused overall on leveraging partnerships to diversify economies and generate employment, and addressed specifically the digital economy, climate-smart energy solutions, human capital development, enhancing the business climate, and industrialization and global value chains.

In 1991 the African Capacity Building Foundation (ACBF) was established by the World Bank, the African Development Bank and UNDP, with the aim of encouraging indigenous research and managerial capabilities, by supporting or creating institutions for training, research and analysis. During 2017–21 the ACBF was implementing a strategy for Africa titled 'Skilled People and Strong Institutions Transforming Africa', focused on four pillars: Enabling effective delivery of continental development priorities; Supporting countries to achieve tangible development results; Enhancing private sector and civil society contributions to sustainable development; and Leveraging knowledge and learning to increase development effectiveness. The Bank supports the Nile Basin Initiative which aims to promote co-operation among basin states of the Nile to achieve sustainable socioeconomic development through the equitable use of its water resources. Other regional initiatives supported by the Bank include the Sub-Saharan Africa Transport Policy Programme, and TerrAfrica, started in October 2005 to support the financing and mainstreaming of country-driven sustainable land and water management activities. The Bank announced an African Climate Business Plan in November 2015, requiring US $16,100m. in funds, to accelerate and enhance resilience to climate change.

CRISIS SUPPORT

The Bank is a lead organization in providing reconstruction assistance following natural disasters or conflicts, usually in collaboration with other UN agencies or international organizations, and through special trust funds.

The Bank's Global Facility for Disaster Reduction and Recovery—GFDRR, established in 2006/07, focuses on, *inter alia,* the following thematic initiatives: promoting open access to risk information; resilient infrastructure; resilient cities; community resilience; resilience to climate change (with a focus on small island states); hydromet services; financial protection; and resilient recovery. In February 2014 a World Bank-GFDRR Disaster Risk Management Hub was inaugurated in Tokyo, Japan. In July 2015 the WBG, with the Governments of Canada, Norway and the USA, launched a Global Financing Facility which aimed to channel US $12,000m. towards reproductive, maternal, newborn, child, and adolescent health care.

In March 2016 the WBG hosted a meeting of UN agencies, multilateral development banks, and other partners, with a focus on humanitarian-development collaboration. The participants determined to strengthen collective action, and proposed the elaboration of a new humanitarian-development partnership. A new Partnership Framework between the Bank and the UN was signed in April 2017 to provide for greater collaboration in building the resilience of vulnerable communities, in particular in crisis-affected situations.

CO-OPERATION WITH OTHER ORGANIZATIONS

The World Bank co-operates with other international partners with the aim of improving the impact of development efforts. Meetings between the governing bodies of the WBG and IMF are convened annually. WBG-IMF Spring Meetings are held in April, normally in Washington, DC, USA, with participation by ministers of finance, central bankers, business executives, representatives of civil society organizations, and academics. The Bank collaborates with the IMF in implementing the HIPC scheme and the two agencies work closely to achieve a common approach to development initiatives. In May 2000 the Bank signed a joint statement of co-operation with the OECD. It holds regular consultations with other multilateral development banks and with the European Union with respect to development issues. The Bank is a partner, with the IMF, the UN Conference on Trade and Development, UNDP, the WTO and the International Trade Commission, in the Enhanced Integrated Framework (EIF) for trade-related assistance to least developed countries (LDCs), which since 2009 has aimed to facilitate greater participation by LDCs in the global trading system; EIF activities are supported by a dedicated EIF Trust Fund. A second EIF phase, supporting 51 beneficiaries, was being implemented during 2016–22. In June 2007 the World Bank and the UN Office on Drugs and Crime launched a joint Stolen Asset Recovery (StAR) initiative, as part of the Bank's Governance and Anti-Corruption strategy. In April 2009 the G20 recommended that StAR review and propose mechanisms to strengthen international co-operation relating to asset recovery. The inaugural Global Forum on Asset Recovery (GFAR) was convened in December 2017, in Washington, DC, with assistance from StAR.

As an implementing agency of the GEF the Bank assists countries to prepare and supervise GEF projects relating to biological diversity, climate change and other environmental protection measures. In September 2007 the Bank's Executive Directors approved a Carbon Partnership Facility and a Forest Carbon Partnership Facility to support its climate change activities. The Bank is a partner agency of the Climate and Clean Air Coalition to Reduce Short Lived Climate Pollutants (SLCPs), which was launched in February 2012 with the aim of combating SLCPs, including methane, black carbon and certain hydrofluorocarbons.

The World Bank hosts the administrative unit of the Global Infrastructure Facility (GIF), which commenced operations in April 2015, tasked with assisting emerging markets and developing economies to generate investment in and to implement infrastructure projects. The GIF partnership included several donor countries, multinational banks and private sector advisers. Eligible projects were to focus on 'climate-smart' investments and those facilitating trade and enhanced interconnectivity. The Bank participates with other multilateral development banks and partners in the annual Global Infrastructure Forum (first convened in April 2016).

The WBG hosts the Public-Private Infrastructure Advisory Facility (PPIAF), a multi-donor facility that was established in 1999 by Japan and the UK to promote engagement in emerging economies by private sector interests.

IBRD Institutions

International Centre for Settlement of Investment Disputes (ICSID): f. 1966 under the Convention of the Settlement of Investment Disputes between States and Nationals of Other States; the Convention was designed to encourage the growth of private foreign investment for economic development, by creating the possibility, always subject to the consent of both parties, for a Contracting State and a foreign investor who is a national of another Contracting State to settle any legal dispute that might arise out of such an investment by arbitration and/or conciliation before an impartial, international forum; the governing body of the Centre is its Administrative Council, composed of one representative of each Contracting State, all of whom have equal voting power; the President of the World Bank is (ex officio) the non-voting Chairman of the Administrative Council; at 1 Oct. 2022 924 cases had been registered with the Centre, of which 635 had been concluded and 289 were pending consideration; mems: 165 (158 Contracting States having signed and ratified the Convention and 7 Signatory States); Sec.-Gen. MEG KINNEAR (Canada); publs *Annual Report, ICSID Caseload Statistics* (2 a year), *ICSID Review—Foreign Investment Law Journal* (2 a year).

Open Learning Campus (OLC): f. Dec. 2015; aims to use and improve e-learning for development; comprises WBx Talks, providing short lessons through, *inter alia,* podcasts, video presentations, webinars and mobile telephone apps; WBa Academy, offering self-paced, customized structured courses; and WBc Connect, providing peer learning and expert advice, and establishing communities of practice; topics covered include climate change; governance; insurance and pensions; urban floods; gender identity and devt; knowledge hubs; and public-private partnerships; the establishment of a devt-focused Solutions Bank is envisaged; the Campus is supported by partner institutions and donor partners; in particular, the Government of South Korea and South Korean institutions have played a leading role in supporting the OLC; publs *Annual Report, Development Outreach* (quarterly), other books, working papers, case studies.

Publications

Africa's Pulse (2 a year).

Commodity Markets Outlook (2 a year).

Digital Development Partnership Annual Interactive Report.

Doing Business.

Global Development Finance (annually).

Global Economic Prospects (2 a year).

Global Financial Development Report (annually).

International Debt Statistics (annually).

MENA Data Book.

Poverty and Shared Prosperity (annually).

Results and Performance of the World Bank Group (annually).

State and Trends of Carbon Pricing.

Sustainable Energy for All: Global Tracking Framework (every 2 years).

The World Bank and the Environment (annually).

World Bank Annual Report.

World Bank Economic Review (3 a year).

World Bank Research Observer.

World Development Indicators (annually).

World Development Report (annually).

Technical papers, regional and country reports and strategy documents, sectoral studies.

Statistics

IBRD LENDING COMMITMENTS, BY SECTOR AND REGION

(projects approved, year ending 30 June; US $ million)

	2019	2020	2021
Agriculture, fishing and forestry	1,025	1,767	1,260
Education	1,875	1,135	2,017
Energy and extractives	2,847	2,053	2,379
Financial sector	2,299	3,702	3,828
Health	1,674	3,980	2,606
Industry, trade and services	2,361	2,208	3,030
Information and communication technologies	611	886	773
Public administration	5,327	4,301	5,666
Social protection	2,115	4,786	4,800
Transportation	1,485	1,323	2,273

—continued	2019	2020	2021
Water, sanitation and waste management	1,571	1,834	1,891
Total	23,191	27,976	30,523
Africa	820	1,725	2,025
East Asia and the Pacific	4,030	4,770	6,753
Europe and Central Asia	3,749	5,699	4,559
Latin America and the Caribbean	5,709	6,798	9,464
Middle East and North Africa	4,872	3,419	3,976
South Asia	4,011	5,565	3,746

Source: World Bank, *Annual Report 2021*.

IBRD AND IDA LENDING IN EASTERN AND SOUTHERN AFRICA BY SECTOR, 1 JULY 2020–30 JUNE 2021

Sector	% of total subregional commitments*
Agriculture, fishing and forestry	7.0
Education	10.0
Energy and extractives	12.0
Financial sector	6.0
Health	10.0
Industry, trade and services	7.0
Information and communication technologies	5.0
Public administration	12.0
Social protection	17.0
Transportation	11.0
Water, sanitation and waste management	3.0
Total	100.0

* Amounting to US $15,614m. (IBRD: $1,525m.; IDA: $14,089m.).

Source: World Bank, *Annual Report 2021*.

IBRD AND IDA LENDING IN WESTERN AND CENTRAL AFRICA BY SECTOR, 1 JULY 2020–30 JUNE 2021

Sector	% of total subregional commitments*
Agriculture, fishing and forestry	10.0
Education	9.0
Energy and extractives	17.0
Financial sector	5.0
Health	10.0
Industry, trade and services	4.0
Information and communication technologies	3.0
Public administration	17.0
Social protection	13.0
Transportation	4.0
Water, sanitation and waste management	10.0
Total	100.0

* Amounting to US $11,455m. (IBRD: $500m.; IDA: $10,955m.).

Source: World Bank, *Annual Report 2021*.

International Development Association—IDA

Address: 1818 H St, NW, Washington, DC 20433, USA.
Telephone: (202) 473-1000; **fax:** (202) 477-6391; **internet:** www.worldbank.org/ida.

IDA began operations in November 1960. Affiliated to the International Bank for Reconstruction and Development (IBRD), IDA advances capital to the poorer developing member countries on more flexible terms than those offered by the IBRD. IDA is a member of the World Bank Group (WBG). From 2013 IDA participated in the first WBG Strategy aimed at reducing extreme poverty and promoting shared prosperity by 2030.

Organization
(October 2022)

Officers and staff of the IBRD serve concurrently as officers and staff of IDA.

President and Chairman of Executive Directors: DAVID MALPASS (USA).

Activities

IDA assistance is aimed at supporting the poverty reduction strategies of the poorer developing countries, i.e. those with an annual gross national income (GNI) per caput of less than US $1,205 in 2021/22. Under IDA lending conditions, credits can be extended to countries whose balance of payments could not sustain the burden of repayment required for IBRD loans. Terms are more favourable than those provided by the IBRD; as at 1 January 2022 the maturity of IDA credits for small economies was 40 years, with a grace period of 10 years; for regular economies 38 years with a grace period of six years; and for so-called blend borrowers (which are entitled to borrow from both IDA and IBRD) 30 years with a five-year grace period.

In 2021/22 74 countries were eligible for IDA assistance, including 15 blend borrowers. Exceptions may be made for countries with GNI greater than US $1,205, but which would otherwise have little or no access to Bank funds.

IDA's development resources are replenished every three years by contributions from the more affluent member countries, which are supplemented by WBG funding and credit repayments. At the same time partner countries review IDA policies and may determine future strategic priorities. The 19th replenishment of IDA funds (IDA19) amounted to US $82,000m., pledged by 52 countries in December 2019. The theme of IDA19 was 'Ten Years to 2030: Growth, People, and Resilience'. In April 2021 the IDA20 replenishment process was launched a year early, with a view to advancing policy and financial support measures for developing nations' COVID-19 pandemic recovery. IDA20, to be implemented during July 2022–June 2025, was finalized in December 2021, at a meeting hosted by Japan in a virtual format. Donor nations pledged $23,400m., contributing to a replenishment package of $93,000m. The special themes for IDA20—under the broad commitment of 'Building Back Better from the Crisis: Towards a Green, Resilient and Inclusive Future'—were climate change; fragility, conflict and violence; gender and development; human capital; and jobs and economic transformation. Debt, technology, governance and institutions and crisis preparedness were identified as priority cross-cutting issues.

In April 2018 IDA issued a five-year bond (its first), raising US $1,500m. from investors globally.

In March 2020 the Boards of Directors of the IBRD and IFC approved an emergency US $14,000m. package comprising fast-track low-cost loans, grants and technical assistance, to support at-risk developing countries in containing and combating the COVID-19 contagion. Some $6,000m. was to be made available in the near term by IDA and the IBRD to support health care activities. In April the WBG, IMF and Group of 20 (G20) leading economies agreed to suspend, for a period of one year from 1 May, the debt service payments of up to 73 eligible developing countries (of which 40 were in Africa); this deadline was subsequently extended to 31 December 2021. On 1 July 2020 the WBG introduced a Sustainable Development Finance Policy for IDA countries, establishing financial incentives for debt and investment transparency.

FINANCIAL OPERATIONS

During the year ending 30 June 2021 new IDA commitments amounted to US $36,028m. for 297 projects, compared with $30,365m. for 298 projects in the previous year. In 2020/21 $6,352m. (representing some 17.6% of lending) was for social protection, $5,572m. (15.5%) was for projects in the area of public administration, $3,840m. (10.7%) was for health initiatives (particularly related to the COVID-19 pandemic), $3,801m. (10.6%) for energy and extractives sector initiatives, $3,585m. (nearly 10%) for education initiatives, $2,912m. (8.1%) for agriculture, $2,367m. (6.6%) for transportation, $2,365m. (6.6%) for water, sanitation and waste management projects, $2,174m. (6.0%) for projects in the industry, trade and services sectors, $1,910m. (5.3%) for financial sector projects, and $1,151m. (3.2%) for information and communications technology initiatives.

Of total IDA assistance during 2020/21 US $14,089m. (39.1%) was for Eastern and Southern Africa and $10,955m. (30.4%) for Western and Central Africa.

In July 2017, under IDA18, an IDA-International Finance Corporation (IFC)-Multilateral Investment Guarantee Agency (MIGA) Private Sector Window (PSW) was established, which aimed to leverage increased private sector investment in IDA-only countries, in particular in fragile and conflict-affected states. The PSW includes a Risk Mitigation Facility, Blended Finance Facility, Local Currency Facility (aimed at reducing currency risk), and a MIGA Guarantee Facility (to expand the coverage of MIGA guarantees); the facilities were to be implemented by IFC on behalf of IDA.

From July 2020 the IDA's Fragility, Conflict and Violence Envelope was assisting fragile states through a Prevention and Resilience Allocation (PRA—targeted at countries deemed to be at risk of descending into large-scale or high-intensity conflict); a Remaining Engaged during Conflict Allocation (RECA); and a Turn Around Allocation (TAA—supporting the implementation of constructive reforms aimed at building resilience in states that were emerging from conflict or from a debilitating social or political crisis).

An IDA Window for Host Communities and Refugees (WHR) supports a UN Comprehensive Refugee Response Framework (CRRF), which aimed to provide long-term development solutions for low-income countries hosting significant influxes of refugees, with a focus on the social and economic inclusion of refugees and on the wellbeing of host communities. Under IDA19 up to US $2,200m. was to be channelled through the WHR, including $1,000m. for projects focused on COVID-19 response and recovery, and under IDA20 up to $2,400m. was to be allocated to the Window.

In December 2011 the Board of Executive Directors approved the establishment of an Immediate Response Mechanism, enabling countries rapidly to access up to 5% of their undisbursed IDA investment project balances in the event of a crisis. IDA's Crisis Response Window (CRW), established in 2009, aims to strengthen the capacity of IDA-eligible countries to address the impact of exceptionally severe natural and economic shocks in a structured and expedited manner, without damaging their long-term development paths. Under IDA20 some US $3,300m. was to be allocated to the CRW.

A new IDA Regional Window was initiated under IDA19, in 2020, to support policy reforms and strategic investments aimed at facilitating regional integration, connectivity and development, and the generation of wider public goods, by taking advantage of economies of scale and collective action. The Regional Window was to provide top-up funding to boost projects in areas including critical infrastructure (for example, digital technology, energy and transport); public goods; human capital; the blue economy; and the specific needs of small islands. Some 75% of funding through the new Window was to be allocated to Africa (with a special focus on the fragile Horn of Africa, Lake Chad area, and Sahel), and the remaining 25% distributed to other regions. Under IDA20 US $6,300m. was allocated to the IDA Scale-Up Window (SUW—introduced in 2017 as the IDA18 Scale-up Facility, and renamed in 2020), with a focus on supporting high quality, transformational development projects; additional short maturity loans were also to be made available within the SUW.

During April–September 2020 the WBG channelled US $195.8m. through a quick-disbursing Pandemic Emergency Financing Facility (PEF—which was operational during June 2017–30 April 2021), to support rapid surge responses to contain and combat the COVID-19 pandemic in 64 developing countries.

The WBG's US $500m. Emergency Locust Response Program (ELRP) was approved by the Board of Executive Directors in May 2020 to extend flexible support, in the form of technical assistance, policy advice, and finance, to states in Africa, Middle East and beyond that were affected or at risk from a recent upsurge in locust swarms. The ELRP has a particular focus on monitoring and controlling locust population growth and preventing the spread of swarms, while mitigating control measure-related risks; restoring the livelihoods of affected households; and building capacity to respond swiftly and efficiently to future outbreaks.

Bespoke ELRP initiatives approved in 2020 included a US $6m. Djibouti Locust Response Project; $63m. Ethiopia Locust Response Project; $43m. Kenya Locust Response Project; $40m. Somalia Shock Responsive Safety Net for Locust Response; and $48m. Uganda Locust Response Project.

Through a WBG multi-donor trust fund on nutrition, IDA supports the Power of Nutrition—an initiative launched in April 2015 by the WBG, UNICEF and partner agencies to finance country-led programmes targeting undernutrition through a combination of public and private contributions.

IDA administers a Trust Fund, which was established in November 1996 as part of a World Bank/International Monetary Fund (IMF) initiative to assist heavily indebted poor countries (HIPCs). IDA's participation in the so-called Multilateral Debt Relief Initiative (MDRI) was approved by the Board of Executive Directors in March 2006 and entered into effect on 1 July. (See IBRD for further details on the HIPC initiative and the MDRI.)

In April 2015 the WBG and partners made a commitment to achieving universal financial inclusion—access by all adults worldwide to a transaction account. The 2017 edition of the World Bank's Global Findex Database (measuring financial inclusion) found that 69% of the global adult population was 'banked' in 2017, compared with 62% in 2014 and with 51% in 2011. The findings of the Database are summarized in the periodic *Little Data Book on Financial Inclusion*.

Publications

ABCs of IDA.
Annual Report.

International Finance Corporation—IFC

Address: 2121 Pennsylvania Ave, NW, Washington, DC 20433, USA.

Telephone: (202) 473-1000; **e-mail:** fjones@ifc.org; **internet:** www.ifc.org.

IFC was founded in 1956 as a member of the World Bank Group (WBG) to stimulate economic growth in developing countries through the direct financing of private sector investments. IFC also mobilizes capital in international financial markets, and provides technical assistance and advice to governments and businesses. From 2013 IFC participated in the first WBG Strategy aimed at reducing extreme poverty and promoting shared prosperity by 2030.

Organization

(October 2022)

IFC is a separate legal entity in the WBG. Executive Directors of the World Bank also serve as Directors of IFC. The President of the World Bank is ex officio Chairman of the IFC Board of Directors, which has appointed him President of IFC. Subject to his overall supervision, the day-to-day operations of IFC are conducted by its staff under the direction of the Executive Vice-President. At 30 June 2021 IFC had 4,283 staff members, of whom 57% were based in field offices.

PRINCIPAL OFFICERS

President: DAVID MALPASS (USA).

Managing Director and Executive Vice-President: MAKHTAR DIOP (Senegal).

Vice-President, Africa: SÉRGIO PIMENTA (France/Portugal).

Director, Eastern Africa: JUMOKE JAGUN-DOKUNMU (based in Nairobi, Kenya).

Director, Southern Africa: KEVIN NJIRAINI (based in Johannesburg, South Africa).

Director, West and Central Africa: ALIOU MAIGA (based in Dakar, Senegal).

Director, North Africa: CHEICK-OUMAR SYLLA (based in Cairo, Egypt).

Activities

IFC aims to advance the economies of developing member countries by lending directly without the need for government guarantees to sustainable private enterprises, and by providing expert advisory services. IFC finances private sector projects either through loans from its own account (known as A-loans); through equity and quasi-equity financing and syndicated loans (B-loans); or through partial credit guarantees and risk management products. IFC also extends funding to financial intermediaries, which then lend onwards to clients. It aims to facilitate the conditions that stimulate the flow of domestic and foreign private investment and generate jobs. IFC may provide finance for a project that is partly state-owned, provided that there is participation by the private sector and that the project is operated on a commercial basis. IFC also mobilizes additional resources from other financial institutions, in particular through syndicated loans, thus providing access to international capital markets. Its range of advisory services aim to improve the investment climate in developing countries. Technical assistance is extended to private enterprises and governments.

To be eligible for financing, projects must be profitable for investors, as well as financially and economically viable; must benefit the economy of the country concerned; and must comply with IFC's environmental and social guidelines. IFC aims to promote best corporate governance and management methods and sustainable business practices, and encourages partnerships between governments, non-governmental organizations and community groups. In 2006 IFC initiated a Sustainability Framework to help to assess the longer-term economic, environmental and social impact of projects; an updated Sustainability Framework came into effect on 1 January 2012. In 2002/03 IFC assisted 10 international banks to draft a voluntary set of guidelines (the Equator Principles), based on IFC's environmental, social and safeguard monitoring policies, to be applied to their global project finance activities. At June 2022 132 financial institutions, in 38 countries, had signed up to the Equator Principles.

IFC's authorized share capital is US $2,580m. In July 2010 the Board of Directors recommended a special capital increase of $130m., to raise authorized capital from $2,450m.; the increase took effect on 27 June 2012, having received the approval of the Board of Governors. A capital increase endorsed by the Board of Governors in October 2018 provided for the conversion of a portion of retained earnings into paid-in capital, and a Selective Capital Increase (SCI) and a General Capital Increase (GCI) that would provide up to $5,500m. in additional paid-in capital; the suspension of IFC grants to the International Development Agency (IDA) after the conclusion of the IDA18 replenishment cycle; and internal reform measures aimed at ensuring increased efficiency. The GCI and SCI took effect on 16 April 2020, followed on 22 April by the initiation of a subscription process. At 30 June 2021 IFC's paid-in capital stood at $20,760m. The World Bank was originally the principal source of borrowed funds, but IFC also borrows from private capital markets. In 2020/21 IFC reported a net income of $4,209m.

An IFC 3.0 Strategy, implemented from 2018, aimed to identify market opportunities, generate markets, and boost investment from private sector sources, with a particular focus on designing profitable initiatives with strong development impacts in regions with high rates of poverty and fragility. In April 2019 IFC adopted a series of Operating Principles for Impact Management, which aimed to promote transparency in investments.

In March 2020 the IFC Board of Directors endorsed (as a component of a US $14,000m. WBG package of assistance) $8,000m. in fast track financing that was intended to help protect economies and livelihoods affected by the COVID-19 pandemic. IFC anticipated that the immense local disruptions and global economic shock resulting from the pandemic crisis would place particular stress on micro, small and medium-sized enterprises, which had small capital bases. During the period 1 April 2020–30 June 2021 IFC financing to counter the impacts of the pandemic amounted to $42,700m., of which 37% was reportedly directed to support the private sector in low-income and fragile or conflict-affected states.

IFC's Global Trade Finance Program (GTFP), founded in 2004, provides guarantees for trade transactions. By 2021 more than 235 eligible financial institutions in 73 countries were participating in the GTFP, through which IFC had issued more than 68,000 guarantees, totalling US $66,500m.

The Banking on Women Global Trade Finance Programme (BOW-GTFP) supports banks participating in the GTFP network to expand trade finance to women-owned SMEs ('WSMEs').

IFC committed US $1,000m. in funds to a Global Trade Liquidity Program (GTLP), which was inaugurated by the WBG in April 2009; by 2021 the GTLP had mobilized support (extended by governments, other development banks and the private sector) of around $53,000m. in a estimated 24,000 trade transactions involving more than 400 financial institutions in 69 emerging markets. In 2009 IFC established a Distressed Asset Recovery Programme (DARP).

During 2020/21 IFC's Asset Management Company (AMC), through 11 investment funds, had raised assets totalling US $10,100m. From 1 February 2020 the AMC—hitherto a wholly-owned subsidiary of IFC—was merged fully into the Corporation. AMC investment funds include the IFC Capitalization Fund, initiated in 2009, which had made 41 investments amounting to $2,800m. by 30 June 2021. The Financial Institutions Growth Fund, established in 2015, had made 12 investment commitments, amounting to $258m., by 30 June 2021. By then the IFC Global Infrastructure Fund, established in 2013, with capitalization of $1,200m., had made 22 investment commitments, with a total value of $702m. IFC's Global Emerging Markets Fund of Funds, which invests mainly in private equity funds in emerging and frontier markets, had made 30 investment commitments totalling $756m. by end-June 2021. An IFC Catalyst Fund was inaugurated in 2012 to invest in private equity funds providing growth capital for companies addressing resource efficiency in emerging markets; by 30 June 2021 it had made 22 investment commitments totalling $386m. A $115m. IFC's Women Entrepreneurs Debt Fund has supported female-owned SMEs since 2016. In 2021 IFC had a portfolio of more than 200 active trust funds.

The AMC also manages IFC's African, Latin American and Caribbean (ALAC) Fund, inaugurated in 2010 to co-invest, with IFC, in equity investments across a wide range of sectors. By 30 June 2021 the ALAC Fund had made 39 investment commitments amounting to US $879m. In 2010 an Africa Capitalization Fund was launched to invest in systemically important commercial banking institutions in Africa; assets under its management totalled $182m. at 30 June 2021, by which time it had made eight investments, totalling $130m. A Middle East and North Africa Fund, with assets of $162m., was established in 2015/16, and by 30 June 2021 had made five investment commitments that totalled $78m.

IFC was tasked with implementing, on behalf of the IDA, the Risk Mitigation Facility, Blended Finance Facility, Local Currency Facility (aimed at reducing currency risk), and MIGA Guarantee Facility (to expand the coverage of MIGA guarantees) that were included in the US $2,500m. IDA-IFC-MIGA Private Sector Window (PSW), inaugurated in July 2017.

In the year ending 30 June 2021 IFC's long-term investment commitments and core mobilization of funds amounted to US $23,305m. for 313 projects (compared with $21,961m. for 282 projects in the previous year). Of the total approved in 2020/21, $12,474m. was for IFC's own account, while $10,831m. was in the form of loan syndications and parallel loans, underwriting of securities issues and investment funds, public-private partnerships, and funds mobilized by the IFC Asset Management Company. Generally, IFC limits its financing to less than 25% of the total cost of a project, but it may take up to a 35% stake in a venture (although never as a majority shareholder). Disbursements amounted to $12,747m. in 2020/21.

In the financial year 2020/21 some US $2,435m. in long-term investment commitments from IFC's own account was allocated to sub-Saharan Africa. IFC's strategic priorities for the region are: to accelerate and deepen support to SMEs; to catalyze and conclude large investment projects; and to bolster reform of the investment climate. In particular, IFC was concerned with the needs of countries emerging from conflict and with the promotion of projects that support cross-border trade and investment. IFC aims significantly to increase its investment in and advisory services to agribusiness operations in order to improve efficiency and counter the escalating cost of food production. In January 2013 IFC and FAO signed a Memorandum of Understanding jointly to promote responsible private investment in agribusiness, and to promote the development of economic opportunities for rural communities. In May 2009 IFC pledged an additional $1,000m. in funding to the region in support of an international initiative, the Joint Action Plan for Africa, to promote trade, to strengthen the financial sector and to increase lending for infrastructure, agribusiness and SMEs in the region affected by the global financial crisis.

IFC's Advisory Services, in the form of advice, dialogue, problem solving and training, aim to promote best practices, improve business standards, increase access to finance, develop a regulatory environment that facilitates entrepreneurship and private sector growth, promote environmental and social sustainability, and enhance infrastructure. IFC undertook more than 800 active Advisory Service projects in more than 100 countries in 2020/21. In that financial year 54% of such projects were implemented in IDA countries, and 21% in fragile and conflict-affected areas, 24% were climate-related, and 42% incorporated efforts aimed at closing economic gaps between men and women. Total expenditure on Advisory Services during 2020/21 amounted to US $244.0m. IFC manages, jointly financed with the World Bank and MIGA, the Foreign Investment Advisory Service (FIAS), which provides technical assistance and advice on promoting foreign investment and strengthening a country's investment framework, at the request of governments.

Of total expenditure on Advisory Services during 2020/21 US $77.4m. was allocated to sub-Saharan Africa.

In April 1989 IFC (with UNDP and the African Development Bank—AfDB) initiated the African Management Services Company (AMSCo): its aim is to help find qualified senior executives from around the world to work with African companies, assist in the training of local managers, and provide supporting services.

In June 2022 IFC co-hosted the annual Africa CEO Forum, in Abidjan, Côte d'Ivoire, with participation that included business leaders, investors, policymakers and heads of state or government from 70 countries.

Publications

Annual Report.
Doing Business (annually).
Lessons of Experience (series).
Other handbooks, discussion papers, technical documents, policy toolkits, public policy journals.

Multilateral Investment Guarantee Agency—MIGA

Address: 1818 H St, NW, Washington, DC 20433, USA.
Telephone: (202) 458-2538; **fax:** (202) 522-0316; **e-mail:** migainquiry@worldbank.org; **internet:** www.miga.org.
MIGA was founded in 1988 as a member of the World Bank Group (WBG). MIGA's mandate is to end extreme poverty and promote shared prosperity by encouraging the flow of foreign direct investment to, and among, developing member countries—through the provision of political risk insurance and investment marketing services to foreign investors and host governments, respectively.

Organization
(October 2022)

MIGA is a legally separate entity within the World Bank Group. It is supervised by a Council of Governors (comprising one Governor and one Alternate of each member country) and an elected Board of Directors (of no less than 12 members).
President: DAVID MALPASS (USA).
Executive Vice-President and CEO: HIROSHI MATANO (Japan).
Regional Head, Africa: NKEM ONWUAMAEGBU.

Activities

The convention establishing MIGA took effect in April 1988. Authorized capital was initially set at 100,000 shares, equivalent to US $1,082m. The convention provided for an automatic increase of capital stock upon the admission of new members. By 30 June 2021 MIGA's capital base comprised 186,665 shares, equivalent to $1,919.6m. Total subscriptions to the capital stock amounted to $1,553.3m., of which $366.3m. was paid-in.

Under MIGA's Strategy and Business Outlook for 2021–23 the Agency aimed to deliver an annual average of US $5,500m.–$6,000m. in guarantees, and committed to increasing its share of investments in low-income countries and fragile situations to 30%–33% (from 25%). Priority areas of focus were to be clean energy, green finance, green buildings, public transportation, and climate-smart agribusiness. During 2021–25 some 35% of guarantees were to be allocated to climate support projects.

Before guaranteeing any investment, MIGA must ensure that it is commercially viable, contributes to the development process and is not harmful to the environment. The MIGA/International Finance Corporation Office of the Compliance Advisor/Ombudsman (established in the fiscal year 1998/99) considers the concerns of local communities directly affected by MIGA- or International Finance Corporation (IFC)-sponsored projects. In November 2010 the Council of Governors endorsed amendments to MIGA's convention (the first since 1988) to broaden the eligibility for investment projects and to enhance the effectiveness of MIGA's development impact. In April 2013 the Board of Directors approved a Conflict-Affected and Fragile Economies Facility (CAFEF), with the aim of providing political risk insurance to enable projects to be implemented in challenging environments that might assist with reconstruction, bring in capital, and generate employment. MIGA issues guarantees and cedes to the CAFEF—for eligible projects—an initial loss layer, of which the

Agency shares a portion. By 2022 MIGA had paid out on 10 claims on its political risk insurance. At that time the amount of insurance available for each project was US $220m., and there was a limit of $720m. in guarantees per country. MIGA works to deter and resolve disputes that might disrupt investments that it has insured, thereby enhancing the safety of investments and also boosting investor confidence.

During the year ending 30 June 2021 MIGA issued investment insurance contracts for 40 projects with a value of US $5,199.2m. (compared with 47 projects valued at $3,961m. in 2019/20). Some 85% of new guarantees went to projects in strategic priority areas, i.e. to International Development Association (IDA) or fragile countries or climate-related initiatives. As at 30 June 2021 guarantees issued by MIGA on behalf of trust funds that it administers had a total outstanding gross exposure of $24.8m. During 1988–2021 the total investment guarantees issued amounted to $64,900m., in support of local initiatives in 119 member countries, as well as regional, multiregional and global projects. As at 30 June 2021 MIGA's gross guarantee exposure stood at a record high of US $23,000m.

An IFC-administered MIGA Guarantee Facility, to fund expansion of the coverage of the agency's guarantees, was included in the IFC-MIGA Private Sector Window (PSW), which was established on 1 July 2017 with allocated funding of US $2,500m.

In April 2020 MIGA initiated a fast-track facility to help counter the COVID-19 emergency in low- and middle-income countries by supporting the purchase of urgent medical supplies, providing working capital for businesses and individuals, and helping to meet governments' funding needs. By 30 June 2021 MIGA had issued US $5,600m. in new guarantees under the new facility, to support 38 projects. In May of that year the Board of Directors approved a new partnership with IFC, in the framework of which MIGA was to extend $1,000m. in new trade finance guarantees to support the poorest countries' recovery from the COVID-19 crisis. In July MIGA and IFC launched a joint initiative supporting trade flows of critical goods—including COVID-19 vaccines and food—in low-income and fragile countries.

MIGA works with local insurers, export credit agencies, development finance institutions and other organizations to support capacity building within the insurance industry and to ensure a level of consistency among insurers. The Agency also offers investment marketing services to help to promote foreign direct investment (FDI) in developing countries and in transitional economies, and to disseminate information on investment opportunities.

MIGA reported in mid-2021 that trade finance in Africa had slumped by around 80% since the onset in early 2020 of the COVID-19 pandemic. In December 2021 the agency led a webinar that addressed means of encouraging a renewed flow of FDI to that continent.

Publications

Annual Report.
MIGA News (online newsletter, every 2 months).
World Investment and Political Risk.
Other guides, brochures and regional briefs.

International Fund for Agricultural Development—IFAD

Address: Via Paolo di Dono 44, 00142 Rome, Italy.
Telephone: (06) 54591; **fax:** (06) 5043463; **e-mail:** ifad@ifad.org; **internet:** www.ifad.org.

IFAD was established in 1977 with a mandate to combat hunger and eradicate poverty on a sustainable basis in the low-income, food-deficit regions of the world. Funding operations were initiated in January 1978.

Organization

(October 2022)

IFAD is governed by its member states, meeting as the Governing Council or Executive Board, while management of the organization is led by its President.

GOVERNING COUNCIL

Each member state is represented in the Governing Council (the Fund's highest authority) by a Governor and an Alternate. Sessions are held annually with special sessions as required. The Governing Council elects the President of the Fund (who also chairs the Executive Board) by a two-thirds' majority for a four-year term. The 45th session of the Council was convened in February 2022, on the theme 'Leveraging innovations and finance for a climate resilient and inclusive recovery'.

EXECUTIVE BOARD

The Executive Board is responsible for the conduct and general operation of IFAD and approves loans and grants for projects; it holds three regular sessions each year. It consists of 18 members and 18 alternates, elected by the Governing Council, who serve for three years. An independent Office of Evaluation reports directly to the Board.

The governance structure of the Fund is based on the classification of members. Membership of the Executive Board is distributed as follows: eight List A countries (i.e. industrialized donor countries), four List B (petroleum-exporting developing donor countries), and six List C (recipient developing countries), divided equally among the Sub-List C categories (i.e. Africa, Europe, Asia and the Pacific, and Latin America and the Caribbean).

President and Chairman of Executive Board: ÁLVARO LARIO (Spain).

Activities

IFAD provides financing primarily for projects designed to improve food production systems and strengthen market access in developing member states, and to strengthen related policies, services and institutions. In allocating resources IFAD is guided by the need to increase food production in the poorest food-deficit countries; the potential for increasing food production in other developing countries; and the importance of ensuring the nutrition, health and education of the poorest, most marginalized people in developing countries, i.e. small-scale farmers, artisanal fishermen, nomadic pastoralists, rural women, and the rural landless. All projects emphasize the participation of beneficiaries in development initiatives, both at local and national level. Issues relating to gender and household food security are incorporated into all aspects of its activities. IFAD recognizes that four-fifths of the Earth's biodiversity is in territories inhabited by Indigenous communities, and that they retain immense inherited local knowledge on means of living and producing food in holistic interdependence with the environment—while also, in the modern era, having experienced external disruption to traditional production and consumption patterns.

In May 2014 the Executive Board endorsed IFAD's Strategic Framework for 2016–25, devised within the context of the UN's 2030 Agenda for Sustainable Development, with its associated set of Sustainable Development Goals (SDGs). Priority areas of the Strategic Framework include the need to maximize IFAD's strategic positioning, to use its comparative advantage in both a leadership and catalytic role; to forge partnerships with governments, rural communities, farmers' organizations, and other partners; to mobilize increased investment for smallholder agriculture; to improve institutional efficiency; to mobilize resources through innovative means; to innovate in all of IFAD's areas of expertise; to continue to mainstream gender equality and women's empowerment, climate-smart agriculture and the sustainable management of natural resources, the promotion of nutrition-sensitive agriculture, and the

development of public-private production partnerships and of inclusive financial services; and to continue to develop South-South and triangular co-operation.

IFAD is a leading repository of knowledge, resources and expertise in the field of rural hunger and poverty alleviation. Through its technical assistance grants IFAD aims to promote research and capacity building in the agricultural sector, as well as the development of technologies to increase production and alleviate rural poverty. Within the strategic context of knowledge management, IFAD has supported initiatives to develop lines of communication between organizations, local agents and the rural poor.

IFAD hosts the secretariat of the International Land Coalition (ILC), a global alliance of more than 300 civil society and intergovernmental organizations that aim to respond to the needs and rights of communities living on and from the land. IFAD advocates for security of land tenure, and for strong land governance, recognizing that small farmers with protected land security have more incentive to invest in their land holdings and improve farming techniques. IFAD also invests in rural water infrastructure, and in technologies that facilitate domestic water supply, agricultural production, and post-harvest processing. Furthermore, the agency invests in strengthening fisheries access rights for fisher communities, and the development of small-scale aquaculture production.

IFAD recognizes that, traditionally, rural women have had limited access to credit, land, information and technologies, and focuses on areas that can empower women economically and socially. IFAD reported female participation in 51% of its projects in 2019. IFAD, FAO, WFP and UN Women implement a Joint Programme on Accelerating Progress towards the Economic Empowerment of Rural Women; in 2022 this was active in Ethiopia, Guatemala, Kyrgyzstan, Liberia, Nepal, Niger and Rwanda.

IFAD hosts the secretariat of the Platform for Agricultural Risk Management (PARM), an initiative of the G7 and G20 that was established in 2013, and was active in 2022 in eight African countries: Cabo Verde, Cameroon, Ethiopia, Liberia, Niger, Senegal, Uganda and Zambia.

IFAD contributes, with FAO, WFP and other agencies, to an Agricultural Market Information System (AMIS), which was initiated by a meeting of ministers responsible for agriculture from G20 countries, held in June 2011 to increase market transparency and to address the stabilization of food price volatility. IFAD, jointly with FAO, WFP, UNICEF and WHO, compiles an annual *State of Food Security and Nutrition in the World* report.

In March 2022 IFAD's President stated concern over the consequences for global staple cereal and fertilizer prices of the Russian Federation's invasion of Ukraine, noting that those two countries normally supplied around one-third of wheat exports to the global market, and that Russia was the largest global producer of fertilizer. In May, in response to the wider impacts of the situation in Ukraine, IFAD launched a Crisis Response Initiative, under which tailored interventions were to be targeted at rural communities—with a particular focus on high-risk countries in the Horn of Africa, southern Africa and the Sahel—to support sustainable food systems, prevent hunger, protect livelihoods and build resilience. Also in May, IFAD, the IMF, World Bank and other international financial institutions collectively issued the Joint International Financial Institution Plan to Address Food Insecurity, with a focus on the following six objectives: (i) support vulnerable people; (ii) promote open trade; (iii) mitigate fertilizer shortages; (iv) support food production now; (v) invest in climate-resilient agriculture for the future; and (vi) co-ordinate for maximum impact. In July negotiations held in İstanbul, Türkiye, under the auspices of the UN and Türkiye, culminated in the conclusion by Russia and Ukraine of a UN-backed agreement aimed at alleviating global food insecurity by enabling the resumption of exports of grain, sunflower oil and other essential goods from Odesa and two other Ukrainian Black Sea ports (that had hitherto been blockaded by Russia), and at facilitating fertilizer and grain exports from Russia (which had been subjected to punitive sanctions).

Since 2016 IFAD has intermittently published a *Rural Development Report*. The 2021 edition, issued in September, was themed 'Transforming food systems for rural prosperity'.

IFAD emphasizes the urgency of developing the sustainable intensification of farming, fishing and food security systems, given the growing and increasingly urbanized global population (requiring ever higher levels of food production), and parallel ongoing environmental degradation and reduction in access to agricultural land and to soil and water resources. The Fund supports projects that are concerned with environmental conservation, in an effort to alleviate poverty that results from the deterioration of natural resources. In addition, it extends environmental assessment grants to review the environmental consequences of projects under preparation. IFAD is an executing agency of the Global Environmental Facility, specializing in the area of combating rural poverty and environmental degradation, and of the Green Climate Fund. It was envisaged that US $500m. would be raised to support 10m. small-scale rural producers under a Rural Resilience Programme (2RP) that was developed in 2020. (2RP superseded a previous Adaptation for Smallholder Agriculture Programme.) In January 2022 the Executive Board approved an ethical investment policy, with an environmental, governance and social focus.

In November 2016 IFAD issued a report which addressed the role played by the sustainable management of drylands in countering the negative impact on food insecurity of land degradation, climate change and drought. In November 2020 IFAD contributed to a report that noted that only 1.7% of climate finance was allocated to support small-scale farmers.

IFAD and the International Center for Tropical Agriculture issued a statement of intent in February 2017 on maximizing co-operation between the two agencies in the development of climate-smart innovations and technologies for use by smallholder farmers.

IFAD supervises projects conceived in the framework of the Global Agriculture and Food Security Programme (GAFSP), a multilateral mechanism established in September 2009 by G20 heads of state and government. IFAD, WFP, FAO, and the UN Secretary-General collectively organized a Food Systems Summit in September 2021, with the aim of raising global awareness of challenges related to the production, processing and consumption of food, and to improving the output of safe, nutritious food. In January 2022, to support the follow-up to the Food Systems Summit, a co-ordination hub was launched, under the joint leadership of IFAD, FAO and WFP, and assisted by a Champions Advisory Group comprising stakeholder representation by, *inter alia*, producers, the private sector, indigenous peoples, youth and women.

In September 2021 IFAD issued a *Stocktake Report on Agroecology in IFAD Operations: An Integrated Approach to Sustainable Food Systems,* its first comprehensive assessment of agroecological practices—which combine traditional farming knowledge with modern scientific innovation, and aim to integrate ecological, social and economic development. The report addressed the efficient use and natural management of resources; diversification and agrobiodiversity; recycling of nutrients, water, biomass and energy; and innovations that link producers and consumers. The Fund reported at that time that agroecology was a component of three-fifths of the Fund's projects.

In November 2017 IFAD, FAO and WFP initiated a roadmap outlining enhanced collaboration in support of South-South and Triangular Co-operation (SSTC), as a means of achieving SDG 2 (on ending hunger). In February 2018 an IFAD/China SSTC Facility was established, with initial Chinese seed funding totalling US $15m. The Facility aimed to mobilize knowledge and resources to accelerate the alleviation of rural poverty, to improve the productivity of rural smallholders, to advance rural transformation, and to promote investments between developing countries. IFAD supports an Agri-Business Capital (ABC) Fund, which was initiated in 2019 to provide loans and equity investments tailored to the requirements of rural farmers' organizations, agribusinesses, small and medium sized enterprises, and financial institutions, with a particular focus on generating jobs for young people.

The IFAD Indigenous Peoples Assistance Facility (IPAF), created in 2007, funds microprojects that aim to build upon the traditional knowledge and natural resources of Indigenous communities and organizations. An IFAD Policy on Engagement with Indigenous Peoples was adopted in 2009. The fifth global meeting of IFAD's Indigenous Peoples' Forum (initiated in 2013) was held in February 2021 on the theme 'The value of indigenous food systems: resilience in the context of the COVID-19 pandemic'.

IFAD funds projects that support small farmers in maximizing the potential of their livestock, for example through the delivery of animal health services, training in best husbandry practices, supplies of credit to enable restocking, and assistance with optimizing the quality of breeds of animal and types of feed.

During 2021 migrant workers reportedly sent remittances to some 800,000 family members in developing countries (many in rural areas), to support, *inter alia*, local education, health and housing requirements. In early 2020, in view of the pandemic emergency, IFAD initiated a #FamilyRemittances campaign (2020–30), promoting the provision of financial services and a reduction of transfer costs to support resilience in the flow of remittances. In June 2021 IFAD hosted (in a virtual format) the seventh session of the Global Forum on Remittances, Investment and Development (GFRID). This launched a new Remittance Community Task Force (RCTF).

A Platform for Remittances, Investments and Migrants' Entrepreneurship in Africa (PRIME Africa) was initiated in 2019, with a view to maximizing the continental impact of remittances. During 2021 remittances exceeding US $95,000m. were sent by migrant workers to and within Africa.

IFAD's multi-donor Facility for Refugees, Migrants, Forced Displacement and Rural Stability (FARMS) aims to enhance social resilience and strengthen the management of natural resources.

IFAD is empowered to make both loans and grants. Loans are available on highly concessional, hardened, intermediate and ordinary terms. New Debt Sustainability Framework (DSF) grant financing was introduced in 2007 in place of highly concessional loans for heavily indebted poor countries (HIPCs). Research and technical assistance grants are awarded to projects focusing on research and training, and for project preparation and development. In order to increase the impact of its lending resources on food production, the Fund seeks as much as possible to attract other external donors and beneficiary governments as cofinanciers of its projects. In 2021 external co-financing amounted to US $1,281.5m., while domestic contributions, i.e. from recipient governments and other local sources, totalled $982.9m.

In November 2006 IFAD was granted access to the core resources of the HIPC Trust Fund, administered by the World Bank, to assist in financing the outstanding debt relief of heavily indebted poor countries. By 31 December 2021 IFAD had provided US $249.3m. in debt relief to the countries eligible for assistance under the initiative. In September 2010, the Executive Board approved the establishment of a Spanish Food Security Cofinancing Facility Trust Fund (the 'Spanish Trust Fund'), which is used to provide loans to IFAD borrower nations. At 31 December 2021 this had total assets of $209.9m.

IFAD's development projects usually include several components, such as infrastructure (e.g. improvement of water supplies, small-scale irrigation and road construction); input supply (e.g. improved seeds, fertilizers and pesticides); institutional support (e.g. research, training and extension services); and producer incentives (e.g. pricing and marketing improvements). IFAD also attempts to enable the landless to acquire income generating assets. By increasing the provision of credit for the rural poor, it seeks to free them from dependence on the capital market and to generate productive activities.

In addition to its regular efforts to identify projects and programmes, IFAD organizes special programming missions to selected countries to undertake a comprehensive review of the constraints affecting the rural poor, and to help countries to design bespoke strategies for resolving these. In general, projects based on the recommendations of these missions tend to focus on institutional improvements at national and local level to direct inputs and services to small farmers and the landless rural poor. Monitoring and evaluation missions are also sent to countries of operations.

During 2021 IFAD approved lending for six projects in Western and Central Africa and seven initiatives in the Eastern and Southern Africa region, involving loans amounting to US $249.4m. and $285.9m., respectively. At the end of 2021 49 programmes and projects were ongoing in 22 Western and Central African countries (representing a total investment of $1,865.2m.) and 46 programmes and projects were being implemented in 17 countries in Eastern and Southern Africa ($1,891.5m.). In March 2021 IFAD finalized the financing arrangements for a $35.7m. contribution to a cofinanced $67.4m. agricultural smallholder project in Zimbabwe. The Fund approved $9.8m. in May 2021 towards supporting a $25.9m. rural livelihoods resilience project in South Sudan, that was being implemented during 2021–27. In June 2021 IFAD approved $21.3m. in financing towards a three-year $58.8m. agricultural emergency support programme for Côte d'Ivoire.

Finance

In accordance with the Articles of Agreement establishing IFAD, the Governing Council periodically undertakes a review of the adequacy of resources available to the Fund and may request members to make additional contributions. In February 2021 member countries pledged US $3,800m. in contributions to IFAD12, covering 2022–24. The provisional regular budget for 2022 amounted to $174.1m.

Publications

Annual Report.

Journal of Law and Rural Development.

Resilient Food Systems.

Rural Development Report.

State of Food Security and Nutrition in the World (annually, with FAO, WFP, UNICEF and WHO).

International Monetary Fund—IMF

Address: 700 19th St, NW, Washington, DC 20431, USA.

Telephone: (202) 623-7000; **fax:** (202) 623-4661; **e-mail:** publicaffairs@imf.org; **internet:** www.imf.org.

The IMF was established at the same time as the World Bank in December 1945, to promote international monetary co-operation, global financial stability, and the expansion and balanced growth of international trade.

Organization

(October 2022)

Managing Director: KRISTALINA GEORGIEVA (Bulgaria).
First Deputy Managing Director: GITA GOPINATH (USA).
Director, African Department: ABEBE AEMRO SELASSIE (Ethiopia).

BOARD OF GOVERNORS

The highest authority of the Fund is exercised by the Board of Governors, on which each member country is represented by a Governor and an Alternate Governor. The Board normally meets once a year. The Board of Governors has delegated many of its powers to the Executive Directors. However, certain important powers including the conditions governing the admission of new members, adjustment of quotas, and the election of Executive Directors remain the sole responsibility of the Board of Governors.

BOARD OF EXECUTIVE DIRECTORS

The 24-member Board of Executive Directors, responsible for the day-to-day operations of the Fund, is in continuous session in Washington, DC, USA. As in the Board of Governors, the voting power of each member is related to its quota in the Fund, but in practice the Executive Directors normally operate by consensus. On 26 January 2016 a reform amendment entered into effect that altered the composition of the Board of Executive Directors in order to increase the representation of emerging dynamic economies and developing countries, as well as determining that the Board be fully elected by member countries or groups of countries.

REGIONAL REPRESENTATION

There is a network of regional offices and Resident Representatives in more than 90 member countries. In addition, special information and liaison offices are located in Tokyo, Japan (for Asia and the Pacific); in New York, USA (for the UN); and in Europe (including in Paris, France; Geneva, Switzerland; and Belgium, Brussels; and—for Central Europe and the Baltic States—in Warsaw, Poland).

Activities

The Fund works to support sustainable growth and to further international monetary co-operation. It extends financial assistance to countries experiencing actual and potential balance of payments difficulties, provides technical assistance and training to strengthen national economic capacities and promotes the dissemination of economic and financial data by its member states. The Fund undertakes regular consultations with its members and monitoring of their economic policies as part of its broader mandate of surveillance and assessment of global macroeconomic and financial stability.

COVID-19 AND RUSSIA–UKRAINE CRISES

In late March 2020 the IMF Managing Director welcomed the efforts of major central banks to ease monetary policy in response to the escalating COVID-19 crisis, and commended fiscal actions implemented by many governments to protect workers and companies in the interim, and to boost health systems. She noted that investors had already withdrawn US $83,000m. from emerging markets, representing the largest ever recorded flight of capital. The Managing Director pledged that, under the unprecedented and extraordinary circumstances, the Fund was ready to deploy all its lending capacity and would increase emergency finance massively. At that time the IMF announced $50,000m. in funding to support poor and middle-income member states with weak health systems to respond to the pandemic; some $10,000m. of this funding was in the form of zero interest rapid emergency loans. Meanwhile, the IMF's Catastrophe Containment and Relief Trust (CCRT), which provides debt relief to countries hit by catastrophic events, was being urgently replenished to enable the poorest economies to maximize and focus all available resources towards combating the pandemic; a first tranche of CCRT

grants was extended in mid-April. Meanwhile, at that time, the Fund, the World Bank Group and the G20 membership agreed a Debt Service Suspension Initiative (DSSI), providing for the temporary suspension of the debt service payments of up to 73 eligible countries (40 of which were in Africa).

In January 2021 the IMF's *World Economic Outlook* estimated that the global economy had contracted by -3.5% in 2020, and noted that women, youth, workers in informal employment, workers in contact-intensive sectors, and people already living in poverty had been particularly adversely affected by the impacts of the pandemic crisis. From June 2021 the IMF Executive Director participated, with the heads of the World Bank, the World Health Organization and the World Trade Organization (WTO), in a Multilateral Leaders Taskforce on vaccines access. They collectively issued a call for action to generate US $50,000m. in new financing to support a comprehensive health, trade and finance roadmap aimed at bringing an end to the COVID-19 crisis, including the implementation of an accelerated co-ordinated strategy to enable the prompt vaccination of people across the whole world against COVID-19. Meanwhile, the IMF was preparing an unprecedented new SDR allocation to assist its member states (see *Special Drawing Rights*). In July 2021 the *World Economic Outlook* noted that access to vaccines represented the principal factor underpinning economic normalization, and a major fault line between advanced and developing economies. The amount of debt service suspended through the DSSI during May 2020–December 2021 (when it expired, having twice been extended, in November 2020 and in April 2021) totalled $12,900m.; 48 of the 73 eligible countries participated in the initiative. During April 2020–9 March 2022 some 31 states received SDR 689.6m. (equivalent to $965.3m.) in debt relief through the CCRT (which had been extended through five tranches). As at 9 March 2022 (the date of the final published update on such support) the IMF was making available to member states financial assistance and debt service relief totalling around $250,000m.

In early March 2022, in response to the Russian Federation's military invasion of Ukraine (initiated in late February), the IMF warned of the 'severe impact' on the global economy of the consequences of the war. Already energy and grain prices were rising, while unprecedented economic, financial and communications sanctions had been imposed against Russia. In addition, a massive refugee crisis was developing beyond Ukraine's borders. National authorities were urged to assist poor households who would be particularly vulnerable to price rise shocks. At that time the Executive Board approved emergency financial support under the Rapid Financing Instrument (q.v.) of SDR 1,005.9m. (some US $1,400m.) to meet Ukraine's urgent balance of payments requirements and help to mitigate the economic impact of the conflict. In April, as a means of channelling donor resources, the Board established a Multi-Donor Administered Account for Ukraine. In May, in response to the wider global impacts of Russia's invasion of Ukraine, the IMF, World Bank and other international financial institutions collectively issued the Joint International Financial Institution Plan to Address Food Insecurity, with a focus on the following six objectives: (i) support vulnerable people; (ii) promote open trade; (iii) mitigate fertilizer shortages; (iv) support food production now; (v) invest in climate-resilient agriculture for the future; and (vi) co-ordinate for maximum impact. The IMF was also to intensify co-operation with other international financial institutions in support of debt restructurings, was to provide emergency assistance where necessary, and was to use a new Resilience and Sustainability Trust (RST) and associated Resilience and Sustainability Facility (RSF) to provide affordable longer term financing for low-income and vulnerable middle-income countries (including small states) that were implementing structural transitions to meet long-term challenges such as pandemic preparedness and climate change adaptation. By the end of April some $40,000m. had been committed by international donors to the RST.

In July 2022 the IMF forecast that global real growth in GDP would decelerate to 3.2% in 2022 (downgraded from a forecast of 3.6% that had been issued in April). Ongoing challenges included economic downturns in the People's Republic of China and Russia; mounting inflation, particularly in the USA and major European economies; and continuing broadly adverse impacts of the conflict in Ukraine. The risks that (in retaliation for economic sanctions imposed against it) Russia might suddenly cease exporting gas to Europe, and that tighter global financial conditions might prompt increased debt distress in emerging market and developing economies were noted.

RESOURCES

Members' fully paid quota subscriptions, in the form of currencies and reserve assets, serve as the principal resources of the IMF. The IMF's resources are held in three accounts: a main General Resources Account; a Special Disbursement Account, in which profits from sales of the Fund's gold are invested; and an Investment

Account. The IMF's quota resources may be supplemented by borrowing.

Special Drawing Rights (SDRs): The SDR was introduced in 1970 as a substitute for gold in international payments, and was intended eventually to become the principal reserve asset in the international monetary system. SDRs are allocated to members in proportion to their quotas. In September 1997 the Executive Board approved a special allocation of SDR 21,400m., in order to ensure an SDR to quota ratio of 29.32%, for all member countries: the ensuing Fourth Amendment to the Articles of Agreement came into effect on 10 August 2009, following its acceptance by 60% of member countries, having 85% of the total voting power, and the special allocation, equivalent to some US $33,000m., was implemented on 9 September. On the basis of recommendations made in April 2009 by the IMFC and by G20 heads of state and government, in response to the then global financial crisis, the Board of Governors also approved a third general allocation of SDRs, amounting to SDR 161,200m., in August 2009: this became available to all members, in proportion to their existing quotas, effective from 28 August. In April 2021 the IMFC urged the IMF to propose a new SDR general allocation amounting to $650,000m. (some SDR 456,000m.) aimed at boosting member countries' reserves and liquidity in the context of the ongoing recovery from the COVID-19 crisis; this was approved by the Board of Governors on 2 August.

The list of currencies and the weight of each in the SDR valuation basket is revised every five years (ongoing valuation period: 1 August 2022–31 July 2027). In November 2015 the Executive Board resolved to incorporate the Chinese renminbi into the valuation basket, with effect from 1 October 2016, in addition to the currencies of the European Economic and Monetary Union (the euro), Japan (yen), the UK (pound sterling) and the USA (US dollar) (which had made up the basket since 1999). The value of the SDR averaged US $1.42451 in 2021; it stood at $1.28068 on 3 October 2022.

Quotas: Each member is assigned a quota related to its national income, monetary reserves, trade balance and other economic indicators. A member's subscription is equal to its quota and is payable partly in SDRs and partly in its own currency. The quota determines a member's voting power, which is based on one vote for each SDR 100,000 of its quota plus the 250 votes to which each member is entitled. A member's quota also determines its access to the financial resources of the IMF, and its allocation of SDRs.

Quotas are reviewed at five-yearly intervals, to take into account the state of the world economy and members' different rates of development. Special increases, separate from each General Review, may be made in exceptional circumstances.

In February 2020 the Board of Governors adopted a Resolution that concluded, with no increase, the Fifteenth General Review of Quotas, and provided guidance for a forthcoming Sixteenth General Review of Quotas (to be concluded by 15 December 2023). At October 2022 total quotas in the Fund amounted to SDR 476,272.0m.

Borrowing: In May 1996 the participants (11 member states and central banks) in the General Arrangements to Borrow (GAB, established in 1962), concluded an agreement in principle to expand resources available for borrowing from SDR 17,000m. to SDR 34,000m., by securing the support of 25 countries with the financial capacity to assist the international monetary system. Consequently the New Arrangements to Borrow (NAB) was approved by the Executive Board in January 1997 and became effective in November 1998. The GAB ended on 25 December 2018 (the participants having agreed in December 2017 that the initiative had only limited usefulness).

In April 2009 G20 heads of state and of government resolved to expand the NAB facility, to incorporate all G20 economies, in order to increase its resources by up to SDR 367,500m. (US $500,000m.). They also agreed to support a general allocation of SDRs amounting to a further $250,000m., and to use additional resources from sales of IMF gold to provide $6,000m. in concessional financing for the poorest countries over the next two to three years. In April 2010 the IMF Executive Board approved the expansion and enlargement of NAB borrowing arrangements to SDR 369,997m.; this came into effect in March 2011. European Union (EU) heads of state and of government agreed in December to allocate to the IMF additional resources of up to $270,000m. in the form of bilateral loans. At meetings held in April and June 2012 G20 member states pledged to increase by more than $456,000m. resources to be made available to the IMF as part of a universal protective firewall to serve the Fund's entire membership. In June the Executive Board approved the modalities to enable bilateral borrowing from member countries as a means of supplementing both quota resources and the institution's standing borrowing arrangements; the Board agreed a new framework in August 2016 to maintain temporary access to bilateral borrowing. During 2021–23 some 40 bilateral borrowing agreements were in effect, with a value of around SDR 135,000m. In February 2016 NAB resources were reduced to SDR 182,000m. However, in January 2020 the IMF Executive Board approved an increase in NAB resources to SDR 364,700m. for the period 2021–25.

LENDING

The Fund makes resources available to eligible members on an essentially short-term and revolving basis to provide temporary assistance to contribute to the solution of their payments problems. The IMF holds both usable currencies (where the external payments position of the issuing member is strong) and unusable (weak) currencies. A member obtaining IMF resources 'purchases'—draws—either SDRs, or else the currency of another member in exchange for an equivalent amount (in SDR terms) of its own currency (so-called exchange purchases). The member then later 'repurchases' its own currency—i.e. reverses the transaction.

Before making a purchase, a member must show that its balance of payments or reserve position makes the purchase necessary. Apart from this requirement, reserve tranche purchases (i.e. purchases that do not bring the Fund's holdings of the member's currency to a level above its quota) are permitted unconditionally. With further purchases, however, the Fund's policy of conditionality means that a recipient country must agree to adjust its economic policies, as stipulated by the IMF. All requests other than for use of the reserve tranche are examined by the Executive Board to determine whether the proposed use would be consistent with the Fund's policies, and a member must discuss its proposed adjustment programme (including fiscal, monetary, exchange and trade policies) with IMF staff. In March 2009 the Executive Board approved reforms to modernize the Fund's conditionality policy, including greater use of pre-set qualification criteria and monitoring structural policy implementation by programme review (rather than by structural performance criteria).

Purchases outside the reserve tranche are made in four credit tranches, each equivalent to 25% of the member's quota; a member must then repurchase its own currency within a specified timescale. A credit tranche purchase is usually made under a Stand-by Arrangement (SBA) with the Fund (the core lending instrument, created in 1952 and revised in 2009), or under the Extended Fund Facility (EFF, launched in 1974). An SBA is normally of one to three years' duration, and the amount is made available in instalments, subject to the member's observance of performance criteria; repurchases must be made within three-and-a-quarter to five years. Repurchases under the EFF must be made within four-and-a-half to 10 years.

Members' annual access to IMF resources is reviewed periodically. In February 2016 the Executive Board set the annual access limit under SBAs and EFF credits (q.v.) at up to 145% of a member's quota, with the cumulative access limit set at 435%. In exceptional circumstances higher access may be permitted.

In January 2010 the Fund introduced new concessional facilities for low-income countries as part of broader reforms to enhance flexibility of lending and to focus support closer to specific national requirements. The three new facilities aimed to support country-owned programmes to achieve macroeconomic positions consistent with sustainable poverty reduction and economic growth. They carried a zero interest rate, although this was to be reviewed every two years. An Extended Credit Facility (ECF) succeeded the former Poverty Reduction and Growth Facility (PRGF, used during 1999–2009) to provide medium-term balance of payments assistance to low-income members. ECF loans were repayable over 10 years, with a five-and-a-half-year grace period. A Stand-by Credit Facility (SCF) replaced the high-access component of a former Exogenous Shocks Facility (operational from January 2006–December 2009) in order to provide short-term balance of payments financial assistance in response to the adverse economic impact of events beyond government control, including on a precautionary basis. SCF loans were repayable over eight years, with a grace period of four years. A Rapid Credit Facility (RCF) was to provide financial assistance to PRGF-eligible members requiring urgent balance of payments assistance, under a range of circumstances. Loans were repayable over 10 years, with a five-and-a-half-year grace period. In November 2011 a Rapid Financing Instrument (RFI) was launched, for which all member states were eligible, and which was designed to support urgent balance of payments requirements, including those arising from exogenous shocks such as commodity price changes, natural disasters, and post-conflict and other extreme situations. Low-income member states may also make use of a non-financial Policy Support Instrument (PSI), providing access to IMF monitoring and other support aimed at consolidating economic performance.

In February 2015 the IMF transformed its Post-Catastrophe Debt Relief Trust, established in 2010 following the devastating earthquake in Haiti, into the CCRT. With a similar objective of providing debt relief to low-income member states in order to free up resources to meet exceptional balance of payments needs, the CCRT incorporated a new window to support states affected by public health crises, in addition to a window to respond to natural disasters.

In May 2017 the Executive Board increased the annual access limit under the RCF and the RFI to 60% (from 37.5%) of a member's quota, in circumstances involving large natural disasters. The limits on access to the Fund's concessional facilities for low-income countries were expanded by 50% in 2015, and by a further one-third in May

2019. Following the onset of the COVID-19 pandemic, the Executive Board approved temporary increases in the annual limit on overall access to resources in the General Resources Account and the Poverty Reduction and Growth Facility Trust (PRGT, established in 1999), and increased access to the RCF's Exogenous Shock window and the RFI's regular window; in September 2020 and in March 2021 the exceptional terms were further extended. In June 2021 temporary increases were also agreed on access to the RCF's and RFI's Large Natural Disaster (LND) windows. In December the Executive Board endorsed temporary increases until 30 June 2023 on access to the RFI's regular window and to the RCF's Exogenous Shock window, and to both instruments' LND windows. In July 2021 normal access to the PRGT was increased to 145% of a member state's quota.

During the period March 2020–March 2022 emergency finance to alleviate the socioeconomic impacts of the COVID-19 pandemic was extended through the RFI to Benin (SDR 82.5m.), the Comoros (SDR 5.9m.), Equatorial Guinea (SDR 47.3m.), Eswatini (SDR 78.5m.), Ethiopia (SDR 300.7m.), Gabon (two instalments of SDR 108m., and a third instalment, of SDR 388.8m.), Lesotho (SDR 23.2m.), Namibia (SDR 191.1m.), Nigeria (SDR 2,454.5m.), Senegal (SDR 215.7m.), the Seychelles (SDR 22.9m.), and South Africa (SDR 3,051.2m.). Through the RCF, SDR 41.3m. had been approved for Benin, SDR 84.3m. for Burkina Faso, SDR 23.7m. for Cabo Verde, SDR 165.6m. and SDR 110.4m. (two instalments) for Cameroon, SDR 27.9m. for the Central African Republic (CAR), SDR 84.1m. and SDR 49.1m. (two instalments) for Chad, SDR 3.0m. for the Comoros, SDR 216.8m. for Côte d'Ivoire, SDR 31.8m. for Djibouti, SDR 15.6m. for The Gambia, SDR 107.1m. for Guinea, SDR 14.2m. for Guinea-Bissau, SDR 542.8m. for Kenya, SDR 11.7m. for Lesotho, two instalments of SDR 122.2m. for Madagascar, SDR 64.4m. and SDR 72.3m. (two instalments) for Malawi, SDR 146.7m. for Mali, SDR 95.7m. for Mauritania, SDR 227.2m. for Mozambique, SDR 83.7m. for Niger, two instalments of SDR 80.1m. for Rwanda, SDR 9.0m. for São Tomé and Príncipe, SDR 107.9m. for Senegal, SDR 103m. and SDR 35.3m. (two instalments) for Sierra Leone, SDR 36.9m. and SDR 123m. (two instalments) for South Sudan, SDR 397.8m. and SDR 265.2m. (two instalments) for Tanzania, and SDR 361m. for Uganda. Meanwhile, Benin, Burkina Faso, Burundi, the CAR, Chad, the Comoros, the Democratic Republic of the Congo, Djibouti, Ethiopia, The Gambia, Guinea, Guinea Bissau, Liberia, Madagascar, Malawi, Mali, Mozambique, Niger, Rwanda, São Tomé and Príncipe, Sierra Leone, Tanzania and Togo had all been had been granted allocations through the CCRT.

In March 2009 the Executive Board introduced a Flexible Credit Line (FCL) facility, which provided credit to countries with very strong economic foundations, but was also to be primarily considered as precautionary. The FCL had a repayment period of up to five years and no access 'cap'. In August 2010 the duration of the FCL, and credit available through it, were increased. In November 2011 a relatively flexible Precautionary and Liquidity Line (PLL) was initiated, which was to be made available to countries 'with sound economic fundamentals' and 'sound policies' that were encountering broadly challenging circumstances—including as insurance against shocks and as a short-term liquidity window. PLL arrangements may have a duration of either six months or one to two years.

In 2019 three-year ECFs were approved for Mali (in August, for SDR 140m.), for São Tomé and Príncipe (in October, for SDR 13.3m.), and for the CAR (SDR 86m.), and for Ethiopia (SDR 1,203m., both in December). Also in December 2019, an SDR 155m. ECF covering 2019–23 was approved for Liberia. In March 2020 the IMF Executive Board approved a 39-month SDR 35m. ECF for The Gambia (augmented by SDR 20m. in January 2021); and a three-year SDR 292.4m. combined ECF/EFF for Somalia—with the aim of simultaneously supporting the Somali authorities' implementation of economic reforms and also catalyzing concessional donor financing, in view of the ongoing coronavirus and desert locust infestation crises. In April the Executive Board augmented by SDR 71.5m. an (originally SDR 176.2m.) ECF that had been agreed for Togo in May 2017. Three-year EFF arrangements were approved in December 2019 for Equatorial Guinea (for SDR 205m.) and Ethiopia (SDR 902m.). In May 2020, bringing to an end a three-year ECF initiated for Benin in April 2017, the Executive Board approved an SDR 76.0m. augmentation to the original SDR 111.4m. arrangement, to address that country's urgent COVID-19-related financing requirements. In late July 2020, in view of socioeconomic pressures arising from the COVID-19 emergency, the ongoing ECF for São Tomé and Príncipe was augmented by SDR 148m., to be disbursed immediately. In early September an (initially SDR 115.9m.) ECF that had been approved for Mauritania in December 2017 was augmented by SDR 20.2m. An (initially SDR 2,673m.) EFF that had been approved for Angola in December 2018 was augmented in September 2020 by SDR 540.4m. An ECF totalling SDR 220m. was approved for Madagascar in March 2021. In June an SDR 1,733.1m. ECF was approved for Sudan, and an SDR 722m. ECF for Uganda. In July ECF and EFF arrangements, amounting to SDR 483m., were approved for Cameroon, and an SDR 407m. ECF and SDR 1,248m.

EFF were agreed for Kenya. An SDR 1,066m. ECF for the DRC and an SDR 74m. EFF for the Seychelles were also endorsed in that month. In December an SDR 392.6m. ECF was approved for Chad and an SDR 197.4m. ECF for Niger.

Under an enhanced heavily indebted poor countries (HIPCs) initiative agreed by the IMF and World Bank in September 1999, countries seeking debt relief were first to formulate, and then successfully to implement for at least one year, a national poverty reduction strategy. (Some 41 HIPCs had been identified, of which 33 were in sub-Saharan Africa.) In September 2005 the IMF and World Bank endorsed a G8 proposal—subsequently referred to as the Multilateral Debt Relief Initiative (MDRI)—to provide additional resources to achieve the full cancellation of debts owed by eligible HIPCs; countries that had reached their completion point were to qualify for immediate assistance. The IMF's Executive Board determined, additionally, to extend MDRI debt relief to all countries with an annual per caput gross domestic product of US $380, to be financed by IMF's own resources. Other financing was to be made from existing bilateral contributions to a PRGF Trust Subsidy Account. The initiative became effective in January 2006. In February 2015, given that there was no outstanding MDRI-eligible debt to the Fund, the IMF Executive Board decided to transfer related funds held in trust to the CCRT.

The Fund's non-financing Policy Coordination Instrument (PCI) enables member states not requiring resources (at the time of approval) to signal commitment to reforms, and also to promote financing from external sources.

In September 2014, in the context of the Third UN International Conference on Small Island Developing States (SIDS), convened in Apia, Samoa, the IMF pledged to continue to provide financial and technical assistance in support of the sustainable economic development of SIDS, which are deemed to be at increased risk of vulnerability to external shocks, and to have an increased likelihood of low economic growth and national debt. Some SIDS, for example those with suspended tourism sectors, were particularly vulnerable to adverse socioeconomic impacts of the COVID-19 crisis. In 2020 the IMF recognized 34 'Small Developing States' (SDS), i.e. states (excluding advanced and fuel exporting economies) with populations smaller than 1.5m. Of these states, 27 were SIDS, two were landlocked, and five were coastal. Fifteen of the SDS, with fewer than 200,000 inhabitants, were classified by the IMF as 'microstates'. There were 12 SDS (all of them SIDS) in the Caribbean, 11 (all SIDS) in the Pacific, seven in Africa, and four in Europe and Asia. The IMF considered one-half of the SDS globally to be offshore financial centres.

The IMF is a partner in the Enhanced Integrated Framework for trade-related assistance to least developed countries (LDCs), a multi-donor programme which aims to support greater participation by LDCs in the global trading system. A Trade Integration Mechanism assists member countries to secure financial support to cover balance of payments shortfalls resulting from multilateral trade liberalization agreements.

SURVEILLANCE

Under its Articles of Agreement, the Fund is mandated to oversee the effective functioning of the international monetary system. The main tools of surveillance are regular, bilateral consultations with member countries conducted in accordance with Article IV of the Articles of Agreement, which cover fiscal and monetary policies, balance of payments and external debt developments, as well as policies that affect the economic performance of a country, such as the labour market, social and environmental issues and good governance, and aspects of the country's capital accounts, and finance and banking sectors. The Executive Board monitors global economic developments and discusses policy implications from a multilateral perspective, based partly on World Economic Outlook reports and Global Financial Stability Reports. In July 2012 the Executive Board adopted a Decision on Bilateral and Multilateral Surveillance (the so-called Integrated Surveillance Decision), which aimed to strengthen the legal framework underpinning surveillance activities. In September the Board endorsed a Financial Surveillance Strategy detailing steps towards further strengthening the financial surveillance framework.

By September 2022 77 countries or territories were active subscribers to the IMF's Special Data Dissemination Standard, initiated in 1996 to enable access to reliable economic statistical information on international capital markets. Of those countries, 29 were subscribing to the supplementary SDDS Plus, which was introduced in 2012 to cover an expanded set of data categories. A Dissemination Standards Bulletin Board aims to ensure that information on SDDS subscribing countries is widely available. Through a General Data Dissemination System (GDDS), established in 1997, the Fund encourages all member countries to improve the production and dissemination of core economic data. In July 2015 the Executive Board approved an enhanced version of the GDDS (e-GDDS), which had 111 active participants by 2022.

The IMF's Financial Sector Assessment Programme (FSAP), initiated in 1999 and strengthened in 2009, aims to promote greater global financial security through the preparation of confidential detailed evaluations of the financial sectors of individual countries.

CAPACITY DEVELOPMENT

Technical assistance is provided by online training courses and engagement, special missions or resident representatives, or through specialized centres.

In October 2002 an East African Regional Technical Assistance Centre (East AFRITAC), based in Dar es Salaam, Tanzania, was inaugurated and West AFRITAC was launched in May 2003, to serve Francophone West African countries. (In 2012 West AFRITAC relocated from Bamako, Mali to Abidjan, Côte d'Ivoire.) AFRITAC West 2, based in Accra, Ghana, to cover the non-Francophone West African countries, commenced operations in December 2013. Central AFRITAC was launched in Libreville, Gabon, in 2007, and AFRITAC South (serving Southern Africa and the Indian Ocean) was inaugurated in October 2011, in Port Louis, Mauritius. An Africa Training Institute, located in Port Louis, was inaugurated in June 2014.

In May 2009 the IMF launched the first of a series of Topical Trust Funds (TTFs—providing support to member states towards addressing economic policy challenges), on Anti-Money Laundering and Combating the Financing of Terrorism. A TTF on Managing Natural Resource Wealth (MNRW-TF) was created in May 2011; a second phase of the MNRW-TF was launched in June 2016. In August 2016 the IMF initiated a Revenue Mobilization Trust Fund. A Financial Sector Stability Fund (FSSF) was established in April 2017, to promote financial inclusion and development.

Publications

Annual Report.
External Sector Report (annually).
F & D—Finance and Development (quarterly).
Fiscal Monitor (2 a year).
Global Financial Stability Report (2 a year).
Handbook on Securities Statistics (published jointly by the IMF, the BIS and the European Central Bank).
Joint BIS-IMF-OECD-World Bank Statistics on External Debt (quarterly).
Regional Economic Outlooks.
World Economic Outlook (2 a year).
Other country reports, staff discussion notes, working papers, economic and financial surveys, occasional papers, pamphlets, books.

Statistics

MEMBERSHIP AND QUOTAS IN AFRICA SOUTH OF THE SAHARA
(million SDR)

Country	October 2022
Angola	740.1
Benin	123.8
Botswana	197.2
Burkina Faso	120.4
Burundi	154.0
Cabo Verde	23.7
Cameroon	276.0
Central African Republic	111.4
Chad	140.2
Comoros	17.8
Congo, Democratic Republic	1,066.0
Congo, Republic	162.0
Côte d'Ivoire	650.4
Djibouti	31.8
Equatorial Guinea	157.5
Eritrea	15.9
Eswatini	78.5
Ethiopia	300.7
Gabon	216.0
The Gambia	62.2
Ghana	738.0
Guinea	214.2
Guinea-Bissau	28.4
Kenya	542.8
Lesotho	69.8
Liberia	258.4
Madagascar	244.4
Malawi	138.8
Mali	186.6
Mauritania	128.8
Mauritius	142.2
Mozambique	227.2
Namibia	191.1
Niger	131.6
Nigeria	2,454.5
Rwanda	160.2
São Tomé and Príncipe	14.8
Senegal	323.6
Seychelles	22.9
Sierra Leone	207.4
Somalia	163.4
South Africa	3,051.2
South Sudan	246.0
Sudan	630.2
Tanzania	397.8
Togo	146.8
Uganda	361.0
Zambia	978.2
Zimbabwe	706.8

World Health Organization—WHO

Address: 20 ave Appia, 1202 Geneva 27, Switzerland.
Telephone: 227912111; **fax:** 227913111; **e-mail:** info@who.int; **internet:** www.who.int.
WHO, established in 1948, is the lead agency within the UN system concerned with the protection and improvement of public health. It co-ordinates and undertakes disease control, prevention and surveillance, promotes lifelong good health, and supports the development of equitable, sustainable health systems.

Organization
(October 2022)

WHO's members gather annually in the World Health Assembly. The day-to-day activities of the organization are led by its Director-General.

WORLD HEALTH ASSEMBLY (WHA)

The Assembly meets once a year (in May) in Geneva, Switzerland, and is responsible for policymaking. It also reviews budgetary contributions; sets the biennial budget; appoints the Director-General; and admits new members. The 75th WHA took place in late May 2022.

EXECUTIVE BOARD

The Board is composed of 34 health experts designated by a member state that has been elected by the WHA to serve on the Board; each expert serves for three years. The Board holds a principal annual meeting every January to agree the agenda of the next WHA, and a second meeting in May to follow up the Assembly. The Board is responsible for putting into effect the decisions and policies of the Assembly.

SECRETARIAT

Within the secretariat are divisions of External Relations and Governance; Business Operations; Data, Analytics and Delivery of

Emergency Preparedness; the Chief Scientist and Science; Universal Health Coverage (UHC) and the Life Course; UHC and Communicable/Non-Communicable Diseases; UHC/Healthier Populations; Antimicrobial Resistance; Access to Medicines and Health Products; and Emergencies Preparedness and Response.

Director-General: Dr Tedros Adhanom Ghebreyesus (Ethiopia).

Deputy Director-General: Dr Zsuzsanna Jakab (Hungary).

Executive Directors: Jane Ellison (UK) (External Relations and Governance), Dr Michael Ryan (Ireland) (Health Emergencies).

PRINCIPAL OFFICES

Each of WHO's six geographical regions has its own organization, consisting of a regional committee representing relevant member states and associate members, and a regional office staffed by experts in various fields of health.

Africa Office: Cité du Djoue, BP 06, Brazzaville, Republic of the Congo; tel. 83-94-02; e-mail afrgocom@who.int; internet www.afro.who.int; Dir Dr Matshidiso Rebecca Moeti (Botswana).

International Health Regulations Coordination—WHO Lyon Office: 24 rue Jean Baldassini, 69007 Lyon, France; tel. 4-72-71-64-70; fax 4-72-71-64-71; e-mail ihrinfo@who.int; internet www.who.int/ihr/lyon/en; supports (with regional offices) countries in strengthening their national surveillance and response systems, with the aim of improving the detection, assessment and notification of events, and responding to public health risks and emergencies of international concern under the International Health Regulations.

WHO Centre for Health Development: I. H. D. Centre Bldg, 9th Floor, 5-1-1 Wakinohama-Kaigandori, Chuo-ku, Kobe, Japan; tel. (78) 230-3100; fax (78) 230-3178; e-mail wkc@who.int; internet extranet.who.int/kobe_centre/en; f. 1995; Dir Dr Sarah Louise Barber (USA).

A new WHO Academy, based in Lyon, France, introduced online courses for health workers from 2021, with the goal of reaching 10m. learners globally by 2023.

Activities

WHO is the UN system's co-ordinating authority for health (defined as 'a state of complete physical, mental and social wellbeing and not merely the absence of disease and infirmity'). WHO's objective is stated in its Constitution as 'the attainment by all peoples of the highest possible level of health'. It aims to provide leadership on global public health matters, in partnership, with other agencies, as well as to help to shape the global health research agenda, and to monitor and assess health trends. WHO provides technical and policy support to member countries and extends aid following emergencies and natural disasters.

WHO supports the pursuit of the Sustainable Development Goals (SDGs), which were designed to contribute—either directly or indirectly—to improved global health. SDG 3 explicitly aimed 'to ensure healthy lives and promote wellbeing for all at all ages', and was underpinned by some 13 health targets to be achieved by 2030. These included reducing the maternal mortality ratio to less than 70 per 100,000 live births; ending preventable deaths of newborns, to at least as low as 12 per 1,000 live births, and lowering the under-five mortality rate to at least as low as 25 per 1,000 live births; ending the epidemics of AIDS, tuberculosis (TB), malaria, and neglected tropical diseases, and combating hepatitis, water-borne diseases and other communicable diseases; reducing by one-third—through prevention and treatment—premature mortality from non-communicable diseases (NCDs), and promoting mental health and wellbeing; ensuring universal access to sexual and reproductive health services; strengthening prevention and treatment of substance abuse; enhancing the implementation of the Framework Convention on Tobacco Control; substantially lowering numbers of deaths and illnesses from hazardous chemicals, environmental pollution and contamination; ensuring UHC, including financial risk protection, and access to high-quality essential healthcare services, essential medicines and vaccines for all; advancing research and development of vaccines and medicines for those communicable and NCDs that mainly impact developing countries, and providing access to affordable essential medicines and vaccines against these; significantly increasing health financing and the recruitment, development and training of the health workforce in developing countries, with a particular focus on least developed countries and small island developing states; strengthening the capacity of all countries, in particular developing countries, for early warning, risk reduction and management of national and global health risks; and reducing by one-half the number of global deaths and injuries arising from road traffic accidents.

General Programme of Work: WHO's 13th General Programme of Work, adopted by the WHA in May 2018 to guide the organization's activities during 2019–23, had a 'triple billion goal', with the following specific objectives: by 2023 1,000m. more people globally were to benefit from UHC; protection against health emergencies was to be improved for 1,000m. people worldwide; and 1,000m. more people were to enjoy enhanced health and wellbeing. WHO welcomed the establishment in May 2020 of the independent Geneva-based grant-making WHO Foundation, which was to support WHO and its implementing partners in delivering the triple billion objectives.

COVID-19 PANDEMIC

On 31 December 2019 WHO's country office in the People's Republic of China reported that a cluster of cases of a viral respiratory illness similar to MERS-CoV (see under *Communicable Respiratory Diseases*) had emerged in Wuhan City, Hubei Province, apparently having been transmitted to humans from infected produce at a local wildlife and seafood market. It was believed to have derived originally from a species of wild bat. On 7 January 2020 the Chinese authorities confirmed that a newly identified coronavirus was in circulation. (In February the highly contagious new virus was officially termed severe acute respiratory syndrome coronavirus 2—SARS-CoV-2—and the disease that it was causing in humans was formally named COVID-19.) Experts were deployed immediately (in January) by WHO to liaise with the Chinese regional authorities. From January WHO liaised with global experts in studying, *inter alia*, the impacts of the emerging virus, means of treating it, vaccine development and testing, regulatory standardization, and optimum preparedness and response mechanisms. WHO issued technical guidance relating to the clinical management of the virus, case definitions, surveillance, infection prevention and control, and reducing zoonotic transmission. It also issued advisory notices for international traffic. WHO's Director-General met with the Chinese President in late January to discuss ongoing collaboration and public health measures to contain the outbreak. On 30 January WHO formally declared the intensifying new coronavirus epidemic to be a Public Health Emergency of International Concern (PHEIC). At the beginning of February WHO launched a preparedness and response plan, with a focus on ending human–human and zoonotic transmission of the virus, protecting frontline health workers, strengthening the capacity of fragile health systems to detect and diagnose the virus and to support patients, and minimizing the social and economic impact of the crisis. An international team of WHO medical experts was deployed to China in early February to investigate containment measures (including enforced quarantine) and other dimensions of the Chinese authorities' management of the outbreak, as well as scientific findings on transmission of the virus. On 11–12 February WHO organized a global research and innovation forum, with a view to identifying research priorities and knowledge gaps relating to the virus. A Global Research Roadmap was formulated to effect a co-ordinated scientific response to the epidemic. Later in February WHO experts led a joint rapid response team, with the European Centre for Disease Prevention and Control, to Italy where a sharp escalation in confirmed cases of COVID-19 had been recorded. On 11 March WHO declared the outbreak to be a pandemic, expressing deep concern at 'the alarming levels of spread and severity'. The declaration was intended to stimulate all governments to adopt new measures to reduce the transmission of the virus and control the epidemic. On 17 March the WHO Director-General emphasized that health authorities should test all suspected COVID-19 patients, with a view to identifying and isolating them and also identifying their contacts. On 23 March the WHO Director-General noted that the pace of the pandemic was accelerating and emphasized the urgent need for the production of protective equipment. By that time many governments were enforcing physical distancing measures, with the aim of containing the social transmission of the SARS-CoV-2 virus and reducing the COVID-19 caseload that risked overwhelming some public health systems.

In mid-April 2020 US President Trump announced the suspension of the USA's mandated and voluntary funding to WHO, pending the conclusion of a review into WHO's relationship with China and accountability in managing the prelude to the COVID-19 pandemic. In May the WHA adopted by consensus a proposal put forward by the European Union (EU) and Australia that an independent, impartial, comprehensive inquiry should be conducted into the origin of and global response to the pandemic, including an assessment of WHO's own performance; accordingly, an Independent Panel for Pandemic Preparedness and Response was initiated, to undertake this evaluation. The WHA also called for an intensification of efforts to contain the pandemic, and for transparent and equitable access to COVID-19-related health technologies, vaccines and treatments.

During March 2020 WHO established, with the UN Foundation and Swiss Philanthropy Foundation, a COVID-19 Solidarity Response Fund, in order to generate donations and funding to support a co-ordinated global response to the pandemic. In late April WHO and partners initiated the Access to COVID-19 Tools (ACT) Accelerator (q.v.), aimed at expediting the development and production of, and promoting equitable global access to, new health diagnostics, therapeutics, health systems and vaccines to combat the pandemic. In early June a US $2,000m. procurement fund was announced to support poorer countries to access COVID-19 vaccines. A WHO scientific brief issued in August noted that priority risk groups for severe COVID-19 illness included elderly people, people with comorbidities and frontline healthcare workers (at increased risk of high exposure to the virus).

From June 2021 WHO's Director-General participated in a Multilateral Leaders Taskforce on vaccines access with the WTO Director-General, IMF Executive Director and World Bank President. A WHO-WTO-World Intellectual Property Organization Trilateral COVID-19 Technical Assistance Platform was initiated in April 2022.

By September 2022 11 COVID-19 vaccines had been validated for emergency use by WHO's Emergency Use Listing (EUL) procedure, which reviews the safety, quality and efficacy of as yet unlicensed vaccines, therapeutics and diagnostics.

The Geneva Package approved in June 2022 by the 12th World Trade Organization (WTO) Ministerial Conference included an agreement that provided for a partial IP waiver under the WTO's 1995 Agreement on Trade-Related Aspects of Intellectual Property Rights to enable developing countries to manufacture and export COVID-19 vaccines. A decision on waiving patents for COVID-19 therapeutics and diagnostics was to be taken before the end of 2022.

According to WHO some 12,677,499,928 COVID-19 vaccine doses had been administered globally at 28 September 2022. Around one-fifth of the doses administered in early 2022 were reported to be booster doses, i.e. reinforcing a completed primary vaccination schedule.

Notable discrepancies have been reported between countries' COVID-19 data methodologies. Data collection on confirmed COVID-19 case numbers has depended upon the extent of national testing programmes, which by 2022 had largely subsided in states with high COVID-19 vaccination coverage, and was from the start of the pandemic very significantly lower across low-income countries. During the initial stages of data collection inconsistencies were reported relating to the inclusion of deaths that had occurred in care homes for the elderly. As at 3 October 2022 some 6,524,568 COVID-19-related deaths had been formally confirmed worldwide, of which 1,047,392 had been recorded in the USA, 685,927 in Brazil, 528,701 in India, 387,559 in the Russian Federation, 330,046 in Mexico, 216,539 in Peru, 190,317 in the United Kingdom, 177,150 in Italy and 158,132 in Indonesia.

ACT Accelerator and Equitable Access to COVID-19 Vaccines:

The ACT Accelerator, initiated in April 2020 by WHO, the European Commission, the Bill & Melinda Gates Foundation, and the French Government, comprises, *inter alia,* Gavi, the Vaccine Alliance, the Coalition for Epidemic Preparedness Innovations—CEPI, other health organizations, the World Bank Group, scientists, governments, civil society representatives, businesses, and philanthropists. It aims to accelerate, collectively, the development and production of tools to combat the COVID-19 pandemic, and to ensure their equitable distribution. Its work has four pillars: diagnostics, treatment, health system strengthening, and vaccines (known as the COVID-19 Vaccines Global Access—COVAX—Facility, and co-led by WHO, Gavi, the Vaccine Alliance, and CEPI. WHO leads the Accelerator's cross-cutting Access and Allocation dimension, which aims to formulate the framework underpinning the fair and equitable allocation of the tools that the Accelerator develops and produces. From 2020 the Accelerator focused intensively on expediting research into and the development of new COVID-19 tests, treatments, health systems, and safe vaccines, and meeting the continuous challenges presented by the evolution of new virus variants. Gavi, the Vaccine Alliance focuses on procurement and delivery for COVAX, and administers the COVAX Facility (the pooled vaccine procurement mechanism that aims to ensure equitable access to vaccines for the 190 economies that participate in COVAX). Gavi also manages the COVAX Advance Market Commitment (AMC—the mechanism that supports the participation of low- and middle-income countries in the Facility). COVAX vaccine research and development is led by CEPI.

A COVID-19 Vaccine Delivery Partnership (CoVDP), comprising WHO, UNICEF and Gavi, the Vaccine Alliance, was launched in January 2022, with a focus on increasing the COVID-19 vaccination rate in 34 AMC-supported countries where, in January, coverage stood at or at less than 10% of the national population (by August COVID-19 vaccination coverage had advanced in 25 of the 34 countries).

The second Global COVID-19 Summit, co-hosted in May 2022 by the USA, Belize, Germany, Indonesia and Senegal, raised new financial commitments totalling US $3,200m. Of the total amount nearly $2,500m. was directly in support of COVID-19 and related response activities, while $712m. was for the Financial Intermediary Fund for Pandemic Prevention, Preparedness and Response (q.v.) that was under development at that time. (The inaugural global summit had been convened in June 2021.) By 1 September 2022 COVAX had supplied 1,630m. COVID-19 vaccine doses to 146

countries, most having been distributed through the AMC. By that time several AMC-supported countries—including Bangladesh, Bhutan, Fiji, the Maldives, Nicaragua, Rwanda, Samoa and Viet Nam—had attained the goal of more than 70% vaccination coverage.

PANDEMIC PREVENTION, PREPAREDNESS AND RESPONSE

A WHO BioHub System for Preparedness and Response to Epidemics and Pandemics, announced in November 2020, aimed to enhance the rapid sharing of viruses and other pathogens between research laboratories worldwide. The first WHO BioHub Facility, based in Switzerland, was initiated in May 2021. A Berlin, Germany-based WHO Hub for Pandemic and Epidemic Intelligence, inaugurated in September, was to support national governments in monitoring emerging variants of concern of COVID-19 (q.v.) and in promptly detecting and responding to pandemic and epidemic risks. In October WHO established a Scientific Advisory Group for the Origins of Novel Pathogens (SAGO), tasked with investigating the origins of the COVID-19 pandemic, and with assessing outbreaks of new diseases with the potential to cause epidemics/pandemics. A special session of the WHA held on 1 December agreed to establish an intergovernmental negotiating body to draft a new international agreement on pandemic prevention, preparedness and response. In March 2022 WHO initiated a Global Genomic Surveillance Strategy for Pathogens with Pandemic and Epidemic Potential, to cover the period 2022–32. In April 2022 a provisional consensus was reached by the ministers responsible for finance of the G20 member states on establishing, under World Bank auspices, a Financial Intermediary Fund for Pandemic Prevention, Preparedness and Response. In May the second Global COVID-19 Summit generated pledges of US $712m. towards the new fund, in addition to previous commitments totalling $250m.

INTERNATIONAL HEALTH REGULATIONS AND EMERGENCY RESPONSE

WHO keeps diseases and other health problems under constant surveillance, promotes the exchange of prompt and accurate information and of notification of outbreaks of diseases, and administers the binding 2005 International Health Regulations, which aim to support the international community in preventing and reacting to severe potentially transboundary public health risks. Within the UN system, WHO co-ordinates the international response to emergencies and natural disasters in the health field, in close co-operation with other agencies. In this context, WHO provides expert advice on epidemiological surveillance, control of communicable diseases, public health information, and health emergency training. Its emergency preparedness activities include co-ordination, policymaking and planning, awareness-building, technical advice, training, publication of standards and guidelines, and research. Its emergency relief activities include organizational support, the provision of emergency drugs and supplies, and conducting technical emergency assessment missions. WHO's *R&D Blueprint* is a global preparedness plan focused on the swift activation of research and development activities during epidemics.

Under the International Health Regulations, states parties are required to follow safeguarding procedures including reporting certain critical public health events to WHO, and WHO may declare as a PHEIC any extraordinary event that represents a public health risk to multiple countries, and which requires intensified mobilization of resources, and a co-ordinated global response, under the guidance of a dedicated International Health Regulations Emergency Committee of relevant experts. During the period 2009–September 2022 seven PHEICs were declared, in respect of outbreaks of H1N1 (swine flu) in 2009, wild poliovirus in 2014, Ebola Virus Disease (EVD) in 2014 and 2019, the Zika virus in 2016, novel coronavirus (COVID-19) in early 2020, and Monkeypox from mid-2022.

WHO's Global Alert and Response framework aims to provide an effective international system for co-ordinated response to epidemics and other public health emergencies. The Global Outbreak Alert and Response Network (GOARN), established in 2000 by WHO and several partner institutions in epidemic surveillance, maintains constant vigilance regarding outbreaks of disease, and links worldwide expertise to provide an immediate response capability. WHO assists member states in the development and implementation of domestic capacities for epidemic preparedness and response through strengthening national laboratory capacities and early warning alert and response mechanisms; supporting training programmes; and promoting standardized approaches in relation to biorisk reduction and epidemic-prone infections. In July 2011 WHO launched the Global Infection Prevention and Control (GIPC) Network, which provides technical support to member states, through the dissemination of epidemic-prone infection prevention and control (IPC) policies and guidance; the compilation of relevant indicators; and generic training curricula.

WHO aims to strengthen the national capacity of member states to reduce the adverse health consequences of disasters, including conflict, natural disasters and food insecurity. In responding to emergency situations, WHO works to develop projects and activities that will assist national authorities in rebuilding or strengthening their own capacity to handle the impact of such situations. In April 2015 WHO initiated a global registry of fast-response Emergency Medical Teams. WHO has also taken into consideration the potential malevolent use of bacteria (such as bacillus anthracis, which causes anthrax), viruses (for example, the variola virus, causing smallpox) or toxins, or of chemical agents, in acts of biological or chemical terrorism.

WHO CHIEF SCIENTIST AND SCIENCE DIVISION

The WHO Chief Scientist and Science Division covers norms and standards, digital health, and research and knowledge.

The inaugural meeting of a WHO Science Council—comprising nine distinguished scientists—was held in April 2021.

WHO works to develop national drugs policies and global guidelines, and promotes the rational use of medicines, and compliance with international drug control requirements. It supports national drug-regulatory authorities and drug-procurement agencies and facilitates international pharmaceutical trade through the exchange of technical information and the harmonization of internationally respected norms and standards.

WHO's so-called Family of International Classifications (WHO-FIC) includes the International Classification of Diseases (ICD), providing an etiological framework of health conditions.

WHO supports member states in the integration of traditional medicine (TM, also referred to as complementary or alternative medicine—CAM) into national healthcare systems and in the appropriate use of traditional medicine, through the provision of technical guidelines, standards and methodologies. WHO's strategy on TM covering the period 2014–23 supports the implementation of action plans and proactive policies aimed at promoting and prioritizing the use of TM. The Jamnagar, Gujarat, India-based WHO Global Centre for Traditional Medicine, inaugurated in April 2022, aims to collate evidence and data on TM products and practices.

In July 2021 WHO issued the first global recommendations on the use of human genome editing for the advancement of public health (for example in supporting more accurately targeted treatments).

UHC AND THE LIFE COURSE

UHC: In December 2016 WHO launched the UHC Data Portal, which tracks what proportion of national populations have access to 16 essential health services, and provides data on the financial impact on households of private health care. In July 2018 WHO, the Organisation for Economic Co-operation and Development (OECD) and the World Bank jointly issued *Delivering Quality Health Services—a Global Imperative for Universal Health Coverage*. The report emphasized that governments should provide strong policies and strategies on national health care, health systems should prioritize competent care and user experience, and citizens should be enabled actively to engage in decisions and in establishing appropriate models of care.

In September 2019 WHO, with 11 other agencies, launched a Global Action Plan for Healthy Lives and Wellbeing for All, under which they pledged to provide more streamlined support to countries' delivery of UHC and of the health-related SDG targets. In late September 2019 the first UN High-level Meeting on UHC was convened, at the UN General Assembly, in New York, USA, with participation by heads of state and of government, other senior political representatives, health leaders, and policymakers. The meeting—taking into account the recommendations of the recent WHO report—adopted a Political Declaration on advancing commitments towards the achievement of UHC. Commitments included the implementation of a recommended additional primary health care investment equivalent to 1% of GDP, the establishment of mechanisms to ensure that no one should suffer financial hardship linked to the cost of health care, and the implementation of interventions to combat diseases, and to protect women's and children's health through accessible essential health services, such as antenatal care, immunization and healthy lifestyle advice. Leaders committed to strengthening their health workforces, health infrastructures, and health governance capacity. They were to present a progress report to the UN General Assembly in 2023.

In November 2020 the 73rd WHA established a Council on the Economics of Health for All, to focus on using investments in health to foster sustainable economic growth; its component 11 leading experts on health and economics were appointed in May 2021.

In December 2021 WHO, with the World Bank, the OECD and other partners issued *Tracking Universal Health Coverage: 2021 Global Monitoring Report*, which found that in 2017 1,900m. people worldwide were confronted with an impoverishing level of personal health expenditure, and 1,400m. with a catastrophic level.

Access to Medicines and Health Technologies: WHO participates in the 'Accelerating Access' initiative, which aims to expand access to care and support, and to advance access to antiretroviral therapy (ART) for people living with the human immunodeficiency virus/acquired immunodeficiency syndrome (HIV/AIDS). It also hosts the secretariat of the International HIV Treatment Access Coalition, founded in December 2002 to facilitate access to ART for people in low- and middle-income countries. In September 2017 a global pricing agreement was announced by UNAIDS and global partners that aimed to accelerate the availability in 92 low- and middle-income countries of an affordable generic single-pill ART treatment regimen containing dolutegravir (DTG), an integrase (viral enzyme) inhibitor that was widely available in most high-income states. In July 2019 WHO declared DTG to be the preferred first- and second-line treatment for all populations, on the basis of new clinical trial evidence assessing its risks versus its benefits.

WHO Patient Safety facilitates the development of patient safety policy and practice across all WHO member states. WHO promotes worldwide co-operation on blood safety and clinical technology, supporting states in ensuring access (based on Voluntary Non-Remunerated Donation) to safe blood, blood products and transfusions, as well as to healthcare technologies.

Life Course and Ageing: WHO supports the Global Strategy for Women's, Children's and Adolescents' Health, which was initiated by the UN Secretary-General in September 2015. The Global Strategy laid out a roadmap that comprised targets aligned with the SDGs—to be achieved by 2030—and was aimed at ending all preventable deaths of women, children and adolescents, and at ensuring that they should thrive and should transform the world. In February 2017 WHO, UNICEF and partners initiated a Network for Improving Quality of Care for Maternal, Newborn and Child Health. In February 2018 WHO released a series of guidelines aimed at establishing global care standards for healthy pregnant women; these aimed to minimize unnecessary medical interventions.

In May 2016 WHO issued guidelines to assist health workers in supporting all girls and women with the physical and mental health consequences of female genital mutilation (FGM)—estimated to number more than 200m. worldwide.

In September 1997 WHO, in collaboration with UNICEF, formally initiated a programme advocating the Integrated Management of Childhood Illness (IMCI). In April 2013 WHO and UNICEF launched an Integrated Global Action Plan for the Prevention and Control of Pneumonia and Diarrhoea, focusing on interventions such as improved nutrition and maintaining a clean environment to protect children from contracting both diseases.

In May 2012 the WHA adopted a resolution on raising awareness of early marriage (entered into by more than 30% of women in developing countries) and adolescent pregnancy, and the consequences thereof for young women and infants.

WHO forecasts that by 2050 nearly 2,000m. people globally will be aged over 60 years. Its Global Network of Age-Friendly Cities and Communities aims to support the creation of environments that would enable older people to remain active and healthy. A UN Decade of Healthy Ageing was being observed during 2021–30, with a focus on age-friendly environments; combating ageism; integrated care; and long-term care.

Immunization and Vaccines: WHO, UNICEF and partners collaborated in reducing the global immunization coverage from 20% in the early 1980s to a targeted rate of 80% by the end of 1990. Some 81% of infants had received three doses of a DTP (diphtheria, tetanus and pertussis) vaccine in 2021, the rate having declined—following the onset of the COVID-19 crisis—from 86% at the end of 2019. WHO's guiding Strategic Advisory Group of Experts (SAGE) on Immunization was established in 1999. WHO's Immunization Agenda 2030 (IA2030) aimed to extend vaccines 'to everyone everywhere' by 2030. WHO is a founding partner of Gavi, the Vaccine Alliance, which was established in 2000 to enhance immunization coverage in developing countries through direct funding and new pricing arrangements with manufacturers.

By the end of 2021 some 350m. people in Africa had received MenAfriVac, a vaccine that was introduced in 2010 to combat Meningitis A infections (which have long-term health impacts on one-fifth of affected patients).

UHC/COMMUNICABLE AND NONCOMMUNICABLE DISEASES

WHO aims to reduce the burden of infectious and parasitic communicable diseases, identifying these as a major obstacle to social and economic progress, particularly in developing countries. Emerging and re-emerging diseases, those likely to cause epidemics, zoonoses (diseases or infections passed from vertebrate animals to humans by means of parasites, viruses, bacteria or unconventional agents), diseases attributable to factors such as environmental changes and changes in farming practices, outbreaks of unknown etiology, and the undermining of some drug therapies by the spread of antimicrobial resistance, are main areas of concern.

In May 2017 the 70th WHA adopted a Global Vector Control Response programme which, during the period 2017–30, was to support countries and development partners in strengthening vector control as a principal means of preventing and addressing outbreaks of communicable diseases.

WHO works with animal health sector partners at the human–animal interface at national level to identify and reduce animal health and public health risks. In 2019 WHO, FAO and the OIE published *A Tripartite Guide to Addressing Zoonotic Diseases in Countries* to support implementation of a multisectoral One Health approach to disease control. In May 2021 WHO, FAO, the UN Environment Programme (UNEP) and the OIE established a One Health High-Level Expert Panel, which was tasked with advancing understanding of the emergence and spread of zoonotic diseases that have the potential to generate human pandemics. In April 2022 the four organizations concluded a Memorandum of Understanding that provided for the establishment of a Quadripartite Collaboration for One Health, which was collectively to address challenges at the human-animal-plant-ecosystem interface.

Combating HIV/AIDS, TB and malaria are organization-wide priorities and, as such, are supported not only by their own areas of work but also by activities undertaken in other areas. TB is the principal cause of death for people infected with the HIV virus and an estimated one-third of people living with HIV/AIDS globally are co-infected with TB. In July 2000 a meeting of the G7 and Russia launched the Global Fund to Fight AIDS, TB and Malaria (as previously proposed by the UN Secretary-General and recommended by the WHA).

Cholera: In October 2017 WHO's Global Task Force on Cholera Control (GTFCC—established in 1992, and relaunched in 2014) issued 'Ending Cholera: A Global Roadmap to 2030', in accordance with which best practices were to be shared, partnerships strengthened and resources aligned, with a view to eliminating cholera in up to 20 affected countries by 2030.

Communicable Respiratory Diseases: From March 2003 WHO co-ordinated an international investigation into Severe Acute Respiratory Syndrome (SARS), a previously unknown atypical coronavirus, and provided logistical, epidemiological and clinical support to combat its spread.

From 2020 WHO was co-ordinating the global response to the COVID-19 pandemic (q.v.).

Influenza: In March 2014 WHO issued an updated version of a *Global Influenza Preparedness Plan* originally launched in 2005. In May 2011 the 64th WHA adopted a Pandemic Influenza Preparedness (PIP) Framework, which aimed to broaden access to anti-influenza vaccines. In March 2019 WHO initiated a Global Influenza Strategy, covering the period 2019–30, with a focus on preventing seasonal influenza (believed to cause up to 650,000 deaths annually), controlling the spread of influenza from animals to humans, and pandemic preparedness. Updated WHO *Guidelines for the clinical management of severe illness from influenza virus infections* were released in March 2022.

Malaria: In October 1998 WHO, jointly with UNICEF, the World Bank and the UN Development Programme (UNDP), formally launched the Roll Back Malaria (RBM) programme. The global multi-stakeholder RBM Partnership aims to mobilize resources and support for controlling malaria. WHO recommends a number of guidelines for malaria control, focusing on the need for prompt, effective antimalarial treatment, and the issue of drug resistance; vector control, including the use of insecticide-treated bed nets; malaria in pregnancy; malaria epidemics; and monitoring and evaluation activities. WHO's Global Technical Strategy for Malaria (GTS), covering the period 2016–30 (and updated in mid-2021) aims—through a continued focus on the promotion of universal access to malaria prevention, diagnosis and treatment; strengthening surveillance; and the achievement of national malaria-free status—to reduce malaria cases globally by 90% by 2030, as well as to eliminate the disease entirely in at least 35 countries by 2030. A complementary RBM advocacy plan: Action and Investment to defeat Malaria 2016–30 (AIM) was being implemented simultaneously. The GTS and AIM were aligned with the SDGs, including SDG 3, Target 3.3. A large-scale clinical trial of the first ever vaccine against malaria (known as RTS,S/AS01 and thought to cause a 30% reduction in deadly severe malaria) was initiated in April 2019 in Malawi, and then extended to Ghana and Kenya—reaching in total 800,000 children. In a landmark decision in October 2021 WHO recommended the widespread preventive use of RTS,S/AS01 among children in sub-Saharan Africa and in other regions with moderate to high malaria transmission (according to a schedule of four doses given from the age of five months). WHO reported in April 2022 that more than 1m. children in Ghana, Kenya and Malawi had already received one or more doses of RTS,S/AS01. By that time funding exceeding US $155m. had been secured from Gavi, the Vaccine Alliance to assist the delivery of the vaccine throughout sub-Saharan Africa.

In December 2021 WHO estimated that in 2020 there were 241m. cases of malaria (compared with 229m. in 2019, and 251m. in 2010), and 627,000 deaths from the disease—representing a sharp increase over 409,000 fatalities in 2019. (Some 585,000 deaths had been reported in 2010.) The increase in recorded cases and deaths (compared with 2019) was attributed to disruption to prevention, diagnosis and treatment services arising from the COVID-19 pandemic. Around 95% of confirmed cases in 2020 occurred in WHO's Africa region; 2% arose in WHO's South East Asia region, where numbers fell from 23m. in 2000 to 5m. in 2020 (India accounted for 83% of the cases reported there in 2020). Some 96% of the caseload in 2020 occurred in 29 countries (with 27% of cases arising in Nigeria, and 12% in the Democratic Republic of the Congo—DRC). It was reported that 222m. insecticide-treated mosquito nets were provided to malaria-endemic countries during 2020. Of 88 malaria-endemic countries that had supplied data for the period 2010–20, 29 had detected resistance to all four of the most frequently used classes of insecticide, and 78 had detected resistance to at least one insecticide class. Funding for anti-malaria drug research and development amounted to US $3,300m. in 2020.

By 2022 WHO had certified two countries in its Africa region as malaria-free: Algeria (in May 2020) and Mauritius (in 1973).

Monkeypox: From mid-2022 WHO and partners supported surveillance of and analysed a multi-country outbreak of monkeypox—a zoonotic infection originating in areas of Central and West Africa—transmission of which, atypically, had recently spread in non-endemic locations. On 23 July, by which time some 16,016 cases and five related fatalities had been confirmed in 75 countries, WHO designated the outbreak as a PHEIC. The most significant caseload was reported from WHO's Europe region. Initial evidence had indicated that undetected transmission in the new locations might have been ongoing for some time. Anti-smallpox vaccines were reported to protect against the disease.

Neglected Tropical Diseases: In November 2020 the WHA endorsed a new roadmap to guide the control, elimination and eradication during 2021–30 of 20 neglected tropical diseases (NTDs) and disease groups. This was to be supported by a Global Strategy on WASH and NTDs (2021–30), addressing cross-sector interaction with water, sanitation and hygiene provision.

An Expanded Special Project for Elimination of NTDs (ESPEN) was launched in mid-2016, to support African countries in the elimination of onchocerciasis ('river blindness', spread by blackflies), lymphatic filariasis and other neglected tropical diseases. WHO's SAFE strategy for the elimination of blinding trachoma—a bacterial tropical disease that causes visual impairment or full blindness in around 1.9m. people—consists of: Surgery; Antibiotics (particularly the mass administration of azithromycin, which is donated by the International Trachoma Initiative); Facial cleanliness; and Environmental improvement (with a focus on improving water and sanitation provision). Ghana and The Gambia were declared trachoma-free in June 2018 and April 2021, respectively.

In May 2019 the WHA launched a Snakebite Envenoming Strategy for Prevention and Control, which set the objective of reducing fatalities and disabilities caused by snakebite by one-half by 2030. Priority was to be placed on improved community-based prevention activities, improved integration of snakebite into health systems, health worker training, diagnosis, treatment, and access to safe, effective and affordable high-quality antivenoms. WHO was to establish a stockpile of antivenoms.

HIV/Hepatitis: WHO supports governments to develop effective health sector responses to the HIV/AIDS epidemic through enhancing their planning capabilities, implementation capacity, and health systems resources. Guidelines on managing the HIV/AIDS epidemic are regularly revised and updated. WHO and other agencies sponsor the Joint UN Programme on HIV/AIDS (UNAIDS, q.v.); the UNAIDS secretariat is based at WHO headquarters. A WHO-UNAIDS HIV Vaccine Initiative was launched in 2000.

The principal goals of UNAIDS are reducing sexual transmission of HIV; preventing HIV among drug users; eliminating new infections among children; increasing access to ART; avoiding TB deaths; eliminating gender inequalities; closing the resources gap; integrating HIV-related services; eliminating travel restrictions on people living with HIV; and eliminating HIV-related stigma and discrimination. In June 2021 the UN General Assembly adopted a Political Declaration on HIV and AIDS: Ending Inequalities and Getting on Track to End AIDS by 2030. This supported a series of evidence-informed targets that were incorporated in UNAIDS' Global AIDS Strategy covering 2021–26. Parallel global strategies on HIV/AIDS, viral hepatitis, and sexually transmitted infections for the period 2022–30 were endorsed by the WHA in May 2022.

In 2020 eight countries globally had achieved the 90-90-90 'Fast-Track' target on HIV treatment (set by UNAIDS in 2014) of, by 2020, at least 90% of people living with HIV being aware of their serostatus (i.e. presence or not in the blood of detectable antibodies to the virus); 90% of these taking ART; and 90% being virally suppressed: Eswatini (98-98-95); Switzerland (93-98-96); Rwanda (93-98-96);

Qatar (93-98-96); Botswana (91-95-98); Slovenia (90-97-96); Uganda (91-98-90); and Malawi (91-94-94). A follow-on 95-95-95 Fast-Track target was to be achieved by 2030, alongside a target of reducing annual new HIV infections by 2030 to 200,000.

In 2020 4.7m. people were reported to be living with HIV/AIDS in western and central Africa, of whom 200,000 were estimated to have been newly infected during that year. Meanwhile some 20.6m. people in eastern and southern Africa were reported to have HIV/AIDS—of whom around 670,000 were newly infected during the year. Around 460,000 deaths were attributed to HIV/AIDS in both regions in 2020. At that time an estimated 78% people living with HIV/AIDS in sub-Saharan Africa, who knew their status, were receiving treatment.

In April 2014 WHO issued its first guidelines on the treatment of chronic Hepatitis C infections, with a view to reducing the number of deaths globally (estimated at up to 500,000 annually) from Hepatitis C-related cirrhosis and cancer of the liver. A *Progress report on HIV, viral hepatitis and sexually transmitted infections*, issued by WHO in July 2019, noted that 257m. people were living with chronic Hepatitis B infection in 2016, and (in 2015) 71m. people had chronic Hepatitis C. A Global Hepatitis Summit was convened in June 2021, in Taipei, Taiwan.

TB: According to WHO estimates, one-quarter of the world's population carries the TB bacillus. In October 2021 WHO reported that during 2020 the COVID-19 pandemic had significantly disrupted the provision of TB diagnosis and treatment services. The number of people worldwide who were newly diagnosed with TB declined from 7.1m. in 2019 to 5.8m. in 2020, while the number of deaths from TB rose, from (among HIV-negative TB patients) 1.2m. in 2019 to 1.3m. in 2020; meanwhile, 214,000 HIV-positive TB patients died in 2020 compared with 209,000 in 2009. Children accounted for 11% of worldwide TB cases in 2020. In that year, by WHO region, 43% of TB cases were in South East Asia, 25% in Africa, and 18% in the Western Pacific. Two-thirds of cases globally in 2020 were concentrated in eight countries: India, China Indonesia, the Philippines, Pakistan, Nigeria, Bangladesh and South Africa.

WHO is actively involved in all aspects of the detection, diagnosis and treatment of TB. Inadequate or inconsistent treatment of the disease has resulted in the development of drug-resistant and, often, incurable strains. In (pre-pandemic, thus more typical) 2019, 500,000 new TB cases were believed to be resistant to the antibiotic rifampicin (known as rifampicin-resistant TB—RR-TB), and 206,030 RR-TB cases were also notified as multidrug-resistant (MDR-TB). Around one-half of the total of MDR-TB cases arise in (descending order of prevalence) India, China and Russia. In 2019 12,350 MDR-TB cases (of which 8,560 were in Europe) were believed to be also extensively drug-resistant TB (XDR-TB), defined as MDR-TB plus resistance to any fluoroquinolone, and to at least one additional 'Group A' (i.e. most potent) second-line treatment of MDR-TB. In March 2019 WHO released new guidance aimed at improving treatment of MDR-TB, entailing a shift to fully oral regimens. In January 2021 WHO introduced a new definition, alongside XDR-TB, of Pre-XDR-TB—'MDR/RR-TB which is also resistant to any fluoroquinolone'—to manage monitoring systems and treatment regimens more precisely. In 2019 61% of bacteriologically confirmed TB cases were also tested for RR-TB (compared with 41% in 2017).

A 'Stop TB' partnership initiative was launched by WHO in 1999 with the World Bank, the US Government and a coalition of NGOs. The Global TB Drug Facility, launched by Stop TB in 2001, aims to increase access to high-quality anti-TB drugs for sufferers in developing countries. A Stop TB Global Drug-resistant TB Initiative was launched in May 2014. In October 2013 WHO and partners launched the 'Roadmap for childhood TB: towards zero deaths', recommending 10 relevant actions. In May 2014 the WHA adopted a Post-2015 Global TB Strategy, aimed at reducing the global incidence of TB by 90% by 2035. The inaugural WHO Global Ministerial Conference on Ending TB in the Sustainable Development Era was held in November 2017, in Moscow, Russia. The first UN high-level meeting on TB, convened in September 2018, adopted a political declaration which launched a set of near-term global targets: treating 40m. TB patients and providing preventive treatment to at least 30m. people with a latent TB infection (during 2018–22); mobilizing at least US $1,300m. annually to support universal access to TB diagnosis, treatment and care; and raising at least $2,000m. annually towards research on TB. The Stop TB coalition was implementing a Global Plan to End TB during 2018–22, which represented a roadmap for pursuing these goals. Vaccination with the bacille Calmette–Guérin (BCG) vaccine can confer protection, especially from severe forms of TB in children. At the end of 2021 the global BCG vaccination coverage rate stood at 84%.

Polio: In 1988 the WHA launched the Global Polio Eradication Initiative (GPEI), which has most recently set a deadline of 2026 to achieve the elimination of poliomyelitis.

In early 2022 the WHO Executive Director stated concern over the international importation of WPV1 from Afghanistan/Pakistan to Lilongwe, the Malawian capital; genomic sequencing of a WPV1 case in a child in Malawi linked the virus to a case that had occurred in

Pakistan in 2019. A campaign was therefore initiated in March to vaccinate 20m. people in Malawi, Mozambique, Tanzania and Zambia. (Africa had in 2020 been declared free of polio.)

At September 2022 27 African states were classified by the GPEI as polio outbreak countries—i.e. having ended indigenous wild poliovirus, but remaining prone to re-infection via the importation of wild or vaccine-derived poliovirus.

Leprosy: WHO is committed to the elimination of leprosy. The use of a highly effective combination of drugs (known as multidrug therapy—MDT) resulted in a reduction in the number of leprosy cases worldwide from 10m.–12m. in 1988 to 121,538 new registered cases in 2020. In that year India accounted for 65,147 of cases, Brazil for 17,979, and Indonesia for 11,173. Clinical trials in humans of the first vaccine against leprosy were initiated in 2016. A Special Rapporteur on the elimination of discrimination against persons affected by leprosy and their family members was appointed by the UN Human Rights Council in 2017. WHO's Global Leprosy Strategy 2021–30 aimed to eliminate the disease by 2030, including through facilitating an uninterrupted supply of cost-free multidrug therapy medicines.

Measles: WHO's Measles and Rubella Strategic Framework covering the period 2021–30 aimed to combat, through routine immunization, deaths from measles (which is particularly dangerous for children under the age of five and malnourished children), and also congenital rubella syndrome. During 2000–18 WHO estimated that effective measles vaccinations had prevented 23m. deaths. By the end of 2018 82 countries were reported to have eliminated measles, and 81 to have eliminated rubella. However, some 207,500 fatal measles cases were recorded by WHO in 2019, a significant increase over 110,000 in 2016. WHO has attributed the rise in part to widespread misinformation about vaccines. At the end of 2021 global coverage with both of two required measles vaccinations together with rubella vaccines stood at 71%. In April 2022 WHO and UNICEF issued a joint warning that COVID-19 pandemic-related disruptions to routine childhood immunisation programmes and increasingly inequitable access to vaccines were undermining worldwide protection from vaccine-preventable diseases: notably, nearly 17,340 cases of measles been reported globally during the first two months of that year, compared with 9,665 cases in January–February 2021. Furthermore, conflict-related population displacement, overcrowding and lack of access to clean water and sanitation risked exacerbating outbreaks of vaccine-preventable diseases.

Buruli Ulcer: In 1998 WHO launched the Global Buruli Ulcer Initiative, which aimed to co-ordinate control of and research into Buruli ulcer, another mycobacterial disease. In July of that year the Director-General of WHO and representatives of more than 20 countries, meeting in Yamoussoukro, Côte d'Ivoire, signed a declaration on the control of Buruli ulcer; a further declaration was signed in March 2009 by WHO's Regional Director for Africa, representatives of affected countries, and other stakeholders.

Ebola Virus Disease (EVD): In the aftermath of the EVD PHEIC declared in West Africa during August 2014–March 2016 WHO supported the Governments of Guinea, Liberia and Sierra Leone in building capacity to break promptly any future chains of transmission, with a focus on prevention, surveillance and response. WHO, with partners, also facilitated survivors' access to medical care and to psychosocial support, and organized screenings aimed at detecting dormant persistent cases of the virus. During late 2013–mid-2016 28,616 EVD cases and 11,319 related deaths were confirmed in West Africa.

WHO has supported the DRC Government in controlling several outbreaks of EVD in recent years, including six during 2018–22.

On 25 June 2020 WHO formally declared the end of the DRC's 10th EVD outbreak, which, during August 2018–early 2020, had resulted in 3,470 confirmed EVD cases and 2,287 related deaths in North Kivu and neighbouring Ituri. During the outbreak more than 303,000 at risk people had been given the vaccine rVSV-ZEBOV-GP, which had been demonstrably effective in preventing EVD infection. Following a visit to the DRC in September 2019, the WHO Director-General noted that the EVD outbreak was a symptom of a deeper structural challenge relating to the need for widespread affordable access to good health services, and emphasized the importance of achieving UHC. On 1 June 2020 the DRC authorities announced that the country's 11th EVD outbreak had commenced, in Bikoro and Mbandaka, Equateur Province; a WHO team was dispatched to help scale up the ongoing national response. By 18 November, when the outbreak was declared to be at an end, 130 cases and 55 deaths had been reported. During the outbreak more than 43,000 people were vaccinated against EVD and 3m. were screened for symptoms at points of control. A 12th EVD outbreak in the DRC occurred during February–May 2021. The 11 confirmed cases in a 13th outbreak that occurred during October–December, in North Kivu, resulted in six fatalities. All four infected people died in the DRC's 14th EVD outbreak, which arose in Equateur during April–July 2022.

In November 2019, for the first time, WHO 'prequalified' a new injectable Ebola vaccine, Ervebo—certifying that it met appropriate standards for quality, safety and (with a success rate of 97%) efficacy. In January 2021 WHO, UNICEF, the International Federation of Red Cross and Red Crescent Societies and Médecins Sans Frontières announced the creation of a global Ebola vaccine stockpile, which was being facilitated with financial assistance from Gavi, the Vaccine Alliance.

In August 2021 a confirmed case of EVD in Côte d'Ivoire was reported to WHO; the infected patient had recently travelled to the Ivorian capital, Abidjan, from Guinea.

Plague: In January 2018 the WHO Director-General presented a vision for ending intermittent epidemics of plague in Madagascar. This included strategic investments in the health system, with a focus on improved access to health care; enhanced preparedness, surveillance and response capabilities, and thoroughly implementing the International Health Regulations. During 2018 104 cases of plague were reported in that country (resulting in five fatalities), compared with 661 cases (87 deaths) in the previous year. Also, 133 cases (and five related deaths) were recorded in the DRC in 2018. The case-fatality ratio for untreated plague is between 30%–100%.

NCDs: The surveillance, prevention and management of NCDs and mental health are organization-wide priorities. Tobacco use, unhealthy diet, harmful use of alcohol and physical inactivity are regarded as common, preventable risk factors for the four most prominent NCDs, i.e. cardiovascular diseases, cancer, chronic respiratory disease and diabetes. It is estimated that these NCDs are collectively responsible for an estimated 35m. deaths—60% of all deaths—globally each year, and that up to 80% of cases of heart disease, stroke and type 2 diabetes, and more than one-third of cancers, could be prevented by eliminating shared risk factors. WHO aims to monitor the global epidemiological situation of NCDs, to co-ordinate multinational research activities concerned with prevention and care, and to analyse determining factors such as gender and poverty.

In March 2018 a WHO Independent Global High-level Commission was inaugurated, tasked with formulating innovative solutions aimed at advancing the prevention and control of NCDs. The Third UN General Assembly High-level Meeting on the Prevention and Control of NCDs was convened in September 2018.

An International Task Force on Obesity aims to encourage the development of innovative policies for managing obesity. In October 2017 WHO issued guidelines aimed at managing childhood obesity, for use by personnel at primary health care facilities. In May 2018 the WHA endorsed a WHO Global Action Plan on Physical Activity (GAPPA), with a focus on promoting healthy lifestyles and increasing inclusive participation.

WHO initiated a Global Diabetes Compact in April 2021, with the aim of supporting effective national diabetes prevention and management programmes. In May the 74th WHA agreed a resolution aimed at enhancing the prevention, diagnosis and control of diabetes and the prevention and management of related risk factors (such as obesity).

WHO's Substance Abuse Programme offers technical support to member countries to address the misuse of all psychoactive substances, irrespective of legal status. In May 2010 WHO endorsed a global strategy to reduce the harmful use of alcohol; this promoted measures including taxation on alcohol, minimizing outlets selling alcohol, raising age limits for those buying alcohol, and the employment of effective measures to deter people from driving while under the influence of alcohol.

In 2012 WHO estimated that tobacco would lead to more than 8m. deaths annually by 2030 (through lung cancer, heart disease, chronic bronchitis and other effects). The Tobacco or Health Programme aims to reduce the use of tobacco, by educating tobacco-users and preventing young people from adopting the habit. In May 1999 the WHA endorsed the formulation of a Framework Convention on Tobacco Control (FCTC) to help to combat the increase in tobacco use; it entered into force in February 2005. A Protocol to Eliminate Illicit Trade in Tobacco Products entered into force on 25 September 2018. The second Meeting of the Parties to the Protocol, held in November 2021, agreed to establish an investment fund to secure financing and strengthen implementation of the Protocol.

UHC/HEALTHIER POPULATIONS

In May 2020 the 73rd WHA adopted a resolution on integrated people-centred eye care (referred to as IPEC), aimed at ensuring the widespread use of IPEC. In May 2021 the 74th WHA resolved that by 2030 global coverage of refractive errors and cataract surgery should increase by 40% and 30%, respectively. During the 75th WHA, in May 2022, a WHO *Eye Care in Health Systems—Guide for Action* was issued.

Climate Change, Health and Environment: In January 2018 WHO and UNEP signed an agreement establishing an extensive new programme of WHO-UN Environment collaboration, comprising joint actions aimed at combating environmental health risks, such as antimicrobial resistance, air pollution, and climate change.

Furthermore, co-ordination was to be strengthened in the areas of waste and chemicals management, food and nutrition, and water quality. A joint work programme was to be developed, and the two agencies were to convene an annual high-level meeting, to follow up progress and make recommendations for advancing the collaboration. In May 2019 the WHA endorsed a Global Strategy on Health, Environment and Climate Change, which aimed to address environmental health risks and challenges until 2030.

WHO's programme area on environmental health addresses the increasing threats to health and wellbeing from a changing environment, especially in relation to air pollution, water quality, sanitation, protection against UV-radiation, management of hazardous waste, chemical safety and housing hygiene. In October–November 2018 WHO, with UNEP and other partners, organized the inaugural Global Conference on Air Pollution and Health; this committed to a goal of reducing deaths from air pollution by two-thirds by 2030. In April 2022 WHO reported that 99% of the global population was breathing air that did not meet WHO's air quality limits on fine particulate matter and nitrogen dioxide.

In 2022 WHO attributed some 829,000 deaths annually to diarrhoea caused by unsafe drinking water, sanitation systems and hand hygiene. Around 2,000m. people worldwide in 2020 were reported to have no access to clean drinking water. In August 2019 WHO released a report on microplastics in drinking water and urged further assessment of the risks posed to human health by microplastics in the environment.

WHO aims to protect human health against risks associated with biological and chemical contaminants and additives in food. With FAO, WHO establishes food standards (through the work of the Codex Alimentarius Commission and its subsidiary committees) and evaluates food additives, pesticide residues and other contaminants and their implications for health. WHO also addresses the methods of producing, processing and preparing foods that contribute to the incidence of foodborne trematode infections (parasitic infections caused by flatworms). WHO's Global Foodborne Infections Network, established in 2001, promotes integrated laboratory-based surveillance and intersectoral collaboration among human health, veterinary and food-related entities.

Finance

A total programme budget of US $4,364.0m. was approved by the WHA in May 2021 for the two years 2022–23. Some $1,168.2m., or 26.8% of regionally allocated expenditure, was provisionally assigned to programmes in Africa.

Publications

Bulletin of the World Health Organization (monthly).

Global Status Report on Alcohol and Health.

Global Tuberculosis Report.

International Classification of Diseases.

International Health Regulations.

International Pharmacopoeia.

International Travel and Health.

Levels and Trends in Child Mortality (every 2 years, with the World Bank and UNICEF).

Model List of Essential Medicines (every 2 years).

Public Health Panorama.

Tracking Universal Health Coverage.

Weekly Epidemiological Record.

WHO Drug Information (quarterly).

WHO Report on the Global Tobacco Epidemic.

World Cancer Report (every 5–6 years).

World Health Report (annually).

World Health Statistics.

World Malaria Report (annually, with UNICEF).

WHO also publishes an *African Health Monitor*.

Technical report series; guidelines; catalogues of specific scientific, technical and medical fields are available.

Associated Agencies

Gavi, the Vaccine Alliance: Global Health Campus, 40 chemin du Pommier, 1218 Grand-Saconnex, Geneva, Switzerland; 2099 Pennsylvania Ave, NW, Suite 200, Washington, DC 20006, USA; tel. 229096500; (202) 478-1050; fax 2229096550; (202) 478-1060; e-mail info@gavi.org; internet gavi.org; f. 2000 by WHO, UNICEF, the World Bank and the Bill & Melinda Gates Foundation as the Global Alliance for Vaccines and Immunization, present name adopted in 2014; aims to improve childhood immunization coverage in developing countries and to accelerate access to new vaccines; promotes specific immunization campaigns and supports the strengthening of health systems and services in low-income countries; works in partnership with govts, international and civil society orgs, research agencies, manufacturers and other private sector bodies; in June 2020 a replenishment meeting, hosted in a virtual format by the UK Government, secured new commitments of US $8,800m. for the period 2021–25; from 2020 Gavi hosted and co-ordinated the COVAX Facility, a mechanism tasked with facilitating rapid, equitable access to COVID-19 vaccines worldwide, and representing the vaccines pillar of the ACT Accelerator (initiated in April, q.v.); Gavi also manages the COVAX Advance Market Commitment, which aims promptly to secure safe, effective doses of COVID-19 vaccines for 92 low- and middle-income countries and economies at the same time as developed states; in Dec. 2021 the Gavi Board agreed to invest $155.7m. during 2022–25 to support the introduction, procurement and delivery of the newly-approved RTS,S vaccine against malaria in endemic African countries; CEO Dr SETH BERKLEY (USA).

Joint UN Programme on HIV/AIDS (UNAIDS): 20 ave Appia, 1211 Geneva 27, Switzerland; tel. 227913666; fax 227914187; e-mail communications@unaids.org; internet www.unaids.org; f. 1996 to lead, strengthen and support an expanded response to the global HIV/AIDS pandemic; guided by UN Security Council Resolution 1308, focusing on the possible impact of AIDS on social instability and emergency situations, and the potential impact of HIV on the health of international peacekeeping personnel; by the Declaration of Commitment on HIV/AIDS agreed in June 2001 by a Special Session of the UN General Assembly on HIV/AIDS, which acknowledged the AIDS epidemic as a 'global emergency'; the Political Declaration on HIV/AIDS, adopted by the June 2006 UN General Assembly High Level Meeting on AIDS; and the June 2016 Political Declaration on HIV and AIDS: On the Fast-Track to Accelerate the Fight Against HIV and to End the AIDS Epidemic by 2030; activities focus on prevention, care and support, reducing vulnerability to infection, and alleviating the socioeconomic and human effects of HIV/AIDS; launched the Global Coalition on Women and AIDS in Feb. 2004; the UNAIDS 2012–26 Strategy was focused on 3 strategic priorities: Maximize equitable and equal access to HIV services and solutions; Break down barriers to achieving HIV outcomes; and Fully resource and sustain efficient HIV responses and integrate them into health, social protection, humanitarian, and pandemic response situations; in July 2020, jtly with WHO and UNDP, UNAIDS initiated a COVID-19 Law Lab initiative, facilitating the sharing of legal documents from more than 190 states, to support the establishment of robust legal frameworks to manage the pandemic; co-sponsors: WHO, UN Women, UNICEF, UNDP, UNFPA, UNODC, the ILO, UNESCO, the World Bank, WFP, UNHCR; Exec. Dir WINNIE BYANYIMA (Uganda).

International Agency for Research on Cancer: 150 Cours Albert Thomas, 69372 Lyon Cedex 08, France; tel. 4-72-73-84-85; internet www.iarc.fr; f. 1965 as a self-governing body within the framework of WHO; organizes international research on cancer; maintains its own laboratories, an IARC Biobank, a web-based Global Cancer Observatory (GCO), and runs a research programme on the environmental factors causing cancer; issues a series of monographs on the identification of carcinogenic hazards to humans and publishes *The Cancer Atlas*, providing an overview of cancer worldwide; mems: 26 countries; Dir Dr ELISABETE WEIDERPASS.

Other UN and Related Organizations Active in the Region

International Court of Justice—ICJ

Address: Peace Palace, Carnegieplein 2, 2517 KJ The Hague, Netherlands.

Telephone: (70) 3022323; **fax:** (70) 3649928; **e-mail:** information@icj-cij.org; **internet:** www.icj-cij.org.

Established in 1945, the Court (composed of 15 judges, each of a different nationality) is the principal judicial organ of the UN. All members of the UN are parties to the Statute of the Court. The Jurisdiction of the Court comprises: cases which the parties refer to it jointly by special agreement; matters concerning which a treaty or convention in force provides for reference to the Court through the inclusion of a jurisdictional clause; and legal disputes between states which have recognized the jurisdiction of the Court as compulsory for specified classes of dispute. Judgments are without appeal, but are binding only for the particular case and between the parties. States appearing before the Court undertake to comply with its Judgment. Advisory opinions on legal questions may also be requested by the General Assembly, the Security Council or, if so authorized by the Assembly, other UN organs or specialized agencies.

At October 2022 16 cases were under consideration, or pending before the Court, including a case brought by The Gambia against Myanmar, within the context of the 1948 UN Convention on the Prevention and Punishment of the Crime of Genocide, a case brought as a Special Agreement by Gabon and Equatorial Guinea requesting the Court to rule on land and maritime delimitation and sovereignty over several islands, and proceedings instituted by Equatorial Guinea (in September 2022) against France, concerning that country's obligations under the United Nations Convention against Corruption. In February 2019, at the request of the UN General Assembly, the Court delivered an advisory opinion on the Legal Consequences of the Separation of the Chagos Archipelago from Mauritius in 1965. This found that the archipelago had been and remained unlawfully occupied by the United Kingdom.

President: JOAN E. DONOGHUE (USA).

Registrar: PHILIPPE GAUTIER (Belgium).

UN Sanctions

The UN Security Council may—as provided for under Chapter VII of the UN Charter—take enforcement measures as a means of targeting regimes and entities that are deemed to threaten international peace and security, in situations where diplomatic efforts aimed at achieving a resolution to the situation have failed. The offending entities are expected to comply with a set of objectives issued by the Security Council aimed at restoring order. Such enforcement measures encompass mandatory economic and trade and/or other sanctions (such as financial or diplomatic restrictions, arms embargoes and bans on travel), and also, in certain cases, international military action. Sanctions committees are established to oversee the implementation of economic or political enforcement measures imposed by the Security Council. In December 2006 an informal working group recommended that resolutions enforcing sanctions should clearly specify intended goals and targets, include incentives to reward partial compliance, and focus in particular on the finances and movements of leaders (so-called smart sanctions). Humanitarian exceptions may now be embodied in Security Council resolutions. The Consolidated Sanctions List comprises all individuals and entities on which the Council has imposed sanctions measures, under all punitive regimes. A Focal Point for De-listing, established in December 2006, by Resolution 1730, receives and processes requests from individuals and entities wishing to be removed from sanctions lists, with the exception of the ISIL (Da'esh) and al-Qa'ida Sanctions List. Since 2005 INTERPOL-UN Security Council Special Notices have been issued for individuals and entities that are subjected to UN sanctions regimes.

Sanctions Committees that were operational in 2022 included:

Security Council Committee established pursuant to Resolution 2374 (2017) concerning Mali.

Security Council Committee established pursuant to Resolutions 1267 (1999), 1989 (2011) and 2253 (2015) concerning ISIL (Da'esh), al-Qa'ida, and associated individuals, groups, undertakings and entities.

Security Council Committee established pursuant to Resolution 2206 (2015) concerning South Sudan.

Security Council Committee established pursuant to Resolution 2127 (2013) concerning the Central African Republic.

Security Council Committee established pursuant to Resolution 2048 (2012) concerning Guinea-Bissau.

Security Council Committee established pursuant to Resolution 1591 (2005) concerning Sudan.

Security Council Committee established pursuant to Resolution 1533 (2004) concerning the DRC.

Security Council Committee established pursuant to Resolution 751 (1992) concerning Somalia.

Office of the Ombudsperson of the 1267/1989/2253 ISIL (Da'esh) and al-Qa'ida Sanctions Committee: Rm TB-08041 D, UN Plaza, New York, NY 10017, USA; f. Dec. 2009; reviews requests from individuals, groups, undertakings or entities seeking to be removed from the Islamic State and al-Qa'ida Sanctions List; by June 2022 91 cases had passed fully through the Ombudsperson process, resulting in the de-listing of 63 individuals and 28 entities; Ombudsperson RICHARD MALANJUM (Malaysia).

International Residual Mechanism for International Criminal Tribunals—IRMCT

Address: Churchillplein 1, 2517 JW, The Hague, Netherlands.
Telephone: (27) 256-5013; **e-mail:** mict-registrythehague@un.org.
Address: Haki Rd, Plot No. 486, Block A, Lakilaki Area, Arumeru District, Arusha, Tanzania.
Telephone: (70) 512-5691; **e-mail:** mict-registryarusha@un.org.

The Mechanism was established by Security Council Resolution 1966 (December 2010) to undertake some essential functions of the so-called International Tribunal for the Prosecution of Persons Responsible for Serious Violations of International Humanitarian Law Committed in the Territory of the Former Yugoslavia (also referred to as the International Criminal Tribunal for the former Yugoslavia—ICTY) and of the International Criminal Tribunal for Rwanda (ICTR) pending and after their closure. The IRMCT comprises a branch that is based in Arusha, Tanzania (which commenced operations on 1 July 2012), and a branch based in The Hague, Netherlands (operational from 1 July 2013). The Mechanism is mandated to conduct any appeals against Tribunal judgments filed following its entry into operation.

The ICTR, established in November 1994 by Security Council Resolution 955 to prosecute persons responsible for genocide and other serious violations of humanitarian law that had been committed during that year in Rwanda, as well as by Rwandans in neighbouring states, was terminated on 31 December 2015. During the course of its operations the ICTR indicted 95 individuals (with two indictments subsequently withdrawn), and—although eight indictees evaded capture—proceedings against 85 of the accused reached conclusion (including five cases that were transferred to other jurisdictions: two to France and three to Rwanda). Some 14 accused were acquitted by the Tribunal. In mid-May 2020 the French authorities arrested Félicien Kabuga, who had been indicted by the ICTR in 1997 on charges relating to genocide and crimes against humanity, including providing financial backing to the perpetrators of the Rwandan atrocities. Shortly afterwards the IRMCT confirmed that the mortal remains of a second fugitive from justice, Augustin Bizimana, a senior minister in Rwanda's interim government during the 1994 genocide, had been identified, having been discovered at a grave site at Pointe Noire, Republic of the Congo. Kabuga was transferred into the custody of the Mechanism in late October 2020, and appeared for the first time there in November where he pleaded not guilty. The trial commenced in September 2022. Intelligence activities to help track and identify the fugitives continued to be undertaken by a specialist IRMCT team. In May 2022 the Court confirmed the death, in 2006, of Protais Mpiranya, who had been a senior commander of the Presidential Guard of the Rwandan Armed Forces during the genocide, and, in 2002, of Lt-Col Phénéas Munyarugarama, who had been accused of committing and inciting genocide in the Bugesara district. Four indictees remained at liberty as at mid-2022, and were to be transferred to Rwandan jurisdiction.

President of the Mechanism: GRACIELA GATTI SANTANA (Uruguay).

Prosecutor of the Mechanism: SERGE BRAMMERTZ (Belgium).

Registrar of the Mechanism: ABUBACARR MARIE TAMBADOU (The Gambia).

Global Crisis Response Group (GCRG) on Food, Energy and Finance

In March 2022 the UN Secretary-General formed the GCRG—guided by a 32-member steering committee comprising leaders of UN agencies and of multilateral development banks—to address the broad global impacts of the ongoing war in Ukraine. A Task Team was established within the GCRG, co-ordinated by the Executive Director of the UN Conference on Trade and Development, to collate and analyse data, and to make policy recommendations along three workstreams, on food, energy and finance.

Office for the Coordination of Humanitarian Affairs—OCHA

Address: United Nations Plaza, New York, NY 10017, USA.
Telephone: (212) 963-1234; **fax:** (212) 963-1312; **e-mail:** unocha@un.org; **internet:** unocha.org.

The Office was established in January 1998 as part of the UN Secretariat, with a mandate to co-ordinate international humanitarian assistance and to provide policy and other advice on humanitarian issues. A complementary service, Reliefweb, provides humanitarian updates on, and analysis of, natural disasters and other crisis situations.

OCHA facilitates inter-agency appeals, which aim to co-ordinate resource mobilization following humanitarian crises. Since 2013 appeals have been formulated within the framework of a Humanitarian Programme Cycle, comprising the following five elements: needs assessment and analysis; strategic response planning; mobilization of resources; implementation and monitoring; and operational evaluation. In December 2021 OCHA issued its Global Humanitarian Overview (2022), comprising country Humanitarian Needs Overviews, 28 Humanitarian Response Plans (HRPs), and nine other response initiatives. At that time OCHA appealed for US $41,000m. to respond to the very urgent needs of 183m. people in 63 countries during 2022. Global requirements are adjusted continuously throughout each year as response initiatives are revised to reflect ongoing needs.

Under the Global Humanitarian Response process for 2022, the most costly response initiatives (as foreseen at December 2021) included an HRP for Ethiopia (requiring US $2,800m.); the Democratic Republic of the Congo HRP ($1,900m.) and Regional Response Plan—RRP ($532m.); the Sudan HRP ($1,900m.); the South Sudan HRP ($1,700m.) and RRP ($805m.); and HRPs for Somalia ($1,500m.) and Nigeria ($1,100m.). As at September 2022 northern Ethiopia and Somalia were designated by the UN as 'corporate emergencies', requiring the urgent focus of all OCHA's sections.

OCHA managed the preparatory process leading to the inaugural World Humanitarian Summit, which was convened in May 2016, in İstanbul, Turkey (Türkiye). Some 55 heads of state and government attending the meeting endorsed a new Agenda for Humanity, incorporating the following five core humanitarian responsibilities: Political leadership to prevent and end conflict; Uphold the norms that safeguard humanity; Leave no one behind; Change people's lives: from delivering aid to ending need; and Invest in humanity.

Under-Secretary-General for Humanitarian Affairs and Emergency Relief Co-ordinator: MARTIN GRIFFITHS (UK).

United Nations Entity for Gender Equality and the Empowerment of Women—UN Women

Address: 405 East 42nd St, New York, NY 10017, USA.
Telephone: (646) 781-4400; **fax:** (646) 781-4444; **internet:** www.unwomen.org.

UN Women was established by the UN General Assembly in July 2010 in order to strengthen the UN's capacity to promote gender equality, the empowerment of women, and the elimination of discrimination against women and girls. It commenced operations on 1 January 2011. In 2021 UN Women helped to stage a Generation Equality Forum which launched a Global Acceleration Plan (GAP) for Gender Equality that was framed around six new multistakeholder Action Coalitions, covering: gender-based violence, economic justice and rights, bodily autonomy and sexual and reproductive health rights, technology and innovation, feminist action for climate justice, and feminist movements and leadership. These were to mobilize civil society, governments, private sector interests and international organizations to advance equality during the period 2021–26.

Executive Director: SIMA SAMI BAHOUS (Jordan).

United Nations Office for Disaster Risk Reduction—UNDRR

Address: 9–11 rue de Varembé, 1202 Châtelaine, Geneva 10, Switzerland.
Telephone: 229178908; **fax:** 227339531; **e-mail:** undrrcomms@un.org; **internet:** undrr.org.

The Office was established in 1999 as an inter-agency secretariat to implement the International Strategy for Disaster Reduction (ISDR), formally adopted by UN member states in 2000. The ISDR was intended to guide and co-ordinate international efforts towards achieving substantive reduction in disaster losses, and building resilient communities and nations as the foundation for sustainable development activities. The Office (known until 2019 as UNISDR) led efforts to formulate a UN Plan of Action on Disaster Risk Reduction for Resilience, which was adopted in 2013.

In March 2015 the Office organized the Third UN World Conference on Disaster Risk Reduction (WCDRR), held in Sendai City, Japan, which adopted the (non-binding) Sendai Framework for Disaster Risk Reduction, covering the period 2015–30. The Sendai Framework listed seven measurable targets, four priorities, and a set of guiding principles related to disaster risk reduction planning, with the aim of lowering during 2020–30 the global mortality rate from disasters, as well as the numbers of people affected by disasters, compared with the rate in 2005–15; reducing disaster-related economic losses; and preventing disaster-related damage to basic services, infrastructure and livelihoods. Furthermore, public access to disaster risk information and early warning systems was to be enhanced. In view of rapidly advancing urbanization globally, the Sendai Framework placed a focus on building safer cities. In 2018 the ISDR adopted a Sendai Framework Monitor, which aimed to track progress in implementing the Framework in the context of 38 globally agreed indicators.

UNDRR serves as the focal point providing guidance for the implementation of the Sendai Framework. It also organizes the biennial sessions of the Global Platform for Disaster Risk Reduction (seventh session: May 2022, in Bali, Indonesia), and promotes information sharing on disaster risk reduction.

Special Representative of the UN Secretary-General for Disaster Risk Reduction: Mami Mizutori (Japan).

United Nations Office for Disarmament Affairs—UNODA

Address: UN Plaza, Rm S-3024, New York, NY 10017, USA.

Fax: (212) 963-4066; **e-mail:** UNODA-web@un.org; **internet:** www.un.org/disarmament.

UNODA—established in 1982 as the UN Department for Disarmament Affairs, with its present name adopted in 2007—works to promote nuclear disarmament and non-proliferation; to strengthen disarmament regimes with regard to biological and chemical weapons and other weapons of mass destruction; and to support disarmament activities relating to conventional weapons, with a particular focus on landmines and small arms.

UNODA maintains subsidiary offices in Geneva, Switzerland; Kathmandu, Nepal; Lima, Peru; Lomé, Togo; and Vienna, Austria.

Under-Secretary-General and High Representative for Disarmament Affairs: Izumi Nakamitsu (Japan).

United Nations Regional Centre for Peace and Disarmament in Africa (UNREC): BP 2705, Lomé, Togo; tel. 22-53-50-00; internet www.unrec.org; f. 1986; provides, often in co-operation with the African Union, substantive support for African states' initiatives towards achieving arms limitations and disarmament.

United Nations Office on Drugs and Crime—UNODC

Address: Vienna International Centre, POB 500, A 1400 Vienna, Austria.

Telephone: (1) 26060-0; **fax:** (1) 263-3389; **e-mail:** unodc@unodc.org; **internet:** www.unodc.org.

The Office was established in November 1997 (as the UN Office of Drug Control and Crime Prevention) to strengthen the UN's integrated approach to issues relating to drug control, crime prevention and international terrorism.

In February 2021 UNODC launched a Strategic Vision for Africa 2030, which aimed to develop innovative ways of strengthening crime and corruption prevention, criminal justice systems, drug control, and relevant legislation in the region. In July 2009 UNODC, other UN agencies, the Economic Community of West African States and INTERPOL launched the West Africa Coast Initiative (WACI), which aimed to build national and regional capacities to combat drug trafficking and organized crime in, initially, four post-conflict countries: Côte d'Ivoire, Guinea-Bissau, Liberia and Sierra Leone. In February 2010 the participating countries signed the 'WACI–Freetown Commitment', endorsing the implementation of the initiative, and agreeing to establish specialized transnational crime units on their territories. WACI activities were subsequently expanded to Guinea.

Executive Director: Ghada Fathi Waly (Egypt).

Office of the United Nations High Commissioner for Human Rights—OHCHR

Address: Palais Wilson, 52 rue de Paquis, 1201 Geneva, Switzerland.

Telephone: 229179220; **e-mail:** infodesk@ohchr.org; **internet:** www.ohchr.org.

OHCHR is a body of the UN Secretariat and is the focal point for UN human rights activities. The Office's Geneva headquarters incorporates the following three divisions: Human Rights Council and Treaty Mechanisms; Thematic Engagement, Special Procedures and Right to Development; and Field Operations and Technical Co-operation. The High Commissioner is the UN official with principal responsibility for UN human rights activities.

As at mid-2022 OHCHR was concerned with 45 thematic mandates (for example addressing the independence of judges and lawyers; rights to freedom of peaceful assembly and of association; arbitrary detention; adequate housing; and obligations relating to the enjoyment of a safe, clean, healthy and sustainable environment).

OHCHR was also concerned as at mid-2022 with 13 country mandates, including for Burundi (mandate established in 2021); the Central African Republic (mandate established in 2013, extended 2021); Eritrea (2012, 2021); Mali (2013, 2022); and Somalia (1993, 2021). The mandate of the UN Working Group of Experts on People of African Descent (established in 2002) was renewed in 2020. At mid-2022 OHCHR was supporting, *inter alia*, a Commission on Human Rights (CoHR) that was examining the situation in South Sudan (following a resolution adopted in March 2016 by the Human Rights Council); an International Team of Experts (ITE) on the Democratic Republic of the Congo (authorized in June 2017 with an initial focus on that country's Kasaï region; in October 2021 the scope of the ITE's mandate was extended to cover the whole country); and an International Commission of Human Rights Experts on Ethiopia (authorized in December 2021). In February 2021 the CoHR on South Sudan welcomed a decision made in late January by the South Sudanese authorities to proceed with the establishment of a Hybrid Court for South Sudan and other transitional justice mechanisms, to facilitate accountability for violations of human rights committed during the conflict (as provided for by a Revitalized Peace Agreement that had been concluded by the parties in September 2018).

High Commissioner: Volker Türk (Austria).

United Nations Human Settlements Programme—UN-Habitat

Address: POB 30030, Nairobi, Kenya.

Telephone: (20) 621234; **fax:** (20) 624266; **e-mail:** infohabitat@unhabitat.org; **internet:** unhabitat.org.

UN-Habitat was established as the UN Centre for Human Settlements, UNCHS-Habitat, in October 1978, on the recommendation of the First UN Conference on Human Settlements, convened in Vancouver, Canada, in May–June 1976. It led the Habitat Agenda, which was adopted as a Global Plan of Action to achieve 'adequate shelter for all' and 'sustainable human settlements development in an urbanizing world' by the Second UN Conference on Human Settlements (Habitat II), convened in İstanbul, Turkey (Türkiye), in June 1996. In January 2002 it became a full UN programme, serving as a focus for human settlements and sustainable urban development activities in the UN system. UN-Habitat leads the delivery of the New Urban Agenda, adopted in October 2016 by Habitat III, held in Quito, Ecuador. A new UN-Habitat Assembly was inaugurated in May 2019.

Executive Director: Maimunah Mohd Sharif (Malaysia).

United Nations Conference on Trade and Development—UNCTAD

Address: 8–14 Palais des Nations, 1211 Geneva 10, Switzerland.

Telephone: 229171234; **fax:** 229070057; **e-mail:** unctadinfo@unctad.org; **internet:** unctad.org.

UNCTAD was established in 1964. It is the principal organ of the UN General Assembly concerned with trade and development, and is the focal point within the UN system for integrated activities relating to trade, finance, technology, investment and sustainable development. It aims to maximize the trade and development opportunities of developing countries, in particular least-developed countries, and to assist them to adapt to the increasing globalization and liberalization of the world economy. UNCTAD undertakes consensus-building activities, research and policy analysis and technical co-operation.

Since 2000 UNCTAD has published an annual *Economic Development in Africa Report*. The 2021 edition focused on trading under the African Continental Free Trade Area.

UNCTAD aims to focus particular attention on the needs of the world's least developed countries (LDCs), of which there were 46 listed in 2022. In June 2018 a Gebze, Türkiye-based Technology Bank for LDCs was inaugurated, tasked with broadening the application of innovation, science and technology in, and serving as a knowledge hub for LDCs. Five UN Conferences on LDCs have been convened under UNCTAD auspices. At the first part of LDC V, held in March 2022, in New York, USA, the Doha Programme of Action for LDCs was adopted. The final part of LDC V was scheduled to be held in Doha, Qatar, in March 2023. In order to graduate from LDC status countries are required to meet at least two of three thresholds relating to gross national income per capita, the Human Assets Index, and the Economic Vulnerability Index; or to at least double the GNI per capita threshold.

In 2022 32 countries in Africa were classified as LDCs. Equatorial Guinea graduated from LDC status in June 2017, Cabo Verde in 2007, and Botswana in 1994. The 32 landlocked developing countries listed by the UN include 16 African countries.

Secretary-General: REBECA GRYNSPAN (Costa Rica).

United Nations Population Fund—UNFPA

Address: 605 Third Ave, New York, NY 10158, USA.

Telephone: (212) 297-5000; **fax:** (212) 370-0201; **e-mail:** hq@unfpa.org; **internet:** www.unfpa.org.

Created in 1967 as the Trust Fund for Population Activities, the UN Fund for Population Activities (UNFPA) was established as a Fund of the UN General Assembly in 1972 and was made a subsidiary organ of the UN General Assembly in 1979, with the UNDP Governing Council (now the Executive Board) designated as its governing body. In 1987 UNFPA's name was changed to the UN Population Fund (retaining the same acronym). UNFPA works to promote reproductive rights, and universal access to sexual and reproductive health, with a particular focus on women, adolescents and youth.

Executive Director: Dr NATALIA KANEM (Panama).

Regional Office for East and Southern Africa: 9 Simba Rd, Sunninghill, Johannesburg 2157, South Africa; tel. (11) 603-5300; fax (11) 297-4951; e-mail esaro.info@unfpa.org; internet esaro.unfpa.org; Dir LYDIA ZIGOMO.

Regional Office for West and Central Africa: Dakar, Senegal; e-mail wcaro.info@unfpa.org; internet wcaro.unfpa.org; Dir ARGENTINA MATAVEL PICCIN.

UN Specialized Agencies and Related Organizations

International Atomic Energy Agency—IAEA

Address: Vienna International Centre, POB 100, 1400 Vienna, Austria.

Telephone: (1) 26000; **fax:** (1) 26007; **e-mail:** official.mail@iaea.org; **internet:** www.iaea.org.

The Agency was founded in 1957 as an autonomous intergovernmental organization, although it is administratively part of the UN system and reports annually to the UN General Assembly. Its main objectives are to enlarge the contribution of atomic energy to peace, health and prosperity throughout the world, and to ensure that materials and services provided by the Agency are not used to further any military purpose.

Several regional nuclear weapons treaties require their member states to conclude Comprehensive Safeguards Agreements with the IAEA, including the African Nuclear-Weapon Free Zone Treaty (Pelindaba Treaty), adopted in 1996, and with 43 states parties at mid-2022.

A Treaty on the Prohibition of Nuclear Weapons entered into force in January 2021.

Director-General: RAFAEL GROSSI (Argentina).

International Civil Aviation Organization—ICAO

Address: 999 University St, Montréal, QC H3C 5H7, Canada.

Telephone: (514) 954-8219; **fax:** (514) 954-6077; **e-mail:** icaohq@icao.org; **internet:** www.icao.int.

ICAO was founded in 1947, on the basis of the Convention on International Civil Aviation, signed in Chicago, in 1944, to develop the techniques of international air navigation and to help in the planning and improvement of international air transport.

In April 2020 ICAO's Governing Council established a COVID-19 Aviation Recovery Task Force (CART), which subsequently released a series of recommendations—to be continuously updated—that were aimed at restarting the international air transport system and at facilitating the global mutual recognition, harmonization and convergence of aviation COVID-19 related measures. By January 2022 ICAO estimated that passenger levels had risen during 2021, compared with the previous year, but were still 49% lower than in (pre-pandemic) 2019. The industry losses as a result of COVID-19 were estimated at that time at US $696,000m.

Secretary-General: JUAN CARLOS SALAZAR GÓMEZ (Colombia).

Eastern and Southern Africa Office: Limuru Rd, Gigiri, POB 46294, Nairobi, Kenya; tel. (20) 7622395; fax (20) 7623028; e-mail icaoesaf@icao.int; internet www.icao.int/esaf.

Western and Central African Office: Leopold Sedar Senghor International Airport, BP 38050, Yoff, Dakar, Senegal; tel. 33-839-2424; fax 33-823-3259; e-mail icaowacaf@icao.int; internet www.icao.int/wacaf.

International Labour Organization—ILO

Address: 4 route des Morillons, 1211 Geneva 22, Switzerland.

Telephone: 227996111; **fax:** 227988685; **e-mail:** ilo@ilo.org; **internet:** www.ilo.org.

The ILO was founded in 1919 to work for social justice as a basis for lasting peace. It carries out this mandate by promoting decent living standards, satisfactory conditions of work and pay and adequate employment opportunities. Activities include the creation of international labour standards; the provision of technical co-operation services; and training, education, research and publishing activities to advance ILO objectives. ILO flagship programmes include the International Programme on the Elimination of Child Labour and Forced Labour (IPEC+); Global Action for Prevention on Occupational Safety and Health (OSH-GAP); and Social Protection Floors for All.

Director-General: GILBERT F. HOUNGBO (Togo).

Regional Office for Africa: CCIA Bldg, rue Jean Paul II, 01 BP 3960 Abidjan 01, Côte d'Ivoire; tel. 20-31-89-00; fax 20-21-28-80; e-mail abidjan@ilo.org; internet www.ilo.org/africa.

International Maritime Organization—IMO

Address: 4 Albert Embankment, London, SE1 7SR, United Kingdom.

Telephone: (20) 7735-7611; **fax:** (20) 7587-3210; **e-mail:** info@imo.org; **internet:** www.imo.org.

The Inter-Governmental Maritime Consultative Organization (IMCO) began operations in 1959, as a specialized agency of the UN to facilitate co-operation among governments on technical matters affecting international shipping. Its main aims are to improve the safety of international shipping, and to control pollution caused by ships. IMCO became IMO in 1982.

In January 2009 a high level subregional meeting of states from the Western Indian Ocean, the Gulf of Aden and Red Sea areas, held under IMO auspices, adopted the Djibouti Code of Conduct concerning the Repression of Piracy and Armed Robbery. Signatories to the Code agreed to co-operate lawfully in the apprehension, investigation and prosecution of people suspected of committing or facilitating acts of piracy; in the seizure of suspect vessels; in the rescue of ships, persons and property subject to acts of armed robbery; and to collaborate in the conduct of security operations. The Doraleh-based Djibouti Regional Training Centre facilitates capacity-building initiatives related to the Code of Conduct. In January 2017 12 states signed the Jeddah Amendment to the Djibouti Code of Conduct, in accordance with which they were to co-operate—supported by IMO and other stakeholders—in developing national and regional capacity to address wider maritime security issues, with a focus on promoting the 'blue economy' and sustainable development of the maritime sector.

IMO supported the Economic Community of West Africa States and the Communauté Economique des Etats de l'Afrique Centrale in drafting the Code of Conduct concerning the Prevention and Repression of Piracy, Armed Robbery against Ships, and Illegal Maritime Activities in West and Central Africa. This was formally adopted at a meeting of regional heads of state convened in June 2013, in Yaoundé, Cameroon, and has subsequently been referred to as the Yaoundé Code of Conduct (YCC). Implementation of the YCC is supported by a Yaoundé-based Interregional Coordination Centre.

Secretary-General: KITACK LIM (Republic of Korea).

International Organization for Migration—IOM

Address: 17 route des Morillons, CP 71, 1211 Geneva 19, Switzerland.

Telephone: 227179111; **fax:** 227986150; **e-mail:** hq@iom.int; **internet:** www.iom.int.

IOM was established in 1951 as the Intergovernmental Committee for Migration (ICM), to address orderly and planned migration meeting the specific needs of emigration and immigration countries; international resettlement; and the voluntary return and reintegration of migrants, refugees and internally displaced persons. ICM's name was changed to IOM in 1989. IOM was admitted as an observer to the UN General Assembly in 1992. In September 2016, at the UN Summit on Addressing Large Movements of Refugees and Migrants, held at the UN General Assembly, in New York, USA, IOM was incorporated into the UN system as a related body. The conference adopted the New York Declaration for Refugees and Migrants, which recognized an unprecedented level of human mobility, and determined to address the root causes of mass migration movements. A commitment was made to negotiate a Global Compact for Safe, Orderly and Regular Migration. The Compact was adopted by an Intergovernmental Conference on International Migration, hosted by Morocco, in December 2018.

Following the onset in November 2020 of armed conflict in the Ethiopian region of Tigray IOM monitored ensuing displacement and humanitarian needs; in 2022, IOM was implementing a major US $129m. humanitarian operation to support nearly 3m. people in Ethiopia. In 2022 IOM also appealed, *inter alia,* for $191m. to fund a Lake Chad Basin Crisis Response Plan; $171m. to assist 2.1m. people in Sudan; $118m. for a Central Sahel Crisis Response Plan; $116m. to support 1.6m. crisis-affected populations in southern areas and vulnerable migrants in Niger; $96m. to assist the Nigerian Government with its response efforts in non-state armed group-affected areas; $82m. to help 1.4m. beneficiaries in Somalia; $72m. to support 734,000 IDPs and local community members in the Democratic Republic of the Congo; and $55m. to assist 800,000 people (including encamped IDPs, returnees, host community members and survivors of human rights abuses) in Burundi. IOM requested funding of $30m. to contribute to Ebola Virus Disease prevention, early detection and response (from a human mobility perspective) throughout sub-Saharan Africa during 2022.

Director-General: ANTÓNIO MANUEL DE CARVALHO FERREIRA VITORINO (Portugal).

International Telecommunication Union—ITU

Address: Place des Nations, 1211 Geneva 20, Switzerland.

Telephone: 227305111; **fax:** 227337256; **e-mail:** itumail@itu.int; **internet:** www.itu.int.

Founded in 1865, ITU became a specialized agency of the UN in 1947. It aims to encourage world co-operation for the improvement and national use of telecommunications to promote technical development, to harmonize national policies in the field, and to promote the extension of telecommunications throughout the world. ITU helped to organize the World Summit on the Information Society, held, in two phases, in 2003 and 2005, and supports follow-up initiatives. ITU has assumed responsibility for issues relating to cybersecurity. In December 2012 a World Conference on International Communications endorsed new International Telecommunication Regulations (ITRs), updating those previously set down in 1988. World Radiocommunication Conferences, World Telecommunication Standardization Assemblies and World Telecommunication Development Conferences are convened regularly.

Secretary-General: HOULIN ZHAO (People's Republic of China) (outgoing), DOREEN BOGDAN-MARTIN (USA) (from 1 Jan. 2023).

United Nations Educational, Scientific and Cultural Organization—UNESCO

Address: 7 place de Fontenoy, 75352 Paris 07 SP, France.

Telephone: 1-45-68-10-00; **fax:** 1-45-67-16-90; **e-mail:** bpi@unesco .org; **internet:** www.unesco.org.

UNESCO was established in 1946 and aims to contribute, through education, the sciences, culture, communication and information, to the building of peace and the eradication of poverty, and to advancing sustainable development and intercultural dialogue.

UNESCO's World Heritage Programme, inaugurated in 1978, aims to protect historic sites and natural landmarks of outstanding universal significance, in accordance with the 1972 UNESCO Convention Concerning the Protection of the World Cultural and Natural Heritage, by providing financial aid for restoration, technical assistance, training and management planning.

In addition to numerous nature reserves and national parks, examples in Africa include Mbanza Kongo—vestiges of the political and spiritual capital of the former Kingdom of Kongo (Angola); the royal palaces of Abomey (Benin); the ancient ferrous metallurgy sites at Douroula, Tiwêga, Yamané, Kindibo and Békuy (Burkina Faso); the Ennedi Massif: Natural and Cultural Landscape (Chad); Sudanese style adobe mosques in northern Côte d'Ivoire; the Modernist African City of Asmara (Eritrea); the rock-hewn churches at Lalibela (Ethiopia; seized in 2021 by Tigrayan rebels); Ivindo National Park; forts, castles and Ashanti traditional buildings in Ghana; Lamu Old Town, and the Thimlich Ohinga Archaeological Site (Kenya); the Royal Hill of Ambohimanga (Madagascar); the Bandiagara cliffs of the Dogon people (Mali); four ancient trading towns in Mauritania; the Sukur Cultural Landscape (Nigeria); Robben Island and the Mapungubwe Cultural Landscape (South Africa); the pyramids at Gebel Barkal and other archaeological sites in the Napatan region (Sudan); the stone town of Zanzibar (Tanzania); and the Great Zimbabwe National Monument. In 2022 the list of World Heritage in Danger included four national parks and reserves in the Democratic Republic of the Congo (DRC); the Niokolo-Koba National Park in Senegal; the Selous Game Reserve in Tanzania; the tombs of Buganda Kings at Kasubi, Uganda; the Rainforests of the Atsinanana in Madagascar; and (owing to conflict in northern Mali) the old town of Djenné and four neighbouring archaeological sites, and the city of Tombouctou and the Tomb of Askia (dating from 1495, and situated in Gao, Mali). In July 2017 the World Heritage Committee removed the Simian National Park (Ethiopia) from the list of sites in danger, given significant management improvements; similarly, the DRC's Salonga National Park was removed in July 2021. Lake Turkana National Parks, in Kenya, were added to that list in 2018, in view of concerns over the impact of the Gilgel Gibe III Dam (on the Omo River, in Ethiopia) on Lake Turkana's flow and ecosystem, and also over threats to the lake posed by Ethiopia's Kuraz Sugar Development Project.

UNESCO's Man and the Biosphere Programme supports a worldwide network of biosphere reserves, which aim to promote environmental conservation and research, education and training in biodiversity and problems of land use (including the fertility of tropical soils and the cultivation of sacred sites). In July 2022 there were 90 biosphere reserves in 33 countries in Africa, including Doumba-Rey (Cameroon), Sena Oura (Chad), Kafue Flats (Zambia), and Middle Zambezi (Zimbabwe), all of which had been newly designated in June of that year. UNESCO also supports a Global Network of National Geoparks (177 in 46 countries at mid-2022). The first sub-Saharan African Geopark was approved by the UNESCO Executive Board in April 2018 in Ngorongoro Lengai, Tanzania. The Ngorongoro Lengai Geopark is noted for its great diversity of wildlife—coexisting with human settlements, and for the Oldoinyo Lengai ('Mountain of God' in the local Masai language) active stratovolcano.

Director-General: AUDREY AZOULAY (France).

UNESCO Dakar: Almadies, Route de la Plage de Ngor, Dakar Senegal; e-mail dakar@unesco.org; internet en.unesco.org/fieldoffice/dakar; serves as the Regional Office for West Africa (Sahel), Burkina Faso, Cabo Verde, Gambia, Guinea-Bissau, Mali, Niger and Senegal; Dir DIMITRI SANGA.

UNESCO Harare: 8 Kenilworth Rd, Newlands, Highlands, Harare, Zimbabwe; e-mail harare@unesco.org; internet en.unesco.org/fieldoffice/harare; serves as the Regional Office for Southern Africa, covering Botswana, Eswatini, Lesotho, Malawi, Mozambique, Namibia, South Africa, Zambia and Zimbabwe; Dir LIDIA BRITO.

UNESCO Multisectoral Regional Office for Central Africa: Rue 1778, Quartier Bastos, Mfoundi, Yaoundé, Cameroon; tel. 222-508-301; e-mail yaounde@unesco.org; internet fr.unesco.org/fieldoffice/yaounde; Dir SALAH KHALED.

UNESCO Multisectoral Regional Office for West Africa: UN House, Plot 617/618, Diplomatic Drive, Central Business District Garki, Abuja, Nigeria; e-mail abuja@unesco.org; internet en.unesco .org/fieldoffice/abuja; Dir MAMADOU LAMINE SOW.

UNESCO Nairobi: United Nations Ave, Gigiri, Nairobi, Kenya; tel. (20) 7622356; e-mail nairobi@unesco.org; internet en.unesco.org/fieldoffice/nairobi; serves as the Regional Office for Eastern Africa, covering Comoros, Djibouti, Eritrea, Ethiopia, Kenya, Madagascar, Mauritius, Rwanda, Seychelles, Somalia, South Sudan, Tanzania and Uganda; Dir Prof. HUBERT GIJZEN.

UNESCO International Institute for Capacity Building in Africa (UNESCO–IICBA): UNECA Compound, Menilik Ave, POB 2305, Addis Ababa, Ethiopia; tel. (11) 5445284; fax (11) 514936; e-mail info.iicba@unesco.org; internet www.iicba.unesco.org; f. 1999 to promote capacity building in the following areas: teacher education; curriculum development; educational policy, planning and management; and distance education; Dir YUMIKO YOKOZEKI.

United Nations Industrial Development Organization—UNIDO

Address: Vienna International Centre, Wagramerstr. 5, POB 300, 1400 Vienna, Austria.
Telephone: (1) 260260; **fax:** (1) 2692669; **e-mail:** unido@unido.org; **internet:** www.unido.org.

UNIDO began operations in 1967 and became a specialized agency in 1985. Its objectives are to promote sustainable and socially equitable industrial development in developing countries and in countries with economies in transition. It aims to assist such countries to integrate fully into global economic system by mobilizing knowledge, skills, information and technology to promote productive employment, competitive economies and sound environment.

Director-General: GERD MÜLLER (Germany).

Universal Postal Union—UPU

Address: POB 312, 3000 Bern 15, Switzerland.
Telephone: 313503111; **fax:** 313503110; **e-mail:** info@upu.int; **internet:** www.upu.int.

The General Postal Union was founded by the Treaty of Bern (1874), beginning operations in July 1875. Three years later its name was changed to the Universal Postal Union. In 1948 UPU became a specialized agency of the UN. It aims to support an efficient, effective and co-ordinated international postal service.

In December 2018 UPU introduced a Financial Inclusion Technical Assistance Facility (FITAF), which was to support projects providing digital financial services support up to 800,000 impoverished and 'unbanked' people (i.e. excluded from more mainstream financial institutions) in Africa, Asia and the Pacific.

In May 2021—in view of a non-binding Advisory Opinion issued in February 2019 by the International Court of Justice, which had found that the United Kingdom was illegally occupying the Chagos Archipielago (constituted since 1965 as the British Indian Ocean Territory), and should return the islands forthwith to Mauritius—the UPU Council of Administration recommended that UPU member states should no longer register, distribute or forward postage stamps issued by the territory. The decision was endorsed by the 27th Universal Postal Congress in August 2021.

Director-General: MASAHIKO METOKI (Japan).

World Intellectual Property Organization—WIPO

Address: 34 chemin des Colombettes, 1211 Geneva 20, Switzerland.
Telephone: 223389111; **fax:** 227335428; **internet:** www.wipo.int.

WIPO was established in 1970. It became a specialized agency of the UN in 1974 concerned with the protection of intellectual property (e.g. patents, trademarks, industrial designs and literary copyrights) throughout the world. WIPO formulates and administers treaties embodying international norms and standards of intellectual property, establishes model laws, and facilitates applications for the protection of inventions, trademarks etc. WIPO provides legal and technical assistance to developing countries and countries with economies in transition and advises countries on obligations under the World Trade Organization's agreement on Trade-Related Aspects of Intellectual Property Rights.

Director-General: DAREN TANG (Singapore).

World Meteorological Organization—WMO

Address: 7 bis, ave de la Paix, 1211 Geneva 2, Switzerland.
Telephone: 227308111; **fax:** 227308181; **e-mail:** cpa@wmo.int; **internet:** www.wmo.int.

WMO was established in 1950 and was recognized as a specialized agency of the UN in 1951, aiming to improve the exchange of information on meteorology, climatology, operational hydrology and related fields. WMO jointly implements, with UNEP, the UN Framework Convention on Climate Change.

In May 2022 WMO released the 2021 edition of its annual *State of the Global Climate*, based on data that had been provided by national meteorological and hydrological services, UN partners, and other scientific institutions and international experts. The report found that new records had been reached in 2021 for ocean heat, ocean acidification, and rises in sea levels. Concentrations of carbon dioxide, methane and nitrous dioxide in the Earth's atmosphere were observed to have been significantly higher in 2020 (respectively 149%, 262% and 123% higher) in comparison with pre-1750 levels (i.e. compared with prior to the commencement of the industrial era). The average global temperature in 2021 was recorded as $1.11°C$ higher than at pre-industrial levels.

Secretary-General: PETTERI TAALAS (Finland).

World Tourism Organization—UNWTO

Address: Capitán Haya 42, 28020 Madrid, Spain.
Telephone: (91) 5678100; **fax:** (91) 5713733; **e-mail:** omt@unwto.org; **internet:** www.unwto.org.

The World Tourism Organization was established in 1975 and was recognized as a specialized agency of the UN in December 2003. It works to promote and develop sustainable tourism, in particular in support of socioeconomic growth in developing countries.

In May 2020 UNWTO released a COVID-19 Tourism Recovery Technical Assistance Package, providing guidance to member states focused on three pillars: economic recovery; marketing and promotion; and institutional strengthening and building resilience (with a particular focus on enhancing public-private partnerships, strengthening crisis management and recovery skills, and promoting collaborative efforts for tourism recovery). An UNWTO Tourism Data Dashboard was developed during the COVID-19 crisis. In January 2022 the UNWTO World Tourism Barometer estimated that international tourist arrivals had totalled 415m. in 2021, compared with 400m. in 2020, and with 1,500m. in (pre-pandemic) 2019.

Secretary-General: ZURAB POLOLIKASHVILI (Georgia).

World Trade Organization—WTO

Address: Centre William Rappard, 154 rue de Lausanne, 1211 Geneva 21, Switzerland.
Telephone: 227395111; **fax:** 227314206; **e-mail:** enquiries@wto.org; **internet:** www.wto.org.

The World Trade Organization was established in 1995 as the successor to the General Agreement on Tariffs and Trade (GATT), overseeing the multilateral trading system. It facilitates negotiations on global trade agreements, monitors the implementation of trade agreements, undertakes dispute procedures, and promotes development, economic reform, as well as trade capacity among developing nations and countries with economies in transition. The WTO participates in the UN Chief Executives Board for Co-ordination as a related organization.

In November 2001 the fourth WTO Ministerial Conference initiated the Doha Round of negotiations on major reform to the international trading system; progress in implementing the Doha Round was, however, subsequently slow. The 12th WTO Ministerial Conference, held in June 2022, agreed a Geneva Package of measures, that included: a decision relating to e-commerce; an agreement on fisheries subsidies; a ministerial declaration on the WTO Response to the COVID-19 pandemic and preparedness for future pandemics; a ministerial decision on the Agreement on Trade-related Aspects of Intellectual Property Rights (which provided for a partial intellectual property waiver to enable developing countries to manufacture COVID-19 vaccines and export them to other developing countries); and a ministerial declaration on the emergency response to food insecurity.

The WTO has 164 member states, including 38 in Africa South of the Sahara.

Director-General: Dr NGOZI OKONJO-IWEALA (Nigeria).

AFRICAN DEVELOPMENT BANK—AfDB

Address: Immeuble du Centre de Commerce International d'Abidjan, ave Jean-Paul II, 01 BP 1387, Abidjan 01, Côte d'Ivoire.

Telephone: 20-26-39-00; **e-mail:** afdb@afdb.org; **internet:** www .afdb.org.

Established in 1964, the Bank began operations in July 1966, with the aim of financing economic and social development in African countries. Non-African countries were admitted to the Bank from 1982. The Bank aims to contribute to development and poverty reduction by mobilizing funds for investment and by providing policy and technical assistance. The Bank and two other institutions, the African Development Fund and the Nigeria Trust Fund, constitute the African Development Bank (AfDB) Group.

REGIONAL MEMBERS

Algeria	Eritrea	Namibia
Angola	Eswatini	Niger
Benin	Ethiopia	Nigeria
Botswana	Gabon	Rwanda
Burkina Faso	The Gambia	São Tomé and
Burundi	Ghana	Príncipe
Cabo Verde	Guinea	Senegal
Cameroon	Guinea-Bissau	Seychelles
Central African	Kenya	Sierra Leone
Republic	Lesotho	Somalia
Chad	Liberia	South Africa
Comoros	Libya	South Sudan
Congo,	Madagascar	Sudan
Democratic	Malawi	Tanzania
Republic	Mali	Togo
Congo, Republic	Mauritania	Tunisia
Côte d'Ivoire	Mauritius	Uganda
Djibouti	Morocco	Zambia
Egypt	Mozambique	Zimbabwe
Equatorial Guinea		

The Bank has 27 non-African members.

Organization

(October 2022)

BOARD OF GOVERNORS

The Board of Governors is the highest policymaking body of the Bank, responsible for electing the Board of Directors and the President. Each member country nominates one Governor, usually its Minister of Finance and Economic Affairs, and an alternate Governor or the Governor of its central bank. The Board meets in ordinary session once a year: the 2022 meeting was held in Abidjan, in May.

BOARD OF DIRECTORS

The 20-member Board of Directors, elected by the Board of Governors for a term of three years, is responsible for the general operations of the Bank and meets on a weekly basis.

ADMINISTRATION

The President—who is elected for a five-year term and serves as the Chairperson of the Board of Directors—is responsible for the organization and the day-to-day operations of the Bank, under the guidance of the Board of Directors. The Bank has the following divisions, each headed by a Vice-President: Power, Energy, Climate, and Green Growth; Agriculture, Human and Social Development; Private Sector, Infrastructure and Industrialization; Regional Development, Integration and Business Delivery; Economic Governance and Knowledge Management; Finance; People and Talent Management; and Technology and Corporate Services.

In 2022 Bank field offices were located in 37 member countries. Four regional hubs have been approved: in Nairobi, Kenya (for East Africa), Centurion, South Africa (Southern Africa), Tunis, Tunisia (North Africa), and in Yaoundé, Cameroon (for Central Africa). The Bank's first external representation office (for Asia) was inaugurated in Tokyo, Japan, in October 2012. An African Natural Resources Centre was established in 2013, at the Bank's headquarters.

President and Chairperson of Board of Directors: Dr AKINWUMI A. ADESINA (Nigeria).

FINANCIAL STRUCTURE

The African Development Bank Group of development financing institutions uses a unit of account (UA), which at December 2021 was valued at US $1.53692.

The capital stock of the Bank was at first exclusively open for subscription by African countries, with each member's subscription consisting of an equal number of paid-up and callable shares. In 1978, however, the Governors agreed to open the capital stock of the Bank to subscription by non-regional states on the basis of nine principles aimed at maintaining the African character of the institution. The decision was finally ratified in May 1982, and the participation of non-regional countries became effective on 30 December. It was agreed that African members should still hold two-thirds of the share capital, that all loan operations should be restricted to African members, and that the Bank's President should always be a national of an African state. In May 1998 the Board of Governors resolved that the non-African members' share of the capital be increased from 33.3% to 40%.

In October 2019 an extraordinary meeting of the Board of Governors approved the Bank's seventh general capital increase, of some US $115,000m. At 31 December 2021, accordingly, the Bank's authorized capital was UA 180,638.83m.; subscribed capital at the end of 2021 was UA 148,473.62m. (of which the paid-up portion was UA 9,958.90m.).

Activities

The Bank's Strategy for 2013–22, adopted in April 2013, focused on achieving inclusive growth and promoting the transition to green growth, with infrastructure development, regional integration, private sector development, governance and accountability, and skills and technology designated as core areas of priority. Further areas of special emphasis included fragile states, gender, agriculture, and food security. The Development and Business Delivery Model that was endorsed by the Board in April 2016 aimed to transform the Bank's internal organization in alignment with its 2013–22 Strategy and the following High 5 priorities: Light up and power Africa, Feed Africa, Industrialize Africa, Integrate Africa, and Improve the quality of life for the people of Africa.

In March 2009 a Coalition for Dialogue on Africa was inaugurated by the Bank, the United Nations (UN) Economic Commission for Africa (ECA) and the African Union (AU). A joint secretariat supports co-operation activities between the three organizations. The AfDB is actively involved in the AU Development Agency (AUDA-NEPAD), which aims to promote sustainable development and eradicate poverty throughout the region. The Bank is a strategic partner in AUDA-NEPAD's African Peer Review Mechanism.

FINANCIAL OPERATIONS

At the end of 2021 the Bank Group had approved total lending of UA 125,461m. for 6,575 operations since the beginning of its activities in 1967. In 2021 the Group approved 196 lending operations amounting to UA 4,506.3m., compared with 217 operations with a value of UA 4,171.1m. in the previous year. Of the total amount approved in 2021, UA 4,085.3m. was for loans and grants, UA 127.6m. for guarantees, and UA 29.9m. for equity participation.

Of the total operations approved in 2021, by High 5 priority sector, UA 1,653.65m. (37%) was for Improve the quality of life for the people of Africa projects; UA 908.00m. (20%) was for Feed Africa initiatives; UA 827.68m. (18%) for Industrialize Africa; UA 697.59m. (16%) for Integrate Africa; and UA 419.36m. (9%) was for Light up and power Africa initiatives. Some 26.1% of expenditure was allocated to transport projects, 19.2% to power, 15.4% to finance, 11.0% to agriculture, and 10.4% to multisector projects. In terms of geographical distribution, 27.1% of approved Bank Group operations in 2021 were allocated to countries in West Africa, 24.1% to East Africa, 19.4% to Southern Africa, 14.2% to North Africa, and 10.8% to countries in Central Africa; furthermore, 4.3% of approvals was for multiregional projects.

African Development Bank: The Bank makes loans at a variable rate of interest, which is adjusted twice a year, plus a commitment fee of 0.75%. Lending approved (including resources allocated under the Post-conflict Country Facility and private and public equity participations) amounted to UA 2,449.1m. for 66 operations in 2021, compared with UA 2,492.7m. for 48 operations in 2020. Since October 1997 fixed and floating rate loans have been made available.

African Development Fund: The Fund commenced operations in 1974. It grants interest-free loans to low-income African countries for projects with repayment over 50 years (including a 10-year grace period) and with a service charge of 0.75% per annum. Grants for project feasibility studies are made to the poorest countries.

In December 2019 a global coalition of donor countries concluded an agreement on ADF-15, replenishing the Fund by US $7,600m. for the period 2020–22.

In 2021 approvals under the ADF amounted to UA 1,263.3m. for 66 projects, compared with UA 938.8m. for 71 projects in the previous year.

Nigeria Trust Fund: The Agreement establishing the NTF was signed in February 1976 by the Bank and the Government of Nigeria. The Fund is administered by the Bank and its loans are granted for up to 25 years, including grace periods of up to five years, and carry 0.75% commission charges and 4% interest charges. The loans are intended to provide financing for projects in co-operation with other lending institutions. The Fund also aims to promote the private sector and trade between African countries by providing information on African and international financial institutions able to finance African trade.

In 2021 one new operation with a value of UA 3.6m. was approved under the NTF, and UA 15.0m. was disbursed.

The AfDB and Nigerian authorities co-manage a Nigeria Technical Co-operation Fund (NTCF), which became operational in 2004 to support regional development initiatives.

REGIONAL DEVELOPMENT, INTEGRATION AND BUSINESS DELIVERY

The Bank, the AU and ECA jointly contribute to Agenda 2063, a long-term vision to guide the economic and social transformation of Africa, within the context of which a series of African Development Goals (ADGs) are to be pursued; Agenda 2063 was adopted by AU heads of state and of government in January 2015. The independent, profit-driven Africa50 Infrastructure Fund—headquartered in Finance City, Casablanca, Morocco—was inaugurated in September 2014, having been endorsed by the Board of Governors in May 2013.

The inaugural meeting of an African Economic Platform (AEP), supporting Agenda 2063, was held in March 2017, in Port Louis, Mauritius.

The AfDB has identified the following as fragile states: Burundi, the Central African Republic, Comoros, the Democratic Republic of Congo (DRC), Côte d'Ivoire, Guinea, Guinea-Bissau, Liberia, Madagascar, Mali, Sierra Leone, Somalia, South Sudan, Sudan, Togo and Zimbabwe. A Transition Support Facility (TSF) was established in 2014. The resources released through the TSF are mainly allocated to capacity-building initiatives, social services projects, and to infrastructure development. In 2021 the Bank approved UA 483.1m. for 29 operations funded through the TSF. Of the total, UA 314.2m. was allocated to 15 operations supporting state-building efforts. The fourth Africa Resilience Forum, themed 'COVID-19 and Beyond: Working Together for a Resilient Continent', was convened by the Bank at the end of September 2021, in a virtual format. In March 2022 the AfDB initiated a new Strategy for Addressing Fragility and Building Resilience in Africa, covering the period 2022–26, with a focus on catalyzing private investment, and strengthening economies, institutional capacity and societies.

In February 2015 the Bank appointed three High-Level Advisers on Fragility, tasked with strengthening its advisory, advocacy and policy leadership role.

An Africa Growing Together Fund was established in 2014, with the People's Republic of China, to co-finance public and private sector projects in support of regional integration and infrastructure development. In July 2017 the AfDB and the Islamic Development Bank concluded an agreement under which they were to provide some US $2,000m. in support of activities aimed at accelerating economic development in Africa, with a particular emphasis on promoting agriculture and food security, energy, and small and medium-sized enterprises (SMEs). An AfDB Microfinance Capacity Building Fund for Africa was launched in 2011.

An AfDB Regional Integration Strategy was being implemented over the period 2018–28, with a focus on enhancing power and infrastructure connectivity; trade and investment; and financial sector integration. An Africa Regional Integration Index, jointly developed by the AfDB, ECA and the AU, was launched in April 2016. The Index aims to measure, systematically (providing data on member states and regional economic communities), regional integration across areas including governance, investment, trade, infrastructure, industry, the free movement of persons, energy, culture and macroeconomic policy convergence. The second edition of the Index, issued in May 2020, found South Africa to be the most regionally integrated African country. It recommended, *inter alia*, enhancing member states' productive, distributive, and marketing capacities; promoting public-private partnerships to strengthen the continental infrastructure; strengthening regional sectoral value-chain frameworks; fully implementing the African Continental Free Trade Area; enhancing workers' technological and other competencies; and promoting the free movement of people on the continent.

Since 1996 the Bank has collaborated closely with international partners, in particular the World Bank, in efforts to address the problems of heavily indebted poor countries (HIPCs—see IBRD). Of the 41 countries identified as potentially eligible for assistance under the scheme, 33 were in sub-Saharan Africa. In April 2006 the Board of Directors endorsed a Multilateral Debt Relief Initiative (MDRI), which provided for 100% cancellation of eligible debts from the ADF, the International Monetary Fund and the International Development Association; the ADF's participation in the MDRI, which became effective in September, was anticipated to provide some UA 5,570m. (US $8,540m.) in debt relief. An AfDB Debt Action Plan was being implemented during 2021–23 to address fiscal and debt stress.

The AfDB's Lusophone Compact, initiated in 2018, is a financing platform engaging the Bank, Portugal and the six Portuguese-speaking African countries—Angola, Cabo Verde, Equatorial Guinea, Guinea-Bissau, Mozambique and São Tomé and Príncipe. In July 2019 the Bank and the Governments of Angola and Portugal signed a Country-Specific Compact under the initiative, which aimed to advance the sustainable development of Angola's private sector. In December 2021 the AfDB and International Finance Corporation concluded a partnership agreement that admitted the latter to the Lusophone Compact.

POWER, ENERGY, CLIMATE AND GREEN GROWTH

In 2012 the Bank initiated, with funding from the Government of Denmark, a Sustainable Energy Fund for Africa (SEFA); in September 2013 the Board approved the conversion of SEFA into a multi-donor trust fund. The Bank's Board of Governors decided in November 2019 to restructure SEFA as a concessional financing facility. Its launch as the SEFA Special Fund was marked by a virtual gathering of donor and development partners, industry representatives and government officials in December 2020. The Bank hosts the secretariats of the African Energy Leaders Group and of the Africa Hub of the UN's Sustainable Energy for All initiative. In December 2016 the Bank's Board of Directors endorsed a trusteeship role for the Bank with respect to the administration and management of the resources of the African Renewable Energy Initiative, which was initiated by the AU in December 2015, with the aim of producing by 2030 some 300 GW of electricity across the continent. The AfDB's New Deal on Energy for Africa and related High 5 priority: Light up and power Africa by 2025 focus on fostering partnerships between governments, the private sector and energy sector initiatives to develop an overarching Transformative Partnership on Energy for Africa, providing innovative financing for the continental energy sector. The third round of the AfDB-designed Africa Energy Market Place (AEMP), a collaborative investment platform within the New Deal on Energy framework, was convened in June 2019, in Abidjan. The AfDB launched an online Africa Energy Portal (AEP) in November 2018. In October 2020 the Bank and AUDA-NEPAD jointly released the recommendations of a baseline study that had examined the planned development of a continental energy transmission grid and market.

In April 2014 the Board of Directors endorsed the establishment of an Africa Climate Change Fund, which is hosted by the Bank, and aims to assist the transition of African countries towards climate-resilient and low-carbon development. The AfDB and Green Climate Fund concluded a partnership agreement in November 2017. The Bank announced in March 2019 that it would commit at least US $25,000m. towards climate finance projects during the period 2020–25. In 2021 the AfDB committed 41% of expenditure to climate-sensitive projects, compared with 9% in 2016. The AfDB's Africa Nationally Determined Contributions Hub supports member states in meeting obligations under the 2015 Paris Agreement on climate change. Secretariat services are provided by the Bank to the Africa Financial Alliance on Climate Change (AFAC), which co-ordinates the mobilization of contributions towards climate action and climate-resistant development by, *inter alia*, African central, commercial and development banks, stock exchanges, funds and insurance companies.

The AfDB has been actively involved in the Africa Carbon Forum process; forums have been convened regularly since September 2008. The 11th forum was held in Accra, Ghana, in March 2019; an Africa Climate Week was observed at that time. The Bank hosts the secretariat of the Congo Basin Forest Fund, which was established in 2008, as a multi-donor facility, with initial funding from Norway and the United Kingdom, to protect and manage the forests in that region.

In March 2000 African ministers responsible for water resources endorsed an African Water Vision and a Framework for Action to pursue the equitable and sustainable use and management of water resources in Africa in order to facilitate socioeconomic development, poverty alleviation and environmental protection. An African Ministers' Council on Water (AMCOW) was established in April 2002 to provide the political leadership and focus for implementation of the Vision and the Framework for Action. AMCOW requested the Bank to establish and administer an African Water Facility Special Fund, in order to provide the financial requirements for achieving their objectives; this became operational in December. In November 2021 the Board of Directors approved a revised version of the African Water Facility Strategy (2017–25). A new five-year strategy, titled 'Towards a Water Secure Africa' was also endorsed. The Bank and the Government of Senegal co-ordinated the ninth World Water Forum, which was held in March 2022, in the Senegalese capital, Dakar.

The AfDB manages the Zimbabwe Multi Donor Trust Fund (ZimFund), established in 2010 to support that country in improving water supply and quality, power services and sanitation facilities. The Bank's Multi-Partner Somalia Infrastructure Fund, which became operational in 2016, supports infrastructure rehabilitation and institution rebuilding.

In December 2015 the Bank joined the Inclusive Green Growth Partnership, a collaboration between the Global Green Growth Institute, UN agencies and multilateral development banks, which aimed to promote social inclusion and green growth at national level. The Bank is also one of the 26 members of the African Green Revolution Forum (AGRF) Partners Group. The 2021 edition of the annual AGRF was hosted by Kenya, in September, on the theme 'Pathways to recovery and resilient food systems'.

At the end of March 2022 the Board of Directors approved a five-year Africa Circular Economy Facility, which was to focus on institutional capacity building to enhance the regulatory framework for relevant innovations; on a business development programme; and on the provision of technical assistance to the African Circular Economy Alliance (founded in 2017 to minimize waste and damage from economic activities in the region).

PRIVATE SECTOR, INFRASTRUCTURE AND INDUSTRIALIZATION

In 1989 the Bank, in co-ordination with the International Finance Corporation and UNDP, created the African Management Services Company (AMSCo), which provides management support and training to private companies in Africa. The Bank is one of three multilateral donors, with the World Bank and UNDP, supporting the African Capacity Building Foundation, which was established in 1991 to strengthen and develop institutional and human capacity in support of sustainable development activities. An Enhanced Private Sector Assistance initiative (EPSA) was established, with support from the Japanese Government, in 2005 to support the Bank's strategy for the development of the private sector. The scheme incorporated an Accelerated Cofinancing Facility for Africa and a Fund for African Private Sector Assistance. In October 2010 the Board of Directors agreed to convert the Fund into a multi-donor trust fund. A fifth phase of EPSA, covering the period 2023–25, was announced by the Bank and Japanese Government in August 2022. In 2014 the Bank established a Private Sector Credit Enhancement Facility (PSF), which aimed to increase private sector financing in low-income member countries. In 2021 UA 43.7m. was approved under the PSF, for three initiatives.

The Bank's Africa Trade Fund, launched in 2012, aims to facilitate the integration of member states and of African regional economic communities into multilateral trading systems.

The Africa Investment Forum (AIF) was established by the Executive Board in October 2016, to act as a platform for international investors. In July 2020 the AIF announced that, under its Unified COVID-19 Response, US $3,790m. would be allocated to addressing the impacts of the COVID-19 crisis across the following priority sectors: agriculture and agro-processing, energy, health, telecommunications, and industry and trade. The fifth AIF was held in a virtual format in March 2022.

The AfDB convened the second conference in April 2017 of the so-called Abidjan Union, a pan-African gathering of representatives of export credit and investments insurance providers.

In June 2018 the AfDB and the World Bank jointly convened Roundtable 2 on Infrastructure Governance and Tools, in Grand Bassam, Côte d'Ivoire, to address the impacts of poor infrastructure governance on economic growth. (Roundtable 1 was held in Cape Town, South Africa, in November 2017.) An Africa Integrity Fund was established in November 2016, to support member states in combating corruption.

The AfDB is an executing agency for and, jointly with the AU Commission and AUDA-NEPAD, leads the Programme for Infrastructure Development in Africa (PIDA), which aims to develop the continental energy, transport, transboundary water resources, and information and communications technologies infrastructures. A second PIDA Priority Action Plan (PIDA PAP 2) was being implemented over the period 2011–30. Since 2005 the AfDB has managed the NEPAD-Infrastructure Project Preparation Facility (NEPAD-IPPF), a multi-donor trust fund. The Bank hosts the secretariat of the Infrastructure Consortium for Africa, which was inaugurated in October of that year by several major African institutions and donor countries to accelerate efforts to develop the region's infrastructure.

In 1990 the Bank established the African Business Round Table (ABR), which is composed of the chief executive officers (CEOs) of Africa's leading corporations, and aims to strengthen Africa's private sector, promote intra-African trade and investment, and attract foreign investment to Africa. The AfDB, jointly with the French media company Groupe Jeune Afrique, organizes the annual Africa CEO Forum. In March 2021 the Africa CEO Forum and International Finance Corporation jointly organized (online) an inaugural Financial Industry Summit, with participation by African financial sector leaders. A new African Financial Industry Barometer, released during the summit, found the top three priorities for financial institutions to be: digitization; operational efficiency; and mastering emerging risks.

In July 2016 the AfDB Executive Board approved an Industrialization Strategy for Africa, covering the period 2016–25; this outlined a roadmap for the implementation of priority programmes aimed at advancing the industrial transformation of the continent.

The Bank's Africa SME Programme provides lines of credit and technical assistance to African local financial institutions to support local businesses. The AfDB does not, however, finance SMEs directly.

AGRICULTURE, HUMAN AND SOCIAL DEVELOPMENT

The Bank's Feed Africa strategy aims to transform continental agriculture into a sustainable, business-oriented, globally competitive, inclusive, employment and wealth generating sector, with a focus on ending extreme poverty; eliminating hunger and improving nutrition; making Africa a net exporter of agricultural commodities; and moving to the top (by market share) of agricultural value chains for processed commodities. In October 2015 a conference on Feeding Africa, held in Dakar, under the auspices of the Bank, adopted an action plan, and endorsed several partnerships aimed at developing agribusiness on the continent. The Bank manages a multi-donor Agriculture Fast Track Fund, which was launched in 2013 to boost continental agribusiness and agricultural infrastructure investments. In February 2018 the Board of Directors approved the establishment of a Rockefeller Trust Fund, which was to have a particular focus on supporting the High 5 priorities: Feed Africa and Improve the quality of life for the people of Africa.

The Bank hosts the secretariat of an African Fertilizer Financing Mechanism (AFFM), established in 2007 to boost agricultural productivity, food security and the sustainable management of natural resources in Africa. The 10th meeting of the AFFM Governing Council, hosted by the Bank in March 2022, urged more continental private sector investment.

The ADB's operational plan under Strategy 2030 for promoting rural development and food security aimed to transform agriculture and to promote sustainable resilient food supply systems, with a focus on the provision of safe, nutritious food, achieving higher incomes for farmers, and generating economic growth in rural areas. The Bank's support for food systems quadrupled from US $409m. in 2010 to $1,200m. in 2020. A Bank seminar on COVID-19-related agricultural issues that was held (virtually) in May 2020 recommended that member states amend their annual budgets to prioritize agriculture production and the expansion of food reserves, and that they focus on developing technology for agriculture production, as a means of building sectoral resilience.

In April 2020 the Bank's Board of Directors approved a US $1.5m. emergency relief grant to support efforts by nine East African countries (co-ordinated by the Intergovernmental Authority on Development) to control severe desert locust swarms that were endangering regional food output and livelihoods.

In May 2022, in response to the wider global impacts of the Russian Federation's invasion of Ukraine, the AfDB, IMF, World Bank and other international financial institutions collectively issued the Joint International Financial Institution Plan to Address Food Insecurity, with a focus on the following six objectives: (i) support vulnerable people; (ii) promote open trade; (iii) mitigate fertilizer shortages; (iv) support food production now; (v) invest in climate-resilient agriculture for the future; and (vi) co-ordinate for maximum impact. Also in May the Bank approved US $1,500m. for a new African Emergency Food Production Facility to counter the disruption to food and fertilizer supplies resulting from the conflict in Ukraine.

An AfDB-supported African Leaders for Nutrition (ALN) initiative was launched in January 2018. In February 2019 the AfDB and AU Commission and partners issued a Continental Nutrition Accountability Scorecard, compiled by the ALN to promote commitments towards ending malnutrition. In September 2020 the ALN called for financing for nutrition to be embedded by governments into national COVID-19 response and recovery plans.

The Bank launched an African Gender Equality Index in May 2015. In March 2016 the Bank and UN Women signed a Memorandum of Understanding (MOU) on jointly advancing gender equality in Africa. In May 2016 the AfDB established an Affirmative Finance Action for Women in Africa (AFAWA) initiative, with a view to raising US $3,000m. towards reducing the risks incurred by commercial banks and microfinance institutions in financing businesses owned by women in the region. In April 2020 the AfDB Board of Directors endorsed a Gender Equality Trust Fund dedicated to supporting the AFAWA agenda. The Bank funds a continental 50 Million African Women Speak Project (50MAWSP), which aims to address specific challenges confronting women, including female entrepreneurs, in securing access to financial and non-financial services. A 50 Million Women Digital Platform was launched in November 2019. In December a digital skills training platform for young people, Coding for Employment, was launched. In December 2020 the Bank's Board of Directors initiated a Gender Strategy for 2021–25, based on three pillars: Empowering women through access to finance and markets; Accelerating employability and job creation for women through skills enhancement; and Increasing women's access to social services through infrastructure. An AfDB People Strategy for 2021–26, fostering resilience and diversity, was also introduced in 2020. In 2021 100% of the Bank's sovereign operations were categorized under its Gender Marker System—a tool for systematizing the mainstreaming of gender in its business processes.

The Bank participates in the Sahel Alliance, established by the European Union in 2017 to promote education and youth employment; agriculture, rural development and food security; energy and climate adaptation; good governance; decentralization and basic services; and internal security, in Burkina Faso, Mali, Mauritania and Niger.

In April 2020 the Bank initiated a US $10,000m. COVID-19 Rapid Response Facility, to support the continental recovery from the impacts of the ongoing public health, social and economic emergency. During 2020 the AfDB Group significantly refocused its lending programme to meet the challenges posed by the pandemic crisis, as a result of which loan approvals declined by 43%, compared with 2019, while disbursements increased by 44%. The 2021 edition of the Bank's annual *African Economic Outlook,* issued in March, urged the acceleration of the delivery of COVID-19 vaccines to Africa, to enable the pandemic to be contained, as a prerequisite for the reinvigoration of economic growth and alleviation of extreme poverty. The need for Africa to develop its own pharmaceutical industry was noted. In February 2022 the Bank's Board of Directors approved a new Strategy for Quality Health Infrastructure in Africa 2022–30 to support national health systems, including through strengthening health information systems, promoting regional collaboration and harmonizing health policies and regulation.

ECONOMIC GOVERNANCE AND KNOWLEDGE MANAGEMENT

The AfDB hosts the African Legal Support Facility, which since 2010 has provided legal advice and technical assistance to African governments negotiating complex commercial transactions.

The Bank Group, with ECA and UNDP, organizes an annual African Economic Conference (AEC), which aims to foster dialogue and the exchange of knowledge on issues affecting the continent. In December 2021 the 16th AEC was held in a hybrid format, in-person in Cabo Verde and virtually, on the theme 'Financing Africa's post-COVID-19 development'.

The Bank provides technical assistance to regional member countries in the form of experts' services, pre-investment feasibility studies and staff training. Much of this assistance is financed through bilateral trust funds contributed by non-African member states. The Bank's African Development Institute provides training and seminars for officials of regional member countries in order to enhance the management of Bank-financed projects and, more broadly, to strengthen national capacities for promoting sustainable development. The Institute also manages an AfDB/Japan Fellowship programme that provides scholarships to African students to pursue further education.

FINANCE

In September 2008 the AfDB supported the establishment of an African Financing Partnership, which aimed to mobilize private sector resources through collaborations with regional development finance institutions. The Bank hosts the secretariat of the Partnership. It hosts the secretariat of the Making Finance Work for Africa Partnership, which was established, by the then G8, in October 2007, in order to support the development of the financial sector in the sub-Saharan region. The AfDB also supports an Africa-USA Partnership on Illicit Finance that was launched in July 2014. Through a Migration and Development Initiative Fund, initiated in 2009, the Bank supports the development of financial services for migrant workers, and facilitates channelling remittances towards productive uses in workers' countries of origin. In 2019 it initiated an Africa

Digital Financial Inclusion Facility, which aimed to promote digital financial tools to ensure engagement by a further 332m. Africans (with a particular focus on women) in the formal economy.

In 2008 the AfDB initiated the African Financial Markets Initiative (AFMI), to support the development of bond markets throughout the continent and to stimulate domestic resource mobilization. In February 2015 an AFMI-Bloomberg African Bond Index was launched. A social bond framework was established in 2017. In March 2020 the Bank issued a US $3,000m. Fight COVID-19 social bond in order to mitigate the potential social and economic impact of the global pandemic on member states. By the end of April this had been further subscribed, at $4,500m.

Publications

AfDB Statistics Pocketbook.

Africa Competitiveness Report (every 2 years).

Africa Economic Brief (monthly).

African Development Report (annually).

African Development Review (3 a year).

African Economic Outlook (annually).

African Statistical Yearbook (with the AU and ECA).

Annual Report.

Capacity Focus (2 a year).

Compendium of Statistics on Bank Group Operations (annually).

Development Effectiveness Review Series.

Other reports, country profiles, working papers, background and Board documents.

Statistics

SUMMARY OF BANK GROUP OPERATIONS

(millions of UA)

	2020	2021	Cumulative total*
AfDB approvals†			
Number	48	66	2,118
Amount	2,492.72	2,449.14	77,326
ADF approvals†			
Number	71	66	3,230
Amount	938.76	1,263.25	40,076
NTF approvals			
Number	—	1	105
Amount	—	3.60	491
Special Funds‡			
Number	38	31	659
Amount approved . .	240.51	263.55	3,672
Group total†			
Number	217	196	6,575
Amount approved . .	4,171.12	4,506.29	125,461

* Since the initial operations of the three institutions (1967 for the AfDB, 1974 for the ADF and 1976 for the NTF).

† Includes loans and grant operations, private and public equity investments, emergency operations, HIPC debt relief, and loan reallocations and guarantees, and the Post-Conflict Country Facility; Group total approvals include those from the Private Sector Credit Enhancement Facility and the Transition Support Facility.

‡ Includes the African Water Facility, the Rural Water Supply and Sanitation Initiative, the Global Environment Facility, the Africa Climate Change Fund, the Climate Investment Funds, the Congo Basin Forest Fund, the Fund for African Private Sector Assistance, the Global Agriculture and Food Security Programme, the Micro Finance Capacity Building Fund, the Migration and Development Initiative Fund, the Sustainable Energy Fund for Africa, the Middle East and North Africa Transition Fund, the Trust Fund for Countries in Transition, the Nigeria Technical Cooperation Fund, and the Zimbabwe Multi-Donor Trust Fund.

BANK GROUP APPROVALS BY HIGH 5 PRIORITY, 2021
(millions of UA)

High 5 Priority	AfDB	ADF	Special resources*	Total
Light up and power Africa	105.88	220.01	93.46	419.36
Power generation, transmission and distribution (conventional)	—	119.84	11.59	31.43
Power generation (renewable)	35.80	52.09	16.04	103.93
Off-grid solutions	—	2.09	—	2.09
Energy sector strengthening and reform	—	15.10	1.98	17.08
Infrastructure for energy sector development	16.65	—	—	16.65
Multisector	70.08	—	—	70.08
Other	—	14.25	63.85	78.10
Feed Africa	421.84	261.75	224.42	908.00
National and regional operations in production and value addition	103.20	89.93	83.95	277.09
Investment in infrastructure	223.51	72.68	51.38	347.57
Agriculture finance and agribusiness environment	63.10	22.35	21.86	107.31
Inclusivity and sustainable development	32.02	76.79	67.23	176.04
Industrialize Africa	734.01	58.29	35.39	827.68
Industrial business environment	70.99	7.00	1.00	78.99
Financial sector and capital markets development	94.79	5.60	25.68	126.07
Enterprise development	279.07	40.14	4.87	324.08
Multi-sector	160.80	3.04	1.00	164.84
Regional environment improvement	128.36	2.50	2.84	133.70
Integrate Africa	120.32	549.00	28.27	697.59
Regional infrastructure connectivity	50.54	533.35	17.67	601.56
Trade facilitation and investment	69.78	15.65	10.60	96.03
Improve quality of life for the people of Africa	1,067.10	174.21	412.35	1,653.65
Water supply and sanitation	246.86	75.25	15.37	337.48
Human and social development	31.44	16.97	20.72	69.13
Multisector	403.89	28.50	305.40	737.79
Other	384.90	53.49	70.86	509.24
Total	2,449.14	1,263.25	793.91	4,506.29

* Including the NTF, PSF, TSF and Special Funds (as defined above).
Source: African Development Bank, *Annual Report 2021*.

AFRICAN UNION—AU

Address: Roosevelt St, W21K19, POB 3243, Addis Ababa, Ethiopia.
Telephone: (11) 5517700; **fax:** (11) 5517844; **e-mail:** dic@africa-union.org; **internet:** au.int.

The Constitutive Act of the African Union entered into force in May 2001. In July 2002 the AU became fully operational, replacing the Organization of African Unity (OAU), which had been founded in 1963. The AU aims to support unity, solidarity and peace among African states; to defend African common positions on issues of shared interest; to promote sustainable development and political and socioeconomic integration; and to encourage human rights, democratic principles and good governance in all member states.

MEMBERS

Algeria	Eritrea	Namibia
Angola	Eswatini	Niger
Benin	Ethiopia	Nigeria
Botswana	Gabon	Rwanda
Burkina Faso*	The Gambia	São Tomé and
Burundi	Ghana	Príncipe
Cabo Verde	Guinea*	Senegal
Cameroon	Guinea-Bissau	Seychelles
Central African	Kenya	Sierra Leone
Republic	Lesotho	Somalia
Chad	Liberia	South Africa
Comoros	Libya	South Sudan
Congo, Democratic	Madagascar	Sudan*
Republic	Malawi	Tanzania
Congo, Republic	Mali*	Togo
Côte d'Ivoire	Mauritania	Tunisia
Djibouti	Mauritius	Uganda
Egypt	Morocco†	Zambia
Equatorial Guinea	Mozambique	Zimbabwe

* On 1 June 2021, following the overthrow in late May by the Malian military of the leadership of Mali's transitional administration, the Peace and Security Council suspended that country's participation in the activities of the AU. Guinea was suspended on 10 September, following the overthrow of President Alpha Condé. On 26 October Sudan was suspended, in response to the removal by that country's military of the civilian transitional government. In January 2022 Burkina Faso was also suspended pending the restoration of constitutional order following a military coup.

† The Sahrawi Arab Democratic Republic (SADR–Western Sahara) was admitted to the OAU in February 1982, following recognition by more than one-half of the member states, but its membership was disputed by Morocco and other countries which claimed that a two-thirds' majority was needed to admit a state whose existence was in question. Morocco withdrew from the OAU with effect from November 1985. In July 2016 a Moroccan special envoy met AU leaders to discuss the possibility of Morocco's accession to the AU; it was readmitted at the 28th session of the Assembly in January 2017. The SADR ratified the Constitutive Act in December 2000 and is a full member of the AU.

Organization
(October 2022)

ASSEMBLY

The Assembly, comprising heads of state and of government, is the supreme organ of the Union and meets usually twice a year to determine and monitor the organization's priorities and common policies and to adopt its annual work programme. Resolutions are passed by a two-thirds' majority, procedural matters by a simple majority. Extraordinary sessions may be convened at the request of a member state and on approval by a two-thirds' majority. The Assembly ensures compliance by member states with decisions of the Union, appoints judges of the African Court of Human and Peoples' Rights, and hears and settles disputes between member states. It may also appoint individual African heads of state and government to lead the implementation of specific high priority AU initiatives. The 35th ordinary session of the Assembly took place in February 2022, in Addis Ababa. The Chairperson of the Assembly is assisted by a four-member Bureau.

Chairperson (2022/23): MACKY SALL (President of Senegal).

EXECUTIVE COUNCIL

The Council consists of ministers responsible for foreign affairs and others and meets at least twice a year, with provision for extraordinary sessions. It prepares meetings of, and is responsible to, the Assembly; determines the issues to be submitted to the Assembly for decision; co-ordinates and harmonizes the policies, activities and initiatives of the Union in areas of common interest to member states; and monitors the implementation of policies and decisions of the Assembly.

PERMANENT REPRESENTATIVES COMMITTEE

The Committee, which comprises ambassadors accredited to the AU, meets at least once a month. It is responsible to the Executive Council, which it advises, and whose meetings, including matters for the agenda and draft decisions, it prepares.

In July 2021 the Chairperson of the AU Commission accepted the credentials of Israel's Ambassador to Ethiopia: the AU's membership was divided in response.

COMMISSION

The Commission is the permanent secretariat of the AU, reporting to the Executive Council. It comprises a Chairperson (elected for a four-year term of office by the Assembly), Deputy Chairperson and six further Commissioners, responsible for: Political Affairs, Peace and Security; Infrastructure and Energy; Health, Humanitarian Affairs and Social Development; Education, Science, Technology and Innovation; Agriculture, Rural Development, Blue Economy and Sustainable Environment; and Economic Development, Trade, Industry and Mining. They are elected on the basis of equal geographical distribution. Members of the Commission serve a term of four years and may stand for re-election for one further term of office. A Panel of Eminent Africans was established to oversee the equitable selection of Commission candidates.

The Commission deals with administrative issues, implements the decisions of the Union, and acts as the custodian of the Constitutive Act and Protocols, and other agreements, and areas where a common position has been established by member states. It has responsibility for the co-ordination of AU activities and meetings.

Chairperson (2021–24): MOUSSA FAKI MAHAMAT (Chad).

Director-General: FATHALLAH SIJILMASSI (Morocco).

Commissioners

Economic Development, Trade, Industry and Mining: ALBERT MUCHANGA (Zambia).

Infrastructure and Energy: Dr AMANI ABOU-ZEID (Egypt).

Political Affairs, Peace and Security: BANKOLE ADEOYE (Nigeria).

Agriculture, Rural Development, Blue Economy and Sustainable Environment: JOSEFA LEONEL CORREA SACKO (Angola).

Health, Humanitarian Affairs and Social Development: CESSOUMA MINATA SAMATE (Burkina Faso).

Education, Science, Technology and Innovation: Prof. MOHAMED BELHOCINE (Algeria).

SPECIALIZED TECHNICAL COMMITTEES

There are specialized committees—comprising member states' ministers and senior officials—for agriculture, rural development, water and environment; communication and information communications technology; defence, safety and security; education, science and technology; finance, monetary affairs, economic planning and integration; gender and women's empowerment; health, population and drug control; justice and legal affairs; migration, refugees and internally displaced persons; public service, local government, urban development and decentralization; social development, labour and employment; trade, industry and minerals; transport, transcontinental and inter-regional infrastructure, energy and tourism; and youth, culture and sports. The Nairobi, Kenya-based African Institute for Remittances—supported by the European Commission, the African Development Bank (AfDB), the World Bank, and the International Organization for Migration—is a Specialized Technical Office of the AU Commission.

PAN-AFRICAN PARLIAMENT

The Pan-African Parliament, established in 2004 and located in Midrand, South Africa, comprises five deputies (including at least one woman) from each AU member state, presided over by an elected President. The President and four Vice-Presidents must equitably represent the five African regions. The Parliament convenes at least twice a year; an extraordinary session may be called by a two-thirds' majority of the members. The Parliament has only advisory and consultative powers; its eventual evolution into an institution with full legislative authority is envisaged. A high-level consultation between the Pan-African Parliament and Speakers of Regional and National Parliaments was convened in September 2022.

JUDICIAL AND HUMAN RIGHTS INSTITUTIONS

African Commission on Human and Peoples' Rights (ACHPR): POB 673, Banjul, The Gambia; tel. 441-05-05; fax 441-05-04; e-mail au-banjul@african-union.org; internet www.achpr.org; f. 1987, in accordance with and a year after the entry into force of the African Charter on Human and Peoples' Rights; the Commission was to promote and protect human rights and basic freedoms and to interpret the provisions of the Charter; it comprises 11 Commissioners, appointed by the AU Assembly for six-year terms in office, who meet at least twice a year; a secretariat provides administrative, technical and logistical support. Recommendations of the Commission are not legally-binding; it may use its 'good offices' to support states to abide by the recommendations. Other subsidiary mechanisms to support the Commission's activities include special rapporteurs, working groups and advisory committees, all of which are required to report regularly on their findings. In 2016 the ACHPR issued a set of Principles and Guidelines on Human Rights while Countering Terrorism in Africa; 71st ordinary session: April–May 2022, in a virtual format.

African Court of Human and Peoples' Rights: POB 6274, Arusha, Tanzania; tel. (27) 2970430; e-mail registrar@african-court.org; internet www.african-court.org; f. Jan. 2004, upon the entry into force in January 2004 of the Protocol to the African Charter on Human and Peoples' Rights (adopted in June 1998); consists of 11 judges, elected by the AU Assembly. Its role is to support the ACHPR and rule on the interpretation and application of the Charter. A Protocol to establish an African Court of Justice was adopted in July 2003 (it entered into effect in February 2009 after receiving the required number of ratifications but has never been operational). In July 2008 the AU summit determined to merge the courts and adopted a Protocol on the Statute of the African Court of Justice and Human Rights; by September 2022 the Protocol had been signed by 33 states and ratified by eight (requiring 15 ratifications to enter into force). By the start of 2016 10 states (Benin, Burkina Faso, Côte d'Ivoire, Ghana, The Gambia, Malawi, Mali, Rwanda, Tanzania and Tunisia) had made formal declarations accepting the competence of the Court to receive cases from individuals and non-governmental organizations located in their territories; however, Rwanda withdrew its declaration in February 2016, Tanzania in November 2019, and Benin and Côte d'Ivoire in April 2020; consequently, in 2022 six declarations remained active.

In February 2020 the AU Assembly adopted the following new entities: the Sudan-based Continental Operational Centre for Combating Irregular Migration; the Mali-based African Centre for Study and Research on Migration; the African Migration Observatory (based in Morocco); the Algeria-based AU Mechanism for Police Co-operation (AFRIPOL); the AU Centre for Post-Conflict Reconstruction and Development (Egypt); and the African Observatory of Science, Technology and Innovation (Equatorial Guinea).

PEACE AND SECURITY COUNCIL

The Protocol to the Constitutive Act of the African Union Relating to the Peace and Security Council of the African Union entered into force on 26 December 2003; the 15-member elected Council was formally inaugurated in May 2004. It acts as a decision making body for the prevention, management and resolution of conflicts.

ECONOMIC, SOCIAL AND CULTURAL COUNCIL

The Economic, Social and Cultural Council, inaugurated in March 2005, comprises representatives of civic, professional and cultural bodies at national, regional and diaspora level. Its main statutory organs are an elected General Assembly; a Standing Committee; a Credentials Committee; and Sectoral Cluster Communities, tasked with formulating opinions and advising on AU decision making.

DEVELOPMENT AGENCY

African Union Development Agency (AUDA-NEPAD): 230 15th Rd, Randjespark, Midrand 1685, South Africa; tel. (11) 2563600; e-mail info@nepad.org; internet www.nepad.org; f. 2018; a successor to the New Partnership for Africa's Development (NEPAD) Planning and Co-ordination Agency, the technical body established in 2010 to implement NEPAD projects—NEPAD having been launched in 2001 as a long-term strategy to promote socioeconomic devt in Africa. A voluntary African Peer Review Mechanism (APRM), established under NEPAD auspices in accordance with a Declaration on Democracy, Political, Economic and Corporate Governance adopted by AU heads of state and government in June 2002, assesses states' conduct in the areas of democracy and political governance; economic governance and management; corporate governance; and socioeconomic governance; by 2022 the APRM had 41 participants; NEPAD's Programme for Infrastructure Development in Africa (PIDA), of which the AfDB is the executing agency, was initiated in 2010 with the aim of developing the continental energy, information and communications technology, transport and transboundary water resources infrastructures; a second PIDA Priority Action Plan (PIDA PAP 2) was being implemented over the period 2011–30, with NEPAD-AUDA as lead co-ordinating agency; in February 2021 AU leaders approved 69 PIDA PAP 2 projects; NEPAD-AUDA launched in March 2021 a Pandemic Resilience Accelerator for African Health-Related Businesses. A Heads of State and Government Orientation Cttee provides leadership to the NEPAD process, determines policies, priorities and programmes of action and, through its Chair., reports directly to the AU Assembly; the UN allocated US $8.2m. in support of the agency under its 2022 budget; CEO Nardos Bekele-Thomas (Niger).

AFRICAN CONTINENTAL FREE TRADE AREA SECRETARIAT

AfCFTA Secretariat: Accra, Ghana; internet au-afcfta.org; f. 2019 to facilitate the implementation of the AfCFTA (q.v.); a Sec.-Gen. was appointed and took office in March 2020; a ceremony was held in Aug. to mark the Secretariat's move into its permanent headquarters in Accra; Sec.-Gen. Wamkele Keabetswe Mene (South Africa).

Activities

In November 1958 Ghana and Guinea (later joined by Mali) drafted a Charter that was to form the basis of a Union of African States. In January 1961 a conference was held at Casablanca, Morocco, attended by the heads of state of Ghana, Guinea, Mali, Morocco, and representatives of Libya and of the provisional government of the Algerian Republic (GPRA). Tunisia, Nigeria, Liberia and Togo declined the invitation to attend. An African Charter was adopted and it was decided to institute an African Military Command and an African Common Market. Between October 1960 and March 1961 three conferences were held by French-speaking African countries, which led to the signing, in September 1961, at Tananarive, Madagascar, of a charter establishing the Union africaine et malgache (later the Organisation commune africaine et mauricienne— OCAM). In January 1962 a conference of the heads of state or representatives of Cameroon, Central African Republic, Chad, Congo-Brazzaville, Congo-Léopoldville, Côte d'Ivoire, Dahomey, Ethiopia, Gabon, Liberia, Madagascar, Mauritania, Niger, Nigeria, Senegal, Sierra Leone, Somalia, Togo and Upper Volta, held in Lagos, Nigeria, established a permanent secretariat and a standing committee of ministers of finance, and accepted a draft charter for an Organization of Inter-African and Malagasy States.

It was the Conference of Addis Ababa, convened in 1963, which finally brought together African states despite the regional, political and linguistic differences that divided them. A ministerial Preparatory Meeting held in mid-May discussed the creation of an Organization of African States; co-operation among African states (in the fields of economic and social affairs, education, culture and science, and collective defence); decolonization; apartheid and racial discrimination; the effects of economic grouping on the economic development of Africa; disarmament; the creation of a Permanent Conciliation Commission; and Africa and the United Nations. The Heads of State Conference that opened on 23 May 1963 drew up the Charter of the Organization of African Unity, which was then signed by the heads of 30 states on 25 May. The Charter was essentially functional and reflected a compromise between the concept of a loose association of states favoured by the Monrovia Group and the federal idea supported by the Casablanca Group, in particular by Ghana.

In May 1994 the Abuja Treaty Establishing the African Economic Community (AEC, signed in June 1991) entered into force. An extraordinary summit meeting, convened in September 1999, in Sirte, Libya, at the request of the then Libyan leader Col Muammar al-Qaddafi, determined to establish an African Union, based on the principles and objectives of the OAU and the AEC, but furthering African co-operation, development and integration. Heads of state declared their commitment to accelerating the establishment of regional institutions as well as the implementation of economic and monetary union, as provided for by the Abuja Treaty.

In July 2000 at a summit meeting of the OAU held in Lomé, Togo, 27 heads of state and of government signed the draft Constitutive Act of the African Union, which was to enter into force after ratification by two-thirds of member states' legislatures; this was achieved in May 2001. The Union was inaugurated, replacing the OAU, on 9 July 2002, at a summit meeting held in Durban, South Africa. During the transitional year, a review of all OAU treaties was undertaken and those deemed relevant were retained by the AU. The AU operates on the basis of both the Constitutive Act and the Abuja Treaty.

In February 2021 the 34th AU Assembly declared the Decade of African Roots and Diasporas, covering 2021–31, with the aim of furthering diaspora engagement in the continental development agenda.

AGENDA 2063

The May 2013 session of the Assembly issued a 50th Anniversary Solemn Declaration, which outlined a vision and series of ideals for the economic and social transformation of the continent over the coming 50 years. These were to be translated into concrete actions and objectives by a joint programme with the AfDB and the UN Economic Commission for Africa (ECA) known as Agenda 2063, within the context of which 20 African Development Goals were to be developed. Endorsed by AU heads of state and of government in January 2015, the finalized Agenda 2063 was underpinned by the following so-called African Aspirations: a prosperous Africa, based on inclusive growth and sustainable development; an integrated, politically united continent, based on the ideals of Pan-Africanism and a vision of Africa's Renaissance; an Africa of good governance, democracy, respect for human rights, justice and the rule of law; a peaceful and secure Africa; a strong continental cultural identity, based on common heritage, values and ethics; people-driven continental development (with a particular focus on women and youth); and Africa as a strong, united, influential global player and partner. In June 2015 the AU summit adopted 'The First Ten-Year Implementation Plan of Agenda 2063 and its Financing Mechanism'. The following were designated as Agenda 2063 flagship initiatives: (i) connecting all African capital cities and commercial centres through an African Integrated High Speed Train Network; (ii) formulating an African Commodities Strategy, aimed at transforming the continent from a supplier of raw materials to an active user—for the economic benefit of Africans—of its own resources; (iii) developing the AfCFTA; (iv) promoting free movement of people and an African passport; (v) silencing guns: ending all conflicts, genocides and gender-based violence, and introducing an African Human Security Index; (vi) implementing the proposed 43,200 KW Grand Inga Dam hydropower project on the River Congo, Democratic Republic of the Congo—DRC, which, it was envisaged, would support regional power pools; (vii) establishing a Single African Air Transport Market; (viii) promoting an annual African Economic Forum; (ix) establishing the proposed African continental financial institutions; (x) putting in place a Pan-African E-Network, including a strong intra-African broadband terrestrial infrastructure; (xi) implementing an Africa Outer Space Strategy, to promote climate forecasting, disaster management, remote sensing, defence and security, and agricultural development; (xii) establishing a Pan African E-University; (xiii) advancing continental cyber security, guided by the (2014) AU Convention on Cyber Security and Personal Data Protection; (xiv) establishing a Great African Museum, guided by the (2006) Charter for African Cultural Renaissance; and (xv) compiling an *Encyclopaedia Africana*, to represent an authoritative and authentic resource on African history and life.

In May 2013 the AfDB endorsed an Africa50 Infrastructure Fund, which was to finance, in partnership with regional institutions, transformational projects with a focus on enhancing the transcontinental infrastructure.

An inaugural African Economic Platform (AEP), supporting Agenda 2063, was held in March 2017, in Port Louis, Mauritius. The AEP, with participation by representatives of government, the public sector, business and academia, aimed to promote economic integration, enhanced intra-African trade, capacity building and skills development.

ECONOMIC DEVELOPMENT, TRADE, INDUSTRY AND MINING

The AU recognizes the following regional economic communities, or RECs, in Africa: COMESA, the EAC, SADC, CEEAC, ECOWAS, IGAD, and the Union of the Arab Maghreb. The inaugural meeting of the AEC took place in June 1997. In July 2007 the ninth AU Assembly adopted a Protocol on Relations between the AU and the RECs, aimed at facilitating the harmonization of policies and ensuring compliance with the schedule of the 1991 Abuja Treaty. Within the framework of the Protocol the AU Commission convenes biannual Joint Coordination Meetings comprising representatives of the AU, RECs, ECA, AfDB, NEPAD and the African Capacity Building Foundation (an AU specialized agency).

In January 2012 AU leaders endorsed an action plan on Boosting Intra-African Trade, which aimed to reduce transit times between member states.

A 2030 Agenda for Africa's industrialization was launched in September 2015. In November 2014 the AU and the AfDB decided that the African Business Round Table (ABR)—comprising the chief executives of Africa's leading corporations, and established by the AfDB in 1990 to strengthen Africa's private sector, promote intra-African trade and investment, and attract foreign investment to the continent—should become an annual meeting of the AU. An AU Summit on Africa's Industrialization and Economic Diversification was to be convened in November 2022, in Niamey, Niger, with a focus on, *inter alia*, aligning skills training with the developing requirements of the labour market; enhancing the continental infrastructure, especially with regard to the energy sector; mobilizing financing for the structural transformation of Africa; promoting commodity-based industrialization; and strengthening continental research and development capabilities.

In June 2022 the AU Commission convened an extraordinary session of the Specialized Technical Committee on Transport, Transcontinental and Interregional Infrastructure, Energy and Tourism to address impacts of the ongoing Russia-Ukraine conflict on the continental energy and infrastructure sectors.

In July 2016 AU heads of state and of government launched an AU Passport policy, with the objective of facilitating the free movement of people on the continent. In late January 2019 the 30th AU Assembly adopted the Protocol to the Treaty Establishing the AEC relating to the Free Movement of Persons, Rights of Residence and Right of Establishment; a draft roadmap to guide the new Protocol's implementation was also adopted at that time. The Protocol was signed by 27 countries at the extraordinary summit held in March; by September 2022 it had been ratified by four states (Mali, Niger, Rwanda, and São Tomé and Príncipe).

The sixth edition of the joint AUC-AfDB *Africa Visa Openness Index*, issued in December 2021, found that in 2021 African nationals could visit around one-half of the continent without a visa, or with the possibility of acquiring one on arrival. E-visas were being offered by 24 African countries.

In February 2009 AU leaders adopted the Africa Mining Vision (AMV), which promotes the contribution of mining to sustainable local development, aiming to ensure that employees and communities benefit from industrial mining enterprises, and that priority is given to the protection of local environments. An African Minerals Development Centre, based in Maputo, Mozambique, with a mandate to implement the AMV, was inaugurated in December 2013.

African Continental Free Trade Area: In January 2012 the 18th summit of AU leaders endorsed a new Framework, Roadmap and Architecture for Fast Tracking the Establishment of a Continental Free Trade Area, and an Action Plan for Boosting Intra-African Trade. The summit determined that the implementation of the AfCFTA process should follow these milestones: the finalization by 2014 of the COMESA-EAC-SADC Tripartite FTA (the so-called TFTA was adopted in June 2015); the completion during 2012–14 of other REC FTAs (not achieved as scheduled); the consolidation of the Tripartite and other regional FTAs into the free trade area initiative during 2015–16; and the establishment of an operational AfCFTA by the end of 2017. The 2012 summit invited ECOWAS, CEEAC, CEN-SAD and the Union of the Arab Maghreb to draw inspiration from the TFTA initiative and to establish promptly a second pole of regional integration, thereby accelerating continental economic integration. The summit also recognized the need to strengthen the AU's institutional framework for sustainable development, deeming that promoting the transition to 'green' and 'blue' economies would accelerate continental progress towards sustainable development. In June 2015 the 25th AU summit launched a series of formal negotiations on the establishment of the AfCFTA. In July 2016 AU heads of state and of government determined to establish a five-member High Level Panel (drawn from all regions) to support the fast tracking of the process. The inaugural Meeting of the AfCFTA Technical Working Groups was convened in February 2017.

In March 2018 the 10th extraordinary summit of AU heads of state and government, convened in the Rwandan capital Kigali, formally initiated the AfCFTA; the Agreement Establishing the AfCFTA was signed by 44 member states. It entered into force on 30 May 2019, and provided for the liberalization of 90% of tariff lines over 10 years for Least Developed Countries (LDCs) and over five years for non-LDCs; trade in sensitive products would be liberalized over 13 years (LDCs) and 10 years (non-LDCs). The AfCFTA was declared operational in early July, at an extraordinary AU summit. At that time it was decided that Ghana would host its secretariat. In early 2020 the Assembly determined that an extraordinary summit should be convened in late May to approve instruments that would enable trading to commence within the AfCFTA on 1 July; the summit and deadline were, however, postponed, in view of the COVID-19 pandemic. In August the AU Commissioner for Trade and Industry emphasized the importance to the continent's recovery from the COVID-19 crisis of implementing the AfCFTA, and the need to boost intra-African trade. In December an extraordinary session of the Assembly confirmed that trading under the AfCFTA would commence on 1 January 2021. By September 2022 the accord had been signed by 54 states, and had been ratified by 43. AfCFTA protocols on e-commerce, competition, investment and intellectual property were under development in 2022.

An online African Trade Observatory (ATO) was launched in July 2019 to support the AfCFTA. The second Intra-African Trade Fair was organized jointly by the AU Commission, Afreximbank, South African Government, and KwaZulu-Natal regional authorities in November 2021, in Durban. In May 2022 a new business-to-business e-commerce platform, the Africa Trade Exchange (ATEX), was initiated to support the implementation of the AfCFTA.

INFRASTRUCTURE AND ENERGY

An African Energy Commission (AFREC) was inaugurated in February 2008, with the aim of increasing co-operation in energy matters between Africa and other regions. At that time a subsidiary African Electrotechnical Standardization Commission also become operational. In June 2021 the AU initiated an African Single Electricity Market (AfSEM). The AU Commission, NEPAD, the AfDB and other partners jointly lead the Africa Renewable Energy Initiative, which was launched in December 2015 to promote the installation of large-scale renewable energy capacity in Africa, with a medium-term objective of achieving the cross-continent generation of at least 300 GW of energy from renewable sources by 2030. In July 2022 the AU Executive Council adopted an African Common Position on Energy Access and Just Transition.

The Bamako Convention on the Ban of the Import into Africa and the Control of Transboundary Movement and Management of Hazardous Wastes within Africa was adopted by OAU member states in 1991 and entered into force in April 1998. By September 2022 it had been signed by 35 states and ratified by 29.

In July 2009 the AU Assembly issued a decision endorsing the establishment of an African Agency for the Protection of Territorial and Economic Waters of African Countries. An African Charter on Maritime Security and Safety and Development in Africa (known as the Lomé Charter) was adopted in October 2016.

In January 2012 the Executive Council endorsed an African Civil Aviation Policy. In January 2018 the 30th AU Assembly adopted a Decision on the Establishment of a Single African Air Transport Market (SAATM). By 2022 the SAATM had 34 participating states that accounted for 89% of intra-African air traffic.

A Pan African E-Network Project was initiated in 2009 to advance continental connectivity. In May 2014 heads of African ICT units adopted a comprehensive Continental ICT Strategy for Africa (CISA), covering the period 2014–24, and focusing on the following themes: post and telecommunications infrastructure; capacity development; e-applications and services; enabling environment and governance; mobilization of resources and partnerships; industrialization; and research and development. A Digital Transformation Strategy for Africa, being implemented during 2020–30, aimed to help build by 2030 a secure Digital Single Market in Africa, and to facilitate the full digital empowerment of all people on the continent.

AGRICULTURE, RURAL DEVELOPMENT, BLUE ECONOMY AND SUSTAINABLE ENVIRONMENT

In July 2003 the second Assembly of heads of state and of government adopted the Maputo Declaration on Agriculture and Food Security in Africa, focusing on the need to revitalize the agricultural sector and to combat hunger on the continent by developing food reserves based on African production. The leaders determined to deploy policies and budgetary resources to remove current constraints on agricultural production, trade and rural development; and to implement the Comprehensive Africa Agriculture Development Programme (CAADP), as an integral programme of NEPAD. The CAADP has agreed the objective of allocating at least 10% of national budgets to investment in agricultural productivity. It aims to achieve dynamic agricultural markets between African countries and regions; good participation in and access to markets by farmers; a more equitable distribution of wealth for rural populations; more equitable access to land, practical and financial resources, knowledge, information, and technology for sustainable development; development of Africa's role as a strategic player in the area of agricultural science and technology; and environmentally sound agricultural production and a culture of sustainable management of natural resources. By 2022 44 AU member states had signed CAADP compacts. A Revised African Convention on the Conservation of Nature and Natural Resources entered into force in July 2016, and had been ratified by 17 member states at September 2022. In September 2021 the AU Commission, through the Department of Agriculture, Rural Development, Blue Economy and Sustainable Environment and the African Land Policy Centre (managed by the AU, AfDB and ECA), issued a draft continental Land Governance Strategy, which aimed to ensure more equitable land governance with secured land rights and tenure.

In June 2015 the AU Executive Council adopted a Regional Nutrition Strategy that covered the period 2016–25. An African Leaders for Nutrition (ALN) initiative was endorsed by AU heads of state and government in January 2018. An African Green Revolution Forum is convened annually (2021: in September, online), under AU auspices, to promote inclusive dialogue on food and nutrition security. The AU, NEPAD-AUDA and ECA prepared an African common position in advance of the UN Food Systems Summit that was convened in September 2021. Meanwhile, an Africa Food Safety Strategy was formulated. An AU High-level Food Security and Nutrition Conference was organized in early October 2022.

In July 2021 the AU Commission initiated a Continental Green Recovery Action Plan, to be implemented during 2021–27, with a focus on strengthening climate finance; assisting the just transition to renewable energy; pursuing nature-based solutions, with a focus on fostering biodiversity; promoting resilient agriculture; and encouraging green and resilient cities. In February 2022 the 35th AU Assembly adopted an AU Climate Change and Resilient Development Strategy and Action Plan to be implemented during the period 2022–32, and an Integrated African Strategy on Meteorology Services (that covered the period 2021–30). An African Green Stimulus Programme and AU Green Recovery Action Plan were also adopted at that time; both were focused on achieving a sustainable continental recovery from the COVID-19 pandemic.

In June 2019 the AU and UNEP jointly organized Africa's inaugural Wildlife Economy Summit, held at Victoria Falls, Zimbabwe, with participation by African heads of state, government ministers, academics, business people and other representatives of civil society.

A Pan African Veterinary Vaccine Centre is based at Debre-Zeit, Ethiopia (and includes an AU COVID-19 Diagnostic Laboratory that was inaugurated in May 2020).

The First Conference of African Ministers of Fisheries and Aquaculture (CAMFA) was convened in September 2010, in Banjul, and CAMFA II was held in March 2014, in Entebbe, Uganda. In January 2011 the Executive Council urged member states to adopt and integrate ecosystem approaches in their national and regional fisheries management plans; to strengthen measures to address illegal, unreported and unregulated (IUU) fishing; and to eliminate barriers to intraregional trade in fish and fishery products.

An AU Africa Blue Economy Strategy—formulated at the instigation of African leaders who participated in a Sustainable Blue Economy Conference held in November 2018, in Nairobi, Kenya—aims to guide the development and utilization of aquatic resources in Africa, within the Agenda 2063 framework. The Strategy was endorsed in February 2020, at a side event of the AU summit meeting. It has five focal areas: fisheries, aquaculture, conservation and sustainable aquatic ecosystems; shipping and transportation, trade, ports, maritime security, safety and enforcement; coastal and maritime tourism, climate change, resilience, environment, and infrastructure; sustainable energy and mineral resources and innovative industries; and policies, governance, employment, job creation, poverty eradication, and innovative financing.

Great Green Wall: In December 2006 the AU adopted the Great Green Wall (GGW) for the Sahara and Sahel Initiative, comprising a set of cross-sectoral actions and interventions, such as tree planting, that were aimed at conserving and protecting natural resources; halting soil degradation and advancing desertification; reducing poverty; and increasing land productivity. The GGW was to cover 7,000 km across 22 countries in the Sahara and Sahel areas, with an initial focus on Burkina Faso, Chad, Djibouti, Eritrea, Ethiopia, Mali, Mauritania, Niger, Nigeria, Senegal and Sudan. The Pan-African Agency for the GGW was established in 2010. In January 2021 the Food and Agriculture Organization of the UN (FAO) confirmed its ongoing commitment to the GGW; at that time the AfDB agreed to mobilize US $6,500m. over the next five years to support several programmes aimed at advancing its implementation.

HEALTH, HUMANITARIAN AFFAIRS AND SOCIAL DEVELOPMENT

On 27 January 2020 the Africa Centres for Disease Control and Prevention (Africa CDC) activated its Incident Management System (IMS)—which is supported by the African Volunteer Health Corps (AVoHC), an entity that facilitates Africa-wide surge staffing during public health crises—to address the viral outbreak that had arisen in the People's Republic of China. On 20 March Africa CDC issued an Africa Joint Continental Strategy for the COVID-19 Outbreak, with the overarching goals of preventing severe illness and death from COVID-19 in member states, and minimizing severe social disruption and economic consequences arising from the pandemic. The Strategy was to be implemented through the Africa CDC IMS and a new Africa Task Force for Novel Coronavirus, and to be supported by an AU COVID-19 Response Fund. The Strategy provided, *inter alia,* for collaboration between member states in maintaining supply chains for shared resources, such as personal protective and laboratory equipment; and for support to laboratories to provide, *inter alia,* quality-assured diagnostic testing, specimen referral testing, and next generation sequencing on COVID-19 specimens. In mid-May the inaugural meeting was convened of an AU Taskforce on COVID-19's Impact on Food Security and Nutrition in Africa, with participation by representatives of the AU Commission, AUDA-NEPAD, the AfDB, FAO, the European Commission and the World Bank. An Africa Medical Supplies Platform (AMSP) was launched by the AU in June to facilitate the ordering of essential medical and related inputs. Also in June the AU initiated a Partnership to Accelerate COVID-19 Testing (PACT). Meanwhile, an Africa Vaccine Strategy was launched, which aimed to secure sufficient supplies of COVID-19 vaccines and to ensure their efficient and fair distribution; a high-level Africa Vaccine Acquisition Task Team (AVATT) was established as a component of the Strategy.

In February 2021 the AU Bureau established a new Commission on African COVID-19 Response, under the leadership of South African President Cyril Ramaphosa, who was designated as the AU Champion on COVID-19. In April 2021 the AU and Africa CDC launched a Partnerships for African Vaccine Manufacturing (PAVM) framework, which aimed to enable the sustainable production of vaccines within Africa. In June AU ministers responsible for finance and the World Bank Group agreed to support an AVATT initiative to purchase and deliver vaccines for up to 400m. people across Africa, with a view to protecting 60% of the continent's population. In February 2022 six member states—Egypt, Kenya, Nigeria, Senegal, South Africa and Tunisia—became the first African recipients of mRNA COVID-19 vaccine technology under a global mRNA technology transfer hub initiative that had been launched in June 2021 by the AU, AU CDC, WHO, ACT Accelerator/COVAX and Medicines Patent Pool.

The AU promotes the eradication of endemic parasitic and infectious diseases and improving access to medicines. An AU African Health Strategy was being implemented during 2016–30; further long-term strategies included a Sexual and Reproductive Health and Rights Continental Policy Framework (accompanied by a Maputo Plan of Action); the Pharmaceutical Manufacturing Plan for Africa (approved in 2007); the African Regional Nutrition Strategy, covering 2015–25; the Abuja Action Plan towards the Elimination of HIV and AIDS, Malaria and Tuberculosis in Africa by 2030 (approved in 2013); the AIDS Watch Africa Strategic Framework aimed at eliminating AIDS, TB and Malaria by 2030 (endorsed in July 2017); and a Catalytic Framework to End AIDS, TB and Eliminate Malaria in Africa by 2030. A Treaty for the Establishment of the African Medicines Agency was adopted by the Assembly in February 2019. It provided for the establishment of the 'AMA' as a specialized AU body to be tasked with expanding the capacity of AU member states and regional economic commissions to regulate and improve access to safe, high-quality and effective medical products. The treaty entered into effect, having received the required 15 ratifications, in November 2021, although no agreement had been reached regarding the host country for the Agency. The first conference of the parties to the Treaty met in June 2022.

In August 2010 the AU and the UN Office for the Coordination of Humanitarian Affairs signed an agreement detailing key areas of future co-operation on humanitarian issues, with the aim of strengthening the AU's capacity in the areas of disaster preparedness and response, early warning, co-ordination, and protection of civilians affected by conflict or natural disaster. In May 2014 a ministerial conference on disaster reduction, held in Abuja, endorsed a Declaration on Africa's Contribution to the Post-2015 Framework for Disaster Risk Reduction. A pan-African meeting was convened in Port Louis, in November 2016, to review progress in the continent of the implementation of the Sendai Framework for Disaster Risk Reduction, covering the period 2015–30, which was adopted in March 2015 by the Third UN World Conference on Disaster Risk Reduction, held in Sendai City, Japan. In January 2016 the AU Assembly endorsed the establishment of an African Humanitarian Agency (AfHA), as well as a Common African Position on achieving effective humanitarian action by 2025. During 2018 the AU, Arab League and UN provided preparatory support in advance of the Seventh Africa-Arab Regional Platform and Sixth High-Level Meeting on Disaster Risk Reduction, which took place in mid-October, in Tunisia. In February 2020 the AU Assembly urged the prompt operationalization of the proposed AfHA. The first biennial *Africa Report on Disaster Risk Reduction* was issued in August 2020.

In July 2004 the Assembly adopted the Solemn Declaration on Gender Equality in Africa (SDGEA), incorporating a commitment to reporting annually on progress made towards attaining gender equality. The first conference of ministers responsible for women's affairs and gender, convened in Dakar, Senegal, in October 2005, adopted the Implementation Framework for the SDGEA, and Guidelines for Monitoring and Reporting on the SDGEA, in support of member states' reporting responsibilities.

At the January 2014 Assembly the Chairperson of the AU Commission appointed a Special Envoy for Women, Peace and Security. In June 2015 the 25th AU summit adopted a common position on ending child marriage. The AU's Saleema Initiative on Eliminating Female Genital Mutilation was launched in February 2019.

An African Committee of Experts on the Rights and Welfare of the Child was established pursuant to the African Charter on the Rights and Welfare of the Child, which was adopted by heads of state and government in July 1990 and entered into force in November 1999. The Committee comprises 11 experts, serving in their personal capacity, who are elected by the AU Assembly. It is supported by a secretariat.

In June 2020 the AU and UNICEF launched a No Name Campaign, which aimed to promote the registration of births in Africa and to ensure children's right to a legal identity. In November, in the context of the No Name Campaign, the AU convened a videoconferenced High Level Political Dialogue on Birth Registration.

An African Youth Charter, which entered into force in August 2010, outlined the basic rights and responsibilities of youths (divided into four main categories: youth participation; education and skills development; sustainable livelihoods; and health and wellbeing) and detailing the obligations of member states towards young people. In January 2017 the AU Assembly adopted a roadmap on Harnessing the Demographic Dividend through Investments in Youth. The first AU Youth Envoy was appointed in November 2018.

A Council of the Peers was established in 2019 that was tasked with collectively championing continental arts, culture and heritage. In October 2020 a Charter for African Cultural Renaissance entered into force. A Technical and Advisory Committee of the Great Museum of Africa (GMA) is tasked with developing the GMA, a project that was to be launched in 2023, in the Agenda 2063 framework, with a view to protecting and promoting African cultural heritage. The GMA was to include an Algeria-based Museum of Africa Permanent Memorial of the Slave Trade.

EDUCATION, SCIENCE, TECHNOLOGY AND INNOVATION

In January 2016 AU heads of state and of government adopted a Continental Education Strategy for Africa, covering the period 2016–25. An AU Scientific, Technical and Research Commission is based in Abuja, and a virtual AU Network of Sciences connects 54 research institutions in Africa and Europe. In January 2016 AU heads of state and of government adopted the first African Space Policy and Strategy, as an initial step towards establishing an AU outer space programme. A statute establishing an African Space Agency entered into force in January 2019.

POLITICAL AFFAIRS, PEACE AND SECURITY

The African Charter on Human and Peoples' Rights, which was adopted by the OAU in 1981 and entered into force in October 1986, provided for the establishment of the African Commission on Human and Peoples' Rights. A Protocol to the Charter, establishing an African Court of Peoples' and Human Rights, was adopted by the OAU Assembly in June 1998 and entered into force in January 2004. In February 2009 a protocol (adopted in July 2003) establishing an African Court of Justice entered into force. A Protocol on the Statute of the African Court of Justice and Human Rights, aimed at merging the African Court of Human and Peoples' Rights and the African Court of Justice, was opened for signature in July 2008. A further Protocol, relating to the Rights of Women, was adopted by the July 2003 Maputo Assembly. An African Charter on the Rights and Welfare of the Child entered into force in November 1999. The sixth annual African Transitional Justice Forum was convened in September 2022, in Lomé, Togo.

In May 2014 the ACHPR adopted a resolution on drafting a protocol to the African Charter on Human and Peoples' Rights with regard to the Right to Nationality in Africa. The ACHPR subsequently advocated for action to address statelessness.

In 1964 the OAU adopted a Declaration on the Denuclearization of Africa, and in April 1996 it adopted the African Nuclear Weapons Free Zone Treaty (also known as the Pelindaba Treaty), which promotes co-operation in the peaceful uses of nuclear energy, and identifies Africa as a nuclear weapons-free zone; the Pelindaba Treaty entered into force in July 2009.

The July 2002 inaugural summit meeting of AU heads of state and of government adopted a Declaration Governing Democratic Elections in Africa, providing guidelines for the conduct of national elections in member states and outlining the AU's electoral observation and monitoring role; an African Charter on Democracy, Elections and Governance entered into force in February 2012.

A Convention Governing the Specific Aspects of Refugee Problems in Africa was adopted by OAU member states in 1969. It entered into force in June 1974 and had been ratified by 46 states at September 2022. The Convention promotes close co-operation with the UN High Commissioner for Refugees (UNHCR). The AU Convention for the Protection and Assistance of IDPs in Africa (the 'Kampala Convention')—the first legally binding international treaty providing legal protection and support to people displaced within their own countries by violent conflict and natural disasters—entered into force in December 2012, and had been ratified by 33 countries by September 2022.

A revised AU Migration Policy Framework (MPFA) and accompanying Plan of Action, covering the period 2018–30, were issued in May 2018 (superseding an original MPFA that had been adopted in 2006). The revised MPFA had the following areas of focus: border management; forced displacement; human rights of migrants; internal migration; inter-state co-operation and partnerships; irregular migration; labour migration; migration data management; and migration and development. The sixth Pan African Forum on Migration (PAFoM VI) was hosted by Senegal, in Dakar, under AU auspices, in September 2021. A Joint Labour Migration Programme for Africa (JLMP), jointly implemented by the AU Commission, International Labour Organization, International Organization for Migration, and ECA, was initiated in January 2015 to improve continental labour migration governance. AU efforts to combat human trafficking are guided by the 2006 Ouagadougou Action Plan to Combat Trafficking in Human Beings.

An AU Convention on Preventing and Combating Corruption entered into force in August 2006, and in May 2009 an associated AU Advisory Board on Corruption was inaugurated. An AU Convention on Cyber Security and Personal Data Protection was adopted in June 2014, and by September 2022 had 13 states parties. In June 2021 the AU Commission, supported by the Council of Europe, organized the second African Cybercrime Forum, in Addis Ababa. (The first had been convened in October 2018.)

In October 2013 an extraordinary summit of the AU Assembly, convened on the theme 'Africa's relationship with the International Criminal Court', determined that—in order to safeguard the constitutional order, stability and integrity of member states—no trial proceedings ought to be commenced or continued before any international court or tribunal against any serving AU head of state or of government, or against anybody acting in such capacity, during her or his term of office. The summit specifically requested the Court to defer until after the expiry of their terms of office the indictments that were issued in 2011 against the serving President of Kenya, Uhuru Muigai Kenyatta, and his Vice-President, William Samoei Ruto, in relation to violent unrest that followed the December 2007 presidential elections there. The summit decided to convene an Executive Council Contact Group to engage with the UN Security Council on all concerns of the AU regarding its relationship with the Court, including the deferral of the Kenyan cases, and the arrest warrant issued by the Court in 2009 against former President Omar al-Bashir of Sudan, concerning his alleged responsibility for the perpetration of war crimes in Darfur. (The Kenyan cases were withdrawn in early 2016.) In January 2017 the 28th AU Assembly adopted a non-binding decision that supported a strategy of collective African withdrawal from the Court. In May, with a view to strengthening relations with Africa, the Court, with support from the Swiss Government, convened (in Dakar) a high-level conference on 'Capacity-building with regard to African judicial systems through effective and dynamic complementarity and co-operation with the International Criminal Court'. In March 2018 a Nigerian national was elected as President of the Court.

The Protocol to the Constitutive Act of the African Union Relating to the Establishment of the Peace and Security Council, adopted by the inaugural AU summit of heads of state and of government in July 2002, entered into force in December 2003, superseding the 1993 Cairo Declaration on the OAU Mechanism for Conflict Prevention, Management and Resolution. The Protocol provides for the development of a collective peace and security framework (known as the African Peace and Security Architecture—APSA). This includes a Peace and Security Council, operational at the levels of heads of state and of government, ministers responsible for foreign affairs, and permanent representatives, to be supported by a five-member advisory Panel of the Wise, a Continental Early Warning System, an African Standby Force (ASF) and a Peace Fund. A Network of African Women in Conflict Prevention and Mediation (FemWise-Africa)—a subsidiary mechanism of the Panel of the Wise—was formally endorsed in July 2017 by AU heads of state and of government. In February 2020 the Assembly requested the AU Commission fully to operationalize FemWise-Africa.

The activities of the AU Peace and Security Council include early warning and preventive diplomacy; peacemaking mediation; peace support operations and intervention; peacebuilding activities and post-conflict reconstruction; and humanitarian action and disaster management. The Council is tasked with implementing the common defence policy of the Union, and ensuring the implementation of the 1999 OAU Convention on the Prevention and Combating of Terrorism (under which signatory states were to exchange information and refrain from granting asylum to terrorists). In April 2017 the AU Chairperson and UN Secretary-General signed a framework agreement aimed at consolidating co-operation between their respective organizations in the area of peace and security. In this context, in September the AU Commissioner for Peace and Security and the UN Assistant Secretary-General for Peacebuilding Support concluded a Memorandum of Understanding (MOU) on a UN-AU Partnership in Peacebuilding. An AU-UN Joint Declaration on Co-operation for AU Peace Support Operations was signed by the AU Commission Chair and the UN Secretary-General in December 2018; this outlined principles to guide future joint responses to conflicts and political crises in Africa. The Fifth AU-UN Annual Conference, convened in December 2021, at the UN's headquarters in New York, USA, reviewed progress achieved in the areas of peace and security and sustainable development, and discussed co-operation on human rights issues.

The AU Non-Aggression and Common Defence Pact, which entered into force in December 2009, stipulates measures aimed at preventing and at peacefully resolving inter- and intra-state conflicts. The Pact states that an act, or threat, of aggression against an individual member state affects all member states.

An AU Policy on Post-Conflict Reconstruction and Development (PCRD) has been pursued since 2006. In July 2012 an African Solidarity Initiative was launched, with the aim of mobilizing support among member states for countries emerging from conflict, in line with the PCRD.

In December 2000 OAU heads of state and of government adopted the Bamako Declaration, concerned with arresting the circulation of small arms and light weapons (SALW) within the continent. It was envisaged that the Central African Convention for the Control of SALW, their Ammunition, Parts and Components that can be used for their Manufacture, Repair or Assembly (Kinshasa Convention), which was adopted by Central African states in April 2010 and entered into force in February 2017, would contribute to the AU's SALW control capacity. In November 2016 the Peace and Security Council adopted an AU Master Roadmap on Practical Steps to Silence the Guns in Africa. In February 2020 the Assembly requested the AU Commission to integrate child protection into the Silencing the Guns agenda. In December of that year the timeframe of the agenda was extended until 2030.

An AU Mechanism for Police Cooperation (AFRIPOL), comprising member states' chiefs of police, was launched in May 2017. In December 2019 an AU Ministerial Meeting adopted the Bamako Declaration on Access to Natural Resources and Conflicts between Communities. African Youth Ambassadors for Peace represent five continental regions. An AU Centre for Post-Conflict Reconstruction and Development was inaugurated in Cairo in December 2021.

In November 2019 the AU and NATO concluded an agreement (updating a previous accord) that was to guide continuing mutual practical and political co-operation, with a focus on developing logistical, operational and capacity-building support.

AU Peace Fund: In July 2016 the AU Assembly agreed on an initial endowment and subsequent 0.2% import levy to support the Peace Fund's activities, which included mediation and preventive diplomacy, institutional capacity and peace support operations. A Board of Trustees was appointed in November 2018, when the Fund was officially inaugurated. It was hoped that US $400m. would be endowed to the Fund by 2023.

During 2004–19 the European Union (EU) channelled €2,700m. in funding for African subregional and national peace and security activities directly to the AU through an African Peace Facility (APF). From January 2021 the EU replaced the APF with two funds with a global scope: a European Peace Facility and a Neighbourhood, Development and International Cooperation Instrument.

African Standby Force (ASF): An extraordinary AU summit meeting, convened in Sirte, in February 2004, adopted a declaration approving the establishment of the multinational ASF, which was to comprise rapidly deployable multidimensional military, police and civilian capabilities, and was to be mandated to undertake observation, monitoring and other peace support missions; to deploy in member states as required to prevent the resurgence or escalation of violence; to intervene as required to restore stability; to conduct post-conflict disarmament and demobilization and other peacebuilding activities; and to provide emergency humanitarian assistance. The Force was to be drawn from five regional brigades: the North Africa Regional Standby Brigade (NASBRIG), the Eastern African Standby Force (EASF), the Force Multinationale de l'Afrique Centrale (FOMAC), the Southern African Development Community (SADC) Standby Brigade (SADCBRIG) and the Economic Community of West African States (ECOWAS) Standby Brigade (ECOBRIG).

In January 2014 AU leaders endorsed the creation of an interim African Capacity for Immediate Response to Crises (ACIRC), to be deployed as a continental rapid reaction force in emergency situations, pending the ASF's full operationalization (which required substantial additional financing). In July 2016 the 27th AU summit authorized the establishment of an AU Special Fund for Prevention and Combating of Terrorism and Violent Extremism; this was to be funded through voluntary donations. An ASF Continental Logistics Base was inaugurated in Douala, Cameroon, in January 2018.

In May 2022 an extraordinary AU summit was convened to address terrorism and unconstitutional changes of government.

Boko Haram: In January 2015 the AU Assembly welcomed ongoing efforts by the Lake Chad Basin Commission (LCBC), and Benin, to eliminate the terrorist grouping Jama'atu Ahlus Sunnah lid Da'awati wal Jihad ('Boko Haram'). In March Boko Haram pledged allegiance to Islamic State, formally becoming Islamic State's West Africa Province—ISWAP. However, a splinter faction subsequently re-identified as Boko Haram. In that month the Peace and Security Council authorized the deployment of a Multinational Joint Task Force, under the operational control of the Commission, which was to combat Boko Haram in north-eastern Nigeria and surrounding border regions. In May 2016 the AU convened in Abuja a Second Regional Security Meeting, at which US $250m. was raised to fund operations against the group. In February 2017 the AU Commissioner for Peace and Security and Chad's Minister of Public Security and Immigration issued a joint communiqué that addressed means—such as temporary detention, deradicalization and community

reintegration—of managing former members of Boko Haram. In late August 2018 an AU-LCBC ministerial conference, held in Abuja, adopted a Regional Stabilization, Recovery and Resilience Strategy for Areas Affected by Boko Haram in the Lake Chad Basin Region. The Strategy was endorsed in December by the AU Peace and Security Council. A Regional Stabilization Facility for Lake Chad was launched by the UN Development Programme in July 2019, in support of the initiative. In July 2021 the Peace and Security Council stated concern over the protracted insecurity in the region, including continuing attacks by non-state actors, abductions of schoolchildren, and the impacts of climate change on many people's livelihoods (for example the impacts on fish production of drying in Lake Chad, and the degradation of pasturelands). The Council noted that the reported death in May of the Boko Haram terrorist leader Abubakar Shekau was prompting a consolidation of the activities of ISWAP.

Burkina Faso: In late January 2022 the Chairperson of the AU Commission strongly condemned a military coup that had overthrown the democratically elected President of Burkina Faso, Roch Marc Christian Kaboré; the mutinous soldiers had reportedly demanded a change of senior military personnel and greater resources to combat Islamist insurgents. Soon afterwards Burkina Faso was suspended from the AU, pending the restoration of constitutional order. The AU pledged to co-operate closely with ECOWAS in seeking a solution to the crisis. In mid-February an interim military junta-appointed president, Lt-Col Paul-Henri Sandaogo Damiba, was inaugurated. A charter detailing a three-year schedule of transition to democratic elections was issued at the beginning of March, and an interim Prime Minister designated soon afterwards. In mid-2022, following the appointment of an ECOWAS Mediator for Burkina Faso, a new timetable was announced, whereby the transition to constitutional rule would be completed in mid-2024. On 30 September 2022 the Chairman of the AU Commission unequivocally condemned a new seizure of power in Burkina Faso, by Captain Ibrahim Traore. Traore, who cited a worsening security situation as the cause of the coup, subsequently committed to the ongoing timetable for a return to constitutional rule.

Cameroon: In November 2019 the AU Commission Chairperson, the Secretary-General of the Organisation Internationale de la Francophonie, and the Secretary-General of the Commonwealth collectively visited Yaoundé, Cameroon, to discuss with national stakeholders the sociopolitical unrest that had escalated from late 2017 in the country's English-speaking North West and South West regions. In February 2020 the AU Assembly commended the Cameroon Government for pursuing measures aimed at achieving a peaceful resolution to the crisis in the anglophone regions—including the adoption of decentralization legislation that conferred a special status to the anglophone regions, and of legislation that promoted traditional national languages, and the use of both English and French as official languages of equal value. The Assembly also welcomed the release by the Cameroon Government of political leaders accused of participating in the organization of illegal demonstrations, and of other individuals who had been prosecuted for crimes committed during the recent unrest.

Central African Republic: In response to mounting sectarian violence and human rights violations caused by a rebel offensive, initiated in December 2012, that culminated in the overturning of the legitimately elected CAR Government of President François Bozizé in March 2013 and the inauguration as President in August of the coup leader Michel Djotodia, the UN Security Council approved, in October, the deployment of a new peacekeeping force to the CAR. During October the AU Peace and Security Council adopted a concept of operations for the consequent AU-led International Support Mission to the CAR (MISCA). The UN Security Council authorized the deployment of MISCA in December. The mission—with support from a strengthened contingent of French troops that had already been stationed in the CAR—was mandated to use all necessary measures to protect civilians, to restore state authority and to support the provision of humanitarian assistance. An existing Mission for the Consolidation of Peace in the CAR (MICOPAX), which had operated under the auspices of the Communauté Economique des Etats de l'Afrique Centrale (CEEAC) since July 2008, transferred authority to MISCA on 19 December. In January 2014 the UN Security Council authorized the deployment of a 1,000-strong EU Mission in the CAR (EUFOR CAR), tasked with securing part of Bangui, the capital, for the conduct of humanitarian operations; this was deployed in April. In April, in view of the continuing crisis in the CAR, the UN Security Council authorized the creation of the UN Multidimensional Integrated Stabilization Mission in the Central African Republic (MINUSCA). MINUSCA took over the military and policing functions of MISCA from mid-September. An International Contact Group on the CAR, chaired by the AU, and with participation by, *inter alia*, the UN, the CEEAC, and the CAR Government, was convened periodically from May 2013–August 2016; in the latter month it was transformed into an International Support Group on the CAR, chaired jointly by the AU and the UN. The AU and the UN both backed an initiative led from early July 2014 by the President of the

Republic of the Congo, Denis Sassou Nguesso, to mediate in the CAR situation, and also supported the implementation of a ceasefire (the 'Brazzaville Agreement') concluded between the parties to the conflict there later in that month. The AU dispatched an observer mission to monitor legislative and presidential elections held in the CAR at the end of December 2015 (these had been postponed from October, owing to a renewed escalation of violent unrest from late September). The AU also welcomed the successful organization—in mid-December, prior to the elections—of a referendum at which the electorate approved a new national Constitution. In view of the annulment in January 2016 of the results of the legislative elections held in the previous month, these were repeated in mid-February, alongside a second round of presidential voting; a further round of legislative elections was held in late March. A new President, Faustin Archange Touadéra, was inaugurated at the end of March, marking the end of the period of transitional governance in the CAR. The CAR was readmitted to full participation in AU activities in the following month.

In July 2017 the AU Commission endorsed an African Initiative for Peace and National Reconciliation in the CAR and supporting Roadmap, which were to be led jointly by the AU, CEEAC and the International Conference on the Great Lakes Region (ICGLR), with the aim of promoting dialogue between the CAR authorities and militant groupings, and achieving long-term national disarmament. In February 2019, after a year of negotiations within the context of the African Initiative, 14 rebel groups and the Government signed, under AU auspices, the Political Agreement for Peace and Reconciliation in the CAR (PAPR-CAR). Representatives of the AU Peace and Security Council and of the Political and Security Committee of the EU visited the CAR in the following month to support the implementation of the new Political Agreement. In February 2020 the AU Assembly urged all CAR stakeholders to ensure that a pending general election should be organized in strict compliance with the February 2019 PAPR-CAR and with domestic CAR laws. President Faustin Touadéra was commended for efforts aimed at promoting inclusive consensus, and in particular for instituting a Peace Agreement-focused dialogue with former national heads of state. An MOU was concluded in mid-2020 between a new AU Military Observers Mission in the CAR (MOUACA) and MINUSCA. Touadéra was re-elected in late December 2020, winning an outright majority at the first round of the presidential poll. In June 2021 the AU Commissioner for Political Affairs, Peace and Security, the UN Under-Secretary-General for Peace Operations, and representatives of CEEAC and the EU collectively visited Bangui with a view to promoting a credible and inclusive political dialogue to consolidate and advance the peace process. In July the Peace and Security Council stated deep concern over worsening insecurity in the CAR, and urged armed groups that had withdrawn from the 2019 PAPR-CAR unconditionally to cease all hostilities and to rejoin the peace process. The Council urged the CAR Government to take all necessary steps to prevent the illegal exploitation of national mineral resources, and to improve the delivery of basic public services to the people of the country. In mid-October 2021 the UN Security Council welcomed the announcement of a ceasefire by Touadéra, following the adoption in by the ICGLR in the previous month of a roadmap aimed at achieving peace in the CAR. A Republican Dialogue on reconciliation, convened in March 2022, was boycotted by most opposition representatives.

Eswatini: At the beginning of July 2021 the Chairperson of the AU Commission stated deep concern over an escalating political and security crisis in Eswatini, where pro-democracy demonstrations were being organized to demand political reforms to the national system of absolute monarchy. Numerous incidents of violent unrest had been reported, and by that time at least 20 activists were believed by the international human rights organization Amnesty International to have been killed (and a further 150 to have been injured) by the national security forces. Curfews had been imposed and schools suspended by the national authorities, with a view to controlling the unrest. The Chairperson strongly condemned all related fatalities and destruction of property. He called for immediate action to protect citizens, and for all national stakeholders to pursue constructive dialogue towards a peaceful resolution of the situation.

Ethiopia: In November 2020 the AU Chairperson appointed three former heads of state as envoys to support efforts to end internal conflict in Tigray, northern Ethiopia. An AU monitoring mission, led by the former President of Nigeria, Chief Olusegun Obasanjo, was invited by the Federal Government of Ethiopia to observe a national general election that was held on 21 June 2021 for 486 of the 547 parliamentary seats. The mission issued a preliminary statement in which it noted that, despite significant political reforms that had been introduced since April 2018 by the incumbent (and re-elected) Ethiopian Prime Minister, Dr Abiy Ahmed, which had enlarged the national political and civic space, several political parties had been banned from participating in the poll and others had boycotted it in response to arrests of opposition figures. The Ethiopian Government was urged to sustain and widen political freedoms, and to advance

national dialogue, reconciliation and inclusivity. The mission concluded that, overall, the electoral process had been conducted in an 'orderly, peaceful and credible' manner, and urged all national stakeholders to remain calm. In early July 2021 the Chairperson of the AU Commission welcomed the formal proclamation of the outcome by the National Electoral Board of Ethiopia, and congratulated Dr Ahmed on the victory of his Prosperity Party. An AU Commission of Inquiry on Tigray was initiated in mid-June, under the auspices of the African Commission on Human and People's Rights, with a mandate to investigate allegations of violations of international human rights law and international humanitarian law there. In late June the Chairperson welcomed the Ethiopian Federal Government's declaration of a humanitarian ceasefire in Tigray. In August the Chairperson appointed Chief Obasanjo as AU High Representative for the Horn of Africa region. The Chairperson welcomed the declaration of an indefinite humanitarian truce in the region, announced by the Ethiopian authorities in March 2022, and urged his High Representative to continue efforts to secure a permanent ceasefire and a political settlement to the conflict. In early October the Chairperson of the AU Commission welcomed agreement by Dr Ahmed and the Tigrayan leadership to participate in high-level peace talks that were to take place in South Africa, and to be mediated by a panel of eminent Africans.

Grand Ethiopian Renaissance Dam (GERD): In mid-2020 the Chairperson of the AU Assembly determined to lead a consultation process aimed at resolving a longstanding dispute concerning Ethiopia's construction of the GERD—on the Blue Nile, the River Nile's main tributary—and its impacts, including potential water losses, on Egypt and Sudan (both downstream Nile countries). The resulting inaugural meeting of the AU Bureau to review progress in Trilateral Negotiations on the GERD was convened in late June. Several meetings were subsequently held, but the negotiations process eventually stalled, with Egypt and Sudan reportedly seeking a legally binding international accord, providing a formal mechanism to resolve future disputes, and Ethiopia unilaterally advocating for a non-binding approach. In September the UN Security Council issued a statement that urged the resumption of constructive negotiations under AU auspices. Electricity production from the GERD commenced in February 2022, and was augmented in August.

Guinea: On 10 September 2021 the AU suspended Guinea, following the overthrow in a military coup of that country's longstanding President Alpha Condé and dissolution of the Guinean Government and of the national Constitution—which, in 2020, against a background of widespread opposition, had been revised to enable Condé to serve a third term of office. Condé was temporarily detained by the military.

Lord's Resistance Army: The Regional Cooperation Initiative for the Elimination of the Lord's Resistance Army (AU RCI-LRA) was authorized by the Peace and Security Council in November 2011, and officially launched in March 2012, comprising: a Joint Coordination Mechanism, based in Bangui, CAR, and chaired by the AU Commissioner for Peace and Security, with participation by the ministers responsible for defence of LRA-affected countries (i.e. Uganda, the CAR, the DRC and South Sudan), and responsibility for strategic coordination with all affected states and actors; a Regional Task Force (AU RTF), with a troop ceiling of 5,000, comprising national contingents from LRA-affected countries; and a Joint Operations Centre, reporting to the RTF Commander. Actions by the AU RCI-LRA reportedly achieved the removal of several LRA commanders, as well as a downward turn in the numbers of LRA abductions and killings, and a significant increase in the number of defections from the rebel grouping. In January 2015 the AU RCI-LRA transferred Dominic Ongwen, a senior LRA commander who had been indicted by the International Criminal Court on charges relating to crimes against humanity, to the custody of the CAR authorities; he was subsequently placed in the custody of the Court. In June 2016 the Ugandan Government announced that it intended to implement a phased withdrawal of Uganda's 2,500 troops from the AU RTF (which at November 2015 comprised 3,085 troops—only around three-fifths of its envisaged configuration). In mid-2016 an AU-UN-EU-US joint technical assessment mission reported that the LRA remained an active threat, and that insecurity in the region was amplified by the presence of other militia—including the ex-Séléka faction (opposed to the CAR Government) and the Janjaweed (active in western Sudan and eastern Chad). It urged the renewal of the mandate of US special forces, which had been deployed to provide logistical support to the AU RTF. In April 2017, however, when the withdrawal of Ugandan forces commenced, the new US Administration terminated US engagement against the LRA. Meanwhile, South Sudan indicated that it would no longer host the AU RTF headquarters (hitherto based in Yambio): therefore, they relocated to Koboko, Uganda, in July. By 2022 the LRA was reported to comprise up to 1,000 combatants in disparate groupings, largely funded through the smuggling of arms and ivory.

Mali: In July 2014 the Chairperson of the AU Commission welcomed the end of the first phase of an inter-Malian dialogue that had been initiated in that month (with participation by a senior AU representative and team of AU experts), and the adoption by the participants of a roadmap towards the achievement of a comprehensive peace settlement. The AU, with ECOWAS, UN, the EU, the Organization of Islamic Cooperation, and other regional stakeholders, participated in the Algerian-led mediation team supporting the so-called Algiers dialogue process, which led to the initialling at the beginning of March 2015—and adoption by all further parties in May and June—of a Mali Peace and Reconciliation Agreement. A high-level meeting on Mali and the Sahel, organized in September 2019 on the sidelines of the UN General Assembly, reaffirmed that the Algiers Agreement remained the cornerstone of resolving the security crisis in Mali.

In December 2019 Malian stakeholders, meeting in Bamako, the national capital, adopted four resolutions, including to hold legislative elections before May 2020, and to follow those with a constitutional referendum. Accordingly (despite the COVID-19 emergency—which was reported to have resulted in a low voter turnout) the parliamentary poll was held in two rounds on, 29 March and 19 April 2020, with the final outcome confirmed on 30 April by Mali's Constitutional Court—which had overturned the results for 31 seats, resulting in the re-election of the political party associated with Mali's President Ibrahim Boubacar Keïta. Subsequently, tensions over the validity of the election results, a dangerous national security situation, and growing economic uncertainty (in particular related to the COVID-19 situation) erupted into large-scale protests in Bamako, which became violent from early July, resulting in 11 fatalities. A newly formed opposition alliance known as the June 5 Movement demanded the resignation of President Keïta. On 18 August Keïta, who was forced to announce his resignation and the dissolution of the Malian Government, the hitherto Malian Prime Minister Boubou Cisse, and other senior government figures were detained by members of the Mali military, and were removed from Bamako to a military base in the nearby settlement of Kati. The AU Chairperson strongly condemned the unconstitutional removal of the government. Pending the restoration of constitutional order, Mali was suspended by the Peace and Security Council from participation in AU processes. The Council demanded the release of Keïta, Cisse and the other forcibly detained government officials. In late August Keïta left Mali to receive medical treatment in the United Arab Emirates. In mid-September the new military leadership determined that an 18-month transitional government would be established pending new national elections. On 25 September Bah N'Daou, a former Minister of Defence, was inaugurated as the civilian transitional President. A charter to govern the transition over the next 18 months was issued at the beginning of October (this extended an amnesty to the leaders of the coup), a 25-member transitional cabinet was appointed on 5 October, and members of the Conseil national de Transition (transitional parliament) were installed in early December. On 9 October the AU reversed Mali's suspension. In mid-November the AU Chairperson visited Mali and met the Malian transitional leadership and senior UN presence. The inaugural meeting of a Transition Support Group on Mali (GST-Mali)—with participation by the AU, ECOWAS, the UN Multidimensional Stabilization Mission in Mali, and other partners—was convened at the end of November, in Bamako. A programme of action for the transition, comprising eight priority actions, including reforms and the organization of a general election at the end of the transition period, was presented to the meeting by the Prime Minister of the transitional government. A second GST-Mali meeting took place in March 2021. In late May the AU and the other the GST-Mali participants stated deep concern at the recent arrest by the Malian military of members of the transitional authorities—including President N'Daou and the interim Prime Minister—and demanded their immediate release. Shortly afterwards the interim President and premier were forced to resign their posts (while continuing to be detained under house arrest). On 1 June the Peace and Security Council once again suspended Mali's AU membership, and called on the Malian military 'urgently and unconditionally' to return to their barracks and to cease interfering in the national political process. The Council warned that, otherwise, punitive sanctions would be imposed. In mid-2022 a new timetable was announced, under which a referendum on a proposed new Constitution would be organized in March 2023, local elections in June, legislative elections during October–November, and a presidential poll would be held in February 2024. The third meeting of the GST-Mali, held in early September, welcomed the lifting of the economic and financial sanctions on Mali by ECOWAS (and also by UEMOA). The fourth GST-Mali session was to be held in Bamako, in early 2023.

Mauritius: In February 2021 the 34th AU Assembly adopted a decision that called on member states to support all regional, international and intergovernmental efforts to enable Mauritius to assert its sovereignty over the Chagos Archipelago, pursuant to an Advisory Opinion issued in February 2019 by the International Court of Justice (ICJ) relating to the legal consequences of the separation of the Chagos Archipelago from Mauritius in 1965 to form the British Indian Ocean Territory. The ICJ had found that the archipelago had been, and remained, unlawfully occupied by the United Kingdom. Its ruling had been endorsed in May 2019 by the UN General Assembly, which had adopted a (non-binding) resolution setting a deadline of 22 November 2019, by which the UK ought to relinquish sovereignty of the islands and return them to Mauritius. The UK, however, had stated that it would continue to administer the territory, and had ignored the deadline. The 34th AU Assembly welcomed a judgment issued in late January 2021 by the International Tribunal for the Law of the Sea (ITLOS), which also found that Mauritius had sovereignty over the Chagos Archipelago, and condemned the continued occupation of the islands by the UK.

Mozambique: At the end of March 2021 the Chairperson of the AU Commission strongly condemned terrorist attacks in Mozambique's Cabo Delgado region (perpetrated by Ahl al-Sunna Wal-Jama'a, associated with Islamic State Central Africa Province), and particularly recent atrocities in the vicinity of the coastal town of Palma. He stated utmost concern at the presence of international terrorist groups in southern Africa, and called for a co-ordinated regional and international response.

Nouakchott Process: In December 2014 the AU Chairperson convened the inaugural summit of countries—Algeria, Burkina Faso, Chad, Côte d'Ivoire, Libya, Mali, Mauritania and Senegal—participating in the so-called Nouakchott Process on the Enhancement of Security Co-operation and the Operationalization of the APSA in the Sahelo-Saharan Region. In April 2017 the AU Peace and Security Council endorsed the strategic concept of operations, and deployment, of a joint counter-terrorism force—the Force conjointe du G5 Sahel (FC-G5S)—which was tasked with combating violent extremist groups operating in the common space of the member states of the G5 Sahel grouping. The deployment of the FC-G5S—to comprise up to 5,000 military and police personnel—was endorsed by the UN Security Council in June; in December the Council authorized the Multidimensional Integrated Stabilization Mission in Mali to provide the FC-G5S with logistical and operational support. In January 2020, at a summit attended in Pau, France, by the G5 Sahel heads of state, President Emmanuel Macron of France and the UN Secretary-General, a Niamey, Niger-based joint command mechanism was established for the FC-G5S and French Opération Barkhane (deployed in the region to support action against terrorist insurgencies). The strategic concept of operations of the FC-G5S was revised at that time. In February the AU Assembly—expressing deep concern over continuing incidents in the Sahel region of terrorism, banditry, cross-border crime and of all forms of trafficking—emphasized the need to support through enhanced financing ECOWAS-led and other regional initiatives aimed at securing peace. In June 2021 the Chairperson of the AU Commission condemned a terrorist attack which caused more than 130 fatalities in Solhan, northern Burkina Faso. In June 2022 Mali's military regime withdrew from the G5 Sahel.

Somalia: A high-level Somalia Security Conference convened in December 2017, in the Somali capital, Mogadishu, addressed the need for representatives of the Somali authorities, the AU, AMISOM, the UN, the EU and other international partners to accelerate the co-ordinated development of a plan to guide a phased transition from AMISOM to a full Somali-led national security architecture. In May 2018 the UN Security Council tasked AMISOM with, *inter alia*, engaging with communities and securing principal supply routes in areas newly recovered from the al-Shabaab ('the Youth') terrorist grouping, securing key population centres, and mentoring the Somali military and police.

In March 2021 the Chairperson of the AU Commission urged stakeholders in Somalia to engage in constructive dialogue—within the framework of a so-called '17 September Agreement' that had been reached in September 2020—to resolve an ongoing impasse over the organization of elections (which were to have been held in February 2021, but had been postponed). In mid-April the AU and international partners collectively stated deep concern over a recent decision by the Somali legislature to replace the 17 September agreement with a different electoral process that entailed a lengthy extension to the current presidential and parliamentary mandates. Later in the month they strongly condemned an eruption of violence in Mogadishu, reiterating that adherence to the 17 September arrangement should represent the only model for the electoral process, and that an extension of government mandates would cause a destabilizing political crisis. They stated particular concern over emerging fragmentation of the Somali National Army into clan-based factions. The former President of Ghana, John Mahama, was appointed in May as the AU High Representative for Somalia to support the political negotiations; on 21 May, however, Mahama resigned, after the Somali authorities opposed his deployment and expressed doubt regarding his impartiality. In mid-2021 representatives of AMISOM, the UN, IGAD and the EU visited Somalia's federal member states with the aim of fostering constructive engagement in the electoral preparations. In September AMISOM and the Somali military initiated a Joint Operations Coordination Centre in Mogadishu. In that month the AU Commission and AMISOM began to provide technical and advisory electoral assistance to the Somali authorities to support legislative elections that were initiated in November. In early March 2022 the AU Peace and Security Council determined to reconfigure AMISOM as the AU Transition Mission in Somalia (ATMIS); this transformation was endorsed on 31 March by the UN Security Council. ATMIS was tasked with reducing the threat posed by al-Shabaab, assisting efforts to build the capacity of the Somali security and police forces, supporting national peacebuilding and reconciliation activities, and with undertaking a phased transfer of security responsibilities to Somalia. Until the end of 2022 the mission was to comprise up to 19,626 uniformed personnel, with a minimum 1,040 police. A phased reduction of total personnel was then envisaged: to 14,626 by September 2023 and to 10,626 by June 2024, with the termination of the mission scheduled for December of that year. In early May 2022 the Chairperson of the AU Commission strongly condemned an al-Shabaab terrorist attack that killed at least 10 Burundian ATMIS troops. In mid-May he congratulated the newly elected President of Somalia, Hassan Sheikh Mohamud (a presidential poll having completed a protracted Somalian electoral process). At the beginning of September a new Head of ATMIS and AU Special Representative to Somalia, Mohammed el-Amine Souef, took office.

South Africa: In mid-July 2021 the Chairperson of the AU Commission condemned an outbreak in South Africa of rioting, looting, destruction of infrastructure, and other violent unrest, which had erupted following the imprisonment of former President Jacob Zuma—who had been convicted of contempt of court following his failure to engage with an inquiry into corruption allegedly perpetrated during his presidency. By that time 72 people had reportedly been killed in the unrest, which had been particularly intense in Zuma's home province of KwaZulu-Natal, and in Gauteng, and around 1,300 people had been detained by the security forces. The Chairperson called for the urgent restoration of peace, stability and order.

South Sudan: In April 2012 the AU High-Level Implementation Panel on Sudan (AUHIP—established in October 2009) presented a draft Joint Decision for Reduction of Tension, providing for the immediate cessation of hostilities and the withdrawal of armed forces of each state from the territory of the other. In accordance with a seven-point Roadmap for Action by Sudan and South Sudan, approved in late April by the AU Peace and Security Council, and aimed at normalizing relations between the two states, both militaries were withdrawn from Abyei by the end of May. (See UN Interim Security Force for Abyei—UNISFA for further details.)

In March 2014 the inaugural meeting took place of an AU Commission of Inquiry into the conflict that had emerged in December 2013 in South Sudan. The Commission met with representatives of the South Sudan Government, the opposition SPLM, and other stakeholders; and with the Intergovernmental Authority on Development (IGAD), the AUHIP and the UN and other relevant bodies. In January 2015 the Commission presented its final report to the AU Peace and Security Council.

In June 2015 Alpha Oumar Konaré—the former President of Mali and former Chairperson of the AU Commission—was appointed to the post of AU High Representative for South Sudan. An AU High-Level Ad Hoc Committee for South Sudan, chaired by South Africa and also comprising Algeria, Chad, Nigeria and Rwanda (the 'C5'), was established by the Peace and Security Council to assist the peace process. In September 2017 the AU Peace and Security Council decided that the AU Commission and Transitional Government of National Unity should urgently conclude an MOU on the establishment of a proposed Hybrid Court for South Sudan to try suspects accused of war crimes, and that the AU Commission should draft punitive sanctions to be applied against all those obstructing a return to peace and security in that country. In January 2018 the AU Assembly commended IGAD for its leadership of the inaugural session of a High Level Revitalization Forum, which had been convened in December 2017 to advance the implementation of the (August 2015) Agreement for the Resolution of the Conflict in South Sudan, and welcomed the signing by stakeholders in South Sudan, during the Forum, of an Agreement of Cessation of Hostilities, Protection of Civilians and Humanitarian Access. In early 2018 the Chairperson of the AU Commission and the UN Secretary-General strongly condemned violations of the December 2017 accord. In September 2018 the Chairperson of the AU Commission welcomed the signature by the parties to the conflict of a new Revitalized Agreement on the Resolution of the Conflict in South Sudan. On 22 February 2020 President Salva Kiir and former Vice-President Riek Machar concluded a power-sharing agreement, formally ending the civil war. In accordance with the accord, a new Revitalized Transitional Government of National Unity (RTGoNU) was established. In that month the AU Assembly urged the international community to extend further logistical, financial and material assistance to the South Sudan Peace Process, and commended the AU C5's ongoing efforts to support South Sudan. The AUHIP has continued to work towards facilitating agreement between South Sudan and Sudan over the future of Abyei. At the beginning of June 2021 a

joint delegation that included representatives of the AU, UN Mission in South Sudan, and IGAD visited Pibor, in eastern South Sudan, where intercommunal violence had recently escalated. In August 2022 the Chairperson of the AU Commission welcomed the adoption by the RTGoNU of an Agreement on the Roadmap to a Peaceful and Democratic End to the Transitional Period in South Sudan; this extended the end of the transitional period by 24 months, to 22 February 2025.

Sudan: In July 2007 the UN Security Council authorized the establishment of a joint AU/UN Hybrid Operation in Darfur (UNAMID), in order to support the implementation and verification of the Darfur Peace Agreement, concluded between parties to the conflict in western Sudan in May 2006. The operation was also mandated to protect civilians, to provide security for humanitarian assistance, to support an inclusive political process, to contribute to the promotion of human rights and rule of law, and to monitor and report on the situation along the borders with Chad and the Central African Republic (CAR). UNAMID assumed command of the existing AU Mission in Sudan in December 2007. A joint AU-UN Chief Mediator was appointed in June 2008. A Joint Support Co-ordination Mechanism Office in Addis Ababa, comprising liaison officers and communications equipment, was established in November to ensure effective consultation between AU headquarters and the UN. In March 2009 an AU High-Level Panel on Darfur was established to address means of securing peace, justice and reconciliation in Darfur. The panel issued a report of its findings and recommendations in October; a key recommendation was the creation of a hybrid court, comprising both AU and Sudanese judges, to prosecute crimes against humanity committed in Darfur. In March 2016 the Sudanese Government signed a Roadmap Agreement for Ending the Conflicts in Sudan, which had been negotiated under the auspices of the AUHIP on Sudan; the Roadmap was adopted by Sudanese opposition groups in early August. In late 2018 UNAMID transferred to the Sudanese Government 10 team sites in eastern and southern Darfur, in accordance with a UN Security Council resolution of July to reconfigure the operation. In January 2019 UNAMID relocated its headquarters from El Fasher to Zalingei, in central Darfur.

In April 2019 the AU Peace and Security Council condemned as unconstitutional the overthrow of President al-Bashir by the Sudanese armed forces and establishment of a military-led transitional government. The Council demanded the introduction of a civilian transitional political authority (to precede national elections) within 15 days, later extended to 60 days, with the threat of suspension from the organization if this was not achieved. At the beginning of June, in response to the forced dispersal by the Sudanese paramilitary Rapid Support Forces (reportedly linked to the Janjaweed militia) and police of a sit-in protest at the Sudanese military headquarters in Khartoum, which had resulted in significant fatalities, the Chairperson of the AU Commission urged that an immediate and transparent investigation should be initiated to ensure accountability for attacks against civilians. He called on Sudan's Transitional Military Council to protect civilians, and reiterated demands that all Sudanese stakeholders should participate in negotiations aimed at achieving an inclusive accord providing for the establishment of the proposed civilian transitional authority. On 6 June—by which time the Rapid Support Forces had reportedly killed more than 100 civilians and negotiations between opposition representatives and the interim military council had stalled—the AU suspended Sudan from participation in its activities, pending the introduction of civilian transitional rule. A political agreement, negotiated under AU auspices, was concluded in July, and a formal power-sharing arrangement was signed in early August. In early September, following the appointment of a new Prime Minister and cabinet, the AU Peace and Security Council resolved to lift Sudan's suspension from the organization. In early September 2020 the Chairperson of the AU Commission welcomed the recent adoption by the SPLM-North faction (active in Darfur) of a statement of principles that backed a peace agreement that had been initialled on 31 August, in Juba, South Sudan, by the Transitional Government of Sudan and five opposition groupings (excluding SPLM-North). UNAMID officially ended its mandated operational phase on 31 December 2020, and entered a final six-month drawdown period on 1 January 2021. Meanwhile, a new UN political mission, the UN Integrated Transition Assistance Mission in Sudan, was established. Almost immediately, from January 2021, intercommunal violence escalated in El Geneina (West Darfur), as well as in Tawila (North Darfur) and East Jebel Marra (South Darfur), generating renewed population displacement in the region.

In mid-September 2021 the Chairperson of the AU Commission condemned an attempt by the military to seize power in Sudan. On 25 October the Transitional Government of Sudan was overthrown in a military coup, the transitional institutions dissolved and the civilian leadership detained. The Chairperson of the AU Commission stated 'deep dismay' at this development, and urged dialogue and the release of all the detained leaders. Although the Prime Minister, Abdalla Hamdok, was released on 26 October, he remained under the 'close surveillance' of the military, and other senior members of the transitional administration continued to be detained. Later that day the Peace and Security Council suspended Sudan, once again, from participation in the organization's activities. Hamdok resigned the premiership in January 2022. In February the 35th AU ordinary Assembly stated deep concern over violent clashes that had intensified since 2021 at the Sudan–Ethiopia border. At the end of March 2022 the international Friends of Sudan Group (including Canada, France, Germany, Italy, the Netherlands, Norway, Saudi Arabia, Sweden, the United Arab Emirates and the United Kingdom) welcomed ongoing collaboration between the AU, IGAD and the UN mission in Sudan (UNITAMS) to facilitate a political process aimed at resolving the political crisis in Sudan. From April the AU, IGAD and UNITAMS initiated a new phase of the process, convening discussions with stakeholders to the Juba Peace Agreement in order to advance more formal political dialogue. They issued a joint statement, as the Trilateral Mechanism, in mid-May urging a lifting of the country's state of emergency and an end to violence on the part of the authorities, and reiterated their support to restoring constitutional order. At the end of May Sudan's military regime issued a decree ending the state of emergency. The Trilateral Mechanism aimed to initiate direct talks between the Sudanese stakeholders.

INTERNATIONAL CO-OPERATION

EU-Africa Summits: In April 2000 the first EU-Africa summit of heads of state and of government was held in Cairo. The second EU-Africa summit meeting was initially to have been held in April 2003 but was postponed, owing to disagreements concerning the participation of President Mugabe of Zimbabwe, against whom the EU had imposed sanctions. Held eventually in December 2007, in Lisbon, Portugal, the summit adopted a Joint Africa-EU Strategy (JAES), outlining a long-term vision of the future partnership between the two regions. Convened in Brussels, Belgium, in April 2014, the fourth EU-Africa summit adopted a Pan-African Programme, which aimed to support the AU's continental integration vision during 2014–20, at a total cost of €845m. The objectives of the programme included improving trade relations and increasing mobility across regions, and strengthening the continental response to transnational challenges, including security, migration and climate change. A Joint Africa-EU Task Force meets regularly to consider areas of co-operation. The fifth EU-Africa summit was convened in November 2017, in Abidjan, Côte d'Ivoire, with a focus on 'Youth'. A joint AU-EU-UN Task Force on Migration was established to address the ongoing migrant crisis in Libya.

The sixth EU-Africa summit was convened in February 2022, in Brussels, Belgium. An €150,000m. Africa-Europe Investment Package was announced, and the EU reaffirmed a commitment to donate 450m. COVID-19 vaccine doses to Africa. An EU-Africa Business Forum was held alongside the summit, in a hybrid (online and in-person) format.

Forum on China-Africa Cooperation: Co-operation between African states and China is undertaken within the framework of the Forum on China-Africa Cooperation (FOCAC). The first FOCAC ministerial conference was held in October 2000, and subsequently conferences have been held every three years. The eighth FOCAC ministerial meeting, held in late November 2021, in Dakar, Senegal, adopted a China-Africa Cooperation Vision 2035; the Dakar Action Plan covering 2022–24 (the first phase of Vision 2035); the Sino-African Declaration on Climate Change; and a general Declaration. Nine programmes were to be implemented under the Dakar Action Plan. These included a medical and health programme, under which, *inter alia,* China was to donate 600m. further COVID-19 vaccine doses to Africa, and to provide 400m. doses through joint Chinese-African production; poverty reduction, agricultural, and trade and investment programmes; a digital innovation programme; green initiatives; capacity building support; cultural initiatives; and a peace and security programme (which was to include military assistance to the AU). Addressing the conference by videolink, China's President Xi Jinping pledged continued support for expanding Africa's local capacity for COVID-19 vaccine production, and to promote vaccine waiver exemptions. A reduced Chinese financial commitment, totalling US $40,000m., was made for 2022–24, compared with $60,000m. in 2019–21. (Concerns over some African nations' debt dependency on China had been raised in recent years.) Themed 'Deepen China-Africa Partnership and Promote Sustainable Development to Build a China-Africa Community with a Shared Future in the New Era', the eighth FOCAC focused on Africa-China co-operation in aligning synergies between the Belt and Road Initiative (launched by China in 2013, with the aim of developing infrastructure and trade along traditional trade routes between Asia, Europe and Africa), the AU's Agenda 2063, the UN's 2030 Agenda for Sustainable Development, and the national development strategies of African states. The seventh China-Africa Business Forum was staged alongside the conference. From 2014 China superseded the USA as Africa's primary source of foreign direct investment.

A Ministerial Forum of China-Africa Health Development was held in October 2016, in Cape Town, South Africa. In August 2018 the interim secretariat of a new China-Africa Environmental Cooperation Centre (approved by the sixth FOCAC, held in December 2015) was inaugurated in Nairobi. An AU office opened in Beijing in October.

An extraordinary China-Africa Summit on Solidarity against COVID-19—jointly proposed by China, the AU and the FOCAC chairmanship—was convened by videoconference in mid-June 2020. The third session of an AU-China Human Rights Dialogue was held (in a virtual format) in September 2021.

AU-Russia Co-operation: The inaugural AU-Russia summit and Russia-Africa Business Forum were organized in October 2019, in Sochi, Russian Federation.

Africa-Caribbean Community: An inaugural Africa-Caribbean Community summit meeting was convened, in a virtual format, in September 2021.

Africa-UN Cooperation: The inaugural AU-UN Periodic Coordination Meeting was convened (in a virtual format) in June 2022.

Finance

In mid-2019 the AU Assembly agreed a budget of US $647m. for 2020, of which $273m. was for peace support operations, $217m. for the programme budget, and $57m. to fund operational expenditure. Some 38% of expenditure (including the whole operating budget) was to be derived from assessed contributions from member states, and the remaining 61% (including 41% of the programme budget) from partners. The AU Foundation, inaugurated in February 2014, aims to mobilize voluntary contributions towards the financing of development priorities throughout the continent.

Publications

African Human Rights Yearbook.
AU Echo.
AU Handbook (annually).

Specialized Agencies

Africa Centres for Disease Control and Prevention (Africa CDC): POB 3243, Addis Ababa, Ethiopia; tel. (11) 5517700; e-mail africacdc@africa-union.org; internet africacdc.org; f. 2017; aims to support AU member states in responding to public health emergencies; comprises Regional Collaborating Centres in Libreville, Gabon (for Central Africa), Nairobi, Kenya (East Africa), Cairo, Egypt (North Africa), Lusaka, Zambia (Southern Africa), and Abuja, Nigeria (West Africa); supports region-wide surveillance, public health information activities, and works to strengthen public health institutes and networks of laboratories; in late Jan. 2020 activated its Incident Management System to address the COVID-19 crisis; undertook to support mem. countries to contain the spread of the virus through training in surveillance, detection, laboratory testing and case management; produced a digest of global guidelines and scientific studies relating to the virus; in March adopted an Africa Joint Continental Strategy for the COVID-19 Outbreak; from Sept. worked with WHO to establish a COVID-19 sequencing network of laboratories; during 2021 a digital CDC COVID-19 Travel Pass was developed; in April 2021 launched, with the AU, a Partnerships for African Vaccine Manufacturing (PAVM) framework; in Feb. extended support to Guinea and Rep. of Congo following new outbreaks of Ebola Virus Disease; organized in Dec. the inaugural International Conference on Public Health in Africa; in July 2022 the AU Exec. Council approved a revised statute of Africa CDC to enable it to become an autonomous health agency; Dir Dr AHMED OGWELL OUMA (acting).

African Academy of Languages (ACALAN): ACI 2000 Hamdallaye, Porte 223, rue 394 Bamako, Mali; tel. 20-29-04-59; fax 20-29-04-57; e-mail info@acalan.tv; internet acalan-au.org; f. 2006; fosters continental integration and devt through the promotion of the use—in all domains—of African languages; aims to restore the role and vitality of indigenous languages (estimated to number around 2,035), and to reverse the negative impact of colonialism on their perceived value; works through a structure of National Language Structures and Vehicular Cross-border Language Commissions; implements a Training of African Languages Teachers and Media Practitioners Project; promotes a Pan-African Masters and PhD Program in African Languages and Applied Linguistics (PANMAPAL), inaugurated in 2006 at the University of Yaoundé 1 (Cameroon), Addis

Ababa University (Ethiopia), and at the University of Cape Town (South Africa); in Feb. 2022 the 35th AU Assembly endorsed Kiswahili as an org.-wide working language; Exec. Sec. Prof. LANG FAFA DAMPHA (The Gambia).

African Capacity Building Foundation (ACBF): 2 Fairbairn Dr., Mount Pleasant, Harare, Zimbabwe; tel. (4) 304663; e-mail root@ acbf-pact.org; internet www.acbf-pact.org; f. 1991 by the World Bank, UNDP, the AfDB, African govts and bilateral donors; designated a specialized agency of the AU in 2017; aims to build sustainable human and institutional capacity for sustainable growth, poverty reduction and good governance in Africa; identifies strategies to support the implementation of the AU's Agenda 2063 strategic framework for the long-term socioeconomic transformation of Africa; hosts the secretariat of an African Think Tank Network, and, since 2014, has organized an annual Africa Think Tank Summit to promote the exchange of innovative solutions and peer learning aimed at advancing Africa's devt agenda; mems: 36 African and 13 non-African govts, the AfDB, World Bank and UNDP; Exec. Sec. Prof. EMMANUEL NNADOZIE (Nigeria).

African Civil Aviation Commission (AFCAC): 1 route de l'Aéroport International LSS, BP 8898, Dakar, Senegal; tel. 33-859-88-00; fax 33-820-70-18; e-mail secretariat@afcac.org; internet www.afcac .org; f. 1969 jtly by the OAU and International Civil Aviation Organization; became an AU specialized agency in 1978; promotes co-ordination and better utilization and devt of African air transport systems and the standardization of aircraft, flight equipment and training progs for pilots and mechanics; organizes working groups and seminars, and compiles statistics; mems: 54 states; Sec.-Gen. ADEFUNKE ADEYEMI.

African Risk Capacity (ARC): Bldg 1, Sunhill Park, 1 Eglin Rd, Sunninghill, 2157 Johannesburg, South Africa; tel. (11) 5171535; e-mail info@arc.int; internet www.africanriskcapacity.org; f. 2012 under the African Risk Capacity Establishment Agreement (which had 34 signatories and had been ratified by 11 states at Sept. 2022); aims to finance risk resistance and contingency measures; uses satellite weather surveillance and World Food Programme-developed software to assess, and disburse immediate funding to, mem. states affected by a natural disaster; in May 2016 the ARC signed MOUs with the AfDB and the Conférence Inter-Africaine des Marchés d'Assurance on future collaboration in planning, preparation and response to extreme weather events and natural disasters; they concluded a further MOU in Aug. 2017 affirming co-operation on strengthening mechanisms to manage weather-related risk; Dir-Gen. IBRAHIMA CHEIKH DIONG (Senegal).

African Telecommunications Union (ATU): ATU Secretariat, POB 35282 Nairobi, 00200 Kenya; tel. (20) 2322120; fax (20) 2322124; e-mail sg@atuuat.africa; internet atuuat.africa; f. 1999 as successor to Pan-African Telecommunications Union (f. 1977); promotes the devt of information communications in Africa, with the aim of making Africa an equal participant in the global information society; works towards universal service and access and full inter-country connectivity; promotes devt and adoption of appropriate policies and regulatory frameworks and the financing of devt; encourages co-operation between mems and the exchange of information; advocates the harmonization of telecommunications policies; mems: 49; 57 assoc. mems comprising fixed and mobile telecoms operators; Sec.-Gen. JOHN OMO (Kenya).

Pan-African Agency of the Great Green Wall (Agence Panafricaine de la Grande Muraille Vert): Lot 414, ilot C, Nouakchott RIM, Mauritania; tel. 45-25-56-88; internet grandemuraillevert.org; f. 2010; co-ordinates implementation of the Great Green Wall initiative; mems: 11 govts; Exec. Sec. Dr IBRAHIM SAID.

Pan-African News Agency (PANAPRESS): BP 4056, Dakar, Senegal; tel. 33-869-12-34; fax 33-824-13-90; e-mail marketing@ panapress.com; internet www.panapress.com; f. 1979 as PanAfrican News Agency, restructured under current name in 1997; regional offices in Khartoum, Sudan; Lusaka, Zambia; Kinshasa, DRC; Lagos, Nigeria; Tripoli, Libya; began operations in May 1983; receives information from national news agencies and circulates news in Arabic, English, French and Portuguese.

Pan-African Postal Union (PAPU): Plot III, Block Z Golf Course, Sekei, POB 6026, Arusha, Tanzania; tel. (27) 2543263; e-mail sc@ papu.co.tz; internet www.upap-papu.africa; f. 1980; facilitates co-operation among mem. states in the improvement of postal services; mems: 45 countries; Sec.-Gen. SIFUNDO CHIEF MOYO (Zimbabwe); publ. *PAPU News*.

Pan African University (PAU) (Université Panafricaine): (Rectorate) BP 5383, Yaoundé, Cameroon; tel. (222) 217090; internet pau-au.africa; f. 2011; Governing Council inaugurated in 2015; aims to develop a network of academic and research centres of excellence across Africa offering postgraduate training in the areas of science, technology, innovation, social sciences and governance; comprises the following specialized institutes: the PAU Institute for Basic Sciences, Technology and Innovation (PAUSTI) (based in Juja, Kenya); PAU Institute for Life and Earth Sciences—including Health and Agriculture (PAULESI) (in Ibadan, Nigeria); PAU Institute for Governance, Humanities and Social Sciences (PAUGHSS) (Yaoundé, Cameroon); the PAU Institute for Water and Energy Sciences—including Climate Change (PAUWES) (Tlemcen, Algeria); and the PAU Virtual and E-University (launched in Dec. 2019) which offers online learning progs; the establishment of a South Africa-based PAU Institute for Space Sciences (PAUSS) was pending.

COMMON MARKET FOR EASTERN AND SOUTHERN AFRICA—COMESA

Address: COMESA Center, Ben Bella Rd, POB 30051, 101101 Lusaka, Zambia.

Telephone: (1) 229725; **fax:** (1) 225107; **e-mail:** info@comesa.int; **internet:** www.comesa.int.

The COMESA treaty was signed by member states of the Preferential Trade Area for Eastern and Southern Africa (PTA) in November 1993. COMESA formally succeeded the PTA in December 1994. COMESA aims to strengthen regional economic and social development, with the ultimate aim of merging with the other regional economic communities of the African Union (AU).

MEMBERS

Burundi	Malawi
Comoros	Mauritius
Congo, Democratic Republic	Rwanda
Djibouti	Seychelles
Egypt	Somalia
Eritrea	Sudan
Eswatini	Tunisia
Ethiopia	Uganda
Kenya	Zambia
Libya	Zimbabwe
Madagascar	

Note: Somalia and Tunisia were admitted as new members in July 2018. COMESA heads of state and of government confirmed in October 2016 that South Sudan was eligible for membership.

Organization

(October 2022)

AUTHORITY

The Authority of the Common Market is the supreme policy organ of COMESA, comprising heads of state or government of member countries. The 21st summit meeting, held in November 2021, was hosted from Cairo, Egypt in a hybrid in-person and virtual format, and addressed the theme 'Building Resilience through Strategic Digital Economic Integration'.

Chair.: ABD AL-FATTAH AL-SISI (President of Egypt).

COUNCIL OF MINISTERS

Each member government appoints a minister to participate in the Council. The Council monitors COMESA activities, including supervision of the Secretariat, recommends policy direction and development, and reports to the Authority.

COMMITTEES

A Committee of Governors of Central Banks advises the Authority and the Council of Ministers on monetary and financial matters. An Intergovernmental Committee drafts programmes and action plans in all other sectors of co-operation, and reviews the development of the Common Market. Technical committees covering all areas of co-operation submit reports and recommendations to the Intergovernmental Committee. A multi-sectoral technical committee on health was established in November 2021.

The Committee on Peace and Security, comprising senior officials from the ministries responsible for foreign affairs from member states, meets at least once a year to address the modalities of peace and security in the region. Recommendations of the Committee are submitted to meetings of the member states' ministers of foreign affairs.

COURT OF JUSTICE

The Court—based in Khartoum, Sudan—is vested with the authority to settle disputes between member states and to adjudicate on matters concerning the interpretation of the COMESA treaty. It is composed of seven judges, who serve terms of five years' duration, and comprises a First Instance division and an Appellate division. In November 2019 the Court introduced revised arbitration rules.

President: LOMBE PHYLLIS CHIBESAKUNDA (Zambia).

SECRETARIAT

COMESA's secretariat, headed by a Secretary-General and supported by two Assistant Secretaries-General, includes the following technical divisions: Gender and Social Affairs; Industry and Agriculture; Infrastructure and Logistics; Information and Networking; and Trade and Customs Services.

Secretary-General: CHILESHE MPUNDU KAPWEPWE (Zambia).

Activities

COMESA promotes economic and social progress, co-operation and integration, and the eradication of poverty, in member states. A medium-term strategic plan guiding COMESA's goals and activities during the period 2021–25 was aligned on the following 'pillars': market integration; physical integration and connectivity; productive integration; and gender and social integration. It recognized the adverse socioeconomic impacts of the COVID-19 pandemic and prioritized, *inter alia*, trade facilitation; infrastructure development; market integration; industrialization, including the advancement of micro, small and medium-sized businesses (MSMEs) and development of regional industrial clusters; resource mobilization; and the development of institutional and regulatory policies.

TRADE, CUSTOMS AND MONETARY AFFAIRS

In October 2000 an extraordinary summit of COMESA heads of state and of government inaugurated a free trade area (FTA), as envisaged under the COMESA treaty, with nine initial members: Djibouti, Egypt, Kenya, Madagascar, Malawi, Mauritius, Sudan, Zambia and Zimbabwe. Burundi and Rwanda became members of the FTA in January 2004; Swaziland (now Eswatini), meanwhile, obtained a derogation enabling it to participate in the FTA as a non-reciprocating member. In March 2014 Ethiopia and Uganda announced that they were committed to ratifying the instruments of accession to the FTA. The DRC joined the FTA in February 2016 and announced immediate tariff reductions of 40%. Trading practices within the FTA have been liberalized, including the elimination by August 2018 of 97.8% of all non-tariff barriers (NTBs), thereby enabling the free internal movement of goods, services and capital. New NTB Regulations, providing guidance on the elimination of barriers, were adopted in December 2015. COMESA technical experts met in September 2019 to address means of further liberalizing the services sector. In March 2021 COMESA launched an NTBs Regional Forum, with participation by national monitoring committees and focal points. As at October 2022 16 of the 19 member states were fully implementing the FTA (including Tunisia, since 2021). At that time members were urged to maximize their usage of available preferences under the FTA, to enhance regional trade integration and resilience.

A COMESA Customs Union (CU), with a common external tariff set at 0% for capital goods and raw materials, 10% for intermediate goods and 25% for finished products, was launched at the 13th annual summit meeting of the Authority, in June 2009. The full operationalization of the CU was, however, delayed. A COMESA Simplified Trade Regime (STR) was launched in 2010, with the aim of reducing trade-related documentation and procedures for small cross-border traders. A Protocol establishing a COMESA Fund, which assists member states in addressing structural imbalances in their economies, came into effect in November 2006. In March 2011 a Nairobi, Kenya-based COMESA Monetary Institute was inaugurated, tasked with enhancing the implementation of a monetary co-operation programme, in support of an eventual monetary union, which COMESA intends to establish by 2030. A regional payments and settlement system (REPSS), headquartered in Lusaka, became operational in October 2012, and facilitates the swift, cost-efficient transfer of funds between traders in COMESA member states through the pre-funding of commercial bank accounts held within,

and guaranteed by, participating central banks. By 31 January 2020 more than US \$138m. in transactions had passed through the REPSS. At that time it had nine participating states: the DRC, Egypt, Eswatini, Kenya, Malawi, Mauritius, Rwanda, Uganda and Zambia, while Burundi, Djibouti, Sudan and Zimbabwe were reportedly in an advanced preparatory stage prior to membership.

In February 2021 COMESA issued a report that focused on the potential of the AfCFTA for stimulating intra-COMESA trade. In September it was noted that intra-COMESA exports with a value of US \$905m. had been lost as a result of measures implemented to contain the spread of COVID-19; the digitalization of trade was recommended. The 21st COMESA summit meeting held in November called for the equitable global distribution of COVID-19 vaccines, especially with regard to Africa, and commended member states such as Egypt, Rwanda and Uganda that were actively undertaking initiatives to produce COVID-19 vaccines. All member states were urged to scale up investment in research and innovation in the health sector. The meeting endorsed the establishment of a new multisectoral technical committee on health.

COMESA's Regional Customs Transit Guarantee Scheme (RCTG-CARNET), launched in 2012, facilitates the movement of goods through the region by providing the necessary customs security and guarantee to transit countries. South Sudan (not yet a member of COMESA) joined the Scheme in May 2016. In March 2021 COMESA and the Africa Export-Import Bank (Afreximbank) signed an agreement under which Afreximbank was to act as a guarantor for RCTG-CARNET. In June 2013 a pilot version of a COMESA Virtual Trade Facilitation System (CVTFS) was launched to cover routes from Mombasa, Kenya to the DRC, Rwanda and Uganda, and in August the CVTFS pilot was extended to cover the Djibouti–Addis Ababa, Ethiopia–Khartoum, Sudan–Juba, South Sudan trade corridor. In accordance with plans to extend the CVTFS further, across the Malawi–Zambia–Zimbabwe trade corridor, the System was established in Malawi in July 2014, and in July 2016 it was extended to the DRC, on the Matadi–Kinshasa Corridor.

A European Union (EU)-funded COMESA Cross Border Trade Initiative was being implemented during May 2018–December 2024.

A COMESA Protocol on the Gradual Relaxation and Eventual Elimination of Visa Requirements ('Visa Protocol') was adopted in 1984. By 2022 only Burundi, Kenya, Rwanda and Zimbabwe were implementing the 2001 Protocol on the Free Movement of Person, Services, Labour and the Right of Establishment and Residence.

A COMESA Statistics Strategy covering the period 2021–25 was focused on advancing regional integration. Statistical data is collated in the online COMSTAT Data Hub.

From 2000 the secretariats of COMESA and SADC undertook a programme of co-operation aimed at reducing the duplication of roles between the two organizations. A co-ordinating task force was established in 2001, and was joined by the East African Community (EAC) in 2005, as the EAC became involved in the Regional Economic Communities co-operation programme.

In October 2008 the first tripartite COMESA-EAC-SADC summit was convened, in Kampala, Uganda, to discuss the harmonization of policy and programme work by the three communities. Leaders of the 26 countries attending the Kampala summit approved a roadmap towards the formation of an FTA and the eventual establishment of a single African Economic Community (a long-term objective of African Union—AU—co-operation). A COMESA-EAC-SADC Joint Competition Authority was established at the tripartite summit. At the second tripartite summit, held in June 2011, in Johannesburg, South Africa, negotiations were initiated on the creation of the COMESA-EAC-SADC Tripartite FTA (TFTA); an agreement establishing the TFTA was concluded in June 2015 (at January 2022 this had 11 ratifications, and required a further three to enter into force). In May 2018 COMESA-EAC-SADC chiefs of immigration authorities met to address means of introducing free movement for business people throughout the TFTA. On 31 July 2020 Tripartite Guidelines for the Movement of Persons, Goods and Services across the Tripartite Region during the COVID-19 Pandemic were introduced, based on guidelines developed by COMESA.

INDUSTRY AND INVESTMENT PROMOTION

In September 2017 COMESA ministers responsible for trade and industry adopted a regional common industrialization policy, covering the period 2017–26.

A COMESA Business Council was inaugurated in 2003, with a mandate to provide a policy and advocacy platform for regional private sector interests. The 13th COMESA Business Forum was organized in July 2018, in Lusaka. In October 2021 the COMESA Competition Commission published draft guidelines on the implementation of organization-wide competition regulations that had been introduced in 2004.

A COMESA Regional Investment Agency (RIA), based in Cairo, Egypt, was inaugurated in June 2006. The COMESA RIA sponsors an annual investment forum, and in May 2013 organized the first Africa Global Business Forum in Dubai, United Arab Emirates, jointly with the Dubai Chamber of Commerce and Industry. An Agreement on the establishment of a COMESA Common Investment Area was adopted by the Authority in May 2007. In September 2016 COMESA and the Rwandan Government organized the inaugural Global Africa Investment Summit, held in Kigali, Rwanda. In February 2014 COMESA heads of state and of government adopted a COMESA SME Strategy, and urged member states to support the participation of female entrepreneurs in policymaking roles.

INFRASTRUCTURE DEVELOPMENT

A COMESA Infrastructure Fund was established in 2012 to support trade-related infrastructure projects in the region. In March 2014 the management of the Fund was transferred to the Eastern and Southern Africa Trade and Development Bank (TDB).

A World Bank Group-assisted COMESA Regional Infrastructure Finance Facility (RIFF) initiative that was underway over the period July 2020–September 2025 comprised a US $325m. Project and Infrastructure Finance Facility (providing long-term finance to projects administered by the TDB); a $75m. COVID Infrastructure Sector SME Response component (with a focus on the renewable energy sector); and a $25m. technical assistance element.

In March 2009 a Regional Association of Energy Regulators for Eastern and Southern Africa was initiated; this comprised 13 full member states by 2022. An Eastern Africa Power Pool (EAPP) has been established by COMESA, comprising Burundi, the DRC, Djibouti, Ethiopia, Kenya, Sudan, Tanzania and Uganda, as well as Libya and Tanzania (not members of COMESA). COMESA and SADC have the joint objective of eventually linking the EAPP and the Southern Africa Power Pool.

In June 2021 COMESA ministers responsible for infrastructure decided to terminate a project that had been initiated in 2000 to establish a regionwide COMESA Telecommunications Company (COMTEL). The COMESA Secretariat was asked to undertake, instead, a study to assess gaps in telecommunications links between member states.

In mid-2016 reforms were initiated to COMESA's Information Resource Center (which was established in 1992), with the aim of creating a virtual knowledge environment. A COMESA Virtual University of Regional Integration was launched in September 2019. By 2022 this was offering a Master's Degree in Regional Integration accredited by Kenya's Kenyatta University, and a similar Degree accredited by the University of Mauritius. The ninth annual COMESA Research Forum was held in September 2022, in Cairo.

The design of a COMESA Digital Free Trade Area (DFTA) was finalized in November 2017, incorporating measures to use digital technology to facilitate cross-border trade, for example electronic certificates of origin or online trademark registrations. In July 2018 the Council of Ministers established a sub-committee to support implementation of the DFTA. A regional Public-Private Dialogue on Digital Financial Inclusion was held in January 2021. In March COMESA reported that digital finance had thrived in the region since the onset of the COVID-19 pandemic, strengthening financial inclusion through the extension of services (such as mobile phone cash transfers) to hitherto unbanked people.

COMESA initiatives to facilitate travel in the region include a scheme for third-party motor vehicle insurance (the Yellow Card Scheme) and a road customs declaration document.

A COMESA Airspace Integration project aims to develop a single, seamless subregional airspace. In July 2014 the inaugural meeting was held, in Kigali, of a steering committee for the project, comprising representatives from Burundi, Egypt, Madagascar, Rwanda and Sudan. In June 2017 a meeting was convened of regional experts determined to undertake a COMESA Seamless Upper Airspace project during 2018–25. A COMESA Airspace Agreement was approved by COMESA ministers of justice in May 2018. In March 2022 COMESA and African Civil Aviation Commission aviation experts met to harmonize their workplans and strengthen institutional arrangements for the implementation of the AU's Single African Air Transport Market initiative (q.v.).

AGRICULTURE, ENVIRONMENT AND NATURAL RESOURCES

COMESA maintains a Food and Agricultural Marketing Information System, providing up-to-date data on the subregional food security situation. A regional food security programme aims to ensure continuous adequate food supplies. A COVID-19 Food Security Response Plan for the region was adopted by the Council of Ministers in November 2020. In September 2022 COMESA and partners launched a digital Regional Food Balance Sheet, which aimed to advance the application of advanced remote sensing and analytical technologies to strengthen food commodity forecasting in the region. The organization supports the establishment of common agricultural standards and phytosanitary regulations throughout the region in order to stimulate trade in food crops. In June 2009 the Alliance for Commodity Trade in Eastern and Southern Africa (ACTESA),

launched in the previous year by COMESA ministers responsible for agriculture with the aim of integrating small farmers into national, regional and international markets, became a specialized agency of COMESA. In March 2010 COMESA and ACTESA signed an agreement aimed at accelerating the implementation of regional initiatives in agriculture, trade and investment. In February 2014 the COMESA Authority adopted a policy on commercial planting, trade and emergency food assistance involving genetically modified organisms. In March 2015 regional experts validated an implementation plan for a COMESA policy on biotechnology and biosafety. A COMESA Seed Harmonization Implementation Plan (COMSHIP) was initiated in November 2019, with a view to enhancing seed production and the competitiveness of the regional seed industry. In December 2021 the COMESA Secretariat, in the context of COMESA's Regional Enterprise Competitiveness and Access to Markets Programme (RECAMP), convened a dialogue on enhancing SMEs' engagement in regional and international fisheries and fish product value chains. In 2022 COMESA was co-ordinating Climate Smart Agriculture (CSA) pilot programmes in Eswatini, Madagascar, Seychelles, Uganda and Zimbabwe.

CLIMATE CHANGE ADAPTATION

Following a recommendation by the AU, in January 2007, that climate change adaptation strategies should be integrated into African national and subregional development planning and activities, COMESA launched a Climate Change Initiative. A COMESA climate action virtual knowledge management portal was initiated in July 2021. In December the COMESA Secretariat organized a regional meeting to validate an implementation plan and resource mobilization strategy for a new COMESA Regional Resilience Framework (RRF); the RRF, which had been finalized in late 2019, was focused on building resistance to climate change and to disasters such as droughts, cyclones, landslides and disease epidemics.

GENDER AND SOCIAL AFFAIRS

The COMESA Secretariat's Gender and Social Affairs division, established in 2008, aims to facilitate increased involvement by COMESA in areas related to social development, including health, education, youth affairs, and migration and labour. A COMESA Social Charter, opened for signature in April 2015, aimed to incorporate social dimensions into the regional integration agenda, through the identification of economic and social rights-related benchmarks. In 2013 a Migration Dialogue from the COMESA Member States was inaugurated. COMESA released the first edition of a *Gender Statistics Bulletin* in March 2018. A Gender Policy Implementation Plan, aimed at strengthening gender mainstreaming at all levels of the organization, was endorsed in November 2021 by the 21st COMESA summit meeting. The 21st summit also endorsed the establishment of a COMESA Youth Advisory Panel. The second annual high-level conference of ministers responsible for youth was convened in July 2022, in Harare, Zimbabwe.

In July 2018 COMESA, the EAC and the Economic Community of West African States launched an African Development Bank-funded online women's economic empowerment project, 50 Million African Women Speak (50MAWS), with the aim of providing financial and other information to women entrepreneurs. A 50MAWS Digital Platform was initiated in November 2019.

GOVERNANCE, PEACE AND SECURITY

Meetings of member states' ministers of foreign affairs address recommendations made by COMESA's Committee on Peace and Security, which met for the first time in 2000. It was announced in September 2002 that the COMESA Treaty was to be amended to provide for the establishment of a formal conflict prevention and resolution structure to be governed by member countries' heads of state. COMESA's programme on Governance, Peace and Security has pillars of conflict prevention, conflict management and post conflict reconstruction.

COMESA participates, with other regional economic communities in the AU's Continental Early Warning System, and has, since 2008, taken part in joint technical meetings and training sessions in this respect. In June 2009 COMESA inaugurated the regional COMWARN early warning system, which was to monitor indicators of vulnerability to conflict in member states. A COMWARN structural vulnerability assessment model has been developed. A COMESA Peace and Prosperity Index tracks drivers associated with peace and prosperity in member states, with input from COMWARN.

A COMESA Committee of Elders, tasked with undertaking preventive peacebuilding assignments, met for the first time in December 2011. In November 2013 COMESA ministers responsible for justice adopted rules of procedure for the Committee of Elders, aimed at guiding its activities. In 2022 the Committee comprised elected members from nine member states.

A COMESA Trading for Peace programme—using trade as a peacebuilding mechanism—is implemented in countries that are emerging from conflict. COMESA's War Economy programme, meanwhile, aims to enhance legal frameworks to support the economies in conflict-affected countries.

In February 2016 COMESA concluded an MOU with the Communauté économique des pays des Grands Lacs aimed at deepening co-operation on economic development, peace and security.

COMESA, the EAC, IGAD, and the Indian Ocean Commission jointly support the Programme to Promote Regional Maritime Security in the Eastern and Southern Africa-Indian Ocean region (MASE), aimed at combating piracy in the Indian Ocean.

Under its programme on democracy and governance COMESA deploys teams of observers to monitor elections held in member states. An AU-COMESA election mission (the first such joint mission) observed the general election that was held in Kenya in August 2022.

Finance

COMESA is financed by member states.

Publications

Annual Report.
e-COMESA Newsletter (weekly).
Key Issues in Integration.
Official Gazette.

COMESA Institutions

Africa Leather and Leather Products Institute (ALLPI): POB 2358, 1110 Addis Ababa, Ethiopia; tel. (11) 4390330; e-mail executive .director@allpi.int; internet www.allpi.int; f. 1990 as the PTA Leather Institute; subsequently renamed as the COMESA Leather and Leather Products Institute, present name adopted in 2018; Exec. Dir Prof. MWINYIKIONE MWINYIHIJA.

African Trade Insurance Agency (ATI): POB 10620, 00100-GPO, Nairobi, Kenya; tel. (20) 2726999; fax (20) 2719701; e-mail info@ ati-aca.org; internet www.ati-aca.org; f. 2001; promotes trade and investment activities throughout the region; mems: 14 African countries, 10 orgs; CEO MANUEL MOSES (Zimbabwe).

Alliance for Commodity Trade in Eastern and Southern Africa (ACTESA): Corporate Park, Alick Nkhata Rd, 10101 Lusaka, Zambia; tel. (21) 1253572; e-mail info@actesacomesa.org; f. 2008, became a specialized agency of COMESA in June 2009; aims to integrate small farmers into national, regional and international markets; a COMESA Regional Policy on Biotechnology and Biosafety was revitalized under ACTESA's auspices from 2020; Pres. JASON SCARPONE; CEO Dr JOHN MUKUKA.

COMESA Business Council: COMESA Centre, Ben Bella Rd, POB 30051, 101101 Lusaka, Zambia; tel. (21) 1229725; e-mail info@ comesabusinesscouncil.org; internet www.comesabusinesscouncil .org; f. 2005 as a private sector policy and advocacy platform; helped to organize in July 2021 a High-Level Public-Private Dialogue

themed 'Towards the COMESA Digital Integrated Common Payment Policy for MSMEs'; CEO DICKSON POLOJI (acting).

COMESA Competition Commission: Kang'ombe House, 5th Floor, Lilongwe 3, Malawi; tel. (1) 772-466; e-mail compcom@ comesa.int; internet comesacompetition.org; f. 2004, began operations 2013; Chief. Exec. WILLARD MWEMBA.

COMESA Federation of National Associations of Women in Business (COMFWB): Off Queens Drive, Area 6, Plot No. 170, POB 1499, Lilongwe, Malawi; tel. (1) 774-656; e-mail info@femcomcomesa .org; internet www.femcomcomesa.org; f. 1993 as the Federation of National Associations of Women in Business in Eastern and Southern Africa—FEMCOM, present name adopted in Aug. 2020; aims to promote progs that integrate women into regional trade and devt activities; co-ordinates implementation of the AUDA-NEPAD-funded Business Incubator for African Women Entrepreneurs programme; 2nd COMFWB Trade Fair held in Sept. 2021; has chapters in all COMESA mem. states (in June 2020 the Zimbabwe chapter established a micro-finance institution, Empowered Woman Excel SACCO, to support local women's economic empowerment); CEO RUTH NEGASH (Eritrea).

COMESA Regional Investment Authority (COMESA-RIA): 3A Salah Salem Rd, Nasr City, 11562 Cairo, Egypt; tel. (2) 4055428; fax (2) 4055421; e-mail info@comesaria.org; internet www.comesaria .org.

Eastern African Power Pool (EAPP): POB 100644, Addis Ababa Ethiopia; tel. (11) 6671669; e-mail eapp@eappool.org; internet eappool.org; in Feb. 2005 ministers responsible for energy from Burundi, the DRC, Egypt, Ethiopia, Kenya, Rwanda and Sudan signed the Inter-Governmental MOU on the establishment of the Eastern Africa Power Pool (EAPP); the EAPP was adopted by COMESA as a specialized institution in 2006; Tanzania, Libya and Uganda joined in 2010, 2011 and 2012, respectively; mems: 11 countries; Sec.-Gen. LEBBI MWENDAVANU KISITU CHANGULLAH (Tanzania).

Eastern and Southern African Trade and Development Bank (TDB): Chaussée Prince Louis, Rwagasore, Bujumbura, Burundi; tel. 22224966; fax 2222498; e-mail info@tdbgroup.org; internet www .tdbgroup.org; f. 1983; fmrly commonly known as the PTA Development Bank, rebranded as the Trade and Development Bank (TDB) in 2017; aims to mobilize resources and finance COMESA activities to foster regional integration, trade and sustainable devt; in March 2014 assumed responsibility for managing the COMESA Infrastructure Fund; in Feb. 2016 concluded an MOU with the Export-Import Bank of China on co-operation in infrastructure, project and trade finance, with a view to promoting the economic and social devt of COMESA mem. states; maintains a further principal office in Reduit, Mauritius, and regional offices in Nairobi, Kenya and Harare, Zimbabwe; auth. cap. US $6,000m.; total assets $7,900m. (30 June 2021); mems: 22 from the Eastern and Southern Africa region, 2 non-regional (Belarus and the People's Rep. of China), 14 institutions; Pres. and CEO ADMASSU TADESSE (Ethiopia).

ZEP-RE (PTA Reinsurance Co): ZEP-RE Pl., Longonot Rd, Upper Hill, POB 42769, 00100 Nairobi, Kenya; tel. (20) 2738221; fax (20) 2738444; e-mail mail@zep-re.com; internet www.zep-re.com; f. 1992, as compagnie de réassurance de la zone d'échanges préférentiels; provides local reinsurance services and training to personnel in the insurance industry; a ZEP-RE Academy, offering training, became operational in 2017; in July 2021 hosted (in a virtual format) the 3rd East African Insurance Regulators' Strategic Forum; Chair. CHRISTABEL BANDA (Zambia); Man. Dir HOPE MURERA (Uganda).

THE COMMONWEALTH

Address: Commonwealth Secretariat, Marlborough House, Pall Mall, London, SW1Y 5HX, UK.

Telephone: (20) 7747-6500; **fax:** (20) 7930-0827; **e-mail:** info@ commonwealth.int; **internet:** www.thecommonwealth.org.

The Commonwealth is a voluntary association of independent sovereign states, comprising about one-third of the world's population, linked by a common history and values. The Commonwealth Secretariat, established in 1965, operates as an intergovernmental organization to promote the principles of the Commonwealth, to support sustainable and equitable development in member countries and to co-ordinate activities and meetings.

MEMBERS IN AFRICA SOUTH OF THE SAHARA

Botswana	Lesotho	Seychelles
Cameroon	Malawi	Sierra Leone
Eswatini	Mauritius	South Africa
Gabon	Mozambique	Tanzania
The Gambia	Namibia	Togo
Ghana	Nigeria	Uganda
Kenya	Rwanda	Zambia

Note: In March 2002 Zimbabwe was suspended from participation in meetings of the Commonwealth; Zimbabwe announced its withdrawal from the Commonwealth in December 2003. In May 2018 it submitted an application to rejoin the grouping. The Gambia rejoined the Commonwealth in February 2018, having previously terminated its membership in October 2013. Gabon and Togo were admitted to the Commonwealth in June 2022.

United Kingdom Overseas Territories

British Indian Ocean Territory
St Helena, Ascension, Tristan da Cunha

Organization

(October 2022)

All Commonwealth countries accept King Charles III as the symbol of the free association of the independent member nations and as such the Head of the Commonwealth. The role is not considered to be a hereditary position, although it was confirmed by consensus in April 2018 that the then heir apparent of Queen Elizabeth II should succeed her as Head of the Commonwealth in due course.

In December 2012 Commonwealth heads of government adopted a non-binding Charter of the Commonwealth defining the core values and aspirations of the grouping. It was signed by Queen Elizabeth II (the then Head of the Commonwealth) in March 2013.

MEETINGS OF HEADS OF GOVERNMENT

Commonwealth Heads of Government Meetings (CHOGMs), normally convened every two years, are private and informal and operate by consensus. The emphasis is on consultation and exchange of views for co-operation. A communiqué is issued at the end of every meeting. The planned 2020 meeting was postponed in view of the COVID-19 pandemic. It was eventually held in Kigali, Rwanda, in late June 2022, and addressed the theme 'Delivering a Common Future: Connecting; Innovating; Transforming'. The next (2024) CHOGM was to be hosted by Samoa.

OTHER CONSULTATIONS

An annual Meeting of Commonwealth Foreign Affairs Ministers is convened in New York, USA, on the sidelines of the UN General Assembly. Commonwealth ministers responsible for finance convene prior to the annual meetings of the International Monetary Fund and the World Bank (2022: mid-October). Commonwealth health ministers meet on the sidelines of the annual World Health Assembly (normally held in May, in Geneva, Switzerland). Ministers responsible for civil society, education, the environment, foreign affairs, gender issues, law, tourism and youth also hold regular meetings. Furthermore, biennial conferences of representatives of Commonwealth small states are convened.

Senior officials—cabinet secretaries, permanent secretaries to heads of government and others—meet regularly in the year between CHOGMs to provide continuity and to exchange views on various developments. A Women's Forum, Youth Forum, Business Forum and People's Forum are organized on the sidelines of each CHOGM. A Commonwealth Day is celebrated annually on the second Monday in March.

COMMONWEALTH SECRETARIAT

The Secretariat organizes consultations between governments and administers programmes of co-operation. Meetings of heads of government, ministers and senior officials decide these programmes and provide overall direction. A Board of Governors, on which all eligible member governments are represented, meets annually to review the Secretariat's work and approve its budget. The Board is supported by an Executive Committee which convenes four times a year to monitor implementation of the Secretariat's work programme. The Secretariat is led by a Secretary-General, elected by heads of government to a normally four-year term of office. The Secretariat has observer status at the UN.

The Secretariat incorporates Directorates of Economic, Youth and Sustainable Development; Governance and Peace; and Trade, Oceans and Natural Resources. There are also divisions and units covering, *inter alia,* corporate business; strategy, portfolio and partnerships; human rights; countering violent extremism; and communications.

On 11 September 2022 the first meeting was held between the Secretary-General and King Charles III, who had acceded to the British throne, as Head of State of 14 other Commonwealth realms, and as the Head of the Commonwealth, upon the death on 8 September of his mother, Queen Elizabeth II (whose reign as British monarch had commenced in February 1952).

Secretary-General: Patricia Scotland (Dominica/UK).

Deputy Secretary-General: Dr Arjoon Suddhoo (Mauritius).

Senior Directors: Dr Ruth Kattumuri (India) (Economic, Youth and Sustainable Development), Paulo Kautoke (Tonga) (Trade, Oceans and Natural Resources), Luis G. Franceschi (Kenya) (Governance and Peace).

Activities

The Commonwealth's Strategic Plan covering the period 2021–25 was formulated in line with the Commonwealth Charter, the UN's 2030 Agenda for Sustainable Development, and the 2015 Paris Agreement on countering climate change. It focused on the following strategic outcomes: Democracy and Governance: greater adherence to Commonwealth values and principles and advancement of good governance; Sustainable Development: working towards sustainable and inclusive economic and social development; Resilience and Climate Action: climate-resilience and low-carbon development to respond to climate and ocean emergencies; and Small and Vulnerable States: addressing their needs and concerns in global governance. Cross-cutting themes were to mainstream gender equality and youth empowerment into Commonwealth planning and programmes, and to enhance the participation of women and young people in all aspects of society.

The June 2022 CHOGM, convened in Kigali, Rwanda, issued a communiqué titled 'Delivering a Common Future: Connecting, Innovating, Transforming', which emphasized, *inter alia,* the importance of international law, and the need sustainably to transform food systems, and to co-operate in facilitating safe, orderly, and regular migration. The meeting also issued the Kigali Declaration on Child Care and Protection Reform, which focused on ending forced labour, modern slavery, human trafficking, and all forms of child labour (including the recruitment and use of child soldiers).

DEMOCRACY, GOVERNMENT AND LAW

Promoting Democracy: Through her good offices the Commonwealth Secretary-General works to promote political dialogue in member states, to foster greater democratic space for political and civil actors, and to strengthen institutions. The Secretary-General's good offices may involve 'behind the scenes' diplomacy, sometimes conducted by Special Envoys, to prevent or resolve conflict and assist other international efforts to promote political stability. Advisers may be appointed in support of the organization's long-term promotion of democracy.

In early 2022 a series of Commonwealth Marlborough Dialogues was initiated, as an international forum for discussion on means of resolving global challenges.

In November 1995 Commonwealth Heads of Government adopted the Millbrook Commonwealth Action Programme on the Harare Declaration, to promote adherence by member countries to the fundamental principles of democracy and human rights (as proclaimed in the Harare Declaration, adopted in October 1991). A Commonwealth Ministerial Action Group on the Harare Declaration (CMAG) was established in December 1995 to implement this process. In March 2002 Commonwealth leaders expanded CMAG's mandate to enable it to consider action against serious violations of the Commonwealth's core values perpetrated by elected administrations as well as by military regimes. In October 2011 the Perth CHOGM agreed a series of reforms aimed at strengthening further the role of CMAG in addressing serious violations of Commonwealth political values; these included clearer guidelines and time frames for engagement when the situation in a country causes concern, with a view to shifting from a reactive to a more proactive role. The unjustified postponement of elections, systematic violation of human rights, abrogation of constitutions, undermining of the rule of law and independence of the judiciary, suppression of media freedoms, and closing of the national political space were specified as events that might cause investigation by CMAG.

CMAG's membership is normally reconstituted every two years. In 2022 it comprised Kenya (Chair), Australia (Vice-Chair), Barbados, Belize, Ghana, Malaysia, Namibia, Samoa and the UK.

The Commonwealth, often working alongside observation teams from regional organizations, monitors the preparations for and conduct of parliamentary, presidential or other elections in member countries at the request of national election management bodies or governments. Furthermore, it offers peer support to enhance the functioning of the electoral process, and assists with the strengthening of institutions between elections. A *Compendium of Commonwealth Good Practice on Election Management* was released in June 2016. In April 2018 the CHOGM held in London and Windsor, UK, agreed updated guidelines on best practice for Commonwealth election observation missions.

In November 2019 a tripartite mission comprising the heads of the Commonwealth, African Union and Organisation Internationale de la Francophonie (OIF) visited Cameroon to discuss with stakeholders the ongoing national political and security crisis, and to promote peacebuilding efforts. In February 2020 the Commonwealth Secretary-General strongly condemned an attack on a North West Cameroon village in which 23 civilians (mainly children) were killed. She urged the Cameroon Government to initiate an impartial investigation into the atrocity.

In July 2021 the Commonwealth called for calm, restraint and tolerance in Eswatini, where a series of pro-democracy demonstrations had been organized to demand political reforms to the national system of absolute monarchy. By that time, according to the international human rights organization Amnesty International, at least 20 activists had been killed and around a further 150 injured by the national security forces. Curfews had been imposed and schools suspended by the national authorities, with a view to controlling the unrest. Numerous reports had emerged of incidents of violence and attacks by protesters against public and private property. In October the Commonwealth Secretary-General held discussions with the Eswatini King, Mswati III. At that time she stated concern over continuing civil unrest in the country, emphasizing the need to accelerate inclusive national dialogue, and reaffirming the organization's readiness to support a resolution of the situation.

In August 2022 a Commonwealth observer mission monitored a general election held in Kenya. A Commonwealth mission was also dispatched to observe the general election held in Lesotho in early October.

Rule of Law: The Commonwealth Secretariat works to strengthen the rule of law underpinning strong and accountable democratic governance in member states. In July 2017 a Commonwealth Office of Civil and Criminal Justice Reform (OCCJR) was inaugurated, to provide member states with expert advice and knowledge on the drafting of fair and effective legislation in support of sustainable development and the rule of law. The OCCJR has established a Legal Exchange database of statutes and model laws to support the formulation of legislation. In May 2004 the Secretariat issued the Commonwealth (Latimer House) Principles, outlining relations between parliament, the judiciary and the executive in member states. In July 2015 the Commonwealth issued a series of guiding principles for member countries on the appointment, tenure of office, and removal of superior court judges. The Commonwealth Secretariat assists in combating corruption and financial and organized crime, in particular transborder criminal activities. A triennial meeting of ministers, Attorneys-General and senior ministry officials concerned with the legal systems in Commonwealth countries is organized by the Secretariat. A Commonwealth Law Ministers Declaration on Equal Access to Justice was issued in November 2019, in Colombo, Sri Lanka; this and an accompanying plan of action were endorsed by the June 2022 Kigali CHOGM. In July 2020 legal experts from Commonwealth member states and partner organizations participated in a webinar that addressed maintaining the rule of law during the COVID-19 pandemic. In February 2021 Commonwealth law ministers noted that the pandemic had advanced the digitalization and modernization of judicial services in member states, including the use of videoconferencing in courts.

The Commonwealth Secretariat provides legal and technical support to member states with regard to the establishment of maritime boundary agreements, and to exercising their rights under international law, as well as to issues related to the law of the sea.

The Commonwealth Secretariat facilitates the exchange of knowledge on human rights matters, raises awareness and promotes human rights education, and strengthens the capacities of member states to participate in the UN's Universal Periodic Review (which assesses, cyclically, the human rights situation in all UN member states). An informal Commonwealth Forum of National Human Rights Institutions aims to promote collaboration and to share best practices.

The Secretariat offers advice, training and other expertise in order to build capacity in the national public institutions of member states. The seventh Commonwealth Ministers for Public Service Forum was held in October 2018, in Guyana.

An Association of Anti-Corruption Agencies in Commonwealth Africa was established in 2011. In February 2013, under the auspices of the Association, an Africa Anti-Corruption Centre was established in Gaborone, Botswana. The 12th Commonwealth Conference of Heads of Anti-Corruption Agencies in Africa was hosted by Rwanda in May 2022, in Kigali, on the theme 'Combating Corruption for Good Governance and Sustainable Development in Africa'.

Commonwealth Cyber Declaration Programme: In April 2018 Commonwealth leaders adopted a Cyber Declaration, which focused on strengthening collective cybersecurity capabilities, with a view to combating the presence in cyberspace of hostile criminal groups and state actors, and promoting the internet as a 'powerful' means of boosting socioeconomic development in member states. The Declaration emphasized the need for common standards and harmonized legal frameworks to guide the development of cyberspace. A UK-funded programme initiated at that time to support the implementation of the Declaration comprises the following four projects: African Cyber Resilience; Electronic Evidence Training in the Caribbean; International Co-operation; and Election Cybersecurity. In December 2019 criminal investigators and prosecutors from Commonwealth countries conducted a collective cybercrime investigation exercise.

Combating Violent Extremism: The Commonwealth Secretariat, the IMF and the UN Office on Drugs and Crime jointly published *Model Legislative Provisions on Money Laundering, Terrorism Financing, Preventative Measures and Proceeds of Crime* in December 2016. In January 2017 a Countering Violent Extremism (CVE) Unit became operational within the Commonwealth Secretariat. In August 2021 the Commonwealth convened a virtual summit that aimed to engage young people in CVE.

ENVIRONMENT AND CLIMATE CHANGE

The November 2015 CHOGM resolved to take action to ensure that average global temperatures remained less than a maximum of 2.0°C above pre-industrial levels and to work towards limiting the ongoing upward trend to 1.5°C. In that month, at the conference of the parties (COP) to the UN Framework Convention on Climate Change (UNFCCC) at which the Paris Agreement on climate change was concluded, a supportive Commonwealth Leaders' Statement on Climate Action was issued. The Commonwealth pursued an active presence at the 26th UNFCCC COP, held in Glasgow, Scotland, in November 2021, and organized workshops and side events, in particular to advance the concerns of its small island member states.

A Commonwealth Environmental Investment Platform links entrepreneurs and companies in the environmental sector to each other, and to international investors. Meeting in September 2019, Commonwealth ministers responsible for the environment, climate and oceans committed to working collectively to address the impacts of climate change, to build resilience, and to collaborate on ocean action. In October 2020 an online Commonwealth Disasters Risk Finance Portal was launched.

An inaugural Commonwealth Sustainable Energy Forum was held in June 2019, at which high-level representatives of member states agreed three pillars of action to support a transition to more efficient, low-carbon and sustainable energy systems: (i) Inclusive Transitions; (ii) Technology and Innovation; and (iii) Enabling Frameworks. These pillars became the foundation of a new Commonwealth Sustainable Energy Transition (CSET) Agenda. The second Forum, held in a virtual format in May 2021, addressed the implementation of the Agenda. CSET Action Groups on Youth, Energy Literacy and Geothermal Energy were launched in June 2022.

Commonwealth Climate Finance Access Hub: In November 2013 Commonwealth heads of government endorsed the establishment of the Hub, to be based in Mauritius, in order to facilitate access to climate finance and technical assistance. The Hub became operational in late 2015 and was formally inaugurated in September 2016. In July it was agreed that the Hub's countries of operation would be expanded from 10 to 39. By 31 December 2021 the Hub had mobilized US $46.4m. in financing, and had approved 36 climate mitigation and adaptation projects.

Commonwealth Blue Charter: In recent years the Commonwealth has actively promoted the concept of the Blue Economy, as a model of sustainable development based on the economic contribution of activities from oceans and coastal waters, such as fishing, marine transport, aquaculture and tourism. In April 2018 Commonwealth heads of government endorsed a Commonwealth Blue Charter, enshrining Commonwealth principles on the governance of the world's oceans. The Charter aimed to provide a framework for co-operation in the effective and sustainable management, protection and preservation of the marine environment. Ten action groups were established to pursue the aims of the Charter, covering: Sustainable Aquaculture; Sustainable Blue Economy; Coral Reef Protection and Restoration; Mangrove Ecosystems and Livelihoods; Ocean Acidification; Ocean and Climate Change; Ocean Observations; Commonwealth Clear Ocean Alliance; Marine Protected Areas; and Sustainable Coastal Fisheries. Some 40 governments have signed up to one or more of the groups. In August 2019 the Commonwealth Secretary-General participated—with representatives of UN and other agencies and of governments—in the inaugural meeting of Ocean Ambassadors, held in Malta. She noted at that time that the Commonwealth accounted for the majority of small island developing states and territories, around one-third of the world's coastal ocean, and for some 42% of coral reefs. In May 2021 the Commonwealth Secretariat launched a web tool and handbook to raise awareness among member states of international funding available to invest in ocean-related initiatives.

Other Natural Resources: The Commonwealth aims to assist member countries in the sustainable management of their natural resources, and provides legal and technical support to formulate and implement relevant policies, best practices, regulatory frameworks, and revenue management mechanisms. The Secretariat notably extends expertise on the development of regulatory and financial frameworks for the developing deep sea mining industry (i.e. the extraction of cobalt, copper, nickel, gold and rare earth elements from the ocean floor).

In June 2022 the Kigali CHOGM adopted the landmark (non-binding) Living Lands Charter: A Commonwealth Call to action on Living Lands (CALL), in which member states committed to safeguarding global land resources and implementing co-ordinated action to address biodiversity loss, climate change and sustainable land management.

SMALL STATES

The Commonwealth aims to address the specific needs of small states, accounting for 32 of the Commonwealth member states, of 42 such states defined globally. It provides technical support and advice, with a focus on trade, vulnerability, environment, politics and economics. In October 2017 the Commonwealth and UNCTAD signed a Memorandum of Understanding on promoting sustainable growth in developing countries, with a special focus on island nations. The fifth Commonwealth Global Biennial Small States Conference (GBSSC—the first having been held in London, in June 2010) was convened in March 2019, in Samoa, on the theme 'Building Resilience Through Disaster Risk Reduction'. The 2019 GBSSC included a training session (organized jointly by the Commonwealth and the World Bank) on the mobilization of disaster finance and management of disaster risk. In July 2020, in view of the COVID-19 pandemic crisis, the Commonwealth Secretary-General urged the reconsideration of present eligibility criteria for debt relief that exempted some vulnerable small island states, noting that no Commonwealth small island states (and only six member states overall) qualified for ongoing IMF COVID-19 debt relief, and that some small states, such as Belize and Jamaica, were not among the 30 Commonwealth states granted temporary debt relief by the Group of 20 (G20) major economies. A Commonwealth study that was issued in June 2021 proposed the development of a new Universal Vulnerability Index, which would use more complex criteria than GDP to assess countries' vulnerability and to determine appropriate accessible levels of international finance. In that month the Commonwealth Secretariat announced that a Commonwealth Tourism Action Plan had been prepared, to support recovery in that sector. In November a Small Island Developing States Clean Energy Toolkit was launched jointly by the Commonwealth and the UN Sustainable Energy for All mechanism.

TRADE AND ECONOMY

The Commonwealth actively supports developing member countries to participate in the multilateral trading system, including in World Trade Organization (WTO) negotiations, and promotes policy discourse on issues related to the WTO's Aid for Trade initiative. Active engagement within the G20 Development Working Group is also pursued, to promote the concerns of small and vulnerable states. In March 2015 the inaugural consultative meeting of a Commonwealth Expert Group on Trade, comprising 27 experts from member states, addressed means of promoting a development-friendly global trading

system. The Commonwealth Secretariat has provided assistance to the African, Caribbean and Pacific (ACP) group of countries in the negotiation of economic partnership agreements with the European Union (EU) and more generally supports developing countries in strengthening their links with international capital markets and foreign investors. A Commonwealth Business Forum, with participation by business leaders and senior government officials, is held on the sidelines of the CHOGM.

In November 2015 a Commonwealth trade-financing facility was established, with the aim of boosting trade and investment flows, with a particular focus on small and developing member countries (which were to be provided with up to US $100m. of seed finance under the facility). The inaugural meeting of Commonwealth ministers responsible for trade, industry and investment, convened in March 2017, in London, pledged to maximize 'Commonwealth advantage' to boost intra-Commonwealth trade. The CHOGM held in April 2018 committed to increasing the value of intra-Commonwealth trade to $2,000,000m. by 2030 (compared with an estimated $600,000m. in 2016).

In October 2020 Commonwealth ministers of finance issued (exceptionally) a joint statement in which they called on the G20, the World Bank, the IMF and the so-called Paris Club of creditors to improve vulnerable countries' access to flexible financing and debt sustainability options, in light of the COVID-19 pandemic. In the following month a Common Framework for Debt Treatment was endorsed by the G20 and Paris Club. In July 2021 a new edition of the *Commonwealth Trade Review* reported on the impact of the pandemic on trade and investment in Commonwealth economies during 2020. GDP overall contracted by some 10% in 2020, while trade losses were estimated at up to US $345,000m.

Connectivity Agenda: In April 2018 Commonwealth heads of state and of government endorsed a Connectivity Agenda for Trade and Investment, with the following focal areas: physical connectivity (i.e. trade facilitation, trade information, and best practice on infrastructure development); digital connectivity; regulatory connectivity; business to business connectivity; supply side connectivity; and inclusive and sustainable trade (emphasizing women's and youth economic empowerment).

A 20-member Commonwealth Digital Connectivity Group promotes the sharing of knowledge, best practices and experiences, with a view to promoting digital development. In February 2020 the Commonwealth released a report titled *The State of the Digital Economy in the Commonwealth*, which found that while 85% of citizens of high-income Commonwealth states had access to the internet, the corresponding proportion from low-income Commonwealth countries amounted to only 18%. Women from poorer countries were found frequently to experience a 'double digital divide', as they were less likely than men to have either internet access or to own a mobile phone. The report noted that such disparities drove economic disadvantages and restricted global economic growth. Governments were urged to pursue policies that promoted digital trade, enhanced access to broadband internet, and advanced up-skilling in technology, science and mathematics. In June 2021 a Commonwealth event was convened (in a virtual format) on the theme 'ICT Infrastructure Development Policy: Supporting Data Innovation and Digital Trade'. A webinar on advancing digital skills among young people was also held in that month. A Commonwealth Digital Hub was initiated in February 2022.

At the April 2018 CHOGM an online Commonwealth Innovation Hub was initiated. This comprised accounts of ideas and innovation from Commonwealth member states; data; knowledge products and toolkits; an innovation lab; and a network of partnerships. In early 2020 a virtual Commonwealth Coronavirus Response Centre was established on the Innovation Hub. In July the Commonwealth Secretariat launched a Commonwealth COVID-19 Dashboard, providing relevant data and analysis.

Public Debt Management Programme: The Commonwealth Secretariat advises member states on the development of sound debt management policies and strategies. Its Commonwealth Meridian specialized debt management tool was introduced in July 2019, and was eventually to supersede the previously developed Debt Recording and Management System (CS-DRMS) (first used in 1985, and updated in 2014). In mid-2020 the Secretariat issued guidelines on the use of Commonwealth Meridian and CS-DRMS in the identification and navigation of optimal available COVID-19-related debt-relief instruments. The Secretariat's Securities Auctioning System, initiated in 2008, supports institutions involved in government securities auctions to manage all phases of that process.

SOCIETY AND YOUNG PEOPLE

The Commonwealth is committed to advancing gender equality and youth empowerment. It advocates for the use of sport to promote development, collaboration and reconciliation.

In July 2020 the Commonwealth heads of state and government noted the likely economic impacts of the COVID-19 crisis on young people, women, girls and other economically marginalized groups.

The leaders emphasized that inclusiveness should be central to economic recovery, social protection, and to the provision of educational and health services. In September the Commonwealth Secretariat and NO MORE Foundation launched a 'Commonwealth Says NO MORE' digital portal, which aimed to support governments, organizations and individuals to prevent and address domestic and sexual violence, particularly in the context of the social isolation and distancing measures that had been widely imposed to contain the COVID-19 pandemic.

Young People: A Commonwealth Youth Programme (CYP), funded by dedicated voluntary contributions from governments, works to promote the involvement of young people in the economic and social development of their countries. The Programme administers a Youth Study Fellowship scheme, a Diploma in Youth Development Work, a Youth Project Fund, a Youth Exchange Programme (in the Caribbean), and a Youth Development Awards Scheme. It also organizes conferences and seminars, conducts research and disseminates information. In April 2018 Commonwealth heads of government agreed that youth priorities should be mainstreamed into member states' national development policies and plans. In 2015 a Commonwealth Young Professionals Programme was initiated, with the aim of encouraging young graduates to contribute to international development. A third edition of the Commonwealth's *Global Youth Development Index* was released in August 2021, assessing progress made (as at 2018—i.e. prior to the onset of the COVID-19 pandemic crisis) for people aged between 15 and 29 in 181 countries with respect to education, employment, equality and inclusion, health, political and civic participation, and peace and security. The first Index had been issued in September 2013. The Commonwealth Youth Forum (which since 1997 has been convened alongside CHOGMs) established a Commonwealth Youth Council (CYC), led by an Executive Committee, in November 2014; a CYC secretariat was inaugurated in Kuala Lumpur, Malaysia, in August 2016. The 10th quadrennial Commonwealth Youth Ministers' Meeting was held in April 2021, in a virtual format. The mental health impact of the COVID-19 pandemic was a focal theme.

Since 2000 Commonwealth Youth Games have been convened at regular (normally four-yearly) intervals.

Gender: Commonwealth Women's Affairs Ministers Meetings (WAMMs) have been held every three years since 1985. The 12th WAMM, held in September 2019, in Nairobi, addressed means of accelerating gender equality and women's empowerment, and gave consideration to a study that outlined progress hitherto achieved in these goals at the national level. The study noted that Rwanda was the only member state to have achieved gender parity in its parliament. A Commonwealth Women Leaders' Summit was convened in July 2016, in London. In December 2020 the Commonwealth Secretary-General issued a statement that warned of the threat posed by the COVID-19 crisis to girls' access to education. Since 2015 a Commonwealth Women's Forum (CWF) has been convened on the sidelines of the CHOGM. The inaugural meeting was held in May 2021 of a Commonwealth Women's Ministers Action Group. In June 2022 the Kigali CHOGM issued a Commonwealth Declaration on Gender Equality and Women's Empowerment.

In May 2015 the Commonwealth Forum of National Human Rights Institutions issued the Kigali Declaration on preventing and eliminating early and forced marriage. The Commonwealth Secretariat was to support member states in implementing the principles enshrined in the Declaration.

Health Policies and Systems: Technical and expert group meetings and workshops are convened regularly to foster co-operation on health matters, and to promote the exchange of health information and expertise. Studies are commissioned, and professional and technical advice is provided to member states. The Secretariat supports the work of regional health organizations. Priority areas of focus are e-health; health worker migration; HIV/AIDS; maternal and child health; non-communicable diseases (NCDs); and mental health. A Commonwealth Advisory Committee on Health addresses public health matters. Since 2015 a Commonwealth Health Hub has provided online support to health professionals and policymakers promoting universal health coverage (UHC) in member countries. In September 2021 the Commonwealth Secretary-General called on the G20 urgently to co-ordinate with the World Health Organization (WHO), WTO, Commonwealth and other agencies to formulate a plan for vaccinating people in the world's 42 smallest states against COVID-19. In May an International Taskforce on Cervical Cancer Elimination in the Commonwealth was inaugurated. A Commonwealth mechanism to track cases of malaria in member states was launched in June. In February 2022 the Commonwealth Secretariat and WHO agreed to strengthen their collaboration in enhancing UHC and resilient health systems in Commonwealth member states, as well as to promote healthy environments and to develop data partnerships. In May the annual meeting of Commonwealth ministers responsible for health issued a joint statement that pledged commitment to achieving vaccine equity, developing resilient health systems, and using digital technology to strengthen health security.

It was reported at the meeting that malaria prevention and treatment services in affected member states had been disrupted during the COVID-19 pandemic, prompting a rise in malaria cases and mortality rates.

In June 2022 Commonwealth heads of government issued the Kigali Declaration on Neglected Tropical Diseases.

Education: An internet-based Commonwealth Education Hub aims to connect education professionals across all member countries. The Commonwealth Secretariat works to improve the quality of and access to basic education in member states; to strengthen science, technology and mathematics education; to improve the quality of management in institutions of higher learning and basic education; to enhance—in accordance with the Pan-Commonwealth Framework on Professional Standards for Teachers and School Leaders—the performance of educational staff; to strengthen examination assessment systems; and to promote the movement of students between Commonwealth countries. Advancing inclusive education—focusing on reaching excluded and underperforming groups—is a priority area of activity. In June 2015 the 19th meeting of Commonwealth ministers responsible for education, in Nassau, Bahamas, established the Commonwealth Education Ministers Action Group (EMAG). The development of a set of universal Commonwealth Quality Standards for Education was announced in June 2016. In February 2017 EMAG endorsed proposals setting out new education policy and curriculum frameworks in member states that aimed to accelerate progress towards achieving the UN's SDGs. An expansion of the number and scope of Commonwealth scholarships was also agreed at that time. Meeting in February 2018, in Nadi, Fiji, Commonwealth education ministers issued the Nadi Declaration: Education Can Deliver, in which they committed to working to ensure 12 years of free, quality education for all. In January 2020 the fifth EMAG meeting reviewed progress in implementing the Nadi Declaration. During that year a set of Educational Guidelines & Resources was added to the Education Hub to assist remote learning during the COVID-19 pandemic. In April 2022 Commonwealth education ministers, meeting in Nairobi, Kenya, emphasized the urgent need to ensure foundational education and skills for all, and determined to explore means of strengthening education financing.

Sport for Development and Peace: The Commonwealth Secretariat promotes sport as a means of advancing development, peacebuilding, health, education, employment creation, human rights and gender equality. A 'Commonwealth Moves' initiative was introduced by the Commonwealth Secretariat in 2020 to promote the importance of sport and exercise to physical and mental health during the COVID-19 crisis. In July a (virtual) Commonwealth Ministerial Forum on Sports and COVID-19, chaired by Kenya, committed to facilitating the safe return of organized sports at all levels, in alignment with WHO and other relevant guidelines. In October a Commonwealth statement was adopted on advancing human rights and addressing discrimination through sport at all levels. The need for investment in the recovery of the sports sector was emphasized.

TECHNICAL ASSISTANCE

Commonwealth Fund for Technical Co-operation (CFTC): f. 1971 to facilitate the exchange of skills between member countries and to promote economic and social devt; it is administered by the Commonwealth Secretariat and financed by voluntary subscriptions from member govts. The CFTC responds to requests from member govts for technical assistance, such as the provision of experts for short- or medium-term projects, advice on economic or legal matters, and training programmes. Public sector devt, allowing member states to build on their capacities, is the principal element in CFTC activities. This includes assistance for improving supervision and combating corruption; improving economic management, for example by advising on exports and investment promotion; strengthening democratic institutions, such as electoral commissions; and improving education and health policies.

Finance

Member governments meet the costs of the Commonwealth Secretariat through discretionary subscriptions on a scale related to income and population.

Publications

Commonwealth Election Reports.
Commonwealth News (weekly e-mail newsletter).
Commonwealth Human Rights Law Digest.
Global Youth Development Index and Report.
Report of the Commonwealth Secretary-General (every 2 years).
Small States Digest (periodic newsletter).
Numerous reports, studies and papers.

Commonwealth Organizations

(in the United Kingdom, unless otherwise stated)

The two principal intergovernmental organizations established by Commonwealth member states, apart from the Commonwealth Secretariat itself, are the Commonwealth Foundation and the Commonwealth of Learning. In June 2016 a new Commonwealth Hub was launched in London, that was to comprise the Commonwealth Games Federation, Commonwealth Local Government Forum, and the Royal Commonwealth Society. In December 2018 the Commonwealth Secretary-General inaugurated a Commonwealth Secretariat Partnerships Strategy, setting out guidelines for engagement with professional or advocacy organizations bearing the Commonwealth's name and associated with or accredited to the Commonwealth. A selection of these (numbering more than 80 in 2022) is listed below.

PRINCIPAL INTERGOVERNMENTAL ORGANIZATIONS

Commonwealth Foundation: Marlborough House, Pall Mall, London, SW1Y 5HY; tel. (20) 7930-3783; fax (20) 7839-8157; e-mail foundation@commonwealth.int; internet commonwealthfoundation.com; f. 1966; intergovernmental body promoting people-to-people interaction, and collaboration within the non-governmental sector of the Commonwealth; supports non-governmental orgs, professional asscns and Commonwealth arts and culture; funds are provided by Commonwealth govts; Dir-Gen. Dr ANNE THERESE GALLAGHER (Australia); publ. *Commonwealth People* (quarterly).

Commonwealth of Learning (COL): 4710 Kingsway, Burnaby, BC V5H 4M2, Canada; tel. (604) 775-8200; fax (604) 775-8210; e-mail info@col.org; internet www.col.org; f. 1987 by Commonwealth Heads of Government to promote the devt and sharing of distance education and open learning resources, including materials, expertise and technologies, throughout the Commonwealth and in other countries; implements and assists with national and regional educational programmes; acts as consultant to international agencies and national govts; conducts seminars and studies on specific educational needs; helps to formulate and facilitates enrolment in massive open online courses (MOOCs); supports a regular Pan-Commonwealth Forum on Open Learning (2022: in Calgary, Canada); core financing for COL is provided by Commonwealth govts on a voluntary basis; mems: 54 countries; Pres. and CEO Prof. ASHA KANWAR; publs *Connections* (3 a year), *Journal of Learning for Development*, *Open Educational Resources: Global Report*.

ADMINISTRATION AND PLANNING

Commonwealth Local Government Forum: Commonwealth House, 55–58 Pall Mall, London, SW1Y 5JH; tel. (20) 7747-6441; e-mail info@clgf.org.uk; internet www.clgf.org.uk; works to promote democratic local govt in Commonwealth countries, and to encourage good practice through confs, research progs and the provision of information; regional offices in Ghana, India and South Africa; mems: 200 in 53 countries; Chair. MPHO MORUAKGOMO (Botswana); Sec.-Gen. LUCY SLACK (UK); publs *Bulletin* (2 a year), *Commonwealth Journal of Local Governance*.

AGRICULTURE AND FORESTRY

Commonwealth Forestry Association: The Crib, Dinchope, Craven Arms, Shropshire, SY7 9JJ; tel. (1588) 672868; fax (870) 011645; e-mail cfa@cfa-international.org; internet www.cfa-international.org; f. 1921; produces, collects and circulates information relating to world forestry and promotes good management, use and conservation of forests and forest lands throughout the world; hosts the secretariat of the Standing Committee on Commonwealth Forestry; mems: 1,200; Pres. JOHN INNES (Canada); publs *International Forestry Review* (quarterly), *CFA Newsletter* (quarterly).

Royal Agricultural Society of the Commonwealth: Royal Highland Centre, Ingleston, Edinburgh, EH28 8NB; tel. (131) 335-6200; e-mail info@therasc.com; internet www.therasc.com; f. 1957; promotes the devt of agricultural shows and good farming practice, in order to improve incomes and food production in Commonwealth countries; mems: 23 countries; Chair. Sir NICHOLAS BACON (UK).

EDUCATION AND CULTURE

Association of Commonwealth Universities (ACU): Woburn House, 20-24 Tavistock Sq., London, WC1H 9HF; tel. (20) 7380-6700; fax (20) 7387-2655; e-mail info@acu.ac.uk; internet www.acu.ac.uk; f. 1913; promotes international co-operation and understanding; provides assistance with staff and student mobility and devt programmes; researches and disseminates information about universities and relevant policy issues; organizes major meetings of Commonwealth universities and their representatives; acts as a liaison office and information centre; administers scholarship and fellowship schemes; operates a policy research unit; mems: more than 500 univs in 50 Commonwealth countries; Sec.-Gen. Dr JOANNA NEWMAN.

Institute of Commonwealth Studies: South Block, 2nd Floor, Senate House, Malet St, London, WC1E 7HU; e-mail ics@sas.ac.uk; internet commonwealth.sas.ac.uk; f. 1949 to promote advanced study of the Commonwealth; provides a library and meeting place for postgraduate students and academic staff engaged in research in this field; offers postgraduate teaching; maintains library comprising 190,000 vols; Dir Dr SUE ONSLOW; publs *Annual Report*, *Newsletter*, *Theses in Progress in Commonwealth Studies*, *Journal of Human Rights in the Commonwealth* (e-journal).

HEALTH AND WELFARE

Commonwealth Medical Association (CMA): c/o International Office, BMA House, Tavistock Sq., London, WC1H 9JP; tel. (777) 351835; e-mail office@commonwealthdoctors.org; internet commonwealthdoctors.org; f. 1952; aims to support and strengthen the capacities of mem. states' national medical asscns; meetings of its Council are held every 3 years; 26th conf.: Nov. 2022, in Kuala Lumpur, Malaysia; mems: 47 medical asscns in 6 regional groupings; Pres. Dr OSAHON ENABULELE (Nigeria).

Commonwealth Pharmacists Association: 66–68 East Smithfield, London, E1W 1AW; tel. (77) 6157-4284; e-mail admin@commonwealthpharmacy.org; internet commonwealthpharmacy.org; f. 1970 (as the Commonwealth Pharmaceutical Association); aims to promote the interests of pharmaceutical sciences and the profession of pharmacy in the Commonwealth; to maintain high professional standards, encourage links between mems and the creation of national asscns; and to facilitate the dissemination of information; holds confs (every 4 years) and regional meetings; mems: pharmaceutical asscns from over 40 Commonwealth countries; Pres. RAO VADLAMUDI (India); Exec. Dir VICTORIA RUTTER (UK); publ. *Quarterly Newsletter*.

Royal Commonwealth Ex-Services League (RCEL): Haig House, 199 Borough High St, London, SE1 1AA; tel. (20) 3207-2413; fax (20) 298-3394; e-mail mgordon-roe@commonwealthveterans.org.uk; internet www.commonwealthveterans.org.uk; f. 1921; links the former service orgs in the Commonwealth and assists former servicemen of the Crown who are resident abroad; holds confs every 5 years; mems: 55 orgs; Sec.-Gen. Lt Col CHRISTOPHER WARREN (UK); publ. *Annual Report*.

Sound Seekers (Commonwealth Society for the Deaf): Studio 410, Pelican House, 144 Cambridge Heath Rd, London, E1 5QJ; tel. (73) 0543-3250; e-mail help@sound-seekers.org.uk; internet www.sound-seekers.org.uk; f. 1959; undertakes initiatives to establish audiology services in developing Commonwealth countries, including mobile clinics to provide outreach services; aims to educate local communities in aural hygiene and the prevention of ear infections and deafness; provides audiological equipment and organizes the training of audiological maintenance technicians; conducts research into the causes and prevention of deafness; CEO KAVITA PRASAD (India).

LAW AND PARLIAMENTARY AFFAIRS

Commonwealth Lawyers Association: c/o Mariner House, 5th Floor, 62 Prince St, Bristol, BS1 4QD; tel. (20) 7841-1075; e-mail info@commonwealthlawyers.com; internet www.commonwealthlawyers.com; f. 1986; seeks to maintain and promote the rule of law throughout the Commonwealth, by ensuring that the people of the Commonwealth are served by an independent and efficient legal profession; upholds professional standards and promotes the availability of legal services; organizes events including a Commonwealth Law Conference every 2 years (2021: Nassau, Bahamas, in Sept.); Pres. BRIAN SPEERS (UK); publ. *The Commonwealth Lawyer Journal*.

Commonwealth Legal Education Association: c/o Commonwealth Secretariat, Marlborough House, Pall Mall, London, SW1Y 5HX; tel. (20) 7747-6415; fax (20) 7004-3649; e-mail clea@commonwealth.int; internet www.clea-web.com; f. 1971; promotes contacts and exchanges and provides information regarding legal education; Gen. Secs PATRICIA MCKELLAR (UK), MICHAEL BROMBY (UK); publs *Commonwealth Legal Education Association Newsletter* (2 a year), *Journal of Commonwealth Law and Legal Education*.

Commonwealth Magistrates' and Judges' Association: Uganda House, 58–59 Trafalgar Sq., London, WC2N 5DX; tel. (20) 7976-1007; fax (20) 7976-2394; e-mail info@cmja.org; internet www.cmja.org; f. 1970; aims to advance the administration of the law by promoting the independence of the judiciary, to further education in law and crime prevention and to disseminate information; organizes an annual conf. and study tours; corporate membership for asscns of the judiciary or courts of limited jurisdiction; assoc. membership for individuals; Pres. CHARLES M. MKANDAWIRE; Sec.-Gen. Dr KAREN

BREWER (UK); publs *Commonwealth Judicial Journal* (2 a year), *CMJA News*.

Commonwealth Parliamentary Association (CPA): Richmond House, Houses of Parliament, London, SW1A 0AA; tel. (20) 7799-1460; fax (20) 7222-6073; e-mail hq.sec@cpahq.org; internet www.cpahq.org; f. 1911; aims to promote understanding and co-operation between Commonwealth parliamentarians; administered by an Executive Committee of 35 MPs; organizes an annual Commonwealth Parliamentary Conf. (2023: Accra, Ghana, in Sept.–Oct.); also regional confs and seminars; convenes an annual Commonwealth Youth Parliament; more than 180 brs in national, state, provincial and territorial legislatures throughout the Commonwealth; Pres. ALBAN BAGBIN (Ghana); Sec.-Gen. STEPHEN TWIGG (UK); publs *The Parliamentarian* (quarterly), *Journal of the Parliaments of the Commonwealth* (quarterly).

MEDIA AND PRESS

Commonwealth Journalists Association (CJA): c/o Canadian Newspaper Association, 890 Yonge St, Suite 200, Toronto, ON M4W 3P4, Canada; tel. (416) 575-5377; fax (416) 923-7206; internet commonwealthjournalists.org; f. 1978; aims to promote co-operation between journalists in Commonwealth countries, organize training facilities and confs, and foster understanding among Commonwealth peoples; 20 affiliates; Pres. CHRIS COBB (Canada); publ. *Newsletter* (3 a year).

SPORT AND YOUTH

Commonwealth Games Federation (CGF): Commonwealth House, 55–58 Pall Mall, London, SW1Y 5JH; tel. (20) 7104-6427; e-mail info@thecgf.com; internet www.thecgf.com; the Games were first held in 1930 and are now held every 4 years; participation is limited to competitors representing the mem. countries of the Commonwealth; 2022 Games: Birmingham, UK (in July–Aug.); mems: 72 affiliated bodies; Pres. Dame LOUISE MARTIN (UK); CEO KATIE SADLEIR (UK).

Commonwealth Students Association (CSA): c/o Commonwealth Secretariat, Marlborough House, Pall Mall, London, SW1Y 5HX; tel. (20) 7747-6462; e-mail youth@commonwealth.int; internet www.commonwealthstudent.org; f. 2012; aims to empower students across the Commonwealth to become partners in delivering SDG 4 ('Ensure inclusive and equitable quality education and promote lifelong learning opportunities for all'), to participate in decision making at the highest levels, and to ensure they are part of education policy formulation, implementation and review; Chair. MUSARRAT MAISHA REZA (Singapore).

Commonwealth Youth Exchange Council (CYEC): Award House, 7–11 St Matthew St, London, SW1P 2JT; tel. (20) 3727-4300; e-mail ival@cyec.org.uk; internet www.cyec.org.uk; f. 1970; promotes contact between groups of young people of the UK and other Commonwealth countries by means of educational exchange visits; provides host govts with technical assistance for delivery of the Commonwealth Youth Forum, held on the sidelines of the CHOGM; administers the Commonwealth Teacher Exchange Programme; mems: 222 orgs, 134 local authorities, 88 voluntary bodies; Dir of Programmes HELEN JONES (UK); publs *Exchange Starter Pack*, *Building Bridges*, *Annual Report*.

In March 2016 a Commonwealth Alliance of Youth Workers (CAYWA) was established.

TRADE AND INDUSTRY

Commonwealth Engineers' Council: c/o Institution of Civil Engineers, One Great George St, London, SW1P 3AA; tel. (20) 7222-7722; fax (20) 7223-1806; e-mail katie.momber@ice.org.uk; internet cec.ice.org.uk; f. 1946; links and represents engineering institutions across the Commonwealth, providing them with an opportunity to exchange views on collaboration and mutual support; holds international and regional confs and workshops; mems: 45 institutions in 44 countries; Pres. PAUL JOWITT.

Commonwealth Enterprise and Investment Council: North Wing, Guildhall, Gresham St, London, EC2V 7HH; tel. (20) 7104-6189; e-mail info@cweic.org; internet www.cweic.org; f. 2014, as a successor to the Commonwealth Business Council; promotes intra-Commonwealth trade and investment and the role of the private sector in devt initiatives; organizes the Commonwealth Business Forum; mems: 52 states; Chair. Lord JONATHAN MARLAND (UK); CEO SAMANTHA COHEN (UK).

Commonwealth Telecommunications Organization (CTO): 64–66 Glenthorne Rd, London, W6 0LR; tel. (20) 8600-3800; fax (20) 8600-3819; e-mail info@cto.int; internet www.cto.int; f. 1967 as an international devt partnership between Commonwealth and non-Commonwealth govts, business and civil society orgs; aims to help to bridge the digital divide and to achieve social and economic devt by delivering to developing countries knowledge sharing programmes in the use of information and communication technologies in the specific areas of telecommunications, broadcasting and the internet; convened in June 2018, in London, jtly with the Commonwealth Secretariat, the 2nd forum of Commonwealth ICT ministers, to discuss recommendations on pan-Commonwealth cyber governance; mems: 37 countries and 3 affiliate member countries; Sec.-Gen. BERNADETTE LEWIS (Trinidad and Tobago); publs *CTO Update* (quarterly), *Annual Report*, *Research Reports*.

RELATIONS WITHIN THE COMMONWEALTH

Commonwealth Countries League (CCL): 29/30 Fitzroy Sq., London, W1T 6LQ; e-mail admin@the-ccl.org; internet www.the-ccl.org; f. 1925; aims to secure equality of liberties, status and opportunities between women and men and to promote friendship and mutual understanding throughout the Commonwealth; promotes women's political and social education and links together women's orgs in most countries of the Commonwealth; supports an associated charity, the Commonwealth Girls Education Fund, to sponsor the secondary education of girls from lower-income backgrounds in their own Commonwealth countries; Pres. DUCHESS WILLIAMS-ALONGA (Bahamas).

Commonwealth War Graves Commission (CWGC): 2 Marlow Rd, Maidenhead, SL6 7DX; tel. (1628) 634221; fax (1628) 771208; e-mail enquiries@cwgc.org; internet www.cwgc.org; casualty and cemetery enquiries: e-mail casualty.enq@cwgc.org; f. 1917 (as Imperial War Graves Commission, present name adopted in 1960); responsible for the commemoration in perpetuity of the 1.7m. mems of the Commonwealth Forces who died during the wars of 1914–18 and 1939–45; provides for the marking and maintenance of war graves and memorials at some 23,000 locations in 150 countries; Dir-Gen. CLAIRE HORTON (UK).

Royal Commonwealth Society (RCS): 40–41 Pall Mall, London, SW1Y 5JH; tel. (20) 3727-4300; e-mail info@royalcwsociety.org; internet www.royalcwsociety.org; f. 1868, present name adopted in 1958; aims to improve the lives and prospects of Commonwealth citizens across the world; the soc. is constituted by Royal Charter and as a charity; organizes meetings and seminars on topical issues, projects for young people, a youth leadership programme; Chair. Dr LINDA YUEH; publs *RCS Exchange* (3 a year), conf. reports.

Victoria League for Commonwealth Friendship: 55 Leinster Sq., London, W2 4PW; tel. (20) 7229-3961; e-mail enquiries@victorialeague.co.uk; internet victorialeague.co.uk; f. 1901; aims to further personal friendship among Commonwealth peoples and to provide hospitality for visitors; maintains Student House, providing accommodation for students from Commonwealth countries; has 7 branches elsewhere in the UK and abroad; Chair. Brig. ANTHONY FAITH; Gen. Man. DOREEN HENRY (UK); publ. *Newsletter*.

ECONOMIC COMMUNITY OF WEST AFRICAN STATES—ECOWAS

Address: ECOWAS Executive Secretariat, 101 Yakubu Gowon Crescent, PMB 401, Asokoro, Abuja, Nigeria.

Telephone: (9) 3147647; **fax:** (9) 3147646; **e-mail:** info@ecowas.int; **internet:** www.ecowas.int.

The Treaty of Lagos, establishing ECOWAS, was signed in May 1975, with the aim of promoting trade, co-operation and self-reliance in West Africa. A revised ECOWAS treaty, to accelerate economic integration and to strengthen political co-operation, was signed in July 1993. This incorporated new provisions for ECOWAS to co-operate in the maintenance of regional peace and security.

MEMBERS

Benin	Ghana	Niger
Burkina Faso*	Guinea*	Nigeria
Cabo Verde	Guinea-Bissau	Senegal
Côte d'Ivoire	Liberia	Sierra Leone
The Gambia	Mali*	Togo

* On 31 May 2021, following the overthrow by the Malian military of the leadership of Mali's transitional administration, that country's membership of ECOWAS was suspended; Guinea's membership was suspended on 8 September, also following a military coup. On 28 January 2022 Burkina Faso was also suspended in response to the overthrow of its democratically elected Government by the military.

Note: A high-level committee was established in December 2017 to consider applications by Morocco, for full membership, Mauritania, for associate membership, and Tunisia, for observer status. All applications remained pending in 2022.

Organization

(October 2022)

AUTHORITY OF HEADS OF STATE AND GOVERNMENT

The Authority is the supreme decision-making organ of the Community, with responsibility for its general development and realization of its objectives. The Chairman is elected annually by the Authority from among the member states. The Authority meets at least once a year in ordinary session, and as required as extraordinary summit meetings. The 61st ordinary session was convened in July 2022, in Accra, Ghana. Extraordinary sessions were convened during 2022 to address the political situations in Mali, Burkina Faso, Guinea and Guinea-Bissau.

Chairperson: Umaro Sissoco Embaló (Pres. of Guinea-Bissau).

COUNCIL OF MINISTERS

The Council meets at least twice a year, and is responsible for the running of the Community; the chairmanship is held by a minister from the same member state as the Chair of the Authority.

ECOWAS COMMISSION

The Commission comprises seven members (reduced in July 2022 from 15): a President, a Vice-President, an Auditor-General, and Commissioners for: Economic Affairs and Agriculture; Human Development and Social Affairs; Infrastructure, Energy and Digitalization; and Political Affairs, Peace, and Security. The members are elected for a four-year term, which may be renewed once only.

President: Dr Omar Alieu Touray (The Gambia).

ECOWAS PARLIAMENT

The inaugural session of the ECOWAS Parliament, based in Abuja, Nigeria, was held in November 2000. The Parliament has 115 seats, and each member is elected for a four-year term. The first ordinary session of the Parliament's fifth legislature opened in May 2021. There is a co-ordinating administrative bureau, comprising a speaker and four deputy speakers.

Speaker: Sidie Mohamed Tunis (Sierra Leone).

ECOWAS COURT OF JUSTICE

The Court of Justice, established in January 2001, is based in Abuja, and comprises seven judges who serve a five-year renewable term of office. The judges hold (non-renewable) tenure for four years. In November 2021 the Speaker of the ECOWAS Parliament urged member states to end a pattern of only partial adherence to rulings

of the Court of Justice. During 2021–March 2022 the Court issued 434 rulings and six advisory opinions.

President: Edward Amoako Asante (Ghana).

Registrar: Dr Yaouza Ouro-Sama.

Activities

ECOWAS promotes regional co-operation and development in economic, social and cultural activities. It is committed to abolishing all obstacles to the free movement of people, services and capital, and to promoting harmonization of agricultural policies; common projects in marketing, research and the agriculturally based industries; joint development of economic and industrial policies and elimination of disparities in levels of development; and common monetary policies.

A revised treaty for the Community was drawn up by an ECOWAS Committee of Eminent Persons in 1991–92, and was signed at the ECOWAS summit conference that took place in Cotonou, Benin, in July 1993. The treaty designated the achievement of a common market and a single currency as economic objectives, while in the political sphere it envisaged the establishment of an ECOWAS parliament, an economic and social council, and an ECOWAS court of justice to enforce Community decisions. The treaty also formally assigned the Community with the responsibility of preventing and settling regional conflicts. At a summit meeting held in Abuja, Nigeria, in August 1994, ECOWAS heads of state and of government signed a protocol agreement for the establishment of a regional parliament. The meeting also adopted a Convention on Extradition of non-political offenders. The new ECOWAS treaty entered into effect in August 1995. A draft protocol providing for the creation of a mechanism for the prevention, management and settlement of conflicts, and for the maintenance of peace in the region, was approved by ECOWAS heads of state and of government in December 1999. In December 2000 Mauritania, a founding member, withdrew from the Community.

In April 2020 an extraordinary session of the ECOWAS Authority, convened by videoconference to address the regional impacts of the COVID-19 pandemic, determined, *inter alia,* to enhance co-operation between the West African Health Organization (WAHO) and the African Union (AU) Africa Centres for Disease Control and Prevention (Africa CDC) and to encourage, where possible, the pooling of purchases of equipment and drugs to combat the disease. Nigeria's President Muhammadu Buhari was appointed as the organization's coronavirus response co-ordinator, and—under his supervision—ministerial co-ordination committees were established to direct the regional pandemic response in the areas of health, finance and transport. In September the ECOWAS Authority urged member states, the ECOWAS Commission and WAHO urgently to advance the regional availability of anti-COVID-19 vaccines and support for regional pharmaceutical industries. The President of the Commission was tasked with appointing a team of specialists to study the feasibility of producing anti-COVID-19 vaccines locally.

In December 2021 the ECOWAS Authority approved a new ECOWAS Vision 2050, focused on the following pillars: peace, security and stability; governance and rule of law; economic integration and interconnectivity; transformation and inclusive and sustainable development; and social inclusion.

ECONOMIC AFFAIRS AND AGRICULTURE

In 1990 ECOWAS heads of state and of government agreed to adopt measures that would create a single monetary zone and remove barriers to trade in goods that originated in the Community. It was announced in September 1992 that, as part of efforts to enhance monetary co-operation and financial harmonization in the region, the West African Clearing House was to be restructured as the West African Monetary Agency (WAMA) tasked with administering an ECOWAS exchange rate system and establishing the single monetary zone. In July 1996 the Authority agreed to impose a common value-added tax on consumer goods, in order to rationalize indirect taxation and to stimulate greater intra-Community trade. On 1 July 1999 regional travellers' cheques entered into circulation. These were issued by WAMA in denominations of a West African Unit of Account and convertible into each local currency at the rate of one Special Drawing Right (see International Monetary Fund—IMF). In December the ECOWAS Authority determined to pursue a 'Fast Track Approach' to economic integration, involving a two-track implementation of related measures. In April 2000 seven member states—Cabo Verde, The Gambia, Ghana, Guinea, Liberia, Nigeria and Sierra Leone—issued the Accra Declaration, in which they agreed to establish a second West African monetary union (the West African Monetary Zone—WAMZ) to co-exist initially alongside the Union Economique et Monétaire Ouest-Africaine—UEMOA, which unites eight, mainly francophone, ECOWAS member states. As preconditions for adopting a single currency and common monetary and exchange rate policy, the member states of the second West African monetary union were to attain a number of criteria (under the supervision of a newly established ECOWAS Convergence Council, comprising member states' ministers responsible for finance and central bank governors), including a satisfactory level of price stability; sustainable budget deficits; a reduction in inflation; and an adequate level of foreign exchange reserves. The two complementary monetary unions were expected to harmonize their economic programmes, with a view to effecting an eventual merger, as outlined in an action plan adopted by ECOWAS and UEMOA in February 2000. The ECOWAS Authority summit held in December, in Bamako, Mali, adopted an Agreement Establishing the WAMZ, approved the establishment of a West African Monetary Institute to prepare for the formation of a central bank, and determined that the harmonization of member countries' tariff structures should be accelerated to facilitate the implementation of the planned customs union. In December 2001 the Authority authorized the establishment during 2002 of an exchange rate mechanism for the proposed region-wide currency; this was achieved in April. In May 2004 ECOWAS and UEMOA signed an agreement that provided for the establishment of a Joint Technical Secretariat to enhance the co-ordination of their programmes. In October 2000 ECOWAS and the EU held their first joint high-level meeting, at which the EU pledged financial support for ECOWAS's economic integration programme, and in April 2001 it was announced that the IMF would provide technical assistance.

Owing to slower than anticipated progress in achieving the convergence criteria required for monetary union, successive deadlines for the inauguration of the WAMZ and launch of the single currency were not met. In October 2011 the Convergence Council adopted supplementary acts to facilitate the process of establishing a single currency. The documents included the Guideline on the Formation of a Multi-year Programme on Convergence with ECOWAS; and the Draft Supplementary Act on Convergence and Macroeconomic Stability Pact among Member States, constituting a formal commitment by signatories to ensure economic policy co-ordination, to strengthen economic convergence and to increase macroeconomic stability. In July 2014 the ECOWAS Commission announced that it had reduced the required macroeconomic convergence criteria for the WAMZ monetary union from 11 to six member states, in order to expedite the process. An ECOWAS common economic, monetary and financial database (ECOBASE), initiated in 2014, was designed to harmonize regional statistical data, in order to advance the monitoring of macroeconomic convergence. In February 2014 a Presidential Task Force was established to further the single currency project (initially comprising the heads of state of Ghana and Niger, the ministers of finance of those countries and ECOWAS central bank governors, later expanded to include the presidents and finance ministers of Côte d'Ivoire, Nigeria and Togo). At its fifth meeting, held in the Ghanaian capital, Accra, in February 2018, the Presidential Task Force urged renewed determination among member states to implement the single currency by 2020 and approved a revised roadmap to achieve that deadline. In December 2018 the ECOWAS Authority authorized the establishment of a committee to name and approve a symbol for the proposed future single currency; the name 'eco' was selected in July 2019. In December the Authority determined that the ECOWAS central bank would be named the Central Bank of West Africa. On 22 December the UEMOA member states and France adopted an agreement that (upon entry into force) would rename the then UEMOA currency (the franc CFA) as the eco, and would reduce its ties to the French Government.

In April 2020 the ECOWAS Authority requested the Convergence Council to give consideration to the implications for regional macroeconomic convergence of the impacts of the COVID-19 pandemic. In September the Authority confirmed that the launch of the common currency in member states would be postponed, noting that this would carry far too much risk, given the adverse economic impacts of the COVID-19 crisis. The Authority stated that the overriding immediate priority of member states was to revive their economies. It also tasked the Commission with supporting the efforts of member states to ensure the suspension of debt servicing obligations, and with negotiating a reduction in the cost of transfers of remittances to member states by the West African diaspora. It was reported in June 2022 that a new deadline of 2027 had been set for the launch of the single currency.

In March 2013 ECOWAS ministers responsible for finance endorsed a five-band regional common external tariff (CET) regime, covering some 5,899 tariff lines, under which a rate of 5% duty was to be applied to 2,146 lines designated as basic raw materials and capital goods; 10% to 1,373 lines designated as intermediate products; and a 20% tariff would be levied on 2,165 lines categorized as final consumer products. A new 1.5% community integration levy

was to replace the existing ECOWAS community levy and UEMOA community solidarity levy, to help to ensure uniformity in port charges. In January of that year a new West African Capital Markets Integration Council was inaugurated, tasked with governing the integration of regional capital markets, and envisaged as a pillar of a proposed West African Common Investment Market. An extraordinary summit of the ECOWAS Authority was convened in October 2013, in Dakar, Senegal, to address in detail matters of critical importance to the consolidation of the regional market, and to the Community levy. The summit meeting endorsed the final structure of the CET and the establishment of a task force on trade liberation. The CET entered into effect on 1 January 2015, and by 2022 was being implemented by Benin, Burkina Faso, Côte d'Ivoire, Ghana, Guinea-Bissau, Mali, Niger, Nigeria, Senegal and Togo.

In January 2003 Community heads of state and of government approved an intraregional ECOWAS Travel Certificate (passport); in 2022 member states were in the process of replacing this with a modernized system of ECOWAS national biometric identity cards. A Customs Code, drafted in consultation with regional governments, customs officials and the private sector, was adopted by ECOWAS heads of state and of government in December 2017. In December 2019 the ECOWAS Authority called on all member states fully to implement free movement, and to make use of the new ECOWAS biometric identity cards. A Brown Card scheme provides recognized third-party liability insurance throughout the region. An ECOVISA project, aimed at harmonizing regional visa processes, was ongoing in 2022.

In April 2020, in response to the COVID-19 pandemic crisis, the Authority agreed that long-term treasury bills and bonds should be issued to finance critical investment needs, to support private sector activities, and to revive economies; that liquidity should be provided through central banks; that assistance should be targeted to the social sector (for example, ensuring internet access and enhancing the provision of distance learning tools) and to ensure social safety nets for the most vulnerable people; as well as to mobilize additional resources from the international community; to support the AU in calling for the cancellation of regional public debt and for the restructuring of private debt; urgently to implement measures aimed at supporting the local production of consumer goods, including agricultural products; to establish a support programme for the health protection equipment and pharmaceutical manufacturing sectors; to avoid imposing intra-regional import restrictions, especially on essential goods; to promote the acceleration of efforts to produce vaccines and effective therapies for COVID-19; and to ensure provision of eventual vaccines at subsidized prices. Economic growth in the ECOWAS region was forecast to rise by 4.8% in 2022, compared with 0.8% in 2020.

An ECOWAS Trade Liberalization Scheme (ETLS) database; ECOWAS Commercial Information System (ECOTIS); and Business Information System (ECOBIZ) are maintained. In June 2020 the website was launched of an EU-funded West African Competitiveness Programme, which includes a West African Competitiveness Observatory, and is orchestrated at the regional level by the ECOWAS Commission, supported by UEMOA.

In November 2014 the Council of Ministers adopted a Regional Strategy for Private Sector Promotion. An ECOWAS Quality Agency was formally constituted in February 2018 during an inaugural ECOWAS Quality Infrastructure Forum, convened in Dakar. ECOWAS maintains an ECOWAS Quality and Industrial Database (ECOQUIB). In July 2021 the inaugural annual General Assembly was convened, in Abuja, of an ECOWAS Trade Promotion Organizations Network, tasked with working alongside the ECOWAS Commission to establish inclusive trade development initiatives throughout the region. In December the Authority adopted an ECOWAS Public Private Partnership (PPP) Policy, aimed at promoting alternative and innovative investment in the region. An ECOWAS Investment Climate Scorecard was initiated in June 2017, under an Improved Business and Investment Climate in West Africa project that was launched in 2014 with the aim of identifying national and regional barriers to investment, tracking proposed reforms to investment policy, and sharing relevant proposed reforms and good practice. In July 2020 ECOWAS launched a website in support of the project.

ECOWAS has a 10% share in a private regional investment bank, Ecobank Transnational Inc., which was founded in 1984 and is headquartered in Lomé.

In June 2010 the Council of Ministers adopted the West African Common Industrial Policy (WACIP) and a related action plan and supplementary acts. WACIP aimed to diversify and expand the regional industrial production base by supporting the creation of new industrial production capacities as well as developing existing capacities.

An ECOWAS automotive industry policy framework, aimed at enhancing member states' national capacities in the areas of vehicle assembling, production and marketing, was validated by a ministerial meeting held in May 2019.

In June 2019 the ECOWAS Authority adopted an ECOWAS Regional Tourism Policy (ECOTOUR), with a focus on developing the region as a competitive tourist destination; a supporting action plan was also adopted, covering the period 2019–29.

From 2013 ECOWAS has implemented a Business Incubators for African Women Entrepreneurs (BIAWE) project, with a particular focus on agri-business, agro-processing and handicrafts. In July 2018 ECOWAS, the East African Community and the Common Market for Eastern and Southern African States launched an African Development Bank-funded online women's economic empowerment project, 50 Million African Women Speak (50MAWS), with the aim of providing financial and other information to women entrepreneurs.

The Community enforces a certification scheme for facilitating the monitoring of animal movement and animal health surveillance and protection in the sub-region. The January 2005 Authority summit endorsed an ECOWAS Regional Agricultural Policy (ECOWAP). ECOWAP 2025, representing an updated version of ECOWAP, was initiated in November 2015. This was supported by a Regional Agricultural Investment and Food Security and Nutrition Plan (RAIFSNP) and National Agricultural Investment and Food Security and Nutrition Plans (NAIFSNPs—implemented by FAO and co-ordinated by the RAAF). A Togo-based ECOWAS Regional Agency for Agriculture and Food (RAAF) was established in September 2013, tasked with implementing the technical aspects of regional investment programmes on agriculture, forestry and livestock. ECOWAS and UEMOA jointly participate in a Food Crisis Prevention Network, which is co-ordinated by the Permanent Interstate Committee on Drought Control in the Sahel, and supported by the OECD's Sahel and West Africa Club. ECOWAS maintains an ECOWAS West Africa Agricultural Sector Information System (ECOAGRIS).

In February 2012 ECOWAS established a Regional Animal Health Centre, hosted by Mali, in Bamako. In June 2022, through the Centre, ECOWAS launched a mass vaccination campaign in member states against Peste des Petits Ruminants, a very contagious disease affecting goats and sheep. The eighth annual meeting of ECOWAS Regional Animal Health Networks (RAHN) was held in September, in Cabo Verde.

A Subregional Action Programme for Combating Desertification in West Africa was initiated in September 2013. The inaugural ECOWAS Hydromet Forum and Disaster Risk Reduction was held in September 2018. In April 2021 the second Forum adopted an ECOWAS Hydromet Initiative, which aimed to strengthen investment in systems that would build resistance against hydrological and meteorological risks; an ECOWAS Disaster Risk Reduction Gender Strategy and Action Plan; and an ECOWAS Flood Risk Management Strategy. An ECOWAS Early Warning Strategic Plan was being implemented during 2022–26.

In March 2010 ECOWAS ministers responsible for agriculture, the environment and water resources adopted a Framework of Strategic Guidelines on the Reduction of Vulnerability and Adaptability to Climate Change in West Africa, outlining the development of regional capacities to build up resilience and adaptation to climate change and severe climatic conditions. ECOWAS supports the development and implementation by member states of Nationally Appropriate Mitigation Actions. An ECOWAS Scientific and Technical Consultative Group on Climate Change (STCGCC) was established in February 2017. An ECOWAS Regional Climate Strategy was under development in 2022.

In September 2013 ECOWAS ministers responsible for forestry and wildlife, gathered in Abidjan, adopted a Convergence Plan for the Sustainable Management and Utilization of Forest Ecosystems in West Africa, to protect regional forests and woodlands, which cover a total surface area of about 72.1m. ha (representing some 14% of the total land area). In April 2019 ECOWAS, FAO (offering technical support) and the Swedish International Development Cooperation Agency (providing US $8m. in funding) agreed collectively to implement a five-year project aimed at strengthening sustainable forest and land management, with a particular focus on transboundary forest threats, in support of the 2013 Convergence Plan.

In July 2019 ECOWAS and UEMOA ministers responsible for the environment, and their counterpart from Mauritania, collectively launched a Programme of Support for the Preservation of Biodiversity and Fragile Ecosystems. In September 2020 the ECOWAS Authority welcomed the adoption of a regional environmental action plan for the period 2020–26.

INFRASTRUCTURE, ENERGY AND DIGITALIZATION

In December 2021 the Authority adopted a long-term ECOWAS Regional Infrastructure Master Plan that was to cover the period 2020–45. The plan was to support 201 projects with a projected total cost of US $122,000m., and included, *inter alia*, 15 road schemes, 13 railway projects, 57 power generation investment initiatives and 31 power transmission projects.

In December 2007, following a recommendation by the Authority, a Togo-based regional airline, ASKY (Africa Sky) was established, which initiated operations in January 2010. In October 2011 West

African ministers responsible for transport concluded a series of measures to establish a common regulatory regime for the airline industry in order to improve the viability of regional airlines and to support regional integration.

A longstanding ECOWAS vision for the development of an integrated regional road network comprises the Trans-West African Coastal Highway, connecting Lagos with Nouakchott, Mauritania (4,767 km), and envisaged as the western part of an eventual Pan-African Highway; and the Trans-Sahelian Highway, linking Dakar (Senegal) with N'Djamena, Chad (4,633 km). In November 2012 ECOWAS and the People's Republic of China concluded an agreement on regional infrastructure development and economic co-operation, which incorporated Chinese support in advancing the Trans-West African Coastal Highway project. In July 2013 the inaugural meeting was convened of an ECOWAS steering committee to guide the implementation of the 1,028 km Abidjan–Lagos corridor road project, linking Lagos (Nigeria), Cotonou (Benin), Lomé (Togo), Accra (Ghana) and Abidjan (Côte d'Ivoire) as well as several other sea ports (forming a section of the Trans-Sahelian Highway). In April 2014 the presidents of Benin, Côte d'Ivoire, Ghana, Nigeria and Togo signed a treaty providing for the establishment of an Abidjan–Lagos corridor management authority, and also providing for the harmonization of trade and transport facilitation procedures along the route, in areas such as customs control, immigration and maritime port facilities. In February 2019 the ECOWAS Commission established a project implementation unit to oversee the Abidjan–Lagos Corridor Highway Development Project. In April 2016 regional ministers responsible for infrastructure, roads and works adopted a Plan of Action for Dakar–Abidjan Corridor Development. A treaty concerning the establishment of a Praia–Dakar–Abidjan Corridor was opened for signature on the margins of the 51st ECOWAS Authority session in June 2017. Cabo Verde joined the scheme in late 2018, incorporating a maritime component. A forum of ECOWAS road infrastructure experts and ministers of justice was convened in March 2017 to address the harmonization of immigration procedures in the context of the overall Trans-Sahelian Highway scheme. A Master Plan for Corridor Development for the West African Growth Ring (covering Cote d'Ivoire, Ghana, Togo and Burkina Faso) was finalized in 2019.

In June 2020 a virtual meeting of a recently established Committee of Experts for Transport, Logistics, Free Movement and Trade in the Fight against the COVID-19 Pandemic strengthened guidelines aimed at the harmonization and facilitation of cross-border trade and transportation throughout the ECOWAS region. In December 2021 the Authority urged member states to ensure that all land borders were reopened from 1 January 2022.

In April 2009 ministers responsible for the development of mineral resources endorsed an ECOWAS Directive on the Harmonization of Guiding Principles and Policies in the Mining Sector. An ad hoc committee convenes periodically to monitor the implementation of the Directive.

An ECOWAS directive on Securitization of Payments Related to Cross-Border Power Trade in West Africa entered into effect on 1 January 2020. In February regional energy ministers, experts and World Bank representatives met to consider related policy.

In 2007 the 600 km West African Gas Pipeline—extending from Lagos, Nigeria, to Takoradi, Ghana—became operational. A study on the feasibility of extending the Pipeline was commissioned in 2015, and the proposed extension has subsequently remained under consideration.

An ECOWAS Energy Protocol, establishing a legal framework for the promotion of long-term co-operation in the energy sector, was adopted in 2003. In May of that year the Community initiated the first phase of ECOWAPP (q.v.), to be implemented in Benin, Côte d'Ivoire, Ghana, Niger, Nigeria and Togo, at an estimated cost of US $335m. A revised masterplan for the advancement of ECOWAPP was being implemented during the period 2019–33. An Accra-based ECOWAS Regional Electricity Regulatory Authority was established in 2008, and a Regional Centre for Renewable Energy and Energy Efficiency (ECREEE) was inaugurated in 2009; ECREEE's secretariat was established in July 2010, in Praia, Cabo Verde. In August 2022 an ECOWAS Regional Off-Grid Electricity Access Project (ROGEAP) was launched in Côte d'Ivoire and The Gambia. An ECOWAS Regional Electricity Code was under development in 2022.

In May 2018 ECOWAS, UEMOA and the EU initiated a regional programme aimed at improving energy governance in West Africa, which aimed to enable the region to meet the challenges that hamper universal access to sustainable energy. In December the ECOWAS Authority endorsed a Master Plan for the Development of Regional Power Generation and Transmission Infrastructure 2019–33 to address the ongoing energy deficit in the region. An updated ECOWAS Energy Policy was being developed in 2022.

A West African Telecommunications Regulators' Assembly (WATRA) was established under ECOWAS auspices in November 2004. The January 2006 summit meeting of the Authority approved a Special Fund for Telecommunications to facilitate improvements to cross-border telecommunications connectivity. In January 2007 ECOWAS leaders adopted a regional telecommunications policy and a regulatory framework that covered areas including interconnection to ICT and services networks, licence regimes, and radio frequency spectrum management. In January 2020 ECOWAS technical experts validated a new ECOWAS Regional Cyber Security and Cybercrime Strategy. ECOWAS helped to organize the inaugural Cyber Africa Forum in June 2021, in Abidjan. ECOWAS supports the West Africa Internet Governance Forum (WAIGF); the 13th annual WAIGF was held by videoconference in July 2021, on the theme 'Digital Inclusion and Access for a Resilient West Africa'.

In September 2021 ECOWAS organized a workshop on digital trade that aimed to build capacity to participate in negotiations on the development of an E-Commerce Protocol to the African Continental Free Trade Agreement (AfCFTA—which entered into force in May 2019). A Regional E-commerce Strategy was under development in 2022. The inaugural meeting of a new ECOWAS Regional Trade Facilitation Committee (established by the Authority in June 2021) was convened in February 2022, in Lomé (Togo).

HUMAN DEVELOPMENT AND SOCIAL AFFAIRS

In February 2020 the ECOWAS Commission inaugurated an ECOWAS Human Resources Training Centre, in Abuja. The Centre was to facilitate sharing knowledge and experience throughout member states, in collaboration with other regional human development stakeholders, including organizations, civil society, and academia.

In December 2018 ECOWAS experts on Science, Technology and Innovation (STI) from member states convened, in Cotonou, to address means of using STI in initiatives to advance sustainable development in the region. ECOWAS organized the inaugural African Forum for Research and Innovation in September 2022, in Abuja. The seventh conference of the Association of West Africa Universities was held in October 2019 at the Université Abomey-Calav. An inaugural West African Arts and Cultural Festival (ECOFEST), on the theme 'Culture as a catalyst for peace, diversity and economic and social integration in West Africa', was to have taken place during 2020, but was postponed in view of the COVID-19 pandemic. In December 2019 the ECOWAS Authority approved a Regional Action Plan for the Return of African Cultural Artefacts to their Countries of Origin, covering the period 2019–23. The inaugural meeting of the monitoring committee for the Action Plan was convened in June 2021. An ECOWAS Youth and Sports Development Centre (EYSDC) was established in 2005.

In 2014 the ECOWAS Commission co-operated with member states and international partners, in particular the World Health Organization (WHO), to control the spread of an outbreak of Ebola Virus Disease (EVD), which had emerged in Guinea in December 2013 and had soon spread to Liberia and Sierra Leone. At the beginning of August 2014 the ECOWAS Commission and WAHO established an Ebola Solidarity Fund, to support affected countries with controlling and eliminating the disease. A meeting of crisis communication and community mobilization experts, held in early October, in Accra, under the auspices of ECOWAS and WAHO, developed a co-ordinated regional emergency communication response strategy on Ebola, that included intensive engagement by the media in disseminating information on preventing and containing the virus. An extraordinary summit meeting of ECOWAS heads of state and of government that was convened, in Accra, in November, determined to implement a regional roadmap on EVD eradication. In September 2019 the ECOWAS Commission organized a meeting to address the lingering economic impacts of the 2014 EVD crisis. In February 2020 an emergency meeting of ECOWAS health ministers was convened to address the activation of regional prevention, surveillance and early detection structures in response to the COVID-19 crisis. In February 2022 ECOWAS ministers responsible for health adopted a WAHO Vision 2030, which focused on accelerating access to inclusive, affordable quality healthcare in the region; advancing effective public health emergency preparedness; and promoting organizational excellence.

The ECOWAS Commission and the International Labour Organization (ILO) undertake joint efforts to address the challenges of child labour in West Africa. The Commission has worked to harmonize national action plans relating to child labour and has developed an ECOWAS Regional Action Plan for the Elimination of Child Labour. ECOWAS and the ILO also collaborated to draft a Decent Work Regional Programme, covering the period 2019–22.

In May 2017 ECOWAS and UNHCR jointly organized a meeting at which an action plan was adopted that aimed to eradicate statelessness in West Africa by 2024. In August 2017 a meeting of ECOWAS heads of immigration services approved the establishment a Nigeria-based Migration Training Academy, with the aim of effectively managing migration and relevant emerging trends. ECOWAS member states participate in the Migration Dialogue for West Africa (MIDWA Process). MIDWA had seven thematic working groups in 2022, covering border management and cross-border crime; the West African diaspora, West African communities and/or nationals;

professional mobility and student exchanges; climate change, land degradation, desertification, environment and migration; migration statistics and data; return, readmission and reintegration; and co-operation and partnership. The fourth MIDWA ministerial meeting, held in July 2020, addressed the impacts of the COVID-19 pandemic on free movement. In late September 2022 an ECOWAS mission was sent to Niger to investigate the situation of migrants trapped there while intending to head onwards to North Africa and Europe.

The ECOWAS Gender Development Centre is based in Dakar. An ECOWAS Child Policy and Strategic Action Plan (2019–30), an ECOWAS Roadmap on Prevention and Response to Child Marriage, and an ECOWAS Declaration on and Common Position against Child Marriage were endorsed in June 2019 by the ECOWAS Authority. (In that year it was reported that nearly 49% of girls below 18 years were married in the region, and that in some member states, in spite of UN guidance, the legal age for marriage remained at below 18 years.) In October 2020 a Working Group Against Gender Based Violence/Violence Against Children was established.

POLITICAL AFFAIRS, PEACE AND SECURITY

In December 1999 ECOWAS heads of state and of government approved a draft protocol to the organization's treaty, providing for the establishment of a Permanent Mechanism for the Prevention, Management and Settlement of Conflicts and the Maintenance of Peace in the Region, an ECOWAS Peace Fund (EPF), and for the creation of a Mediation and Security Council, to comprise representatives of 10 member states, elected for two-year terms. The Council was to be supported by an advisory Council of Elders (also known as the Council of the Wise), initially comprising 32 eminent statesmen from the region; this was inaugurated in July 2001. A Supplementary ECOWAS Protocol on Democracy and Good Governance was adopted in 2001. In January 2003 the Council of Elders was recomposed as a 15-member body with a representative from each member state. A new statute governing the work of the Council of Elders was adopted in May 2016. The EPF became fully operational in May 2006. In December a Technical Committee of Experts on Political Affairs, Peace and Security was established as a subsidiary body of the Mediation and Security Council.

In January 2008 the ECOWAS Mediation and Security Council adopted an ECOWAS Conflict Prevention Framework (ECPF). ECPF national plans of action were initiated in ECOWAS member states in January 2019; the development of a second generation of plans of action was discussed by an ECPF-civil society meeting that was held in July 2021. In June 2016 ECOWAS heads of state and of government adopted the ECOWAS Political Framework for Security Sector Reform and Governance. In February 2017 the ECOWAS Council of Ministers adopted an action plan on women, peace and security, to cover the period 2017–22. A new ECOWAS Peace and Security Architecture and Operations (EPSAO) was initiated in October 2019.

An ECOWAS Warning and Response Network assesses threats to regional security. In June 2004 the Community approved the establishment of the ECOWAS Standby Force (ESF), comprising 6,500 troops, including a core rapid reaction component, the ECOWAS Task Force, numbering around 2,770 soldiers (deployable within 30 days). The ECOWAS Defence and Security Commission subsequently approved the operational framework for the ESF. During 2012 the ESF was deployed in Mali. In late December 2016 the Authority authorized the Force to intervene in The Gambia to uphold the democratic transfer of presidential power.

In January 2005 the Authority approved the establishment of a Bamako-based humanitarian depot and of a Freetown, Sierra Leone-based logistics depot. An ECOWAS Emergency Response Team was established in 2007. An ECOWAS Model for National Disaster Management Agencies was agreed in October 2015 by the relevant ministers from member states.

In June 2006 the Authority adopted the ECOWAS Convention on Small Arms and Light Weapons, their Ammunitions and other Materials, with the aim of regulating the importation and manufacture of such weapons. The ECOWAS Small Arms Control Programme was inaugurated in that month, based in Bamako, to improve the capacity of national and regional institutions to reduce the proliferation of small weapons across the region. During 1999 ECOWAS member states established the Intergovernmental Action Group Against Money Laundering in Africa (GIABA) to combat drug trafficking and money laundering throughout the region; a revised regulation for GIABA, adopted by the Authority in January 2006, expanded the Group's mandate to cover regional responsibility for combating terrorism.

In July 2009 ECOWAS, the UN Office on Drugs and Crime (UNODC), other UN agencies, and INTERPOL launched the West Africa Coast Initiative (WACI), which aimed to build national and regional capacities to combat drug trafficking and organized crime in, initially, four pilot post-conflict countries: Côte d'Ivoire, Guinea-Bissau, Liberia and Sierra Leone. In February 2010 the pilot countries signed the WACI-Freetown Commitment, endorsing the implementation of the initiative, and agreeing to establish specialized transnational crime units on their territories. WACI's Programme Advisory Committee adopted a revised operational strategy for the Initiative in November 2015. In September 2016 ECOWAS and UNODC signed a Letter of Co-operation reaffirming their collaboration. In that month ECOWAS ministers responsible for justice and the interior adopted an Action Plan on the Fight against Illicit Drug Trafficking, related Organized Crime, Corruption and Terrorism, as well as Drug Abuse in West Africa. A West African Epidemiology Network on Drug Use (WENDU) project has national focal points in each member state, as well as in Mauritania. In March 2022 ECOWAS organized the inaugural Regional Multi-Stakeholder Dialogue on Addressing Transnational Organised Crime, at which a new West African Research Network on Organised Crime was launched.

An ECOWAS Counter-Terrorism Strategy and Implementation Plan, and Political Declaration on a Common Position against Terrorism, were endorsed by the Authority in February 2013. In December 2017 the ECOWAS Authority urged member states to increase information sharing and mutual intelligence as a means of combating terrorist networks active in the region. In this regard it instructed the ECOWAS Commission to monitor the effective implementation of the EU-supported West African Police Information System (WAPIS). In September 2019 an extraordinary ECOWAS summit on terrorism adopted a priority action plan to guide regional efforts to combat terrorism during 2020–24 (with a particular focus on the Sahel). The ECOWAS leaders determined to mobilize up to US $1,000m. during the implementation of the plan, to be paid into a common fund, to support national and joint military action against terrorist groupings in the region. The action plan, with a total budget of $2,300m., was approved by the Authority in December 2019.

In June 2019 the ECOWAS Authority stated support for the Accra Initiative, a collective collaboration on combating security issues (such as terrorism, illegal mining, and drug and weapon trafficking) that was initiated in November 2017 by Benin, Burkina Faso, Côte d'Ivoire, Ghana and Togo. (Mali and Niger subsequently joined.) Subsequently three security operations were implemented under the Initiative: Koudanlgou 1, in May 2018, Koudanlgou II, in November, and Koudanlgou III, in November 2019. Islamist extremist militancy had significantly encroached from Mali into Burkina Faso from 2018–19.

In March 2008 an ECOWAS Network of Electoral Commissions (ECONEC), comprising heads of member states' institutions responsible for managing elections, was established, to provide electoral support to member states and also to serve as a regional platform for the exchange of best practices in the management of elections. An ECOWAS Gender and Elections Strategic Framework and Action Plan, covering the period 2017–22, was adopted by the ECOWAS Council of Ministers in February 2017.

ECOWAS monitoring teams were deployed to observe the second phase of a presidential election that was held in Niger, in February 2021, a presidential poll that took place in Benin in April, and Cabo Verde's presidential election held in October.

ECOWAS developed, at the request of the Authority in June 2013, a Sahel Strategy, which is overseen by the ECOWAS Sahel Strategy Co-ordination Platform, and aims to counter weak governance, poverty, terrorism, organized crime and trafficking in the region. In November 2015 the Platform recommended that a socioeconomic database of the Sahel region should be developed.

In March 2014 the Chairman of the Authority condemned violent acts being perpetrated in northern Nigeria by the terrorist group Boko Haram. (In March 2015 Boko Haram pledged allegiance to Islamic State, formally becoming Islamic State's West Africa Province—ISWAP. However, a splinter faction subsequently re-identified as Boko Haram. The Boko Haram insurgency also spread to adjacent areas of Cameroon, Chad and Niger.) In December 2015 the Authority commended the efforts of the Joint Multinational Force, deployed by the Lake Chad Basin Commission member states against the terrorist threat. In December 2016 the Assembly decided to establish a special solidarity fund to assist victims of terrorism, and urged the international community to support efforts by President Buhari of Nigeria to facilitate rehabilitation and reconstruction in affected communities in north-eastern areas of that country. In May 2017 the ECOWAS Commission welcomed an augmentation in EU support for combating poverty, noting that this was a powerful means of arresting violent insurgencies that were destabilizing the region.

ECOWAS and the Communauté Economique des Etats de l'Afrique Centrale (CEEAC) held their first joint Summit on Peace, Security, Stability and the Fight against Terrorism and Violent Extremism in July 2018, in Lomé, Togo. The two organizations determined to conclude a mutual Criminal Cooperation Agreement, and to establish a ministerial committee to follow up future joint decisions on collaboration.

Burkina Faso: In late January 2022 ECOWAS condemned a military coup that had removed from power the democratically elected President of Burkina Faso, Roch Marc Christian Kaboré. The mutinous soldiers had reportedly demanded a change of senior military

personnel and greater resources to combat Islamist insurgents. On 28 January an extraordinary session of the Assembly suspended Burkina Faso's membership of the organization. A further extraordinary meeting, held in early February, called on the Burkinabè military regime to establish transitional authorities and a schedule that would facilitate the promptest possible return to constitutional order. The ECOWAS Commission was instructed to establish a monitoring mechanism, including AU and UN participation, to address the situation continuously. In mid-February an interim military junta-appointed president, Lt-Col Paul-Henri Sandaogo Damiba, was inaugurated. A charter detailing a three-year schedule of transition to democratic elections (deemed too long by ECOWAS) was issued at the beginning of March, and an interim Prime Minister designated soon afterwards. In late March an extraordinary session of the ECOWAS Authority imposed punitive financial and economic sanctions against Burkina Faso, A further extraordinary session held in early June reiterated concern at the length of the transition period, and appointed former Nigerian President Mahamadou Issoufou as ECOWAS Mediator for Burkina Faso. In mid-June the Mediator undertook his first working visit to Burkina Faso; at that time he noted that 40% of Burkinabè territory was outside state control. A new timetable whereby the transition to constitutional rule would be completed in mid-2024 was endorsed in early July 2022 by the ECOWAS Authority; the financial and economic sanctions imposed in March were consequently withdrawn at that time. At the beginning of October the ECOWAS Authority strongly condemned a new seizure of power in Burkina Faso, on 30 September, by Captain Ibrahim Traore. Traore, who cited a worsening security situation as the root cause of the coup, subsequently committed to the ongoing timetable for a return to constitutional rule.

The Gambia: In mid-December 2016 the Chairperson of the ECOWAS Authority led an inconclusive high-level mediating mission to The Gambia with a view to ensuring a peaceful transfer of power, following the rejection by that country's incumbent head of state, Yahya Jammeh, of the results of a presidential election held at the beginning of that month. A second unsuccessful mission, led by President Buhari of Nigeria, took place in mid-January 2017. Buhari urged all parties to pursue inclusive dialogue and to respect the national Constitution. Jammeh, meanwhile, was attempting at that time to have the election results overturned by The Gambia's Supreme Court, and on 18 January the Gambian legislature approved a decision by President Jammeh to impose a state of emergency and the extension by 90 days of Jammeh's term of office. On the evening of 19 January—the scheduled presidential inauguration date, on which Adama Barrow was sworn in during a ceremony in neighbouring Senegal—ECOWAS member states deployed a 7,000-strong joint military force to The Gambia with an initial mandate to ensure the peaceful transfer of power to President Barrow. Following further mediation under ECOWAS auspices—led by (former) President Alpha Condé of Guinea and the President of Mauritania, Mohamed Ould Abdel Aziz—Jammeh eventually agreed on 21 January to stand down, while refusing to acknowledge that he had been defeated in the December 2016 election. President Barrow returned to The Gambia in late January 2017, and legislative elections were successfully organized there in early April. In July the ECOWAS force in The Gambia was recast as a peace support mission (the ECOWAS Mission in the Gambia—ECOMIG). In September a senior ECOWAS representative participated in the formal launch of a new Security Sector Reform (SSR) process in that country.

In May 2019 the ECOWAS Commission, The Gambia and Germany's Ministry for Economic Cooperation and Development initiated a new Gambia Stabilization Fund, based in Banjul, the capital of The Gambia. The President of the ECOWAS Commission participated in a delegation that visited The Gambia in late November-early December 2020 to address, *inter alia,* domestic security sector reforms and local impacts of the COVID-19 pandemic. In December 2021, following the successful staging of presidential elections early in the month, the Authority determined to transform ECOMIG into a police mission, with effect from January 2022.

Guinea: On 8 September 2021 the ECOWAS Authority convened an emergency, virtual meeting to consider recent events in Guinea, where the military had arrested President Alpha Condé and dissolved the Government. ECOWAS leaders determined to suspend Guinea's membership, pending an agreement to restore constitutional rule, and to send a high-level mission to that country. (In 2020, against a background of widespread opposition, the Guinean Constitution had been revised to enable Condé to serve a third term of office.) A further emergency meeting of the Authority, held on 16 September, demanded the immediate and unconditional release of President Condé, and emphasized to the members of a newly installed Guinean Comité National de Rassemblement et de Développement (CNRD) that they were both individually and collectively responsible for Condé's safety. The Authority took note of CNRD's decision to hold consultations with national and international stakeholders to address Guinea's socio-political situation. In December 2021 the Authority welcomed a recent decision of the transitional authorities to permit Condé finally to return to his home in the Guinean capital Conakry, but stated great concern that no schedule for a return to constitutional order had yet been published. In early January 2022 the Authority reiterated concern over the slow pace of the transition process, regretting the continuing failure to agree an electoral calendar or to install a National Council of Transition. In the following month the Authority formally requested the Transitional Authority to provide ECOWAS with an acceptable timetable for restoring constitutional order. An extraordinary meeting of the Authority held in June emphasized continued concern at the length of the transition period. In July the 61st ordinary session of the ECOWAS Authority set a deadline of 1 August for the establishment of an acceptable transition timetable. At that time the former President of Benin Thomas Yayi Boni was appointed as ECOWAS Mediator for Guinea. In September an extraordinary session of the Authority noted that little progress had been made, and imposed a broad raft of diplomatic, financial and economic sanctions against Guinea. The ongoing efforts of the ECOWAS Mediator were commended.

Guinea-Bissau: In June 2016, following popular protests in response to a decision in May by President José Mário Vaz of Guinea-Bissau to dissolve the Government and appoint a new Prime Minister, the ECOWAS Authority designated a high-level mediation mission. In September, under the auspices of the mission, a roadmap was finalized, defining six steps aimed at resolving the crisis. Actions to be taken included convening a roundtable dialogue of national stakeholders; ensuring the functioning of a consensual inclusive government until legislative elections scheduled to be held in 2018; reforming the national Constitution, electoral law, territorial administration, and legislation on political parties; and strengthening of the justice system; reforming the defence and security sectors; and deploying an ECOWAS monitoring and evaluation mechanism to ensure the full implementation of the roadmap. In October, as the first phase of the roadmap, an inclusive dialogue was convened in Conakry, Guinea, by the (former) Guinean President Alpha Condé (appointed as the ECOWAS Mediator for the Guinea-Bissau crisis): the dialogue gathered together stakeholders from Guinea-Bissau, and adopted the Conakry Agreement on the implementation of the roadmap. ECOWAS, the AU, the Community of Portuguese Speaking Countries, the EU and the UN collectively participate in the Group of Five in Bissau format for co-operation on pursuing stability in Guinea-Bissau.

In December 2017 the ECOWAS Authority expressed deep regret at the continuing political impasse in Guinea-Bissau, and requested the ECOWAS mediators to organize talks with national stakeholders aimed at expediting the implementation of the Conakry Agreement within one month, while giving warning that any stakeholders who continued to obstruct the political process would be subjected to punitive sanctions. In February 2018 ECOWAS proceeded to impose sanctions—including freezes on assets and travel bans—on 19 politicians and businessmen from Guinea-Bissau (including a son of President Vaz), whom it deemed responsible for undermining the implementation of the Conakry Agreement. In view of the delay in implementing the Agreement, the mandate of the ECOWAS Mission in Guinea-Bissau (ECOMIB, present in that country since May 2012) was repeatedly extended. In April 2018 an extraordinary meeting of the ECOWAS Authority noted the recent appointment by consensus of Aristide Gomes as Prime Minister, and plans for forthcoming legislative elections in that country in November. In July the Authority expressed concern at the slow pace of implementation of the schedule for preparing the planned elections. An ECOWAS mission observed the legislative elections, which were eventually held in March 2019 (having been postponed from November 2018). In June 2019 the Authority—while noting that President Vaz's constitutionally mandated term of office had ended on 23 June—welcomed forthcoming presidential elections to be held in November, and called for a new Government, under the premiership of Aristides Gomes, to be put in place by 3 July.

In November 2019 ECOWAS convened an extraordinary summit following the decision by President Vaz in late October to dismiss Prime Minister Gomes and his Cabinet and appoint a new premier. The Authority condemned the political developments, but determined to pursue preparations for the scheduled presidential election and to reinforce ECOMIB to uphold security in the country. A 75-member mission was deployed to monitor the election, the first round of which was held at the end of November. ECOWAS observers also monitored the second round of voting, conducted in late December, which was won by (retired army general and former premier) Umaro Sissoco Embaló. The result was upheld in January 2020 by the National Electoral Commission, which rejected an objection made by the runner up, Domingos Simões Pereira (also a former Prime Minister). However, Pereira's political party also registered a complaint at the Supreme Court over the verification process. At that time an extraordinary meeting of the ECOWAS Authority welcomed the peaceful conduct of the 2019 elections and the conclusion reached by the ECOWAS monitors that the electoral process had been

effected in a transparent and fair manner, and requested the Supreme Court to finalize its work promptly to enable normalization of the political arena. In April 2020, although the Supreme Court had not yet delivered a verdict, the ECOWAS Authority formally acknowledged Sissoco Embaló as President. (In February Embaló, supported by an armed guard, had—in contravention of the national Constitution—conducted a self-investiture as President.) The Authority issued a road map for the resolution of the political crisis, emphasizing the urgency of conducting, and submitting to a referendum, a review of the national Constitution. In early September the ECOWAS Authority determined to withdraw ECOMIB from Guinea-Bissau, and stated that it would guide the national Government through the constitutional reform process.

In February 2022 the ECOWAS Authority strongly condemned a recent attempt by heavily armed gunmen (allegedly linked to illicit drug trafficking networks) to overthrow President Embaló and determined to deploy a new stabilization force to protect peace and democracy in the country.

Mali: ECOWAS, with the AU, the UN, the EU, the Organization of Islamic Cooperation, and regional governments, participated in a mediation team that supported the so-called Algiers dialogue process, which led to the initialling at the beginning of March 2015—and adoption by further opposition parties in May and June—of a Mali Peace and Reconciliation Agreement. In October 2017, under ECOWAS auspices, a regional conference on the security situation in the Sahel and West Africa was convened in Bamako, Mali; this adopted the Bamako Declaration, which urged increased operational co-operation and enhanced sharing of information between the international forces active in that region.

In December 2019 Malian stakeholders, meeting in Bamako, adopted four resolutions, including to hold legislative elections before May 2020, and to follow those with a constitutional referendum. Accordingly, the parliamentary poll was held in two rounds, on 29 March and 19 April 2020, with the final outcome confirmed on 30 April by Mali's Constitutional Court—which had overturned the results for 31 seats, leading to the re-election of the political party associated with Mali's President Ibrahim Boubacar Keïta. Subsequently, tensions over the validity of the election results, a dangerous national security situation, and growing economic uncertainty (complicated by the COVID-19 crisis) erupted into large-scale, violent protests in Bamako. President Keïta dissolved the controversial Constitutional Court in early July. On 23 July an ECOWAS presidential mission to Mali—led by the ECOWAS Special Envoy and Mediator for Mali, former President of Nigeria Goodluck Jonathan—proposed the formation of a government of national unity, addressing the 31 disputed parliamentary seats, and the reconstitution of the Constitutional Court. The proposals were, however, rejected by a newly formed major opposition alliance known as the June 5 Movement, which was demanding the resignation of President Keïta. On 18 August Keïta—who was forced to announce his resignation and the dissolution of the elected Malian Government—Prime Minister Boubou Cisse, and other senior government figures were detained by members of the Mali military, and were removed from Bamako to a military base in the nearby settlement of Kati. In immediate response, ECOWAS suspended Mali from participation in its decision-making bodies, determined to pursue a sanctions regime against all those involved in the coup, and halted financial flows between the other member states to Mali. Furthermore, all land and air borders were closed between Mali and the other ECOWAS member states. In late August Keïta left Mali to receive medical treatment in the United Arab Emirates. In mid-September the new military leadership determined that an 18-month transitional government would be established pending new national elections. A meeting held on 15 September between the ECOWAS Authority and a delegation from the National Committee for the Salvation of the People (CNSP—established to govern Mali temporarily after the coup), examined a CNSP roadmap on the transition to the resumption of constitutional governance. The Authority decided that the President and Prime Minister of the proposed Malian Transitional Government should be civilians; that the CNSP should be dissolved upon the establishment of the Transitional Government; and that elections should be held within 18 months of the date of the meeting. On 25 September Bah N'Daou, a former Minister of Defence, was inaugurated as the civilian transitional President. A charter to govern the transition over the next 18 months was issued at the beginning of October (this extended an amnesty to the leaders of the coup), and, following the appointment on 5 October of a 25-member transitional cabinet, the Authority withdrew the sanctions regime against Mali, and urged international donors to support the transitional administration. The inaugural meeting of a Transition Support Group on Mali (GST-Mali)—with participation by representatives of ECOWAS, the AU, the UN Multidimensional Stabilization Mission in Mali (MINUSMA), and other partners—was convened at the end of November, in Bamako. In early December 2020 members of the Conseil national de Transition (transitional parliament) were installed. A second GST-Mali meeting took place in

March 2021. On 24 May ECOWAS and the other GST-Mali participants stated deep concern at the recent arrest by the Malian military of members of the transitional authorities—including the interim President and Prime Minister—and demanded their immediate release. Shortly afterwards the interim President and premier were forced to resign their posts (while continuing to be detained under house arrest). An extraordinary summit of the Authority, convened on 31 May, in Accra, strongly condemned the recent coup, called for the immediate nomination of a new Prime Minister, and once again suspended Mali's participation in ECOWAS's institutions. A monitoring mechanism was to be established to ensure that the next presidential election should proceed as scheduled (for 27 February 2022). In mid-June 2021 the Authority noted the recent appointment of a new civilian Prime Minister and formation of a new transitional Government in Mali.

Meeting in an extraordinary session in early January 2022, the ECOWAS Authority deeply deplored the failure of the Malian regime to take necessary steps to ensure the organization of the planned presidential poll prior to its scheduled date (27 February), and noted that, instead, the authorities had unacceptably scheduled the election to take place after a delay of some years. Therefore, the Authority added additional economic and financial sanctions against Mali and its transitional authorities. In February the Malian military regime enacted an extension of the transition period that would enable it to maintain power for up to five years. Visiting Mali in late February the ECOWAS Special Envoy and the Malian regime stated continuing commitment to pursuing dialogue. At the beginning of July the ECOWAS Authority withdrew economic and financial sanctions from Mali, in view of a newly announced timetable under which a referendum on a proposed new Constitution would be organized in March 2023, local elections in June, legislative elections during October–November, and a presidential poll would be held in February 2024. (However, Mali's suspension from active participation in ECOWAS institutions continued.) A terrorist assault perpetrated against the Kati military base (near Bamako) in late July 2022 was deplored by the ECOWAS Commission. The third meeting of the GST-Mali, held in early September, welcomed the lifting of the economic and financial sanctions on Mali by ECOWAS (and also by UEMOA). The fourth GST-Mali session was to be held in Bamako, in early 2023. Later in September 2022 an extraordinary session of the ECOWAS Authority strongly condemned the ongoing detention in Mali since July, despite regional mediation efforts, of 46 Ivorian soldiers, and called for their immediate release. (While the Côte d'Ivoire authorities stated that the soldiers had been sent to provide logistical support to MINUSMA, they were suspected by Mali of being mercenaries.) The ECOWAS Authority determined to send a high-level mission to Mali (comprising the leaders of Ghana, Senegal and Togo) to secure the soldiers' release.

Piracy in the Gulf of Guinea: In April 2011 ECOWAS initiated a series of measures to combat an increased incidence of piracy, in co-operation with the CEEAC. In October the UN Security Council adopted Resolution 2018 which urged ECOWAS, CEEAC and the Gulf of Guinea Commission to develop a comprehensive regional action plan against piracy and armed robbery at sea. Accordingly, in June 2013 regional heads of state attending a summit held in Yaoundé, Cameroon, formally adopted and opened for signature a Code of Conduct concerning the Prevention and Repression of Piracy, Armed Robbery against Ships, and Illegal Maritime Activities in West and Central Africa, that had been drafted by ECOWAS and CEEAC and the Gulf of Guinea Commission. In June 2014 the three organizations signed an agreement on the establishment of a Yaoundé-based Inter-regional Coordination Centre for Maritime Safety and Security in Central and West Africa. An ECOWAS Integrated Maritime Strategy (EIMS) and Implementation Plan were adopted by the Authority in March 2014. In May 2015 ECOWAS inaugurated a new Multinational Maritime Coordination Centre, in Cotonou, Benin; the Centre was to address maritime issues, including security threats, arising in the territorial waters of Benin, Niger, Nigeria and Togo. Meeting in July 2019, in Accra, the Chiefs of Naval staff of Ghana, Côte d'Ivoire, Guinea and Sierra Leone, as well as Liberia's Chief of Coast Guard and the Burkinabè High Commander of the National Gendarmerie concluded a Memorandum of Understanding guiding collaboration on joint maritime operations in the ECOWAS maritime zone.

Finance

Under the revised treaty, signed in July 1993, ECOWAS was to receive revenue from a community tax, based on the total value of imports from member countries. In March 2013 ECOWAS ministers responsible for finance agreed that a 1.5% community integration levy should be agreed as a replacement for the existing ECOWAS community levy and UEMOA community solidarity levy. In practice Nigeria provides around two-thirds of the annual budget. In April 2020, at the time of the onset of the COVID-19 crisis, the ECOWAS Authority reiterated a commitment (previously made at the height of the 2014 West African Ebola outbreak) to allocate a minimum of 15% of their annual budgets towards strengthening public health care systems. The 2022 budget, approved by the ECOWAS Parliament in December 2021, amounted to 393.6m. West African Units of Account. An ECOWAS Regional Stabilization Fund was established in 2019.

Publications

Annual Report.
Convergence Report (annually).

Specialized Agencies

ECOWAS Bank for Investment and Development (EBID): BP 2704, 128 blvd du 13 janvier, Lomé, Togo; tel. 22-21-68-64; e-mail bidc@bidc-ebid.org; internet www.bidc-ebid.org; f. 2001, replacing the former ECOWAS Fund for Co-operation, Compensation and Development; has two windows covering private sector promotion, and public sector devt; focuses on the following sectors: agriculture and rural devt; water supply and sanitation; environment; social affairs; art and culture; urban planning and habitat; industry and mining; transport; energy; finance; hotels and tourism; and information and communication technologies; loans are normally denominated in units of account (UA), equivalent to the IMF's Special Drawing Right (exceptionally, when mobilized locally, loans may be denominated in local currencies); auth. cap. UA 1,000m., of which UA 301.1m. was paid-up (31 Dec. 2020); Chair. Dr Olavo Avelino Garcia Correia (Cabo Verde); Pres. Dr George Agyekum Nana Donkor (Ghana).

West African Health Organization (WAHO): 01 BP 153 Bobo-Dioulasso 01, Burkina Faso; tel. (226) 20-97-01-00; fax (226) 20-97-57-72; e-mail wahooas@wahooas.org; internet www.wahooas.org; f. 2000 by merger of the West African Health Community (f. 1978) and the Organization for Co-ordination and Co-operation in the Struggle against Endemic Diseases (f. 1960); aims to harmonize mem. states' health policies and to promote research, training, the sharing of resources and diffusion of information; from 2020, in response to the COVID-19 pandemic, WAHO distributed diagnostic test kits and personal protective equipment for healthcare workers to member states, and developed operational guides and training on treating the virus; maintains an online ECOWAS COVID-19 Dashboard; in Aug. 2021 convened, jtly with the ECOWAS Parliament, a virtual high-level meeting to address the elimination of malaria; guided since Feb. 2022 by a WAHO Vision 2030; Dir-Gen. Dr Melchior Athanase Joël C. Aïssi (Benin); publ. *Annual Report*.

West African Monetary Agency (WAMA): 11–13 ECOWAS St, PMB 218, Freetown, Sierra Leone; tel. (22) 232482; fax (22) 223943; internet amao-wama.org; f. 1975 as West African Clearing House; agreement founding WAMA signed by governors of ECOWAS central banks in March 1996; administers transactions between its eight mem. central banks in order to promote subregional trade and monetary co-operation; administers ECOWAS travellers' cheques scheme; mems: Banque Centrale des Etats de l'Afrique de l'Ouest (serving Benin, Burkina Faso, Côte d'Ivoire, Guinea-Bissau, Mali, Niger, Senegal, Togo) and the central banks of Cabo Verde, The Gambia, Ghana, Guinea, Liberia, Nigeria and Sierra Leone; Dir-Gen. Momodu Bamba Saho (The Gambia); publ. *Annual Report*.

West African Monetary Institute (WAMI): Gulf House, Tetteh Quarshie Interchange, Cantonments 75, Accra, Ghana; tel. (30) 2743801; fax (30) 2743807; e-mail info@wami-imao.org; internet www.wami-imao.org; f. Dec. 2000, by the ECOWAS Authority; working to prepare for the establishment of an ECOWAS central bank (in Dec. 2019 the Authority resolved that the bank should be named the Central Bank of West Africa); Dir-Gen. Dr Olorunsola E. Olowofeso (Nigeria).

West African Power Pool (ECOWAPP): 06 BP 2907, Zone des Ambassades, PK 6 Cotonou, Benin; tel. 21-37-41-95; fax 21-37-41-96; e-mail info@ecowapp.org; internet www.ecowapp.org; f. 1999; approved as a Specialized Agency in Jan. 2006; aims to facilitate the integration of the power systems of mem. nations into a unified regional electricity market; 16th WAPP General Assembly: held in Nov. 2021, in Ouagadougou, Burkina Faso; 29 mem. utilities; Sec.-Gen. Ki Apollinaire Siengui (Senegal); publ. *WAPP Newsletter*.

EUROPEAN UNION—EU

In December 2001 the European Council adopted the Declaration on the Future of the European Union, which aimed to reform EU institutions to ensure the smooth functioning of the Union after enlargement. The full text of the draft constitutional treaty was submitted to the Council of the European Union (often known as the Council) in July 2003. At a summit meeting held in Brussels in June 2004, the heads of state and of government of the then 25 EU member states approved the draft constitutional treaty, which was formally signed in Rome in October by the heads of state or of government of the 25 member states and the three candidate countries of Bulgaria, Romania and Turkey (now known as Türkiye). However, the treaty remained subject to ratification by each member nation (either by a vote in the national legislature or by a popular referendum), and in May and June 2005 it was rejected in national referendums held in France and the Netherlands, respectively.

At an informal summit of the European Council held in Lisbon, Portugal, in mid-October 2007, agreement was reached at an Inter-governmental Conference on the final text of a new reform treaty. The resulting Treaty of Lisbon amending the Treaty on European Union and the Treaty establishing the European Community was signed in Lisbon, on 13 December, by the heads of state or of government of the now 27 member states. The Treaty of Lisbon retained much of the content of the abandoned constitutional treaty. In June 2008 voters in Ireland, which was constitutionally bound to conduct a popular referendum on the issue, rejected ratification of the treaty. Consequently, in December the European Council agreed to a number of concessions, including the removal of a provision in the treaty for a reduction in the number of European Commissioners. A new referendum, held in Ireland in October 2009, approved the treaty. By early November all EU member states had ratified the Treaty of Lisbon, which entered into force on 1 December. The Treaty of Rome was duly renamed the Treaty on the Functioning of the European Union, with references to the European 'Community' changed to the 'Union'.

Meetings of the principal organs take place in Brussels, in Luxembourg and in Strasbourg, France. The Treaty of Lisbon cre-ated a High Representative of the Union for Foreign Affairs and Security Policy (appointed by the European Council by qualified majority with the agreement of the President of the Commission) to represent the EU internationally, combining the former roles of EU Commissioner responsible for external relations and EU High Rep-resentative for the Common Foreign and Security Policy (although foreign policy remains subject to a national veto). The Lisbon Treaty also provided for the creation of a new permanent President of the European Council, elected by the European Council; the creation of this role aimed to promote coherence and continuity in policymaking. The system of a six-month rotating Presidency was retained for the different formations of the Council of the European Union (except for the External Relations Council, chaired by the High Representative). A new system of fixed 18-month troikas (groups of three presidencies) was introduced, sharing the presidencies of most configurations of the Council, to facilitate overall co-ordination and continuity of work. The Lisbon Treaty provided for a revised system of qualified majority voting in the Council. The European Parliament's legislative powers were consolidated under the Lisbon Treaty, which granted the Parliament the right of co-decision with the Council in an increased number of policy areas, giving it a more prominent role in framing legislation. The maximum number of seats in the European Parlia-ment was raised to 751 from 2014.

The Lisbon Treaty sought to improve democracy and transparency within the Union, introducing the right for EU citizens to petition the Commission to introduce new legislation and enshrining the prin-ciples of subsidiarity (that the EU should only act when an objective can be better achieved at supranational level, implying that national powers are the norm) and proportionality (that the action should be proportional to the desired objective). National parliaments are given the opportunity to examine EU legislation to ensure that it rests within the EU's remit, and legislation may be returned to the Commission for reconsideration if one-third of member states find that a proposed law breaches these principles. The Treaty of Lisbon enabled enhanced co-operation for groups numbering at least one-third of the member states. The treaty provided a legal basis for an EU defence force, with a mutual defence clause, and stipulated that the EU has the power to sign treaties and sit on international bodies as a legal entity in its own right. The new framework also provided for the establishment of a European Public Prosecutor's Office to combat EU fraud and cross-border crime and the right to dual citizenship (i.e. of the EU as well as of a member state). Article 50 of the Treaty of Lisbon provides for a member state to withdraw from the Union if it so wishes, 'in accordance with its own constitutional requirements'. Such a member state must notify the European Council of its intention, thereby formally invoking Article 50. If a withdrawing member state later wishes to apply to rejoin the EU, its application

will be considered as that of a third country (under Article 49 of the Treaty of Lisbon).

Presidency of the Council of the European Union: Czech Republic (July–December 2022); Sweden (January–June 2023); Spain (July–December 2023).

President of the European Council: CHARLES MICHEL (Belgium).

High Representative of the Union for Foreign Affairs and Security Policy: JOSEP BORRELL FONTELLES (Spain).

Sub-Saharan Africa

In June 2000, meeting in Cotonou, Benin, heads of state and of government of the EU and African, Caribbean and Pacific (ACP) states concluded the 20-year Cotonou Agreement, which officially entered into force on 1 April 2003. (Previously, the principal means of co-operation between the EC and developing countries were the Lomé Conventions concluded in 1975–89.) A financial protocol attached to the Cotonou Agreement indicated the funds available to the ACP through the European Development Fund (EDF), the main instrument for EU aid for development co-operation in ACP countries. A revised agreement was signed in mid-2005, providing for free trade arrangements with the most developed ACP countries. In 2010 negotiations were concluded on a second revision of the Cotonou Agreement, which was signed in Ouagadougou, Burkina Faso, in June.

The Cotonou Agreement was due to expire in February 2020 (subsequently extended); negotiations on future relations with the ACP states commenced in September 2018. The ninth summit of ACP leaders was held in Nairobi, Kenya, in December 2019. The Nairobi Nguvu Ya Pamoja declaration was endorsed, setting out the ACP's position on issues including good governance, security and the environment, and detailed commitments by ACP leaders. Agreement was reached on significant revisions to the Georgetown Agreement (which formally constituted the ACP in 1975). From 5 April 2020, in conformity with the provisions of the revised Georgetown Agree-ment, the ACP states became collectively known as the Organisation of African, Caribbean and Pacific States (OACPS). An OACPS-EU Partnership Agreement was initialled in mid-April 2021.

Meanwhile, the first summit representing the institutionalization of Africa-EU dialogue was convened in April 2000, in Cairo, Egypt. At the second Africa-EU summit, held in December 2007 in Lisbon, Portugal, a Joint Africa-EU Strategy was adopted, providing an overarching long-term framework for future political co-operation. The first action plan of the Joint Strategy identified eight areas for strategic partnership during 2008–10: peace and security; demo-cratic governance and human rights; trade, regional integration and infrastructure; achievement of the UN Millennium Development Goals (MDGs); energy; climate change; migration, mobility and employment; and science, information society and space. The action plan for 2011–13 largely retained the focus of the previous plan. At the fourth Africa-EU summit, held in Brussels in April 2014, a political declaration was adopted by heads of state and of govern-ment. The action plan for 2014–20 identified five strategic areas of focus, which replaced the eight previous areas: peace and security; democracy, good governance and human rights; human develop-ment; sustainable and inclusive development, together with growth and continental integration; and global and emerging issues. Joint Annual Forums were to be introduced, and the summit also adopted a declaration on migration and mobility, and plans, *inter alia*, to combat illegal migration and human trafficking and to improve international protection. In August the EU launched a Pan-African Programme, which was allocated a budget of €845m. for 2014–20, to facilitate implementation of the Joint Africa-EU Strategy. In Novem-ber 2017 the fifth Africa-EU summit was held in Abidjan, Côte d'Ivoire, with the theme 'investing in youth for a sustainable future'. A declaration was adopted establishing joint priorities in four prin-cipal areas: investment in people through education and training; strengthening resilience, peace, security and governance; mobility and migration; and economic investment. A country-specific Exter-nal Investment Plan sought to promote investment in African states to stimulate growth and employment, and to combat irregular migration. A joint statement was also adopted on human rights in Libya, condemning the treatment of migrants and refugees by criminal organizations. In March 2020 the Commission proposed a new Comprehensive Strategy with Africa, based on five priority areas: a partnership for green transition and energy access; a part-nership for digital transformation; a partnership for sustainable growth and jobs; a partnership for peace and security governance; and a partnership on migration and mobility. The sixth EU-Africa summit took place in Brussels in February 2022, following delays resulting from the COVID-19 crisis. EU and African Union leaders agreed on a new Joint Vision for 2030, supported by the Global Gateway Africa-Europe Investment Package totalling some €150,000m.

The Council has adopted specific strategies and action plans for the Horn of Africa (East Africa), the Gulf of Guinea and for security and development in the Sahel. The EU also maintains several missions in Africa. Operation EU NAVFOR Somalia was established in 2008 in support of UN Security Council resolutions aimed at deterring and repressing acts of piracy and armed robbery in waters off the coast of Somalia, and protecting vulnerable vessels in that area (including vessels delivering humanitarian aid to displaced persons in Somalia). In February 2010 the Council established the EU Training Mission for Somalia (EUTM Somalia). The establishment of EUCAP Sahel Niger was approved by the Council in July 2012, as a training, advisory and assistance mission aimed at augmenting the capacity of Niger's security forces to combat terrorism and organized crime. In the same month EUCAP Nestor (now EUCAP Somalia) was established to support the rule of law in Somalia and the maritime capacity of Djibouti, Kenya, Seychelles and Tanzania, complementing the EU's anti-piracy naval force ATALANTA (EU NAVFOR Somalia) and EUTM Somalia. EUTM Mali was launched in February 2013 to increase the military efficacy of that country's armed forces, in an effort to facilitate the restoration of Mali's territorial integrity, under civilian leadership. In April 2014 a civilian mission, EUCAP Sahel Mali, was established to help to support the security situation in Mali. In April 2016 the Council agreed to dispatch a military training mission to the Central African Republic (CAR), known as EUTM RCA; the EU suspended the work of EUTM RCA in the CAR in December 2021 amid concerns that mercenaries employed by a Russian private contractor, the Wagner Group, and accused of human rights violations were working closely with CAR military forces. EUTM Mali and EUCAP Sahel Mali were partially suspended in April 2022. Meanwhile, a military training mission in Mozambique (EUTM Mozambique) was established in October 2021.

In September 2015 the European Commission announced that it was to create an Emergency Trust Fund for stability and addressing root causes of irregular migration and displaced persons in Africa. The Fund, established in November, focuses assistance on the regions of the Sahel and Lake Chad, the Horn of Africa and North Africa, and seeks to help to strengthen the rule of law, improve socioeconomic opportunities and develop migration management policies. By January 2021 254 programmes had been approved, totalling some €4,900m.

FRANC ZONE

internet: www.tresor.economie.gouv.fr/tresor-international/la-zone-franc.

MEMBERS

Benin	Equatorial Guinea
Burkina Faso	France
Cameroon	Gabon
Central African Republic	Guinea-Bissau
Chad	Mali
Comoros	Niger
Congo, Republic	Senegal
Côte d'Ivoire	Togo

The former French West and Equatorial African territories are grouped within the two currency areas that existed before independence, each group having its own variant on the franc CFA, issued by a central bank: the franc de la Communauté Financière Africaine ('franc CFA de l'Ouest'), issued by the Banque Centrale des Etats de l'Afrique de l'Ouest—BCEAO, and the franc Coopération financière en Afrique Centrale ('franc CFA central'), issued by the Banque des Etats de l'Afrique Centrale—BEAC. In 1981 the Banque Centrale des Comores introduced a Comoros franc. In accordance with an agreement adopted in December 2019, in Abidjan, Côte d'd'Ivoire, by France and the Union Economique et Monétaire Ouest-Africaine (UEMOA), it was envisaged that the franc CFA would be superseded by a new West African currency, the eco. An agreement providing for reform of the historic monetary arrangements was ratified by France's Assemblée nationale (lower legislative assembly) in November 2020, and in January 2021 by its Sénat (upper house). Ratification in signatory African states was, however, delayed. (See *The 2019 Monetary Co-operation Agreement.*)

Equatorial Guinea, formerly a Spanish territory, joined the zone in January 1985, and Guinea-Bissau, a former Portuguese territory, joined in May 1997.

BACKGROUND

From 1 January 2002, when European economic and monetary union was finalized and the French franc withdrawn from circulation, the franc CFA and Comoros franc became officially pegged to the euro, at a fixed rate of exchange. Arrangements previously concluded between France and the Franc Zone remained in force that provided the Franc Zone currencies with unlimited convertibility into euros, at a fixed exchange rate, guaranteed by the French Treasury; central issuing banks were based in each group of member countries, and the Comoros—with overdraft facilities provided by the French Treasury, and monetary reserves held mainly in the form of euros. The BCEAO and the BEAC were authorized to hold up to 35% of their foreign exchange holdings in currencies other than the euro; one-half of foreign reserves were required to be held by the Banque de France, receiving 0.75% interest from the French Treasury.

In 1990 the Franc Zone governments agreed to develop an economic union, with integrated public finances and common commercial legislation. In April 1992, at a meeting of Franc Zone ministers, a treaty on the insurance industry was adopted, providing for the establishment of a regulatory body for the industry, the Conférence Intrafricaine des Marchés d'Assurances (CIMA), and for the creation of a ministerial council for the insurance industry, with its secretariat in Libreville, Gabon. A code of conduct for members of CIMA entered into force in February 1995. At the meeting held in April 1992 ministers also agreed that a further council of ministers should be created to monitor the social security systems in Franc Zone countries. A programme drawn up by Franc Zone finance ministers concerning the harmonization of commercial legislation in member states through the establishment of l'Organisation pour l'Harmonisation en Afrique du Droit des Affaires (OHADA) was approved by the Franco-African summit in October. A treaty to align corporate and investment regulations was signed by 11 member countries in October 1993. The member governments co-operated in countering money laundering.

THE 2019 MONETARY CO-OPERATION AGREEMENT

On 21 December 2019 the ministers responsible for finance of the UEMOA member states and their French counterpart signed a Monetary Co-operation Agreement that, upon its full entry into force, would provide for a new currency, the eco, to replace the franc CFA. (The negotiation of the Agreement had been instigated at the request of the UEMOA member states.) The eco was to be pegged to the euro with a fixed exchange rate and an unlimited and unconditional guarantee of convertibility provided by France (to continue to support UEMOA's macroeconomic stability). A dedicated agreement defining the guarantee mechanism and specifying the terms under which the guarantee might be triggered was signed by the BCEAO and the French authorities in December 2020. The Monetary Co-operation Agreement was endorsed by France's Assemblée nationale on 10 November, and by the Sénat on 28 January 2021. From 2020 France ceased participating in governance of the zone, and the BCEAO was no longer obliged to centralize its foreign exchange reserves with the French Treasury. Progress in ratifying the Agreement was, however, delayed in the UEMOA region, which was focused on addressing the economic uncertainty posed by the onset in 2020 of the COVID-19 pandemic. In December 2021 the BCEAO estimated that—having been fuelled by a gradual strengthening of domestic demand—the overall economic growth of the UEMOA member states had rebounded to 6.7% (year on year) in the third quarter of that year, compared with very subdued growth of only 0.9% in 2020. However, accelerating price rises were noted across the region, reflecting a global trend. During the first half of 2022 the value of the CFA franc against the US dollar markedly declined, in view of the CFA franc's pegging to the euro, which in mid-July fell below parity with the US dollar for the first time in two decades (a slight upwards trend subsequently occurred).

CURRENCIES OF THE FRANC ZONE

1 franc CFA = €0.00152. CFA stands for Communauté financière africaine in the West African area and for Coopération financière en Afrique centrale in the Central African area. Used in the monetary areas of West and Central Africa, respectively.

1 Comoros franc = €0.00203. Used in the Comoros, where it replaced the franc CFA in 1981.

CENTRAL ISSUING BANKS

Banque Centrale des Comores: pl. de France, BP 405, Moroni, Comoros; tel. (773) 1002; fax (773) 0349; internet www .banque-comores.km; f. 1981; Gov. Dr IMANI YOUNOUSSA.

Banque Centrale des Etats de l'Afrique de l'Ouest (BCEAO): ave Abdoulaye Fadiga, BP 3108, Dakar, Senegal; tel. 33-839-05-00; fax 33-823-83-35; e-mail mail.bceao@bceao.int; internet www.bceao .int; f. 1962; central bank of issue for the mems of UEMOA; from 2020 foreign exchange reserves were no longer required to be centralized (as hitherto) with the Banque de France; in March 2020 BCEAO and UEMOA agreed to channel 196,600m. francs CFA to support the containment of the COVID-19 pandemic crisis in the region; mems: Benin, Burkina Faso, Côte d'Ivoire, Guinea-Bissau, Mali, Niger, Senegal, Togo; Gov. JEAN-CLAUDE KASSI BROU (Côte d'Ivoire); publs *BCEAO studies and research papers, Economic Outlook.*

Banque des Etats de l'Afrique Centrale (BEAC): 736 ave Mgr François Xavier Vogt, BP 1917, Yaoundé, Cameroon; tel. 223-40-30; fax 223-33-29; e-mail beac@beac.int; internet www.beac.int; f. 1972 as the central bank of issue of Cameroon, Central African Republic, Chad, Rep. of the Congo, Equatorial Guinea and Gabon; a monetary market, incorporating all national financial institutions of the BEAC countries, came into effect on 1 July 1994; Gov. ABBAS MAHAMAT TOLLI (Chad); publs *Rapport Annuel, Situation comptable* (monthly).

OTHER FRANC ZONE INSTITUTIONS

Banque de Développement des Etats de l'Afrique Centrale (BDEAC): blvd Denis Sassou N'Guesso, BP 1177, Brazzaville, Republic of the Congo; tel. 426-83-00; fax 281-18-80; e-mail bdeac@ bdeac.org; internet www.bdeac.org; f. 1975; auth. cap. 1,200,000m. francs CFA (increased in 2014 from 250,000m.); shareholders: Cameroon, Central African Rep., Chad, Rep. of the Congo, Gabon, Equatorial Guinea, the AfDB, BEAC, France, Libya, Kuwait; Pres. DIEUDONNÉ EVOU MEKOU (Cameroon).

Banque Ouest-Africaine de Développement (BOAD): 62 ave de la Libération, BP 1172, Lomé, Togo; tel. 22-21-59-06; fax 22-21-52-67; e-mail boadsiege@boad.org; internet www.boad.org; f. 1973; established to promote the balanced devt of mem. states and the economic integration of West Africa; promotes small and medium-sized businesses; public-private partnerships; agricultural resilience and food security; sustainable energy and electricity infrastructure devt; climate adaptation; issued in Jan. 2021 its inaugural sustainability bond, aimed at funding sustainable development initiatives; auth. cap. 1,155,000m. francs CFA; mems: Benin, Burkina Faso, Côte d'Ivoire, Guinea-Bissau, Mali, Niger, Senegal, Togo; Pres. SERGE EKUÉ (Benin); publs *Rapport Annuel, BOAD en Bref* (quarterly).

Bourse Régionale des Valeurs Mobilières (BRVM): 18 rue Joseph Anoma, BP 3802, Abidjan 01, Côte d'Ivoire; tel. 20-32-66-85; e-mail brvm@brvm.org; internet www.brvm.org; f. 1998; regional electronic stock exchange; Man. Dir EDOH KOSSI AMENOUNVE; publs *Monthly Bulletins, Quarterly Statistics.*

Communauté Economique et Monétaire de l'Afrique Centrale (CEMAC): BP 969, Bangui, Central African Republic; tel. 21-61-47-81; fax 70-14-15-66; internet www.cemac.int; f. 1998; formally inaugurated as the successor to the Union Douanière et Economique de l'Afrique Centrale (UDEAC, f. 1966) at a meeting of heads of state held in Malabo, Equatorial Guinea, in June 1999; aims to promote the process of subregional integration within the framework of an economic and monetary union; CEMAC was also to comprise a parliament and a subregional tribunal; UDEAC established a common external tariff for imports from other countries and administered a common code for investment policy and a Solidarity Fund to counteract regional disparities of wealth and economic devt; in Oct. 2017 CEMAC mem. states issued a formal declaration that an agreement concluded in June 2013 to abolish visa requirements between mem. states for citizens in possession of biometric identification documentation had been fully ratified; an extraordinary summit of CEMAC heads of state was convened in Aug. 2021, with participation by the Pres. of the World Bank and the Man. Dir of the IMF, to assess the subregional macroeconomic situation, and to consider appropriate measures to strengthen

regional resilience and recovery from the COVID-19 pandemic crisis; a CEMAC Business Energy Forum is convened annually; mems: Cameroon, Central African Rep., Chad, Rep. of the Congo, Equatorial Guinea, Gabon; Pres. DANIEL ONA ONDO (Gabon).

Union Economique et Monétaire Ouest-Africaine (UEMOA): 380 ave Prof. Joseph Ki-Zerbo, BP 543, Ouagadougou 01, Burkina Faso; tel. 25-31-88-73; fax 25-31-88-72; e-mail commission@uemoa .int; internet www.uemoa.int; f. 1994; promotes regional monetary and economic convergence, and envisages the eventual creation of a subregional common market; the Ouagadougou-based UEMOA Court of Justice (f. 1995) arbitrates disputes between mem. states, and between the Union and other bodies; a preferential tariff scheme, eliminating duties on most local products and reducing by 30% import duties on many Union-produced industrial goods, became operational on 1 July 1996; in addition, from 1 July, a community solidarity levy of 0.5% (increased to 1% in December 1999) was imposed on all goods from third countries sold within the Union, in order to strengthen UEMOA's capacity to promote economic integration; in June 1997 UEMOA heads of state and govt agreed to reduce import duties on industrial products originating in the Union by a further 30%; an inter-parliamentary cttee, recognized as the predecessor of a UEMOA legislature, was inaugurated in Mali, in March 1998; mem. states adopted a treaty on the establishment of a UEMOA parliament in Jan. 2003; on 1 Jan. 2000 internal tariffs were eliminated on all local products (incl. industrial goods) and an external tariff system, in 5 bands of between 0% and 20%, was imposed on goods deriving from outside the new customs union; Guinea-Bissau and Mali joined the arrangement in 2003; a High-level Committee on Food Security monitors the regional food and nutrition security situation and promotes policies aimed at addressing structural causes of food crises; UEMOA and ECOWAS jtly participate in a Food Crisis Prevention Network, which is co-ordinated by the Permanent Interstate Committee on Drought Control in the Sahel, and supported by the OECD's Sahel and West Africa Club; an advisory Labour and Social Dialogue Council was established in March 2009; also in that month UEMOA adopted a regional initiative for sustainable energy, aiming to meet all regional electricity needs by 2030; in May 2018 UEMOA and ECOWAS jtly initiated an EU-supported programme aimed at improving energy governance in West Africa; a subsidiary mortgage refinancing institution (Caisse Régionale de Refinancement Hypothécaire de l'UEMOA—CRRH-UEMOA) was established in July 2010; by end-2018 UEMOA had contributed nearly €800,000 to the trust fund supporting the Force conjointe du G5 Sahel (FC-G5S—tasked with combating violent extremist groups operating in the G5 Sahel common space); in July 2019 UEMOA and ECOWAS ministers responsible for the environment, and also their counterpart from Mauritania, jtly launched a Programme of Support for the Preservation of Biodiversity and Fragile Ecosystems; on 21 Dec. 2019 UEMOA and France adopted an agreement that (upon full entry into force) was to provide for a new currency, the eco, to replace the franc CFA; in March 2021 UEMOA and the BOAD adopted a draft bilateral co-operation agreement on accelerating the digital transformation of the UEMOA area; in Jan. 2022 Mali was suspended and sanctioned, given that the military junta that took power there in Aug. 2020 had still not yet organized democratic elections; Mali lodged an appeal with the UEMOA Court of Justice in Feb. 2022; in March the Court ruled that some economic sanctions against Mali should be suspended, on humanitarian grounds: these were eventually withdrawn in July 2022, following the agreement of a timetable under which a referendum on a new constitution would be organized in Mali in March 2023, and presidential elections would be held there in Feb. 2024; mems: Benin, Burkina Faso, Côte d'Ivoire, Guinea-Bissau, Mali (suspended), Niger, Senegal, Togo; Pres. ABDOULAYE DIOP (Senegal).

At a summit meeting in December 1981 leaders of the former UDEAC agreed in principle to establish an economic community of Central African member states: the Communauté Economique des Etats de l'Afrique Centrale began operations in 1985, and includes the members of CEMAC, and also Burundi, Rwanda, São Tomé and Príncipe and the Democratic Republic of the Congo.

INTERGOVERNMENTAL AUTHORITY ON DEVELOPMENT—IGAD

Address: ave Georges Clemenceau, BP 2653, Djibouti.
Telephone: 21354050; **fax:** 21356994; **e-mail:** info@igad.int; **internet:** igad.int.

IGAD was established in 1996 to supersede the Intergovernmental Authority on Drought and Development (IGADD, which, in turn had been founded in 1986 to combat the effects of aridity and desertification arising from the severe drought and famine that has periodically affected the Horn of Africa). IGAD aims to co-ordinate the sustainable socioeconomic co-operation and development of member countries, to strengthen food security and environmental protection, to combat the effects of drought and desertification, and to promote regional security.

MEMBERS

Djibouti	Kenya	South Sudan*	Uganda
Ethiopia	Somalia	Sudan	

*South Sudan was temporarily suspended in December 2021 because of unpaid dues.

Eritrea, which joined in 1993 following its proclamation as an independent state, has not participated in the activities of IGAD since 2007, when it suspended itself from the organization. In August 2011 the IGAD Council of Ministers—accusing the Eritrean regime of supporting groups that were destabilizing the region, notably al-Shabaab—rejected an attempt by Eritrea to reactivate its membership, and instead demanded the imposition of further UN sanctions against the country. However, in November 2018 IGAD's Executive Secretary welcomed the withdrawal of the UN sanctions, in view of a recent improvement of relations between Eritrea and Ethiopia, Somalia, and Djibouti.

Organization

(October 2022)

ASSEMBLY

The Assembly, consisting of heads of state and of government of member states, is the supreme policymaking organ of the Authority. It holds a regular summit meeting, normally at least once a year, and extraordinary sessions as required. The chairmanship of the Assembly rotates among the member countries on an annual basis.

COUNCIL OF MINISTERS

The Council of Ministers, which meets twice a year, is composed of the minister responsible for foreign affairs and one other minister from each member state. It formulates policy and approves the work programme and the annual budget of the Secretariat.

COMMITTEE OF AMBASSADORS

The Committee of Ambassadors comprises the ambassadors or plenipotentiaries of member states that are accredited to Djibouti (i.e. the host country of IGAD's headquarters). It convenes as regularly as required to advise and assist the Executive Secretary concerning the interpretation of policies and guidelines and the realization of the annual work programme.

SECRETARIAT

The secretariat is headed by an Executive Secretary, who is appointed by the Assembly for a term of four years, renewable once. In addition to the Office of the Executive Secretary, the secretariat comprises the following divisions, each headed by a director: Health and Social Development; Economic Co-operation; Agriculture and Environment; and Peace and Security.

Executive Secretary: WORKNEH GEBEYEHU (Ethiopia).

INTER-PARLIAMENTARY UNION OF IGAD (IPU-IGAD)

A Protocol establishing the IPU-IGAD, signed in February 2004 by the participants in the first meeting of regional speakers of parliament, entered into force in November 2007. The first meeting of an IPU-IGAD Executive Council was convened in May 2008.

IGAD PARTNERS FORUM

Meetings between IGAD ministers responsible for foreign affairs and the IGAD Partners' Forum (IPF), comprising the grouping's donors, are convened periodically to discuss issues such as food security and humanitarian affairs. The first conference aimed at facilitating engagement between development partners and all IGAD programmes, divisions and specialized institutions was convened in September 2017.

Activities

A strategy to guide IGAD's activities during 2021–25 focused on the following pillars: (i) agriculture, natural resources and environment; (ii) economic co-operation; (iii) health and social development; (iv) peace and security, and humanitarian affairs; and (v) corporate development services. Emphasis was to be placed on: Response to crises; Revitalization of regional integration; Reform to enhance organizational efficiency; and Results. The strategy was the first to contribute to a longer-term IGAD Vision 2050 development agenda.

ECONOMIC CO-OPERATION

IGAD supports the development of the regional infrastructure, particularly in the areas of transport and communications, to promote foreign, cross-border and domestic trade and investment opportunities. IGAD seeks to harmonize national transport and trade policy and thereby to facilitate the free movement of people, goods and services. In February 2020 a Protocol on Free Movement of Persons in the IGAD Region was endorsed by ministers responsible for internal affairs and labour. In April 2019 IGAD's Executive Secretary signed a contract enabling the development of a new IGAD Regional Infrastructure Master Plan (IRIMP). This was to cover energy, transport, information technologies, and transboundary water resources. A roundtable conference to support implementation of the IRIMP was held in Nairobi, Kenya, in November 2021.

Infrastructure projects under way in the region include the construction of missing segments of the Trans-African Highway and the Pan African Telecommunications Network; the removal of barriers to trade and communications; improvements to ports and inland container terminals; and the modernization of railway and telecommunications services. IGAD has promoted the upgrading of the Djibouti–Addis Ababa (Ethiopia)–Juba (South Sudan)–Kampala (Uganda) transport corridor.

An IGAD Sustainable Tourism master plan was being implemented during the period 2013–23. An IGAD Business Forum was organized in May 2021, in Addis Ababa.

In May 2021 IGAD and the UN Capital Development Fund agreed to co-operate to harmonize policy across the IGAD member states on remittances (i.e. cross-border payments made by diaspora migrants working outside their country of origin).

AGRICULTURE AND ENVIRONMENT

About 80% of the IGAD region is classified as arid or semi-arid, and some 40% of the region is unproductive. Meanwhile, seasonal flooding has intensified in recent years. An IGAD Food Security and Nutrition Response Strategy, launched in August 2020, aimed to support vulnerable populations through enhancing the regional co-ordinated response capacity to withstand multiple concurrent shocks (outbreaks of diseases, desert locust infestations, and climatic disasters); extending targeted humanitarian and livelihood assistance; improving longer-term nutrition security; and enhancing regional trade and market access.

In February 2020 participants in the 34th IGAD extraordinary summit, held in Addis Ababa, stated alarm at the speed and extent of an invasion of locusts that was plaguing member states, and agreed proactively to share best practices and information on eradicating the infestation, via the IGAD Secretariat. A virtual meeting held in late May of IGAD ministers responsible for agriculture and livestock, their counterparts from Saudi Arabia and Yemen, and representatives of desert locust control organizations, agreed to strengthen co-ordination between the IGAD and Arabian peninsula countries in desert locust surveillance, control operations, contingency planning, and infestation mapping. It was noted that the impact of the desert locust infestation on the agricultural planting season, as well as flooding and the COVID-19 pandemic, represented a very significant threat to food security, nutrition and livelihoods. A joint statement issued in July by IGAD and UN agencies emphasized the continuing urgent 'triple threat', and called for collaborative strategic interventions. In June 2021 an IGAD Ministerial Conference on the Sustainable Management of Desert Locusts, and other Transboundary Pests—with participation by the ministers of agriculture from member states and Yemen—endorsed a regional roadmap on the control of transboundary pests and established an Inter-regional Pests Early Warning System, to facilitate the prompt exchange of information on the emergence of desert locusts and other pests between countries in the Horn of Africa and the Arabian peninsula.

In November 2011 IGAD and partner countries agreed the institutional arrangements for implementing a Horn of Africa IGAD Drought Disaster Resilience and Sustainability Initiative (IDDRSI): Ending Drought Emergencies, which had been launched in September. The meeting also agreed to establish an IDDRSI Platform, intended as an enhanced partnership with donors facilitating long-term investment to end the recurrence of drought emergencies. A Platform Steering Committee was constituted in February 2013. The Initiative aims to achieve drought-resistant communities, institutions and ecosystems in the IGAD region by 2027. In December 2016 IGAD heads of state and of government authorized the establishment of a multi-donor trust fund, under the management of the IDDRSI Platform. In January 2017, within the IDDRSI framework, a European Union (EU)-funded Collaboration in Cross-Border Areas of the Horn of Africa Region project was initiated. A new IDDRSI strategy to cover the period 2019–24 identified the following priority intervention areas: Natural resources and environmental management; Market access, trade and financial services; Enhanced production and livelihoods diversification; Disaster risk management; Research, knowledge management and technology transfer; Peacebuilding, conflict prevention and resolution; Co-ordination, institutional strengthening and partnerships; and Human capital, gender and social development. In April 2022 IGAD issued a warning of impending disaster given the escalating severe drought in the subregion. In the following month IGAD convened a high-level ministerial meeting, attended by representatives of international partner organizations, to discuss measures to enhance resilience and to ensure food security. The eighth IDDRSI Platform General Assembly, convened in July, in Addis Ababa, noted that the region was suffering the most extreme drought for four decades, had also been affected by severe flooding since 2019, and was vulnerable to compounding factors such as ongoing global political and economic instability. The Assembly meeting appealed to humanitarian actors to extend the necessary resources to address persisting food insecurity in the region; called on the IGAD Secretariat, member states and development partners to intensify regional, climate-smart resilience investments; asked Platform members to support the effective regulation of cross-border pastoralist mobility (to prevent conflict); and urged the strengthening of anticipatory early action.

Ministers responsible for biodiversity, environment and natural resources adopted an IGAD Regional Biodiversity Protocol in July 2017, as well as related strategies addressing conservation of transboundary wildlife and sharing of biodiversity benefits, control and management of invasive species, and the national application of relevant regional, continental and global legislation. A Horn of Africa Wildlife Enforcement Network, established in November of that year as the regional anti-wildlife trafficking framework, is managed by the IGAD Secretariat.

In October 2015 the IGAD Center for Pastoral Areas and Livestock Development established a Regional Export Quarantines Network. In December IGAD and the Food and Agriculture Organization of the United Nations (UN) jointly initiated a regional project 'Improving Supply of Safe and Quality Livestock and Meat Exported from the Horn of Africa to Middle East and Gulf Countries'. An IGAD regional Livestock Identification and Traceability Systems legal framework was initiated in May 2016. An IGAD Regional Animal Welfare Strategy and an Action Plan were validated in August.

IGAD has placed a focus on developing the contribution of fish resources in arid and semi-arid areas to strengthening local food security and the diversification of livelihoods. An IGAD regional fisheries and aquaculture strategy and action plan was approved in March 2016. The Strengthening Trans-Boundary Water Governance and Cooperation in the IGAD Region programme, initiated in December of that year, aimed to enhance regional and local level frameworks for collaboration and dispute mitigation. In January 2022 the second IGAD Water Dialogue Forum was convened, in Entebbe, Uganda, on the theme 'Groundwater for resilience'.

During 2021 IGAD organized workshops that aimed to advance the sustainable development and management of two transboundary fishing areas: the Baro-Akobo-Sobat River Basin (shared by Ethiopia and South Sudan), and the Lake Turkana Basin (Ethiopia/Kenya).

In October 2021 a three-year IGAD Blue Economy Project was launched, with a focus on enhancing Blue Economy governance; compiling an inventory of plastic and chemical sea pollutants; developing measures to alleviate the impacts of these on aquatic biodiversity and ecosystems; and undertaking marine biodiversity situation analyses. An IGAD Blue Economy Strategy (2021–25) was initiated in April 2022.

An IGAD Land Policy Initiative (IGAD LPI), being implemented in the context of the African Union (AU)'s 2009 Land Declaration on Land Issues and Challenges in Africa, focuses on, *inter alia*, land and natural resources degradation; land tenure insecurity; the

disproportionately weak land rights of youth, women, pastoralists and other vulnerable groups; land governance and migration; land and conflict; and food insecurity.

An IGAD Regional Forestry Policy and Strategy was adopted by ministers responsible for forestry in March 2020.

Other activities to improve food security and preserve natural resources have included the introduction of remote-sensing services; the development of a Livestock Marketing Information System and of a Regional Integrated Information System; the establishment of training and credit schemes for fishers; research into the sustainable production of drought-resistant, high-yielding crop varieties; livestock vaccine production; the control of environmental pollution; the promotion of alternative sources of energy in the home; the promotion of community-based land husbandry; training programmes in grain marketing; and the implementation of the International Convention to Combat Desertification.

HEALTH AND SOCIAL DEVELOPMENT

In early 2020 the IGAD Executive Secretary established an IGAD Taskforce on COVID-19, mandated to collect information and best practices, to develop policies, and to formulate emergency response plans to combat the regional spread of the disease. In July the 36th extraordinary meeting of IGAD heads of state and government called for the adoption of regional guidelines on the harmonization and facilitation of cross-border transport operations, and welcomed the establishment of a new IGAD Emergency Fund (for the control of pandemic diseases). In December IGAD heads of state and government urged the international community to facilitate the timely and equitable distribution of safe and affordable COVID-19 vaccines. An inaugural IGAD Scientific Virtual Conference on Pharmaceutical Manufacturing was held in November 2021, at which means of developing a regional pharmaceutical production capacity were explored. The establishment of an IGAD Centre for Health Emergency Preparedness and Response, to be hosted by Sudan, was pending in 2022.

In May 2020 IGAD initiated a Regional Education Policy Framework, supporting the expansion of accessible, inclusive, high-quality education throughout the member states. The inaugural consultative meeting of a new Board of IGAD Council of Higher Education was convened in July 2021.

In December 2009 the first IGAD Women's Parliamentary Conference, convened in Addis Ababa, adopted a declaration on the Enhancement of Women's Participation and Representation in Decision-Making Positions. An IGAD Women and Peace Forum Board was inaugurated in October 2015. In March 2020 IGAD's Executive Secretary noted the need to redress persisting gender inequalities relating to women's education and health outcomes, as well as asset ownership.

In February 2016 an IGAD study was published on *Human Smuggling and Trafficking on the Horn of Africa–Central Mediterranean Route*, addressing organized irregular migration flows from member states into Europe. In November an IGAD Sectoral Ministerial Committee on Migration was inaugurated. An IGAD support platform was established in December 2019 to co-ordinate assistance to and long-term solutions for refugees in the region. In mid-2020 IGAD launched consultations with member states on harmonizing the regional collection and use of data on migration. The inaugural *IGAD Migration Statistics* report was issued in April 2022.

PEACE AND SECURITY

IGAD promotes conflict prevention, management and resolution through dialogue. It aims to restore peace and stability to member countries affected by conflict, in order that resources may be diverted for development purposes.

The Executive Secretary of IGAD participated in the first summit meeting of all East African heads of state and of government, convened in April 2005 in Addis Ababa. The meeting agreed to establish an Eastern African Standby Force (EASF), which was to form the regional component of the AU Standby Force. The EASF was declared ready to deploy in January 2015.

In April 2009 a meeting of IGAD ministers responsible for justice approved draft IGAD conventions on extradition, and on draft mutual legal assistance.

The IGAD Security Sector Programme (ISSP), which was launched in October 2011, focuses on initiatives in the areas of counterterrorism; transnational organized crime; maritime security; and capacity building of security institutions. In May 2015 IGAD and the Committee of Intelligence and Security Services of Africa concluded an agreement governing future co-operation in developing an intelligence exchange mechanism.

In February 2017 IGAD's Djibouti-based Center of Excellence for Preventing and Countering Violent Extremism (inaugurated in October 2016) validated a Regional Strategy on Preventing Violent Extremism/Countering Violent Extremism (the PVE/CVE Strategy). In September 2017, in Addis Ababa, IGAD organized the inaugural meeting of a Strategic Dialogue Forum in the Horn of Africa, which was conceived as a means for IGAD to take a more proactive role in promoting peace, security and development in the region. The first meeting of the steering committee of a new IGAD programme on Promoting Peace and Stability in the Horn of Africa Region was convened in February 2019.

In May 2019 the Committee of Ambassadors endorsed a Protocol on Preventive Diplomacy and Mediation, which was to guide member states in efficiently and transparently designing interventions and deploying envoys or mediators with the aim of preventing, managing and resolving conflicts in the region. In August the Committee endorsed draft guiding principles and rules of procedure to underpin the establishment of an IGAD Governance Forum (IGF). The IGF, which aimed to provide a policy framework and to act as a co-ordination mechanism to promote good governance and democratic elections throughout the region, was launched in Entebbe (Uganda) in April 2021. The third IGAD-UN conference on peace and security matters was convened in March 2020.

IGAD Election Observation Missions (EOMs) may be deployed to monitor elections in member states: in August 2022 IGAD dispatched a 24-member EOM to observer a general election in Kenya.

The establishment of a Nairobi-based IGAD Leadership Academy was pending in 2022.

Red Sea and Gulf of Aden: IGAD's membership includes four maritime littoral states, with, notably, Djibouti strategically located at the narrow Bab-el-Mandeb strait, connecting the Gulf of Aden and Red Sea. Maritime terrorism and crimes—such as piracy, illegal fishing, arms- and drug-trafficking, and the dumping of toxic waste—are emphasized as threats to regional security. An IGAD Integrated Maritime Strategy (IGAD IMS) was being implemented during 2015–30, with a focus on enhancing maritime governance; maritime infrastructures and critical routes; sustainable development and protection of the marine environment; maritime research and mapping; and the maritime economy. IGAD is the lead co-ordinating agency of the regional Programme to Promote Maritime Security in the Eastern and Southern Africa-Indian Ocean ('MASE'), aimed at combating piracy in the Indian Ocean. In June 2013 an agreement on maritime security was concluded between IGAD and the EU.

In February 2019 the IGAD Council of Ministers decided to establish an IGAD Task Force on the Red Sea and Gulf of Aden. The Force, which met for the first time in April, under the leadership of an IGAD Special Envoy for the Red Sea, Gulf of Aden and Somalia, was mandated to assess and advise on the implementation of relevant Council decisions, and to promote a common position and chart a plan of action to address challenges and opportunities in the Red Sea and the Gulf of Aden area. The fourth meeting of the Task Force was held in July 2021, in Bishoftu, Ethiopia.

Eritrea and Ethiopia: Following the violent escalation of a border dispute between Eritrea and Ethiopia in mid-1998 IGAD supported efforts by the Organization of African Unity (now AU) to mediate a ceasefire between the two sides. This was achieved in mid-2000. In September 2018 IGAD welcomed the recent adoption (on 5 September) of a Joint Declaration on the Comprehensive Cooperation between Ethiopia, Eritrea and Somalia. It was envisaged that the accord might hasten Eritrea's readmission to IGAD. In early November 2020 IGAD stated concern at mounting internal conflict in Ethiopia (government forces having launched a military intervention in the Tigray region) and urged conciliatory dialogue. In December the 38th extraordinary session of IGAD's heads of state and government stressed the need for constitutional order, stability and unity in Ethiopia, and welcomed a recent agreement permitting unimpeded access for humanitarian support to Tigray. In August 2022 IGAD's Executive Secretary expressed profound concern at reports of an escalation of hostilities in the Tigray border zone, and called for an immediate ceasefire. In the following month he welcomed indications that parties to the Ethiopian conflict would commit to negotiations under AU auspices.

Somalia: In May–August 2000 a conference aimed at securing peace in Somalia was convened in Arta, Djibouti, under the auspices of IGAD. The conference appointed a transitional Somali legislature, which then elected a transitional national president. The IGAD summit meeting, held in Khartoum, Sudan, in November, welcomed the conclusion in September of an agreement on reconciliation between the new Somali transitional administration and a prominent opposition alliance, and appointed a special envoy to implement IGAD's directives concerning the Somali situation. The second Somalia reconciliation conference was initiated in October 2002, in Eldoret, Kenya, and relocated to Nairobi in February 2003. In January 2004 the Nairobi conference determined to establish a new parliament; this was inaugurated in August. In January 2005 IGAD heads of state and of government authorized the deployment of a Peace Support Mission to Somalia (IGASOM) to assist the transitional federal authorities there, pending the subsequent deployment of an AU peace force; in January 2007, however, the AU Peace and Security Council authorized the deployment of the AU Mission in Somalia (AMISOM) in place of the proposed IGASOM. An IGAD Facilitator for Somalia Peace and Reconciliation was appointed in

December 2008. The Kampala Accord, signed in June 2011 by the President of the Somali transitional federal authorities and the Speaker of the transitional legislature, and related roadmap on its implementation, determined that IGAD and the East African Community (EAC), with UN and AU co-operation, should establish a political bureau to oversee and advance the Somali peace process. An extraordinary session of the Authority, convened in January 2012, endorsed an IGAD Somalia Inland Strategy and Action Plan to Prevent and Counter Piracy. (IGAD is a member of the International Contact Group on Piracy off the Coast of Somalia.) In December IGAD adopted a Grand Stabilization Plan for South Central Somalia, under the auspices of the IGAD Facilitator.

In May 2013 an extraordinary IGAD summit, convened in Addis Ababa, requested the Somali Federal Government to chart a process, with IGAD support, to provide for the establishment of an interim administration in the autonomous Juba region. This was endorsed by an agreement concluded between the Government and the newly elected Juba authorities in August. In September 2014 IGAD, with help from the UN and the EU, facilitated a reconciliation conference of Jubaland communities that was hosted, in Kismayo, by the Somali authorities. A permanent regional legislature was inaugurated in April 2015; Jubaland presidential elections were conducted in August.

An IGAD extraordinary summit convened in September 2016, in the Somali capital, Mogadishu, endorsed the outcome of a Somali National Leadership Forum (held in August) on a roadmap towards forthcoming elections. The legislative elections were held in October–November, and a new Somali Federal Parliament was inaugurated in late December. A presidential election was held in February 2017. In March an extraordinary summit, convened in Nairobi to address the large Somali displaced and refugee population throughout the region, adopted the Nairobi Comprehensive Plan of Action for Durable Solutions for Somali Refugees. A new IGAD Special Envoy for Somalia was appointed in June. In October IGAD expressed horror at recent al-Shabaab terror attacks perpetrated in Mogadishu that had resulted in at least 587 fatalities. In December a power-sharing agreement, negotiated under the auspices of IGAD, was signed by the leaders of Somalia's Galmudug State (which had been created in July 2015) and the Sufi-based paramilitary grouping Ahlu Sunna Wal Jama'a (which has opposed the al-Shabaab insurgency); this was, however, subsequently abandoned. In July 2018 a joint IGAD-UN Assistance Mission in Somalia was dispatched to Garowe, Hargeisa, Puntland and Somaliland, to explore means of achieving a peaceful resolution of an escalation of tension in the Tukaraq area. The IGAD Executive Secretary condemned a major terrorist atrocity committed against targets in Mogadishu in October. In October 2019 he deplored an attack against UN and AMISOM facilities again in the Somali capital. In August 2020 IGAD and other international partners issued a statement that called for the participation of all Somali leaders in pending consultations on developing electoral modalities—in relation to advancing the preparation of legislative and presidential elections that had been postponed from November 2020 to February 2021. The partners also offered to facilitate the process. In February 2021, following the further postponement of the planned elections, IGAD welcomed an agreement reached by the Federal Government of Somalia and Council of Presidential Candidates on a number of issues relating to security, public safety, and to upholding the right of peaceful assembly. Tensions mounted, however, culminating in violent protests following a decision in April to extend President Farmajo's term in office by two years. In early May IGAD expressed support for the resumption of dialogue, following the parliamentary annulment of the extension, and commended all parties for the conclusion of a political agreement reached on 27 May. In mid-2021 representatives of IGAD, AMISOM, the UN and the EU visited Somalia's federal member states with the aim of fostering constructive engagement in the electoral preparations. In December IGAD organized a capacity building workshop that developed a roadmap for enhancing intergovernmental relations and systems in Somalia's federal structure. Legislative elections were initiated in Somalia in November. In January 2022 IGAD's Executive Secretary strongly condemned a terrorist attack that caused several fatalities in Mogadishu. On 1 April AMISOM was superseded by an AU Transition Mission in Somalia. A new Parliament was inaugurated in April, and the electoral process was completed in mid-May following the election and swearing in of a new President, Hassan Sheikh Mohamud. IGAD's Executive Secretary offered the organization's full support to the new government, and commended former President Farmajo for facilitating a peaceful transition of power.

South Sudan: Following the referendum on self-determination for South Sudan, held in January 2011, and South Sudan's consequent attainment of independence in July, the new nation was admitted to IGAD in November. In April 2012 IGAD's Executive Secretary expressed deep concern at escalating conflict between Sudan and South Sudan, and urged the two sides to adhere to a Memorandum of Understanding (MOU) signed in February on non-aggression and co-operation. From 2013 sectarian conflict between forces loyal to the President, Salva Kiir Mayardit, and those supportive of the Vice-President, Riek Machar, undermined the security of South Sudan.

In December 2013 IGAD established a Mediation Process for South Sudan—under the leadership of three newly appointed special envoys to South Sudan—tasked with brokering a ceasefire between government and opposition forces and pursuing a dialogue for inclusive and sustainable peace. An extraordinary summit meeting on South Sudan, held in January 2014, welcomed the signing in that month by the South Sudan authorities and armed militants of a Cessation of Hostilities Agreement (COHA) and of a further accord relating to the status of detainees. The meeting urged the expeditious implementation of the agreements, and, in that respect, directed IGAD's special envoys to establish an IGAD Monitoring and Verification Mechanism (IGAD MVM) in South Sudan. IGAD leaders met once again in an extraordinary summit in mid-March to assess progress made by the IGAD mediation team in South Sudan. They welcomed the adoption in February by the parties to the conflict in South Sudan of a follow-up 'Implementation Modalities' document, and authorized the prompt deployment of a regional Protection and Deterrent Force as part of the IGAD MVM. (The Force was deployed from June.) IGAD MVM activities commenced in South Sudan at the beginning of April. Priority IGAD monitoring and verification teams—MVTs—were also deployed from April. An extraordinary summit of IGAD heads of state and of government, convened in June, welcomed the conclusion in early May by the South Sudanese President and opposition leadership of an agreement on ending the conflict in South Sudan. In late August an extraordinary summit meeting deplored numerous violations by all parties of agreements signed to date; demanded full co-operation with the MVTs; welcomed the recent conclusion by all parties of the Implementation Matrix to the January COHA; and endorsed arrangements to establish a new negotiation political dispensation for South Sudan, which was to outline a transitional governance agenda, and also arrangements for a transitional government of national unity. (At the end of August the main opposition grouping denied having signed the Implementation Matrix, although this was contested by IGAD, and the special envoys urged all the parties to the conflict to adhere to it.) An IGAD summit meeting held in early November demanded that both the South Sudanese Government and the opposition cease hostilities with immediate effect, and threatened the imposition of collective IGAD sanctions should this not happen. In February 2015 the South Sudanese President and main opposition leader signed a document that recommitted the parties to the conflict to implementing all previously signed accords, with the aim of establishing a transitional government by early July, and reaching an agreement by 5 March on facilitating this process; the IGAD secretariat released a statement in early March, however, regretting that this initial deadline had not been met. In June an expanded negotiating mechanism, IGAD Plus, was agreed upon by the conflicting sides, to comprise, in addition to the special envoys, representatives of the AU, the EU, the UN, the IPF, the People's Republic of China, and the so-called Troika of Norway, the United Kingdom and the USA. A new compromise peace agreement, based on the protracted negotiations with all stakeholders to the conflict, was issued in July. In August a fourth phase of peace talks, under the IGAD Plus formation, was initiated, resulting in all parties signing a new Agreement on the Resolution of the Conflict in South Sudan (ARCSS). IGAD MVM was transformed at this time into the Ceasefire and Transitional Security Arrangements Monitoring Mechanism (CTSAMM). In November IGAD appointed chairpersons to lead the CTSAMM and a Joint Monitoring and Evaluation Commission (JMEC) on the Peace Agreement on South Sudan, also established to oversee the implementation of the accord. In January 2016 IGAD ministers responsible for foreign affairs noted only limited implementation, hitherto, of ARCSS, and urged representation on the JMEC by all relevant South Sudanese political organizations. The Transitional Government of National Unity of South Sudan—with Kiir remaining as President and Machar returning to the administration as First Vice-President (a newly established post)—was appointed at the end April and was to remain in power pending elections to be held in 2018. In mid-May 2016 IGAD mediators deplored an escalation of fighting in South Sudan since late April. The mediators also stated deep concern at restrictions imposed by government forces on the MVTs' freedom of movement.

An extraordinary summit of IGAD leaders held in July 2016, in Nairobi, to address a deterioration in the security situation in South Sudan, strongly condemned a recent escalation of violent conflict in Juba, which had resulted in significant fatalities, injuries, and destruction of properties. The summit demanded an immediate ceasefire; the re-opening—under the protection of the UN Mission in South Sudan (UNMISS)—of Juba International Airport; the immediate return of all armed forces and weaponry to barracks; the opening of humanitarian corridors; an urgent revision of the mandate of UNMISS to enable the establishment of an intervention brigade; those responsible for the breakdown of law and order to be made accountable for their actions; and the immediate implementation of the security arrangements provided for under the August

2015 Agreement. In August 2016 an IGAD Plus extraordinary summit issued a communiqué in which it expressed deep concern over the grave conflict-related humanitarian situation and population displacement in South Sudan, and reiterated strong condemnation of the recent outbreak of violent conflict in Juba, as well as the targeting of diplomatic, UN and humanitarian personnel. The summit meeting also endorsed a proposal of East African Chiefs of Defence that a Regional Protection Force should be deployed under the remit of UNMISS. Consequently, in mid-August—taking note of IGAD's recommendation—the UN Security Council authorized the deployment of a 4,000-strong Regional Protection Force within UNMISS, tasked with creating a secure environment in and around Juba, and—in response to extreme circumstances—elsewhere in South Sudan. Having initially rejected the immediate deployment of the Force, the South Sudanese authorities eventually granted consent in September. An IGAD-AU-UN joint consultative meeting convened in January 2017 pledged continued collective commitment to pursuing a lasting peace in South Sudan. The 31st extraordinary IGAD summit meeting, held in June, welcomed a national dialogue process that was launched in late May by President Kiir, and urged that this should be inclusive and transparent. The summit commended a recent announcement by President Kiir of a ceasefire, and urged armed opposition forces to renounce violence. It expressed regret at the lengthy delay in fully deploying the new Regional Protection Force. (The phased deployment of the Force eventually began in early August.) The IGAD leaders determined to convene promptly a High-Level Revitalization Forum (HLRF) of the parties to the August 2015 Agreement on the Resolution of the Conflict in South Sudan and appointed a new IGAD Special Envoy for South Sudan. The Forum convened for its inaugural session in Addis Ababa, in December 2017, attended by representatives of all parties to the conflict, IGAD Plus observers and civil society organizations. A new Agreement on Cessation of Hostilities, Protection of Civilians, and Humanitarian Access was concluded. From early 2018, however, repeated violations of the accord were reported. The second phase of the HLRF on South Sudan, convened in February under the auspices of IGAD, reaffirmed commitment to the December 2017 Agreement. In late January 2018 an extraordinary session of the IGAD Council of Ministers determined that punitive sanctions should be imposed against individuals found to have violated the Agreement, and that violators would also be referred to the AU Peace and Security Council. A further extraordinary meeting of the Council in late March reaffirmed this position. Nevertheless, violent conflict intensified in the first half of 2018, particularly in Central Equatoria, Jonglei and Unity states. On 12 September, following extensive engagement by IGAD and regional leaders, with support from the AU and other partners, the parties to the conflict, gathered in Addis Ababa during the 33rd extraordinary session of the IGAD Assembly, adopted a Revitalized Agreement on the Resolution of the Conflict in South Sudan (R-ARCSS). The inaugural meeting was held in early December of a new Technical Boundary Committee, comprising members appointed by the IGAD member states and the (UK-USA-Norway) Troika, and supported by an international expert appointed by the UN. Its first task was to map and report to the IGAD mediation process on the tribal areas of South Sudan as they stood on 1 January 1956.

In May 2019 the parties to the R-ARCSS extended the pre-transition stage of the agreement by six months, until November, at which time a 36-month transition period was to commence, with elections scheduled to be held 60 days prior to the transition period's end. Several pre-transition stage tasks, including the cantonment, screening, training and unification of forces, and the determination of the number and borders of states, remained to be finalized. At that time the IGAD Council of Ministers cited insufficient political will and funding as challenges to the implementation of the R-ARCSS. Militant groupings that were not signatories to the R-ARCSS reportedly remained active in Central Equatoria region, in particular in the Yei area. In November parties to the R-ARCSS agreed to extend the pre-transition stage for a further 100 days. On 22 February 2020 Kiir and Machar concluded a power-sharing agreement, formally ending the civil war. Accordingly, a new Revitalized Transitional Government of National Unity (RTGoNU) was established, including Machar and other opposition leaders as Vice-Presidents. The IGAD Executive Secretary congratulated President Kiir and First Vice-President Machar, and other South Sudanese leaders, on the formation of the RTGoNU in mid-March. An extraordinary meeting of the IGAD Council of Ministers held by videoconference in April called on stakeholders in South Sudan promptly to reconstitute the Transitional National Legislative Assembly, in accordance with provisions of the R-ARCSS. In view of the ongoing threats to the implementation of the peace process posed by the public health and socioeconomic impacts of the COVID-19 emergency, and also by the continuing regional desert locust invasion, the Council of Ministers decided to work closely with the South Sudanese Government to mobilize regional and international material and financial assistance. In May, in the context of combating the spread of COVID-19, the IGAD Special Envoy for South Sudan urged an immediate cessation of inter-communal and all other forms of violence, to ensure access to health care and the protection of frontline health workers. In late August the IGAD Executive Secretary issued an appeal for support for response and rehabilitation activities that were ongoing in areas of South Sudan (particularly the Jonglei, Upper Nile and Warrap regions) that had been devastated by flooding. IGAD organized a national consultative meeting on halting the illicit circulation of small arms and light weapons in Sudan that was held in December. In March 2021 the IGAD Special Envoy congratulated RTGoNU and opposition factions for recommitting to the 2017 cessation of aggression agreement and to substantive political negotiations. At the beginning of June 2021 a joint delegation that included representatives of IGAD, the AU, and UNMISS visited Pibor, in eastern South Sudan, where intercommunal violence had recently escalated. In mid-September a peace mission comprising delegates from IGAD, UNMISS and other partners visited Tambura, in Western Equatoria, where since June some 80,000 people had been displaced by conflict. In August IGAD and UNMISS stated concern at divisions that had emerged within Riek Machar's Sudan People's Liberation Movement/Army-in-Opposition (SPLM/A-IO), that had led to unrest in Magenis, Upper Nile. IGAD's Executive Secretary and the IGAD Special Envoy for South Sudan undertook a three-day fact-finding mission to South Sudan in that month, during which they met President Kiir and First Vice-President Machar. South Sudan was temporarily suspended from participation in IGAD in December 2021 for non-payment of dues. In 2022 IGAD was supporting efforts to implement in full the R-ARCSS, amid ongoing intercommunal violence in the country. In July the 39th extraordinary IGAD summit called on all stakeholders to draft a roadmap setting out clear benchmarks and timelines to support the completion of the 36-month transition period. In the following month the RTGoNU adopted an Agreement on the Roadmap to a Peaceful and Democratic End to the Transitional Period in South Sudan; this extended the end of the transitional period to 22 February 2025.

Sudan: In April 2019, following the overthrow of President Omar al-Bashir by the Sudanese armed forces and the establishment of a military-led transitional regime in Khartoum, IGAD offered its support, in co-operation with the AU, in enabling Sudanese stakeholders to ensure a peaceful transition to the restoration of civil political authority. In early July the IGAD Executive Secretary welcomed the conclusion of an agreement by the Transitional Military Council of Sudan and the opposition that laid the framework for a return to civilian rule. In mid-August he congratulated the Sudanese people on the delivery of a constitutional decree on power sharing, and welcomed the appointment of Abdallah Hamdok as Prime Minister of the newly established Transitional Government of Sudan. IGAD welcomed the initialling on 31 August 2020, in Juba, South Sudan, of a peace agreement between the Transitional Government of Sudan and five opposition groupings. In December the 38th extraordinary session of IGAD heads of state and government commended the signature in October of the Juba Peace Agreement by the Transitional Government of Sudan and two further opposition militias. The IGAD leaders also welcomed ongoing Sudan–South Sudan co-operation in seeking long-term solutions for subregional population displacement. The IGAD Executive Secretary, and Norway, the UK and USA (the Troika countries) co-signed the Juba Peace Agreement in June 2021 as guarantors.

In September 2021 IGAD condemned an attempt by the military to seize power in Sudan. On 25 October the Transitional Government of Sudan was overthrown in a military coup, the transitional institutions dissolved and the civilian leadership detained. IGAD's Executive Secretary stated alarm at this development, condemned any attempt to undermine the transitional authorities, and demanded the release of all the detained leaders. Although the Prime Minister, Abdalla Hamdok, was released on 26 October, he remained under the 'close surveillance' of the military, and other senior members of the transitional administration continued to be detained. In November the Executive Secretary welcomed an agreement by the military to reinstate Prime Minister Hamdok and to release all political leaders detained in the coup. An IGAD mission visited Sudan in January 2022 to pursue dialogue with all parties, following Hamdok's resignation at the start of the year. In February IGAD organized a

workshop in Nyala, with participation by representatives of local authorities, that extended technical assistance on conflict prevention, management and mediation, and peacebuilding. The detention of opposition supporters contributed to ongoing political protests and unrest. From April IGAD, with the UN mission in Sudan (UNITAMS) and the AU, undertook discussions with stakeholders to the Juba Peace Agreement in order to advance more formal political dialogue. They issued a joint statement, as the Trilateral AU-IGAD-UN Mechanism, in mid-May urging a lifting of the country's state of emergency and an end to violence on the part of the authorities, and reiterated their support for restoring constitutional order. At the end of May IGAD's Executive Secretary welcomed a decree issued by Sudan's military regime that ended the state of emergency.

Publications

Annual Report.

IGAD Migration Statistics.

IGAD News (2 a year).

Specialized Institutes

IGAD Climate Prediction and Application Centre (ICPAC): POB 10304, 00100 Nairobi, Kenya; tel. (20) 3514426; e-mail info@ icpac.net; internet www.icpac.net; f. 1989 as the Drought Monitoring Centre and subsequently renamed; became an IGAD specialized institution in 2007 (and designated in 2016 as a World Meteorological Org. Regional Climate Centre); aims to enhance subregional and national capacities to utilize climate knowledge for the provision of climate information and prediction, and early warning, and for advancing sustainable devt; offers open access to a Data Center and other sources of environmental monitoring and observation; organizes a regular ICPAC Greater Horn of African Climate Outlook Forum; an IGAD Regional Climate Change Strategy was being implemented during 2016–30; in Sept. 2021 launched an online East Africa Drought Watch system; joined the global Risk-informed Early Action Partnership in March 2022; mems: Burundi, Djibouti, Eritrea, Ethiopia, Kenya, Rwanda, South Sudan, Sudan, Somalia, Tanzania, Uganda; Dir Dr GULEID ARTAN (Somalia).

IGAD Conflict Early Warning and Response Mechanism (CEWARN): POB 58652, Addis Ababa, Ethiopia; tel. (11) 6614488; fax (11) 6614489; e-mail cewarn@cewarn.org; internet cewarn.org; f. 2002; aims to prevent and mitigate violent conflict in the IGAD mem. states; has directed particular attention to cross-border pastoralist and related conflicts; the regional strategy for conflict early warning and response launched by IGAD in Sept. 2012 provided for the strengthening of CEWARN to address a broader range of national and transboundary security factors, such as competition for natural resources and land; migration; displaced populations; internal and international boundaries; climate; environment; ethnicity and religion; and economic variations; works through a network of Conflict Early Warning and Response Units, national research institutes, and field monitors and conducts conflict profiling and scenario building exercises to secure accurate and up-to-date data on situations; a CEWARN Rapid Response Fund was established in 2009 to provide grants for short-term peacebuilding initiatives; Dir CAMLUS OMOGO; publ. *Conflict Early Warning in the Horn* (issued in April 2021).

Other IGAD specialist institutes are the IGAD Center for Pastoral Areas and Livestock Development, the IGAD Center of Excellence in Preventing and Countering Violent Extremism, and the IGAD Sheikh Technical Veterinary School. In December 2020 IGAD heads of state and government endorsed a ministerial decision made in 2013 to establish an IGAD Disaster Operations Centre and IGAD Disaster Response Fund.

INTERNATIONAL CRIMINAL COURT—ICC

Address: Oude Waalsdorperweg 10, 2597 AK The Hague, Netherlands.

Telephone: (70) 5158515; **fax:** (70) 5158555; **e-mail:** otp .informationdesk@icc-cpi.int; **internet:** www.icc-cpi.int.

The ICC was established by the Rome Statute of the International Criminal Court, which was adopted by 120 states participating in a United Nations (UN) Diplomatic Conference in July 1998. The Statute (and therefore also the ICC's temporal jurisdiction) entered into force on 1 July 2002. At October 2022 the Statute had 123 states parties.

Amendments to the Rome Statute that were adopted in December 2017 extended its scope to cover the use of non-detectable fragment weapons; blinding laser weapons; and biological and toxic weapons. In July 2018 amendments entered into effect that characterized the use of certain weaponry during non-international conflict as a war crime, and defined international aggression as the use of armed force by a state against the sovereignty, territorial integrity or political independence of another, or in any other manner inconsistent with the UN Charter. A further amendment (adopted in December 2019) designated the deliberate starvation of civilians in a non-international conflict as a war crime. In March 2021 an ICC Case Law Database was launched. A revised version of the *Code of Judicial Ethics of the International Criminal Court* entered into force in early October 2022.

The Court comprises the Presidency (consisting of a President and first and second Vice-Presidents), Chambers (including a Pre-Trial Chamber, Trial Chamber and Appeals Chamber) with 18 permanent judges, Office of the Prosecutor (comprising the Prosecutor and up to two Deputy Prosecutors), and Registry. The judges must each have a different nationality and equitably represent the major legal systems of the world, a fair geographical distribution, and a fair proportion of men and women. They are elected by the Assembly of States Parties to the Rome Statute from two lists, the first comprising candidates with established competence in criminal law and procedures and the second comprising candidates with established competence in relevant areas of international law, to terms of office of three, six or nine years. The President and Vice-Presidents are elected by an absolute majority of the judges for renewable three-year terms of office. The Prosecutor is elected by an absolute majority of states parties to the Rome Statute to a non-renewable nine-year term of office. In March 2021 the Court appointed a Focal Point for Gender Equality.

The Court has established a Trust Fund for Victims (TFV) to finance mandated reparations (including compensation, restitution, or rehabilitation), and other assistance, for victims (individuals or groups of individuals) of crimes under the jurisdiction of the Court. The Fund is administered by an independent board of directors and secretariat, led by an Executive Director. By December 2021 the ICC had issued four decisions on reparations for victims, relating to the convictions of Thomas Lubanga, Germain Katanga and Bosco Ntaganda (see *Situation in the Democratic Republic of the Congo—DRC*), and of Ahmad al-Mahdi (see *Situation in Mali*). Collective service-based reparations to victims provide education and training (aimed at advancing socioeconomic prospects); income-generating activities; pensions; subsistence allowances; and psychological and physical health care. During 2021 the TFV financed community peacebuilding and other projects in the Central African Republic (CAR), Côte d'Ivoire, DRC, Georgia, Kenya, Mali and northern Uganda. The Fund's reserve for reparations totalled €3.2m. in 2021.

By October 2022 31 cases had been brought before the ICC for investigation. Two preliminary investigations were underway at that time.

In January 2017 the 28th African Union (AU) Assembly adopted a non-binding decision that supported a strategy of collective African withdrawal from the Court. Various diplomatic efforts have subsequently been undertaken with a view to strengthening relations between the Court and Africa.

In June 2019 representatives of African parties to the Rome Statute, the ICC, the TFV, the AU, the European Union and the Organisation de la Francophonie collectively participated in a Retreat, in Addis Ababa, Ethiopia, with a view to strengthening dialogue on the mandate and activities of the ICC.

In October 2016 Burundi announced its intention to withdraw from the Rome Statute, the first country ever to do so; this took effect in October 2017. Later in October 2016, South Africa and then The Gambia determined to withdraw, also with a year's notice. In February 2017, however, a newly elected administration in The Gambia rescinded that country's notice. In the same month the South African high court found the government's withdrawal to be unconstitutional and invalid, and consequently it was revoked in March.

THE COURT
(October 2022)

	Term ends*
President: PIOTR HOFMAŃSKI (Poland) . . .	2024
First Vice-President: LUZ DEL CARMEN IBAÑEZ CARRANZA (Peru)	2027
Second Vice President: ANTOINE KESIA-MBE MINDUA (DRC)	2024
MARC PERRIN DE BRICHAMBAUT (France) . . .	2024
BERTRAM SCHMITT (Germany)	2024
PÉTER KOVÁCS (Hungary)	2024
CHANG-HO CHUNG (Republic of Korea)	2024
SOLOMY BALUNGI BOSSA (Uganda)	2027
TOMOKO AKANE (Japan)	2027
REINE ALAPINI-GANSOU (Benin)	2027
KIMBERLY PROST (Canada)	2027
ROSARIO SALVATORE AITALA (Italy)	2027
JOANNA KORNER (United Kingdom)	2030
GOCHA LORDKIPANIDZE (Georgia)	2030
MARÍA DEL SOCORRO FLORES LIERA (Mexico) . .	2030
SERGIO GERARDO UGALDE GODINEZ (Costa Rica) .	2030
MIATTA MARIA SAMBA (Sierra Leone)	2030
ALTHEA VIOLET ALEXIS-WINDSOR (Trinidad and Tobago)	2030

* Each term ends on 10 March of the year indicated.

Prosecutor: KARIM A. A. KHAN (UK).

Registrar: PETER LEWIS (UK).

PRELIMINARY EXAMINATION

Nigeria: opened in November 2010; addresses alleged crimes against humanity (namely: murder and persecution) or war crimes committed in the Niger Delta, Nigeria's Middle-Belt states and in the context of armed conflict between Boko Haram and the Nigerian security forces.

CLOSED INVESTIGATIONS

Gabon: in September 2018 the ICC Prosecutor ended an investigation by the Court into the 2016 post-election violence in Gabon, citing a lack of subject matter jurisdiction, finding there to be no reasonable basis to construe as crimes against humanity (as covered by the Rome Statute) acts committed either by the Gabonese security forces or by members of the opposition, and determining that the crime of incitement to genocide had not been committed during the election campaign.

Guinea: in September 2022, in view of the initiation of trial proceedings at the national level, the Prosecutor closed a preliminary investigation that had been opened in October 2009 into alleged crimes against humanity committed in Guinea on 28 September 2009 (when a peaceful opposition protest was crushed by the country's Presidential Guard, resulting in numerous fatalities and incidents of sexual violence).

SITUATIONS

Uganda: referred to the Court in January 2004 by the Ugandan Government; the ICC Prosecutor agreed to open an investigation into the situation in July; relates to the long-term unrest in the north of the country; in October 2005 the Court unsealed warrants of arrest (issued in July) against five commanders of the Ugandan Lord's Resistance Army (LRA), including the LRA leader, Joseph Kony; proceedings against two of the accused were subsequently terminated following confirmation of their deaths; in January 2015 Dominic Ongwen, one of the accused (and, notably, a former child soldier), surrendered to US forces in the CAR and was transferred to the custody of the Court; his trial commenced in December 2016; in February 2021 he was found guilty on 61 counts that encompassed war crimes and crimes against humanity committed in northern Uganda between 1 July 2002 and 31 December 2005, including atrocities perpetrated against civilians during attacks on IDP camps in 2003–04; conscripting children aged below 15 years and deploying them militarily; and sexual and gender based crimes—he was convicted, *inter alia*, of inflicting 'forced pregnancy', the first ever such conviction by the Court; he was sentenced, in May 2021, to 25 years in prison.

Democratic Republic of the Congo (DRC): referred in April 2004 by the DRC Government; the ICC Prosecutor agreed in June to open an investigation into the situation; relates to alleged crimes committed since 1 July 2002; in March 2006 Thomas Lubanga Dyilo, a DRC militia leader, was arrested by the DRC authorities and transferred to the Court, thereby becoming the first ICC indictee to be captured; Lubanga was charged with conscripting child soldiers; in July 2007 warrants of arrest were issued for the DRC rebel commanders Germain Katanga and Mathieu Ngudjolo Chui; Katanga was transferred into the custody of the Court in October 2007 and Ngudjolo Chui in February 2008; in April 2008 the Court unsealed a warrant of arrest for the rebel leader Bosco Ntaganda, relating to the exploitation of children under the age of 15 years as soldiers during 2002–03, in Ituri; a second warrant for Ntaganda, expanding upon the original charges, was issued in July 2012; in that same month a warrant was issued for the arrest of Sylvestre Mudacumura, the commander of the Democratic Forces for the Liberation of Rwanda, relating to war crimes (specifically cruel treatment; attacking civilians; mutilation; outrages against personal dignity; rape; torture; murder; destruction of property; and pillaging) allegedly committed during the period 20 January 2009–30 September 2010; Lubanga's trial—the first conducted by the Court—commenced in January 2009; Lubanga was found guilty in March 2012, in the first verdict given by the Court, and in July of that year he was sentenced to 14 years' imprisonment (the Court's Appeals Chamber upheld the sentence in December 2014); the trial in the case of Katanga and Ngudjolo Chui commenced in November 2009; Ngudjolo Chui was acquitted of all charges of war crimes and crimes against humanity in December 2012 (an appeal by the Office of the Prosecutor against the acquittal was rejected in February 2015 by the Appeals Chamber); in March 2014 Katanga was found guilty of four counts of war crimes and one of crimes against humanity, and in May he was sentenced to 12 years' imprisonment (nearly seven years already spent in detention were to be deducted from this); in November 2015 a Panel of the Appeals Chamber reviewed Katanga's sentence and reduced it by three years and eight months; in April 2016 the ICC presidency agreed that Katanga might be tried on additional charges by the DRC authorities; in March 2017 the Court awarded individual and collective reparations to 297 victims of Katanga's crimes; most of the reparations order against Katanga was upheld by the Appeals Chamber in March 2018; in December 2011 charges relating to crimes against humanity and other war crimes were withdrawn against Callixte Mbarushimana, an alleged rebel leader who had been arrested by the French authorities in October 2010 and transferred to the custody of the Court in January 2011; in March 2013 Gen. Ntaganda surrendered to the US embassy in Kigali, Rwanda and was transferred to the custody of the Court; his trial commenced in September 2015, and in July 2019 he was found guilty of the commission of war crimes and crimes against humanity; he was sentenced to 30 years imprisonment in November (he subsequently initiated an appeal against the verdict); in March 2021 the Court authorized the payment of reparations totalling US $30m. to the victims of Ntaganda's atrocities; in September 2022 the Appeals Chamber determined that a new reparations order should be issued in the Ntaganda case, finding several errors in the basis for the 2021 judgment, including that it had not made an appropriate determination of the number of potentially eligible or actual victims, and had not sufficiently elaborated the concept of transgenerational harm.

Central African Republic (CAR) (I): referred in January 2005 by the CAR Government; the ICC Prosecutor agreed to open an investigation into the situation in May; relates to war crimes and crimes against humanity allegedly committed during the period October 2002–March 2003; in May 2008 the Court issued a warrant of arrest for Jean-Pierre Bemba Gombo, the leader of the Mouvement du Libération du Congo (the 'Banyamulenge'); Bemba was transferred into the custody of the Court in July 2008, and his trial commenced in November 2010; in March 2016 the Court declared Bemba guilty of two counts of crimes against humanity and three counts of war crimes; he was sentenced in June to 18 years' imprisonment; in October Bemba, Narcisse Arido, Jean-Jacques Mangenda Kabongo, Aimé Kilolo Musamba and Fidèle Babala Wandu were found guilty of corruptly influencing witnesses at Bemba's trial; the Appeals Chamber upheld the convictions against them, in respect of most of the charges, in March 2018; in June the Appeals Chamber overturned Bemba's convictions for war crimes and crimes against humanity, finding that he had been wrongly convicted for specific criminal acts that were outside the scope of the charges confirmed against him and that the original verdict had erroneously assessed that Bemba had not attempted to halt crimes perpetrated by his subordinates; in September Bemba, Kabongo and Musamba received one-year sentences (considered already served) in respect of the 2016 charges relating to obstructing the administration of justice.

CAR (II): referred in May 2014; the ICC Prosecutor agreed in September to open an investigation into the situation; relates to war crimes and crimes against humanity allegedly committed in the CAR since 1 August 2012 (and ongoing), including torture, murder, persecution, forced displacement, rape, pillaging, attacks against humanitarian missions, and the use in combat of children aged under 15 years; in November 2018 Alfred Yekatom, alleged to be responsible for crimes against humanity and war crimes in the CAR between December 2013 and August 2014, surrendered to the Court; in the following month, Patrice-Edouard Ngaïssona, accused of similar crimes, was arrested in France and transferred to the custody of the Court; a Pre-Trial Chamber determined, in February 2019, to join the two cases; the two defendants' trial commenced in February 2021; in January 2019 a sealed arrest warrant was issued for Mahamat Said Abdel Kani, a military commander accused of committing war crimes and crimes against humanity in Bangui in 2013; Said was transferred to the Court by the CAR authorities in January 2021; in Dec. the Court confirmed the charges against Said and committed him to trial (this opened in September 2022); in July 2022 a public redacted version was issued of an arrest warrant issued in January 2019 against Mahamat Nouradine Adam, the CAR government minister responsible for security, emigration, immigration and public order during March–August 2013, who was accused of committing war crimes and crimes against humanity at that time.

Darfur, Sudan: referred to the Court in March 2005 by the UN Security Council following publication of the report of an International Commission of Inquiry on Darfur; the ICC Prosecutor agreed to open an investigation relating to the situation prevailing in Darfur since 1 July 2002; the UN Secretary-General handed the Prosecutor a sealed list of 51 names of people identified in the report as having committed crimes under international law; in April 2007 the Court issued warrants for the arrests of Ahmad Harun, a former Sudanese government minister, and Muhammad Ali Abd-al-Rahman ('Ali Kushayb'), a leader of the Sudanese Janjaweed militia, who were both accused of perpetrating war crimes and crimes against humanity; in July 2008 the Prosecutor presented evidence that Sudan's President Omar al-Bashir had been responsible for committing crimes against humanity and genocide in Darfur; an arrest warrant for al-Bashir was issued by the Court in March 2009; a second arrest warrant for al-Bashir was issued in July 2010, charging him with genocide against three ethnic groups in Darfur; in May 2009 a summons was issued against the militia leader Bahr Idriss Abu Garda, who appeared voluntarily before the Court later in that month; the Pre-Trial Chamber examining the Garda case declined, in February 2010, to confirm the charges against him; in June Abdallah Banda Abakaer Nourain and Saleh Mohammed Jerbo Jamus surrendered voluntarily to the Court, having been accused, with Abu Garda, of attacking the Haskanita AU camp in September–October 2007 and causing the deaths of 12 peacekeeping troops; they were not, however, taken into the custody of the Court; the charges against Abdallah Banda were confirmed in March 2011, while proceedings against Jerbo were terminated in October 2013 on the basis of strong evidence that he had died in the previous April; in March 2012 the Court issued an arrest warrant for the Sudanese Minister of Defence, Abdelrahim Mohamed Hussein, for crimes against humanity and war crimes committed during August 2003–March 2004, when he was the country's minister for the interior; in September 2014 the Court issued an arrest warrant against Abdallah Banda, who had not presented before the Court, and whose scheduled trial commencement date (in November) had, therefore, been vacated; in December 2014 the Prosecutor—citing inaction by the UN Security Council in pressing for the enforcement of the arrest warrant against al-Bashir—suspended the investigation into the situation in Darfur; in July 2017 a Pre-Trial Chamber of the Court found that South Africa had failed to comply with its obligations under the Rome Statute by refraining from arresting al-Bashir and surrendering him to the Court when he visited South Africa in June 2015 to attend an AU summit meeting; the Chamber decided, however, not to refer South Africa onwards to the Assembly of States Parties or to the UN Security Council; in December 2017 a Pre-Trial Chamber assessed that Jordan had also failed to abide by its obligations under the Statute by not detaining al-Bashir in March, on the occasion of his attendance at a League of Arab States summit meeting; the Chamber referred Jordan to the Assembly of States Parties and to the UN Security Council; the decision to refer Jordan to the Security Council was, however, overturned by the Appeals Chamber in May 2019; in April 2019 al-Bashir was deposed and detained by Sudan's armed forces; in February 2020 Sudan's transitional government indicated that it would transfer al-Bashir and other indictees into the custody of the Court; in June Ali Kushayb was transferred into the custody of the Court, having reportedly surrendered to the authorities in the CAR; a request for his interim release was rejected by the Court's Appeals Chamber in October; a confirmation of charges hearing against Ali Kushayb took place in May 2021, and the charges were confirmed by Pre-Trial Chamber II in July; his trial commenced in April 2022.

Kenya: in November 2009 the Presidency of the Court decided to assign the situation in Kenya, relating to violent unrest that followed the December 2007 presidential elections, to a Pre-Trial Chamber; on

31 March 2010 Pre-Trial Chamber II granted the Prosecution authorization to open an investigation *proprio motu* into the situation of Kenya; in March 2011 the ICC issued summonses for six Kenyans alleged to be criminally responsible for crimes against humanity, and in April the six accused presented voluntarily to the Court; charges against four of the six: William Samoei Ruto, Joshua arap Sang, Francis Kirimi Muthaura and Uhuru Muigai Kenyatta were confirmed in January 2012; in March, however, the Court Prosecutor filed to withdraw the charges against Muthaura; Kenyatta was elected as President of Kenya in March 2013; he assumed office, with Ruto as his Vice-President, in early April; trial proceedings against Ruto and arap Sang commenced in September; a warrant against Walter Osapiri Barasa, accused of offences against the administration of justice (i.e. attempting corruptly to influence witnesses) was unsealed in October 2013; Kenyatta's trial was postponed during 2014 pending the gathering of information and evidence; President Kenyatta was ordered to attend a public status conference on 8 October, and thus became the first serving head of state to appear before the Court; in early December the Trial Chamber refused a request from the Prosecution for a further adjournment of the trial; given the lack of sufficient evidence and 'non-compliance' by the Kenyan authorities in providing relevant information; the Prosecutor subsequently withdrew all charges against Kenyatta; in March 2015 the Court agreed that the charges be withdrawn; proceedings against Ruto and arap Sang were terminated in April 2016; in September a trial chamber of the Court determined that Kenya had failed to comply with its obligations to co-operate with the Court, and referred the matter to the Assembly of States Parties to the Rome Statute; a warrant of arrest was issued under seal in March 2015 against Paul Gicheru and Philip Kipkoech Bett, who were charged with corruptly influencing witnesses; in November 2020 Gicheru surrendered to the Netherlands authorities, and was promptly delivered into the custody of the Court; in December a Pre-Trial Chamber severed the (hitherto conjoined) charges against Gicheru and Bett; on 28 January 2021 Gicheru was granted an interim release order, under which he was permitted to return temporarily to Kenya; his trial opened in February 2022.

Côte d'Ivoire: in October 2011 an ICC Pre-Trial Chamber agreed, at the request of the Prosecutor, to commence an investigation into alleged crimes committed in Côte d'Ivoire between 28 November 2010 and 12 April 2011, during a period of civil unrest resulting from disputed presidential election results; in November the former president, Laurent Gbagbo, who had been in Ivorian custody since April, was transferred to the Court to face charges of crimes against humanity; a warrant for the arrest of his wife, Simone Gbagbo, was issued in February 2012 and made public in November; in May 2015 the Appeals Chamber upheld a decision on the admissibility of the case against Mme Gbagbo; this, however, was challenged by the Côte d'Ivoire authorities, which had opted to try her in that country (in March Mme Gbagbo had been sentenced by a national court to 20 years imprisonment on charges related to the 2010–11 disturbances); in February 2012 the Court expanded the scope of the Côte d'Ivoire investigation to include crimes within the jurisdiction of the Court allegedly committed during the period 19 September 2002–28 November 2010; in September 2013 the Court unsealed an arrest warrant, initially issued in December 2011, against Charles Blé Goudé for four counts of crimes against humanity; in March 2014 Goudé surrendered to the Côte d'Ivoire authorities and was transferred to the Court; in June 2014 a Pre-Trial Chamber confirmed four charges of crimes against humanity against Laurent Gbagbo; trial proceedings against both men commenced in January 2016; in January 2019 the Court acquitted Gbagbo and Blé Goudé, having determined that the charges against them had not been proven; the Prosecutor filed a notice of appeal against this decision in September; the Appeals Chamber upheld their acquittal at the end of March 2021; the arrest warrant for Mme Gbagbo was vacated by the Court in July.

Mali: in January 2013, following a request made in July 2012 by the Government of Mali, the Prosecutor launched a formal investigation into atrocities allegedly perpetrated since the start of that year by armed militants in northern areas of Mali; in August 2016 Ahmad al-Mahdi (a senior member of an Islamist armed group that had occupied areas in northern Mali) pleaded guilty as charged with respect to the destruction of cultural artefacts (the first guilty plea registered by the Court, and the first individual to receive a war crimes charge relating to the destruction of historic heritage); he received a nine-year term of imprisonment in September; in August 2017 the Court imposed a reparations order on al-Mahdi, amounting to €2.7m., to recompense members of the Tombouctou community for the degradation that he had caused; in March 2018 most of the reparations order against al-Mahdi was upheld by the Appeals Chamber; in May 2019 the Court announced that al-Mahdi had been transferred, in August of the previous year, to serve his sentence in Scotland, UK; al-Hassan ag Abdoul Aziz ag Mohamed ag Mahmoud ('al-Hassan') was transferred to the ICC on 31 March, shortly after an arrest warrant had been issued that accused him of

war crimes and crimes against humanity, of being the former *de facto* head of Islamic police in Tombouctou, of participating in the destruction of cultural heritage there, and of implementing a policy of enforced marriage that led to the sexual enslavement of women and girls; al-Hassan's trial commenced in July 2020.

Burundi: in October 2017 the Prosecutor authorized a *proprio moto* investigation into alleged crimes against humanity perpetrated in Burundi, or by Burundian nationals outside Burundi, during the period 26 April–26 October 2017 (the day prior to Burundi's withdrawal from the Rome Statute).

At October 2022 the following suspects remained outside the custody of the Court: Joseph Kony, Vincent Otti (Uganda); Sylvestre Mudacumura (DRC); Omar al-Bashir, Abdallah Banda, Ahmad Harun, Abdelrahim Hussein (Sudan); Walter Barasa, Philip Kipkoech Bett (Kenya); Saif al-Islam Gaddafi (Libya).

Finance

The programme budget for the International Criminal Court for 2022 amounted to €154.9m.

Publications

Chambers Practice Manual.
ICC Weekly Update (electronic publication).
Booklets, factsheets, official records.

Hybrid International Criminal Courts

Extraordinary African Chambers in the Courts of Senegal

Address: Sicap Keur Gorgui Lot R111, BP 25832, Senegal.
Telephone: 33-869-00-20; **internet:** www.chambresafricaines.org.

The Extraordinary African Chambers became operational in February 2013, on the basis of an accord adopted in August 2012 by the African Union (AU) and the Government of Senegal, to try the former President of Chad, Hissène Habré (who had been resident in Senegal), on charges of having committed—as a member of a 'joint criminal enterprise'—crimes against humanity and torture, and—on the grounds of his presidential responsibility—war crimes, in Chad during the period 7 June 1982–1 December 1990 (i.e. the duration of his term in office as President of Chad); around 40,000 people were reported to have been killed as a result of his alleged crimes. The Chambers represented the first 'universal jurisdiction' criminal process in Africa, with grave crimes allegedly committed in one territory being tried, by judges of various (African) nationalities, in another, under the overall stewardship of the AU. The AU Commission appointed the judges of the tribunal from among its member states. Formal proceedings against Habré commenced in July 2015 and concluded in February 2016. In May the Court found Habré guilty in respect of crimes committed against humanity, summary executions, torture and rape, and sentenced him to life imprisonment. An appeal against the verdict was lodged by Habré in June, and was heard in January 2017. In April the Court overturned Habré's rape conviction, while upholding the remaining convictions and ordering that 82,000,000m. francs CFA should be paid in reparations to his victims. Habré died in August 2021.

Residual Special Court for Sierra Leone

Address: POB 19536, 2500 CM The Hague, Netherlands.
Telephone: (70) 5128481; **e-mail:** info@rscsl.org; **internet:** www.rscsl.org.

In December 2013 a 16-member Residual Special Court assumed responsibility for the ongoing commitments of the Special Court for

Sierra Leone, which had concluded its mandate to prosecute those 'bearing the greatest responsibility for committing violations against humanitarian law' committed in the territory of Sierra Leone since 20 November 1996. The final judgment in the case of Charles Taylor, who became the first former head of state to be found guilty of charges relating to war crimes and crimes against humanity by an international court, was issued in September 2013. The Residual Special Court, based in The Hague, was authorized to oversee witness protection and sentencing appeals. It has jurisdiction to try Maj. Johnny Paul Koroma, who, although declared dead in June 2003, remained, pending verification, an indictee of the Court charged with crimes against humanity and war crimes. By 2022 three people convicted of having perpetrated war crimes in Sierra Leone had been granted conditional early release (having become eligible following the completion of two-thirds of their sentences); five other convicts remained imprisoned. The Residual Special Court maintains an office in Freetown, Sierra Leone, that provides witness and victim support.

President of the Court: Pierre G. Boutet (Canada).

Prosecutor: James C. (Jim) Johnson (USA).

Registrar: Binta Mansaray (Sierra Leone).

Principal Defender: Ibrahim Yillah (Sierra Leone).

Special Criminal Court in the Central African Republic (CAR)

Address: Palais de Justice de Bangui, CAR.

Telephone: 75-20-39-50; **e-mail:** info@cps-rca.cf.

The Special Criminal Court, comprising national and international judges, was established in June 2015 to hold accountable those guilty of grave crimes against humanity committed in the CAR since 2003 who were not already under the jurisdiction of the ICC. The Court was to work in close co-operation with the ICC. The Court's Special Prosecutor was appointed in February 2017, and its inaugural session was held in October 2018. Preliminary investigations into 10 cases were undertaken in 2020. In May nine members of a militia grouping were arrested and brought into custody of the Court, charged with attacks against civilians in the eastern Haut-Mbomou prefecture. The Court's first trial opened in September 2022.

Special Prosecutor: Toussaint Muntazini Mukimapa (Democratic Republic of the Congo).

President: Michel Landr Louanga.

ISLAMIC DEVELOPMENT BANK—IsDB

Address: POB 5925, Jeddah 21432, Saudi Arabia.

Telephone: (12) 636-1400; **fax:** (12) 636-6871; **e-mail:** info@isdb.org; **internet:** www.isdb.org.

The Bank was established following a conference of ministers of finance of member countries of the then Organization of the Islamic Conference (now Organization of Islamic Cooperation), held in Jeddah in December 1973. Its aim is to encourage the economic development and social progress of member countries and of Muslim communities in non-member countries, in accordance with the principles of the Islamic *Shari'a* (sacred law). The Bank formally opened in October 1975. The Bank and its associated entities—the International Islamic Trade Finance Corporation (ITFC), Islamic Research and Training Institute, Islamic Corporation for the Development of the Private Sector, and Islamic Corporation for the Insurance of Investment and Export Credit—constitute the Islamic Development Bank (IsDB) Group.

MEMBERS

There are 57 members (see *Financial Structure*).

Organization

(October 2022)

BOARD OF GOVERNORS

Each member country is represented by a governor, usually its minister of finance, and an alternate. The Board of Governors is the supreme authority of the Bank, and meets annually. The 2022 meeting was held in Sharm el-Sheikh, Egypt, in June.

BOARD OF EXECUTIVE DIRECTORS

The Board consists of 18 members, one-half of whom are appointed by the nine largest subscribers to the capital stock of the Bank; the remaining nine are elected by Governors representing the other subscribers. Members of the Board of Executive Directors are elected for three-year terms. The Board is responsible for the direction of the general operations of the Bank.

ADMINISTRATION

President of the Bank and Chairman of the Board of Executive Directors: Dr Muhammed Sulaiman Al Jasser (Saudi Arabia).

Vice-President, Country Programmes: Dr Mansur Muhtar (Nigeria).

Vice-President, Finance: Zamir Iqbal (Pakistan).

REGIONAL OFFICES

In accordance with a policy of decentralization introduced in 2017, by 2022 the IsDB had regional hubs based in Abuja, Nigeria; Almatı, Kazakhstan; Cairo, Egypt; Dakar, Senegal; Jakarta, Indonesia; Kuala Lumpur, Malaysia; Rabat, Morocco; and Ankara/İstanbul, Türkiye.

Senegal: 18 blvd de la République, BP 6253 Dakar; tel. 33-889-11-44; fax 33-823-36-21; e-mail RODK@isdb.org.

FINANCIAL STRUCTURE

The Bank's unit of account is the Islamic Dinar (ID), which is equivalent to the value of one Special Drawing Right (SDR) of the International Monetary Fund. (The average value of the SDR in 2021 was US $1.42451.) In 2016 the Bank introduced the solar year, i.e. corresponding to 1 January–31 December, as the basis of its accounting series; prior to that its reports refer to the lunar year ('Hirja': H). The Bank's authorized capital is ID 100,000m. In December 2020 the Board of Governors approved an a 6th General Capital Increase, raising subscribed capital by ID 5,500m. to ID 55,500m. At 31 December 2021 total committed subscriptions amounted to ID 50,260.5m.

SUBSCRIPTIONS

(million Islamic Dinars, as at 31 December 2021)

Afghanistan	9.9	Malaysia	823.1
Albania	9.2	Maldives	25.8
Algeria	1,285.6	Mali	50.9
Azerbaijan	50.9	Mauritania	35.8
Bahrain	72.5	Morocco	256.7
Bangladesh	510.0	Mozambique	25.8
Benin	58.2	Niger	90.2
Brunei		Nigeria	3,874.5
Darussalam	128.4	Oman	142.6
Burkina Faso	90.2	Pakistan	1,285.6
Cameroon	128.4	Palestine	19.6
Chad	9.8	Qatar	3,632.4
Comoros	13.0	Saudi Arabia	11,896.8
Côte d'Ivoire	13.0	Senegal	147.8
Djibouti	5.0	Sierra Leone	18.2
Egypt	3,579.7	Somalia	5.0
Gabon	54.6	Sudan	233.0
The Gambia	25.8	Suriname	9.2
Guinea	45.9	Syrian Arab	
Guinea-Bissau	5.0	Republic	18.5
Guyana	2.5	Tajikistan	18.2
Indonesia	1,138.0	Togo	18.2
Iran	4,174.6	Tunisia	71.6
Iraq	135.1	Türkiye (Turkey)	3,263.8
Jordan	219.8	Turkmenistan	5.0
Kazakhstan	54.0	Uganda	69.0
Kuwait	3,500.0	UAE	3,799.5
Kyrgyzstan	25.8	Uzbekistan	13.4
Lebanon	35.8	Yemen	258.6
Libya	4,771.7		

Activities

The Bank provides interest-free loans—adhering to the Islamic principle that forbids usury. It prioritizes support for infrastructural projects that are expected to have a marked impact on long-term socioeconomic development; provision of technical assistance (e.g. for feasibility studies); equity participation in industrial and agricultural projects; leasing operations, involving the leasing of equipment such as ships, and instalment sale financing; and profit-sharing operations. Funds not immediately needed for projects are used for foreign trade financing.

The IsDB's Member Country Partnership (MCP) Strategy, initiated in 2010, aims to strengthen dialogue with individual member countries and thus to contribute more effectively to their medium- and long-term development plans. New Global Value Chain-driven MCP strategies (GVC-MCPs) were introduced in 2020 for Guinea, Indonesia, Niger, Nigeria and Senegal. In May 2017 the Board of Governors endorsed a President's Five-Year Program ('P5P'), that had been initiated by the Bank's President to accelerate the implementation of the IsDB's 10-Year Strategy (2015–25). The main focus of the Strategy was fostering economic growth through the promotion of solidarity, connectivity and Islamic finance. A new IsDB business model was introduced in 2020 (with a focus on market efficiency, stimulating local supply chains and job creation). In September 2021 the Bank initiated a new Resilience Index to assist economic policymakers. A (digital) e-Disbursement Platform was also initiated in that month to facilitate more efficient tracking of disbursements.

During 1976–2021 the Bank Group approved a total of ID 112,175.9m. (equivalent to some US $160,267.8m.) for 11,066 operations. In 2021 the Bank approved a net total of ID 6,272.5m., of which ordinary capital resources (OCR) accounted for ID 1,403.5m. ($1,993.7m.). The three principal beneficiaries of Bank approvals in 2021 were Egypt (28.7%), Pakistan (13.7%) and Bangladesh (8.8%). The principal sectoral distribution of OCR approvals in 2021 was as follows: transport 36.4%, agriculture 14.7%, water, sanitation and urban services 13.8%, education 11.9%, energy 11.4%, and health 8.6%.

Trade Financing: In June 2005 the Board of Governors approved the establishment of the ITFC as an autonomous trade promotion and financing institution within the Bank Group; its inaugural meeting was held in February 2007. Through direct or co-financing the ITFC supports the development of intra-OIC trade. The Bank also finances other trade financing operations, including the Islamic Corporation for the Development of the Private Sector (ICD) and the Awqaf Properties Investment Fund (APIF). In addition, a Trade Co-operation and Promotion Programme supports efforts to enhance trade among member countries of the Organization of Islamic Cooperation (OIC). In 2021 trade financing approved through the ITFC amounted to ID 4,594.0m., and operations approved by the ICD totalled ID 174.1m. The APIF approved ID 16.6m. in co-financing for four new projects in that year.

Islamic Financial Markets: The Bank mobilizes resources from the international financial markets through the issuance of the *Shari'a*-compliant International Islamic Sukuk bond (launched in 2003). In November 2019 the Bank introduced a new Sustainable Finance Framework, under which funding raised through the Sukuk bond method was to be directed to green initiatives. A COVID-19 Sustainability Sukuk was issued in June 2020. The Bank's Kuala Lumpur, Malaysia-based Islamic Financial Services Board (IFSB)—which commenced operations in March 2003—acts as an international standard-setting body for regulatory and supervisory agencies (81 at June 2021) connected to the Islamic financial services industry. The IFSB maintains a database of Prudential and Structural Islamic Financial Indicators, and the IsDB has worked to improve the dissemination of relevant information. In early 2020 the IsDB established a Working Group to Study the Impact of the COVID-19 Pandemic on the Islamic Finance Industry.

The 15th IsDB Global Forum on Islamic Finance was convened in August 2021, in a virtual format, on the theme 'The Role of Islamic Finance in Post-COVID-19 Economic Recovery of IsDB Member Countries'. A *Reference Guide: Islamic Finance for Infrastructure PPP Projects* was issued at that time jointly by the IsDB and World Bank.

COVID-19 Pandemic: In March 2020 the Bank established a US $730m. Strategic Preparedness and Response Facility to extend financing, in the form of grants, trade finance, lending and risk insurance, for targeted interventions, including the purchase of medical equipment, disease surveillance, community awareness and social safety nets. In early April the IsDB Board of Executive Directors approved a Strategic Preparedness and Response Programme (SPRP) for the COVID-19 Pandemic, to which the Bank had committed $4,430m. in funding by the end of 2021. Referred to as '3Rs', the Programme had three pillars: Response Track 1 (R1): focused on providing immediate emergency support; Restore Track 2

(R2): medium-term financing for trade and small and medium-sized businesses to promote activities in strategic supply chains; and Restart Track 3 (R3): long-term support to build resilient economies. An IsDBG Vaccine Access (IVAC) Facility was established within the SPRP framework, covering vaccine deployment, procurement, and manufacturing support. By the end of 2021 the Bank had approved three IVAC-funded projects, in Guinea, Kyrgyzstan and Pakistan. A COVID-19 Global Coordination Platform was also launched to facilitate the efficiency of health supplies procurement supply chains; from mid-2020 the UN Office for Project Services joined the Platform. In June 2020 the IsDB issued a $1,500m. International Islamic Sukuk bond (q.v.) to fund part of its COVID-19 response. In February 2021 the Bank and the ITFC signed an accord jointly to facilitate a recently introduced COVID-19 Restore Program (based on R2 of the SPRP), and to support the ongoing P5P.

Technical Assistance: During 1976–2021 the Bank approved 2,231 technical assistance operations, with a cumulative value of ID 1,500.4m. (equivalent to US $2,180.1m.). In 2021 19 new operations were approved through the Bank's Technical Cooperation Programme, amounting to $498,700; a total of $1.5m., was approved for 'Reverse Linkage' projects, which facilitate the transfer of expertise, knowledge and technology between member states; and $434,500 was allocated in grants to support short-term technical co-operation interventions. In March 2018 the Board of Executive Directors approved the establishment of a Public-Private Partnerships (PPP) Advisory Facility, to promote PPP-based infrastructure development in member states.

Human Development: The Islamic Solidarity Fund for Development (ISFD), established in 2005, extends concessionary loans and grants aimed at promoting human development and pro-poor economic growth, and has a particular focus on education and health care; by 2021 the Fund had approved ID 773.2m. (including ID 44.4m. during that year) for poverty alleviation initiatives. In 2019 the ISFD initiated a new scholarship programme to advance the educational opportunities of eligible students from least developed countries.

In January 2020 the IsDB and the World Food Programme signed a Memorandum of Understanding (MOU) on co-operation in identifying alternative financing mechanisms and opportunities for collaboration on humanitarian and development projects, with a particular focus on nutrition, food security, agriculture, rural development, and human capital and institutional development. In July the Bank and FAO concluded an MOU on strengthening co-operation through the implementation during 2020–22 of a joint action plan with a focus on agriculture-related business development, capacity building and technical assistance.

In February 2021 the IsDB and ICD agreed to enhance the efforts of the IsDB Group Business Forum (known as THIQAH) to attract private sector and market resources.

In June 2017 the IsDB and the UN determined to intensify collaboration in implementing the UN Sustainable Development Goals (SDGs, being implemented globally during 2015–30).

Science, Technology and Innovation: In September 2017 the IsDB established a US $500m. Transform Fund, which was to provide seed capital to start-up businesses and small and medium-sized enterprises for initiatives with a focus on innovation, science and technology, with the wider aim of accelerating progress towards the attainment of the UN SDGs. At the beginning of April 2020 the Bank announced that, through the Transform Fund, it would provide financial support to innovations with a focus on, *inter alia,* health supply chain management and low cost rapid testing, that would help to control the spread of and reduce the negative socioeconomic impacts of COVID-19. In February 2018 the Bank launched Engage, an internet hub that aimed to link innovators in developing countries with funding and with market opportunities, also as a means of promoting the SDGs through science and technology. The IsDB gives prizes for science and technology to promote excellence in education, research and development.

Communities Outreach Programme: The Bank's Communities Outreach Programme (initiated in 1400H as the Special Assistance Programme) supports the economic and social development of minority Muslim communities in non-member countries, in particular in the education and health sectors. It also aims to provide emergency aid in times of natural disasters, and to assist Muslim refugees throughout the world. A Special Account Resources Waqf Fund finances such operations. By 31 December 2021 the Waqf Fund had resources of some ID 772.4m. In September 2022 the Bank and the UN High Commissioner for Refugees (UNHCR) agreed to establish a new Global Islamic Fund for Refugees.

Other Assistance Activities: The IsDB implements scholarship programmes, technical co-operation projects, and a sacrificial meat utilization project (distributing meat sacrificed by pilgrims to needy beneficiaries). In addition, the Bank supports recovery, rehabilitation and reconstruction efforts in member countries affected by natural disasters or conflict.

In July 2017 the IsDB and the African Development Bank concluded an agreement under which they were to provide some US $2,000m. in support aimed at accelerating economic development in Africa.

Publications

Annual Report.

SDG Digest (3–4 a year).

Technical and industry sector reports, investor presentations, guidance notes.

Statistics

CUMULATIVE OPERATIONS APPROVED
(1 January 1976–31 December 2021)

Type of operation	Number of operations	Amount (million Islamic Dinars)
Project financing . .	2,944	41,733.4
Technical assistance . .	2,231	1,500.4
Trade financing* . .	4,036	67,771.6
Special assistance . .	1,855	1,170.4
Total†	11,066	112,175.9

* Including operations by the ITFC, the ICD, Treasury operations, and the APIF.

† Excluding cancelled operations.

Source: Islamic Development Bank, *Annual Report 2021*.

Bank Group Entities

International Islamic Trade Finance Corporation (ITFC): POB 55335, Jeddah 21534, Saudi Arabia; tel. (12) 646-8337; fax (12) 637-1064; e-mail itfc@itfc-idb.org; internet www.itfc-idb.org; f. 2007; commenced operations Jan. 2008; aims to promote trade and trade financing in Bank mem. countries, to facilitate access to public and private capital, and to promote investment opportunities; the ITFC's Cooperation and Promotion Program (TCPP) supports the design and implementation of trade-related technical assistance progs; during 2021 the ITFC approved ID 4,594.0m. for trade financing operations; auth. cap. US $3,000m.; CEO HANI SALEM SONBOL.

Islamic Corporation for the Development of the Private Sector (ICD): POB 54069, Jeddah 21514, Saudi Arabia; tel. (12) 644-1644; fax (12) 644-4427; e-mail icd@isdb.org; internet www .icd-ps.org; f. 1999; aims to identify opportunities in the private sector, provide financial products and services compatible with Islamic law, to mobilize additional resources for the private sector in mem. countries, and to encourage the devt of Islamic financing and capital markets; approved projects and capital increases amounting to ID 174.1m. in 2021; the Bank's share of the capital is 50%, mem. countries' share 30%, and that of public financial institutions of mem. countries 20%; auth. cap. US $4,000m.; mems: 54 countries, the Bank and 5 public financial institutions; CEO and Gen. Man. AYMAN SEJINY.

Islamic Corporation for the Insurance of Investment and Export Credit (ICIEC): POB 15722, Jeddah 21454, Saudi Arabia; tel. (12) 644-5666; fax (12) 637-9755; e-mail ICIEC-Communication@ isdb.org; internet iciec.isdb.org; f. 1994; aims to promote trade and promote foreign investment in mem. countries, through the provision of export credit and investment insurance services; has a representative office in Dubai, United Arab Emirates; new insurance commitments amounted to ID 2,198.1m. in 2021; auth. cap. ID 400m.; mems: 47 countries; CEO OUSSAMA ABDEL RAHMAN KAISSI.

Islamic Development Bank Institute (IsDBI): 8111 King Khalid St, Jeddah 22332–2444, Saudi Arabia; tel. (12) 636-1400; fax (12) 637-8927; e-mail isdbi-info@isdb.org; internet www.isdbinstitute .org; f. 1981 as the Islamic Research and Training Institute, present name adopted in 2021; aims to undertake research enabling economic, financial and banking activities to conform to Islamic law, and to provide training for staff involved in devt activities in the Bank's mem. countries; also organizes seminars and workshops, and holds training courses aimed at furthering the expertise of govt and financial officials in Islamic developing countries; Dir-Gen. Dr SAMI AL-SUWAILEM (acting); publs *Annual Report, Islamic Economic Studies Journal* (2 a year), various research studies, monographs, reports.

ORGANIZATION OF ISLAMIC COOPERATION—OIC

Address: Medina Rd, Sary St, POB 178, Jeddah 21411, Saudi Arabia.

Telephone: (12) 651-5222; **fax:** (12) 651-2288; **internet:** www .oic-oci.org.

The OIC was formally established, as the Organization of the Islamic Conference, at the first conference of Muslim heads of state convened in Rabat, Morocco, in September 1969. The first conference of Muslim ministers responsible for foreign affairs, held in Jeddah, Saudi Arabia, in March 1970, established the General Secretariat—which became operational in May 1971. In June 2011 the 38th ministerial conference changed the name of the organization to the Organization of Islamic Cooperation (abbreviated, as hitherto, to OIC).

MEMBERS

Afghanistan	Indonesia	Qatar
Albania	Iran	Saudi Arabia
Algeria	Iraq	Senegal
Azerbaijan	Jordan	Sierra Leone
Bahrain	Kazakhstan	Somalia
Bangladesh	Kuwait	Sudan
Benin	Kyrgyzstan	Suriname
Brunei Darussalam	Lebanon	Syrian Arab
Burkina Faso	Libya	Republic*
Cameroon	Malaysia	Tajikistan
Chad	Maldives	Togo
Comoros	Mali	Tunisia
Côte d'Ivoire	Mauritania	Türkiye (Turkey)
Djibouti	Morocco	Turkmenistan
Egypt	Mozambique	Uganda
Gabon	Niger	United Arab
The Gambia	Nigeria	Emirates
Guinea	Oman	Uzbekistan
Guinea-Bissau	Pakistan	Yemen
Guyana	Palestine	

* Suspended from participation in the activities of the OIC and from all its subsidiary organs and specialized and affiliated institutions since August 2012, in view of the Syrian Government's violent suppression of opposition elements and related acts of violence against civilian communities.

Note: Observer status has been granted to Bosnia and Herzegovina, the Central African Republic, the Russian Federation, Thailand, the 'Turkish Republic of Northern Cyprus', the Moro National Liberation Front (MNLF) of the southern Philippines, the United Nations (UN), the African Union (AU), the Non-Aligned Movement, the League of Arab States, the Economic Cooperation Organization and the Parliamentary Union of OIC member states. The revised OIC Charter, endorsed in March 2008, made future applications for OIC membership and observer status conditional upon Muslim demographic majority and membership of the UN.

Organization

(October 2022)

SUMMIT CONFERENCES

The supreme body of the organization is the Conference of Heads of State ('Islamic summit'), which first met in 1969, in Rabat, Morocco. Ordinary summit conferences are normally held every three years, while extraordinary conferences may be convened as necessary. The 14th ordinary summit was convened in May–June 2019, in Makkah, Saudi Arabia; the 15th was expected to be held in The Gambia.

CONFERENCE OF MINISTERS OF FOREIGN AFFAIRS

Conferences take place annually, to consider the means of implementing the general policy of the OIC, although they may also be convened for extraordinary sessions.

GENERAL SECRETARIAT

The executive organ of the organization, the General Secretariat is headed by a Secretary-General (who is elected by the Conference of Ministers of Foreign Affairs for a five-year term, renewable only once) and four Assistant Secretaries-General (similarly appointed).

In March 2013 a specialized Peace, Security and Mediation Unit was opened at the General Secretariat. In October 2017 an Information Resource Centre was inaugurated, comprising a business centre, training unit, section on seminars and workshops, and archives area.

Secretary-General: HISSEIN IBRAHIM TAHA (Chad).

At the summit conference in January 1981 it was decided that an International Islamic Court of Justice should be established to adjudicate, using Islamic *Shari'a* principles, in disputes between member countries. Experts met in January 1983 to draw up a constitution for the court; however, by 2022 it was not yet in operation.

EXECUTIVE COMMITTEE

The Executive Committee follows up resolutions of OIC conferences. It comprises representatives of the OIC host country, the OIC General Secretariat, and the summit conference and ministerial conference troikas made up of member countries equally representing the OIC's African, Arab and Asian membership.

COMMITTEE OF PERMANENT REPRESENTATIVES

The Committee, comprising member states' accredited Permanent Representatives to the OIC, meets intermittently.

STANDING COMMITTEES

Standing Committee for Economic and Commercial Co-operation (COMCEC): f. 1981; Chair. RECEP TAYYIP ERDOĞAN (President of Türkiye).

Standing Committee for Information and Cultural Affairs (COMIAC): f. 1981; Chair. MACKY SALL (President of Senegal).

Standing Committee for Scientific and Technological Co-operation (COMSTECH): f. 1981; Chair. Dr ARIF ALVI (President of Pakistan).

There is also a standing committee on Al-Quds (relating to the status of Jerusalem). Other committees include the Islamic Peace Committee, the Permanent Finance Committee, the Committee of Islamic Solidarity with the Peoples of the Sahel, and the Committee on UN reform. In addition, there is an Islamic Commission for Economic, Cultural and Social Affairs, and there are several OIC Contact Groups, including on Peace and Dialogue, Mali, Muslims in Europe, Sierra Leone, and Somalia. A Commission of Eminent Persons was inaugurated in 2005.

INDEPENDENT PERMANENT HUMAN RIGHTS COMMISSION (IPHRC)

Secretariat: 2550 Khalij Al Qamar, al-Hamra District, Jeddah 23212 6885, Saudi Arabia; e-mail info@oic-iphrc.org; internet oic-iphrc.org; f. 2011 to promote the civil, political, social and economic rights enshrined in the covenants and declarations of the OIC, and in universally agreed human rights instruments, in conformity with Islamic values; inaugural session convened in Jakarta, Indonesia, in Feb. 2012; OIC human rights instruments include the Covenant on the Rights of the Child in Islam (2005), and the OIC Declaration on Human Rights (initially adopted in 1990, as the Cairo Declaration on Human Rights in Islam, and amended in 2020 to align with 'universal human rights standards'); 19th regular session: May 2022, themed 'The Role of National Human Rights Institutions in the Promotion and Protection of Human Rights in the OIC Countries'; the IPHRC comprises 18 commissioners, equally representing Africa, Asia and the Middle East; Exec. Dir MARGHOOB SALEEM BUTT (Pakistan).

Activities

The OIC's aims, as proclaimed in the Charter (adopted in 1972, with revisions endorsed in 1990 and 2008), are:

(i) to promote Islamic solidarity among member states;

(ii) to consolidate co-operation among member states in the economic, social, cultural, scientific and other vital fields, and to

arrange consultations among member states belonging to international organizations;

(iii) to endeavour to eliminate racial segregation and discrimination and to eradicate colonialism in all its forms;

(iv) to take necessary measures to support international peace and security founded on justice;

(v) to co-ordinate efforts to safeguard the Holy Places, to support the struggle of the people of Palestine and help them to regain their rights and liberate their land;

(vi) to strengthen the struggle of all Muslim people with a view to safeguarding their dignity, independence and national rights;

(vii) to create a suitable atmosphere for the promotion of co-operation and understanding among member states and other countries.

At the second Islamic summit conference (Lahore, Pakistan, 1974), the Islamic Solidarity Fund was established, together with a committee of representatives that later evolved into the Islamic Commission for Economic, Cultural and Social Affairs. Subsequently, numerous other subsidiary bodies were set up.

In April 2016 the 13th OIC summit adopted OIC-2025, a 10-year plan of joint Islamic action, which included goals for collaboration in the following areas: the environment, climate change and sustainability; combating extremism, sectarianism and Islamophobia; peace and security; poverty alleviation; trade, investment and finance; agriculture and food; employment infrastructure and industrialization; science, technology and innovation; education; health; the advancement and empowerment of women; family welfare and social security; joint Islamic humanitarian action; human rights, good governance and accountability; and developing communications and digital information structures.

In May 2022 an inaugural OIC-US Strategic Dialogue was convened in Washington, DC, USA. The meeting addressed ongoing crises in Africa, Asia and the Middle East, and means of combating extremism.

ECONOMIC AFFAIRS

In 1991 22 OIC member states signed a Framework Agreement on a Trade Preferential System among the OIC Member States (TPS-OIC); this entered into force in 2003, and was envisaged as representing the first step towards the eventual establishment of an Islamic common market. Rules of origin for the TPS-OIC were adopted in September 2007, and a Protocol on the Preferential Tariff Scheme for TPS-OIC (PRETAS) entered into force in February 2010. In April 2016 the 10th OIC summit endorsed the goal that by 2025 some 25% of member states' trade should be intra-Islamic. OIC has pursued efforts to enhance the role of the private sector through the promotion of intra-OIC small and medium-sized enterprise clusters, in sectors including agro-food processing, and transportation and logistics.

In July 2020 the OIC Secretariat and Islamic Chamber of Commerce, Industry and Agriculture met (virtually) to consider the promotion of Islamic microfinance and proposed establishment of family banks (aimed at strengthening women's access to finance) in Burkina Faso, Chad, Mali, Mauritania and Niger.

An International Islamic Business and Finance Summit, known as the KazanSummit, has been organized annually since 2009, in Kazan, Russian Federation, by the OIC and the Russian Government (14th edition: May 2023). In March 2017 an OIC-People's Republic of China Forum was convened in Beijing, China. The 17th OIC Trade Fair was held in June 2022, in Dakar, Senegal. A World Islamic Economic Forum is convened intermittently.

The fourth session of the Islamic Conference of Labour Ministers held in Jeddah, in February 2018, welcomed an OIC Labour Market Strategy. Ministers adopted an OIC Agreement on Mutual Recognition Arrangement of the Skilled Workforce, as well as an OIC Standard Bilateral Agreement on the Exchange of Manpower.

An inaugural OIC International Forum on Islamic Tourism was convened in June 2014. An Islamic Conference of Tourism Ministers meets regularly (2022: in June, in Baku, Azerbaijan).

CULTURE, SOCIAL AND FAMILY AFFAIRS

OIC's Directorate of Culture, Social and Family Affairs comprises two separate departments, the Cultural Affairs Department, which focuses on Islamic cultural issues, the protection of Islamic sites and interfaith dialogue, and the Social and Family Affairs Department. In December 2007 the OIC organized the first International Conference on Islamophobia, aimed at addressing concerns that alleged instances of defamation of Islam appeared to be increasing worldwide (particularly in Europe). OIC leaders denounced stereotyping and discrimination, and urged the promotion of Islam by Islamic states as a 'moderate, peaceful and tolerant religion'. An Islamic Observatory on Islamophobia, established in 2007, has issued regular reports on intolerance against Muslims; the 14th covered the period December 2020–January 2022. The inaugural meeting of an OIC Ministerial Contact Group for Muslims in Europe was held in October 2016. In June 2019 the OIC issued the first edition of an *International Islamic Encyclopedia of Tolerance*. In the following month the inaugural meeting of a new OIC Contact Group on Peace and Dialogue agreed a comprehensive Plan of Action on Islamophobia, Religious Discrimination, Intolerance and Hatred Towards Muslims, to cover the period 2020–23. Under the Plan the Islamophobia Observatory and relevant multilateral co-operation were to be strengthened.

An OIC Plan of Action for the Advancement of Women in Member States was adopted in November 2016 by the sixth session of the Ministerial Conference on Women. The eighth Ministerial Conference, convened in July 2021, in Cairo, Egypt, urged member states to ensure that national social protection programmes were supporting people affected by the COVID-19 pandemic, including those working in the informal sector, and especially women and girls. The ninth Conference of Muslim Women Parliamentarians was organized in January 2020, in Ouagadougou, Burkina Faso.

In December 2012 the statute of a proposed OIC Women Development Organization (WDO) was opened for signature. The inaugural meeting of a OIC Women's Advisory Council was convened in May 2017, in Istanbul. In September the OIC Secretary-General and the Executive Director of UN Women signed a Memorandum of Understanding on Inter-Institutional Co-operation, to cover co-ordination on the advancement of women; the eradication of poverty; sustainable development; and the promotion of good governance and the rule of law.

The fourth session of the Islamic Conference of Ministers of Youth and Sports, convened in April 2018, in Baku (Azerbaijan), adopted an OIC Youth Strategy and an OIC Sports Strategy. (The first youth and sports ministerial conference took place in April 2005.)

HUMANITARIAN ASSISTANCE

OIC's Department of Humanitarian Affairs works to co-ordinate the delivery of emergency relief and rehabilitation assistance to Muslim communities affected by conflict or natural disasters. It also promotes efforts to strengthen disaster risk reduction and response strategies. In May 2016 an agreement was concluded between the OIC and the Qatari authorities to establish a new OIC Humanitarian Funds secretariat in Doha (Qatar).

In September 2019 the Islamic Development Bank (IsDB) and UN Children's Fund (UNICEF) jointly established a Global Muslim Philanthropy Fund for Children (GMPFC), which was to enable various traditional forms of Muslim philanthropy—such as voluntary 'Sadaqah' donations, Waqf endowments, and obligatory 'Zakat' financing—to support IsDB and UNICEF emergency response and development initiatives in OIC member states. The OIC Secretary-General participated in the second Riyadh International Humanitarian Forum, hosted by Saudi Arabia in early March 2020.

In September 2022 the OIC General Secretariat welcomed an agreement by the Islamic Development Bank and the UN High Commissioner for Refugees to establish a new Global Islamic Fund for Refugees.

SCIENCE AND TECHNOLOGY

The OIC supports education in Muslim communities, and was instrumental in the establishment of Islamic universities in Niger and Uganda, the American Islamic College of Chicago (USA), and the Islamic Solidarity Centre in Guinea-Bissau.

The First Islamic Summit on Science and Technology, hosted by Kazakhstan in September 2017, at the level of heads of state and of government, adopted an OIC Science and Technology Agenda 2026 initiative. A Second Islamic Summit on Science and Technology, hosted by the UAE in a virtual format in June 2021, issued the Abu Dhabi Declaration on Science, Technology and Innovation: Opening New Horizons, which, *inter alia,* supported ongoing research by member states into vaccines, encouraged further innovation, and determined to boost investment in science, technology, engineering and mathematics (STEM) studies (with a particular focus on girls and women).

In March 2012 OIC ministers responsible for water approved the OIC Water Vision 2025, providing a framework for co-operation in maximizing the productive use of members' water resources. The inaugural meeting of an OIC Water Council was held in November 2017. In October 2019 the eighth Islamic Conference of Environment Ministers, convened in Rabat, Morocco, gave consideration to a Draft Strategy for the Activation of the Role of Cultural and Religious Factors in Protecting the Environment and Achieving Sustainable Development in the Islamic World.

In October 2013 Islamic ministers responsible for health, meeting in Jakarta, adopted the OIC Strategic Health Programme of Action, covering the period 2014–23, and also a plan providing a framework for focused national actions to enable the implementation of the Programme. In February 2014 the OIC inaugurated an Islamic International Advisory Group on Polio Eradication (its sixth session was held in September 2019). The sixth session of the Islamic Conference of Health Ministers, meeting in Jeddah, in December 2017, urged the OIC General Secretariat to strengthen the capacities of mechanisms enabling the implementation, measurement and assessment of the ongoing 2014–23 Programme of Action. The First Meeting of OIC National Medication Regulatory Authorities was held in September 2018, in Indonesia. A voluntary civilian OIC humanitarian medical corps and an OIC internet health portal were developed in that year.

POLITICAL AFFAIRS

The OIC gives support to member countries in regaining or maintaining political stability. An OIC Contact Group on Peace and Conflict Resolution was inaugurated by the 13th OIC summit in April 2016 (renamed the Contact Group on Peace and Dialogue in January 2019), and in the following month the first consultative session was convened of an OIC Wise Persons Council and group of Special Envoys of the Secretary-General, representing the guiding tier of a new OIC mechanism for conflict resolution and peace-building. The First OIC Member States Conference on Mediation was convened in November 2017, in Istanbul. The inaugural meeting of an OIC Contact Group of Friends of Mediation was held in September 2018. In March 2019 the Council of Foreign Ministers issued a resolution on enhancing the OIC's mediation capabilities.

Within the framework of a Memorandum of Understanding concluded in 2015 between the OIC and the European Union (EU), the fifth OIC–EU senior officials' meeting was convened in March 2022, in Jeddah. This addressed issues in the social, cultural, humanitarian, political and economic spheres, including women's empowerment, education, health, post-COVID-19 recovery, interfaith dialogue, Islamophobia, and the observation of elections. The situations in Afghanistan, Palestine, the Sahel and Yemen, and of the Royingya in Myanmar were given particular attention.

In March 2022 the OIC Secretary-General strongly condemned a series of terrorist attacks against targets in Somalia, including against the airport in that country's capital, Mogadishu, and against a female parliamentarian. In that month he appointed a Special Envoy to Africa. In May the OIC General Secretariat welcomed the election of Hassan Sheikh Mohamud as the new President of Somalia.

The inaugural OIC-USA Strategic Dialogue, convened in Washington, DC, in May 2022, addressed, *inter alia,* the situation of Muslim communities and other minorities in non-OIC member states, combating hate speech and Islamophobia, religious freedoms, freedom of expression, gender equality and human rights.

In early October 2022 the OIC General Secretariat condemned a forced transfer of power in Burkina Faso on 30 September, and urged stakeholders there to ensure a prompt return to constitutional rule.

Mali: In April 2012 the OIC Secretary-General expressed 'total rejection' of the proclamation by militants in northern Mali of an independent homeland of Azawad. In February 2013 the 12th OIC summit issued a declaration in which it strongly condemned the activities of terrorist groups and movements in Mali, including attacks on communities and the destruction of cultural sites, and also condemned the threat to security and stability posed by transnational organized crime and drug-trafficking networks. The summit determined to establish an OIC Contact Group on Mali, to monitor future developments. The inaugural meeting of the Contact Group was held in May. The OIC Secretary-General commended the peaceful conduct of the presidential election held in Mali in late July and early August, and in May 2015 the OIC Contact Group on Mali welcomed the conclusion of a Mali Peace and Reconciliation Agreement. In December 2014 the OIC participated in the inaugural meeting of the Nouakchott Process on the Enhancement of Security Co-operation in the Sahel Region, an initiative of the AU. In June 2018 the OIC Secretary-General stated concern over the recent eruption of violent events Bamako, Mali's capital; he urged restraint by all parties. In August he commended the calm completion of presidential elections in that country. In mid-August 2020 the OIC Secretary-General expressed concern over the (forced) resignation of the legitimate President of Mali, Ibrahim Boubacar Keïta, and dissolution of the Malian Government. He urged all stakeholders in Mali to pursue a resolution to the national crisis through dialogue. The new military leadership determined in mid-September that an 18-month transitional administration would be established pending new national elections. In late May 2021 the OIC General Secretariat stated concern over the arrests by the Malian military of several members of the transitional authorities—including the interim President and Prime Minister, who were forced to resign their posts (while continuing to be detained under house arrest). In August the OIC General Secretariat strongly condemned terrorist shootings in the Malian communities of Daoutegeft, Karou and Ouatagouna and Daoutegeft, which had caused numerous fatalities. In January 2022 the OIC General Secretariat noted that it was following developments in Mali with concern: at that time the Malian military junta had postponed for several years elections that were to have been held in February. In August the General Secretariat strongly condemned a terrorist attack that was perpetrated in the Malian town of Tessit. In the following month a high-level OIC delegation attended the third meeting, held in Lomé, Togo, of the Transition Support Group on Mali (GST-Mali, led by the AU, Economic Community of West African States and UN).

Combating Terrorism: In December 1994 OIC heads of state adopted a Code of Conduct for Combating International Terrorism, and an OIC Convention on Combating International Terrorism was adopted in 1998. In April 2009 the heads of law enforcement agencies in OIC member states, gathered in Baku, adopted the Baku Declaration on co-operation in combating transnational organized crime, including international terrorism, extremism, aggressive separatism and human trafficking. The OIC has repeatedly urged the worldwide adoption of a clear definition of terrorism. In April 2016 the 13th OIC summit emphasized the need to draft a comprehensive Islamic strategy to combat terrorism and extremism, and for the OIC to play a leading role in global action to avert extremism.

Finance

The OIC's activities are financed by mandatory contributions from member states.

Subsidiary Organs

International Islamic Fiqh Academy: Al Madinah Al Munawarah Rd, Al Faisaliyyah, Jeddah 23442, Saudi Arabia; tel. (12) 690-0347; fax (12) 697-9329; e-mail info@iifa-aifi.org; internet www.iifa-aifi.org; f. 1983; concerned with the study and evolution of Islamic jurisprudence; 57 states; Gen. Sec. Prof. KOUTOUB MOUSTAPHA SANO.

Islamic Centre for Development of Trade: Tour des Habous, ave des FAR, 20000 Casablanca, Morocco; tel. (52) 2314974; fax (52) 2310110; e-mail icdt@icdt-oic.org; internet www.icdt-cidc.org; f. 1983; supports regular commercial contacts, harmonizes policies and promotes investments among OIC mems; 57 mem. states; Dir-Gen. LATIFA EL BOUADELLAOUI; publs *Tijaris: International and Inter-Islamic Trade Magazine* (every 2 months), *Inter-Islamic Trade Report* (annually).

Islamic Solidarity Fund: Abbas al-Halawani, AR Rawdah District, Jeddah 23434, Saudi Arabia; tel. (12) 698-1296; fax (12) 256-8185; e-mail mail@isf-fsi.org; internet www.isf-fsi.org; f. 1974; aims to meet the needs of Islamic communities by providing emergency aid and the funds to build mosques, Islamic centres, hospitals, schools and univs; in March 2022 helped to initiate a Global Islamic Fund for Refugees; Exec. Dir Dr HIBA AHMED.

Islamic University of Technology (IUT): Board Bazar, Gazipur 1704, Dhaka, Bangladesh; tel. (2) 9291254; fax (2) 9291260; e-mail vc@iut-dhaka.edu; internet www.iutoic-dhaka.edu; f. 1981 as the Islamic Centre for Technical and Vocational Training and Research, named changed to Islamic Institute of Technology in 1994, present name adopted in 2001; aims to develop human resources in OIC mem. states, with special reference to engineering, technology and technical education; 57 mem. states; Vice-Chancellor Prof. MOHAMMAD RAFIQUL ISLAM (Bangladesh); publs *Journal of Engineering and Technology* (quarterly), *News Bulletin* (annually), *News Letter* (6 a year), annual calendar and announcement for admission, reports, human resources development series.

Research Centre for Islamic History, Art and Culture (IRCICA): Alemdar Cad. 15, Bâbıâlî Girişi, 34110 Cağaloğlu Fatih, Istanbul, Türkiye; tel. (212) 4020000; fax (212) 2584365; e-mail ircica@ircica.org; internet www.ircica.org; f. 1979; organizes regional congresses in Asia, Africa, the Middle East and Europe; Dir-Gen. Prof. Dr MAHMUD EROL KILIÇ; publs *Newsletter* (3 a year), monographical studies.

Statistical, Economic and Social Research and Training Centre for Islamic Countries (SESRIC): Kudüs Cad. No. 9, Diplomatik Site, 0645 Ankara, Türkiye; tel. (312) 4686172; fax (312) 4673458; e-mail oicankara@sesric.org; internet www.sesric.org; f. 1978; SESRIC's mandate is to collate, process and disseminate socioeconomic statistics and information on, and for the utilization of, its mem. countries; to study and assess economic and social devts in mem. countries with the aim of helping to generate proposals for advancing co-operation; and to organize training activities; the Centre also acts as a focal point for technical co-operation activities between the OIC system and related UN agencies, and prepares economic and social reports and background documentation for OIC meetings; Dir-Gen. NEBIL DABUR (Türkiye); publs *Statistical Yearbook on OIC Member Countries*, *Journal of Economic Cooperation* (quarterly), *OIC Economic Outlook* (annually).

Specialized Institutions

Islamic Broadcasting Union (IBU): POB 6351, Jeddah 21442, Saudi Arabia; tel. (12) 672-1121; fax (12) 672-2600; e-mail ibu@ibuj.org; internet www.ibuj.org; f. 1975; Pres. Dr AMRU EL-LEITHI (Mauritania).

Islamic Organization for Food Security (IOFS): Astana, Kazakhstan; tel. (72) 999900; fax (72) 999975; e-mail info@iofs.org.kz; internet www.iofs.org.kz; f. 2013; aims to co-ordinate, provide technical advice on, and implement OIC policies on agriculture, rural devt and food security; also tasked with mobilizing financial resources for developing agriculture and enhancing food security in OIC mem. states; in Sept. 2017 concluded a co-operation framework with the Arab Organization for Agricultural Development; in Oct. 2021 the 8th OIC Ministerial Conference on Food Security and Agricultural Development tasked the IOFS with establishing an OIC Food Security Reserve System; Dir-Gen. YERLAN A. BAIDAULET.

Islamic World Educational, Scientific and Cultural Organization (ICESCO): BP 2275, Rabat 10104, Morocco; tel. (5) 37566052; e-mail pcontact@icesco.org; internet icesco.org; f. 1982 as Islamic Educational, Scientific and Cultural Org., present name adopted in 2020; mems: 54 states; Dir-Gen. SALIM BIN MOHAMMED AL-MALIK (Saudi Arabia); publs *ICESCO Newsletter* (quarterly), *ICESCO Journal of Science and Technology*, *The Societies We Want*.

OIC Union of News Agencies (OIC-UNA): POB 5054, Jeddah 21422, Saudi Arabia; tel. (12) 665-2056; fax (12) 665-9358; e-mail Info@una-oic.org; internet www.iinanews.org; f. 1972 as the International Islamic News Agency (IINA), present name adopted in 2017; distributes news and reports daily on events, in Arabic, English and French; mems: 57 countries; Dir-Gen. MOHAMMED AL-YAMI (Saudi Arabia).

Science, Technology and Innovation Organization (STIO): c/o COMSTECH Secretariat, 33 Constitution Ave, G-5/2, Islamabad, Pakistan; tel. (51) 9220681; fax (51) 9211115; e-mail comstech@comstech.org; internet www.comstech.org; f. 2010; mandated to implement science, technology and innovation (STI)-related resolutions and decisions, in accordance with the provisions of the OIC Charter; promotes STI activities in mem. states and co-operation and co-ordination between states; Dir-Gen. (and CEO of COMSTECH) Dr M. IQBAL CHOUDHARY (Pakistan).

The Islamic Development Bank is also an OIC Specialized Institution.

Affiliated Institutions

International Association of Islamic Banks (IAIB): King Abdulaziz St, Queen's Bldg, 23rd Floor, Al-Balad Dist, POB 9707, Jeddah 21423, Saudi Arabia; tel. (12) 651-6900; fax (12) 651-6552; f. 1977; links financial institutions operating on Islamic banking principles; mems: 192 banks and other financial institutions in 34 countries.

Islamic Chamber of Commerce, Industry and Agriculture: POB 3831, Clifton, Karachi 75600, Pakistan; tel. (21) 35874910; fax (21) 35870765; e-mail info@iccia.com; internet iccia.com; f. 1979; aims to promote trade and industry among mem. states; comprises national chambers or feds of chambers of commerce and industry; mems: 57; Pres. ABDULLAH SALEH ABDULLAH KAMEL; Sec.-Gen. YOUSEF HASAN KHALAWI.

Islamic Committee of the International Crescent: POB 17434, Benghazi, Libya; tel. (61) 2238080; fax (61) 2220037; e-mail info@icic-oic.org; internet icic-oic.org; f. 1979; aims to attempt to alleviate the suffering caused by natural disasters and war; from 2020 extended humanitarian support to efforts to control the COVID-19 emergency in Libya, Palestine, Syria and Yemen; Pres. ALI MAHMOUD BUHEDMA (Libya); Exec. Dir MOHAMED H. ELASBALI.

Islamic Solidarity Sports Federation: 8535 al Wadi, Ar Rafiah, Riyadh 12752, Saudi Arabia; tel. (11) 480-8986; fax (11) 482-2145; e-mail info@issf.sa; internet issf.sa; f. 1981; organizes the Islamic Solidarity Games (Sept. 2021: Konya, Türkiye); mems: 57 National Olympic Cttees; Pres. Prince ABDULAZIZ BIN TURKI AL-FAISAL (Saudi Arabia); Sec.-Gen. MOHAMMED SALEH AL-GARNAS (Saudi Arabia).

Islamic University in Uganda: POB 2555, Kumi Rd, Mbale, Uganda; tel. (77) 8007077; e-mail registrar@iuiu.ac.ug; internet www.iuiu.ac.ug; f. 1988; aims to meet the educational needs of Muslim populations in English-speaking African countries; second campus in Kampala; mainly financed by the OIC; Rector ISMAIL SSIMBWA GYAGENDA.

Islamic University of Niger: BP 11507, Niamey, Niger; tel. 20-72-39-03; fax 20-73-37-96; e-mail unislamsay@gmail.com; internet www.universite-say.com; f. 1986; provides courses of study in *Shari'a*

(Islamic law) and Arabic language and literature; also offers courses in pedagogy and teacher training; receives grants from the Islamic Solidarity Fund and contributions from OIC mem. states; Rector Dr JAMEL BEN TAHAR.

OIC Computer Emergency Response Team (OIC-CERT): c/o CyberSecurity Malaysia, 7 Jalan Tasik, The Mines Resort City, 63000 Seri Kembangan, Selangor Darul Ehsan, Malaysia; e-mail secretariat@oic-cert.org; internet www.oic-cert.org; f. 2009; aims to promote the exchange of information, to prevent cyberterrorism and computer crimes, and to advance education and technological research and devt; mems: 24.

Organization of Islamic Capitals and Cities (OICC): POB 13621, Jeddah, Saudi Arabia; tel. (12) 698-1953; fax (12) 698-1053; e-mail webmaster@oicc.org; internet oicc.org; f. 1980; aims to preserve the identity and the heritage of Islamic capitals and cities; to achieve and enhance sustainable devt in mem. capitals and cities; to establish and develop comprehensive urban norms, systems and plans to serve the growth and prosperity of Islamic capitals and cities and to enhance their cultural, environmental, urban, economic and social conditions; to advance municipal services and facilities; to support mem. cities' capacity-building progs; and to consolidate fellowship between mems and co-ordinate the scope of co-operation; mems: 141 capitals and cities, 8 observer mems and 14 assoc. mems, in 54 countries across Asia, Africa, Europe and South America; Sec.-Gen. OMAR ABDULLAH.

Organization of the Islamic Shipowners' Association: POB 14900, Jeddah 21434, Saudi Arabia; tel. (12) 663-7882; fax (12) 660-4920; e-mail mail@oisaonline.com; internet www.oisaonline.com; f. 1981; aims to promote co-operation among maritime cos in Islamic countries; in 1998 mems approved the establishment of the Bakkah Shipping Co, to enhance sea transport in the region; mems: 34; Sec.-Gen. Dr ABDULLATIF A. SULTAN.

World Federation of Arab-Islamic Schools: Flat 2, Area 1, Block 38, 10th District, Nasr City, Cairo, Egypt; e-mail tshawi@hotmail.com; f. 1976; supports Arab-Islamic schools worldwide and encourages co-operation between the institutions; promotes the dissemination of the Arabic language and Islamic culture; supports training progs; regional offices in Malaysia, Pakistan and Saudi Arabia.

Other OIC-affiliated institutions are: the Association of Tax Authorities of Islamic Countries; Federation of Consultants from Islamic Countries; General Council for Islamic Banks and Financial Institutions; International Islamic University Malaysia; Islamic Conference Youth Forum for Dialogue and Cooperation; International Union of Muslim Scouts; Islamic World Academy of Sciences; Organisation of Islamic Cooperation Broadcasting Regulatory Authorities Forum; Real Estate Union in Islamic States; and the Standards and Metrology Institute for Islamic Countries.

SOUTHERN AFRICAN DEVELOPMENT COMMUNITY—SADC

Address: SADC Secretariat, Plot No. 54385, Private Bag 0095, Gaborone, Botswana.

Telephone: 3951863; **fax:** 3972848; **e-mail:** registry@sadc.int; **internet:** www.sadc.int.

The first Southern African Development Co-ordination Conference (SADCC) was held in July 1979, to harmonize development plans and to reduce the region's economic dependence on South Africa. In August 1992 the 10 member countries of the SADCC signed a Treaty establishing the SADC, which replaced the SADCC upon its entry into force in October 1993. The Treaty places binding obligations on member countries, with the aim of promoting economic integration towards a fully developed common market. The Treaty was amended in 2001 to institutionalize closer social and political co-operation.

MEMBERS

Angola	Lesotho	Seychelles
Botswana	Madagascar	South Africa
Comoros	Malawi	Tanzania
Congo, Democratic	Mauritius	Zambia
Republic	Mozambique	Zimbabwe
Eswatini	Namibia	

Organization
(October 2022)

SUMMIT MEETING

Heads of state and of government or their representatives meet at least once a year. The meeting is the supreme policymaking organ of SADC and is responsible for the appointment of the Executive Secretary. It is managed by a troika system, comprising the current, incoming and previous chairpersons. The 42nd regular summit was hosted by the Democratic Republic of the Congo (DRC) in its capital Kinshasa, in August 2022.

Chairperson: (2022–23) FELIX TSHISEKEDI (President of the DRC).

SUMMIT TROIKA OF THE ORGAN

The troika, comprising the Organ on Politics, Defence and Security's current, incoming and outgoing chairpersons, manages the Organ and reports directly to the SADC Summit.

Chairperson of the Organ: (2022–23) Dr HAGE G. GEINGOB (President of Namibia).

COUNCIL OF MINISTERS

Representatives of SADC member countries at ministerial level meet twice a year to oversee the functioning and development of the organization.

SECTORAL AND CLUSTER MINISTERIAL COMMITTEES

These Committees, comprising ministers from each member state, provide policy guidance to the Secretariat, oversee the core areas of integration, and, each in their area of competence, monitor the implementation of the Regional Indicative Strategic Development Plan. The following Cluster Ministerial Committees were active in 2022: Food, Agriculture, Natural Resources and Environment; Infrastructure and Services; Trade, Industry, Finance and Investment; Politics, Defence and Security; Legal Affairs and Judicial matters; and Social and Human Development and Special Programmes (i.e. education; HIV and AIDS; labour; employment; and gender).

STANDING COMMITTEE OF SENIOR OFFICIALS

The Committee, comprising senior officials, usually from the ministry responsible for economic planning or finance, acts as the technical advisory body to the Council. It meets twice a year.

SECRETARIAT

The Secretariat is headed by an Executive Secretary, who directly oversees the Organ on Politics, Defence and Security Affairs; a Gender Unit; an Internal Audit and Risk Management Unit; a Macro-economic Convergence Surveillance Unit; a Communication and Public Relations Unit; and a Legal Unit. A Deputy Executive Secretary for Regional Integration and Corporate Affairs oversees the Directorates of Industrial Development and Trade; Finance, Investment and Customs; Infrastructure and Services; Food, Agriculture and Natural Resources; Social and Human Development; and Policy, Planning and Resource Mobilization. The Deputy Executive Secretary for Corporate Affairs oversees Directorates of Budget and Finance; and Human Resources and Administration; and also units concerned with conference services; procurement; and information and communications technologies.

Executive Secretary: ELIAS MPEDI MAGOSI (Botswana).

Deputy Executive Secretary (Regional Integration): Dr THEMBINKOSI MHLONGO (South Africa).

Deputy Executive Secretary (Corporate Affairs): JOSEPH ANDRÉ NOURRICE (Seychelles).

SADC TRIBUNAL

The creation of an SADC Tribunal was provided for under the Treaty establishing SADC and facilitated by a protocol adopted in 2000. A 10-member Tribunal, located in Windhoek, Namibia, was eventually inaugurated in November 2005. In 2010—following a Tribunal judgment that declared as invalid and as a contravention of the SADC Treaty actions by the Zimbabwe Government to expropriate private land without compensation—the SADC summit meeting suspended the functioning of the Tribunal pending a review of its operations and terms of reference. In August 2012 SADC heads of state and of government determined to limit jurisdiction of a new Tribunal to disputes between member states arising from the Treaty, excluding individuals or private companies from seeking its arbitration. In August 2014 SADC heads of state and government adopted a protocol establishing a new Tribunal with more limited powers. By 2022, however, this protocol had not entered into force, and the Tribunal remained suspended. In December 2018 South Africa's Constitutional Court ruled that the role of that country's President in the SADC's decision to abolish the original Tribunal and to sign the replacement protocol was unconstitutional and 'irrational', and he was therefore directed to remove his signature from the 2014 protocol—it was withdrawn in August 2019. In June 2019 the Tanzania High Court ruled against that Government's participation in the 2010 decision to suspend the original Tribunal.

Activities

In July 1979 the first Southern African Development Co-ordination Conference (SADCC) was attended by delegations from Angola, Botswana, Mozambique, Tanzania and Zambia, with participation by representatives from donor governments and international agencies. In April 1980 a regional economic summit was held in Lusaka, Zambia. The meeting approved the Lusaka Declaration, a statement of strategy with the aim of reducing regional economic dependence on South Africa, then in its apartheid period. The 1986 SADCC summit meeting recommended the adoption of economic sanctions against South Africa but failed to establish a timetable for doing so.

In January 1992 a meeting of the SADCC Council of Ministers approved proposals to transform the organization—by then expanded to include Lesotho, Malawi, Namibia and Swaziland (now Eswatini)—into a fully integrated economic community, and in August the Treaty establishing SADC was signed. Post-apartheid South Africa became a member of SADC in August 1994, thus strengthening the objective of regional co-operation and economic integration. Mauritius became a member in August 1995. In September 1997 SADC heads of state agreed to admit the DRC and Seychelles as members of the Community; Seychelles withdrew, however, in July 2004. Madagascar was admitted in August 2005, and Comoros in August 2017.

In March 2001 heads of state and of government endorsed an SADC Common Agenda, which covered the promotion of poverty reduction measures and of sustainable and equitable socioeconomic development, the advancement of democratic political values and systems, and the consolidation of peace and security. Furthermore, the establishment of an integrated committee of ministers was authorized, mandated to formulate and oversee a Regional Indicative Strategic Development Plan (RISDP), intended as the key policy framework for managing the SADC Common Agenda; the finalized RISDP (which was open to subsequent revision) was approved by SADC heads of state and of government in August 2003. An updated RISDP covering 2020–30, and an SADC Vision 2050—together forming part of an SADC Post-2020 Agenda—were approved by the summit meeting held in August 2020. The RISDP (2020–30) was based on the 'foundation' of Peace, Security and Good Governance, and comprised three interrelated 'pillars': Industrial Development and Market Integration; Infrastructure Development in Support of Regional Integration; and Social and Human Capital Development. Gender, Youth, Environment and Climate Change, and Disaster Risk Management were cross-cutting components.

In March 2020 an emergency meeting of SADC ministers responsible for health agreed to share data and to collaborate in responding to the COVID-19 pandemic. In early April the SADC Council of Ministers adopted a set of guidelines aimed at facilitating and harmonizing the flow of critical services and essential goods in the region during the crisis. A virtual extraordinary meeting of SADC health ministers that was held in May 2021 addressed the need to strengthen collective efforts to secure access to COVID-19 vaccines. In August the incoming SADC Chairperson, Dr Lazarus Chakwera (the President of Malawi) emphasized the unacceptability of unequal global access to the vaccines.

TRADE, INDUSTRY, FINANCE AND INVESTMENT

The SADC Protocol on Trade, providing for the establishment of a regional free trade area (FTA), through the gradual elimination of tariff barriers, entered into force in January 2000 (and was subsequently amended). Some 85% of intra-SADC trade tariffs were withdrawn by 1 January 2008, and the SADC FTA was formally inaugurated in August. (Angola and the DRC remained outside of the FTA in 2022, having not yet signed the Protocol.) In January 2012 the

withdrawal of tariffs for sensitive products was finalized. A Protocol on Trade in Services was adopted in the following August; it entered into effect in January 2022. The planned SADC customs union had not yet been effected by 2022. Monetary union and a single currency were to be introduced following its establishment. Technical working groups were created in November 2007 to facilitate the development of policy frameworks in legal and institutional arrangements; revenue collection, sharing and distribution; policy harmonization; and a common external tariff. In March 2016 a Trade Facilitation Programme (TFP) was introduced; in November 2021 the TFP was extended until 2030 by ministers responsible for trade. An SADC Electronic Certificate of Origin (e-CoO) entered into effect in September 2022, under the TFP.

In October 2018 an SADC Real Time Gross Settlement System (SADC-RTGS) multi-currency platform was initiated to facilitate more efficient regional payment transactions. By 2022 all SADC member states (other than Comoros) and 85 banks were participating in the SADC-RTGS.

In 2005 an SADC Protocol on Facilitation of Movement of Persons entered into force. A Labour Migration Action Plan that was being implemented during the period 2020–25 aimed to enhance the regional framework for the transfer of skills and for matching labour demand and supply. SADC Guidelines on Portability of Social Security Benefits were introduced in December 2020.

In May 2022 the SADC, European Union and Germany initiated a new digital Corridor Trip Monitoring System, which was to facilitate more rapid cross-border truck movements at land borders in Southern and East Africa.

In August 2007 SADC heads of state and of government determined that industrialization should be the principal focus of the regional economic integration agenda, and mandated the Ministerial Task Force, accordingly, to develop a long-term SADC Industrialization Strategy and Roadmap covering (in three phases) the period 2015–63. This was endorsed by an extraordinary summit convened in April 2015, and subsequently launched in August, with the aim of ensuring that member states exploited their diverse natural resources to the greatest potential. An annual SADC Industrialization Week was initiated in 2016, supported by SADC and the Southern Africa Business Forum. In March 2017 the SADC Ministerial Task Force on Regional Economic Integration endorsed an action plan to support the implementation of the Strategy and Roadmap, including the regular convening of an Industrial Development Forum to review progress. In August the 37th ordinary SADC summit addressed the promotion of private sector partnerships aimed at developing regional industry and value chains, and urged that related projects should be implemented in the following focus areas: agro-processing, energy, minerals, and pharmaceuticals. In August 2019 the 39th summit approved a Protocol on Industry, and—stating great concern over the slow growth in intra-SADC trade—determined to accelerate the implementation of the SADC's 2015–63 Industrialization Strategy.

The SADC region is rich in natural resources. In February 2000 a Protocol on Mining entered into force, providing for the harmonization of policies and programmes relating to the development and exploitation of mineral resources in the region, with a view to harnessing the mining sector to alleviate poverty and generate prosperity. SADC aims to stimulate increased local and foreign investment in the sector, through the assimilation and dissemination of data and the promotion of prospecting activities. Other objectives include the improvement of industry training, increasing the contribution of small-scale mining, reducing the illicit trade in gemstones and gold, increasing co-operation in mineral exploration and processing, and minimizing the adverse impact of mining operations on the environment. SADC supports the Kimberley Process Certification Scheme to prevent trade in illegally mined rough diamonds.

During the period January 2015–March 2022 an EU-funded SADC Trade Related Facility (SADC TRF) provided some €18.5m. in technical support towards the implementation of member states' commitments under both the SADC Protocol on Trade and a regional Economic Partnership Agreement (EPA) that entered into force in October 2016 between the EU and an SADC sub-group comprising Botswana, Lesotho, Mozambique, Namibia, South Africa and Swaziland (now Eswatini). The remaining SADC member states belonged to other EPA negotiating blocs. SADC has worked with other subregional organizations to establish a common position on co-operation between African ACP (African, Caribbean and Pacific) countries and the EU. A new ACP-EU Partnership Agreement was initialled in 2021, and was to replace the Cotonou Agreement (which had governed ACP-EU co-operation since June 2000). In August 2019 three EU-funded SADC programmes were approved, on improving the investment and business environment; trade facilitation; and support to industrialization and the productive sectors (SIPS).

In May 2016 SADC member states' competition authorities concluded a Memorandum of Understanding (MOU) governing interagency co-operation on competition policy, law and enforcement.

In August 2006 SADC heads of state and of government adopted a Protocol on Finance and Investment. The document, regarded as constituting the main framework for economic integration in Southern Africa, outlined, *inter alia,* how the region intended to proceed towards monetary union.

In August 2008 an SADC Protocol on Science, Technology and Innovation was adopted, to promote the development and harmonization of regional science and technology activities.

In May 2020 SADC issued a *COVID-19 SADC Economy Report,* which outlined policy recommendations to support member states with building economic resilience and safeguarding citizens from the socioeconomic impacts of the ongoing pandemic. These included the strengthening of early warning, response and mitigation structures for pandemics and other disasters, and developing roadmaps and action plans with a focus on reviving economies, strengthening economic resilience and improving competitiveness. In August SADC heads of state and of government received a report addressing the sectoral socioeconomic impacts of the COVID-19 crisis, and approved remedial measures proposed therein. The summit also endorsed a new SADC Macroeconomic Convergence Surveillance Mechanism.

INFRASTRUCTURE AND SERVICES

An SADC Regional Infrastructure Development Master Plan: Vision 2027, intended to be the basis for infrastructure-related co-operation and planning, was adopted in August 2012 by SADC heads of state and of government. The Master Plan—which was to be implemented in three phases—was envisaged as an element of a broader Tripartite Interregional Infrastructure Master Plan with the Common Market for Eastern and Southern African (COMESA) and the East African Community (EAC). An SADC Project Preparation Development Facility (SADC PPDF) extends grants to member states to advance the implementation of initiatives aimed at improving the transboundary water, energy, transport and ICT infrastructures. In August 2022 the PPDF approved funding totalling US $20.2m. to support the preparation of 12 projects in the region's transport, water and energy sectors. It was announced in March of that year that 63 infrastructure projects had been initiated in the SADC region under the Programme for Infrastructure Development in Africa of the African Union (AU).

An SADC Protocol on Transport, Communications and Meteorology, adopted in August 1996, provided for an integrated regional transport policy, an SADC Regional Trunk Road Network, and harmonized regional policies relating to maritime and inland waterway transport; civil aviation; regional telecommunications; postal services; and meteorology. An Integrated Transport Committee, and other sub-committees representing the sectors covered by the Protocol, have been established. A Southern African Telecommunications Regional Authority was created in January 1997. In March 2001 an Association of Southern African National Road Agencies was founded to foster the development of an integrated regional road transportation system. The 2012 Master Plan incorporated the long-term implementation of 72 infrastructure projects, with a particular focus on three principal transport corridors connecting points of production in member states to sea ports (these being: the Maputo Corridor; North-South Corridor; and Dar-es-Salaam Corridor).

An SADC Regional Information Infrastructure was adopted in December 1999, with the aim of linking member states by means of high-capacity digital land and submarine routes. In September 2017 SADC ministers responsible for Information and Communications Technology (ICT) adopted a Declaration on the Fourth Industrial Revolution, which emphasized the use of digital technology as a cross cutting tool for socioeconomic transformation. A Fourth Industrial Revolution Task Team was established. SADC supports the normally annual Southern Africa Internet Governance Forum (SAIGF).

Areas of activity in the energy sector include joint petroleum exploration; training programmes for the petroleum sector and studies for strategic fuel storage facilities; promotion of the use of coal; development of hydroelectric power and the co-ordination of SADC generation and transmission capacities; new and renewable sources of energy, including pilot projects in solar energy; assessment of the environmental and socioeconomic impact of wood fuel scarcity and relevant education programmes; and energy conservation. The Southern African Power Pool (SAPP), approved in 1995 by SADC ministers responsible for energy, has the goal of linking all member states into a single electricity grid; utilities participating in SAPP aim to provide an economical and reliable electricity supply to consumers in the region. SADC and COMESA have the joint objective of eventually linking SAPP and COMESA's Eastern Africa Power Pool. Within the framework of SADC's energy programme a Zambia–Tanzania–Kenya Interconnector project has been initiated. It was envisaged that the project, together with an Angola–Namibia interconnector and the construction of a new power transmission line in Mozambique and Malawi, would achieve the full integration of all mainland SADC member states into the SAPP upon its completion, scheduled for October 2023. In August 2017 SADC heads of state and of government determined that an SADC Natural Gas Committee should be established, tasked with promoting the role of natural gas

in regional industrial development. An SADC Centre for Renewable Energy and Energy Efficiency (SACREEE) was inaugurated in Windhoek, in October 2018.

An SADC Protocol on the Development of Tourism entered into force in 2002, and an amended Protocol was adopted in September 2009, with a view to using southern Africa's potential as a tourism destination as a tool for sustainable development. SADC has organized trade fairs and investment forums. The Regional Tourism Organization for Southern Africa (RETOSA), established in 1997, is administered jointly by SADC, national tourism authorities and private sector operators. In July 2016 SADC ministers responsible for tourism agreed that RETOSA should focus on private-sector-led marketing, while SADC would co-ordinate the development and implementation of regional tourism policies.

SADC promotes 18 Transfrontier Conservation Areas (TFCAs)—i.e. terrestrial and marine conservation environments straddling international borders (including in partnership with non-SADC states)—as premier regional tourist and investment destinations. In September 2021 SADC and partners launched a €100m. SADC TFCA Financing Facility.

The TFCAs include: Ais/Richtersveld (in Namibia and South Africa), Kgalagadi (Botswana, Namibia and South Africa), Limpopo-Shashe (Botswana, South Africa and Zimbabwe), the Great Limpopo Transfrontier Park (Mozambique, South Africa and Zimbabwe), Lubombo (Mozambique, South Africa and Swaziland), Maloti-Drakensburg (Lesotho and South Africa), and Kavango-Zambezi (envisaged as the largest conservation area in the world, straddling the borders of Angola, Botswana, Namibia, Zambia and Zimbabwe), the Iona-Skeleton Coast (Angola and Namibia), Liuwa Plain-Kamela (Zambia and Angola), the Lower Zambezi-Mana Pools (Zambia and Zimbabwe), Niassa-Selous (a woodland ecosystem, Mozambique and Tanzania), Mnazi Bay-Quirimbas (Mozambique and Tanzania), the Mayombe Forest (Angola, the DRC, the Republic of the Congo and Gabon), and Chimanimani (Zimbabwe and Mozambique).

SADC aims to promote equitable distribution and effective management of the region's water resources, around 70% of which are shared across international borders. A Revised Protocol on Shared Watercourses came into force in September 2003 (updating an earlier Protocol from April 1998). An SADC Regional Water Policy was adopted in August 2005 as a framework for providing the sustainable and integrated development, protection and utilization of national and transboundary water resources. In September 2016 an SADC Groundwater Management Institute was inaugurated, based at the University of the Free State, Bloemfontein, South Africa, to promote sustainable groundwater management throughout the region.

FOOD, AGRICULTURE AND NATURAL RESOURCES

The Directorate of Food, Agriculture and Natural Resources aims to develop, co-ordinate and harmonize policies and programmes on natural resources management and agriculture, with a focus on sustainability.

In August 2014 the 34th SADC summit meeting approved a Protocol on Environmental Management for Sustainable Development. An SADC Protocol on Wildlife Conservation and Law Enforcement entered into effect in November 2003, and a Protocol on Forestry entered into force in 2009. SADC's Plant Genetic Resources Centre, based near Lusaka, aims to collect, conserve and utilize indigenous and exotic plant genetic resources and to develop appropriate management practices. In August 2017 SADC heads of state and of government adopted an SADC Protocol on Plant Variety Production and Charter Establishing the SADC Seed Centre. In May 2020 SADC ministers responsible for agriculture and food security, and for fisheries and aquaculture approved an SADC Animal Genetic Resources Conservation and Utilization Strategy. A parallel SADC Regional Strategy on Plant Genetic Resources Conservation and Utilisation was being implemented during 2020–30. Meeting in May 2022, in Lilongwe, Malawi, to review policies and strategies for advancing food production and security, SADC ministers responsible for agriculture and food security, and for fisheries and aquaculture approved guidelines on handling plant genetic resources.

The Gaborone-based SADC Centre for Coordination of Agricultural Research and Development for Southern Africa (CCARDESA), established in 2010, aims to harmonize agricultural research and development across the region; it maintains an online knowledge hub. An SADC Regional Agricultural Policy was approved by the SADC Council in 2014. Agricultural programmes have aimed to strengthen the capacity of the livestock sector, control various pests and livestock diseases, and (with a view to reducing the regional dependency on rain-fed agricultural production) to enhance irrigation development and water management. In September 2022 SADC and the Food and Agriculture Organization of the UN (FAO) established an SADC Agricultural Information Management System (SADC AIMS), with the aim of collating data to enhance evidence-based policy making.

An SADC Fisheries Protocol that entered into force in August 2003 incorporated measures to promote the management of fisheries resources; the protection of the aquatic environment, and of artisanal and subsistence fisheries; and to combat illegal, unregulated and unreported (IUU) fishing activities in regional waters. In August 2017 the Council of Ministers agreed to establish an SADC Regional Monitoring, Control and Surveillance Coordination Centre to combat IUU, and in June 2019 the Council determined to incorporate into the Centre mechanisms of the FISH-i Africa Task Force (established in 2012 by eight western Indian Ocean countries to counter IUU). At the end of March 2022 the SADC and African Development Bank jointly launched the Programme for Improving Fisheries Governance and Blue Economy Trade Corridors (ProFishBlue), which aimed to foster the sustainable management of regional fisheries resources. An SADC Regional Aquaculture Strategy and Action Plan were being implemented during the period 2016–26 to support the sustainable development of that sector.

In October 2019 the SADC and African Risk Capacity concluded an MOU on enhancing regional resilience. An SADC Regional Climate Change Strategy and Action Plan were finalized in June 2015. The SADC Climate Services Centre (established in 1990 as the Drought Monitoring Centre) organizes an annual Southern African Regional Climate Outlook Forum (SARCOF), which assesses seasonal weather prospects. SARCOF-26, convened in late August 2022, in a virtual format, forecast average to above-average rainfall for the last quarter of 2022 and first quarter of 2023.

A regional Food and Nutrition Security Strategy covering the period 2015–25 was endorsed by SADC heads of state and of government in August 2014. The SADC Secretariat and the World Food Programme concluded an MOU in 2019 aimed at consolidating co-operation in the area of regional food and nutrition security; they also established a joint technical team to operationalize the accord. Commitment to the MOU was confirmed in September 2022. The SADC Secretariat implements a Regional Vulnerability Assessment and Analysis (RVAA) programme, which assists member states to conduct their own annual vulnerability audits. Analysis of the results is synthesized into a biannual *SADC Regional State of Food and Nutrition Security and Vulnerability in Southern Africa Report.* In September 2020 the SADC Secretariat, the FAO Subregional Office for Southern Africa and the International Red Locust Control Organization for Central and Southern Africa initiated a joint technical co-operation project aimed at eradicating an outbreak of migratory locusts that was affecting cereal output and pastures in Botswana, Malawi, Namibia, South Africa and Zambia. In November SADC initiated a US $20m. appeal to fund locust control activities. In July 2021 the RVAA launched a new Online Vulnerability Atlas, collating data on regional food, nutrition and livelihoods security. In the following month an SADC *Synthesis Report on the State of Food and Nutrition Security in Southern Africa* estimated that 47.6m. people in the region were food insecure—some 34.3% above the five-year average.

SOCIAL AND HUMAN DEVELOPMENT

An SADC Protocol on Health entered into force in August 2004. In August 2000 the Community adopted a set of guidelines to underpin any future negotiations with major pharmaceutical companies on improving access to and reducing the cost of drugs to combat HIV/AIDS. In July 2003 an SADC special summit issued the Maseru Declaration on HIV/AIDS, identifying priority areas for action, including prevention, access to testing and treatment, and social mobilization. In June 2013 the SADC Secretariat, in co-operation with the UN Development Programme, formulated a set of indicators aimed at mainstreaming HIV awareness in the following five sectors: economic development; finance; infrastructure; local government; and works and planning. In September 2020 national AIDS co-ordinating agencies in SADC member states convened to take stock of the ongoing HIV response in the context of the COVID-19 pandemic. SADC supports efforts to control tuberculosis (TB) in the SADC region, and to address challenges posed by the emergence of Multidrug Resistant TB (MDR-TB) and Extensive Drug Resistant TB (XDR-TB) strains. In August 2018 SADC heads of state and government adopted the Windhoek Declaration on Eliminating Malaria in the SADC Region by 2030. An SADC Pharmaceutical Business Plan, launched in August 2017, aimed to promote research, to harmonize essential medicine lists and standard treatment guidelines, and to strengthen regional regulatory capacity and supply chain management systems. The Business Plan also provided for the establishment of a regional databank of African traditional medicines and medical plants. In June 2021 it was reported that SADC's EU-funded SIPS programme would support private sector participation in regional pharmaceutical and medical value chains. In August 2022 the SADC Secretariat launched a five-year SADC Hygiene Strategy, with a focus on preventing the spread of communicable diseases (such as COVID-19) in the region. The annual SADC Healthy Lifestyles Day, held (since 2008) on the last Friday of February, aims to raise regional awareness on the prevention of non-communicable diseases (NCDs), which are predicted to become

the leading cause of death in Africa by 2030. An SADC Protocol on Combating Illicit Drugs entered into force in March 1999.

In July 2000 an SADC Protocol on Education and Training, which was to provide a legal framework for co-operation in this sector, entered into force. SADC administers an intraregional education and skills development programme, supports distance learning, and operates a scholarship and training awards programme. An SADC Technical Committee on Higher Education and Training and Research and Development was established in 2012. The creation of an SADC University of Transformation, to provide technical vocational training, was endorsed by the 38th SADC summit, in August 2018. In April 2020 SADC and UNESCO adopted a joint statement and action plan aimed at ensuring continuity of learning while educational establishments in the region remained closed as a means of containing the COVID-19 pandemic.

SADC seeks to promote employment and to harmonize legislation concerning labour and social protection.

In August 2018 a Revised SADC Protocol on Gender and Development entered into force that set targets on gender equality and provided for gender-responsive legislation, policies and programmes.

POLITICS, DEFENCE AND SECURITY

In June 1996 SADC heads of state and of government, meeting in Gaborone inaugurated the Organ on Politics, Defence and Security (OPDS). The stated objectives of the Organ were, *inter alia,* to safeguard the people and development of the region against instability arising from civil disorder, inter-state conflict and external aggression; to undertake conflict prevention, management and resolution activities, by mediating in inter-state and intra-state disputes and conflicts, pre-empting conflicts through an early warning system and using diplomacy and peacekeeping to achieve sustainable peace; to promote the development of a common foreign policy, in areas of mutual interest, and the evolution of common political institutions; to develop close co-operation between the police and security services of the region; and to encourage the observance of universal human rights. A Protocol on Politics, Defence and Security Co-operation—overseen by an Inter-state Politics and Diplomacy Committee—regulates the structure, operations and functions of the Organ. (The Protocol entered into force in March 2004.) Peace, Security and Good Governance are described as the foundation of the RISDP (2020–30).

The March 2001 extraordinary SADC summit adopted a Declaration on Small Arms, promoting the curtailment of the proliferation of and illicit trafficking in light weapons in the region. A Protocol on the Control of Firearms, Ammunition and Other Related Materials was adopted in August of that year. In January 2002 SADC heads of state and government adopted a Declaration against Terrorism. In August 2011 they endorsed an SADC Maritime Security Strategy, and in 2015 they approved an SADC Regional Counter-Terrorism Strategy. A Dar es Salaam, Tanzania-based SADC Regional Counter Terrorism Centre was inaugurated in February 2022.

In August 2003 SADC heads of state and of government adopted an SADC Mutual Defence Pact, incorporating the principle of collective self-defence and the objectives of promoting regional stability and security. The SADC Standby Force (SADC SF), authorized by SADC heads of state and government in August 2007, represents a pillar of the AU's African Standby Force, and was declared in July 2016 to have attained full operational capacity status. A Rasea, Botswana-based SADC SF regional logistics depot was to become operational in 2023. SADC's Regional Peacekeeping Training Centre was established in June 1999 and since August 2005 has been directed by the SADC Secretariat. An SADC Mine Action Committee, to support demining activities, is also maintained.

The SADC's mediation, conflict prevention and preventive diplomacy structures also comprise a Panel of Elders and a Mediation Support Unit. The inaugural meeting of an SADC Mediation Reference Group was held in May 2015.

In August 2004 SADC heads of state and government adopted a Protocol on Principles and Guidelines Governing Democratic Elections, which advocated full participation by citizens in the political process; freedom of association; political tolerance; elections at regular intervals; equal access to the state media for all political parties; equal opportunity to exercise the right to vote and be voted for; independence of the judiciary; impartiality of the electoral institutions; the right to voter education; the respect of election results proclaimed to be free and fair by a competent national electoral authority; and the right to challenge election results as provided for in the law. Regional elections are monitored by SADC Election Observation Missions (SEOMs). An SADC Electoral Advisory Council (SEAC) became operational in April 2011.

In August 2012 SADC leaders urged Rwanda to denounce militants of the Kivu-based 23 March Movement (M23), which had became highly active in north-eastern DRC, clashing with government forces and causing mass population displacement. A meeting of the OPDS troika, convened in September, urged the parties to the conflict in eastern DRC to seek a negotiated resolution. In December an extraordinary summit of SADC heads of state and of government agreed in principle to deploy SADCBRIG in eastern DRC, within the framework of a neutral international force that had been proposed by the International Conference of the Great Lakes Region (ICGLR). In February 2013 the leaders of 11 African countries (including Angola and South Africa), meeting in Addis Ababa, Ethiopia, signed the Peace, Security and Cooperation Framework (PSCF) for the DRC and the Region; with the UN, the AU and the ICGLR, SADC subsequently acted as a guarantor of the Framework. In March the UN Security Council authorized the establishment of a Force Intervention Brigade (FIB), to be operational in eastern DRC under the auspices of the UN Organization Stabilization Mission in the DRC (MONUSCO); from May the new Brigade was deployed, in the form of a 3,069-strong SADCBRIG force, comprising troops from Malawi, South Africa and Tanzania. In November the DRC armed forces, with FIB assistance, gained control over former M23 strong-holds, causing the remaining M23 combatants to flee and the M23 leaders to declare the end of its rebellion in eastern DRC. In November–early December a so-called Kampala dialogue took place between the DRC Government and the M23, culminating in the signing, under the auspices of SADC and the ICGLR, of final declarations by the parties. In July 2016 SADC participated in an inter-Congolese national dialogue led by the AU. In the following month SADC leaders condemned the massacre perpetuated by the partly Islamist Allied Democratic Forces (ADF) in eastern DRC, noting that the ADF was a terrorist grouping that posed a danger to the wider region. In October SADC congratulated all parties in the DRC for concluding an agreement to establish a transitional coalition government. The OPDS sent a fact-finding mission in that month to assess political and security developments in the DRC, and a follow-up mission in April 2017. In August SADC heads of state and of government appointed a Special Envoy to the DRC. In December the SADC Executive Secretary condemned an attack in Semuliki, eastern DRC, that resulted in the deaths, among others, of 15 FIB peacekeepers. During November–December an SEAC team undertook a technical assessment mission to the DRC in advance of elections that were scheduled to be held by the end of 2018. The Executive Secretary led a political assessment mission to the DRC in January–February 2018, and an SADC liaison office was opened in the capital Kinshasa in March. In mid-2018 a joint SADC-UN task force was deployed to review the FIB; it recommended reconfiguring the Brigade to achieve a more agile and flexible structure. A 94-member SEOM was deployed to the country to oversee campaigning and voting in the presidential, legislative and provincial elections that were held on 30 December. In early January 2019 the OPDS, following disputed results of the presidential poll, recommended all parties to pursue negotiations to establish a government of national unity. An SADC 'double troika' summit of heads of state and government, convened in Addis Ababa, Ethiopia, in mid-January, to address the situation in the DRC, reaffirmed its commitment to supporting the DRC's political processes, and to the goal of supporting the neutralization of the militant insurgency in that country. At that time the ICGLR, SADC and AU Chairpersons determined to dispatch a joint high-level delegation to the DRC to liaise with national stakeholders on means of resolving the post-electoral crisis. Soon afterwards, however, despite continuing evidence of irregularities in the electoral process, Félix Tshisekedi was declared the victor in the presidential poll and promptly inaugurated. In August the 39th SADC summit noted continuing acts of extremism and terrorism in the DRC, in particular in the Beni area of North Kivu, and agreed to co-operate closely with the ICGLR to advance security stabilization efforts in the Great Lakes Region. In August 2020 the OPDS protested a unilateral UN decision to reconfigure the FIB and to include non-SADC forces in the format, with the aim of enhancing its effectiveness. Eventually, in November, however, a special summit of the Organ approved the amendments. The revitalized FIB comprised three SADC region battlegroups (from Malawi, Tanzania and South Africa) and four Quick Reaction Forces ('QRFs', from Kenya, Nepal, South Africa and Tanzania), as well as new intelligence units. In April 2022 SADC and other PSCF guarantors strongly condemned attacks in eastern DRC perpetrated by former M23 militants, urged them to silence their guns, and reiterated commitment to supporting progress towards peace in that country. (In April 2022, following the DRC's admittance to the EAC in March, that body determined to organize a dialogue with armed groups active in eastern areas of the DRC, and to deploy a force there should the militants fail to comply.)

In February 2019 the SADC Chairperson urged the withdrawal of international sanctions still imposed on Zimbabwe. This stance was reiterated in August by SADC heads of state and of government participating in the 39th summit meeting. They noted the adverse impacts of the sanctions on the Zimbabwean economy and on the wider region, and determined that SADC member states would collectively protest the sanctions annually on 25 October, pending their withdrawal.

The assassination in early September 2017 of Lt-Gen. Khoantle Motšomotšo, the incumbent Commander of the LDF, and of two

senior LDF officers, led the OPDS Chair. immediately to send a ministerial-level fact finding mission to Lesotho. A double troika summit of SADC heads of state and government that was convened in mid-September strongly condemned the murders, and urged the Lesotho authorities to restore law and order forthwith and to accelerate investigations into both the recent atrocity and into the June 2015 assassination, by the Lesotho security forces, of the Commander of the Lesotho Defence Force (LDF), Maaparankoe Mahao. The summit also authorized the deployment of an SADC contingent force, consisting of intelligence, military, security, and civilian experts, which was tasked with providing support to the Lesotho Government by facilitating the establishment of a secure environment to support the conduct of a multi-stakeholder dialogue and the implementation of constitutional, parliamentary, judicial, security sector and public service reforms. The ministerial fact finding mission reported to the summit on the still volatile security situation in that country. The new SADC Preventive Mission in the Kingdom of Lesotho (SAPMIL) was deployed to Lesotho from early December 2017. The Executive Secretary undertook a follow-up mission to SAPMIL in February 2018. The SADC Facilitator to Lesotho helped to organize a Lesotho National Leaders Forum in August, in Maseru: this adopted the Lesotho National Leaders Forum Declaration on Comprehensive Reforms, including a commitment promptly to convene a National Dialogue aimed at advancing the ongoing political reforms process. SAPMIL was formally closed down in November. In August 2019 the 39th SADC summit welcomed the enactment of legislation in Lesotho that provided for the creation of a National Reforms Authority. In August 2022 the 42nd summit commended the ongoing efforts of the SADC Facilitator, and approved the establishment of an oversight committee for the reforms process in Lesotho, comprising the SADC Panel of Elders and the SADC Mediation Reference Group (q.v.). A SEOM was deployed to observe legislative elections held in Lesotho in early October 2022.

In late March 2021 President Mokgweetsi Masisi of Botswana (the Chair. of the OPDS) condemned recent terrorist attacks (perpetrated by Ahl al-Sunna Wal-Jama'a, associated with Islamic State Central Africa Province) that had caused numerous civilian deaths in the coastal town of Palma, Cabo Delgado, northern Mozambique, and had also prompted significant population displacement. At the beginning of April President Masisi and President Emmerson Mnangagwa of Zimbabwe met in the Zimbabwean capital, Harare, to discuss a regional response to the worsening security situation in Cabo Delgado—where a violent insurgency had persisted since 2017; an OPDS technical deployment to Mozambique was authorized. On the basis of the OPDS report, in June 2021 SADC heads of state and government authorized the immediate deployment of an SADC Mission in Mozambique (SAMIM) to combat terrorism and violent extremism. Rwanda also committed to sending troops to work alongside the mission. The mandate of the mission was extended in October. An extraordinary summit meeting, convened in January 2022, reiterated support for the SAMIM and the grouping's commitment to securing peace in Cabo Delgado. It was reported in September that the SAMIM was being reformed to incorporate, as well as a military component, multidimensional civilian, police and correctional services dimensions.

Against the background of an escalating political and security crisis in Eswatini, where pro-democracy demonstrations were being organized to demand political reforms to the national system of absolute monarchy, in July 2021 the Chairperson of the OPDS stated concern over numerous reported incidents of violence. He urged protesters not to attack public and private property, and called on the national security forces to exercise restraint. The OPDS Chair. urged that grievances should be addressed through established structures, and called on the Eswatini authorities to initiate an open national dialogue to support a resolution of the crisis. An SADC fact-finding mission was dispatched briefly to Eswatini to assess the situation, and to encourage a calm national dialogue. In October the OPDS troika sent a Special Envoy to meet with the authorities in that country.

An SADC SEOM observed the general election that was held in Angola in August 2022.

An SADC Regional Disaster Preparedness and Response Strategy was adopted in November 2016. In August 2019 the 39th summit directed the SADC Secretariat to accelerate the operationalization of an SADC Disaster Preparedness and Response Mechanism. An SADC Emergency Response Team (a part of the Mechanism) has been developed. In June 2021 an SADC Humanitarian and Emergency Operations Centre (SHOC) was inaugurated in Nampula, Mozambique.

EXTERNAL RELATIONS

In April 2006 SADC adopted the Windhoek Declaration, providing a framework for co-operation and dialogue between SADC and its international co-operation partners (ICPs), with the aim of facilitating the implementation of the SADC Common Agenda. At the end of 2021 nine SADC-ICP thematic groups were active.

A (normally) biennial SADC-EU Ministerial Political Dialogue is convened. In 2021 this was conducted in a virtual format, in June.

In 2001 a task force was established to co-ordinate a programme of co-operation between SADC and COMESA, and in 2005 EAC became incorporated into the process, which was led thereafter by the COMESA-EAC-SADC Task Force. In October 2008 the first tripartite COMESA-EAC-SADC summit was convened, in Kampala, Uganda, to discuss the harmonization of policy and programme work by the three regional economic communities. The Kampala summit approved a roadmap towards the formation of a single free trade area. At the second tripartite summit, held in June 2011, in Johannesburg, negotiations were initiated on the establishment of the proposed COMESA-EAC-SADC Tripartite Free Trade Area (TFTA). In January 2012 AU leaders endorsed a Framework, Roadmap and Architecture for Fast Tracking the Establishment of a Continental FTA (referred to as AfCFTA), and an Action Plan for Boosting Intra-African Trade, which planned for the consolidation of the TFTA with other regional FTAs into the AfCFTA initiative. An agreement establishing the TFTA was concluded in June 2015, and was to enter into force following ratification by three-quarters of the TFTA states. On 31 July 2020 Tripartite Guidelines for the Movement of Persons, Goods and Services across the Tripartite Region during the COVID-19 Pandemic were introduced.

In July 2018 an MOU on military co-operation, under which development projects were envisaged, was adopted by the SADC and the Russian Federation. A further bilateral MOU, on basic principles of co-operation, was concluded in October. An SADC Investment Forum was organized in the Russian capital, Moscow in that month.

In August 2022 the 42nd SADC summit reaffirmed the organization's commitment to non-alignment with respect to conflicts occurring outside Africa, and stated objections to the targeting of the African continent for punitive measures under the recently introduced US 'Countering Malign Russian Activities in Africa Act'.

Finance

In March 2022 the Council of Ministers approved a budget totalling US $87.4m. for 2022–23, of which $50.7m. was to be funded by member states and $36.7m. by international co-operating partners.

Publications

Annual Report.

Climate Outlook Update (quarterly).

Inside SADC (monthly).

SADC Agromet Update (6 a year).

Other thematic reports, assessments, bulletins (including an *SADC Regional Response to COVID-19 Pandemic Bulletin* series).

Associated Body

SADC Parliamentary Forum: 578 Love St, off Robert Mugabe Ave, Windhoek, Namibia; tel. (61) 2870000; fax (61) 254642; e-mail info@sadcpf.org; internet www.sadcpf.org; f. 1996; aims to promote democracy, human rights and good governance throughout the SADC region, ensuring fair representation for women; endorsed in Sept. 1997 by SADC heads of state as an autonomous institution; a training arm of the Forum, the SADC Parliamentary Leadership Centre, was established in 2005; the Forum deploys missions to monitor parliamentary and presidential elections in the region and to guide the pre- and post-election phases; adopted, in March 2001, Electoral Norms and Standards for the SADC Region; progs are also undertaken in the areas of democracy and governance; HIV/AIDS and public health; regional devt and integration; gender equality and empowerment; ICT; and parliamentary capacity devt; the Forum is funded by mem. parliaments, govts and charitable and international orgs; in Nov. 2021 the Forum validated a Model Law addressing gender-based violence; in Aug. 2022 the 42nd SADC summit meeting adopted an Agreement Amending the SADC Treaty on Transformation of the SADC Parliamentary Forum into an SADC Parliament; mems: national parliaments of SADC countries, representing more than 3,500 parliamentarians; Sec.-Gen. BOEMO MMANDU SEKGOMA (Botswana).

Agriculture, Food, Forestry and Fisheries

(For organizations concerned with agricultural commodities, see Commodities)

Africa Rice Center (AfricaRice): AfricaRice Headquarters, 01 BP 4029, blvd François Mitterrand, Cocody, Abidjan 01, Côte d'Ivoire; tel. 22-48-09-10; fax 22-44-26-29; e-mail AfricaRice@cgiar.org; internet www.africarice.org; f. 1971 (as the West Africa Rice Development Association, present name adopted in 2009 as scope of membership and activities expanded to pan-African); participates in the network of agricultural research centres supported by the Consultative Group on International Agricultural Research; aims to contribute to food security and poverty eradication in poor rural and urban populations, through research, partnerships, capacity strengthening and policy support on rice-based systems; promotes sustainable agricultural devt based on environmentally sound management of natural resources; maintains research stations in Benin, Ghana, Liberia, Madagascar, Nigeria, Senegal, Sierra Leone and Tanzania; provides training and consulting services; mems: 28 countries; Dir-Gen. Dr HAROLD ROY-MACAULEY (Sierra Leone); publs *Annual Report*, *Program Report* (annually), training series, proceedings, leaflets.

African Agricultural Technology Foundation: POB 30709, Nairobi 00100, Kenya; tel. (20) 4223700; e-mail aatf@aatf-africa.org; internet www.aatf-africa.org; f. 2003; aims to facilitate and promote public-private partnerships for the access and delivery of agricultural technologies for use by resource-poor smallholder farmers in sub-Saharan Africa; Chair. OUSMANE BADIANE (Senegal); Exec. Dir Dr CANISIUS KANANGIRE (Rwanda).

African Union-Interafrican Bureau for Animal Resources (AU-IBAR): Kenindia Business Park Museum Hill, Westlands Rd, POB 30786, Nairobi, Kenya; tel. (20) 3674000; fax (20) 3674341; e-mail ibar.office@au-ibar.org; internet www.au-ibar.org; f. 1951 as Interafrican Bureau of Epizootic Diseases; works to develop animal resources for Africa through supporting and empowering AU mem. states and Regional Economic Communities; Dir Dr NICK NWANKPA (acting).

CAB International (CABI): Nosworthy Way, Wallingford, Oxon, OX10 8DE, United Kingdom; tel. (1491) 832111; fax (1491) 833508; e-mail enquiries@cabi.org; internet www.cabi.org; f. 1930 as the Imperial Agricultural Bureaux (later Commonwealth Agricultural Bureaux), present name adopted in 1986; aims to improve human welfare worldwide through the generation, dissemination and application of scientific knowledge in support of sustainable devt; places particular emphasis on sustainable agriculture, forestry, human health and the management of natural resources, with priority given to the needs of developing countries; a separate microbiology centre, in Egham, Surrey (UK), undertakes research, consultancy, training, capacity building and institutional devt measures in sustainable pest management, biosystematics and molecular biology, ecological applications and environmental and industrial microbiology; compiles and publishes extensive information (in a variety of print and electronic forms) on aspects of agriculture, forestry, veterinary medicine, the environment and natural resources, and rural devt in developing countries; maintains regional centres in Brazil, the People's Rep. of China, Ghana, India, Kenya, Malaysia, Pakistan, Switzerland, Trinidad and Tobago, the UK, Zambia and the USA; mems: 49 countries and territories; Chair. ROGER HORTON; CEO Dr DANIEL ELGER (UK).

Consultative Group on International Agricultural Research (CGIAR): CGIAR System Management Office, 1000 ave Agropolis, 34394 Montpellier, France; tel. 4-67-04-75-75; fax 4-67-04-75-83; e-mail contact@cgiar.org; internet www.cgiar.org; f. 1971, under the sponsorship of the World Bank, FAO and the UN Development Programme; supports international agricultural research aimed at improving crops and animal production in developing countries, and works in partnership with govts, international and regional orgs, private businesses and foundations to support 15 research centres; in 2010 a CGIAR Fund was established to administer donations to the various progs, while a Consortium, governed by a 10-mem. board, was established to unite the strategic and funding supervision of the research centres; a Science Council was also established to promote the quality, relevance and impact of science in CGIAR and to advise on strategic scientific issues; CGIAR was granted international org.

status in 2012; in June 2016 CGIAR funders and centres approved a new CGIAR System Framework, under which representatives of funders and of developing countries were to meet in a System Council, comprising up to 20 voting mems; the inaugural meeting of the Council was held in July, in Paris; a further reform process, to unify governance, funding and strategic objectives under the brand One CGIAR, was underway in 2022; its new portfolio of initiatives was introduced in July, under the theme of 'Transforming Food, Land, and Water Systems in a Climate Crisis'; Exec. Dir of the CGIAR System Council ELWYN GRAINGER-JONES (UK).

Desert Locust Control Organization for Eastern Africa (DLCO-EA): POB 4255, Addis Ababa, Ethiopia; tel. (1) 461477; fax (1) 460296; e-mail dlc@ethionet.et; internet www.dlco-ea.org; f. 1962; aims to promote effective control of the desert locust in the region and to conduct research into the locust's environment and behaviour; also assists mem. states in the monitoring, forecasting and extermination of other migratory pests; mems: Djibouti, Eritrea, Ethiopia, Kenya, Somalia, South Sudan, Sudan, Tanzania, Uganda; Dir Dr STEPHEN WANGAI NJOKA (Kenya); publs *Desert Locust Situation Reports* (monthly), *Newsletter* (quarterly), technical reports.

Global Pulse Confederation: internet globalpulses.com; f. 1965, as Int. Pulses Trade and Industry Confederation; organizes regular confs (2022: in Cancún, Mexico, in Dec.), and events to celebrate World Pulses Day (held annually on 10 Feb.); mems: 24 nat. asscns; Pres. CINDY BROWN; Exec. Dir RANDY DUCKWORTH (USA).

Indian Ocean Tuna Commission (IOTC): POB 1011, Victoria, Mahé, Seychelles; tel. 4225494; fax 4224364; e-mail secretariat@iotc.org; internet www.iotc.org; f. 1996; mandated to work for the conservation and management of tuna and tuna-like species in the Indian Ocean; a revised convention was adopted in 2018; mems: Australia, People's Rep. of China, Comoros, Eritrea, France, Guinea, India, Indonesia, Iran, Japan, Kenya, Rep. of Korea, Madagascar, Malaysia, Maldives, Mauritius, Mozambique, Oman, Pakistan, Philippines, Seychelles, Sierra Leone, Somalia, South Africa, Sudan, Sri Lanka, Tanzania, Thailand, UK, Yemen, European Union; co-operating non-contracting parties: Bangladesh, Djibouti, Liberia, Senegal; Chair. JUNG-RE RILEY KIM (Republic of Korea); Exec. Sec. CHRISTOPHER O'BRIEN (Australia).

International Crops Research Institute for the Semi-Arid Tropics (ICRISAT): Patancheru, Telangana 502 324, India; tel. (40) 30713071; fax (40) 30713074; e-mail icrisat@cgiar.org; internet www.icrisat.org; f. 1972; aims to promote the genetic improvement of crops and for research on the management of resources in the world's semi-arid tropics, with the aim of reducing poverty and protecting the environment; research covers all physical and socioeconomic aspects of improving farming systems on unirrigated land; maintains regional centres in Nairobi, Kenya (for Eastern and Southern Africa) and in Bamako, Mali (for Western and Central Africa); Dir-Gen. Dr JACQUELINE D'ARROS HUGHES (UK); publs *ICRISAT Report* (annually), information and research bulletins.

International Institute of Tropical Agriculture (IITA): Oyo Rd, PMB 5320, Ibadan, Nigeria; tel. (2) 700800; fax (2) 7113786; e-mail iita@cgiar.org; internet www.iita.org; f. 1967; principal financing arranged by the Consultative Group on International Agricultural Research and several NGOs for special projects; research programmes comprise crop management, improvement of crops and plant protection and health; conducts a training programme for researchers in tropical agriculture; maintains a virtual library and an image database; administers Research Stations, Research Sites and Regional Administrative Hubs in 15 African countries; Dir-Gen. Dr NTERANYA SANGINGA (Democratic Republic of the Congo); publs *Annual Report*, *R4D Review* (2 a year), *BOT Newsletter* (quarterly), technical bulletins, research reports.

International Livestock Research Institute (ILRI): POB 30709, Nairobi 00100, Kenya; tel. (20) 4223000; fax (20) 4223001; e-mail ilri-kenya@cgiar.org; internet www.ilri.org; f. 1995 to supersede the International Laboratory for Research on Animal Diseases and the International Livestock Centre for Africa; conducts laboratory and field research on animal bioscience, animal science for sustainable productivity, BecA-ILRI Hub, feed and forages bioscience, food safety and zoonoses, livelihoods, gender and impact, livestock systems and environment, policy, trade and value chains, vaccine biosciences, biosciences facilities; carries out training progs for scientists and technicians; maintains a specialized science library; Chair. ELSA MURANO; Dir-Gen. JIMMY SMITH (Canada); publs

Annual Report, *Livestock Research for Development* (newsletter, 2 a year).

International Plant Protection Convention, Secretariat: Vialle delle Terme di Caracalla, 00153 Rome, Italy; tel. (06) 5705-4812; e-mail ippc@fao.org; internet www.ippc.int; f. 1992; provides operational support to the IPPC (adopted first in 1951 and revised in 1997), including the formulation of international standards for phytosanitary measures, exchanging plant health information and providing other policy guidelines; inaugural International Plant Health Conference: Sept. 2022, in London, UK; Sec. OSAMA EL-LISSY (USA).

International Red Locust Control Organization for Central and Southern Africa (IRLCO-CSA): POB 240252, Ndola, Zambia; tel. (21) 2651264; fax (21) 2650117; e-mail admin@redlocust.org.zm; f. 1971; established to strengthen the control locusts in Eastern, Central and Southern Africa; also assists in the control of African army-worm and quelea-quelea; mems: 6 countries; Dir MOSES OKHOBA; publs *Annual Report*, *Quarterly Report*, scientific reports.

Permanent Interstate Committee on Drought Control in the Sahel (Comité permanent inter-états de lutte contre la sécheresse au Sahel—CILSS): POB 7049, Ouagadougou 03, Burkina Faso; tel. (226) 25-49-96-00; e-mail administration.se@cilss.int; internet www.cilss.int; f. 1973; aims to combat the effects of chronic drought in the Sahel region, by improving irrigation and food production, halting deforestation and creating food reserves; maintains a regional food security surveillance system; initiated a series of projects to improve food security and to counter poverty, entitled Sahel 21; the heads of state of all mems have signed a convention for the establishment of a Fondation pour le Développement Durable du Sahel; maintains the Institut du Sahel at Bamako (Mali) and centre at Niamey (Niger); provides technical co-ordination of the UEMOA-ECOWAS Food Crisis Prevention Network (which is also supported by the OECD's Sahel and West Africa Club); mems: Benin, Burkina Faso, Cabo Verde, Chad, Côte d'Ivoire, The Gambia, Guinea, Guinea-Bissau, Mali, Mauritania, Niger, Senegal, Togo; Exec. Sec. DJIMÉ ADOUM (Chad); publ. *Newsletter CILSS*.

World Organisation for Animal Health (Organisation mondiale de la santé animale—OIE): 12 rue de Prony, 75017 Paris, France; tel. 1-44-15-18-88; fax 1-42-67-09-87; e-mail oie@oie.int; internet www.oie.int; f. 1924 as Office International des Epizooties, present name adopted in 2003; objectives include promoting international transparency of animal diseases; collecting, analysing and disseminating scientific veterinary information; providing expertise and facilitating international co-operation in the control of animal diseases; promoting veterinary services; providing new scientific guidelines on animal production, food safety and animal welfare; launched in May 2005, jtly with FAO and WHO, a Global Strategy for the Progressive Control of Highly Pathogenic Avian Influenza (H5N1), and, in partnership with other orgs, has convened confs on avian influenza; in May 2017 the OIE adopted its first global strategy on animal welfare; a significant increase in cases of African Swine Fever was reported by the OIE in 2019–22, across most regions; maintains the World Animal Health Information System (WAHIS); in April 2022 the OIE, WHO, UNEP and FAO concluded an MOU that provided for the establishment of a Quadripartite Collaboration for One Health, which was collectively to address challenges at the human-animal-plant-ecosystem interface; OIE experts work in a network of 51 collaborating centres and 260 reference laboratories (covering 119 diseases); mems: 182 countries; Dir-Gen. Dr MONIQUE ELOIT (France); publs *Disease Information* (weekly), *World Animal Health* (annually), *Scientific and Technical Review* (3 a year), other manuals, codes, etc.

Arts and Culture

Afro-Asian Writers' Association: f. 1958; reactivated in Aug. 2013 when an Exec. Board met in Hanoi, Viet Nam; mems: writers' orgs in 67 countries; publs *Lotus Magazine* (quarterly in English, French and Arabic), *Afro-Asian Literature Series* (in English, French and Arabic).

Pan-African Writers' Association (PAWA): PAWA House, Roman Ridge, POB C456, Cantonments, Accra, Ghana; tel. (21) 773062; fax (21) 773042; e-mail afronomiks@gmail.com; internet www.panafricanwritersassociation.org; f. 1989; aims to link African creative writers, defend the rights of authors and promote awareness of literature; mems: 61 nat. writers' asscns in the continent.

Commodities

African Oil Palm Development Association (AFOPDA): 15 BP 341, Abidjan 15, Côte d'Ivoire; tel. 21-25-15-18; fax 20-25-47-00;

f. 1985; seeks to increase production of, and investment in, palm oil; mems: Benin, Cameroon, Democratic Rep. of the Congo, Côte d'Ivoire, Ghana, Guinea, Nigeria, Togo.

African Petroleum Producers' Association (APPA): 76 ave Amilcar Cabral, Area 3, Poto-Poto, Centre-Ville-Brazzaville, Republic of the Congo; tel. 563-59-27; e-mail info@apposecretariat.org; internet apposecretariat.org; f. 1987; aims to reinforce co-operation among regional petroleum producing countries and to stabilize prices; Council of Ministers responsible for the hydrocarbons sector meets twice a year; holds regular African Petroleum Congress and Exhibition (CAPE); mems: Algeria, Angola, Benin, Cameroon, Chad, Democratic Rep. of the Congo, Rep. of the Congo, Côte d'Ivoire, Egypt, Equatorial Guinea, Gabon, Libya, Niger, Nigeria, South Africa; Pres. (2022) DIAMANTINO PEDRO AZEVEDO (Angola); Sec.-Gen. Dr OMAR FAROUK IBRAHIM (Niger); publ. *APPA Bulletin* (2 a year).

Common Fund for Commodities (CFC): Rietlandpark 301, 6th Floor, Quintet Officepark, IBFD Bldg, 1019 DW Amsterdam, Netherlands; tel. (20) 5754949; fax (20) 6760231; e-mail managing.director@common-fund.org; internet common-fund.org; f. 1989 as the result of an UNCTAD negotiation conf.; finances orgs and enterprises engaged in commodity value chains in its mem. countries and provides for a measurable social and environmental return; mems: 101 countries and 9 institutional mems; Man. Dir Sheikh MOHAMMED BELAL (Bangladesh); publ. *CFC Newsletter* (2 a year).

East Africa Tea Trade Association: POB 85174-80100, Tea Trade Centre, 1st Floor, Nyerere Ave, Mombasa, Kenya; tel. (41) 2228460; fax (41) 2225823; e-mail info@eatta.co.ke; internet www.eatta.com; f. 1957; brings together producers, brokers, buyers and packers; administers tea auctions and conducts marketing campaigns; mems: 267 in 10 countries; Chair. GIDEON MUGO (Kenya); Man. Dir EDWARD K. MUDIBO.

Gas Exporting Countries Forum (GECF): POB 23753, Tornado Tower, 47th–48th Floors, West Bay, Doha, Qatar; tel. 44048400; fax 44048415; internet www.gecf.org; f. 2001; aims to represent and promote the mutual interests of gas exporting countries, and to promote dialogue between gas producers and consumers; a ministerial meeting is convened annually; the inaugural meeting of heads of state was convened in Doha in 2011; the Forum became a partner in the Joint Oil Data Initiative in April 2014; in Oct. 2019 concluded an accord on future co-operation with OPEC; 6th GECF Summit was held in Feb. 2022, in Doha, on the theme 'Natural Gas: Shaping the Energy Future'; mems: Algeria, Bolivia, Egypt, Equatorial Guinea, Iran, Libya, Nigeria, Qatar, Russian Fed., Trinidad and Tobago, Venezuela; observers: Angola, Azerbaijan, Iraq, Malaysia, Mozambique, Norway, Peru, United Arab Emirates; Sec.-Gen. MOHAMED HAMEL (Algeria); publs *Annual Statistical Bulletin*, *Global Gas Outlook 2050*.

Inter-African Coffee Organization (IACO) (Organisation Inter-Africaine du Café—OIAC): BP V210, Abidjan, Côte d'Ivoire; tel. 20-21-61-31; fax 20-21-62-12; e-mail IACO_OIAC@aviso.ci; internet www.iaco-oiac.org; f. 1960; founded to adopt a common policy on the marketing and consumption of coffee; aims to foster greater collaboration in research technology transfer through the African Coffee Research Network; seeks to improve the quality of coffee exports, and implement poverty reduction programmes focusing on value-added products and the manufacturing of green coffee; mems: 25 coffee producing countries in Africa; Sec.-Gen. SOLOMON RUTEGA (Uganda).

International Cocoa Organization (ICCO): POB 1166, Abidjan 06, Côte d'Ivoire; tel. 22-51-49-50; fax 22-51-49-79; e-mail info@icco.org; internet www.icco.org; f. 1973 under the 1st International Cocoa Agreement, 1972; the ICCO supervises the implementation of the agreements, and provides mem. govts with up-to-date information on the world cocoa economy; the 7th International Cocoa Agreement (2010) entered into force in Oct. 2012; mems: 21 exporting and 28 importing countries, plus the European Union; Chair. ANNE LUGON-MOULIN (Switzerland); Exec. Dir MICHEL ARRION (Belgium); publs *Quarterly Bulletin of Cocoa Statistics*, *Annual Report*, *World Cocoa Directory*, studies on the world cocoa economy.

International Coffee Organization (ICO): 222 Gray's Inn Rd, London, WC1X 8HB, United Kingdom; tel. (20) 7612-0600; fax (20) 7612-0630; e-mail info@ico.org; internet www.ico.org; f. 1963 under the International Coffee Agreement, 1962, which was renegotiated in 1968, 1976, 1983, 1994, 2001 and 2007; aims to improve international co-operation and provide a forum for intergovernmental consultations on coffee matters; to facilitate international trade in coffee by the collection, analysis and dissemination of statistics; to act as a centre for the collection, exchange and publication of coffee information; to promote studies in the field of coffee; and to encourage an increase in coffee consumption; a World Coffee Conference is normally convened every 4–5 years (5th Conf. scheduled to have been held in Bengaluru, India, in Sept. 2020, postponed owing to the COVID-19 pandemic); mems: 49 (42 exporting countries; 7 importing countries and the European Union); Exec. Dir VANÚSIA NOGUEIRA (Brazil); publs *Coffee Market Report* (monthly), *Annual Review*.

International Network for Bamboo and Rattan (INBAR): POB 100102, 8 Fu Tong Dong Da Jie, Wang Jing Area, Chaoyang District, Beijing 100102, People's Republic of China; tel. (10) 6470-6161; fax (10) 6470-2166; e-mail info@inbar.int; internet www.inbar.int; f. 1997; promotes the use of bamboo and rattan to foster sustainable devt and environmentally sound economic policies; maintains regional offices in Addis Ababa, Ethiopia; Kumasi, Ghana; Quito, Ecuador; and New Delhi, India; mems: 48; Dir-Gen. ALI MCHUMO.

International Rubber Study Group: 51 Changi Business Park Central 2, Unit 6, 4/5 The Signature, Singapore 486066; tel. 65880463; fax 65880468; e-mail secgen@rubberstudy.com; internet www.rubberstudy.com; f. 1944; serves as a forum for the discussion of problems affecting synthetic and natural rubber; provides statistical and other general information on rubber; organizes World Rubber Summits; mems: govts of Cameroon, Côte d'Ivoire, India, Nigeria, Russian Fed., Singapore, Sri Lanka, and the European Union; 120 industry mems; Sec.-Gen. SALVATORE PINIZZOTTO; publs *Rubber Statistical Bulletin* (every 2 months), *Rubber Industry Report* (every 2 months), *Proceedings of World Rubber Summits* (annually), *World Rubber Industry Outlook* (2 a year), *World Rubber Statistics Handbook*.

International Sugar Organization: 1 Canada Sq., Canary Wharf, London, E14 5AA, United Kingdom; tel. (20) 7513-1144; fax (20) 7513-1146; e-mail info@isosugar.org; internet www.isosugar.org; administers the International Sugar Agreement (1992), with the objectives of stimulating co-operation, facilitating trade and encouraging demand; aims to improve conditions in the sugar market through debate, analysis and studies; serves as a forum for discussion; holds annual seminars and workshops; sponsors projects from developing countries; mems: 87 countries producing some 86% of total world sugar; Exec. Dir JOSÉ ORIVE (Guatemala); publs *Sugar Year Book*, *Statistical Bulletin*, *Monthly Market Report*, *Quarterly Market Outlook*, seminar proceedings.

International Tea Committee Ltd (ITC): 21–24 Millbank, 1st Floor, Millbank Tower, London, SW1P 4QP, United Kingdom; tel. (20) 3627-0898; e-mail inteacom@globalnet.co.uk; internet inttea .com; f. 1933 to administer the International Tea Agreement; now serves as a statistical and information centre; in 1979 membership was extended to include consuming countries; producer mems: nat. tea boards or asscns in Bangladesh, People's Rep. of China, India, Indonesia, Kenya, Malawi, Sri Lanka, Tanzania; consumer mems: Tea Association of the USA Inc., Irish Tea Trade Association, the Tea Association of Canada; publs *Annual Bulletin of Statistics*, *Monthly Statistical Summary*.

International Tobacco Growers' Association (ITGA): Avda 1 de Maio 99, 1D, 6000-086 Castelo Branco, Portugal; tel. (272) 092583; e-mail itga@tobaccoleaf.org; internet www.tobaccoleaf.org; f. 1984; provides a forum for the exchange of views and information of interest to tobacco producers; holds annual meeting; mems: 24 countries producing over 80% of the world's internationally traded tobacco; Pres. ABIEL M. KALIMA BANDA (Malawi); Chief Exec. MERCEDES VÁZQUEZ; publs *ITGA Crop Monitor* (quarterly), *Tobacco Courier*, *Tobacco Monitor* (monthly), interactive Atlas, reports and research papers.

International Tropical Timber Organization (ITTO): International Organizations Center, 5th Floor, Pacifico-Yokohama, 1-1-1, Minato-Mirai, Nishi-ku, Yokohama 220-0012, Japan; tel. (45) 223-1110; fax (45) 223-1111; e-mail itto@itto.int; internet www.itto.int; f. 1985 under the International Tropical Timber Agreement (ITTA, 1983); provides a forum for consultation and co-operation between countries that produce and consume tropical timber, and is dedicated to the sustainable devt and conservation of tropical forests; promotes exports of tropical timber and timber products from sustainably managed resources; encourages, through policy and project work, forest management, conservation and restoration, the further processing of tropical timber in producing countries, and the gathering and analysis of market intelligence and economic information; the most recently revised treaty, ITTA 2006, entered into effect in Dec. 2011; 58th session of the annual International Tropical Timber Council: Nov. 2022, in Yokohama, Japan; mems: 36 producing and 38 consuming countries and the European Union; Exec. Dir SHEAM SATKURU (Malaysia); publs *Review and Assessment of the World Timber Situation* (every 2 years), *Market Information Service* (every 2 weeks), *Tropical Forest Update* (quarterly), technical reports.

Kimberley Process: internet www.kimberleyprocess.com; launched following a meeting of Southern African diamond producing states, held in May 2000 in Kimberley, South Africa, to address means of halting the trade in 'conflict diamonds' (also referred to as 'blood diamonds') and of ensuring that revenue derived from diamond sales would henceforth not be used to fund rebel movements aiming to undermine legitimate govts; in Dec. of that year a landmark UN General Assembly resolution was adopted supporting the creation of an international certification scheme for rough diamonds; accordingly, the Kimberley Process Certification Scheme (KPCS), detailing requirements for controlling the production of and trade in 'conflict-free' rough diamonds, entered into force on 1 Jan. 2003; issues warnings over fraudulent KPCS certificates in circulation; suspended the membership of the Central African Republic during 2013–15; Venezuela was suspended during 2008–16; participating countries, with industry and civil society observers, meet twice a year; working groups and cttees also convene frequently; implementation of the KPCS is monitored through 'review visits', annual reports, and through ongoing exchange and analysis of statistical data; it was estimated in 2022 that participating states accounted for 99.8% of global rough diamond production; mems: 56 participants representing 82 countries (the European Union is a single participating mem. representing its 27 mem. states), and 4 observers (incl. the World Diamond Council); chaired, on a rotating basis, by participating mems (2022: Botswana; 2023: Zimbabwe).

World Diamond Council: 580 Fifth Ave, 28th Floor, New York, NY 10036, USA; tel. (212) 575-8848; fax (212) 575-8187; e-mail communications@worlddiamondcouncil.org; internet www .worlddiamondcouncil.com; f. 2000, by a resolution passed at the World Diamond Congress, convened in July by the World Federation of Diamond Bourses, with the aim of promoting responsibility within the diamond industry towards its stakeholders; lobbied for the creation of a certification scheme to prevent trade in 'conflict diamonds', and became an observer of the ensuing Kimberley Process Certification Scheme, launched in Jan. 2003; in Oct. 2002 approved—and maintains—a voluntary System of Warranties, enabling dealers, jewellery manufacturers and retailers to pass on assurances that polished diamonds derive from certified 'conflict-free' rough diamonds, with the aim of extending the effectiveness of the Kimberley Process beyond the export and import phase; mems: 40 diamond and jewellery industry orgs; Pres. EDWARD ASSCHER; Exec. Dir ELODIE DAGUZAN (France).

Economic and Sustainable Development Co-operation

African Training and Research Centre in Administration for Development (Centre Africain de Formation et de Recherche Administratives pour le Développement—CAFRAD): Tangier, 90000 Morocco; tel. (539) 322707; fax (539) 325785; e-mail cafrad@ cafrad.org; internet cafrad.org; f. 1964 by agreement between Morocco and UNESCO; undertakes research into administrative problems in Africa and documents results; provides a consultation service for govts and orgs; holds workshops to train senior civil servants; organizes webinars and seminars; mems: 36 African countries; Dir-Gen. Dr STÉPHANE MONNEY MOUANDJO (Cameroon); publs *African Administrative Studies* (2 a year), *Research Studies*, *Newsletter* (online), Collection: *Etudes et Documents*, *Répertoires des Consultants et des institutions de formation en Afrique*.

African-Asian Rural Development Organization (AARDO): No. 2, State Guest Houses Complex, Chanakyapuri, New Delhi 110 021, India; tel. (11) 26877783; fax (11) 26115937; e-mail aardohq@ aardo.org; internet www.aardo.org; f. 1962; aims to promote social change and develop participative co-operation among its mems; provides assistance in evolving an integrated approach, as the crucial pre-requisite in rural Asia and Africa; facilitates exchange of knowledge, best practices and technical assistance concerning rural and agricultural devt among its mems; provides technical and financial support to its mem. countries to undertake pilot projects; organizes training, study visits, deputation of experts; holds international workshops and seminars; awards more than 389 training fellowships at institutes in Bangladesh, Rep. of China, Egypt, India, Rep. of Korea, Malaysia, Nigeria, Pakistan, Philippines, Thailand and Zambia; mems: 17 African countries, 14 Asian countries, 2 assoc. mems; Sec.-Gen. MANOJ NARDEOSINGH (Mauritius); publs *African-Asian Journal of Rural Development* (2 a year), *Annual Report*, *AARDO Newsletter* (quarterly).

Arab Bank for Economic Development in Africa (Banque Arabe pour le Développement Economique en Afrique—BADEA): Sayed Abdar-Rahman el-Mahdi St, POB 2640, Khartoum 11111, Sudan; tel. (1) 83773646; fax (1) 83770600; e-mail badea@badea.org; internet www.badea.org; f. 1973 by mem. states of the Arab League; provides loans and grants to sub-Saharan African countries to finance devt projects; in Nov. 2020 BADEA, the African Export-Import Bank and the International Islamic Trade Finance Corporation initiated a US $1,500m. Collaborative COVID-19 Pandemic Response Facility, which aimed to support African countries in addressing the pandemic; during 2020 the Bank approved commitments totalling $780.4m., including $300.0m. for 19 public sector projects, $95.5m. for 4 private sector operations, $375.0m. for 8 trade finance operations, and $9.9m. for 28 technical assistance operations; Chair. Dr FAHAD ALDOSSARI (Saudi Arabia); Dir-Gen. Dr SIDI OULD TAH

(Mauritania); publs *Annual Report*, *Co-operation for Development* (quarterly), studies on Afro-Arab co-operation.

BRICS: informal grouping of large emerging economies, comprising Brazil, the Russian Federation, India, the People's Republic of China, and South Africa (which together accounted for more than 40% of the global population in 2020); known as BRIC prior to the accession of South Africa in Dec. 2010; convened an inaugural summit of heads of state and of govt in June 2009, in Yekaterinburg, Russia, at which principles for future co-operation and devt were adopted; a 2nd summit was held in April 2010, in Brasília, Brazil; and a 3rd in Sanya, China, in April 2011, which adopted the Sanya Declaration, outlining the future deepening of co-operation in areas including trade, energy, finance and industry; a 4th summit, convened in New Delhi, India, in March 2012, directed mem. state ministers responsible for finance to examine the feasibility of establishing a Development Bank to mobilize resources in support of infrastructure and sustainable devt projects in BRICS economies, other emerging economies, and developing countries, with the aim of supplementing the existing efforts of multilateral and regional financial institutions; the creation of the Bank (as well as of a BRICS Business Council) was approved in principle in March 2013; leaders attending the 6th summit, held in Fortaleza, Brazil, in July 2014, concluded an accord establishing the New Development Bank, which was launched, in Shanghai, China, in July 2015; the 11th summit meeting, held in Nov. 2019, in Brasília, pledged continuing support to the WTO as the focal point of the multilateral trading system, emphasizing the importance of avoiding unilateral and protectionist measures; welcomed the establishment of a BRICS Women's Business Alliance; noted ongoing progress in collectively drafting a BRICS Customs Mutual Administrative Assistance Agreement, and in developing a BRICS Authorized Economic Operator Program—which was to facilitate mutual recognition of controls and economic operators; a dialogue with the BRICS Business Council was held prior to the 11th summit, and the BRICS Business Forum was staged concurrently; the 12th summit was hosted by Russia in a virtual format in Nov. 2020; the 13th was hosted by India, again in a virtual format, in Sept. 2021 on the theme 'BRICS@15: Intra-BRICS cooperation for continuity, consolidation and consensus'; a BRICS Vaccine R&D Center was launched in March 2022; meetings of BRICS ministers responsible for foreign affairs are held every Sept. on the sidelines of the UN General Assembly; regular meetings are also convened of ministers responsible for finance and economics, security, agriculture, trade, communications and ICT, and health; in Sept. 2018 BRICS communications and ICT ministers resolved to support co-operation between small, micro and medium enterprises in mem. states, and agreed a Partnership on New Industrial Revolution (PartNIR) agenda, which aimed to strengthen co-operation with regard to innovation, digitalization and industrialization; a Digital BRICS Task Force was established to co-ordinate PartNIR activities; a BRICS Plus initiative, introduced in 2017, promotes engagement with other emerging economies; granted observer status at the UN General Assembly in Dec. 2018; mems: Brazil, People's Rep. of China (holding the rotating chair. in 2022), India, Russian Fed., South Africa (chair.: 2023).

Club du Sahel et de l'Afrique de l'Ouest (Sahel and West Africa Club): c/o OECD, 2 rue André Pascal, 75775 Paris, Cedex 16, France; tel. 1-45-24-82-00; e-mail swac.contact@oecd.org; internet www.oecd.org/swac; f. 1977 as Club du Sahel, present name and structure adopted in April 2001; an informal discussion forum for exchange of ideas and experience between OECD donor agencies and African recipients; aims to create, promote and facilitate links between the countries of the OECD and West Africa, and between the private and public sectors in order to improve the efficiency of devt aid; mems: 13 nat. and int. orgs, 3 observers; Hon. Pres. IBRAHIM ASSANE MAYAKI (Niger).

Co-Prosperity Alliance Zone (COPAZ): f. 2007; aims to combat poverty through socioeconomic devt; mems: Benin, Ghana, Nigeria, Togo.

Coalition for Dialogue on Africa (CoDA): ECA New Bldg, 4th Floor, Menelik Ave, POB 3001, Addis Ababa, Ethiopia; tel. (11) 15445540; fax (11) 15443715; internet codafrica.org; f. 2009; brings together African stakeholders and policymakers; policy-oriented, working in collaboration with regional and international orgs to address issues relating to security, peace, governance and devt; sponsored by the AU Commission, ECA and the AfDB; a CoDA office was established at the AU Commission headquarters, in Addis Ababa, in Jan. 2018; Exec. Dir SOUAD ADEN-OSMAN.

COMESA-EAC-SADC Tripartite Secretariat: Bldg 41, 1st Floor, CSIR Campus, Meiring Naude Rd, Brummeria, Pretoria, 0001 South Africa; tripartite co-operation, aiming to advance regional integration through the harmonization of the trade and infrastructure devt programmes of these regional economic communities, was initiated in 2005 (a COMESA-SADC task force having been active during 2001–05); a Tripartite Task Force—led by the Secretaries-General of COMESA and the EAC, and the Executive Secretary of SADC—has

convened regularly thereafter; the inaugural Tripartite Summit, organized in Oct. 2008, in Kampala, Uganda, approved a roadmap towards the formation of a single Tripartite FTA (TFTA) and the eventual establishment of a single African Economic Community; at the 2nd summit, held in June 2011, in Johannesburg, South Africa, negotiations were initiated on the establishment of the proposed TFTA; in accordance with a Framework, Roadmap and Architecture for Fast Tracking the Establishment of a Continental FTA (referred to as CFTA), and an Action Plan for Boosting Intra-African Trade, adopted by African Union leaders in Jan. 2012, an agreement establishing the TFTA was signed in June 2015, by heads of state and government meeting in Sharm el-Sheik, Egypt (by March 2022 the agreement had been signed by 22 mem. states, and ratified by 11, requiring a further 3 to enter into force); it was envisaged that, on entry into force, the TFTA would be consolidated with other regional FTAs into the CFTA initiative; in May 2018 EAC-COMESA-SADC chiefs of immigration authorities met to address means of introducing free movement for business people in the TFTA; on 31 July 2020 new Tripartite Guidelines for the Movement of Persons, Goods and Services across the Tripartite Region During the COVID-19 Pandemic were approved (based on guidelines developed by COMESA).

Commission Internationale du Bassin Congo-Oubangui-Sangha (CICOS) (International Commission of the Congo-Oubangui-Sangha Basin): internet www.cicos.int; f. 2007; promotes inland navigation and integrated water resources management along the Congo River watershed; mems: Angola, Cameroon, Central African Rep., Democratic Rep. of the Congo, Rep. of the Congo, Gabon; Sec.-Gen. JUDITH ENAW EFUNDEM AGBORN.

Communauté Economique des Etats de l'Afrique Centrale (CEEAC) (Economic Community of Central African States): BP 2112, Libreville, Gabon; tel. 01-44-47-31; fax 01-44-47-32; e-mail contact@ceeac-eccas.org; internet ceeac-eccas.org/en/; f. 1983, operational 1 Jan. 1985; aims to promote co-operation between mem. states by abolishing trade restrictions, establishing a common external customs tariff, linking commercial banks, and setting up a devt fund; works to promote regional security; in June 2002 CEEAC heads of state and govt adopted a protocol providing for the establishment of a Council for Peace and Security in Central Africa (including a Defence and Security Commission), as well as a subregional multinational force (FOMAC), and the Early Warning Mechanism of Central Africa; a CEEAC Parliament was inaugurated in Malabo, Equatorial Guinea, in April 2010; the Central African Power Pool (q.v.) was est. in 2003 as a specialized agency of CEEAC; from July 2008–Dec. 2013 deployed the Mission for the Consolidation of Peace in the CAR—MICOPAX; participated from May 2013 in meetings of the International Contact Group on the CAR, and has from Aug. 2016 been part of the successor International Support Group on the CAR; in June 2013 CEEAC participated, with ECOWAS and the Gulf of Guinea Commission, in a regional summit on maritime safety and security, convened in Yaoundé, Cameroon, which adopted a Code of Conduct concerning the Prevention and Repression of Piracy, Armed Robbery against Ships, and Illegal Maritime Activities in West and Central Africa; in Sept. 2014, under the auspices of the 3 orgs, an Interregional Coordination Centre for Maritime Safety and Security in Central and West Africa was inaugurated, in Yaoundé; in 2015 formally adopted the Migration Dialogue for Central African States (MIDCAS); 8th extraordinary session of heads of state and of govt, held in Libreville, in Nov. 2016, expressed support for a CEEAC-AU-UN mediation initiative between the CAR Government and armed groups in support of the demobilization and repatriation process in that country; a jt CEEAC-ECOWAS Summit on Peace, Security, Stability and the Fight against Terrorism and Violent Extremism, convened in July 2018, in Lomé, Togo, determined to formulate a mutual Criminal Cooperation Agreement and to establish a ministerial cttee to follow up decisions on collaboration; in Dec. 2019 CEEAC heads of state and of govt determined to transform the Secretariat of the org. into a Commission, and to introduce a streamlined regional peace and security framework; the new structure was initiated on 1 Sept. 2020; heads of state and of govt convened in a virtual format summit in July of that year; mems: 11 countries; Pres. GILBERTO DA PIEDADE VERISSIMO (Angola).

Community of Sahel-Saharan States (Communauté des états Sahelo-Sahariens—CEN-SAD): Pl. d'Algeria, POB 4041, Tripoli, Libya (since 2019 operating from interim offices in N'Djamena, Chad); e-mail censad_sg@yahoo.com; f. 1998 (fmrly known as COMESSA); aims to strengthen co-operation between signatory states in order to promote their economic, transportation, communications, social and cultural integration and to facilitate conflict resolution and poverty alleviation; partnership agreements have been concluded with the African Union, the European Union, ECOWAS, FAO, CILSS and BADEA; the 7th meeting of CEN-SAD ministers responsible for defence was convened in Abuja, Nigeria, in June 2018, to discuss, *inter alia,* the risk posed by the deliberate recruitment by Islamic State of insurgents in Nigeria and other mem. states; organized in April 2021 a high-level meeting on counter terrorism; the Sec.-Gen. visited Libya in March 2022 to advance the return of the org. to its Tripoli Headquarters; mems: Benin, Burkina Faso, Central African Republic, Chad, Comoros, Côte d'Ivoire, Djibouti, Egypt, Eritrea, The Gambia, Ghana, Guinea, Guinea-Bissau, Libya, Mali, Mauritania, Morocco, Niger, Nigeria, Senegal, Sierra Leone, Somalia, Sudan, Togo, Tunisia; Sec.-Gen. BRIGI RAFINI (Niger).

Conseil de l'Entente (Entente Council): 01 BP 3734, angle ave Verdier/rue de Tessières, Abidjan 01, Côte d'Ivoire; tel. 22-50-92-02; fax 20-33-11-49; e-mail secretariatexecutif@conseil-entente.org; internet www.conseildelentente.org; f. 1959 to promote economic devt in the region; the Council's Mutual Aid and Loan Guarantee Fund (Fonds d'entraide et de garantie des emprunts) was created to finance devt projects, including agricultural projects, support for small and medium-sized enterprises, vocational training centres and research into new sources of energy; a Convention of Assistance and Co-operation was signed in Feb. 1996; supports infrastructure devt in mem. countries; the 12th Council of Ministers meeting, held in Dec. 2017, in Lomé, Togo, adopted a strategic plan covering 2018–22, welcomed the recent establishment of a trilateral task force to promote co-operation between the Conseil de l'Entente, ECOWAS and the ACP states, and issued a statement that strongly condemned human trafficking, gross violations of human rights, and other slavery-like practices being perpetrated in Libya; in March 2022 the Exec. Sec. led a delegation to Burkina Faso, to assess the situation there following the military coup that had taken place in Jan; mems: Benin, Burkina Faso, Côte d'Ivoire, Niger, Togo; Exec. Sec. MARCEL AMON TANOH (Côte d'Ivoire); publ. *Rapport d'activité* (annually).

Conseil Ouest et Centre Africain pour le Recherche et le Développement Agricoles (West and Central African Council for Agricultural Research and Development): 7 ave Bourguiba, BP 48, Dakar, Senegal; tel. and fax 33-869-96-18; e-mail secoraf@coraf.org; internet www.coraf.org; f. 1987; aims to achieve a sustainable reduction of poverty through agricultural devt and growth in West and Central Africa; mems: 23 countries; Chair. Dr ANGELA MARIA P. BARRETO DA VEGA MORENO; Exec. Dir Dr ABDOU TENKOUANO.

Developing Eight (D-8): Darüşşafaka Cad., Seba Center 45, Istinye, 34460 Istanbul, Türkiye; tel. (212) 3561823; fax (212) 3561829; e-mail secretariat@developing8.org; internet www.developing8.org; f. 1997; aims to foster economic co-operation between mems and to strengthen the role of developing countries in the global economy; project areas include trade; agriculture and food security; transportation; industrial devt; energy and minerals; tourism; and health; granted observer status at the UN in Oct. 2014; in April 2015 announced a partnership with UNIDO that aimed to accelerate inclusive, sustainable industrial devt through the promotion of trade capacity building and entrepreneurship in mem. states; the implementation phase of the D-8 Preferential Trade Agreement (signed in 2006) entered into effect on 1 July 2016; a D-8 Charter entered into force on 1 Sept. 2017; the 9th summit meeting, convened in Oct. in Istanbul, decided to establish a D-8 Project Support Fund, a D-8 Research and Development Centre, and a Hamadan, Iran-based D-8 University; the 10th summit meeting, hosted by Bangladesh in April 2021, adopted a D-8 Decennial Roadmap for 2020–30, which included the goal (to be achieved by 2030) of increasing the volume of intra-D-8 trade to 10% of the organization's total trade; during phase 1 of the Roadmap, covering 2020–22, new projects were to be developed; these were to be implemented during phase 2 (2023–27); and were to be reviewed during phase 3 (2028–30); a single card payment system (the 'DP8') has been envisaged, with the aim of facilitating intra-D-8 commerce; mems: Bangladesh, Egypt, Indonesia, Iran, Malaysia, Nigeria, Pakistan, Türkiye; Sec.-Gen. ISIAKA ABDULQADIR IMAN (Nigeria).

East African Community (EAC): POB 1096, Arusha, Tanzania; tel. (27) 2162100; fax (27) 2162190; e-mail eac@eachq.org; internet www.eac.int; f. 2001, following the adoption of a treaty on political and economic integration (signed in Nov. 1999) by the heads of state of Kenya, Tanzania and Uganda, replacing the Permanent Tripartite Commission for East African Co-operation (f. 1993) and reviving the former East African Community (f. 1967, dissolved 1977); Rwanda and Burundi formally became mems of the Community on 1 July 2007, Sudan was admitted in March 2016; initial areas for co-operation were to be trade and industry, security, immigration, transport and communications, and promotion of investment; further objectives were the elimination of trade barriers and ensuring the free movement of people and capital within the grouping; a customs union came into effect on 1 Jan. 2005; an East African Legislative Assembly and an East African Court of Justice were inaugurated in 2001; in April 2006 heads of state agreed that negotiations on a common market would commence in July; the Protocol on the Establishment of the EAC Common Market entered into force on 1 July 2010; the 15th ordinary summit, held in Kampala, Uganda, in Nov. 2011, signed a protocol on the establishment of an East African Monetary Union which envisaged a single currency; it was envisaged in early 2021 that an East African Monetary Institute would be inaugurated on 1 July; a progress report on the

establishment of an East African Federation was considered at an extraordinary summit meeting, held in April 2014, which then instructed the Council to initiate a process of drafting a Constitution; a Regional Vision for Socioeconomic Transformation and Development (Vision 2050), was launched in Aug. 2015; in late 2015 President Museveni of Uganda, on behalf of the EAC, led an Inter-Burundi Dialogue with participation by Burundi stakeholders; in March 2016 the EAC appointed the (late) fmr President of Tanzania, Benjamin Mkapa, as the Facilitator of the Dialogue, under Museveni's guidance; an extraordinary EAC summit convened in Dec. adopted a roadmap to guide the negotiations process; the process was supported by the AU and by the fmr Office of the Special Envoy of the UN Secretary-General in Burundi; the Inter-Burundi Dialogue talks were suspended in mid-2019, reportedly owing to continuing intransigence by the Burundian authorities; a general election was held in Burundi in May 2020; an EAC e-passport was launched at the 17th ordinary summit meeting, held in March 2016, and was issued from 1 Jan. 2017; in Nov. 2017 an EAC Energy Security Policy Framework was adopted; EAC has since 2005 participated in the COMESA-EAC-SADC Tripartite Secretariat, with a view to advancing regional co-operation; in March 2014 signed a Memorandum of Understanding with the Economic Community of the Great Lakes Countries to strengthen co-operation between the orgs and enhance regional integration; negotiations on an Economic Partnership Agreement (EPA) with the European Union were concluded in Oct. 2014; upon entry into force this was to provide immediate duty- and quota-free access for all EAC exports to the EU market, and a gradual, partial opening of the EAC market for EU exports; in Feb. 2019 EAC heads of state agreed that each mem. state might sign and pursue implementation of the EPA without full approval of the grouping; the 4th EAC Arts and Culture Festival (JAMAFEST) was held in Sept., in Dar-es-Salaam, Tanzania; in March 2020 a ministerial meeting formulated a Community COVID-19 Response Plan to ensure collaboration in containing the virus and in mitigating the impacts of the pandemic; the regular 2021 summit meeting convened, in a virtual format, in Feb., directed the Council to undertake a verification mission to the Democratic Rep. of the Congo (DRC) with regard to its membership application; the mission reported its findings to an extraordinary summit, held in Dec., which upheld the application; the DRC was admitted as the EAC's 7th mem. in late March 2022; an inaugural EAC Head of States Conclave on the DRC, held in April, in Nairobi, invited armed groups active in the DRC to participate in an EAC-mediated dialogue; in June EAC heads of state agreed to deploy a regional force to eastern areas of the DRC, tasked with supporting efforts to restore and maintain peace and security; mems: Burundi, Democratic Rep. of the Congo, Kenya, Rwanda, South Sudan, Tanzania, Uganda; Chair. EVARISTE NDAYISHIMIYE (Burundi); Sec.-Gen. Dr PETER MATHUKI (Kenya).

Economic Community of the Great Lakes Countries (Communauté Economique des Pays des Grands Lacs—CEPGL): POB 58, Gisenyi, Rwanda; tel. 788307061; e-mail info@cepgl.org; internet www.cepgl.org; f. 1976; main organs: annual Conference of Heads of State, Council of Ministers of Foreign Affairs, Permanent Executive Secretariat, Consultative Commission, Security Commission, 3 Specialized Technical Commissions; 4 CEPGL specialized agencies were established: a regional electricity co (SINELAC) at Bukavu, Democratic Rep. of the Congo (DRC)—through which the Ruzizi III hydroelectric power project is underway; an energy centre at Bujumbura, Burundi; the Institute of Agronomic and Zootechnical Research, Gitega, Burundi; and the Banque de Développement des Etats des Grands Lacs at Goma, DRC; in March 2014 signed a Memorandum of Understanding (MOU) with the East African Community to strengthen co-operation between the orgs and enhance regional integration; and in Feb. 2016 concluded an MOU with COMESA focused on economic integration, and peace and security; in April 2018 the Exec. Sec. urged mem. states to invest financially in the org. and to initiate a renaissance of CEPGL activities, noting that the last meeting of heads of state had been held in 2007 and the last ministerial session in 2014; mems: Burundi, Democratic Rep. of the Congo, Rwanda.

Gambia River Basin Development Organization (Organisation pour la mise en valeur du fleuve Gambie—OMVG): BP 2353, 50 rue de Ouakam, Stèle Mermoz, Immeuble Serigne Bassirou Mbacké, Dakar, Senegal; tel. 33-859-28-80; fax 33-864-29-88; e-mail omvg@omvg.sn; f. 1978 by Senegal and The Gambia; Guinea joined in 1981 and Guinea-Bissau in 1983; a masterplan for the integrated devt of the Kayanga/Geba and Koliba/Corubal river basins has been developed, encompassing a projected natural resources management project, and a hydraulic devt plan for the Gambia river has been formulated; it was envisaged that Guinea's Samba Ngallo Dam project would provide hydroelectricity to The Gambia, thereby connecting that country to the OMVG interconnection grid; maintains a documentation centre; High Commr LANSANA FOFANA.

Group of 15 (G15): f. 1989 by 15 developing nations during the 9th summit of the Non-Aligned Movement; retains its original name although membership has expanded; promotes co-operation to address the global economic and political situation; liaises with other groupings, incl. G7; mems: Algeria, Argentina, Brazil, Chile, Colombia, Egypt, India, Indonesia, Iran, Jamaica, Kenya, Malaysia, Mexico, Nigeria, Senegal, Sri Lanka, Venezuela, Zimbabwe.

Group of 77 (G77): United Nations Secretariat Bldg, Rm S-0518, New York, NY 10017, USA; tel. (212) 963-4777; fax (212) 963-3515; e-mail secretariat@g77.org; internet www.g77.org; f. 1964 by the 77 signatory states of the Joint Declaration of the Seventy-Seven Countries (the G77 retains its original name, owing to its historic significance, although its membership has expanded); the inaugural ministerial meeting, held in Algiers, Algeria, in Oct. 1967, adopted the Charter of Algiers as a basis for G77 co-operation; subsequently, G77 Chapters were established with liaison offices in Geneva (UNCTAD), Nairobi (UNEP), Paris (UNESCO), Rome (FAO/IFAD), Vienna (UNIDO), and the Group of 24 (G24) in Washington, DC (IMF/World Bank); as the largest intergovernmental org. of developing states in the UN the G77 aims to enable developing nations to articulate and promote their collective economic interests and to improve their negotiating capacity within the UN system; an inaugural South Summit, bringing together all G77 heads of state and govt, was convened in Havana, Cuba, in April 2000; a 2nd Summit was held in Doha, Qatar, in June 2005; in Sept. 2006 G77 ministers responsible for foreign affairs, and the People's Rep. of China, endorsed the establishment of a Consortium on Science, Technology and Innovation for the South; G77 approves funds allocated through the Perez-Guerrero Trust Fund for South-South Cooperation (PGTF, f. 1983); during 1986–2021 some 379 projects, with a cumulative value of US $15.9m., were approved through the PGTF; an annual meeting of G77 foreign ministers is held at the start (in Sept.) of the regular session of the UN General Assembly; an Intergovernmental Follow-up and Coordination Committee on South-South Cooperation meets every 2 years; periodic sectoral ministerial meetings are organized in preparation for UNCTAD sessions and prior to the UNIDO and UNESCO General Conferences, and with the aim of promoting South-South co-operation; other special ministerial meetings are also convened periodically; mems: 134 countries; chairmanship rotates annually on a regional basis (2022: Pakistan).

Indian Ocean Commission (IOC) (Commission de l'Océan Indien—COI): Blue Tower, 3rd Floor, rue de l'Institut, BP 7, Ebene, Mauritius; tel. 402-6100; fax 465-6798; e-mail secretariat@coi-ioc.org; internet commissionoceanindien.org; f. 1982; promotes regional co-operation, particularly in economic devt; projects include tuna fishing devt, protection and management of environmental resources and strengthening of meteorological services; tariff reduction is also envisaged; an Anti-Piracy Unit was established within the secretariat in 2011; organizes an annual regional trade fair; participates with the Caribbean Community and the Secretariat of the Pacific Regional Environment Programme in a Climate Resilient Islands Partnership; mems: the Comoros, France (representing the French Overseas Department of Réunion), Madagascar, Mauritius, Seychelles; Sec.-Gen. VÉLAYOUDOM MARIMOUTOU (France); publ. *La Lettre de l'Océan Indien.*

Indian Ocean Rim Association (IORA): Nexteracom Tower 1, 3rd Floor, Ebene, Mauritius; tel. 454-1717; fax 468-1161; e-mail hq@iora.net; internet www.iora.int; f. 1997 as the Indian Ocean Rim Association for Regional Co-operation, present name adopted in 2013; aims to promote the sustained and balanced devt of the region and of its mem. states and to create common ground for regional economic co-operation, *inter alia,* through trade, investment, infrastructure, tourism, and science and technology; the third IORA Ministerial Blue Economy Conference (BEC-3) was held in Sept. 2019; the inaugural Leaders' summit meeting was held in Jakarta, Indonesia, in March 2017; IORA working groups on maritime safety and security and on the blue economy held inaugural meetings in Aug. and Dec. 2019, respectively; the 8th Indian Ocean Dialogue—IOD—was held, in a virtual format, in Dec. 2021, on the theme 'Post Pandemic Indian Ocean: Leveraging Digital Technologies for Health, Education, Development and Trade in IORA Member States' (inaugural IOD convened in 2014); an IORA Action Plan on Maritime Safety and Security was being implemented during 2022–26; mems: Australia, Bangladesh, Comoros, France (representing the French Overseas Department of Réunion), India, Indonesia, Iran, Kenya, Madagascar, Malaysia, Maldives, Mauritius, Mozambique, Oman, Seychelles, Singapore, Somalia, South Africa, Sri Lanka, Tanzania, Thailand, United Arab Emirates, Yemen. Dialogue Partner countries: People's Rep. of China, Egypt, Germany, Italy, Japan, Rep. of Korea, Türkiye, UK, USA. Observers: Indian Ocean Research Group Inc., Western Indian Ocean Marine Science Asscn; Sec.-Gen. SALMAN AL-FARISI (Indonesia).

International Think Tank for Landlocked Developing Countries (ITTLLDC): UN House, United Nations St 14, Sükhbaatar District, 14201 Ulaanbaatar, Mongolia; tel. (11) 351971; fax (11) 322127; e-mail thinktank@land-locked.org; internet land-locked.org; f. 2017, with the entry into force of the Multilateral Agreement for the Establishment of an International Think Tank for LLDCs;

aims, through high-quality research and advocacy, to enhance the capacity of landlocked developing countries to benefit from international trade, with the objective of advancing human development and reducing poverty; granted observer status at the UN General Assembly in Dec. 2018; mems: Afghanistan, Armenia, Azerbaijan, Bhutan, Burkina Faso, Ethiopia, Kazakhstan, Kyrgyzstan, Lao People's Democratic Rep., Mongolia, Nepal, Niger, Paraguay, Tajikistan; Exec. Dir DULGUUN DAMDIN-OD (Mongolia).

Lake Chad Basin Commission (LCBC): BP 727, N'Djamena, Chad; tel. 52-41-45; fax 52-41-37; e-mail info@cblt.org; internet www.cblt.org; f. 1964 to encourage co-operation in developing the Lake Chad region and to promote the settlement of regional disputes; work programmes emphasize the regulation of the utilization of water and other natural resources in the basin; also co-ordinates devt projects and research; in March 2014 LCBC ministers responsible for defence, and their counterpart in Benin, agreed to develop a concept of operations for a Multinational Joint Task Force, to combat arms trafficking, terrorism and cross-border attacks in the sub-region (with particular reference to the terrorist activities of the militant northern Nigeria-based grouping Boko Haram, and ongoing violent conflict in the Central African Republic); in Oct. an extraordinary meeting of Commission heads of state (plus Benin) agreed to reinforce jt intelligence and operational capabilities; to put in place a collective border surveillance mechanism; and promptly to develop a subregional common defence strategy; the co-ordinated deployment of national Task Force units commenced in late 2015 (the legal modalities of the collective military co-operation were authorized by the AU Peace and Security Council in Jan. of that year); the LCBC and other agencies participated in May 2016 in an AU Regional Security Summit, held in Abuja, Nigeria, to consider progress achieved towards neutralizing Boko Haram; in 2018 the LCBC and UNESCO initiated a programme (known as BIOPALT) aimed at preserving the biosphere and heritage of Lake Chad; in May 2018 the inaugural meeting of governors of territories bordering Lake Chad established a Lake Chad Basin Governors' Forum, to advance collective efforts to promote peace and sustainable devt regionally; in Aug. an LCBC-AU ministerial conf., held in Abuja, adopted a Regional Stabilization, Recovery and Resilience Strategy for Areas Affected by Boko Haram in the Lake Chad Basin Region; in July 2019 a Regional Stabilization Facility for Lake Chad was launched by UNDP in support of the initiative; in mid-March 2022 adopted a regional action plan to support the implementation of the Regional Stabilization, Recovery and Resilience Strategy during 2022–24; convenes an annual regular summit of heads of state; mems: Cameroon, Central African Rep., Chad, Libya, Niger, Nigeria; observers: Egypt, Democratic Rep. of the Congo, Rep. of Congo, Sudan; Exec. Sec. MAMMAN NUHU (Nigeria); publ. *Bibliographie générale de la CBLT* (2 a year).

Lake Tanganyika Authority (LTA) (Autorité du Lac Tanganyika): BP 4910, Ngagara, Bujumbura, Burundi; tel. 22273582; e-mail info@lta-alt.org; internet www.lta-alt.org; f. 2008; implements a regional integrated management programme to co-ordinate the implementation of the 2003 Convention on the Sustainable Management of Lake Tanganyika; aims to support local climate change adaptation initiatives, to support sustainable fisheries, and to combat ecological threats to Lake Tanganyika such as biological invasion; launched in July 2019 a European Union-funded (€6.9m.) 4-year Lake Tanganyika Regional Water Management Project; mems: Burundi, Democratic Rep. of the Congo, Tanzania, Zambia; Exec. Dir SYLVAIN TUSANGA MUKANGA.

Lake Victoria Basin Commission (LVBV): Off Kenyatta Highway, New Nyanza Regional Headquarters, 13th Floor, POB 1510-40100, Kisumu, Kenya; tel. (57) 2026344; fax (57) 2026324; e-mail lvbc@lvbcom.org; internet www.lvbcom.org; f. 2004; specialized agency of the East African Community; aims to co-ordinate sustainable devt and management of the Lake Victoria Basin (the world's second largest freshwater body); implements an Engaging Private Sector for Green Growth in Lake Victoria Basin initiative, Lake Victoria Environment Programme Lake Victoria Water and Sanitation Programme, and Planning for Resilience in East Africa through Policy, Adaptation, Research and Economic Development initiative; mems: Burundi, Kenya, Rwanda, Tanzania, Uganda.

Limpopo Watercourse Commission (LIMCOM): Avda 24 de Julho 370, Maputo, Mozambique; f. 2006 to co-ordinate the management of the Limpopo watercourse; in early 2019 formalized a co-operation mechanism to promote the management of surface water and groundwater resources, with a focus on the Ramotswa, Tuli Karoo, and Limpopo Aquifer Basin transboundary aquifers; mems: Botswana, Mozambique, South Africa, Zimbabwe.

Liptako-Gourma Integrated Development Authority (LGA): POB 619, 417 ave Kwamé N'krumah, Ouagadougou, Burkina Faso; tel. (3) 30-61-48; internet www.liptakogourma.org; f. 1970; in 1986 undertook a study on devt of water resources in the basin of the Niger river (for hydroelectricity and irrigation); in 2004 signed a co-operation agreement with the Niger Basin Authority; an extraordinary summit meeting held in Jan. 2017, in Niamey, Niger, authorized the establishment of a multinational jt force tasked with combating militant and terrorist activities in the Liptako-Gourma area; in April representatives of the LGA and the Lake Chad Basin Commission met, in N'Djamena, Chad, to consider regional security matters; the LGA force was absorbed in 2017 as a component of the Force conjointe du G5 Sahel (FC-G5S)—an initiative of the G5 Sahel tasked with combating violent extremist groups operating in the G5 common space; mems: Burkina Faso, Mali, Niger.

Mano River Union (MRU) (Union du Fleuve Mano): 32/c Fudia Terrace, Spur Loop Western Area, Freetown, Sierra Leone; internet mru.int; f. 1973; founded to establish a customs and economic union between mem. states to accelerate devt via integration; a common external tariff was instituted in 1977; intra-union free trade was officially introduced in May 1981; the Union was inactive for 3 years until mid-1994, owing to regional conflict and disagreements regarding funding; a revised security structure was approved in 2000; in Aug. 2001 mins responsible for foreign affairs, security, internal affairs and justice, meeting as the Joint Security Committee, resolved to deploy jt border security and confidence-building units, and to work to re-establish the free movement of people and goods; implements progs in institutional revitalization and restructuring; peace and security; economic devt and regional integration; and social devt; in Oct. 2013, as requested in recent resolutions of the UN Security Council, the Union adopted a Strategy for Cross-border Security; in July 2014 the Union convened an emergency summit, in Conakry, Guinea, with participation by the World Health Organization (WHO) Dir-Gen., to consider measures to address the ongoing intensive outbreak in Guinea, Liberia and Sierra Leone of Ebola Virus Disease (EVD); an EVD Outbreak Response Plan in West Africa was adopted; an extraordinary summit meeting was convened in June 2015 to further efforts to support a subregional post-Ebola socioeconomic recovery programme; signed a Memorandum of Understanding (MOU) with ECOWAS in Jan. 2015, and concluded an MOU in Feb. 2017 with the UN Economic Commission for Africa's Subregional Office for West Africa; in Feb. 2021 held a high-level planning meeting with the UN Office for West Africa and the Sahel to review a jt work plan, to assess the impact of COVID-19 on the sub-region and to enhance their partnership; mems: Côte d'Ivoire, Guinea, Liberia, Sierra Leone; Sec.-Gen. Dr MEDINA A. WESSEH.

Niger Basin Authority (Autorité du Bassin du Niger): BP 729, Niamey, Niger; tel. 20-72-43-95; fax 20-72-42-08; internet www.abn .ne; f. 1964 (as River Niger Commission; present name adopted in 1980) to harmonize national programmes concerned with the River Niger Basin and to execute an integrated devt plan; compiles statistics; regulates navigation; runs projects on hydrological forecasting, environmental control; in April 2018 launched jtly with AfDB the US $300m. Programme for the Integrated Development and Adaptation to Climate Change in the Niger Basin (PIDACC), which was to promote the devt of mechanisms to address the environmental depletion of the Niger River Basin; the 13th summit meeting was held in a virtual format in June 2021; mems: Benin, Burkina Faso, Cameroon, Chad, Côte d'Ivoire, Guinea, Mali, Niger, Nigeria; Exec. Sec. ABDERAHIM BIRÉMÉ HAMID (Chad).

Nile Basin Initiative (NBI): POB 192, Entebbe, Uganda; tel. (41) 7705000; e-mail nbisec@nilebasin.org; internet www.nilebasin.org; f. 1999; aims to achieve sustainable socioeconomic devt through the equitable use and benefits of the Nile Basin water resources and to create an enabling environment for the implementation of programmes with a shared vision; highest authority is the Nile Basin Council of Ministers (COM); other activities undertaken by a Nile Basin Technical Advisory Committee; in March 2015 Egypt, Ethiopia and Sudan signed a declaration of principles, which provided for priority to be given to downstream Nile countries with regard to power generated by Ethiopia's controversial Grand Renaissance Dam project; an extraordinary COM meeting was held in Entebbe, in March 2017, to facilitate Egypt's full resumption of activities in the org. (it having been suspended in 2010); the inaugural NBI summit of heads of state was convened in June 2017; a Regional HydroMet Project, to facilitate the exchange of data and monitoring information among mems, was launched in Dec. 2019; mems: Burundi, Democratic Rep. of the Congo, Egypt, Ethiopia, Kenya, Rwanda, South Sudan, Sudan, Tanzania, Uganda; observer: Eritrea; Chair. MANOAH PETER GATKUOTH (South Sudan); Exec. Dir SYLVESTER ANTHONY MATEMU (Tanzania); publ. *Corporate Report* (annually).

OPEC Fund for International Development (OFID): Parkring 8, 1011 Vienna, Austria; tel. (1) 515-64-0; fax (1) 513-92-38; internet www.ofid.org; f. 1976 by mem. countries of OPEC; aims to provide financial co-operation and assistance in support of social and economic devt in low-income countries, and to promote co-operation between OPEC countries and other developing states; in 2021 OFID's total approvals amounted to US $1,483m., for 47 projects in more than 30 countries; mems: Algeria, Ecuador, Gabon, Indonesia, Iran, Iraq, Kuwait, Libya, Nigeria, Saudi Arabia, United Arab Emirates, Venezuela; Dir-Gen. Dr ABDULHAMID ALKHALIFA (Saudi Arabia); publs *OFID Quarterly*, *Annual Report*.

Orange-Senqu River Commission (ORASECOM): Block A, 66 Corporate Park, cnr Von Willich/Lenchen Sts, Centurion, Gauteng, South Africa; tel. (12) 6636826; fax (12) 3367565; internet orasecom .org; f. 2000; studies uses of the Orange-Senqu river system, addresses flood management and flow monitoring requirements, aims to strengthen regional socioeconomic co-operation; in Sept. 2018 undertook a groundwater survey of the Orange-Senqu river system; mems: Botswana, Lesotho, Namibia, South Africa.

Organisation of African, Caribbean and Pacific States (OACPS): 451B ave Georges Henri, 1200 Brussels, Belgium; tel. (2) 743-06-00; fax (2) 735-55-73; e-mail info@acp.int; internet www .acp.int; f. 1975, in accordance with the founding Georgetown Agreement, as the African, Caribbean and Pacific Group of States (ACP), with the aim of promoting devt in mem. states; in Dec. 2019 the 9th summit of ACP heads of state and govt, held in Nairobi, Kenya, endorsed revisions to the Georgetown Agreement that, *inter alia,* renamed the org., entering into effect on 5 April 2020; in Sept. 2018 the (then) ACP Group initiated negotiations with the EU on drafting a successor agreement to the 2003 Cotonou Agreement governing EU-ACP devt co-operation, which was scheduled to expire at the end of Feb. 2020 (in turn, the Cotonou Agreement had seceded the 1975 Lomé Conventions as the mutual co-operation basis); in Feb. 2020 both sides agreed to extend the existing Agreement until the end of the year, and in Dec. a further extension was approved; in Dec. 2020, meeting virtually, the OACPS Council of Ministers endorsed a new draft ACP-EU Partnership Agreement; a finalized version of the text was initialled in April 2021; the OACPS Council of Ministers convenes two ordinary annual sessions; sectoral ministerial meetings on trade and on culture are also held; mems: 48 African, 16 Caribbean and 15 Pacific states; Sec.-Gen. GEORGES REBELO PINTO CHIKOTI (Angola).

Organization for the Development of the Senegal River (Organisation pour la mise en valeur du fleuve Sénégal—OMVS): Immeuble OMVS, Rocade Fann Bel-air Cerf volant, Dakar, Senegal; tel. 33-859-81-82; e-mail omvssphc@omvs.org; internet www.omvs .org; f. 1972; aims to promote the use of the Senegal river for hydroelectricity, irrigation and navigation; the Djama dam in Senegal provides a barrage to prevent salt water from moving upstream, and the Manantali dam in Mali is intended to provide a reservoir for irrigation of about 375,000 ha of land and for production of hydroelectricity and provision of year-round navigation for ocean-going vessels; 2 cos were formed in 1997 to manage the dams: Société de gestion de l'énergie de Manantali and Société de gestion et d'exploitation du barrage de Djama; OMVS plans to develop a €990m. dam and hydroelectric plant at Koukoutamba, Guinea, were ongoing in 2022; in Sept. 2018 OMVS initiated a Typha Combustible Construction West Africa project, with the aim of reducing the hitherto uncontrolled proliferation of typha (bulrush) plants in the Senegal River Basin, and to promote the devt of typha-based fuels; mems: Guinea, Mali, Mauritania, Senegal; High Commissioner HAMED DIANE SEMEGA.

Pan-African Institute for Development (PAID): 5 route des Morillons, 1211 Geneva, Switzerland; tel. 227336016; fax 227330975; e-mail sg-paid-ipd@hotmail.ch; internet paidafrica.org/ paidwa; f. 1964; gives training to people from African countries involved with devt at grass-roots, intermediate and senior level; emphasis is given to management and financing; agriculture and rural devt; gender issues; promotion of small and medium-sized enterprises; training policies and systems; environment, health and community devt; research, support and consultancy services; and specialized training; there are 4 regional institutes: Central Africa (Douala, Cameroon), Sahel (Ouagadougou, Burkina Faso), West Africa (Buéa, Cameroon), Eastern and Southern Africa (Kabwe, Zambia) and a European office in Geneva, Switzerland; Sec.-Gen. EMMANUEL KAMDEM (Cameroon); publs *Newsletter* (2 a year), *Annual Progress Report*, *PAID Report* (quarterly).

Partners in Population and Development (PPD): PPD Secretariat Bldg Complex, Block-F, Plots-17/ B & C, Agargaon Administrative Zone, Dhaka 1212, Bangladesh; tel. (2) 9117842; fax (2) 9117817; e-mail partners@ppdsec.org; internet www .partners-popdev.org; f. 1994; aims to implement the decisions of the International Conference on Population and Development, held in Cairo, Egypt in 1994, in order to expand and improve South-South collaboration in the fields of family planning and reproductive health; administers a Visionary Leadership Programme, a Global Leadership Programme, a Scholarship Programme and other training and technical advisory services; in April 2018 concluded a Memorandum of Understanding (MOU) with UNFPA to strengthen South-South co-operation in population and devt; an MOU was signed with the League of Arab States in Dec. 2020; mems: 27 developing countries from Asia, Africa, Latin America and the Middle East; Chair. LINDIWE ZULU (South Africa); Exec. Dir ADNENE BEN HAJ AISSA.

SEED Initiative: POB 30552, 00100 Nairobi, Kenya; tel. (20) 7621234; fax (20) 7624489; internet www.seed.uno; f. 2002 by

UNEP, UNDP and IUCN at the World Summit on Sustainable Development in Johannesburg, South Africa; aims to support local and small-scale entrepreneurships that integrate business practice with social and environmental sustainability; a mem. of the Green Economy Coalition; active in Ghana, India, Indonesia, Malawi, South Africa, Thailand, Uganda, Zambia, Zimbabwe; Chair. CRISPIN RAPINET; Exec. Dir ARAB HOBALLAH.

Union of the Arab Maghreb (Union du Maghreb arabe—UMA): 73 rue Tensift, Agdal, Rabat, Morocco; tel. (53) 7681371; fax (53) 7681377; e-mail sg.uma@maghrebarabe.org; internet www .maghrebarabe.org; f. 1989; aims to encourage jt ventures and to create a single market; structure comprises a council of heads of state (meeting annually), a council of ministers responsible for foreign affairs, a follow-up committee, a consultative council of 30 delegates from each country, a UMA judicial court, and 4 specialized ministerial commissions; chairmanship rotates annually between heads of state; a Maghreb Investment and Foreign Trade Bank, funding jt agricultural and industrial projects, has been established and a customs union created; mems: Algeria, Libya, Mauritania, Morocco, Tunisia; Sec.-Gen. Dr TAYEB AL-BAKOUSH (Tunisia).

United Nations African Institute for Economic Development and Planning (IDEP) (Institut africain de développement économique et de planification): rue du 18 Juin, BP 3186, Dakar, Senegal; tel. 33-823-10-20; fax 33-822-29-64; e-mail idep@unidep.org; internet www.unidep.org; f. 1963 by UN ECA to train economic devt planners, conduct research and provide advisory services; mems: 53 mem. states; Dir KARIMA BOUNEMRA BEN SOLTANE.

World Economic Forum: 91–93 route de la Capite, 1223 Cologny/ Geneva, Switzerland; tel. 228691212; fax 227862744; internet www .weforum.org; f. 1971; comprises commercial interests gathered on a non-partisan basis, under the stewardship of the Swiss Government, with the aim of improving society through economic devt; convenes an annual meeting in Davos-Klosters, Switzerland; also holds a regular World Economic Forum on Africa (2019: held in Cape Town, South Africa, in Sept.); organizes the following programmes: Technology Pioneers; Women Leaders; a Network of Global Future Councils; New Champions; and Young Global Leaders; and aims to mobilize the resources of the global business community in the implementation of initiatives including the Global Health Initiative, the Disaster Relief Network, and the G20/International Monetary Reform Project; compiles a Global Competitiveness Index; in 2018 the Forum opened a Centre for the Fourth Industrial Revolution, in San Francisco, CA, USA, as a focal point for international dialogue regarding the impact of advanced technologies, and a Centre for Cybersecurity, located in Geneva, Switzerland; in Jan. 2019 launched a Global Humanitarian Action Executive Alliance and in Aug. initiated an Africa Growth Platform to support small, start-up enterprises; the Essential Digital Infrastructure and Services Network (EDISON) Alliance was initiated by the Forum in Feb. 2021, to promote cross-sectoral collaboration in advancing equitable global access to the digital economy; the Forum is governed by a guiding Foundation Board, an advisory International Business Council, and an administrative Managing Board; regular mems: reps of 1,000 leading commercial cos in 56 countries worldwide; selected mem. cos taking a leading role in the movement's activities are known as 'partners'; Exec. Chair. KLAUS MARTIN SCHWAB (Switzerland); publ. *The Global Competitiveness Report*.

Zambezi Watercourse Commission (ZAMCOM): 128 Samora Machel Ave, Harare, Zimbabwe; tel. (24) 2253361-3; e-mail zamcom@ zambezicommission.org; internet www.zambezicommission.org; f. 2004 to oversee the management of the Zambezi watercourse, became operational in 2014; manages the Zambezi Water Resources Information System to support local planning processes; mems: Angola, Botswana, Malawi, Mozambique, Namibia, Tanzania, Zambia, Zimbabwe; Exec. Sec. FELIX M. NGAMLAGOSI (Tanzania).

Economics and Finance

Afreximbank: 72B el-Maahad el-Eshteraky St, Heliopolis, Cairo 11341, Egypt; tel. and fax (2) 24564100; e-mail info@afreximbank .com; internet afreximbank.com; f. 1993 as the African Export Import Bank, in accordance with an agreement concluded by multilateral orgs and mem. states; commenced operations 1994; aims to promote and finance trade within and beyond Africa; organized (in Cairo) in Dec. 2018, jtly with the AU Commission, the inaugural Intra-African Trade Fair; the 2nd Fair was held in Nov. 2021, in Durban, South Africa; in March 2021 operationalized a US $1,000m. AfCFTA Adjustment Facility which was to enable AU mem. states to manage losses in tariff revenues arising from the initiation of trading under the African Continental Free Trade Area; the Bank established, in March 2020, a Pandemic Trade Impact Mitigation Facility, with funds of up to $3,000m., to support mems confronting economic, financial and health crises as a result of the COVID-19 pandemic;

later in that year the Bank offered guarantees of up to $2,000m. under a new financing facility to support the procurement of COVID-19 vaccines; in Nov. Afreximbank, BADEA, and the International Islamic Trade Finance Corporation initiated a $1,500m. Collaborative COVID-19 Pandemic Response Facility, which aimed to support African countries in addressing the pandemic; a General Capital Increase of $6,500m. was approved at the Bank's annual meeting in July 2021; in March 2022 Afreximbank launched a $4,000m. Ukraine Crisis Adjustment Trade Financing Programme for Africa (UKAFPA) to support the regional response to impacts of the war in Ukraine, particularly the rising cost of fertilizer, fuel and grain imports; brs are located in Côte d'Ivoire (Abidjan), Cameroon (Yaoundé, opened in 2021), Kenya (Nairobi), Nigeria (Abuja) and Zimbabwe (Harare); mems: 51 participating or shareholder states; Pres. Dr BENEDICT OKEY ORAMAH (Nigeria).

African Insurance Organization (AIO): 30 ave de Gaulle, BP 5860, Douala, Cameroon; tel. 233-42-01-63; fax 233-43-20-08; e-mail info@africaninsurance.net; internet www.african-insurance.org; f. 1972; aims to promote the expansion of the insurance and reinsurance industry in Africa, and to increase regional co-operation; holds annual conf., periodic seminars and workshops, and arranges meetings for reinsurers, brokers, consultants and regulators in Africa; has established African insurance 'pools' for aviation, petroleum and fire risks, and created asscns of African insurance educators, supervisory authorities and insurance brokers and consultants; mems: 354 from 48 countries in Africa and 16 assoc. mems from 10 overseas countries; Sec.-Gen. JEAN BAPTISTE NTUKAMAZINA (Rwanda); publs *African Insurance Annual Review*, *African Insurance Bulletin*.

African Reinsurance Corporation (Africa-Re): Africa Re House, Plot 1679, Karimu Kotun St, Victoria Island, PMB 12765, Lagos, Nigeria; tel. (1) 4616820; fax (1) 2800074; e-mail info@ africa-re.com; internet www.africa-re.com; f. 1976; its purpose is to foster the devt of the insurance and reinsurance industry in Africa and to promote the growth of national and regional underwriting capacities; auth. cap. US $500m.; mems: 42 countries, 114 African insurance and reinsurance cos, African Development Bank (AfDB), PROPARCO, IRB-Brasil Re, Fairfax, AXA; Chair. MOHAMED AHMED MAAIT; Man. Dir and CEO CORNEILLE KAREKEZI; publs *The African Reinsurer* (annually), *Africa Re Newsletter* (quarterly), *Risk Watch* (quarterly).

African Rural and Agricultural Credit Association (AFRACA): POB 41378-00100, Nairobi, Kenya; tel. (72) 6080454; e-mail afraca@africaonline.co.ke; internet africa.org; f. 1977; aims to develop the rural finance environment by adopting and promoting policy frameworks and assisting sustainable financial institutions to increase outreach; mems: more than 150 in 27 African countries, including central, commercial and agricultural banks, microfinance institutions, and national progs working in the area of agricultural and rural finance in the continent; Chair. Dr JESIMEN T. CHIPIKA; Sec.-Gen. THOMAS T. ESSEL; publs *Afraca Workshop Reports*, *Rural Finance Experience*.

Asian Infrastructure Investment Bank (AIIB): B9 Financial St, Xicheng District, Beijing, People's Republic of China; tel. (10) 83580000; e-mail information@aiib.org; internet www.aiib.org; f. 2015; aims to finance projects focused on infrastructure devt and regional connectivity in the Asia-Pacific area; Articles of Agreement entered into effect in Dec. 2015 (having been ratified by 17 signatory states with 50.1% of capital subscriptions); inaugural meeting of Bd of Dirs convened in Jan. 2016; 6th regular annual meeting held in a virtual format, in Oct. 2021; in April 2016 signed a co-financing framework agreement with the World Bank to provide for joint implementation of projects; Memorandums of Understanding with the ADB, the EBRD and the EIB were signed in May; in July 2021 the AIIB approved a US $100m. loan for Rwanda, to support the Rwanda Digital Acceleration Project—representing the Bank's first funding operation in sub-Saharan Africa; total subscriptions $96,964.7m. (Aug. 2022); mems: 92 (and 13 approved prospective mems); Pres. JIN LIQUN (People's Republic of China).

Association of African Central Banks (AACB): Ave Abdoulaye Fadiga, BP 3108, Dakar, Senegal; tel. 33-839-08-84; fax 33-839-08-01; e-mail spabca@bceao.int; internet www.aacb.org; f. 1968; aims to increase co-operation and trade among mem. states and strengthen monetary and financial stability in the African continent; administers an African Monetary Co-operation Programme; mems: 39 African central banks representing 37 states; Chair. BUAH SAIDY (Gambia); Exec. Sec. DJOULASSI KOKOU OLOUFADE.

Association of African Development Finance Institutions (AADFI): Immeuble AIAFD, blvd Latrille, rue J61, Cocody Deux Plateaux, 06 BP 321 Abidjan 06, Côte d'Ivoire; tel. 22-52-79-40; fax 22-52-25-84; e-mail info@adfi-ci.org; internet www.adfi-ci.org; f. 1975; aims to promote co-operation among financial institutions in the region in matters relating to economic and social devt, research, project design, financing and the exchange of information; mems: 59 in 43 African and non-African countries; Chair. THABO

THAMANE (Botswana); Sec.-Gen. CYRIL A. OKOYE; publs *Annual Report*, *AADFI Information Bulletin* (quarterly), *Finance and Development in Africa* (2 a year).

East African Development Bank: 4 Nile Ave, POB 7128, Kampala, Uganda; tel. (417) 112900; fax (41) 4253585; e-mail enquiry@eadb.org; internet eadb.org; f. 1967 by the former East African Community to promote regional devt; Rwanda became a member of the Bank in 2008; equity is also held by the AfDB and other institutional investors; mems: Kenya, Tanzania, Rwanda, Uganda; 9 institutional shareholders; Dir-Gen. VIVIENNE YEDA APOPO (Kenya).

Equator Principles Association: e-mail secretariat@equator-principles.com; internet www.equator-principles.com; f. July 2010; aims to administer and develop further the Equator Principles, first adopted in 2003, with the support of the International Finance Corporation, as a set of industry standards for the management of environmental and social risk in project financing; 4th version of the Equator Principles (EP4) was launched in Nov. 2019; holds an annual meeting and workshop; mems: 134 signed-up financial institutions from 38 countries.

Financial Action Task Force (FATF) (Groupe d'action financière—GAFI): 2 rue André-Pascal, 75775 Paris Cedex 16, France; tel. 1-45-24-90-90; fax 1-44-30-61-37; e-mail contact@fatf-gafi.org; internet www.fatf-gafi.org; f. 1989, on the recommendation of the G7; mandated to develop and promote policies to combat money laundering and the financing of terrorism; formulated 40 recommendations for countries worldwide to implement in order to combat money laundering and the financing of terrorism and proliferation; these are periodically revised; established partnerships with regional task forces in the Caribbean, Asia-Pacific, Central Asia, Europe, East and South Africa, and the Middle East, and Central and North Africa; has developed terrorist financing-related risk indicators; mems: 37 state jurisdictions, the European Commission, the Cooperation Council for the Arab States of the Gulf; 1 observer country, 9 regional assoc. mems and 23 observer orgs; Pres. (1 July 2022–30 June 2024) T. RAJA KUMAR (Singapore); Exec. Sec. VIOLAINE CLERC (France); publ. *Annual Report*.

Fonds Africain de Garantie et de Co-opération Economique (FAGACE) (African Guarantee and Economic Co-operation Fund): 01 BP 2045 RP, Cotonou, Benin; tel. 21-30-03-76; fax 21-30-02-84; e-mail courriel.fagace@le-fagace.org; internet www.le-fagace.org; f. 1977, commenced operations in 1981; guarantees loans for devt projects, provides loans and grants for specific operations and supports national and regional enterprises; mems: 14 African countries; Dir-Gen. MINAFOU FANTA COULIBALY-KONE (Côte d'Ivoire).

Group of 20 (G20): internet www.g20.org; f. Sept. 1999; established initially as an informal deliberative forum of ministers responsible for finance and central bank governors representing both industrialized and 'systemically important' emerging market nations; aims to strengthen the international financial architecture and to foster sustainable economic growth and devt; an extraordinary meeting of heads of state and of govt to discuss extreme concerns regarding global financial markets and the world economy was convened in Washington, DC, USA, in Nov. 2008; a further summit meeting, held in London, United Kingdom, in April 2009, issued as its final communiqué a Global Plan for Recovery and Reform; detailed declarations were also issued on measures agreed to deliver substantial resources (of some US $850,000m.) through international financial institutions; as a follow-up to the London meeting, G20 leaders gathered in Pittsburgh, PA, USA, in Sept. 2009; the meeting adopted a Framework for Strong, Sustainable, and Balanced Growth and resolved to expand the role of the G20 to be at the centre of future international economic policymaking; summit meetings were held in June 2010, in Canada, and in Nov., in Seoul, Rep. of Korea; the 6th G20 summit, held in Cannes, France, in Nov. 2011, concluded an Action Plan for Growth and Jobs, and addressed measures to secure financial stability in some countries using the euro; the 7th summit, convened in Los Cabos, Baja California Sur, Mexico, in June 2012, further considered means of stabilizing the eurozone, with a particular focus on reducing the borrowing costs of highly indebted mem. countries; an SME Finance Forum was launched in that year; in Sept. 2013 11 heads of state and govt participating in the summit meeting held in St Petersburg, Russia, issued a statement condemning an alleged chemical attack perpetrated against civilians in Ghouta, Syria, on 21 Aug., and urging a strong international response; the meeting also adopted a new Base Erosion and Profit Shifting Action Plan, developed by the OECD with the aim of combating corporation tax avoidance globally; in Feb. 2016 G20 ministers responsible for finance and central bank governors (FMCBG) met in Shanghai, People's Rep. of China, to discuss policy options to counter a deceleration in global economic growth; the 2016 summit meeting was held in Sept., in Hangzhou; a G20-Africa Partnership conf. was convened in June 2017, in Berlin, Germany; in a communiqué issued by the 2017 summit meeting, held in July, in Hamburg, Germany, 19 of the participating leaders (excluding US Pres. Trump) renewed commitment to implementing the 2015 Paris Agreement on climate change; the communiqué also noted the right of countries to protect their markets with 'legitimate trade-defence instruments'; the 2018 summit, convened in late Nov.–early Dec., in Buenos Aires, Argentina, released a communiqué in which, *inter alia,* participating leaders reaffirmed commitment to improving the rules-based international order and pledged support to 'necessary' reform to the functioning of the WTO; the 2019 G20 summit, convened in June, in Osaka, Japan, noted the recent intensification of geopolitical and trade tensions, reaffirmed support for reform of the WTO (including with a view to enhancing its dispute settlement system), endorsed a series of G20 Principles on Artificial Intelligence (based on principles formulated by the OECD), determined to promote cross-border data exchange, agreed to work towards eliminating marine plastic litter by 2050, and made a collective statement on combating exploitation of the internet for terrorism/violent extremism; an emergency summit was held in mid-March 2020, in a virtual format, to discuss the COVID-19 pandemic; a further virtual summit, convened subsequently to address the co-ordination of related medical and economic planning, issued a statement committing to close collaboration in sharing data, research and best practices and to the financing of pandemic response efforts; leaders endorsed measures being taken by central banks to safeguard their economies, and pledged $5,000,000m. in funding to combat the impacts of the coronavirus emergency; in April G20 finance ministers and central bank governors endorsed a G20 Action Plan on supporting the global economy in relation to measures imposed to counter COVID-19; the meeting announced a temporary Debt Service Suspension Initiative (DSSI), providing for the world's poorest countries to freeze repayment of official bilateral credit, with effect from 1 May; in mid-July the (virtual) FMCBG meeting pledged to continue to deploy all possible policy tools to alleviate the impacts of the ongoing global crisis; Saudi Arabia hosted that year's summit, in a virtual format, in Nov.; the meeting endorsed a Common Framework for Debt Treatments beyond the DSSI, to provide structural support, on a case-by-case basis, as requested, to LDCs with unsustainable debt; in May 2021 a G20 Global Health Summit, convened in Rome, Italy, adopted the Rome Declaration, which included commitments to common principles aimed at overcoming the COVID-19 crisis and preparing for and preventing future disease pandemics; in July the FMCBG meeting gave support to a proposal—that had been agreed by the G7 leadership in June and subsequently endorsed by OECD mem. states—to introduce a minimum global corporate tax rate of 15%; in July the G20 finance ministers also notably endorsed for the first time the taxation of carbon dioxide emissions ('carbon pricing'), as a tool for addressing climate change; a G20 summit meeting was held in late Oct., in Rome; leaders agreed to implement the 15% global corporate tax rate by 2023; they also resolved to accelerate efforts to achieve global net zero greenhouse gas emissions, to continue to mobilize climate finance commitments, to increase the provision of and access to COVID-19 vaccines for low- and middle-income countries and to establish a G20 Joint Finance-Health Task Force to formulate a mechanism to fund pandemic prevention, preparedness and response; the amount of debt service suspended through the DSSI during May 2020–Dec. 2021 (when it expired, having been twice extended, in Nov. 2020 and April 2021) totalled $12,900m.; 48 of the 73 eligible countries participated in the initiative; the April 2022 FMCBG meeting, convened in a hybrid virtual and in-person format hosted from Washington, DC, considered the humanitarian and economic impacts (incl. upwards pressure on energy and food prices) of the ongoing war in Ukraine; several reps, incl. those of the EU, Canada, France, UK and USA, removed themselves from the meeting during an address by the Russian Fed.'s delegate, in protest at that country's aggression against Ukraine; a provisional consensus was reached on establishing, under World Bank auspices, a new Financial Intermediary Fund for Pandemic Prevention, Preparedness and Response; a meeting of G20 foreign ministers, convened in early July, in Bali, Indonesia, with Russian participation, considered (without achieving consensus) the impacts on global energy and food security of the Russia–Ukraine war; Russia's foreign minister withdrew from a session in response to criticism of Russia's military and territorial aggression; a summit of G20 heads of state and govt was to be held in Bali in Nov. 2022; parallel meetings to promote dialogue and engagement with different groups are held concurrently with the summit gatherings, including with representatives of the private sector (Business 20), civil society (Civil 20), labour orgs (Labour 20), women (Women 20), tourism and young people (Youth 20); since 2012 the Think 20 (T20) network of think tanks and research institutes from the G20 mem. states has offered research-based policy proposals to the G20 leaders, providing both continuity between presidencies and focusing on developing issues; mems: Argentina, Australia, Brazil, Canada, People's Rep. of China, France, Germany, India, Indonesia, Italy, Japan, Rep. of Korea, Mexico, Russian Fed., Saudi Arabia, South Africa, Türkiye (Turkey), UK, USA and the European Union; observers: Netherlands, Spain; the presidency rotates among the participating states on an annual basis (Nov. 2021–Nov. 2022: Indonesia).

Intergovernmental Group of 24 (G24) on International Monetary Affairs and Development: 700 19th St, NW, HQ1 Rm 2-588, Washington, DC 20431, USA; tel. (202) 623-6101; fax (202) 623-6000; e-mail g24@g24.org; internet www.g24.org; f. 1971; aims to co-ordinate the position of developing countries on monetary and devt finance issues; operates at the political level of ministers responsible for finance and governors of central banks; in April 2022, in the context of the COVID-19 pandemic, called for more widespread global attention to debt vulnerability, and recommended the creation of an inclusive forum to reconsider the suitability of the global international financial and economic architecture and its ability to respond quickly and fairly to global crises; mems (Africa): Algeria, Côte d'Ivoire, Democratic Rep. of the Congo, Egypt, Ethiopia, Gabon, Ghana, Kenya, Morocco, Nigeria, South Africa; (Latin America and the Caribbean): Argentina, Brazil, Colombia, Guatemala, Ecuador, Haiti, Mexico, Peru, Trinidad and Tobago, Venezuela; (Asia and the Middle East): Egypt, India, Iran, Lebanon, Pakistan, Philippines, Sri Lanka, Syrian Arab Rep.; the People's Rep. of China has the status of special invitee at G24 meetings; G77 participant states may attend G24 meetings as observers, 11 institutional and 5 country observers; Chair. SERGIO RECINOS (Guatemala); Dir MARILOU UY.

Islamic Financial Services Board: Sasana Kijang, Level 5, Bank Negara Malaysia, 2 Jalan Dato Onn, 50840 Kuala Lumpur, Malaysia; tel. (3) 91951400; fax (3) 91951405; e-mail ifsb_sec@ifsb.org; internet www.ifsb.org; f. 2002; aims to formulate standards and guiding principles for regulatory and supervisory agencies working within the Islamic financial services industry; has developed, in co-operation with the Basel Committee on Banking Supervision, Core Principles for Islamic Finance Regulation (CPIFR); Guiding Principles on *Shari'a* Governance Systems for Institutions offering Islamic Financial Services, and Guiding Principles on Governance for *Takâful* Undertakings (Islamic insurance) were adopted in Dec. 2009; Guiding Principles for *Retakâfu* (Islamic reinsurance) adopted in April 2018; mems (full, assoc. and observers): 188, incl. 81 regulatory and supervisory authorities, 10 orgs, 97 financial institutions, professional firms, industry associations and stock exchanges in 57 jurisdictions; Chair. REZA BAQIR (Pakistan); Sec.-Gen. Dr BELLO LAWAL DANBATT (Malaysia); publ. *IFSB Bulletin* (3 a year).

New Development Bank: 1600 Gouzhan Rd, Pudong, Shanghai 200120, People's Republic of China; tel. (21) 80211800; fax (21) 80211990; e-mail info@ndb.int; internet www.ndb.int; f. July 2015 (founding agreement signed in July 2014, in Fortaleza, Brazil, by mem. govts of the BRICS grouping); aims to mobilize resources for infrastructure and sustainable devt projects in BRICS and other emerging economies and developing countries, complementing the existing efforts of multilateral and regional financial institutions for global growth and devt; an NDB African Regional Centre was inaugurated in Sandton, South Africa, in Aug., an NDB Americas Regional Office was established in São Paulo, Brazil, in July 2018, and a new Moscow, Russia-based NDB Eurasian Regional Centre was approved in Dec. 2019; in March 2020 the Bd of Dirs approved the Bank's largest ever loan, of some RMB 7,000m. (approx. US $987m.), to assist the Chinese authorities to combat the COVID-19 contagion and mitigate some of the social and economic consequences in the 3 provinces most affected (a further RMB 7,000m. loan was extended to China in March 2021); an Emergency Assistance Facility was established by the Bank in April 2020, with some $10,000m. of funding, to extend COVID-19 related loans for healthcare, social safety nets and economic recovery; 7th annual meeting held in a virtual format in May 2022; in 2021 undertook an expansion of its membership: Bangladesh and United Arab Emirates acceded in Sept. and Oct., respectively; Uruguay was approved as a prospective mem. in Sept., and Egypt was admitted in Dec., although full membership was pending their deposit of accession; new transactions in the Russian Fed. were suspended in March 2022; mems: Bangladesh, Brazil, People's Rep. of China, India, Russian Fed., South Africa, United Arab Emirates; Pres. MARCOS TROYJO (Brazil); Dir CHENG ZHIJUN.

Paris Club (Club de Paris): 139 rue de Bercy, Télédoc 551, 75572 Paris Cedex 12, France; internet www.clubdeparis.org; f. 1956; informal group of official creditors; aims to formulate co-ordinated and sustainable solutions to the payment difficulties experienced by debtor countries; in 2020 agreed, with the G20, a debt service initiative (operational until 31 Dec. 2021) to suspend repayments of bilateral official debt by the world's poorest countries; in Nov. 2020 the Paris Club and G20 endorsed a Common Framework for debt treatment beyond the DSSI, to provide structural support, on a case-by-case basis, as requested, to LDCs with unsustainable debt (it was subsequently reported that LDCs that applied to the Framework were liable to be downgraded by international credit rating agencies); by Sept. 2022 the Paris Club had concluded 478 agreements with 102 debtor countries, treating a total value of US $612,000m. of debt; mems: 22; Chair. EMMANUEL MOULIN; Sec.-Gen. PHILIPPE GUYONNET DUPÉRAT (France).

Vulnerable Twenty Group (V20): 2E Maison de la Paix, Chemin Eugène-Rigot, 1202 Geneva, Switzerland; e-mail secretariat@V-20 .org; internet www.v-20.org; f. 2015, in accordance with a proposal outlined in the Costa Rica Action Plan of the Climate Vulnerable Forum (CVF); comprises the ministers responsible for finance of mem. states of the CVF, with the following objectives: to promote the mobilization of both public and private climate finance; to exchange and share best practices on the financial and economic aspects of climate action; to develop new approaches to climate finance; and to undertake collective action, including jt advocacy; 4th ministerial dialogue held in Bali, Indonesia, in Oct. 2018; a Climate Vulnerable Forum-V20 Joint Multi Donor Fund was launched in Dec. 2020; inaugural (virtual) climate vulnerables' finance summit held in July 2021; in June 2022 the V20 reported that during 2000–19 climate change had eradicated one-fifth of vulnerable countries' wealth, and demanded the creation of a dedicated international funding mechanism to support their adaptation to the climate crisis; chair. rotates (mid-2022–mid-2024: Ghana); mems: 48 (Afghanistan, Bangladesh, Barbados, Bhutan, Burkina Faso, Cambodia, Colombia, Comoros, Costa Rica, Democratic Rep. of the Congo, Dominican Rep., Ethiopia, Fiji, The Gambia, Ghana, Grenada, Guatemala, Haiti, Honduras, Kenya, Kiribati, Lebanon, Madagascar, Malawi, Maldives, Marshall Islands, Mongolia, Morocco, Nepal, Niger, Palau, Palestine, Papua New Guinea, Philippines, Rwanda, Saint Lucia, Samoa, Senegal, South Sudan, Sri Lanka, Sudan, Tanzania, Timor-Leste, Tunisia, Tuvalu, Vanuatu, Viet Nam, Yemen).

West African Bankers' Association (WABA): 11–13 Ecowas St, PM Bag 1012, Freetown, Sierra Leone; tel. (22) 226752; fax (22) 229024; e-mail sbalde@waba-abao.org; internet www.waba-abao .org; f. 1981; aims to strengthen links between banks in West Africa, to enable exchange of information, and to contribute to regional economic devt; holds annual general assembly; mems: 217 commercial banks in 15 West African countries; Sec.-Gen. AGBAI ABOSI; publ. *West African Banking Almanac.*

Education

Association for the Development of Education in Africa: Immeuble CCIA, Abidjan Plateau, Ave Jean-Paul II, 01 BP 1387, Abidjan 01, Côte d'Ivoire; tel. 20-26-56-74; e-mail adea@afdb.org; internet www.adeanet.org; f. 1988 as Donors to African Education, present name adopted in 1995; aims to enhance collaboration in the support of African education; promotes policy dialogue and undertakes research, advocacy and capacity building in areas of education in sub-Saharan Africa through progs and working groups comprising representatives of donor countries and African ministries of education; serves 87 ministries of education in Africa; Exec. Sec. ALBERT NSENGIYUMVA; publ. *Kibare: Non-formal Education and Literacy Journal.*

Association of African Universities (AAU) (Association des universités africaines): POB 5744, Accra-North, Ghana; tel. (21) 774495; e-mail info@aau.org; internet www.aau.org; f. 1967; aims to promote exchanges, contact and co-operation among African univ. institutions and to collect and disseminate information on research and higher education in Africa; convenes a General Conference every 4 years (2017: Accra, Ghana, in June, also marked 50th anniversary celebrations); mems: 416; Pres. Prof. SAEED BAKRI OSMAN (Sudan); Sec.-Gen. Prof. OLUSOLA BANDELE OYEWOLE (Nigeria); publ. *AAU Newsletter* (3 a year).

Pan-African Association for Literacy and Adult Education: rue 10, Bldg 306, POB 21783, Ponty, Dakar, Senegal; tel. 33-825-48-50; fax 33-824-44-13; e-mail anafa@sentoo.sn; f. 2000 to succeed African Asscn for Literacy and Adult Education (f. 1984); Co-ordinator Dr LAMINE KANE (Senegal).

Southern and Eastern Africa Consortium for Monitoring Educational Quality: Plot 4775, Notwane Rd, Gaborone, Botswana; tel. 3552055; fax 3184535; e-mail info@sacmeq.org; internet www.sacmeq.org; f. 1995; aims to undertake integrated research and training activities in order to develop the capacities of education planners to enhance the evaluation and monitoring of the condition of schools and the quality of education; receives technical assistance from UNESCO International Institute for Educational Planning (IIEP); mems: Ministries of Education in 16 countries of the region; Chair. Dr JOYCE NDALICHAKO (Tanzania); Dir TOZIBA MASALILA (Botswana).

West African Examinations Council (WAEC) (Conseil des examens de l'Afrique orientale): POB GP 125, Accra, Ghana; tel. (30) 2248967; fax (30) 2222905; internet www.waecheadquartersgh.org; f. 1952; administers prescribed examinations in mem. countries; aims to harmonize examinations procedures and standards; offices in each mem. country and in London, UK; mems: The Gambia, Ghana, Liberia, Nigeria, Sierra Leone; Chair. BABOUCARR BOUY; Registrar Dr IYI UWADIAE (Nigeria).

Environment and Energy

African Conservation Foundation: POB 189, Buéa, Cameroon; e-mail info@africanconservation.org; internet www .africanconservation.org; f. 1999 as a regional network for information exchange and capacity building towards environmental conservation; aims to improve management and utilization of natural resources to reconcile devt needs with biodiversity conservation; Conservation Dir AREND DE HAAS.

Central African Power Pool (CAPP): Namemba Tower, 14th Floor, Brazzaville, Republic of the Congo; f. 2003 as a specialized agency of the Communauté Economique des Etats de l'Afrique Centrale (CEEAC); oversees the implementation of energy-related policy, monitoring, and infrastructure devt, and the organization of electric energy exchanges and related services in the CEEAC region; mems: 10 central African states.

Central African Forests Commission (Commission des Forêts d'Afrique Centrale—COMIFAC): BP 20818 Yaoundé, Cameroon; tel. 222-21-35-12; e-mail comifac@comifac.org; internet www.comifac .org; f. 2005; promotes the sustainable management of forest ecosystems; mems: Burundi, Cameroon, Central African Rep., Chad, Democratic Rep. of the Congo, Rep. of the Congo, Gabon, Equatorial Guinea, Rwanda, São Tomé and Príncipe; Pres. JULES DORET NDONGO; Exec. Sec. HERVÉ MARTIAL MAIDOU.

Climate Vulnerable Forum (CVF): Office of the President, International Convention Center, POB 2, Majuro, MH 96960, Marshall Islands; tel. (625) 2233; e-mail info@thecvf.org; internet www.thecvf .org; f. 2009; inaugural meeting, held in Nov. 2009, in Malé, Maldives, adopted a joint Declaration expressing alarm at the fast pace of human-induced climate change; in Nov. 2011 adopted a 14-point Declaration of the CVF; launched a trust fund in Sept. 2012; the inaugural meeting of the Vulnerable Twenty Group of CVF ministers of finance was held in Oct. 2015; a CVF-V20 Joint Multi Donor Fund was launched in Dec. 2020; chair. rotates (mid-2022–mid-2024: Ghana); mems: 55 countries; publ. *Climate Vulnerability Monitor*.

Conservation International: 2011 Crystal Drive, Suite 600, Arlington, VA 22202, USA; tel. (703) 341-2400; e-mail community@conservation.org; internet www.conservation.org; f. 1987; aims to demonstrate to govts, institutions and corporations that sustainable global devt is necessary for human wellbeing, and provides strategic, technical and financial support to partners at local, national and regional level to facilitate balancing conservation actions with devt objectives and economic interests; focuses on the following priority areas: biodiversity hotspots (36 threatened habitats that cover just 2.3% of the Earth's surface yet hold at least 50% of plant species and some 42% of terrestrial vertebrate species); high biodiversity wilderness areas (5 areas retaining at least 70% of their original vegetation: Amazonia; the Congo Basin; New Guinea; North American deserts; and the Miomo-Mopane woodlands and savannas of Southern Africa); and oceans and seascapes; maintains offices in around 30 countries worldwide; partners: govts, businesses, local communities, non-profit orgs and univs worldwide; Chair. PETER SELIGMANN (USA); CEO M. SANJAYAN.

International Energy Forum (IEF): POB 94736, Diplomatic Quarter, Riyadh 11614, Saudi Arabia; tel. (11) 481-0022; fax (11) 481-0055; e-mail info@ief.org; internet www.ief.org; f. 1991 to promote dialogue on energy matters; ministers responsible for energy affairs from states accounting for about 90% of global oil and gas supply and demand convene, usually, every 2 years; a meeting of the International Business Energy Forum, attended by CEOs of leading energy cos, precedes the gathering; since 2005 the IEF secretariat has co-ordinated the work of the Joint Oil Data Initiative (JODI), formally established as a multi-agency permanent reporting mechanism in 2002; an annual symposium with OPEC and the International Energy Agency has been held since 2011; signed an MOU with IRENA in Jan. 2020 to promote greater collaboration between the orgs; mems: 71 states, including the mems of OPEC and the IEA; Sec.-Gen. JOSEPH MCMONIGLE (USA).

International Renewable Energy Agency (IRENA): Masdar City, POB 236, Abu Dhabi, United Arab Emirates; tel. (2) 4179000; e-mail info@irena.org; internet www.irena.org; f. 2009 at a conf. held in Bonn, Germany; aims to promote the devt and application of renewable sources of energy; to act as a forum for the exchange of information and technology transfer; and to organize training seminars and other educational activities; inaugural Assembly convened in April 2011; 12th Assembly held in Jan. 2022, in Abu Dhabi, UAE; hosts SEforALL's Renewable Energy hub; signed an MOU with IEF in Jan. 2020; initiated in Jan. 2021 a Global High-Level Forum on Energy Transition; promotes 3 subregional Clean Energy Corridors; mems: 167 (incl. the European Union); Dir-Gen. FRANCESCO LA CAMERA (Italy); publ. *World Energy Transitions Outlook*.

International Solar Alliance (ISA): Surya Bhawan, National Institute of Solar Energy Campus, Gwal Pahari, Faridabad-

Gurugram Rd, Gurugram, 122003 Haryana, India; tel. (124) 2853090; e-mail info@isolaralliance.org; internet isolaralliance.org; f. 2015, as a coalition of solar resource rich countries; aims to increase the use of solar energy to meet energy needs of mem. and prospective mem. countries in an equitable and sustainable manner, and to provide a platform for collaboration; granted observer status at the UN General Assembly in Dec. 2021; mems: 86 signatory countries; Dir-Gen. Dr AJAY MATHUR (India); publs *ISA Programmes*, *ISA Journals*.

IUCN—International Union for Conservation of Nature: 28 rue Mauverney, 1196 Gland, Switzerland; tel. 229990000; fax 229990002; e-mail mail@iucn.org; internet www.iucn.org; f. 1948, as the International Union for Conservation of Nature and Natural Resources; supports partnerships and practical field activities to promote the conservation and sustainable use of natural resources, to secure the conservation of biological diversity; develops programmes to protect and sustain the most important and threatened species and ecosystems and assists govts to devise and carry out national conservation strategies; incorporates the Species Survival Commission, a science-based network of volunteer experts aiming to ensure conservation of present levels of biodiversity; compiles the annually updated Red List of Threatened Species; by 2022 the list had determined some 41,000 species of animals, plants and fungi (representing 28% of all species assessed) to be vulnerable, endangered or close to extinction; from July 2021 a new IUCN Green Status of Species was used for the first time, as a standard to measure how near a species is to being fully ecologically functional across its range, and how successful conservation action has been; at that time Green Status assessments were presented for 181 species; also maintains a Green List of Protected and Conserved Areas; in 2022 the IUCN was working to develop its lists into a broad Barometer of Life, involving assessments of at least 160,000 species (at that time it was managing data from more than 134,400 species); maintains a conservation library and documentation centre and units for monitoring traffic in wildlife; organizes a World Conservation Congress every 4 years (2021: Marseilles, France, in Sept.); the 2021 World Conservation Congress voted decisively in favour of a resolution that called for a global moratorium on deep seabed mining, in view of potential risks posed by such activities to oceanic biodiversity and ecosystems; mems: 1,400 mem. orgs, agencies and asscns in some 170 countries; Pres. RAZAN AL MUBARAK (United Arab Emirates); Dir-Gen. Dr BRUNO OBERLE (Switzerland); publs *World Conservation Strategy*, *Caring for the Earth*, *Green List of Protected and Conserved Areas*, *Red List of Threatened Plants*, *Red List of Threatened Species*, *United Nations List of National Parks and Protected Areas*, *World Conservation* (quarterly), *IUCN Today*.

Organization of the Petroleum Exporting Countries (OPEC): Helferstorferstr. 17, 1010 Vienna, Austria; tel. (1) 211-12-3302; e-mail prid@opec.org; internet www.opec.org; f. 1960; aims to unify and co-ordinate mems' petroleum policies and to safeguard their interests generally; holds regular conferences of mem. countries to set reference prices and production levels; conducts research in energy studies, economics and finance; provides data services and news services covering petroleum and energy issues; in Dec. 2016 signed a Declaration of Cooperation with 11 non-mem. oil producing countries (together styled 'OPEC+') to help to stabilize the global petroleum market through production adjustments; the inaugural OPEC-Africa Energy Dialogue was convened in June 2021, with participation by the African Energy Commission, African Petroleum Producers' Organization, and African Refiners and Distributors Association; mems: 13 states, incl., Angola, Rep. of Congo, Equatorial Guinea, Gabon, Nigeria; the OPEC+ states incl. South Sudan and Sudan; Sec.-Gen. HAITHAM AL-GHAIS (Kuwait); publs *Annual Report*, *Annual Statistical Bulletin*, *OPEC Bulletin* (10 a year), *Monthly Oil Market Report*, *World Oil Outlook* (annually).

Permanent Okavango River Basin Water Commission (OKACOM): POB 25741, Plot 25019, Old Lobatse Rd, Gaborone, Botswana; tel. 3161593; fax 3700231; e-mail okasec@okacom.org; internet www.okacom.org; f. 1994; monitors transboundary issues in the Okavango Delta (which represents the world's third largest wetlands site) and facilitates an ongoing dialogue among the basin's stakeholders; has task forces on biodiversity, hydrology and on institutional matters; mems: Angola, Botswana, Namibia; Exec. Sec. PHERA S. RAMOELI.

Regional Integrated Multi-Hazard Early Warning System for Africa and Asia (RIMES): Asian Institute of Technology campus, Klong Luang, Pathumthani 12120, Thailand; tel. (2) 516-5900; fax (2) 516-5902; internet www.rimes.int; f. 2005; evolved from the efforts of countries in Africa and Asia, in the aftermath of the 2004 Indian Ocean tsunami, to establish a regional early warning system within a multi-hazard framework for the generation and communication of early warning information, and capacity building for preparedness and response to transboundary hazards; mems: 12 states and 19 collaborating countries; Chair. Dr MADHAVAN NAIR RAJEEVAN (India).

Small Island Developing States Sustainable Energy and Charter Resilience Organization (SIDS DOCK): Belmopan, Belize; tel. (501) 822-1104; e-mail secretariat@sidsdock.org; internet sidsdock.org; f. 2009; aims to connect the energy sector of small island developing states (SIDS) with global markets, providing greater access to finance, technologies and carbon in order to support sustainable economic development and to address adaptation to climate change; awarded observer status at the UN General Assembly in 2020; mems: 17; Chair. RONALD J. JUMEAU (Seychelles).

Sustainable Energy for All (SEforALL): Andromeda Tower, 15th Floor, Donau-City-Str. 6, 1220 Vienna, Austria; e-mail info@seforall .org; internet www.se4all.org; f. 2011, as an initiative of the UN Secretary-General; works towards the attainment of Sustainable Development Goal 7, i.e. to secure by 2030 universal access to modern energy sources, to increase, by 50%, the use of renewable energy, and to enhance energy efficiency worldwide; aims to develop international partnerships and funding arrangements in support of these objectives; in 2016 established a Co-ordination Cttee to maintain a close working relationship with the UN and to co-ordinate activities; in response to the COVID-19 pandemic SEforALL focused work on sustainable cold chain infrastructure (in support of equitable vaccine distribution), the power needs of healthcare facilities, and incorporating sustainable energy into recovery plans; organizes a regular Forum (2022: Kigali, Rwanda); Chair. of Admin. Bd FRANCESCO STARACE; CEO (and Special Rep. of the UN Sec.-Gen. for Sustainable Energy for All) DAMILOLA OGUNBIYI (Nigeria).

Volta Basin Authority (Autorité du Bassin de la Volta): POB 13621, Ouagadougou 10, Burkina Faso; tel. (25) 376067; e-mail secretariat@abv.int; internet abv.int; f. 2006; supports the harmonization of national policies governing integrated water resources management in the Volta basin; co-ordinates studies and research on the supply of water to local communities, irrigation, fishing and conservation of aquatic systems, and hydropower production; an Observatory for Water Resources and Related Ecosystems was planned by the Authority; mems: Benin, Burkina Faso, Côte d'Ivoire, Ghana, Mali, Togo; Exec. Dir ROBERT DESSOUASI.

Wetlands International: POB 471, 6700 AL Wageningen, Netherlands; tel. (318) 660910; fax (318) 660950; e-mail post@wetlands.org; internet www.wetlands.org; f. 1995 by merger of several regional wetlands orgs; aims to protect and restore wetlands, their resources and biodiversity through research, information exchange and conservation activities; supports implementation of the 1971 Ramsar Convention on Wetlands as one of its 6 int. org. partners; mems: 24 countries and 9 NGOs; CEO JANE MADGWICK.

World Coal Association (WCA): e-mail info@worldcoal.org; internet www.worldcoal.org; represents industry leaders committed to building a sustainable global future for coal, promoting a modern coal value chain, fostering innovation, and supporting global economic and environmental goals; mems: 17 corp mems and 12 assoc mems; Chair. JULY NDLOVU (Zimbabwe); Sec.-Gen. MICHELLE MANOOK.

Governance and Security

African Association for Public Administration and Management (AAPAM): 132 Fuchsia Close, POB 48677, 00100 GPO, Nairobi, Kenya; tel. (20) 2629650; e-mail aapam@aapam.org; internet www.aapam.org; f. 1971 to promote good practices, excellence and professionalism in public administration through training, seminars, research; convenes regular confs to share learning experiences among mems, and an annual Roundtable Conference (2022: in Nov.–Dec.); funded by membership contributions, govt and donor grants; mems: 500 individual, 50 corp., 15 nat. chapters; Pres. Dr ROLAND MSISKA (Zambia); Sec.-Gen. GEORGE K. SCOTT (Uganda); publs *Newsletter* (quarterly), *Annual Seminar Report*, *African Journal of Public Administration and Management* (2 a year).

African Parliamentary Union: BP V314, Abidjan, Côte d'Ivoire; tel. 20-30-39-70; fax 20-30-44-05; e-mail upa1@aviso.ci; internet www.apunion.org; f. 1976 (as Union of African Parliaments); aims to promote democracy and to facilitate interaction between African legislators and parliamentary institutions; mems: 41 parliaments; Pres. MOHAMED ALI HOUMED (Djibouti); Sec.-Gen. GADO BOUBACAR IDI.

Afro-Asian Peoples' Solidarity Organization (AAPSO): 89 Abdel Aziz Al-Saoud St, POB 11559-61 Manial El-Roda, Cairo, Egypt; tel. (2) 3636081; fax (2) 3637361; e-mail aapso@idsc.net.eg; internet www.aapsorg.org; f. 1958; acts always and for the peoples of Africa and Asia in support of genuine independence, sovereignty, socioeconomic devt, peace and disarmament; holds General Congress normally every 2 years; mems: nat. cttees and affiliated orgs in 90 countries and territories, assoc. mems in Europe and Latin America; Pres. HELMY AL-HADIDI; Sec.-Gen. NOURI ABDEL RAZZAK HUSSEIN

(Iraq); publs *Solidarity Bulletin* (monthly), *Socio-Economic Development* (3 a year).

Coalition for the Sahel: f. Jan. 2020, in Pau, France, by the heads of state of the G5 Sahel countries and of France; aims to provide a framework for co-operation with a wider grouping of international partners to counter terrorism in the sub-region, to strengthen the capacities of G5 states to impose order within all their territories, and to harness humanitarian and devt assistance; High Rep. ADOUM DJIMÉ (Chad).

Comunidade dos Países de Língua Portuguesa (CPLP) (Community of Portuguese-speaking Countries): rua de S. Mamede (ao Caldas) 21, 1100-533 Lisbon, Portugal; tel. (21) 392-8560; fax (21) 392-8588; e-mail comunicacao@cplp.org; internet www.cplp.org; f. 1996; aims to produce close political, economic, diplomatic and cultural links between Portuguese-speaking countries and to strengthen the influence of the Lusophone Commonwealth within the international community; Lisbon-based CPLP Parliamentary Assembly inaugurated in Nov. 2007; in Nov. 2010 adopted, jtly with ECOWAS, the CPLP-ECOWAS roadmap on reform of the defence and security sector in Guinea-Bissau; in April 2017 the CPLP Exec. Sec. held consultations with national and international stakeholders in Guinea-Bissau to address an ongoing paralysis of the political process in that country; a jt military exercise, Exercício FELINO, is conducted periodically by mem. states; summit meeting normally held every 2 years (13th was convened in Luanda, Angola, in July 2021, having been postponed by one year as a result of COVID-19); a CPLP strategic plan was being implemented during 2016–26; in July 2019, with the Food and Agriculture Organization of the UN, opened a new Training Centre for Sustainable Family Farming, based in São Tomé and Príncipe; mems: Angola, Brazil, Cabo Verde, Equatorial Guinea, Guinea-Bissau, Mozambique, Portugal, São Tomé and Príncipe, Timor-Leste; 19 assoc. observers; Exec. Sec. ZACARIAS DA COSTA (Timor-Leste).

East African Legislative Assembly: POB 1096, AICC Bldg, Arusha, Tanzania; tel. (27) 2162126; fax (27) 2162179; e-mail eala@eachq.org; internet www.eala.org; f. 2001; established under the East African Community's founding Treaty as the legislative organ of the Community; the 4th tenure of the Assembly commenced in Dec. 2017; 52 mems (45 elected and 7 ex officio); Speaker Rt Hon. MARTIN NGOGA (Rwanda).

G5 Sahel: ILOT ZRA 742 BIS, rue Monotel, Tevragh Zeina, Nouakchott, Mauritania; tel. (222) 45-25-7730; e-mail contact@g5sahel.org; internet www.g5sahel.org; f. 2014; aims to promote security, devt, good governance and resilience in the Sahel region; a UN-supported G5 unit is tasked with preventing extremist radicalization; determined in Feb. 2017 to establish a counter-terrorism force—Force conjointe du G5 Sahel (FC-G5S)—tasked with combating violent extremist groups operating in the G5 common space; the FC-G5S was to comprise up to 5,000 military and police personnel; in April the AU Peace and Security Council endorsed the strategic concept of operations of the FC-G5S and authorized its deployment, which was then endorsed by the UN Security Council in June; it was announced in Aug. that the FC-G5S had become operational; a co-ordinated operation along Mali's borders with Burkina Faso and Niger was undertaken in early Nov.; in Dec. the UN Security Council determined to extend further technical support to the force; a FC-G5S Trust Fund has been established; a G5 Sahel summit convened in July 2018, on the sidelines of the 31st AU summit, designated a new FC-G5S Force Cmmdr; in Jan. 2020, at a summit attended in Pau, France, by the G5 Sahel heads of state, Pres. Emmanuel Macron of France and the UN Sec.-Gen., a Niamey, Niger-based jt command mechanism was established between the FC-G5S and French Opération Barkhane (deployed in the region to support action against terrorist insurgencies); the strategic concept of operations of the FC-G5S was revised at that time; the meeting endorsed the establishment of a new Coalition for the Sahel, as a collaborative framework between the G5 Sahel and international partners to promote peace, stability and devt assistance throughout the sub-region; in March the Force initiated Operation Sama in the Sahel region; the 6th ordinary G5 Sahel summit, held in Feb., in Nouakchott, agreed to create a G5 Sahel Exec. Secretariat; the 7th summit was hosted by Chad, in N'Djamena, in Feb. 2021; in Feb. 2022 Pres. Macron announced that Opération Barkhane was to be withdrawn from Mali (this was undertaken by Aug.); Mali withdrew from the G5 Sahel in June; mems: Burkina Faso, Chad, Mauritania, Niger; Sec. ERIC YEMDAOGO TIARÉ.

Gulf of Guinea Commission (Commission du Golfe de Guinée—CGG): Largo Primeiro de Maio, Torres Dipanda, 9° Andar, Luanda, Angola; tel. 237-13-87; fax 233-76-61; e-mail cgg@cggrps.org; internet cggrps.org; f. 2001; aims to promote co-operation among mem. countries, and the peaceful and sustainable devt of natural resources in the sub-region; in June 2013 the CGG participated, with ECOWAS and CEEAC, in a regional summit on maritime safety and security, convened in Yaoundé, Cameroon, which adopted a Code of Conduct concerning the Prevention and Repression of Piracy, Armed

Robbery against Ships, and Illegal Maritime Activities in West and Central Africa; in Sept. 2014, under the auspices of the 3 orgs, an Inter-regional Coordination Centre for Maritime Safety and Security in Central and West Africa was inaugurated, in Yaoundé; mems: Angola, Cameroon, Democratic Rep. of Congo, Rep. of the Congo, Equatorial Guinea, Gabon, Nigeria, São Tomé and Príncipe; Exec. Sec. Florentina Adenike Ukonga (Nigeria).

International Conference on the Great Lakes Region (ICGLR) (Conference internationale sur la region des grands lacs): POB 7076, 38 blvd du Japon, Bujumbura, Burundi; tel. 22256824; fax 22256828; e-mail secretariat@icglr.org; internet www.icglr.org; f. 2006 following the signing of the Security, Stability and Development Pact for the Great Lakes Region at the 2nd summit meeting of the International Conference on the Great Lakes Region, held in Dec., in Nairobi, Kenya; the UN Security Council proposed in 2000 a Great Lakes Conference to initiate a process that would bring together regional leaders to pursue agreement on a set of principles and to articulate programmes of action to help to end the cycle of regional conflict and establish durable peace, stability, security, democracy and devt in the whole region; the inaugural summit meeting was convened in Dar es Salaam, Tanzania, in Nov. 2004; the Pact on Security, Stability and Development in the Great Lakes Region (adopted by ICGLR heads of state and govt in Dec. 2006; entered into force in June 2008) provides a legal framework for the org.'s activities; 10 protocols that were also adopted in 2006 address: democracy and good governance; judicial co-operation; non-aggression and mutual defence in the Great Lakes Region; the illegal exploitation of natural resources; the prevention of the crime of genocide, war crimes, crimes against humanity and all forms of discrimination; prevention and suppression of sexual violence against women and children; protection and assistance to IDPs; property rights of returning persons; and management of communication and information; the Executive Secretariat of the org. was inaugurated in May 2007 (main divisions and assoc. programmes of action: Peace and Security, Democracy and Good Governance, Economic Development and Regional Integration, Humanitarian and Social Issues, and Gender, Women and Children); subsidiary institutions incl. the Lusaka, Zambia-based ICGLR Levy Mwanawasa Regional Centre for Democracy and Good Governance; ICGLR Regional Training Facility (based in Kampala, Uganda, and focused on sensitizing police units, and judicial and other officials to addressing cases of sexual violence); Joint Intelligence Fusion Centre; Expanded Joint Verification Mechanism (Goma, Democratic Rep. of the Congo—DRC); monitors and investigates security incidents); and the Joint Follow-up Mechanism (Kasese, Uganda; comprises counter-terrorism experts); a Special Fund of Reconstruction and Development, hosted by the AfDB, was established in 2008; launched in 2009 the ICGLR Regional Initiative against the Illegal Exploitation of Natural Resources (known as the ICGLR RINR, and governed by a Regional Steering Cttee), which aims to break the link between revenues from illegal mining and the financing of rebel groups; in Dec. 2010 ICGLR heads of state and govt signed the Lusaka Declaration, identifying specific tools for the formation of an ICGLR RINR-related regional control mechanism, which incl. the establishment of an ICGLR Regional Certification Mechanism (ICGLR RCM) for natural resource supply chains (the RCM provides assurance to purchasers that gold, tantalum, tin and tungsten extracted in ICGLR mem. states have been sourced, transported, and exported legally); harmonization of national legislation; creation of a regional database on mineral flows; formalization of the artisanal mining sector; and establishment of a whistle-blowing mechanism; from 2012 the Conference worked to mediate between govt and rebel forces fighting in eastern DRC; agreement was reached in early Nov. to establish an Expanded Joint Verification Mechanism, to counter rebel groups fighting in that region; an emergency summit meeting was convened in Nov., in Kampala, Uganda, following the advance by the 23 March Movement ('M23') grouping to take control of the provincial capital, Goma; in Feb. 2013 the leaders of 11 African countries signed the Peace, Security and Cooperation Framework (PSCF) for the DRC and the Region, which aimed to stabilize the Great Lakes region; with the UN, the African Union and SADC, the ICGLR was tasked with guaranteeing the Framework; the signatories to the Framework committed to protect the future territorial sovereignty and the peace and stability of the DRC; an intervention brigade was mandated by the UN Security Council in the following month to target militias in eastern DRC; following the declaration by the M23, in early Nov., of the end of its rebellion in eastern DRC, a so-called Kampala dialogue was convened between the DRC Govt and the M23 leadership in Nov.–early Dec., culminating in the signing, under the auspices of the ICGLR and SADC, of final declarations by the parties, providing for, *inter alia,* an envisaged process of disarmament of former M23 combatants; in Jan. 2019 the ICGLR expressed concern at the outcome of the presidential part of a general election held on 30 Dec. 2018 in the DRC, and recommended a recount of votes cast; in mid-Jan. 2019, stating serious concern over the conformity of the official provisional result, the ICGLR, SADC

and AU determined to dispatch a jt high-level delegation to the DRC to liaise with national stakeholders on means of resolving the post-electoral crisis; soon afterwards, however, despite continuing evidence of irregularities in the electoral process, Félix Tshisekedi was declared the victor in the presidential poll and promptly inaugurated; 8th ordinary summit meeting was held in Nov. 2020, in a virtual format; a mini summit of heads of state held in April 2021 initiated a working group to draft recommendations to guide consultations with armed groups in the CAR; an ICGLR workshop organized in late Aug.–early Sept. prepared a series of recommendations on strengthening the implementation of the ICGLR RINR, incl. an emphasis on combating impunity for those engaged in natural resources-related crimes; adopted in mid-Sept. a roadmap towards achieving peace in the CAR; in Nov. issued a statement that welcomed the political agreement concluded between the General Commander of the Sudanese armed forces and head of that country's transitional govt that aimed to restore civilian rule (following a military coup perpetrated in Oct. against the transitional authorities); in April 2022 the ICGLR and other PSCF guarantors strongly condemned attacks in eastern DRC perpetrated by former M23 militants, urged them to silence their guns, and reiterated commitment to supporting progress towards peace in that country; COVID-19, HIV/AIDS, refugees, preventing sexual and gender-based violence, and promoting the disarmament, demobilization, and reintegration of former militants were cross-cutting themes of the ICGLR's activities in 2022; maintains centres in Goma, DRC, and Lusaka, Zambia; mems: Angola, Burundi, Central African Rep., Democratic Rep. of Congo, Rep. of the Congo, Kenya, Rwanda, South Sudan, Sudan, Tanzania, Uganda, Zambia; Exec. Sec. João Samuel Caholo (Angola).

Inter-Parliamentary Union (IPU): 5 chemin du Pommier, CP 330, 1218 Le Grand-Saconnex/Geneva, Switzerland; tel. 229194150; fax 229194160; e-mail postbox@mail.ipu.org; internet www.ipu.org; f. 1889; aims to promote peace, co-operation and representative democracy by providing a forum for multilateral political debate between representatives of national parliaments; Fifth World Conference of Speakers of Parliament was initiated as a virtual event in Aug. 2020 and was concluded in Vienna, hosted by the Austrian Govt, in Sept. 2021; mems: nat. parliaments of 178 sovereign states; 14 inter-parliamentary asscns as assoc. mems; Pres. Duarte Pacheco (Portugal); Sec.-Gen. Martin Chungong (Cameroon); publs *Annual Report, IPU Information Brochure* (annually), *Women in Parliament* (annually), *IPU Strategy.*

League of Arab States (Arab League): POB 11642, Arab League Bldg, Tahrir Sq., Cairo, Egypt; tel. (2) 575-0511; fax (2) 574-0331; e-mail communication.dept@las.int; internet www.lasportal.org; f. 1945; aims to strengthen mutual ties and to co-ordinate policies and activities to support the common good of all the Arab countries; mems: 22 states, incl. Comoros, Somalia, Sudan; Sec.-Gen. Ahmed Aboul Gheit (Egypt).

Organisation Internationale de la Francophonie (International Organization of La Francophonie—La Francophonie): 19–21 ave Bosquet, 75007 Paris, France; tel. 1-44-37-33-00; fax 1-45-79-14-98; internet www.francophonie.org; f. 1970 as l'Agence de coopération culturelle et technique; promotes co-operation among French-speaking countries in the areas of education, culture, peace and democracy, and technology; implements decisions of the Sommet francophone; technical and financial assistance supports projects in every mem. country, mainly to aid rural people; a Parliamentary Assembly of the Francophonie is also based in Paris; 17th summit was held in Yerevan, Armenia, in Oct. 2018; the 18th meeting was scheduled to be convened in Djerba, Tunisia, in Nov. 2022 (postponed from 2020); in Nov. 2020 Burundi was readmitted after a 4-year suspension; signed a Memorandum of Understanding with the World Health Org. in April 2021; in early June Mali was suspended from participation in the org. following the detention of that country's interim leaders by the military; mems: 54 mem. states and regional authorities, 27 countries with observer status and 7 assoc. mems; Sec.-Gen. Louise Mushikiwabo (Rwanda); publ. *Journal de l'Agence de la Francophonie* (quarterly).

Industrial and Professional Relations

African Regional Organization of ITUC (ITUC-Africa): Route Internationale d'Atakpamé, POB 44101, Lomé, Togo; tel. 225-07-10; fax 225-61-13; e-mail info@ituc-africa.org; internet www.ituc-africa .org; f. 2007; mems: 17m. workers and 101 affiliated trade unions in 51 African countries; Gen. Sec. Kwasi Adu-Amankwah (Ghana).

Business Africa: c/o Federation of Kenya Employers (MEF), Waajiri House, 48311-00100 Nairobi, Kenya; tel. (20) 2721929; fax (20)

2720295; e-mail info@businessafrica-emp.org; internet www
.businessafrica-emp.org; f. 1986, as Pan-African Employers' Confederation; organized inaugural Employers' Summit in May 2016;
mems: in 45 countries; Sec.-Gen. JACQUELINE MUGO (Kenya).

Organisation of African Trade Union Unity (OATUU): POB
M386, Accra, Ghana; tel. (30) 7011033; e-mail oatuughana@gmail
.com; internet oatuu.org; f. 1973 as a single continental trade union
org., independent of international trade union orgs; has affiliates
from all African trade unions. Congress, the supreme policymaking
body, is composed of 4 delegates per country from affiliated national
trade union centres, and meets at least every 4 years; the General
Council, composed of representatives from each affiliated trade
union, meets annually to implement Congress decisions and to
approve the annual budget; mems: 61 affiliated nat. trade union orgs
in 54 independent African countries; Sec.-Gen. AREZKI MEZHOUD
(Algeria); publ. *The African Worker*.

Law

African Intellectual Property Organization (Organisation Africaine de la Propriété Intellectuelle—OAPI): 158 pl. de la Prefecture,
Yaoundé, Cameroon; tel. 22-20-57-00; e-mail oapi@oapi.int; internet
www.oapi.int; f. 1962; supports the technological devt of mem. states
and promotes the application of patent rights; mems: 17 African
states; Dir-Gen. DENIS LOUKOU BOHOUSSOU (Côte d'Ivoire).

**African Society of International and Comparative Law
(ASICL):** Private Bag 520, Kairaba Ave, KSMD, Banjul, The
Gambia; tel. 375476; fax 375469; e-mail africansociety@aol.com;
f. 1986; promotes public education on law and civil liberties; aims to
provide a legal aid and advice system in each African country, and to
facilitate the exchange of information on civil liberties; publ. *African
Journal of International and Comparative Law* (quarterly).

Asian-African Legal Consultative Organization (AALCO): 29–
C, Rizal Marg, Diplomatic Enclave, Chanakyapuri, New Delhi
110021, India; tel. (11) 24197000; fax (11) 26117640; e-mail mail@
aalco.int; internet www.aalco.int; f. 1956; considers legal problems
referred to it by mem. countries and serves as a forum for Afro-Asian
co-operation in international law, including international trade law,
and economic relations; provides background material for confs,
prepares standard/model contract forms suited to the needs of the
region; promotes arbitration as a means of settling international
commercial disputes; trains officers of mem. states; has permanent
UN observer status; has established International Commercial
Arbitration Centres in Kuala Lumpur, Malaysia; Cairo, Egypt;
Lagos, Nigeria; and Tehran, Iran; mems: 47 countries; Sec.-Gen. Dr
KAMALINNE PINITPUVADOL (Thailand).

East African Court of Justice: EAC Headquarters, 1st Floor,
Africa Mashariki Rd, POB 1096, Arusha, Tanzania; tel. (27) 2506093;
fax (27) 2509493; e-mail eacj@eachq.org; internet eacj.org; f. 2001;
established under the Treaty for the Establishment of the East
African Community (EAC) with responsibility for ensuring compliance with the Treaty; Pres. Justice NESTOR KAYOBERA; Registrar
YUFNALIS N. OKUBO (Kenya).

International Criminal Police Organization (INTERPOL):
200 quai Charles de Gaulle, 69006 Lyon, France; tel. 4-72-44-70-
00; fax 4-72-44-71-63; internet www.interpol.int; f. 1923, reconstituted 1946; promotes co-operation and mutual assistance between
police forces in different countries; centralizes records and information on international criminals; operates a global police communications network linking all mem. countries; co-ordinates and
supports international law enforcement operations; in June 2021
est. I-Familia—a global dna kinship matching database, aimed at
advancing the identification of missing persons; provides targeted
training to police around the world; holds a General Assembly
annually (2022: New Delhi, India, in Oct.), and organizes regular
regional meetings; mems: 195 countries; Pres. Maj.-Gen. AHMED
NASSER AL-RAISI (United Arab Emirates); Sec.-Gen. JÜRGEN STOCK
(Germany); publ. *Annual Report*.

International Development Law Organization (IDLO): Viale
Vaticano 106, 00165 Rome, Italy; tel. (06) 40403200; fax (06)
40403232; e-mail info@idlo.int; internet www.idlo.int; f. 1983;
enables govts and empowers people to reform laws and strengthen
institutions to promote peace, justice, sustainable devt and economic
opportunities; provides technical legal assistance and capacity devt
at national and local level; activities include Policy Dialogues,
Technical Assistance, Global Network of Alumni and Partners,
Training Programs, Research and Publs; maintains a branch office in
The Hague, Netherlands, and field offices for Afghanistan, Kenya,
Kyrgyzstan, Mongolia, South Sudan and Tajikistan; mems: 37
parties; Dir-Gen. JAN BEAGLE (New Zealand).

International Tribunal for the Law of the Sea (Tribunal international du droit de la mer): Am Internationalen Seegerichtshof 1,
22609 Hamburg, Germany; tel. (40) 35607-0; fax (40) 35607-275;
e-mail itlos@itlos.org; internet www.itlos.org; f. 1996; responsible for
interpreting the UN Convention on the Law of the Sea (UNCLOS)
and adjudicating disputes brought by states parties to the Convention on matters within its jurisdiction; in Jan. 2021 (in the context of a
maritime border dispute between the Maldives and Mauritius) the
Tribunal ruled that the Chagos Archipelago came under the
sovereignty of Mauritius, and concluded that the United Kingdom
was unlawfully occupying the islands—confirming a previous
related ruling of the International Court of Justice and resolution
of the UN General Assembly; 21 judges; Pres. ALBERT J. HOFFMANN
(South Africa); Registrar XIMENA HINRICHS OYARCE (Chile).

Permanent Court of Arbitration: Peace Palace, Carnegieplein 2,
2517 KJ, The Hague, Netherlands; tel. (70) 3024165; fax (70)
3024167; e-mail bureau@pca-cpa.org; internet pca-cpa.org; f. 1899
(by the Convention for the Pacific Settlement of International
Disputes); provides for the resolution of disputes involving combin-
ations of states, private parties and intergovernmental orgs, under
its own rules of procedure, by means of arbitration, conciliation and
fact-finding; also develops model state contracts, for example for
projects relating to infrastructure and natural resources; operates a
secretariat, the International Bureau, which has provided registry
services and legal support to ad hoc tribunals and commissions, incl.
the Eritrea–Ethiopia Boundary Commission, f. in Dec. 2000, to rule
on the demarcation of the Eritrea–Ethiopia border, in accordance
with a peace accord that ended the 1998–2000 active Eritrea–
Ethiopia conflict; in April 2002 the Boundary Commission issued a
'final and binding' verdict, awarding territory to both parties;
Ethiopia, however, refused at that time to accept the Commission's
designation of the border town of Badme as Eritrean; in Nov. 2006 the
Commission stated that should no final agreement on border
demarcation be reached between the two parties by Nov. 2007, the
boundary would stand as directed by an annex to the statement; on
30 Nov. 2007, no such agreement having been reached, the boundary
outlined in the annex became binding; on 5 June 2018 the
administration of the recently elected Ethiopian Prime Minister
Abiy Ahmed Ali agreed that it would fully accept and implement a
peace arrangement with Eritrea based on the Commission's rulings,
incl. the transfer of the disputed town of Badme to Eritrea; mems:
govts of 122 countries; Sec.-Gen. Dr MARCIN PIOTR CZEPELAK
(Poland).

Medicine and Health

Global Fund to Fight AIDS, Tuberculosis and Malaria: Global
Health Campus, 40 chemin de Pommier, 1218 Grand-Saconnex
Geneva, Switzerland; tel. 587911700; e-mail website@
theglobalfund.org; internet www.theglobalfund.org; f. 2002; the
Global Fund operates as a partnership between govts, the private
sector, civil society and local communities; it mobilizes and invests
funds to support countries to implement disease prevention programmes, as well as to treat and care for people affected by the
diseases; in Sept. 2022 the 7th donor replenishment conf., held at the
UN's headquarters in New York, USA, generated pledged contributions of more than US $14,250m. for the 3-year period 2022–25; Exec.
Dir PETER SANDS (UK).

Organisation panafricaine de lutte contre le SIDA (OPALS):
15–21 rue de L'École de Médecine, 75006 Paris, France; tel. 1-43-26-
72-28; internet www.opals.asso.fr; f. 1988; disseminates information
relating to the treatment and prevention of AIDS; provides training
of medical personnel; promotes co-operation between African medical centres and specialized centres in the USA and Europe; Pres.
Prof. MARC GENTILINI (France); Exec. Dir GEOFFROY BESSAUD.

**Organization for Co-ordination in the Struggle against
Endemic Diseases in Central Africa** (Organisation de
coordination pour la lutte contre les endémies en Afrique Centrale—OCEAC): BP 288, Yaoundé, Cameroon; tel. 222-23-22-32;
fax 222-23-00-61; e-mail contact@oceac.org; internet www.oceac
.org; f. 1965; aims to standardize methods of controlling endemic
diseases, to co-ordinate national action, and to negotiate programmes of assistance and training on a regional scale; mems:
Cameroon, Central African Rep., Chad, Rep. of the Congo, Equatorial
Guinea, Gabon; Exec. Sec. Dr CONSTANT ROGER AYENENGOYE; publ.
Bulletin de Liaison et de Documentation (quarterly).

Société de neuro-chirurgie de langue française (Society of
French-speaking Neuro-Surgeons): e-mail elazhari.a@gmail.com;
internet www.snclf.org; f. 1949; holds annual convention and
congress; mems: 450; Pres. PHILIPPE CORNU (France); Sec.-Gen.
ABDESSAMAD EL AZHARI (Morocco); publ. *Neurochirurgie* (6 a year).

Posts and Telecommunications

Regional African Satellite Communications System (RAS-COM): 2 ave Thomasset, BP 3628, Abidjan 01, Côte d'Ivoire; tel. 20-22-36-83; fax 20-22-36-76; e-mail rascomps@africaonline.co.ci; internet www.rascom.org; f. 1992; aims to provide telecommunications facilities to African countries; supports a regional satellite communication system; mems: 45 African countries.

Southern African Telecommunications Association (SATA): Av. Martires de Inhaminga 170–3, POB 2677, Maputo, Mozambique; tel. 21302195; fax 21431288; e-mail sata@sata-sec.net; internet www.sata-sec.net; f. 1980; aims to improve regional co-operation among mems of the Southern Africa Development Community and to address common issues in the telecommunications industry; mems: 17 regional telecommunications cos; Exec. Sec. and CEO JACOB MUNODAWAFA (Zimbabwe).

Press, Radio and Television

African Union of Broadcasting (AUB): ave Carde, Immeuble CSS, 1 étage, BP 3237, Dakar, Senegal; tel. 33-821-16-25; fax 33-821-59-70; e-mail contact@uar-aub.org; internet www.uar-aub.org; f. Nov. 2006, superseding the Union of National Radio and Television Organizations of Africa (f. 1962); co-ordinates radio and television services, including monitoring and frequency allocation, the exchange of information and coverage of national and international events among African countries; mems: 50 orgs and 6 assoc. mems; CEO GRÉGOIRE NDJAKA (Cameroon).

Federation of African Journalists (FAJ): Maison de la Presse 5, rte de la Corniche 0, Médina, Dakar, Senegal; internet www.africanjournalists.org; f. 2007; defends the freedom of the press, and addresses professional issues affecting journalists; supports a network encompassing the West African Journalists Association, the Southern African Journalists Association, the Eastern African Journalists Association, the Association of Media Professionals Unions of Central Africa, and the Network of North African Journalists; Pres. ABDULWAHEED ODUSILE (Nigeria).

International Council of French-speaking Radio and Television Organizations (Conseil international des radios-télévisions d'expression française): 52 blvd Auguste-Reyers, 1044 Brussels, Belgium; tel. (2) 732-45-85; fax (2) 732-62-40; e-mail cirteff@rtbf.be; internet cirtef.com; f. 1978; mems: 50 orgs and 2 assoc. mems; Sec.-Gen. LOÏC CRESPIN.

International Federation of Journalists (IFJ): 155 rue de la Loi, 1040 Brussels, Belgium; tel. (2) 235-22-00; fax (2) 235-22-19; e-mail ifj@ifj.org; internet www.ifj.org; f. 1926; aims to improve the working conditions of journalists and the quality of journalism through training progs and advocacy campaigns in the defence of rights related to the media; conducts international campaigns on journalists' safety, press freedom, public service values, editorial independence, ethics, gender equality, children's rights, tolerance and the right to decent working conditions; maintains 5 regional offices; mems: 187 trade unions and assocs in more than 140 countries; Pres. DOMINIQUE PRADALIÉ (France); Gen. Sec. ANTHONY BELLANGER.

Southern African Broadcasting Association (SABA): Windhoek, Namibia; tel. (61) 2912068; e-mail sabanews@hotmail.co.uk; f. 1993; promotes quality public broadcasting; facilitates training of broadcasters at all levels; co-ordinates broadcasting activities in the SADC region; organizes radio news exchange service; produces television and radio progs; Pres. STANLEY BENJAMIN SIMILO.

Religion

All Africa Conference of Churches (AACC): Waiyaki Way, POB 14205, 00800 Westlands, Nairobi, Kenya; tel. (20) 4441483; e-mail secretariat@aacc-ceta.org; internet www.aacc-ceta.org; f. 1963; an organ of co-operation and continuing fellowship among Protestant, Orthodox and independent churches and Christian Councils in Africa; 11th Assembly: Kigali, Rwanda, in June 2018; mems: 152 churches and affiliated Christian Councils in 39 African countries; Gen. Sec. Rev. Dr FIDON MWOMBEKI (Tanzania).

Muslim World League (MWL) (Rabitat al-Alam al-Islami): POB 537, Makkah, Saudi Arabia; tel. (12) 5309444; fax (12) 5601319; e-mail info@themwl.org; internet www.themwl.org; f. 1962; aims to advance Islamic unity and solidarity, and to promote world peace and respect for human rights; provides financial assistance for education, medical care and relief work; organized an international conf. in March 2017 on 'Ideological trends between freedom of expression and the rulings of *Shari'a* (Islamic law)'; in April 2020 donated US $1m. to assist the UN Relief and Works Agency for Palestinian Refugees in the Near East's operations to manage local impacts of the COVID-19 pandemic; 44 offices worldwide, 3 councils, 3 subsidiary bodies; Sec.-Gen. Dr MOHAMMED BIN ABDULKARIM AL-ESSA; publs *Al-Rabita Arabic*, *Muslim World League Journal* (monthly, English and Arabic).

World Council of Churches (WCC): 150 route de Ferney, Postfach 2100, 1211 Geneva 2, Switzerland; tel. 227916111; fax 227910361; e-mail info@wcc-coe.org; internet www.oikoumene.org; f. 1948 to promote co-operation between Christian Churches and to prepare for a clearer manifestation of the unity of the Church; activities are grouped under the following programmes: Unity, Mission and Ecumenical Relations; Public Witness and *Diakonia*; and Ecumenical Formation; holds Assembly normally every 8 years; 11th Assembly: Karlsruhe, Germany, in Aug.–Sept. 2022; mems: 350 Churches in more than 110 countries; Gen. Sec. Rev. Prof. Dr IOAN SAUCA (Romania) (acting, until 31 Dec. 2022), Rev. Prof. Dr JERRY PILLAY (South Africa) (from 1 Jan. 2023); publs *Current Dialogue* (2 a year), *Ecumenical Review* (quarterly), *International Review of Mission* (quarterly).

Science

African Minerals and Geosciences Centre: POB 9573, Dar es Salaam, Tanzania; tel. (22) 2650-347; fax (22) 2650-319; e-mail seamic@seamic.org; internet www.seamic.org; f. 1977 (as the Southern and Eastern Mineral Centre—SEAMIC, membership limited to Eastern and Southern African countries until 2007; subsequently opened to all African countries, present name adopted in 2015) to promote socioeconomic and environmentally responsible mineral sector devt in the region and to provide advisory and consultancy services in the fields of the geosciences, mineral mining and mineral processing; provides advisory and consultancy services in exploration geology, geophysics, geochemistry, mining and mineral processing; archives and processes geospatial data; organizes training courses in the areas of geoinformatics; provides minerals related specialized laboratory services; mems: Angola, Comoros, Ethiopia, Kenya, Mozambique, Tanzania, Sudan, Uganda; Dir-Gen. IBRAHIM SHADDAD (Sudan); publ. *Seamic Newsletter* (2 a year).

Association for Tropical Biology and Conservation (ATBC): POB 13916, Gainesville, FL 32604, USA; e-mail director@tropicalbio.org; internet tropicalbiology.org; f. 1963 as the Asscn for Tropical Biology, present name adopted in 2002; aims to promote research and to foster exchange of ideas among biologists working in tropical environments; holds annual Congress (2022: Cartagena, Colombia, in July); mems: 900 in 65 countries; Pres. BETH KAPLIN (USA); Exec. Dir LÚCIA G. LOHMANN; publ. *Biotropica* (2 a year).

United Nations University Institute for Natural Resources in Africa (UNU/INRA): International House, Annie Jiagge Rd, University of Ghana, Legon, Accra, Ghana; tel. (30) 2213850; fax (30) 2500396; e-mail inra@unu.edu; internet inra.unu.edu; f. 1986 as a research and training centre of the United Nations University (Tokyo, Japan); operational since 1990; aims at human resource devt and institutional capacity building through co-ordination with African universities and research institutes in advanced research, training and dissemination of knowledge and information on the conservation and management of Africa's natural resources and their rational utilization for sustainable devt; has operating units in Cameroon, Côte d'Ivoire, Namibia, Senegal and Zambia; Dir Dr FATIMA DENTON; publ. *Annual Report*.

Social Sciences

African Centre for Applied Research and Training in Social Development (ACARTSOD): Africa Centre, Wahda Quarter, Zawia Rd, POB 80606, Tripoli, Libya; tel. (21) 4835103; fax (21) 4835066; e-mail fituri_acartsod@hotmail.com; f. 1977 under the jt auspices of the ECA and OAU (now AU); aims to promote and co-ordinate applied research and training in social devt, and to assist in formulating national devt strategies; Exec. Dir Dr AHMED SAID FITURI.

Council for the Development of Social Science Research in Africa (CODESRIA): ave Cheikh, Anta Diop X Canal IV, BP 3304, CP 18524, Dakar, Senegal; tel. 33-825-98-22; fax 33-825-12-89; internet www.codesria.org; f. 1973; promotes research, organizes confs, working groups and information services; mems: research institutes and univ. faculties and researchers in African countries; Pres. ISABEL CASIMIRO (Mozambique); Exec. Sec. Dr GODWIN MURUNGA (Kenya); publs *Africa Development* (quarterly), *CODESRIA Bulletin* (quarterly), *African Journal of International Affairs* (2 a year), *Journal of African Transformation* (2 a year), *African*

Sociological Review (2 a year), *Afrika Zamani* (annually), *Identity, Culture and Politics* (2 a year), *Afro-Arab Selections for Social Sciences* (annually), directories of research.

International African Institute (IAI): School of Oriental and African Studies, Thornhaugh St, Russell Sq., London, WC1H 0XG, United Kingdom; tel. (20) 7898-4420; e-mail iai@soas.ac.uk; internet www.internationalafricaninstitute.org; f. 1926; established to promote the study of African peoples, their languages, cultures and social life in their traditional and modern settings; organizes an international seminar prog. bringing together scholars from Africa and elsewhere; links scholars in order to facilitate research projects, especially in the social sciences; Chair. Prof. ALCINDA HONWANA; publs *Africa* (quarterly), *Africa Bibliography* (annually).

Southern African Research and Documentation Centre (SARDC): 15 Downie Ave, POB 5690, Harare, Zimbabwe; tel. (4) 791141; e-mail sardc@sardc.net; internet www.sardc.net; f. 1985; aims to enhance and disseminate information on political, economic, environmental, cultural and social developments in southern Africa; Chair. Prof. PETER H. KATJAVIVI; publs *Southern Africa Today*, *The Zambezi*.

Social Welfare and Human Rights

Amnesty International: 1 Easton St, London, WC1X ODW, United Kingdom; tel. (20) 7413-5500; fax (20) 7956-1157; e-mail contactus@amnesty.org; internet www.amnesty.org; f. 1961; an independent, democratic, self-governing worldwide movement of people who campaign for internationally recognized human rights, such as those enshrined in the Universal Declaration of Human Rights; undertakes research and action focused on preventing and ending grave abuses of the rights to physical and mental integrity, freedom of conscience and expression, and freedom from discrimination, within the context of its work impartially to promote and protect all human rights; major policy decisions are taken by an International Council comprising representatives from all nat. sections; financed by donations; no funds are sought or accepted from govts; mems: more than 7m. individuals; nationally organized sections in 70 countries and pre-section co-ordinating structures in another 22 countries; Sec.-Gen. AGNES CALLAMARD (France); publs *Annual Report*, *International Newsletter* (monthly), *The Wire* (quarterly), country reports.

International Federation of Red Cross and Red Crescent Societies (IFRC): POB 303, 1211 Geneva 19, Switzerland; tel. 227304222; fax 227304200; e-mail secretariat@ifrc.org; internet www.ifrc.org; f. 1919; aims to prevent and alleviate human suffering; conducts relief operations for refugees and victims of disasters, co-ordinates relief supplies and assists in disaster prevention; supports humanitarian activities by national Red Cross and Red Crescent societies; pan-African conferences of national Red Cross and Red Crescent societies are convened every 4 years under the joint auspices of the IFRC and the host government (9th conf.: Abidjan, Côte d'Ivoire, in April 2017); mems: 190 nat. socs; Pres. FRANCESCO ROCCA (Italy); Sec.-Gen. JAGAN CHAPAGAIN (Nepal); publs *Annual Report*, *Red Cross Red Crescent* (quarterly), *Weekly News*, *World Disasters Report*, *Emergency Appeal*.

Médecins Sans Frontières (MSF): 78 rue de Lausanne, CP 116, 1211 Geneva 21, Switzerland; tel. 228498484; fax 228498488; e-mail office-gva@geneva.msf.org; internet www.msf.org; f. 1971; independent medical humanitarian org. composed of physicians and other mems of the medical profession; aims to provide medical assistance to victims of war and natural disasters; operates longer-term progs of nutrition, immunization, sanitation, public health, and rehabilitation of hospitals and dispensaries; awarded the Nobel Peace Prize in 1999; in mid-2014, in response to the most intensive outbreak of Ebola Virus Disease (EVD) hitherto recorded, in Guinea, Liberia and Sierra Leone opened EVD treatment centres in Guéckédou, Guinea, and in Kailahun, Sierra Leone; mounted a response also to the EVD emergency that emerged in North Kivu and Ituri, DRC, from Aug. 2018; in 2020 MSF initiated new projects and adapted existing progs to respond to the COVID-19 pandemic; priority areas of focus included the protection of most at-risk and otherwise vulnerable people, including in countries with systemically fragile health provision, and protecting healthcare workers; mems: 24 asscns in more than 69 countries worldwide; Int. Pres. Dr CHRISTOS CHRISTOU (Greece); publs *International Activity Report* (annually), *Dispatches* (quarterly).

Mixed Migration Centre: 23 ave de France, Geneva, Switzerland; e-mail info@mixedmigration.org; internet www.mixedmigration.org; f. 2011 to provide assistance to agencies and institutions with the management of mixed migration; conducts research and analysis on migration flows and estimates (incl. through the Mixed Migration Monitoring Mechanism initiative—the 4Mi), and co-ordinates humanitarian assistance; aims to stimulate debate and foster policy

devt on mixed migration; regional hubs provide focused research, and cover Asia, East Africa and Yemen, Europe, Latin America and the Caribbean, the Middle East, North Africa, and West Africa; Head BRAM FROUWS; publs *Mixed Migration Review* (annually), research papers, thematic reports.

Shack/Slum Dwellers International (SDI): POB 13033, Mowbray, 7705 Cape Town, South Africa; tel. (21) 4474016; fax (21) 4482434; e-mail info@sdinet.org; internet sdinet.org; f. 1996; a transnational network of local shack/slum dweller orgs; mems: community-based orgs in 32 countries; Chair. JOSEPH MUTURI (Kenya); Sec. EMILY MOHOHLO (South Africa).

Sightsavers: Bumpers Way, Bumpers Farm, Chippenham, Wiltshire, SN14 6NG; tel. (1444) 446600; e-mail info@sightsavers.org; internet www.sightsavers.org; f. 1950; name changed from Royal Commonwealth Society for the Blind to present name in 1986; works to prevent blindness and restore sight in developing countries, and to provide education and community-based training for incurably blind people; operates in collaboration with local partners in some 30 developing countries, with high priority given to training local staff; Chair. Sir CLIVE JONES (UK); publ. *Sightsavers News*.

Union Africaine de la Mutualité (African Union of Mutuals): rue Aram, Lot 14, Secteur 7, Hay Riad, Rabat, Morocco; tel. and fax (5) 37570988; internet www.uam.org.ma; f. 2007; promotes co-operation among African companies concerned with health care and social insurance; mems: 40 orgs in 17 African countries; Pres. ABDELMOULA ABDELMOUMNI (Morocco); Sec.-Gen. CLARISSE KAYO MAHI (Côte d'Ivoire).

Sport and Recreations

Confederation of African Football (Confédération africaine de football—CFA): 3 Abdel Khalek Sarwat St, El Hay El Motamayez, POB 23, 6th October City, Egypt; tel. (2) 38247272; fax (2) 38247274; internet www.cafonline.com; f. 1957; promotes football in Africa; organizes inter-club competitions and Cup of Nations (2022: Cameroon, in Jan.–Feb.); General Assembly held every 2 years; mems: nat. asscns in 54 countries; Pres. PATRICE MOTSEPE (South Africa); Sec.-Gen. VERON MOSENGO-OMBA (Democratic Republic of the Congo); publ. *CAF News* (quarterly).

Fédération Internationale de Football Association (FIFA) (International Federation of Association Football): FIFA-Str. 20, POB 8044, Zürich, Switzerland; tel. 432227777; fax 432227878; internet www.fifa.com; f. 1904; aims to promote the game of association football and foster friendly relations among players and national asscns; to control football and uphold the laws of the game as laid down by the International Football Association Board; to prevent discrimination of any kind between players; and to provide arbitration in disputes between national asscns; organizes several global competitions, most notably the FIFA World Cup, held every 4 years (2022: Qatar, in Nov.–Dec.); the FIFA Congress meets annually; the Fed.'s 37-mem. Council is the main decision making body between meetings of the Congress; in Jan. 2017 the FIFA Council determined to expand participation in the FIFA World Cup to 48 teams (from 32) with effect from 2026; a proposal to bring this forward with effect from the Qatar tournament in 2022 was rejected in May 2019; the 68th Congress, held in June 2018, determined that the 2026 World Cup would be held in Canada, the USA and Mexico; in Feb. 2022, in response to the Russian Fed.'s military invasion of Ukraine, FIFA and UEFA jtly suspended Russian national and club teams from participation in international competition football; FIFA Women's World Cup 2023 (the 9th edition of the tournament) was to be jtly hosted, in July–Aug., by Australia and New Zealand; mems: 211 nat. asscns, 6 continental confeds (the nat. asscns of Kenya and Zimbabwe were suspended from Feb. 2022, in response to alleged third party interference in their operations); Pres. GIANNI INFANTINO (Switzerland); Sec.-Gen. FATMA SAMBA DIOUF SAMOURA (Senegal); publs *FIFA News* (monthly), *FIFA Magazine* (every 2 months), *FIFA Directory* (annually), *Laws of the Game* (annually), *Competitions' Regulations*, *Technical Reports* (before and after FIFA competitions).

International Association of Athletics Federations (IAAF): 6–8 Quai Antoine 1er, BP 359, 98007 Monte Carlo Cedex, Monaco; tel. 93-10-88-88; fax 93-15-95-15; e-mail info@iaaf.org; internet www.iaaf.org; f. 1912 (as International Amateur Athletic Fed.) to ensure co-operation and fairness and to combat discrimination in athletics; present name adopted in 2001; compiles athletic competition rules and organizes championships at all levels; frames regulations for the establishment of world, Olympic and other athletic records; settles disputes between mems; affiliates national governing bodies; and conducts a programme of devt including courses for coaching, judging and other aspects of the sport; Congress convenes every 2 years, prior to the World Championships (2019: Doha, Qatar, in Oct.); in Nov. 2015 a report of an independent commission established by the World Anti-Doping Agency criticized the IAAF for failing to implement adequate anti-doping measures, thus enabling many athletes in violation of drug rules to compete in major athletic tournaments during the period 2001–12; the Russian Athletics Federation (RusAF) was provisionally suspended in Nov. 2015 by the IAAF Council, having been declared non-compliant with the provisions of the World Anti-Doping Code; a 2nd report, issued in Jan. 2016, made several serious allegations against the IAAF, including corrupt practices at the highest level under its previous presidency; in June, in advance of the Summer Olympic Games (held in Aug.) RusAF's suspension from the IAAF was prolonged; prospective Russian participants in the Games were required, therefore, to demonstrate individually their drug-free status; mems: nat. asscns in 214 countries and territories; Pres. Lord SEBASTIAN COE (UK); publs *IAAF Handbook* (every 2 years), *IAAF Statistical Book* (2 a year), *IAAF Directory* (annually), *IAAF Lists* (annually), *New Studies in Athletics* (quarterly).

International Automobile Federation (Fédération Internationale de l'Automobile—FIA): 8 pl. de la Concorde, 75008 Paris, France; tel. 1-43-12-44-55; fax 1-43-12-44-66; internet www.fia.com; f. 1904; manages world motor sport and organizes international championships; also campaigns to improve road safety and to reduce road fatalities globally through FIA Action for Road Safety; promotes sustainable motoring through FIA Action for Environment; promotes women's participation in motor sport; and campaigns against the use of prohibited drugs in motor sport; in May 2018 concluded an MoU with the World Bank and the International Transport Forum to establish the first regional Road Safety Observatory in Africa; mems: more than 244 motoring and motor sport clubs and asscns in 146 countries; Pres. MOHAMMED BEN SULAYEM (UAE); Sec.-Gen. (Sport) PETER BAYER; Sec.-Gen. (Mobility) ONIKA MILLER (acting).

International Cricket Council: POB 500070, St 69, Dubai Sports City, Emirates Rd, Dubai, United Arab Emirates; tel. (4) 382-8800; fax (4) 382-8600; e-mail enquiry@icc-cricket.com; internet www.icc-cricket.com; f. 1909; the governing body for international cricket; mems: 12 full mems, 94 assoc mems; Chair. GREG BARCLAY (New Zealand); CEO GEOFF ALLARDICE (Australia); publs *Annual Report*, *Playing Handbook* (annually).

International Olympic Committee (IOC): Château de Vidy, 1001 Lausanne, Switzerland; tel. 216216111; fax 216216718; internet www.olympic.org; f. 1894 to ensure the regular celebration of the Olympic Games; the IOC is the supreme authority on all questions concerning the Olympic Games and the Olympic movement; established the independent World Anti-Doping Agency (WADA) in 1999; Olympic Games are held every 4 years—winter games 2022: Beijing, People's Rep. of China, 2026: Milan and Cortina d'Ampezzo, Italy; summer games 2020: Tokyo, Japan (rescheduled owing to the COVID-19 pandemic, and held in July–Aug. 2021), 2024: Paris, France; mems: 206 national Olympic cttees; Pres. THOMAS BACH (Germany); publs *Newsletter* (weekly), *Olympic Review* (quarterly).

Technology

African Regional Centre for Technology: Imm. Fahd, 17th Floor, blvd Djilly Mbaye, BP 2435, Dakar, Senegal; tel. 33-823-77-12; fax 33-823-77-13; e-mail arct@orange.sn; internet www.crat-arct .org; f. 1977; aims to encourage the devt of indigenous technology and to improve the terms of access to imported technology; assists the establishment of national centres; mems: govts of 31 countries.

Regional Centre for Mapping of Resources for Development (RCMRD): POB 632, 00618 Ruaraka, Nairobi, Kenya; tel. (20) 2680748; fax (20) 2680747; e-mail rcmrd@rcmrd.org; internet www.rcmrd.org; f. 1975, present name adopted in 1997; provides services for the professional techniques of map-making and the application of satellite and remote sensing data in resource analysis and devt planning; undertakes research and provides advisory services to African govts; mems: 20 signatory govts; Dir-Gen. Dr EMMANUEL NKURUNZIZA (Rwanda).

Regional Centre for Training in Aerospace Surveys (RECTAS) (Centre Regional de Formations aux Techniques des leves aerospatiaux): PMB 5545, Ile-Ife, Nigeria; tel. (708) 2869-116; e-mail adewaleakingbade@gmail.com; internet www.rectas.org; f. 1972; provides training, research and advisory services in aerospace surveys and geoinformatics; administered by the ECA; mems: 8 govts; Exec. Dir Dr A. O. AKINGBADE (Nigeria).

Tourism

Africa Tourism Association (ATA): 99 Wall St, 1855, New York, NY 10036 USA; tel. (917) 745-5310; e-mail info@ataww.org; internet www.africatourismassociation.org; f. 1975, as the Africa Travel Association; aims to promote travel and tourism to Africa and to

strengthen intra-Africa partnerships; holds an annual World Tourism Conference and Presidential Forums on Tourism; in 2010 signed a Memorandum of Understanding with the African Union; mems: 20 corps, 12 nat., and 40 allied cos.

Kavango Zambezi Transfrontier Conservation Area (KAZA TFCA): POB 821, Kasane, Botswana; tel. 6251332; internet www .kavangozambezi.org; f. 2011, having been developed under the auspices of the Southern Africa Development Community; promotes the sustainable management of the Kavango Zambezi ecosystem, the transfrontier conservation area's cultural heritage, and local tourism; mems: Angola, Botswana, Namibia, Zambia, Zimbabwe.

World Indigenous Tourism Alliance (WINTA): 1 Manapouri Lane, Aotea, Porirua, 5024 New Zealand; tel. (21) 402419; e-mail secretariat@winta.org; internet www.winta.org; f. 2012; provides a forum for Indigenous groups to share experiences and protect and promote their interests within the tourism industry; aims to advocate in support of Indigenous peoples wishing to develop responses to issues and opportunities arising from existing and proposed tourism devts and trends of global interest; 2nd biennial World Indigenous Tourism Summit: Perth, Australia, in Nov. 2021; Chair. BEN SHERMAN.

Trade and Industry

African Organisation for Standardization (ARSO): POB 57363-00200, Nairobi, Kenya; tel. (20) 2224561; e-mail info@arso-oran.org; internet www.arso-oran.org; f. 1977; promotes standardization and conformity assessment in Africa, and co-ordinates participation in international standardization activities; mems: 37 African states; Pres. CHARLES BOOTO À NGON (Cameroon); Sec.-Gen. Dr HERMOGÈNE NSENGIMANA (Rwanda); publs *African Standardization Watch* (quarterly), *ARSO Catalogue of Regional Standards* (annually), *ARSO Annual Report*.

African Regional Intellectual Property Organization (ARIPO): 11 Natal Rd, Belgravia, POB 4228, Harare, Zimbabwe; tel. (4) 79406568; fax (4) 794072; e-mail mail@aripo.org; internet www.aripo.org; f. 1976; grants patents, registers industrial designs, utility models, trademarks, traditional knowledge, promotes copyright and promotes devt and harmonization of laws concerning industrial property; mems: Botswana, Cabo Verde, Eswatini, The Gambia, Ghana, Kenya, Lesotho, Liberia, Malawi, Mauritius, Mozambique, Namibia, Rwanda, São Tomé and Príncipe, Seychelles, Sierra Leone, Somalia, Sudan, Tanzania, Uganda, Zambia, Zimbabwe; Dir-Gen. BEMANYA TWEBAZE (Uganda); publs *ARIPO Magazine* (quarterly), *Journal* (monthly).

African Water and Sanitation Association (AfWASA): 05 BP 1910, Abidjan 05, Côte d'Ivoire; tel. 22-49-96-11; fax 21-24-26-29; e-mail contact@afwa-hq.org; internet www.afwa-hq.org; f. 1980 as the Union of African Water Suppliers; restructured and renamed the African Water Association in 2003, present name adopted in 2021; facilitates co-operation between public and private bodies concerned with water supply and sewage management in Africa; promotes the study of economic, technical and scientific matters relating to the industry; encourages the exchange of information on methods, processes and procedures of drinking water production, supply and sanitation; a Scientific and Technical Council meets 2–3 times a year; Congress normally held every 2 years (20th: Kampala, Uganda, in Feb. 2020; 21st scheduled to be held in Abidjan, in Feb. 2023); mems: 205 orgs, institutes or cos working in the sector in 41 countries; Exec. Dir SYLVAIN USHER; publ. *AFWA News Magazine* (quarterly).

Association of Power Utilities of Africa (APUA): Abidjan, Côte d'Ivoire; tel. 22-51-61-00; fax 22-51-61-19; e-mail secgen@apua-asea .org; internet www.apua-asea.org/updea/ang; f. 1970 (as the Union of Producers, Conveyors and Distributors of Electric Power in Africa, present name adopted in 2012); aims to study tech. matters and to promote efficient devt of enterprises in this sector; operates training school in Côte d'Ivoire; holds annual congress (2022: Dakar, Senegal, in July); mems: 58 active and 27 affiliate cos in 42 countries; Pres. PAPA MADEMBA BITEYE (Senegal); Dir-Gen. ABEL DIDIER TELLA; publs *UPDEA News Bulletin*, technical papers.

Federation of West African Chambers of Commerce and Industry (FEWACCI): 101 Yakubu Gowon Cres., Asokoro District, PMB 401, Abuja, Nigeria; tel. 7035130060; e-mail info@fewacci.com; internet www.fewacci.com; f. 1974; brings together the National Chambers of Commerce of ECOWAS mem. states; Pres. FAMAN TOURE (Côte d'Ivoire).

Southern African Customs Union (SACU): Private Bag 13285, Windhoek, Namibia; tel. (61) 2958000; fax (61) 245611; e-mail info@sacu.int; internet www.sacu.int; f. 1910, later reconstituted by new SACU Agreements signed in 1969 and 2002; provides common pool of customs, excise and sales duties, according to the relative volume of trade and production in each country; goods are traded within the union free of duty and quotas, subject to certain protective measures for less developed mems; the Customs Union Commission meets quarterly in each of the mems' capital cities in turn; mems: Botswana, Eswatini, Lesotho, Namibia, South Africa; Exec. Sec. PAULINA MBALA ELAGO.

Transport

African Airlines Association: POB 20116, Nairobi 00200, Kenya; tel. (20) 2320144; fax (20) 6001173; e-mail afraa@afraa.org; internet www.afraa.org; f. 1968; aims to give African air companies expert advice in technical, financial, juridical and market matters; to improve air transport in Africa through inter-carrier co-operation; and to develop manpower resources; mems: 45 nat. carriers, representing 85% of African airlines; Pres. (2022) KANE IBRAHIMA; Sec.-Gen. ABDERAHMANE BERTHÉ; publs *Newsletter*, *Africa Wings*, reports.

Agency for the Safety of Air Navigation in Africa and Madagascar (ASECNA) (Agence pour la Sécurité de la Navigation Aérienne en Afrique et Madagascar): 32–38 ave Jean Jaurès, BP 3144, Dakar, Senegal; tel. 33-849-66-00; fax 33-823-46-54; internet www.asecna.aero; f. 1959; organizes air-traffic communications in mem. states; co-ordinates meteorological forecasts; provides training for air-traffic controllers, meteorologists and airport fire-fighters; ASECNA is under the authority of a cttee comprising ministers of civil aviation of mem. states; mems: Benin, Burkina Faso, Cameroon, Central African Rep., Chad, Comoros, Rep. of the Congo, Côte d'Ivoire, Equatorial Guinea, France, Gabon, Guinea Bissau, Madagascar, Mali, Mauritania, Niger, Senegal, Togo; Dir-Gen. MOHAMED MOUSSA.

Airlines Association of Southern Africa (AASA) : 32–38 ave Jean Jaurès, BP 3144, Dakar, Senegal; tel. 33-849-66-00; fax 33-823-46-54; internet www.aasa.za.net; f. 1970; represents the mutual interests of its regional mems; works together with leaders of the aviation industry and senior public and govt officials on policy, regulatory, planning, operational, safety, security and financial matters affecting the overall profitability of the airlines and their continued sustainability; leads and co-ordinates the airline industry position on airport, airspace and civil aviation issues, as well as consumer legislation, environmental and tourism matters; mems: 21 airlines, 38 assoc; Chair. ELMAR CONRADIE; CEO AARON MUNETSI.

International Transport Forum: 2 rue André Pascal, 75775 Paris Cedex 16, France; tel. 1-45-24-97-10; fax 1-45-24-97-42; e-mail contact@itf-oecd.org; internet www.itf-oecd.org; f. 2006 by a decision of the European Conference of Ministers of Transport (f. 1953) to broaden membership; aims to create a safe, sustainable, efficient, integrated transport system; hosts an annual Forum in Liepzig, Germany, in May; organizes roundtable discussions, seminars and working group meetings; in May 2018 concluded an MoU with the World Bank and the International Automobile Federation to establish the first regional Road Safety Observatory in Africa; mems: 62 countries; Sec.-Gen. Dr YOUNG TAE KIM (Republic of Korea); publs *Annual Report*, various statistical publs and surveys.

Youth and Students

Pan-African Youth Union (Union pan-africaine de la jeunesse): Khartoum, Sudan; tel. (960) 184-833; fax (183) 526-695; e-mail info@pyu.org; internet pyu.org; f. 1962; encourages the participation of African youth in socioeconomic and political devt and democratization; organizes confs and seminars, youth exchanges and youth festivals; mems: youth groups in 54 African countries and liberation movements; Pres. JULIANA RATOVOSON (acting); publ. *MPJ News* (quarterly).

World Alliance of Young Men's Christian Associations: 1 chemin de Mouille-Galand, 1214 Vernier, Switzerland; tel. 228495100; fax 228495110; e-mail office@ymca.int; internet www.ymca.int; f. 1844; represents the YMCA movement at global level, strengthens its effectiveness and co-operation between national and regional asscns, advocates on youth issues, co-ordinates YMCA emergency response initiatives; organizes World Council every 4 years (2022: in July, in a hybrid in-person and virtual format, hosted from Aarhus, Denmark); mems: YMCAs in 119 countries; Pres. PATRICIA PELTON (Canada) (2018–22); Sec.-Gen. CARLOS SANVEE (Togo); publ. *YMCA World* (quarterly).

World Organization of the Scout Movement (WOSM): Suite 3, Level 17, Menara Sentral Vista, 150 Jalan Sultan Abdul Samad Brickfields, 50470 Kuala Lumpur, Malaysia; tel. (3) 2276-9000; fax (3) 2276-9089; e-mail worldbureau@scout.org; internet www.scout.org; f. 1907; works to promote unity and understanding of scouting throughout the world; to develop good citizenship among young people by promoting service, co-operation and leadership; and to provide aid and advice to mems and potential mem. asscns; the World Scout Bureau (Geneva, Switzerland) has regional offices in Belgium, Egypt, Kenya, Panama, the Philippines, Switzerland and Ukraine; mems: 171 national scout orgs in more than 200 countries and territories; Sec.-Gen. AHMAD ALHENDAWI (Jordan); publs *Triennial Report*, *WorldScoutInfo*.

MAJOR COMMODITIES OF AFRICA

Note: For each of the commodities in this section, there is a statistical table relating to recent levels of production and another table relating to prices on world markets. Each production table shows estimates of output for the world and, generally, for sub-Saharan Africa. In addition, the table lists the main regional producing countries and, for comparison, the leading producers from outside the continent.

ALUMINIUM AND BAUXITE (Aluminium or aluminum, *Al*)

Aluminium (known as aluminum in the USA and, generally, Canada) is the second most abundant metallic element in the earth's crust after silicon, comprising about 8% of the total. However, it is much less widely used than steel, despite having about the same strength and only half the weight. Aluminium has important applications as a metal because of its lightness, ease of fabrication and other desirable properties. Other products of alumina (aluminium oxide trihydrate, into which aluminium ore is refined) are materials in refractories, abrasives, glass manufacture, other ceramic products, catalysts and absorbers. Alumina hydrates are used for the production of aluminium chemicals, fire retardant in carpet backing, and industrial fillers in plastics and related products. Bauxite is the principal aluminium ore. Nepheline syenite, kaolin, shale, anorthosite and alunite are all potential alternative sources of alumina, but these are not currently economic to process. Of all bauxite mined, approximately 85% is converted to alumina (Al_2O_3) for the production of aluminium metal. The developing countries, in which at least 70% of known bauxite reserves are located, supply some 60% of the ore required. According to the US Geological Survey (USGS), in 2021 32% of potential world bauxite resources were located in Africa, 23% in Oceania, 21% in Latin America and the Caribbean, and 18% in Asia.

The industry is structured in three stages: bauxite mining, alumina refining, and smelting. After mining, bauxite is fed direct to process if mine-run material is adequate (as in Jamaica), or else it is crushed and beneficiated. Where the ore 'as mined' presents handling problems, or weight reduction is desirable, it may be dried prior to shipment. The alumina is separated from the ore by the Bayer process, through precipitation from a chemical solution. The ratio of bauxite to alumina is approximately 1.95:1. The smelting of the aluminium from alumina is generally by electrolysis in molten cryolite. Owing to the high consumption of electricity by the smelting process, alumina is usually smelted in areas where low-cost electricity is available. However, most of the electricity now used in primary smelting in the Western world is generated by hydroelectricity—a renewable energy source.

Production of Bauxite
(crude ore, '000 metric tons)

	2018	2019	2020	2021*
World total (excl. USA).	340,000	387,000	391,000	391,000
Sub-Saharan Africa . .	60,356	70,834	89,042	n.a.
Leading sub-Saharan African producers				
Ghana	1,011	1,200*	1,000*	n.a.
Guinea*†	57,000	67,000	86,000	85,000
Sierra Leone . . .	1,938	1,884	1,342	n.a.
Leading non-African producers				
Australia	95,948	105,544	104,328	110,000
Brazil†	32,377	31,938	31,000*	32,000
China, People's Republic.	77,170	105,000*	92,700*	86,000
India	23,229	22,321	20,200*	22,000
Indonesia	13,243	16,593	20,800*	18,000
Jamaica†	10,058	9,020	7,546	5,800
Kazakhstan	5,700	4,118	5,000*	5,200
Malaysia*	500	900	500	n.a.
Russian Federation . .	5,651	5,574	5,570	6,200

* Estimated production.
† Dried equivalent of crude ore.

Source: US Geological Survey.

The World Market and the Region The high degree of 'vertical integration' (i.e. the control of successive stages of production) in the industry means that a significant proportion of trade in bauxite and alumina is in the form of intra-company transfers. The increasing tendency to site alumina refineries near to bauxite deposits has also resulted in a shrinking bauxite trade, but there is a growing free market in alumina, serving the needs of the increasing number of independent (i.e. non-integrated) smelters. The major markets for aluminium are in transportation, packaging, building and construction, electrical and other machinery and equipment, and consumer durables. Although the production of aluminium is energy intensive, its light weight results in a net saving, particularly in the transportation industry, where the use of the metal as a substitute for steel, in particular in the manufacture of road motor vehicles and components, is well established. Aluminium is valued by the aerospace industry for its weight saving characteristics and for its low cost relative to alternative materials. Aluminium-lithium alloys command considerable potential for use in this sector, although the traditional dominance of aluminium in the aerospace industry has been challenged since the 1990s by 'composites' such as carbonepoxy, a fusion of carbon fibres and hardened resins, the lightness and durability of which can exceed that of many aluminium alloys. The recycling of aluminium is economically, as well as environmentally, desirable, as the process uses only 5% of the electricity required to produce a similar quantity of primary aluminium. Recycling is of commercial significance in many countries, but the world leaders were Brazil, Japan and Argentina in the late 2010s.

According to industry sources, in 2020 the largest bauxite-producing companies in the world, based on production volumes, were Rio Tinto Group (Australia/United Kingdom—the aluminium-related business is based in Canada, until 2015 under the name Rio Tinto Alcan), Alcoa (USA), Aluminium Corporation of China Ltd (Chinalco—especially its listed subsidiary, Chalco), United Company RUSAL (Russian Federation) and Hydro (Norway—Norsk Hydro). Many of the other major companies are located in countries boasting the availability of cheap power: Dubai Aluminium Co, China Power Investment Co, BHP Billiton (Australia/United Kingdom—in 2015 BHP bauxite and aluminium interests were spun off into a separate company, South32), Shandong Xinfa Aluminum and Electricity Group (People's Republic of China) and Aluminium Bahrain BSC, or Alba. In 2020, according to industry analysts, based on primary aluminium production output, the largest companies were Chalco, Hongqiao (People's Republic of China), United Company RUSAL (Russian Federation), Shandong Xinfa (People's Republic of China) and Rio Tinto.

In 2021, according to USGS estimates, the People's Republic of China alone provided 57% of world smelter production of primary aluminium (39.0m. metric tons of a world total of 68.0m. tons), followed by India (6%), the Russian Federation and Canada (5% each), the United Arab Emirates (4%) and Australia and Bahrain (2% each). China displaced the USA as the most significant country for the international aluminium industry in the 2000s, accounting for about two-fifths of both consumption and production globally by 2013. By 2018, according to the USGS, the country accounted for 18% of semi-fabricated aluminium material imports (down from 33% in 2017). The USA was for many years the world's principal producing country, but in 2001 US output of primary aluminium was surpassed by that of Russia and of China. By 2021 the USA had fallen to ninth place among world producers (level with Iceland). In the same year, when smelter output was less than one-half that of 2015, production of primary aluminium by China was estimated to be close to 45 times that of the USA.

Guinea possessed about 23% of the world's known bauxite reserves in 2021, according to estimates by the USGS. The country is the world's leading exporter of bauxite, mainly because other producers export more refined aluminium. Guinea once ranked second in the world, after Australia, in terms of ore production. Exports of aluminium ore and concentrate dominate the Guinean economy. In 2021 exports of aluminium ores and concentrates, valued at US $3,524m., contributed 47% of Guinea's total revenue from foreign sales. Compagnie des Bauxites, CBG, accounted for 78% of bauxite production capacity in Guinea, while United Company RUSAL's Alumina Co of Guinea (ACG) operated the country's only alumina refinery near its Friguia mine until it closed in 2012. The refinery reopened in mid-2018. Contingent on returning political stability, international interest remained strong into the second half of the 2010s, but more in bauxite mining than ore processing, despite the Government being keen to encourage investment in refineries. In mid-2019 Emirates Global Aluminium (EGA—of the United Arab Emirates) announced its first exports of bauxite ore (from its Guinea Alumina Corporation—GAC). The GAC project, reported to have cost some $1,400m. by mid-2019, represented the largest investment in undeveloped areas in Guinea for 40 years, and followed the same company's introduction of its Al Taweelah refinery there in April. Mine production in Guinea had not been too badly affected by outbreak of Ebola virus disease in West Africa from December 2013, because the minerals sector companies adopted robust measures to ensure continued output. From 2011 the Government was attempting to deal with governance issues in the mining sector and to instil investor confidence, and although international investment in bauxite mining continued, commodity prices remained problematic. Furthermore, popular impatience with alleged corruption and the failure of mining revenues to make any discernable difference to the lives of Guineans broke out in several days of rioting in the bauxite hub city of Boké in late April 2017, with protests triggered by a power failure and fuelled by complaints about pollution.

Cameroon traditionally receives bauxite or alumina from Guinea for its smelter, but has its own extensive bauxite deposits, estimated at some 1,200m. metric tons, which await commercial exploitation. Compagnie Camérounaise de l'Aluminium, in which Rio Tinto and the Government have shares, produces primary aluminium at Edéa. Most significant mineral deposits in Cameroon are yet to be fully developed. Meanwhile, the country produced an estimated 70,000 tons of primary aluminium in 2020. Tanzania produces a small amount of bauxite (7,000 tons in 2018, but no mining output in 2019–20), while Malawi's reserves of bauxite, located at Mulanje, have remained unexploited because of a lack of available power supply (an electricity grid connection with Mozambique remains the best hope to resolve the issue). The readier availability of energy in Mozambique enabled the major aluminium smelter project (Mozal), which was formally inaugurated in 1998, although the country is not a significant producer of bauxite (an estimated 5,000 metric tons in 2020, from the operations of Zimbabwean company E. C. Meikles in Manica province). The smelter was the largest single investment project in the country, and it cast its first aluminium in 2000, using alumina from Australia. Expansion of the smelter required contracts for secure and long-term electricity supplies from South Africa. Mozambique remains Africa's second largest producer of primary aluminium (some 571,000 tons in 2020), after South Africa. In 2021 exports of aluminium and articles thereof (mainly to Europe) contributed 22% of Mozambique's total export revenue (it was 62% in 2008). South Africa has no significant bauxite reserves, but also produces primary aluminium from imported alumina. In 2014 BHP Billiton closed one of the country's two smelters at Richards Bay (Bayside), but retained the larger Hillside plant, run by South32 from 2015. Primary aluminium production in South Africa was 717,000 tons in 2020. Power supply reliability was an issue for the industry; alumina is mainly imported from Guinea. The value of South Africa's exports of aluminium and articles thereof amounted to US $1,881m. in 2021.

Ghana's bauxite reserves have been estimated at 780m. metric tons. The country produces bauxite, and has a smelter that produces aluminium, but it has no refinery, so alumina has to be imported back into the country. The Government has therefore long been interested in developing a fully integrated system in Ghana. Bosai Minerals Group of China bought the Ghana Bauxite Co in 2010, having expressed support for an integrated aluminium industry, but the feasibility of that remained problematic, given anxieties about secure energy provision. The smelter at Tema, operated by the Volta Aluminium Co (Valco), is one of the largest in Africa, having a capacity of 200,000 metric tons, but at its peak production had absorbed 65% of the country's electricity consumption. The plant was taken over by the Government in 2008, after it closed following several years of severe power shortages resulting from the effect of drought on the hydroelectric supply. Operations resumed in 2011, and in 2020 the smelter produced an estimated 30,000 tons of primary aluminium (compared to 42,000 tons one year earlier). Meanwhile, Sierra Leone had for a time displaced Ghana as Africa's second largest bauxite producer, but output there fell in the 2010s. The country's only mine was owned by Alum SA of Romania. Bauxite output increased substantially in recent years, to reach 1.9m. tons in 2018, before falling back down to 1.3m. tons in 2020.

Global Forum The International Aluminium Institute (IAI), based in London, UK, is a global forum of producers of aluminium dedicated to the development and wider use of the metal. In 2022 the IAI had 24 member companies, representing every part of the world, including Russia and China, and responsible for more than 60% of global bauxite, alumina and aluminium production.

Aluminium Price on the London Metal Exchange
(average settlement price, US $ per metric ton)

	Average	High	Low
2005	1,898.31	(December) 2,247.45	(June) 1,731.30
2010	2,173.12	(December) 2,350.67	(June) 1,931.39
2015	1,664.68	(April) 1,819.19	(November) 1,467.89
2019	1,794.49	(March) 1,871.21	(October) 1,725.96
2020	1,703.99	(December) 2,014.67	(April) 1,459.93
2021	2,472.85	(October) 2,934.39	(January) 2,003.98

Source: World Bank, *Commodity Price Data* (Pink Sheet).

Prices The international benchmark price for aluminium cited here and by the World Bank is the average settlement price (unalloyed primary ingots, high grade—minimum 99.7% purity) traded on the London Metal Exchange (LME). Aluminium prices were particularly affected by the global recession precipitated by the international financial crisis of 2008, with the average price falling to US $1,664.83 per metric ton for 2009, the lowest level since 2003. Recovery was strong, but average annual prices declined in 2011–13; an improvement in 2014 was not sustained into 2015–16, and in November of the earlier year prices reached the lowest nominal monthly price in six years. Meanwhile, the average annual price in 2016 was its lowest since 2003. A recovery took prices generally upwards over 2017–18 (reaching their highest point since early 2012 in October 2017—$2,131 per ton). However, prices began to fall again in late 2018 and continued to decline throughout 2019 and the first half of 2020. From early 2021 prices had begun to recover, rising throughout the year and into early 2022; by March of the latter year the price was averaging $3,498 per ton (the highest monthly price since June 1988); the high prices were a consequence of higher input costs (specifically fuel, caused by the ongoing Russia–Ukraine conflict) leading to supply disruption in many regions. Prices dropped over the next few months (to $2,431 per ton in August) as primary aluminium output in China increased significantly, reaching record highs in April.

CASSAVA (Manioc, Tapioca, Yuca) (*Manihot esculenta*)

Cassava is a perennial woody shrub, up to 5 m in height, which is cultivated mainly for its enlarged starch-rich roots, although the young shoots and leaves of the plant are also edible. The plant can be harvested at any time from seven months to three years after planting. A native of South and Central America, cassava is now one of the most important food plants in all parts of the tropics (except at the highest altitudes), having a wide range of adaptation for rainfall (500–8,000 mm per year). Cassava is also well adapted to low-fertility soils, and grows where other crops will not. It is produced mainly on marginal agricultural land, with virtually no input of fertilizers, fungicides or insecticides.

The varieties of the plant fall into two broad groups, bitter and sweet cassava, formerly classed as two separate species, *Manihot utilissima* and *M. dulcis* or *aipi*. The roots of the sweet variety are usually boiled and then eaten. The roots of the bitter variety are either soaked, pounded and fermented to make a paste (such as 'fufu' in West Africa), or given an additional roasting to produce 'gari'. They can also be made into flour and starch, or dried and pelletized as animal feed.

The cassava plant contains two toxic substances, linamarin and lotaustralin, in its edible roots and leaves, which release the poison hydrocyanic acid, or cyanide, when plant tissues are damaged. Sweet varieties of cassava produce as little as 20 mg of acid per kg of fresh roots, whereas bitter varieties may produce more than 1,000 mg per kg. Although traditional methods of food preparation are effective in reducing cyanogenic content to harmless levels, if roots of bitter varieties are underprocessed and the diet lacks protein and iodine (as occurs during famines and wars), cyanide poisoning can cause fatalities. Despite the disadvantages of the two toxins, some farmers prefer to cultivate the bitter varieties, possibly because the cyanide helps to protect the plant from potential pests, and possibly because the texture of certain food products made from bitter varieties is preferred to that of sweet cassavas.

Cassava, which was introduced to Africa from South America in the 16th century, is the most productive source of carbohydrates and produces more calories per unit of land than any cereal crop. Although the nutrient content of the roots consists almost entirely of starch, the leaves are high in vitamins, minerals and protein and, processed as meal or eaten as a fresh vegetable ('saka saka'), provide a useful source of nutrition in many parts of Africa, especially in the Democratic Republic of the Congo (DRC), the Congo basin generally, Sierra Leone, Malawi, Mozambique, Niger, Tanzania and Uganda. A plot of cassava may be left unattended in the ground for two years after maturity without deterioration of the roots. As the plant is also resistant to prolonged drought it is valued as a famine reserve. The roots are highly perishable after harvest, however, and if not consumed immediately must be processed (into flour, starch, pellets, etc.). Cassava pellets are processed through grinding and extrusion from the original cassava chips (dried chopped and chipped roots) or processed into pellets in advance of drying. Pellets give off less dust and are therefore less polluting; they are also more compact and more uniform, making transportation easier and cheaper. Tapioca starch (sometimes called tapioca flour) is a starch extracted from cassava by washing and pulping—usually made from the fresh root by grating, mixing with water, sedimentation and drying—whereas cassava flour is the peeled, dried and ground root. Starch for ethanol production is usually made from cassava chips, either through wet milling or dry grinding. Tapioca starch is widely used in food processing and other industries, while chips and pellets are mainly used as animal feed.

While the area under cassava has expanded considerably through the 2000s, there is increasing concern that the rapid expansion of cassava root planting may threaten the fertility of the soil and subsequently other crops. Under cropping systems where no fertilizer is used, cassava is the last crop in the succession because of its particular adaptability to infertile soils and its high nutrient use efficiency in yield terms (although there is now evidence to suggest that cassava yields increase with the use of fertilizer). Soil fertility is not threatened by cassava itself, but rather by cultivation systems that dispense with fertilizers.

Production of Cassava
('000 metric tons)

	2017	2018	2019	2020
World total	280,521	290,616	299,028	302,662
Sub-Saharan Africa* .	170,939	185,366	191,675	193,625
Leading African producers				
Angola	8,327	8,731	9,000	8,782*
Congo, Democratic Republic . . .	37,700	38,873	40,050	41,014*
Ghana	19,009	20,846	19,368*	21,812*
Mozambique . . .	3,867	6,346	6,019	5,404*
Nigeria	55,069	55,868*	59,412*	60,002*
Tanzania	4,025	8,372	8,184	7,550*
Leading non-African producers				
Brazil	18,502	17,877	17,593	18,205
Cambodia*	7,500	7,500	7,500	7,664
China, People's Republic*	4,866	4,887	4,876	4,876
India	4,171	4,950	4,976	5,043
Indonesia . . .	19,054	16,119	16,350	18,302
Thailand	30,495	29,368	31,080	28,999
Viet Nam	10,268	9,847	10,175	10,488

* FAO estimate(s).

Source: FAO.

The World Market and the Region As a staple source of carbohydrates in the tropics, cassava is an essential part of the diet of about 600m. people. In 2020 it was harvested from an estimated 22.5m. ha in sub-Saharan Africa (cassava is barely grown in North Africa), and it may provide more than one-half of the calorific requirements of the vast population of the continent. The area in sub-Saharan Africa from which cassava was harvested in 2020 amounted to more than three-quarters (80%) of the area harvested worldwide in that year, and Africa's output accounted for more than one-half (64%) of estimated world production. Most of the African crop is produced by subsistence farmers and is traded domestically: only a small quantity enters world trade, mainly dried or as cassava starch (South-East Asia, notably Thailand, dominates the export markets). The expansion of production from the mid-1980s was driven by demand for food consumption. Attempts undertaken in a number of African countries to increase the use of cassava as a feedstuff have met with only limited success, owing to cassava chips and pellets' uncompetitiveness relative to imported feedstuffs. Little cassava production is exported.

Pests and diseases can cause yield losses of up to one-half the cassava crop in Africa. From the early 1970s African production was seriously undermined by mealybug infestation. Indigenous to South America, the mealybug (*Phenacoccus manihoti*) encountered few natural enemies in Africa, and by about 1992 had infested almost all African cassava growing areas. In 1981 the parasitic wasp *Epidinocarsis lopezi* was introduced into Nigeria from Paraguay to attack the mealybug, and by 1990 it was successfully established in 25 African countries. The introduction of natural enemies, such as *E. lopezi*, has brought about a 95% reduction in mealybug damage to cassava crops. The green spider mite (*Mononychellus tanajoa*), another threat to cassava cultivation, has also been successfully combated by the introduction of a natural enemy, the phytoseiid mite (*Typhlodromalus aripo*), which by 1997 had established a presence over 400,000 sq km in West Africa and in 1999 was reported to have reduced the presence of the green spider mite by up to 70% in some regions. Overall, there was reported to have been a 50% reduction in green spider mite damage to cassava crops owing to the introduction of natural predators. In the 2010s major threats include the variegated grasshopper, *Zonocerus variegatus*, and African cassava leaf mosaic disease (CMD), which, like the green spider mite, deprives the plant of chlorophyll and causes low yields. CMD is carried by white-fly (*Bemisia tabaci*), which also spreads the less prevalent but more serious cassava brown streak disease (CBSD) that has afflicted eastern Africa (Tanzania especially). At the start of the 2010s CMD and CBSD were together costing African farmers about US $1,000m. per year. Resistance to CMD has been developed, but

control strategies for CBSD, which is highly infectious, mutates rapidly and difficult to detect, have thus far been far less effective. In 2015, as reported by FAO, the disease was described as one of the most important biotic threats to world food security, although by 2017 the use of genomic techniques had improved hopes of bringing CBSD under timely control. Pest and diseases, in combination with poor husbandry, have in the past led to substantial yield losses in African cassava crops. Other diseases include cassava bacterial blight, cassava anthracnose disease and root rot.

In the 21st century there has been interest in the utilization of cassava as an industrial raw material as well as a food crop. Cassava has the potential to become a basic energy source for ethyl alcohol (ethanol), a substitute for petroleum; 'alcogas' (a blend of cassava alcohol and petrol) can be mixed with petrol to provide motor fuel, while the high protein residue from its production can be used for animal feed. There is some anxiety, however, about the implications of such a development for food security. The possibility of utilizing cassava leaves and stems (which represent about 50% of the plant and are normally discarded) as cattle feed concentrates has also been receiving scientific attention.

Regional Research Institute The International Institute of Tropical Agriculture (IITA) is based in Ibadan, Nigeria. To combat losses from diseases and pests, in addition to the measures described above, IITA has conducted numerous projects, including programmes to develop (for resistance to pests and diseases) new (in some cases high yielding) varieties of cassava in Africa's cassava belt. Notably, distribution of cassava varieties resistant to CMD brought under control the most recent outbreak of the disease which began in Uganda in the 1990s, and led to a recovery of cassava crops to pre-epidemic levels by the 2010s. Countries in which the IITA operated regional hubs or stations in mid-2021 included Benin, Burundi, Cameroon, the Democratic Republic of the Congo (DRC), Ghana, Kenya, Malawi, Mozambique, Nigeria, Rwanda, Tanzania, Uganda and Zambia. The IITA has many international donors, and funding from and numerous links and partnerships with other organizations, networks and research establishments.

Cassava Price
(tapioca chips, US $ per metric ton)

	Average	High	Low
2018 .	231	(April) 252	(December) 214
2019 .	224	(July) 238	(February) 209
2020 .	238	(December) 268	(April) 219
2021 .	256	(February) 263*	(August) 250†

* Also March.
† Also September, October and December.

Source: Thai Tapioca Trade Association.

Prices In 2000 the average price of hard cassava pellets (f.o.b. Bangkok, Thailand) was US $55 per metric ton. Steady increases took this average to $111 per ton in 2005. Figures from the Thai Tapioca Trade Association have been used to calculate the average annual export price for tapioca (cassava) chips or hard pellets since 2010 (f.o.b. Koh Sichang, Thailand). Average monthly prices peaked in July 2015, then fell into the start of 2016 and again at the beginning of 2017, before recovering by the end of that year. The price continued to climb in 2018–21; by July 2022 the price had reached $280 per ton. Prices are also quoted for cassava starch (but are not given here).

CHROMIUM (Cr)

Chromium, historically used as an alloying element, is a hard, lustrous metal, the name of which derives from the Greek *kroma* (colour). It is only obtained from chromite (the name applied both to the metal-bearing mineral and to the ore containing that mineral—the terms chromite ore, chromium ore and chrome ore are used interchangeably). About 91% of total demand for chromite is from the metallurgical industry, some 5% from the chemical industry and about 4% from the refractory and foundry industries. For the metallurgical industry, most chromite ore is smelted in an electric arc furnace to produce ferrochromium or ferrochrome, an alloy with iron. Within this industry the major use of chromium remains as an alloying element—it is essential to the composition of stainless steel, which is valued for its toughness and resistance to most forms of corrosion. Chromium chemicals are also used for wood preservation, dyeing and tanning. Chrome plating is a popular way of enhancing the appearance of motor vehicles, kitchen appliances, etc. Chromite is also used as a refractory mineral.

The US Geological Survey (USGS) estimated world reserves to be at least 570m. metric tons of shipping-grade chromite ore in 2021, including Kazakhstan with 230m. tons, South Africa with 200m. tons, India with 100m. tons, Turkey (Türkiye from 2022) with 26m. tons, Finland with 13m. tons and the USA with 620,000 tons. What the USGS describes as the world's resources of shipping-grade chromite ore (i.e. not only economic reserves) are reckoned to be greater than 12,000m. tons, 95% located in southern Africa and Kazakhstan. South Africa is the leading producer of chromite ore supplies and of ferrochromium. South African charge-grade, high-carbon ferrochromium (which has a chromium content of 52%–55%) has been replacing the more expensive high- and low-carbon ferro-chromiums (which have a chromium content of 60%–70%) since the development, during 1965–75, of the argon-oxygen decarbonizing process.

Production of Chromium Ore
('000 metric tons, gross weight)

	2017	2018	2019	2020
World total	43,000	48,200	46,400	37,000
Sub-Saharan Africa . .	20,594	20,875	20,730	14,510
Sub-Saharan African producers				
Madagascar	208	109	76	60*
South Africa	18,680	18,983	19,084	13,243
Sudan	32	27	20*	10*
Zimbabwe	1,674	1,756	1,550	1,197
Leading non-African producers				
Albania	808	1,143	1,288*	913
Brazil*	450	450	450	400
Finland	1,954	2,211	2,415	2,293
India	3,478*	4,076	4,139	2,500*
Kazakhstan	6,313	6,689	7,019	7,000*
Oman	453	885	608	367
Russian Federation . .	496	511	510	500*
Türkiye	7,850	10,757	8,666	8,000*

2021 (gross weight, '000 metric tons, estimates): World 41,000 (South Africa 18,000; India 3,000, Kazakhstan 7,000, Türkiye 7,000).
* Estimated production.

Source: US Geological Survey.

The World Market and the Region As with the ore, South Africa is one of the world's dominant ferrochromium producers, accounting for an estimated 2.7m. tons, or 21% of world output, in 2020. In the same year Zimbabwe, the only other African producer, contributed 1% of estimated world ferrochromium production. South Africa's ferrochromium sector has benefited historically from its access to inexpensive supplies of electrical energy, and from low labour costs, but in the 2000s the sector was beset by power supply problems. The impact of international boycotts and trade bans, and of civil disturbances, on South Africa's ferrochrome industry in the 1980s led to the development of new production capacity, generally close to ore deposits, in Brazil, Finland, Greece, India, Sweden and Turkey (subsequently Türkiye). After 1993, however, the implementation of political change in South Africa acted to consolidate the country's pre-eminence in international ferrochromium markets. While South Africa is the world's leading producer of chromite ore, it is not its largest exporter (India, Kazakhstan and Türkiye have all exported more historically) since it processes much of its production. The world's principal importer of chromite ore is the People's Republic of China, which is also the largest producer of ferrochromium (an estimated 45% in 2020). From 2000 ferrochromium plants were increasingly developed in South Africa's Bushveld Complex—more than 80% of the world's chromite ore resources are located in southern Africa, associated with the Complex and the Great Dyke of Zimbabwe—while ferrochromium producers also sought to make greater use of chromite ore generated as a by-product of platinum mining. According to the USGS, South African production of ferrochromium peaked at an estimated 3.9m. tons in 2018. The value of exports of chromium ores and concentrates in 2021 amounted to some US $1,944m. (1.6% of the total value of exports in that year). South Africa exported 85% of ferrochromium production in 2014, as well as 27% of chromite ore production. Domestic consumption of chromium ore had been challenged by Chinese demand and problems with electricity for the ferrochromium industry. The inadequacy of transport infrastructure, as well as electricity supply, and concerns about the environmental impact of chromite ore mining have all confronted the industry in the 21st century. The largest chromite and ferrochromium producer in South Africa, and the world, is Glencore Xstrata, its joint venture partner in South Africa being the local Merafe Resources. Samancor Chrome is South Africa's second chromite ore and ferrochromium producer.

Zimbabwe's ferrochromium industry was beset into the 2000s by problems arising from the currency exchange rate, by inadequate power supplies and by deficiencies in rail transportation. However, Zimbabwe is believed to have the world's second largest reserves of chromium. In 2013 a number of local co-operatives and small-scale miners dominated ore extraction on the Great Dyke of Zimbabwe, but the largest single companies were Zimbabwe Mining and Smelting Co (Zimasco), with operations near Darwendale, Lalapanzi, Mutorashanga, Ngezi and south of Shurugwi, and, far smaller, Zimbabwe Alloys (Zim Alloys), with the Inyala mine. The Zimasco plant is the main ferrochromium producer; national output recovered from a level of some 72,000 metric tons in 2009, during a world recession, to some 146,000 tons in 2010, then fluctuating at that sort of level until a sharp increase to 214,110 tons in 2014. Output fell substantially in 2016, to just 78,200 tons, before regaining lost ground in 2018–19, reaching 311,500 tons in the latter year; but output was just 134,000 tons in 2020. Six companies apart from Zimasco and Zim Alloys operate smelters in Zimbabwe.

Sudan has been gradually increasing its relatively minor production of chromite ore, while Madagascar reopened its Bemanevika mine (with a remaining estimated production life of 15 years) in 2009, so that output soon recovered from the 60,000 metric tons low point of that year. In 2010 Nigeria found that its chromite deposits in the Anka area of Zamfara state were exploitable, and future production there was considered a possibility.

Chromite Ore and Ferrochromium Prices
(US import values, annual averages, US $ per metric ton)

	Chromite ore	Ferrochromium
2005	110	1,300
2010	212	2,564
2015	216	2,593
2019	248	2,094
2020	179	1,878
2021	210	2,400

Source: US Geological Survey.

Prices Chromite and ferrochrome prices tend to be negotiated on a private contract basis, although some publications produce indicator prices. The USGS provides a series of average annual import values that can provide an index for the movement of international prices: gross quantity of chromite ore (44% Cr_2O_3 f.o.b. South Africa) and the chromium content of ferrochromium (high-carbon, containing 49% to 51% chromium).

COBALT (*Co*)

Cobalt is usually mined as a by-product of another metal; in the case of African cobalt, this is principally copper, although cobalt is also produced from nickel-copper-cobalt ores in Botswana and Zimbabwe and from platinum ores in South Africa. It is rarely mined as the primary product of an ore, and is found in very weak concentration, generally 0.1%–0.5%. The ore must be crushed and ground after mining, and subjected to a flotation process to obtain the concentrate. In the mid-1990s it was predicted that a new method of extraction, known as pressure acid leaching, would substantially increase the rate of recovery of cobalt as a by-product when laterite nickel ore is treated. In the first decades of the 2000s, however, this process was still not widely applied.

Traditional cobalt mining may eventually be complemented, and perhaps superseded, by the wide-scale retrieval of manganese nodules from the world's seabeds. It is estimated that the cobalt content of each nodule is about 0.25%, although nodules recovered from the Pacific Ocean in 1983 had a cobalt content of 2.5%. Ferromanganese crusts, containing extractable cobalt, have been identified at relatively shallow depths within the USA's exclusive economic zones, which extend 370 km (200 nautical miles) into US coastal waters. Some of the most valuable cobalt-bearing nodules were considered to be those in the Pacific Ocean around the Cook Islands, where estimates of the cobalt resource were placed as high as 32m. metric tons. Nodules off Namibia were thought to have a lesser, though still significant, cobalt content. However, the full exploitation of seabed resources such as these is thought likely to remain impracticable for many years to come.

Production of Cobalt Ore
(cobalt content, metric tons)

	2016	2017	2018	2019
World total	112,000	126,000	148,000	144,000
Sub-Saharan Africa . .	75,357	87,335	110,838	106,320
Sub-Saharan African producers				
Botswana	248	0	0	0
Congo, Democratic Republic*	68,000	80,000	104,000	100,000
Madagascar*	3,800	3,600	3,300	3,400

—continued		2016	2017	2018	2019
South Africa*	. . .	2,300	2,300	2,300	2,100
Zambia	. . . .	600*	990	835	420
Zimbabwe .	. . .	409	445	403	400*
Leading non-sub-					
Saharan African					
producers					
Australia	. . . .	5,140	5,034	4,878	5,742
Brazil .	. . . .	852*	185	0*	30*
Canada	. . . .	4,216†	3,704	3,279	3,336
China, People's Republic*		2,300	2,500	2,000	2,500
Cuba* .	. . . .	3,900	3,900	3,500	3,800
Morocco*	. . . .	1,600	2,300	2,300	2,300
New Caledonia*	. .	3,390	2,780	2,100	1,700
Papua New Guinea	. .	2,191	3,308	3,275	2,911
Philippines*	. . .	4,000	4,600	4,750	5,100
Russian Federation*	.	5,500	5,900	6,100	6,300

2020 ('000 metric tons, estimates): World 142.0 (Congo, Democratic Republic 98.0, Madagascar 0.9; Australia 5.6, Canada 3.7, China, People's Republic 2.2, Cuba 3.8, Papua New Guinea 2.9, Philippines 4.5, Russian Federation 9.0). **2021** ('000 metric tons, estimates): World 170.0 (Congo, Democratic Republic 120.0, Madagascar 2.5; Australia 5.6, Canada 4.3, China, People's Republic 2.2, Cuba 3.9, Papua New Guinea 3.0, Philippines 4.5, Russian Federation 7.6).
* Estimated production.
† Preliminary figure.

Source: US Geological Survey.

The World Market and the Region The principal uses of cobalt are in the manufacture of rechargeable batteries and in superalloys (mainly for aircraft engines), but it is also used for hard and wear resistant materials, as a catalyst, in ceramics, enamels, pigments and colours (9%), and for magnets, among many other uses. The USA remains the world's principal consumer of cobalt, especially in superalloys for the aerospace industry. In 2021 the Democratic Republic of the Congo (DRC) possessed almost one-half of the world's identified economic cobalt reserves (46%, according to estimates by the US Geological Survey—USGS). These reserves, associated with the country's copper deposits, also have the highest grade of the metal, with up to six metric tons of cobalt produced with every 100 tons of copper. The DRC, therefore, is by far the largest producer and exporter of cobalt ore in the world, although its production of the refined metal is less significant. In 2019 the USGS estimated that the People's Republic of China was the largest producer of refined cobalt in the world, followed by Finland, Canada, Norway and Japan. Given the sheer scale of resources in the DRC, the country is likely to remain fundamental to the international cobalt market.

The mining, marketing and export of cobalt from the DRC was conducted by a state monopoly, La Générale des Carrières et des Mines (Gécamines), but from 2008 a large refinery of Katanga Mining was also in operation. Between 2010 and 2015 there were plans for several new projects, including two new mines, two new refineries, and enhanced capacity at several existing refining and processing facilities. Artisanal miners have been responsible for much of the DRC's mined output of cobalt ore production since the 1990s, gathering by hand cobalt-rich ores containing the mineral heterogenite. Many of these ores have been exported, via intermediaries and illegally, in particular to India and the People's Republic of China. Much of China's cobalt refining industry is supplied with Congolese ore or, increasingly, semi-processed cobalt. In 2015 the USGS reported that only 5% of Congolese mine production was exported as refined cobalt, although it reported that refined cobalt production had increased by 140% in 2017. In 2020, according to official preliminary figures, cobalt exports accounted for 16% of the DRC's total export revenues, whereas copper exports accounted for 68%. Despite the use by the Government of export bans to encourage refining, the industry remained constricted by the country's chronic power shortage. In August 2019 Glencore (of Switzerland/UK) announced that it would be closing the Mutanda mine, which accounts for some 20% of global cobalt production, for a period of two years, citing its unprofitability. However, in mid-2021 Glencore announced that it was planning to reopen the mine, and in mid-2022 its staged restart suggested production would reach 10,000 tons for the year.

Since the early 1980s Zambia has promoted the expansion of its cobalt production in an attempt to offset declines in copper output, with varying degrees of success. Zambia remains a significant producer of refined cobalt, although according to the USGS, in 2015 production fell by almost 31%. Production recovered substantially in 2016, with output increasing by some 58%, but fell thereafter, reaching just 1,500 metric tons in 2019 (less than one-third its 2016 level). Exports of cobalt contributed 1.7% of Zambia's total exports in 2016. In the following year export earnings from cobalt increased by 10.5%, notwithstanding a decline in actual export

volumes during the year (owing to an increase in commodity prices.) In 2015 Zambia accounted for 4% of total exports of cobalt and copper. Elsewhere in Africa, cobalt was being produced as a by-product of other mining operations in South Africa. That country also produced some refined cobalt, as did Uganda. In 1992–2013 cobalt was extracted from stockpiles of cobaltiferous concentrate at the old Kilembe copper-cobalt mine in south-western Uganda (where operations had ceased in 1977). With the Kilembe stockpile about to be exhausted, in 2013 the Government secured a commitment to investment in reopening mining operations from Chinese company Tibet Hima, but the 25-year contract was cancelled in 2018 owing to alleged breaches of the concession agreement. In 2010, according to data cited by the USGS, Ugandan cobalt exports contributed 1.1% of total export revenue. Botswana tends to export its cobalt ore to Norway and Zimbabwe for refining. In 2011 a refinery project was abandoned, owing to escalating costs and interruptions to power supply in the area; only smelting takes place in the country. In 2016 Botswana's smelter production declined by 11%, according to the USGS, and no cobalt ore production was reported in 2017–18. Neighbouring Zimbabwe also produces some cobalt ore. In Madagascar, the operator of the Ambatovy nickel laterite project is Canada's Sherritt International. Construction of what is set to become one of the world's biggest nickel laterite mines was slowed by escalating costs, but an operating licence was granted in September 2012 and commercial production began in 2014, with output eventually expected to reach 5,600 tons per year. With development costs of almost $7,000m., the mine represented the largest ever foreign investment in Madagascar. Nickel-cobalt deposits were first identified in north-western Tanzania in the early 1990s, and have since been the object of detailed exploration. Cobalt reserves, estimated initially at about 20,000 tons, remained unexploited there as of 2022 (construction of a mine at Kabanga is anticipated), as did reserves identified in Côte d'Ivoire.

Global Forum The Cobalt Institute (CI—formerly the Cobalt Development Institute, CDI), an association of producers, users and traders of cobalt, was founded in 1982, and in 2022 comprised 47 members.

Cobalt Prices
(annual averages, US $ per lb)

		LME (cash)	USA (spot)
2005	. . . . .	—	15.80
2010	. . . . .	—	20.85
2015	. . . . .	12.90	13.44
2019	. . . . .	14.88	16.95
2020	. . . . .	14.21	15.70
2021	. . . . .	22.00	23.00

Source: US Geological Survey.

Prices There have been different price references for cobalt, but a useful indicator was formed with the launch of a cobalt contract on the London Metal Exchange (LME) in 2010. Under the LME contract, cobalt was traded in lots consisting of four 250-kg drums (one metric ton) of minimum 99.3% cobalt, delivered by brand, with impurities identified, to warehouses in Baltimore (USA), Rotterdam (Netherlands) and Singapore. Trading was by 'open outcry' ring trading, as well as electronically and by telephone. The prices determined in the ring were intended to be used by the industry as a reference price. It remained unclear whether the market would adapt in the long term to this type of regulated pricing model for trading 'spot' and future contracts, but interest remained strong. The LME contracts began trading during 2010, so the first annual average indicator price cited by the USGS was for 2011 (US $16.01 per lb), the mean of the cash buyer price and cash seller and settlement price (minimum 99.3% cobalt briquettes, cathode, ingot, or rounds). The USGS also gives an average annual import price into the USA 'spot' price for minimum 99.8% cobalt cathode, as reported by *Platts Metals Week*, now *Platts Metals Daily*). Prices are given in US dollars per avoirdupois pound. In 2017 prices for cobalt more than doubled, the steep increases attributed to strong customer demand and limited supply on the spot market. The price continued to increase in 2018, but fell for a period in 2019 until news of Glencore's temporary closure of the Mutanda mine was announced. The mid-2021 announcement that the mine would be reopened, civil unrest in South Africa (a major supply route for the DRC's mined output), COVID-related restrictions on production in the DRC, and strong demand in the electric vehicle sector, all pushed prices higher in 2021. Prices remained high in 2022 as a consequence of the Russian Federation's renewed armed invasion of Ukraine—this development deterring some buyers from breaking Western sanctions imposed on trade with that country in order to source supplies there.

COCOA (*Theobroma cacao*)

The cacao or cocoa tree, up to 14 m tall, originated in the tropical forests of South America. The first known cocoa plantations were in southern Mexico around AD 600, although the crop may have been cultivated for some centuries earlier. Cocoa first came to Europe in the 16th century. The Spanish and Portuguese introduced cocoa into Africa—on the islands of Fernando Póo (now Bioko), in Equatorial Guinea, and São Tomé and Príncipe—at the beginning of the 19th century. At the end of the century the tree was established on the African mainland, first in Ghana and then in other West African countries. Cultivated cocoa trees may be broadly divided into three groups. Most cocoas belong to the Amazonian Forastero group, which now accounts for more than 80% of world cocoa production. It includes Amelonado varieties, suitable for chocolate manufacturing, and widely cultivated in Brazil and in West Africa. Criollo cocoa is rarely grown and is used only for luxury confectionery. The third group is Trinitario—descending from a cross between the Criollo and Forastero varieties, first grown in Trinidad (Trinidad and Tobago)—which comprises about 15% of world output and is cultivated mainly in Central America and the northern regions of South America.

Cocoa is now widely grown in the tropics, usually at altitudes less than 300 m above sea-level, where it needs a fairly high rainfall and good soil. The cocoa tree has a much shallower tap root than, for example, the coffee bush, making cocoa more vulnerable to dry weather. Cocoa trees can take up to four years from planting before producing sufficient fruit for harvesting. They may live to 80 years or more, although the fully productive period is usually about 20 years. The tree is highly vulnerable to pests and diseases, and it is also very sensitive to climatic changes. Its fruit is a large pod, about 15–25 cm in length, which at maturity is yellow in some varieties and red in others. The ripe pods are cut from the tree, where they grow directly out of the trunk and branches. When opened, cocoa pods disclose a mass of seeds (beans) surrounded by white mucilage. After harvesting, the beans and mucilage are scooped out and fermented. Fermentation lasts several days, allowing the flavour to develop. The mature fermented beans, dull red in colour, are then dried, ready to be bagged as raw cocoa which may be further processed or exported. Much cocoa processing takes place in importing countries, notably the USA and the Netherlands. The processes include shelling, roasting and grinding the beans. The primary product of grinding is chocolate liquor, a part of which is sold directly to chocolate manufacturers; the remainder is then processed further, in order to extract a fat—cocoa butter—and chocolate powder. Almost half of each bean after shelling consists of cocoa butter. Cocoa powder for use as a beverage is largely fat free. Cocoa is a mildly stimulating drink, because of its caffeine content, and, unlike coffee and tea, is highly nutritious. The most important use of cocoa liquor is in the manufacture of chocolate, of which it is the main ingredient. About 90% of all cocoa liquor produced is used in chocolate making, for which extra cocoa butter is added, as well as other substances, such as sugar and, in the case of milk chocolate, milk. Cocoa butter is also used in cosmetic products, while the by-products of cocoa beans—the husks and shells—are used to make fertilizers and animal feed.

Production of Cocoa Beans

('000 metric tons)

	2017	2018	2019	2020
World total . . .	5,259	5,516	5,615	5,757
Sub-Saharan Africa* .	3,756	3,783	3,794	3,938
Leading African producers				
Cameroon† . . .	246	250	280	290
Côte d'Ivoire . . .	2,034	2,113	2,235	2,200
Ghana†	969	905	812	800
Nigeria*	325	340	348	340
Uganda†	35	35	35	35
Leading non-African producers				
Brazil	236	239	259	270
Colombia	89	98	102	63
Dominican Republic . .	87	86	76	78
Ecuador	206	235	284	328
Indonesia	591	767	774	739
Mexico	27	28	28	29
Papua New Guinea† . .	37	33	36	38
Peru	122	135	142	160

* FAO estimates.
† Unofficial figures.

Source: FAO.

The World Market and the Region In the 2000s mounting concerns about European Union (EU) and US moves to permit chocolate manufacturers to substitute vegetable fats for some of the cocoa solids and cocoa fats used in the manufacture of chocolate products were alleviated to an extent by consumer demand for high cocoa-content products (driven by perceived health benefits and the promotion of refined flavours) and the growing interest in organic produce. According to the International Cocoa Organization (ICCO), such changes in consumption have mainly benefited the economies of those countries recognized by the International Cocoa Council (ICC) as exporters of premium cocoa (Colombia, Costa Rica, Dominica, the Dominican Republic, Ecuador, Grenada, Indonesia, Jamaica, Madagascar, Papua New Guinea, Peru, Saint Lucia, São Tomé and Príncipe, Trinidad and Tobago, and Venezuela). At the same time as this qualitative shift in consumption, which has expanded existing, saturated markets, increased consumption in emerging and newly industrialized countries, in particular in the Russian Federation and in Asia, has sustained demand for bulk cocoa. Another development has been the combination of growing consumer concerns about poverty in less developed countries with a more organized fair trade movement, which has established steady growth in sales of fair trade products since the early 1990s, mainly in Europe.

The cocoa production chain is extremely labour-intensive: the International Cocoa Organization (ICCO) estimated that in the 2000s some 3m. smallholders accounted for 90% of output worldwide. Large-scale plantations are found only in Brazil and Indonesia. The cocoa processing industry, meanwhile, is highly concentrated. In the 2000s the ICCO reckoned that the three major companies (Archer Daniels Midland—ADM and Cargill of the USA, and Barry Callebaut of Switzerland) processed about 40% of global cocoa production. Into the 2010s further consolidation took place. In July 2013 Barry Callebaut bought the cocoa unit of Petra Foods of Singapore, making the Swiss company the world's largest cocoa processor (alone accounting for 25% of the global market). Later that year Cargill was reported to be negotiating to buy the cocoa and chocolate business of ADM, which would have created another giant to challenge Barry Callebaut and caused concern to competition authorities in Europe and the USA. In the event, ADM sold its chocolate interests to Cargill (the deal was cleared by the authorities in July 2015) and its cocoa business to Olam International Ltd (Singapore), another major cocoa trader along with Ecom Agroindustrial Corporation (Switzerland).

In 2020, according to FAO, the most important producing area in the world was Africa, which accounted for 68% of total output, followed by Latin America and the Caribbean, at 17%, and South-East Asia and Oceania, at 14%. In 2020 Africa accounted for 70% of foreign sales of cocoa beans worldwide, by volume, Latin America and the Caribbean 12% (the balance includes re-exports) and South-East Asia and Oceania 9%. According to estimated ICCO figures, the largest single producer of cocoa beans in 2020/21 (the cocoa year runs October–September) was Côte d'Ivoire, with a forecast 2.2m. metric tons, followed by Ghana with 1.0m. tons, Ecuador with 365,000 tons, Cameroon and Nigeria with 290,000 tons each, and Brazil with 200,000 tons; the largest Latin American producers were Ecuador and Brazil. World output of cocoa beans was put at 5.24m. tons in 2020/21 (compared with 4.73m. tons in 2019/20, and 4.78m. tons in 2018/19), with output in 2021/22 forecast to drop to 4.92m. tons; ICCO figures for production tend to be lower than those of the FAO. Only about two-fifths of the processing (grinding) of cocoa beans still takes place in the country of origin (45% in 2020/21, according to ICCO estimates), with Côte d'Ivoire accounting for 12% of the world total of 4.97m. tons, just ahead of the Netherlands also with an estimated 12%, Indonesia with 10%, Germany with 9% and the USA with 8%. Overall, Europe accounted for 36% of grindings, with Asia and Oceania 24%, Africa 21% and the Americas 20%. Global consumption of chocolate products is dominated by the European Union (EU—more than one-half) and by Northern America (one-quarter).

Cocoa is the most valuable agricultural export commodity in West Africa. Recorded world exports of cocoa beans, according to FAO, were 4.12m. metric tons in 2020, of which sub-Saharan African countries accounted for 70%. The world's leading exporters of cocoa beans in 2020 were Côte d'Ivoire (1.6m. tons), Ghana (520,470 tons—some of the cocoa comes from other countries in the region) and Ecuador, which is the world's largest non-African producer-exporter, with 323,399 tons. Cameroon (312,912 tons) is also a significant exporter. In 2020 the next largest exporter in the world was Belgium (223,497 tons), followed by Nigeria (216,676 tons). The Democratic Republic of Congo and Uganda are usually the next most important African exporters, but other, non-African countries, such as Malaysia, Peru and the Dominican Republic, are more significant. In 2008 the number of cocoa farms in West Africa was estimated at 1.2m.–1.5m., with an average size of 3–5 ha, employing 10.5m. workers in total. Côte d'Ivoire has been the leading producer in both regional and world terms since it overtook Ghana in 1977. Cocoa superseded coffee as Côte d'Ivoire's main cash crop at the beginning of the 1980s. In 2021 51% of the country's export revenue was derived from cocoa beans and cocoa manufactures.

Cocoa is traditionally Ghana's most important cash crop, occupying more than one-half of all the country's cultivated land. In the mid-

1960s Ghana was the world's leading producer, accounting for more than one-third of world production. From the mid-1970s to the mid-1990s, however, Ghana's cocoa production underwent a sharp decline. This contraction of the country's cocoa industry has been attributed to growing competition from Côte d'Ivoire and to mismanagement. The decline was exacerbated by the smuggling of cocoa to neighbouring countries, where higher prices were obtainable. The spread of plant diseases, particularly black pod and swollen shoot, also inhibited recovery. Government attempts to liberalize the sector and to revive the industry began to have some effect in the early 2000s, assisted to some extent by political instability in Côte d'Ivoire. According to FAO, the country provided 13% of world exports in 2020. Although cocoa was overtaken in 1992 by gold as Ghana's main export commodity, it regained its pre-eminence in 2003–06, only to be displaced again thereafter. In 2021, despite strong gold sales and some years of substantial petroleum exports, sales of cocoa beans and cocoa products still accounted for 21% of Ghana's export revenue. Ghana has also invested considerably in processing facilities, as part of an attempt to add value to its exports. Between 2004/05 and 2013/14 Ghanaian grindings of cocoa beans almost tripled, from 80,000 tons to an estimated 234,000 tons; grindings were forecast at 320,000 tons in 2021/22, a 6% global share. Among the smaller African producers, cocoa exports are a significant component of the economies of Cameroon (where they contributed 16% of total export revenue in 2021) and of São Tomé and Príncipe (where they contributed 60% of total export revenue in 2021). Cocoa exports also remain important to, but by no means dominate, Togo's foreign trade. Although cocoa is still the main export crop in Nigeria (which itself is Africa's fourth largest producer), its significance to the economy has been eclipsed by petroleum, and the same can be said of Equatorial Guinea.

International Associations In accordance with the first International Cocoa Agreement (ICCA—see below), the International Cocoa Organization (ICCO) was established in 1973. The ICCO was originally based in London, United Kingdom, but in April 2017 moved to Abidjan, Côte d'Ivoire. Under the 2001 sixth ICCA, at October 2010 the membership of the Agreement, and hence of the Organization, comprised 44 countries (15 exporting members, 29 importing members), representing about 85% of world cocoa production and some 60% of world cocoa consumption. The European Union (EU) was also an intergovernmental party to the 2001 Agreement, but the USA, a leading importer of cocoa, was not a member, nor was Indonesia. Membership of the 2010 ICCA, however, included Indonesia (the third largest producer in the world) and Venezuela among the 21 exporting members by the end of January 2017; the 30 importing members included all 28 (at that time) EU members and Switzerland, as well as the Russian Federation (but not, still, the USA). The governing body of the ICCO is the International Cocoa Council (ICC), established to supervise implementation of the ICCA. The ICC is also based in Abidjan. The Cocoa Producers' Alliance (COPAL), with headquarters in Lagos, Nigeria, had 10 members as of 2022: Brazil, Cameroon, Côte d'Ivoire, the Dominican Republic, Gabon, Ghana, Malaysia, Nigeria, São Tomé and Príncipe, and Togo. The alliance was formed in 1962 with the aim of preventing excessive price fluctuations by regulating the supply of cocoa. Members of COPAL currently account for about three-quarters of world cocoa production. COPAL has acted in concert with successive ICCAs.

ICCO Cocoa Price
(ICCO daily price, selected quotations, US $ per metric ton)

		Average	High	Low
2005	.	1,538	(March) 1,755	(November) 1,443
2010	.	3,133	(January) 3,525	(September) 2,910
2015	.	3,135	(November) 3,361	(April) 2,868
2019	.	2,341	(December) 2,445	(August) 2,195
2020	.	2,370	(February) 2,716	(July) 2,102
2021	.	2,427	(October) 2,568	(July) 2,327

Source: World Bank, *Commodity Price Data* (Pink Sheet).

Prices The principal centres for cocoa trading in the industrialized countries are the London Cocoa Terminal Market, in the UK, and the New York Coffee, Sugar and Cocoa Exchange, in the USA. The ICCO daily price is based on the average of the first three positions on the terminal markets of New York and London (nearest three future trading months). Prices were at their highest in the late 1970s, even in nominal terms, when they reached an annual average of US $3.79 per kilogram ($3,790 per metric ton) in 1977 and $3.29 per kg in 1979. Prices only moved above $3.00 per kg again in the 2000s ($3.13 per kg in 2010). Average monthly prices fell as low as $2.02 per kg in February 2013, but recovered and fluctuated thereafter. The UK's referendum vote in favour of leaving the EU in June 2016 had an impact on the London price, pushing daily prices up near their late 1970s levels for a time, but because of the severe decline in the value

of the British currency—cocoa is one of the few commodities still denominated in the pound sterling—the dollar price fell. This price trend was exacerbated by a surplus in supply. The average monthly price rose throughout most of 2019 and into early 2020, peaking at $2.72 per kg ($2,716 per ton) in February (its highest level in almost three and a half years). Prices fluctuated in 2021, and had fallen again by the middle of 2022, reaching $2.31 per kg ($2,313 per ton) in August.

The International Cocoa Agreements World prices for cocoa are highly sensitive to changes in supply and demand, making its market position volatile. Negotiations to secure international agreement on stabilizing the cocoa industry began in 1956. Full-scale cocoa conferences, under UN auspices, were held in 1963, 1966 and 1967, but all proved abortive. A major difficulty was the failure to agree on a fixed minimum price. In 1972 the fourth UN Cocoa Conference took place in Geneva, Switzerland, and resulted in the first International Cocoa Agreement (ICCA), adopted by 52 countries, although the USA, the world's principal cocoa importer at that time, did not sign. The ICCA took formal effect in October 1973, bringing into existence the ICCO, based in London. Agreements followed in 1979, in 1981 (plus an extension) and in 1987, attempting to use quotas and a buffer stock to support the agreed prices. The buffer stock (which ceased to operate during 1983–88) and other financial operations under the fourth ICCA contributed to problems in the price stabilization mechanism. The fourth ICCA was extended for a two-year period from October 1990, although the suspension of the economic clauses rendered the agreement ineffective in terms of exerting any influence over cocoa market prices.

A fifth ICCA was delayed by agreement to extend the fourth ICCA for a further year (until October 1993), because of disagreements about the export quota system and the disposition of cocoa buffer stocks. In July 1993 terms were finally agreed for a new ICCA, to take effect from October, subject to its ratification by at least five exporting countries (accounting for at least 80% of total world exports) and by importing countries (representing at least 60% of total imports). Unlike previous commodity agreements sponsored by the UN, the fifth ICCA aimed to achieve stable prices by regulating supplies and promoting consumption, rather than through the operation of buffer stocks and export quotas. The new ICCA took effect in February 1994, to operate until 1998, although it was subsequently extended until September 2001. Stocks reduction and limitation were complemented by a number of other measures to achieve a closer balance of production and consumption. In April 2000 the ICCO agreed to implement measures to remedy low levels of world prices, centring on the elimination of sub-grade cocoa in world trade, which was perceived to be having a damaging effect on prices.

A sixth ICCA was negotiated in February 2001. It aimed not only for stable prices through the regulation of supplies and the promotion of consumption, but for the development of a sustainable cocoa economy. The Agreement took provisional effect on 1 October 2003, for an initial five-year period; it was twice extended for two years, latterly from 1 October 2010. In November 2005, on its ratification by the Dominican Republic, the sixth ICCA entered definitively into force (the first time that this had happened). The Agreement was to remain open to new signatories until 2010, and was extended to when the next Agreement was due to enter into force. A seventh ICCA was signed in Geneva on the last day of the UN Cocoa Conference of 21–25 June 2010. It was opened for signature on 1 October for two years (subsequently extended to 2026). Previous agreements had been for five years, with extensions possible, but the 2010 Agreement was to be in effect for 10 years, provisionally from 1 October 2012, with the possibility of two four-year extensions, recognizing the perceived success of the existing regime.

COFFEE (*Coffea*)

The coffee plant is an evergreen shrub or small tree, generally 5–10 m in height, indigenous to Asia and tropical Africa. Wild trees grow to 10 m, but cultivated shrubs are usually pruned to a maximum of 3 m. The dried seeds (beans) are roasted, ground and brewed in hot water to provide one of the most popular of the world's non-alcoholic beverages. Coffee is drunk in every country in the world, and its consumers comprise an estimated one-third of the world's population. Although it has little nutrient value, coffee acts as a mild stimulant, owing to the presence of caffeine, an alkaloid also present in tea and cocoa.

There are about 40 species of *Coffea*, most of which grow wild in the eastern hemisphere. The two species of economic importance are *C. arabica* (native to Ethiopia), which in the mid-2010s accounted for about 60% of world production, and *C. canephora* (the source of Robusta coffee), which accounted for almost all of the remainder. Arabica coffee is more aromatic, but Robusta, as the name implies, is a stronger plant. Coffee grows in the tropical belt, between 20°N and 20°S, and from sea-level to as high as 2,000 m above. The optimum growing conditions are found at 1,250–1,500 m above sea-level, with an average temperature of around 17°C and an average annual rainfall of 1,000–1,750 mm. Trees begin bearing fruit three to five years after planting, depending upon the variety, and give their maximum yield (up to 5 kg of fruit per year) from the sixth to the 15th year. Few shrubs remain profitable beyond 30 years.

Arabica coffee trees are grown mostly in the American tropics and supply the largest quantity and the best quality of coffee beans. The yield of Arabica trees has a propensity to follow a biennial cycle, whereby a heavy crop alternates with a light crop. In Africa and Asia Arabica coffee is vulnerable in lowland areas to a serious leaf disease, and consequently cultivation has been concentrated in highland areas. Some highland Arabicas, such as those grown in Kenya, are renowned for their high quality. The Robusta coffee tree, grown mainly in East and West Africa, and in the Far East, has larger leaves than Arabica, but the beans are generally smaller and of lower quality and, consequently, fetch a lower price. However, Robusta coffee has a higher yield than Arabica, as the trees are more resistant to disease. It can also be grown at lower elevations than Arabica, from 500 m to 1,500 m above sea level. Robusta varieties are popular among multinational roasters and soluble ('instant') coffee producers.

Each coffee berry, green at first but red when ripe, usually contains two beans (white in Arabica, light brown in Robusta) which are the commercial product of the plant. To produce the best quality Arabica beans—known in the trade as 'mild' coffee—the berries are opened by a pulping machine and the beans fermented briefly in water before being dried and hulled into green coffee. Much of the crop is exported in green form. Robusta beans are generally prepared by dry-hulling. Roasting and grinding are usually undertaken in the importing countries, for economic reasons, and because roasted beans rapidly lose their freshness when exposed to air. Apart from beans, coffee produces a few minor by-products. When the coffee beans have been removed from the fruit, what remains is a wet mass of pulp and, at a later stage, the dry material of the 'hull' or fibrous sleeve that protects the beans. Coffee pulp is used as cattle feed; the fermented pulp makes a good fertilizer; and coffee bean oil is an ingredient in soaps, paints and polishes.

More than one-half of the world's coffee is produced on smallholdings of less than 5 ha. In most producing countries, and especially in Africa, coffee is almost entirely an export crop, with little domestic consumption (with the exception of Ethiopia). Green coffee accounts for about 80% of all the coffee that is exported, with coffee extract for flavouring, and soluble and roasted coffee comprising the balance. Tariffs on green/raw coffee are usually low or non-existent, but those applied to soluble coffee may be as high as 30%. The USA is the largest single coffee importer, according to the US Department of Agriculture—USDA, although its volume of coffee purchases was overtaken in 1975 by the combined imports of the (then) nine countries of the European Community (EC, now the European Union—EU). As an indicator, in the first four months of the 2020/21 crop year the USA accounted for 22% of world coffee imports, with the EU on 60%. Sub-Saharan Africa has no significant importers.

Production of Green Coffee Beans

('000 bags, each of 60 kg, coffee years)

	2017/18	2018/19	2019/20	2020/21*
World total . . .	163,693	172,461	164,953	175,347
Sub-Saharan Africa . .	17,354	18,620	18,686	18,514
Leading African producers				
Cameroon	370	310	268	280
Côte d'Ivoire . . .	1,624	2,175	1,929	1,775
Ethiopia	7,347	7,511	7,343	7,375
Kenya	790	930	844	775
Madagascar . . .	404	379	383	370
Tanzania . . .	783	1,175	926	900
Uganda	4,597	4,704	5,509	5,620
Leading non-African producers				
Brazil	52,740	65,131	58,211	69,000
Colombia	13,824	13,866	14,100	14,300
Honduras	7,560	7,153	5,931	6,100
India	5,813	5,325	4,988	5,700
Indonesia	10,852	9,618	11,433	12,100
Mexico	4,485	4,351	3,985	4,000
Peru	4,279	4,263	3,836	3,800
Viet Nam	33,432	30,283	30,487	29,000

* Estimated figures.

Source: International Coffee Organization.

The World Market and the Region After petroleum, coffee is the major raw material of world trade, and it is the single most valuable agricultural export of the tropics. In the 2010s about 26m. small producers worldwide depended on coffee. Coffee is the most important cash crop of Latin America, with a number of countries

heavily dependent on it as a source of foreign exchange. Of the estimated total world crop of coffee beans in 2020/21, Latin American and Caribbean countries accounted for 61% (Brazil alone contributed 39% of the world total). Africa, which formerly ranked second, was overtaken in 1992/93 by Asian producers; in 2020/21 African producers accounted for 11% of the estimated world coffee crop, compared with 25% for countries in eastern Asia and Oceania—Far East and Australasia. India harvested a further 3% of the world coffee crop in the same year; the only other producer in South Asia was Sri Lanka, not a member of the International Coffee Organization—ICO. (The above shares have been calculated on the basis of data released by the ICO for production of 'all exporting countries'. Non-members of the ICO accounted for 6% of the world coffee crop in 2013/14, but were not subsequently cited separately.) The 2014/15 harvest was lower than it would otherwise have been, because of continuing problems with coffee rust disease in Brazil and other countries, but higher output in Asia and Africa in 2015/16 and recovery in Brazil from 2016/17 pushed world harvests up gradually through 2020/21. Reports in 2021 indicated, however, that severe droughts had significantly hindered Brazilian production, placing upward pressure on global prices (see below).

Robusta coffee beans, which are more suitable for the production of 'instant' coffee or coffee for flavouring, etc., are favoured by multinational roasters and 'instant' coffee producers because of the lower cost and less volatile price. Soluble ('instant') coffee accounted for about 12.5% of all coffee exports in 2000–11. In the mid-2000s four main roaster companies (Kraft Foods, Nestlé, Procter & Gamble, and Sarah Lee) purchased more than 50% of global Robusta coffee production. Some predicted a shift towards more mass Arabica purchases from 2014 by the large roasting companies. According to ICO estimates, in 2020/21 Robusta accounted for 36% of coffee on the international market.

Africa's largest exporter, and the fifth largest in the world in 2020/21, was Uganda (4.5% of global exports), followed by Ethiopia (2.2%). In the 20th century Côte d'Ivoire was long Africa's leading coffee producer, and coffee was the country's leading cash crop until 1980, when cocoa supplanted it—in 2021 exports of coffee accounted for just 0.2% of the country's total export revenue. Despite a programme of replanting in the 1990s, more than 60% of Côte d'Ivoire's coffee trees were reported in 2005 to be over 30 years old, and the country also suffered from political and military disruption, which affected the maintenance of coffee plantations. Production reached a nadir in 2010, and exports in 2011, but recovery began thereafter, and the country was the continent's fourth largest exporter in 2020/21. Ethiopia is the continent's largest producer and had consistently high exports in the 2000s and into the 2010s, despite significant domestic consumption. The country also emerged as the major regional producer of Arabicas. The contribution of coffee to total export earnings had declined into the 2000s, representing only about 39% in 2002 and falling to 23% by 2009. Coffee sales recovered somewhat in recent years, representing 39% of the value of total exports in 2021.

The African countries that have traditionally been most dependent on coffee as a source of foreign exchange are Burundi and Uganda. In 2002 coffee sales accounted for three-quarters of Burundi's total export revenue, although this was just 25% by 2021. The proportion varied considerably, depending on international coffee prices. In Uganda coffee provided about 35% of export earnings in 2021. The country was traditionally Africa's leading exporter of coffee, but only the continent's second largest producer. The coffee sector in Rwanda, which contributed more than 60% of export revenue in 1991, was severely affected by civil war, and in 1994 the bulk of the crop was lost. Rwanda's coffee output—which consists mainly of Arabicas—began to recover only in the early 2000s. Despite contributing about 56% of Rwanda's total export earnings in 1999, coffee was overtaken by tea as the major cash crop in 2000. Depending on the relative international prices, as well as production, coffee and tea were each in some years the leading agricultural export; in 2021 coffee exports accounted for 21% of total exports, a little more than tea in that year (making it the country's most important cash crop).

Among other African countries where coffee is an important export are Tanzania, Kenya, Cameroon, Togo, Ghana and the Central African Republic. Madagascar is not a significant exporter, but it is (along with Rwanda) Africa's sixth largest producer; like Guinea and the Democratic Republic of the Congo, Madagascar is not a member of the ICO. Angola was formerly the world's leading exporter of Robusta coffee, but production during 1975–95 was severely disrupted by civil conflict. The full rehabilitation of Angola's coffee industry depended on an enduring political and military settlement, and even then was expected to span many years.

International Associations The International Coffee Organization (ICO) was established in London, UK, in 1963 under the first International Coffee Agreement (see below). At February 2022, the ICO consisted of 42 exporting members (Venezuela acceded in October 2017) and seven importing members (33 importing nations in all, because one member was the 27-country EU); a further three countries had signed the seventh ICA but had not yet completed all membership procedures, while four more countries had not signed. In February 2017 Turkey (Türkiye from 2022) withdrew from the ICO, while the USA left in June 2018 and Paraguay in November 2019. In addition, there was an Association of Coffee Producing Countries (ACPC), also based in London, but it closed in 2002, and there is still an Inter-African Coffee Organization (IACO), based in Côte d'Ivoire (see below).

ICO Coffee Price
(ICO average annual indicator, US $ per metric ton)

							Arabicas	Robustas
2005	.	.	.	.	.	.	2,532	1,115
2010	.	.	.	.	.	.	4,320	1,736
2015	.	.	.	.	.	.	3,526	1,941
2019	.	.	.	.	.	.	2,880	1,622
2020	.	.	.	.	.	.	3,324	1,516
2021	.	.	.	.	.	.	4,512	1,981

Source: World Bank, *Commodity Price Data* (Pink Sheet).

Prices Coffee is traded on a number of exchanges worldwide. The ICO has two main indicator prices, one for Arabica beans (other mild Arabicas, average New York and Bremen/Hamburg markets, ex-dock) and the other for Robusta beans (Robustas, average New York and Le Havre/Marseilles markets, ex-dock). In the 2010s coffee again approached price levels similar to those experienced in the late 1970s, but only at current prices. Moreover, that is mainly true of the Arabica price, because the differential from the Robusta price has become more pronounced, although the indicators to some extent echo each other's movement on a price graph: the all-time coffee price peak was in April 1977, the average monthly price for Arabicas reaching US $7.00 per kg (the Robusta price peaked at $6.88); the 2011 peak for Arabicas was $6.62 per kg in April (but for Robustas, $2.69 per kg in May); and the 2014 peak was $4.97 per kg in October (for Robustas, $2.33 per kg in April). Prices tended downwards from 2014, the Arabica price reaching an average monthly price of $3.20 per kg in January 2016 (the price had been lower in January 2014 and the months before), and the Robusta price $1.63 per kg in February 2016 (a level not seen since May 2010). The Arabica recovery peaked at $4.06 per kg in November but oversupply placed downward pressure on prices in 2017–19. Prices had recovered somewhat by late 2019, and grew throughout 2020–21. There was continued strong growth in the first half of 2022 on the back of historically high fuel prices (largely a result of sanctions and supply concerns following the Russian Federation's renewed armed invasion of Ukraine) impacting transportation costs. By February the average price of Robustas and Arabicas had reached their highest levels in over a decade; by August, however, prices had fallen back slightly to average, respectively, $2.42 per kg and $5.92 per kg.

The International Coffee Agreements Effective international attempts to stabilize coffee prices began in 1954, when a number of producing countries made a short-term agreement to fix export quotas. After three such agreements, a five-year International Coffee Agreement (ICA), covering both producers and consumers and introducing a quota system, was signed in 1962. This led to the establishment in 1963 of the ICO. Successive ICAs took effect in 1968, 1976, and 1983. The system of export quotas to stabilize prices was eventually abandoned in July 1989, contributing to a crisis in coffee prices as oversupply undermined market stability. In October 1993 the USA withdrew from the ICO (it did not rejoin it until 2005), which was increasingly perceived at that time to have been eclipsed by the Association of Coffee Producing Countries (ACPC—see below). In 1994 the ICO agreed provisions for a new five-year ICA (later extended), again with primarily consultative and administrative functions, and a successor ICA took effect provisionally in October 2001, and definitively in May 2005. By May 2007 the new ICA had been endorsed by 74 of the 77 members (45 exporting countries, 32 importing countries) of the International Coffee Council (ICC), the highest authority of the ICO. A seventh ICA, agreed between the 77 members of the ICC, was formally adopted in September 2007. The new agreement reiterated the objectives contained in the sixth ICA, emphasizing the need to support the advancement of a sustainable coffee economy to benefit small-scale farmers. It established in particular a Consultative Forum of Coffee Sector Finance that was to facilitate access to financial and market information in the coffee sector, and a Promotion and Market Development Committee that was to co-ordinate information campaigns, research and studies.

The ICAs are concerned with maintaining a stable price environment for the worldwide coffee market, but numerous and various disagreements led to the collapse of the quota system and of the extant ICA's economic provisions. The failure to agree on a new formulation for quotas and the existence of high stock levels combined to keep coffee prices at historic 'lows' in the early 1990s. In September 1993 the Latin American producers announced the formation of an ACPC to implement an export withholding, or coffee

retention, plan. In the following month the 25-member Inter-African Coffee Organization (IACO) agreed to join the Latin American producers in a new plan to withhold 20% of output whenever market prices fell below an agreed level. With the participation of Asian producers, a 28-member ACPC, with headquarters also in London, was formally established in August (its signatory member countries numbered 28 in 2001, 14 of which had ratified). Production by the 14 ratified members in 1999/2000 accounted for 61.4% of coffee output worldwide. In the meantime the ACPC coffee retention plan had come into operation in October 1993 and gradually generated improved prices. Ultimately, however, the ACPC was unable—even with the support of non-members—to bring about lasting price stability by pursuing coffee/export-retention strategy. In October 2001 the ACPC announced that it would dissolve itself in January 2002, its relevance compromised by breaches of the retention plan and poor finances. Meanwhile, in May 2001 the collapse in the price of coffee had been described as the most serious crisis in a global commodity market since the 1930s, with prices at their lowest level ever in real terms. The collapse of the market was regarded, fundamentally, as the result of an ongoing increase in world production at twice the rate of growth in consumption, this oversupply having led to an overwhelming accumulation of stocks. (In this connection, some observers highlighted the role of Viet Nam, which had substantially increased its production and exports of coffee in recent years: by mid-2000 Viet Nam had overtaken Indonesia to become the world's leading supplier of Robusta coffee and was rivalling Colombia as the second largest coffee producing country overall.) In early July 2001 the price of the Robusta coffee contract for September delivery fell below US $540 per metric ton, marking a record 30-year 'low'. At about the same time the ICO recorded its lowest composite price ever. Despite a recovery beginning in October, the average composite price recorded by the ICO for 2001 was 29% lower than the average composite price recorded in 2000. In 2001 coffee prices were at their lowest level since 1973 in nominal terms, and at a record low level in real terms. Although prices began to recover slowly, the low returns for producers in the early 2000s created what was sometimes called the 'coffee crisis'. In its review of the 2004/05 crop year, the ICO noted that the crisis in the coffee economy of exporting countries had abated somewhat, although oversupply of Robustas and augmented demand for Arabicas increased the differential between the two prices. Against this background, the seventh ICA sought to protect not only markets, but farmers, in future.

COPPER (*Cu*)

Copper is a reddish-orange metal (copper compounds, by contrast, often give a blue or green colour to minerals) in use even before the 'Bronze Age', the characteristic metal of which was obtained by the addition of tin to copper. The ores containing copper are mainly copper sulphide or copper oxide. They are mined both underground and by open-cast or surface mining. After break-up of the ore body by explosives, the lumps of ore are crushed, ground and mixed with reagents and water, in the case of sulphide ores, and then subjected to a flotation process by which copper-rich minerals are extracted. The resulting concentrate, which contains about 30% copper, is then dried, smelted and cast into anode copper, which is further refined to about 99.98% purity by electrolysis (chemical decomposition by electrical action). The cathodes are then cast into convenient shapes for working or are sold as such. Oxide ores, less important than sulphides, are treated in ways rather similar to the solvent extraction process described below.

Two alternative copper extraction processes were developed in the 20th century. The first of these techniques, and of little importance in the industry, is known as the 'Torco' (treatment of refractory copper ores) segregation process, which can be used for extracting copper from silicate ores that were previously not treatable. A commercial plant was operated in Zambia from the 1960s, until 1983, and another in Mauritania in the 1970s. The second, and relatively low-cost, technique is the solvent extraction process. This is suited to the treatment of very low-grade oxidized ores and is used on both new ores and waste dumps that have accumulated over previous years from conventional copper working. The copper in the ore or waste material is dissolved in acid, and the copper-bearing leach solution is then mixed with a special organic-containing chemical reagent which selectively extracts the copper. After allowing the two layers to separate, the layer containing the copper is separated from the acid leach solution. The copper is extracted from the concentrated leach solution by means of electrolysis to produce refined cathodes.

The World Market and the Region Copper is ductile, resists corrosion, and is an excellent conductor of heat and electricity. Its industrial uses are mainly in the electrical industry (about 60% of copper is made into wire for use in power cables, telecommunications, domestic and industrial wiring) and the building, engineering and chemical industries. Bronzes and brasses are typical copper alloys used for both industrial and decorative purposes. There are, however, substitutes for copper in almost all of its industrial uses, and in recent years aluminium has presented a challenge in the electrical

Production of Copper Ore
(copper content, '000 metric tons)

	2018*	2019	2020	2021*
World total . . .	20,400	20,400	20,600	21,000
Sub-Saharan Africa‡ .	2,084	2,087	2,430	2,630
Leading sub-Saharan African producers				
Congo, Democratic Republic . .	1,226	1,290	1,600	1,800
Zambia	854	797	853	830
Leading non-African producers				
Australia	920	934	885	900
Canada	543	573	585	590
Chile	5,832	5,790	5,730	5,600
China, People's Republic .	1,591	1,680	1,720	1,800
Mexico	751	715	733	720
Peru	2,437	2,460	2,150	2,200
Russian Federation . .	751†	801	810†	820
USA	1,220	1,260	1,200	1,200

* Preliminary figures.
† Estimated production.
‡ Figures represent the sum of output in listed countries.

Source: US Geological Survey.

and transport industries. The major copper importing countries are the People's Republic of China, the member states of the European Union (EU), Japan and the USA. According to the International Copper Study Group (ICSG), worldwide usage of refined copper reached a new record in 2021 of 25.3m. metric tons (provisional figure), with usage slightly up in the first five months of 2022 compared with the previous year. In 2021 Asia accounted for 73% of refined usage and Europe 16%. The largest copper mining companies in the world are CODELCO (Chile), Freeport-McMoRan (USA), Glencore (Switzerland/UK) and BHP Billiton (Australia/UK).

Proven world reserves of copper were estimated by the USGS at 880m. metric tons (copper content) in 2021. In that year about 2.4% of the world's total reserves were located in Zambia, where copper production is the mainstay of the economy, and copper sales at one time accounted for some 85% of export earnings. Production of refined copper in Zambia had entered a gradual decline in the mid-1980s; dwindling ore grades, high extraction costs, transport problems, shortages of foreign exchange, equipment and skilled labour, lack of maintenance and labour unrest combined to make the copper industry seem an unstable basis for the Zambian economy. However, following a change of government in 1991, a number of remedial measures were implemented. Before being overtaken by Canada in 1983, Zambia ranked second only to Chile among the world's copper exporters, but it fell also behind Peru in 2010. Zambian copper exports are predominantly in refined but unwrought form (Zambian smelter production totalled a preliminary 828,700 metric tons in 2018, refinery production a preliminary 425,000 tons). Copper and articles thereof provided 76% of Zambia's export income in 2021.

Even before the Zairean (Congolese) civil conflict, which began in 1993 and was renewed in 1998, led to the suspension of much of the country's normal mining activity, the copper industry in what is now the Democratic Republic of the Congo (DRC) had become increasingly vulnerable to competition from other producers, such as Chile, which have established new open-cast, low-cost mines. The DRC had placed greater emphasis on efforts to increase refined production capacity, but war had an impact on facilities and infrastructure. In 2021 copper ores and concentrates accounted for 4% of total exports of US $673m. (although exports of copper and articles thereof—principally refined copper—contributed 57% of the value of total exports). South Africa is the continent's other main producer, although from the 1980s copper output was affected by declining grades of ore, leading to mine closures and a reduction in the level of operations. The country had a number of smelters (producing a preliminary 70,000 metric tons in 2018) and refineries (an estimated 65,000 tons). South African exports of copper ores and concentrates earned $250m. in 2021 (copper and articles thereof earned $972m.). Namibia derived more than 10% of its total export revenue from copper in the late 1980s, but recorded a fluctuating performance into the 2000s, with global economic conditions and mine flooding in 2008 closing much of the industry until 2011 (when only 3,370 tons were produced, with a preliminary 15,177 tons by 2018). Smelter production depended on imported concentrates for some years. In Botswana copper and nickel are mined at Selebi-Phikwe, and high-grade copper ore deposits have also been identified in the Ghanzi area. The country mined some 38,000 tons in 2014, almost double the 2011 output, but by 2018 output had fallen to just 1,462 tons—largely a result of its smelter

closing down in 2016. In the same year exports of copper-nickel matte contributed only about 3% of Botswana's total export revenue—but this fell to almost negligible amounts in 2017–21. In 2006, in response, partly to the high price of copper on international markets, Wambao Shinex of China (51%) and Zimbabwe Mining Development Corpn (49%) formed Zimbao Mining Ventures, in order to assess the potential for reopening Zimbabwe's Mhangura and Sanyati copper mines and the country's smelter and refining complex at Lomangundi. Copper mining and refined copper production recovered more emphatically in the 2010s (mined output was a preliminary 9,077 tons of copper concentrates in 2018, with refined production falling to zero). From 2007 Mauritania was producing a significant amount of copper in concentrates from the Guelb Moghrein mine, 250 km northeast of Nouakchott; output in 2018 was a preliminary 28,137 tons. In 2018 Tanzanian production of copper concentrates and bullion (doré) stood at a preliminary 10,000 tons.

International Association The ICSG, initially comprising 18 producing and importing countries, was formed in 1992 to compile and publish statistical information and to provide an intergovernmental forum on copper. In 2022 ICSG members and observers totalled 24 countries, plus the EU, accounting for more than 80% of world trade in copper. The ICSG, which is based in Lisbon, Portugal, does not participate in trade or exercise any form of intervention in the market.

Copper Price on the London Metal Exchange
(average settlement price, US $ per metric ton)

	Average	High	Low
2005 .	3,678.88	(January) 3,170.00	(December) 4,576.78
2010 .	7,534.78	(December) 9,147.26	(June) 6,499.30
2015 .	5,510.46	(May) 6,294.78	(December) 4,638.83
2019 .	6,010.15	(March) 6,439.46	(August) 5,709.44
2020 .	6,173.77	(December) 7,772.24	(April) 5,057.97
2021 .	9,317.05	(May) 10,161.97	(January) 7,972.15

Source: World Bank, *Commodity Price Data* (Pink Sheet).

Prices There is no international agreement between producers and consumers governing the stabilization of supplies and prices. Although most of the world's supply of primary and secondary copper is traded direct between producers and consumers, prices quoted on the London Metal Exchange (LME), the New York Commodity Exchange (COMEX) and the Shanghai Futures Exchange (SHFE) provide the principal price setting mechanism for world copper trading. The World Bank cites the average settlement price of Grade 'A' copper (minimum purity 99.9935%) traded on the LME.

Along with other commodities, copper experienced exceptionally high prices into the beginning of 2008, until economic recession occasioned by the global financial crisis of that year set in. In real terms at least, the price did not exceed the record levels of early 1974, which had collapsed with the onset of the oil crisis of that year. In nominal terms, the average annual copper price in 1974 was only US $2,058.5 per metric ton (monthly averages peaked in April at $3,031.8 per ton), and compared with, in 2008, $6,955.8 per ton (peaking in April at $8,684.93 per ton). Copper recovered to a new nominal record in 2011, the monthly average peaking at an all-time high, at current prices, of $9,867.6 per ton in February, with the highest daily price reaching over $10,100 per ton. Prices tended downwards thereafter, albeit with some short-lived recoveries, reaching the lowest monthly price in almost seven years in January 2016; prices were up and down in 2016–19 and into early 2020, reaching just $5,058.0 in April of the latter year. However, from mid-2020 prices began to increase substantially, reaching $10,231 per ton by March 2022, the highest monthly average on record. High prices were attributed to falling inventories and higher demand as many countries emerged from economic restrictions associated with the COVID-19 pandemic. However, the price had fallen significantly, back to $7,982 per ton, by August.

COTTON (*Gossypium*)

Cotton is the name given to the soft hairs that grow on the epidermis of the seed of the plant genus *Gossypium*. The most important of the four species cultivated for fibre is *G. hirsutum*, upland cotton, which originated in Mexico and now accounts for about 90% of the cotton harvest. *G. barbadense* is the extra long staple cotton, originating in Peru and accounting for a further 5%–8%; it is generally known by a number of names, such as Pima, American or Creole cotton and, with a reputation for quality, Egyptian and Sea Island cotton. The two Old World commercial species are *G. arboreum*, the tree cotton of South Asia, and *G. herbaceum* or Levant cotton.

The initial development of the cotton fibres takes place within a closed pod, called a boll, which, after a period of growth of about 50–75 days (depending upon climatic conditions), opens to reveal white tufts of cotton hair. After the seed cotton has been picked, the cotton fibre, or lint, has to be separated from the seeds by means of a mechanical process, known as ginning. (Cotton has been cultivated since antiquity, but the invention of the cotton gin revolutionized production costs and led to it becoming the natural fibre most widely used in clothing.) Depending upon the variety and growing conditions, it takes about three metric tons of seed cotton to produce one ton of raw cotton fibre. After ginning, a fuzz of very short cotton hairs remains on the seed. These are called linters, and may be removed and used in the manufacture of paper, cellulose-based chemicals, explosives, etc. The remaining cottonseed can have an oil extracted, the residual meal or cake being used for animal feed, etc.

About one-half of the cotton produced in the world is used in the manufacture of clothing, about one-third is used for household textiles and the remainder is used for numerous industrial products (tarpaulins, rubber reinforcement, abrasive backings, filters, high-quality papers, etc.). The official cotton 'season' (for trade purposes) runs from 1 August to 31 July of the following year, and quantities are measured in both metric tons and bales; for statistical purposes, one bale of cotton is 226.8 kg (500 lb) gross or 217.7 kg (480 lb) net. The price of a particular type of cotton depends upon its availability relative to demand and upon characteristics related to yarn quality and suitability for processing. These include fibre length, fineness, cleanliness, strength and colour. The most important of these is length. Generally, the length of the fibre determines the quality of the yarn produced from it, with the longer fibres being preferred for the finer, stronger and more expensive yarns.

Production of Cotton
('000 metric tons, USDA estimates)

	2018/19	2019/20	2020/21	2021/22*
World total	25,736	26,118	24,248	25,246
Sub-Saharan Africa . .	1,691	1,811	1,542	1,792
Leading sub-Saharan African producers				
Benin	305	310	316	309
Burkina Faso . . .	185	192	207	209
Cameroon	131	140	148	139
Chad	7	46	51	65
Côte d'Ivoire . . .	204	216	220	229
Mali	277	294	65	311
Nigeria	51	44	76	76
Sudan	109	131	131	131
Tanzania	79	130	47	56
Zimbabwe	44	40	53	47
Leading non-African producers				
Australia	479	136	610	1,197
Brazil	2,830	3,000	2,356	2,613
China, People's Republic .	6,042	5,933	6,423	5,879
India	5,661	6,205	6,009	5,334
Pakistan	1,655	1,350	980	1,306
USA	3,999	4,336	3,181	3,815
Uzbekistan	603	531	686	588

* Preliminary.

Source: US Department of Agriculture.

The World Market and the Region Cotton is the world's leading textile fibre. However, with the increased use of synthetics, cotton's share in the world's total consumption of fibre declined from 48% in 1988 to about 31% in 2012. About one-third of the decline in its market share was attributed to increases in the real cost of cotton relative to prices of competing fibres, and the remaining two-thirds to other factors, for example greater use of chemical fibre filament yarn (yarn that is not spun but is extruded in a continuous string) in domestic textiles, such as carpeting. In the 21st century, two important factors in the international trade in cotton have been output in the USA, which is among the world's leading producers without the matching levels of consumption, and the Chinese market (although officially enforced limits on the use of cotton in the People's Republic of China had ramifications for the international market). According to data compiled by the US Department of Agriculture (USDA), consumption of cotton worldwide had reached a record peak of 27.0m. metric tons in 2006/07, only for the greatest contraction in cotton consumption since the Second World War (by some 11%) to be precipitated after the world financial crisis in 2008 triggered a crash in commodity prices and a global economic recession. Consumption had recovered to 26.2m. tons by 2018/19, and continued to grow slightly to 26.5m. tons in 2021/22. The largest cotton consumers are China (31% of the world total in 2021/212) and India (21%); Pakistan, Bangladesh, Türkiye (Turkey before 2022) and Viet Nam are among other important consumers. China was for a time overwhelmingly the largest importer of cotton, but in 2015/16–2017/18 was displaced by both Bangladesh and Viet Nam. China regained its place as the largest importer of cotton in 2018/19, but could not maintain that

position in 2019/20, when it was overtaken once more by Bangladesh. However, China was by far the largest importer again in 2020/21, and in 2021/22 it bought 19% of global imports (down from 54% in 2011/12). Bangladesh also purchased 19% in that year, followed by Viet Nam (16%), Türkiye, Pakistan, Indonesia and India. The world's principal exporters of cotton are the USA (33% in 2021/22), Brazil (17%), Australia and India (10%), and Benin and Greece (3% each); Uzbekistan is also traditionally an important exporter, as are Burkina Faso and Mali.

Cotton is a major source of income and employment for many developing countries, both as a primary product and, increasingly, through sales of yarn, fabrics and finished goods. The countries of francophone West Africa are, generally, significant exporters of cotton. Cotton is usually the principal commercial crop, in terms of foreign exchange earnings, in Benin, Burkina Faso, the Central African Republic, Chad, Mali, Mozambique, Sudan and Togo. It is also important in Senegal (although less than in the 20th century) and in Tanzania, in East Africa. In the early 2000s more than 90% of cotton entering the world market from sub-Saharan Africa came from the francophone countries of the CFA franc zone. The largest producer and exporter of cotton in sub-Saharan African—indeed, in the whole continent from 2008/09, owing to poor harvests in Egypt—is usually Burkina Faso. Burkina Faso was the 15th largest producer in the world in 2021/22; it exported 174,182 tons in that same production year, making it Africa's fourth largest and the world's ninth largest exporter. In 2021/22 Burkina Faso's exports were surpassed by those of Benin (304,819 tons), Côte d'Ivoire (295,675 tons) and Mali (239,501 tons). Cameroon, Sudan and Chad also exported significant volumes. In addition, Togo, Zimbabwe, Mozambique, Zambia, Uganda, Tanzania, Malawi and Nigeria were notable exporting producers. Ethiopia has an important cotton harvest but mainly for its domestic market, having exported little since 2014. For many years in the 20th century Sudan was the largest cotton producer in sub-Saharan Africa. However, from the 1970s the industry was adversely affected by domestic difficulties resulting from climatic factors, an inflexible, government dictated marketing policy and crop infestation by whitefly. The area under cotton cultivation in Sudan had declined dramatically by the late 1990s. It was not until the early 2000s that improved levels of output seemed likely to be sustained; indeed, Sudan increased its output more than fourfold between 2014/15 and 2020/21, for example. In the latter year it was the region's sixth largest producer.

Global Forum The International Cotton Advisory Committee (ICAC), an intergovernmental body, established in 1939, with its headquarters in Washington, DC, USA, publishes statistical and economic information and provides a forum for consultation and discussion among its members. The ICAC had 26 member governments at August 2022.

Cotton Price (Cotlook 'A')
(US $ per metric ton)

	Average	High	Low
2005 .	1,217	(October) 1,283	(January) 1,130
2010 .	2,283	(December) 3,703	(January) 1,706
2015 .	1,552	(May) 1,606	(January) 1,485
2019 .	1,717	(April) 1,924	(August) 1,560
2020 .	1,586	(December) 1,786	(April) 1,401
2021 .	2,231	(November) 2,790	(January) 1,923

Source: World Bank, *Commodity Price Data* (Pink Sheet).

Prices Although co-operation in cotton affairs has a long history, there have been no international agreements governing the cotton trade. Proposals to link producers and consumers in price stabilization arrangements have been opposed by the USA (the world's largest cotton exporter), and by Japan and the European Union (EU). Liverpool, United Kingdom, is the historic centre of cotton-trading activity, and international cotton prices are still collected by organizations located there. However, almost no US cotton has been imported through Liverpool in the 2000s, and consumption in the textile industry in the United Kingdom has fallen to negligible levels. The Cotton Outlook (Cotlook) 'A' index has long since changed from Liverpool quotations, then in August 2004 from c.i.f. Northern Europe to C/F Far East. The cotton quality base for the index is middling upland cotton, 1–3/32 inch. A decline in world cotton stocks in 2010 limited supplies, not only maintaining prices at high levels, but creating problems for indexing. From 22 June the usual Cotlook 'A' index was suspended, owing to a lack of quotations on offers, and the new 'A' forward index was then relied on. The World Bank cites the Cotlook 'A' figures, which recorded average monthly prices as being weaker in the second half of 2015 through to the end of the first quarter of 2016, strengthening and then stabilizing in the second half of the year, before rising to a peak in May 2017. The second half of 2017 saw a decline in average monthly prices, but prices peaked once more in June 2018 at $2.15 per kg (the highest such figure since April

2012). However, prices fell again in the second half of 2018, through 2019 and into 2020, before rising from the second half of the year. Prices continued to increase throughout 2021 and the first half of 2022, reaching $3.61 per kg ($3,610 per metric ton) by May, the highest level in 11 years—largely a consequence of low crop yields in a number of Indian producer states—before falling to $2.74 per kg ($2,743 per metric ton) in August.

DIAMONDS

Diamonds are a crystalline form of carbon, and are the hardest naturally occurring substance. They are of two categories: gem qualities (among the most prized gemstones used in jewellery), which are superior in terms of colour or quality; and industrial quality, about one-half of the total by weight, which are used for high-precision machining or crushed into an abrasive powder called boart (bort). The primary source of diamonds is a rock known as kimberlite, occurring in volcanic pipes, which may vary in area from a few hectares to more than 100 ha, and volcanic fissures, which are considerably smaller. Among the indicator minerals for kimberlite are chrome diopside, pyrope garnet, ilmenite and zircon. Few kimberlites contain diamonds, and in ore that does, the ratio of diamond to waste is about one part per 20m. There are four methods of diamond mining, of which open-cast mining is the commonest; diamonds are also recovered by underground, alluvial and, increasingly, offshore mining. The diamond is separated from its ore by careful crushing and gravity concentration, which maximizes the diamond's high specific gravity in a process called dense media separation.

The size of diamonds and other precious stones is measured in carats. One metric carat is equal to 0.2 gram, so one ounce avoirdupois equals 141.75 carats.

Diamonds can also be formed artificially, although these are usually very small. Synthetic diamonds form the bulk of industrial use (99%), although since the end of the 20th century production of gem-quality synthetic diamonds of appreciable size has been possible. However, synthetic gemstone diamonds amount to only a few thousand carats per year (compared with some 90m. carats of natural gemstones); many of the so-called fancy diamonds, which are coloured other than clear, through yellow to brown, are synthetic—only 0.01% of natural diamonds are fancy. Production of synthetic diamonds, almost all of which are destined for industrial use, usually amounts to between 25 and 30 times the output of natural diamonds annually: 14,600m. carats in 2019, compared with 138m. carats of natural diamonds (40% industrial), according to the latest available figures from the US Geological Survey (USGS). The People's Republic of China is, overwhelmingly, the principal producer of synthetic diamonds (91% of 2011 production; the USA produced 2.2% and nine other countries the rest—these USGS figures exclude production by Germany and the Republic of Korea). In Africa, only South Africa produces synthetic diamonds (1.4% in 2011). The principal market for synthetic diamonds remains the USA. Synthetic diamonds are produced by simulating geological formation under high-pressure, high-temperature (HPHT) conditions, or by chemical vapour deposition (CVD). Although the largest volume of diamond production and commerce is for industrial purposes, the gemstone market accounts for some 90% of the value traded. Sub-Saharan Africa, therefore, which produces about one-half (44% in 2019—an estimated 47% from the top four African producers alone in 2021) of the world's natural diamonds is the vital region in the diamond commodity market.

In 2018, according to the USGS, De Beers (Switzerland/South Africa) and Alrosa (Russian Federation) are the world's principal diamond-producing companies, with De Beers producing 23% of total global quantity of natural diamonds and 33% of the total value, and Alrosa 24% and 22%, respectively. Rio Tinto (United Kingdom/ Australia) is responsible for 12% of global production quantity and 5% of value. In 2013 operators on the Chiadzwa alluvial fields in Zimbabwe contributed 8% of quantity and 4% of value, while the Catoca mine in Angola was itself responsible for about 5% of not only production quantity but value, given the high proportion of gemstones found.

The World Market and the Region Africa is the major producing region for natural diamonds, although Australia joined the ranks of the major producers in 1983, and the Argyle open-cast diamond mine, in Western Australia, became the world's largest producing mine and the main source of industrial diamonds—output is predominantly of industrial-grade diamonds, with some lower-quality gem diamonds and a few pink diamonds. In 1998 Australian diamond production represented almost one-third of world output by volume, but in the 2000s its pre-eminence was increasingly challenged by Botswana, the Democratic Republic of the Congo (DRC) and the Russian Federation, reflecting a sharp decline in output at Argyle. Australia's gemstone production collapsed almost entirely in 2007. Of the other major producers, Russia produced more gem diamonds than industrial ones, but of a comparable order of output, while Botswana produced mainly gemstones and the DRC mainly industrial diamonds. Canada is almost entirely, and Angola

Production of Uncut Diamonds
(gem and industrial stones, million metric carats)

	2016	2017	2018	2019
World total	127.0	151.0	147.0	138.0
Sub-Saharan Africa . .	59.1	67.8	66.5	60.3
Leading sub-Saharan African producers				
Angola	9.0	9.4	8.4	9.1
Botswana*	21.0	22.9	24.5	23.7
Congo, Democratic Republic* . . .	15.6	19.1	15.1	13.5
Namibia	1.7	1.9	2.4	2.0
South Africa* . . .	8.3	9.7	9.9	7.2
Zimbabwe*	2.1	2.5	3.3	2.1
Other leading producers				
Australia*	14.0	17.1	14.1	13.0
Canada	13.0	23.2	23.2	18.6
Russian Federation* .	40.3	42.7	43.2	45.3

2020 (million carats): World 45 (Botswana 5, Congo, Democratic Republic 10, South Africa 2, Zimbabwe 2; Australia 11, Russian Federation 14). **2021** (million carats, estimates): World 45 (Botswana 6, Congo, Democratic Republic 11, South Africa 2, Zimbabwe 2; Australia 8, Russian Federation 15).
* Estimated production.

Source: US Geological Survey.

predominantly, a gemstone producer; by contrast, industrial diamond output accounted mostly for increased production in Zimbabwe from 2010. In 2019 Africa accounted for 46% of gem diamond production and 41% of natural industrial diamond production.

The continent's wealth in natural diamonds accounts for the dominance in the international trade of the great South African mining and trading house of De Beers. Founded in the late 19th century, De Beers Consolidated Mines Ltd controlled 90% of world diamond production by the beginning of the 1900s and proceeded to dominate the international trade in diamonds for the rest of that century. The company maintained a cartel by persuading or coercing independent producers to sell through its single marketing channel, while underpinning its control of supply by stockpiling. The Diamond Corporation, formed in 1930 by the major diamond producers, acted as the single channel through which most of the world's rough diamond production would be sold. To stabilize the market, the corporation put surplus output into reserve, to be sold at a time when conditions were favourable. The corporation was one of a group of companies, based in London, United Kingdom, that constituted the Central Selling Organisation (CSO). Until the 1990s the CSO dealt with about 90% of the world natural diamond trade, but De Beers' monopoly was challenged by Russian and Canadian interests, as well as by its loss of control of Australian output. Competition authorities were increasingly critical of the De Beers system, with its Russian deals attracting legal complications in Europe into the 2000s. Finally, in mid-2000 De Beers announced the abandonment of its monopoly of world diamond supply, in favour of adopting a more profitable demand-led business model; the 'historical' diamond stockpile had been sold off within four years. The successor to the CSO, the Diamond Trading Company (DTC), is still the leading marketing channel for natural diamonds, accounting for 40%–50% of the international trade in the 2000s. The parent company has been a Swiss-domiciled corporation, De Beers Centenary AG, since 1990, with De Beers Consolidated Mines retaining only the South African interests. De Beers still dominates the main national diamond ventures, joint ventures with the respective Governments, in Botswana and Namibia.

In terms of value, Botswana now ranks as the world's second largest producer of diamonds (behind the Russian Federation), which are the country's principal source of export earnings, normally accounting for up to three-quarters of export receipts and for as much as one-half of government revenues. In 2021 the value of Botswana's exports (f.o.b.) of diamonds represented 84% of the total value of the country's merchandise exports. In the mid-2010s diamonds were reckoned to account for about 30% of GDP, although a sharp decline in the value of sales threatened the Botswanan economy into the end of the decade. The mines are all open-cast, but the feasibility of eventual underground mining at Jwaneng (considered the world's richest diamond mine, based on the value of recovered diamonds) was being explored. Most diamond mining operations in Botswana are conducted by the Debswana Diamond Co (Pty) Ltd, which is owned equally by the Botswana Government and De Beers Centenary AG. Debswana is expected to be able to maintain diamond output at its 2002 level until around 2030. A new sales agreement with the Government announced in September 2011 consolidated the company's position and also provided for the DTC to move its hitherto London-based sales and aggregation functions to the country from 2013. Almost three-quarters (70%) of Botswana's natural diamond production in 2019 consisted of gemstones.

By the early 2010s almost all diamond output in the Democratic Republic of the Congo (DRC), which is mainly derived from alluvial mining operations in Kasai Oriental, consists of industrial diamonds, of which the DRC (as Zaire) was the world's principal producer until it was overtaken by Australia in 1986. In the 1990s as much as 50% of the DRC's production of gem- or near-gem-quality stones was smuggled out of the country. In the 2010s, the DRC was Africa's leading producer of industrial natural diamonds; globally, its main rivals are the Russian Federation and Australia. The Société Minière de Bakwanga (MIBA), in which the Government has an 80% share, holds the DRC diamond monopoly; MIBA accounted for 27% of annual capacity until the mid-2000s, the rest being artisanal. Since 2001, after some engagement with Zimbabwean military and Israeli interests, MIBA has operated an open-bidding and free market sales and export system. Artisanal production has been boosted by greater domestic political stability and by the implementation of the Kimberley Process (see below). The main MIBA site is at Mbuyi-Mayi. Almost all DRC diamond mining depended on artisanal production. In 2021 the value of the DRC's foreign sales of diamonds, at an estimated US $67m., represented only 0.4% of its total export revenue (down from 61% in 2003, although that is largely because other exports have increased in importance in the intervening period).

De Beers Consolidated Mines Ltd contributed the overwhelming bulk of South Africa's diamond production. According to official sources, South Africa usually exports more rough diamonds than it produces domestically because of the re-export of imported diamonds supplied by the DTC to its clients—'sightholders'—and of diamonds imported by dealers and cutters. The country is the only African producer of synthetic diamonds, providing some 60m. carats annually, according to the USGS. Angola's diamond output, which totalled 2.4m. carats in 1974, subsequently fell sharply as a consequence of the civil war. Production recovered substantially into the 2000s, and diamonds contributed 10.4% of the country's total export earnings in 2001, although its share declined once petroleum exports became more important in the late 2000s. (In 2021 exports of diamonds accounted for 4.6% of Angola's export earnings.) Most Guinean production, principally gemstones, is alluvial and artisanal. Namibian production, also mainly of gem-quality, suffers from high recovery costs, and the country has extensive offshore deposits. In 1994 the Namibian Government and De Beers established the Namdeb Diamond Corpn (Pty) Ltd, which is the country's leading producer. In 2005, according to the Bank of Namibia, the diamond sector accounted for 41% of Namibia's total export earnings and contributed 10% of the country's GDP; in 2021 diamonds accounted for 10% of the value of exports.

Other than the Democratic Republic of the Congo, Angola, Guinea and the Republic of the Congo, African countries whose diamond industries became tainted by the trade in 'conflict diamonds' were Sierra Leone, Côte d'Ivoire and Liberia. The Central African Republic was troubled more by the loss of diamond revenues to smuggling, as artisanal production was sold abroad illegally, but it hoped to benefit from certification (see below). In May 2013, however, diamond exports from the country were banned under the certification process, in an attempt to prevent 'conflict diamonds' sales financing the civil war; the export ban was only lifted in June 2016. In 2021—three years after the end of the ban—the country exported diamonds to the value of $5.1m., equivalent to 5.7% of the total value of exports that year. From 2010 Zimbabwean diamond production increased dramatically, despite international controversy over illicit diamond trading and dubious military involvement, and into the mid-2010s the country was exceeding Angolan production—although production fell dramatically in 2014–16, with Angolan production once more surpassing it. Production did recover some lost ground in 2017–19. Diamonds are still an important commodity to Zimbabwe's export earnings (2.7% of the total value of exports in 2021). By contrast, countries such as Tanzania have strong and yet non-controversial production. The Mwadui diamond pipe in Tanzania was one of the world's largest producing pipes, covering an area of 146 ha. Tanzania's diamond output was 838,000 carats in 1971, but by the late 1980s exports from Mwadui had effectively ceased. Following extensive rehabilitation, mining at Mwadui, and exports, recommenced in 1995. The country's main producer recently has been the Williamson mine—mainly gem-quality stones. Diamonds contributed just 0.1% of Tanzania's export revenues in 2021. Ghana, which once had a flourishing diamond sector, regained fairly steady production for most of the 2000s. Lesotho has a small industry, while Mauritania and Mozambique both have hopes of benefiting from the exploitation of diamond reserves.

Prices Rough diamonds, of which there are currently more than 5,000 categories, were traditionally sold by the CSO in mixed packages 10 times each year at regular sales, known as 'sights', in London, Johannesburg, South Africa, and Lucerne, Switzerland. Gems accounted for about 20% of total sales by weight, but, it was

Diamond Price
(imports to the USA, US $ per carat)

		Annual average
2005	. . . .	12.55
2010	. . . .	18.78
2015	. . . .	17.50
2019	. . . .	5.80
2020	. . . .	8.40
2021	. . . .	12.00

Source: US Geological Survey.

estimated, more than 90% by value. After being sold by the CSO, gem diamonds were sent to be cut and polished in preparation for jewellery manufacture. The leading cutting centres were in Antwerp, Belgium, Mumbai, India, New York, USA, and Tel-Aviv, Israel; this last opened an exchange for 'raw', or uncut, diamonds in 1993, with the intention of lessening the dependence of Israeli cutters on allocations from the CSO and purchases from the small, independent diamond exchange in Antwerp. However, by 2003 it was reported that 92% of the world's diamonds were cut and polished in Surat, India; higher grade diamonds tended to be dealt with in the older centres. Antwerp is the leading trading bourse.

As there are so many varieties of diamond, changes to prices (quoted in US dollars) effected by the CSO and its successor, the DTC, represent averages only. There are wide discrepancies in price, depending on such factors as rarity, colour and quality. The level of the price for diamonds can be indicated by volume sales at the DTC, or by the unit value of South African diamond exports, but the USGS cites the value of imports to the USA.

'Conflict Diamonds', Certification and the World Diamond Council In the 1990s the increasing role of the world diamond trade in the financing of guerrilla insurgencies in Africa, with particular reference to Angola, Sierra Leone and the DRC, prompted the UN Security Council in June 1998 to adopt a resolution (No. 1173) requiring that international markets ensure that illicitly exported diamonds from these areas did not enter world trade. These 'conflict diamonds' were defined as diamonds that had been either mined or stolen by rebels in opposition to the legitimate government of a country (about 3.7% of world diamond production in 1999, according to De Beers).

Despite the efforts to stem the trade in 'conflict diamonds', outlets for smuggled stones continued to operate, principally in Antwerp, Belgium, in Mumbai (Bombay), India, and in Tel-Aviv, Israel, while illicit output from guerrilla-controlled regions of Angola was marketed under false certification provided mainly by outlets in Côte d'Ivoire, Guinea and Liberia. In May 2000 southern African producing countries initiated what was termed the Kimberley Process, with the objective of ending the commercialization of 'conflict diamonds'. Endorsed in December by the UN General Assembly, and subsequently expanded to involve, as of August 2013, some 54 participants representing 81 countries (including the European Union, whose 28 members count as a single participant), the Kimberley Process has established the Kimberley Process Certification Scheme (KPCS), which has since 1 January 2003 imposed strict standards on all of its participants in respect of trade in rough diamonds. In July 2000 representatives of the World Federation of Diamond Bourses and the International Diamond Manufacturers Association resolved to implement a certification system that would allow rough diamonds to be monitored direct from mines to trading centres. At the same time the World Diamond Council (WDC) was established in order to implement and monitor the certification system, with a complementary warranties system of its own. Both the UN Security Council (in 2003) and the UN General Assembly (in 2000—see above—and 2004) have adopted resolutions supporting the Kimberley Process. In 2013, according to the WDC, 99.8% of rough diamonds were certified under the KPCS. Both the UN and some non-governmental organizations, however, have documented anomalies within the Kimberley Process, alleging a failure to address non-compliance, and with some in 2010, for instance, urging a widening of the definition of 'conflict diamonds'. In December 2011 one organization, Global Witness, even withdrew from the KPCS, alleging that the system was not working.

Action was also taken at the country and company level. Although considerable technical difficulties exist in the identification of diamonds originating in conflict areas, De Beers, as the principal conduit for African diamond sales, implemented a range of measures to comply with UN Resolution 1173. In 2000 the company went so far as to introduce documentation guaranteeing customers that none of its marketed diamonds emanated from conflict areas of Africa. There was a particular problem in Angola. The report of a UN sanctions committee explicitly cited the Presidents of Togo and Burkina Faso, as well as Belgian, Bulgarian and Ukrainian officials, who were all accused of involvement in the illicit diamond trade and of providing military assistance to the União Nacional para a Independência

Total de Angola (UNITA). As a result, the Diamond High Council in Antwerp entered into an origin verification agreement with the Angolan Government, which also initiated the restructuring of its national industry. In December 2002, following the death of the leader of UNITA, Jonas Savimbi, the UN Security Council voted to end the sanctions that it had applied to UNITA's diamond mining and selling operations; none the less, it was widely recognized that UNITA continued to dispose of large quantities of 'conflict diamonds'. Given civil conflict in the Central African Republic and the temptation of armed groups to finance their activity through illegal diamond sales, diamond exports from the country were banned in 2013–16. Greater compliance with certification standards around the world continued to be encouraged by the Kimberley Process, which was again endorsed by the UN General Assembly in February 2017. In August 2022 it was reported that the USA and other Western opponents of the Russian Federations's renewed armed invasion of Ukraine in the same year were seeking to classify Russian diamonds as 'conflict diamonds' in light of the ongoing hostilities.

GOLD (*Au*)

Gold minerals commonly occur in quartz, and are also found in alluvial deposits and in rich, thin underground veins. In South Africa gold occurs in sheets of low-grade ore (reefs) which may be at great depths below ground level. Gold is associated with silver, which is the commonest by-product of gold mining. Uranium oxide is another valuable by-product, particularly in the case of South Africa. Depending upon its associations, gold is separated by cyaniding, or else is concentrated and smelted. Gold is a dense, malleable metal, bright yellow in colour, and is one of the least reactive chemical elements.

Gold, silver and platinum are customarily measured in troy weight. A troy pound (now obsolete) contains 12 ounces, each of 480 grains. One troy oz is equal to 31.1 grams (1 kg = 32.15 troy oz), compared with the avoirdupois oz of 28.3 grams. Gold purity is measured in carats, in parts per 24, with 24 carats being pure gold (for gemstones and pearls, a carat is a unit of weight).

In modern times the principal function of gold has been as bullion in reserve for bank notes issued. From the early 1970s, however, the USA actively sought to 'demonetize' gold and so to make it simply another commodity. This objective was later adopted by the International Monetary Fund (IMF), which has attempted to end the position that gold occupied for many years in the international monetary system (see below). Gold remains an important investment commodity.

Production of Gold Ore
(metric tons, gold content)

	2017	2018	2019	2020
World total . . .	3,576.3	3,652.8	3,597.2	3,478.1
Africa	902.2	934.6	939.5	931.0
Leading African producers				
Burkina Faso . . .	74.6	78.0	83.1	93.4
Congo, Democratic Republic	47.0	63.0	62.9	60.9
Ghana	133.3	149.1	142.4	138.7
Mali	73.9	88.3	96.8	93.8
South Africa . . .	154.0	128.0	111.3	99.2
Sudan	88.0	76.6	78.0	83.8
Tanzania	54.6	46.3	46.5	45.9
Leading non-African producers				
Australia	292.5	313.0	325.1	327.8
Brazil	95.4	96.7	100.4	107.0
Canada	171.2	188.9	182.9	170.6
China, People's Republic .	429.1	404.1	383.2	368.3
Indonesia	117.6	153.0	92.3	100.9
Kazakhstan . . .	67.2	73.9	74.6	78.4
Mexico	119.6	118.4	109.0	101.6
Peru	166.6	162.6	143.3	97.8
Russian Federation . .	280.7	295.4	329.5	331.1
USA	236.3	224.9	200.4	190.2
Uzbekistan . . .	90.0	92.0	94.6	101.6

2021 (metric tons, gold content, estimates): Ghana 130, South Africa 100, Sudan 90; Australia 330, China, People's Republic 370, Russian Federation 300; World total (incl. others) 3,000.

Sources: Thomson Reuters GFMS; US Geological Survey.

The World Market and the Region As a portable real asset which is easily convertible into cash, gold is widely esteemed as a store of value. Another distinguishing feature of gold is that new production in any one year is very small in relation to existing stocks.

Much of the world's gold is in private bullion stocks, held for investment purposes, or is hoarded as a 'hedge' against inflation. Private investment stocks of gold throughout the world are estimated at 15,000–20,000 metric tons, much of it held in East Asia and India. By the beginning of 2013 the end of the decade-long bull run was apparent, as the gold price faltered. According to the World Gold Council, the first quarter of 2022 saw strong growth in gold demand; compared to the same period in the previous year, demand was up by 34%. The average price rose by 8% compared with the previous quarter as a result of the resurgent conflict in Ukraine and historically high inflation. Investors of exchange traded products (ETPs) increased global holdings by some 269 metric tons over the quarter, in contrast to just 174 tons of outflows during 2021 as a whole. Notwithstanding higher demand overall, jewellery consumption declined by 7% compared with the first quarter of 2021—owing largely to lower demand in the People's Republic of China and India. Although gold bar and coin investment was down by some 20% compared with the first quarter of 2021—when investment reached historically high levels—the 282 tons were still 11% above the five-year quarterly average for this market. Meanwhile, in the first quarter of 2022 gold demand in the technology segment (principally electronics) registered its highest first quarter figure since 2018 (82 tons).

Gold reserves were discovered near Johannesburg, South Africa, in 1884, and their exploitation formed the basis of the country's subsequent economic prosperity. For more than 100 years South Africa was the world's leading gold producer. In 2007, however, the country relinquished primacy to China, where output had been rising steadily since 1999. China's position was confirmed in 2008 (when it accounted for 12% of world production, in which year the USA also exceeded South African production. By 2020 the output of 10 countries exceeded that of South Africa (including Ghana, Africa's largest producer). South Africa achieved its peak gold production in 1970, mining some 1,000 metric tons in that year. From the mid-1980s in particular the South African gold industry was adversely affected by the rising costs of extracting generally declining grades of ore from ageing and increasingly marginal (low return) mines. Additionally, the level of world gold prices was not sufficiently high to stimulate the active exploration and development of new mines. The share of gold in South Africa's export revenue accordingly declined. and in 1989 the commercial profitability of South African gold production was for the first time exceeded by profits from mining activities other than gold. In 2006, for the first time since 1925, South Africa produced less than 300 tons of gold (295.7 tons). Lower grades of ore, new safety procedures but continuing concerns, power and other infrastructural problems, skills shortages and issues with organized labour all contributed to steadily declining production. By 2008 South Africa's contribution to global mined production of gold had fallen to below one-10th for the first time in more than a century, having provided two-thirds in 1970. In 2021 gold still contributed 6.0% of South Africa's total export revenue. That process of decline has also been accompanied by substantial increases in world output, as new capacity has been brought into production in other countries.

From 2009 rising gold production elsewhere in Africa began to compensate for the continuing contraction in South African mining of the metal. Ghana, formerly a significant African producer of gold, had from 1990 begun to reverse a long period of decline, and by the end of the decade and into the new century was secure in its position as the second largest producer on the continent. By 2018 it had overtaken South Africa as the continent's largest producer, a position it maintained in 2019–20. In 2021 exports of gold accounted for about 27% of Ghana's total export revenue, which was down from 64% in 2010, despite continuing strength in the international gold price, because significant hydrocarbons exports began in the latter year. As petroleum exports became stronger and more consistent, so did gold's share stabilize in 2014. Gold production in Mali increased substantially from 1997, reflecting the exploitation of deposits at Sadiola Hill, and from 2009 was bolstered to an extent by increasing production at new mines. Most mining operations were located in the south of the country, so activity was little affected by the political upheavals in 2012. In 2021 gold was still overwhelmingly Mali's most important source of export revenue, accounting for 82% of the country's total export earnings. Artisanal production (31% of the total in 2016) boosted gold output in 2015–20 in particular; however, there was a drop in artisanal exports in 2020 as a result of the COVID-19 pandemic and ongoing political instability. (A military coup had unseated President Ibrahim Boubacar Keïta that year and forced the dissolution of the country's parliament.) Meanwhile Tanzania had began to challenge Mali for third place among African producers, its first large-scale gold mine commenced operations in 1998. A subsequent mine, the Geita project, is the largest producer of gold in East Africa. Tanzania recorded an increase of almost 87% in its output in 2000, and in 2001 production almost doubled. Production thus rose from 17.2 metric tons in 2000 to peaks of 49.3 tons in 2005 and 49.6 tons in 2011, but output was vulnerable to labour disputes, problems with the encroachment of artisanal miners, high inflation and, increasingly, low-grade or depleted resources. By 2020 Tanzania ranked as only the continent's eighth largest producer. The Democratic Republic of the Congo (DRC) was Africa's sixth largest producer of gold in 2020, although there were concerns about the prevalence of 'conflict' gold serving to finance armed groups.

Burkina production had risen slowly through the 2000s, and in 2008 five large-scale mines came into production in Burkina Faso. In mid-2010 the Inata mine of Avocet Mining and the Essakane mine of IAMGOLD began commercial production, alone contributing almost one-third of Burkinabè output in that year and accounting for most of the boost in 2011 production. By 2020 the country was Africa's fourth largest producer. Equipment issues sometimes limited output, but the general impact on national exports was apparent: the contribution of gems and precious metals (overwhelmingly gold) went from 2% in 2007 to 75% by 2012—gold provided 77% of the value of total exports in 2021. In Guinea, meanwhile, output declined from 2008 onwards. The country continued to slip down the rankings of African gold producers into the 2010s; the most notable of the challengers was Sudan, where the high gold price encouraged a leap in production from 2009 (output peaked at 88.0 tons in 2018). Sudan, the DRC and Ethiopia all relied on artisanal production to boost output. Zimbabwean gold production also increased, doubling between 2008 and 2011. Gold had been overtaken in 1980 by tobacco as the country's major source of foreign exchange, and the gold mining industry had contracted substantially, not helped by political and economic problems in the country. Contracting output had fallen as low as 8.9 tons by 2008 (taking Zimbabwean gold production to its lowest level in 90 years), before gradual recovery. In 2020 Zimbabwe produced 40.9 metric tons of gold. Ethiopia and Eritrea also produced some gold; the former's output had reached 10.0 tons in 2020.

Côte d'Ivoire's Tongon mine poured its first gold in November 2010, and the increasing production from it more than offset interruptions to supply from other mines owing to civil unrest in 2011. National output reached a record 36.4 metric tons in 2020, putting the country in 10th place among African gold producers. Commercial production at the Sabodala open-pit mine in Senegal began in 2009, taking that country's gold output from 0.1 tons annually to a peak of 17.3 tons in 2019; production was 15.8 tons in the following year. Mauritania's output increased from less than 1.0 tons annually to 1.9 tons in 2007 and 15.6 tons in 2020. The only significant North African producer is Egypt, which produced 14.1 tons in 2020 (from negligible production as late as 2009). Liberia began commercial production at its New Liberty mine during 2016; ccording to USGS figures, the country produced an estimated 4.9 tons in 2019. Less significant African producers included Zambia (4.5 tons in 2019—USGS figures), Niger and, for the first time in 2013, Gabon, where the new Bakoudou-Magnima operation produced 1 ton of gold.

International Association The World Gold Council (WGC), founded in 1987, is an international association of gold producing companies which aims to promote gold as a financial asset and to increase demand for the metal. The WGC, based in London, United Kingdom, had 32 corporate members in 2022.

Gold Prices on the London Bullion Market
(afternoon 'fixes', US $ per troy oz)

	Average	Highest	Lowest
1990 .	383.59	n.a.	n.a.
2000 .	279.11	(7 February) 312.70	(27 October) 263.80
2010 .	1,224.52	(9 November) 1,421.00	(5 February) 1,058.00
2015 .	1,160.06	(22 January) 1,295.75	(17 December) 1,049.40
2019 .	1,392.60	(4 September) 1,546.10	(23 April) 1,269.50
2020 .	1,769.59	(6 August) 2,067.15	(19 March) 1,474.25
2021 .	1,798.60	(4 January) 1,943.20	(30 March) 1,683.95

Gold Prices in Various Currencies
(annual averages, per troy oz)

	Rand per kg*	Yen per gram*	Rupees per 10 grams (Mumbai)
1990 .	31,893	1,784	3,406
2000 .	62,173	967	4,518
2010 .	287,568	3,444	18,368
2015 .	473,944	4,513	26,484
2016 .	589,454	4,354	29,653
2017 .	538,028	4,531	29,153
2018 .	538,141	4,503	30,841

* Prices calculated using London exchange rates and the afternoon 'fix'.

Source: Thomson Reuters GFMS.

Prices The unit of dealing in international gold markets is the 'good delivery' gold bar, weighing about 400 oz (12.5 kg). The principal centres for gold trading are London, Hong Kong and Zürich, Switzerland. The dominant markets for gold futures (buying and selling for future delivery) are the New York Commodity Exchange (COMEX) in the USA and the Tokyo Commodity Exchange (TOCOM) in Japan. A small group of dealers meets twice on each working day (morning and afternoon) to 'fix' the price of gold in the London Bullion Market (LBM), and the first table above is based on the second of these daily 'fixes'. During any trading day, however, prices may fluctuate above or below these levels. (A new LBM Association gold price was launched on 20 March 2015, to be operated by an independent third-party provider, ICE Benchmark Administration—IBA.) Prices in other markets and other currencies vary. In real terms, the average annual London gold price has never exceeded its 1980 height of US $1,765.83 per troy oz (at constant 2014 prices); the London price fell to $695.02 per oz in 1990 and $383.73 per oz in 2000, reaching its lowest point in 2001 ($362.43 per oz). The rise in the average annual price of gold through the 2008 collapse in commodity prices and the onset of global recession was even more pronounced at constant prices than in nominal terms, reaching a peak of $1,720.86 per oz in 2012. The financial crisis had prompted many investors to seek refuge in the traditional haven of gold, disrupting the typical alignment of the gold price with petroleum prices, which was therefore less apparent from October 2008 for a time.

Gold: Monetization and Demonetization During the 19th century gold was increasingly adopted as a monetary standard, with prices set by governments. In 1919 the Bank of England allowed some South African gold to be traded in London 'at the best price obtainable'. The market was suspended in 1925–31, when sterling returned to a limited form of the gold standard, and again in 1939–54. In 1934 the official price of gold was fixed at US $35 per troy oz and, by international agreement, all transactions in gold had to take place within narrow margins around that price. In 1960 the official gold price came under pressure from market demand. As a result, an international gold 'pool' was established in 1961 at the initiative of the USA. Originally a consortium of leading central banks with the object of restraining the London price of gold in case of excessive demand, it later widened into an arrangement by which eight central banks agreed that all purchases and sales of gold should be handled by the Bank of England. However, growing private demand for gold continued to exert pressure on the official price, and the gold 'pool' was ended in 1968, in favour of a two tier price system. Central banks continued to operate the official price of $35 per oz, but private markets were permitted to deal freely in gold. However, the free market price did not rise significantly above the official price. In August 1971 the USA announced that it would cease dealing freely in gold to maintain exchange rates for the dollar within previously agreed margins. This 'floating' of the dollar against other major currencies continued until December, when it was agreed to raise the official gold price to $38 per oz. Gold prices on the free market rose to $70 per oz in August 1972. In February 1973 the US dollar was devalued by a further 10%, the official gold price rising to $42.22 per oz. Thereafter the free market price rose even higher, reaching $127 per oz in June 1973. In November it was announced that the two tier system would be terminated, and from 1974 governments were permitted to value their official gold stocks at market prices.

In 1969 the IMF had introduced a new unit for international monetary dealings, the special drawing right (SDR), with a value of US $1.00, and the first allocation of SDRs was made on 1 January 1971. The SDR was linked to gold at an exchange rate of SDR 35 per troy oz, but this came under pressure from the devaluations of the US currency, and in July 1974 the direct link between the SDR and the US dollar was ended. Instead, the SDR was valued in terms of a weighted 'basket' of national currencies. At the same time the official gold price of SDR 35 per troy oz was retained as the IMF's basis for valuing official reserves. In 1976 the membership of the IMF agreed on proposals for far reaching changes in the international monetary system. These reforms, which were implemented on a gradual basis during 1977–81, included a reduction in the role of gold in the international system and the abolition of the official price of gold. A principal objective of the IMF plan was achieved in April 1978, when central banks were able to buy and sell gold at market prices. The physical quantity of reserve gold held by the IMF and member countries' central banks as national reserves has subsequently fallen (see below). The USA still maintains the largest national stock of gold, although the volume of its reserves has been substantially reduced. At the end of 1949 US gold reserves were 701.8m. oz, but since the beginning of the 1980s the level has been in the range of 261.4m.–264.6m. oz. At July 2021 US gold reserves reportedly stood at 8,133 tons, or 261.5m. oz.

During 1996 substantial amounts of gold bullion, jointly exceeding 500 metric tons, were sold by the central banks of Belgium and the Netherlands, and the Swiss National Bank announced its intention to allocate part of its gold reserves to fund a new humanitarian foundation. In the same year the UK first suggested a scheme to use some sales of IMF gold to finance debt relief for the world's poorest countries, principally in Africa. In July 1997 the Reserve Bank of Australia announced that it had disposed of more than two-thirds of its bullion holdings (reducing its reserves from 247 tons to 80 tons) over the previous six months. National sales of gold became far more common and, in response to concerns that the official sector's unco-ordinated gold sales were depressing gold prices, in 1999 the European Central Bank (ECB), in a joint statement with the central banks of Switzerland and 13 members of the European Union (Sweden, the UK and the 11 countries then in the eurozone), announced a five-year moratorium on new sales of gold held in official reserves. Total gold reserves held by the 15 signatory banks totalled 16,336 metric tons, accounting for around 48% of global gold reserves. The agreement—referred to as the Central Bank Gold Agreement (CBGA) and also known as the Washington Agreement on gold—allowed impending sales that had already been decided to proceed, although total sales were not to exceed 400 tons per year over the five-year period. The announcement also stated that gold would remain an important element of global monetary reserves. The European agreement was generally welcomed for removing uncertainty from the gold market, although the permitted rate of sales (400 tons per year) was more than 100% greater than the average net sales by the signatory countries in 1989–98. In March 2004 the renewal of the CBGA was announced, to cover the five-year period from September 2004 to September 2009, without the UK but with Greece as a new signatory. The second CBGA ended the moratorium on sales not already decided, and annual sales quotas were raised to 500 tons in order to take into account the consolidation of the price of gold that had occurred. Slovenia became a signatory of the second CBGA in December 2006, immediately prior to its adoption of the euro as its currency. Cyprus and Malta likewise became CBGA signatories on adopting the euro in January 2008, as did Slovakia in January 2009. The third CBGA entered effect at the end of September 2009, with the same signatories as those to the second agreement. Under the new CBGA, covering the five-year period to 2014, the cap on annual sales was again reduced to 400 tons (with the signatories noting that the intention of the IMF to sell 403 tons of gold could be accommodated within the overall quotas). Despite speculation that the low level of official sales made a fourth CBGA unnecessary, a new five-year agreement was concluded in May 2014 and it took effect on 27 September; the cap on sales was removed, but this marked the end of the era of significant official gold sales. It was reported in mid-2019 that the ECB and 21 other European central banks would not be renewing the CBGA for a fourth time, citing the maturity of the gold market as the reason for its decision.

GROUNDNUT (Peanut, Monkey Nut, Earth Nut) (*Arachis hypogaea*)

The groundnut or peanut is not a true nut, although the underground pod, which contains the kernels, forms a more or less dry shell at maturity. The plant is a low growing annual herb introduced from South America, and resembles the indigenous African Bambarra groundnut (*Vigna subterranea*), which it now outnumbers. Groundnuts that come to market generally consist of one of the four main types: runner, Spanish, Virginia and Valencia.

Each groundnut pod contains between two and four kernels, enclosed in a reddish skin. The kernels are highly nutritious because of their high content of both protein (about 30%) and oil (40%–50%). In tropical countries the crop is grown partly for domestic consumption and partly for export. Whole nuts of selected large dessert types, with the skin removed, are eaten raw or roasted. Peanut butter is made by removing the skin and germ and grinding the roasted nuts. The most important commercial use of groundnuts is the extraction of oil. Groundnut oil is used as a cooking and salad oil, as an ingredient in margarine, and, in the case of lower quality oil, in soap manufacture. According to the US Department of Agriculture (USDA), the world's most produced vegetable oils are palm oil and soybean oil, then rapeseed oil and sunflowerseed oil, and distantly followed by palm kernel oil, groundnut oil and cottonseed oil (then coconut oil and olive oil). Consumption followed a similar pattern, but in terms of world exports palm oil was by far the most important vegetable oil, with groundnut oil eighth of the nine listed by USDA for 2021/22. Oilseed production, however, in volume terms, is dominated by soybean, followed by rapeseed, cottonseed, sunflowerseed and groundnut, then palm kernel and copra.

An oilcake, used in animal feeding, is manufactured from the groundnut residue left after oil extraction. However, trade in this groundnut meal is limited by health laws in some countries, as groundnuts can be contaminated by a mould which generates toxic and carcinogenic metabolites, the most common and most dangerous of which is aflatoxin B_1. The European Union (EU) has banned imports for use as animal feed of oilcake and meal which contain more than 0.03 mg of aflatoxin per kg. The meal can be treated with ammonia, which both eliminates the aflatoxin and enriches the cake. Groundnut shells, which are usually incinerated or simply discarded as waste, can be converted into a low-cost organic fertilizer, which has been produced since the early 1970s.

Production of Groundnuts
(in shell; '000 metric tons)

	2017	2018	2019	2020
World total . . .	48,441	51,472	49,544	53,638
Sub-Saharan Africa* .	14,741	16,609	16,362	16,581
Leading sub-Saharan African producers				
Cameroon† . . .	480	480	500	500
Mali	301	491	369	260
Nigeria	4,521	4,600*	4,461*	4,493*
Senegal	1,405	1,501	1,421	1,797
Sudan	1,648†	2,884	2,828	2,773
Tanzania† . . .	650	670	680	690
Other leading producers				
Argentina	1,031	921	1,337	1,285
China, People's Republic.	17,092	17,332	17,520	17,993†
India	7,462	9,253	6,727	9,952
Indonesia	849	886	1,175	860*
Myanmar	1,583	1,562	1,616	1,647*
USA	3,228	2,493	2,480	2,782
Viet Nam	460	457	443	425

* FAO estimate(s).

† Unofficial figure(s).

Source: FAO.

The World Market and the Region Since the late 20th century more than 90% of the world's groundnut output has come from developing countries. Groundnuts are the most important of Africa's oilseeds and form the chief export crop of The Gambia and, traditionally, Senegal (which still exports groundnut oil in reasonable quantities). According to USDA, sub-Saharan Africa's exports accounted for 20% of the world total in 2021/22; only 6% of African production was exported in that year. Sub-Saharan Africa accounted for about one-fifth (19% in 2021/22) of world production of groundnut oil. The world's largest exporters of groundnut oil were Brazil, Argentina, India, Mali, Senegal, Nicaragua, the USA and Sudan. Many of the large African producers provided increasingly for domestic consumption. In 2018 exports of groundnuts and groundnut products contributed just 3% of The Gambia's total revenue from exports (including re-exports) after a declining trend (although this figure was based on total exports that were less than one-half of the previous year). The Gambia exported no groundnuts in 2019–20. Malawi, an erratic but often strong exporter, earned 2% of the value of its exports from groundnuts in 2021. Nigeria, Africa's largest producer by some margin, was chiefly engaged in feeding only its own burgeoning internal market by the 2010s, and the country had become less relevant to international markets, except in the export of groundnuts. The traditional West African groundnut states were reinforced by production in the Sahel and southern Africa, although both were vulnerable to devastation by drought, as was the case in Sudan.

Regional Council The African Groundnut Council was founded in 1964 to advise its member producing countries (The Gambia, Mali, Niger, Nigeria, Senegal and Sudan) on marketing policies. It is based in Kano, Nigeria (having relocated from Lagos in 2005), and has a sales promotion office in Geneva, Switzerland. Western Europe, particularly France, has traditionally been the principal market for African groundnuts.

Groundnut and Groundnut Oil Prices
(annual averages, US $ per metric ton)

	Groundnuts	Groundnut oil
2005	874.22	1,170.98
2010	1,240.66	1,400.99
2015	1,304.87	1,377.96
2019	1,337.81	1,407.37
2020	1,838.67	1,697.81
2021	1,555.04	2,075.09

Source: World Bank, *Commodity Price Data* (Pink Sheet).

Prices Groundnuts are traded unprocessed or as the oil. The international indicator prices here are for US runner peanuts (40/50, unshelled) (c.f.r. north-west Europe). The groundnut oil import price (f.o.b. south-east) is generally more volatile than that for groundnuts. The average monthly price for groundnuts grew throughout 2016 and into 2017. Prices declined once more from early 2017 and into much of 2018, but recovered substantially in late 2019 and early 2020—averaging US $2,050 per ton in April–June, the highest level since January 2013. However, the average monthly price for groundnuts was generally lower thereafter; it reached $1,625 per ton in August 2022. Meanwhile, the price of groundnut oil had reached $2,146 per ton by August 2022. The increased price of the latter was attributed, initially in 2021, to greater consumer demand during periods of government-enforced 'lockdown' around the world (to contain the COVID-19 pandemic), as households traditionally consume groundnut oil—this in preference to commercially favoured oils such as palm oil, which experienced significant price declines as restaurants and hotels remained closed. Sustained price growth in 2022 was largely the result of the ongoing war in Ukraine (usually a significant exporter of sunflower oils), which caused supply disruptions and placed upward pressure on the price of edible oils, as a consequence of which demand for compressed oils (such as groundnut oil manufactures) increased.

IRON ORE (Iron, *Fe*)

Iron is, after silicon and aluminium, the third most abundant metallic element in the earth's crust, and its ore volume production is far greater than that of any other metal. Some ores contain 70% iron, while a grade of only 25% is commercially exploitable in certain areas. The main economic iron-ore minerals are magnetite and haematite, which are used almost exclusively to produce pig-iron and direct-reduced iron (DRI—also known as sponge iron). These comprise the principal raw materials for the production of crude steel (which makes up about 95% of global metal production).

Most iron ore is processed after mining to improve its chemical and physical characteristics, and is often agglomerated by pelletizing or sintering. The transformation of the ore into pig-iron is achieved through reduction by coke in blast furnaces; the proportion of ore to pig-iron yielded is usually about 1.5:1 or 1.6:1. Pig-iron is used to make cast iron and wrought iron products, but most of it is converted into steel by removing most of the carbon content. Particular grades of steel (e.g. stainless) are made by the addition of ferro-alloys such as chromium, nickel and manganese. From the 1990s processing technology was being developed in the use of high-grade ore to produce DRI, or sponge iron, which, unlike the iron used for traditional blast furnace operations, requires no melting or refining. The DRI process, which is based on the use of natural gas, expanded rapidly in Venezuela, but, owing to technological limitations, is not expected within the foreseeable future to replace more than a small proportion of the world's traditional blast furnace output. Venezuela and Mexico were the leading producers of DRI into the beginning of the 21st century, but India became increasingly the world's largest single producer from 2003 (Venezuelan production fell dramatically in the 2010s). The energy-rich Middle East and North Africa was the leading producing region for DRI.

Production of Iron Ore
(iron content, '000 metric tons, estimates)

	2016	2017	2018	2019
World total	1,460,000	1,500,000	1,520,000	1,520,000
Sub-Saharan Africa* .	54,548	60,180	56,889	51,482
Principal Sub-Saharan African producers				
Liberia	878	1,210	2,460	2,560
Mauritania . . .	8,290	7,320	6,694	7,625
Sierra Leone . . .	2,380	4,050	535	97
South Africa . . .	43,000	47,600	47,200	41,200
Leading non-African producers				
Australia	531,075	548,297	562,137	568,965
Brazil	268,000	289,000	293,000	258,000
Canada†	28,100	30,200	31,500	35,200
China, People's Republic .	228,118	215,989	209,311	219,000
India‡	114,000	125,000	127,000	148,000
Russian Federation .	59,647	56,074	56,700	64,287
Ukraine	39,300	37,900	37,800	39,500
USA	26,400	30,300	31,300	29,800

2020 (usable ore, gross weight, million metric tons): South Africa 56; Australia 912, Brazil 388, China, People's Republic 360, India 204, Russian Federation 100; World total (incl. others) 2,470. **2021** (usable ore, gross weight, million metric tons, estimates): South Africa 61; Australia 900, Brazil 380, China, People's Republic 360, India 240, Russian Federation 100; World total (incl. others) 2,600.

* Sum of the output in the listed countries; data on the small amounts produced in Kenya, Nigeria, Togo and Uganda are insufficient for inclusion.

† Estimated production.

‡ Production based on Indian fiscal year starting 1 April.

Source: US Geological Survey.

The World Market and the Region As the basic feedstock for the production of steel, iron ore is a major raw material in the world economy and in international trade. After petroleum, the iron ore trade is the second largest commodity market by value (but still generally equivalent to less than one-10th of the crude market). Mining the ore usually involves substantial long-term investment, so until about 2010 up to 60% of trade was conducted under long-term contracts, while the mine investments were financed with some participation from consumers. Stability was undermined by the arrival of the People's Republic of China on the international markets; in 2004 China surpassed Japan as the world's leading importer, and its burgeoning internal market ended a system based on steady slow growth in the iron ore mining sector. After the international financial crisis in 2008 particularly, but also given preceding commodity price fluctuations, producers became frustrated with the inflexibility of long-term contracts and began to favour quarterly and then monthly average-based contracts, or 'spot' pricing, thereby fuelling a derivatives market (see below).

The international trade in iron ore expanded in 2019. In that year, on the basis of data compiled by the USGS, a little more than one-half of world exports of iron ore were provided by Australia (54%) and almost one-quarter by Brazil (24%), followed by South Africa (4%). India, previously an important exporter, faced problems in dealing with illegal mining from 2010 and exports collapsed (see below). According to data from the UN Conference on Trade and Development (UNCTAD) Trust Fund Project on Iron Ore Information, between 2001 and 2010 four countries—the People's Republic of China, Japan, the Republic of Korea (South Korea) and Germany—had consistently accounted for more than two-thirds of all world imports of iron ore; over that period, however, China's share in the world total had gone from 19% to 59%, while Japan's share declined from 26% to 13%, South Korea's from 9% to 5% and Germany's from 8% to 4%. Iron ore exports globally had doubled between 1999 and 2008, mainly owing to increased demand from China. The three largest iron ore producing companies in the world in 2020 were Vale (300m. tons annually), Rio Tinto (286m. tons) and BHP Billiton (248m. tons). The three companies are even more significant in export markets, controlling 57% of the world seaborne trade of iron ore in 2011. The fourth largest producer, Fortescue Metals Group of Australia, increased output significantly in the first half of the 2010s, and by 2014 the top four companies were reckoned to control almost 70% of seaborne iron ore demand.

Iron ore is widely distributed throughout Africa, with several countries having substantial reserves of high-grade deposits (60%–68% iron). Africa was expected to be supplying about 10% of the world's iron ore supply by 2025 (compared with 4% in 2010), as well as processing more ore domestically. One of the world's largest unexploited iron ore deposits (with estimated resources of more than 560m. metric tons, with a metal content of 64%) is located at Bélinga, in remote north-east Gabon. In August 2022 it was reported that a joint venture had been agreed between Fortescue Metals (Australia) and the Government of Gabon to begin development of the 4,500-sq km area. The deal for the Bélinga iron ore project included a US $90m. exploration programme. Annual output from the Bélinga project was ultimately expected to reach 20m.–30m. tons of ore. In Senegal, the development of the country's Falémé iron ore project and accompanying infrastructure was also mired in controversy and delay. Côte d'Ivoire's as yet unexploited resources of iron ore were estimated at 3,000m. tons (40% iron) in 2003. Tata Steel agreed at the end of 2007 to conduct exploratory and feasibility work on the Mount Nimba deposit. The Mount Nimba iron ore reserves, estimated at 1,000m. tons, extended into two other countries—Liberia and Guinea—and the Côte d'Ivoire mine was at one time expected to begin production in 2016, but market conditions militated against this, as well as the failure to build, as yet, a railway to a new port at San Pedro. ArcelorMittal began iron ore production at the Liberia site in September 2011, while the first iron ore mine in Guinea commenced operations in mid-2012. Other iron ore reserves in Guinea include the Pic du Fon deposit, totalling an estimated 1,200m. tons, at Simandou, one of the world's few remaining unexploited iron ore resources and probably to be the largest integrated iron ore mine and infrastructure project in Africa. Allegations of corruption (BSG Resources of Switzerland was accused of obtaining the rights corruptly, an official inquiry finding the company guilty in 2014), court cases and reassessment of mining policies by the new regime frustrated the development of the deposits and first shipments seemed unlikely before the end of the decade. Meanwhile, in 2009 Xstrata of Switzerland announced investment of $50m. in exploration of the Zanaga iron ore deposits in the Republic of the Congo.

The continent's leading producer of iron ore is South Africa, and that country's export sales are mainly destined for Pacific Rim countries. In 2021 iron ore exports earned 8% of total export revenues; a further 5% of total income from exports was earned from iron and steel. The country's two principal iron ore concerns, Kumba Iron Ore (KIO) and Assmang, both continued to invest in iron ore production in South Africa. Highveld is also an important iron ore miner, and there are two other, smaller operations.

Among the African producers of iron ore, the country most dependent on the mineral as a source of foreign exchange is Mauritania, which still derived 55% of its total export earnings from shipments of iron ore in 2021, despite notable petroleum production, which began in 2006, and the increase in gold exports, for example. The Société Nationale Industrielle et Minière (SNIM), which has sole responsibility for iron ore production and beneficiation, operated a mining centre at the northern town of Zouérate, three open-pit iron ore mines and transport infrastructure including a railway linking the mining centre with port facilities at Nouadhibou. Investment in existing sources of output, as well as new projects, continued into the 2010s. Kenya produces a small amount of iron ore, while iron ore deposits in Nigeria seem barely to be exploited; unofficially estimated in 1999 to exceed 3,000m. metric tons, mining commenced in 1986, but in the 2010s remained at a low level. In 1980 deposits estimated at 20m. tons of ore (50% iron) were identified in the west of Zambia, but these remained unexploited more than 40 years later. Tanzania has ore reserves estimated at 45m. tons (52% iron) at Liganga and 8m. tons (40% iron) in the Uluguru Mountains. Zimbabwean production, exceeding 350m. tons in some years until 2005, declined thereafter, and was put at just 50m. tons in 2007 and one-half of that amount in 2008 (the last recorded year of production). Iron ore mining in Angola was beset by civil conflict and was abandoned in 1975. Angola holds considerable ore production stockpiles, but the resumption of export trade in the ore depends on the eventual rehabilitation of the 520-km rail link between mines at Cassinga and the coast. The revived Marampa mine and the new Tonkolili project in Sierra Leone helped to fuel high growth in the country from 2011 and accounted for an estimated 16% of gross domestic product just before they closed, owing to financial problems in 2015. The ore deposits have an iron content of 69%, which tempted Chinese firm Shandong Iron and Steel into taking over and resuming operations in 2016, although it was announced in August 2019 that the Government had cancelled its operating licence. Liberia has abandoned stockpiles of iron ore from the old Yekepa works, but also the Mount Nimba iron ore reserves in the west of the country. ArcelorMittal Liberia assumed responsibility for mining these, under a 2005 agreement with the Government, and it expected its mines' capacity to be 15m. tons of iron ore concentrate per year from 2015. Madagascar has an iron ore deposit at Bekipsa, the rights to which are held by Canadian company Cline.

International Association The Association of Iron Ore Exporting Countries (Association des Pays Exportateurs de Minerai de Fer—APEF) was established in 1975 to promote close co-operation among members, to safeguard their interests as iron ore exporters, to ensure the orderly growth of international trade in iron ore, and to secure 'fair and remunerative' returns from its exploitation, processing and marketing. Since 1975 APEF, which also collects and disseminates information on iron from its secretariat in Geneva, Switzerland, has had nine members: Algeria, Australia, Chile, India, Mauritania, Peru, Sierra Leone, Tunisia and Venezuela.

Iron Ore Price
(average settlement price, US $ per metric ton)

	Average	High	Low
2005*	65.00	—	—
2010	145.86	(April) 172.47	(January) 125.72
2015	55.85	(January) 68.23	(December) 40.05
2019	93.85	(July) 120.24	(January) 76.16
2020	108.92	(December) 155.43	(April) 84.73
2021	161.71	(June) 214.43	(November) 96.24

* Annual contract price (Brazil to Europe, f.o.b., $ per ton).

Source: World Bank, *Commodity Price Data* (Pink Sheet).

Prices Until 2009 world reference prices for iron ore were decided annually at a series of meetings between producers and purchasers (the steel industry accounts for about 95% of all iron ore consumption), but when China failed to agree prices with major producers, and with 'spot' prices for iron ore soaring in the latter half of that year when miners were still selling at prices agreed in March, the system effectively collapsed in 2010. The USA and the republics of the former USSR, although major steel producers, rely on domestic ore production and had taken little part in the price negotiations. It was generally accepted that, because of its diversity in form and quality, iron ore was ill-suited to price stabilization through an international buffer stock arrangement.

Given the complexity of the old pricing system, a general trend can be indicated from the prices cited by the World Bank—the average 'spot' price per dry metric ton (cost and freight) to China of iron ore (fines, 62% *Fe*) of any origin. By the 2000s Chinese demand was the principal determinant of prices in the international iron ore trade, although various fears about prospects for growth in the world

economy have contributed to price volatility. With supply problems easing by 2015, as new capacity finally began to enter production, prices were tending downwards until the end of 2015, only strengthening into 2016 in line with renewed Chinese demand. The December 2015 average monthly price was the lowest figure since December 2004; prices improved generally over 2016 but were erratic throughout 2017 and 2018. Prices began to climb from early 2019, but fell back down in the second half of that year and the first half of 2020; from the middle of 2020 and through the first half of 2021, however, prices increased substantially, to reach $214 per ton in June, their highest ever level. The rising prices were attributed to strong demand from China, and mine closures in Brazil and China putting further pressure on existing supply constraints. Prices fell dramatically thereafter; the average price was $109 per metric ton in August.

MAIZE (Indian Corn, Mealies) (*Zea mays*)

Maize is one of the world's three principal cereal crops, with wheat and rice. Originally from the Americas, maize has been dispersed to many parts of the world. The principal varieties are dent maize (which has large, soft, flat grains) and flint maize (which has round, hard grains). Dent maize is the predominant type worldwide, but flint maize is widely grown in southern Africa. Maize may be white or yellow (there is little nutritional difference), but the former is preferred for human consumption in Africa. Maize is an annual crop, planted from seed, and matures within three to five months. It requires a warm climate and ample water supplies during the growing season. Genetically modified varieties of maize, with improved resistance to pests, are now being cultivated, particularly in the USA and also in Argentina and the People's Republic of China. However, further development of genetically modified maize may be slowed by consumer resistance in importing countries and doubts about its environmental impact.

Maize is an important foodstuff in regions such as sub-Saharan Africa and the tropical zones of Latin America, where the climate precludes the extensive cultivation of other cereals. It is, however, inferior in nutritive value to wheat, being especially deficient in lysine, and tends to be replaced by wheat in diets when the opportunity arises. In many African countries the grain is ground into a meal, mixed with water, and boiled to produce a gruel or porridge. In other areas it is made into (unleavened) corn bread or breakfast cereals. Maize is also the source of an oil used in cooking.

The high starch content of maize makes it highly suitable as a compound feed ingredient, especially for pigs and poultry. Animal feeding is the main use of maize in the USA, Europe and Japan, and large amounts are also used for feed in developing countries in the Far East, South Asia, Latin America and, to some extent, in North Africa. Maize has a variety of industrial uses, including the preparation of ethyl alcohol (ethanol), which may be added to petrol to

Production of Maize
('000 metric tons, USDA estimates)

	2018/19	2019/20	2020/21	2021/22*
World total	1,128,741	1,122,735	1,129,443	1,218,757
Sub-Saharan Africa	76,430	80,006	85,856	87,332
Leading sub-Saharan African producers				
Ethiopia	10,120	9,636	10,557	9,400
Kenya	4,014	3,582	3,789	3,100
Malawi	2,698	3,392	3,692	4,581
Mali	3,625	3,817	3,517	3,588
Nigeria	11,000	12,700	12,400	12,745
South Africa	11,824	15,844	16,951	16,300
Tanzania	6,273	5,652	6,711	7,000
Zambia	2,395	2,004	3,387	3,620
Leading non-African producers				
Argentina	51,000	51,000	52,000	53,000
Brazil	101,000	102,000	87,000	116,000
Canada	13,885	13,404	13,563	13,984
China, People's Republic	257,174	260,779	260,670	272,552
European Union	64,351	66,742	67,440	70,979
India	27,715	28,766	31,647	33,000
Indonesia	12,000	12,000	12,600	12,700
Mexico	27,671	26,658	27,346	27,550
Philippines	7,608	8,030	8,352	8,300
Russian Federation	11,415	14,275	13,872	15,225
Serbia	7,400	7,500	8,100	6,000
Ukraine	35,805	35,887	30,297	42,126
USA	364,262	345,962	358,447	383,943

* Preliminary figures.

Source: US Department of Agriculture.

produce a blended motor fuel. Maize is also a source of dextrose and fructose, which can be used as artificial sweeteners, many times sweeter than sugar. The amounts of maize used for these purposes depend, critically, on its price to the users relative to that of petroleum, sugar and other potential raw materials. Maize cobs, previously discarded as a waste product, may be used as feedstock to produce various chemicals (e.g. acetic acid and formic acid).

The World Market and the Region The USA is by far the largest producer of maize (in years of drought or excessive heat, US output can fall dramatically) and the People's Republic of China, whose maize output has been expanding rapidly, is the second largest producer—its harvest doubled in 2000–13. China's production, however, is mainly destined for the domestic market, whereas US output makes the country generally the world's largest exporter by far (except in 2012/13). Figures from the US Department of Agriculture (USDA) for 2021/22 showed that US exports provided 31% of total world sales abroad, while Brazil provided 22%, Argentina 20% and Ukraine 12%. Brazilian exports that year were three times their level in 2015/16 when there had been a poor harvest. The world's principal maize importer is Japan, though it was surpassed by Mexico in 2017/18–2021/22, according to preliminary figures. The volume of Japanese imports remained stable through the 2000s, as the domestic livestock industry was rationalized to compete with imported meat. Japanese imports of maize totalled about 15.4m. metric tons in 2021/22. The European Union (EU), meanwhile, imported 16.0m. tons in 2021/22, mostly from Ukraine. Apart from Japan and Mexico, rapidly growing livestock industries elsewhere in East Asia made the region the major world market for maize, although in terms of individual countries the Republic of Korea (South Korea) generally qualifies as the other important market for maize (11.7m. tons in 2021/22). Egypt, by far the largest importer in the African continent, imported 9.2m. tons in 2021/22, putting it in sixth place (with Viet Nam) among world importers, with Iran (8.5m. tons) and Colombia (6.0m. tons) also significant customers in that year.

Maize imports by sub-Saharan Africa vary from around 1m. metric tons annually in years of good crops to far higher amounts after droughts. In 1992/93, for example, these imports exceeded 8m. metric tons, most of which entered through South African ports, either for that country's own use or for onward transport overland to neighbouring countries. In 2021/22, according to USDA, sub-Saharan African imports of maize totalled 2.9m. tons, which was significantly lower than the century's peak of 5.2m. tons six years earlier. Apart from Egypt, most maize in Africa is grown south of the Sahara. Maize is not grown under irrigation in most of sub-Saharan Africa, as scarce water supplies are reserved instead for export crops with a higher value. Yields are therefore low. In many countries in the region commercial farming is hindered by the lack of foreign exchange to buy essential equipment, as well as fuels and fertilizers. In addition, transport difficulties make marketing expensive and uncertain. In much of Africa maize is a subsistence crop.

South Africa, which grows both white corn (for human consumption) and yellow corn (for animal feed), is traditionally the region's largest producer. It was formerly an exporter of both types (except in years of severe drought), but market deregulation in 1997 altered the economic basis of commercial maize production. In the absence of government support, domestic maize is not competitive with imported maize in the feed mills of the coastal regions, with the result that sowings, particularly of yellow corn, have fallen. White corn production usually exceeds local food requirements, the surplus being exported to neighbouring food-deficit countries. South African production increased by almost 80% in 2008 (wiping out the bulk of imports). Southern Africa in general suffered from some years of drought in the 2010s, which affected maize harvests in South Africa, but they were showing signs of recovery by 2016/17 when output rose to 17.6m. metric tons, from just 8.2m. tons the previous year. Output fell in the next two years but recovered in 2019/20–2021/22 to reach 16.3m. tons in the latter year. South African maize exports averaged above 2m. tons per year in the 2010s, but from 2014/15 fell to less than 1m. tons, only to recover to 2.3m. tons in 2016/17. In 2021/22 exports reached an estimated 3.2m. tons. Imports increased from negligible levels to 2.2m. tons in 2015/16 and then declined once again in 2016/17–2017/18; it was estimated that South Africa imported almost no maize at all in 2019/20–2021/22. In Zimbabwe maize is the main staple food. The country's maize crop, like that of South Africa, is often affected by drought. Traditionally, after good harvests Zimbabwe was able to export its surplus of maize. In 2000 the country still exported 107,000 tons of maize, mainly to other sub-Saharan countries, but thereafter, however, Zimbabwe's agricultural sector was severely disrupted by the deteriorating economic, social and political situation in the country. Exports ceased, and imports were necessary to sustain supplies in most years after 2001. However, Zimbabwean maize output in 2021/22 recovered to 2.7m. tons, which represented a three-fold increase compared with the previous year, with imports falling as a result to less than 0.1m. tons in the same year. Zambia (which in 2021/22 exported 400,000 tons), Tanzania and Malawi are more consistent in producing surplus production for export. Maize is also Kenya's main food crop. Output is erratic,

depending strongly on weather conditions, and tends to conform to a 'boom-and-bust' pattern. Imports are required in most seasons, especially when, as in recent years, the subsistence needs of refugee camps add to domestic food requirements. Maize is one of Nigeria's main subsistence crops, and is traded locally—mainly outside the official market economy. In the past, an important end use of maize in Nigeria was for brewing of beer, but since a ban on imports of barley and barley malt was revoked in 1998 breweries have used less maize. Nigerian production rose steadily from the beginning of the 2000s, to peak at 7.1m. tons in 2006 (FAO), eclipsing South Africa, which had had a poor harvest, as the region's major producer in that year. Generally, it remained the region's second producer, but the potential for output growth had been hindered by marketing difficulties and shortages of essential agricultural inputs, such as fertilizers, but newly introduced maize varieties helped improve yields. Ethiopia, Ghana and Mozambique are all important producers, mainly for domestic markets.

Global Forum The International Grains Council (IGC) is based in London, United Kingdom. The new Grains Trade Convention entered into force in July 1995, giving what used to be the International Wheat Council a wider mandate to consider all coarse grains as well as wheat (rice was added to the definition of grains from 1 July 2009 and oilseeds from 1 July 2013). In July 2022 the IGC consisted of 29 members and the EU.

Maize (Corn) Price
(US $ per metric ton)

		Average	High	Low
2005	.	98.67	(July) 107.52	(February) 94.14
2010	.	185.91	(December) 250.38	(June) 152.75
2015	.	169.75	(July) 179.60	(August) 162.59
2019	.	170.07	(June) 195.08	(September) 157.26
2020	.	165.47	(December) 198.77	(May) 143.91
2021	.	259.55	(May) 305.31	(January) 234.47

Source: World Bank, *Commodity Price Data* (Pink Sheet).

Prices Export prices of maize are mainly influenced by the level of supplies and demand in the USA, and the intensity of competition between the exporting countries. The price of US No. 2 Yellow Corn (f.o.b. Gulf ports) first rose above US $200 per metric ton in January 2008, but global recession pushed it below that mark again from October until September 2010 (in terms of average monthly prices). Prices then rose sharply for a time, reaching above $300 per ton in April–August 2011 and again in July 2012–March 2013, only to dip below $200 per ton for three months from November to February 2014 and to remain below that level from July 2014. Indeed, prices remained below $180 per ton thereafter, tending generally downwards and reaching a low point in September 2017. The average monthly price fell in the second half of 2018, but recovered in early 2019, before falling again for the remainder of 2019 and much of 2020. The price began to rise in 2021, reaching an eight-year high in May 2021, and rose rapidly again thereafter. By April 2022 the price was averaging $348.17 per ton, the highest monthly level in history, and largely a result of the Russian Federation's renewed armed invasion and effective blockade of Ukraine (a major grain exporter) in that year. However, there were hopes that a potential global humanitarian crisis in those less developed countries where wheat and maize imports from Ukraine were a critical food staple might be averted following reports, in July 2022, of a UN-backed agreement, brokered by Türkiye between the Russian Federation and Ukraine, to allow the resumption of grain exports from Ukrainian Black Sea ports. Later that month the first grain exports since February were allowed to leave the Ukrainian port of Odessa, with the first grain shipment arriving in Djibouti in late August, in which month the price had fallen to average $289.84 per ton.

Maize and grain prices were also generally projected to increase in line with the expanding market for ethanol, which is closely linked to the price of petroleum. New energy legislation in 2007, in both the EU and the USA, stipulated the greater use of biofuels for motor vehicles. According to the World Bank, the share of global maize production used for ethanol increased from 2.5% in 2000 to 11.0% in 2007, and the trend remained evident thereafter. However, maize-based ethanol production was still a heavily subsidized industry in the USA, and it remained a costly and relatively inefficient substitute for its sugar-based equivalent (see below). Critics remained sceptical regarding the long-term prospects for the industry, especially as sugar-based ethanol was already being produced more cheaply in Latin America.

MANGANESE (*Mn*)

Manganese is a silvery grey metal that is obtained from various ores containing such minerals as hausmannite, manganite and pyrolusite. The ore is usually washed or hand sorted and then smelted with iron and carbon to make ferromanganese (80% manganese), in which form it is chiefly used to alloy into steel, manganese steel being particularly hard and tough. The other main manganese alloy is silicomanganese (68% manganese). Almost 95% of manganese produced is thus used in the manufacture of steel, which, on average, consumes about 6 kg of manganese per metric ton. Electrolytic manganese is used to make stainless steel and in the aluminium industry. Minor uses of manganese as oxides are in dry cell batteries, paints and varnishes, and in ceramics and glass making. Manganese is the world's fourth most consumed metal by weight.

Extensive accumulations of manganese in marine environments have been identified. The characteristic occurrences are as nodules on deep ocean floors and as crusts on sea mounts at shallower depths. Both forms are oxidic and are often termed 'ferromanganese' because they generally contain iron and manganese. The main commercial interest in both types of deposit derives from the copper, nickel and cobalt contents also present, which represent large resources of these metals. Attention was focused initially on nodules, of which the Pacific Ocean encompasses the areas with the densest coverage and highest concentration of potentially economic metals. However, the exploitation of nodules has, to date, been impeded by legal, technical and economic factors.

Production of Manganese Ore
(manganese content, '000 metric tons)

	2018	2019	2020	2021*
World total . . .	19,400	20,600	18,900	20,000
Sub-Saharan Africa† .	9,500	10,913	10,451	11,640
Leading African producers				
Gabon	2,336	2,759	3,314	3,600
Ghana	1,364	1,554	637	640
South Africa* . . .	5,800	6,600	6,500	7,400
Leading non-African producers				
Australia	3,475	3,177	3,331	3,300
Brazil	1,281	1,452	494	400
China, People's Republic.	1,427	1,206	1,336	1,300
India	1,217	963	632	600
Kazakhstan* . . .	143	152	158	160
Malaysia*	492	441	347	360
Mexico	209	202	198	200
Ukraine*	517	574	578	670

* Estimated production.
† Figures are the sum of output in the listed countries. Small quantities of manganese ore, included in the world total, are also produced in Burkina Faso, Côte d'Ivoire, Namibia, Sudan and Zambia.

Source: US Geological Survey.

The World Market and the Region According to the International Manganese Institute, in 2020 the manganese industry experienced a considerable contraction: manganese ore production worldwide totalled 20m. metric tons in that year (down 7% compared to 2019); manganese content is usually a little over 30% of the total. Of total 2020 world production of manganese alloys, some 77% was accounted for by silicomanganese, 18% by high carbon ferromanganese and the rest (6%) by refined ferromanganese. In 2011 22m. tons of manganese ore entered international trade, China alone accounting for 60% of world imports. Australia, Brazil, Gabon, Ghana and South Africa together accounted for 88% of the seaborne supply of manganese ore. India is no longer a significant exporter.

In 2021 world reserves of manganese were estimated by the USGS at 1,500m. metric tons, of which about 43% were located in South Africa, 18% in each of Brazil and Australia and 9% in Ukraine. About 74% of the world's identified manganese resources were in South Africa. Development of manganese resources generally and of the Kalahari Manganese Field (KMF) from the 2000s was dominated by two established companies, Assmang and Samancor, and Kalahari Resources. Transport infrastructure was to be expanded in anticipation of the increased production from the KMF that new exploration was expected to generate. The Government also attempted to promote greater local beneficiation of ore into value added products—South Africa's traditional policy has been to maximize export revenues by shipping as much manganese as possible in processed ferroalloy form. The country is sub-Saharan Africa's only producer of manganese alloys, with the 2020 output of the country's electric furnaces amounting to 122,000 tons in gross weight of ferromanganese (3% of world production) and 108,000 tons of silicomanganese (1%). Output of high-carbon ferromanganese fell in 2020, as it did in all major producer countries.

Gabon, Africa's second major producer of manganese ore, had estimated reserves totalling 61m. metric tons in 2021 (compared with South Africa's 640m. tons). Gabon's Moanda mine is operated by Compagnie Minière de l'Ogooué (Comilog), a subsidiary of France's

Eramet SA. All exports reportedly pass through Owendo Port, near Libreville. However, increases in production from Moanda were limited by the capacity of the railway link to the coast, which Eramet was committed to upgrading. According to the USGS, a seven-year modernization programme was underway in 2018. Chinese companies were also hoping to exploit manganese near Ndjole, while other operators also joined the Gabonese market in the 2010s. Exports of manganese ores and concentrates (including ferruginous manganese ores and concentrates) contributed 23% of Gabon's total export revenue in 2021, compared with crude petroleum on 61% (the country's timber resources used to earn more than manganese). Plans exist to produce ferromanganese in Gabon, but electricity production is inadequate to achieve this aim. Manganese nevertheless directly accounted for about 6% of Gabonese gross domestic product (2013 figure).

Ghana benefited from government measures to revive manganese operations in the 2010s, assisted by loan finance from the World Bank. In 2017 Ghana Manganese came into Chinese ownership when TMI (Ningxia Tianyuan Manganese Industry Co) bought it. China has traditionally purchased exports of manganese carbonate ore from Ghana, but Chinese demand for manganese metal increased into the 2010s. Burkina Faso has deposits of manganese ore sufficient to establish it as a minor regional producer. In 2020 it produced about 13,000 metric tons of manganese (metal content) and granted the rights to develop the rich reserves at Tambao to Romanian investors. The Democratic Republic of the Congo (DRC), once a significant source of manganese exports, has mined only on a sporadic basis since 1980. In Côte d'Ivoire, a new mine operated by Taurian Resources began production in 2007 (the country produced 525,000 tons in 2020), but a mine opened in Zambia in March of the same year was closed by the Government in May for environmental and safety reasons. The USGS reported that the country produced 82,000 metric tons in 2020. A new mine planned in Cameroon, according to the USGS, was delayed as a result of global economic conditions after 2008.

Manganese Ore Prices
(contained manganese, US $ per metric ton unit, unless otherwise indicated)

	UNCTAD*	US ports	China
2005 .	1,569.2	—	—
2010 .	2,990.8	8.45	7.23
2015 .	1,799.2	3.53	3.22
2019 .	n.a.	6.60	5.63
2020 .	n.a.	n.a.	4.59
2021 .	n.a.	n.a.	5.20

* US $ per metric ton of electrolytic manganese flake.

Sources: UNCTAD and USGS.

Prices The average annual indicator price cited by the UN Conference on Trade and Development (UNCTAD—for a pure form of the metallic element produced by electrolysis, in flakes, 99.7% manganese, free market, in warehouse) fell steadily each month after September 2014 to reach an average of US $1,488 per metric ton of manganese flake in November 2015; the average price then rose to a peak of $2,630 per ton by December 2016, falling back to $1,739 per ton by July 2017. The USGS gives two import prices for metallurgical ore (46%/48% manganese): an estimated price c.i.f. at US ports; and, taken from CRU *Ryan's Notes*, CNF (cost and freight) China price, which represents costs paid by a seller to ship manganese ore by sea to a Chinese port (i.e. excludes insurance).

MILLET AND SORGHUM

Millet and sorghum are often grouped together in economic analyses of world cereals, not because of any affinity between the two grains—in fact they are quite dissimilar—but because in many developing countries both are subsistence crops that are little traded. Figures for the production of the individual grains should be treated only as broad estimates in most cases. Data cover only crops harvested for grain.

Data on millet relate mainly to the following: cat-tail millet (*Pennisetum glaucum* or *P. typhoides*), also known as bulrush millet, pearl millet or, in India and Pakistan, as 'bajra'; finger millet (*Eleusine coracana*), known in India as 'ragi'; common or bread millet (*Panicum miliaceum*), also called 'proso'; foxtail millet (*Setaria italica*), or Italian millet; and barnyard millet (*Echinochloa crusgalli*), also often called Japanese millet.

Sorghum statistics refer mainly to the several varieties of *Sorghum vulgare*, known by various names such as great millet, Guinea corn, kafir or kafircorn (*caffrorum*), milo (in the USA and Argentina), feterita, durra, jowar, sorgo or maicillo. Other species included in the table are Sudan grass (*S. sudanense*) and Columbus grass or sorgo negro (*S. almum*). The use of grain sorghum hybrids has resulted in a considerable increase in yields in recent years.

Millet and sorghum are cultivated particularly in semi-arid areas where there is too little rainfall to sustain maize and the temperature is too high for wheat. These two cereals constitute the staple diet of people over large areas of Africa, India, the People's Republic of China and parts of the former USSR. They are usually consumed as porridge or unleavened bread. Both grains have good nutritional value, but are less palatable than wheat, and tend to be replaced by the latter when circumstances permit. In many African countries sorghum is used to make beer. Sorghum is also produced and used in certain countries in the western hemisphere (particularly Argentina, Mexico and the USA), where it is used mainly as an animal feed, although the high tannin content of some varieties lowers their value as a feed grain.

Millet and sorghum are grown largely for human consumption, but are gradually being replaced by wheat and rice as those cereals become more widely available. Only low-grade sorghum is used for animal feed in Africa, but some is used for starch when maize is in short supply. Apart from food and animal feed requirements, sorghum is used in a number of countries in Asia and Africa for the production of beers and other alcoholic liquors.

Production of Millet
('000 metric tons)

	2017	2018	2019	2020
World total	28,813	31,632	28,333	30,464
Sub-Saharan Africa* .	12,730	15,978	13,658	13,795
Leading sub-Saharan African producers				
Burkina Faso . . .	828	1,189	970	957†
Chad	660	757	718	687
Ethiopia	1,031	1,036	1,126	1,219
Mali	1,493	1,840	1,879	1,921
Niger	3,790	3,856	3,270	3,509
Nigeria	1,500	2,119†	2,000†	2,000†
Senegal	875	898	807	1,145
Sudan	878	2,647	1,133	485
Tanzania	309	316	386	325†
Leading non-African producers				
China, People's Republic .	2,548	2,342	2,300†	2,300†
India	11,557	11,633	10,236	12,490
Nepal	307	314	314	321
Pakistan	339	350	384	266
Russian Federation . .	316	217	440	396
USA	338	263	377	209

* FAO estimates.
† Unofficial figure.

Production of Sorghum
('000 metric tons)

	2017	2018	2019	2020
World total	57,754	60,128	57,363	58,706
Sub-Saharan Africa* .	26,972	29,306	27,381	26,733
Leading sub-Saharan African producers				
Burkina Faso . . .	1,366	1,930	1,872	1,840†
Cameroon* . . .	1,200	1,200	1,200	1,215
Chad	946	988	973	970
Ethiopia	5,169	5,024	5,266	5,058
Mali	1,423	1,470	1,511	1,823
Niger	1,945	2,100	1,897	2,132
Nigeria	6,939	6,800†	6,665†	6,362†
Sudan	4,156*	5,435	3,714	2,538
Leading non-African producers				
Argentina	2,527	1,563	1,601	1,830
Australia	994	1,257	1,160	397
Brazil	2,224	2,281	2,672	2,769
China, People's Republic .	2,465	2,909	3,600†	3,550†
India	4,568	4,803	3,475	4,770
Mexico	4,853	4,531	4,353	4,704
USA	9,192	9,271	8,673	9,474

* FAO estimate(s).
† Unofficial figure.

Source: FAO.

The World Market and the Region World trade in sorghum ranges between 5m. and 10m. metric tons per year, but since the mid-2000s has tended to be closer to the lower end of this range, reflecting the small volume of exportable supplies (around 7.9m. tons in 2020). The principal exporter is usually the USA, which in recent decades has, on average, accounted for more than four-fifths of total world exports and holds the greater part of world sorghum stocks. In 2012, however, export volumes had fallen by more than two-fifths; in 2020, however, the USA's exports almost tripled, to account for 83% of world exports, while the other major exporter in that year, Argentina, provided 6% of the sorghum on the international market. Australia, traditionally an important exporter, only accounted for 2% of world exports in 2020—which was less than one-quarter of the total in the previous year. Japan and Mexico were two of the main sorghum markets (buying, respectively, 6% and 5% of world imports) in 2020. However, the People's Republic of China was the principal importer of sorghum, accounting for 70% of world imports in the same year. Mexico's annual sorghum purchases tended to average more than 2m. tons annually in the 2000s, less into the 2010s (only 0.3m. tons in 2020—around one-half of the 2019 level), but they vary as they depend upon the size of the domestic crop and on the relative prices of sorghum and maize. Imports of sorghum by sub-Saharan Africa were about 0.7m. tons in 2020, or 10% of the world total. Very little millet enters world trade (511,252 tons in 2020), worth US $190m., according to the Food and Agriculture Organization of the United Nations (FAO).

Sorghum (Milo) Price
(US $ per metric ton)

	Average	High		Low	
2005 .	96	(July)	106	(January)	90
2010 .	165	(December)	222	(June)	131
2015 .	202	(March)	228	(November)	169
2019 .	162	(February)	170	(August)	148
2020 .	172	(December)	288	(February)	164
2021 .	342	(May)	396	(September)	297

Source: World Bank, *Commodity Price Data* (Pink Sheet).

Prices Export prices for sorghum tend closely to follow those of maize—sorghum is generally slightly cheaper, although for most of the period from 2000 until January 2008 it was a little more expensive (until the spike and then crash in commodity prices). The US sorghum export price of No. 2 Yellow Milo (f.o.b. US Gulf Ports) reached US $214 per ton in 2008. During the first half of 2008 the average monthly price of sorghum had increased very considerably, from $187 per ton in January to $262 per ton in June. The fall in commodity prices in the second half of the year, particularly in the last quarter, hit sorghum harder than maize. Prices reached another peak in 2011, then tended to fall and in September 2016 the average monthly price was its lowest since mid-2010. Average monthly prices increased gradually in 2017 and early 2018. Prices fluctuated from mid-2018 until mid-2019, but remained steady until the first half of 2020, when the price increased substantially. Prices continued to rise in 2021–22 on the back of extraordinarily high demand in the People's Republic of China, reaching $396 per ton in May 2021 (its highest level on record to date), before softening in the second half of the year. Concerns surrounding the supply of grain and cereals following the Russian Federation's renewed armed invasion of Ukraine in 2022 pushed prices up once more (to $380 per ton in May), but these had fallen back to $316 per ton by July. Since relatively little millet enters international trade, no reliable export price series can be established.

OIL PALM (*Elaeis guineensis*)

The oil palm is a tree native to West Africa, and grows wild in tropical forests along the coast of that region. The palm fruit is a red colour, about the size of a big plum, and grows in large clusters that can contain hundreds of fruit and usually weighs between 40 kg and 50 kg. The entire fruit is of use commercially; palm oil is made from its pulp, and palm kernel oil from the seed. Palm oil is a versatile product and, because of its very low acid content (4%–5%), it is almost all used in food. It is used in margarine and other edible fats; as a 'shortener' for pastry and biscuits; as an ingredient in ice cream and chocolate; and in the manufacture of soaps and detergents. Palm kernel oil, which is a lauric oil, and so is similar to coconut oil, is also used for making soaps and fats. The sap from the stems of the tree can be used to make palm wine, an intoxicating beverage. Most processing is done near to where the oil palms are harvested, so the production figures cited tend to be for palm oil and for palm kernels, the latter giving an indication of the number of fruit harvested—for every 100 kg of palm fruit bunches, 22 kg of palm oil and 1.6 kg of palm kernel oil can typically be produced.

Palm oil can be produced virtually through the year once the palms have reached oil bearing age, which takes about five years. The palms continue to bear oil for 30 years or more and the yield far exceeds that of any other oil plant, with one ha of oil palms producing as much oil as six ha of groundnuts or 10–12 ha of soybeans. However, it is an intensive crop, needing considerable investment and skilled labour.

Production of Palm Kernels
('000 metric tons, USDA oilseed estimates)

	2018/19	2019/20	2020/21	2021/22
World total . . .	19,462	19,323	19,041	20,068
Sub-Saharan Africa . .	1,276	1,359	1,301	1,393
Leading African producers				
Benin	5	5	5	5
Cameroon	145	145	145	145
Congo, Democratic Republic	46	46	47	47
Côte d'Ivoire . . .	120	127	132	139
Ghana	80	75	75	75
Guinea	53	53	53	53
Nigeria	800	880	815	900
Leading non-African producers				
Colombia	328	306	289	313
Guatemala . . .	200	170	170	175
Indonesia . . .	10,900	11,250	11,460	12,000
Malaysia . . .	5,154	4,746	4,344	4,650
Papua New Guinea . .	176	160	162	165
Thailand	870	750	790	830

Source: US Department of Agriculture.

Production of Palm Oil
('000 metric tons, USDA estimates)

	2018/19	2019/20	2020/21	2021/22
World total . . .	74,286	73,125	73,173	76,120
Sub-Saharan Africa . .	3,013	3,059	3,273	3,423
Leading sub-Saharan African producers				
Angola	53	54	55	55
Benin	70	70	70	70
Cameroon	385	420	465	465
Congo, Democratic Republic	293	294	300	300
Côte d'Ivoire . . .	514	525	550	575
Ghana	379	365	365	365
Guinea	50	50	50	50
Nigeria	1,130	1,140	1,275	1,400
Leading non-African producers				
Colombia	1,632	1,529	1,558	1,747
Ecuador	584	509	465	380
Guatemala . . .	862	862	865	880
Indonesia . . .	41,500	42,500	43,500	45,300
Malaysia . . .	20,800	19,255	17,854	18,300
Papua New Guinea . .	705	575	600	625
Thailand	3,034	2,652	2,963	3,150

Source: US Department of Agriculture.

The World Market and the Region During the 1980s palm oil accounted for more than 15% of world production of vegetable oils, second only to soybean oil. Largely driven by high levels of demand in Asia, especially in the People's Republic of China, palm oil production increased considerably, to account for often more than one-third of world vegetable oils (36% in 2021/22, according to the US Department of Agriculture—USDA, compared with 28% soybean oil and 14% rapeseed oil; palm kernel oil accounts for a further 4%). In world markets for vegetable oils, the dominance of palm oil was even more marked: in 2021/22 palm oil accounted for 57% of all exports of vegetable oils globally (palm kernel oil 4%). In that year the equivalent of 61% of palm oil production worldwide entered international markets. The main producers of palm oil are now Asian. Indonesia replaced Malaysia as the world's leading individual producer in 2005/06, while in the following year Thailand definitively replaced Nigeria in third place; from 2012/13 Colombia even took fourth place from Nigeria. Indonesia and Malaysia likewise dominate export markets, with Guatemala, Colombia and Papua New Guinea following them distantly in 2021/22. In some years Thailand is an important exporter. India, China and the member countries of the European Union (EU) are the chief importers. The principal consumers of palm

oil are Indonesia (25% of world domestic consumption in 2021/22) and India (12%), followed by the member countries of the EU (8%) and China (7%).

In Africa a large proportion of oil palms still grow in wild groves, and the bulk of oil production is for local consumption. In export terms, Africa has since 1980 accounted for less than 3% of world trade in palm oil, and in 2021/22 sub-Saharan African exports comprised 2.2% of the world market. Côte d'Ivoire and Benin were by far the largest African exporters, followed by Kenya. Nigeria had been the world's leading producer of palm oil until overtaken by Malaysia in 1971. The loss of Nigeria's market dominance was, in part, a result of civil war and the authorities' failure to help replace old, unproductive trees (an estimated 70% of production came from smallholders), but remediation policies could not compensate for growing internal consumption. Nigeria's reliance on imports subsequently grew, and increases in domestic production now tend to be used for import substitution rather than to boost exports. Nigeria is the world's fifth largest producer of palm oil, but mainly participates in the international trade as an importer. In 2021/22 Nigeria (equally with Djibouti and Mozambique) was sub-Saharan Africa's fourth largest importer. The largest importer was Kenya, on 22% of the region's total imports, followed by South Africa and Tanzania, on 11% and 10%, respectively. Many of Africa's largest producers are not significant exporters of palm oil, using it instead in manufacturing, whether for domestic consumption or export at that stage.

Benin is not now a major producer of palm oil, but is an entrepôt for surrounding countries and, therefore, one of Africa's largest exporters. In Benin, where the oil palm was traditionally a staple crop of the national economy, oil palm plantations and natural palm groves covered some 450,000 ha in the 1990s, but only an estimated 18,000 ha in 2002 (figure from the Food and Agriculture Organization of the United Nations—FAO); by 2020 this figure had recovered to an estimated 35,170 ha. Benin was an important exporter of palm oil in the 2010s, but much was the production of neighbouring countries; it accounted for 17% of sub-Saharan African exports in 2021/22, according to USDA. Côte d'Ivoire had become Africa's principal palm oil producer-exporter in the mid-2000s, but the country certainly no longer attained the rank of fourth largest exporter in the world as it did throughout most of the 1990s. More than one-half of Côte d'Ivoire's palms were planted in 1965–70 and had passed their peak of productivity by the end of the 1990s. Management and financial difficulties during the 1990s, as well as declining world prices for palm oil, led to the scaling down of a replanting programme. Plans to increase production in the 2000s were interrupted by civil conflict, but in 2021/22 Côte d'Ivoire sold more palm oil (46%) than any other sub-Saharan African country. Other than Benin, Kenya, Ghana, Djibouti, South Africa and Nigeria were the next largest exporters of palm oil in 2021/22, but in far smaller volumes. Much production among the smaller producers was to satisfy domestic demand, such as the output of Guinea, sub-Saharan Africa's 10th largest producer in 2021/22, but not an exporter.

Oil Palm Oils Prices
(US $ per metric ton)

	Palm oil	Palm kernel oil
2005	450.56	630.82
2010	933.02	1,187.41
2015	663.39	903.35
2019	601.37	665.39
2020	751.77	824.07
2021	1,130.58	1,533.08

Source: World Bank, *Commodity Price Data* (Pink Sheet).

Prices Internationally, palm oil is faced with sustained competition from the other major edible oils—soybean, rapeseed and sunflower oils—and these markets are subject to a complex and changing interaction of production, stocks and trade. Two main distinguishing features have traditionally characterized palm oil relative to its competitors: a very high trade-to-production ratio, far greater than that of comparable crops; and the geographical concentration of both production and trade, for both of which Indonesia and Malaysia account for approximately 90%. Palm oil has enjoyed a long-term price advantage over its principal competitor, soybean oil, which has enabled it to achieve a very high degree of market penetration. It is only in the 21st century—since about 1999—that the prices recorded for palm oil have consistently exceeded the long-term trend, reflecting new demand for feedstocks for biodiesel production. Even so, palm oil is the lowest priced vegetable oil, and it is, in the opinion of many market analysts, the most competitive biodiesel feedstock. However, its utilization for this purpose has remained very low compared with, in particular, rapeseed oil, which enjoys a high level of subsidization in the member states of the European Union (EU), where it is the principal biodiesel feedstock. The average import price (c.i.f. Rotterdam) of Malaysian crude palm oil was just US $600 per metric ton (monthly average) in September 2015, but strengthened through 2016 to peak at $825 per ton in January 2017; the trend was lower for the rest of that year and through 2018. The price reached just $535 per ton in December of that year, its lowest level since October 2006. By the end of 2019 it had only improved marginally, but the price began to improve in the second half of 2020; from February 2021 the average monthly price stayed above $1,000 per ton, reaching $1,136 per ton by August. The usually more volatile average import price (c.i.f. north-west Europe) of Malaysian palm kernel oil was just $735 per ton in August 2015, but it rose and also peaked in January 2017, at $1,737 per ton, before falling for the rest of that year and through 2018. Prices remained low in 2019, but showed signs of recovery by the end of the year. Prices trended upwards in 2020–21, with the average price breaching and then staying above $1,000 per ton; prices continued their steep rise in the first half of 2022 (maintaining the wider trend of vegetable oil inflation), reaching $2,443 per ton in February (the highest level ever recorded), but prices had fallen back down to $1,173 per ton by August.

PETROLEUM

Crude oils, from which petroleum fuel is derived, consist essentially of a wide range of hydrocarbon molecules which are separated by distillation in the refining process. Refined oil is treated in different ways to make the different varieties of fuel. More than four-fifths of total world oil supplies are used as fuel for the production of energy in the form of power or heating.

Petroleum, together with its associated mineral fuel, natural gas, is extracted both from onshore and offshore wells in many areas of the world. The dominant producing region is the Middle East, whose proven reserves in December 2020 accounted for 48.3% of known world deposits of crude petroleum and natural gas liquids. The Middle East accounted for 31.2% of estimated world output in 2021. Africa (including North Africa) contained 16,572m. metric tons of proven reserves (7.2% of the world total) at the end of 2020, and accounted for 8.2% (344,733m. tons) of estimated world production in the following year.

From storage tanks at the oilfield wellhead, crude petroleum is conveyed, frequently by pumping for long distances through large pipelines, to coastal depots where it is either treated in a refinery or delivered into bulk storage tanks for subsequent shipment for refining overseas. In addition to pipeline transportation of crude petroleum and refined products, natural (petroleum) gas is, in some areas, also transported through networks of pipelines. Crude petroleum varies considerably in colour and viscosity, and these variations are a determinant both of price and of end use after refining.

The most important of the petroleum products is fuel oil, composed of heavy distillates and residues, which is used to produce heating and power for industrial purposes. Products in the kerosene group have a wide number of applications, ranging from heating fuels to the powering of aviation gas turbine engines. Gasoline (petrol) products fuel internal combustion engines (used mainly in road motor vehicles), and naphtha, a gasoline distillate, is a commercial solvent that can also be processed as a feedstock. Propane and butane, the main liquefied petroleum gases, have a wide range of industrial applications and are also used for domestic heating and cooking.

Petroleum is the leading raw material in international trade. Worldwide demand for this commodity totalled an estimated 94.1m. barrels per day (b/d) in 2021, an increase of 6.0% compared with the previous year. The world's 'published proven' reserves of petroleum and natural gas liquids at 31 December 2020 were estimated to total 244,421m. metric tons, equivalent to 1,732,366m. barrels (1 metric ton is equivalent to approximately 7.3 barrels, each of 42 US gallons or 34.97 imperial gallons, i.e. 159 litres).

Production of Crude Petroleum
('000 metric tons, including natural gas liquids and oil from shale, estimates)

	1985	1995	2005	2021
World total	2,791,547	3,279,064	3,931,638	4,221,366
Africa	257,982	336,281	464,481	344,733
Leading African producers				
Algeria	47,061	55,811	86,438	58,174
Angola	11,452	31,173	62,434	56,607
Chad	0	0	9,108	6,118
Congo, Republic . . .	5,937	9,267	12,567	14,020
Egypt	45,067	46,588	33,167	29,601
Equatorial Guinea . .	0	347	17,469	6,432
Gabon	8,626	17,756	13,498	9,038
Libya	48,391	67,893	81,966	59,650
Nigeria	73,832	95,061	121,144	77,929

—continued	1985	1995	2005	2021
South Sudan	0	0	0	7,516
Sudan	0	99	14,466	3,157
Other leading producers				
Brazil	29,470	37,504	88,981	156,792
Canada	85,685	111,906	142,679	267,096
China, People's Republic .	124,900	149,020	181,353	198,881
Iran	110,351	185,457	207,871	167,658
Iraq	69,839	26,026	89,934	200,829
Kazakhstan	22,660	20,633	61,493	85,989
Kuwait	55,489	104,889	130,411	131,093
Mexico	145,854	150,213	186,491	96,486
Norway	39,211	138,400	138,434	93,796
Qatar	15,318	21,831	52,559	73,320
Russian Federation . .	542,306	310,749	474,819	536,446
Saudi Arabia . . .	172,072	431,263	516,628	515,023
United Arab Emirates .	55,960	114,411	136,553	164,381
United Kingdom . .	127,611	129,894	84,721	40,865
USA	498,705	383,554	308,988	711,125
Venezuela	91,504	155,325	169,409	33,408

Source: BP, *Statistical Review of World Energy 2022.*

The World Market and the Region Nigeria's first petroleum discovery was made in the Niger Delta region in 1956, and exports began in 1958. Production and exports increased steadily until output was disrupted by the outbreak of civil war in 1967. After the end of hostilities in 1970, Nigeria's petroleum production greatly increased, and it became the country's major industry. After Libya restricted output in 1973, Nigeria became Africa's leading petroleum producing country. Being of low sulphur content and high quality, Nigerian petroleum is much in demand on the European market. Nigeria's proven reserves were estimated to be 4,978m. metric tons at 31 December 2020. The state petroleum enterprise, the Nigerian National Petroleum Corpn (NNPC), operates refinery facilities at Port Harcourt (I and II), Kaduna and Warri. According to the *Oil and Gas Journal*, Nigeria's crude oil distillation capacity amounts to some 423,750 b/d (as of early 2020)—including the privately operated Ogbele field in Rivers State. However, according to the NNPC, operational capacity at Nigeria's refineries was less than 15% in 2016, owing to deficient management, and fire and theft, and sabotage, compounded by the frequent unavailability of sufficient supplies of crude after attacks on the country's oil infrastructure (see below). Since an amnesty was declared in late 2009 between militants and the Government—militants exchanged weapons for money and training opportunities—attacks had declined and companies have been able to rebuild infrastructure. Indeed, the rise in overall production in 2010 was attributed to the amnesty. However, it was reported that between January and October 2013 renewed attacks, kidnappings and vandalism at onshore and shallow offshore fields in the Niger Delta were of equal severity to those of 2008–09, when supply disruptions were at record highs. The deteriorating situation was attributed to the country's ongoing failure to stimulate significant economic development. In fact it was reported that acts of sabotage had increased in 2016. In September of that year a group calling itself the Niger Delta Avengers claimed responsibility for the destruction of a Shell-operated pipeline used for exports in the south of the country. It was reported that for a few months in 2016 production fell by some 700,000 b/d (close to a 30-year low). In mid-2019 Shell reported that in the Niger Delta region alone it had lost around 11,000 b/d to theft from its crude pipelines during 2018 (an increase from the 9,000 b/d loss in 2017). President Muhammadu Buhari had initially responded to such attacks by changing the payment process for amnesty beneficiaries—instead of paying former militant leaders (who were tasked with distributing funds), the scheme was to pay beneficiaries directly. Moreover, disbursements were diminishing, and for a time in 2016 they were halted altogether. (Payments resumed in August, while it was reported in mid-2017 that President Buhari had approved an additional US $100m. for the programme, which represented a significant increase compared with the 2016 budget.) In the first half of 2017 calm returned to the Delta and production increased in response to a shift in government policy which saw Vice-President Oluyemi Oluleke Osibajo (deputizing for President Buhari, who was on extended medical leave) visit the region regularly and meet with local community leaders. Over the whole year, output rose by 4.5% compared with 2016. Following three consecutive years of growth, production in 2020 dropped by 12.6%, although falling output in this instance was the result of depressed industrial output globally—a consequence of the COVID-19 pandemic—and concomitant lower demand. However, production fell once more in 2021 (by 11.6%), a result of poor maintenance and infrastructure inefficiency. As a member of the Organization of the Petroleum Exporting Countries (OPEC), Nigeria is supposed to be bound by the production quotas (which remained in place in mid-2022), capping its production (in August 2022) at 1.83m. b/d, although its production levels remained well below that. During the course of the 'OPEC+' agreement (see below), Nigeria (in common with other members) had frequently exceeded its production quota, and has been accused of tending to classify some of its output as 'lease condensate', which is not subject to the quota restriction. Indeed, at the latest field to come online (the deep-water Engina project in January 2019), it was suggested that the crude was labelled as a condensate—despite its reported characteristics placing it firmly in the medium, sweet categories.

Nigeria depends on imports to meet national demand for petroleum products; in 2021 imports of petroleum oils and oils obtained from bituminous minerals (excluding crude) constituted 30% of total imports (by value) in the year. As part of a wider process of reform of the country's petroleum sector, the Government planned to address the shortcomings of the refining sector through a programme of privatization and by removing subsidies that encouraged producers of crude petroleum to supply foreign refineries at the expense of local ones. It was reported in mid-2012 that then-President Goodluck Jonathan and his Cabinet had approved the Petroleum Industry Bill, which aimed for transparency in the petroleum sector (through the industry 'watchdog' the National Petroleum Regulator) and privatization of the refining sector; the bill also included tax and royalty reforms. However, some international oil companies were concerned that the legislation would undermine the fiscal viability of certain projects. In August 2021 President Buhari finally signed into law the Petroleum Industry Bill, a month after it had been passed by both the Senate and the House of Representatives. Furthermore, the Nigerian Government passed the Finance Act in January 2020. One likely repercussion of the Act was an increase in the cost of doing business (including for petroleum corporations) in the country. Meanwhile, Buhari had appointed a minister responsible for the petroleum portfolio in late 2015, following the dismissal of a number of the NNPC's executive directors and the dissolution of its corporate board. In July of the following year Buhari removed the deputy oil minister from his position as managing director of NNPC, a move welcomed by industry analysts as a positive development—although the latter continued to chair the board of directors. In mid-2016 the NNPC announced provisional agreements with Chinese companies to upgrade existing oil and gas infrastructure. The agreements were reported to be worth some US $80,000m. and included pledges to upgrade refineries and build new pipelines. In 2021, of crude oil exports valued at some US $36,256m., most sales came from European markets (including 13% from Spain, 6% from the Netherlands, 6% from France and 5% from Italy), 20% from India, 6% from Canada and 5% from Indonesia. The largest African customer was South Africa, which purchased some 4% of Nigerian crude oil exports. In 2021 the value of exports of crude petroleum accounted for about 76% of the total value of exports. According to projected data published by the IMF, petroleum had been expected to contribute just 36.7% of federal government revenue in 2020 (down from 57.6% in 2018).

As in many significant petroleum producing nations, equitable distribution of Nigeria's oil wealth has been negligible, and in spite of the country's high ranking among the world's major exporters of petroleum, it was estimated by the World Bank that in 2022 four out of 10 Nigerians were living in poverty. The operations of multinational oil companies—notably Royal Dutch/Shell—in the Niger Delta have increasingly become the focus of local politically and environmentally motivated opposition. This is frequently expressed in acts of sabotage carried out against pipelines and other oil infrastructure, and in the kidnapping of expatriate oil workers in the Delta. The Movement for the Emancipation of the Niger Delta is prominent among groups that have claimed responsibility for kidnappings and acts of sabotage in recent years. In 2010 the explosion at BP's Deepwater Horizon petroleum exploration platform in the Gulf of Mexico and the resulting environmental catastrophe there refocused international attention on environmental damage due to oil production/exploration in other locations, including the Niger Delta, where heavy contamination has occurred regularly for 50 years, and where there were, according to the Nigerian National Oil Spill Detection and Response Agency, more than 2,400 oil spills between 2006 and 2010. In December 2011 Royal Dutch/Shell's Bonga field experienced its worst spill for a decade, affecting 150 km–200 km of Nigeria's coastline. It was reported in mid-2021 that Royal Dutch/Shell had agreed to pay communities in southern Nigeria $111m. in compensation relating to oil spills and resulting environmental damage dating back to 1970—although the company continues to deny responsibility, blaming spills on sabotage during the country's civil war in 1967–70. Earlier in the year a Dutch appeals court had rejected the company's defence following a 13-year court battle with Nigerian farmers (two claimants had died during the protracted legal process). Corruption allegations were made against Shell in early 2017 relating to the company's acquisition of rights to an undeveloped oil block (OPL 245), which were awarded to Shell in 2002. Correspondence seized by Dutch investigators appeared to suggest that Shell (and Eni, of Italy) had engaged with a former Nigerian oil minister and businessman who—with his company Malabu—had owned the rights to the block since 1998.

Allegations surround a payment of $1,100m., made ostensibly to the Nigerian Government, but part of which Shell acknowledged in April 2017 would be paid directly to Malabu. An Italian court acquitted Eni, Shell and their managers in early 2021. Meanwhile the block remained undeveloped as of mid-2022.

Angola, which joined OPEC as its 12th member in January 2007, made its first petroleum discovery in 1955 near Luanda. However, Cabinda province has a major offshore deposit, in production since 1968, which now forms the basis of the country's oil industry. Output from Cabinda was briefly disrupted by the country's civil war, but has proceeded uninterrupted since 1977 and has risen steadily since 1982. Since the late 1980s production of crude petroleum has risen more than fourfold. The Angolan economy is heavily dependent on the petroleum industry. The African Development Bank estimated that the sector contributed 30% of the country's GDP in 2017. In 2007–12 a number of deep-water offshore projects were brought into operation, though production has not surpassed 2008 levels—when output reached 93.1m. metric tons. In 2021 Angola obtained 82.4% of its total foreign earnings from crude petroleum. Angola's proven oil reserves were assessed at 1,050m. metric tons at 31 December 2020. Domestic consumption of crude petroleum has been forecast to increase in coming years, but is at present sufficiently low to allow most of the country's output to be exported. The vast majority of Angola's crude export sales in 2021 were made to countries in the Asia-Pacific region—primarily the People's Republic of China (some 71% of the total value of crude petroleum exports); some 7% and 3% of Angola's crude oil sales went to India and Thailand, respectively, in the same year. Also in 2021, Chinese imports of Angolan crude amounted to 2.0m. tons, while India imported some 198,837 tons; US imports of Angolan crude amounted to 41,352 tons in the same year. Italy and Singapore were also major customers for Angolan crude. Plans exist to augment the annual capacity of Angola's refinery at Luanda, which stood at about 65,000 b/d in 2019, although, according to the Energy Information Administration (EIA) of the US Department of Energy, it typically operates well below capacity. The national oil company, Sociedade Nacional de Combustíveis de Angola (SONANGOL), is constructing a new refinery, SonaRef, at the coastal city of Lobito. The new refinery, with planned daily capacity of 200,000 b/d, will be able to process heavy crudes such as those produced from Angola's Kuito and Dalia fields. The facility's construction was continuing in 2016, until August, when building work was suspended to reassess the project. None the less, the project was scheduled for completion by 2025. Meanwhile, it was reported in mid-2022 that the US-led Quanten Consortium had committed US $3,500m. to the Soyo oil refinery project in Zaire province. This refinery—with capacity of 100,000 b/d—is also expected to be completed by 2025. Construction of the Malongo refinery—which will enable Angola to refine its domestic crude—began in September 2020 and was expected to be completed in 2024. Meanwhile, under presidential decree, in mid-2016 President José Eduardo dos Santos had appointed his daughter, Isabel dos Santos, as head of SONANGOL—following his dismissal of the entire board of directors in April of that year. (Following President dos Santos's decision not to seek re-election in August 2017, however, his successor as President, João Lourenço, removed her from the SONANGOL post in November of the same year, replacing her with Carlos Saturnino—who was then himself fired in May 2019 in response to fuel shortages, and was replaced by Gaspar Martins.) In January 2020 Isabel dos Santos was reported to be under investigation for possible involvement in allegations of corporate mismanagement and misappropriation of funds during her time as head of the state oil company. It was reported in mid-2021 that dos Santos had been ordered by the International Court of Arbitration in the Netherlands to return to SONANGOL her 6% stake (some $500m. in shares) in Portuguese oil company Galp due to alleged illegality in its initial acquisition. Despite historically low prices for crude, between 2015 and 2017 SONANGOL was estimated to have reduced its debt from some $13,600m. to $9,800m. It was reported in mid-2017 that in response to flat oil prices and much needed upstream investment, SONANGOL was undergoing a restructuring; indeed, President Lourenço merged the petroleum and mining ministries soon after his inauguration. The President was also planning the establishment of a regulatory body in 2019—the Agência Nacional de Hidrocarbonetos e Biocombustíveis (ANHB)—to oversee production-sharing agreements with investors and thereby free SONANGOL to focus on commercial activities, but this still required amendments to the Petroleum Activities Law. International oil companies which were reported to be active in Angola's oil industry in 2010, via joint ventures or production sharing agreements with SONANGOL, included China's state petroleum company SINOPEC, BP, Chevron, Eni, Total, ExxonMobil, and China National Offshore Oil Corpn (CNOOC). Two projects came online in 2014: Cravo, Lirio, Orquidea and Violeta (CLOV), operated by Total of France and with production capacity of 160,000 b/d, began commercial operations in June; while the West Hub, operated by Eni of Italy and with capacity of 100,000 b/d, came online in December. Angolan fuel prices are among the lowest in the world, a situation attributed to a system of government subsidies, including those related to electricity generation. From 1 January 2016, however, a significant reduction in subsidies resulted in an 80% increase in the price of diesel, and a 39% increase in the price of gasoline.

Other significant African petroleum producers include Equatorial Guinea, the Republic of Congo, Gabon and Chad. At December 2020 Equatorial Guinea's proven reserves were assessed at 149m. metric tons; in the following year it ranked as the sixth largest producer in sub-Saharan Africa. The oil and gas industry regularly contributes more than 90% of the country's annual GDP, while annual exports of crude petroleum were worth 61% of the total value of exports in 2021. Together with natural gas, petroleum is usually responsible for more than 90% of total government revenue. All of Equatorial Guinea's production is located offshore. The Republic of the Congo, meanwhile, with proven recoverable reserves estimated at 407m. tons in December 2020, ranked as the third largest producer in sub-Saharan Africa in the following year. In 2021 Congo's crude petroleum exports accounted for some 45% of the country's total foreign export sales. Gabon, whose recoverable reserves were estimated at 274m. tons at 31 December 2020 (the fifth largest reserves in sub-Saharan Africa), earned some 61% of its total foreign income from crude petroleum sales, mostly to China, in 2021.

Sudan and the Secession of the South In 1998 Sudan, a relatively minor producer with estimated proven reserves of some 360m. metric tons in that year, finalized an agreement with four foreign companies to construct a 1,600-km pipeline to convey output from western Sudan to a terminal at Bachair, south of Port Sudan. The pipeline, with the capacity to carry 450,000 b/d, was inaugurated in mid-1999, and petroleum production subsequently rose rapidly to total an estimated 23.4m. tons in 2009 and 22.8m. tons in 2010. However, production fell significantly in 2011 and 2012, to just 14.3m. and 5.1m. tons, respectively. Output has remained low in subsequent years, reaching 3.6m. tons in 2019, 3.1m. tons in 2020 and 3.2m. tons in 2021. The decline was largely the result of political and logistical difficulties surrounding South Sudan's secession from Sudan in 2011. (South Sudan produces most of the area's petroleum—see below.) Owing to limited resources, the Sudan National Petroleum Corpn (SUDAPET) has frequently collaborated in joint exploration and production ventures with foreign companies, retaining minority stakes in these projects. Among the foreign companies active in Sudan's oil sector are CNPC, Oil and Natural Gas Corpn of India and Petronas of Malaysia. Activity in the petroleum industry in the south has been complicated by conflicting claims to ownership of resources by northern and southern authorities—NILEPET is South Sudan's counterpart of SUDAPET. Sudan's refining facilities are state-owned, with the Khartoum oil refinery (the location of 36m. barrels, or 80%, of national refining capacity) being operated as a joint venture between a Sudanese government vehicle and CNPC. A smaller facility is operated at Port Sudan. In 2015, according to the USGS, Sudan's petroleum sector contributed 2.0% to the country's GDP. Meanwhile, the country exported no crude petroleum in 2013 as a result of South Sudan's secession, which had a devastating effect on its economy. (Exports of crude petroleum subsequently contributed 19% of the total value of the country's foreign export sales in 2021, with lower production mitigated by significantly higher prices for crude in that year, which meant export receipts were some 46% higher than the previous year.) Sudan's proven reserves were estimated at 202m. tons at the end of 2020. The manner in which both the production of and exploration for petroleum in Sudan had hitherto been conducted had allegedly involved the Government in human rights abuses, including the forced evacuation of populations living in the vicinity of potentially lucrative oilfields. In late 2006 the US Government had proscribed investment by US individuals and organizations in Sudan's petroleum and petrochemical industries, a measure that was intended, in part, to counter the alleged use of petroleum derived revenues to fund the conflict in Darfur. Shortly before US President Barack Obama left office in 2017, he signed an executive order temporarily suspending sanctions against Sudan, meaning its petroleum resources could be sold on the global market. The sanctions were due for permanent revocation six months later, but in July of that year US President Donald Trump extended the deadline by three months, by executive order. It was eventually announced in October that a number of the sanctions imposed by the USA had been eased (though some remained in place). In early 2020 it was finally reported that the USA had ended sanctions on 157 Sudanese enterprises. As a result of this development, analysts were optimistic that the sector would now attract foreign investment. To this end, the Sudanese Government had offered up tenders to 15 exploration blocks in November 2017, and a further 10 blocks in March 2019. Following the removal from power of Sudanese President Omar Hassan Ahmad al-Bashir, a Sudanese transitional government, led by Prime Minister Abdalla Hamdok, requested the country's removal from the US list of state terrorist sponsors, a move which would enable renewed access to international financing; in December 2020 the country was formally removed from the list.

At the time of the official declaration of independence of South Sudan from the Republic of Sudan on 9 July 2011, it was unclear how the northern and southern regions would handle the division of petroleum resources: the land-locked southern region produced most of the area's petroleum, but all of the refineries and export pipelines were located in the north, as was the main port. It was estimated by the IMF that petroleum contributed around 76% of total government revenues in South Sudan in 2015–16. At the end of 2011 SUDAPET's assets in South Sudan were nationalized and transferred to NILE-PET. At 31 December 2020 South Sudan's reserves were estimated at 472m. metric tons. In the following year—the 10th year for which data were available—South Sudan's petroleum output was estimated to be 7.5m. metric tons, up from 6.8m. tons in 2016. Poor production in 2012 (just 1.5m. tons) was blamed on South Sudan's imposed halt on output at the end of January 2012. Officials pointed to the high transit fees Sudan was attempting to impose to make up for its lost oil revenue following secession as the reason for South Sudan's action. (The former was reportedly demanding US $32–$36 per barrel, while South Sudan was offering less than $1 per barrel.) Following more than a year of negotiations, South Sudan restarted production in April 2013, although bilateral arrangements were considered fragile. Considerable disagreement centres around support for rebel groups. The Sudanese Government threatened to cut off access to two main pipelines that export South Sudanese crude from June 2013 in response to South Sudan's alleged support for rebels accused of plotting to overthrow the administration in Khartoum. In September 2018 and January 2019 South Sudan supported marginal increases in its production by reopening two previously closed fields: Toma South and Unity. South Sudan passed the Petroleum Act in 2012, which established the National Petroleum and Gas Corporation (NPGC)—the country's main policy-making body responsible for approving oil and gas agreements for the Government. In 2015 the country enacted (though only implemented in part) the Petroleum Revenue Management Act, which is aimed at reducing mismanagement and bribery in the petroleum sector, and encouraging efficient use of revenues in the future. In March 2021 operation of a small refinery in Bentiu, near the international border with Sudan, commenced, while a larger refinery at Thiangrial in the Upper Nile region was under construction in mid-2021. Meanwhile, deliberations were continuing on the construction of a 3,600-km pipeline to Lamu port in Kenya in order to reduce the country's reliance on Sudan's pipeline infrastructure—although analysts were not optimistic that it would be built in the near future, given the fragile security situation. The origin of disputed shipments of crude continued to damage relations between the two countries in early 2012, while a civil war in South Sudan—which began in late 2013 and only ended in early 2020—further threatened already intermittent supply. Following the signing of a power-sharing and ceasefire agreement between the Government and rebels in August 2018 and the formation of a unity government in February 2020, however, South Sudanese officials were hopeful that the potential improvement in the security situation would attract foreign investment in the sector. Indeed, the country launched its first exploration licensing round in 2021, with five licences offered.

Traditionally, petroleum exports from Sudan and South Sudan have been sold almost exclusively to Asian markets. However, following the shutdown in South Sudanese production in 2012 (see above), the contribution to Chinese imports of crude petroleum—China being Sudan and South Sudan's largest purchaser—fell to just 1% (compared with 5% in 2011). In 2021 80.9% of the value of South Sudan's exports were derived from crude petroleum, with China purchasing some 77% and Italy 23%. Exports of crude petroleum totalled some 337,000 b/d in 2011, but this fell significantly after South Sudan's secession, to just 65,000 b/d in 2012; Sudan and South Sudan exported about 132,000 b/d of crude oil in 2021.

Organization of the Petroleum Exporting Countries (OPEC) International petroleum prices are strongly influenced by the Organization of the Petroleum Exporting Countries (OPEC), founded in 1960 in Baghdad, Iraq. Its purpose is to co-ordinate the production and marketing policies of those countries with substantial net petroleum exports in order to secure stable and fair prices for producing countries, a regular supply of petroleum for consuming countries and a return on capital for countries and corporations that invest in the industry. OPEC came under scrutiny in the 1970s when Arab countries imposed an oil embargo (in 1973), which led to a steep rise in prices on world markets. The embargo—initiated by the Organization of Arab Petroleum Exporting Countries (OAPEC)—was initiated in response to US involvement in the Yom Kippur War. In the meantime, however, the USA had withdrawn from the Bretton Woods Accord, which led to the floating of the US dollar (and other currencies) and an increase in US dollar reserves. The resultant devaluing of that currency meant that petroleum producing countries were receiving less real income from their exports (since petroleum, at this time, was priced and traded in US dollars). OPEC subsequently released a statement confirming that it would henceforth peg the price of a barrel of oil against the price of gold.

OPEC member countries experienced severe economic setbacks in the mid-1980s as prices dropped substantially (by as much as two-thirds). The overall decline in prices was attributed to an oversupply of petroleum and significantly reduced consumer demand. Prices recovered somewhat in the late 1980s, but only to around one-half of the record levels seen at the start of the decade. Recovery was encouraged by the introduction of a production ceiling and the OPEC reference 'basket' (ORB) for pricing. The 1990s was a comparatively stable decade, although Iraq's invasion of Kuwait and the resultant Gulf War created some volatility in world markets. However, the decade was characterized by general weakness in pricing, with particularly mild winters in the northern hemisphere countries in the late 1990s causing prices to drop to 1986 levels. None the less, crude prices strengthened and then stabilized in the early 2000s, before reaching record levels later in the decade (see below). Following historically low prices for crudes in 2015–16, OPEC and non-OPEC producers agreed in late 2016 to reduce output for the first time since the global financial crisis in 2008. Saudi Arabia, which had been most significantly impacted by the low prices, assumed the largest reduction in output, while Russia, the UAE, Kuwait and Qatar also agreed to reduced production quotas. Nigeria and Libya were granted exemptions. The deal (often referred to as 'OPEC+') has since been extended multiple times. (Meanwhile, production in the USA increased significantly during the same period, overtaking that of both Saudi Arabia and the Russian Federation.) Production quotas remained in place as of July 2022, although Western sanctions on Russian exports (imposed in response to Russia's renewed armed invasion of Ukraine in 2022) and unplanned outages (particularly in Nigeria) meant modest production gains among the alliance in the first half of the year still fell short of the negotiated increases in quota thresholds (particularly in Saudi Arabia and the UAE), placing upward pressure on prices. Indeed, the European Union (EU) announced that it would phase out imports of Russian refined crude products altogether by the end of 2022. Iran, Libya and Venezuela continued to be exempt from the production quotas. In mid-2022 US President Biden visited Saudi Arabia in an effort to persuade the authorities there to increase production further, and thereby attempt to regulate spiralling prices, but the cartel's response in early August—agreement to an insignificant increase in output—was considered unlikely to impact the market in a meaningful way. Conversely, in June 2020 OPEC production had reached its lowest level in nearly 30 years as members sought to reverse the plummeting prices of crude (a consequence of the global contraction in industrial activity during attempts to contain the COVID-19 pandemic). The strategy of OPEC+ to stockpile supplies during the pandemic, however, resulted in rapid price recovery from May 2021, when quotas began to increase once again. By May of the following year prices were at an almost 10-year high.

OPEC distinguishes between founder members and full members. At mid-2022 it had 13 members in total. Nigeria joined OPEC in 1971; the other African members are Algeria, Angola, the Republic of Congo, Gabon and Libya. (Gabon terminated its membership in 1997, but rejoined in 2016.)

Regional Association The (then) four African members of OPEC (Algeria, Gabon, Libya and Nigeria) formed the African Petroleum Producers' Association (APPA) in 1987. Angola, Benin, Cameroon, Chad, the DRC, the Republic of Congo, Côte d'Ivoire, Egypt, Equatorial Guinea, Ghana, Mauritania, South Africa and Sudan subsequently joined the association, in which Tunisia has observer status. Apart from promoting co-operation among regional producers, the APPA, which is based in Brazzaville, Republic of the Congo, co-operates with OPEC in stabilizing oil prices.

Price History of the OPEC 'Basket' of Crude Oils
(US $ per barrel)

		Average	High	Low
2011	.	107.46	(April) 118.09	(January) 92.83
2012	.	109.45	(March) 122.97	(June) 93.98
2013	.	105.87	(February) 117.75	(May) 100.65
2014	.	96.29	(June) 107.89	(December) 59.46
2015	.	49.49	(May) 62.16	(December) 33.64
2016	.	40.76	(December) 51.67	(January) 26.50
2017	.	52.43	(December) 62.06	(June) 45.21
2018	.	69.78	(October) 79.39	(December) 56.94
2019	.	64.04	(April) 70.78	(January) 58.74
2020	.	41.47	(January) 65.10	(April) 17.66
2021	.	69.89	(October) 82.11	(January) 54.38

Source: OPEC, *Annual Reports* and *Monthly Oil Market Reports*.

Prices The growth in petroleum prices continued apace in 2011, with the average price of the OPEC reference 'basket' (ORB) rising by 38.7%. The global economy grew by 3.6% in 2011 in spite of fiscal conservatism in many countries. Export driven countries once again performed well, but OECD countries—especially Japan, which weathered an earthquake and associated tsunami and nuclear disaster in March of that year that pushed the country into recession—again struggled to maintain growth. Overall demand declined during the

year, as the financial crisis undermined consumer confidence in OECD and non-OECD countries alike. US demand was especially weak, as high retail prices for gasoline led to lower consumption. The significant increase in prices during the year was attributed mostly to ongoing violence in Libya, which severely disrupted exports. All 'basket' components performed well in 2011, with African crudes performing particularly well. In that year the average price of Brent crude reached US $111.36 per barrel, which represented growth of just less than 40% compared with 2010. There was international concern over the volatility of prices in the first half of 2012, as the ORB moved from $124 per barrel to less than $90 per barrel, in spite of steady supply levels (including a recovery in Libyan production). The average price of the ORB grew by 1.9% compared with the previous year. Global economic growth decelerated to 3.0%, with the People's Republic of China alone contributing around one-third. The moderate growth was attributed to the ending of financial assistance packages in many developed economies, and the resulting decline in petroleum demand among OECD countries. However, demand in non-OECD countries remained robust, growing by 1.2m. b/d. In Japan, however, crude petroleum consumption increased by 36% as nuclear power plants remained closed and the country sought an alternative electricity supply. Price growth over the year was attributed to resurgent turmoil in the Middle East and supply disruptions in the North Sea fields. The price of Brent crude in 2012 was 0.2% higher than in 2011, averaging $111.63 for the year. The world economy demonstrated some growth in the first half of 2013, but gathered momentum in the second half. Global economic growth slowed to 2.9% in the year overall, while the fluctuation in petroleum prices witnessed in 2012—causing a great deal of market volatility—was largely avoided. Overall world demand for crude increased in 2013 (by some 1.3m. b/d), aided in OECD countries by optimism in manufacturing and other industrial sectors. Japanese demand, meanwhile, declined during the year as it relied more heavily on natural gas and coal for its energy needs, although this was partly offset by increased naphtha consumption resulting from growth in the petrochemical industry. In 2013 the average price of the ORB declined by 3.3%. Following strong growth early in the year (supported by healthy demand and ongoing maintenance issues in the North Sea), petroleum prices declined in the third quarter, following the publication of poor economic data from the USA and China, the world's two largest consumers. Ongoing economic problems in the eurozone and record inventories in the USA also exerted downward pressure on prices later in the year. The price of Brent crude averaged $108.62 per barrel in 2013, which represented a fall of 2.7% compared with the previous year.

The price of the ORB declined significantly in 2014, by 9.0% compared with 2013. Following minimal movement in the first half of the year, prices declined precipitously from June over concerns of oversupply and subdued growth in demand. Surges in Libyan production appeared to justify such concerns, placing crude stocks at levels higher than they had been for five and a half years, while the drop in demand was also attributed to weaker than expected economic data in China and Europe, and ongoing maintenance to refineries. At the end of the year the ORB price reached its lowest point for more than five years; in fact it lost almost one-half of its value during the course of 2014. The ORB price continued to fall in early 2015 as a result of oversupply: it reached a six-year low in January of US $44.38 per barrel (the seventh consecutive month of decline), before picking up in February. The price of Brent crude averaged just $52.41 in 2015, which represented a decline of almost 50% compared with the previous year's average. The average price of the ORB, meanwhile, fell to $49.49. Oversupply (which had persisted for some 18 months) and ongoing concerns about a slowing Chinese economy were identified as contributing to the steep decline in prices, as was the strength of the US dollar over the same period. The price of the ORB fell sharply again at the beginning of 2016 (by some 21%), to just $26.50 per barrel. The price represented its lowest value since September 2003. However, it recovered somewhat in the first half of the year. The significant decline in prices in January was again attributed to a weaker Chinese economy, a reduction in demand owing to lower seasonal heating requirements (a consequence of a milder northern-hemisphere winter), and ongoing global oversupply. Prices were steady in the second half of the year, until December, when the average price of the ORB rose by some 20%—the first time in 18 months that the price had averaged more than $50 per barrel. News of cooperation between OPEC and non-OPEC producers to rebalance the market (specifically to remove some 1.8m. b/d from the market) led to the steep rise in prices over the month, though the yearly average for 2016 was still the lowest for 12 years.

The global economy was generally strong in 2017, which resulted in higher prices for petroleum; global GDP growth was estimated at 3.7% for the year. Economies in China, the USA and the EU had demonstrated forward momentum and increased demand, however, price growth was slow in the first half of the year, and weakened somewhat in June–July—a temporary trend attributed to oversupply and high inventories among producing countries. Damage sustained in the Gulf of Mexico as a result of Hurricanes Harvey,

Irma and Maria in the second half of the year, however, raised supply concerns and caused a sharp rise in prices. By November the price of the ORB had risen more than 35% since June, to over US $60 per barrel. From June 2018 the ORB included Congolese Djeno crude in its pricing for the first time, a result of the Republic of Congo's recent accession to OPEC. The price of the ORB remained historically low in that year, although it grew steadily through most of 2018 (increasing by 33.1% year on year) before recording a sharp drop in the final two months. Global economic growth remained steady at 3.6% (slightly down from 2017), although ongoing trade tensions between the USA and China began to impact the latter country, which witnessed a deceleration in growth to its lowest level since 2008. The price of the ORB reached $79.39 per barrel in October, an increase attributed to positive market sentiment, which was supported by the voluntary production adjustments by OPEC member countries under the Declaration of Cooperation (global stocks were at their lowest since 2014), and increased global demand—up by some 1.43m. b/d over the year. Prices dropped once more from October, with analysts pointing to the easing of supply disruptions and the expectation of a reduction in demand resulting from weak economic growth forecasts—prompted, in part, by continuing US–China tensions over trade. Moreover, higher-than-expected crude production in the USA in particular led to fears of oversupply, with the average price of the ORB falling to just $56.94 per barrel in December. Global economic growth in 2019 was lower than in the previous two years, which was attributed to a slow-down in global trade—a result of ongoing trade disputes involving the USA—as well as lower growth in emerging markets. India in particular registered GDP growth some 2% lower than a year earlier. Demand for crude petroleum and prices over the year were consequently lower than the previous year. Prices in particular were negatively affected by trade disputes between the USA and China. None the less, price growth in the first half of the year was strong (the ORB reached $70.78 per barrel in April), before concerns over global demand led to considerable declines in the second half of the year (prices reached just $59.62 per barrel in August).

As the COVID-19 pandemic took hold in the first half of 2020, however, crude petroleum prices entered a precipitous decline; the average price of the ORB was just US $17.66 per barrel in April, its lowest level in almost two decades. The plummeting prices were the result of historically low demand (as much industrial production ground to a halt), oversupply and dire predictions of global economic performance. (It was reported that the world economy shrank by 3.5% over the year.) However, by the end of 2020 the ORB and Brent crude prices had recovered substantially (as many countries relaxed the 'lockdown' measures introduced earlier in the year in an attempt to halt the spread of the virus, and supply cuts among OPEC members and non-members alike began to have an effect), averaging $49.17 per barrel and $50.22 per barrel, respectively, in December. Notwithstanding these gains, the average price for the ORB for the year was its lowest since 2016. Prices showed strong growth through most of 2021—with its average year-to-date price in October some 68% higher than one year earlier—on the back of a stronger than expected economic performance by many major economies in the second half of 2020, US supply disruptions resulting from severe winter weather, strong demand in advance of the summer driving season (in the northern hemisphere) and declining stocks in many important consuming countries in 2021. Global economic growth was revised upwards to 5.8%, supporting the price recovery; US, Chinese and Indian growth rates were estimated at 5.7%, 8.1% and 8.3%, respectively. The price of Brent crude increased by some 64% in 2021 to average $70.95 per barrel for the year, its highest level since 2018. The first half of 2022 was characterized by historically high crude prices, a consequence of the resurgent conflict in Ukraine, and the imposition, in response, by many important consumers (including the USA and the European Union—EU) of sanctions on Russian fuel exports—although the EU continued to be the largest importer of Russian fossil fuels (chiefly natural gas). By June the average price for the ORB was $117.72 per barrel. Compared with the previous year, the average price for 2022 thus far was 65% higher than at the same point in 2021. The price of Brent crude averaged $117.50 per barrel over the same month. Consumption was projected to remain robust throughout the year, particularly as Chinese authorities began to ease renewed restrictions introduced to control a new wave of the COVID-19 pandemic (this relaxation was almost certain to support an increase in industrial activity) and also because of the advent of the summer driving season in the USA. However, prices and supplies remained vulnerable to ongoing concerns over inflation (in the USA, to May 2022 the price of gasoline had increased by almost 50% compared with the same period of 2021), a possible return to containment measures in response to emerging COVID-19 variants and increasing military and geopolitical tensions in Europe. In July the average price for the ORB had fallen to $108.55 per barrel, while the price of Brent crude averaged $105.12 per barrel (some 10% lower than the previous month). The declines were attributed to negative outlooks in the global economy and likely reduced demand.

PLATINUM (*Pt*)

Platinum is one of a group of six related metals known as the platinum-group metals (PGM), which also includes palladium, rhodium, ruthenium, iridium and osmium. In nature, platinum is usually associated with the sulphides of iron, copper and nickel. Depending on the relative concentration of the PGM and copper and nickel in the deposit, platinum is either the major product or a by-product of base metal production. PGM are highly resistant to corrosion, and do not oxidize in air. They are also extremely malleable and have a high melting point, giving them a wide range of industrial uses. Platinum itself is grey-white in colour and popular for jewellery. Alloyed platinum is hard and heavy, and it is the least chemically reactive of the metals. As with gold, platinum's traditional units are troy ounces (oz), but production figures are given in kilograms; 1 oz is equivalent to 31.103 g, and there are 32,151 oz in 1 metric ton.

Production of Platinum
(kg, platinum content)

	2017	2018	2019	2020
World total . . .	185,000	190,000	186,000	166,000
Leading African producers				
South Africa	132,500	137,053	132,989	111,993
Zimbabwe	14,257	14,703	13,857	15,005
Leading non-African producers				
Canada*	7,600	7,600	7,300	7,000
Russian Federation* .	22,000	22,000	24,000	23,000
USA†	4,000*	4,160	4,150	4,200

2021 ('000 kg, platinum content, estimates): South Africa 130.0, Zimbabwe 15.0; Canada 6.0, Russian Federation 19.0, USA 4.2; World total (incl. others) 180.0.

* Estimated production.

† Platinum produced from gold-copper and nickel ores are excluded.

Sources: US Geological Survey.

The World Market and the Region Although widely employed in the petroleum refining and petrochemical sectors, the principal industrial use for platinum is in catalytic converters in motor vehicles (which reduce pollution from exhaust emissions), which, from 2004, generally accounted for almost one-half of global platinum consumption (down to 40% in 2018, given the challenge of palladium as an alternative). Since the 1990s most Western countries and many others have implemented legislation to neutralize vehicle exhaust gases, and this necessitates the fitting of catalytic converters, using platinum, rhodium and palladium, to vehicles. The resultant increase in demand for automotive emission control catalysts (autocatalysts) generated a rising trend in the consumption of platinum, rhodium and palladium during and since the 1990s, in particular as further restrictions on emissions were introduced. The increasing use of autocatalysts, principally by US and European motor vehicle manufacturers, was reflected in a strong advance in autocatalyst demand for platinum into the 2000s. Almost one-half of platinum use in autocatalysts was once accounted for by Europe, but that proportion is declining. Palladium use in autocatalysts (80% of palladium consumption in 2018) was increasing more rapidly than that of platinum, in particular in North America, while in the longer term new technologies in motor vehicles threatened the need for autocatalysts. Platinum is also a precious metal and some is traded as bullion, but it is rather more popular in jewellery (27% of platinum consumption in 2018). Until the growth in demand for autocatalysts, Japan was the world's main consumer of platinum, its jewellery industry absorbing 19% of total global demand in 1999. However, Japanese demand for platinum jewellery fell steadily through the 2000s and, from 2001, Chinese jewellery demand was a challenger, in some years exceeding European autocatalyst demand.

World production of PGM generally is dominated by South Africa, which traditionally accounted for about three-quarters of supplies of platinum—the proportion has declined in the 2000s. More accurate assessment of global production has been possible since 2005, when official data relating to Russian PGM were declassified. The Russian Federation is the world's largest producer of mined palladium (except in 2015, when South African output exceeded that of Russia) and the second largest producer of platinum. Canada was once the third largest producer of platinum, mined as a by-product of nickel production, but in 2009 was displaced by Zimbabwe. The next largest platinum producer was the USA. The world's five leading platinum mining companies in 2018 were Anglo American Platinum Ltd (Amplats) of South Africa, Impala Platinum Holdings Ltd (Implats) of South Africa, Sibanye-Stillwater of South Africa, Lonmin PLC of the United Kingdom and South Africa, and OJSC MMC Norilsk

Nickel of Russia. The South African industry has been affected in the 2010s by labour unrest (including strike action in 2014, which lowered output for the year), greater enforcement of safety standards in mines, possible ownership legislation and power supply issues. In 2021 South Africa's exports (f.o.b.) of platinum (unwrought, powder, or semi-manufactured) contributed 18.7% of the country's total export earnings. It was reported in mid-2022 that Amplats earnings had nearly halved in the first six months of the year (down 43%) compared with the first half of 2021, as a result of supply chain challenges and electricity disruptions in South Africa—the national power utility had implemented significant rotational power rationing ('loadshedding') throughout the country in the first half of the year. Moreover, refined production of PGM had also declined (by 19%) in the first six months of 2022.

Zimbabwe, the only other significant African producer, boasts sizeable deposits of PGM. In 2017 an implementation of the 2008 'indigenization' legislation (proposing the transfer of 51% of all foreign owned companies in the country to Zimbabwe nationals) seemed to have been agreed. (The Government of new Zimbabwean President Emmerson Mnangagwa, elected in July 2018, subsequently indicated that the 51% local stakeholder stipulation would indeed apply to the gold and platinum industries.) Negotiations about the compliance details gazetted in 2011 dragged on for some years, though by 2013 all three companies involved had allocated equity to local community, employee and national trusts. The Government favoured a greater degree of domestic beneficiation of PGM ores and, in April 2017, agreed the construction of a smelter in the country (apparently using the new Kell process, which is considered cheaper) with Pallinghurst Resources (since renamed Gemfields) of the UK. To avoid the risks of a perceived 'asset grab' against the major multinational companies, the indigenization obligation would be satisfied by having to supply the ore to the new refinery; Amplats later reported that it would be excused the requirement to supply the government smelter because it was already building its own (since completed in 2019). Notwithstanding the devastating economic effects of the COVID-19 pandemic, it was reported in mid-2020 that the largest mining company in Zimbabwe (Zimplats—the Zimbabwean offshoot of Implats) had posted a 38% increase in revenue for the year ending 30 June 2020. It was reported in early 2022 that Implats would be investing close to US $80m. in the Bimha mine, following the recent completion of a $100m. reconstruction project at the mine (which had collapsed in 2014). Meanwhile, the power issue in southern Africa remained problematic. PGM occur as trace element by-products associated with nickel production in Botswana, but the country produces more palladium than platinum. Elsewhere in Africa, there are known or probable deposits of platinum in Ethiopia, Kenya and Sierra Leone.

Whereas PGM are produced in Canada and Russia as by-products of copper and/or nickel mining, PGM in South Africa are produced as the primary products, with nickel and copper as by-products. Another fundamental difference between the platinum deposits in South Africa and those in Russia and Canada is the ratio of platinum to palladium. In South Africa the percentage of platinum contained in PGM has, to date, exceeded that of palladium, although the ratio tended to favour palladium in new mines that were brought into production from the early 1990s (see below). In the Russian Federation, Canada and the USA there is a higher proportion of palladium than platinum.

Prices for Platinum and Palladium
(London market*, afternoon 'fixes', annual and monthly averages, US $ per troy oz)

	Platinum (London)	High month	Low month	Palladium (London)
2005 .	897	—	—	201
2010 .	1,609	(April) 1,716	(October) 1,520	525
2015 .	1,053	(January) 1,243	(December) 859	692
2019 .	863	(September) 944	(January) 807	1,537
2020 .	883	(December) 1,026	(April) 754	2,193
2021 .	1,090	(May) 1,214	(December) 940	2,398

* London Platinum and Palladium Fixing Co Ltd for prices before 1 December 2014 and the London Bullion Market Association (LBMA) platinum or palladium price from 1 December 2014.

Source: London Bullion Market Association.

Prices International commodity prices for platinum (and palladium) are based on the afternoon 'fix' on the London Platinum and Palladium Market (LPPM) or, from 1 December 2014, on the London Bullion Market in the UK, cited in US dollars per troy oz. A twice-daily quotation of platinum prices began in London in 1973 (the main London and Zurich, Switzerland, dealers agreeing certain common standards in 1979), but the system was only formalized as the LPPM in 1987, with quotations upgraded to full fixings in 1989. In that year the nominal London platinum price was US $507.3 per oz, a level that

was not exceeded until 2000 (in real terms, the 1989 price was not exceeded until 2004, but subsequently rose to a new peak in 2011). The average annual London platinum price, together with the highest and lowest average monthly prices in each year, are cited in the table (above), along with the corresponding London palladium price (also based on the afternoon 'fix' and given in US dollars per troy oz). Both platinum and palladium are industrial metals, but platinum in particular is a precious metal and can be an investment resource.

RICE (*Oryza*)

Rice is an annual grass belonging to the same family as (and having many similar characteristics to) small grains such as wheat, oats, rye and barley. It is principally the semi-aquatic nature of rice that distinguishes it from other grain species, and this is an important factor in determining its place of origin. In Africa and Asia unmilled rice is referred to as 'paddy', although 'rough' rice is the common appellation in the West. After removal of the outer husk, it is called 'brown' rice. After the grain is milled to varying degrees to remove the bran layers, it is called 'milled' rice. Since rice loses 30%–40% of its weight in the milling process, most rice is traded in the milled form to save shipping expenses.

There are two cultivated species of rice, *Oryza sativa* and *O. glaberrima*. Originating in tropical Asia, *O. sativa* is widely grown in tropical and semi-tropical areas, while the cultivation of the native *O. glaberrima* is limited to the high rainfall zone of West Africa. In Africa rice is grown mainly as a subsistence crop, principally by smallholder farmers of whom a disproportionate number are women. Methods of cultivation differ from region to region and yields tend to be low by world standards. Rice is a staple food in several African countries, including Côte d'Ivoire, The Gambia, Guinea, Guinea-Bissau, Liberia, Madagascar, Senegal and Sierra Leone. In West African countries generally rice is a staple food of 40% of the population. As a consequence of population growth and increased dietary preference for rice, sub-Saharan African demand for consumption increased rapidly in the late 20th century. Most of the varieties of rice cultivated in Africa originated in Asia and are relatively new to the region, so suitable high-yielding varieties only began to be propagated from the 1990s (see below).

Production of Milled Rice
(estimates, '000 metric tons)

	2018/19	2019/20	2020/21	2021/22*
World total . . .	498,219	499,150	509,262	513,654
Sub-Saharan Africa . .	20,117	20,742	20,595	20,732
Leading sub-Saharan African producers				
Côte d'Ivoire . . .	1,304	1,225	962	1,078
Guinea	1,544	1,715	1,909	1,921
Madagascar . . .	2,579	2,708	2,708	2,560
Mali	2,059	2,077	1,957	1,570
Nigeria	5,294	5,314	5,148	5,255
Senegal	821	786	918	940
Sierra Leone . . .	920	948	958	964
Tanzania	2,254	2,293	2,310	2,525
Leading non-African producers				
Bangladesh . . .	34,909	35,850	34,600	35,850
Brazil	7,140	7,602	8,001	7,344
China, People's Republic .	148,490	146,730	148,300	148,990
India	116,480	118,870	124,370	129,660
Indonesia . . .	34,200	34,700	34,500	34,400
Japan	7,657	7,611	7,573	7,640
Myanmar	13,200	12,650	12,600	12,352
Philippines . . .	11,732	11,927	12,416	12,600
Thailand	20,340	17,655	18,863	19,650
USA	7,107	5,877	7,224	6,090
Viet Nam	27,344	27,100	27,381	27,069

* Preliminary.

Source: US Department of Agriculture.

The World Market and the Region The bulk of rice production is consumed in the producing countries, and international trade generally accounts for less than 10% of world output. Governments are the principal (but not exclusive) traders, and four countries dominate the export market in most years: Thailand, Viet Nam, the USA and India. Thailand became the world's leading rice exporter in 1981, and rice has remained the country's principal agricultural export commodity. Thailand's dominance in the world rice market has come under increasing pressure, although it still provided some 7.0m. metric tons of milled rice to world markets in 2021/22 (13% of global exports, according to provisional figures from the US

Department of Agriculture—USDA); a controversial subsidy introduced in 2011 (known as the rice pledging scheme) left the country with fewer exports and high stocks, without any increase in the export price, because India (ending a non-basmati rice export ban in the same year) and Viet Nam supplied the balance to world markets. By selling stocks at aggressive prices, Thailand briefly regained its position as the leading rice exporter in 2013/14, but India was then again ahead, as it had been for some years. In 2021/22 USDA put Indian exports at 21.0m. tons or 40% of the milled rice market and Viet Nam's share at 12%; Pakistan was the next largest exporter, at 8%, then the USA (5%), followed by Myanmar and the People's Republic of China (4% each). The role of China in international rice markets changed significantly in the early 21st century. In 2000 it was the third largest rice exporter (supplying 13% of world trade), but it experienced a period of being far less significant in global markets in the latter part of the first decade of the century as it largely satisfied its own needs. In the 2010s, however, China's policy of support for the price of domestic rice not only encouraged high levels of production, but the importation of cheaper foreign rice. Rice exports remained healthy, but the country became not only a net importer of rice, but the world's largest importer. In 2021/22 China accounted for almost 11% of global purchases—up from the 5% two years earlier. The second largest importer in that year was the Philippines (6%), followed by Nigeria (4%).

World rice production is therefore dominated by the Asian region (East, South and South-East Asia produced 89% of the world's total in 2021/22). African rice production increased steadily from the 1970s, but increased dependence on imports resulted in a reduction in domestic production (although this began to recover in the 2000s). Sub-Saharan African output accounted for only some 4.0% of total world output in 2021/22 (compared with 7.1% of global domestic consumption). As the bulk of rice production is consumed mainly in the producing countries, the market is subject to great volatility and fluctuating prices. Only 2% of the sub-Saharan African rice crop entered international trade in 2021/22—few African countries export much rice, apart from Egypt, which is the continent's largest producer. Sub-Saharan Africa is a substantial net importer of rice, although the volume growth in imports was held in check by the impact of higher world rice prices on the depleted foreign exchange reserves of many African importing countries: sub-Saharan Africa bought 32% of global imports in 2021/22, according to USDA. The major African importers include Nigeria, Côte d'Ivoire, Senegal and South Africa. In 2021/22 Nigeria was the world's third largest importer, accounting for 2.2m. tons or 4% of the total in international trade. Madagascar, the world's largest consumer of rice in per caput terms, has not yet achieved its goal of self-sufficiency in rice, although steadily improving harvests from 2002/03 put this aim within reach. The country began to challenge Nigeria for its position as sub-Saharan Africa's largest rice producer from the mid-2000s.

Regional Research Organization The development of HYV counts among the activities of the Africa Rice Center (AfricaRice), formed by the producing countries in 1971 as the West Africa Rice Development Association (WARDA, which acronym it retained until 2009). The grouping had 28 members in 2022. From the beginning of 2005 the organization transferred its operations to Cotonou, Benin, from its headquarters in Bouaké, Côte d'Ivoire, owing to ongoing political instability in the latter country, but in 2015 announced that it would begin a phased return of its headquarters and activities to Côte d'Ivoire during that year. Research staff are based in Benin, Côte d'Ivoire, Nigeria, Senegal and Tanzania, conducting scientific research on crop improvement and providing technical assistance, with the aim of advancing the region towards eventual self-sufficiency in rice production. Since 2000 several New Rice for Africa (NERICA) cultivation projects have been initiated. The NERICA varieties have been developed by what is now AfricaRice, and it is hoped that their adaptation to West African growing conditions will increase their yields by at least 25%, compared with conventional rice crops. The next stage, in the following decade, was the introduction of the Advanced Rices for Africa (ARICA).

Rice Price
(US $ per metric ton)

	Average	High	Low
2005 .	286	(April) 297	(July) 277
2010 .	489	(January) 569	(June) 440
2015 .	386	(January, February) 420	(September) 357
2019 .	418	(December) 432	(March) 406
2020 .	497	(April) 564	(February) 450
2021 .	458	(February) 557	(September) 400*

* Also November and December.

Source: World Bank, *Commodity Price Data* (Pink Sheet).

Prices Rice was not exempt from the rapid expansion in global commodity prices seen from late 2007 and into the first half of 2008.

Market observers placed the extraordinarily high levels to which international prices of rice rose in the first half of 2008 in the context of a rising trend in the prices of basic food commodities—in particular wheat, soya, maize, rape and palm oil—that had been apparent for two years, as supply failed to keep pace with increasing demand for food, given a generally higher standard of living in developing countries, especially in Asia. A high level of speculative investment in agricultural commodities also contributed, because they had come to be viewed as a refuge from rising inflation and the weakness of the US dollar (for a three-month period in the first half of 2008 rice reportedly became the agricultural 'market of choice' for speculative funds). Domestic inflation or the need to placate social unrest also prompted export curbs or other restrictions imposed by some major rice-exporting countries. Such policies—with some countries reducing exports and others increasing imports—are of particular significance because of the small proportion of world rice production that enters world trade. Given such restrictions, notably in India, rice prices remained firm after the general commodity price correction in the second half of 2008. Using the price of Thai milled white rice (5% broken—indicative survey price, government standard, f.o.b. Bangkok) as an indicator, average monthly prices peaked in April 2008 at US $907 per metric ton (187% higher than one year previously and 141% higher than even at the beginning of the year—the average price for 2008 was $650 per ton). In April–June 2014 and April 2015 for one year average monthly prices fell below $400 per ton (for the first time since January 2008). Prices recovered in late 2017 and were generally higher through 2020–21 (staying above the $400 per metric ton threshold). Following depressed prices in the final months of 2021, the average price rose in early 2022; by August, however, the price had fallen once again, to average $431 per ton.

SUGAR

Sugar is a sweet crystalline substance which may be derived from the juices of various plants. Chemically, the basis of sugar is sucrose, one of a group of soluble carbohydrates which are important sources of energy in the human diet. It can be obtained from trees, including the maple and certain palms, but virtually all manufactured sugar is derived from two plants, sugar beet (*Beta vulgaris*) and sugar cane, a giant perennial grass of the genus *Saccharum*.

Sugar cane, found in tropical areas, grows to a height of up to 5 m (16 ft). The plant is native to Polynesia, but its distribution is now widespread. It is not necessary to plant cane every season as, if the root of the plant is left in the ground, it will grow again in the following year. This practice, known as 'ratooning', may be continued for as long as three years, when yields begin to decline. Cane is ready for cutting 12–24 months after planting, depending on local conditions. More than one-half of the world's sugar cane is still cut by hand, but rising costs are hastening the change to mechanical harvesting. The cane is cut as close as possible to the ground, and the top leaves, which may be used as cattle fodder, are removed.

After cutting, the cane is loaded by hand or by machine into lorries (trucks) or trailers and towed directly to a factory for processing. Sugar cane deteriorates rapidly after it has been cut and should be processed as soon as possible. At the factory the cane passes first through shredding knives or crushing rollers, which break up the hard rind and expose the inner fibre, and then to squeezing rollers, where the crushed cane is subjected to high pressure and sprayed with water. The resulting juice is heated and lime is added for clarification and the removal of impurities. The clean juice is then concentrated in evaporators. This thickened juice is next boiled in steam heated vacuum pans until a mixture or 'massecuite' of sugar crystals and 'mother syrup' is produced. The massecuite is then spun in centrifugal machines to separate the sugar crystals (raw cane sugar) from the residual syrup (cane molasses).

After the milling of sugar, the cane has dry fibrous remnants known as bagasse, which is usually burned as fuel in sugar mills. Bagasse can also be pulped and used for making fibreboard, particle board and most grades of paper. As the costs of imported wood pulp have risen, cane growing regions have turned increasingly to the manufacture of paper from bagasse. In view of rising energy costs, some countries (such as Cuba) have encouraged the use of bagasse as fuel for electricity production in order to conserve foreign exchange expended on imports of petroleum. Other by-products can be utilized as an animal feed or distilled into alcoholic beverages (notably in Brazil).

The production of beet sugar follows the same process as sugar from sugar cane, except that the juice is extracted by osmotic diffusion. Its manufacture produces white sugar crystals that do not require further refining. In most producing countries, it is consumed domestically, but any fall in the production of beet sugar by the European Union (EU) can mean that it becomes a net importer of white refined sugar. Beet sugar accounted for about one-fifth of estimated world sugar production (21% in 2021/22), according to the US Department of Agriculture (USDA). The production data in the first table, therefore, is for sugar cane, covering all crops harvested, except crops grown explicitly for feed. The second table covers the production of raw sugar by the centrifugal process (including beet sugar). While global output of non-centrifugal sugar (i.e. produced from sugar cane which has not undergone centrifugation) is not insignificant, it tends to be destined for domestic consumption. The main producer of non-centrifugal sugar is India, where it is known as gur, but countries such as Brazil and Colombia are also significant producers.

Most of the raw cane sugar produced in the world is sent to refineries outside the country of origin, unless the sugar is for local consumption. Cuba, Thailand, Brazil and India are among the few cane producers that export part of their output as refined sugar. The refining process further purifies the sugar crystals and eventually results in finished products of various grades, such as granulated, icing or castor sugar. The ratio of refined to raw sugar is usually about 0.9:1.

In the closing decades of the 20th century sugar encountered increased competition from other sweeteners, including maize-based products, such as isoglucose (a form of high-fructose corn syrup, or HFCS), and chemical additives, such as saccharine, aspartame (APM) and xylitol. APM was the most widely used high-intensity artificial sweetener in the early 1990s, its market dominance then came under challenge from sucralose, which is about 600 times as sweet as sugar (compared with 200–300 times for other intense sweeteners) and is more resistant to chemical deterioration than APM. In 1998 the US Government approved the domestic marketing of sucralose, the only artificial sweetener made from sugar. Sucralose was stated to avoid many of the taste problems associated with other artificial sweeteners. From the late 1980s research was conducted to formulate means of synthesizing thaumatin, a substance derived from the fruit of the West African katemfe plant, *Thaumatococcus daniellii*, which is about 2,500 times as sweet as sugar. As of 2005, the use of thaumatin had been approved in the EU, Israel and Japan, while in the USA its use as a flavouring agent had been endorsed. By 2011 sugar use was resurgent because of health concerns about other sweeteners—for example, sugar producers attempted to preserve this advantage in the US courts by preventing the Corn Refiners Association from renaming HFCS 'corn sugar'.

The World Market and the Region Production of sugar cane is dominated by Latin America and the Caribbean, which usually grows about one-half of the world total: 52% in 2020, according to the Food and Agriculture Organization of the United Nations (FAO—South America 45%, Central America 6% and the Caribbean 1%). South Asia grew 25% of the world's sugar cane, eastern Asia and Oceania—the Far East and Australasia—16% and Africa 5% (sub-Saharan Africa 4%). The area under sugar cane cultivation in the whole of Latin America and the Caribbean more than doubled in the 40 years from the late 1960s, but the Caribbean declined in importance to sugar production, with the area harvested in Central America increasing by 76% and that in South America more than fourfold. Moreover, South America enjoyed productive yields, whereas the Caribbean yield was the lowest in the world. According to USDA,

Production of Sugar Cane
('000 metric tons)

	2017	2018	2019	2020
World total	1,835,890	1,935,215	1,955,308	1,869,715
Sub-Saharan Africa* .	76,402	79,574	80,235	79,961
Leading sub-Saharan African producers				
Eswatini*	5,676	5,685	5,737	5,699
Kenya	4,752	5,262	4,606	6,800
Mauritius	3,713	3,155	3,405	2,621
South Africa . . .	17,388	19,302	19,242	18,220
Sudan	6,482†	6,084†	5,449†	5,192*
Zambia*	4,366	4,630	4,682	4,827
Zimbabwe	3,101†	3,583†	3,562†	3,590*
Other leading producers				
Argentina*	19,386	9,141	18,375	18,046
Australia	36,561	33,507	32,415	30,283
Brazil	758,646	747,557	753,470	757,117
China, People's Republic .	104,404	108,097	109,388	108,121
Guatemala . . .	25,951	27,665	27,249	28,350*
India	306,069	379,905	405,416	370,500
Indonesia	28,000†	29,500†	29,100†	28,914*
Mexico	56,955	56,842	59,334	53,953
Pakistan	83,333	67,174	66,380	81,009
Philippines . . .	29,287	24,731	20,719	24,399
Thailand	93,088	135,074	131,002	74,968
USA	30,153	31,336	28,973	32,749

* FAO estimate(s).
† Unofficial figure.
Source: FAO.

Production of Centrifugal Sugar
(raw value, '000 metric tons)

	2018/19	2019/20	2020/21	2021/22*
World total† . . .	179,158	166,576	181,010	181,184
Sub-Saharan Africa . .	7,762	7,840	7,565	7,519
Leading sub-Saharan African producers				
Eswatini	747	673	690	615
Kenya	500	600	710	700
Mauritius	350	360	300	300
Mozambique . . .	430	450	455	455
South Africa . . .	2,257	2,295	2,106	1,906
Sudan	600	500	350	500
Uganda	480	485	485	500
Zambia	440	435	440	450
Zimbabwe	453	442	409	408
Leading non-African producers				
Australia	4,725	4,285	4,335	4,120
Brazil	29,500	30,300	42,050	35,350
China, People's Republic .	10,760	10,400	10,600	9,600
European Union . . .	16,750	17,040	15,913	16,505
India	34,300	28,900	33,760	36,880
Mexico	6,812	5,596	6,058	6,537
Pakistan	5,270	5,340	6,505	7,140
Russian Federation . .	6,080	7,800	5,625	6,000
Thailand	14,581	8,294	7,587	10,230
USA	8,164	7,392	8,376	8,373

* Advance estimates.

† Including sugar beet production ('000 metric tons): 39,553 in 2018/19 (China, People's Republic 1,320, EU 16,531, Pakistan 60, Russian Federation 6,080, USA 4,481); 40,692 in 2019/20 (China, People's Republic 1,400, EU 16,807, Pakistan 60, Russian Federation 7,800, USA 3,946); 38,098 in 2020/21 (China, People's Republic 1,500, EU 15,689, Pakistan 60, Russian Federation 5,625, USA 4,619); 38,471 in 2021/22 (China, People's Republic 900, EU 16,280, Pakistan 60, Russian Federation 6,000, USA 4,766).

Source: US Department of Agriculture.

exports of (centrifugal) sugar from Latin American and Caribbean countries contributed 51% of total world sales abroad in 2021/22, compared with 23% from eastern Asia and Oceania, notably Thailand and Australia. Some major Asian producers such as China are net importers; South Asia, likewise, is a net importer, despite India being the second largest producer in the world. The main importing regions were eastern Asia and Oceania (34% in 2021/22, mainly Indonesia and China) and the Middle East and North Africa (23%).

In Africa ethanol has been blended with gasoline (petrol) for use in fuel for motor vehicles in Kenya, Malawi and Zimbabwe, but Zimbabwe is the only one of those countries to have required it, legally, to be used. In 2008 the World Bank estimated that Mozambique, Tanzania and other African countries had large cultivable areas that could be used for sugar cane ethanol production without directly displacing food crop production. By then, however, the promotion of biofuels was becoming increasingly controversial. In April 2008 a report compiled by the World Bank argued that the drive for biofuels by the US and European governments had been the most important factor responsible for the rapid increase in the prices of internationally traded food commodities since 2002. In the same month a UN report warned that unchecked expansion of the production of biofuel jeopardized food security in developing countries, not only by raising food prices, but also by making 'substantial demands on the world's land and water resources at a time when demand for both food and forest products is also rising rapidly'. The UN urged governments to put in place regulations to manage the growth of the biofuel industry.

Sugar cane production in sub-Saharan Africa accounts for only a small share of global output (4.3% in 2020), but the rate of growth in sugar output increased between the mid-1990s and the mid-2000s, in response to an increase in regional sugar consumption, as well as a consequence of national sugar expansion programmes that aimed to boost exports—a number of African sugar producing least developed countries (LDCs) gained duty- and quota-free access to the EU sugar market from 1 October 2009, under the EBA (Everything But Arms) regulation (see below). According to preliminary figures from USDA, in 2021/22 sub-Saharan Africa's contribution to world sugar exports was 3.3% of the total. South Africa is usually the continent's largest exporter, in 2021/22 accounting for 28% of all sub-Saharan African exports of centrifugal sugar (some 595,000 metric tons). However, this volume of exports represented only one-third of the level achieved just two years earlier, when the country sold 1.5m. tons of sugar abroad (42% of sub-Saharan exports in that year). The next largest regional exporters in 2021/22 were Eswatini selling 524,000 tons and Nigeria 350,000 tons, while Mauritius exported 305,000 tons in that year. Eswatini and other neighbouring countries have provided South Africa with increased competition in its domestic market, because of free trade agreements in the context of the Southern African Customs Union (SACU) and the Southern African Development Community (SADC). Mozambique, Zimbabwe, Sudan, Zambia and Malawi were also important exporters.

Sugar is the staple product in the economies of Mauritius and Réunion, although output is vulnerable to climatic conditions, as both islands are subject to cyclones. In Mauritius, cane and beet sugar sales accounted for about 10% of the island's revenue from exports in 2021. Increasingly, the island was exporting refined sugar, boosted by a 2010 agreement with the European Union (EU). In Réunion, sales of sugar (together with rum) provided 24% of export income in 2021. The expansion of sugar output, however, was subsequently impeded by unfavourable weather, and by the pressure on agricultural land use from the increasing demands of road construction and housing. Mozambique's sugar industry, formerly the country's primary source of foreign exchange, has begun to surmount the ill effects of many years of disruption and neglect. Considerable Mauritian and South African investment following the resolution of internal civil conflict made possible the rehabilitation both of cane growing and of four of the country's six sugar complexes. Production of raw centrifugal sugar increased rapidly after the conclusion of the peace agreement, rising from 39,000 metric tons in 1998 to about 265,000 tons in 2005, its highest level for 30 years, according to the National Sugar Institute. Increased investment in the second half of the 2000s restored the country as a net exporter. However, in 2021/22 the country exported just 60,000 tons of sugar. South Africa is an important preferential export market, favourable prices being regulated under SACU. In 2021 cane and beet sugar provided 3.5% of Malawi's revenue from foreign sales (although this was 48% below the level achieved in 2020); the differing fortunes of commodity prices mean the country's most valuable agricultural export after tobacco varies between sugar, tea and coffee, with groundnuts (peanuts) also beginning to challenge. Zambia and Zimbabwe have also launched rehabilitation and expansion programmes. In 2021/22 Zimbabwe exported some 101,000 tons of sugar.

Outside southern Africa, Tanzania sought to develop its sugar sector during the 1990s, with the aim of reducing reliance on imports from Malawi and Zambia. Domestic demand for raw sugar outstrips production, but Tanzania usually exports some sugar each year (10,000 metric tons in 2015/16, but none the following six years) to the EU and had expanded its sugar industry to take advantage of improved EU market access under the EBA regulation. Uganda increased production too during the 2000s, while Ethiopian production was reckoned to be steady, but with rising domestic consumption having put an end to exports in 2007—any fall in production, such as in 2014/15, increased imports. Kenya's rising output of centrifugal sugar made the country one of sub-Saharan Africa's largest producers, but a negligible exporter. In Sudan one of the world's largest single sugar projects was inaugurated in 1981 at Kenana, on the eastern bank of the White Nile, south of Khartoum. The Kenana Sugar Co (in which the governments of Sudan, Kuwait and Saudi Arabia are the major shareholders), comprising an estate and processing facilities, was instrumental in the elimination of the drain on reserves of foreign exchange of sugar, which was, until the mid-1980s, Sudan's costliest import item after petroleum. Regeneration of the industry and the construction of a second growing and refining facility in the White Nile region, north of the Kenana site, improved production, but from 2008/09 Sudan was a net importer. Its exports, however, are of refined sugar and remain important. Sudan was not only sub-Saharan Africa's second largest producer of centrifugal sugar, but its largest producer of refined sugar; following the secession of South Sudan in mid-2011, with its rich petroleum reserves, the Government had ambitions to expand the sugar sector. In West Africa, the most important sugar producer and exporter is Nigeria, but its interests are in refined sugar. Sugar cane grows wild throughout Nigeria, and domestic production has not been developed, so the country's sugar industry depends on imports, mainly from Brazil, Guatemala and the EU. In 2005 one sugar refinery was reported to be in operation in Nigeria. The country has a large domestic market. Imports reached 1.9m. tons in 2021/22, according to USDA.

International Associations and Agreements In 1958 the first International Sugar Agreement (ISA) was negotiated. A second ISA, which came into effect in 1969, established the International Sugar Organization (ISO—see below) to administer the agreement. The implementation of a third ISA, which took effect in 1978, was supervised by an International Sugar Council (ISC), which was empowered to establish price ranges for sugar trading and to operate a system of quotas and special sugar stocks. Owing to the reluctance of the USA and of European Communities (EC—now the EU) countries (which were not party to the agreement) to accept export controls, the ISO ultimately lost most of its power to regulate the market, and since 1984 the activities of the organization have been restricted to recording statistics and providing a forum for discussion between producers and consumers. Subsequent ISAs, without effective regulatory powers, have been in operation since 1985. At the end of 1992 the USA withdrew from the ISO, following a disagreement over the formulation of members' financial contributions. Special arrangements for the sugar trade were incorporated into the successive Lomé Conventions that were in operation from 1975 between the EU and a group of African, Caribbean and Pacific (ACP) countries. A special protocol on sugar, forming part of each Convention, required the EU to import specified quantities of raw sugar annually from ACP countries. In June 1998, however, the EU indicated its intention to phase out preferential sugar prices paid to ACP countries within three years. Under the terms of the Cotonou Agreement, a successor to the fourth Lomé Convention covering the period 2000–2020, the protocol on sugar was to be maintained initially, but would become subject to review within the framework of negotiations for new trading arrangements (negotiations for more WTO-compatible Economic Partnership Agreements—EPAs began in 2002). In 2001 the EU Council adopted the EBA (Everything but Arms) regulation, whereby the least developed countries were granted unlimited duty-free access to the EU for all goods except arms and ammunition. EBA was to apply to sugar from October 2009. Meanwhile, in September 2007 the EU Council of Ministers criticized the protocol on sugar on the grounds that it was not compatible with EU sugar reforms (themselves undertaken in response to upheld complaints before the WTO by Australia, Brazil and Thailand about export subsidies for the ACP countries) and did not take into account the specific needs of different ACP regions. The EU offered duty- and quota-free access to the ACP countries after 2015, in compensation for the loss of subsidies and quotas. A transitional period from October 2009 until September 2015 was to effect the progressive removal of reciprocal trade barriers. However, there was concern that the benefits that ACP countries were intended to derive from unlimited access to the EU market would be undermined by falling sugar prices. It was also uncertain whether some countries that had refused to embrace the EPA arrangements, such as Malawi, would be allowed to continue trading under EBA in order to take advantage of unrestricted access to the EU market sooner (i.e. from 2009 instead of 2015), while sugar prices were still guaranteed to be maintained at a relatively high level. On the basis of data for 2009, the 86 members of the ISO together contributed 83% of world sugar production and 95% of world exports of sugar; ISO members additionally accounted for 69% of global sugar consumption and 47% of world imports. At August 2022 the ISO had 87 members (Madagascar joined in 2014, and the United Kingdom acceded to the ISO independently in 2021), including both the EU and its 27 member states. The ISO is based in London, United Kingdom.

Sugar Prices
(annual averages, US $ per metric ton)

		ISA (World)	USA	EU
2005	.	218	469	665
2010	.	469	792	442
2015	.	296	547	363
2019	.	280	577	366
2020	.	283	595	373
2021	.	390	740	386

Source: World Bank, *Commodity Price Data* (Pink Sheet).

Prices In tandem with world output of cane and beet sugars, stock levels (of centrifugal sugar) are an important factor in determining the prices at which sugar is traded internationally. These stocks, which were at relatively low levels in the late 1980s, had increased significantly, if not consistently, by the 1990s. Stocks increased fairly steadily after 2000, with a peak at some 49m. metric tons at the end of 2014/15, before decreasing over the next two years. Stocks reached a new peak of 54m. tons by the end of 2018/19.

The World Bank records three sugar prices, to reflect the major markets. The world price that it quotes is the ISA daily price for raw sugar (f.o.b., stowed at greater Caribbean ports); the US price is for sugar under nearby futures contract (c.i.f.); and the increasingly anachronistic EU-negotiated import price for raw, unpackaged sugar from African, Caribbean and Pacific (ACP) countries under the Lomé Conventions (c.i.f., European ports). Following lower production in 2015/16, output rose significantly in 2016/17–2018/19 (on the back of near-record production in India and Thailand), while consumption remained steady over the same period—causing a weakening of world prices. In 2020, average prices trended upwards before steadying. It was reported that recovering petroleum prices and an expected sugar supply deficit were pushing prices upwards again in 2021, with these continuing to rise in the first half of 2022 (fuelled by reports of Brazil's slow start to the 2022 harvest and a move by the Indian Government to cap exports); by August of the latter year the ISA world price had reached US $394 per metric ton, while the US price was $782 per ton and the EU price had declined to $331 per ton.

TEA (*Camellia sinensis*)

Tea is a beverage made by infusing in boiling water the dried young leaves and unopened leaf-buds of the tea plant, an evergreen shrub or small tree. Black (known as red tea in China) and green tea are the most common finished products (white, yellow, oolong and post-fermented tea are also well known). Black tea, which has greater longevity, accounts for the bulk of the world's supply, and is associated with machine manufacture and plantation cultivation, which guarantees an adequate supply of leaf to the factory. Green tea, produced mainly in the People's Republic of China and Japan, is grown mostly on smallholdings, and much of it is consumed locally. There are two main varieties of tea, the China and the Assam, although hybrids may be obtained, such as Darjeeling; leaf size is also important, varying between the large Assam leaf and the small China leaf, with a medium Cambodian leaf. In this survey, wherever possible, data on production and trade relate to made tea, i.e. dry, manufactured tea. Where figures have been reported in terms of green (unmanufactured) leaf, appropriate allowances have been made to convert the reported amounts to the approximate equivalent weight of made tea.

The tea plant can grow up to 16 m, but cultivated ones are usually kept at about waist height, because the leaves and buds harvested are the top 3–5 cm of the plant (known as flushes), every week to a fortnight. Once picked, tea leaves are withered, to preserve them, while black tea is oxidized using either what is known as the orthodox treatment or the CTC (crush, tear, curl) method—the latter means of breaking the leaves also produces the fannings or dust grades that are commonly used in tea bags—before being dried and graded.

Production of Made Tea
('000 metric tons)

	2017	2018	2019	2020
World total	6,299.4	6,650.6	7,761.7	7,024.0
Sub-Saharan Africa . .	677.5	772.2	730.8	837.5
Leading African producers				
Kenya	439.9	493.0	458.9	569.5
Malawi*	47.4	48.1	48.1	47.9
Rwanda	27.9	31.1	30.4*	33.6
Tanzania	41.5	55.4	61.7*	46.1*
Uganda	50.1	74.2	60.3	63.4*
Zimbabwe* . . .	3.8	3.5	3.9	3.7
Leading non-African producers				
Argentina	366.2	369.6	375.1	335.2
China, People's Republic .	2,460.4	2,610.4	2,777.2	2,970.0
India	1,325.1	1,338.6	1,390.1	1,424.7*
Indonesia	146.3	140.2	128.7	138.3
Japan	82.0	86.3	81.7	69.8
Sri Lanka	307.7	303.8	300.1	278.5
Türkiye	234.0	270.0	261.0	255.0
Viet Nam	260.0	270.0	234.1	240.5

* FAO estimate(s).

Source: FAO.

The World Market and the Region Of the world tea crop, according to the Food and Agriculture Organization of the United Nations (FAO), 30% was sold abroad in 2020 (compared with 45% in 2004). Tea production worldwide has increased every year of the 21st century (except 2006, when it fell slightly), up to and including 2019, but the growth in exports has been more erratic. Since 2005 the People's Republic of China has been the largest producer of tea in the world. Tea exports reached a then record level of 2.05m. metric tons in 2013, although it had declined to only 1.85m. tons in 2015 before recovering in 2016–17, to a new record level of 2.14m. tons in the latter year. Exports grew to 2.14m. tons in 2020. The major exporting countries, Kenya, China, Sri Lanka and India, have long dominated the market. China and India both have large domestic markets for their tea, but still export substantial amounts. In 2020 Kenya provided 27% of world exports, China 16%, Sri Lanka 13% and India 10% (the next largest exporters were Viet Nam, with 6%, and Uganda, Argentina and the United Arab Emirates, with some 3% each).

For much of the 20th century India and Sri Lanka were the two leading exporters of made tea, with approximately equal sales. During the 1960s India and Sri Lanka together exported more than two-thirds of all the tea sold by producing countries, but their joint foreign sales gradually declined during the 1970s, until they came to constitute less than one-half of world exports (in 2019 some

21%). Over the years Sri Lankan sales came to exceed those of India by a comfortable margin (Indian exports had been exceeded by those of Sri Lanka throughout much of the 2000s—and, indeed, by those of China). Exports by Sri Lanka took primacy in 1997–2004. Kenya was the main tea exporter in 2005–10, but was overtaken by China, India and Sri Lanka the following year. However, in 2013 its foreign sales reached a record high of 448,809 metric tons, which was almost 50% higher than the previous year. Exports by India have been surpassed by those of China (whose sales include a large proportion of green tea) in every year since 1996; in 2011 China resumed its place as Asia's largest tea exporter for the first time in centuries, although Sri Lanka interrupted that order again the following year. A newer challenge to the four principal exporters came from Viet Nam, which became the world's fifth largest seller of tea on the international market from 2000, exporting almost three times as much as the Far East's next largest exporter, Indonesia, in 2020. In 2011 Argentina had exceeded Indonesian sales to become the world's sixth largest exporter for the first time, maintaining that position in 2012–19, and becoming the world's seventh largest exporter in 2020. In 2016–20 Uganda was estimated to have sold more tea abroad than Indonesia (and more than Argentina in the latter year). In 2020 Malawi's foreign sales of tea also exceeded those of Indonesia.

For many years the United Kingdom was the largest single importer of tea. From the late 1980s consumption and imports expanded significantly in developing countries (notably in countries of the Middle East) and, particularly, in the USSR, which in 1989 overtook the United Kingdom as the world's principal tea importer. However, internal factors following the break-up of the USSR in 1991 caused a sharp decline in tea imports by its successor republics; as a result, the United Kingdom regained its position as the leading tea importer in that year. In 1992–99 the United Kingdom remained the principal destination of tea exports. Since 2000, however, imports by the Russian Federation have exceeded those of the United Kingdom by a substantial and, generally, increasing margin (except in 2001, when the United Kingdom briefly regained its position as the principal importer). In 2020 the Russian Federation imported 151,441 metric tons of tea, accounting for 8% of the world market, although Pakistan was the largest importer (a position it had maintained since 2016), buying 254,406 tons. Next, in terms of imports, came the United Kingdom with 129,865 tons and the USA with 107,414 tons. Other major importers of tea in 2020 were Egypt, the United Arab Emirates, Morocco and Iran.

African exports accounted for 36% of the world total in 2020 (and a record of 766,770 metric tons). Of total African exports in 2020, 75% came from Kenya. Since 2007 Kenya has consistently been the largest tea exporting nation. In the 1990s and 2000s the conservation of tea supplies by India, in order to satisfy rising domestic consumption, enabled Kenya to replace India as the UK's principal supplier. In 1999 Kenya provided 50% of British tea imports (by volume), but the proportion varied (46% in 2015). Kenya's tea sales provided 18% of its total export receipts in 2021, making tea the country's most valuable export crop. In 2020 some 269,400 ha in Kenya were planted with tea, an increase of 124% since 2000.

Malawi, with an estimated 18,108 ha under tea in 2020, according to the FAO, is generally considered to be Africa's second largest producer and exporter of tea, although Ugandan production surpassed that of Malawi in 2008 and in most years from 2012, and Ugandan exports exceeded Malawi's every year from 2010. Malawian exports in 2020 totalled only some 46,923 metric tons, still accounting for 6% of all African tea exports in that year. In 2021 exports of tea accounted for 7% of Malawi's total export earnings. A great increase in Ugandan exports from 2007 challenged Malawi's position as Africa's second tea exporter. Prior to the regime of Idi Amin and the nationalization of tea plantations in 1972, Uganda had been second only to neighbouring Kenya among African producers. Uganda's tea exports were negligible by the early 1980s, but, following agreements between tea companies and the subsequent Ugandan governments, exports were resumed. There has been a sustained recovery since 1990, when sales of tea totalled only 4,760 tons. In 1994 Uganda's exports of tea reached their highest annual total since 1977. Exports in subsequent years advanced strongly, sometimes varying, but reaching a new record of 72,454 tons in 2020 (9% of the African total). In 2021 tea exports were reported to contribute just 1.5% of the country's total export earnings. Still in East Africa, Tanzania's exports of tea advanced significantly during the 1990s, generally moving above 25,000 tons annually into the 2010s—until 2019–20, when exports fell back to 18,879 tons in the latter year. Foreign sales of tea contributed 0.5% of Tanzania's total revenue from exports in 2021. Tea has traditionally made a significant contribution to the export earnings of Burundi and Rwanda, whose foreign sales were 9,122 tons and 15,309 tons, respectively, in 2020 (the latter country also Africa's fifth largest exporter). Since 1997 Rwanda's tea industry has recovered from the disruption caused by civil unrest during 1993–96. In 2008 surging international commodity prices sent exports of tea to 32% of all exports, up from 17% in the previous year, but the share was a more usual 9% in 2014. Tea provided 21% of total export earnings in Burundi in 2021.

Zimbabwe has long been ahead of Burundi in the ranking of Africa's largest exporters of tea. Historically, however, tea has not been a significant cash crop in Zimbabwe—in 2000 it accounted for only about 1% of the country's total export earnings (and this contribution declined to just 0.3% in 2021). Cameroon, the Democratic Republic of the Congo, Ethiopia, Mauritius, Mozambique and South Africa also export some tea.

International Associations An International Tea Agreement (ITA), signed in 1933 by the governments of India, Ceylon (now Sri Lanka) and the Netherlands East Indies (now Indonesia), established the International Tea Committee (ITC), based in London, UK, as an administrative body. Although ITA operations ceased after 1955, the ITC has continued to function as a statistical and information centre. In 2022 there were eight producer/exporter members (the tea boards or associations of Bangladesh, India, Indonesia, Kenya, Malawi, Sri Lanka and Tanzania, and the China Chamber of Commerce of Import and Export of Foodstuffs, Native Produce and Animal By-products), four consumer members (the tea associations of Canada, Ireland, Italy and the USA), 25 associate members and 49 corporate members. In 1969 the Food and Agriculture Organization of the United Nations (FAO) formed a Consultative Committee on Tea (renamed Intergovernmental Group on Tea in 1970), and an exporters' group, meeting under this committee's auspices, set voluntary export quotas in an attempt to avert an overall long-term decline in the real price of tea. This succeeded in raising prices for two years, but collapsed subsequently as (mainly) African countries—Kenya in particular—opposed efforts to restrict their rapidly increasing production. The regulation of tea prices is further complicated by the perishability of tea, which impedes the effective operation of a buffer stock.

Tea Prices
(annual averages, US $ per metric ton)

	Three auctions*	Colombo	Mombasa
1990 .	2,056	1,877	1,486
2000 .	1,876	1,793	2,029
2005 .	1,647	1,843	1,478
2010 .	2,885	3,290	2,560
2015 .	2,777	2,975	2,965
2019 .	2,563	3,101	2,211
2020 .	2,699	3,404	2,007
2021 .	2,689	3,126	2,112

* Three auction average for Kolkata, Colombo and Mombasa/ Nairobi.

Source: World Bank, *Commodity Price Data* (Pink Sheet).

Prices Much of the tea traded internationally is sold by auction, principally in the exporting countries. Until declining volumes brought about their termination in June 1998 (Kenya having withdrawn in 1997, and a number of other exporters, including Sri Lanka and Malawi, having established their own auctions), the weekly London auctions in the UK had formed the centre of the international tea trade.

The World Bank provides a number of tea price indexes. The first gives a world price, citing a three auction average, based on quotations at Kolkata (India), Colombo (Sri Lanka) and Mombasa/Nairobi (Kenya). As noted above, Colombo is the largest single auction site for tea in Asia, and the price given is another arithmetic average, this time of weekly quotes for all tea (Sri Lanka, all origins). The Mombasa auctions, dealing in tea from 12 countries, provide the third price, an average of weekly quotes for all tea of African origin. There is also a small auction at Limbe in Cameroon.

TOBACCO (*Nicotiana tabacum*)

Tobacco originated in South America and was used in rituals and ceremonials or as a medicine; it was smoked and chewed for centuries before its introduction into Europe, the Middle East, Africa and South Asia in the 16th century. The generic name *Nicotiana* denotes the presence of the alkaloid nicotine in its leaves. The most important species in commercial tobacco cultivation is *N. tabacum*. Another species, *N. rustica*, is widely grown, but on a smaller scale, to yield cured leaf for oriental tobacco, snuff or simple cigarettes and cigars.

Commercially grown tobacco (from *N. tabacum*) can be divided into four major types—flue cured (e.g. Virginia, the most grown tobacco variety in the world), air cured (including burley, cigar, light and dark), fire cured and sun cured (including oriental)—depending on the procedures used to dry or 'cure' the leaves. Each system imparts specific chemical and smoking characteristics to the cured leaf, although these may also be affected by other factors, such as the type of soil on which the crop is grown, the type and quantity of fertilizer applied to the crop, the cultivar used, the spacing of the crop in the field and the number of leaves left at topping (the removal of

the terminal growing point). Each type is used, separately or in combination, in specific products. All types are grown in Africa.

As in other major producing areas, local research organizations in Africa have developed new cultivars with specific desirable chemical characteristics, disease resistance properties and improved yields. The principal tobacco research centres are in Zimbabwe, Malawi and South Africa. Since the late 20th century efforts have been made to develop low-cost sources of tobacco in Tanzania and, later, in Swaziland and Mozambique.

In Malawi, South Africa and, to a lesser extent, Zambia and Tanzania, tobacco is grown mainly as a direct labour crop on large farms, some capable of producing as much as 250 metric tons of cured leaf per year. In other parts of Africa, however, tobacco is a smallholders' crop, with each farmer cultivating, on average, 1 or 2 ha of tobacco as well as essential food crops and, usually, other cash crops. Emphasis has been placed on improving yields by the selection of cultivars, by the increased use of fertilizers, by the reduction of crop loss (through the use of crop chemicals) and by reducing hand labour requirements through the mechanization of land preparation and the use of crop chemicals. Where small farmers are responsible for producing the crop, harvesting remains a manual operation, as the area under tobacco and their limited financial means preclude the adoption of mechanical harvesting devices.

Production of Tobacco
(unmanufactured, farm sales weight, '000 metric tons)

	2017	2018	2019	2020
World total	6,294	6,120	6,458	5,886
Sub-Saharan Africa . .	506	677	654	679
Leading sub-Saharan African producers				
Malawi	83	95	100*	94*
Mozambique	95	115	142	159*
Tanzania*	90	93	91	91
Uganda*	32	32	32	32
Zambia	20	25	30*	26*
Zimbabwe	111	240	185	203
Leading non-African producers				
Argentina	117	104	108*	109*
Bangladesh	92	89	129	86
Brazil	866	756	770	702
China, People's Republic .	2,391	2,241	2,612	2,134
India*	752	774	758	761
Indonesia	181	195	197	200*
Korea, DPR*	83	84	84	83
Pakistan	100	107	104	133
Türkiye	94	75	70	77
USA	322	242	212	177

* FAO estimate(s).

Source: FAO.

The World Market and the Region Between one-third and two-fifths of world tobacco production are traded internationally. Until 1993, when it was overtaken by Brazil, the USA was the world's principal tobacco exporting country. Since 1993 Brazil has consolidated its position as the world's leading exporter of tobacco, largely at the expense of the USA and Zimbabwe. Brazil's share of global exports of unmanufactured tobacco increased in volume from 13% in 1993 to about one-quarter from the mid-2000s (21% in 2020). The principal type of tobacco commercially cultivated in Africa is flue cured, of which Malawi and Zimbabwe are the dominant regional producers. The tobacco sector formerly normally accounted for about almost one-half of Zimbabwe's total agricultural earnings, and in 2021 unmanufactured tobacco provided 13% of the country's export revenue. The Zimbabwean tobacco crop, of which 98% has traditionally been exported, is highly regarded for its quality and flavour, and its marketability has been assisted by its relatively low tar content. Output was affected in the early 2000s by the programme of land reform pursued by the Government. In 2005 the number of farmers engaged in tobacco production exceeded 30,000, while the area planted to tobacco was 51,167 ha in the same year; this figure had more than doubled by 2020, reaching 104,759 ha in that year. The increase in the number of farmers reflects an officially encouraged transfer away from the large-scale, estate-based cultivation of tobacco to a smallholder-based sector. As a consequence of land reform, many former estate cultivators of tobacco were reported to have relocated to countries such as Zambia and Mozambique and to have resumed large-scale tobacco cultivation there. Improved prospects for the industry in Zimbabwe were helped by reform of the public subsidy systems on which the sector was reliant and, crucially, by the decision to pay farmers in foreign currency, which helped maintain prices and stability. The tobacco industry was recovering by the 2010s, therefore, with Chinese buyers of increasing importance; they accounted for 32.8% of unmanufactured tobacco sales in 2021.

Malawi is reckoned to be the most tobacco dependent economy in the world. In the mid-1990s Malawi obtained as much as 70% of its export revenue from tobacco, exporting more than 98% of the mainly flue cured, fire cured and burley varieties that it produced. Thereafter, output, especially of burley tobacco, of which Malawi formerly supplied about one-fifth of world output, declined; the country remained the world's largest producer of burley, which accounted for some 88% of sales by volume in the 2015 Malawi auction season, the bulk of the rest being flue cured. From the early 2000s, however, Malawi was reported to have benefited indirectly from the problems of the tobacco sector in Zimbabwe, and to have attracted increased investment from multinational tobacco companies. In 2021 the country earned 58% of the value of its total exports from unmanufactured tobacco. Three-quarters of employment was reckoned to depend to some extent on the tobacco industry. The industry was badly affected by controversy and recriminations over low prices, with a 2011 collapse in sales leading the authorities to blame a cartel of international buyers for allegedly keeping prices down, while the buyers in turn blamed the Government's failure to ensure the quality of the leaf. Attention was also focused on the widespread practice of smuggling, and the sale of Malawian tobacco in Zambia and Zimbabwe, where prices were better, leaving the Government deprived of revenue. Sales recovered from 2012, although in 2013 Zimbabwean sales abroad exceeded those of Malawi. Moreover, weaker prices after 2014 hit Malawi hard.

Tanzania contributes a small, but increasing, and significant quantity of flue cured tobacco to the world market, and in 2021 exports of unmanufactured tobacco contributed 2% of the country's total. The sector had been encouraged to expand by the potential of the People's Republic of China to offset the decline in traditional markets, in particular given that by 2013 it had become apparent that official European Union efforts to discourage smoking would limit the purchase of tobacco from the developing world. Between 2008 and 2014 Tanzania's export volumes exceeded those of Mozambique, but Mozambican exports have generally been greater in subsequent years. Mozambique was sub-Saharan Africa's third largest exporter of unmanufactured tobacco after Zimbabwe and Malawi in 2020, followed by Tanzania, Zambia and Kenya. Tobacco production in Nigeria is fairly static, and its flue cured crop is entirely reserved for local consumption. Kenya has greatly increased its output of flue cured leaf since commencing tobacco exports in 1984, and tobacco cultivation has increased in importance in Uganda, as a result of a government programme to offset declining earnings from coffee. Exports of manufactured and unmanufactured tobacco contributed 2% of Uganda's total export earnings in 2021. There are also small exports of flue cured tobacco from Sierra Leone. Nigeria, Malawi and South Africa account for the African crop of sun cured and air cured types of tobacco. Modest quantities of oriental tobacco are cultivated in Malawi and South Africa. Côte d'Ivoire also produces some tobacco.

International Association The International Tobacco Growers' Association (ITGA), with headquarters in Castelo Branco, Portugal, was formed in 1984 by growers' groups in Argentina, Brazil, Canada, Malawi, the USA and Zimbabwe. In 2022 its members numbered 24 countries, including Kenya, Malawi, South Africa, Tanzania, Zambia and Zimbabwe. ITGA members account for more than 80% of the world's internationally traded tobacco. The Association provides a forum for the exchange of information among tobacco producers, conducts research and publishes studies on tobacco issues.

Tobacco Price
(US $ per metric ton)

	Average	High	Low
2005 .	2,790	(December) 2,946	(January) 2,696
2010 .	4,333	(January) 4,466	(April) 4,180
2015 .	4,908	(May) 5,018	(December) 4,790
2019 .	4,579	(January) 4,805	(December) 4,316
2020 .	4,336	(February) 4,442	(December) 4,200
2021 .	4,155	(October) 4,242	(August) 3,973

Source: World Bank, *Commodity Price Data* (Pink Sheet).

Prices According to the World Bank, general US import prices (c.i.f.) for unmanufactured tobacco of any origin soon recovered from the commodity slump of late 2008 and early 2009, and the average annual price continued to rise until 2011. Prices were fairly stable in 2015, but weakened towards the end of the year and into 2016. From mid-2017 prices climbed steadily, reaching their highest level since May 2015 in August 2018 (US $4,984 per ton), before falling through most of 2019. Prices were steady through most of 2020, only falling below $4,200 per ton in the first two months of 2021. Prices fluctuated in the second half of 2021, but stayed above $4,100 per ton in the first

half of 2022; the average monthly price had recovered to $4,263 per ton by April, before falling back to $4,143 per ton in August.

URANIUM (*U*)

Uranium occurs in a variety of ores, often in association with other minerals, such as gold, phosphate and copper, and may be mined by open-cast, underground or *in situ* leach methods, depending on the circumstances. An increasing proportion of uranium is produced through *in situ* leaching (57% in 2019). The concentration of uranium that is needed to form an economic mineral deposit varies widely, depending upon its geological setting and physical location. Average ore grades at operating uranium mines vary from 0.03% U to as high as 15% U, but are most frequently less than 1% U. South Africa produces uranium concentrates as a by-product of the mining of gold and copper, and possesses uranium conversion and enrichment facilities. Both copper mining and the exploitation of phosphates by wet (phosphoric acid-yielding) processes offer a more widespread potential for by-product uranium production.

Uranium is principally used as a fuel in nuclear reactors for the production of electricity. There were 437 commercial nuclear reactors operable in 32 countries worldwide at 1 August 2022, generating 10% of the world's electricity; 59 more reactors were under construction, with 89 more in planning stages. Enriched uranium is used as fuel in most nuclear power stations and in the manufacture of nuclear weapons. With regard to the latter, however, the abandonment of East–West confrontation and the conclusion of a series of nuclear disarmament treaties between the USA and Russia (and other former Soviet republics) in the late 20th century led to the release from military stockpiles of substantial quantities of uranium for civil energy programmes (although renewed geopolitical tensions between East and West following the Russian Federation's military invasion of Ukraine in 2022—and the strategic targeting of the Zaporizhzhya nuclear power plant in Ukraine—gave rise to concerns that the threat of global nuclear conflict had returned). In 2019, according to data cited by the World Nuclear Association (WNA), the world's known recoverable resources of uranium (defined as reasonably assured resources plus estimated additional resources, recoverable up to a cost of US $130 per kg) totalled about 6.15m. metric tons of metal content; some 28% of world resources were located in Australia, 15% in Kazakhstan, 9% in Canada, 8% in Russia, 7% in Namibia, and 5% each in South Africa and Brazil.

Production of Uranium
(uranium content of ores, metric tons)

	2018	2019	2020	2021
World total . . .	54,154	54,742	47,731	48,332
Africa	8,782	8,805	8,654	8,386
African producers				
Namibia	5,525	5,476	5,413	5,753
Niger	2,911	2,983	2,991	2,248
South Africa* . . .	346	346	250	385
Leading non-African producers				
Australia	6,517	6,613	6,203	4,192
Canada	7,001	6,938	3,885	4,693
China, People's Republic*	1,885	1,885	1,885	1,885
Kazakhstan . . .	21,705	22,808	19,477	21,819
Russian Federation . .	2,904	2,911	2,846	2,635
Ukraine	790	800	744	455
USA	582	58	6	8
Uzbekistan* . . .	3,450	3,500	3,500	3,500

* Estimates.

Source: World Nuclear Association.

The World Market and the Region Uranium's strategic military value led to intense prospecting activity in the 1940s and 1950s, but the market was later depressed as government purchasing programmes ceased. Uranium demand fell in the late 1960s and early 1970s, until industrialized countries responded to the 1973–74 petroleum crisis by intensifying their civil nuclear power programmes. Anticipated strong demand for rapidly expanding nuclear power further improved the uranium market until the early 1980s, when lower-than-expected growth in electricity consumption forced nuclear power programmes to be restricted, leaving both producers and consumers with high levels of accumulated stocks requiring liquidation. A number of mining operations were also scaled down or closed. The market was further depressed in the aftermath of the accident in 1986 at the Chornobyl (Chernobyl) nuclear plant in Ukraine (then part of the USSR). Following a decade of declining output, mined production began to increase from 1993, a general trend it maintained into the 2010s (although global production fell in 2017–18 and 2019–21).

Kazakhstan and Canada are the world's largest uranium producers. The five largest mines in the world in 2021 were Cameco's Cigar Lake (10% of world mine output) in Canada, Kazatomprom and Cameco's Inkai in Kazakhstan (7%), Swakop Uranium's Husab in Namibia (7%), Uranium One and Kazatomprom's Karatau in Kazakhstan (5%) and China National Nuclear Corporation's Rössing in Namibia (5%). The seventh largest mine ranked by the WNA was the Arlit or SOMAIR mine (4%) of French company Orano, in Niger. The largest companies in the world in the same year were Kazatomprom (of Kazakhstan, accounting for 25% of world output), Orano (formerly Areva until early in 2018—9%), Canada-based Uranium One (9%), which is owned by ARMZ Uranium Holding of Russia, Cameco (Canada, 9%) and the China General Nuclear (9%).

Uranium production has been an important component of the South African mining industry since uranium extraction began in 1951, with output reaching a record 6,146 tons in 1980. South Africa's production has subsequently declined sharply, and has been overtaken by that of Namibia, Niger and, in 2010–13, Malawi. Namibia's exports of ores and concentrates of uranium and thorium do not contribute significantly to its export revenues—some US $282,000 in 2021. Deliveries of ore from what was then the world's largest open-pit uranium mine, at Rössing, had begun in 1976. In 2021 Rössing, operated by Rio Tinto (United Kingdom), was Africa's second largest uranium mine (5% of global output). Rising extraction at the new Langer Heinrich open-pit mine (opened in 2006), boosted Namibian production from 2008. Niger's SOMAIR mine was in 2021 the world's third largest open-pit mine. (The largest was Husab in Namibia.) In 2021 uranium and thorium ores and concentrates provided 29% of Niger's export earnings, although receipts were 37% less than one year earlier. Uranium exploration in Niger had started in the 1950s, around the Aïr mountains near Agadez, with production commencing at the Arlit mine in 1971. Niger's other main uranium mine, where operations commenced in 1978, is the Compagnie Minière d'Akouta (COMINAK) mine at Akouta (2% of global output in 2017), also one of Africa's largest. However, the COMINAK mine ceased operations at the end of March 2021 due to the depletion of its reserves, subdued uranium prices and high operating costs. Like Namibia, Niger was compelled from the early 1990s to restructure and streamline its uranium operations. In 2011 the country became Africa's largest and the world's fourth largest producer. The Arlit open-pit mine (operated by Société des Mines de l'Aïr, or SOMAIR, a subsidiary of Orano) ranked just outside the world's top 10 uranium producing mines in 2021. Gabon, which commenced uranium production in 1958, possesses six identified deposits containing sufficient reserves to support 30 years' output at production rates achieved during the mid-1990s. However, the depressed level of uranium prices in the late 1990s, with little prospect of recovery in the short term, prompted French interests, exploiting the deposits in conjunction with the Government of Gabon, to terminate uranium mining operations there from early 1999, leaving Namibia, Niger and South Africa as the only regional producers for the next 10 years. Interest remained in Gabon's Mounana uranium mine, but it was as yet unexploited. However, a uranium mine at Kayelekera in Malawi began production in 2009, increasing output sixfold in 2010 to exceed South African production, only for the weaker uranium price to prompt Australian parent company Paladin to suspend operations at the mine in February 2014. In 2013 uranium or thorium ores and concentrates had provided 11% of total Malawian exports, but less than 3% in 2014 and none from 2015.

Uranium has also been found, but has been hitherto unexploited, in a number of African countries. In Botswana, the first uranium mine in the country received environmental clearance in 2016; A-Cap of Australia was granted the licence later that year, but due to weak uranium prices commercial production was not expected to begin before the end of 2022. In the Central African Republic, a mine opened in 2010, with full production initially expected from 2014, but the controversial Areva project was subsequently abandoned. Other countries included the Democratic Republic of the Congo, Guinea, Equatorial Guinea, Mali, Mauritania, Nigeria, Tanzania (infrastructure construction was expected at several sites in 2013–18, but in mid-2017 Russian state nuclear corporation Rosatom suspended construction of the Mkuju River uranium project for at least three years owing to the underperforming uranium market), Zambia (an Australian company was investigating uranium recovery at a copper mine) and Zimbabwe.

International Associations The World Nuclear Association (WNA), which succeeded the Uranium Institute in 2001, is a global industrial organization that seeks to promote the peaceful use of nuclear power worldwide as a sustainable source of energy. The WNA concerns itself with all stages of the nuclear fuel cycle, including the mining of uranium, its enrichment, the manufacture of nuclear plants and the safe disposal of spent fuel. The Euratom Supply Agency (ESA), established in 1960 under the European Communities' Euratom Treaty, operates in areas connected with atomic energy, including research, the formulation of safety standards, and the peaceful uses of nuclear energy. Its main duty is to coordinate the supply of nuclear fuels (source materials and special fissile materials) in the European Union (EU), while ensuring a regular and equitable supply of ores and nuclear fuels to all users.

ESA Uranium Prices
(natural uranium, annual averages, € per kg)

		Multi-annual contracts index	Spot contracts	New multi-annual contracts (MAC-3)
1990	.	60.00	19.75	—
2000	.	37.00	22.75	—
2005	.	33.56	44.27	—
2010	.	61.68	79.48	78.12
2015	.	94.30	88.73	88.53
2018	.	73.74	44.34	74.19
2019	.	79.43	55.61	80.00
2020*	.	71.37	n.a.	75.51

* The spot price was not calculated because there were not enough transactions (fewer than 3) to calculate the index.

Source: Euratom Supply Agency.

Prices The market for uranium is small, comprising only about 100 buyers worldwide, according to industry sources. Marginal trading, to which 'spot' prices for uranium apply, accounts for only a small proportion of the total quantity of the metal traded, but spot prices nevertheless provide a reference price for long-term contracts concluded between miners and utilities. According to the WNA, very high prices for uranium in the 1970s were succeeded by very low prices in the early 1990s, to the extent that spot prices fell below the cost of production in most mines. In 1996 spot prices reportedly recovered to the extent that most mines were able to produce at a profit. That recovery, however, was succeeded by a further decline which lasted until late 2003. Prices began to rise thereafter, and interest in uranium mining accordingly increased. The ESA provides three price series for natural uranium (U_3O_8) delivered to EU utility companies: the long-term price based on the weighted average of the price for uranium delivered under multi-annual contracts; the average weighted spot price of uranium; and the so-called MAC-3 or new multi-annual index, a weighted average of uranium prices paid under multi-annual contracts concluded or amended in the previous three years. All prices are given in euros per kg of uranium and in US dollars per lb of U_3O_8. The MAC-3 price series began in 2009 (€63.49 per kg, or US $34.06 per lb). In 2020 the multi-annual contracts index recorded an average annual price of $31.36 per lb, the spot contracts index was unavailable and the MAC-3 was $33.17 per lb (for euro price per kg, see table).

WHEAT (*Triticum*)

The most common species of wheat (*Triticum vulgare*) includes hard, semi-hard and soft varieties which have different milling characteristics but which, in general, are suitable for bread making. Another species, *T. durum*, is grown mainly in semi-arid areas, including North Africa and the Mediterranean. This wheat is very hard and is suitable for the manufacture of semolina. In North Africa, in addition to being used for making local bread, semolina is the basic ingredient of pasta and couscous. A third species, spelt (*T. spelta*), is also included in production figures for wheat. It is grown in very small quantities in parts of Europe and is used mainly as animal feed.

Production of Wheat
('000 metric tons, USDA estimates)

	2018/19	2019/20	2020/21	2021/22*
World total	730,920	761,612	774,276	779,243
Sub-Saharan Africa . .	8,283	8,431	9,456	9,369
Leading sub-Saharan African producers				
Ethiopia	4,838	5,315	5,479	5,520
Kenya	337	366	405	250
Nigeria	60	60	55	90
Rwanda	13	16	13	13
South Africa . . .	1,868	1,535	2,120	2,257
Sudan	702	726	751	600
Tanzania	57	63	85	100
Zambia	114	152	192	206
Zimbabwe	170	95	213	210
Leading non-African producers				
Australia	17,598	14,480	31,923	36,300
Canada	32,352	32,670	35,183	21,652

—continued	2018/19	2019/20	2020/21	2021/22*
China, People's Republic.	131,441	133,600	134,250	136,946
European Union . . .	123,124	138,799	126,691	138,289
India	99,870	103,600	107,860	109,586
Pakistan	25,076	24,349	25,248	27,464
Russian Federation . .	71,685	73,610	85,352	75,158
Ukraine	25,057	29,171	25,420	33,007
USA	51,306	52,581	49,751	44,790

* Preliminary figures.

Source: US Department of Agriculture.

The World Market and the Region Wheat is the principal cereal in international trade. According to data from the US Department of Agriculture (USDA), in 2021/22 the European Union (EU) and the People's Republic of China each accounted for 18% of world wheat production, with India accounting for 14%. France and Germany were the EU's main producers; according to FAO, in 2020 France accounted for 24% of EU output (4% of the world total), Germany 18%, Poland 10% and the United Kingdom 8%. The EU was also the leading exporter of wheat for three consecutive production years until 2016/17, when it was third, because the USA, traditionally the world's leading exporter, reclaimed the top position. However, in 2017/18 the Russian Federation became the leading exporter. The EU regained the top position in 2019/20, but was overtaken by Russia once more in 2020/21; Russia remained the largest exporter in 2021/22, when it contributed a 17% share of international trade (with the EU exporting around 15% and the USA 11%). The strength of Russia as an exporter is that it has a relatively small internal market, as do Ukraine (10%) and Canada (8%). Russia and Ukraine alone account for close to one-third of total wheat supplies on the global market. Meanwhile, Australia saw its exports of wheat more than double in 2020/21, and exports increased again in 2021/22, when it contributed 14% of the global total. Any significant decline in production in the other major producers, notably China and India, can impact hugely on world trade through their consequent need for greater imports. In 2021/22 USDA estimated the largest importing region, by far, to be the Middle East and North Africa (31% of world imports), followed by South-East Asia (14%), sub-Saharan Africa (as defined by USDA, all African states except the five Mediterranean littoral countries— 13%), East Asia (11%), South America (8%) and, higher than usual in that year (India replenishing stocks after poor harvests in previous years), South Asia (8%). Developed countries were formerly the principal consumers of wheat, but the role of developing countries as importers has been steadily increasing and they now regularly account for approximately two-thirds of world imports.

World consumption, which has, in the long term, been increasing at a similar rate to production, varies much less from year to year than the wheat harvest. Wheat food use has been expanding at the expense of rice: its growth is associated with rising consumer incomes and an increasing number of fast-food outlets. Substantial amounts of wheat are used for animal feed in Europe and, when prices are favourable, in North America. Substantial quantities were also used for feed in the 1980s in what was then the USSR, but this volume decreased sharply in response to the diminution in livestock numbers. Some wheat is used for feed in Japan, while the Republic of Korea (South Korea) imports wheat for feed when prices are low in comparison with those of coarse grains such as sorghum and maize (corn). According to USDA, domestic consumption of wheat was highest in the EU until 2010/11, but is now generally exceeded by East Asia and, from 2016/17, South Asia. At 2021/22 the largest consuming region was East Asia (21%), followed by South Asia (20%), the Middle East and North Africa (14%) and the EU (14%).

In Africa, wheat is principally grown in the south and east of the continent, often at high altitudes where conditions are less humid. South Africa was traditionally the main regional producer, but it was surpassed by Ethiopia in 2003/04 (according to USDA), hitherto the second largest regional producer. Ethiopia, however, grows for a domestic market, while South Africa is the more important exporter of wheat (205,000 tons in 2021/22—17% of the sub-Saharan total), although on a small scale compared with major producers elsewhere in the world. The continent's principal exporter, on paper, was Nigeria (50% of the sub-Saharan total), because it had taken on a similar role to Côte d'Ivoire as a re-exporter for West Africa. In some other wheat producing countries (e.g. Tanzania and Zimbabwe) the crop is grown mainly on large commercial farms and, with the benefit of irrigation, usually yields well. Efforts to produce wheat in tropical countries such as the Democratic Republic of the Congo (DRC) and Nigeria have shown mixed results. In the case of the DRC, production declined at least partially because of the prevalence of civil unrest rather than purely agricultural considerations. Zimbabwean wheat output, similarly, was negatively affected by the Government's land reform programme in the 2000s. By the 2010s the country's wheat output was recovering. Indeed, in 2021/22, according to preliminary USDA figures, the country produced 210,000 tons (compared to just 62,000 tons five years earlier). The surge in output was attributed to a

Government scheme that brought in private sector investment and expertise (including much-needed machinery and financing). Lesotho, although a much smaller country, is an elevated one with a suitable climate for growing wheat. The country produced just 6,000 tons in 2021/22. Harvests in southern Africa in the mid-2010s were generally severely reduced because of sustained drought caused by the El Niño weather phenomenon. In 2021/22 Eritrea and Uganda each grew some 25,000 tons of wheat, Mali grew 21,000 tons and Mozambique produced 15,000 tons. The only other sub-Saharan grower of wheat of any significance was Sudan (most of the country's wheat growing areas are outside what became South Sudan in July 2011), although it exported little. Rwanda increased its wheat production in the 2000s, in particular latterly, reaching a peak of 90,684 tons in 2011, although according to USDA output since then has dropped.

Global Forum The International Grains Council (IGC) is based in London, United Kingdom. It is the successor body of the International Wheat Council (IWC). From 1949 nearly all world trade in wheat was conducted under the auspices of successive international agreements, administered by the IWC. The early agreements involved regulatory price controls and supply and purchase obligations, but such provisions became inoperable in more competitive market conditions, and were abandoned in 1972. The IWC subsequently concentrated on providing detailed market assessments to its members and encouraging them to confer on matters of mutual concern. A new Grains Trade Convention, which entered into force in July 1995, gave the renamed IGC a wider mandate to consider all coarse grains as well as wheat (rice was added to the definition of grains from 1 July 2009 and oilseeds from 1 July 2013). This facilitates the provision of information to member governments, and enhances their opportunities to hold consultations. In addition, links between governments and industry are strengthened at an annual series of grain conferences sponsored by the IGC. In August 2022 the IGC consisted of 29 member countries, plus the EU.

Wheat Price
(US $ per metric ton)

	Average	High	Low
2005 .	152	(October) 168	(April) 141
2010 .	224	(December) 307	(June) 158
2015 .	204	(January) 248	(September) 173
2019 .	202	(January) 219	(August) 181
2020 .	232	(November) 273	(June) 198
2021 .	315	(November) 379	(March) 273

Source: World Bank, *Commodity Price Data* (Pink Sheet).

Prices Hard Red Winter is one of the most widely traded wheat varieties. The export price of US No. 1 Hard Red Winter (ordinary protein, delivered at Gulf ports for prompt or 30 days shipment) is cited by the World Bank as an indicator. Average monthly prices ended below US $300 per metric ton for the first time in 18 months at the end of 2013 and remained below that level from July 2014. One year later average monthly prices fell below $200 per ton and stayed below that level for the whole of 2017 (with the exception of July). The price began to recover in early 2018, but by mid-2019 the price had fallen below $200 per ton for the second time that year. Prices recovered strongly thereafter, reaching their highest level in five years—$225 per ton—in January 2020. Prices continued to increase throughout 2021 and the first half of 2022; in May of the latter year the price soared to $522 per metric ton, by far its highest level on record—fuelled by Russia's renewed military invasion of Ukraine (and the resultant supply disruptions in the latter country as the ongoing hostilities resulted in an effective blockade of Ukrainian ports, preventing crucial grain exports) and an Indian export ban (intended to regulate inflated domestic prices)—and prompting widespread fears of a developing global humanitarian crisis in many countries, including those in sub-Saharan Africa, where these wheat imports were a critical food staple. However, in July 2022 the UN and Türkiye brokered an agreement between the Russian Federation and Ukraine to allow the resumption of grain exports from Ukrainian Black Sea ports. Later that month the first grain exports since February were allowed to leave the Ukrainian port of Odessa. By August 2022 the price had declined substantially, to $383 per ton.

The Food Aid Conventions and the Food Assistance Convention Since 1967 a series of Food Aid Conventions (FACs), linked to the successive Wheat and Grains Trade Conventions, have ensured continuity of supplies of food aid in the form of cereals to countries in need. Under the last FAC, negotiated in 1999, the donor countries (including the member states of the EU) pledged to supply a minimum of some 5m. metric tons of food aid annually to developing countries, with priority given to least developed countries and other low-income food-importing countries. Aid was provided mostly in the form of cereals, and all aid given to least developed countries was in the form of grants. The FAC sought to improve the effectiveness, and increase the impact, of food aid by improved monitoring and consultative procedures. In mid-2004 FAC members undertook a renegotiation of the 1999 FAC in order 'to strengthen its capacity to meet identified needs when food aid is the appropriate response'. However, it was decided that this renegotiation should await the conclusion of discussions on trade-related food aid issues in agriculture negotiations at the World Trade Organization. Meanwhile, it was agreed to extend the 1999 FAC for two years from July 2005; further, one-year extensions were agreed subsequently and it only finally expired on 30 June 2012. In December 2010 formal negotiations on the future of the FAC had commenced, so the extensions were to give the discussions a fair chance of fruition. A new Food Assistance Convention was adopted in London on 25 April 2012, and was open for signature from 11 June to the 34 signatories and the EU. It came into force on 1 January 2013 (after ratification by six signatories—Canada, Denmark, the EU, Japan, Switzerland and the USA), and from that date was open to other signatories. Rather than focusing only on certain specified food items (expressed in wheat-equivalent tons), the new instrument focused on 'nutritious food', leaving it up to the parties to express commitments in wheat tons or monetary terms, as part of the mechanisms for information sharing and registration of undertakings.

ACKNOWLEDGEMENTS

We gratefully acknowledge the assistance of the following organizations in the preparation of this section: Centro Internacional de Agricultura Tropical; De Beers; Euratom Supply Agency; Food and Agricultural Organization of the United Nations (FAO); Thomson Reuters GFMS (formerly Gold Fields Mineral Services Ltd); International Cocoa Organization; International Coffee Organization; International Copper Study Group; International Cotton Advisory Committee; International Monetary Fund; International Aluminium Institute; International Rice Research Institute; International Tobacco Growers' Association; US Department of Agriculture (USDA); US Department of Energy; US Geological Survey, US Department of the Interior; World Bank; World Gold Council and World Nuclear Association.

CALENDARS

The Islamic Calendar

The Islamic era dates from 16 July 622, which was the beginning of the Arab year in which the *Hijra* ('flight' or migration) of the prophet Muhammad (the founder of Islam), from Mecca to Medina (in modern Saudi Arabia), took place. The Islamic or *Hijri* Calendar is lunar, each year having 354 or 355 days, the extra day being intercalated 11 times every 30 years. Accordingly, the beginning of the *Hijri* year occurs earlier in the Gregorian Calendar by a few days each year. Dates are reckoned in terms of the *anno Hegirae* (AH) or year of the Hegira (*Hijra*). The Islamic year AH 1444 began on 30 July 2022.

The year is divided into the following months:

1. Muharram	30 days	7. Rajab	30 days
2. Safar	29 days	8. Shaaban	29 days
3. Rabia I	30 days	9. Ramadan	30 days
4. Rabia II	29 days	10. Shawwal	29 days
5. Jumada I	30 days	11. Dhu'l-Qa'da	30 days
6. Jumada II	29 days	12. Dhu'l-Hijja	29 or 30 days

The *Hijri* Calendar is used for religious purposes throughout the Islamic world.

PRINCIPAL ISLAMIC FESTIVALS

New Year: 1st Muharram. The first 10 days of the year are regarded as holy, especially the 10th.

Ashoura: 10th Muharram. Celebrates the first meeting of Adam and Eve after leaving Paradise, also the ending of the Flood and the death of Hussain, grandson of the prophet Muhammad. The feast is celebrated with fairs and processions.

Mouloud (Birth of Muhammad): 12th Rabia I.

Leilat al-Meiraj (Ascension of Muhammad): 27th Rajab.

Ramadan (Month of Fasting).

Id al-Fitr or Id al-Saghir (The Small Feast): Three days beginning 1st Shawwal. This celebration follows the constraint of the Ramadan fast.

Id al-Adha or Id al-Kabir (The Great Feast, Feast of the Sacrifice): Four days beginning on 10th Dhu'l-Hijja. The principal Islamic festival, commemorating Abraham's sacrifice and coinciding with the pilgrimage to Mecca. Celebrated by the sacrifice of a sheep, by feasting and by donations to the poor.

	AH 1443	AH 1444	AH 1445
New Year	9 Aug. 2021	30 July 2022	19 July 2023
Ashoura	18 Aug. 2021	8 Aug. 2022	28 July 2023
Mouloud	18 Oct. 2021	9 Oct. 2022	27 Sept. 2023
Leilat al-Meiraj	1 March 2022	18 Feb. 2023	8 Feb. 2024
Ramadan begins	3 April 2022	23 March 2023	12 March 2024
Id al-Fitr	3 May 2022	22 April 2023	10 April 2024
Id al-Adha	10 July 2022	29 June 2023	17 June 2024

Note: Local determinations may vary by one day from those given here.

The Ethiopian Calendar

The Ethiopian Calendar is solar, and is the traditional calendar of the Ethiopian Church. New Year (1st Maskarem) usually occurs on 11 September Gregorian. The Ethiopian year 2015 began on 11 September 2022.

The year is divided into 13 months, of which 12 have 30 days each. The 13th and last month (Paguemen) has five or six days, the extra day occurring in leap years.

The months are as follows:

1. Maskarem	5. Tir	10. Sene
2. Tikimit	6. Yekatit	11. Hamle
3. Hidar	7. Megabit	12. Nahasse
4. Tahsas	8. Maiza	13. Paguemen
	9. Ginbat	

The Ethiopian Calendar is used for most purposes, religious and secular, in Ethiopia.

RESEARCH INSTITUTES
ASSOCIATIONS AND INSTITUTIONS STUDYING AFRICA

AUSTRALIA

Australian Institute of International Affairs (AIIA): Stephen House, 32 Thesiger Court, Deakin, ACT 2600; tel. (2) 6282-2133; e-mail communications@internationalaffairs.org.au; internet www.internationalaffairs.org.au; f. 1924 as a br. of Chatham House (UK); present name adopted in 1933; brs in all states; Pres. ALLAN GYNGELL; Exec. Dir Dr BRYCE WAKEFIELD; publs include *Australian Journal of International Affairs* (5 a year), *Australia in World Affairs* and book series.

Indian Ocean Research Group (IORG): POB 884, Cottesloe, WA 6011; e-mail sanjaychaturvedi@sau.ac.in; f. 2002; Chair. Prof. SANJAY CHATURVEDI; publ. *Journal of the Indian Ocean Region* (3 a year).

AUSTRIA

Österreichische Forschungsstiftung für Internationale Entwicklung (ÖFSE) (Austrian Foundation for Development Research): 1090 Vienna, Sensengasse 3; tel. (1) 317-40-10; e-mail office@oefse.at; internet www.oefse.at; f. 1967; documentation and information on devt aid and developing countries, particularly in relation to Austria; Chair. ULRICH BRAND; Dir Dr WERNER RAZA; publs include *Österreichische Entwicklungspolitik* (annual), *ÖFSE Forum*, working and briefing papers, and policy notes,.

Österreichische Gesellschaft für Aussenpolitik und die Vereinten Nationen (ÖGAVN) (Foreign Policy and United Nations Association of Austria): 1010 Vienna, Hofburg/Stallburg, Reitschulgasse 2/2; e-mail office@oegavn.org; internet www.oegavn.org; f. 1945 as Österreichische Liga für die Vereinten Nationen; merged with Österreichischen Gesellschaft für Außenpolitik und Internationale Beziehungen in 2008; lectures, discussions; Pres. Dr WOLFGANG SCHÜSSEL; *Magazin Society* (annual).

BELGIUM

Académie Royale des Sciences d'Outre-Mer/Koninklijke Academie voor Overzeese Wetenschappen (Royal Academy for Overseas Sciences): ave Circulaire 3, 1180 Brussels; tel. (2) 790-39-02; e-mail contact_raos@kaowarsom.be; internet www.kaowarsom.be; f. 1928 as Institut Royal Colonial Belge; present name adopted in 1959; promotion of scientific knowledge of overseas areas, especially those with special devt problems; Pres. SYLVIE PEPERSTRAETE; Perm. Sec. Prof. PHILIPPE DE MAEYER; publ. *Bulletin des Séances/Mededelingen der Zittingen* (online, 4 a year).

Bibliothèque Foreign Affaires: c/o Bibliothèque Royale de Belgique, Mont des Arts, 1000 Brussels; tel. (2) 519-54-71; e-mail contemporarybooks@kbr.be; internet www.kbr.be; f. 1885; large collections in the fields of African history, ethnography, economics, politics and devt co-operation; relocated to KBR (fmrly Bibliothèque Royale de Belgique) in 2017; Dir DAMIEN ANGELET.

Centre d'Etudes du Développement: Université catholique de Louvain, IACCHOS-DVLP, 1 pl. Montesquieu, 1348 Louvain-La-Neuve; tel. (32) 10-47-21-11; e-mail stephanie.lorent@uclouvain.be; internet www.uclouvain.be; f. 1961; Dir-Gen. Prof. AN ANSOMS.

Institut voor Ontwikkelingsbeleid (IOB) (Institute for Development Policy): University of Antwerp, Stadscampus, Lange Sint-Annastraat, 2000 Antwerp; tel. (3) 265-57-70; e-mail iob@uantwerp.be; internet www.uantwerpen.be/nl/overuantwerpen/faculteiten/iob/over-iob; f. 1965; focuses on economic, political and social aspects of devt policy and management, particularly on the African Great Lakes region; ; Chair. DANNY CASSIMON; publs research reports and papers.

Institut Royal des Relations Internationales (IRRI) (EGMONT): 24A rue des Petits Carmes, 1000 Brussels; tel. (2) 223-41-14; e-mail info@egmontinstitute.be; internet www.egmontinstitute.be; f. 1947; research in international relations, economics, law and politics; Dir-Gen. POL DE WITTE; Dir NINA WILÉN; publs include *Studia Diplomatica* (quarterly) and policy briefs.

Koninklijk Museum voor Midden-Afrika/Musée Royal de l'Afrique Centrale (AfricaMuseum): Leuvensesteenweg 13, 3080 Tervuren; tel. (2) 769-52-11; e-mail info@africamuseum.be; internet www.africamuseum.be; f. 1897; collections of prehistory, ethnography, nature, arts and crafts; geology, mineralogy, palaeontology; zoology (entomology, ornithology, mammals, reptiles, etc.); history; economics; Dir-Gen. GUIDO GRYSEELS; publ. *Africana Linguistica* (annual).

BOTSWANA

Botswana Institute for Development Policy Analysis (BIDPA): BIDPA House, Plot 134, Tshwene Dr., Millennium Office Park, PMB BR29, Gaborone; tel. 3971750; e-mail info@bidpa.bw; internet bidpa.bw; f. 1995; Exec. Dir Dr GLORIA SOMOLEKAE (acting).

BRAZIL

Centro de Estudos Africanos (African Studies Centre): University of São Paulo, Av. Prof. Luciano Gualberto 315, 05508-900 São Paulo, SP; tel. (11) 2648-0608; e-mail cea@usp.br; internet cea.fflch.usp.br; f. 1969; promotes the study of African societies and their devt; Dirs Prof. Dr MARINA DE MELLO E SOUZA, Prof. Dr ROSANGELA SARTESCHI; publ. *Africa: Revista do Centro de Estudos Africanos da USP* (annual).

Centro de Estudos Afro-Orientais (CEAO) (Afro-Oriental Studies Centre): Praça Inocêncio Galvão, 42, Largo Dois de Julho, 40060-055 Salvador-BA; tel. (71) 3283-5509; e-mail ceao@ufba.br; internet ceao.ufba.br; f. 1959; African, Oriental and Afro-Brazilian studies; Co-ordinator JOILSON RODRIGUES DE SOUZA; publ. *Afro-Asia* (biannual).

Núcleo de Estudos Afro-Brasileiros (NEAB) (Centre for Afro-Brazilian Studies): Centro de Letras e Ciências Humanas, Universidade Estadual de Londrina, CP 10011, CEP 86057-970 Londrina, PR; tel. (43) 3371-4599; e-mail neab@uel.br; internet www.uel.br/neab; f. 1985 as Núcleo de Estudos Afro-Asiáticos; Co-ordinator Dr MARLEIDE RODRIGUES DA SILVA PERRUDE.

CANADA

Canadian Association of African Studies (CAAS): Institute of African Studies, 439 Paterson Hall, 1125 Colonel By Dr., Carleton University, Ottawa, ON K1S 5B6; tel. (613) 520-2600; e-mail caasacea@caas-acea.org; internet caas-acea.org; f. 1970; Pres. NDUKA OTIONO; publs include *Canadian Journal of African Studies* (English and French—3 a year), *CAAS Newsletter* (online; English and French—irreg.).

Canadian International Council: 5305 River Bldg, Carleton University, 1125 Colonel By Dr., Ottawa, ON K1S 5B6; tel. (613) 903-4011; e-mail ottawa@thecic.org; internet thecic.org; f. 1928; research in international relations; Pres. BEN ROWSWELL; publs include *International Journal* (quarterly), *Behind the Headlines* (paper series).

Co-operation Canada: 39 McArthur Ave, Ottawa, ON K1L 8L7; tel. (613) 241-7007; e-mail info@cooperation.ca; internet cooperation.ca; f. 1968 as the Canadian Council for International Co-operation; present name adopted in 2020; information and training centre for international devt and forum for voluntary agencies; 93 mem. orgs; Co-Chair. EILEEN ALMA, RICHARD VEENSTRA; CEO KATE HIGGINS; publs include *Au Courant* (2 a year).

The Harriet Tubman Institute for Research on Africa and its Diaspora: 321 York Lanes, York University, 4700 Keele St., Toronto, ON M3J 1P3; tel. (416) 736-2100; e-mail tubman@yorku.ca; internet www.yorku.ca/research/tubman; f. 2007; studies the global diaspora of Africans and their descendants; Dir GERTRUDE MIANDA; publ. *Journal of African and Black Diasporic Studies*.

Institute for the Study of International Development (ISID): 3610 McTavish St, 2nd Floor, Montréal, QC H3A 1Y2; tel. (514) 398-4804; e-mail info.isid@mcgill.ca; internet www.mcgill.ca/isid; f. 2008; Found. Dir Prof. PHILIP OXHORN; Dir ERIK MARTINEZ KUHONTA; publs include policy briefs, newsletters and annual reports.

International Development Research Centre (IDRC): POB 8500, Ottawa, ON K1G 3H9; tel. (613) 236-6163; e-mail info@idrc.ca; internet www.idrc.ca; f. 1970 by the Govt with the mission to support research in developing countries to promote growth and development; regional offices in Kenya, Jordan, Senegal, Uruguay and India; Pres. JEAN LEBEL; publ. *IDRC Bulletin* (English and French—monthly).

PEOPLE'S REPUBLIC OF CHINA

China Institutes of Contemporary International Relations (CICIR): A2 Wanshousi, Haidian, Beijing 100081; tel. (10) 8418640; internet www.cicir.ac.cn; f. 1980; research on international devt and peace issues; Pres. YUAN PENG; publ. *Contemporary International Relations* (bimonthly).

Institute of West-Asian and African Studies, Chinese Academy of Social Sciences (IWAAS—CASS): 1 National Stadium

North Rd, Chaoyang District, Beijing 100101; tel. (10) 87421043; internet iwaas.cass.cn; f. 1961; Dir-Gen. LI XINFENG; publs include *West Asia and Africa* (Chinese, with summary in English—6 a year), monographs and reports.

CZECH REPUBLIC

Ústav mezinárodních vztahů (Institute of International Relations): Nerudova 3, 118 50 Prague 1; tel. 251108111; e-mail iir@iir.cz; internet www.iir.cz; f. 1957; over 100,000 vols of monographs, proceedings, yearbooks, etc. and 300 periodicals; Dir Dr ONDŘEJ DITRYCH; publs include *Mezinárodní politika / International Politics* (in Czech—monthly), *Mezinárodní vztahy / Czech Journal of International Relations* (in Czech, Slovak and English—quarterly), *New Perspectives* (in English—quarterly).

DENMARK

Danish Institute for International Studies (DIIS): Gl. Kalkbrænderi Vej 51A, 2100 Copenhagen K; tel. 45-32-69-87-87; e-mail diis@diis.dk; internet www.diis.dk; f. 2003; independent research institution engaged in research on foreign policy, security and devt; library of over 80,000 vols; Chair. HENRIK HALKIER; Dir KRISTIAN FISCHER; publs include *DIIS Reports, DIIS Working Papers, DIIS Policy Briefs, DIIS Longreads*.

FRANCE

Académie des Sciences d'Outre-mer: 15 rue La Pérouse, 75116 Paris; tel. 1-47-20-87-93; e-mail vbenichou@academiedoutremer.fr; internet www.academieoutremer.fr; f. 1922; library of approx. 130,000 documents, incl. 115,000 monographs, 4,600 periodicals; Perm. Sec. PIERRE GÉNY; publs include *Mondes et Cultures* (annual), *Les Annales, Hommes et Destins: dictionnaire biographique d'outre-mer*.

Les Afriques dans le Monde (LAM): 11 allée Ausone, Domaine universitaire, 33607 Pessac; tel. 5-56-84-42-82; e-mail communication.lam@sciencespobordeaux.fr; internet www.lam .sciencespobordeaux.fr; f. 2011 following the merger of the Centre d'Etude d'Afrique Noire (CEAN) and the Centre d'Etudes et de Recherches sur les Pays d'Afrique Orientale (CREPAO); Dir DAVID AMBROSETTI.

Centre d'Etudes et de Recherches sur le Développement International (CERDI): Université d'Auvergne, 26 ave Léon Blum, BP 320, 63000 Clermont-Ferrand Cedex 1; tel. 4-73-17-74-08; e-mail webmestre.cerdi@udamail.fr; internet cerdi.uca.fr; f. 1976; covers all aspects of economic devt; Head Prof. GRÉGOIRE ROTA-GRAZIOSI; publs include *Revue d'économie du développement* (in French—biannual), working papers and series.

Institut Français des Relations Internationales (Ifri): 27 rue de la Procession, 75740 Paris Cedex 15; tel. 1-40-61-60-00; e-mail accueil@ifri.org; internet www.ifri.org; f. 1979; international politics and economy, security issues, regional studies; comprises the African Studies Center (f. 2007); Founder/Exec. Chair. THIERRY DE MONTBRIAL; Dir THOMAS GOMART; publs include *Politique Etrangère* (quarterly), *Rapport annuel mondial sur le système économique et les stratégies (Ramses)* (annual), notes and policy briefs.

Institut des Mondes Africains (IMAF): Campus Condorcet, RCI 3, Bâtiment Recherche Sud 5, cours des Humanités, 93300 Aubervilliers Cedex; tel. 1-88-12-02-24; e-mail c.vincenti@univ-amu.fr; internet www.imaf.cnrs.fr; f. 2014 following the merger of Centre d'Etudes des Mondes Africains (CEMAf), Centre d'Etudes Africaines (CEAf) and Centre d'Histoire Sociale de l'Islam Méditerranéen (CHSIM); Dir HELENA VEZZADINI, FABIENNE SAMSON; publs include *Politique africaine, Afriques* (annual), *Cahiers d'études africaines* (in French and English).

Institut de Recherche pour le Développement (IRD): 44 blvd de Dunkerque, CS 90009, 13572 Marseille Cedex 02; tel. 4-91-99-94-87; e-mail presse@ird.fr; internet www.ird.fr; f. 1943, reorg. 1982 and 1998; Chair. and CEO Dr VALÉRIE VERDIER.

Musée de l'Homme: 17 pl. du Trocadéro, 75116 Paris; tel. 1-44-05-72-72; e-mail presse.mdh@mnhn.fr; internet www.museedelhomme .fr; f. 1938, reorg. 2015; library of 35,000 vols, 800 periodicals and 30,000 offprints; ethnography, physical anthropology, prehistory; Dir ANDRÉ DELPUECH.

Société des Africanistes (SDAF): Musée du quai Branly, 222 rue de l'Université, 75343 Paris; tel. 1-56-61-71-17; e-mail africanistes@ yahoo.fr; internet africanistes.org; f. 1930; Pres. FRANÇOISE LE GUENNEC-COPPENS; publs include *Journal des Africanistes* (biannual), monthly newsletters and memoirs.

Société Française d'Historie d'Outre-mer (SFHOM): BP 50026, 75228 Paris Cedex 05; tel. 6-86-37-49-64; e-mail outremers.sfhom@ gmail.com; internet www.sfhom.com; f. 1912 as Société d'histoire des colonies françaises; 500 mems; Pres. Prof. HUGUES TERTRAIS; Sec.-Gen. GUILLAUME DENGLOS; publ. *Outre-Mers. Revue d'histoire* (biannual).

GERMANY

Deutsche Gesellschaft für Auswärtige Politik eV (German Council on Foreign Relations): Rauchstr. 17/18, 10787 Berlin; tel. (30) 2542310; e-mail info@dgap.org; internet www.dgap.org; f. 1955; promotes research on international politics, security and defence, migration, climate; develops German expertise in foreign policy; library of over 85,000 vols and 200 periodicals; approx. 2,800 mems; Pres. Dr THOMAS ENDERS; Dir and CEO Dr GUNTRAM WOLFF; publs include *Internationale Politik* (in German), *Internationale Politik Quarterly* (in English),.

GIGA Institute of African Affairs: Neuer Jungfernstieg 21, 20354 Hamburg; tel. (40) 42825523; e-mail iaa@giga-hamburg.de; internet www.giga-hamburg.de/iaa; f. 1963; conducts research on sub-Saharan Africa; Dir Prof. Dr MATTHIAS BASEDAU; publs include *Africa Spectrum* (3 a year), *GIGA Focus Afrika, GIGA Working Paper Series*.

ifo Institut (Institute for Economic Research): Universität München, Poschingerstr. 5, 81679 Munich; tel. (89) 92240; e-mail ifo@ifo.de; internet www.ifo.de; f. 1949 following the merger of Süddeutsche Institut für Wirtschaftsforschung and Forschungsstelle für Wirtschaftsbeobachtung; Pres. Prof. Dr CLEMENS FUEST; publs.

informationsstelle südliches afrika eV (issa) (Information Centre on Southern Africa): Königswinterer Str. 116, D-53227 Bonn; tel. (228) 464369; e-mail info@issa-bonn.org; internet www .issa-bonn.org; f. 1971; research, documentation and information on southern Africa; focuses on the devt of countries in the Southern African Development Community (SADC); Co-Chairs BRIGITTE REINHARDT, KLAUS-DIETER SEIDEL; publs include *Afrika Süd* (6 a year), book series and dossiers.

Institut für Afrikastudien: Leipzig University, Geisteswissenschaftliches Zentrum, Beethovenstr. 15, 04107 Leipzig; tel. (341) 9737030; e-mail mgrosze@uni-leipzig.de; internet www.gko .uni-leipzig.de/institut-fuer-afrikastudien; f. 1960; fmrly Institut für Afrikanistik; present name adopted in 2017; Dir Prof. Dr DMITRI VAN DEN BERSSELAAR.

GHANA

African Center for Economic Transformation (ACET): 7 Yiyiwa St, Abelemkpe, Accra; tel. (24) 2436858; e-mail info@ acetforafrica.org; internet acetforafrica.org; f. 2008; offers policy advice to African countries for developing their economies; Pres. and Founder Dr K. Y. AMAOKO; publs include *The West Africa Trends Newsletter, African Transformation Report* (irreg.), policy briefs.

Danquah Institute: Second Norla St, Labone, Accra; tel. (30) 2737479; e-mail info@localhost; internet danquahinstitute.com; f. 2008; promotes the Danquah-Busia-Dombo ideology; Chair. Prof. AARON MICHAEL OQUAYE; Exec. Dir Dr ANTOINETTE TSIBOE-DARKO (acting).

HUNGARY

Africa Research Institute: Doctoral School on Safety and Security Sciences, Bánki Donát Faculty of Mechanical and Safety Engineering, Obuda University, Népszínház str. 8, 1081 Budapest, Hungary; tel. (1) 666-5345; publ. *Journal of Central and Eastern European African Studies* (quarterly).

Magyar Tudományos Akadémia Közgazdaság- és Regionális Tudományi Kutatóközpont Világgazdasági Intézet (Institute of World Economics of the Centre for Economic and Regional Studies of the Hungarian Academy of Sciences): 1097 Budapest, 4 Tóth Kálmán St; tel. (1) 309-2643; e-mail vgi.titkarsag@krtk.mta.hu; internet www.vki.hu; f. 1973 as the Világgazdasági Kutatóintézet (Institute for World Economics); present name and structure adopted in 2012; Dir PÉTERNÉ TÖLGYESSY MAGDOLNA SASS.

INDIA

Centre for African Studies: University of Mumbai, Area Studies Bldg, opp. Ranade Bhavan, Vidyanagari Campus, Santacruz (E), Mumbai 400 098; tel. (22) 26543000; e-mail director@cas.mu.ac.in; internet mu.ac.in/department-of-african-studies; f. 1971; Dir Dr RENU MODI; publ. *African Currents* (2 a year).

Centre for African Studies: School of International Studies, Jawaharlal Nehru University, New Mehrauli Rd, New Delhi 110 067; tel. (11) 26704607; e-mail akdubey@mail.jnu.ac.in; internet www.jnu.ac.in/sis/cas; f. 1969; interdisciplinary centre for study of Africa; Chair. Prof. AJAY KUMAR DUBEY.

African Studies Association of India (ASA): Centre for African Studies, 351-School of International Studies, Jawaharlal Nehru University, New Mehrauli Rd, New Delhi 110 067; tel. (11) 26704607; e-mail office@africanstudies.in; internet www .africanstudies.in; f. 2003 to foster and promote the study, knowledge and understanding of African affairs in India and Indian affairs in Africa through research and studies; Chair.

SHASHANK; Pres. RUCHITA BERI; publs incl. *Africa Review* (3 a year) and *Insight on Africa* (biannual).

Centre of Arabic and African Studies (CAAS): School of Language, Literature and Culture Studies, Jawaharlal Nehru University, New Mehrauli Rd, New Delhi 110 067; tel. (11) 26704253; e-mail chair_caas@mail.jnu.ac.in; internet www.jnu.ac.in/sllcs/caas; f. 1971 as Center of African and Asian Languages; present name adopted in 1996; provides courses in Hebrew and Swahili; Chair. Prof. RIZWANUR RAHMAN; publ. *Dirasat Arabiah*.

Centre for Development Studies: Prasanth Nagar, Ulloor, Thiruvananthapuram 695 011; tel. (471) 2448881; e-mail rec@cds.ac.in; internet www.cds.edu; f. 1970; instruction and research in disciplines relevant to economic devt; library of 138,075 vols, 18,072 journal bound vols, 85 print journals and 21,951 working papers; Chair. Prof. SUDIPTO MUNDLE; Dir Prof. SUNIL MANI; publs include *CDS Chronicle* (quarterly), working papers, annual reports, commentary series.

Department of African Studies: Faculty of Social Sciences, University of Delhi, New Delhi 110 007; tel. (11) 27666673; e-mail depttafrica9@gmail.com; internet as.du.ac.in; f. 1954; Head of Dept Prof. GAJENDRA SINGH.

Indian Council for Cultural Relations (ICCR): Azad Bhavan, Indraprastha Estate, New Delhi 110 002; tel. (11) 23370229; e-mail presidentoffice.iccr@gov.in; internet www.iccr.gov.in; f. 1950; library includes a collection of approx. 10,000 vols and MSS in Arabic, Persian, Urdu, etc. called Gosha-e-Azad; Pres. Dr VINAY SAHASRA-BUDDHE; Dir-Gen. KUMAR TUHIN; publs include *Indian Horizons* (quarterly), *Gangananchal* (in English and Hindi—irreg.).

Indian Council of World Affairs (ICWA): Sapru House, Barakhamba Rd, New Delhi 110 001; tel. (11) 23317246; e-mail dg@icwa .in; internet www.icwa.in; f. 1943; statutory institution for the study of Indian and international issues; library of over 152,000 vols, incl. periodicals, maps, microfiches, press clippings, and UN and EU documents; also possesses over 39,000 bound journals; Pres. JADGEEP DHANKHAR; Dir-Gen. VIJAY THAKUR SINGH; publs include *India Quarterly*, *Sapru House Papers* (annual), issue briefs, books.

IRAN

Institute for Political and International Studies (IPIS): Shaheed Bahonar St, Shaheed Aghaii Ave, POB 19395-1793, Tajrish, Tehran; tel. (21) 22802641; e-mail info@ipis.ir; internet www.ipis.ir; f. 1983; research and information on international relations, foreign policy, economics, culture and law; Pres. MUHAMMAD HASSAN SHAYKH AL-ISLAMI; publs include *History of Foreign Relations* (quarterly), *Journal of Foreign Policy* (quarterly).

ISRAEL

Harry S. Truman Research Institute for the Advancement of Peace: The Hebrew University of Jerusalem, Mt Scopus, Jerusalem 9190501; tel. (2) 5882300; e-mail truman@savion.huji.ac.il; internet truman.huji.ac.il; f. 1965; conducts a broad range of research relating to the advancement of peace in the Middle East and the non-Western world, incl. Africa, Asia and Latin America; Head Prof. IFAT MAOZ.

Institute of Asian and African Studies: The Hebrew University of Jerusalem, Mt Scopus, Jerusalem 91905; tel. (2) 5883581; e-mail nissim.otmazgin@mail.huji.ac.il; internet www.hum.huji.ac.il; f. 1926 as the Institute of Oriental Studies; incorporates Max Schloessinger Memorial Foundation; studies of medieval and modern languages, culture, and history of Middle East, Asia and Africa; Dir Prof. NISSIM OTMEZGIN.

Moshe Dayan Center for Middle Eastern and African Studies: Gilman 419, Tel Aviv University, Ramat-Aviv, Tel Aviv 69978; tel. (3) 6409100; e-mail dayancen@tauex.tau.ac.il; internet dayan.org; f. 1959; Dir Prof. UZI RABI; publs include *Current Contents of Periodicals on the Middle East* (6 a year), *Jihadiscope* (online—weekly), *Ifriqiya: Africa Research and Analysis* (in English—bimonthly), *MDC Occasional Papers* (biannual).

ITALY

Istituto per gli Studi di Politica Internazionale (ISPI): Palazzo Clerici, Via Clerici 5, 20121 Milan; tel. (02) 8633131; e-mail ispi .segreteria@ispionline.it'; internet www.ispionline.it; f. 1934 for the promotion of the study of international relations; conducts research, documentation and training; Pres. Dr GIAMPIERO MASSOLO; publs include *Relazioni Internazionali* (6 a year), dossiers, reports, policy briefs.

The Johns Hopkins University School of Advanced International Studies (SAIS Europe): The Johns Hopkins University, SAIS, Via B. Andreatta 3, 40126 Bologna; tel. (051) 2917838; e-mail sais.eu.admissions@jhu.edu; internet sais.jhu.edu; f. 1955; graduate studies in international affairs; Dir MICHAEL G. PLUMMER.

JAPAN

Institute of Developing Economies, Japan External Trade Organization (IDE—JETRO): 3-2-2 Wakaba, Mihama-ku, Chiba-shi, Chiba 261-8545; tel. (3) 3582-5511; e-mail info@ide.go.jp; internet www.ide.go.jp; f. 1958 as the Institute of Developing Economies; merged with JETRO 1998; library of 640,295 vols, 3,727 periodicals and 81,715 bound periodicals (2018); Pres. KYOJI FUKAO; publs *Ajia Keizai* (in Japanese—quarterly), *The Developing Economies* (in English—quarterly), *Africa Report* (in Japanese—annual).

The Japan Institute of International Affairs (JIIA) (Nihon Kokusai Mondai Kenkyusho): Toranomon Mitsu Bldg, 3rd Floor, 3-8-1, Kasumigaseki, Chiyoda-ku, Tokyo 100-0013; tel. (3) 3503-7261; e-mail jiiajoho@jiia.or.jp; internet www.jiia.or.jp; f. 1959; Chair. MOTOYUKI OKA; Pres. KENICHIRO SASAE; publs include *Kokusai Mondai / International Affairs* (10 a year), *Japan Review* (quarterly), *AJISS-Commentary*.

Nihon Afurika Gakkai (Japan Association for African Studies): c/o Dogura and Co Ltd, 1–8, Nishihanaikecho, Koyama, Kita-ku, Kyoto 603-8148; tel. (75) 451-4844; e-mail info@african-studies.com; internet african-studies.com; f. 1964; promotes multi-disciplinary African studies; over 800 mems; Pres. MOTOJI MATSUDA; publs include *Afurika Kenkyu / Journal of African Studies* (biannual), *Kaiho* (annual).

Research Institute for Languages and Cultures of Asia and Africa: Tokyo University of Foreign Studies, Asahi-cho 3-11-1, Fuchu, Tokyo 183-8534; tel. (42) 330-5600; e-mail ilcaa@aa.tufs.ac .jp; internet www.aa.tufs.ac.jp; f. 1964; Dir IZUMI HOSHI; publs *Asian and African Languages and Linguistics* (annual), *Journal of Asian and African Studies* (biannual).

KENYA

African Economic Research Consortium (AERC): Middle East Bank Towers Bldg, 3rd Floor, Jakaya Kikwete Rd, Nairobi; tel. (20) 2734150; e-mail communications@aercafrica.org; internet aercafrica .org; f. 1988 to inform economic policies in sub-Saharan Africa; integrates economic policy research, postgraduate training and policy outreach; Chair. Prof. ERNEST ARYEETEY; Exec. Dir Prof. NJUGUNA NDUNG'U.

British Institute in Eastern Africa (BIEA): Laikipia Rd, Kileshwa, POB 30710, Nairobi; tel. (20) 8155186; e-mail office@biea.ac .uk; internet biea.ac.uk; f. 1959 as the British Institute of History and Archaeology in East Africa; ; under the aegis of the British Academy in London (UK); Dir Dr JANE HUMPHRIS; Country Dir Dr DAMARIS PARSITAU; publs *Azania: Archaeological Research in Africa* (4 a year), *Journal of Eastern African Studies* (4 a year), *BIEA Annual Report*.

Institute of Economic Affairs (IEA Kenya): CK Garden House, 5th Floor, 1st Ngong Ave, POB 53989, Nairobi; tel. (20) 2721262; e-mail admin@ieakenya.or.ke; internet ieakenya.or.ke; f. 1994; CEO KWAME OWINO.

Kenya Institute for Public Policy Research and Analysis (KIPPRA): Bishops Garden Towers, 2nd Floor, Bishops Rd, POB 56445-00200, Nairobi; tel. (20) 4936000; e-mail admin@kippra.or.ke; internet kippra.or.ke; f. 1997; Chair. Dr BENSON A'. ATENG; Exec. Dir Dr ROSE NGUGI; publs include *Kenya Economic Report* (annual), *KIPPRA Policy Monitor*, policy briefs, discussion papers, working papers.

MAURITANIA

Centre for Strategies for the Security in Sahel Sahara (Centre 4 S): Tevragh Zeina, Nouakchott; e-mail contact@centre4s.org; internet www.newcentre4s.org; covers studies on the Sahel and Sahara region; Pres. AHMEDOU OULD ABDALLAH.

MOROCCO

Institut des Études Africaines (IEA): ave Allal el-Fassi,, Madinat el-Irfane, Agdal, BP 8968, Rabat; tel. (61) 641094; e-mail webmaster@um5.ac.ma; internet iea.um5.ac.ma; f. 1987; promotes research on Africa in the field of social sciences; covers political, economic, social, cultural and spatial changes in Africa; Dir MOHAMMED DAFIR EL-KETTANI (acting); publs include *Revue Marocaine des Etudes Africaines / Moroccan Journal of African Studies*, book series.

NAMIBIA

Institute for Public Policy Research (IPPR): 70–72 Frans Indongo St, POB 6566, Windhoek; tel. (61) 240514; e-mail info@ ippr.org.na; internet ippr.org.na; f. 2001; researches social, political and economic issues affecting devt in Namibia; Dir GRAHAM HOPWOOD.

NETHERLANDS

ActionAid (AA): Stadhouderskade 60, POB 10707, 1001 ES, Amsterdam; tel. (20) 5206210; e-mail info@actionaid.nl; internet www.actionaid.nl; f. 1997 as NiZA: Nederlands Instituut voor Zuidelijk Afrika; joined ActionAid International in 2007; present name adopted in 2012; promotes democracy in southern Africa; Dir MARIT MAIJ; publs *Zuidelijk Afrika*, *NiZA Informatie* (quarterly), *Niza Cahiers* and reports of seminars and conferences.

African Studies Centre Leiden (ASCL): Wassenaarseweg 52, 2333 AK, Leiden; POB 9555, 2300 RB, Leiden; tel. (71) 5273354; e-mail asc@ascleiden.nl; internet www.ascleiden.nl; f. 1947 to carry out research on sub-Saharan Africa in the social sciences, and to disseminate information on African affairs; fmrly known as Afrika-Instituut; library of approx. 100,000 vols, 2,200 films, over 400 serial subscriptions and 500 maps, and 9,500 microfiches; Dir Prof. MARLEEN DEKKER; publs include *African Dynamics* (annual), *Afrika-Studiecentrum Series* (2–3 titles a year) and *Africa Yearbook*, *ASCL Infosheets*, *African Postal Heritage*, book series, occasional papers, maps.

International Institute of Social Studies of the Erasmus University Rotterdam (ISS): Kortenaerkade 12, 2518 AX, The Hague; POB 29776, 2502 LT, The Hague; tel. (70) 4260460; e-mail info@iss.nl; internet www.iss.nl; f. 1952; postgraduate instruction, research and consultancy in devt studies; library of 100,000 vols, approx. 120,000 e-periodicals and over 350 online databases; Rector Prof. INGE HUTTER; publs *Development and Change* (6 a year), *DevISSues* (irreg.), working papers.

Netherlands-African Business Council: Prinses Beatrixlaan 582, 2595 AM, The Hague; tel. (70) 3043618; e-mail info@nabc.nl; internet nabc.nl; f. 1946; over 250 mem. cos; Chair. FRANK NAGEL; Man. Dir ROSMARIJN FENS.

NIGERIA

Center for the Study of the Economies of Africa (CSEA): 4 Dep St, off Danube St, Maitama, Abuja; tel. (9) 2914822; e-mail enquiries@cseaafrica.org; internet cseaafrica.org; f. 2008; Exec. Dir CHUKWUKA ONYEKWENA; publs include *Nigeria Economic Update*, policy briefs, working and discussion papers.

NORWAY

Norsk Utenrikspolitisk Institutt (Norwegian Institute of International Affairs): C. J. Hambros Plass 2D, 0164 Oslo; POB 7024 St Olavs Plass, 0130 Oslo; tel. 22994000; e-mail post@nupi.no; internet www.nupi.no; f. 1959; Chair. KARL ERIK HAUG; Dir ULF SVERDRUP; publs include *Internasjonal Politikk* (quarterly), *Nordisk Østforum* (quarterly), *Forum for Development Studies* (3 a year), *NUPI Notat* and *NUPI Rapport* (research reports).

POLAND

Chair of African Languages and Cultures, University of Warsaw: 02-630 Warsaw, Tyniecka 15/17; tel. (22) 5520517; e-mail afrykanistyka.orient@uw.edu.pl; internet www.afrykanistyka.uw.edu.pl; f. 1977; postgraduate studies and research in linguistics, literature, history, sociology and ethnology; library of over 10,000 vols and 500 periodicals; Head Dr BEATA WÓJTOWICZ; publ. *Studies of the Department of African Languages and Cultures*.

Wydział Geografii i Studiów Regionalnych (Faculty of Geography and Regional Studies): 00-927 Warsaw, Krakowskie Przedmiescie 30; tel. 5520668; e-mail swz.wgsr@uw.edu.pl; internet wgsr.uw.edu.pl; f. 1977; interdisciplinary research on developing countries; Dean Prof. MACIEJ JĘDRUSIK; publs include *Miscellanea Geographica: Regional Studies on Development* (quarterly, in English), *Studies in Geography*.

PORTUGAL

Centro de Estudos Africanos da Universidade do Porto (CEAUP) (African Studies Centre of the University of Porto): Via Panorâmica s/n, 4150-564 Porto; tel. (22) 6077141; e-mail ceaup@letras.up.pt; internet www.africanos.eu; f. 1997; research and postgraduate courses in African Studies; Pres. RUI DA SILVA; publs include *Africana Studia*, *Estudos Africanos* (monograph series), *Experiências de África*, *Journal of US-Africa Studies* (biannual).

Centro de Estudos Internacionais (Centre for International Studies): CEI-IUL (ISCTE-IUL), Av. das Forças Armadas, 1649-026 Lisbon; tel. (21) 0464029; e-mail cei@iscte.pt; internet cei.iscte-iul.pt; f. 2013; interdisciplinary research in social sciences, international relations and economy; Dir LUÍS NUNO RODRIGUES; publs include *Cadernos de Estudos Africanos*, occasional paper series.

Centro de Estudos Sobre África e do Desenvolvimento (CEsA) (Centre of African and Development Studies): Instituto Superior de Economia e Gestão, Rua Miguel Lupi 20, 1249-078 Lisbon; tel. (21) 3925983; e-mail comunicacao@cesa.iseg.ulisboa.pt; internet cesa.rc.iseg.ulisboa.pt; f. 1982; conducts research and holds seminars; Dir LUÍS MAH; publs include *Mundo Crítico*, policy briefs, working papers, books.

Centro de Intervenção para o Desenvolvimento Amílcar Cabral (CIDAC) (Amilcar Cabral Information and Documentation Centre): Rua Tomás Ribeiro, 3°–9° esq., 1069-069 Lisbon; tel. (21) 3172860; e-mail cidac@cidac.pt; internet www.cidac.pt; f. 1974; Pres. CRISTINA MARIA GUERRA DA CRUZ.

RUSSIAN FEDERATION

Institute for African Studies, Russian Academy of Sciences: 123001 Moscow, 30/1 Spiridonovka; tel. (495) 690-63-85; e-mail info@inafr.ru; internet www.inafran.ru; f. 1959; Dir IRINA ABRAMOVA; publs include *Journal of the Institute for African Studies*, *Asia and Africa Today* (monthly).

Institute of Asian and African Studies: 125009 Moscow, ul. Mokhovaya 11; tel. (495) 629-43-49; e-mail office@iaas.msu.ru; internet iaas.msu.ru; f. 1956 as Institute for Oriental Languages; present name adopted 1972; Pres. (vacant); Dir Prof. ALEXEY ALEXANDROVICH MASLOV.

Primakov Institute of World Economy and International Relations (IMEMO): 117997 Moscow, ul. Profsoyuznaya 23; tel. (499) 120-52-36; e-mail imemoran@imemo.ru; internet www.imemo.ru; f. 1956; Dir ALEXANDER DYNKIN; publs include *Mirovaya Economika I Mezhdunarodnye Otnosheniya* (monthly), *Analysis and Forecasting: IMEMO Journal*.

Moscow State Institute of International Relations (MGIMO): 119454 Moscow, Vernadskogo pr. 76; tel. (495) 299-40-49; e-mail international@inno.mgimo.ru; internet www.mgimo.ru; f. 1944; library of over 770,000 vols and periodicals; Rector ANATOLY TURKUNOV; publs include *MGIMO Review of International Relations*, *Mezhdunarodnaya analitika* (4 a year), *MGIMO Journal*.

SENEGAL

Council for the Development of Social Science Research in Africa (CODESRIA): ave Cheikh Anta Diop, angle Canal IV, BP 3304, Dakar; tel. 33-825-98-22; e-mail codesria@codesria.sn; internet codesria.org; f. 1973; pan-African org; Pres. Prof. ISABEL MARIA ALÇADA PADEZ CORTESÃO CASIMIRO; Exec. Sec. Dr GODWIN R. MURUNGA; publs include *Africa Development* (quarterly), *African Sociological Review* (biannual), *African Journal of International Affairs* (biannual), *CODESRIA Bulletin* (6 a year), *Journal of Higher Education in Africa* (biannual), *Africa Media Review* (3 a year), *Africa Review of Books* (biannual), *The African Anthropologist* (biannual), *Afrika Zamani* (annual) and *Identity, Culture and Politics: An Afro-Asian Dialogue* (biannual).

Timbuktu Institute (African Center for Peace Studies): Sacré-Coeur 3, CP 10700, BP 15177, Dakar; tel. 39-827-34-91; e-mail contact@timbuktu-institute.org; internet timbuktu-institute.org; f. 2016; Regional Dir Dr BAKARY SAMBE; publ *Lettres de l'observatoire*.

SOUTH AFRICA

Africa Institute of South Africa: HSRC Bldg, 134 Pretorious St, Pretoria 0002; Private Bag X41, Pretoria 0001; tel. (12) 3169700; e-mail mchipu@hsrc.ac.za; internet www.ai.org.za; f. 1960; undertakes research and collects and disseminates information on all aspects of continental Africa and its offshore islands, with particular focus on politics, economics and devt issues; Exec. Dir Prof. CHERYL HENDRICKS; publs include *Africa Insight* (quarterly).

The Brenthurst Foundation: 6 St Andrew's Rd, Parktown, Johannesburg; POB 61631, Marshalltown 2107; tel. (11) 2742000; internet thebrenthurstfoundation.org; f. 2004; works on African policy matters to strengthen Africa's economic performance; Dir GREG MILLS.

Harvard University Center for African Studies, Africa Office: Rosebank Office Park, Block C, 1st Floor, 181 Jan Smuts Ave, Parktown, North Johannesburg; tel. (21) 2142790; e-mail africaoffice@harvard.edu; internet africa.harvard.edu; f. 2017; br. of the Harvard University Center for African Studies (USA); Dir NTHATISI QUELLA.

Centre for Advanced Studies of African Society (CASAS): 7 Nursery Rd, Rondebosch, POB 358, Cape Town 7701; tel. (21) 6899217; e-mail casas@casas.co.za; internet www.casas.uwc.ac.za; f. 1997; Dir Prof. KWESI PRAH.

Centre for African Studies: Harry Oppenheimer Institute Bldg, 3rd Floor, University of Cape Town, Private Bag, Rondebosch 7701; tel. (21) 6504034; e-mail cas-africas@uct.ac.za; internet www.africanstudies.uct.ac.za; f. 1976; incorporates the Harry Oppenheimer Inst. for African Studies; promotes comparative study of Africa and research; offers multidisciplinary courses at postgraduate level;

Dir Prof. LUNGISILE NTSEBEZA (acting); publs include *Social Dynamics* biannual).

Human Sciences Research Council (HSRC): 134 Pretorius St, Private Bag X41, Pretoria; tel. (12) 3022000; internet hsrc.ac.za; f. 1968; conducts large-scale, policy-relevant, social-scientific projects for public sector users, non-governmental organizations and international devt agencies; CEO Prof. LEICKNESS CHISAMU SIMBAYI (acting).

Institute of Race Relations: 222 Smit St, 21st Floor, Braamfontein, Johannesburg 2000; POB 291722, Melville 2109; tel. (11) 4827221; e-mail info@irr.org.za; internet irr.org.za; f. 1929 as the South African Institute of Race Relations; research, education, publishing; Chair. ROGER CRAWFORD; Pres. RUSSELL LAMBERTI; CEO Dr JOHN ENDRES; publs include *FreeFACTS* (monthly), and *South Africa Survey* (annual).

Institute for Security Studies (ISS): Brooklyn Court, Block C, 361 Veale St, New Muckleneuk, Pretoria 0181; Brooklyn Sq., POB 1787, Pretoria 0075; tel. (12) 3469500; e-mail iss@issafrica.org; internet issafrica.org; f. 1991; brs in Kenya, Ethiopia and Senegal; Exec. Dir FONTEH AKUM; publs *South African Crime Quarterly*, *Africa Report* (series).

National Research Foundation: CSIR Complex, Meiring Naudé Rd, Brummeria, POB 2600, Pretoria 0001; tel. (12) 4814000; e-mail info@nrf.ac.za; internet www.nrf.ac.za; f. 1999; govt agency, responsible for supporting and promoting research; Chair. Dr NOMPUME-LELO OBOKOH; Pres. and CEO Dr FULUFHELO NELWAMONDO.

South African Institute of International Affairs (SAIIA): East Campus, University of the Witwatersrand, Johannesburg; tel. (11) 3392021; e-mail media@saiia.org.za; internet saiia.org.za; f. 1934; independent public policy think tank advancing a well-governed, peaceful, economically sustainable and globally engaged Africa; Nat. Chair. FRED PHASWANA; CEO ELIZABETH SIDIROPOULOS; publs include *South African Journal of International Affairs* (4 a year).

SPAIN

Africa Fundación Sur (Africa South Foundation): Gaztambide 31, 28015 Madrid; tel. 915497787; e-mail correo@africafundacion.org; internet cidafucm.es; f. 1979; library of over 20,000 documents; Dir LAZARO BUSTINCE SOLA; publs include *Noticias de Africa* (monthly), *Cuadernos*.

Colegio Mayor Universitario Nuestra Señora de Africa: Avda Ramiro de Maeztu s/n, Ciudad Universitaria, 28040 Madrid; tel. 915540104; e-mail info.africa@eoi.es; internet www.eoi.es/es/colegios-mayores/africa; f. 1964; attached inst. of the Complutense Univ. of Madrid and the Spanish Ministry of Foreign Affairs; linguistic studies and cultural activities; Dir JOSÉ PÉREZ ARÉVALO.

SWEDEN

Institutet för Internationell Ekonomi (Institute for International Economic Studies): Stockholm University, 106 91 Stockholm; tel. (8) 162000; e-mail hanna.weitz@iies.su.se; internet www.su.se/institute-for-international-economic-studies; attached to Stockholm Univ.; f. 1962; Dir Prof. JAKOB SVENSSON.

Nordiska Afrikainstitutet (The Nordic Africa Institute): POB 1703, 751 47 Uppsala; tel. (18) 4715200; e-mail nai@nai.uu.se; internet www.nai.uu.se; f. 1962; research, documentation and information centre for contemporary African affairs, publication work, lectures and seminars; library of approx. 80,000 vols on politics, economics, contemporary history, anthropology, literature and other social sciences, and approx. 210 periodicals on Africa and devt issues; Dir THERÉSE SJÖMANDER MAGNUSSON; publs include *Africa Now* (book series), *Current African Issues* (policy dialogue series), working papers, policy notes.

Utrikespolitiska Institutet (UI) (Swedish Institute of International Affairs): Drottning Kristinas väg 37, 114 28 Stockholm; POB 27035, 102 51 Stockholm; tel. (8) 51176800; e-mail info@ui.se; internet www.ui.se; f. 1938; Dir JAKOB HALLGREN; publs include *UI Papers*, *UI Briefs*, *UI Reports*.

SWITZERLAND

Institut de Hautes Etudes Internationales et du Développement (IHEID) (Geneva Graduate Institute): Maison de la paix, rue Eugène-Rigot 2, CP 1672, 1211 Geneva 1; tel. (22) 9085700; e-mail info@graduateinstitute.ch; internet graduateinstitute.ch; f. 1927; a centre of higher education and research into devt problems of Africa, Latin America, Asia and Eastern Europe; conducts courses, seminars and practical work; Dir MARIE-LAURE SALLES; publs include *Revue Internationale de Politique de Développement*, *Itinéraires*.

UNITED KINGDOM

African Studies Association of the United Kingdom (ASAUK): SOAS University of London, 10 Thornhaugh St, London, WC1H 0XG;

tel. (20) 7074-5176; e-mail secretary@asauk.net; internet asauk.net; f. 1963 to advance academic studies relating to Africa by providing facilities for the interchange of information and ideas; works in collaboration with the Royal African Society; Pres. OLA UDUKU; Hon. Sec. Dr DAVID KERR.

Centre for the Study of African Economies (CSAE): Dept of Economics, University of Oxford, Manor Rd Bldg, Manor Rd, Oxford, OX1 3UQ; tel. (1865) 271084; e-mail csae.enquiries@economics.ox.ac.uk; internet www.csae.ox.ac.uk; f. 1986; Dir Prof. STEFAN DERCON; publ. *Journal of African Economies* (quarterly).

Centre of African Studies: Alison Richard Bldg, 7 West Rd, Cambridge, CB3 9DT; tel. (1223) 334396; e-mail centre@african.cam.ac.uk; internet www.african.cam.ac.uk; f. 1965; affiliated with the Univ. of Cambridge; Dir Dr BRONWEN EVERILL.

Centre of African Studies: University of Edinburgh, Chrystal MacMillan Bldg, 15A George Sq., Edinburgh, EH8 9LD; tel. (131) 651-3060; e-mail african.studies@ed.ac.uk; internet www.sps.ed.ac.uk/centre-african-studies; f. 1962; undergraduate and postgraduate studies on Africa; Dir Dr HAZEL GRAY; publs include occasional paper series and annual conference proceedings.

Centre of African Studies: SOAS University of London, 10 Thornhaugh St, Russell Sq., London, WC1H 0XG; tel. (20) 7898-4370; e-mail cas@soas.ac.uk; internet www.soas.ac.uk/cas; f. 1965; co-ordinates interdisciplinary study, research and discussion on Africa; Chair. Dr WAYNE DOOLING; Dir Prof. ADAM HABIB; publ. *Africa News* (newsletter).

Department of African Studies and Anthropology, University of Birmingham: The University of Birmingham, Arts Bldg, Edgbaston, Birmingham, B15 2TT; tel. (121) 4145128; e-mail dasaadmin@contacts.bham.ac.uk; internet www.birmingham.ac.uk; f. 1963; Head Dr JESSICA JOHNSON.

Institute of Commonwealth Studies (ICWS): School of Advanced Study, University of London, Senate House, Malet St, London, WC1E 7HU; tel. (20) 7862-8844; e-mail ics@sas.ac.uk; internet commonwealth.sas.ac.uk; f. 1949; promotes advanced study of the Commonwealth and its member nations; provides a library and meeting place for postgraduate students and academic staff engaged in research in this field; offers postgraduate teaching; library of over 190,000 vols, over 9,000 periodicals and an archive of 230 collections; Dir Dr SUE ONSLOW.

Institute of Development Studies (IDS): University of Sussex, Brighton, East Sussex, BN1 9RE; tel. (1273) 606261; e-mail ids@ids.ac.uk; internet www.ids.ac.uk; f. 1966; research, training, postgraduate teaching, advisory work, information services; Dir Prof. MELISSA LEACH; publ. *IDS Bulletin*.

International African Institute (IAI): SOAS University of London, Thornhaugh St, Russell Sq., London, WC1H 0XG; tel. (20) 7898-4420; e-mail iai@soas.ac.uk; internet internationalafricaninstitute.org; f. 1926 to facilitate research on Africa; Chair. Prof. ALCINDA HONWANA; publs include *Journal of African Cultural Studies*, *Africa Bibliography* (annual), monograph and reprint series.

Leeds University Centre for African Studies: University of Leeds, Leeds, West Yorkshire, LS2 9JT; tel. (113) 3435069; e-mail african-studies@leeds.ac.uk; internet lucas.leeds.ac.uk; f. 1964; a liaison unit for all depts with African interests; organizes public seminars and conferences and a book donation scheme for African university theatre arts depts; Dir Prof. ADRIAAN VAN KLINKEN; publ. *Leeds African Studies Bulletin* (annual).

Overseas Development Institute (ODI): 203 Blackfriars Rd, London SE1 8NJ; tel. (20) 7922-0300; e-mail odi@odi.org.uk; internet www.odi.org; f. 1960 as a research centre and forum for the discussion of devt issues and problems; Chair. Sir SUMA CHAKRABARTI; CEO SARA PANTULIANO; publs include *Development Policy Review* (quarterly), *Disasters* (quarterly).

Royal African Society: SOAS University of London, 10 Thornhaugh St, London, WC1H 0XG; tel. (20) 7074-5176; e-mail ras@soas.ac.uk; internet royalafricansociety.org; f. 1901; Chair. ARUNMA OTEH; Dir Dr NICHOLAS WESTCOTT; publs include *African Affairs* (quarterly), *African Arguments* (monthly).

Royal Institute of International Affairs (Chatham House): 10 St James's Sq., London, SW1Y 4LE; tel. (20) 7957-5700; e-mail contact@chathamhouse.org; internet www.chathamhouse.org.uk; f. 1920; independent body, which aims to promote the study and understanding of international affairs; Chair. Sir NIGEL SHEINWALD; Dir and CEO BRONWEN MADDOX; publs include *International Affairs* (6 a year), *The World Today* (6 a year), *Journal of Cyber Policy* (3 a year), *Expert Perspectives*.

School of International Development: University of East Anglia, Norwich Research Park, Norwich, NR4 7TJ; tel. (1603) 456161; e-mail dev.general@uea.ac.uk; internet www.uea.ac.uk/dev; f. 1967; library of over 800,000 books and 97,500 periodicals; Head Prof. LAURA CAMFIELD.

SOAS University of London: Thornhaugh St, Russell Sq., London, WC1H 0XG; tel. (20) 7637-2388; e-mail press@soas.ac.uk; internet www.soas.ac.uk; f. 1916 as School of Oriental and African Studies, adopted present name in 2013; research and expertise in Africa, Asia and the Middle East; library of over 1.5m. volumes, periodicals and audiovisual materials in 400 languages; Dir Prof. ADAM HABIB; publs include *The Bulletin* (3 a year), *Journal of African Law* (3 a year).

UNITED STATES OF AMERICA

Action Africa Inc: 2903 Mills Ave, NE, Washington, DC 20018; tel. (202) 529-8350; e-mail info@africaaction.org; internet www .africaaction.org; f. 2000; supports political, economic and social justice in Africa and, through the provision of information and analysis, aims to encourage positive US and international policies on African issues; Pres. Dr CHRIS N. EGBULEM.

Africa-America Institute: 1 Grand Central Pl., 60 E 42nd St, Suite 1700, New York, NY 10165-6222; tel. (212) 949-5666; e-mail aainy@ aaionline.org; internet www.aaionline.org; f. 1953; organizes training programmes and offers devt assistance; Pres. and CEO KOFI APPENTENG.

Africa Center for Strategic Studies: National Defense University, 300 Fifth Ave, Bldg 20, Fort Lesley J. McNair, Washington, DC 20319-5066; tel. (202) 685-6813; e-mail isacoffj@ndu.edu; internet africacenter.org; f. 1999; supports the devt of US strategic policy towards Africa by providing academic programmes, fostering awareness of and dialogue on US strategic priorities and African security issues; Dir AMANDA J. DORY.

African Studies Association (ASA): c/o African Studies Asscn, Rutgers University, The State University, Livingston Campus, 54 Joyce Kilmer Ave, Piscataway, NJ 08854-8045; tel. (848) 445-8173; e-mail secretariat@africanstudies.org; internet africanstudies.org; f. 1957; Pres. OUSSEINA ALIDOU; Exec. Dir ALIX SABA (acting); publs include *African Studies Review* (3 a year), *ASA News* (biannual), *History in Africa* (annual/biannual).

African Studies Center (ASC): Boston University, 232 Bay State Rd, Boston, MA 02215; tel. (617) 353-7303; e-mail ascinfo@bu.edu; internet www.bu.edu/africa; f. 1953; research and teaching on archaeology, African languages, anthropology, economics, history, geography and political science of Africa; library of 200,000 vols; Dir MARK C. STORELLA; publs include *International Journal of African Historical Studies* (3 a year), working papers, discussion papers.

African Studies Center: Michigan State University, 427 N Shaw Lane, Rm 100, East Lansing, MI 48824; tel. (517) 353-1700; e-mail africa@msu.edu; internet africa.isp.msu.edu; f. 1960; offers instruction in 30 African languages; library of approx. 270,000 vols, periodicals, maps, films, archives, and microform units; Dir Dr JAMIE MONSON; publs include *African Rural and Urban Studies* (3 a year), *Northeast African Studies* (biannual).

African Studies Program: 1 Ohio University, Yamada Int. House, Athens, OH 45701; tel. (740) 593-1832; e-mail african.studies@ohio .edu; internet www.ohio.edu/cis/african; African politics, education, economics, geography, community health, anthropology, languages, literature, philosophy and history; Dir Dr GHIRMAI NEGASH.

African Studies Program: University of Wisconsin-Madison, 205 Ingraham Hall, 1155 Observatory Dr., Madison, WI 53706; tel. (608) 262-2380; e-mail asp@africa.wisc.edu; internet africa.wisc.edu; library of over 500,000 vols and serials and 270,000 monographs; Dir LUÍS MADUREIRA; publs include *African Economic History* (annual), *Ghana Studies* (annual), monograph series and rare language guides.

Brookings Institution: 1775 Massachusetts Ave, NW, Washington, DC 20036-2188; tel. (202) 797-6000; e-mail media@brookings .edu; internet www.brookings.edu; f. 1916; research, education, and publishing in economics, govt and foreign policy; Co-Chair GLENN HUTCHINS, SUZANNE NORA JOHNSON; Pres. AMY LIU (acting); publs include *Brookings Papers on Economic Activity* (biannual), *Economia* (biannual).

Center for African Studies (CAS): Stanford University, 615 Crothers Way, 100 Encina Commons, Stanford, CA 94305-6045; tel. (650) 736-6253; e-mail africanstudies@stanford.edu; internet africanstudies.stanford.edu; f. 1963; African languages, society, culture, foreign policy and social and behavioural sciences; Dir JOEL CARBITA; Assoc. Dir LAURA HUBBARD.

Center for African Studies: University of Florida, 427 Grinter Hall, 1523 Union Rd, Gainesville, FL 32611; tel. (352) 392-2183; e-mail agoldmn@ufl.edu; internet africa.ufl.edu; Dir Dr ALIOUNE SOW (acting); Assoc. Dir TODD H. LEEDY; publs include *African Studies Quarterly*, *CAS Weekly Bulletin*, *African Business Update* (biweekly).

Center for African Studies: University of Illinois 125 Coble Hall, 801 S Wright St, Champaign, IL 61820; tel. (217) 333-6335; e-mail african@illinois.edu; internet afrst.illinois.edu; f. 1970; Dir TERESA ANN BARNES; publ. *Habari Newsletter*.

Center for International Studies (CIS): Massachusetts Institute of Technology, 77 Massachusetts Ave, E40-400, Cambridge, MA 02139-4307; tel. (617) 253-8093; e-mail cis-info@mit.edu; internet cis.mit.edu; f. 1951; Dir RICHARD J. SAMUELS; publ. *précis* (biannual).

Council on Foreign Relations (CFR): 58 East 68th St, New York, NY 10065; tel. (212) 434-9400; e-mail communications@cfr.org; internet www.cfr.org; f. 1921; Pres. RICHARD N. HAASS; publs include *Foreign Affairs* (bimonthly) and *Backgrounders*.

Harvard University Center for African Studies: 1280 Massachusetts Ave, 3rd Floor, Cambridge, MA 02138; tel. (617) 495-5265; internet africa.harvard.edu; f. 1969 as Cttee on African Studies; research and teaching on topics related to Africa; Dir EMMANUEL K. AKYEAMPONG.

Human Rights Watch: 350 Fifth Ave, 34th Floor, New York, NY 10118-3299; tel. (212) 290-4700; e-mail hrwnyc@hrw.org; internet www.hrw.org; f. 1978 as Helsinki Watch; Exec. Dir TIRANA HASSAN (acting).

Hutchins Center for African and African American Research: 104 Mount Auburn St, 3R, Cambridge, MA 02138; tel. (617) 495-8508; internet hutchinscenter.fas.harvard.edu; research on the history and culture of people of African descent across the world, forum for collaboration and the ongoing exchange of ideas; art exhibitions, publications, research projects, archives, readings, conferences, and new media initiatives; part of Harvard Univ; Dir Prof. HENRY LOUIS GATES, Jr; Exec. Dir ABBY WOLF.

Institute of World Affairs (IWA): 2445 M St, NW, Washington, DC 20037; tel. (571) 214-5293; e-mail info@iwa.org; internet www.iwa .org; f. 1924; conducts seminars on international issues; Pres. Dr HRACH GREGORIAN; publs include monographs and opinion pieces.

James S. Coleman African Studies Center: University of California, 10244 Bunche Hall, 405 Hilgard Ave, Los Angeles, CA 90095-1310; internet www.international.ucla.edu/asc; f. 1959; Co-Dirs ANDREW APTER, HAROLD TORRENCE; publs include *African Arts* (quarterly), *UFAHAMU* (quarterly), *Marcus Garvey Papers*.

John L. Warfield Center for African and African American Studies (WCAAAS): University of Texas, 210 W 24th St, Austin, TX 78705; tel. (512) 471-1784; e-mail blackstudies@austin.utexas.edu; internet liberalarts.utexas.edu/caaas; f. 1969; Dir MINKAH MAKALANI.

Princeton Institute for International and Regional Studies: Louis A. Simpson International Bldg, Princeton University, Princeton, NJ 08544; tel. (609) 258-7497; e-mail piirs@princeton.edu; internet piirs.princeton.edu; f. 2003; Dir DEBORAH J. YASHAR; publ. *World Politics* (quarterly).

Princeton School of Public and International Affairs: Bendheim Hall, Princeton University, Princeton, NJ 08540; tel. (609) 258-5633; e-mail extaff@princeton.edu; internet wws.princeton.edu; f. 1930; fmrly Woodrow Wilson School of Public and International Affairs; present name adopted in 2020; Dean AMANEY A. JAMAL.

Schomburg Center for Research in Black Culture: 515 Malcolm X Blvd, New York, NY 10037; tel. (917) 275-6975; e-mail scgenref@nypl.org; internet www.nypl.org/locations/schomburg; f. 1925; a research unit of the New York Public Library; Dir JOY L. BIVINS; publ. *Africana Heritage* (newsletter).

SELECT BIBLIOGRAPHY (BOOKS)

See also bibliographies at end of relevant chapters in Part Two.

Abdulahi, A. *Governance and Internal Wars in Sub-Saharan Africa: Exploring the Relationship*. London, Adonis & Abbey Publishers, 2007.

Abegunrin, O. *Africa in Global Politics in the Twenty-First Century: A Pan-African Perspective*. London, Palgrave Macmillan, 2013.

Abrahamsen, R. *Conflict and Security in Africa*. Woodbridge, James Currey, 2013.

Achebe, C. *Africa: Altered States, Ordinary Miracles*. London, Portobello Books Ltd, 2008.

Adebajo, A., and Rashid, I. (Eds). *West Africa's Security Challenges: Building Peace in a Troubled Region*. Boulder, CO, Lynne Rienner Publishers, 2004.

Adebajo, A., and Whiteman, K. (Eds). *The EU and Africa: From Eurafrique to Afro-Europa*. New York, Columbia University Press, 2012.

Adebanwi, W. (Ed.). *The Political Economy of Everyday Life in Africa: Beyond the Margins*. Woodbridge, James Currey, 2017.

Everyday State and Democracy in Africa: Ethnographic Encounters Athens, OH, Ohio University Press, 2022.

Adejumobi, S. (Ed.). *Democratic Renewal in Africa: Trends and Discourses*. New York, Palgrave Macmillan, 2015.

Adetula, V., Bereketeab, R., and Obi, C. (Eds). *Regional Economic Communities and Peacebuilding in Africa: Lessons from ECOWAS and IGAD*. Abingdon, Routledge, 2020.

Affi, L., Tønnessen, L., and Tripp, A. M. (Eds). *Women & Peacebuilding in Africa*. Martlesham, Boydell & Brewer, 2021.

Agence Française de Développement and Dunod Editeur. *Atlas of Africa: New Perspectives on the Continent*. Abingdon, Routledge, 2021.

Agyeman, O. *Africa's Persistent Vulnerable Link: Global Politics*. New York, New York University Press, 2001.

The Failure of Grassroots Pan-Africanism: The Case of the All-African Trade Union Federation. Lanham, MD, Lexington Books, 2003.

Ahluwalia, P., Bethleham, L., and Ginio, R. (Eds). *Violence and Non-Violence in Africa*. Abingdon, Routledge, 2007.

Airewele, P. S., and Endozie, R. K. *Reframing Contemporary Africa: Politics, Economics, and Culture in the Global Era*. Washington, DC, CQ Press, 2010.

Ajakaiye, D. O., and Oyejide, T. A. (Eds). *Trade Infrastructure and Economic Development*. Abingdon, Routledge, 2011.

Akeya Agnango, G. (Ed.). *Issues and Trends in Contemporary African Politics*. New York, Peter Lang, 2003.

Alao, A. *Natural Resources and Conflict in Africa: The Tragedy of Endowment*. Rochester, NY, University of Rochester Press, 2015.

Amoah, M. *Nationalism, Globalization, and Africa*. London, Palgrave Macmillan, 2011.

Anderson, D., and Rolandsen, Ø. (Eds). *Politics and Violence in Eastern Africa: The Struggles of Emerging States*. Abingdon, Routledge, 2017.

Andrews, N., Khalema, N., and Assié-Lumumba, N. (Eds). *Millennium Development Goals (MDGs) in Retrospect: Africa's Development Beyond 2015*. Berlin, Springer, 2015

Anseeuw, W., and Alden, C. (Eds). *The Struggle over Land in Africa: Conflicts, Politics & Change*. Cape Town, HSRC Press, 2010.

Arriola, L., Johnson, M., and Phillips, M. (Eds). *Women and Power in Africa Aspiring, Campaigning, and Governing*. Oxford, Oxford University Press, 2021.

Aryeetey, E., Devarajan, S., Kanbur, R., and Kasekende, L. (Eds). *The Oxford Companion to the Economics of Africa*. Oxford, OUP, 2012.

Aryeetey, E., and Nissanke, M. *Financial Integration and Development: Liberalization and Reform in Sub-Saharan Africa*. London, Routledge, 1998.

Asante, M. K. *The History of Africa: The Quest for Eternal Harmony*. London, Routledge, 2007.

Asante, S. K. *Regionism and Africa's Development*. London, Palgrave Macmillan, 1997.

Ascher, W., and Mirovitskaya N. (Eds). *The Economic Roots of Conflict and Cooperation in Africa (Politics, Economics, and Inclusive Development)*. New York, Palgrave Macmillan, 2016.

Assensoh, A. B., and Alex-Assensoh, Y. M. *African History and Politics*. London, Palgrave Macmillan, 2003.

Ayittey, G. B. N. *Africa Unchained*. New York, Palgrave Macmillan, 2005.

Bachelard, J. *Governance Reform in Africa: International and Domestic Pressures and Counter-Pressures*. Abingdon, Routledge, 2016.

Badri, B., and Tripp, A. M. *Women's Activism in Africa: Struggles for Rights and Representation*. London, Zed Books, 2017

Bakut, B. T., and Dutt, S. *Africa at the Millennium*. London, Palgrave Macmillan, 2000.

Banham, M. (Ed.). *Southern Africa*. Oxford, James Currey, 2004.

Banini, D. *Geopolitical Political Rivalries for Africa's Natural Resources: West and East Collision in Africa*. Munich, GRIN, 2013.

Barrett, C. B., Little, P., and Carter, M. (Eds). *Understanding and Reducing Persistent Poverty in Africa*. London, Routledge, 2007.

Bassey, C., and Oshita, O. (Eds). *Conflict Resolution, Identity Crisis, and Development in Africa*. Lagos, Malthouse Press, 2007.

Bayart, J.-F. *The State in Africa: The Politics of the Belly*. 2nd edn. Cambridge, Polity Press, 2009.

État et religion en Afrique Paris, Karthala, 2018.

Bekker, S., Croese, S., and Pieterse, E. (Eds).*Refractions of the National, the Popular and the Global in African Cities*. Cape Town, African Minds, 2021.

Belshaw, D., and Livingstone, I. *Renewing Development in Sub-Saharan Africa*. London, Routledge, 2001.

Benabdallah, L. *Shaping the Future of Power: Knowledge Production and Network-Building in China-Africa Relations*. Ann Arbour, MI, University of Michigan Press, 2020.

Bereketeab, R. (Ed.). *The Horn of Africa: Intra-State and Inter-State Conflicts and Security*. London, Pluto Press, 2013.

Self-Determination and Secession in Africa: The Post-Colonial State. Abingdon, Routledge, 2014.

National Liberation Movements as Government in Africa. Abingdon, Routledge, 2017.

Berger, I., and White, E. F. *Women in Sub-Saharan Africa: Restoring Women to History*. Bloomington, IN, Indiana University Press, 1999.

Berkeley, B. *The Graves Are Not Yet Full: Race, Tribe and Power in the Heart of Africa*. Oxford, Basic Books, 2003.

Besada, H. G. (Ed.). *Governing Natural Resources for Africa's Development*. Abingdon, Routledge, 2016.

Bhalla, S. S. *Imagine There's No Country: Poverty, Inequality and Growth in the Era of Globalization*. Washington, DC, Institute for International Economics, 2002.

Binns, T., Dixon, A., and Nel, E. *Africa: Diversity and Development*. Abingdon, Routledge, 2012.

Bleck, J., and van de Walle, N. (Eds). *Electoral Politics in Africa since 1990: Continuity in Change*. Cambridge, Cambridge University Press, 2016.

Birmingham, D. *The Decolonization of Africa*. Athens, OH, Ohio University Press, 1996.

Bond, P. *Looting Africa: The Economics of Exploitation*. London, Zed Books, 2006.

Booth, D., and Cammack, D. *Governance for Development in Africa: Solving Collective Action Problems*. London, Zed Books, 2013.

Boulden, J. *Dealing with Conflict in Africa*. 2nd edn. New York, Palgrave Macmillan, 2004.

Brass, J. *Allies or Adversaries: NGOs and the State in Africa*. New York, Cambridge University Press, 2016.

Bratton, M. *Voting and Democratic Citizenship in Africa*. Boulder, CO, Lynne Rienner Publishers, 2012.

Brautigam, D. *The Dragon's Gift: The Real Story of China in Africa*. New York, Oxford University Press, 2010.

Brems, E., Corradi G., and Schotsmans, M. (Eds). *International Actors and Traditional Justice in Sub-Saharan Africa: Policies and Interventions in Transitional Justice and Justice Sector Aid*. Cambridge, Intersentia, 2015.

Brett, P., and Gissel, L. E. *Africa and the Backlash Against International Courts*. London, Zed Books, 2020.

Brioni, S., and Gulema, S. (Eds). *The Horn of Africa and Italy: Colonial, Postcolonial and Transnational Cultural Encounters*. New York, Peter Lang, 2018.

Broadman, H. G. *Africa's Silk Road: China and India's New Economic Frontier*. Washington, DC, World Bank Publications, 2007.

Brosig, M. (Ed.). *Cooperative Peacekeeping in Africa: Exploring Regime Complexity*. Abingdon, Routledge, 2015.

Brune, S., et al. *Africa and Europe: Relations of Two Continents in Transition*. Hamburg, LIT Verlag, 1994.

Burgis, T. *The Looting Machine: Warlords, Oligarchs, Corporations, Smugglers, and the Theft of Africa's Wealth*. New York, PublicAffairs, 2015.

Calamitsis, E. A. *Adjustment and Growth in Sub-Saharan Africa*. Washington, DC, IMF Publications, 2000.

Calderisi, R. *The Trouble with Africa: Why Foreign Aid Isn't Working*. New York, Palgrave Macmillan, 2006.

Carey, K., Gupta, S., and Jacoby, U. *Sub-Saharan Africa: Forging New Trade Links with Asia*. Washington, DC, IMF Publication Services, 2007.

Carmody, P. *Neoliberalism, Civil Society and Security in Africa*. London, Palgrave Macmillan, 2007.

    The New Scramble for Africa. Cambridge, Polity Press, 2011.

    The Rise of the BRICS in Africa: The Geopolitics of South-South Relations. London, Zed Books, 2013.

Carmody, P., Kragelund, P., and Reboredo, R. *Africa's Shadow Rise: China and the Mirage of African Economic Development*. London, Zed Books, 2020.

Carrier, N., and Klantschnig, G. *Africa and the War on Drugs*. London, Zed Books, 2012.

Chabal, P., et al. *A History of Postcolonial Lusophone Africa*. London, Hurst and Co., 2002.

Chafer, T., and Cumming, G. (Eds). *From Rivalry to Partnership?: New Approaches to the Challenges of Africa*. London, Ashgate Publishing, 2011.

Chafer, T., and Keese, A. (Eds). *Francophone Africa at Fifty*. Manchester, Manchester University Press, 2013.

Chan, S. *African Political Thought: An Intellectual History of the Quest for Freedom*. London, Hurst & Co., 2021.

Chanie, P., and Mihyo, P. (Eds). *Thirty Years of Public Sector Reforms in Africa. Selected Country Experiences*. Kampala, Fountain Publishers, 2013.

Charbonneau, B. *France and the New Imperialism: Security Policy in Sub-Saharan Africa*. Abingdon, Routledge, 2016.

Cheeseman, N. *Democracy in Africa: Successes, Failures, and the Struggle for Political Reform*. New York, Cambridge University Press, 2015.

Cheeseman, N. (Ed.) *The Oxford Encyclopedia of African Politics*. Oxford, Oxford University Press, 2020.

Cheeseman, N., Lynch, G., and Willis, J. *The Moral Economy of Elections in Africa: Democracy, Voting and Virtue*. Cambridge, Cambridge University Press, 2020.

Cheeseman, N., Anderson, D., and Scheibler, A. (Eds). *Routledge Handbook of African Politics*. Abingdon, Routledge, 2013.

Cheru, F., and Obi, C. (Eds). *The Rise of China and India in Africa: Challenges, Opportunities and Critical Interventions*. London, Zed Books, 2010.

Cheru, F., and Modi, R. *Agricultural Development and Food Security in Africa*. London, Zed Books, 2013.

Chiwandamira, L., and Makaula, M. (Eds). *Perspectives on African Governance*. Cape Town, Institute for Democracy in South Africa, 2006.

Choucane-Verdier, A. *Libéralisation financière et croissance économique: le cas de l'Afrique subsaharienne*. Paris, L'Harmattan, 2001.

Chrétien, J.-P. *The Great Lakes of Africa: 2,000 Years of History*. New York, Zone, 2003.

Christiaensen, L., and Demery, L. *Down to Earth: Agriculture and Poverty Reduction in Africa*. Washington, DC, World Bank Publications, 2007.

Clapham, C. *Africa and the International System: The Politics of State Survival*. Cambridge, Cambridge University Press, 1996.

    The Horn of Africa: State Formation and Decay. London, Hurst & Co., 2017.

Clarke, D. *Africa: Crude Continent: The Struggle for Africa's Oil Prize*. London, Profile Books, 2010.

    Africa's Future: Darkness to Destiny. London, Profile Books, 2014.

Clarke, J. F. *Political Reform in Francophone Africa*. Boulder, CO, Westview Press, 1996.

Cole, R., and De Blij, H. J. *Survey of Sub-Saharan Africa: A Regional Geography*. New York, Oxford University Press Inc, 2006.

Collins, R. O., and Burns, J. M. *A History of Sub-Saharan Africa*. Cambridge, Cambridge University Press, 2007.

Cooke, J., and Goldwyn, D. *Africa's New Energy Producers: Making the Most of Emerging Opportunities*. Washington, DC, Center for Strategic & International Studies, 2015.

Cooper, F. *Africa Since 1940: The Past of the Present*. Cambridge, Cambridge University Press, 2002.

Coppedge, M., et al (Eds). *Varieties of Democracy: Measuring Two Centuries of Political Change*. Cambridge, Cambridge University Press, 2020.

Coquery-Vidrovitch, C. *African Women: A Modern History*. Boulder, CO, Westview Press, 1997.

    History of African Cities South of the Sahara. Princeton, NJ, Markus Wiener, 2006.

Cotula, L. *The Great African Land Grab?* London, Zed Books, 2013.

Coulibaly, S. *Coups d'Etat: Légitimation et démocraties en Afrique*. Paris, L'Harmattan, 2012.

Cowan, M., and Laakso, L. *Multiparty Elections in Africa*. Oxford, James Currey, 2002.

Cramer, C., Sender, J., and Oqubay, A. (Eds). *African Economic Development: Evidence, Theory, Policy*. Oxford, Oxford University Press, 2020.

Cruise O'Brien, D., et al. (Eds). *Contemporary West African States*. Cambridge, Cambridge University Press, 1990.

Curtin, P., et al. *African History*. London, Longman, 1995.

Dago, F. *Politics, Economics and Development in Sub-Saharan Africa*. Twickenham, Athena Press, 2004.

David, J. (Ed.). *Africa and the War on Terrorism*. London, Ashgate Publishing, 2007.

Davids, Y., et al. *Measuring Democracy and Human Rights in Southern Africa*. Uppsala, Nordic Africa Institute, 2002.

Davidson, B. *Let Freedom Come*. Boston, MA, Little, Brown & Co, 1989.

    The Black Man's Burden: Africa and the Curse of the Nation-State. Oxford, James Currey, 1992.

    African Civilization Revisited. Trenton, NJ, Africa World Press, 1993.

    Africa in History: Themes and Outlines. London, Simon and Schuster, 1995.

Debrun, X., Masson, P. R., and Pattillo, C. A. *Monetary Union in West Africa: Who Might Gain, Who Might Lose, and Why?* Washington, DC, IMF Publication Services, 2003.

Decalo, S. *Coups and Military Rule in Africa: Motivations and Constraints*. Newhaven, CT, Yale University Press, 1990.

Decker, C., and McMahon, E. *The Idea of Development in Africa: A History*. Cambridge, Cambridge University Press, 2020.

Deegan, H. *Africa Today: Culture, Economics, Religion, Security*. Abingdon, Routledge, 2009.

Dent, C. M. (Ed.). *China and Africa Development Relations*. Abingdon, Routledge, 2011.

Derrick, J. *Africa's 'Agitators': Militant Anti-Colonialism in Africa and the West, 1918–1939*. New York, Columbia University Press, 2013.

Devereux, S., and Getu, M. (Eds). *Informal and Formal Social Protection Systems in Sub-Saharan Africa*. Kampala, Fountain Publishers, 2013.

De Waal, A. *Famine Crimes: Politics and the Disaster Relief Industry in Africa*. Oxford, James Currey, 1997.

Diakité, T. *50 ans après, l'Afrique* Paris, Arléa, 2011.

Diamond, L., and Plattner, M. F. (Eds). *Nationalism, Ethnic Conflict and Democracy*. Baltimore, MD, Johns Hopkins University Press, 1997.

Diawara, M. *In Search of Africa*. Cambridge, MA, Harvard University Press, 1998.

Dibie, R. (Ed.). *Non-governmental Organizations and Sustainable Development in Sub-Saharan Africa*. Lanham, MD, Lexington Books, 2007.

Dickovick, J. T., and Wunsch, J. S. (Eds). *Decentralization in Africa: The Paradox of State Strength*. Boulder, CO, Lynne Rienner Publishers, 2014.

Dinar, A., Hassan, R., Mendelsohn, R., Benhin, J., et al. *Climate Change and Agriculture in Africa: Impact Assessment and Adaptation Strategies*. London, Earthscan, 2008.

Diop, M.-C., and Diouf, M. *Les Figures du politique en Afrique: Des pouvoirs hérités aux pouvoirs élus*. Paris, Éditions Karthala, 1999.

Diouf, M. *L'Afrique dans la mondialisation*. Paris, L'Harmattan, 2002.

Dowden, R. *Africa: Altered States, Ordinary Miracles*. London, Portobello Books, 2007.

Doss, A. *A Peacekeeper in Africa: Learning from UN Interventions in Other People's Wars*. Boulder, CO, Lynne Rienner, 2020.

Dwyer, M., and Molony, T. (Eds). *Social Media and Politics in Africa: Democracy, Censorship and Security*. London, Zed Books, 2019.

Ecker, O. *Economics of Micronutrient Malnutrition: The Demand for Nutrients in Sub-Saharan Africa*. New York, Peter Lang, 2009.

Ehui, F. T. *L'Afrique noire: De la superpuissance au sous-développement*. Abidjan, Nouvelles Editions Ivoiriennes, 2002.

Elischer, S. *Political Parties in Africa: Ethnicity and Party Formation*. Cambridge, Cambridge University Press, 2013.

Salafism and Political Order in Africa. Cambridge, Cambridge University Press, 2021.

Ellis, S. *Africa Now: People, Policies, Institutions*. Oxford, James Currey, 1996.

Seasons of Rains: Africa and the World. London, Hurst & Co., 2011.

Endo, M., Neocosmos, M., and Onoma, A.K. (Eds). *African Politics of Survival: Extraversion and Informality in the Contemporary World*. Bamenda, Langaa Research and Publishing Common Initiative Group, 2021

Engel, U., and Gomes Porto, J. *Africa's New Peace and Security Architecture (Global Security in a Changing World)*. London, Ashgate Publishing, 2010.

Englebert, P. *State Legitimacy and Development in Africa*. Boulder, CO, Lynne Rienner Publishers, 2000.

Epprecht, M. *Sexuality and Social Justice in Africa: Rethinking Homophobia and Forging Resistance*. London, Zed Books, 2013.

Estache, A., and Wodon, Q. *Infrastructure and Poverty in Sub-Saharan Africa*. Washington, DC, World Bank Publications, 2007.

Everill, B., and Kaplan, J. (Eds) *The History and Practice of Humanitarian Intervention and Aid in Africa*. Basingstoke, Palgrave Macmillan, 2013.

Eyene-Mba, J. *Afrique sur le chemin de la croissance et de l'évolution*. Paris, L'Harmattan, 2003.

Fage, J. (updated by Tordoff, W.). *A History of Africa*. London, Frank Cass, 2001.

Falola, T. *Nationalism and African Intellectuals*. Rochester, NY, University of Rochester Press, 2001.

Falola, T., and Achberger, J. (Eds). *The Political Economy of Development and Underdevelopment in Africa*. Abingdon, Routledge, 2013.

Falola, T., and Essien, K. *Pan-Africanism, and the Politics of African Citizenship and Identity*. Abingdon, Routledge, 2013.

Falola, T., and Hamel, N. (Eds). *Disability in Africa Inclusion, Care, and the Ethics of Humanity*. Rochester, NY, University of Rochester Press, 2021.

Falola, T., and Kalu, K. *Africa and Globalization: Challenges of Governance and Creativity*. London, Palgrave Macmillan, 2018.

Falola, T., and Mbah, E. *Contemporary Africa: Challenges and Opportunities*. New York, Palgrave Macmillan, 2014.

Falola, T., and Salau, M. B. (Eds) *Africa in Global History A Handbook*. Berlin, De Gruyter Oldenburg, 2021.

Falola, T., and Usman, A. (Eds). *Movements, Borders, and Identities in Africa*. Rochester, NY, University of Rochester Press, 2009.

Ferguson, J. *Global Shadows: Africa in the Neoliberal World Order*. Durham, NC, Duke University Press, 2006.

Finaldi, G. M. *Italian National Identity in the Scramble for Africa*. New York, Peter Lang, 2009.

Fisher. J. *East Africa after Liberation: Conflict, Security and the State since the 1980s*. Cambridge, Cambridge University Press, 2020.

Fisher. J., and Wilén, N. *African Peacekeeping*. Cambridge, Cambridge University Press, 2022.

Francis, D. J. *Uniting Africa: Building Regional Peace and Security Systems*. London, Ashgate Publishing, 2006.

French, H. W. *A Continent for the Taking: The Tragedy and Hope of Africa*. New York, Alfred A. Knopf, 2004.

China's Second Continent: How a Million Migrants Are Building a New Empire in Africa. New York, Alfred A. Knopf, 2014.

Born in Blackness: Africa, Africans, and the Making of the Modern World, 1471 to the Second World War. New York, Liveright, 2021.

Freund, B. *The Making of Contemporary Africa*. London, Palgrave Macmillan, 1998.

Fuller, B. *Government Confronts Culture: The Struggle for Local Democracy in Southern Africa*. London, Garland Science, 1999.

Funke, N. *The New Partnership for Africa's Development (NEPAD): Opportunities and Challenges*. Washington, DC, IMF Institute, 2003.

Gabay, C., and Death, C. *Critical Perspectives on African Politics*. Abingdon, Routledge, 2014.

Gassama, M. (Ed.). *50 ans après, quelle indépendance pour l'Afrique?* Paris, Philippe Rey, 2010.

Gbaguidi, N. A. (Ed.). *La Réparation du Dommage Ecologique dans l'Espace Francophone: Cas du Bénin, de la Roumanie, du Sénégal et du Togo*. Paris, L'Harmattan, 2016.

Gebissa, E. *Leaf of Allah: Khat and Agricultural Transformation*. Oxford, James Currey, 2005.

Geda, A. *Finance and Trade in Africa*. London, Palgrave Macmillan, 2002.

Ghaia, D. *Renewing Social and Economic Progress in Africa*. London, Palgrave Macmillan, 2000.

Gidron, Y. *Israel in Africa Security, Migration, Interstate Politics*. London, Zed Books, 2020.

Gil, N., Stafford, A., and Musonda, I. (Eds). *Duality by Design: The Global Race to Build Africa's Infrastructure*. Cambridge, Cambridge University Press, 2019.

Gilbert, E., and Reynolds, J. *Africa in World History*. 2nd edn. Harlow, Prentice Hall, 2007.

Glawion, T. *The Security Arena in Africa: Local Order-Making in the Central African Republic, Somaliland, and South Sudan*. Cambridge, Cambridge University Press, 2020.

Gow, J., Olonisakin, F., and Dijxhoorn, E. (Eds). *West African Militancy and Violence*. Abingdon, Routledge, 2013.

Grilli, M., and Gerits, F. (Eds). *Visions of African Unity: New Perspectives on the History of Pan-Africanism and African Unification Projects*. Cham, Palgrave Macmillan, 2021.

Grosh, B., and Mukandala, R. *State-Owned Enterprises in Africa*. Boulder, CO, Lynne Rienner Publishers, 1994.

Gulliver, P. H. (Ed.). *Tradition and Transition in East Africa*. London, Routledge, 2004.

Gumede, W. *The Democracy Gap: Africa's Wasted Years*. London, Zed Books, 2012.

Gunning, J. W., and Oostendorp, R. *Industrial Change in Africa*. London, Palgrave Macmillan, 2001.

Gyimah-Boadi, E. *Democratic Reform in Africa: The Quality of Progress*. Boulder, CO, Lynne Rienner Publishers, 2004.

Hall, R., Scoones, I., and Tsikata, D. *Africa's Land Rush: Rural Livelihoods and Agrarian Change*. Woodbridge, James Currey, 2015.

Harel, X., and Hofnung, T. *Le scandale des biens mal acquis. Enquête sur les milliards volés de la Françafrique*. Paris, La Découverte, 2011.

de Haas, M., and Frankema, E. (Eds). *Migration in Africa Shifting Patterns of Mobility from the 19th to the 21st Century*. Abingdon, Routledge, 2022.

Hargreaves, J. D. *Decolonization in Africa*. 2nd edn, Abingdon, Routledge, 2016.

Harmon, S. A. *Terror and Insurgency in the Sahara-Sahel Region: Corruption, Contraband, Jihad and the Mali War of 2012–2013*. Abingdon, Routledge, 2016.

Harms, R. *Land of Tears*. New York, Basic Books, 2019.

Harris, G. (Ed.). *Achieving Security in Sub-Saharan Africa: Cost Effective Alternatives to the Military*. Pretoria, Institute for Security Studies, 2004.

Havinden, M., and Meredith, D. *Colonialism and Development: Britain and its Tropical Colonies*. London, Routledge, 1993.

Havnevik, K., et al. (Eds). *African Agriculture and the World Bank: Development or Impoverishment?* Uppsala, Nordic Africa Institute, 2007.

Heilbrunn, J. R. *Oil, Democracy, and Development in Africa*. New York, Cambridge University Press, 2014.

Hentz, J. J. (Ed.). *Routledge Handbook of African Security*. Abingdon, Routledge, 2013.

Herbst, J. *States and Power in Africa: Comparative Lessons in Authority and Control*. Princeton, NJ, Princeton University Press, 2000.

Herbst, J., and Mills, G. *The Future of Africa: A New Order in Sight?* Oxford, Oxford University Press, 2003.

Africa's Third Liberation. Johannesburg, Penguin, 2012.

Hiscox, M. J. *International Trade and Political Conflict: Commerce, Coalitions and Mobility*. Princeton, NJ, Princeton University Press, 2002.

Hoag, H. J. *Developing the Rivers of East and West Africa: An Environmental History*. London, Continuum Publishing Corpn, 2013.

Honohan, P., and Beck, T. *Making Finance Work for Africa*. Washington, DC, World Bank Publications, 2007.

Hope, K. R., and Chikulo, B. C. *Corruption and Development in Africa*. London, Palgrave Macmillan, 1999.

House-Soremekun, B., and Falola, T. *Globalization and Sustainable Development in Africa*. Rochester, NY, University of Rochester Press, 2016.

Howe, H. M. *Ambiguous Order: Military Forces in African States*. Boulder, CO, Lynne Rienner Publishers, 2005.

Huband, M. *The Skull beneath the Skin: Africa and the Cold War*. Boulder, CO, Westview Press, 2002.

Hugon, P. *La zone franc à l'heure de l'Euro*. Paris, Editions Karthala, 1999.

Hyden, G., and Bratton, M. (Eds) *Governance and Politics in Africa*. Boulder, CO, Lynne Rienner Publishers, 1992.

Jackson, D. R, *US Foreign Policy in The Horn of Africa: From Colonialism to Terrorism*. Abingdon, Routledge, 2018.

Jackson, R., and Rosberg, C. *Personal Rule in Black Africa*. Berkeley, CA, University of California Press, 1982.

Jackson, T. *Management and Change in Africa*. London, Frank Cass, 2004.

Jacquemot, P. *L'Afrique des possibles, les défis de l'émergence*. Paris, Karthala, 2016.

Jamieson, D. T., et al. (Eds). *Disease and Mortality in Sub-Saharan Africa*. 2nd edn. Washington, DC, World Bank Publications, 2006.

Janis, M. *Africa After Modernism: Transitions in Literature, Media, and Philosophy*. London, Routledge, 2007.

Jarpa Dawuni, J. (Ed.) *Gender, Judging and the Courts in Africa*. Abingdon, Routledge, 2021.

Jerven, M. *Poor Numbers: How We Are Misled by African Development Statistics and What To Do About It*. Ithaca, NY, Cornell University Press, 2013.

Africa: Why Economists Get it Wrong. London, Zed Books, 2015.

The Wealth and Poverty of African States: Economic Growth, Living Standards and Taxation since the Late Nineteenth Century. Cambridge, Cambridge University Press, 2021.

Juma, C. *The New Harvest: Agricultural Innovation in Africa*. 2nd edn. Oxford, Oxford University Press, 2015.

Kabbaj, O. *The Challenge of African Development*. Oxford, Oxford University Press, 2003.

Kamate, E. *Quel développement pour l'Afrique?* Mali, Editions Jamana, 1997.

Kane, I., and Mbelle, N. *Towards a People-Driven African Union: Current Obstacles and New Opportunities*. Oxford, Oxfam Publishing/Open Society Institute's Africa Governance Monitoring and Advocacy Project/African Network on Debt and Development, 2007.

Kayizzi-Mugerwa, S., et al. *Towards a New Partnership with Africa*. Uppsala, Nordic Africa Institute, 2000.

Keller, E. J. *Identity, Citizenship, and Political Conflict in Africa*. Bloomington, IN, University of Indiana Press, 2014.

Kelsall, T. *Business, Politics and the State in Africa: Challenging the Orthodoxies on Growth and Transformation*. London, Zed Books, 2013.

Kemper, S. *A Labyrinth of Kingdoms: 10,000 Miles through Islamic Africa*. New York, W. W. Norton & Co, 2012.

Khadiagala, G. (Ed.). *War and Peace in Africa's Great Lakes Region*. London, Palgrave Macmillan, 2017.

Khisa, M., and Day, C. (Eds.). *Rethinking Civil-Military Relations in Africa: Beyond the Coup d'Etat*. Boulder, CO, Lynne Rienner Publishers, 2022.

Kidanu, A., and Kumssa, A. (Eds). *Social Development in Africa*. Nairobi, United Nations Centre for Regional Development Africa Office, 2001.

Kieh, G. K., and Agbese, P. O. (Eds). *Reconstituting the State in Africa*. London, Palgrave Macmillan, 2007.

Reconstructing the Authoritarian State in Africa. Abingdon, Routledge, 2013.

Kingma, K. *Demobilization in Sub-Saharan Africa*. London, Palgrave Macmillan, 2000.

Konaté, M. *L'Afrique noire est-elle maudite?* Paris, Fayard, 2010.

Kornegay, F. A. (Ed.) *Africa and the World: Navigating Shifting Geopolitics*. Johannesburg, Mapungubwe Institute for Strategic Reflection, 2020.

Koser, K. (Ed.). *New African Diasporas*. London, Routledge, 2003.

Kouvouama, A. *Modernité africaine: Les figures du politique et du religieux*. Congo, Editions Paari, 2002.

Kroslak, D. *France's Role in the Rwandan Genocide*. London, Hurst & Co., 2007.

Kwaa Prah, K. *The State of the Nation*. Cape Town, Centre for Advanced Studies of African Society, 2008.

Lamphear, J. *African Military History*. London, Ashgate Publishing, 2007.

Large, D. *China and Africa: The New Era*. Chichester, Wiley, 2021.

Lata, L. *Peacekeeping As State Building: Current Challenges for the Horn of Africa*. Trenton, NJ, Africa World Press, 2011.

Lawrence, P., and Thirtle, C. *Africa and Asia in Comparative Economic Perspective*. London, Palgrave Macmillan, 2001.

Lebeau, Y., Niane, B., Piriou, A., and de Saint Marie, M. *Etat et acteurs émergents en Afrique*. Paris, Editions Karthala, 2003.

Lehman, H. P. *Japan and Africa: Globalization and Foreign Aid in the 21st Century*. Abingdon, Routledge, 2011.

Lekha Sriram, C., Martin-Ortega, O., and Herman, J. (Eds). *Peacebuilding and Rule of Law in Africa: Just Peace?* Abingdon, Routledge, 2010.

Leonard, D. K., and Straus, S. *Africa's Stalled Development: International Causes and Cures*. Boulder, CO, Lynne Rienner Publishers, 2003.

Levine, D. H. and Nagar, D. (Eds). *Region-Building in Africa: Political and Economic Challenges*. Basingstoke, Palgrave Macmillan, 2016.

Le Vine, V. T. *Politics in Francophone Africa*. Boulder, CO, Lynne Rienner Publishers, 2007.

Levitt, J. I. *Illegal Peace in Africa: An Inquiry into the Legality of Power Sharing with Warlords, Rebels, and Junta*. Cambridge, Cambridge University Press, 2012.

Lewis, P. *Africa: Dilemmas of Development and Change*. Boulder, CO, Westview Press, 1998.

Linberg, S. I. *Democracy and Elections in Africa*. Baltimore, MD, Johns Hopkins University Press, 2006.

Lombe, M., and Ochumbo, A. (Eds). *Children and AIDS: Sub-Saharan Africa*. Abingdon, Routledge, 2015.

Lopes, C. *Africa in Transformation: Economic Development in the Age of Doubt*. Cham, Palgrave Macmillan, 2018.

Lugan, B. *Décolonisez l'Afrique!* Paris, Editions Ellipses, 2011.

Lumumba-Kasongo, T. *Political Re-Mapping of Africa: Transnational Ideology and Re-definition of Africa in World Politics*. Lanham, MD, University Press of America, 1993.

The Dynamics of Political and Economic Relations between Africa and the Foreign Powers: A Study in International Relations. Westport, CT, Praeger, 1998.

The Rise of Multipartyism and Democracy in the Context of Contemporary Global Change: The Case of Africa. Westport, CT, Praeger, 1998.

Japan-Africa Relations. New York, Palgrave Macmillan, 2010.

Lumumba-Kasongo, T., Gahama, J. (Eds). *Peace, Security and Post-conflict Reconstruction in the Great Lakes Region of Africa*. Dakar, CODESRIA, 2017.

Lundahl, M. (Ed.). *From Crisis to Growth in Africa*. London, Frank Cass, 2001.

McClendon, G. H., and Riedl, R. B. *From Pews to Politics: Religious Sermons and Political Participation in Africa*. Cambridge, Cambridge University Press, 2019.

McDonald, D. (Ed.). *On Borders: Perspectives on Internal Migration in Southern Africa*. New York, St Martin's Press, 2000.

Machacek, E. *Sustainable Development in Western Anglophone Africa*. Munich, GRIN, 2011.

McNamee, T., and Muyangwa, M. (Eds). *The State of Peacebuilding in Africa: Lessons Learned for Policymakers and Practitioners*. Cham, Palgrave Macmillan, 2021.

Magyar, K. P., and Conteh-Morgan, E. *Peacekeeping in Africa*. London, Palgrave Macmillan, 1998.

Mahadevan, V. *Contemporary African Politics and Development: A Comprehensive Bibliography, 1981–1990*. Boulder, CO, Lynne Rienner Publishers, 1995.

Makgetlaneng, S. *Kwame Nkrumah and the Pan-African Ideal: Debates and Contestations*. Pretoria, Institute for Preservation and Development, 2021.

Makhan, V. *Economic Recovery in Africa*. London, Palgrave Macmillan, 2002.

Makinda, S. M., and Wafula Okumu, F. (Eds). *The African Union: Challenges of Globalization, Security, and Governance*. London, Routledge, 2009.

Mamdami, M., and Wamba dia Wamba, E. *African Studies in Social Movements and Democracy*. Dakar, CODESRIA, 1995.

Mangala, J. *New Security Threats and Crises in Africa: Regional and International Perspectives*. London, Palgrave Macmillan, 2011.

Mangala, J. (Ed.). *Africa and the European Union: A Strategic Partnership*. New York, Palgrave Macmillan, 2013.

Manning, P. *Francophone Sub-Saharan Africa 1880–1995*. Cambridge, Cambridge University Press, 1999.

The African Diaspora: A History Through Culture. New York, Columbia University Press, 2009.

Mano, W. (Ed.). *Racism, Ethnicity and the Media in Africa: Mediating Conflict in the Twenty-First Century*. London, I. B. Tauris, 2015.

Mapako, M., and Mbewe, A. (Eds) *Renewables and Energy for Rural Development in Sub-Saharan Africa*. London, Zed Books, 2013.

Mason, R., and Mabon, S. (Eds). *The Gulf States and the Horn of Africa: Interests, Influences and Instability*. Manchester, Manchester University Press, 2022.

Masson, P., et al. *Monetary Union in West Africa (ECOWAS)*. Washington, DC, IMF Publications, 2001.

Matondi, P. B., Havnevik, K., and Beyene, A. *Biofuels, Land Grabbing and Food Security in Africa*. London, Zed Books, 2011.

Mawere, M., Taranhike, D., and Lessem, R. (Eds). *Nhakanomics: Harvesting Knowledge and Value for Re-generation Through Social Innovation*. Masvingo, Africa Talent Publishers, 2019.

Mawere, M., Chazovachii, B., and Machingura, F. (Eds). *COVID-19 and the Dialectics of Global Pandemics In Africa: Challenges, Opportunities and the Future of the Global Economy in the Face of COVID-19*. Bamenda, Langaa Research and Publishing Common Initiative Group, 2021.

Mazama, A. (Ed.). *Africa in the 21st Century: Toward a New Future*. Abingdon, Routledge, 2007.

Mazibuko, Z. (Ed.). *Epidemics and the Health of African Nations*. Johannesburg, Mapungubwe Institute for Strategic Reflection, 2019.

Medard, J.-F. (Ed.). *Etats d'Afrique Noire: Formation, mécanismes et crises*. Paris, Editions Karthala, 1994.

Mehler, A., Melber, H., and van Walraven, K. (Eds). *Africa Yearbook: Politics, Economy and Society South of the Sahara 2006*. Leiden, Brill, 2007.

Melber, H. *The Rise of Africa's Middle Class: Myths, Realities and Critical Engagements*. London, Zed Books, 2017.

Melber, H., et al. *The New Partnership for African Development (NEPAD): African Perspectives*. Uppsala, Nordic Africa Institute, 2002.

Mengisteab, K., and Hagg, G. (Eds). *Traditional Institutions in Contemporary African Governance*. Abingdon, Routledge, 2017.

Meredith, M. *The Fate of Africa: A History of the Continent Since Independence*. Revised edn. New York, Public Affairs, 2011.

The Fortunes of Africa: A 5,000 Year History of Wealth, Greed and Endeavour. London, Simon & Schuster Ltd, 2014.

Merlin, P. *L'Afrique peut gagner*. Paris, Editions Karthala, 2001.

Migani, G. *La France et l'Afrique sub-saharienne, 1957–1963*. New York, Peter Lang, 2008.

Mills, G. *Expensive Poverty: Why Aid Fails and How it Can Work*. Johannesburg, Pan Macmillan South Africa, 2021.

Mills, G., Herbst, J., Obasanjo, O., and Davis, D. *Making Africa Work: A Handbook*. London, Hurst & Co., 2017.

Mlambo, N. *Violent Conflicts, Fragile Peace: Perspectives on Africa's Security Problems*. London, Adonis & Abbey Publishers, 2007.

Moghalu, K. C. *Emerging Africa: How the Global Economy's 'Last Frontier' Can Prosper and Matter*. London, Penguin, 2014.

Monga, C. *The Anthropology of Anger: Civil Society and Democracy in Africa*. Boulder, CO, Lynne Rienner Publishers, 1996.

Monga, C., and Yifu Lin, J. (Eds). *The Oxford Handbook of Africa and Economics: Volume 1: Context and Concepts*. Oxford, Oxford University Press, 2015.

The Oxford Handbook of Africa and Economics: Volume 2: Policies and Practices. Oxford, Oxford University Press, 2015.

Moorcraft, P. *Total Onslaught: War and Revolution in Southern Africa 1945–2018*. Barnsley, Pen & Sword Military, 2018.

Moss, T. J. *African Development: Making Sense of the Issues and Actors*. Boulder, CO, Lynne Rienner Publishers, 2007.

Moyo, B. *Africa in Global Power Play: Debates, Challenges and Potential Reforms*. London, Adonis & Abbey Publishers, 2007.

Moyo, D. *Dead Aid: Why Aid is Not Working and How There is Another Way for Africa*. London, Penguin, 2009.

Moyo, I., Nshimbi, C. C., and Laine, J. P (Eds). *Migration Conundrums, Regional Integration and Development Africa-Europe Relations in a Changing Global Order*. Singapore, Springer Nature Singapore, 2020.

Muchie, M. (Ed.). *The Making of the African Nation: Pan-Africanism and the African Renaissance*. London, Adonis & Abbey Publishers, 2005.

Mulinge, M. M. and Getu, M. (Eds) *Impacts of Climate Change and Variability on Pastoralist Women in Sub-Saharan Africa*. Kampala, Fountain Publishers, 2013.

Munier, N. *The Political Economy of the Kimberley Process*. Cambridge, Cambridge University Press, 2020.

Murithi, T. *The African Union: Pan-Africanism, Peacebuilding and Development*. London, Ashgate Publishing, 2005.

Murithi, T. (Ed.). *Handbook of Africa's International Relations*. Abingdon, Routledge, 2013.

The Politics of Transitional Justice in the Great Lakes Region of Africa. Johannesburg, Fanele, 2016.

Mwakikagile, G. *Africa at the End of the Twentieth Century: What Lies Ahead*. Dar es Salaam, New Africa Press, 2013.

Mwandosya, M. *Daraja Juu Ya Mto Nile (Bridge Across the Nile)*. Dar es Salaam, E &D Vision Publishing, 2015.

Ncube, M. and Lufumpa, C. (Eds) *The Emerging Middle Class in Africa*. Abingdon, Routledge, 2014.

Ndikumana, L., and Boyce, J. K. *Africa's Odious Debts: How Foreign Loans and Capital Flight Bled a Continent*. London, Zed Books, 2011.

Ndikumana, L., and Boyce, J. K. (Eds). *On the Trail of Capital Flight from Africa: The Takers and the Enablers*. Oxford, Oxford University Press, 2022.

Ndulo, M., and Grieco, M. *Failed and Failing States: The Challenges to African Reconstruction*. Cambridge, Cambridge Scholars Publishing, 2010.

Ndulu, B. J., et al. *The Political Economy of Economic Growth in Africa, 1960–2000*. Cambridge, Cambridge University Press, 2007.

The Political Economy of Economic Growth in Africa, 1960–2000: Volume 2. Cambridge, Cambridge University Press, 2015.

Nhema, A., and Tiyambe Zeleza., P. (Eds). *The Roots of African Conflicts: The Causes and Costs*. Oxford, James Currey, 2008.

The Resolution of African Conflicts: The Management of Conflict Resolution and Post-Conflict Reconstruction. Oxford, James Currey, 2008.

Niang, A. *The Postcolonial African State in Transition: Stateness and Modes of Sovereignty*. London, Rowman and Littlefield, 2018.

Niehof, A., Gabriel, R., and Gillespie, S. (Eds). *AIDS and Rural Livelihoods: Dynamics and Diversity in Sub-Saharan Africa*. Abingdon, Routledge, 2010.

Noman, A., and Stiglitz, J. E. *Industrial Policy and Economic Transformation in Africa*. New York, Columbia University Press, 2015.

Nordic Africa Institute. *Regionalism and Regional Integration in Africa*. Uppsala, Nordic Africa Institute, 2001.

Nugent, P. *Africa Since Independence*. London, Palgrave Macmillan, 2004.

Ohaegbelum, F. U. *U.S. Policy in Postcolonial Africa: Four Case Studies in Conflict Resolution*. New York, Peter Lang, 2004.

Okafor, O. C. *The African Human Rights System, Activist Forces and International Institutions*. Cambridge, Cambridge University Press, 2007.

Okech, A. (Ed.). *Gender, Protests and Political Change in Africa*. Cham, Palgrave Macmillan, 2020.

Okoth, G. P. (Ed.). *Africa at the Beginning of the 21st Century*. Nairobi, University of Nairobi Press, 2000.

Oladejo, M. T., Okoli-Uwajumogu, N., and Tijani, O. A. (Eds). *Social Protection in Africa: A Study of Paradigms and Contexts* Ibadan, Reamsworth Publishing, 2019.

Oliver, R., and Atmore, A. *Africa Since 1800*. 5th edn. Cambridge, Cambridge University Press, 2005.

Oliver, R., and Fage, J. D. *A Short History of Africa*. London, Penguin Books, 1988.

Olowu, D., and Sako, S. (Eds) *Better Governance and Public Policy*. Bloomsfield, CT, Kumarian Press, 2003.

Olukoshi, A. *The Politics of Opposition in Contemporary Africa*. Uppsala, Nordic Africa Institute, 1998.

Olukoshi, A., and Laakso, L. (Eds). *Challenges to the Nation-State in Africa*. Uppsala, Nordic Africa Institute, 1996.

Olutayo, A., and Adeniran, A. (Eds). *Regional Economic Communities: Exploring the Process of Socio-economic Integration in Africa*. Dakar, CODESRIA, 2015.

Omeje, K. (Ed.) *Peacebuilding in Contemporary Africa: In Search of Alternative Strategies*. Abingdon, Routledge, 2018.

Onyeiwu, S. *Emerging Issues in Contemporary African Economies: Structure, Policy, and Sustainability*. London, Palgrave Macmillan, 2015.

Opalo, K. O. *Legislative Development in Africa: Politics and Post-colonial Legacies*. Cambridge, Cambridge University Press, 2019.

Oqubay, A., and Yifu Lin, J. (Eds). *China–Africa and an Economic Transformation*. Oxford, Oxford University Press, 2019.

Oshikoya, T. (Ed.). *Monetary and Financial Integration in West Africa*. Abingdon, Routledge, 2010.

Padayachee, V. (Ed.). *The Political Economy of Africa*. Abingdon, Routledge, 2010

Pakenham, T. *The Scramble for Africa*. 2nd edn. Avon Books, New York, 1992.

Paice, E. *Youthquake: Why African Demography Should Matter to the World*. London, Head of Zeus, 2021.

Palmer, E. *Africa: An Introduction*. Abingdon, Routledge, 2021.

Parker, J., and Rathbone, R. *African History: A Very Short Introduction*. Oxford, Oxford University Press, 2007.

Parker, J., and Reid, R. (Eds). *The Oxford Handbook of Modern African History*. Oxford, Oxford University Press, 2013.

Pathe Gueye, S. *Du bon usage de la démocratie en Afrique*. Dakar, Nouvelles Editions Africaines du Sénégal (NEAS), 2003.

Patterson, A. S. *The African State and the AIDS Crisis*. London, Ashgate Publishing, 2005.

    The Politics of AIDS in Africa. Boulder, CO, Lynne Rienner Publishers, 2006.

Paulson, J. A. *African Economies in Transition*. London, Palgrave Macmillan, 1999.

Peterson, D. *Africa's Totalitarian Temptation: The Evolution of Autocratic Regimes*. Boulder, CO, Lynne Rienner Publishers, 2019.

Pfister, R. *Apartheid South Africa and African States: From Pariah to Middle Power, 1961–1994 (International Library of African Studies, Vol. 14)*. London, I. B. Tauris, 2005.

Philips, J. E. (Ed.). *Writing African History*. Rochester, NY, University of Rochester Press, 2006.

Pigeaud, F., and Sylla, N. S. *Africa's Last Colonial Currency: The CFA Franc Story*. London, Pluto Press, 2021.

Pitcher, M. A. *Party Politics and Economic Reform in Africa's Democracies*. Cambridge, Cambridge University Press, 2012.

Poku, N., and Mdee, A. *Politics in Africa: A New Introduction*. London, Zed Books, 2011.

Prah, M. *Insights into Gender Equity, Equality and Power Relations in Sub-Saharan Africa*. Kampala, Fountain Publishers, 2013.

Prunier, G. *Africa's World War: Congo, the Rwandan Genocide, and the Making of a Continental Catastrophe*. Oxford, Oxford University Publishing, 2011.

Radelet, S. *Emerging Africa: How 17 Countries Are Leading the Way*. Washington, DC, Center for Global Development, 2010.

Raine, S. *China's African Challenges*. London, International Institute For Strategic Studies, 2009.

Ramani, S. *Russia in Africa: Resurgent Great Power or Bellicose Pretender?* London, Hurst & Co., 2022.

Rankhumise, S. P., and Mahlako, A. (Eds). *Defence, Militarism, Peace Building and Human Security in Africa*. Pretoria, Africa Institute of South Africa, 2005.

Reid, R. J. *A History of Modern Africa: 1800 to the Present*. Chichester, Wiley-Blackwell, 2011.

Reno, W. *Warlord Politics and African States*. Boulder, CO, Lynne Rienner Publishers, 1999.

Resnick, D., and van de Walle, N. (Eds). *Democratic Trajectories in Africa: Unravelling the Impact of Foreign Aid*. Oxford, Oxford University Press, 2013.

Riedl, R. *Authoritarian Origins of Democratic Party Systems in Africa*. New York, Cambridge University Press, 2014.

Robinson, D. *Muslim Societies in African History*. Cambridge, Cambridge University Press, 2004.

Rossi, B. *From Slavery to Aid. Politics, Labour, and Ecology in the Nigerien Sahel, 1800-2000*. Cambridge, Cambridge University Press, 2015.

Rotberg, R. I. (Ed.). *Battling Terrorism in the Horn of Africa*. Washington, DC, Brookings Institution Press and the World Peace Foundation, 2005.

    Africa Emerges: Consummate Challenges, Abundant Opportunities. Cambridge, Polity, 2013.

Rukato, H. *Future Africa: Prospects for Democracy and Development under NEPAD*. Trenton, NJ, Africa World Press, 2009.

Ryan, O. *Chocolate Nations: Living and Dying for Cocoa in West Africa*. London, Zed Books, 2011.

Sachs, J. *The End of Poverty*. London, Allen Lane, 2005.

Salih, M. A. (Ed.). *African Political Parties: Evolution, Institutionalisation and Governance*. Sterling, VA, Pluto Press, 2003.

    African Parliaments: Between Governance and Government. Cape Town, Human Sciences Research Council Press, 2006.

Sall, A. (Ed.). *Africa 2025: What Possible Futures for Sub-Saharan Africa?* Pretoria, Unisa Press, 2003.

Saul, J. S. *Decolonization and Empire: Contesting the Rhetoric and Reality of Resubordination in Southern Africa*. London, The Merlin Press, 2007.

Saunders, C., Dzinesa, G., and Nagar, D. (Eds). *Region-building in Southern Africa: Progress, Problems and Prospects*. London, Zed Books, 2012.

Schomerus, M. *The Lord's Resistance Army Violence and Peacemaking in Africa*. Cambridge, Cambridge University Press, 2021.

Schouten, P. *Roadblock Politics: The Origins of Violence in Central Africa*. Cambridge, Cambridge University Press, 2022.

Schraeder, P. *African Politics and Society: A Mosaic in Transformation*. Boston, MA, Wadsworth, 2003.

Schraeder, P. (Ed.) *Understanding Contemporary Africa*. 6th edn. Boulder, CO, Lynne Rienner Publishers, 2020.

Schwab, P. *Africa: A Continent Self-Destructs*. London, Palgrave Macmillan, 2003.

Scoones, M., and Wolmer, W. *Pathways of Change in Africa*. Oxford, James Currey, 2002.

Sherwood, M., and Adi, H. *Pan-African History*. London, Frank Cass, 2003.

Shillington, K. *History of African*. 4th edn. London, Red Globe Press, 2018.

Shorter, A. *East African Societies*. London, Frank Cass, 2004.

Siebels, D. *Maritime Security in East and West Africa: A Tale of Two Regions*. Cham, Palgrave Pivot, 2019.

Sindayigaya, J.-M. *Mondialisation: Le nouvel esclavage de l'Afrique*. Paris, L'Harmattan, 2000.

Skard, T. *Continent of Mothers, Continent of Hope: Understanding and Promoting Development in Africa Today*. London, Zed Books, 2003.

Smith, G. *Where Credit Is Due. How Africa's Debt Can Be a Benefit, Not a Burden*. London, Hurst & Co., 2021.

Smith, M. S. *Beyond the 'African Tragedy': Discourses on Development and the Global Economy*. London, Ashgate Publishing, 2006.

Soares, B. (Ed.). *Islam and Muslim Politics in Africa*. London, Palgrave Macmillan, 2007.

Söderbaum, F., and Tavares, R. (Eds). *Regional Organizations in African Security*. Abingdon, Routledge, 2011.

Solhjell, R. *Dimensions of African Statehood: Everyday Governance and Provision of Public Goods*. Abingdon, Routledge, 2019.

Solomon, H. *Terrorism and Counter-Terrorism in Africa: Fighting Insurgency from Al Shabaab, Ansar Dine and Boko Haram*. Basingstoke, Palgrave Macmillan, 2015.

Souare, I. K. *Africa in the United Nations System, 1945–2005*. London, Adonis & Abbey Publishers, 2006.

Souare, I. K. (Ed.). *Electoral Violence and Post-Electoral Arrangements in Africa (African Renaissance, Vol. 5, Nos 3–4)*. London, Adonis & Abbey Publishers, 2009.

Southall, R. *Liberation Movements in Power: Party and State in Southern Africa*. Woodbridge, James Currey, 2016.

Southall, R., and Melber, H. (Eds). *Legacies of Power: Leadership Change and Former Presidents in African Politics*. Cape Town, Human Sciences Research Council Press, 2006.

Soyinka, W. *Of Africa*. New Haven, CT, Yale University Press, 2012.

Sparks, D. (Ed.) *The Blue Economy in Sub-Saharan Africa: Working for a Sustainable Future*. Abingdon, Routledge, 2021.

Sriram, C. S., Martin-Ortega, O., and Herman, J. (Eds). *Peacebuilding and Rule of Law in Africa: Just Peace?* Abingdon, Routledge, 2016.

Stapleton, J. *Africa: War and Conflict in the Twentieth Century*. Abingdon, Routledge, 2018.

Stock, R. *Africa South of the Sahara*. London, Frank Cass, 1995.

Stolte, C. *Brazil's Africa Strategy: Role Conception and the Drive for International Status*. New York, Palgrave Macmillan, 2016.

Subramanian, A. *Africa's Trade Revisited*. Washington, DC, IMF Publications, 2001.

Suttner, R. (Ed.). *Africa in the New Millennium*. Uppsala, Nordic Africa Institute, 2001.

Tadele, G., and Kloos, H. (Eds). *Vulnerabilities, Impacts and Responses to HIV/AIDS in Sub-Saharan Africa*. Basingstoke, Palgrave Macmillan, 2013.

Taylor, I. *The Forum on China-Africa Cooperation (FOCAC)*. Abingdon, Routledge, 2012.

    Africa Rising? BRICS - Diversifying Dependency. Woodbridge, James Currey, 2014.

African Politics: A Very Short Introduction. Oxford, Oxford University Press, 2018

Taylor, I., and Williams, P. (Eds). *Africa in International Politics.* London, Routledge, 2004.

Teferra, D. (Ed.). *Funding Higher Education in Sub-Saharan Africa.* Basingstoke, Palgrave Macmillan, 2013.

Themnér, A. (Ed.). *Warlord Democrats in Africa: Ex-Military Leaders and Electoral Politics.* London, Zed Books, 2017.

Thomas, C., and Wilkin, P. (Eds). *Globalization, Human Security and the African Experience.* Boulder, CO, Lynne Rienner Publishers, 1999.

Thomson, A. *An Introduction to African Politics.* London, Routledge, 2004.

Thurston, A. *Jihadists of North Africa: Local Politics and Rebel Groups.* Cambridge, Cambridge University Press, 2020.

Tilley, H. *Africa as a Living Laboratory: Empire, Development, and the Problem of Scientific Knowledge, 1870–1950.* Chicago, IL, The University of Chicago Press, 2011.

Tiyambe Zeleza, P. *Africa and the Disruptions of the Twenty-First Century.* Dakar, CODESRIA, 2021.

Tordoff, W. *Government and Politics in Africa.* Basingstoke, Macmillan, 1997.

Totte, M., Dahou, T., and Billaz, R. *La décentralisation en Afrique de l'Ouest.* Paris, Editions Karthala, 2003.

Turshen, M. *Gender and the Political Economy of Conflict in Africa: The Persistence of Violence.* Abingdon, Routledge, 2017

Tvedt, T. *The River Nile in the Post-Colonial Age.* London, I. B. Tauris, 2009.

Twaddle, M. *The Making of Modern Africa: 1787 to the Present.* Oxford, Oxford University Press, 2004.

Udogu, E. I. *African Renaissance in the Millennium: The Political, Social and Economic Discourses on the Way Forward.* Lanham, MD, Lexington Books, 2007.

Utas, M. (Ed.). *African Conflicts and Informal Power: Big Men and Networks.* London, Zed Books, 2012.

Van Buuren, M., et al. (Eds). *State Recognition and Democratization in Sub-Saharan Africa: A New Dawn for Traditionalist Authorities?* London, Palgrave Macmillan, 2007.

Van Eerd, J. *The Quality of Democracy in Africa: Opposition Competitiveness Rooted in Legacies of Cleavages.* Cham, Springer International Publishing, 2017.

Van Reisen, M., Mawere, M., Stokmans, M., and Gebre-Egziabher, K. (Eds). *Roaming Africa: Migration, Resilience and Social Protection.* Bamenda, Langaa Research and Publishing Common Initiative Group, 2019.

Van de Walle, N. *African Economies and the Politics of Permanent Crisis, 1979–1999.* Cambridge, Cambridge University Press, 2001.

Venter, A. *Portugal's Guerrilla Wars in Africa: Lisbon's Three Wars in Angola, Mozambique and Portuguese Guinea 1961-74.* Solihull, Helion & Co, 2017.

Villalón, L. A. (Ed). *The Oxford Handbook of the African Sahel.* Oxford, Oxford University Press, 2021.

Villalón, L. A., and Idrissa, R. (Eds). *Democratic Struggle, Institutional Reform, and State Resilience in the African Sahel.* Lanham, MD, Rowman & Littlefield, 2020.

Wallerstein, I. *Africa: The Politics of Independence and Unity.* Lincoln, NE, University of Nebraska Press, 2006.

Warner, J., Cummings, C., Nsaibia, H., and O'Farrell, R. *The Islamic State in Africa The Emergence, Evolution, and Future of the Next Jihadist Battlefront* London, Hurst & Co., 2021.

Weinreb, A., and Trinitapoli, J. *Religion and AIDS in Africa.* New York, Oxford University Press, 2012.

Whitaker, B. E., and Clark, J. F. *Africa's International Relations: Balancing Domestic and Global Interests.* Boulder, CO, Lynne Rienner Publishers, 2018.

Whitehouse, B. *Migrants and Strangers in an African City: Exile, Dignity, Belonging.* Bloomington, IN, Indiana University Press, 2012.

Williams, P. D. *War and Conflict in Africa.* Cambridge, Polity Press, 2011.

Wills, A. J. *An Introduction to the History of Central Africa.* Oxford, Oxford University Press, 1985.

Wilson, Z. *The United Nations and Democracy in Africa: Labyrinths of Legitimacy.* Abingdon, Routledge, 2009.

Wohlgemuth, L., et al. *Institution Building and Leadership in Africa.* Uppsala, Nordic Africa Institute, 1998.

Wood, G., and Brewster, C. *Industrial Relations in Africa.* London, Palgrave Macmillan, 2007.

Woodward, P. *Crisis in the Horn of Africa: Politics, Piracy and the Threat of Terror.* London, I. B. Tauris, 2012.

World Economic Forum. *The Africa Competitiveness Report 2009.* Oxford, Oxford University Press, 2009.

Yalae, P. *The Road to a New Africa: An Essay to the African People.* New York, Random House Ventures, 2003.

Ylönen, A. and Záhořík, J. (Eds). *The Horn of Africa since the 1960s: Local and International Politics Intertwined.* Abingdon, Routledge, 2017.

Young, C. *The Postcolonial State in Africa: Fifty Years of Independence, 1960–2010.* Madison, WI, University of Wisconsin Press, 2012.

Young, T. (Ed.). *Readings in African Politics.* Bloomington, IN, Indiana University Press, 2003.

Zartman, W., et al. *Europe and Africa: The New Phase.* Boulder, CO, Lynne Rienner Publishers, 1992.

Zeilig, L. *Revolt and Protest: Student Politics and Activism in Sub-Saharan Africa.* London, I. B. Tauris, 2007.

Zeleza, P. T., and Eyoh, D. (Eds). *Encyclopedia of Twentieth-Century African History.* London, Routledge, 2003.

SELECT BIBLIOGRAPHY
(PERIODICALS)

Africa: International African Institute, SOAS, Thornhaugh St, Russell Sq., London, WC1H 0XG, UK; tel. (20) 7898-4420; e-mail africa@internationalafricaninstitute.org; internet www.internationalafricaninstitute.org; f. 1928; study of African societies and culture; also annual bibliography; Co-Editors JULIE ARCHAMBAULT, Dr MAXIM BOLT, Prof. JOOST FONTEIN, ASONZEH UKAH; 5 a year.

Africa Confidential: 37 John's Mews, London, WC1N 2NS, UK; tel. (20) 7831-3511; e-mail subscriptions@africa-confidential.com; internet www.africa-confidential.com; f. 1960; political and economic news and analysis; Editor PATRICK SMITH; fortnightly.

Africa Development (Afrique et Développement): Council for the Development of Social Science Research in Africa (CODESRIA), ave Cheikh Anta Diop, Canal IV, BP 3304, Dakar 18524, Senegal; tel. 33-825-9822; e-mail publications@codesria.org; internet codesria.org; f. 1976; in French and English; Editor-in-Chief IBRAHIM OANDA OGACHI; quarterly.

Africa Education Review: 4 Park Sq., Milton Park, Abingdon, Oxfordshire, OX14 4RN, UK; tel. (20) 8052-0500; e-mail enquiries@taylorandfrancis.com; internet www.tandfonline.com/journals/raer20; f. 1972 as Educare; Editor-in-Chief M. LETSEKA; 6 a year.

Africa Health: African Centre for Global Health and Social Transformation, Plot 13B, Acacia Ave, POB 9974, Kampala, Uganda; tel. (41) 4237225; e-mail africahealth@achest.org; internet africa-health.com; f. 1978; Editor BRYAN PEARSON; 6 a year.

Africa Insight: Africa Institute of South Africa, HSRC Bldg, 134 Pretorious St, Pretoria 0002, South Africa; tel. (12) 3169762; e-mail rlepule@hsrc.ac.za; internet www.ajol.info/index.php/ai; f. 1971; Editor SOLANI NGOBENI; quarterly.

Africa Renewal/Afrique Renouveau: Africa Section, Dept of Global Communications, 10th Floor, United Nations, New York, NY 10017, USA; tel. (212) 963-6857; e-mail africarenewal@un.org; internet www.un.org/africarenewal; f. 1987; fmrly Africa Recovery; Man. Editor KINGSLEY IGHOBOR; monthly.

The Africa Report: 57 bis rue d'Auteuil, 75016 Paris, France; tel. 1-44-30-19-60; e-mail editorial@theafricareport.com; internet www.theafricareport.com; Editor-in-Chief PATRICK SMITH; Man. Editor NICHOLAS NORBROOK.

Africa Research Bulletin: The Atrium, Southern Gate, Chichester, PO19 8SQ, UK; tel. (1865) 778315; e-mail editors@africaresearch.co.uk; internet onlinelibrary.wiley.com; f. 1964; separate bulletins on political and economic topics; Editor VERONICA HOSKINS; monthly.

Africa Spectrum: GIGA German Institute of Global and Area Studies, Leibniz-Institut für Globale und Regionale Studien, Institute of African Affairs, Neuer Jungfernstieg 21, Hamburg 20354, Germany; tel. (40) 42825522; e-mail afrika-spectrum@giga-hamburg.de; internet journals.sagepub.com/home/afr; f. 1966; articles in English; Editors-in-Chief TIM GLAWION, LEONARDO R. ARRIOLA; 3 a year.

Africa Today: AMC House, 3rd Floor, Suite 6, 12 Cumberland Ave, London, NW10 7QL, UK; tel. (20) 8838-5900; e-mail publisher@africatoday.com; internet www.africatoday.com; f. 1995; Founder and Publr KAYODE SOYINKA; monthly.

Africa Today: Suite 3081, 355 North Jordan Ave, Bloomington, IN 47405, USA; tel. (812) 855-8817; e-mail afrtoday@indiana.edu; internet www.iupress.org/journals/africatoday; f. 1954; Editors TAVY DE LACY AHERNE, BETH BUGGENHAGEN, SERGIO FERNANDEZ, MARIA GROSZ-NGATÉ, LAUREN M. MACLEAN, ALLISON MARTINO, ESI THOMPSON; quarterly.

African Administrative Studies: Centre Africain de Formation et de Recherche Administratives pour le Développement (CAFRAD), blvd Mohammed V, Pavillon International, BP 1796, Tangier, 90001 Morocco; tel. (53) 9322707; e-mail cafrad@cafrad.org; internet www.cafrad.org; f. 1964; biannual.

African Affairs: Royal African Society, SOAS, 10 Thornhaugh St, London, WC1H 0XG; tel. (20) 7074-5176; e-mail ras@soas.ac.uk; internet royalafricansociety.org; f. 1901; social sciences and history; Co-Editors RICARDO SOARES DE OLIVEIRA, AMBREENA MANJI, GEORGE BOB-MILLIAR, SCOTT STRAUS; quarterly.

African Agenda: Third World Network-Africa, 9 Asmara St, East Legon, POB AN19452, Accra, Ghana; tel. (30) 2511189; e-mail africanagenda@twnafrica.org; internet www.twnafrica.org; f. 1994; analysis of economic and social issues; Editor-in-Chief YAO GRAHAM; Editor CORNELIUS ADEDZE.

African Arts: James S. Coleman African Studies Center, 10244A Bunche Hall, Box 951310, University of California, Los Angeles, CA 90095-1310, USA; tel. (310) 825-1218; e-mail afriartsedit@international.ucla.edu; internet www.international.ucla.edu/asc/africanarts; f. 1967; Exec. Editor LESLIE ELLEN JONES; quarterly.

African and Black Diaspora: 4 Park Sq., Milton Park, Abingdon, Oxon, OX14 4RN, UK; tel. (20) 8052-0500; e-mail enquiries@taylorandfrancis.com; internet www.tandfonline.com/journals/rabd20; f. 2008; locates the movt of African-descended populations in the context of globalized and transnational spaces; Editors Dr FASSIL DEMISSIE, Dr SANDRA JACKSON; 3 a year.

The African Book Publishing Record (ABPR): Petit Bersac, 24600 Ribérac, France; tel. 5-53-90-55-76; e-mail africanbookpublishingrecord@gmail.com; internet www.degruyter.com/view/j/abpr; f. 1975; bibliographic listings, book reviews, articles and information on book trade activities in Africa; Editor CÉCILE LOMER; 4 a year.

African Business: 7 Coldbath Sq., London, EC1R 4LQ, UK; tel. (20) 7841-3210; e-mail editorial@icpublications.com; internet africanbusinessmagazine.com; f. 1978; economics, business, commerce and finance; sister publs include New African Magazine and Magazine de l'Afrique ; Editor DAVID THOMAS; monthly.

African Farming and Food Processing: Alain Charles Publishing Ltd, University House, 11–13 Lower Grosvenor Pl., London, SW1W 0EX, UK; tel. (20) 7834-7676; e-mail post@alaincharles.com; internet www.africanfarming.net; f. 1980; Editor MADHURI RAMESH; 6 a year.

African Finance Journal (AFJ): The Cliffs Unit 13 Tygerfalls Niagara Way Bellville 7535, Cape Town, South Africa; POB 3628, Bellville 7536, South Africa; tel. (21) 9146778; e-mail info@africagrowth.com; internet www.africagrowth.com/afj.htm; f. 1999; publ. by the Africagrowth Institute and the African Finance Asscn; finance, accounting and economics; Exec. Editor NICHOLAS BIEKPE; Co-Editor KALU OJAH; biannual.

African Historical Review: 4 Park Sq., Milton Park, Abingdon, Oxon, OX14 4RN, UK; tel. (20) 8052-0500; e-mail enquiries@taylorandfrancis.com; internet www.tandfonline.com/journals/rahr20; f. 1969 as Kleio: A Journal of Historical Studies from Africa; present name adopted in 2007; Editor Dr SIPOKAZI MADIDA (acting); biannual.

African Identities: 4 Park Sq., Milton Park, Abingdon, Oxon, OX14 4RN, UK; tel. (20) 8052-0500; e-mail enquiries@taylorandfrancis.com; internet www.tandfonline.com/journals/cafi20; f. 2003; social, political and cultural expressions of African identity; Editor PAL AHLUWALIA; 4 a year.

African Journal of AIDS Research (AJAR): 4 Park Sq., Milton Park, Abingdon, Oxon, OX14 4RN, UK; tel. (20) 8052-0500; e-mail enquiries@taylorandfrancis.com; internet www.tandfonline.com/journals/raar20; f. 2002; Editor-in-Chief ALAN WHITESIDE; 4 a year.

African Journal on Conflict Resolution: ACCORD, Private Bag X018, Umhlanga Rocks 4320, South Africa; tel. (31) 5023908; e-mail info@accord.org.za; internet www.accord.org.za/publications/ajcr; f. 1999; publ. by the African Centre for the Constructive Resolution of Disputes (ACCORD); conflict transformation in Africa; Chief Editor Dr CEDRIC DE CONING; Man. Editor ANDREA PRAH; biannual.

African Journal of Health Sciences: Kenya Medical Research Institute, POB 54840, 00200 Nairobi, Kenya; tel. (20) 2722541; e-mail africanjournal@kemri.org; internet www.ajhsjournal.org; f. 1994; Editor-in-Chief Dr PETER WANZALA; bimonthly.

African Journal of International and Comparative Law: Edinburgh University Press, The Tun-Holyrood Rd, 12-2F Jackson's Entry, Edinburgh, EH8 8PJ, UK; tel. (131) 650-4218; e-mail journals@eup.ed.ac.uk; internet www.euppublishing.com/loi/ajicl; f. 2005; in English and French; Gen. Editors Prof. RACHEL MURRAY, Dr KOFI OTENG KUFUOR; quarterly.

African Review: A Journal of African Politics, Development and International Affairs: Dept of Political Science and Public Administration, University of Dar es Salaam, POB 35042, Dar es Salaam, Tanzania; tel. 659632365; e-mail theafricanreview@udsm.ac.tz; internet brill.com/tare; f. 1971; Chief Editor Prof. ALEXANDER BONIFACE MAKULILO; biannual.

African Review of Business and Technology: Alain Charles Publishing Ltd, University House, 11–13 Lower Grosvenor Pl., London, SW1W 0EX, UK; tel. (20) 7834-7676; e-mail post@alaincharles.com;

internet www.africanreview.com; f. 1965; Publr NICK FORDHAM; Editor ROBERT DANIELS; 11 a year.

African Security: Taylor & Francis Inc, 530 Walnut St, Suite 850, Philadelphia, PA 19106, USA; tel. (215) 207-0050; e-mail enquiries@ taylorandfrancis.com; internet /www.tandfonline.com/journals/ uafs20; Editors-in-Chief W. ANDY KNIGHT, TEMITOPE ORIOLA; 4 a year.

African Security Review: 4 Park Sq., Milton Park, Abingdon, Oxon, OX14 4RN, UK; tel. (20) 8052-0500; e-mail enquiries@ taylorandfrancis.com; internet www.tandfonline.com/journals/ rasr20; f. 1992; African human security issues; Editor Dr LISA OTTO, Prof. ANDREAS VELTHUIZEN; 4 a year.

African Studies: 4 Park Sq., Milton Park, Abingdon, Oxon, OX14 4RN, UK; tel. (20) 8052-0500; e-mail enquiries@taylorandfrancis .com; internet www.tandfonline.com/journals/cast20; f. 1921 as Bantu Studies; present named adopted in 1942; social and cultural studies of southern Africa; Editors CLAUDIA GASTROW, KHWEZI MKHIZE, SENAYON OLAOLUWA, MARGOT RUBIN; 4 a year.

African Studies Review: Rutgers University, 54 Joyce Kilmer Ave, Piscataway, NJ 08854-8045; tel. (848) 445-8173; e-mail usjournals@ cambridge.org; internet www.cambridge.org/core/journals/ african-studies-review; f. 1956; Editor-in-Chief BENJAMIN N. LAWRANCE; 4 a year.

Africanus: Journal of Development Studies: University of South Africa, POB 392, Unisa 0003, South Africa; tel. (12) 3376155; e-mail africanus1@unisapressjournals.co.za; internet upjournals .co.za/index.php/Africanus; f. 1972; devt issues; Editor Prof. VUSI GUMEDE; biannual.

Afrika Süd: informationsstelle südliches afrika eV, Königswinterer Str. 116, D-53227 Bonn, Germany; tel. (228) 464369; e-mail info@ afrika-sued.org; internet www.afrika-sued.org; f. 1972; politics, economics, social and military affairs of southern Africa and German relations with the area; Editor-in-Chief LOTHAR BERGER; 6 a year.

Afrika und Übersee, Journal of African Languages and Cultures: Asien-Afrika-Institut, Abteilung für Afrikanistik und Äthiopistik, Edmund-Siemers-Allee 1, 20146 Hamburg, Germany; tel. (40) 428382579; e-mail afrikaunduebersee@uni-hamburg.de; internet journals.sub.uni-hamburg.de/hup1/afrikaunduebersee; f. 1910 as Zeitschrift für Kolonialsprachen; African languages and linguistics and their social and historical contexts; in German, English and French; Editor-in-chief Prof. Dr ROLAND KIESSLING; Co-Editors Prof. Dr HENNING SCHREIBER, Prof. Dr LUDWIG GERHARDT; biannual.

Afrique Agriculture: BP 90146, 57004 Metz, Cedex 1, France; tel. 3-87-69-18-18; internet www.afrique-agriculture.org; f. 1975; Editor-in-Chief ANTOINE HERVÉ; bimonthly.

Afrique-Asie: 3 rue de l'Atlas, 75019 Paris, France; tel. 1-42-38-14-50; internet www.afrique-asie.fr; f. 1969; Dir MAJED NEHMÉ; monthly.

Afrique Contemporaine: c/o Agence Française de Développement, 5 rue Roland-Barthes, 75598 Paris Cédex 12, France; tel. 1-53-44-36-12; e-mail afcontemporaine@gmail.com; internet afrique -contemporaine.info; f. 1962; political, economic and sociological studies; Editor-in-Chief MARC-ANTOINE PÉROUSE DE MONTCLOS; biannual.

Afrique Expansion: 4629 rue Louis-B-Mayer, Suite 201, Laval, QC, H7P 6G5, Canada; tel. (450) 902-0527; e-mail info@afriqueexpansion .com; internet afriqueexpansion.com; f. 1995; communications; Editor GERBA MALAM.

Afrique Magazine: 31 rue Poussin, 75016 Paris, France; tel. 1-53-84-41-81; e-mail redaction@afriquemagazine.com; internet afriquemagazine.com; f. 1983; African current affairs; Editor-in-Chief ZYAD LIMAM; monthly.

Agrekon: 4 Park Sq., Milton Park, Abingdon, Oxon, OX14 4RN, UK; tel. (20) 8052-0500; e-mail enquiries@taylorandfrancis.com; internet www.tandfonline.com/journals/ragr20; a journal of the Agricultural Economics Asscn of South Africa; Editor-in-Chief Prof. JOHANN KIRSTEN; 4 a year.

Botswana Notes and Records: The Botswana Society, POB 71, Gaborone, Botswana; tel. 3554448; e-mail botsoc@info.bw; internet journals.ub.bw; f. 1969; Editor CHRISTIAN JOHN MAKGALA; annual.

Bulletin of SOAS: SOAS, Thornhaugh St, Russell Sq., London, WC1H 0XG, UK; tel. (20) 7898-4064; e-mail bulletin@soas.ac.uk; internet www.cambridge.org/core/journals/bulletin-of-the-school -of-oriental-and-african-studies; f. 1917; Editor Dr AYMAN SHIHADEH; 3 a year.

Cahiers d'Etudes Africaines: IMAf-Bâtiment de recherche Sud, 4126, 5 rue des Humanités, 93300 Aubervilliers Cedex, France; e-mail cahiers-afr@ehess.fr; internet journals.openedition.org/etudes africaines; f. 1960; publ. by Éditions de l'EHESS; in French and English; Editor-in-Chief ELOI FICQUET; quarterly.

Canadian Journal of African Studies (Revue canadienne des études africaines—CJAS): 4 Park Sq., Milton Park, Abingdon, Oxon, OX14 4RNP, UK; tel. (20) 8052-0500; e-mail enquiries@taylorandfrancis .com; internet www.tandfonline.com/journals/rcas20; f. 1967; in

French and English; a journal of Canadian Asscn of African Studies; Co-ordinating Editor BELINDA DODSON; Man. Editor MARTIN EVANS; 3 a year.

Communicatio: 4 Park Sq., Milton Park, Abingdon, Oxon, OX14 4RN, UK; tel. (20) 8052-0500; e-mail enquiries@taylorandfrancis.com; internet www.tandfonline.com/journals/rcsa20; f. 1975; South African journal for communication theory and research; Editor-in-Chief Prof. VIOLA C. MILTON; 4 a year.

Communications Africa: Alain Charles Publishing Ltd, University House, 11–13 Lower Grosvenor Pl., London, SW1W 0EX, UK; tel. (20) 7834-7676; e-mail circulation@alaincharles.com; internet www .communicationsafrica.com; f. 1991; telecommunications, broadcasting and information technology; in French and English; Editor VAUGHAN O'GRADY; 6 a year.

Contemporary Journal of African Studies: Institute of African Studies, University of Ghana, POB LG73, Accra, Ghana; tel. (21) 4979233; e-mail cjaseditor@ug.edu.gh; internet www.ajol.info/index.php/ contjas; f. 1965; fmrly Research Review of the Institute of African Studies; Editor-in-Chief Prof. AKOSUA ADOMAKO AMPOFO; biannual.

Critical Arts: 4 Park Sq., Milton Park, Abingdon, Oxon, OX14 4RN, UK; tel. (20) 8052-0500; e-mail enquiries@taylorandfrancis.com; internet www.tandfonline.com/journals/rcrc20; f. 1980; transdisciplinary epistemologies, debates on Africa and the South; Co-Editors KEYAN G. TOMASELLI, LAUREN DYLL; 6 a year.

Development Policy Review: Overseas Development Institute, 203 Blackfriars Rd, London, SE1 8NJ, UK; tel. (20) 7922-0300; e-mail publications@odi.org; internet www.odi.org; f. 1960; Lead Editor ANNALISA WIGGINS; Editor DEBORAH EADE; 6 a year.

Development Southern Africa (DSA): 4 Park Sq., Milton Park, Abingdon, Oxon, OX14 4RN, UK; tel. (20) 8052-0500; e-mail enquiries@taylorandfrancis.com; internet www.tandfonline.com/ journals/cdsa20; f. 1984; articles on policy solutions to local and regional socioeconomic development challenges; Editor MARIÉ KIRSTEN; 6 a year.

English Academy Review: Journal of English Studies (EAR): 4 Park Sq., Milton Park, Abingdon, Oxon, OX14 4RN, UK; tel. (20) 8052-0500; e-mail enquiries@taylorandfrancis.com; internet www .tandfonline.com/journals/racr20; f. 1983; publ. on behalf of the English Academy of Southern Africa; articles on African languages and book reviews; Editor-in-Chief SOPELEKAE MAITHUFI; biannual.

English Studies in Africa: 4 Park Sq., Milton Park, Abingdon, Oxon, OX14 4RN, UK; tel. (20) 8052-0500; e-mail enquiries@ taylorandfrancis.com; internet www.tandfonline.com/journals/ reia20; f. 1958; covers the study of world literature in English within African contexts and promotion of African literature; Man. Editors KARL VAN WYK, GRACE MUSILA; biannual.

Estudios de Asia y África: El Colegio de México, AC, Carretera Picacho Ajusco 20, Ampliación Fuentes del Pedregal, Tlalpan 14110, Ciudad de México, Mexico; tel. (55) 5449-3000; e-mail reaa@colmex .mx; internet estudiosdeasiayafrica.colmex.mx/index.php/eaa; f. 1966 as Estudios Orientales; present name adopted in 1975; Editor CYNTHIA GODOY; quarterly.

Horn of Africa Bulletin: Life and Peace Institute, Kungsängsgatan 17, SE 753 22 Uppsala, Sweden; tel. (18) 660130; e-mail info@ life-peace.org; internet www.life-peace.org; f. 1989; 6 a year.

Indilinga: African Journal of Indigenous Knowledge Systems (IAJIKS): POB 266, Msunduzi, Pietermaritzburg 3231, South Africa; tel. (33) 3413447; e-mail qmkabela@gmail.com; internet www.ajol .info/index.php/indilinga/index; f. 2002; issues relating to the transmission and recognition of traditional knowledge systems; Editor-in-Chief Dr QUEENETH MKABELA; biannual.

International Development Policy (Revue internationale de politique de développement): CP 1672, 1211 Geneva 1, Switzerland; tel. (22) 9084364; e-mail frances.rice@graduateinstitute.ch; internet journals.openedition.org/poldev; f. 2010; Editor-in-Chief UGO PANIZZA; 2–3 a year.

International Journal of African Historical Studies: African Studies Center, Boston University, 232 Bay State Rd, Boston, MA 02215, USA; tel. (617) 353-7306; e-mail ascpub@bu.edu; internet www.bu .edu/africa/publications/ijahs; f. 1968 as *African Historical Studies*; present name adopted in 1972; Editor Dr MICHAEL DIBLASI; 3 a year.

International Journal of African Renaissance Studies (IJARS): 4 Park Sq., Milton Park, Abingdon, Oxon, OX14 4RN, UK; tel. (20) 8052-0500; e-mail enquiries@taylorandfrancis.com; internet www .tandfonline.com/journals/rars20; f. 2006; covers multi-, inter- and transdisciplinary approaches in studying the African Renaissance; Editor SIPHAMANDLA ZONDI; biannual.

Jeune Afrique L'Intelligent: Groupe Jeune Afrique, 57 bis rue d'Auteuil, 75016 Paris, France; tel. 1-44-30-19-60; e-mail redaction@jeuneafrique.com; internet www.jeuneafrique.com; f. 1960; Man. Editor AMIR BEN YAHMED; monthly.

Journal of African Business: Taylor & Francis Inc, 530 Walnut St, Suite 850, Philadelphia, PA 19106, USA; tel. (215) 625-8900; e-mail enquiries@taylorandfrancis.com; internet /www.tandfonline.com/journals/wjab20; official journal of the International Academy of African Business and Development; Editor MOSES ACQUAAH; 4 a year.

Journal of African Cultural Studies: 4 Park Sq., Milton Park, Abingdon, Oxon, OX14 4RNP, UK; tel. (20) 8052-0500; e-mail enquiries@taylorandfrancis.com; internet www.tandfonline.com/journals/cjac20; f. 1988 as African Languages and Cultures; present name adopted in 1998; literature, performance arts, visual arts, music, media, sociolinguistics and gender; Editor CARLI COETZEE; 4 a year.

Journal of African Economies: Oxford University Press, Great Clarendon St, Oxford, OX2 6DP, UK; tel. (1865) 353907; e-mail jnl.info@oup.co.uk; internet academic.oup.com/jae; f. 1992; publ. on behalf of the Centre for the Study of African Economies; Editor FRANCIS TEAL; 5 a year.

Journal of African Elections (JAE): EISA, POB 740, Auckland Park 2006, South Africa; tel. (11) 3816000; e-mail publications@eisa.org; internet eisa.org.za/jae.php; f. 1996; Editor DENIS KADIMA; biannual.

Journal of African History: SOAS, Thornhaugh St, Russell Sq., London, WC1H 0XG, UK; tel. (20) 7637-2388; e-mail journals@cambridge.org; internet www.cambridge.org/core/journals/journal-of-african-history; f. 1960; Editors Prof. SHANE DOYLE, Prof. MARISSA MOORMAN, Prof. MOSES OCHONU, DANIEL MAGAZINER; 3 a year.

Journal des Africanistes: Société des Africanistes, Musée du Quai Branly, 222 rue de l'Université, 75007 Paris, France; tel. 1-56-61-71-17; e-mail africanistes@yahoo.fr; internet journals.openedition.org/africanistes; f. 1931 as *Journal de la Société des Africanistes*; present name adopted in 1976; in English and French; Editor-in-Chief LUC PECQUET; biannual.

Journal of Asian and African Studies (JAAS): SAGE Publications Ltd, 1 Oliver's Yard, 55 City Rd, London, EC1Y 1SP, UK; tel. (20) 7324-8500; internet journals.sagepub.com/home/jas; f. 1965; Editor NIGEL C. GIBSON; 8 a year.

Journal of Black Studies: SAGE Publications Ltd, 305 Seventh Ave, 15th Floor, New York, NY 10001, USA; tel. (212) 741-2247; internet journals.sagepub.com/home/jbs; f. 1970; Editors AMA MAZAMA, MOLEFI KETE ASANTE; bimonthly.

Journal of Central and Eastern European African Studies (JCEEAS): Africa Research Institute, Doctoral School on Safety and Security Sciences, Bánki Donát Faculty of Mechanical and Safety Engineering, Óbuda University, Népszínház str. 8, 1081 Budapest, Hungary; tel. (1) 666-5345; internet jceeas.bdi.uni-obuda.hu/index.php/jceeas/index; Editorial Head JÁNOS BESENYŐ; Publr ZOLTÁN RAJNAI; quarterly.

Journal of Contemporary African Studies (JCAS): 4 Park Sq., Milton Park, Abingdon, Oxon, OX14 4RN, UK; tel. (20) 8052-0500; e-mail enquiries@taylorandfrancis.com; internet www.tandfonline.com/journals/cjca20; Chief Editor NTHABISENG MOTSEMME; 4 a year.

The Journal of Development Studies: 4 Park Sq., Milton Park, Abingdon, Oxon, OX14 4RN, UK; tel. (20) 8052-0500; e-mail enquiries@taylorandfrancis.com; internet www.tandfonline.com/journals/fjds20; f. 1964; Man. Editors JENNIFER BRASS, LISA CHAUVET, LISA CHAUVET, DAVID FIELDING, OLIVER MORRISSEY, RICHARD PALMER-JONES, EMMANUEL TEITELBAUM; 12 a year.

Journal of Eastern African Studies: 4 Park Sq., Milton Park, Abingdon, Oxon, OX14 4RN, UK; tel. (20) 8052-0500; e-mail enquiries@taylorandfrancis.com; internet www.tandfonline.com/journals/rjea20; f. 2007; publ. of the British Institute in Eastern Africa; Man. Editor JASON MOSLEY; 4 a year.

The Journal of Imperial and Commonwealth History: 4 Park Sq., Milton Park, Abingdon, Oxon, OX14 4RN, UK; tel. (20) 8052-0500; e-mail enquiries@taylorandfrancis.com; internet www.tandfonline.com/journals/fich20; f. 1972; Editors Prof. STEPHEN HOWE, Prof. PHILIP MURPHY; 6 a year.

Journal for Islamic Studies: Centre for Contemporary Islam, Rm 5.48, Leslie Social Science Bldg, Upper Campus, University of Cape Town, Private Bag, Rondebosch 7701, South Africa; tel. (21) 6503889; e-mail dllcat004@myuct.ac.za; internet www.cci.uct.ac.za/cci/publications/jis/overview; Chief Editor ANDREA BRIGAGLIA; annual.

Journal of Islamic Studies: Oxford Centre for Islamic Studies, Marston Rd, Oxford, OX3 0EE, UK; tel. (1865) 618500; e-mail publications@oxcis.ac.uk; internet academic.oup.com/jis; f. 1990; all aspects of Islam; Editor-in-Chief Dr FARHAN AHMAD NIZAMI; 3 a year.

Journal of Literary Studies (JLS) (Tydskrif vir Literatuurwetenskap): Dept of Afrikaans and Theory of Literature, Winnie Madikizela-Mandela Bldg, 10-80 Unisa Preller St, Muckleneuk Ridge, Pretoria 0002, South Africa; e-mail jls1@unisapressjournals.co.za; internet unisapressjournals.co.za/index.php/jls; f. 1985; provides a forum for the discussion of literary theory, methodology, research and related matters; in English and Afrikaans; fmrly publ. by Taylor & Francis, UK; Editor Prof. RICHARD ALAN NORTHOVER; quarterly.

Journal of Modern African Studies: Cambridge University Press, The Edinburgh Bldg, Shaftesbury Rd, Cambridge, CB2 8BS, UK; tel. (1223) 326070; e-mail journals@cambridge.org; internet www.cambridge.org/core/journals/journal-of-modern-african-studies; f. 1963; current issues in African politics, economies, societies and international relations; Editor EBENEZER OBADARE; quarterly.

Journal of the Musical Arts in Africa (JMAA): 4 Park Sq., Milton Park, Abingdon, Oxon, OX14 4RN, UK; e-mail enquiries@taylorandfrancis.com; internet www.tandfonline.com/journals/rmaa20; a publ. of the NISC (Pty) Ltd and South African College of Music, University of Cape Town; Editors-in-Chief WILHELM DELPORT, ANRI HERBST; biannual.

The Journal of Peasant Studies (JPS): 4 Park Sq., Milton Park, Abingdon, Oxon, OX14 4RN, UK; tel. (20) 8052-0500; e-mail enquiries@taylorandfrancis.com; internet www.tandfonline.com/journals/fjps20; f. 1973; Editors SATURNINO M. BORRAS, Jr, SHAILA SESHIA GALVIN, JACOBO GRAJALES, RUTH HALL, SERGIO SAUER, ANNIE SHATTUCK; 7 a year.

Journal of Religion in Africa: Brill, Plantijnstraat 2, 2321 JC, Leiden, Netherlands; tel. 715353500; e-mail sales@brill.com; internet brill.com/view/journals/jra/jra-overview.xml; f. 1967; Exec. Editor ELIAS BONGMBA; 4 a year.

Journal of Social Development in Africa: School of Social Work, University of Zimbabwe, Private Bag 66022, Kopje, Harare, Zimbabwe; tel. (24) 3552682; e-mail editormanagingeditor@jsda.msu.ac.zw; Editor VICTOR MUZVIDZIWA; biannual.

Journal of Southern African Studies (JSAS): 4 Park Sq., Milton Park, Abingdon, Oxon, OX14 4RN, UK; tel. (20) 8052-0500; e-mail enquiries@taylorandfrancis.com; internet www.tandfonline.com/journals/cjss20; f. 1974; Co-Chair. SARA RICH DORMAN, BRIAN RAFTOPOULOS; 6 a year.

Journal for the Study of Religion: Dept of Religious Studies, Rm 5.40, Leslie Social Science Bldg, Upper Campus, University of Cape Town, Private Bag, Rondebosch 7701, South Africa; tel. (21) 6503452; e-mail journalforthestudyofreligion@gmail.com; internet www.ajol.info/index.php/jsr/index; Editor-in-Chief Dr JOHANNES A. SMIT; biannual.

Language Matters: 4 Park Sq., Milton Park, Abingdon, Oxon, OX14 4RN, UK; tel. (20) 8052-0500; e-mail enquiries@taylorandfrancis.com; internet www.tandfonline.com/journals/rlms20; f. 1991 as English Usage in Southern Africa; present name adopted in 1993; multilingualism in Africa; Editor LAWRIE BARNES; 3 a year.

New African: 7 Coldbath Sq., London, EC1R 4LQ, UK; tel. (20) 7841-3210; e-mail editorial@africasia.com; internet newafricanmagazine.com; f. 1966; politics and general interest; Editor ANVER VERSI; monthly.

Nigrizia: Vicolo Pozzo 1, 37129 Verona, Italy; tel. (45) 8092390; e-mail redazione@nigrizia.it; internet www.nigrizia.it; f. 1883; Dir GIUSEPPE CAVALLINI; monthly.

Nordic Journal of African Studies: NARN, Box 631, 751 26 Uppsala, Sweden; e-mail njas-info@njas.fi; internet www.njas.fi/njas; f. 1992 by the Nordic Association of African Studies; publ. by the Nordic Africa Research Network since 2018; online-only; Editors-in-Chief Dr THERA CRANE, Dr JONNA KATTO; 4 a year.

Politikon: South African Journal of Political Studies: 4 Park Sq., Milton Park, Abingdon, Oxon, OX14 4RN, UK; tel. (20) 8052-0500; e-mail enquiries@taylorandfrancis.com; internet www.tandfonline.com/journals/cpsa20; f. 1974; primarily South African politics; Editor CHRISTOPHER AFOKE ISIKE; 4 a year.

Politique Africaine: 22–24 blvd Arago, 75013 Paris, France; tel. 1-43-31-15-59; internet www.politique-africaine.com; f. 1981; political science and international relations; Editor-in-Chief VINCENT FOUCHER; quarterly.

Red Cross, Red Crescent: BP 303, 1211 Geneva 19, Switzerland; tel. (22) 7304222; e-mail rcrcmagazine@ifrc.org; internet www.rcrcmagazine.org; Arabic, English, French and Spanish edns; Editor-in-Chief MALCOLM LUCARD; 3 a year.

Research in African Literatures (RAL): The Ohio State University, 486 University Hall, 230 North Oval Mall, Columbus, OH 43210, USA; tel. (614) 292-9735; e-mail ral@osu.edu; internet iupress.org/journals/ral; f. 1970; Editor KWAKU LARBI KORANG; quarterly.

Review of African Political Economy (ROAPE): 4 Park Sq., Milton Park, Abingdon, Oxon, OX14 4RN, UK; tel. (20) 8052-0500; e-mail website.editor@roape.net; internet roape.net; f. 1974; publ. by Taylor and Francis (UK); Chair. of Editorial Working Group HANNAH CROSS; quarterly.

Revue Internationale des Études du Développement: Institut d'Etude du Développement Economique et Social, 45 bis ave de la Belle Gabrielle, 94736 Nogent sur Marne Cédex, France; tel. 1-43-92-72-02; e-mail revdev@univ-paris1.fr; internet iedespubli.hypotheses.org/la-revue; f. 1960 as Revue Tiers Monde; present name adopted in 2017; devt studies; in French, English and Spanish; Editorial Co-ordinator BÉATRICE TROTIER-FAURION; quarterly.

Safundi: The Journal of South African and American Studies: 4 Park Sq., Milton Park, Abingdon, Oxon, OX14 4RN, UK; tel. (20) 8052-0500; e-mail enquiries@taylorandfrancis.com; internet www.tandfonline.com/journals/rsaf20; f. 2000; Lead Editor SHANE GRAHAM; Co-Editors RITA BARNARD, CHRISTOPHER LEE, SIMON VAN SCHALKWYK; quarterly.

Scrutiny2: 4 Park Sq., Milton Park, Abingdon, Oxon, OX14 4RN, UK; tel. (20) 8052-0500; e-mail enquiries@taylorandfrancis.com; internet www.tandfonline.com/journals/rscr20; f. 1996; theoretical and practical concerns in English studies in southern Africa, particularly tertiary education; Man. Editors DEIRDRE BYRNE, GREGORY GRAHAM-SMITH; 3 a year.

Social Dynamics: 4 Park Sq., Milton Park, Abingdon, Oxon, OX14 4RN, UK; tel. (20) 8052-0500; e-mail enquiries@taylorandfrancis.com; internet www.tandfonline.com/journals/rsdy20; f. 1975; publ. on behalf of the Centre for African Studies, Cape Town (South Africa); all aspects of humanities and social sciences, with focus on the African continent; Editors CHRISTOPHER OUMA, BERNARD DUBBELD, LAUREN PAREMOER; 3 a year.

South African Historical Journal: 4 Park Sq., Milton Park, Abingdon, Oxon, OX14 4RN, UK; tel. (20) 8052-0500; e-mail enquiries@taylorandfrancis.com; internet www.tandfonline.com/journals/rshj20; incorporated the Journal of Natal and Zulu History in 2022; Co-ordinating Editors PRINISHA BADASSY, THULA SIMPSON, SANDRA SWART, LAURA PHILLIPS, NICHOLAS SOUTHEY; quarterly.

South African Review of Sociology (SARS): 4 Park Sq., Milton Park, Abingdon, Oxon, OX14 4RN, UK; tel. (20) 8052-0500; e-mail enquiries@taylorandfrancis.com; internet www.tandfonline.com/journals/rssr20; f. 1990 as the South African Journal of Sociology; fmrly known as Society in Transition; present name adopted in 2005; Editorial Collective Prof. DAVID COOPER, TAWANDA NYAWASHA, NOMKHOSI GAMA; 4 a year.

Southern African Linguistics and Applied Language Studies: 4 Park Sq., Milton Park, Abingdon, Oxon, OX14 4RN, UK; tel. (20) 8052-0500; e-mail enquiries@taylorandfrancis.com; internet www.tandfonline.com/journals/rall20; f. 1983 as the South African Journal of Linguistics; fmrly known as the Southern African Journal of Applied Language Studies; present name adopted in 2001; provides a forum for research on all southern African languages; Editor-in-Chief Prof. JOHANITA KIRSTEN; 4 a year.

Third World Quarterly (TWQ): 4 Park Sq., Milton Park, Abingdon, Oxon, OX14 4RN, UK; tel. (20) 8052-0500; e-mail enquiries@taylorandfrancis.com; internet www.tandfonline.com/journals/ctwq20; f. 1978; associated with the Third World Thematics journal; Editor SHAHID QADIR; 12 a year.

Vostok/Oriens (The East): Russian Academy of Sciences, 107031 Moscow, ul. 12 Rozhdestvenka, Russian Federation; tel. (495) 625-51-46; e-mail vostok.o@yandex.ru; internet vostokoriens.ru; f. 1955; publ. by the Institute of Oriental Studies and the Institute of African Studies of the Russian Academy of Sciences; text in Russian, summaries in English; Editor-in-Chief Dr VITALY NAUMKIN; 6 a year.

INDEX OF REGIONAL ORGANIZATIONS

(Main reference only)